ARCTIC OCEAN
Barents Sea
Kara Sea
Laptev Sea
East Siberian Sea
FINLAND
RUSSIA
ESTONIA
LATVIA
LITHUANIA
BELARUS
UKRAINE
MOLDOVA
ROMANIA
BULGARIA
KOSOVO
MACEDONIA
GREECE
Black Sea
GEORGIA
ARMENIA
AZERBAIJAN
TURKEY
CYPRUS
SYRIA
LEBANON
ISRAEL
JORDAN
IRAQ
IRAN
KUWAIT
BAHRAIN
QATAR
SAUDI ARABIA
UNITED ARAB EMIRATES
OMAN
YEMEN
Persian Gulf
Red Sea
Arabian Sea
EGYPT
SUDAN
ERITREA
DJIBOUTI
Somaliland
ETHIOPIA
SOMALIA
UGANDA
KENYA
DEMOCRATIC REPUBLIC OF THE CONGO
RWANDA
BURUNDI
TANZANIA
SEYCHELLES
COMORO ISLANDS
MALAWI
ZAMBIA
MOZAMBIQUE
ZIMBABWE
BOTSWANA
MADAGASCAR
MAURITIUS
Réunion
SWAZILAND
LESOTHO
SOUTH AFRICA
KAZAKHSTAN
Aral Sea
Caspian Sea
UZBEKISTAN
KYRGYZSTAN
TURKMENISTAN
TAJIKISTAN
AFGHANISTAN
PAKISTAN
MONGOLIA
PEOPLE'S REPUBLIC OF CHINA
NEPAL
BHUTAN
BANGLADESH
INDIA
MYANMAR (BURMA)
LAOS
THAILAND
VIETNAM
CAMBODIA
Bay of Bengal
MALDIVES
SRI LANKA
INDIAN OCEAN
Sea of Okhotsk
Bering Sea
Aleutian Islands
DEMOCRATIC PEOPLE'S REPUBLIC OF KOREA
REPUBLIC OF KOREA
Sea of Japan
JAPAN
Yellow Sea
East China Sea
Taiwan
Hong Kong
Macau
South China Sea
PHILIPPINES
Spratly Islands
Philippine Sea
Northern Marianas
PALAU
Caroline Islands
FEDERATED STATES OF MICRONESIA
MARSHALL ISLANDS
PACIFIC OCEAN
BRUNEI
MALAYSIA
SINGAPORE
Celebes Sea
INDONESIA
EAST INDIES
TIMOR-LESTE
PAPUA NEW GUINEA
MELANESIA
NAURU
Gilbert Islands
KIRIBATI
Phoenix Islands
SOLOMON ISLANDS
TUVALU
Wallis & Futuna
VANUATU
FIJI
Coral Sea
TONGA
New Caledonia
Great Barrier Reef
Norfolk Island
AUSTRALIA
Tasman Sea
North Islands
Chatham Islands
NEW ZEALAND
South Islands
ANTARCTICA

POLITICAL HANDBOOK OF THE WORLD 2010

POLITICAL HANDBOOK OF THE WORLD 2010

EDITED BY

Arthur S. Banks
Thomas C. Muller
William R. Overstreet
Judith F. Isacoff

A Division of SAGE
Washington, D.C.

Political Handbook of the World 2010

Editors: Arthur S. Banks, Thomas C. Muller, William R. Overstreet, Judith F. Isacoff
Associate Editors: Tony Davies, Thomas Lansford
Assistant Editor: Robin Best, Michael D. McDonald
Contributing Editors: Thomas Carson, Anastazia Skolnitsky Clouting, Mary H. Cooper, Melissa Doak, James Frusetta, Doug Goldenberg-Hart, Ioannis Grigoriadis, Alison Hawkes, Stephen Hoadley, Adam Isacson, Michael Keller, Jennifer Schuett, Roger Smith, Nancy Rhea Steedle
Production Assistant: Kathleen Stanley

CQ Press

Sponsoring Editor: Doug Goldenberg-Hart
Associate Editor: Andrea Cunningham
Project Assistants: Laura Masterson, Gregory Rees
Editorial Director, Reference Information Group: Andrea Pedolsky
Managing Editor: Steve Pazdan
Production Editor: Allyson Rudolph
Copy Editors: Sarah Bright, Kathleen Savory, Mary Sebold, Anna Socrates, Robin Surratt, Tracy Villano
Manager, Electronic Production: Paul P. Pressau
Online Edition: Andrew Boney, Jerry Orvedahl, Mary Grace Palumbo
President and Publisher: John A. Jenkins

CQ Press
2300 N Street, NW, Suite 800
Washington, DC 20037

Phone: 202-729-1600; toll-free, 1-866-4CQ-PRESS (1-866-427-7737)

Web: www.cqpress.com

Cover design: TGD Communications
Composition: C&M Digitals (P) Ltd.

∞ The paper used in this publication exceeds the requirements of the American National Standard for Information Sciences—Permanence of Paper for Printed Library Materials, ANSI Z39.48-1992.

Printed and bound in the United States of America

14 13 12 11 10 1 2 3 4 5

ISBN: 978-1-60426-736-5
ISSN: 0193-175X

Publishing history continues on page 1932, which is to be considered an extension of the copyright page.

CONTENTS

GOVERNMENTS

INTERGOVERNMENTAL ORGANIZATIONS

APPENDIXES

INTERGOVERNMENTAL ORGANIZATION ABBREVIATIONS

Country membership in an intergovernmental organization is given in one of two locations: Appendix C lists membership of the United Nations and its specialized and related agencies; non-UN memberships are listed at the end of each country section, under Intergovernmental Representation, using the abbreviations below. An asterisk indicates a nonofficial abbreviation. In the individual country sections, associate memberships are in italics.

*AC	Arctic Council
ACS	Association of Caribbean States
ADB	Asian Development Bank
*AfDB	African Development Bank
*AFESD	Arab Fund for Economic and Social Development
ALADI	Latin American Integration Association
AMF	Arab Monetary Fund
AMU	Arab Maghreb Union
APEC	Asia-Pacific Economic Cooperation
ASEAN	Association of Southeast Asian Nations
AU	African Union
BADEA	Arab Bank for Economic Development in Africa
BCIE	Central American Bank for Economic Integration
BDEAC	Central African States Development Bank
BIS	Bank for International Settlements
*BLX	Benelux Economic Union
BOAD	West African Development Bank
BSEC	Organization of the Black Sea Economic Cooperation
*CAEU	Council of Arab Economic Unity
CAN	Andean Community of Nations
Caricom	Caribbean Community and Common Market
CBSS	Council of the Baltic Sea States
CDB	Caribbean Development Bank
CEEAC	Economic Community of Central African States
CEI	Central European Initiative
CEMAC	Central African Economic and Monetary Community
*CENT	Council of the Entente
CEPGL	Economic Community of the Great Lakes Countries
CERN	European Organization for Nuclear Research
*CEUR	Council of Europe
CILSS	Permanent Inter-State Committee on Drought Control in the Sahel
CIS	Commonwealth of Independent States
Comesa	Common Market for Eastern and Southern Africa
CPLP	Community of Portuguese Speaking Countries
*CWTH	Commonwealth
EAC	East African Community
EADB	East African Development Bank
EBRD	European Bank for Reconstruction and Development
ECO	Economic Cooperation Organization
ECOWAS	Economic Community of West African States
EFTA	European Free Trade Association
EIB	European Investment Bank
ESA	European Space Agency
EU	European Union
Eurocontrol	European Organization for the Safety of Air Navigation
GCC	Gulf Cooperation Council
G-7	Group of Seven
G-8	Group of Eight
G-10	Group of Ten
G-20	Group of Twenty
*IADB	Inter-American Development Bank
IDB	Islamic Development Bank
IEA	International Energy Agency
IGAD	Inter-Governmental Authority on Development
Interpol	International Criminal Police Organization
IOC	Indian Ocean Commission
IOM	International Organization for Migration
IOR-ARC	Indian Ocean Rim Association for Regional Cooperation
LAS	League of Arab States (Arab League)
Mercosur	Southern Cone Common Market
*MRU	Mano River Union
*NAM	Nonaligned Movement
NATO	North Atlantic Treaty Organization
*NC	Nordic Council
NIB	Nordic Investment Bank
OAPEC	Organization of Arab Petroleum Exporting Countries
OAS	Organization of American States
OECD	Organization for Economic Cooperation and Development
OECS	Organization of Eastern Caribbean States
*OIC	Organization of the Islamic Conference
OIF	International Organization of the Francophonie
OPANAL	Agency for the Prohibition of Nuclear Weapons in Latin America and the Caribbean
OPEC	Organization of the Petroleum Exporting Countries
OSCE	Organization for Security and Cooperation in Europe
PC	Pacific Community
*PCA	Permanent Court of Arbitration
PIF	Pacific Islands Forum
SAARC	South Asian Association for Regional Cooperation
SADC	Southern African Development Community
SCO	Shanghai Cooperation Organization
SELA	Latin American Economic System
SICA	Central American Integration System
UEMOA	West African Economic and Monetary Union
*WCO	World Customs Organization/Customs Co-operation Council
WEU	Western European Union
WTO	World Trade Organization

PREFACE

In October 2008 the Nobel Committee awarded the world's most prestigious peace prize to Finland's former president Marrti Ahtisaari, citing his more than three decades of work in conflict resolution on several continents. A year later, in contrast, the Nobel Peace Prize went to a new participant in international politics, Barack Obama, who had occupied the office of U.S. president for less than ten months. The committee lauded Obama's "extraordinary efforts to strengthen international diplomacy and cooperation between peoples."

Early in President Obama's Nobel lecture on December 9, 2009, he acknowledged that many regarded the Nobel Committee's decision as premature and considered others—for example, humanitarian workers and those "who have been jailed and beaten in the pursuit of justice"—more deserving. He also spoke frankly about the central paradox surrounding the award: In addition to being the Nobel Peace Prize recipient, he was commander in chief of a country that was engaged in two wars, in Iraq and Afghanistan. Indeed, only eight days before his Nobel address he had called for committing an additional 30,000 U.S. troops, for a total of about 100,000, to the eight-year-old Afghan conflict.

The Nobel Committee's gesture of support for a "new climate in international politics" came at the end of a decade that some commentators disparaged as "the aughts" for its dearth of positive developments. The "00s" had begun with considerable apprehension over a "Y2K" millennial software meltdown that never materialized, as "1999" reset to "2000" with few glitches. At the same time, much of the world appeared inattentive to what would prove to be a far more substantial threat: the lethal growth of terrorism on the part of Islamic militants, which on September 11, 2001, claimed nearly 3,000 lives and provided the decade with its most indelible image, the collapse of the World Trade Center's twin towers in New York City, brought down by airline hijackers in a suicide mission linked to Osama bin Laden's al-Qaida. The shorthand "9/11" soon became common parlance, signifying the potentially devastating impact of "nonstate actors" who, whether devoted to jihad or some other cause, had the capacity to operate without regard for geopolitical boundaries or governments. For the balance of the decade suicide bombings and other terrorist assaults were never far from the headlines. Islamic terrorists, some of them homegrown, would later strike successfully, although not at such a high cost as on 9/11, in the United Kingdom, Spain, and elsewhere in the West as well as across a swath of Asia, from the Middle East through Indonesia and the Philippines.

As an immediate consequence of 9/11, the administration of President George W. Bush spearheaded the multinational invasion of Afghanistan, where the fundamentalist Taliban government permitted al-Qaida to operate. Eighteen months later, in March 2003, the United States launched a considerably larger military force against Iraq, which President Bush had characterized in January 2002 as part of an "axis of evil" that also included Iran and North Korea. Although the invasion of Iraq quickly succeeded in ousting strongman Saddam Hussein from power in Baghdad, it also destabilized Iraqi society. The occupying forces not only failed to locate the ostensible raison d'être for the invasion—stockpiled weapons of mass destruction (WMDs), which proved to be nonexistent—but also failed to bring with them a coherent plan for maintaining order and reestablishing civil society, thereby contributing to a protracted insurgency and sectarian bloodshed that would continue for the rest of the decade.

Meanwhile, the Bush administration refused to negotiate bilaterally with North Korea, which confirmed its entry into the company of nuclear powers with a successful underground nuclear explosion in October 2006. Washington also accused Iran of assisting terrorists and of using its efforts to develop civilian nuclear power as a cover for a nuclear weapons program—a charge lent at least some credence by Tehran's secrecy and failure to be forthcoming with the International Atomic Energy Agency (IAEA), which, along with its director general, Mohamed ElBaradei of Egypt, had won the 2005 Nobel Peace Prize for efforts to prevent the military use of nuclear energy.

President Obama's first year in office therefore found him dealing with the war in Afghanistan, the war in Iraq, erratic behavior from North Korea, the issue of Iran's nuclear status, and the continuing terrorist threat. There were numerous attacks around the world in 2009, including a car bombing in Spain by the Basque separatist ETA that injured some 60 people and the bombing of two Jakarta hotels in Indonesia that killed 9 and injured more than 50. However, the nexus of terrorist activity, excluding Afghanistan and Iraq, was Pakistan, which found itself confronted not only by the efforts of the jihadist *Tehrik-e-Taliban Pakistan* (TTP) to establish dominion and impose sharia (Islamic law) in the Swat valley of the North-West Frontier Province, but also by reprisals for its attempts to exert military control in tribal areas where al-Qaida and the Taliban had been taking advantage of the porous border with Afghanistan since 2001. Reprisals indiscriminately targeting civilians as well as the military and police also came in response to missile strikes launched by unmanned U.S. drones, one of which killed TTP leader Baitullah Mahsud, the alleged mastermind behind one of the decade's most consequential assassinations, that of former Pakistani prime minister Benazir Bhutto in December 2007.

In addition to addressing Islamic terrorism and nuclear proliferation, Obama's Nobel lecture focused on conflicts within countries—ethnic and sectarian clashes, secessionist movements, and insurgencies—and the chaos created by failed states. These are conflicts in which, he noted, "many more civilians are killed than soldiers; the seeds of future conflict are sown, economies are wrecked, civil societies torn asunder, refugees amassed, children scarred." He went on to argue that attendant violations of international law demand a principled international response and that armed intervention may be necessary and morally justified if nonmilitary measures, such as stiff sanctions, fail.

The decade 2000–2009 provided ample examples to support Obama's concerns:

- In Myanmar (Burma), where a repressive junta kept 1991 Nobel Peace Prize laureate Aung San Suu Kyi under house arrest for most of the decade
- In the failed state of Somalia, where "terrorism and piracy are joined by famine and human suffering"
- In the Democratic Republic of the Congo, where throughout the decade contending forces committed what Obama characterized as "systematic rape" and preyed on tribal

animosities in an effort to control the country's natural wealth

- In Sudan's Darfur region, where during the new century an estimated 200,000 died and 2.5 million were uprooted, and where the presidency continued to be held by Umar al-Bashir, whom prosecutors at the International Criminal Court charged with genocide
- In Sri Lanka, where a separatist insurgency fought for more than a quarter of a century by the Liberation Tigers of Tamil Eelam (LTTE) was finally defeated by government forces in May 2009, but not before tens of thousands of civilians had been killed and both sides had repeatedly been accused of human rights violations that included torture, rape, assassination, and extrajudicial killings

Turning to the prospects for building "a just and lasting peace," Obama called for imposing sanctions severe enough to change the behavior of noncompliant governments. He also advocated honoring the inherent rights of individuals, such as freedom of speech, religion, and assembly, and ensuring the opportunity for citizens to freely choose their leaders.

In the latter regard, the previous decade had recorded notable accomplishments, including the independence of Timor-Leste (East Timor) from Indonesia in 2002 and the return of limited self-rule to Northern Ireland in 2007. Also in Indonesia, impetus for settling a long-standing separatist conflict in Aceh Province had arisen from a catastrophe: the tsunami that struck the Indian Ocean on December 26, 2004, killing at least 230,000 people, the majority of them in Aceh. Partly as a result of mediation by Marrti Ahtisaari's Crisis Management Initiative team, Jakarta approved an autonomy statute for Aceh in 2006, bringing a formal end to the 30-year conflict. Other noteworthy developments in 2000–2009 included the 2003 "Rose Revolution" in Georgia, the 2004 "Orange Revolution" in Ukraine, and the 2005 "Tulip Revolution" in Kyrgyzstan, although electoral politics in Kyrgyzstan, in particular, subsequently failed to meet fully democratic standards.

In 2008, as the decade approached its close, "change" became a common electoral theme, bringing into power a spate of opposition parties, including, in the United States, Barack Obama's Democratic Party. In 2009, however, "stability" appeared to be key in a number of elections. Notable second-term victories were won by the center-right government of Chancellor Angela Merkel in Germany and the multiparty coalition of Prime Minister Manmohan Singh in India, who thereby became the first Indian prime minister since Jawaharlal Nehru (1946–1964) to continue in office following completion of a full first term. Among the industrialized countries, Japan offered the most noteworthy counter to the trend as the Democratic Party of Japan ousted the Liberal Democratic Party, whose rule had been almost continuous for over half a century. The switchover was hardly a surprise, however, as polling had predicted the results more than two years before the election.

Incumbent presidents were also reelected in Afghanistan and Iran in 2009, but large segments of the populace in both countries rejected the vote counts as fraudulent. In Afghanistan, Hamid Karzai, heading a government allegedly rife with corruption, claimed an outright victory but ultimately succumbed to international pressure and agreed to a runoff against his leading opponent, Abdullah Abdullah. Expressing concerns over fairness and transparency, Abdullah ultimately dropped out of the November contest, which was canceled. In Iran, the leading challenger to President Mahmoud Ahmadinejad, opposition figure Mir-Hossein Mousavi, refused to accept the June election results, which gave him only 34 percent of the vote versus the incumbent's 62 percent. But Ahmadinejad had the crucial support of Supreme Religious Leader Ayatollah Seyed Ali Khamenei, who directed an often violent crackdown against Mousavi supporters and other opposition demonstrators. Defying authorities, antigovernment protesters repeatedly took to the streets throughout the rest of the year.

Among 2009's other significant election results, Benjamin Netanyahu returned as Israeli prime minister, heading a conservative coalition government that assumed a hardened stance toward creation of a Palestinian state and that, ignoring international objections, soon authorized construction of additional Jewish housing units in the West Bank and East Jerusalem. Those decisions and the latest denunciation of Israeli intentions by the Palestinian Authority and the Hamas-led government in Gaza undermined efforts to restart the Middle East peace process.

In Africa, the leader of a 2008 coup in Mauritania, Mohamed Ould Abdelaziz, was elected to his country's presidency in July 2009. At the same time, in Guinea-Bissau the orderly conduct of a two-round presidential election in June–July (won by Malam Bacai Sanhá) garnered wide international praise, coming as it did only weeks after the assassination of the country's president and most senior politician, João Bernardo Vieira.

In the Americas, the president of Honduras, José Manuel Zelaya, was deposed on June 28 and forced into exile in an action that was widely condemned internationally but was characterized by his opponents as authorized by the constitution. In his three years in office Zelaya had introduced an increasingly leftist agenda, and he had recently called for revising the constitution. The previously scheduled election for Honduras's next president took place on November 29 and was won by the opposition National Party's Porfirio Lobo Sosa, but at the end of the year, with Zelaya still sequestered in the Brazilian embassy in Tegucigalpa after stealing back into the country in September, the crisis remained unresolved.

In addition to championing human rights and free elections, in his Nobel lecture President Obama identified economic opportunity and economic security as features of a just peace. (Twice in the past decade the peace prize has been awarded for achievements related to economic opportunity and sustainable development: in 2004, to the Kenyan Wangari Muta Maathai, founder of the environmental Green Belt Movement, and in 2006, to Bangladeshi economist Muhammad Yunus and the Grameen Bank for their work in offering microcredit loans, primarily to poor women.) However, economic opportunity and security were in relatively short supply in 2009 as the world attempted to recover from the worst recession since the Great Depression of the 1930s.

Beginning in September 2008 with a "credit crisis" that washed over the global banking and financial sectors, market downturns wiped out sizable portions of personal and institutional wealth and forced governments to rethink the basic underpinnings of their economies. The crisis had been precipitated in the United States and other developed economies by the rupture of a housing market bubble and its impact on largely unregulated, complex financial instruments. With striking speed, bank nationalizations, surreally priced bailouts, and massive stimulus packages collectively totaling trillions of dollars became the standard approaches for preventing complete implosion of the world economy.

According to the International Monetary Fund (IMF), the world economy contracted by 1.1 percent in 2009, although the downturn was not distributed evenly. In fact, many countries in Africa and Asia, despite experiencing drops in GDP growth rates, avoided falling into recession. The hardest hit countries were often developed economies: GDP fell by 2.7 percent in the United States, by 4.4 percent in the United Kingdom, by 5.3 percent in Germany, and by 5.4 percent in Japan. Every country in the European Union except Poland was in recession for the year as a whole, with the hardest hit being the Baltic republics of Estonia (–14 percent), Latvia (–18 percent), and Lithuania (–18.5 percent). Even the world's most vibrant economies, China (8.5 percent GDP growth) and India (5.4 percent), saw their rates of expansion slow from previous highs.

By mid-2009 economic data indicated that the "Great Recession" was technically over in many of the affected economies, but year-end IMF forecasts for 2010 predicted continuing recession in other countries and slow growth in most. Moreover, the return to modest growth was widely labeled as a "jobless recovery," especially in the

United States, where unemployment remained at 10 percent and where, for the decade as a whole, no net job growth had occurred.

Both the Nobel Committee, in announcing its 2009 award, and President Obama, in his Nobel lecture, called attention to another crisis, namely climate change. In a major end-of-decade event, the UN-sponsored Climate Change Conference—formally, the 15th Conference of the 193 Parties to the United Nations Framework Convention on Climate Change (UNFCCC) and the 5th Meeting of the 189 Parties to the 1997 Kyoto Protocol—met December 7–18, 2009, in Copenhagen, Denmark. The conference was originally called to conclude negotiations on a new agreement targeting cuts in carbon dioxide and other greenhouse emissions, but for a time it appeared that the conferees would fail to reach agreement on a final communiqué, let alone a treaty. At the eleventh hour, however, President Obama (visiting Europe for the second time in less than two weeks) met behind the scenes with the leaders of China, Brazil, India, and South Africa and emerged with a compromise agreement, the Copenhagen Accord.

The accord, which Obama himself characterized as "an imperfect framework," called for cooperation in reducing greenhouse gases "with a view" toward keeping the global temperature from rising no more than 2 degrees Celsius above preindustrial levels. In addition, wealthier countries agreed to provide $10 billion annually for three years to fund the efforts of poorer countries to develop clean energy and to redress the impact of global warming. By 2020, $100 billion a year is to be made available. Critics, citing the lack of legally binding provisions and specific emission-reduction targets, immediately dismissed the accord as toothless.

The year, and the decade, came to a close with the threat of Islamic terrorism once again commanding the headlines. On December 25, 2009, a would-be suicide bomber nearly succeeded in blowing up a U.S. passenger plane over Detroit, Michigan, despite all of the airport screening procedures and other precautions that had been instituted in the wake of 9/11. The alleged bomber, a Nigerian who had apparently been recruited while a student in the United Kingdom and was later reportedly trained by al-Qaida in Yemen, boarded a plane in Lagos, Nigeria, and then transferred to the U.S.-bound flight in Amsterdam, Netherlands, carrying in his clothing an explosive compound that he ignited but failed to detonate as the aircraft, with 289 passengers aboard, began its landing procedures.

Traditionally, the *Handbook* editors have used these prefaces to welcome the emergence of newly independent nations, particularly when independence has been embraced by the international community through such actions as quick admission to the United Nations. A global consensus has yet to be reached, however, regarding Kosovo, which declared its independence from Serbia in February 2008 after years of conflict between the Muslim majority in Kosovo and the strongly nationalist Serbian population. For the 2009 edition, the *Handbook* editors decided to include a separate article on Kosovo. We based our decision primarily on the fact that more than 50 countries had recognized Kosovo but also on our assessment that readers would best be served by having a consolidated analysis and history of the complicated developments concerning Kosovo. That rationale continues to hold for the present edition, but this decision should not be construed as evidence that we support Kosovo's side in the recognition dispute with Serbia. We remain neutral on that issue, as we also do in regard to two pro-Russian separatist regions in Georgia—South Ossetia and Abkhazia—that also declared independence in 2008. For this edition at least, both remain covered in the article on Georgia. (It is worth noting that while Kosovo has been recognized, as of January 12, 2010, by 65 countries and Taiwan, Abkhazia and South Ossetia have been recognized only by Nauru, Nicaragua, Russia, and Venezuela.)

In attempting to assess, in highly compressed form, the past and present politics of the global community, CQ Press and the editors of the *Handbook* continue a publishing tradition extending from 1928, when the Council on Foreign Relations prepared *A Political Handbook of the World*, edited by Malcolm W. Davis and Walter H. Mallory. (The book's history is outlined on page 1932.) This is the fifth edition published by CQ Press, now a division of SAGE Publications. The *Handbook* is now also available in an online edition.

The articles on individual countries are presented in alphabetical order based on their customary names in English. Their official names, if differing from the customary, are also provided, in both English and the national language or languages. If a country has related territories, they are treated together at the end of the country article. In the case of politically divided China and Korea, a discussion of matters pertaining to the nation as a whole is followed by separate articles on the People's Republic of China and Taiwan, in the first instance, and on the Democratic People's Republic of Korea (North Korea) and the Republic of Korea (South Korea), in the second. We have elected to include one territory without a permanent population and government (Antarctica). At the end of the country articles we have also included an article on the Palestinian Authority/Palestine Liberation Organization (PA/PLO), now no longer denied a territorial base, but whose status with regard to much of the West Bank and East Jerusalem is still evolving.

For this edition, the *Handbook* editors have attempted to cover national elections for all of 2009. This information is incorporated within the regular text wherever possible or in headnotes at the beginning of the country articles for elections that occurred in the latter part of the year.

The intergovernmental organizations selected for treatment are presented in a separate alphabetical sequence based on their official (or, in a few cases, customary) names in English. A list of member countries of most organizations is printed within each article; for the UN and its specialized agencies, the memberships are given in Appendix C. Non-UN intergovernmental organization memberships for individual countries are listed at the end of each country section, in conformity with the list of IGO abbreviations (see page ix). We have explicitly limited this section to groups that have memberships composed of more than two states, governing bodies that meet with some degree of regularity, and permanent secretariats or other continuing means for implementing collective decisions.

CQ Press gratefully acknowledges The Research Foundation of the State University of New York at Binghamton for its longtime support of this work and its integral role, from 1975 until 2005, in maintaining the *Handbook*'s strong legacy of readership and editorial standards. Special thanks are extended to Stephen A. Gilje, associate vice president for research at Binghamton University; Paul C. Parker, associate vice president for research administration; Michael D. McDonald and David H. Clark, former chairs of the Department of Political Science; and Benjamin Fordham, chair of the Department of Political Science.

GOVERNMENTS

AFGHANISTAN

Islamic Republic of Afghanistan

Note: Following the August 20, 2009, presidential balloting, President Hamid Karzai was initially credited with a first-round victory with 54.6 percent of the vote. However, runner-up Abdullah Abdullah alleged that massive fraud had occurred, and most international observers concluded that the poll had at least been significantly flawed. An audit reduced Karzai's total to just below 50 percent, and a runoff with Abdullah was scheduled for November 7 (unless the two contenders negotiated a coalition government, as suggested by the United States and other Western countries). However, declaring that fraud was again inevitable, Abdullah withdrew from the runoff, and Karzai was inaugurated for another five-year term on November 19, along with First Vice President Mohammad Qasim Fahim and Vice President Mohammad Karim Khalili. Karzai subsequently proposed a new cabinet, although many of his choices were challenged in the legislature.

Political Status: Republic established following military coup that overthrew traditional monarchy in July 1973; constitution of 1977 abolished and the Democratic Republic of Afghanistan announced following left-wing coup of April 27, 1978; successor regime established following coup of December 27, 1979, but effectively overthrown on April 16, 1992; successor regime effectively overthrown by the Taliban in late September 1996 but claimed to remain legitimate government; interim administration installed in December 2001 following overthrow of the Taliban; transitional government installed in June 2002; new constitution providing for multiparty democracy approved by a *Loya Jirga* (Grand National Council) on January 4, 2004; permanent government of the renamed Islamic Republic of Afghanistan established by inauguration of the president on December 7, 2004, and the cabinet on December 23.

Area: 249,999 sq. mi. (647,497 sq. km.).

Population: 13,051,358 (1979C), excluding an estimated 2.5 million nomads; 25,375,000 (2008E, including nomads). Nomads and refugees in western Pakistan and northern Iraq at one time totaled more than 5 million, many of whom have returned to Afghanistan.

Major Urban Centers (2005E): KABUL (3,082,000), Kandahar (341,000), Herat (268,000), Mazar-i-Sharif (197,000).

Official Languages: Pushtu, Dari (Persian); in addition, the 2004 constitution authorized six minority languages (Baluchi, Nuristani, Pamiri, Pashai, Turkmen, and Uzbek) to serve as official third languages in the areas where the majority speaks them.

Monetary Unit: Afghani (market rate December 1, 2009: 45.50 afghanis = $1US).

President: *(See headnote.)* Hamid KARZAI (nonparty); appointed chair of a new interim administration at the UN-sponsored Bonn Conference on December 5, 2001, and inaugurated on December 22 for a six-month term (for a detailed description of the complicated issue of the leadership of Afghanistan prior to Karzai's inauguration, see the 2000–2002 *Handbook*); elected president of a new transitional government by an "emergency" *Loya Jirga* on June 13, 2002, and inaugurated on June 19 for a term that was initially scheduled not to exceed two years; elected by popular vote on October 9, 2004, and sworn in for a five-year term on December 7. (President Karzai's term was scheduled to expire on May 21, 2009, but new presidential elections were postponed until August 20 due to security concerns and organizational difficulties. The Supreme Court proposed that Karzai remain in his post until the election.)

Vice Presidents: *(See headnote.)* Ahmad Zia MASOUD (First Vice President) and Mohammad Karim KHALILI (Second Vice President); elected on October 9, 2004, and inaugurated on December 7 for a term concurrent with that of the president. (For a detailed description of the prior vice-presidential situation, see the 2000–2002 *Handbook.*)

THE COUNTRY

Strategically located between the Middle East, Central Asia, and the Indian subcontinent, Afghanistan is a land marked by physical and social diversity. Physically, the landlocked country ranges from the high mountains of the Hindu Kush in the northeast to low-lying deserts along the western border. Pushtuns (alternatively Pashtuns or Pathans) constitute the largest of the population groups, followed by Tajiks, who speak Dari (an Afghan variant of Persian); others include Uzbeks, Hazaras, Baluchis, and Turkmen. The Kuchi peoples, primarily Pushtuns and Baluchis who maintain a centuries-old nomadic lifestyle, reportedly number 1.3–1.5 million. Tribal distinctions (except among the Tajiks) may cut across ethnic cleavages, while religion is a major unifying factor. Approximately 90 percent of the people profess Islam (80 percent Sunni and the remainder Shiite [mostly from the Hazara population]). Prior to the Taliban takeover in 1996, women constituted a growing percentage of the paid workforce in urban areas, particularly in health services and education, although female participation in government was minuscule. In the countryside the role of women has for a long time been heavily circumscribed by traditional Islamic fundamentalist strictures, which the Taliban movement also imposed on the urban population. The interim administration of December 2001, transitional government of June 2002, and permanent government of December 2004 all included women, while a significant number of seats were reserved for women in the new National Assembly inaugurated in late 2005. However, Amnesty International concluded in early 2006 that the status of women had not improved nearly as much as had been anticipated following the fall of the Taliban, with rape, abduction, and forced marriage still commonplace, particularly beyond Kabul.

Afghanistan is one of the world's poorest countries, with a per capita GNP of less than $200 a year in 2004. Nearly 80 percent of the labor force is engaged in agriculture (largely at a subsistence level). Current government subsidies are aimed at the production of pomegranates, nuts, grapes, apricots, and saffron for export. The country's extensive mineral deposits are largely unexploited, except for natural gas. Industry is virtually nonexistent. One major source of income is opium; as much as 90 percent of the world's heroin reportedly originates in Afghanistan. In 2007 it was reported that 2006 had seen record opium production—up 25 percent from 2005. About 12 percent of the population reportedly was engaged in opium activities, valued at about $3 billion annually, compared to "legal" exports valued at less than $200 million. Most of the opium production is currently concentrated in the south and southwest. Government poppy eradication efforts have been moderately successful elsewhere, although many former poppy farmers have reportedly turned to cultivating cannabis, of which Afghanistan is now also one of the world's leading exporters.

The rate of childhood death (mostly from preventable diseases) is among the highest in the world, and the illiteracy rate is estimated to be more than 70 percent. Nearly all girls and two-thirds of boys reportedly did not attend school under the Taliban regime, the former in large part because of the Taliban policy against education for women. (It was reported in 2007 that some 5 million children were enrolled, compared to only 900,000 under the Taliban.) Life expectancy is only 45 years, an estimated 50 percent of the population lives in poverty, and 75 percent of the population lacks access to safe water. In addition, unemployment is high, and much of the country has inadequate electrical grids, sewerage, roads, and other public services. Economic development is hampered by the fact that much of the nation's wealth is concentrated in the hands of powerful warlords backed by private militias.

For many years the Soviet Union was Afghanistan's leading trade partner, while development aid from the West and from such international agencies as the Asian Development Bank was suspended as a result of the Soviet military intervention in late 1979. Thereafter, more than 20 years of civil war and subsequent turmoil left an estimated 2 million dead and much of the country in ruins. The Taliban government, which spent most of its energy following its partial takeover in 1996 in an attempt to secure complete control of the country, was described as having "no apparent economic program."

Western nations were eager in 1997 and early 1998 to see a resolution to the Afghan conflict so that progress could be made in laying oil and gas pipelines across the country from the huge and largely unexploited fields in Central Asia. However, alternate plans were subsequently adopted to run the pipelines through other countries as fighting continued in Afghanistan. Renewed Western interest in cross-Afghanistan pipelines returned following the overthrow of the Taliban in late 2001 and the subsequent installation of a transitional government of national unity. However, the most immediate concerns

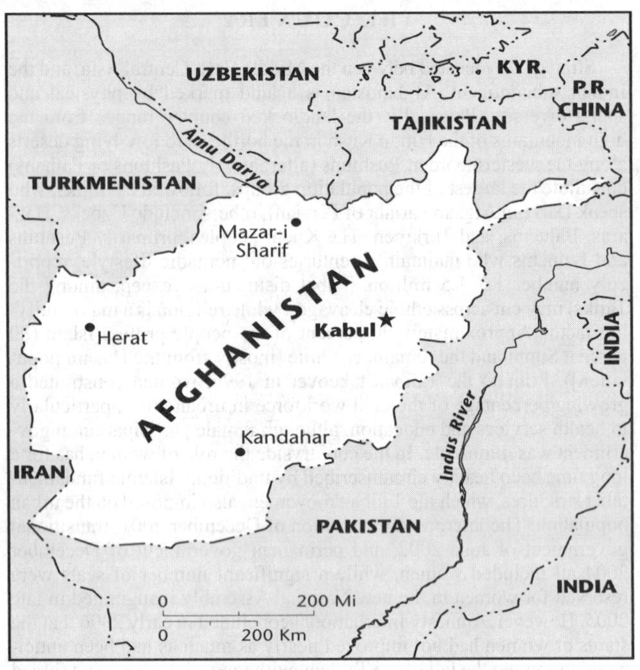

of the new administration were to start rebuilding the nation's infrastructure, facilitate the return of millions of refugees from neighboring countries, and remove land mines. (Observers described Afghanistan as the most heavily mined country in the world.)

The United States, which led the military campaign that deposed the Taliban, was accused in some circles of losing its focus on Afghanistan in 2002–2003 as attention shifted to events involving Iraq. However, in 2004 the United States allocated $1.8 billion for reconstruction in Afghanistan and also increased the number of U.S. troops dedicated to fighting Taliban and al-Qaida remnants in Afghanistan. Overall, Western donors pledged $8.2 billion in new aid at a conference in April 2004, which also endorsed the Karzai administration's economic plans. Although private foreign investors remained leery of ongoing security problems and perceived deep-seated corruption at all levels of authority, in general, the transitional government received praise for its "crisis management" during 2002–2004. Following its installation in late 2004, the new permanent administration pledged to pursue long-term stability and economic expansion through the promotion of free-market activity.

The International Monetary Fund (IMF) in early 2006 estimated economic growth at 8 percent in the 2004–2005 fiscal year and nearly 14 percent in 2005–2006. However, journalists described the country as having "no viable economy" and noted that the government continued to rely on foreign aid for nearly all of its budget and on foreign troops for its security.

A survey in 2006 indicated that oil and gas reserves might be significantly larger than anticipated, while deposits of coal, copper, gold, gemstones, iron ore, and marble also awaited exploitation. Meanwhile, some 60 countries in 2006 pledged an additional $10.5 billion in aid for reconstruction over the next five years under an Afghanistan Compact, which also called for additional reforms by the government. The IMF also approved a three-year lending program valued at $1.2 billion. However, corruption, the deteriorating security situation, and poor governmental administration continued to hamper distribution of aid resources. Private investment also slumped by 50 percent in 2007 as a consequence of the Taliban insurgency, which continued to rely on "taxes" on opium for much of its financing. The "narco-economy" continued to dominate in 2008, annual production having increased 34 percent in 2007 over 2006 levels.

The IMF argued in 2008 that Western institutions "had not taken root," with corruption being rampant in many sectors, particularly the judiciary. The Fund also criticized the government for failing to enact tax reforms deemed necessary to support the "anemic" private sector. On a more positive note, a state-owned Chinese company announced plans to invest $3 billion over the next five years to exploit what was believed to be the second largest copper deposit in the world.

An Afghan Support Conference in June 2008 pledged an additional $15–20 billion for development, although participants acknowledged that much aid to date had been wasted. Subsequently, the IMF reported GDP growth of 7.5 percent for 2008, although progress in that regard was countered by inflation of more than 24 percent for the year, fueled by rising food and energy prices. Meanwhile, the government estimated that more than 2 million people remained unemployed as economic revitalization efforts suffered from an intensified insurgency by the Taliban.

GOVERNMENT AND POLITICS

Political background. The history of Afghanistan reflects the interplay of a number of political forces, the most important of which traditionally were the monarchy, the army, religious and tribal leaders, and foreign powers. The existence of the country as a political entity is normally dated from 1747, when the Persians were overthrown and Ahmad Shah DURANI established the foundations of an Afghan empire. His successors, however, proved relatively ineffective in the face of dynastic and tribal conflicts coupled in the 19th century with increasingly frequent incursions by the Russians and British. The latter wielded decisive influence during the reign of ABDUR RAHMAN Khan and in 1898 imposed acceptance of the Durand line, which established the country's southern and eastern borders but which, by ignoring the geographic distribution of the Pushtun tribes, also laid the foundation for subsequent conflict over establishment of a Pushtunistan state. Emir AMANULLAH succeeded in forcing the British to relinquish control over Afghan foreign affairs in 1919 and attempted to implement such reforms as modern education, women's rights, and increased taxation before being forced to abdicate under pressure from traditional leaders.

The outbreak of World War II severely damaged the economy: markets were lost and access to imports and credit was cut off. Subsequently, dissent among intellectuals and failure to resolve the Pushtunistan issue led to a crisis of leadership. Prince Sardar Mohammad DAOUD, designated prime minister in 1953, succeeded in obtaining economic aid from both the United States and the Soviet Union, while modernization of the army helped to alleviate the threat posed by tribes hostile to the government. Politically, however, Daoud was autocratic, ignoring the legislature, jailing his critics, and suppressing opposition publications. His dismissal in 1963 was followed by a series of moves toward a more modern political system, including the promulgation of a new constitution in 1964 and the holding of parliamentary elections in 1965. Nevertheless, problems were subsequently encountered, including recurrent famine; a worsening financial situation; increased restiveness on the part of the small, educated middle class; and a sense of impatience with civilian rule. The distress led in 1973 to a military coup, the overthrow of the monarch (Mohammad ZAHIR SHAH), and the return of Daoud as president of a newly proclaimed republic.

On April 27, 1978, in the wake of unrest stemming from the assassination of a prominent opposition leader in Kabul, the Daoud regime was overthrown in a left-wing coup led by the deputy air force commander, Col. Abdul KHADIR. On April 30 a newly constituted Revolutionary Council designated Nur Mohammad TARAKI, secretary general of the formerly outlawed People's Democratic Party of Afghanistan (PDPA), as its president and announced the establishment of the Democratic Republic of Afghanistan, with Taraki as prime minister. On March 27, 1979, Taraki yielded the office of prime minister to party hard-liner Hafizullah AMIN while remaining titular head of state by virtue of his presidency of the Revolutionary Council.

It was officially announced on September 16, 1979, that the PDPA Central Committee had unanimously elected Amin as its secretary general, and shortly thereafter the Revolutionary Council designated him to succeed Taraki as president. While Kabul radio reported on October 9 that Taraki had died after "a severe and prolonged illness," foreign observers generally assumed that the former president had succumbed on September 17 to wounds received three days earlier during an armed confrontation at the presidential palace. Subsequent reports suggested that a Soviet-backed effort by Taraki to remove the widely disliked Amin as part of a conciliatory policy toward rebel Muslim tribesmen had, in effect, backfired. Such suspicions intensified when the Soviet Union airlifted some 4,000–5,000 troops to Kabul on December 25–26, which resulted in Amin's death and replacement on December 27 by his longtime PDPA rival, Babrak KARMAL, theretofore living under Soviet protection in Czechoslovakia. Karmal proved scarcely more acceptable to the rebels than Amin, however, his regime being supported primarily by the continued presence of Soviet military personnel (estimated to number more than 110,000 by mid-1982). During the ensuing three years, the level of Soviet military involvement increased because of continued resistance throughout the country by mujahidin (holy warriors) guerrillas (funded in part by the United States), operating largely from rural bases and supplied from Pakistan, where more than 3 million Afghans had sought refuge. However, in 1985 a semblance of constitutional government was restored. A partially elected *Loya Jirga* was convened on April 23, the first such assemblage in eight years. It promptly endorsed the Soviet presence, while elections for local village councils were held from August through October, despite disruptions attributable to mujahidin activity. Based in Peshawar, Pakistan, the seven leading mujahidin groups formed an Islamic Alliance of Afghan Holy Warriors (*Ittehad-i-Islami Afghan Mujahidin*) in May 1985 to coordinate resistance to the Moscow-backed regime in Kabul.

On May 4, 1986, after a visit to the Soviet Union for what were described as medical reasons, Karmal stepped down as PDPA secretary general in favor of the former head of the state intelligence service, Mohammad NAJIBULLAH (Najib). On November 20 Karmal asked to be relieved of his remaining government and party posts, being succeeded as head of the Revolutionary Council by Haji Mohammad CHAMKANI, who was, however, designated only on an acting basis.

In December 1986 the PDPA Central Committee endorsed Najibullah's plan for "national reconciliation," calling for a cease-fire, political liberalization, and the formation of a coalition government. Although the seven-party mujahidin alliance refused to negotiate and intense fighting continued, the government promoted its democratization campaign in 1987 by legalizing additional political parties, drafting a new constitution providing for an elected national legislature, and conducting local elections. However, in practical terms there was little challenge to Najibullah's consolidation of power: the Revolutionary Council on September 30, 1987, unanimously elected him as its president, and on November 30 the *Loya Jirga,* having approved the new constitution, named him as the first president of the republic ("Democratic" having been deleted from the country's name).

On April 14, 1988, Afghanistan, Pakistan, the Soviet Union, and the United States concluded a series of agreements providing for a Soviet troop withdrawal within one year. Elections to the new National Assembly (*Meli Shura*) were held the same month, although the government was unable to convince the mujahidin to participate. On May 26 the Revolutionary Council dissolved itself in deference to the assembly, and, in a further effort by the government to reduce the appearance of PDPA dominance, Mohammad Hasan SHARQ, who was not a PDPA member, was appointed chair of the Council of Ministers to replace Soltan Ali KESHTMAND.

The Soviet troop withdrawal was completed on February 15, 1989, prompting significant political moves by both the government and mujahidin. Najibullah quickly dropped all non-PDPA members from the Council of Ministers; concurrently, a state of emergency was declared, and a new 20-member Supreme Council for the Defense of the Homeland was created to serve, under Najibullah's leadership, as the "supreme military and political organ" for the duration of the emergency. On February 21 Keshtmand effectively resumed the duties of prime minister through his appointment as chair of the Council of Ministers' Executive Committee.

For their part, the mujahidin vowed to continue their resistance until an Islamic administration had been installed in Kabul. On February 24, 1989, the rebels proclaimed a "free Muslim state" under an Afghan Interim Government (AIG) headed by Imam Sibghatullah MOJADEDI as president and Abdul Rasul SAYAF as prime minister. However, the widespread belief that the rebels would quickly vanquish the Najibullah regime proved incorrect, despite two reported coup plots in December and a nearly successful uprising led (in apparent collusion with rebel fundamentalist Gulbuddin HEKMATYAR) by the hard-line defense minister, Lt. Gen. Shahnawaz TANAI, in March 1990.

On May 7, 1990, President Najibullah named Fazil Haq KHALIQYAR, a former minister-advisor in the Executive Council, to succeed Keshtmand as prime minister. Half of the members of the cabinet subsequently named by Khaliqyar were described as politically "neutral." On May 28–29 the *Loya Jirga* convened in Kabul to reiterate its commitment to private sector development and to ratify a number of reform-oriented constitutional amendments.

On May 27, 1991, Najibullah announced that his government was prepared to observe a cease-fire with the mujahidin to permit implementation of a peace plan advanced by UN secretary general Javier Pérez de Cuéllar that would entail an end to external involvement in Afghan affairs and provide for nationwide balloting to choose a new government. Two months later, the AIG stated that it "had recognized positive points" in the UN proposal. Consequently, on September 1 the United States and the Soviet Union declared that they were halting arms supplies to the combatants. Trilateral discussions among U.S., Soviet, and mujahidin representatives were subsequently held on the transfer of power to an interim regime that would oversee elections within two years. The fundamentalists, however, continued to call for Najibullah's immediate removal and the scheduling of an earlier poll.

On March 19, 1992, mujahidin hard-liners rejected an offer by Najibullah to yield effective authority to an interim administration, reiterating their demand that he resign. By early April, on the other hand, a pronounced shift in the balance of power had emerged in the strategic northern city of Mazar-i-Sharif, where local militias were forming alliances with moderate mujahidin units. The realignment cut across both government and insurgent groupings, inaugurating a new cleavage between southern Pushtun fundamentalists led by Hekmatyar and non-Pushtun northerners under the command of Ahmed Shah MASOUD.

On April 16, 1992, Najibullah submitted his resignation and sought refuge at the UN office in Kabul after four of his top generals had deserted to Masoud. Within a week, the eastern city of Jalalabad became the last provincial capital to fall to joint mujahidin, militia, and former government forces (including supporters of both Hekmatyar and Masoud, who thereupon initiated a successful assault on Kabul. On April 24 the leaders of six rebel groups met in Peshawar, Pakistan, to announce the formation of a 51-member Islamic Jihad Council (IJC), headed by Imam Mojadedi, to assume power in the capital. After two months the IJC was to be replaced by an interim administration under Burhanuddin RABBANI, with Hekmatyar as prime minister and Masoud as defense minister. However, Hekmatyar refused to participate, proceeding instead to launch an attack on his erstwhile allies. In three days of heavy fighting, Hekmatyar's troops were unable to defeat the Masoud coalition, and on April 28 Mojadedi arrived to proclaim the formation of an Islamic republic. Meanwhile, Hekmatyar's forces continued to ring Kabul's southern and eastern outskirts, threatening to launch another offensive if Masoud did not break with the non-mujahidin northerners (particularly with Gen. Abdul Rashid DOSTAM, an Uzbek, who had served under the former Communist regime). Subsequently, on May 25, Masoud and Hekmatyar agreed to halt hostilities and hold elections in six months. Even while they were talking, however, clashes were reported between units loyal to Hekmatyar and Dostam. In early June, fighting also broke out between Iranian-backed Hazara Shiites and Saudi Arabian–backed Sunni units loyal to Masoud. Reportedly the Shiites had demanded a minimum of eight ministerial posts in the Mojadedi government.

Although initially indicating that he wished to continue as acting president beyond his two-month mandate, Mojadedi stepped down on June 28, 1992, in favor of Rabbani. Concurrently, Hekmatyar agreed to the appointment of his deputy, Ustad FARID, as prime minister of an interim cabinet. Formally invested on July 6, Farid was forced from office a month later, after heavy fighting had erupted in Kabul between pro- and anti-Rabbani groups, including a massive artillery bombardment by Hekmatyar's forces that caused more than 1,800 deaths.

On October 31, 1992, a Leadership Council, self-appointed five months earlier and chaired by Rabbani, extended the interim president's mandate beyond its four-month limit, permitting Rabbani to convene a Council of Resolution and Settlement in late December that elected him to a two-year term as head of state. Thereafter, Kabul was the scene of renewed fighting, culminating in a peace accord concluded by Rabbani and Hekmatyar in Islamabad, Pakistan, on March 7, 1993. The pact was endorsed by all but one of the major mujahidin leaders. On March 8 Hekmatyar accepted appointment as prime minister, although differences immediately arose over the assignment of portfolios. On May 24, after further fighting in Kabul, a new cease-fire was announced, under which Masoud agreed to resign as defense minister and turn the ministry over to a tripartite commission. The principal obstacle having been overcome, a coalition cabinet was reportedly sworn in at an undisclosed location on June 17. However, the new administration was never effectively implemented in view of continued conflict between forces loyal to Rabbani and Hekmatyar, with General Dostam switching sides to join forces with Hekmatyar in fighting in Kabul and elsewhere in early 1994.

In late June 1994 Rabbani's troops succeeded in sweeping most Hekmatyar and Dostam units from the capital, and in mid-July the Organization of the Islamic Conference (OIC) reported that all parties had agreed to a peace process. Concurrently, however, reports circulated that Pakistan's Inter-Services Intelligence (ISI) was supplying large quantities of arms and ammunition to Hekmatyar, who commenced a systematic bombardment of Kabul after the Supreme Court had extended Rabbani's presidential mandate for an additional six months without granting a similar extension of Hekmatyar's prime ministerial mandate.

On August 28, 1994, Maulawi Mohammad Nabi MOHAMMAD of the moderate Islamic Revolutionary Movement was named chair of a *Loya Jirga* convening commission in preparation for national elections. On November 6 Rabbani and his supporters accepted a modified version of a UN peace plan that called for a commission on which the principal mujahidin units would have equal representation, with Rabbani subsequently announcing his willingness to step down as soon as "reliable mechanisms for a transfer of power" were in place.

Meanwhile the balance of power within Afghanistan was disrupted by an incursion of several thousand young Taliban (Islamic students) supported by Pakistan's fundamentalist *Jamiat-ul-Ulema-e-Islam* (Assembly of Islamic Clergy) and led by Maulana Fazlur RAHMAN. In November 1994 Taliban forces captured the city of Kandahar and initiated an antidrug crusade throughout the opium-growing province of Helmand. The success of the new group appeared to reflect a major shift by Pakistan's ISI away from Hekmatyar and gave rise to speculation that the new element in Afghanistan's domestic turmoil might force a truce between Hekmatyar and Rabbani.

After winning control of a third of the country's provinces, the Taliban by late February 1995 had driven Hekmatyar from his base in Charosyab, ten miles south of Kabul, and proceeded to advance on the capital. However, on March 11 the student militia suffered its first major defeat at the hands of Rabbani and Masoud and was subsequently forced to yield Charosyab to government forces. Routed in the east, the Taliban launched an offensive against the western city of Herat. That initiative also failed when Masoud dispatched a number of fighter-bombers and some 2,000 troops to aid in the city's defense. Further Taliban defeats followed, while the anti-Rabbani mujahidin front collapsed with Hekmatyar's withdrawal to the eastern city of Jalalabad and Dostam's unwillingness to commit his forces to battle.

On June 9, 1995, a truce was declared between government and Taliban forces. However, the Taliban mounted a major offensive in September that yielded the capture of Herat. On November 7 President Rabbani offered to resign if the Taliban agreed to a cease-fire and "foreign interference" (presumably by Pakistan in support of the Taliban) were to end. Thereafter, fighting intensified in the vicinity of Kabul, followed by peace talks in which the government succeeded in reaching an accommodation with Hekmatyar (although not with his erstwhile mujahidin allies) providing for joint military action against the Taliban and for governmental power-sharing. Under a peace accord signed on May 24, 1996, the supporters of Rabbani and Hekmatyar undertook to cooperate on the organization of new elections and to establish "genuine Islamic government," with Rabbani continuing as president and Hekmatyar being restored to the premiership. In accordance with the agreement, Hekmatyar was formally reappointed prime minister on June 26. Among the first actions of the restored prime minister were the closure of cinemas and the banning of music on radio and television on Sundays, on the grounds that such activities were contrary to Islamic precepts. However, underscoring the potential for a new round of conflict, Hekmatyar's former anti-Rabbani mujahidin allies suspended Hekmatyar from membership of the coordination council established by the four main fundamentalist movements in 1994 under the leadership of former interim president Sibghatullah Mojadedi (leader of the National Liberation Front).

More ominously for the new government, the predominantly Sunni Taliban guerrillas, still strongly backed by Pakistan, continued to make military advances in July and August 1996, and by early September they controlled 18 of the country's 30 provinces. The eastern city of Jalalabad, the country's second largest, was captured on September 11, whereupon Taliban forces pursued retreating government troops to Kabul and mounted a new onslaught on the capital. After heavy fighting on the eastern side of the city, resistance crumbled, and the government fled. By September 25 Taliban units were in complete control of Kabul, where on September 27 a six-member Provisional Council was installed under the leadership of Mullah Mohammad RABBANI (not related to the ousted president). Meanwhile, Mullah Mohammad OMAR (the spiritual leader of the Taliban) assumed the status of de facto head of state. Among the first acts of the new rulers was to seize Najibullah, the former president, from the UN compound in which he had lived since April 1992 and to execute him in summary fashion, together with his brother Shahpur AHMADZAY (who had served as his security chief) and two aides. Mullah Rabbani justified the executions on the grounds that the former president had been "against Islam, a criminal, and a Communist."

After a period of disorganization, the ousted government of Burhanuddin Rabbani relocated to northern Afghanistan, where a military alliance of the regrouped government troops under Masoud's command, the forces loyal to General Dostam, and Hazara fighters served to block the Taliban offensive. The military situation remained effectively stalemated until May 1997, when Gen. Abdul Malik PAHLAWAN, who had apparently ousted General Dostam as leader of the National Front forces, invited the Taliban troops into the alliance's stronghold in Mazar-i-Sharif. However, just as the Taliban takeover of the entire country seemed imminent, General Pahlawan's forces suddenly turned on the Taliban, killing, according to subsequent reports, some 2,000–3,000 Taliban fighters. Anti-Taliban groups, including, significantly, Hekmatyar's Islamic Party, subsequently coalesced as the United National Islamic Front for the Salvation of Afghanistan (UNIFSA) and retained effective control of the north for the rest of the year. Collaterally, General Dostam, who had fled the country in June after General Pahlawan's "coup," returned to Afghanistan in late October to wrest control of the Uzbek forces from Pahlawan, who apparently fled to Turkmenistan. Meanwhile, Mullah Omar was named emir of the Islamic Emirate of Afghanistan that was proclaimed by the Taliban on October 26, 1997.

In early 1998 the Taliban and UNIFSA appeared willing to consider a negotiated settlement, agreeing in principle to establish a joint council of religious scholars to assist in the process. However, the Taliban olive branch did not extend to the Hazara Shiite community in central Afghanistan, where the regime was enforcing an economic blockade that was said to be threatening famine. Consequently, despite UN, U.S., and OIC mediation efforts, the peace talks quickly broke down, and heavy fighting resumed. The Taliban launched what its supporters hoped would be a final offensive to secure total control of the country in mid-July, and Mazar-i-Sharif fell from UNIFSA hands in mid-August. However, as Taliban forces approached the northern borders, neighboring countries sent troops to defend their own territory from possible Taliban incursions and also provided assistance to the beleaguered UNIFSA fighters. In addition, Iran, angered over the killing of eight of its diplomats during the recent fighting and concerned over the threat to the Afghan Shiite community, amassed some 250,000 soldiers along its border with Afghanistan, raising fears of a full-blown regional war. Further complicating matters, on August 20 U.S. cruise missiles struck camps in Afghanistan believed to be part of the alleged terrorist network run by Osama BIN LADEN. (The attack was ordered as retaliation for the bombing of U.S. embassies in Kenya and Tanzania earlier in the month, in which Washington suspected bin Laden's followers to have been involved.) Bin Laden's presence in Afghanistan subsequently proved to be a barrier to Taliban attempts to gain additional international recognition. However, after the government rejected Western calls for bin Laden's extradition, an Afghan court in November ruled that the United States had not produced evidence of his complicity in the embassy bombings and permitted him to remain in the country as long as he or his followers did not use it as a base for terrorist activity.

In July 1999 U.S. president Bill Clinton imposed economic sanctions on Afghanistan as the result of the Taliban's unwillingness to turn over bin Laden. Four months later, at Washington's urging, the UN Security Council directed UN members to freeze overseas assets of the Taliban government and to halt all flights to Afghanistan to pressure Kabul regarding bin Laden as well as to protest the perceived mistreatment of women, other human rights abuses, and ongoing opium production. (One correspondent for the *Christian Science Monitor* described the Taliban as having achieved the "rare feat of provoking the hostility of all five permanent members of the Security Council." China, for example, reportedly expressed concern about Taliban influence on Islamic unrest within its borders, while Russia went so far as to threaten to bomb Afghanistan if Kabul provided support to Chechen rebels or Islamist insurgents in neighboring Central Asian countries.) For their part, Taliban leaders appeared to remain preoccupied with attempting to secure control of the approximately 10 percent of the country in the northeast still in the hands of opposition forces. Major Taliban offenses were launched in the summers of 1999 and 2000, each being repulsed (after heavy fighting and large-scale civilian dislocation) by fighters, now referenced as the Northern Alliance, led by Ahmed Shah Masoud. Consequently, in September 2000 discussion was reported on yet another peace plan, under which Masoud would have been given special administrative powers in an autonomous northeastern region.

Negotiations between the Northern Alliance and the Taliban continued for the rest of 2000; however, they ultimately failed, and sporadic heavy fighting ensued in the first part of 2001. Meanwhile, the UN rejected a suggestion from the Taliban that bin Laden be tried in an Islamic country by Islamic religious leaders. Further complicating matters for the Taliban, Mullah Mohammad Rabbani, by then routinely referred to as chair of the Taliban's "council of ministers," died on April 15 of natural causes. Although he had been the architect of many of the harsh strictures imposed on the population by the Taliban, Rabbani had been viewed by the international community as more approachable than most of the other Taliban leaders. He was also generally well respected within Afghanistan for the prominent role he had played while a member of the Islamic Party in the mujahidin war against the Soviets. Most of Rabbani's duties were assumed by the vice chair of the ministerial council, Mohammed Hassan AKHUND, but no formal appointment to the chair was announced.

The Taliban launched a major attack against the Northern Alliance in June 2001 and once again appeared dedicated to the pursuit of a final, complete military victory. However, such hopes were irrevocably compromised by the terrorist attacks on September 11 in the United States, which the George W. Bush administration quickly determined to be the work of bin Laden's al-Qaida. Washington immediately demanded that bin Laden be turned over for prosecution or else military action would be initiated to remove him by force from Afghanistan. Intense debate was reported within the Taliban leadership on the issue, and efforts were made to forge a compromise under which, for example, bin Laden might be tried in a third country. However, President Bush declared the U.S. terms to be "nonnegotiable," and Mullah Omar finally decided that the Taliban would take a stand in defense of its "guest." Consequently, after having secured broad coalition support for the action, the United States, declaring that it was acting in self-defense, launched Operation Enduring Freedom on October 7 against al-Qaida and Taliban targets. By that time, it was clear that the assault was intended not only to destroy al-Qaida but also to produce a new regime in Afghanistan, Washington having concluded that al-Qaida and the Taliban were now "one and the same."

Heavy bombing by U.S. aircraft and cruise missiles quickly shattered the minimal infrastructure available to the Taliban military, while Omar's call on October 10 to the rest of the Muslim world for assistance in countering the U.S. invasion elicited little response. The attention of the military campaign shifted later in the month to bombing al-Qaida and Taliban troops in the north to support a ground assault by the Northern Alliance. After a disorganized start, the anti-Taliban forces, substantially rearmed and resupplied by the United States and its allies, assumed an offensive posture at the end of October and drove toward the capital with few setbacks, as many warlords previously aligned with the Taliban defected to the Northern Alliance. The first big prize, Mazar-i-Sharif, fell on November 9, and Kabul was surrounded by November 11. The swiftness of the Taliban collapse apparently surprised coalition military planners, and confusion reigned over how control of the capital would be achieved, U.S. policy-makers being aware of the complicated political overtones involved in the establishment of a new Afghan government. Despite apparent U.S. wishes to the contrary, the Northern Alliance moved into Kabul November 12–13, and the administration of Burhanuddin Rabbani announced it was reassuming authority, at least over the territory now controlled by the Northern Alliance.

Formal definition of the status of the Rabbani administration and governmental responsibility throughout the country overall remained ill-defined following the fall of Kabul, pending the results of a UN-sponsored conference that convened in Bonn, Germany, on November 27, 2001, to negotiate a power-sharing, post-Taliban government that would bridge the nation's myriad cleavages. In addition to UNIFSA/Northern Alliance officials, attendees at the conference included representatives from the so-called Rome Group (supporters of Afghanistan's former king, Mohammad Zahir Shah), the Peshawar Group (Afghan exiles who had been living in Pakistan), and a delegation of pro-Iranian refugees and exiles who had been centered in Cyprus. No Taliban officials were invited to participate.

Initial negotiations at the Bonn Conference proved difficult regarding the issues of proposed international peacekeepers for Afghanistan (opposed by the Northern Alliance) and the selection of the head of the planned interim government. A collapse of the talks appeared possible over the latter when it became apparent that the choice would not be Rabbani or the 84-year-old ex-king. However, the conference on December 3, 2001, agreed upon Hamid KARZAI, an obscure former deputy minister with U.S. backing. Karzai was formally appointed on December 5 as chair of an interim administration that would eventually include a 29-member cabinet that had been carefully crafted to include as broad an ethnic base as possible. The Bonn Declaration that concluded the conference on December 5 authorized the interim government for only six months, by which time an emergency *Loya Jirga* was to have established a new transitional government to prepare for free elections of a permanent government. The conference participants also agreed that a UN peacekeeping force would be stationed in Kabul, although details on its mandate and size were left for further negotiation.

Meanwhile, as plans for the installation of the interim administration proceeded, the military campaign against the remaining Taliban and al-Qaida forces continued unabated. After a sustained U.S. bombing campaign, the Taliban surrendered its last remaining stronghold in Kandahar to the UNIFSA/Northern Alliance on December 7, 2001, although Mullah Omar and a number of Taliban ministers escaped capture, perhaps as part of controversial secret negotiations. The air assault subsequently focused on the cave complexes in Tora Bora, southwest of Jalalabad, where it was estimated that as many as 1,700 al-Qaida and Taliban fighters may have died before the complex was overrun. However, bin Laden escaped, fleeing, apparently, to the remote tribal areas across the border in Pakistan.

Karzai and his interim cabinet were inaugurated on December 22, 2001, in a ceremony in Kabul that featured a role for Rabbani as "outgoing president." Notable attendees included General Dostam, who had earlier threatened to boycott the proceedings because he did not believe the Uzbek community was sufficiently represented in the government. On December 26 Dostam accepted a post as vice chair of the interim administration and deputy defense minister.

On January 10, 2002, final agreement was reached on the deployment of an International Security Assistance Force (ISAF), directed by the UN to assist in providing security in Kabul and surrounding areas but not to become involved outside that region. In May the mandate of the ISAF (comprising some 4,500 troops from 19 countries at that point) was extended for another six months, some Western leaders reportedly pressing for its eventual extension to other areas of the country. Meanwhile, U.S. ground forces (upwards of 7,000 strong) remained in Afghanistan to conduct mopping-up activities against remnants of the Taliban and al-Qaida. No timetable was set for withdrawal of the American troops.

Former king Zahir Shah, who had returned to Afghanistan in April, was given the honor of opening the emergency *Loya Jirga* in Kabul on June 12, 2002. On June 13 Karzai received about 80 percent of the votes against two minor candidates in the balloting for president of the new transitional government, all potential major opponents (including Zahir Shah) having removed themselves from contention. On its final day (June 19) the *Loya Jirga* also endorsed, by a show of hands, the partial cabinet announced by Karzai. However, the council adjourned without having made a decision on the makeup of a proposed transitional legislature. The transitional government was authorized to hold power for up to two years, with a constitutional *Loya Jirga* to be convened in approximately 18 months to adopt a new constitution that would provide the framework for new elections by June 2004.

In April 2003 President Karzai appointed a 33-member constitutional commission that in November drafted a new basic law calling for a multiparty system headed by a president with broad powers and a mostly elected bicameral legislature. A *Loya Jirga* approved the constitution, with modifications, on January 4, 2004 (see Constitution and government, below, for details). Although both presidential and legislative elections were initially scheduled for June 2004, they were postponed due to difficulties in completing voter registration and other electoral arrangements. Presidential balloting was finally held on October 9, with Karzai winning in the first round of balloting with 55.4 percent of the vote. Authority was formally transferred from the transitional administration upon Karzai's inauguration on December 7; Karzai appointed a new "reconstruction" cabinet on December 23. Balloting for the new National Assembly was held in the last quarter of 2005 (see Legislature, below), and most proposed members of a new cabinet were installed on May 2, 2006. However, five positions remained unfilled until August 7 due to objections within the *Wolesi Jirga* (dominated by conservatives) to the initial appointees. Friction between the legislative and executive branches intensified in May 2007 when the *Wolesi Jirga* attempted to impeach two of Karzai's ministers in the wake of the forced repatriation to Afghanistan of Afghan refugees in Iran. The Supreme Court subsequently ruled that the impeachments were invalid.

Constitution and government. Following their takeover of power in Kabul in September 1996, the Taliban quickly installed a six-member Provisional Council in Kabul that subsequently grew in stages into a full-fledged Council of Ministers. However, government decision-making authority appeared to remain in the hands of a small Taliban consultative council in Kandahar, the headquarters of the movement's spiritual leader (and emir of the Islamic Emirate of Afghanistan proclaimed in October 1997), Mullah Mohammad Omar, who served, among other things, as de facto head of state and commander in chief of the armed forces.

The constitution approved in January 2004 provided for a Western-style democracy with a strong central government headed by a popularly elected president (limited to two five-year terms) and a National Assembly (see Legislature, below, for details). The *Loya Jirga* (comprising the current members of the assembly and the chairs of the proposed elected provincial and district councils) was institutionalized as the "highest manifestation of the people of Afghanistan" and given full responsibility to amend the constitution, prosecute the president if necessary, and "make decisions relating to independence, national sovereignty, territorial integrity, and other supreme interests of the country." The new basic law enshrined Islam as the state religion but guaranteed freedom for other religions. Equal rights were guaranteed for men and women, as were freedoms of expression and association (see the introductory text under Political Parties and Groups, below, for details). Provisions were also made for an independent human rights commission and an independent judiciary headed by a Supreme Court comprising presidential appointees subject to confirmation by the lower house of the assembly. (The constitution called for a committee to be established to oversee the "implementation" of a Constitutional Court, but no action had been taken in that regard as of early 2009, despite regular confrontation between the legislature and the government on constitutional issues.)

The new constitution authorized the establishment of the Islamic Transitional State of Afghanistan pending what were expected to be simultaneous presidential and legislative elections. However, in view of the subsequent delay in holding assembly balloting, the transitional state was declared to have concluded with the inauguration in December 2004 of President Karzai to head the administration of the newly renamed Islamic Republic of Afghanistan. The process of "institution-creating" culminated in the election of provincial councils and the lower house of the new National Assembly on September 18, 2005 (see Legislature, below, for details).

Critics have become increasingly vocal recently in challenging the basic law, with its enshrinement of a strong presidential system, as "inappropriate" for dealing with the country's myriad ethnic and regional divisions. Northern groups that spearheaded the overthrow of the Taliban in particular have called for decentralization and reduction of presidential authority in favor of a parliamentary system.

Foreign relations. Afghan foreign policy historically reflected neutrality and nonalignment, but by the mid-1970s Soviet economic and military aid had become paramount. After the April 1978 coup, the Taraki government, while formally committed to a posture of "positive nonalignment," solidified relations with what was increasingly identified as "our great northern neighbor." Following what was, for all practical purposes, Soviet occupation of the country in late 1979, the Karmal regime asserted that Soviet troops had been "invited" because of the "present aggressive actions of the enemies of Afghanistan" (apparently an allusion to the United States, China, Pakistan, and Iran, among others)—a statement that proved unconvincing to most of the international community. The UN General Assembly called for the immediate and unconditional withdrawal of the Soviet forces, and many other international bodies supported the UN position. Most nations refused to recognize the Kabul regime; exceptions included India, which participated in a joint Indo-Afghan communiqué in early 1985 expressing concern about "the militarization of Pakistan."

In early 1986, following the accession to power in the Soviet Union of economy-conscious Mikhail Gorbachev, Moscow indicated a willingness to consider a timetable for withdrawal of its troops, conditioned on withdrawal of international support for the mujahidin. The signature of an Afghan-Pakistani agreement (guaranteed by the Soviet Union and the United States) called for mutual noninterference and nonintervention. Accompanying accords provided for the voluntary return of refugees and took note of a time frame established by Afghanistan and the Soviet Union for a "phased withdrawal of foreign troops" over a nine-month period commencing May 15. However, the agreements did not provide for a cease-fire, with both the United States and Pakistan reserving the right to provide additional military supplies to the Afghan guerrillas if Moscow continued to provide arms to Kabul.

In late 1990 the United States and the Soviet Union agreed on a policy of "negative symmetry," whereby both would cease supplying aid to their respective Afghan allies in expectation that the aid suspension would necessitate a cease-fire between the government and the rebels. Upon implementation of the mutual suspension in September 1991, even fundamentalist rebel leaders reportedly declared that they welcomed the end of foreign "interference." However, by early 1995 it was apparent that involvement by external powers had by no means ceased, although it was being conducted far less visibly than during the Najibullah era. Former students from Islamic seminaries in Pakistan launched the Taliban movement, with one observer initially characterizing the seminarians as "cannon fodder" in a Pakistani effort to reopen vital highway shipping routes to Tajikistan and beyond. Countering Pakistan's support of the Taliban was Indian aid to Rabbani and Masoud, particularly the provision of military aircraft that were crucial to the defense of Herat. For his part, General Dostam, the northern Uzbek warlord, had long been backed by Russia and Uzbekistan.

Washington initially exhibited a somewhat surprisingly warm stance toward the Taliban takeover in late 1996, reportedly out of the hope that it offered Afghanistan a chance for "stability" after 17 years of civil war. However, the U.S. posture cooled significantly during 1997 because of the Taliban's human rights record and harsh religious strictures, with U.S. secretary of state Madeleine Albright strongly criticizing the Taliban policies toward women. Meanwhile, Russia and members of the Commonwealth of Independent States (CIS), including Tajikistan and Uzbekistan, issued a stern warning to the Taliban in early 1997 not to attempt to spread militant fundamentalist influence beyond the Afghan borders. Collaterally, Iran displayed its support for the Shiite population in the Hazara region, which was aligned with the anti-Taliban forces.

During a regional tour in March 2006, U.S. president George W. Bush consulted with President Karzai and President Musharraf of Pakistan on the delicate issue of the perceived use of Pakistani border areas by remnants of al-Qaida and the Taliban. Karzai later in the year claimed that Pakistan was not doing enough to curb the insurgents, who had made significant advances in southern Afghanistan.

In April 2007 U.S. officials noted what they described as the "unhealthy" involvement by Iran in Afghanistan, asserting that Iranian weapons were finding their way into the hands of Taliban insurgents. Iran denied providing the weapons, and independent analysts questioned whether Iran, which had been strongly anti-Taliban in 2001, would now be supplying the Taliban. For his part, Iranian president Mahmoud Ahmedinejad visited Afghanistan for the first time in August, at which time he signed a number of cooperation agreements with the Afghan government and pledged significant reconstruction aid.

In October 2007 Jaap de Hoop Scheffer, the secretary general of the North Atlantic Treaty Organization (NATO), urged NATO members to increase their troop commitments in order to combat the strengthening insurgency in Afghanistan. U.S. officials subsequently echoed that sentiment, suggesting that some European NATO members were underestimating the magnitude of the threat that a "destabilized" Afghanistan would present to them. However, disagreement continued within the alliance, as several leading European governments maintained their stance that resources should be earmarked primarily for political and economic reconstruction rather than counterinsurgency.

The situation in Afghanistan remained a primary focus of NATO's attention into the first half of 2009, with the new Obama administration in the United States describing conditions as "extremely perilous." Although President Barack Obama received pledges for only a minor number of new troops, the European NATO members strongly supported his call for a regional strategy to contain disruptions in Afghanistan and Pakistan. In that vein, it was reported that President Karzai had established a good relationship with new Pakistani president Asif Ali Zardari, who had campaigned on an anti-Taliban platform.

Current issues. Most of Afghanistan appeared in late 2001 to celebrate the collapse of the Taliban government, which had imposed a "joyless existence" on the population and fostered extreme international isolation. The festive mood was tempered, however, by the knowledge that many of the important components of the new interim government had been part of the disastrous mujahidin regime in the first half of the 1990s that had created the opportunity for the Taliban to flourish in the first place. In addition, much of the country outside the capital remained under the control of warlords with very little inclination to acquiesce to a strong centralized government. The daunting task of maintaining stability under severe ethnic, regional, and religious strains fell to Hamid Karzai, a "moderate" Muslim whose emergence as the choice to head the interim administration had surprised most observers.

In May 2003 U.S. defense secretary Donald Rumsfeld declared that only "pockets of resistance" remained within Afghanistan and that reconstruction was the transitional administration's appropriate priority. However, a resurgence in the second half of the year of Taliban guerrilla attacks on U.S. and government forces killed hundreds. President Karzai also had to contend with outbreaks of fighting between various warlords' militias, many of whom were resisting the new UN/Afghan demobilization and disarmament campaign. When Karzai dropped Vice President Mohammad Qasim FAHIM (a northern commander) as a running mate for the 2004 presidential campaign, many of the northern tribal leaders threw their support to Mohammad Yunos QANUNI, who finished second in the balloting with 16.3 percent of the vote. As a result, the election revealed a continued north/south divide that still threatened national unity.

At his inauguration in December 2004, President Karzai pledged to combat the "mortal threat" of drug production and trafficking, to fight systemic poverty, and to promote "governmental accountability." Toward those ends, his new cabinet appeared to rely more heavily on technocrats than had his previous administration, although critics noted that most "power portfolios" remained in the hands of Pushtuns.

The frequency of rebel attacks remained relatively low for a number of months after the 2004 presidential poll, but the Taliban-led insurgency reintensified in the spring of 2005. In an apparently related vein, a special *Loya Jirga* endorsed Karzai's plan for a continued "strategic partnership" with the United States and NATO, although it was unclear if the final arrangements would include permanent U.S. military bases in Afghanistan.

The elections for the lower house of the National Assembly (*Wolesi Jirga*) and provincial councils in September 2005 received widespread international attention as a pivotal moment in the nation's democratization efforts. The successful candidates to the *Wolesi Jirga* represented a broad spectrum of the population, from mujahidin (including deeply conservative tribal leaders) to communists to reformists to former members of the Taliban. The *Wolesi Jirga* adopted an independent stance in April 2006, when under the leadership of Qanuni (narrowly elected speaker the previous December) it announced it would vote separately on each of Karzai's proposed cabinet appointments. (Five were subsequently rejected.)

As part of the Afghanistan Compact, negotiated with international donors, the administration in early 2006 agreed to improve human rights, combat corruption, eliminate illegal militias, counter the booming trade in narcotics, and "restore a functioning economy." Pledges were also made to triple the size of the Afghan army (from 24,000 in 2006 to 70,000 in 2009) and to establish a judiciary appointed on merit rather than tribal or religious status.

The Taliban guerrilla campaign continued into 2006, particularly in the south. (More than 1,600 people, including 60 Americans, died from conflict-related violence in 2005.) NATO (in command of the ISAF since August 2003) in early 2006 announced plans to increase the force from 8,500 to 16,000. Many of the new troops were to be deployed in the "volatile" south, a departure from the ISAF's previous primary role as a peacekeeping and security mission around Kabul and in "stable" northern regions. The U.S.-led Combined Forces Command Afghanistan formally transferred control of six southern provinces to NATO/ISAF at the end of July, and in October NATO assumed responsibility for security throughout the country. By that time the ISAF forces had grown to 31,000, including many U.S. soldiers previously under direct U.S. command. However, the United States retained control over some 8,000 of its troops for counterterrorism activities and for training Afghan soldiers and police.

In one of the bloodiest periods since the fall of the Taliban in 2001, Taliban guerrillas regained control of a number of southern villages in the second half of 2006, and the rate of suicide attacks escalated throughout the country. Some observers suggested that the Taliban movement was conducting an at least partially successful battle for the "hearts and minds" of southerners, who had reportedly been angered by the loss of civilian lives during NATO and U.S. military operations. Disagreement was reported within NATO over the degree of effort to be allocated toward the anti-insurgency campaign versus reconstruction, much of the population having reportedly grown pessimistic as a result of the lack of progress in the latter.

In view of deteriorating security, economic, and political conditions, President Karzai in June 2007 urged the Taliban and other rebel fighters to negotiate an end to the violence. However, guerrilla attacks continued, with armor-piercing explosives and improvised explosive devices inflicting increasingly greater damage on Afghan, NATO, and U.S. forces.

The Taliban insurgency intensified in 2007–2008, particularly in the south and east, despite several major anti-Taliban campaigns by the ISAF and Afghan troops. The UN estimated that 5,000 people (including 2,100 civilians) had died in 2008 as a result of the conflict, which was marked by numerous suicide attacks and roadside bombings. Some analysts suggested that half of the country was under Taliban "influence," although others said a more accurate figure would be 10 percent, with 30 percent under government control and the remainder ruled by warlords or other local leaders. Not surprisingly, the Karzai administration faced increasing criticism for its inability to restore order, curb corruption, slow opium production, or protect local officials and public servants from the insurgents' assassination campaign. Facing what pessimistic observers described as the prospect of Afghanistan becoming a "failed state," the United States pledged more troops, citing, among other things, the pressing need for proper training of the police forces, currently often dominated by local militias. U.S. forces also launched guided-munitions attacks against suspected Taliban sites inside Pakistan, while Afghan and Pakistani officials attempted to negotiate a joint approach to dealing with their troubled border region. Meanwhile, in November 2008, in what was considered another overture to the Taliban, President Karzai again offered to conduct peace talks with any group that "accepts the constitution."

The Taliban continued to exercise substantial control over the southern provinces in early 2009, while a spate of suicide bombings spread to Kabul and other cities throughout the country. With the level of violence at its highest since 2001, international pressure grew for negotiations toward a peace settlement with "moderate" elements within the Taliban. President Obama urged a comprehensive regional strategy to undercut support for militants in Afghanistan and Pakistan through diplomacy and development as well as enhanced military strength as needed. Obama ordered more than 20,000 additional U.S. troops to be deployed to Afghanistan, in part to provide additional security for presidential elections scheduled for August 20. Although President Karzai was still widely considered the front-runner in the presidential campaign, significant challenges were deemed possible from several of his former cabinet allies. *(See headnote.)*

POLITICAL PARTIES AND GROUPS

Resistance to the Taliban was coordinated at first by the Supreme Defense Council, formed in October 1996 by the Islamic Afghan Society, the National Front, and the Islamic Unity Party. The umbrella organization's name was changed to the United National Islamic Front for the Salvation of Afghanistan (UNIFSA) in mid-1997 to reflect the addition of new members (including the National Islamic Front) as well as expansion of the alliance's mandate to cover political as well as military initiatives. UNIFSA, with heavy U.S. military and financial support, spearheaded the overthrow of the Taliban in late 2001.

The new constitution approved in January 2004 provided for freedom of association, with political parties being authorized if they had no military or paramilitary structures and their platforms were not "contrary to the principles of Islam." Parties based on ethnicity, language, religious sects, or regions were also prohibited. Many small parties applied for legal status in 2004 and 2005, contributing to highly fluid and often confusing conditions in the run-up to the legislative balloting of September 2005. Some 80 parties were subsequently registered. However, party influence remained minimal, particularly in the *Wolesi Jirga,* where all candidates in the 2005 elections had technically run as independents.

National Understanding Front—NUF (*Jabha-i-Tafahon-i-Milli*). Launched in early 2005 by some 11 political parties, the NUF was described by one reporter as the "first attempt to forge a serious opposition" to the Karzai administration. NUF chair Mohammad Yunos Qanuni had finished second in the 2004 presidential poll after leaving his post as planning minister in the Karzai cabinet (see Current issues, above, for additional information).

The leaders of the NUF announced that their first goal was to achieve parliamentary power in the National Assembly balloting scheduled for September 2005. They accused the Karzai administration of having failed to combat corruption in government, indicated opposition to the presence of foreign troops in Afghanistan, and called for the adoption of a proportional voting system in the assembly. However, some observers described the Front as comprising "incongruous factions" that might lack sustained cohesion.

It was estimated the candidates aligned with the NUF gained 60–80 seats in the balloting for the *Wolesi Jirga* in 2005, thereby securing the front's position as the main opposition to the Karzai administration. Qanuni was subsequently elected as speaker of the *Wolesi Jirga,* after which he announced his resignation as chair of the NUF.

Leaders: Ahmad Shah AHMADZAY, Mohammad MOHAQEQ, Najia ZHARA, Mohammad Ali JAWID, Mustapha KAZEMI.

New Afghanistan Party (*Hizb-i-Afghanistan-i-Nawin*). Formed by Mohammad Yunos Qanuni in advance of his 2004 presidential campaign, this party was among the core components at the formation of the NUF. Qanuni, an ethnic Tajik, was considered the most formidable political rival to President Karzai.

Leader: Mohammad Yunos QANUNI (Speaker of the *Wolesi Jirga* and 2004 presidential candidate).

Islamic Unity Party of the People of Afghanistan (*Hizb-i-Wahdat-i-Islami Mardom-i-Afghanistan*). A primarily Shiite offshoot of the Islamic Unity Party, this organization is led by Mohammad Mohaqeq, a former member of the Karzai administration who left the government in 2004 in a dispute of unclear origin with President Karzai. Mohaqeq, an ethnic Hazara, finished third (as an independent) in the 2004 presidential election, with 11.7 percent of the vote. He was elected to the *Wolesi Jirga* in 2005.

Leader: Mohammad MOHAQEQ.

National Islamic Empowerment Party (*Hizb-i Iqtedar-i-Milli-Islami*). The formation of this party was reported in early 2006 under the leadership of Ahmad Shah Ahmadzay, a deputy chair of the NUF previously referenced as leader of the Islamic Power Party. Ahmadzay, a religious conservative, ran as an independent in the 2004 presidential election on a platform of opposition to the presence of U.S. forces in Afghanistan.

Leaders: Ahmad Shah AHMADZAY, Mustapha KAZEMI.

Other components of the NUF reportedly included the **Afghanistan Ethnic Unity Party** (*Hizb-i-Wahdat-i-Aqwam-i-Afghanistan*), led by Nasrullah BARAKZAI; the **Afghanistan National Independence Party** (*Hizb-i-Istiqlal-i-Milli Afghanistan*), led by Taj Mohammad WARDAK; the **Afghanistan Islamic Peace and Brotherhood Party** (*Hizb-i-Sulh wa Ukhwat-i-Islami Afghanistan*), led by Qadir Imami GHORI; a faction of the **Islamic Movement Party of Afghanistan** (*Hizb-i-Harakat-i-Islami-i-Afghanistan*), led by Mohammad Ali JAWID; a faction of the **Islamic Revolutionary Movement Party** (*Hizb-i-Harakat-i-Inqilah-i-Islami*), led by Ahmad NABI; the **National Islamic Party of Afghanistan** (*Hizb-i-Milli-Islami-i-Afghanistan*), led by Ustad Mohammad AKBARI and Rohullah LOUDIN; and the **New Islamic Party of Afghanistan** (*Hizb-i-Islami-i-Afghanistan Jawan*), led by journalist Sayed Jawad HUSSEINI.

Islamic Afghan Society (*Jamaat-i-Islami Afghanistan*). The Islamic Afghan Society draws most of its support from Tajiks in the northern part of the country. It was long the most effective rebel force in the Panjsher Valley, and it engaged in heavy combat with Soviet forces in 1985, including sporadic invasions of Soviet Tajikistan.

Internal disagreement over relations with the Islamic Party threatened to splinter *Jamaat* in 1990, when military commander Ahmed Shah Masoud temporarily parted company with political leader Burhanuddin Rabbani in rejecting an appeal to aid the Islamic Party's offensive against Kabul. In October, Masoud, long a leading military figure, gained additional prominence when he chaired a *shura* (assembly) of Afghan military chiefs.

Forces loyal to Rabbani fled from the Taliban offensive against Kabul in September 1996, subsequently coalescing under Masoud's command in the north, where, in conjunction with other anti-Taliban militias, they fought the Taliban to a stalemate. Masoud's forces were estimated to number 12,000–15,000 in the fall of 2001, having weathered heavy Taliban offensives during the summers of the past three years.

Masoud was killed in an attack by suicide bombers disguised as journalists on September 10, 2001. The assassination was widely attributed to al-Qaida as a prelude to the terrorist attacks in the United States the following day. Mohammad Qasim FAHIM, who became one of the top leaders in the subsequent expulsion of the Taliban, succeeded Masoud as military commander of the Northern Alliance.

Rabbani, whose government had maintained the recognition of many countries throughout the Taliban regime, returned to Kabul in mid-November 2001 to resume the exercise of presidential authority. He reportedly hoped that the subsequent Bonn Conference would appoint him as president of the proposed new interim administration, and he only reluctantly accepted the appointment of Hamid Karzai after holding up the conference for several days in apparent protest to being sidelined. Any remaining short-term political aspirations on Rabbani's part were also put on hold at the *Loya Jirga* in July 2002, where Rabbani endorsed Karzai's election as president of the new transitional government. Fahim, however, was named vice president and minister of defense, establishing himself as one of the administration's dominant figures. Rabbani supported Karzai in the 2004 presidential election even though Fahim was dropped from the Karzai ticket. Rabbani was elected to the *Wolesi Jirga* in 2005 and briefly campaigned for election as the speaker of that body before deferring to Yunos Qanuni.

In the spring of 2007 Rabbani spearheaded the formation of a new group—the **United National Front** (UNF), which brought together mujahidin, former communists, members of the royal family, and other diverse elements in pursuit of national unity, reconstruction, and establishment of a federal system under which governors and provincial councils would be directly elected and the national government would operate on a parliamentary rather than a presidential system. Members of the UNF reportedly included *Wolesi Jirga* speaker Qanuni, first vice president of the republic Ahmad Zia Masoud, Gen. Abdul Rashid Dostam (leader of the National Front [below] and a top military adviser to President Karzai), Mustapha Kazemi (a leader of the National Islamic Empowerment Party), representatives of the National Congress Party of Afghanistan, Mustapha ZAHIR (grandson of the former king), several cabinet members, and a number of legislators. The new grouping, primarily representing non-Pushtun northerners, immediately was perceived as the dominant political force in the *Wolesi Jirga*. It strongly supported a proposed national amnesty bill, not surprisingly considering the number of warlords and others with major roles in past conflicts involved in its formation. Saying that military defeat of the Taliban was impossible, Rabbani invited the Taliban and other antigovernment forces to lay down their arms and join the UNF in pursuit of national unity. Although the UNF remained formally supportive of President Karzai in early 2008, it subsequently instigated a legislative confrontation with the administration.

By early 2009 the UNF was considered likely to present the most significant challenge to Karzai in the presidential polling scheduled for August. In April, Vice President Masoud announced he would not be a candidate, observers suggesting that Dr. Abdullah ABDULLAH, a former minister of foreign affairs, had thereby become the most likely UNF nominee.

Leaders: Burhanuddin RABBANI (Former President of Afghanistan), Abdul Hafez MANSUR, Munawar HASAN (Secretary General).

National Front (*Jumbish-i-Milli*). The *Jumbish-i-Milli* is a primarily Uzbek grouping formed by Gen. Abdul Rashid Dostam, who had been a military commander in the Najibullah government before aligning himself with Ahmed Shah Masoud in 1992. In early 1994 Dostam broke with Masoud to join forces with Gulbuddin Hekmatyar's *Hizb-i-Islami* and Abdul Ali Mazari's *Hizb-i-Wahdat* in an anti-Rabbani alliance. He did not, however, support those groups in decisive encounters in March 1995, thereby contributing to their defeat. Following the Taliban takeover of Kabul in 1996, General Dostam initially played an important role in the anti-Taliban alliance (see Political background, above). However, it was reported that he and his remaining forces had retreated to Uzbekistan following the Taliban offensive of the second half of 1998, and his influence had declined significantly by mid-2000.

Dostam returned to Afghanistan in March 2001 and rejoined the Northern Alliance. The general subsequently remained closely aligned with Burhanuddin Rabbani during the overthrow of the Taliban and strongly objected to the selection at the Bonn Conference of Hamid Karzai over Rabbani as president of the new interim government in December. Initially, it appeared that Dostam's disgruntlement would prove a threat to stability, but he accepted positions as vice chair of the interim administration and deputy minister of defense in late December, thereby calming the situation. General Dostam, burdened with a reputation for military ruthlessness and political shiftiness, was not included in the July 2002 cabinet.

Running as an independent, Dostam finished fourth in the 2004 presidential poll, with 10 percent of the vote. In April 2005 he became the chief of staff of the high command of the armed forces in Karzai's administration, seen as a largely symbolic post. However, in early 2007 he joined the UNF (above), which called for a reduction in presidential authority. Dostam's supporters subsequently had a number of confrontations with government officials, and several Tajik ministers were removed from the cabinet in 2008.

Leaders: Gen. Abdul Rashid DOSTAM, Azizullah KARQAR, Sayyed NUROLLAH, Faysollah ZAKI, Abdul Majid ROZI.

Islamic Unity Party of Afghanistan (*Hizb-i-Wahdat-i-Islami Afghanistan*). The *Hizb-i-Wahdat* was launched in mid-1987 by eight Iran-based groups. (See the list in the 2008 *Handbook.*) Also known as the Tehran Eight, the group claimed at its inception to represent an estimated two million Shiite Afghan refugees in Iran. During 1992 and early 1993 it joined with Hekmatyar's *Hizb-i-Islami* in a number of clashes with Rabbani's *Jamaat-i-Islami* and the Saudi-backed *Ittihad-i-Islami. Hizb-i-Wahdat*'s principal leader, Abdul Ali MAZARI, was killed on March 13, 1995, reportedly in a helicopter crash south of Kabul after having been captured by the Taliban militia.

Hizb-i-Wahdat was an important component of UNIFSA in that it represented the Hazara Shiite community in central Afghanistan. As of early 1998 the Hazaras were reportedly exercising autonomous government control in the Hazarajat region while contributing substantially to the anti-Taliban military alliance in the north. However, Taliban forces pushed *Hizb-i-Wahdat* out of most of the populated areas in the region (including the important city of Bamiyan) in September 1998. In consonance with the ouster of the Taliban by the UNIFSA/Northern Alliance in late 2001, *Hizb-i-Wahdat* regained control of much of central Afghanistan, and party leader Karim Khalili was named as a vice president in the transitional government installed in June 2002. He was elected as second vice president of the republic in 2004.

Leaders: Karim KHALILI (Second Vice President of the Republic), Ayatollah FAZL.

National Islamic Front (*Mahaz-i-Milli-i-Islami*). The most left-leaning of the moderate groups, the National Islamic Front had refused to join the Supreme Council in 1981 because not all of the participants had agreed to the election of people's representatives to a provisional government. In November 1990 party leader Pir Sayed Ahmad Gailani endorsed a reported U.S.-Soviet peace plan that would have left the Najibullah regime in power after the two countries withdrew their support for the combatants. Thereafter, at a meeting in Geneva, Switzerland, Gailani allegedly turned down an offer by Najibullah to assume control of the government, suggesting instead the return of Mohammad Zahir Shah, the former monarch.

Gailani, the spiritual leader of the Sufi Muslims, served in the Rabbani cabinet from 1992 to 1996, he and his supporters relocating to Cyprus following the Taliban takeover. They subsequently served as the core component of the so-called Cyprus Group at the 2001 Bonn Conference, where the front continued to display a proroyalist orientation. Gailani was elected chair of a prominent faction in the *Meshrano Jirga* in 2007.

Leader: Pir Sayed Ahmad GAILANI.

Islamic Party (*Hizb-i-Islami*). Drawing most of its support from Pushtuns in the southeastern part of the country, the Islamic Party was one of the largest and most radical of the mujahidin groups and often engaged in internecine clashes with former allies including, most notably, the *Jamaat-i-Islami.* Its principal leader, Gulbuddin Hekmatyar, was known to have ties to both Iran and Libya in the 1970s and early 1980s, although they subsequently were believed to have weakened.

Hekmatyar was named prime minister following an all-party accord in March 1993 but was at that stage deeply opposed to the Rabbani presidency; Hekmatyar's appointment lapsed in mid-1994. Thereafter, his supporters maintained a partial siege of Kabul until forced to withdraw after a decisive defeat in March 1995. This experience eventually impelled Hekmatyar to break ranks with other mujahidin leaders by reaching his own accommodation with the government in May 1996, enabling him to resume the premiership from June until the overthrow of the government in September. Hekmatyar's decision to align his forces with those of Ahmed Shah Masoud and General Dostam was considered an important factor in their subsequent ability to stall the Taliban offensive in the north in 1997. However, Hekmatyar and the Islamic Party were described in 1998 as only nominally associated with UNIFSA and apparently not playing a major role in the remaining military opposition to the Taliban. Interviewed in Iran in mid-2000, Hekmatyar called on the Taliban to establish a provisional government including opposition representatives pending national elections, describing the civil war as benefiting only "foreign forces."

In the fall of 2001 Hekmatyar adopted a strongly anti–Northern Alliance stance and urged support for the Taliban against a U.S. invasion. Hekmatyar returned to Afghanistan in early 2002 but remained noticeably outside the negotiations toward a government of national unity. Considered a threat to the stability of the interim administration, Hekmatyar was reportedly the target of an unsuccessful assassination attempt in May on the part of the United States through the use of an unmanned, aerial drone. Hekmatyar subsequently reportedly fled to Iran, but he was eventually expelled from that country. Having returned to Afghanistan, he was labeled a terrorist because of attacks on U.S. and Afghan forces. In early 2005 it appeared that some Islamic Party adherents had begun peace negotiations with the Karzai administration, although Hekmatyar (who rejected an apparent amnesty offer) and others remained committed to jihad (holy war) until U.S. forces were removed from Afghanistan and an "Islamic system" was installed.

Party members opposed to Hekmatyar's hard line participated (reportedly with some success) in the 2005 legislative balloting. Meanwhile, an arrest warrant reportedly remained in effect for Hekmatyar, while his supporters, now considered allied with the Taliban (and possibly al-Qaida) and reportedly sometimes operating out of Pakistan, participated in attacks on government and NATO forces in the north in 2006–2007. There were reports in 2008 of negotiations between the Karzai administration and Hekmatyar regarding a possible cessation of hostilities.

Leaders: Gulbuddin HEKMATYAR (Former Prime Minister), Mohammad Yunos KHALES, Haroun ZARGHUN.

Islamic Unity (*Ittihad-i-Islami*). Ultra-orthodox Sunni Muslims backed by Saudi Arabia formed the *Ittihad-i-Islami.* Like the other fundamentalist formations, it long opposed Westernizing influences in pursuing what it viewed largely as an Islamic holy war against Soviet-backed forces. One of its leaders, Abdul Rasul Sayaf, headed the Islamic Alliance of Afghan Holy Warriors at its inception in 1985.

The party endorsed President Karzai in the 2004 presidential campaign. Subsequently, Sayaf, described as an "archconservative," was elected to the *Wolesi Jirga* in 2005 and was only narrowly defeated for the speaker's position. (Reports have differed on Sayaf's recent formal party affiliation.)

Leader: Abdul Rasul SAYAF (Former Prime Minister of Government-in-Exile).

National Liberation Front (*Jabh-i-Nijat-i-Milli*). The National Liberation Front was formed to support Afghan self-determination and the establishment of a freely elected government. Its leader, Sibghatullah Mojadedi, was chair of the moderate opposition bloc in the late 1980s. Subsequently, Mojadedi served as interim president from April to June 1992, before becoming a prominent opponent of the succeeding Rabbani government. Immediately following the Taliban takeover of Kabul in September 1996, it was reported that Mojadedi had announced his support for the new government. However, he was subsequently described as having moved to Egypt, from where he was "abstaining" from the conflict between the Taliban and its opponents. Mojadedi supported Hamid Karzai in the 2004 presidential campaign and was later named chair of the fledgling national reconciliation commission. He was also elected as speaker of the *Meshrano Jirga* in late 2005.

Leaders: Imam Sibghatullah MOJADEDI (Former President of Government-in-Exile and Speaker of the *Meshrano Jirga*), Dr. Hashimatullah MOJADEDI.

Homeland Party (*Hizb-i-Watan*). Previously known as the People's Democratic Party of Afghanistan (PDPA), which dominated national political affairs during the late 1970s and most of the 1980s (see Political background, above), the Homeland Party adopted its new name at its second congress in June 1990. Although not formally dissolved following the fall of the pro-Soviet regime, the group's subsequent activity was limited to meetings of international communist organizations. It was reported in 2003 that the interim government had refused a request from the Homeland Party for legal status, and party adherents subsequently appeared to have launched several new groupings. Former PDPA members reportedly participated in the formation of the UNF in 2007.

National Solidarity Movement of Afghanistan (*Nahzat-i Hambastagi-i Milli Afghanistan*). This party is led by Ishaq Gailani, who was a candidate for president in 2004 prior to withdrawing in support of Hamid Karzai.

Leader: Ishaq GAILANI.

Afghan Nation (*Afghan Mellat*). Established during the reign of King Zahir Shah in support of Pushtun nationalism, this grouping (also referenced as the Social Democratic Party of Afghanistan) reportedly factionalized in the early 2000s. One faction, which supported Hamid Karzai in the 2004 presidential campaign, is led by Anwar al-Haq Ahadi, who was named minister of finance in the December 2004 cabinet.

Leader: Anwar al-Haq AHADI (President).

National Congress Party of Afghanistan (*Hizb-i Kongra-i Milli-i Afghanistan*). This party was launched in April 2004 in support of the presidential candidacy of moderate Abdul Latif Pedram, who finished fifth in the October poll with 1.37 percent of the vote. Pedram, a former journalist and professor, proposed the establishment of a federal system in Afghanistan.

Leaders: Abdul Latif PEDRAM, Nasir OJABER.

National Movement of Afghanistan (*Hizb-i Nahzat-i Milli-i Afghanistan*). Primarily supported by Tajiks, *Nahzat* was launched by Ahmad Wali Masoud following the death of his brother, Ahmed Shah Masoud, the legendary mujahidin military leader. The party factionalized in 2004 when *Nahzat* member Yunos Qanuni ran against Hamid Karzai in the 2004 presidential campaign, while another Masoud brother, Ahmad Zia Masoud, was one of Karzai's vice presidential running mates.

Leaders: Ahmad Wali MASOUD (Party Leader), Ahmad Zia MASOUD (Vice President of the Republic).

Other recently launched parties include the **Afghanistan Independence Party** (*Hizb-i-Istiqlal-i Afghanistan*), led by Ghulam Faruq NEJRABI, who won 0.3 percent of the vote in the 2004 presidential poll on a platform that rejected all "direct or indirect influence" on the part of "foreigners," including aid organizations; the **Democracy and Progress Movement of Afghanistan** (*Nahzat-i-Faragir-i Democracy wa Taraqi-i-Afghanistan*), led by Mohammad BUZGAR; the **Freedom Party** (*Hizb-i Azadi*), led by Gen. Abdul MALEK, a former leader of the National Front; the **Islamic Justice Party of Afghanistan** (*Hizb-i Adalat-i Islami-i Afghanistan*), which, under the leadership of Mohammad Kabir MARZBAN, also supported President Karzai in the 2004 campaign; the **National Awareness and Deliverance Movement of Afghanistan** (*Hizb-i Nahzet-i Bedari Milli Falah-i Afghanistan*), launched in late 2007 by a group of national legislators and government officials under the leadership of Mohammad Yasin HABIB; the **National Freedom Seekers Party** (*Hizb-i Azadi Khwahan-i Maihan*), led by Abdul Hadi DABIR, an independent presidential candidate in 2004; the **National Movement for Peace** (*Jumbish-i Milli-i Solk*), led by Shahnawaz TANAY, a former defense minister in the Communist regime; **National Need**, formed in February 2008 to focus on women's rights under the leadership of legislator Fatima NAZARI; the **National Party** (*Hizb-i Milli*), led by Abdul Rashid ARYAN, a former member of the PDPA and member of the cabinet during Communist rule; the **National Unity Movement** (*Tabrik-i-Wahdat-i Milli*), led by Mahmud GHAZI and Homayun Shah ASEFI; the **People's Islamic Movement of Afghanistan** (*Harakat-i Islami-i Mardon-i Afghanistan*), led by Hosayn ANWARI, the minister of agriculture in the transitional government; the **Republican Party** (*Hizb-i Jamhuri Khwahan*), led by Sebghatullah SANJAR, who supported Hamid Karzai in the 2004 presidential election; and the **Youth Solidarity Party of Afghanistan** (*Hizb-i-Hambastagi-i Milli-i Jawanan-i Afghanistan*), which, under the leadership of Mohammed Jamil KARZAI, supported President Karzai in the 2004 election.

Movement Formerly in Power:

Taliban. Translated as "seekers" or "students," the Persian *taliban* was applied to a group of Islamic fundamentalist theology students from Pakistan who swept through southern Afghanistan during late 1994 in a campaign pledged to rid the country of its contending warlords and introduce "genuine" Islamic rule. In a statement issued in connection with U.S. congressional hearings on Afghanistan in June 1996, the Taliban movement listed its basic demands as including the resignation of President Rabbani, the demilitarization of Kabul, the formation of a national security force, and the convening of an elected assembly of the Afghan people charged with forming "a national Islamic government." The group's seizure of power in Kabul three months later gave it the opportunity to implement this program. Previous assessment of the Taliban as espousing a less ferocious brand of fundamentalism than the ousted regime was speedily revised in light of its imposition of strict Islamic law (sharia) and summary execution of opponents.

The Taliban militia launched several offensives in late 1996 and 1997 designed to win complete control of the country but was unable to defeat opposition forces in the north or maintain command of the Hazara region west of Kabul. In part, resistance to the Taliban was based on ethnicity or religion: in the north the opposition militias comprised Uzbeks and Tajiks, who had long been wary of domination by Pushtuns (the core Taliban ethnic group), while the Hazara-Taliban split pitted Shiite versus Sunni Muslims. Despite international criticism, the Taliban leaders in 1997 exhibited little moderation in their harsh interpretation of sharia, described as "medieval" by some observers, particularly regarding strictures on women. Meanwhile, the Taliban's spiritual guide, Mullah Mohammad Omar, was described as a reclusive leader who rarely left Kandahar (where the movement was launched) and who, following Taliban interpretation of religious law, never permitted himself to be photographed. A small consultative council located in Kandahar reportedly advised Omar.

Although the Taliban nearly succeeded in the first half of 2001 in efforts to push opposition forces completely out of Afghanistan, the regime's fortunes reversed dramatically as the result of the terrorist attacks in the United States in September. Washington quickly blamed the al-Qaida network of Osama bin Laden (see below) for the hijackings and demanded that the Taliban turn their "guest" over for prosecution or face U.S. military intervention. Although some Taliban leaders reportedly argued that the U.S. demand should be met, Omar and other hard-liners refused and thereby sealed the movement's fate. Following the Taliban's final military defeat at the hands of the Northern Alliance in late December, Omar and a number of Taliban ministers were reported to have fled to Pakistan.

Although many observers predicted the total collapse of the Taliban in the wake of its fall from power, the movement subsequently regrouped and launched a series of deadly guerrilla attacks against U.S. troops and the new Afghan army. Mullah Omar, believed at that point to be operating as the head of a ten-man Taliban leadership council, called for a jihad against all foreign forces and vowed to "punish" Afghans who supported the Karzai administration. The Taliban failed in an announced plan to disrupt the October 2004 presidential election but intensified attacks in mid-2005, apparently in an effort to complicate the upcoming legislative balloting. Although some former Taliban leaders by that time reportedly had entered into negotiations with the government toward a possible peace settlement, Mullah Omar maintained his hard line, rejecting an apparent amnesty offer from administration representatives. Some reports attributed the 2005 attacks to a "Neo-Taliban," while it was also clear that several Taliban splinter groups were operating, raising questions about the cohesiveness and precise leadership of the movement. Meanwhile, the United States, convinced of Mullah Omar's ties to al-Qaida, continued to offer a $10 million reward for his capture.

Several former Taliban commanders were reportedly elected to the *Wolesi Jirga* in September 2005, while a number of other former members of the movement had reportedly been released from custody in return for their commitment to "peace." Nevertheless, attacks attributed to the Taliban grew in number in late 2005 and early 2006, most of them emulating the roadside bombings and suicide attacks so prevalent in Iraq at that time. By then the Taliban movement was described as having significant ties to drug smuggling and was characterized as still representing a significant "menace" in parts of southern Afghanistan.

The Taliban insurgency, fueled by the use of sophisticated new weaponry, escalated steadily for the remainder of 2006 and the first half of 2007, resulting in the takeover (sometimes temporarily) by the Taliban of a number of villages and other rural areas in the south. Afghan, NATO, and U.S. officials alleged that Taliban forces were operating with impunity out of remote border areas in Pakistan. Western analysts estimated the Taliban's strength in 2006 at 6,000 fighters (up from 2,000 only a year earlier), while the Taliban claimed control of 12,000 fighters. In early 2007 Omar said he had not seen bin Laden since 2001 and indicated the Taliban had no direct alliance with al-Qaida, other than the shared goal of the expulsion of foreign forces from Afghanistan. The Taliban leader again refused an invitation to peace talks with the Karzai administration.

Mullah DADULLAH, described as the Taliban's senior military commander in Afghanistan, was killed in a NATO/government attack in May 2007. He was apparently succeeded by his brother, Mansur DADULLAH, who was reported in December to have been removed from his post by Mullah Omar in a policy dispute.

President Karzai reportedly offered cabinet posts to Taliban leaders in late 2007 in return for a cease-fire, prompting mixed responses from the insurgents. Meanwhile, the Taliban, responsible for the kidnapping of a group of South Korean missionaries in mid-2007, continued the campaign of suicide bombing into early 2008. In March Taliban leaders clearly indicated that their single goal was the exit of U.S.-led forces from Afghanistan and that the movement sought "positive relations" with neighboring countries, including Iran, and would consider negotiations with the Karzai administration. The announcement appeared to underscore a schism between at least some of the Taliban and al-Qaida, supporters of the latter having criticized the Taliban for a perceived lack of fervor in regard to "global jihad." The Taliban faction led by Jalaluddin Haqqani and his son, Sirajuddin HAQQANI, subsequently announced its "brotherly ties" with al-Qaida. Supporters of the Haqqanis reportedly were responsible for much of the insurgency in southeastern Afghanistan, apparently benefitting from the use of bases in Pakistan, where several Taliban branches were operating, including one led by Baitullah Mehsud. (For additional information on Taliban activities in Pakistan, see the section on the *Tehrik-e Taliban Pakistan* under Political Parties and Groups in the article on Pakistan.) Meanwhile, Taliban attacks continued in Afghanistan into early 2009, the movement's success apparently prompting the Karzai administration to offer more olive branches to "moderate" Taliban supporters. At that point, some analysts concluded that a significant percentage of the Taliban rank and file might be interested in a negotiated peace settlement. In addition, it was reported that areas recently placed under Taliban control were not being subjected to social constraints as strict as those imposed by the earlier Taliban administration.

Leaders: Mullah Mohammad OMAR (Spiritual Leader and Former Emir of the Self-proclaimed Islamic Emirate of Afghanistan), Laftullah HAKIMI (Self-proclaimed Spokesperson for the "Neo-Taliban"), Qari Mohammad Yousuf AHMADI, Muhammad HANIF, Jalaluddin HAQQANI (Military Commander).

Terrorist Group:

Al-Qaida (The Base). Al-Qaida is the network established in the 1990s by Osama bin Laden in pursuit of his goal of getting U.S. forces out of Saudi Arabia. Bin Laden, a member of one of the wealthiest Saudi families, had participated personally and financially in the mujahidin guerrilla campaign against Soviet forces in Afghanistan. Having returned to his native land following the Soviet withdrawal from Afghanistan in 1989, bin Laden subsequently focused his fundamentalist fervor on the buildup of U.S. forces in Saudi Arabia in connection with the invasion of Kuwait by Iraqi forces and the subsequent Desert Storm counterattack. Bin Laden reportedly urged the Saudi royal family to reject the U.S. forces, and he adopted an antimonarchical stance when his recommendations were rebuffed. In 1991 bin Laden moved his operations to Sudan, his attacks on the Saudi government becoming more scathing after he was stripped of his citizenship in 1995 for "irresponsible behavior," a reference to his having made large sums of money available to militant Islamic causes in a number of countries.

Under heavy pressure from the United States, the Sudanese government expelled bin Laden in 1996, and he established a base in Afghanistan, where he reportedly helped to finance the Taliban takeover. Bin Laden also declared war on the "occupying American enemy" in Saudi Arabia, which he blamed for the perceived repression and corruption on the part of the Saudi government.

In February 1998 al-Qaida joined with several other regional militant organizations to form an International Islamic Front, which urged Arabs to kill "Americans and their allies" until U.S. "hegemony" in the Gulf was dismantled. U.S. officials subsequently accused bin Laden's "terrorist network" of masterminding the embassy bombings in Kenya and Tanzania on August 7, and American cruise missiles attacked suspected bin Laden camps in Afghanistan two weeks later. Several alleged supporters of bin Laden were arrested in the United States on conspiracy and terrorism charges later in the year, while bin Laden was indicted in absentia. An Afghan court ruled in November that Washington had failed to present credible evidence of bin Laden's guilt; he was therefore permitted to remain in Afghanistan, although the government officially cautioned him against using his base there to coordinate terrorist activity in other countries.

In March 2000 Jordan announced the arrest of some 28 alleged bin Laden followers on charges of conspiring to conduct a terrorist campaign in the kingdom. Arrests were subsequently also made in the United Kingdom and Germany in what officials described as an international crackdown on groups affiliated with the bin Laden network. Four of his alleged associates were charged in connection with the 1998 embassy bombings (they were subsequently sentenced to life in prison), and al-Qaida was also considered at the time a prime suspect in the bombing of the USS *Cole* in Yemen in October 2000 (see article on Yemen for details).

Immediately following the terrorist attacks in the United States on September 11, 2001, Washington described bin Laden as the mastermind of the conspiracy that had left nearly 3,000 Americans dead. The U.S. government unsuccessfully pressed the Taliban government to turn over bin Laden and his associates for prosecution before launching Operation Enduring Freedom in Afghanistan and its "war on terrorism" throughout the world. A reward of $25 million was offered for bin Laden, U.S. president George W. Bush declaring the al-Qaida leader would be brought to justice "dead or alive."

Al-Qaida forces fought alongside the Taliban army against advances by the Northern Alliance from October to December 2001, most analysts concluding that al-Qaida had become the main financial backer of the Taliban and its strongest military component. Mohammed ATEF, an al-Qaida military commander, was killed in a November 14 U.S. air strike, and many al-Qaida fighters died during heavy bombing of their cave complex in Tora Bora in the second half of December. Most analysts subsequently concluded that bin Laden had escaped to the "anarchic tribal areas" of western Pakistan along with a number of other al-Qaida leaders, one of whom—Abu ZUBAYDAH—was captured in Pakistan in March 2002 and turned over to the United States. Even though al-Qaida had obviously suffered major losses at the hands of U.S. forces, the international community remained extremely wary of the group's ongoing potential to conduct new terrorist activity. Underscoring the breadth of al-Qaida's appeal to a certain segment of the Muslim population, it was reported that the alleged al-Qaida prisoners being held by the United States at the Guantánamo Bay naval base had come from more than 40 countries.

In early 2003 a purported audiotape from bin Laden called upon all Muslims to fight against any U.S.-led action in Iraq, although the tape also described Iraqi president Saddam Hussein and his administration as "apostates." In March U.S. officials announced that more than half of al-Qaida's "senior operatives" had been killed or captured, including Khalid Shaikh MOHAMMAD (considered one of the masterminds of the September 11, 2001, attacks on the United States), who was arrested in Pakistan. (In March 2007 Mohammad confessed to his role in the U.S. attacks and some 30 other terrorist operations around the world, although skeptics wondered if the confession had been unduly affected by his treatment in U.S. custody.) U.S. forces continued their assault on al-Qaida along the border with Pakistan in mid-2003, Pakistan having also sent soldiers to its side of the border to apply similar pressure. In response, in September Ayman al-Zawahiri (reportedly bin Laden's top lieutenant—see Holy War under Illegal Groups in the article on Egypt for additional information) urged Pakistanis to overthrow President Pervez Musharraf. Two assassination attempts against Musharraf were reported late in the year.

In April 2004 another bin Laden tape suggested that al-Qaida would no longer support terrorist attacks in Europe if European governments agreed to remove their military forces from Iraq and Afghanistan. (Many observers had suggested a possible link between al-Qaida and the train bombing in Madrid, Spain, the previous month.) The European leaders immediately rejected the "offer," although political events in Spain were dramatically affected by the train attacks (see article on Spain).

In June 2004, in response to the killing of a kidnapped American, Saudi Arabian security forces killed several leaders of a group calling itself "al-Qaida in the Arabian Peninsula," including Abdelaziz Issa Abdul-Mohson al-MUQRIN. At the same time, followers of Abu Musab al-ZARQAWI, a Jordanian militant heading a group called Tawhid, were reportedly conducting many of the insurgent attacks against U.S. and Iraqi targets in Iraq. Consequently, questions were raised concerning the extent to which bin Laden exercised control over al-Qaida adherents in particular and militant Islamists in general. However, in October al-Zarqawi declared his allegiance to bin Laden, who subsequently endorsed al-Zarqawi as the al-Qaida leader in Iraq. (See article on Iraq for further information on the campaign conducted in Iraq under al-Zarqawi's purported leadership.)

Bombings in Egypt and London in July 2005 were considered by some observers to have links to al-Qaida. Subsequently, al-Zarqawi claimed direct responsibility for a series of bombings in Jordan in November as part of an apparent campaign to broaden his campaign beyond Iraq. (Some reports referred to al-Zarqawi's group as "al-Qaida in Mesopotamia.") However, a degree of friction was reported between al-Zarqawi and al-Zawahiri over al-Zarqawi's apparent endorsement of attacks on Shiites in Iraq and the beheading of hostages. For most of 2005 al-Zawahiri served as the primary al-Qaida spokesperson outside of Iraq, conducting what was described as a "political" campaign to gain greater support throughout the Muslim world. Among other things, al-Zawahiri was the target of a U.S. missile attack on a Pakistani village in January 2006. Meanwhile, Pakistani authorities insisted that Abu Hamza RABIA, described as "number three" in the al-Qaida hierarchy, had been killed in December by Pakistani security forces.

An audiotape released in December 2005 represented the first apparent public message from bin Laden in a year. The tape reportedly offered a vague truce to the United States if all U.S. troops were withdrawn from

Afghanistan and Iraq. Washington immediately dismissed the proposal, announcing it would never "negotiate" with al-Qaida. The United States continued to proclaim that al-Qaida was in complete disarray, despite bin Laden's pledge that additional major attacks were being planned. Most analysts concluded that bin Laden and al-Zawahiri remained "deeply hidden" in the Pakistani border area as of spring 2006. Al-Zarqawi was killed in a U.S. air strike in Iraq in June.

Bin Laden subsequently accused the United States of "waging war against Islam," and al-Zawahiri in mid-2006 urged Afghans to "rise up" against the "infidel invaders," i.e., U.S. and NATO forces. It was widely accepted that al-Qaida subsequently continued to operate out of the "lawless tribal areas" of Pakistan. However, al-Qaida also intensified its efforts to serve as an umbrella organization for Islamic militants in other countries in the Middle East, East Africa, North Africa, and other regions. Among other things, a "merger" was announced in September between al-Qaida and the Salafist Group for Preaching and Combat in Algeria, which was later renamed the al-Qaida Organization in the Islamic Maghreb (see Illegal Groups in article on Algeria for details). Al-Qaida later was believed to be seeking affiliation with "franchises" in Kashmir, Lebanon, Libya, Somalia, Syria, and other places. Some analysts suggested that al-Qaida was moving away from an emphasis on direct action of its own and toward pursuing broader ideological influence on small local movements, supported by increasingly effective use of media technology and the Internet. However, in early 2007 UK terrorism experts warned that al-Qaida was still capable of "devastating attacks" and that its networks, now apparently "radiating" from "secure hideouts" in Pakistan, remained "incredibly resilient." Al-Zawahiri pledged that anti-U.S. attacks would increase unless U.S. forces ceased military action in Muslim countries. He also criticized the leaders of Egypt for "collaborating" with the United States and Israel.

U.S. forces attacked suspected al-Qaida targets in Somalia in early 2007 in conjunction with the entry of Ethiopian forces into that country to support the Somali government against Islamic militants. Over the next year arrests related to al-Qaida conspiracies were reported in Morocco, Kenya, Jordan, Italy, the United Kingdom, Yemen, Germany, Austria, Denmark, Azerbaijan, Turkey, and Belgium, while several attacks in Algeria, Yemen, and Mauritania were attributed to al-Qaida sympathizers. Al-Qaida was also described at the end of the year as "fortifying" its connections with antigovernment militants in Pakistan, bin Laden having called for the overthrow of the "infidel" President Musharraf.

In early 2008 analysts pointed out the "robust media and propaganda capability" of al-Qaida, which was increasingly relying on audio- and videotape recordings for recruitment. Much of that campaign was aimed at young people in Iraq, although al-Qaida supporters in that country had come under significant pressure from former Sunni insurgent groups who had realigned themselves with U.S. forces.

Shortly after being inaugurated in early 2009, U.S. president Barack Obama declared that his administration would give priority to efforts to "disrupt, dismantle, and defeat al-Qaida in Pakistan and Afghanistan," and in April U.S. drone missiles attacked suspected al-Qaida sites in Pakistan. Meanwhile, al-Qaida reiterated its support for militant groups in Sudan, Somalia, and other parts of the Horn of Africa.

Leaders: Osama BIN LADEN, Ayman al-ZAWAHIRI.

LEGISLATURE

Following the overthrow of the Taliban in late 2001, an "emergency" *Loya Jirga* (Grand National Council) was held June 12–19, 2002, as authorized by the Bonn Conference of November–December 2001, to establish a transitional government. The *Loya Jirga* comprised more than 1,500 delegates, about two-thirds of whom were indirectly elected to represent various civic, business, academic, and religious organizations. The remaining delegates were selected by a special commission (appointed as part of the Bonn agreement) to represent minority groups and women.

A new *Loya Jirga* convened in December 2003 to consider a new proposed constitution drafted by a constitutional commission appointed by President Karzai in April. The *Loya Jirga* comprised 500 delegates—450 elected by representatives of the previous *Loya Jirga* and 50 appointed by the president. As approved on January 4, 2004, the new constitution provided for a bicameral **National Assembly** (*Shoray-i-Milli*).

House of Elders (*Meshrano Jirga*). The upper house comprises 102 members: 34 indirectly elected for three-year terms by provincial councils; 34 appointed by the president for five-year terms; and (eventually) 34 indirectly elected by district councils for four-year terms. The first elections to the 34 provincial councils were held on September 18, 2005, and those councils subsequently each elected one permanent member of the *Meshrano Jirga* from among its ranks. In addition, the provincial councils each elected a temporary delegate to the *Meshrano Jirga* to serve on an interim basis in the place of the members slated to be elected by district councils. (Due to difficulties in establishing final boundaries for the proposed districts, balloting for the district councils was postponed.) The upper house convened for the first time on December 19, following the announcement of President Karzai's appointments. (Among other things, the president is required to ensure that there are at least 17 women in the *Meshrano Jirga,* as well as 2 Kuchi representatives and 2 representatives of the disabled population.)

Speaker: Iman Sibghatullah MOJADEDI.

House of the People (*Wolesi Jirga*). The lower house of the assembly comprises 249 members who are directly elected for a five-year term in single-round balloting. Each of the country's 34 provinces has 2 or more *Wolesi Jirga* representatives, based on population. Voters cast a single vote for one candidate in their province. Seats for the most part are allocated to the top vote-getters in each province until that province's seats are filled. However, the constitution requires that at least 68 members of the lower house be women; therefore, some women are named to seats despite having lower vote totals than candidates who would have otherwise qualified. In addition, 10 seats are reserved for Kuchi nomads, which can also alter the regular distribution of seats. The first election was held on September 18, 2005. Candidates (approximately 2,775) ran as independents, although a number of them appeared easily identifiable as members of various political parties. The lower house convened for the first time on December 19.

Speaker: Mohammad Yunos QANUNI.

CABINET

[as of April 1, 2009] *(See headnote.)*

President	Hamid Karzai (Pushtun)
First Vice President	Ahmad Zia Masoud (Tajik)
Second Vice President	Mohammad Karim Khalili (Hazara)
Senior Minister	Hedayat Amin Arsala
Ministers	
Agriculture, Irrigation, and Livestock	Mohammad Asif Rahimi
Borders and Tribal Affairs	Abdul Karim Barahowie
Communications and Information Technology	Amirzai Sangin
Commerce and Industry	Wahidullah Shahrani
Counter-Narcotics	Gen. Khodaidad
Defense	Gen. Abdurrahim Wardak
Economy	Mohammed Jalil Shams
Education	Farooq Wardek
Finance	Omar Zakhilwal
Foreign Affairs	Rangin Dadfar Spanta
Haj and Islamic Affairs	Nematullah Shahrani
Higher Education	Muhammad Azam Dadfar
Information, Culture, and Tourism	Abdul Karim Khuram
Interior	Mohammad Hanif Atmar
Justice	Sarwar Danish
Martyrs, Disabled, Social Affairs, and Labor	Noor Mohammed Qarqeen
Mines	Muhammad Ibrahim Adel
Minister of State for Parliamentary Affairs	Mohammad Anwar Jigdalak
Public Health	Dr. Mohammad Amin Fatimie
Public Welfare	Sohrab Ali Saffary
Refugees	Abdul Karim Barahui
Rural Rehabilitation and Development	Mohammad Ehsan Zia
Transportation and Civil Aviation	Hamidullah Farooqi
Urban Development	Yousef Pashtun
Water and Energy	Mohammad Ismael Khan
Women's Affairs	Husn Banu Ghazanfar [f]

[f] = female

COMMUNICATIONS

Reporters Without Borders initially described the development of a degree of press freedom as one of the "few achievements" of the Afghan government following the fall of the Taliban in 2001. However, the journalism watchdog described the situation in Afghanistan as "fragile" in view of the deteriorating security situation and pressure from conservative elements inside and outside the government.

The legislature approved a new media law, supported mainly by the mujahidin and religious conservatives, in mid-2007, that although ostensibly providing for freedom of the press, was viewed in some circles as presenting curbs on journalists. President Karzai declined to sign the bill into law at the end of the year. A revised media law was adopted by the legislature in 2008, and press advocates indicated a greater degree of support for the new version than for the previous one. However, Karzai had not signed it as of early 2009, his critics suggesting that the administration was interested in instituting stronger governmental control of the media than the legislation would permit. Meanwhile, Reporters Without Borders argued that press freedom was declining, in part due to threats and violence against journalists from many quarters. Attention focused on the case of a journalism student sentenced to 20 years in prison for blasphemy in connection with an article that Afghan authorities characterized as critical of the Koran's precepts regarding women. In a similar vein, the government commission that oversees the media reportedly filed charges against several newspaper journalists and television stations for "anti-Islamic" reporting or broadcasting.

Press. Widespread civil war and other fighting in the 1980s and 1990s adversely affected the publication of many newspapers. Several hundred new papers were launched following the overthrow of the Taliban government, but many subsequently folded due to economic problems. Many ongoing papers reportedly survive thanks to direct assistance from the government, myriad "political-military powers," or nongovernmental organizations. Newspapers currently published in Kabul include *Anis* (Friendship), a long-standing, government-funded daily published primarily in Dari; the *Kabul Times,* another state-owned daily (in English); *Erada,* an independent daily; *Arman-i Milli* (National Aspiration), an independent daily; *Hewad* (Homeland), a state-run daily; *Estah,* a state-owned daily; *Cheragh* (Light), an independent daily; *Payam-i-Mujahid* (Holy Warrior's Message), an independent, pro-mujahidin weekly; *Kilit* (Key, 13,000); *Rah-i Nejat,* an independent daily; *Roznawa-i Afghanistan* (The Daily Afghanistan), an independent daily; *Milli Jarida,* independent; *Hasht-i Sobh,* an independent, "secular" daily; *Weesa* (Thrust), an independent daily; *Erada* (Will), an independent daily; *Shahadat,* a daily affiliated with the Islamic Party; the *Kabul Weekly,* independent; *Mosharekat-i Milli* (National Participation), a "progovernment" weekly affiliated with the Islamic Unity Party of Afghanistan; and *Iqtedar-i Milli* (National Empowerment), a weekly affiliated with the National Islamic Empowerment Party. The government also publishes the daily *Itefaq-e Islam* in Herat.

News agencies. The official domestic facility is the Bakhtar News Agency. There are also a number of private news agencies.

Broadcasting and computing. Following the Taliban takeover, Radio Afghanistan was redesignated the Voice of Sharia, and Kabul TV was shut down. Television service was resumed on a limited basis in the capital in 2001. State-run Radio/Television Afghanistan (RTA) resumed broadcasting following the overthrow of the Taliban in 2001. (The legislature has proposed a new media law that would accord the RTA "independent" status.) Several influential private stations have also been launched (including *Aina,* the "youth-oriented" *Emrooz, Shamshad,* and *Tolo*), as have a number of private radio stations. In May 2005 the Karzai administration, facing criticism for using the national radio and television stations for public relations purposes, announced plans to establish independent agencies to oversee the stations, but no action had been taken in that regard by early 2008. As of 2008 there were 18.4 Internet users per 1,000 inhabitants.

INTERGOVERNMENTAL REPRESENTATION

Ambassador to the U.S.: Said Tayeb JAWAD.

U.S. Ambassador to Afghanistan: Karl Winfrid EIKENBERRY.

Permanent Representative to the UN: Zahir TANIN.

IGO Memberships (Non-UN): ADB, CP, ECO, IDB, Interpol, IOM, NAM, OIC, WCO.

ALBANIA

Republic of Albania
Republika e Shqipëri

Political Status: Independent state since 1912; Communist regime established in 1946; interim democratic constitution adopted April 29, 1991; permanent constitution approved by national referendum on November 22, 1998, and signed into law by the president on November 28.

Area: 11,100 sq. mi. (28,748 sq. km.).

Population: 3,069,275 (2001C); 3,187,000 (2008E).

Major Urban Centers (2005E): TIRANË (TIRANA, 387,000), Durrës (107,000), Elbasan (90,000), Shkodër (83,000), Vlorë (80,000), Korçë (53,000).

Official Language: Albanian.

Monetary Unit: Lek (market rate December 1, 2009: 92.24 lekë = $1US).

President: Bamir TOPI (formerly Democratic Party of Albania); elected in the fourth round of voting by the People's Assembly on July 20, 2007, and sworn in for a five-year term on July 24, succeeding Gen. (Ret.) Alfred MOISIU (formerly Socialist Party of Albania). (Upon election the president is constitutionally required to discard formal party affiliation.)

Prime Minister: Sali BERISHA (Democratic Party of Albania); nominated by the president on September 3, 2005 (following the legislative elections of July 3), approved by the People's Assembly on September 10, and inaugurated on September 11 to succeed Fatos Thanos NANO (Socialist Party of Albania); nominated for a second term in office by the president on September 9, 2009 (following the legislative elections of June 28), approved by the People's Assembly on September 16, and inaugurated to head a new coalition government on September 17.

THE COUNTRY

The Republic of Albania, one of the smallest and least advanced of European nations, is located at the mouth of the Adriatic, where it is flanked by Serbia and Montenegro on the north, Macedonia on the east, and Greece on the southeast. A mountainous topography has served to isolate the population and retard both national unity and development. The two main ethnic-linguistic groups—the Ghegs north of the Shkumbin River and the Tosks south of that river—together embrace 97 percent of the population. Albanian (*shqip*) is an independent member of the Indo-European language group. There are two dialects corresponding to the ethnic division, the Tosk dialect being in official use. A majority of the population has traditionally been Muslim, but in 1967 Albania was proclaimed an atheist state and religious observances were proscribed until April 1991. (Recent estimates describe 70 percent of the population as "nominally" Muslim, 20 percent Orthodox Christian, and 10 percent Roman Catholic.) Because the country has one of Europe's highest population growth rates, some 60 percent of its inhabitants are reported to be under 26 years of age. More than 20 percent of the successful candidates in the 1991 balloting for the People's Assembly were women, but only eight women were elected in 2001 and ten in 2005. There is only one woman in the current cabinet.

Throughout the Communist era, agriculture was dominated by state farms and collectives. In mid-1991, however, the new government adopted a policy of gradually returning the land to peasant ownership or control, yielding a pattern of excessively small holdings with overall productivity one-tenth that of the European Union (EU). Nearly all farmland is now privately owned, and agriculture, primarily at the subsistence level, accounts for roughly a quarter of GDP, although a significant percentage of food and other basic goods is imported. Chrome,

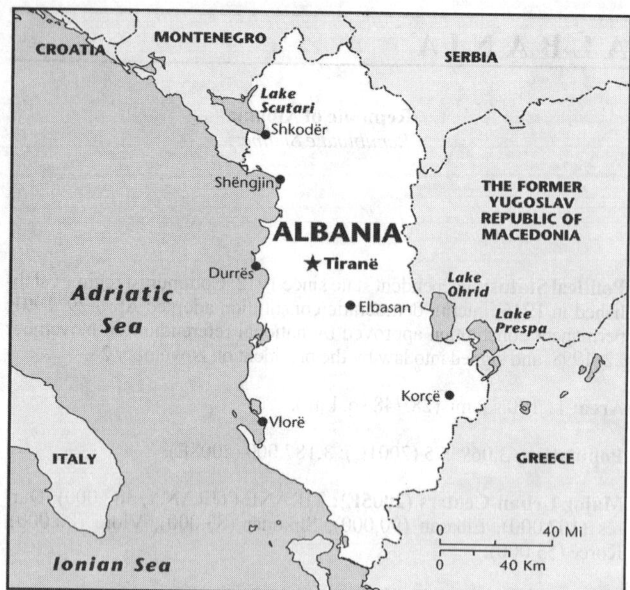

nickel, and copper are mined, although the mining sector remains significantly outdated despite recent interest from foreign investors. Industry accounts for about 20 percent of GDP; textiles are a significant export, while the fledgling fishing sector has been targeted for government support. Remittances from workers abroad (an estimated 800,000 in Italy, Greece, and other Western European countries) continue to underpin the Albanian economy. The leading trading partners are Italy and Greece, with whom traditional links were revived in the wake of the Communist collapse.

With per capita income estimated at no more than $340 in 1993, Albania was classified as Europe's only "least developed" country. The demise of the socialist system had yielded soaring inflation, paralysis in the industrial sector, massive unemployment, and a huge state budget deficit. Subsequently, however, Albania temporarily became one of Europe's fastest-growing economies, achieving GDP growth of 11 and 8 percent in 1993 and 1994, respectively, albeit from a very low base. Although the discovery in 1995 of new oil reserves offered promise of greater self-sufficiency, the economy was devastated in late 1996 and early 1997 by the collapse of the "pyramid" financial schemes that had attracted heavy investment from much of the population. (It was subsequently estimated that Albanians were bilked of $1.2 billion through the schemes.) Consequently, GDP contracted by 7 percent in 1997 before rebounding to a robust annual average of nearly 8 percent growth in 1998–2000.

Annual per capita income had reportedly risen significantly by 2005, in part due to GDP growth that had averaged 6 percent annually for several years. Moreover, annual inflation was running at only a little over 2 percent, partly in response to the government's tight fiscal policies. Nevertheless, Albania remained one of the poorest countries in Europe, with the informal sector (i.e., the untaxed sector) reportedly outstripping the formal sector.

Despite political discord in Albania in the late 1990s and first half of the 2000s, international lenders such as the International Monetary Fund (IMF) and the World Bank continued to support the government's recovery programs. The IMF praised the government for "steadfast pursuit of sound macroeconomic policies" while urging focus on what was generally conceded to be widespread fraud and corruption, particularly in the customs service and judiciary. Albania's hopes for eventual EU accession also appeared to depend on, among other things, establishment of sufficient border controls to combat trafficking in drugs and arms, successful completion of bank reform currently underway under international supervision, further privatization of inefficient state-run enterprises, and "good governance" on the national and local levels. Other government priorities included modernization of the port in Durrës (as part of the "Corridor VIII" project, a transportation route running from the Black Sea through Bulgaria and Macedonia to Albania's Adriatic coastline), additional infrastructure improvements, and development of the energy sector. The government also pledged to promote the fledgling tourist industry and otherwise attract foreign investment by encouraging "more modern business practices." However, the IMF in 2006 described the business climate as still "relatively uninviting" and called for better enforcement of property rights. Meanwhile, heavy migration from the poor mountainous regions to urban areas compromised basic services and complicated an already unsatisfactory (by Western standards) electoral process (see Current issues, below).

It was reported in 2007 that annual per capita income had risen to $5,200, although significant disparities remained in regard to the distribution of wealth. Despite having fallen steadily since 2000, unemployment remained high at more than 13 percent. Other problems included droughts in 2007–2008 that reduced the production of hydroelectric plants by as much as two-thirds. The government proposed the construction of a nuclear power plant to help deal with future electrical shortfalls. GDP growth reached 6 percent in 2008, and the Albanian government forecast similar growth for 2009. However, the IMF offered a conservative estimate of only 0 to 1 percent growth for 2009 in the context of the global economic decline. One concern noted by the IMF was an ongoing sharp drop in remittance payments from Albanians working abroad.

GOVERNMENT AND POLITICS

Political background. Following almost 450 years of Ottoman suzerainty, Albania was declared independent in 1912, but its central government remained weak, despite the coup and proclamation of a monarchy in 1928 by President Ahmet Bey ZOGU, who ruled as King Zog until Italian invasion and annexation in 1939. During the later stages of World War II, the Communist-led National Liberation Front under Gen. Enver HOXHA assumed control of the country, proclaiming its liberation from the Axis powers on November 29, 1944. Hoxha's provisional government obtained Allied recognition in November 1945 on the condition that free national elections be held. On December 21 a Communist-controlled assembly was elected, and the new body proclaimed Albania a republic on January 11, 1946. The Albanian Communist Party, founded in 1941, became the only authorized political organization in a system closely patterned on other communist models. Renamed the Albanian Party of Labor (*Partia e Punës e Shqipërisë*—PPS) in 1948, its Politburo and Secretariat wielded decisive control.

Despite extensive second-echelon purges from 1972 to 1977, very little turnover in the top political leadership occurred prior to a number of Politburo changes announced in November 1981, at the conclusion of the Eighth PPS Congress. Shortly thereafter, on December 17, Mehmet SHEHU, who had served as chair of the Council of Ministers since 1954, was officially reported to have committed suicide at "a moment of nervous distress." (Three years later, party officials declared that Shehu had been "liquidated" because he had interfered with the "unbreakable unity of the party with the people.") On November 22, 1982, a newly elected People's Assembly named Ramiz ALIA to succeed Haxhi LLESHI as president of its Presidium (head of state), while an ensuing reorganization of the Council of Ministers was widely interpreted as a purge of former Shehu supporters.

On April 11, 1985, after a prolonged illness that had kept him from public view for nearly a year, Hoxha died of a heart condition. Two days later, Alia (who had assumed a number of Hoxha's functions during the party leader's illness) became only the second individual to be named PPS first secretary since World War II.

As late as January 1990 President Alia displayed a hard-line posture in regard to the pace of change in Eastern Europe. In April, however, he proclaimed an end to Albania's policy of diplomatic isolation, and in early May the People's Assembly approved a number of major reforms, including an end to the ban on religious activity, liberalization of the penal code, increased autonomy in enterprise decision making, and the right to passports for all Albanians over the age of six. On December 11, following widespread popular demonstrations, liberalization was further advanced by a declaration that other parties would be recognized, with the Democratic Party of Albania (*Partia Demokratike e Shqipërisë*—PDS), the country's first opposition formation in 46 years, being launched the following day.

Student-led demonstrations in the capital on February, 20, 1991, prompted Alia to declare presidential rule and, two days later, to appoint a provisional government headed by the politically moderate Fatos Thanos NANO. At multiparty balloting on March 31 and April 17 the Communists secured 168 of 250 legislative seats, largely on the basis of their strength in rural areas, while the opposition PDS won 75. The restructured assembly fell into discord at its opening session because of a PDS boycott prompted by the killing of four party members on April 2. On May 9 the president nonetheless appointed Nano to head a new all-PPS government. A fresh wave of street violence ensued, and on June 5 a respected economist, Ylli BUFI, was named to head an interim coalition that was installed on June 12, coincident with redesignation of the PPS as the Socialist Party of Albania (*Partia Socialiste e Shqipërisë*—PSS). The new administration contained 12 representatives from the PSS, 7 from the PDS, and 5 from smaller groups that had failed to win assembly seats.

On December 4, 1991, the PDS announced that it was withdrawing from the government coalition because of foot dragging by the PSS in regard to political reform. Two days later Prime Minister Bufi resigned in favor of Vilson AHMETI, the first non-Marxist government head since World War II. On December 22, ten days after a rally of 20,000 people called for his resignation, President Alia agreed to the scheduling of a new general election.

At two-stage balloting on March 22 and 29, 1992, the PDS won close to a two-thirds majority in a reduced assembly of 140 seats, and on April 3 Alia resigned. Elected by the assembly as Albania's new head of state on April 9, PDS leader Sali BERISHA immediately named Aleksander MEKSI to succeed Ahmeti as prime minister of a tripartite administration that included representatives of the smaller Social Democratic Party of Albania (*Partia Socialdemokrat e Shqipërisë*—PSDS) and Albanian Republican Party (*Partia Republikane Shqiptare*—PRS), in addition to three independents.

In September 1992 former president Alia was placed under house arrest after reportedly being charged with abuse of power and misuse of state funds, while in July 1993 Nano was charged with corruption during his brief premiership. In 1994 both former leaders received substantial prison sentences. (Alia was released in July 1995, although he was rearrested in February 1996 on charges of "genocide" and "crimes against humanity." See PSS in Political Parties, below, for details on the resolution of those charges.) Collaterally, the Albanian authorities also took action against the Democratic Union of the Greek Minority (*Omonia*); although prison terms for five *Omonia* leaders were later rescinded, a further crackdown against Greek separatists was mounted in March 1995.

President Berisha suffered an unexpected rebuff on November 6, 1994, when a referendum on a post-Communist constitution yielded a 53.9 percent majority against the proposed draft (which in October had failed to secure the required two-thirds legislative majority). The president responded by carrying out a major ministerial reshuffle on December 4. Although the PRS and the PSDS announced their withdrawal from the government, the two PSDS cabinet members promptly formed the breakaway Social Democratic Union of Albania (*Bashkimi i Social Demokratiket i Shqipërisë*—BSDS) and remained in their posts. The reshaped administration retained a comfortable parliamentary majority and derived some benefit from an economic upturn in 1994 and 1995.

A controversial Genocide Law enacted in September 1995 authorized the barring from public life until 2002 of Communist-era officials found to have committed crimes against humanity for political, ideological, or religious motives, while associated legislation adopted in November provided for the "screening" of the past records of senior political and other figures. Under these measures, some 70 opposition candidates (notably of the ex-Communist PSS) were barred from standing in the legislative elections held May–June 1996.

The first-round balloting on May 26, 1996, was so riddled with malpractice and fraud (as confirmed by international observers) that the main opposition parties boycotted the second round on June 2, as protest demonstrations in Tirana and elsewhere were broken up with considerable police brutality. The official results of the balloting gave the PDS 122 of the 140 seats, with 10 going to the PSS and the other 8 being shared by three parties. The PDS thus acquired substantially better than the two-thirds majority required for passage of constitutional amendments, one of its campaign pledges having been to draw up a fully democratic post-Communist constitution. The substantially changed government sworn in on July 12, under the continued premiership of Meksi, contained 22 PDS representatives, with two posts going to the reinstated PRS and one to the BSDS.

The collapse in early 1997 of the so-called pyramid financial schemes pushed the country to the brink of anarchy, and pressure mounted on President Berisha to resign and call new elections. On February 11 the PRS withdrew from the government, and, with dissent growing even within his own PDS, Berisha on March 1 conceded and ordered the resignation of the government. However, on March 2 the government declared a state of emergency, and, as "rebels" seized control of about one-third of the nation (primarily in the south), Berisha turned to security forces and "northern vigilantes" to defend the regime. Berisha was reelected president (unopposed) by the assembly on March 3, and he soon offered amnesty to the southern rebels and began negotiations with the opposition, which included the ad hoc Forum for Democracy, led by a number of former political prisoners. The opposition demanded Berisha's resignation, early elections, and installation of a government of technocrats to deal with economic problems. Berisha, also under pressure from the EU and the Organization for Security and Cooperation in Europe (OSCE), on March 12 announced the formation of an interim "government of reconciliation." The cabinet, led by the PSS's Bashkim FINO as the new prime minister, included all the major parties. However, Berisha refused to resign as president unless he was repudiated in an election, and the southern rebels declined to lay down their arms until he resigned.

In the face of that impasse, the UN Security Council on March 29, 1997, endorsed a proposal by the OSCE that affirmed the right of self-selected nations to accept the Albanian government's call for foreign military intervention. Fearing that refugees, disorder, and a torrent of smuggled weapons would spill into adjoining states unless the Albanian conflict was resolved, eight nations in mid-April sent a total of about 5,900 troops to Albania under "Operation Alba," designed to help provide humanitarian aid and keep the peace pending new elections. Meanwhile, Leka ZOGU, exiled son of King Zog, had returned to Albania on April 13 to campaign for a return of the monarchy. However, in a national referendum on June 29, a monarchy proposal was endorsed by only one-third of the voters.

New legislative elections were conducted on June 29, 1997, after a compromise was reached on enlargement of the assembly to include additional proportional representation. In balloting that was marred by violence but was ultimately deemed "reasonably free and fair" by the OSCE, the PSS overwhelmed the PDS by better than a three-to-one margin (101 seats to 28, including the results of runoff balloting in July). After a period of uncertainty as to his intentions, President Berisha resigned on July 23, and the assembly elected Rexhep MEJDANI (secretary general of the PSS) to succeed him the next day. PSS chair Fatos Nano (freed from jail during the recent domestic unrest and subsequently officially pardoned by Berisha) was again sworn in as prime minister on July 25, heading a coalition government of the PSS, the PSDS, the Party of the Democratic Alliance (*Partia e Alenca Demokratike*—PAD), the Albanian Agrarian Party (*Partia Agrare e Shqipërisë*—PAS), and the Union for Human Rights Party (*Partia e Bashkimi për te Drejtat e Njeriut*—PBDNj). Former prime minister Fino of the PSS was named deputy prime minister. Meanwhile, Operation Alba was concluded.

Although the southern rebellion subsided following the installation of the new PSS-led government in 1997, conflict erupted again in August 1998 when six members of the PDS were arrested on charges relating to the repression of the domestic unrest the previous year. In addition, the killing of a prominent PDS activist, Azem HAJDARI, on September 12 outside PDS headquarters prompted thousands of PDS-led protesters to march on government buildings in Tirana the following day. Gunfire was exchanged, and Nano and his cabinet were forced to flee their offices and go into hiding. Demonstrations continued for several days (some 7 people died and nearly 80 were injured) as Berisha called for the resignation of Nano, who in turn accused his PDS adversary of attempting a coup. However, the international community, fearful that Albania was about to repeat the civil strife of 1997, strongly pressured both camps to negotiate a settlement. Order was consequently restored, in part due to Berisha's plea for calm.

Prime Minister Nano resigned on September 28, 1998, and was succeeded by PSS Secretary General Pandeli MAJKO, who was sworn in on October 2 after receiving the endorsement of the PSS as well as President Mejdani. Majko's cabinet, as approved by the assembly on October 8, comprised the same five parties as the previous government. In keeping with one of Majko's declared priorities, a long-delayed constitutional referendum was held on November 22, the new basic law (see Constitution and government, below) receiving a reported 93.5 percent approval level in a turnout of just above 50 percent of the voters.

The appointment of Majko (at 30 years old, then the youngest prime minister in Europe) was initially perceived as a potentially stabilizing influence, particularly since he had no association with previous Communist governments. However, conflict with the "old guard" quickly surfaced, and Majko stepped down in late October 1999 after losing a

PSS leadership battle with Nano. He was succeeded by Deputy Prime Minister Ilir META, whose revamped cabinet easily secured assembly endorsement despite a boycott of the vote by most legislators from the PDS-led Union for Democracy and the United Albanian Right.

The legislative election of June 24 and July 8, 2001, saw the PSS retain a majority, but with fewer seats. Despite PDS complaints of ballot-rigging and other irregularities, international observers regarded the campaign and balloting as fundamentally free and fair. Prime Minister Meta, having renegotiated a coalition agreement with the PSDS, PAD, PAS, and PBDNj, won a parliamentary endorsement for his new cabinet on September 12.

Following sustained friction between him and PSS leader Nano, Prime Minister Meta resigned on January 29, 2002. On February 7 the president invited former prime minister Majko to form a cabinet, which, as endorsed by the assembly on February 22, comprised the same five parties as the outgoing government.

Extensive squabbling over the nomination of the next president of the republic resulted in the selection of a compromise candidate—Gen. (Ret.) Alfred MOISIU—who was endorsed by both the PSS and the PDS. (Moisiu secured 97 of 140 votes in the assembly, comfortably above the required three-fifths [84] majority that was required.) Moisiu took office on July 24, 2002, and the following day Prime Minister Majko retired to make way for Nano, after the PSS had voted to make Nano its parliamentary leader. Nano's new cabinet was sworn in on August 1; it included the PSS, PAS, and PBDNj, but not the PSDS, which objected to losing the post of deputy prime minister.

Former Prime Minister Meta was persuaded to join the July 2002 cabinet as deputy prime minister and foreign affairs minister. However, Meta quit the government a year later, prompting another severe internal PSS dispute that culminated in Meta and a group of PSS legislators forming a new party called the Socialist Movement for Integration (*Lëvizja Socialiste për Integrim*—LSI). Meanwhile, in late December 2003 Nano appointed a new cabinet that included the PSDS and the PBDNj and was also supported by several small parliamentary parties.

The PDS and its allies in the new Alliance for Freedom, Justice, and Welfare (*Aleanca për Liri, Drejtësi, dhe Mirëqenie*—ALDM) secured 74 seats in the July 3, 2005, legislative balloting. Despite initial protests from the PSS over the conduct of the poll, PDS leader Sali Berisha was approved as the new prime minister by an 84–53 vote in the assembly on September 10. Berisha was inaugurated the following day as head of a center-right coalition government that comprised the PDS, Agrarian Environmental Party (*Partia Agrare Ambientaliste*—PAA), PBDNj, and members of two ALDM components (the PRS and the New Democrat Party [*Partia Demokrate e Re*—PDr]).

Local elections were initially planned for mid-2006, but the PSS, led by new Chair Edi RAMA, and other opposition parties threatened to boycott the balloting unless broad electoral changes were implemented. A six-month dispute ensued, leading international organizations (including the EU, North Atlantic Treaty Organization [NATO], OSCE, and the Council of Europe) to warn that Albania's "political maturity" was in question. An agreement was finally reached among the warring political parties in January 2007 to hold the elections on February 18. Although voting was conducted peacefully, international observers described the balloting as another "missed opportunity" for Albania to improve its electoral reputation, noting shortcomings in both preparation and vote counting. Both the government and the opposition attempted to portray the results as a victory for their side, although the PSS-led opposition won a majority of municipal elections, including eight of the nine largest cities (the PDS winning Shkodër). Prime Minister Berisha, acknowledging the need for additional reform, reshuffled his cabinet in March as attention turned toward the presidential election scheduled for midyear.

Divisions between the left and right continued in the 2007 presidential election. No suitable consensus candidate could be found, although the military representative to NATO, Brigadier General Arjan ZAIMI, was proposed as such by the opposition. When the PDS rejected Zaimi, the opposition boycotted the first two rounds of voting, preventing any candidate from achieving the 84 votes necessary for victory. Bamir TOPI of the PDS and Fatos Nano (standing as an independent) dominated the first rounds. In the third round some opposition lawmakers attended the proceedings for the first time, and Neritan ÇEKA of the DPA was added as a candidate. Since the constitution requires that new elections for the assembly must be called if five rounds of voting in the assembly fail to elect a president, additional members of the opposition attended the fourth round on July 20 in order to prevent such a development. Five voted in favor of Topi, who was elected with the support of 85 out of the 90 members present.

The PDS and its allies in the Alliance for Changes (*Aleanca për Ndryshim*—AN) won a plurality of 70 seats in the June 28, 2009, assembly election. On September 17 Prime Minister Berisha formed a new coalition government that included AN parties and the small Socialist Alliance for Integration (*Aleanca Socialiste për Integrim*—ASI).

Constitution and government. A constitution adopted in December 1976 did not significantly alter the system of government introduced three decades earlier. Under its provisions, the former People's Republic of Albania was redesignated as the Socialist People's Republic of Albania and the PPS was identified as "the sole directing political power in state and society." Private property was declared to be abolished, as were the "bases of religious obscurantism"; financial dealings with "capitalist or revisionist monopolies or states" were also outlawed. Under the interim basic law of April 1991, all of these stipulations were abandoned, with the country's name being foreshortened to "Republic of Albania."

The constitution that was approved in a national referendum on November 22, 1998, and signed into law by the president on November 28 codified many of the changes implemented in 1991. The new basic law was described as a "Western-style" document modeled most directly on the German and Italian examples. It describes Albania as a "democratic republic" in which individual human rights (including religious freedom) are guaranteed, as are those of ethnic minorities. Private property rights are also protected, and emphasis is given to a "market-oriented" economy.

The supreme organ of government is the unicameral People's Assembly, none of whose members can be nominated by groups representing ethnic minorities. The assembly elects the republic's president, who is precluded from holding party office and is limited to two five-year terms. (In 2007 Prime Minister Berisha proposed a change to direct popular election of the president, but no action was taken on the matter because of concerns that insufficient time existed to implement the change before the upcoming election.) The powers of the president, particularly those regarding the authority to govern by decree in times of emergency, were substantially diluted in the 1998 constitution. Responsibility for day-to-day governmental administration rests with the Council of Ministers, whose head serves as prime minister. The prime minister is appointed by the president, who, upon the proposal of the prime minister, also nominates the Council of Ministers for approval by the assembly. Should the assembly endorse a nonconfidence motion in the Council of Ministers, the president is directed to appoint a new prime minister in an effort to nominate an acceptable council.

The judiciary includes a Supreme Court and district and local courts. For purposes of local administration, Albania is divided into 36 districts (*rrethët*), the municipality of Tirana, over 200 localities, and 2,500 villages. Local councils, elected by direct suffrage for three-year terms, are the governing bodies in each subdivision.

Foreign relations. Prior to the democratic liberalization of the early 1990s, Albania's pursuit of an antirevisionist and anti-imperialist foreign policy was long conditioned by geography and shifting relationships among external Communist powers. (For a description of the country's four principal phases in dealings with the outside world from the end of World War II to the late 1980s, see the 2007 *Handbook*.)

Negotiations with the Federal Republic of Germany yielded an agreement in September 1987 to establish diplomatic links after Albania abandoned its insistence on reparations for World War II damage. During the same month Greece announced the end of a state of war that had technically existed since an Italian invasion from Albania in October 1940. The action was preceded by a settlement of border issues that effectively voided Athens' long-standing claim to a portion of southern Albania (known to the Greeks as Northern Epirus) populated by a sizable ethnic Greek community.

Albania's transition to multiparty democracy in 1990 and 1991 brought about a transformation in its external relations. In July 1990, it was announced that diplomatic relations were to be reestablished with the Soviet Union after a break of 29 years, and in August Albania was granted observer status at the Vienna talks of the Conference on Security and Cooperation in Europe (CSCE, precursor of the OSCE) and declared that it would sign the Nuclear Non-Proliferation Treaty. On March 15, 1991, formal relations with the United States, severed since 1939, were restored, paving the way for a visit by U.S. Secretary of State James Baker, who was greeted by some 300,000 cheering residents of Tirana on June 22. Diplomatic relations were restored with

Britain in May, Albania became a full member of the OSCE in June, and relations with the Vatican were reestablished in July.

In the wake of perceived Western indifference to the growing threat to ethnic Albanians and other Muslims in former Yugoslavia, particularly in the Yugoslavian province of Kosovo and in Macedonia, Albania was reportedly admitted to the Organization of the Islamic Conference (OIC) in December 1992. The OIC membership subsequently became controversial: in mid-1998 Prime Minister Nano argued that appropriate legal steps had not been taken regarding the original application for membership and that Albania's accession had not been official. In part, Nano's position was apparently influenced by his preference for orienting Albania toward Europe rather than the Islamic world. In that context, his government launched, with U.S. assistance, a crackdown on Islamic fundamentalists in 1998. Following Nano's resignation in September, government officials indicated that Albania was prepared to "reactivate" relations with the OIC, which subsequently offered broad support for Albania's role in housing the primarily Muslim Kosovo refugees in 1999. In May 1999 President Berisha appealed to the United States and NATO to dispatch forces to Kosovo to prevent "ethnic cleansing" of Albanians.

Relations with Greece worsened in the post-Communist era due to a mass exodus of ethnic Greeks from Albania, attendant border incidents, and renewed Albanian fears of Greek territorial designs. Despite the signature of a series of cooperation agreements by the Albanian and Greek prime ministers in May 1993, tensions flared again in April 1994 as a result of the killing of two Albanian border guards during a raid by activists of the Greek-based Northern Epirus Liberation Front (NELF). Further deterioration caused by an Albanian crackdown on alleged ethnic Greek subversives was partially reversed by a visit to Tirana by the Greek foreign minister in March 1995 and by collateral Greek action against NELF militants. The improvement in bilateral relations yielded a Greek-Albanian friendship treaty in March 1996 that called for cooperation in various fields, as well as mutual respect for the rights of minorities. (Although the question of illegal Albanian immigration subsequently became a significant domestic political issue in Greece, it did not emerge as a significant issue in bilateral relations.)

Albania became a signatory of NATO's Partnership for Peace in February 1994, while Council of Europe membership was conferred in June 1995. A U.S.-Albanian military cooperation agreement was signed in October 1995, following an official visit to Washington by President Berisha a month earlier, and a U.S. military aid package worth over $100 million was approved in April 1996. Meanwhile, Albania's relations with Italy and other EU countries continued to be complicated by the role of Albanian Adriatic ports as staging areas for illegal immigrants of various origins seeking to reach Western Europe. In addition, the presence of significant ethnic Albanian populations in neighboring countries prompted discussions in some circles over the possibility of a "Greater Albania," particularly with respect to Kosovo and the western regions of Macedonia. In late 1998 and early 1999 Prime Minister Majko carefully endorsed Western policy regarding Kosovo, agreeing that the province should seek autonomy within Yugoslavia, not independence, despite significant sentiment within the Albanian populace for the latter. Not surprisingly, the government strongly endorsed the military campaign that NATO launched against Serbia in late March 1999, although the initiative produced an influx of some 450,000 refugees from Kosovo. A NATO force of more than 5,000 personnel was stationed in Albania until September 1999 in connection with the anti-Serbian operation, Albania subsequently expressing the hope that support for NATO in the campaign would facilitate Albania's eventual accession to that alliance. During the ethnic fighting in neighboring Macedonia in 2001, Prime Minister Meta also made his intentions clear: although supportive of the cause of ethnic Albanian rights, he condemned violent acts, rejected militant calls for border changes, and disavowed any interest in formation of a "Greater Albania."

Possibly in continued appreciation of NATO's action to protect the ethnic Albanian population in Kosovo, Albania supported the U.S./UK-led invasion of Iraq in 2003 and contributed a small contingent of troops to the NATO mission in Afghanistan. Collaterally, the Nano government, keenly focused on potential accession to the EU, maintained its distance from the independence movement among ethnic Albanians in Kosovo. In early 2006 new Prime Minister Berisha referred to the "will for independence" among the population in Kosovo, perhaps thereby signaling a shift in attitude from the previous administration regarding that delicate issue. U.S. President George W. Bush was popularly received in a June 2007 visit to Tirana, at which he stated support for an independent Kosovo. On February 18, 2008, Albania was one of the first states to formally recognize the independence of Kosovo.

Albania signed a Stabilization and Association Agreement with the EU in June 2006, and at the April 2008 Bucharest Conference NATO formally tendered an accession invitation to Albania. Full membership in NATO was tentatively planned for 2009, with the proviso that the Albanian Armed Forces be reformed as a "professional military" (as defined by NATO) by 2010, with aid and advice from the U.S. Defense Department. (Some 250 Greek military advisors were also authorized to participate in the modernization program.) Meanwhile, in 2007 Albania became the first country under the Chemical Weapons Convention of 1997 to completely destroy its stockpiles of chemical weapons.

On April 1, 2009, Albania formally became a member of NATO. Albania's Stabilization and Accession Agreement with the EU entered in to force on the same day, prompting its formal application on April 28 for full EU membership.

Current issues. Although domestic political differences are less volatile than in 1997–1998, the political divide—particularly between the PSS and PDS—remains a critical aspect of domestic affairs. The PSS, PDS, and a number of smaller parties pledged prior to the July 2005 assembly elections to wage a "fair campaign" under guidelines developed in cooperation with the OSCE and the Council of Europe. Despite an initial statement by Prime Minister Nano that results showing a PDS victory were "unacceptable" and "illegitimate," he formally accepted the results in early September, allowing the first peaceful transfer of power in Albania since the fall of Communism. The 2007 municipal and presidential elections demonstrated continued polarization in politics, however. The EU accession progress report of 2007 noted that there remained "little progress towards constructive consensus between political parties on implementing reforms." In April 2008 proposals to switch parliamentary elections to a proportional system divided into 12 regions that would decrease the power of smaller parties were jointly supported by the PSS and PDS but were opposed by smaller parties.

Corruption also remains a significant issue, exacerbated by questions over the independence of the judiciary. Several arrests and investigations of government officials in 2007–2008 suggested continued corruption in government. In September 2007 seven members of the ministry of public works were arrested (including a deputy minister for transport and the head of the roads department) following a scandal concerning the bidding process for highway renovation contracts. In November the justice minister resigned over allegations of corruption and favorable contracts in the prison system, while an investigation of the taxation police in December resulted in a new series of arrests. At the same time, Prosecutor General Theodhori SOLLAKU was removed by the president in November 2007 and replaced by Edi RAMA, resulting in criticism that the executive under Berisha was attempting to limit the judiciary's role in investigating members of his own government. Such sentiment intensified in June 2008 following allegations that Berisha's nominations for the Albanian supreme court had agreed to provide him immunity from prosecution.

The issue of corruption received international attention following explosions at the Gerdac ammunition site on March 15, 2008, which killed 26, wounded more than 300, and damaged 5,500 houses. The depot was a site for the demilitarization of aging ammunition stockpiled during the Communist era and now being dismantled for scrap. Domestic criticism focused on unsafe working conditions, questions over corruption in the awarding of contracts, and the slow process of compensating victims. Defense Minister Fatmir MEDIU resigned in the wake of the crisis.

Questions of political divides in Albania were renewed following the adoption of a new electoral code in 2009. Domestic nongovernmental organizations and foreign observers questioned whether the code would impair the ability of smaller parties to compete with the PDS and PSS. Proposed reforms such as the mandatory use of new identification cards for voters were put into place slowly, and some phrases in the law (such as stipulated quotas of female assembly candidates for parties) were worded in a manner open to interpretation. Not surprisingly, the June 28 assembly elections produced a broad decline in the fortunes of smaller parties, despite the involvement of nearly every such party in large electoral coalitions. The election proved unusually close, however, and the PSS refused to initially recognize the validity of the results and requested recounts in selected districts, thereby delaying the announcement of a new PDS-led government until September.

POLITICAL PARTIES

Until December 1990, when the first opposition party was recognized, Albania accorded a monopoly position to the Albanian Party of Labor (*Partia e Punës e Shqipërisë*—PPS), which served as the core of the Democratic Front of Albania (*Fronti Demokratik ë Shqipërisë*—FDS), a mass organization to which all adult Albanians theoretically belonged. Although numerous parties were registered in 1991 and the first half of 1992, the People's Assembly in July 1992 banned all parties identifiable as "fascist, antinational, chauvinistic, racist, totalitarian, communist, Marxist-Leninist, Stalinist, or Enverist," the last in reference to former Communist leader Enver Hoxha. However, the 1992 law was revised in 1998 to repeal the ban against communist parties (among other things), although proscription was maintained against "antinational, anti-Albanian, antidemocratic, and totalitarian" groups. There are no current restrictions on parties based on ethnicity, religion, or regional status, as long as such parties do not denigrate other groups.

Government Parties:

Alliance for Changes (*Aleanca për Ndryshim*—AN). The AN is considered an outgrowth, at least in part, of the rightist "Grand Alliance" that was formed for the February 2007 municipal elections under the leadership of the PDS. The alliance also included the PRS, PDK, PAA, PBD, PLL, BLD, and other small groups. Earlier, the BLD, PBK, PRS, PDK, PBD, PLDLNj, and PDr had formed the PDS-supportive Alliance for Freedom, Justice, and Welfare (*Aleanca për Liri, Drejtësi, dhe Mirëqenie*—ALDM) for the 2005 assembly elections. (See PDS below for information on related electoral arrangements.) Due to the PDS support, the ALDM received 33 percent of the proportional vote in the 2005 poll and was accorded 18 assembly seats (PRS, 11; PDr, 4; PDK, 2, and BLD, 1), subsequently joining the PSD in forming a government.

Other small parties in the AN, all of which polled under 1 percent of the vote, included the **Christian Democratic League** (*Lidhja Demokristiane Shqiptare*—LDK), led by Nikolle LESI; the **Party of New Albanian European Democracy** (*Partia Demokracia e Re Europiane Shqiptare*—PDRESH), led by Koçi TAHIRI; the **New Party of Denied Rights** (*Partia e të Drejtave të Mohuara e Re*—PDMeRE), led by Fatmir HOXHA; the **Alliance for Democracy and Solidarity** (*Aleanca për Demokraci dhe Solidaritet*—ADS), led by Gaqo APOSTOLI; the **Ora of Albania** (*Partia Ora e Shqipërisë*—POSH), led by Zef SHTJEFNI; and the **Party Forca Albania** (*Partia Forca Albania*—PFA), led by Iledin PILLATI. The AN secured 46.9 percent of the nationwide vote in the 2009 assembly elections and won 70 seats.

Democratic Party of Albania (*Partia Demokratike e Shqipërisë*—PDS). The PDS, launched in December 1990, sought protection of human rights, a free-market economy, and improved relations with neighboring states. Serious tensions in the PDS following the 1992 elections were highlighted by the departure of six moderate leftists in July 1992 to form the PAD (below), after which the PDS-led government was accused of authoritarian leanings. The party leadership responded by expelling several rightists, who later formed the ultranationalist PDDS (see PDr below).

In March 1995 Eduard SELAMI was dismissed as PDS chair for criticizing President Berisha's effort to secure approval of a new constitution by referendum. His acting successor, Tritan SHEHU, was formally installed in April 1996, as the PDS launched an election campaign advocating lower taxes and more privatization. Later the same month, Selami and seven members of the PDS national council, including Secretary General Tomor DOSTI, were ousted. Although the party's landslide victory in the May–June balloting was tarnished by evidence of widespread voting irregularities, a new PDS-dominated government took office in July. However, the PDS was crushed in the legislative elections of June–July 1997, dropping from 122 to 28 seats. (The PDS participated in the 1997 balloting in a Union for Democracy [*Bashkimi për Demokraci*—BD] coalition that also included the PLL, BSDS, PDK, PBD, a number of other small parties, and various cultural associations. The BD won only 31 seats, including the 28 PDS seats. Meanwhile, another smaller conservative grouping—the United Albanian Right [*Djatha e Bashkuar e Shqipërisë*—DBS]—won 4 seats. Members of the DBS included the PBK, PRS, PDDS, and LD [See under PDr below].)

PSS/PDS friction continued following the 1997 balloting, reportedly fueled by animosity between Berisha and the PSS's Fatos Nano. Consequently, the PDS boycotted most legislative activity. Six high-ranking PDS members were arrested in August 1998 on charges related to suppression of the 1997 domestic unrest, and the tension between the two leading parties almost erupted into civil war in September after Azem Hajdari, a controversial PDS legislator and Berisha protégé, was assassinated outside PDS headquarters in Tirana. Although Hajdari's murder remained unsolved, an extraordinary PDS congress voted in July 1999 to end the party's ten-month assembly boycott. Subsequently, Berisha was able to beat back a challenge from Genc POLLO, leader of the PDS reform wing, for the party's chair at the October 1999 regular congress. In January 2001 Pollo finally broke from the PDS and established the Democrat Party (PD, see below).

Prior to the 2001 legislative balloting, the PDS organized the Union for Victory *(Bashkimi për Fitore)* coalition with the PLL, BLD, PBK, and PRS. The coalition was largely a successor to the Union for Democracy of 1997. The Union for Victory was a more successful effort than its predecessor in organizing all the leading conservative elements and secured 46 seats. (Berisha claimed that massive irregularities had cost the PDS and its allies many other seats.)

The PDS signed electoral cooperation agreements for the July 2005 legislative balloting with seven small groupings that had coalesced as the ALDM (above). Under the unique arrangements, the PDS presented one candidate in each of the 100 single-member constituencies, although 15 of those candidates reportedly were in fact members of various ALDM components. Collaterally, the PDS urged its supporters to vote for the ALDM in the national proportional balloting.

In 2007 PDS candidate Bamir Topi was elected president of Albania following four rounds of voting by the national assembly. Topi accordingly resigned his party membership in a show of impartiality, although he subsequently maintained close political relations with Prime Minister Berisha.

In October 2008 the New Democrat Party (*Partia Demokrate e Re*—PDr) merged into the PDS. Also referenced simply as the Democrat Party (*Partia Demokrate*—PD), the PDr, originating in the reform wing of the PDS, was organized in January 2001 by former PDS leader Genc Pollo, who had already established a six-member reformist group in the People's Assembly. The new formation also incorporated the former Movement for Democracy (*Lëvizja për Demokraci*—LD) and the Democratic Party of the Right of Albania (*Partia Demokratike e Djatha e Shqipërisë*—PDDS), both of which were participants in 1997's United Albanian Right. The PDr won six seats in the 2001 assembly balloting. In 2002 former LD leader Dashamir Shehi (then the PDr secretary general) and several other PDr legislators attempted unsuccessfully to push Pollo out of the PDr leadership. Shehi and the others subsequently formed a new party (see PDRn, under PLL, below). As part of the ALDM, the PDr secured four seats in the proportional component of the July 2005 assembly balloting, and Pollo was named to the new PDS-led cabinet in September.

In 2009 the PDS campaigned on a platform of further integration with Europe, citing the government's success in achieving admission into NATO early that year. The party won 68 of the AN's 70 seats in the June assembly balloting and 40 percent of the vote nationwide.

Leaders: Sali BERISHA (Prime Minister and Chair), Genc POLLO (Deputy Prime Minister and Former Chair of the PDr), Jozefina TOPALLI (Chair of the Presidency of the People's Assembly), Astrit PATOZI (Vice Chair, Parliamentary Leader), Ridvan BODE (Secretary General).

Liberal Democratic Union (*Bashkimi Liberal Demokrat*—BLD). The BLD was launched as the Social Democratic Union of Albania (*Bashkimi i Social Demokratikët i Shqipërisë*—BSDS) in January 1995 by Teodor Laço and Vullnet ADEMI, formerly of the PSDS, who had opted to remain in the government in the December 1994 reshuffle, notwithstanding the decision of the parent party to go into opposition. Laço retained his post in the government appointed in July 1996, even though the BSDS had won no seats in the May–June election. His moderating influence was also apparent in late 1998 and early 1999, when he encouraged the Union for Democracy to end its legislative boycott, arguing it could serve more effectively as a genuine opposition party via full parliamentary participation. By then, the party had been transformed into the BLD.

Leaders: Arjan STAROVA (Chair), Teodor LAÇO.

National Front Party (*Partia Balli Kombëtare*—PBK). The PBK is descended from the anticommunist wing of the National Front created in 1942 to oppose Axis occupation. The then PBK leader, Abaz Ermenji, returned to Albania in October 1995 after 49 years in exile. The party won three of the United Albanian Right's four seats to the assembly in the 1997 election. In 2002 Ermenji was defeated in his attempt to retain the PBK leadership.

Reports surrounding the July 2005 legislative poll referenced electoral cooperation between the PBK (under Adriatík Alimadhi's leadership) and the PDS. However, other reports also referenced PDS cooperation with the **Democratic National Front Party** (*Partia Balli Kombëtar Demokrat*—PBKD), which had reportedly been formed in 1998 by Hysen SELFO, former deputy chair of the PBK who had been expelled from the parent group as a result of conflict with Ermenji. Negotiations toward a merger were conducted in 2005 between the PBK and PBKD (now led by Artur ROSHI) but ultimately failed. The relationship between the two parties subsequently remained unclear, and even regional media reports frequently conflated or confused the two groups.

Leaders: Adriatík ALIMADHI, Abaz ERMENJI (Chair), Shkelqim ROQI.

Albanian Republican Party (*Partia Republikane Shqiptare*—PRS). Third-ranked in the 1991 balloting, the PRS is an urban formation with links to the Italian Republican Party, from which it appears to have drawn financial support. The first PRS congress in June 1992 was marred by a major split, resulting in the creation of distinct centrist and right-wing groups.

The PRS withdrew from the ruling coalition in December 1994, criticizing the government's "shortcomings" but pledging itself to "constructive" opposition. It was reinstated with two posts in the government appointed in July 1996, despite winning only three seats in the preceding assembly election. The PRS again exited the government in February 1997 and, amid growing public disorder, called for it to resign. The party secured one of the United Albanian Right's four seats in the 1997 balloting for the assembly.

Early in November 1997, PRS Chair Sabri Godo denounced the PDS at a PRS party congress and said conservatives should rally around the PRS, which could become a "third force" against communism. Saying his legislative duties kept him too busy to lead his party, Godo relinquished the chair to a 32-year-old, Fatmir Mediu. However, Godo continued to serve as chair of the parliamentary constitutional commission that drafted the new basic law implemented in November 1998. Mediu was appointed to the PDS-led cabinet in September 2005, the PRS having secured 11 seats in the July legislative balloting as part of the ALDM. In March 2008 Mediu resigned as defense minister following the Gerdac disaster. In the 2009 assembly election the PRS won 1 seat and 2 percent of the nationwide vote.

Leaders: Fatmir MEDIU (Chair), Sabri GODO (Former Chair), Çerçiz MINGOMATAJ, Arian MADHI (Parliamentary Leader).

Party of the Democratic Alliance (*Partia e Aleanca Demokratike*—PAD). The PAD was launched in October 1992 by a number of parliamentarians, including PDS cofounder Gramoz PASHKO, in opposition to what was termed the "autocratic rule" of President Berisha. One of the PAD's activists was killed on January 14, 1994, during a rally that had generated what the government termed "pro-Serbian statements." Several prominent PAD candidates were barred (because of their allegedly Communist past) from the 1996 legislative balloting, which the PAD contested unsuccessfully as part of the PQ alliance with the PSDS. The party won 2 assembly seats in the 1997 election (having presented its own candidates for that balloting) and joined the new PSS-led government. It remained in the government after the 2001 election, at which it took 3 seats. However, a split in the party left its status in the government in limbo in 2002. One faction, led by Arben Imani and including at least one legislator, announced in May that it was taking the PAD out of the Alliance of State on the grounds that effective governance was being compromised by PSS infighting. However, another faction, led by Neritan Çeka, reaffirmed its support for the government and named new members to fill the party vacancies created by the "defection" of Imani and his supporters. The factionalization continued into 2005 with Çeka and his supporters cooperating informally with the PSS while Imani's group aligned with the PDS. Competing, at least partially, as an ally of the PSS, the PAD secured 3 proportional seats (on a vote share of 4.8 percent) in the July 2005 legislative poll.

Gramoz Pashko died in a helicopter crash in July 2006. In 2008 the PAD began talks with the LSI to join a new left-leaning coalition as a "third force" in domestic politics, following a cited rift with the leadership of the PSS. In 2009, however, the PAD joined the AN.

Leaders: Neritan ÇEKA, Arben IMANI.

Party for Justice and Integration (*Partia për Drejtësi dhe Integrim*—PDI). Formed in 2005 as a center-right party for the protection of human rights, the PDI represents the interests of the Cham minority. Ethnically Albanian, the group possesses a distinct regional identity; many of its members are expatriates from Greece, which expelled much of its Cham population during the Greek Civil War. The party is concentrated in a small number of districts, and, benefiting from the new regional electoral arrangements, it won a seat in the 2009 assembly elections, although it secured less than 1 percent of the nationwide vote.

Leader: Tahir MHUEDINI (Chair).

Movement of Legality Party (*Partia Lëvizja e Legalitetit*—PLL). The PLL was founded in 1991 as the political wing of the monarchist movement, which has marginal support in Albania but some following among Albanians living abroad. Leka ZOGU, son of the late King Zog (who fled the country in 1939) briefly attended the movement's 50th anniversary celebrations in Tirana in November 1993. Zogu, having returned to Albania to rally support for a referendum on the monarchy (held simultaneously with the June 29, 1997, assembly election), subsequently went back to South Africa and was later threatened with arrest, should he return to Albania, for leading an armed rally in Tirana at which there was a fatal shoot-out. Reporting on the early balloting, Prime Minister Fino initially estimated that 53 percent favored a monarchy, but official results subsequently put the figure at 33 percent, which the PLL insisted was a fraudulent count. The PLL won 3 seats in the collateral assembly election.

Leka Zogu and a group of his supporters were arrested in South Africa in early 1999 on charges of illegal possession of a large cache of weapons. Meanwhile, the government alleged that PLL supporters had in effect been involved in a coup attempt. In late 1999 Zogu was sentenced in absentia by a court in Tirana to three years in prison, and the assembly defeated an amnesty motion in his case in mid-2000.

However, Leka Zogu was permitted by invitation of the assembly to return to Albania in mid-2002 as a "common citizen." Although he initially indicated he would not pursue a political career, in mid-2004 he launched a Movement for National Development (*Lëvizja për Zhvillim Kombëtar*—LZhK) that comprised the PLL, the Conservative Party, and the small **Renewal Democratic Party** (*Partia Demokratika e Rinovor*—PDRn), led by Dashamir Shehi, who had recently split from the PDr. The LZhK's "law and order" platform for the 2005 legislative balloting called for anticorruption measures (including judicial reform) and pursuit of integration with the EU and NATO. Zogu also endorsed independence for Kosovo, although he retreated from previous support for formation of a "Greater Albania."

In early 2007 Zogu announced that he was formally withdrawing his affiliations with the PLL and LZhK on the grounds that a king should "stand above politics." The LZhK, which had emerged as a minor political party in its own right, joined the PL, below, for the 2009 assembly poll, in which the PLL took less than 1 percent of the nationwide vote.

Leader: Ekrem SPAHIA (Chair).

Macedonian Alliance for European Integration (*Aleanca e Maqedonasve për Integrim Evropian*—AMIE; in Macedonian, *Makedonska Alijansa za Evropska Integracija*). Launched in mid-2005, this grouping was described as the first "ethnically-based" party to be registered. It pledged to support the interests of the Macedonian minority in Albania. In 2007 the group claimed that the government had exerted pressure on its supporters in municipal elections. In the 2009 elections the AMIE took less than a tenth of a percent of the nationwide vote.

Leader: Kimet FETAHU.

Agrarian Environmental Party (*Partia Agrare Ambientaliste*—PAA). The PAA is a successor rubric for the Albanian Agrarian Party (*Partia Agrare e Shqipërisë*—PAS), which upon its formation in 1991 called for the privatization of all previously collectivized property, credit arrangements for farmers, and job stimulation for those thrown out of work by the collapse of collectivization. The PAS won 1 seat in the 1997 assembly election and three in 2001. The PAA was given a deputy ministerial post in the December 2003 PSS-led cabinet.

Although the PAA continued to cooperate with the PSS for the July 2005 assembly poll (at which the PAA secured 4 seats in the proportional balloting [on a vote share of 6.6 percent]), Lufter Xhuveli accepted a post in the new PDS-led government formed in September.

Leaders: Lufter XHUVELI (Chair), Petrit GJONI (Parliamentary Leader)

Socialist Alliance for Integration (*Aleanca Socialiste për Integrim*—ASI). Formed in late 2008 in an attempt to build a left-leaning "third force" in Albanian politics, the ASI included, in addition to the LSI and LDLNj, the **Real Socialist Party '91** (*Partia Socialiste e Vërtetë '91*—PSV '91), led by Petro KOÇI; the **Green Party** (*Partia e Gjelbër*—PGj), led by Edlir PETANAJ; the **Party for the Protection of Immigrants' Rights** (*Parti për Mbrojtjen e të Drejtave të Emigrantëve*—PMDE), led by Ymer KURTI; and the **New Tolerance of Albania Party** (*Partia Tolerancë e Re e Shqipërisë*—PTR), led by Avdi KECI. The ASI as a whole secured 5.5 percent of the nationwide vote and four seats in the 2009 assembly balloting.

Socialist Movement for Integration (*Lëvizja Socialiste për Integrim*—LSI). A left-of-center splinter from the PSS, the LSI was launched under the leadership of former prime minister Ilir Meta, who had been feuding with PSS leader Nano for several years. Nine PSS legislators reportedly joined the LSI, which ran separately from all other parties in the 2005 legislative poll, securing five seats (four on a vote share of 8.4 percent in the proportional balloting). The LSI agreed to join the PSS-led opposition coalition for the February 2007 local balloting but broke with the PSS in 2008 and led the formation of the ASI. In the 2009 assembly balloting the LSI garnered 5 percent of the nationwide vote and secured all of the ASI's four seats. Announcements in early July 2009 stated that the LSI would support a PDS-led AN government, but as of August the precise delineation of such a deal had not been determined, including whether the LSI would be represented in the cabinet and whether other ASI members would also lend their support.

Leaders: Ilir META (Chair and Former Prime Minister), Pellumb XHUFI (Deputy Chair), Ndre LEGISI.

Human Rights League Party (*Partia Lëvizja për te Drejtat dhe Lirite e Njeriut*—LDLNj). The LDLNj is led by Ligoraq Karamelo, a former legislator and former member of the PBDNj. Among other things, Karamelo in early 2006 joined other activists in criticizing the PBDNj and *Omonia* for failing to address the concerns of the Greek minority adequately.

Leader: Ligoraq KARAMELO

Opposition Parties:

Unification for Changes (*Bashkimi për Ndryshim*). This PSS-led coalition is a continuation of the 2007 "Union for the Future" alliance that was formed for the 2007 municipal balloting. In addition to the PSS, that alliance included the PSDS, LSI, PAD, and PDSSh.

The Unification for Changes won 45.3 percent of the vote in the 2009 assembly elections and secured 66 seats.

Socialist Party of Albania (*Partia Socialiste e Shqipërisë*—PSS). The PSS is a successor to the Communist Party of Albania (*Partia Komuniste e Shqipërisë*—PKS), which was launched in November 1941 under the supervision of Yugoslav emissaries and became the ruling single party following World War II. The PKS was renamed the Albanian Party of Labor (*Partia e Punës e Shqipërisë*—PPS) in 1948.

In 1990 the PPS Central Committee proposed a number of drastic changes in the country's constitution, including a provision that would prohibit the president of the republic from serving as party first secretary. In accordance with this requirement, President Alia stepped down as first secretary on May 4, 1991. A month earlier, at the conclusion of the country's first multiparty balloting since World War II, the PPS had won a better than two-thirds majority in the new People's Assembly. However, due to subsequent popular unrest, it was forced to participate in a "nonpartisan" governing coalition on June 12, at which time it adopted its current name. In light of these developments, a rump group organized the new Albanian Communist Party (see PKS, below).

At the March 1992 general election the PSS won only 38 of 140 seats with 25 percent of the vote. As a result, Alia resigned as president of the republic, and the party, for the first time, moved into opposition. Alia and his successor as party leader, Fatos Thanos Nano, were both arrested in mid-1993, Nano being convicted in April 1994 of having mishandled $8 million in Italian aid funds during his 1991 incumbency as prime minister. His 12-year prison sentence was upheld by the Supreme Court in August, prior to which Alia and nine former colleagues had also received prison sentences. Alia was released in July 1995, but he was imprisoned (along with several other members of his former administration) in February 1996 on charges of "genocide" and "crimes against humanity" in connection with the alleged killing or internment of Albanians who had attempted to flee the country during his tenure. Nano also remained in prison during the May–June 1996 election, from which many PSS candidates were barred because of their Communist affiliations. Opposition protests over the conduct of the balloting were headed by the PSS, which was officially credited with ten seats despite boycotting the second round.

In a communication from his prison cell in July 1996, Nano proposed that the PSS should become a genuinely reformist party and drop all references to Marxism in its constitution. In the rebellion of early 1997 (see Political background, above), Nano and Alia escaped from prison along with hundreds of others. Nano was subsequently pardoned by President Berisha, who was under pressure to include the PSS in an interim "government of reconciliation." Meanwhile, Alia fled the country, returning in December after having been declared innocent of all outstanding charges by the Albanian courts in October.

The PSS, showing its greatest strength in the south, swept to victory in the 1997 elections, taking 101 seats, which, with 18 seats secured by five allies (the PSDS, PAD, PAS, PBDNj, and PUK [see below]) in an Alliance of State coalition, gave the party a secure margin for amending the constitution. Following severe political turmoil in 1998, Nano resigned his PSS chair in early 1999. However, although he had announced he would launch a new political movement that, among other things, would be "neither communist nor anticommunist," Nano made a comeback at the October PSS Congress, defeating Majko for the chair by a vote of 291–261. PSS Deputy Chair Ilir Meta was subsequently selected to be the new prime minister by a vote of 68–45 in the PSS steering committee over Makbule ÇEÇO, the governor of Tirana, who was designated to be deputy prime minister.

At the 2001 national election the PSS barely retained its majority, winning 73 seats in a downsized People's Assembly. However, Nano was reelected chair of the PSS at a December 2003 congress that also demanded that PSS legislators toe the party line on major votes or else quit the party. Meta and a number of PSS legislators subsequently left the PSS to form the LSI (below).

The PSS in early 2005 reportedly announced plans to contest the July legislative poll under informal cooperative arrangements with the PSDS, PAS, PBDNj, and a faction of the PAD. As part of that pact, the PSS called upon its supporters to vote for the smaller parties in the nationwide proportional balloting. However, that initiative was undercut by the fact that each party presented a separate nationwide list, thereby precluding the kind of cohesion exhibited by the PDS-aligned ALDM (above). In addition, the PSS presented its own candidate in each single-member constituency, sometimes in direct competition with candidates from its "allies."

Following the defeat of the PSS in the July 2005 balloting, Nano resigned as the PSS chair in September. He was succeeded by Edi Rama (the mayor of Tirana), who defeated former president Mejdani for the post.

Following its 2005 electoral defeat (which the party ascribed to fraud), the PSS in 2006 led the opposition in demanding broad electoral changes for the scheduled municipal elections (see Current issues, above). In forming a left-wing coalition for the February 2007 municipal balloting, the PSS reportedly agreed to give its smaller partners greater representation among joint candidates than had been offered in the ill-fated 2005 negotiations. Tensions between pro-Rama and pro-Nano factions increased in 2007 when Rama denied political backing for Nano's bid for the presidency. In September 2007 Nano announced his resignation from the party and the establishment of a new party, the **Movement for Solidarity,** although it subsequently failed to emerge as a significant political force.

Although initially supportive of the new electoral code approved in 2008, the PSS subsequently accused the ruling PDS of failing to implement some aspects of electoral reform. Following the release of preliminary results of the June 2009 assembly elections, the PSS condemned the results as fraudulent. Rama continued to reject the results into August, calling for early elections for a new assembly. His stance contributed to increasing calls within the party for his resignation, and a struggle for party leadership was widely expected at an extraordinary PSS congress scheduled for late August. The party won 65 of the BN's 66 seats in the June assembly balloting and 41 percent of the vote nationwide.

Leaders: Edi RAMA (Chair and Mayor of Tirana), Gramoz RUÇI (Former Secretary General), Valentina LESKAJ, (Parliamentary Leader).

Social Democratic Party of Albania (*Partia Socialdemokrat e Shqipërisë*—PSDS). The PSDS was launched in 1991 on a platform of moderate socialism; it finished third at the 1992 poll, winning 7 assembly seats, and became a junior partner in the new government headed by the PDS. Following the president's November 1994 referendum defeat, the PSDS officially withdrew from the coalition, although the 2 cabinet representatives previously associated with the party opted to retain their portfolios as members of the breakaway BSDS.

The PSDS formed an alliance, called the Pole of the Center (*Poli i Quendres*—PQ), with the PAD for the 1996 legislative poll as a centrist alternative to the ruling PDS on the right and the PSS on the left; the PQ secured no seats in that election. However, the PSDS offered some joint candidates with the PSS for the June 1997 balloting, in which nine PSDS members were elected, and the PSDS joined the subsequent coalition government. After winning four seats at the 2001 election, it again joined the government. The PSDS declined to join the July 2002 cabinet because it was not offered the post of deputy prime minister that it had previously held. However, the PSDS returned to the cabinet in December 2003, and, despite his steady criticism of perceived administration failures, PSDS Chair Skënder Gjinushi said the party would support the PSS-led government in the run-up to the July 2005 legislative poll and beyond. The PSDS secured 7 seats (on a vote share of 13 percent) in the proportional component of the 2005 balloting.

Leaders: Dr. Skënder GJINUSHI (Chair and Former Deputy Prime Minister), Engjell BEJTJA (General Secretary).

Union for Human Rights Party (*Partia e Bashkimi për te Drejtat e Njeriut*—PBDNj). The PBDNj was established in February 1992 following the enactment of legislation banning parties based on "ethnic principles." The new law was aimed in particular at the **Democratic Union of the Greek Minority** (*Bashkimia Demokratik i Minoritet Grek*), referenced as *Omonia,* the transliteration of the Greek word for "harmony." The PBDNj became the electoral successor of *Omonia,* winning two assembly seats in March 1992 against *Omonia*'s five seats in 1991.

Representing the southern ethnic Greek community, *Omonia* had been formed by clandestine opponents of the former regime in December 1989 and was officially launched a year later under the leadership of Theodori BEZHANI and Sotiris KYRIAZATIS. Presumed to have strong links to several parties in Greece, particularly New Democracy, *Omonia* contended that any territorial change between Albania and Greece should come only from negotiation and agreement, publicly distancing itself from such militant ethnic Greek groups as the **Northern Epirus Liberation Front** (NELF). *Omonia* nevertheless attracted the wrath of Albanian nationalists, and six prominent *Omonia* members were among many ethnic Greeks detained in May 1994 in a government crackdown on suspected subversion.

The PBDNj was credited with winning 3 assembly seats in 1996 and 4 in 1997. It joined the PSS-led coalition in July 1997, a decision reportedly opposed by some members of *Omonia,* which had maintained a separate identity as a cultural organization despite usually close ties with the PBDNj. Vasil MELO, then leader of the PBDNj, defended the 1998 constitution as providing sufficient protection for minorities, although *Omonia* leaders in January 2000 called for greater attention to minority issues, particularly the provision of educational services in Greek where appropriate. *Omonia* was led at the time by Vangjel Dule, elected in 1998 following a leadership crisis that had resulted in the removal of Kyriazatis in 1996.

The PBDNj won 3 proportional seats, with 2.6 percent of the vote, at the 2001 election. Dule was elected chair of the PBDNj at a party congress in February 2002 that Melo derided as "illegitimate and manipulated." The PBDNj was given one portfolio in the December 2003 cabinet led by the PSS.

It was reported in early 2005 that *Omonia,* under the leadership of Jani JANI, had decided to present its own candidates for the July assembly poll after an absence of 14 years from the electoral process. *Omonia* reportedly agreed to support the PBDNj in the proportional balloting in return for the PBDNj's support for some *Omonia* candidates in the single-member districts. After securing 2 proportional seats (on a vote share of 4.1 percent), the PBDNj was given the ministry of labor, social affairs, and equal opportunities in the new PDS-led cabinet. In the 2009 elections it won over 1 percent of the vote and secured a single seat in the assembly.

Leaders: Vangjel DULE (President), Leonard SOLIS (Deputy Chair), Vasilis BOLLANO (Mayor of Himare).

G99 (*Grupim 99*—G99). Formed in 2008 by members of the MJAFT! ("Enough!") nongovernmental organization, the G99 is predominantly a party of younger Albanians who grew to adulthood after 1991. The party's platform is broadly social democratic, advocating both reform within Albania and youth participation in politics. Although polling well in late 2008 and early 2009, the party took less than 1 percent of the nationwide vote in the June 2009 elections.

Leader: Erion VELIAJ (Chair).

Social Democracy Party of Albania (*Partia Demokracia Sociale e Shqipërisë*—PDSSh). Formed in April 2003 by several disgruntled members of the PSDS (including Paskal Milo, a former member of the PSDS presidency), the PDSSh described itself as a center and center-left grouping devoted to the concerns of a populace that was "tired of the left's unkept promises." The PDSSh subsequently appeared to move in and out of the PSS-led Coalition for Integration, although it was reportedly supportive of the coalition during the run-up to the July 2005 legislative balloting. The PDSSh secured 2 proportional seats (on a vote share of 4.3 percent) in the 2005 assembly balloting. In the 2009 assembly elections it polled approximately 2 percent of the nationwide vote but failed to secure any seats.

Leader: Paskal MILO (Chair).

Other Parties that Participated in the 2009 Assembly Elections:

Pole of Freedom (*Poli i Lirisë*—PL). The PL was founded by the PDK as a center-right "third force" in domestic politics in 2009 in opposition to both the PDS and PSS. The PDK was joined by the PBD, which, like the PDK, had left an earlier alliance with the PDS, as well as several smaller parties: the **Movement for National Development** (*Lëvizja për Zhvillim Kombëtar*—LZhK), a royalist party led by Dashamir SHEHI (see PLL, above, for details); the **Conservative Party** (*Partia Konservatore*—PKons), led by Armando RUÇO; the **Democratic Reform Party** (*Partia e Reformave Demokratike Shqiptare*—PRDSh), led by Skender HALILI; and the **Path of Freedom Party** (*Partia Rruga e Lirisë*—PRrL), led by Shukrane MUDA. The PL overall won less than 2 percent of the nationwide vote in the 2009 assembly balloting, with the PDK and LZhK obtaining most of this support and the remaining parties taking less than a tenth of a percent each.

Christian Democratic Party of Albania (*Partia Demokristiane e Shqipërisë*—PDK). A member of the 1977 Union for Democracy coalition, the PDK drew support mainly from Shkodër and other northern Catholic towns. It won 1 percent of the vote in the 2001 legislative poll. The then chair of the PDK, Zef BUSHATI, was appointed Albania's ambassador to the Vatican in 2002 and was succeeded as PDK leader by Nikolle LESI, a well-known editor. The PDK secured two seats in the 2005 assembly who had recently left the New Democratic Party (PDr). In November 2007 Lesi split with the party and founded the **Albanian Christian Democratic Movement**, stating his intention to draw from PDK supporters and compete in the 2009 parliamentary elections.

A local PDK party head was assassinated by a bomb attack in June 2009, although it was not confirmed that the attack was politically motivated.

Leader: Nard NDOKA (Chair).

Democratic Union Party (*Partia Bashkimi Demokrat*—PBD). Another member of the 1977 Union for Democracy coalition, the PBD captured 0.6 percent of the vote in the 2001 general election and 0.5 percent in 2005. In 2009 it declined further, taking less than a tenth of a percent of the nationwide vote.

Leader: Ylber VALTERI.

Law and Justice Party (*Partia Ligj dhe Drejtësi*—PLiDr). Founded in February 2009 by defectors from the PDS, the PLiDR is a center-right party with an anticorruption and "law and order" agenda. Running without coalition partners, it secured less than 1 percent of the vote in the June assembly elections.

Leader: Spartak NGJELA (Chair), Gilman BAKALLI (Secretary).

Other Parties Participating in the 2005 Assembly Elections:

Albanian Communist Party (*Partia Komuniste e Shqiptare*—PKSH). The PKSH was organized in 1991 by a rump of the PPS after the parent group adopted the PSS rubric. Although accorded legal recognition in November 1991, the PKS was subsequently outlawed by the mid-1992 ban on "extremist" organizations. When the 1992 law was repealed in April 1998, the PKS was in effect reregistered. It won about 0.9 percent of the vote in 2001 and 0.7 percent in 2005.

Leader: Hysni MILLOSHI.

Albanian Homeland Party (*Partia Shqiptare Atdheu*—PShA). Initially denied legal status in 2004 on the grounds that it was a religion-based (Muslim) grouping, the PShA was subsequently permitted by the Court of Appeals to register for the 2005 assembly balloting. The leader of the PShA, Artan Shaqiri, a prominent young religious leader, called, among other things, for the introduction of religious education into the Albanian school system.

Leader: Artan VUCAJ.

Party of National Unity (*Partia e Unitetit Kombëtar*—PUK). Organized in June 1991 by former Communists, the PUK forged links with Kosovo's Albanian community. Its posture of extreme nationalism was said to be supported, in part, by Albanian "Mafia" groups in Turkey and elsewhere. PUK leader Idajet Beqiri was sentenced to a six-month prison term in July 1993 for asserting that President Berisha sought to create a fascist dictatorship. In January 1996 Beqiri was again arrested, this time charged with crimes against humanity as a communist-era prosecutor. However, he was subsequently pardoned along with members of the PSS. (Beqiri has subsequently also been referenced as a leader of the underground AKSh, below.)

The PUK earned one seat in the 1997 election as a member of the PSS-led Alliance of State. It won only 0.2 percent of the vote and no seats in 2001.

The PUK participated in the 2005 assembly elections with several other small parties in a coalition called the **Albanian Social Parties and National Unity Party** (*Partite e Spektrit dhe Partia e Unitetit Kombëtar*—PSS + PUK). Other components of the coalition included the **Environmentalist Party** (*Partia Ambientaliste*—PA), led by Nasi BOZHEKU; the **Albanian Party of Labor** (*Partia Punëtore Shqiptare*—PPS), led by Xhevdet PATAJ; and the **Party for the Defense of Workers' Rights** (*Partia për Mbrojtjen e te Drejtave te Punëtorëve*—PMDP), led by Ymer KURTI and Kadri Mehmat ISUFAG.

Leader: Idajet BEQIRI (Chair).

(For a list of other small parties that participated in the 2005 elections, see the 2007 *Handbook*.)

Underground Group:

Albanian National Army (*Armata Kombëtare Shqiptare*—AKSh). Described as a "loosely organized criminal extremist group" by the U.S. government, the AKSh promotes establishment of a "Greater Albania" to include the current Albania, Kosovo, and portions of western Macedonia, southern Serbia, and southern Montenegro. It is reportedly a major component of the cross-national Albanian National Unification Front (*Frontit për Bashkimin Kombëtare Shqiptar*—FBKSh). The UN Mission in Kosovo has declared the AKSh to be a terrorist organization. Macedonian courts have also sentenced several purported AKSh members to prison for alleged participation in bomb attacks in Macedonia in 2003. After being active in Kosovo, Macedonia, and Serbia in the first years of the current decade, the AKSh was reported in 2004 to have gone "completely underground" following the arrest by NATO of several AKSh leaders.

In December 2004 one AKSh leader, Gafur Adili, was placed under house arrest in Tirana for his alleged encouragement of AKSh members to "intervene" in Macedonia. Meanwhile, another reported AKSh leader, Idajet Beqiri, was released from prison in Tirana after the Court of Appeals overturned his conviction for "inciting interethnic hatred." (Beqiri had been arrested in Germany and extradited to Albania.)

In late 2005 Serbian representatives claimed that the FBKSh/AKSh had perpetrated a number of attacks on Serbs in Kosovo. For his part, Adili reportedly said that he believed an ethnic war would be "inevitable" in Kosovo if that province was granted independence. In November 2007 Macedonian security forces engaged an "armed criminal" group reportedly linked to the AKSh, killing eight and seizing several truckloads of weapons.

Leaders: Gafur ADILI, Idajet BEQIRI.

LEGISLATURE

The unicameral **Assembly of Albania** (*Kuvendi i Shqipërisë*), named the People's Assembly (*Kuvënd Popullore*) until 2006, comprises 140 deputies serving four-year terms. Prior to 2009, 100 members were directly elected from single-member constituencies in single-round plurality balloting. The remaining 40 members were selected by proportional representation from party or coalition lists in a single nationwide constituency, assuming a minimum vote share of 2.5 percent for individual parties and 4 percent for coalitions. However, under constitutional amendments approved in April 2008, all 140 seats are now allocated via a regional proportional system. The country is divided into 12 electoral regions (corresponding to the country's administrative regions) with varying numbers of assembly seats depending on population (e.g., the Kukes region elects only 4 seats, while the Tirane region elects 32).

All parties, including those in coalitions, present their own candidate lists, and voters cast a single vote for an individual party in their district. Most parties also register as members of coalitions, and the total votes received by the individual parties in a coalition are added together to produce that coalition's vote percentage in a region. (Although the normal electoral threshold is 3 percent for parties and 5 percent for coalitions, regions with small numbers of assembly seats may have a higher "natural threshold" [the percentage of votes required to gain 1 seat]). A coalition's seats within a region are distributed to the individual parties within the coalition in proportion to the votes garnered by the individual parties in that region.

Following the election of June 28, 2009, the seats were distributed as follows: the Alliance for Changes, 70 seats (the Democratic Party of Albania, 68; the Albanian Republican Party, 1; the Party for Justice and Integration, 1); the Unification for Changes, 66 (the Socialist Party of Albania, 65; the Union for Human Rights Party, 1); and the Socialist Alliance for Integration, 4 (the Socialist Movement for Integration, 4).

Chair of Presidency: Jozefina TOPALLI.

CABINET

[as of September 17, 2009]

Prime Minister	Sali Berisha (PDS)
Deputy Prime Minister	Ilir Meta (LSI)
Ministers	
Agriculture, Food, and Consumer Protection	Genc Ruli (PDS)
Defense	Arben Imami (PDS)
Economy, Trade, and Energy	Dritan Prifti (LSI)
Education and Science	Myqerem Tafaj (PDS)
Environment, Forestry, and Water Administration	Fatmir Mediu (PRS)
European Integration	Majlinda Bregu (PDS) [f]
Finance	Ridvan Bode (PDS)
Foreign Affairs	Ilir Meta (LSI)
Health	Petrit Vasili (LSI)
Interior	Lulëzim Basha (PDS)
Justice	Bujar Nishani (PDS)
Labor, Social Affairs, and Equal Opportunities	Spiro Ksera (LDLNj)
Public Works, Transport, and Telecommunications	Sokol Olldashi (PDS)
State and Parliament Relations	Genc Pollo (PDS)
Tourism, Culture, Youth, and Sports	Ferdinand Xhaferri (PDS)

[f] = female

COMMUNICATIONS

Albanian newspapers tend to be highly politicized in their reporting, whether they are independent or represent a political party, although a degree of nonpartisan journalism has emerged in connection with the country's recent political liberalization. In addition, the People's Assembly voted on September 4, 1997, to protect freedom of the press, replacing a 1993 law that restricted access to information and made editors liable for heavy fines if they published "punishable material." International observers described coverage of the 2005 legislative elections as "generally balanced." However, the OSCE and the U.S. State Department expressed concern that the government had "attempted to assert greater control" over the media during the 2009 campaign. Among other things, the new electoral code provided for greater public airtime for larger parliamentary parties and those currently holding seats in the assembly. Meanwhile, in January 2009 domestic media watchdogs argued that government action against the newspaper *Tema,* apparently as a result of articles critical of Prime Minister Berisha, had created an atmosphere of media repression.

Press. The following are published in Tirana: *Koha Jonë* (Our Time, 10,500), influential independent daily; *Zëri i Popullit* (Voice of the People, 7,000), PSS daily; *Rilindja Demokratike* (Democratic Revival, 5,000), PDS daily; *Bashkimi* (Unity, 5,000); *Republika* (Republic, 5,000), PRS daily; *Progresi Agrar* (Agrarian Progress), twice-weekly PAS organ; *Albanian Daily News,* daily in English; *Gazeta Shqiptare* (Albanian Gazette, 12,500), independent daily; *Shekulli* (22,000), independent daily; *Korrieri* (5,000), independent daily; *Tema* (5,000), daily; *Ekonomia* (500), daily; *Panorama,* daily; *Klan,* weekly.

News agency. The principal source for both domestic and foreign news is the official Albanian Telegraph Agency (*Agjensi Telegrafike Shqiptar*—ATS).

Broadcasting and computing. Radio and Television of Albania (*Radio Televizioni Shqiptare*), a government facility, dominates broadcasting. Radio Tirana transmits internationally in a number of languages. There is a largely state-financed national television station (TVSH) and several privately owned national television stations, including *TV Arberia, TV Klan,* and *Top Channel.* As of 2008 there were 238.6 Internet users per 1,000 inhabitants. In May 1997 the assembly passed a law providing for private ownership of radio and television stations, although a government commission controls licensing.

INTERGOVERNMENTAL REPRESENTATION

Ambassador to the U.S.: Aleksander SALLABANDA.

U.S. Ambassador to Albania: John L. WITHERS II.

Permanent Representative to the UN: Ferit HOXHA.

IGO Memberships (Non-UN): BSEC, CEI, CEUR, EBRD, Eurocontrol, IDB, Interpol, IOM, OIC, OIF, OSCE, NATO, WCO, WTO.

ALGERIA

Democratic and Popular Republic of Algeria
al-Jumhuriyah al-Jazairiyah
al-Dimuqratiyah al-Shabiyah

Political Status: Independent republic since July 3, 1962; one-party rule established by military coup July 5, 1965, and confirmed by constitution adopted November 19, 1976; multiparty system adopted through constitutional revision approved by national referendum on February 23, 1989; state of emergency declared for 12 months by military-backed High Council of State on February 9, 1992, and extended indefinitely on February 9, 1993; three-year transitional period declared by High Security Council effective January 31, 1994, as previously endorsed by National Dialogue Conference; constitutional amendments approved by national referendum on November 28, 1996, in advance of return to elected civilian government via multiparty local and national legislative elections in 1997.

Area: 919,590 sq. mi. (2,381,741 sq. km.).

Population: 29,100,867 (1998C); 34,985,000 (2008E).

Major Urban Centers (2005E): EL DJAZAIR (Algiers, 1,532,000), Wahran (Oran, 724,000), Qacentina (Constantine, 475,000). In May 1981 the government ordered the "Arabizing" of certain place names that did not conform to "Algerian translations."

Official Language: Arabic (French and Berber are also widely spoken. However, in December 1996 the National Transitional Council adopted legislation banning the use of French in the public sector as of July 5, 1998, with the exception that universities were given until July 5, 2000, to switch to the use of Arabic only. In the wake of unrest in Berber areas, the government announced in October 2001 that the Berber language—Tamazight—would be elevated to a "national" language.)

Monetary Unit: Dinar (official rate December 1, 2009: 72.12 dinars = $1US).

President: Abdelaziz BOUTEFLIKA (National Liberation Front—FLN); declared winner of controversial election of April 15, 1999, and sworn in for a five-year term on April 27 to succeed Maj. Gen. (Ret.) Liamine ZEROUAL (nonparty), who in September 1998 had announced his intention to resign prior to the scheduled completion of his term in November 2000; reelected (due to internal FLN disputes, as the candidate of the National Democratic Rally [RND] and the Movement for a Peaceful Society [MSP]) on April 8, 2004, and sworn in for a second five-year term on April 19; reelected (as the candidate of the FLN, RND, and MSP) for a third five-year term on April 9, 2009.

Prime Minister: Ahmed OUYAHIA (National Democratic Rally); appointed by the president on June 23, 2008, to succeed Abdelaziz BELKHADEM (National Liberation Front); reappointed on November 16, 2008, and April 27, 2009.

THE COUNTRY

Located midway along the North African littoral and extending southward into the heart of the Sahara, Algeria is a Muslim country of Arab-Berber population, Islamic and French cultural traditions, and an economy in which the traditional importance of agriculture has been replaced by reliance on hydrocarbons, with petroleum and natural gas now accounting for more than 95 percent of exchange earnings. Women currently make up approximately 20 percent of the work force, although, providing a sharp contrast with the rest of the Arab world, they constitute more than half of the nation's lawyers, judges, and university students. There are 30 women in the 389-member national assembly.

For nearly two decades following independence Algeria was perceived by many as a model for Third World liberation movements: the socialist government attended to social welfare needs, while the economy grew rapidly as oil prices rose in the 1970s. Subsequently, declining oil revenues and poor economic management led to major setbacks. Once nearly self-sufficient in food, the country became highly dependent on foreign imports. Other problems included 25 percent unemployment, high population growth (more than one-half of the population is under 20 years old), an external debt estimated at more than $26 billion, a severe shortage of adequate housing, a widespread perception of corruption among government officials, and a spreading black market.

In the mid-1980s the government began to impose budget austerity while attempting to reduce state control of large industries and agricultural collectives, boost nonhydrocarbon production, and cultivate a free-market orientation. The pace of economic reform accelerated following an outbreak of domestic unrest in late 1988, which also precipitated the launching of what was initially considered one of the continent's "boldest democratic experiments." Although political liberalization was seriously compromised during the 1990s by confrontation with the Islamic fundamentalist movement, the government persevered with its new economic policies, thereby gaining partial rescheduling of the external debt and additional credits from the International Monetary Fund (IMF) and the World Bank. Meanwhile, as mandated by the IMF, privatization accelerated, the collateral loss of some 400,000 jobs in the public sector contributing to growing popular discontent with fiscal policy. Burgeoning terrorist activity in the second half of the 1990s impaired foreign investment in a number of sectors, but it did not affect activity in the oil and gas fields in the southern desert, where oil reserves were estimated at about 16 billion barrels.

GDP growth of more than 5 percent was reported for 2004 and 2005, supported primarily by high oil and gas prices. Although growth slowed to 2 percent in 2006, a significant budget surplus continued to permit large-scale spending increases designed to create jobs (official unemployment remained at more than 17 percent, with some observers suggesting the actual level could be twice that figure) and improve the housing and transportation sectors. Efforts were also launched to attract additional foreign investment to the nonhydrocarbon sector, although the IMF cautioned that substantial reform and modernization were still required in the banking system. International financial institutions also urged the government to speed up its privatization program, described as having stalled recently in the wake of the budget surpluses and a lingering fondness among the population (as well as a number of government leaders) for public benefits associated with the socialist past. Meanwhile, Algeria signed an association agreement with the European Union in September 2005 and subsequently intensified its efforts to gain membership in the World Trade Organization.

Real GDP growth of 4.6 percent and 3.0 percent was reported for 2007 and 2008, respectively, as the nonhydrocarbon sector grew by 6 percent each year. Inflation remained manageable at 3.5 percent in 2008, although high unemployment (particularly among young people) and the severe housing shortage continued to resist an intensified public spending campaign. Growth of 2.5 percent was predicted for 2009, with Algeria appearing relatively insulated from the global financial crisis because of its public control of the banking system, negligible external debt, and ongoing budget surplus.

GOVERNMENT AND POLITICS

Political background. Conquered by France in the 1830s and formally annexed by that country in 1842, Algeria achieved independence as the result of a nationalist guerrilla struggle that broke out in 1954 and yielded eventual French withdrawal on July 3, 1962. The eight-year war of liberation, led by the indigenous National Liberation Front (*Front de Libération Nationale*—FLN), caused the death of some 250,000 Algerians, the wounding of 500,000, the uprooting of nearly 2 million others, and the emigration of some 1 million French settlers. The new Algerian regime was handicapped by deep divisions within the victorious FLN, particularly between commanders of the revolutionary army and a predominantly civilian political leadership headed by Ahmed BEN BELLA, who formed Algeria's first regular government and was elected to a five-year presidential term in September 1963. Despite his national popularity, Ben Bella's extravagant and flamboyant style antagonized the army leadership, and he was deposed (and imprisoned) in June 1965 by a military coup under Col. Houari BOUMEDIENNE, who assumed power as president of the National Council of the Algerian Revolution.

During 1976 the Algerian people participated in three major referenda. The first, on June 27, yielded overwhelming approval of a National Charter that committed the nation to the building of a socialist society, designated Islam as the state religion, defined basic rights of citizenship, singled out the FLN as the "leading force in society," and stipulated that party and government cadres could not engage in "lucrative activities" other than those afforded by their primary employment. The second referendum, on November 17, approved a new constitution that, while recognizing the National Charter as "the fundamental source of the nation's policies and of its laws," assigned sweeping powers to the presidency. The third referendum, on December 10, reconfirmed Colonel Boumedienne as the nation's president by an official majority of 99.38 percent. Two months later, in the first legislative election since 1964, a unicameral National People's Assembly was established on the basis of a candidate list presented by the FLN.

President Boumedienne died on December 27, 1978, and he was immediately succeeded by assembly president Rabah BITAT, who was legally proscribed from serving as chief executive for more than a 45-day period. Following a national election on February 7, 1979, Bitat yielded the office to Col. Chadli BENDJEDID, who had emerged in January as the FLN presidential designee during an unprecedented six-day meeting of a sharply divided party congress.

At a June 1980 FLN congress, President Bendjedid was given authority to select members of the party's Political Bureau, and on July 15 he revived the military General Staff, which had been suppressed by his predecessor after a 1967 coup attempt by Col. Tahir ZBIRI. As a further indication that he had consolidated his control of state and party, Bendjedid on October 30 pardoned the exiled Zbiri and freed former president Ben Bella from house detention. (The latter had been released from 14 years' imprisonment in July 1979.)

Bendjedid was unopposed in his reelection bid of January 12, 1984, and on January 22 he appointed Abdelhamid BRAHIMI to succeed Col. Mohamed Ben Ahmed ABDELGHANI as prime minister. Thereafter, the regime was buffeted by deteriorating economic conditions, growing militancy among Islamic fundamentalists and students, and tension within the government, the FLN, and the army over proposed economic and political liberalization. The political infighting limited the effectiveness of reform efforts, critics charging that many of those entrenched in positions of power were reluctant to surrender economic and social privileges.

The pent-up discontent erupted into rioting in Algiers in early October 1988 and quickly spread to other cities, shattering Algeria's reputation as an "oasis of stability" in an otherwise turbulent region. Upwards of 500 persons died when the armed forces opened fire on demonstrators in the capital, while more than 3,000 were arrested. President Bendjedid thereupon adopted a conciliatory attitude, converting what could have been a challenge to his authority into a mandate for sweeping economic and political change. In a referendum on November 3, voters overwhelmingly approved a constitutional amendment reducing the FLN's political dominance by assigning greater responsibility to the prime minister and making him accountable to the assembly. Two days later, Bendjedid appointed Kasdi MERBAH, described as a "determined" proponent of economic liberalization, as the new ministerial leader, and on November 9 Merbah announced a cabinet from which a majority of the previous incumbents were excluded. Collaterally, the president instituted leadership changes in the military and the FLN, the latter agreeing late in the month to open future legislative elections to non-FLN candidates. On December 22 Bendjedid was reelected to a third five-year term, securing a reported 81 percent endorsement as the sole presidential candidate.

The FLN's status was eroded further by additional constitutional changes in February 1989 that provided, among other things, for multiparty activity (see Constitution and government, below). Seven months later, arguing that economic reforms were not being implemented quickly enough, Bendjedid named Mouloud HAMROUCHE, a longtime political ally, to succeed Merbah as prime minister.

A multiparty format was introduced for the first time in elections for municipal and provincial councils on June 12, 1990. Contrary to expectations, the Islamic Salvation Front (*Front Islamique du Salut*—FIS), the country's leading Islamic fundamentalist organization, obtained 53 percent of the popular vote and a majority of the 15,000 seats being contested. Responding to demands from the FIS and other opposition parties, President Bendjedid announced in April 1991 that two-stage national legislative elections, originally scheduled for 1992, would be advanced to June 27 and July 18, 1991. However, the FIS called a general strike on May 25 to demand additional electoral law changes, the immediate application of sharia (Islamic religious law), the resignation of Bendjedid, and the scheduling of new presidential elections. Clashes in the capital between fundamentalists and police intensified in early June, leaving at least seven dead, and on June 5 Bendjedid declared a state of emergency, ordered the army to restore order, and postponed the legislative poll. He also called upon the foreign minister, Sid Ahmed GHOZALI, to form a new government.

On June 18, 1991, Ghozali, described as a "technocrat" committed to economic and political reform, announced his cabinet (the first since independence not to be dominated by FLN leaders) and pledged "free and clean" parliamentary elections by the end of the year. The schism between the government and the fundamentalists remained unbridged, however, and top FIS leaders and hundreds of their followers were arrested when new violence broke out in Algiers in early July.

Following a period of relative calm, the state of emergency was lifted on September 29, 1991, and two-round elections to a 430-seat assembly were scheduled for December 26, 1991, and January 16, 1992. Again testifying to the remarkable surge in fundamentalist influence, FIS candidates won 188 seats outright in the first round (compared to 25 for the Berber-based Socialist Forces Front [*Front des Forces Socialistes*—FFS] and only 15 for the FLN). With the FIS poised to achieve a substantial majority (possibly even the two-thirds majority needed for constitutional revision), Bendjedid initiated talks with the fundamentalists regarding a power-sharing arrangement.

On January 11, 1992, Bendjedid, apparently under pressure from military leaders upset with his accommodation of the FIS, submitted his resignation. The High Security Council (*Haute Conseil de Securité*—HCS), composed of Ghozali and other top officials, including three senior military leaders, announced that it had assumed control to preserve public order and protect national security. (According to the constitution, the assembly president was mandated to assume interim presidential duties, but it was revealed that the assembly had been dissolved by a secret presidential decree on January 4. Although the president of the Constitutional Council was next in the line of temporary succession, the council deferred to the HCS upon Bendjedid's resignation, reportedly ruling that "prevailing conditions" were not covered by the basic law.)

On January 12, 1992, the HCS canceled the second stage of the legislative election and nullified the results of the first stage. Two days later it announced that it had appointed a five-man High Council of State (*Haute Conseil d'État*—HCE) to serve as an interim collegial presidency. Mohamed BOUDIAF, vice president of the country's wartime provisional government, was invited to return from 28 years of exile in Morocco to assume the chair of the new body.

Following its "soft-gloved coup" in early 1992, the military launched what was described as an "all-out war" against the fundamentalist movement, arresting numerous FIS leaders (including moderates who had been counseling against violent confrontation) in addition to some 500 other FIS members. Bloody demonstrations throughout Algeria erupted shortly thereafter, and on February 9 the HCE declared a new 12-month state of emergency. With most constitutional rights effectively suspended by the declaration, the government intensified its anti-FIS campaign, while militant fundamentalists initiated guerrilla activity against police and security forces. The unrest continued following Ghozali's reappointment on February 23, even relatively moderate fundamentalists being driven underground by a March decision of the Algerian courts, acting on an HCE petition, to ban the FIS as a legal party. Meanwhile, the nonfundamentalist population, apparently fearing political, legal, and social constraints should the FIS come to power, reportedly accepted the military intervention with relief.

HCE Chair Boudiaf was assassinated on June 29, 1992, while addressing a rally in the eastern city of Annaba. Official investigators subsequently concluded there was a broad conspiracy behind the attack without being able to identify those involved. Suspects ranged from militant fundamentalists to members of the "power elite" who may have felt threatened by Boudiaf's anticorruption efforts. (Only one person was arrested in connection with the incident—a member of the presidential guard who was convicted in June 1995 following a trial that shed little light on his motives or possible coconspirators.) On July 2 the HCS named Ali KAFI, the secretary general of the National Organization of Holy Warriors (a group of veterans from the war of independence) as Boudiaf's successor. Prime Minister Ghozali, blaming corrupt government officials and radical fundamentalists equally for the country's disorder, resigned on July 8. He was replaced on the same day by Belaid ABDESSELAM, longtime industry and energy minister under former president Boumedienne.

On February 9, 1993, the HCE extended the state of emergency indefinitely, declaring that steps toward restoration of an elected civilian government would be taken only after successful completion of the "antiterrorist" crackdown. Four months later the HCE presented a blueprint for constitutional change, promising a democratic Muslim state and a free-market economy. In keeping with the new economic thrust, Prime Minister Abdesselam, viewed as strongly oriented towards state control of heavy industry, was replaced on August 21 by Redha MALEK, an advocate of privatization and other forms of liberalization geared to winning debt rescheduling from international creditors.

In October 1993 the HCE appointed an eight-member Committee for National Dialogue to negotiate an agreement on the nation's political future among the legal political parties, labor organizations, and trade and professional groups. However, talks were constrained by a mounting conviction among party leaders that full-scale civil war loomed unless the FIS was brought into the negotiations, a step the regime refused to accept. Consequently, the National Dialogue Conference held in Algiers in January 1994 was boycotted by nearly all the political parties, and its influence was extremely limited. The conference had been expected to name a president to succeed the HCE but failed to do so, reportedly because the military would not grant sufficient authority to a civilian leader. Therefore, on January 27 the HCS announced the appointment of Maj. Gen. (Ret.) Liamine ZEROUAL as president, his inauguration four days later coinciding with the dissolution of the HCE. Zeroual, who retained his former position as defense minister, was authorized to govern (in conjunction with the HCS) for a three-year transitional period, initial reports indicating he would seek a settlement with the FIS.

With debt rescheduling negotiations at a critical juncture, President Zeroual reappointed Prime Minister Malek on January 31, 1994, despite

Malek's hard line regarding the FIS. Malek resigned on April 11, following the announcement of preliminary agreement with the IMF; he was replaced by Mokdad SIFI, who had held a number of ministerial posts recently. On April 15 Sifi announced the formation of a new government, described as largely comprising "technocrats" who would concentrate on economic recovery while leaving political and security issues to the president and the HCS. One month later the military-dominated regime set up an appointive National Transitional Council to act in a quasi-legislative capacity prior to elections tentatively scheduled for 1997. However, most of the leading parties boycotted the body, severely undercutting its claim to legitimacy.

A number of groups (including, significantly, the FIS, FLN, and FFS) drafted a proposed national reconciliation pact in Rome in late 1994 and early 1995. The plan called for cessation of antigovernment violence, release of fundamentalist detainees, recognition of the FIS, and inauguration of a national conference to establish a transitional government pending new national elections. Despite strong international endorsement of the proposal, the government quickly rejected it on the ground that no "credible" truce could be achieved. Further illustrating the sway held by the military's hard-liners, security forces subsequently launched a massive campaign against the Armed Islamic Group (*Groupe Islamique Armé*—GIA) and other militant factions that had claimed responsibility for a series of bombings and assassinations. At the same time, the Zeroual administration reportedly continued negotiations with the FIS in the hope that the front's supporters could be reintegrated into normal political processes. However, the talks collapsed in mid-1995, and the regime subsequently began to implement its own schedule for a gradual return to civilian government.

The first stage of the transition was a presidential election conducted on November 16, 1995, in which Zeroual, running as an independent but with the support of the military, was elected to a five-year term with 61 percent of the vote. His closest competitor, Sheikh Mahfoud NAHNAH of the moderate fundamentalist Hamas Party, secured 25 percent of the vote, followed by Saïd SAADI of the Berber Rally for Culture and Democracy (*Rassemblement pour la Culture et la Démocratie*—RCD), with 9 percent, and Nourreddine BOUKROUH of the Algerian Renewal Party (*Parti pour le Renouveau de l'Algérie*—PRA), with 4 percent. President Zeroual's resounding first-round victory was initially seen as easing the "sense of crisis" somewhat, much of the electorate having apparently endorsed his continued hard line toward the militants. Zeroual, whose platform contained strong anticorruption language, was also reportedly perceived as a buffer, to a certain extent, against complete domination of political affairs by military leaders. As anticipated, Prime Minister Sifi submitted his resignation following the successful completion of the election, and on December 31 President Zeroual appointed Ahmed OUYAHIA, former director of the president's office, to succeed Sifi. The government that was announced on January 5, 1996, included several members from Hamas and the PRA, seemingly as a "reward" for their participation in the presidential poll, which had been boycotted by several major legal parties (including the FLN and the FFS) in protest over the lack of an agreement with the FIS.

In mid-1996 President Zeroual proposed a number of constitutional amendments granting sweeping new powers to the president and banning political parties based on religion (see Constitution and government, below). Some 38 parties and organizations endorsed the proposals, although the absence of several major legal groupings (including the FFS and RCD) and, of course, the FIS (which would have been precluded from any eventual legalization under the revisions) undercut the impact of the accord. The government subsequently reported that 85 percent of those voting in a national referendum on November 28 had supported the changes in the basic law. However, opposition leaders and some international observers questioned those results and described the government's claim of an 80 percent vote turnout as vastly inflated.

A new wave of antiregime attacks broke out shortly after the constitutional referendum of November 1996 and reached an unprecedented scale in July–August, despite (or perhaps because of) recent national legislative balloting and other progress toward full return to elected civilian government. Nevertheless, the administration proceeded with its timetable in 1997. New assembly elections were held on June 5, the balloting being dominated by the recently established, progovernment National Democratic Rally (*Rassemblement National et Démocratique*—RND), with 156 seats, followed by the Movement for a Peaceful Society (*Mouvement pour une Société Paisible*—MSP, as Hamas had been renamed) with 69 seats, and the FLN with 62. The MSP and the FLN subsequently agreed to join a new RND-led coalition government, which was announced on June 25 under the continued direction of Prime Minister Ouyahia. The RND also secured most of the seats in municipal elections conducted on October 23, although some were allocated to other parties after a judicial review of allegations of widespread fraud made by a number of groups, including the MSP and the FLN. The political transition was completed on December 25, 1997, with indirect elections to the Council of the Nation (the new upper house in the legislature), the RND winning 80 of the 96 contested seats. By that time, however, despite the progress on the institutional front, the wave of domestic violence had reached an unprecedented level.

As of early 1998 the government reported that about 26,000 people had died during the six-year insurgency, although other observers estimated the figure to be as high as 80,000. A special UN commission that visited Algeria at midyear placed the blame for the violence squarely on "Islamic terrorists" and argued that the Zeroual regime deserved international and domestic support. However, human rights organizations strongly criticized the UN report for inadequately addressing the harsh retaliatory measures on the part of government security forces. In that context, it appeared that differences of opinion had emerged within the military and political elite over how to proceed vis-à-vis the fundamentalists. Hard-liners subsequently appeared to continue to dominate that debate, possibly contributing to the surprise announcement in September by Zeroual (seen as having come to favor a dialogue with moderate Islamist leaders) that he would leave office prior to the completion of his term.

The April 15, 1999, presidential election proved to be highly controversial, as six of the seven candidates quit the race shortly before the balloting out of conviction that the poll had been rigged in favor of the military's preferred candidate, Abdelaziz BOUTEFLIKA, who had served as foreign minister in the 1960s and 1970s but had been on the political sidelines for 20 years. Despite the opposition's demand for a postponement, the election proceeded as scheduled, Bouteflika being credited with 74 percent of the vote.

Following surprisingly long negotiations, President Bouteflika named Ahmed BENBITOUR, a former foreign minister who was described as a close friend of the president's, as prime minister on December 23, 1999. On the following day, Benbitour formed a new government that included seven parties, all of whom remained in the cabinet named by Ali BENFLIS after he replaced Benbitour in late August 2000. However, the RCD left the coalition in May 2001 as the result of severe unrest within the Berber community (see Current issues, below).

The FLN dominated the May 30, 2002, legislative balloting, securing 199 seats, while the RND declined to 47. Prime Minister Benflis was reappointed on June 1, and on June 17 he formed a new government comprising FLN, RND, and MSP ministers.

Further successes by the FLN in the October 2002 assembly elections appeared to kindle presidential aspirations in Benflis, who was dismissed by President Bouteflika on May 5, 2003; Ahmed Ouyahia returned to the prime ministerial post he had held from 1995 to 1998. In September 2003 Bouteflika also dismissed several pro-Benflis cabinet ministers, exacerbating tensions that subsequently split the FLN into two camps (see FLN under Political Parties and Groups, below, for details). The FLN dispute resulted in confusing circumstances under which Bouteflika was reelected (with 85 percent of the vote) on April 8, 2004, as the candidate of the RND and MSP, while Benflis secured only 6.4 percent of the vote as the nominal FLN candidate.

The president dismissed Prime Minister Ouyahia on May 24, 2006, and replaced him with Abdelaziz BELKHADEM, the secretary general of the FLN. The cabinet appointed by Belkhadem the next day was largely unchanged.

Although the FLN's representation declined to 136 seats in the May 17, 2007, assembly poll, the FLN/RND/MSP coalition retained a strong legislative majority. The three parties formed a new government on June 4, again under Belkhadem's leadership.

On June 23, 2008, President Bouteflika again appointed Ouyahia as prime minister. Ouyahia announced a reshuffled cabinet that included former prime minister Belkhadem as a minister of state and personal representative of the president. Following controversial constitutional revision to permit him to run for a third term, Bouteflika was easily reelected on April 9, 2009, with 90.2 percent of the vote.

Constitution and government. The 1976 constitution established a single-party state with the FLN as its "vanguard force." Executive powers were concentrated in the president, who was designated president of the High Security Council and of the Supreme Court, as well as commander in chief of the armed forces. He was empowered to appoint one or more vice presidents and, under a 1979 constitutional amendment that reduced his term of office from six to five years, was obligated to name a prime minister. He also named an 11-member High Islamic Council selected from among the country's "religious personalities." The 1976 document also stipulated that members of the National People's Assembly would be nominated by the FLN and established a judicial system headed by a Supreme Court, to which all lower magistrates were answerable.

In late 1983, as part of a decentralization move, the number of administrative departments (*wilayaat*) was increased from 31 to 48, each continuing to be subdivided into districts (*dairaat*) and communes. At both the *wilaya* and communal (town) levels there were provisions for popular assemblies, with an appointed governor (*wali*) assigned to each *wilaya.* The various administrative units were linked vertically to the minister of the interior, with party organization paralleling the administrative hierarchy.

On January 16, 1986, a referendum approved a new National Charter that, while maintaining allegiance to socialism and Islam, accorded President Bendjedid greater leeway in his approach to social and economic problems, particularly in regard to partial privatization of the "inefficient" public sector. Additional constitutional changes were approved by referendum on November 3, 1988. The revisions upgraded the prime minister's position, declaring him to be the "head of government" and making him directly responsible to the assembly. In effect, the change transferred some of the power previously exercised by the FLN to the assembly, particularly in light of a decision later in the month to permit non-FLN candidates in future elections. The role of the FLN was further attenuated by reference to the president as the "embodiment of the unity of the nation" rather than "of the unity of the party and the state."

Another national referendum on February 23, 1989, provided for even more drastic reform. It eliminated all mention of socialism, guaranteed the fundamental rights "of man and of the citizen" as opposed to the rights of "the people," excised reference to the military's political role, and imposed stricter separation of executive, legislative, and judicial powers. In addition, the FLN lost its "vanguard" status with the authorization of additional "associations of a political nature." Continuing the transfer to a multiparty system, the assembly on July 2 established criteria for legal party status (see Political Parties and Groups, below), and on July 19 it adopted a new electoral law governing political campaigns. The new code established multimember districts for local and national elections, with any party receiving more than 50 percent of the votes to be awarded all the seats in each. However, reacting to complaints from newly formed opposition parties, the government in March 1990 approved a system of proportional representation for the June municipal elections. After intense debate, the electoral law was further changed in 1991 to provide for two-round balloting in single-member districts in future assembly elections.

In announcing a one-year state of emergency in February 1992, the newly formed High Council of State suspended a number of key constitutional provisions, and over the next ten months it ordered the dissolution of nearly 800 municipal assemblies controlled by the FIS since the 1990 elections. In furtherance of its antifundamentalist campaign, the High Council of State in October also created three secret courts in which persons over 16 years of age charged with "subversion" or "terrorism" could be sentenced without the right of appeal. The state of emergency was extended indefinitely in February 1993, a transitional government being named a year later for a three-year period leading to proposed multiparty elections and a return to civilian leadership.

The electoral code was amended in 1995 to provide for multicandidate presidential elections, in two rounds if no candidate received a majority in the first round. Potential candidates were required to obtain the signatures of 75,000 voters to be placed on the ballot, and anyone married to a foreigner was precluded from running.

In connection with the planned transition to civilian government, the Zeroual administration in the spring of 1996 proposed a number of constitutional amendments, which were approved by national referendum on November 28. Among other things, the amendments banned political parties from referencing religious or ethnic "identities," while codifying Islam as the state religion and Arabic as the official national language. The president was given authority to govern by decree in certain circumstances and to appoint one-third of the members of the Council of Nations, a new upper house in the Parliament. That second provision was viewed as one of the most significant aspects of the new charter because it gave the president effective blocking power on legislation. (New laws require the approval of three-quarters of the Council of Nations.) A Constitutional Council was established in April 1998, while a juridical State Council was installed two months later. In November 2008 Parliament eliminated the previous two-term presidential limit and formally reinstalled the position of prime minister (as opposed to "head of government").

Foreign relations. Algerian foreign relations have gone through a series of changes that date back to the preindependence period, formal contacts with many countries having been initiated by the provisional government created in September 1958. Foreign policy in the immediate postindependence period was dominated by President Ben Bella's anti-imperialist ideology. The period immediately following the 1965 coup was essentially an interregnum, with President Boumedienne concentrating his efforts on internal affairs. Following the Arab-Israeli War of 1967, Boumedienne became much more active in foreign policy, with a shift in interest from Africa and the Third World to a more concentrated focus on Arab affairs. After the 1973 Arab-Israeli conflict, the theme of "Third World liberation" reemerged, reflecting a conviction that Algeria should be in the forefront of the Nonaligned Movement. Subsequently, Algeria joined with Libya, Syria, the People's Democratic Republic of Yemen, and the Palestine Liberation Organization to form the so-called "Steadfastness Front" in opposition to Egyptian-Israeli rapprochement. However, in conjunction with a softening Arab posture toward Egypt, Algiers resumed full diplomatic relations with Cairo in November 1988.

A major controversy erupted following division of the former Spanish Sahara between Morocco and Mauritania in early 1976. In February the Algerian-supported Polisario Front (see under Morocco: Disputed Territory) announced the formation of a Saharan Arab Democratic Republic (SADR) in the Western Sahara that was formally recognized by Algeria on March 6; subsequently, a majority of other nonaligned states accorded the SADR similar recognition. However, the issue split the Organization of African Unity (OAU), with Morocco withdrawing from the grouping in 1984 in protest over the seating of an SADR delegation. Concurrently, relations between Algeria and Morocco deteriorated further, with President Bendjedid pledging full support for Mauritania's "territorial integrity" and Morocco referring to the Polisarios as "Algerian mercenaries." Relations improved significantly in late 1987, however, and in May 1988 Rabat and Algiers announced the restoration of formal ties, jointly expressing support for settlement of the Western Saharan problem through a self-determination referendum. Subsequent progress in Morocco-Polisario negotiations permitted Algiers to concentrate on a long-standing foreign policy goal: the promotion of economic, social, and political unity among Maghrebian states (see separate section on Arab Maghreb Union).

The victories of the Islamic fundamentalist movement in Algeria's 1990 and 1991 elections were characterized as generating "shock waves throughout northern Africa." The governments of Egypt, Libya, Morocco, and Tunisia (all struggling to contain fundamentalist influence) were reported to be greatly relieved by the military takeover in January 1992 and supportive of Algiers' anti-FIS campaign. The government/fundamentalist schism also led in March 1993 to the severing of ties with Iran, which the administration accused of supporting local terrorist activity. France, concerned over the possible influx of refugees should a fundamentalist government be established in Algiers, also supported the military regime.

President Bouteflika met with U.S. President George W. Bush in Washington in June 2001, their talks centering on energy issues rather than, as some reformists had hoped, democratization or good governance. Bouteflika returned to the United States late in the year to pledge Algeria's support for Washington's recently launched war on terrorism. Among other things, the aftermath of the September 11, 2001, attacks in the United States appeared to shine a more positive light, in the minds of many international observers, on the hard line adopted by the Algerian regime toward militant fundamentalism since 1992. In consonance with its renewed U.S. ties, the Algerian government refused in 2003 to permit domestic protests against U.S. actions in Iraq.

In March 2003 French President Jacques Chirac made the first formal state visit by a French leader to Algeria since the war of independence. The Algerian population warmly greeted Chirac, who pledged further "reconciliation" initiatives. However, relations with France deteriorated in early 2005 when the French parliament endorsed a bill that recognized the "positive role" that colonization had played in Algeria. President Bouteflika subsequently demanded that France formally apologize for its actions in Algeria, and a proposed French/Algerian "friendship treaty" remained unsigned. New French President Nicolas

Sarkozy visited Algeria in December 2007; he described the colonial past as "profoundly unjust" but declined to offer the apology sought by Algerians. Meanwhile, a number of French-Algerian business contracts were reportedly negotiated as Sarkozy promoted his vision for an economic "Mediterranean Union" involving 21 countries.

Morocco has also been reported to be seeking improved ties with Algeria recently, but the Algerian government remains committed to a self-determination referendum in the Western Sahara. Consequently, the border between Algeria and Morocco stayed closed as of mid-2009, although interest in negotiations on the issue appeared to have intensified.

Current issues. Facing an extremely difficult task in convincing the Algerian populace and the international community of the legitimacy of the April 1999 presidential poll, President Bouteflika moved quickly to establish his leadership credentials by, among other things, announcing plans for a "civil concord," which proposed amnesty for most fundamentalist militants in return for their permanent renunciation of violence and surrender of arms. The pact easily secured legislative approval in the summer and was endorsed by 98 percent of those voting in a national referendum on September 16. By the end of the cutoff date for the amnesty in mid-January 2000, upwards of 6,000 guerrillas had reportedly accepted the government's offer. However, most of them came from the FIS-affiliated Islamic Salvation Army, which had already been honoring a cease-fire since 1997. Significantly, the GIA rejected the peace plan, and deadly attacks and counterattacks continued on a nearly daily basis throughout the summer of 2000.

Despite the partial success of the civil concord, some 2,700 deaths were reported in 2000 from the ongoing conflict, and an upsurge of antigovernment violence was reported in December. In early 2001 President Bouteflika promised an "iron fist" in dealing with the remaining militants. However, the government faced a new crisis in April when riots broke out within the Berber population in the Kabylie region after a young man died under inadequately explained circumstances while in police custody. Government forces responded with a harsh crackdown, and some 1 million demonstrators reportedly participated in the antiregime protests that ensued in the Kabylie region and other areas, including Algiers. More than 60 people were killed and 2,000 injured in the clashes, which, fueled by economic malaise and long-standing concern over the authoritarian rule of what one journalist described as the "overwhelming power of an opaque military leadership," continued into 2002, prompting the leading Berber parties (the FFS and the RCD) to boycott the national legislative poll on May 30.

Deadly bomb attacks continued in 2003, mostly the work of the GIA offshoot called the Salafist Group for Preaching and Combat (*Groupe Salafiste pour la Prédication et le Combat*—GSPC). However, the level of violence was greatly reduced from its height earlier in the decade (as one reporter put it, dozens killed per month rather than dozens per day). Most observers credited President Bouteflika's resounding reelection in April 2004 to popular appreciation of the improved security situation, along with recent economic advances and Algeria's renewed international status in connection with the U.S.-led war on terrorism.

A January 2005 accord between the government and Berber representatives called for enhanced economic support for Berber areas and appeared to reduce unrest within the Berber community. Even more significant was a national referendum on September 29 that overwhelmingly endorsed the government's proposed national charter for peace and reconciliation. The charter called for amnesty for most of the Islamic militants involved in the civil war that had started in 1991, although leaders of the "insurrection" were barred from future political activity. Collaterally, the charter praised the role of the army in the conflict, effectively eliminating any possibility that excesses on the part of the security forces would be investigated. (It was estimated that 6,000–20,000 Algerians had "disappeared" as the result of the army's anti-insurgency measures.) Most major political parties supported the charter, and President Bouteflika staked his political future on its passage. The government reported a 97 percent yes vote and an 80 percent turnout, although the latter figure was broadly discounted by opponents of the initiative as well as some independent analysts. (It was noted that turnout in Berber regions appeared to be less than 20 percent.) Despite protests over the perceived heavy-handedness of the government in stifling effective opposition to the charter, the consensus appeared to be that the vote was a clear indication that the majority of Algerians were prepared to put the matter behind them. (It was estimated that the conflict had cost more than $30 billion and left 150,000–200,000 people dead.) However, the state of emergency remained in effect "until terrorism is completely defeated."

After several months of debate, the legislature approved the details of the peace and reconciliation charter in February 2006, and in March several thousand "Islamist" prisoners were released. A $400 million fund was established to provide compensation to the civil war's victims, although they were precluded from filing other legal claims against the government. Critics of the plan denounced it for "sheltering" the military and security forces and demanded a more intensive, "South African–style" truth and reconciliation approach under which the facts of individual cases would be revealed prior to the issuance of pardons.

The government offered remaining militants six months to accept the amnesty offer, but the GSPC, now formally aligned with al-Qaida (as Al-Qaida in the Islamic Maghreb [AQIM], see Political Parties and Groups, below), stepped up its attacks in late 2006–early 2007, targeting Western business interests as well as Algerian police. The spate of bombings appeared to undercut the turnout (35 percent) for the May 2007 assembly balloting, as did what was widely perceived to be popular discontent with the political process as a whole. Nearly 1 million ballots were spoiled by voters, apparently to protest the entrenched status of the ruling coalition. Critics were also discouraged by the reappointment of most of the incumbent ministers in the cabinet reshuffle of June 4 and by the FLN/RND/MSP domination of the November local elections. Attention subsequently focused on a series of deadly bomb attacks (including an assassination attempt against the president) that continued throughout 2008 and into 2009.

Parliament approved the elimination of presidential term limits by a vote of 500–21 in November 2008, thereby clearing the way for President Bouteflika to seek a third term. Opposition parties (notably the RCD and FFS) characterized the changes as enshrining a "lifetime president" and charged the administration with "political and spiritual bankruptcy." For his part, Bouteflika announced a five-year, $150 billion economic stimulus plan designed to promote small- and medium-sized enterprises and alleviate unemployment running at more than 50 percent among young people. He also pledged to continue the pursuit of national reconciliation, although a spate of deadly AQIM attacks had triggered recent intensification of the government's antiterrorist campaign.

Bouteflika's reelection in April 2009 was a foregone conclusion, especially since a boycott led by the RCD and FFS left him with only five minor challengers. The government reported a turnout of 74.5 percent, although the opposition described that figure as obviously inflated.

POLITICAL PARTIES AND GROUPS

From independence until 1989 the National Liberation Front was the only authorized political grouping, Algeria having been formally designated as a one-party state. Under constitutional changes approved in 1989, however, Algerians were permitted to form "associations of a political nature" as long as they did not "threaten the basic interests of the state" and were not "created exclusively on the basis of religion, language, region, sex, race, or profession." To operate legally, parties were also required to obtain government permits. Subsequently, constitutional amendment of November 1996 and electoral law revision of February 1997 further restricted parties from referencing religion, ethnicity, or race. A number of existing groups were deregistered for failure to adapt to the changes by the deadline of April 1997. In addition, other parties were told to disband in May 1998, either for failing to have the minimum of 2,500 members or for violating other new regulations. Twenty-four parties participated in the 2007 legislative balloting.

Government Parties:

National Liberation Front (*Front de Libération Nationale*—FLN). Founded in November 1954 and dedicated to socialism, nonalignment, and pan-Arabism, the FLN led the eight-year war of independence against France. Although weakened by factionalism and disagreement over the role of the army in politics, the front subsequently assumed complete control of Algerian political and governmental affairs.

By the late 1980s a cleavage was apparent within the FLN between an "old guard," dedicated to the maintenance of strict socialist policies, and a group, led by President Bendjedid, favoring political and economic liberalization. The reformers having manifestly gained the ascendancy, Mohamed Cherif MESSAADIA, the front's leading socialist ideologue, was dismissed from the ruling Politburo in early November 1988. Subsequently, during the party congress in Algiers November 27–28, the Politburo itself was abolished, and the office of secretary general was dissociated from that of state president. (Bendjedid, however, was named to the newly created post of FLN president.) The delegates also voted to democratize the filling of FLN organs, approved the chief executive's proposals for economic reform, and nominated Bendjedid as sole candidate for a third presidential term. Although not specifically empowered by the congress to do so, the Central Committee in June 1989 endorsed the creation of a multiparty system, some continued opposition to Bendjedid's political and economic reforms notwithstanding.

Following the FLN's poor showing (about 34 percent of the popular vote) in the June 1990 municipal elections, a number of government officials were dismissed from the Politburo amid intense debate over how to check the rapid erosion of the front's influence. In late June 1991 Bendjedid resigned as FLN president, and several other members of his administration relinquished their party posts as part of the government's effort to distance itself from FLN control. However, Abdelhamid MEHRI, Bendjedid's brother-in-law and close associate, was subsequently reelected FLN secretary-general.

Further illustrating the rapid decline in its electoral potency, the FLN won only 15 seats on the basis of a 24 percent vote share in the December 1991 first-round legislative poll. The party was subsequently reported to be divided over Bendjedid's resignation as president of the republic and the assumption of power by the High Security Council. Subsequently, however, the FLN Central Committee announced it would support the High Council of State, assuming adherence to that council's pledge to return the nation to a democratic process.

By late 1994 the FLN was firmly in the opposition camp, its leaders joining with those of the FIS, FFS, and other parties in negotiating a proposed plan for a return to civilian government. At the urging of Secretary General Mehri, the FLN formally endorsed a boycott of the 1995 presidential election, although it appeared that many party members voted anyway, a large percentage of their support reportedly going to President Zeroual. Mehri was subsequently dismissed as secretary general in January 1996 by the FLN Central Committee, and his successor, Boualem BENHAMOUDA, quickly distanced the FLN from the FIS and other antiregime groupings.

The 1995 electoral boycott having been widely acknowledged as a mistake, the FLN participated full force in the three 1997 elections and accepted junior partner status in the RND-led coalition government formed in June. However, despite the solidly proadministration stance of the FLN leaders, it was reported that a "reformist" faction, led by former prime minister Mouloud Hamrouche, continued to promote, among other things, a negotiated settlement with the FIS.

The 1998 FLN congress reelected Secretary General Benhamouda, thereby underlining the party's return to a "conservative tendency." The FLN nominated military-backed Abdelaziz Bouteflika as its official candidate for the April 1999 presidential election, although a segment of the party supported Hamrouche, who ran as an independent and subsequently indicated his intention to form a new party. Benhamouda, viewed as a longstanding "rival" to Bouteflika, resigned as secretary general in September 2001; the post was later filled by Prime Minister Ali Benflis.

Following the resurgence of the FLN in the May 2002 assembly balloting (199 seats [to lead all parties] on a 35 percent vote share) and the October 2002 municipal elections, Benflis was reelected as FLN secretary general at a July 2003 congress, which also installed a pro-Benflis Central Committee. By that time it was clear that Benflis (who had been dismissed as prime minister in April 2003) planned to run for president in 2004, thereby causing a rupture in the FLN between his supporters and those of President Bouteflika. The FLN convention in December 2003 selected Benflis as the party's standard-bearer, but an Algerian court (apparently under pressure from the Bouteflika administration) "annulled" that nomination and ordered FLN funds frozen. After Benflis secured only 8 percent of the vote in the April 2004 balloting, he resigned as FLN secretary general. At a party congress in February 2005, Bouteflika was named "honorary president" of the party, his supporters having clearly regained party control. In addition, Abdelaziz Belkhadem, described as close to Bouteflika and a potential link to the moderate Islamic movement, was reelected as secretary general. Belkhadem was named prime minister in May 2006. The FLN fell to 136 seats in the 2007 legislative poll (on a vote share of 35 percent), losing its majority but retaining government control with its coalition partners—the RND and MSP.

Leaders: Abdelaziz BOUTEFLIKA (President of the Republic), Abdelaziz BELKHADEM (Secretary General and Former Prime Minister), Abdelaziz ZIARI (President of the National People's Assembly), Saïd BOUHADJA (Parliamentary Leader).

National Democratic Rally (*Rassemblement National et Démocratique*—RND). Launched in February 1997 in support of the policies of President Zeroual, the RND dominated the subsequent assembly, municipal, and Council of the Nation balloting, in part due to substantial financing and other assistance from sitting government officials, many of whom ran for office under the RND banner. Formally committed to pluralism, a "modern" economy (including emphasis on privatization), and "social justice," the RND was widely viewed primarily as a vehicle for entrenched authority to participate in an expanding democratic process without facing a genuine threat to its hold on power.

A serious split developed in the party over whom to support in the April 1999 presidential balloting. Consequently, Tahar BENBAIBECHE, who had complained that military leaders had been inappropriately pressuring the RND to back Abdelaziz Bouteflika, was dismissed as secretary general in January 1999 and replaced by Ahmed Ouyahia, who had recently resigned as prime minister. Ouyahia quickly announced that Bouteflika, the official candidate of the FLN, enjoyed the support of most of the RND.

By early 2002 the RND was described as having failed to attract as much popular support as originally expected, apparently because of the party's ongoing ties to the military, and the RND's representation in the assembly fell from 156 to 47 in the 2002 balloting.

Ouyahia returned to the prime ministership in April 2003, and the RND supported Bouteflika in the 2004 presidential poll. However, Ouyahia was dismissed as prime minister in May 2006, apparently because he was considered a potential rival to Bouteflika. Although the RND subsequently remained in the FLN-led cabinet, Ouyahia, a hard-liner in regard to proposed reconciliation with Islamist militants, continued to challenge Bouteflika on several issues. The RND's legislative representation increased to 61 in the 2007 balloting on a vote share of 15.7 percent.

Ouyahia was again named prime minister in June 2008, having reportedly spent the previous two years concentrating on strengthening the RND.

Leaders: Ahmed OUYAHIA (Prime Minister and Secretary General), Abdelkader BENSALAH (Speaker of the Council of the Nation), Mouloud CHORFI.

Movement for a Peaceful Society (*Mouvement pour une Société Paisible/Harakat Mujitamas al-Silm*—MSP/Hamas). Formerly known as the Movement for an Islamic Society (*Mouvement pour une Société Islamique*—MSI) or Hamas (an acronym from that grouping's name in Arabic), the MSP adopted its current rubric in 1997 in light of new national restrictions on party references to religion. The MSP is a moderate Islamic fundamentalist organization distinct from the more militant Palestinian formation also known as Hamas. It advocates "coexistence" with groups of opposing views in a democratic political structure and the introduction "by stages" of an Islamic state that would maintain "respect for individual liberties." Although it was reported in early 1992 that some Hamas members had been arrested in the sweeping antifundamentalist campaign, the government subsequently returned to its position that the grouping represented an acceptable moderate alternative to the FIS. Subsequently, Sheikh Mohamed BOUSLIMANI, a founder of Hamas, was killed in late 1993, while another leader, Aly AYEB, was assassinated in September 1994, the attacks being attributed to radicals opposed to Hamas's ongoing dialogue with the government.

Hamas leader Sheikh Mahfoud NAHNAH, who had announced his support for the regime's "antiterrorist" campaign but had described the nation as stuck "in a political dead end" in view of the "lack of trust between people and authority," received 25 percent of the vote in the 1995 presidential election. After finishing second in the June 1997 legislative balloting, the MSP joined the subsequent RND-led coalition government, a decision that was described as putting the party's "credibility on the line" vis-à-vis the more hard-line grouping, the MR (or *Nahda*, see below), which was competing for Islamic support.

Nahnah attempted to run in the April 1999 presidential balloting, but his candidacy was disallowed, ostensibly on the ground that he had not provided proof he had participated in the country's "war of independence" as required of all presidential contenders under the 1996 constitutional revision. Nahnah died in July 2003 after a long illness.

The MSP, which had seen its assembly representation fall from 69 to 38 in the 2002 balloting, supported President Bouteflika in the 2004 presidential campaign. Not surprisingly, MSP leader Bouguerra Soltani also strongly endorsed the 2005 national charter on peace and reconciliation. The MSP, whose campaign focused on economic diversification, increased its legislative representation to 52 in the 2007 balloting on a vote share of 13.4 percent. Soltani served in the cabinet until April 20009, when he left the government to focus on MSP affairs. By that time, a group of MSP members who opposed Soltani's strong support for the Bouteflika administration had announced formation of a splinter group named the **Call and Change Movement.**

Leaders: Bouguerra SOLTANI (President), Abderrahmane SAIDI, Ahmed ISSAAD, Djemaa NACER.

Other Legislative Parties:

Workers' Party (*Parti des Travailleurs*—PT). The Trotskyist PT was one of the groups that signed the proposed national reconciliation pact in early 1995. It secured four seats in the June 1997 assembly balloting and subsequently continued to urge the government to negotiate with the FIS. The PT improved dramatically to 21 seats in the 2002 assembly balloting on a vote share of 4.8 percent. PT leader and women's rights activist Louisa Hannoun, described as the first woman to run for president in the Arab world, won 1.2 percent in the vote in the 2004 poll. The PT secured 26 seats in the 2007 legislative poll on a vote share of 6.7 percent, while Hannoun finished second in the 2009 presidential balloting with 4.2 percent of the vote.

Leaders: Louisa HANNOUN, Djelloul DJOUDI.

Rally for Culture and Democracy (*Rassemblement pour la Culture et la Démocratie*—RCD). Formed in February 1989 to represent Berber interests, the RCD proclaimed its commitment to "economic centralism," linguistic pluralism, and separation of the state and Islamic religion. It won 2 percent of the votes in the June 1990 municipal balloting.

In early 1994 Mohamed Ouramadane TIGZIRI, the RCD's national secretary, was assassinated, apparently as part of the militant fundamentalist campaign against groups such as the RCD that advocated a secular, Western-style political system. The RCD's strongly antifundamentalist leader, Saïd Saadi, was also subsequently prominent in the Berber Cultural Movement, described by the *New York Times* as having evolved into an influential political group in its campaign to have the Berber language sanctioned for use in schools and other public forums. Saadi captured 9 percent of the votes in the 1995 presidential poll, having been assured of the lion's share of Berber votes because of the boycott by the FFS, the RCD's primary competitor for support within that ethnic group. The RCD secured 19 seats in the June 1997 assembly elections but boycotted the December balloting for the new Council of the Nation. The RCD also announced in early 1999 that it was boycotting the upcoming presidential election. However, surprising many observers, the RCD subsequently joined the government coalition of December 1999, the party reportedly having become "increasingly closer" to President Bouteflika. The RCD left the coalition in May 2001 in the wake of severe government/Berber friction, and it boycotted the 2002 national and local elections. Saadi won 1.9 percent of the vote in the 2004 presidential poll.

The RCD strongly condemned the national charter for peace and reconciliation that was approved in 2005. The party also charged the government with fraud in regard to the official vote turnout for the related referendum. Meanwhile, another Berber grouping (the **Movement for the Autonomy of Kabylie** [MAK], led by singer Ferhat MEHENNI) also rejected the charter as an exercise in "self-amnesty" by the Algerian authorities.

The RCD rejoined the electoral process for the 2007 legislative balloting, winning 19 seats on a vote share of 4.9 percent. However, it boycotted the 2009 presidential poll (as did the MAK), Saadi describing the current political situation as a "pitiable and dangerous circus."

Leaders: Saïd SAADI (President), Mohcene BELABES.

Algerian National Front (*Front National Algérien*—FNA/*Jabhah al-Wataniyah al-Jazairiyah*). Organized in June 1999 in support of the "downtrodden," the FNA, describing itself as "republican and democratic," received official recognition the following November. It won 8 seats in the 2002 legislative poll on a 3.2 percent vote share. However, the proposed presidential bid in 2004 of the FNA leader, Moussa Touati, was rejected by the Constitutional Council. The FNA won 3.3 percent of the vote in the 2007 legislative poll, securing 13 seats. Touati, characterized during the campaign as a nationalist, won 2.3 percent of the vote in the 2009 presidential election.

Leader: Moussa TOUATI.

Renaissance Movement (*Mouvement de la Renaissance/Harakat al-Nahda*—MR/*Nahda*). Previously called the Islamic Renaissance Movement (*Mouvement de la Renaissance Islamique/Harakat al-Nahda al-Islamiyya*—MRI/*Nahda*), the party dropped the "Islamic" portion of its rubric in early 1997 to conform to new national regulations. Initially a small, moderate fundamentalist grouping, *Nahda* was promoted in the mid-1990s by the government as a legal alternative to the banned FIS. The grouping performed "surprisingly well" in the June 1997 legislative balloting, finishing fourth with 34 seats. By that time *Nahda* had adopted a tougher stance than the other main legal Islamic party (the MSP), and its leaders ultimately declined to participate in the new RND-led coalition government.

A *Nahda* congress in early 1998 reportedly directed that some authority previously exercised by long-standing leader Sheikh Abdallah Djaballah be turned over to Secretary General Lahbib Adami. The apparent rivalry between the two came to a head late in the year when Adami announced that the party had agreed to support Abdelaziz Bouteflika, the military-backed FLN candidate, in the upcoming presidential balloting. Djaballah consequently left *Nahda* in January 1999 and formed the MRN (below), taking nearly half of the 34 *Nahda* assembly representatives with him. *Nahda* fell to only 1 seat in the 2002 assembly poll before rebounding slightly to 5 seats in 2007 on a vote share of 1.3 percent. The party boycotted the 2009 presidential poll.

Leaders: Fatah REBAI, Lahbib ADAMI (Secretary General).

Republican National Alliance (*Alliance Nationale Républicaine*—ANR). The ANR was formed in early 1995 by several former government officials, including Redha Malek, prime minister in 1993–1994, and Ali Haroun, a member of the 1992–1994 collective presidency. Formally opposed to any compromise with the Islamic fundamentalist movement, the ANR was considered a vehicle for a presidential bid by Malek. However, Malek was prevented from contesting the 1995 election because he failed to obtain the required 75,000 signatures of support. Malek was reelected chair of the party by the June 1996 ANR congress in Algiers, which also elected a new 145-member National Council.

Despite retaining a seat in the cabinet, the ANR in early 2002 was described as "steering clear" of the upcoming legislative poll. However, it won four seats in the 2007 poll on a vote share of 1.0 percent.

Leaders: Redha MALEK (Chair), Ali HAROUN.

Movement of National Harmony (*Mouvement de l'Entente Nationale*—MEN). The MEN secured 1.9 percent of the vote in the 2002 assembly balloting and 1.0 percent in 2007 (good for four seats).

Leaders: Ali BOUKHAZNA, Amar LASSOUED.

Algerian Renewal Party (*Parti pour le Renouveau de l'Algérie*—PRA). A moderate Islamic group that first surfaced during the October 1988 demonstrations, the PRA announced in 1989 that it would concentrate on economic issues, particularly a fight to end "state capitalism and interventionism." PRA leader Noureddine Boukrouh, described as a "liberal businessman," won 4 percent of the votes in the 1995 presidential election. Although the government disallowed Boukrouh's candidacy for the 1999 presidential election, citing insufficient signatures of support, Boukrouh joined the coalition government announced in December 1999. The PRA secured 2.2 percent of the vote in the 2002 assembly balloting and 1.0 percent in 2007 (securing four seats).

Leaders: Noureddine BOUKROUH, Yacine TORKMANE.

Movement for National Reform (*Mouvement pour la Réforme Nationale*—MRN). The MRN, also known as *Islah* (Arabic for "reform"), was launched in early 1999 to promote the presidential campaign of Sheikh Abdallah DJABALLAH, who had recently split from *Nahda*. The MRN, supportive of eventual establishment of an "Islamic State," won 43 seats in the 2002 assembly balloting, thereby becoming the largest opposition grouping. Djaballah won 4.9 percent of the vote in the 2004 presidential poll.

Dissent within the MRN over Djaballah's reported "autocratic" style subsequently led to his ouster from the party, which fell dramatically to only three seats in the 2007 legislative poll on a vote share of 0.8 percent. New MRN leader Mohamed Djahid Younsi, described as lacking the popular appear of Djaballah, secured only 1.4 percent of the vote in the 2009 presidential balloting.

Leaders: Mohamed Djahid YOUNSI, Djamel ABDESSALAM.

***Ahd* 54.** A small, nationalist party, *Ahd* 54 (*Ahd* is Arabic for "oath," reportedly a reference to principles espoused at the beginning of the war of independence) secured 0.9 percent of the vote in the 2002 assembly balloting. Its leader, human rights activist Mohamed Ali Fawzi Rebaine, won 0.7 percent of the vote in the 2004 presidential poll. The party secured two seats in the 2007 assembly poll on a vote share of 0.5 percent, and Rebaine, reportedly facing internal party criticism, won 0.9 percent of the vote in the 2009 presidential election.

Leaders: Mohamed Ali Fawzi REBAINE, Toufik CHELLAL.

National Party for Solidarity and Development (*Parti National pour la Solidarité et le Développement*—PNSD). The center-right PNSD won a reported 1.6 percent of the popular vote in the June 1990 municipal elections. It secured 1.8 percent of the vote in the 2002 assembly poll and, according to preliminary results, 0.5 percent in 2007 (good for two seats).

Leader: Mohamed Cherif TALEB (President).

Patriotic Republican Rally (*Rassemblement Patriotique Républicain*—RPR). The RPR is a successor to the Algerian Movement for Justice and Development (*Mouvement Algérien pour la Justice et le Développement*—MAJD), a reformist group launched in November 1990 by former prime minister Kasdi Merbah, who had resigned in October from the FLN Central Committee. Merbah, a staunch antifundamentalist, was assassinated in August 1993, the government accusing Islamic militants of the act. However, no group claimed responsibility for the killing, and observers pointed out that Merbah had a broad spectrum of enemies. In 1999 the government listed the RPR as the successor to the MAJD. The RPR secured two seats in the 2007 assembly poll on a vote share of 0.5 percent.

Leader: Abd al-Kader MERBAH (President).

Democratic and Social Movement (*Mouvement Démocratique et Social*—MDS). The MDS rubric reportedly was recently adopted by the grouping formerly known as Challenge (*Ettahaddi*). Dedicated to "the revolutionary transition of Algeria to modernity and progress," *Ettahaddi* had been launched in January 1993 as successor to the Socialist Vanguard Party (*Parti de l'Avant-Garde Socialist*—PAGS). The PAGS had emerged in 1966 as an illegal, but generally tolerated, heir to the Algerian Communist Party (*Parti Communiste Algérien*—PCA), which had been proscribed shortly after independence. Supportive of the Boumedienne government but less so of the Bendjedid administration, the PAGS reportedly applauded the 1988 unrest as helpful in its effort to "reestablish itself," particularly among labor unionists. It offered a limited number of candidates in the 1990 municipal elections, without success, and boycotted the 1991, 1997, and 2002 legislative elections as well as the 1999 presidential poll. However, the MDS was credited with winning one seat in the 2007 assembly balloting.

Leader: Hachemi CHERIF (Secretary General).

Other small parties winning representation in the 2007 balloting included the **National Movement for Nature and Development** (*Mouvement National pour la Nature et le Développement*—MNND), led by Abderrahman AKIF; the **Movement for Youth and Democracy** (*Mouvement pour la Jeunesse et la Démocratie*—MJD); the ***Infitah* Movement** (*Mouvement El Intifah*); the **National Front of Independents for Concord** (*Front National des Indépendants pour la Concorde*—FNIC); the **National Movement of Hope** (*Mouvement National d'Esperance*—MNE), led by Mohamed HADEF; the **Algerian Rally** (*Rassemblement Algérien*—RA); and the **Democratic National Front** (*Front National Démocratique*—FND), led by Sassi MABROUK.

Other Parties that Competed in 2007 Legislative Elections:

Progressive Republican Party (*Parti Républicain Progressiste*—PRP). The PRP won three seats in the 1997 assembly balloting but failed to secure representation in 2002 or 2007.

Leader: Idriss KHADIR.

Socialist Workers Party (*Parti Socialist des Travailleurs*—PST). Legalized in early 1990, the Trotskyite PST supports "radical socialism," nonpayment of Algeria's external debt, and secular government. The PST boycotted the 2002 assembly balloting but participated (without success) in the 2007 poll.

Leader: Chawki SALHI.

Other Parties:

Socialist Forces Front (*Front des Forces Socialistes*—FFS). Long a clandestine group, the predominantly Berber FFS was legalized in November 1989. Having earned the enmity of the government in 1985 when he briefly formed a "united front" with Ben Bella's MDS (above) to oppose the FLN, the FFS leader, revolutionary hero Hocine Aït-Ahmed, remained in Swiss exile until December 1989. The FFS boycotted the 1990 municipal elections but, after failing to create a multiparty coalition to "block" the FIS, presented over 300 candidates in the December 1991 legislative balloting on a platform that endorsed a "mixed economy," greater regional autonomy, and official recognition of the Berber language. The FFS won 25 seats (second to the FIS) on a 15 percent vote share in the first election round, Aït-Ahmed strongly criticizing cancellation of the second prior to returning to self-imposed exile in Switzerland. The FFS subsequently joined the FIS and the FLN as the leading proponents of the unsuccessful January 1995 peace plan and boycotted the 1995 presidential balloting. However, Aït-Ahmed then called for "conciliation" talks with the government in apparent recognition of the Zeroual regime's strengthened position following the election.

Aït-Ahmed, hitherto FFS general secretary, was elected to the newly created post of party president at the March 1996 FFS congress in Algiers. Dueling with the RCD for support within the Berber community, the FFS secured 20 seats in the June 1997 assembly balloting but was not invited to participate in the new RND-led government because of the FFS's insistence that negotiations should proceed with the goal of incorporating the FIS into the legal political process. A special congress in February 1999 nominated Aït-Ahmed as the FFS candidate for the upcoming presidential balloting, despite the reported poor health of the aging leader, who had recently returned from his self-imposed exile. A May 2000 congress reelected Aït-Ahmed as FFS president amid reports of deepening divisions within the party.

In the wake of severe unrest in Berber areas, the FFS boycotted the 2002 assembly balloting. The FFS also called for a boycott of the 2005 referendum on the national charter for peace and reconciliation, arguing that the charter would "consecrate impunity" for perpetrators of violent crimes on both sides of the recent conflict.

The FFS boycotted the 2007 assembly poll, although some members, opposed to Aït-Ahmed's hard line in the matter, reportedly ran as independents. The party also boycotted the 2009 presidential election.

Leaders: Hocine AÏT-AHMED (President of the Party and 1999 presidential candidate), Karim TABBOU.

Fidelity (*Wafa*). Organized by former foreign affairs minister Ahmed Taleb Ibrahimi following his 1999 presidential campaign in the hope of coordinating nationalist and Islamist opposition groups, *Wafa* was subsequently denied recognition by the government on the grounds that it was essentially an FIS "clone." Ibrahimi was rejected by the Constitutional Council as a presidential candidate in 2004 and subsequently threw his support behind Ali Benflis. Former *Wafa* leader Mohamed Said, described as a moderate Islamist, finished last in the 2009 presidential balloting with 0.9 percent of the vote as the candidate of the unrecognized **Party of Freedom and Justice.**

Leaders: Ahmed Taleb IBRAHIMI, Mohammed SAID, Rashid LERARRI.

Democratic Front (*Front Démocratique*—FD). An anti-Bouteflika grouping, the FD elected former prime minister Sid Ahmed Ghozali as its chair during the May 2000 inaugural congress. Ghozali was not permitted by the Constitutional Council to run in the 2004 presidential election, and he subsequently announced he was supporting Ali Benflis in that campaign.

Leader: Sid Ahmed GHOZALI (Chair).

Illegal Groups:

Islamic Salvation Front (*Front Islamique du Salut*—FIS). The FIS was organized in early 1989 to represent the surging Islamic fundamentalist movement. Capitalizing upon strong antigovernment sentiment, it won control of a majority of town and departmental councils in the June 1990 municipal elections. Apparently to permit the broadest possible support for its effort to win national legislative control, the FIS leadership was subsequently reluctant to define its goals in specific terms. However, a significant proportion of the front's supporters appeared committed to the adoption and enforcement of sharia throughout Algeria's theretofore relatively secular society and the imposition of measures such as the segregation of the sexes in schools and the workplace, a ban on alcohol consumption, and obligatory veils for women. FIS leaders also made it clear that a national fundamentalist government, even one that came to power through a multiparty election, would not feel bound to maintain a "Western-style" democracy.

In June 1991 FIS leader Dr. Abassi Madani, Ali Belhadj (his deputy), other members of the party's Constitutional Council, and hundreds of FIS followers were arrested on charges of fomenting an "armed conspiracy against the security of the state" in connection with violent demonstrations in Algiers and other cities. Although hard-line FIS factions reportedly called for continued protest and an election boycott unless the detainees were released, the FIS ultimately participated in the December 26 legislative balloting under the leadership of the moderate Abdelkader HACHANI.

After winning 188 seats in the first round of the 1991 assembly poll, the FIS prepared to assume national political leadership, Hachani attempting to reassure the nonfundamentalist population that the FIS would "persuade, not oblige people into doing what we say." However, the party's plan to mount the world's first Islamic state via the ballot box was thwarted by the military takeover of the Algerian government in early January 1992. Nearly all of the remaining FIS national leaders, including Hachani, were subsequently arrested, as were hundreds of its local and provincial officials, with upwards of 30,000 FIS followers reportedly being placed in desert detention camps. In addition, Algerian courts in March formally banned the FIS as a political party upon petition of the High Council of State, which also ordered the dissolution of many municipal councils under FIS control and their replacement by appointed bodies. The front was subsequently reported to be sharply divided between members remaining faithful to the group's official commitment to nonviolence and more radical adherents prepared to "move from words to rifles." It was generally believed that the latter were responsible for a number of attacks on Algerian security personnel during the rest of the year and for the subsequent emergence of armed groups such as the AIS and the GIA (below).

In July 1992 Madani and Belhadj were sentenced to 12 years in prison for conspiring against the authority of the state, five other leaders receiving shorter terms. In the wake of Liamine Zeroual's appointment as president in early 1994, sporadic negotiations were reported between the government and the FIS, many reports suggesting that a breakthrough was imminent in mid-1995. However, the government finally declared the talks deadlocked, allegedly over the failure of the FIS leaders to renounce antiregime violence unequivocally. Consequently, no FIS participation was permitted in the 1995 presidential balloting, the front calling upon supporters to boycott the election as a way of embarrassing the government. That strategy backfired, however, as heavy voter turnout and Zeroual's strong showing served to undercut the front's insistence that it still held majority popular support.

The government released Madani on July 15, 1997, one week after Hachani had been freed when a court found him guilty of "inciting rebellion" in 1992 but sentenced him to time served. However, the nature of subsequent FIS-government talks was unclear, and Madani was placed under house arrest in September after he had called for UN mediation of the Algerian political impasse. Not surprisingly, the FIS urged its supporters to boycott the October local elections.

FIS leaders expressed the hope that President Bouteflika's civil concord of the second half of 1999 would lead to legalization of the party (perhaps under a different name). Meanwhile, the circumstances surrounding the assassination of Hachani in Algiers in November 1999 were unclear, although the government attributed the murder to the GIA.

FIS leaders Madani and Belhadj were released from house arrest and prison, respectively, in July 2003, the former subsequently settling in Qatar. Both men were barred from political activity.

Rabeh Kebir, a longstanding FIS leader, returned to Algeria in September 2006 after 14 years in exile in Germany. He announced his support for the nation's current reconciliation program and indicated a desire to become involved in legal political affairs, thereby divorcing himself from other "historic" FIS figures such as Madani and Belhadj. Anwar Haddam, another former FIS leader, in early 2007 expressed similar sentiments, although he remained in the United States. Meanwhile, Belhadj described the national reconciliation program as a "trick" that was designed primarily to protect the military from further investigation regarding its activities in the antifundamentalist campaign. (Belhadj had earlier urged Muslims to join the jihad against U.S.-led forces in Iraq.)

The FIS called for a boycott of the May 2007 assembly elections as well as, after failing to get some of its members on the lists of legal parties, the November local elections.

Leaders: Dr. Abassi MADANI (in Qatar), Ali BELHADJ, Abdelkader BOUKHAMKHAM, Sheikh Abdelkader OMAR, Abdelkrim Ould ADDA (Foreign Spokesperson), Rabeh KEBIR, Anwar HADDAM (in the United States).

Islamic Salvation Army (*Armée Islamique du Salut*—AIS). The AIS, also previously referenced as the Armed Islamic Movement (*Mouvement Islamique Armée*—MIA), was an underground fundamentalist organization formed in response to the banning of the FIS in 1992. It was often described as the "military wing" of the FIS, although there were occasional reports of policy differences between the leaders of the two groups.

Initially, the AIS was formally committed to antiregime military activity, although, unlike the GIA (below), it attacked only "official" military and police targets. (Shortly after the formation of the AIS, its fighters, estimated at about 10,000 strong, were reported to be operating under a unified command with GIA guerrillas, but extensive fighting, apparently emanating from disputes over tactics, broke out between the two groups in early 1994.) In early 1995 AIS leaders called for dialogue with the government, indicating that they would accept any "peace settlement" negotiated by the FIS. The AIS declared a "cease-fire" in antigovernment attacks as of October 1, 1997, apparently to disassociate itself from the shocking (even by recent Algerian standards) wave of violence gripping the country.

In June 1999 the AIS agreed to a permanent cease-fire in connection with President Bouteflika's plans for a civil concord that included an amnesty for most AIS members and the restoration of their civil and political rights. In January 2000 AIS leader Madani MEZRAG signed documents formalizing the elements of the concord and announced the "dissolution" of the AIS, some 1,500 AIS members having reportedly been declared eligible for amnesty. Mezrag supported President Bouteflika's reelection bid in 2004 and endorsed the 2005 national charter for peace and reconciliation, indicating his desire to help form a new legal party among former FIS/AIS supporters. Mezrag participated in the May 2007 assembly elections as a candidate of the FLN.

Armed Islamic Group (*Groupe Islamique Armé*—GIA). The GIA was an outgrowth of antigovernment violence that first broke out in the mid-1980s around the city of Blida. In the 1990s the group emerged as the most militant of the underground fundamentalist organizations, its targets including police, government officials, journalists, feminists, and foreigners. Vehemently anti-Western, the group reportedly supported establishment of an Iranian-style "theocracy" in Algeria and firmly rejected dialogue with the military-backed Zeroual regime.

The GIA guerrilla force was once estimated at 2,500–10,000 fighters, some known as "Afghanis" in reference to their having fought with the mujahidin in Afghanistan. In early 1994 the group was reportedly in control of many rural areas and several urban districts. However, the government subsequently claimed that its intensive "antiterrorist" campaign had significantly weakened the GIA. Moreover, many GIA leaders were killed by security forces or rival Islamists. In addition, one leader, Sheikh Abdelhaq LAYADA, was arrested in Morocco in 1993 and extradited to Algeria, where he was sentenced to death following his conviction on terrorism charges (see below for information on his subsequent release).

In mid-1995 the GIA was placed on the U.S. State Department's list of "terrorist" organizations. Although deemed by mid-1996 to be stronger militarily than the AIS, the GIA was believed to have lost much of whatever popular support it might once have commanded as the result of its assassination campaign and sometimes indiscriminate bomb attacks.

The GIA was broadly accused of the bulk of the terrorist incidents of 1997–2000, most of which occurred in central Algeria, where the group's influence was considered the strongest. As the attacks grew more random and increasingly targeted civilians, some observers suggested that discipline had broken down within the GIA, a correspondent for the *New York Times* describing the group as a "loose organization of roving bandits, including outlaws with little or no ideological commitment to Islam."

GIA leader Antar ZOUABI strongly rejected the government's amnesty offer included in President Bouteflika's civil concord of the second half of 1999, and most GIA fighters reportedly followed his lead. Zouabi was reportedly killed by security forces in February 2002; Rachid Abou TOURAB was subsequently reported to have been selected as the new GIA leader. Meanwhile, like the GSPC (below, under AQIM), the GIA was included on the list of "terrorist" organizations subject to asset seizure by the United States as part of the war on terrorism announced after the September 11, 2001, attacks.

Noureddine BOUDIAFI reportedly assumed leadership of the GIA in 2004; however, he was subsequently arrested, and the GIA mantle reportedly fell to Younes CHAABANE, who was killed during a security sweep in early 2005. By that time, the government was describing the GIA as "nearly extinct."

Layada was released from prison in early 2006, apparently as part of the national peace and reconciliation process. Although some GIA fighters reportedly remained active at that point, having been blamed by the government for at least one attack in mid-2005, no further GIA activity was subsequently reported through mid-2009.

Al-Qaida in the Islamic Maghreb (AQIM). The AQIM is a successor to the Salafist Group for Preaching and Combat (*Groupe Salafiste pour la Prédication et le Combat*—GSPC), which was established in 1999 by members of the GIA who were opposed to the parent group's targeting of civilians but remained committed to attacks on military sites and personnel. The GSPC was included on the list of proscribed organizations published by the United States following the September 11, 2001, terrorist attacks.

By 2003 the GSPC was one of the few Islamist groups "still fighting," hard-liner Nabil SAHRAOUI having supplanted GSPC founder Hassan HATAB as leader of the group. In October 2003 Sahraoui said that the GSPC supported Osama bin Laden's *jihad* against "the American heretics," and the GSPC was held responsible for several attacks on Algerian forces in 2003–2004. However, Sahraoui was killed by the Algerian army in June 2004, analysts suggesting that GSPC forces had dwindled to 400–450 guerrillas by that time. Another GSPC leader, Amari SAIFI, was taken into custody in late 2004 and subsequently sentenced to life imprisonment.

In late 2005 Hassan Hattab, one of the founders of the GSPC, said he believed most GSPC supporters were now willing to consider an amnesty agreement. However, he later withdrew his support for the nation's new reconciliation charter. In September 2006 Ayman al-Zawahiri, bin Laden's deputy, announced a "blessed union" between al-Qaida and the GSPC, indicating that French and U.S. supporters of the Algerian regime would be targeted. Although the government announced that several hundred GSPC fighters had been killed recently, the GSPC claimed responsibility for a series of attacks in late 2006–early 2007. Prompting even greater concern among Western leaders over the possible expansion of GSPC activity to Europe, the GSPC announced in early 2007 that it was adopting the AQIM rubric in support of an eventual Islamic state across North Africa.

The "rebranding" of the GSPC as the AQIM was perceived as a rejuvenation effort, and the AQIM subsequently became the "most active" militant group in North Africa. After claiming responsibility for attacks in April 2007 that killed more than 30 people, the AQIM warned voters not to participate in the May legislative poll.

AQIM leader Abdelmalek Droukel was sentenced in absentia in June by an Algerian court to 20 years in prison, while Hattab was also convicted in absentia of terrorist activity. However, Hattab in September reportedly surrendered to pursue amnesty, the government describing him at that time as "repentant." (Hattab issued appeals in 2008 and 2009 for his former GSPC comrades to cease their attacks.)

Apparently bolstered by recruits (some from neighboring countries) enflamed by anti-Western sentiment regarding Iraq, the AQIM claimed responsibility for a number of attacks throughout the rest of 2007 (including double suicide bombings in December that killed 17 UN personnel and more than 20 others) and early 2008. The group, relying on tactics (notably suicide bombings) similar to those used by insurgents in Iraq, also vowed to target multinational companies in Algeria. Most analysts concluded that the AQIM suffered heavy losses in the intensified government campaign of late 2008–early 2009, although it remained a potent force not only in Algeria but also in neighboring countries, having called for attacks on Westerners throughout the world.

Leader: Abdelmalek DROUKEL (Abu Musab ABDULWAHOOD).

Defenders of the Salafi Call (*Dhanat Houmet Daawa Salafia*). One of the few Islamist militant groups active in Algeria as of 2005, this "Taliban-trained" grouping, another offshoot of the GIA, was reported to comprise about 150–250 fighters in western Algeria. Like the GSPC, it has been declared a terrorist organization by the United States.

Leader: Mohammed BENSLIM.

LEGISLATURE

The 1996 constitution provided for a bicameral **Parliament** (*Barlaman*), consisting of a restructured National People's Assembly and a new upper house, the Council of the Nation. The first round of multiparty balloting for a new 430-member assembly was held December 26, 1991, with the Islamic Salvation Front (FIS) winning 188 seats, the Socialist Forces Front (FFS) 25, the FLN 15, and independents 3. A runoff round involving the top two vote-getters in the remaining districts was scheduled for January 16, 1992. However, the second poll was canceled on January 12 by the High Security Council, which also declared the results of the first round invalid.

In April 1992 the High Council of State announced the appointment of a 60-member National Consultative Council (*Majlis al-Shoura al-Watani*) to serve in an advisory capacity to the government pending new assembly elections. The National Dialogue Conference of early 1994, in turn, authorized the appointment of a three-year National Transitional Council (*Conseil National de Transition*—CNT), which at its initial sitting in May encompassed 63 seats filled by parties, 85 by professional associations and trade unions, and 30 by government nominees, with 22 reserved for nonparticipating secular parties. The CNT was dissolved on May 18, 1997, in preparation for the elections to the bodies authorized by the new constitution.

Council of the Nation (*Majlis al-Umma/Conseil de la Nation*). The upper house has 144 members, 96 (2 from each *wilaya*) elected in secret ballot by an electoral college of the members of local councils and communal and *wilayaat* assemblies and 48 appointed by the president. The term of office is six years, although one-half of the initial members (elected on December 25, 1997) served only three years to permit 50 percent replenishment of the council every three years from that point. Following the balloting of December 30, 2003, the distribution of the elected seats was as follows: National Democratic Rally, 52; National Liberation Front, 31; Movement for a Peaceful Society, 10; Movement for National Reform, 2; Socialist Forces Front, 1. The most recent balloting for indirectly elected seats was held December 28, 2006.

Speaker: Abdelkader BENSALAH.

National People's Assembly (*Majlis Ech Chaabi al-Watani, Assemblée Popularie Nationale*). The lower house has 389 members, 381 representing the 48 *wilayaats* (each of which has at least 4 representatives) according to population, and 8 (4 in Europe and 4 in other Arab nations) elected by Algerians living abroad. Members are elected for a five-year term on a proportional basis from lists presented by parties or independents. Following the election of May 17, 2007, the distribution of seats (according to preliminary results) was as follows: National Liberation Front, 136; National Democratic Rally (RND), 61; Movement for a Peaceful Society, (MSP), 52; Workers' Party, 26; Rally for Culture and Democracy, 19; Algerian National Front (FNA), 13; National Movement for Nature and Development, 7; Renaissance Movement, 5; Movement for Youth and Democracy, 5; Republican National Alliance, 4; Movement of National Harmony, 4; Algerian Renewal Party, 4; Movement for National Reform, 3; *El Infitah* Movement, 3; National Front of Independents for Concord, 3; *Ahd* 54, 2; National Party for Solidarity and Development (PNSD), 2; National Movement of Hope, 2; Patriotic Republican Rally, 2; Algerian Rally, 1; National Democratic Front, 1; Democratic and Social Movement, 1; and independents, 33. In early 2008 the legislature's Web site reported the same seat distribution except for 62 seats for the RND, 51 for the MSP, 15 for the FNA, and none for the PNSD.

President: Abdelaziz ZIARI.

CABINET

[as of July 1, 2009]

Prime Minister	Ahmed Ouyahia (RND)
Ministers of State	Abdelaziz Belkhadem (FLN)
	Noureddine Yazid Zerhouni (FLN)
Ministers	
Agriculture and Rural Development	Rachid Benaissa
Commerce	El Hachemi Djaaboub (MSP)
Culture	Khalida Toumi [f]
Energy and Mining	Chakib Khelil
Finance	Karim Djoubi
Fishing and Marine Resources	Smaïl Mimoune
Foreign Affairs	Mourad Medelci
Health, Population, and Hospital Reform	Said Barkat
Higher Education and Scientific Research	Rachid Harraoubia (FLN)
Housing and Urban Affairs	Noureddine Moussa
Interior and Local Collectives	Noureddine Yazid Zerhouni (FLN)
Industry and the Promotion of Investment	Abdelhamid Temmar
International Local Collectives	Noureddine Yazid Zerhouni (FLN)
Justice, Keeper of the Seals	Tayeb Belaiz
Labor, Employment, and Social Security	Tayeb Louh (FLN)
National Education	Boubakeur Benbouzid (RND)
National Solidarity, Family, and Overseas Community	Djamal Ould-Abbes (FLN)
Posts and Information and Communications Technologies	Hamid Bessallah
Public Works	Amar Ghoul (MSP)
Relations with Parliament	Mahmoud Khedri (FLN)
Religious Affairs and Endowments	Bouabdallah Ghlamallah (RND)
Small- and Medium-sized Enterprises and Crafts	Mustapha Benbada (MSP)
	Chérif Rahmani
Territorial Management, Environment, and Tourism	El Hadi Khaldi (FLN)
Training and Professional Education	Amar Tou (FLN)
Transportation	
War Veterans	Mohamed Cherif Abbas (RND)
Water Resources	Abdelmalek Sellal
Youth and Sports	Hachemi Djiar (FLN)
Ministers Delegate	
Family and Women's Affairs	Nouara Saâdia Djaffar (RND) [f]
Local Collectives	Daho Ould Kablia
Maghreb and African Affairs	Abdelkader Messahel (FLN)
National Defense	Gen. (Ret.) Abdelmalek Guenaïzia
Rural Development	Rachid Benaissa (FLN)
Scientific Research	Souad Bendjaballah [f]
Secretary General of the Government	Ahmed Noui
Secretary of State in Charge of Communications	Azzedine Mihoubi

[f] = female

COMMUNICATIONS

After a long period of strict control of national and foreign media activities, the government introduced a new Information Code in mid-1989 that formally ended the state media monopoly and accorded journalists greater freedom of expression. It was succeeded in March 1990 by a more stringent code that mandated imprisonment for journalists who "offended" Islam or any other religion; the new regulations also stipulated that all new periodicals be printed in Arabic. However, those strictures were not rigorously implemented, and an information "explosion" subsequently took place in the increasingly independent press. By mid-1991 there were reportedly more than 110 daily, weekly, and monthly periodicals, many of them fostered by a government program under which journalists in state-owned enterprises were offered a sum equal to two years' salary to help establish private publications. However, most of the new papers continued to be printed on government presses, which enabled the administration to suspend their issuance during the early phase of the 1991 state of emergency. Significant restrictions, largely directed at the Islamic fundamentalist press, were imposed following the declaration of a state of emergency in early 1992. In addition, journalists were permitted to report on "security matters" only with government authorization and only using information released by the state, stories on antigovernment activity consequently becoming quite limited. In part because they were often perceived as "apologists" for the government, journalists were subsequently targeted by fundamentalist radicals.

New restrictions, including harsh penalties in a revised penal code, have been imposed on the press in recent years, prompting protests from both domestic and international journalism organizations. Among other things, opposition candidates complained during the 2002 and 2007 election campaigns about the high level of control exercised by the administration of President Bouteflika over all aspects of the media. Journalists have subsequently been jailed regularly for what the government calls "libel" or "defamation" but what free press advocates describe as legitimate criticism of officials. In addition, conflict continued between the media and the government in regard to how terrorist activities should be covered.

Press. It is currently estimated that approximately 50 daily papers are published, many of them receiving much of their advertising revenue from state agencies and thereby being subject to heavy government influence. The following are dailies published in Algiers unless otherwise noted: *el-Moudjahid* (The Fighter, 26,000), former FLN organ in French; *al-Chaab* (The People, 15,000), former FLN information journal in Arabic; *Le Soir de l'Algérie* (82,000), in French; *Al Khabar* (The News, 460,000), in Arabic; *El Watan* (The Nation, 128,000), in French; *Le Jeune Indépendant* (14,000), in French; *La Nouvelle République* (12,000), in French; *Al Djazair News* (11,000), in Arabic; *Le Matin*, in French; *La Tribune* (16,000), in French; *Liberté* (120,000), in French; *Le Quotidien d'Oran* (Wahran, 110,000), in French; *Ech Chououk* (Sunrise, 208,000); *al-Nasr* (Victory, 19,000), published in Arabic in Qacentina; *El Bilad* (Country, 16,000), in Arabic; *al-Fadjr* (Dawn, 12,000); *L'Expression* (30,000), in French; and *Le Jour d'Algerie*, in French.

News agencies. The domestic agency is the Algerian Press Service (*Wikalat al-Anba al-Jazairiyah/Algérie Presse Service*—APS). A number of foreign agencies maintain offices in Algiers, and there is one privately owned domestic news service.

Broadcasting and computing. The government announced it was decreasing its control over broadcasting services in 2000, although it retained a supervisory role and government influence remains dominant through the state-run national radio and television companies, which broadcast in Arabic, French, and Tamazight. Algerians seeking unfiltered news reportedly rely heavily on foreign satellite channels. As of 2008 there were 119.3 Internet users per 1,000 inhabitants.

INTERGOVERNMENTAL REPRESENTATION

Ambassador to the U.S.: Abdallah BAALI.

U.S. Ambassador to Algeria: David D. PEARCE.

Permanent Representative to the UN: Mourad BENMEHIDI.

IGO Memberships (Non-UN): AfDB, AFESD, AMF, AMU, AU, BADEA, BIS, IDB, Interpol, IOM, LAS, NAM, OAPEC, OIC, OPEC, WCO.

ANDORRA

Principality of Andorra
Principat d'Andorra (Catalan)
Principalité d'Andorre (French)
Principado de Andorra (Spanish)

Political Status: Sovereign "Parliamentary Co-Principality," with the President of the French Republic and the Spanish Bishop of Urgell possessing certain powers as joint heads of state under constitution approved March 14, 1993, with effect from May 4.

Area: 180 sq. mi. (467 sq. km.).

Population: 72,320 (2003C); 87,000 (2008E). Since 1986, the population has nearly doubled, with native Andorrans now constituting only a third of the total.

Major Urban Center (2005E): ANDORRA LA VELLA (22,000).

Official Language: Catalan (French, Spanish, and Portuguese are also used).

Monetary Units: There is no local currency. The French franc and the Spanish peseta both circulated until 2002, when Andorra adopted the euro (market rate December 1, 2009: 1 euro = $ 1.51US).

French Co-Prince: Nicolas SARKOZY; became Co-Prince May 16, 2007, upon inauguration as President of the French Republic.

Permanent French Delegate: Christian FRÉMONT.

Spanish Episcopal Co-Prince: Mgr. Joan Enric VIVES Sicilia; became Co-Prince May 12, 2003, upon induction as Bishop of See of Urgell.

Permanent Episcopal Delegate: Nemesi MARQUES Oste.

Head of Government (*Cap del Govern*): Jaume BARTUMEU Cassany (Social Democratic Party) elected for a four-year term by the General Council on June 3, 2009, following the legislative balloting of April 26 and sworn in on June 5 to succeed Albert PINTAT Santolària (Liberal Party of Andorra); named a new government on June 8, 2009.

THE COUNTRY

A rough, mountainous country of limited dimensions, Andorra is set in a large drainage area of the Pyrenees between France and Spain. The main stream is the Riu Valira, which has two branches and six open basins. The indigenous residents are of Catalan stock and represent about one-third of the population; foreign residents include Spaniards (about 43 percent of the total population), Portuguese (11 percent), and French (7 percent). Virtually all of the inhabitants are Roman Catholic. The traditional mainstays of the economy were sheep farming and animal husbandry, but tourism, which accounts for 80 percent of GDP, and the transshipment of goods are presently the most important sources of income. Apart from the transmission of power from a hydroelectric plant at Les Escaldes to southern France and the Spanish province of Barcelona, the main exports are machinery and electrical goods, paper, graphic arts products, textiles, foodstuffs, tobacco products, and cattle. The main trading partners are Spain and France, with Andorra having gained a reputation as "the Hong Kong of the Pyrenees" because of money laundering and other services attractive to financiers from nearby countries. Andorra's status as a duty-free principality has also reportedly generated a substantial contraband trade, particularly involving tobacco.

Andorra experienced steady economic growth from the late 1980s into the early 1990s, with negligible unemployment (a steady influx of foreign workers having been required to fill jobs in the booming tourism sector). Growth slowed in the mid-1990s, primarily as a result of the international economic downturn, the related drop in consumer demand in Spain and France, and a decline in tourist arrivals. However, the economy subsequently improved, and GDP grew by an annual average of more than 3.5 percent in 2005–2008.

In 2008 the Andorran government, in an effort to offset some effects of the worldwide recession, opened the country to foreign investors in an unprecedented manner, replacing the limit of one-third ownership for foreign investors with a new limit of 49 percent for main industries and 100 percent for new industries the government hoped to nurture, such as those in the technology sector.

Although the government continued to report "zero" unemployment in 2008, a modest amount of joblessness had apparently developed by early 2009 in connection with the global financial downturn. Decline was registered in the tourist industry, which accounts for 60 percent of the country's GDP, and in the banking sector. Meanwhile, in response to years of intense international pressure concerning the country's "tax haven" status, the government in March 2009 agreed to revise its tax secrecy laws (see Current issues, below, for details.)

GOVERNMENT AND POLITICS

Political background. Andorra is the last independent survivor of the *Marca Hispanica* (or March states), a series of several former Spanish countries that served as buffer states and were established by Charlemagne around 800 A.D. to keep the Muslim Moors from advancing into Christian France. Charlemagne, who granted a charter to the Andorran people in return for their fighting the Moors, is credited as the founder of the country. The unique political structure of Andorra dates from 1278, when an agreement on joint suzerainty (a *paréage*) was reached between the French count of Foix, whose right ultimately passed to the president of the French Republic, and the Spanish bishop of the nearby See of Urgell. The first personal meeting between co-princes since 1278 occurred on August 25, 1973, when President Georges Pompidou and Bishop Joan MARTI y Alanís met at Cahors, France, to discuss matters affecting the future of the principality, while on October 19, 1978, President Valéry Giscard d'Estaing and Mgr. Martí y Alanís attended 700th anniversary ceremonies at Andorra la Vella.

Under new constitutional arrangements (see below) that included, on December 9, 1981, the principality's first nonstaggered legislative election, the General Council, on January 8, 1982, named Oscar RIBAS Reig to a four-year term as Andorra's first head of government. Ribas Reig resigned on April 30, 1984, as the result of a lengthy dispute over tax policy, the council on May 21 electing as his successor Josep PINTAT Solans, who was redesignated following a general election in December 1985.

Ribas Reig returned to power after balloting on December 10, 1989, and in 1990 Andorra obtained its first penal code, providing, among other things, for the abolition of the death penalty. Ribas Reig again resigned in January 1992 after conservatives had blocked his effort to introduce a constitution that would legalize parties and trade unions, and guarantee civil rights. Retaining office as the result of legislative balloting on April 5 and 12, he announced that the new council's principal task would be to draft a basic law for submission to a popular referendum. The process was completed on March 14, 1993, when, in a turnout of 76 percent of the 9,123 eligible voters, 74.2 percent approved what was in effect Andorra's first written constitution. The adoption of the new basic law represented a conscious attempt by progressive elements led by Ribas Reig to bring Andorra into line with other European states in terms of prescribed civil and social rights, although in many respects the principality remained a feudalistic state whose social practices were governed by clerical canons of morality and whose politics were often determined by family loyalties.

In Andorra's first multiparty elections, held on December 12, 1993, Ribas Reig's National Democratic Grouping (*Agrupament Nacional Democràtic*—AND) emerged as the strongest party in the General Council, with Ribas Reig being reelected head of government on January 19, 1994. These victories confirmed the ascendancy of the modernizing political forces led by Ribas Reig, who said that his new government would give priority to fiscal and tax reforms and to the development of tourism. Nevertheless, in the emerging new party structure, conservative elements retained considerable influence in the General Council, and on November 25, following rejection of his 1995 budget, Ribas Reig again resigned and was succeeded on December 21 by Marc FORNÉ Molné of the Liberal Union (*Unió Liberal*—UL), the second-largest party in the General Council. Communal elections in

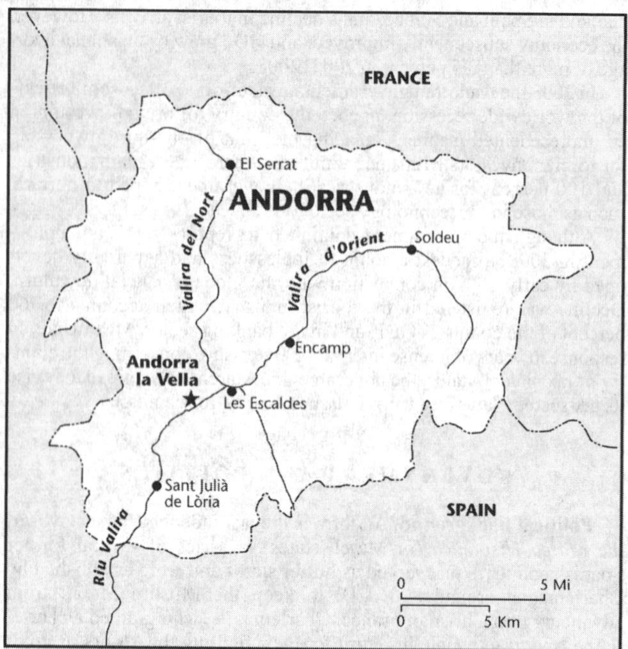

December 1995 were notable for returning two women mayors, who broke the previous male mayoral monopoly.

Following premature dissolution of the General Council on January 1, 1997, new legislative balloting was conducted on February 16, with the UL capturing 16 seats to 6 for the AND and Forné being reelected as head of government by the new council on March 21; the new cabinet took office on April 4. Forné was reelected for another term following new balloting for the General Council on March 4, 2001, at which his Liberal Party of Andorra (*Partit Liberal d'Andorra*—PLA), as the UL had been renamed, captured 15 seats, the AND having splintered into two new parties, which together had gained 11 seats. A new PLA government was appointed on April 9.

The PLA won 14 seats in the April 24, 2005, General Council poll under the leadership of Albert PINTAT Santolària, who was subsequently elected as head of government with the support of the Andorran Democratic Center (*Centre Demòcrata Andorrà*—CDA). However, the victory was tempered by the success of the Social Democratic Party (*Partit Socialdemòcrata*—PS), which, under the leadership of Jaume BARTUMEU Cassany (who had served as finance minister in the early 1990s), increased its seat total from 6 to 11. The cabinet was reshuffled on May 2.

In the legislative elections on April 26, 2009, the PS and its parish allies won a plurality of 14 seats with 45 percent of the vote in the nationwide balloting. After failing to gain formal support for a new government from the recently formed Andorra for Change (*Andorra pel Canvi*—APC), which won 3 seats, the PS was left without a major ally in the General Council. The first balloting for head of government failed to produce a winner, as Bartumeu received 14 votes to 11 for Joan GABRIEL Estany, who had been selected as the PLA candidate when Pintat declined to run for reelection. (The APC abstained from the voting.) Bartumeu, however, was elected in the second ballot (in which a winner is determined by a majority of the votes cast, compared to the first ballot, in which a majority of the full membership is required) on June 3 with 14 votes, the APC again abstaining. On June 9 Bartumeu formed a new cabinet comprising members of the PS and several independents.

Constitution and government. The 1993 document defines Andorra as an independent "parliamentary co-principality" in which sovereignty is vested in the people (i.e., Andorran citizens), although the Spanish and French co-princes remain joint heads of state, with defined and largely symbolic powers. The text provides for an independent judiciary, civil rights, and elections by universal suffrage (of citizens) to the legislative General Council. For the first time, membership in political parties and trade unions is permitted, and the government is empowered to raise revenue by taxation and other means. As joint suzerains, the French president and the bishop of Urgell are represented respectively by the prefect of the French department of Pyrenees-Orientales and the vicar general of the Urgell diocese. Their resident representatives in Andorra bear the titles of *viguier de France* and *veguer Episcopal*.

Under a Political Reform Law approved after a stormy legislative debate in November 1981, a head of government (*cap del govern*) was created for the first time, while the former first and second syndics were redesignated as syndic general (chair) and sub-syndic (sub-chair) of the General Council, with the *syndic général* remaining, by protocol, the higher-ranked official. Legislators were formerly elected every two years for staggered four-year terms; under the 1981 reform, the council as a whole sits for four years, designating the head of government (who appoints a cabinet) for a like term.

Women were enfranchised in 1970 and in 1973 were permitted to stand for public office. Second-generation Andorrans were allowed to vote in 1971 and first-generation Andorrans over the age of 28 were accorded a similar right in 1977.

The judicial structure is relatively simple. The *viguiers* each appoint two civil judges (*battles*), while an appeals judge is appointed alternately by each co-prince. Final appeal is either to the Supreme Court in Perpignan, France, or to the Ecclesiastical Court of the Bishop of La Seu de Urgell, Spain. Criminal law is administered by the *Tribunal de Corts,* consisting of the *battles,* the appeals judge, the *viguiers,* and two members of the General Council (*parladors*).

Local government functions at the district level through parish councils, whose members are selected by universal suffrage. At the lower levels there are *communs* and *corts*. The former are ten-member bodies elected by universal suffrage; the latter are submunicipal advisory bodies that function primarily as administrators of communal property.

Foreign relations. On January 1, 1986, Spain joined France as a member of the European Community (EC), subsequently the European Union (EU), but it was not until September 1989 that an Andorran customs union with the EC was negotiated. Approval of the agreement by the General Council in March 1990 yielded the country's first international treaty in more than 700 years, the union coming into effect on July 1, 1991. Substantially more indicative of emerging international status was Andorra's admission to the UN on July 28, 1993.

On June 3, 1993, Andorra signed friendship and cooperation treaties with France and Spain, and on October 2 President Mitterrand paid an official visit to the principality. On November 10, 1994, Andorra became the 33rd full member of the Council of Europe.

In 2005 Andorra expanded its cooperation with the EU in a variety of areas, including the environment, public health, transportation, and communications. Also in 2005 China promised cooperation with Andorra on trade and tourism and praised Andorra for its support of the "one-China" policy. Relations with China were strengthened even further in 2007 when Andorra, endorsing China's position, opposed Taiwan's entry into the UN under the name Taiwan. Closer to home, Andorra signed an agreement with Portugal to allow free movement of citizens between the two countries, similar to agreements Andorra has with Spain and France. Andorra also signed an agreement with Luxembourg to avoid double taxation of their citizens, a partnership similar to Andorra's arrangements with Spain, Portugal, and France.

In 2008 Andorra continued to expand its diplomatic contact by establishing relations with Oman, the United Arab Emirates, and Kazakhstan. The following year Andorra established relations with Myanmar, whose military rulers have been soliciting ties with smaller countries in order to break Myanmar's diplomatic isolation and project a softer image.

Current issues. In November 1998 EU finance ministers focused on the formulation of a common method for taxing nonresident bank accounts, particularly in neighboring non-EU countries such as Andorra where bank secrecy rules attract foreign money. The banking sector continued to receive scrutiny in 1999 and 2000, and the Organization for Economic Cooperation and Development (OECD) in June 2000 included Andorra in its list of 35 "tax havens" that could face sanctions unless new standards were established regarding greater transparency in the financial sector and the exchange of information with other countries.

Following the 2001 legislative election the PLA's success (43 percent in the nationwide balloting) was seen as an indication of the electorate's desire for stability. The issues of money laundering and tax evasion, however, continued to frustrate the government.

It was unclear whether the international financial issues played a significant role in the 2005 legislative balloting. Although the PLA lost its majority, it asserted that the vote (in which it still won a plurality of 14 seats) represented an endorsement of recent policies, particularly regarding further integration "to some degree" with the EU, which it favored. For its part, the surging PS accused the PLA of failing to keep past electoral promises. (Forné, constitutionally prohibited from serving another term as head of government, also lost his legislative seat when the PS won the seats from his parish.)

A degree of accommodation on tax issues was achieved in a mid-2005 accord with the EU under which Andorran banks agreed to charge a withholding tax on foreign deposits rather than reveal secret information about the accounts. As of mid-2008, however, Andorra remained one of only three countries on the OECD's "uncooperative" list.

In March 2009 Head of Government Pintat promised to make the requested changes to bank secrecy laws by September 1. His pledge to meet OECD standards regarding the exchange of financial information was enough to have the OECD move Andorra from its "black list" to the "grey list" (those countries that have committed to the global rules but not yet enacted the necessary legislation.) French President Nicolas Sarkozy subsequently threatened to resign as co-prince of Andorra if the reforms were not implemented by November.

In the run-up to the June 2009 legislative election, observers described a general dissatisfaction with the PLA's delay in making necessary change to the banking laws, which was perceived as contributing, in part, to the country's economic malaise during the recent global economic downturn. Possibly sensing an impending defeat, Pintat chose not to seek reelection, though he was eligible for a second term. Meanwhile, the PS's Bartumeu appeared to strike a chord with the electorate by promising to continue bank reform, institute an income tax and a value-added tax, and pursue full membership of the EU. Following the election, the opposition APC (which ran as a free-market, centrist party and won 3 seats in the General Council), deprived the PS (which controlled 14 of the 28 seats in the council) of a legislative majority by declining the PS's invitation to form a coalition government. Nonetheless, the election was a triumph for Bartumeu, a founding member of the PS, who had seen his party grow until it had been able to overtake the PLA, which had been in control of the government for 14 years.

POLITICAL PARTIES

Although political parties were technically illegal until March 1993, various unofficial groupings had contested elections in the 1970s and 1980s. The December 1993 balloting was the first held under multiparty auspices, with 18 associations of various kinds presenting or endorsing candidates.

Government and Government-Supportive Parties:

Social Democratic Party (*Partit Socialdemòcrata*—PS). The PS was established by Jaume Bartumeu Cessany in 2000 when the National Democratic Grouping (*Agrupament Nacional Democràtic*—AND) split into two new parties. The center-left AND, formed in 1979, had emerged as the strongest party in the December 1993 elections, winning eight seats and 26.4 percent of the vote on a platform of modernization. Its leader, Oscar Ribas Reig, therefore remained head of government (having first attained the post in 1982) with the support of the New Democracy (*Nova Democràcia*—ND), which had been founded prior to the 1993 balloting, at which it won 5 seats on a 19.1 percent vote share. However, Ribas was forced to resign in November 1994 when the coalition collapsed. The AND was definitively relegated to second-party status in the February 1997 General Council balloting, when it won 4 national seats (based on 28 percent of the vote) and the 2 seats from the parish of Encamp. The strength of the party, which appeared to have subsumed the ND, fell to 2 seats on a 17 percent share of national balloting in 1997.

Bartumeu has steered the left-of-center party since its inception, increasing its representation in consecutives elections. The PS won 6 seats in the March 2001 legislative balloting, 4 of them on a 28 percent vote share in the national polling. In 2005 the party improved significantly to 12 seats, largely owing to voter dissatisfaction with Andorra's reputation as a tax haven and the seeming reluctance of the PLA to deal effectively with the problem. A housing shortage also contributed to the PS's performance.

In 2009 the PS campaigned (in alliance with the GUPI in Ordino parish and with independents in other parishes) as "PS, The Alternative," capturing 45.8 percent of the national vote and 14 seats (6 on the national level and the 2 seats from each of the parishes of Encamp, Ordino, Andorra la Vella, and Escaldes-Engordany). Upon his installation as the new head of government, Bartumeu, among other things, pledged to work toward full membership for Andorra in the EU.

Leaders: Jaume BARTUMEU Cassany (Head of Government), Francesc RODRÍGUEZ Rossa (Parliamentary Leader).

Parochial Union of Independents Group (*Grup d'Unió Parroquial Independents*—GUPI) The progressive GUPI is active only in the parish of Ordino. It contested the Ordino parish seats unsuccessfully in alliance with the PS in 2005 but won the seats in 2009 (again in alliance with the PS) on a vote share of 41 percent in the parish.

Leader: Esteve LOPEZ Montanya.

Other Parliamentary Parties:

Reformist Coalition (*Coalició Reformista*—CR). The PLA-led CR was formed for the 2009 elections, at which it won 32.3 percent of the vote and 11 seats (5 national seats and the 2 seats from each of the parishes of Canillo, La Mariana, and Sant Julià de Lòria).

Leader: Joan GABRIEL Estany (Leader of the PLA and Parliamentary Leader).

Liberal Party of Andorra (*Partit Liberal d'Andorra*—PLA). The PLA was initially launched as the Liberal Union (*Unió Liberal*—UL) prior to the December 1993 legislative poll, at which the UL won five seats and 22 percent of the vote. After a year of opposition, the right-of-center formation came to power in December 1994. Its constituent **Liberal Party** (*Partit Liberal*—PL) joined the Liberal International in 1994.

The UL and its parish allies won 16 seats (6 national and 10 parish) in the February 1997 legislative elections. (The parish seats were won by groups that campaigned under their unique local party rubrics.) The working majority for Head of Government Marc Forné Molné was subsequently improved when councilors representing the Union of the People of Ordino (*Unió del Poble d'Ordino*—UPd'O) joined the UL in forming a parliamentary faction in the General Council. (The now-defunct UPd'O had won the two parish seats from Ordino in the 1997 poll.)

The UL adopted the PLA rubric prior to the March 2001 legislative balloting, at which it won 15 seats. The PLA secured 41.2 percent of the national vote in the 2005 legislative poll and 14 seats (6 national and 8 parish). After ten years as head of government, the PLA's Forné was not allowed to seek a second term. He was succeeded by Albert Pintat Santolària, whose new government was supported in the legislature by the CDA (see NC, below). Surprisingly, Pintat opted not to seek reelection in 2009, and he was succeeded as party leader by Joan Gabriel Estany.

Leaders: Joan GABRIEL Estany (Parliamentary Leader and 2009 candidate for head of government), Albert PINTAT Santolària (Former Head of Government).

New Centre (*Nou Centre*—NC). The Christian-democratic NC was recently formed through the merger of the Andorran Democratic Centre (*Centre Demòcrata Andorrà*—CDA) and the conservative Century 21 (*Segle 21*). The CDA was established in 2000 as the Democratic Party (*Partit Demòcrata*—PD), the second party to spin off from fragmentation of the AND. The PD won five seats in the 2001 legislative poll, three of them on a 22.4 percent vote share in the national constituency. The CDA secured two seats in the national poll of 2005 on an 11 percent vote share; it participated in that balloting in coalition with Century 21. The CDA subsequently agreed to support the new PLA government in the legislature.

NC leader Enric Tarrado Vives served as only a "supplementary" candidate on the CR's 2009 list.

Leader: Enric TARRADO Vives (Leader of Party and 2005 candidate for head of government).

Independents of Ordino (*Independents d'Ordino*). This group is active only in the parish of Ordino, in which it unsuccessfully contested the parish seats in the 2009 election in what appeared to be an at least informal electoral arrangement within the CR. (The

CR presented formal CR candidates in balloting in all parishes except Ordino.)

Leader: Bernadeta GASPÀ Bringueret (Former Deputy Speaker of Parliament).

Lauredian Union (*Unió Laurediana*). This group is a local conservative party from the parish of Sant Julià de Lória, where it won the two parish seats in the 2001 legislative balloting. Those successful candidates subsequently joined the PLA parliamentary group in the General Council. There was no reference to the Union in the 2005 legislative poll, and it appeared that the party had been absorbed into the PLA. The two successful candidates in the parish balloting in 2009 in Sant Julià de Lòria, however, were elected on a CR-Lauredian Union ticket.

Andorra for Change (*Andorra pel Canvi*—APC) The APC was formed in 2008 under the leadership of Juan Eusebio Nomen Calvert, a Spanish businessman, in reaction to international pressure for Andorra to reform its tax code and discourage the country's status as a tax haven. Despite its name, the party is committed to retaining the country's tax haven structure and also believes that the nation's current tax system should not be altered.

In the 2009 elections the APC secured three seats on a vote share of 18.9 percent nationwide, a significant showing for its first electoral foray. (The APC ran in alliance with the UNP in the parish of Encamp and with the RD in the parish of Escaldes-Engordany.) The APC subsequently declined an invitation from the PS to participate in a coalition government and abstained from voting for the head of government in the General Council, Nomen announcing that his party's stance would be neither progovernment nor opposition, but "bipartisan."

Leader: Juan Eusebio NOMEN Calvert (Parliamentary Leader and 2009 candidate for head of government).

Other Parties that Participated in the 2009 Parliamentary Elections:

Greens of Andorra (*Verds D'Andorra*—VA). The VA is a left-leaning party that emphasizes a commitment to both social justice and environmentalism, which it sees as linked and necessary to a decent social order. The party ran for the first time in the 2005 legislative poll and secured 3.5 percent of the vote (no seats). The results were similar in 2009, when it obtained 3.8 percent of the vote and no seats in the legislature.

Leader: Isabel LOZANO Muñoz (candidate for head of government in 2005 and 2009).

National Union of Progress (*Unió Nacional de Progrés*—UNP). The UNP, concerned with issues of social justice, emerged in 2007. It garnered only 0.8 percent of the nationwide vote in the 2009 elections, in which it contested the balloting in the parish of Encamp in alliance with the APC.

Leader: Tomas PASCUAL Casabosch.

Democratic Renovation (*Renovació Democràtica*—RD). The RD won 6.2 percent of the vote (no seats) in the 2005 legislative balloting. It apparently participated in a joint list with the PS called the PS/RD Alternative (*L'Alternativa PS/RD*) in four parishes in the 2005 poll, and several reports indicated that one of the parish seats nominally won by the PS in fact was won by a member of the RD. In the 2009 elections the RD backed the AFC, with which it joined in an alliance to contest (unsuccessfully) the balloting in the parish of Escaldes-Engordany.

Leader: Ricard de HARO Jiménez.

LEGISLATURE

The **General Council** (*El Consell General*) is a unicameral body consisting of 28 members. Fourteen councilors are elected from national party lists in proportion to the percent of votes received by the parties participating in nationwide balloting. The country is divided into seven administrative districts called parishes, and the remaining 14 councilors are elected in separate parish voting. The party with a plurality in each of the parishes wins that parish's 2 seats. Although all major parties run candidates for the national seats, not all compete in the parish elections, while others compete in the parish elections in alliance (formal or informal) with local parish parties.

In the most recent election of April 26, 2009, The distribution of seats was as follows: Social Democratic Party and its allies, 14 (6 national seats and 8 parish seats); Reform Coalition, 11 (5, 6); and Andorra for Change, 3 (3, 0).

Speaker: Josep DALLERÈS Codina.

CABINET

[as of September 1, 2009]

Head of Government	Jaume Bartumeu Cassany (PS)
Executive Council	
Economy and Finance	Pere López Agràs (PS)
Education and Culture	Susanna Vela Palomares (ind.) [f]
Foreign Affairs	Xavier Espot Miró (ind.)
Health	Cristina Rodríguez Galan (ind.) [f]
Interior	Víctor Naudi Zamora (PS)
Justice	Jaume Bartumeu Cassany (PS)
Territorial Development, Environment, and Agriculture	Vicenç Alay Ferrer (PS
Head of the Office of the President of the Executive Council	Marian Sanchiz Rego [f]
Secretary General	Alexandre Cucurella Rossell

[f] = female

COMMUNICATIONS

Freedom of the press is fully guaranteed under Andorran law.

Press. The domestic press consists of two dailies, *Diari d'Andorra* (Andorran Diary, 3,000) in Andorra la Vella and *El Periòdic d'Andorrá* (Andorran Newspaper) in Escaldes-Engordany, plus the weeklies *Poble Andorra* (Andorran People, 3,000), *Informacions* (News), and *7 Dies* (7 Days), all issued in Andorra la Vella. In addition, French and Spanish newspapers have long circulated in the principality.

Broadcasting and computing. In 1981 the question of control over Andorran airwaves resulted in the government ordering the principality's two radio stations, the French-owned *Sud-Radio* and the commercial, privately owned Spanish *Radio Andorra,* off the air. The dispute arose over the co-princes' refusal to permit effective nationalization of the broadcast facilities, which had extensive audiences in both France and Spain. Under a compromise approved by the General Council in September, the right of the Andorran people to operate (but not necessarily own) radio stations was acknowledged, and the General Council was granted full sovereignty over any stations broadcasting solely within Andorra. In 1984 *Radio Andorra* returned to the air, with an *Antena 7* television facility initiating programs of Andorran interest from the Spanish side of the border in 1987. In January 1991 a domestic service, *Televisióde Andorra,* initiated four hours of daily programming. *Ràdio i Televisió d'Andorra* (Andorran Radio and Television) has been the public service broadcaster since 2000 and operates *Ràdio Nacional d'Andorra* (RNA) and *Andorra Televisió* (ATV). As of 2008 there were 700.4 Internet users per 1,000 inhabitants.

INTERGOVERNMENTAL REPRESENTATION

Andorra's quite limited foreign relations are largely conducted through the French co-prince, although it maintains a number of embassies, particularly in Europe.

Ambassador to the U.S. and Permanent Representative to the UN: Narcís CASAL DE FONSDEVIELA.

U.S. Ambassador to Andorra: (Vacant).

IGO Memberships (Non-UN): CEUR, Interpol, OIF, OSCE, WCO.

ANGOLA

Republic of Angola
República de Angola

Political Status: Formally independent upon departure of the Portuguese High Commissioner on November 10, 1975; government of the Popular Movement for the Liberation of Angola (MPLA) recognized by the Organization of African Unity on February 11, 1976; peace accord signed with rebel National Union for the Total Independence of Angola on June 1, 1991; multiparty democratic system approved by constitutional amendment on August 26, 1992.

Area: 481,351 sq. mi. (1,246,700 sq. km.).

Population: 5,646,166 (1970C); 17,623,000 (2008E). A census launched in 1982 was never completed, and no subsequent enumeration has been undertaken; the 2008 figure is an extrapolation from recent UN estimates.

Major Urban Center (2005E): LUANDA (urban area, 2,825,000).

Official Language: Portuguese (although most Angolans speak tribal languages).

Monetary Unit: Kwanza (market rate December 1, 2009: 87.47 kwanzas = $1US).

President: José Eduardo DOS SANTOS (Popular Movement for the Liberation of Angola); designated by the Central Committee of the Popular Movement for the Liberation of Angola—Labor Party (MPLA-PT) and sworn in September 21, 1979, following the death of Dr. António Agostinho NETO on September 10; confirmed by an extraordinary congress of the MPLA-PT on December 17, 1980; reconfirmed in 1985 and 1990; mandate extended following popular election on September 29–30, 1992, and extended indefinitely by presidential order on January 29, 1999.

Prime Minister: Antonio Paulo KASSOMA (Popular Movement for the Liberation of Angola); appointed by the president on September 30, 2008, and sworn in the same day to succeed Fernando ("Nando") Da Piedade Dias DOS SANTOS (Popular Movement for the Liberation of Angola); formed government on October 1, 2008.

THE COUNTRY

The largest of Portugal's former African possessions, Angola is located on the Atlantic Ocean, south of the Congo River. The greater part of its territory is bounded on the north and east by the Democratic Republic of the Congo (DRC, formerly Zaire), on the southeast by Zambia, and on the south by Namibia. It also includes the small enclave of Cabinda in the northwest (bordered by the Republic of the Congo and the DRC), where important offshore oil deposits are being exploited (see Separatist Groups under Political Parties, below). The overwhelming proportion of Angola's people are Bantus, who comprise four distinct tribal groups: the Bakongo in the northwest, the Kimbundu in the north-central region inland from Luanda, the Ovimbundu in the south-central region, and the Chokwe in eastern Angola. No native language is universally spoken, Portuguese being the only tongue not confined to a specific tribal area. Women have traditionally experienced equality with men in subsistence activities, and they were estimated to constitute 46 percent of the workforce in 1996.

Because of its rail links with Zaire, Zambia, Zimbabwe, Mozambique, and South Africa, the port of Lobito served as a leading outlet for much of Central Africa's mineral wealth until independence was declared in 1975. Thereafter, civil war crippled the Benguela Railway and devastated much of the formerly prosperous economy, including the export of diamonds and coffee. Guerrilla activity resulted in massive migration of peasant farmers to cities or neighboring countries, and, despite its potential as a breadbasket for southern Africa, Angola became dependent on food imports to stave off widespread famine. In addition, black market activity flourished, contributing to a substantial degradation of the local currency. Although the government attempted to stimulate the economy by reducing state control over industry and agriculture, its efforts were hampered by corruption, bureaucratic inefficiency, and the allocation of more than half of its income to military expenditure. Only oil kept the economy afloat, generating more than 85 percent of revenue and attracting private foreign investment. Vowing to promote a "mixed economy" with additional free-market influence, Angola became a member of the International Monetary Fund (IMF) and the World Bank in 1989, although assistance from those institutions was constrained prior to initial accommodation with leading rebel forces in June 1991.

The subsequent 18-month cease-fire, as well as military actions against other insurgents in the oil-rich Cabindan province, raised hopes for economic as well as political stability. However, such optimism was dashed in late 1992 by the outbreak of postelectoral violence, and in early 1993 coffee and cotton production were described as nonexistent, while oil and diamond extraction were severely constrained. Thereafter, in response to the 1994 peace accord and appeals from both government and rebel leaders, a conference sponsored by the European Union (EU) yielded pledges of nearly $1 billion to facilitate recovery from the country's 20 years of military devastation. During 1995–1997, Angola enjoyed average annual real GDP growth of approximately 10 percent; furthermore, inflation fell dramatically in 1997–1998. However, with the return of civil war in late 1998, the government's economic energies again turned to fueling its war efforts.

In early 2000 the United Nations estimated that 4 million Angolans (approximately one-third of the population) had been directly affected by the conflict and that half of those individuals were "internally displaced." (Angola's massive repatriation program was reported to have officially ended in March 2007 with the return of some 400,000 refugees.) On a more positive note, the dos Santos government reported that GDP had grown in real terms by 3.5 percent in 1999, largely due to oil-related production. However, inflation remained out of control at 3,000 percent annually before declining to 305 percent in 2000 and 125 percent in 2001. New French investment pushed oil production to nearly 900,000 barrels per day in late 2001, underscoring the country's prominence in that sector. (Angola, already a major oil exporter to the United States and the second leading producer, next to Nigeria, in sub-Saharan Africa, was estimated to have reserves of more than 12.5 billion barrels.)

Despite its oil wealth, Angola remained in severe economic and social distress as of 2002, when the long-standing civil war finally concluded, leaving the nation's infrastructure in ruins and sapping government resources that might otherwise have gone to the health and education sectors. Life expectancy was estimated at less than 40 years, while 65 percent of the population lived below the poverty line. In addition, the IMF suspended its assistance after the war's end, citing, among other things, a lack of fiscal accountability on the part of the government. (Analysts suggested that billions of dollars in oil revenues had disappeared from government coffers and were hidden in secret offshore bank accounts.) Beginning in 2004 the government worked with the IMF on a plan to restore aid, President dos Santos continuing to resist meeting IMF conditions for fiscal transparency and accountability. The IMF did, however, commend government officials for their commitment to lowering inflation, which averaged around 10 percent annually in 2005 and 2006, and the World Bank gave aid to the government to reduce the spread of AIDS, malaria, and tuberculosis.

By 2007, the government and transnational companies had embarked on massive initiatives to further exploit not only Angola's oil reserves but also its significant deposits of diamonds, gold, uranium, iron ore, and other minerals and ores. China, in particular, was one of Angola's major creditors, prompting criticism from the West that Angola was relying on Chinese loans as an alternative to the World Bank. Major improvements to infrastructure, including an overhaul of the Benguela Railway and the construction of a new airport and a "mega-city" south of Luanda—all backed by Chinese financing—were under way in 2007. Also, the state-owned diamond company formed a partnership with leading foreign diamond producers for development rights. Meanwhile, average annual GDP growth, bolstered by the oil and non-oil sectors, averaged just under 19 percent annually for 2007–2008, according to the IMF, placing Angola among the fastest-growing

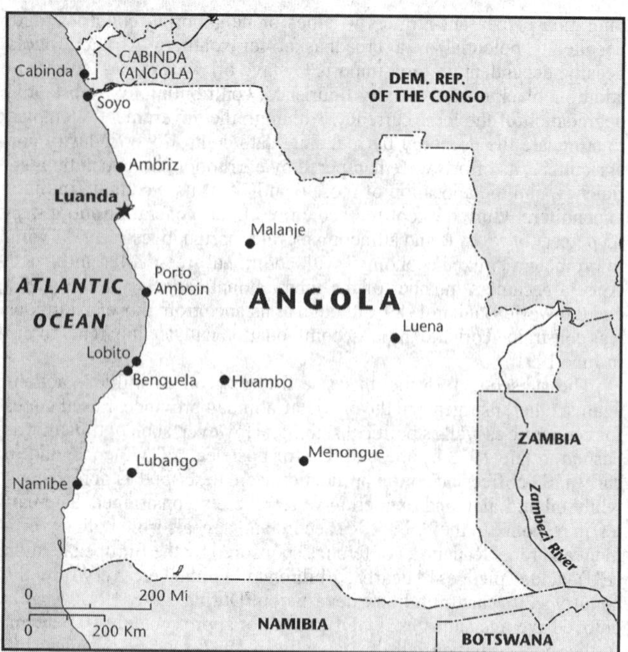

economies in Africa. However, falling oil prices and a decline of 30 percent in exports due to the global economic recession led to a downward revision of annual growth estimates, possibly to 6 percent in 2009 and 2010. In an effort to strengthen the economy, the government in 2009 undertook a $42 billion spending plan aimed primarily at improving housing, health, and education.

GOVERNMENT AND POLITICS

Political background. Portuguese settlements were established in eastern Angola in the late 15th century by navigators seeking trade routes to India, but the territory's present boundaries were not formally established until the Berlin Conference of 1884–1885. In 1951 the colony of Angola became an Overseas Province of Portugal and was thus construed as being an integral part of the Portuguese state.

Guerrilla opposition to colonial rule broke out in 1961 and continued for 13 years, despite a sizable Portuguese military presence. At the time of the 1974 coup in Lisbon, there were three principal independence movements operating in different parts of Angola. The National Front for the Liberation of Angola (*Frente Nacional para a Libertação de Angola*—FNLA), which had established a government-in-exile in Zaire in 1963 under the leadership of Holden ROBERTO, controlled much of the north; the Soviet-backed Popular Movement for the Liberation of Angola (*Movimento Popular de Libertação de Angola*—MPLA), led by Dr. Agostinho NETO, controlled much of the central region plus Cabinda; the third group, the National Union for the Total Independence of Angola (*União Nacional para a Indepêndencia Total de Angola*—UNITA), operated in eastern and southern Angola under the leadership of Dr. Jonas SAVIMBI. On January 15, 1975, the three leaders signed an agreement with Portuguese representatives calling for the independence of Angola on November 11 (the 400th anniversary of the founding of Luanda). The pact provided for interim rule by a Portuguese high commissioner and a Presidential Collegiate consisting of one representative from each of the three liberation movements. During succeeding months, however, the FNLA and UNITA formed a tacit alliance against the MPLA, whose forces at the time of independence controlled the capital. On November 10 the Portuguese high commissioner departed after a brief ceremony in Luanda, and at midnight Neto proclaimed the establishment, under MPLA auspices, of the People's Republic of Angola. On November 23 the FNLA-UNITA announced the formation of a rival Democratic People's Republic of Angola, with the central highlands city of Huambo (formerly *Nova Lisboa*) as its capital.

Within a month of independence, some two dozen nations had recognized the MPLA government, although the Organization of African Unity (OAU, subsequently the African Union—AU) had urged all countries to withhold recognition until formation of a coalition government. Meanwhile, Cuba had dispatched upwards of 18,000 troops in support of the MPLA. The revelation that American money and equipment were being channeled to FNLA forces through Zaire posed the additional risk of a U.S.-Soviet confrontation. By late December the Cuban troops, equipped with Soviet armored vehicles and rocket launchers, had helped turn the tide in favor of the MPLA, and some 4,000–5,000 South African troops operating in support of the Huambo regime were substantially withdrawn a month later. In early February 1976 the MPLA launched a southern offensive that resulted in the capture of Huambo and other key cities, prompting declarations by the FNLA and UNITA that their forces would thenceforth resort to guerrilla warfare. On February 11 the OAU announced that the MPLA government had been admitted to membership, following formal recognition of the Neto regime by a majority of OAU member states.

The FNLA and UNITA continued to resist government and Cuban units from 1976 to 1978, and in early 1979 they announced the formation of a joint military force. Nevertheless, it subsequently appeared that Roberto's FNLA had been virtually annihilated in the north and that only UNITA was offering organized opposition to the Luanda regime.

On September 10, 1979, President Neto died in Moscow, where he had been undergoing medical treatment. He was succeeded on September 21 by José Eduardo DOS SANTOS (the minister of planning) as chief of state, head of government, and chair of the ruling party, which had been renamed the MPLA–Labor Party (*MPLA–Partido Trabalhista*—MPLA-PT).

In September 1984 the remaining 1,500 guerrillas and 20,000 civilian members of *Conselho Militar para a Resistência de Angola* (COMIRA), which had been founded by former FNLA members, surrendered to the Luanda government under a 1979 amnesty provision; its military members were integrated into the MPLA-PT forces. However, the confrontation with UNITA settled into an intractable civil war: the U.S.-backed rebels, charged with brutal intimidation of the peasantry, continued to dominate much of the countryside, while the government, supported by 50,000 Cuban troops and extensive Soviet aid, retained control of most urban areas.

With more than 300,000 people dead, an estimated 1.5 million dislocated, and the country's economy and social infrastructure in shambles, attention in the late 1980s turned to negotiation of a political settlement to the military stalemate. One major breakthrough was an agreement in late 1988 on curtailment of foreign military involvement in Angola. Domestic reconciliation proved more difficult, however, as a much-publicized cease-fire brokered by Zairean president Mobutu at a meeting attended by the leaders of 16 African nations in mid-1989 lasted only a few weeks. Despite further fighting, government-UNITA talks continued, yielding, with the involvement of both U.S. Secretary of State James Baker and Soviet Foreign Minister Aleksandr Bessmertnykh, a peace settlement signed in Washington on June 1, 1991, that provided for a multiparty election in late 1992. Responsibility for monitoring the accord and organizing elections was assigned to the Joint Political and Military Commission (*Comissão Comun Politica e Militar*—CCPM), consisting of Portuguese, U.S., USSR, MPLA-PT, and UNITA representatives, which was bolstered in June by the arrival of a 600-member United Nations Angola Verification Mission (UNAVEM).

In July 1992 dos Santos named former planning minister Fernando José França Dias VAN-DÚNEM to the recently restored prime ministerial post, without, however, relinquishing his powers of executive leadership. Thereafter, despite clashes between MPLA-PT and UNITA supporters, preelectoral activity continued, including the emergence of a number of opposition political parties and the return to Luanda of former MPLA-PT adversaries Holden Roberto and Jonas Savimbi.

On August 26, 1992, the MPLA-PT endorsed constitutional revisions formalizing the government's dedication to a democratic system. Subsequently, the party also dropped "Labor Party" from its name. On September 8 dos Santos and Savimbi agreed to form a postelection unity government based on voting percentages derived from the balloting later that month. On September 28 the Angolan Armed Forces (FAA), drawn from the MPLA's Popular Armed Forces for the Liberation of Angola (FAPLA) and UNITA's Armed Forces for the Liberation of Angola (FALA), was inaugurated. However, at 8,000 troops, the FAA was far below its projected troop strength, a shortfall consistent with reports that entire UNITA units remained intact outside the capital.

Although 11 presidential candidates and 18 political parties participated in balloting on September 29–30, 1992, the polling was dominated by dos Santos, Savimbi, and their respective parties. On September 30 Savimbi, facing certain defeat, rejected the conclusions of international observers by declaring the balloting "rigged" and stated that he would "not accept defeat." By mid-October widespread violence was reported in the countryside, while for the first time UNITA and MPLA units clashed in the capital. Election results released on October 17 confirmed the MPLA's near 2-to-1 legislative victory, although dos Santos's 49.57 percent share of the presidential vote was constitutionally insufficient to avoid a second round against Savimbi, whose 40.07 percent vote share eclipsed nine other candidates by a wide margin. No presidential repolling occurred, as Savimbi's forces returned to military confrontation.

By October 1992 the MPLA-UNITA struggle had reached a previously unmatched intensity. On November 26 UNITA legislators boycotted the inaugural convention of the National Assembly, and, despite a new cease-fire agreement the following day, the fighting continued. On December 2 a transitional government was named, headed by Marcelino José Carlos MOCO, who had been appointed by dos Santos on November 27. Although dominated by MPLA members, the "unity" government provided for the participation of five opposition parties, featuring most prominently UNITA, which was assigned one full ministry and four deputy posts. Five days later UNITA agreed to join the government, and on December 20 the rebels reportedly accepted yet another peace plan, which was again ignored.

By mid-January 1993 tens of thousands of people had been reported killed, with Savimbi's forces on the defensive. On January 26 UN Secretary General Boutros Boutros-Ghali warned that if fighting continued, the remaining UN peacekeepers would be removed upon expiration of their mandate on April 30. The following day peace talks in Addis Ababa, Ethiopia, were abandoned. On March 6 UNITA recaptured its headquarters in Huambo after a pitched, 55-day battle that left over 12,000 dead, including 5,000 civilians. In addition to leaving the insurgents in control of over 70 percent of Angolan territory, the victory was described as pivotal to UNITA's transformation from a guerrilla force to a conventional army. Furthermore, UNITA's military advantage was evidenced by the government's subsequent willingness to make concessions at peace talks that opened on April 13 in Côte d'Ivoire. In mid-May the government agreed to a peace plan brokered by the UN, the United States, Russia, and Portugal that incorporated UNITA's demand for decentralized power sharing under a national unity government. However, days later, UNITA rejected the agreement.

In response to UNITA's continued intransigence, the United States on May 18, 1993, announced its intention to recognize the dos Santos government, formally signaling an end to its support for UNITA. Subsequently, UNITA intensified its military activities, capturing oil-rich Soyo on May 26. On June 2 the UN Security Council unanimously declared UNITA responsible for the breakdown of peace negotiations and extended the UNAVEM mandate until July 15, albeit with a sharply reduced staff. In mid-July the UN continued the UNAVEM mandate until September 15 and threatened to impose an embargo on UNITA unless the rebels agreed to honor the 1991 accord, respect the 1992 elections, and enact a verifiable cease-fire. Heavy fighting nonetheless continued, and on August 20 the World Food Program agreed to a six-month emergency food operation to help alleviate the suffering from what one observer described as the "world's worst war." On September 20 UNITA announced a unilateral cease-fire; nevertheless, its military activities escalated, and on September 26 the UN imposed an embargo on oil and arms sales to the rebels. On October 30 and 31 UNITA agreed to withdraw from territory it had seized after the 1992 elections. However, the MPLA dismissed UNITA demands that "thousands of military prisoners" be released, UN forces be encamped in all towns it vacated, and UNITA fighters be integrated on an equal basis with government troops into an Angolan army.

In November 1993 a fresh round of peace talks opened in Lusaka, Zambia, and were reportedly going well until government negotiators insisted that UNITA civilian supporters be disarmed. Although the demand precipitated a temporary suspension of the talks, another cease-fire agreement was reported on December 10 to be near completion. However, three days later, the negotiations were again suspended after UNITA accused the government of attempting to kill Savimbi in a bombing raid.

"Lusaka-2" negotiations were launched on January 5, 1994, with negotiators concluding an agreement on fundamental principles of national reconciliation on February 17. In March the government was reported to have offered four secondary ministerial posts to UNITA, which countered with a demand for the key portfolios of defense, interior, and finance. In late April agreement was reached on second-round conclusion of the presidential balloting that had been repudiated by UNITA in September 1992, although a deadlock ensued at midyear over UNITA's insistence that it be awarded the governorship of Huambo province. On September 5 the two sides agreed to a renewal of UNAVEM, whose existing mandate was scheduled to expire on September 30, and on October 31 they initialed a new peace agreement under which UNITA would be awarded 11 government portfolios and three provincial governorships. Nonetheless, heavy fighting continued, and on November 8 the rebel stronghold of Huambo again fell to government troops. Despite the absence of Savimbi, who was reported to have been wounded in an incident involving his own bodyguard, the latest peace accord was formally signed in Lusaka on November 20. On February 8, 1995, the UNAVEM mandate was extended for another six months amid evidence of tensions within UNITA because of hard-line opposition to Lusaka-2.

It was not until May 6, 1995, that a long-awaited meeting between dos Santos and Savimbi took place in Lusaka, at the conclusion of which the UNITA leader accepted his opponent as "president of my country." While there was no public mention at the meeting of demobilization of UNITA's guerrilla army, Savimbi later declared in talks with South African President Mandela that his group's revival of hostilities in late 1992 had been "stupid," and on May 31 the advance units of a projected 7,460-member UNAVEM peacekeeping force arrived in Angola.

On June 17, 1995, it was confirmed that Savimbi had been offered a vice presidency. While there was no immediate response from the UNITA leader, he was reported during a second meeting with dos Santos in Gabon, on August 10 to have accepted, subject to a number of "understandings" that included a role in defining economic policy. On the other hand, Radio Angola announced prior to a joint appearance by the two rivals at the Brussels donor conference in September that Savimbi would not assume office until the demobilization or integration of UNITA military units had been completed in early 1996. The latter process was halted in December after government troops launched a new offensive in northern Angola but was resumed on the basis of a new timetable negotiated with Luanda on January 9, 1996.

The new timetable was immediately disregarded by UNITA, only about 8,000 of whose 62,000-strong army had reported to UN-supervised confinement camps by mid-February 1996. Direct talks between dos Santos and Savimbi were held in Libreville, Gabon, on March 1, and the two leaders agreed that a government of national unity would be formed within four months and that a 90,000-member national army would be created from existing guerrilla forces. A further agreement on May 24 specified an immediate start to the integration of UNITA soldiers into a national force and the disarming of all civilians. Meanwhile, the UNAVEM mandate had been renewed on May 8, this time for only a two-month period.

The new agreements produced no greater urgency on UNITA's part, so that by the end of May 1996 only some 23,000 UNITA forces had been confined. Losing patience with the slow rate of compliance, President dos Santos on June 8 appointed a new government in which Van-Dúnem (then assembly speaker) returned to the premiership. Charged in particular with launching an urgent assault on corruption and government inefficiency, the new ministerial list contained no UNITA representatives, although government spokesmen stressed that UNITA would be included as soon as it had honored its undertakings under the 1994 Lusaka agreement. The UN Security Council renewed the UNAVEM mandate in July and again in October, the second extension including a warning to UNITA that sanctions would be imposed on the group if it failed to comply with the Lusaka agreement promptly. On November 13, 1996, the National Assembly, citing a lack of electoral preparations, adopted a constitutional revision that extended its mandate for a period of two to four years. On December 12 the UNAVEM mandate was extended to February 28, 1997, and the following day UNAVEM officials declared that UNITA had fulfilled its obligations as delineated by the Lusaka accord; however, the desertion of approximately 15,000 UNITA members from confinement centers coupled with reports of UNITA's involvement in the fighting in Zaire rekindled concerns regarding Savimbi's dedication to the peace process. Subsequently, implementation of the peace accord stalled in the first quarter of 1997, as Savimbi formally rejected the offer of a vice presidential appointment and demanded instead a role as "principal adviser" and the establishment of a "joint basic government." Both requests were promptly dismissed by the dos Santos government, which further asserted that Savimbi remained unwilling to relinquish rebel-held territory and completely disarm his forces.

On a more positive note, on April 9, 1997, the National Assembly met for the first time with its full complement of UNITA legislators and approved legislation naming Savimbi the "Leader of the Largest Opposition Party." On the same day, dos Santos took the first formal step toward the establishment of a unity government, naming Van-Dúnem as prime minister of the Unity and National Reconciliation Government (*Governa da Unidade e da Reconciliação Nacional*—GURN), which included 11 UNITA members.

On August 31, 1998, the dos Santos administration announced that UNITA's legislators and cabinet members had been suspended because of UNITA's failure to adhere to the dictates of the Lusaka accord. However, most of the UNITA representatives were reported to have resumed their duties in September, some now apparently operating under the rubric of the new UNITA-Renewal faction (see UNITA under Political Parties). With relations between the government and the Savimbi faction of UNITA having deteriorated into full-scale war, dos Santos formed a new government on January 30, 1999, in which he left the prime minister's post unfilled and assumed the responsibilities of head of the government pending the "return of constitutional normality." The new cabinet included several UNITA-Renewal representatives but no Savimbi supporters. Dos Santos also announced he had taken over direct control of the armed forces as the government pursued what it hoped would be a final offensive against Savimbi's fighters.

In early 1999 the UN condemned the two combatants, asserting that their desire for a military conclusion to the strife had caused a humanitarian disaster; following the expiration of the mandate of the UN Observer Mission at Angola (UNOMA) on February 26, the peacekeepers were withdrawn. Meanwhile, heavy fighting continued, and by May approximately 10,000 people had been killed and 1 million dislocated.

By mid-1999 UNITA forces had reportedly closed to within 40 miles of Luanda; however, the government unleashed a fierce offensive highlighted by relentless air strikes. Reportedly aided by Western intelligence, government forces captured Bailundo in October, and in December UNITA forces fled from Jamba in the face of a government attack that originated, in part, from Namibia. For its open support of Luanda, Namibia suffered a wave of UNITA attacks. On the political front, President dos Santos continued to reach out to opposition party leaders in Luanda while at the same time remaining adamantly opposed to suggestions that he reopen negotiations with Savimbi.

In March 2000 the Angolan conflict once again captured international attention when the UN Sanctions Committee on Angola issued a report accusing individuals and institutions in nearly a dozen countries of ignoring sanctions against supplying or trading with the UNITA rebels. The document underscored the UN's efforts to tighten the application of sanctions, with the ultimate goal of derailing UNITA's war-making capabilities. (UNITA earlier had suffered another blow to its already severely tarnished image when the Southern African Development Community [SADC] had formally branded Savimbi as a "war criminal.")

Significantly increased pressure on the government to resume peace negotiations was reported in 2001 from civic and religious groups as well as small opposition parties, a growing number of critics suggesting that the MPLA was using Savimbi and UNITA to distract attention from the administration's long-standing inability to effectively confront the nation's social woes. Savimbi declared himself available for new power-sharing talks, but dos Santos, apparently buoyed by recent military successes, adopted a hard line, demanding that UNITA forces lay down their arms as a precondition to negotiations. By the end of the year, government forces were reportedly in control of more than 90 percent of the country, UNITA having once again been reduced to waging a guerrilla campaign.

Savimbi was killed in a government ambush on February 22, 2002. On April 4, two days after the National Assembly had approved an amnesty for all participants in the long-standing civil war who now accepted a negotiated settlement, the government and UNITA signed a cease-fire that provided for disarmament of UNITA, integration of UNITA fighters into the Angolan military, and UNITA's return to normal political party activity.

In August 2002 the UN Security Council authorized the creation of the UN Mission in Angola (UNMA) to assist the government and UNITA in implementing the peace plan. An August 2 ceremony in Luanda formally marked the integration of 5,000 UNITA soldiers into the Angolan army. Declaring an end to the "exceptional period" that had existed since 1999, President dos Santos on December 6 appointed Fernando Da Piedade Dias DOS SANTOS as prime minister. Collaterally, the administration, UNITA, and small opposition parties reportedly agreed on the delineation of authority between the president and the prime minister.

The end of the civil war did not result in an immediate resolution concerning elections, and President dos Santos postponed balloting in December 2006 and December 2007. With some 8 million people reportedly having been registered to vote, a new National Assembly poll, the first since 1992, was finally held on September 5–6, 2008. The MPLA won 81.64 percent of the vote, while UNITA received 10.36 percent, with a small number of seats going to the FNLA and minor parties. Women won 82 seats. The president appointed Antonio Paulo KASSOMA as prime minister on September 30, and Kassoma named a new MPLA-dominated government on October 1. In December President dos Santos said that presidential and municipal elections, which had been anticipated in 2009, would not be held until a new constitution was promulgated.

Constitution and government. Under the 1975 constitution as amended, the government was headed by a president who also served as chair of the MPLA. In the event of presidential disability, the MPLA Central Committee was authorized to designate an interim successor, thus reinforcing the role of the party as the people's "legitimate representative." In December 1978 the positions of prime minister and deputy prime minister were abolished, while in November 1980 the legislative Council of the Revolution was replaced as the "supreme organ of state power" by the National People's Assembly, whose members were indirectly designated at meetings of locally elected provincial delegates. (The Council of the Revolution, subsequently renamed the Council of the Republic, continued to function as an advisory body.)

In late 1990 the government committed itself to a new constitution that would permit multiparty presidential and legislative elections. UNITA representatives were invited to help draft the document under the peace accord of June 1, 1991. Thus, on February 1, 1992, UNITA representatives (who boycotted a multiparty conference held January 14–26) agreed with the government that the September election would be held on the basis of proportional representation and that the post-electoral executive would be elected for a five-year term, while the assembly would serve for four years.

On August 26, 1992, the MPLA approved a revised constitution that, in addition to the February 1 stipulations, provided for a presidentially appointed prime minister to head a transitional government; the abolition of the death penalty; and, in keeping with the removal of "People's" from the Republic's formal name, the deletion of all constitutional references to "popular" and "people" as reflecting former Marxist tendencies. A new constitutional committee was established by the assembly in 1998 to address issues such as whether federal governors and the prime minister should be popularly elected and what authority should be invested in the latter. Negotiations between the government and the UNITA-led opposition on a new constitution began following the peace accord of 2002, but progress has continued at a slow pace. By the end of 2004, the National Assembly had abolished the Constitutional Commission (the object of a boycott by the opposition), announcing that constitutional revision would henceforth be handled by a government-dominated assembly committee. On December 15, 2008, the assembly voted to form a new Constitutional Commission, comprising 45 members—35 from the MPLA, 6 from UNITA, and the remainder from smaller parties. A draft constitution was expected within six months.

The country is divided into 18 provinces (*províncias*) administered by centrally appointed governors, with legislative authority vested in provincial assemblies. The provinces are further divided into councils (*concelhos*), communes (*comunas*), circles (*círculos*), neighborhoods (*bairros*), and villages (*povoações*).

Foreign relations. On June 23, 1976, the United States exercised its right of veto in the Security Council to block Angolan admission to the United Nations. The stated reason was the continued presence in Angola of a sizable Cuban military force. On November 19, however, the United States reversed itself, citing "the appeals of its African friends," and Angola was admitted on December 1. Senegal, the last black African state to withhold recognition of the MPLA-PT government, announced the establishment of diplomatic relations in February 1982, while the People's Republic of China, long an opponent of the Soviet-supportive regime, established relations in late 1983.

Relations with Portugal were suspended briefly in late 1976 and remained relatively cool prior to a June 1978 agreement providing for the mutual repatriation of Angolan and Portuguese nationals. Subsequently, relations were again strained by allegations of Portuguese-based exile support for UNITA rebels, although efforts were made to restore previously substantial trade links between the two countries.

Relations have fluctuated with neighboring Zaire (restyled the Democratic Republic of the Congo in 1997), which charged the Neto government with providing support for rebel incursions into Shaba (formerly Katanga) Province in March 1977 and May 1978. Shortly thereafter, President Mobutu agreed to end his support for anti-MPLA forces based in Zaire, in return for a similar pledge from President Neto regarding Zairean dissidents sited in Angola. In October 1979 the presidents of Angola, Zaire, and Zambia signed a more extensive trilateral nonaggression pact in Ndola, Zambia. Despite these agreements and a Kinshasa-Luanda security pact signed in early 1985, periodic accusations of Zairean support for Angolan insurgents continued to issue from Luanda.

In the south, Luanda's support for the South West African People's Organization (SWAPO), which began operating from Angolan bases in the mid-1970s, resulted in numerous cross-border raids by South African defense forces deployed in Namibia. On the other hand, despite periodic encouragement of UNITA and an unwillingness to establish formal relations prior to the withdrawal of Cuban troops, both the Carter and Reagan administrations in the United States made overtures to Luanda, citing the need for Angolan involvement in the Namibian independence process. In early 1985 statements by dos Santos indicating a willingness to negotiate on Cuban troop withdrawal were offered by Washington as evidence of its "constructive engagement" policy in southern Africa. All contacts, however, were suspended by Angola later in the year following U.S. congressional repeal of the "Clark Amendment" banning military aid to the insurgents, with repeated military activity by Pretoria having already reduced Luanda's willingness to negotiate.

A series of meetings in 1988 concluded with the signing of two accords (one a tripartite agreement among Angola, Cuba, and South Africa, and the other a bilateral agreement between Angola and Cuba) for the phased withdrawal of Cuban forces, coupled with South African acceptance of a 1978 Security Council resolution calling for UN-supervised elections for an independent Namibia. Under the withdrawal provisions, to be monitored by UNAVEM, half of the Cubans were to leave by November 1989, with the remainder to depart by July 1991. For its part, Pretoria agreed to end military assistance to the UNITA rebels, while insisting that Luanda would be in violation of the accord if it permitted African National Congress (ANC) guerrillas to use its territory as a staging area for infiltration into Botswana, Namibia, or South Africa. (For the Namibia portion of the settlement, see articles on Namibia and South Africa.) In January 1989, three months ahead of schedule, Cuban troops began their withdrawal, although South Africa's apparent adherence to the accord was offset by a reported doubling of U.S. aid to the rebels.

In the wake of the June 1991 peace settlement, Washington pledged $30 million to assist UNITA in its transformation from a military organization into a political party, and, following a September summit meeting between presidents dos Santos and George H. W. Bush, the United States reiterated its intent to restrict trade and investment until after multiparty elections. Nevertheless, dos Santos, citing a U.S. offer of humanitarian aid, electoral assistance, and the potential for postelection aid, stated that relations had reached a "turning point."

Resurgence of the Angolan civil war in late 1992 revived allegations by both combatants of military and financial intervention by neighboring states. Progovernment officials accused South Africa and Zaire of supporting UNITA efforts, while Namibia challenged UNITA to prove its allegation that Namibian forces were fighting alongside government troops.

Angola's foreign relations in 1993 were dominated by international efforts to thwart UNITA's widely condemned aggression and aid those adversely affected by the civil war. Most dramatically, on May 18 the United States announced its intention to recognize the Luanda government. The U.S. decision came after much exhortation by South Africa and Mozambique, both of whom feared that UNITA's refusal to accept the 1992 poll results might undermine their own election plans. Thereafter, France, Russia, and the United Kingdom announced that they were negotiating arms sales with the government.

Although both the MPLA and UNITA denied involvement in the fighting in Zaire in early 1997, observers there reported that MPLA units had provided at least rearguard and logistical assistance to Laurent Kabila's fighters, while UNITA forces had suffered heavy casualties fighting alongside the Mobutu regime's ultimately unsuccessful defenders. Meanwhile, in Luanda, government officials announced a reordering of their diplomatic priorities, with major emphasis being placed, in order of importance, on relations with the United States, France, and Angola's Asian economic partners. In late October President dos Santos hosted a summit of the leaders of the Republic of the Congo, Democratic Republic of the Congo (DRC), and Gabon during which the four presidents agreed to isolate UNITA as well as the Cabindan guerrillas.

In 1998 Luanda alleged that Burkina Faso, Rwanda, Togo, Uganda, and Zambia were either supplying the UNITA rebels or offering them safe haven. Meanwhile, international attention focused on Angola's prominent role in the civil wars in the DRC and the Republic of the Congo. President dos Santos sought to justify Angola's involvement there as an attempt to help prevent a "bloodbath" and expansion of the fighting. In September, Angola, the DRC, and the Republic of the Congo signed a border security agreement. Meanwhile, Namibia's willingness to let anti-UNITA troops operate from within its borders proved pivotal to Luanda's military successes in late 1999.

In December 1999 the Portuguese legislature approved a "vote of protest" against Angola's ongoing fighting, thus prompting Luanda to register its own complaint that Lisbon was attempting to interfere in its affairs. Thereafter, international attention turned to a UN investigation into alleged efforts by UNITA supporters to circumvent sanctions against supplying or trading with UNITA.

Following the mid-2002 peace accord in Angola, U.S. President George W. Bush welcomed President dos Santos at the White House, underscoring, among other things, the importance of Angolan oil to the United States. At the same time, ties between Angola and China intensified, resulting in major Chinese investment in Angolan oil production, and in 2006 dos Santos agreed to work with Venezuelan President Hugo Chávez on oil and natural gas exploration in Angola. (In the midst of the oil boom, the Organization of Petroleum Exporting Countries [OPEC] admitted Angola as a new member in 2007.)

Meanwhile, tensions increased on the border between Angola and the DRC in 2006 and early 2007, partially resulting from an incident in which Angolan security forces allegedly crossed into DRC villages and killed 11 Congolese diamond prospectors.

In 2008 the United States strengthened relations with Angola, providing ships and radar in an effort to stem the growing problem of piracy. Angola's relations with Cuba warmed in 2009 following talks between President dos Santos and Raúl Castro in Luanda.

Current issues. Almost immediately after the death of UNITA's Jonas Savimbi in February 2002, it became clear that most Angolans were more than ready for the nearly three-decade-long civil war to come to an end. The transformation of UNITA into a functioning political party and the reintegration of UNITA forces into the military and civil society occurred surprisingly swiftly and smoothly. (It was estimated that 500,000–1 million people had died in the conflict, with 4–5 million having been internally or externally dislocated.) Attention soon turned to plans for a return to a normal political process, including the writing of a new constitution in order to permit national elections. In 2005 the MPLA remained strongly entrenched politically, despite regularly facing charges of corruption and economic mismanagement, particularly in regard to oil revenues. One example of alleged corruption involved a line of credit from China meant for public works projects that some suggested was being used as a "political slush fund" for future elections. Meanwhile, progress toward constitutional reform and elections slowed in 2005 as President dos Santos backed away from his initial affirmation that elections would be held in 2006. Sharp increases in oil revenues helped solidify the current administration's power, enabling it to rebuff opposition parties' attempts to impose political reforms.

In 2006 President dos Santos responded to severe criticism from the IMF and others by pledging greater transparency in governmental affairs, and he subsequently made public general information about state finances and some of the signing bonuses granted to oil companies, as well as the amounts targeted for the regions in which they would be working. The administration also embarked, with the assistance of foreign investors, on a series of massive projects to rebuild the nation's infrastructure, with dos Santos contending that roads and railways needed to be rebuilt before any elections were held, in part to facilitate voter registration.

Despite the apparent economic boom (with oil production reported near 2 million barrels per day in 2007), observers cautioned that poverty was increasing, with much of the population still lacking basic services. The return of hundreds of thousands of refugees from the war put a further strain on services. In the wake of a cholera epidemic in 2006, critics blamed government corruption for the substandard living conditions that contributed to the spread of disease.

Attention in 2008 turned to the long-delayed legislative elections, finally scheduled for September. Of 34 parties that sought to contest the elections, only 10 parties and 4 coalitions were approved by the Constitutional Court in July, just five days before the start of the official month-long campaign. UNITA, in particular, and other opposition parties were highly critical of the government's actions, including the transfer of oversight authority from the National Electoral Commission to a government commission that did not include any opposition members; delayed state funding for the political parties contesting the elections; government dominance of the media to convey pro-MPLA messages; and the arrests of and attacks against numerous UNITA supporters at rallies in mid-August. The election itself was allegedly fraught with irregularities, various monitoring groups reporting intimidation, bribes, and other problems. A formal complaint about the voting process filed by UNITA was rejected on September 8 by the elections commission. Ultimately, the elections were generally assessed by the international community as a major step toward democracy and stability in the country. With the MPLA having won an overwhelming majority, President dos Santos's new prime minister, Antonio Paulo Kassoma named an enlarged cabinet comprised almost entirely of MPLA members, the few UNITA ministers from the previous government being dismissed. One notable appointment outside of the party was that of António Bento Bembe, former leader of the separatist group Front for the Liberation of the Cabinda Enclave (*Frente de Libertação do Enclave de Cabinda*—FLEC), as minister without portfolio. (FLEC disbanded in 2007 following the signing of a peace agreement between Cabinda and the government; see Separatist Groups, below.)

The MPLA's margin of victory reportedly surprised even its most loyal backers, the mandate seen as granting President dos Santos and the governing party overwhelming control in writing a new constitution. In December 2008 parliament approved a new Constitutional Commission, made up primarily of MPLA members, to rework a draft constitution drawn up by the previous legislature. Of greatest concern to opposition parties was the commission's consideration of options that would adopt a parliamentary system of governance, with a prime minister as head of state and a president indirectly elected; or a system in which parliament elects the president, who would effectively operate as a prime minister. The opposition argued that either option would be unconstitutional and would virtually ensure dos Santos's reelection. The Constitutional Committee, meanwhile, invited proposals from citizens, civil societies, and other non-state groups. President dos Santos, for his part, announced that presidential and (the first) municipal elections, widely anticipated in 2009, would not take place until a new constitution was promulgated. Meanwhile, in 2009 the registration process began for Angolans living abroad in anticipation of their being able to vote in the next elections (see Legislature, below.)

Turning his attention to the global economic downturn in 2009, President dos Santos said the government would try to create more jobs, improve Angolans' standard of living, and maintain political stability and a democratic society. Meanwhile, the salaries of legislators were tripled "in a bid to ensure their loyalty," according to published reports. Pope Benedict XVI, on a visit to Angola in March, which drew the largest crowd of his weeklong Africa trip, called for the country to make better use of its diamond and oil wealth to foster "peace and understanding" among its citizens. The pontiff also met with President dos Santos and spoke out against corruption in Africa.

POLITICAL PARTIES

Angola was a one-party state for the first 16 years of its independence; however, in 1990 the government agreed to institute a multiparty electoral system, and, under legislation of March 26, 1991, more than 30 groups expressed interest in achieving formal party status. Thereafter, the imposition of strict registration guidelines limited participation in the September 1992 legislative balloting to 18 parties. (For information on several subsequent pro- and antigovernment coalitions, see the 2000–2002 *Handbook.*)

Ten individual parties and four coalitions contested the legislative elections of September 2008, participation again being limited by the Constitutional Court, which also deregistered numerous minor parties after the balloting.

Government Party:

Popular Movement for the Liberation of Angola (*Movimento Popular de Libertação de Angola*—MPLA). Organized in 1956, the Soviet-backed MPLA provided the primary resistance to Portuguese colonial rule in central Angola prior to independence. During its first national congress December 4–11, 1977, the party was formally restructured along Marxist-Leninist lines and redesignated as the MPLA–Labor Party (*MPLA–Partido Trabalhista*—MPLA-PT).

Reflecting the dos Santos administration's increasingly pragmatic approach to economic problems, the party's second congress in 1985 adopted a resolution promoting several "Western-style" reforms, without, however, altering its alliance with Cuba and the Soviet Union or its hostility to the United States and South Africa regarding the UNITA insurgency (below). At its third congress, held December 4–10, 1990, the MPLA-PT abandoned Marxism-Leninism in favor of "democratic socialism" and endorsed multiparty elections in the wake of a peace settlement with UNITA. In consonance with those decisions, the party decided to drop "Labor Party" from its name prior to the 1992 elections.

Dos Santos was reelected as MPLA president at the 1998 and 2003 congresses, apparently positioning himself at the latter for a run in the presidential election (reportedly postponed until 2009). In 2006 and 2007 the MPLA held a series of meetings with opposition groups to discuss its National Consensus Agenda for the country's long-term development.

The 2008 legislative elections proved to be something of a turning point for the MPLA, which, according to observers benefited from the public's fear that the economic boom days would end if the MPLA was not reelected. The party pledged to strengthen parliament's authority while still ensuring an "active role" for the president. With its overwhelming victory in the elections, on which it reportedly spent an estimated $8.7 million—more than seven times the total spent by the 13 other parties and coalitions—the MPLA no longer needed to include UNITA in the government, the latter's members being replaced when a new government was installed in October. The party's greater dominance also underscored its potential role in rewriting the constitution, as in 2009 parliament formed a committee, comprised largely of MPLA members, to begin considering proposed changes.

Leaders: José Eduardo DOS SANTOS (President of the Republic and President of the Party), Antonio Paulo KASSOMA (Prime Minister), Roberto de Antonio Victor de ALMEIDA (Vice President of the Party), António Domingos Pitra da Costa NETO, João Manuel Gonçalves LOURENÇO, Julião Mateus PAULO (Secretary General).

Other Legislative Parties:

National Union for the Total Independence of Angola (*União Nacional para a Independência Total de Angola*—UNITA). Active primarily in southern Angola prior to the Portuguese withdrawal, UNITA, whose support is centered within the Ovimbundu ethnic group, joined with the FNLA in establishing an abortive rival government in Huambo in November 1975 and subsequently engaged in guerrilla operations against Luanda. Although its ideology was of Maoist derivation, the party's image within black Africa suffered because of U.S. and South African military assistance. In late 1982 UNITA leader Jonas SAVIMBI asserted that no basic ideological differences separated UNITA and the MPLA-PT and that the removal of all Cuban troops would lead to negotiations with the government. Although his subsequent avowals of "anti-communism" and increased solicitation of aid from Pretoria and Washington reportedly generated internal dissent, Savimbi remained in control.

In the peace accord of June 1, 1991, UNITA agreed to recognize the legitimacy of the dos Santos government until the holding of multiparty elections in September 1992. In March 1992 two of UNITA's most senior officials, Secretary General Miguel NZAU PUNA and Gen. Tony da Costa FERNANDES, left the party, ostensibly to focus on problems involving their native enclave of Cabinda. Late in the month, however, the two issued a statement in Paris charging UNITA with political killings and other human rights abuses. At midyear the party's election hopes were dealt another blow when Savimbi reportedly announced that a UNITA-led government would be composed of only black members, thus exacerbating the fear already existing in the mixed-race and Portuguese communities. Following the September election, Savimbi's rejection of the results and reports of UNITA military activities generated domestic and international condemnation. UNITA officials, however, blamed MPLA supporters for initiating the violence that broke out in Luanda in mid-October. In May 1993 UNITA's rejection of a peace plan that reportedly addressed most of Savimbi's demands appeared to reflect a split within the group between pro-negotiation moderates and fight-to-the-end hard-liners.

Meanwhile, on the diplomatic front, UNITA negotiators rejected demands in 1993 that its troops be withdrawn to their May 1991 positions, claiming that it feared MPLA reprisals against its supporters in the contested areas. In September the rebel leadership agreed to recognize the 1992 election results. Thereafter, in late 1993 and into 1994, UNITA, propelled by Savimbi's apparently undiminished desire to rule Angola, continued its pattern of simultaneous diplomatic negotiations and military offensives.

On November 15, 1994, UNITA's Secretary General Eugénio Manuvakola signed a truce on behalf of the rebels with the government. However, in February 1995 UNITA hard-liners were reported to be dissatisfied with the peace agreement, which was to have come into effect on November 22, and Manuvakola was replaced as secretary general by Gen. Paulo Lukamba Gato.

In addition to the four senior cabinet posts awarded the group in April 1997, UNITA representatives were also named to seven deputy ministerial positions. Amid speculation that UNITA was preparing to return to war, reports circulated at midyear that the group's military high command was planning on moving to the panhandle region along the Zambian border. Subsequently, General Manuvakola broke with the group, denouncing its hostile intentions.

Meanwhile, observers reported that a gap had developed between UNITA officials participating in the government in Luanda and those in Savimbi's inner circle, with the former attempting to distance themselves from the latter's confrontational stances. Evidence of the group's factionalization became apparent in February 1998 when the Luanda-based members ignored a Savimbi dictate to vote against a budget proposal. Thereafter, with the country once more poised for civil war, pro-Savimbi UNITA members fled Luanda in July, and, on August 31, the government announced the temporary suspension of UNITA representatives from the government and the assembly. In September, Jorge Alicerces VALENTIM, a UNITA cabinet minister, announced that he and a number of other UNITA ministers and parliamentarians had aligned with General Manuvakola. Furthermore, the dissidents announced the suspension of Savimbi and, under the banner of UNITA-Renewal (UNITA-*Renavado*), appointed an interim group to lead the party until the convening of its next congress. Thereafter, a third UNITA strain emerged under the leadership of Abel Chivukuvuku, the party's parliamentary leader, and Armindo KASSESSA, both of whom had rejected UNITA-Renewal's entreaties. Chivukuvuku, reportedly popular with both UNITA military leaders and international mediators, was reelected to his legislative post in late October in what observers described as a direct "slap" at Valentim.

In January 1999, delegates aligned with UNITA-Renewal elected General Manuvakola president of the party. Meanwhile, Savimbi dismissed the Luanda-based factions as "irrelevant." Thereafter, the government intensified its efforts to persuade UNITA militants to disarm and play a role in the political process.

Following Savimbi's death in February 2002, UNITA quickly negotiated an accord with the government that ended the long civil war and provided for the integration of about 5,000 UNITA fighters into the Angolan armed forces. The peace agreement also permitted reunification of the various UNITA factions, General Manuvakola suspending his UNITA-Renewal leadership to facilitate that initiative.

Again acting as a regular political party, UNITA elected its former representative in Paris, Isaias Samakuva, as its new president in June 2003. (Samakuva defeated General Gato, who had served as interim leader since Savimbi's death.) In 2004 UNITA announced it was forming the Campaign for a Democratic Angola with some seven small parties in preparation for the next elections. In 2005 Samakuva announced his intention to run for the presidency. Meanwhile, a rift developed in the party after Valentim was removed from his ministry post in 2005 and briefly suspended after publicly criticizing party leaders. He claimed party leaders were delaying his appointment to the assembly, though he was subsequently seated in April 2005. The following year he and three other UNITA members of parliament were expelled from the party for again speaking out against the party leadership. At the same time, General Manuvakola was suspended from the party for 12 months. In March 2007 the party claimed that Samakuva was the target of an assassination attempt by police when he was visiting a province east of the capital; the police who reportedly fired shots at the local party headquarters were arrested. In July Samakuva was reelected party president, handily defeating Chivukuvuku.

By the end of 2007, UNITA was becoming more vocal in its criticism of the long-delayed elections, claiming that the government had stepped up its brutal crackdown on political opponents in the countryside as "deliberate acts to postpone democracy."

In the run-up to the 2008 legislative elections, UNITA claimed intimidation, including suspension of the party-line radio station, and attacks against its supporters. Meanwhile, rifts developed within the party, resulting in Jorge Valentim's reported defection to the MPLA. Following the elections, in which UNITA received only 10.39 percent of the vote and 16 seats—a distant second to the MPLA—*Africa Confidential* said the party was put "on a level with other, previously insignificant opposition parties." However, unlike in the 1990s, UNITA accepted the results (after a complaint it had lodged about the balloting was rejected by the court), helping, observers said, to pave the way toward establishment of a peaceful democratic state after years of civil war. Subsequently, the three UNITA members of the cabinet were removed by Prime Minister Kassoma in October 2008, when he named a new government almost entirely comprised of MPLA members.

Leaders: Isaias SAMAKUVA (President), Ernesto MULATO (Vice President), Abel CHIVUKUVUKU, Gen. Paulo Lukamba GATO, Gen. Eugénio MANUVAKOLA, Alcides SAKALA, Camalata NUMA (Secretary General).

National Front for the Liberation of Angola (*Frente Nacional para a Libertação de Angola*—FNLA). Organized as a resistance group in 1962 in northern Angola, the FNLA was consistently the most anti-communist of the three major groups until the collapse of its forces in the late 1970s.

The FNLA was inactive throughout most of the 1980s; however, in 1991 longtime leader Holden Roberto announced his intention to seek the presidency and stated that the FNLA deserved to be accorded its earlier de facto parity with the MPLA-PT and UNITA. Nevertheless, in presidential and legislative balloting in September 1992 the FNLA fared poorly, with Roberto being held to 2.11 percent of the presidential vote and the party securing only 5 assembly seats.

In February 1999, delegates elected Lucas Ngonda party president. In addition, the party held balloting to fill its Central Committee and declared its willingness to participate in the government. The October 2004 congress reportedly agreed to have Roberto lead the party for the next ten months in an effort to reduce lingering friction between the FNLA's old guard and younger members. However, friction increased in 2005 with division over Roberto's suspension of Secretary General Francisco MENDES in September, and the majority's discontent with Roberto's failure to hold another congress to elect new leadership. While Roberto was out of the country in June 2006, reportedly for medical treatment, a party congress was convened by dissidents who elected Ngonda as the faction's president. Supporters of Roberto, under the leadership of Ngola Kabango in Roberto's absence, contended that only the legitimate president—Roberto—could convene a party congress. In March 2007, while the two factions were still awaiting a ruling on the status of the congress from Angola's high court, Roberto, 83, announced he was stepping down from an active role in politics and would not run for party chair at the next congress. He died in August 2007. Despite continuing rifts with the Ngonda faction, Kabango, who had been named interim chair following Roberto's death, was elected party chair at an extraordinary congress in November 2007. In July 2008 the Constitutional Court ruled that the Ngonda faction was illegal, thus solidifying Kabango's leadership. Soon afterward, attention turned to preparations for the legislative elections in which the FNLA placed fourth with 1.1 percent of the vote.

Leaders: Ngola KABANGO (Chair), Paulo JOAQUIM (Secretary General).

Social Renewal Party (*Partido Renovador Social*—PRS). The PRS finished third in the legislative balloting of September 1992 by winning 6 assembly seats. At a congress in 1999 Eduardo Kwangana was reportedly elected to lead the PRS; however, the incumbent party chief, António João Machicungo, rejected the polling, arguing that

Kwangana's supporters had ignored party statutes in an effort to gain control of the grouping. In 2006, Machicungo again rejected the December congress of the Kwangana faction as "illegal and undemocratic" and appealed for a ruling from the high court.

In July 2008 the Constitutional Court ruled in favor of Kwangana over the Machicungo faction. In the September elections, the PRS won 3.2 percent of the vote, and Kwangana was among eight party members to secure a seat in parliament.

Leaders: Eduardo KWANGANA, Lindo Bernardo TITO (Chair), António João MACHICUNGO.

New Democracy Electoral Union (*Nova Democracia União Eleitoral*—ND). Most of the six small parties comprising the ND, legally registered in July 2008, formerly were among the 14 parties that made up a coalition called the **Civil Opposition Parties** (*Partidos de Oposição Civis*—POC). The parties comprising ND are the **Movement for Angolan Democracy;** the **Independent Social Party of Angola** (*Movimento para Democracia de Angola*—MPDA); the **National Union for Democracy;** the **Liberal Socialist Party;** the **Angolan Union for Peace, Democracy, and Development;** and the **National Independent Alliance of Angola.**

The ND won 1.2 percent of the vote to secure 2 national assembly seats in the 2008 legislative elections.

Leader: Quintino MOREIRA (President of MPDA).

Other Parties and Groups That Participated in the 2008 Legislative Elections:

Note: All of the parties in this section (except for the PDP-ANA) were deregistered by the Constitutional Court in December 2008 for having failed in the September assembly balloting to meet the threshold required for continued recognition (0.5 percent of the national vote).

Democratic Party for Progress–Angolan National Alliance (*Partido Democrático para Progresso–Aliança Nacional Angolano*—PDP-ANA). The PDP-ANA is a right-of-center humanist grouping previously led by a prominent university professor, Mfulumpinga Lando VICTOR, who was formerly affiliated with the FNLA. In mid-1992 Victor was named as a presidential candidate; however, there were no reports of his having received any votes in the September balloting in which the party secured 1 assembly seat. Victor, a prominent opposition leader, was killed by unidentified gunmen during an attack in Luanda in July 2004. Sediangani Mbimbi, who had been acting president, was elected president of the party in April 2005, defeating Malungo Belo.

The PDP-ANA received 0.51 percent of the vote in the 2008 legislative elections, narrowly reaching the threshold required to maintain its legal party status. In 2009 the party suspended secretary general Malungo Belo Honoré for allegedly mismanaging campaign funds.

Leaders: Sediangani MBIMBI (President), Malungo Belo HONORÉ (Secretary General).

Democratic Renewal Party (*Partido Renovador Democrático*—PRD). The PRD was formed by survivors and sympathizers of the dissident Nito ALVES faction of the MPLA-PT, whose abortive 1977 coup attempt led to a violent purge of the parent party leadership. In September 1991 the PRD was the first party sanctioned by the Supreme Court to begin gathering the signatures necessary to secure legal status. In February 2008, at the first party congress held since 1996, Luís da Silva Dos Passos was reelected president.

The PRD received 0.22 percent of the vote in 2008.

Leaders: Luís da Silva DOS PASSOS (President and 1992 presidential candidate), Noy da COSTA (Secretary General).

Liberal Democratic Party (*Partido Liberal Democrático*—PLD). The PLD won 3 legislative seats in the 1992 poll, party leader Anália de Victoria PEREIRA finishing 10th in the 11-candidate presidential field. Pereira, who was renominated as party leader in July 2005 and was considered a possible candidate for the presidency in the next election, died of illness in Portugal in January 2009.

The PLD received 0.33 percent of the vote in 2008.

Party of the Alliance of the Youth, Workers, and Farmers of Angola (*Partido da Aliança da Juventude, Operários e Camponeses de Angola*—PAJOCA). The PAJOCA earned 1 seat in the legislative poll of September 1992 but received 0.24 percent of the vote, and thereby no seats, in 2008.

Leaders: ANDRE, David MENDES, Alexandre Sebastião.

Angola Democratic and Progress Support Party (*Partido de Apoio Democrático e Progresso de Angola*—PADEPA). PADEPA's initial effort to organize a demonstration against a fuel-price hike in early 2000 was thwarted by the government but subsequently served as the impetus for a larger protest march soon thereafter.

In August 2005 a senior party member was sentenced to 45 days in prison for an unauthorized protest outside parliament after his party was excluded from a panel set to supervise the next elections.

Following a party congress in November 2007 in which party president Carlos LEITÃO was expelled, a rift developed between his supporters and those of Silva Cardosa. In the run-up to the 2008 legislative election, the Constitutional Court ruled in favor of Cardosa. The party received just 0.27 percent of the 2008 vote.

Leader: Silva CARDOSA (President)

Front for Democracy (*Frente para a Democracia*—FpD). Founded in 1992, the FpD advocates autonomy for Cabina. It won one seat in the 1992 National Assembly elections as part of the AD—*Coligação*. The FpD received 0.27 percent of the vote in the 2008 legislative election.

Leaders: Filomena Viera LOPES (President), Nelson PESTANA

Democratic Angola–Coalition (*Angola Democrática Coligação* [AD—*Coligação*]). This coalition, led by Kengele JORGE, has been described as a group of young activists who promote democracy and ecology. In 2008 it included the **Angolan National Ecological Party,** the **Angola National Democratic Convention,** and **Angola's Democratic Unification;** the coalition won 0.29 percent of the 2008 legislative vote.

Angolan Fraternal Forum Coalition (*Fórum Fraternal Angolano Coligação*—FOFAC). This electoral group, formed in 1997, was led in 2008 by Artur Quixona FINDA with the goals of promoting economic equality and reforming political and public institutions. It included the **Angolan People's Conservative Party,** the **Workers Democratic Party,** the **Social Democracy Juvenile Party,** and the **National Front for the Democratic Development of Angola.** The coalition received 0.17 percent of the vote in 2008.

Electoral Political Platform (*Plataforma Politica Eleitoral*—PPE). The PPE coalition, which included nine small parties, was chaired by José João MANUEL. Its platform focused on industrial development and government reforms. It received 0.19 percent of the vote in 2008.

Other Parties:

Angolan Democratic Forum (*Forum Democrático Angolano*—FDA). The FDA was organized by UNITA dissident and peace activist Jorge Chicoti to protest human rights abuses by the parent group and was registered in February 1992. Its ranks included a number of Angolan students overseas. The FDA secured 1 assembly seat in the September 1992 balloting.

The FDA's Paulo Tjipilica held the justice ministry in the MPLA-led cabinet until 2005, when he was named the country's first ombudsman. Meanwhile, Chicoti continued to serve as deputy minister of foreign affairs. Little party activity was reported from 2006 to 2008, and the party subsequently was reported to be defunct.

Leaders: Jorge Rebelo Pinto CHICOTI (President), Paulo TJIPILICA, Manuel Adão DOMINGOS (Secretary General).

Angolan National Democratic Party (*Partido Nacional Democrático de Angola*—PNDA). Originally styled the Angolan National Democratic Convention (*Convenção Nacional Democrática de Angola*—CNDA), the PNDA in September 1992 supported the presidential candidacy of Daniel Julio CHIPENDA, an independent who had reportedly left the MPLA in protest over the party's decision to present dos Santos as its standard-bearer. Chipenda captured only 0.52 percent of the presidential vote, with the PNDA winning 1 assembly seat.

In 2008 the party was among several smaller parties ruled ineligible to contest the legislative elections.

Leaders: Geraldo Pereira João da SILVA (President), Pedro João ANTÓNIO (Secretary General).

Social Democratic Party (*Partido Social Democrático*—PSD). The PSD secured 1 assembly seat in September 1992, while its presidential candidate, Bengue Pedro JOÃO, won less than 1 percent of the vote. In 2005 the party elected Nzuzi Nsumbo as its president.

Leaders: Nzuzi NSUMBO (President), Dr. José Manuél MIGUEL.

Democratic Alliance of Angola (*Aliança Democrática de Angola*—ADA). Although garnering less than 1 percent of the vote, the ADA was able to win 1 assembly seat in September 1992.

Leader: Simba da COSTA.

Angolan Democratic Party (*Partido Democrático Angolano*—PDA). PDA leader António Alberto Neto finished third in the September 1992 presidential balloting, albeit with a vote share of 2.16 percent, far behind dos Santos and Savimbi. In 2008 the PDA was among numerous parties whose bid to contest the legislative elections was rejected by a newly appointed Constitutional Court in July.

Leader: António Alberto NETO.

Former Separatist Groups:

Since the early 1960s a number of groups have been active under the banner of the **Front for the Liberation of the Cabinda Enclave** (*Frente de Libertação do Enclave de Cabinda*—FLEC) in the oil-rich province of Cabinda, a sliver (7,300 sq. km.; 2,819 sq. mi.) of land between the Republic of the Congo and what is now the Democratic Republic of the Congo (formerly Zaire). The original FLEC was founded in August 1963 by Luis Ranque FRANQUE, who, encouraged by Portuguese authorities to continue separatist activities, refused to join other Angolan independence movements. In 1974 the Front's attempts to gain military control of the enclave were rebuffed by the MPLA and, in 1975, the movement broke into three factions: FLEC–Ranque Franque; FLEC-Nzita, led by Henrique Tiaho NZITA; and FLEC-Lubota, led by Francisco Xavier LUBOTA. In November 1977 a splinter group styling itself the Military Command for the Liberation of Cabinda was organized, while in June 1979 the Armed Forces for the Liberation of Cabinda established another splinter, the Popular Movement for the Liberation of Cabinda (*Movimento Popular de Libertação de Cabinda*—MPLC). In the 1980s FLEC-UNITA, or UNIFLEC, was reported to be operating in Cabinda with South African assistance; however, the group's activities ceased following withdrawal of Pretoria's aid. In the early 1990s two other groups, the National Union for the Liberation of Cabinda (*União Nacional de Libertação de Cabinda*—UNLC), led by Lumingu Luís Caneiro GIMBY, and the Communist Committee of Cabinda (*Comité Comunista de Cabinda*—CCC), led by Kaya Mohamed YAY, were linked to separatist activities.

Anxious to create ties to the economically important region, both the government and UNITA named Cabindans to leadership positions in their parties. Nevertheless, in July 1991 a joint MPLA-PT/UNITA offensive was launched in Cabinda to eradicate the terrorists. Meanwhile, although past attempts to unify the numerous FLEC factions had proven short-lived, it was reported that four of the identifiable groups (FLEC-Lubota, the UNLC, CCC, and FLEC-R [*Renovada*]) were attempting to form a united front, FLEC-Nzita reportedly refusing to participate.

In mid-May 1993 FLEC responded to the U.S. recognition of Luanda by declaring that it did not extend to Cabinda and warning that "all those people with companies in Cabinda must choose between supporting the extermination of the Cabindan people or leaving the territory." Following UNITA's capture of Soyo in northwestern Angola in late May, the government, fearing a pact between the separatists and rebels, was alleged to be attempting to form an alliance with a FLEC-R opponent, the **FLEC-Armed Forces of Cabinda** (*Forcas Armadas de Cabinda*—FLEC-FAC), which was reportedly being led by Henrique Tiaho Nzita; his son, Emmanuel NZITA; and José Liberal NUNO. However, after a new guerrilla offensive in Cabinda from mid-1995, government and FLEC-R representatives meeting in Windhoek, Namibia, in April 1996 concluded a cease-fire agreement that was thought likely to be observed by the other FLEC factions. However, such optimism proved ungrounded as the government subsequently was unable to reach an agreement with the FLEC-FAC or Francisco Xavier Lubota's **Democratic Front of Cabinda** (*Frente Democrática de Cabinda*—FDC).

In September 1996 FLEC-R's Central Council advised its president, Jose Tiburcio LUEMBA, and a second party leader, Jorge Victor GOMES, not to attend a meeting in Brazzaville, Congo, with government officials. Their decision to ignore the committee led to their ouster on January 24, 1997. Subsequently, António Bento BEMBE, theretofore party secretary general, and Arture TCHIBASSA, described by *Africa Confidential* as the group's "founder and most powerful leader," were named party president and secretary general, respectively.

Meanwhile, in early 1997 heightened military and political activity was reported in the enclave as the government launched an offensive aimed at dismantling the military capabilities of the separatists. With FLEC-R's cease-fire having formally lapsed in January, its newly installed, more militant leadership also acknowledged having increased its military operations. In 1998 skirmishes between the militants and government forces reportedly intensified as the latter sought to neutralize its opponents (both FLEC and UNITA) in the region. In the early 2000s, analysts suggested that the proliferation of FLEC-related groupings had resulted in confusion among Cabinda's 400,000 inhabitants, most of whom apparently would opt for independence or at least autonomy if offered a choice.

The Angolan government launched what was reportedly considered a successful campaign against the Cabindan fighters in late 2002, following conclusion of the peace accord with the much larger UNITA forces. However, tension regarding "the forgotten war" continued into 2005. By that time FLEC-R and FLEC-FAC had reportedly agreed to operate together as FLEC, with Tiaho Nzita as the group's leader and Bembe as secretary general. Although FLEC apparently indicated a willingness to negotiate with the government, no cease-fire had been achieved by February 2005, when a mass rally in Cabinda again underscored popular support for "self-rule." Meanwhile, an unprecedented strike by Catholic clergy fueled further unrest in 2005 after the Vatican sought to replace a retiring bishop with a non-Cabindan.

In a setback to FLEC, Bembe was arrested in mid-2005 in the Netherlands, where he had been invited by the Dutch foreign ministry to participate in peace negotiations regarding the situation in Cabinda. Bembe, who had been arrested for his alleged role in the kidnapping of an American oil company employee several years earlier, was released on bail but disappeared near the end of 2005. Meanwhile, Tchibassa was serving a 24-year sentence in the United States on the same charge. A few months later Bembe surfaced in the Republic of the Congo as Angola's negotiator, representing FLEC and a coalition referenced as the **Cabinda Forum for Dialogue**, on behalf of peace in Cabinda.

On August 1, 2006, a peace agreement was signed by the Angolan government and the Forum, representing some members of FLEC, the Catholic church, and civic groups. The agreement, approved by the assembly on August 10, officially ended 31 years of war in Cabinda and accorded it special status under the constitution. The Memorandum of Understanding, as the agreement was called, also provided amnesty for the rebels who disarmed, and in January 2007, FLEC was officially disbanded, with many of its members drafted by the national police and the FAA. The U.S. government was reported to have "strongly supported" the agreement. On the other hand, Nzita, who was in exile in Paris, and other FLEC and Forum members who had demanded independence for Cabinda, claimed that Bembe had no authority to negotiate on behalf of FLEC.

In late 2008 reports surfaced of cross-border "incursions" by Angolan troops into the Democratic Republic of the Congo (DRC) and by former FLEC fighters into Cabinda from the DRC. A former FLEC fighter was killed and several Cabindan refugees were wounded, allegedly by Angolan troops in a village in the DRC. Reportedly, several hundred Cabindans were forced from camps inside their territory due to the incursions by Angolan soldiers and by small groups of FLEC fighters from the Republic of the Congo and the DRC. The Angolan forces were said to be countering attempts by FLEC-Nzita fighters to "create havoc" in Cabinda.

Following the 2008 legislative elections and the appointment of a new prime minister, former FLEC leader António Bento Bembe was named to the new government installed on October 1.

LEGISLATURE

In accordance with the 1975 constitution, as amended, a 223-member National People's Assembly (*Assembleia Nacional Popular*) with a three-year term of office was elected in 1980 as successor to the Council of the Revolution, which had served as a legislature since formation of the republic. Subsequent balloting was deferred until late 1986, when the legislative term was extended to five years and the number of deputies increased to 289. The list of candidates, all members of the Popular Movement for the Liberation of Angola—Labor Party (MPLA-PT), was drawn up by the assembly's Permanent Commission.

In late 1990 the MPLA-PT approved liberalization measures providing for election of a restyled **National Assembly** (*Assembleia Nacional*) on a multiparty basis. The size of the assembly was reduced to 223 seats; three of those seats were reserved for overseas Angolans, but by mutual agreement of the parties, they were not filled in the balloting of September 29–30, 1992, in which the MPLA (which had dropped "Labor Party from its name) secured 129 seats, followed by the National Union for the Total Independence of Angola (UNITA) with 70 seats and a number of smaller parties.

On November 13, 1996, the assembly overwhelmingly approved a constitutional revision extending the current legislature's mandate (due to expire on November 26) for a minimum of two and a maximum of four years. On April 9, 1997, the assembly met for the first time with the full complement of UNITA representatives in attendance. However, the status of the UNITA contingent became clouded in 1998 as relations between UNITA and the government deteriorated. The government announced on August 31, 1998, that the UNITA legislators had been suspended, although many were subsequently permitted to reassume their seats under an agreement between the government and UNITA-Renewal, the new UNITA faction opposed to longtime UNITA leader Jonas Savimbi. At the same time, some of the UNITA legislators restated their allegiance to Savimbi. Following Savimbi's death in February 2002, the UNITA factions reunified as part of the broad peace accord with the government.

Though the government in 2004 announced plans to hold new assembly balloting in September 2006, legislative elections were subsequently postponed until September 5–6, 2008, when 220 members were elected for four-year terms, the 3 seats for overseas Angolans again left vacant due to difficulties in conducting balloting for those seats. Ninety seats were filled by proportional representation at the provincial level (5 seats in each of the 18 provinces), while 130 were filled via proportional representation in a single nationwide constituency, the nationwide results based on the total votes gained by parties at the provincial level. The seat distribution was as follows: MPLA, 191 (107 national, 84 provincial); UNITA, 16 (14, 2); Social Renewal Party, 8 (5, 3); National Front for the Liberation of Angola, 3 (2, 1); and New Democratic Coalition, 2 (2, 0).

President: Fernando Da Piedade Dias DOS SANTOS.

CABINET

[as of September 1, 2009]

President	José Eduardo dos Santos (MPLA)
Prime Minister	Antonio Paulo Kassoma (MPLA)
Ministers	
Agriculture and Rural Development	Alfonso Canga
Commerce	Maria Idalina de Oliveira Valente (MPLA) [f]
Culture	Rosa Maria Martins da Cruz e Silva [f]
Defense	Gen. Kundi Pahiama (MPLA)
Economy	Manuel José Nunes Júnior (MPLA)
Education	António Burity da Silva (MPLA)
Energy	Emanuela Afonso Viera Lopes [f]
Environment	Maria de Fátima Monteiro Jardim (MPLA) [f]
Family and the Promotion of Women	Genoveva da Conceição Lino (MPLA) [f]
Finance	Eduardo Leopoldo Severin de Morais
Fisheries	Salomão Luheto Xirimbimbi (MPLA)
Foreign Affairs	Assunção Afonso dos Anjos (MPLA)
Former Combatants and Veterans Affairs	Pedro José Van-Dúnem (MPLA)
Geology and Mines	Makenda Ambroise (MPLA)
Health	José Viera Dias Van-Dúnem (MPLA)
Hotels and Tourism	Pedro Mutindi (MPLA)
Industry	Joaquim Duarte da Costa David (MPLA)
Interior	Gen. Roberto Leal Monteiro (MPLA)
Justice	Guilhermina Contreiras da Costa Prata (MPLA) [f]
Ministers Without Portfolio	António Bento Bembe Francisca do Espírito Santo de Carvalho Almeida (MPLA) [f]
Petroleum	José Maria Botelho de Vasconcelos (MPLA)
Planning	Ana Afonso Dias Lourenço (MPLA) [f]
Public Administration, Employment, and Social Security	António Domingos Pitra da Costa Neto (MPLA)
Public Works	Francisco Higino Carneiro (MPLA)
Science and Technology	Maria Cândida Teixeira (MPLA) [f]
Social Assistance and Reintegration	João Baptista Kussumua (MPLA)
Social Communication (Information)	Manuel Rabelais (MPLA)
Telecommunications and Information Technology	José Carvalho da Rocha
Territorial Administration	Virgílio Ferreira Fontes Pereira (MPLA)
Transport	Augusto da Silva Tomás (MPLA)
Urban Affairs and Housing	Diekunpuna Sita José
Youth and Sports	Gonçalves Manuel Muandumba
Secretaries of State	
Higher Education	Adão Gaspar Pereira do Nascimento
Rural Development	Maria Filomena de Fátima Lobão Telo Delgado (MPLA) [f]

[f] = female

COMMUNICATIONS

Following nationalization of the press in 1976, the government required all news disseminated by the media to conform to official policy. The government announced that press liberalization would be addressed in the course of a constitutional review launched in late 1990. However, domestic and international watchdog groups strongly criticized the government between 2000 and 2001 for tightening controls on the media and otherwise pressuring journalists. The negotiation of a proposed new press law was one of the major areas of disagreement between the government and opposition parties in 2004 as plans were made for the next national elections. However, in February 2006 the National Assembly approved the new press law, granting freedom of the press by prohibiting censorship and revoking the state's monopoly over television and news agencies. Despite the new law, however, the press was not necessarily deemed free.

In the run-up to the 2008 legislative elections, the government suspended *Radio Despertar*, the voice of the opposition National Union for the Total Independence of Angola (*União Nacional para a Independencia Total de Angola*—UNITA), for allegedly broadcasting beyond its range. In a further crackdown on press freedom, the minister of social communications in August announced that criticism of the government would no longer be tolerated. "State media have come under tighter control," according to *Africa Confidential*, as several independent newspapers were accused of defamation, and a journalist was sentenced to six months in prison and fined $9,000 as a result of complaints filed by the government. Nevertheless, private newspapers and radio and television stations, geared to younger, middle-class audiences and with greater Portuguese influence, began to appear in 2009.

Press. The following are Portuguese-language dailies published in Luanda: *O Jornal de Angola* (42,000) and *Diário da República* (8,500), government news sheet. *Correio da Semana*, a weekly, is published in Luanda by the owners of *O Jornal*. Independent weeklies include *Agora, Semanario Angolense*, and *Folha 8*.

News agencies. The domestic facility is the formerly government-operated Angolan News Agency (*Agência Noticiosa N'gola*

Press—ANGOP). A limited number of foreign agencies maintain offices in Luanda.

Broadcasting and computing. The principal broadcasting services are *Radio Nacional de Angola* and *Televisão Popular de Angola*, both formerly controlled by the government. Other services are the independent *Radio Eclesia* and *Radio Despertar*, a pro-UNITA station. As of 2008 there were 30.5 Internet users per 1,000 inhabitants.

INTERGOVERNMENTAL REPRESENTATION

Ambassador to the U.S.: Josefina Pitra DIAKITE.

U.S. Ambassador to Angola: Dan MOZENA.

Permanent Representative to the UN: Ismael Abrão Gaspar MARTINS.

IGO Memberships (Non-UN): AfDB, AU, BADEA, CEEAC, CPLP, Interpol, IOM, NAM, SADC, WCO, WTO.

ANTARCTICA

Political Status: Normally uninhabited territory, subject to overlapping claims of national sovereignty that remain in suspense under provisions of the Antarctic Treaty signed December 1, 1959.

Area: 4,826,000 sq. mi. (12,500,000 sq. km.).

Population: Various nations operating research stations under terms of the Antarctic Treaty maintain a transient population of about 3,000 (during the Antarctic summer); in addition, a limited number of treaty signatories (including the United States) maintain year-round stations populated by limited personnel.

Political Institution: In 2004 an Antarctic Treaty Secretariat was established in Buenos Aires, Argentina (see Posttreaty developments, below).

Executive Secretary: Johannes HUBER (Netherlands).

Political background. The most isolated and inhospitable of the world's continents, Antarctica remained outside the mainstream of exploration and colonial exploitation until the early 20th century. British explorer Capt. James Cook first sailed south of the Antarctic Circle in 1773, and in the following century ships from such countries as the United Kingdom, France, Russia, and the United States visited the coastal areas. Between 1900 and 1914 explorers Roald Amundsen of Norway (the first, in 1911, to reach the South Pole), Robert F. Scott and Ernest H. Shackleton of the United Kingdom, Douglas Mawson of Australia, and others penetrated the interior of the continent. This era saw the first territorial claims and the start of commercial Antarctic whaling. Competition for Antarctic territory increased in the interwar decades, while scientific exploration was aided by new technology, chiefly the airplane. Contention over territorial claims further intensified during and after World War II, but the coming of the International Geophysical Year (IGY) (July 1, 1957–December 31, 1958) brought the beginnings of a new, cooperative, nonpolitical approach to Antarctic problems.

Territorial claims. Prior to the conclusion of the Antarctic Treaty of 1959, the political geography of Antarctica followed the conventional 19th-century pattern of national claims to sovereignty over areas largely unexplored and unsettled. Such claims, advanced by seven governments, took the form of wedge-shaped sectors extending inward from the coast to the South Pole.

The overlapping claims of the United Kingdom, Argentina, and Chile in the area of the Antarctic Peninsula, the most northerly and accessible area of the continent, have been in dispute since the 1940s. The British claim is based on its early discovery and occupation, while those of Chile and Argentina are based on the "contiguity" principle, involving a southward extension of their national territories. The two latter claims overlap, but Argentina and Chile have consistently presented a united front in opposition to the British claim.

The remaining sector claims have occasioned no serious disputes. Norway's claim is based on coastal reconnaissance in the 1930s, France's on the 1840 expedition of Jules d'Urville. The Australian claim, assigned by the United Kingdom in 1936, is based on both exploration and "contiguity," while the "contiguous" area claimed by New Zealand resulted from conveyance by the United Kingdom in 1923. This sector provides the best access to the interior of the continent by way of the Ross Ice Shelf.

The unclaimed "Pacific Sector" (sometimes called Marie Byrd Land) has the most inaccessible coastline of the entire continent and was tacitly awarded to the United States because of Adm. Richard Byrd's work in that area. U.S. personnel are located primarily in the vicinity of the Palmer Peninsula in the northwest, at McMurdo Station near the Ross Ice Shelf, and at the Amundsen-Scott South Pole facility. As originally enunciated by Secretary of State Charles Evans Hughes in 1924, however, U.S. Antarctic policy has consistently denied the principle of valid sovereignty without actual settlement. While reserving all rights accruing from its discoveries and exploration, the United States has made no territorial claims and has refused to recognize those of any other nation.

The Soviet Union, which returned to the area during the IGY, established seven year-round scientific bases, including those in the Australian and Norwegian areas and in the Antarctic Peninsula; in 1993, however, the successor Russian Federation withdrew from Vostok Station, theretofore the only non-U.S. permanent installation on the Polar Plateau, which was subsequently maintained as an international research base. Russia, like the United States, has rejected all claims to territorial sovereignty, which are tabulated (roughly clockwise from the Greenwich meridian) below:

Queen Maud Land (Norway)	20°W	to	45°E
Australian Antarctic Territory (Australia)	45°E	to	136°E
Adélie Land (France)	136°E	to	142°E
Australian Antarctic Territory (Australia)	142°E	to	160°E
Ross Dependency (New Zealand)	160°E	to	150°W
"Pacific Sector" (unclaimed)	150°W	to	90°W
Antártida Chilena (Chile)	90°W	to	53°W
British Antarctic Territory (UK)	80°W	to	20°W
Antártida Argentina (Argentina)	74°W	to	25°W

The Antarctic Treaty. The IGY shifted the emphasis in Antarctic development to international cooperative scientific research. Under the IGY program 11 nations operated research stations: Argentina, Australia, Belgium, Chile, France, Japan, New Zealand, Norway, the Soviet Union, the United Kingdom, and the United States. Between 200 and 300 scientists and technical personnel participated in Antarctic projects in the fields of geology, terrestrial and upper atmospheric physics, biology, glaciology, oceanography, meteorology, and cartography. Following this effort, a conference of the same 11 nations and South Africa was held in Washington, D.C., on U.S. initiative in October 1959 to formalize continued scientific cooperation in Antarctica and to prohibit military use of the area. The resulting treaty, which was signed December 1, 1959, and entered into force June 23, 1961, set forth the following major principles applicable to the area south of 60 degrees south latitude:

1. *Peaceful purposes*. Article I of the treaty specifies that "Antarctica shall be used for peaceful purposes only" and specifically prohibits such measures as establishing military bases, carrying out military maneuvers, and testing weapons. Other articles prohibit nuclear explosions and the disposal of radioactive waste material (Article V) and confer on each contracting party a right to have duly designated observers inspect Antarctic stations, installations and equipment, and ships and aircraft (Article VII).

2. *Freedom of scientific investigation*. Articles II and III provide for continued freedom of scientific investigation and for cooperation toward that end, including the exchange of information, personnel, and scientific findings, and the encouragement of working relations with United Nations Specialized Agencies and other interested international

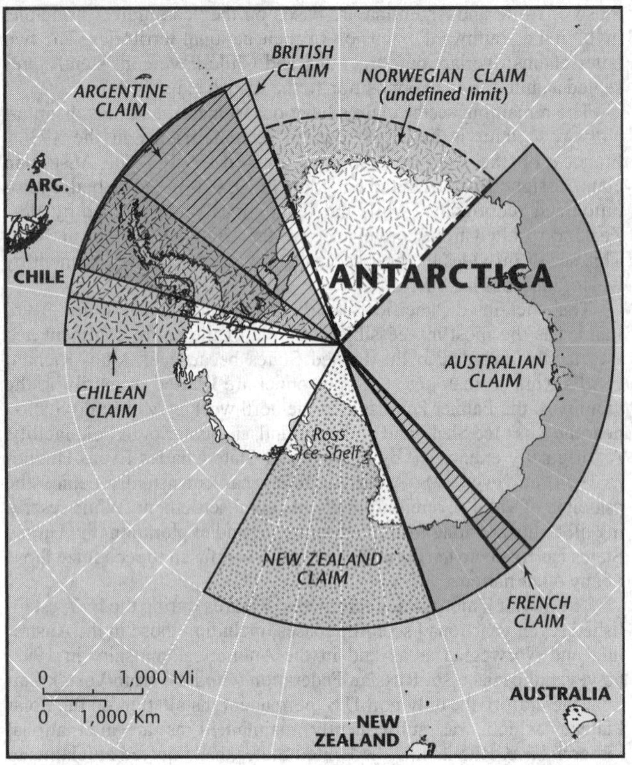

organizations. There are also provisions for periodic consultations among the signatory powers.

3. *"Freezing" of territorial claims.* Article IV stipulates (1) that the treaty does not affect the contracting parties' prior rights or claims to territorial sovereignty in Antarctica, nor their positions relative to the recognition or nonrecognition of such rights or claims by others; and (2) that activities taking place while the treaty is in force are not to affect such claims, and no new claims may be asserted (or existing claims enlarged) during the same period.

The treaty is open to accession by any UN member state or any other state acceptable to the signatory powers, although the treaty makes a distinction between "consultative parties" (signatories that engage in Antarctic scientific activities and participate in consultative meetings) and "nonconsultative parties" (those that have only acceded to the treaty and do not attend the meetings). As of January 1, 2009, there were 28 consultative parties, including the original 12 signatories plus Poland (1977), the Federal Republic of Germany (1981 [absorbed the German Democratic Republic (1987) in 1990]), Brazil (1983), India (1983), China (1985), Uruguay (1985), Italy (1987), Spain (1988), Sweden (1988), Finland (1989), the Republic of Korea (1989), Peru (1989), Ecuador (1990), the Netherlands (1990), Bulgaria (1998), and the Ukraine (2004), while the 19 acceding parties (apart from the 15 that subsequently moved into consultative status) included Austria, Belarus, Canada, Colombia, Cuba, the Czech Republic, Denmark, Estonia, Greece, Guatemala, Hungary, the Democratic People's Republic of Korea, Monaco, Papua New Guinea, Romania, Slovakia, Switzerland, Turkey, and Venezuela.

The duration of the treaty is indefinite, but provision was made for modification by unanimous consent at any time and for a review of its operation at the call of any consultative member after 30 years (i.e., after June 23, 1991). The United States, among others, has carried out a number of inspections under Article VII and has declared itself satisfied that the provisions of the treaty are being faithfully observed.

Economic potential. It was long assumed that Antarctica's mineral resources (including coal, oil, gold, platinum, tin, silver, molybdenum, antimony, and uranium) would remain technologically unexploitable for an indefinite period, but the discovery of iron deposits in the Prince Charles Mountains bordering on the Indian Ocean, coupled with the possibility that similar deposits may lie in the Shackleton Range near the Weddell Sea, led to concern that political cooperation might yield to economic rivalry.

A number of governments and private corporations have expressed interest in pressing the search for petroleum, although the per-barrel cost of tapping any reserves is estimated at almost twice the current sales value. With the sharp increase of oil prices in 2008, it was felt this might change. Attention has also been focused on potential offshore oil and natural gas deposits and on the harvesting of krill, a small crustacean that is the major living marine resource of the region and a potentially important source of protein. Those states currently fishing for krill include Germany, Japan, Poland, Russia, and Taiwan.

Posttreaty developments. At a meeting held May 7–20, 1980, in Canberra, Australia, 15 treaty members (the original 12 plus Poland and East and West Germany at that time) approved the final draft of the Convention on the Conservation of Antarctic Marine Living Resources, which was signed September 11 and, having been ratified by a majority of the participating governments, came into force April 7, 1982. The accord called for the establishment in Hobart, Tasmania, of both a scientific committee to set quotas for the harvesting of krill, and an international commission responsible for conducting studies of Antarctic species and the food chain, recommending conservation measures, and supervising adherence to the convention. The area covered by the document extends beyond that specified in the 1959 treaty to roughly the "Antarctic Convergence"—where warm and cold waters meet and thus form a natural boundary between marine communities. The convention did not, however, meet the expectations of conservationists. In particular, a report issued by the International Institute for Environment and Development criticized the accord for requiring consensus decisions, which might hinder effective action; for being unenforceable with regard to nonsignatories; and for failing to recognize that even minimal harvesting of krill might irreparably harm the Antarctic ecosystem. In March 1978, the Convention for the Conservation of Antarctic Seals, which was negotiated among the treaty members but is open for signature by nontreaty parties as a separate and independent agreement, preceded the Marine Resources Convention.

The establishment of an International Minerals Regime was discussed at the 11th Consultative Meeting in Buenos Aires, June 23–July 7, 1981; at the 12th Consultative Meeting in Canberra, September 13–27, 1983; and at a series of special consultative sessions between 1981 and 1987. The talks yielded approval of a convention on the Regulation of Antarctic Mineral Resource Activities at a meeting of 33 Antarctic Treaty members held May 2–June 2, 1988. The convention, which required ratification by 16 signatories (including the Soviet Union and the United States and all countries having territorial claims) to come into effect, was bitterly attacked by environmental groups, including the Cousteau Society and Greenpeace, which called for the designation of Antarctica as a "World Heritage Park"; by late 1990 the convention was effectively doomed because of the declared unwillingness of Australia, France, and New Zealand to become ratifying states.

For years, developing countries have demanded full international control over the region, a proposal to such effect being advanced by Malaysia at the 1982 session of the UN General Assembly. The matter was further debated at the General Assembly's 1983 session, culminating December 15 in a directive to Secretary General Pérez de Cuéllar to prepare "a comprehensive, factual and objective study on all aspects of Antarctica, taking fully into account the Antarctic Treaty system and other relevant factors."

The 13th Consultative Meeting in Brussels, Belgium, October 4–18, 1985, focused primarily on the growing environmental impact of scientific activity in the region. Specifically, the group decided to limit access to 13 special scientific zones and 3 environmental areas—a 75 percent increase in such restricted areas. Subsequently, a report of the World Commission on Environment and Development, chaired by Norway's Gro Harlem Brundtland, called in 1987 for more joint scientific activities in the area, stringent safeguards to protect the continent's environment, and closer working relations among parties to the Antarctic Treaty and other groups within and outside the UN system with responsibilities for science and technology, conservation, and environmental management.

The 15th Consultative Meeting in Paris, France, October 9–21, 1989, was dominated by the opponents of the minerals treaty and their efforts to have the continent declared a global "wilderness reserve." Because of a deadlock on the issue, it was agreed that special consultative meetings would be convened in 1990 to create a "comprehensive protection system in Antarctica." Concurrently, crew members of the

Greenpeace vessel *Gondwana* issued a critical report on the waste disposal practices of scientific stations along the Antarctic Peninsula and indicated that Greenpeace would resume its environmental policing during the ensuing year.

Between November 16 and December 6, 1990, representatives of 34 signatory states met in Vina del Mar, Chile, to draft a protocol on environmental protection for the continent that would effectively supplant the 1988 convention. Unable to reach agreement on the duration of a moratorium on mining activity, the parties scheduled a further meeting in Madrid, Spain, in April 1991, at which a 50-year period was agreed upon after Japan had abandoned an appeal for limited mining. Subsequently, an apparent failure of communication within the U.S. administration precluded formal action as scheduled on June 23, although President George H. W. Bush, in response to an outcry from environmental groups, stated on July 4 that the United States would endorse the protocol. His only stipulation was that a two-thirds vote of full treaty members for lifting the ban after 50 years replace a unanimity requirement for such action. The change being made, the document was signed on October 4 during ceremonies in Madrid. However, two problems remained: (1) the possibility that one or more signatories might not ratify the accord, and (2) the absence of a legal mechanism to prevent nonsignatories from initiating mining activity.

The 16th Consultative Meeting was held in Bonn, Germany, October 7–18, 1991. No calls having been issued for treaty review, the principal achievement of the meeting was healing rifts in the membership caused by the dispute over the mining agreement. Not surprisingly, adoption of the moratorium convention plus the end of the Cold War yielded a substantial decline in funding for Antarctic activity. As a U.S. spokesperson put it, "We've been living on a tripod—geopolitics, future uses of Antarctica, and research. Now two of the three legs have been taken away from us." Thus, four of nine former Soviet research stations were closed by late 1991, while Poland, which had been a leader in marine biology, cut its Antarctic staff by three-quarters. Subsequently, it appeared that the countries with the strongest commitments to Antarctica might be Argentina and Chile, both acting on the basis of nationalistic rather than scientific motivation.

The 17th Consultative Meeting in Venice, Italy, November 11–20, 1992, yielded a number of recommendations on environmental monitoring and data management, revised descriptions and proposed management plans for Specially Protected Areas, and established a new group of specialists on global change and international Antarctic programs.

Major topics of discussion during the 18th Consultative Meeting in Kyoto, Japan, April 11–22, 1994, centered on drafting an environmental protection protocol and creating an international mechanism for the certification of tourist groups. While only 50,625 tourists had visited Antarctica by late 1993, the number of summer voyages had surged from only a handful in the late 1950s to more than 50 in the 1992–1993 season, with the potential for a damaging impact on the natural habitat.

The 40-member International Whaling Commission voted May 26, 1994, to bar commercial whaling in a vast area around Antarctica. While largely symbolic in the short term because of an existing worldwide whaling moratorium, the ban would leave nearly a quarter of the world's oceans off-limits to whalers should the moratorium be rescinded.

During the 19th Consultative Meeting in Seoul, Korea, May 8–19, 1995, significant progress was reported on entry into force of the environmental protocol, with 16 of the 26 consultative parties having ratified the document. The meeting also continued examination of the impact of tourism and other nongovernmental activity on Antarctica. However, lack of consensus over its location continued to block establishment of an Antarctic Treaty Secretariat, which was described as a "high priority for most delegations." The principal difficulty was the British objection to Buenos Aires as the site, when Argentina's offer was the only one on the table.

The 20th Consultative Meeting in Utrecht, the Netherlands, April 29–May 10, 1996, focused largely on technical issues. The meeting did, however, endorse the desirability of information exchanges between Antarctic and Arctic groups, given the projected establishment of an Arctic Council. It was reported that 22 of the (then) 26 consultative parties had ratified the environmental protocol, while discussion continued on the impact of tourism on the Antarctic ecosystem and on what instruments might be necessary to establish a treaty secretariat.

The 21st Consultative Meeting in Christchurch, New Zealand, May 19–30, 1997, was again devoted primarily to technical issues, including rules of procedure for the environmental protocol. By December, with action by Japan, all of the consultative parties had ratified the protocol, thus permitting the document to become law, effective January 14, 1998.

In mid-1997 Russia announced further cuts in its Antarctic program: crews at its Bellingshausen and Myrny stations would be drastically reduced, while its Molodyozhnaya facility in eastern Antarctica would be closed in 2 to 3 years, leaving the Progress Station, some 800 miles away, as its main base in the region. Subsequently, in a ceremony held in Christchurch February 20, 1998, the U.S. Navy formally ended its 43-year role of moving people and supplies between Antarctica and the outer world. Air support of American stations was transferred to the 109th Air Wing of the New York National Guard, with on-site operations continuing under authority of the National Science Foundation.

The 22nd Consultative Meeting in Tromsø, Norway, May 25–June 5, 1998, yielded further discussion of the environmental protocol and establishment of a protocol committee. Also addressed was what action members would take in the event of oil spills in the region.

In their first gathering on the continent, 24 signatories of the Antarctic Treaty met January 27, 1999, at the U.S. McMurdo Station to reaffirm their commitment to preservation of the polar ecosystem, including both the land and surrounding seas. During the meeting, scientists warned of the potential melting of the West Antarctica Ice Shelf, which would have disastrous consequences for a number of low-lying Pacific island countries; furthermore, should the meltdown involve the entire ice sheet (including the currently more stable eastern portion), the world's oceans would rise by some 60 meters, causing Gulf Stream disturbances that could lead to a new European ice age.

Environmental issues were again featured during the 23rd Consultative Meeting in Lima, Peru, May 24–June 4, 1999. For lack of a venue, there was no full meeting of treaty members in 2000, although the third session of the Committee for Environmental Protection met during a Special Consultative Meeting at The Hague, September 11–15. The 24th Consultative Meeting, held in St. Petersburg, Russia, July 9–20, 2001, was most noteworthy for the United Kingdom's announcement that it was no longer opposed to locating the Antarctic Treaty's permanent secretariat in Buenos Aires, following a commitment from Argentina to transfer control of its Antarctic bases from military to civilian control. The United Kingdom had previously blocked the proposal, which required consensus, as a consequence of the 1982 Falklands War, and some analysts suggested that the UK decision was also facilitated by a secret agreement in which Argentina agreed to "demilitarize" its status in Antarctica by closing three of its six permanent bases there.

No major decisions were made at the 25th Consultative Meeting in Warsaw, Poland, September 10–20, 2002. The 26th Consultative Meeting in Madrid, Spain, June 9–20, 2003, however, dealt with a number of problems arising from tourism and illegal fishing in the region.

Final details on a secretariat, including the appointment of an executive secretary, were worked out during the 27th Consultative Meeting in Cape Town, South Africa, May 24–June 4, 2004, with the secretariat being launched shortly thereafter. The Cape Town participants also agreed to designate the McMurdo Dry Valleys (an ice-free zone sheltered by the Transantarctic Mountains) as an Antarctic Specially Managed Area (ASMA) within which human activity would be strictly limited.

The 28th Consultative Meeting in Stockholm, Sweden, June 6–17, 2005, featured, after 13 years of negotiation, a Liability Annex to the Environmental Protocol, under which those active in Antarctica who fail to take "prompt and effective response action to environmental emergencies arising from [their] activities" would be held liable for the cost of response actions taken by others. However, the agreement required approval by all of the contracting parties before it could come into effect.

A major focus of the 29th Consultative Meeting in Edinburgh, Scotland, June 12–23, 2006, was the International Polar Year 2007–2008, sponsored by the International Council for Science (ICSU) and the World Meteorological Organization (WMO). Hailed as the largest internationally coordinated scientific research effort in 50 years, its aim was to educate the public in polar issues, while paving the way for more than 200 projects by the next generation of Arctic and Antarctic scientists.

Discussion of the International Polar Year continued at the 30th Consultative Meeting in New Delhi, India, April 30–May 11, 2007. Delegates also addressed the problem of increasing Antarctic tourism, which had more than quadrupled over the last decade.

The management of tourism continued at the 31st Consultative Meeting in Kiev, Ukraine, May 31–June 14, 2008, although most of the discussion focused on the impact of climate change on the Antarctic ecosystem.

Current issues. Antarctica received widespread international attention in early 2002 when an ice shelf the size of the U.S. state of Rhode Island collapsed during a 35-day period, generating several thousand icebergs amid projections that continued shrinkage of the shelves could lead to a drastic increase in sea levels, with incalculable climatic change worldwide. Collaterally, the WMO reported that the hole in the ozone layer above Antarctica had grown to the largest level ever recorded. A subsequent survey in 2004 revealed that the Antarctic ice cap was one-tenth smaller and half the thickness as measured 30 years earlier, and in early 2008 British scientists reported that a massive fracture at the edge of the Wilkins Ice Shelf threatened collapse of the entire shelf, an area roughly the size of the U.S. state of Connecticut. The sobering reality was that global warming was proceeding at a much faster rate at the poles than elsewhere, a team of Australian scientists reporting in mid-2008 that the Antarctic oceans were warming 50 percent faster than previously estimated, with consequences that would entail widespread climate changes stemming from a catastrophic rise in sea levels.

ANTIGUA AND BARBUDA

Political Status: Former British dependency; joined West Indies Associated States in 1967; independent member of the Commonwealth since November 1, 1981.

Area: 171.5 sq. mi. (444 sq. km.), encompassing the main island of Antigua (108 sq. mi.) and the dependent islands of Barbuda (62 sq. mi.) and Redonda (0.5 sq. mi.).

Population: 77,426 (2001C); 89,000 (2008E).

Major Urban Center (2005E): ST. JOHN'S (22,700).

Official Language: English.

Monetary Unit: East Caribbean Dollar (official rate December 1, 2009: 2.70 EC dollars = $1US).

Sovereign: Queen ELIZABETH II.

Governor General: Louise LAKE-TACK; inaugurated on July 17, 2007, to succeed Sir James B. CARLISLE.

Prime Minister: Winston Baldwin SPENCER (United Progressive Party); sworn in March 24, 2004, following election of March 23, succeeding Lester Bryant BIRD (Antigua Labour Party); reappointed following election of March 12, 2009.

THE COUNTRY

Located in the northern part of the Caribbean's Lesser Antilles, the islands of Antigua and Barbuda are populated largely by blacks whose ancestors were transported as slaves from western Africa in the 17th and 18th centuries. Minorities include descendants of British colonial settlers, Portuguese laborers, and Lebanese and Syrian traders. Anglican Protestantism and Roman Catholicism claim the largest number of adherents, although a wide variety of other denominations exist, and complete religious freedom prevails.

Agriculture dominated the economy until the 1960s, when a pronounced decline in sugar prices led to the abandonment of most cane fields and increased reliance on tourism, which currently accounts for about 60 percent of GDP. The harbor at St. John's, long used as a dockyard for the British Navy, is a port of call for 11 major shipping lines, while a modern air facility, featuring a Canadian-financed terminal complex, is served by 6 international carriers. Although real GDP rose by an average of 4.5 percent during 2000–2007, while inflation averaged less than 2.0 percent through the same period (the lowest in the region), the country has long faced a variety of economic problems, including high external debt and damage from a series of severe hurricanes, and growth declined to 2.1 percent in 2008, while inflation rose to 3.0 percent. As a result, Antigua and Barbuda have undertaken efforts to promote agriculture, particularly livestock raising and produce cultivation; expand the fishing industry; and, most recently, develop an Internet gambling industry (see Foreign relations and Current issues, below).

GOVERNMENT AND POLITICS

Political background. Colonized by Great Britain in the early 17th century after unsuccessful efforts by Spain and France, Antigua became a founding member of the Federation of the West Indies in 1958, following the introduction of ministerial government two years earlier. Together with its northern dependency, Barbuda, it joined the West Indies Associated States in 1969 as an internally self-governing territory with a right of unilateral termination, which it exercised on November 1, 1981. At independence, Premier Vere C. BIRD Sr., whose Antigua Labour Party (ALP) had returned to power in 1976 and was victorious in the election of April 1980, became prime minister. In the election on April 17, 1984, the ALP swept all the Antiguan seats in the House of Representatives, with Bird forming a new government two days later.

In 1987 Prime Minister Bird resisted demands that his son, Vere C. BIRD Jr., be dismissed as public works minister in the wake of an official inquiry that had charged him with conduct "unbecoming a minister of government" in connection with the funding of an airport rehabilitation project. The issue led to a split within the Bird family. The prime minister's second son, Deputy Prime Minister Lester Bryant BIRD, joined a "dissident majority" of eight officials, including Education Minister Reuben HARRIS, who announced a campaign to rid the country of "family government."

For its part, the opposition seemed unable to capitalize on the intra-ALP cleavage. Efforts to form an antigovernment alliance before the 1989 election proved unavailing, as a result of which the ALP retained power in the March 9 vote by winning 15 of 17 legislative seats.

In February 1990 Education Minister Harris continued his attack on his government colleagues by suggesting that corrupt practices might be involved in a scheme to lease 400 acres of land in his district to a group of Hong Kong investors for the construction of a tourist facility. Far more embarrassing was the revelation in early May that a shipment of arms that Israeli authorities said had been approved for sale to the Antiguan government had turned up at the ranch of a notorious Colombian drug trafficker. After it became known that his name was on the purchase order held by Israel, Vere Bird Jr. was obliged to leave the cabinet. In August, Lester Bird announced that the cabinet's "deep sense of shame and outrage" had yielded agreement on a government cleanup and on November 13 the prime minister announced his reluctant acceptance of all major recommendations of a committee of inquiry, including the banning from public office of his eldest son, whom the report had castigated as a "thoroughly unprincipled man."

In the course of a cabinet reshuffle on March 15, 1991, Prime Minister Bird assumed the finance portfolio and in a subsequent parliamentary presentation gave a summary rather than a detailed account of his budget proposals. In response, four government ministers, including Deputy Prime Minister Lester Bird, resigned after branding the action unconstitutional, both of the younger Birds, for quite different reasons, thus having left the government.

A new scandal erupted in January 1992, when the opposition weekly *Outlook* accused Prime Minister Bird of having pocketed a government check for $25,000 that was to have covered unspecified medical expenses incurred by the cousin of a longtime live-in companion. The charges provoked a general strike as well as widespread civil unrest that included arson attacks on a number of public and private buildings. The prime minister responded with an announcement that he would not seek reelection in 1994, although Lester Bird, who had returned to the cabinet as external affairs minister, was unable to muster sufficient support at a party convention in May to stand forth as a certain successor to

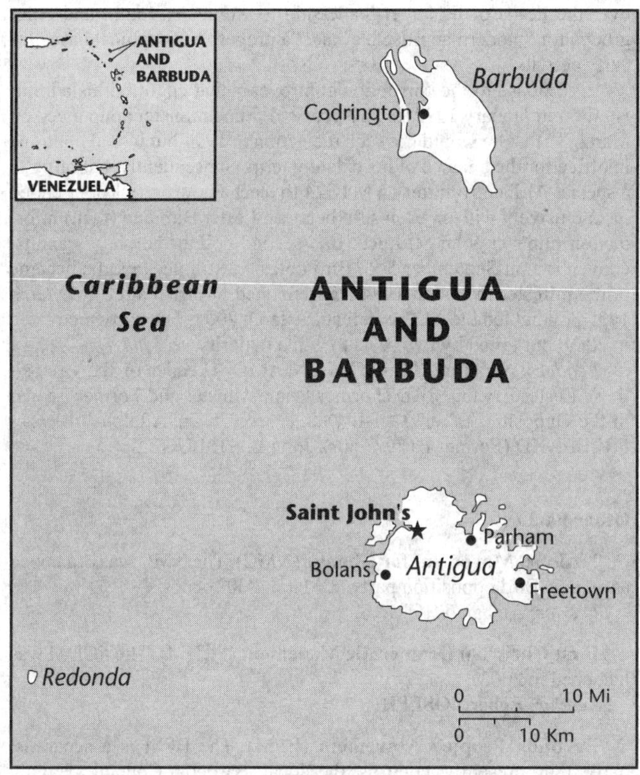

his father. He was, however, successful in a second leadership bid in September after gaining the support of Vere Bird Jr., who had previously endorsed his opponent.

The ALP won its fifth consecutive general election in legislative balloting on March 8, 1994, albeit with a reduced majority of 11 of 17 seats. Two days later, Lester Bird announced the formation of a new government that included John ST. LUCE, his most recent challenger for the party leadership, while generating some surprise by excluding his brother Vere Bird Jr. The ALP majority in the House of Representatives increased to 12 seats in the election of March 9, 1999. Vere Bird Sr. died on June 28, 1999.

In the wake of long-standing charges of corruption involving senior ministers, the ALP was decisively defeated in the election of March 23, 2004, with Lester Bird among those losing their House seats. On March 24, Winston Baldwin SPENCER, leader of the United Progressive Party (UPP) was sworn in as the new prime minister. Spencer remained in office after the election of March 12, 2009, on the basis of parliamentary representation that had plummeted to a bare majority of nine seats.

Constitution and government. Although the opposition Progressive Labour Movement (PLM) had campaigned for a unicameral legislature elected by proportional representation, the independence constitution retained the existing bicameral legislature composed of an appointed Senate and a House of Representatives elected from single-member constituencies (16 on Antigua and 1 on Barbuda) for a 5-year term, subject to dissolution. Of the 17 senators, 11 are selected in consultation with the prime minister, 4 in consultation with the leader of the opposition, 1 on the advice of the smaller island's Barbuda Council, and 1 at the governor general's discretion. Executive power is exercised by a Council of Ministers headed by a prime minister and responsible to Parliament. The constitutional independence of the judiciary is reinforced by the fact that Antigua and 5 neighboring states (Dominica, Grenada, St. Kitts-Nevis, St. Lucia, and St. Vincent) participate equally in a Supreme Court, which encompasses a Court of Appeal with a High Court, one of whose judges is resident in Antigua and presides over a Court of Summary Jurisdiction. District courts deal with minor offenses and civil actions involving not more than EC$500.

While Antigua and Barbuda constitute a nominally unitary state, secessionist sentiment has long been pronounced on the smaller island. Premier Bird initiated, before independence, a limited devolution of powers to the Barbuda Council, which contains nine directly elected members in addition to a government nominee and the Barbuda parliamentary representative. However, in early 2000 Barbudans complained of the government's handling of their affairs through a single ministry (Home Affairs), and in March the Commonwealth appointed two members to review relations between the council and the government. Among other things, the council had called for establishment of a federal system under which Barbuda would have a legislative assembly with full authority over its internal affairs. In late 2000 the Commonwealth review commission rejected that proposal, although officials from Barbuda pledged to pursue the issue. Meanwhile, St. John's endorsed the creation of a new joint consultative committee of representatives from both islands to oversee a proposed five-year development plan for Barbuda, and in 2004 the Spencer administration established a separate Barbuda Affairs ministry, which, however, was abandoned in 2009

Foreign relations. In 1965 (then) Chief Minister Bird, a strong believer in regional cooperation, played a leading role in organizing the Caribbean Free Trade Association (Carifta), predecessor of the Caribbean Community and Common Market (Caricom). Upon independence, Antigua became a member of the Commonwealth and, shortly thereafter, the 157th member of the United Nations. Subsequently, St. John's accepted observer status within the Nonaligned Movement, viewing the latter as a "viable alternative [to] . . . confrontation between the superpowers." However, in January 1982 the prime minister called on the United States to protect the Caribbean against foreign subversive elements. Antigua is also an active member of the Organization of Eastern Caribbean States (OECS), which provided troops in support of the U.S. invasion of Grenada in October 1983. The swing to the right continued in 1985, with St. John's agreeing to the establishment of a U.S.-backed regional military training base on the main island and the use of existing U.S. bases for regional security exercises.

In April 1999 the government announced an overhaul of its banking supervision board after foreign banks had been warned of dealing with local institutions because of money-laundering charges. In November the government said it had uncovered one such scheme and in April 2000 it agreed to adopt a number of UN-sponsored measures to prevent abuses of its offshore facilities.

In mid-2003 the Bird administration filed an appeal with the World Trade Organization (WTO) against restrictions on Internet gambling by U.S. consumers. Nine months later, in a landmark decision, the WTO ruled in favor of Antigua, stating that the restrictions were inconsistent with U.S. obligations under the General Agreement on Trade in Services (GATS), and in April 2005 the WTO ordered the United States to either lift its ban or remove a "discriminatory exemption" for horse-race betting.

Current issues. The major issue facing Antigua and Barbuda in 2009 was the blow to its financial sector from charges filed in February by the U.S. Securities and Exchange Commission (SEC) that Antigua's leading private investor, the Texas-based Sir Robert Allen Stanford, had engaged in fraud of a "shocking magnitude." While Stanford insisted that he was guilty of no wrongdoing, including allegedly running a Ponzi scheme, the government felt obliged to transfer the assets of the Bank of Antigua to a semi-governmental Eastern Caribbean Amalgamated Financial Company.

Meanwhile, the WTO gambling controversy remained unresolved. The United States refused to comply with the WTO's order on the ground that to do so would violate a number of state laws, and the U.S. Congress responded by passing an "Unlawful Internet Gambling Enforcement Act" that specifically banned Internet gambling and horse-race betting within the United States but failed to limit application of the law to offshore locations. As a result, the WTO took the unusual action of awarding Antigua and Barbuda the right to violate U.S. copyright restrictions on goods such as films and music up to a value of $21 million a year (far less than the $3.4 billion in damages that the island nation had sought).

POLITICAL PARTIES

Government Party:

United Progressive Party (UPP). The UPP was launched in March 1992 by merger of the Progressive Labour Movement (PLM), the United National Democratic Party (UNDP), and the Antigua Caribbean

Liberation Movement (ACLM). The action came in the wake of involvement by the three groups in antigovernment demonstrations triggered by the January corruption scandal.

In power from 1971 to 1976 under its (then) leader George WALTER, the PLM was organized in 1970 as the political affiliate of the Antigua Workers' Union (AWU), which had emerged in the wake of a 1967 split in the Antigua Trades and Labour Union (AT&LU). The PLM delegation to the December 1980 independence talks in London refused to sign the conference report following rejection of proposals that included guarantees related to human rights and the right to strike, the adoption of proportional representation and a unicameral legislature, and assurances of greater local autonomy for Barbuda. In 1984 the party lost the three parliamentary seats it had won four years earlier, but with no parties other than the ruling ALP represented in the lower house, the PLM insisted that it remain the "official opposition."

The UNDP was formed in early 1986 by merger of the United People's Movement (UPM) and the National Democratic Party (NDP). The UPM had been organized in 1982 by former PLM leader Walter, who had been forced to withdraw from active politics in February 1979 after his conviction of mishandling state finances while premier from 1971 to 1976. The decision was reversed several days after the 1980 election, Walter subsequently accusing the new PLM leadership of efforts to exclude him. With considerable support from AWU members, who had been omitted from the PLM delegation to the independence talks, Walter announced that the UPM would be devoted to social democracy and to returning the country "to the hands of Antiguans"—a reference to extensive foreign participation in the economy. Ironically, in late 1982 a government official accused Walter of accepting financial support from Venezuela in return for a pledge of greater cooperation with Caracas should the UPM win power. The UPM secured no parliamentary representation in 1984 and Walter assumed no public role in forming the UNDP, reportedly because of the negative impact it might have in launching the new formation. The NDP was organized by a group of business leaders in early 1985. Initially perceived as a conservative alternative to both the ALP and the ACLM (below), it subsequently attempted to forge links with the leftist opposition in an effort to soften its image as a party of the middle-class. However, elements within the NDP, as well as within the ACLM, were reportedly opposed to the latter's inclusion in the UNDP, which secured one parliamentary seat in 1989.

Originally known as the Afro-Caribbean Liberation Movement, the ACLM was a "new left" organization that contested the 1980 election, winning less than 1 percent of the vote and obtaining no parliamentary seats. In 1982 ACLM accusations of government corruption in regard to the sale of passports and the alleged "disappearance" of loan funds resulted in a police raid on the offices of the party's newspaper, the *Outlet*, where classified documents were discovered, in violation of the Official Secrets Act. Subsequently, party leader Tim HECTOR and a number of others were arrested and fined for violations of the Newspaper Registration Act and the Public Order Act. In 1985 Hector was sentenced to six months imprisonment on charges of "undermining confidence in a public official," after publishing criticism of several government ministries; he remained free on bail while his appeal was heard, and in May 1986 his conviction was overturned by the High Court, which ruled the relevant section of the Public Order Act to be unconstitutional. The ACLM presented no candidates for the 1984 balloting; in 1989 it gained only 2 percent of the vote and won no seats. Hector died in November 2002.

The UPP won only 4 lower house seats in 1999 but held a commanding majority of 13 seats after the 2004 balloting, with former opposition leader Baldwin Spencer being named prime minister. The UPP majority declined to 9 seats in 2009.

Leaders: Winston Baldwin SPENCER (Prime Minister), Wilmoth DANIEL (Deputy Prime Minister), Charlesworth SAMUEL (Agriculture Minister), Leon SYMISTER (Chair).

Opposition Party:

Antigua Labour Party (ALP). In power from 1967 to 1971 and a decisive victor in subsequent balloting in 1976, 1980, 1984, and 1989, the ALP has long been affiliated with the AT&LU. By the early 1980s, however, questions had arisen as to the viability of its grassroots linkages. In accepting redesignation as party chair in June 1984, the incumbent prime minister's son, Lester Bird, adopted a posture of appealing over the heads of the older leadership to women's, youth, and other groups for "modern approaches" and "a proper philosophical base" for party activity.

In response to the corruption controversy that engulfed his administration in January 1992, the 82-year-old prime minister announced on March 30 that he would not seek reelection in 1994 but would continue in office for the balance of his existing term. Subsequently, balloting in a special ALP convention on May 24 to elect a new party leader ended inconclusively with an even split between Lester Bird and (then) information minister John St. Luce. In a second poll at the party's annual convention on September 5–6, Bird defeated St. Luce, and he became prime minister in March 1994. He remained in office after the March 1999 poll but led the ALP to defeat in March 2004. The party recovered in 2009, but failed by two seats to win a majority.

Leaders: Steadroy ("Cutie") BENJAMIN (Leader of the Opposition), Lester Bryant BIRD (Former Prime Minster and Former Leader of the Opposition), Vere C. BIRD Jr. (Party Chair), Adolphus Eleazer FREELAND (Former Party Chair), John E. ST. LUCE.

Other Parties:

National Movement for Change (NMC). The NMC was organized as an anti-Bird opposition party in March 2002.

Leader: Alistair THOMAS.

First Christian Democratic Movement (FCDM). The FCDM was launched in 2003.

Leader: Egbert JOSEPH.

Barbuda People's Movement (BPM). The BPM is a separatist party that presently controls the local Barbuda Council. Having rejected the independence agreement, party leader Hilbourne Frank asserted in early 1982 that parliament's passage of a bill altering land-tenure practices and permitting individual ownership "erodes the traditional, customary and constitutional authority handed down to the Council and the people of Barbuda." Frank was elected Barbuda's parliamentary deputy on March 9, 1989, while the BPM swept all four local Council contests at balloting on March 23 to win full control of the 9 elective seats. In March 1997 the party won all 5 seats up for reelection, thereby retaining full control of the body. BPM retained Barbuda's parliamentary seat in 2009.

Leaders: Thomas Hilbourne FRANK, Fabian JONES (Chair).

Barbuda People's Movement for Change (BPMC). Launched in 2004 as the successor to the former Organization for National Reconstruction (ONR), the BPMC favors self-government for Barbuda.

Leader: Arthur SHABAZZ-NIBBS.

A number of additional parties emerged prior to the 2004 election, including the **Antigua Freedom Party** (AFP), led by George (Rick) JAMES; the **Democratic People's Party** (DPP), led by Sherfield BOWEN; the **National Labour Party** (NLP); and the **Organization for National Development** (OND), a breakaway faction of the UPP currently led by Melford NICHOLAS.

LEGISLATURE

The **Parliament** is a bicameral body consisting of an appointed Senate and a directly elected House of Representatives.

Senate. The upper house has 17 members named by the governor general: 11 (including at least 1 from Barbuda) appointed on advice of the prime minister, 4 named after consultation with the leader of the opposition, 1 recommended by the Barbuda Council, and 1 chosen at the governor general's discretion.

President: Hazelyn Mason FRANCIS.

House of Representatives. The lower house has 17 members chosen every 5 years (subject to dissolution) from single-member constituencies, plus the attorney general, ex officio. At the most recent election of March 12, 2009, the UPP won 9 seats; the ALP, 7; and the BPM, 1.

Speaker: Giselle ISAAC-ARRINDELL.

CABINET

[as of September 1, 2009]

Prime Minister	Winston Baldwin Spencer
Deputy Prime Minister	Wilmoth Daniel
Ministers	
Agriculture, Lands, Housing, and the Environment	Hilson Baptiste
Education, Gender, Sports, and Youth Affairs	Dr. Jacqui Quinn-Leandro [f]
Finance, Economy, and Public Administration	Harold E.E. Lovell
Foreign Affairs and Foreign Trade	Winston Baldwin Spencer
Health, Social Transformation, and Consumer Affairs	Wilmoth Daniel
Legal Affairs and Attorney General	Justin L. Simon
National Security	Dr. Leon Errol Cort
Tourism, Civil Aviation, and Culture	John Maginley
Works and Transport	Trevor Myke Walker

[f] = female

COMMUNICATIONS

Press. Freedom of the press is constitutionally guaranteed. The following are published in St. John's: *The Worker's Voice* (6,000), the twice-weekly organ of the ALP and AT&LU; *The Outlet* (5,500), the ACLM weekly; *The Nation* (1,500), the government weekly; *Antigua Sun*, daily; *Rappore*, the UPP weekly.

News Agency. There is no domestic facility. Most media rely on the regional Caribbean News Agency (CANA) for international coverage.

Broadcasting and computing. Radio ZDK is a private station broadcasting from St. John's. The government-operated Antigua and Barbuda Broadcasting Service (ABBS) transmits over one radio station and one TV facility, the latter providing the most sophisticated full-color service in the Commonwealth Caribbean. Other radio facilities include Voice of America, BBC Caribbean, and Deutsche Welle relays, plus a religious station, Caribbean Radio Lighthouse; additional television service is provided by privately owned CTV Entertainment Systems. As of 2008 there were 750.3 Internet users per 1,000 inhabitants.

INTERGOVERNMENTAL REPRESENTATION

Ambassador to the U.S.: Deborah Mae LOVELL.

U.S. Ambassador to Antigua and Barbuda: (Vacant).

Permanent Representative to the UN: John William ASHE.

IGO Memberships (Non-UN): ACS, Caricom, CDB, CWTH, Interpol, NAM, OAS, OECS, OPANAL, WTO.

ARGENTINA

Argentine Republic
República Argentina

Political Status: Independent republic proclaimed 1816; under military regimes 1966–1973 and 1976–1983; current constitution adopted August 22, 1994.

Area: 1,068,013 sq. mi. (2,766,889 sq. km.), excluding territory claimed in Antarctica and the South Atlantic.

Population: 36,260,130 (2001C); 39,870,000 (2008E).

Major Urban Centers (2005E): BUENOS AIRES (12,704,000), Córdoba (1,315,000), Rosario (908,000), La Plata (581,000).

Official Language: Spanish.

Monetary Unit: Peso (official rate December 1, 2009: 3.81 pesos = $1US).

President: Cristina FERNÁNDEZ de Kirchner (Justicialist Party–Victory Front); elected on October 28, 2007, and inaugurated for a four-year term on December 10, 2007, succeeding Néstor Carlos KIRCHNER (Justicialist Party).

Vice President: Julio César Cleto COBOS (Radical Civic Union for Kirchner–Victory Front); elected on October 28, 2007, and inaugurated for a term concurrent with that of the president on December 10, 2007, succeeding Daniel Osvaldo SCIOLI (Justicialist Party).

THE COUNTRY

Second in size among the countries of South America, the Argentine Republic includes the national territory of Tierra del Fuego and claims certain South Atlantic islands (including the Falklands, known to Argentines as the Malvinas) as well as portions of Antarctica. The country extends 2,300 miles from north to south and exhibits a varied climate and topography, including the renowned pampas, the fertile central plains. The population is largely Caucasian but of diverse national origin. Spaniards and Italians predominate, but there are also large groups from other Western and Eastern European countries, as well as Middle Easterners of both Arab and Jewish descent. Although Spanish is the official language, English, Italian, German, and French are also spoken. More than 90 percent of the population is Roman Catholic. According to the 2001 census, literacy was greater than 97 percent.

Women pursue professional careers in great numbers. With the exception of both wives of former president Juan Perón, women have historically been minimally represented in government, although a women's group called "*Las Madres de la Plaza de Mayo*" was at the forefront of opposition to the former military regime. In the 2007 presidential election, a woman, Cristina FERNÁNDEZ de Kirchner, was elected president. In the upper house, 27 of 77 members are women, and in the lower house, 99 of 277 members are women.

Argentina has traditionally enjoyed one of the highest per capita incomes in South America but for a number of years were subject to rampant inflation that escalated to more than 1,000 percent in early 1985, necessitating a drastic currency revision as part of a series of "war economy" measures. Inflation fell to an annualized rate of 50 percent the following year but escalated to an unprecedented rate of nearly 5,000 percent in 1989 despite several attempted stabilization programs. However, a currency convertibility plan introduced in March 1991 (under which the peso was pegged to the U.S. dollar) subsequently eliminated hyperinflation (which declined steadily to a remarkable low of 0.1 percent in 1996) and prompted a surge of investment. The currency change also required the imposition of conservative banking measures, including higher interest rates.

GDP, which had fallen by an average of 0.4 percent annually in 1980–1990, rose by an average of 5.3 percent annually during 1990–1998. However, international financial crises in 1997–1999 tested the convertibility law, and, in part due to the government's refusal to devalue the peso, the economy subsequently suffered more than three years of recession, with unemployment rates ranging between 14 to 19 percent. In a move that generated substantial global attention, the government in late 2001 announced a moratorium on repayments of $155 billion in public debt. (Formal default on the debt front was averted in mid-2002 with a $550 million repayment to the Inter-American Development Bank [IADB], although no progress was registered in talks with private bondholders, to whom an overwhelming proportion of the loans was owed.) Meanwhile, the peso was devalued in January 2002 and allowed to float in February in an effort to spur growth.

The economy experienced a severe decline of 11.0 percent in 2002, but it rebounded to growth of 8.8 percent in 2003 and 9.0 percent in 2004, with the government holding firm to an offer to settle on a 70 percent write-down of the privately held bonds' nominal value. In early March 2005 Argentina reached agreement with three-quarters of its private creditors on a write-down of approximately $100 billion, and in late December the country paid off its outstanding debt of $9.8 billion to the International Monetary Fund (IMF), with the Kirchner administration concurrently declaring that it was severing relations with the IMF. Significantly, growth averaged 8 percent per year in 2003–2006, and unemployment, which had been mired in double digits for nearly a decade, fell to 8.7 percent at the end of that period. However, the administration's fiscal policies also led to rising inflation, which reached 9.8 percent in 2006. Many analysts have questioned the accuracy of official inflation figures, instead reporting double-digit inflation rates. While the government reported a 7.2 percent inflation rate in 2008, the actual figure, according to private economists, was somewhere near 20 percent. Annual GDP growth in 2008 was a robust 7.4 percent, though unemployment rates of 7.3 percent were recorded. In response to the global economic crisis in late 2008 the Fernández government pushed through the legislature a stimulus package that included $21 billion in new public-works spending backed by the nationalization of ten private pension funds.

As a result of the worldwide recession, annual GDP growth in 2009 was forecast at 2 percent. Meanwhile, what analysts described as the worst drought in a generation severely affected the agricultural sector in 2009.

GOVERNMENT AND POLITICS

Political background. Following the struggle for independence from Spain in 1810–1816, Argentina experienced a period of conflict over its form of government. The provinces advocated a federal system to guarantee their autonomy, while Buenos Aires favored a unitary state in which it would play a dominant role. A federal constitution was drafted in 1853, but Buenos Aires refused to ratify the document until its 1859 defeat in a brief war. Following a second military reversal in 1880, the territory was politically neutralized by being designated a federal district.

The early years of the 20th century were dominated by the Conservative Party (*Partido Conservador*—PC). However, the reformist Radical Civic Union (*Unión Cívica Radical*—UCR) successfully pressed in 1912 for a liberal electoral law that resulted in the election of UCR leader Hipólito IRIGOYEN as president in 1916. Faced with mounting economic problems, the Irigoyen government was overthrown and replaced by the nation's first military regime in 1930.

The election of Augustín P. JUSTO to the presidency in 1932 launched a second period of Conservative rule that lasted until 1943, when the military again intervened. Gen. Juan Domingo PERÓN Sosa was elected chief executive in 1946, inaugurating a populist dictatorship that was eventually overthrown in 1955. His second wife, María Eva Duarte de PERÓN (better known as Eva Perón or Evita) was an active participant. She initiated the Eva Perón Foundation with donations and funds coerced from the private sector, which helped to improve the lives of the poor. Juan Perón's influence over the political arena can hardly be exaggerated, as it was during his government and through his leadership that unions were recognized as legitimate political actors and that the "masses" (known as the *descamisados* or "shirtless ones") were incorporated into political strategies. Women's suffrage was introduced in 1951 after a strong campaign by Evita, who died of cancer in 1952. In the following years Juan Perón relied more on cooptation and coercion than on democratic representation, and he struggled when economic growth slowed and the politicized masses had minimal institutional channels to accommodate them. During his term in office, a divorce law was promulgated with Perón's approval, an act which put him at odds with the Catholic Church, who actively campaigned for his removal. Peron's loss of control was noted by elites, who supported the military coup that removed him in 1955. Subsequent military and democratic governments attempted to "ban" Peronism, but it remained the country's most powerful ideological influence.

In the March 1973 general election, which ended seven years of military rule, the Peronist Dr. Héctor J. CÁMPORA emerged victorious. Four months later Cámpora resigned to force a new election in which Perón would be eligible as a candidate. The new round of balloting, held in September, returned the former president to power with an overwhelming majority after 18 years of exile. Following his inauguration, Perón was plagued by factionalism within his movement and by increasingly widespread opposition from guerrilla groups. After his death on July 1, 1974, he was succeeded by his second wife, Isabel (born María Estela) Martínez de PERÓN, who had been elected vice president the preceding September. Isabel Perón's turbulent presidency was terminated on March 24, 1976, by a three-man military junta, which on March 26 designated Lt. Gen. Jorge Rafael VIDELA as her replacement.

In December 1976 General Videla stated that his government was "very close to final victory" over left-wing terrorists, most prominently the so-called *Montonero* guerrillas and the People's Revolutionary Army. The military government embarked on a campaign of repression, described as the "dirty war," that killed or "disappeared" as many as 30,000 people, the vast majority of whom were not involved with guerrilla groups.

Earlier, in an apparent consolidation of power by Videla, a number of rightist officers were retired and replaced by moderates. On May 2, 1978, the government announced that while Videla had been redesignated as president for a three-year term retroactive to March 29, he would cease to serve as a member of the junta following his military retirement on August 1. The pattern was repeated with the retirement of Lt. Gen. Roberto Eduardo VIOLA as army commander and junta member as of December 31, 1979, and his designation to succeed Videla in March 1981. Buffeted by health problems and an inability to deal with a rapidly deteriorating economy, Viola stepped down as chief executive on December 11, and he was succeeded 11 days later by the army commander, Lt. Gen. Leopoldo Fortunato GALTIERI, who continued as a member of the junta, along with Adm. Jorge Isaac ANAYA and Lt. Gen. Basilio Arturo LAMI DOZO, commanders of the navy and air force, respectively.

The region and the world were shaken by a brief but intense conflict with Great Britain that erupted in 1982 as the result of a 149-year dispute over ownership of the Falkland Islands (*Islas Malvinas*), located in the South Atlantic about 400 miles northeast of Tierra del Fuego. Argentina invaded the islands on April 2, prompting the dispatch of a British armada that succeeded in regaining control with the surrender of about 15,000 Argentine troops at the capital, Stanley, on July 15 (see Contested Territory, below). Branded as having sold out the country by his conduct of the war, Galtieri resigned on June 17 and was succeeded immediately as army commander by Maj. Gen. Cristino NICOLAIDES and on July 1 as president by Gen. Reynaldo Benito Antonio BIGNONE.

In the face of an economic crisis and mounting pressure from the nation's political parties, Bignone announced in February 1983 that elections for a civilian government would be advanced to the following October.

In balloting for national, provincial, and municipal authorities on October 30, 1983, the UCR, under the leadership of Raúl ALFONSÍN Foulkes, scored a decisive victory, winning not only the presidency but a majority in the Chamber of Deputies. Following pro forma designation by the electoral college, Alfonsín and his vice-presidential running mate, Víctor MARTINEZ, were sworn in for six-year terms on December 10.

On November 3, 1985, at the first renewal of the lower house in 20 years, the UCR marginally increased its majority, largely at the expense of the *oficialista* wing of the Peronist party (see Justicialist Party [*Partido Justicialista*—PJ], under Political Parties, below). On September 6, 1987, on the other hand, the Radicals were reduced to plurality status, with most of the Peronist gains again being registered by the movement's *renovadores* faction, whose principal leaders Antonio CAFIERO (governor of Buenos Aires) and Carlos Saúl MENEM (governor of La Rioja) emerged as the leading Peronist contenders for presidential nomination. In the primary balloting in July 1988, Menem and the UCR's Eduardo César ANGELOZ were formally selected as their parties' standard-bearers for the presidential poll, which yielded a Peronist victory on May 14, 1989.

Although not scheduled to be inaugurated until December 10, Menem and his running mate, Eduardo Alberto DUHALDE, were sworn in on July 8, following congressional acceptance of their predecessors' early resignations. The unprecedented early transfer resulted from suddenly escalating commodity prices in late May that necessitated the declaration of a state of siege to contain widespread food riots. However, Menem's standing in the opinion polls, which had reached a peak of 74 percent in September, plunged to a low of 31 percent by the end of the year because of his inability to halt the downward economic spiral.

In early December 1990 the army responded to the country's economic problems, as well as to the imprisonment of officers associated with the "dirty war" of 1976–1983, with its fourth revolt in three years. The government moved quickly, however, to counter the dissidents, who had seized the army headquarters in central Buenos Aires immediately prior to a state visit by U.S. President George H. W. Bush. The uprising was reportedly staged by a nationalist military faction headed by (former) Colonel Mohamed Alí SEINELDIN, who was under arrest at the time. Thereafter, despite widespread popular opposition, Menem issued pardons for a number of former presidents and military leaders convicted of criminal acts during the period of military rule, as well as for former *Montonero* guerrilla leader Mario FIRMENICH and several others.

Largely because of continued implementation of stringent economic reforms, including the introduction of full currency convertibility in March, inflation plunged in 1991, yielding an unexpectedly strong Peronist showing in a series of provincial and federal legislative elections between August and October. One of the victors was Vice President Duhalde, who resigned his federal post on December 5 to assume the governorship of Buenos Aires province.

In mid-1993 President Menem indicated that, subsequent to forthcoming congressional balloting, he might call a national referendum on constitutional reform, the most important component of which would permit him to seek reelection. However, as the Peronists secured an unprecedented victory at the poll of October 3, on November 14 Menem and opposition leader Alfonsín concluded a "Democratic Pact" (Olivos Pact) (see Constitution and government, below) that made the referendum unnecessary.

At Constituent Assembly balloting on April 10, 1994, both of the leading formations experienced setbacks. The Peronists were held to a plurality of 136 seats on a 37.7 percent share of the vote, while the UCR won 75 seats on a 19.9 percent vote share. The most striking gain was registered by the left-of-center Broad Front (*Frente Grande*—FG) coalition, which captured 31 seats as contrasted with only 3 chamber seats in 1993.

In the general election of May 14, 1995, Menem surpassed poll projections by easily winning direct election to a new four-year mandate on a 49.8 percent vote share—20.6 percent more than that of his nearest competitor, José Octavio BORDON, who headed a recently formed leftist coalition (the Front for a Country in Solidarity [*Frente del País Solidario*—Frepaso]), that included the FG. By contrast, the UCR candidate, Horatio MASSACCESI, came in third with 17.1 percent of the vote. The PJ, as the Peronists were formally known, also won control of a majority of lower house seats and 9 of 14 contested provincial governorships. Further rounds of regional balloting later in the year gave the PJ control of 14 of the country's 23 provinces; 5 of the remainder were won by the UCR and 4 by provincial parties. However, in a dramatic reversal in Buenos Aires' first-ever mayoral election on June 30, 1996, the UCR candidate, Fernando DE LA RÚA swept to victory with a 39.8 percent vote share, while the incumbent, Jorge DOMINGUEZ, placed third in the four-candidate field with 18.8 percent.

At nationwide balloting on October 26, 1997, the Peronists lost control of the Chamber of Deputies by winning only 51 of 127 contested seats; the opposition UCR and Frepaso secured 46 seats in coalition and an additional 17 seats on separate lists.

On October 24, 1999, opposition presidential candidate de la Rúa defeated the PJ's Duhalde with a 48.5 percent vote share. In simultaneous balloting for 130 of 257 Chamber of Deputies' seats, representation of the president-elect's Alliance for Work, Justice and Education (*Alianza por Trabajo, Justicia y Educación*—ATJE) rose to 127, which, with the support of third-party allies, gave it a working majority.

In addition to continuing economic malaise, the de la Rúa administration was shaken by a bribery scandal in September 2000 that prompted a cabinet reshuffle on October 5. Protesting the retention of two ministers who had been implicated in the affair, Vice President Carlos Alberto ALVAREZ resigned the following day, his Senate presidency being assumed by the president pro tempore, Mario Aníbal LOSADA.

In the congressional balloting on October 14, 2001, the Peronists regained control of both houses, the ATJE winning only 88 of 257 Chamber and 25 of 72 Senate seats. Two months later, on December 20, President de la Rúa resigned in the face of widespread public protests and generalized disorder sparked by a sharp and severe economic decline, and Senate President Ramón PUERTA became his successor on an acting basis. On December 23 a special joint session of legislators and provincial governors elected the Peronist governor of San Luis, Adolfo RODRÍGUEZ Saá, as interim chief executive. Rodríguez Saá was popularly applauded when he immediately declared a moratorium on the payment of Argentina's international debt, but many established politicians did not back him on the measure. Rodríguez Saá resigned on December 30, his office devolving briefly on the president of the Chamber of Deputies, Eduardo CAMAÑO, before passing by another joint election to former vice president Eduardo Duhalde on January 1, 2002. Duhalde quickly ended the convertibility regime and allowed the peso to float. He chose Néstor Carlos KIRCHNER, a governor from the remote province of Santa Cruz, as his preferred successor, rejecting Menem. In first-round presidential balloting on April 27, 2003, former president Menem narrowly outpolled Kirchner, a fellow Peronist, with a plurality of 24.3 percent. On May 14, however, Menem withdrew from a runoff after it became apparent that Kirchner would be supported by the other minor candidates. Kirchner and his running mate, Daniel SCIOLI, were subsequently inaugurated on May 25.

Before the legislative poll of October 23, 2005, Kirchner waged a bitter struggle with his immediate predecessor, Duhalde, over control of the PJ, while launching on August 24 a Victory Front grouping to contest constituencies where his supporters did not possess majorities. The strategy yielded a substantial victory for the *kirchneristas*, who won 69 of 127 contested seats in the Chamber of Deputies and 17 of 24 in the Senate.

In August 2006 the congress voted to give President Kirchner expanded powers, including the ability to make alterations in the budget without congressional approval and to issue executive decrees. Concurrently, Kirchner agreed to make Supreme Court Judicial nominations more transparent and to reduce the size of the court from 9 to 5 (reversing the Menem expansion in 1990). He also reduced the size of the Magistrates' Council from 20 to 13 members, 5 of whom he appoints.

Although President Kirchner's approval rating stood at 60 percent in July 2007, he declined to stand in the upcoming election, announcing on July 1 that his wife, Senator Cristina Fernández de Kirchner, would be a candidate to succeed him, fueling speculation that the presidential couple aimed to circumvent constitutional convention by holding rotating presidencies the maximum number of terms, effectively holding collective leadership during both their tenures in the office.

Other presidential candidates included former finance minister Roberto LAVAGNA, who enjoyed the backing of some more conservative PJ dissidents, including the Duhalde family, and some UCR members. Meanwhile, powerful anti-Kirchner Peronists, including former presidents Menem and Puerta, decided to support their candidate, Alberto Rodríguez Saá.

In the presidential election of October 28, 2007, Senator Fernández de Kirchner secured 44.9 percent of votes, precluding a recount by exceeding the 40 percent threshold requirement to become Argentina's first elected woman president. Her nearest rival, Elisa María Avelina CARRIÓ, of the Alternative for a Republic of Equals (*Alternativa para una República de Iguales*—ARI), represented the Civic Coalition (*Coalición Cívica*—CC) with a 23.0 percent vote share, followed by Roberto Lavagna, of the Concertation Alliance (*Alianza Concertación UNA*—AC) with 16.9 percent. Minor party candidates included Alberto José Rodríguez Saá, representing the Union and Liberty Party (*Alianza Frente Justicia Union y Libertad*—JUL) with 7.7 percent of votes, and Néstor PITROLA, representing the Worker's Party (*Partido Obrero*—PO) with 6.2 percent.

Legislative elections for half of the Chamber of Deputies and one-third of the Senate were also held on October 28, 2007. They returned pluralities for the Victory Front (*Frente para la Victoria*—FPV) (see Legislature, below). Pro-government parties gained seats in both houses, while the center-left CC was the only opposition party to make any gains. Others, particularly the Radical Civic Union and the Republican Proposal, lost ground.

In March 2009 partial legislative elections originally scheduled for October 25 were moved up to June 28 after the legislature approved the change proposed by President Fernández de Kirchner.

Constitution and government. After Argentina returned to civilian rule in 1983, most of the constitutional structure of 1853 was reintroduced. The president and vice president were again designated for nonrenewable 6-year terms by an electoral college chosen on the basis of proportional representation, with each electoral district having twice as many electors as the combined number of senators and deputies. The National Congress consisted of a 46-member Senate, one-third being replenished every three years, and a 254-member Chamber of Deputies, one-half being elected every 2 years. The judicial system encompassed a Supreme Court, federal appeals courts, and provincial structures including supreme and subsidiary judicial bodies.

In 1993 President Carlos Menem negotiated an agreement (in what became known as the Olivos Pact [Democratic Pact]) on constitutional change that would allow reelection of the president in exchange for reducing the presidential mandate from six to four years. The pact also reduced some of the powers of the president over other branches.

The constitution of August 1994 provided for direct election of the president and vice president for four-year terms, with the possibility of one consecutive renewal. (First-round election requires a 45 percent majority [40 percent in the event of a gap greater than 10 percent between the two leading contenders].) Newly created was the post of cabinet chief (*jefe de gabinete*), a coordinating position filled by presidential appointment, subject to recall by an absolute majority of each of the legislative chambers.

The number of senators from each province was increased from two to three under the 1994 basic law revisions, the added member to represent the leading opposition party or group. The senatorial mandate, on the other hand, was shortened from nine years to six, with replenishment of one-third by direct election every two years commencing in the year 2001. The Chamber of Deputies continued to be renewed by halves every two years.

The 1994 basic law provided for an auditor general nominated by the largest opposition party and for a people's defender (ombudsman) appointed for a once-renewable five-year term by a two-thirds vote of each legislative chamber. It also affirmed Argentina's sovereignty over the Malvinas, South Georgia, and South Sandwich islands.

There are now 23 provinces (Tierra del Fuego having been upgraded from the status of a National Territory in 1991), plus the Federal District of Buenos Aires. The provinces elect their own governors and legislatures and retain those powers not specifically delegated to the federal government; in practice, however, there has been a history of substantial federal intervention in provincial affairs. Included in the current constitution is a provision that the mayor of Buenos Aires (formerly a presidential appointee) also be directly elected.

Province and Capital	*Area (sq. mi.)*	*Population (2008E)*
Buenos Aires (La Plata)	118,843	15,108,000
Catamarca (Catamarca)	38,540	389,000
Chaco (Resistencia)	38,468	1,053,000
Chubut (Rawson)	86,751	464,000
Córdoba (Córdoba)	65,161	3,354,000
Corrientes (Corrientes)	34,054	1,014,000
Entre Ríos (Paraná)	29,427	1,258,000
Formosa (Formosa)	27,825	540,000
Jujuy (San Salvador de Jujuy)	20,548	681,000
La Pampa (Santa Rosa)	55,382	335,000
La Rioja (La Rioja)	35,649	342,000
Mendoza (Mendoza)	58,239	1,734,000
Misiones (Posadas)	11,506	1,079,000
Neuquén (Neuquén)	36,324	551,000
Río Negro (Viedma)	78,383	601,000
Salta (Salta)	59,759	1,225,000
San Juan (San Juan)	33,257	698,000
San Luis (San Luis)	29,632	439,000
Santa Cruz (Río Gallegos)	94,186	226,000
Santa Fé (Santa Fé)	51,354	3,259,000
Santiago del Estero (Santiago del Estero)	52,222	866,000
Tierra del Fuego (Ushuaia)	8,074	127,000
Tucumán (San Miguel de Tucumán)	8,697	1,478,000
Federal District		
Distrito Federal (Buenos Aires)	77	3,079,000

Foreign relations. Argentina has traditionally maintained an independent foreign policy and has been reluctant to follow U.S. leadership in hemispheric and world affairs. Argentina claims territory in the Antarctic (see article on Antarctica) and, despite the outcome of the 1982 war with Britain, continues to assert its long-standing claim to sovereignty over the Falklands (*Islas Malvinas*). The latter has won support at the UN General Assembly, which, since the cessation of hostilities, has repeatedly called on the claimants to initiate negotiations on a peaceful resolution of the dispute.

Relations with Chile became tense following the announcement in May 1977 that a panel of international arbitrators had awarded Chile the ownership of three disputed islands in the Beagle Channel, just north of Cape Horn. As in the case of the Falklands, there is evidence of petroleum in the area. Argentina formally repudiated the decision in January 1978. A subsequent 19-month mediation effort by Pope John Paul II resulted in a proposal that endorsed the awarding of the three islands to Chile while limiting the assignment of offshore rights on the Atlantic side of the Cape Horn meridian. The proposal was rejected by the Argentine junta but accepted by Raúl Alfonsín before his election as president of Argentina, and a treaty ending the century-old dispute was narrowly ratified by the Argentine Senate in March 1985. Additional border issues were ostensibly resolved by an agreement between presidents Menem of Argentina and Frei of Chile in 1991, but its terms drew opposition in both countries because of an "additional protocol" concluded by the two chief executives in late 1996. It was not until June 1999 that ratifications were completed on the Continental Glaciers Treaty that resolved the last remaining border dispute between the two countries.

For nearly a decade Argentina was embroiled in a dispute with Brazil over water rights on the Paraná River. In October 1979, however, both countries joined Paraguay in signing an agreement that not only resolved differences over Brazil's Itaipú Dam, the world's largest, but also freed the way for cooperative exploitation of the Uruguay River. Economic linkage between the continent's two largest states was further enhanced on December 10, 1986, with the signing by presidents Alfonsín and Sarney of 20 accords launching an ambitious economic integration effort. Under the plan, a customs union was established for most capital goods as of January 1, 1987, with cooperation in the exchange of food products, the promotion of bilateral industrial ventures, the establishment of a $200 million joint investment fund, and joint energy development (including a new $2 billion hydroelectric facility) to follow. President Sanguinetti of Uruguay, who was at the meeting, pledged his "determined support" for the move and agreed to a series of ministerial-level talks designed to pave the way for his country's participation in the integration process. The result was the signing in Asunción, Paraguay, on March 26, 1991, of a four-nation treaty (including the host country) providing for the formation of the Southern Cone Common Market (*Mercado Común del Cono Sur*—Mercosur).

In 1988 Argentina and Brazil agreed to cooperate in the nuclear power industry. While neither was a signatory of the Nuclear Non-Proliferation Treaty (see article on the International Atomic Energy Agency), the two countries formally rejected the development of nuclear weaponry in a July 1991 accord that also banned the introduction of such arms from external sources. In addition, the Argentine Chamber of Deputies, after a lengthy delay, voted in November 1993 to ratify the 1967 Treaty of Tlatelolco (see article on the Agency for the Prohibition of Nuclear Weapons in Latin America and the Caribbean), which bans nuclear weapons from the continent.

Although insisting during the 1989 presidential campaign that Argentina would recover the Falklands "even if blood has to be spilled," Menem subsequently indicated that he was prepared to engage in a "civilized dialogue" with Britain, particularly if the latter were to abandon its economic zone around the islands. In mid-October the first direct talks between the two countries in five years were held in Madrid, Spain. At the conclusion of a second round of talks in Madrid on February 15, 1990, an agreement was reached to restore full diplomatic relations.

Argentina's relations with the United States, traditionally cordial, markedly improved in the 1990s during the Menem administration. Cooperation expanded in such areas as trade and security, with Washington in 1997 even naming Argentina the United States's only "Major Non-NATO Ally" in the hemisphere, a designation that eased the flow of several types of security assistance.

By contrast, fresh tension erupted in August 1993 as the result of a suggestion that the Falkland Islanders be given cash awards by Buenos Aires to lift their opposition to Argentine sovereignty claims, coupled with the introduction by Britain of a new fishing licensing regime for the waters around South Georgia and the South Sandwich Islands. No sooner was an agreement reached in settlement of the latter controversy than a British geological survey suggested that the undersea oil potential in the Falklands area appeared to be substantially greater than in Britain's North Sea fields. The result was a major agreement signed in New York in September 1995 for joint oil and gas exploration in a 7,000-square-mile area southwest of the disputed islands (see Contested Territory, below).

In October 1998 President Menem traveled to Britain for the first such visit by an Argentine chief executive in four decades. Although he insisted during his stay that the question of sovereignty over the Falklands remained nonnegotiable, tension between the former combatants manifestly eased, and in mid-December the administration of Prime Minister Tony Blair announced that the British arms embargo would be relaxed, save for material that would put the disputed territory at renewed risk. In mid-1999 an agreement was reached on the restoration of air traffic with the mainland and a resumption of visits to the territory by Argentina. However, the dispute over sovereignty remained unresolved and the issue was not discussed during a visit by Blair (the first by a British prime minister) in August 2001. The Argentinian hard line continued under President Kirchner, who, in April 2005, emphasized his government's commitment to "full recovery" of the islands, albeit "through dialogue and peace."

The U.S. image in Argentina declined during the 2000s along with President Menem's popularity, which plummeted after Argentina's 2001 economic crisis. Because of the George W. Bush administration's initial opposition to a multibillion-dollar bailout, Latin American opinion polls consistently showed Argentinians holding the region's lowest opinion of the United States. Ultimately, however, the United States came out in favor of $8 billion in new IMF loans for Argentina, in addition to the nearly $14 billion Argentina had received eight months earlier.

Relations with Brazil reached their warmest with a state visit by Brazilian President Lula da Silva in October 2003 but declined thereafter. With growth in Argentine exports to Brazil in 2003–2004 scarcely more than 10 percent of Brazil's to Argentina, Buenos Aires complained of Mercosur's "economic asymmetries." Argentina also objected to Brazil's posture as regional leader in its bid for a seat on the UN Security Council. Brazilian-Argentine relations subsequently continued to decline as Argentina turned much of its trade attention toward Venezuela, with whom Kirchner, as a "progressive Peronist," desired closer ties.

Argentina and Venezuela became involved in the proposed development of a South American development bank that would be an alternative to the U.S.-dominated IADB; the two countries also urged the creation of an organization of petroleum- and gas-producing countries in South America. Concurrently, Venezuela agreed to supply lower-priced oil to Argentina, and the Venezuelan government bought $3.1 billion of Argentine bonds.

Relations between Venezuela and Argentina were strained on November 18, 2006, when an Argentine judge issued warrants for former Iranian president Akbar Rafsanjani and eight other former Iranian officials for allegedly backing the bombing of a Jewish community center in Buenos Aires on July 18, 1994, that killed 85 people. The judge argued that the Lebanese group Hezbollah had been implicated in the bombing and that the Iranian officials were potentially liable because of their financial support of Hezbollah. Venezuela president Hugo Chávez's unwavering support for the Iranian republic led Kirchner's housing secretary, Luis D'ELÍA, considered pro-Chávez, to critique the warrant as "an American-Israeli military aggression against the Islamic republic." D'Elía was subsequently dismissed.

The ties between Argentina and Venezuela remained warm, however. This negatively affected U.S.-Argentine relations, especially after the Argentine government, in March 2007, hosted Chávez in Buenos Aires for a counter rally to the simultaneous visit of U.S. President George W. Bush to Uruguay.

Relations have also worsened quite significantly with Uruguay recently as a result of Argentine opposition to the decision of a Finnish company (Botnia) to invest in a pulp mill along the Uruguay River, which forms the border between the two countries. (The project was supported by a US$170 million loan from the World Bank.) Argentine protestors insisted that the mill would bring pollution and that Argentina should have been consulted on the project. Protests included the blockade of bridges between Argentina and Uruguay. The Spanish company Ence subsequently decided to move a related project to a less controversial section of Uruguay, but Botnia and Uruguayan president Tabaré Vazquez did not appear willing to back down. President Néstor Kirchner, his wife, President-elect Cristina Fernández de Kirchner, Tabaré Vazquez, and the King of Spain met in Santiago, Chile, in the first week of November 2007 to discuss the Uruguayan pulp mill. The following week, while negotiations continued in Chile, Vazquez closed the Uruguayan border with Argentina and gave the green light for the inauguration of the mill. Upon learning of the decision, the Argentine government left the negotiating table. The dispute remained unresolved in 2008, when in October Vásquez played a leading (and successful) role in opposition to Néstor Kirchner's bid to head a new regional political body, the South American Union of Nations (Unasur). During her campaign for the presidency, Fernández de Kirchner traveled to Germany and Austria to promote foreign investment and her profile abroad, meeting with the presidents of Brazil, Venezuela, and Bolivia. She visited the United States after her election. President Fernández de Kirchner also attended the Grupo Rio summit in El Salvador on March 7, 2008, which allowed regional leaders to defuse the crisis caused by Colombia's pursuit of FARC rebels within Ecuadorian borders (see Colombia entry). While the president's efforts to encourage negotiation had been supported by the U.S. embassy in Buenos Aires, U.S. Secretary of State Condoleezza Rice pointedly skipped Argentina in a regional tour later that month. Observers attributed the snub to U.S. displeasure regarding Argentina's deepening relationship with Venezuela, a key player viewed by the United States as a provocative force in the crisis.

President Fernández de Kirchner sought to further expand ties with Venezuela and Cuba in 2009, signing numerous energy, agricultural, and industrial agreements with the former and signing more bilateral agreements with the latter. She also visited ailing former Cuban leader Fidel Castro. Fernández de Kirchner also devoted much of her address at the April 2009 Summit of the Americas to a call for normalizing U.S.-Cuban relations.

In February 2009, Argentina had a minor diplomatic dispute with the U.S. administration of President Barack Obama when U.S. Central Intelligence Agency (CIA) Director Leon Panetta, in his first press conference, speculated that the political and economic stability of Argentina, Ecuador, and Venezuela) were likely in jeopardy due to the world economic crisis. Panetta subsequently apologized for his remarks.

Current issues. In addition to fostering economic recovery, President Nestor Kirchner was widely credited with challenging the impunity granted by the Menem administration to those involved in the authoritarian excesses during the 1976–1983 junta rule. The president called for the prosecution of numerous officials who had been covered by the previous amnesty agreement, while in 2005 the Supreme Court annulled several amnesty laws that had protected low-ranking officers who had argued they had acted in due obedience during the "dirty war." That decision led to many trials, including that of Julio SIMÓN, a former police sergeant, who was sentenced to 25 years in prison for kidnapping and torture. Problems arose in the case of Miguel ETCHECOLATZ, police commissioner in Buenos Aires province during the period in question. He was sent to prison for life on the evidence provided by more than 130 people. However, on the day before his 2007 testimony, a witness for the prosecution went missing and was presumed dead, leading many to question the accountability of the current police force. Kirchner was subsequently perceived as being less successful in dealing with impunity in regard to current malfeasance than in regard to earlier actions.

The challenge to impunity most prominently led to the overturning of pardons of Jorge VIDELA, the first leader of the military junta, and Albano HARGUINDEGUY and José Martínez de HOZ, former interior and economic ministers, respectively. With about 200 other people arrested and scheduled to be tried for crimes related to the military period, Kirchner focused on righting historical injustices as a legacy of his administration. However, critics of Kirchner pointed to the "lopsided" direction of the subsequent prosecutions, noting that Montoneros and other leftist revolutionaries remained protected from arrest. (Kirchner was close to several ex-Montoneros, as were other members of his administration.) Meanwhile, in a more surprising move, Argentine officials asked Spanish authorities to detain former president Isabel Perón for human rights investigations. She has been largely perceived to have had no control over the government when she was president from 1974 to 1976, and she has denied any knowledge of the activities under investigation. By mid December 2007, the former commander of the Army, Cristino Nicolaides, received 25 years in prison. Another seven members of the same battalion received between 20 and 25 years in prison for kidnapping and torture during the "dirty war."

President Néstor Kirchner left office with a high approval rating, Argentines having given him credit for helping the country recover from the economic crisis in 2001. His popularity allowed him to rule in part by decree in 2006 and 2007, and to push through changes to the makeup of the Supreme Court and Magistrates' Council. It also allowed Kirchner to designate his wife, Cristina Fernández de Kirchner as his successor.

In the run-up to the 2007 presidential election, Guido Alejandro Antonini Wilson, a businessman holding joint U.S.-Venezuelan citizenship, arrived in Buenos Aires in August with $800,000 in his suitcase. By the time his trip was made public, Antonini had already returned to Miami, Florida, where he cooperated with U.S. authorities by implicating those who had ordered him to deliver the funds. According to the U.S. Federal Bureau of Investigation (FBI) records, the money was earmarked for Fernández de Kirchner's campaign, a charge denied by the Argentine government

Subsequently, Cristina Fernández de Kirchner, a career politician and prominent senator from Santa Cruz, won easily in the October 2007 presidential balloting. Following his wife's election, former president Kirchner in late January 2008 announced his candidacy for president of the PJ, prompting the Argentine press to question his suddenly expanded financial assets, particularly in real estate. The opposition CC said that it was considering setting up an inquiry on the Kirchners' holdings.

Soaring energy and commodity prices pushed inflation upward in 2008, presenting a major challenge to the new Fernández de Kirchner government. The president's initiative to raise taxes on agricultural exports in an effort to increase the domestic food supply and hold down prices was met with universal opposition by agricultural interests. Four months of massive protests occurred throughout the country, blocking more than 300 roads. Critics argued that the law hurt small producers as well as big agribusinesses, while the president retorted that the farmers were "greedy" and trying to "keep food from the tables of the poor." Following the departure of the independent economy minister, Martín Lousteau, the legislature rejected the president's export tax plan on July 17, after a tied vote on the bill was dramatically broken by her erstwhile ally, Vice President Julio César Cleto COBOS (see Political parties, below). The failure of the legislation was viewed as a significant check on the influence of Fernández de Kirchner, and observers predicted she would labor to rule by consensus without the support enjoyed by her predecessor and husband. On July 23, days after the defeat, cabinet chief Alberto Fernández stepped down and was replaced by the 36-year-old mayor of Tigre, Sergio MASSA. President Fernández de Kirchner's continuing disputes with the agricultural sector prompted a number of legislators, primarily from agricultural provinces, to leave the pro-government coalition though they did not abandon their party affiliations.

Meanwhile, concern grew among investors in 2008 over the poor quality of official economic statistics and the government's earlier decision to extend the "economic emergency" law of 2002, which gave the government the right to freeze tariffs on utilities and to renegotiate privatization agreements. Labor leaders accused the government of failing to bargain with them in good faith by relying on the allegedly faulty data in determining inflation-adjusted raises.

Public unrest grew in late 2008, following the release of 20 naval officers who had been held for more than two years awaiting trial for "dirty war" crimes. Their release was quickly suspended. Around the same time, Gen. Jorge Rafael Videla, the former military junta leader, was transferred from house arrest to prison.

The global economic crisis, which spread throughout the world in late 2008, did not spare Argentina. Conditions were exacerbated by a severe drought that greatly reduced wheat, corn, and cattle output. President Fernández de Kirchner sought to cushion the impact of both crises by increasing government spending through fiscal stimulus packages; a $3.5 billion package was approved in December 2008. Subsequently, the government, with the approval of congress, nationalized pension funds of $25 billion in an effort to stimulate the construction and real estate sectors and, according to President Fernández de Kirchner, to protect workers' pensions from the global financial crisis. Meanwhile, critics claimed that the move only took money away from workers.

In March 2009, arguing that the severity of the economic crisis did not allow for a protracted campaign, President Fernández de Kirchner in a surprise announcement asked the congress to move the October legislative elections up to June 28, a move that had been initiated by the mayor of Buenos Aires in an effort, he said, to increase transparency and democratic quality. Following congressional approval of the new date, critics, mainly Peronists, charged that the earlier election date was designed to deny the opposition time to consolidate alliances, and if the balloting were held later, the downturn in the economy might be significant enough to erode some of the president's support and possibly result in an opposition majority in the congress. As the elections approached, candidates began making a central issue of escalating urban crime, primarily related to the drug trade, with an increasing number of violent robberies and homicides prompting a series of public protests in Buenos Aires. In response, municipal officials and opposition leaders proposed tougher measures, such as security cameras, increased police presence, and walls between neighborhoods. Though the central government subsequently deployed more police to crime-ridden Buenos Aires neighborhoods, the number of police killings increased. The opposition, meanwhile, criticized the president for claiming that the media had exaggerated the problem, and they disputed government statistics showing only modest increases in crime. Meanwhile, security and crime became the signature issues of Francisco de NARVÁEZ, a wealthy businessman and Republican Proposal (PRO) Peronist challenger to former president Kirchner, who was seeking a chamber seat in the 2009 legislative election.

In the run-up to the 2009 elections, accusations of political malfeasance marked the increasingly acrimonious campaign. Opposition candidates were judicially disqualified for not having met the two-year residency requirements, but were unable to get former president Kirchner's candidacy disqualified for the same reason. Just weeks before the poll, a judge called on opposition candidate Narváez to testify in a drug trafficking case, citing a mobile phone in Narváez's name from which calls were allegedly made to an incarcerated drug kingpin. The candidate denied the charges and accused the judge of being under the government's political influence. Observers, meanwhile, described the election as a referendum on the left-leaning government and its efforts to exert greater control over the economy, according to the Associated Press.

POLITICAL PARTIES

A ban on political activity, imposed by the military on its return to power in March 1976, was formally lifted by President Bignone at his inauguration on July 1, 1982, and more than 300 national and regional groups participated in the general election of October 30, 1983. However, two formations, the UCR and the Justicialist Liberation Front

(Peronist) shared 92 percent of the vote. At the legislative balloting of November 3, 1985, the combined vote share of the UCR and Peronists dropped to 77 percent, with "orthodox" and "renewing" factions of the latter (alone or in alliance with smaller parties) presenting separate lists in most districts. At the midterm lower house poll of September 6, 1987, the two major groups drew more than 79 percent of the vote, although the UCR slipped from majority to plurality status by retaining only 117 of 254 seats. The combined vote of the two parties in the presidential balloting of May 14, 1989, was a little more than 84 percent, with the Peronists outpolling the UCR in 23 of 24 electoral districts. (The UCR has been affiliated with the Socialist International, the world body of socialist parties, since 1996.)

On August 3, 1997, the two main opposition parties (the UCR and Frepaso, below) announced an Alliance for Work, Justice, and Education (*Alianza por Trabajo, Justicia y Educación*—ATJE) for the October legislative poll and the 1999 presidential balloting. Although the ATJE was received with varying degrees of enthusiasm by provincial leaders, it outpolled the Peronists by nearly 10 percent in the 1997 election, depriving the latter of their legislative majority. In addition to winning the presidency in 1999, the ATJE secured a near majority of lower house seats with the absence of upper house balloting, leaving PJ control of the Senate undisturbed. Since then, however, the Peronists have been dominant, particularly the Victory Front (FPV), the "*kirchenismo*" wing founded in 2003 to sustain the presidential candidacy of Néstor Kirchner, which also attracted the support of the "K Radicals"—those UCR members who supported Fernández de Kirchner in the 2007 presidential elections. The former governor of Mendoza, Julio César Cleto COBOS, one of five UCR-affiliated governors who declared their support for Kirchner, ran in the ticket with Fernández de Kirchner under "UC for K-Victory Front."

Cobos, together with four other governors, was subsequently expelled from the UCR, though the party reversed itself in early 2009 and left the door open for Cobos' return.

Federal Parties with Legislative Seats as of January 2008:

Justicialist Party (*Partido Justicialista*—PJ). What was formerly the Justicialist Nationalist Movement (*Movimiento Nacionalista Justicialista*—MNJ) grew out of the extreme nationalist Peronist (also known as *laborista*) movement led by General Juan Perón from 1946 to 1955. Formally dissolved after its leader went into exile, the Peronists regrouped, in alliance with a number of smaller parties, as the Justicialist Liberation Front (*Frente Justicialista de Liberación*—Frejuli) before the 1973 election. Frejuli's victorious candidate, Héctor Cámpora, subsequently resigned to permit the reelection of Perón, who had returned in 1972. The movement's nominal leader, Isabel Perón, who was ousted as her husband's successor in 1976 and confined to prison and house arrest for five years thereafter, was permitted to go into exile in July 1981.

The Peronists (as they are still popularly known) have experienced a number of internal cleavages, including one occasioned by the *corrientes renovadoras* ("current of renewal"), which was initially launched by a group of moderate trade unionists and students calling for a more democratic party structure.

Senator Vicente Saadi resigned as the first PJ vice president following the 1985 legislative election, reportedly because of the movement's poor showing. In December 1985 the *renovadores* appointed a leadership of their own, headed by Antonio CAFIERO, Carlos GROSSO, and Carlos Saúl Menem. However, a cleavage subsequently developed within the dissident troika, Cafiero boycotting a *renovador* congress in Tucumán, while Grosso withdrew from the meeting because of a dispute over the timing of internal party elections.

Following the party's relatively poor showing in the 1987 election, Senator Saadi resigned as PJ president, paving the way for a "unity slate" that awarded the group's presidency and vice presidency to Cafiero and Menem, respectively. Menem defeated Cafiero as the party's 1989 standard-bearer at a PJ presidential primary on July 9, 1988, and led the party, campaigning with minor party allies as the Justicialist Front of Popular Unity (*Frente Justicialista de Unidad Popular*—Frejupo), to a conclusive victory in the nationwide balloting of May 14, 1989.

The party contested the partial legislative elections of 1991, 1993, and 1995 under the *Partido Justicialista* rubric, although the total number of "*Justicialista*" seats resulting from each poll included seats held by affiliated Peronist groups. In 1995 President Menem secured reelection to a foreshortened term of four years on a 49.8 percent vote share while the PJ won its first absolute majority in the Chamber of Deputies. In 1997 the party's lower house representation was reduced to 118 of 257 seats. With Menem ineligible to run for a third term, the party lost the presidency in 1999 and was reduced to second place in the Chamber of Deputies with 110 seats. It recovered its majority in both houses on October 14, 2001, despite its leader's arrest, four months earlier, on charges of UN arms embargo violations.

Menem secured a plurality in the 2003 presidential poll, but he withdrew from a runoff when it became apparent that he could not defeat Néstor Kirchner in a two-man race. Late in the year, after taking up residence in Chile, Menem was charged with tax fraud; however, the case was dismissed in May 2004. Menem returned to Argentina in December 2004, secured election to the Senate on a "best loser" basis in October 2005, and vowed to contest the 2007 presidential election.

Before the 2005 congressional balloting, the PJ split into two principal factions, a **Victory Front** (*Frente para la Victoria*—FPV), launched by President Kirchner, and a **Federal Peronist** (*Peronismo Federal*—PF) grouping headed by former president Duhalde. In addition, former presidents Menem and Rodríguez Saá campaigned as leaders of a distinctly minor **Justicialist Loyalty and Dignity** (*Lealtad y Dignidad Justicialista*—LDJ) faction. Several members of the UCR formed a coalition with the FPV for the 2007 elections. As part of the FPV electoral ballot, the PJ secured 42 Senate and 129 Chamber seats after the election, a decisive majority in both houses. The president received 44.9 percent of the votes.

Former president Néstor Kirchner, Buenos Aires governor Daniel SCIOLI, and cabinet chief Sergio MASSA, the leaders of the PJ list of candidates in the June 2009 legislative elections, were widely accused of developing a strategy in which they would use their popularity and name-recognition to win seats for the party, then step down and assume their former positions, allowing lesser-known replacements to succeed them and maintain a strong Peronist presence in the legislature.

Leaders: Cristina Fernández de KIRCHNER (President of the Republic, PJ-FPV), Néstor Carlos KIRCHNER (Former President of the Republic, PJ-FPV), Eduardo Alberto DUHALDE (Former President of the Republic, PF), Carlos Saúl MENEM Former President of the Republic, LDJ), and Adolfo RODRÍGUEZ Saá (Former President of the Republic, LDJ).

Civic Coalition (*Coalición Cívica*—CC). The CC, a coalition of political parties, nongovernment organizations, and public personalities, was created on April 11, 2007, by Elisa Carrió. The coalition includes the ARI, Union for Everybody (*Unión por Todos*—UPT), some members of the Socialist Party, and the UCR. The CC secured 2 seats in the upper house and 18 in the lower house.

Leaders: Elisa CARRIÓ (2000, 2003, and 2007 presidential candidate and President of the Civic Coalition), Patricia BULLRICH (President of Union for Everybody), Margarita STOLBIZER

Radical Civic Union (*Unión Cívica Radical*—UCR). The UCR, whose history dates from the late 19th century, represents the moderate left in Argentine politics. In the period following the deposition of Juan Perón, the party split into two factions, the People's Radical Party (*Unión Cívica Radical del Pueblo*—UCRP) and the Intransigent Radical Party (*Unión Cívica Radical Intransigente*—UCRI), led by former presidents Arturo ILLÍA and Arturo FRONDIZI, respectively. The UCR reemerged following the legalization of parties in 1971 and remained relatively unified during the 1973 presidential candidacy of Dr. Ricardo BALBÍN but suffered a number of internal cleavages thereafter. Balbín was instrumental in organizing the 1981 five-party alignment to press for a return to civilian rule but died in September, leaving the party without a unified leadership. Largely because of the personal popularity of its presidential candidate, Raúl Alfonsín, the party led the 1983 balloting with 51.8 percent of the vote, winning, in addition to the presidency, a majority in the Chamber of Deputies. Subsequently, internal dissention diminished, the *balbinista* faction concluding a late 1984 alliance with left-leaning elements, while the long-standing policy of incompatibility between government and party roles was abandoned with the designation of President Alfonsín as ex officio party leader. In early 1986, as the issue of presidential succession loomed, a new rivalry emerged between former labor minister Juan Manuel Casella, the apparent *alfonsinista* front-runner, and the influential governor of Córdoba province, Eduardo Angeloz, with the latter being designated the UCR candidate at internal party balloting in July 1988, but losing to the MNJ's Carlos Menem in May 1989.

In October 1991, following the poor showing of candidates he had endorsed for recent provincial elections, Alfonsín submitted his resignation as party president, while announcing the formation of an internal faction, the Movement for Social Democracy (*Movimiento por la Democracia Social*—MDS), devoted to defending traditional UCR "social-democratic" principles. He was reelected party leader by an overwhelming margin in November 1993.

In the 1995 presidential poll, UCR nominee Horatio MASSACESSI placed a distant third, with a 17.1 percent vote share; in the legislative balloting the party retained second rank, though its representation fell from 83 to 69 seats. Alfonsín again resigned on September 27, 1995, and was replaced on November 17 by Rodolfo TERRANGO.

For the legislative election of October 26, 1997, an alliance with a left-of-center electoral coalition styled the Front for a Country in Solidarity (*Frente del País Solidario*—Frepaso) yielded 46 of 127 contested seats, while the UCR secured 12 seats running separately. The alliance candidate, Fernando De La Rúa, won the presidency in 1999, but he resigned in December 2001 because of the economic crisis. The UCR's share of the presidential vote plummeted to 2.3 percent in 2003. It remained the second-ranked congressional party after the 2005 balloting, albeit with only 39 of 257 lower house seats.

The centralization of power in the hands of president Kirchner, his increased ability to control governors, and his progressive politics have made him very popular among so-called "K Radicals" in the UCR recently. Others in the party preferred either supporting Roberto Lavagna (apparently still formally a member of the PJ) in the 2007 presidential balloting or presenting a candidate from the UCR ranks. After considerable negotiation, it was determined that Lavagna would run as a candidate of the UCR in an alliance with Just Society Peronists (Duhalde). Within the UCR, Lavagna had strong support from former president Alfonsín. The UCR decided not to run a candidate for president and ultimately coalesced behind Roberto Lavagna, who received 16.9 percent of the votes. The party lost 5 seats in the Senate and 16 in the Chamber of Deputies, leaving it with 8 senators and 24 deputies in the lower house.

The UCR expelled former governor and newly inaugurated vice president Cobos and four other governors who supported Kirchner in the elections. On March 15, 2008, under the banner of "K Radicals" Cobos urged like-minded politicians to join an Official National Concertation (*Concertación Nacional Oficial*) and to persuade the UCR leadership not to expel them, but to support formation of a new Radicals for Concertation grouping. Cobos was reinstated by the UCR in early 2009, reportedly in response to a dying wish from former president Raúl Alfonsín, who had died in March.

The UCR and CC struck an agreement in late April to form a partial coalition, presenting a unified list of candidates for the June 2009 legislative elections in 11 provinces.

Leaders: Angel ROZAS, Mario LOSADA (Former President of the Party), Leopoldo Raúl Guido MOREAU (2003 presidential candidate).

Alternative for a Republic of Equals (*Alternativa por una República de Iguales*—ARI). The ARI was organized in mid-2000 by the left-wing UCR defector, Elisa Carrió. Affiliating with the new formation, which secured 1 Senate and 31 Chamber seats in October 2001, was the Democratic Socialist Party (*Partido Socialista Democrático*—PSD), Carrió ran fourth in the 2003 presidential election, with a 14.2 percent vote share and second in the 2007 presidential election, with a 23.0 percent vote share.

The ARI was decimated in the 2003 congressional poll but recovered marginally to win 8 lower house seats in 2005. In 2007 the ARI formed a coalition with the PS (below). Some members ran under ARI, securing three Senate and nine Chamber seats.

Leader: Elisa CARRIÓ (2000, 2003, and 2007 presidential candidate and President of the Party)

Union for Everybody (*Unión por Todos*—UPT) was founded in 2002 by Patricia Bullrich, a former minister who held the social security portfolio in 2000 and the labor portfolio in 2001. The party joined the CC for the 2007 election.

Leader: Patricia BULLRICH (President).

Socialist Party (*Partido Socialista*—PS). The PS was launched in 2003 by merger of the PSD (under ARI, above) and the Popular Socialist Party (*Partido Socialista Popular*—PSP), which had been reorganized as the Argentine affiliate of Socialist International. Rubén Héctor Guistinian ran in the ticket with Elisa Carrió in 2007, while the PS presented a separate, independent ballot for the legislative polls that year, securing 10 seats in the Chamber of Deputies. In Buenos Aires province only, the PS agreed to participate in an opposition coalition, along with CC and UCR, to present candidates for the June 2009 legislative elections.

Leaders: Rubén Héctor GIUSTINIANI (PSP), Hermes Juan BINNER.

Republican Proposal (*Propuesta Republicana*—PRO). A center-right group based in Buenos Aires, PRO was launched before the 2005 election by businessman Mauricio Macri. It was able to capitalize on a center-left cleavage between the FPV and ARI to win 34 percent of the vote in the federal capital. In the 2007 balloting, Macri was elected mayor of Buenos Aires.

Ricardo López Murp, the party's candidate for president in the 2007 election, received less than a 2 percent vote share, while the party lost 2 of its 11 Chamber seats in that year's legislative balloting.

The party was mounting a well-funded campaign to gain seats in the June 2009 legislative elections, with millionaire businessman Francisco De Narváez, a dissident Peronist leading the list of candidates for the Chamber of Deputies in a loose coalition between the PRO and several dissident Peronist groups.

Leader: Mauricio MACRI.

Recreate for Growth Party (*Partido para Recrear el Crecimiento*—RECREAR). RECREAR is a conservative formation that contested the 2003 election in an alliance with a number of provincial parties styled the *Movimiento Federal para Recrear el Crecimiento*—MFRC (Federal Movement to Recreate Growth) that continued into the 2005 poll. The movement's leader, Ricardo López Murphy, formerly a right-wing member of the UCR, placed third in the 2003 presidential balloting. RECREAR entered a political alliance with PRO ahead of the 2007 polls.

Leaders: Ricardo López MURPHY (President), Ricardo URQUIZA (Secretary).

Action for the Republic–New Direction (*Acción por la República–Nueva Dirección*—AR-ND). The AR-ND was formed in 1997 as an electoral alliance of the AR, which had been launched by former economic minister Domingo Cavallo in support of his bid for a congressional seat, and the ND, a Buenos Aires–based party founded in 1996. The grouping won 9 lower house seats in 1997 and 12 in 1999, only one of which it retained in 2005.

Leaders: Armando Caro FIGUEROA (AR), Gustavo BÉLIZ (ND), Domingo CAVALLO (1999 presidential candidate).

Republican Force (*Fuerza Republicana*—FR). The FR was organized before the 1989 national balloting by a retired army general, Antonio Domingo Bussi, who hoped to covert the formation into "a great national party" before the expiration of Carlos Menem's term in 1995. The party won three lower house seats from the northwestern province of Tucumán in October 1993 and added a fourth in May 1995. In July 1995 Bussi won the Tucumán governorship, but he was suspended in April 1998 when confronted with impeachment proceedings because of an undeclared foreign bank account. The vote against removal subsequently fell short, and Bussi was reinstated. The party's lower house representation was reduced to two in 1997, with the same number (elected in 2003) remaining in 2005. The party held two senate seats in 2008.

Leader: Gen. (Ret.) Antonio Domingo BUSSI (Former Governor of Tucumán).

Minor and Regional Parties with Legislative Seats as of January 2008:

Minor and regional groups winning congressional representation in 2007 included **Buenos Aires for Everybody in Southern Project** (*Buenos Aires Para Todos en Proyecto Sur*—BATPS), 1 seat; the Buenos Aires–based **Blue and White Union** (*Unión Celeste y Blanca*—UCB), 4 seats; the **Civic Front for Santiago** (*Frente Cívico por Santiago*—FCS), 6 seats; the Catamarca-based **Civic and Social Front** (*Frente Cívico y Social*—FCS), 3 seats; the Rio Negro-based **Concertation for the Desarrollo** (*Alianza Concertación para El Desarrollo*—ACD), 1 seat; the **Concordia Renewal Front**, (*Frente Renovador de la Concordia*—FRC), 1 seat; the **Córdoba Union Alliance** (*Alianza Unión Córdoba*—AUC), 1 seat; the **Democratic Mendoza** (*Demócrata Mendoza*—DM), 1 seat; the Buenos Aires city–based **Dialogue for**

Buenos Aires (*Diálogo por Buenos Aires*—DPBA), 1 seat; Entre Ríos–based **Entrerian Concertation** (*Concertación Entrerriana*—CE), 1 seat: the Buenos Aires province–based **Federalist Unity** (*Unidad Federalista*—UF) 2 seats; the Catamarca-based **For the Truth** (*Por la Verdad*—PLV), 1 seat; the Corrientes–based **Front for Everybody** (*Frente de Todos*—FT), 3 seats; the Buenos Aires–based **Front for Citizens' Rights** (*Frente por los Derechos Ciudadanos*), 1 seat; the Buenos Aires–based **Independent Movement** (*Movimiento Independiente*—MI), 1 seat; the **Justice, Union and Liberty Front** (*Frente Justicia, Unión y Libertad*—FJUL), 6 seats; **Liberal Party of Corrientes** (*Partido Liberal de Corrientes*—PLC), 1 seat; the Córdoba-based **Memory and Democracy** (*Memoria y Democracia*—MD), 1 seat; the Buenos Aires–based **National Justicialist** (*Justicialista Nacional*—JN), 1 seat; the Corrientes-based **New Party**, 1 seat; the Córdoba-based **New Front**, 1 seat; the Córdoba-based **New Party against Corruption, for Honesty and Transparency** (*Partido Nuevo contra la Corrupción, por la Honestidad y la Transparencia*—PNCHT), 2 seats; the Buenos Aires–based **National Syndicalist** (*Nacional Sindical*—NS), 1 seat; the **Neuquén Popular Movement** (*Movimiento Popular Neuquino*—MPN), 4 seats; the Misiones-based **Peronist Dignity** (*Dignidad Peronista*—DP), 1 seat; the Buenos Aires–based **Peronist Guard** (*Guardia Peronista*—GP), 1 seat; the San-Luis–based **Production and Labor Front** (*Frente Producción y Trabajo*—FPT), 1 seat; the Buenos Aires–based **Popular and Social Encounter** (*Encuentro Popular y Social*—EPS), 4; the Buenos Aires–based **Recreate for Growth** (*Recrear Para el Crecimiento*—RPC), 2 seats; the **Salta Renewal** (*Renovador de Salta*—SR), 3 seats; the Buenos Aires city–based **Social Encounter Network** (*Red de Encuentro Social*—RES), 4 seats; the **Federal Consensus** (*Consenso Federal*—CF), 4 seats; the **Justicialist Republican Party** (*Justicialista Republicano*—JR), 1 seat.

Other Parties:

A number of additional parties have been active in recent years, but the current status of most is unclear. See earlier editions of the *Handbook* for listings.

LEGISLATURE

Argentina's bicameral **National Congress** (*Congreso Nacional*) was dissolved in March 1976 and reconstituted after the election of October 30, 1983.

Senate (*Senado*). Before adoption of the 1994 constitution, the upper house consisted of 2 senators elected for nine-year terms by each of the 23 provincial legislatures, plus 2 from the federal district named by an electoral college, the body being replenished by thirds every three years. The 1994 basic law increased the membership to 72 (3 from each of the 23 provinces and 3 from the federal district of Buenos Aires.) Since 2001, one-third of the seats have been renewed every two years for six-year terms.

Elections were held on October 28, 2007. Seats were distributed as follows: the Justicialist Party—Victory Front and its allies, 42 seats; the Civic Coalition, 2; the Radical Civic Union, 7; the Civic and Social Front, 2; the Civic Front for Santiago, 2; the Concordia Renewal Front, 2; the Republican Force, 2; the Union for a Republic of Equals, 2; Concertation for the Desarollo, 1; Cordoba Union Alliance, 1; Federalist Unity, 1; Front for Everybody, 1; Movement for a Viable Santiago, 1; Neuquén New Front, 1; New Party, 1; Popular Movement, 1; Production and Labor Front, 1; Salta Renewal, 1; Socialist Party, 1.

Elections for one-third of the Senate were scheduled for June 28, 2009.

President: Julio César Cleto COBOS.

Chamber of Deputies (*Cámara de Diputados*). The lower house currently consists of 257 deputies, directly elected for four years, with approximately one-half reelected every two years.

Parliamentary balloting occurred on October 28, 2007. The distribution of seats was as follows: the Justicialist Party—Victory Front and its allies, 131 seats; the Civic Coalition, 18; the Radical Civic Union, 24; the Socialist Party, 10; the Alternative for a Republic of Equals, 9; Republican Proposal, 9; Civic Front for Santiago, 6; Of the Concertation, 6; Justice, Unity, and Liberty Front, 6; Popular and Social Encounter, 6; Blue and White Union, 4; Neuquén Popular Movement, 3; Civic and Social Front, 2; Front for Everybody, 2; New Party against Corruption, for Honesty and Transparency, 2; Salta Renewal, 2; Buenos Aires in the Southern Project, 1; Democratic Mendoza, 1; Dialogue for Buenos Aires, 1; Entrerian Concertation, 1; Federalist Unity, 1; For the Truth; 1; Front for Citizens Rights, 1; Justicialist Republican Party, 1; Independent Movement, 1; Liberal Party of Corrientes, 1; Memory and Democracy, 1; National Justicialist, 1; National Syndicalist, 1; Peronist Dignity, 1; Peronist Guard, 1; Production and Labor Front, 1; the Recreate for Growth Party, 1. Realignments have made assessments of party strength difficult.

Elections for one-half of the Chamber were scheduled for June 28, 2009.

President: Eduardo FELLNER.

CABINET

[as of June 1, 2009]

President	Cristina Fernández de Kirchner [f]
Vice President	Julio César Cleto Cobos (UCR)
Chief of Cabinet	Sergio Massa (PJ)
Ministers	
Defense	Nilda Garré [f]
Economy and Public Finance	Carlos Rafael Fernández (PJ)
Education	Juan Carlos Tedesco (PJ)
Federal Planning and Public Investment	Julio Miguel de Vido (PJ)
Foreign Relations, International Trade, and Worship	Jorge Enrique Taiana
Interior	Aníbal Florencio Randazzo (PJ)
Justice, Security, and Human Rights	Aníbal Domingo Fernández (PJ)
Labor, Employment, and Human Resources	Carlos Alfonso Tomada (PJ)
Production	Débora Giorgi (PJ) [f]
Public Health	Graciela Ocaña [f]
Social Development and Environment	Alicia Kirchner (PJ) [f]
Science and Technology	Lino Barañao (PJ)
Secretaries	
Secretary General of the Presidency	Oscar Parrilli (PJ)
Secretary of State Intelligence	Hector Icazuriaga (PJ)
Legal and Technical Secretary	Carlos Alberto Zannini (PJ)
Military House (Casa Militar)	Col. Alejandro Guillermo Graham
Secretary of Culture	José Nun (PJ)
Secretary of Tourism	Carlos Enrique Meyer (PJ)
Secretary of Prevention of Drug Addiction and Battle against Drug-Trafficking	José Ramón Granero (PJ)
Secretary of Communication	Enrique Raúl Albistur (PJ)
Secretary of Environment and Sustainable Development	Homero Biblioni (PJ)

[f] = female

COMMUNICATIONS

The impact of Argentina's traditionally influential news media has been substantially reduced in recent years. There were numerous newspaper closings during the Peronist revival, while official censorship and personal attacks on journalists further inhibited the media before the restoration of civilian rule in 1983. Before the October 1993 legislative election, attacks on journalists had become increasingly prevalent, while economic difficulties had drastically curtailed the circulation of virtually all leading papers, except for *Clarín,* which, having diversified into radio and television, had emerged as the country's foremost media power. The Kirchners have maintained a strained relationship with

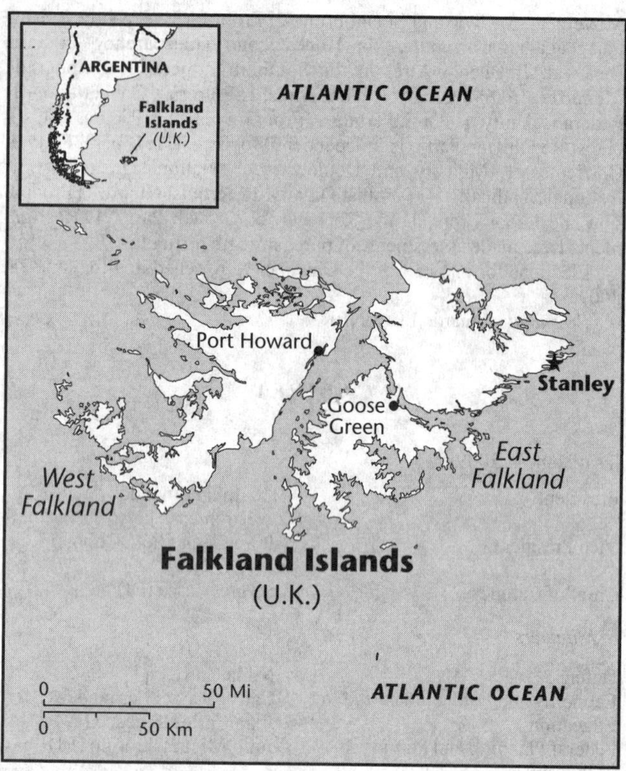

Argentina's media, which they reportedly view as being aligned with the opposition. The media's principal complaints have been difficulties in accessing information and the government's withholding of official advertisements from critical media outlets.

Press. Unless otherwise noted, the following are Spanish-language dailies published in Buenos Aires: *Clarín* (700,000 daily, 1,000,000 Sunday), reportedly the world's largest-selling Spanish-language paper; *La Nación* (630,000 daily, 835,000 Sunday), founded 1870; *Crónica* (330,000 daily, 450,000 Sunday); *Página 12* (280,000), a highly regarded investigative paper launched in 1987; *Diario Popular* (140,000); *El Cronista Comercial* (63,000); *La Razón* (60,000); *La Prensa* (50,000), founded 1869; *Buenos Aires Herald* (22,500), in English.

News agencies. The domestic agencies include *Diarios y Noticias* (DyN), *Noticias Argentinas* (NA), and the official *Agencia TELAM.* There are also a number of foreign agencies with bureaus in Buenos Aires.

Broadcasting and computing. Broadcasting is supervised by the *Secretaría de Communicaciones* and the *Comité Federal de Radiodifusión* (Comfer). Nearly two-thirds of the more than 120 radio stations and 29 of the 44 television stations are privately owned. *Radio Nacional* is an official government service providing local, national, and international programming. Government-owned commercial radio and television stations are grouped under the *Dirección General de Radio y Televisión,* while most privately owned stations belong to the *Asociación Radiodifusoras Privadas Argentinas* (ARPA) and the *Asociación de Teleradiodifusoras Argentinas* (ATA). As of 2008 there were 281.1 Internet users per 1,000 inhabitants.

INTERGOVERNMENTAL REPRESENTATION

Ambassador to the U.S.: Hécto Marcos TIMERMAN.

U.S. Ambassador to Argentina: Vilma S. MARTÍNEZ.

Permanent Representative to the UN: Jorge ARGÜELLO.

IGO Memberships (Non-UN): AfDB, ALADI, BCIE, BIS, CAN, G-20, IADB, Interpol, IOM, Mercosur, OAS, OPANAL, PCA, SELA, UNASUR, WCO, WTO.

CONTESTED TERRITORY

Falkland Islands (*Islas Malvinas*). First sighted by an English vessel in the late 17th century and named after the incumbent treasurer of the Royal Navy, the Falkland Islands were later styled Les Malouines (from which the Spanish *Las Malvinas* is derived) by a group of French settlers who transferred their rights to Spain in 1766. A British settlement, recognized by Spain in 1771, was withdrawn in 1774, the islands being uninhabited at the time of Argentine independence in 1816. The new government in Buenos Aires claimed the territory by right of colonial succession in 1820, although a group of its nationals were forcibly expelled in 1832, before a reaffirmation of British sovereignty in 1833. Argentine claims to the smaller South Georgia and South Sandwich islands, several hundred miles to the southeast, were not formally advanced until 1927 and 1948, respectively. The question of the legal status of the territories, collectively encompassing about 6,000 square miles (16,058 sq. km.), became the subject of extensive negotiations initiated under UN auspices in 1966 and extending to early 1982. The British claim is based on continuous occupation since 1833 and the manifest sentiment of the 2,900 inhabitants (primarily sheepherders domiciled on East and West Falkland) to remain British subjects.

The immediate precipitant of the 1982 conflict was the arrival in South Georgia on March 19 of a group of workers to dismantle an old whaling station, in the course of which the Argentine flag was raised. Following a British protest to the UN Security Council, Argentinian troops landed on the Falklands on April 2 and quickly overcame resistance by a token force of Royal Marines. South Georgia and South Sandwich were seized on April 3. Two days later the lead ships of a British armada sailed from Portsmouth, England, participating in the recovery of South Georgia on April 25 and 26. On May 21 about 5,000 British troops began landing at San Carlos Bay on the northwestern coast of East Falkland, initiating an operation that culminated in the surrender of the main Argentine force in Stanley on June 14. Overall, the campaign cost 254 British and 750 Argentinian lives and heavy material losses, including that of Argentina's only heavy cruiser, the *General Belgrano*, and, on the British side, of two destroyers and two frigates. Subsequently, Argentina and 19 other Latin American countries submitted the Falkland issue to the UN General Assembly, although no de jure resolution of the sovereignty issue has yet been forthcoming.

During 1985 President Alfonsín repeatedly expressed alarm at the construction of an airport (approximately the size of that at Point Salines in Grenada) on Mount Pleasant and named as his government's priority "the demilitarization of the South Atlantic." A more serious problem arose in 1986 with a British announcement in late October that it would establish a 200-mile "exclusive economic zone," measured from the shore of the islands, as of February 1, 1987, thereby overlapping a 200-mile zone previously claimed by Argentina off its continental mainland. However, the effect of the action was subsequently diluted by a British foreign ministry declaration that it would police the new zone (impinging largely on fishing) only up to the limit of the previously established 150-mile Falkland Islands Interim Conservation and Management Zone (FICZ), measured from the center of the islands. As part of the agreement concluded in Madrid in February 1990, Britain also yielded (save for fishing) on the 150-mile zone, allowing Argentine ships and planes to approach within 50 and 75 miles, respectively, of the islands without prior permission. (For additional details, see United Kingdom: Related Territories.)

In April 1990 the Argentine Congress, in what was termed a "purely symbolic act," approved the inclusion of the Falklands in the (then) national territory of Tierra del Fuego. Subsequently, a series of "technical" discussions were held between Argentine and British representatives to prevent overfishing in the waters surrounding the islands. The Falklanders protested their exclusion from the talks, which yielded an agreement in December on a third-party fishing ban in the portion of the 200-mile economic zone that did not overlap the corresponding Argentine limit.

Argentina and Britain in September 1991 reached new accords that liberalized military restrictions imposed by Britain in the aftermath of the 1982 conflict; Argentine authorities insisted, however, that the action should not be construed as implying relinquishment of their country's claim to the islands. Thus in early January 1992 President Menem proposed that the jurisdictional conflict be settled through international arbitration, in much the same manner as the earlier border dispute with Chile. However, despite an assertion in May 1993 that recovery of the islands remained a "strategic" part of Argentina's foreign policy, he appeared unwilling to press the matter, lest it reverse the recent improvement in relations with London.

Following the Argentine reaffirmation of sovereignty over the Falklands in its 1994 constitution, Britain began patrolling the nonoverlapping portion of the "gap" between the 150- and 200-mile zones. British authorities responded to Argentine complaints that the new policy was an act of "reprisal" for the constitutional claim by insisting that they were simply attempting to deny unlicensed fishing vessels a staging area for intrusion into British- and Argentine-controlled areas.

During 1995 the question of oil rights supplanted that of fishing. On September 27, following a meeting between Argentine and British representatives in Madrid, the two countries signed an agreement in New York on the extraction of oil in waters surrounding the archipelago. Under the accord, Britain will earn two-thirds and Argentina one-third of the royalties from drilling east of the islands, while the two will share equally in the yield from extraction off the Argentine coast in the west. UCR legislators immediately charged that the Menem government had "ceded a measure of sovereignty" by agreeing to the lower share in the east, while the government insisted that its participation implied recognition of the Argentinian claim.

In May 1996 Foreign Minister Guido DI TELLA announced that Argentina would "never consent" to the Falklands becoming an independent state. The declaration came after Britain and the Falkland Island Council had urged the UN Special Committee on Decolonization to adopt a resolution on self-determination for the territory (an action that the UN body has been unwilling to pursue). In mid-1997 the committee cited its long-standing opposition to the "colonial situation" in the islands by reissuing an appeal to the two governments to resolve the dispute by peaceful negotiations.

In July 1999 Britain agreed to lift restrictions on travel by Argentine citizens to the islands and to reestablish Chilean flights to the mainland, which had been suspended by Santiago following the March detention in London of its former president Augusto Pinochet. In a further sign of improved relations, the British and Argentine navies conducted in November their first joint naval exercise since the 1982 war.

On July 19, 2000, the European Court of Human Rights in Strasbourg, France, dismissed as too late a lawsuit by Argentinians seeking compensation from Britain for the deaths of relatives killed when British forces sank the cruiser *General Belgrano.* Lawyers for the plaintiffs stated that they would pursue the matter at the World Court in The Hague, The Netherlands. As part of the suit, the plaintiffs had sought the extradition of former British prime minister Margaret Thatcher to stand trial for "aggravated homicide and war crimes." Subsequently, in a mark of improved relations, Argentina and Britain signed an agreement in early 2001 that permitted Argentinian planes to fly to the islands for the first time in nearly two decades.

In April 2004 Argentinian president Kirchner reaffirmed his government's commitment to regaining sovereignty over the islands through "dialogue and peace." The administration in 2005 also criticized the inclusion of the islands in the proposed new European Union (EU) constitution, arguing that the sovereignty question remained unsettled.

During events in 2007 commemorating the 25th anniversary of the 1982 war, Argentinian officials again accused the UK of "illegitimate occupation" of the islands. Perhaps in view of upcoming elections, President Kirchner appeared to adopt a hard line, unilaterally canceling some previous oil exploration agreements with the UK and revoking charter flights from the islands to the mainland. Meanwhile, although the issue of sovereignty remained nonnegotiable, the UK administration called for "constructive ties" in the hope of resolving lingering hostility. Popular opinion in Argentina remained highly supportive of Kirchner's position, although the inhabitants of the islands reportedly continued to evince no opposition to their UK status. (One recent report estimated that the islanders enjoyed an annual GDP per capita of approximately $50,000 [among the highest in the world] based largely on the sale of licenses for fishing and oil exploration.)

ARMENIA

Republic of Armenia
Hayastani Hanrapetoutioun

In October 2009 the governments of Armenia and Turkey signed an agreement calling for the reopening of their border (closed since 1993) and establishment of normal diplomatic relations. The accord also called for an international commission to be established to review archives relating to the deaths of Armenians in 1915 (see Political background and Foreign relations for details). However, the agreement did not address the controversial issue of Nagorno-Karabakh. Parliamentary approval (by no means assured) was required in both countries for the agreement to be implemented.

Political Status: Armenian Republic established on November 29, 1920; joined the Union of Soviet Socialist Republics (USSR) as part of the Transcaucasian Soviet Socialist Republic on December 30, 1922; became a constituent republic of the USSR on December 5, 1936; independence declared September 23, 1991, following national referendum of September 21.

Area: 11,506 sq. mi. (29,800 sq. km.).

Population: 3,210,606 (2001C); 3,225,000 (2008E).

Major Urban Centers (2005E): YEREVAN (1,102,000), Gumayri (formerly Leninakan, 149,000).

Official Language: Armenian.

Monetary Unit: Dram (official rate December 1, 2009: 384.00 drams = $1US).

President: Serzh SARKISIAN (Republican Party of Armenia); directly elected in first round of balloting on February 19, 2008, and inaugurated for a five-year term on April 9 in succession to Robert KOCHARIAN (nonparty).

Prime Minister: Tigran SARKISIAN (Republican Party of Armenia); appointed (as an independent) by President Serzh Sarkisian on April 9, 2008, following Serzh Sarkisian's inauguration as president the same day; formed new government on April 21, 2008. (Serzh Sarkisian [Republican Party of Armenia] had been appointed prime minister by President Kocharian on April 5, 2007, following the death on March 25 of Prime Minister Andranik MARKARIAN [Unity/Republican Party of Armenia].)

THE COUNTRY

The eastern portion of what became (c. 301 AD) the world's earliest Christian state, contemporary Armenia has Georgia, Azerbaijan, Iran, and Turkey as its northern, eastern, southern, and western neighbors, respectively. Its population is more than 93 percent ethnic Armenian, the principal minorities (less than 3 percent each) being Azerbaijanis, Kurds, and Russians. Although more than a third of Armenians reside in the capital, Yerevan, agriculture remains a leading economic activity. Crops include grain, potatoes, sugar beets, grapes, and a variety of other fruits and vegetables. Refined diamonds, crayfish, and brandy are among the major exports, while the technology sector has grown rapidly recently under the influence of Western investment.

Output declined substantially as a result of a massive earthquake in 1988, the onset of conflict with Azerbaijan the following year, and the effects of post-Communist economic restructuring. GDP underwent a 67 percent contraction between 1992 and 1993, and industry was reported to have virtually ceased by early 1993, with an estimated two-thirds of the country's workforce being unemployed. A partial recovery yielded GDP growth of 5 percent in 1994 and 1995, albeit with little tangible improvement in general economic and social conditions. GDP growth surpassed 6 percent in 1996 and 1997, earning Armenia continued support from financial institutions such as the International Monetary Fund (IMF), which had approved its first loan in 1996 to support Armenia's economic reform program, including massive privatization of state enterprises. However, the long-standing

dispute with Azerbaijan over Nagorno-Karabakh continued to cause difficulties. (Armenia has controlled that enclave in Azerbaijan since 1994. See Political background and Foreign relations, below, and the article on Azerbaijan for details.) In addition, widespread poverty, rising unemployment, and a huge trade deficit reportedly fueled discontent over the effects of shifting to a free-market economy, particularly the uneven distribution of wealth. Hope for improvement in part focused on the U.S. plan for an oil pipeline from the Caspian Sea through Armenia to a Turkish port on the Mediterranean, which, if constructed, would mean a windfall in transit fees to Armenia. (Reportedly at Azerbaijan's request, oil pipelines in the region subsequently skirted Armenia.)

GDP grew by an average of 12 percent annually from 2001 to 2005, fueled by an export boom, expanding foreign investment in the food-processing sector, and Armenia's admission to the World Trade Organization (WTO) in 2003. Inflation for the same period averaged less than 3 percent annually. The "remarkable" economic performance was attributed to "prudent" fiscal policy. However, concern continued over the poverty level (33 percent of the population reportedly lived below the poverty line in 2006) and unemployment (officially 10 percent but possibly double that figure in the estimation of some independent observers). In addition, the IMF argued that Armenia would not reach its "full potential" until a resolution was achieved in the dispute over Nagorno-Karabakh, which, among other things, had led Azerbaijan and Turkey to close their borders with Armenia, thereby costing Armenia much-needed market access. A settlement of that conflict was also considered crucial for Armenia to achieve its long-term goal of membership in the European Union (EU), which as of 2005 was additionally demanding immediate and substantial political reform in the face of what was widely judged to be Armenia's poor record regarding genuine democratization, protection of human rights, and press freedom.

Annual GDP growth of 12–14 percent was achieved in 2006 and 2007, as an ongoing boom in the construction and service sectors more than made up for manufacturing stagnancy. Meanwhile, Armenia made little progress in reducing its energy dependency on Russia, while Russian businesses also continued to dominate the nonenergy sector in Armenia, having secured complete or partial ownership of many recently privatized entities.

GDP growth fell to 6.8 percent in 2008 (coming to a complete halt in the fourth quarter) under the influence of the global economic crisis, which, among other things, adversely affected the mining industry and other export sectors. Meanwhile, inflation rose to nearly 9 percent for the year, and unemployment increased substantially. After approving a regular three-year lending agreement in November 2008, the IMF in March 2009 announced additional "anticrisis" lending to assist the government in restoring confidence in the currency and financial system while also increasing social spending.

GOVERNMENT AND POLITICS

Political background. Ruled at various times by Macedonians, Romans, Persians, Byzantines, Mongols, Turks, and Russians, the territory of the present republic was obtained by Russia from Persia in 1828. A western region was controlled (prior to their defeat in World War I) by the Ottoman Turks, who engaged in what Armenians have called a systematic campaign of genocide between 1894 and 1922. (Armenians estimate that 1.5 million people died during the period in question, and they continue to press for international acknowledgment that genocide had indeed taken place. For its part, Turkey has strongly resisted the genocide label, claiming that the loss of life was much less than estimated by Armenians. The issue has received renewed international attention in recent years; the French parliament in January 2001 officially accepted the genocide description, thereby prompting economic retaliation from Turkey.) Under the 1918 Treaty of Brest-Litovsk, Russian Armenia became an independent republic under German auspices before emerging as the core of a revived Greater Armenia under the 1920 Treaty of Sèvres. Shortly thereafter, the Russian component came under Communist control and was designated a Soviet Socialist Republic in December 1922, western Armenia having been returned to Turkey.

In 1988 ethnic turmoil erupted in the form of protests by Armenians over the status of their compatriots in the Azerbaijani autonomous *oblast* (region) of Nagorno-Karabakh. In February 1988 the *oblast* council requested that the territory be transferred to Armenian administration. The ensuing year was punctuated by ethnic violence, and in November 1989 the Armenian Pan-National Movement (*Hayots Hamazgain Sharzhum*—HHSh) was organized in support of "genuine sovereignty" for the Armenian people and resolution of the Nagorno-Karabakh dispute.

In early 1990 the Armenian Supreme Soviet proclaimed its right to veto legislation approved by Moscow after the Presidium of the USSR Supreme Soviet had ruled as unconstitutional a late 1989 declaration of a "unified Armenian republic" that included the Azerbaijani-held region. The action prompted demonstrations by Azerbaijani nationalists in Baku, and communal violence ensued, leading Moscow to dispatch military units in an attempt to restore order. Fighting nonetheless intensified along the border of the two republics during the following months. In July 1990 a newly elected Armenian Supreme Soviet refused to comply with a directive from USSR President Mikhail Gorbachev banning local "armed formations," and on August 23 it issued a declaration of Armenian "independent statehood," which did not, however, call for immediate secession from the Soviet Union.

In mid-April 1991 the Armenian government moved to nationalize the property of the republican Armenian Communist Party (*Hayastani Komunistakan Kusaktsutiun*—HKK), whose first secretary, Stepan POGOSIAN, resigned in favor of Aram SARKISIAN on May 14. At a congress on September 7, following the failure of the hard-line coup in Moscow and coincident with an Armenian Supreme Soviet vote to establish a directly elected presidency, the HKK voted to disband. In a referendum two weeks later, 94.39 percent of those participating voted for full independence, which was declared by the Armenian Supreme Soviet on September 23. Subsequently, on October 16, the incumbent Supreme Soviet chair, Levon TER-PETROSIAN, was elected president of the republic, with Gagik HAROUTIUNIAN becoming vice president and, additionally, acting prime minister, following the resignation of Vazgen MANUKIAN on September 25. On July 30, 1992, the vice president yielded the prime ministerial post to Khosrov HAROUTIUNIAN (no relation).

On February 2, 1993, President Ter-Petrosian dismissed Prime Minister Haroutiunian for having criticized government economic policies, and a successor administration under Hrand BAGRATIAN was inducted on February 16. The opposition parties thereupon pressed for new elections, mounting large antigovernment demonstrations in the capital in 1993 and 1994; however, the Ter-Petrosian administration remained firmly in control, despite a deteriorating economic situation and no progress in resolving the Nagorno-Karabakh dispute.

In Armenia's first postindependence election on July 5, 1995 (with reruns being held for some 40 seats on July 29), a six-party Republic bloc headed by Ter-Petrosian's HHSh won a substantial legislative majority, while a constitutional referendum the same day gave 68 percent endorsement to a new post-Soviet text conferring enhanced powers on the president. The fairness of the electoral process was questioned by international observers, partly because the government had suspended the opposition Armenian Revolutionary Federation (*Hai Heghapokhakan Dashnaktsutyun*—HHD/*Dashnak*) in December 1994, thereby preventing it from contesting the election as a party.

President Ter-Petrosian was reelected outright in the first-round balloting on September 22, 1996, with the official results giving him 51.75 percent of the vote. His nearest challenger was former prime minister Vazgen Manukian of the National Democratic Union of Armenia (*Azgayin Zhoghovrdavarakan Miutiun*—AZhM), who was credited with 41.29 percent. Claims by Manukian and other opposition leaders of widespread electoral fraud in the incumbent's favor triggered several days of protests in Yerevan, during which demonstrators clashed violently with security forces. After the incidents, many opposition party members, including Manukian, were arrested. Although those prisoners received amnesty in mid-1997, various appeals filed by opposition leaders asking for annulment of the presidential elections were rejected. Meanwhile, observers from the Organization for Security and Cooperation in Europe (OSCE) confirmed that "very serious breaches" of Armenian electoral law had occurred. (The European Parliament subsequently passed a resolution challenging the legitimacy of the elections and called for a new round of voting.)

On November 4, 1996, the president appointed Armen SARKISIAN, the former ambassador to the United Kingdom, to succeed Bagratian as prime minister. The latter had resigned his post, ostensibly for personal reasons but perhaps under the influence of growing popular discontent over the effects of the government's economic reforms, which, although underpinning solid GDP growth, had also produced lower wages and higher unemployment. Sarkisian himself resigned on March 6, 1997; ill health was given as the cause of the resignation, although conflict between the popular prime minister and President Ter-Petrosian was widely believed to have been an underlying factor. Sarkisian was replaced on March 20 by Robert KOCHARIAN, the president of the self-proclaimed Republic of Nagorno-Karabakh (see article on Azerbaijan).

President Ter-Petrosian appeared to step in political quicksand in September 1997 when he suggested that he would consider an arrangement in which an autonomous Nagorno-Karabakh would remain a part of Azerbaijan. The president's perceived willingness to compromise, based on his belief that Armenia's economic potential was being held hostage to the conflict, put him at increasingly greater odds with Prime Minister Kocharian. Ter-Petrosian resigned on February 3, 1998, apparently under pressure from hard-line military leaders, who by that time were widely believed to wield the strongest authority in Armenia. Although the constitution provided for the speaker of the National Assembly to assume the presidency temporarily under such circumstances, the speaker, Babken ARARKTSIAN, also resigned his post, leaving Kocharian, as prime minister, to serve as acting president pending new elections.

Twelve candidates contested the first round of presidential balloting on March 16, 1998, with Kocharian and Karen DEMIRCHIAN, who had led Armenia under Communist rule for 14 years (1974–1988), finishing in the top two spots. In the runoff poll on March 30, Kocharian was elected with 60 percent of the vote, although Demirchian challenged the accuracy of the count. On April 10 Kocharian named Economy and Finance Minister Armen DARBINIAN, a young (age 33) and reform-minded economist, as prime minister.

Having been embroiled in a series of conflicts with the assembly, President Kocharian called for early legislative elections to be held on May 30, 1999. Some 21 parties and blocs registered for the balloting, many of them bearing little resemblance to previous formations. The most prominent coalition was the Unity bloc, comprising Demirchian's People's Party of Armenia (*Hayastani Zhoghovrdakan Kusaktsutiun*—HZhK) and Vazgen SARKISIAN's Republican Party of Armenia (*Hayastani Hanrapetakan Kusaktsutiun*—HHK). The bloc secured 42 percent of the nationwide proportional vote and a total of 55 seats in the new assembly. Demirchian was elected speaker of the assembly on June 10, and the following day Kocharian announced the appointment of Sarkisian, a former defense minister widely believed to have been involved in the "ouster" of President Ter-Petrosian, as prime minister. Many incumbents were retained in Sarkisian's Unity-led government (formed June 15), which also included representatives from *Dashnak* and a number of independents.

Hope subsequently grew that Armenia was set for a period of much-needed political stability, but such optimism was dashed on October 27, 1999, when gunmen seized the assembly and killed Prime Minister Sarkisian, Demirchian, and five other government officials. Certain observers have suggested there was a link between a perceived softening on Kocharian's part in regard to Nagorno-Karabakh and the assassinations, the gunmen being described in some quarters as hard-line nationalists. Others theorized the killings were part of a "delusional" coup attempt, whereas statements from the attackers, who said Sarkisian was the primary target, condemned "corruption" and "poor leadership" within the government. On November 3 President Kocharian named Aram SARKISIAN, Vazgen's brother, as the new prime minister.

A new cabinet (including members of Unity, *Dashnak*, the AZhM, and the reconstituted HKK [which had finished second in the May 1999 legislative balloting]) was announced on February 28, 2000, with significant friction in determining the structure and membership of the government being reported between Prime Minister Sarkisian and President Kocharian. Sarkisian also continued to criticize the president regarding the prosecution of the assassination case, and tension rose even higher in March when Kocharian issued several decrees asserting his right to appoint senior military officers. Impeachment proceedings against Kocharian were considered in the assembly in April but were not pursued, in part, apparently, because the president had appointed members of the Yerkrapah Union of Karabakh War Veterans, an important HHK power base, to top army posts. The infighting culminated in Kocharian's dismissal of Sarkisian on May 2 and his appointment of the HHK's Andranik MARKARIAN as prime minister on May 12. On May 20 Markarian announced a new cabinet, although many incumbents were retained. Kocharian said he hoped the changes would eliminate the "intrigues" that he described as barring government effectiveness. However, news reports throughout the summer and early fall focused on the perceived deterioration of relations between the two parties in the Unity coalition, which finally collapsed in mid-2001 (see Political Parties, below).

Tensions persisted in 2001, and mass demonstrations in the fall called for President Kocharian's resignation, while opposition parties attempted (unsuccessfully) to have the assembly consider an impeachment motion. Kocharian's critics accused him of adopting a "Russian-style" authoritarian approach designed, among other things, to harass his opponents and muzzle the press.

Amid continuing political and public discord, Kocharian was credited with 49.48 percent of the vote against eight other candidates in the first round of presidential balloting on February 19, 2003. He defeated HZhK leader Stepan DEMIRCHIAN with 67.5 percent of the vote in the runoff poll on March 5. However, those results were strongly contested by opposition parties, as were the official results of the May 25 assembly elections that were again dominated by propresidential parties. Prime Minister Markarian formed a new cabinet (comprising members of the HHK and the Country of Law [*Orinats Yerkir*—OY] party) in June. The OY withdrew from the coalition in May 2006.)

Prime Minister Markarian died on March 25, 2007, and on April 5 President Kocharian appointed Defense Minister Serzh SARKISIAN (who had joined the HHK the previous year) as the new prime minister pending assembly balloting already scheduled for May 12. Following that balloting (in which the HHK and its allies won a substantial majority), Kocharian reappointed Sarkisian, who formed a new government that included ministers from the HHK, HHD-*Dashnak*, and the new Prosperous Armenia (*Bargavach Hayastan*—BH) party. In the wake of his controversial election as president (see Current issues, below) on February 19, 2008, Sarkisian on April 9 named Tigran SARKISIAN, previously the head of the central bank, as the new prime minister. Tirgan Sarkisian, an independent, on April 21 formed a new government that included several other independents as well as ministers from the HHK, HHD-*Dashnak*, BH, and OY. However, *Dashnak* left the coalition on April 27, 2009, in protest over what it perceived to be an "unacceptable" framework agreement moving toward improved relations with Turkey (see Foreign relations, below).

Constitution and government. A new constitution approved by referendum on July 5, 1995, replaced the existing Soviet-era text by providing for a strong presidential system of government balanced by separation of powers, strengthened independence of the judiciary, and the creation of a Constitutional Court. Directly elected for a maximum of two five-year terms, the president has the right to appoint the prime minister and other government ministers, subject to approval by the National Assembly. The president can also dissolve the assembly and call new elections, although a veto on legislation can be overridden by simple majority in the assembly (instead of the two-thirds majority required previously).

Administratively, Armenia is divided into ten centrally controlled provinces or regions (*marzes*) plus the capital of Yerevan. The legal system is headed by the Court of Cassation and the Constitutional Court. Magistrates' Courts are currently envisioned to take over the handling of civil lawsuits and minor crimes from the Courts of First Instance, which will be reserved for serious offenses.

Following his election in 1998, President Kocharian appointed a commission to propose constitutional revision that would dilute presidential authority. However, the commission's recommendations, published in 2001, would not have transferred nearly enough power to the assembly to satisfy opposition parties, who demanded the right to present their own plan for consideration by national referendum. Concurrent with legislative balloting in 2003, a national referendum was held on several constitutional issues, including the removal of a ban on dual citizenship, the specific conditions under which the president could dissolve the National Assembly, and whether to reduce the number of deputies in the assembly from 131 to 101. The referendum failed because the requisite turnout threshold was not met.

A national referendum on November 27, 2005, approved a number of constitutional amendments designed to reduce the powers of the president and strengthen the legislature and the judiciary. Among other things, the changes were intended to curb the president's previously essentially unchecked power to appoint and dismiss judges.

Foreign relations. Armenia was a founding member of the Commonwealth of Independent States (CIS) in December 1991. By early 1992 diplomatic relations had been established with a number of Western countries, including the United States, as well as with China and Japan. Armenia had also become a member of the Conference on Security and Cooperation in Europe (CSCE, subsequently the OSCE). On March 2, 1992, Armenia was admitted to the United Nations, with membership in the IMF and World Bank following soon thereafter.

Armenia's major international issue since independence has been the status of Nagorno-Karabakh in Azerbaijan, a dispute that extends back to the early 20th century (see Political background in article on Azerbaijan) and that played an important role in the Armenian independence movement in the late 1980s and early 1990s (see Political background, above). In May 1992 Armenian forces captured Azerbaijan's last major urban stronghold in the region and proceeded to open a corridor to Armenia proper. Concurrently, an attack was launched on the Azerbaijani enclave of Nakhichevan near Armenia's border with Turkey. Azerbaijan subsequently counterattacked in Nagorno-Karabakh and by early July had recaptured most of its northern sector, which, however, returned to Armenian control in ensuing months. Meanwhile, under a May 1992 agreement among Russia and five other CIS members (Azerbaijan not included), the signatories had pledged to provide assistance in the event of threats to each other's security. Armenia appealed to the pact after an Azerbaijani attack on one of its border villages in early August, receiving a manifestly cool response from Moscow, where there was little support for the proposed transfer of Armenian-populated Nagorno-Karabakh from Azerbaijan to Armenia. At the same time, Armenian forays into Nakhichevan raised the possibility of Turkish involvement, despite a pledge by Ankara to refrain from action that might lead to a wider conflict between the region's Christians and Muslims.

In May 1993 Armenia and Azerbaijan agreed to a cease-fire brokered by the United States, Russia, and Turkey that called for Armenian withdrawal from recently conquered Azerbaijani territory and the launching of peace talks in Geneva, Switzerland, under the auspices of the CSCE. However, the agreement was repudiated by the Nagorno-Karabakh leadership, and by mid-June Armenian forces had resumed military activity that left them in effective control of much of southwestern Azerbaijan.

On May 5, 1994, talks sponsored by the CIS Inter-Parliamentary Union in Bishkek, Kyrgyzstan, yielded a cease-fire protocol, which Azerbaijan belatedly signed three days later. A follow-up agreement was concluded in Moscow on May 11, although the Azerbaijani opposition criticized the pact as implying de facto recognition of the self-proclaimed Republic of Nagorno-Karabakh. Yet another accord on May 16 called for the deployment to the disputed territory of some 1,800 CIS peacekeepers under a Russian commander, but the placement of the troops was deferred because of an Azerbaijani objection to the size of the Russian component. Subsequently, whereas the military advantage had appeared to lie with Azerbaijan in early 1994, a CIS-brokered cease-fire in July left the Armenians in control of much of the disputed territory.

In late 1994 both sides accepted (in principle) a Budapest summit conference decision that 3,000 CSCE peacekeeping troops be deployed in Nagorno-Karabakh, subject to approval by the UN Security Council and formal cessation of hostilities by the contending parties. The Budapest decision represented the first potential peacekeeping venture by the CSCE/OSCE; it was further agreed that the force would be multinational, with no one country contributing more than 30 percent of the total. However, although the Russian government had endorsed the Budapest agreement, it reportedly was reluctant to accept the deployment of a genuinely multinational force in one of the former Soviet republics, and no peacekeeping troops were subsequently dispatched. Meanwhile, the Russian defense ministry estimated that some 18,000 people had died in the Armenia-Azerbaijan conflict since its inception.

Efforts to establish a lasting cease-fire on the basis of the December 1994 accord were set back in May 1995 when Armenia withdrew from the negotiating process, charging Azerbaijani involvement in a bomb attack by Georgian Azerbaijanis that severed a pipeline carrying vital gas supplies to Armenia from Turkmenistan. Talks resumed in September but made little progress, complicated by Nagorno-Karabakh's unilateral declaration of independence in March 1996. Despite calls by the Armenian opposition for the new entity to be recognized, the Ter-Petrosian government reacted cautiously, saying that recognition would not be extended by Yerevan until at least one other country had done so.

The appointment of Robert Kocharian, the president of the self-declared Republic of Nagorno-Karabakh, as the new prime minister of Armenia on March 20, 1997, seriously increased the tension between Armenia and Azerbaijan. Although some observers expressed the hope that the maneuver might provide renewed energy to negotiations, Azerbaijan quickly accused Armenian president Ter-Petrosian of "provocation" in the matter, and in mid-April fighting between Armenian and Azerbaijani forces broke out in two locations along the frontier. In late May the OSCE submitted a draft peace plan that proposed giving Nagorno-Karabakh autonomous status within Azerbaijan. The plan also called for the withdrawal of Armenian forces from five districts in Azerbaijan. Meanwhile, Prime Minister Kocharian announced that his government did not rule out the possibility of annexing Nagorno-Karabakh.

Following Armenia's 1999 legislative poll, international pressure continued to mount for a permanent resolution of the situation in Nagorno-Karabakh, one U.S. plan calling for the region to attain the status of an autonomous republic (with its own army and currency) within Azerbaijan. Washington reportedly offered financial incentives to both sides of the dispute, since a resolution would have facilitated construction of a pipeline to transport the anticipated flow of Caspian Sea oil from Azerbaijan through Armenia to a Turkish port on the Mediterranean Sea, thereby avoiding other routes preferred by Moscow. Such discussions also touched on the ongoing question of Armenia's international orientation; a number of Armenians reportedly supported the HKK's call for participation in the fledgling Union of Belarus and Russia (see article on Belarus for details), while others urged a more "multifaceted" approach that would provide additional ties with the West. As a result, Armenia announced it did not intend to pursue full NATO membership, although it had joined NATO's Partnership for Peace Program in 1994.

Armenia's relations with Russia subsequently remained strong. A 1997 treaty permitted Russia to maintain military bases in Armenia for up to 25 years and to continue to "guarantee" Armenia's security. (As of 2008, some 6,000 Russian troops remained stationed in Armenia.) In addition, in 2001 the two countries signed a ten-year economic agreement, while in September 2003 Armenia transferred control of its sole remaining nuclear power plant to Russia.

In January 2004 the United States agreed to provide some $75 million in aid to Armenia, including $5 million for humanitarian assistance in Nagorno-Karabakh and $2.5 million in military aid. Perhaps in response to the U.S. assistance, Armenia deployed 46 noncombat troops to Iraq in January 2005 to support the U.S.-led coalition. (The Armenian troops were withdrawn in late 2008.)

In August 2004 Armenia and China initiated a series of military cooperation discussions that included the expansion of Chinese training of Armenian military personnel. On another front, plans were announced in December 2004 for construction of a gas pipeline from Iran to Armenia. (In 2006 Armenia announced that Russia would be a joint owner of the proposed pipeline, which was completed in 2007.) Meanwhile, relations between Armenia and Turkey remained strained. Turkey refused efforts to finalize the border between the two states because of the continuing presence of Russian troops along the border areas. In addition, Armenia continued to press for Turkish recognition that the Ottoman killing of Armenians in the late 19th and early 20th centuries had been a genocide. Turkey also demanded that Armenia renounce any claims to territory in eastern Turkey.

In mid-2007 President Kocharian stated that Armenia currently had no intention of pursuing NATO membership, stressing instead Armenia's ties to Russia, for whom NATO expansion remained an anathema, and to Iran, an important trading partner. Kocharian also indicated that the government was "realistic" regarding Armenia's poor prospects for receiving an EU accession invitation in the foreseeable future.

Relations with Turkey began to improve significantly in the second half of 2008 as new Armenian president Serzh Sarkisian met several times with his Turkish counterpart, Abdullah Gül. Their discussions culminated in a Russian-mediated declaration in November pledging intensified negotiations toward a political resolution that would lead Turkey to reopen the border and, among other things, possibly permit Armenia to participate in the lucrative oil and gas pipelines from the Caspian to the West. (Analysts suggested that the recent war between Russian and Georgian forces in South Ossetia had underscored the vulnerability of such pipelines and revealed the need for "diversification.") In April 2009 Sarkisian and Gül announced a framework agreement that outlined a "road map" toward a final settlement. Although few details subsequently emerged, it appeared that a special commission was envisioned to investigate the events of 1915. Significantly, new U.S, president Barack Obama, a previous supporter of a controversial resolution in the U.S. Congress that would label the killings genocide, opted not to use that word in hailing the apparent progress toward normalization of relations between Turkey and Armenia. It was also still unclear if a final settlement would be possible without resolution of the impasse over Nagorno-Karabakh. Meanwhile, Armenia was one of six countries targeted by the EU's new "Eastern Partnership," which hoped to draw the countries into deeper ties with the West without implying that full membership was in the offing. At the same time, Armenia concluded several joint infrastructure agreements with Iran and received a $500-million emergency loan from Russia.

Current issues. Widespread demonstrations organized by the opposition in April 2004 were suppressed, sparking condemnation from the Council of Europe, the U.S. State Department, and international human rights organizations. The domestic campaign to force President Kocharian's resignation ultimately failed, in part, apparently, because of new legislation passed in May that placed substantial restrictions on the right to demonstrate.

The United States and the Council of Europe supported the constitutional amendments presented by the government for a national referendum on November 27, 2005, on the grounds that the revisions represented a significant first step on the road to democratic reform, most importantly through the dilution of presidential authority. However, most opposition parties called for a boycott of the balloting, and street protests were organized during the prereferendum campaign, although they did not reach the organizers' hopes regarding size or intensity. (Some leaders of the opposition concluded that Armenians were not yet ready for the kind of mass movements that had recently toppled strong-arm governments in Georgia, Kyrgyzstan, and Ukraine.)

The government announced a 65 percent turnout and a 93 percent "yes" vote in the 2005 referendum, claiming that voters had clearly indicated their support of the Kocharian administration's policies. Unfortunately for the government, however, international observers quickly concluded that the balloting had been rigged, primarily through ballot-stuffing. In early 2006 EU representatives expressed doubts about the government's "commitment to democracy" and called for broad political reform. For their part, domestic critics of the government suggested that the country was in fact regressing in regard to democratization and human rights, although public discontent was tempered by the country's undeniably excellent economic progress in recent years.

The United States in 2006 announced that additional aid to Armenia would be tied to intensified attention to political rights on the part of the Armenian government. Additionally, the Council of Europe indicated that assembly elections in May 2007 needed to be demonstrably democratic before further integration of Armenia into Europe would be considered. Some experts concluded that the HHK's control might be seriously challenged in the legislative election, since polls showed significant public discontent over perceived ongoing corruption. However, the opposition failed to coalesce into an effective electoral alliance, and following his reappointment in June, Prime Minister Sarkisian dampened the hopes of political reformers by announcing that his new government's focus would be on economic development, not democratic refinements.

Former president Ter-Petrosian, who had spent the previous decade in "academic seclusion," dramatically altered the political landscape in September 2007 when he announced plans to compete in the 2008 presidential election. Ter-Petrosian adopted a populist platform (apparently to attract support from those who had benefited little from the recent economic advances) and attracted large crowds to his rallies. When preliminary results of the February 2008 balloting indicated that Prime Minister Sarkisian had secured a first-round victory with 52.8 percent of the vote (compared to 21.5 percent for Ter-Petrosian, who ran as an independent, and 16.7 percent for the OY's Arthur BAGHDASARIAN), protesters filled the streets on the capital demanding an annulment of the poll. Opposition leaders accused the government of physically intimidating their supporters, bribing voters, and committing massive poll fraud. The antigovernment demonstrations intensified after the Constitutional Court validated the election results, and violent street battles erupted on March 1 when police used force against the protesters. Ten people died in the conflict, and more than 130 were injured, prompting President Kocharian to declare a 20-day state of emergency and direct the army to restore order. The crackdown also included the detention of many opposition leaders and heavy restrictions on the media, further blackening the country's image internationally. For their part, most Western capitals adopted a muted stance regarding the government's approach, apparently out of concern that instability in Armenia might exacerbate tensions in an already tumultuous region.

At his inauguration in April 2008, President Sarkisian called for national reconciliation, and restrictions were finally lifted on public demonstrations in June. However, the opposition remained highly skeptical of the government's intentions, and Ter-Petrosian insisted that a genuine dialogue would be possible only if his supporters were released from jail. Although detainee trials continued throughout the summer, the assembly established an ad hoc commission in June to investigate the electoral violence, which many neutral observers attributed to what one correspondent for *Radio Free Europe/Radio Liberty* described as the "unjustifiable overreaction" of the police. Mass protests continued on a regular basis until October, when Ter-Petrosian called for a moratorium on further demonstrations. By the spring of 2009, it was apparent that Ter-Petrosian and his supporters were focusing on the ballot box, not street "revolution," to effect regime change, beginning with the May 31 municipal elections. Among the developments upon which the opposition hoped to capitalize were the nation's recent economic decline (marked by, among other things, a major currency devaluation in March that prompted widespread panic buying of consumer staples) and reported friction within the government coalition. For his part, President Sarkisian acknowledged that police had not acted with "sufficient professional skill" during the 2008 protests but ruled out a general amnesty for detainees until all trials were completed. Meanwhile, the assembly report on the matter was delayed until at least September.

In assessing his first year in office in late April 2009, President Sarkisian described improved relations with Turkey (see Foreign relations, above) as his most important accomplishment to date. However, the dialogue with Turkey cost his coalition the support of the nationalistic *Dashnak* party, which withdrew from the cabinet over fears that the rapprochement might lead to a "whitewash" of the 1915 events and unacceptable compromise regarding Nagorno-Karabakh. (See article on Azerbaijan for details on progress regarding the latter issue.) Meanwhile, the HHK retained the mayor's post in the May 31 balloting in Yerevan, although international observers cited irregularities in the poll.

POLITICAL PARTIES

New legislation required all political parties to reapply for registration in November 2002. As of 2006 there were reportedly 74 legal parties. Twenty-two parties and one coalition contested the 2007 legislative elections.

The Unity (*Miasnutiun*) coalition was launched in early April 1999 by the People's Party of Armenia (HZhK) and the Republican Party of Armenia (HHK) in preparation for the upcoming legislative poll. Unity was described as a "marriage of convenience" that hoped to capitalize on the resurgent popularity of the HZhK's Karen Demirchian and the "political machine" of the HHK's Vazgen Sarkisian. The coalition of the left-leaning HZhK and the center-right HHK necessitated a "vague" campaign platform, although Unity broadly pledged to use government economic intervention to offset some of the problems associated with the free-market transition of the 1990s.

Unity won nearly 42 percent of the proportional vote in the May 1999 legislative balloting and, with support from independent legislators, subsequently controlled a comfortable parliamentary majority and formed a new government under Sarkisian's leadership, while Demirchian was elected speaker of the assembly. However, following the assassination of both leaders in October 1999, tension between the two Unity partners bubbled to the surface. Meanwhile, Unity's parliamentary strength had been eroded by the defection of a group of legislators opposed to the majority's willingness to cooperate with President Kocharian. HZhK leaders described Unity as defunct in mid-2001, and the HHK ran on its own in the 2003 elections.

The HZhK subsequently was at the center of a new opposition coalition, the Justice (*Artarutiun*) bloc, formed in early 2003 by opposition groups and parties to oppose the propresidential parties in the legislative elections. Other parties in the bloc included the AZhM, HDK, Republic, the National Democratic Party, the Social-Democratic Hnchakian Party, the National Democratic Alliance, and the Union for Constitutional Rights, whose sole member of the assembly, Hrant KHACHATARIAN, reportedly stepped down as party leader in 2006. The Justice bloc gained 14 seats in the May 2003 legislative balloting, and it subsequently represented one of the two main opposition parties to Kocharian and led a series of demonstrations and protests against the government. The bloc called for a boycott of the November 2005 constitutional referendum and accused the government of massive fraud regarding the official results of the vote. Justice was subsequently plagued by infighting, and it disintegrated prior to the 2007 legislative poll.

An important opposition bloc called the **Armenian National Congress** (ANC) was formed by supporters of former Armenian president Levon Ter-Petrosian in August 2008. Ter-Petrosian, whose defeat in the February presidential election had prompted widespread anti-administration protests, announced that the ANC did not intend to try to topple the government by force but planned a "civilized" electoral struggle, beginning with the municipal elections due in May 2009, in which Ter-Petrosian was an unsuccessful candidate for mayor of Yerevan. Some 16 parties and civic organizations reportedly participated in the launching of the ANC, including the HHSh, HZhK, and Republic.

Government Parties:

Republican Party of Armenia (*Hayastani Hanrapetakan Kusaktsutiun*—HHK). The HHK was launched in November 1998 as a merger of the small Republican Party (a founding member of the Republic bloc, see HHSh, below) and the Yerkrapah Union of Karabakh War Veterans, which had recently become influential in the National Assembly as well as in the national cabinet and a number of local administrations. Vazgen Sarkisian, the leader of Yerkrapah and defense minister in the Darbinian cabinet, was selected to lead the HHK, which he said would be dedicated to free economic competition, a stance that appeared somewhat at odds with the HZhK, its subsequent partner in the Unity coalition. Sarkisian also indicated he believed the HHK would serve as the future core of political support for President Kocharian, although ten Yerkrapah hard-liners subsequently dissociated themselves from the president in reaction to what they perceived as a softening of his position regarding Nagorno-Karabakh. A degree of appeasement appeared to develop in March 2000 when Kocharian appointed Yerkrapah leaders to a number of important military posts, although ten Yerkrapah legislators reportedly left the HHK parliamentary bloc because of the conflict. Meanwhile, Kocharian had accepted the HHK's nomination of Andranik Markarian as prime minister in May 2000 after nearly six months of political instability precipitated by the October 1999 assembly shootings in which Sarkisian was among those killed.

The HHK supported incumbent president Kocharian in the 2003 presidential balloting, and the party became the largest party in the assembly by gaining 33 seats in the 2003 legislative poll. Serzh Sarkisian, the influential defense minister, in mid-2006 announced his official alignment with the HHK, positioning himself as the leading candidate for the party's 2008 presidential nomination. Meanwhile, Yerkrapah leaders announced they would not endorse any parties for the 2007 legislative balloting.

The HHK secured 65 seats in the 2007 assembly poll. The **Powerful Homeland** (*Hzor Hayrenik*—HH) party, formed in 1997 under the leadership of Varden VARAPETIAN, was credited with 1 of the seats from the HHK's proportional list, as was the **Democracy and Labor** party, led by Spartak MELIKYAN.

The HHK's Sarkisian, who had been named prime minister in April 2007, was elected president of the republic in February 2008, being credited (controversially) with 52.8 percent of the first-round votes.

The HHK's Tigran TOROSIAN resigned as speaker of the assembly in September 2008 in the wake of party and policy disputes. He also left the HHK, declaring that he would subsequently serve in the assembly as an independent. Prime Minister Tigran Sarkisian, previously an independent, joined the HHK in November 2009.

Leaders: Serzh SARKISIAN (Chair and President of the Republic), Tigran SARKISIAN (Prime Minister), Razmik ZOHRABIAN (Deputy Chair), Gagik BEGLARIAN (Mayor of Yerevan), Hovik ABRAHAMYAN (Speaker of the National Assembly), Galust SAHAKYAN (Parliamentary Leader).

Prosperous Armenia (*Bargavach Hayastan*—BH). Formed in 2006 by wealthy businessman Gagik Tsarukian, the pro-Kocharian BH claimed a membership of more than 200,000. The new party called for greater cooperation with the United States and NATO as well as the promotion of "political pluralism" within Armenia. In late 2006 critics accused Prosperous Armenia of attempting to buy votes by supplying free medical services and other assistance to poor voters. The BH became the second-largest party in the 2007 assembly balloting. (The chair of the **Social-Democratic Hnchakian Party**, Ernest SOGHOMONYAN, was elected on the BH's proportional list. However, his party was subsequently reported to be one of the founders of the opposition ANC in 2008.)

Leaders: Gagik TSARUKIAN (Parliamentary Leader), Arevik PETROSYAN (Deputy Speaker of the National Assembly), Vartan VARTANIAN.

Country of Law (*Orinats Yerkir*—OY). Formed in 1998, the Country of Law party was subsequently reported to enjoy the support of the influential interior minister Serzh Sarkisian, a native of Nagorno-Karabakh believed to have been instrumental in pressuring President Ter-Petrosian to resign earlier in the year. Describing itself as a centrist grouping, the Country of Law party won 5.28 percent of the votes in the proportional component of the May 1999 legislative poll. The party supported President Kocharian in the 2003 presidential balloting and secured 19 seats in the subsequent legislative elections.

Artur Baghdasarian, the party's leader, resigned as speaker of the assembly in May 2006 and announced that the Country of Law was withdrawing from the cabinet over an apparent foreign policy dispute with President Kocharian. (Baghdasarian was reportedly viewed as too pro-NATO by the president.) A number of Country of Law party legislators reportedly later quit the party, while Sarkisian soon thereafter joined the HHK.

The OY won 16 seats in the 2007 assembly poll, and the charismatic Baghdasarian, running on a populist platform, was credited with 16.7 percent of the vote in the 2008 presidential balloting, having reportedly angered some government critics for having failed to support the candidacy of former president Ter-Petrosian. Despite its former differences with the HHK, the OY joined the new HHK-led government in June 2008.

Leaders: Artur BAGHDASARIAN (Chair and Former Speaker of the Assembly), Heghine BISHARYAN (Parliamentary Leader).

Other Parliamentary Parties:

Armenian Revolutionary Federation (*Hai Heghapokhakan Dashnaktsutyun*—HHD/*Dashnak*). Originally founded in 1891, the HHD was the ruling party in pre-Soviet Armenia and retained a substantial following in the Armenian diaspora after it was outlawed by the Bolsheviks in 1920. Reestablished in 1991 as a nationalist and socialist opposition party, the HHD (popularly known as *Dashnak*) nominated the actor Sos SARKISIAN in the October 1991 presidential election, but he received only 4 percent of the vote. In 1992 the party struck a public chord with its criticism of the government's conduct of the war in Nagorno-Karabakh. The government responded by alleging that the HHD leaders in exile had for many years cooperated with Soviet security authorities.

In late December 1994 the HHD was suspended by presidential decree on the grounds that it had engaged in terrorism, political assassination, and drug trafficking. It was therefore unable to contest the July 1995 election as a party. Although more than 100 *Dashnak* candidates stood as individuals in the majoritarian component of the balloting, only 1 candidate was elected. In March 1996, 31 party members were put on trial in Yerevan, charged with involvement in an abortive coup attempt at the time of the 1995 poll. However, the imprisoned HHD leaders were released in February 1998, and *Dashnak* was subsequently permitted to reregister as a legal party, several *Dashnak* members being named to the April cabinet.

Dashnak secured 7.83 percent of the vote in the proportional component of the May 1999 legislative poll, and the party accepted two cabinet posts in 2001. The HHD endorsed President Kocharian in the 2003 presidential election. It secured 11 seats in the May 2003 legislative elections and joined the subsequent Unity government.

In 2006 *Dashnak* announced its "dissatisfaction" with the current "state of affairs" and indicated it would not back the HHK's presumptive nominee, Serzh Sarkisian, in the 2008 presidential campaign. However, the party remained in the HHK-led coalition government. Vakan Hovkannisian, the HHD's presidential candidate in 2008, received 6.2 percent of the votes.

Dashnak subsequently remained what one analyst described as "the most opposition-minded of the progovernment forces," and in late April 2009 it withdrew from the government in opposition to, among other things, the recent rapprochement with Turkey (see Foreign relations, above). *Dashnak* leaders announced plans to cooperate with Heritage as opposition forces in the assembly but said *Dashnak* would not align with the recently formed ANC. (Although the three *Dashnak* cabinet ministers resigned from the government, *Dashnak* committee chairs in the assembly decided to retain their posts.)

Leaders: Ruben HAGOBIAN (Chair), Hrant MARKARIAN (Former Chair), Hrayr KARAPETIAN, Armen RUSTAMIAN, Gino MANOIAN, Vakan HOVKANNISIAN (2008 presidential candidate and Parliamentary Leader).

Heritage (*Zharangutiun*). This party is led by outspoken former foreign minister Raffi Hovanisian, an Armenian from the United States who was precluded from pursuing his goal of campaigning for the Armenian presidency in 2003 because of citizenship issues. Heritage won seven seats in the 2007 assembly poll, having campaigned on a pro-Western platform that called for greater integration by Armenia into European institutions.

Heritage supported former president Levon Ter-Petrosian in his controversial 2008 presidential race and called for support of the "opposition" in the May 2009 municipal elections. However, Heritage did not specifically endorse Ter-Petrosian's new ANC.

Leaders: Raffi HOVANISIAN, Hovsep KHURSHUDIAN (Spokesperson), Vardan KHACHATRYAN.

Alliance (*Dashink*). Formed in November 2005 by former Nagorno-Karabakh strongman Gen. Samvel Babayan, Alliance described itself as a "neutral" party that favored decentralization and judicial reform. (Babayan, who had led the army in Nagorno-Karabakh in 1993–1999, was released from prison in September 2004 after having been given a 14-year sentence in 2000 for alleged participation in an assassination plot against Arkady Ghukasian, the prime minister of Nagorno-Karabakh.) Babayan joined the Republic party in 2001 but left that group in 2005 to launch Alliance, which won 1 seat in the 2007 assembly poll on a platform perceived as anti-Kocharian.

Leaders: Gen. Samvel BABAYAN, Martun GRIGORYAN.

Other Parties Participating in the 2007 Legislative Elections:

People's Party of Armenia (*Hayastani Zhoghovrdakan Kusaktsutiun*—HZhK). The HZhK was formed in 1998 by former Communist leader Karen Demirchian following his defeat in the March presidential election, which he described as fraudulent. Demirchian had served as first secretary of the Armenian Communist Party from 1974 until 1988, when he was dismissed by Mikhail Gorbachev for his perceived failure to combat the nationalist movement in Armenia. Although Demirchian was subsequently considered a "political has-been," he made a remarkable comeback with his 1998 presidential campaign, which apparently struck a chord with those elements of the populace who yearned for the security of the Soviet era.

Demirchian campaigned for the May 1999 legislative poll on a pledge to slow down liberalization in order to protect the populace from economic dislocation, his popularity being deemed the primary reason for Unity's success. Following his assassination in October, Demirchian was succeeded as party leader by his son, Stepan, and as speaker of the assembly by Armen KHACHATRIAN, himself a subject of controversy within the fragile Unity coalition.

Stepan Demirchian subsequently displayed increasingly anti-Kocharian sentiment, and the HZhK in 2001 announced the end of Unity, calling the HHK a "stooge" for President Kocharian. Demirchian was the HZhK's candidate in the 2003 presidential election; he finished second with 32.5 percent of the vote in the second round. The HZhK subsequently led the Justice bloc in the 2003 assembly poll (see introductory text, above), but Demirchian failed in his efforts to convince other parties to form a new antigovernment electoral alliance for the 2007 balloting after the Justice bloc collapsed.

Leaders: Stepan DEMIRCHIAN (Chair), Hmayak HOVANISSIAN.

Democratic Party of Armenia (*Hayastani Demokratakan Kusaktsutiun*—HDK). The HDK was founded in late 1991 as self-proclaimed successor to the once-dominant HKK following the latter's suspension in September 1991, after which many of the HKK's senior members switched allegiance to the ruling HHSh (see below). Weakened by the revival of the HKK for the 1995 legislative balloting, the HDK managed only a 1.8 percent vote share and no seats.

In 1996 the HDK was prominent in opposition calls for the government to recognize the self-declared independence of Nagorno-Karabakh. It was a strong supporter of Robert Kocharian in the 1998 presidential election, its leader, Aram G. Sarkisian (not to be confused with former prime minister Aram Sarkisian [see Republic, below]), subsequently becoming an influential foreign policy adviser to the new president. The HDK secured less than 1 percent of the proportional vote in the May 1999 legislative balloting.

Leader: Aram G. SARKISIAN (Chair).

Republic (*Hanrapetutiun*). This party was formed in 2001 by former members of the HHK, including Albert Bazeyan (the former mayor of Yerevan) and Aram Sarkisian (prime minister for six months in 1999–2000 following the assassination of his brother, Prime Minister Vazgen Sarkisian). Republic was subsequently referred to as one of the most strongly anti-Kocharian parties, calling, among other things, for a more pro-Western orientation for the government, including support for Armenia's eventual accession to the EU and NATO. The party vehemently opposed the 2005 constitutional referendum and in early 2006 continued to press for "regime change" prior to the legislative elections of 2007. Meanwhile, Bazeyan had left Republic in late 2005 (see National Revival, below) in opposition to what he reportedly perceived to be Aram Sarkisian's "radical" antigovernment stance. In late 2006 Sarkisian claimed there would be a "revolution" if opposition parties were not successful in the 2007 legislative elections. However, Republic, which had won a seat in the 2003 assembly poll, failed to secure representation in 2007.

Leaders: Aram SARKISIAN (Chair and Former Prime Minister), Suren ABRAKAMIAN (Former Mayor of Yerevan).

National Democratic Party. Although it participated in the Justice bloc in the 2003 legislative elections, this party reportedly withdrew from the bloc in late 2005 after having been "censured" by the other members for failing to support the boycott of the November constitutional referendum. Shavarsh Kocharian, the "notably pro-Western" leader of the party, reportedly described other Justice leaders as "too radical." Running on its own, the party failed to secure representation in the 2007 assembly poll.

Leader: Shavarsh KOCHARIAN.

National Revival. Formed in November 2005 by dissenters from the Republic party, National Revival announced it would oppose the Kocharian administration but without the "radical antigovernment discourse" and strongly pro-Western tilt of Republic.

Leaders: Albert BAZEYAN (Former Mayor of Yerevan), Vagharshak HARUTIUNIAN (Former Defense Minister).

National Unity Party (*Azgayin Miabanutiun*). This nationalist party was formed in 1997 under the leadership of former Yerevan mayor Artashes Geghamian. The party supported continued close ties with Russia as well as further integration into the institutions of Europe. Geghamian placed third in the first round of the 2003 presidential balloting with 16.9 percent of the vote. In the subsequent legislative elections, the National Unity Party secured 8.8 percent of the vote and 9 seats in the assembly, but the party boycotted the assembly from February 2004 to September 2005. After the party failed to secure representation in the 2007 assembly poll, Geghamian was credited with only 0.46 percent of the votes in the 2008 presidential balloting.

Leaders: Artashes GEGHAMIAN (Chair and 2003 and 2008 presidential candidate), Aleksan KARAPETIAN (Deputy Chair).

Armenian Pan-National Movement (*Hayots Hamazgain Sharzhum*—HHSh). The HHSh was founded in November 1989 by proindependence leaders of the then-ruling Communist Party, including Levon Ter-Petrosian, who had been a key member of the unofficial Karabakh Committee seeking the transfer of the Armenian-populated enclave of Nagorno-Karabakh from Azerbaijan to Armenia. Advocating Armenia's withdrawal from the USSR, the HHSh swept the May 1990 legislative elections and subsequently led Armenia to full independence. Following dissolution of the Communist Party, Ter-Petrosian in October 1991 secured a presidential mandate through direct election by an 83 percent majority. As the governing party, the HHSh insisted that the conflict with Azerbaijan be pursued to a successful conclusion, including the transfer of Nagorno-Karabakh, with territorial adjustments to make it contiguous with Armenia proper.

The HHSh was the driving force in 1995 in the formation of the Republic bloc (*Hanrapetutiun*), an electoral coalition that also included the Liberal Democratic Party; the Republican Party, led by A. NAVASARDIAN; the Social-Democratic Hnchakian Party; and the **Armenian Christian Democratic Union**, led by Azat ARSHAKIAN. The Republic bloc took a 42.7 percent vote share in the 1995 proportional balloting and won some two-thirds of the assembly seats by virtue of its dominance of the contests in the single-member districts.

During 1996 and 1997 the HHSh suffered serious internal problems and splits. Discord also permeated the party in regard to Ter-Petrosian's resignation in February 1998. Among those facing criticism was Vano Siradeghyan, accused of ordering politically motivated killings while he was interior minister from 1992 to 1996. Following an effort by reformist legislators to remove his parliamentary immunity, Siradeghyan left the country in January 1999. Nevertheless, he was reelected HHSh chair in absentia in March.

The HHSh won only 1.17 percent of the vote in the proportional component of the May 1999 legislative balloting, although Siradeghyan was easily elected in his race for the seat in a single-member district. Siradeghyan's parliamentary immunity was subsequently lifted, and he was reported to have again gone into exile. In 2002 the HHSh absorbed the small **National Democratic Party–21st Century**, which was led by former national security minister Davit SHAHNAZARIAN, who had campaigned for the presidency in 1998.

Although he has retained a low public profile in the 2000s, Ter-Petrosian, running as an independent, finished second (with 21.5 percent of the vote), in the 2008 presidential election, although he and his supporters claimed victory (see Current issues, above). His supporters reportedly included a dissident HHSh faction called **Armat** (Root), which, under the leadership of Babken ARARKTISIAN and Aleksandr ARZUMANIUM, was reportedly attempting to reduce the influence of Siradeghyan and bring the HHSh back from the "political wilderness." In 2008 Ter-Petrosian and his supporters launched the new ANC opposition grouping (see above).

Leaders: Levon TER-PETROSIAN (Former President of the Republic), Vano SIRADEGHYAN (in exile), Ararat ZURABIAN, Aran MANUKIAN.

Armenian Communist Party (*Hayastani Komunistakan Kusaktsutiun*—HKK). Having secured the second-largest number of legislative seats in the 1990 election, the Soviet-era HKK voted to disband in September 1991 under heavy government pressure, some of its remaining adherents regrouping in the HDK (above). Permitted to resume activities in 1994, the HKK took a 12.1 percent vote share in the July 1995 legislative balloting, winning 7 seats, while HKK leader Sergey BADALIAN secured 6.3 percent of the votes in the September 1996 presidential election and 11 percent in the first round of the 1998 balloting.

Calling for Armenian reintegration with Russia and Belarus for security and economic reasons, the HKK secured 12.1 percent of the vote in the proportional component of the May 1999 legislative poll. Following Badalian's death from a heart attack in November 1999, Vladimir Darbinian was elected as the HKK's new first secretary, and the party reportedly accepted several portfolios in the February 2000 cabinet reshuffle.

Several members were expelled from the HKK in 2001 for suggesting greater cooperation with the government; they reportedly later announced the launching of a "renewed" HKK. In the 2003 legislative elections, the HKK received 2 percent of the vote and, therefore, no seats in the assembly, having supported some candidates from other parties in the balloting and, according to one self-assessment, having "disoriented" its "electorate." Several communist splinters, including the **United Communist Party** (led by Yuri MANUKIAN), were reportedly preparing to present candidates in the 2007 legislative poll, while Ruben Tovmasian, described as the HKK's leader as of 2006, announced the HHK would run on its own.

Leaders: Ruben TOVMASIAN, Vladimir DARBINIAN, Sanatruk SAHAKIAN.

New Times (*Nor Zhamanakner*). The recently formed New Times party in early 2006 was described as a member of the "radical opposition" calling for regime change and early elections. Its leader, Aram Karapetian, backed former president Ter-Petrosian in the February 2008 presidential election, and Karapetian was one of the opposition leaders arrested following the subsequent disturbances.

Leader: Aram KARAPETIAN.

Other parties that participated unsuccessfully in the 2007 assembly elections included the **United Labor Party** (*Miavorvats Ashkhatankayin Kusaksutiun*—MAK), which had won 6 assembly seats in 2003 under the leadership of wealthy businessman Gurgen ARSENIAN; the **Conservative Party**; the **Youth Party of Armenia**; the **Marxist Party of Armenia**; the **Democratic Homeland** party; the **Progressive Party of Armenia**, founded prior to the 2003 elections; the **Democratic Way** party; and the **People's Christian Democratic Renaissance** party.

Other Parties and Groups:

National Democratic Union of Armenia (*Azgayin Zhoghovrdavarakan Miutiun*—AZhM). The AZhM was formed by Vazgen Manukian following his resignation as prime minister and withdrawal from the HHSh in September 1991. In mid-1994 the AZhM organized large-scale demonstrations against the Yerevan government. It took 7.5 percent of the vote in the 1995 assembly election, securing 5 seats.

In 1996 Manukian challenged the official results of presidential balloting, in which he was runner-up to the incumbent with 41 percent of the vote. The AZhM leader won 12.2 percent of the vote in the first round of the 1998 presidential poll, while the party, described as displaying a center-right orientation, secured 5.17 percent of the vote in the proportional component of the May 1999 legislative balloting, just barely surpassing the threshold required to gain representation. The AZhM accepted a cabinet post in 2000, although significant opposition to that decision was reported within the party's rank-and-file. In the 2003 presidential elections, Manukian received less than 1 percent of the vote. In 2006 he indicated that the AZhM would boycott the 2007 legislative balloting unless additional political reform was enacted. Manukian garnered 1.3 percent of the vote in the 2008 presidential poll.

Leaders: Vazgen MANUKIAN (Chair), Arshak SADOYIAN.

National Self-Determination Union (NSDU). Formed in 1987 as a clandestine proindependence grouping by anti-Soviet dissident Paruyr Hairikian, the NSDU won 5.6 percent of the proportional vote and three seats overall in the 1995 legislative balloting, subsequently providing support for Presidents Ter-Petrosian and Kocharian. The party's Self-Determination Union and Bloc, which also included the **Motherland-Diaspora Union,** secured only 2.29 percent of the proportional vote in the 1999 legislative balloting. In 2000 Hairikian, a survivor of 17 years in a Soviet labor camp, was named a presidential adviser in the area of constitutional reform. However, he resigned that post in May 2002 and said that Kocharian should not be reelected in 2003 because of his failure to follow through with his 1998 campaign pledges. For the 2003 assembly elections the NDSU led a coalition called the Liberal Bloc, which also included the **Free Armenia Mission** (*Azat Hyat Arakelutin*), led by Ruben MNATSAKANIAN, and **Intellectual Armenia** (*Mtavorakan Hayastan*—MH).

Leader: Paruyr HAIRIKIAN.

Stability (*Kazunitiun*). Formed primarily by independents elected in single-member districts in the May 1999 legislative poll, the Stability parliamentary faction was reported initially to control 22 assembly seats and was generally supportive of the Unity government. In May 2000 Stability leaders indicated an interest in formalizing the faction as a political party that would evince a social-democratic orientation in support, among other things, of a stronger governmental role in managing the economy. Two Stability members were reportedly named to the May 2000 cabinet, one of whom was apparently dismissed in 2001.

Leader: Vartan AYVAZIAN.

Dignified Future (*Arzhanapativ Apaga*). Led by prominent sociologist Lyudmila Harutiunian and described as having ties to (then) prime minister Armen Darpinian, Dignified Future was credited with 3.27 percent of the proportional vote in the May 1999 legislative election. In the 2003 legislative balloting, Dignified Future led a coalition called Dignity, Democracy, and Motherhood, which secured 2.8 percent of the vote.

Leader: Lyudmila HARUTIUNIAN.

Solidarity. A recently formed small party that supported the constitutional referendum of 2005, Solidarity is led by Andranik Manukian, who served as transport and communications minister in 2006–2007.

Leader: Andranik MANUKIAN.

Successful parties in 2003 also included the **All Armenian Labor Party**, which won 1 seat. Other parties that contested the 2003 legislative elections but failed to secure representation included the **Democratic Liberal Party** (*Ramakavar-Azatakan*), founded in 1991 and led by Rouben MIRZAKHANIAN (in 2008 it was reported that this party had merged with the Progressive Party of Armenia); the **Liberal Democratic Union of Armenia,** created in 2001 and led by Seyran AVAGIAN; the **Labor, Law, and Unity Party** (*Iravunk ev Miabanutiun*), led by Miran MOVSESIAN; and the **Union of Producers and Women** (AKM), which was formed in March 2003 by a coalition of trade unions, business leaders, the **Advanced United Communist Parties of Armenia** (*Hayastani Arajadimakan Miatsial Komunistakan Kusaktsutiun*—HAMKK), and the **Women of the Armenian Land** (*Anayk Hayots Ashkhari*). The AKM secured 2 percent of the vote in the 2003 balloting.

Other recently formed parties include the **Liberal Progressive Party**, led by pro-Western "oppositionist" Hovannes HOVANNISIAN (in 2000 it was reported that Hovannisian had been elected president of the newly formed **Liberal Party of Armenia**, of which the Liberal Progressive Party had served as one of the founders); the **Motherland Party,** led by Karine TUMANIAN; the **Union for Armenia; Fatherland and Honor,** a hard-line nationalist party (led by Garnik MARKARIAN and Vastan MALKHASIAN) opposed to concessions regarding Nagorno-Karabakh; the **Association for Armenia,** led by former prosecutor Aghvan HOVSEPIAN and Vahram BAGHDASARIAN; and the ultranationalist **Armenian Aryan Union,** led by Armen AVESTISIAN, who was jailed in 2005 for making allegedly anti-Semitic statements; and the **Labor-Socialist Party**, founded in 2004 as a successor to the Socialist Party.

LEGISLATURE

The 1995 constitution provided for a unicameral **National Assembly** (*Azgayin Zhoghov*) elected by direct vote for a four-year term. Following several revisions of its composition, the assembly currently comprises 131 members, 41 elected on a first-past-the-post system from single-member districts and 90 on a proportional basis from a national constituency. Parties must secure 5 percent of the vote and coalitions 7 percent to gain representation in the proportional component of the balloting. The most recent election, held May 12, 2007, yielded the following distribution of seats: Republican Party of Armenia (HHD), 65 (41 in the proportional vote, 24 in the single-member districts); Prosperous Armenia (BH), 25 (18, 7); the Armenian Revolutionary Federation, 16 (16, 0); the Country of Law, 9 (8,1); Heritage, 7 (7, 0); the Alliance party, 1 (0, 1); and independents 8 (0, 8). (Two members from small parties secured seats as candidates on the HHK proportional list, as did one member from a small party on the BH proportional list. In addition, all of the parties that successfully contested the proportional balloting included elected candidates who were not formal members of the parties.)

Speaker: Hovik ABRAHAMYAN.

CABINET

[as of December 1, 2009]

Prime Minister	Tigran Sarkisian (HHK)
Deputy Prime Minister	Armen Gevorgyan (ind.)
Ministers	
Agriculture	Gerasim Alaverdyan (OY)
Culture	Hasmik Poghosyan (ind.) [f]
Defense	Gen. Seyran Ohanyan (ind.)
Diaspora	Hranush Hacobyan (HHK) [f]
Economy	Nerces Yeritzyan (HHK)
Education and Science	Armen Ashtoyen (HHK)
Emergency Situations	Mher Shageldyan (OY)
Energy and Natural Resources	Armen Movsissyan (HHK)
Environmental Protection	Aram Harutyunian (HHK)
Finance	Tigran Davtyan (ind.)
Foreign Affairs	Edvard Nalbanian (ind.)
Health	Dr. Harutyun Kushkyan (HHK)
Justice	Gevorg Danielyan (HHK)
Labor and Social Affairs	Mkhitar Mnatsakanyan (HHK)
Sport and Youth Affairs	Armen Grigoryan (BH)
Territorial Administration	Armen Gevorgyan (ind.)
Transport and Communication	Gurgen Sarkisian (OY)
Urban Development	Vardan Vardanyan (BH)

[f] = female

COMMUNICATIONS

After a sustained period of relative tolerance of dissent on the part of the government, media have been subjected to increasing governmental pressure in recent years, prompting sharp criticism from domestic journalists and international watchdog organizations. In March 2006 the U.S. State Department described press freedoms as "limited," in part in response to the government's perceived tight control of the media during the run-up to the November 2005 constitutional referendum. The OSCE in late 2006 expressed concern over reported acts of violence against journalists. Additional restrictions were instituted in 2007, particularly on foreign media, and the state of emergency of March 2008 included a ban on publication or broadcast of news perceived to be critical of the government and a block on independent Internet sites. Although some of the more draconian measures were subsequently lifted, journalists continued to charge that they were being "muzzled," and more than 20 violent attacks against journalists were reported in 2008.

Press. Although there were more than 90 newspapers published in Armenia prior to independence, most were controlled by the Communist Party and affiliated organizations. A number of new papers were launched in the 1990s, some as independents and others as party or government organs. One leading paper at the present is *Hayastani Hanrapetoutioun* (Republic of Armenia), founded in 1990 by the Supreme Council and published daily in Armenian in Yerevan. (A sister paper in Russian, *Respublika Aremeniya*, is also published, although it was reportedly beset by financial problems in the fall of 2000.) Other papers published daily in Yerevan in Armenian (unless otherwise indicated) include the following: *Aravot* (Morning), independent; *Azg* (The Nation); *Hayk* (Armenia), the weekly organ of the Armenian Pan-National Movement that resumed publication in September 2006 after a seven-year absence and is currently perceived as an opposition paper; *Haykakan Zhamanak*, described as critical of the government; *Iravunk*, independent biweekly associated with the Union of Constitutional Law; *Molorak* (Planet); *168 Zham*; *Charrord Ishkhanutian*, an opposition paper; *A1+*, independent; *Jamanak Yerevan*, independent; *Yerkis* (Country), published weekly (circulation 2,500) by the HHD; *Aizhm*, AZhM weekly; *Hraparak*, an opposition paper; *Golos Armenii*, in Russian; and *Hayots Ashkhar*, described as progovernment.

News agency. The dominant domestic facility is the government-controlled Armenian Press Agency (Armenpress), headquartered in Yerevan. Several private agencies have also been established recently, including the influential ARMINFO News Agency and *Armenia Today*, a widely used online news service.

Broadcasting and computing. Radio Yerevan and Armenian TV broadcast from Yerevan in Armenian and a number of other languages. Broadcasting licenses are controlled by the National Commission on Television and Radio, and several independent television stations have been shut down by the government in recent years. Most current broadcasters are considered loyal to the government. As of 2008 there were 62.1 Internet users per 1,000 inhabitants.

INTERGOVERNMENTAL REPRESENTATION

Ambassador to the U.S.: Tatoul MARKARIAN.

U.S. Ambassador to Armenia: Marie L. YOVANOVITCH.

Permanent Representative to the UN: Garen NAZARIAN.

IGO Memberships (Non-UN): BSEC, CEUR, CIS, EBRD, Eurocontrol, Interpol, IOM, OSCE, WCO, WTO.

AUSTRALIA

Commonwealth of Australia

Political Status: Established as a federal state under democratic parliamentary regime in 1901.

Area: 2,966,136 sq. mi. (7,682,300 sq. km.).

Population: 19,855,288 (2006C); 21,320,000 (2008E). The 2006 figure is not adjusted for underenumeration, estimated at 1.9 percent in the 2001 census.

Major Urban Centers (including suburbs, 2006 census): CANBERRA (323,056), Sydney (4,119,190), Melbourne (3,592,591), Brisbane (1,763,131), Adelaide (1,105,839), Perth (1,445,078), Hobart (200,525), Darwin (105,991).

Official Language: English.

Monetary Unit: Australian Dollar (market rate December 1, 2009: 1.08 dollars = $1US).

Sovereign: Queen ELIZABETH II.

Governor General: Quentin BRYCE; formerly governor of Queensland; sworn into office September 5, 2008, replacing Maj. Gen. Michael JEFFERY.

Prime Minister: Kevin RUDD (Australian Labor Party); sworn in December 3, 2007, following the general election of November 24 2007, succeeding John Winston HOWARD (Liberal Party of Australia), who had served as prime minister since 1996.

THE COUNTRY

Lying in the Southern Hemisphere between the Pacific and Indian oceans, Australia derives its name from the Latin *australis* (southern). A country of continental size, with an area slightly less than that of the contiguous United States, Australia includes the separate island of Tasmania in the southeast and small outlying islands in the Tasman Sea and Indian Ocean. It is the driest of the inhabited continents, with the inner third of its territory a desert ringed by another third of marginal agricultural lands. The population is concentrated in the coastal areas, particularly in the southeastern states of New South Wales and Victoria. Persons of British extraction now comprise less than half of the total population; the majority includes a sizable group of immigrants of predominantly Western and Southern European origins and a substantial proportion of East and South Asians (including refugees from Indochina), whose admission since December 1988 has been subject to strict financial and skill-based entry standards. There are also an estimated 300,000 Aboriginal people. In 2008 women constituted 45 percent of the labor force, concentrated mainly in retail sales, health care, real estate, and education. As of April 2009 two women were serving as state governors, in New South Wales and Queensland, and a third had been elected premier of Queensland. In 2008 a woman was appointed governor general of Australia.

Traditionally dependent on exports of wool and wheat, the Australian economy industrialized rapidly after World War II, with subsequent expansion based on extensive mineral resources, including iron ore, bauxite, coal, nickel, gold, silver, copper, uranium (the world's largest deposits), oil, and natural gas. Agriculture employs 3.6 percent of the labor force but contributes only 2.5 percent of GDP, whereas the industrial sector as a whole employs about 21 percent of workers and accounts for about 26 percent of GDP. Leading exports include manufactures, fuels, food and live animals, and metalliferous ores. Principal trading partners are Japan, China, the United States, South Korea, Singapore, and New Zealand.

In late 1991 Australia began a recovery from its worst postwar recession and commenced a decade and a half of continuous economic expansion. Growth in 2007 was a respectable 3.9 percent despite a severe drought. Growth slowed to 0.6 percent in 2008, however, with negative growth of 0.1 percent registered in the final quarter. The IMF forecast a decline of 1.4 percent in 2009 and the Federal Treasurer forecast a decline of 0.5 percent in 2009–2010. Unemployment, which had eased to 4.4 percent in November 2007, the lowest rate in three decades, rose to 4.9 percent by February 2009 and was predicted to climb to 8.3 percent by 2010. Contrary to predictions, in the third quarter of 2009 the economy registered net growth, and Treasurer Wayne SWAN announced that the recession was over for Australia.

GOVERNMENT AND POLITICS

Political background. The Commonwealth of Australia was formed on January 1, 1901, by federation of the former British colonies of New South Wales, Queensland, South Australia, Tasmania, Victoria, and Western Australia, all of which became federal states. Two territorial

units were added in 1911: the vast, underpopulated, and undeveloped area of the Northern Territory and the Australian Capital Territory, an enclave created within New South Wales around the capital city of Canberra. The small Jervis Bay Territory was added to the latter in 1915 to afford the capital direct sea access.

Political power since World War II has been exercised largely by three leading parties: the Australian Labor Party (ALP) on the one side and the Liberal Party of Australia (LPA), in alliance with the National Party (formerly the National Country Party), on the other. The Liberal–National Country coalition ruled from 1949 to 1972 and again from 1975 to 1983. Under Robert James Lee (Bob) HAWKE, former head of the Australian Council of Trade Unions, Labor achieved a decisive lower house victory in the election of March 1983, although it was unable to win effective control of the Senate. Additional victories followed in 1984, 1987, and 1990, when Hawke secured an unprecedented fourth term. In December 1991 Paul KEATING supplanted Hawke as party chief, and in March 1993 Keating went on to achieve an unexpected fifth consecutive election victory for Labor, with a slightly increased majority in the House of Representatives, although neither of the leading parties won control of the Senate.

In 1993–1994 the Keating government made progress in addressing the contentious issue of Aboriginal land rights. Reform legislation followed a High Court ruling of June 1992—the "Mabo judgment"—that effectively overturned the concept of Australia as a *terra nullius* (uninhabited land) at the time of 18th-century European settlement. Despite determined opposition and the longest Senate debate (nearly 50 hours) in Australian history, the government secured passage on December 22, 1993, of a Native Title Act that would permit Aboriginal people to press claims to as much as 10 percent of the country's land. Other settlements followed, such as the September 2006 court decision that granted the Nyoongar people native title to Perth.

In federal balloting on March 2, 1996, Keating's party lost to John HOWARD's Liberals and their National Party allies. Commanding 94 of the 148 lower house seats, the first Liberal-National government since 1983 took office on March 4 under Howard. Keating immediately stepped down as ALP leader in favor of Kim BEAZLEY.

In September 1996 Queensland representative Pauline HANSON, in a highly charged speech to the lower house, condemned Asian immigration and set off an escalating debate not only over immigration by non-Europeans but also of affirmative action and funding for Aboriginal social programs. Three months later the High Court ruled on an appeal lodged in part by the Wik people of Queensland, deciding that Aboriginal peoples could claim leased pastoral lands provided that such claims did not substantially interfere with the rights of the leaseholders. Furthermore, in May 1997 a national human rights commission condemned the forced placement of Aboriginal children in white foster homes, an assimilationist practice that had involved some 100,000 children (the "stolen generation") up through the 1960s. Although Prime Minister Howard offered a personal apology for the removal of the children from their parents, the government refused to make a formal apology and rejected proposals for compensation.

Meanwhile, under pressure from their rural-based coalition partner the Nationalists, the Liberal-led government had proposed legislation to limit the effect of the "Wik judgment" by increasing pastoralists' control over leased land. Howard staked his government's survival on the issue and persuaded the Senate on July 8, 1998, to pass the Native Title Amendment Bill, which it had previously rejected twice. He then called an early election for October 3 and his coalition again prevailed at the polls, but with a reduced total of 83 seats in the House. Despite an impressive showing in Queensland's June state elections, Pauline Hanson's One Nation party failed in its bid for greater federal representation, with Hanson losing her House seat and the party electing only one senator.

Riding a tide of popular support for its recently tightened immigration policy, coupled with a strong economy and public backing for the United States following the September 11, 2001, al-Qaida attacks in New York and Washington, Prime Minister Howard's Liberal-National coalition won a third term in the election of November 10, when it captured 81 of 150 House seats.

Despite public disapproval of the Howard government's participation in the March 2003 U.S.-led invasion of Iraq, Howard announced that he would seek a fourth term as prime minister in the 2004 election. On February 5, 2003, for the first time in over a century, the Senate had passed, 34–31, a symbolic no-confidence motion. The opposition move came in response to the government's decision to dispatch troops to staging areas in the Middle East. A similar motion in the House was defeated by the Liberal–National majority.

On October 9, 2004, Howard led his coalition to a bigger-than-expected electoral victory, increasing the Liberal–National total in the lower house and also, for the first time during his tenure, claiming a majority in the Senate.

After three further years of controversial Howard leadership, the electorate on November 24, 2007, delivered a strong verdict in favor of the Labor Party, which achieved an additional 5.7 percent and 23 new House seats over its 2004 performance. Prime Minister Howard was unseated after 11 years in his post, and the Labor leader Kevin RUDD was sworn as prime minister on December 3. The first-count party votes were distributed as follows: Labor Party, 43.4 percent; Liberal Party, 36.6 percent; Australian Greens, 7.8 percent; National Party, 5.5 percent; Family First, 2.0 percent; Australian Democrats, 0.7 percent; minor parties, 1.8 percent; and independents, 2.2 percent. Redistribution of votes to parties gaining seats in the House of Representatives gave Labor 52.7 percent and 83 seats and the Liberal-National Coalition 47.3 percent and 65 seats. Independents won 2 seats. No other party won seats in the House. The Senate, in contrast, remained dominated by the Liberal–National coalition, which had a total of 37 seats (including 1 held by the allied Country Liberal Party) to Labor's 32 seats.

Constitution and government. The Federal Constitution of July 9, 1900, coupled a bicameral legislative system patterned after that of the United States with the British system of executive responsibility to Parliament. The governor general, most of whose actions are circumscribed by unwritten constitutional convention, represents the crown and is advised by a Federal Executive Council that includes all federal ministers. Most other links to the monarchy were severed in 1986, with the assent of Queen ELIZABETH II. At a referendum held November 6, 1999, 55 percent of voters rejected adopting a republican form of government that would have replaced the British monarch and the governor general with a president chosen by a two-thirds majority of Parliament. (An even larger majority, 61 percent, defeated a proposed constitutional preamble that would have recognized the Aboriginal population as "the nation's first people.") Responsibility for defense, external affairs, foreign trade, and certain other matters is entrusted to the federal government, residual powers being reserved to the states.

The prime minister, who is the leader of the majority party (or coalition) in the Federal Parliament (the House of Representatives), is assisted by a cabinet selected from the membership of the House and Senate. The Senate is composed of no fewer than 6 (currently 12) senators from each of the six states, with 2 additional senators each from the Australian Capital Territory (ACT) and the Northern Territory. Approximately half of the Senate is renewed every three years. The House of Representatives is to have approximately twice as many members as the Senate. House membership is proportional to population, although no state can be allotted fewer than five representatives. Save in cases of early dissolution, the House is elected for a period of three years and must initiate all measures dealing with revenue and taxation. The entire Senate may be elected at once in the event of a "double dissolution," normally on the advice of the prime minister triggered by Senate intransigence in regard to government measures, as occurred in both 1983 and 1987.

The judicial system is comprised of the High Court of Australia, the Federal Court of Australia, state and territorial courts, and lower (magistrates') courts. Under legislation enacted in 1976, the High Court remains responsible for interpreting the Constitution while also maintaining original and appellate jurisdiction in certain areas. Established in 1977, the Federal Court has jurisdiction in a number of matters previously under the purview of the High Court in addition to replacing the Australian Industrial Court and the Federal Court of Bankruptcy.

For the most part, state governments are patterned after the federal government. Each state has an elected premier, an appointed governor, and (with the exception of Queensland) a bicameral legislature. The more important activities of the state governments are in the areas of health, public safety, transportation, education, and public utilities. In 1974 the partially elected advisory councils of the Northern and Capital territories were replaced by fully elected legislative assemblies, and in 1978 a wide range of internal authority was transferred to the Northern Territory government. The ACT became self-governing in 1988, at which time the previously incorporated Jervis Bay Territory reverted to a separate status. The governor general is empowered to make ordinances governing Jervis Bay, 90 percent of which has been granted to the Wreck Bay Aboriginal Community. In 1995 the Wreck Bay Aboriginal Community Council was granted limited authority to enact by-laws.

In an October 1998 referendum 53 percent of voters in the Northern Territory rejected a statehood proposal, even though opinion polls had indicated 80 percent support for becoming the seventh state. Analysts attributed the defeat, in part, to concern over taxation and a loss of federal funding.

State and Capital	*Area (sq. mi.)*	*Population (2008E)*
New South Wales (Sydney)	309,498	6966,000
Queensland (Brisbane)	666,872	4,263,000
South Australia (Adelaide)	379,922	1,603,000
Tasmania (Hobart)	26,177	498,000
Victoria (Melbourne)	87,876	5,290,000
Western Australia (Perth)	975,096	2,144,000
Territory and Capital		
Australian Capital Territory (Canberra)	899	344,000
Northern Territory (Darwin)	519,768	216,000
Jervis Bay Territory	28	499

Foreign relations. Australia's foreign policy, traditionally based on loyalty to Great Britain and the Commonwealth, adjusted to the realities of declining British power and the rising importance of Asia. Australia's long-standing commitment to internationalism has been expressed by active membership in the United Nations, in such regional security organizations as ANZUS (in partnership with the United States and New Zealand) and the Five Power Defence Arrangements (with Britain, Singapore, Malaysia, and New Zealand), and in such economic cooperation institutions as the World Trade Organization (WTO), the International Monetary Fund (IMF), the World Bank, the Asian Development Bank, and economic aid agencies.

During the 1970s Australia sought to delineate a foreign policy more independent of Britain and the United States. Almost immediately after assuming office in 1972, Labor Prime Minister E. Gough WHITLAM, an outspoken critic of U.S. policy in Vietnam, established diplomatic relations with the People's Republic of China, East Germany, and North Vietnam. His successor, Liberal Prime Minister Malcolm FRASER, improved relations with Washington. Following the refusal by New Zealand in 1985 to allow a U.S. Navy warship to visit without an affirmation that no nuclear weapons were on board, the ANZUS Treaty became "inoperative." Australia reinforced its security cooperation with the United States in the form of annual AUSMIN (Australia-U.S. ministerial) talks and enhanced exercises and military exchanges. John Howard formed a close personal relationship with U.S. President George W. Bush, committed Australian troops to the invasion of Iraq in 2003, and joined the U.S.-led Proliferation Security Initiative. Kevin Rudd came to office pledging to withdraw Australian combat troops from Iraq, which he did by December 2008, leaving only a small training contingent at the request of President Bush. Following a March 2009 meeting with President Barack Obama, Rudd committed to a troop increase in Afghanistan of 450 to reinforce the approximately 1,100 deployed at that time. A further 800 Australian troops are deployed in other parts of the Middle East.

Although deciding to allow port access to U.S. Navy vessels without requiring declarations that they carried no nuclear weapons, the government in late 1986 responded to widespread antinuclear sentiment by ratifying the South Pacific Forum's Treaty of Rarotonga, which declared a nuclear-weapons-free zone in the region. In addition, the government's vocal opposition to French nuclear testing in the South Pacific, despite Australia's export of uranium to France and elsewhere, generated a diplomatic dispute between the two countries. Relations with Paris subsequently warmed when the French terminated nuclear-arms testing in the Pacific in 1996 and the two governments agreed on policies to protect Antarctic resources.

In recent years Australia has devoted increasing attention to its nearby Asian and Pacific neighbors. In November 1989 Prime Minister Hawke hosted the launching of the Asia-Pacific Economic Cooperation (APEC), a forum for regional trade liberalization. His successor, Prime Minister Keating, played an active role in securing agreement at the 1994 Bogor, Indonesia, APEC meeting to achieve regional free trade by 2020. At the next meeting in 1995 Australia persuaded other regional governments to condemn France for resuming Pacific nuclear tests. In the 1990s Japan and China emerged as Australia's two most valuable trade partners. The Howard government initiated trade and investment facilitation negotiations with China, South Korea, Thailand, Singapore, Malaysia, and Indonesia aimed at eventual conclusion of free trade agreements. In November 2007 Australia and China signed a Nuclear Material Transfer Agreement and a Nuclear Cooperation Agreement regulating export of uranium. In April 2008 the new prime minister, Kevin Rudd, conducted a lengthy state visit to China, reiterated Australia's commitment to the on-going free trade negotiations, and announced an agreement with Beijing on cooperation on climate change and environmental policy. In August Rudd attended the Beijing Olympics despite calls for a boycott over China's controversial policies in Tibet. The Australian Defence White Paper of May 2009, foreshadowing Australia's acquisition of new weapons platforms and land-attack missiles, and reportedly responding to China's on-going arms buildup, drew an angry reaction from a senior Chinese navy officer, who characterized Australia's plans as "dangerous" and risking a regional arms race. The signing of a deal in August whereby ExxonMobil would supply PetroChina with liquefied natural gas from Western Australia worth $41 billion over two decades marked a warming of the relationship.

Relations with Papua New Guinea, a former Australian-administered territory, improved significantly following the approval in 1985 of a treaty demarcating the maritime border in the Torres Strait, although difficulties subsequently emerged over access to traditional fishing grounds in the area. In early 1998 Australia greeted the conclusion of a peace treaty (brokered by New Zealand) between the Papua New Guinea government and rebels on Bougainville by offering troops to monitor the agreement. In late 2003 Australia agreed to send some 200 police and civil servants to help Papua New Guinea combat crime. In 2006, however, Canberra criticized both Papua New Guinea and Solomon Islands for assistance given to Australian fugitive Julian MOTI in his effort to evade prosecution for alleged child sex crimes. Papua New Guinea sent the Australian police and officials home after local politicians objected to the alleged interference in domestic affairs. Harmony was restored by the election of new leaders in Honiara and Canberra.

Political turmoil in nearby Pacific islands led Australia in 2003 to initiate the Regional Assistance Mission to Solomon Islands (RAMSI) and to dispatch troops and police to restore order and support the elected government after a flare-up of inter-island ethnic hostility and lawlessness. Subsequently, Australia provided aid and seconded police and civilian experts to strengthen the government of the islands. Prime Minister Rudd visited Honiara in March 2008 to encourage the new government led by Prime Minister Derek Sikua. The Australian presence in 2009 numbered approximately 140 Defence Force personnel, 210 police, and 169 civilian specialists.

Fiji's December 2006 coup triggered an Australian cutoff of military links, imposition of travel restrictions on the interim government's leaders, and selective reduction of aid. In the Pacific Island Forum and Commonwealth meetings Rudd advocated deadlines for a return to civilian constitutional democracy by means of an election in 2009 and supported suspension of Fiji from both bodies when the deadlines were not met. Junta leader Commodore Frank Bainimarama blamed Australia's sanctions for imposing economic hardship on Fiji.

In December 1995 Australia and Indonesia signed a security cooperation agreement providing for consultation in the event of "adverse challenges." In January 1999, however, in a major policy shift, the Howard administration stated that it would back an "act of self-determination" for East Timor (now Timor-Leste), a former Portuguese colony that Indonesia had annexed in 1976. When an August 30 independence referendum passed in Timor-Leste, precipitating widespread violence by pro-Indonesia militia, Australia negotiated the formation of an 8,000-person peacekeeping force (International Force for East Timor, INTERFET) and committed 5,000 Australian troops. The peacekeeping deployment, approved by the United Nations Security Council, restored order and supervised the emergence of an independent Timor-Leste in 2002. Humiliated, Indonesia's president annulled the 1995 security treaty. By mid-2001 Jakarta appeared ready to restore relations, as indicated by the first visit by an Indonesian head of state, President Abdurrahman Wahid, to Australia in a quarter century, which was followed by Prime Minister Howard's reciprocal visit. Thereafter, however, relations were strained by Jakarta's inability (or unwillingness) to stem the flow of asylum seekers embarking by boat from Indonesia to Australia's outer territories. Relations were further complicated by terrorism, particularly the actions of *Jemaah Islamiah,* an Indonesian-based militant Muslim group responsible for the October 12, 2002, bombing of a Bali tourist resort that cost 184 lives, including 88 Australians.

Relations between Jakarta and Canberra took a more positive turn when the Howard government responded quickly to the Indian Ocean tsunami disaster of December 2004 by offering Indonesia the largest aid package in Australian history, worth A$1 billion over five years. Australian military personnel were also dispatched to aid stricken areas. In November 2006 Australia and Indonesia signed a new agreement on security cooperation despite Jakarta's displeasure, earlier in the year, at Canberra's decision to grant visas to 43 asylum seekers from the Indonesian province of Papua, where a separatist movement remains active. Relations were further improved by visits to Jakarta by the new prime minister, Kevin Rudd, and two of his senior ministers in June 2008 and the hosting in Canberra of the 9th Australia-Indonesia Ministerial Forum in November, at which time a five-year 2.5 billion Australian dollar aid package was announced. The two countries now have cooperative programs in trade and economic development, counterterrorism and security, illegal fishing, people smuggling, avian influenza, climate change, and interfaith dialogue. Relations with the newly independent government of Timor-Leste have generally been positive despite a dispute over the maritime border in the Timor Sea. Although Timor-Leste was to receive the vast majority of royalties from hydrocarbon extraction in a Joint Petroleum Development Area, it sought to revise a 2003 agreement that would give it only 20 percent of the larger Greater Sunrise field, which lies mostly within territory claimed by Australia. Border talks began in November 2003. The Howard government insisted on retaining the border as delineated by a 1972 agreement with Indonesia, and the Timor-Leste government accused Australia of delaying tactics, bad faith, and bullying. In January 2006 the disputants signed an agreement to share revenue equally from the disputed Greater Sunrise block, designated the Joint Petroleum Development Area, with resolution of the border issue deferred for 50 years. Australia and Timor-Leste have negotiated agreements on trade, development, illegal migration, people smuggling, counterterrorism, and security. In response to an assassination attempt against Timor-Leste's president, Australia in early 2008 dispatched an additional 200 troops and 70 police to shore up the International Stabilization Force that underpins the United Nations Mission in Timor-Leste. The additional troops were withdrawn when the security situation stabilized; Australia's contribution in 2009 stood at approximately 650 Defence Force personnel and 50 federal police plus civilian specialists.

In April 2008 Australia gained control of an additional 2.5 million square kilometers of seabed, including rights to exploit oil, gas, and minerals, according to a ruling by the UN Commission on the Limits of the Continental Shelf (CLCS). Parts of the new jurisdiction were expected to be designated as protected maritime areas.

For more than a decade, illegal immigration to Australia has been controversial not only domestically but also internationally. The issue flared up in 2001 when the Howard government, facing reelection, hardened its position on illegal immigrants. Beginning in August the navy was instructed to intercept refugee-laden boats attempting to land on Australia's northern islands, such as Christmas Island and Ashmore Reef. International headlines were made when a Norwegian freighter, the *MV Tampa,* rescued some 450 people from a sinking ferry but was denied permission to bring them to an Australian port. In September both the Liberals and Labor supported adoption of strict measures that included reduced rights of appeal for rejected immigration applications and legislation eliminating the right of those landing on Australia's off-shore islands to lodge asylum claims.

The intercepted asylum-seekers, many of whom had fled Afghanistan or Iraq, were placed in detention centers in the Australian outback or were transported to facilities in Nauru and Manus Island, Papua New Guinea, pending resolution of their cases. Australia met all costs for this offshore internment of nearly 700 asylum-seekers, which was called the "Pacific solution". In the following five years many internees were accepted by Australia or third countries such as New Zealand and Sweden, but the majority were repatriated.

Meanwhile, in March–April 2002, violent riots, arson, and episodes of self-inflicted injury broke out at several detention centers within Australia, including the isolated Woomera facility. In August 2003 the High Court ruled that the government could not detain refugees indefinitely, and the government, while remaining firm on nonadmission of illegal migrants, in 2004 and 2005 made concessions in response to judicial and public concern. These included offers of up to A$10,000 to hundreds of Afghan detainees to encourage voluntary repatriation, the speeding of asylum hearings, the release of women and children from detention during the review process, and later the closing of the Woomera center, the upgrading of the others, and establishment of a new center on Christmas Island.

A cabinet reshuffle in late January 2007 saw the departure of Sen. Amanda VANSTONE as minister of the Department of Immigration and Multicultural Affairs, who had frequently been the target of opposition criticism in connection with Australia's harsh refugee interception and detention policies. The new Rudd government in February 2008 closed the Australian-sponsored camps on Nauru and Manus islands and terminated the "Pacific solution."

Current issues. The run-up to the 2007 general election produced vigorous debate and criticism of the Howard government. Campaign issues included Howard's widely unpopular support of U.S. policy in Iraq, controversial workplace legislation that had been adamantly opposed by trade unions, and economic uncertainties related to competition from Asia, weaknesses in the U.S. economy, and the high value of the Australian dollar. In addition, a prolonged drought and dire warnings of future water shortages were contributing to a wider public dialogue about the environment and global warming. Prime Minister Howard, who was a skeptic on the climate change issue, refused to sign the Kyoto Protocol, and instead joined with the United States, China, Japan, South Korea, and India in the less-ambitious Asia-Pacific Partnership on Clean Development and Climate. His opponent, Kevin Rudd, in contrast, pledged to join the Kyoto initiative and did so on December 3, 2007 soon after becoming prime minister.. In 2008 Rudd initiated legislation to set up a Carbon Pollution Reduction Scheme and require industrial emitters to bid for permits. On August 13, 2009, the Senate rejected the legislation by 42 votes to 30 but climate change minister Penny WONG pledged to re-introduce it, with amendments, in October. Moreover the Rudd government announced that in upcoming international negotiations in Copenhagen in December Australia would commit to a unilateral reduction of greenhouse gas emissions of 5 per cent below the 1990 level by 2020 and consider increasing that percentage to up to 25 percent if other states reduced their emissions correspondingly.

Other initiatives by the Rudd government in its first months in office included refusing to sell uranium ore to India until it signed the

Nuclear Non-Proliferation Treaty (NPT), allowing unions more latitude in workplace bargaining, and initiating a comprehensive review of environmental and water resource policy. On February 15, 2008, Rudd offered a formal apology in Parliament to aborigines for injustices by past governments, but he did not propose any specific measures of restitution. In April 2009, however, Rudd reversed the Howard government's prior disapproval of the UN-sponsored Declaration on the Rights of Indigenous Peoples and endorsed it.

Rudd also indicated that transforming Australia into a republic would appear on his government's agenda but would not be an urgent priority. The Rudd government appointed Queensland Governor Quentin BRYCE as governor general, effective on September 4, 2008. She became the first woman to achieve Australia's highest post, and was also reported to favor republicanism. Liberal Party leader Malcolm TURNBULL, who assumed leadership of the opposition in September 2008, was also an avowed republican. But public support for republicanism eased to 45 percent in early 2009 from a prior high of 54 percent, and Rudd indicated that there would be no referendum on the issue during his first term.

In September 2008 the Victoria state court found seven Muslim defendants guilty of membership in a terrorist association and planning a bombing campaign aimed at forcing the withdrawal of Australian troops from Iraq, and in August 2009 further arrests were made, reportedly thwarting an attack on an army facility.

The 2008 budget provided incentives to foreign investors and funds to modernize the infrastructure and develop renewable energy sources. It also raised the immigration target to 300,000 and foreshadowed a guest worker scheme for Pacific islanders. The May 2009 budget increased funding for public works, communications, energy, education, health, and clean energy technology. Taxes were not raised and an unprecedented deficit of A$57.6 billion was projected, drawing criticism from the opposition.

The Defence White Paper issued the same month prescribed an annual increase in defence spending of 3 percent and acquisition of top-of-the-line strike aircraft, heavy destroyers, submarines, missiles, and attack drones. Opposition leaders queried how these weapons would be paid for and Asian leaders wondered who they might be used against.

POLITICAL PARTIES

Government Party:

Australian Labor Party (ALP). The oldest of the existing political parties, with a continuous history since the 1890s, the ALP began as the political arm of the trade union movement, to which it still has close ties. Present policies include support for extensive social services, the pursuit of racial and sexual equality, a more independent foreign policy, and restriction of the constitutional role of the British monarch. It is ambivalent about expanded immigration. It has long been divided between a moderate, pragmatic wing, which commands a majority in terms of parliamentary representation, and a dogmatically socialist, trade union–oriented left wing, which tends to be more strongly entrenched in the party organization.

First in office in 1904, the ALP formed the government from 1941 to 1949 and then languished in opposition until E. Gough Whitlam led the party to victory in 1972. The governor general's dismissal of his administration in 1975, subsequent to Senate rejection of the proposed national budget, was followed by electoral defeat, but the ALP returned to power in 1983 under the leadership of Robert (Bob) Hawke, who also won the three succeeding elections in 1984, 1987, and 1990.

On December 1991 Hawke was challenged by his treasurer, Paul Keating, and lost a caucus vote in an unprecedented defeat of an incumbent prime minister. Despite economic recession, record unemployment, and a series of financial scandals, the ALP won a fifth term on March 13, 1993, increasing its tally in the 147-member House of Representatives to 80 seats.

The ALP failed to win the March 1996 election, however, following which Keating resigned as party leader and was succeeded by former deputy prime minister Kim Beazley. In the national election of October 1998 the party narrowly missed gaining a parliamentary majority and remained in opposition. In the 2001 election the ALP's House representation fell by 2, to 65 seats. A day after the national loss, Kim Beazley resigned as party leader and was replaced by Simon CREAN, who in turn resigned in November and was succeeded by Mark LATHAM.

In the 2004 general election the ALP lost ground in the lower house, winning only 60 seats, and in January 2005, citing health reasons, Latham resigned his party and legislative posts. He was succeeded by former party leader Beazley, who was unopposed for the post following the withdrawals of Kevin Rudd and Julia Gillard. In early December 2006, however, Rudd mounted a successful challenge to Beazley, whom he defeated 49–39. Shortly thereafter, Beazley announced that he would retire from politics in 2007.

In contrast to its lack of success at the national level, the ALP in the period 2002–2009 controlled all six state governments and both self-governing territories.

In the 2007 general election Labor won 52.7 percent of the consolidated party vote and 83 seats in the House of Representatives and was able to form a government. Labor also won 40.5 percent in the election for half of the Senate, bringing its total seats to 32, equal to that of the Liberal Party. However, following the Western Australia state election of September 2008, Labor was overpowered by a Liberal-National coalition, its first loss of power at the state level since 2002. But in the March 2009 Queensland state election Labor prevailed over the Liberal–National coalition by 50 seats to 35 in the 89-seat parliament, and Anna BLIGH became the state's first elected woman premier.

Leaders: Linda BURNEY (National President), Kevin RUDD (Leader and Prime Minister), Julia GILLARD (Deputy Leader and Deputy Prime Minister), Chris EVANS (Leader in the Senate), Karl BITAR (National Secretary).

Major Opposition Party:

Liberal Party of Australia (LPA). The LPA, a successor to the United Australia Party, was founded in 1944 by Sir Robert MENZIES, who served as prime minister in 1939–1941 and 1949–1966. It represents an amalgamation of traditional liberals and conservatives with strong ties to the business community. The Liberals have a record of conservative financial policies, economic stability, counterinflationary measures, and cooperation with the Commonwealth and the United States.

After losing its legislative majority to Labor in 1983 after governing for eight years under Prime Minister Malcolm Fraser, the LPA recouped some of its losses in the 1984 election. Its popular leader, Andrew PEACOCK, resigned in September 1985 because of the rejection of his candidate for deputy leader and was succeeded by John Howard. Peacock regained the leadership following the unexpected ouster of Howard in May 1989. He again stepped down after the party's 1990 defeat and was succeeded by John HEWSON.

After the failure of the Liberal-National coalition's March 1993 bid to unseat Labor, Hewson was replaced in May by Alexander DOWNER, a monarchist from the Liberal patrician wing who was nevertheless an economic centrist and more progressive than many of his colleagues on such social issues as race relations, immigration, and homosexuality. However, public gaffes and declining support for the LPA in polls obliged Downer to resign in January 1995, enabling the more conservative Howard to return to party leadership.

A declared monarchist and "Thatcherite," Howard moved to a more centrist stance for the March 1996 federal election, leading the Liberals to a landslide lower house victory and forming a government that again included the National Party. His decision to call an early election for October 1998 resulted in a loss of 11 House seats from the 1996 total of 75. At the 2001 election the Liberals moved up to 68 House seats.

In October 2004 the party exceeded expectations not only by gaining 6 house seats but also by picking up 2 Senate seats, thereby giving the LPA–NPA coalition an upper house majority. In June 2005 the Liberals elected their first woman party president, Chris McDiven.

In the 2007 general election the Liberals suffered a negative swing of 4.2 percent of the popular vote, winning only 36.6 percent and 55 seats in the House of Representatives. In the Senate, newly won and holdover seats totaled 32, equal to that of Labor. Following the election, in which he lost his House seat, John Howard announced his retirement from the party leadership. He was replaced by former minister of defence Brendon NELSON, whose leadership proved lackluster. In September 2008 Malcolm Turnbull, former minister for environment and water resources, was selected as party leader. Also in September the Liberals in coalition with the Nationals won 28 seats in the state election in Western Australia and formed a government, tipping out Labor, which had won the prior two elections. This election also broke Labor's monopoly of all federal and state governments. But in Queensland in March 2009 the coalition was less successful in the state election, winning only 37 out of 89 seats, and was denied power for the fifth straight time as Labor formed a state government.

Leaders: Malcolm TURNBULL (Federal Liberal Party Leader and Leader of the Opposition), Julie BISHOP (Deputy Party Leader and Deputy Leader of the Opposition), Alan STOCKDALE (Federal President), Nick MINCHIN (Liberal Party Leader in the Senate), Helen COONAN (Deputy Party Leader in the Senate), Brian LOUGHNANE (Federal Director).

Other Parliamentary Parties:

National Party of Australia (NPA or The Nationals). Founded in 1920 as the Country Party and then known as the National Country Party from 1975 until 1982, the NPA assumed its present name in 1983 in an effort to widen its appeal beyond its rural roots. Conservative in outlook, the party's policies traditionally reflected rural and farming interests such as guaranteed farm prices, tax rebates for capital investment and conversion to electricity, and soil conservation. Precluded by its limited constituency from winning a majority in the House, it has a long history of alliance with the United Australia Party and its successor, the Liberal Party. Although tensions have periodically surfaced on policy issues and the allocation of safe seats, the conservative John Howard's recovery of the Liberal leadership in January 1995 heralded improved relations between the coalition partners, who returned to government in March 1996. The NPA lost 3 House seats in October 1998, retaining a total of 16.

On June 30, 1999, the party chief and deputy prime minister, Tim FISCHER, announced his decision to resign and his deputy John ANDERSON became party leader and deputy prime minister. The Nationals lost 3 House seats at the November 2001 election and another seat in October 2004, but it added 2 Senate seats, thereby helping the Liberal-National bloc retain a slim majority in the upper house.

In June 2005, Anderson was succeeded by the party's deputy leader, Mark VAILE. In the 2007 general election the National Party gained 5.5 percent of the vote and won 10 seats in the House of Representatives. In the Senate it won 2 seats, for a total of 4. Vaile retired and Warren Truss was chosen to succeed him. The Nationals succeeded in winning four seats in the Western Australia state election in September 2008 and joined the Liberals to form a government. The Liberal–National coalition was unsuccessful in displacing Labour in the Queensland state election of March 2009.

Leaders: Warren TRUSS (Party Leader), Nigel SCULLION (Deputy Party Leader), John TANNER (Federal Party President), Brad HENDERSON (Federal Party Director), Barnaby JOYCE (Party Leader in the Senate), Pam STALLMAN (Federal Party Secretary).

Country Liberals. Established in the Northern Territory in 1974 as the Country Liberal Party (CLP), the conservative CLP constituted an amalgamation of the Country Party of Sam CALDER and supporters of the Northern Territory's Liberal Party branch. At the territory's first Legislative Assembly election, in 1974, the CLP won 17 of 19 seats. In 1979 it established close official ties to both the LPA and the NPA. At various times CLP members of Parliament have chosen to sit with both those federal parties.

Following the October 2004 election, the CLP continued to hold 1 seat in the federal House of Representatives and 1 seat in the Senate. At a territorial election in June 2005 the CLP lost 6 of the 10 seats it had held in the territorial legislature but raised its total to 11 in the subsequent election. The party won no federal seats in the 2007 general election, but Sen. Nigel SCULLION's term continued until June 2011. In December 2008 the party voted to change its name to Country Liberals.

Leaders: Rick SETTER (President), Barry DENSLEY (Vice President), Richard TEO (Vice President), Bob JOHNSTON (Director), Graeme LEWIS (Treasurer), Nigel SCULLION (Deputy Leader of the Nationals in the Senate), Terry MILLS (Leader of the Opposition in the Northern Territory Legislature).

Australian Greens. Preferring not to be called a "party," the Australian Greens is a confederation of the following autonomous environmental groups: **ACT Greens** (Australian Capital Territory), **The Greens NSW** (New South Wales), **Queensland Greens, Greens SA** (South Australia), **Tasmanian Greens, NT Greens** (Northern Territory), the **Victorian Greens**, and the **Greens (WA)** (Western Australia). From its founding in 1990 until October 2003, the Greens (WA) was organizationally separate from the federal Greens, although closely allied. It had held a federal Senate seat from 1993 until 1998. In a September 2003 ballot 80 percent of those voting endorsed formally joining the Australian Greens.

Although the Greens had not won election to the House of Representatives until a by-election victory by Michael ORGAN in 2002 (a seat they failed to retain in 2004), they have had a presence in the Senate since 1996, when party leader Bob Brown was elected from Tasmania. A second seat was added in 2001, and total representation was doubled at the 2004 election, when they captured 7.5 percent of the first-preference vote, for third place behind the Liberal-National coalition and Labor. In October 2003 the Greens' Bob Brown and Kerry NETTLE were suspended from the House for a day for interrupting U.S. President George W. Bush during his address to Parliament.

In the 2007 general election the Greens attracted 7.8 percent of the vote but won no seats in the House of Representatives. In the Senate election they garnered 9.0 percent of the vote and won 2 seats, for a total of 5.

Leaders: Adam BANDT (National Convenor), Emma YOUNG (National Secretary), Bob BROWN (Party Leader in the Senate), Christine MILNE (Senator from Tasmania), Rachel SIEWERT and Scott LUDLAM (Senators from Western Australia), Sarah HANSON-YOUNG (Senator from South Australia).

Australian Democrats (AD). The social democratic AD was organized in 1977 by former Liberal cabinet minister Donald L. CHIPP and some members of the Australia Party, a small reformist group. By increasing its Senate representation from 2 seats to 5 at the October 1980 national election, it secured the balance of power in the upper house, a position that it maintained until the 2004 elections. In October 1996 the party lost its leader, Sen. Cheryl KERNOT, arguably the most prominent woman politician in Australia in her day, through defection to the ALP, whereupon Meg LEES became parliamentary party leader.

Sharp divisions over the 10 percent goods and services tax (GST) and other issues roiled the party from 1999 to 2001 and led to Lees's displacement in April 2001 by GST opponent Natasha STOTT DESPOJA who in turn resigned her party post in August, to be succeeded on an interim basis by Sen. Brian GREIG. In October Sen. Andrew BARTLETT was named parliamentary leader, but he stepped down in December 2003 after an altercation with another senator. He was replaced by Sen. Lyn ALLISON. Meanwhile, in April 2003 Lees had formed the Australian Progressive Alliance (APA), but she failed to win reelection in 2004 and the APA was deregistered at the end of her senatorial term.

At the October 2004 federal election the Democrats saw their senatorial delegation halved and their percentage of the first-preference vote drop to 2.1 percent. Although Stott Despoja won a Senate seat, the party's deputy leader in the upper house, Aden RIDGEWAY—only the second Aboriginal candidate ever to win election to Parliament—was defeated in a reelection bid.

In the 2007 general election the Democrats attracted only 0.7 percent of votes and won no seats in the House of Representatives or the Senate. When the terms of four senators who took their seats in 2004 expired on June 30, 2008, the Democrats were left with no federal parliamentary seats.

Leaders: Aron PAUL (National President); Casey BALK, Clinton BARNES, Mayo MATERAZZO, Julia MELLAND, James PAGE (Deputy National Presidents); Anton PRANGE (National Secretary).

Family First Party (FFP). Initially organized in South Australia, where Andrew Evans, an Assemblies of God pastor, was elected to the upper house of the legislature in early 2002, the FFP quickly attracted wider support because of its appealing family values orientation. In August 2004, soon after organizing at the federal level, it named Andrea MASON the first indigenous woman to head an Australian party.

Despite its Christian roots, the party insists that it is not only a Christian party but seeks to cross religious as well as social and ethnic lines. The party supports ecologically sustainable development, the war on terrorism (although it initially opposed involvement in the war in Iraq), mandatory filtering of the Internet by service providers, and requiring women who seek publicly funded abortions to first receive counseling. In 2004 both the Liberals and Labor sought its support. The FFP won one Senate seat in the October federal election.

In the 2007 general election the FFP attracted 2.0 percent support in the House election and 1.6 percent in the Senate election but won no seats. The term of its sole senator runs until June 2011.

Leaders: Andrew EVANS (Federal President), Steve FIELDING (Leader of Family First Federal Party), Dennis HOOD (South Australia State Leader).

Other Parties:

One Nation. Formed in April 1997 by Pauline Hanson (and later called "Pauline Hanson's One Nation" for a time), One Nation quickly became the rallying point for Australians skeptical of non-European immigration, Aboriginal welfare programs, and trade liberalization. It nevertheless suffered significant setbacks in the October 1998 national election, at which it won only a single Senate seat despite having captured 11 of 89 seats, on a first-preference vote share of 23 percent, in Queensland's state legislature in June. Hanson herself lost her House seat in the October balloting, at which the party as a whole won 8.4 percent of first-preference votes.

Although Hanson was reelected party leader in February 1999, by late in the month dissatisfaction with what some members called the party's "autocratic and undemocratic structure" had led the majority of its recently elected Queensland state representatives to bolt or be dismissed from the party. In December 1999 five of the legislators formed the City Country Alliance (CCA).

In early October 2000 Hanson forced the expulsion of a party cofounder, David OLDFIELD, over his participation in forming a new No GST Party with David ETTRIDGE, another One Nation cofounder. The party's disintegration accelerated after that, and in the November 2001 federal election it took only 4.3 percent of the House votes. In January 2002 Hanson resigned as leader. In August 2003 both she and Ettridge were convicted of electoral fraud in connection with the party's registration in Queensland in 1997. They were sentenced to three years in prison, but the convictions were quashed by the Queensland Court of Appeals.

By then, most One Nation members of various state legislatures had been defeated or had left the party. Following the 2004 state election, One Nation held only one seat in the Queensland legislature, and in the 2004 federal election its sole senator, Len HARRIS, was defeated. Hanson herself, running as an independent, was also defeated in a Senate bid. David Oldfield, then head of the New South Wales One Nation, announced in 2005 that he would sit as an independent in the NSW upper house.

In February 2005 One Nation lost its federal registration. Its membership had dropped by then to 200–300. In September 2006 it retained its 1 seat in the Queensland legislature. From that time the One Nation party has had no national leadership organization, only state leaders.

In the 2007 general election One Nation gained 0.3 percent of votes for the House and 0.4 percent for the Senate but won no seats. Pauline Hanson stood in the Queensland Senate election at the head of her new **Pauline's United Australia Party,** which she had launched in May, but with only 4 percent of the vote she failed to gain a seat. In the March 2009 Queensland state election the last sitting member of One Nation, Rosa Lee LONG, lost her House seat, marking the end of One Nation representation in any national or state legislature. Pauline Hanson, standing as an independent, was also unsuccessful.

Leaders: James CASSIDY (National Secretary), Stan BATTEN (National Registered Officer), Rod EVANS (National Party Agent). James SAVAGE (Queensland Party President),), Neil GILOUR (Western Australia Party President).

Australia has many smaller parties, some operating at the state level and others focusing on single issues. Other minor parties that nominated candidates for the November 2007 general election but won no seats (and had no Senate seats carrying over from the 2004 election) included the **Australian Shooters Party,** the **Careers Alliance,** the **Christian Democratic Party (Fred Nile Group),** the **Citizens Electoral Council,** the **Climate Change Coalition,** the **Conservatives for Climate and Environment,** the **Democratic Labor Party,** the **Fishing and Lifestyle Party, Hear Our Voice,** the **Liberty and Democracy Party,** the **Non-Custodial Parents Party (Equal Parenting),** the **Nuclear Disarmament Party, Senator-On-Line,** the **Socialist Alliance,** the **Socialist Equity Party,** and **What Women Want.**

Of the small leftist parties that did not contest the 2004 or 2007 federal elections, the best known is the **Communist Party of Australia** (CPA), which in 1996 changed its name from the Socialist Party of Australia (a 1971 splinter from the original, defunct CPA). The CPA is currently led by longtime activist Hannah MIDDLETON (General Secretary) and Vinnie MOLINA (President).

LEGISLATURE

The Australian **Federal Parliament** is a bicameral legislature with an upper chamber (Senate) and a lower chamber (House of Representatives), both elected by direct universal suffrage.

Senate. The Senate currently consists of 76 members (12 from each state plus 2 each from the Australian Capital Territory and the Northern Territory), who are elected from state or territorial lists by proportional representation for staggered six-year terms. Balloting is normally conducted every three years for one-half of the Senate, at the same time as the elections for the House of Representatives. A Senate vacancy is filled by a member of the party holding the seat. Following the election of 38 senators on November 24, 2007 (with effect from July 1, 2008), the Senate had the following distribution of seats: Australian Labor Party, 32; Liberal Party, 32; Australian Greens, 5; National Party, 4; Country Liberal Party, 1; Family First Party, 1; independent, 1, with no changes as of April 2009.

President: John HOGG.

House of Representatives. The present House consists of 150 representatives elected from single-member constituencies by preferential balloting (progressive elimination of lowest-ranked candidates with redistribution of preferences until one candidate secures a majority). Members are elected for three-year terms, subject to dissolution. The election of November 24, 2007, produced the following distribution of seats: Australian Labor Party, 83; Liberal Party, 55; National Party, 10; independents, 2. By-elections in June and September 2008 altered the distribution to Labor, 83; Liberal, 55; National, 9; independents 3.

Speaker: Harry JENKINS.

CABINET

[as of September 24, 2009]

Prime Minister	Kevin Rudd
Deputy Prime Minister	Julia Gillard [f]
Cabinet Ministers	
Agriculture, Fisheries, and Forestry	Tony Burke
Broadband, Communications, and the Digital Economy	Stephen Conroy
Climate Change and Water	Penny Wong [f]
Defense	John Faulkner
Education	Julia Gillard [f]
Employment and Workplace Relations	Julia Gillard [f]
Environment, Heritage, and the Arts	Peter Garrett
Families, Housing, Community Services, and Indigenous Affairs	Jenny Macklin [f]
Finance and Deregulation	Lindsay Tanner
Financial Services, Superannuation and Corporate Law	Chris Bowen
Foreign Affairs	Stephen Smith
Health and Aging	Nicola Roxon [f]
Human Services	Chris Bowen
Immigration and Citizenship	Chris Evans
Innovation, Industry, Science, and Research	Kim Carr
Infrastructure, Transport, Regional Development, and Local Government	Anthony Albanese
Resources and Energy	Martin Ferguson
Social Inclusion	Julia Gillard [f]
Tourism	Martin Ferguson
Trade	Simon Crean
Attorney General	Robert McClelland
Special Minister of State and Cabinet Secretary	John Faulkner
Treasurer	Wayne Swan
Outer Ministers	
Aging	Justine Elliot [f]
Competition Policy and Consumer Affairs	Chris Emerson
Defense Personnel, Materiel, and Science	Warren Snowdon
Early Childhood Education, Childcare, and Youth	Kate Ellis [f]

CABINET

Employment Participation	Mark Arbib
Home Affairs	Brendan O'Connor
Housing	Tanya Pilbersek [f]
Indigenous Health, Rural and Regional Health and Regional Services Delivery	Warren Snowden
Small Business, Independent Contractors, and the Service Economy	Craig Emerson
Sport	Kate Ellis [f]
Status of Women	Tanya Plibersek [f]
Superannuation and Corporate Law	Chris Bowen
Veterans' Affairs	Alan Griffin

[f] = female

COMMUNICATIONS

In recent years an increasing number of newspapers and broadcasting stations have been absorbed by media groups, the two principal ones being Rupert Murdoch's News Corporation, whose media interests extend to the United Kingdom and United States (where it now has its corporate headquarters), and John Fairfax Holdings. In October 2006 the Howard government successfully pushed for further media deregulation, although the Federal Parliament balked at permitting a single company to own all three of a community's or region's main newspaper, radio, and television outlets.

Press. Newspapers are privately owned and almost all are published in the state capitals for intrastate readers; News Corporation's *Australian* and Fairfax's *Australian Financial Review* are the only genuinely national daily newspapers. The leading dailies are as follows: *Herald Sun* (Melbourne, 540,000 daily, 510,000 Saturday), sensationalist; *Daily Telegraph* (Sydney, 400,000 daily, 340,000 Saturday), tabloid; *Sydney Morning Herald* (Sydney, 225,000 daily, 380,000 Saturday), oldest morning newspaper (founded 1831), conservative; *Courier-Mail* (Brisbane, 220,000 daily, 330,000 Saturday); *Advertiser* (Adelaide, 200,000 daily, 270,000 Saturday), tabloid; *Age* (Melbourne, 200,000 daily, 300,000 Saturday), independent; *West Australian* (Perth, 200,000 daily, 390,000 Saturday), conservative; *Australian* (Sydney, Adelaide, Perth, Melbourne, Townsville, Brisbane, 130,000 daily; 290,000 Saturday, published as *Weekend Australian*), first national daily; *Brisbane News* (Brisbane, 120,000); *Australian Financial Review* (Sydney, 85,000); *Mercury* (Hobart, 50,000 daily, 65,000 Saturday), conservative; *Canberra Times* (Canberra, 40,000 daily, 70,000 Saturday), conservative; *Northern Territory News* (Darwin, 20,000 daily, 30,000 Saturday). The leading Sunday papers are *Sunday Telegraph* (Sydney, 700,000); *Sunday Mail* (Brisbane, 610,000); *Sun-Herald* (Sydney, 580,000); *Sunday Times* (Perth, 350,000); *Sunday Mail* (Adelaide, 320,000); *Sunday Tasmanian* (Hobart, 60,000); *Sunday Territorian* (Darwin, 25,000).

News agencies. The domestic agency is the Australian Associated Press (AAP), a Reuters-affiliated international news service owned by the country's principal metropolitan dailies; in addition, most leading foreign agencies maintain bureaus in the Sydney area.

Broadcasting and computing. The federal Australian Communications and Media Authority licenses and regulates radio and television stations. The principal source for public radio and television is the Australian Broadcasting Corporation; there is also a public Special Broadcasting Service that offers programming in some 60 languages. Commercial broadcasting covers the spectrum, including satellite, cable, and pay-TV, although there are only three free national television stations. As of 2008 there were 719.8 Internet users per 1,000 inhabitants.

INTERGOVERNMENTAL REPRESENTATION

Ambassador to the U.S.: Dennis James RICHARDSON.

U.S. Ambassador to Australia: (Vacant).

Permanent Representative to the UN: Gary Francis QUINLAN.

IGO Memberships (Non-UN): ADB, ANZUS, APEC, BIS, CP, CWTH, EBRD, G-20, IEA, Interpol, IOM, IOR-ARC, OECD, PC, PCA, PIF, WCO, WTO.

RELATED TERRITORIES

Ashmore and Cartier Islands Territory. The Ashmore Islands (comprising Middle, East, and West islands) and Cartier Island, totaling about 0.36 square miles, are situated in the Indian Ocean about 200 miles off the northwestern coast of Australia. All are uninhabited save for a seasonal presence. Under the Ashmore and Cartier Islands Acceptance Act (effective May 10, 1934), it was intended that the territory be administered by Western Australia, but by a 1938 amendment to the act it was formally annexed to the Northern Territory. Since July 1978 Ashmore and Cartier have been under the direct administration of the Australian government, with oversight currently falling under the Attorney General's Department. Two oilfields, Challis and Jabiru, are located near the islands, and in April 2005 the Australian government included an area near Ashmore and Cartier among 29 new offshore exploration sites open for bidding by the petroleum industry.

In May 1996 officials from Australia and Indonesia visited the territory during discussions on the maritime boundary. International attention has since been drawn to Ashmore by "people smuggling" of refugees seeking Australian residency. To counter the flow, in 2001 Parliament passed legislation that excised the territory from the country's migration zone, thereby removing the right of refugees who land there to apply for asylum.

Australian Antarctic Territory. A legacy of British claims, the Australian Antarctic Territory encompasses two sectors of Antarctica extending from 45 to 136 degrees east longitude and from 142 to 160 degrees east longitude. Together these sectors comprise almost 2.5 million square miles, or nearly 50 percent of the continent. The provisions of the Antarctic Treaty of 1959 have placed the area in a state of suspended sovereignty, although nominally the laws of the Australian Capital Territory are in effect. Australian activities in the Territory are administered by the Australian Antarctic Division of the Department of the Environment, Water Resources, Heritage, and the Arts.

In 1991 an international treaty banned all mining in the Antarctic, including the Australian Antarctic Territory and the adjacent continental shelf.

In December 1999 the Howard administration announced that it planned to survey the Antarctic continental shelf beyond Australia's 200-mile exclusive economic zone (EEZ). Under the UN Convention on the Law of the Sea (UNCLOS), international acceptance of the survey results would grant Australia exclusive rights to explore the seabed in the delineated area, which may extend as far as an additional 150 nautical miles. The Howard government noted, however, that the effort to exercise its sovereignty rights under UNCLOS did not signal any shift in policy toward the 50-year moratorium on mining the continental shelf.

A more recent concern has been whaling by Japanese ships within the EEZ, particularly in the Australian Whale Sanctuary, which was established in 2000 under the Environment Protection and Biodiversity Conservation Act of 1999. As part of the International Polar Year 2007–2008 Australian scientists are participating in over 60 projects, including a Census of Antarctic Marine Life.

Christmas Island. Named by a British captain on December 25, 1643, Christmas Island, with an area of about 52 square miles, is located in the Indian Ocean about 230 miles south of Java, Indonesia. It was annexed by the United Kingdom in 1888 but was not inhabited by a significant number of people until the late 1890s, when Chinese workers were brought in to mine phosphate. The Japanese occupied the crown colony during World War II and imprisoned many of the residents.

Australia took over administration of Christmas Island from Singapore in 1958. A 2001 census recorded 1,508 persons, 70 percent of whom were Chinese and 10 percent, Malays. The balance of residents were predominantly of European descent. The chief government official, the administrator of the Indian Ocean Territories, is responsible to the federal Attorney General's Department. The nine-member Christmas Island Shire Council, established in 1992 as successor to the Christmas Island Services Corporation, provides municipal-type services and economic management.

On May 7, 1994, an unofficial referendum on secession was sponsored by the Union of Christmas Island Workers. While the result was negative, the poll served to point out widespread frustration over a number of issues, including a housing shortage. A subsequent referendum on November 6, 1999, returned a 62 percent vote favoring self-government.

The only nonservice industry on the island, the extraction of nearly exhausted phosphate deposits, was previously under management of the British Phosphate Commission, the shareholders being Australia, New Zealand, and the United Kingdom. However, in June 1991, after a number of reorganizations, a new corporation, Phosphate Resources Ltd., was formed by mine workers to exploit existing sites. In 2006 controversy persisted over the company's recent request to extend mining into a previously untouched rainforest.

The Australian government has encouraged other private commercial activities to broaden the economic base, including a tourist hotel and casino complex. The Christmas Island Resort opened in 1993 but closed in April 1998, laying off some 320 workers. Also in 1998, the government selected the Asia Pacific Space Centre Pty. Ltd. consortium (APSC) to build a satellite-launching facility on the island. In April 2000 the APSC bought the resort property to use for housing, but by 2004 construction of the launch facility was behind schedule. In 2000 Canberra had pledged A$100 million for the space project and infrastructure, but by 2004 only some A$300,000 had been spent, for road design work. No significant progress occurred in 2005 or after. A proposal to upgrade the island's airport to take larger aircraft remains in the planning phase.

Beginning in early 1999 Christmas Island witnessed a wave of illegal immigrants smuggled by boat from nearby Indonesia attempting to enter Australia. In November 1999 alone, nearly 1,000 people landed, while hundreds drowned attempting the passage. A decision by Canberra not to allow some 430 mainly Afghan refugees rescued by the freighter *Tampa* to land in August 2001, and Parliament's subsequent removal of Christmas Island from Australia's immigration zone, led to wide international criticism of the Howard government's increasingly tough anti-immigration policies. Some undocumented migrants were subsequently brought to a detention facility at Phosphate Hill. In 2007 construction commenced on a new Christmas Island Immigration Reception and Processing Center, designed to accommodate up to 1100 persons. Local residents, including the president of the Shire Council, opposed the expanded facility, fearing that it might be used to hold suspected terrorists and would deter tourists. The center was closed in February 2008 when the Rudd government terminated the "Pacific solution" of offshore detention but it reopened in September to accommodate a surge of unauthorized persons entering Australian waters. By September 2009, more than 700 refugees were lodged there for processing following Navy interception of boats from Sri Lanka and Indonesia.

Administrator: Brian James LACY.

President of the Shire Council: Gordon THOMSON.

Chief Executive Officer: Paul MABERLY.

Cocos (Keeling) Islands. The Cocos Islands, discovered in 1609 by Capt. William Keeling of the British East India Company, consists of two copra-producing atolls of 27 islands that were transferred from Singapore to Australia in 1955. They are located in the Indian Ocean about 580 miles southwest of Java and have an area of about 5.5 square miles. In 1978 John Clunies-Ross, the descendant of a Scottish sea captain who was granted authority over the islands by Queen Victoria in 1886, yielded his claim after agreeing to financial compensation of $7 million.

The population of the islands at the 2001 census was 618: some 500 on Home Island, where virtually all the inhabitants are Muslims of Malay extraction, and the balance on West Island, where mainly federal government employees and their families reside. By 2006, the total had dropped to an estimated 587. The islands have no significant industry apart from the production of coconuts and copra. In early 2000 plans to open a casino were scrapped.

In a referendum conducted on April 6, 1984, an overwhelming majority of the inhabitants voted for integration with Australia rather than free association or independence. While Australia's administrator of the Indian Ocean Territories remains the chief executive officer of the islands, a seven-member Cocos (Keeling) Islands Shire Council with municipal-level powers was established in 1993 under the Territories Law Reform Act of 1992. For voting purposes, the islands are treated as part of Australia's Northern Territory.

In 2001 the territory was removed from Australia's migration zone to deter asylum seekers, a number of whom were being held at a former quarantine facility. The refugees were later moved to the Christmas Island Immigration Reception and Processing Center, as were subsequent illegal arrivals, most recently in April 2009.

Administrator: Brian James LACY.

President of the Shire Council: Shane CHARISTON.

Coral Sea Islands Territory. The Coral Sea Territory was created in 1969 as a means of administering a number of very small islands and reefs east of Queensland. Except at a weather station on Willis Island, there are no inhabitants. In 1997 the Coral Sea Islands Act of 1969 was amended to include Elizabeth and Middleton reefs, in the Tasman Sea. The widely scattered islands and reefs of the territory are under the jurisdiction of the Attorney General's Department.

Heard Island and McDonald Islands. Heard and the McDonalds, totaling about 150 square miles and located about 2,500 miles southwest of Fremantle in Western Australia, serve primarily as scientific stations. There are no permanent inhabitants, and the islands are administered by the Australian Antarctic Division of the Department of the Environment, Water, Heritage, and the Arts.

In recent years poaching of Patagonian toothfish in the vicinity has led to increased patrolling of nearby waters. In August 2003 a Uruguayan-registered trawler was apprehended with an illegal toothfish cargo, and in November three crewmen were convicted, fined, and deported. A year earlier, Australia had established a fully protected marine reserve second in size only to the Great Barrier Reef Marine Park.

Norfolk Island. Located about 1,000 miles east of Queensland, Norfolk Island has an area of 14 square miles and a population (2006E) of 2,300. The island is the second-oldest British settlement in the South Pacific, having been discovered by Captain James Cook in 1774 and occupied as a penal colony a few weeks after the founding of Sydney in 1788. Slightly less than half of its inhabitants are descendants of *Bounty* mutineers who moved from Pitcairn in 1856. Tourism is the principal industry, accommodating some 40,000 visitors a year.

The island was supported by grants from Canberra until 1979, when the arrangements were altered by the Norfolk Island Act to provide Australian support for administrative staff, with the remainder of expenses to be met as much as possible from local sources, including tourism. Under the act, a nine-member Norfolk Island Legislative Assembly is elected for a three-year term; its leadership constitutes an Executive Council with cabinetlike functions. The most recent islandwide election occurred on March 21, 2007. An Australian administrator is named by the governor general and is responsible to the federal government. Norfolk has no formal parties, the principal division being between Islanders (of Pitcairn descent) and Mainlanders (Australians and New Zealanders). The main political issue has long been whether Norfolk is an integral part of Australia, as argued by Canberra, or whether the Pitcairners are an indigenous people and have a right of self-determination.

In 1999 Canberra introduced legislation intended to further integrate the island, prompting a charge of "bloodless ethnic cleansing" from Norfolk leaders and an August vote by the local assembly for immediate and full internal self-government.

In March 2003, in the context of increasing criticism from Canberra over the need for governmental reform, the Legislative Assembly amended the island's electoral framework by requiring enrolled voters to be Australian, New Zealand, or British citizens. The assembly also reduced the residency requirement from 900 days to one year. A subsequent report by the Parliament's External Territories Committee alleged that some Norfolk officials had resorted to such tactics as intimidation, arson, and phone tapping to gain political or financial advantages.

In a December 2005 report, "Norfolk Island Financial Stability: The Challenge—Sink or Swim," a parliamentary committee recommended that Norfolk's taxation and welfare systems be brought into the commonwealth's systems. A year later, however, Canberra reversed course after receiving assurances from the island government that it would continue economic and financial reforms. The issue had contributed to the ouster of Chief Minister Geoffrey GARDNER by the Legislative Assembly on June 2, 2006. His replacement, David BUFFETT, was described as more amenable to negotiating with Canberra. Buffett lost his seat in the election of March 21, 2007, and the new Legislative Assembly on March 28, 2007, chose André Neville Nobbs as the new chief minister. In October 2008 Interior Minister Bob DEBUS, indicting the Norfolk Island government for falling behind in provision of basic services and risking financial insolvency, warned that it could become a "failed state." The Norfolk Island government responded on December 29, with its *Submission to the Commonwealth on Governance Issues,* building on its *Submission to the Senate Select Committee on State Government Financial Management* of August 28, 2008, both of which argued for continued autonomy and exemption from personal income taxes. In March 2009, the Legislative Assembly approved an administrative complaints system and tabled a proposal to extend the jurisdiction of the Commonwealth ombudsman to Norfolk Island. In June the Assembly introduced a budget incorporating further tax reforms but not a personal income tax regime.

Administrator: Owen WALSH.

Chief Minister: André Neville NOBBS.

AUSTRIA

Republic of Austria
Republik Österreich

Political Status: Federal republic established in 1918; reestablished in 1945 under Allied occupation; independence restored under Four-Power Treaty of July 27, 1955.

Area: 32,376 sq. mi. (83,853 sq. km.).

Population: 8,032,926 (2001C); 8,379,000 (2008E). The 2001 figure includes foreign workers.

Major Urban Centers (2005E): VIENNA (1,554,000), Graz (222,000), Linz (178,000), Salzburg (142,000), Innsbruck (112,000).

Official Language: German.

Monetary Unit: Euro (market rate December 1, 2009: 1 euro = $1.51US).

Federal President: Heinz FISCHER (Austrian Social Democratic Party); elected on April 25, 2004, and sworn in for a six-year term on July 9 to succeed Thomas KLESTIL (nonparty), who had been constitutionally precluded from running for a third term and who had died on July 6.

Federal Chancellor: Werner FAYMANN (Austrian Social Democratic Party); invited by the president on October 8, 2008, to form a new government following the legislative election of September 28 and sworn in on December 2, 2008, to succeed Alfred GUSENBAUER (Austrian Social Democratic Party).

THE COUNTRY

Situated at the crossroads of Central Europe, Austria is topographically dominated in the south and west by the Alps, while its eastern provinces lie within the Danube river basin. The vast majority of the population is of Germanic stock, but important ethnic enclaves exist, including a Slovene minority in the province of Carinthia, which borders Slovenia to the south, and a Croatian minority in Burgenland, a province bordering Hungary. Approximately 75 percent of the population is Catholic, although religious freedom is guaranteed. An influx of immigrants from southeastern Europe and Turkey over the last 20 years has created a small (4 percent) but growing Muslim minority, mostly concentrated in Vienna and Vorarlberg. Women made up 45 percent of the official labor force in 2005, concentrated in sales, agriculture, and unskilled manufacturing; women currently hold about 27 percent of Federal Assembly seats. The Austrian literacy rate is over 97 percent, and life expectancy is over 77 years for men and 83 years for women.

Austria has a mixed economy with highly organized and powerful national-level business and labor associations that have worked with the government to preserve economic growth and a social safety net in a "social partnership." Despite recent privatizations, the state still owns or holds major shares in several large industries. Although limited in scope by the mountainous terrain, agriculture continues to provide much of the domestic food requirements, with an emphasis on grains, livestock, and dairy products. Agriculture accounts for about 2 percent of GDP, the industrial sector accounts for 31 percent, and services for more than 67 percent.

During the 1970s Austria's 3.4 percent average annual growth rate was one of the highest among industrialized countries. It fell back to 2 percent annually during the 1980s, but Austrian business garnered a larger share of world trade, and by 1986 Austrian investment abroad exceeded capital inflow for the first time. With the collapse of Eastern European Communism in 1989, the country was favorably positioned to regain its historic role as a pivotal economic power in the region. Exports to Eastern Europe increased rapidly during the 1990s, and Austrian firms were heavily involved in new joint ventures in the Czech Republic, Slovakia, and Hungary.

Real GDP grew by more than 2 percent annually from 2004 to 2005, with inflation averaging 2 percent during the same period. Results for 2006 and 2007 were even stronger: in 2006 GDP growth was 3.2 percent, inflation was 1.7 percent, and unemployment was 4.7 percent, and in 2007 GDP growth hovered at 3 percent, inflation rose moderately to 2.2 percent, and unemployment dipped to 4.3 percent. In 2008 the economy started strong, but as the global financial crisis set in the economic indicators came down: GDP grew by only 1.6 percent, with all forecasts for 2009 predicting a significant economic contraction. The downturn reversed the upward trend in inflation (3.2 percent in 2008) but threatened to sharply drive up the unemployment rate (under 4 percent in 2008).

The center-right/far-right governments of 2000 to early 2007 deemphasized the "social partnership" by pursuing conservative economic policies, including deregulation, pension reform, control of budget deficits, and privatization of selected state-run enterprises. The government also approved sharp cuts in corporate taxes, in part to help the economy "compete" effectively following the admission to the European Union (EU) in May 2004 of four neighboring countries (the Czech Republic, Hungary, Poland, and Slovakia) with historically lower tax rates. The left-center coalition government sworn in January 2007 shifted the balance back toward more social spending but with a commitment to reducing public budget deficits below EU thresholds. The new government formed in late 2008 moved back even further in the direction of the social partnership; it forecasts increases in public expenditure and debt in 2009 and 2010 to mitigate the impact of the global financial crisis.

EU expansion boosted the Austrian banking sector and presented promising trade opportunities. Building on the success of the 1990s, much of Austria's recent economic growth was fueled by expanded investment and trade with Eastern and Central European states beyond its immediate neighbors. With the severe contraction in world markets in late 2008, however, the Austrian finance sector was hobbled by substantial loan portfolios held by their subsidiaries in these countries, many of which presented the greatest credit default risks in the EU.

GOVERNMENT AND POLITICS

Political background. Austria was part of the Habsburg-ruled Austro-Hungarian Empire until the close of World War I, the Austrian republic being established in November 1918. Unstable economic and political conditions led in 1933 to the imposition of a dictatorship under Engelbert DOLLFUSS, while civil war in 1934 resulted in suppression of the Social Democratic Party and Dollfuss's assassination by National Socialists. Hitler invaded Austria in March 1938 and formally incorporated its territory into the German Reich.

With the occupation of Austria by the Allies in 1945, a provisional government was established under the Social Democrat Karl RENNER. Following a general election in November 1945, Leopold FIGL formed a "grand coalition" government based on the Austrian People's Party (*Österreichische Volkspartei Partei*—ÖVP) and the Austrian Social Democratic Party (*Sozialdemokratische Partei Österreichs*—SPÖ). The coalition endured under a succession of chancellors until 1966, when the ÖVP won a legislative majority and Josef KLAUS organized a single-party government. In 1970 the SPÖ came to power as a minority government under Bruno KREISKY. Subsequent elections in 1971, 1975, and 1979 yielded majority mandates for Chancellor Kreisky.

Following legislative balloting on April 24, 1983, in which the SPÖ failed to retain clear parliamentary control, Kreisky resigned in favor of Vice Chancellor Fred SINOWATZ, who formed a coalition government on May 24 that included three members of the third-ranked Freedom Party of Austria (*Freiheitliche Partei Österreichs*—FPÖ).

In a runoff election on June 8, 1986, that attracted world attention because of allegations concerning his service in a German unit guilty of demonstrable atrocities in the Balkans during World War II, former UN secretary general Kurt WALDHEIM, an independent supported by the ÖVP, defeated the SPÖ candidate, Kurt STEYRER, for the Austrian presidency. In protest, Chancellor Sinowatz and three other cabinet members resigned, a new SPÖ-FPÖ government being formed under the former finance minister, Franz VRANITZKY, on June 16.

The government collapsed in mid-September 1986 after the FPÖ elected Jörg HAIDER, a far-right nationalist, as its chair, thereby rendering it unacceptable as a coalition partner for the SPÖ. At the ensuing lower house election of November 23, the SPÖ lost 10 seats, though retaining a slim plurality, and on January 14 Vranitzky formed a new "grand coalition" with the ÖVP. The coalition continued with a somewhat restructured cabinet following legislative balloting on October 7, 1990, that yielded a substantial gain for the nationalist FPÖ opposition. The FPÖ continued to gain strength in a series of provincial elections in 1991, and its 16.4 percent support in the first round of presidential elections on April 26, 1992, was assumed to have provided the margin that enabled the ÖVP candidate, Thomas KLESTIL, to defeat the SPÖ's Rudolf STREICHER in a runoff vote on May 24.

Provincial elections in early 1994 yielded significant gains for the FPÖ, mainly at the expense of the ÖVP. In June the government achieved one of its key aims, when a referendum gave a decisive two-to-one verdict in favor of accession to the EU, despite opposition from the FPÖ and The Greens (*Die Grünen*). In October, however, the coalition parties were chastened by federal election results showing postwar percentage lows for both, while the FPÖ made further gains. In the absence of any acceptable alternative (and to keep the FPÖ out of office), the SPÖ and the ÖVP agreed to continue their coalition under Vranitzky's chancellorship.

The SPÖ-ÖVP government achieved its central policy objective when Austria became an EU member on January 1, 1995; however, Chancellor Vranitzky's authority was subsequently undermined by the resignation of four disaffected SPÖ ministers in March and by a major dispute between the coalition parties on budget deficit reduction measures. An accommodation proving unattainable, the government resigned on October 12, with an early election called for December 17. Contrary to forecasts, the balloting yielded gains for both the SPÖ and the ÖVP, the former appreciably so, while the FPÖ lost ground. After lengthy negotiations, the SPÖ and ÖVP succeeded in resolving their differences, enabling Vranitzky to enter his fifth term as chancellor on March 12, 1996.

In the first direct election for the European Parliament in October 1996, the SPÖ (with 29.1 percent of the vote) finished second to the ÖVP (29.6 percent), while the FPÖ secured a surprisingly high 27.6 percent. The relatively poor showing by the SPÖ was subsequently seen as a factor in Chancellor Vranitzky's resignation on January 18, 1997, in favor of Finance Minister Viktor KLIMA, who made substantial changes in the SPÖ ministerial contingent in the government formed on January 29.

On April 19, 1998, President Klestil, running as an independent with the support of the ÖVP and the FPÖ, was reelected with 63.4 percent of the vote, leaving four other candidates far behind.

The federal election of October 3, 1999, ended the "grand coalition" of the SPÖ and ÖVP when the FPÖ placed second, with 27 percent of the vote, virtually tied with the ÖVP. (The SPÖ secured a plurality with more than 33 percent, but it was the party's worst postwar showing up to that point.)

Among other things, the former coalition partners could not agree on how to deal with a troublesome budget deficit. Consequently, after three months of negotiations, the ÖVP turned to the FPÖ, notwithstanding the threat of sanctions by the EU, which was alarmed by the anti-immigration and anti-EU rhetoric of FPÖ populist Haider, who resigned as party leader amid a storm of international criticism. A center-right/far-right coalition of the ÖVP and FPÖ was subsequently sworn in on February 4, 2000, with the ÖVP's Wolfgang SCHÜSSEL as chancellor.

In early September 2002, Susanne RIESS-PASSER, the vice chancellor and leader of the FPÖ, resigned both posts following a rebellion within the FPÖ led by Haider, who opposed the government's decision to forestall planned tax cuts in the wake of severe flooding in August. Announcing that the ÖVP could no longer work with the FPÖ, Chancellor Schüssel dissolved the National Council, and new elections were held on November 24. The ÖVP won a plurality of 79 seats, and Schüssel intensely pursued a coalition government with either the SPÖ or The Greens. Those efforts ultimately failed, however, and Schüssel was forced to turn again to the FPÖ, a new ÖVP-FPÖ government being installed on February 23, 2003.

In presidential elections on April 25, 2004, Heinz FISCHER of the SPÖ defeated the ÖVP's Benita FERRARO-WALDNER by 52.4 percent to 47.6 percent. Outgoing President Klestil, who was constitutionally precluded from seeking a third term, died on July 6, and Schüssel temporarily assumed the duties of president until Fischer was inaugurated on July 9.

In April 2005 the FPÖ was replaced as the junior coalition partner by the new Alliance for the Future of Austria (*Bündnis Zukunft Österreich*—BZÖ), formed by former FPÖ members, including Haider, who had recently been marginalized in the FPÖ.

The SPÖ won a slim plurality over the ÖVP in the legislative balloting of October 1, 2006, with 35.3 percent of the vote versus 33.5 percent for the ÖVP, and the SPÖ's Alfred GUSENBAUER was sworn in as chancellor on January 11, 2007, to head another SPÖ-ÖVP "grand coalition" government with seven members from each party in the cabinet. Three months of difficult negotiations were required to revive the "grand coalition." As part of the agreement, the SPÖ dropped demands to cancel a Eurofighter airplane contract. In addition, the SPÖ compromised on the issue of eliminating university tuition fees recently instituted. Instead of their abolition, the government announced that some fees would be waived if students engaged in public service. Meanwhile, the ÖVP compromised on a number of its campaign pledges by accepting minimum wage legislation, increased social spending, and greater investment in public education. Tax and pension reforms, however, were retained. Additionally, both parties agreed to continue pursuing administrative reforms across the federal and provincial civil services. The government also pledged to develop a climate protection strategy.

Within months tensions between the coalition partners flared, as the SPÖ defense minister renewed threats to cancel the Eurofighter contract and Chancellor Gusenbauer and former chancellor Schüssel (as leader of the ÖVP parliamentary group) engaged in a bitter verbal battle over which leader better embodied moral leadership. Going forward, the uneasy partners managed to reach consensus on policies emphasizing development of a high-technology- and knowledge-centered economy via increased public funding for research and development, but they fought publicly over when and how to implement tax reforms and budget priorities. Tensions were exacerbated by two parliamentary investigations launched by opposition parties, with support of the SPÖ, targeting the conduct of the previous ÖVP-led government.

After a year and a half of bitter infighting over policy matters and jockeying for advantage between the two coalition partners, Wilhelm MOLTERER, the vice chancellor and chair of the ÖVP, announced that his party was pulling out of the government on July 7, 2008. This triggered the dissolution of the National Council, and new elections were subsequently scheduled for September. Chancellor Gusenbauer announced that he would not seek another term.

Former chancellor Fred Sinowatz died on August 11, 2008.

In final results of the legislative balloting on September 28, 2008, the SPÖ won a slim plurality with 29.3 percent of the national vote as the ÖVP lost ground to the other right-of-center parties the FPÖ and the BZÖ with turnout at over 78 percent of registered voters. A new SPÖ-ÖVP coalition government under new party leadership was sworn in on December 2 with the SPÖ's Werner FAYMANN as the new chancellor.

In the June 7 European Parliament elections the SPÖ posted its worst percentage in the postwar era with just 23.8 percent of the votes cast with 42 percent turnout, nearly ten percentage points below the party's 2004 results. The ÖVP won a plurality with 30.6 percent, securing six seats to the SPÖ's four seats. List Dr. Martin won 18.1 percent with three seats. The FPÖ doubled its percentage from 2004 with 12.7 percent of the vote and two seats. The Greens secured 9.7 percent of the vote for two seats, while the BZÖ fell below the 5 percent threshold.

Constitution and government. Austria's constitution, adopted in 1920 and amended in 1929, provides for a federal democratic republic embracing nine provinces (*Länder*), including Vienna, which also serves as the capital of Lower Austria. Although most effective power is at the federal level, the provinces have considerable latitude in local administration. The national government consists of a president whose functions are largely ceremonial, a cabinet headed by a chancellor, and a bicameral Federal Assembly (*Bundesversammlung*). The chancellor is appointed by the president from the party with the strongest representation in the lower house, the National Council (*Nationalrat*); the upper house, the Federal Council (*Bundesrat*), which represents the provinces, is restricted to a review of legislation passed by the National Council and, for the most part, has only delaying powers, although approval of the assembly in full sitting is required in certain situations.

Each province has an elected legislature (*Landtag*) and an administration headed by a governor (*Landeshauptmann*) designated by the legislature. The judicial system is headed by the Supreme Judicial Court (*Oberster Gerichtshof*) for civil and criminal cases and includes two other high courts, the Constitutional Court (*Verfassungsgerichtshof*), which decides constitutional issues, and the Administrative Court (*Verwaltungsgerichtshof*), which reviews disputes involving actions of government ministries. The judges who serve on these courts are appointed by the president for specified terms. There are also four higher provincial courts (*Oberlandesgerichte*), 17 provincial and district courts (*Landes-und Kreisgerichte*), and numerous local courts (*Bezirksgerichte*).

Province and Capital	*Area (sq. mi.)*	*Population (2008E)*
Burgenland (Eisenstadt)	1,531	281,000
Carinthia (Klagenfurt)	3,681	560,000
Lower Austria (administered from Vienna)	7,402	1,604,000
Salzburg (Salzburg)	2,762	531,000
Styria (Graz)	6,327	1,207,000
Tirol (Innsbruck)	4,883	704,000
Upper Austria (Linz)	4,625	1,409,000
Vorarlberg (Bregenz)	1,004	366,000
Vienna	160	1,678,000

A two-year commission studying constitutional reform known as the "Austria Convention" submitted a report to the National Council in January 2005. Any further action on its recommendations is subject to legislation by the National Council. Changes to the constitution require a two-thirds majority in that chamber; if the proposed changes affect the competencies of the provinces, the Federal Council must also approve the changes with a two-thirds majority. In May 2007 the government, possessing the necessary two-thirds vote, lowered the voting age to 16 years, set the minimum age to stand for election at 18 years old (35 for presidential candidates), and changed the terms of office for members of the *Nationalrat* to five years, instead of the previous four years.

Foreign relations. The Austrian State Treaty of 1955 ended the four-power occupation of Austria; reestablished the country as an independent, sovereign nation; and forbade any future political or economic union with Germany. In October 1955 the Federal Assembly approved a constitutional amendment by which the nation declared its permanent neutrality, rejected participation in any military alliances, and prohibited the establishment of any foreign military bases on its territory. In November 1990 a number of treaty articles (primarily involving relations with Germany) were declared obsolete by the Austrian government because of the recent political and legal changes in Eastern Europe, although the document's major provisions, including a ban on the acquisition of nuclear, biological, and chemical weapons, were reaffirmed.

The European Community (EC, subsequently the EU) opened a bilateral mission in Vienna in April 1988, and, despite manifest Soviet displeasure, Austria formally submitted an application to join the EC in July 1989. While EC membership remained the priority, Austria also cultivated relations with postcommunist Central and Eastern Europe, taking a lead in the Central European Initiative (CEI) established in March 1992 on the basis of earlier regional cooperation. Intended to counter the economic power of the reunited Germany, the CEI grouping corresponded in part with the old Habsburg domains and was thus seen by some as the embryo of a resurgent Austrian economic empire.

On the basis of terms agreed upon in March 1994 and strongly recommended by the government, accession to the EU was endorsed by Austrian voters in a referendum on June 12 by a convincing margin of 66.4 to 33.6 percent. On January 1, 1995, Austria (together with Finland and Sweden) ceased to be on the European Free Trade Association (EFTA) side of the European Economic Area (EEA) table, where it had sat for just a year, and instead became a full EU member.

On February 10, 1995, Austria joined the Partnership for Peace program of the North Atlantic Treaty Organization (NATO). It also obtained observer status at the Western European Union (WEU), while stressing that it would retain its long-standing neutrality. In April 1995 Austria became a signatory of the Schengen Accord, which provided for free movement among a number of EU states, and in November it agreed to contribute 300 soldiers to the NATO-commanded Implementation Force (IFOR) in Bosnia-Herzegovina.

Austria's role in a united Europe took center stage in 1998. In March Austria was 1 of 11 nations recommended for inclusion in the EU's Economic and Monetary Union (EMU), which became effective January 1, 1999. With a budget deficit of 2.7 percent of GDP for 1997, Austria was well within the 3 percent EMU criteria established by the Maastricht Treaty. However, Austria's role in the "new Europe" did not include full membership in an expanding NATO, but Austria expanded its cooperation with NATO via participation in the International Security Assistance Force (ISAF) peacekeeping mission to Afghanistan beginning in late 2001. Austria also has representatives in additional international peacekeeping initiatives, including ongoing missions to the Althea region of Bosnia and Herzegovina, Chad, and the police and civilian mission in Kosovo.

Austria has been instrumental as a diplomatic leader in "bridge building to the East," by brokering integration of Eastern European and Southeastern European governments and economies with the rest of Europe via formal ties and by facilitating informal exchanges of commercial leaders, students, and government officials with these former communist states. In the late 1990s, however, the influx of migrants and refugees from Eastern Europe and the former Yugoslavia prompted the Austrian government to tighten restrictions on immigration. In addition, the success of the radical FPÖ in Austria's 1999 elections prompted renewed questions about Austria's commitment to European integration and created image problems for Vienna reminiscent of the Kurt Waldheim years. Following the formation of a governing coalition that included the anti-immigrant FPÖ in 2000, the EU imposed diplomatic sanctions against Austria. France and Belgium were among the strongest backers of the sanctions, but by May 2000 at least six EU members reportedly were looking for a face-saving way to end them, especially as Vienna threatened to block EU reforms and EU enlargement. On September 12 the EU lifted the sanctions but pledged to monitor the activities of the FPÖ. Subsequently, the National Council approved the EU's Treaty of Nice in November 2001. However, even though recent election results showed that most Austrians rejected antiforeigner extremism and xenophobia, immigration issues remained highly sensitive. In October 2003 the government adopted what were widely described as the most restrictive asylum laws in the EU.

The Austrian legislature in May 2005 ratified the proposed EU constitution (although a majority of the Austrian public appeared to be against the measure). By 2005 Austria had regained what one journalist described as "surprising international respectability" only five years after falling into the status of "pariah state" because of the FPÖ. Nevertheless, Austria's credibility in European diplomatic circles was shaken somewhat at an October 2005 meeting of EU foreign ministers called to clear remaining hurdles to opening accession talks with Turkey.

Austria attempted to put the brakes on full EU membership for Turkey, proposing instead a "privileged partnership" status. The Turkish accession enjoyed little popular support in Austria, and the radical-right anti-immigrant parties had called for a popular referendum on the question. At the Luxembourg meeting, however, Austria withdrew its veto once it secured concessions that Croatia's case for EU membership would be put on a faster track (Croatia is within Austria's cultural and economic sphere of influence in south-central Europe).

Popular support for the EU continued to decline in Austria with the rapid expansion of EU membership, rejection of the EU constitutional referenda in France and the Netherlands in 2005, high-profile squabbling over EU budgets, and high domestic unemployment attributed to the influx of foreign workers. In January 2006 the ÖVP-BZÖ government announced that it would extend until 2009 labor restrictions on citizens from new EU members. During the 2006 elections the campaign rhetoric of the right-wing parties focused on opposition to continued immigration (with a pronounced anti-Muslim overtone), continued opposition to Turkish membership in the EU, and a backlash against further EU expansion or integration. Given the political stalemate between the two governing parties in the aftermath of the election, both felt constrained to avoid major policy shifts over these issues. A shortage of skilled laborers in 2007, which hurt Austrian firms, prompted an announcement by the SPÖ-ÖVP government that more than 50 skilled job categories would have their restrictions relaxed by 2008. Unskilled workers on the other hand had labor restrictions extended to 2011.

The Austrian Parliament ratified the revived attempt to formalize EU institutional arrangements, known as the Treaty of Lisbon and designed to replace the failed constitution, in April 2008. Public discontent with the Lisbon treaty was on the rise, however, after Irish voters rejected it in a referendum. This prompted a shift from the SPÖ leadership over whether future EU treaties would be subject to a popular referendum (see Current issues below).

Austria was under pressure from the United States in early 2007 to suspend contact between Austrian energy firms and Iran over natural gas exports from Iran to Austria set to begin in 2012. (The United States had asked EU nations to cut economic ties with Iran as punishment for the controversial Iranian nuclear program.)

Austria's relationship with its northern, eastern, and southern neighbors is influenced by its strong commercial ties to their economies and by environmental issues posed by the energy and environmental policy legacies of the communist era. Controversy flared up over the Temelin nuclear power plant in the Czech Republic in early 2007. (The plant, only 40 miles from the Austrian border, had been a source of friction since 2000.) Austrian Chancellor Gusenbauer met with his Czech counterpart in Prague to discuss the plant's safety and management, and the two leaders agreed to establish a joint Czech-Austrian commission to oversee operation of the facility. However, a leak of radioactive water from the facility occurred on the same day as the bilateral meeting, and news of the incident did not emerge from the Czech Republic for several days. The reports sparked new protests from Austrian antinuclear demonstrators at the Czech border (and in response, a blockade of the Austrian border organized by the Czech ultra-rightists) and complaints from Chancellor Gusenbauer over Czech reluctance to share information. The Slovakian government announced plans to begin construction of two new nuclear reactors at the Mochovce power plant as well as a new reactor at the Bohunice plant in 2009. Chancellor Faymann visited Bratislava in April 2009, registering Vienna's concern that these plants were a security and safety risk. Environmental issues also shaped recent exchanges with Hungary. Faymann discussed pollution remediation on the Raba River and Austria's plans to construct a waste incinerator in Heiligenkreuz near the border with Hungary.

Austria recognized Kosovo's independence from Serbia in 2008. The Serbian government recalled its ambassador in protest. Relations got a boost in April 2009 when Serbian President Boris Tadić came to Vienna on a state visit to discuss Serbia's EU integration one week after the Serbian foreign minister had visited.

In 2009 a cost savings recommendation by the Science and Research Ministry to pull out of the European Organization for Nuclear Research (CERN) was overruled by Chancellor Faymann on the grounds that Austria's longstanding membership in the organization and reputation were paramount considerations.

The Austrian government secured a nonpermanent seat on the UN Security Council for a two-year term from 2009 to 2010.

Current issues. The SPÖ–ÖVP grand coalition government led by Chancellor Alfred Gusenbauer was crippled by infighting between the two parties during its 18 months in office over tax, pension, and health policy issues. The final blow came when Chancellor Gusenbauer and transport minister Werner Faymann, feeling pressure from the growing public dissatisfaction with the Austrian government's pro-EU stance, published a letter in a "Euroskeptic" newspaper calling for public referenda on any future decisions relating to the EU constitution. ÖVP Vice Chancellor Wilhelm Molterer declared that "enough is enough" and pulled his party's ministers out of the coalition. The snap elections that followed set off a chain reaction that almost overnight remade the top leadership of nearly all of Austria's political parties.

The September 28, 2008, election results left both parties with diminished voting blocs in the National Council and weak governing mandates. The election and its aftermath unfolded, however, just as global financial markets were sliding into crisis. These circumstances increased the pressure on the rival parties to form a government quickly to deal with the fallout in the banking and securities markets. Faymann, the new SPÖ head and chancellor-designate, spurned any opportunity to form a government with the resurgent right-wing parties in favor of a restyled SPÖ–ÖVP coalition arranged with new ÖVP leader Josef Pröll, with whom he had a good personal relationship. The split of the cabinet ministries among the two parties was nearly the same as in the previous government, but some portfolios were shifted, and the new cabinet personnel were more closely tied to the consensual social partnership style that prevailed before 2000. The document formalizing the agreement between the two parties, however, was over 250 pages long and included a measure agreeing that no EU treaty referenda would be held unless both partners were in favor. (The ÖVP's long-standing foreign minister Ursula PLASSNIK resigned over the EU referenda compromise.) The new government instituted two new stimulus measures, on top of a September 2008 preelection measure, to aid the ailing banking sector and to invest in infrastructure projects. Income tax reforms (which reduced tax receipts) were implemented in January 2009, and the combined effect of the stimulus measures and tax reforms drove up public sector deficit projections for 2009 and 2010.

Provincial elections are scheduled for 2010 in Vienna.

POLITICAL PARTIES

Government Coalition:

Austrian Social Democratic Party (*Sozialdemokratische Partei Österreichs*—SPÖ). Formed in 1889 as the Social Democratic Party and subsequently redesignated the Austrian Socialist Party (*Sozialistische Partei Österreichs*) before reassuming its original name in 1991, the SPÖ represents the overwhelming majority of workers and part of the lower middle class; as such, it advocates progressive taxation, high social expenditure, and economic planning. However, the SPÖ renounced state ownership as a necessary element of a democratic socialist economy in 1978. After serving as junior coalition partner to the ÖVP from 1947 to 1966, the SPÖ returned to office as a minority government in 1970 under Bruno Kreisky, who won an absolute majority in 1971 and retained it in the 1975 and 1979 elections. Losing its overall majority in 1983, the SPÖ formed a coalition with the FPÖ, with Kreisky yielding the chancellorship and party leadership to Fred Sinowatz, who resigned in June 1986 over the Waldheim affair and was replaced by Franz Vranitzky.

In September 1986, in light of the FPÖ's sharp swing to the right, the SPÖ terminated the government SPÖ-FPÖ coalition, but it lost ground in resultant elections, opting in January 1987 to re-form a "grand coalition" with the ÖVP. This provoked the resignation of Kreisky as SPÖ honorary chair, on the grounds that Vranitzky had turned his back on socialism in favor of the "banks and bourgeoisie." Nonetheless, a party congress in October gave qualified support to the government's privatization program.

The "grand coalition" was maintained after the 1990 election, with the SPÖ remaining the largest party; it was also preserved after the October 1994 balloting, when the SPÖ vote slipped to a postwar low of 34.9 percent, and after the December 1995 election, when the SPÖ recovered to 38.1 percent.

Following the SPÖ's relatively poor performance in the October 1996 balloting for the European Parliament, Vranitzky in January 1997 resigned as chancellor and was succeeded by Viktor Klima, who was also elected to replace Vranitzky as SPÖ chair at a special party congress in April.

In the parliamentary elections of October 1999, the SPÖ representation fell from 71 to 65 seats on a vote share of 33 percent, although the

SPÖ retained a legislative plurality. After months of negotiations with the ÖVP, the grand coalition collapsed, reportedly over the unwillingness of the labor wing of the SPÖ to agree to budget cuts necessary to keep deficit spending within bounds. In February 2000 Klima resigned as party chair.

The SPÖ improved to 36.5 percent of the vote and 69 seats in the November 2002 elections, although it lost its legislative plurality to the ÖVP. In 2004 Heinz Fischer became the first member of the SPÖ in 30 years to be elected to the nation's largely ceremonial presidency, while the SPÖ's Gabi BURGSTALLER was elected governor of Salzburg after decades of conservative control of that province. The provincial turnover continued in late 2005 with the election of Franz VOVES as governor of Styria province, leaving the SPÖ with four of the nine provincial governorships, and costing the ÖVP its majority in the Federal Council in 2006.

Following its success in the October 2005 provincial elections the SPÖ enjoyed a slight lead over the ÖVP in national opinion polls, but the surge in popular opinion shrunk to a virtual tie in early 2006 amid a deepening banking fraud scandal associated with the BAWAG bank owned by the Austrian Trade Union Federation, which has close ties to the SPÖ. A government investigation revealed in March 2006 that the bank had averted failure via a massive loan guarantee from the trade union federation's strike fund. A subsequent poll revealed that most Austrians believed that SPÖ Chair Alfred Gusenbauer had knowledge of the events surrounding the bailout.

In response to the 2005 energy price and supply disruptions across Europe, the SPÖ leadership in early 2006 announced a renewable energy initiative as part of the party's platform for the parliamentary elections later in the year. As the October election drew nearer, Gusenbauer pledged that an SPÖ government would cancel the recent Eurofighter jet procurement contract, eliminate the university tuition fees introduced by the conservative government, increase benefits for certain pensioners, and improve public education.

The SPÖ won a narrow plurality in the October 1, 2006, balloting, securing 68 seats in the lower house with 35.3 percent of the vote. Gusenbauer's handling of the subsequent negotiations for the new SPÖ-ÖVP coalition drew significant criticism from within SPÖ ranks, specifically his concession of strategic cabinet posts to the ÖVP, as well as his abandonment of campaign promises regarding the Eurofighter contract and other social democratic goals (see Current issues, above). Gusenbauer also was criticized from within and outside the party for his mild response to the release of photos of FPÖ leader Heinz-Christian Strache taking part in paramilitary exercises and allegedly using a neo-Nazi greeting, which Gusenbauer characterized as "youthful pranks."

Dissatisfaction with Gusenbauer's handling of the coalition relationship with the ÖVP continued to grow in party ranks during 2007: it grew louder when the coalition infighting increased in 2008, hurting the SPÖ's standing in public opinion polls. After the SPÖ suffered setbacks in the provincial elections in Lower Austria (down 8 percent from the 2003 election) and Tirol (down 10 percent from 2003) in the first half of 2008, Gusenbauer agreed to step down as party chair in June. He ceded control to a new party leader, Werner Faymann, the minister for transport. When the coalition government collapsed in July, Gusenbauer announced that he would not seek reelection. Faymann was officially approved as leader by the party with over 98 percent support on August 8.

Faymann delivered a plurality of 29.3 percent for the SPÖ in the September 2008 election, but the percentage was the lowest postwar tally ever for the party, with the right-wing parties receiving the biggest percentage increases, making the victory somewhat hollow. After successfully brokering a new coalition government with the ÖVP, installed in December, Faymann called on party loyalists to close ranks and support him at a meeting commemorating the party's founding in Hainfeld.

The SPÖ retained Hannes Swoboda as its top candidate for the June 2009 European parliamentary elections.

In provincial elections in Salzburg and Carinthia on March 1, 2009, the SPÖ lost more ground to right-wing parties. In Salzburg the SPÖ won a slim plurality but lost two seats, both of which were picked up by the FPÖ. In Carinthia the party had a nearly 10 percent drop in support. These poor results came on the heels of the 2008 loss in Lower Austria, where 4 seats were lost to the FPÖ. Provincial elections in Vorarlberg and Upper Austria held in September continued the poor poll results for the SPÖ. In Vorarlberg the SPÖ slid from second to fourth place (while the FPÖ doubled its share of the vote and moved into second place). In Upper Austria the party suffered its worst defeat ever with 25 percent of the vote and a loss of 14 seats, its worst defeat ever in the province and a full 13 percentage points below the vote percentage in the previous election. The stinging defeats in the 2009 provincial elections undermined Faymann's position as party leader as criticism from the SPÖ ranks over the losses, especially to the benefit of the FPÖ, grew louder.

Leaders: Werner FAYMANN (Federal Chancellor and Chair of the Party), Heinz FISCHER (President of the Republic), Laura RUDAS and Günther KRÄUTER (Vice Chairs), Bettina STADLBAUER (Federal Executive Director), Reinhard BUCHINGER (General Secretary), Alfred GUSENBAUER (Former Federal Chancellor), Doris BURES, Helmut FIALA, Josef CAP, Hannes SWOBODA, Gabi BURGSTALLER.

Austrian People's Party (*Österreichische Volkspartei Partei*—ÖVP). Catholic in origin, the ÖVP developed out of the prewar Christian Social Party. Dominated by farmers and businesspeople, it advocated a conservative economic policy and strongly supported EU accession. The dominant government party from 1946 to 1970, the ÖVP was thereafter in opposition for 16 years, with longtime party chair Aloïs Mock standing down in 1980 following provincial election reverses. Damaged by its support of Kurt Waldheim at the 1986 presidential poll, the party lost ground in November legislative balloting and opted to return to a "grand coalition" as junior partner to the SPÖ. The coalition was maintained despite further losses in 1990 and 1994 (the overall decline being only partially disguised by the easy victory of ÖVP nominee Thomas Klestil in the 1992 presidential poll).

The ÖVP's 1994 vote share of 27.7 percent was a postwar low, with the party close to being overtaken on the right by the radical FPÖ (see below). The setback led to the ouster of Vice Chancellor Erhard BUSEK as party chair in April 1995 and the appointment of Wolfgang Schüssel as his successor, although the coalition with the SPÖ was maintained. ÖVP ministers precipitated the collapse of the coalition in October and an early election in December, at which the ÖVP vote unexpectedly improved to 28.3 percent. The "grand coalition" with the SPÖ was resumed in March 1996. However, the party slipped in the October 1999 parliamentary election to less than 27 percent, tied for second place with the FPÖ at 52 seats each. Schüssel, favoring reforms that a divided SPÖ would not accept, became a reluctant partner with the FPÖ and was sworn in as chancellor on February 4, 2000 (see Political background, above, for subsequent developments).

The ÖVP's results in the provincial elections in October 2005 were mixed. The party increased its share in Vienna to 49 percent but lost control over the provincial assembly and governorship to the SPÖ in Styria. Its national coalition partner, the BZÖ, fared badly, however, undermining confidence that the ÖVP-BZÖ coalition could survive the next parliamentary election. The party's national poll numbers eroded in 2006 because of persistent high unemployment, opposition to its attempts to reform the pension system, and the negative impact of allegations that work visas were sold at Austrian embassies when Schüssel served as foreign minister in the mid-1990s. Eventually, even the SPÖ's troubles with the BAWAG bank fraud came back to haunt Schüssel's government, which shouldered the blame for lax oversight of the banking sector and suspicion that the ÖVP manipulated the investigation to maximize the political damage to the SPÖ.

In the October 1, 2006, balloting, the ÖVP received 33.5 percent of the national vote, a loss of more than eight percentage points off its 2002 results. The party's poor showing in the 2006 balloting spurred a leadership shift, and Schüssel resigned as party leader in January 2007 after declining a position in the new cabinet. However, Schüssel took control of the ÖVP parliamentary group, a position previously held by Wilhelm Molterer, who succeeded Schüssel as party leader.

Molterer became vice chancellor in the SPÖ-ÖVP coalition government with the finance portfolio. The ÖVP also secured the foreign affairs, economics, and interior ministries, giving the junior member of the coalition the most prestigious cabinet posts, and leverage in cabinet negotiations with the SPÖ. Molterer, with Schüssel maintaining party discipline in the lower house, pushed Gusenbauer and the SPÖ hard in negotiations over government policy, raising tensions within the grand coalition, but generally winning the battle for public support in opinion polls.

In the 2008 provincial elections the ÖVP managed a slight increase in its share of the vote in Lower Austria, but lost 9.5 percent in Tirol from the 2003 election results, largely due to the challenge posed by an ex-ÖVP partisan, Fritz Dinkhauser (see below). In April former minister and EU commissioner Franz Fischler called for Schüssel to step down as leader of the parliamentary group, claiming that Schüssel was interfering with Molterer's ability to operate effectively as vice chancellor in negotiations with the SPÖ, but the ÖVP cabinet ministers closed ranks and defended Schüssel's role.

The ÖVP received only 26 percent of the national vote in the September 2008 legislative election, which was scheduled after Molterer's withdrawal of the ÖVP ministers from the cabinet in July. A lackluster campaign and disappointment over the party's poor results (in the face of major gains by the right-wing FPÖ and BZÖ), however, led Molterer to step down as party leader immediately after the balloting, ceding control to Josef Pröll. Pröll was confirmed as party leader with nearly 90 percent of the votes cast at a party conference in Wels on November 28. Pröll's ascension to the leadership swept away the cadre of party leaders closely allied with Schüssel and Molterer. His good personal relations with SPÖ chancellor-designate Faymann helped propel the ÖVP's negotiations with the SPÖ to form the new coalition government. Three ÖVP executive committee members, however, voted against participating in a new coalition.

In March 2009 Pröll announced that Ernst Strasser, a former cabinet minister, would head the party's list for the June European parliamentary elections, with the previous top ÖVP choice, MEP Othmar KARAS now listed second.

In the 2009 provincial elections the ÖVP either held onto its seats or lost little ground to right-wing parties, avoiding the large drop in support experienced by the SPÖ.

Leaders: Josef PRÖLL (Vice Chancellor and Chair of the Party), Aloïs MOCK (Honorary Chair of the Party), Karlheinz KOPF (Vice Chair and Leader of the Parliamentary Group), Maria FEKTER, Johanna MIKL-LEITNER, and Günther PLATTER (Vice Chairs), Fritz KALTENEGGER (General Secretary), Wolfgang SCHÜSSEL (Former Federal Chancellor), Erwin PRÖLL, Wilhelm MOLTERER.

Opposition Parties:

Freedom Party of Austria (*Freiheitliche Partei Österreichs*—FPÖ). Formed in 1956 as successor to the League of Independents, which drew much of its support from former National Socialists, the FPÖ in the early 1970s moderated its extreme right-wing tendencies in favor of an essentially liberal posture. Its coalition with the SPÖ after the 1983 election, the first time that it had participated in a federal administration, collapsed as the result of the election of rightist Jörg Haider as party chair in 1986. Nonetheless, the FPÖ made substantial gains at the expense of both the SPÖ and the ÖVP in the National Council balloting of November 1986 and at provincial elections in March 1989. On the basis of a platform stressing opposition to immigration from Eastern Europe, it nearly doubled its lower house representation in 1990, almost entirely at the expense of the ÖVP.

In November 1992 the FPÖ launched an "Austria First" campaign for a referendum on the immigration issue, which was rejected in September 1993 by a large majority in the legislature. Three months later, moderate elements broke away to form the Liberal Forum (see below), which subsequently replaced the FPÖ as the Austrian affiliate of the Liberal International. Haider's anti-EU stance failed to prevent a decisive referendum vote in favor of entry in June 1994; in the October federal election, however, the FPÖ advanced further, its 22.5 percent vote share enabling Haider to claim that he was on course to win the chancellorship. In January 1995 the party attempted to broaden its appeal by forming a "citizens' movement," *Die Freiheitlichen* (Freedom Movement), that rejected "old-style party politics."

Although the FPÖ unexpectedly fell back to 21.9 percent in the December 1995 federal balloting and remained in opposition, it rebounded to capture nearly 28 percent of the vote in the October 1996 elections to the European Parliament. In March 1999 the party won the regional election in Carinthia, Haider's home province, with 42 percent of the vote. It was the first time the party had won a provincial election. Haider's victory was capped in April by his election as governor by the Carinthian legislature, which had been dominated by the SPÖ for about 50 years.

The FPÖ tied for second with the ÖVP in the October 1999 parliamentary election, picking up 12 seats to bring its total to 52. The disintegration of the grand coalition allowed the FPÖ to join the government, but only after agreeing with the ÖVP to end its opposition to EU membership and EU enlargement. When this failed to satisfy the FPÖ's critics abroad, Haider resigned as party leader, effective May 1, 2000, in favor of a Haider loyalist. Political analysts viewed this as a purely tactical move.

The party lost significant ground at provincial elections in Styria, Burgenland, and Vienna in late 2000 and early 2001. It also performed poorly in the November 2002 legislative balloting (18 seats on a 10.2 percent vote share), the June 2004 poll for the European Parliament (6.3 percent of the vote), and the March 2005 municipal elections in Lower Austria. As a result, the FPÖ announced that many "far-rightists" were being removed from top party posts. In the ensuing internal struggle, however, Haider and his supporters (who advocated maintaining the coalition government with the ÖVP) lost the battle and immediately quit the FPÖ to form the BZÖ (see below), the FPÖ thereby losing most of its legislative representation and all its cabinet ministries.

Now led by the new party chair Heinz-Christian Strache (elected on April 23, 2005, at the party congress in Salzburg) the FPÖ contested the provincial elections in October 2005 on an anti-immigration and anti-EU platform in a bid to recapture the support of its right-wing populist base. This strategy moved the FPÖ to the right of the BZÖ, which had a more pragmatic approach because of its membership in the government. In the Vienna provincial election the FPÖ won 15 percent of the vote, but in Styria, a traditional FPÖ stronghold, the party failed to win any representation in the provincial assembly. In early 2006 the party launched a national petition for a referendum on the EU-related issues regarding Turkish admission to the EU as well as Austria's continued neutrality and its level of participation in the EU.

Strache's strategy for the FPÖ 2006 national election campaign emphasized anti-immigrant and anti-Muslim themes, as well as continued opposition to Turkish entry into the EU. The results of the balloting left the party tied with The Greens as the third largest block in the lower house with 21 seats and 11 percent of the national vote share, slightly improved from 2002, and well ahead of the BZÖ in the competition for right-wing populist support in every province except Carinthia, home province of former FPÖ and BZÖ party chair Jörg Haider.

Strache was widely condemned by political opponents and opinion leaders in the center and on the left after the emergence of photos in early 2007 showing Strache participating in paramilitary exercises and allegedly giving a neo-Nazi salute. Strache denied having any ties to neo-Nazis.

The FPÖ opposed the ratification of the Lisbon treaty in 2008 and advocated that the decision be put before the electorate in a referendum. In the provincial elections the FPÖ saw gains over its 2003 results of 6 percent in Lower Austria and nearly 5 percent in Tirol. This was consistent with national opinion poll results showing some voters turning to the FPÖ as an alternative to the ÖVP or BZÖ.

The FPÖ, which along with the BZÖ was the main beneficiary of voter frustration over infighting within the grand coalition and voter backlash against immigration and the Lisbon Treaty, won 17.5 percent of the national vote in the September 2008 legislative election. The strong national results for the FPÖ and BZÖ (when combined, the parties drew 28.2 percent of the vote, a full point more than the ÖVP) led to speculation that the two parties might reunite. Strache made several overtures to this effect, first after the death of BZÖ leader Jörg Haider in October 2008, and again following the provincial elections in Carinthia and Salzburg in March 2009 (in the Salzburg provincial election the FPÖ won 13 percent of the vote and gained two additional seats for a total of five). The new BZÖ leadership, reluctant to lose its identity after the death of party leader Haider, rebuffed Strache each time.

Strache was reelected party leader for the third time with 97 percent of the ballots cast at a party conference on May 16, 2009. Earlier in February Strache announced that Andreas Mölzer would head the party's ticket for the European parliamentary elections.

The tone of the FPÖ campaign rhetoric drew intense criticism in the run-up to the European parliamentary elections. The party's campaign advertisements declared that the FPÖ would veto Turkey and Israel for EU membership and its posters declared that the party would keep "The West in Christian Hands." Muslim and Christian leaders condemned the introduction of religious symbols and rhetoric into the campaign, as did President Heinz Fischer. SPÖ leader Chancellor Werner Faymann accused the FPÖ of anti-Semitism (since Israel was not a candidate for EU membership), and the head of the ÖVP European Parliament list said the words were "on the border of Nazism." Strache countered that it was insulting to accuse the FPÖ of anti-Semitism; party secretary Herbert Kickl dismissed the criticism from the SPÖ as anxiety over the SPÖ's recent setbacks to the FPÖ.

Following the FPÖ's gains in the June European parliamentary elections, the party scored impressive results in the September provincial elections in Vorarlberg and Upper Austria. In both instances the FPÖ nearly doubled its share of the vote and gained seats, largely at the expense of the SPÖ.

Leaders: Heinz-Christian STRACHE (Chair of the Party), Hans WEIXELBAUM (Vice Chair), Herbert KICKL and Harald VILIMSKY (General Secretaries), Andreas MÖLZER.

Alliance for the Future of Austria (*Bündnis Zukunft Österreich*—BZÖ). Disgruntled FPÖ members, including all of the FPÖ cabinet ministers and most of the FPÖ legislators, launched the BZÖ in April 2005. The BZÖ, which elected prominent right-winger Jörg Haider as its chair, therefore became the junior partner in an ÖVP-BZÖ coalition government and averted a fall of the coalition government that would have triggered early national elections. In the same month Siegfried Kampl, a BZÖ member from Carinthia who was scheduled to assume the rotating presidency of the Federal Council in July 2005, tarred the new party's image by denouncing deserters from the Nazi-era Austrian armed forces. Amid a storm of protest Kampl pledged to resign his seat but reneged on the promise in May 2005, and he subsequently resigned his membership in the BZÖ.

In the October 2005 provincial elections the BZÖ secured less than 2 percent of the vote in Vienna (and thus no representatives) and also failed to win any seats in the Styrian provincial assembly. The poor results immediately cast doubt on the BZÖ's potential fortune in the October 2006 national polls, specifically its ability to win the 4 percent needed to retain seats in the parliament. Following the provincial elections Haider made overtures to reunite with the FPÖ but was rebuffed.

Responding to the success of the populist antiforeigner appeals of the FPÖ, in December 2005 the BZÖ stepped up calls for expulsion of any foreigners who were unemployed or charged with a crime, stricter enforcement of immigration quotas, government approval of Muslim religious instructors, and greater school emphasis on the integration of foreign-born students.

Haider announced his intent to resign as national party chair in late 2005 and finally stepped down in May 2006. Acting Chair Peter Westenthaler was formally elected chair at a party congress in Salzburg on June 23, 2006. Westenthaler reiterated the party's call for enforcement of immigration restrictions and deportation of long-term unemployed immigrants as well as opposition to EU expansion to include Turkey. In the October 2006 balloting the BZÖ polled just over the 4 percent threshold, with 4.1 percent of the national vote.

The BZÖ, like the FPÖ, opposed the ratification of the Lisbon treaty in 2008 and supported calls for putting the decision before the voters in a national referendum. The BZÖ made overtures to the SPÖ in 2008 with a promise to support an SPÖ minority government or perhaps form an alliance in government, but with so few seats in the lower house, deep distrust and disdain from the other opposition parties (The Greens and the FPÖ), and no momentum to get past 4 percent support in national polls or recent provincial elections, there was little chance that such an alliance would succeed.

Party leader Peter Westenthaler was convicted of perjury in July 2008 and forced to step down. In a bid to revive the party's electoral fortunes in the run-up to the September 28 snap election, the BZÖ executive committee voted on August 8, 2008, to bring back Jörg Haider to replace Westenthaler as party leader. Party members ratified this decision unanimously at a meeting in late August. The move produced the best national election result to date for the party with a 10.7 percent margin. Immediately thereafter Haider and FPÖ leader Heinz-Christian Strache worked out an agreement on draft economic measures to spur growth for submission to the five parliamentary parties, but Haider subsequently died in a car accident on October 11. Stefan Petzner, a protégé of Haider, was named acting party leader.

Petzner, however, was forced by BZÖ party officials to step down on November 19. Vice Chair Hubert Scheibner became the new acting leader. Permanent party leadership elections were held in late April, when Josef Bucher, a leader of the parliamentary group in the National Council, was elected leader with over 99 percent of the votes cast. Ewald Stadler was chosen to lead the party's list for the European parliamentary election.

The BZÖ won a huge victory in the Carinthian provincial elections in March 2009 by securing nearly 45 percent of the vote. Its vote share in the September provincial elections in Vorarlberg and Upper Austria, however, failed to crest the 5 percent threshold for securing seats in the provincial legislatures.

Leaders: Josef BUCHER (Chair of the Party), Hubert SCHEIBNER, Gerald GROSZ, Ursula HAUBNER and Uwe SCHEUCH (Vice Chairs), Stefen PETZNER and Martin STRUTZ (Secretaries General), Manfred STROMBERGER (Federal Executive Manager), Peter WESTENTHALER, Ewald STADLER.

The Greens (*Die Grünen*). Austria's principal ecology-oriented party, *Die Grünen* was organized as the Green Alternative (*Die Grüne* Alternative—GAL) during a congress in Klagenfurt on February 14 and 15, 1987, of three groups that had jointly contested the 1986 election: the **Austrian Alternative List** (*Alternative Liste Österreichs*—ALÖ), a left-wing formation with links to the West German Greens; the **Citizens' Initiative Parliament** (*Bürgerinitiative Parlament*—BIP); and the **United Greens of Austria** (*Vereinte Grünen Österreichs*—VGÖ). After failing in a bid to retain its organizational identity, the VGÖ withdrew, leaving the GAL, with seven National Council deputies, one seat short of the minimum needed to qualify as a parliamentary group. The party overcame the difficulty in 1990 by winning ten seats, with three more being added in 1994 on a 7 percent vote share before declining to 4.8 percent and nine seats in December 1995. In 1993 it adopted its present name but continued to offer national candidate lists as The Greens–The Green Alternative. A July 2001 party congress passed a new platform based on core principles of ecology, solidarity, autonomy, grassroots democracy, nonviolence, and feminism.

Die Grünen became the fourth-largest parliamentary party following the October 1999 election when it gained 5 additional seats, for a total of 14, with 7.4 percent of the vote. It improved to 9.5 percent of the vote and 17 seats in 2002.

In the run-up to the October 2006 national balloting, The Greens' platform emphasized an energy policy that moved away from oil and nuclear power; investment in "green jobs" and education; priority for women's rights, social justice, and organic foods; and a global foreign policy that repudiated the "xenophobic" stance on the EU and the status of immigrants.

Die Grünen polled 11 percent of the national vote, securing 21 seats, the same number as the FPÖ and a high-water mark for the party. Twelve of The Greens' delegates to the lower house were women, giving them the only party bloc where women outnumber men. In 2008 The Greens joined the two right-wing parties in calling for a parliamentary inquiry into the allegations of misconduct in the Interior Ministry during the ÖVP-led governments. In the provincial elections The Greens generally lost ground over their showing in 2003, despite signs in public opinion polls that the party was benefiting from public frustration with the infighting between the grand coalition parties at the national level. However, in the Graz municipal election in January, The Greens nearly doubled their share of the vote from the 2003 balloting.

Long time party leader Alexander VAN DER BELLEN stepped down as party chair after The Greens' poor results in the September 2008 balloting. The Greens finished with the lowest margin of all the parliamentary parties with 10.4 percent. Eva Glawischnig replaced Van der Bellen as chair.

Ulrike Lunacek won the party's top spot in the European Parliament candidate list.

The Greens lost some ground in the early 2009 provincial elections in terms of the percentage of votes won, but the slide had little effect on the seats secured in the provincial legislatures. In the September provincial elections The Greens held their vote percentages steady and retained their seats.

Leaders: Eva GLAWISCHNIG (Chair), Michaela SBURNY (Federal Executive Manager), Maria VASSILAKOU (Deputy Federal Speaker), Werner KOGLER (Leader of Parliamentary Group), Daniela GRAF, Andreas PARRER, Peter PILZ, Sigrid PILZ, Johannes RAUCH, Ulrike LUNACEK.

Other Parties or Groups That Contested the 2008 Election:

Liberal Forum (*Liberales Forum*—LiF). The LiF was founded in February 1993 by five FPÖ deputies opposed to the party's nationalist agitation, among them the FPÖ presidential candidate in 1992, Heide SCHMIDT. In the October 1994 federal balloting, the LiF limited the gain for its parent party by winning 11 seats on a 5.9 percent vote share, although it slipped to 5.5 percent and 10 seats in December 1995. Party Leader Schmidt ran in the presidential election of April 1998 and came in a distant second (with 11.4 percent of the vote) in a field of five. She resigned her leadership position when the party lost all 10 seats in 1999 on a vote share of 3.65 percent, less than the 4 percent threshold required for representation. The LiF managed to secure only 0.1 percent of the vote in 2002.

The LiF did not contest the October 2006 national poll under its own banner, but Alexander Zach, the party chair, was elected to the National Council on the SPÖ list, and caucused with SPÖ delegates.

In the September 2008 election the LiF drew more than 1 percent of the vote in every province for a total of 2 percent of the national vote.

On October 25, 2008, the LiF reorganized under new leadership selected at a meeting held in Vienna. The party announced in 2009 that it would not run any candidates in the European parliamentary election.

Leaders: Werner BECHER (Chair), Amir AHMED and Gabriele METZ (Vice Chairs).

Austrian Citizens Forum Liste Fritz Dinkhauser (*Bürgerforum Österreich Liste Fritz Dinkhauser*—FRITZ). Led by its namesake, a former ÖVP partisan unhappy about the ÖVP's close ties with farm interests, FRITZ scored a major victory in the 2008 provincial election in Tirol by garnering 18 percent of the vote and winning seven seats in the provincial assembly, two more than the SPÖ.

In the September 2008 national election FRITZ received 1.76 percent of the national vote, drawing votes from every province, with strong support in Tirol and Vorarlberg, but well below the 4 percent threshold for securing seats in the National Council. In January 2009 Dinkhauser announced that the forum would not field candidates for the European parliamentary election in June of that same year.

Leaders: Fritz DINKHAUSER, Stefan ZANGERL

Austrian Communist Party (*Kommunistische Partei Österreichs*—KPÖ). The KPÖ, founded in 1918, supports nationalization, land reform, and a neutralist foreign policy. Its strength lies mainly in the industrial centers and in trade unions, but it has not been represented in the legislature since 1959 and obtained only 0.3 percent of the vote in 1994, 0.5 percent in 1999, and 0.6 percent in 2002. The KPÖ did, however, surpass the BZÖ vote total in the October 2005 provincial election in Vienna, finishing in fifth place to the BZÖ's sixth place, but well short of the 5 percent necessary to win representation in the provincial assembly.

In the October 2006 national election the KPÖ won just over 1 percent of the national vote. Results in the September 2008 election were slightly worse, with the party capturing only 0.76 percent of the national vote and just over 1 percent of the vote in Vienna and Styria provinces.

The KPÖ was part of the European Left grouping for the European parliamentary elections, with Günther Hopfgartner as the party's candidate for the June balloting.

Leaders: Walter BAIER (Chair), Melina KLAUS, Günther HOPFGARTNER.

Independent Citizens' Initiative Saves Austria (*Unabhängige Bürgerinitiative Rettet Österreich*—RETTÖ). The RETTÖ group, founded by Wilfried AUERBACH, claimed not to be a party but instead an independent movement of citizens skeptical of the established Austrian political parties and of EU-imposed policies not subject to approval by Austrian citizens. The group's manifesto opposed extremism, fanaticism, and violence, including Austrian participation in foreign military operations. Moreover, the group opposed certain "hazardous technologies," including nuclear energy and genetic engineering. The group drew a small fraction of votes in every province in the 2008 legislative elections but ultimately polled only 0.74 percent of the total national vote.

Leaders: Karl W. NOWAK, Gerhard REITER, Brigitte FLEISCHHACKER.

The Christians (*Die Christen*—DC). A conservative religious party founded in October 2005 and registered in January 2006 that contested the provincial elections in Lower Austria and Tirol in 2008 but failed to win any seats. In the September 2008 national election DC secured 0.6 percent of the national vote and over 1 percent in Vorarlberg province.

Leader: Alfons ADAM.

Other parties that contested the 2008 balloting in one or more provinces but failed to win 0.1 percent of the national vote included the **Socialist Left Party** (*Sozialistische Links Partei*—SLP), launched in 2000 by disaffected members of the SPÖ seeking a more radical socialist alternative; **Animal Rights Party** (*Tierrechtspartei mensch-umwelt-tierschutz*—SLP) led by Ralph CHALOUPEK; and **Liste Stark** (STARK).

Other Parties:

List Dr. Martin (*Liste Dr. Martin*). In the 2004 balloting for the European Parliament, two Austrian seats (on a 14 percent vote share) were won by an independent list headed by Hans-Peter Martin, a member of the European Parliament since 1999 who had gained significant attention for his campaign against the perceived exorbitant financial allowances accorded some of his peers.

In the 2006 legislative balloting the list won 2.8 percent of the vote, short of the 4 percent necessary to secure seats in the assembly.

Leader: Dr. Hans-Peter MARTIN (Chair).

LEGISLATURE

The bicameral **Federal Assembly** (*Bundesversammlung*) consists of a Federal Council (upper house) and a National Council (lower house).

Federal Council (*Bundesrat*). The upper chamber as of 2009 consisted of 62 members representing each of the provinces on the basis of population, but with each province having at least three representatives. Chosen by provincial assemblies in proportion to party representation, members serve for terms ranging from five to six years, depending on the life of the particular assembly. The presidency of the council rotates among the nine provinces for a six-month term. In the council as of June 2009, the Austrian Social Democratic Party held 27 seats; Austrian People's Party, 27; The Greens, 3; the Freedom Party of Austria, 2; The Alliance for the Future of Austria, 2; and List Fritz Dinkhauser, 1 seat.

President: Harald REISENBERGER (through June 2009).

National Council (*Nationalrat*). The lower chamber consists of 183 members elected by universal suffrage from 25 electoral districts for maximum terms of five years. At the most recent election of September 28, 2008, the Austrian Social Democratic Party won 57 seats; Austrian People's Party, 51; the Freedom Party of Austria, 34; The Alliance for the Future of Austria, 21; and The Greens, 20.

President: Barbara PRAMMER.

CABINET

[as of June 1, 2009]

Chancellor	Werner Faymann (SPÖ)
Vice Chancellor	Josef Pröll (ÖVP)
Ministers	
Agriculture, Forestry, Environment, and Water Management	Nikolaus Berlakovich (ÖVP)
Defense and Sports	Norbert Darabos (SPÖ)
Economic Affairs, Family, and Youth	Reinhold Mitterlehner (ÖVP)
Education, Arts, and Culture	Claudia Schmied (SPÖ) [f]
Finance	Josef Pröll (ÖVP)
Foreign Affairs	Michael Spindelegger (ÖVP)
Health	Alois Stöger (SPÖ)
Interior	Maria Fekter (ÖVP) [f]
Justice	Claudia Bandion-Ortner (ind.) [f]
Labor, Social Affairs, and Consumer Protection	Rudolf Hundstorfer (SPÖ)
Science and Research	Johannes Hahn (ÖVP)
Transportation, Innovation, and Technology	Doris Bures (SPÖ) [f]
Women and Civil Service	Gabriele Heinisch-Hosek (SPÖ) [f]

[f] = female

COMMUNICATIONS

All news media operate freely and without government restrictions, though the establishment in 2000 of a media regulatory bureau to monitor the "objectivity" of radio and television journalists alarmed libertarians.

Press. The following are published daily in Vienna, unless otherwise noted: *Kronen Zeitung* (1,080,500 daily, 1,332,400 Sunday), independent; *Der Kurier* (385,000 daily, 607,000 Sunday), independent; *Kleine Zeitung* (Graz and Klagenfurt, 259,000), independent; *Salzburger Nachrichten* (Salzburg, 70,700 daily, 100,300 Sunday), independent; *Ober Österreichische Nachrichten* (Linz, 120,000), independent; *Tiroler Tageszeitung* (Innsbruck, 100,000), independent; *Die Presse* (73,000), independent; *Der Standard* (100,000 daily, 152,000 Sunday); *Neue Zeit* (Graz, 71,000), Socialist; *Vorarlberger Nachrichten* (Bregenz, 65,000); *Wiener Zeitung* (22,000), government organ, world's oldest daily (f. 1703); *Kärtner Tageszeitung* (Klagenfurt, 36,000), Socialist.

News agencies. The domestic agency is *Austria Presse-Agentur* (APA); numerous foreign agencies also maintain bureaus in Vienna.

Broadcasting and computing. The Austrian Broadcasting Company (*Österreichischer Rundfunk*—ÖRF), which operates television and radio media, is state owned but protected in its operation from political interference under the broadcasting law. In October 1989 the government moved to end the ÖRF's monopoly by licensing private broadcasting. Currently, there is one national commercial television broadcast service, and one national commercial radio network competing with the ÖRF public broadcasting services. Regional television and radio broadcasting are well established and largely owned by the media companies affiliated with the regional newspapers. Cable and satellite television bring diverse programming options, and all European channels are available in accordance with EU law.

As of 2008 there 712.1 were Internet users per 1,000 inhabitants.

INTERGOVERNMENTAL REPRESENTATION

Ambassador to the U.S.: Christian PROSL.

U.S. Ambassador to Austria: William Carlton EACHO III.

Permanent Representative to the UN: Thomas MAYR-HARTING.

IGO Memberships (Non-UN): ADB, AfDB, BIS, CEI, CERN, CEUR, EBRD, EIB, ESA, EU, Eurocontrol, IADB, IEA, Interpol, IOM, OECD, OSCE, PCA, WCO, WTO.

AZERBAIJAN

Azerbaijan Republic
Azerbaycan Respublikasy

Political Status: Azerbaijan Republic established under Turkish auspices in May 1918; joined the Union of Soviet Socialist Republics as part of the Transcaucasian Soviet Federated Republic on December 30, 1922; became separate Soviet Socialist Republic on December 5, 1936; independence declared August 30, 1991, and confirmed October 18, 1991; new constitution providing for a strong presidential system adopted by national referendum on November 12, 1995, and entered into force November 27.

Area: 33,436 sq. mi. (86,600 sq. km.).

Population: 7,953,000 (1999C); 8,709,000 (2008E).

Major Urban Center (2005E): BAKU (1,820,000).

Official Language: Azeri (Azerbaijani).

Monetary Unit: Manat (official rate December 1, 2009: 1.25 manats = $1 US). A new manat, equivalent to 5,000 old manats, was introduced in January 2006.

President: Ilham ALIYEV (New Azerbaijan Party); elected by popular vote on October 15, 2003, and sworn in for a five-year term on October 31 to succeed Heydar ALIYEV (New Azerbaijan Party); reelected on October 15, 2008, and inaugurated for another five-year term on October 24.

Prime Minister: Artur RASIZADE (New Azerbaijan Party); appointed acting prime minister by the president on July 20, 1996, to succeed Fuad KULIYEV (New Azerbaijan Party), who had resigned July 19; confirmed as prime minister by the president on November 26, 1996; reappointed by the president on October 23, 1998; resigned on August 4, 2003, but reappointed on an acting basis on August 6; reappointed in full capacity by the president on November 4, 2003; reappointed by the president and confirmed by the National Assembly on October 28, 2008, following the presidential election of October 15.

THE COUNTRY

Home to a largely Turkic-speaking population, Azerbaijan is bordered by Georgia on the northwest, Russia on the north, the Caspian Sea on the east, Iran on the south, and Armenia on the west. Within its territory is the predominantly Armenian enclave of Nagorno-Karabakh, which has been the focus of intense conflict since independence. Azerbaijan also controls the noncontiguous, but largely Azeri, autonomous region of Nakhichevan on the southwestern border of Armenia. Shiite Muslims constitute the majority of the country's population, although the percentage of Sunnis (located primarily in the north) has risen recently. Ethnic Azeris make up an estimated 90 percent of the population. Minorities include Avars, Tsakhurs, and Lezgins in the north, among whom a degree of support is reported for a possible alignment with similar populations in Russia's southern Dagestan. Women are generally underrepresented in government; there are no women in the current cabinet and only 14 women in the National Assembly.

The capital of Azerbaijan, Baku, is located on the Caspian's Apsheron Peninsula, one of the world's oldest oil-producing regions, the proceeds from which made Baku one of Europe's richest cities in the years before World War I. Agriculture employs 40 percent of the labor force but accounts for only 6.0 percent of GDP, with crops including wheat, barley, potatoes, cotton, tobacco, rice, and tea. The country's mineral resources, which, in addition to petroleum, include natural gas, iron, zinc, copper, lead, and cobalt, support a number of manufacturing industries. Oil and gas account for 50 percent of GDP and 90 percent of exports. Annual per capital income was estimated at $3,500 in 2008.

The war with Armenia over Nagorno-Karabakh absorbed 25 percent of the state budget in the early 1990s, amid GDP contraction of some 60 percent between 1990 and 1994 and attendant widespread impoverishment. Since 1994 Nagorno-Karabakh, which represents some 14 percent of Azerbaijan's territory, and several contiguous provinces (constituting an additional 8 percent of Azerbaijani territory) have been under Armenian control. Meanwhile, Azeri refugees from Nagorno-Karabakh and surrounding regions (estimated at more than 750,000) reside in camps throughout the rest of the country awaiting a permanent settlement of the conflict and possible return to their former homes. Azerbaijan is also home to an estimated 220,000 Azeri refugees from Armenia proper.

Little immediate progress was made toward a market economy following the 1994 cease-fire in Nagorno-Karabakh, although in 1995 Azerbaijan obtained its first loans from the International Monetary Fund (IMF) to support economic transition amid hopes that Western exploitation of the country's oil reserves would yield major financial benefits. Meanwhile, the non-oil sector essentially stagnated in the late 1990s, with widespread corruption reported at all levels of government.

In April 1999 a 515-mile oil pipeline from Baku to the Black Sea port of Supsa, Georgia, was opened amid great fanfare. Attention subsequently focused on a Western-backed oil pipeline of even greater capacity from Baku through Georgia to the Mediterranean port of Ceyhan, Turkey (see below).

The second phase of the country's privatization program, launched in mid-2000, was directed toward major state enterprises in the energy, telecommunications, and transportation sectors. Relations with the IMF subsequently remained mixed, the fund suspending some of its support in 2002 and 2003 because of the government's failure to implement several promised reforms. Meanwhile, Transparency International ranked

Azerbaijan as one of the most corrupt countries in the world (95th out of 102 countries).

The IMF reported progress in the privatization of small- and medium-sized enterprises in 2005 but called for significant additional reform in the energy, financial, and business sectors. As did many other international institutions, the IMF also criticized the dearth of "good governance" on the part of Azerbaijan's Aliyev regime.

The $4 billion, 1,000-mile oil pipeline from the Caspian to Turkey was completed in May 2005 by a consortium that included British Petroleum as the largest shareholder. The pipeline, which began operating in June 2006, was ultimately expected to pump 1 million barrels per day, with some experts predicting it could eventually be extended under the Caspian to Kazakhstan, providing the West with even greater access to Caspian oil without dealing with Russia or Iran.

GDP rose by 24.3 percent in 2005, 31 percent in 2006, and more than 20 percent in 2007, making Azerbaijan's economy the fastest growing in the world. The booming oil sector fueled the growth, aided since 2007 by the opening of gas export lines from large deposits recently discovered in the Caspian Sea region. (After many years of gas dependency on Russia, Azerbaijan is now considered a potential gas supplier for Europe, also trying to reduce its reliance on Russia.) In response to higher revenues, the government has dramatically increased expenditures since 2005 in an effort to combat poverty (which still afflicts one-third of the population), reinvigorate agriculture (the country had been known as the "vegetable garden" of the Union of Soviet Socialist Republics [USSR]), and rehabilitate dilapidated railways, roads, and water distribution networks. Meanwhile, the IMF has called for additional structural reform to support the non-oil sector and other liberalization to facilitate Azerbaijan's proposed accession to the World Trade Organization. Other analysts have described Azerbaijan as a prime candidate to suffer the "oil curse" under which similarly positioned nations have failed to capitalize effectively on economic potential because of a lack of transparency in governmental activities and systemic corruption.

GDP growth declined to 11 percent in 2008 under the influence of falling oil prices, poor economic conditions in Russia (a key trading partner), and the global slowdown in general. Meanwhile annual inflation remained at approximately 20 percent. The IMF predicted that growth would fall to 2.5 percent in 2009, although Azerbaijan was expected to weather the international economic storm better than many countries.

GOVERNMENT AND POLITICS

Political background. Historic Azerbaijan spanned the area of the present republic plus a somewhat larger region located in northern Iran. Persia and the Ottoman Empire competed for the territory in the 16th century, with the former gaining control in 1603. The northern sector, ceded to Russia in the early 19th century, joined Armenia and Georgia in a short-lived Transcaucasian Federation after the 1917 Bolshevik Revolution. Azerbaijan proclaimed its independence the following year but was subdued by Red Army forces in 1920. In 1922 it entered the USSR as part of the Transcaucasian Soviet Federal Republic, becoming a separate Soviet Socialist Republic (SSR) in 1936. Whereas the largely Armenian-populated enclave of Nagorno-Karabakh had been ceded to the new Armenian SSR in 1920, three years later, at Joseph Stalin's direction, it was returned to the Azerbaijan SSR. In 1924 the western enclave of Nakhichevan was also placed under Azerbaijan's jurisdiction (this step was approved by Turkey in its capacity as a regional guarantor power under the 1921 Treaty of Kars).

In 1989, as the Communist monolith began to crumble, a secessionist Azerbaijan Popular Front (*Azerbaycan Xalq Cebhesi*—AXC) emerged that was the object of intense repression by Soviet troops. Meanwhile, conflict had erupted with neighboring Armenia regarding the status of Nagorno-Karabakh (see article on Armenia for additional information), and the Azerbaijan Communist Party (*Azerbaycan Kommunist Partiyasi*—AKP) was able to deflect support from the nationalists by strongly opposing any compromise involving the enclave. As a result, the Communists were clear victors in elections to the republican Supreme Soviet on September 30 and October 14, 1990.

In March 1991 it was reported that 93 percent of those voting in a national referendum in Azerbaijan had approved the draft "Union Treaty" proposed by Mikhail Gorbachev for the continuation of a Union of Soviet Republics with additional rights being extended to the constituent republics. (Armenia declined to conduct a referendum on the matter for fear the new treaty would compromise its claim to Nagorno-Karabakh.) However, the chair of the Azerbaijan Supreme Soviet, Ayaz Niyaz Ogly MUTALIBOV, subsequently appeared to side with hard-liners who in mid-August in Moscow attempted a coup aimed at stopping Gorbachev's reforms. When the coup failed, Mutalibov denied having supported the initiative and resigned his post as first secretary of the AKP, apparently to show his solidarity with demonstrators clamoring for independence and separation from Communist rule.

On August 30, 1991, the Azerbaijani Supreme Soviet voted to "restore the independent status of Azerbaijan." Opposition groups called for a delay in the presidential election scheduled for September 8, but Mutalibov insisted the balloting be held. As a result of an opposition boycott, Mutalibov, describing himself as a "new Communist," was elected as the sole candidate. On October 10 the Azerbaijan Supreme Soviet passed legislation providing for the formation of a national defense force, and on October 18 it unanimously approved the Constitutional Act on the State Independence of the Republic of Azerbaijan, which reaffirmed the independence announcement of August 30. However, the administration flatly rejected the opposition's demands for new legislative elections.

President Mutalibov resigned on March 6, 1992, because of his government's inability to protect the Azeri minority in Nagorno-Karabakh from Armenian guerrilla attacks; Yagub MAMEDOV was named his interim successor. However, following a major reversal for Azerbaijani forces in Nagorno-Karabakh, a quorumless legislature voted on May 14, 1992, to restore Mutalibov to the presidency. The action triggered a clash between ex-Communists and AXC supporters that resulted in Mutalibov again being toppled on May 15. Four days later the Supreme Soviet voted to disband in favor of an AXC-dominated National Assembly, and on June 7 the AXC candidate, Abulfaz Ali ELCHIBEY, easily defeated four competitors in a new round of presidential balloting.

In 1993 President Elchibey came under increasing pressure for his government's failure to evict Armenian forces from Nagorno-Karabakh, and in early June a domestic insurrection was launched by the garrison in the country's second-largest city, Gyandzha. On June 16 the president left Baku for Nakhichevan as rebel units, commanded by Col. Surat GUSEINOV, approached the capital. On June 18 Heydar ALIYEV, formerly AKP first secretary, who as leader of the New Azerbaijan Party (*Yeni Azerbaycan Partiyasi*—YAP) had been installed as parliamentary chair on June 15, declared that, because of Elchibey's "inexplicable and unwarranted absence," he had assumed

"the duties and responsibilities of the presidency of Azerbaijan." On June 30 Aliyev named Col. Guseinov to head a new government. In popular balloting on October 3, YAP candidate Aliyev was confirmed as president, officially winning 98.8 percent of the vote.

Following a further power struggle, President Aliyev on October 6, 1994, dismissed Guseinov as prime minister, in favor of Fuad KULIYEV (theretofore a deputy premier), while stressing that he (Aliyev) was head of the government. The president described the outgoing cabinet as "a den of criminals" and indicated that treason charges would be laid against Guseinov, who had fled to Russia. (Guseinov was extradited to Azerbaijan in 1996 and was sentenced to life imprisonment in early 1999 following his conviction on more than 40 charges.)

A new crisis erupted in March 1995 when rebel interior ministry forces led by Deputy Interior Minister Ravshan JAVADOV staged an attempted coup, which was put down with numerous fatalities, including that of Javadov. Amid the turbulence, President Aliyev accused Russia of plotting to destabilize his government in concert with hard-line exiles, notably Mutalibov. According to Baku authorities, the effort reflected Moscow's anger at a Caspian Sea oil-exploitation agreement that Azerbaijan had signed in September 1994 with a consortium of oil companies led by British Petroleum, a charge that the Russian foreign ministry rejected as groundless.

Internal instability and stringent registration requirements resulted in only eight parties contesting the first round of legislative balloting on November 12, 1995; the exclusion of a dozen opposition parties and other factors led a monitoring mission from the United Nations and the Organization for Security and Cooperation in Europe (OSCE) to conclude that the election had been less than fair. The official results (including runoff contests for 15 seats in February 1996) gave the ruling YAP and its allies a massive majority in the new 125-member assembly. In a referendum held simultaneously with the initial assembly balloting, a new constitution establishing a presidential republic was reported to have secured 91.9 percent approval.

The legislative balloting of November 1995 and February 1996 served to entrench the Aliyev regime, which became noticeably more vigorous in its actions against those seeking to challenge its hold on power. It was assisted in this endeavor by traditionally compliant courts, which handed down a series of harsh sentences, including the death penalty, for opposition activists convicted of subversion. It also received unprecedented support from Russia, which Aliyev had previously castigated for harboring Azerbaijanis plotting to overthrow his government. In April 1996 ex-president Mutalibov and former defense minister Rakhim GAZIYEV were both arrested in Moscow, the latter being quickly extradited to Baku (where two months earlier a military court had sentenced him to death for high treason), while the former escaped extradition only on a legal ruling by the Russian procurator general.

The shift in Russian policy reflected a partial resolution in October 1995 of the dispute with Azerbaijan about the exploitation of Caspian oil reserves, in particular, the route by which the oil would be piped to Western markets. As ratified by the Azerbaijani National Assembly in November 1994, the $7.5 billion agreement signed with a Western-led consortium in September 1994 had included Lukoil of Russia (with a 10 percent stake). Nevertheless, Moscow had rejected its legitimacy, arguing that the Caspian Sea was the joint possession of its five littoral states (Azerbaijan, Iran, Kazakhstan, Russia, and Turkmenistan) and that each should share in its exploitation. Further complications had ensued from Azerbaijan's granting an increased stake in the venture to Turkey in April 1995, much to the chagrin of Iran. In the October 1995 announcement, however, Russian concerns were substantially met, the consortium agreeing that two pipelines from the Caspian Sea would be used, one an upgrade of the existing pipeline running through Russian territory to the Black Sea and the other a new pipeline through Georgia and thence potentially to Turkey. The U.S. government was reported to have played a significant role in the pipeline-route decision and in securing the exclusion of Iran from the consortium. In the latter regard, Azerbaijan was later able to make partial amends by allocating the Iranians a 10 percent stake in the next phase of Caspian oil development.

Internal instability continued to complicate President Aliyev's efforts to steer Azerbaijan to a negotiated settlement of the Nagorno-Karabakh conflict under the auspices of the OSCE. Several cease-fire agreements in 1993 and 1994 had proved abortive, not least because the opposition AXC had assailed associated provisions as amounting to de facto recognition of Nagorno-Karabakh as a separate entity. Against this background, the Baku government had resisted a May 1994 plan from the Commonwealth of Independent States (CIS) for the deployment of a predominantly Russian peacekeeping force and had achieved a diplomatic victory in December, when it was agreed that a 3,000-strong multinational OSCE force would be sent, with no one country providing more than 30 percent of the total. However, subsequent efforts to establish a permanent cease-fire had made little progress by May 1995, when Armenia withdrew from the talks, charging Azerbaijani involvement in a Georgian Azeri bombing that severed a pipeline carrying vital gas supplies to Armenia from Turkmenistan. Talks resumed under OSCE auspices in September but were complicated by the issuance of a unilateral declaration of independence by the Karabakh Armenians in March 1996, an action that drew predictably fierce condemnation from Azerbaijan.

The Kuliyev government came under increasing criticism in 1996, not least from President Aliyev, for the slow pace of economic reform, particularly the privatization program. Matters came to a head with an announcement on July 19 that the president had accepted the prime minister's resignation "on health grounds" and had also dismissed several senior economic ministers and state managers. The following day Artur RASIZADE was appointed to the premiership, while Nadir NASIBOV became chair of the State Privatization Committee.

On January 24, 1997, Azerbaijani officials claimed that a coup attempt against President Aliyev, allegedly involving supporters of former president Mutalibov, former prime minister Guseinov, and a number of foreign intelligence officers, had been prevented in October 1996. Subsequently, after fighting had broken out in April and May in Nagorno-Karabakh, the OSCE submitted a draft peace plan for the region, proposing that the enclave be given autonomous status within Azerbaijan. However, the appointment of Robert Kocharian (the president of the self-declared Republic of Nagorno-Karabakh) as the prime minister of Armenia and the election of Arkady GHUKASIAN to replace him as the president of the disputed republic on September 1 were rejected by Azerbaijani officials as "intolerable provocations." On October 16 President Aliyev claimed that an agreement had been reached to settle the conflict on the basis of the proposals put forward by the OSCE, and on November 17 Ghukasian indicated that his government might agree to a step-by-step settlement of the conflict provided that the status of the region was determined in advance. However, no progress was achieved during the remainder of the year, and the ascendancy of hard-liner Kocharian in the Armenian government in February 1998 (see article on Armenia) seemed to place further impediments in the way of a final negotiated settlement. In November 1998 the OSCE presented a new peace proposal that called for a "common state" between Azerbaijan and Nagorno-Karabakh. Armenia and the leadership of Nagorno-Karabakh welcomed the proposal, whereas Azerbaijani foreign minister Tofiq ZULFUGAROV said on November 20 that the idea was unacceptable because it represented a threat to Azerbaijan's territorial integrity and national sovereignty.

Aliyev was reelected to another five-year term on October 11, 1998, although many prominent politicians and opposition parties boycotted the balloting to protest the government's stranglehold on the national election commission. The opposition also alleged fraud in the counting of ballots, which officially showed Aliyev gaining 76 percent of the vote against four other candidates and thereby surpassing the two-thirds threshold required to eliminate the need for a second round of balloting. Although the cabinet resigned on October 20 (as constitutionally required following a presidential election), Aliyev reappointed Prime Minister Rasizade on October 23. Many incumbents were also subsequently returned to the cabinet, although the process dragged on for several months.

Western leaders, hopeful that political liberalization in Azerbaijan would facilitate the exploitation of oil and gas, pressured the government to revamp its electoral code so that the municipal elections in December 1999 would be fully contested by opposition parties. However, many parties boycotted the polling, while those opposition groups that participated cited massive irregularities, which exacerbated antigovernment discontent that culminated in April 2000 in mass demonstrations calling for Aliyev to resign. The government's initial response was a crackdown that included a number of arrests. However, in June the president announced the release of some 87 political prisoners, a decision that was apparently designed to facilitate Azerbaijan's accession to the Council of Europe. (The membership was formally approved in January 2001; similar concurrent action regarding Armenia led some analysts to suggest that a military solution in Nagorno-Karabakh had thereby become even less likely.)

Controversy again surrounded the November 2000 assembly elections, as the government initially barred some parties and blocs from contesting the proportional component of the poll. International pressure influenced the administration to relent at the last minute, but the parties involved argued that their prospects had already been irrevocably compromised. (The YAP dominated the election by winning 75 seats.) Many observers also described the balloting as seriously flawed, and the election commission significantly revised the results of the proportional balloting.

President Aliyev held several face-to-face talks with President Kocharian of Armenia in the first half of 2001, prompting reports of a possible settlement regarding Nagorno-Karabakh. No breakthrough occurred, however, and Kocharian subsequently declared it was "unthinkable" that Nagorno-Karabakh would return to any degree of control by Azerbaijan; meanwhile, the government of Azerbaijan and its internal critics found at least one issue upon which they agreed—that they would not accept a "defeatist" solution in Nagorno-Karabakh.

The Constitutional Court ruled in 2002 that President Aliyev was eligible to run for a third term in 2003 on the grounds that his first term should not count toward the two-term limit because he had been elected to it prior to the constitutional revision of 1995. Campaign issues included the growing influence of Islamist groups in Azerbaijan (which had prompted the government to institute more extensive oversight of religious organizations) as well as continued accusations against the administration of human rights violations, such as harassment of opposition parties and torture and other mistreatment of political prisoners.

In April 2003 President Aliyev collapsed twice during a televised speech, and he later announced he would not run for reelection in October. On August 4 Prime Minister Rasizade announced his resignation, purportedly for health reasons. President Aliyev's son, Ilham ALIYEV, was appointed as the new prime minister, but on August 6 he announced he was taking an unpaid leave of absence to participate in the presidential campaign. Rasizade returned to the prime minister's post in an acting capacity.

Ilham Aliyev won the presidency in first-round balloting on October 15, 2003, securing 79.5 percent of the votes. Second place went to Isa GAMBAR, leader of the New Equality Party (*Yeni Musavat Partiyasi*—YMP), with 12 percent of the vote. (Opposition groups and a number of international observers decried the election as neither free nor fair.) Rasizade returned to the premiership in a permanent capacity as head of a reshuffled cabinet on November 4. Charges of massive irregularities also surrounded the November 2005 assembly elections, at which the YAP and its supporters again gained an overwhelming majority.

On October 15, 2008, President Aliyev was reelected for a second five-year term, being credited with 88.7 percent of the vote against six other minor candidates, none of whom received more than 3 percent of the vote. The major opposition parties boycotted the election, which international observers characterized as not fully democratic. On October 28 the assembly approved Prime Minister Rasizade's reappointment by a vote of 101–2; all but one of the incumbent ministers were also reappointed to the cabinet.

On July 19, 2007, Bako SAHAKIAN (a former national security chief for the de facto Armenian government in the region) was elected president of Nagorno-Karabakh with the support of the Democratic Artsakh Party (led by outgoing president Arcadiy GHUKASIAN). Following Sahakian's inauguration on September 7, the legislature of Nagorno-Karabakh unanimously approved the appointment of Arayik HARUTIUNIAN as prime minister in succession to Anushavan DANIELIAN. In late 2008 Sahakian welcomed the resumption of talks between Armenian and Azerbaijani leaders regarding Nagorno-Karabakh (see Current issues, below) but asked that his administration be accorded full negotiating status (denied to date) in future discussions.

Constitution and government. After nearly four years under a modified Soviet-era constitution (an interim 50-member legislature replacing the former 360-seat Supreme Soviet in May 1992), Azerbaijan adopted a new basic law on November 12, 1995, that provided for a strong presidency. Executive power is vested in a popularly elected head of state who appoints the prime minister and other cabinet members, subject to approval by the National Assembly, the 125-member legislative authority. Until 2009 presidents were limited to two five-year terms. However a national referendum in March approved constitutional amendments that, among other things, eliminated presidential term limits. In other respects, preindependence administrative structures remain largely intact. The judicial system includes a Constitutional Court, Supreme Court, and High Economic Court.

The country includes two autonomous regions: Nagorno-Karabakh, an Armenian-populated enclave that has been the object of military contention with Armenia since 1990; and Nakhichevan, a largely Azeri-populated enclave within Armenia that has also been a source of military confrontation (see Armenia article). The Azerbaijani Assembly approved a new constitution for Nakhichevan in late 1998, formalizing its autonomous status despite objection from some legislators concerned that such action was setting a troublesome precedent.

A national referendum on controversial constitutional revisions was approved by a reported 84 percent "yes" vote on August 24, 2002. Opposition groups strongly objected to a provision designating the presidentially appointed prime minister as the presidential successor in case of the incapacitation or death of the president. The constitutional successor previously had been the speaker of the assembly, and critics of President Aliyev argued that the change had been implemented to permit him to handpick his successor. They also strongly protested the elimination of partial proportional representation beginning with the 2005 assembly elections.

Foreign relations. Although Azerbaijan participated in the formal launching of the CIS in December 1991, its legislature voted against ratification of the CIS foundation documents on October 7, 1992. In late 1991 Azerbaijan was admitted to the Organization of the Islamic Conference, and by early 1992 it had established diplomatic relations with a number of foreign countries, including the United States. On March 2 it was admitted to the UN, with membership in the IMF and the International Bank for Reconstruction and Development following on September 18. Azerbaijan's closest emerging links, however, were with Iran (because of a shared Shiite faith) and Turkey (because of a common Turkic ancestry). During a regional summit in Tehran in February 1992, Azerbaijan joined with the four Central Asian republics of Kyrgyzstan, Tajikistan, Turkmenistan, and Uzbekistan in gaining admission to the long-dormant Economic Cooperation Organization that had been founded by Iran, Pakistan, and Turkey in 1963.

Meanwhile, an additional threat to regional stability had been posed by the emergence of conflict in Nakhichevan. While troops of the former Soviet army remained stationed along the border with Turkey and Iran, an increasing number of clashes between Armenian and Azerbaijani militias were erupting in the northern portion of the region. Following Heydar Aliyev's assumption of the Azerbaijani presidency in mid-1993, direct talks were initiated with Karen BABURYAN, the president of the Karabakh parliament. Subsequently, after a meeting between Aliyev and Russian President Boris Yeltsin in Moscow on September 6, the Azerbaijan Assembly endorsed CIS membership, although the government steadfastly distanced itself from Russian-led CIS security plans.

Azerbaijan concluded a ten-year friendship and cooperation treaty with Turkey in February 1994 and became a signatory of NATO's Partnership for Peace in May. In the latter month it also became an observer member of the Nonaligned Movement. In May 1997 Turkey and Azerbaijan issued a joint declaration condemning "Armenian aggression" in Nagorno-Karabakh and asking Armenia to withdraw its troops from the region.

In January 2001 Russian President Vladimir Putin visited Azerbaijan, the two countries agreeing in principle on demarcation of the Caspian seabed border and signing numerous other cooperation protocols. (In February 2004 Azerbaijan and Russia signed the Moscow Declaration, which confirmed earlier agreements and pledged further bilateral cooperation regarding security, economic development, and other issues.) Azerbaijan's relations with the West also subsequently improved, particularly after Baku agreed to support Washington's antiterrorism initiatives following the attacks in the United States on September 11, 2001. In January 2002 a grateful U.S. president George W. Bush lifted the partial economic sanctions that had been imposed on Azerbaijan as the result of Azerbaijan's blockade of Armenia in connection with the Nagorno-Karabakh dispute. The United States also provided humanitarian aid and granted Azerbaijan most-favored-nation trade status. Subsequently, Azerbaijan lent some 159 troops to the U.S.-led occupying forces in Iraq in 2003. In 2004 Washington, seen as interested in using improved ties with Azerbaijan as a counter to potential Russian dominance in the region, signed a security cooperation agreement with Baku. (See Current issues, below, for subsequent developments.) Meanwhile, the Aliyev administration reportedly remained strongly interested in cooperation with the European Union (EU), in part because it considered the Armenian force in Nagorno-Karabakh to be essentially a Russian proxy. (Azerbaijan was one of six former Soviet republics invited to participate in the EU's "Eastern Partnership" in 2009.)

In May 2005 the defense ministers of Azerbaijan and Iran signed a security cooperation agreement, the two countries having previously (in 2002) agreed to build a joint natural gas pipeline and to facilitate the transport of goods. However, strains developed in the relationship between the two countries in 2007 when Azerbaijani security forces arrested a group of men who were allegedly plotting to overthrow the government with support from members of Iran's Revolutionary Guards Corps (see Political Parties and Groups, below). Meanwhile, attempting to maintain its delicate balancing act as a bridge between East and West, Azerbaijan as of early 2008 indicated it had no plans to seek full NATO membership (so as not to offend Russia). Concurrently, Russia continued to offer its radar base in Azerbaijan for potential United States use as part of a possible compromise regarding the Bush administration's controversial missile-defense initiative. For its part, Washington praised Azerbaijan for its assistance in combating Islamic militancy and promoted Azerbaijan as a key transit route for the rapidly increasing delivery of oil and gas to the West from the Caspian region. However, Azerbaijan diverged significantly from U.S. policy by refusing to accept the recent independence declaration by Kosovo, declaring the separatist initiative "illegal," apparently out of concern that Kosovo's independence would influence the situation in Nagorno-Karabakh.

Azerbaijan's East-West balancing act became even more difficult as a result of the Georgian-Russian conflict in South Ossetia in mid-2008, which to many analysts indicated that increased Russian pressure could be expected throughout the Caucusus region. In a perhaps related vein, it was reported in early 2009 that talks were underway for delivery of natural gas, highly coveted by the EU, from Azerbaijan to Russia. Azerbaijan's other international focus at that time was the recent improvement in relations between Armenia and Turkey (see Foreign relations in article on Armenia for details). Azerbaijani officials insisted that no final agreement should be reached for the reopening of the Armenian-Turkish border without a resolution of the situation in Nagorno-Karabakh, which had triggered the border's closure 15 years earlier. (See headnote in article on Armenia.)

Current issues. The brief elevation of Ilham Aliyev to the post of prime minister in August 2003 was widely perceived as a heavy-handed measure designed to ensure that he would succeed his father as president. Large-scale demonstrations broke out to protest the action, prompting what critics called brutal suppression by security forces. The presidential balloting in October was also widely criticized for failing to meet international standards. However, despite ongoing negative reaction in Western capitals, Ilham Aliyev's administration maintained its hard line, quashing political protests and imposing restrictions on the media. Human rights groups estimated that more than 1,000 people were arrested, including a number of prominent officials from opposition parties. Numerous violations, including voter intimidation and ballot-box tampering, were also alleged in the December 2004 local elections, which were boycotted by most opposition groups, including the YMP. Meanwhile, the government condemned as illegal the June 2005 legislative balloting in Nagorno-Karabakh in which the ruling pro-Armenian government secured a majority.

Most international observers and numerous domestic analysts (including some associated with the government) strongly condemned the way the November 2005 assembly poll in Azerbaijan was conducted. The opposition Freedom (*Azadliq*) coalition charged that ballot-stuffing, vote-buying, intimidation of voters by the government, and fraudulent tallying had cost it many assembly seats. *Azadliq* organized mass demonstrations in Baku throughout November, its supporters wearing orange in an apparent attempt to duplicate the so-called Orange Revolution that had toppled the government of Ukraine a year earlier. However, support for regime change reportedly did not nearly reach critical mass, despite Azerbaijan's ongoing reputation as what one *Financial Times* contributor described as a "highly corrupt post-Soviet state." The OSCE bluntly reported that the assembly elections had failed to meet international standards, while other observers used stronger language such as "electoral crime" and "rigged elections." The United States and the EU also criticized the government over its handling of the balloting, although, as one journalist put it, "not too loudly." (The opposition suggested that criticism has been toned down in recognition of Western military and energy interests in Azerbaijan.)

Despite the claim from Aliyev's critics that the United States was guilty of using a double standard by glossing over Azerbaijan's lack of democratic progress, Aliyev was invited to Washington to meet with President Bush in the spring of 2006. Topics included Azerbaijan's ongoing support for the U.S.-led war on terrorism and the growing importance of Azerbaijan as an air transit route for shipment of U.S. supplies to Afghanistan. In addition, Aliyev called for a peaceful settlement to U.S. tensions with Iran, which is home to a significant population of ethnic Azeris and with which Azerbaijan has strong diplomatic and economic ties. Later in the year Aliyev underscored his commitment to greater cooperation with the EU and NATO.

The November 2006 municipal elections did little to improve Azerbaijan's dismal reputation regarding genuine democratization, as government repression of the press and opposition parties appeared, if anything, to intensify. Most of the opposition boycotted the balloting to protest the lack of electoral reform and failure of the government to appoint an independent election commission. Meanwhile, human rights activists expressed increasing concern about conditions in Azerbaijan, while Western capitals, including Washington, pressed for reforms in the judiciary and relaxation of curbs on the media and opposition activity. (Some analysts argued that strong-arm tactics by the Aliyev administration and widespread corruption might create fertile conditions for militant Islamic fundamentalists. In that regard, Azerbaijani security forces announced a number of arrests in 2007 [see Political Parties and Groups, below, for details].)

For his part, President Aliyev was reportedly taking advantage of the Caspian oil boom to, among other things, strengthen the military, which has been described as sufficiently upgraded to offer a genuine challenge to Armenian forces in Nagorno-Karabakh. Little progress was achieved in 2005 to early 2008 toward a permanent resolution of the dispute, despite numerous bilateral meetings and ongoing involvement by international mediators, most of whom appeared to favor the withdrawal of Armenian troops from the enclave in favor of international peacekeeping forces pending an eventual self-determination vote. (In December 2006 a referendum among the Armenian population currently residing in Nagorno-Karabakh had given a reported 99 percent approval to a "constitution" designating the territory as a sovereign state, as proposed by Arkady Ghukasian, then the "president" of Nagorno-Karabakh. The legitimacy of the referendum was rejected by all the leading international organizations involved in the search for a political settlement.)

New Armenian president Serzh Sarkisian in early 2008 announced that his administration considered the independence of Nagorno-Karabakh to be irreversible, and the new administration in the disputed region maintained a similarly hard line. For his part, President Aliyev offered little compromise in the matter as he geared up for his reelection campaign.

All major opposition parties boycotted the October 2008 presidential balloting, claiming that the government continued to repress genuine dissent and that electoral participation was "pointless." The OSCE noted "improvements" over previous elections but concluded that the conduct of the poll still failed to meet a number of "democratic commitments." However, most analysts concluded that President Aliyev would have been reelected even in a "real" election, considering the nation's recent extraordinary economic advances and the fractionalization of the opposition. Aliyev's critics appeared increasingly impotent in March 2009 when the government reported a 92 percent "yes" vote in a national referendum on constitutional amendments that, among other things, eliminated the two-term presidential limit, thereby appearing to pave the way for Aliyev's potential "life presidency." The Council of Europe strongly condemned the constitutional revision, but overall Western criticism remained muted, perhaps in part so as not to jeopardize recent advances in regard to Nagorno-Karabakh. Following several informal meetings in the second half of 2008, the Armenian and Azerbaijani presidents signed a declaration (the first such document in 15 years) calling for a peaceful resolution of that so-called frozen conflict. For their part, Azerbaijani officials called for the immediate withdrawal of Armenian forces from the buffer zone around Nagorno-Karabakh while negotiations continued regarding Nagorno-Karabakh proper. In the spring of 2009 it was reported that conceptual breakthroughs had been achieved but that technical implementation remained the subject of disagreement. Little progress was reported throughout the rest of the year.

POLITICAL PARTIES AND GROUPS

Following the achievement of independence in 1991, Azerbaijan moved to a limited multiparty system, qualified by the exigencies of the ongoing war with Armenia, internal political conflict, and the continuing dominance of the state bureaucracy by former functionaries of the long-dominant Azerbaijan Communist Party (*Azerbaycan Kommunist Partiyasi*—AKP). A number of opposition blocs were organized in advance of the November 2005 assembly poll, although their effectiveness was limited. (For information on several opposition groups, now apparently defunct, from the late 1990s and early 2000s, see the 2007 *Handbook.*)

Government and Government-Supportive Parties:

New Azerbaijan Party (*Yeni Azerbaycan Partiyasi*—YAP). The YAP was founded by Heydar Aliyev in September 1992 as an alternative to the then-ruling AXC (see below) following his exclusion from the June 1992 presidential election because he was over a newly decreed age limit of 65. At the time, Aliyev held the presidency of the Azerbaijani enclave of Nakhichevan, previously having been a politburo member of the Soviet Communist Party and first secretary of the party in Azerbaijan (from 1969). He had also served as a Soviet deputy premier until he was dismissed by Mikhail Gorbachev in 1987 for alleged corruption. Aliyev used the YAP to rally opposition against the AXC government of Abulfaz Ali Elchibey, who was deposed in June 1993 with assistance from Nakhichevan military forces. Elected interim head of state, Aliyev won a presidential election in October 1993 (for which the 65-year age limit had been rescinded), being credited with 98.8 percent of the vote.

Amid a fragile internal security situation and with the major opposition parties barred from participation, the YAP and its allies secured an overwhelming parliamentary majority at legislative balloting in November 1995 and February 1996, and Aliyev was reelected president on October 11, 1998. Aliyev was also reelected YAP chair at the December 1999 party congress, while his son Ilham was chosen as a deputy chair in what was viewed as the first step in establishing himself as his father's successor. Ilham Aliyev was elevated to first deputy chair at the YAP's November 2001 congress, which also unanimously reelected Heydar Aliyev as party chair and 2003 presidential candidate.

Following the decline of his father's health in early 2003, Ilham Aliyev assumed control of the YAP. Heydar Aliyev died on December 12, 2003.

Ilham Aliyev was elected president of the republic in the controversial 2003 presidential poll, while the YAP retained overwhelming control (with the support of many so-called independents) in the 2005 assembly balloting. As of 2006 the YAP claimed a membership of 400,000.

Leaders: Ilham ALIYEV (President of the Republic and Party Chair), Artur RASIZADE (Prime Minister), Oqtay ASADOV (Speaker of the National Assembly), Mehriban ALIYEVA, Ali AHMADOV (Executive Secretary)

Smaller parties allied with the YAP for National Assembly elections have included the **Azerbaijan Independent Democratic Party** (*Azerbaycan Müstaqil Demokrat Partiyasi*—AMDP), led by Leyla YUNUSOVA; the **Independent Azerbaijan Party** (*Müstaqil Azerbaycan Partiyasi*—MAP), led by Nizami SULEYMANOV, who contested the 1992 and 1998 presidential elections, coming in third in the latter with 8.6 percent of the votes; the **Motherland Party** (*Anavatan Partiyasi*—AP), modeled on the Turkish party of the same name and led by Fazail AGAMALY and Yusuf CUNAYDIN; and **United Azerbaijan** (*Azerbaycan Vahid*—AV), whose leader, Kerrar ABILOV, had received a 0.3 percent presidential vote share in 1993.

Other Parties:

Freedom (*Azadliq*). An opposition bloc formed by the AXC, YMP, ADP, and LPA prior to the 2005 assembly balloting, *Azadliq* called for regime change in the apparent hope of igniting antigovernment sentiment similar to the kind that had peacefully toppled strong-arm regimes in several other former Soviet states recently. However, *Azadliq*'s results in the elections were disappointing, leaders claiming that their campaign efforts had been repressed by the government and that massive fraud had occurred in counting the votes. The AXC and ADP consequently decided to boycott the May 2006 reballoting in ten districts, although the YMP agreed to participate, putting the future effectiveness of the coalition in doubt, as did the fractionalization of the ADP (see below). The AXC subsequently boycotted assembly activity, while the YMP and the ADP reportedly separated from *Azadliq*.

As of the spring of 2008 the active members of *Azadliq* reportedly comprised the AXC, LPA, and the **Citizens and Development Party**, formed in 2006 by Ali ALIYEV and other former AMİP members. (The latter group was also referenced in some news reports as the Civic Democratic Party.) *Azadliq* boycotted the 2008 presidential poll.

Azerbaijan Popular Front Party (*Azerbaycan Xalq Cebhesi*—AXC). The AXC was launched in 1989 as an opposition movement urging reform by the Communist regime. Spanning a range of political currents and led by philosophy teacher Abulfaz Ali Elchibey, the movement evinced a broadly pan-Turkic orientation, supporting irredentist calls for the acquisition of Azerbaijani-populated areas of Iran.

In January 1990 some 150 AXC activists and others were killed by security forces in Baku and elsewhere in disturbances arising from AXC-led anti-Armenian demonstrations. Allowed to contest the Supreme Soviet elections of September–October 1990, the AXC-led opposition won only 45 of the 360 seats. Together with other opposition parties, the AXC boycotted the direct presidential poll of September 1991, but it subsequently forced the resignation of President Mutalibov in March 1992. In a further presidential election in June 1992, Elchibey was elected with 59 percent of the vote against four other candidates.

Replaced as head of state by Heydar Aliyev of the YAP in June 1993, Elchibey fled to Nakhichevan, and the AXC boycotted the September presidential election won by Aliyev. The authorities subsequently launched a crackdown against the AXC, raiding its headquarters in Baku in February 1994 and arresting a large number of its supporters. In May 1995 Elchibey repeated his call for a "greater Azerbaijan" to include Azerbaijani-populated northern Iran.

In January 1995, some 20 AXC members received jail sentences for antistate offenses, and in February the former AXC defense minister, Rakhim GAZIYEV, was sentenced to death in absentia for alleged high treason. Two months later, he was extradited to Baku from Moscow, and he was subsequently jailed, his sentence having been changed to life imprisonment.

In the November 1995 assembly election, the AXC was credited with winning three proportional seats on a national vote share of 10 percent, its tally increasing to four in the runoff balloting in February 1996. (The official name of the grouping was apparently changed prior to the 1995 balloting to the Azerbaijan Popular Front Party [AXCP]; subsequent reports have regularly referenced both the original and new names.) Elchibey returned to Azerbaijan from exile in October 1997, but he and the AXC boycotted the 1998 presidential poll.

Internal division between Elchibey's conservative or "traditionalist" wing and a faction of young reformers continued despite Elchibey's death in late August 2000. Deputy Chair Mirmahmud FATTEYEV reportedly signed a cooperation agreement with the YMP on behalf of the conservative faction for the November legislative balloting, an initiative that was criticized by the reformist wing, led by Deputy Chair Ali Kerimli and Asim MOLLAZADE, which preferred cooperation with the Civil Solidarity Party (below).

The AXC presidential candidate in 2003, Qudrat Muzaffar HASANQULIYEV, won only 0.4 percent of the vote. However, several AXC reformists, including Kerimli, were reportedly leading in districts for which the voting was annulled following the November 2005 legislative poll. In mid-2008 Kerimli, criticizing President Aliyev's "fully-fledged authoritarian regime," announced the AXC would boycott the October presidential balloting so as not to be part of the "illusion" of democracy. (The government had refused for two years to permit Kerimli to leave Baku.)

Leaders: Ibrahim IBRAHIMLI (Chair), Hasan KERIMOV (Deputy Chair), Ali KERIMLI (Head of "Reformist" Faction), Alimammud NURIEV, Mirmahmud MIRALIOGLU (Head of "Traditionalist" Faction), Fuad MUSTAFAYEV (Deputy Chair).

Liberal Party of Azerbaijan (LPA). Formed in 1995, the LPA was initially reported to have been involved in the formation of the New Policy bloc (see AMİP, below) for the 2005 assembly poll. However, subsequent reports indicated that the party had decided to cooperate (as the leader of a National Unity Movement) with *Azadliq* for the election. Lala Shovket Haciyeva, an LPA leader, was described in some reports as having won an assembly seat, which she reportedly refused to accept as an antigovernment protest. The LPA called for a boycott of the 2008 presidential poll.

Leaders: Lala SHOVKET HACIYEVA, Avaz TEMIRKHAN.

New Equality Party (*Yeni Musavat Partiyasi*—YMP). Indirectly descended from the pre-Soviet *Musavat* nationalists, the pan-Turkic and Islamist YMP (often referenced as *Musavat*) was founded in June 1992 and was closely allied with the 1992–1993 AXC government. In sharp conflict with the succeeding Aliyev regime, the party was barred from the first round of legislative elections in November 1995, although YMP chair Isa Gambar, a former speaker of the assembly, won a constituency seat in the February 1996 runoff balloting. The YMP boycotted the 1998 presidential balloting, and although it participated in the 2000 legislative poll (winning two seats), the YMP subsequently called for a boycott of the assembly. (According to some reports, the successful YMP candidates refused to follow the decree and were expelled from the party.)

Gambar placed second in the 2003 presidential balloting with 12.1 percent of the vote, with *Musavat* reportedly being perceived as significantly weakened by the government crackdown that followed that election. Following the November 2005 assembly poll, Gambar announced that the YMP would participate in the May 2006 reballoting, indicating that the YMP would withdraw from *Azadliq* over the issue. Gambar reportedly had concluded that Azerbaijan was not ready for the large-scale protests that had toppled governments in other former Soviet countries recently. Significant leadership infighting was subsequently reported within *Musavat*, with Gambar alleging that government repression had left the populace afraid to support opposition parties. In calling for a boycott of the 2008 presidential balloting, Gambar charged the Aliyev regime with not even bothering "to imitate democratic elections."

Leaders: Isa GAMBAR (Chair), Fakhreddin ABBASLI, Arif GACILI, Arif HACIYEV, Rauf ARIFOGLU, Niyazi IBRAHIMOV (General Secretary).

Democratic Party of Azerbaijan (*Azerbaycan Demokrat Partiyasi*—ADP). An opposition grouping launched in February 2000, the ADP includes among its leaders Rasul GULIEV, who lived in the United States following his resignation as speaker of the assembly in 1996. The new party issued a joint statement in April 2000 with the AMİP (see below) strongly criticizing the Aliyev regime. Subsequently, the government accused ADP supporters of having planned a coup on behalf of Guliev and issued a warrant for his arrest.

The ADP was initially declared ineligible for the November 2000 legislative balloting, but the ban was lifted shortly before the election. In 2004, the chair of the party's Supreme Council (Nuraddin MAMMADLI) and several other ADP members defected to the AXC.

Guliev attempted to return to Azerbaijan in 2005 to run as a candidate in the November assembly elections, but his plane was denied landing rights. Subsequently, ADP Deputy Chair Sardar Calaloglu reportedly appeared headed for victory in the assembly poll, but the results in his district were annulled. An ADP leadership struggle was subsequently reported between Calaloglu and close associates of Guliev, prompting the defection of some party members to other opposition groups. Internal friction continued into 2007 within the ADP, with Calaloglu's faction, which called for "constructive dialogue" with the YAP, subsequently appearing to gain control of the party and Guliev announcing plans to launch a new party called **Open Society**. It was reported in 2008 that the ADP had split from *Azadlig* and was involved in negotiations with other parties (including the YMP and the AMİP) regarding the proposed formation as a new bloc called the Consultative Center of the Opposition.

Leaders: Sardar CALALOGLU (Chair), Sharvarsh KOCHARYAN.

Civil Solidarity Party (*Vatandaş Hamrayliyi Partiyasi*—VHP). Founded in 1992 to support "progress toward a democratic society," the VHP was credited with securing 1 seat in the 1995–1996 legislative balloting. It subsequently was routinely referenced as a participant in various opposition groupings and activities and won 3 legislative seats in 2000. The VHP chair secured 1 percent of the vote in the 2003 presidential balloting.

Leader: Sabir RUSTAMKHANLY (Chair).

Azerbaijan National Independence Party (*Azerbaycan Milli İstiqlal Partiyasi*—AMİP). The AMİP was founded in July 1992 by Etibar Mamedov, who had been a prominent leader of the then-ruling AXC but had defected in light of resistance to his hard-line nationalist approach to the conflict with Armenia over Nagorno-Karabakh. Mamedov backed Heydar Aliyev's accession to power in June 1993 but declined to join the new cabinet. Thereafter, the AMİP vigorously opposed the government's support for deployment of Russian troops in Azerbaijan to help guarantee a Nagorno-Karabakh settlement. The party was officially credited with winning 3 seats in the 1995–1996 assembly elections on the basis of a national vote share of 9 percent. Theretofore regarded as part of the "loyal opposition," the party became strongly critical of the Aliyev regime in 1996. Mamedov came in second in the presidential election of October 1998 with 11.6 percent of the votes.

A number of AMİP supporters were given prison sentences in early 1999 for their role in demonstrations in Baku in November 1998 protesting the government's handling of the recent presidential election. In 2000 the AMİP accused the government of being authoritarian and "antinational."

Mamedov finished fourth in the 2003 presidential balloting. In February 2005 an AMİP congress elected Ali Nader Aliev as the new party chair, Mamedov being named honorary chair.

The AMİP subsequently served as a core component of the **New Policy** (*Yeni Siyasat*—YeS) electoral bloc, which also reportedly included several civic and professional groups; the **Social-Democratic Party** (*Sosial-Demokratik Partiya*—SDP), led by Araz ALIZADE; the **Azerbaijan National Movement Party,** led by Samir JAFAROV; the **Union of Free Democrats,** launched in March 2004 by former deputy prime minister Ali MASIMOV; and supporters of Nazim IMANOV, who had left the AMİP following the 2003 presidential election. The YeS declared itself to be a "third force" in politics, supporting "evolutionary" rather than "revolutionary" change. Ayaz Mutalibov, the former president of Azerbaijan who has been living in Russia, was permitted to run as a YeS candidate in the 2005 assembly poll, even though he reportedly faced possible arrest if he returned to Azerbaijan.

Friction was reported within the AMİP in early 2006 as Mamedov and Aliev held rival congresses, and YeS suspended its activities in the summer. The AMIP boycotted the 2008 presidential election.

Leaders: Ayaz RUSTAMOV (Chair), Ali Nader ALIEV (Former Chair), Etibar MAMEDOV (Honorary Chair).

Civic Unity Party (*Ventendash Birliyi Partiyasi*—VBP). At the launching of the VBP in May 2000, its chair was announced as Iqbal AGAZADE. However, at a congress in December, the VBP elected ex-Azerbaijani president Ayaz Mutalibov, in exile in Russia, as its chair. As of May 2001, the party had reportedly split into two factions, one headed by Agazade, who accused the other, headed by Mutalibov, of pursuing "Russian interests" to the detriment of Azerbaijan. (Agazade had been elected to the assembly in November 2000, having been referenced variously as an independent, as a member of the "non-Mutalibov faction of the VBP," or as a member of a VBP splinter called the **National Unity Party**.)

In July 2002 the government accused Mutalibov and a group of supporters of plotting a coup attempt in late 2001. The VBP derided the charges and demanded that the government permit the safe return of Mutalibov to Azerbaijan. In 2005 Mutalibov ran as an assembly candidate in the YeS electoral bloc (see AMİP, above), while Agazade was elected as a candidate of the **Hope Party** (*Ümid Partiyasi*—UP), of which he was described as chair. Mutalibov as of the spring of 2008 remained in exile, from where he reportedly was serving as chair of a **Social Democratic Party**. Agazade, the head of the assembly's human rights committee, secured 2.9 percent of the vote in the 2008 presidential election as UP candidate.

Azerbaijan United Communist Party (*Azerbaycan Vahid Kommunist Partiyasi*—AVKP). The AVKP was founded in November 1993 as the successor to the AKP, which had governed the republic during the Soviet era, latterly under the hard-line rule of Ayaz Mutalibov. In elections to the 360-member Azerbaijan Supreme Soviet in 1990, the AKP won 280 of the 340 contested seats, and Mutalibov was reelected president in September 1991 in direct balloting that was boycotted by the opposition. As a result of military setbacks in Nagorno-Karabakh, Mutalibov was forced to resign in March 1992, and he fled to Russia after a brief return to power in May. The AKP was effectively suspended under the subsequent AXC government; nevertheless, party members remained preponderant in the state bureaucracy, and AKP deputies continued to regard the 1990 Supreme Soviet as the legitimate legislative body. The relaunching of the party in November 1993 under the AVKP rubric was aimed at rallying these elements in opposition to the YAP government.

On September 1, 1995, the Supreme Court banned the AVKP for alleged antistate activities (such as advocating the restoration of the Soviet Union), but the decision was reversed later in the month. As a result, the party was able to contest the November election, albeit unsuccessfully.

The Communists were subsequently described as severely factionalized. The **Azerbaijan Communist Party-2** (AKP-2) was recognized as a legal party, and it put forward Firudin HASONOV as a presidential candidate in 1998, although he received less than 1 percent of the vote. Meanwhile, Sayad SAYADOV led a hard-line faction, and Ramiz AHMEDOV led a pro-Russian group reportedly allied with the Communist Party of the Russian Federation. (Mutalibov has lived in exile in Moscow since May 1992, although there has been a campaign recently for his political rehabilitation within Azerbaijan. See VPB, above, for additional information.)

Although the faction led by Sayadov reportedly announced in mid-2000 that it was changing its name to the Communist Workers Party, news reports surrounding the November legislative balloting regularly referenced the old AKP rubric. Sayadov's faction was generally identified with the AVKP, while Ahmedov's faction was routinely referenced under the old AKP rubric. Another group of AVKP members reportedly left the party in 2000 to form a small Stalinist party (led by Telman NURULLAYEV) called the **Communist Party of Azerbaijan.** Ahmedov died in September 2007, prompting additional turmoil within the Communist ranks.

Leader: Rauf GURBANOV (Chair).

Justice (*Adalat*). Formed in November 2000 under the leadership of former ADP chair Ilyas Ismayilov, *Adalat* was reportedly supported mainly by judges and law enforcement officials. (Ismayilov had been a minister of justice in the early 1990s.)

Leaders: Ilyas ISMAYILOV (Chair and Member of the Assembly), Isa MIRZEYEV.

Parties receiving 1 seat in the November 2000 assembly balloting were the progovernment **Alliance for Azerbaijan Party**, led by Abutalyb SAMADOV; the **Compatriot Party** (*Yurddash Partiyasi*), an opposition grouping led by Mais SAFARLI; and the progovernment **Social Welfare Party**, led by Khanhuseyn KAZYMLY, who received 0.2 percent of the vote in the 1998 presidential election. (The latter party also won 1 seat in the 2005 assembly poll.)

Other parties that won a single seat in the 2005 assembly balloting included the **Azerbaijan Democratic Reforms Party;** the **United Azerbaijan Popular Front Party,** founded in 2002 under the leadership of Gudrat HASANGULIYEV, who was credited with 2.3 percent of the vote in the 2008 presidential poll; and the **Great Creation Party,** founded in 2003 under the leadership of Fazil Mustafayev GAZAMFAROGLU, who received 2.5 percent of the vote in the 2008 presidential election.

Other parties participating in the 2005 assembly balloting included the **Azerbaijan Evolution Party,** founded in 1996 under the leadership of Teyub GANIEV; the **Progress Party,** founded in 2001 under the leadership of Cingiz DAMIROGLU, who in early 2008 was reportedly involved in efforts to forge a new opposition coalition in advance of the October presidential poll; the **Great Azerbaijan Party,** founded in 2003 under the leadership of Elshad MUSAYEV; the **People's Party,** led by Panah HUSEYNOV; the **People's Republican Party,** whose inaugural congress in August 2005 elected Hurru ALIYEV as chair; the **Democratic Azerbaijan World Party** (*Demokratik Azerbaycan Dünyasi Partiyasi*), led by Mammad ALIZADE; the **Azerbaijan Democratic Enlightenment Party,** led by Rufiz GONOGOV; the **Unity Party** (*Birlik Partiyasi),* led by Hussein ARTIKOGLU and Tahir KARIMLI; and the **Azerbaijan National Statehood Party,** led by Sabir TARVERDIYEV and Neimat PANAKHLY.

A grouping called **Azerbaijan's Path** was recently launched under the leadership of former prosecutor Ilgar GASYMOV with the aim of promoting a "favorable" solution to the conflict in Nagorno-Karabakh that would rectify conditions for the Azerbaijanis who had been forced from that enclave. A number of ADP defectors reportedly joined the grouping in 2006. Other parties referenced recently include the **Party for Democratic Reforms**, led by Asim MOLLAZADE; the **National Democratic Party**, led by Iskander HAMIDOV; the **National Revival Movement**, led by Faraj GULIYEV. Small parties participating in the 2008 presidential balloting included the **Modern Musavat Party**, whose chair, Hafiz HAJIYEV, was credited with 0.7 percent of the vote; and the **Liberal Democratic Party**, whose chair, Fuad ALIYEV, won 0.8 percent of the vote.

In mid-2000 the **Karabakh Liberation Organization**, which claimed a membership of 10,000 under the leadership of Akif NAGIYEV, was denied party status in view of its military orientation. Meanwhile, several members of **Allah's Army** (*Jeyshullah*), a Wahhabi opposition guerrilla movement that has operated in Azerbaijan since 1996 under the leadership of Mubariz ALIYEV, were convicted on terrorism charges in October 2000. Aliyev received a life sentence. Following protests in the outskirts of Baku in 2002, members of the **Islamic Party of Azerbaijan** were briefly imprisoned. Movsum SAMEDOV succeeded Gadjiaga NURI as chair of the grouping in 2007.

In early 2007 security forces arrested some 15 men accused of fomenting antigovernment activity through a militant Islamist group identified by the government as the **Northern Madhi Army** under the leadership of Said DADASBEYLI, a young cleric. The Azerbaijani and U.S. governments alleged that the group had ties to the Quds Force of Iran's Revolutionary Corps and was plotting to install a religious regime in Azerbaijan. However, Dadasbeyli's attorneys described the allegations as groundless, adding that Dadasbeyli and his supporters were devoted entirely to charity work. All of the detainees received prison sentences upon their conviction on various charges in December.

LEGISLATURE

The unicameral **National Assembly** (*Milli Majlis*) created under the 1995 constitution is elected for a five-year term and has 125 members elected in single-member districts in single-round balloting. (Prior to 2005, 25 of the 125 members were elected from party lists by proportional representation [6 percent threshold] in a single nationwide constituency.) The most recent balloting was held on November 6, 2005. However, the results were annulled in 10 of the 125 districts. Although it was clear that the New Azerbaijan Party and its supporters had been credited with winning an overwhelming majority of the 115 seats that were certified, reports varied on exact figures as well as on the role of some of the small parties. Following are the results as provided by the OSCE, referencing official results as provided by the electoral commission of Azerbaijan: New Azerbaijan Party (YAP), 56; Freedom, 6 (New Equality Party, 5; Azerbaijan Popular Front Party, 1); Motherland Party, 2; Civil Solidarity Party (VHP), 2; Hope Party, 1; Social Welfare Party, 1; Azerbaijan Democratic Reforms Party, 1; United Azerbaijan Popular Front Party, 1; Civic Unity Party, 1; Great Creation Party, 1; independents, 43. (Many of the candidates elected as independents were reportedly allied with the YAP.) Preliminary results from the May 13, 2006, reballoting for 10 seats indicated that the YAP and independents allied with it had won an additional 8 seats. The VHP and the Justice (*Adalat*) party each reportedly won 1 of the remaining 2 seats.

Speaker: Oqtay ASADOV.

CABINET

[as of May 1, 2009]

Prime Minister	Artur Rasizade
First Deputy Prime Minister	Yagub Eyyubov
Deputy Prime Ministers	Elchin Efendiyev
	Ali Hasanov
	Abid Sharifov
Ministers	
Agriculture	Ismat Abbasov
Communications and Information Technology	Ali Mamad Abbasov
Culture and Tourism	Abulfaz Garayev
Defense	Lt. Gen. Safar Abiyev
Defense Industries	Yavar Camalov
Ecology and Natural Resources	Huseyn Bagirov
Economic Development	Sahin Mustafayev
Education	Misir Mardanov
Emergencies	Kyamaleddin Heydarov
Finance	Samir Sharifov
Foreign Affairs	Elmar Mammadyarov
Industry and Energy	Natiq Aliyev
Internal Affairs	Lt. Gen. Ramil Usubov
Justice	Fikrat Mammadov
Labor and Social Security	Fizuli Alekperov
National Security	Eldar Makhmudov
Public Health	Oqtay Siraliyev
Taxation	Fazil Mamedov
Transportation	Ziya Arzuman Mammadov
Youth and Sports	Azad Ragimov

COMMUNICATIONS

A new media law entered into force in early 2000, its restrictions drawing significant domestic and international criticism. Among other things, the legislation permitted the government to close media outlets under certain circumstances. International organizations guarding the rights of journalists subsequently expressed growing concern over the treatment of reporters in Azerbaijan. In addition, journalists demonstrated in early 2006 against what they charged was ongoing harassment and intimidation on the part of the government. Their allegations were echoed by Reporters Without Borders, the Council of Europe, the OSCE, and Freedom House, which also decried the increased occurrences of violence against journalists and the government's proclivity for arresting reporters perceived to be aligned with opposition parties. However, the government continued its heavy-handed tactics into 2007 as a number of prominent journalists were sentenced on what were widely viewed as questionable charges. Concurrently, more than 20 journalists sought political asylum in other countries. President Aliyev pardoned most of the imprisoned journalists in December, although journalism watchdogs subsequently reported that the media remained muzzled in the run-up to the October 2008 presidential election. (Analysts estimated that only 5 percent of the media could accurately be described as independent at that point.) Among other things, the government was widely accused of censoring Internet access.

In 2009 Reporters Without Borders alleged that journalists who criticized the Aliyev regime faced real danger, with several reporters remaining in custody. Meanwhile, the government early in the year announced that foreign organizations (such as *Radio Free Europe/ Radio Liberty*, *Voice of America*, and the *British Broadcasting Corporation)* would no longer be able to broadcast over national frequencies, which government critics described as yet another effort to suppress divergent views. Critics also expressed strong concern over the government's subsequent support for an amendment to the media law that would permit suspension of media outlets for vaguely defined abuses of power.

Press. Prior to independence in the early 1990s, more than 150 newspapers were published in Azerbaijan, most of them in Azeri. The sector subsequently grew even further for most of the rest of the decade, as the government displayed a relatively tolerant attitude toward criticism. However, conditions changed dramatically at the end of the decade (see above), and major opposition dailies issued in Baku such as *Azadliq* (Freedom) and the sister publications *Gundelik Azerbaycan* (Daily Azerbaijan, in Azeri) and *Realni Azerbaycan* (Real Azerbaijan, in Russian) have been routinely targeted by the government. Other opposition papers that have been affected by the crackdown and concurrent arrests include *Nota Bene, Mukhalifat, Yeni Musavet* (a weekly based in Nakhichevan), *Bizim Yol, Hurriyet* (aligned with the Democratic Party of Azerbaijan), and the independent weekly *Monitor,* whose editor, Elmer HUSEYNOV, was murdered in 2005. Other papers include *Azerbaijan*, government daily in Azeri and Russian; *Bakinskii Bulvard*, opposition organ; *Respublika* (Republic), government daily; *Halq Gazeti*, government-owned; *Uch Nogte; Zaman; Zerkalo*, independent daily in Russian; *525-Gazeti,* independent daily; *Azerbaijan Gonjlari* (Youth of Azerbaijan), weekly; *Ses*, a daily aligned with the governing New Azerbaijan Party); *Sanat* (Industry), independent fortnightly; and *Tazadlar* (Contrasts), independent. Circulations in general are small, with readership mostly confined to urban areas.

News agency. The government facility is the Azerbaijan State News Agency (Azer TAJ), headquartered in Baku; private independent organizations include the Turan News Agency, which was evicted from its offices by the government in late 2006.

Broadcasting and computing. Radio Baku and Azerbaijan National Television (AzTV) broadcast from Baku in Azeri and a number of other languages. (The state network was described in 2006 as having a "distinctly Soviet-era" approach.) According to recent OSCE reports, there are some 47 television and radio stations providing national or regional coverage. Licensing is controlled by the National Radio and Television Council. Privately owned stations include Lider TV, Space TV, ANS, Khazar TV, and ATV. A public service station called Public TV was inaugurated in mid-2005. Analysts described broadcasting prior to the November 2005 elections as generally favoring the government, with television serving as the primary source of information for most of the population. ANS, considered the most important independent television station, was briefly closed by the government in late 2006 to early 2007. Subsequently, the OSCE described broadcast coverage of the 2008 presidential campaign as lacking "vibrant political discourse." As of 2008 there were 280 Internet users per 1,000 inhabitants.

INTERGOVERNMENTAL REPRESENTATION

Ambassador to the U.S.: Yashar ALIYEV.

U.S. Ambassador to Azerbaijan: (Vacant).

Permanent Representative to the UN: Agshin MEHDIYEV.

IGO Memberships (Non-UN): ADB, BSEC, CEUR, CIS, EBRD, ECO, IDB, Interpol, IOM, OIC, OSCE, WCO.

BAHAMAS

Commonwealth of the Bahamas

Political Status: Independent member of the Commonwealth since July 10, 1973.

Area: 5,380 sq. mi. (13,935 sq. km.).

Population: 303,611 (2000C); 336,000 (2008E).

Major Urban Center (2005E): NASSAU (227,000).

Official Language: English.

Monetary Unit: Bahamian Dollar (principal rate December 1, 2009: 1.00 dollars = $1US).

Sovereign: Queen ELIZABETH II.

Governor General: Arthur Dion HANNA; inaugurated on February 1, 2006, succeeding Dame Ivy DUMONT.

Prime Minister: Hubert Alexander INGRAHAM (Free National Movement); served as prime minister 1992–1997; returned to office on May 4, 2007, in succession to Perry G. CHRISTIE (Progressive Liberal Party), following election of May 2.

THE COUNTRY

The Commonwealth of the Bahamas encompasses a group of about 700 flat, coral islands stretching from the western Atlantic near Florida to the Caribbean Sea. Geomorphically an extension of the Little and Great Bahama banks, the archipelago features as its principal components New Providence and Grand Bahama. The islands have a temperate climate with modest rainfall but lack sufficient fresh water, much of which must be imported. Most Bahamians (85 percent) are descendants of former slaves. The most important religious denominations are Anglican, Baptist, Methodist, and Roman Catholic.

Banking and tourism have long been mainstays of the Bahamian economy. One of the first—and the largest—of the offshore tax havens, the country has more than 300 financial institutions, including more than 100 Eurocurrency branches of foreign banks; there are currently no corporate, capital gains, or personal income taxes. Extensive resort facilities typically attract in excess of 2.5 million tourists annually, while oil refining and transshipment has emerged as an important industry. During 1990–1993, however, tourist bookings and sugar production declined sharply, with the economy contracting by 2 percent in 1992 and 1993; further declines in 1994 and early 1995 were attributed primarily to fewer calls by cruise ships, although arrivals by air set a new record in 1995. Real GDP grew by 5.9 percent in 1999, before dropping to 1.9 percent growth in 2000 and collapsing to -0.8 percent in 2001. Recovery thereafter yielded 4.2 percent growth in 2006, despite a major blow to the economy in September 2004 when Hurricane Frances caused more than $200 million in damage. Another severe decline in growth, to 0.7 percent in 2008, reflected the impact of the global recession.

GOVERNMENT AND POLITICS

Political background. A landfall of Columbus in 1492 and subsequently inhabited by a variety of private settlers, the Bahamas suffered harassment by the Spanish and by pirates until becoming a British Crown Colony in 1717. During the U.S. Civil War the islands enjoyed a degree of prosperity as a base for blockade runners. Similar periods of prosperity occurred during the U.S. prohibition era and following World War II.

After more than two centuries of colonial rule, constitutional changes were negotiated in 1964 that called for the establishment of internal self-government with a bicameral legislature and a prime minister. These changes were implemented following an election in 1967 that resulted in a victory for the Progressive Liberal Party (PLP) under the leadership of Lynden O. PINDLING. Local government authority was broadened in 1969, and independence, which was not supported by the opposition Free National Movement (FNM), was formally granted on July 10, 1973. In the parliamentary elections of 1982 and 1987, the PLP retained control of the House of Assembly, although falling short of the three-fourths majority it had previously enjoyed. The quarter-century Pindling era came to an end in the balloting of August 19, 1992, with the FNM, led by Hubert A. INGRAHAM, winning 33 of 49 lower house seats. The FNM retained control by a substantially wider margin on March 14, 1997, winning 34 seats in a reduced House of 40 members, with an additional seat added in a by-election in September. However, it suffered a decisive reversal in the May 2, 2002, balloting, winning only 7 seats compared to 29 for the PLP, led by Perry G. CHRISTIE. The FNM returned to power after the election of May 2, 2007, at which, for the first time, a governing party was ousted after only one five-year term.

Constitution and government. Under the 1973 constitution, executive authority is vested in the queen (represented by a governor general with largely ceremonial powers) and the prime minister, who serves at the pleasure of the elective House of Assembly, in which legislative authority is concentrated; the appointive upper house (Senate) of the bicameral Parliament has limited functions.

Internal administration is based on the natural division into island groupings. Islands other than New Providence and Grand Bahama are administered by centrally appointed commissioners, despite a program that was launched in early 2000 to transfer authority over the smaller entities to elected local officials. The judicial system is headed by a Supreme Court and a Court of Appeal, although certain cases may be appealed to the Judicial Committee of the Privy Council in London; there also are local magistrates' courts. On the outer islands the local commissioners have magisterial powers.

In March 2006 British law lords invalidated Bahamian capital punishment as inhumane and degrading. But with polls showing overwhelming public support for executing convicted murderers, the action was seen as likely to trigger debate over retention of the Privy Council as the country's court of final appeal.

Foreign relations. Bahamian foreign relations have been determined in large part by the islands' proximity to Cuba, Haiti, and the United States. A long-standing dispute with Cuba over territorial fishing rights led in May 1980 to a Cuban MiG aircraft sinking a Bahamian patrol vessel that had apprehended two Cuban fishing boats for poaching. Havana subsequently agreed to pay compensation of $5.4 million and apologized for the involuntary violation of Bahamian sovereignty. In regard to Haiti, the Pindling government periodically attempted to deport illegal aliens, who were estimated to constitute more than 10 percent of the resident population; progress was reported to have been made with Haiti on the issue before the fall of the Duvalier regime, although criticism of treatment accorded the aliens continued thereafter. In May 1994 a group of 239 Haitians were returned to Haiti after being declared "economic refugees," while 17 listed as "political refugees" were refused entry for national security reasons. Terming illegal immigration as "the single greatest threat to our system of orderly development," the government declared an amnesty for the illegal residents in October and November, during which about 2,000 registered for government-assisted repatriation. An agreement with the Haitian government in January 1995 provided for the return of several thousand additional aliens of whom about 1,200 had departed (most involuntarily) by mid-February. The influx of illegals nonetheless continued, with nearly 16,000 reportedly apprehended in Bahamian waters during 2000–2008.

In May 1997, citing the "overwhelming size, economic strength, and expanding political influence" of mainland China, diplomatic relations were transferred from Taipei to Beijing, although an embassy in the Chinese capital was not opened until January 2006. Relations with the United States have been generally cordial, although periodically strained by U.S. accusations of high-level Bahamian participation in drug trafficking.

The Bahamas is a member of the United Nations, the Commonwealth, and the Organization of American States (OAS). It participates in the Caribbean Community and Common Market (Caricom) as a member of the Community but not the Common Market. Thus, it elected not to join the more integrated Caricom Single Market (CSM) at the latter's launching on January 30, 2006.

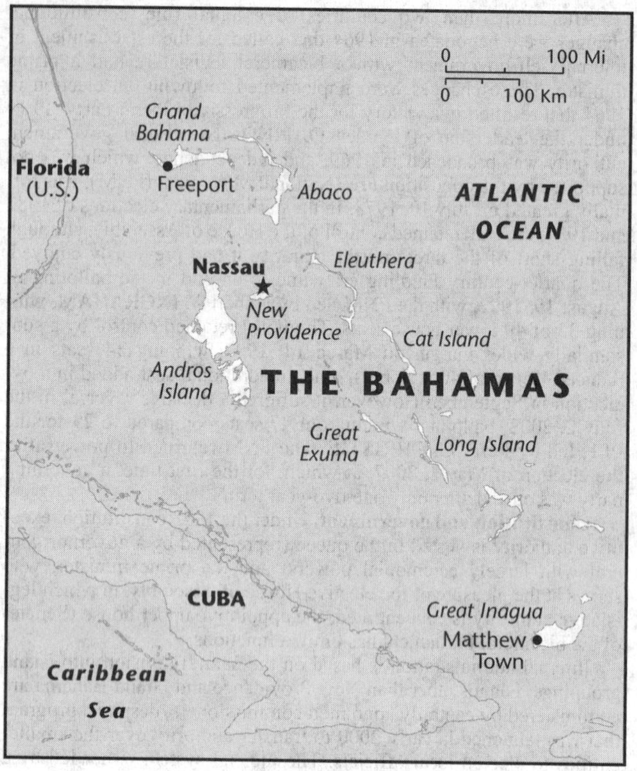

Current issues. In a move coincident with, but not directly linked to the Privy Council's abolition of the death penalty (see Constitution and government, above), a Constitutional Commission recommended in March 2006 that the British monarch be replaced as head of state by a Bahamian selected by the two legislative chambers. However, no action had been taken with matter by mid-2009.

In the run-up to the 2007 election, both the FNM and PLP pledged to curb illegal immigration and fight crime, while a major issue for Ingraham was his contention that the Christie government had been selling too much land to foreign investors, who had been allowed to reap handsome returns at the expense of Bahamians. Some progress was subsequently made on the repatriation of illegals to Haiti, although the homicide rate of 22 per 100,000 was deemed four times that acceptable by worldwide standards.

POLITICAL PARTIES

Government Party:

Free National Movement (FNM). The FNM was founded in 1972 by amalgamation of the United Bahamian Party (UBP) and a number of anti-independence dissidents from the PLP. In 1979 it was reconstituted as the Free National Democratic Movement (FNDM) by merger with the Bahamian Democratic Party (BDP), which had been organized in late 1976 when five FNM parliamentary deputies withdrew from the parent group. Before the 1982 election, which the party contested under its original name, it was joined by the two remaining representatives of the Social Democratic Party (SDP), which had been founded by BDP dissidents in late 1979 and had been recognized thereafter as the official opposition. Following the 1987 balloting, Kendal G.L. ISAACS resigned as parliamentary leader, the party's chair (and founder), Sir Cecil Wallace-Whitfield, being designated his successor; Sir Cecil, who died in May 1990, was in turn succeeded by Hubert A. INGRAHAM, a former independent MP who had joined the party only a month before. Isaacs died in May 1996.

Sir Orville A.T. (Tommy) Turnquest was elected "leader-designate" of the FNM in August 2001, Ingraham having previously announced his plans to retire from politics following the general election in 2002, at which time the party lost its majority and went into opposition. Ingraham returned to politics in mid-2005 and was designated opposition leader in the House of Assembly before returning as prime minister in May 2007.

Leaders: Hubert A. INGRAHAM (Prime Minister and Party Leader), Brent T. SYMONETTE (Deputy Party Leader).

Opposition Party:

Progressive Liberal Party (PLP). A predominantly black-supported party, the PLP was formed in 1953 in opposition to the policies of business interests who then controlled the government. The party was a leading supporter of the independence movement and endorses policies promoting tourism and foreign investment while at the same time preventing land speculation and providing more opportunity for indigenous Bahamians. Although subject to some internal dissent, the PLP secured commanding parliamentary majorities in 1972, 1977, 1982, and 1987 but lost by a better than two-to-one margin in 1992. Following the further loss of all but 6 seats on March 14, 1997, Lynden PINDLING resigned as party leader and on July 7 announced his retirement from parliamentary politics (he died in August 2000). The party returned to power under Perry G. Christie in the election of May 3, 2002, before losing to the FNM in 2007.

Leaders: Perry G. CHRISTIE (Former Prime Minister and Leader of the Party), Raynard S. RIGBY (Chair).

Other Groups:

Coalition Plus Labour (CPL). The CPL was formed before the 2002 election as an alliance of three recently organized small groups: the **Bahamas Freedom Alliance** (BFA), led by D. Halston MOULTRIE; the **Coalition for Democratic Reform** (CDR), led by Bernard NOTTAGE; and the **People's Labour Movement** (PLM). It failed to secure legislative representation.

LEGISLATURE

The **Parliament** consists of an appointed Senate with limited powers and a directly elected House of Assembly.

Senate. The upper house consists of 16 members, 9 of whom are appointed on the advice of the prime minister, 4 on the advice of the leader of the opposition, and 3 on the advice of the prime minister and others whom the governor general may wish to consult.

President: Lynn HOLOWESKO.

House of Assembly. The lower house presently consists of 41 members directly elected on the basis of universal suffrage for five-year terms (subject to dissolution). In the most recent election of May 2, 2007, the Free National Movement won 23 seats and the Progressive Liberal Party, 18.

Speaker: Alvin SMITH.

CABINET

[as of June 1, 2009]

Prime Minister	Hubert A. Ingraham
Deputy Prime Minister	Theodore Brent Symonette
Ministers	
Agriculture and Marine Resources	Lawrence Cartwright
Education	Carl Bethel
Environment and Maritime Affairs	Earl Deveaux
Finance	Hubert A. Ingraham
Foreign Affairs	Theodore Brent Symonette
Health	Hubert A. Minnis
Housing and National Insurance	Alfred Kenneth Russell
Labor and Social Development	Dion Foulkes
National Security	Orville Alton Thompson (Tommy) Turnquest
Public Works and Transport	Neko Grant
Tourism and Aviation	Vincent Vanderpool-Wallace
Youth, Sports, and Culture	Desmond Bannister
Attorney General	Michael Barnett

CABINET

Ministers of State

Culture	Charles Maynard
Immigration	Brannville McCartney
Lands and Local Development	Byran Woodside
Without Portfolio	Loretta Butler-Turner [f]
	Zhivargo Laing
	Phenton Neymour

[f] = female

COMMUNICATIONS

Press. The following are published daily in Nassau, unless otherwise noted: *Nassau Guardian* (14,100); *Nassau Daily Tribune* (12,000); *Freeport News* (Freeport, 4,000); *Bahama Journal; Official Gazette*, a weekly government publication. In August 1998 the *Tribune* concluded a partnership agreement with the *Miami Herald* to produce a combined edition of the two papers.

Broadcasting and computing. The government-owned Broadcasting Corporation of the Bahamas operates two commercial radio stations in Nassau and one in Freeport. Bahamas Television began broadcasting from Nassau in 1977, while the Canadian-owned Cable Bahamas commenced cable TV transmission in March 1995; the nation also receives U.S. television directly from Florida. As of 2008 there were 315.4 Internet users per 1,000 inhabitants.

INTERGOVERNMENTAL REPRESENTATION

Ambassador to the U.S.: Cornelius A. SMITH.

U.S. Ambassador to the Bahamas: Nicole A. AVANT.

Permanent Representative to the UN: Paulette BETHEL.

IGO Memberships (Non-UN): ACS, Caricom, CDB, CWTH, IADB, Interpol, IOM, NAM, OAS, OPANAL, SELA, WCO.

BAHRAIN

Kingdom of Bahrain
al-Mamlakah al-Bahrayn

Political Status: Independent emirate proclaimed August 15, 1971; constitution adopted December 6, 1973; constitutional monarchy established on February 14, 2002, under constitutional amendment decreed by the emir in purported accordance with National Action Charter endorsed by national referendum on February 14–15, 2001.

Area: 258 sq. mi. (668 sq. km.).

Population: 650,604 (2001C); 786,000 (2008E). Both figures include non-nationals (approximately 264,000 in 1999).

Major Urban Centers (2005E): MANAMA (152,000); Muharraq (119,000).

Official Language: Arabic.

Monetary Unit: Dinar (official rate December 1, 2009: 1 dinar = $2.65US).

Sovereign: King Sheikh Hamad ibn Isa Al KHALIFA, descendant of a ruling dynasty that dates from 1782; succeeded to the throne as emir on March 6, 1999, upon the death of his father, Sheikh Isa ibn Salman Al KHALIFA; proclaimed himself king under constitutional amendment adopted on February 14, 2002.

Heir to the Throne: Crown Prince Sheikh Salman ibn Hamad Al KHALIFA.

Prime Minister: Sheikh Khalifa ibn Salman Al KHALIFA, uncle of the emir; appointed January 19, 1970, by his brother, then-emir Sheikh Isa ibn Salman Al KHALIFA; continued in office upon independence.

THE COUNTRY

An archipelago of some 33 largely desert islands situated between the Qatar peninsula and Saudi Arabia, the Kingdom of Bahrain consists primarily of the main island of Bahrain plus the smaller islands of Muharraq, Sitra, and Umm-Nassan. Summer temperatures often exceed 100 degrees (F), and annual rainfall averages only about four inches; however, natural springs provide sufficient water. The predominantly Arab population is about two-thirds indigenous Bahraini, with small groups of Saudi Arabians, Omanis, Iranians, Asians, and Europeans. An estimated 65 percent consists of Shiite Muslims, while 30 percent, including the royal family, adheres to the Sunni sect.

Oil, produced commercially since 1936, and natural gas account for some 65 percent of the government's income, although recoverable petroleum reserves may be exhausted in 15 to 20 years. (As of 2008 Bahrain was producing 48,500 barrels per day, while its total reserves were estimated at about 125 million barrels.) Additional revenue is derived from operation of the Aluminum Bahrain smelter, one of the largest nonextractive enterprises in the Gulf area, and from one of the Middle East's largest oil refineries, devoted largely to processing crude (about 150,000 barrels per day) from Saudi Arabia. Bahrain also has been a prominent financial center for many years; its more than 50 offshore banks handle much of the region's oil-related wealth.

Aided by financial support from Saudi Arabia, Kuwait, and the United Arab Emirates, the government upon independence began to establish an extensive network of social services, including free education and medical care, and in 1982 mounted an ambitious program for infrastructure development and improvements in agriculture and education. An economic downturn in the mid-1980s, caused by declining foreign aid, appeared to have been reversed by the end of the decade; however, the Gulf crisis precipitated by the August 1990 Iraqi invasion of Kuwait generated additional economic problems for the emirate as aid from Gulf neighbors was severely constrained and offshore banking activity fell sharply. In response, the government intensified its campaign to promote development of new small- and medium-scale industries, in large part by loosening restrictions on private foreign investment. The economy rebounded in the mid-1990s under the influence of steady oil revenue. Subsequently, falling oil prices in 1998 led to a 3 percent decline in GDP for the year and intensified concern over the government's budget deficit, and observers suggested that a growing segment of the population (particularly those under 27 years of age, who make up 70 percent of the total) was at risk of becoming economically disenfranchised. However, the economy rebounded strongly in 1999 as the result of the sharp turnaround in oil prices and the subsequent positive response from foreign investors. GDP growth subsequently remained strong, averaging more than 5 percent annually in 2000–2004. The International Monetary Fund (IMF) described the economy as "one of the most advanced in the region," although unemployment remained a significant concern, and a number of observers warned that entrenched poverty (primarily within the Shiite population) still presented a threat to political and social stability. High oil prices were the primary factor in GDP growth averaging 5.8 percent annually in 2005–2006, with increased non-oil revenue and continued low inflation. Also, a construction boom in 2006 saw progress in the development of a major financial center and a causeway linking Bahrain and Qatar.

GDP growth of just under 7 percent was recorded in 2007, while declining global oil prices led to slower growth, averaging about 4.5 percent annually in 2008–2009. The government has been focusing on diversification, with particular attention devoted to the service sector, as well as to improving subsidies and incentives in the agriculture sector. Meanwhile, construction of one of the world's largest causeways—linking Bahrain and Qatar—was scheduled to begin in 2009. Annual growth was expected to remain stable at about 4.5 percent in 2010.

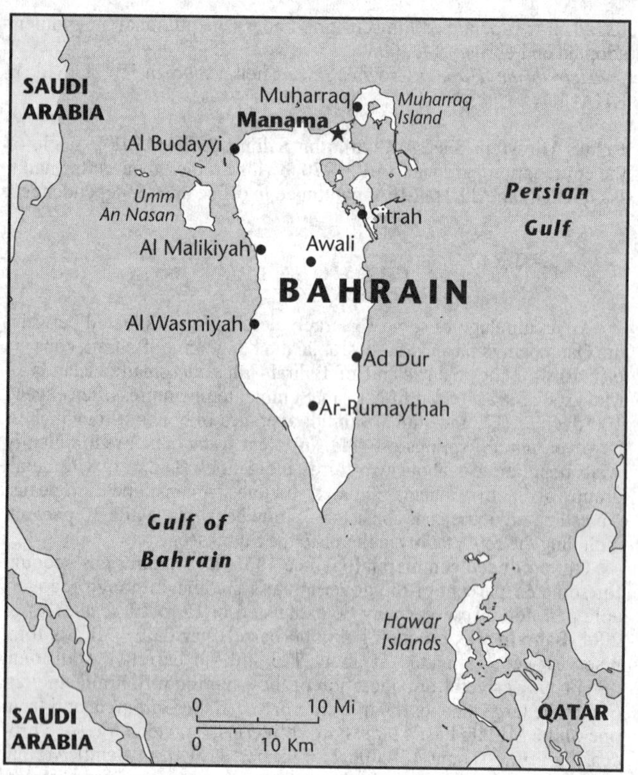

GOVERNMENT AND POLITICS

Political background. Long ruled as a traditional monarchy, Bahrain became a British protectorate in 1861 when Britain concluded a treaty of friendship with the emir as part of a larger effort to secure communication lines with its Asian colonies. The treaty was modified in 1892, but little evolution in domestic politics occurred prior to the interwar period. In 1926 Sir Charles BELGRAVE was appointed adviser to the emir, providing guidance in reform of the administrative system—an especially important step in light of accelerated social change following the discovery of oil in 1932. Belgrave continued to have a direct and personal effect on Bahraini policy until his departure in 1957, the result of Arab nationalist agitation that began in 1954 and reached a peak during the 1956 Anglo-French action in Egypt. Incipient nationalists also provoked disturbances in 1965 and in 1967, following the second Arab-Israeli conflict.

In 1968 Britain announced that it would withdraw most of its forces east of Suez by 1971, and steps were taken to prepare for the independence of all of the British-protected emirates in the Persian Gulf. Initially, a federation composed of Bahrain, Qatar, and the seven components of the present United Arab Emirates was envisaged. Bahrain, however, failed to secure what it considered an appropriate allocation of seats in the proposed federation's ruling body and declared separate independence on August 15, 1971.

Despite nominal efforts at modernization, such as the creation of an Administrative Council following the 1956 disturbances and a quasi-ministerial Council of State as its successor in 1970, virtually absolute power remained in the hands of the emir until the adoption in 1973 of the country's first constitution, which provided for a partially elected National Assembly. However, total control quickly returned to the royal family when the emir, describing the new legislative body as "obstructionist," ordered its dissolution in August 1975.

Although initially less intense than in other regional countries, rebellious sentiments among some of the majority Shiites, resentful of Sunni rule, precipitated conflict following the Iranian revolution of 1979 and the accompanying spread of Islamic fundamentalism. In December 1981 the government declared that it had thwarted a conspiracy involving the Iranian-backed Islamic Front for the Liberation of Bahrain (IFLB). That plot and the discovery in February 1984 of a rebel arms cache resulted in numerous arrests, the banning of a Shiite religious organization (the Islamic Enlightenment Society), and the issuance of compulsory identity cards to nationals and resident aliens. The government subsequently maintained a tight rein on the activity of fundamentalists, a number of whom were arrested in 1992 for belonging to illegal organizations. In January 1993, apparently in response to Western calls for political liberalization, the emir established a Consultative Council of 30 "elite and loyal men," including some former National Assembly members.

A wave of clashes with security forces erupted during the summit of the Gulf Cooperation Council (GCC) in Manama in December 1994, following the arrest of Sheikh Ali SALMAN, a religious leader who had demanded more jobs for Shiites. In January 1995 Salman and two followers were deported to Dubai and thereafter granted temporary asylum in Britain. However, after the emir complained of "meddling by foreign countries in our internal affairs," in an implicit reference to Iran, further disturbances occurred in March in which a police officer was killed. In April two people were killed and dozens injured during a raid on the home of another opposition cleric, Sheikh Abd al-Amir al-JAMRI, and on May 2 ten Shiites, including Jamri, received jail terms for property damage resulting from the December and January outbreaks.

Sheikh Jamri was released on September 25, 1995, following the initiation of reconciliation talks between the government and the Shiite opposition. However, a new outbreak of violence in early 1996 prompted the rearrest of Jamri and seven followers. Additional arrests were made in February after a series of bombings in the capital. Following further bombings in early 1996, the government announced on June 3 that it had foiled an allegedly Iranian-backed plot to seize power and that more than 80 of those involved had been arrested. Recalling its ambassador from Tehran, Bahrain claimed that the Iranian authorities had hatched the plot with a Bahraini branch of the Lebanon-based Hezbollah (Party of God), whose members had been trained in Iran and had been the principal instigators of the recent unrest among Bahraini Shiites. Denying the Bahraini charges, Iran responded by withdrawing its ambassador from Manama while offering to mediate between the government and the Shiite opposition. Meanwhile, apparently responding to international pressure for political liberalization throughout the Gulf, the emir in September appointed an expanded 40-member Consultative Council.

Sheikh Isa ibn Salman Al KHALIFA, the emir of Bahrain since 1961, died of a heart attack on March 6, 1999. He was immediately succeeded by his son and longtime heir apparent, Sheikh Hamad ibn Isa Al KHALIFA, who was reportedly more reform-minded than his father. A new cabinet was appointed on May 31, although it comprised most members of the previous government, including his uncle, Prime Minister Sheikh Khalifa ibn Salman Al KHALIFA. In November 2000 the emir appointed a 46-member Supreme National Committee to draft a National Action Charter that would serve as a blueprint for political development and democratization. Although some members reportedly resigned over alleged "interference" by the emir, the draft charter was endorsed by a reported 98.4 percent in a national referendum on February 14–15, 2001. A year later the emir decreed constitutional amendments that incorporated the charter's provisions, including the establishment of a constitutional monarchy in which authority was to be shared by a bicameral National Assembly and the former emir (now to bear the title "king"). As the first step in the progressive (by regional standards) democratization process, local elections were held in May 2002, with a number of opposition political "associations" or "societies" participating. However, several such groups boycotted the October balloting for the Chamber of Deputies to protest the king's decision that the assembly's upper house, the Consultative Council, would continue to be appointed rather than elected.

Several political associations participated in two rounds of municipal elections and balloting for the Chamber of Deputies on November 25 and December 2, 2006. In the Chamber of Deputies, opposition Shiites increased their representation, securing 17 seats (compared to 7 in 2002), while Sunnis, many supportive of the government, retained control by winning 22 seats (see Current issues, below). One woman, who ran uncontested, was among those elected to the lower house. The king appointed new members to the Consultative Council on December 5, and his cabinet reshuffle of December 11 included for the first time a former member of the Islamic National Accord Society (INAS). The prime minister retained his post.

In January 2008 the king moved to consolidate the royal family's control of the military by appointing his eldest son, Crown Prince Sheikh Salman ibn Hamad Al KHALIFA, as deputy commander in chief of the army. He also replaced the defense minister with the state minister for defense, Sheikh Muhammad ibn Abdullah Al KHALIFA.

Constitution and government. In December 1972 the emir convened a Constituent Council to consider a draft constitution that provided for a National Assembly composed of a cabinet (which had replaced the Council of State in 1971) and 30 members elected by popular vote. The constitution was approved in June 1973 and became effective December 6, 1973, and an election was held the following day. However, the assembly was dissolved in August 1975, with the emir suspending the constitutional provision for an elected legislative body. The Consultative Council named in January 1993 was established by the emir's decree, observers predicting it would operate on a "trial basis" before provision for it or some other such body was incorporated into the constitution. At the time of the appointment of the council in September 2000, the government announced plans to conduct elections in 2004 for the next council. Meanwhile, the emir in April had decreed the establishment of a new Supreme Council for Economic Development to oversee the privatization of some state-owned industries.

The constitutional amendments of February 2002 proclaimed the country a "constitutional monarchy" based on separation of powers, the rule of law, respect for human rights, and freedom of association. In addition, the changes in the basic law provided for formation of a bicameral legislature; women were empowered not only to vote but also to run for office. However, critics accused King Hamad of reserving too much authority for himself. (The king was designated head of state and commander in chief of the armed forces and was given uncontested power to appoint cabinet ministers, judges, and members of the upper house in the new National Assembly.)

The legal system is based on sharia (canonical Muslim law); the judiciary includes separate courts for members of the Sunni and Shiite sects. A constitutional court was established in July 2002.

The six main towns serve as bases of administrative divisions that are governed by municipal councils.

Foreign relations. Since independence, Bahrain has closely followed Saudi Arabia's lead in foreign policy. However, it was more moderate than most other Arab states in its support of the Palestine Liberation Organization and in condemning the Israeli–Egyptian peace treaty of 1979.

Generally regarded as the most vulnerable of the Gulf sheikhdoms, Bahrain was a target of Iranian agitation and territorial claims following the overthrow of the shah. Although Manama adopted a posture of noncommitment at the outbreak in 1980 of the Iran–Iraq war, it subsequently joined the other five members of the GCC in voicing support for Iraq. A security treaty with Saudi Arabia was concluded in December 1981, and in February 1982 the foreign ministers of the GCC states announced that they would actively oppose "Iranian sabotage acts aimed at wrecking the stability of the Gulf region." To this end, Bahrain joined with the other GCC states in annual joint military maneuvers. The spirit of cooperation was jolted in April 1986, however, by Bahrain's conflict with Qatar over a small uninhabited island, Fasht al-Dibal, that had been reclaimed from an underlying coral reef for use as a Bahraini coast guard station. Following a brief takeover by Qatari armed forces, an agreement was reached to return the site to its original condition. In January 1989 the two countries agreed to mediation by Saudi Arabia to resolve other territorial problems, including Bahrain's claim to Zubara, the ancestral home of the Al Khalifa family on the Qatari mainland. Nonetheless, in mid-1991 Qatar instituted a suit at the International Court of Justice (ICJ), claiming sovereignty not only over Fasht al-Dibal, but another reef, Qitat Jaradah, and the larger Hawar Island. Following the ICJ's March 2001 ruling on the dispute (wherein Zubara was awarded to Qatar and Fasht al-Dibal, Qitat Jaradah, and Hawar Island to Bahrain), relations between the two countries improved significantly.

Relations with Washington have long been cordial, and in October 1991, following the UN action against Iraq, Bahrain and the United States signed a defense cooperation agreement, similar to one concluded between the United States and Kuwait, that provided for joint military exercises and authorized the storage of equipment and the use of port facilities by U.S. forces. The Gulf crisis was seen as having provided the government with a powerful means of surmounting Sunni Arab fears that an ongoing U.S. presence would promote unrest among the country's numerically predominant Shiite population, and in October 1995 Manama announced it had granted the United States permission to base 30 military aircraft in Bahrain. Meanwhile, the emirate and its GCC associates continued to seek regional security arrangements that would dilute domestic political pressure on individual members regarding military ties with the West. However, upon ascending to power in March 1999, Sheikh Hamad quickly pledged to maintain the close ties that his father had established with the Western powers. Subsequently, Bahrain signed a free trade agreement with the United States, whose naval base in Bahrain remained an important component of U.S. military force in the Gulf. Anti-American sentiment has remained relatively low in Bahrain, although protests broke out in May 2004 against attacks by U.S. forces on Shiite "holy cities" in Iraq. In late 2005 Bahrain was reported to have lifted its ban on imports of Israeli products as a result of pressure from the United States under terms of the free trade agreement. However, conflicting reports emerged over the status of Bahrain's Israeli Boycott Office, with U.S. officials contending it had been closed in advance of implementation of the free trade agreement in 2006, while other reports stated that Bahrain's boycott was still in effect, in compliance with Arab League dictates (see Current issues, below). In November 2007, Bahrain participated in the Middle East peace summit aimed at helping to resolve the Israeli-Palestinian conflict, hosted by the United States in Annapolis, Maryland.

Iran's president, Mahmoud Ahmadinejad, visited Bahrain in November 2007 to ease tensions following verbal confrontations between Iran and the United States that had prompted fears of a military buildup in the Gulf region. In 2008, Bahrain announced that it would join other Arab countries in a plan to develop nuclear energy for civilian purposes.

In February 2009 tensions again flared with Iran following an Iranian official's comment about Bahrain's sovereignty that was perceived as an insult by a delegation from Bahrain. The remark prompted Bahrain to suspend a gas import deal with Tehran. A week later President Mahmoud Ahmadinejad reiterated Iran's respect for Bahrain's sovereignty in a letter to the king, but the situation was exacerbated when Iran announced its naval vessels were ready to move beyond the Gulf into the Indian Ocean. Observers said hostile moves by Iran were seemingly connected to the possibility of direct negotiations with the United States over Iran's nuclear program. Iran's preference was to engage in these talks alone, observers said, and its hostile actions were a way of warning Bahrain and other Gulf states not to interfere.

Current issues. Critics of Sheikh Isa's domestic policies (particularly the repression of dissent emanating from the Shiite population and secular liberals since the 1996 disturbances) expressed the hope in 1999 that the new emir, Sheikh Hamad, would prove more open to dialogue and compromise. Among other things, Shiite leaders called for the release of Sheikh Jamri, the popular cleric who in 1999 was sentenced to ten years in jail on charges of inciting unrest and operating illegally on behalf of a foreign power. Opposition groups also continued to lobby for restoration of an elected legislature, release of all political prisoners and the return of exiled dissidents—demands that attracted significant international support. The emir pardoned the sheikh almost immediately after his sentencing, albeit not before coercing a "humiliating confession" from Jamri. (Jamri died of a heart attack in December 2006.) Opposition groups welcomed the emir's decision in November to release a number of detainees, but they claimed that numerous other political prisoners remained in jail. They also were only cautiously supportive of the government's decision to include women for the first time in the new Consultative Council appointed in September 2000 and its announcement that membership of the next council would be determined through the ballot box. However, some of those concerns were alleviated by the referendum on the National Action Charter in February 2001. The emir also reduced tensions between his administration and its opponents by visiting Shiite-dominated areas, issuing a general amnesty for political detainees, permitting the return of prominent dissidents from exile, and repealing a number of hard-line security measures.

Although Sheikh Hamad promoted his constitutional amendments of February 2002 as moving Bahrain toward the status of a "modern democracy," complaints quickly arose within the opposition camp. Most importantly, opponents decried Hamad's decree that only the lower house of the National Assembly would be elected, with the upper house appointed by the king having an effective veto over legislation. (Critics called that decision a violation of the intent of the 2001 National Action Charter.) King Hamad also was strongly attacked for a 2002 decree granting immunity to any security personnel or government officials accused of torture or other human rights violations prior to 2001. A number of public protests subsequently broke out, many of them among Shiites who continued to feel repressed by the royal family and Sunnis in general. In the wake of a boycott by several prominent political "societies" (see Political Groups, below), the turnout for the October 2002 balloting for the Chamber of Deputies was only 53 percent (down from more than 80 percent for the May municipal elections). International observers also began to question the government's enthusiasm for reform, particularly when Abd al-Hadi al-KHAWAJA (the executive director of the Bahrain Center for Human Rights [BCHR]) was arrested in late 2004 for criticizing Prime Minister Salman. (Khawaja was pardoned by the king following his conviction, but the BCHR remained closed.) Concerns also were raised about the new antiterrorism law proposed by the government in 2005, opponents describing the language in the bill as being so broad as to permit the detention of any government critic.

While political societies continued to increase in number, in mid-2005 the king ratified a law placing more restrictions on the societies, specifically barring them from receiving funding from foreign sources and raising the minimum age for membership from 18 to 21. Also prohibited were political associations based on "class or profession, sectarian or geographical" groupings, drawing immediate criticism from the societies and prompting large public protests that carried over into early 2006. Nevertheless, most of the political societies, including several that had boycotted the 2002 elections, agreed to register in accordance with the new law while continuing to promote full-fledged party empowerment and preparing to participate in the elections. In August 2006 the government announced tiered financial support for political groups, depending on size of membership, number of representatives in the legislature, and number of women representatives. Another decision by the government in 2006 to help former political exiles on humanitarian grounds was "cautiously welcomed" by social activists.

Tensions escalated between Shiites and Sunnis in advance of the 2006 parliamentary elections, with reports of confrontations between Shiite villagers and government security forces early in the year. Additionally, observers reported that Sunnis were becoming increasingly alarmed over Iranian influence that they believed could lead to a "Shiite crescent" in the region. Further, a pre-election "political firestorm" was ignited by a former government official's report alleging a secret plan to promote sectarian discrimination against Shiites and to rig the elections. Following balloting for the Chamber of Deputies (see Legislature, below) and the gains made by the main Shiite opposition group, the INAS, the government was encouraged that tensions might ease. Observers noted, however, that about three-quarters of the successful candidates, including both Sunnis and Shiites, were described as Islamists, underscoring the electoral failure of liberal tendencies. INAS members briefly boycotted the opening session of the National Assembly on December 15 but joined the swearing-in ceremonies on December 18. INAS leaders said the boycott was prompted by the reappointment of government officials whose names allegedly were linked to the scandal.

Attention in mid-2007 turned to the government's imposition of an annual income tax, Bahrain becoming the first country in the region to institute such a levy. Despite the objections of trade unions, religious leaders, and some political groups, the tax went into effect in June, with a deduction of 1 percent from the paychecks of some 100,000 workers. Religious officials said the tax was unfair because exemptions were granted to the military and to elected officials, and they said it was against Islamic precepts to take the money without workers' permission. Part of the revenue was to be used for a program to help relieve unemployment.

In December 2007, 39 people were arrested following a week of antigovernment demonstrations in villages near the capital. Increasing economic disparity between Shiites and the Sunni ruling family was said by observers to have been one of the reasons for the demonstrations.

In an unprecedented move, Bahrain in 2008 named a Jewish ambassador to the U.S., Huda Ezra Ebrahim NONOO. She is a member of the legislature and secretary general of the Bahrain Human Rights Watch Society.

In 2009 sectarian tensions heightened following the arrests of some 35 Shiite activists, including Abduljalil ALSINGACE and Husayn MUSHAYMA of the Movement of Liberties and Democracy–Bahrain (*Haq*) and a Shiite cleric, all of whom were accused of attempting to overthrow the government and plan terror attacks. The defendants claimed they had been tortured, and their arrests prompted three days of protests in the capital in advance of their trial. The government alleged that the defendants had received military training in Syria in 2008. Alsingace claimed the government was trying to quash dissent against its policies, which he claims marginalize Shiites. Several opposition groups joined the INAS in calling for the release of the alleged plotters, while some observers said the arrests and prosecution raised serious questions about democratic reforms promoted by the National Action Charter.

POLITICAL GROUPS

Political parties are proscribed in Bahrain. At the first National Assembly election in 1973, however, voters elected ten candidates of a loosely organized Popular Bloc of the Left, while such small clandestine groups as a Bahraini branch of the Popular Front for the Liberation of Oman and the Arabian Gulf (PFLOAG), apparently consisting mainly of leftist students, subsequently continued to engage in limited activity. During the 1994 disturbances, a Shiite opposition group, the Islamic Front for the Liberation of Bahrain (IFLB), insisted that security forces were arresting its followers "at random" and condemned deportations of regime opponents.

Reports in the first half of the 1990s concerning activity on behalf of Shiites focused on Hezbollah, based in Lebanon and believed to be financed by Iran. The government charged that a Hezbollah-Bahrain was formed in Iran in 1993 and contributed to anti-regime activity, including the alleged coup attempt of 1996.

Although the constitutional amendment of February 2002 did not lift the ban on political parties, several "groups" and "societies" were subsequently legalized in line with the democratic reforms. Staffed largely by formerly exiled opposition figures who had returned to Bahrain following the amnesty issued by the king in February 2002, those groups and associations "unofficially" endorsed candidates in local elections in May. In 2005 some groups registered under the new political associations law (see Political background, above) and entered candidates in the 2006 parliamentary elections. The political associations appeared to be functioning as de facto political parties, although parties remain formally banned.

Islamic National Accord Society (INAS). Referenced as *"al-Wifaq"* ("accord"), this Shiite grouping is led by cleric Sheikh Ali Salman, a former prominent member of the Bahrain Freedom Movement. *Al-Wifaq*, reported to be the country's largest opposition group, was credited with winning upward of 70 percent of the seats in the municipal elections of May 2002. However, the INAS boycotted the October 2002 national balloting to protest some of the king's constitutional amendments that *al-Wifaq* leaders considered inimical to genuine power-sharing (see Current issues, above). In 2004 it was reported that a number of INAS members split off to form a new **Justice and Development Society,** which INAS loyalists said would divide and weaken the Shiites. (While the Justice and Development Society pledged to participate in the 2006 national poll, the group apparently was dissolved sometime before the election.) In 2005 INAS decided to register as called for under the new political associations law, despite objecting to provisions of the law. A number of members resigned in protest over the registration, and subsequently, Sheikh Ali Salman was appointed the group's first secretary general, underscoring his increasing status in the society. The group greatly increased the Shiite representation (to 42.5 percent) in the 2006 Chamber of Deputies elections. Though Salman had been widely regarded as the candidate to win the post of speaker of the chamber, the incumbent was reelected.

In 2007 Sheikh Ali Salman tried to intervene with the king and stop the imposition of the annual income tax above, despite the group's initial support for such a levy. After heavy criticism from religious leaders and others, Sheikh Ali Salman took a new tack with the government, reaching an agreement on an increase in public sector salaries.

In 2009 the group called for an ad hoc national committee to address the turmoil surrounding the arrest of several Shiite leaders (see Current issues, above).

Leaders: Husayn al-DAIHI (Deputy Secretary General), Sheikh Ali SALMAN (Secretary General).

Progressive Democratic Forum (PDF). This group was launched by former members of the Marxist **National Liberation Front of Bahrain** (NLFB)—active mainly in exile since the 1950s—upon their return to Bahrain in 2002 following reforms by King Hamad. The PDF subsequently registered as an official group. In 2005 the group was one of nine that urged the king to suspend the new political associations law and to institute more democratic reforms. The PDF unofficially supported candidates in the 2002 and 2006 balloting for the Chamber of Deputies.

Leader: Hassan MADAN.

National Islamic Society (*Al Menbar*). This Sunni group, reported to be part of the political wing of the Muslim Brotherhood, won representation in the 2006 parliamentary election.

In 2007 the group pressed for reinstituting censorship in advance of publication and prison sentences for journalists who allegedly disparaged Islam. In 2009 *Al Menbar* called for a national dialogue in connection with the arrest of several Shiite leaders.

Leaders: Salah ALI (President), Abdullahtif al-SHAIKH, and Ali AHMAD.

Al-Asala. A progovernment Sunni Salafi society of some 240 members, *al-Asala* was the first political society to register under the new political associations law. It secured five seats in the 2006 parliamentary elections and reportedly formed an alliance with the National Islamic Society to offset gains by Shiite groups in the Chamber of Deputies.

Leader: Ghanion al-BUANEEN.

Al-Mithaq. Established in 2005, *al-Mithaq* ("covenant") backed the National Action Charter and the government's decision to offer financial support to political groups since the new political associations law banned them from receiving money from foreign sources. Other societies criticized *al-Mithaq*'s position, saying its support for the government hindered other groups' attempts to expand democracy. *Al-Mithaq*'s only candidate for the 2006 parliamentary election withdrew before the poll.

Leaders: Ahmad JUMA (President), Muhammad JANAHI (Secretary General).

National Democratic Action Society (*Waad*). This leftist, nationalist group boycotted the October 2002 balloting for the Chamber of Deputies. However, in 2005 its members voted in favor of registering under the new political associations law despite having vowed months earlier to challenge some aspects of the law. The group failed to win seats in the 2006 parliamentary election.

Group leader Ibrahim Sharif was injured in clashes with police at an opposition rally in May 2007.

Leaders: Ibrahim SHARIF (President), Ibrahim Kamal al-DEEN (Vice President), Abdul Rahman al-NUAIMI.

Islamic Arab Democratic Society (*Wasat*). A Pan-Arab opposition group, *Wasat* ("center") fielded candidates in the 2002 parliamentary election. In 2005 the group participated in protests aimed at the political associations law and continued to press for amendments to the law through the legislature.

Leader: Jassem al-MEHZEA.

National Justice Movement (*Adalah*). This opposition group announced its formation in March 2006 to offset the influence of the INAS and to give more weight to secular groups. The group, whose focus was naturalization and constitutional issues, was highly critical of government actions against Islamists alleged to be jihadists. The group, which is reportedly pro al-Qaida, supported candidates who ran as independents in the 2006 parliamentary election.

Leader: Abdullah HASHIM.

Islamic Action Society. This grouping was formed by followers of Shiite religious scholar Muhammad Mahdi al-SHIRAZI. It was initially led by Sheikh Muhammad Ali Mahfuz, a former leader of the IFLB. The Islamic Action Society, which supported political reforms and was seen as furthering the aims of the IFLB, boycotted the 2002 elections but supported candidates who ran as independents in the 2006 parliamentary election.

In 2007 the group's leader, Sheikh Muhammad Al Mahfud, participated in a demonstration against Bahrain's increasing poverty, a protest that turned violent when police confronted the picketers. Al Mahfud criticized the government for its lack of sound economic policies and requested that the government increase the minimum wage to help raise workers' standard of living.

Leader: Sheikh Muhammad Al MAHFUD.

Bahrain Freedom Movement (BFM). Based in London in the 1990s under the leadership of Mansur al-JAMRI (the son of popular Shiite leader Sheikh Abd al-Amir al-Jamri), the BFM called for "passive resistance" on the part of the Bahraini populace to pressure the government into adopting "democratic reforms."

Some members of the London-based BFM returned to Bahrain in 2002, including former BFM leader Majid al-AWALI, who was named to the new cabinet in November. However, other BFM members remained in exile in London, criticizing King Hamad for orchestrating a "constitutional putsch." The group continued to be active in its criticism of the government in early 2006, with one senior member calling for a boycott of the next elections. In 2007 group members participated in demonstrations protesting the detention of a Shiite cleric who had been detained at the Manama airport following his visit to Iran. The demonstration turned violent when police tried to break it up. Observers said the government did not want any protests taking place while Bahrain hosted a major automobile race.

Leader: Said Al SHEHABI (in London).

Movement of Liberties and Democracy–Bahrain (*Haq*). This mostly Shiite separatist group, which was formed in 2005 after its members broke away from the INAS, does not recognize the country's constitution. In 2006 the group participated in several protest rallies and boycotted the Chamber of Deputies elections.

In February 2007 group leader Husayn Mushayma and two other political activists, including the head of the Bahrain Center for Human Rights, were arrested. They were set to face trial on charges that included plotting to overthrow the government, but the king subsequently pardoned them. Mushayma, Abduljalil Alsingace, and other Shiites faced trial again in 2009 (see Current issues, above).

Leaders: Abduljalil ALSINGACE, Husayn MUSHAYMA (Secretary General).

Other political societies active in 2006 included the Baathist Democratic National Rally, the leftist Progressive Democratic Society, Constitutional Rally, and National Free Thought.

LEGISLATURE

The first election to fill 30 non-nominated seats in the **National Assembly** was held December 7, 1973. In addition to the elected members, who were to serve four-year terms, the assembly contained 14 cabinet members (including 2 ministers of state). The assembly was dissolved on August 26, 1975, on the grounds that it had indulged in debates "dominated by ideas alien to the society and values of Bahrain."

In January 1993 the emir appointed a 30-member Consultative Council to contribute "advice and opinion" on legislation proposed by the cabinet and, in certain cases, suggest new laws on its own. In accordance with reforms announced in April 1996, the emir appointed new 40-member councils on September 28, 1996, and September 27, 2000. (The council appointed in 2000 included women for the first time.)

The king dissolved the Consultative Council on February 14, 2002, in anticipation of the establishment of the new bicameral National Assembly (*Majlis al-Watani*) provided for in the constitutional revision of the same day.

Consultative Council (*Majlis al-Shura*). The upper house comprises 40 members appointed by the king for a four-year term. The first appointments, including six women as well as representatives of the Christian and Jewish communities, were made by King Hamad on November 16, 2002. The king appointed 40 new members on December 5, 2006.

Speaker: Ali Saleh Abdullah al-SALEH.

Chamber of Deputies (*Majlis al-Nuwwab*). The lower house comprises 40 members directly elected on a majoritarian basis for a four-year term. In the most recent elections on November 25, 2006, with runoff balloting on December 2, the seat distribution was as follows: Islamic National Accord Society (INAS), 17 seats; the National Islamic Society, 7; the *Al-Asala*, 5; and independents, 11 (one of the independents was described as firmly aligned with INAS).

Speaker: Khalifa al-DHAHRANI.

CABINET

[as of September 1, 2009]

Prime Minister	Sheikh Khalifa ibn Salman Al Khalifa
Deputy Prime Ministers	Sheikh Ali ibn Khalifa Al Khalifa
	Sheikh Muhammad ibn Mubarak Al Khalifa
	Jawad Salim al-Urayid
Ministers	
Commerce and Industry	Hassan ibn Abdullah Fakhro
Education	Majid ibn Ali al-Nuaimi
Finance	Sheikh Ahmed ibn Muhammad Al Khalifa

Foreign Affairs	Sheikh Khalid ibn Ahmad ibn Muhammad Al Khalifa
Health	Faisal ibn Yaqoub al-Hamar
Housing	Sheikh Ibrahim ibn Khalifa al-Khalifa
Information	Mai Al Khalifa [f]
Interior	Sheikh Rashid ibn Abdullah Al Khalifa
Justice and Islamic Affairs	Sheikh Khalid ibn Ali Al Khalifa
Labor	Majid ibn Mushin al-Alawi
Municipalities and Agricultural Affairs	Mansur ibn Rajab
Oil and Gas	Abdullahussain ibn Ali Mirza
Prime Minister's Court Minister	Sheikh Khalid ibn Abdullah Al Khalifa
Social Affairs	Fatima al-Balushi [f]
Works, in charge of Electricity and Water Authority	Fahmi ibn Ali al-Jawder
Ministers of State	
Cabinet Affairs	Sheikh Ahmad ibn Atayatallah Al Khalifa
Defense	Sheikh Muhammad ibn Abdullah Al Khalifa
Foreign Affairs	Nizar Al Baharna
Shura Council and Parliamentary Affairs	Abdulaziz al-Fadhil

[f] = female

COMMUNICATIONS

Until recently, the ruling family strongly censored all media; the Bahraini press was described by a correspondent for the *Financial Times* as "fawning." Some progress toward media freedom has been noted since early 2001 in line with recent democratic reforms, although "draconian" regulations remained formally in place, including Internet censorship. In 2009 it was reported that the information ministry had significantly expanded its Web censorship.

Press. The following newspapers are published in Manama unless otherwise noted: *Akhbar al-Khalij* (Gulf News, 30,000), first Arabic daily, founded 1976; *al-Ayam* (The Days, 21,400), independent daily in Arabic; *al-Adhwaa* (Lights, 16,000), Arab weekly; *Bahrain Tribune* (12,500), sister paper to *al-Ayam* in English; *Gulf Daily News* (11,000), daily in English; *Al Watan* (The Nation, started in 2005), daily in Arabic; *Sada al-Usbu* (Weekly Echo, 5,000), Arabic weekly; *al-Bahrain al-Yawm* (Bahrain Today, 5,000), Arabic weekly, published by the Ministry of Information; and *al-Wasat* (described as the "first truly independent" paper in Bahrain).

News agencies. The official national facility is the Bahrain News Agency; *Agence France-Presse*, the Associated Press, the Gulf News Agency, and Reuters maintain offices in Manama.

Broadcasting and computing. The Bahrain Radio and Television Corporation (BRTC), established in 1993 as an independent entity that transmits in Arabic and English, and Radio Bahrain (Radiyu al-Bahrayn), an English-language commercial station, are the principal sources of radio programs and were received by approximately 355,000 sets in 1999. Bahrain's first private radio station began broadcasting in 2005 as The Voice of Tomorrow (Sawt Al Ghad), focusing on sports and entertainment. The government-operated Bahrain Television (Tilifiziyun al-Bahrayn), which has provided commercial programming in Arabic since 1973, added an English-language channel in 1981. As of 2008 there were 519.5 Internet users per 1,000 inhabitants.

INTERGOVERNMENTAL REPRESENTATION

Ambassador to the U.S.: Huda Ezra Ebrahim NONOO.

U.S. Ambassador to Bahrain: Joseph Adam ERELI.

Permanent Representative to the UN: Tawfeeq Ahmed ALMANSOOR.

IGO Memberships (Non-UN): AFESD, AMF, BADEA, GCC, IDB, Interpol, LAS, NAM, OAPEC, OIC, WCO, WTO.

BANGLADESH

People's Republic of Bangladesh
Ganaprojatantri Bangladesh

Political Status: Independent state proclaimed March 26, 1971; de facto independence achieved December 16, 1971; republican constitution of December 16, 1972, suspended following coup of March 24, 1982, but restored on November 10, 1986; parliamentary system (abandoned in favor of presidential system in January 1975) restored by referendum of September 15, 1991; state of emergency in effect from January 11, 2007, until December 17, 2008.

Area: 55,598 sq. mi. (143,999 sq. km.).

Population: 129,247,233 (2001C); 149,939,000 (2008E). Both figures include adjustments for underenumeration.

Major Urban Centers (2005E): DHAKA (Dacca, 6,788,000), Chittagong (2,640,000), Khulna (881,000).

Official Language: Bangla (Bengali).

Monetary Unit: Taka (official rate December 1, 2009: 69.09 takas = $1US).

President: Mohammad Zillur RAHMAN (Awami League); as the only candidate, declared president-elect by the Election Commission on February 11, 2009, and sworn in the following day for a five-year term, succeeding Iajuddin AHMED (nonparty), whose term had been extended beyond the expiration date of September 5, 2007, given the absence of a sitting National Parliament to conduct a presidential election.

Prime Minister: Sheikh HASINA Wajed (Awami League); previously held office in 1996–2001; sworn in on January 6, 2009, following the general election of December 29, 2008, succeeding Chief Adviser (head of caretaker government) Fakhruddin AHMED, who had served in that capacity from January 12, 2007. (As constitutionally mandated, Prime Minister Begum Khaleda ZIA [Bangladesh Nationalist Party] had stepped down on October 27, 1996, upon completion of the parliamentary term, with President Iajuddin AHMED initially serving as chief adviser.)

THE COUNTRY

Located in the east of the Indian subcontinent, Bangladesh comprises a portion of the historic province of Bengal (including Chittagong) in addition to the Sylhet district of Assam. Except for a short boundary with Myanmar in the extreme southeast, the country's land frontier borders on India. Endowed with a tropical monsoon climate, Bangladesh possesses rich alluvial plains dominated by the Ganges and Brahmaputra rivers. One of the world's most densely populated independent countries, with over 1,000 people per square kilometer of land, it is ethnically homogeneous: 98 percent of the people are Bengali and speak a common language. Urdu-speaking, non-Bengali Muslim immigrants from India, largely Bihari, comprise 1 percent; the remaining 1 percent includes assorted tribal groups, of which one of the most important is the Chakma of the Chittagong Hill Tracts. Bangladesh contains more Muslim inhabitants than any other country except Indonesia and Pakistan, with nearly 90 percent of its people professing Islam. Most of the remainder are Hindu. Women constitute about 25 percent of the economically active population, more than half in the agricultural sector. Although women remain underrepresented in politics, since 1991 two women have alternated as prime minister.

Bangladesh continues to rank as one of the world's poorest countries. Slightly under half of the labor force is engaged in agriculture, which now accounts for about 19 percent of the GDP. Rice, sugarcane, pulses, and oilseeds are among the leading food crops. Although industry

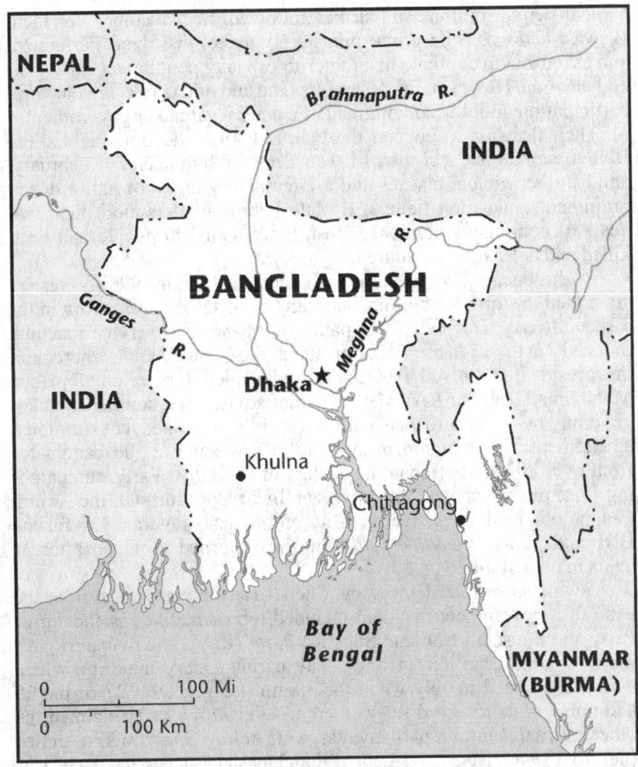

contributes about 29 percent of GDP, it employs only 13 percent of the paid labor force. Textiles and related articles, especially ready-made garments, account for two-thirds of merchandise export earnings. Exported jute and jute goods, once mainstays of the economy, are now surpassed in value by sales of frozen fish and shrimp. Bangladesh is deficient in most natural resources except hydrocarbon reserves.

The 2001–2006 elected government embarked on a program of structural changes, including the closure or privatization of state-owned manufacturing enterprises and nationalized commercial banks, tax administration reform, and trade reform. Those policies were largely continued under the caretaker government of October 2006–January 2009. GDP growth consistently registered between 6.0 and 6.6 percent in fiscal years (July–June) 2004–2008, largely fueled by exports, remittances, and domestic activity, although the gains were partially offset by consumer price inflation that reached 10 percent in 2008 because of rising costs for food and fuel. In 2006 Bangladeshi economist Mohammad YUNUS was awarded the Nobel Peace Prize for innovative work in extending microcredit, primarily to poor women. As many of 70 million Bangladeshis had reportedly benefited from miniloans given by his Grameen Bank.

The country's low-lying coastal region is extremely vulnerable to natural disasters, as evidenced by annual monsoon flooding and devastating cyclones, one of which, in 1991, is estimated to have killed upward of 150,000 persons and left more than 10 million homeless. Installation of a sophisticated storm-alert system in 1992 has reduced the death toll from subsequent cyclones, but weather-related devastation remains a frequent occurrence. A cyclone on November 15, 2007, killed over 3,200 people.

GOVERNMENT AND POLITICS

Political background. When British India was partitioned into independent India and Pakistan in August 1947, Bengal was divided along communal lines. Predominantly Hindu West Bengal was incorporated into India, while predominantly Muslim East Bengal was joined with the Sylhet district of Assam as the Eastern Province of Pakistan.

During the 1960s Bengali resentment over major disparities in development expenditure and representation in the public services intensified, and in 1966 Sheikh Mujibur RAHMAN (Mujib), president of the East Pakistan branch of the Awami League, called for a constitutional reallocation of powers. The sheikh's subsequent arrest helped coalesce Bengali opinion against the Pakistani president, Ayub Khan, who was forced from office in March 1969.

Ayub's successor, Gen. Yahya Khan, endorsed a return to democratic rule, and during the 1970 electoral campaign Sheikh Mujib and his party won 167 of 169 seats allotted to East Pakistan in a proposed National Assembly of 313 members. The issue of power distribution remained unresolved, however, and postponement of the National Assembly session on March 1, 1971, led to massive civil strife in East Pakistan. Three weeks later, Sheikh Mujib was again arrested and his party banned. Martial law was imposed following disturbances in Dhaka, and civil war ensued. India, having protested against suppression of the eastern rebellion and the resultant influx of millions of refugees, declared war on Pakistan on December 3, 1971, and the allied forces of India and Bangladesh defeated Pakistani forces in the East on December 16. The new but war-ravaged nation of Bangladesh emerged on the same day.

Upon his return from imprisonment in West Pakistan, Sheikh Mujib assumed command of the provisional government and began restructuring the new state along socialist lines that featured a limitation on large landholdings and the nationalization of banks, insurance companies, and major industries. During July and August 1974 the already fragile economy was devastated by floods that led to famine and a cholera epidemic. Following a period of near-anarchy, a state of emergency was declared on December 28. Four weeks later, on January 25, 1975, a Constituent Assembly revised the constitution to provide for a presidential form of government and the adoption of a one-party system under the rubric of the *Bangladesh Krishak Sramik Awami* League (Baksal), an all-encompassing socialist "political platform."

On August 15, 1975, a group of pro-Pakistan, Islamic right-wing army officers mounted a coup, in the course of which Sheikh Mujib, his wife, and five of their children were killed. The former minister of trade and commerce, Khandakar Moshtaque AHMED, was sworn in as president and on August 20 assumed the power to rule by martial law. On November 3 the new president was himself confronted with a rebellion led by Brig. Khalid MUSHARAF, the pro-Indian commander of the Dhaka garrison. Three days later President Ahmed vacated his office in favor of the chief justice of the Supreme Court, Abu Sadat Mohammad SAYEM, and on November 7 Musharaf was killed during a left-wing mutiny led by Col. Abu TAHER. As a result, President Sayem announced that he would assume the additional post of chief martial law administrator, with the army chief of staff, Maj. Gen. Ziaur RAHMAN (Zia), and the heads of the air force and navy as deputies. Vigorous action was taken against those implicated in the November 7 mutiny, and Colonel Taher was hanged.

Although President Sayem announced in mid-1976 that his government would honor former president Ahmed's pledge to hold a general election by the end of February 1977, he reversed himself in November. Shortly thereafter, he transferred the office of chief martial law administrator to Ziaur Rahman, and in April 1977 he resigned the presidency, having nominated the general as his successor. President Zia was confirmed in office by a nationwide referendum in May. In June he designated the former special assistant to President Sayem, Abdus SATTAR, as vice president.

President Zia announced in April 1978 that a presidential election would be held in June, to be followed by a parliamentary election. Opposition allegations of polling irregularities notwithstanding, Zia was credited with a near three-to-one margin of victory over his closest rival in the presidential balloting and was sworn in for a five-year term. A new Parliament dominated by Zia's Bangladesh Nationalist Party (BNP) was elected in February 1979, and in April a civilian cabinet with Shah Azizur RAHMAN as prime minister was announced.

The Zia government encountered continuing unrest, including several coup attempts and a major uprising by tribal guerrillas in the southeastern Chittagong Hill Tracts in early 1980. On May 30, 1981, long-standing differences within the army precipitated the assassination of President Zia in the course of an attempted coup in Chittagong. The alleged leader of the revolt, Maj. Gen. Mohammad Abdul MANZUR, was killed while fleeing the city on June 1, most of the army having remained loyal to Acting President Sattar. The former vice president was elected to a five-year term as Zia's successor in November, subsequently designating Mirza Nurul HUDA as his deputy while retaining Azizur Rahman as prime minister.

Following a period in which the military, led by its chief of staff, Lt. Gen. Hossain Mohammed ERSHAD, pressed for a campaign to counter "political indiscipline, unprecedented corruption, a bankrupt economy, [and] administrative breakdown," the armed forces again intervened on March 24, 1982, suspending the constitution, ousting the Sattar government, and installing Ershad as chief martial law administrator. Three days later, on Ershad's nomination, Abul Fazal Mohammad Ahsanuddin CHOWDHURY, a retired Supreme Court judge, was sworn in as the nation's eighth president.

In September 1983, in an effort to bring an end to martial law, two broad opposition alliances—one headed by the Awami League under President Mujib's daughter, Sheikh Hasina WAJED, and the other led by the BNP under President Zia's widow, Begum Khaleda ZIA, and former president Sattar—formed a 22-party Movement for the Restoration of Democracy (MRD). In November a regime-supportive People's Party (*Jana Dal*) was formed under President Chowdhury, who resigned his office in December in favor of Ershad. General Ershad was reconfirmed as president by referendum in March 1985. The promotion of a "transition to democracy" was announced by a *Jana Dal*-centered National Front in August.

On January 1, 1986, coincident with revocation of a ban on political activity, it was announced that the National Front had been converted into a proregime National Party (*Jatiya Dal*), and in early March President Ershad scheduled parliamentary balloting for late April. Initially, the leading opposition groups refused to participate without a full lifting of martial law. Subsequently, both the Awami League alliance and the fundamentalist Bangladesh Islamic Assembly (*Jamaat-i-Islami Bangladesh*), but not the BNP, agreed to compete in an election rescheduled for May.

Despite widespread unrest, the *Jatiya Dal* won a narrow majority of legislative seats, and a new government took office in July 1986 that included as prime minister Mizanur Rahman CHOWDHURY, then leader of a minority conservative faction of the Awami League. Subsequently, General Ershad formally joined the government party to permit his nomination as its presidential candidate, and in October he was credited with winning 84 percent of the vote. In November, having secured parliamentary ratification of actions taken by his administration since March 1982, Ershad announced the lifting of martial law and restoration of the amended 1972 constitution.

In January 1987 the Awami League, which was now under the undisputed "Mujibist" leadership of Sheikh Hasina, withdrew from parliamentary proceedings in response to President Ershad's projection of an enhanced political role for the military. Subsequently, the League joined with the BNP, *Jamaat-i-Islami,* and a group of Marxist parties in supporting a series of strikes and demonstrations, prompting the government to declare a nationwide state of emergency in late November. In December the president dissolved Parliament. None of the leading opposition parties presented candidates for the legislative election of March 1988, in which the government officially swept more than 80 percent of the seats.

In August 1989 it was announced that Moudud AHMED, who had succeeded Chowdhury as prime minister in March 1988, had been appointed vice president in succession to A.K.M. Nurul ISLAM; concurrently, Deputy Prime Minister Kazi Zafar AHMED was named to succeed Moudud Ahmed as titular chief of government.

In October 1990 the student wings of both the BNP and the Awami League launched a series of antiregime demonstrations in Dhaka that soon mushroomed into nationwide strikes and riots. President Ershad's declaration of a state of emergency on November 27 was generally ignored by increasingly violent mass protesters, and in early December 19 MPs from the president's own party resigned their seats. With army officers having indicated that they were unwilling to take control of the country, Ershad announced his intention to resign. On December 5 the principal opposition formations nominated Shahabuddin AHMED, theretofore chief justice of the Supreme Court, as successor to the beleaguered head of state, who named Ahmed vice president (hence next in line to the presidency) prior to withdrawing from office.

At the legislative election of February 1991, the BNP won a sizable plurality of seats, enabling it, with the support of the *Jamaat-i-Islami,* to claim a majority when the 30 additional seats reserved for women were distributed by the newly elected Parliament. In March the BNP's Khaleda Zia was sworn in as prime minister, although her political mandate was constitutionally limited to offering "advice" to the president. Voters approved the return to a Westminster-style parliamentary system in a referendum on September 15, and Khaleda Zia became, effectively, the executive through her reappointment as prime minister four days later. A month later the legislature filled the substantially weakened presidency by electing the BNP's Abdur Rahman BISWAS.

Beginning in May 1994 with a legislative boycott, the Awami League and other opposition parties began demanding new elections. Violent demonstrations and strikes followed. In November President Biswas, acting on the prime minister's advice, dissolved Parliament and asked Zia to continue in an interim capacity pending an early general election. However, the Awami League and others rejected electoral participation until the appointment of a neutral caretaker government.

Their decision to boycott the February 1996 election enabled the BNP to win all but 2 of the 214 seats declared by the end of February, amid further violent clashes and the temporary arrest of half a dozen prominent opposition figures. By late February, after more than two years of continuous political unrest, more than 100 people had been killed and at least 1,000 injured.

At the opening of the new Parliament in March 1996, protesters attempted to storm the building as Prime Minister Zia was sworn in for a second term. However, near-paralysis of the civil service machine induced Zia to resign as prime minister at the end of March, whereupon the president dissolved Parliament and named former chief justice Mohammad Habibur RAHMAN as chief adviser of a neutral caretaker government, in accordance with a recently instituted constitutional amendment. The election of June 1996 saw some 2,500 candidates from over 80 parties (including Ershad of the *Jatiya* Party, campaigning from prison) contest the 300 seats. In a record turnout, the Awami League obtained a decisive plurality of 146 seats (against 116 for the BNP and 32 for the *Jatiya Dal*) and thus returned to power after 21 years in opposition.

Vowing to restore democracy, Sheikh Hasina was sworn in at the head of a government that also included representatives of the *Jatiya* Party and the small National Socialist Party (Rab). Their support gave the new administration an immediate parliamentary majority, which was consolidated in July when the Awami League took 27 of the 30 additional seats reserved for women and the *Jatiya* Party claimed the other 3. In a unanimous parliamentary vote in July, Shahabuddin Ahmed (nonparty) was elected president of Bangladesh in succession to Biswas, thus returning to the post he had previously held on a transitional basis following the demise of the Ershad regime in December 1990.

In its first year in office, the Hasina government moved to resolve a major disagreement with India over water rights to the Ganges (see Foreign relations, below) and, as it had also pledged in the 1996 campaign, to settle the rebellion led by the Chakma tribal group in the Chittagong Hill Tracts. Despite vehement objections from the BNP-led opposition, an accord with the Chittagong insurgents was finally reached in December 1997, bringing to a close a conflict that may have cost 20,000 lives.

The government had released former president Ershad from prison in January 1997, thereby fulfilling a commitment that had won Sheikh Hasina the *Jatiya* Party's support after the June 1996 election. In March 1998, however, the *Jatiya* Party left the coalition, in part over objections to the Chittagong peace agreement. In May, despite opposition-led strikes and demands that legislative action on the accord be deferred, the Awami League majority passed four Chittagong implementation bills.

Beginning in December 1998, opposition efforts to force Sheikh Hasina's government to step down escalated. The four-party alliance of the BNP, the *Jamaat-i-Islami,* the *Jatiya* Party, and the Islamic Unity Front (*Islami Oikya Jote*—IOJ) persistently boycotted parliamentary sessions and conducted a campaign of demonstrations and *hartals* (organized disruptions). The opposition also protested the nationwide municipal council elections of February 1999, which went ahead as scheduled, but not without violent altercations that injured over 1,000 people.

On July 13, 2001, in accordance with the constitution, Parliament was dissolved, having completed its five-year term—the first to do so in 30 years. Collaterally, Sheikh Hasina and her cabinet stepped down, and a caretaker government headed by Chief Adviser Latifur RAHMAN, a retired chief justice, was named on July 16. With many observers citing national concern over civil violence as a primary factor, in the balloting on October 1 Khaleda Zia's BNP won a massive victory, capturing 191 of 300 seats. Sheikh Hasina's Awami League took only 62 seats. On October 10 Khaleda Zia was sworn in as the head of a BNP cabinet that also included two members of the *Jamaat-i-Islami*.

On September 6, 2002, Iajuddin AHMED, a nonpartisan with close ties to the BNP, assumed office as Bangladesh's largely ceremonial president, having been declared elected by the Election Commission the previous day upon the technical disqualification of the two other candidates. Ahmed's predecessor, A.Q.M. Badruddoza CHOWDHURY, had served in office from November 14, 2001, until pressured to resign by the BNP on June 21, 2002, because he had not marked the May 30 anniversary of Ziaur Rahman's death with an obligatory visit to the slain president's grave.

The Zia government stepped down at the end of the parliamentary term on October 27, 2006, but with the government and the opposition having failed to agree on the makeup of a caretaker government that would hold office until the election scheduled for January 22, 2007, President Ahmed took on the additional role of chief adviser. Accusing Ahmed and the Election Commission of favoring the BNP, and questioning the validity of the existing inflated election roll, a "Grand Alliance" of the Awami League, its allies, and most other opposition parties announced in early January that it would boycott the election. At the same time, the opposition stepped up pressure on the caretaker administration with an increasingly strident series of demonstrations, strikes, and disruptions. In response, on January 11, with the tacit support of Army Chief of Staff Lt. Gen. Moin AHMED and the rest of the military leadership, President Ahmed instituted a state of emergency, indefinitely postponed the election, and announced his resignation as chief adviser. The next day, he named an economist and former central bank governor, Fakhruddin AHMED, to head a new caretaker administration.

By mid-2007 some 190,000 people had been arrested during the state of emergency, and the national Anti-Corruption Commission (ACC) and other authorities, operating under emergency power rules (EPRs), continued to file corruption cases against prominent politicians, businessmen, and former government ministers—some 170 in all—many of whom were held without bail into mid-2008. Allegations of extortion, graft, illegally amassing wealth, and concealing financial information were the most common charges. The military-backed government arrested former prime ministers Sheikh Hasina and Khaleda Zia on July 16 and September 3, 2007, respectively. The archrivals were both charged with corruption and other offenses allegedly committed during their terms in office. Other prominent detainees included the Awami League secretary general, Abdul JALIL, and Khaleda Zia's elder son and heir-apparent, Tarique RAHMAN. In addition, Sheikh Hasina and other Awami leaders faced a murder charge in connection with the October 2006 deaths of *Jamaat-i-Islami* members during rioting in the capital.

Meanwhile, the caretaker government continued to prepare a new voter roll. In July 2008 the Election Commission announced that the roll, numbering some 80 million registrants (down by 13 million from the previous listing), had been completed. Less than a month later, elections were held in four cities and nine municipalities, and although all candidates were required to run as independents under the EPRs, AL members reportedly won in all but one of the localities.

With a legislative election having been scheduled for December, Khaleda Zia was released on bail on September 9, 2008, it having become apparent to the caretaker government that, given wide popular support for both her and Shiekh Hasina, no legitimate election could be conducted without their presence. Sheikh Hasina, who had been released on June 12 to undergo medical treatment in the United States, returned to Bangladesh on November 6.

Sheikh Hasina's Awami League and its allies won an overwhelming victory in the election of December 29, 2008, taking 263 seats to 33 for the BNP-led four-party alliance. A new government under Hasina took office on January 6, 2009. A month later, the Election Commission named the Awami League's unopposed presidential candidate, 79-year-old Mohammad Zillur RAHMAN, to succeed Iajuddin Ahmed as head of state.

Constitution and government. The constitution of December 1972 has been subjected to numerous revisions, the most important being the adoption of a presidential system in January 1975 and a return to the earlier parliamentary form in September 1991. At present, the essentially titular president is elected for a once-renewable five-year term by the Parliament (*Jatiya Sangsad*), from which the prime minister and all but one-tenth of the other ministers must be drawn. The president appoints as prime minister the individual who commands a legislative majority. Under the 13th Constitutional Amendment, adopted unanimously by the Parliament in 1996, the president has authority to create a nonparty caretaker government for a three-month interim period beginning with a dissolution of Parliament and concluding after a general election.

The unicameral legislature, which has a five-year mandate, contains 300 seats filled by direct election from single-member constituencies. Legislators lose their seats if they defect from their parties. A 2004 constitutional amendment reserves an additional 45 seats for women, who are chosen by the directly elected members. The 45 seats are proportionally distributed among the parliamentary parties.

The Supreme Court is divided into a High Court, with both original and appellate jurisdiction, and an Appellate Division that hears appeals from the High Court. Other courts are established by law. Under an ordinance approved in February 2007 by the interim Council of Advisers, authority over lower judges and magistrates was removed from the executive branch and delegated to higher courts.

Bangladesh comprises 6 administrative divisions (Barisal, Chittagong, Dhaka, Khulna, Rajshahi, and Sylhet), 64 districts (*zillas*), over 500 towns (*thanas*), over 4,400 unions, and some 87,000 villages. In addition, there are 4 metropolitan cities and over 100 other municipalities.

Foreign relations. Bangladesh joined the United Nations in 1974, when the People's Republic of China, an ally of Pakistan, withdrew its objections. It is now a member of all UN Specialized Agencies as well as the Commonwealth, various Islamic groups, the South Asian Association for Regional Cooperation (SAARC) and the SAARC-sponsored South Asia Free Trade Area (SAFTA).

The government of Mujibur Rahman committed itself to neutralism and nonalignment. At the same time, Bangladesh acknowledged natural ties of geography, culture, and commerce with India, and in March 1972 the two countries signed a 25-year treaty of friendship, cooperation, and peace. Relations with Pakistan, initially characterized by mutual hatred and suspicion, slowly improved, with Islamabad according Bangladesh diplomatic recognition in February 1974.

A lingering source of tension between Bangladesh and Pakistan involves the status of what now totals 300,000 Biharis, many of whom supported Pakistan during the independence struggle in 1971 and whom Pakistan agreed to "repatriate" from Bangladesh but did not. In August 1992 the 21-year stalemate appeared broken, but a repatriation program was suspended after Pakistan's prime minister Benazir Bhutto took office in 2003, effectively stranding the Biharis in over 100 refugee camps. A May 2003 High Court ruling paved the way for Biharis to become citizens. In September 2007 the interim government announced that those Biharis who were born in Bangladesh or who were minors when independence occurred, and who willingly chose to remain in Bangladesh, would be entered on the voter lists for the upcoming parliamentary elections. In May 2008 the High Court ruled that some 150,000 Biharis were entitled to citizenship, but only 22,000 signed up to vote in the December national election.

Dhaka also has been burdened, to a lesser extent, by Rohingya Muslims who fled Myanmar's western Rakhine (Arakan) State in the 1990s. At its peak in 1992, the Rohingya flight numbered over 250,000. An agreement between Dhaka and Yangon led to repatriation by mid-1997 of all but about 21,000 Rohingyas. Repatriation resumed in November 1998, but Myanmar again suspended the operation a month later. In January 2000 it refused to accept 14,000 of the Muslim refugees, whom it claimed were not from Myanmar. In April 2004 Yangon once again agreed to the repatriation of the remaining Rohingyas, but most have refused to leave or their return has not been authorized by Myanmar officials. (At least one estimate has placed the number of unregistered Rohingya refugees in Bangladesh at over 200,000.) The 2006–2007 interim government in Dhaka called for the United Nations to join Bangladesh and Myanmar in a tripartite initiative to resolve the issue. In April 2009 the new government's foreign minister, Dipu MONI, indicated a willingness to assist Myanmar.

In 1976 Bangladesh lodged a formal complaint at the United Nations alleging excessive Indian diversion of water from the Ganges at the Farakka barrage, and in 1980 India's unilateral seizure of two newly formed islands in the Bay of Bengal further complicated relations. Despite opposition objections, the Hasina government and India finally concluded a Ganges pact in December 1996. An Indo-Bangla Joint Rivers Commission now meets regularly, and in October 2003 the two countries signed a water-sharing agreement for the Teesta and six other rivers.

Meeting in April 2003, representatives of India and Bangladesh agreed to move forward on delineating the final five kilometers of their mutual border and to discuss exchange of enclaves. (There are over 100 Indian enclaves in Bangladesh and 50 Bangladeshi enclaves in India.) A related source of contention has been competing claims to a 50-hectare shoal in Parshuram. Border security has also been a persistent irritant. Members of the Indian Border Security Force and the Bangladesh Rifles (BDR) have frequently exchanged fire over perceived territorial violations. The worst northern border clash in 25 years occurred in April 2001, resulting in nearly 20 fatalities. In 2005 illegal immigration, smuggling, and the cross-border activities of Indian separatists led India to begin construction at the border of a barbed-wire fence, to which Dhaka strongly objected. If completed, the fence is expected to traverse over 2,000 miles. A 1991 agreement calls for the mutual return of illegal migrants, a principal concern being fleeing Indian insurgents from Assam, Manipur, and Tripura. (The Indian government has recently asserted that antigovernment elements maintain some 140 camps in Bangladesh.) Until the 1997 Chittagong accord, the presence in India of, at one point, up to 65,000 Chakma refugees had also caused tension. In the months following the peace agreement, the 30,000 remaining refugees returned to Bangladesh.

In January 1998 the prime ministers of Bangladesh, India, and Pakistan met in Dhaka for the first of what promised to be an annual series of "business summits," and in March 1999 Bangladesh hosted the second summit of the fledgling D-8 (Developing Eight) group of Islamic nations. The D-8 was organized in 1997 by Bangladesh, Egypt, Indonesia, Iran, Malaysia, Nigeria, Pakistan, and Turkey to advance cooperation in trade and other economic matters. The sixth summit convened in Kuala Lumpur, Malaysia, in July 2008.

A brief visit to Dhaka by U.S. president Bill Clinton on March 20, 2000—the first by a U.S. chief executive to Bangladesh—was protested by both leftists and Muslim clerics. During the visit Sheikh Hasina urged that Lawful Permanent Resident status be given to some 50,000 undocumented Bangladeshis living in the United States.

Current issues. With bitter rivals Sheikh Hasina and Khaleda Zia still dominating their parties, despite corruption allegations against both that were ultimately dropped, many observers questioned the ultimate effectiveness of the limited anticorruption and governmental reforms introduced under the interim administration. Although the ACC continued to function, there were clear indications, early in Sheikh Hasina's new administration, that its purview had narrowed considerably and that few high-level politicians and businessmen would be prosecuted.

The overwhelming AL victory stood as clear evidence that Bangladeshis had tired of the corruption rampant under the preceding Khaleda Zia government. Perhaps for that reason, Prime Minister Hasina selected a cabinet that bypassed almost all of her previous ministerial appointments, reducing the possibility that her new administration would be tied to past corruption allegations. The cabinet also marked a first in that women ministers, though few in number, held a majority of the key portfolios: Hasina herself held defense; Dipu Moni, foreign affairs; Sahara KHATUN, home affairs; and Motia CHOWDHURY, agriculture.

In late January 2009, following Parliament's unanimous passage (with the opposition absent) of a resolution calling for the prosecution of "war criminals" during the independence struggle, the Hasina government ordered that suspects be prevented from leaving the country. Although a broad amnesty had been granted in 1973, it excluded anyone suspected of murder, rape, arson, and various other offenses. More than 1,500 individuals could be targeted, including the leadership of the *Jamaat-i-Islami.*

The new government faced its first dramatic challenge in late February 2009 when paramilitary troops belonging to the BDR, the country's border guards, mutinied against their regular-army officers. The complaints involved pay, corruption, and mistreatment. Following a February 26 televised warning from the prime minister, some 900 mutineers surrendered, although at least that many escaped. Shortly thereafter, government forces began recovering some 75 bodies, 57 of them slain officers, within the BDR headquarters complex. As of late September, legal proceedings against the alleged mutineers were continuing. As many as 3,500 individuals could be prosecuted.

POLITICAL PARTIES

Political party activity has typically been curtailed or proscribed during periods of martial law or during states of emergency, most recently in 2007–2008. On March 8, 2007, the interim government banned political activity, but on September 9 Chief Adviser Ahmed announced that the offices of major parties would be permitted to reopen and that indoor party activities could resume even though many leaders of major parties, including former ministers, had been detained or charged with corruption. From December 12 the interim government permitted parties to begin holding outdoor campaign rallies, and the state of emergency was lifted effective December 17

The current election law states that to be registered, a party (1) must have won, in any election since independence, at least one parliamentary seat or at least 5 percent of the vote in at least one constituency, or (2) must maintain central officers and a central committee as well as a presence in at least 10 administrative districts and 50 localities. In addition, the party constitution must disavow discrimination on the basis of religion, race, caste, language, or gender, and provisions must be in place for women to hold at least one-third of committee positions by 2020.

A total of 107 parties sought recognition for the December 2008 general election, but the Election Commission registered only 39. (Many Islamic parties refused to open their ranks to non-Muslims and to women, resulting in their disqualification.) The poor electoral showing of most registered parties—the 25 at the bottom of the results collectively accounted for under 2.5 percent of the vote—led to proposals for tightening registration requirements before the next general election.

Governing and Major Allied Parties:

Awami League (AL) A predominantly middle-class party organized in East Pakistan in 1948 under Sheikh Mujibur Rahman (Mujib), the Awami (People's) League was, with Indian support, a major force in the drive for independence. Although formally disbanded by President Moshtaque Ahmed in 1975, it remained the best-organized political group in the country and served as the nucleus of a Democratic United Front that supported the presidential candidacy of Gen. Mohammad Ataul Ghani Osmani (National People's Party) in 1978.

During 1980–1981 a major cleavage developed between a majority faction, which elected Mujib's daughter, Sheikh Hasina Wajed, as its leader in February 1981, and a right-wing minority faction led by Mizanur Rahman Chowdhury, who accepted appointment as prime minister of the Ershad government in July 1986 and later joined Ershad's *Jatiya Dal.* Committed to socialism, secularism, and a "Westminster-style" parliamentary system, Sheikh Hasina's AL participated in the legislative election of May 1986 but boycotted most parliamentary proceedings and the March 1988 poll. It contested the election of February 1991 but was runner-up to the Khaleda Zia's BNP. In 1991 the *Bangladesh Krishak Sramik Awami* League (Baksal), a left-wing faction that had broken away in 1984 under the leadership of Abdur RAZZAQ, returned to the parent organization. (In 1997 Baksal was reestablished by new leaders.)

Following the ultimately successful campaign to bring about the resignation of the BNP government, the League emerged victorious from the June 1996 election and thus took office for the first time since 1975, with a plurality of 146 seats of the 300 elected, to which it added 27 of the 30 seats reserved for women and thereby achieved a majority. At the October 2001 election the party suffered a devastating defeat, winning only 62 legislative seats. Sheikh Hasina nevertheless maintained firm control of the party apparatus, and in December 2002 she was reelected party president. At a party rally in August 2004 she was among the 200 injured by a grenade attack that cost nearly two dozen lives.

After the 2001 election the AL headed a 14-party opposition "combine" that also included an 11-party leftist alliance, the National Socialist Party (Inu), and the National Awami Party (NAP). In January 2007 the 14-party grouping's decision to boycott the upcoming parliamentary election led directly to President Ahmed's decision to step down as chief adviser of the caretaker government and to postpone the poll. Subsequently, a group of reformers emerged in opposition to the continued dominance of Sheikh Hasina.

On June 12, 2008, after 11 months in detention while facing corruption charges, Sheikh Hasina was paroled to receive medical treatment in the United States for eye, ear, and circulation conditions. She returned to Bangladesh on November 6 to lead the AL alliance into the December legislative election, at which the AL won 49 percent of the vote and 230 of 300 seats. Hasina thereby returned as prime minister, but in choosing her cabinet she bypassed nearly all members of her previous administration in favor of younger ministers. Hasina's return to power ensured that the corruption charges against her would not be pursued.

Leaders: Sheikh HASINA Wajed (Prime Minister and Party President), Mohammad Zillur RAHMAN (President of Bangladesh), Tofael AHMED, M. Abdul JALIL (General Secretary), Syed Ashraful ISLAM (Acting Secretary General).

Jatiya Party (JP). The current *Jatiya (*National) Party traces its origin to the *Jatiya Dal,* which was initially launched in August 1985 as the National Front, a somewhat eclectic grouping of right-wing Muslims and Beijing-oriented Marxists who rejected the confrontational politics of their former alliance partners in favor of cooperation with President Ershad. The Front embraced the People's Party (*Jana Dal*), founded in 1983 by President Chowdhury; the United People's Party (UPP), then led by Kazi Zafar Ahmed; the Democratic Party (*Ganatantrik Dal*), led by Sirajul Hossain KHAN and Nasrullah KHAN; the Bangladesh Muslim League (BML), led by Tofazzal ALI; and a dissident faction of the Bangladesh Nationalist Party (BNP) led by former prime minister Azizur Rahman. It was declared to have been converted into a unified party on January 1, 1986, although the BML and the UPP subsequently functioned as independent parties.

Following the May 1986 election, the *Jatiya Dal* held 178 of 300 directly elective legislative seats, plus all 30 indirectly elected women's seats. In 1988, with neither of the leading opposition parties competing, it won 250 elective seats. The party participated in the election of February 1991 "for the sake of democracy," despite corruption charges that had been brought against most of its top leadership, including General Ershad. He was placed in detention in December 1990 and convicted of a variety of offenses during 1991–1993.

In September 1993 a number of party dissidents announced the formation of a *Jatiya* Party (National) under the nominal chairmanship of Ershad (from his prison cell). Ershad's wife, Raushan, became a member of its presidium. Having participated in the opposition boycott of the February 1996 election, the party won 32 elective seats in the June balloting and opted to join a coalition government headed by the Awami League, in part on the understanding that Ershad would be released on parole. This decision, taken by Ershad, provoked dissension and led to the resignation of former vice president Moudud Ahmed, who later joined the BNP. In January 1997 Ershad was released from detention, but conflict continued within the party. In June a dissident group led by Kazi Zafar Ahmed and Shah Moazzem HOSSAIN formed the *Jatiya* Party–Zafar-Moazzem.

In March 1998 the *Jatiya* Party left the government, although its lone minister, Anwar Hossein Manju, decided to stay in the cabinet. Collaterally, Ershad removed him as the party's secretary general. At a "unity conference" in December Ershad and the Zafar-Moazzem splinter mended their rift, but in April 1999 a meeting of party dissidents led by Manju and Vice Chair Mizanur Rahman Chowdhury "expelled" Ershad and formed their own *Jatiya* Party—see JP(M), below.

In November 1999 former prime minister Kazi Zafar Ahmed was tried in absentia for corruption and received a 15-year sentence, while in August 2000 Ershad lost an appeal of a corruption conviction and was ordered back to prison by the High Court. In November Ershad began serving a 5-year sentence (reduced from 7) for a corruption conviction, but he was released on bail in April 2001. In August Ahmed returned from Australia to appeal his conviction, and he remained a key Ershad ally.

With the October 2001 election approaching, Ershad began distancing the party from his opposition partners, with the intention of campaigning independently even though he himself was barred from running. His decision led to yet another rift, with the party's ousted secretary general, Naziur Rahman Manjur, forming another *Jatiya* offshoot in April (see BJP, below). Now identified as the *Jatiya* Party (Ershad), the parent group won 14 seats in the October election.

In June 2002 the right-wing *Jatiya Ganatantrik* Party (Jagpa), led by Shafiul Alam Prodhan, and the Progressive Nationalist Party (*Progatishil Jatiyabadi Dal*—PJD), led by Shawkat Hossain Nilu, merged into the *Jatiya* Party (Ershad). Jagpa had originated in the 1990s; the PJD was organized prior to the 1986 election by BNP dissidents. Both later joined Ershad's *Jatiya* Party in the Islamic National Unity Front (*Islami Jatiya Oikya* Front), which Ershad and Pir Fazlul KARIM established to contest the 2001 elections. Also identified with the Front were the Islamic Constitution Movement (see under the BKA, below) and the Alhaj Zamir ALI faction of the **Bangladesh Muslim League** (BML), both of which ran a few parliamentary candidates under their own banners.

In anticipation of the 2007 general election, Ershad initially tried to reunite the various *Jatiya* parties and forge a coalition substantial enough to challenge the BNP and the Awami League. He suffered a setback, however, when Shafiul Alam Prodhan left to establish a new Jagpa (below). Subsequently, Nilu also departed and formed the current National People's Party (NPP, below). At the same time, Ershad had to confront a well-publicized rupture with his second wife, Bidisha, whom he had promoted within the party. (Ershad's first wife, Raushan, to whom he has remained married, continues to play a significant role in the party.)

Throughout much of 2006 observers speculated as to whether Ershad would join the Awami League–led opposition alliance or cut a deal with the BNP. Despite four acquittals in August–September 2006, Ershad continued to face several corruption charges, which he wanted dropped. In the end, however, he sided with the opposition and in early January 2007 announced that he, too, would boycott the election set for January 22.

In mid-2007 the party once again appeared on the verge of a split. In late June Raushan Ershad, senior member of the party presidium, announced that she was assuming the chair in an acting capacity. At the end of the month former president Ershad announced his intention to retire as party leader and named as acting chair former foreign minister Anisul Islam Mahmud. In September eight reform-minded presidium members, including former party adviser Kazi Firoz RASHID, were dropped from the leadership for undermining party discipline and violating its constitution.

In late 2008 the JP (Ershad) was formally registered simply as the *Jatiya* Party. Speculation over whether Ershad would join the Awami-led Grand Alliance persisted nearly until voting day. In the end, the JP ran with the AL, winning 7 percent of the vote and 27 seats and then joining the government. Speculation that the new AL-led government would put forward Ershad for the presidency proved incorrect.

Leaders: Lt. Gen. (Ret.) Mohammad ERSHAD (Former President of the Republic), Begum Raushan ERSHAD, Anisul Islam MAHMUD (Acting Chair), Kazi Zafar AHMED, Ruhul Amin HAWLADER (Secretary General).

National Socialist Party (*Jatiya Samajtantrik Dal*—Jasad). Jasad, which is sometimes referenced as the JSD (Inu), is one of the two principal splinters from the JSD that originated as a Scientific Socialists (*Boigyanik Samajtantrabadi*) faction within the Awami League in the early postindependence period. The largely student group, led by Abdur Rab and Shajahan SIRAJ, defected from the AL in 1972. Many of its leaders were arrested following President Zia's assumption of power. It was reinstated as a legal entity in November 1978, although several leaders were not released from detention until March 1980.

Differences within the JSD over participation in a loosely formed 10-party opposition alliance contributed to a November 1980 split that resulted in formation of the Bangladesh Socialist Party (BSD, below). In 1983–1985 the party was a prominent member of the 15-party anti-Ershad coalition led by the AL.

In May 1986 separate electoral lists were presented by supporters of Rab and Siraj. Subsequently, the JSD (Rab) remained an autonomous party, winning one seat in June 1996 (and joining the government), by which time the Siraj faction had become part of the *Gano* Forum (below). A third faction led by Hasanul Haq Inu joined the Left Democratic Front (LDF; see under the Communist Party of Bangladesh, below). Siraj later joined the BNP, while the Rab and Inu factions reached an accommodation that reunited the rest of the party.

The party failed to win any parliamentary seats in October 2001, after which the Inu and Rab factions reestablished separate identities as the JSD (Inu) and the JSD (Rab)—for a discussion of the latter, see the JSD (Ziku), below. In the 2008 general election Jasad won three seats (despite running only 6 candidates and obtaining only 0.6 percent of the vote) as part of the Awami-led Grand Alliance.

Leaders: Hasanul Haq INU (Chair), Mainuddin Khan BADAL (Executive President), Syed Zafar SAJJAD (General Secretary).

Bangladesh Workers' Party (BWP). The BWP began as a pro-Soviet offshoot of the United People's Party (UPP). Having opposed formation of a front with Ziaur Rahman, the BWP left the UPP in the late 1970s and in 1983 joined the anti-Ershad movement. It was a founding member of the Left Democratic Front (LDF) in 1994.

For the 2008 general election the BWP participated in the Grand Alliance, winning 2 seats in Parliament.

Leaders: Rashed Khan MENON (Chair), Fazle Hossain BADSHA, Bimal BISWAS (Secretary General).

Liberal Democratic Party (LDP). In late October 2006 former president A.Q.M. Chowdhury, joined by BNP dissident Oli Ahmed, announced formation of the LDP, which, in most respects, was a continuation of Chowdhury's previous party, the Alternative Stream Bangladesh (BDB, below). By June 2007 differences over the leadership had led to a rupture between Chowdhury and Ahmed factions, resulting in Chowdhury's reviving the BDB.

In February 2008 the LDP and the *Samyabadi Dal* of Dilip Barua (see CPB-ML, below) announced their intention to present identical proposals on electing a new parliament when participating in the ongoing "dialogue" with the Elections Commission. Both ultimately joined the Awami alliance. The LDP won one parliamentary seat in the December election.

Leaders: Oli AHMED (Chair), Jahanara BEGUM (Secretary General).

Communist Party of Bangladesh (Marxist-Leninist)—CPB-ML (*Bangladesher Samyabadi Dal [Marxbadi-Leninbadi]*). Dating from 1971 and frequently referred to as simply the *Samyabadi Dal,* the branch of the CPB-ML led by Dilip Barua began as a Maoist formation. In 1983, however, it adopted a pro-Soviet posture. It supported the 15-party AL alliance in the anti-Ershad Movement for the Restoration of Democracy (MRD) and later participated in the LDF and the 11-party leftist opposition to the Zia government of 2001–2006.

For the 2008 parliamentary election the CPB-ML joined the Awami-led alliance. Despite winning no legislative seats, the party's longtime leader, Dilip Barua, was awarded a cabinet post.

Leader: Dilip BARUA (Minister of Industry).

Four-Party Opposition Alliance:

Bangladesh Nationalist Party—BNP (*Bangladesh Jatiyabadi Dal*). The BNP was formally launched in September 1978 by various groups that had supported President Zia in his election campaign. During 1978–1980 a number of defectors from other parties joined the government formation. In 1983 a BNP-led seven-party coalition helped form the anti-Ershad MRD.

The main body of the party, led by Zia's widow, Begum Khaleda Zia, refused to participate in the parliamentary poll of May 1986, the presidential balloting of October 1986, or the legislative election of March 1988. In 1989 the party was divided into a majority group led by Khaleda Zia and a dissident bloc led by former BNP secretary general A.K.M. Obaidur RAHMAN. Khaleda Zia was installed as prime minister following the 1991 elections, after which parliamentary deputies were advised that factionalism would no longer be tolerated.

The BNP won only 116 seats in the June 1996 election, Khaleda Zia becoming leader of an opposition "combine" that also included as principal participants the *Jamaat-i-Islami* and the Islamic Unity Front (IOJ). Following its March 1998 departure from the government, the *Jatiya* Party joined the alliance.

The BNP's October 2001 election victory saw Khaleda Zia's return to the prime minister's office on the strength of a 191-seat parliamentary majority, plus an additional 23 seats won by its three allied parties, the JI, BJP, and IOJ (all below). In June 2002 Zia named a son, Tarique Rahman, as joint secretary general of the BNP.

With Khaleda Zia facing imminent arrest by the interim government, on September 2, 2007, she named Khander Delwar Hossain as acting secretary general, replacing Abdul Mannan BHUIYAN, whom she expelled for "antiparty" activities along with Joint Secretary General Ashraf HOSSAIN. On October 29 a majority of the party's Standing Committee named M. Saifur Rahman as acting chair and Hafizuddin Ahmed as acting secretary general, both "reformers" who, along with Bhuiyan and Ashraf Hossain, demanded greater democracy within the party. An adviser to the former prime minister, Hannan Shah, emerged as leader of the pro-Zia faction. With the Election Commission having invited the reform faction to represent the BNP in the commission's planned dialogue with leading parties, the issue of party leadership was brought before the High Court, which in April 2008, without addressing the legitimacy of either faction's claims to supremacy, ruled that the Election Commission invitation to the reformers was not illegal.

Talks between the Zia and Saifur Rahman factions led to a May report that the party would unite, but differences then surfaced between Zia loyalists Hannan Shah and Delwar Hossain. The release of Zia on bail in September appeared to calm the internal disputes, although the reformers were mostly passed over in selecting candidates for the December 2008 election. Having been released on bail, Zia again led the party into the parliamentary voting, but the BNP came away with only 30 seats and a 33 percent vote share.

Leaders: Begum Khaleda ZIA (Former Prime Minister and Chair of the Party), Hannan SHAH (Adviser), Tarique RAHMAN (Senior Joint Secretary General), Nazrul Islam KHAN (Joint Secretary General), M. Saifur RAHMAN, Brig. Gen. (Ret.) Hafizuddin AHMED, Khander Delwar HOSSAIN (Secretary General).

Jamaat-i-Islami (JI). Tracing its origins to prepartition India, where the *Jamaat-i-Islami* (Islamic Assembly) was established in 1941 under Syed Abul Ala MAUDUDI, the Bangladeshi JI descends from the East Pakistan wing of the postpartition Pakistani party. Banned after the 1971 war of independence for its alleged pro-Pakistani leanings, the *Jamaat-i-Islami* Bangladesh was permitted to resume political activities later in the decade, and its leader, Golam AZAM, returned from self-imposed exile.

JI Bangladesh ran fourth in the 1991 balloting, winning 18 parliamentary seats. After the 1996 election, in which it won only 3 seats, the party actively opposed the Awami League government. In October 2001 it captured 17 seats and joined the new Khaleda Zia government.

In seeking registration for the December 2008 parliamentary election, the JI dropped the word "Bangladesh" from its name and made a number of changes in its constitution to comply with the electoral law. For example, non-Muslims may now become members.

Party President Matiur Rahman Nizami and Secretary General Ali Ahsan Muhammad Mujahid were jailed in November 2008 in connection with corruption charges, but both were released on bail a week later. Nizami had already spent two months in jail earlier in the year, before a court ordered his release on bail. At the election the JI won only 2 seats. Since then, JI leaders have been targeted by those seeking to pursue war crimes trials for offenses allegedly committed during the independence war.

Leaders: Matiur Rahman NIZAMI (Party President), Abul Katam Muhammad YUSUF (Senior Vice President), Ali Ahsan Muhammad MUJAHID (Party Secretary General).

Bangladesh Jatiya Party (BJP). Initially identified at its formation in April 2001 as the *Jatiya* Party (M-N) in honor of its initial president, M.A. Matin, and its prime mover, Naziur Rahman MANJUR, the party was often referenced leading up to the October 2001 parliamentary election as the *Jatiya* Party (Naziur). Since that election, in which it won four seats, it has most often been identified as the BJP. (For a history of the parent *Jatiya* Party's formation and complicated history, see the JP, above.)

In March–April 2005 differences between Manjur and Matin erupted. The warring leaders tried to expel each other following what Matin characterized as an "anticoalition" speech by Manjur, who had attacked the BNP's deference to *Jamaat-i-Islami* and the latter's alleged contacts with Islamic extremists. Manjur, in turn, accused Matin of "antiorganizational activities." In early March the BJP's secretary general, Kazi Firoz Rashid, and other party leaders had defected to the JP. After that, Matin and Manjur headed separate wings.

In April 2008 Manjur died at age 59. He was succeeded as leader by Andalib Rahman. For the December 2008 election the two wings were registered as separate parties. The Naziur-Rahman branch won one seat as the **Bangladesh Jatiya Party–BJP;** the Matin branch, running simply as the **Bangladesh Jatiya Party,** won none.

Bangladesh Jatiya Party–BJP Leaders: Andalib RAHMAN (Chair of the Party and Member of Parliament), Saifur RAHMAN (Secretary General)

BJP (Matin) Leaders: M.A. MATIN (Chair), A.B.M. Gulam MUSTAFA (Secretary General).

Islamic Unity Front (*Islami Oikya Jote*—IOJ). A fundamentalist organization that has urged the adoption of Islamic law, the IOJ was highly critical of Sheikh Hasina's secularist policies during her first term in office. After the June 1996 election, it participated in the BNP-led opposition, although its sole member of Parliament, Golam Sarwar HIRU, was threatened with expulsion by the IOJ leadership for breaking party discipline. In October 2001 it won two seats but was offered no cabinet posts. Afterward, as in the BJP, some elements of the IOJ were increasingly dissatisfied with the BNP's alleged deference to *Jamaat-i-Islami*.

Already divided into two principal factions, the party split further in 2005. In May 2006 the third faction, led by Misbahur Rahman Chowdhury and Mufti Izharul Islam, attacked the governing alliance for corruption, nepotism, and misrule and announced formation of a separate noncommunal *Bangladesh Islami Oikya Jote* (BIOJ) that subsequently aligned with the Awami League.

In the December 2008 election the IOJ won no seats.

Leaders: Shaikhul Hadith Muhammad AZIZUL HAQ (Faction Chair), Abdur RAB YUSUFI (Secretary General of Azizul Haq Faction), Fazlul Huq AMINI (Faction Chair), Abdul Latif NEJAMI (Secretary General of Amini Faction).

Other Center and Center-Left Parties and Alliances:

Alternative Stream Bangladesh (*Bikalpa Dhara Bangladesh*—BDB). The BDB was launched in May 2004 by former president and BNP leader A. Q. M. Badruddoza Chowdhury. In 2005, looking toward the next parliamentary election, the BDB reached a "strategic understanding" with the Awami League. In October 2006, however, Chowdhury dissolved the BDB and replaced it with a new Liberal Democratic Party (LDP, above). By June 2007, however, the LDP had split, which led Chowdhury to revive the BDB.

In October 2007 Chowdhury proposed that resolution of the country's political crisis required a "government of national consensus" that would include all major parties and govern for ten years. With the December 2008 general election approaching, he instead proposed organizing a "third force" of parties to oppose both the AL and the BNP. The resultant **Jatiya Jukta Front** (JJF), announced in November, was the latest in a series of similar groupings (including the *Jatiya Oikya* Front, which the BDB had helped organize in preparation for the canceled January 2007 election). Parties associated with the JJF, none of which won more than 0.03 percent of the vote, also included the Gano Forum (below); the **Peasants' and Workers' People's League** (*Krishak Sramik Janata League*—KSJL), which had been established in December 1999 by Kader SIDDIQUI, a former AL stalwart who won the KSJL's only parliamentary seat in October 2001; the **Progressive Democratic Party** (*Progotishil Ganatantrik Dal*—PGD), founded in July 2007 by Ferdous Ahmed QURESHI; the **Bangladesh Kalyan Party,** led by Syed Muhammad IBRAHIM; and the unregistered **Bangladesh Labor Party,** led by Sekander ALI. The JJF identified itself as an "alliance for change" and campaigned for reform, an end to corruption, and an end to poverty.

Leaders: A.Q.M. Badruddoza CHOWDHURY (Chair), Maj. Abdul MANNAN.

Gano Forum. The leftist *Gano* (People's) Forum was launched in August 1993 by a breakaway Awami League faction that declared as its objectives "violence-free politics, economic progress at the grassroots, and basic amenities for all." It initially absorbed the faction of the National Socialist Party (JSD, above) led by Shajahan Siraj. In 1997 a JSD-Siraj emerged from the Forum as a separate organization, but Siraj subsequently joined the BNP. The Forum's secretary general, Saifuddin Ahmed MANIK, died in February 2008.

In 2008, although initially allied with the Awami League, the Forum's president was critical of Sheikh Hasina's alleged corruption. The parties' relationship withered as a result, with Kamal Hossain urging formation of a front that would unite democratic progressive, noncommunal forces for the December election. In November the Forum joined the BDB in forming the "third force" *Jatiya Jukta* Front, but in the December election the Forum won only 0.01 percent of the vote.

Leaders: Dr. Kamal HOSSAIN (President), Pankaj BHATTACHARYA, Abdur RAUF, Mostafa Mohsin MONTU, Mofizul Islam Khan KAMAL.

Jatiya Party (Manju)—JP(M). The JP(M) began as the JP (Mizan-Manju), which was formed in April 1999 when a "special council" held by rebellious members of General Ershad's *Jatiya* Party broke from his leadership, charging him with undemocratic tendencies and with corruption during his years as the country's president. Among those condemning Ershad was former prime minister (and party vice chair) Mizanur Rahman Chowdhury. Another factor in the break was Ershad's removal from all party offices of Anwar Hossain Manju, who had stayed in the Hasina cabinet despite the JP's departure from the government in March 1998. The new grouping included 11 members of Parliament, all of whom objected to Ershad's recent alliance with the BNP. Shortly before the October 2001 election, Chowdhury, the party chair, left to join the Awami League, and the JP(M) won only 1 seat. In April 2004 Manju denied participating in reunification efforts by Ershad.

In June 2007 Manju was convicted in absentia of possessing foreign liquor and, pending appeal, faced a 5-year prison sentence. He has also been convicted of amassing wealth illegally and accepting kickbacks., offenses for which he has been sentenced to 13 years and 7 years, respectively.

In December 2008 the JP(M) ran as an ally of the Awami League but won no seats.

Leaders: Anwar Hossain MANJU (Chair), Sheikh Shahidul ISLAM (Secretary General).

National People's Party—NPP (*Jatiya Janata Party*). A social democratic party organized in 1978, the NPP supported the candidacy of its founder, Gen. Mohammad Ataul Ghani OSMANI, in the 1978 and 1981 presidential elections. Following Osmani's death in 1985, the group split into a number of factions. In the October 2001 election three personalist factions ran a total of six candidates, none successfully.

In July 2007 former leader of the JP(Nilu) faction, Shawkat Hossain Nilu, launched a new NPP, but the party won only 0.02 percent at the polls in December.

Leader: Shawkat Hossain NILU (Chair).

Bangladesh National Awami Party (NAP). Founded by the late Maulana Abdul Hamid Khan BHASANI, the original NAP was the principal opposition party prior to the 1975 coup. Thereafter it underwent numerous cleavages, the main splinters being the NAP-Bhasani (NAP-B) and the NAP-Muzaffar (NAP-M).

The NAP-B began as a pro-Beijing grouping that participated in a five-party left-wing Democratic Front (*Ganatantrik Jote*), which was organized in 1979. The NAP-M began as a pro-Moscow splinter. Both NAP factions later joined the Awami League alliance within the anti-Ershad MRD.

In 2008 the Election Commission registered the Muzaffar branch as the **Bangladesh National Awami Party** (BNAP) and the Bhasani branch as the **Bangladesh National Awami Party–Bangladesh NAP**, the former of which was allied with the Awami League.

BNAP Leaders: Muzaffar AHMED (President), Enamul HAQUE (Secretary General).

Bangladesh NAP Leaders: Sheikh Anwarul HAQUE (President), Mohammad Abdul MATIN (Secretary General).

National Socialist Party–Ziku (*Jatiya Samajtantrik Dal*—JSD or JSD [Ziku]). The JSD (Ziku) began as the Abdur Rab faction of the JSD (for details, see Jasad, above). More recently, with Rab having formed a new political forum, the **Unity for Political Reforms** (UPR), the JSD (Rab) has usually been referenced as the JSD (Ziku).

In September 2006 the JSD (Rab) and the UPR joined two other parties in announcing formation of the *Sangskarbadi Jukta Front* (SJF) to contest the anticipated January 2007 parliamentary election. Based on the nationalist Bengali *Jukta Front* of the 1950s, the SJF called for national unity, adoption of a bicameral legislature, governmental decentralization, people's participation, and economic policies based on the people's welfare.

In the December 2008 election the JSD (Ziku) won only 0.04 percent of the vote.

Leaders: Nur Alam ZIKU (President), Abdur RAB (Adviser), Abdul Malek RATAN (General Secretary).

Among the other parties belonging to or supporting the AL-led "Grand Alliance" in 2008 were the **Bangladesh Islami Oikya Jote** (BIOJ; see the IOJ, above), led by Misbahur Rahman CHOWDHURY and Mufti Izharul ISLAM; the **Communist Center** (*Communist Kendra*), led by Asit Baran ROY; the **Ganatantri Party**, led by Mohammad Afzal HOSSAIN since the December 2008 death of Mohammad Nural ISLAM; the moderate **Islamic Front Bangladesh;** the **People's Freedom League** (*Gano Azadi* League), led by Abdus SAMAD, and the moderate Islamic **Zaker Party** of Mustafa Amir FAISAL.

The **United Citizens Movement** (*Oikyaboddho Nagorik Andolon*—ONA), led by Quazi Faruque AHMED, was organized in October 2008 on the basis of a nongovernmental organization, *Proshika,* dedicated to serving the poor and ensuring democratic rights. It won 0.01 percent of the December parliamentary vote.

Left and Far-Left Parties:

Communist Party of Bangladesh (CPB). Originally the Communist Party of East Pakistan, the pro-Moscow CPB was often banned, following independence, during periods of military and rightist rule. The party held its first congress since 1974 in February 1980 and participated in the opposition alliance of the same year.

The CPB was a leading component of the Patriotic Democratic Front from 1991 until formation of the Left Democratic Front (LDF) in 1994 by the CPB, CPB-ML, BWP, BSD, JSD-Inu, the Unifying Process (*Oikya Prokria*), and the Workers' and Peasants' Socialist Party (*Sramik Krishak Samajbadi Dal*—SKSD). The LDF served as the core of an 11-party leftist opposition alliance after the 2001 election.

In the 2008 parliamentary election the CPB ran about 40 candidates but won only 0.06 percent of the vote.

Leaders: Manjural Ahsan KHAN (President), Mujahidul Islam SELIM (General Secretary).

Bangladesh Socialist Party (*Bangladesh Samajtantrik Dal*—BSD). The BSD, formed following a 1980 split in the JSD (see Jasad, above), itself subsequently split into factions. In October 2004 one of the faction leaders, A.F.M. Mahbubul Haq, was seriously injured by unidentified assailants.

In September 2007 BSD leader Khalequzzaman announced formation of an 11-member **Democratic Left Alliance** (DLA) that, intending to engage in "bold politics based on ideology," included many of Bangladesh's more radical leftist parties. Most participants were not previous members of the LDF, and only the BSD was registered for the December 2008 election. Among the other DLA participants are a branch of the CPB-ML, the **Communist Party of Bangladesh (Marxist-Leninist-Maoist)**—CPB-MLM (*Bangladesher Samyabadi Dal [Marxbadi-Leninbadi-Maobadi]*); the **Democratic Workers' Party** (*Ganotantrik Majdur Party*), led by Abdus SALAM and Zakir HOSSAIN; the **National People's Front** (*Jatiya Gano Front*), led by Tipu BISWAS; the **People's Solidarity Movement** (*Gano Sanghati Andolon*), led by Julhasnain BABU; and the **Revolutionary Unity Front** (*Biplobi Oikya Front*), led by Mushrefa MISHU. Khalequzzaman agreed to serve as DLA convener.

Leaders: KHALEQUZZAMAN Bhuiyan (Central Convenor), Bazlur Rashid FIROZ, A.F.M. Mahbubul HAQ (BSD Mahbub).

Revolutionary Workers Party of Bangladesh (*Bangladesher Biplobi Workers Party*—BBWP). The BBWP was formed in 1994 as a splinter from the BWP (above). Frequently allied with the CPB, it ran in a handful of constituencies in the December 2008 election, winning under 0.01 percent of the vote. In addition to calling for equal rights for minorities and women, an end to poverty, food security, and employment opportunity, its election manifesto targeted corruption, "black money holders," terrorists, and "mafias."

Leaders: Khandaker Ali ABBAS (President), Saiful HUQ (General Secretary).

The Maoist **Proletarian Party of East Bangla** (*Purba Banglar Sharbahara* Party—PBSP) dates back to 1971 but has split into several factions. One leader, Abdur Rashid MALITHA (also known as Dada TAPAN), was reportedly killed by security forces in June 2008. A number of other outlawed communist groups also exist.

Other Right and Center-Right Parties:

Bangladesh Caliphate Movement (*Bangladesh Khelafat Andolon*—BKA). The Caliphate Movement was founded in 1981 to support the unsuccessful campaign for the presidency of its leader, Maulana Mohammed Ullah Hafezji HUZUR, who ran again in 1986. In 1993 it participated in formation of the National Democratic Alliance (NDA), which included nearly a dozen conservative Islamic parties. The BKA staunchly opposed the U.S. invasions of Afghanistan in 2001 and Iraq in 2003.

In November 2006, looking toward the parliamentary election scheduled for early 2007, the BKA joined the Islamic Constitution Movement (*Islami Shashantantra Andolon*) of Syed Fazlul KARIM, which was registered in 2008 as the **Islami Andolon Bangladesh,** and the **Jamiat-e-Ulama-e-Islam Bangladesh** in forming a Three-Party Islamic Movement that was intended to counter *Jamaat-i-Islami.*

In July 2008 the BKA called for prohibiting women from serving as head of state or government. In the December election it won only 0.02 percent of the vote.

Leaders: Maulana Ahmadullah ASHRAF, Maulana Zafrullah Mohammad KHAN (Secretary General).

Bangladesh Tariqat Federation (BTF). Formation of the BTF was announced in October 2005 by Najibul Bashar MAIZBHANDARI. Formerly an official of the BNP, he resigned in September 2005 over the party's alliance with *Jamaat-i-Islami* and the latter's alleged involvement in recent bombings of shrines. In 2006 it joined in forming the *Jatiya Oikya Front.*

In the 2008 general election the BTF won 0.03 percent of the vote.

Leader: Maulana Syed Rezaul Haque CHANDPURI (Secretary General).

Jatiya Ganatantrik Party (Jagpa). The current right-wing Jagpa was reestablished by Shafiul Alam Prodhan upon his departure from General Ershad's JP. The preceding Jagpa, dating from the 1990s, had merged into the Ershad's party in 2002. For the 2008 parliamentary election Jagpa ran in alliance with the BNP.

Leader: Shafiul Alam PRODHAN.

Islamic Democratic Party (IDP). In November 2008 the Election Commission refused to register the new IDP, which had been established by individuals previously associated with the banned militant organization *Harkat-ul-Jihad Islami* (HuJI; see below). In April 2009 the government included the IDP as well as the HuJI on a watch list of suspected militant organizations.

Leaders: Sheikh Abdus SALAM, Kazi Azizul HUQ.

Chittagong Groups:

Chittagong Hill Tracts People's Solidarity Association (*Parbattya Chattagram Jana Sanghati Samity*—PCJSS). Formed in 1972 under the leadership of Manabendra Narayan LARMA, a former member of Parliament, the PCJSS long opposed the influx of Bengali settlers into the Chittagong Hill Tracts. Consisting mainly of Chakma tribesmen, the organization formed a military wing, the *Shanti Bahini* (Army of Peace), under Larma's brother Jytrindriyo (also know as Shantu Larma) in 1973. In 1982 a PCJSS faction led by Priti Kumar CHAKMA left the parent grouping; many of its supporters, but not Chakma, surrendered to the government in 1985.

M.N. Larma was killed in November 1983 by a rival group, with his brother leading subsequent negotiations with Dhaka and concluding a peace agreement in December 1997. The accord included amnesty for all members of the PCJSS, including the *Shanti Bahini,* and granted the Hill Tracts limited autonomy over regional affairs. Some of the more militant Chakma guerrillas objected, however, demanding full autonomy and stating that they would continue the insurgency. Subsequent clashes with the PCJSS occurred.

In February 1999 it was announced that Larma would assume a status equal to that of a minister of state in the Hasina government, effective upon his formally taking office as chair of the interim Chittagong Hill Tracts Regional Council. The 21-member Council was installed on May 2, 1999, and the PCJSS held its first party congress in November. Subsequently, Larma demanded that the Khaleda Zia government fully implement the 1997 accord, including ending discrimination, distributing development money, and permitting greater local control. In December 2006 he threatened to take up arms again if the next government failed to do so.

In July 2007 the party's secretary general, Satyabir DEWAN, was sentenced to 17 years in prison for possession of an unlicensed weapon and ammunition. In mid-March 2009 Shantu Larma and 13 others were accused of attempting to murder Chandra Shekhar CHAKMA, a reformist who was shot in January.

Leaders: Jytrindriyo Bodhipriyo (Shantu) LARMA (President), Rupayan DEWAN (Vice President).

Movement for Equal Privileges (*Sama Adhikar Andolon*—SAA). The SAA, an organization formed by Bangladeshi settlers, initially opposed the Chittagong settlement but has since argued for peaceful coexistence with tribal groups.

Leader: Sahaz UDDIN.

United People's Democratic Front (UPDF). The UPDF was formally organized in late 1998 by opponents of the 1997 Chittagong settlement who demanded full regional autonomy. Some of those claiming allegiance to the UPDF have since been responsible for killings, kidnappings, and other criminal acts and have repeatedly clashed with central government officials and the PCJSS. The party held its first congress in November 2006.

Leaders: Prasit Bikash KHISHA (President), Rabi Shankar CHAKMA (General Secretary).

Militant Islamic Groups:

The country's first militant Islamic groups were apparently organized as part of the anti-Soviet war effort in Afghanistan. Chief among these was the Bangladesh branch of the international **Harkat-ul-Jihad Islami** (HuJI), the existence of which was long denied by Dhaka authorities. As a consequence, the HuJI was not banned until October 2005 despite its links to al-Qaida. In the meantime, many of its members had branched out and helped found other militant organizations, including the **Shahadat al-Hikma**, which was banned in 2003. In August 2006, under the name **Sachetan Islami Janata** (Enlightened Islamic People), members of the HuJI held a meeting at Dhaka's largest mosque. Efforts were reportedly under way to convince the government that the new group was not a terrorist organization.

On December 23, 2008, the HuJI's Mufti Abdul HANNAN and 2 others were sentenced to hang for their involvement in a May 2004 grenade attack on a former British high commissioner. Hannan and 13 others have also been charged in connection with a grenade attack on an Awami League rally that left 24 dead in August 2004. In April 2009 Hannan was also indicted in connection with a 2001 bombing that killed 10.

Two closely linked banned organizations, the **Jamaat-ul-Mujahidin Bangladesh** (JMB) and the **Jagrata Muslim Janata Bangladesh** (JMJB), have attracted considerable recent attention, especially following the coordinated explosion of some 460 crude bombs on August 17, 2005. Leaflets apparently left by the JMB at bomb sites demanded the adoption of strict Islamic law. Among those sought by authorities in the aftermath were JMB leader Maulana Abdur RAHMAN and JMJB operations chief Siddiqul ISLAM (alias Bangla BHIA). Both also were implicated by the government in two courthouse bombings in November 2005 that killed two judges. The JMB and JMJB reportedly merged in October 2005. Abdur Rahman and Siddiqul Islam were both captured in March 2006 and sentenced to death in May. They and four other JMB members were executed on March 29, 2007.

Their clandestine nature makes it difficult to obtain definitive information on militant Islamic groups. At present, there may be as many as 30 groups, although some may be using alternate names and may have overlapping memberships.

LEGISLATURE

The **Parliament** (*Jatiya Sangsad*, or House of the Nation) is a unicameral body of 345 seats: 300 filled by direct election for a five-year term, subject to dissolution, and 45 indirectly elected seats reserved for women and filled on a proportional basis among represented parties. In the election of December 29, 2008 (including a January 12, 2009, vote in one district), the Awami League and its "Grand Alliance" allies won 263 seats (Awami League, 230; *Jatiya* Party (JP), 27; National Socialist Party, 3; Workers Party of Bangladesh, 2; Liberal Democratic Party, 1); the Four-Party Alliance, 33 (Bangladesh Nationalist Party [BNP], 30; *Jamaat-i-Islami,* 2; Bangladesh *Jatiya* Party, 1); and independents, 4. The 45 seats reserved for women were filled as follows on March 19, 2009: Awami League, 36; BNP, 5; JP, 4.

Speaker: Abdul HAMID.

CABINET

[as of October 1, 2009]

Prime Minister	Shiekh Hasina Wajed [f]
Ministers	
Agriculture	Motia Chowdhury [f]
Civil Aviation and Tourism	G. M. Kader (JP)
Commerce	Lt. Col. (Ret.) Faruq Khan
Communications	Syed Abul Hossain
Cultural Affairs	Abul Kalam Azad
Defense	Shiekh Hasina Wajed [f]
Education	Nurul Islam Nahid
Establishment	Sheikh Hasina Wajed [f]
Expatriates' Welfare and Overseas Employment	Khandakar Mosharraf Hossain
Finance	Abul Maal Abdul Muhit
Fisheries and Livestock	Abdul Latif Biswash
Food and Disaster Management	Abdur Razzak
Foreign Affairs	Dipu Moni [f]
Health and Family Welfare	A.F.M. Ruhul Haq
Home Affairs	Sahara Khatun [f]
Housing and Public Works	Sheikh Hasina Wajed [f]
Industry	Dilip Barua (CPB-ML)
Information	Abul Kalam Azad
Jute and Textiles	Abdul Latif Siddiqui
Labor and Employment	Khandakar Mosharraf Hossain
Land	Rezaul Karim Hira
Law, Justice, and Parliamentary Affairs	Shafiq Ahmed
Local Government, Rural Development, and Cooperatives	Syed Ashraful Islam
Planning	Air Vice Mar. (Ret.) A.K. Khandoker
Posts and Telecommunications	Razi Uddin Ahmed Raju
Power, Energy, and Mineral Resources	Sheikh Hasina Wajed [f]
Primary and Mass Education	Nurul Islam Nahid
Religious Affairs	Sheikh Hasina Wajed [f]
Roads, Railways, and Bridges	Syed Abul Hossain
Shipping	Mohammad Shajahan Khan
Social Welfare	Enamul Huq Mustafa Shahid
Water Resources	Ramesh Chandra Sen
Women's and Children's Affairs	Sheikh Hasina Wajed [f]
Ministers of State (Independent Charge)	
Chittagong Hill Tracts Affairs	Dipanker Talukdar
Environment and Forests	Hasan Mahmud
Liberation War Affairs	Capt. (Ret.) A.B.M. Tazul Islam
Communication Technology	Yafes Osman
Science and Information	Yafes Osman
Youth and Sports	Ahad Ali Sarker

[f] = female

Note: Unless otherwise indicated, ministers belong to the Awami League.

COMMUNICATIONS

Freedom of the press is guaranteed by the constitution, but in 1998 four journalists were charged with treason for printing an allegedly divisive report about the country's defense forces. Print outlets are privately owned, although intimidation by the police and political partisans, especially Islamists and Maoists, remains common, particularly in rural areas. The 2003 annual report by Reporters Without Borders described Bangladesh as "by far the world's most violent country for journalists." In contrast, the 2008 report noted a "sharp decrease" in death threats and assaults against reporters, although it added that the military and the government were attempting to silence independent journalists. Self-censorship was increasingly common.

Press. Circulation figures are often unreliable. The following are among the dozens of dailies, all published in Bangla in Dhaka unless otherwise noted: *Dainik Ittefaq* (260,000), progovernment; *Daily Prothom Alo* (220,000), independent; *Dainik Inqilab* (150,000), Islamist; *Dainik Janakantha* (100,000), independent, also published in other cities; *Sangbad* (70,000); *Dainik Bangla* (70,000); *Dainik Bhorer Kagoj* (50,000); *Dainik Purbanchal* (Khulna, 40,000); *Bangladesh Observer* (35,000), in English; *Daily Star* (30,000), in English.

News agencies. The principal domestic news agency, located in Dhaka, is the government-owned Bangladesh News Agency (*Bangladesh Sangbad Sangstha*—BSS). In addition, many of the leading foreign agencies maintain offices in the capital.

Broadcasting and computing. The government-controlled *Bangladesh Betar* network operates domestic radio stations in Dhaka, Chittagong, Khulna, and other leading cities. Bangladesh Television, also operated by the government, remains the only domestic terrestrial television source, although private satellite and cable services are available in some urban areas. Indian television signals can also be received.

As of 2008 there were 3.5 Internet users per 1,000 inhabitants.

INTERGOVERNMENTAL REPRESENTATION

Ambassador to the U.S.: Akramul QADER.

U.S. Ambassador to Bangladesh: James Francis MORIARTY.

Permanent Representative to the UN: Abulkalam Abdul MOMEN.

IGO Memberships (Non-UN): ADB, CP, CWTH, IDB, Interpol, IOM, IOR-ARC, NAM, OIC, SAARC, WCO, WTO.

BARBADOS

Political Status: Independent member of the Commonwealth since November 30, 1966.

Area: 166 sq. mi. (431 sq. km.).

Population: 250,010 (2000C); 275,000 (2008E). The 2000 figure does not include an adjustment for underenumeration.

Major Urban Center (2005E): BRIDGETOWN (urban area, 142,000).

Official Language: English.

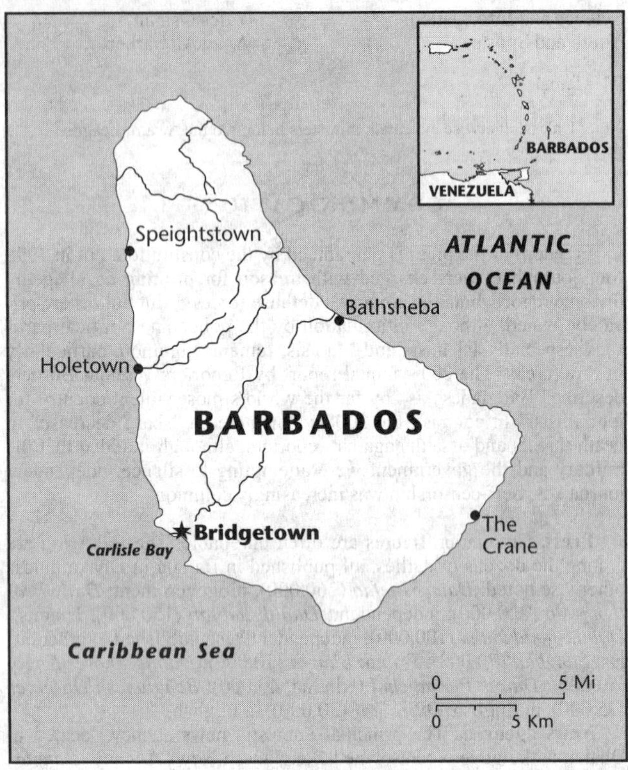

Monetary Unit: Barbados Dollar (official rate December 1, 2009: 2.00 dollars = $1US).

Sovereign: Queen ELIZABETH II.

Governor General: Sir Clifford HUSBANDS; succeeded Dame Ruth Nita BARROW, who died December 19, 1995.

Prime Minister: David THOMPSON (Democratic Labour Party); sworn in January 16, 2008, following election of January 15, succeeding Owen Seymour ARTHUR (Barbados Labour Party).

THE COUNTRY

Geographically part of the Lesser Antilles, Barbados also is the most easterly of the Caribbean nations. The island enjoys an equable climate and fertile soil, approximately 85 percent of the land being arable. Population density is among the world's highest, although the birth rate has declined in recent years. Approximately 80 percent of the population is of African origin, and another 15 percent is of mixed blood, with Europeans representing only 5 percent of the total; nonetheless, there is a strong and pervasive sense of British tradition and culture. The Anglican Church enjoys official status, but other Protestant, Roman Catholic, and Jewish groups are active. The island historically has been dependent on sugar, which still is a major contributor to the economy. Tourism is the leading source of foreign exchange, while manufacturing, especially that geared toward fellow members of the Caribbean Community, also is an important source of income. After modest advances in 1988 and 1989 the economy was buffeted by the onset in 1990 of a series of reversals that led to a 4 percent decline in real GDP during 1992. In 1993 unemployment soared to 25.5 percent (the highest in 15 years), although GDP registered a healthy advance of more than 3.0 percent. In 1998 GDP growth increased further to 4.2 percent, before falling to 3.2 percent in 1999 and a record low of –3.4 percent in 2001 before recovering to an average of 3.8 percent for 2003–2007, with, however, an average increase of 4.4 percent in inflation over the same period. In 2008, reflecting the global decline, GDP growth plummeted to 0.7 percent, while inflation soared to 9.0 percent.

In a 2003 United Nations Development Program (UNDP) report, Barbados retained its status as the highest-ranked developing country in the world, with a Human Development Index (HDI) score close to that of several developed nations.

GOVERNMENT AND POLITICS

Political background. Historically a planter-dominated island, and often called the "Little England" of the Caribbean, Barbados has been molded by a British tradition extending back to 1639. In 1937 economic problems caused by the fluctuating price of sugar led to demonstrations in Bridgetown, which resulted in the establishment of a British Royal Commission to the West Indies. The commission proved instrumental in bringing about social and political reform, including the introduction of universal adult suffrage in 1951. The island was granted full internal sovereignty ten years later.

Barbados played a leading role in the short-lived West Indies Federation (1958–1962) and supplied its only prime minister, Sir Grantley ADAMS. The collapse of the federation and the inability of Barbadian leaders to secure the establishment of an Eastern Caribbean Federation as a substitute left independence within the Commonwealth, which was achieved on November 30, 1966, as the only viable alternative. An election held November 3, 1966, confirmed the dominant position of the Democratic Labour Party (DLP), whose leader, Errol Walton BARROW, had been named premier in 1961 and was reappointed prime minister in 1971.

In an election held September 2, 1976, the opposition Barbados Labour Party (BLP) upset the DLP, and Barrow's 15-year rule ended the following day with the designation of Sir Grantley's son, J.M.G.M. ("Tom") ADAMS, as prime minister. In voting that was extremely close in many constituencies, the BLP retained its majority on June 18, 1981. Adams died in March 1985 and was succeeded by his deputy, H. Bernard ST. JOHN, who was unable to contain deepening fissures within the party. As a result, the DLP won a decisive legislative majority of 24–3 in balloting on May 28, 1986, with a new Barrow administration being installed the following day. Barrow died suddenly on June 1, 1987, and was succeeded on the following day by Lloyd Erskine SANDIFORD, who led the party to victory on January 22, 1991, with a reduced margin of ten seats in the lower House of Assembly.

After losing a legislative confidence vote on June 7, 1994, over his appointment of a new chief executive of the Barbados Tourism Authority (BTA), Sandiford dissolved the House of Assembly and called for a premature general election on September 6. The result was an overwhelming defeat for the DLP, with the newly installed BLP leader, Owen S. ARTHUR, being named to head a government that was sworn in on September 12. The BLP inflicted a shattering 26–2 defeat on its opponent in the election of January 20, 1999, with analysts crediting the victory to a buoyant economy. Riding a wave of favorable public opinion, Arthur was elected to a third term at an early vote on May 21, 2003.

At the most recent poll of January 15, 2008, the DLP returned to power under the leadership of David THOMPSON, winning 20 of 30 lower house seats.

Constitution and government. The Barbados governmental structure is modeled after the British parliamentary system. The queen remains titular head of state and is represented by a governor general with quite limited functions. Executive authority is vested in the prime minister and his cabinet, who are collectively responsible to a bicameral legislature. The upper house of the legislature, the Senate, is appointed by the governor general after consultation with the government, the opposition, and other relevant social and political interests. The lower house, the House of Assembly, sits for a maximum term of five years. The franchise is held by all persons 18 years of age and older, and voting is by secret ballot.

The judicial system embraces lower magistrates, who are appointed by the governor general with the advice of the Judicial and Legal Service Commission, and a Supreme Court, encompassing a High Court and a Court of Appeal. The chief justice is appointed by the governor general on the recommendation of the prime minister after consultation with the leader of the opposition.

Previously elected local government bodies were abolished in 1969 in favor of a division into 11 parishes, all of which (in addition to the municipality of Bridgetown) are now administered by the central government.

Foreign relations. Barbados has pursued an active, but nonaligned, posture in United Nations, Commonwealth, and hemispheric affairs. After participating for some years in the Organization of American States' (OAS) ostracism of Cuba, Barbados reestablished relations with Havana in 1973, although still enjoying cordial relations with the

United States. In December 1979, in a move characterized by Prime Minister Adams as an act of "East Caribbean defence cooperation," Barbados dispatched troops to St. Vincent to help maintain order while St. Vincent police were deployed in containing an uprising on the Grenadines' Union Island. Relations with neighboring Grenada, on the other hand, deteriorated following installation of the leftist regime of Maurice Bishop in St. George's in March 1979, and the Adams government participated in the U.S.-led invasion precipitated by the coup of October 1983. This action, while strengthening Bridgetown's relations with the United States, strained its links with the United Kingdom and, perhaps more seriously, with Trinidad, which claimed that the operation was undertaken without properly consulting all members of the Caribbean community.

Despite his government's difficulties, Prime Minister Adams was widely perceived as a regional leader, his death being described as "leaving a power vacuum in the Caribbean." Subsequently, Barbados moved even closer to the United States. Despite outspoken dissatisfaction with the level of aid provided by the U.S. Caribbean Basin Initiative, the island was designated in early 1985 as the center of the U.S.-funded Regional Security System (RSS), which conducted military maneuvers in the eastern Caribbean the following September. Even before Adams's death, however, the idea of providing the RSS with a 1,000-man rapid deployment force had quietly been dropped. Following the DLP's 1986 victory, Prime Minister Barrow joined James Mitchell of St. Vincent in opposing the conclusion of a formal RSS treaty, stating in a letter to six regional chief executives that his government would rely instead on a 1982 memorandum of understanding that provided for cooperation in a number of nonmilitary activities such as drug control, prevention of smuggling, and maritime conservation and training.

In August 1998 the government announced that henceforth it would place more emphasis on its relations with Asia and the Pacific. Concurrently, indicating that the "basic focus" of its foreign policy would be economic, Barbados established a consular office in Geneva to coordinate relations with the World Trade Organization.

Indicative of a shift from Washington to Havana, Prime Minister Arthur signed a number of economic accords with Cuba in mid-1999, while accepting Cuba's highest decoration, the José Martí award, for opposing the continued U.S. blockade of the Castro regime.

In 2004 the Arthur administration reiterated its long-standing objection to a maritime treaty between Trinidad and Venezuela that purportedly assigned to the signatories "an enormous part of Barbados' and Guyana's maritime territory" and declared that it would follow Guyana in taking the dispute to the United Nations under the UN Convention on the Law of the Sea (UNCLOS). The action came after the arrest of two Barbadian fishermen in what were alleged to be Trinidadian waters and appeared linked to the allocation of regional offshore oil and gas exploration blocks. The dispute appeared to be resolved in early 2007, following a ruling by the Permanent Court of Arbitration at The Hague, which established a maritime boundary roughly halfway between the two countries. However, in mid-2008 Venezuela complained that 2 of 26 offshore blocks in Barbados's recent oil bidding tender were within Venezuelan territorial waters, a claim that Bridgeport termed "baseless".

Current issues. In May 1995 Prime Minister Arthur appointed a ten-member Constitutional Review Commission to propose reforms aimed at building a "new, just and humane society," and in July 1996 the commission began a review of issues that included assessment of the link to the British Crown. Underlying the inquiry was rising concern over the role of Britain's Privy Council, which had recently tightened procedures for executions in capital cases, with both parties adopting an essentially republican posture during the 1994 electoral campaign. Assembly debate began in mid-2000 on the commission's report, which recommended a move to republic status, under which an indirectly elected president would serve as head of state while most governmental authority would remain with the prime minister. In early 2005 Arthur pledged that a referendum (endorsed by his party's 2003 election manifesto) would be included in the next election. However, in December 2007 Deputy Prime Minister Mia MOTTLEY announced, without explanation, that action in the matter would be further postponed.

Two concerns, apart from oil concession rights, surfaced in the wake of the 2008 electoral campaign: the impact of the global recession, particularly as it affected the tourist industry; and the failure of Barbadian immigration laws to stem what was perceived as a heightened influx of foreign criminals associated with the drug trade.

POLITICAL PARTIES

For most of the period since independence, the Barbados Labour Party and the Democratic Labour Party exhibited similar labor-oriented philosophies with political contests turning mainly on considerations of personality. Recently, however, the DLP has adopted a somewhat right-of-center posture that appears to have influenced the launching of the National Democratic Party (below) as a third force in island politics.

Government Party:

Democratic Labour Party (DLP). A moderate party founded in 1955 by dissident members of the BLP, the DLP has, for most of its existence, been closely allied with the country's principal labor group, the Barbados Workers' Union. In the 1971 election the party obtained 18 of 24 legislative seats, but it retained only 7 in 1976; its representation rose to 10 in 1981. Former prime minister Errol W. Barrow resigned as DLP leader following the 1976 reversal but returned to the party presidency in mid-1980. After the 1981 defeat, he again stepped down as president while remaining in Parliament as leader of the opposition.

In 1985, in the wake of Tom Adams's death, continued recession, and the likelihood of an early election, Barrow advanced an essentially conservative program including privatization of state enterprises, cutbacks in public works, sale of the government's share in a number of corporate sectors, and the introduction of business incentives. However, the new platform also deplored Bridgetown's involvement in U.S. strategic interests and called for dissolution of the RSS.

Barrow returned as prime minister in 1986, but he died the following year; his deputy, Erskine Sandiford, assumed leadership of the government and the party. Former finance minister David Thompson was named to succeed Sandiford after the party's electoral loss in September 1994. The party's legislative representation plummeted to two seats in January 1999. Thompson resigned as party president in September 2001; he was succeeded by Clyde MASCOLL, an economist, who was not a member of the Assembly. The party continued in opposition after the 2003 poll, with a net gain of five House seats and Mascoll assuming the opposition leadership in the lower house.

In August 2005 Thompson returned to the party presidency, defeating the incumbent, Sen. Freundel Stuart, by an Annual Conference vote of 345–164. He was reconfirmed by a party poll in November, after some members had indicated a preference for Mascoll. Mascoll reacted to his defeat by resigning from the party in January 2006, and he was promptly named to a BLP cabinet post. Thompson consequently became opposition leader and succeeded Owen Arthur as prime minister following the DLP's electoral victory in January 2008.

Leaders: David THOMPSON (Prime Minister and President of the Party), Sen. Freundel STUART (Deputy Prime Minister and Former President of the Party).

Opposition Party:

Barbados Labour Party (BLP). Founded in 1938, the BLP is the oldest of the leading parties. After dominating Barbadian politics in the 1950s under the leadership of Sir Grantley Adams, it went into opposition, winning nine seats in 1966, three of which were lost in 1971. It returned to power in 1976 under Sir Grantley's son, J.M.G.M. ("Tom") Adams, and retained its majority in the election of June 18, 1981. The party split into a number of factions after the death of the younger Adams in 1985, thereby contributing to the defeat of the St. John government a year later. Former foreign minister Henry FORDE, named to succeed St. John as parliamentary leader in October 1986, declared that the party would have to be rebuilt as a "highly decentralized" organization featuring "mass democracy in the formation of policy." Forde was succeeded in July 1993 by Owen Arthur, who led the party to victory 14 months later. The BLP retained power in an electoral landslide on January 20, 1999, winning 26 of 28 lower house seats, 3 of which were lost in 2003.

Although Archer remained personally popular, the BLP was decisively defeated at the early election of January 15, 2008, after which its leader, while retaining his legislative seat, announced his retirement from active politics.

Leaders: Mia MOTTLEY (Party Chair and Leader of the Opposition), Owen Seymour ARTHUR (Former Prime Minister), William DUGUID (General Secretary).

Other Parties:

National Democratic Party (NDP). The NDP was launched on February 1, 1989, following the withdrawal of former finance minister Richie Haynes and three other MPs from the DLP. Haynes, who had earlier criticized the Sandiford administration for raising taxes in violation of a 1987 campaign pledge, declared that the new party would strive for a "just and caring society" with "efficiency and integrity in public affairs." The NDP lost all four of its seats in January 1991; one that was regained in September 1994 was lost in January 1999.

In mid-1997 several NDP figures rejoined the DLP, although most of its founding members indicated that they would remain with the dissident formation.

Leaders: Dr. Richard (Richie) HAYNES (Former Leader of the Opposition), Edgar BOURNE, Richard BYER.

Minor parties include the **People's Progressive Movement** (PPM), founded in 1979 and led by Eric SEALY; the left-wing **Workers' Party of Barbados** (WPB), founded in 1985 by Dr. George BELLE; and the leftist **People's Empowerment Party** (PEP), launched in 2006 by Roberty (Bobby) CLARKE, former leader of the Movement for National Liberation (Monali).

LEGISLATURE

The bicameral **Parliament** consists of an appointed Senate and an elected House of Assembly.

Senate. The Senate consists of 21 members appointed by the governor general; 12 are appointed on advice of the prime minister, 2 on advice of the leader of the opposition, and 7 to represent social, religious, and economic interests.

President: Branford TAITT.

House of Assembly. The House currently consists of 30 members elected for five-year terms by direct popular vote. In the most recent election of January 15, 2008, the Democratic Labour Party won 20 seats, and the Barbados Labour Party, 10.

Speaker: Michael CARRINGTON.

CABINET

[as of June 1, 2009]

Prime Minister	David Thompson
Deputy Prime Minister	Freundel Stuart
Ministers	
Agriculture	Sen. Haynesley Benn
Economic Affairs and Empowerment, Innovation, Trade, Industry, and Commerce	Dr. David Eastwick
Education and Human Resource Development	Ronald Jones
Environment, Water Resources, and Drainage	Dr. Denis Lowe
Family, Youth Affairs, and Sports	Dr. Esther Byer-Suckoo [f]
Foreign Affairs and Foreign Trade	Sen. Maxine McClean [f]
Health	Donville Inniss
Home Affairs and Attorney General	Freundel Stuart
International Business and International Transport	George Hutson
Social Care, Constituency Empowerment, and Rural and Urban Development	Christopher (Chris) Sinckler
Transport and Works	John Boyce
Ministers of State	
Parliamentary Secretary in the Prime Minister's Office	Sen. Irene Sandiford-Garner [f]
Prime Minister's Office, with Responsibility for Finance, Investment, Telecommunications, and Energy	Sen. Darcy Boyce
Prime Minister's Office, with Responsibility for Labour and Immigration	Sen. Arni Walters

[f] = female

COMMUNICATIONS

All news media are free of censorship and government control.

Press. The following are privately owned and published in Bridgetown: *Daily Nation* (32,000 daily; 52,000 Sunday, published as *Sunday Sun*); *The Beacon* (15,000), weekly BLP organ; *Barbados Advocate* (15,000 daily; 21,000 Sunday), independent; *Action*, weekly. In addition, an *Official Gazette* is issued Monday and Thursday.

News agencies. The regional Caribbean News Agency (Cana) is headquartered in St. Michael; Spain's *Agencia EFE* also is represented in Barbados.

Broadcasting and computing. Barbados Rediffusion Service, Ltd., has operated a wired radio system since the 1930s, and the government-owned Caribbean Broadcasting Corporation (CBC) has offered a wireless system since 1963. The Voice of Barbados, privately owned, began broadcasting in 1981, while Barbados Broadcasting Service (BBS), also private, began transmission in late 1982. In addition, a multidenominational religious system has sought licensing. The CBC operates the only television service, apart from two cable channels. As of 2008 there were 736.7 Internet users per 1,000 inhabitants.

INTERGOVERNMENTAL REPRESENTATION

Ambassador to the U.S.: John BEALE.

U.S. Ambassador to Barbados: (Vacant).

Permanent Representative to the UN: Christopher Fitzherbert HACKETT.

IGO Memberships (Non-UN): ACS, Caricom, CDB, CWTH, IADB, Interpol, NAM, OAS, OPANAL, SELA, WCO, WTO.

BELARUS

Republic of Belarus
Respublika Belarus

Political Status: Formerly the Byelorussian Soviet Socialist Republic, a constituent republic of the Union of Soviet Socialist Republics (USSR); declared independence on August 25, 1991; current constitution declared to be in force by the government on November 27, 1996, following approval by national referendum on November 24.

Area: 80,155 sq. mi. (207,600 sq. km.).

Population: 10,045,237 (1999C); 9,606,000 (2008E).

Major Urban Center (2005E): MINSK (Miensk, 1,775,000).

Official Languages: Belarusan and Russian (the latter being the first language of most inhabitants).

Monetary Unit: Belarusan Ruble (official rate December 1, 2009: 2,783.00 rubles = $1US). On January 2, 2009, the ruble was devalued by 20.5 percent against the dollar and pegged to a basket comprising, in equal weight, the euro, the dollar, and the Russian ruble.

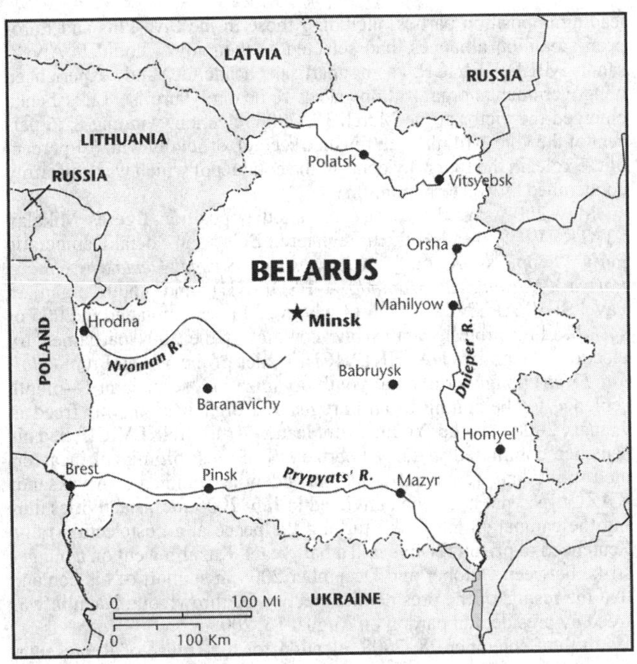

President: Alyaksandr LUKASHENKA; elected in popular runoff balloting on July 10, 1994, and inaugurated for a five-year term on July 20, succeeding Mechyslaw HRYB (Mechislav GRIB), who, as chair of the Supreme Council, had theretofore served as head of state; term extended to 2001 by constitutional referendum of November 1996; reelected on September 4–9, 2001, and inaugurated on September 20; reelected for a third term on March 19, 2006, and sworn in on April 8.

Prime Minister: Syarhey SIDORSKY (Sergei SIDORSKY); named acting prime minister on July 10, 2003, by the president, who had dismissed Prime Minister Henadz NAVITSKI (Gennady NOVITSKY) on the same day; endorsed as prime minister by the House of Representatives on December 19, 2003, and appointed to that post by the president later that same day; reconfirmed on April 17, 2006.

THE COUNTRY

Located east of Poland in the western region of the former Soviet Union, Belarus is bordered on the north by Latvia, on the northwest by Lithuania, on the east by the Russian Federation, and on the south by Ukraine. Approximately 78 percent of its population is Belarusan, 13 percent Russian, 4 percent Polish, and 3 percent Ukrainian. The predominant religion is Eastern Orthodox, with another 10 percent of the population professing Roman Catholicism. A 2002 law prohibits publication and missionary work by churches that have not been registered for at least 20 years. Women make up 53 percent of the labor force. Following the September–October 2008 legislative elections, women held 32 percent of the seats in the lower house and 34 percent of the seats in the upper house.

Agriculture, which continues to be dominated by state and collective farms, and forestry account for about 14 percent of employment and 9 percent of GDP, overall output having declined significantly during the 1990s. The leading crops include grains (rye, oats, wheat), potatoes, and sugar beets, while extensive forests support a major timber industry. Industrial output includes machinery, chemicals, processed foods, and wood and paper products, with industry as a whole employing 35 percent of the workforce and contributing about 40 percent of GDP. Belarus is generally considered "the most unreformed" of the former European Soviet republics, and the state continues to control most assets and economic activity. The private-sector share of GDP stands at about 25 percent.

The postindependence economy suffered a significant contraction that averaged nearly 14 percent of GDP annually in 1993–1995. GDP growth in the latter half of the 1990s was sporadic, peaking at 11.4 percent in 1997 but declining to 3.4 percent in 1999, and inflation was a major problem. Consumer prices soared by 182 percent in 1998 and 251 percent in 1999, largely as a consequence of the 1998 Russian ruble crisis; shortages of food and other essential goods occurred, and the value of the Belarusan ruble plummeted. The subsequent Russian recovery benefited foreign trade, while the value of the Belarusan currency was stabilized in September 2000 by adoption of a unified exchange rate. From 2004 through 2006 growth averaged about 10 percent annually and inflation steadily declined, dropping to 7 percent in 2006. In 2007 the growth rate remained high at 8 percent, while inflation rose to 12 percent, partly as a consequence of dramatically increased costs for hydrocarbons shipped from Russia. GDP expanded by 10.5 percent in 2008, with inflation reaching 15 percent, but a sharp downturn was predicted for 2009 as a consequence of the ongoing international financial crisis.

GOVERNMENT AND POLITICS

Political background. Merged with Poland in the 16th century after a lengthy period of Lithuanian rule, Byelorussia became part of the Russian Empire as a result of the Polish partitions of 1772, 1793, and 1795. A major battlefield during World War I, the region was reconquered by Red Army troops following a declaration of independence in 1918 and became a constituent republic of the USSR in 1922. In 1939 a western area that had been awarded to Poland in 1921 was reclaimed and incorporated into the Byelorussian SSR.

On July 27, 1990, Byelorussia emulated a number of its sister republics by issuing a declaration of sovereignty. On August 25, 1991, following the abortive Moscow coup against USSR President Mikhail Gorbachev, the Byelorussian Communist Party was suspended, and the Supreme Soviet proclaimed the republic's "political and economic independence." On September 18 its name was changed to Belarus, and Stanislau SHUSHKEVICH was designated chair of the Supreme Soviet (head of state), succeeding Nicholai DEMENTEI, who had been obliged to resign after displaying support for the Moscow hard-liners. Belarus hosted the December 8 tripartite meeting with Russia and Ukraine that proclaimed the demise of the Soviet Union.

Belarus became fully independent with virtually all of its Soviet-era power structure and personnel still in place. In 1992 disputes between the government and the non-Communist opposition became more heated. While the Supreme Soviet voted to lift the suspension of the Communist Party, its property remained under state ownership. Strains then intensified between Shushkevich, a free-market nationalist, and the chair of the Council of Ministers, Vyacheslau KEBICH, a veteran Communist who favored state control of the economy and close ties with Moscow. In January 1994 Shushkevich's opponents won legislative approval of a censure motion that accused him of "personal immodesty" (i.e., corruption). Shushkevich resigned and was succeeded on January 28 by Mechyslaw HRYB (Mechislav GRIB), a former Communist apparatchik who shared Kebich's enthusiasm for closer economic and military cooperation with Russia.

In the first round of balloting for the newly created office of president on June 23, 1994, Alyaksandr LUKASHENKA, a pro-Russian anticorruption campaigner, topped a six-man field with 44.8 percent of the vote. Lukashenka, running as an independent, went on to defeat Kebich by a near 6–1 margin in a two-way second-round poll on July 10. Lukashenka's nomination of Mikhail CHYHIR (CHIGIR) as prime minister secured legislative approval on July 21.

Despite opposition calls for an early legislative poll, the preindependence Supreme Council, which had been elected in April 1990, concluded its five-year term. At the legislative election of May 14 and 28, 1995, only 119 of the 260 seats were filled, well short of the two-thirds constitutionally required for a quorum.

The 119 deputies included contingents of Communists, Agrarians, and conservative independents, almost all supportive of the government's pro-Russian line and unenthusiastic about market reform. President Lukashenka wanted the outgoing Soviet-era legislature to reduce the quorum requirement in the new body to two-fifths (i.e., to 104) so that the seated deputies could conduct legislative business. Even though their mandate had expired, the majority of the outgoing legislators preferred to maintain the status quo pending new elections for the unfilled seats. The political impasse was eased somewhat when further elections in November and December increased the number of seats properly filled to 198. The Communists and Agrarians ended up with a substantial majority of party-based seats, although the largest number

(95) went to "unaffiliated" candidates, most of whom were thought to support the president.

In the context of an ongoing dispute with the Constitutional Court and his opponents in the Supreme Council over what they charged were his efforts to "rule by decree," in mid-1996 President Lukashenka proposed sweeping constitutional revisions. Prime Minister Chyhir resigned on November 18 to protest Lukashenka's plans, the president naming Deputy Prime Minister Syarhey LING to serve as acting prime minister. Six days later, over 70 percent of the voters approved an amended constitution in a highly controversial referendum that strengthened the presidency and extended Lukashenka's term from five to seven years, until 2001. On November 27, rejecting assertions that the referendum results were undemocratic and the official tally padded, the government declared the amended constitution in force.

Among other things, the document provided for a new, bicameral National Assembly, although more than 40 members of the Supreme Council refused to recognize the referendum's legitimacy and continued to meet in rump sessions as the former legislature's "13th convocation." In January 1997 the defiant legislators initiated a shadow cabinet, the Public Coalition Government–National Economic Council (subsequently the National Executive Council—NEC). On January 15 President Lukashenka announced a cabinet reshuffle that was formally confirmed on February 19 by the new lower house, the House of Representatives, which comprised those legislators who had been elected to the Supreme Council in 1995 and who accepted the legitimacy of the new constitution.

On January 10, 1999, 43 members of the rump Supreme Council announced a "presidential" election for May 16, in conformance with the 1994 constitution. Organizations supporting the move included the three largest opposition parties. By March exiled opposition leader Zyanon PAZNYAK and former prime minister Chyhir had been certified as presidential candidates by the opposition's Central Electoral Commission (CEC). Ultimately, however, the CEC was forced to declare the results of the May balloting invalid because of official harassment, resultant organizational difficulties, and Paznyak's decision to withdraw over procedural objections.

On February 18, 2000, President Lukashenka replaced Prime Minister Ling with Vladimir YERMOSHIN, the chair of the Minsk Executive Committee (mayor). He was confirmed on March 14 by the House of Representatives.

Controversial elections to the House took place on October 15, 2000, although much of the opposition, linked through a Coordinating Council of Democratic Forces, called for a boycott. Only about 50 of the 562 official candidates for office represented the opposition, many others having been disqualified on technicalities or intimidated into withdrawing. Following a second round on October 29, the election results were declared valid in 97 of 110 constituencies, with the remaining seats being filled in March–April 2001.

Although most of the opposition united behind Uladzimir HANCHARYK (Vladimir GONCHARIK) of the Belarusan Federation of Trade Unions for the presidential election of September 4–9, 2001, President Lukashenka claimed some 76 percent of the disputed vote. Inaugurated on September 20, he nominated a new prime minister, Henadz NAVITSKI (Gennady NOVITSKY), on October 1. Formation of a new Council of Ministers was concluded by mid-December.

On July 10, 2003, President Lukashenka dismissed Prime Minister Navitski and several agricultural officials and named a deputy prime minister, Syarhey SIDORSKY, to head the cabinet in an acting capacity. Sidorsky's elevation to prime minister was completed on December 19, following endorsement by a 111–9 vote of the House of Representatives earlier in the day.

During the second half of 2003 opposition forces began organizing for the 2004 legislative election. The principal alliances to emerge from the process were the Popular Coalition "Five-Plus" and the European Coalition "Free Belarus."

On September 7, 2004, Lukashenka announced that the October 17 balloting also would include a referendum on ending the two-term limit for presidents. Although the opposition united in an effort to defeat the constitutional change, the referendum easily passed, according to the official results, thereby permitting Lukashenka to seek a third term in 2006. The simultaneous election for the House of Representatives saw the opposition parties shut out: of the 110 contested seats, only 12 were won by party candidates, all of them government supportive.

Although President Lukashenka's term was not due to expire until September 2006, on December 16, 2005, the legislature unanimously endorsed holding the next presidential election six months early. At a National Congress of Democratic Forces, held October 1–2, 2005, the leading opposition parties, including those in the Five-Plus and European Coalition alliances, had selected as their joint candidate Alyaksandr MILINKEVICH, a nonpartisan academic and experienced nongovernmental organization leader. To no one's surprise, Lukashenka emerged the victor at the March 19, 2006, election, winning 82.6 percent of the vote. Milinkevich finished second, officially with 6.1 percent of the vote, in the four-way contest, the conduct of which was uniformly condemned by Western monitors.

May 2007 saw the release of jailed opposition figures Mikalay STATKEVICH, head of the unregistered Belarusan Social Democratic Party "People's Assembly" (*Belaruskaya Satsyal-Demakratychnaya Partya "Narodnaya Hramada"*—BSDP-NH), and youth organizer Pavel SEVYARYNETS, both of whom had been convicted in 2005 of spearheading protests against the conduct of the 2004 parliamentary elections. Dzmitryy DASHKEVICH, leader of the Young Front (*Malady Front*) nongovernmental youth organization, serving an 18-month sentence for belonging to an unregistered organization, was freed in January 2008. Another Young Front leader, Artur FINKEVICH, had his sentence commuted in early February. The most prominent incarcerated politician remained 2006 presidential candidate Alyaksandr KAZULIN, who had been convicted in July 2006 for his activities during the campaign and for disturbing the peace at a postelection rally. Sentenced to prison for five and a half years, Kazulin went on a hunger strike between October and December 2006 in support of his demand that the results of the presidential election be thrown out. Kazulin was freed by presidential pardon on August 16, 2008.

In the September 28, 2008, election for the House of Representatives the opposition once again failed to win any seats. Monitors from the Organization for Security and Cooperation in Europe (OSCE) noted "minor improvements" in the conduct of the election but continued to criticize Belarus for its failure to meet democratic commitments.

Constitution and government. After a two-year gestation period, a new constitution secured legislative approval on March 15, 1994, and entered into force on March 30. It provided for an executive president to be directly elected for a once-renewable five-year term, and assigned him powers that included serving as commander in chief; declaring a state of emergency; and appointing the prime minister, cabinet, and judges. Under constitutional amendments approved in May 1995, the president was also given the authority to dissolve the legislature "in the event of systematic or gross violation of the constitution." The legislature was the unicameral, 260-member Supreme Council, also directly elected for a five-year term. A Constitutional Court of 11 judges served as the final authority on legislative and executive acts, although its status was brought into question by the creation in April 1996 of a separate Constitutional Council attached to the presidency. An impeachment law adopted on February 1, 1995, specified that the president could be removed from office by a two-thirds majority of the legislature.

The powers of the presidency were vastly expanded by referendum on November 24, 1996. Revisions to the constitution extended the current president's term of office and gave him the authority to nullify decisions of local councils, set election dates, and call parliament into session as well as dissolve it. The president also was empowered to appoint half the members of the Constitutional Court, as well as the chief justice, and officials of the Central Electoral Commission. The unicameral legislature was replaced by a two-chamber body comprising an upper Council of the Republic and a lower House of Representatives. A referendum on October 17, 2004, eliminated the two-term limitation on the presidency.

Under a simplification of local government structures given legislative approval in 1994, village and some town councils were abolished, while district and regional councils were made less bureaucratic. By a decree of November 1994, the president assumed the authority to appoint and dismiss senior local government officials in the country's six regions (*voblasti*) and the municipality (*horad*) of Minsk, the aim being to create a "vertical chain of power."

Foreign relations. Although not then an independent country, Byelorussia was accorded founding membership in the United Nations in a move by the Western Allies to reconcile the USSR's Joseph Stalin to the creation of a world organization that would appear to have a built-in anti-Soviet majority. In contrast, it did not join the International Monetary Fund (IMF) and World Bank until July 1992. By then, independent Belarus had been recognized by a wide variety of foreign governments and had become a founding member of the Commonwealth of Independent States (CIS).

After protracted diplomatic exchanges, Belarus ratified a series of agreements by which it renounced its inherited nuclear weapons. Under one of the accords, signed in Washington on July 22, 1992, the U.S.

government pledged $59 million to assist in dismantling about 80 Belarus-based SS-25 missiles. In November 1996 Russia reported that it had removed the last nuclear missiles from Belarus.

Under a December 1993 agreement Russia obtained the right to guide seven CIS members, including Belarus, in defense policy. Belarus nevertheless joined the Partnership for Peace program of the North Atlantic Treaty Organization (NATO) in January 1995, although it proceeded more slowly than many other countries in negotiating the specifics of its participation in the program.

In February 1995 Belarus and Russia signed a friendship and cooperation treaty aimed at achieving a degree of bilateral reintegration. Among other things, the pact provided for joint border protection and the eventual creation of a single administration to run an economic and monetary union. This then led to the signing in Moscow on April 2, 1996, of a far-reaching Treaty on the Formation of the Community of Sovereign Republics (CSR), which envisioned military and political cooperation as well as economic union. Russian Prime Minister Viktor Chernomyrdin became the first chair of the CSR executive committee upon entry into force of the treaty in August. Provision also was made for the eventual establishment of a CSR Supreme Council (comprising governmental and legislative leaders of both nations) to serve as the grouping's ruling body, assisted by a CSR Parliamentary Assembly consisting of an equal number of representatives from the Belarusan and Russian legislatures.

Russian President Boris Yeltsin and Belarusan President Lukashenka attempted to reinvigorate the stalled integration process on April 2, 1997, by signing a revised treaty and initialing a lengthy "Charter of the Union" that, although watered down somewhat at the last minute, provided specifics regarding the extent and timing of integration. Despite opposition from various constituencies in both countries, the two presidents on May 23 signed the charter, which formally came into effect on June 11, following ratification by the Belarusan and Russian legislatures. All citizens of both nations were declared "citizens of the Community," and other countries were pointedly invited to join. The union remained largely symbolic, however, despite the new Parliamentary Assembly's December approval of the first CSR budget, with financing for military cooperation and anticrime and customs measures.

On December 8, 1999, Yeltsin and Lukashenka signed yet another agreement, a Treaty on the Creation of a Union State, that was quickly passed by the legislatures of both countries. Although specifying that Russia and Belarus would retain sovereignty and "territorial integrity," the document, like its predecessors, called for establishing joint executive and legislative bodies; a common currency; a joint taxation system; and coordinated defense, foreign, and economic policies. On April 25, 2000, the Council of Ministers of the Union met for the first time.

A monetary union was to have been established by January 2005, but adoption of a single currency was repeatedly postponed, in part because of a failure to agree on what compensation Belarus would receive to offset the consequent economic damage. In January 2007 Boris Gryzlov, speaker of Russia's lower house, also cited the absence of a free trade zone as an impediment. In the meantime, negotiations continued on a constitutional draft, but basic issues remained unresolved, including, especially, questions related to sovereignty. The cooperative atmosphere was also clouded by differences related to Belarus's purchase of hydrocarbons from Russia and transit fees imposed by Minsk on Russian oil headed to other European countries.

In early 2006 the Russian natural gas monopoly, Gazprom, demanding an end to the generous energy subsidy enjoyed by Belarus, sought to bring gas prices in line with what other former Soviet states paid. Belarus argued that this was counter to union agreements and could quintuple gas prices. In December, with the existing gas contract due to expire, the dispute grew increasingly rancorous, although it was ultimately settled on the last day of the year. Belarus agreed to a new contract under which gas prices would more than double in 2007 and continue to rise thereafter, until reaching parity with European prices in 2011. Belarus also agreed to sell Gazprom a 50 percent stake in the country's second export pipeline (Gazprom already owned the other). In the new year President Lukashenka condemned Russia's "unfriendly steps" and threatened to impose transit fees on Russian oil exports, although the latter issue was apparently settled by a January 2007 agreement. Following a two-day visit to Belarus by Russian President Vladimir Putin in mid-December 2007, the Lukashenka regime received a $1.5 billion stabilization loan from Moscow that was intended to cushion the dramatically higher price of Russian natural gas.

Relations with Western European countries and institutions long suffered because of their objections to the Lukashenka regime's political practices. Efforts to mediate between Lukashenka and the opposition and to encourage free and fair elections were unavailing despite initiatives by the "parliamentary troika" of the European Parliament, the Parliamentary Assembly of the OSCE, and the Parliamentary Assembly of the Council of Europe (PACE).

In October 2002 the last foreign member of the OSCE Advisory and Monitoring Group (AMG) in Belarus was obliged to leave the country due to the expiration of her visa. The Lukashenka regime, alleging that the AMG had repeatedly aided the opposition and interfered in the country's internal affairs, demanded revision of the mission's mandate. In late December the OSCE and Belarus agreed to scrap the AMG and establish in its place a new OSCE Office in Minsk to assist "in further promoting institution building," to help with economic and environmental activities, and to monitor events.

In February 2003 the OSCE Parliamentary Assembly restored Belarus's membership, but in the same month the European Parliament adopted a resolution that criticized the Lukashenka regime for an adverse human rights climate and "indiscriminate attacks" on opponents, journalists, human rights activists, and others. In March 2005 the European Parliament labeled the government a dictatorship. In October 2006 it awarded Alyaksandr Milinkevich its Sakharov Prize for Freedom of Thought, the most prestigious human rights award in the European Union (EU). Two months later, the outgoing EU president, Finnish Prime Minister Matti Vanhanen, described Belarus as "a black hole on the face of European democracy." (For the most recent EU-Belarus developments, see Current issues, below.)

At about the same time, the United States imposed tightened sanctions directed primarily against Belarus's state-owned petrochemical company. The dispute escalated into a diplomatic spat in March 2008, when Washington and Minsk recalled their respective ambassadors and Lukashenka ordered the downsizing of U.S. embassy staff. On April 30 the government labeled ten U.S. diplomats personae non gratae and ordered them to leave Belarus. Accusations were also made that the United States had set up a spy ring in Belarus.

Current issues. According to an OSCE report on the March 2006 presidential election, the "abuse of state power intensified and fundamental freedom and civil and political rights were violated as a matter of routine." In the weeks following the election, between 500 and 1,000 protesters were arrested, with at least 400 being quickly convicted and sentenced for their activities. One consequence was a decision by the EU to impose travel bans on some 40 Belarusan officials. In November 2007 the UN General Assembly's Social, Humanitarian, and Cultural Committee, voting 86–32 (with 76 abstentions), approved a resolution requesting the General Assembly to state its concern regarding the Belarusan government's human rights violations, including arbitrary detentions, lack of due process, and closed political trials.

On March 25, 2008, Minsk police broke up an unauthorized gathering of some 3,000 demonstrators who had come together to mark the 90th anniversary of the declaration of an independent republic of Belarus. Some of the demonstrators were beaten, 88 were detained, and 70 were quickly given short jail terms or fined. On March 27 state security personnel arrested some 30 journalists ostensibly as part of an ongoing investigation. The Belarusan Journalists' Association charged, however, that the arrests were in retaliation for reports about the March 25 demonstration.

As 2008 progressed, the Lukashenka regime appeared more interested in currying favor with the EU, which in turn appeared more willing to reduce Belarus's isolation despite continuing concerns over human rights abuses. Most observers attributed these changes by both Belarus and the EU to a cooling of relations with a more assertive Russia. Moscow, for its part, appeared particularly miffed at Minsk for its failure to recognize the self-declared independence of the Russian-backed Georgian breakaway regions of South Ossetia and Abkhazia.

An October 2008 decision by the EU foreign ministers to suspend the 2006 travel restrictions against all but five of the affected Belarusan officials drew the criticism of most Belarusan opposition leaders. Then in February 2009 Javier Solana, EU high commissioner for foreign policy and security, became the highest ranking EU official ever to visit Belarus. Solana met with opposition leaders and representatives of civil society as well as President Lukashenka. The visit was taken as a sign that the EU's proposed Eastern Partnership (EaP) program with Armenia, Azerbaijan, Georgia, Moldova, and Ukraine might be expanded to include Belarus, a move that the EU member states then approved in March. A month later, the European Parliament endorsed a resolution that was described as representing "pragmatic engagement" with Minsk, which was in turn expected to introduce electoral reforms and relax restrictions on associations, the right of assembly, and the media. On April 26–28 Lukashenka, taking advantage of the suspension of the travel ban, visited Italy, where he met with Prime Minister Silvio Berlusconi and Pope Benedict XVI. It was Lukashenka's first visit to Western Europe in a decade.

On the economic front, in October 2008 Minsk approached the IMF for a stabilization loan, which was approved in the amount of nearly $2.5 billion in January 2009. In return for the loan, which was intended to help offset the negative consequences of the international economic recession, the Lukashenka government agreed to devalue the ruble, tighten fiscal policy, and undertake various measures to liberalize the economy. Even so, growth for 2009 was expected to drop to 1–2 percent after averaging nearly 10 percent a year in 2004–2008. In April, commenting on his country's relations with Russia, President Lukashenka said that no one in his government opposed closer integration but that he wanted "more clarity and transparency in our relations." He added that he did not understand Russia's decision to close its markets to Belarusan exports. Regarding accusations by the Russian media that he had "sold himself" to the West, Lukashenka noted that the EU now accounts for over 50 percent of Belarusan trade, necessitating closer dealings.

POLITICAL PARTIES

As in post-Soviet Russia, top Belarusan officials have generally avoided direct involvement in political party activity while in office, despite (or because of) their earlier associations with the Soviet-era Communist Party. Unlike in Russia, however, where party politics has often dominated proceedings in the powerful State Duma, under the disputed 1996 constitution the less powerful Belarusan legislature has been controlled by Lukashenka loyalists rather than by party caucuses.

In Belarus political and personal support for the head of state and prime minister has often coalesced in broad alliances of assorted parties, nongovernmental organizations, and interest groups. The Popular Movement of Belarus (*Narodni Dirzhenie Belarusi*—NDB), organized in 1992, embraced both the hard-line left and the pan-Slavic right on a joint platform advocating maintenance of close relations with Russia and resistance to Western capitalist encroachment. It supported the conservative prime minister, Vyacheslau Kebich, against the reformist head of state, Stanislau Shushkevich, in 1992–1993, as well as Kebich's unsuccessful presidential candidacy in 1994. During the Lukashenka era the NDB gave way to the Belarusan Popular Patriotic Union—BPPU (*Belaruski Narodna Patryatychny Sayuz*), which was established in September 1998 by some 20 government-supportive parties and groups, many of them former NDB participants. Founding members of the BPPU included the Communist Party of Belarus (KPB) and the Liberal Democratic Party of Belarus (LDPB).

Opposition policy coordination has often been lacking despite unifying efforts spearheaded by the largest parties: the Belarusan Popular Front "Revival" (NFB-A), the United Civic Party of Belarus (AHPB), and the Belarusan Social Democratic Party "People's Assembly" (BSDP-NH). In January 1997, in the wake of the disputed November 1996 constitutional referendum, the NFB-A, the AHPB, the Agrarian Party of Belarus (APB), the Party of Communists of Belarus (PKB), and other anti-Lukashenka organizations established a "shadow" cabinet, the Public Coalition Government–National Economic Council (PCG-NEC), under Genadz KARPENKA, that in October 1997 was reorganized as a National Executive Committee (NEC). After Karpenka's death in April 1999, the NEC was led by his former deputy, Mechyslaw Hryb.

In late January 1999 a Congress of Democratic Forces of Belarus met in an attempt to consolidate the opposition. This led in mid-February to the establishment of a Coordinating Council of Democratic Forces (CCDF), which had already existed since at least 1997 on a more informal basis. "Founding" groups were the NFB-A, the AHPB, the BSDP- NH, the Association of Nongovernmental Organizations, the Charter-97 (*Khartiya-97*) human rights group, and the Congress of Democratic Trade Unions; other participants have included the Belarusan Labor Party (BPP), the Belarusan Social Democratic Assembly (BSDH), and the Belarusan Women's Party "Hope" (BPZ-N). Chaired by the AHPB's Anatol LYABEDZKA, the CCDF called for a boycott of the November 2000 legislative election, but the effort was only partially successful. In August 2001, with the presidential election approaching, the CCDF suspended its activities, but it was revived in January 2002.

Under a presidential decree issued in January 1999, all 27 officially registered political parties, all public associations, and all trade unions were required to reregister under stricter standards regarding, for example, national membership. Only 17 parties met the new criteria when the reregistration period expired in August; most of the others had not applied, while the Party of Common Sense (*Partya Zdarovaga Sensu*—PZS) and the Belarusan Christian Democratic Unity (*Belaruskaya Khrystsiyanska Demakratychnaya Zluchnasts*—BKDZ) were denied official recognition for technical reasons. In 1998 half a dozen other small parties had already been disbanded by order of the Supreme Court.

In mid-2003, looking toward the parliamentary balloting scheduled for October 2004, opposition elements began organizing alliances. The largest of these, encompassing the AHPB, the BSDH, the NFB-A, the PKB, and the BPP as well as a number of smaller parties and nongovernmental organizations, adopted the name Popular Coalition "Five-Plus" (*"V-Plyus"*) in early November. Despite ideological and other differences, the participating organizations endorsed a uniform "Five Steps to a Better Life" platform that emphasized economic and social dignity for everyone, job creation and worker protection, self-governance and equality before the law, budget transparency and an end to official corruption, and "mutually beneficial friendly relations with all neighboring and EU countries." At the same time, a European Coalition "Free Belarus" (*"Svabodnaya Belarus"*) was taking shape under the leadership of the BSDP-NH, the BPZ-N, the Charter-97, a number of youth groups, and assorted public associations. On September 13, 2004, shortly after Lukashenka announced that a referendum on repealing the two-term limit for presidents would be included on the October ballot, the two alliances plus the Young Belarus (*Maladaya Belarus*) youth coalition and the Republic (*Respublika*) faction of opposition deputies in the House of Representatives announced that they would campaign jointly against the change under the slogan "Say No! to Lukashenka."

The only major party boycotting the October 2004 election and referendum was the Conservative-Christian Party of the Belarusan Popular Front (KKhP-NFB), but none of the opposition parties, and none of the few *Respublika* incumbents who were permitted to contest the election, won seats. Only 12 were won by declared party candidates, all of them government supportive.

In November 2004 most opposition leaders agreed that they would select a single candidate for the 2006 presidential contest. Late in the same month they organized a Permanent Council of Democratic Forces that included the original Five-Plus members (technically minus the BPP, which had been deregistered by the government), the Free Belarus parties, the Belarusan Green Party, the Public Youth Organization "Civil Forum," the Young Front, and various nongovernmental organizations. At a National Congress of Democratic Forces, held October 1–2, 2005, in Minsk, this "unified opposition" endorsed the unaffiliated Alyaksandr Milinkevich as their 2006 presidential candidate by a narrow margin over the AHPB's Lyabedzka. Shortly after the congress the PKB's chair, Syarhey KALYAKIN, assumed leadership of the Political Council of the **United Democratic Forces** (UDF), which was later led by Milinkevich. At a second national congress, held May 26–27, 2007, however, the opposition voted to replace Milinkevich with a four-person rotating leadership from the AHPB, NFB-A, PKB, and Alyaksey Kazulin's Belarusan Social Democratic Party "Assembly" (BSDP-H). The following August, those four parties, the BPZ, the BPZ-N (liquidated by the government in September 2007), a founding committee for a new Labor Party, and Pavel Sevyarynets's as-yet-unregistered Belarusan Christian Democracy agreed to work together in preparation for contesting the next legislative election. Milinkevich, heading the unregistered Movement for Freedom, and several other leaders declined to participate. They argued that the opposition should press the government for democratic reforms before agreeing to take part in the vote. According to the Central Election Commission, 56 of 263 candidates for the September 2008 election were UDF members, but none won.

At present, parties must have offices in Minsk and at least four regional capitals. In addition, official party offices are prohibited from being located in residences or residential complexes, which has placed a considerable burden on some of the cash-strapped opposition groups. As of January 2006, prior to the most recent presidential election, there were 17 registered parties in Belarus.

Leading Progovernment Parties:

Agrarian Party of Belarus (*Agrarnaya Partya Belarusi*—APB). The APB was founded in 1994 in opposition to the restoration of peasant land ownership in Belarus, as advocated by the Belarusan Peasants'

Party (*Belaruskaya Syalarskaya Partya*—BSP), which was deregistered in 1999. The APB returned 33 candidates in the 1995 legislative balloting and later attracted 13 "unaffiliated" deputies to its group in the Supreme Council, of which party chief Semyon SHARETSKY was elected chair.

The party ruptured in 1996, with Sharetsky and his supporters disavowing the results of the November constitutional referendum. Sharetsky continued as the chair of the opposition's reconstituted Supreme Council but, fearing for his safety, ultimately fled to Lithuania in July 2000. On March 31 a congress of the APB had pledged its loyalty to President Lukashenka. In 2004 the APB won 3 House seats but in 2008 it held only one.

In March 2008, at the party's fifth convention, Mikhail Rusy, a member of the House of Representatives and a former minister of agriculture, was unanimously elected chair. His predecessor, Mikhail SHYMANSKI, chose not to seek reelection.

Leader: Mikhail RUSY (Chair).

Communist Party of Belarus (*Kommunisticheskaya Partya Belarusi*—KPB). The Soviet-era Communist Party had originated as a regional committee of the Russian Social Democratic Labor Party (formed in 1904). Established as the ruling party of the Soviet Socialist Republic of Byelorussia in 1920, the party suffered heavily during the terror of the 1930s and thereafter remained wholly subservient to Moscow. The conservative Minsk leadership miscalculated, however, when it backed the abortive coup by hard-liners in Moscow in August 1991. In the immediate aftermath, many party officials were ousted, independence from the USSR was declared, and the party itself was suspended, its property being nationalized. The party was subsequently legalized as the Party of Communists of Belarus (PKB, below) and backed the ouster of reformist head of state Stanislau Shushkevich in January 1994. Embracing the concept of multipartyism, the PKB contested the mid-1994 presidential elections in its own right by supporting Vasil NOVIKAU, who placed last of six in the first round with only 4.6 percent of the vote. Nevertheless, the Communists' strong organization enabled them to win 42 seats in the 1995 Assembly election, a plurality that later rose to 44 because of accessions by independents.

Tensions in the party were revealed in September 1996 when First Secretary Syarhey Kalyakin was publicly criticized by several other party leaders for aligning with opponents of President Lukashenka. The factionalization culminated with a pro-Lukashenka group headed by Viktar CHYKIN readopting the KPB designation at a congress in November, while Kalyakin's supporters continued to operate as the PKB. The KPB subsequently endorsed the president's push for reintegration with Russia, and in 1998 Chykin was chosen as leader of the BPPU. Nevertheless, at its August 2000 congress the party paradoxically claimed to be part of the opposition. At the October 2004 general election the KPB won eight seats in the House of Representatives.

In March 2005 Tatsyana Holubeva was named chair, the previous party chief, Valery ZAKHARCHENKA, having died in July 2004. In the 2008 election for the House of Representatives, the KPB won six seats.

Leader: Tatsyana HOLUBEVA (Tatyana GOLUBEVA, Chair).

Liberal Democratic Party of Belarus (*Liberalna-Demakratychnaya Partya Belarusi*—LDPB). Registered in March 1994 under the leadership of Vasil KRYVENKA, the LDPB views itself as the Belarusan counterpart of Russia's ultranationalist Liberal Democratic Party and therefore advocates close links with Russia. It subsequently allied with pro-Lukashenka forces as a founding member of the BPPU. By March 1999, however, responding in part to what it considered unfair official tactics against its candidates for local soviets, the party distanced itself from other presidential supporters, claiming that democratic elections were impossible.

The LDPB initially refused to participate in the opposition boycott of the October 2000 House of Representatives election, but it withdrew from the voting before the second round because of alleged electoral violations. It subsequently announced that it would rejoin the opposition Coordinating Council. Reelected chair of the party at a congress in August 2000, Syarhey Haydukevich described himself as Lukashenka's "very decent rival" for the presidency in 2001, and in late November he announced plans to create a center-left electoral bloc, the New Belarus Unity, to support his candidacy. In the September 2001 poll he officially won only 2.5 percent of the vote.

At an extraordinary convention in September 2003, supporters of the party's deputy chair, Aleh MARKEVICH, voted their opposition to Haydukevich's leadership, but the Ministry of Justice subsequently ruled in the chair's favor. Other efforts to wrest the party from Haydukevich in 2005 and 2006 also failed.

The LDPB won one House seat in October 2004. In 2006 Haydukevich again sought the presidency and finished third, with 3.5 percent of the vote. A party congress in February 2008 reelected Haydukevich and again designated him as the party's candidate for president in the next election. In September 2008 none of the party's eight candidates for the House won.

Leader: Syarhey HAYDUKEVICH (Sergei GAIDUKEVICH, Chair).

Leading Opposition Organizations:

Belarusan Popular Front "Revival" (*Narodni Front Belarusi "Adradzhennie"*—NFB-A). The NFB-A was launched in June 1989 at a conference in Vilnius, Lithuania, of pro-independence groups. They chose as their leader Zyanon Paznyak, an archaeologist who in 1988 had published evidence of mass graves found at Kurapaty, near Minsk, on the site of a detention/execution camp established on Stalin's orders in 1937. In the April 1990 Supreme Soviet elections in Belarus, the NFB-A won only 34 of 360 seats against an entrenched Communist hierarchy. In August 1991 it welcomed the declaration of independence. The NFB-A defines itself as a broad popular movement with a "closely integrated" political party, the **Party of the Belarusan Popular Front,** which was established in 1993.

The issuance of a warrant for his arrest after an antigovernment demonstration in April 1996 caused NFB-A Chair Paznyak to flee abroad. Granted asylum by the United States, he was reelected chair in absentia at the party congress in June 1997 and later agreed to serve as the NFB-A standard-bearer in the controversial symbolic presidential election in May 1999. (In 1994 he had won 13.9 percent of the first-round presidential vote.)

A major split in the party occurred following a July 31–August 1, 1999, congress, at which neither Paznyak nor his principal challenger, Deputy Chair Vintsuk Vyachorka, received sufficient votes to resolve a leadership dispute occasioned by Paznyak's continuing exile and his alleged authoritarianism. With another leadership vote expected in October, the party ruptured; at a congress on September 26, 1999, the Paznyak supporters "renamed" the party the Conservative-Christian Party of the BNF (KKhP-NFB, below). A month later the rump NFB-A elected Vyachorka as its new chair.

In 2005 Vyachorka was one of the early supporters behind Alyaksandr Milinkevich's quest for the presidency in 2006. In January 2007, however, the party distanced itself from Milinkevich's effort to establish a United For Freedom opposition movement. A party congress in December 2007 elected Lyavon Barshchewski as successor to Vyachorka.

Leaders: Lyavon BARSHCHEWSKI (Chair); Vintsuk VYACHORKA (First Deputy Chair); Ales MIKHALEVICH, Yuryy HUBAREVICH, Viktar IVASHKEVICH, and Alyaksey YANUKEVICH (Deputy Chairs).

Belarusan Social Democratic Assembly (*Belaruskaya Satsyal-Demakratychnaya Hramada*—BSDH). The BSDH held its founding congress in February 1998 under the leadership of former Supreme Council chair Stanislau Shushkevich, who called for restoration of the 1994 constitution. The new formation attracted many members of the Belarusan National Party (*Belaruskaya Natsyanalnaya Partya*—BNP), including its chair, Anatol ASTAPENKA. (The BNP was not reregistered in 1999.)

In 2003 the United Social Democratic Party (USDP), led by Alyaksey Karol, merged into the BSDH. Karol's party had been denied registration following its August 2002 formation through merger of a faction of the Belarusan Women's Party "Hope" (BPZ-N, below) and the unregistered Belarusan Social Democratic Party (*Belaruskaya Satsyal-Demakratychnaya Partya*—BSDP). The BSDP, dating from December 2001, had been formed by Karol and other defectors from the BSDP-NH (below).

In April 2005, over Shushkevich's objection, elements of the BSDH, including Alyaksey Karol's supporters, voted to merge with the BSDP-NH (see BSDP-H, below). Shushkevich's supporters ultimately retained control of the party, however, and he continued his efforts to seek the presidency in 2006. One of four candidates selected to vie for the endorsement of the unified opposition, Shushkevich withdrew before the secret balloting by the National Congress of Democratic Forces in October 2005.

First Deputy Leader Syarhey SKRABETS announced in March 2009 that he was leaving the party because of differences involving the next national presidential election and "international issues."

Leader: Stanislau SHUSHKEVICH (Chair).

Belarusan Social Democratic Party "People's Assembly" (*Belaruskaya Satsyal-Demakratychnaya Partya "Narodnaya Hramada"*—BSDP-NH). The original BSDP was founded in 1991 as a latter-day revival of the Revolutionary *Hramada* Party (founded in 1902), which spearheaded the early movement for the creation of a Belarusan state but was outlawed following declaration of the Soviet Socialist Republic in January 1919. The revived party participated initially in the opposition NFB-A, but it contested the 1995 legislative election in its own right, winning two seats and later increasing its parliamentary group to 15 members. In 1996 it absorbed the Party of Popular Accord (PPA), which dated from 1992, although some members of the latter rejected the merger and went on to form the Social Democratic Party of Popular Accord (see Other Parties, below).

The party organized unsanctioned anti-Lukashenka rallies in 1996–1999, for which party leader Mikalay Statkevich was jailed repeatedly. Tactical differences with other opposition parties emerged in 2000, with Statkevich opposing the boycott of the October legislative election and advocating nomination of a single opposition candidate—one acceptable to Communists and nationalists alike—to run against Lukashenka in 2001.

In December 2004, seeking to bring together the country's moderately leftist parties, Statkevich led formation of an organizational committee for a "United Social Democratic Party of Belarus." At the same time, opposition was growing within the BSDP-NH to his allegedly autocratic style and his strong support for Belarusan EU membership. Dissident elements led by Anatol Lyawkovich attempted to expel Statkevich and key supporters, who responded in kind. In January 2005 the Ministry of Justice ruled in favor of the dissidents, who formally retained title to the party, but Statkevich's supporters claimed control of the party at a February 2005 congress. In April the anti-Statkevich elements of the BSDP-NH, having been joined by elements of the BSDH, voted to drop "People's" from their party's name, as demanded by the Justice Ministry, and become the Belarusan Social Democratic Party "Assembly" (BSDP-H, below). Statkevich's BSDP-NH remained unregistered.

In May 2005 Statkevich was convicted of participating in illegal protests against the conduct of the October 2004 election and was sentenced to three years' detention and community service. He was transferred to house arrest in November 2005, but the conviction meant that he was ineligible to run for president in 2006. He was released in May 2007. The party held a "founding" conference in November 2007, but as of April 2009 the government had not permitted it to register.

Into early 2008 Statkevich remained aloof from the decision of other UDF participants to present a joint candidate list for the September 2008 parliamentary election, arguing that the opposition should pressure the government for democratic reforms before agreeing to participate in the poll. Statkevich himself was not permitted to contest the election, in part because of his "criminal" record. The party has participated in an informal pro-EU "European Coalition," which also includes the unregistered Party of Freedom and Progress (below) and the Young Front.

Leaders: Mikalay (Mikola) STATKEVICH (Chair); Alyaksandr ARASTOVICH, Alaksey HAWRUTSIKAW, and Syarhey KULINICH (Deputy Chairs).

Belarusan Social Democratic Party "Assembly" (*Belaruskaya Satsyal-Demokratychnaya Party "Hramada"*—BSDP-H). Formation of the BSDP-H, by factions of the BSDH and the BSDP-NH, was announced in early 2005. Initially led by Anatol Lyawkovich, the party initially retained "People's" as part of its title but soon dropped it to comply with a Justice Ministry decision. Alyaksandr Kazulin, a former rector of Belarusan State University who had recently joined the BSDP-NH, assumed leadership of the party in April 2005. He had hoped to accomplish a full merger of the BSDP-NH and BSDH but was ultimately opposed by BSDH leader Stanislau Shushkevich as well as by BSDP-NH leader Mikalay Statkevich, who had originally supported the idea. Kazulin's supporters included former BSDH deputy chair Mechyslaw Hryb. In September 2005 the Permanent Council of Democratic Forces rejected Kazulin and his party's participation in the October National Congress of Democratic Forces, the BSDH having accused him of playing a divisive role.

Kazulin was officially registered as a presidential candidate in February 2006. He finished last in the four-way contest, with only 2.2 percent of the vote. In July he was convicted of disturbing the peace and other charges and sentenced to five and a half years in prison. In October, hoping to draw international attention to Belarus and demanding that the results of the presidential election be declared invalid, he began a hunger strike that lasted more than seven weeks.

Meeting in December 2006 in Ukraine, the leaders of the BSDP-H, the BPZ-N, and the PKB agreed to form the Union of Left Parties (ULP),with Kazulin as honorary chair. Named as his deputies were the chairs of the three founding parties plus Alyaksandr Bukhvostau of the liquidated Belarusan Labor Party. The Justice Ministry has refused to register the ULP. Having mended fences with most of the other leading opposition parties, which had made Kazulin's release from prison a key demand, the BSDP-H now actively participates in the United Democratic Forces.

In April 2008 Mechyslaw Hryb was elected secretary general of the party. In early August, however, a party congress replaced Kazulin as chair by the former acting chair, Anatol Lyawkovich. Kazulin's supporters, including former deputy chair Ihar RYNKEVICH and members of the For In-Party Democratization faction, described the move as a "staff coup," while Kazulin, shortly after his release from prison on August 16, described it as a "pure betrayal."

Leader: Anatol LYAWKOVICH (Anatoly LEVKOVICH, Chair).

Conservative-Christian Party of the Belarusan Popular Front (*Konservativnaya Khrystsiyanska Partiya–Narodni Front Belarusi*—KKhP-NFB). The strongly nationalist KKhP emerged from a congress held in September 1999 by supporters of Zyanon Paznyak within the NFB-A. It was registered as a party in February 2000. The party staunchly opposed the Lukashenka regime and union with Russia and has attacked OSCE efforts to mediate between the opposition and the government as lending legitimacy to the present regime. The KKhP was a principal organizer of an "All-Belarusan Congress" that met on July 29, 2000, in Minsk and condemned any agreements that would result in a loss of Belarusan independence and sovereignty. Paznyak was reelected party leader in December 2003.

The party boycotted the October 2004 election, the only significant opposition party to do so. As expected, Paznyak later stated that he would run for president in 2006, but in January 2006, from exile in the United States, he endorsed conducting a "people's vote." The plan called for anti-Lukashenka voters to cast fake ballots, leave with the real ballots, and submit the latter to an independent commission as evidence of opposition to the incumbent. The party's seventh congress, held in May 2006, overwhelmingly endorsed Paznyak's reelection as chair.

Leaders: Zyanon PAZNYAK (Chair, in exile), Yuras BELENKI (Acting Chair).

Movement for Freedom (*Rukh "Za Svabodu"*). Organized by former opposition presidential candidate Alyaksandr Milinkevich, the anti-Lukashenka Movement for Freedom is a Western-oriented association, not a political party per se. In December 2007 the Supreme Court upheld the decision of the Justice Ministry to deny registration to the organization on the grounds that its most recent founding conference had failed to obtain a permit from local authorities and had therefore violated the Mass Events Law. The government had previously rejected the movement's application in July, citing an inadequate charter. In August 2008 the Supreme Court backed the decision of the Ministry of Justice not to register Milinkevich's movement., but registration was finally granted in mid-December 2008. Milinkevich has already stated that he plans to seek the presidency again at the next election.

Leaders: Alyaksandr MILINKEVICH (Chair), Viktar KARNYAYENKA and Yuryy HUBAREVICH (Deputy Chairs).

Party of Communists of Belarus (*Partya Kamunistau Belaruskaya*—PKB). The PKB originated as the refashioned Soviet-era Communist Party, but in November 1996 a major split occurred over whether to support President Lukashenka. As a result, the Lukashenka supporters became the Communist Party of Belarus (KPB, above), with the opposition faction retaining the PKB designation.

While not opposed to closer ties with Russia, the PKB rejects Soviet-style rule and loss of Belarusan sovereignty. It has called for democratic reforms, including reduction of presidential powers and transfer of authority to soviets. It condemned the 2000 House of Representatives election as a "farce," despite polling better than expected. Party leader Syarhey Kalyakin was initially a presidential candidate in 2001 but withdrew in a show of unity behind Vladimir Goncharik.

Looking toward the 2006 presidential race, Kalyakin was again named as the party's preferred candidate. Following the October 2005 decision of the unified opposition to support Alyaksandr Milinkevich, Kalyakin became a leading figure in the Milinkevich campaign.

In July 2006 a Communist congress was held ostensibly to reunite the PKB and KPB, but Kalyakin described the effort as a government-backed attempt to liquidate his party. Two months later the Justice Department asked the Supreme Court to deregister the PKB because it no longer met membership requirements. In September 2007 the Supreme Court ordered the party to suspend its activities for six months because of registration violations.

Leaders: Syarhey KALYAKIN (Chair), Alena SKRYHAN (Central Committee Secretary).

United Civic Party of Belarus (*Abyadnanaya Hramadzyanskaya Partya Belarusi*—AHPB). The promarket AHPB was founded in October 1995 as a merger of several groups—most notably the professional/technocratic United Democratic Party of Belarus (*Abyadnanaya Demakratychnaya Partya Belarusi*—ADPB), led by Alyaksandr DABRAVOLSKY—that had contested the first round of that year's legislative balloting in an alliance called the Civic Accord Bloc. The leader of the merged party, Stanislau BAHDANKEVICH, had recently been dismissed as president of the National Bank after disagreeing with President Lukashenka's pro-Russian policies. (The ADPB itself had been formed in 1990 as a merger of three prodemocracy groupings, including Communists for Perestroika and the Democratic Party, and had initially been a constituent of the opposition NFB-A.) In the 1995 legislative balloting the AHPB won nine seats in its own right, forming the Civic Action parliamentary group, which rose to 18 members with the adhesion of "unaffiliated" deputies. It subsequently continued its anti-Lukashenka stance, organizing demonstrations against the government and boycotting the 2000 legislative election.

Anatol Lyabedzka was reelected party chair in May 2004 and was subsequently endorsed as the party's 2006 presidential candidate. At the opposition's National Congress in October 2005, he finished second to Alyaksandr Milinkevich, 391 votes to 399, in balloting to select the unified opposition's candidate. Lyabedzka was again reelected chair in May 2006. Although the government has not yet actively pursued his prosecution for allegedly libeling President Lukashenka in 2004, criminal cases against him remain open.

A party activist, Andrey KLIMAW, was sentenced to two years in prison in August 2007 for using the party's Web site to promote the overthrow of the government. His sentence was commuted in February 2008. Klimaw had been imprisoned in 1998–2002 for embezzlement and forgery—politically motivated charges, according to his supporters—and had been detained from June 2005 until December 2006 for organizing an antigovernment march in March 2005.

Leaders: Anatol LYABEDZKA (Anatol LEBEDKO, Chair); Stanislaw BAHDANKEVICH, Alyksandr DABRAVOLSKI, Valyantsina PALEVIKOVA, and Yaraslau RAMANCHUK (Deputy Chairs).

Other Registered Parties:

Belarusan Green Party (*Belaruskaya Partya "Zyaleny"*—BPZ). The BPZ was established in 1994 by ecological activists. It supported the Five-Plus alliance in 2004 and the presidential candidacy of Alyaksandr Milinkevich in 2006. Both the BPZ and another environmental party, the **Belarusan Ecological Party of the Greens,** were subsequently threatened with liquidation by the Justice Department for failing to meet all requirements of the political party law. In 2008 the BPZ participated in the UDF's selection of a joint candidate list for the next parliamentary election.

Leader: Aleh NOVIKAU (Chair).

Other recently active parties include the pro-Lukashenka **Belarusan Patriotic Party** (*Belaruskaya Patryatychny Partya*—BPP); the pro-Lukashenka **Belarusan Social-Sporting Party** (*Belaruskaya Satsyalna-Sportyunaya Partya*—BSSP), which lost its one House seat in 2004; the **Republican Party** (*Respublikanskaya Partya*—RP), founded in 1994; the pro-Lukashenka **Republican Party of Labor and Justice** (*Respublikanskaya Partya Pratsy i Spravyadlivasti*—RPPS), founded in 1993; and the **Social Democratic Party of Popular Accord** (*Satsyal Demakratychnaya Partya Narodnay Zgody*—SDPNZ), formed in 1997 by former members of the Party of Popular Accord who had opposed the latter party's 1996 absorption by the BSDP-NH.

Unregistered and Deregistered Parties:

Belarusan Christian Democracy (*Belaruskaja Hhristsijanskaja Demakratija*—BHD). In September 2007 youth leader Pavel Sevyarynets was named one of five coleaders at a founding conference for the BHD association, which intended ultimately to organize a political party of the same name. (The BHD mirrors the name of a pre–World War II party.) Meanwhile, the BHD was included among the opposition organizations supporting a joint UDF candidate list for the October 2008 lower house election. In March 2009 the BHD applied for registration as a party.

Leader: Pavel SEVYARYNETS (Coleader).

Party of Freedom and Progress (*Partya Svabody i Pragrzsu*—PSP). The government has repeatedly denied registration to the PSP, which held its initial congress in November 2003 under the leadership of Uladzimir Navasyad, who at that time was a member of the House of Representatives. Its fourth and most recent "founding congress" was planned for April 2009.

Leader: Uladzimir NAVASYAD (Chair).

The **Belarusan Labor Party** (*Belaruskaya Partya Pratsy*—BPP), established in 1993 by Alyaksandr BUKHVOSTAU, a leader of the country's independent trade union movement, had its registration canceled by the Supreme Court in August 2004 over technical irregularities. The social-democratic Belarusan Women's Party "Hope" (*Belaruskaya Partya Zhanchyn "Nadzeya"*—BPZ-N), founded in 1994, was liquidated in September 2007. A former leader, Valyantsina Palevikova, is currently a deputy chair of the AHPB. After the October 2004 election the BPZ-N, then led by Valyantsina MATUSEVICH, had joined the BSDP-NH in seeking to unify the country's social-democratic parties. At the party's fifth congress, held in September 2006, Matusevich stepped down as party chair and was succeeded by Alena YASKOVA.

LEGISLATURE

The controversial amended constitution of November 1996 provided for abolishing the unicameral Supreme Council and establishing a two-chamber **National Assembly** (*Natsionalnoye Sobrani*) consisting of a House of Representatives and a Council of the Republic. Although the referendum approving the constitution was declared "nonbinding" by the Constitutional Court and denounced as illegitimate by some opposition parties, a majority of the Supreme Council members on November 28 voted to abolish the Council and appointed themselves to the new House of Representatives. For a time, an anti-Lukashenka rump continued to meet as the Supreme Council, arguing that it remained the legitimate legislature.

Council of the Republic (*Soviet Respubliki*). The upper house has up to 64 members: 8 elected by local soviets from each of the country's 6 regions and the municipality of Minsk, plus 8 appointed by the president. The most recent elections occurred October 3–10, 2008, with 55 of the 56 elective seats being filled. An additional seat was filled by presidential appointment. As of April 2009 the membership was 58, including the Council president and deputy president.

President: Boris BATURA.

House of Representatives (*Palata Predstaviteley*). The constitutional revisions of November 1996 provided for direct election of a 110-member lower house for a four-year term. More than 100 members of the former Supreme Council met for the first time as the new House shortly after voting to abolish the Supreme Council on November 28, 1996.

The most recent election took place on September 28, 2008. The vast majority of the winning candidates were Lukashenka loyalists who had run without party affiliation. The Central Electoral Commission described 7 of the winners as party candidates: Communist Party of Belarus, 6; Agrarian Party of Belarus, 1.

Speaker: Uladzimir ANDREYCHANKA.

CABINET

[as of September 15, 2009]

Prime Minister	Syarhey Sidorsky
First Deputy Prime Minister	Uladzimir Syamashka
Deputy Prime Ministers	Ivan Bambiza
	Viktar Bura
	Andriy Kobyakov
	Uladzimir Patupchyk
Ministers	
Agriculture and Food	Syamyon Shapira
Architecture and Construction	Alyaksandr Selyaznyou
Communications and Information Technology	Mikalay Pantsyaley
Culture	Pavel Latushka
Defense	Col. Gen. Leanid Maltsau
Economy	Mikalay Zaychanka
Education	Alyaksandr Radzkow
Emergency Situations	Col. Enver Baryyew
Energy	Alyaksandr Azyarets
Finance	Andrey Kharkovets
Foreign Affairs	Syarhey Martynaw
Forestry	Pyotr Syamashka
Health	Vasily Zharko
Housing and Municipal Services	Uladzimir Belakhvostau
Industry	Alyaksandr Radzevich
Information	Uladzimir Rusakevich
Interior	Anatol Kulyashow
Justice	Viktar Halavanov
Labor and Social Security	Uladzimir Patupchyk
Natural Resources and Environmental Protection	Uladzimir Tsalka
Revenue and Taxes	Hanna Dzyayko [f]
Sport and Tourism	Aleh Kachan
Trade	Valyantsin Chekanaw
Transportation and Communications	Ivan Shcherba

[f] = female

COMMUNICATIONS

Although media independence and the freedom to disseminate information are protected by the constitution and in law, the government continues to control electronic news transmission and newspaper distribution. Independent, opposition publications have been subjected to a variety of threats and pressures, including confiscation of printing equipment by tax authorities and allegations of libeling or defaming President Lukashenka and other officials. Journalists have been jailed and publications fined, leading the international Committee to Protect Journalists to rank Belarus among the ten "worst places to be a journalist."

In June 2008 the National Assembly passed a revised media law that further restricted media. Media regulations were extended to Web sites, and rules governing accreditation of journalists and registration of outlets were expanded.

Press. The following are published daily in Minsk in Belarusan, unless otherwise noted: *Sovetskaya Belorussiya* (Soviet Byelorussia, 430,000), government organ, in Russian; *Respublika* (Republic, 120,000), government organ, in Belarusan and Russian; *Vechernii Minsk* (Evening Minsk, 110,000), in Russian; *Narodnaya Hazeta* (People's Newspaper, 90,000), government organ, in Belarusan and Russian; *Zvyazda* (Star, 90,000), government organ; *Narodnaya Volya* (People's Will, 27,000), independent, in Belarusan and Russian. In addition to *Narodnaya Volya,* which has been repeatedly targeted by the government, leading opposition publications include *Belorusskaya Delovaya Gazeta* (Belarusan Business News).

News agencies. The domestic facility is the Belarus Information Agency (Belta, originally the Belarus Telegraphy Agency), headquartered in Minsk. The Belarusan Information Company (BelaPAN) also provides news and other services.

Broadcasting and computing. Broadcasting continues to be dominated by the National State Television and Radio Company, which operates all national television services Smaller, private stations broadcast in the larger cities. In 2003, transmission facilities previously used by major Russian TV channels were assigned by the government to regional usage.

The government is the only legal Internet service provider. As of 2008 there were 321 Internet users per 1,000 inhabitants.

INTERGOVERNMENTAL REPRESENTATION

Ambassador to the U.S.: (Vacant).

U.S. Ambassador to Belarus: (Vacant).

Permanent Representative to the UN: Andrei DAPKIUNAS.

IGO Memberships (Non-UN): CEI, CIS, Interpol, IOM, NAM, OSCE, PCA, WCO.

BELGIUM

Kingdom of Belgium
Koninkrijk België (Dutch)
Royaume de Belgique (French)
Königreich Belgien (German)

On November 25, 2009, King Albert accepted the resignation of Prime Minister Herman Van Rompuy, who had earlier been selected to be the first permanent president of the European Council. The king appointed former prime minister Yves Leterme of the Christian Democratic and Flemish party as prime minister on the same day. Leterme's new government was approved by the House of Representatives on November 27 by a vote of 82–53.

Political Status: Independence proclaimed October 4, 1830; monarchical constitution of 1831 most recently revised in 1970.

Area: 11,781 sq. mi. (30,513 sq. km.).

Population: 10,296,350 (2001C); 10,708,000 (2008E).

Major Urban Centers (2005E): BRUSSELS (urban area, 999,000), Antwerp (urban area, 457,000), Ghent (230,000), Charleroi (200,000), Liège (185,000), Bruges (117,000), Namur (106,000).

Official Languages: Dutch, French, German.

Monetary Unit: Euro (market rate December 1, 2009: 1 euro = $1.51US).

Sovereign: King ALBERT II; ascended the throne on August 9, 1993, following the death of his brother, King BAUDOUIN.

Heir to the Throne: Prince PHILIPPE, son of the king.

Prime Minister: *(See headnote.)* Herman VAN ROMPUY (Christian Democratic and Flemish); designated by the king to form a new government on December 28, 2008, and sworn in as head of an ongoing five-party cabinet two days later, succeeding Yves LETERME (Christian Democratic and Flemish), whose resignation had been accepted by the king on December 22.

THE COUNTRY

Wedged between France, Germany, and the Netherlands, densely populated Belgium lies at the crossroads of Western Europe. Its location has contributed to a history of ethnic diversity, as manifested by linguistic and cultural dualism between the Dutch-speaking north (Flanders) and the French-speaking south (Wallonia). The Flemings and Walloons constitute 58 percent and 31 percent of the total population, respectively, with 11 percent being effectively bilingual; most of the remainder are a small German-speaking minority located along the eastern border. In contrast to the linguistic division, 75 percent of the population is Roman Catholic, with small minorities of Jews, Protestants, and Muslims.

The economy is largely dominated by the service sector, which provides 74 percent of GDP and employs 73 percent of the nation's labor force. Belgium's industry, responsible for less than 24 percent of GDP, was traditionally concentrated in textiles, steel, and glass, but emphasis has shifted to production of machinery, fabricated metals, food, and chemicals. Agriculture occupies less than 2 percent of the labor force and accounts for only 1.4 percent of GDP, although it supplies three-quarters of food requirements. Unemployment has hovered around 8 percent since 2000.

Labor force participation rates have grown from 50 to 60 percent in recent decades but remain among the lowest in the industrialized world, with participation rates below one-third for those under the age of 25 and over the age of 55. Women constitute approximately 44 percent of the labor force. In government, women currently occupy 35.3 percent of the seats in the Chamber of Representatives and 38 percent of the seats in the Senate. Women hold the portfolios of 5 of 15 cabinet ministries, and 1 of 7 secretaries of state is female.

A substantial regional imbalance exists between the more modern, industrialized Flanders and the French-speaking Wallonia, home to older, declining enterprises. This disparity was accentuated by the move to a federal governmental structure in the early 1990s, despite government efforts to reduce the imbalance.

Moderate but steady economic growth prevailed during most of the two decades after World War II, but the annual increase in GDP fell to an average of less than 2 percent in the decade following the OPEC-induced "oil shock" of 1973–1974. Higher growth in the late 1980s was accompanied by a persistent 10 percent unemployment rate and was followed by recession, with unemployment rising to 12 percent in 1993. Growth of some 2 percent a year resumed in 1994–1995, and expansion continued at a solid rate throughout the rest of the decade.

GDP growth averaged 1 percent in 2001–2003, increasing to 2–3 percent annually in 2004–2007. Spiking oil prices, turmoil in global financial markets, and the political stalemate over forming a government after the June 2007 election contributed to a slowdown in growth to 1.2 percent in 2008. Other problematic issues included a sharp rise in inflation through 2008, an unemployment rate continuing to hover around 8 percent, and an aging population. GDP was projected to decline by as much as 2.5 percent in 2009.

GOVERNMENT AND POLITICS

Political background. After centuries of Spanish and Austrian rule and briefer periods of French administration, Belgium was incorporated into the Kingdom of the Netherlands by the Congress of Vienna in 1815. Independence was proclaimed on October 4, 1830, and Prince LEOPOLD of Saxe-Coburg was elected king in 1831, although Belgian autonomy was not formally recognized by the Netherlands until 1839. In the 20th century the country was subjected to German invasion and occupation during the two world wars.

Since World War II, Belgium has been governed by a series of administrations based on one or more of its three major political groups: Christian Democratic, Socialist, and Liberal. Beginning in the early 1960s, however, the traditional system was threatened by ethnic and linguistic antagonism between the Dutch- and French-speaking regions. By a series of constitutional amendments in 1970–1971, substantial central government powers were to be devolved to regional councils for Flanders, Wallonia, and Brussels (nominally bilingual but in fact largely French speaking), while German speakers also were recognized as forming a distinct cultural community.

Following up on the earlier constitutional revision, Belgium's major parties, after years of discord, agreed under the Egmont Pact of 1977 to establish a federal system based on Flanders, Wallonia, and Brussels. However, in August 1978 the Supreme Court ruled that certain aspects of the plan were unconstitutional, and on October 11 the government of Prime Minister Léo TINDEMANS was forced to resign. At the ensuing general election of December 17 the distribution of seats in the Chamber of Representatives remained virtually unchanged, and on April 3, 1979, a new center-left government was formed under Dr. Wilfried MARTENS of the Christian People's Party (*Christelijke Volkspartij*—CVP) that included five of the six participating parties in the outgoing government.

In early January 1980 Prime Minister Martens, bowing to militant Flemish pressure, announced the postponement of self-government for Brussels while committing his government to the establishment of regional bodies for Flanders and Wallonia. In response, representatives of the Democratic Front of French Speakers (*Front Démocratique des Francophones*—FDF) withdrew on January 16, leaving the government without the two-thirds majority needed for constitutional revision and forcing its resignation on April 9. Nonetheless, Martens succeeded in forming a "grand coalition" on May 18 that included representatives of the two Liberal parties—the Flemish Liberals and Democrats (*Vlaamse Liberalen en Demokraten*—VLD) and the Liberal Reformation Party (*Parti Réformateur Libéral*—PRL)—as well as the CVP; the Christian Social Party (*Parti Social Chrétien*—PSC); and two Socialist formations, the *Parti Socialiste* (PS) and the *Socialistische Partij* (SP). Requisite constitutional majorities thus having been restored, the government was able to secure parliamentary approval during July and August 1980 to establish councils for the Dutch- and French-speaking regions.

Alleviation of the constitutional crisis brought to the fore a number of long-simmering differences on economic and defense policies. As a result, the government resigned on October 4, 1980, and 12 days later Martens announced the formation of a center-left coalition (CVP, PSC, SP, and PS). On April 8, 1981, Martens stepped down as prime minister in favor of the CVP's Mark EYSKENS, but a general election on November 8 yielded little in the way of party realignment in either legislative house. Eventually, on December 17, Martens secured approval for a center-right administration that included both Liberal parties (the VLD and PRL) while excluding the Socialists. Having introduced an economic austerity program, the coalition marginally increased its majority in parliamentary balloting on October 13, 1985, a new government (Martens's sixth) being sworn in on November 28.

In the late 1980s linguistic controversy erupted again over specifics of regionalization. Particularly controversial was the status of a group of villages in southeastern Flanders (Les Fourons/Voeren) whose French-speaking majority doggedly resisted the authority of the surrounding Dutch-speaking region. Amid fierce interparty discord, Martens was again forced to resign on October 15, 1987. In the ensuing election of December 13 the Christian parties lost ground, and the Socialists achieved a plurality for the first time since 1936. A 144-day impasse followed, with Martens responding on May 6, 1988, to the king's request to form a new five-party government that encompassed the Christian parties, the Socialists, and the Flemish nationalist People's Union (*Volksunie*—VU), while again excluding the Liberals.

In September 1991 the VU ministers withdrew over an arms export controversy. As a result, Prime Minister Martens stepped down for the seventh time, precipitating a general election on November 24, at which the four remaining coalition parties all lost seats without collateral gains by the opposition Liberal parties. Against a groundswell of anti-immigration sentiment, the main victor was the militant Flemish Bloc (*Vlaams Blok*—VB), which overtook the less extreme VU; two environmental parties also registered substantial gains. Another lengthy interregnum ensued before the CVP's Jean-Luc DEHAENE succeeded in forming a four-party Christian-Socialist administration (Belgium's 35th since World War II) on March 7, 1992.

Although the Dehaene government lacked the two-thirds parliamentary majority required to enact constitutional amendments, the St. Michael Accords of September 29, 1992, enabled it to win a historic vote on February 6, 1993; by dint of support from the VU and the Ecologists, the government mustered the necessary Chamber majority for a constitutional amendment transforming Belgium from a unitary state into a federation of its linguistic communities. The decision was formally confirmed by the Chamber on July 14.

On July 31, 1993, a reign that had spanned more than four decades came to an end with the death of King BAUDOUIN. His brother, Prince ALBERT of Liège, was crowned on August 9.

Belgium was saved from having to find a new prime minister when the Franco-German nomination of Dehaene as European Union (EU) Commission president was vetoed by Britain in June 1994 on the grounds that he was too federalist. Meanwhile, the ruling coalition had been weakened by the Agusta-Dassault scandal, involving the PS's alleged receipt of some $3.2 million in kickbacks for expediting the award of military contracts to Italian and French firms in 1988–1989. The allegations later extended to the Flemish socialists (SP), notably to former prime minister Guy SPITAELS and to Willy CLAES, who had been economics minister in 1988 and who was appointed North American Treaty Organization (NATO) secretary general in September 1994. Accordingly, the Agusta affair figured prominently in the campaign for early general elections held on May 21, 1995, the first under the new federal constitution. The government parties again secured about 50 percent of the vote among them, and Dehaene was reappointed prime minister on June 23 at the head of the same four-party coalition (CVP, PSC, PS, and SP), although with some personnel changes. The government subsequently faced severe difficulties in attempting to meet the criteria for participation in the EU's Economic and Monetary Union (EMU), and related job and spending cuts precipitated widespread public-sector protest strikes in 1995 and 1996.

In October 1995 the Belgian lower house voted to lift the parliamentary immunity of Claes, so that he could be brought to trial on Agusta-Dassault affair charges. As a consequence, he resigned as NATO secretary general, and in December 1998 he and a dozen other individuals were convicted of corruption, with Claes receiving a suspended three-year sentence.

Not surprisingly, the 1999 national electoral campaign largely focused on high-level corruption and law enforcement concerns as well as on the merits of further devolution to Flanders, Wallonia, and Brussels. In late May, however, attention dramatically shifted with the revelation that for two months the government had delayed notifying the public that a factory had distributed animal feed contaminated by the chemical dioxin, a suspected carcinogen. Amid considerable confusion about the extent of the contamination and what steps were needed to ensure a safe food supply, the Dehaene government was voted out of office in balloting on June 10.

In balloting on June 13, 1999, Prime Minister Dehaene's CVP lost 7 of the 29 lower house seats it had won in 1995, permitting the VLD, with 23 seats, to fashion a 94-seat, six-party majority coalition with the PS, SP, PRL, and two environmental parties, the Ecologists (*Ecologistes Confédérés pour l'Organisation de Luttes Originales*—ECOLO) and Live Differently (*Anders Gaan Leven*—Agalev). The new prime minister, VLD leader Guy VERHOFSTADT, became Belgium's first Liberal prime minister in more than a century. His "blue-red-green" coalition cut broadly across ideological lines, bringing together the rightist Liberals, the Socialists, and the Greens, while excluding the Christian Democrats from the national government for the first time in 40 years. He and his cabinet were sworn in on July 12.

Although the new government survived its first year in office without encountering a new crisis, the electorate remained fractured along ethnic, linguistic, regional, and ideological lines. At the October 2000 local elections most of the government parties fared well, but the far-right VB captured the headlines by achieving larger gains, including winning one-third of the votes in Antwerp, the country's second-largest city. Often compared ideologically to Austria's Freedom Party, the VB had campaigned on a separatist and anti-immigrant platform at a time when Belgians were increasingly concerned about the steady influx of aliens.

Prime Minister Verhofstadt's refusal to send troops to support U.S.-UK actions in Iraq apparently contributed to the success of the VLD and its coalition partners in the May 18, 2003, general elections. Unemployment, national security, and taxes also played prominent roles in the campaign, although the leading parties differed only slightly in their approach to those issues. Following the elections, Verhofstadt remained in office as head of another coalition government that comprised the VLD, PS, the Socialist Party–Different (*Socialistische Parti—Anders*—SP.A), the Reformist Movement (*Mouvement Reformateur*—MR), and SPIRIT (*Sociaal, Progressief, International, Regionalistisch, Integraal-democratisch en Toekomstgericht*—SPIRIT).

Prime Minister Verhofstadt's party, running under the banner of "Open VLD," fell to third place in Flanders in the June 10, 2007, legislative balloting and finished in fourth place overall in the Chamber of Representatives. The leading vote getter was the electoral coalition of the Christian Democratic and Flemish (*Christen-Democratisch en Vlaams*—CD&V), as the CVP had been renamed in 2001, and the conservative New Flemish Alliance (*Nieuw-Vlaamse Alliante*—N-VA), which had been established in 2001 as a partial successor to the VU. Negotiations on a new government proved difficult, and Verhofstadt led a transition government from June to December and an interim government (authorized solely to handle pressing budget matters) from December to March 2008 (see Current issues, below, for details). With some analysts questioning the long-term viability of Belgium's political structure, the CD&V's leader, Yves LETERME, finally formed a five-party government (CD&V, MR, Open VLD, CDH, and PS) on March 20, 2008. Following ten months of complicated political developments (including the N-VA's decision in September to withdraw its support for the government), Leterme resigned in December (see Current issues, below, for details). He was succeeded by the CD&V's Herman VAN ROMPUY, whose government (sworn in on December 23) comprised the same five parties as Leterme's administration.

Constitution and government. Belgium's constitution of 1831 (as amended) provides for a constitutional monarchy with a parliamentary form of government (voting being compulsory). Executive power is theoretically exercised by the monarch, who is head of state, but actual power rests with the prime minister and the cabinet, both responsible to a bicameral legislature. There are 15 members in the cabinet, 7 from each of the two language communities plus the prime minister. Formally, the cabinet is called the Council of Ministers, and the cabinet plus the secretaries of state form the executive branch, termed the Council of Government. The judicial system, based on the French model, is headed by the Court of Cassation, which has the power to review any judicial decision; it may not, however, pass on the constitutionality of legislation, for which advisory opinions may be sought from a special legal body, the Council of State. There also are assize courts, courts of appeal, and numerous courts of first instance and justices of the peace.

Male primogeniture was eliminated from the law of succession in 1991.

The ethnic-linguistic reorganization finally enacted in 1993 involved the creation of three self-governing regions—Dutch-speaking Flanders, French-speaking Wallonia, and bilingual Brussels—each with directly elected assemblies of 124 (including 6 from Brussels), 75, and 75 members, respectively. There also are cultural councils for the Dutch-speaking and French-speaking communities (the former being identical with the Flanders assembly and the latter being indirectly constituted by the Wallonia assembly members and 19 members of the Brussels assembly), as well as a 25-member directly elected cultural council for the small German-speaking minority in eastern Belgium. The regional governments of Flanders, Wallonia, and Brussels are responsible to the respective assemblies, exercising broad social and economic powers; only defense, foreign relations, and monetary policy are reserved to the federal government, the size of which has been reduced as responsibilities have been devolved to the regions. Also reduced, as of the 1995 election, was the size of the central legislature (see Legislature, below). Local administration is based on ten regions and nearly 600 communes.

Foreign relations. Originally one of Europe's neutral powers, Belgium has been a leader in international cooperation since World War II. It was a founding member of the United Nations (UN), NATO, the Benelux Union, and all of the major West European regional organizations. Its only overseas possession, the former Belgian Congo, became independent in 1960, while the Belgian-administered UN Trust Territory of Ruanda-Urundi became independent in 1962 as the two states of Rwanda and Burundi.

Belgium contributed to the U.S.-led multinational coalition that liberated Kuwait in early 1991. In September 1991 Belgian troops were sent to Zaire (now the Democratic Republic of the Congo) to oversee the evacuation of Belgian nationals from that strife-torn state, the action marking an effective end to Belgium's close relationship with its former colony. Belgian nationals also came under serious threat when Rwanda descended into bloody anarchy in April 1994. (In 2007 a former Rwandan army major was convicted in the killing of 10 Belgian peacekeepers in 1994.)

The cornerstone of Belgium's external policy remains active participation in the EU. Having initially expressed some misgivings about the rapid reunification of Germany in 1990, Belgian political leaders agreed for the most part that European integration was the best means of preventing any revived threat from Belgium's powerful eastern neighbor. Belgium was a prime proponent of the Schengen accord providing for the abolition of border controls between certain EU members, as inaugurated in March 1995, although in November 2000 the Verhofstadt government, responding to anti-immigrant sentiment and a rising number of asylum cases, announced that it favored tighter restrictions. (In the spring of 2005 the Belgian Parliament approved the proposed new EU constitution.)

In late 2001 the Verhofstadt government hailed a 35-country agreement on international diamond certification as a necessary step toward ending the illegal trafficking in so-called conflict, or "blood," diamonds. A UN report had criticized the Antwerp diamond market, the largest in the world, for "lax controls and regulations" that permitted gem transactions to finance wars in Africa. By the time of the 2001 agreement, Belgium had already signed certification agreements with Angola, Botswana, the Democratic Republic of the Congo, Guinea, and Sierra Leone.

The Verhofstadt administration sided with many other European governments in opposing the U.S./UK-led invasion of Iraq in 2003. However, relations with Washington subsequently improved when Belgium agreed to send fighter planes to Afghanistan to help provide security for elections.

Belgium irritated both the United States and Israel with its laws that allowed individuals to file cases in Belgian courts for crimes against humanity by individuals outside of Belgian jurisdiction. Palestinians and Lebanese living in Belgium brought a case against Israeli Prime Minister Ariel Sharon in 2001, and cases were brought against U.S. President George W. Bush and British Prime Minister Tony Blair in 2003 in connection with the war in Iraq. The cases were all ultimately dismissed, and the law was amended in 2004 to make such charges more difficult to bring. Under the revised law, complainants must show a direct link between themselves and the alleged crime. In addition, if the alleged crimes occurred outside Belgium and the accused are not Belgian, the government can refer the cases to the International Criminal Court in the Netherlands.

In 2006 Belgium agreed to help NATO financially but not with more troops as worldwide requests for more peacekeepers increased.

Current issues. The aging workforce and rising pension costs have received sustained attention over the past decade. In 2005 the government proposed raising the minimum retirement age from 58 to 60, starting in 2008, and limiting certain long-standing retirement benefits. In response, hundreds of thousands of workers initiated the first general strike in 12 years.

The issue of employment remained at the forefront even as the Belgian economy strengthened during the early years of Prime Minister Verhofstadt's second term. In 2006 the government eased restrictions on immigrants from Eastern Europe in an effort to fill jobs. Later that year, thousands of Belgians demonstrated in Brussels in what was reported to be a show of solidarity with some 4,000 auto workers facing layoffs by Volkswagen. A seven-week strike ended in early 2007 after Volkswagen guaranteed that 2,000 jobs would be saved.

The campaign for the June 2007 legislative elections raised divisive questions about constitutional reform, including proposed continued devolution of economic policy, which Walloon interests feared would mean a diminution of subsidies from the federal level. Other matters receiving attention included employment and retirement policies, energy supplies, health care reform, and the generosity of state welfare system.

Following the June 2007 legislative balloting Prime Minister Verhofstadt accepted responsibility for the poor showing of the Open VLD and resigned his premiership. However, he agreed to stay on in a caretaker capacity while negotiations for a new government got underway. Initially, CD&V leader Yves Leterme was expected to form a cross-language, Christian-Liberal Coalition of the CD&V/N-VA, CDH, Open VLD, and MR. However, by mid-August the negotiations had collapsed over cross-community disagreement on constitutional reform. (Leterme had campaigned on a platform of greater regional autonomy on tax and employment policies. Other divisive issues, in addition to proposed increased economic policy control for regional governments, included the proposed separation of the Halle-Vilvorde area from the Brussels Capital region. Such a move would have meant that French-speaking Belgians in the area would have had only Flemish parties from which to choose in elections.) Leterme began another series of exploratory discussions in September, but in December he once again declared failure. Since the caretaker administration held no effective power to make or change policy, Verhofstadt in December formed an emergency interim government of limited powers, which received a vote of confidence in the legislature on December 23. (Leterme assumed the post of deputy prime minister with responsibility for the budget, which was the primary focus of the interim government.)

The protracted negotiations on a permanent government in the second half of 2007 and early 2008 represented a major crisis, some analysts wondering whether Belgium might dissolve as a single nation over the matter. (The nine months of talks before installation of a permanent government shattered the previous record of 148 days [following the 1988 election].) The five-party coalition of March 2008 appeared to at least temporarily prevent such a development, the new Leterme government agreeing to greater regional autonomy over industrial policy, housing, and agriculture. However, other contentious matters, such as proposed regional self-rule on tax and employment matters, were left for subsequent discussion.

Prime Minister Leterme offered his resignation on July 14, 2008, when he described the disagreement in his government over proposed additional devolution of power to Flanders as "irreconciliable." (The CD&V strongly endorsed devolution, which was opposed equally as vehemently by the French-speaking parties, representing Walloon interests.) The king, however, declined to accept Leterme's resignation, asking the government to concentrate on other matters while a new three-member mediation committee attempted to come up with fresh proposals regarding devolution.

In early autumn 2008, Fortis, a major financial services group in all three Benelux countries, found itself awash in toxic assets. After the Dutch government decided to nationalize Fortis's operations in the Netherlands, the Belgian government took temporary control of Fortis Belgium and decided to sell a major portion of it to BNP Paribus of France. Fortis shareholders sued to stop the sale, and the Court of Appeals agreed to block it until the shareholders had the opportunity to vote on the matter in February 2009. On December 18 a letter from the head of the Court of Cassation to the president of the Chamber of Representatives alleged that Leterme's office had intervened with the Court of Appeals with the intention of preventing the decision that was ultimately rendered. Calls for Leterme's resignation were swift, and on December 19 Leterme submitted his resignation. The king accepted the resignation on December 23 but asked the government to stay on as a caretaker until a new government could be formed.

Upon his inauguration on December 30, 2008, new prime minister Herman Van Rompuy faced significant constitutional difficulties over the language divide and major policy challenges from fallout over the global financial crisis. However, his prospects were bolstered by the fact that he was respected by Flemish and French speakers and, as a former finance and budget minister, appeared to have as good a set of policy credentials as any politician in the country to manage the economic difficulties. He was able to put the Fortis question behind him in April 2009 when shareholders approved a 75 percent sale of Fortis holdings to BNP Paribus, with the remaining 25 percent staying under control of the Belgian government. The June 7, 2009, balloting for the EU Parliament showed no signs of shifting voter sentiments as the major parties held the seats they occupied before the election, with only the newly formed List Dedecker party gaining one seat at the expense of the Flemish Interest.

POLITICAL PARTIES

Belgium's leading parties were long divided into French- and Dutch-speaking sections, which tended to subscribe to common programs for general elections. Beginning in the late 1960s the cleavages became more pronounced, leading eventually to formal separation as the country moved to a federal structure. Collaterally, the dominance of the three principal groupings (Christian Democratic, Socialist, and Liberal) has been eroded somewhat by an increase in the strength of numerous smaller ethnic and special interest groups.

Government Parties:

Christian Democratic and Flemish (*Christen-Democratisch en Vlaams*—CD&V). The CD&V was called the Christian People's Party (*Christelijke Volkspartij*—CVP) until September 2001. The CVP and the PSC (see CDH, below) were joint heirs to the former Catholic Party (*Parti Catholique Belge*—PCB), which traced its origins to 1830 and traditionally upheld the position of the Catholic Church in Belgium. The PCB included representatives of commercial and manufacturing interests as well as of the working classes. Following World War II the PCB was reshaped into two wings, the CVP and PSC, which remained closely linked until the 1960s. Both Christian parties are now nondenominational and, with substantial representation from the Catholic Trade Union Federation (the country's largest labor organization), favor a variety of social and economic reforms. Consistently the plurality parliamentary party until 1999, the CVP provided the prime minister in a long series of coalitions, with Wilfried Martens serving for 13 years until 1992. Following its 1993 congress, the CVP committed itself to "refocus on renewal." Its lower house vote share of 17.2 percent and its 29 seats gave it plurality status in May 1995, but it fell to 22 seats and a 14.1 percent share in June 1999, as a consequence of which Prime Minister Jean-Luc Dehaene resigned. The party's current designation was formally adopted at a party congress on September 29, 2001.

The CD&V defined itself as a moderate alternative to the Verhofstadt government in the 2003 general elections. However, the party's very public stance favoring Turkey's accession to the EU apparently cost it some vote share. Following the 2003 losses, Yves Leterme was named party chair, succeeding Stefaan DE CLERCK. In the June 2004 balloting for the European Parliament, the CD&V allied itself with the N-VA (below).

The CD&V did very well in the 2004 regional Flemish elections, reestablishing itself as the largest party in Flanders. Following the election, Leterme resigned as party chair to become the Flemish prime minister. The CD&V repeated its performance in the 2006 local elections, once again in alliance with the N-VA.

In the June 2007 parliamentary elections the CD&V/N-VA alliance won the largest vote share, 18.5 percent, and the most seats, 30. In the nine months of protracted negotiations to form a new government, party leader and prospective prime minister Leterme twice resigned his *formateur* duties, being unable to bridge the gulf between Flemish and Francophone parties over constitutional changes that would bolster Flemish regional governmental authority. Successful negotiations concluded in February 2008, and Leterme was sworn in as prime minister on March 20 as head of a five-party government. However, he resigned the following December (see Political background and Current issues, above for details) and was succeeded as prime minister by the CD&V's Herman Van Rompuy.

Leaders: Herman VAN ROMPUY (Prime Minister), Steven VANACKERE (Deputy Prime Minister), Marianne THYSSEN (Chair), Kris PEETERS (Minister-President Flemish Community and Flanders Region).

Reformist Movement (*Mouvement Reformateur*—MR). The MR was formed in March 2002 through the merger of the Liberal Reformation Party (*Parti Réformateur Libéral*—PRL), the Democratic Front of French Speakers (*Front Démocratique des Francophones*—FDF), and the Citizens' Movement for Change (*Mouvement des Citoyens pour le Changement*—MCC).

The PRL had been formed in May 1979 under the leadership of Jean GOL by merger of the Party of Walloon Reform and Liberty (*Parti des Réformes et de la Liberté en Wallonie*—PRLW) and the Brussels-based Liberal Party (*Parti Libéral*—PL). Electorally weaker than its Flemish counterpart, the PRL was in government in 1981–1988 but slipped to a vote share of 8.2 percent in the 1991 Chamber elections. In 1995 it campaigned with the FDF on a joint list that captured 10.3 percent of the Chamber vote and 18 seats. PRL leader Gol (a former deputy premier) died in September 1995 and was succeeded by Louis MICHEL.

The FDF, a formation of French-speaking Brussels interest groups founded in 1964, sought to preserve the French character of the Belgian capital. It participated in a center-left coalition in 1977–1980 to help enact the Egmont Pact on devolution, under which Brussels became a separate (bilingual) region, but it made little progress in the 1980s. The FDF won only a 1.5 percent vote share in the 1991 balloting.

Disavowing the role of a traditional party, the MCC was organized by Gérard DEPREZ in March 1998, after his January expulsion from the PSC (below). The MCC was formally constituted the following October.

At the 1999 general election the PRL again joined with the FDF as well as with the recently formed MCC. The joint federation list won 18 lower house seats on a 10.1 percent vote share, and the PRL then elected to join the Verhofstadt government. In December 2000 the PRL president, Daniel DUCARME, announced his intention to start the MR, which in 2002 became the country's second largest Liberal party. The MR had a respectable showing in the 2003 balloting (24 seats and an 11.4 percent vote share) and ran second to the PS in the 2004 provincial and 2006 local elections. In the 2007 Chamber balloting the MR won the second largest number of seats, 23, with a 12.5 percent vote share.

Leader: Didier REYNDERS (President of the Party and Deputy Prime Minister).

Socialist Party (*Parti Socialiste*—PS). Until formal separation in October 1978 the PS was the dominant French-speaking wing of the historic Belgian Socialist Party (*Parti Socialiste Belge*—PSB), an evolutionary Marxist grouping organized in 1885 as the *Parti Ouvrier Belge*. Both the PS and the SP had trade union roots and are essentially pragmatic in outlook, concentrating on social welfare and industrial democracy issues within a free-enterprise context.

Becoming the largest lower house bloc in the 1987 elections (for the first time since 1936), the two Socialist parties joined a center-left coalition but lost ground in the 1991 balloting, the PS vote slipping to 15.6 percent. It remained in the federal government and also headed the regional governments of Wallonia and Brussels, but from 1993 it was badly compromised by defense-related bribery scandals, which necessitated the resignations of several senior PS figures. It won a lower house vote share of 11.9 percent (for 21 seats) in 1995. Despite retaining only 19 seats on 10.2 percent of the vote in 1999, it remained in the new VLD-led government. The PS won 11 seats in the upper house and 25 seats in the lower house in the 2003 elections and secured the largest vote and seat shares in Wallonia in the 2004 provincial elections. By 2005, however, corruption scandals touched the party again, forcing the resignation of Jean-Claude VAN CAUWENBERGHE as Minister-President of the Walloon Region. In the 2006 municipal elections the PS lost ground but held its first-place standing in the Walloon region. Still suffering from the scandals, the PS vote share fell by more than 2 points, to 10.9 percent, and its seats by 5, to 20, in the 2007 Chamber balloting.

Leaders: Elio DI RUPO (President), Christie MORREALE (Vice President), Laurette ONKELINX (Deputy Prime Minister), Véronique Paulus DE CHÂTELET (Governor Brussels-Capital Region), Charles PICQUÉ (Minister-President Brussels Capital Region), Rudy DEMOTTE (Minister-President French Community and Walloon Region), Karl-Heinz LAMBERTS (Minister-President German Community).

Flemish Liberals and Democrats (*Vlaamse Liberalen en Demokraten*—VLD). In 1961 Belgium's traditional Liberal Party changed its name to the Party for Freedom and Progress (*Partij voor Vrijheid en Vooruitgang*—PVV), its Flemish wing becoming autonomous in 1970. Having participated in various coalitions in the 1970s, both the PVV and its Walloon counterpart were in government with the CVP and PSC in 1981–1988. They were regarded as occupying the coalition's right wing, in part because of their reluctance to accept federalization. In the 1991 Chamber balloting the PVV increased its vote share to 11.9 percent but remained in opposition. In November 1992 it opted for the VLD designation, to which it appended "Citizens' Party" (*Partij van de Burger*).

A smaller-than-anticipated rise to 13.1 percent of the Chamber vote (for 21 seats) in 1995 prompted the resignation of Guy Verhofstadt as party president. However, in June 1997 he was reelected as party president after only one round of voting, and he completed his comeback by being named prime minister after the June 1999 election, at which the VLD led all parties with 14.3 percent of the Chamber vote and 23 seats.

During the 2003 election campaign, the VLD continued to emphasize deregulation and tax reduction, while arguing that new EU legislation should demonstrate it would not diminish the purchasing power of European citizens or have a negative impact on employment.

In 2004 the VLD did poorly in regional elections, falling from second to third place among Flemish political parties.

In 2006 a major rift developed between the VLD and its coalition partner the Socialist Party (PS) over a parole case involving Justice Minister Laurette Onkelinx, a member of the PS. Ultimately, the two groups resolved their differences. Later that year, further tensions within the VLD resulted in the expulsion of conservative member Jean-Marie Dedecker, who vowed to form a new right-wing party before the next federal elections and founded List Dedecker (see below). In local elections of October 8, 2006, the VLD had a weaker showing than expected, particularly in Flemish areas, with Verhofstadt calling the results "disappointing." Gains made by the right-wing Flemish Interest (VB) cost the VLD some representation. In an effort to stem the loss of support, the VLD contested the June 2007 parliamentary elections under the banner of Open VLD after absorbing two smaller parties—Alive and Liberal Appeal. The alliance failed to prevent losses as the Open VLD received 11.8 percent of the vote, down from 15.4 percent the VLD alone won in 2003, resulting in 18 seats, 7 fewer than in 2003.

Leaders: Bart SOMERS (President), Guy VERHOFSTADT (Former Prime Minister), Karel DE GUCHT (Deputy Prime Minister).

Alive (*Vivre Intensement vers l'Avenir de Notre*—VIVANT). Charging that the traditional Belgian parties had not addressed the problems of average workers transitioning from an industry-based to a service-based economy, VIVANT won 2.1 percent of the lower house vote in 1999 but declined to 1 percent in 2003. The party also did poorly in regional elections in 2004. In the 2006 local elections Alive polled well in the Brussels region. In March 2007 it was absorbed into Open VLD.

Leaders: Roland DUCHATELET (Former President), Joseph MEYER (Former Political Coordinator).

Democratic Humanist Center (*Centre Démocrate Humaniste*—CDH). This party was originally called the Christian Social Party (*Parti Social Chrétien*—PSC), the French-speaking (Walloon) counterpart of the CVP. (The PSC and the CVP established autonomy in the late 1960s and formally separated in 1972.) The substantially smaller PSC was subsequently a junior partner in coalitions headed by the CVP, its vote share falling to 7.8 percent in the 1991 national balloting and 7.7 percent of the Chamber vote (for 12 seats) in 1995. At the 1999 election the PSC saw its vote share drop to 5.9 percent (10 seats) despite efforts to redefine itself as a "party-movement" with a broader focus on mediating between civil society and the state. In May 2002 a PSC congress agreed to adopt the CDH rubric. The name change apparently reflected a desire to emphasize the party's support for social welfare and high levels of government intervention in the economy as well as a "Christian ethic" to guide public and private actions. In the 2006 local elections the CDH made a strong comeback in French regions. It won two seats in the 2007 balloting for the Chamber of Representatives on a vote share of 6.1 percent.

Leaders: Joëlle MILQUET (President of the Party and Deputy Prime Minister), Andre ANTOINE (First Vice President), Melchior WATHELET (Second Vice President).

Opposition Parties:

Flemish Interest (*Vlaams Belang*—VB). This grouping was formally known as the Flemish Bloc (*Vlaams Blok*—VB), which contested the election of December 1978 as an alliance of the National Flemish Party (*Vlaamse Nationale Partij*—VNP) and the Flemish People's Party (*Vlaamse Volkspartij*—VVP). The right-wing VB was formally constituted as a unified party in May 1979. Capitalizing on an upsurge in anti-immigrant sentiment, it increased its lower house representation sixfold (to 12) in 1991, with a 6.6 percent vote share, ahead of the more moderate People's Union (VU; see N-VA, above). In the 1994 local elections the VB won a 29 percent plurality in Antwerp but was excluded from the mayorship by the other parties. Its share of the Chamber vote in 1995 was 7.8 percent, for 11 seats, rising to 9.9 percent and 15 seats in 1999. In the October 2000 local elections the VB made additional gains, prompting the Flemish *De Morgen* paper to comment, "One in three Antwerp citizens believes in fear, intolerance, unadulterated racism, and law and order."

The party became increasingly nationalistic in the 2003 election campaign, decrying the "Islamization of Europe" and calling for independence for the Flemish part of Belgium. After the Flemish Bloc won 18 seats in the Chamber vote, the Supreme Court upheld a lower court's decision that the bloc's policies violated antiracist laws. Consequently, the bloc disbanded in November and reformed as Flemish Interest, but only after running a vigorous campaign in the June 2004 balloting for the European Parliament and winning the second highest vote share among all Belgian parties. Under the Flemish Interest banner, the VB held its position in the 2006 municipal elections and again in the 2007 parliamentary balloting, recording a 12 percent vote share. However, other parties continued to exclude Flemish Interest from government as an extension of the "*cordon sanitaire*" that had been applied to the Flemish Bloc. (Karel DILLON, the founder and honorary president of the VB, died in April 2007.)

Leaders: Bruno VALKENIERS (President), Filip DEWINTER, Geof ANNEMANS (Political Secretary).

Socialist Party–Different (*Socialistische Parti—Anders*—SP.A). Originally known as the Socialist Party (*Socialistische Partij*—SP), this grouping was until October 1978 the Dutch-speaking wing of the historic Belgian Socialist Party. Until 2008 it had participated in all coalitions involving its French-speaking counterpart while becoming markedly less supportive of state ownership than the PS. It slipped to a 12 percent vote share in the 1991 national balloting and won 12.6 percent (for 20 lower house seats) in May 1995. The SP also was heavily implicated in the Agusta bribery scandal, its former chair, Frank VANDENBROUCKE, becoming the most senior ministerial casualty when he was obliged to resign as deputy prime minister and foreign minister in March 1995. Party Chair Louis TOBBACK, who had been named deputy prime minister and interior minister in April 1998, resigned in September after a Nigerian was killed in custody while resisting forcible deportation.

At the June 1999 balloting the SP won only 14 Chamber seats on 9.6 percent of the vote but was able to negotiate a role in the VLD-led coalition government that was formed in July. The SP appended the term *Anders* to its name in August 2001 and then also adopted the additional alternative designation "Social Progressive Alternative" (*Sociaal Progressief Alternatief*).

Positioning itself as a prolabor and environmentally friendly party, the SP.A (which also vigorously opposed the U.S.-led invasion of Iraq) ran in coalition with SPIRIT (see Flemish Progressives, below) in the 2003 general election. The SP.A did very well, increasing its share of the national vote from 9.4 to 14.9 percent and its seats from 14 to 23. As a result, the SP.A continued as part of the VLD-led government.

Although the SP.A gained votes and seats in the 2004 regional elections for the Flemish Parliament, the party performed below expectations. In 2005 party president Steve STEVAERT resigned to become governor of Limburg; he was succeeded for a brief period by Caroline Gennez until the election of Johan VANDE LANOTTE in October, 2005. Vande Lanotte led the party into the June 2007 federal elections and stirred controversy when he raised doubts about whether the 1915 killing of Armenians by the Turks was genocide, as the Belgian Parliament had declared, with the support of the SP.A forerunner SP, in a 1998 resolution. The SP.A again aligned with SPIRIT for the 2007 federal election, the alliance losing much of what had been gained in the 2003 federal balloting by securing only 10.3 percent of the vote and 14 seats. On June 11, 2007, the day after the balloting, Vande Lanotte resigned as party president and was replaced by Gennez.

Leaders: Caroline GENNEZ (President), Dirk VAN DER MAELEN (Vice President), Alain ANDRÉ (National Secretary).

Social Liberal Party (*Sociaal-Liberale Partij*—SLP). The SLP is the rubric adopted in late 2008 by the party known since April 2008 as the Flemish Progressives (*Vlaams Progressieven*—VP) and before that as SPIRIT (*Sociaal, Progressief, International, Regionalistisch, Integraal-democratisch en Toekomstgericht*—SPIRIT). The "Social, Progressive, International, Regionalist, Integrally Democratic and Forward-Looking" SPIRIT was established in November 2001 following the demise of the People's Union (VU). It represented the merger of the VU's progressive "Group of the Future" (*Toekomstgroep*) with the VU's 1999 electoral partner, the left-leaning Complete Democracy for the 21st Century (*Integrale Democratie voor de 21ste Eeuw*—ID21), which dated from 1998. A number of key members of the VU's "middle group" also joined the SPIRIT, which adopted "Free Flemish, European, Global Democrats" as a descriptive and vowed to reject participation in politically expedient alliances. The new party claimed two senators and four Chamber deputies as members.

Following its successful coalition in the 2003 general elections with the SP.A, the SPIRIT joined the new cabinet at the secretary of state level. In the 2006 local elections and the 2007 legislative elections, SPIRIT again ran in coalition with the SP.A, finding mixed results in 2006 and disappointing results in 2007. (None of the alliance's successful Chamber candidates came from SPIRIT, which claimed one senator.)

Leaders: Geert LAMBERT (President), Els VAN WEERT (Vice President).

Ecologists (*Ecologistes Confédérés pour l'Organisation de Luttes Originales*—ECOLO). Formed in 1978, the Walloon-based ECOLO, which takes a libertarian approach to environmentalism, won 5 Chamber seats in 1985, 2 of which were lost in 1987. It recovered strongly in 1991, capturing 10 lower house seats and a 5.1 percent vote share, which slipped to 4 percent and 6 seats in 1995. In June 1999 the party advanced to 7.4 percent and 11 seats, thereafter joining the new VLD-led government. However, it was dropped from the government following its disappointing performance in the 2003 general election. ECOLO suffered a small setback in the 2006 local elections but rebounded in the 2007 federal balloting, winning a 5.1 percent vote share, up 2 points over 2003, and 8 seats, 4 more than in 2003.

Leaders: Isabelle DURANT, Jean-Michael JAVAUX, and Claude BROUIR (Federal Secretaries).

New Flemish Alliance (*Nieuw-Vlaamse Alliantie*—N-VA). The N-VA was established in mid-October 2001 by the largest, most conservative faction of the recently defunct People's Union (*Volksunie*—VU). Also known as the Flemish Free Democrats (*Vlaamse Vrije Democraten*), the nationalist VU had been founded in 1954 and had championed an autonomous Flanders within a federal state. After steady electoral advance on a "socially progressive, tolerant, modern, and forward-looking platform," the VU first entered the government in 1977–1978 in a center-left coalition that enacted key stages of regional devolution under the Egmont Pact. This was regarded as insufficient by its militant wing, which later joined the Flemish Bloc (VB). The VU was again in government in 1988–1991 but was overtaken by the VB in the 1991 elections, when it slipped to 5.9 percent of the lower house vote. The VU secured 4.7 percent of the vote in 1995 and claimed five seats, but advanced to 5.6 percent and eight seats in a 1999 coalition with the ID21 (see Flemish Progressives, below). Intraparty ideological differences led to the VU's demise in the summer of 2001, shortly after it had been embarrassed by the forced resignation of Johan SAUWENS, interior minister of the Flemish regional government, because of his association with a pro-Nazi organization.

The N-VA's principal goal is formation of an independent Flanders republic. Regarded as the heir of the VU (but having rejected *Nieuwe Volksunie* as its name), the N-VA also attracted members of the VU's middle wing, while the more liberal "Future" wing subsequently joined the ID21 in establishing SPIRIT. Like its predecessor, the N-VA adamantly rejects the far-right posture of Flemish Interest and frames its argument for Flemish independence on the basis of international law and the principle of self-determination.

In the federal elections in 2003 the N-VA won only 5 percent of the vote and a single seat in the Chamber. In February 2004 the party formed an alliance with the CD&V and won six seats in the Flemish Parliament. In the 2006 local elections and the 2007 legislative elections, the N-VA joined forces with the CD&V. Although the N-VA declined to join the cabinet formed in March 2008 because the government program did not go far enough on questions of economic policy autonomy for Flanders, the party initially pledged to support the Leterme government. (The N-VA at that point claimed six members in the lower house and one senator.) However, frustrated over the lack of progress on the further devolution of powers to the regions, the N-VA withdrew its pledge of support for the government in September.

Leaders: Bart DE WEVER (Chair), Bart DE NIJN (Secretary).

List Dedecker (*Lijst Dedecker*). The List Dedecker was established in January 2007 by Jean-Marie Dedecker after he was expelled from the VLD in 2006. (Dedecker had fiercely campaigned against SP.A candidates in the recent municipal elections and had strongly [and very publicly] criticized the VLD's subsequent decision to form a coalition with the SP.A in the municipality of Ostend.) Dedecker initially sought a place in the pro-Flemish independence N-VA, but this threatened the N-VA alliance with the CD&V because the CD&V objected to Dedecker's membership. By early spring 2007 two Flemish Interest members of parliament had joined List Dedecker, and in May an SP.A senator joined the new party. List Dedecker contested the 2007 federal elections on a market-liberal platform of lower tax rates and reduced unemployment benefits along with a pro-Flemish independence stand favoring self-determination for the province and an end to the *cordon sanitaire* that excludes Flemish Interest from government. The 2007 federal elections proved a success for List Dedecker as the party won a 4.0 percent vote share and 5 Chamber seats, as well as 1 senate seat.

Leaders: Jean-Marie DEDECKER (President), Ivan SABBE (Secretary), Jurgen VERSTREPEN (Under-Secretary).

Green! (*Groen!*). ECOLO's Flemish counterpart, this party was formally known as Live Differently (*Anders Gaan Leven*—Agalev), which obtained 4 lower house seats in the 1985 balloting, 6 in 1987, and 7 in 1991, when its vote share was 4.9 percent. Agalev fell back to 4.4 percent of the Chamber vote (for 5 seats) in 1995. Loosely allied with the VLD and ECOLO, Agalev won 7 percent of the vote in 1999 and then joined the governing coalition. The new party name was adopted in November 2003, Agalev having won no seats in the May general election.

In 2003 the party also gave permission to local divisions to form alliances with other parties. In November 2003 the party replaced Dirk HOLEMANS as party leader with Vera Dua. In the 2006 local elections Green! fared well in Brussels. The party also improved in the 2007 parliamentary election, winning 4.0 percent of the vote and four Chamber seats.

Leaders: Mieke VOGELS (President), Wouter VAN BESIEN (Vice President).

National Front (*Front National*—FN). Inspired by the French party of the same name and based in the Walloon community, the right extremist FN was founded in 1983 on a platform of opposition to non-European immigration. It won one Chamber seat in 1991 with 1.1 percent of the vote and took two seats on 2.3 percent of the lower house vote in 1995. In 1999 it fell back to one seat and 1.5 percent of the vote. After the 2003 elections it held one Chamber seat and two senate seats. Party leader Daniel Féret was sentenced in 2006 to 250 hours of community service (helping immigrants) after he was found guilty of inciting racial hatred. The court also ruled he could not stand in elections for 10 years, and he lost his seat in parliament. Féret said he would consider seeking asylum in Russia. Despite these setbacks, the FN held its 2.0 percent vote share in the 2007 Chamber balloting, securing one seat.

Leader: Daniel HUYGENS (President).

Other Parties:

Belgium's smaller political parties include the nationalist **New Belgian Front** (*Front Nouveau de Belgique/Front Nieuw België*—FNB), established in 1997 by former FN member Marguerite BASTIEN and currently led by François-Xavier ROBERT. Among a number of Walloon regionalist parties is the **Rally Wallonia-France** (*Rassemblement Wallonie-France*—RWF), which was founded in November 1999 by the merger of three small parties supporting unification with France: the Walloon Rally (*Rassemblement Wallon*—RW); the Walloon Democratic Alliance (*Alliance Démocratique Wallonne*—ADW), a 1985 splinter from the RW; and the Walloon Movement for the Return to France (*Mouvement Wallon pour le Retour à la France*—MWRF). The RWF Brussels branch is the *Rassemblement Bruxelles-France* (RBF). The party leadership includes Claude THAYSE (President) and Paul-Henri GENDEBIEN (Founding President). Other small Walloon formations include the leftist **Walloon Party** (*Parti Wallon*—PW), which was founded by merger in 1985 and which won 0.2 percent of the lower house vote in 1999.

Parties representing the German-speaking community include the **Party of Belgian German-Speakers** (*Partei der Deutschsprächigen Belgier*—PDB), founded in 1971 and currently led by Guido BREUER. Parties of the left include the Wallonia-based **Communist Party** (*Parti Communiste*—PC), led by Pierre BEAUVOIS, and the Flanders-based **Communist Party** (*Kommunistische Partij Vlaanderen*—KP), led by Jaak PERQUY. Both trace their origins to the historic Belgian Communist Party (*Parti Communiste de Belgique/Kommunistische Partij van België*—PCB/KPB) founded in 1921. The Maoist **Belgian Party of Labor** (*Partij van de Arbeid van België/Parti du Travail de Belgique*—PvdA/PTB), led by Peter MERTENS, was established in 1979 in opposition to the Eurocommunist line of the PCB/KPB.

LEGISLATURE

The bicameral **Parliament** (*Federale Parlament/Parlement Fédérale*) consists of a Senate and a Chamber of Representatives, both elected for four-year terms and endowed with virtually equal powers. The king may dissolve either or both chambers on the advice of the prime minister.

Senate (*Senaat/Sénat*). The upper house consists of 71 members, of which 40 are directly elected (25 from Flanders, 15 from Wallonia), 21 are indirectly elected (10 each by the Flemish Council and the French Council, and 1 by the German Council), and 10 are appointed by the elected senators (6 Flemish and 4 Walloon). At least six of the Walloon senators must be legally resident in Brussels, as must at least one of the Flemish senators. In addition, the reigning monarch's children or Belgian heirs are senators by right from the age of 18, with voting rights from the age of 21. Following the election of June 10, 2007, the distribution of seats (with directly elected seats in parentheses) was as follows: the coalition of Christian Democratic and Flemish and the New Flemish Alliance, 14 (9); Reformist Movement, 11 (6); Open Flemish Liberals and Democrats, 9 (5); Flemish Interest, 8 (5); Socialist Party (Walloon), 8 (4); the coalition of the Socialist Party-Different and SPIRIT, 7 (4); Democratic Humanist Center, 5 (2); Ecologists, 5 (2); Green!, 2 (1); National Front, 1 (1); and List Dedecker 1 (1).

President: Armand DE DECKER.

Chamber of Representatives (*Kamer van Volksvertegenwoordigers/Chambre des Représentants*). The lower house consists of 150 deputies directly elected by proportional representation and compulsory adult suffrage from multimember electoral districts. Each district's complement of deputies is in proportion to population. The election of June 10, 2007, yielded the following distribution of seats: the coalition of Christian Democratic and Flemish and the New Flemish Alliance, 30; Reformist Movement, 23; Socialist Party (Walloon), 20; Open Flemish Liberals and Democrats, 18; Flemish Interest, 17; the coalition of the Socialist Party-Different and SPIRIT, 14; Democratic Humanist Center, 10; Ecologists, 8; List Dedecker 5; Green! 4; and National Front 1.

President: Patrick DEWAEL.

CABINET

[as of June 1, 2009] *(see headnote)*

Prime Minister	Herman Van Rompuy (CD&V)
Deputy Prime Ministers	Karel De Gucht (Open VLD)
	Laurette Onkelinx (PS) [f]
	Didier Reynders (MR)
	Joëlle Milquet (CDH) [f]
	Steven Vanackere (CD&V)
Ministers	
Agriculture, Self-Employed, and Science Policy	Sabine Laruelle (MR) [f]
Civil Service and Public Enterprises	Steven Vanackere (CD&V)
Climate and Energy	Paul Magnette (PS)
Development Cooperation	Charles Michel (MR)
Defense	Pieter De Crem (CD&V)
Employment and Equal Opportunities	Joëlle Milquet (CDH) [f]
Enterprise and Simplification	Vincent Van Quickenborne (Open VLD)
Finance	Didier Reynders (MR)
Foreign Affairs	Karel De Gucht (Open VLD)
Interior	Guido De Padt (Open VLD)
Justice	Stefaan De Clerk (CD&V)
Migration and Asylum Policy	Annemie Turtelboom (Open VLD) [f]
Pensions and Social Integration	Marie Arena (PS) [f]
Social Affairs and Public Health	Laurette Onkelinx (PS) [f]
Secretaries of State	
Budget and Family Policy	Melchior Wathelet Jr. (CDH)
Combating Fraud	Carl Devlies (CD&V)
Combating Poverty	Jean-Marc Delizée (PS)
Disabled Persons	Julie Fernandez-Fernandez (PS) [f]
European Affairs	Olivier Chastel (MR)
Finance	Bernard Clerfayt (MR)
Mobility	Etienne Schouppe (CD&V)

[f] = female

COMMUNICATIONS

Under the basic law of May 18, 1960, information transmission (i.e., news and current affairs) cannot be censored by the government.

Press. The following are published daily in Brussels, unless otherwise noted: *Krantengroep De Standaard* (including *De Gentenaar* of Ghent, *Het Nieuwsblad,* and *De Standaard,* 370,000), in Dutch, independent; *Het Laatste Nieuws* (310,000), in Dutch, independent; *Le Soir* (180,000), in French, independent; *La Meuse* (Liège, including *La Lanterne* of Brussels, 130,000), in French, independent; *Gazet van Antwerpen* (Antwerp, 120,000), in Dutch, Christian Democratic; *Het Volk* (Ghent, 120,000), in Dutch, Christian Democratic; *La Libre Belgique* (including *Gazette de Liège,* 80,000), in French, independent; *La Dernière Heure* (70,000), in French, Liberal.

News agencies. The official agency is Agence Télégraphique Belge de Presse/Belgisch Pers-telegraafagentschap (Agence Belga/Agentschap Belga); private facilities include Centre d'Information de Presse (Catholic), Agence Europe, and Agence Day. Numerous foreign agencies also maintain bureaus in Belgium.

Broadcasting and computing. The French-language Radio-Télévision Belge de la Communauté Française (RTBF), the Dutch-language Vlaamse Radio- en Televisieomroep (VRT), and the German-language Belgisches Rundfunk- und Fernsehzentrum (BRF) are government-owned systems operated by cultural councils, under grants made by Parliament. As of 2008 there were 688.6 Internet users per 1,000 inhabitants.

INTERGOVERNMENTAL REPRESENTATION

Ambassador to the U.S.: Jan MATTHYSEN.

U.S. Ambassador to Belgium: Howard G. GUTMAN.

Permanent Representative to the UN: Jan GRAULS.

IGO Memberships (Non-UN): ADB, AfDB, BIS, BLX, BOAD, CERN, CEUR, EBRD, EIB, ESA, EU, Eurocontrol, G-10, IADB, IEA, Interpol, IOM, NATO, OECD, OIF, OSCE, PCA, WCO, WEU, WTO.

BELIZE

Political Status: Former British dependency; became independent member of the Commonwealth on September 21, 1981.

Area: 8,867 sq. mi. (22,965 sq. km.).

Population: 240,204 (2000C); 324,000 (2008E).

Major Urban Centers (2005E): BELMOPAN (13,600), Belize City (62,300).

Official Language: English. Spanish is the country's second language, and a form of English creole is widely spoken.

Monetary Unit: Belize Dollar (official rate December 1, 2009: 1.95 dollars = $1US).

Sovereign: Queen ELIZABETH II.

Governor General: Sir Colville YOUNG; sworn in November 17, 1993, following the resignation of Dame Minita Elvira GORDON.

Prime Minister: Dean BARROW (United Democratic Party); sworn in on February 8, 2008, succeeding Said MUSA (People's United Party), following legislative election of February 7.

THE COUNTRY

Located on the Caribbean coast of Central America, bordered by Mexico's Yucatan Peninsula on the north and by Guatemala on the west and south, Belize is slightly larger than El Salvador but with less than 3 percent of the latter's population. Most of the inhabitants are of mixed ancestry. Mestizos of Spanish and Mayan Indian derivation comprise the largest part of the population (48.7 percent), while Creole descendants of African slaves and English settlers form the second largest group (24.9 percent). Other smaller ethnic groups include Amerindians (mainly Mayans), African Caribbeans (*Garifunas*), Asians, German Mennonites, and others of European descent. Roman Catholics constitute the largest religious group (60 percent), with roughly equal numbers (14 percent each) of Anglicans and Methodists.

Approximately three-quarters of the country is forested, but the quality of its timber has been depleted by more than two centuries of exploitation by British firms, and in 1992 the government banned the export of ziricote and rosewood lumber. Less than a fifth of the country's arable land, located primarily in the south, is under cultivation. The economy suffers from chronic trade deficits. Nearly one-quarter of the country's population lives in Belize City, where living conditions are poor. However, despite the poor living conditions, school attendance is high and adult literacy is more than 90 percent.

Economic growth, as reported by the International Monetary Fund (IMF), averaged 2.9 percent during 1993–1998, before rising to 6.5 percent in 1999 and 10.4 percent in 2000. After several years of deflation (averaging 0.8 percent in 1997–1998), inflation of 1.0 percent was recorded in 2000. The economy was severely battered by a hurricane in October 2001, but poverty levels remained static between 1996 and 2002 at 33.5 percent.

The principal export commodities are agricultural, particularly bananas, sugar, and citrus, which accounted for nearly half of the country's exports in 2005. GDP growth in 2005 receded to 3.0 percent, despite the discovery of an oil field in Spanish Lookout in western Belize, and rebounded to 5.6 percent in 2006. However, GDP growth in 2007 dropped to 2.2 percent, as a result of the impact of Hurricane Dean in August 2007 on agriculture and tourism, as well as a leveling off of oil production. Several years of robust economic growth, however, had a positive effect on gross national income, which was US$8,600 per capita in 2008, up sharply from US$3,940 per capita in 2004. In February 2007 the government succeeded in restructuring its debt payments, lowering debt servicing costs and partially stabilizing the economy. In 2008, the damage from two tropical storms was estimated to be 4.8 percent of GDP; nevertheless, GDP rose that year by 3 percent, boosted by foreign investments and increased oil extraction. Although inflation surged in summer 2008, by year's end it had declined to 4.5 percent. The IMF predicted inflation would decrease to 2.5 percent in 2009, but that the unemployment rate would rise above 9.5 percent. The IMF approved US$6.9 million in emergency aid to Belize in February 2009 to help the country recover from the damage from the 2008 tropical storms. During the first quarter of 2009, the economy contracted by 2.2 percent, mostly due to effect of the worldwide recession, including a drop in consumer spending and tourism, and a smaller than average banana crop.

GOVERNMENT AND POLITICS

Political background. Initially colonized in the early 17th century by English woodcutters and shipwrecked sailors, the territory long known as British Honduras became a Crown dependency governed from Jamaica in 1862 and a separate colony in 1884. The country's western boundary was delineated in an 1859 convention that was repudiated by Guatemala in 1940 (see Foreign relations, below). Internal self-government was granted under a constitution effective January 1, 1964, and the official name was changed to Belize in June 1973. Although the dispute with Guatemala remained unresolved, independence was granted on September 21, 1981, with Great Britain agreeing to provide for the country's defense "for an appropriate period." At independence, George Cadle PRICE, who had served continuously in an executive capacity since his designation as first minister in 1961, was named prime minister.

In the country's first postindependence election on December 14, 1984, the electorate expressed its apparent weariness of more than three decades of rule by Price's People's United Party (PUP), turning by a substantial margin to the more conservative United Democratic Party (UDP) led by Manuel A. ESQUIVEL. However, in balloting on September 4, 1989, PUP returned to power, winning 15 of 28 legislative seats in a narrow electoral victory (50.3 to 48.4 percent) over the incumbent UDP. The UDP's loss was linked, in part, to popular disenchantment with its economic policies, which Price had castigated as "savage economic liberalism."

Buoyed by sweeping victories in a 1993 parliamentary by-election in January and local government balloting in April, Prime Minister Price called a snap lower house election for June 30. This proved a mistake, as the opposition UDP captured 16 of 29 seats, returning Esquivel to government leadership. However, PUP swept municipal balloting on March 11, 1997, winning all seven town boards, and went on to a conclusive victory in the lower house poll of August 27, 1998, winning 26 of 29 seats. Shortly thereafter Said MUSA was named to succeed Esquivel as prime minister, and he remained in office following the PUP victory in the election on March 5, 2003.

After the 2003 elections, public support for PUP declined substantially amid a weakening economy and allegations of financial mismanagement and corruption. (See Current issues, below.) The UDP won 64 of 67 seats in the municipal elections on March 1, 2006. This landslide foreshadowed the UDP victory in the February 2008 general elections, in which the party gained secured 25 seats in the House of Representatives and ended ten years of rule by the PUP. UDP party leader Dean BARROW was sworn in as prime minister on February 8 and named a UDP cabinet four days later. The UDP's electoral success continued in 2009 when it again swept municipal elections (see Current issues, below).

Constitution and government. With modifications appropriate to Britain's yielding of responsibility in the areas of defense, foreign affairs, and the judiciary, Belize's 1981 constitution is structured after its 1964 predecessor. The British Crown is represented by a governor general of Belizean citizenship who must act, in most matters, on the advice of a cabinet headed by a prime minister. The National Assembly, with a normal term of five years, is a bicameral body currently encompassing a 31-member House of Representatives elected by universal adult suffrage, plus the speaker, if not an elected member, and an appointed Senate of 13 members. Cabinet members may be drawn from either house, except that the finance minister must sit in the House of Representatives, where all money bills originate.

The governor general is empowered to appoint a 5-member Elections and Boundaries Commission and, on the advice of the prime minister, 8 members of a 13-member Public Services Commission (the remaining members serving ex officio). The judicial system includes a Supreme Court as superior court of record, whose chief justice is appointed on the advice of the prime minister after consultation with the leader of the opposition; and a Court of Appeal, from which final appeal may, in certain cases, be made to the Judicial Committee of the UK Privy Council. There also are courts of summary jurisdiction and civil courts in each of the six districts into which the country is divided for administrative purposes.

In the nation's first ever referendum on February 7, 2008, voters were also asked whether they thought the Senate should be directly elected. While 61.5 percent of voters supported the measure, the prime minister rejected the results, preventing the implementation of the proposed reform.

Foreign relations. Belize became a full member of the Commonwealth upon independence and was admitted to the United Nations in September 1981, despite a Guatemalan protest that the "unilateral creation" of an independent state in disputed territory constituted "an invitation to third powers to become protectors of Belize" and thus make Central America "an area for ambitions and confrontation." Guatemala had long contended that its dispute was with Britain, not with Belize. Guatemalan leaders claimed that their country's repudiation in 1940 of the Belizean boundary set forth in the 1859 convention was justified because of Britain's failure to fulfill certain treaty obligations, including a commitment to construct a road from Belize City to the border to provide northern Guatemala with access to the Caribbean. Thus, under its 1945 constitution, Guatemala claimed British Honduras, as Belize was first known, as part of its national territory.

Progress toward resolution of the problem was attempted in a tripartite "Heads of Agreement" document drafted in London on March 11, 1981, with Guatemala yielding on the territorial issue and Belize abandoning certain maritime claims as a means of granting Guatemala "permanent and unimpeded access" to its relatively isolated port of Puerto Barrios on the Gulf of Honduras. However, the agreement angered elements within both Belize and Guatemala. The British government announced that it would proceed with independence on September 21, 1981, despite the lack of formal settlement.

The immediate postindependence period yielded further negotiations between the three countries and an increase in external support for Belize. In 1982 Guatemala called for renewed discussions with Britain, and tripartite talks were reopened in January 1983 but broke down immediately because of Belize's continued refusal to cede any territory. More inconclusive discussions were held in Miami, Florida, in April 1987.

In May 1988 a Joint Permanent Commission was established, with Guatemala appearing to yield in its demand for a land corridor across Belize in return for the right of free transit and guaranteed access to Belizean waters. Collaterally, British aid for road improvements on the Guatemalan side of the border was seen as a means of securing token compliance with the 1859 treaty, which lay at the heart of the dispute. The commission subsequently held a number of "positive and cordial" meetings, including a session in Miami in February 1989, which concluded with a call for talks "at a higher level" to settle on the details of a draft treaty.

In May 1990 tension again flared in the form of a clash between residents of Belize's Toledo district and Guatemalan agricultural workers who had unknowingly planted crops on the Belizean side of the border. The incident prompted a meeting between Guatemalan president Vinicio Cerezo Arévalo and Prime Minister Price on the Honduran island of Roatán on July 9, at the conclusion of which "significant progress" was reported in reaching a solution to the lengthy impasse.

In January 1991 Belize was admitted to the Organization of American States after the Guatemalan president-elect, Jorge Serrano Elías, indicated that his administration would continue talks aimed at settling the controversy. One month after his inauguration, Serrano asserted that "Belize has the recognition of the international community" and again committed himself to a resolution. Shortly thereafter, however, his foreign minister, Alvaro Arzú, insisted that Guatemala did not recognize Belize's independence and continued to lay claim to the territory. Less than six months later Serrano overruled Arzú by announcing that his administration recognized "the right of the Belizean people to self-determination" and on September 5 extended diplomatic recognition to Belmopan. Termination of the lengthy dispute was reinforced in November 1992 by the Guatemalan Constitutional Court, which upheld Serrano's action in a 4–3 vote, and on April 16, 1993, the two countries reached agreement on a nonaggression pact during a meeting in Miami. On May 13 the United Kingdom announced that its army garrison and jet aircraft would be withdrawn by August 1994.

The rapprochement with Guatemala came after Belize had agreed to reduce its southern territorial limit by three miles and to grant its neighbor access to the sea from the northern department of Petén. Belize also ceded the use of port facilities in Stann Creek and the right to participate in offshore ventures, such as oil exploration, in Belize's 12-mile economic zone. Criticism of the accord ensued in both countries: Guatemalan foreign minister Arzú resigned after insisting that Serrano's action was unconstitutional, while a faction of the Belizean UDP, the National Alliance for Belizean Rights, argued that the maritime provisions would have adverse consequences, particularly for fishermen. During another round of territorial negotiations in Miami on November 20, 1998, the Belizean delegation rejected a Guatemalan proposal that the underlying dispute be resolved by an international court, but the two governments did agree to establish a mixed commission to deal with a variety of issues concerning the rights of their respective citizens.

Following a number of border incidents, agreement was reached in September 2002 to deploy OAS observers to the disputed area pending the holding of a referendum on the issue in both countries. However, the accord was repudiated by Guatemala in August 2003, and in May 2004 new discussions were launched at OAS headquarters in Washington, D.C., to find an "equitable and permanent solution" to the controversy.

After lengthy negotiations, an Agreement on a Framework of Negotiations and Confidence Building Measures between Belize and Guatemala was signed on September 8, 2005. The document provided for a bilateral commission to undertake cooperative projects and develop a solution to the territorial dispute. Evidence of the thaw in relations was provided in October 2005 by the conclusion of the first bilateral trade accord between the two countries and again in July 2006 when they endorsed a preliminary trade agreement that would allow 150 products to be traded duty-free. Despite these positive steps a final resolution to the territorial dispute could not be reached, and on November 19, 2007, the OAS recommended that the dispute be settled by the International Court of Justice (ICJ).

In December 2008, officials from Belize and Guatemala signed an agreement to allow the ICJ to rule on the territorial dispute, pending referendums in both countries to ratify the agreement. The president of the Guatemala Congress visited Belize in March 2009 to discuss arrangements for the referendum to be held simultaneously in both countries, perhaps as soon as early 2010.

Current issues. In February 2008 the UDP took power after a landslide victory in the general elections. The PUP government under Prime Minister Said Musa had been plagued with rumors of financial mismanagement and corruption, leading to a drop in popularity after their victory in the 2003 general elections. Among other accusations, the PUP administration lost large sums of social security funds in risky investments, some of which were run by party supporters. More controversy ensued in 2007, when it was learned that Musa had secretly assumed the debts of the private United Health Service without the approval of the House of Representatives. Additional allegations charged that the PUP was buying votes with disbursements of housing loans from a \$10 million grant from Venezuela.

After the decisive UDP victory in 2008, more details about the PUP's secrecy and financial mismanagement emerged. A \$10 million Venezuelan grant had been given out in housing grants and loans in the period immediately before the elections, even though the finance minister was not constitutionally permitted to give out monies exceeding \$500,000 with approval of the National Assembly. It was subsequently revealed that Venezuela had actually loaned Belize \$20 million, not \$10 million, as previously reported. The additional monies had been used to pay off a debt of the United Health Service held by the Belize Bank, rather than to finance a sports stadium and new home construction, as specified in the agreement between the two governments. In March 2008 new evidence confirmed that the Taiwanese government had loaned an additional \$10 million to Belize when the Musa government had requested help after Hurricane Dean. This money also had been deposited against the United Health Service debt. Barrow subsequently pressured the Belize Bank to return the \$20 million that was deposited there against the United Health Service debt. Former prime minister

Musa and his housing minister, Ralph FONESCA, were charged with theft and released on $100,000 bail on December 2008. Both men appeared before the courts in the following months.

The UDP decisively won municipal elections held in March 2009, winning 64 of 67 available seats in the two city and seven town councils of Belize. Three seats were won by PUP candidates in Orange Walk Town. Four third parties ran candidates: Vision for the People (VIP), People's National Party, Congress of the Punta Gorda People, and the Benque Association. VIP performed the best, emerging as a strong force to be contended with in future elections. Only 37 percent of the electorate voted in the election.

In March 2009, charges against Fonesca were dismissed. Supreme Court hearings on Musa's case were held in April. In May 2009, the Supreme Court of Belize ruled that the loan note signed by Musa with the Belize Bank for US $17.2 on behalf of the United Health Service was unlawful because any loan agreement of that size had to be approved by the National Assembly. The Belize government demanded the Belize Bank return the money paid to satisfy the voided loan. In June, the Court ruled that there was insufficient evidence to put Musa on trial. In August 2009, the London Court of International Arbitration dismissed all claims of the Belize Bank to the $20 million.

POLITICAL PARTIES

Government Party:

United Democratic Party (UDP). The UDP was formed in 1974 by merger of the People's Democratic Movement, the Liberal Party, and the National Independence Party. A largely Creole grouping, the party boycotted the preindependence constitutional discussions and the independence ceremonies on the grounds that assurances of continued support by Britain were vague and uncertain. In January 1983 Manuel Esquivel was named party leader in succession to Theodore ARANDA, who withdrew from the UDP while retaining his parliamentary seat. Aranda later formed the center-right Christian Democratic Party before joining PUP in mid-1987.

After securing an unexpectedly lopsided victory in the balloting of December 14, 1984, Esquivel became head of the first non-PUP government since independence. In December 1986 the UDP triumphed again, winning all nine seats on the Belize City Council. Hampered by opposition criticism of its economic policies, the UDP lost its legislative majority in the September 1989 balloting and failed to retain a single council seat the following December.

The UDP won only 3 of 29 seats in the election of August 27, 1998, and lost all 7 seats in Belmopan's first municipal poll on March 1, 2000, while retaining control in only one of seven other municipalities. Although the party lost to the PUP by a wide margin in March 2003, it secured an overwhelming victory in the municipal poll of March 2006 when it won 64 of 67 seats. This overwhelming victory was a precursor to the UDP's huge victory in the February 2008 general elections, when it won 25 of the available 31 lower house seats after campaigning on an anticorruption platform. The UDP statement of philosophy affirms the party's commitment to social justice. Barrow promised in his inaugural address to combat the corruption of the previous administration, reduce the cost of living and unemployment, distribute land to the poor, and expand free public education.

The UDP's political dominance continued in March 2009 when it again won the majority of seats in the municipal elections.

Leaders: Dean BARROW (Prime Minister and Party Leader), Gaspar VEGA (Deputy Prime Minister).

Opposition Party:

People's United Party (PUP). Founded in 1950 as a Christian Democratic group, PUP was dominant for most of the period after the achievement of internal self-government in 1964. After 34 years in office (largely under colonial administration), PUP was decisively defeated in the December 1984 election. Following the election, the (then current) PUP chair and right-wing faction leader Louis SYLVESTRE resigned from the party. At a January 1986 "Unity Congress," the leader of the left-wing faction, Said Musa, was elected party chair, while the leader of the rump right-wing faction, Florencio MARÍN, was elected deputy chair.

Promising a liberalized media policy and an expanded state role in the economy, PUP regained legislative control in the September 1989 election, before again losing it in the early vote of June 1993.

In May 1996 deputy chair Marín resigned, prompting speculation that he was positioning himself for a power struggle with Musa for the party leadership post. In balloting at the party's national convention on November 10, Musa outpolled Marín, 358 to 214, to capture the top PUP slot. Musa became prime minister following the party's landslide victory on August 27, 1998. Musa remained prime minister when the PUP won a comfortable victory in the general election five years later, on March 5, 2003.

The PUP's overwhelming loss in municipal elections in 2006 indicated that the PUP might lose power in the upcoming 2008 general elections. Prime Minister Musa called early elections, which were held on February 7, 2008. After the PUP won only 6 of the 31 seats in that election, Musa resigned his position as PUP party leader on February 13, 2008. On March 30 the PUP held a convention to elect a new leader. After bitter infighting within the party, John Briceño, who had been deputy leader of the party since 2006, defeated the PUP leadership's candidate, Francis FONESCA. The party won only 3 out of 67 seats in the municipal elections of March 2009.

Leaders: Said John BRICEÑO (Party Leader), Henry USHER (Secretary General).

Other Parties Contesting the 2008 Elections:

Vision Inspired by the People (VIP). The VIP first fielded candidates in the 2003 Belmopan City Council Elections, capturing 20 percent of the vote. Encouraged by those results, the VIP decided to field candidates in the 2008 general elections. Ten VIP candidates ran for seats in the legislature, campaigning on the need to attain what they called the "five pillars of nationhood": national unity, a culture of productivity, a family life environment, social justice, and fair representation in government. VIP favored giving the electorate more political power, endorsing an elected Senate, proportional representation in the House of Representatives, and stronger referendum powers and recall power. The VIP failed to win any seats in the 2008 election. In the municipal elections in Belmopan in 2009, 3 of the 7 VIP candidates earned more votes than PUP candidates. Despite the strong showing, the VIP failed to win any municipal seats.

Leaders: Paul M. MORGAN Sr. (Chair), Hubert ENRIQUEZ (Secretary General).

People's National Party (PNP). The PNP was organized in February 2007 and launched on February 18 in San Antonio, a village populated almost exclusively by indigenous Maya. PNP campaigned in the 2008 general elections under the banner of the National Belizean Alliance (NBA). The NBA was an alliance between the PNP, the We the People Reform Movement, and Christians Pursuing Reform. Both the PNP and the NBA were headed by Wil Maheia. The PNP stands for the elimination of government corruption and sustainable development. The PNP ran three candidates in the 2008 general elections but won no seats. The PNP held their town council convention, open to all residents of Punta Gorda Town, on November 29, 2008 and selected 7 candidates to run in the March 2009 municipal elections. All candidates were defeated.

Leader: Wil MAHEIA (Party Leader).

National Reform Party (NRP). The NRP, a Christian conservative party, was founded in 2006. In 2007 it announced it would run a full slate of 31 candidates for the general elections in 2008. However, on January 19, 2008, NRP presented only 11 candidates for election. The party platform emphasized the supremacy of God, the family as the cornerstone of society, zero tolerance for governmental corruption, and the need to substantially raise the minimum wage. The NRP secured no seats in the 2008 balloting and fielded no candidates in the 2009 municipal elections

Leader: Cornelius DUECK (Party Leader).

Congress of the Punta Gorda People (CPGP). The CPGP ran three candidates in the 2009 municipal elections in Punta Gorda, winning no seats.

Leader: Herman Marion LEWIS (Party Leader).

LEGISLATURE

The Belize **National Assembly** is a bicameral body consisting of an appointed Senate and a directly elected House of Representatives, both serving five-year terms, subject to dissolution.

Senate. The upper house currently has 12 members, plus the Senate president. The governor general appoints 6 members on the advice of the prime minister, 3 on the advice of the leader of the opposition, and 3 on the advice of various sectors of society. In 2009 one member represented the Belize Council of Churches and the Evangelical Association of Churches, one member represented the Belize Chamber of Commerce and Industry and the Belize Business Bureau, and one member represented the National Trade Union Congress and the Civil Society Steering Committee.

President: Andrea GILL.

House of Representatives. In 2005 a reorganization of electoral districts increased the number of districts from 29 to 31. The 31 members of the lower house, one representing each district, are elected by universal adult suffrage for five-year terms. In the election of February 13, 2008, the United Democratic Party won 25 seats, while the People's United Party won 6.

Speaker: Emil ARGUELLES.

CABINET

[as of August 1, 2009]

Prime Minister	Dean Barrow (UDP)
Deputy Prime Minister	Gaspar Vega (UDP)
Ministers	
Agriculture and Fisheries	Rene Montero (UDP)
Civil Aviation	Manuel Heredia Jr. (UDP)
Culture	Manuel Heredia Jr. (UDP)
Economic Development, Commerce, Industry, and Consumer Protection	Erwin Contreras (UDP)
Education	Patrick Faber (UDP)
Finance	Dean Barrow (UDP)
Foreign Affairs and Foreign Trade	Wilfred Elrington (UDP)
Health	Pablo Marin (PUP)
Housing and Urban Development	Michael Finnegan (UDP)
Human Development and Social Transformation	Peter Eden Martinez (UDP)
Labour, Local Government, and Rural Development	Gabriel Martinez (UDP)
Natural Resources and Environment	Gaspar Vega (UDP)
National Security	Carlos Perdomo (UDP)
Public Service, Governance Improvement, and Elections and Boundaries	John Saldivar (UDP)
Public Utilities, Transport, Communications, and National Emergency Management	Melvin Hulse (UDP)
Tourism	Manuel Heredia Jr. (UDP)
Works	Anthony "Boots" Martinez (UDP)
Youth, Sports and Information and Broadcasting	Elvin Penner (UDP)
Attorney General	Wilfred Elrington (UDP)
Ministers of State	
Human Development	Juan Coy (suspended until September 17, 2009)
	Edmond George Castro
Works	Michael Hutchinson
Labor, Local Government and Rural Development	
Health	Arthur William Roches
Natural Resources and the Environment	Mark Pech

[f] = female

COMMUNICATIONS

Press. Freedom of the press is constitutionally guaranteed. The following are published in Belize City: *Amandala* (40,000), independent; *The Reporter* (7,000), pro-UDP; *The Belize Times* (6,000), PUP organ; *The Guardian,* UDP organ; *Government Gazette.*

Broadcasting and computing. The Belize Broadcasting Network (BBN) provides daily programming on a semicommercial basis in English and Spanish; formerly government-operated, the BBN was privatized in November 1998. In mid-1986 the government issued licenses to eight operators for 14 privately owned television channels retransmitting U.S. satellite programs, all of which technically had been operating illegally previously. Two additional licenses for the operation of nationwide television services were issued in late 1994. As of 2008 there were 113.1 Internet users per 1,000 inhabitants.

INTERGOVERNMENTAL REPRESENTATION

Ambassador to the U.S.: Nestor E. MENDEZ.

U.S. Ambassador to Belize: Vinai K. THUMMALAPALLY.

Permanent Representative to the UN: (Vacant).

IGO Memberships (Non-UN): ACS, Caricom, CDB, CWTH, IADB, Interpol, IOM, NAM, OAS, OPANAL, PCA, SELA, SICA, WCO, WTO.

BENIN

Republic of Benin
République du Bénin

Political Status: Independent Republic of Dahomey established August 1, 1960; military regime established October 26, 1972, becoming Marxist one-party system 1972–1975; name changed to People's Republic of Benin on November 30, 1975; name changed further to Republic of Benin on February 28, 1990, by National Conference of Active Forces of the Nation, which also revoked constitution of August 1977; multiparty constitution approved by popular referendum on December 2, 1990.

Area: 43,483 sq. mi. (112,622 sq. km.).

Population: 6,769,914 (2002C); 9,315,000 (2008E).

Major Urban Centers (2005E): PORTO NOVO (240,000), Cotonou (789,000).

Official Language: French.

Monetary Unit: CFA franc (official rate December 1, 2009: 434.59 CFA francs = $1US). The CFA franc, previously pegged to the French franc, is now permanently pegged to the euro at 655.957 CFA francs = 1 euro.

President: Boni YAYI (nonparty); elected in second-round balloting on March 19, 2006, and inaugurated for a five-year term on April 6 to succeed Brig. Gen. (Ret.) Mathieu KÉRÉKOU.

Prime Minister: (Vacant). (Adrien HOUNGBÉDJI [Party of Democratic Renewal] had been appointed prime minister by the president on April 8, 1996; however, following Houngbédji's resignation on May 8, 1998, President Kérékou did not name a successor, the post not being constitutionally required. President Yayi also did not include a prime minister in the cabinets he named in April 2006, June 2007, and October 2008.)

THE COUNTRY

The elongated West African state of Benin (formerly Dahomey) lies between Togo and Nigeria, with a southern frontage on the South Atlantic and a northerly bulge contiguous with Burkina Faso and Niger. The country's population exhibits a highly complex ethnolinguistic structure, the majority falling within four major tribal divisions: Adja,

Bariba, Fon, and Yoruba. The principal tribal languages are Fon and Yoruba in the south and Bariba and Fulani in the north. Approximately 70 percent of the people are animists, the remainder being almost equally divided between Christians (concentrated in the south) and Muslims (concentrated in the north). The labor force includes nearly three-quarters of the adult female population, which is concentrated primarily in the cultivation of subsistence crops. Female participation in government has traditionally been minimal; the first female cabinet member was named in 1989.

Benin is one of the world's poorest countries, with an average per capita wage of only $3 per day. It has been reported recently that 60 percent of adults are illiterate, while only 50 percent of school-age children attend school. The country also ranks near the bottom in other "quality of life" measures, a high rate of population growth having hindered recent antipoverty initiatives. The economy is based primarily on agriculture, with cotton accounting for 40 percent of GDP and more than 75 percent of export volume. Other exports include textiles, cocoa, and various oilseeds. Benin's major trading partner, France, subsidizes current expenses as well as basic development. Black-market activity is widespread, and contraband trade, especially with Nigeria, is a significant source of income for many Beninois. Small deposits of oil and gas have been located, although exploitation has been minimal and significant impact from that sector on the economy is not currently anticipated.

The government adopted a strongly Marxist orientation in the mid-1970s but thereafter moved to privatize a number of state-run companies in an effort to counter high external debt, corruption, and severe economic stagnation. In addition, wide-ranging austerity measures were adopted, facilitating international aid agreements but also contributing to social unrest. In 1998 the International Monetary Fund (IMF) reported that Benin's implementation of a structural adjustment program in the mid-1990s had resulted in "real income growth, a decline in inflation, and a reduction in internal and external imbalances." Additional debt relief was announced in mid-2000, although concern was expressed in some quarters that the nation's poor were not benefiting from economic advancement. In that context, opposition surfaced to IMF/World Bank insistence on further privatization of state-controlled enterprises, particularly in the cotton and power sectors, out of fear for the loss of jobs and an increase in prices. GDP growth averaged more than 5 percent annually from 2000 through 2003, and in 2003 the World Bank approved $460 million in debt relief for Benin, in part due to economic reforms, including improved tax collection, instituted by the government.

The IMF described Benin's economic performance since 2003 as "subdued," although GDP growth rose to 3.8 percent in 2006 due to a strengthened cotton market. The fund called for revitalization of the stalled privatization campaign and other renewed structural reform.

GDP grew by 4.6 percent in 2007 and 5.3 percent in 2008, in part due to increased construction, higher agricultural output, and port improvements in Cotonou. However, inflation rose to an annual rate of nearly 8 percent by the end of 2008 under the influence of higher food and fuel prices. The IMF described the government's economic policies as "broadly satisfactory" but continued to press for reform in the cotton sector and banking system.

GOVERNMENT AND POLITICS

Political background. Under French influence since the mid-19th century, the territory then known as Dahomey became self-governing within the French Community in December 1958. However, Dahomey permitted its community status to lapse upon achieving full independence on August 1, 1960. During the next 12 years personal and regional animosities generated five military coups d'état, most of them interspersed with short-lived civilian regimes.

The country's first president, Hubert MAGA, was overthrown in October 1963 by Col. Christophe SOGLO, who served as interim head of state until the election in January 1964 of Sourou-Migan APITHY. In December 1965, after a series of political crises and a general disruption of civilian government, Soglo again assumed power as president of a military-backed regime. Another military coup, led by Maj. Maurice KOUANDÉTÉ on December 17, 1967, ousted Soglo and established an interim regime under Lt. Col. Alphonse ALLEY. Following an abortive attempt at a new election in May 1968, the former foreign minister, Dr. Émile-Derlin ZINSOU, was appointed president of a civilian administration. In December 1969 the Zinsou government was overthrown by Kouandété, and military rule was reinstituted. After another failed election in March 1970, the military established a civilian regime based on the collective leadership (Presidential Council) of the country's three leading politicians: Justin AHOMADEGBE, Apithy, and Maga. On October 26, 1972, following an unsuccessful coup attempt by Kouandété in February, the triumvirate was overthrown by (then) Maj. Mathieu KÉRÉKOU. The new president abolished the Presidential Council and Consultative Assembly and established a Military Council of the Revolution committed to a division of posts on the basis of regional equality.

On December 3, 1974, President Kérékou declared that Dahomey was to become a "Marxist-Leninist state," and two days later he announced that the nation's banks, insurance companies, and oil distribution facilities would be nationalized. Subsequently, he ordered the establishment of "Defense of the Revolution Committees" in all businesses to "protect the revolution from sabotage." On November 30, 1975, the country was styled a "people's republic" (to reflect the ideology officially embraced a year earlier) and was renamed Benin, after an African kingdom that had flourished in the Gulf of Guinea in the 17th century. The Benin People's Revolutionary Party (*Parti de la Révolution Populaire du Bénin*—PRPB) was established as the nucleus of a one-party system the following month. In August 1977 a new basic law was promulgated to reflect a commitment to three stages of development: a "revolutionary national liberation movement," a "democratic people's revolution," and a "socialist revolution."

In January 1977 a group of mercenaries had been repulsed by government forces in a brief but pitched battle in Cotonou. A UN mission of inquiry subsequently reported that the invaders had been flown in from Gabon under the command of an adviser to Gabonese President Bongo. The incident provoked an angry exchange between Presidents Kérékou and Bongo at a summit of the Organization for African Unity (OAU) in July 1978, after which Bongo ordered the expulsion of some 6,000 Benin nationals from Gabon. Most of the mercenaries as well as 11 Benin "traitors" (including former president Zinsou in absentia) were condemned to death in May 1979.

President Kérékou was redesignated for a five-year term as head of state and government on July 31, 1984, having launched a government austerity program that included the proposed privatization of many parastatal enterprises that had not responded to a recent campaign to improve efficiency and curtail corruption.

Unrest intensified among students, teachers, and civil servants in early 1989 as the government, facing a severe cash shortage, withheld scholarship and salary checks. The PRPB nonetheless maintained complete control of legislative balloting on June 18, the single list that was advanced being credited with 89.6 percent voter approval. Subsequently, on August 2, Kérékou, the sole candidate, was reelected to another five-year presidential term by a reported 192–2 assembly vote.

In response to continued difficulties that included damaging charges of official corruption and widespread opposition to an IMF-mandated structural adjustment program, the government convened an unprecedented joint session of the PRPB Central Committee, the National Revolutionary Assembly Standing Committee, and the National Executive Council (cabinet) in late 1989. That meeting followed the lead of Eastern-bloc countries by abandoning formal adherence to Marxism-Leninism. It also called for a national conference in early 1990 to consider constitutional reforms. The resultant National Conference of Active Forces of the Nation met on February 19–28, 1990. Assuming the unexpected posture of a "sovereign" body, the conference revoked the 1977 basic law, dropped the word "People's" from the country's official name, dissolved the existing legislature, and named Nicéphore SOGLO, a former World Bank official, as interim prime minister pending the formation of a "transitional government." President Kérékou, after initially terming the proceedings a "civilian coup d'état," endorsed the conference's decisions and was designated to remain head of state with the defense portfolio (but not command of the armed forces) removed from his jurisdiction.

A 50-member High Council of the Republic (*Haut Conseil de la République*—HCR) was installed on March 9, 1990, to replace the former National Revolutionary Assembly. Three days later a new government, containing no carryovers from the previous administration, was announced. In April the preliminary text of a new constitution providing for a multiparty system was submitted to the HCR. After being presented for public comment and revision, it was approved by a reported 80 percent of those participating in a December 2 referendum.

In parliamentary balloting on February 17, 1991, none of two dozen competing parties secured a majority, the leading party winning only 11 of 64 seats. Subsequently, in a second-round presidential poll on March 24, Prime Minister Soglo was elected president, defeating Kérékou, who became the first incumbent chief executive in mainland Africa to fail in a reelection bid. General Kérékou's decision to run for reelection had been unexpected, having been announced less than a month before the presidential balloting. In an unusual appeal to the electorate, he had asked "forgiveness" from those who had suffered from "deplorable and regrettable incidents" during his 17 years of military-Marxist rule. The transitional government, in one of its concluding actions, responded to the mea culpa by granting immunity to Kérékou for any crimes committed while in office.

First results of the legislative election of March 28, 1995, showed opponents of President Soglo with a majority of seats. After repolling in 13 constituencies on May 28, the opposition held a 16-seat advantage in the assembly.

On January 17, 1996, the assembly rejected the administration's 1996 budget, and, in response, President Soglo issued an edict enacting the budget, insisting that failure to implement his plan would imperil approximately $500 million of international assistance. Shortly thereafter, former president Kérékou announced his intention to contest the presidential elections scheduled for March, alleging that the incumbent's economic policies had devastated Benin's poor. Kérékou joined a field of seven other contenders, including Soglo, former assembly president Adrien HOUNGBÉDJI of the Party of Democratic Renewal (*Parti du Renouveau Démocratique*—PRD), and Bruno AMOUSSOU, Houngbédji's assembly successor and leader of the Social Democratic Party (*Parti Social-Démocrate*—PSD).

President Soglo secured a slim lead over former president Kérékou (35.69 percent to 33.94) in the first round of presidential balloting on March 3, 1996. However, both Houngbédji and Amoussou, third and fourth place finishers, respectively, urged their parties to support Kérékou, and in second-round balloting on March 18 the former president was returned to power with a vote share of 52.49 percent. On April 1 the Constitutional Court rejected Soglo's claim that he had been the victim of polling fraud and a "vast international plot," and on April 6 Kérékou was officially inaugurated. On April 8 the new president named an 18-member government headed by Houngbédji in the reestablished post of prime minister. Houngbédji's PRD controlled the most cabinet portfolios, with four, while Amoussou's PSD was second, with three.

In early May 1998 President Kérékou met with the leaders of a number of small opposition parties and reportedly pledged to increase their representation in his government. On May 8 Prime Minister Houngbédji and his PRD colleagues quit the government amid speculation that they were about to be demoted in a cabinet reshuffling. Six days later the president named a new government that did not include a prime minister.

In legislative balloting on March 30, 1999, opponents of the president, led by Soglo's Renaissance Party (*Renaissance du Bénin*—RB) and the PRD, captured a one-seat majority (42 to 41) in the assembly. (The RB, PRD, and their allies performed well in the pivotal capital region, while supporters of President Kérékou dominated balloting in the north.) Confronted with a choice between assuming their newly won legislative seats or remaining in the government, six legislators-elect subsequently quit their cabinet posts. On June 22 Kérékou named a new government that included representatives from ten presidential-supportive parties (up from seven). The PSD controlled the most posts (four), followed by the Action Front for Renewal and Development-Alafia (*Front Action pour la Renouvellement et le Développement-Alafia*—FARD-Alafia), which assumed two. No opposition members were included in the cabinet.

Seventeen candidates contested the first round of presidential balloting on March 4, 2001, with Kérékou finishing first with 45 percent of the vote, followed by Soglo (27 percent), Houngbédji (13 percent), and Amoussou (8 percent). However, Soglo challenged the results of the first round and refused to participate in the runoff, as did Houngbédji. Consequently, the balloting on March 22 pitted Kérékou against Amoussou, with the president easily winning another term by an 84–16 percent vote.

The country's continuing north-south split was apparent in the December 2002–January 2003 municipal elections, in which the president's supporters won about 50 percent of the seats while the opposition secured the mayorships in Cotonou and Porto Novo. However, significant economic growth and increased political stability appeared to solidify Kérékou's popularity prior to the March 30, 2003, National Assembly balloting, in which propresidential parties won 52 of 83 seats, marking the first time since 1990 that a president could count on a solid legislative victory. Kérékou replaced about half the ministers in a June reshuffle, but he again declined to appoint a prime minister.

In the first round of presidential balloting on March 5, 2006, Boni YAYI, a prominent economist and regional banking executive, led 26 candidates with 35.6 percent of the vote. He was followed by Houngbédji (24 percent), Amoussou (15.3 percent), and Léhady SOGLO (the son of former president Soglo), who secured 8.5 percent of the vote. Yayi scored a landslide victory over Houngbédji in the runoff on March 19 with 75 percent of the vote. The new cabinet, appointed on April 8, was comprised of a number of technocrats, although the PSD and RB also were reportedly represented.

In balloting for the National Assembly on March 31, 2007, the propresidential Cauri Forces for an Emerging Benin (*Force Cauris pour un Bénin Émergent*—FCBE) secured 35 of 83 seats, followed by the Alliance for a Democratic Dynamic (*Alliance pour une Dynamique Démocratique*—ADD) with 20 seats and the PRD with 10 seats. Legislators from a number of smaller parties subsequently announced they would support President Boni Yayi in the assembly, thereby giving him a working legislative majority. Yayi announced a reshuffled cabinet on June 17, most of the ministers being described as nonparty technocrats.

In the wake of declining support for his administration, President Yayi announced a major cabinet reshuffle on October 23, 2008. However, several important opposition groups declined to participate, thereby compromising Yayi's hope for a government of national unity.

Constitution and government. The Marxist-inspired *Loi Fondamentale* of 1977 was rescinded in February 1990 by the National Conference, which authorized the formation of the High Council of the Republic to exercise legislative power during the transition to a new regime. The constitution approved by referendum on December 2, 1990, instituted a multiparty presidential system headed by an executive elected for a five-year, once-renewable term, with National Assembly deputies serving four-year terms. (Presidential candidates must be between 40 and 70 years of age and have been a citizen for 10 years.) The new basic law also provided for a Constitutional Court, a Supreme Court, a High Court of Justice, an Economic and Social Council, and an Audiovisual Authority.

The country is divided into 12 provinces (6 prior to 1997), which are subdivided into 86 districts and 510 communes. (Legislation is currently under consideration to increase the number of provinces [or "departments"] to 21.) Local administration is assigned to elected provincial, district, town, and village councils.

Foreign relations. Throughout the Cold War era Benin adhered to a nonaligned posture, maintaining relations with a variety of both Communist and Western governments. Traditionally strong military and economic ties with France were reaffirmed during meetings in 1981 and 1983 between Presidents Kérékou and Mitterrand, following a revision of treaty relations in 1975.

Although its early regional links were primarily with other francophone states, Benin later sought to consolidate its interests with the broader African community. Relations with Nigeria, initially strained by Nigeria's expulsion of foreign workers in the mid-1980s, subsequently improved to the point that Kérékou felt obliged in July 1990 to deny rumors that Benin was to become Nigeria's 22nd state. Subsequent trade between the two countries allegedly occurred primarily in the "informal sector dominated by smuggling and unrecorded business," and in early 2000 Nigeria urged Benin to remove the remaining "obstacles to free trade."

Benin has been a strong supporter of multilateral development through the Economic Community of West African States, while bilateral ventures have been initiated with Ghana, Mauritania, and Togo. However, a confrontation developed between Benin and Niger in mid-2000 over Lété and some 25 other islands in the Niger River, where sovereignty had been disputed for four decades. In April 2002 the two countries agreed to submit the case to the International Court of Justice (ICJ), although the two countries in June had reached a tentative agreement to redraw the border to settle other disputes. Improved relations also were apparent in the initiation of joint border patrols and an agreement among Benin, Ghana, Nigeria, and Togo to build an oil pipeline through their countries. On a negative regional note, Chad temporarily severed economic ties with Benin in 2003 after Benin's government granted asylum to a group of exiled Chadian opposition figures.

Relations between Benin and the United States underwent a dramatic improvement in 2003 when the two countries agreed to cooperate on security and military issues. (The United States also announced more than $300 million in aid in early 2006 for port rehabilitation and the promotion of small businesses.) Benin also has recently become more involved in regional security, participating in several recent regional peacekeeping missions, including those in the Democratic Republic of the Congo, Liberia, and Côte d'Ivoire.

In July 2005 the ICJ allocated Lété (the most important of the disputed islands) to Niger, along with 15 of the other 25 islands. Also in 2005, Nigeria agreed to cede seven villages along its disputed border with Benin to Benin; collaterally, Benin ceded three villages to Nigeria. Meanwhile, a border dispute resurfaced between Benin and Burkina Faso, with Benin claiming sovereignty over territory beyond the Pendjari River. Burkina Faso contended the river constituted the border. In early 2008 the two countries decided to establish a joint commission to oversee infrastructure development in the region. Collaterally, each agreed to withhold any "visible sovereignty act" (such as deployment of police or military forces) in the disputed territory, while residents were authorized to vote in the country of their choice.

In late 2008 Benin signed several cooperation agreements with China involving, among other things, a proposed new bridge in Cotonou. Bilateral agreements with India were also announced in 2009, President Yayi collaterally indicating Benin would support India's bid for a permanent seat on the UN Security Council.

Current issues. Some observers worried that President Kérékou (constitutionally precluded from seeking a third term) might attempt to extend his tenure, particularly when he announced that the government did not have sufficient funds to conduct the March 2006 balloting. However, Kérékou ultimately accepted a peaceful democratic transition, resisting (apparently under heavy European pressure) the "temptation" to which a number of West African leaders had recently succumbed to remain in power through heavy-handed measures. With both Kérékou (Benin's leader for 28 of the last 33 years) and former president Soglo (precluded from another presidential bid because of his age) out of the picture, the campaign drew 26 hopefuls, including a number of independents who apparently believed that the electorate was ready to move beyond oldtime politics and concentrate on the troubled economy. Among the independents was Boni Yayi, who recently had resigned after 12 years as head of the West African Development Bank. The political newcomer pledged to combat corruption, promote small- and medium-sized businesses (particularly in the food-processing sector), and increase budget allocations for education and youth employment programs. His landslide victory also was attributed in part to the fact that he was of mixed tribal descent, had been born in the country's "middle belt," and was a Christian from a predominantly Muslim family, which helped him bridge the ethnic, geographic, and religious divides so prevalent in previous elections. In addition, Yayi, an economic advisor in the Soglo administration in the early 1990s, was viewed as a "modernizer" whose regional contacts would prove useful in helping Benin to deal with its "economically aggressive" neighbors (most notably Nigeria). Among other things, the presidential results were seen as a severe blow to the traditional political class, although the third peaceful transfer of power in 15 years contributed to Benin's status as a regional leader in regard to democratization.

The atmosphere in Benin reportedly remained "cautiously optimistic" one year into Yayi's tenure, although the calm was shattered briefly in March 2007 when gunmen opened fire on a presidential motorcade. (Yayi, who was unhurt, blamed "criminals" who felt threatened by his anticorruption campaign, which had included audits of many state-run enterprises.) The March 2007 assembly poll revealed a modicum of support for Yayi's initiatives as the FCBE and other propresidential parties secured a legislative majority. However, public opinion appeared to turn against the administration prior to the April 2008 local elections, which were dominated by opposition parties. The electorate's concerns reportedly included ongoing corruption among police and port administrators, slow progress in proposed road construction, and rising food and fuel prices. The political deadlock subsequently intensified as the FCBE could no longer muster a working majority in the assembly, which, among other things, refused to approve Yayi's proposed budget.

The president in September 2008 called upon opposition groups to join the FCBE in a new national unity government, but most major opposition parties declined the invitation. Consequently, activity in the assembly was severely compromised through the first half of 2009 as neither the government nor the opposition could muster an effective majority.

POLITICAL PARTIES AND GROUPS

On April 30, 1990, at the conclusion of a closed-door congress in Cotonou, the ruling Benin People's Revolutionary Party (*Parti de la Révolution Populaire du Bénin*—PRPB) voted to dissolve itself. The PRPB had been the country's only authorized political formation from its December 1975 founding until installation of the Soglo government in March 1990. Delegates to the congress approved the launching of a new grouping, the Union of the Forces of Progress, to replace the PRPB.

By 2002 there were reportedly more than 160 registered parties, a total that, according to a number of Benin's political observers, presented a hindrance to political development. A number of parties and civic organizations that supported President Kérékou formed the Union for the Benin of the Future (*Union pour le Bénin du Futur*—UBF), which served as the core component of the Presidential Movement (*Mouvement Présidential*—MP) that dominated the 2003 legislative balloting. Included in the UBF were the PSD, RDL-Vivoten, FARD-Alafia, and NCC. It was reported that some 120 groups supported the MP. Subsequently, the UBF, under the leadership of Joseph GANAHO, reported in late 2004 that a number of small parties had disbanded and merged into the UBF. However, references to the UBF ceased in late 2005 as it became clear that the Kérékou government was coming to an end.

The formation of the Coordination of Political Forces for 2006 was announced in early 2005 by some ten "propresidential" parties and groups. The leader of the alliance, Idrissou IBRAHIMA, secured less than 1 percent of the vote in the first round of the 2006 presidential balloting.

A number of small parties that supported President Yayi launched an umbrella electoral grouping called the Cauri Force for an Emerging Benin (FCBE, see below) in advance of the 2007 legislative poll. Meanwhile, the major opposition parties (the PRD, PSD, RB, and MADEP) have recently aligned as the so-called Group of Four (G4), which in 2008 announced plans to coordinate its 2011 presidential campaign with the G13 (see below) and the FC. Although that association appeared to be the most promising opposition coordination in many years, analysts cautioned that agreement on a single presidential candidate could prove highly contentious.

Legislative Parties and Groups:

Cauri Force for an Emerging Benin (*Force Cauris pour un Bénin Émergent*—FCBE). The FCBE coalition was formed in January 2007 by some 20 small parties (some referenced below) that supported President Yayi, who remained officially an independent. The FCBE secured 35 seats in the March assembly poll (on a vote share of 23 percent) and joined with a number of small parties to give Yayi a working legislative majority. However, the FCBE did more poorly than expected in the April 2008 local elections, and several FCBE legislators reportedly defected to the new G-13 (see below). Additional division was reported within the FCBE in the first half of 2009.

Party of Democratic Renewal (*Parti du Renouveau Démocratique*—PRD). Led by (then) National Assembly president Adrien Houngbédji, the PRD won 9 legislative seats in 1991 and 19 in 1995, its support centering in the south around Porto Novo. Houngbédji finished third in the first round of presidential balloting in March 1996 with

18.72 percent of the vote. Subsequently, the PRD's support proved pivotal to Mathieu Kérékou in the second round of balloting, and the new president rewarded the party by appointing Houngbédji as prime minister and naming four other PRD members to his new cabinet.

In May 1998 Houngbédji and his PRD colleagues resigned from the government amid reports that the president was preparing to demote them in a cabinet reshuffling. The PRD was subsequently allied with a number of other parties in an anti-Kérékou coalition in mid-2000. However, the groups were unable to agree on a joint presidential candidate for 2001. In February 2003 Houngbédji was elected mayor of Porto Nova, but he lost the assembly president's position in April 2003. He finished second to Boni Yayi in the 2006 presidential runoff with 25 percent of the vote. The PRD was considered "neutral" (i.e., in neither the presidential nor the opposition camps) in the 2007 legislative elections, in which it secured ten seats. However, Houngbédji subsequently became increasingly critical of President Yayi's administration, and the PRD reportedly made significant gains in the April 2008 municipal balloting.

Leader: Adrien HOUNGBÉDJI (Former President of the National Assembly, Former Prime Minister, 2006 presidential candidate, and Mayor of Porto Novo).

Alliance for a Democratic Dynamic (*Alliance pour une Dynamique Démocratique*—ADD). The ADD was formed prior to the March 2007 legislative poll by the following three parties and other small opposition groups. The alliance finished second in the assembly balloting with 20 seats (on a vote share of 17 percent).

Social Democratic Party (*Parti Social-Démocrate*—PSD). In June 1995 the PSD's leader and former presidential candidate, Bruno Amoussou, captured the assembly presidency. Thereafter, in March 1996 Amoussou failed to advance beyond the first round of presidential balloting; however, for rallying behind Mathieu Kérékou, the PSD was awarded cabinet posts in April. Amoussou, described by *Africa Confidential* as a "kingmaker" for his role in the 1996 election and strongly positioned in the cabinet, enjoyed solid backing in portions of southern Benin.

Amoussou finished third in the first round of the 2006 presidential election with 15.3 percent of the vote as a candidate of an alliance of parties. The alliance supported Boni Yayi in the second round and reportedly secured four seats (two for the PSD) in Yayi's new cabinet. However, by 2008 the PSD was firmly in the opposition camp. (Amoussou is currently precluded from a presidential bid in 2011 because he is over the age of 70.)

Leaders: Bruno AMOUSSOU (Coordinator and 2006 presidential candidate), Felix ADIMI (First Vice Chair of the National Executive Committee), Emmanuel GOLOU (Parliamentary Leader).

Renaissance Party (*Renaissance du Bénin*—RB). The PRB was founded in March 1992 by Rosine Soglo, the wife of (then) President Nicéphore Soglo. In July 1993 President Soglo announced his intention to "come down into the arena" to help the RB serve as a "catalyst" for Benin's democracy movement, and in July 1994 he assumed leadership of the party. On October 1, 1994, the RB absorbed the small Pan-African Union of Democracy and Solidarity (*Union Panafricaine de la Démocratie et la Solidarité*—UPDS), but it managed to gain only 20 of 83 legislative seats in two rounds of balloting in March and May 1995.

Among the reasons cited for President Soglo's electoral defeat in his 1996 reelection bid was his increasing reliance on a small circle of family members and the exclusion of the supporters who had helped him capture the presidency. Furthermore, his followers' strident attacks on President Kérékou were described as having backfired on Soglo's campaign.

In August 1998 RB dissidents led by Nicolas TCHOTCHONE left the party and formed the **African Movement for Development and Integration** (*Mouvement Africain pour le Développement et l'Intégration*—MADI), with Tchotchone calling for the establishment of a "new economic and political order."

In February 2003 Nicéphore Soglo was elected mayor of Cotonou. After the March 2003 assembly elections, the RB became the largest opposition party, with 15 seats.

With Nicéphore Soglo unable to run because of his age (over 70), the RB presented his son, Léhady Soglo, as its 2006 presidential candidate. Léhady Soglo finished fourth in the first round of balloting with 8.5 percent of the vote. The PRB was reportedly given one seat in the new cabinet formed by President Boni Yayi following the election.

In early 2008 Nicéphore Soglo criticized President Bayi for a perceived lack of commitment to "genuine democracy." The RB secured a majority of the council seats in Cotonou in the April 2008 municipal balloting. Subsequently, Léhady was considered one of the leading contenders for the opposition's proposed joint candidate to challenge Yayi in 2011.

Leaders: Nicéphore SOGLO (President of the Party, Former President of the Republic, 2001 presidential candidate, and Mayor of Cotonou), Léhady SOGLO (Deputy Mayor of Cotonou and 2006 presidential candidate), Rosine SOGLO (Chair).

African Movement for Democracy and Progress (*Mouvement Africain pour la Démocratie et le Progrès*—MADEP). Led by Séfou Fagbohoun, a wealthy businessman, the MADEP captured 6 seats in the 1999 legislative elections and in 2003 became the second-largest propresidential party, after the UBF. The MADEP's Antoine Kolawolé Idji finished fifth in the first round of the 2006 presidential poll with 3.25 percent of the vote. Corruption charges were subsequently filed by the government against Fagbohoun, but he was released from jail in mid-2008 when the courts decided not to proceed with the case for lack of evidence. The MADEP was subsequently described as highly factionalized as several members accepted portfolios in the new Yayi cabinet in October.

Leaders: Séfou FAGBOHOUN (Chair), Antoine Idji Kolawolé IDJI (Former Speaker of the National Assembly and 2006 presidential candidate), Christophe Kint AGUIAR (Secretary General).

Eleven legislators from small parties agreed to support President Yayi in the assembly following the March 2007 legislative elections. Their parties (which had also supported Yayi in the 2006 presidential poll) included the **Coalition for an Emerging Benin** (*Coalition pour un Bénin Émergent*—CBE); the **Hope Force** (*Force Espoir*—FE); the **National Union for Democracy and Progress** (*Union National pour la Démocratie et le Progrès*—UNDP), led by Janvier YAHOUEDÉOU, who reportedly had become disenchanted with the Yayi administration by early 2009; the **Party for Democracy and Social Progress** (*Parti pour la Démocratie et le Progrès*—(PDPS); the **Renewal Alliance** (*Alliance du Renouveau*—AR); and **Restore Hope** (*Restaurer l'Espoir*—RE), led by Candida AZANAI, who had recently left the RB.

Other successful small parties in the 2007 legislative poll included the **Alliance of the Forces of Progress** (*Alliance des Forces du Progrès*—AFP), led by Valentin Aditi HOUDE; the **Key Force** (*Force Clé*—FC), led by Eric HOUNDATE; and the **Union for Relief** (*Union pour la Relève*—UPR), led by Salifou ISSA. In 2008 it was reported that a number of legislators had formed, under Issa's leadership, an influential **Group of 13** (G13), which was a focus of President Yayi's national unity discussions in September. After declining the invitation to join Yayi's new cabinet, the G13, which primarily represents business interests, joined the G4, FC, and other small parties in pledging to cooperate in the campaign to unseat Yayi in 2011. Many analysts concluded that the G13's favored candidate would be Bio TCHANE (the president of the West African Development Bank), who reportedly enjoyed the support of Benin's former president Mathieu Kérékov.

Other Parties and Groups:

Rally of Liberal Democrats for National Reconstruction (*Rassemblement des Démocrates Libéraux pour la Reconstruction Nationale*—RDL-Vivoten). Led by Sévérin Adjovi, an advocate for the reelection of former president Kérékou, the RDL-Vivoten secured 3 seats in the 1993 legislative balloting. Adjovi served as minister of defense from 1996 to May 1998, at which time he was named minister of communications, culture, and information.

In the 1999 legislative balloting the RDL-Vivoten reportedly campaigned along with four other groups under the banner of the **Movement for Citizens' Commitment and Awakening** (*Mouvement pour l'Engagement et le Réveil des Citoyens*—MERCI).

Adjovi secured 1.8 percent of the vote in the first round of presidential balloting in 2006.

Leader: Sévérin ADJOVI (2006 presidential candidate).

Action Front for Renewal and Development-Alafia (*Front Action pour la Renouvellement et le Développement–Alafia*—FARD-Alafia). At its launching in 1994 as a self-described "national unity party," FARD-Alafia claimed to control five National Assembly seats, which increased to ten in 1995.

In September 1995 FARD-Alafia's leader, Dr. Alafia Saka Saley, called for a grassroots campaign to persuade former president Kérékou to compete in the 1996 presidential elections. At a party congress in April 1997 Jerome Saka Kina captured the secretary general's post, succeeding Saley.

In June 1998 FARD-Alafia suffered the defection of parliamentarians who were subsequently reported to have formed a new grouping, called Car-DUNYA.

Leaders: Jerome Saka KINA (Secretary General), Dr. Alafia Saka SALEY.

Our Common Cause (*Notre Cause Commune*—NCC). The NCC was founded as a vehicle for the presidential ambitions of Albert Tévoédjré, a former deputy director of the International Labour Organisation. Formally registered as a separate party, the NCC won six assembly seats in February 1991, with its leader placing third in the March presidential contest.

In November 1995 the NCC announced its support of former president Kérékou in the upcoming presidential campaign, surprising some observers at the pairing of the northern military leader with Tévoédjre, a purportedly "radical" southerner. In April 1996 Kérékou named Tévoédjre to his new government.

In late March 1997 a group of NCC dissidents, including Vice Chair Gratien Pognon, attempted to remove Tévoédjre from the party chairmanship. Accusing Tévoédjre of "single-handedly" controlling the party, the dissidents elected François Tankpinou as the new chair. However, the legality of their efforts was immediately challenged by Tévoédjre, who argued that the steering committee voting for his dismissal had lacked a quorum. Subsequent reports regularly referenced Tankpinou as the NCC chair, however.

Leader: François TANKPINOU (Chair).

Alliance (*Alliance*). The Alliance was a grouping of three propresidential parties formed prior to the 2003 legislative elections. The component parties were the **Congress of the People for Progress** (*Congrès du Peuple pour le Progrès*—CPP), led by Sédégnon ADANDE-KINTI; the **Movement for Development Through Culture** (*Mouvement pour le Développement par Culture*—MDC), led by Codjo ACHODE; and the **Party of the Beginning** (*Parti du Salut*—PS), led by Damien Alahassa. The CPP ran on its own in the 2007 legislative elections.

Leader: Damien ALAHASSA.

Star Alliance (*Alliance Etoile*—AE). A platform for northern political figures, the AE includes **The Greens** (*Les Verts*) and the **Union for Democracy and National Solidarity** (*Union pour la Démocratie et la Solidarité Nationale*—UDSN), led by Adamou N'DIAYE. The AE secured four seats in the March 1999 poll, and thereafter an AE representative was named to the cabinet. The AE backed an opponent of the PSD's Amoussou in a contest for the assembly presidency and was subsequently excluded from the government named in June 1999. In the 2003 elections, the AE won three seats.

Leader: Sacca LAFIA (Chair and Parliamentary Leader).

New Alliance (*Nouvelle Alliance*—NA). Led by Soulé Dankoro, the NA won two seats in the 2003 legislative elections. Dankoro won less than 1 percent of the vote in the first round of the 2006 presidential balloting.

Leader: Soulé DANKORO.

Communist Party of Benin (*Parti Communiste du Bénin*—PCB). Founded in 1977 as the Communist Party of Dahomey (*Parti Communiste du Dahomey*—PCD) and informally functioning for the next 12 years as the sole opposition grouping, the PCB filed for legal recognition in early June 1993. In 1990 the party had boycotted the National Conference, labeling it a "plot between French imperialism and its Beninois lackeys."

Theretofore in opposition, the PCB allied itself with propresidential forces in May 1995, and in first-round presidential balloting in March 1996 PCB First Secretary Pascal Fatondji secured 1.3 percent of the vote. The PCB called for a boycott of the 2001 presidential balloting.

Leader: Pascal FATONDJI (First Secretary and 1996 presidential candidate).

Other groups (in addition to the AFP and FC) allied with President Kérékou prior to his retirement in 2006 included the **Alliance for Democracy and Progress** (*Alliance pour la Démocratie et le Progrès*—ADP), led by Sylvain Adekpedjou AKINDES; the **Chameleon Alliance** (*Alliance Caméléon*—AC); the **Impulse for Progress and Democracy** (*Impulsion pour le Progrès et la Démocratie*—IPD), led by Théophile NATA; the **Movement for Development and Solidarity** (*Mouvement pour le Développement et la Solidarité*—MDS); the **Rally for Democracy and Progress** (*Rassemblement pour la Démocratie et le Progrès*—RDP); the **Rally for the Nation** (*Rassemblement pour la Nation*—RPN), led by De Sodji Zanclan ABEO; and the **Together Party.** In the 2003 legislative balloting, the AFP, FC, IPD, MDS, and RDP all captured seats. The IPD presented candidates in the 2007 legislative elections, as did a number of new small parties, including the **Belier Social Democratic Party** (*Parti Social Démocrate Le Belier*—PSD–Belier); the **Movement of Benin, Struggle Against Poverty** (*Movement du Bénin, Lutte Contre la Pauvreté*—MBLCP); and the **Union of Citizen Forces** (*Union des Forces Citoyennes*—UFC). New alliances presenting candidates included the **Awakening Alliance** (*Alliance Le Réveil*—AR), led by Martin Dohou AZONHIHO; the **Cauri Alliance for Change** (*Alliance Cauris pour le Changement*—ACC), led by Codjo ACHODÉ, a participant in the former MP; the **National Alliance for Change** (*Alliance Nationale pour le Changement*—ANC), founded by Philippe ABOUMON and other former MP supporters; and the **Alliance for the Defense of Change** (*Alliance pour la Défense du Changement*—ADC), led by former Kérékou supporter Touré MERE.

The **African Congress for Democracy** (*Congrès Africain pour la Démocratie*—CAD) presented Lionel Jacques AGBO as its presidential candidate in 2006. The candidate of the **Rally of Liberal Democrats–Heviosso** (*Rassemblement des Démocrats Libéraux–Heviosso*) was Leandre DJAGOUE. Agbo and Djagoue each received less than 1 percent of the vote in the first round. Meanwhile, the candidate of the **Movement for an Alternative for the People**, Lazare SÉHOUÉTO, finished sixth in the first round with 2.1 percent of the vote.

LEGISLATURE

National Assembly (*Assemblée National*). Benin's unicameral legislature currently includes 83 deputies serving four-year terms and elected by party-list proportional representation in 24 constituencies. At the most recent election of March 31, 2007, the propresidential Cauri Force for an Emerging Benin won 35 seats; the Alliance for a Democratic Dynamic, 20; the Party of Democratic Renewal, 10; the Key Force, 4; the Union for Relief, 3; the National Union for Democracy and Progress, 2; the Coalition for an Emerging Benin, 2; the Alliance of the Forces of Progress, 1; the Party for Democracy and Social Progress, 1; and Restore Hope, 1.

President: Mathurin NAGO.

CABINET

[as of May 1, 2009]

President	Boni Yayi
Ministers of State	
Economic Forecasting, Development, and Evaluation of Public Action	Pascal Irénée Koupaki
National Defense	Issifou Kogui N'Douro
Ministers	
Administrative and Institutional Reform	Joseph Ahanhanzo
Agriculture, Husbandry, and Fisheries	Roger Dovonou
Commerce	Christine Ouinsavi [f]
Culture, Literacy, and Promotion of National Languages	Galiou Soglo
Decentralization, Local Collectives, and Territorial Management	Alassane Seidou
Economy and Finance	Soulé Mana Lawani
Environment and Protection of Nature	Justin Adamaï [f]
Family and Children's Affairs	Mamatou Marie Djossou [f]
Foreign Affairs, African Integration, Francophony, and Béninois Abroad	Jean-Marie Ehouzou
Health	Issofou Takpara

Higher Education and Scientific Research	François Abiola
Industry	Grégoire Akofodji
Interior and Public Security	Armand Zinzindohoue
Justice, Legislation, Human Rights, and Keeper of the Seals	Victor Topanou
Labor and Public Affairs	Christopher Kint Aguiar
Microfinance and the Employment of Women and Youth	Rékyath Madougou [f]
Mining and Petroleum Research	Barthélemy Kassa
Mines, Energy, and Water Resources	Sacca Lafia
Primary Education	Felicien Zacharie
Relations with Institutions	Zacharie Baba Body
Secondary Education and Professional Formations	Bernard Lani Davo [f]
Small- and Medium-Sized Enterprises	Léandre Houaga
Sports and Leisure	Etienne Kossi
Tourism and Handicrafts	Mamata Bako Djaouga [f]
Urban Development, Housing, Land Reform, and the Fight against Coastal Erosion	François Gbenoukpo Noudegbessi

Ministers Delegate

Communication and Information Technologies	Désiré Adadja
Maritime Affairs and Past Reform	Issa Badarou
Transportation, Civil Aviation, and Public Works	Nicaise Fagnon

[f] = female

COMMUNICATIONS

Censorship was extensive prior to liberalization that was codified in the 1990 constitution. Press freedoms are currently considered among the most liberal in Africa, although several suspensions of media outlets and arrests of journalists have been reported recently. Media activity, except for radio broadcasts, are concentrated in the south of the country.

Press. It is currently estimated that more than 30 daily newspapers are published. Some receive state subsidies. Local businesspeople and politicians reportedly own many papers, leading to a perceived "credibility gap." Dailies published in Cotonou in French include *La Nation* (4,000); *Le Matinal* (5,000), progovernment; *Le Matin* (1,500), independent; *Fraternité* (1,500), independent; *Le Republicain*, independent; *Le Point Au Quotidien* (2,000), independent; *L'Autre Quotidien; Les Echos du Jour* (3,000), independent; *L'Aurore* (1,500); *Le Béninois; Nouvelles Mutations; La Dépêche du Soir; Le Progrès; L'Oeil du Peuple; La Nouvelle Tribune; Le Soleil; Le Nouvel Espoir; La Gazette du Golfe; L'Option Hebdo* and *L'Information*.

News agency. The *Agence Bénin-Presse* operates as a section of a government ministry.

Broadcasting and computing. Broadcasting is regulated by an autonomous (albeit government-appointed) High Authority for Audio-visual and Communication (HAAC). The government's *Office de Radio-diffusion et de Télévision du Bénin* broadcasts in French, English, and a number of indigenous languages throughout the country. There are also several private television stations and more than 30 private radio stations. As of 2008 there were 18.5 Internet users per 1,000 inhabitants.

INTERGOVERNMENTAL REPRESENTATION

Ambassador to the U.S.: Segbe Cyrille OGUIN.

U.S. Ambassador to Benin: James KNIGHT.

Permanent Representative to the UN: (Vacant).

IGO Memberships (Non-UN): AfDB, AU, BADEA, BOAD, CENT, ECOWAS, IDB, Interpol, IOM, NAM, OIC, OIF, PCA, UEMOA, WCO, WTO.

BHUTAN

Kingdom of Bhutan
Druk-yul

Political Status: Independent parliamentary monarchy; first formal constitution adopted June 2, 2008.

Area: 18,147 sq. mi. (47,000 sq. km.).

Population: 672,425 (2005C); 777,000 (2008E). The census, described by the government as representing the total resident population, includes 552,996 citizens as well as a "floating population" of 37,453—presumably temporary or short-term residents. In contrast, the United Nations Population Division estimated the 2005 population to be 2.16 million.

Major Urban Center (2005C): THIMPHU (98,676, district).

Official Language: Dzongkha.

Monetary Unit: Ngultrum (official rate December 1, 2009: 46.31 ngultrum = $1US). The ngultrum is at par with the Indian rupee, which circulates freely within the country.

Monarch: Dasho Jigme Khesar Namgyel WANGCHUK; proclaimed king (*Druk Gyalpo*) on December 14, 2006, upon the voluntary abdication of his father, Jigme Singye WANGCHUK; crowned as constitutional monarch on November 6, 2008.

Prime Minister: Jigme Yoser THINLEY (Bhutan Peace and Prosperity Party); nominated by his party on April 5, 2008, following the National Assembly election of March 24; received royal imprimatur and assumed office on April 9 in succession to Kinzang DORJI, who had headed a small caretaker cabinet since the resignation on July 31, 2007, of Chair of the Cabinet Khandu WANGCHUK.

THE COUNTRY

The Kingdom of Bhutan is situated in the eastern Himalayas between Tibet and India. Mountainous in the north and heavily forested in the south, the country's terrain has served to isolate it from the rest of the world. In recent decades official census results have been challenged, particularly by people of Nepalese extraction (Lhotshampas), who appear to constitute 40 percent or more of the population. The principal Bhutanese communities are the Sarchops (an estimated 30 percent) and the ruling Ngalung Drukpas of West Bhutan (15 percent). Four main languages are spoken: Dzongkha (the official language) in the north and west, Bumthangkha in the central section, Sarachapkha in the east, and Nepali in the west and south. The *Druk Kargue* sect of Mahayana Buddhism is the official state religion, and Buddhist priests (*lamas*) exert considerable political influence. The *lamas*, numbering about 3,500, are distributed in 8 major monasteries (*dzongs*) and 200 smaller shrines (*gompas*). Most of the Nepalese are Hindu. Women, who constitute about 37 percent of the economically active population, play a minimal role in governance.

The economy remains largely agrarian. About 44 percent of the paid labor force engages in agriculture and animal husbandry, which account for about 22 percent of the GDP. The main crops are maize, rice, and other cereals; potatoes and other tubers and roots; and apples and other fruits. Industry, contributing about 38 percent of GDP and employing 17 percent of the workforce (mostly in construction), is led by production of hydroelectric power and by food and distillery operations. Electricity is now the leading source of nonservice export earnings—in 2007 nearly five times as much electricity was exported as was consumed domestically—followed in importance by cement and calcium carbide. Particleboard is also important, but the export of raw timber was banned in 1999. India remains Bhutan's principal trading partner.

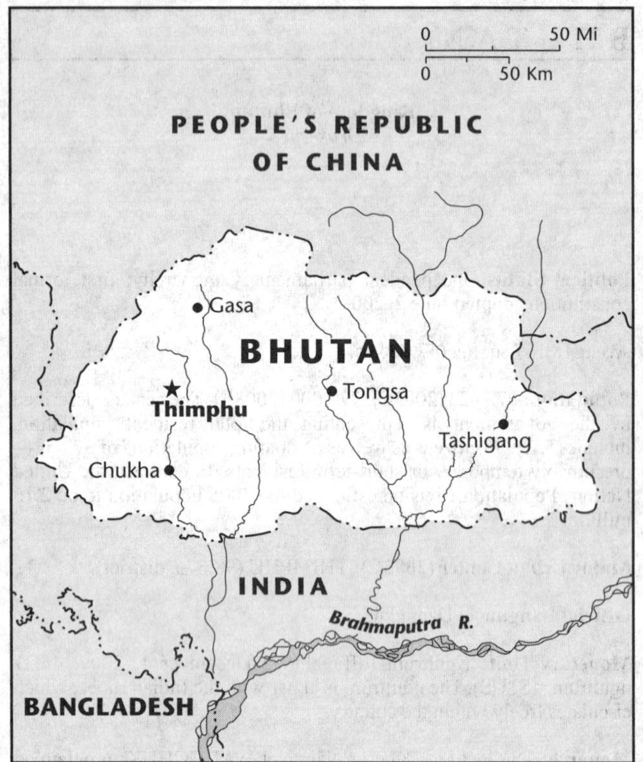

With support from the World Bank group and other international donors, transportation, power, and communications have improved dramatically since the 1960s. Nevertheless, poverty afflicts 23 percent of the population and remains widespread in rural areas. The Tenth Five-Year Plan (July 2008–June 2013) includes among its goals poverty alleviation, reduced unemployment, road construction, and rural electrification. (Bhutan's development philosophy has as its overall goal improving "Gross National Happiness.") Since 1999 GDP growth has typically been in the 6–9 percent range, peaking at 10.9 percent in 2002 and achieving an 8.5 percent rate in 2006. The kingdom remains heavily dependent on foreign grants, which accounted for nearly 37 percent of government income in 2007, down from 48 percent in 2006.

GOVERNMENT AND POLITICS

Political background. A consolidated kingdom since the mid-16th century, Bhutan is presently governed by a fourth-generation hereditary monarch referred to as the *Druk Gyalpo* (Dragon King). Historically, the country was ruled by a dyarchy of temporal and spiritual rajas, but in 1907 Ugyan WANGCHUK was established on the throne with British assistance. British guidance of Bhutan's external affairs, which began in 1865 in exchange for a financial subsidy, was confirmed by treaty in 1910. India succeeded to the British role by a treaty concluded August 8, 1949, in which India pledged not to interfere in Bhutanese internal affairs. Bhutan agreed to be "guided" by Indian advice in its external relations.

The post–World War II era witnessed increased social and political change, primarily at the initiative of King Jigme Dorji WANGCHUK, who ascended the throne in 1952. Considerable unrest resulted from some of these policies, and in 1964 Prime Minister Jigme Polden DORJI was assassinated. Nonetheless, the king pursued his policy of modernization, establishing a Royal Advisory Council in 1965 and a Council of Ministers three years later, when a High Court was also created. Western-educated Jigme Singye WANGCHUK succeeded his father as monarch on July 24, 1972.

From the late 1980s a resurgence of democracy in Nepal generated increased restiveness by Bhutan's large Nepalese immigrant community, particularly after the monarch's launching of a national integration (*Driglam Namzha*) drive that mandated the wearing of traditional Bhutanese dress and proscribed the teaching of Nepali in the schools. Based in the country's southern regions, the Nepalese agitation spawned a number of political groups, including the Bhutan People's Party (BPP) in 1990. Violent outbreaks accelerated what had initially been a small refugee problem, and by 1993 some 80,000 or more Bhutanese of Nepalese extraction had relocated to seven camps in eastern Nepal run by the Office of the United Nations High Commissioner for Refugees (UNHCR).

In October 1993 representatives of Bhutan and Nepal held the first in a series of ministerial-level meetings to work toward resolution of the problem. Further rounds of talks in 1994 yielded agreement that a Joint Verification Team would categorize the refugees according to whether they were bona fide Bhutanese nationals, non-Bhutanese refugees from elsewhere, Bhutanese emigrants who had forfeited citizenship, or criminals. Meanwhile, a number of ethnic Nepalese leaders, most prominently Tek Nath RIZAL of the BPP, had been sentenced by Bhutan's High Court to life imprisonment or other lengthy terms for terrorist activities. Intermittent violence by "antinationals" (*ngolops*), as they were branded by Bhutanese authorities, continued in the south as succeeding rounds of bilateral discussions made little progress. Rizal and 40 other political prisoners were released in December 1999, by which time the number of refugees had surpassed 100,000.

On October 22, 2003, Nepal and Bhutan proclaimed an agreement that would permit repatriation of approximately three-fourths of the ethnic Nepalese living at the Khudunabari refugee camp in Nepal. The repatriation was expected to begin in early 2004, but an incident in Khudunabari, during which refugees allegedly assaulted Bhutanese members of the Joint Verification Team, led Thimphu to cancel the repatriation. In September 2006 the two countries' foreign ministers agreed to a renewal of talks in November, but Nepal, in the midst of a domestic crisis, later requested a postponement. (For subsequent developments, see Current issues, below.)

On June 16, 1998, the king announced his intention to dissolve the cabinet for the first time since he ascended the throne. In accordance with a royal edict (*kasho*), on July 1 the National Assembly approved the formation of a partially elected cabinet to assume most of the king's administrative duties and powers. On July 20 the king formally handed governmental authority over to the new cabinet, which included six ministers who had been nominated by the king and elected for five-year terms by secret ballot of the assembly. Thenceforth, the cabinet chair rotated annually among ministers.

On July 10, 2003, the king announced portfolio assignments for a new ten-member cabinet, which assumed office on August 30 with Jigme THINLEY as chair. Yeshey ZIMBA, minister of trade and industry, took over as chair on August 18, 2004, and he was succeeded by the minister of health and education, Sangay NGEDUP, on September 5, 2005. The minister of foreign affairs, Khandu WANGCHUK, assumed the chair on September 7, 2006.

In the context of discussions over a proposed constitution that would establish a "democratic constitutional monarchy" in 2008, the king announced in December 2005 his intention to abdicate before then in favor of his eldest son, Crown Prince Jigme Khesar Namgyel WANGCHUK. Accordingly, the king, himself only 51, stepped down from the throne on December 14, 2006, a year earlier than had been expected, to afford his 26-year-old son the chance to gain "valuable experience" prior to implementation of the constitution.

Cabinet Chair Wangchuk and six other ministers resigned on July 31, 2007, to prepare for contesting Bhutan's first multiparty, democratic legislative elections. Kinzang DORJI, minister for works and human settlements, was named by the king to head a small caretaker cabinet.

Following a lengthy preparatory process that included the registration in 2007 of Bhutan's first political parties and a two-round mock legislative election to help educate the populace, voters on March 24, 2008, elected the 47 members of a new National Assembly. The Bhutan Peace and Prosperity Party (*Druk Phuensum Tshogpa*—DPT), led by former cabinet chair Jigme Thinley, took 45 seats, with the other 2 being won by the People's Democratic Party (PDP) of Sangay Ngedup. On December 31, 2007, and January 28, 2008, voters cast ballots for the 20 elective, nonpartisan members of the new Parliament's upper house, the National Council. Thinley took office as prime minister on April 9.

Constitution and government. Bhutan's movement toward adoption of its first written constitution began with a 1998 royal edict in which the king, at his own instigation, surrendered his role as head of government and established a partially elected cabinet (*Lhengye Zhungtsho*) with a five-year term of office. Ultimate responsibility for the country's sovereignty and security continued to be vested in the king as head of state, but the National Assembly (*Tshongdu*

Chhenmo) was authorized to approve or reject the king's ministerial nominations by secret ballot. The cabinet chair (the head of government) served a one-year term, with the position rotating among elected ministers. As in the past, the cabinet also included, ex officio, the 9 members of the Royal Advisory Council (*Lodoi Tsokda*, established in 1965), who also sat in the partially elected National Assembly. In July 1998 the assembly accepted the authority to remove the king by a two-thirds vote.

In late 2001 the king announced that work had begun on drafting a formal constitution. The first draft was published in 2005. Following an extended period of national consultation, a slightly revised, 35-article third draft was presented in August 2007. With the written constitution yet to be adopted, the electoral process begun in 2007 and concluded in March 2008 was authorized by royal decree. Formal adoption of the constitution occurred early in the parliamentary term.

The most controversial provisions of Bhutan's draft constitution concern citizenship. To be a citizen an individual must be the child of two Bhutanese parents or must have been officially registered as a resident on or before December 31, 1958. To be eligible for naturalization an individual must have resided in Bhutan for at least 15 years; have committed no criminal offenses; be able to speak and write Dzongkha; have a "good knowledge" of the country's culture and history; and "have no record of having spoken or acted against the King, the Country, and the People of Bhutan." Most of the ethnic Nepalese community are thereby excluded from citizenship.

Bhutan is now a constitutional monarchy that separates powers into executive, legislative, and judicial branches. The *Druk Gyalpo* remains head of state but must step down upon reaching the age of 65; in another break with tradition, females are included in the line of succession, although a male heir, even if younger, takes precedence. The bicameral Parliament has a 25-member National Council as an upper house and a new National Assembly as the lower. Members of the National Assembly (a maximum of 55) are elected through single-member constituencies in two stages: first, a primary round in which all registered political parties may compete, followed by a second round contested by the two parties that receive the most primary votes. Both houses serve five-year terms, although the National Assembly is subject to early dissolution in the event of a political impasse. Dissolution requires concurrence by two-thirds of the National Assembly's members and the monarch. As in nearby Bangladesh, interim governments will be responsible for holding elections following all parliamentary dissolutions. The monarch is empowered to declare a state of emergency for up to 21 days, with a two-thirds vote of Parliament, sitting in joint session, then needed to extend it.

The leader or nominee of the majority party in the National Assembly becomes prime minister (subject to a two-term limit), with the monarch naming other ministers on the recommendation of the prime minister. The National Assembly and National Council, sitting in joint session, may override a monarchical veto by a two-thirds vote. By a three-fourths vote and with popular concurrence in a national referendum, they may force the king to abdicate. The judicial system comprises a Supreme Court, a High Court, district courts, and other lower courts.

The constitution describes Buddhism as "the spiritual heritage" of the country but guarantees freedom of religion as well as freedom of speech, press, and assembly.

The country is divided into 20 administrative districts (*dzongkhags*). Villages are grouped into counties (*gewogs*). The constitution specifies the election of assemblies at all levels of government.

Foreign relations. Historically, Bhutan's external relations were conducted largely through the Indian government, although the 1949 treaty that required Thimphu to seek "advice" from New Delhi in foreign affairs came under periodic criticism. Bhutan's establishment of diplomatic relations with Bangladesh in 1980 was Thimphu's first effort to deal directly with a third country, although it had acted independently of India in several international forums, including the UN General Assembly. On February 8, 2007, during a visit by the king to New Delhi, Bhutan and India signed a revised India-Bhutan Friendship Treaty that eliminated the reference to Indian guidance in foreign affairs. The treaty was quickly ratified by both countries and entered into force on March 5. In May 2008 Manmohan Singh became the first Indian prime minister to visit Bhutan in 25 years. His visit included an address to a joint session of Parliament.

Since 1980 Bhutan has joined a number of multilateral bodies, including the World Bank, the International Monetary Fund, and the Asian Development Bank. In 1983 it participated with Bangladesh, India, the Maldives, Nepal, Pakistan, and Sri Lanka in the establishment of a committee that subsequently evolved into the South Asian Association for Regional Cooperation (SAARC). In 2005 the seven reached agreement on establishing a South Asia Free Trade Area, which became operational in 2006.

In late 2003 Bhutan moved to resolve a decade-old problem involving Indian separatists who were using bases in southeastern Bhutan to mount cross-border raids. Altercations with Bhutanese police also had occurred. In mid-December, in its first large-scale mission since the 1865 Anglo-Bhutanese war, the Royal Bhutanese Army attacked some 30 camps occupied by an estimated 3,000 Assamese and Bodo separatists associated with three militant Indian movements: the United Liberation Front of Assam, the National Liberation Front of Bodoland, and the more recently organized Kamatapur Liberation Organization. In February 2004 India reported that over 400 insurgents had been killed in the successful offensive, which had extended into the new year.

Since the 1980s Bhutan and China have held discussions to resolve a border controversy that is linked to the Chinese-Indian dispute over portions of Arunachal. A government report on the Sino-Bhutanese talks presented to the National Assembly in 1995 said that Chinese territorial claims included some 270 square kilometers in the western sector and somewhat more in the northern sector, to which Bhutan had responded with counterclaims. Seventeen rounds of border talks had been held through April 2004, at which time the two sides agreed to form a technical expert group for purposes of demarcation.

Current issues. Ideologically, both contesting parties in the March 2008 legislative election were royalist and supported the "four pillars" of gross national happiness: sustainable and equitable economic development, conservation, cultural preservation and promotion, and good governance. The DPT, however, was apparently viewed by many voters as the establishment party, closest to the monarchy, and thus won 45 constituencies. The PDP came away with only 2 seats, raising the question of how it could function effectively as the opposition. The chair of the constitutional drafting committee argued, however, that the country's constitution would prevent a "tyranny of the majority" through its system of checks and balances, including the review powers of the National Council, the king's authority to call a national referendum, and the right of legislators to vote their conscience regardless of party affiliation. In addition to approving the constitution, the new Parliament's main tasks included completing work on the Tenth Five-Year Plan (2008–2013), which includes among its goals expansion of hydroelectricity, faster development in industry and agriculture, and a cut in the poverty rate from one in four to one in six.

In late May 2007, in a demonstration timed to coincide with the mock parliamentary runoff, thousands of ethnic Nepalese refugees attempted to cross the narrow strip of India separating Nepal and Bhutan, but their passage was prevented by Indian troops, who used tear gas and live ammunition to turn back the marchers. Some 60 Nepalese were injured and 2 killed. Thimphu has refused to talk directly to refugee groups, insisting that most of the refugees are not legitimately Bhutanese and arguing that the refugee camps have been infiltrated by Maoists and others who wish to overthrow the government. Many Nepalese leaders, including Tek Nath Rizal, have pressed for India to get involved, to no avail, while in January 2006 the UNHCR asked Nepal to grant refugees permission to leave the camps for third countries. In October 2006 the United States offered to admit 60,000 of the Nepalese, but most ethnic leaders, fearing a divided community, rejected the proposal. In March 2008, however, with the UNHCR reporting that some 25,000 ethnic Nepalese had already applied to emigrate, the first 120 left for the United States. Other countries that have agreed to admit the refugees include Australia, Canada, Denmark, the Netherlands, New Zealand, and Norway, but in far smaller numbers. According to a UNHCR spokesperson, as of September more than 4,800 had left for the United States, 131 for Australia, and 129 for New Zealand.

POLITICAL PARTIES

Until 2007, Bhutan had no legal parties. Under the 2008 constitution political parties are permitted as long as their membership is not based on "region, sex, language, religion, or social origin." Members of the royal family, appointed government officials, members of the police force and the military, members of the clergy, and civil servants are prohibited from participation in parties, all of which must meet registration requirements. Only members may contribute money to a party. The two parties contesting the March 2008 election, the *Druk Phuensum Tshogpa* (DPT) and the People's Democratic Party (PDP), had no significant ideological differences. Both were considered royalist, as were two other parties, the Bhutan People's United Party (BPUP) and the Bhutan National Party (BNP), that failed to meet registration requirements.

Registered Parties:

Bhutan Peace and Prosperity Party (*Druk Phuensum Tshogpa*—DPT). Formation of the DPT by merger of the Bhutan People's United Party (BPUP) and an offshoot, the All People's Party (APP), was announced in late July 2007, following the decision of a handful of cabinet ministers to resign their posts and unite for the first multiparty assembly election in 2008. Shortly after the DPT's formation, however, personality differences led a faction headed by Sigay DORJI and Penjore DORJI to reestablish the BPUP, but in November the Election Commission rejected the registration application on the grounds that the BPUP had no clear ideology or mission and that it lacked "credible leadership."

Hallmarks of the DPT platform included fighting poverty and fostering equitable development, in keeping with the four pillars of "gross national happiness." In the March 2008 election the DPT won 67 percent of the vote and 45 National Assembly seats.

Leaders: Jigme Yoser THINLEY (Prime Minister and President of the Party), Yeshey ZIMBA (Minister of Works and Human Settlements and Officiating President of the Party), Khandu WANGCHUK (Minister of Economic Affairs), Thinley GYAMTSHO (Secretary).

People's Democratic Party (PDP). The PDP was established in March 2007 under the leadership of former chair of the Council of Ministers Sangay Ngedup and became the country's first registered party in September. Promoting "well being for everyone" through such measures as economic development, expansion of basic infrastructure, and improved access to health care, the PDP was initially viewed as likely to win the March 2008 National Assembly election. It nevertheless managed to capture only 2 seats.

At the annual PDP meeting in March 2009, Ngedup formally stepped down as party chair, having taken responsibility for the party's poor showing in the 2008 election. The PDP general secretary, Lam KEZANG, had already resigned.

Leaders: Tshering TOBGAY (Opposition Leader and Party Chair), Sangay NGEDUP (Vice Chair), Damcho DORJI (Vice Chair and Member of the National Assembly), Sonam JATSHO (General Secretary).

Ethnic Nepalese Formations:

The groups below, based abroad, represent the ethnic Nepalese community. In general, they support a limited constitutional monarchy, a parliamentary system, and equal rights for all ethnic groups, but there are differences regarding the issue of repatriation versus resettlement in third countries.

National Front for Democracy in Bhutan (NFDB). Formed in July 1996 (and also known as the United Front for Democracy), the NFDB is a coalition of prodemocracy groupings—the BPP, DNC-Democratic, and BGNLF—which operates mainly from Nepal but also, under some limitations, from India. It has organized numerous protests at the Nepal-India border, in part to call attention to its demand that India intervene on behalf of the refugees. Members have repeatedly been arrested as a result of NFDB activities.

Having rejected the draft constitution proposed by the Bhutanese government, in July 2006 the National Front made public its own "parallel constitution." In May 2007 the NFDB organized an effort by thousands of ethnic Nepalese to leave Nepal and enter Bhutan by crossing the narrow Indian corridor between the two, but the marchers were forcibly turned back by Indian troops. Initial reports stated that 2 ethnic Nepalese had died and that another 60 were injured.

Thinley Penjore, who had served as the NFDB's chair since its formation, stepped aside in March 2008 and was succeeded by Balaram Poudel of the BPP.

Leaders: Balaram POUDEL (Chair); Jagirman LAMA, Thinley PENJORE, and D.B. Rana SAMPANG (Vice Chairs); Narad ADHIKARI (Spokesperson).

Bhutan People's Party (BPP). With backing from the Nepali Congress and the Communist Party of Nepal (Marxist-Leninist), the BPP evolved in 1990 from the still-extant People's Forum for Human Rights. It was formally banned after disturbances in southern Bhutan in September 1990. The BPP subsequently became a leading component of the Appeal Movement Coordination Council (AMCC), which organized a number of refugee marches and protests.

The party's founder, Tek Nath Rizal, having been imprisoned since 1989 and sentenced to life in 1993 for "masterminding" antinational activities, was released by the king in December 1999 but barred from political activity. In January 2000 the BPP president, R. K. BUDHATHOKI, described the release as part of a conspiracy to damage Rizal's popularity. Budhathoki was assassinated in Nepal in September 2001.

Leader: Balaram POUDEL (Chair).

Druk National Congress–Democratic (DNC-Democratic). Founded on June 16, 1994, by Rongthong Kinley DORJI, leader of the Sarchop community in Bhutan, the **Druk National Congress** (DNC) operated in Bhutan until 1995, when the regime began to limit its activities. A split in the party was reported in 2001, with one faction remaining loyal to Dorji and another naming Chheku DUKPA as leader. Thimphu has repeatedly demanded Dorji's extradition from India.

Although Dorji remains leader of the DNC, a splinter, the DNC-Democratic appears to be more prominent.

Leaders: Thinley PENJORE (President), Narad ADHIKARI (General Secretary).

Bhutan Gorkha National Liberation Front (BGNLF). Organized in December 1994, the BGNLF has called for constitutional protection of ethnic Nepalese, immediate repatriation of refugees, greater representation in the National Assembly, and establishment of an independent judiciary. The group has often organized demonstrations on the Indian border and has attempted to lead refugees into Bhutan. It has at least two main factions.

Leaders: D.B. Rana SAMPANG, Aaiman RAI.

Bhutan National Democratic Party (BNDP). Founded in February 1992 by former government officials of Nepalese ethnic origin, the party was banned shortly afterward. The BNDP was the driving force in the Bhutan Coalition for the Democratic Movement (BCDM), which received backing from the Communist Party of India–Marxist for a series of protest actions on the Bhutanese border in 1995–1996. Longtime leader R.B. BASNET died in August 2007.

Leaders: Dev Narayan Singh DHAKAL (Founding General Secretary), Hari Prasad ADHIKARI (General Secretary).

Communist Party of Bhutan (Marxist-Leninist-Maoist). The Communist Party was reportedly formed in 2003 in the Bhutanese refugee camps in Nepal. It has close links to the Communist Party of Nepal (Maoist). In December 2007 30 alleged members were sentenced to between five and nine years in prison for subversive activities, including recruiting members. Some recent reports have claimed that a group called the **Bhutan Tiger Force** (BTF) is the party's military wing; others have identified the military wing as the **United Revolutionary Front of Bhutan** (URFB). In 2007 the government identified the BTF as possibly responsible for a series of minor bombings. Responsibility for four coordinated bombings in January 2008 was claimed by the URFB. Reports have suggested that the CPB (MLM) may also have links to various militant separatist groups in India's Assam.

Leader: VIKALPA.

In addition, various expatriate human rights organizations—all of which the Bhutanese government classifies as political and therefore bans—have been operating abroad. In July 2003 seven of them banded together to organize the **Human Rights Council of Bhutan** (HRCB) under the chairmanship of Tek Nath Rizal, whose status as leader of the human rights community was further solidified in March 2006, when he was selected to head a new **Bhutanese Movement Steering Committee.** Founding groups in the HRCB were the **Bhutanese Refugees Representative Repatriation Committee** (BRRRC), chaired by Rizal; the **Bhutanese Refugee Women Forum** (BRWF), led by Garima ADHIKARI (Coordinator); the **Center for Protection of Minorities and Against Racism and Discrimination** (CEMARD Bhutan), led by Rakesh CHHETRI (Executive Director); the **Association of Human Rights Activists of Bhutan** (AHURA Bhutan), led by Ratan

GAZMERE (Chief Coordinator); the **Human Rights Organization of Bhutan** (HUROB), led by S. B. SUBBA; the **People's Forum for Human Rights in Bhutan** (PFHRB), formed in 1989 by Rizal and later led by D. P. KAFLE; and the **Students Union of Bhutan** (SUB), represented by Mukti GURUNNG.

LEGISLATURE

Until 2008 the National Assembly was a unicameral legislature of 150 members, including 100 elected district representatives, the 6 indirectly elected members of the Royal Advisory Council (formally abolished under the 2008 constitution), 10 members chosen by religious bodies, the 10 members of the Council of Ministers, and 24 senior civil servants designated by the king. Members served overlapping three-year terms. Under a June 30, 2007, electoral law instituted by royal decree, Bhutan set about instituting a bicameral **Parliament** (*Chitshog*) in accordance with the constitution that was formally adopted in 2008. Candidates for both houses must have a university degree.

National Council (*Gyalyong Tshogde*). The upper house of Parliament comprises 25 members, 20 elected on a nonpartisan basis (1 from each district) and 5 appointed by the king. Fifteen seats were filled at voting on December 31, 2007. Voting in the other 5 districts was postponed until January 29, 2008, because of an insufficient number of candidates. The king named his appointees on March 30. All members serve five-year terms. In addition to its regular legislative duties, the National Council is regarded as a "house of review" on security and sovereignty matters. It is not subject to early dissolution.

Chair: Namgay PENJORE.

National Assembly (*Gyalyong Tshogdu*). The lower house may have up to 55 members, all elected on a partisan basis from single-member constituencies (a minimum of 2 and a maximum of 7 per *dzongkhag*). All candidates must belong to political parties. Members serve five-year terms, subject to early dissolution. Defection to another party is prohibited.

Elections are to be held in two stages. If there are more than two registered parties, all participate in a "primary round," with the two parties winning the most votes then entering the general election. No primary round was needed in 2008. In the election for a 47-member house on March 24, 2008, the Bhutan Peace and Prosperity Party won 45 seats and the People's Democratic Party, 2.

Speaker: Jigme TSHULTIM.

CABINET

[as of October 1, 2009]

Prime Minister	Jigme Yoser Thinley
Council of Ministers	
Agriculture	Pema Gyamtsho
Economic Affairs	Khandu Wangchuk
Education	Thakur Singh Powdyel
Finance	Wangdi Norbu
Foreign Affairs	Ugyen Tshering
Health	Zangley Dukpa
Home and Cultural Affairs	Minjur Dorji
Information and Communications	Nandalal Rai
Labor and Human Resources	Dorji Wangdi
Works and Human Settlements	Yeshey Zimba

COMMUNICATIONS

The media were operated by the government until October 1992, when the king decreed that they should be granted greater independence. The government nevertheless continues to influence content. A media bill passed in 2006 restricts cross-ownership of media and requires equitable treatment of parties and candidates during election campaigns.

Press. Before 2006 the country's only newspaper was *Kuensel* (Clarity, Thimphu, 17,000), founded in 1967 as a bimonthly government bulletin but now an autonomous, government-subsidized daily published in English, Dzongkha, and Nepali. In early 2006 the country's first two private newspapers were licensed: *Bhutan Times* (Thimphu), twice weekly in English; *Bhutan Observer* (Thimphu), weekly, in English and Dzongkha. The country's first daily, *Bhutan Today* (Thimphu), in English, was launched in late October 2008.

Broadcasting and computing. The Bhutan Broadcasting Service (BBS), an autonomous agency, transmits radio signals; it began limited television service in Thimphu in 1999. In early 2006 the BBS announced that its television broadcasts now reached the entire country. The BBS and the privately run United Cable TV offer limited cable service. The nation's television sets also can receive transmissions from India and Bangladesh.

As of 2008 there were 65.5 Internet users per 1,000 inhabitants.

INTERGOVERNMENTAL REPRESENTATION

Diplomatic relations between Bhutan and the United States are conducted through the government of India.

Permanent Representative to the UN: Lhatu WANGCHUK.

IGO Memberships (Non-UN): ADB, CP, Interpol, NAM, SAARC, WCO.

BOLIVIA

Republic of Bolivia
República de Bolivia

Political Status: Independent republic proclaimed 1825; civilian government reestablished in October 1982 after virtually constant military rule since September 1969; present constitution promulgated on February 7, 2009.

Area: 424,162 sq. mi. (1,098,581 sq. km.).

Population: 8,274,325 (2001C); 10,039,000 (2008E).

Major Urban Centers (2005E): LA PAZ (administrative capital, 826,000), Sucre (judicial capital, 231,000), Santa Cruz (1,337,000), Cochabamba (583,000), Oruro (209,000).

Official Languages: Spanish, Aymará, Quechua (Aymará and Quechua were adopted as official languages in 1977).

Monetary Unit: Boliviano (market rate December 1, 2009: 7.02 bolivianos = $1US).

President: Juan Evo MORALES Ayma (Movement to Socialism); elected December 18, 2005, and inaugurated January 22, 2006, for a five-year term, succeeding Interim President Eduardo RODRÍGUEZ Veltsé (Nonparty).

Vice President: Álvaro GARCÍA Linera (Movement to Socialism); elected December 18, 2005, and inaugurated January 22, 2006, for a term concurrent with that of the president. (The office had been vacant since assumption of the presidency by Carlos Diego MESA Gisbert on October 17, 2003.)

THE COUNTRY

A country of tropical lowlands and *pampas* flanked by high mountains in the west, landlocked Bolivia is noted for a high proportion of Indians (predominantly Aymará and Quechua), who constitute more than 60 percent of the population, although their integration into the

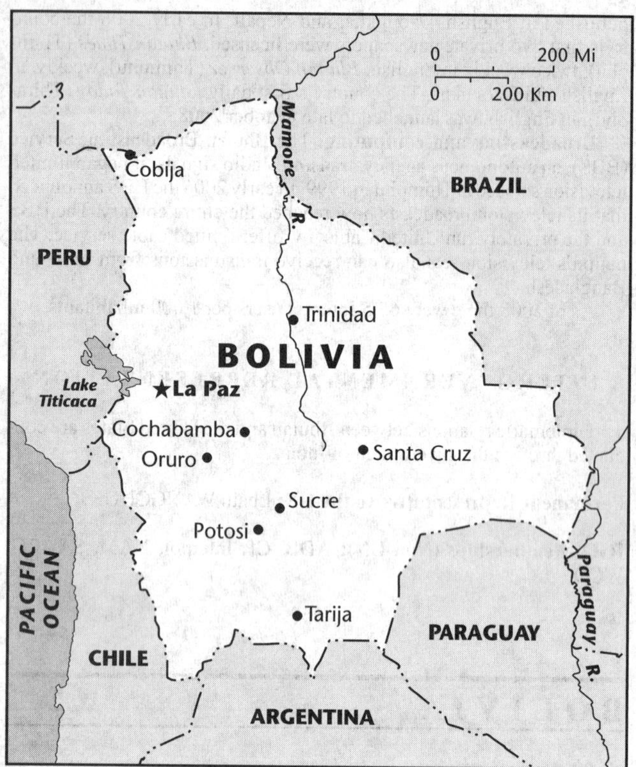

country's political and economic life progressed slowly until recently. Women constitute approximately 39 percent of the labor force, with roughly equal numbers in agricultural, manufacturing, clerical, and service activities. Spanish, the sole official language until 1977, is the mother tongue of less than 40 percent of the people, while Roman Catholicism is the predominant religion.

Although providing only one-sixth of Bolivia's gross national product, agriculture employs about half the population, mostly on a subsistence level. The main crops are soybeans, cotton, coffee, sugar, wheat, barley, and corn. According to recent estimates, only 10 percent of the nation's farming families own 90 percent of arable land, a situation the current administration plans to alter through a controversial land distribution plan (see Current issues, below). Tin mining has been a traditional mainstay of the economy, although the state-owned mines have long been wracked by labor difficulties. The country holds an estimated 50 percent of the world's lithium reserves in the saltpans of its southern Andean plains. Other significant metal exports include silver, zinc, and tungsten. Bolivia also reportedly controls one of the world's largest unexploited reserves of iron ore. A limited number of large-scale gold mines have operated around the country since 2002, with the largest to date beginning production in 2008.

Natural gas surpassed tin as the leading export commodity in 1982. Gas reserves (estimated as the second largest in Latin America) are located primarily in the eastern lowlands, exacerbating a long-standing divide between the poorer western highlands (populated mainly by Indians) and the richer east (populated mainly by people of European descent and mestizos). Based on the rapidly growing gas and agricultural sectors, the department of Santa Cruz and other lowland departments have served as the country's "economic engine" for several decades. Petroleum production peaked in 1974. A leading contributor to the underground economy has long been coca leaf production, with the overwhelming proportion of annual output entering the cocaine trade. In the late 1980s, about 400,000 persons in the Chapare region alone were engaged in coca cultivation, with total income from drug trafficking estimated at more than $2.5 billion. U.S.-backed efforts at coca eradication, chiefly by means of crop substitution, fluctuated thereafter.

After inflation exploded to a then world record of 24,000 percent in 1985, it fell steadily to 6.5 percent in 1998 under the influence of a sustained austerity program. However, the measures taken to counter it also brought about higher unemployment, which reached 25 percent in the 1990s. The economy consistently expanded for most of the 1990s followed by a period (1999–2003) when annual growth declined due to political turmoil and growing social tensions. Subsequently, annual GDP growth recovered to more than 4 percent in 2005. Sixty percent of all citizens lived below the poverty line in 2006, with that number rising to more than 80 percent in rural areas. The International Monetary Fund (IMF), while citing Bolivia's "macroeconomic stability," noted in 2006 and 2007 that economic advancement had only marginally assisted the poor. The new leftist government announced a massive poverty-reduction program designed, among other things, to create jobs and provide better public services.

In 2008 Bolivia had an annual GDP growth of 5.9 percent, owed largely to sharp increases in revenue from hydrocarbon and mineral exports. The same growth pushed unemployment to a low of 7.5 percent, and the IMF noted that the country's overall fiscal position had improved. Though an inflation rate of 14 percent was reported, it was projected to decline to 8.9 percent in 2009.

In the wake of the global economic downturn, revised estimates in the first quarter of 2009 forecast a contraction of GDP growth to 1.4 percent in 2009 due to slowing private investment and consumption. The Morales administration announced stimulus measures to counter the worldwide recession, saying that the government would spend $1.9 billion to improve infrastructure and services, along with another $1 billion in the hydrocarbons sector. The administration rebuffed an IMF recommendation to increase privatization and instead embarked on a controversial program of partial nationalization of the gas and mining sectors (see Current issues, below).

GOVERNMENT AND POLITICS

Political background. Bolivia's history since its liberation from Spanish rule in 1825 has been marked by recurrent domestic instability and frequent conflicts with neighboring states, especially Chile, Peru, and Paraguay. Increased unrest in the mid-20th century prompted a seizure of power in April 1952 by the reform-minded Nationalist Revolutionary Movement (*Movimiento Nacionalista Revolucionario*—MNR), which proceeded to carry out a thoroughgoing social and political revolution under the leadership of presidents Víctor PAZ Estenssoro and Hernán SILES Zuazo, who alternately dominated the political scene in four-year terms from 1952 to 1964. MNR rule was cut short in November 1964, when the vice president, Gen. René BARRIENTOS Ortuño, acting in the midst of widespread disorder, assumed power by a military coup. After serving with Gen. Alfredo OVANDO Candía as co-president under a military junta, Barrientos resigned to run for the presidency and was elected in July 1966. Supported by the armed forces and a strong coalition in Congress, his regime encountered intense opposition from the tin miners, who charged repression of workers' unions. A southeastern jungle uprising led by Castroite revolutionary Ernesto "Ché" GUEVARA in 1967 resulted in Guevara's death at the hands of government troops and the capture of guerrilla ideologist Régis DEBRAY.

President Barrientos was killed in a helicopter crash in April 1969, and Vice President Luis Adolfo SILES Salinas succeeded to the presidency. Siles was deposed the following September by the military, which installed Barrientos's former co-president, Ovando Candía, as chief executive. Back-to-back coups occurred in October 1970, the first led by Gen. Rogelio MIRANDA and the second by Gen. Juan José TORRES. The Torres regime came to power with the support of students, workers, and leftist political parties. It was accompanied by continuing instability, the nationalization of properties (both foreign and domestic), and the creation in 1971 of an extraconstitutional "Popular Assembly" of trade-union leaders, Marxist politicians, and radical students led by Juan LECHIN Oquendo of the tin-miners' union. In August 1971 the armed forces, in alliance with the MNR and the Bolivian Socialist Falange (*Falange Socialista Boliviana*—FSB), deposed Torres and appointed a government under Col. Hugo BÁNZER Suárez. Two years later the MNR withdrew from the coalition, and, after an abortive revolt the following November, Bánzer rescinded an earlier pledge to return the nation to civilian rule in 1975.

In November 1977 President Bánzer again reversed himself, announcing that a national election would be held on July 9, 1978. After balloting marked by evidence of massive fraud, the military candidate, Gen. Juan PEREDA Asbún, was declared the winner over his closest competitor, former president Siles Zuazo. However, faced with a suddenly unified opposition, Pereda was forced to call for an annulment.

President Bánzer then declared that he would not remain in office beyond August 6, and on July 21 Pereda was installed as Bolivia's 188th head of state. Pereda was himself ousted on November 24 by Brig. Gen. David PADILLA Arancibia, who promised to withdraw following an election on July 1, 1979.

At the 1979 election, Siles Zuazo, the nominee of a center-left coalition, obtained a bare plurality (36.0 percent to 35.9 percent) over former president Paz Estenssoro, who headed a new MNR coalition that included a number of leftist groups. Called on to decide the outcome because of the lack of a majority, the Congress was unable to choose between the front-runners and on August 6 designated Senate President Walter GUEVARA Arce to serve as interim executive pending a new presidential election in May 1980.

Guevara was ousted on November 1, 1979, in a military coup led by Col. Alberto NATUSCH Busch, who was himself forced to resign 15 days later in the face of widespread civil disorder, including a paralyzing general strike in La Paz. On November 16 the Congress unanimously elected the president of the Chamber of Deputies, Lidia GUEILER Tejada, to serve as the country's first female executive for an interim term expiring August 6, 1980.

In the national election on June 29, 1980, Siles Zuazo again secured the largest number of votes while failing to win an absolute majority. As a result, before the new Congress could meet to settle on a winner from among the three leading candidates, the military, on July 17, once more intervened, forcing the resignation of Gueiler the following day in favor of a "junta of national reconstruction" that included Maj. Gen. Luis GARCIA MEZA Tejada (sworn in as president on July 18), Maj. Gen. Waldo BERNAL Pereira, and Vice Adm. Ramiro TERRAZAS Rodríguez.

During the following year the regime was divided because of differences within the military and internationally isolated because of charges that certain of its members were actively engaged in the drug trade. In early 1981 revolts broke out at the military academy in La Paz and in Cochabamba, southeast of the capital, while former presidents Natusch and Bánzer were both exiled in mid-May for plotting against the government. On May 26 García Meza resigned as army commander and as junta member, naming Gen. Humberto CAYOJA Riart as his successor in both posts; three days later Admiral Terrazas resigned as navy commander and junta member in favor of Capt. Oscar PAMMO Rodríguez. On June 27 General Cayoja was arrested for involvement in a plot to remove García Meza from the presidency, Brig. Gen. Celso TORRELIO Villa being designated his successor. On August 4, following a rebellion in Santa Cruz, the president resigned in favor of General Bernal, who, in turn, yielded the office of chief executive to General Torrelio on September 4.

Amid growing economic difficulty, labor unrest, pressure from the parties, and lack of unity within the military, President Torrelio announced that a constituent assembly election would be held in 1984. The increasingly beleaguered government issued a political amnesty in late May 1982 and authorized the parties and trade unions to resume normal activity. On July 19 General Torrelio was ousted in favor of Gen. Guido VILDOSO Calderón, who announced, following a meeting of armed forces commanders on September 17, that the Congress elected in 1980 would be reconvened to name a civilian president. The lengthy period of military rule formally ended on October 10 with the return to office of Siles Zuazo and the concurrent installation of Jaime PAZ Zamora as vice president.

During the ensuing two years, numerous government changes proved incapable of reversing steadily worsening economic conditions, and in November 1984 Siles Zuazo announced that he would retire from the presidency following a general election in mid-1985. In the balloting on July 14, 1985, former president Bánzer of the right-wing Nationalist Democratic Action (*Acción Democrática Nacionalista*—ADN) obtained a narrow plurality (28.6 percent) of the votes cast, while the MNR of runner-up Paz Estenssoro won a plurality of congressional seats. In a second-round poll in Congress on August 5, Paz Estenssoro secured a clear majority over his ADN competitor. He was inaugurated for his fourth presidential term on August 6 in the country's first peaceful transfer of power since his succession of Siles Zuazo exactly 25 years earlier.

While successful in virtually eliminating one of history's highest rates of inflation, the new administration proved unable to resolve a wide range of other economic difficulties that included massive unemployment (generated, in part, by a crippling decline in world tin prices) and an illegal cocaine trade that provided half the country's export income. The public responded on December 6, 1987, by rejecting most government candidates in municipal balloting that yielded impressive gains for both the rightist ADN and the Movement of the Revolutionary Left (*Movimiento de la Izquierda Revolucionaria*—MIR).

As in 1985 the results of the nationwide balloting of May 7, 1989, were inconclusive. MNR candidate Gonzalo ("Goni") SANCHEZ DE LOZADA Bustamente obtained a slim plurality (23.1 percent) in the presidential poll over the ADN's Bánzer (22.7 percent) and the MIR's Paz Zamora (19.6 percent). A period of intense negotiation ensued that yielded a somewhat improbable pact of "national unity" between the right-wing ADN and the left-of-center MIR on August 2 and the congressional selection four days later of Paz Zamora to head an administration in which 10 of 18 cabinet posts were awarded to the ADN. The unusual accord (which excluded the MNR) was seen, in part, as a continuation of long-standing personal animosity between former president Bánzer and MNR leader Sánchez de Lozada. Bánzer claimed as his reward the chair of an interparty Political Council of Convergence and National Unity (*Consejo Superior de Unidad y Convergencia*), which some interpreted as the effective locus of power within the MIR-ADN coalition.

In the nationwide poll of June 6, 1993, Sánchez de Lozada again defeated Bánzer, this time by a sufficiently impressive margin to ensure designation by Congress under a new procedure that confined its options to the two front-runners. In the legislative balloting, the MNR obtained an equally improved plurality (69 of 157 seats overall) that yielded a preinaugural governing pact between the MNR, the rightist Civic Solidarity Union (*Unión Cívica Solidaridad*—UCS), and the leftist Free Bolivia Movement (*Movimiento Bolivia Libre*—MBL). The UCS withdrew from the coalition in September 1994, apparently because of government concessions to labor in furtherance of its antidrug campaign; however, the party rejoined the coalition in June 1995.

The 1997 candidacy of the ADN's Bánzer was aided by the withdrawal of the highly respected René BLATTMANN Bauer, in favor of the relatively colorless Juan Carlos DURAN. Despite his advanced age of 71 and former role as a military dictator, Bánzer led the June 1 poll with 22.3 percent of the vote and ensured his congressional designation by entering into a post-election coalition with the MIR, the UCS, and the fourth-ranked Conscience of the Fatherland (*Conciencia de Patria*—Condepa). Overall, the group controlled 96 of 130 seats in the Chamber of Deputies and 24 of 27 in the Senate. Following a leadership dispute within Condepa in mid-1998, its two cabinet members resigned, and Bánzer dropped the party from the ruling coalition. An ailing Bánzer resigned on August 7, 2001, and was succeeded by Vice President Jorge Fernándo QUIROGA Ramírez to serve for the balance of the presidential term to August 2002.

In the election of June 30, 2002, the MNR, in alliance with the MBL, won pluralities of 11 Senate and 36 Chamber seats, while Sánchez de Lozada outpolled Movement to Socialism (*Movimiento al Socialismo*—MAS) leader Evo MORALES by a bare 1.5 percent margin in presidential balloting and was reappointed by Congress on August 4. The ensuing year was marked by turmoil on a number of fronts, including opposition to the U.S.-backed coca eradication program, anger at the plight of the landless, objections to the export of natural gas to Chile, and discontent with tax increases and a number of recent privatizations. On October 13, 2003, Vice President Carlos MESA Gisbert withdrew his support for the president, and on October 17, amid widespread clashes between security forces and demonstrators, Sánchez de Lozada was forced to resign and flee the country. Mesa assumed the presidency, naming a new and formally nonpartisan cabinet.

President Mesa resigned on June 6, 2005, in the wake of widespread unrest over the nation's hydrocarbon policies and related autonomy pressure in several regions, most notably Santa Cruz. After the president of Congress and the president of the Chamber of Deputies had removed themselves from the official line of succession to permit a compromise with the MAS (the party most directly involved in the protests), Supreme Court Justice Eduardo RODRÍGUEZ Veltsé was named interim president by the Congress. Rodríguez promptly announced an interim cabinet and launched negotiations for a new election schedule that would fill the presidential and vice-presidential vacancies and select a new Congress. However, a dispute erupted over a constitutionally mandated redistribution of seats to reflect demographic changes recorded by the 2001 census.

A congressional effort to sidestep the redistricting issue by decreeing that elections called for December 4 would be based on the 1992 census was voided by the Constitutional Court on September 22, 2005. On November 1, Rodríguez issued a constitutionally questionable decree redistricting the legislative seats, and on December 18 MAS

leader Morales won the presidency, defeating his closest competitor, former president Quiroga, by securing an unanticipated 53.7 percent of the vote. (Morales was the first presidential contender since the end of military rule in 1982 to gain a majority in the national poll and thereby secure victory without congressional action.) In the congressional races, the MAS won control of the lower house with a 72-seat majority, while running a close second to Quiroga's Social Democratic Power (*Poder Democrático Social*—Podemos) in the Senate. However, the MAS won the prefectures (governorships) in only three of the nine departments in concurrent balloting.

As requested by the Morales administration, Congress in March 2006 authorized the election of a Constituent Assembly to rewrite the constitution. In balloting on July 2, the MAS secured 137 of 255 seats in the assembly, while in concurrent balloting on a referendum regarding proposed greater regional autonomy, the five western departments (La Paz, Oruro, Potosi, Chuquisaca, and Cochabamba) voted no and the four eastern departments (Santa Cruz, Tarija, Beni, and Pando) voted yes. Autonomy was thereby not granted to any of the departments, the National Elections Court (*Corte Nacional Electoral*—CNE) having previously ruled (much to the consternation of the easterners) that a majority of voters nationwide needed to approve the measure for it to be adopted in any department. (The national no vote totaled 57 percent.)

President Morales appointed a new cabinet with a "distinct leftist tilt" on January 24, 2007, in the midst of a severe east/west schism regarding constitutional revision and other issues (see Current issues, below). The president reshuffled the cabinet on January 24, 2008, following the Constituent Assembly's approval of the text for a new constitution, which was approved in a national referendum on January 25, 2009 (see Current issues, below, for details). The cabinet was reshuffled in February 2009 and included three new ministries: Autonomy; Cultures and Transparency; and the Fight Against Corruption.

Constitution and government. The constitution of February 1967 was Bolivia's 16th since independence. It vested executive power in a popularly elected president and legislative authority in a bicameral Congress. Suspended in 1969, it was reinstated in 1979, the country having been ruled during the intervening decade by presidential decree; the constitution remained technically in effect following the 1980 coup subject to military contravention of its terms and was restored to full force upon the return to civilian rule in October 1982.

Under the 1967 basic law the president was directly elected for a four-year term if the recipient won an absolute majority of votes; otherwise, Congress made the selection from among the three leading candidates. However, given the selection in 1989 of the third-ranked contender, congressional leaders in mid-1990 agreed on a revision that limited Congress to choosing between the plurality candidate and the runner-up. In 1997 the term of office was extended to five years, with a limit of only one term.

The bicameral legislature consists of a 27-member Senate and a 130-member Chamber of Deputies, both directly elected for five-year terms. The judicial system is headed by a Supreme Court whose 12 members divide into four chambers: two for civil cases, one for criminal cases, and one for administrative cases. There is a District Court in each territorial department as well as provincial and local courts to try minor offenses.

There are nine territorial departments, each administered by a prefect (governor), who was appointed by the central government until first-ever direct elections were held for the posts in December 2005. Although the 1967 constitution called for the biennial election of municipal councils (empowered to supplant the president in the designation of mayors), implementing legislation was deferred until 1986, with local balloting being conducted in December 1987 for the first time in 39 years.

In July 1996 the government secured approval from the Chamber of Deputies for a constitutional amendment on redistribution of seats in the chamber, giving added representation to the more populous and powerful departments of La Paz and Santa Cruz at the expense of the peripheral departments of Chuquisaca, Pando, and Potosi. Agreement also was reached on the first-ever introduction of single-member constituencies.

Congress, under pressure from the Morales administration, passed a resolution in March 2006 calling for a 255-member elected constituent assembly to rewrite the Bolivian constitution beginning August 6, 2006, following direct elections on July 2, 2006, for the assembly delegates. The assembly was given a one-year mandate, after which its proposals were to be presented for a national referendum. Little progress was reported within the assembly throughout most of 2007, as government and opposition members argued over procedures. The Morales administration was pursuing, among other things, revisions to basic law that would permit presidents to serve more than one term as well as codification of the government's plans to redistribute land to the benefit of the Indian population and to give indigenous populations the power to conduct political and economic affairs according to their traditions. Meanwhile, opposition parties (dominant in the resource-rich eastern lowlands) called for greater regional autonomy, the establishment of elected regional legislatures, and other decentralization measures that would weaken the power of the president.

On December 9, 2007, the Constituent Assembly approved a new charter that was to have been subject to national referendum in 2008 but was pushed back to 2009. A new constitution was approved by 61.4 percent of voters in a national referendum on January 25, 2009, and promulgated on February 7.

Foreign relations. Throughout most of the modern era, Bolivia's relations with its immediate neighbors have been significantly influenced by a desire to regain at least a portion of the maritime littoral that was lost to Chile in the War of the Pacific (1879–1884). In February 1975 relations with Chile were resumed after a 12-year lapse, Chile announcing that an "agreement in principle" had been negotiated between the two countries whereby Bolivia would be granted an outlet to the sea (*salida al mar*) along the Chilean-Peruvian border in exchange for territory elsewhere. However, definitive resolution of the issue was complicated in late 1976 by a Peruvian proposal that the corridor from Bolivia be linked to an area north of the city of Arica (obtained by Chile as a consequence of the war) that would be under the three nations' joint sovereignty. The proposal was based on a 1929 treaty that provided that any cession of former Peruvian territory must be approved by Peru. (For developments from 1976 to 1994, see the 2007 *Handbook*.) In 2006, Evo Morales became the first president-elect in more than half a century to invite Chile's president to attend his inauguration, while insisting that restoration of full diplomatic relations would be contingent on Chile's acceding to Bolivia's demand for a sovereign corridor to the sea. During July of that year, Morales and Chilean President Bachelet reached agreement on an "agenda" for resolving the territorial issue, and by early 2007 it was reported that the "cold war" between the two countries had clearly been replaced by a period of confidence building.

Under the Bánzer dictatorship, Bolivia pursued an anti-communist and pro-U.S. line in inter-American affairs, although links with the United States were tenuous during most of the period of military rule because of the alleged involvement of senior officials in the cocaine trade. Relations with Colombia, Ecuador, Peru, and Venezuela were severed after the 1980 coup.

In July 1992 Bolivia applied for membership in the recently launched Southern Cone Common Market (Mercosur), while indicating that it wished to retain the membership in the Andean Pact. Subsequently, the Sánchez de Lozada administration endorsed a proposal to construct a 1,360-mile natural gas pipeline from Santa Cruz to São Paulo, Brazil, as well as a joint venture with Paraguay to develop a waterway for oceangoing ships from Bolivia to the Atlantic. While flow through the gas line following its inauguration in mid-1999 was far less than anticipated, talk of a second line arose in the wake of additional gas discoveries in Bolivia and a substantial increase in projected Brazilian demand. Meanwhile, the route of a pipeline to the coast to permit gas exports to Mexico and the United States became a major factor in domestic politics.

In an elaborate demonstration of reconciliation that included an exchange of trophies between former opponents in the bloody Chaco War of 1932–1935, President Wasmosy of Paraguay visited La Paz in August 1994. Subsequently, at the conclusion of a Rio Group meeting on September 10, Sánchez de Lozada signed a free-trade agreement with Mexican President Salinas de Gortari.

In 1996 Bolivia and the United States issued seemingly divergent assessments of the coca eradication campaign, the former insisting that a targeted reduction of 5,000–8,000 hectares for the year would be reached, and the latter claiming that the area under cultivation had remained constant during an eight-year period. (The statements were not incompatible, as land taken out of production could have been offset by new plantings elsewhere.) A revised U.S. estimate in mid-1997 contended that the total area under cultivation had increased by 27 percent during the preceding decade, and under a new cooperation agreement signed in late August the United States cut its farmer compensation funding by half. In September 2001 Bolivia conceded that claims by former president Bánzer that most illegal plantations had been eradicated were in error and that about 6,000 hectares (rather than 600) remained under cultivation. In late 2002, amid reports that new plantings were far outstripping eradication, U.S. satellite imagery placed the figure at 24,400 hectares. By 2007, estimates indicated Bolivia's coca production had increased to around 29,000 hectares, 5 percent more than the year before, though still significantly lower than production in the 1990s. The country's potential for cocaine production amounted to 104-120 metric tons the same year, ranking Bolivia as the world's third-largest cocaine producer and coca cultivator. Total area under coca cultivation and cocaine refinement increased steadily beginning in 2000.

President Morales, while urging decriminalization of coca cultivation and its removal from the UN list of banned substances, indicated in 2006 that he opposed both processing the leaf into cocaine and trafficking in the drug. Before his inauguration, Morales embarked on a whirlwind international tour that took him to ten countries, including Brazil, Cuba, Venezuela, China, and Spain. Warmly greeted in Cuba and Venezuela for his stand against "American imperialism," he was coolly received in Spain, whose officials were uneasy about his plans for greater control of the energy industry.

In early 2006 (then) U.S. secretary of defense Donald Rumsfeld described the election of Morales, whose campaign had showcased anti–United States rhetoric, as "clearly worrisome," and the United States quickly announced plans to reduce military aid to Bolivia. However, any potential gap from that decision was apparently resolved by Bolivia's conclusion of a military agreement with Venezuela, which was reportedly greeted with concern in neighboring Peru and Paraguay. Venezuelan President Hugo Chávez, of whom Morales was considered a close ally, also pledged massive aid to Bolivia for the construction of hospitals and other social needs. In addition, Morales and Chávez negotiated a "people's trade area" with Cuba. (The pact, called the the Bolivarian Alternative for the Americas (ALBA), was signed on April 29, 2006, as a counter to the U.S. Free Trade Agreement of the Americas and focused on enhancing social programs and economic cooperation between the signatories.) On the other hand, Morales, revealing a pragmatic approach that his critics had not anticipated, declined to follow Chávez's decision to withdraw from the Andean Community of Nations. He also toned down his criticism of the United States, and met with U.S. officials to mend relations following protests on the U.S. embassy that turned violent on June 9, 2008. The Bolivian government expelled the U.S. ambassador on September 10 after declaring him persona non grata for fomenting opposition to the Morales administration. The U.S. government responded the next day by expelling the Bolivian ambassador. (Both offices remained vacant in 2009.)

On May 23, 2008, Bolivia became a member of the Union of South American Nations (Unasur). In November the U.S. government suspended Bolivia from participating in the Andean Trade Promotion and Drug Eradication Act, a U.S. trade preference program that gives countries incentives to develop economic alternatives to drug production. Bolivia was suspended for alleged noncompliance with law enforcement efforts

In April 2009 officials from Chile and Bolivia reached an initial agreement to resolve disputed rights to the Silala River. The deal was meant to compensate Bolivia for Chile's use of the water.

In what was hailed as a historic event, Bolivia and Paraguay signed an agreement on April 27, 2009, that officially ended their long-standing border dispute over the Chaco region, which had triggered a war in the 1930s. The agreement reconfirmed the border as it had been designated in a 1938 treaty, giving a larger portion of the area to Paraguay. Improved bilateral relations followed the resolution.

Current issues. Few countries have matched Bolivia's unhappy record of political instability, which yielded nearly 200 chief executives in its first century and a half of independence. There were 13 presidents from 1969 to 1982 alone, the most durable incumbency being that of General Bánzer (1971–1978), while eight more followed in 1983–2006. Given the magnitude of the victory, there was hope that the pattern might be broken with the 2006 election of Evo Morales as the first indigenous chief executive.

President Mesa won approval of a somewhat ambiguous five-part hydrocarbons referendum in July 2004 that called for "using gas as a strategic resource to recover sovereign and viable access to the sea" (a reference to the dispute with Chile, see Foreign relations, above). Also approved were recovery of "all hydrocarbons at the wellhead" and the levying of taxes up to 50 percent on oil and gas production.

The referendum, as presented, had been opposed by the eastern, natural-gas producing department of Santa Cruz. The *cruceños*, who included most of the country's European descendants, contrasted their region of "productive Bolivia" with the Inca-dominated "conflictive Bolivia" of the western highlands; by mid-2004 they were calling for regional autonomy, if not secession. In January 2005 Santa Cruz announced the formation of an autonomous regional government. President Mesa responded by terming the unconstitutional action as "one of the gravest and most difficult situations that Bolivia has ever had to face."

In 2006 President Morales attempted to defuse the divisive hydrocarbon issue, endorsing nationalization while insisting that it did not mean "confiscation or exportation," only that "control of the resources at the wellhead" would no longer be retained by private companies.

In May 2006, Morales sent soldiers to occupy 32 privately owned oil and gas fields. Arguing that foreign corporations had been plundering what rightfully belonged to the Bolivian people, Morales gave the companies six months to renegotiate their contracts or face eviction. Instead of the 50 percent return that he had campaigned on in 2005, Morales now wanted foreign corporations to return 82 percent of their oil and gas revenue to Bolivia. Morales's bid to nationalize Bolivia's energy industry stirred anguish among the country's private developers, especially those in neighboring Brazil, whose state company Petrobras was the largest foreign investor in Bolivia. However, within weeks Brazilian President Luiz da Silva and Morales agreed to resolve the issue "rationally." (In 2007 Petrobras agreed to sell its two refineries in Bolivia to the Bolivian government for $112 million.)

Also beginning in 2006, Morales announced a plan for wide-scale land reform and redistribution to the country's indigenous rural workers, an issue perhaps even more divisive within the eastern regions of the country than the nationalization of natural gas and oil. Under the plan, 12 million state-owned acres would be redistributed initially, followed by the seizure and redistribution of privately owned land deemed "unproductive" because it was not used for farm production. The government contended that the legal ownership of much of the eastern lowlands under consideration was dubious because it had been acquired illegally by wealthy landowners under the Bánzer dictatorship. Vice President Alvaro Garcia Linera attempted to assuage fears among Santa Cruz landowners by giving them the opportunity to legalize their deeds and retain property that was under cultivation. Ultimately, the government's plan called for about 48 million acres to be redistributed by 2011, with limits to be placed on the size of private holdings.

Despite their initial outcries over the new hydrocarbon proposals and threats to withdraw from Bolivia, the foreign energy companies in October 2006 negotiated agreements whereby they would continue their activities while ceding a much larger share of the profits to the government. Although Bolivia's state-owned energy company was given formal control of hydrocarbon operations, it was widely agreed that it lacked the resources to develop the gas sector on its own. In addition, soaring global gas prices made it much easier for both sides to reach agreement on the allocation of revenues. President Morales was credited with having adopted a more pragmatic approach toward this issue than originally anticipated in many quarters, a development that prompted criticism from the far left. Meanwhile, Morales pledged that nationalization of a sort would proceed in the mining, telecommunications, and other sectors, although deadlines were not imposed as the government sought additional foreign investment.

The president's other proposed major policy thrust—land redistribution—was one of the main topics of discussion in the Constituent Assembly that was elected in mid-2006 with a mandate to draft a new constitution (see Constitution and government, above). The assembly did not begin work in earnest until spring 2007 because of the insistence of MAS, Morales's party, that individual components of the draft constitution be approved by majority vote in the assembly rather than the two-thirds vote demanded by the opposition. (Morales lost that battle.) The assembly also grappled with the complicated issue of greater regional autonomy, which agribusiness leaders in the eastern lowlands had demanded. Much of the population in the eastern departments appeared to support increased autonomy, particularly because it would mean greater local control of resource revenues. The movement for more autonomy burst out into large-scale anti-Morales demonstrations in several cities earlier in the year. Due to the contentiousness of the issues, the assembly was unable to meet its August deadline and its mandate was extended until December. Tensions resulting from the polarization of the country were heightened throughout the latter part of the year as the homes of politicians aligned with Morales, trade unions, and other public offices were the targets of bomb attacks.

On December 9, 2007, despite a boycott by the opposition party Podemos, the Constituent Assembly approved a new charter. However, one key article failed to garner the required two-thirds vote—a provision defining the "unproductive land holdings" that were key to the president's controversial redistribution plan. That article was to be the subject of a referendum in 2008 and, if approved, the entire proposed constitution would then have to be adopted by the Constituent Assembly and another referendum held on the entire charter. Articles approved in the charter included those allowing two consecutive presidential terms of five years each; increased power for the indigenous people; abolition of the Senate; and greater state control over natural resources. Days later, thousands of supporters of Morales demonstrated in favor of the new charter, while thousands in opposition protested in the streets.

In January 2008 Morales met with the opposition governors in an effort to overcome the impasse but was unsuccessful. Further undermining Morales's plan to redistribute the country's wealth, the National Electoral Court in March postponed indefinitely the president's proposed constitutional referendum, which had been scheduled for May 4. As tensions continued to mount, the prosperous department of Santa Cruz voted for autonomy—seen as a largely symbolic move—by over 85 percent on May 5, prompting violent protests between groups on either side of the issue. In June two of the poorer departments, Beni and Pando, also voted for greater autonomy; a subsequent referendum in Tarija, a region that contains 85 percent of the country's natural gas reserves, also supported greater autonomy. While President Morales declared all of the votes illegal, they underscored the seemingly intractable differences between the eastern lowland regions, which opposed Morales's redistribution plans, and the poverty-stricken western regions, where most of the indigenous population resides. In the wake of the political stalemate, Morales announced a referendum on his own government and on eight of the nine provincial governors. (A recall referendum was not held in the remaining province where a governor had been recently elected.) Morales received the support of 67 percent of voters during the August 10 recall referendum. Two of the governors who had been critics of the Morales administration lost their posts, while the four most powerful opposition governors kept their seats. On September 20 a group of 20 indigenous political workers were killed in the northern province of Pando. The province's opposition governor, Leopoldo Fernandez, was accused of orchestrating the killings and was arrested. Morales named a military leader to restore order in the province and to try to control drug traffickers working in the region.

On a more positive note, in a referendum on January 25, 2009, voters approved by nearly 62 percent a new constitution. The changes allowed Morales to seek election for a second term, instituted new legal rights to 36 indigenous groups, and gave the government greater control over Bolivia's natural resources. In a separate question posed on a specific constitutional amendment designed to limit large-scale land ownership, more than 80 percent of voters approved putting a ceiling of 5,000 hectares on any individual's land holdings. Voters also overwhelmingly backed the lesser of two options to cap ownership. But in a sign that divisions remained between the wealthy eastern and poorer western regions, four eastern departments voted against the constitutional changes.

Constitutional amendments also changed Bolivia's governance structure, establishing four tiers of local autonomy—departmental, regional, municipal and indigenous. The national government's role was altered to set policies governing foreign relations, energy, economics, and security. The senate was increased from 3 senators in each of the 9 departments, to 4 per department, for a total of 36. New provisions also established that supreme court judges be elected instead of appointed by congress. In addition, future constitutional amendments will require a two-thirds majority of congress.

The firing and arrest on January 30, 2009, of Santos RAMIREZ, a Morales supporter and president of the state-owned oil and gas company Yacimientos Fiscales Petrolíferos de Bolivia, made public the turmoil and corruption at the highest levels of business and government in the country. It helped neither popular confidence nor investment in Bolivia's hydrocarbon sector, analysts said. Police accused the company's ex-president of offering $3 million in bribes and linked him to an ongoing murder investigation. The company's three previous leaders were also fired for alleged corruption or incompetence.

In February 2009 the Morales government seized 36,000 hectares from several large landowners in the Alto Parapeti region as its first move to redistribute land. A month later, the president held a ceremony on one of the confiscated ranches and handed out titles to 34 indigenous people and poor farmers. Bolivia's new constitution limits land ownership to 5,000 acres and permits reclamation by the government if it deems the land is not being used to its full potential or for other social reasons, a measure that drew strong opposition from eastern landowners.

Following the installation of a new government in February 2009, leftist groups that supported the president criticized the new cabinet, saying that the changes amounted to name-swapping and continued to leave poor people without representation in the governent. On April 7 Morales sent a bill to Congress that sought, among other things, to change electoral law based on the new constitution by redrawing voting districts and assigning more seats to the rural and majority indigenous areas. The lower house, with a MAS majority, quickly approved the legislation, while the opposition Podemos-controlled Senate blocked it from moving forward, saying it would give MAS complete control over both houses. To protest the Senate's refusal to cooperate, Morales went on a hunger strike beginning April 9. That public move, combined with negotiations that ultimately reduced the number of seats in the lower chamber, thus giving indigenous politicians a voting advantage, garnered enough support for the measure to be approved by the Senate. The new law, signed by Morales on April 14, set the next general elections for December 6 and gave Bolivians living outside the country the right to vote.

On May 3, 2009, Morales officially opened a military and police command base near the restive city of Santa Cruz, which has been the center of calls for separation from Bolivia and opposition to his government. During remarks at the opening, Morales said the base was built specifically to reinforce government armed forces and deal with local separatism and terrorism. In the run-up to December elections, President Morales instituted several social programs. One offered cash incentives to expectant mothers for going to regular pre- and post-natal medical checkups. The cash transfer program is expected to reach 250,000 women. A second gives money to people over age 65, and a third offers money as an incentive to poor children to keep them from dropping out of school.

POLITICAL PARTIES

Of approximately 60 political parties in Bolivia, the leading contenders in 1985 were the MNR and the ADN, with the MIR emerging as a threat to both in 1989. The MIR joined with the ADN in a Patriotic Accord (*Acuerdo Patriótico*—AP) electoral coalition in 1993. In 1997 the MIR, UCS, and Condepa formed an alliance with the ADN that yielded the designation of Hugo Bánzer Suárez as president. The 2002 poll was narrowly won by an alliance of the MNR and five minor parties. In 2005 most of the traditional parties were eclipsed by the triumph of Morales's MAS.

Government and Government-Supportive Parties:

Movement to Socialism (*Movimiento al Socialismo*—MAS). Traditionally a minor leftist grouping, the MAS contested the 1997 election as a component of the United Left (below). In 2002 it emerged as the leading opposition group with 8 Senate and 27 Chamber seats. Militant coca-grower leader Evo Morales, an Aymara Indian, was "adopted" by the MAS for the 2002 presidential campaign, placing second to the MNR's Sánchez de Lozado. The party led all others in the 2004 municipal elections, winning 13 departmental capitals.

Morales won the presidency with 53.7 percent of the vote in 2005, and the MAS secured a comfortable majority in the Chamber of Deputies. The party also won the prefectures of the departments of Chuquisaca, Oruro, and Potosi.

The MAS won a majority in the July 2006 balloting for the Constituent Assembly established to propose constitutional revision and subsequently established ties with the MBL (below) and other small parties to extend its influence in that assembly.

The party came under increasing scrutiny as the fallout widened from the scandal involving the state oil company (see Current issues, above). On March 11, 2009, MAS dismissed both the oil company president and party founding member Santos Ramírez. Critics alleged that Morales gave high-ranking positions to the party faithful rather than to qualified professionals. Rifts also began to emerge within MAS as Morales reallocated seats to his indigenous Indian support base.

With the promulgation of a new constitution in 2009, Morales was given the opportunity to run for a second term. By instituting healthcare, welfare, and other social programs with revenues from the hydrocarbon sector, Morales seemed likely to be reelected in December, analysts speculated.

Leaders: Juan Evo MORALES Ayma (President of the Republic), Álvaro GARCÍA Linera (Vice President of the Republic), Silvia LAZARTE (President of the Constituent Assembly), Gerardo GARCÍA, Roman LOAYZA.

Free Bolivia Movement (*Movimiento Bolivia Libre*—MBL). A breakaway faction of the MIR, sometimes styled the Leftist Revolutionary Movement–Free Bolivia (*Movimiento de Izquierda Revolucionaria–Bolivia Libre*—MIR-BL), the MBL was formed in January 1985. It was a member of the IU before the municipal elections of December 1989. The party secured four lower house seats in 1997. In 2002 it entered into an electoral alliance with the MNR.

The MBL, centered in the department of Cochabamba, cooperated with the MAS in the 2006 balloting for the Constituent Assembly, securing eight seats.

Leaders: Franz BARRIOS, Orlando CEVALLOS.

Opposition Parties:

Social and Democratic Power (*Poder Democrático Social*—Podemos). The right-wing Podemos was launched in 2005 under the leadership of former president and former ADN leader Jorge Quiroga before the December 2005 balloting, at which it won a plurality of Senate seats and placed second to the MAS in the Chamber of Deputies. Quiroga, who enjoyed strong support within the business community, also finished second in the concurrent presidential race with 28.6 percent of the vote, while Podemos won the prefectures of the departments of La Paz, Beni, and Pando. Podemos, in many respects considered an "extension" of the ADN, won 60 seats in the 2006 balloting for the Constituent Assembly, calling for constitutional change that would strengthen the legislature at the expense of the president and provide for the direct election of more officials. In 2007 Quiroga accused the Morales administration of "undemocratic behavior."

In March 2009 Senate president Oscar Ortiz threatened to leave Podemos after rifts developed in the party when a majority agreed to a compromise with the governing MAS party. Thirteen of the party's members of parliament said they would join Ortiz in a new party. Ortiz and his supporters, all from the Santa Cruz area, mounted strong opposition to the administration's agenda. On May 22, 2009, the group began to organize a party under the name **People's Consensus** (*Consenso Popular*). The group was expected to make public its bid for the presidency on June 15.

Leaders: Jorge Fernándo "Tuto" QUIROGA Ramírez (Former President of the Republic), Fernando MESSMER, Rubén DARÍO Cuéllar, Carlos Alberto GOITIA.

National Unity Front (*Frente Unidad Nacional*—UN). The UN was launched in late 2003 by cement magnate Samuel Doria Medina, a defector from the MIR (below), who called for equal representation of men and women in the new group and economic policies favoring "those entrepreneurs who generate employment and are absent from national decision-making." Doria Medina ran third in the 2005 presidential poll with 7.8 percent of the vote. The UN won 8 seats in the 2005 balloting for the Chamber of Deputies and the same number in the 2006 poll for the Constituent Assembly.

As the global financial crisis worsened, the UN called for an end to political struggles to focus on shoring up the flagging economy and creating jobs. Doria Medina invited former presidents Carlos Mesa Gisbert and Eduardo Rodríguez Veltzé, former vice president Víctor Hugo Cárdenas, and Potosi mayor René Joaquino to unify their efforts to defeat the president.

Leaders: Samuel DORIA Medina Arana, José VILLAVICENCIO (Former President of the Senate), Ricardo POL.

Nationalist Revolutionary Movement (*Movimiento Nacionalista Revolucionario*—MNR). Founded in 1941 by Víctor Paz Estenssoro, the original MNR ruled from 1952 until 1964 but was outlawed for a time after the 1964 coup. It joined with the FSB (see ADN, below) and others in a National Popular Front in support of the Bánzer coup in 1971 but withdrew two years later. The MNR spawned a number of other parties as a result of leadership disputes and contested the 1978 election as the leading component of an electoral coalition styled the Historic Nationalist Revolutionary Movement (*Movimiento Nacionalista Revolucionario* Histórico—MNRH), after failing to negotiate an accord with the moderately leftist Democratic and Popular Union (UDP, under MNRI, below). The MNRH in turn contested the 1979 and 1980 elections as the core party of the Alliance of the Nationalist Revolutionary Movement (*Alianza de Movimiento Nacionalista Revolucionario*—A-MNR). Although tendered left-wing congressional support in defeating General Bánzer for the presidency in August 1985, Paz Estenssoro subsequently concluded a political accord with the ADN (below) to facilitate implementation of a hard-line economic stabilization program. The MNR was decisively defeated in most of the municipal contests of December 6, 1987, and was unable to retain the presidency despite recovery to marginal front-runner status at the general election of May 7, 1989. Three months later Paz Estenssoro, who had been living in the United States since the inauguration of his nephew as president of the republic, announced that he was resigning the party leadership. The decision was formalized at a party congress in mid-1990 by the election of Gonzalo Sánchez de Lozada as his successor. During the congress the 84-year-old MNR founder attempted to heal a breach between a group of "renewalists" headed by Sánchez de Lozada and a "traditionalist" faction led by former vice president Julio GARRET. (Paz Estenssoro died on June 7, 2001.)

On October 27, 1992, Sánchez de Lozada resigned as MNR president and withdrew from the 1993 presidential election campaign after reportedly receiving a death threat from an MNR congressional deputy. However, he resumed both activities on November 20 and subsequently served as chief executive from 1993 to 1997. Reelected in 2002, he was forced to resign in October 2003. The party was virtually annihilated in the 2004 municipal balloting. In the December 2005 poll it secured 1 Senate and 7 Chamber seats, while its presidential candidate secured 6.5 percent of the vote. The MNR, currently described as a "traditionalist" and right-wing grouping, won 8 seats on its own in the 2006 balloting for the Constituent Assembly and apparently shared 10 other seats in alliance with other parties. The party's influence has been on the steady decline and the party is now in the process of reorganizing its leadership and direction.

Leaders: Michiaki NAGATANI Morishita (2005 presidential candidate), Eduardo YÁNEZ, Mirta QUEVADO Acalinovic.

Other Parties that Contested Recent Elections:

New Republican Force (*Nueva Fuerza Republicana*—NFR). The NFR is a group led by Manfred Reyes Villa, who supported Bánzer in 1997. It elected 2 senators and 25 deputies in 2002 but fared poorly in the 2004 municipal balloting and elected none of its congressional candidates in 2005, its presidential candidate in the latter year securing only 0.7 percent of the vote.

Reyes Villa was elected prefect of the department of Cochabamba in 2005 under the banner of the **National Union Alliance** (*Alianza de Unidad Nacional*—AUN), which also won 8 seats in the 2006 Constituent Assembly balloting.

Leaders: Manfred REYES Villa (2002 presidential candidate), Adm. (Ret.) Gildo ANGULA Cabrera (2005 presidential candidate).

Pachakuti Indigenous Movement (*Movimiento Indígena Pachakuti*—MIP). The MIP was formed before the 2002 poll by Felipe Quispe ("Mallku"), executive secretary of the United Confederation of Bolivian Peasant Workers (*Confederación Unica de Trabajadores Campesinos de Bolivia*—CUTCB) and a former member of the EGTK (below). Quispe won 2.2 percent of the vote in the 2005 presidential balloting.

Leader: Felipe QUISPE Huanca ("Mallku").

Civic Solidarity Union (*Unión Cívica Solidaridad*—UCS). The UCS is an outgrowth of the National Civic Union (*Unión Cívica Nacional*—UCN), founded in 1988 to promote the presidential aspirations of right-wing industrialist Max FERNÁNDEZ Rojas. The group was first registered under its present name for the December 1989 municipal balloting, in which it ran a surprising third, winning 22.8 percent of the vote. The party also ran third in the June 1993 national poll with 13.1 percent.

In May 1994 continuance of the UCS as an MNR government partner appeared threatened by an unheralded pact concluded by the president with Julio MANTILLA and Ivo KULJIS, the leaders, respectively, of two UCS splinters, the **Popular Patriotic Movement** (*Movimiento Popular Patriótico*—MPP) and the **Unity and Progress Movement** (*Movimiento de Unidad y Progreso*—MUP). Four months later, in what was interpreted as a reaction to the administration's pact with the Bolivian Workers' Confederation, Fernández announced that the UCS was withdrawing from the government coalition. However, a group of dissidents led by Edgar Talavera refused to join in the walkout, and in June 1995 the party rejoined the coalition. Fernández died in a plane crash the following November. The party backed Kuljis for president in 1997 because Johnny Fernández, one of the party's founders, was too young to stand as a candidate. Immediately before the 2002 election, the Constitutional Tribunal overturned an Electoral Court ban on Fernández's presidential candidacy because of tax arrears.

The party's future is currently in doubt because of its inability to win any municipal council seats in 2004, to secure legislative representation in 2005, or to gain seats in the 2006 balloting for the Constituent Assembly.

Leader: Johnny FERNÁNDEZ Saucedo (2002 presidential candidate).

Nationalist Democratic Action (*Acción Democrática Nacionalista*—ADN). The ADN was formed in early 1979 by Hugo Bánzer Suárez under the slogan "peace, order, and work." Bánzer ran third in presidential balloting in both 1979 and 1980. He secured a plurality of the popular vote in 1985 but was defeated by Paz Estenssoro in a congressional runoff. Following the election, the ADN concluded a somewhat fragile legislative alliance, the Democratic Pact (*Pacto pour la Democracia*) with the MNR, which was reaffirmed after both parties had experienced losses in the December 1987 municipal balloting. The alliance was broken by the ADN in early February 1989 to permit the party to campaign separately in the run-up to the May balloting, at which Bánzer ran a close second in the presidential race. In August the party concluded a "national unity" pact with the MIR (below), being awarded 10 of 18 cabinet posts in the Paz Zamora administration. Subsequently, the ADN, the MIR, and the PDC (below) jointly contested the December 1991 municipal elections under a Patriotic Agreement (*Acuerdo Patriótico*—AP) rubric, after having announced their support of Bánzer as their 1993 presidential candidate. The FRI (below) joined the AP for the June 1993 balloting, in which the former chief executive again placed second.

The AP was dissolved in August 1993, while in November Bánzer resigned as ADN leader and announced his retirement from public life. However, in February 1995, shortly after Paz Zamora of the MIR had ended his withdrawal from politics, Bánzer followed suit. He won a plurality in the balloting of June 1997 and was returned to the presidency with the support of the MIR, the UCS, and Condepa.

In mid-1999 Otto RITTER, leader of the **Bolivian Socialist Falange** (*Falange Socialista Boliviana*—FSB), a minor ADN ally, stated that Bánzer was unfit to rule and called for his resignation. As a result, the FSB's sole congressional deputy (elected on the ADN list) was expelled from the alliance. Bánzer resigned the presidency on August 7, 2001, and died on May 5, 2002.

Before the 2005 election, former president Jorge Fernándo Quiroga, an ADN leader, withdrew from the party to form Podemos (above), taking many of the ADN members with him. (Quiroga had reportedly concluded that the ADN rubric was too closely associated in the public consciousness with Bánzer.) The rump ADN failed to secure representation in the 2006 balloting for the Constituent Assembly.

Leaders: Ronald MACLEAN (2002 presidential candidate), Mauro BERTERO.

Patriotic Democratic Transformation (*Transformacíon Democrática Patriótica*—Tradepa). Tradepa was launched in August 2005 to represent retired military officers. It failed to secure representation in the 2006 balloting for the Constituent Assembly.

Leader: Luis GEMIO.

Movement of the Revolutionary Left (*Movimiento de la Izquierda Revolucionaria*—MIR). Affiliated with the Socialist International, the MIR is a non-communist Marxist party that organized as a splinter of the PDC and has a history of cooperation with the MNRI. It joined the UDP coalition before the 1978 election and its leader, Jaime Paz Zamora, ran for the vice presidency in 1979 and 1980. He assumed the office in 1982. The MIR withdrew from the government in January 1983 but returned in April 1984. In mid-December Paz Zamora resigned as vice president to qualify as a presidential candidate in 1985. In addition, several members left the MIR in 1985 to form the MBL (above), Paz Zamora's supporters subsequently referencing themselves as the MIR–New Majority (MIR–*Nueva Mayoría*—MIR-NM). The MIR was surprisingly successful in the December 1987 municipal balloting and, although running third in the national poll of May 1989, was awarded the presidency as the result of its "national unity" pact with the ADN. The party supported the ADN's Bánzer as a member of the AP in 1993. Paz Zamora entered into "permanent retirement" in March 1994 but returned to public life less than a year later, following the December 1994 arrest on drug-trafficking charges of the MIR's (then) secretary general, Oscar Eid Franco.

The MIR–NM won one seat in the 2006 balloting for the Constituent Assembly.

Leader: Jaime PAZ Zamora (Former President of the Republic and 1997 and 2002 presidential candidate).

Left Revolutionary Front (*Frente Revolucionario de Izquierda*—FRI). The FRI is led by Oscar Zamora Medínaceli, who once headed the Marxist-Leninist Bolivian Communist Party (*Partido Comunista Boliviano Marxista-Leninista*—PCB-ML), a pro-Communist China offshoot of the PCB, and was subsequently a founder of the MIR. For the 1985 elections Zamora Medínaceli formed an alliance with the MNR and was rewarded with the Senate presidency. In 1989 he backed the MIR-ADN coalition and was named labor minister in the government of his nephew, Paz Zamora. He resigned the labor portfolio in November 1992, ostensibly to campaign for president in 1993, but instead he accepted the vice-presidential slot on the ticket headed by the ADN's Bánzer. Subsequently, he became mayor of Tarija. An MNR-FRI alliance won eight seats in the 2006 balloting for the Constituent Assembly.

Leaders: Oscar ZAMORA Medinacelli, Dr. Manuel MORALES Dávila.

Christian Democratic Party (*Partido Demócrata Cristiano*—PDC). The PDC is a somewhat left-of-center Catholic party, a right-wing faction of which supported the Bánzer regime. It joined the A-MNR before the 1979 election. In early 1982 (then) PDC leader Benjamín Miguel Harb, in an apparent reference to right-wing elements within the MNR, indicated that the party would henceforth refuse to cooperate with other parties that "lack a democratic vocation." In November the party joined the UDP coalition, one of its members accepting the housing portfolio in the Siles Zuazo government. However, the PDC withdrew from the coalition in October 1984. Although the party won no legislative seats as an ally of the ADN in May 1989, its 1985 presidential candidate, Dr. Luis Ossio Sanjinés, was elected vice president of the republic as a result of its adherence to the ADN-MIR pact in August. The party campaigned as a member of the AP in 1993.

It was reported in 2005 that the PDC was one of the founding components of Podemos, although details were limited.

Leader: Jorge SUAREZ Vargas.

Other parties and groups active in recent elections include the **21st Century Alliance** (*Alianza Siglo XXI*), led by Pablo Mauricio IPIÑA Nagel; the **Agrarian Patriotic Front of Bolivia** (*Frente Patriótico Agropecuario de Bolivia*—FrePAB), whose presidential candidate—Eliceo RODRÍGUEZ Pari—won 0.3 percent of the vote in 2005; **Autonomy for Bolivia** (*Autonomía para Bolivia*—APB), which won the prefecture of the department of Santa Cruz in December 2005 and 3 seats in the 2006 Constituent Assembly elections; the **AYRA Movement** (*Movimiento AYRA*), which secured 2 seats in the Constituent Assembly in 2006; the **Citizens Action Movement** (*Movimiento de Acción Ciudadana*—MAC), which ran unsuccessfully in the Constituent Assembly balloting; **Citizens Democratic Convergence** (*Convergencia Democrática Ciudadana*—CDC), which ran unsuccessfully in the 2006 elections for the Constituent Assembly; **Local Autonomy** (*Autonomía Vecinal*—AVE), a Beni-based grouping led by Erwin Rivero ZIEGLER; the **Movement for Bolivian Integration** (*Movimiento de Integración Boliviana*—MIBOL); the **Movement of Patriotic Social Union** (*Movimiento de Unidad Social Patriótica*—MUSPA), led by Juan Gabriel BAUTISTA; the **National Concertation** (*Concertación Nacional*—CN), a Christian evangelist grouping founded in 2005 under the leadership of Antonio FANOLA Aliaga that secured 5 seats in the 2006 Constituent Assembly elections; the **Original Popular Movement** (*Movimiento Originario Popular*—MOP), which won 3 seats in the Constituent Assembly from the department of Podosi; the **Path to Change** (*Camino al Cambria*—CC), which won the prefecture of the department of Tarija in 2005; the **Progress Plan** (*Plan Progresso*—PP), which had initially been reported as a component of Podemos but was subsequently ruled by the election commission not to have participated officially in that grouping; the **Regional Autonomy Movement** (*Movimiento Autónomo Regional*—MAR), which failed to gain representation in the 2006 Constituent Assembly elections; the **Social Alliance** (*Alianza Social*—AS), a Potosi-based grouping that was granted legal status in 2006 and also won 6 seats in the same year's balloting for the Constituent Assembly; the **Social Union of the Workers of Bolivia** (*Unión Social de Trabajadores de Bolivia*—USTB), whose presidential candidate—Nestor GARCÍA Rojas—won 0.3 percent of the vote in 2005; and the **Without Fear Movement** (*Movimiento Sin Miedo*—MSM), a "progressive" grouping led by Juan DEL GRANADO Cosío.

Other Parties:

Leftist Nationalist Revolutionary Movement (*Movimiento Nacionalista Revolucionario de Izquierda*—MNRI). An offshoot of the MNR, the MNRI was the principal element in the organization of the center-left Democratic and Popular Union (*Unión Democrática y Popular*—UDP) before the 1978 balloting. Its presidential candidate, Hernán Siles Zuazo, obtained electoral pluralities in 1979 and 1980 and returned as the country's chief executive in October 1982. Faced with insurmountable economic problems, the president announced in November 1984 that he would cut short his term by one year. The party, which had suffered the defection of its secretary general three months earlier, split into a number of factions, including the center-right **Nationalist Revolutionary Movement–April 9 Revolutionary Vanguard** (*Movimiento Nacionalista Revolucionario–Vanguardia Revolucionaria 9 de Abril*—MNR-V) and the **Leftist Nationalist Revolutionary Movement–One** (*Movimiento Nacionalista Revolucionario Izquierdo–Uno*—MNRI-1), each of which campaigned separately thereafter.

Leaders: Dr. Hernán SILES Zuazo (Former President of the Republic), Federico ALVAREZ Plata (Secretary General).

Conscience of the Fatherland (*Conciencia de Patria*—Condepa). Condepa was formed in 1988 by popular singer and La Paz broadcast personality Carlos PALENQUE Avilés, who attracted widespread notoriety in November of that year by airing a "friendly" interview with the "king of cocaine," Roberto SUÁREZ. The party's ten-member congressional delegation supported Paz Zamora's selection as president in August 1989. Condepa won a plurality of votes in the 1989 municipal balloting in La Paz but was denied the mayoralty when the MNR cast two swing council votes for the ADN-MIR candidate. It ran fourth in the 1991 municipal poll, winning overall 12.5 percent of the vote but scored a victory in La Paz, with 26.4 percent. It placed fourth in the 1993 legislative balloting, winning an overall total of 14 seats, which increased to 17 in 1997. Palenque Avilés died on March 8, 1997; his successor as party leader, Remedios Loza, was the first indigenous woman to run for president.

Condepa participated in the Bánzer coalition government until August 6, 1998, when, in the wake of the withdrawal of its two ministers, it was expelled because of what the president termed internal strife that detracted from "the image a serious administration must have."

Leaders: Remedios LOZA (1997 presidential candidate), Nicolas Felipe VALDIVA Almanza.

United Left (*Izquierda Unida*—IU). The IU advanced Ramiro Velasco of PS-1 as its presidential candidate in the 1993 balloting, in which it lost all 10 of its existing legislative seats; it regained 4 in 1997. The IU long had a substantial following in the extra-legislative **Assembly for the Sovereignty of the People** (*Asamblea por la Soberanía del Pueblo*—ASP), led by Evo MORALES, who was presented as a 2002 presidential candidate by the MAS (above).

Leaders: Alejo VELEZ (1997 presidential candidate), Germán GUTTIEREZ, Marcos DOMIC (1997 vice-presidential candidate and IU coordinator).

Patriotic Alliance (*Alianza Patriótica*—AP). The AP (not to be confused with the *Acuerdo Patriótico*, above, under ADN) is an outgrowth of the former Workers and Masses Front (*Frente Obreroy de Masas*—FOM), a dissident MIR group also referenced as MIR-Masas and long linked to the Bolivian Workers' Central. It was launched as an electoral coalition in the late 1980s by a number of leftist groups, including the **Patriotic Axis of Convergence** (*Eje de Convergencia Patriótica*—ECP), which remained active in 1998.

Leader: Walter DELGADILLO Terceros.

Socialist Party–One (*Partido Socialista–Uno*—PS-1). The PS-1 was organized in 1971 by a group seeking a return to the policies of former president Ovando Candía. A relatively small party, it nonetheless obtained about 7 percent of the vote in 1979 and 8 percent in 1980. Its presidential candidate on both occasions, Marcelo Quiroga Santa Cruz, was murdered during the 1980 coup. It won 5 congressional seats in 1985, although being credited with only 2.2 percent of the vote. There also is a dissident *Partido Socialista-Uno-Marcelo Quiroga*, led by José María PALACIOS.

Leaders: Ramiro VELASCO (1985 and 1993 presidential candidate), Roger CORTEZ, Walter VAZQUEZ.

Bolivian Communist Party (*Partido Comunista de Bolivia*—PCB). A group with ties to the former Soviet Union formally organized in 1952, the PCB lost much of its influence because of a failure to support the *guevarista* insurgents in the mid-1960s. Subsequently, it joined the UDP coalition, losing further support within the labor movement because of its participation in the Siles Zuazo government. At a contentious party congress in February 1985, Simón Reyes Rivera was named to succeed Jorge Kolle Cueto as PCB secretary general. Shortly thereafter a minority faction, also styling itself the *Partido Comunista de Bolivia*, split from the parent group under Carlos Soria Galvarro.

Leaders: Simón REYES Rivera (Former Secretary General), Marcos DOMICH (Secretary General), Carlos SORIA Galvarro (minority faction leader).

Socialist Party (*Partido Socialista*—PS). A PCB splinter, the PS was launched in 1989 as the Socialist Vanguard of Bolivia (*Vanguardia Socialista de Bolivia*—VSB), which obtained 1.4 percent of the presidential vote in 1997. It secured one lower house seat in 2002.

Leader: Jeres JUSTINIANO (1997 presidential candidate).

Túpaj Katari Revolutionary Movement (*Movimiento Revolucionario Túpaj Katari*—MRTK). Formerly a member of the A-MNR, the MRTK is one of several small *campesino* formations, including the splinter MRTK-L and the guerrilla EGTK (below).

Leaders: Juan CONDORI Uruchi (President), Genaro FLORES Santos (1985 presidential candidate).

Túpaj Katari Revolutionary Movement–Liberation (*Movimiento Revolucionario Túpaj Katari–Liberación*—MRTK-L). The MRTK-L outpolled its parent party in 1985, winning 2 congressional seats, both of which were lost in 1989. In late 1992 the MNR sought to "balance" its 1993 presidential ticket by selecting the MRTK-L's Víctor Hugo Cárdenas as Gonzalo Sánchez de Lozada's running mate.

On the eve of the government's first redistribution of land to indigenous people in February 2009, Morales's supporters attacked Cardenas's family and seized his property. Later, Cardenas, an Aymara Indian and outspoken critic of the socialist elements in the new constitution, said he would challenge President Evo Morales in the December 2009 presidential election.

Leaders: Víctor Hugo CÁRDENAS Conde (Former Vice President of the Republic), Norberto PÉREZ Hidalgo (Secretary General).

Revolutionary Vanguard of 9 April (*Vanguardia Revolucionaria 9 de Abril*—VR-9). The VR-9 is a small grouping formed following the fractionalization of the MNRI (above). The party was highly critical of the ADN-MIR policies (particularly the coalition's effort to seek a postponement of the 1989 municipal balloting).

Leaders: Dr. Carlos SERRATE Reich, Roberto CROFF Centeno (Secretary General).

Other Groups:

Túpaj Katari Guerrilla Army (*Ejército Guerrillero Túpaj Katari*—EGTK). Not to be confused with either the MRTK or MRTK-L, the EGTK was a terrorist group believed to be responsible for more than 30 bombings as well as the assassination of an ADN member of Congress in November 1992. Three months earlier its leader, Felipe Quispe Huanca, had been apprehended by police.

In November 1995 a "manifesto" purportedly issued jointly by the EGTK and the **Nestor Paz Zamora Commission** (*Comisión Néstor Paz Zamora*—CNPZ), which had been identified with the celebrated kidnapping of businessman Jorge LONSDALE in 1990, claimed responsibility for the kidnapping of former planning minister Samuel DORIA Medina. However, Raquel GUTIÉRREZ, an imprisoned EGTK leader, insisted that her group had abandoned armed activity in 1992 and had no links to the CNPZ. The government last reported alleged EGTK activity in 1997, and the group has been considered defunct since at least then.

Alvaro García Linera, elected vice president of the republic in 2005, was once an EGTK member, having served five years in prison in the 1990s for guerrilla activity. Several former EGTK members were reportedly involved in radical leftist political action in the department of Cochabamba in early 2007.

Camba Nation (*Nación Camba*). Formed in the early 2000s in support of autonomy (if not independence) for Santa Cruz and other eastern departments, Camba Nation ("Camba" is a nickname for residents of Santa Cruz or, more broadly, "lowlanders") currently claims a membership of about 40,000. The government alleges that the group has armed itself for possible military confrontation, but Camba leaders insist they are committed to pursuit of their goals through peaceful means only.

Leader: Sergio ANTELO.

LEGISLATURE

The bicameral Bolivian **Congress** (*Congreso*) currently sits for five years. The most recent election was held on December 18, 2005.

Senate (*Senado*). The upper house consists of 27 members, 3 from each department, elected for terms concurrent with those of the Chamber of Deputies. In each department delegation, 2 seats are held by the majority party or group, while 1 is reserved for the minority. After the 2005 election, Social and Democratic Power held 13 seats; the Movement to Socialism, 12; the Nationalist Revolutionary Movement, 1; and the National Unity Front, 1.

President: Óscar ORTIZ Antelo.

Chamber of Deputies (*Camara de Diputados*). The lower house currently consists of 130 members elected in a mixed majoritarian/ proportional system by universal and direct suffrage for five-year terms from 70 single-member constituencies and 9 multimember constituencies. Following the 2005 election, the Movement to Socialism held 72 seats (45 majoritarian, 27 proportional); Social and Democratic Power, 43 (22, 21); the National Unity Front, 8 (1, 7); and the Nationalist Revolutionary Movement, 7 (2, 5).

President: Edmundo NOVILLO Aguilar.

CABINET

[as of June 1, 2009]

President	Juan Evo Morales Ayma
Vice President	Álvaro García Linera
Ministers	
Autonomy	Carlos Romero
Cultures	Pablo Groux
Economy and Public Finance	Luis Alberto Arce Catacora
Education	Roberto Aguilar
Environment and Water	Rene Gonzalo Orellana Halkyer
Foreign Affairs	David Choquehuanca Cespedes
Health and Sport	Ramiro Tapia
Hydrocarbons and Energy	Oscar Coca Antezana
Interior	Octavio Alfredo Rada Vélez
Justice	Celima Torrico Rojas [f]
Labor	Calixto Chipana
Legal Defense of the State	Héctor Arce
Mining and Metallurgy	Luís Alberto Echazú Alvarado
National Defense	Walker San Miguel Rodriguez
Planning and Sustainable Development	Noel Aguirre
Presidency	Juan Ramón Quintana Taborga
Production and Micro-enterprise	Susana Rivero Guzmán [f]
Public Services and Public Works	Walter Delgadillo Júvenal
Rural Development and Land	Julia Ramos [f]
Transparency and the Fight against Corruption	Nardy Suxo

[f] = female

COMMUNICATIONS

All news media are privately owned. Although strict censorship was often enforced under past military governments, Bolivia currently rates among the highest countries in Latin America in various press freedom indexes.

Press. The following papers are published daily in La Paz, unless otherwise noted: *El Diario* (55,000); *La Razón* (35,000); *Los Tiempos* (Cochabamba, 19,000), independent; *El Mundo* (Santa Cruz, 15,000), business oriented; *Jornada* (12,000), independent; *El Deber* (Santa Cruz); *La Prensa*; *El Nacional*.

News agencies. The domestic facility is the *Agencia de Noticias Fides* (ANF); a number of foreign agencies, including AFP, ANSA, and AP, maintain bureaus in La Paz.

Broadcasting and computing. Bolivia has numerous radio and television outlets. As of 2008 there were 108.3 Internet users per 1,000 inhabitants.

INTERGOVERNMENTAL REPRESENTATION

Ambassador to the U.S.: (Vacant).

U.S. Ambassador to Bolivia: (Vacant).

Permanent Representative to the UN: (Vacant).

IGO Memberships (Non-UN): ALADI, CAN, IADB, Interpol, IOM, Mercosur, NAM, OAS, OPANAL, PCA, SELA, WCO, WTO.

BOSNIA AND HERZEGOVINA

Republic of Bosnia and Herzegovina
Republika Bosna i Hercegovina (BiH)

Constituent "Entities":
Federation of Bosnia and Herzegovina
Federacija Bosne i Hercegovine (FBiH)

Serb Republic of Bosnia and Herzegovina
Republika Srpska Bosne i Hercegovine (RS)

Political Status of the Republic of Bosnia and Herzegovina (BiH): Former constituent republic of the Socialist Federal Republic of Yugoslavia; declared independence on March 3, 1992. (The Dayton agreement of November 21, 1995, specified that the institutions of the existing republic's government were to function until the holding of countrywide elections, after which a new central government would be formed with joint FBiH-RS participation and retention of purely internal functions by each of the two constituent "entities." The existence of a single state of Bosnia and Herzegovina and other provisions of the Dayton accords were confirmed by an international treaty signed in Paris, France, on December 14. Elections were held on September 14, 1996, and the central and entity governments were subsequently established in stages.)

Political Status of the Federation of Bosnia and Herzegovina (FBiH): Federation of the areas of the BiH containing majority Bosniac (Muslim) and Croat populations authorized by framework agreement of March 18, 1994, which envisaged the federation as a sovereign nation that would pursue a loose political confederation with Croatia; federation agreement "reinforced" by the Dayton accord of November 10, 1995, with permanent territorial boundaries established by the Dayton accord of November 21, under which, in revision of the 1994 agreement, it was decided that the FBiH would be an entity within the BiH.

Political Status of the Serb Republic (RS): Proclaimed by leaders of Serbian-held areas of the republic on March 27, 1992; established (under revised territorial boundaries) as an entity of the BiH under the Dayton accord of November 21, 1995.

Area (BiH): 19,741 sq. mi. (51,129 sq. km.). At the launching of the FBiH in 1994 the area under its control totaled some 30 percent of the former area of the BiH, the balance being under Serb control. Under the Dayton accord of November 21, 1995, approximately 51 percent of the country's total area was assigned to the FBiH and the remaining 49 percent to the RS.

Population (BiH): 4,377,033 (1991C); 3,521,000 (2008E, including nonresidents).

Major Urban Centers (2005E): SARAJEVO (380,000), Banja Luka (165,000).

Official Languages: Serbian, Croat, Bosnian.

Monetary Unit: Convertible Mark (official rate December 1, 2009: 1.29 convertible marks = $1US).

Presidency of the BiH: Željko KOMŠIĆ (Croat Member, Social Democratic Party of Bosnia and Herzegovina), who succeeded Ivo Miro JOVIĆ (Croatian Democratic Union of Bosnia and Herzegovina); Nebojša RADMANOVIĆ (Serb Member, Alliance of Independent Social Democrats), who succeeded Borislav PARAVAC (Serbian Democratic Party of Bosnia and Herzegovina); and Haris SILAJDŽIĆ (Bosniac Member, Party for Bosnia and Herzegovina), who succeeded Sulejman TIHIĆ (Party of Democratic Action). The three members of the presidency were elected for four-year terms on October 1, 2006, and sworn in on November 6. The chair of the presidency rotates among them every eight months.

President of the FBiH: Borjana KRIŠTO (Croatian Democratic Union), a Croat; elected by the FBiH House of Representatives on February 21, 2007, and confirmed for a four-year term by the FBiH House of Peoples on February 23, succeeding Niko LOZANČIĆ (Croatian Democratic Union).

Vice Presidents of the FBiH: Mirsad KEBO (Party of Democratic Action), a Serb, and Spomenka MIČIĆ (Party for Bosnia and Herzegovina), a Bosniac; elected by the FBiH House of Representatives on February 21, 2007, and confirmed by the FBiH House of Peoples on February 23 for terms concurrent with that of the president, succeeding Desnica RADIVOJEVIĆ (Party of Democratic Action) and Sahbaz DŽIHANOVIĆ (Party for Bosnia and Herzegovina), respectively.

President of the RS: Rajko KUZMANOVIĆ (Alliance of Independent Social Democrats), a Serb; elected December 9, 2007, and sworn into office on December 28, following the death of President Milan JELIĆ (Alliance of Independent Social Democrats) on September 30 and the interim presidency of RS National Assembly Speaker Igor RADOJIČIĆ (Alliance of Independent Social Democrats).

Vice Presidents of the RS: Davor ČORDAŠ (Croatian Democratic Union), a Croat, and Adil OSMANOVIĆ (Party of Democratic Action), a Bosniac; elected on October 1, 2006, and sworn in on November 9 for terms concurrent with that of the president of the RS. Čordaš succeeded Ivan TOMLJENOVIĆ (Social Democratic Party of Bosnia and Herzegovina). Osmanovic, now serving his second term, was first elected on October 5, 2002, succeeding Dragan ČAVIĆ (Serbian Democratic Party of Bosnia and Herzegovina).

Prime Minister of the BiH (Chair of the BiH Council of Ministers): Nikola ŠPIRIĆ (Alliance of Independent Social Democrats); endorsed by the BiH presidency on January 4, 2007, following the general election of October 5, 2006, and elected by the BiH House of Representatives on January 11, succeeding Adnan TERZIĆ (Party of Democratic Action); resigned November 1, 2007, over objections to reforms proposed by the high representative of the international community; resignation accepted by the central presidency on November 12, although he and the full Council of Ministers continued to serve pending confirmation of a successor; renominated by the leading parties on December 11, endorsed by the presidency on December 27, and reconfirmed by the BiH House of Representatives on December 28.

Prime Minister of the FBiH: Mustafa MUJEZINOVIĆ (Party of Democratic Action); nominated on June 11, 2009, and confirmed by the FBiH House of Representatives on June 25, following the resignation of Nedžad BRANKOVIĆ (Party of Democratic Action) on May 27.

Prime Minister of the RS: Milorad DODIK (Alliance of Independent Social Democrats); nominated by the president of the RS on February 4, 2006, and confirmed by the National Assembly on February 28, succeeding Pero BUKEJLOVIĆ (Serbian Democratic Party of Bosnia and Herzegovina), whose government had lost a no-confidence vote in the National Assembly on January 26; reconfirmed on November 30, 2006, following the election of October 1.

THE COUNTRY

A virtually landlocked Balkan country with less than eight miles of Adriatic coastline, Bosnia and Herzegovina is bordered on the west and north by Croatia, and on the east by Serbia and Montenegro (see map).

The capital, Sarajevo, is located in the northern Bosnian region, while Mostar is the principal town in the Herzegovinian south. Serbo-Croat is the principal language of an otherwise diverse population encompassing approximately 1.9 million Muslim Slavs (Bosniacs), 1.4 million Eastern Orthodox Serbs, and 820,000 Roman Catholic Croats. Women make up about 37 percent of the active labor force and 14 percent of the national House of Representatives.

In 2007 the agricultural sector accounted for about 10 percent of GDP, compared to 26 percent for industry and 64 percent for services. Timber is an important product in the north, in addition to maize, wheat, and potatoes, while the largely deforested south yields tobacco and various fruits and vegetables. Natural resources include fairly extensive deposits of lignite, iron ore, bauxite, manganese, and copper, as well as considerable hydroelectric capacity. Industrial output is low, however, and the economy overall compares unfavorably with those of most other regional republics. Leading industrial exports include base metals and related products, machinery and mechanical appliances, mineral products, textiles and footwear, and wood and wood products.

The GDP contracted by some 80 percent as a result of the internal conflict of 1991–1995, which destroyed much of the infrastructure and displaced several million people. Growth was rapid following the November 1995 peace accords—the GDP grew in real terms by 86 percent in 1996, 37 percent in 1997, and 10 percent in 1998—but much of the expansion was fueled by over $5 billion in foreign aid from donors such as the European Union (EU), the United States, the World Bank, and the International Monetary Fund (IMF). The introduction of the convertible mark and the establishment of countrywide customs procedures in 1998 were seen as significant steps in bonding the economies of the two political entities, the Federation of Bosnia and Herzegovina and the Serb Republic, although the latter continued to lag behind in development. Lenders have encouraged privatization of government-controlled enterprises in order to attract private external investment.

Since 2000, annual GDP growth has held roughly in the 4–6 percent range, peaking at 6.3 percent in 2004 and nearly equaling that rate in 2006. Unemployment remains high, however, at an unofficially estimated 20 percent. Inflation, which accelerated after the introduction in January 2006 of a value-added tax, dropped back to under 2 percent in 2007 but was expected to rise again in 2008. In an October 2006 assessment the IMF concluded that the country's economic successes "continue to be hostage to fundamental political and economic imbalances," including "weak institutions and lack of political will."

GOVERNMENT AND POLITICS

Political background. Settled by Slavs in the 7th century, Bosnia annexed what came to be known as Herzegovina in the mid-15th century, with both subsequently being conquered by the Turks. At the 1878 Congress of Berlin the territories were placed under the administration of Austria-Hungary, which continued to recognize Turkish sovereignty until formal annexation in 1908. The June 1914 assassination of the Austrian imperial heir in Sarajevo by a Serbian nationalist led directly to the outbreak of World War I. In 1918 the country became part of the Kingdom of the Serbs, Croats, and Slovenes, which was officially renamed Yugoslavia in October 1929. In November 1945 Bosnia and Herzegovina became one of the six constituent republics (along with Croatia, Macedonia, Montenegro, Serbia, and Slovenia) of the Communist-ruled Federal People's Republic of Yugoslavia.

During November–December 1990, in the constituent republic's first multiparty balloting since World War II, the three leading nationalist parties (appealing to Bosniacs, Serbs, and Croats) won an overwhelming collective majority in the restructured 240-member bicameral assembly, limiting the previously dominant League of Communists to only 19 seats. In a separate poll on November 18, the three groups also captured all 7 seats in the republican presidency. A month later the three announced that Alija IZETBEGOVIĆ, a Bosniac, would become president of the state presidency; Jure PELIVAN, a Croat, would become prime minister; and Momčilo KRAJIŠNIK, a Serb, would become president (speaker) of the assembly.

Declarations of independence by Croatia and Slovenia on June 25, 1991, precipitated incursions into both by the Serb-dominated Yugoslav army, and by early September fighting had spread to Bosnia and Herzegovina. On September 12 a Serbian "autonomous province" was proclaimed on the border with Montenegro, with a number of interior "autonomous regions" being announced by Serb militants later in the month.

At a referendum on February 29–March 1, 1992, in Bosnia and Herzegovina, 99.4 percent of the participants endorsed secession from Yugoslavia, although most Serbs boycotted the poll; on March 3 President Izetbegović issued a proclamation of independence. Subsequently, on March 18, leaders of the country's three main ethnic groups concluded an agreement in Sarajevo that called for division of Bosnia and Herzegovina into three autonomous units based on the "national absolute or relative majority" in each locality. However, most Serbs continued to insist that Bosnia and Herzegovina be included in Yugoslavia, while many Bosniacs, despite the Sarajevo accord, also called for rejection of the division along ethnic lines.

On March 27, 1992, Bosnian Serbs proclaimed a "Serb Republic of Bosnia and Herzegovina" with Dr. Radovan KARADŽIĆ as its president. As ethnic conflict mounted, the UN Security Council in April authorized the deployment of a sizable UN Protection Force (UNPROFOR), although its mandate was to facilitate the distribution of humanitarian aid rather than to engage in active peacekeeping. Subsequently, the Serbs tightened their grip on eastern Bosnia and stepped up their attack on Sarajevo. By mid-May the siege of the capital had created severe shortages of food and medical supplies, with Foreign Minister Haris SILAJDŽIĆ appealing to the Security Council for the creation of "security zones" similar to those used to protect Kurds in Iraq after the 1991 Gulf war. On June 26 the Security Council issued an ultimatum to the Serbs to place their heavy weapons under UN control or face international military action to open Sarajevo's airport to relief supplies.

By late 1992 Serbian nationalists controlled approximately 70 percent of Bosnia and Herzegovina, with Croatian forces holding much of the remainder. In March 1993 agreement appeared to have been reached among President Izetbegović, Bosnian Serb leader Karadžić, and Bosnian Croat leader Mate BOBAN on a peace plan advanced by former U.S. secretary of state Cyrus R. Vance (on behalf of the UN) and Britain's Lord Owen (on behalf of the European Community) to create a new decentralized state divided into ten semiautonomous provinces. The plan was repudiated, however, by the self-styled Bosnian Serb parliament on April 2. On June 7 the Bosnian government felt obliged to cooperate with a UN Security Council resolution that would recognize Bosniac "safe areas" in the six enclaves of Bihać, Goražde, Sarajevo, Srebrenica, Tuzla, and Žepa.

Shortly thereafter, in negotiations chaired by Lord Owen and former Norwegian foreign minister Thorvald Stoltenberg (the new UN mediator), a provisional agreement was reached in Geneva that envisaged the division of Bosnia and Herzegovina into three ethnically based states under a federal or confederal constitution. By November, however, the viability of the Owen-Stoltenberg plan for a "Union of Three Republics" had evaporated, with Bosnia Serb leader Karadžić calling for a currency union between the Bosnian Serb Republic and Serbia proper, Izetbegović insisting that the Croats guarantee Bosniac access to the Adriatic, and intra-Muslim conflict in the northwestern enclave of Bihać yielding the proclamation of an "Autonomous Province of Western Bosnia" under the leadership of dissident Bosnia presidency member Fikret ABDIĆ. In addition, Serbian forces had renewed their bombardment of Sarajevo, while fighting between Croats and Bosniacs continued in Mostar.

On February 8, 1994, hard-line Bosnian Croat leader Boban resigned as president of the separatist "Croatian Republic of Herceg-Bosna," which had been proclaimed in August 1993, and on February 24 Bosnian government and Croat forces agreed to a general cease-fire. On February 28, in the first offensive action by NATO in its 44-year history, allied aircraft enforcing a "no-fly zone" over Bosnia and Herzegovina shot down four Serbian attack aircraft. At a Washington ceremony hosted by U.S. President Bill Clinton on March 18, Bosnian and Croatian representatives signed a framework agreement for a federation of the Bosnian Muslim and Croat populations, together with a preliminary accord on establishment of a loose confederation involving the proposed federation and Croatia. On March 24 the Assembly of the Bosnian Serb Republic declined to endorse the plan.

On May 30, 1994, Krešimir ZUBAK, a Bosnian Croat, was elected to a six-month term as president of the new Federation of Bosnia and Herzegovina (FBiH), with Haris Silajdžić, who had been named prime minister of Bosnia and Herzegovina in October 1993, being designated the FBiH's prime minister. However, at the expiration of his term on November 30, Zubak refused to step down, arguing that if the presidency passed to the Bosniac vice president, Ejup GANIĆ, no major office would then be held by an ethnic Croat. Despite the impasse, both

Croat and Bosniac leaders reaffirmed their support for the FBiH on February 5, 1995.

An international "Contact Group" (France, Germany, Russia, the United Kingdom, and the United States) on July 6, 1994, presented a package of peace proposals that called for awarding 51 percent of Bosnian territory to the Muslim-Croat FBiH, with key areas placed under protection of either the UN or the EU. While the plan would have permitted the Serbs to retain a number of "ethnically cleansed" areas, they would have been obliged to cede about a third of their currently held territory to the FBiH. Although branded as "seriously flawed," the plan was accepted by the Bosnian government, but, as in the case of the Vance-Owen and Owen-Stoltenberg plans, it was rejected by the Serbs, who continued to insist on Serb access to the Adriatic, control of Sarajevo, and the right to confederate areas under their control with Serbia and Montenegro.

A four-month cease-fire began at the end of 1994, but it failed to break the political logjam. New fighting in May 1995 led to further Bosnian Serb advances and renewed heavy shelling of Sarajevo, to which the external powers responded by calling a UN/NATO air strike on an ammunition dump near Pale (the Bosnian Serb capital) on May 25. The Bosnian Serb military reacted by taking some 400 UN peacekeepers as hostages to deter additional strikes, thereby creating a major international crisis. Intensive negotiations led to the phased release of all the UN hostages by early July 1995.

By then, a Bosnian government offensive around Sarajevo had petered out, and Bosnian Serb forces were on the advance in eastern Bosnia, threatening the three Muslim-populated safe areas close to the Serbian border (Srebrenica, Žepa, and Goražde). Srebrenica was overrun by the Bosnian Serbs on July 11, with most of its Muslim population fleeing or disappearing, despite the presence of 200 inadequately armed UNPROFOR troops in the town. (The world subsequently learned that some 7,500 Muslim men and boys had been massacred—the worst such incident in Europe since the end of World War II.) On July 25, with Žepa also having fallen to the Bosnian Serbs, NATO announced detailed plans for the protection of Goražde, the largest eastern safe area.

The killing of 37 people in a Sarajevo market on August 28, 1995, provoked NATO to launch "Operation Deliberate Force," involving heavy air strikes against Serb positions. A U.S. initiative secured the signature of a 60-day cease-fire agreement on October 5. This was followed on November 1 by the launching of new talks at a Dayton, Ohio, air base. The negotiations produced several historic accords among Presidents Franjo Tudjman of Croatia, Slobodan Milošević of Serbia, and Izetbegović of the Republic of Bosnia and Herzegovina, the last of which had continued to function in tandem with the FBiH's new government. On November 10 Tudjman and Izetbegović agreed to "reinforce" the provisions of the 1994 federation agreement, the resultant government having exercised little real authority. In addition, the Croatian and Bosnian leaders accepted the "reunification" of Mostar to serve as the capital of the FBiH. Finally, on November 21 a comprehensive settlement was reached regarding the permanent political status of Bosnia and Herzegovina, and the agreement was formally signed in Paris on December 14.

The Dayton accords specified that Bosnia and Herzegovina would remain a single state under international law but would be partitioned into Bosniac-Croat and Serb "entities" that would enjoy substantial autonomy. The FBiH was awarded 51 percent of the country's territory, including all of Sarajevo, while the Serb Republic (RS) obtained 49 percent, including several areas once inhabited by Bosniacs. All the parties undertook to cooperate with the International Criminal Tribunal for the former Yugoslavia (ICTY), which had been established in The Hague by decision of the UN Security Council in 1993. Those indicted by the tribunal were to relinquish public office. Final authority to interpret the nonmilitary terms of the agreement in Bosnia and Herzegovina was granted to the Office of the High Representative of the International Community, whose head would be endorsed by the Security Council after nomination by a Peace Implementation Council of 55 governments and multilateral organizations.

Compliance with the agreement was to be assured by the speedy deployment of a 60,000-strong Implementation Force (IFOR), which would operate under NATO command but would draw contingents from non-NATO countries and be subject to UN authorization. Including some 20,000 U.S. troops (the first American ground involvement in Bosnia and Herzegovina), IFOR began to arrive at the end of 1995, replacing the ill-starred UNPROFOR contingent. A quick cessation of open hostilities and the withdrawal of opposing forces to the designated cease-fire lines were achieved by the end of January 1996, although interethnic clashes and altercations with IFOR occurred throughout the year. The tensest situations involved the ethnically mixed cities of Brčko and Mostar, the latter split between Bosniacs and Croats in the FBiH.

In late January 1996 Hasan MURATOVIĆ (nonparty) was installed as prime minister of the Republic of Bosnia and Herzegovina in succession to Silajdžić, while Izudin KAPETANOVIĆ became prime minister of the FBiH. The previous month Rajko KASAGIĆ had been elected the new prime minister of the RS; however, as a moderate favored by Western governments, Kasagić quickly came into conflict with the RS president, Radovan Karadžić, who in May 1996 announced Kasagić's dismissal and replacement by Gojko KLIČKOVIĆ, a hard-liner. This controversial action served to intensify international pressure for the ouster of Karadžić, one of several prominent Bosnian Serbs indicted for alleged war crimes by the ICTY and therefore disqualified from public office under the Dayton agreement. After failed efforts by the first high representative, Carl Bildt, U.S. negotiators stepped in and, with Belgrade's backing, secured the formal resignation of Karadžić from all his offices on July 19, with Vice President Biljana PLAVŠIĆ taking over as acting president of the RS.

At the same time, evidence began to mount that atrocities had been committed during the recent hostilities. The discoveries served to intensify calls for those responsible to be brought before the UN tribunal, which began its first actual trial of a suspect in May 1996. In addition to Karadžić, the 75 persons indicted by the tribunal by mid-1996 included Gen. Ratko MLADIĆ, the Bosnian Serb military commander; Mico STANŠIĆ, the Serbian secret police chief; and a number of prominent Bosnian Croats.

Karadžić's departure from office (although not from dominant influence in the RS) unblocked the political obstacles to presidential and legislative elections supervised by the Organization for Security and Cooperation in Europe (OSCE). Within the FBiH, former prime minister Silajdžić mounted a challenge to President Izetbegović, seeking to rally moderate nonsectarian opinion to his new Party for Bosnia and Herzegovina (*Stranka za Bosnu i Hercegovinu*—SBiH). In the RS, the new acting president, Biljana Plavšić, also succeeded Karadžić as presidential candidate of the Serbian Democratic Party of Bosnia and Herzegovina (*Srpska Demokratska Stranka Bosne i Hercegovine*—SDS).

Despite last-minute controversies and much confusion, the elections went ahead on September 14, 1996, involving what OSCE officials described as the most complex popular consultation in the history of democracy. The official results confirmed the dominance of the main nationalist parties of the three ethnic groups, namely the Bosniac Party of Democratic Action (*Stranka Demokratske Akcije*—SDA), the Serb SDS, and the Croatian Democratic Union of Bosnia and Herzegovina (*Hrvatska Demokratska Zajednica Bosne i Hercegovine*—HDZ). In the contests for the three-member presidency of the state, President Izetbegović of the SDA took 80 percent of the Bosniac vote, Momčilo Krajišnik of the SDS took 67 percent of the Serb vote, and Krešimir Zubak of the HDZ took 89 percent of the Croat vote. In the legislative contests, the SDA achieved a plurality in the national House of Representatives and a majority in the lower house of the FBiH, while the SDS won a majority in the Serb Assembly. In the RS's presidential election, Plavšić was confirmed in office with 59 percent of the vote.

The worst fighting since the signature of the Dayton agreement erupted in mid-November 1996, on the eastern line of separation, as Bosnian Serbs mounted armed resistance to Bosniacs who were attempting to return to their former homes. In early December NATO authorized a new Stabilization Force (SFOR) to take over when the IFOR mandate expired on December 20. The SFOR was given an 18-month mandate, with 17 non-NATO countries also agreeing to contribute to its total of 31,000 personnel.

On December 12, 1996, the collective presidency appointed the SBiH's Silajdžić and Boro BOSIĆ of the SDS to cochair the new six-member Council of Ministers of the Republic of Bosnia and Herzegovina. Five days later the leaders of the previous Bosnian Republic formally transferred authority to the new FBiH, while Bosnian Croats collaterally announced that the Croatian Republic of Herceg-Bosna had ceased to exist. On December 18 the House of Representatives of the FBiH elected Edhem BIČAKČIĆ of the SDA as prime minister of the FBiH's Council of Ministers; also during December, the National Assembly of the RS reconfirmed the SDS's Kličković as prime minister of the RS. The central government was formally approved by the national House of Representatives on January 3, 1997.

An indirect presidential election in the FBiH was held on March 18, 1997, Krešimir Zubak having continued to hold the office until then, despite his elevation to the central presidency the previous fall. Vladimir ŠOLJIĆ of the HDZ, representing Croats, was elected as the new FBiH president, while Ejup Ganić of the Bosniac SDA was elected vice president. Under the power-sharing arrangement in the FBiH constitution, the two men would exchange positions on January 1, 1998, with Ganić serving out the remaining year of the presidential term.

Meanwhile, political affairs in the RS had been complicated by a power struggle between President Plavšić's Banja Luka faction and the Karadžić-led Pale faction of the SDS. Plavšić and Krajišnik signed a peace accord mediated by Serbian President Milošević in Belgrade in September 1997. As part of their agreement, new elections were held for the RS's National Assembly in late November. The SDS and its coalition allies from the Serb Radical Party of the Serb Republic (*Srpska Radikalna Stranka Republike Srpske*—SRS) fell three seats short of a majority, and initial parliamentary sessions were unable to agree upon a government. When a coalition of all other parties in the assembly finally selected a pro-Western moderate, Milorad DODIK of the Party of Independent Social Democrats (*Stranka Nezavisnih Socijaldemokrata*—SNSD), as the new prime minister on January 18, 1998, the SDS and SRS deputies temporarily walked out and vowed to ignore all new legislation.

A new cabinet for the RS was sworn in on January 31, 1998, but there were no Muslims among the ministers nor any representatives from Karadžić's stronghold in Pale. The assembly further underscored its majority stance against Karadžić by voting to transfer the RS's seat of government from Pale to Banja Luka, where Plavšić supporters dominated. In June the assembly also endorsed a no-confidence motion against Assembly Speaker Dragan KALINIĆ and Deputy Speaker Nikola POPLAŠEN, both hard-liners, and elected moderates to replace them.

Another full round of state and entity elections took place on September 12–13, 1998, nationalist candidates performing well in most executive races despite a moderate decline in support for nationalist parties in the three legislatures. Izetbegović easily won reelection to the Bosniac seat on the central presidency as the candidate of the SDA-backed Coalition for a Unified and Democratic Bosnia and Herzegovina (*Koalicija za Cjevolitu Demokratsku Bosnu i Hercegovinu*—KCD), while hard-liner Ante JELAVIĆ of the HDZ secured the Croat seat. However, in a result that was widely applauded in the West, Momčilo Krajišnik was defeated for the Serb seat by Živko RADIŠIĆ of the new *Sloga* (Accord) coalition, which comprised Plavšić's recently established Serbian People's Alliance (*Srpski Narodni Savez*—SNS), Radišić's Socialist Party of the Serb Republic (*Socijalisticka Partija Republike Srpske*—SPRS), and Dodik's SNSD.

At the same time, Western officials were dismayed by Poplašen's victory over Plavšić in the race for president of the RS. Following the election, the assembly rejected Poplašen's first two nominees to replace Prime Minister Dodik. On March 5, 1999, Carlos Westendorp, who had succeeded Bildt as high representative, announced the "dismissal" of Poplašen as president for "abuse of power" in his attempt to oust Dodik. Poplašen refused to accept the directive, his position having been strengthened by Serb anger (even among moderates) over the ruling by an international arbitration panel that the city of Brčko, which had been under de facto Serbian control, should be designated as a "neutral" (multiethnic) city under the central presidency.

On December 28, 1998, the central presidency named Silajdžić to continue as a cochair of the central Council of Ministers and nominated Svetozar MIHAJLOVIĆ of *Sloga* and the SNS to succeed hard-liner Bosić as the Serb cochair. However, Mihajlović's appointment was strongly criticized by the SDS and Poplašen, and the central House of Representatives did not confirm the appointments until February 3, 1999.

In August 1999 Wolfgang Petritsch, the Austrian ambassador to Yugoslavia and EU special envoy for Kosovo, was named to succeed High Representative Westendorp, and in October he prohibited Poplašen and two other SRS officials from competing in local and general elections scheduled for 2000. At the same time, he rejected the application of Serb Vice President Mirko SAROVIĆ of the SDS to become the RS's president, and the office therefore remained vacant for another 14 months. In the FBiH, Vice President Ejup Ganić rotated to the presidency on January 1, 2000, exchanging offices with Ivo ANDRIĆ-LUŽANSKI (HDZ); the two had been elected to the rotating offices by the FBiH Parliament on December 11, 1998.

On April 12–13, 2000, the Republic of Bosnia and Herzegovina's Parliamentary Assembly voted to abandon the practice of having two chairs head the Council of Ministers. Instead, as with the collective presidency, the leadership would rotate among the three ethnic constituencies every eight months. The decision was partly a response to acrimonious differences between Cochairs Mihajlović and Silajdžić, the former having accused the latter of, among other things, "war-mongering" and attempting to undermine ethnic parity. In May the presidency nominated independent economist Spasoje TUŠEVLJAK, a Serb, as prime minister, and he was confirmed on June 6, succeeding Silajdžić and Mihajlović.

Meanwhile, the SPRS's differences with Dodik had led it to announce its withdrawal from the RS's *Sloga* government in February 2000. Despite losing a September 7 no-confidence vote, 43–1, in the 83-member National Assembly, Dodik stated that he would remain in office until the November 11 election, at which he was challenging Sarović for the presidency of the RS.

On October 14, 2000, Minister of Human Rights and Refugees Martin RAGUŽ of the HDZ was nominated to succeed national Prime Minister Tuševljak, collateral with Živko Radišić's rotation to the chair of the collective presidency in succession to Alija Izetbegović, who had decided to retire from office. (Tuševljak and Radišić, both Serbs, were prohibited from filling the two positions simultaneously.) The House of Representatives confirmed Raguž on October 18.

The parliamentary elections of November 11, 2000, saw many voters move away from hard-line nationalist parties at the central level and in the FBiH, the principal beneficiary being the new multiethnic Social Democratic Party of Bosnia and Herzegovina (*Socijaldemokratska Partija Bosne i Hercegovine*—SDP), which pulled even with the Bosniac SDA and surpassed both the Serb SDS and the Croat HDZ. In the RS, however, the SDS continued its dominance, easily winning a plurality in the legislature and seeing its candidate for president, Vice President Sarović, defeat Prime Minister Dodik 2–1. Sarović took office on December 16, and a week later he nominated a centrist, Mladen IVANIĆ of the year-old Party for Democratic Progress of the Serb Republic (*Partija Demoktatskog Progresa Republika Srpska*—PDP), as Serb prime minister. Confirmed on January 12, 2001, the multiparty Ivanić government included at least one member of the SDS, Trade Minister Goran POPOVIĆ. Less than a week later, however, in response to wide international criticism and, more specifically, U.S. threats to cut off aid if the SDS remained in the government, Popović resigned. Although refusing to identify his other ministers' party affiliations, Ivanić announced that they would not participate in partisan activity while in office.

With the 42 seats in the central House of Representatives distributed among 13 parties after the November 2000 election, the SDP, with 9 seats, had announced that it was prepared to open negotiations on forming a government with all but the main nationalist parties—the SDA (8 seats), the SDS (6 seats), and the HDZ (5 seats). Led by the SDP chair, Zlatko LAGUMDŽIJA, an Alliance for Change (*Alijanse za Promene*) was established on January 13, 2001, encompassing the SDP, the SBiH, and eight other parties. Together, they controlled 17 seats in the House, and on February 22, with the support of several moderate Serb parties, the SDP's Božidar MATIĆ won parliamentary approval of a multiparty Council of Ministers. Prime Minister Matić, a Bosniac, had been nominated by a majority of the collective presidency—over the objections of the HDZ's Ante Jelavić—after the House of Representatives rejected the redesignation of the Croat Raguž on February 7.

On July 1, 2000, a sharply divided central Constitutional Court had ruled that the country's constitution extended the constituent status of all three major ethnic communities throughout the entire country and required that the separate constitutions of the FBiH and the RS be brought into line with the central document. The plurality Bosniac constituency praised the decision, whereas the smaller Serb and Croat constituencies feared a loss of concessions that had been recognized in Dayton.

Under the leadership of copresident Jelavić, on October 28, 2000, some nine Croat parties formed an unofficial Croatian National Assembly (*Hrvatskih Narodnog Sabora*—HNS), which on March 3, 2001, declared a boycott of the FBiH government as well as establishment of a "Croatian self-administration" for cantons having Croat majorities. Jelavić stated that the HNS would consider revoking the self-administration edict if the government met a list of demands, including rescindment of recent changes that had been made by the OSCE to electoral rules. Those changes allowed all members of the FBiH's ten cantonal assemblies, whatever their ethnicity, to elect the Croat members of the central government's upper parliamentary chamber, the House of Peoples, thereby increasing the prospects of multiethnic parties and potentially diminishing the power of the HDZ. On March 7 High Representative Petritsch removed Jelavić from the central presidency because of his involvement in the autonomy movement, which violated the Dayton agreement.

Confronted by nearly universal condemnation, including that of the government in Zagreb, on March 16, 2001, the HNS announced a two-month postponement in self-rule, and on March 20 the new House of Peoples was constituted as scheduled. A week later the central House of Representatives elected Jozo KRIŽANOVIĆ (SDP) to Jelavić's former seat in the collective presidency, and Beriz BELKIĆ (SBiH) to the Bosniac seat, replacing Halid GENJAC (SDA), who for five months had served as Alija Izetbegović's interim replacement.

Meanwhile, on February 27–28, 2001, the FBiH Parliament had elected two members of the Alliance for Change, Karlo FILIPOVIĆ of the SDP and Safet HALILOVIĆ of the SBiH, to the FBiH's rotating presidency/vice presidency. The previously announced departure from office on January 11, 2001, of Prime Minister Bičakčić had also opened the way for the Alliance (with some 70 seats in the 140-seat House of Representatives) to forge the FBiH's first nonnationalist government, which won lower-house approval on March 12. Headed by Prime Minister Alija BEHMEN of the SDP, the cabinet was dominated by the SDP and the SBiH but also included several independents.

On June 22, 2001, central Prime Minister Matić resigned following the failure of the Parliamentary Assembly to pass an elections bill designed to address the Constitutional Court's concerns about ethnic constituencies. Passage also would have opened the way for Bosnia and Herzegovina's admission to the Council of Europe. On July 10 the central presidency nominated as Matić's replacement the SDP's Lagumdžija, who had been serving as foreign minister. Legislative confirmation followed on July 18. Lagumdžija was succeeded in the rotating post on March 15, 2002, by Dragan MIKEREVIĆ of the PDP.

On April 19, 2002, a month before being succeeded as high representative by Lord Paddy Ashdown of the United Kingdom, Wolfgang Petritsch promulgated constitutional amendments and electoral law changes for the FBiH and the RS, neither of which, in his assessment, had mustered sufficient legislative support for achieving the ends outlined in the July 2000 Constitutional Court decision. With the overarching goal of instituting political equality among Serbs, Croats, and Bosniacs, Petritsch's revisions mandated significant changes to the structure of the entities' legislatures as well as requirements that all ethnic groups be represented at all levels of government.

Overall, in the general election of October 5, 2002, the three principal nationalist parties—the Bosniac SDA, the Serb SDS, and the Croat HDZ (in coalition with other, smaller Croat parties)—had the greatest success in the national and entity legislative contests in addition to sharing the tripartite presidency. On October 28 Dragan ČOVIĆ (HDZ), Mirko Sarović (SDS), and Sulejman TIHIĆ (SDA) were inaugurated as the triumvirate, although Sarović's tenure was brief: he resigned on April 2, 2003, after being implicated in the sale of armaments to Iraq, despite a UN embargo, and in efforts by Bosnian military intelligence agents to spy on NATO and EU personnel. Sarović was succeeded a week later by Borislav PARAVAC (SDS).

Dragan ČAVIĆ (SDS) was inaugurated as president of the RS on November 28, 2002. Niko LOZANČIĆ (HDZ) was sworn in on January 27, 2003, as president of the FBiH, following his election (despite a lack of Serb support in the House of Peoples) by the new FBiH Parliament. Also in January, new national and RS prime ministers—Adnan TERZIĆ (SDA) and Dragan Mikerević (PDP), respectively—won legislative approval. A new FBiH prime minister, Ahmet HADŽIPAŠIĆ (SDA), was confirmed in February.

Objecting to High Representative Ashdown's recent dismissals of Serb officials for noncooperation with the ICTY, Serb Prime Minister Mikerević resigned in December 2004 and was succeeded in February 2005 by Pero BUKEJLOVIĆ (SDS). Less than two months later, on March 29, Ashdown dismissed the Croat member of the national presidency, Dragan Čović, who had refused to step down voluntarily in response to corruption allegations dating back to his 2000–2003 tenure as FBiH deputy prime minister. His replacement, Ivo Miro JOVIĆ (HDZ), was confirmed by the national Parliamentary Assembly in early May.

Meeting in Washington on November 22, 2005, to mark the tenth anniversary of the Dayton accords, leaders from Bosnia's three principal ethnic groups, pressured by the EU as well as the United States, agreed that they would take "first steps" toward comprehensive institutional reforms, including the abandonment of the tripartite republican presidency. Signatories to the "Washington declaration" included the three copresidents and leaders from eight parties: the Serbian SDS, SNSD, and PDP; the Bosniac SDA, SBiH, and SDP; and the Croat HDZ and an ally, the Croatian National Union (*Hrvatska Narodna Zajednica*—HNZ). Nevertheless, on April 26, 2006, the constitutional reform package fell two votes short of the required two-thirds majority in the national House of Representatives, primarily because of opposition from most Croatian members and the SBiH.

Led by the SNSD, on January 26, 2006, opposition forces in the Serb National Assembly ousted the Bukejlović government by passing a no-confidence motion 44–29. Crucial support for the motion came from the PDP, which had withdrawn from the SDS-led administration in late November 2005, citing the slow pace of reform. The SDS subsequently indicated that it would join the opposition at both the national and RS levels. On February 4 Serb President Čavić designated a former prime minister, the SNSD's Milorad Dodik, to form a new government, which was endorsed by the National Assembly on February 28.

The general election of October 1, 2006, at the national, entity, and cantonal levels concluded with significant changes in executive leadership. Former prime minister Haris Silajdžić (SBiH) returned to power by handily defeating the incumbent Bosniac member of the presidency, Sulejman Tihić, with 62 percent of the vote. In addition, Nebojša RADMANOVIĆ (SNSD) captured the Serb seat from the SDS, while the Croat seat was won by the multiethnic SDP's Željko KOMŠIĆ, who defeated incumbent Ivo Miro Jović of the HDZ and Božo LJUBIĆ of the new Croat splinter party HDZ 1990. Another incumbent, the SDS's Dragan Čavić, lost his post as RS president to the SNSD's Milan JELIĆ, who, in a crowded field, took 49 percent of the vote to Čavić's 29 percent.

In legislative contests, the clearest victor was the SNSD, which came within a single seat of capturing a majority in the RS National Assembly—an accomplishment that solidified the preeminence of its leader, RS Prime Minister Dodik, among Serb politicians. In the 42-seat national House of Representatives, no party dominated: the SDA won 9; the SBiH, 8; and the SNSD, 7. In the FBiH, the SDA retained its plurality, but the SBiH made significant gains and the Croat vote split between alliances led by the HDZ and the HDZ 1990.

In early 2007 the tripartite national presidency nominated the SNSD's Nikola ŠPIRIĆ as prime minister of the republic, and the House of Representatives concurred on January 11. The Špirić government encompassed a total of seven parties: the SDA, SBiH, SNSD, HDZ, HDZ 1990, PDP, and People's Party "Working for Prosperity" (*Narodna Stranka "Radom za Boljitak"*—NS-RzB). In the FBiH, it wasn't until February 21, 2007, that the FBiH House of Representatives elected Borjana KRIŠTO (HDZ) as FBiH president, and achieving lower-house approval of a new FBiH government took even longer. On March 23 the latest high representative, Christian Schwarz-Schilling of Germany, nullified the previous day's confirmation of a new cabinet and reinstated Hadžipašić's caretaker administration because the vetting process for five ministerial nominees had not been formally completed. Following replacement of the initial candidate for interior minister, the new FBiH cabinet, headed by Prime Minister Nedžad BRANKOVIĆ (SDA), won approval by the legislature on March 30.

On November 1, 2007, Nikola Špirić resigned as central prime minister over his objections to governmental reforms announced in October by the latest high representative of the international community, Miroslav Lajčák of Slovakia. The principal procedural change involved a new method of calculating a quorum in governmental sessions and in the legislature so that ministers and legislators who objected to policies and proposed legislation could no longer obstruct consideration "through pure absence." On November 12 the collective presidency of the republic accepted Špirić's resignation. Following lengthy negotiations, however, the principal national parties agreed to accept Lajčák's reforms, and in early December Špirić was nominated by the SNSD, with the support of the other leading parties, to continue as prime minister. He was reconfirmed by the BiH House of Representatives on December 28.

The president of the Serb Republic, Milan Jelić, died on September 30, 2007. An early presidential election, held December 9, contested by ten candidates, was won by the SNSD's Rajko KUZMANOVIĆ with 42 percent of the vote. He assumed office on December 28.

On May 27, 2009, the FBiH prime minister, Nedžad Branković, resigned, having been indicted in April for abuse of office. He allegedly used government funds to purchase an apartment but resisted resigning until the SDA chair, Sulejman Tihić, who had called for him to step down, won reelection to the party's top post. The nomination of Branković's replacement, Mustafa MUJEZINOVIĆ (SDA), was endorsed by the legislature on June 25.

Meanwhile, the International Criminal Tribunal in The Hague continued its work, although some cases have been transferred to the War Crimes Chamber of Bosnia's State Court, which issued its first verdict in April 2006. On September 27, 2006, the ICTY sentenced former SDS member of the presidency Momčilo Krajišnik to 27 years imprisonment (reduced to 20 years in 2009) for crimes that included murder, persecution, and extermination (but not genocide). Earlier, in February 2003, it had sentenced former Serb president Biljana Plavšić to 11 years in prison as a consequence of her having pleaded guilty to crimes against humanity. In April 2004 Jadranko PRLIĆ, who had served as the president of the self-proclaimed Bosnian Croat state of Herceg-Bosna, surrendered to the ICTY, which had indicted him for persecution of Muslims. His trial began in April 2006 and was expected to continue into 2010. On July 21, 2008, a Serbian security team arrested the "most wanted" Bosnian, Radovan Karadžić, in a Belgrade suburb. The following day a judge ordered his transfer to The Hague to stand trial for genocide, crimes against humanity, and war crimes. As of September 2009 the Karadžić case was expected to begin trial proceedings shortly.

Constitution and government. The Dayton peace agreement of November 1995 laid down a new constitutional structure under which the Republic of Bosnia and Herzegovina, while having a single sovereignty, was to consist of two "entities," namely the (Bosniac-Croat) Federation of Bosnia and Herzegovina, and the Serb Republic (*Republika Srpska*) of Bosnia and Herzegovina. Responsibilities accorded to the central republican government include foreign relations, trade and customs, monetary policy, international and interentity law enforcement, immigration, international and interentity communications and transportation, interentity policy coordination, and air traffic control. The institutions of the central republic include a three-person presidency (one Bosniac, one Croat, and one Serb), a Council of Ministers, a bicameral legislature, a judicial system, and a central bank. The presidency has exclusive control over foreign affairs and the armed forces, while the chair of the Council of Ministers (prime minister), who is appointed by the presidency and confirmed by the House of Representatives, is the head of government.

The judicial branch is headed by a State Court (with criminal, administrative, and appellate divisions), which began functioning in January 2003. A nine-member Constitutional Court (four judges nominated by the FBiH House of Representatives, two by the Serb National Assembly, and three noncitizens nominated by the president of the European Court of Human Rights in consultation with the presidency) also functions at the national level, while both entities have their own court systems. A High Judicial Council, with participation by international jurists, screens candidates for judicial and prosecutorial positions.

Government functions not specifically vested in the Republic of Bosnia and Herzegovina are regarded as the responsibility of the entities, although some of these may eventually revert to the central administration by agreement of the parties. The Dayton agreement provides for the protection of human rights and the free movement of people, goods, capital, and services throughout the country. It also commits the entities to cooperate with the orders of the UN International Criminal Tribunal in The Hague and to accept binding arbitration in the event of their being unable to resolve disputes. Any person indicted by the tribunal or the Bosnian justice system may not hold appointed or elected office.

In 2000 the Constitutional Court ruled that all citizens should have equal standing throughout the country, which resulted in an April 2002 decision by the high representative to amend the FBiH and RS constitutions. As a consequence, proportional ethnic representation was mandated at all levels of government and the judiciary. In addition, with effect from the October 2002 election, the FBiH's bicameral parliament was reconfigured, and a new Council of Peoples, with limited powers, was established in the RS. (See the discussion of the various legislative bodies in the Legislatures section, below.)

The Muslim-Croat federation agreement of March 18, 1994, provided that indirectly elected representatives of the two ethnic communities would serve alternate one-year terms as president and vice president, although no change in the initial appointments of May 1994 were made prior to the September 1996 legislative elections. From 2002, however, the president serves a four-year term, supported by two vice presidents from the other two communities. The president nominates a government headed by a prime minister for legislative endorsement. Ministers must have deputies who are not from their own constituent group. Local government is based on ten cantons, each with its own elected assembly, and municipalities, each with an elected council and mayor. The judiciary includes both Constitutional and Supreme courts as well as cantonal and municipal courts. There is also provision for a Human Rights Court.

The government of the Serb Republic of Bosnia and Herzegovina, declared in March 1992 and recognized under the 1995 Dayton accords, is headed by a directly elected president. Since 2002 he has been assisted by two vice presidents, instead of one, representing the other ethnic communities. The National Assembly, directly elected by proportional representation, elects the prime minister upon the nomination of the president. The separate Council of Peoples, elected by the ethnic caucuses of the National Assembly, was first constituted in 2003. At the local level, administration is based on municipalities, each with an elected assembly and a mayor. The judiciary is headed by a Supreme Court and a Constitutional Court and also includes district and basic courts.

At present, the entire executive, legislative, and judicial structure, at both the central and entity levels, is subject to decisions by the Office of the High Representative of the International Community, a position established to oversee implementation of the Dayton accords. The high representative, who is nominated by an international Peace Implementation Council and confirmed by the UN Security Council, has broad powers to issue decrees, dismiss officials who violate the accords, and establish civilian commissions. As of late 2007, high representatives had imposed over 800 laws and decrees.

Foreign relations. On December 24, 1991, prior to its declaration of independence, Bosnia and Herzegovina joined Croatia, Macedonia, and Slovenia in requesting diplomatic recognition from the European Community (EC, later the EU). However, the first foreign power to recognize its sovereignty was Bulgaria on January 16, 1992, with the EC according recognition on April 6 and the United States taking similar action the following day. On May 22 Bosnia and Herzegovina was admitted to the UN, thereby qualifying for immediate membership in the Conference on Security and Cooperation in Europe (CSCE, subsequently the OSCE).

Regionally, Bosnia and Herzegovina became a member of the Central European Initiative (CEI), originally formed in 1989 as a "Pentagonal" group of Central European states committed to mutual and bilateral economic cooperation; however, development of relations with the Council of Europe and other bodies was stalled by the unresolved internal conflict. (Membership in the Council of Europe was achieved in April 2002.) In the wider international arena, the Sarajevo government obtained some diplomatic backing from the Nonaligned Movement, and, as an observer at the Organization of the Islamic Conference (OIC) summit in December 1994, President Izetbegović received numerous pledges of financial and other support from member states. On December 14, 1995, the Bosnian and rump Yugoslav governments accorded one another formal recognition.

Both the RS and the FBiH signed "special relations" treaties with their ethnic confreres in Yugoslavia and Croatia, respectively, even though such treaties were considered by some to be in conflict with both the Dayton accords and the Bosnian constitution. In addition, an agreement was negotiated between the Republic of Bosnia and Herzegovina and Croatia in 1998 providing each country with trade advantages. The FBiH also concluded an agreement (despite some opposition from Bosniac leaders) establishing extensive cooperation with Croatia. Formal diplomatic relations were established with Yugoslavia in December 2000. The first summit of the presidents of Yugoslavia, Croatia, and Bosnia and Herzegovina (including the two entity presidents) convened in Sarajevo on June 15, 2002, although a number of difficult issues, including dual citizenship for ethnic Croats and Serbs, were not addressed. A dual citizenship agreement with Yugoslavia (now the separate republics of Montenegro and Serbia) was concluded in October 2002, and one with Croatia dates from August 2005.

In June 2004 NATO reduced its troop level from 12,000 to 7,000, and six months later, on December 4, the SFOR mission concluded. At that time the EU's newly established EUFOR assumed the peacekeeping mandate, utilizing basically the same troops. (Two years earlier an EU Police Mission had replaced the UN Mission in Bosnia and Herzegovina [UNMIBH], which the UN had described as "the most extensive police reform and restructuring mandate ever undertaken by the United Nations.") A total of 22 EU member states and 11 other countries pledged personnel for EUFOR's "Operation Althea." On February 28, 2007, in view of the improved security situation, the EU confirmed that it would reduce its troop level to 2,500. The U.S. military presence in Bosnia, once numbering 700, was reduced to about 250 personnel in late 2004. Their responsibilities focused on military training, the search for suspected war criminals, and antiterrorism. Following the handover to Bosnia of NATO's base in Tuzla in July 2007, the U.S. military presence has amounted to a few intelligence officers who work with NATO.

Given strong objections within the RS and the Serbian community at large, as of mid-2009 Bosnia and Herzegovina had declined to recognize the independence of Kosovo, which had declared its separation from Serbia on February 17.

Current issues. When High Representative Miroslav Lajčák introduced a revised quorum system in October 2007 to expedite consideration of reform proposals—especially those related to centralized police structures, as demanded by the EU for completion of a Stabilization and Association Agreement (SAA)—he precipitated Prime Minister Špirić's resignation and what many Bosnians regarded as the most serious political crisis since completion of the Dayton accords.

In the end, leading parties on all three sides of the ethnic triangle agreed that completing an SAA with the EU was paramount, and they therefore acquiesced to Lajčák's plan in order to facilitate the necessary reforms. Crucially, a sufficient number of Serb representatives also agreed to the elimination of a separate Serb police force. Following adoption of an "action plan" for police reform, the SAA was initialed on December 4, 2007. On April 10, 2008, by a vote of 22–19–1, the BiH House of Representatives passed the Law on Independent and Supervisory Bodies of the Police Structure and the Law on the Directorate for the Coordination of Police Bodies and Agencies for Support to the Police Structure. The upper house concurred on April 16, removing the last major obstacle to signature of the SAA by the EU member states. As a result, the SAA was signed on June 16. In addition to viewing the SAA as a first step toward joining the EU, the Bosnian government hoped it would more immediately facilitate improved trade relations and access to development capital.

At nationwide local elections held October 5, 2008, the major ethnic parties continued their dominance: Milorad Dodik's SNSD more than doubled the number of mayoralties it holds in the RS, while Sulejman Tihić's SDA and Dragan Čović's HDZ dominated in the FBiH. Two weeks later, former U.S. Balkan envoy Richard Holbrooke and former high representative Paddy Ashdown warned in Britain's *The Guardian* that a lack of attention by the United States and a "distracted" international community in general could lead to another Balkan crisis. They accused Milorad Dodik of positioning the RS for secession "if the opportunity arises" and added that Haris Silajdžić was exploiting ethnic tensions.

In a November 8, 2008, meeting in the Prud district of Odžak, Dodik, Čović, and Tihić agreed on a set of principles (the Prud Agreement) for altering the BiH constitution, conducting a population census, dividing state property, and determining the legal status of Brčko. All three ethnic leaders acknowledged that further movement toward EU membership depends on resolving constitutional issues, especially strengthening central structures and bringing the constitution into line with the European convention on human rights. Strengthening central institutions will necessitate changes at the entity level, the principal proposal being reorganization into four territorial divisions, although ethnic Serbians have made it clear that they will not accept any redefinition of RS boundaries. On March 27, 2009, the newest high representative, Valentin Inzko of Austria, took office, pledging to help the country "pick up the pace" toward "EU integration," although no one viewed rapid progress on the constitutional issues as an easy undertaking.

On July 22, 2009, by a vote of 28–7, the BiH House of Representatives (reportedly under pressure from the United States and others) voted to remove the SDA's Tarik SADOVIĆ from his position as BiH deputy prime minister and minister for security. He had been accused of ignoring an annex to the Dayton accords that called for deporting foreign Islamic elements who had entered Bosnia to fight in the 1992–1995 civil war. The SDA then nominated its new deputy chair, Sadik AHMETOVIĆ, as Sadović's successor, but Prime Minister Nikola Špirić, to the consternation of SDA chair Tihić, delayed the appointment, insisting that filling vacancies in the leadership of various government agencies should have priority. Tihić responded by accusing Špirić of obstructionism and deliberately weakening state institutions in an effort to demonstrate that they cannot function.

The Office of the UN High Commissioner for Refugees (UNHCR) has estimated that of the 2.2 million who fled the strife of the early 1990s, about 1.03 million have returned. Of those, fewer than half have "accessed their property rights" or otherwise returned to their place of origin in Bosnia and Herzegovina. This suggests that many have relocated to communities where they are in the ethnic majority. At the end of 2008, some 125,000 individuals remained internally displaced.

POLITICAL PARTIES

For four and a half decades after World War II, the only authorized political party in Yugoslavia was the Communist Party, which was redesignated in 1952 as the League of Communists of Yugoslavia (*Savez Komunista Jugoslavija*—SKJ). In 1989 noncommunist groups began to emerge in the republics, and in early 1990 the SKJ approved the introduction of a multiparty system, thereby effectively triggering its own demise. In Bosnia and Herzegovina the party's local branch was succeeded by the League of Communists of Bosnia and Herzegovina–Party of Democratic Changes (SK BiH-SDP; see SDP, below). Since then, political parties have flourished.

During the 1990s a number of coalitions emerged to contest elections at the central and entity levels. The most prominent, the Coalition for a Unified and Democratic Bosnia and Herzegovina (*Koalicija za Cjevolitu i Demokratsku Bosnu i Hercegovinu*—KCD), was formed prior to the 1997 balloting for the Serb National Assembly by the Party of Democratic Action (SDA), the Party for Bosnia and Herzegovina (SBiH), the Civic Democratic Party (GDS), and the Liberal Party (LS). It won 16 seats at that poll and then, in the September 1998 elections, emerged as the leading group in both the central House of Representatives and the FBiH House of Representatives, while finishing second in the Serb National Assembly. In addition, its candidate for the Bosniac seat on the central presidency, Alija Izetbegović of the SDA, was elected with nearly 87 percent of the vote within the ethnic group and 31 percent of the overall national vote (the most of any candidate). The KCD failed to hold together, however, as the other participants moved further away from the strongly nationalist SDA.

Another coalition, Accord (*Sloga;* also translated as Unity), was established in June 1998 to present joint moderate candidates in the September election, in which Živko Radišić of *Sloga*'s Socialist Party of the Serb Republic (SPRS) won the Serb central presidential seat with 51.2 percent of the ethnic vote and 21.8 percent of the national total. However, *Sloga* leader Biljana Plavšić of the Serbian People's Alliance (SNS) was defeated in her attempt at reelection as president of the RS. Milorad Dodik, the leader of a third *Sloga* party, the Party of Independent Social Democrats (SNSD), served as prime minister of the RS from January 1998 until after the November 2000 election. By then, *Sloga* had dissolved.

No broad coalitions emerged to fight the November 2000 elections, but as a consequence of subsequent efforts to prevent the strongly nationalist SDA, Croatian Democratic Union (HDZ), and Serbian Democratic Party (SDS) from maintaining their predominance, on January 13, 2001, ten moderate parties signed an agreement to establish the Alliance for Change (*Alijanse za Promene*). Initial participants were the Social Democratic Party of Bosnia and Herzegovina (SDP), the SBiH, the New Croatian Initiative (NIH), the GDS, the Croatian Peasants' Party (HSS), the Bosnian-Herzegovinian Patriotic Party (BPS), the Republican Party, the Liberal Democratic Party (LDS), and two pensioners' parties. With the support of a number of other moderate parties, the Alliance, led by the SDP and the SBiH, won control of the central and FBiH parliaments and by late March held the Bosniac and Croat seats in the central presidency, the offices of president and vice president of the FBiH, and the premierships of both the central government and the FBiH. In June 2002 it was announced that the Alliance had disbanded, most of its component parties having decided against a coalition approach to the October elections.

In all, nearly 50 parties and a dozen coalitions (several involving the HDZ in combination with various other Croat parties) competed in the October 2006 national, entity, and cantonal elections.

Parties Represented in the Central House of Representatives:

Party of Democratic Action (*Stranka Demokratske Akcije*—SDA). Organized in May 1990 by Alija Izetbegović, Fikret Abdić (later of the DNZ, below), and others, the SDA is a nationalist grouping representing Bosniacs. Favoring both decentralization and a unitary state, it obtained substantial pluralities in the 1990 legislative and presidency elections, thereafter dominating the republican government (in coalition with other parties) despite being weakened in April 1996 by formation of the breakaway Party for Bosnia and Herzegovina (SBiH, below).

With the party having performed poorly at local elections, in April 2000 it registered a vote of no confidence in the leadership of its deputy chairs, Halid Genjac and Ejup Ganić, who were replaced in May by Edhem Bičakčić, the FBiH prime minister, and Sulejman Tihić. At virtually the same time the party expelled Ganić for refusing to resign as president of the FBiH, a position he had assumed on a rotational basis at the end of 1999 after having served a year as vice president. In October 2000 the SDA's dominant figure, Alija Izetbegović, left the collective presidency, citing age and ill health, with Genjac assuming the Bosniac seat on an interim basis. Izetbegović died in 2003.

In the November 2000 election the SDA remained the strongest party in the FBiH, winning 38 seats in the House of Representatives on a 27 percent vote share. In the simultaneous balloting for the central House of Representatives, it finished second, with about 20 percent of the vote and 8 seats, while in the RS it captured 6 National Assembly seats. In January 2001 Prime Minister Bičakčić left the office he had held for four years to resume his position as general manager of the state electricity company, but shortly thereafter High Representative Wolfgang Petritsch dismissed him because of corruption allegations.

The SDA emerged from the 2002 elections as the dominant Bosniac party, winning a leading 10 seats in the national House of Representatives, capturing twice as many seats as any other party and 33 percent of the vote in the downsized FBiH House of Representatives, and retaining its status as the leading Bosniac party in the RS. In addition, Party Chair Tihić won the Bosniac seat in the national presidency. New national and FBiH coalition governments were then formed under the SDA's Adnan Terzić and Ahmet Hadžipašić, respectively.

The SDA lost ground in the October 2006 elections, when the SBiH's Haris Silajdžić easily foiled Copresident Tihić's reelection bid and its delegation in the FBiH lower house fell to 28 (based on a 25 percent vote share)—still a plurality, but only 4 seats more than the SBiH. It retained 9 seats in the national House of Representatives and remained in the central government, but lost the prime ministership. In 2008 an intraparty leadership dispute involved supporters of Tihić and Vice Chair Bakir IZETBEGOVIĆ, son of the party's founder. Both sought to head the party at a congress in May 2009, as did Deputy Chair Adnan Terzić. The moderate Tihić won a third four-year term, taking 57 percent of the vote. There had been considerable speculation that should Izetbegović's bid fail, he would establish his own party, but he instead indicated that he planned to remain in his father's party.

Leaders: Sulejman TIHIĆ (Former Copresident of the Republic and Chair of the Party); Mustafa MUJEZINOVIĆ (FBiH Prime Minister); Asim SARAJLIĆ (Deputy Chair); Sadik AHMETOVIĆ, Sanjin HALIMOVIĆ, Šemsudin MEHMEDOVIĆ, and Senad ŠEPIĆ (Vice Chairs); Adil OSMANOVIĆ (RS Vice President and Party Vice Chair); Amir ZUKIĆ (Secretary General).

Party for Bosnia and Herzegovina (*Stranka za Bosnu i Hercegovinu*—SBiH). The SBiH was launched in April 1996 by Haris Silajdžić, who had resigned as prime minister of the central government in January after disagreeing with fundamentalist elements of the ruling SDA. The new party aimed to appeal to all ethnic communities and had some success in the September 1996 balloting, winning 10 seats in the FBiH House of Representatives and two in the central House of Representatives, while Silajdžić polled 14 percent in the presidential contest.

Silajdžić returned to the copremiership of the central government in January 1997 and continued in that office until the April 2000 passage of a new Council of Ministers law and the resultant appointment of a single prime minister, Spasoje Tuševljak, two months later. In the November 2000 elections, the SBiH captured 5 seats in the central House of Representatives (on a 12 percent vote share) and 21 seats in the FBiH's lower house (with a 15 percent vote share). It also won 4 seats in the RS's National Assembly. In January 2001 it joined the SDP as a leading force behind formation of the antinationalist Alliance for Change, and in late February the FBiH House of Representatives confirmed the party's secretary general, Safet Halilović, as vice president for a year in the FBiH's rotating presidency/vice presidency.

Silajdžić announced his retirement from politics in September 2001 but in 2002 ran for the Bosniac seat in the state presidency, finishing a close second with 35 percent support. The SBiH won 6 seats in the national House of Representatives, second to the SDA, and 15 seats in the FBiH lower house, while retaining its 4 seats in the Serb National Assembly. Following the elections, the SBiH joined in the governing coalitions at the national and entity levels.

Silajdžić, who was reelected head of the SBiH in May 2006, completed a return to power with his victory in the October 2006 contest for the Bosniac seat in the central presidency. At the same time, the SBiH saw its electoral support rise to 8 seats in the national House and 24 seats in the FBiH lower house, posing a direct challenge to the SDA's continuing leadership. Unlike the SDA, the SBiH supported the police reforms passed in April 2008.

Leaders: Haris SILAJDŽIĆ (Copresident of the Republic and Party Chair); Safet HALILOVIĆ (Former FBiH President and Vice Chair of the Party); Beriz BELKIĆ, Gavrilo GRAHOVAC, and Zdenka MERDŽAN (Vice Chairs); Munib JUSUFOVIĆ (Secretary General).

Alliance of Independent Social Democrats (*Savez Nezavisnih Socijaldemokrata*—SNSD). The SNSD was formally established in 1996 as the Party (*Stranka*) of Independent Social Democrats and adopted its present name in May 2002, upon completion of a merger with the Democratic Socialist Party (*Demokratska Socijalistička Partija*—DSP), a dissident offshoot of the Socialist Party of the Serb Republic (SPRS, below).

After participating in the NSSM-SMP electoral alliance in 1996 (see the SPRS), the SNSD ran its own candidates in the November 1997 balloting for the RS National Assembly, winning two seats. The SNSD's leader, Milorad Dodik, was subsequently elected prime minister of the RS, pledging to conduct governmental affairs on a nonpartisan basis. The SNSD improved to 6 seats in the 1998 election for the National Assembly. In December 1999 the Social Liberal Party (*Socijalno-Liberalna Stranka*—SLS) merged with the SNSD, with its former leader, Rade DUJAKOVIĆ, being named an SNSD deputy chair.

Prime Minister Dodik finished second in the RS's presidential contest in November 2000, winning about 26 percent of the first-preference vote. At the central level, the SNSD competed in alliance with the DSP, but the coalition managed to win only a single seat in the House of Representatives. In the RS, running on its own, the SNSD tied for second with the Party for Democratic Progress of the Serb Republic (PDP, below), taking 11 seats in the National Assembly.

In October 2002 Nebojša Radmanović, who had been expelled from the SPRS and then helped form the DSP before the latter's merger with the SNSD, finished second in the balloting for the Serb seat in the national presidency, winning 20 percent of the vote. The party finished second in the balloting for the Serb National Assembly, winning 19 seats, while its candidate for president of the RS, Milan Jelić, likewise came in second. The SNSD also won 3 seats in the national House of Representatives and 1 in the FBiH House.

In January 2006 the SNSD, as the leading opposition party in the Serb National Assembly, introduced a no-confidence motion against the SDS-led government of the RS. With the support of the PDP (below), the motion passed and the government fell. In early February the SNSD's Dodik was designated prime minister.

In the October 2006 elections the SNSD's performance overshadowed those of the other Serb parties, thereby confirming Dodik's rise to prominence. The party picked up 4 more seats in the central House of Representatives and won a near-majority of 41 seats in the RS National Assembly, taking 43 percent of the vote and far outdistancing the second-place SDS. In addition, Radmanović captured the Serb seat in the central presidency from the SDS, while Jelić defeated the incumbent, the SDS's Dragan Čavić, for the RS presidency. Jelić died in September 2007 and was succeeded by Rajko Kuzmanović.

In preparation for the 2010 elections, Prime Minister Dodik indicated that the SNSD would form an alliance with the SPRS and DNS (both below).

Leaders: Milorad DODIK (Prime Minister of the RS and Chair of the Party), Nebojša RADMANOVIĆ (Copresident of the Republic and Executive Board President), Rajko KUZMANOVIĆ (RS President), Nikola ŠPIRIĆ (Prime Minister of the Republic and Party Vice Chair), Igor RADOJIČIĆ (Speaker of the RS National Assembly and Party Vice Chair), Rajko VASIĆ (General Secretary).

Social Democratic Party of Bosnia and Herzegovina (*Socijaldemokratska Partija Bosne i Hercegovine*—SDP, or *Socijaldemokrati*). The multiethnic SDP was formed in February 1999 as a merger of the Democratic Party of Socialists (*Demokratska Stranka Socijalista*—DSS) and the Social Democrats of Bosnia and Herzegovina (*Socijaldemokrati Bosne i Hercegovine*). The two had reportedly been pressured by social democratic parties in Western European countries to coalesce in order to better oppose the nationalist parties dominating affairs in Bosnia and Herzegovina.

Also styled the Socialist Democratic Party (*Socijalistička Demokratska Partija*—SDP), the DSS had been formed in June 1990, initially as the Democratic Socialist League of Bosnia and Herzegovina (*Demokratski Socijalistički Savez Bosne i Hercegovine*—DSS-BiH). As such, it was the successor to the local branch of the former ruling "popular front" grouping, the Socialist League of the Working People of Yugoslavia (*Socijalistički Savez Radnog Narodna Jugoslavija*—SSRNJ). Later, it absorbed the League of Communists of Bosnia and Herzegovina–Party of Democratic Changes (*Savez Komunista Bosne i Hercegovine–Stranka Demokratskih Promjena*—SK BiH-SDP), which had resulted from reorganization of the republican branch of the SKJ after its withdrawal from the federal party in March 1990. Subsequently, the DSS was a member of the United List (ZL; see HSS, below) but left after the September 1996 elections.

The Social Democrats of Bosnia and Herzegovina was the new name adopted in May 1998 by the former Union of Bosnian Social Democrats (*Zajednica Socijalistička Demokratska Bosna*—ZSDB), led by Selim BESLAGIĆ. The ZSDB was originally established in September 1990 as the Alliance of Reform Forces of Yugoslavia (*Savez Reformskik Snaga Jugoslaviji za Bosnu i Hercegovinu*—SRS-BiH), the local affiliate of the postcommunist Alliance of Reform Forces that had been launched by the federal prime minister, Ante Marković, several months earlier. Beslagić, a Muslim, subsequently emerged as one of the country's leading proponents of a multiethnic approach to government and culture.

With firm support from most of the international community, the SDP made major inroads against the nationalists in the local elections of April 2000 and then at the balloting for the central and FBiH legislatures in November 2000. Nationally, the SDP won a slim plurality (9 of the 42 lower house seats) in November, while it finished second, with 37 seats, in the FBiH's House of Representatives. With the party president, Zlatko Lagumdžija, having spearheaded formation of the Alliance for Change in January 2001, SDP leaders quickly assumed leading positions at both governmental levels. By late March they held the Croat seat in the central presidency, the presidency of the FBiH, and both prime ministerships.

By 2002, however, the SDP had lost considerable ground to the more nationalist parties. Following the October 2002 election, the SDP held only 4 seats in the national House of Representatives, 15 seats in the downsized FBiH House, and no major executive office (except for Vice President Ivan TOMLJENOVIĆ in the RS). A former FBiH prime minister, Alija Behmen, had finished third among Bosniac candidates for the state presidency.

Partly as a consequence of the poor showing at the polls, the party split over the issue of whether to join nationalist-led coalition governments. Opponents retained control of the party, which led a dissident group to establish the Social Democratic Union (SDU, below) in December 2002. At its third congress, held in February 2005, the SDP reelected President Lagumdžija.

In October 2006 a party vice chair, Željko Komšić, won the Croat seat of the state presidency with 40 percent of the vote, defeating the HDZ incumbent, Ivo Miro Jović. Legislatively, the party made only marginal gains, winning 5 seats in the national House and 17 in the FBiH House. It then chose to remain outside the national and entity governments. The SDP's Slobodan Popović finished fourth in the December 2007 election to replace the deceased RS President Jelić, winning 2.1 percent of the vote.

At the party's fifth congress, held March 14–15, 2009, Lagumdžija was reelected party president after 23 other potential candidates withdrew.

Leaders: Zlatko LAGUMDŽIJA (Former Prime Minister of the Republic of Bosnia and Herzegovina and President of the Party); Željko KOMŠIĆ (Copresident of the Republic and Party Vice President); Denis BEĆIROCIĆ, Mirsad DJAPO, and Damir HADŽIĆ (Vice Presidents); Nermin NIKŠIĆ (General Secretary).

Croatian Democratic Union of Bosnia and Herzegovina (*Hrvatska Demokratska Zajednica Bosne i Hercegovine*—HDZ). The HDZ was launched in August 1990, reportedly on the initiative of its counterpart in Croatia. It ran third in the 1990 balloting and joined the postelection government. Serious strains developed when the party spearheaded the declaration of the ethnic Croat Republic of Herceg-Bosna in 1993, headed by HDZ leader Mate Boban. Under pressure from Zagreb, the party participated in the creation of the FBiH in March 1994, following which Boban was replaced as HDZ leader. In the September 1996 post-Dayton legislative balloting, the HDZ had no serious challengers where the voters were Croats.

Prior to the September 1998 elections a number of HDZ candidates were banned from competing by the OSCE for what was perceived as "blatant support" from Croatian television. Nevertheless, the party emerged as the second largest grouping (behind the KCD) in the Houses of Representatives of the state and the FBiH, and its chair, Ante Jelavić, a former defense minister of the FBiH, was elected to the Croat seat on the central presidency, with nearly 53 percent of the Croat vote.

On March 7, 2001, the Office of the High Representative dismissed Jelavić from the presidency because of the support he had voiced, in violation of the Dayton agreement, for the unofficial Croatian National Assembly's declaration of "Croatian self-administration." He had been reelected party chair at a congress in July 2000, by which time the party had drafted a new statute severing its connection to Croatia's HDZ. (The latter party, following the death of Croatian President Tudjman in December 1999, had already discontinued its ideological and financial support of the Bosnian HDZ.)

At the November 2000 general election the party remained the leading Croat formation despite winning only 5 seats in the central House of Representatives. It fared better in the FBiH election, finishing third, with 25 seats in the lower house, but it was excluded from the new Alliance for Change government. On February 7, 2001, the Alliance and other parties in the state-level House of Representatives also rejected the collective presidency's nomination of the HDZ's Martin Raguž to be sole prime minister of Bosnia and Herzegovina. Raguž, who had been serving as prime minister under a rotation system since October 18, 2000, subsequently served as coordinator of the "Croatian self-administration."

In the October 2002 elections the HDZ's Dragan Čović easily won the Croat seat in the collective presidency, capturing 62 percent of the Croat vote as the candidate of the Coalition (*Koalicija*) formed by the HDZ and the small Croatian Demo-Christians (HD; see HDZ 1990, below). At the FBiH level the Coalition also included the **Croatian National Union** (*Hrvatska Narodna Zajednica*—HNZ, also translated as the Croatian People's Community), now led by Milenko BRKIĆ, with a fourth partner, the Croatian Christian Democratic Union (HKDU; see HDZ 1990), joining in the RS. The Coalition won 4 seats in the national House of Representatives and finished second, with 16 seats, to the SDA in the FBiH House. In January 2003 the FBiH Parliament elected the HDZ's Niko Lozančić as the FBiH president. In 2004 a number of HDZ hard-liners left the party and formed the more militant Croatian Bloc (HB, below).

In October 2004 Jelavić, former FBiH president Ivo Andrić-Lužanski, and five other Croats pleaded not guilty to charges stemming from the 2001 declaration of Croat self-administration. A year later Jelavić fled to Croatia to avoid incarceration for embezzlement of aid funds in the 1990s. Because of his dual citizenship, Croatia would not extradite him.

A party session in June 2005 elected ousted national copresident Dragan Čović party president by a vote of 283–258 over Božo Ljubić. (Čović's predecessor, Bariša ČOLAK, had withdrawn from the contest following criticism of his leadership.) The contest did not settle the differences between the Čović and Ljubić factions, however, and in April 2006 the party split in half, with supporters of Ljubić and Martin Raguž forming the HDZ 1990. The immediate consequence was evident in the results of the October 2006 election, when the HDZ 1990, in coalition with several other Croat parties, siphoned off nearly half of the HDZ-HNZ's support, costing Ivo Miro Jović his position as national copresident and resulting in the HDZ's winning only 3 seats in the national House of Representatives. In the FBiH House of Representatives the coalition of the HDZ, HNZ, and Croatian Party of Rights (HSP) won only 8 seats. In the RS, the HDZ participated, without success, in the Croat Coalition for Equality along with the HNZ, the New Croatian Initiative (NHI; see HSS-NHI, below), and the HSP–Djapić-Dr. Jurišić (below).

Dragan Čović's corruption trial concluded in November 2006 with his sentencing to five years in prison for corruption and abuse of power. A month later he was released on bail, and in September 2007 an appellate court ordered a retrial.

Efforts by some Croats to promote reunification of the HDZ and the HDZ 1990 have not yet succeeded in large part because of animosity between the two parties' leaders. Ivo Sanader, the prime minister of Croatia, has suggested that a reunified party could be headed by Dragan VRANKIĆ , the BiH minister of finance.

Leaders: Dragan ČOVIĆ (Former National Copresident and President of the Party), Niko LOZANČIĆ (Former FBiH President and Party Deputy President), Borjana KRIŠTO (FBiH President and Party Vice President), Marinko ČAVARA and Rade BOŠNJAK (Vice Presidents).

Serbian Democratic Party of Bosnia and Herzegovina (*Srpska Demokratska Stranka Bosne i Hercegovine*—SDS). Formed in July 1990, the SDS quickly established itself as the main political organ of the Serbian population. Almost from the birth of the party, hard-line nationalists began purging more moderate factions. The party was technically banned in 1992, after its electoral victories in 1990, due to the role of party leader Radovan Karadžić in the war. In August 1995 Karadžić was indicted for war crimes and thus became, under the later Dayton accords, ineligible to hold office. Nevertheless, he was reelected as party president in June 1996 and named as its nominee for president of the RS. Bowing to joint U.S.-Serbian pressure, however, he soon stepped down from his party office and relinquished the party's presidential nomination to the new acting RS president, Biljana Plavšić. Those changes notwithstanding, the SDS remained essentially under the control of Karadžić.

A split subsequently opened up between the more moderate Banja Luka faction of the SDS, led by Plavšić, and the hard-line Pale faction of Karadžić and Momčilo Krajišnik (then the Serb member of the copresidency). The fissure caused a constitutional crisis and resulted in the expulsion of Plavšić from the SDS and the formation of her own party, the Serbian People's Alliance (SNS; see discussion under the DNS, below). Once the conflict was resolved, the SDS saw its representation drop precipitously (from 45 to 24 out of 83) in the November 1997 balloting for the RS National Assembly, allowing the opposition to exclude the SDS from government for the first time.

Dragan Kalinić was named chair of the SDS in June 1998, shortly after his controversial dismissal as speaker of the National Assembly. Kalinić subsequently accused Plavšić and her supporters of conducting an anti-SDS "witch hunt" in the media. In the September 1998 election the party's representation fell even further in the National Assembly (to 19). Krajišnik, who also had the support of the Serb Radical Party (SRS, below), was defeated in his campaign for reelection to the central presidency, securing 45 percent of the votes within the Serb population. However, the SDS supported the successful candidate in the race for president of the RS—Nikola Poplašen of the SRS.

In the November 2000 elections the SDS again easily finished first in Serb National Assembly balloting, capturing 31 seats on a 38 percent vote share, and its candidate for president of the RS, Serb Vice President Mirko Sarović, also proved successful, winning 50 percent of the vote and narrowly avoiding a runoff. When the new National Assembly convened, Kalinić was again chosen as speaker. At the central level, the SDS won 6 seats in the House of Representatives on a 15 percent vote share.

Although Sarović attempted to distance himself and the party from the extreme nationalism of the past and from Karadžić, many observers remained skeptical of statements from the SDS leadership that Karadžić no longer held sway behind the scenes. On April 3, 2000, former member of the presidency Krajišnik was arrested by the SFOR and quickly transported to The Hague, where he pleaded not guilty to charges that included crimes against humanity and violations of the Geneva Convention. (His trial opened in February 2004 and concluded with a guilty verdict in September 2006, when he was sentenced to 27 years in prison. The sentence was reduced to 20 years in 2009.)

In the October 2002 general election the SDS remained the leading Serbian party at the national level, winning five seats in the House of Representatives and the Serb seat in the collective presidency, and retained both the presidency of the RS and a plurality in the Serb National Assembly. In April 2003, however, Mirko Sarović stepped down from the tripartite national presidency over allegations related to a spying scandal and violations of a UN embargo against arms sales to Iraq. He was arrested in November 2005 on corruption charges but was acquitted in October 2006.

In July 2008 Radovan Karadžić was captured by Serbian security forces in a Belgrade suburb, but a number of other internationally indicted Bosnian Serbs remained at large. Noncooperation had prompted the Office of the High Representative to dismiss dozens of Serb officials, including then party chair Dragan Kalinić, for noncompliance with the ICTY. Kalinić's successor, Dragan Čavić, was formally elected to the chair in March 2005. In January 2006, as a consequence of the Serbian National Assembly's vote of no confidence in the Pero Bukejlović government, the SDS moved into the role of what Čavić termed "constructive opposition" at both the national and entity levels.

In October 2006 Čavić, winning only 29 percent of the vote, lost his bid for reelection as RS president, while the party's candidate for the Serb seat on the national copresidency, Mladen Bosić, also finished second. The SDS won only 3 seats in the national House of Representatives and dropped to 17 seats in the RS National Assembly, as a consequence of which Čavić lost an intraparty confidence vote in November and resigned as chair. On December 16 Bosić was elected to the chair, pledging to introduce reforms before a full party assembly in 2007. In late June Bosić was overwhelmingly reelected.

In March 2007, with the Constitutional Court having ruled that Dragan Kalinić's rights had been violated by former high representative Ashdown, speculation increased that the former SDS leader, who had been living in Belgrade, Serbia, would attempt a return to power. The SDS was widely viewed as split between factions loyal to Kalinić and Čavić. That conflict led to the formation in 2008 of the **Social Democratic Party of Bosnia and Herzegovina 1990** (SDS 1990) by a group of Kalinić supporters under Miladin NEDIĆ. They felt that Čavić and Bosić had led the SDS away from the party's "original principles" and were contributing to the "disappearance" of the RS. A more serious rupture occurred in December 2008, when Čavić left to form the Democratic Party (DP, below). A month earlier, Bosić had been reelected party chair.

With an eye toward the 2010 election cycle, in 2009 the SDS was considering offering joint candidates with the PDP and the SRS (both below) as part of an effort to unseat the SNSD's Dodik.

Leaders: Mladen BOSIĆ (Chair), Ognjen TADIĆ (2007 RS presidential candidate), Vukota GOVEDARICA.

Croatian Democratic Union 1990 (*Hrvatska Demokratska Zajednica 1990*—HDZ 1990). The HDZ 1990 was organized on April 8, 2006, by disaffected members of the HDZ who wished to return to the democratic, conservative, and Christian principles that underlay the foundation of the parent party. The leadership also wished to restore a closer relationship with Croatia's HDZ and rejected proposed constitutional changes, which the Bosnia HDZ had endorsed, that were designed to strengthen the central government.

The HDZ 1990 contested the October 2006 election at the head of the **Croat Unity** (*Hrvatsko Zajedništvo*—HZ) coalition, which also included the Croatian Peasants' Party of Bosnia and Herzegovina (HSS, below); the Croat Democratic Union of Bosnia and Herzegovina (HDU, below); the **Croatian Christian Democratic Union** (*Hrvatska Kršćanska Demokratska Unija*—HKDU), led by Ivan MUSA, a vocal advocate of separation from the FBiH; and the **Croatian Demo-Christians** (*Hrvatski Demokršćani*—HD), led by Ivan MILIĆ. (In 2002 the HD had been allied with the HDZ, as had the HKDU in the Serb Republic; running independently, the right-wing, nationalist HKDU had won one seat in the FBiH lower house, as it had in 2000.) Ljubić finished third in the race for the Croat seat in the copresidency, but his presence may have been the principal factor in defeating the incumbent, the HDZ's Ivo Miro Jović. The coalition won two seats in the national House of Representatives and seven in the FBiH House.

Leaders: Božo LJUBIĆ (President), Martin RAGUŽ (Deputy President), Slavica JOSIPOVIĆ (HDZ Leader in the FBiH House of Representatives).

Bosnian-Herzegovinian Patriotic Party (*Bosanskohercegovačka Patriotska Stranka*—BPS). The BPS won two seats in the FBiH's House of Representatives in 1998, while its candidate for the Bosniac seat on the central presidency, Sefer Halilović, a former commander of the Bosnia and Herzegovina army, finished third with 5.7 percent of the vote. At the November 2000 elections the BPS won one seat in the national House of Representatives and two in the FBiH's lower house. It subsequently joined the Alliance for Change, and Halilović was named to the Behmen cabinet in the FBiH.

In October 2002 the BPS won only one seat in the FBiH's lower house. Its candidate for the Bosniac seat in the state presidency, Emir ZLATAR, won less than 2 percent of the vote.

On November 15, 2005, the ICTY acquitted Halilović of charges related to the killing of Croatian civilians by troops under his command. He had surrendered to the ICTY in September 2001. He has since argued for membership in both the EU and NATO.

In the October 2006 election, running as the **Bosnian-Herzegovinian Patriotic Party–Sefer Halilović,** the party won one seat at the national level and four in the FBiH lower house.

Leader: Sefer HALILOVIĆ.

Democratic Party (*Demokratska Partija*—DP). Formation of the center-right DP was announced by Dragan Čavić in December 2008, upon his departure from the SDS. He described the new party as an effort to reinvigorate the opposition to Prime Minister Dodik. Strongly pro-Dayton, the party was registered in January 2009.

Momčilo Novaković, theretofore the head of the SDS deputy group in the national House of Representatives, left the SDS in January 2009 because of disagreements with party leader Mladen Bosić. Soon after, he joined the DP, which also initially attracted two members of the RS lower house.

Leaders: Dragan ČAVIĆ (Former President of the RS), Momčilo NOVAKOVIĆ.

Democratic People's Alliance of the Serb Republic (*Demokratski Narodni Savez Republike Srpske*—DNS). The DNS (also translated as the Democratic National Alliance or the Democratic People's Union) was established on June 16, 2000, by anti-Plavšić members of the Serbian People's Alliance of the Serb Republic (*Srpski Narodni Savez Republike Srpske*—SNS) following their failed attempt to oust her as party leader. Ideologically moderate, the DNS parted ways with the SNS primarily for reasons of personality. In the November 2000 elections it failed to win a seat in the central House of Representatives but took three in the Serb National Assembly, one more than the SNS.

In 2002 the DNS won three seats in the Serb legislature but none nationally. (The SNS won only one seat and became defunct following Plavšić's sentencing by the ICTY in 2003.) The DNS candidate for the Serb seat in the national presidency, Milorad COKIĆ, finished far down the list, with only 3 percent support. The party chair, Dragan KOSTIĆ, was equally unsuccessful in his bid for president of the RS.

Following the October 2006 general election, at which the DNS won one seat in the central House of Representatives and four in the RS National Assembly, the party's current chair, Marko Pavić, agreed that the DNS would continue in the SNSD-led RS government of Milorad Dodik. The DNS has consistently rejected any constitutional change that would reduce the authority of the RS. It voted against the 2008 police reforms.

Leaders: Marko PAVIĆ (Chair), Nedeljko ČUBRILOVIĆ (RS Minister of Transport and Communications).

Democratic People's Union of Bosnia and Herzegovina (*Demokratska Narodna Zajednica Bosne i Hercegovine*—DNZ). A Muslim party, the DNZ was launched in April 1996 by Fikret Abdić as the successor to his Muslim Democratic Party (*Muslimanska Demokratska Stranka*—MDS), which had been founded in 1993 in the Muslim-populated northern town of Bihać. A former chicken farmer, Abdić had been a member of the state presidency for the ruling SDA but later cooperated with the Bosnian Serbs in the defense of Bihać, until its capture by government forces in August 1994. Earlier, he had attempted to proclaim an "Autonomous Province of Western Bosnia."

Abdić won 6.2 percent of the vote in the 1998 balloting for the Bosniac seat on the central presidency. The party also captured one seat in the national House of Representatives and three in the FBiH House, retaining all four in 2000. In July 2001 Abdić went on trial in Croatia, where he had resided since 1995, charged with war crimes dating back to 1992–1995. Found guilty in July 2002 and sentenced to 20 years in prison, Abdić chose to run for the national presidency from his prison cell while appealing the conviction; he finished fourth, with 4 percent of the Bosniac vote. At the same time, the DNZ won one seat in the state House of Representatives and two in the FBiH's lower house (as it also did in October 2006). Abdić's sentence was reduced to 15 years by the Croatian Supreme Court in March 2005, but with the verdict having been confirmed, he resigned as DNZ president in May.

Leader: Rifet DOLIĆ (President).

Party for Democratic Progress of the Serb Republic (*Partija Demoktatskog Progresa Republika Srpska*—PDP). The founding congress of the PDP was held on September 26, 1999, under the leadership of prominent economist Mladen Ivanić, a centrist. After having registered a modest success in the April 2000 local elections, the PDP finished in a tie for second in the November balloting for the Serb National Assembly, winning 11 seats. In the election for the central House of Representatives, the party won 2 seats. A month later RS President Mirko Sarović nominated Ivanić as prime minister of the Serb entity. In 2001 the PDP joined the Alliance for Change.

In October 2002 the PDP won two seats in the national House of Representatives and finished third in the RS lower house, with nine seats. Its candidate for president of the RS, Dragan Mikerević, also finished third, with 8 percent of the vote, but he was subsequently named prime minister of the entity. He resigned in December 2004 to protest recent dismissals by the Office of the High Representative and related "threats and ultimatums" by the West. In November 2005 the PDP withdrew its support from the SDS-led Bukejlović government, which fell in January 2006. A month later, the PDP joined Milorad Dodik's new multiparty cabinet.

In October 2006 the PDP won one seat in the national House of Representatives and eight in the RS Assembly. In addition to participating in Dodik's reshuffled RS cabinet, it was one of seven parties forming a coalition government at the national level. In December 2007 Ivanić ran third, with 17 percent of the vote, in the RS presidential contest. Two months earlier, he and 12 others had been charged with corruption during his tenure as RS prime minister. The trial concluded in June 2008 with Ivanić's conviction for negligence, although he was acquitted of all other charges. Sentenced to a year and a half in prison, he launched an appeal.

In February 2009 the PDP withdrew from the RS government and joined the opposition, largely because of objections to domination by the SNSD.

Leaders: Mladen IVANIĆ (Former Prime Minister of the RS and Chair of the Party), Dragan MIKEREVIĆ (Former Prime Minister of the RS), Zoran TEŠANOVIĆ (2006 candidate for the Serb seat on the Copresidency), Nevenka TRIFKOVIĆ (General Secretary).

People's Party "Working for Prosperity" (*Narodna Stranka "Radom za Boljitak"*—NS-RzB). A Croat party established in mid-2002, the NS-RzB joined with the HDU (below) to form the Economic Bloc "Croat Democratic Union for Prosperity" (*Ekonomski Blok HDU–Za Boljitak*) prior to the October elections; the bloc's sole successful candidate was the NS-RzB's Mladen Potočnik, who subsequently became leader of the Republican Party (below). The Economic Bloc's candidate for the Croat seat in the presidency, NS-RzB leader Mladen Ivanković-Lijanović, finished second, with 17 percent support. In March 2005 he was charged in the scandal that led to the dismissal of the Croatian member of the state presidency, Dragan Čović, but he was acquitted in 2006 for lack of evidence.

In the October 2006 elections Ivanković-Lijanović ran for the Croat seat on the national Presidency, finishing fourth. The party's candidate for the Bosniac seat, Muhamed ČENGIĆ, also finished fourth, while the nominee for the Serb seat, Ranko BAKIĆ, came in sixth. The NS-RzB won one seat in the national House of Representatives and three in the FBiH lower house. It then joined in forming the seven-party national coalition government.

Leaders: Mladen IVANKOVIĆ-LIJANOVIĆ, Anton JOSIPOVIĆ (2007 RS presidential candidate).

Other Parties Represented in the FBiH House of Representatives:

Bosnian Party (*Bosanska Stranka*—BOSS). BOSS won one seat in the FBiH's House of Representatives in the September 1998 balloting. In 2000 it won two seats in the FBiH's lower house and then added one more in 2002, when it also won one seat in the state-level lower house. Its candidate for the state presidency, Faruk BALIJAGIĆ, won only 2 percent of the Bosniac vote.

In October 2006 BOSS and the Social Democratic Union (SDU, below) ran in coalition as the **Patriotic Bloc BOSS-SDU BiH** (*Patriotski Blok BOSS-SDU BiH*), which won three FBiH seats but failed to win at the national level. Its candidate for the Bosniac seat on the central presidency, Mirnes Ajanović, finished third, with 8 percent of the vote. Its candidate for the Serb seat, Slavko DRAGIČEVIĆ, won only 2 percent.

Leader: Mirnes AJANOVIĆ (Chair).

Croat Democratic Union of Bosnia and Herzegovina (*Hrvatska Demokratska Unija Bosne i Herzegovine*—HDU). The HDU was organized in May 2002 by Miro Grabovac Titan and other former members of the HDZ who sought a less nationalist posture. For the October 2002 elections the HDU joined forces with the NS-RzB (above) in forming the Economic Bloc "Croat Democratic Union for Prosperity," which won one seat in the national legislature and two in the FBiH lower house. In the RS the Croatian Peasants' Party (HSS, below) also participated in the Economic Bloc.

In 2006 the HDU ran as part of the Croat Unity coalition (see HDZ 1990, above), which won seven FBiH lower house seats.

Leader: Miro GRABOVAC TITAN (President).

Croatian Party of Rights of Bosnia and Herzegovina–Djapić-Dr. Jurišić (*Hrvatska Stranka Prava Bosne I Hercegovine–Djapić-Dr. Jurišić*—HSP–Djapić-Dr. Jurišić). Closely linked to Anto Djapić's HSP in Croatia, the rightist, nationalist HSP won two seats in both the 1996 and 1998 balloting for the FBiH's House of Representatives. In 2000 it dropped to one seat, which it retained in 2002 as part of a coalition with the **United Croatian Party of Rights** (*Ujedinjena Hrvatska Stranka Prava*—UHSP). By then, however, differences had already emerged among various Croatian "parties of rights," which led, in part, to the formation, prior to the October 2002 elections, of a Croatian Rights Bloc (*Hrvatska Pravaški Blok*—HPB). The latter, led by Željko KOROMAN, won one FBiH seat.

A further split developed between HSP factions loyal to Zdravko HRSTIĆ and Zvonko Jurišić, which led to formation of the separate HSP–Djapić-Dr. Jurišić. At the October 2006 elections a coalition with the NHI (see HSS-NHI, below), the **Croat Coalition for Equality** (*Hrvatska Koalicija za Jednakopravnost*), won one seat in the FBiH House of Representatives. Jurišić finished fifth in the balloting for the Croat seat on the tripartite presidency, with 7 percent support.

A **Posavina Croatian Party of Rights** (Posavina HSP) was established under the leadership of Andrija MENDES in June 2008 and then aligned with the HSS-NHI (below) in Brčko.

Leaders: Zvonko JURIŠIĆ (Chair), Stanko PRIMORAC (Member of the FBiH House of Representatives).

Croatian Peasants' Party of Bosnia and Herzegovina–New Croatian Initiative (*Hrvatska Seljačka Stranka Bosne i Hercegovine–Nova Hrvatska Inicijativa*—HSS-NHI). The HSS-NHI was established in late September 2007 by merger of the HSS and the NHI. At the time, the party claimed to be second in membership to the HDZ among Croat parties.

Affiliated with a similar party in Croatia, the HSS had been formed in the early 1990s by moderate Croat leader Ivo Komšić, who was named to the collective presidency in November 1993. Komšić subsequently played a significant role in negotiations leading up to the 1995 Dayton accords, and in 1996 he was the candidate for the Croat seat on the new central presidency from the United List (*Združema Lista*—ZL), a coalition of five parties devoted to a multiethnic approach to affairs in Bosnia and Herzegovina. (Otherwise, the parties in the ZL—the HSS, the Muslim Bosniac Organization [*Muslimanska Bošnjačka Organizacija*—MBO], the Republican Party [below], and the two predecessors of the SDP, the Democratic Party of Socialists [DSS] and the Union of Bosnian Social Democrats [ZSDB]—spanned the political spectrum in orientation.) Komšić finished second in his race, while the ZL's candidate for the Bosniac seat on the central presidency, Sead Avdić (later of the SDP, SDU, and BHSD), finished fourth. Meanwhile, the ZL secured seats in all three legislatures. Komšić later joined the SDU.

The HSS won one seat in the FBiH's House of Representatives in both 1998 and 2000. In January 2000 it participated in forming the Alliance for Change. In October 2002 it retained its FBiH seat, as it did in 2006, running as part of the Croat Unity coalition (see HDZ 1990, above). In March 2005, looking toward the 2006 elections, the HSS and four other small, moderate opposition parties—the NHI, the Liberal Democratic Party (LDS), the Civic Democratic Party (GDS), and a pensioners' party—had signed a cooperation statement, but no coalition resulted.

The NHI had been founded in June 1998 by Krešimir Zubak, a former Croat member of the central presidency, and a group of supporters who had recently left the HDZ. Zubak described the NHI as "Christian Democratic" in orientation and committed to peaceful political existence with Muslims and Serbs, in contrast to the HDZ, which he described as still in pursuit of political separation. Zubak finished third in the race for the Croat seat on the central presidency in the September balloting, while the NHI secured representation in all three legislatures.

In the November 2000 elections the NHI held its single seats at the national and RS levels but fell from four to two seats in the FBiH's House of Representatives. The NHI joined the Alliance for Change in early 2001 and accepted ministerial posts in the resultant national and FBiH governments. At the October 2002 election the NHI won one seat in the national House of Representatives, two in the FBiH lower house (one representative was dismissed in March 2003 by the Office of the High Representative because of corruption allegations), and one in the Serb National Assembly. Its candidate for the Croat seat in the state presidency, Mijo ATIĆ, finished a distant third. In March 2004 Atić and a number of other NHI leaders attempted to remove Zubak from the party leadership, but Zubak was reelected at a party assembly, prevailing 173–31 over Drago VRBIĆ. In 2006 the NHI ran in coalition with the HSP–Djapić-Dr. Jurišić (above) but failed to retain any seats at the national or entity levels.

Shortly before announcement of the HSS-NHI merger, the HSS had joined the HDZ, HDZ 1990, HKDU, HSP–Djapić-Dr. Jurišić, and NS-RzB in crafting the "Kresevo Declaration" in an effort to present a united Croat front. The declaration called for abolishing the entities, establishing minimum ethnic quotas in Bosnia's legislatures, and maintaining ethnic parity in executive and judicial offices.

In late March 2008 Marko Tadić unexpectedly stepped down as HSS-NHI president.

Leaders: Ivan KRNDELJ (President), Krešimir ZUBAK (Chair), Marko TADIĆ.

Social Democratic Union of Bosnia and Herzegovina (*Socijaldemokratska Unije Bosne i Hercegovine*—SDU). The SDU was organized in December 2002 by former members of the SDP who, following losses at the polls in October, had failed to change the party's policy of nonparticipation in nationalist-dominated governing coalitions. Among those forming the SDU was Sead Avdić, who was named the new party's president but in late 2003 announced his decision to sit in the national House of Representatives as an independent. He subsequently formed the Free Democrats (below).

In the October 2006 elections the SDU ran in partnership with the BOSS (above) as the Patriotic Bloc, which won three seats in the FBiH House of Representatives. In October 2007 a dispute over party leadership erupted. Sejfudin Tokić, who refused to recognize his dismissal by the party board and his replacement by Ivo Komšić, retained control.

Leaders: Sejfudin TOKIĆ (Chair), Ivo KOMŠIĆ (Deputy Chair).

Other Parties Represented in the RS National Assembly:

Serb Radical Party of the Serb Republic (*Srpska Radikalna Stranka Republike Srpske*—SRS). Related to the Serbian Radical Party in Serbia, the SRS is widely seen as an extension of the Pale faction of the SDS. It increased its electoral performance in the November 1997 National Assembly election, gaining 8 seats, for a total of 15, before declining to 11 in 1998. The SRS supported the SDS's Momčilo Krajišnik in the 1998 campaign for the Serb seat on the central presidency, with the SDS in turn supporting the SRS's Nikola Poplašen in his successful run for president of the RS.

On March 5, 1999, the Office of the High Representative removed Poplašen from the presidency for abuse of power, which included efforts to dismiss Prime Minister Dodik. Poplašen refused to step down, however, and the office remained vacant until December 2000. Moreover, in November 1999 the high representative prohibited the SRS from participating in the April 2000 local elections and the November 2000 general election, citing obstruction of the Dayton accords by party leaders. As a consequence, a number of party members ran for office under the banners of other Serb parties.

Reelected president of the party in May 2002, Poplašen stepped down less than a month later so that the SRS could compete in the October election. (Earlier, the high representative had announced that parties would be ineligible if their official leadership included individuals who had been banned from holding office.) In the general election the SRS won one seat in the national House of Representatives and four seats in the Serb National Assembly. Ognjen Tadić, the SRS candidate for the Serb seat in the national presidency, finished third, while Radislav Kanjerić finished fifth in the election for president of the RS.

In December 2002 the party split, primarily over the issue of support for inclusion of the Bosniac SDA in the Serb government. The more nationalist group, which included Kanjerić and Tadić, ultimately established the SRS "Dr. Vojislav Šešelj" (SRS-VŠ, below). The other faction, based in Banja Luca, elected a new leadership and retained three of the four SRS deputies in the National Assembly.

In the October 2006 elections the SRS won only two seats in the RS National Assembly.

Leader: Milanko MIHAJLICA (Chair).

Socialist Party of the Serb Republic (*Socijalistička Partija Republike Srpske*—SPRS). Founded in June 1993, the SPRS was affiliated with Slobodan Milošević of Yugoslavia and his Socialist Party, although one wing of the party was very close to other social democratic parties in Europe. The SPRS was the driving force behind the Peoples' Union for Peace–Union for Peace and Progress (*Narodni Savez za Mir–Savez za Mir i Progres*—NSSM-SMP), an alliance of five parties that competed in the 1996 elections for the central and RS legislatures, winning two seats in the former and ten in the latter. However, the NSSM-SMP did not subsequently compete as an alliance. Running on its own, the SPRS secured nine seats in the National Assembly of the RS in 1997, improving to ten in 1998, at which time its president, Živko Radišić, was elected to the presidency of the Republic of Bosnia and Herzegovina as the *Sloga* candidate.

In February 2000 the party leadership decided to withdraw from the governing coalition in the RS. Observers attributed the move in part to Prime Minister Dodik's dismissal of his deputy prime minister, Tihomir GLIGORIĆ of the SPRS, in January. A number of opponents of the withdrawal were soon expelled from or left the party voluntarily to form the DSP (see SNSD, above). In late April the country's collective presidency nominated Gligorić for the post of central prime minister, but the nomination was withdrawn in early May without a vote in the House of Representatives, support being insufficient for confirmation. In the November 2000 elections the SPRS won one seat at the central level and four in the RS's National Assembly.

In February 2002 Živko Radišić was ousted as party president and replaced by Petar Djokić. In May Radišić formally resigned from the SPRS and subsequently joined the newly organized People's Party of Socialists (*Narodna Partija Socijalista*—NPS), which prompted the SPRS to request that he step down as the Serb member of the national presidency.

In the October 2002 elections the SPRS won one seat in the national House of Representatives and three in the Serb National Assembly. Its candidate for the national presidency, Dargutin ILIĆ, won under 4 percent of the Serb vote, while Djokić, its candidate for president of the RS, won 5 percent.

In January 2006, contrary to a directive from the party leadership, National Assembly members Nedjo DJURIĆ and Dragutin ŠKREBIĆ voted against the no-confidence motion that ousted the Bukejlović government in the RS. The party then expelled them. Shortly before the October 2006 elections, in which the SPRS won three seats in the RS lower house, Gligorić defected to the SNSD. Following the balloting, the party remained in the SNSD-led Dodik government.

Leaders: Petar DJOKIĆ (President), Predrag GLUHAKOVIĆ (RS Minister for Trade and Tourism), Živko MARJANAC (Secretary General).

Additional Parties:

Civic Democratic Party of Bosnia and Herzegovina (*Gradjanska Demokratska Stranka Bosne i Hercegovine*—GDS). The centrist GDS participated in the KCD alliance in 1997–1998. In November 2000 it won a single seat in the FBiH's House of Representatives, after which it joined in forming the Alliance for Change. It again won one FBiH seat in October 2002 but none in 2004.

Leader: Ibrahim SPAHIĆ.

Croatian Bloc of Bosnia and Herzegovina (*Hrvatski Blok Bosne i Hercegovina*—HB). In mid-2004 a number of former hard-line members of the HDZ left the party to form the HB, which is closely connected to the HB in Croatia. Marko TOKIĆ, a former HDZ secretary general whom the Office of the High Representative had banned from politics for attempting to organize Croat self-rule, was considered a behind-the-scenes actor in forming the group. The HB has been one of the strongest supporters of establishing a third, Croat entity. In 2006 it contested some cantonal races but chose not to compete at higher levels.

Leader: Mario VASILJ (Chair).

Free Democrats (*BH Slobodni Demokrati*—BHSD). The Free Democrats was established in May 2005 under the leadership of Sead Avdić, a former speaker of the national House of Representatives. After having been reelected to the lower house in October 2002 as a member of the SDP, he left that party in late 2002 and was elected president of the newly formed SDU (above). Only a year later, he decided to sit in the House of Representatives as an independent. At the BHSD's founding convention Avdić described the new party as social democratic and committed to human rights and a market economy. It opposed the constitutional reforms proposed in 2006.

Leader: Sead AVDIĆ (President).

Liberal Democratic Party (*Liberalno Demokratska Stranka*—LDS). Formation of the centrist LDS was announced in May 2000 by the Liberal Party of Bosnia and Herzegovina (*Liberalna Stranka Bosne i Hercegovine*—LS-BiH) and the Liberal Bosniac Organization (*Liberalna Bošnjačka Organizacija*—LBO). A formal unification congress was held a month later. The new party won one seat in the FBiH's House of Representatives in November 2000 and subsequently joined in formation of the Alliance for Change. It again won one FBiH seat in 2002, while the party's chair took 1 percent of the Bosniac vote for the state presidency. In 2006 the party fared poorly, losing its seat amid indications that the chair, Rasim KADIĆ, intended to step down.

Leader: Lamija TANOVIĆ (Chair).

Republican Party (*Republikanska Stranka*—RS). The Republican Party was formed in 1993 by Stjepan KLJUIĆ, who had been elected to Bosnia-Herzegovina's collegial presidency in 1990 as a representative of the HDZ but had become unhappy at the parent party's identification with ethnic Croat aims. Thus, the present party strongly favors a multiethnic state.

In 1998 the Republicans and the Liberal Bosniac Organization, campaigning as the Center Coalition (*Koalicija Centra*—KC), won one seat in the FBiH House of Representatives. Human rights activist Senka NOŽICA won 3.1 percent of the vote as the Republican candidate for the Croat seat on the central presidency.

In August 2000 the Republicans and the Liberal Social Party (*Liberalno Socijalna Partija*—LSP) agreed to run jointly in the November elections, in which the Republicans again won one seat in the FBiH's lower house. The party then joined the Alliance for Change in January 2001. In October 2002 the party failed to hold its FBiH seat; Kljuić won 5 percent of the Croat vote for the central presidency. In 2003 he became a foreign policy adviser to the HDZ's winning candidate, Dragan Čović. Party President Mladen Potočnik was elected in 2002 to the national House of Representatives from the Economic Bloc "Croat Democratic Union for Prosperity."

In January 2006 the Republican Party joined four other small organizations in forming the **Alliance of Parties of the Political Center** (*Savez Stranaka Političkog Centra*—SSPC), which voiced support for a new constitution and rapid integration into NATO and, in the next decade, the EU. Partners in the SSPC included the **Bosnian Podrinje People's Party** (*Bosansko Podrinjska Narodna Stranka*—BPNS), led by Seid KARIĆ, and the **Bosnia-Herzegovina Party of Rights** (*Bošanskohercegovačka Stranka Prava*—BHSP), led by Besim ŠARIĆ. None won national- or entity-level legislative seats in October 2006.

Leader: Mladen POTOČNIK (President).

Serb Radical Party "Dr. Vojislav Šešelj" (*Srpska Radikalna Strana "Dr. Vojislav Šešelj"*—SRS-VŠ). The SRS-VŠ resulted from a split in the SRS (above) following the October 2002 elections. The more nationalist Bijeljina-based SRS faction, led by national presidency candidate Radislav Kanjerić and Serb presidential candidate Ognjen TADIĆ, opposed inclusion of the Bosniac SDA in the new Serb entity government.

In November 2003 the Kanjerić wing held a founding assembly for the new party. Named in honor of the ultranationalist Serb leader Vojislav Šešelj, who had been indicted as a war criminal by the ICTY, the party was initially known as the Serb Radical Alliance "Dr. Vojislav Šešelj" (*Srpski Radikalni Savez "Dr. Vojislav Šešelj"*). One of the four SRS members elected to the Serb National Assembly in 2002 chose to join the SRS-VŠ.

In 2006 Kanjerić finished fifth in voting for the Serb seat on the collective presidency. In December 2007 the party's candidate for the RS presidency, Mirko BLAGOJEVIĆ, finished fifth, winning 1.8 percent of the vote.

Leader: Radislav KANJERIĆ (President).

LEGISLATURES

The 1995 Dayton accords provided for a bicameral Parliamentary Assembly (*Parlamentarna Skupština*) of the Republic of Bosnia and Herzegovina, a bicameral Federation Parliament (*Parliamenta Federacije*) of the Federation of Bosnia and Herzegovina, and a unicameral

National Assembly of the Serb Republic of Bosnia and Herzegovina. A second legislative body for the RS was created by constitutional amendment in 2002.

In addition to competing in multimember constituencies, parties may submit separate lists of candidates for compensatory seats that are awarded as needed to ensure proportionality of representation in the central and entity lower houses. In the October 2006 elections the threshold for obtaining compensatory seats was 3 percent of the vote.

Parliamentary Assembly of the Republic of Bosnia and Herzegovina:

House of Peoples (*Dom Naroda*). The upper chamber has 15 members: 5 Bosniacs and 5 Croats elected by their respective ethnic caucuses in the House of Peoples of the FBiH, and 5 Serbs elected by the National Assembly of the RS. All members serve four-year terms. The office of speaker rotates every eight months among three members, one from each ethnic community. The upper house was most recently constituted on March 14, 2007, with the following party breakdown:

Bosniacs: Party of Democratic Action, 3 seats; Party for Bosnia and Herzegovina, 1; Social Democratic Party of Bosnia and Herzegovina, 1.

Croats: Croatian Democratic Union of Bosnia and Herzegovina, 3; Croatian Democratic Union 1990, 2.

Serbs: Alliance of Independent Social Democrats, 3; Party for Democratic Progress of the Serb Republic, 1; Serbian Democratic Party of Bosnia and Herzegovina, 1.

Speakers: Ilija FILIPOVIĆ, Dusanka MAJKIĆ, Sulejman TIHIĆ.

House of Representatives (*Zastupnički Dom/Predstavnički Dom*). The lower chamber consists of 42 directly elected members (28 from the FBiH and 14 from the RS), who serve four-year terms. The office of speaker rotates every eight months among three members, one from each ethnic community. The balloting of October 1, 2006, yielded the following results: Party of Democratic Action, 9 seats (7 direct, 2 compensatory); Party for Bosnia and Herzegovina, 8 (6, 2); Alliance of Independent Social Democrats, 7 (6, 1); Social Democratic Party of Bosnia and Herzegovina, 5 (4, 1); Coalition of the Croatian Democratic Union of Bosnia and Herzegovina and the Croatian National Union, 3 (2, 1); Serbian Democratic Party of Bosnia and Herzegovina, 3 (3, 0); Croat Unity (Coalition of the Croatian Democratic Union 1990, the Croatian Peasants' Party of Bosnia and Herzegovina, the Croatian Christian Democratic Union, the Croat Democratic Union of Bosnia and Herzegovina, and the Croatian Demo-Christians), 2 (1, 1); Bosnian-Herzegovinian Patriotic Party–Sefer Halilović, 1 (0, 1); Democratic People's Alliance of the Serb Republic, 1 (0, 1); Democratic People's Union of Bosnia and Herzegovina, 1 (1, 0); Party for Democratic Progress of the Serb Republic, 1 (0, 1); People's Party "Working for Prosperity," 1 (0, 1).

Speakers: Beriz BELKIĆ, Niko LOZANČIĆ, Milorad ŽIVKOVIĆ.

Federation Parliament:

House of Peoples of the Federation (*Dom Naroda Federacije*). The upper chamber comprises 58 members (17 Bosniacs, 17 Croats, 17 Serbs, and 7 others) indirectly elected by the entity's ten cantonal assemblies. The current House began its constituting session on January 25, 2007, but with only 50 seats filled because of an insufficient number of candidates for the Serb and "other" delegates. (The preceding House had faced a similar difficulty.) The following party breakdown reflects the full complement of 58 seats: Social Democratic Party of Bosnia and Herzegovina, 12; Party of Democratic Action, 11; Party for Bosnia and Herzegovina, 8; Croatian Democratic Union of Bosnia and Herzegovina, 7; Croat Unity (Coalition of the Croatian Democratic Union 1990, the Croatian Peasants' Party of Bosnia and Herzegovina [HSS], the Croatian Christian Democratic Union, the Croat Democratic Union of Bosnia and Herzegovina, and the Croatian Demo-Christians), 5, including 2 held separately by the HSS; Alliance of Independent Social Democrats, 4; People's Party "Working for Prosperity," 4; Coalition for Equality (Croatian Party of Rights–Djapić-Jurišić and the New Croatian Initiative), 2; Democratic People's Union of Bosnia and Herzegovina, 2; Patriotic Bloc BOSS-SDU, 2; and Bosnian-Herzegovinian Patriotic Party–Sefer Halilović, 1.

Speakers: Besim IMAMOVIĆ, Stjepan KREŠIĆ, Drago PUZIGAĆA.

House of Representatives of the Federation (*Predstavnički/Zastupnički Dom Federacije*). The lower chamber has 98 directly elected members. The balloting of October 1, 2006, resulted in the following distribution of seats: Party of Democratic Action, 28 (23 direct, 5 compensatory); Party for Bosnia and Herzegovina, 24 (19, 5); Social Democratic Party of Bosnia and Herzegovina, 17 (13, 4); Coalition of the Croatian Democratic Union of Bosnia and Herzegovina, the Croatian National Union, and the Croatian Party of Rights, 8 (7, 1); Croat Unity (Coalition of the Croatian Democratic Union 1990, the Croatian Peasants' Party of Bosnia and Herzegovina, the Croatian Christian Democratic Union, the Croat Democratic Union of Bosnia and Herzegovina, and the Croatian Demo-Christians), 7 (5, 2); Bosnian-Herzegovinian Patriotic Party–Sefer Halilović, 4 (1, 3); Patriotic Bloc (Bosnian Party and Social Democratic Union of Bosnia and Herzegovina), 3 (1, 2); People's Party "Working for Prosperity," 3 (3, 0); Democratic People's Union of Bosnia and Herzegovina, 2 (2, 0); Alliance of Independent Social Democrats, 1 (1, 0); Coalition for Equality (Croatian Party of Rights–Djapić-Jurišić and the New Croatian Initiative), 1 (1, 0).

Speakers: Marinko ČAVARA, Safet SOFTIĆ, Vesna SARADŽIĆ.

Legislative Bodies of the RS:

Council of Peoples (*Vijeće Naroda*). The Council of Peoples, which was established as part of the constitutional amendments implemented in 2002, has limited powers on "issues of vital national interest," its primary mandate being to ensure that no ethnic group is disadvantaged by legislative acts of the National Assembly. Its 28 members (8 Serbs, 8 Bosniacs, 8 Croatians, and 4 others) are elected by the respective ethnic caucuses in the National Assembly. The first Council was constituted on March 20, 2003, after a delay caused by difficulties related to selection of Bosniac delegates. The constituting session of the second Council convened on December 4, 2006. Party representation was as follows: Alliance of Independent Social Democrats, 13; Party of Democratic Action, 4; Party for Bosnia and Herzegovina, 3; New Croatian Initiative, 2; Party for Democratic Progress of the Serb Republic, 2; Democratic People's Alliance of the Serb Republic, Serbian Democratic Party of Bosnia and Herzegovina, Social Democratic Party of Bosnia and Herzegovina, and Socialist Party of the Serb Republic, 1 each.

Chair: Dževad OSMANČEVIĆ.

National Assembly of the Serb Republic (*Narodna Skupština Republike Srpske*). The lower house consists of 83 directly elected members. The election of October 1, 2006, yielded the following distribution of seats: Alliance of Independent Social Democrats, 41 (32 direct, 9 compensatory); Serbian Democratic Party of Bosnia and Herzegovina, 17 (13, 4); Party for Democratic Progress of the Serb Republic, 8 (6, 2); Democratic People's Alliance of the Serb Republic, 4 (3, 1); Party for Bosnia and Herzegovina, 4 (3, 1); Party of Democratic Action, 3 (1, 2); Socialist Party of the Serb Republic, 3 (3, 0); Serb Radical Party of the Serb Republic, 2 (2, 0); Social Democratic Party of Bosnia and Herzegovina, 1 (1, 0).

Speaker: Igor RADOJIČIĆ.

CABINETS

Republic of Bosnia and Herzegovina

[as of September 25, 2009]

Prime Minister	Nikola Špirić (SNSD)
Deputy Prime Ministers	Dragan Vrankić (HDZ)
	(Vacant)
Ministers	
Civil Affairs	Sredoje Nović (SNSD)
Defense	Selmo Cikotić (SDA)
European Integration	Nikola Špirić (SNSD)
Finance and Treasury	Dragan Vrankić (HDZ)
Foreign Affairs	Sven Alkalaj (SBiH)
Foreign Trade and Economic Relations	Mladen Zirojević
Human Rights and Refugees	Safet Halilović (SBiH)
Justice	Bariša Čolak (HDZ)
Security (Acting)	Mijo Krešić (HDZ)
Transport and Communications	Rudo Vidović (HDZ 1990)

Note: As of late September 2009, Sadik Ahmetović, the SDA nominee for minister of security and deputy prime minister, had yet to be appointed and confirmed.

Federation of Bosnia and Herzegovina

[as of September 25, 2009]

Prime Minister	Mustafa Mujezinović (SDA)
Deputy Prime Ministers	Gavrilo Grahovac (SBiH)
	Vjekoslav Bevanda (HDZ)
Ministers	
Agriculture, Water Management, and Forestry	Damir Ljubić (HDZ 1990)
Culture and Sports	Gavrilo Grahovac (SBiH)
Development, Entrepreneurship, and Crafts	Velimir Kunić (SNSD)
Displaced Persons and Refugees	Edin Mušić (SDA)
Education and Science	Meliha Alić (SBiH) [f]
Energy, Mining, and Industry	Vahid Hećo (SBiH)
Environment and Tourism	Nevenko Herceg (HDZ)
Finance	Vjekoslav Bevanda (HDZ)
Health	Safet Omerović (SBiH)
Interior	Muhidin Alić (SBiH)
Issues of Veterans and Disabled Veterans	Zahid Crnkić (SDA)
Justice	Feliks Vidović (HDZ)
Labor and Social Policy	Perica Jelečević (HDZ 1990)
Trade	Desnica Radivojević (SDA)
Transport and Communications	Nail Šećkanović (SDA)
Urban Planning	Haris Kafedžić (nominee, SDA)

Serb Republic of Bosnia and Herzegovina

[as of September 25, 2009]

Prime Minister	Milorad Dodik (SNSD)
Deputy Prime Ministers	Jasna Brkić (ind.) [f]
	Anton Kasipović (ind.)
Ministers	
Administration and Local Government	Zoran Lipovac (ind.)
Agriculture, Water Management, and Forestry	Radivoje Bratić (SNSD)
Economic Affairs and Coordination	Jasna Brkić (ind.) [f]
Economy, Energy, and Development	Slobodan Puhalac (SNSD)
Education and Culture	Anton Kasipović (ind.)
Family, Youth, and Sports	Proko Dragosavljević (ind.)
Finance	Aleksandar Džombić (SNSD)
Health and Social Welfare	Ranko Škrbić (SNSD)
Interior	Stanislav Čadjo (SNSD)
Justice	Džerard Selman (SBiH)
Labor and Veterans	Rade Ristović (SNSD)
Refugees and Displaced Persons	Omer Branković (SDA)
Science and Technology	Bakir Ajanović (ind.)
Trade and Tourism	Predrag Gluhaković (SPRS)
Transport and Communications	Nedeljko Čubrilović (DNS)
Urbanism, Civil Engineering, and Ecology	Fatima Fetibegović (ind.) [f]

[f] = female

COMMUNICATIONS

Throughout the Bosnian conflict media were dominated by nationalist elements, and incidents of violence or intimidation against journalists by government functionaries, police, and fervent nationalists continued to be reported in subsequent years. In June 2000 a group of editors protested that "every form of pressure" was being brought to bear against freedom of the press. In 2005, however, the French organization Reporters Without Borders ranked Bosnia and Herzegovina among those newly independent countries that are "very observant of press freedom."

Press. The following newspapers are dailies published in Sarajevo, unless otherwise noted: *Dnevni Avaz* (Daily Voice, 40,000), Bosniac; *Slobodna Bosna* (Free Bosnia, 30,000), weekly; *Dani* (Days, 25,000), weekly; *Oslobodjenje* (Liberation, 15,000), Bosniac; *Jutarnje Novine* (Morning News, 10,000), Bosniac; *Glas Srpski* (Serbian Voice, Banja Luca, 7,000), former government organ privatized in 2008, Serbian; *Nezavisne Novine* (Independent News, Banja Luca, 7,000), Serbian; *Dnevni List* (Daily Paper, Mostar), Croatian.

News agencies. Based in Sarajevo, the Federal News Agency (*Federalna Novinska Agencija*—Fena) was established in 2001 by merger of the Bosniac BH Press and the Mostar-based News Agency of the Croatian People in Bosnia and Herzegovina (HABENA). Other news organizations include the government-run Serbian Press Agency (*Srpska Novinska Agencija*—SRNA) and the private Independent News Agency (ONASA).

Broadcasting and computing. In 2001 the Office of the High Representative established a Communication Regulatory Agency for broadcasting. The nationwide broadcasting facility is the Radio and Television of Bosnia and Herzegovina (*Radiotelevizija Bosne i Hercegovine*—BHRT), which operates BH TV1 and BH Radio 1. A 2005 media law specifies that BH TV1 equally serve the three principal ethnic communities from three centers located in Sarajevo, Banja Luca, and Mostar. The FBiH and the RS also support public services. There are, in addition, roughly 200 private radio and television stations, most with limited range; some are controlled by the leading Bosniac, Croatian, and Serb political parties.

As of 2008 there were 346.6 Internet users per 1,000 inhabitants.

INTERGOVERNMENTAL REPRESENTATION

Ambassador to the U.S.: Mitar KUJUNDZIĆ.

U.S. Ambassador to Bosnia and Herzegovina: Charles Lewis ENGLISH.

Permanent Representative to the UN: Ivan BARBALIĆ.

IGO Memberships (Non-UN): BIS, CEI, CEUR, EBRD, Eurocontrol, Interpol, IOM, OSCE, WCO.

BOTSWANA

Republic of Botswana

Note: In balloting on October 16, 2009, for the 57 elected seats in the National Assembly, the ruling Botswana Democratic Party was credited with winning 45 seats; the Botswana National Front, 6; the Botswana Congress Party, 4; the Botswana Alliance Movement, 1; and independents, 1. President Seretse Ian Khama was sworn in for a five-year term on October 20, and the following day he appointed a new cabinet, which retained incumbents in many key positions.

Political Status: Independent republic within the Commonwealth since September 30, 1966. **Area:** 231,804 sq. mi. (600,372 sq. km.).

Population: 1,680,863 (2001C); 1,697,000 (2008E).

Major Urban Centers (2005E): GABORONE (213,000), Francistown (91,000), Molepolole (64,000), Selebi-Pikwe (54,000).

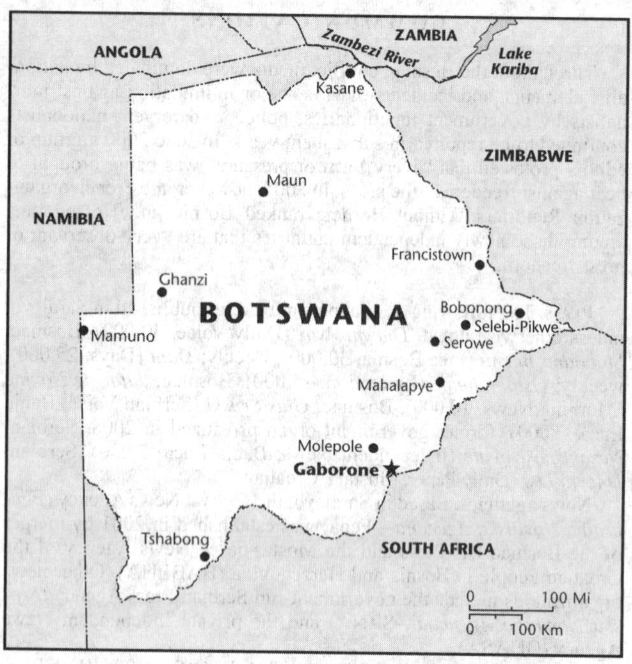

Official Language: English (SeTswana is widely spoken).

Monetary Unit: Pula (official rate December 1, 2009: 6.56 pula = $1US).

President: *(See headnote.)* Lt. Gen. (Ret.) Seretse Ian KHAMA (Botswana Democratic Party); appointed to a five-year term on April 1, 2008, by President Festus MOGAE (Botswana Democratic Party), who retired the same day after having served as president since April 1, 1998; sworn in on April 1 with a new government.

Vice President: Lt. Gen. (Ret.) Mompati MERAFHE (Botswana Democratic Party); appointed to a five-year term by the president on April 1, 2008, to succeed Lt. Gen. (Ret.) Seretse Ian KHAMA (Botswana Democratic Party), who had been elevated to the presidency on April 1.

THE COUNTRY

Landlocked Botswana, the former British protectorate of Bechuanaland, embraces a substantial area of desert, swamp, and scrubland situated on a high plateau in the heart of southern Africa. The country is bordered on the west by Namibia, on the south by South Africa, and on the northeast by Zimbabwe, with a narrow strip adjacent to Zambia in the north. The population is divided into eight main tribal groups, the largest of which is the Bamangwato (including an estimated 39,000 "San," or "bushmen," only 3,000 of whom continue to live in traditional nomadic fashion in the Kalahari desert). A majority of the people follow ancestral religious practices, but about 15 percent are Christian. Due in part to the large-scale employment of males in neighboring South African mines, 80 percent of households are headed by women who, however, cannot hold land title or control their crops, and therefore are denied access to funds and equipment under rural development programs. Female representation among senior officials has been limited.

At the time of independence Botswana was one of the world's poorest countries, dependent on stock-raising for much of its income because of an extremely dry climate that made large-scale farming difficult. Subsequent mineral discoveries initiated economic growth and raised real GDP growth to an annual average of more than 8 percent from the 1970s through the mid-2000s. Botswana is one of the world's largest producers of diamonds, exports of which provide 75 percent of foreign exchange, 50 percent of government revenue, and 33 percent of gross domestic product. While extractive activity (also involving copper-nickel matte and coal) has yielded infrastructural gains, food production has remained a problem. Although a large majority of the workforce is involved in subsistence agriculture, the largely barren soil has led to a dependence on imported food that is only slowly being overcome. The government's free-enterprise orientation and conservative monetary policies have attracted substantial foreign aid. Meanwhile, the lucrative diamond industry has enabled the government to amass large financial reserves, although international advisers have urged diversification in order to insulate the economy from fluctuations in global demand for diamonds. In response, the government has created the International Financial Services Center (IFSC), which has launched a number of projects to attract foreign investment and companies.

Current government programs focus on agricultural improvements, educational expansion, the promotion of tourism, revitalization of the public sector, and efforts to promote investment in the private sector in the hope that diversification would counteract growing unemployment (24 percent in 2006) among unskilled workers. Inflation has recently averaged about 8 percent annually, and employment growth has been slow, with civil service jobs accounting for most of the increase. Although annual GDP growth averaged 4.5 percent from 2004 to 2008, the International Monetary Fund (IMF) continued to emphasize the need for Botswana to reduce poverty and unemployment, and make greater progress in structural reforms. Diversification became a key focal point of the government's fiscal strategy in 2009 in the midst of the global economic crisis, as the demand for diamonds decreased. Though the government began a joint mining company with diamond giant De Beers, some 1,500 miners lost their jobs due to retrenchment and mine closings. Another 1,500 jobs were also lost in the first two months of the year. GDP growth for 2009 declined to about 1 percent, but a more optimistic forecast of about 4.5 percent annual growth was anticipated in 2010. On a more positive note, about $50 million in U.S. aid in 2009 bolstered Botswana's efforts to combat HIV/AIDS. The country has one of the most successful treatment programs in Africa.

GOVERNMENT AND POLITICS

Political background. A British protectorate from 1885, Botswana achieved independence within the Commonwealth on September 30, 1966, under the leadership of Sir Seretse KHAMA and has subsequently been regarded as a showplace of democracy in Africa. Following the National Assembly election of October 20, 1979, in which his Botswana Democratic Party (BDP) won 29 of 32 elective seats, President Khama was given a fourth five-year mandate. His death on July 13, 1980, led to the selection of Ketumile Joni MASIRE, vice president and minister of finance and development planning, to fill the remainder of the presidential term. Both Masire and Vice President Peter S. MMUSI were reappointed following the legislative election of September 8, 1984. However, the opposition Botswana National Front (BNF) showed surprising strength (20.2 percent) in that election and in simultaneous municipal balloting. In the election of October 7, 1989, the BNF vote share increased to 26.9 percent (as contrasted with 64.8 percent for the BDP), although its representation fell from 5 (after a December by-election) to 3. Presenting himself as the sole candidate, President Masire was reconfirmed by the assembly and sworn in for a third term on October 10. On March 8, 1992, Mmusi, under pressure because of alleged corruption, resigned the vice presidency in favor of Festus MOGAE, who retained his position as finance minister.

On May 12, 1993, representatives of the BDP, BNF, and four other parties met in Francistown to debate a recently released BNF proposal for electoral reform that included calls for the establishment of a multipartisan electoral commission to replace the existing presidentially appointed body and a lowering of the voting age from 21 to 18. Rebuffed by the government, the BNF declared six months later that it had tentatively decided to boycott the next election. Subsequently, however, it reversed itself, winning 13 legislative seats (to the BDP's 26) in the balloting of October 15, 1994. While the BDP's majority was sufficient to ensure the capture of all four nominated seats following President Masire's election to a third full term, the party's 53.1 vote share was the lowest in its 28 years of rule.

The unexpected gains of the BNF in 1994 were achieved despite rejection by the High Court in Lobatse of an opposition demand that the poll be canceled because of electoral roll deficiencies that allegedly favored the BDP. Contributing to the reduction in the BDF's majority were a series of corruption scandals, economic recession (triggered by declining diamond production and virtual collapse of the construction industry), and rising unemployment within a rapidly expanding urban population. Tensions generated by this combination erupted into serious antigovernment rioting in Gaborone in February 1995.

In late 1997 President Masire announced his intention to resign as head of state on March 31, 1998, and endorsed the succession of Vice President Mogae. Masire resigned as scheduled at an official ceremony that coincided with the conclusion of U.S. President Bill Clinton's visit to Botswana. On April 1 Mogae was inaugurated, and he announced the formation of a new cabinet on the same day. Two days later the new president nominated Lt. Gen. (Ret.) Seretse Ian KHAMA, son of Botswana's first president, to be his vice president. Khama, who had resigned from the military on March 31 to accept an appointment as minister of presidential affairs and public administration, captured a legislative by-election victory on July 6 (assembly membership being a prerequisite for the vice presidential slot) and, following assembly approval, assumed his new post on July 13. In new legislative balloting on October 16, 1999, the BDP secured 33 of 40 elective seats, and Mogae was consequently sworn in for a five-year presidential term. Mogae announced a new cabinet on October 21, retaining Khama as vice president (and thereby the heir apparent as the next BDP presidential contender).

The BDP maintained its legislative dominance in the October 2004 assembly balloting, and President Mogae was sworn in for another five-year term on November 1. He reshuffled the cabinet on January 21, 2007.

President Mogae stepped down from his post on April 1, 2008, and handed over authority to his vice president, Seretse Ian Khama, who was inaugurated the same day. Khama immediately appointed Foreign Minister Mompati MERAFHE, also of the BDP, as vice president and named a new government.

Constitution and government. The 1966 constitution provides for a president who serves as head of state and government, a parliament consisting of a National Assembly and a consultative House of Chiefs, and a judicial structure embracing a High Court, a Court of Appeal, and a Magistrate's Court in each district. The National Assembly encompasses 57 directly elected members, who vote on four additional nominated members. Sitting as an electoral college, the assembly elects the president for a term coincident with its own. (In August 1997 the assembly approved by two-thirds majority a bill limiting the president to two five-year terms.) The House of Chiefs acts as a consultative body on matters of native law, customs, and land, and also deliberates on constitutional amendments. The president can delay for up to six months, but not veto, legislation.

In June 1996 the government accepted opposition demands for an independent electoral commission and agreed to consider lowering the voting age from 21 to 18 and granting proxy votes to Botswanans living abroad. The latter two measures, in addition to a bill designating the vice president as the president's successor, were approved by popular referendum in October 1997.

At the local level, Botswana is divided into nine districts and five towns, all governed by councils. Chiefs head five of the district councils, elected leaders the remaining four. The districts impose personal income taxes to generate revenue, the local funding being supplemented by central government grants.

Foreign relations. Although generally pro-Western in outlook, Botswana belongs to the Nonaligned Movement and has consistently maintained diplomatic relations with members of the former Soviet bloc as well as with the People's Republic of China. Botswana's relations with South Africa, its major trading partner and the employer of over half its nonagricultural work force, have been problematic. While avoiding official contacts with Pretoria and participating as one of the six Front-Line States (also including Angola, Mozambique, Tanzania, Zambia, and Zimbabwe) opposing minority rule in southern Africa, it attempted to maintain peaceful coexistence with its neighbor prior to the abandonment of apartheid. Tensions heightened in 1985, however, when South African Defense Forces (SADF) mounted a cross-border attack on alleged havens for the African National Congress (ANC), killing 15 people. Botswana subsequently vowed not to condone any "terrorist activity" from its territory and forced numerous ANC adherents to leave the country. Following another SADF raid near Gaborone in May 1986, the Masire government informed the other Front-Line States that it "would not stand in the way" of those who might wish to initiate economic sanctions against South Africa. Despite its denunciation of three more SADF raids, Gaborone announced a joint Botswanan/South African resource development project in 1988, further underlining what critics termed Botswana's contradictory position as a member of both the South African Customs Union (SACU) and the anti-apartheid South African Development Coordination Conference (SADCC, subsequently the Southern African Development Community—SADC), whose headquarters were in Gaborone.

In 1992 the Namibian government, under pressure from opposition politicians to clearly demarcate its borders, claimed a small island in the Chobe River that had previously been assumed to be part of Botswana. The two sides signed an agreement in 1996 providing for the dispute to be submitted to the International Court of Justice (ICJ). Subsequently, in the wake of tension generated by Botswana's buildup of sophisticated weaponry, both countries, under the aegis of the Namibian and Botswanan Joint Commission on Defense and Security, agreed in 1998 to resolve border disputes through diplomatic solutions. In late 1999 the territorial dispute was resolved when the ICJ ruled in favor of Botswana.

In 2002 Botswana and Namibia agreed to the repatriation of some 2,000 Namibian refugees in Botswana, while in 2003 the two countries established an eight-member commission to begin final demarcation of the border. The reported influx of some 100,000 refugees from Zimbabwe led the Botswanan government in 2004 to enact a number of measures, including the erection of an electric fence in some areas, designed to increase border security. By 2006 it was estimated that nearly a half-million Zimbabwean immigrants were living in Botswana.

In 2007 a new border crossing linking Botswana, South Africa, and Namibia was opened at a wildlife park, easing access for travelers. In a move cited by observers as further bolstering cooperation between Botswana and Namibia, the two countries signed a Walvis Bay port agreement in February 2008. Later that year, Botswana's relations with Zimbabwe were severely strained following President Khama's public criticism of the lack of a power-sharing deal by President Mugabe following internationally disputed elections in Zimbabwe.

Current issues. In the October 1999 election, the recent splintering of the BNF (see Political Parties, below) precluded effective opposition to the BDP, especially when the rump BNF failed to reach an agreement with the new Botswana Alliance Movement (BAM). Following the election, President Mogae pledged that the government would continue the defense buildup of recent years while also addressing the problems of burgeoning unemployment among young people and the AIDS epidemic.

Attention in 2001 was focused on the "land invasion" crisis in neighboring Zimbabwe (see article on Zimbabwe), negative publicity in the matter having adversely affected tourism in Botswana. President Mogae was among the leaders of several nations who pressured Zimbabwean President Mugabe to accede to the "rule of law" regarding land ownership in order to calm the turmoil. Mogae also attempted to facilitate a resolution to the civil war in the Democratic Republic of the Congo, which had contributed to an intensified campaign by nongovernmental organizations to convince potential diamond buyers to avoid gems emanating from areas of conflict. Among other things, the government feared that legitimate producers, such as those in Botswana, were being unfairly penalized by the antidiamond initiative. Meanwhile, on the domestic front, a degree of ethnic tension, previously not considered a problem, arose in 2001, particularly in regard to the Kalangas, who made up only 10 percent of the population but reportedly held a majority of judicial posts. A national referendum in November endorsed revision of judiciary regulations; changes included an increase in the retirement age. Critics of the measures argued they were designed to fortify the Kalanga judicial influence.

Since 2001 the government has been challenged by domestic and international critics of its decision to forcibly resettle the last remaining bushmen out of the Central Kalahari Game Reserve. Some observers charged that the government's relocation initiative was designed to permit expanded mining in the tribal lands, several diamond companies holding prospecting rights in the reserve. By 2005 some 3,000 bushmen had been relocated, although others had resisted the government's financial inducements and pressure tactics. In 2006 tensions escalated amid allegations of police brutality and arrests of some bushmen on charges of illegal hunting practices. The government denied mistreating the bushmen and said that those arrested had given up traditional hunting practices in favor of using modern guns and vehicles. In December the high court ruled in favor of the bushmen, but the government said that it would not provide basic services, such as water, in the park and that it would still require the bushmen to provide proof that their hunting was for sustenance.

Botswana has been one of the countries in the region most severely affected by AIDS. (In 2006 one in three adults was reported to have the disease.) In the region, the country has been a leader in offering free AIDS drugs and making treatment available to most of the population.

On the political front, President Mogae said in early 2006 that he would not seek a third term. Since his term expired in 2008 and elections were not due until 2009, observers were forecasting Vice President Khama's early ascension to the presidency, in accordance with the automatic succession clause in the constitution. While the opposition called for direct election of the president, the ruling BDP did not take up the call, and President Mogae also opposed popular balloting. On April 1, 2008, Mogae, as expected, handed over power to Khama, 55, the smooth transition of power indicative of Botswana's "model democracy," according to *Africa Confidential*. Khama, the son of the country's founding leader, Sir Seretse Khama (a former commander of the Botswana Defense Force), immediately named Foreign Affairs Minister Lt. Gen. (Ret.) Mompati Merafhe as vice president. In 2009 attention turned to the legislative scheduled for October. The global economic downturn and a consequent decline in diamond sales were seen as potentially critical factors in the upcoming elections, as reduced government revenue could force spending cuts—a move that observers said could bolster the opposition. At least one grouping of political parties had formed an electoral alliance by March (see BCP, below), while other parties began preparing their election strategy in earnest by mid-year. *(See headnote.)*

POLITICAL PARTIES

Government Party:

Botswana Democratic Party (BDP). Founded in 1962 as the Bechuanaland Democratic Party, the BDP has been the majority party since independence. It advocates self-development on a Western-style democratic basis, cooperation with all states, and multiracialism. In June 1984 the BDP's president, Sir Ketumile Joni Masire, announced measures to "democratize" party nominations through a revamped primary system. However, all candidates remained subject to approval by a central committee dominated by government ministers.

During a BDP congress in July 1993 divisions within the party widened when Peter Mmusi and Daniel Kwelagobe, both of whom had been forced to resign from the government in 1992 for alleged involvement in a land transaction scandal, were elected chair and secretary general, respectively, while traditional southern leaders failed to secure leadership positions. Immediately thereafter, the Mmusi/Kwelagobe faction was reported to be in conflict with the party's "Big Five" cabinet members, led by Lt. Gen. Mompati S. Merafhe, who represented the BDP's patronage, cattle-raising wing. Mmusi died in October 1994 and was eventually succeeded as BDP chair by Ponatshego KEDIKILWE, the minister of presidential affairs and public administration. The government reshuffling in late 1997 was reportedly hailed by party officials for balancing the number of northern and southern ministers.

On March 31, 1998, Masire resigned from both his national and party presidency posts, and on April 1 Festus Mogae assumed both positions. The BDP maintained its dominance in the 1999 assembly poll by securing 57 percent of the vote.

With Mogae's nomination of Lt. Gen. Seretse Ian Khama as the vice president of the republic, and thus the possible "heir," the factionalized structure of the BDP became more apparent. In June 2000 Kedikilwe resigned as minister of education, observers noting that Kedikilwe and BDP Secretary General Daniel K. Kwelagobe were uneasy with Khama, who had publicly called them the "old guard." However, at the party congress in July 2001 a compromise averted a possible crisis, and Khama was elected vice chair of the party, while Kedikilwe and Kwelagobe both kept their positions.

Kedikilwe was replaced by Khama as chair of the BDP at the 2003 congress, following which the party remained divided into two camps. One was led by Foreign Affairs Minister Mompati S. Merafhe and Education Minister Jacob NKATE, both of whom had supported Khama at the 2003 congress. The other faction was led by Kedikilwe and Kwelagobe. Discord between the factions was renewed at the July 2005 congress, but Kwelagobe managed to fend off a challenge for his post from Local Government Minister Margaret NASHA after Khama intervened on his behalf in an effort to keep peace in the party. All remaining top party positions went to the pro-Khama faction, with Nkate retained as deputy secretary general.

Strife continued to increase to the point that in early December 2005 the BDP High Command ordered the dissolution of party factions. The so-called K-K faction (Kedikilwe-Kwelagobe) refused to disband, upholding its battle over cabinet posts and insisting on a meeting with President Mogae to push for power sharing at all levels of government. The rift was unabated in 2007, despite the factions having held numerous sessions to "preach unity." On a more positive note for the party, the BDP was the overwhelming winner in the March 5 by-elections. With the prospect of Khama's ascendance to the presidency, the party was still divided in the run-up to its congress, with some asking why Khama did not voluntarily step down as chair. By July 2007, however, relative peace reportedly prevailed within the party, in part due to Kedikilwe and Kwelagobe having been given cabinet posts. Khama retained his position as party chair, and in 2008 the K-K faction was deemed to be defunct. However, observers said it was unlikely that Khama could unify the party ahead of the 2009 elections: In March, *Africa News* reported, "The factions have reappeared and are here to stay."

Leaders: Lt. Gen. (Ret.) Seretse Ian KHAMA (President of the Republic and Chair of the Party), Lt. Gen. Mompati S. MERAFHE, (Vice President of the Republic and Vice Chair of the Party), Festus MOGAE (Former President of the Republic), Sir Ketumile Joni MASIRE (Former President of the Republic), Batlang Comma SERENA (Executive Secretary), Kentse RAMMIDI (Deputy Secretary General), Jacob NKATE (Secretary General).

Other Legislative Parties:

Botswana National Front (BNF). The BNF is a leftist party organized after the 1965 election. Its principal leader, Dr. Kenneth KOMA, was the only candidate to oppose Seretse Khama for the presidency in 1979, but he failed to retain his assembly seat. The party's share of the vote increased to 20 percent in the 1984 election, with its legislative representation growing from two to four; it also won control of the Gaborone city council.

In the late 1980s a number of right-wing members of the BNF defected to the BDP in response to the BNF's left-wing, procommunist orientation. In the wake of the October 1989 election, in which BNF assembly representation was reduced to three, Koma characterized its activists as "social democrats" who are "not Marxists." In the 1989 poll the BNF gained control of two local councils, including the capital, despite a loss of membership to two new splinter groups.

In August 1990 the BNF joined with the Botswana Progressive Union (BPU) and BPP (below) in forming a joint "Unity in Diversity" committee, which was formalized as a Botswana People's Progressive Front (BPPF) in October 1991. In 1993, however, Front members could not agree on whether they should boycott the next election if their demands for electoral reform were not met. As a result, the BNF contested the October 1994 poll in its own right, substantially increasing its vote share to 37.7 percent and winning 13 elective seats, including all 4 in Gaborone.

In mid-1998 the BNF was severely weakened by the withdrawal of a faction (reportedly including 11 legislators) led by Michael Kitso DINGAKE, who subsequently helped to form the Botswana Congress Party (BCP, below). The BNF was initially described in early 1999 as negotiating participation in the new Botswana Alliance Movement (BAM, below). However, delivering a blow to opposition legislative hopes of cutting into the BDP majority, the BNF ultimately decided to run its own candidates in all districts, securing six seats on 26 percent of the vote.

Although he did not take responsibility for the defeat, Koma announced in January 2000 that he would step down as the party's president. At a November 2001 congress, Otsweletse Moupo beat Peter WOKO, who was supported by Koma, and became the new BNF leader. Koma was expelled in 2002 for reportedly encouraging factionalism and moved on to help form the New Democratic Front (NDF) with other BNF dissidents in 2003 (see below).

In the 2004 elections, the BNF secured 12 seats. Following the election, a rift emerged within the party between supporters of Moupo and those of BNF Vice President Kopano LEKOMA, who unsuccessfully challenged Moupo at the party conference in July 2005. In 2007 the party continued to be divided between those who backed Moupo and others who supported either Kathleen Letshabo or Bucks MOLATLHEGI, but ultimately Moupo prevailed.

In 2008 Moupo expelled the party's national chair, Nehemiah MODUBULE, and several other members for starting a faction within the BNF called the **United Socialist Party** (PUSO), and he suspended the faction for six months. In June the PUSO's suspension was lifted, but BNF leaders did not change their stance on Modubule's status. The expelled members sought reconciliation with the party in 2009, but observers said it was highly unlikely that their request would be considered. Meanwhile, Modubule said he would still stand as a candidate in the upcoming general election.

Leaders: Otsweletse MOUPO (President), Olebile GABORONE (Vice President), Moeti MOHWASA, Mokgweetsi KGOSIPULA (Deputy Secretary General), Mohammad KHAN (Secretary General).

Botswana Congress Party (BCP). The BCP was formally registered in June 1998 by a group of BNF legislators interested in pursuing more centrist policies than the left-leaning parent grouping (personal animosity between BNF leader Kenneth Koma and dissident leader Michael Dingake also reportedly contributed to the rupture). The BCP secured 12 percent of the vote in the 1999 legislative poll but only one seat, Dingake theorizing the party had been punished by the voters for splitting the opposition ranks. In 2002 the BCP was reportedly engaged in unity talks with the BAM (below).

The party retained one seat in the 2004 election, and in 2005 it continued talks with the BAM and the BPP about a possible electoral coalition.

While the party suffered a number of defections (factionalism cited as the main reason) in early 2006, some 45 new members joined, including 3 from the BDP. In 2006 the BCP and the NDF signed a collateral agreement aimed at a more unified opposition.

In advance of the 2009 general election, the BCP, BAM, and NDF entered into an electoral coalition known as Pact, naming BCP leader Gilson Saleshando as its presidential candidate. The prodemocracy Pact feared the governing BDP's militaristic leanings, according to Saleshando.

Leaders: Gilson SALESHANDO (President), Kesitegile GOBOSWANG (Vice President), Taolo LUCAS (Secretary General).

Other Parties That Contested the 2004 Legislative Elections:

Botswana Alliance Movement (BAM). The BAM was formed by the BPU, led by D.K. KWELE; the **Independent Freedom Party** (IFP), led by Motsamai K. MPHO (BIP) and Leach TLHOMELANG (BFP); the **United Action Party** (UAP), launched by a group of BDP dissidents, including Lepetu Setshwaelo; and the BPP (below) for the 1999 legislative balloting. The BAM secured only 5 percent of the votes (and no seats) in that poll after having failed to convince other anti-BDP parties, most notably the BNF, to join in a single opposition electoral coalition. Lepetu Setshwaelo served as the BAM's presidential candidate in 1999. The BAM was reportedly involved in unity talks with the BCP during 2001. Although the parties did not merge before the 2004 elections (in which BAM received 2.84 percent of the vote and no seats in the assembly), talks continued about an electoral alliance between the BAM and other opposition groups, most notably the BCP, in advance of the 2007 by-election (which was ultimately dominated by the BDP) and the 2009 legislative elections.

The BPP left the BAM prior to the 2004 election but in 2006 met with the BAM, the BCP, and the BNF for unity talks. In 2009 the BAM joined an electoral coalition called Pact, which included the BCP and the NDF.

Leaders: Lepetu SETSHWAELO (Chair), Lethogile SETHOKO, Matlhomola MODISE (Secretary General).

Botswana People's Party (BPP). Founded in 1960 and for some years the principal minority party, the northern-based BPP advocates social democracy and takes a pan-Africanist line. It contested the 1994 election, winning no assembly seats on a vote share of 4.6 percent. The BPP was reportedly in disarray for most of 2000–2001. President Knight MARIPE resigned in July 2000, announcing that he had "nothing to offer" to the party. According to the *Africa News*, ten members of the party's National Executive Council, including former chair Kenneth MKHWA and former secretary general Matlhomola MODISE, were expelled in November for "having failed to carry out a resolution which directed the party to withdraw from the BAM." The party left BAM prior to the 2004 legislative elections. The BPP gained only 1.91 percent of the vote and therefore no seats in the legislative balloting. After initially balking at unity terms, the BPP in October 2005 signed on to a memorandum of agreement with the BCP, BAM, and BNF to cooperate in ousting the BDP in 2009. Secretary General Cornelius GOPOLANG resigned in 2007, citing personal reasons; observers reported he was not happy with the party's failure to act on major issues.

Leaders: Bernard BALIKANI (President), Edward MPOLOKA (Secretary General).

New Democratic Front (NDF). Formed in 2003 by dissidents from the BNF, including former BNF leader Kenneth Koma, the NDF is a center-left, social-democratic party. In the 2004 legislative elections, the NDF secured less than 1 percent of the vote. Koma stepped up in October 2005 to assist an NDF candidate in a by-election and was among those pushing for a unified opposition to unseat the BDP. In 2009 the NDF joined the BCP and the NDF in an electoral coalition in advance of the general elections scheduled for October 30–November 1.

Leaders: Dick BAYFORD, Phillip MONOWE (Secretary General).

Marx, Engels, Lenin, Stalin Movement of Botswana (MELS). Also reportedly referenced as the Mars Movement of Botswana, MELS presented two unsuccessful candidates in the 1999 legislative balloting, receiving only 0.1 percent of the vote. In the 2004 election, MELS again received 0.1 percent of the vote. The party received nine votes in the March 5, 2007, by-election dominated by the BDP.

Leader: Themba JOINA.

Other Parties:

Botswana Labour Party (BLP). Formed in September 1989 by former members of the BNF, the Labour Party espoused a program of neither "communism" nor "capitalism." The party did not offer candidates in 1989 or 1994. It was reportedly considering an alliance with the USP and SDP for the 1999 legislative balloting, but the initiative did not come to fruition.

Leader: Lenyeletse KOMA.

Other registered parties in 2004 included the **Social Democratic Party** (SDP), led by Rodgers SEABUENG; and the **Botswana Workers Front** (BWF), led by Mothusi AKANYANG. In 2009, the **Green Party of Botswana**, headed by Benjamin SEGOBAETSO, cast its support behind several members who were expelled from the BNF in 2008, including its national chair, Nehemiah Modubule. The Green Party called for a boycott of the 2009 general elections.

LEGISLATURE

The **Parliament** consists of an elective National Assembly with legislative powers and a consultative House of Chiefs. The next assembly elections were scheduled to be held in October 2009.

House of Chiefs. The House of Chiefs is a largely advisory body of 15 members: the chiefs of the 8 principal tribes, 4 elected subchiefs, and 3 members selected by the other 12. Constitutional revision in late 2006 increased the size of the upper house to 35.

Chair: Chief Kgosi SEEPAPITSO IV.

National Assembly. The National Assembly, which sits for a five-year term, currently consists of 57 (raised from 40 in 2002) directly elected and 4 nominated members, in addition to the speaker and the (nonvoting) attorney general; the president serves ex officio. In the most recent general election on October 30, 2004, the seat distribution was as follows: the Botswana Democratic Party 44 seats; the Botswana National Front, 12; and the Botswana Congress Party, 1. The next election was scheduled for October 16, 2009. *(See headnote.)*

Speaker: Patrick BALOPI.

CABINET

[as of September 1, 2009]

President	Lt. Gen. (Ret.) Seretse Ian Khama
Vice President	Lt. Gen. (Ret.) Mompati Merafhe
Ministers	
Agriculture	Christian De Graaf
Communications, Science, and Technology	Pelonomi Venson-Moitol [f]

Conservation, Wildlife, and Tourism	Onkokame Mokaila
Defense, Justice, and Security	Dikgakgamatso Seretse
Education	Jacob Nkate
Finance and Development Planning (Acting)	Kenneth Matambo
Foreign Affairs and International Cooperation	Phandu Skelemani
Health	Lesego Motsumi [f]
Labor and Home Affairs	Peter Siele
Lands and Housing	Nonofo Molefhi
Local Government	Margaret Nasha [f]
Mines, Energy, and Water Resources	Ponatshego Kedikilwe
Presidential Affairs and Public Administration	(Vacant)
Trade and Industry	Neo Moroka
Works and Transport	Johnny Swartz
Youth, Sports, and Culture	Gladys Kokorwe [f]

Assistant Ministers

Agriculture	Shaw Kgathi
Education	Lebogang Mamokalale
Finance and Development Planning	Samson Guma
Health	Gaotihaetse Matihabaphiri
Labor and Home Affairs	Olifant Mfa
Local Government, Lands, and Housing	Ambrose Masalila
Trade and Industry	Gobopang Lefhoko
Works and Transport	Frank Ramsden

[f] = female

COMMUNICATIONS

While the constitution provides for freedom of expression, the government in 1997 introduced a draft bill to the legislature that included provisions for strict governmental control of the fledgling mass communications industry. In response to domestic and international criticism, the bill was withdrawn. A new draft was presented in 2001, but it also faced criticism, especially from the International Federation of Journalists (IFJ). It claimed that the proposed Press Council would be given "extensive powers to impose fines and jail terms on journalists and publishers." In May the government banned government advertising in the *Botswana Guardian* and the *Midweek Sun* after materials critical of the vice president had appeared in both papers. The papers sued the government, and in September the Botswana High Court ruled that the advertising ban was unconstitutional and violated the papers' freedom of expression. In an unprecedented move, the Botswana Media Workers Union was formed in 2005 to promote freedom of expression.

A Media Practitioners Act, promulgated in December 2008, drew sharp criticism from the media and opposition political parties, as well as some members of the governing Botswana Democratic Party. Journalists feared the new law would restrict their work, according to the Associated Press. The law, which requires journalists to get approval of a state-run media council in order to work, also grants the same council the authority to impose fines of more than $600 and prison terms of up to three years. Members of the media challenged the law in court in March 2009.

Press. All papers are published in Gaborone, except as noted: *Botswana Daily News/Dikgang Tsa Gompieno* (50,000), published by the Department of Information and Broadcasting in English and SeTswana; *Kutlwano* (23,000), published monthly by the Department of Information and Broadcasting in English and SeTswana; *The Reporter/Mmegi* (24,000), weekly; *Botswana Guardian* (17,000), weekly; *The Gazette* (16,000), weekly; *Midweek Sun* (13,800), weekly; *Northern Advertiser* (Francistown, 5,500), weekly; *Botswana Advertiser*, weekly; *Mmegi Monitor*, weekly; *Sunday Standard*, weekly; *The Voice*, bi-monthly; *The Mirror*, bi-monthly.

News agency. The Botswana Press Agency (BOPA) was established in Gaborone in 1981.

Broadcasting and computing. The government-owned Radio Botswana operates six stations broadcasting in English and SeTswana to approximately 252,000 radio receivers. A number of private stations were expected to be launched in the wake of a recent government decision to terminate its monopoly. The TV Association of Botswana operates two low-power transmitters near Gaborone that relay programs from South Africa. In July 2000 the first state-owned television channel went on the air. As of 2008 there were 62.5 Internet users per 1,000 inhabitants.

INTERGOVERNMENTAL REPRESENTATION

Ambassador to the U.S.: Lapologang Caesar LEKOA.

U.S. Ambassador to Botswana: Stephen James NOLAN.

Permanent Representative to the UN: Charles Thembani NTWAAGAE.

IGO Memberships (Non-UN): ADB, AU, BADEA, CWTH, Interpol, NAM, SADC, WCO, WTO.

BRAZIL

Federative Republic of Brazil
República Federativa do Brasil

Political Status: Independent monarchy proclaimed 1822; republic established 1889; current constitution promulgated October 5, 1988.

Area: 3,286,470 sq. mi. (8,511,965 sq. km.).

Population: 183,888,841 (2007C), 191, 931,000 (2008E). The 2008 figure is extrapolated from government estimates, the 2007 figure apparently reflecting substantial underenumeration.

Major Urban Centers (2005E): BRASILIA (federal district, 2,231,000), São Paulo (10,278,000), Rio de Janeiro (6,094,000), Salvador (2,673,000), Belo Horizonte (2,375,000), Recife (1,501,000), Belém (1,397,000), Pôrto Alegre (1,387,000).

Official Language: Portuguese.

Monetary Unit: Real (market rate December 1, 2009: 1.72 reals = $1US).

President: Luiz Inácio ("Lula") DA SILVA (Workers' Party); elected in runoff balloting on October 27, 2002, and inaugurated on January 1, 2003, for a four-year term, succeeding Fernando Henrique CARDOSO (Brazilian Social Democratic Party); reelected in runoff balloting on October 29, 2006, and inaugurated for another four-year term on January 1, 2007.

Vice President: José ALENCAR Gomes da Silva (Liberal Party); elected in runoff balloting on October 27, 2002, and inaugurated on January 1, 2003, for a term concurrent with that of the president, succeeding Marco Antônio de Oliveira MACIEL (Liberal Front Party); reelected (Brazilian Republican Party) in runoff balloting on October 29, 2006, and inaugurated for a term concurrent with that of the president on January 1, 2007.

THE COUNTRY

The population of South America's largest country, which occupies nearly half the continent, is approximately 50 percent Caucasian, 43 percent biracial, 7 percent Afro-Brazilian, and less than 0.5 percent Indigenous and Asian, according to the 2006 census. The Caucasians are mainly of Portuguese descent but include substantial numbers of

Belgian, Dutch, German, Italian, and Spanish immigrants. There are also small Arab, Japanese, and Chinese minorities. In general, Brazilian identity is based on economic and not racial status. Roman Catholicism is by far the predominant religion (73 percent), with evangelical Protestantism making substantial gains (around 15 percent). Women make up 35 percent of the paid labor force, a majority in domestic service, with one-quarter estimated to be unpaid agricultural workers. Although women have been minimally represented in political life, a few from powerful families have managed to occupy high-level government and party positions.

The Brazilian economy was traditionally based on one-crop agriculture under the control of a landed aristocracy. In recent years, however, substantial diversification has occurred, with coffee, which once accounted for 50 percent of the nation's exports, falling to a low of 2.7 percent in 1992 before recovering to 6.3 percent in 1995. Soybeans, cotton, sugar, and cocoa are other important commodities. In industry, textiles remain important, while iron, steel, petroleum, and paper production have grown significantly; in addition, Brazil's arms industry is now an important source of export income. Numerous minerals are mined commercially, including quartz, chromium, manganese, gold, and silver.

In the 1980s, due to depressed commodity prices, government stabilization programs were unable to reduce high levels of inflation and external debt (in excess of $100 billion). By January 1987 inflation had spiraled to an annualized rate of 500 percent, and in late February the government suspended foreign debt payments. The moratorium ended with a highly favorable refinancing agreement in November 1988, but by March 1990 prices had risen by more than 3,900 percent during the preceding 12 months, prompting incoming President Fernando COLLOR de Mello to advance a radical fiscal package designed to bring inflation under control. The short-term result was dramatic: a single-digit monthly rate by May. However, by July double-digit figures had returned, continuing into 1991, and yielding an increase for the year of more than 480 percent, followed by further escalation to 1,128 percent in 1992 and 2,600 percent in 1993. Following the adoption of an economic stabilization program and the introduction of another new currency (the real) in mid-1994, inflation for the year fell to about 24 percent with economic growth registering 5.7 percent, the highest since 1986. The architect of the "Real Plan"—Finance Minister Fernando Henrique CARDOSO—was elected president in 1994 and reelected in 1998, largely as a result of his success in stabilizing the economy, based primarily on linking the real's value to the dollar. Turbulence in international financial markets forced a costly devaluation in 1999, but Brazil's economy recovered relatively quickly.

Annual GDP growth in 2003–2006 averaged approximately 2.5 percent annually, lower than the Latin American average. However, price stability and the direct transfer of government resources to the poor were widely considered to have significantly alleviated the maldistribution of wealth.

In 2007-2008 annual growth averaged 5 percent, owing in large part to what was described as a "booming" domestic market, as well as increased revenues from ethanol, iron ore, and agriculture. Trade diversification helped Brazil avoid devastating effects of the global financial crisis, according to analysts, who also cited Brazil's $281 billion stimulus package and subsequent $3.6 billion in tax cuts to "jump start" the economy. Consequently, Brazil's economy was expected to contract only about 0.5 percent in 2009, and the country was widely expected to fare much better than most during the worldwide recession. In July the finance minister said the economy was already recovering, allowing for the creation of 500,000-700,000 jobs in 2009. After a reported second quarter GDP growth of 1.9 percent the government revised earlier economic forecasts to predict 1 percent growth in 2009.

GOVERNMENT AND POLITICS

Political background. Ruled as a Portuguese colony from 1500–1815, Brazil retained its monarchical institutions as an independent state from 1822 until the declaration of a republic in 1889. The constitution was suspended in 1930 as the result of a military coup d'état led by Getúlio VARGAS, whose dictatorship lasted until 1945. Enrico DUTRA, Vargas, Juscelino KUBITSCHEK, and Jânio QUADROS subsequently served as elected presidents. In 1961 Quadros resigned and was succeeded by Vice President João GOULART. Goulart's leftist administration, after being widely criticized for inflationary policies, governmental corruption, and prolabor and alleged pro-communist tendencies, was overturned by the military in March 1964. Marshal Humberto de Alencar CASTELLO BRANCO, who served as president from 1964 to 1967, vigorously repressed subversive and leftist tendencies, instituted a strongly anti-inflationary economic policy, and reestablished governmental authority on a strictly centralized basis. Brazil's 13 political parties were dissolved in 1965, and political freedom was drastically curtailed by an "institutional act" whose main provisions were later incorporated into a constitution adopted under presidential pressure in 1967. Direct presidential elections were abolished, the president was given sweeping powers to regulate the press, and formal political activity was limited to two newly authorized parties—the progovernment National Renewal Alliance (*Aliança Renovadora Nacional*—Arena) and the opposition Brazilian Democratic Movement (*Movimento Democrático Brasileiro*—MDB).

The policies of Castello Branco were continued under Artur da COSTA E SILVA (1967–1969) and Emílio Garrastazú MEDICI (1969–1974), rising political dissatisfaction with authoritarian rule being countered in December 1968 by the president's assumption of virtually unlimited powers that were retained for nearly a decade thereafter. Despite periodic disturbances, the ease with which power was passed to President Ernesto GEISEL in early 1974 suggested that the military and its allies were still firmly in control. However, at a November legislative election the opposition MDB obtained approximately one-third of the seats in the Chamber of Deputies and 16 of 20 seats that were up for election in the Senate. Four years later the MDB won a clear majority of votes cast but failed to capture either house because of electoral arrangements favoring the government party.

On March 15, 1979, João Baptista FIGUEIREDO was sworn in for a six-year term as Geisel's hand-picked successor, after electoral college designation five months earlier by a vote of 355–226 over the MDB candidate, Gen. Euler Bentes MONTEIRO. In November Arena and the MDB were dissolved under a policy of political relaxation (*abertura*) that permitted the emergence of a more broad-ranged party spectrum.

Despite electoral procedures that favored its newly established Social Democratic Party (*Partido Democrático Social*—PDS), the government failed to gain a majority of lower house seats in the legislative poll of November 15, 1982. Subsequently, Tancredo NEVES of the Party of the Brazilian Democratic Movement (*Partido do Movimento*

Democrático Social—PMDB) defeated PDS nominee Paulo MALUF in the electoral college balloting of January 15, 1985, but was unable to assume office because of illness. His vice-presidential running mate, José SARNEY Costa of the Liberal Front Party (*Partido dâ Frente Liberal*—PFL), became acting president on March 15 and succeeded to the presidency at Neves's death on April 21. Sarney negotiated a somewhat fragile coalition between the PMDB and the PFL, the former securing a 53 percent majority and the coalition 77 percent of lower house seats in the legislative election of November 15, 1986. During the ensuing three years, despite promulgation of a new, substantially liberalized constitution in October 1988, Sarney's popularity eroded sharply, with leftist parties registering significant gains in November municipal elections.

In early 1989 Fernando COLLOR de Mello, the young and relatively obscure governor of Alagoas, the country's second-smallest state, presented himself as presidential candidate of the newly launched National Reconstruction Party. Running on a free enterprise platform, Collor won a plurality in a field of 24 contenders in first-round balloting on November 15 and obtained a 53 percent vote share to defeat Luiz Inácio ("Lula") da SILVA, leader of the socialist Workers' Party (*Partido dos Trabalhadores*—PT), in a runoff on December 17.

In April 1992 President Collor reshuffled his cabinet, dismissing a number of ministers accused of corrupt practices. A month later the president came under fire as the result of charges that his former campaign manager, Paulo César Cavalcante FARIAS, had operated a vast extortion network, part of the proceeds of which were intended to finance a reelection bid. On August 26 a lengthy congressional probe concluded that the president knew of the $330 million "PC scheme" ("*esquema PC*") but had done nothing to deter it. As a result, the Chamber of Deputies on September 29 voted 441–38 to impeach Collor, with Vice President Itamar Augusto Cautiero FRANCO being sworn in as his acting successor on November 2. Ten days later Collor was indicted on criminal charges, and on December 29 he resigned in favor of Franco, who was immediately invested for the remaining two years of the presidential term.

During 1994 the poll ratings of presidential candidate Fernando Henrique CARDOSO proved inversely proportional to a decline in inflation, for which he, as former finance minister, was given credit. Thus, Cardoso, who had trailed his principal opponent, Lula da Silva, by 22 percentage points in early July, gradually overtook the PT leader to win the presidential vote on October 3 with an absolute majority of 54.3 percent. Concurrently, Cardoso's Brazilian Social Democratic Party (*Partido da Social Democracia Brasiliera*—PSDB) and its coalition partners (PFL, the Brazilian Labor Party [*Partido Trabalhista Brasiliero*—PTB], and the Liberal Party [*Partido Liberal*—PL]) won congressional pluralities of sufficient magnitude to give the new president broad support for a constitutional reform program.

In mid-December 1994 the Supreme Court acquitted Collor of personal involvement in the illegal financial scheme that had forced him to resign in 1992. In the wake of the ruling, Brazil's attorney general announced that he would bring unrelated charges of embezzlement against the former president. For his part Collor indicated that he viewed the court's action as total vindication and vowed to reenter politics at the conclusion of an eight-year ban from public office. (Collor was acquitted of the new charges in January 1998. He was elected to the senate in 2006.)

Following his inauguration on January 1, 1995, President Cardoso appointed members of four parties (the PSDB, PFL, PTB, and PMDB) to his cabinet, and pledged to move forward on a number of policy fronts that included the breakup of the state's oil and telecommunications monopolies, civil service and land reform, and a series of fiscal measures that included deindexation of wages and revision of the tax system. Despite substantial opposition from a variety of affected interests, on June 4, 1997, Cardoso was able to secure final legislative approval of a constitutional amendment permitting him to seek reelection in 1998.

On October 4, 1998, Cardoso became the first Brazilian president to win a second term. In addition, his five-party coalition (which now included the Brazilian Progressive Party [*Partido Progressista Brasiliero*—PPB]) won 377 of 513 seats in the Chamber of Deputies, thereby gaining the minimum three-fifths majority needed for constitutional revision, while losing only 1 of 69 seats previously held in the Senate. Cardoso named a new cabinet on January 1, 1999, which included the five parties in the previous government and the addition of the small Popular Socialist Party (*Partido Popular Socialista*—PPS). However, the PTB resigned from the government in March when its sole representative was replaced as budget minister amid severe economic turmoil.

During 2000 the country was threatened by a wave of political scandals. Adding to President Cardoso's woes was an energy crisis in early 2001 that necessitated power rationing, and by midyear the PSDB's candidate as his successor, José SERRA, claimed a poll rating of only 4.2 percent, as opposed to 31.3 percent for the PT's Lula da Silva.

In first-round presidential balloting on October 6, 2002, Lula da Silva won 46.4 percent of the vote, and went on to defeat Serra in an October 27 runoff with 61.4 percent. During the ensuing two years, the president countered most regional critics by retaining broad public support, while the PT increased the number of cities under its control from 187 to 411 in municipal elections held in October 2004.

In 2005 PTB leader Roberto JEFFERSON accused the PT of making monthly payments to its allies in Congress in return for passing legislation. Those accused, many of them allies of President Lula da Silva, included former PT president José GENOINO and eight ministers. While the ministers resigned to be eligible to participate in upcoming elections, some later faced criminal charges (see Current issues, below). Despite the PT's alleged links to the corruption scandal, Lula da Silva was reelected in two rounds of balloting in 2006. He defeated six challengers in the first-round on October 1 but fell short, with 48.6 percent of the vote, of the 50 percent needed to avoid a second round. His closest rival, the PSDB's Geraldo ALCKMIN, won 41.6 percent. Heloísa HELENA of the P-SOL was a distant third with 6.9 percent; all remaining candidates trailed with 2.6 percent or less. In the runoff on October 29, President Lula da Silva won a landslide victory with 60.8 percent of the vote, while Alckmin received 39.2 percent. Meanwhile, the PMDB overtook the PT in the October 1 Chamber of Deputies elections, 89 seats to 83. Two-thirds of the governors elected on October 1 were reportedly supportive of the Lula da Silva administration.

In October 2007, in what was hailed as a landmark decision, the Supreme Court effectively banned lawmakers from changing party affiliation once elected, excepting specific, limited circumstances (e.g., if a party changed its ideology), thus ending lawmakers' propensity to change affiliation with some frequency. Additionally, the ruling required parties to maintain identical coalitions at both the national and regional levels, making it more difficult for governments to build coalitions.

The cabinet was reshuffled in March 2007, with further minor reshuffles later in the year and in the first half of 2008.

Constitution and government. On September 2, 1988, after 19 months of sharp disputes and major shifts in party alliances, the Congress, acting as a Constituent Assembly, approved a new basic law encompassing 246 articles covering a wide range of social and economic issues, including a 40-hour work week, minimum wages, health and pension benefits, access to education, maternity and paternity leaves, labor autonomy and the right to strike, Indian rights, and protection of the environment.

The 1988 document provided for a president to be directly elected for a nonrenewable five-year term (reduced to four years in May 1994), with Brazilians in an April 1993 plebiscite decisively rejecting a return to either a parliamentary or monarchical form of government. In addition, provisions for referenda and "popular vetoes" on proposed and enacted legislation, respectively, were introduced, as well as provisions for "popular initiative" of draft bills for congressional consideration. An amendment ratified on June 5, 1997, authorized reelection of the president, as well as of state governors and mayors.

The existing bicameral National Congress, consisting of a Senate and Chamber of Deputies, was retained, with the Congress gaining added power in regard to budget preparation, foreign debt agreements, and the drafting of legislation. The judicial system, headed by a Supreme Court whose members must be approved by the Senate, gained substantial administrative and financial autonomy. There are also federal courts in the state capitals, a Federal Court of Appeals, and special courts for dealing with military, labor, and electoral issues.

Brazil is divided into 26 states and the Federal District of Brasília. The states, which have their own constitutions, legislatures, and judicial systems, may divide or join with others to form new states. Thus, the former state of Guanabara merged with Rio de Janeiro in 1975, the new state of Mato Grosso do Sul was formed out of the southern part of Mato Grosso in 1979, and the former territory of Fernando de Noronha was included in Pernambuco under the 1988 constitution.

State and Capital	Area (sq. mi.)	Population (2006E)
Acre (Rio Branco)	59,343	709,000
Alagoas (Maceió)	11,238	3,119,000
Amapa (Macapá)	54,965	659,000
Amazonas (Manaus)	605,390	3,479,000
Bahia (Salvador)	218,912	14,219,000
Ceará (Fortaleza)	56,253	8,459,000
Espírito Santo (Vitória)	17,658	3,577,000
Goiás (Goiânia)	131,339	5,953,000
Maranhão (São Luís)	127,242	6,346,000
Mato Grosso (Cuiabá)	348,040	2,964,000
Mato Grosso do Sul (Campo Grande)	138,021	2,364,000
Minas Gerais (Belo Horizonte)	226,496	19,962,000
Pará (Belém)	481,404	7,391,000
Paraíba (João Pessôa)	20,833	3,677,000
Paraná (Curitiba)	76,959	10,639,000
Pernambuco (Recife)	39,005	8,680,000
Piauí (Teresina)	97,017	3,094,000
Rio de Janeiro (Rio de Janeiro)	16,855	15,918,000
Rio Grande do Norte (Natal)	20,528	3,125,000
Rio Grande do Sul (Pôrto Alegre)	108,369	11,198,000
Rondônia (Pôrto Velho)	92,039	1,619,000
Roraima (Boa Vista)	86,880	427,000
Santa Catarina (Florianópolis)	36,802	6,141,000
São Paulo (São Paulo)	95,852	42,281,000
Sergipe (Aracajú)	8,441	2,059,000
Tocantins (Miracema do Tocantins)	107,075	1,387,000
Federal District		
Distrito Federal (Brasília)	2,237	2,485,000

Foreign relations. Long a leader in the inter-American community, Brazil has traditionally been aligned in international affairs with the United States, which is its major trading partner. However, the conclusion of a 1975 nuclear-plant agreement with West Germany in the wake of the Geisel government's refusal to sign the 1968 UN Treaty on the Non-Proliferation of Nuclear Weapons (NPT), coupled with problems arising from increased coffee prices and the stand on human rights by the administration of President Jimmy Carter, led to a degree of estrangement between the two countries. In March 1977, largely in reaction to the human-rights criticism, Brazil canceled a 25-year-old military assistance treaty with the United States. As a result, Brazil's arms industry became one of the fastest-growing sectors of the economy, with customers including Iran, Libya, and Saudi Arabia, resulting in Brazil becoming among the largest arms dealers in the world in 2007. While improved Washington-Brasília relations during the administration of President Ronald Reagan led to the signing of a military cooperation agreement in February 1984, controversy continued over an "understanding" that Washington would be allowed to monitor the sale of Brazilian arms using U.S. technology. Subsequently, differences arose over Brazilian import restrictions on U.S. computer software, which Washington charged as encouraging piracy of the programs, while in mid-1988 Reagan announced a projected $200 million in trade sanctions because of Brazil's refusal to accord patent protection to U.S. pharmaceutical and chemical products.

On July 3, 1978, a Treaty of Amazon Cooperation (Amazon Pact) was signed with Bolivia, Colombia, Ecuador, Guyana, Peru, Suriname, and Venezuela. The pact was criticized as lacking in detail on substantive development of the Amazon basin. In turn, Brazil has strongly objected to "foreign meddling" in the region. (In 2008 president Lula da Silva claimed sole responsibility for the protection and conservation of the Amazon.)

Relations with Argentina, which had been strained due to a series of disputes over the development of the hydroelectric potential of the Paraná River, improved in late 1979 with the conclusion of a tripartite accord involving the two countries and Paraguay. More conclusive evidence of realignment within the Southern Cone was provided by a visit of President Figueiredo to Buenos Aires in May 1980 (the first by a Brazilian head of state in 30 years), during which a total of ten intergovernmental agreements were signed, embracing such traditionally sensitive areas as arms manufacture, nuclear technology, and exploitation of the hydroelectric resources of the Río Uruguay. During the 1982 Falkland Islands war Brazil joined with its regional neighbors in supporting Argentina, while the Brazilian embassy in London represented Argentine interests in the British capital. However, Brazil's posture throughout was distinctly muted, partly because of traditional rivalry between the continent's two largest countries and partly because of an unwillingness to offend British financial interests, which were viewed as critical to resolution of Brazil's foreign debt problems.

The 1983 election of Raul Alfonsín to the Argentine presidency served to dampen rapprochement with Buenos Aires because of the new chief executive's well-publicized links to Brazilian opposition leaders; however, by mid-1984 the situation had improved and a number of trade and cooperation agreements were concluded after Brazil's return to civilian rule in early 1985. Economic ties were further enhanced on December 10, 1986, with the signing by presidents Sarney and Alfonsín of 20 accords launching an ambitious integration effort intended to eventuate in a Latin American common market. Under the plan, a customs union was established for most capital goods as of January 1, 1987, with cooperation in the exchange of food products, the promotion of bilateral industrial ventures, the establishment of a $200 million joint investment fund, and joint energy development (including a new $2 billion hydroelectric facility) to follow. In 1988 Brazil and Argentina agreed to cooperate in the nuclear power industry, although (without endorsing the NPT) formally rejecting the development of nuclear weaponry in a July 1991 accord that also banned the introduction of such arms from external sources. In mid-1990 they responded positively to U.S. President George H. W. Bush's call for a regional free trade zone and announced that an Argentine-Brazilian common market would be launched by December 1994. The latter initiative was broadened to include Paraguay and Uruguay in a treaty concluded in March 1991 to create, by the original target date, a Southern Cone Common Market (*Mercado Común do Cono Sur*—Mercosur).

Diplomatic relations with Cuba were restored in June 1986, after a 22-year rupture, and in July 1988, during a five-day official visit to China by President Sarney, a number of bilateral agreements were announced, including a $150 million joint venture to launch two low-orbit sensoring satellites by 1994.

In January 1992 gold miners along the sparsely populated border of Brazil and Venezuela sparked a flare-up between the two countries. Several months earlier a government drive to clear the area for a planned Yanomami Indian homeland caused many of the miners to cross into Venezuela, where a number of jungle airstrips were created that were subsequently attacked by Venezuelan aircraft. On June 3–14, 1992, Brazil drew international attention by hosting the largest gathering of world leaders in history for the United Nations Earth Summit in Rio de Janeiro (see United Nations Environment Development Programme, under UN General Assembly: Special Bodies).

In May 1994 Brazil extended its 1991 nuclear accord with Argentina by signing an amended version of the 1967 Tlatelolco Treaty proscribing the use of nuclear weapons in Latin America and the Caribbean (see IGO entry under OPANAL). At the first Summit of the Americas in 1995, a meeting of the heads of state of every Latin American nation except Cuba, the United States proposed a Free Trade Area for the Americas (FTAA), which Brazil supported with the stipulation that the issue of U.S. agricultural subsidies be addressed.

During 1997 a number of trade problems emerged with fellow Mercosur member Argentina, including the imposition by the Argentine Senate in early September of a 20 percent import tax on Brazilian sugar. Nonetheless, U.S. President Bill Clinton hailed Mercosur as a steppingstone to a FTAA during a visit to Brazil in mid-October. In what was billed as a "mini-Maastricht" pact, Brazil and Argentina agreed in mid-1999 to adopt mutually compatible mechanisms of fiscal restraint, with a view to moving toward a common currency within Mercosur. In March 2000 Brazil went further by calling for early negotiation of a South American Free Trade Agreement during an economic summit in Brasília in late August. However, the meeting became preoccupied with concerns over U.S. military policy toward Colombia. At the 2005 Summit of the Americas, Brazil, along with four other Latin American nations, rejected the U.S.-backed FTAA, reflecting the change in Brazil's leadership and the regional shift to more leftist politics.

President Lula da Silva has made the diversification of Brazil's foreign relations a priority, expanding and improving relations throughout Africa and with China.

Given the oil wealth of Venezuela and President Hugo Chávez's criticism of ethanol, President Lula da Silva has often been at loggerheads with the Venezuelan president. Brazilian relations with Bolivia have also suffered due to Chávez's support for Bolivian president Evo Morales. More recently, Chávez and Lula da Silva have maintained cordial relations and in 2006 cooperated on the construction of various large projects, such as a $1.2 billion bridge over the Orinoco River to facilitate the transport of Brazilian goods to Venezuelan ports.

Various international agencies increased pressure on Brazil in 2007 to halt the deforestation of rainforests in the Amazon. Meetings between U.S. president George W. Bush and Lula da Silva in March 2007 concentrated on promoting ethanol and reducing tariffs in the United States. At a South American energy summit on April 15, Chávez backed away from criticism of ethanol, but Brazil was stung by a Venezuelan-Bolivian-Argentine proposal for an Organization of Gas Producing and Exporting Countries of South America.

In cooperation with Venezuela, Brazil led efforts to found the South American Defense Council in May 2008 under the umbrella Union of South American Nations (Unasur), which was also established that year.

The Lula da Silva administration has maintained cordial relations with the United States, while at the same time engaging in friendly relations with U.S. adversaries Venezuela and Cuba. Lula da Silva met with U.S. president Barack Obama three times in early 2009 in an effort to promote Brazil as the leading country in the region and a close ally of the United States.

Current issues. President Lula da Silva's overwhelming reelection victory in 2006 was attributed in large part to his administration's having reduced inflation, maintained economic stability, and fostered the direct transfer of government resources to some 11 million of Brazil's poorest families.

Corruption charges linked to the alleged bribing of legislators in 2006 continued to plague the government and prompted thousands to demonstrate against president Lula da Silva in August 2007. That same month, the Supreme Court indicted a dozen politicians, including Lula da Silva's chief of staff and José Genoino, the former PT president, for allegedly buying votes in the legislature. In September the Senate narrowly rejected a call by a congressional ethics committee to expel Senate president Renan CALHEIROS for allegedly violating Senate rules on accepting money from private companies seeking government contracts. Calheiros, a close ally of Lula da Silva, denied all charges. He resigned as Senate president on December 4 before a vote on whether to expel him. By a vote of 48-29, with 4 abstentions, the Senate found him not guilty of corruption, and he retained his seat. Similar abuse of power allegations had resulted in the earlier dismissal of Finance Minister Antonio PALOCCI, said to be among the most influential of Lula da Silva's allies, and the minister of social welfare and PT president, Ricardo BERZIONI, among others.

In 2008 attention turned to the conservation of the Amazon as a major political issue, as Green Party founder Carlos MINC defected to the PT and was named minister of the environment. However, plans for the construction of a hydrodam and a power plant in the Amazon upset many environmentalists and indigenous groups, leading to violent protests in 2008. (As of 2009 the issue remained unresolved.)

Despite the global economic recession, the Lula da Silva administration continued to project the impression that Brazil's economy was not significantly affected. As a result the president's popularity is projected to remain high, according to observers. Though ineligible to run for reelection due to term limits, the president's popularity, if maintained, would bode well for the PT in the 2010 elections. However, in 2009 the expected PT candidate, Dilma Vana ROUSSEFF Linhares, whom Lula da Silva supported, was diagnosed with lymphoma, raising doubts as to her candidacy and the ability of the PT to maintain its leadership role. The PT had yet to choose a candidate in mid-2009, which analysts said gave other parties an advantage going into campaign season. As of August 2009 parties had not chosen their official candidates for the election, but polls showed the governor of the state of Sao Paulo, Jose Serra of the PSDB, to be the most popular candidate. Frontrunners for the PT candidacy included former finance minister Antonio Palocci and Education Minister Fernando Haddad.

POLITICAL PARTIES

All of Brazil's parties were dissolved by decree in 1965, clearing the way for establishment of a single government party, the National Renewal Alliance (*Aliança Renovadora Nacional*—Arena), and a single opposition party, the Brazilian Democratic Movement (*Movimento Democrático Brasileiro*—MDB), which began organizing in 1969. In the November 1978 election Arena retained control of both houses of Congress but was substantially outpolled in the popular vote by the MDB. Both groups were formally dissolved on November 22, 1979, after enactment of legislation sanctioning a more liberal party system. Under the new arrangement, parties were required to swear allegiance to the "democratic system," give six months' prior notice of a national congress, and win 5 percent of the total vote to retain legal status. For the indirect presidential balloting in 1985, a Democratic Alliance (*Aliança Democrática*) was formed, composed of the PFL and PMDB (below), in support of the candidacy of Tancredo Neves. However, neither Alliance partner was firmly committed to the leadership of Neves's successor, while President Sarney called for a "National Pact" centered on the non-*Malufista* wing of his preelection Social Democratic Party (PDS, under PP, below).

On May 9, 1985, Congress enacted a bill that restored direct presidential elections and legalized all political parties, a move presumed to be directed mainly at the theretofore proscribed Brazilian Communist Party (*Partido Comunista Brasiliero*—PCB), which had been publicly running candidates under the PMDB banner. On the other hand, a law passed before the 1990 balloting required that a party have at least 300,000 members to qualify for formal registration.

A 2007 court ruling restricted officials' ability to change party affiliations and parties' ability to form coalitions (see Political Background above). However, in 2009 Brazil still had more than 20 registered political parties, most of which were involved in loosely defined and frequently changing coalitions at the regional and local levels.

Government Parties:

Workers' Party (*Partido dos Trabalhadores*—PT). Long endorsing "a pure form of socialism" that rejected orthodox Marxism, the PT made important gains in the 1985 municipal balloting, electing Maria Luisa FONTONELLE as one of the country's first two women mayors in Ceará's capital, Fortaleza, and winning 20 percent of the vote in São Paulo. It increased its lower house representation from 14 to 19 in 1986, while retaining its single Senate seat. During the 1987–1988 controversy over the duration of President Sarney's mandate and the possible introduction of a parliamentary system of government, the PT came out strongly in favor of immediate presidential elections with the avowed intention of running PT president Lula da Silva as its candidate. The party registered significant gains in the November 1988 municipal balloting, securing, most notably, the election of Luiza Erundina as São Paulo's first woman mayor. In late 1991, at the party's first congress since its founding a decade earlier, the Lula da Silva-led majority voted to abandon its former advocacy of "democratic socialism" and the "dictatorship of the proletariat" in favor of coexistence (not excluding cooperation) with other groups, both socialist and nonsocialist. Lula da Silva was runner-up to Collor de Mello in the 1989 presidential poll and placed second behind Fernando Henrique Cardoso in 1994. Failing again in 1998, he was victorious in 2002, although the PT was held to a 91-seat plurality in the Chamber of Deputies.

Following Lula da Silva's inauguration in 2003, the party shifted from a leftist-Socialist to a more center-left social democratic orientation, which spurred internal debate and the expulsion of four dissident legislators, including Heloísa Helena, who subsequently founded the PSOL (below). Further turmoil within the party occurred during a corruption scandal in 2005, which resulted in the replacement of several high-ranking party officials. Nevertheless, Lula da Silva was reelected with an overwhelming mandate in 2006, and PT deputies under investigation were reelected in concurrent legislative elections. However, the PT trailed the PMDB in number of legislative seats In 2008 the party lost the mayoral election in Sao Paolo; it does hold governorships in the most populous states.

Leaders: Luiz Inácio ("Lula") DA SILVA (President of the Republic), Ricardo BERZOINI (President), Marco Aurélio GARCIA (Vice President).

Brazilian Republican Party (*Partido Republicano Brasileiro*—PRB). The PRB was formed in 2005 as a successor to the Municipal Renewal Party (*Partido Municipalista Renovador*—PMR), which was established following the 2005 corruption scandals by Brazil's leading evangelical group, the Universal Church of the Kingdom of God (*Igreja Universal do Reino de Deus*—IURD). The IURD is a well-known Pentecostal group, with branches in 172 countries, headed by an entrepreneurial "bishop," Edir Macedo. The PRB, however, has been described as being more driven by pragmatism than by ideology, though a party that defends the interests of the church. The PRB has supported the Lula da Silva presidency on the basis of its concern for social democracy and eliminating inequality.

Leaders: Vitor Paulo dos SANTOS (President), José ALENCAR (Vice President of the Republic), Edir MACEDO (IURD leader), Jorge PINHEIRO (Coordinator).

Party of the Brazilian Democratic Movement (*Partido do Movimento Democrático Brasiliero*—PMDB). Rejecting government strictures against the adoption of names implying continuity with earlier party groups, the PMDB was launched in 1979 by about 100 federal deputies and 20 senators representing the more moderate elements of the former MDB. In late 1981 it was enlarged by merger with the Popular Party (*Partido Popular*—PP), a center-right grouping, most of whom had also been affiliated with the MDB. As the party reorganized to prepare for the 1986 congressional balloting, a conservative faction, *Grupo Unidade*, insisted that PP elements (which opposed recent PMDB initiatives for land reform and tax revision) were underrepresented in the party and issued an unsuccessful challenge to Ulysses GUIMARÃES for the party presidency. The PMDB won a majority in both houses of Congress and 22 of 23 state governorships in the November 1986 election.

The party became increasingly divided in 1987, with leftists, organized as the Progressive Unity Movement (*Movimento da Unidade Progressiva*—MUP), proposing a "grand leftist front" that would include "nonradicalized" factions of the PT and the PDT (below) to campaign for truncation of Sarney's term and an immediate presidential election. By early 1988 the *históricos* (constituting a majority within the party, but not within the Constituent Assembly) were also pressing for a break with the Sarney government; in June most of the dissidents withdrew to form the PSDB (below). Following the October 1990 balloting the PMDB held plurality status in both the senate and chamber with 26 and 109 seats, respectively. In March 1991 the 20-year party leadership of Ulysses Guimarães came to an end with the election of Orestes QUERCIA to succeed him as president. Guimarães was killed in a helicopter crash on October 12, 1992. Quércia resigned on April 26, 1993, in response to allegations of corruption during his recent term as governor of the state of São Paulo, although subsequently he presented himself as a candidate for the federal presidency in 1994.

The largest single contributor to the Franco coalition, the PMDB in 1994 won 9 of 26 gubernatorial contests and secured a plurality of seats in both houses of Congress. Retaining its preeminence in the senate, it fell to third place in the chamber in 2002. It participated in the Lula da Silva government until the party officially withdrew its support in late 2004, although its cabinet representatives chose to remain in office.

Opting not to field a presidential candidate in 2006, the party joined coalitions at the state and national levels. It held a plurality in the chamber following the 2006 election, and was brought back into government in 2007, its members having been appointed to several ministry posts. Considerable opposition to these appointments was reported within the party, but overall the party's "amorphous" ideology and preference for being in office allowed for continued support for the Lula da Silva government.

Leaders: Michel TEMER (President), Itamar FRANCO (Former President of the Republic), Íris de ARAÚJO (First Vice President), Garibaldi ALVES Filho (Former President of the Senate), Mauro LOPES (Secretary General).

Progressive Party (*Partido Progressista*—PP). The PP designation was adopted in 2003 by the former Brazilian Progressive Party (*Partido Progressista Brasiliero*—PPB), which had been launched in 1995 as a merger of the Progressive Renewal Party (*Partido Progressista Reformador*—PPR), led by Paulo Salim Maluf, then mayor of São Paulo; the Progressive Party (*Partido Progressista*—PP), led by Alvaro DIAS; and the Progressive Republican Party (*Partido Republicano Progressista*—PRP).

The PP, which favors economic reform, secured a seat in the Senate in the 2006 election, while its representation in the chamber fell from 49 to 42 seats. Former party president Pedro Corréa, accused in a vote-buying scandal, was expelled from his chamber seat in March 2006. Four members of the PP were among 12 indicted on corruption charges by the Supreme Court in August 2007.

Leaders: Francisco DORNELLES (President), Benedito DOMINGOS (Secretary General).

Green Party (*Partido Verde*—PV). Organized largely by a group of PMDB deputies, the PV was legalized in 1988. PV president Fernando Gabeira, a former guerrilla who campaigned for mayor of Rio de Janeiro in 1986 under the PT banner, left the party in 2002 to join the PT but returned to the PV in 2006. The party, which primarily promotes sustainable development, more than doubled its chamber representation in 2006 over 2002, when it had held 5 seats. In 2008 Green Party co-founder Carlos Minc defected to the PT and was appointed minister of the environment.

Leaders: José Luiz de França PENNA (President), Fernando GABEIRA, Carla PIRANDA (Secretary General).

Democratic Labor Party (*Partido Democrático Trabalhista*—PDT). The PDT is a left-wing party organized by Leonel da Moira BRIZOLA, who served as governor of Rio Grande do Sul and leader of the pre-1965 Brazilian Labor Party, following his return on September 5, 1979, after 15 years in exile. In the 1982 balloting Brizola, who was known to hold presidential aspirations, won the state governorship of Rio de Janeiro; before Neves's election, he attempted unsuccessfully to form a new socialist party and after the president-elect's death led the campaign for direct presidential balloting in 1988. In the November 1985 municipal balloting, the PDT won mayoralties in Pôrto Alegre and—more importantly—Rio de Janeiro, while Brizola regained the state governorship in 1990. Brizola waged losing battles for president in 1989 and 1994, and was Lula da Silva's running mate in the 1998 contest. He died on June 21, 2004.

While the party's strength has been in local elections, the PDT won 24 seats in the chamber in the 2006 balloting. In concurrent presidential balloting, Cristovam Buarque, received 2.6 percent of the vote in the first round.

Leaders: Carlos LUPI (President), Cristovam BUARQUE (2006 presidential candidate), Manoel DIAS (Secretary General).

Brazilian Socialist Party (*Partido Socialista Brasileiro*—PSB). The PSB, which has been described by observers as more pragmatic than other socialist parties in the country, withdrew from the Franco government coalition in August 1993. It won two state governorships in 1994 and that same year was part of a broad coalition that supported Lula da Silva's presidential bid.

In 2009 the party held 27 seats in the chamber and 3 in the Senate, as well as 2 state governorships

Leaders: Eduardo CAMPOS (President), Roberto AMARAL (Vice President), Ciro GOMES, Renato CASAGRANDE (Secretary General).

Communist Party of Brazil (*Partido Comunista do Brasil*—PCdoB). An offshoot of the PCB, the PCdoB was formed in 1961 as a Maoist group in support of rural guerrilla operations against the military. In August 1978 it publicly expressed its support for the Albanian Communist Party in its break with the post-Maoist Chinese leadership. In the mid-1980s, the party was instrumental in promoting huge demonstrations against the military regime. In 1994 the PCdoB endorsed Lula da Silva in his initial bid for the presidency, and has continued to support him. The party, whose platform calls for a socialist Brazil that is "truly democratic and sovereign," won 13 chamber seats in 2006.

Leaders: Renato REBELO (President), Renildo CALHEIROS (Vice President).

Brazilian Labor Party (*Partido Trabalhista Brasileiro*—PTB). The PTB was organized in 1980 by a niece of former president Getúlio Vargas. It attained a degree of visibility in 1985 by supporting Jânio Quadros in his successful mayoral bid. The PTB was a member of the Cardoso coalition government installed in 1994 but withdrew from the cabinet in March 1999. It withdrew from the Lula da Silva administration in June 2005 when its leader, Roberto Jefferson Monteiro Francisco, initiated the charges of high-level corruption. Jefferson was later forced to step down as party president after his expulsion from congress for attacking his colleagues "without proof." He faced charges in 2007 in connection with the alleged vote-buying scandal two years earlier. Meanwhile, Walfrido dos Mares GUIA, a key minister who was the president's liaison with congress, resigned in November 2007 in the wake of a money-laundering investigation.

Leaders: José MÚCIO Monteiro Francisco (President), Luis Antônio FLEURY Filho, Fernando COLLOR de Mello (former President of the Republic), Antônio Carlos De Campos MACHADO (Secretary General).

Other Legislative Parties:

Brazilian Social Democratic Party (*Partido da Social Democracia Brasileira*—PSDB). The PSDB was launched in June 1988 by a number of center-left congressional deputies from the PMDB's *histórico* faction, plus others (under PP, above), the PFL, the PTB and the PSB (above). The new alignment issued a manifesto calling for social justice, economic development, land reform, and environmental protection. In addition, it pledged to call for a plebiscite on establishment of a parliamentary system within the next four years. In 1994 and 1998 it joined with the PMDB, the PFL, the PTB, and the PL (below), in supporting the successful presidential bids of Fernando Henrique Cardoso.

The PSDB has suffered since the Cardoso administration in terms of finding a presidential candidate who could unify the party. Lackluster party support for José Serra in 2002 and Geraldo Alckmin (a former governor of São Paulo) in 2006 was a major problem. Among other divisive factors, party president Tasso Jereissati, former party president Eduardo AZEREDO, and party official Aécio Neves have criticized the party as being too centered on São Paulo. The internal divisions and Lula da Silva's shift toward pro-São policies have made it difficult for the PSDB to mount an effective opposition effort.

In 2007 Azeredo was implicated in a fraudulent campaign finance scheme. As of 2009 the party held 65 seats in the chamber and 15 in the Senate.

Leaders: Tasso JEREISSATI (President), Fernando Henrique CARDOSO (Honorary President; Former President of the Republic), José SERRA (Governor of São Paulo), Aécio NEVES (Governor of Minas Gerais), Geraldo ALCKMIN (2006 presidential candidate), Eduardo PÃES (Secretary General).

Democrats 25 (*Democratas 25*—DEM25). The Democrats is the name adopted in 2007 by the **Liberal Front Party** (*Partido da Frente Liberal*—PFL), which contested the 2006 elections under the PFL rubric. The PFL was formed in 1984 as a faction (under PP, above) that was opposed to the presidential candidacy of Paulo Maluf (later, of the PP). The PFL organized as a separate entity before the 1985 electoral college balloting, in which it supported Tancredo Neves as a member of the *Aliança Democrática*. In the 1986 balloting it became the second-largest party in Congress. In September 1987 the PFL announced its withdrawal from the alliance, thus formally terminating its link with the PMDB, although it decided the following month to continue its support of party cofounder, then-president of the republic, José Sarney, until after approval of the new constitution. As of early 1992 it was the largest progovernment formation in the Chamber of Deputies and subsequently became the largest component of the Cardoso coalition.

The PFL withdrew from the coalition government in March 2002 to protest an official investigation into the business dealings of Roseana SARNEY, the PFL's 2002 presidential candidate. Sarney withdrew from the race in April, and the PFL subsequently threw its support behind Ciro GOMES, then of the PPS (below). The PFL supported the PSDB's Geraldo Alckmin in the 2006 presidential balloting. The party became the second largest in the Senate in 2006, with 18 seats; it won 65 seats in the chamber. Also, party member José Roberto Arruda was elected governor of the Federal District in 2006.

In 2007 the PFL, now the Democrats 25, revised its leadership structure to address a "new Brazil." The Democrats have favored a more "balanced" and moderate form of government versus the Lula da Silva administration's move toward populism. The "25" in the party name refers to the party's electoral code.

Leaders: Rodrigo MAIA (President), Antonio Carlos MAGALHÃES Neto, Marco MACIEL, Jorge BORNHAUSEN, Jayme CAMPOS (Secretary General).

Liberal Party (*Partido Liberal*—PL).Founded in 1985, the PL was a tradesmen's party committed to free enterprise and a "more just" wages policy. In 2005 party president Valdemar da Costa Neto resigned from congress after acknowledging his role in a corruption scandal, though he denied accepting bribes. In 2007 several members of the PL were accused of taking bribes in exchange for political support in Congress.

Leaders: César Gaviria TRUJILLO, Cecillia López, Carlos Arturo PIEDRAHITA, José Noé RIOS.

Socialist Peoples Party (*Partido Popular Socialista*—PPS). The PPS was launched in January 1992 as successor to the Brazilian Communist Party (*Partido Comunista Brasileiro*—PCB), which had been formed in 1922 but enjoyed only nine years of legal existence thereafter. In June 1991 the PCB elected a "renewalist" leadership and argued that it was "no longer necessary [for] a Marxist to be a Communist." In furtherance of this posture, the party voted to confine Marxism-Leninism to the status of "historic relevance" and authorized the pursuit of socialism by democratic means. In 2004 the party withdrew from the governing coalition and subsequently expelled party leader Ciro Gomes, who had decided to remain in his cabinet post. Gomes then joined the PSB.

Leaders: Roberto FREIRE (President), *Fernando SANT'ANNA (Honorary President),* Rubens BUENO (General Secretary).

Christian Social Party (*Partido Social Cristão*—PSC). The PSC was launched in 1970 as the Democratic Republican Party (*Partido Democrático Republicano*—PDR); it adopted the PSC rubric in 1985. In the 1990s the party formed a secret coalition with President Durán Ballén in support of market reforms aimed at modernizing the Brazilian economy.

Leaders: Vítor Jorge Abdala NOSSIES (President), Antonio OLIBONI (General Secretary).

Socialist and Liberty Party (*Partido do Socialismo e da Libertade*—P-SOL). A far-left formation, the PSOL was launched in June 2004 by Heloísa Helena, who had been expelled from the PT in late 2003 for voting against the government. She was subsequently joined by a number of other PT defectors.

The PSOL follows an ideology similar to that of the PCdoB and the PSTU. It has benefited from the public perception that its members have been considered "honest politicians." Helena secured 6.8 percent of the vote in the first round of the 2006 presidential balloting.

Leader: Heloísa HELENA (President; 2006 presidential candidate).

Party for the Rebuilding of the National Order (*Partido de Reedificação da Ordem Nacional*—PRONA). PRONA is a far-right grouping founded in 1989 by a São Paulo cardiologist, Enéas Ferreira Carneiro, who was the party's candidate in the country's first presidential election that year. He ran for various offices over the years and in 2006 was elected as a deputy, securing one of his party's 2 seats. He died in May 2007.

The party reportedly disbanded in 2007 and joined members of the Liberal Party to form the **Party of the Republic** (*Partido da República*—PR), led by Sergio TAMER.

Other parties represented in the legislature are: the **National Mobilization Party** (*Partido da Mobilização Nacional*—PMN), led by Oscar Noronha FILHO; the **Christian Labor Party** (*Partido Trabalhista Cristão*—PTC); the **Humanist Party of Solidarity** (*Partido Humanista da Solidariedade*—PHS), led by Paulo Roberto MATOS; the **Party of the Nation's Retirees** (*Partido dos Aposentados da Nação*—PAN), led by Dreyfus Bueno RABELLO; the **Labor Party of Brazil** (Partido Trabalhista do Brasil– PtdoB), led by Luis Henrique de Oliveira RESENDE; and the **Renewed Brazilian Workers Party** (*Partido Renovador Trabalhista Brasileiro*—PRTB), led by José Levy Fidelix DA CRUZ.

Other Parties That Contested the 2006 Elections:

Other parties that contested the 2006 elections include the **Socialist Party of Unified Workers** (*Partido Socialista dos Trabalhadores Unificado*—PSTU), led by José Maria DE ALMEIDA; the **Christian Social Democratic Party** (*Partido Social Democrata Cristão*—PSDC), led by José Maria EYMAEL (2006 presidential candidate); the **Social Liberal Party** (*Partido Social Liberal*—PSL), led by Luciano Caldas BIVAR (2006 presidential candidate); the **Progressive Republican Party** (*Partido Republicano Progressista*—PRP), led by Ovasco Roma ALTIMARI and Ana Maria RANGEL (2006 presidential candidate); the **National Workers Party** (*Partido Trabalhista Nacional*—PTN), led by José Masci DE ABREU; and the **Workers' Cause Party** (*Partido da Causa Operáia*—PCO), led by Rui Costa PIMENTA (2006 presidential candidate).

LEGISLATURE

The bicameral **National Congress** (*Congresso Nacional*) consists of a Federal Senate and a Chamber of Deputies, both of which are directly elected by universal suffrage. The two houses, sitting together, form a Constituent Assembly for purposes of constitutional revision.

Federal Senate (*Senado Federal*). The upper house currently consists of 81 members (3 for each state, plus 3 for the Federal District) elected for eight-year terms, with one-third and two-thirds, respectively, elected every four years. Senators are elected in single-round plurality voting. Voters vote for one candidate when one-third of the membership is renewed, and two candidates when two-thirds of the membership is renewed.

Following the balloting of October 1, 2006, for one-third of the seats, the distribution of seats in the full senate was as follows: the Liberal Front Party, 18 (6 won in 2006); Party of the Brazilian Democratic Movement, 15 (4); Brazilian Social Democratic Party, 15 (5); Workers' Party, 11 (2); Democratic Labor Party, 5 (1); Brazilian Labor Party, 4 (3); Brazilian Socialist Party, 3 (1); Liberal Party, 3 (1); Communist Party of Brazil, 2 (1); Progressive Party, 1 (1); Socialist Peoples Party 1(1); and Renewed Brazilian Workers Party, 1 (1).

President: José SARNEY.

Chamber of Deputies (*Câmara dos Deputados*). Seats in the lower house are allocated on a population basis, their 513 current occupants serving four-year terms. Members are directly elected via party-list proportional balloting from 27 multimember constituencies (1 for each state and 1 for the Federal District).

In the most recent balloting on October 1, 2006, the seat distribution was as follows: the Party of the Brazilian Democratic Movement, 89 seats; Workers' Party, 83; Brazilian Social Democratic Party, 65; Liberal Front Party, 65; Progressive Party, 42; Brazilian Socialist Party, 27; Democratic Labor Party, 24; Liberal Party, 23; Brazilian Labor Party, 22; Socialist Peoples Party, 21; Green Party, 13; Communist Party of Brazil, 13; Christian Social Party, 9; Christian Labor Party, 4; Socialist and Liberty Party, 3; National Mobilization Party, 3; Humanist Party of Solidarity, 2; Party for the Rebuilding of the National Order, 2; Labor Party of Brazil, 1; Brazilian Republican Party, 1; and Party of the Nation's Retirees, 1.

(Changes in memberships have traditionally been known to occur with some frequency due to the Brazilian penchant for shifting political affiliations.)

President: Michel TEMER.

CABINET

[as of August 1, 2009]

President	Luiz Inácio ("Lula") da Silva (PT)
Vice President	José Alencar (PRB)
Chief of Civilian Cabinet	Dilma Rousseff (PT)
Secretary General of the Presidency	Luiz Dulci (PT)
Ministers	
Agrarian Development	Guilherme Cassel (PT)
Agriculture, Livestock, and Food Supply	Reinhold Stephanes (PMDB)
Cities	Márcio Fortes de Almeida (PP)
Communications	Hélio Costa (PMDB)
Culture	João Luiz Silva Ferreira (Juca Ferreira) (PV)
Defense	Nelson Jobim (PMDB)
Development, Industry, and Commerce	Miguel Jorge (ind.)
Education	Fernando Haddad (PT)
Environment	Carlos Minc (PT)
Finance	Guido Mantega (PT)
Foreign Affairs	Celso Luiz Nunes Amorim (ind.)
Health	José Gomes Temporão (PMDB)
Justice	Tarso Genro (PT)
Labor and Employment	Carlos Lupi (PDT)
Mines and Energy	Edison Lobão (PMDB)
National Integration	Geddel Vieira Lima (PMDB)
Planning, Budget, and Management	Paulo Bernardo Silva (PT)
Science and Technology	Sérgio Machado Rezende (PSB)
Social Development and the Fight against Hunger	Patrus Ananías (PT)
Social Security and Assistance	José Barroso Pimentel (PT)
Sport	Orlando Silva Júnior (PCdoB)
Tourism	Luiz Eduardo Pereira Barretto Filho (PT)
Transport	Alfredo Pereira do Nascimento (PRB)
Secretaries with Ministerial Status	
Agriculture and Fisheries	Altemir Gregolin (PT)
Human Rights	Paulo de Tarso Vannuchi (PT)
Institutional Relations	José Múcio Monteiro (PTB)
Institutional Security in the Office of the President	Gen. Jorge Armando Felix (ind.)
Policies to Promote Racial Equality	Martvs Antonio Alves das Chagas (PT) [f]
Social Communication	Franklin de Sousa Martins (ind.)
Strategic Affairs in the Office of the President	Roberto Mangabeira Unger
Women's Rights	Nilcéa Freire (PT) [f]

[f] = female

COMMUNICATIONS

Brazil has a vigorous and extensive news media network, which was subject to censorship, though somewhat relaxed after 1978, during the period of military rule. The Sarney government announced the end of political constraints in March 1985 and virtually all forms of media control have been banned under the 1988 constitution. However, in 2007, violence against journalists seemed to be surging, given the fatal beating of a journalist who reported on allegations of financial irregularities, and the attempted murder of a radio broadcaster. In 2008 the watchdog Reporters Without Borders reported that President Lula da Silva continued to back laws promoting freedom of the press.

Press. No Brazilian newspaper enjoys truly national distribution. The following are Portuguese-language dailies, unless otherwise noted: *O Estado de São Paulo* (São Paulo, 491,000 daily, 460,000 Sunday), independent; *O Globo* (Rio de Janeiro, 350,000 daily, 600,000 Sunday), conservative; *Fôlha de São Paulo* (São Paulo, 320,000 daily, 500,000 Sunday); *O Dia* (Rio de Janeiro, 250,000 daily, 500,000 Sunday), popular labor; *Notícias Populares* (São Paulo, 150,000); *Jornal do Brasil* (Rio de Janeiro, 107,000 daily, 145,000 Sunday), Catholic conservative; *Ultima Hora* (Rio de Janeiro, 57,000); *Diário de Pernambuco* (Recife, 31,000), oldest paper in Latin America (founded 1825), independent.

News agencies. There are a number of domestic agencies, including *Agência Globo* and *Agência Jornal do Brasil*, both headquartered in Rio de Janeiro; *Agência ANDA*, headquartered in Brasília; and *Agência o Estado de São Paulo* and *Agência Fôlha de São Paulo*. Numerous foreign agencies also maintain bureaus in Brasília, Rio de Janeiro, and São Paulo.

Broadcasting and computing. The government's National Telecommunications Department (*Departamento Nacional de Telecomunicações*—Dentel) oversees television and radio broadcasting. Most of the country's nearly 3,000 radio stations are commercial, but several are owned by the government or the Catholic Church. Most of the more than 260 television stations are organized into a national association, *Associação Brasileira de Emissoras de Rádio e Televisão* (ABERT), and a number of regional groups. Among the television networks, TV Globo dominates with an audience share of about 70 percent. As of 2008 there were 375.2 Internet users per 1,000 inhabitants.

INTERGOVERNMENTAL REPRESENTATION

Ambassador to the U.S.: Antonio de Aguiar PATRIOTA.

U.S. Ambassador to Brazil: (Vacant).

Permanent Representative to the UN: Maria Luiza Ribiero VIOTTI.

IGO Memberships (Non-UN): AfDB, ALADI, BIS, CAN, CDB, CPLP, G-20, IADB, Interpol, IOM, Mercosur, OAS, OPANAL, PCA, SELA, Unasur, WCO, WTO.

BRUNEI

State of Brunei Darussalam
Negara Brunei Darussalam

Political Status: Formerly a constitutional monarchy in treaty relationship with the United Kingdom; independent sultanate proclaimed January 1, 1984.

Area: 2,226 sq. mi. (5,765 sq. km.).

Population: 332,844 (2001C); 405,000 (2008E).

Major Urban Center (2005E): BANDAR SERI BEGAWAN (30,000).

Official Language: Malay (English is widely used).

Monetary Unit: Brunei Dollar (market rate December 1, 2009: 1.38 dollars = $1US). The Brunei dollar is at par with the Singapore dollar.

Head of State and Prime Minister: Sultan Sir Haji HASSANAL BOLKIAH Muizzaddin Waddaulah; ascended the throne October 5, 1967, upon the abdication of his father, Sultan Sir Haji Omar ALI SAIFUDDIN; crowned August 1, 1968; assumed office of prime minister at independence, succeeding former chief minister ABDUL AZIZ bin Umar.

Heir Apparent: Crown Prince Haji al-Muhtadee BILLAH, eldest son of the sultan; installed as crown prince August 10, 1998.

THE COUNTRY

Brunei consists of two jungle enclaves on the north coast of Borneo. About three-fourths of its population is Malay; the remainder is largely Chinese or other indigenous tribes. Malay is the official language, but the use of English is widespread. A majority of the inhabitants follow Islam, the official religion; smaller groups are Buddhist, Confucian, Christian, and pagan.

Brunei's per capita income is one of the highest in East Asia. Its wealth is derived from royalties on oil produced by Brunei Shell Petroleum and Brunei Shell Marketing, in both of which the government now holds a 50 percent interest, and on liquefied natural gas (LNG) produced primarily by Brunei LNG, in which the government holds a 50 percent interest and Shell and Mitsubishi of Japan each hold 25 percent. Oil and gas account for over half of real GDP, over 90 percent of government tax revenues, nearly 90 percent of nontax revenue, and 95 percent of exports, the leading markets being Japan, Indonesia, and South Korea.

Concern over declining oil reserves has led the government to accelerate diversification in such areas as tourism, fishing, and trade and to initiate privatization of such government services as electricity, water, and telecommunications. Government service nevertheless remains the second largest contributor to GDP. Private sector growth has been slowed not only by restrictions on foreign investment but also by an inability to equal the high remuneration paid to public sector workers. In May 2006 the home affairs minister announced that the sultan had liberalized rules governing foreign permanent residency for foreign nationals with Bruneian spouses and for individuals who contribute to economic development and growth.

Agriculture and fishing contribute only 1 percent of GDP but account for over 4 percent of employment, while the largest nonpetroleum component of the industrial sector is construction (3 percent of GDP, 25 percent of employment). Manufactures include food and beverages, garments, wood products, and building materials. Nongovernment employment is dominated by temporary residents, who account for nearly three-fourths of all private sector employment. Consistent GDP growth in the mid-1990s was reversed in 1998 because of falling world oil prices, the impact of a regional financial crisis, and the collapse of Brunei's largest nonpetroleum enterprise, the Amedeo Development Corporation, an investment and construction company. Growth averaged about 3 percent annually in 1999–2003 before falling to 0.5 percent in 2004–2005 as the oil and gas sector upgraded its facilities. Growth recovered to 5.1 percent in 2006 before dropping back to an estimated 0.4 percent in 2007. Initial projections for 2008 anticipated a negative growth rate, but that was before oil prices soared to record levels.

GOVERNMENT AND POLITICS

Political background. Brunei became a British protectorate in 1888 and was administered from 1906 to 1959 by a British resident. Sultan Sir Haji Omar ALI SAIFUDDIN, 28th in a line of hereditary rulers dating from the 15th century, promulgated Brunei's first written constitution in 1959, creating a framework for internal self-government while retaining British responsibility for defense and external affairs.

At voting in August–September 1962, all 10 elective seats in a 21-member Legislative Council were won by the left-wing Brunei People's Party (*Parti Rakyat Brunei*—PRB), led by A.M.N. AZAHARI, which sought a unitary state that would include the adjacent British territories of North Borneo (subsequently Sabah) and Sarawak. In December a rebellion was launched by the PRB-backed North Borneo Liberation Army, which, with Indonesian support, proclaimed a "revolutionary State of North Kalimantan." The revolt was quickly suppressed, however, and Azahari was granted political asylum by Indonesia.

A plan to join the Federation of Malaysia was accepted by the sultan in 1963 but later rejected because of disagreements regarding Brunei's position within the federation and the division of its oil royalties. Following talks with the British Commonwealth secretary in 1964, the sultan introduced constitutional reforms to allow a limited form of ministerial government, and a new general election was held in March 1965. Britain continued to press for a more representative government, however, and on October 4, 1967, the sultan, personally unwilling to accept further change, abdicated in favor of his 22-year-old son, Crown Prince HASSANAL BOLKIAH, who was crowned on August 1, 1968.

In early 1970 the constitution was suspended and the Legislative Council was reconstituted as an entirely appointive body, the sultan subsequently ruling primarily by decree. In 1971 renegotiated arrangements with Great Britain gave the sultan full responsibility for internal order but left the British with responsibility for external affairs. An agreement on formal independence, concluded in London on June 30, 1978, specified that Britain's responsibilities for Brunei's defense and foreign affairs would terminate at the end of 1983. Formal treaty signing on January 7, 1979, came only after Indonesia and Malaysia had given assurances that Brunei's sovereignty would be respected and that the sultan's opponents would not be allowed to maintain guerrilla bases in either country.

On January 1, 1984, after proclaiming independence, the sultan assumed the office of prime minister and announced a cabinet dominated by the royal family. In the early 1990s he attempted to shed his earlier "playboy" image in support of a new and demonstrably conservative ideology that blended elements of Bruneian Malay culture with the role of the monarch as defender of Islam (*Melayu Islam Beraja*).

In 1998 Sultan Hassanal Bolkiah removed his younger brother, Prince Muda Haji JEFRI BOLKIAH, as chair of the Brunei Investment Agency (BIA) and as head of the Amedeo Development Corporation, which Jefri had started in 1994. Brunei's largest nonpetroleum company, Amedeo had collapsed at an estimated cost of $16 billion, and the resultant scandal, compounded by Jefri's notoriously lavish lifestyle, caused a major rift in the royal family.

On July 15, 2004, the sultan announced that the Legislative Council would reconvene shortly. On September 25 the newly appointed members met to consider constitutional amendments, including provisions for a partially elected council, which were approved by Hassanal Bolkiah on September 29. A major cabinet reshuffle on May 30, 2005—the first in 17 years—included the elevation of Crown Prince Haji al-Muhtadee BILLAH to the new post of senior minister in the Prime Minister's Office. On September 2 the sultan appointed a new, 29-member Legislative Council. The most recent cabinet reshuffle, involving three ministries, occurred in August 2008.

Constitution and government. Many provisions of the 1959 constitution have been suspended since 1962; others were effectively

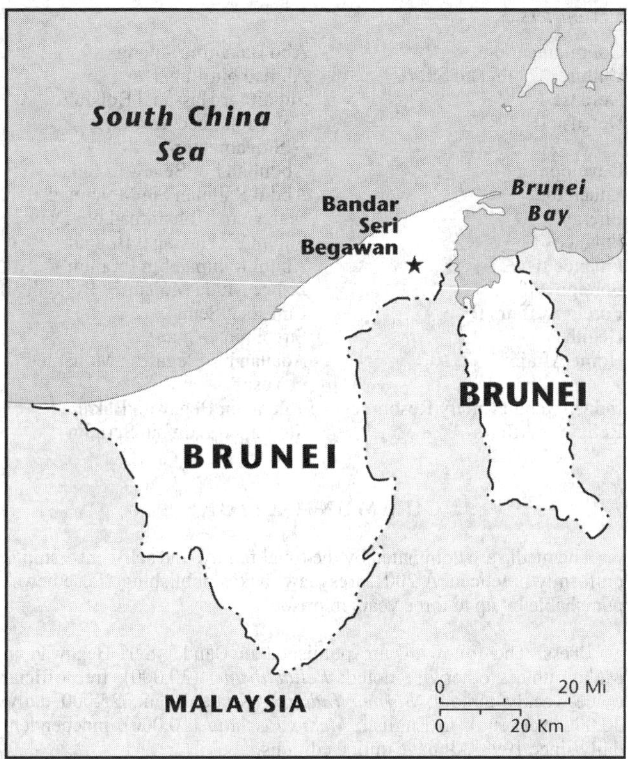

superseded upon independence. The sultan, as head of state, presides over a Council of Cabinet Ministers and is advised by a Legislative Council, a Privy Council to deal in part with constitutional issues, and a Religious Council; the basic law also provides for a Council of Succession. The Legislative Council is currently wholly appointive, but the amendments approved in September 2004 authorize the future election of 15 members to a 45-member body. The judicial system includes a High Court, a Court of Appeal, and magistrates' courts; there are also religious courts from which the Religious Council hears appeals.

For administrative purposes Brunei is divided into four districts, each headed by a district officer responsible to the sultan. District councils with a minority of elected members advise the district officers on local affairs. Subdivisions include some three dozen *mukims*, each headed by a *penghulu* (chieftain), and villages, each led by a *ketua* (headman).

Foreign relations. Upon independence, Brunei became a member of the Commonwealth and in January 1984 joined the Association of Southeast Asian Nations (ASEAN) as its sixth member. Soon after, it was admitted to the Organization of the Islamic Conference (OIC). In 1984 it became a member of the United Nations and in 1985 joined the International Monetary Fund and World Bank. In 1989 it became a founding member of the Asia-Pacific Economic Cooperation (APEC) group.

The sultan moved quickly at independence to transfer the bulk of Brunei's substantial investment portfolio from British management to the newly established BIA. In the defense sphere, however, a 1983 agreement provided for British Army Gurkhas to be stationed in Brunei under British command, on the understanding that their sole function was to protect the country's oil and gas installations (i.e., they could not be used by the sultan for internal security purposes). Originally concluded for a five-year term, the agreement has been periodically extended.

Brunei's relations with Indonesia and Malaysia were long marred by territorial claims and support offered to the sultan's political opponents. In addition, Malaysia regularly called upon Britain to "decolonize" Brunei and backed UN resolutions pressuring London to sponsor UN-supervised elections in the sultanate. Brunei, meanwhile, continued to claim sovereignty over Limbang, the area of Sarawak separating the nation's two regions. In the second half of the 1970s, however, relations between the neighbors improved, and in 1980 Hassanal Bolkiah paid the first official visit by a sultan to Malaysia in 17 years. In 1984 he met in Jakarta with Indonesian President Suharto, and in 1989 he made his first official visit to the neighboring Malaysian state of Sarawak. In 1995 the foreign ministers of Brunei and Malaysia held an inaugural joint commission meeting, at which agreement was reached on adoption of a bilateral approach to resolution of the Limbang issue.

In 1997, in the midst of the regional economic crisis, Brunei attempted to support its neighbors by pledging over $1 billion in loans to Jakarta and by buying Malaysia's ringgit and the Singapore dollar on foreign-exchange markets. More recently, the government participated in formation of the Brunei-Indonesia-Malaysia-Philippines–East ASEAN Growth Area (BIMP-EAGA), which held its fifth summit in February 2009. The group's subregional development roadmap for 2006–2010 emphasizes improved air and sea links as well as trade and investment. Brunei is also a member of the Trans-Pacific Partnership, with Chile, New Zealand, and Singapore—prospective members include Australia, Peru, the United States, and Vietnam—and a participant in the Gas Exporting Countries Forum (GECF). At a December 2008 meeting in Moscow, Russia, GECF decided to formalize its structure and membership.

A continuing foreign policy concern has been the status of the reputedly oil-rich Spratly Islands, portions of which Brunei, China, Malaysia, Philippines, Taiwan, and Vietnam all claim.

Current issues. All of the constitutional changes of September 2004 were proposed by the sultan, and they largely served to codify his authority, including his absolute control of governmental administration. To date, the provision for restoring elective members to the Legislative Council has not been pursued. Moreover, outspoken critics of the regime continue to face the prospect of prosecution under the country's Internal Security Act.

In November 2007 the United Kingdom Privy Council, in its capacity as Brunei's highest appeals court, ruled in favor of Hassanal Bolkiah in his decade-long effort to force Prince Jefri to return state assets. In 2000, in an out-of-court settlement, Jefri had agreed to return assets valued at $6–8 billion, including international hotels and other real estate, and collections of automobiles, jewels, and art. In June 2008 a London High Court judge issued a bench warrant for Jefri's arrest when he failed to appear in court to answer charges that he concealed bank accounts and accessed frozen funds. Jefri fled England to avoid a possible two-year jail term and took up residence in the Philippines.

POLITICAL PARTIES

Political parties were essentially moribund for most of the quarter-century after the failed 1962 rebellion. A Brunei People's Independence Front (*Barisan Kemerdekaan Rakyat*—Baker), formed in 1966 by amalgamation of a number of earlier groups, was deregistered because of inactivity in early 1985. A Brunei People's National United Party (*Parti Perpaduan Kebangsaan Rakyat Brunei*—Perkera), founded in 1968, had also stopped functioning. The moderate Islamist Brunei National Democratic Party (*Parti Kebangsaan Demokratik Brunei*—PKDB) and the Brunei National United Party (PPKB, below) were accorded legal recognition in 1985 and 1986, respectively. In 1988, however, the government confirmed that it had dissolved the PKDB, while the PPKB disappeared from view until 1995. After that, two additional parties, the National Development Party (PPK) and the People's Awareness Party (Pakar), were registered, but neither challenged the government. In 2007 both the PPKB and Pakar were deregistered, leaving the PPK as the only officially recognized party. Membership and activities are strictly regulated by the Registrar of Societies. Civil servants are banned from political activity, and members of deregistered parties are prohibited from joining other parties for three years.

Registered Party:

National Development Party (*Parti Pembangunan Kebangsaan*—PPK). The PPK was registered on August 31, 2005, under the leadership of Muhammad Yassin Affandi, 83, former leader of the PRB (below) who had been imprisoned from 1962 to 1973 and again in 1997–1999. The PPK quickly established branches in the country's four districts and announced its intention to work as a government "partner." The party held its third congress in June 2998, at which time Affandi proposed that Brunei replace Malaysia as coordinator of the International Monitoring Team that has been overseeing a temporary peace between the Philippine government and the Mindanao-based Moro Islamic Liberation Front (MILF). The MILF politely replied that it preferred that Malaysia continue in that role.

Leaders: Muhammad Yassin AFFANDI (AFANDY) (President), Abdullah Rahman YUSOF (Permanent Chair), Aminorrashid GHAZALI (Secretary General).

Recently Deregistered Parties:

Brunei National United Party (*Parti Perpaduan Kebangsaan Brunei*—PPKB). Formed in late 1985 under the leadership of Mohamed Hatta ZAINAL ABIDIN, the PPKB was an offshoot of the PKDB, led by Abdul LATIF Hamid and Abdul LATIF Chuchu. The PKDB was banned early in 1988 and the Latifs were detained, whereupon the PPKB also ceased to function.

In February 1995 the PPKB received authorization to hold a general assembly in which Latif Chuchu was elected party president (the other Latif had died in 1990). However, conditions attached to his release from detention obliged Latif Chuchu to resign, and the party remained largely inactive until another general meeting was permitted in April 1998, at which time Zainal Abidin was elected party president. In 2005 Latif Chuchu was allowed to resume party activities.

Also identified in English as the Brunei Solidarity National Party, the PPKB supported the concept of a Malay-dominated, Muslim monarchy but has also called for democratic reforms, including open legislative elections. In February 2008 the minister of home affairs rejected an appeal of a November 2007 decision by the Registrar of Societies to deregister the party for having failed to submit required reports.

People's Awareness Party (*Parti Kesedaran Rakyat*—Pakar). Also translated as the People's Consciousness Party, Pakar was established in May 2000 but was threatened with deregistration in 2004 for failure to meet technical requirements. Subsequently, a serious rift developed between factions loyal to the party's president, MAIDIN Haji Ahmad, and its secretary general, Jumat bin Haji IDRIS, which led the factions to hold competing meetings in March 2005. For a time, Idris claimed the presidency, but in August 2005 the factions agreed to mend the rift. In March 2007, however, the party was deregistered because of a leadership dispute.

Exile Formation:

Brunei People's Party (*Parti Rakyat Brunei*—PRB). Formerly a legal party that was deeply involved in the 1962 insurgency, the PRB has since been supported by a somewhat shadowy membership of about 100 individuals, most of them living as exiles in Indonesia or Malaysia. News reports from the June 2006 general session of Malaysia's Pan-Malaysian Islamic Party noted the attendance of PRB representatives.

Over the years, the sultan has pardoned a number of participants in the 1962 rebellion, including former PRB leader Muhammad Yassin Affandi, who was released in August 1999 and formed the PPK in 2005. A party founder, A.M.N. Azahari, died in exile in May 2002.

LEGISLATURE

There is no legislature per se. At present, legislation is enacted by proclamation. A 21-member advisory **Legislative Council** (*Majlis Meshuarat Negeri*), a wholly nonelective body that incorporates all cabinet members, met in September 2004, two decades after last convening. It quickly approved constitutional amendments, including a provision for the future election of 15 representatives to an expanded 45-member body. On September 1, 2005, the sultan dissolved the Legislative Council, and on September 2 he appointed a new 29-member council, which has subsequently met regularly.

Speaker: KAMALUDIN Al Haj.

CABINET

[as of October 1, 2009]

Prime Minister	Sultan Sir Hassanal Bolkiah
Senior Minister in the Prime Minister's Office	Prince Al-Muhtadee Billah
Ministers	
Communications	Abu Bakar bin Apong
Culture, Youth, and Sports	Ahmad bin Jumat
Defense	Sultan Sir Hassanal Bolkiah
Defense II	Col. Mohamed Yasmin Singamanteri
Development	Abdullah bin Begawan Bakar
Education	Abdul Rahman bin Mohamed Taib
Energy	Maj. Gen. Mohammad bin Daud
Finance	Sultan Sir Hassanal Bolkiah
Finance II	Abdul Rahman bin Ibrahim
Foreign Affairs	Prince Muda Mohamed Bolkiah
Foreign Affairs II	Lim Jock Seng
Health	Suyoi bin Osman
Home Affairs	Adanan bin Begawan Mohamed Yusof
Industry and Primary Resources	Yahya bin Begawan Bakar
Religious Affairs	Mohamed Zain bin Serudin

COMMUNICATIONS

The media are dominated by the royal family, and self-censorship is uniformly practiced. A 2001 press law makes publishing "false news" punishable by up to three years in prison.

Press. The following are published in Bandar Seri Begawan in Malay, unless otherwise noted: *Pelita Brunei* (30,000), free official twice-weekly tabloid; *Borneo Bulletin* (Kuala Belait, 25,000 daily, 30,000 weekend), in English; *Media Permata* (10,000), independent daily since 1998. All have online editions.

Broadcasting and computing. The government-controlled Radio Television Brunei offers the only local radio and television broadcasts, but private cable and satellite service is available. As of 2008 there were 553.2 Internet users per 1,000 inhabitants.

INTERGOVERNMENTAL REPRESENTATION

Ambassador to the U.S.: Dato Yusoff Abd HAMID.

U.S. Ambassador to Brunei Darussalam: William Edward TODD.

Permanent Representative to the UN: Latif TUAH.

IGO Memberships (Non-UN): APEC, ASEAN, CWTH, IDB, Interpol, NAM, OIC, WCO, WTO.

BULGARIA

Republic of Bulgaria
Republika Balgariya

Political Status: Communist constitution of May 18, 1971, substantially modified on April 3, 1990; present name adopted November 15, 1990; current democratic constitution adopted July 12, 1991.

Area: 42,823 sq. mi. (110,912 sq. km.).

Population: 7,928,901 (2001C); 7,595,000 (2008E). More than 900,000 Bulgarians have emigrated since 1989.

Major Urban Centers (2005E): SOFIA (1,194,000), Plovdiv (337,000), Varna (323,000), Bourgas (213,000), Rousse (182,000).

Official Language: Bulgarian.

Monetary Unit: Lev (official rate December 1, 2009: 1.29 leva = $1US). The lev is pegged to the euro, which Bulgaria hopes to adopt as its official currency in 2012, at the rate of 1.9558 leva = 1 euro.

President: Georgi PARVANOV (elected as the candidate of the Bulgarian Socialist Party [BSP], from which he resigned following his election); sworn in for a five-year term on January 19, 2002, and assumed office on January 22, having been popularly elected in the second round of presidential balloting on November 18, 2001, succeeding Petar STOYANOV (originally Union of Democratic Forces, later independent); reelected (as an independent with the support of the BSP and other parties) in second-round balloting on October 29, 2006, and inaugurated for a second five-year term on January 22, 2007.

Vice President: Angel MARIN (Bulgarian Socialist Party); sworn in January 19, 2002, and assumed office on January 22 for a term concurrent with that of the president, succeeding Todor KAVALDZHIEV (Union of Democratic Forces); reelected on October 29, 2006.

Chair of the Council of Ministers (Prime Minister): Boiko BORISOV (Citizens for European Development of Bulgaria); nominated by the president following the legislative elections of July 5, 2009, and inaugurated on July 27 (following approval that day of his proposed cabinet by the National Assembly) in succession to Sergei STANISHEV (Bulgarian Socialist Party).

THE COUNTRY

Extending southward from the Danube and westward from the Black Sea, Bulgaria occupies a key position in the eastern Balkans adjacent to Macedonia, Romania, Serbia, Greece, and Turkey. Like Greece and Macedonia, the country includes portions of historic Macedonia, and tensions with neighboring states long existed because of the commonly held position in Bulgaria that all Slavic-speaking inhabitants of Macedonia are ethnic Bulgarians. More than 83 percent of Bulgaria's population is considered ethnically Bulgarian, while there are sizable minorities of Turks (about 9.4 percent) and Roma (officially 350,000 but unofficially estimated at more than 800,000). The predominant language is Bulgarian, a component of the southern Slavic language group. While religious observances were discouraged under the communist regime, the principal faith remains that of the Bulgarian Orthodox Church; there is also a substantial Muslim minority (estimated at 800,000), in addition to small numbers of Catholics, Protestants, and Jews.

Traditionally an agricultural country, Bulgaria achieved a measure of industrialization after World War II under a series of five-year plans. As a result, machine building, ferrous and nonferrous metallurgy, textile manufacturing, and agricultural processing grew in importance, with agriculture accounting for only 14 percent of GDP by the end of communist rule in 1990. Subsequently, reforms were introduced that included the removal of price subsidies on many basic commodities, currency flotation, privatization of land and small businesses, and decentralization of state enterprises. The transition proceeded slowly, however, and economic problems were exacerbated by the dismemberment of the Soviet Union, which had long taken about 60 percent of the country's exports. GDP declined by an estimated 15–20 percent in 1992, and unemployment rose to 15 percent. One percent growth was reported in 1994 (Bulgaria being among the last former communist-bloc countries to register such recovery), although inflation worsened to 122 percent and unemployment to 20 percent. Deterioration in the first half of 1996, exacerbated by corruption and entrenched resistance to economic change, brought Bulgaria to the brink of financial collapse: the value of the lev plummeted, banks failed, inflation soared, basic commodities were in short supply, and the prospect of debt default loomed. As a consequence, GDP fell by a further 7 percent in 1997, and the consumer price index soared by 550 percent as a new government scurried to implement a "shock" package of economic reforms that included faster privatization. In a remarkably rapid turnaround, aided by assistance from the International Monetary Fund (IMF), the World Bank, and others, growth resumed in 1998 and reached 5 percent in 2000. The IMF and other international institutions praised the center-right governments of 1997–2005 for tight fiscal policies that, among other things, reduced the ratio of public debt to GDP, limited budget deficits, improved the investment climate (in part through privatization of public enterprises), and generally facilitated economic stability. Nevertheless, collateral constriction of labor, health, educational, and other benefits generated unrest within a significant portion of the populace. The Socialist-led government installed in 2005 loosened fiscal policies, generating concern on the part of the IMF.

Aided by expanding industrial and tourism sectors, annual GDP growth averaged more than 5.5 percent in 2004–2006, while unemployment (18 percent in 2003) declined to just under 10 percent in late 2006 and the government recorded its third consecutive year of budget surpluses. However, inflation remained worrisome at 6.8 percent in 2006, and the IMF and other Western institutions intensified their calls for additional reform in the health and educational sectors and for more effective antipoverty policies on the part of the administration. Foreign investors also complained of inordinate bureaucratic delays in getting permits for new businesses. Despite substantial questions in those areas as well as the lack of progress in combating corruption and organized crime, Bulgaria was admitted to the European Union (EU) on January 1, 2007. (See current issues, below, for additional information.) With a per capita income of less than one-third that of Western European nations, Bulgaria thereupon became the poorest EU member. Critics of its EU accession also described Bulgaria as a "hub" for trafficking in drugs and weapons.

GDP growth reached 6.2 percent in 2007 and 6 percent in 2008, while unemployment dropped below 7 percent, the lowest rate since 1990, in 2008. Inflation, however, registered 9.8 percent in 2007 (led by food prices [up 25 percent] and housing prices [up 34 percent]) and 7.8 percent in 2008, fueling populist sentiment that blamed the increases on EU accession. The IMF projected GDP contraction of as much as 7 percent in 2009, primarily as a result of the global economic crisis.

GOVERNMENT AND POLITICS

Political background. Bulgarian kingdoms existed in the Balkan Peninsula during the Middle Ages, but the Ottoman Empire ruled the area for 500 years prior to the Russo-Turkish War of 1877–1878; full independence was not achieved until 1908. Long-standing territorial ambitions led to Bulgarian participation on the losing side in the Second Balkan War (1913) and in both world wars. Talks aimed at the country's withdrawal from World War II were interrupted on September 5, 1944, by a Soviet declaration of war, followed by the establishment four days later of a communist-inspired "Fatherland Front" government.

The monarchy was rejected by a 92 percent majority in a disputed referendum held September 8, 1946, after which King SIMEON II, who had come to the throne at age six in 1943, went into exile. A "People's Republic" was formally established on December 4, 1947, under the premiership of Georgi DIMITROV, who died in 1949. Communist rule was consolidated under the successive regimes of Vulko CHERVENKOV and Anton YUGOV. From 1954 until his ouster in November 1989, Todor ZHIVKOV, occupying various positions within the government and party hierarchies, maintained his status as Bulgaria's leader while continuing the pro-Soviet policies instituted by his predecessors.

The collapse of East European communism did not become a factor in Bulgarian politics until November 3, 1989, when upwards of 9,000 demonstrators marched in Sofia in the first prodemocracy rally in the country's postwar history. One week later a number of key Politburo changes were announced, including the replacement of Zhivkov as party general secretary by the reformist foreign minister, Petur MLADENOV. On November 17 the National Assembly named Mladenov to succeed Zhivkov as head of state, and the following day 50,000 persons assembled in the capital to applaud the new government. On December 13 Zhivkov was formally expelled from the party. Subsequently, the former leader was indicted on a variety of charges that included misappropriating state property, inciting ethnic hostility, and abusing his powers of office. (He was convicted of embezzlement and sentenced to seven years imprisonment on September 1, 1992. He died in 1998, having been released from house arrest the previous year.)

In multiparty elections held on June 10 and 17, 1990, the Bulgarian Socialist (formerly Communist) Party (*Balgarska Sotsialisticheska Partiya*—BSP) captured a majority of National Assembly seats, with the recently launched Union of Democratic Forces (*Sayuz na Demokratichni Sili*—SDS) trailing by nearly 100 seats. Subsequently, President Mladenov was obliged to resign on July 6 in the wake of evidence that he had endorsed the use of tanks to crush an antigovernment demonstration in late 1989. After nearly a month of political stalemate, the assembly elected SDS chair Zhelyu ZHELEV as Mladenov's successor on August 1. On September 19, after efforts to form a coalition had failed, a new all-Socialist cabinet was announced under the continued premiership of Andrei LUKANOV (first appointed in February 1990). However, Lukanov resigned on November 29 after two weeks of street protests and a four-day general strike. On December 7 a politically independent judge, Dimitur POPOV, was named premier designate, and on December 20 he succeeded in forming a coalition administration that included eight Socialists, four representatives of the SDS, and three Agrarians.

Despite a boycott by many opposition parliamentarians, who demanded a referendum in the matter, a democratic constitution was adopted on July 12, 1991, followed by a new legislative poll on October 13. Emerging with a narrow four-seat plurality, the SDS, with support from the ethnically Turkish Movement for Rights and Freedoms (*Dvizhenieza Prava i Svobodi*—DPS), installed Filip DIMITROV on November 8 as head of the country's first wholly non-communist government since World War II.

On January 19, 1992, in the second round of Bulgaria's first popular presidential poll, Zhelev was reelected to a five-year term. The SDS depended on parliamentary support from the DPS, and, not surprisingly, confirmation of the new Dimitrov administration was accompanied by reversal of a ban, introduced by the communists, on optional Turkish-language instruction in the secondary schools.

In March 1992 the National Assembly completed work, initiated a year earlier, on land privatization, providing for all agricultural cooperatives to be phased out and permitting foreign investors to participate, as minority members, in joint land ventures with Bulgarians. However, other promised reforms remained stalled, including a decommunization bill, amid serious labor unrest and a growing conflict between President Zhelev and the Dimitrov government over their respective responsibilities. The SDS tried to respond by organizing pro-Dimitrov rallies, but a DPS decision on September 23 to withdraw its support from the government proved fatal. On October 28 the government was defeated 121–111 on a nonconfidence motion and was obliged to resign. An interregnum ensued, during which the BSP wasted its constitutional opportunity to nominate a successor premier. The initiative passed to the DPS, which nominated the president's economic adviser, Lyuben BEROV, to form a nonparty administration of "national responsibility." Somewhat unexpectedly, with the backing of BSP and SDS dissidents, Berov obtained parliamentary approval on December 30 by 124 votes to 25, with the bulk of the SDS deputies abstaining.

The longevity of the Berov administration was assisted by the increasing disarray of the SDS, growing conflict between Zhelev and the SDS, defections to the government side, and the preference of the BSP for a government that it could influence and control rather than for official power as such. However, Berov was incapacitated by a heart attack on March 8, 1994, and President Zhelev announced on April 2 that he was withdrawing political support from the government because of the slow pace of privatization and a failure to attract foreign investment. The ailing Berov sought to regain the initiative on June 28 by launching a much-delayed mass privatization scheme for some 500 state-owned companies; finance officials also successfully concluded a rescheduling of Bulgaria's $10 billion external debt, enabling IMF and World Bank credit lines to be reactivated. Political pressure nevertheless mounted on the government, which resigned on September 2. Attempts by the president to find an alternative were thwarted by the preference of the BSP and the SDS for early elections, pending which a caretaker cabinet was installed on October 18 under Bulgaria's first woman prime minister, Reneta INDZHOVA.

In the legislative poll of December 18, 1994, Bulgarian voters continued the East European trend of restoring ex-communist parties to power, according the BSP and two minor party (Agrarian and Ecoglasnost Political Club [*Politicheski klub Ekoglasnost*—PKE]) allies an overall majority of 125 of the 240 seats. By contrast, the SDS obtained only 69, its electoral appeal having been eroded by the decision of several of its factions to stand independently. As a result, 35-year-old BSP leader Zhan VIDENOV was sworn in on January 26, 1995, as prime minister of a government that included two members of the Bulgarian Agrarian National Union–People's Union (*Balgarski Zemedelski Naroden Sayuz–Naroden Sayuz*—BZNS-NS), one PKE member, and several nonparty technocrats reputed to favor market reforms. At that stage less than 40 percent of state-owned land had been restored to private ownership, and only 35 of the country's 3,000 large- and medium-sized industrial enterprises had been privatized.

Party politics in 1996 focused on the presidential election in November, for which incumbent Zhelyu Zhelev declared his candidacy. Because Zhelev had fallen out with the SDS since his 1992 election, the opposition held a primary to find a joint candidate, with Zhelev running as the nominee of the People's Union (*Naroden Sayuz*—NS) coalition and the SDS endorsing Petar STOYANOV, a little-known lawyer. The outcome of the primary balloting on June 1 was a decisive 65.7 percent majority for Stoyanov, who thereupon received Zhelev's endorsement. The ruling coalition parties supported the BSP foreign minister, Georgi PIRINSKI, but his candidacy was effectively blocked by a controversial Constitutional Court ruling on July 23 that, having been born in the United States of Bulgarian émigré parents, he did not meet the constitutional requirement of being Bulgarian by birth. On September 2 the Supreme Court rejected the BSP's appeal, and the BSP culture minister, Ivan MARAZOV, was drafted as a replacement. Stoyanov was subsequently the easy victor, heading the first-round balloting on October 27, 1996, with 44.1 percent of the vote and then obtaining 60 percent in a two-way runoff against Marazov on November 3.

In the wake of Stoyanov's victory, Videnov resigned as prime minister and leader of the BSP on December 21, 1996, the assembly accepting his resignation on December 28. The SDS immediately called for the installation of a caretaker government pending proposed early assembly elections. However, the BSP, ignoring massive public demonstrations in support of the SDS proposal, insisted upon its right (as leading parliamentary party) to name a new prime minister, and on January 7, 1997, it tapped Interior Minister Nikolai DOBREV to succeed Videnov. Public opposition again quickly erupted, and on January 11 President Zhelev announced he would not invite Dobrev to form a new government, arguing that such a government would not be viable. Consequently, the government was stalemated when Stoyanov took office on January 22, 1997. After weeks without a prime minister and a siege of the assembly by SDS supporters, the BSP in early February finally agreed to allow Stoyanov to appoint an interim government, which, as announced on February 12, was led by Stefan SOFIANSKI, the mayor of Sofia. The interim government immediately initiated economic reforms designed to stabilize the currency and control food and fuel shortages while preparing for new assembly elections on April 19. In that balloting, the SDS-led United Democratic Forces (*Obedineni Demokratichni Sili*—ODS) scored a massive victory, securing 137 seats to 58 for the BSP-led Democratic Left (*Demokratichna Levitsa*—DL). ODS leader Ivan KOSTOV, an economist and former finance minister, was named prime minister on May 21, pledging that his new cabinet would steadfastly pursue the reforms launched by Sofianski.

Although the economy experienced a remarkably swift turnaround, the Kostov government's standing in the polls had declined by early 2001, in large part because the economic gains had not produced a notable advance in living standards. By April, with a general election only two months away, the BSP was presenting a serious challenge to Kostov's incumbency. However, on April 6 the political landscape underwent a tectonic shift when the former king, Simeon SAXE-COBURG-GOTHA, after 55 years in exile, announced formation of a National Movement Simeon II (*Natsionalno Dvizhenie Simeon Tvori*—NDST) that would contest the National Assembly election. Although the party was refused registration on technical grounds, two small parties agreed to register for the election as a coalition under the NDST designation, thereby providing visibility to a slate of candidates loyal to Simeon. Immediately, Kostov's ODS and the BSP-led Coalition for Bulgaria (*Koalitsiya za Balgariya*—KzB) saw their poll standings plummet, and in the June 17 balloting the NDST secured 120 of the assembly's 240 seats. The ODS and the KzB trailed with 51 and 48 seats, respectively. Although Simeon had not run for office himself, on July 12, as expected, he received the coalition's endorsement as prime minister. Picked by President Stoyanov to form a cabinet, the former king, having adopted the common name Simeon SAKSKOBURG-GOTSKI (see National Movement for Stability and Progress [*Natsionalno Dvizhenie za Stabilnost i Vazhod*—NDSV], as the NDST has been renamed, under Political Parties, below, for additional information on this name usage), received legislative endorsement on July 24. The first former Eastern European monarch to assume a republican office, he was sworn in as the head of an NDST-dominated Council of Ministers that included two DPS and two BSP members. (Despite the participation of the BSP members in the cabinet, the BSP said it had made no political commitment to the government and would in fact remain in "constructive opposition.")

In presidential balloting on November 11, 2001, President Stoyanov, running as an independent but with NDST support, won only 35 percent of the vote on a low voter turnout of 39 percent. His chief rival, BSP Chair Georgi PARVANOV, took 36 percent and in second-round balloting on November 18 won with 54 percent.

On July 16, 2003, Prime Minister Sakskoburggotski announced a cabinet reshuffle and expansion designed, among other things, to facilitate Bulgaria's planned accession to the EU and the North Atlantic Treaty Organization (NATO). However, in March 2004 the NDST/DPS coalition became a minority government when a group of NDST legislators left that grouping to launch a new party called New Time. Although New Time supported the government in several subsequent no-confidence votes, in early February 2005 it joined the opposition parties in demanding the government's resignation for having failed to achieve its promises of 2001. However, New Time ultimately voted against a no-confidence motion on February 11 (thereby preserving the coalition) as part of an accord whereby New Time joined the cabinet in a February 21 reshuffle.

The BSP-led KzB led all parties by winning 82 seats in the assembly balloting on June 25, 2005. After seven weeks of difficult negotiations, BSP leader Sergei STANISHEV was inaugurated on August 16 as head of a center-left KzB/NDST/DPS coalition government.

President Parvanov received 64 percent of the vote against six opponents in the first round of presidential balloting on October 22, 2006. However, since the turnout was less than 50 percent, a second round was held on October 29, with Parvanov being reelected (the first post-communist president to achieve that feat) with 76 percent of the vote over Volen SIDEROV of the ultranationalist National Union Attack (*Natsionalno Obedinenie Ataka*).

The recently formed Citizens for European Development of Bulgaria (*Grazhdani za Evropejsko Razvitie Balgarija*—GERB) achieved a spectacular victory in the July 5, 2009, assembly balloting by winning a plurality of 116 of 240 seats. (The nearest competitor was the KzB, with 40 seats.) After two weeks of negotiations failed to produce agreement on a formal coalition government, GERB founder Boiko BORISOV was sworn in as prime minister on July 27 after his all-GERB cabinet had been approved by a vote of 162–78 in the assembly. Although technically a minority government, Borisov's cabinet enjoyed the pledged legislative support (for the time being, at least) of *Ataka*, the SDS-led Blue Coalition (*Sinyata Koalitsiya*—SK), and the new Order, Law, and Justice party (*Red, Zakonnost, i Spravedlivost*—RZS), all of whose members voted in favor of the new government.

Constitution and government. The constitution of July 1991 describes Bulgaria as a republic with a democratic parliamentary form of government. It guarantees freedom of association, religion, and opinion, while supporting an economy based on "market forces" and a respect for private property. It provides for a president and vice president, elected jointly for no more than two five-year terms by majority vote of at least 50 percent of those eligible to cast ballots (a second ballot, if necessary, is confined to the top two tickets from the first round). The president nominates the chair of the Council of Ministers (prime minister), who must be confirmed (and can ultimately be dismissed) by the National Assembly. The assembly, popularly elected for a four-year term, is a unicameral body of 240 members, who may not concurrently hold ministerial office. The highest judicial organs are a Supreme Court of Cassation, which oversees application of the law by lower courts, and a Supreme Administrative Court, which rules on the legality of acts by government organs. There is also a Constitutional Court that interprets the basic law and rules on the constitutionality of legislation and decrees. At the local level Bulgaria encompasses 28 administrative regions, each headed by a governor appointed by the Council of Ministers. There are nearly 300 elected municipal councils, each of which appoints a mayor as chief administrative officer for the duration of its four-year term.

The National Assembly may amend the constitution by the casting of majorities of 75 percent on three separate days. On September 24, 2003, the assembly passed the first constitutional amendments to the 1991 constitution, giving life tenure to magistrates and granting them immunity against charges except in cases of criminal misconduct or abuse of office. (The changes were part of a broader effort to harmonize the legal system with EU standards.)

Foreign relations. A longtime Bulgarian alignment with the Soviet Union in foreign policy reflected not only the two countries' economic and ideological ties, but also traditional ties stemming from Russian assistance in Bulgarian independence struggles. In January 1977 Bulgaria's network of relations with West European governments was completed by an exchange of ambassadors with post-Franco Spain. Ties between Bulgaria and the Vatican, broken in 1949, were restored in December 1990, despite allegations of involvement by the (then) hard-line communist regime in an attempt on the pope's life in 1981.

Bulgarian-Turkish relations have fluctuated. Following the establishment of the communist regime in 1947, 150,000 ethnic Turks emigrated in 1950–1951 and 100,000 more in 1968–1978. Subsequent efforts toward assimilation of those that remained (including the forced adoption of Bulgarian names) generated pronounced tension with Ankara. Bulgaria emphatically rejected all "Turkish accusations" in the matter, calling the Bulgarian Turks "a fictitious minority" and claiming that the name changes were merely those of Bulgarians voluntarily reversing a process mandated during Ottoman rule.

In May 1989, following a series of clashes between ethnic protestors and security police in the Islamic border region, a large number of Bulgarian Muslims took advantage of newly issued passports to cross into Turkey. However, in August Ankara closed the border to stem an influx that had exceeded 310,000. In late December, following the downfall of the Zhivkov regime, National Assembly Chair Stenko TODOROV told a group of Turkish demonstrators in Sofia that henceforth "everybody in Bulgaria [would] be able to choose his name, religion, and language freely."

In October 1991 the Bulgarian and Greek prime ministers signed a 20-year friendship treaty, with Greece offering support for its neighbor's application to join the European Community (EC, subsequently the EU). However, relations with Greece cooled in January 1992, following the inclusion of Macedonia in the former Yugoslav republics to which Bulgaria accorded recognition. Greece, which had long refused to acknowledge a separate Macedonian nationality (whereas Bulgaria had traditionally contended that all Macedonians were ethnically Bulgarians), responded by appealing to its EC partners to limit or halt aid to Bulgaria. In a related vein, Bulgaria entered into a 10-year friendship and cooperation treaty with the Russian Federation later in the year during a visit to Sofia by President Yeltsin (who two days later confirmed Moscow's recognition of Macedonia).

In March 1993 Bulgaria completed negotiations on an association agreement with the EU and the same month signed a free trade agreement with the European Free Trade Association (EFTA). In February 1994 it became a signatory of NATO's Partnership for Peace, and in May it was one of nine East European states to become an "associate partner" of the Western European Union (WEU). Meanwhile, an exchange of high-level visits with Russia in September 1995 confirmed the stability of bilateral relations, although a reference by President Yeltsin in March 1996 to the possibility of Bulgaria joining an economic union of the former Soviet bloc sparked a furor in Sofia, with the Videnov government denying allegations by President Zhelev that it had held clandestine talks with Moscow.

In February 1997 the caretaker government of Stefan Sofianski announced its intention to seek full membership for Bulgaria in NATO. That position was reaffirmed by incoming Prime Minister Kostov in April, when he also said Bulgaria would seek EU membership. Although NATO did not include Bulgaria in the "first wave" of new members approved in June, the alliance subsequently indicated that Bulgaria was a "strong contender" for the next round of expansion. Meanwhile, Bulgaria was also left off the EU's "fast track" membership list approved in 1997; however, EU officials said it was only a matter of "when" and not "if" Bulgaria would eventually join, assuming continued economic reform on the part of the government. In January 1999 Bulgaria became a member of the Central European Free Trade Agreement (CEFTA, see Foreign relations in article on Poland).

In February 1999 Bulgaria appeared to have resolved its last major outstanding regional dispute when it reached agreement with Macedonia concerning the language to be used in bilateral accords. A number of agreements had been held up for six years because of Bulgaria's insistence that Macedonian was a dialect of Bulgarian and not a language in its own right. (The issue reflected deeper concerns regarding the status of self-described Macedonians in Bulgaria as well as the two countries' concern over each other's possible territorial claims). In an apparent easing of Bulgaria's stance, the 1999 accord authorized the use of the languages recognized by each country's constitution. Several bilateral accords were subsequently concluded, including one providing for military cooperation. Relations with Turkey were also described in early 1999 as greatly improved, border demarcation issues having been resolved and the Turkish business sector having found significant investment opportunities in the vastly improved Bulgarian economy.

Early in 2000 Bulgaria began formal accession talks with the EU, but it remained a "second tier" prospect. In May the National Assembly approved a resolution, 189–3, to pursue membership in the EU as well as NATO.

At NATO's Prague Summit in November 2002, Bulgaria was one of seven Central and Eastern European states invited to join the alliance. As part of its preaccession protocols (signed in May 2003), Bulgaria subsequently enacted a series of military reforms. The National Assembly formally endorsed NATO accession by a vote of 226–4 on March 18, 2004, and Bulgaria joined the alliance on March 29.

Perhaps in consonance with the NATO developments, the Saksko-burggotski government supported the U.S.-led invasion of Iraq in 2003. In return, the United States provided guarantees on the repayment of Iraq's foreign debt to Bulgaria (these payments had been suspended since 1990). After the fall of the regime of Saddam Hussein, Bulgaria deployed one of the largest contingents in the U.S.-led coalition (some 500 troops, the last elements withdrawn in December 2008).

On the other major international front, Bulgaria completed the final "chapters" in negotiations toward EU accession in late 2004, and in April 2005 a treaty was signed whereby it was envisioned that Bulgaria would become a member of the EU as of January 1, 2007. However, that date was contingent on Bulgaria making promised reforms designed to combat corruption (and collateral organized crime), address lingering human rights concerns (particularly regarding minorities), and continue its progress toward meeting the EU's economic criteria. (See Current issues, below, for information on Bulgaria's subsequent accession to the EU.)

Allegations arose in 2005 that secret U.S. prisons had operated in Bulgaria and that Bulgaria had permitted use of its airports by U.S. planes transferring prisoners to other undisclosed locations as part of the controversial U.S. "rendition" program. However, Bulgarian officials denied the allegations, although in 2006 Bulgaria announced an agreement under which U.S. forces would be allowed to use several military airfields and bases in Bulgaria for at least the next ten years. It was also reported that NATO bases in Bulgaria had been authorized for use in any potential NATO operations in the Caucasus region.

One of the more perplexing issues in Bulgarian foreign policy was resolved in July 2007 when six Bulgarian nurses were expatriated to Bulgaria from Libya. The nurses had been sentenced to death on charges of having deliberately infected Libyan children with HIV in 1999. (The Libyan government alleged that the children had been infected in a botched effort to discover a cure for AIDS, while the nurses insisted the children had arrived in their care already infected.) The EU, with particular involvement by French President Nicolas Sarkozy, played an instrumental role in negotiating the commutation of the sentence to life imprisonment, to be served in Bulgaria (the government of which pardoned the nurses upon their arrival.)

In March 2009 Bulgaria increased its contribution toward the NATO mission in Afghanistan to 820 soldiers..

Current issues. The NDST had fallen sharply in public opinion polls leading up to the 2005 assembly elections, despite having scored significant successes with the country's accession to NATO in 2004 and progress toward EU accession. Among other things, the NDST-led government was apparently widely perceived as having been ineffective in combating corruption and organized crime. In addition, average Bulgarians reportedly were disappointed that the "prosperity" promised through the implementation of IMF reforms had failed to trickle down to needy segments of the population such as pensioners. The administration also faced the penchant of Bulgarian voters to force change at every election (no post-Communist government has been reelected). Consequently, the assembly campaign was tumultuous, particularly after the emergence of *Ataka,* an extreme right-wing grouping with populist overtones. (*Ataka* campaigned on an antiminority/antiimmigrant platform that also proposed severing ties with NATO, the EU, and the IMF.)

Seven coalitions or parties (including *Ataka*) secured seats in the June 2005 assembly poll, making for the "most fragmented" legislature in history. Not surprisingly, it proved difficult for the BSP-led KzB to form a new government. The NDST rejected initial overtures from the KzB, insisting that Sakskoburggotski should remain as prime minister. The KzB subsequently proposed a minority government with the DPS, but the assembly rejected that concept. As international pressure for a resolution grew amid concern that Bulgaria's proposed EU accession was being threatened by the instability, the NDST eventually agreed to join the KzB and DPS in a cabinet led by the BSP's young (38 years old), "reform-minded" leader, Sergei Stanishev. The new administration immediately announced that maintaining the EU accession schedule was its top priority, although most observers agreed that little progress had been achieved by mid-2006 regarding judicial reform, corruption, and organized crime

President Parvanov's reelection in October 2006 was considered a triumph for pro-EU forces, although analysts noted that no strong center-right candidate had emerged and that low voter turnout probably indicated continued popular discontent over "unfulfilled promises of improved living conditions." EU officials subsequently criticized Bulgaria for myriad problems, including unacceptable farm and food-processing standards, poor aviation controls, inadequate money-laundering policies, and ineffective governmental administration in general, the latter raising concerns over whether the necessary structures were in place for distribution of upcoming EU aid. However, noting the country's recent economic progress and announcing it did not want to discourage reformers by delaying accession, the EU in September declared that Bulgaria, as well as Romania, which was facing similar problems, would be admitted as scheduled on January 1, 2007, even though some members of the European Parliament bluntly described Bulgaria as "not ready."

EU accession was reportedly met with "relief" on the part of the Bulgarian government and appeared broadly welcomed by the populace, despite populist sentiment against certain accession standards (such as the closure of two reactors at the Kozloduy nuclear power facility). However, the EU imposed stringent safeguards in connection with the accession, announcing that EU assistance to Bulgaria (estimated at nearly $900 million for the first year) might be withheld unless quick progress was made in combating corruption and organized crime. The EU also warned that Bulgarian court rulings might not be accepted throughout the union unless Bulgaria adopted wide-ranging police, prosecutorial, and judicial reforms. In addition, some EU countries quickly imposed restrictions on the number of immigrant workers they would accept from Bulgaria. Although Prime Minister Stanishev announced that the "modernization" of Bulgaria in many aspects would be his administration's priority, in May 2008 the EU froze funds allocated for infrastructure projects in Bulgaria. In addition, over $300 million in EU development funding was withdrawn in November.

Frustration with the existing political parties (perceived as ineffective in combating corruption and organized crime) was a major issue in the dramatic July 2009 assembly balloting, in which the BSP produced its worst performance since 1989, the NDSV (as the NDST had been renamed) collapsed completely by failing to win any seats, and the SDS continued to decline. Meanwhile, the new GERB, a center-right anti-corruption party led by the popular mayor of Sofia, Boiko Borisov, soared to a near legislative majority. Other contributing factors in GERB's ascendance were the recent economic contraction (after several years of high growth) and scandals involving Ahmed DOGAN, the leader of the DPS (see DPS, below under Political Parties, for details). Analysts concluded that anger over Dogan influenced a higher than expected turnout (60 percent) as non-Turkish voters punished the parties (the BSP and NDSV) that had granted the DPS key roles in recent governments.

Upon assuming the premiership, Borisov announced that his administration's priorities would be to make Bulgaria "worthy" of its EU status, expand cooperation with NATO, pursue judicial reform, and initiate intensified anticorruption measures. However, skeptics warned that the "gentlemen's agreement" for legislative support for GERB from the SK, RZS, and *Ataka* (whose major bond appeared to be dislike of the BSP) could prove fragile if the new government failed to produce quick results.

POLITICAL PARTIES

Prior to the political upheaval of late 1989, Bulgaria's only authorized political parties were the Bulgarian Communist Party (BKP) and the Bulgarian Agrarian National Union (*Balgarski Zemedelski Naroden Sayuz*—BZNS), which formed the core of the Fatherland Front (*Otechestven Front*), a communist-controlled mass organization that also included the trade unions, the communist youth movement, and individual citizens. In the wake of the ouster of longtime BKP leader Todor Zhivkov in 1989, a large number of opposition groups surfaced, while the BKP changed its name to the Bulgarian Socialist Party (BSP). Since then, parties and coalitions have proliferated. By 2004 there were some 80 registered parties, and a new electoral law was approved prior to the 2005 assembly poll with the intent of reducing the number of small parties. Among other things, parties were required to provide signatures of support from at least 5,000 people. Financial deposits were also required of any party presenting legislative candidates, with the deposits being returned only if the party secured more than 1 percent of the national vote. As a result, although 42 parties or coalitions had participated in the 2001 assembly balloting, their number fell to 22 in 2005 and 20 in 2009.

Government and Government-Supportive Parties:

Citizens for European Development of Bulgaria (*Grazhdani za Evropeisko Razvitie Balgariya*—GERB). Initially formed as a nonprofit association in early 2006, GERB officially registered as a party in December with the intention of uniting other center-right parties and organizations. Boiko Borisov, the popular mayor of Sofia, was one of the group's founders. The party's platform focused on combating corruption and organized crime while supporting "civil liberties" and business-friendly economic policies. GERB showed significant strength by winning over 21 percent and 24 percent of the vote in the 2007 and 2009 European Parliament elections, respectively. The party's success in casting itself as an alternative to the political establishment culminated in its plurality victory (116 seats and 43 percent of the national vote) in the July 2009 assembly balloting, following which Borisov formed a GERB government.

Leaders: Boiko BORISOV (Prime Minister), Tsvetan TSVETANOV (Chair).

Order, Law and Justice (*Red, Zakonnost, i Spravedlivost*—RZS). The center-right RZS was founded in opposition to the BSP-led government in December 2005 by dissidents from the BZNS-NS (see ZNS, below). Among other things, the new party called for intensified anticorruption measures. In the first round of the 2006 presidential balloting, RZS candidate (and former constitutional judge) Georgi MARKOV received 2.7 percent of the vote.

The RZS won ten seats (on a vote share of 4.8 percent nationwide) in the July 2009 assembly elections and subsequently pledged at least six months of "unconditional" support for the new GERB government.

Leaders: Yane YANEV (chair); Georgi MARKOV.

Blue Coalition (*Sinyata Koalitsiya*—SK). Established prior to the 2009 European Parliament and national parliamentary elections, the SK is a successor (in part, at least) to the SDS-led United Democratic Forces (*Obedineni Demokratichni Sili*—ODS), the "anti-Communist," primarily center-right formation that was launched by a number of groups opposed to the BSP-led government elected in 1994. In an unusual procedure, the ODS conducted a primary in June 1996 to determine its presidential candidate, the two contenders being Petar Stoyanov of the SDS and incumbent President Zhelyu Zhelev, the nominee of the People's Union (*Naroden Sayuz*—NS), an alliance of the BZNS-NS and the DP. (The NS had secured 18 seats on a vote share of 6.5 percent in the 1994 assembly elections.) Stoyanov easily defeated Zhelev and went on to victory in the November national election. As configured for the presidential balloting, the ODS included not only the SDS and the NS but also the Movement for Rights and Freedom (DPS, below). The DPS, however, opted out of the coalition for the April 1997 legislative balloting, in which the ODS won a majority of 137 assembly seats and presented Ivan Kostov of the SDS as the next prime minister. The reconfigured ODS won only 51 seats on an 18.2 percent vote share in the June 2001 election, prompting Kostov's resignation. For the November 2001 presidential election, Stoyanov chose to run as an independent, although he received the ODS's endorsement.

The ODS subsequently suffered severe factionalization, most notably when Kostov and his supporters left the SDS in February 2004 to form the DSB (below). In addition, the NS left the ODS in March 2004 to form its own legislative grouping, claiming 11 seats. The ODS fell to 20 seats on a 7.7 percent vote share in the 2005 assembly poll, when its components were the SDS, DP, DG, and the small **National Democratic Party** (*Natsionalna Demokraicheska Partiya*—NDP).

The ODS was transformed into the SK for the 2009 elections, the most important change being the inclusion of the DSB. The coalition was initially buffeted by problems in registering with the electoral commission (later resolved) due to ongoing leadership conflicts within the SDS. Campaigning on an anticorruption, progrowth platform, the SK won 15 seats (on a nationwide vote share of 7.2 percent) in the July 2009 assembly elections and subsequently pledged to support (at least temporarily) the new GERB government, based on what SK leaders called "coinciding goals" and antipathy toward the BSP.

Leader: Petar STOYANOV.

Union of Democratic Forces (*Sayuz na Demokratichnite Sili*—SDS). The SDS was launched in late 1989 as a loose opposition coalition of intellectual, environmental, trade union, and other groups. Chaired by Zhelyu Zhelev (a dissident philosophy professor of the Zhivkov era), the SDS entered into talks with the government and negotiated arrangements for multiparty elections in June 1990, which were won by the BSP. Nevertheless, the new assembly elected Zhelev as president of Bulgaria in August 1990, while SDS opposition forced the resignation of the BSP government in November and its replacement by a coalition that included SDS members.

Dissension between moderate and radical elements resulted in the presentation of three distinct SDS lists in the election of October 1991: the main SDS-Movement, the SDS-Centre, and the SDS-Liberals. The outcome was a narrow plurality for the main SDS, which won 110 of the 240 seats and 34.4 percent of the vote, with neither of the other SDS lists gaining representation. The main SDS proceeded to form Bulgaria's first wholly noncommunist government since World War II, headed by Filip Dimitrov, with the external support of the ethnic Turkish DPS. In direct presidential elections in January 1992, Zhelev secured a popular mandate, winning 53 percent of the second-round vote. However, serious strains quickly developed between the president and Prime Minister Dimitrov, while the SDS assembly group became racked with dissent. The government fell in October 1992 and was replaced by a nonparty administration under Lyuben Berov, with the support of some 20 SDS dissidents.

Seen as increasingly conservative, the anti-Berov SDS in mid-1993 mounted demonstrations against President Zhelev for his alleged backing of "recommunization," but defections of left-inclined deputies reduced SDS assembly strength to below that of the BSP by early 1994. In June the remaining SDS deputies launched a boycott of the assembly, prompting the resignation of the Berov government in September. However, an assembly poll in December resulted in defeat for the grouping, which moved quickly to install

Ivan Kostov (a former finance minister) as its new leader on December 29, 1994. With 69 of the 240 assembly seats, it formed the principal opposition to the BSP-led government.

The SDS led the protests against the BSP in early 1997, finally forcing the calling of early elections. In preparation for the April balloting, an SDS conference in February 1997 approved the reformation of the coalition into a political party. (For a list of the members of the SDS prior to its establishment as a single party, see the 1997 *Handbook.*) Following the electoral loss of June 2001, Ivan Kostov resigned as party chair and was replaced by a former chief secretary, Ekaterina MIKHAILOVA. Although regarded as a "natural partner" by the NDST, the SDS declined to join the Sakskoburggotski government, at least in part because it objected to inclusion of an ethnic formation, the DPS. Nadezhda Mikhailova, the ODS parliamentary leader, was elected chair at the March 2002 SDS congress.

In 2004 the SDS was divided by a leadership struggle between Kostov and Nadezhda Mikhailova. At a January 2004 meeting, Mikhailova was reelected as party leader, prompting Kostov and a group of 26 SDS legislators to leave the SDS on February 23 (see DSB, below). The SDS was therefore left with only 14 legislative seats. In October 2005 Mikhailova was defeated in her bid to retain the SDS leadership by Petar Stoyanov, the former president of Bulgaria. Following the party's poor performance (no seats) in the 2007 balloting for the European Parliament, Plamen YUROKOV was elected SDS chair. Yurokov was in turn succeeded in late 2008 by Martin Dimitrov, whose close relationship with the DSB's Ivan Kostov reportedly caused dissent within the SDS. (Yurokov was one of the opponents of ties with the DSB.)

Leaders: Martin DIMITROV (Chair), Nadezhda MIKHAILOVA (Former Chair), Yordan BAKALOV (ODS Parliamentary Leader)

Democrats for a Strong Bulgaria (*Demokrati za Silna Balgariya*—DSB). Dissatisfaction with the leadership of the SDS prompted party leader and former prime minister, Ivan Kostov, and SDS Deputy Chair Ekaterina Mikhailova to quit the SDS and form the DSB in February 2004. Twenty-six deputies left the SDS to help launch the DSB. Campaigning on a strongly "anti-communist" (and thereby anti-BSP) platform, the center-right DSB won 17 seats on a 6.4 percent vote share in the 2005 assembly elections. Facing a drop in the polls following the 2005 assembly elections, the DSB joined the SDS and others in the SK for the 2009 assembly elections.

Leaders: Ivan KOSTOV (Chair and Former Prime Minister), Ekaterina MIKHAILOVA (Deputy Chair).

Bulgarian Social Democratic Party (*Balgarska Sotsialdemokraticheska Partiya*—BSDP). A member of the Socialist International, the BSDP traces its descent from the historic party founded in 1891 and more especially from the secession of its nonrevolutionary wing in 1903. Left-wing Social Democrats participated in the Communist-led Fatherland Front that came to power in 1944, the BSDP being merged with the Communist Party in 1948. Over the next four decades exiles kept the party alive as the Socialist Party, which was reestablished in Bulgaria in 1989 under the leadership of Petar DERTLIEV, a veteran of the pre-1948 era. In March 1990 the party reinstated the BSDP title in view of the imminent decision of the Communist Party to rename itself the BSP. As a component of the SDS, the BSDP took 29 seats in the June 1990 assembly election. The following month Dertliev was the initial SDS candidate for the presidency, but he subsequently withdrew in favor of Zhelyu Zhelev.

The BSDP supported the decision of some SDS elements to enter a BSP-dominated coalition government in December 1990 but thereafter came into conflict with the promarket policies of the SDS leadership, arguing that privatized industries should become cooperatives where possible. In the October 1991 assembly election the BSDP headed a separate SDS-Centre list, which failed to surmount the 4 percent barrier. The BSDP backed Zhelev's successful candidacy in the January 1992 direct presidential balloting and thereafter sided with the president against the SDS minority government. From March 1993, seeking to establish a credible third force between the BSP and an SDS seen as moving to the right, the BSD launched a series of center-left alliances, culminating in the **Democratic Alternative for the Republic** (*Demokratichna Alternativa za Republikata*—DAR). The BSDP, however, joined the SDS-led ODS for the April 1997 legislative balloting, although only 1 of the 137 successful ODS candidates belonged to the BSDP.

Late in 1998 the BSDP split, and Petar Dertliev led a wing of the party into the opposition. That group joined the United Labor Bloc (OBT) in establishing a Social Democratic Union (Balgarska Sotsialdemokraticheska Sayuz—BSDS) in preparation for the 1999 local elections. Dertliev died in November 2000.

In the 2001 legislative election the Social Democrats remained fractured. One of the principal branches renegotiated its standing within the ODS, the former Dertliev wing joined the KzB, and another "united group" participated in the coalition led by the BEL (below). The claim to status as the "legitimate" BSDP remained contentious prior to the 2005 assembly balloting, with a faction led by Petar AGOV running as part of the KzB and a faction led by Yordan NIHRIZOV reportedly participating in the ODS. (Some reports indicated that Nihrizov's supporters had earned the "official" right to the BSDP rubric in 1997, with Agov's supporters subsequently sometimes being referred to as the Party of the Bulgarian Social Democrats (PBS, see below.) Both Agov and Nihrizov won seats in the 2005 assembly elections.

United Agrarians (*Obedineni Zemedeltsi*—OZ). The OZ was founded in 2008 after a split within the BZNS-NS (see ZNS, below).

Leader: Anastasia DIMITROVA-MOSER (Chair).

Radical Democratic Party (*Radikaldemokraticheska Partiya*—RP). A historic Bulgarian liberal party of the early 20th century, the RP was reestablished in 1989.

National Union Attack (*Natsionalno Obedinenie Ataka*). The "ultra-nationalistic" *Ataka* was formed under the leadership of controversial television journalist Volen Siderov in April 2005 by several movements and parties that opposed NATO, EU, and IMF membership for Bulgaria. *Ataka* also demanded the abolition of the DPS (the leading ethnic Turkish party) for being "unconstitutional." This, along with Siderov's controversial writings on alleged conspiracies within Freemasonry and Judaism, contributed to the broad perception of *Ataka* as a right-wing, antiminority formation. (One of the group's slogans was "Bulgaria for the Bulgarians.") *Ataka* also opposed the participation of Bulgarian troops in the U.S.-led operation in Iraq and demanded that the sale of Bulgarian lands to foreigners be banned. Surprising most observers (many of whom condemned *Ataka*'s leadership for engaging in "hate speech"), *Ataka* finished fourth in the June 2005 assembly poll, securing 21 seats on an 8 percent vote share. *Ataka*'s surge continued in the 2006 presidential race, in which Siderov garnered 21 percent and 24 percent of the vote in the first and second rounds, respectively. Siderov's campaign again targeted the Muslim and Roma minorities, earning him a "racist" label. However, he also reportedly attracted support for "populist" rhetoric that criticized recent government cutbacks and economic reform, notably the privatization of state-run enterprises. *Ataka* won 2 seats in the 2009 European Parliament balloting and finished fourth in the 2009 assembly poll with 21 seats (10 percent of the votes nationwide). Siderov subsequently announced that *Ataka* would support the new GERB government, at least temporarily.

Leader: Volen SIDEROV (President and 2006 presidential candidate).

Opposition Parties:

Coalition for Bulgaria (*Koalitsiya za Balgariya*—KzB). Established in preparation for the 2001 legislative election, the KzB was the descendant of the BSP-led but less inclusive Democratic Left (*Demokratichna Levitsa*—DL). The DL had been formed prior to the 1996 presidential election by the BSP, the Ecoglasnost Political Club (PKE), and the BZNS-AS (see below), which had contested the 1994 legislative election in alliance and had then formed the subsequent government under the BSP's Videnov. The three-party coalition saw its representation fall from 125 seats in 1994 to 58 in 1998. In May 2000 the PKE left the DL.

In November 2000 the parliamentary delegations of the BSP, the BSDP, the OBT, and the PDSD announced a cooperative agreement that led in January 2001 to formal establishment of a New Left political program. On January 25 the formation was announced of the more encompassing KzB, which won 48 seats in the 2001 assembly balloting. At that time its membership comprised the BSP, at least one faction of the BZNS-AS, the BSDP, PDSD, KPB, the United Labor Bloc (OBT), and the Alliance for Social Liberal Progress (*Alians za Sotsialliberalen Progress*—ASLP). However, the OBT left the KzB for the Coalition of the Rose in early 2005, and there were no reports concerning the ASLP as far as the 2005 KzB structure was concerned. The KzB (then comprising the BSP, BZNS-AS, BSDP, PDSD, KPB, ZPB, DSH, and the Roma Party) won 82 seats in the 2005 assembly elections on a 31 percent vote share, having campaigned on a platform pledging, among other things, to promote higher wages and additional jobs for Bulgarian workers.

In the 2009 assembly balloting, the KzB, incorporating the six parties below, won 40 seats (on a nationwide vote share of 19 percent), losing more than half of the seats it had won in 2005. The KzB subsequently announced it would serve as "strong opposition" to the new GERB government.

Leaders: Sergei STANISHEV (Former Prime Minister), Angel NAYDENOV (Former Parliamentary Leader).

Bulgarian Socialist Party (*Balgarska Sotsialisticheska Partiya*—BSP). The BSP resulted from a change of name by the Bulgarian Communist Party (*Balgarska Komunisticheska Partiya*—BKP) on April 3, 1990. The BKP traced its origins to an ideological split in the old Social Democratic Party, the dissidents withdrawing in 1903 to form the Bulgarian Workers' Social Democratic Party, which became the Communist Party in 1919. Banned in 1924, the party came to power in 1944 in the wake of the Red Army's military success and, in coalition with other "progressive" forces, took full control from 1946. Todor Zhivkov became leader in 1954, maintaining a rigid pro-Soviet orthodoxy almost until his ouster in November 1989. The BKP's "leading role" in state and society was terminated on January 1990, when an extraordinary party congress renounced "democratic centralism," restructured its leadership bodies, and endorsed "human and democratic socialism" in the context of a "socially oriented market economy."

As the BSP, the party retained a legislative majority at multiparty elections in June 1990, but in December it accepted a coalition under the premiership of the opposition SDS. At a new poll in October 1991 a BSP-led alliance was narrowly defeated by the SDS, the BSP thus going into opposition for the first time since 1944. In a leadership contest at a BSP congress in December, Zhan Videnov, advocate of a "modern left-socialist party," easily defeated a reformist social democratic opponent. In December 1992 most BSP deputies backed the formation of the nonparty Berov government, under which the party reasserted its influence. In further elections in December 1994, the BSP, joined by the PKE and the BZNS-AS, won an overall assembly majority, with 43.5 percent of the vote.

A major national financial crisis in May 1996 accentuated underlying divisions within the coalition, with the two smaller partners threatening to leave the government unless personnel changes were made. Within the BSP a powerful conservative wing attached the blame to the Videnov modernizers and to over-hasty economic liberalization, whereas the Videnov supporters cited entrenched Soviet-era personnel and attitudes. Seeking to occupy the middle ground in the controversy, Videnov also came under attack from the BSP right-wing, organized as the Association for Social Democracy.

When Videnov resigned from the premiership in December 1996, he also relinquished his role as party chair, an extraordinary BSP congress subsequently selecting Deputy Chair Georgi Parvanov as his successor. Although new elections were also held for the BSP Supreme Council and its 15-member Executive Board, hard-liners continued to dominate both bodies. They insisted on trying to exercise the BSP's right to choose a new prime minister, despite massive public demonstrations in support of installation of an interim government pending early elections (see Political background, above). However, the prime minister-designate, Interior Minister Nikolai Dobrev, finally capitulated in early February 1997 to pressure for the BSP to relinquish its mandate, his decision to go against the party hard-liners being widely praised domestically and internationally as preventing further severe political conflict and possibly even civil war.

Following the Democratic Left's poor showing in the April 1998 legislative balloting, the BSP leadership announced it would support the new ODS government's economic reform policies but would oppose the Bulgarian bid for NATO membership. Continued friction was subsequently reported between Parvanov's moderate camp and party hard-liners, the latter enjoying the support of the large number of pensioners and veterans in the BSP. In May 2000 Parvanov, now backing integration into NATO, was easily reelected chair, although the party's electoral defeat in June 2001 led a faction headed by the former parliamentary chair, Krasimir PREMYANOV, to call for Parvanov's resignation. The Sakskoburggotski cabinet of July 2001 included two members of the BSP (later reduced to one), but the party itself remained outside the government, choosing to abstain during the July 24 confirmation vote in the National Assembly.

Designated on September 30, 2001, as the BSP presidential candidate, Parvanov won in second-round balloting in November, after which he resigned from the party in the interest of national unity. He was succeeded as BSP leader by Sergei Stanishev, who was named prime minister following the 2005 assembly poll, the BSP having embraced "Euro-style socialism" and having for the most part removed hard-line communists from influential party positions.

Leaders: Sergei STANISHEV (Chair and Former Prime Minister), Georgi PIRINSKI, Rumen Stoyanov OVCHAROV.

Bulgarian Agrarian National Union "Aleksandur Stamboliyski" (*Balgarski Zemedelski Naroden Sayuz "Aleksandar Stamboliyski"*—BZNS-AS). The BZNS-AS is one of several current groups claiming direct descent from the historic BZNS that had been founded in 1899. The BZNS's most prominent leader, Aleksandur Stamboliyski, was an Agrarian prime minister killed in a right-wing coup in 1923. After World War II, a pro-communist rump BZNS was allowed pro forma assembly and government representation as part of the Fatherland Front, usually holding the agriculture portfolio. Asserting its independence as communism began to crumble, the BZNS replaced longtime leader Petur TANCHEV in November 1989 and refused to join the Lukanov government of February 1990. Nevertheless, the anti-Communist BZNS-Nikola Petkov faction broke away to join the opposition SDS.

The rump BZNS won 16 assembly seats in June 1990 but lost them all in October 1991. A complex sequence of abortive unity schemes and further splits ensued in Agrarian ranks, one outcome being the creation of the BZNS-AS, which contested the 1994 elections in alliance with the victorious BSP. The BZNS-AS also participated in the Democratic Left for the 1996 presidential balloting.

It was reported that an "1899" faction of the BZNS-AS, led by Dragmir SHOPOV, participated in the KzB for the 2001 assembly elections. However, reports about the 2005 assembly balloting indicated no participation by the 1899 faction, with the KzB apparently claiming the support of the BZNS-AS faction led by Svetoslav Stoyanov SHIVAROV.

Party of Bulgarian Social Democrats (*Partiya Balgarski Sotsialdemokrati*—PBS). The PBS claims descent from the 19th-century Bulgarian Socialist party of the same name and is considered an offshoot of the BSDP.

Leader: Georgi ANASTASOV

Communist Party of Bulgaria (*Komunisticheska Partiya na Balgariya*—KPB). The KPB, established in 1997, supported EU accession and a mixed economy.

Leader: Aleksandur PAUNOV (First Secretary).

Movement for Social Humanism (*Dvizhenie za Sotsialen Humanizam*—DSH). The DSH was launched in 1995 by BSDP dissidents.

Leader: Alexander RADOSLAVOV.

Roma Party (*Roma Partiya*). This grouping was launched in March 2001 by some nine nonparty Roma advocacy groups and three parties.

Leader: Toma TOMOV.

Movement for Rights and Freedoms (*Dvizhenie za Prava i Svobodi*—DPS). Representing the Turkish minority, the DPS won 23 assembly seats in June 1990. It became the swing party in October 1991 by winning 24 seats and in late 1992 played a crucial role in the ouster of the SDS government and the advent of the nonparty Berov administration. The DPS was weakened in 1993 by defections and splits as well as by the emigration to Turkey of many of its supporters, and its representation fell to 15 seats on a 5.4 percent vote share in December 1994. However, the DPS polled strongly in ethnic Turkish areas in local elections in October–November 1995, winning 26 mayoralties. In 1996 the DPS participated in the ODS in support of the presidential candidacy of Petar Stoyanov.

A split was reported in the DPS in early 1997 over the decision by Ahmed Dogan not to remain aligned with the ODS for the April legislative balloting and instead to form a broad Alliance for National Salvation (*Obedinenie za Natsionalno Spasenie*—ONS). As configured for the 1997 legislative balloting, the ONS also included an ideologically incongruous mix of small liberal centrist, environmental, and monarchist parties. The ONS nevertheless secured 19 seats in the 1997 balloting, as compared to 15 for the DPS in 1994. The ONS broadly supported the ODS government for most of the rest of the year before the DPS in December charged Prime Minister Kostov with pursuing "populist measures, rather than reforms."

In preparation for the 1999 local elections the DPS helped establish the Liberal Democratic Union (see Liberal Union in the 2007 *Handbook*). Following the 2001 legislative election, a dispute between Dogan and former deputy chair Osman Oktay over party direction threatened a split in the DPS, which had been invited to join the Sakskoburggotski government as a junior partner. In July 2003 several members of the DPS (including Oktay) who were reportedly disillusioned with the party's leadership helped to launch a new party, the Democratic Wing Movement (see Coalition of the Rose, below).

For the 2001 assembly elections, the DPS led a coalition that also included the Liberal Union (*Liberalen Sayuz*—LS; see the 2007 *Handbook*) and Euroroma (see below); the coalition won 21 seats. In 2005 the DPS, running on its own, secured 34 seats on a vote share of 13 percent.

In 2009 statements by Dogan ignited controversy and populist anger among ethnic Bulgarian voters. Among other things, Dogan had allegedly described himself as a "king-maker" in past coalition governments and alluded to his extensive authority in the dispersal of government funds. He also reportedly said that he had possessed the power in the past to stir ethnic conflict in Bulgaria but had held his hand. The DPS also suffered from perception that the party was involved in government corruption scandals, many circulating around the ministry of agriculture. Some domestic analysts accordingly suggested that "anti-Doganism" was an important factor in the decline of its government partners (the KzB and the NDSV) in the 2009 assembly elections, although the DPS, maintaining its base within the Turkish population, itself placed third, winning 38 seats (up from 34 in 2005) with a vote share of 14.5 percent nationwide.

Leaders: Ahmed DOGAN (President, Parliamentary Leader), Kasim DAL, Remzi OSMAN.

Other Parties and Coalitions Participating in the 2009 Legislative Elections:

Liberal Initiative for Democratic European Development (*Liberalna Initsiativa za Demokratichno Evropeisko Razvitie*—LIDER). A conservative, probusiness party, LIDER, roughly translated as "Leader," was founded in 2007 by energy magnate Hristo Kovachki. (The short form of the party's name is universally used by the Bulgarian media and election officials.) After nearly winning a European Parliament seat in the June 2009 elections with almost 6 percent of the vote, LIDER joined with the NV in an electoral coalition (named LIDER) for the July assembly balloting. The coalition, however, won only 3 percent of the vote nationwide and therefore no seats.

Leaders: Kancho FILIPOV (Chair), Mariya PIRGOVA (Vice Chair), Hristo KOVACHKI.

New Time (*Novoto Vreme*—NV). A center-right group, New Time was launched in March 2004 by 11 legislative deputies from the NDST to protest the perceived slow implementation of reforms and Prime Minister Sakskoburggotski's willingness to compromise with the socialist parties in the assembly.

Leaders: Miroslav SEVLIEVSKI, Emil KOSHLUKOV, Borislav TSEKOV.

National Movement for Stability and Progress (*Natsionalno Dvizhenie za Stabilnost i Vazhod*—NDSV). The NDSV is the recently adopted rubric for the National Movement Simeon II (*Natsionalno Dvizhenie Simeon Tvori*—NDST), which was formed in April 2001 by the former king, Simeon Saxe-Coburg-Gotha (an English translation of the family's original German name), a month after he had returned from exile in Spain. On April 28, however, the Supreme Court upheld an April 23 ruling by the Sofia City Court denying registration to the NDST party because it failed to meet legal requirements. In order to get on the ballot for the June National Assembly election, the former monarch's supporters quickly negotiated an arrangement with two small, officially sanctioned parties, the **Party of Bulgarian Women** (PBZh) and the **Movement for National Revival "Oborishte"** (which refers to the site of a 19th-century uprising against the Ottomans), whereby they agreed to contest the election as the NDST. Thus, the NDST was registered as a coalition by the Central Election Commission on May 2. In the June balloting, the formation won 120 seats and a 42.7 percent vote share, far outdistancing its opponents. Simeon II, who was not himself a parliamentary candidate, subsequently accepted the nomination as prime minister. (It was announced that the former king had adopted the common name Sakskoburggotski for the premiership. However, even government sources continued to refer to him regularly as Prime Minister Saxe-Coburg-Gotha or Prime Minister Saxe-Coburg, usages that also subsequently prevailed in news reports.)

The NDST was formally registered as a political party in April 2002, and the prime minister was elected as party leader after initially indicating he would not pursue that post in the interest of party unity.

Five NDST legislators had left the party in March 2002 to protest their leader's perceived failure to follow up on his campaign promises, while 11 others formed New Time (above) in 2004. The NDST fell to 53 seats (on a vote share of 20 percent) in the 2005 assembly elections. In June 2007, although Sakskoburggotski was reelected as party leader to deemphasize his role in the movement and broaden its appeal, the group formally changed its name to the NDSV, replacing "Simeon II" with "Stability and Progress." However, factionalization continued within the party, and 17 NDSV MPs quit the party in May 2008 to form a parliamentary faction called Bulgarian New Democracy (BND) under the leadership of former defense minister Nikolay SVINAROV and Borislav RALCHEV. The BND registered as a party and participated (unsuccessfully) on its own in the June 2009 European Parliament elections. It was subsequently reported that the BND was interested in joining the SK for the July assembly balloting; it appeared that formal linkage was not achieved, although BND leaders urged party members to vote for the SK. Meanwhile, the rump NDSV continued its precipitous decline by garnering only slightly more than 3 percent of the assembly vote nationwide, thereby failing to win any seats. Sakskoburggotski subsequently resigned as party leader.

Leaders: Milen VELCHEV, Marina DIKOVA, Nedelchev MOLLOV.

The Greens (*Zelenite*). Founded in May 2008, the Greens was established by a group of NGOs as a rival to the existing ZPB in support of "moral and ethical principles" relating to the environment, human rights, democracy, and economic life. The party placed ninth in the 2009 assembly elections with 0.5 percent of the vote nationwide.

Leaders: Denica PETROVA, Andrei KOVACHEV, Petko KOVACHE (Co-Chairs)

Euroroma (*Evroroma*). A "sociopolitical" organization formed to support the interests of the Roma minority throughout the region, Euroroma competed as a political party in the 2005 assembly balloting in Bulgaria, securing slightly more than 1 percent of the vote.

Leader: Vassil BOYANOV.

Political Movement "Social Democrats" (*Politichesko Dvizhenie "Sotsialdemokrati"*—PDSD). The PDSD was established in 2000 following a split within the Euroleft (BEL, below, under BSD) over the parent group's direction and leadership. The new formation pledged to advance social democratic interests as well as openness and accountability in government. It participated in the 2005 assembly elections as a member of the KzB.

Leader: Nikolay KAMOV.

Other parties and coalitions that competed unsuccessfully in the 2009 assembly elections included the **Coalition "For the Homeland"** (*Koalitsiya "Za Rodinata"*—KzR), a grouping of the **Democratic Civil Initiative** (*Demokratichna Grazhdanska Initsiativa*—DGI), led by Stefan PEEV, and **New Leaders** (*Novite Lideri*—NL), led by Ivanka ANGELOVE-MITEVA; the **Bulgarian Left Coalition** (*Balgarskata Lyava Koalitsiya*—BLK), a grouping of the **Bulgarian Left, Fatherland Party,** and **Party of Bulgarian Communists**; the **Union of the Patriotic Forces "Defense"** (*Sayuz na Patriotichnite Sili*

"Zashtita"—SPSZ), led by Yoli ABADZHIEV; the **Other Bulgaria** (*Drugata Balgariya*—DB), an emigrants' interests party led by Bozhidar TORNALEV; the **Party of the Liberal Alternative and Peace** (*Partiya na Liberalnata Alternativa i Mira*—PLAM), led by Nikolai NINOV; the **Union of the Bulgarian Patriots** (*Obedinenie na Bulgarskite Patrioti*—OBP), led by Yordan VELICHKOV; and the **National Movement for the Salvation of the Fatherland** (*Natsionalno Dvizhenie za Spasenie na Otechestvo*—NDSO), led by Todor RASHEV.

Other Parties:

Agrarian People's Union (*Zemedelski Naroden Sayuz*—ZNS). The ZNS was formed in 2006 as an offshoot of the Bulgarian Agrarian National Union–People's Union (*Balgarski Zemedelski Naroden Sayuz–Naroden Sayuz*—BZNS-NS). The BZNS-NS was one of several factions claiming descent from the BZNS, a major Bulgarian political party in the beginning of the 20th century that also held power briefly after World War I. Marginalized in power but still widely popular following the 1923 coup, the BZNS was subsequently co-opted into the Communist-led Fatherland Front, with much of its prewar leadership emigrating abroad.

Among the figures contesting for leadership of the BZNS after 1989 was Anastasia DIMITROVA-MOSER, the daughter of G. M. DIMITROV, a prewar Agrarian leader who had emigrated to the United States after World War II. Dimitrova-Moser became leader of the BZNS-Nikola Petkov (named after an Agrarian leader who was executed in 1947) in February 1992. The Petkov group was then a member of the SDS, but the latter became increasingly divided after it lost power in December 1992, with the result that Dimitrova-Moser led a section of the BZNS-NS into a separate alliance with the DP. The BZNS-NS launched the NS coalition with the DP in 1994 and participated in the ODS in the 1997 and 2001 assembly polls before serving as the core component of the **Bulgarian People's Union** (*Balgarski Naroden Sayuz*—BNS) for the 2005 legislative elections. The BNS, a center-right grouping that also included the VMRO (below) and the **Union of Free Democrats** (*Sayuz na Svobodnite Demokrati*—SSD), won 13 assembly seats on a 5.2 percent vote share. (The SSD's leader, former prime minister Stefan Sofianski, was among those elected on the BNS ticket.)

Following a leadership struggle at the May 2006 party congress, the BZNS-NS fragmented into two wings. Former party leader Dimitrova-Moser led one wing to found the new **United Agrarians** (OZ, above), while Stefan Lichev led other factions in formation (or renaming) of the ZNS. In 2009 the ZNS joined other BZNS-derived parties to form the *Koalitsiya BZNS,* but its registration to participate in the 2009 assembly elections was ruled invalid by the Central Electoral Commission because of problems with the required number of signatures.

Leader: Stefan LICHEV (Chair).

Coalition "Forward" (*Koalitsiya "Napred"*—KN). The KN was formed in December 2008 by the two parties below, LIDER (see above), the ZNS (see above), and the small **Unified People's Party** (*Edinna Narodna Partiya*—ENP). LIDER left the coalition in April 2009, with the reduced coalition contesting the June 7 European Parliament elections. Later in June the ZNS also left the coalition. The VMRO and the DG subsequently attempted to register as a coalition for the July 5 parliamentary elections but were rejected due to registration errors.

Internal Macedonian Revolutionary Organization (*Vatreshna Makedonska Revolutsionerna Organizatsiya*—VMRO). Founded in 1996, the VMRO drew on the heritage of the 19th-century Macedonian revolutionary organization to emerge as the most successful nationalist political party until *Ataka.* The VMRO participated in an electoral coalition with the DG (below) in the 2001 assembly elections before helping to launch the BNS in 2005.

Leader: Krassimir KARAKACHANOV.

Saint George Day Movement (*Dvizhenie Gergyovden*—DG). The recently formed DG participated in the 2001 assembly poll in a coalition with the VMRO that secured 3.6 percent of the vote, reportedly appealing to young liberal voters. After joining the ODS for the 2005 assembly balloting, the DG returned to its affiliation with the VMRO for the 2005 polls.

Leader: Lyuben DILOV Jr.

Green Party in Bulgaria (*Zelena Partiya na Balgariya*—ZPB). Established in 1989, the environmentalist ZPB participated in the 1990 elections in coalition with the SDS. The ZPB was split in 1991 by the formation of the now-defunct Ecoglasnost Political Club (*Politicheski klub Ekoglasnost*—PKE) and subsequently participated in several widely varied electoral alliances, including the KzB in the 2005 assembly elections.

Leader: Aleksandur KARAKACHANOV.

Democratic Party (*Demokraticheska Partiya*—DP). Descended from the conservative Christian party of the same name founded in 1896, the DP was revived in 1989 and joined the opposition SDS. Following the SDS victory in the October 1991 elections, the DP's president, Stefan SAVOV, was elected president of the National Assembly. However, he resigned in September 1992 after being named in a censure motion that was tabled by the BSP and supported by some SDS deputies. (Savov died in January 2000.) The DP formed the NS with the BZNS-NS in 1994 and participated in that grouping as part of the ODS in the 1997 and 2001 assembly balloting. However, following the apparent collapse of the NS, the DP served as a single component of the ODS for the 2005 poll, though leaving the ODS parliamentary group later that year. It did not compete in the 2009 elections.

Leader: Aleksander PRAMATARSKI (Chair).

Bulgarian Business Bloc (*Balgarski Biznes Blok*—BBB). The BBB was founded in November 1990 by leading businessman Valentin MOLLOV as a right-wing, promarket formation advocating the conversion of Bulgaria into a tariff- and tax-free zone. It won 1.3 percent of the vote (and no seats) in the 1991 election but attracted growing support under the new leadership of the charismatic Georgi Ganchev, a former fencing champion. In the December 1994 assembly election the BBB broke through to representation, winning 4.7 percent of the vote and 13 of the 240 seats. Ganchev finished third in the first round of the 1996 presidential poll (with 22 percent of the vote). The BBB captured 12 assembly seats in 1997, although several defections were subsequently reported in the wake of dissent over BBB policy. In effect, the party split, with Ganchev and Hristo Ivanov both claiming to be chair. In early 1999 it was reported that the BBB was no longer formally represented in the assembly, all of its former legislators apparently having either joined other parties or decided to serve as independents. In 2001 Ganchev contested the presidency as the candidate of the Georgi Ganchev Bloc (*Blokat na Zhorzh Ganchev*—BZG), and he led a new grouping (the National Patriotic Association) in the 2005 legislative poll, cooperating with the Coalition of the Rose.

United Macedonian Organization—Party for Economic Development and Integration. Founded in February 1998 and based in the Pirin region, near the border with Macedonia, this party is generally referred to as **OMO "Ilinden"** (*Obedineta Makedonska Organizatsiya "Ilinden,"* the fourth word being a reference to a failed 1903 Macedonian uprising begun on the feast day of St. Elijah, August 2). The party won three seats in the 1999 municipal elections before being banned by the Constitutional Court in February 2000 as a group "directed against Bulgaria's sovereignty." In 2006 the organization's right to register as a political party was upheld by the European Court of Human Rights, and in 2008 the European Commission requested to review the government's current steps on adhering to the ECHR's ruling.

Leaders: Ivan SINGARIYSKI, Ivan GARGAVELOV (Secretary).

Coalition of the Rose (*Koalitsiya na Rozata*—KzR). Formed prior to the 2005 assembly balloting, the Coalition of the Rose was perceived as a primarily left-wing grouping, although it cooperated with a number of "diverse" elements in the elections. Included in the latter were the **National Patriotic Alliance** (led by Georgi GANCHEV, the former leader of the BBB [above]) and the **Democratic Wing Movement** (lead by Turkish leader Osman OKTAY, who had split from the DPS in 2003). The coalition secured 1.3 percent of the vote in 2005.

Leaders: Krustyo PETKOV, Aleksander TOMOV.

Bulgarian Social Democracy (*Balgarska Sotsialdemokratsia*—BSD). The BSD was formed in early 2003 by the BEL, the Bulgarian United Social Democrats, and others. The new formation reportedly did well in the 2003 municipal elections.

Leader: Aleksander TOMOV.

Bulgarian Euroleft (*Balgarska Evrolevitsa*—BEL). The BEL, social-democratic in orientation, was organized as the

Euroleft Coalition (*Koalitsiya Evrolevitsa*—KEL) prior to the April 1997 legislative balloting under the leadership of former deputy prime minister Aleksander Tomov. Tomov, along with a group of supporters, had broken from the BSP in 1994 to compete in elections under the banner of the Civic Union of the Republic, which narrowly missed achieving the 4 percent threshold for representation. The ranks of the KEL were enlarged by more BSP defectors in the wake of the collapse of the Videnov government, as well as by recruits from other leftist organizations. The KEL won 14 seats in the 1997 poll, subsequently solidly aligning itself with the ODS in support of economic reform as well as EU and NATO membership for Bulgaria. It became a formal political party at a congress in March 1998, subsequently operating as the BEL, which in December agreed to participate with the Social Democratic Union (BSDS) in the 1999 local elections.

For the 2001 assembly poll the BEL served as the core component of a three-party, left-wing electoral coalition that also included the **Bulgarian United Social Democrats** (a BSDP splinter led by Vulkana TODOROVA) and a faction of the BZNS led by Georgi PINCHEV. The BEL was subsequently described as the "backbone" of the BSD.

Leader: Aleksander TOMOV.

United Labor Bloc (*Obedinen Blok na Truda*—OBT). Formed by trade unionists in May 1997 to represent the interests of "the middle class," the OBT in December 1998 announced an electoral accord with the Dertliev branch of the BSDP for the 1999 local elections. The OBT was a member of the KzB for the 2001 legislative poll, and OBT leader Krustyo Petkov secured one of the KzB seats. However, Petkov (also head of the influential Confederation of Independent Trade Unions) left the KzB in April 2005 in favor of participation in the Coalition of the Rose.

Leaders: Krustyo PETKOV (Chair), Rumen GEORGIEV.

National Movement of Rights and Freedoms (*Natsionalno Dvizhenie za Prava i Svobodi*—NDPS). The NDPS, said to have significant support in northeastern Bulgaria, was formed in 1998 as a breakaway from the DPS under the leadership of Gyuner Tahir. The NDPS was initially slated to participate in the ODS for the 2001 assembly elections, but shortly before the balloting Tahir announced that the NDPS was severing its ties to that coalition because the ODS had failed to honor an agreement regarding the status of NDPS candidates.

Leader: Gyuner TAHIR.

Grigor VELEV, a professor running as the candidate of the **All Bulgaria Association of Bulgarian Nationalists,** received 0.7 percent of the vote in the first round of presidential balloting in 2006. (For a list of small groups that unsuccessfully contested the 2001 and 2005 legislative elections as well as information on several other minor parties, see the 2007 and 2009 *Handbooks.*)

LEGISLATURE

The **National Assembly** (*Narodno Sabranie*) is a unicameral body of 240 members elected for four-year terms. Prior to 2009, all members were proportionally elected from party lists on a district basis. However, changes to the electoral law in April 2009 provided for election of 31 of the 240 members through first-past-the post voting in 31 single-member districts. The remaining 209 members continued to be elected on a proportional basis from 31 districts. The districts are the same for the single-mandate and proportional balloting—1 district for each of the country's 28 administrative regions (including the cities of Sofia and Plovdiv) and 2 additional districts for Sofia and 1 additional seat for Plovdiv. The number of proportional seats in districts ranges from 3 to 12, depending on population. (The decision to have the single-mandate constituencies correspond to the proportional constituencies was controversial, since it meant that some single-mandate members represent four times as many constituents as some other single-mandate members.) Independents may contest the single-mandate voting, but the proportional voting is limited to lists from parties or coalitions. Voters receive two ballots: one for the single-member mandate in their district and one for the proportional seats in their district. Although the proportional seats are distributed according to the results within each district, a party or coalition must receive at least 4 percent of the nationwide vote to be eligible for proportional seats from any district.

In the most recent balloting of July 5, 2009, the Citizens for European Development of Bulgaria won 116 seats (90 proportional, 26 single-mandate); the Coalition for Bulgaria, 40 (all proportional); the Movement for Rights and Freedoms, 38 (33 proportional, 5 single-mandate); the National Union Attack, 21 (all proportional); the Blue Coalition, 15 (all proportional); and Order, Law, Justice, 10 (all proportional).

Chair: Tsetska TSCHAEVA.

CABINET

[as of August 1, 2009]

Prime Minister	Boiko Borisov
Deputy Prime Ministers	Simeon Djankov
	Tsvetan Tsvetanov
Ministers	
Agriculture and Forestry	Miroslav Naydenov
Culture	Vezhdi Rashidov
Defense	Nikolay Mladenov
Economy and Energy	Traicho Traikov
Education, Youth and Science	Yordanka Fandakova [f]
Environment and Water	Nona Karadjova
Finance	Simeon Djankov
Foreign Affairs	Rumiana Jeleva [f]
Health	Bozhidar Nanev
Interior	Tsvetan Tsvetanov
Justice	Margarita Popova [f]
Labor and Social Policy	Totyu Mladenov
Physical Education and Sports	Svilen Neykov
Regional Development and Public Works	Rosen Plevneliev
Transport, Information Technology and Communications	Aleksandar Tsvetkov
Without Portfolio	Bozhidar Dimitrov

[f] = female

Note: All of the above are members of the Citizens for Economic Development of Bulgaria.

COMMUNICATIONS

In April 2004 Freedom House described the press as only "partially free" in Bulgaria because of government control of state media and reported that Bulgaria was one of the few countries in the world in which press freedom had declined recently. In 2009 *Reporters Without Borders* said that conditions had deteriorated even further recently, in part due to violence and other pressure against journalists from organized crime.

Press. The following are dailies published in Sofia unless otherwise indicated: *Trud* (Labor, 105,000); *24 Chasa* (24 Hours, 80,000); *168 Chasa* (168 Hours, 61,000), weekly; *Noshten Trud* (Night Labor, 40,000); *Kapital* (Capital, 30,000); *Dnevnik* (Journal, 15,000); *Pozvanete* (Plovdiv); *Monitor; Sega; Duma; Pari.*

News agencies. The official facility is the Bulgarian Telegraph Agency (*Balgarska Telegrafna Agentsiya*—BTA). A number of foreign agencies, including *Agence France-Presse* and Reuters, maintain offices in Sofia. Recent years have seen the emergence of private Internet-based agencies such as Novinite.com, Focus.com, and News.bg, each of which provide Bulgarian and English news services.

Broadcasting and computing. Broadcast media laws were approved in 1997 providing for an independent, seven-member National Council for Radio and Television appointed by the National Assembly and the president. Directors of national radio and television are nominated by nongovernmental journalism organizations and approved by the council. In January 2001 about 200 Bulgarian journalists accused the council of violating procedures and demanded its resignation.

In the dominant public sector, *Balgarsko Natsionalno Radio* (BNR) operates four national networks, while *Balgarska Natsionalno Televiziya* (BNT) transmits over two channels. The most influential nationwide private television stations are bTV and Nova. Radio Darik is an important private radio station. Foreign satellite channels can also be received, including Cable News Network (CNN). As of 2008 there were 348.6 Internet users per 1,000 inhabitants.

INTERGOVERNMENTAL REPRESENTATION

Ambassador to the U.S.: Latchezar PETKOV.

U.S. Ambassador to Bulgaria: (Vacant).

Permanent Representative to the UN: Rayko Strahilov RAYTCHEV.

IGO Memberships (Non-UN): BIS, BSEC, CEI, CERN, CEUR, EBRD, EIB, Eurocontrol, Interpol, IOM, NATO, OIF, OSCE, PCA, WCO, WTO.

BURKINA FASO

Political Status: Became independent as the Republic of Upper Volta on August 5, 1960; under largely military rule 1966–1978; constitution of November 27, 1977, suspended upon military coup of November 25, 1980; present name adopted August 4, 1984; multiparty constitution adopted by popular referendum on June 2, 1991.

Area: 105,869 sq. mi. (274,200 sq. km.).

Population: 13,730,258 (2006C); 14,539,000 (2008E).

Major Urban Center (2005E): OUAGADOUGOU (1,150,000).

Official Language: French.

Monetary Unit: CFA franc (official rate December 1, 2009: 434.59 CFA francs = $1US). The CFA franc, previously pegged to the French franc, is now permanently pegged to the euro at 655.957 CFA francs = 1 euro.

President: Capt. Blaise COMPAORÉ (Congress of Democracy and Progress); leader of military coup that overthrew Cdr. Thomas SANKARA on October 15, 1987; popularly elected (as leader of the Popular Front) to a seven-year term on December 1, 1991; reelected to another seven-year term on November 15, 1998; reelected to a five-year term on November 13, 2005.

Prime Minister: Tertius ZONGO (Congress of Democracy and Progress); appointed by the president on June 4, 2007, to succeed Ernest Paramanga YONLI (Congress of Democracy and Progress), who had resigned the previous day following the legislative elections of May 6; formed new government on June 10, 2007.

THE COUNTRY

A land of arid savannas drained by the Mouhoun (Black), Nazinon (Red), and Nakambe (White) Volta rivers, Burkina Faso occupies a bufferlike position between the other landlocked states of Mali and Niger on the west, north, and east, and the coastal countries of Côte d'Ivoire, Ghana, Togo, and Benin on the south. The most prominent of its numerous African population groups is the Mossi, which encompasses an estimated 50–70 percent of the population and has dominated much of the country for centuries. Other tribal groups include the Bobo, located near the western city of Bobo-Dioulasso, and the Samo. It is currently estimated that 50 percent of the population adheres to Islam, 40 percent to traditional tribal religions, and 10 percent to Christianity (primarily Catholicism). Women have traditionally constituted over half the labor force, producing most of the food crops, with men responsible for cash crops. Captain Compaoré's 1987 dismissal of a number of women appointed by his predecessor to politically influential posts was consistent with customary law that was described as "unfavorable" to female property and political rights. However, subsequent cabinets have usually included several female ministers, and there are 13 women in the current legislature.

The former Upper Volta is one of the poorest countries in Africa, with a GNP per capita estimated at $300 and an average life expectancy of less than 50 years. In addition, its illiteracy rate (more than 70 percent) is among the highest in the world. Over 80 percent of the population is engaged in subsistence agriculture; cotton, karité nuts, shea nuts, livestock, and peanuts are exported. (Cotton reportedly accounts for some 75 percent of exports and 30 percent of GDP, and Burkina Faso is the largest cotton producer in sub-Saharan Africa.) Mineral deposits, mainly manganese, remain largely unexploited due to a lack of transportation facilities, although a number of gold mines are currently being established and uranium exploration has also proved promising. Industry, consisting primarily of the production of textiles and processed agricultural goods, makes only a small contribution to the GNP. Remittances from Burkinabè working in nearby countries contribute significantly to the economy.

Since 1991 the government has adhered to a structural adjustment plan dictated by the International Monetary Fund (IMF) focusing on redirecting the economy from a "centralized to market-oriented one." In mid-2000 the IMF and the World Bank announced a $700 million debt relief package for Burkina Faso, contingent in part on further privatization and implementation of poverty-reduction policies. In the wake of additional reform by the government, the IMF endorsed debt relief of some $195 million in 2002.

GDP grew by more than 6 percent annually in 1996–2006, although growth was dampened toward the end of that period by low cotton prices and regional turmoil and fell to 4.2 percent in 2007. Development programs focused on the construction of rural roads and the expansion of irrigation systems, while the IMF called for strengthening of the government's fiscal management (including improved tax administration) and intensification of policies designed to promote the private sector. Social spending by the government also increased significantly, although an estimated 42 percent of the population continued to live in poverty.

Superior agricultural production underpinned GDP growth of 5.0 percent in 2008, although rising food and fuel prices prompted protest demonstrations early in the year. Growth was expected to slow in 2009 under the influence of falling cotton prices and the effects of the global financial crisis; consequently, the IMF pledged additional emergency lending.

GOVERNMENT AND POLITICS

Political background. Under French control since 1896, what was then known as Upper Volta gained separate identity in March 1959 when it became an autonomous state of the French Community under Maurice YAMÉOGO, leader of the Voltaic Democratic Union (*Union Démocratique Voltaïque*—UDV) and a political disciple of President Félix Houphouët-Boigny of Côte d'Ivoire. Under Yaméogo's leadership, Upper Volta became fully independent on August 5, 1960. Though reelected for a second term by an overwhelming majority in 1965, Yaméogo was unable to cope with mounting student and labor dissatisfaction, and he resigned in January 1966. Lt. Col. Sangoulé LAMIZANA, the army chief of staff, immediately assumed the presidency and instituted a military regime.

Faithful to his promise to restore constitutional government within four years, President Lamizana submitted a new constitution for popular approval in December 1970 and sponsored a legislative election in which the UDV regained its pre-1966 majority. Gérard Kango OUÉDRAOGO was invested as prime minister by the National Assembly in February 1971, while Lamizana was retained as chief executive for a four-year transitional period, after which the president was to be popularly elected. However, on February 8, 1974, the army, under General Lamizana, again seized control to prevent the political rehabilitation of ex-president Yaméogo. Declaring that the takeover was aimed at saving the country from the threat of squabbling politicians, Lamizana suspended the 1970 constitution, dissolved the National Assembly, and dismissed the cabinet. A new government was formed on February 11,

with Lamizana continuing as president and assuming the office of prime minister.

In the wake of a ministerial reorganization in January 1977, the president announced that a constitutional referendum would take place by midyear, followed by legislative and presidential elections at which he would not stand as a candidate. The referendum was held November 27, with a reported 97.75 percent of the voters endorsing a return to democratic rule. Lamizana reversed himself, however, and announced his candidacy for the presidency in 1978. Rejecting an appeal by opponents that he abandon his military rank and campaign as a civilian, Lamizana retained his office in a runoff on May 29 after having obtained a plurality in first-round balloting on May 14. Earlier, on April 30, the regime-supportive UDV–African Democratic Assembly (UDV–*Rassemblement Démocratique African*—UDV-RDA) obtained a near-majority in a reconstituted National Assembly, which on July 7 designated Dr. Joseph Issoufou CONOMBO as prime minister.

Despite restrictions imposed on all but the leading political groups, Upper Volta remained one of only two multiparty democracies (the other being Senegal) in former French Africa until November 25, 1980, when the Lamizana regime was overthrown in a military coup led by former foreign minister Col. Sayé ZERBO. Officials of the ousted government, including the president and the prime minister, were placed under arrest, while a Military Committee of Recovery for National Progress (*Comité Militaire de Redressement pour le Progrès National*—CMRPN) suspended the constitution, dissolved the legislature, and banned political activity. A 17-member Council of Ministers headed by Colonel Zerbo as both president and prime minister was announced on December 7.

Accusing Zerbo of having "made the paramilitary forces an agent of terror," a group of noncommissioned officers mounted a coup on November 7, 1982, that installed Maj. Jean-Baptiste OUÉDRAOGO, a former army medical officer, as head of what was termed the People's Salvation Council (*Conseil de Salut du Peuple*—CSP). On August 4, 1983, Ouédraogo was in turn overthrown in a brief rebellion led by Capt. Thomas SANKARA, who had been named prime minister in January, only to be arrested, along with other allegedly pro-Libyan members of the CSP, in late May. Immediately after the August coup, Sankara announced the formation of a National Revolutionary Council (*Conseil National de la Révolution*—CNR) with himself as chair. A year later, following two failed counter-coup attempts, the name of the country was changed to Burkina Faso, a vernacular blend meaning "democratic and republican land of upright men."

In the wake of a state visit by Libya's Col. Muammar al-Qadhafi in December 1985, Commander Sankara declared that his country had "gone beyond the era of republics." He therefore proclaimed the establishment of a Libyan-style "Jamahiriya" system aimed at linking national government policy to the wishes of the population as expressed through local people's committees.

Sankara was killed in a coup led by his second-in-command, Capt. Blaise COMPAORÉ, on October 15, 1987. Following the execution of a number of former government officials, Compaoré and his "brothers-in-arms," Maj. Jean-Baptiste LINGANI and Capt. Henri ZONGO, charged that Sankara had been a "madman" who had planned to consolidate power under a one-party system. Faced with substantial domestic hostility, Compaoré pledged to continue the "people's revolution," naming himself head of a Popular Front (*Front Populaire*—FP) administration. In March 1988 Compaoré announced a major government reorganization (see Constitution and government, below), and, vowing to carry on the "rectification program" begun with the October coup, he appealed to elements that Sankara had labeled "entrenched interest groups"—labor unions, tribal chieftaincies, conservative civilians, and the military elite. However, Compaoré's efforts, hailed by some as welcome relief from Sankara's chaotic governing style, lacked his predecessor's wide popular appeal.

In September 1989 Lingani and Zongo, who had been named first and second deputy chairs, respectively, of the FP three months earlier, were arrested and summarily executed on charges of "betraying" the regime by attempting to blow up the plane on which Compaoré was returning from a state visit to the Far East. Three months later, another coup attempt was allegedly foiled by the president's personal guard, with the government subsequently denying press reports that several persons had been executed for involvement in the plot.

The first FP congress, held in early 1990, included representatives of a variety of unions and political groups and drafted a democratic constitution. On June 11 Compaoré dissolved the government and announced the opening of a 24-party consultative assembly to discuss implementation of the new basic law. The following day, however, 13 opposition parties walked out of the assembly when the government rejected their demands that the body be granted sovereign status and be expanded to include trade unionists, traditional leaders, and human rights organizations. Consequently, on June 16 Compaoré named a 34-member transitional government consisting of 28 ministers and 6 secretaries of state, 21 of whom were members of the FP's core formation, the Organization for People's Democracy–Labor Movement (*Organisation pour la Démocratie Populaire–Mouvement Travailliste*—ODP-MT). However, three opposition members withdrew prior to the first cabinet meeting, and they were followed on August 17 by three more, including Herman YAMÉOGO (son of Upper Volta's first president), who had been assigned the agriculture portfolio only three weeks earlier.

In September 1990 Compaoré, who had resigned from the military as required by the new constitution, announced his presidential candidacy. Thereafter, in the run-up to the presidential balloting, clashes intensified between the FP and opposition forces. On September 25 much of the opposition, loosely joined in a Coalition of Democratic Forces (*Coalition des Forces Démocratiques*—CFD), threatened to boycott elections if a national conference was not held. Compaoré responded by offering to hold a referendum on Burkina's transitional institutions. However, at the urging of government supporters, the proposal was quickly withdrawn. Thus, all four opposition presidential nominees boycotted the December 1 balloting, in which Compaoré, running unopposed, won a renewed seven-year mandate. Subsequently, the proposed new constitution was approved by an assembly of 2,000 provincial delegates on December 15 and adopted by popular referendum on June 2, 1991.

Prospects for a representative legislature were dampened when only a quarter of the known parties indicated a willingness to participate in the projected January 1992 legislative poll. At the core of the complaint was the government's refusal to convene a national conference endowed with plenary powers to oversee the transition to a wholly democratic system. In mid-December 1991 opposition leaders had rejected an overture by President Compaoré to participate in a less authoritative National Reconciliation Forum, and the assemblage that was ultimately convened on February 11, 1992, was suspended nine days later because of a disagreement over live radio coverage of its deliberations. Therefore, only 27 of 62 registered parties participated in the balloting that was eventually conducted on May 24, the ruling ODP-MT winning an overwhelming majority of seats.

On June 15, 1992, Compaoré dissolved the transitional government, and the following day he named economist Youssouf OUÉDRAOGO as prime minister. The cabinet named by Ouédraogo on June 20 included representatives from 7 parties, although 13 of the 22 portfolios were awarded to the ODP-MT.

Prime Minister Ouédraogo resigned on March 17, 1994, after the mid-January devaluation of the CFA franc and subsequent collapse of a wage agreement with the trade unions. Three days later President Compaoré appointed Roch Marc Christian KABORÉ, theretofore minister of state in charge of relations with institutions, as Ouédraogo's successor.

On February 6, 1996, Prime Minister Kaboré resigned to assume the vice presidency of the Congress of Democracy and Progress (*Congrès pour la Démocratie et le Progrès*—CDP), a newly formed government grouping created by the ODP-MT and a number of other groups. Kaboré, who was also named special advisor to the president, was replaced on the same day by Kadré Désiré OUÉDRAOGO, theretofore deputy governor of the Central Bank of West African States.

In January 1997 the assembly approved constitutional amendments that abolished provisions limiting the number of presidential terms (previously two). The opposition strongly protested the change, arguing it was designed to insure Compaoré the presidency for as long as he desired.

In legislative balloting on May 11, 1997, the dominance of the pro-Compaoré groupings was underlined by the CDP's capture of 97 of 111 seats, a majority that swelled to 101 in June following elections in four constituencies where earlier results had been invalidated. On June 11 the president reappointed Ouédraogo prime minister and named a cabinet that was largely unchanged.

In April 1998 the Compaoré government announced the establishment of an independent electoral commission and charged it with organizing the presidential polling scheduled for late 1998. The government asserted that the creation of the commission was a sign of a willingness to install transparent electoral procedures. However, that assessment was rejected by many of the leading opposition groups, which, under the banner of the February 14 Group (*Groupe du 14 Février*—G14), a newly created coalition, subsequently vowed to boycott the balloting unless further reforms were implemented. In September President Compaoré met with opposition leaders in an unsuccessful effort to break the impasse; consequently, in presidential polling on November 15, the incumbent easily secured a second term, overwhelming several minor party candidates.

Violent antigovernment protests broke out throughout the country in mid-December 1998 following the discovery of the bodies of Norbert ZONGO (a prominent independent journalist) and two colleagues in a burned vehicle outside of Ouagadougou. Zongo, a vocal critic of the administration, had reportedly been investigating the role the president's brother, François COMPAORÉ, had allegedly played in the death of one of Zongo's assistants. Subsequently, the president appointed an independent judicial commission to investigate the journalists' deaths; nevertheless, demonstrations continued through the first part of 1999.

On January 8, 1999, Prime Minister Ouédraogo and his government issued their pro forma resignations, as required by the constitution following presidential balloting. However, on January 11 Ouédraogo was reappointed by the president, and the government announced on January 15 was only slightly reshuffled.

In May 1999 the judicial commission issued a report that implicated the Presidential Guard in the Zongo killings. Antigovernment unrest subsequently intensified, and the leaders of a number of opposition groups were detained. The CDP dismissed the commission's findings as reflecting "partisan" concerns; nevertheless, President Compaoré created a 16-member Council of Elders on May 21 and asked its members (including three former heads of government) to help create an environment for "reconciliation and social peace." In August the council called for the establishment of a national unity government. Two months later, Prime Minister Ouédraogo reshuffled the cabinet, bringing into its ranks members of two theretofore opposition groups. However, members of the so-called "radical opposition" refused to participate, dismissing the government's entreaties as disingenuous and asserting that the political crisis would continue until those responsible for political killings were brought to justice.

In November 1999 Compaoré established two new bodies, the Consultative Commission on Political Reforms and the National Reconciliation Commission, which he charged with drafting "concrete proposals" for resolving the continuing imbroglio. However, opposition members refused to assume the seats set aside for them in the Consultative Commission, complaining that the president had reneged on an alleged pledge to make the commission's findings binding.

Antigovernment demonstrations continued through the end of 1999, and in the first days of 2000 the opposition criticized the administration's call for early legislative elections and condemned the "culture of impunity" engendered by the president. In late January 2000 CDP activists held a proreform rally, insisting that such efforts were the only way to derail the opposition's movement toward a "democratic coup d'état." The government subsequently announced plans for municipal elections to be held in late July, but the balloting was later delayed in view of opposition complaints about voter registration and electoral procedures.

In August 2000 three soldiers from the Presidential Guard were given prison sentences for having tortured one of Zongo's assistants to death in 1998. Subsequently, in October, the university in Ouagadougou was shut down by the government in response to several months of protests by students, teachers, and unions. After the government agreed to most of the protesters' demands, the university was reopened in December.

The municipal elections of September 2000 appeared to underscore the division between the moderate and radical opposition parties, as some of the latter refused to participate. On November 6, 2000, Prime Minister Ouédraogo resigned, and on November 7 the president appointed one of the ministers from the CDP, Ernest Paramanga YONLI, as the new prime minister. The CDP subsequently signed a "Protocol of Agreement" with a number of parties that consequently accepted posts in the new cabinet formed on November 12, their inclusion being seen by some analysts as evidence of a new atmosphere of compromise and easing of tensions, as well as the split structure of the opposition.

In February 2001, in a further development on the prosecution of the political killings, a warrant officer was charged with the murder of Zongo. Implying that the investigations of the political killings had produced tangible results, the government organized a "National Day of Forgiveness" in March with the hopes of reconciling with the more radical opposition parties. However, the Party for Democracy and Progress (*Parti pour la Démocratie et le Progrès*—PDP), the Social Forces Front (*Front des Forces Sociales*—FFS), and several other parties refused to take part in the event.

Facing increased domestic and international criticism, the government authorized several significant electoral reforms prior to the 2002 assembly balloting, including a revision of the proportional voting system that had previously favored the CDP (it had won 69 percent of the vote in the 1997 balloting but had been awarded 97 of 111 seats). The measures appeared to produce the desired effect, as the CDP majority fell to 57 seats in the May 5 elections. The leading opposition parties were the Alliance for Democracy and Federation/African Democratic Rally (*Alliance pour la Démocratie et la Fédération/Rassemblement Démocratique Africaine*—ADF/RDA) with 17 seats and the PDP/Socialist Party (PDP/*Parti Socialiste*—PDP/PS) with 10 seats. However, unlike the November 2000 cabinet, the new cabinet named by Prime Minister Yonli on June 11 did not include members of the opposition.

Following a controversial ruling by the Constitutional Court that permitted him to seek another term (see Current issues, below), President Compaoré was reelected with 80 percent of the vote against 12 other candidates in balloting on November 13, 2005. He subsequently reappointed Prime Minister Yonli to head a new government which, as formed on January 7, 2006, was again dominated by the CDP, although several small parties that had supported Compaoré in the presidential poll were also included.

In balloting for the Assembly of People's Deputies on May 6, 2007, the CDP rebounded to secure 73 of 111 seats, followed by the ADF/RDA with 14 seats and some 11 small parties with 1–5 seats each. Prime Minister Yonli resigned on June 3, and the following day President Compaoré named Tertius ZONGO, the country's ambassador to the United States, to the post. The cabinet was reshuffled on June 10; it remained dominated by the CDP.

Constitution and government. After the 1977 constitution was suspended in November 1980, a period of uncertain military rule followed, yielding, in August 1985, a revised government structure intended to promote "the Burkinabè identity." (See the 2007 *Handbook* for details.)

A new government was formed on October 31, 1987, two weeks after Sankara's overthrow. However, it was not until March 1988 that Captain Compaoré's Popular Front (FP) announced that Sankara's Revolutionary Defense Committees (which had assumed power at the local level) had been abolished and replaced by Revolutionary Committees.

Described as "mass socio-professional organizations," the new committees were mandated to meet every two years to modify FP programs, define the country's political orientation, and oversee admission into the FP. Although mimicking Sankara's call for extensive citizen involvement in government, the new regime ordered the banning of all political parties that did not align with the FP. Subsequently, the ban was relaxed for all but the most virulent opposition formations, and in August 1990 a commission was charged with drafting a new constitution. The multiparty document approved by popular referendum on June 2, 1991, provided for a separation of powers, a president and legislature elected by universal suffrage for seven- and five-year terms, respectively, and the establishment of an independent judiciary. The president has the right to name a prime minister, who must, however, be acceptable to the legislature. In April 2000 the Assembly of People's Deputies passed a law reducing the president's term from seven to five years, with a maximum of two terms. The new law did not affect the length of President Compaoré's current term. It also did not address the issue of "retroactivity," which led supporters of Compaoré to declare that he was eligible to run for a third term in 2005 (see Current issues, below). The country's Supreme Court is split into four separate courts, namely, the Constitutional Court, the Court of Appeals, the Council of State, and the government audit office.

Administratively, the country is divided into provinces, which are subdivided into departments, arrondissements, and villages. Local elections were held in April 2006 for 49 "urban communes" and 302 "rural communes."

Foreign relations. Upper Volta had consistently adhered to a moderately pro-French and pro-Western foreign policy, while stressing the importance of good relations with neighboring countries. However, after the 1983 coup, relations between Burkina Faso and France cooled, a result primarily of France's unease over Commander Sankara's vigorous attempts to rid the country of all vestiges of its colonial past (made manifest by the 1984 change in country name, the adoption of radical policies modeled on those of Ghana and Libya, and the widely publicized arrests of allegedly pro-French former government officials and trade unionists accused of plotting against the Sankara regime). Subsequent relations with francophone neighbors remained less than uniformly cordial, in part because of Sankara's blunt style in attacking perceived government corruption throughout the region and his strong ideological opinions.

In December 1985 a 20-year-long controversy involving the so-called Agacher Strip at Burkina's northern border with Mali yielded four days of fighting with approximately 300 dead on both sides. However, a ruling from the International Court of Justice (IGJ) on December 22, 1986, which awarded the two countries roughly equal portions of the disputed territory, largely terminated the unrest. Relations with another neighbor, Togo, were strained in 1987 over allegations of Burkinabè complicity (heatedly denied) in a September 1986 coup attempt against Togolese President Eyadema.

The October 1987 coup in Burkina Faso was manifestly welcomed by the region's most respected elder statesman, President Houphouët-Boigny of Côte d'Ivoire, with whom Captain Compaoré had long enjoyed close personal relations. Subsequently, in an attempt to gain recognition of his government and to repair strained ties with "Western-leaning" neighbors, Compaoré traveled to 13 countries during his first year in power. The long-standing border dispute with Mali was formally resolved in early 1988, followed by a resumption in relations with Togo and a border agreement with Ghana. Nevertheless, Compaoré also continued to maintain communist ties: in September 1988 he signed cooperation agreements with North Korea, and in September 1989 he was the first head of state to visit China following the crushing of that country's prodemocracy movement.

In September 1992 Malian president Alpha Oumar Konaré met in Ouagadougou with Compaoré to reactivate bilateral cooperation and to address Burkina's policy of allowing Tuaregs from Mali and Niger refuge in northern Burkina. On November 5 the United States recalled its ambassador to Burkina Faso, accusing the Compaoré government of continuing to supply arms to Charles Taylor's Liberian rebel forces despite Washington's earlier warnings about Ouagadougou's "destabilizing" involvement with Taylor.

On February 2, 1994, Ouagadougou reestablished relations with Taiwan after a 20-year lapse, thus precipitating China's suspension of relations one week later. Meanwhile, regional relations were dominated by the Tuareg dilemma, and in October Ouagadougou was the host site for successful negotiations between the Niger government and its Tuareg rebels. On a far less positive note, the refugee crisis along Burkina's border with Mali was exacerbated by intensified fighting between Tuaregs and Malian government forces. In January 1995 the United Nations reported that the number of Malian Tuareg refugees in Burkina Faso had risen to 50,000, up from 9,000 in 1993. In October Ouagadougou announced plans to send troops to join ECOMOG forces in Liberia, saying it had changed its policy because the peacemaking effort there appeared "more credible than previous ones."

Regional cooperation efforts topped Burkina's foreign policy agenda in 1996, Ouagadougou reaching agreement with Niger in March on the repatriation of that country's refugees. In March 1997 Burkina was the site for joint military exercises with Benin, Togo, and France, while in 1998 Compaoré hosted summits for representatives of combatants in the Eritrean and Ethiopian border conflict as well as participants in the civil war in the Democratic Republic of the Congo. Burkinabè troops also participated in the UN-sponsored peacekeeping mission in the Central African Republic from 1997 to 2000.

In November 1999 a violent land dispute erupted in Côte d'Ivoire between Ivorians and Burkinabè, and by the end of the year approximately 12,000 of the Burkinabè had crossed back into Burkina in search of refuge. Following a coup attempt in Côte d'Ivoire in January 2001, the two countries' relations were strained even further, as some Ivorian authorities unofficially implied that Burkina Faso may have been behind the overthrow effort. The Ivorian government subsequently began forced deportations of Burkinabè who lived or were working in Côte d'Ivoire. Estimates were that 20,000 Burkinabè expatriates were expelled by 2002. Throughout 2002 and into 2003, the Ivorian government continued to blame its neighbor for promoting unrest, and there was another massive wave of Burkinabè refugees. The Compaoré government officially closed the border in September 2002 but reopened it a year later. By 2003, some 350,000 Burkinabè had fled Côte d'Ivoire. In 2003 Compaoré hosted a summit with his Ivorian counterpart and representatives of the main rebel groups in Côte d'Ivoire in an effort to improve bilateral relations. The government also banned several Ivorian rebel groups from using Burkina Faso to undertake political activities in Côte d'Ivoire. However, in October it was reported that the alleged leader of a coup plot in Burkina Faso had been in contact with officials in Togo and Côte d'Ivoire, further straining relations between the Compaoré administration and those two nations. In 2004 Burkinabè opposition leaders called for an investigation into the possibility that Compaoré had provided support for antigovernment activity in Côte d'Ivoire, Mauritania, and other places. However, Compaoré's regional reputation improved significantly when he played a prominent role in facilitating the negotiated settlements in Togo in 2006 and Côte d'Ivoire in March 2007. At the same time, however, tension was reported along Burkina Faso's border with Niger, both countries suggesting that the ICJ attempt to resolve a dispute that has "simmered" since 2000. Subsequently, a border dispute with Benin appeared headed toward a peaceful compromise (see Foreign affairs in the article on Benin for details).

Current issues. In early 2005 President Compaoré announced he would be a candidate for reelection despite the two-term limit implemented in 2000. (Compaoré's position was that the term limits could not be applied retroactively, meaning that, in theory, he was eligible for two more terms.) Not surprisingly, opposition leaders (already angered by the May 2004 reversal of election rules that had favored anti-CDP forces in the 2002 assembly poll) demanded that the Constitutional Court reject Compaoré's candidacy. However, the court quickly dismissed their demand, paving the way for Compaoré's landslide victory in November. Although his opponents cited numerous alleged irregularities, observers from the AU and other organizations described the poll as generally fair. Compaoré, in power for 18 years, clearly benefited from the failure of the opposition to coalesce behind a single candidate, while improved economic conditions also appeared to generate popular support for the incumbent. Meanwhile, another topic of discussion at that point was the possibility that Compaoré might be investigated by the UN court preparing to prosecute former Liberian president Charles Taylor for his alleged war crimes in Sierra Leone. (Critics alleged that Compaoré may have assisted Taylor in arming and training rebels in Sierra Leone.) However, regional pressure on Compaoré subsequently appeared to decline in view of his mediation efforts regarding Côte d'Ivoire and Togo.

Although opposition parties had hoped that the April 2006 municipal balloting would offer them a better chance for success than previous elections, the CDP continued its dominance, securing about two-thirds of the seats. The opposition was also unable to present a strong challenge in the May 2007 assembly poll, although the administration was facing criticism for the dismissal (in mid-2006) of charges against the former head of the presidential guard in regard to the murder of journalist Norbert Zongo in 1998. The government had also come under fire for its handling of clashes in December 2006 between police and disgruntled soldiers, which, according to some analysts, underscored the "fragile state of democracy" in the country and potential threats to Compaoré from elements of the military. For its part, the international community appeared to welcome the results of the assembly election (described by observers from the African Union as generally "free and transparent") as offering the best hope for continued "stability" and continued market-oriented economic growth. However, that premise faced a challenge in February–March 2008 when rapidly increasing food and fuel prices prompted several significant protests and riots, leading to the arrest of nearly 200 people. Several students were also injured in clashes with security forces in June while demonstrating for greater financial support from the government.

President Compaoré, who considered himself eligible to run for a fourth term, had not officially announced his candidacy for the 2010 poll as of mid-2009. However, most analysts concluded he would run and win without much difficulty since he continued to enjoy the support of Western donors, and the opposition, despite new efforts to coalesce, remained weak.

POLITICAL PARTIES

Prior to the 1980 coup the governing party was the Voltaic Democratic Union–African Democratic Assembly (*Union Démocratique Voltaïque–Rassemblement Démocratique Africain*—UDV-RDA), an outgrowth of the Ivorian RDA. In opposition were the National Union for the Defense of Democracy (*Union Nationale pour la Défense de la Démocratie*—UNDD), organized by Herman Yaméogo and the Voltaic Progressive Front (FPV), a socialist grouping led by Joseph KI-ZERBO that contained a number of UDV-RDA dissidents. Most such individuals subsequently left the country, Ki-Zerbo having been accused of planning a coup against Thomas Sankara in May 1984.

Political party activity was suspended in the immediate wake of Sankara's overthrow in 1987, although several groups maintained a highly visible identity, most importantly the Patriotic League for Development (*Ligue Patriotique pour le Développement*—Lipad), a Marxist organization that had been founded in 1973. In March 1988 Captain Compaoré declared that while his recently created Popular Front should not be construed as a political party, separate parties would be permitted to operate within it. A year later an apparent attempt was made to create a single government party (ODP-MT, below). In a return pendulum swing, the Popular Front was described on the eve of its first congress in March 1990 as consisting of "four national unions and seven political groups," although details regarding some of the components were sparse. In addition, it was reported that a number of nonlegalized (but otherwise unidentified) opposition groups had been invited to send representatives to the congress.

The June 1991 constitution provided for multiparty activity, and 44 parties had been recognized by November. References to the Popular Front appeared to have been dropped following the formation of the Congress of Democracy and Progress (CDP) in February 1996. Subsequently, the opposition mantle appeared to have been assumed in 1998 by the February 14 Group (*Groupe du 14 Février*—G14), a coalition that included the ADF/RDA, PAI, PDP, and FFS. (For additional information on the G14 and several other opposition coalitions in 1998–2005, see the 2007 *Handbook*.)

Government and Government Supportive Parties:

Congress of Democracy and Progress (*Congrès pour la Démocratie et le Progrès*—CDP). The CDP was formed on February 6, 1996, as a result of an agreement between the ODP-MT and a number of other parties, including the CNPP-PSD, the **Rally of Independent Social Democrats** (*Rassemblement des Social-Démocrates Indépendants*—RSI), the **Group of Revolutionary Democrats** (*Groupement des Démocrates Révolutionnaires*—GDR), and the **Movement for Socialist Democracy** (*Mouvement pour la Démocratie Socialiste*—MDS). The Compaoré government's commitment to the new grouping was highlighted by the assignment of ODP-MT Executive Committee Chair Arsène Bongnessan Yé and Prime Minister Roch Marc Christian Kaboré to the CDP's presidency and vice presidency, respectively. (Some news reports described the CDP as a "merger" of the various parties, indicating that they might not retain autonomous identities within the Congress. Following is information on the OPD-MT and the CNPP-PSD as they existed immediately prior to the formation of the CDP. For information on the history of the RSI, GDR, MDS, and a number of other small parties reported to have joined the CDP, see the 2000–2002 *Handbook*.)

At a CDP congress on August 1, 1999, party delegates elected Kaboré to the newly created post of national executive secretary, a position that superseded both the party presidency and secretary generalship. Kaboré's ascendancy to the CDP's top post was described by some observers as evidence of a triumph for party moderates over hardliners. Kaboré and the moderates appeared to extend their influence even further when he was elected as the new assembly president following the May 2002 legislative balloting. In June 2005 the CDP selected Compaoré as its candidate in the upcoming presidential balloting.

In 2008 President Compaoré's brother, François COMPAORÉ, was named head of a new Associative Federation for Peace and Progress with Blaise Compaoré (*Fédération Associative pour la Paix et le Progrès avec Blaise Compaoré*—FEDAP-BC), which was reportedly organized as a fund-raising vehicle for the president and, eventually, his brother, who was considered the next likely president of Burkina Faso. Friction was reported in the CDP in 2009 between the FEDAP-BC and a party faction led by Simon Compaoré (the mayor of Ouagadougou [no relation to the president] and Salif DIALLO, who was recently dismissed from the cabinet.

Leaders: Capt. Blaise COMPAORÉ (President of Burkina Faso), Tertius ZONGO (Prime Minister), Marc Christian Roch KABORÉ (National Executive Secretary of the Party and President of the National Assembly), Simon COMPAORÉ (Mayor of Ouagadougou), Pierre Joseph Emmanuel TAPSOBA.

Organization for People's Democracy–Labor Movement (*Organisation pour la Démocratie Populaire–Mouvement Travailliste*—ODP-MT). The leftist ODP-MT was launched on April 15, 1989, as a means of unifying "all political tendencies in the country." Most prominently associated with the new formation were the Union of Burkinabè Communists (*Union des Communistes Burkinabè*—UCB) and a number of dissidents from the former Union of Communist Struggles from which the UCB had earlier split.

During a congress in Ouagadougou in March 1991, the ODP-MT endorsed Compaoré's candidacy in the forthcoming presidential balloting and formally abandoned Marxism-Leninism in favor of free enterprise and a market economy. Meanwhile, in anticipation of multiparty elections, the ODP-MT moved to position itself as an independent grouping within the Popular Front, thus abandoning efforts to present the image of a nonhierarchical coalition.

In early 1996 the ODP-MT renounced its status as a "revolutionary party of the democratic masses" to become a "social democratic" party, shortly thereafter spearheading the formation of the CDP.

Leaders: Marc Christian Roch KABORÉ, Capt. Arsène Bongnessan YÉ, Naboho KANIDOUA (General Secretary).

National Convention of Progressive Patriots–Social Democratic Party (*Convention Nationale des Patriotes Progressistes–Parti Social-Démocrate*—CNPP-PSD). The CNPP-PSD was expelled from the Popular Front in March 1991 for criticizing ODP-MT policies and calling for a national conference. The party subsequently emerged as the opposition's most powerful force, winning 12 assembly seats as runner-up to the ODP-MT in May 1992.

The CNPP-PSD's decision to join its former Popular Front allies in the formation of the CDP in early 1996 was considered a major political victory for the Compaoré administration.

Leaders: Mamadou SIMPORÉ, Moussa BOLY.

Alliance for Democracy and Federation/African Democratic Rally (*Alliance pour la Démocratie et la Fédération/Rassemblement Démocratique Africaine*—ADF/RDA). The ADF and RDA announced their merger in May 1998. The ADF had been formed in December 1990 by Herman Yaméogo, whose previous party had been expelled from the Popular Front in July 1990, largely because of criticism from intraparty critics of Yaméogo.

In February 1991 the ADF called for an immediate amnesty for all political prisoners, the appointment of a transitional government, and "democratization" of the press. By midyear Yaméogo had emerged as the opposition's most prominent government critic. Subsequently,

Yaméogo announced his presidential candidacy; however, he and the other opposition candidates subsequently withdrew from the December 1 balloting. Somewhat inexplicably, Yaméogo joined the cabinet as a minister of state in February 1992.

The party participated in the May 1992 legislative poll, capturing four seats, and in June Yaméogo was redesignated minister of state. In legislative balloting in May 1997 the ADF captured only two seats, and Yaméogo was not included in the cabinet named in June. A leading component of the February 14 Group, the ADF boycotted the 1998 presidential elections.

Formed in 1946 as an outgrowth of the Ivorian RDA, the RDA was a partner in the ruling UDV-RDA grouping that was unseated by the 1980 coup. The party captured six seats in the May 1992 balloting, and an RDA member, Clement SANOU, was included in the government named in June. Compaoré's appointment of Sanou was greeted with suspicion, however, with *Africa Confidential* suggesting that the president was attempting to create friction within the RDA. The RDA presented candidates in slightly more than half of the polling districts in 1997, retaining only two seats.

The Party of the Convergence of Liberties and Integration (*Parti de la Convergence pour les Libertés et l'Integration*—PCLI) joined the ADF/RDA subsequent to the 1998 merger. The ADF/RDA signed a protocol with the CDP and others and was given cabinet posts in November 2000, although it returned to formal opposition status following the May 2002 legislative poll, in which it finished second to the CDP. Leadership disagreements within the ADF/RDA in 2003 led Yaméoga to quit the party and form the UNDD (below). Subsequently, the ADF/RDA supported President Compaoré in his reelection bid in 2005, and ADF/RDA leader Gilbert Ouédraogo was appointed to the new cabinet in January 2006. The ADF/RDA finished second to the CDP in the April 2006 municipal elections as well as in the May 2007 legislative poll, having endorsed Compaoré's economic policies.

Leaders: Gilbert Noël OUÉDRAOGO (President), Gérard Kango OUÉDRAOGO (Honorary President), Dabo HAMADOU (Vice President).

Union for the Republic (*Union pour le République*—UPR). The recently formed UPR finished third in the April 2006 municipal balloting, having campaigned on a platform that pledged to address the needs of rural areas. As of the end of 2006 it was reported that six members of the assembly had joined the UPR, which subsequently finished third in the May 2007 assembly balloting with five seats.

Leader: Toussaint Abel COULIBALY.

Other Legislative Parties:

Union for Rebirth/Sankarist Movement (*Union pour la Renaissance/Mouvement Sankariste*—UNIR/MS). Formed in 2000 under the leadership of Bénéwendé Sankara, the UNIR/MS won three seats in the 2002 assembly elections. In addition, Sankara, a lawyer and prominent human rights activist, finished second in the 2005 presidential poll with 4.95 percent of the vote. He currently chairs the opposition's faction in the assembly, which claimed 11 members as of early 2009.

In March 2009 the UNIR/MS launched the **Union for Rebirth/Sankarist Party** (*Union pour la Renaissance/Parti Sankariste*—UNIR/PS) in conjunction with the CPS (below) and some members of the FFS (below). Bénéwendé Sankara was named president of the new party's national executive secretariat, while the FFS's Nestor BASSIERE was named vice president. Sankara was also chosen by a party congress as the UNIR/PS candidate for the 2010 presidential poll. He subsequently announced the formation of a new bloc called the **Consultation of the Parties of the Opposition** (*Concertation des Parties de l'Opposition*—(CPO) which reportedly included most of the members of the G14, all of the opposition parliamentarians, and the MPS/PF. The UNDD, RDEB, and other small parties were also invited to join the CPO in backing a single presidential candidate.

Leader: Bénéwendé Stanislas SANKARA (2005 presidential candidate).

Convention of the Democratic Forces of Burkina (*Convention des Forces Démocratiques du Burkina*—CFD-B). The CFD-B was formed in advance of the 2007 assembly elections by the **Convention for Democracy and Federation** (*Convention pour la Démocratie et la Fédération*—CDF), led by Amadou Diemdioda Dicko; the **Convention for Democracy and Liberty** (*Convention pour la Démocratie et la Liberté*—CDL), led by Kiello Célestin Dabiré; the **Rally for Independent Forces/Party of the Youth of Burkina** (*Rassemblement des Forces Indépendantes/Parti des Jeunes du Burkina*—RFI/PJB), led by Ali Diaby KASSAMBA; and the Greens of Burkina.

The CDF had been one of the parties that had formed the Coalition of Democratic Forces (*Coalition des Forces Démocratiques*—CFD) prior to the 2002 legislative poll. Other members of the CFD included the UVDB (see Greens of Burkina, below), the MTP, and a number of smaller parties, including the **Refuser's Front/African Democratic Rally** (*Front de Refus/Rassemblement Démocratique Africain*—FR/RDA), a breakaway faction of the RDA whose leader, Frederic Fernand GUIMA, had finished third in the 1998 presidential balloting. The new RDEB (see below), formed in October 2002, effectively became (apparently) a member of the CFD in October 2002, when Ram Ouédraogo quit the UVDB but remained as the national coordinator of the CFD. The CFD secured five seats in the 2002 assembly balloting, and it was reported that the primary education and literacy cabinet post was awarded to a CFD member in June. However, the formal status of the CFD's relationship to the Compaoré administration remained unclear.

The CFD-B secured 3 seats in the May 2007 legislative balloting, some news reports indicating a degree of cooperation between it and the ruling CDP.

Leaders: Amadou Diemdioda DICKO (President), Kiello Célestin DABIRÉ (Vice President).

Greens of Burkina (*Les Verts du Burkina*). This party is a partial successor to the Union of Greens for the Development of Burkina (*Union des Verts pour le Développement du Burkina*—UVDB), launched in 1991. UVDB leader Ram Ouédraogo had the distinction of being the first opposition member to announce his presidential candidacy in 1991. However, prior to the December balloting, he withdrew at the same time as the other opposition candidates.

In 1998 Ouédraogo campaigned for the presidency on a UVDB platform highlighted by a call for the elevation of water management issues to the forefront of national policymaking concerns. He finished second in the November presidential balloting, garnering just 6.61 percent of the vote. In October 1999 Ouédraogo was named a minister of state in the Kadré Ouédraogo government. He kept his position after the formation of the new government in November 2000 but was not retained in June 2002.

Following the 2002 legislative balloting, disagreements broke out over the scope of cooperation between the UVDB and other opposition parties, and Ouédraogo left the UVDB to form the RDEB (below). The rump UVDB subsequently adopted the party's current rubric, although leadership of the group remained unclear and a UVDB was listed as presenting candidates on its own in the 2007 assembly balloting.

Party for Democracy and Socialism (*Parti pour la Démocratie et la Socialisme*—PDS). After gaining representation in the 2002 assembly balloting, the PDS reportedly presented Philippe Ouédraogo, formerly of the PAI (below), as its 2005 presidential candidate. He finished fourth with 2.28 percent of the vote.

Leaders: Félix SOUBEIGA, Ba SAMBO.

Party for Democracy and Progress/Socialist Party (*Parti pour la Démocratie et le Progrès/Parti Socialiste*—PDP/PS). The PDP was launched in May 1993 by Joseph KI-ZERBO in the aftermath of a struggle that erupted when a parliamentary coalition between Ki-Zerbo's Union of Independent Social Democrats (*Union des Sociaux-Démocrates Indépendants*—USDI) and the CNPP-PSD splintered following the retirement of the latter's leader. Ki-Zerbo had previously been linked to the Voltaic Progressive Front (*Front Progressiste Voltaïque*—FPV), which he and a group of UDV-RDA dissidents had formed prior to the 1980 coup. The socialist-oriented FPV was proscribed until early 1991, when its longtime leader was given amnesty; he returned from eight years in exile the following September.

The PDP, operating under the umbrella of the February 14 Group, boycotted the 1998 presidential elections. In May 2001 the PDP merged with the Burkinabè Socialist Party (*Parti Socialiste Burkinabè*—PSB), and the present name was adopted. Led by François Ouédraogo, the PSB was a breakaway formation from the PAI.

Under the leadership of Ki-Zerbo, described as one of the fiercest critics of the Compaoré administration, the PDP/PS boycotted the 2000 municipal elections. However, the party presented candidates in the May 2002 assembly balloting, increasing its representation from six to ten. Disaffected PDP/PS members in 2002 formed a **People's Movement for Socialism/Federal Party** (*Mouvement du Peuple pour le Socialisme/Parti Féderal*—MPS/PF), which, under the leadership of Emile PARÉ, subsequently launched an electoral coalition with PAREN (below). Ali Lankoandé finished sixth (with 1.74 percent of the vote) as the candidate of the PDP/PS in the 2005 presidential election. Ki-Zerbo died in December 2006. The PDP/PS won two seats in the 2007 assembly poll.

Leaders: Sébastien ZABSONRE (General Secretary), François OUÉDRAOGO, Ali LANKOANDÉ (2005 presidential candidate), François KABORÉ.

Rally for the Development of Burkina (*Rassemblement pour le Développement du Burkina*—RDB). The recently launched RDB finished fourth in the April 2006 municipal balloting and won two seats in the 2007 assembly poll.

Leader: Saidou Célestin COMPAORÉ.

Union of Sankarist Parties (*Union des Parties Sankaristes*—UPS). The UPS was formed prior to the 2007 assembly poll by the following groups and the **Convergence of Hope** (*Convergence de l'Espoir*), led by Jean Hubert BAZIÉ; the **Movement of Diverse Sankarists** (*Mouvement des Sankaristes Divers*—MSD), led by Joseph OUÉDRAOGO; and the **Party for National Unity and Development** (*Parti pour l'Unité Nationale et le Développement*—PUND). Ouédraoga, described as the president of the UPS, opposed participation in the formation of the UNIR/PS in 2009 by the CPS and members of the FFS. The UPS and FFS rumps subsequently indicated they would continue to operate outside the UNIR/PS despite having lost many members of the new party.

Convention of Sankarist Parties (*Convention des Partis Sankaristes*—CPS). Also referenced as the Sankarist Panafrican Convention (*Convention Panafricaine Sankariste*), the CPS was formed in mid-1999 by the BSB, the **United Social Democracy Party** (*Parti de la Démocratie Sociale Unifié*—PDSU), a breakaway faction of the FFS, and other small groups. The CPS signed a protocol with the CDP and others and was given cabinet posts in November 2000, a decision that reportedly caused internal CPS tensions.

Leader: Ernest Nongona OUÉDRAOGO (President).

Burkinabè Socialist Bloc (*Bloc Socialiste Burkinabè*—BSB). The BSB traces its lineage to the Democratic and Popular Rally–Thomas Sankara (*Rassemblement Démocratique et Populaire–Thomas Sankara*—RDP-TS), a clandestine resistance movement formed by supporters of the former president following the October 1987 coup. RDP-TS members were subsequently absorbed into the Sankarist Movement (*Mouvement Sankariste*—MS), an anti-Compaoré group, which was formed on August 4, 1988, the "revolution's" fifth anniversary. The MS, in turn, gave rise in November 1991 to the BSB (led by Ernest Nongoma Ouédraogo), which opposed Compaoré but was not part of the prodemocracy opposition.

The BSB boycotted the May 1992 assembly election, although one of its members, the **United Forces** (*Forces Unies*—FU), broke ranks to contest the poll. In August 1995 Ouédraogo was sentenced to six month's imprisonment for allegedly accusing Compaoré of fraudulently amassing a personal fortune. Because of his conviction, Ouédraogo was forbidden from participating in the 1997 legislative elections; however, in March 1998 Compaoré pardoned him.

Leader: Ernest Nongoma OUÉDRAOGO.

Social Forces Front (*Front des Forces Sociales*—FFS). A purported "Sankarist" group, the FFS was launched in October 1996. In 1998 the FFS gained national attention for its vocal role in the February 14 Group. The government accused FFS leader Norbert Tiendrébéogo of being involved in a coup plot in 2003, but Tiendrébéogo was subsequently exonerated. Tiendrébéogo finished seventh in the 2005 presidential poll with 1.6 percent of the vote.

Leaders: Norbert Michel TIENDRÉBÉOGO (President and 2005 presidential candidate), Drissa KOMO (Vice President).

Party for National Renaissance (*Parti pour la Renaissance Nationale*—PAREN). This party was launched in 1989 by Laurent Bado, who claimed that PAREN was neither socialist nor capitalist, but rather "Africanist." In August 2003 PAREN and the MPS/PF (above, under PDP/PS) announced they had formed an electoral coalition called the **United Opposition of Burkina** (*Opposition Burkinabè Uni*—OBU). However, Bado was described as the PAREN candidate when he finished third in the 2005 presidential poll with 2.61 percent of the vote.

Leaders: Laurent BADO (2005 presidential candidate), Baniou BADO.

African Party for Independence (*Parti Africaine pour l'Indépendance*—PAI). Prior to Sankara's overthrow, the PAI's leader, Soumane Touré, was reportedly targeted for execution by the UCB. Despite Touré's reported allegiance to the Compaoré regime, the PAI joined the opposition February 14 Group in early 1998. However, in August the PAI withdrew from the coalition, a schism having emerged in the party between factions led by Touré, who favored participating in the November presidential polling, and Philippe Ouédraogo, who agreed with boycott plans. At a September 13 meeting, Touré was ousted by Ouédraogo, and the group subsequently announced plans to observe the boycott. Rejecting this decision, Touré claimed that he and his followers represented the "true PAI" and continued to use the rubric. In November 2000 Touré's wing signed a protocol with the CDP and others and was given cabinet posts. Ouédraogo's wing stayed in opposition, however. The two factions subsequently fought over the right to use the PAI rubric.

The PAI won five seats in the 2002 assembly balloting, and it was reported that a PAI member was named to the June 2002 cabinet as minister of animal resources. However, apparently underscoring continued PAI disputes, Philippe Ouédraogo was subsequently described as the leader of a strongly anti-Compaoré faction in the assembly known as the Justice and Democracy Parliamentary Group.

Two PAI ministers were reportedly dismissed from the cabinet in September 2005 in an apparent response by Compaoré to Touré's announcement that he intended to oppose Compaoré in the upcoming presidential election. (Touré finished eighth in that poll with 1.12 percent, while Ouédraogo ran as the candidate of the PDS [above]).

Leaders: Soumane TOURÉ (2005 presidential candidate), Zegouma SAMOU.

Other parties that won seats in the 2007 assembly balloting included the **Popular Rally of Citizens** (*Rassemblement Populaire des Citoyens*—RPC), led by Antoine OUARE; and the **Union for Democracy and Social Progress** (*Union pour la Démocratie et le Progrès Social*—UDPS), led by Fidèle AIEN and Baba OUATTARA.

Other Parties and Groups:

Rally of the Ecologists of Burkina (*Rassemblement des Ecologistes du Burkina*—RDEB). A moderate green party, the RDEB was formed by former UVDB leader Ram Ouédraogo in October 2002. He finished fifth in the 2005 presidential balloting with 2.03 percent of the vote. The RDEB presented candidates on its own (unsuccessfully) for the 2007 legislative poll.

Leader: Ram OUÉDRAOGO (President and 2005 presidential candidate).

National Union for Democracy and Development (*Union Nationale pour la Démocratie et le Développement*—UNDD). The UNDD was launched in mid-2003 by Herman Yaméogo, one of the country's leading opposition figures, following a leadership squabble within the ADF/RDA. Among other things, Yaméogo had been accused by other ADF/RDA members of acting "too independently." The UNDD selected Yaméogo as its 2005 presidential candidate, but Yaméogo and the party formally withdrew the candidacy to protest the decision by the Constitutional Court to permit President Compaoré to run for another term. The UNDD called for "civil disobedience" in view of the court's ruling. The UNDD was described in late 2006 as controlling six assembly seats, although it failed to gain representation in the 2007 assembly balloting.

Leaders: Herman YAMÉOGO (Chair), Mathieu N'DO.

Movement for Tolerance and Progress (*Mouvement pour la Tolérance et le Progrès*—MTP). The moderate Sankarist MTP was formed as an "anti-imperialist and national-progressive" grouping in late 1990. Its leader, Emmanuel Nayabtigungu Congo Kaboré, is a former CNR general secretary of government who has called for the maintenance of good relations with the Compaoré administration. To that end, in 1999 Kaboré accepted a post in the government. He kept his position after the formation of the new government in November 2000, but as was the case with other "opposition" ministers, he was not retained in the June 2002 cabinet. Kaboré finished last in the 2005 presidential poll with 0.31 percent of the vote. Although the MTP had participated in the CFD for the 2002 legislative elections, it presented (without success) candidates on its own in some regional constituencies in the 2007 assembly balloting.

Leaders: Emmanuel Nayabtigungu Congo KABORÉ (Secretary General and 2005 presidential candidate).

Minor parties that gained representation in the assembly in the May 2002 elections included: the **Alliance for Progress and Freedom** (*Alliance pour le Progrès et la Liberté*—APL), led by Joséphine TAMBOURA-SAMA; the **National Convention of Progressive Democrats** (*Convention Nationale des Démocrates Progressistes*—CNDP), formed in 2000 and led by Alfred KABORÉ; the **Patriotic Front for Change** (*Front Patriotique pour le Changement*—FPC), a Sankarist party led by Tahirou Ibrahim ZON; and the **Union of Independent Progressive Democrats** (*Union des Démocrates et Progressistes Indépendants*—UDPI), which was formed in 2000 by dissidents from the G14 under the leadership of Longo DONGO.

New parties credited with legislative seats as of late 2006 included the **Party of Concord and Progress** (*Parti pour la Concorde et le Progrès*—PCP); the **Sankarist Democratic Front** (*Front Démocratique Sankariste*—FDS), which split from the CPS in 2004 under the leadership of Fidèle Meng-Néré KIENTÉGA and Inoussa KABORÉ; the **Union of Patriots for Development** (*Union des Patriotes pour le Développement*—UPD); the **Rally of Democrats for the Faso** (*Rassemblement des Démocrates pour la Faso*—RDF); and the **Convergence for Social Democracy** (*Convergence pour la Démocratie Sociale*—CDS), formed in 2002 by a split in the UDPI and led by Valére SOMÉ.

Other parties that participated in the 2002 elections but failed to gain representation included the **National Democratic Party** (*Parti Démocratique National*—PDN), led by Karamoko KONÉ; the **Party for Progress and Social Development** (*Parti pour le Progrès et le Développement Social*—PPDS), led by Basile COMBARY; the **Unified Socialist Party** (*Parti Socialiste Unifié*—PSU), formed in 2001 by Benoît LOMPO; and the **Democrats and Patriots Group** (*Groupe des Démocrates et Patriotes*—GDP), led by Issa TIENDRÉBÉOGO.

Other small parties that participated in the 2005 presidential elections included the **Burkinabè Party for Refounding** (*Parti Burkinabè pour la Refondation*—PBR), whose candidate, Gilbert BOUDA, finished ninth with 1.04 percent of the vote; the **Socialist Alliance** (*Alliance Socialiste*—AS), whose candidate, Parqui Emile Paré, finished tenth with 0.87 percent of the vote (the AS comprised Paré's MPS/PF and the PSU); and the **Union for Democracy and Development** (*Union pour la Démocratie et le Développement*—UDD), whose candidate, Toubé Clément DAKIO, secured 0.37 percent of the vote.

Other minor parties and groups (in addition to the REDB, UNDD, APL, PCP, and MPS/PF) that unsuccessfully presented candidates in the national constituency in the 2007 assembly balloting included the **Alliance of Patriotic Citizens** (*Alliance des Citoyens Patriotes*—ACP), led by Ousmana DIALLO and Boubacar DICKO; the **Alliance for Democracy of Faso** (*Alliance pour la Démocratie du Faso*—ADEFA), led by Boureima OUÉDRAOGO; the **Ecologist Party for the Development of Burkina** (*Parti Écologiste pour le Développement du Burkina*—PEDB), led by Assista TRAORE/DIARRA; and the **Republican Party for Integration and Solidarity** (*Parti Républicain pour l'Integration et la Solidarité*—PARIS), led by Jean NIKIEMA. A number of other parties also presented candidates unsuccessfully in the regional constituencies.

LEGISLATURE

The former National Assembly (*Assemblée Nationale*) was dissolved following the 1980 coup, and no successor body was established under the Sankara regime. The 1991 constitution provided for an Assembly of People's Deputies with a five-year mandate, balloting for which was initially scheduled for January 12, 1992, but subsequently postponed until May 24. The current basic law also provides for a second, consultative chamber (General Conference of the Nation [*Conférence Générale de la Nation*]), which had not been formally constituted as of mid-2009.

Assembly of People's Deputies (*Assemblée des Députés Populaires*). In January 1997 the assembly approved a constitutional amendment increasing its seat total from 97 to 111. Election (for five-year terms) is conducted via a party-list proportional system that was revised in advance of the 2002 balloting with the goal of greater opposition representation. Ninety deputies were elected in 2002 from 15 electoral districts (reduced from the previous 45 districts), and 21 deputies were elected from a national list. Fifteen legislators were elected from the national constituency in 2007, while 96 were elected from 13 multimember constituencies corresponding to the country's 13 regions.

The distribution of seats following the election of May 6, 2007, was as follows: Congress of Democracy, 73 (64 regional, 9 national); Alliance for Democracy and Federation/African Democratic Rally, 14 (12, 2); Union for the Republic, 5 (4, 1); Union for Rebirth/Sankarist Movement, 4 (3, 1); Convention of the Democratic Forces of Burkina, 3 (2, 1); Party for Democracy and Socialism, 2 (1, 1); Party for Democracy and Progress/Socialist Party, 2 (2, 0); Rally for the Development of Burkina, 2 (2, 0); Union of Sankarist Parties, 2 (2, 0); Party for National Renaissance, 1 (1, 0); Popular Rally of Citizens, 1 (1, 0); Union for Democracy and Social Progress, 1 (1, 0); and African Party for Independence, 1 (1, 0).

President: Roch Marc Christian KABORÉ.

CABINET

[as of May 1, 2009]

Prime Minister	Tertius Zongo
Ministers	
Agriculture, Hydraulics, and Water Resources	Laurent Sedgo
Animal Resources	Sékou Bâ
Basic Education and Literacy	Marie Odile Bonkoungou [f]
Civil Service and Administrative Reform	Sougalo Ouattara
Commerce and Promotion of Enterprise and Crafts	Mamadou Sanou
Culture, Tourism, Communication, and Government Spokesperson	Fillippe Savadogo
Defense	Yéro Boly
Economy and Finance	Lucien Marie Noel Bembamba
Environment and Quality of Life	Salifou Sawadogo
Foreign Affairs and Regional Cooperation	Bedouna Alain Yoda
Health	Seydou Bouda
Housing and Urban Planning	Vincent T. Dabilougou
Infrastructure and Access	Seydou Kaboré
Justice and Keeper of the Seals	Zakalia Koté
Labor and Social Security	Jerôme Bougouma
Mines, Quarries, and Energy	Abdoulaye Abdoulkader Cissé
Office of the President (Analysis and Planning)	Gueda Jacques Ouédraogo
Postal Service, Information Technology, and Communication	Noel Kaboré
Promotion of Human Rights	Salamata Sawadoga [f]
Promotion of Women	Céline M. Yoda [f]
Relations with Parliament	Tibo Cecile Beloum [f]
Secondary and Higher Education and Scientific Research	Joseph Pare
Security	Emile Ouédraoga
Social Action and National Solidarity	Pascaline Tamini [f]
Sports and Leisure	Mori Ardouma Jean-Pierre Palm
Territorial Administration and Decentralization	Clément P. Sawadogo
Transportation	Gilbert G. Noël Ouédraogo
Youth and Employment	Justin Koutaba
Ministers Delegate	
Agriculture	Abdoulaye Combary
Budget	Marie Thérèse Drabo [f]
Literacy and Nonformal Education	Ousseni Tamboura
Local Collectives	Toussaint Abel Coulibaly
Regional Cooperation	Minata Samate [f]
Technical and Professional Education	Maxime Some
Secretary General of the Government and the Council of Ministers	Amadou Adrien Kone

[f] = female

COMMUNICATIONS

A Press Code adopted in 1993 ostensibly provided for a "free and transparent press" following decades of near-total state domination of the media. However, although a number of independent media outlets have since been established and the press is described as "generally free," controversial provisions in the Press Code (providing penalties for journalists deemed guilty of publishing "false information") have been used by the government to close radio stations and arrest journalists. Consequently, "self-censorship" is considered to be widespread. International and domestic observers also strongly criticized the government's handling of the investigation into the death of journalist Norbert Zongo in 1998 (see Political background and Current issues, above), and the lack of a resolution in the case prompted a mass protest demonstration in December 2008 on the tenth anniversary of the event.

Press. The following are published in Ouagadougou (unless otherwise noted): *Observateur Paalga* (New Observer 10,000), independent (but progovernment) daily; *Le Journal du Jeudi* (Thursday Journal, 8,000), independent, satirical weekly; *Sidwaya* (Truth, 10,000), government daily; *Sidwaya Hebo* (Weekly Truth, 3,000), government weekly; *Le Pays* (The Country, 8,000), independent (but pro-opposition) daily; *L'Indépendant* (The Independent, 12,000), independent weekly; *L'Observateur Dimanche* (Sunday Observer, 4,000), independent weekly; *L'Express du* Faso (The Express of Faso), independent daily published in the city of Bobo-Bioulasso; *L'Opinion* (Opinion, 5,000); *San Finna*, opposition weekly with connections to the National Union for Democracy and Development; *Le Reporter*, described as critical of the government; and *L'Évenement*, independent published twice a month.

News agencies. The state-owned *Agence d'Information du Burkina* (AIB), a successor to *Agence Burkinabè de Presse* (ABP), is the domestic facility; *Agence France-Presse*, Reuters, and other international agencies also maintain offices in Ouagadougou.

Broadcasting and computing. There are more than 70 radio stations, including the state-owned *Radio National du Burkina*. Television broadcasting remains relatively undeveloped; as of mid-decade there were one state-owned station (*Television Nationale du Burkina Faso*) and three private stations. As of 2008 there were 9.2 Internet users per 1,000 inhabitants.

INTERGOVERNMENTAL REPRESENTATION

Ambassador to the U.S.: Paramanga Ernest YONLI.

U.S. Ambassador to Burkina Faso: Gayleatha Beatrice BROWN.

Permanent Representative to the UN: Michel KAFANDO.

IGO Memberships (Non-UN): AfDB, AU, BADEA, BOAD, CENT, CILSS, ECOWAS, IDB, Interpol, IOM, NAM, OIC, OIF, PCA, UEMOA, WCO, WTO.

BURUNDI

Republic of Burundi
Republika y'u Burundi (Kirundi)
République du Burundi (French)

Political Status: Independent state since July 1, 1962; military control imposed November 28, 1966; one-party constitution adopted by referendum of November 18, 1981; military control reimposed following coup of September 3, 1987; multiparty constitution adopted March 13, 1992, following referendum of March 9; military rule reimposed following coup of July 25, 1996; transitional constitution signed into law June 6, 1998; new transitional constitution providing for a three-year transitional period adopted October 27, 2001; new constitution (institutionalizing Hutu/Tutsi power sharing) approved by national referendum on February 28, 2005; transitional period concluded with local and national elections in June–September 2005.

Area: 10,747 sq. mi. (27,834 sq. km.).

Population: 5,139,073 (1990C); 8,556,000 (2008E).

Major Urban Center (2005E): BUJUMBURA (407,000). (In 2007 the government announced plans to move the capital to the centrally located city of Gitega, although it presented no schedule for such a transfer.)

Official Languages: Kirundi, French (Swahili is also spoken).

Monetary Unit: Burundi Franc (official rate December 1, 2009: 1,230.50 francs = $1US).

President: Pierre NKURUNZIZA (Hutu from the National Council for the Defense of Democracy–Forces for the Defense of Democracy); elected by the Parliament on August 19, 2005, and inaugurated for a five-year term on August 26 in succession to Domitien NDAYIZEYE (Front for Democracy in Burundi).

First Vice President (In Charge of Political and Administrative Affairs): Dr. Yves SAHINGUVU (Tutsi from the Union for National Progress); inaugurated in November 9, 2007, following appointment by the president and approval by the Parliament the previous day to succeed Martin NDUWIMANA (Tutsi from the Union for National Progress), who had resigned on November 7.

Second Vice President (In Charge of Social and Economic Affairs): Gabriel NTISEZERANA (Hutu from the National Council for the Defense of Democracy–Forces for the Defense of Democracy); approved by the Parliament (upon nomination by the president) on February 8, 2007, to succeed Marina BARAMPAMA (National Council for the Defense of Democracy–Forces for the Defense of Democracy), who had been dismissed on February 8.

THE COUNTRY

Situated in east-central Africa (bordered by Rwanda, Tanzania, and the Democratic Republic of the Congo), Burundi, one of Africa's smallest nations, is a country of grassy uplands and high plateaus. It is one of the most densely populated countries on the continent, with over 400 persons per square mile. There are three main ethnic groups: the Hutu (Bahutu), who constitute 84 percent of the population; the Tutsi (Batutsi, Watutsi), who are numerically a minority (15 percent) but have long dominated the country politically, socially, and economically; and the Twa, or pygmies (1 percent). A majority of the population is nominally Christian, primarily Roman Catholic. Women account for almost half of the labor force, although they are concentrated in subsistence activities, with men predominant in paid labor. Female representation in politics and government was traditionally minimal, although the prime minister from July 1993 to February 1994 was a woman. Under the constitution adopted in 2005 significant female representation is guaranteed in the Parliament and in the cabinet.

One of the world's least-developed countries, Burundi remains dependent on agriculture. More than 80 percent of its inhabitants are farmers, primarily at the subsistence level, and coffee accounts for more than 70 percent of export earnings. The small industrial sector consists for the most part of agricultural processing. Small quantities of cassiterite, gold, columbite-tantalite, and wolframite are extracted, while exploitation of a major deposit of nickel and potentially significant reserves of phosphate, petroleum, and uranium await construction of transport infrastructure. (Exploration licenses have recently been issued.)

Officials from the International Monetary Fund (IMF) in 1992 reported that the second phase of an economic reform program had produced "progress toward sustainable economic growth." However, the outbreak of civil conflict in 1993 and the subsequent withdrawal of international assistance yielded negative growth in 1993–1995.

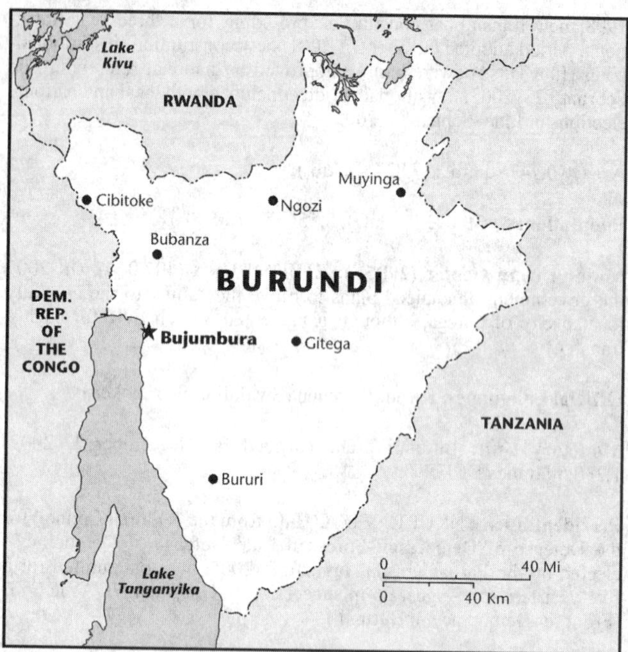

Following the military coup in July 1996, the nation's already extremely unstable security and economic conditions deteriorated even further. Among other things, civil strife constrained the government's ability to collect revenues, as did smuggling.

The transitional government installed in late 2001 under a new power-sharing agreement (see Political background, below) immediately launched an appeal for international aid to assist reconstruction, combat what was described as an "alarming level of poverty," and facilitate the expected repatriation of hundreds of thousands of refugees from neighboring countries. Modest recovery ensued, albeit from a very low base. The relative political stability also permitted the deployment of regional peacekeepers and the resumption of foreign aid by the IMF, the World Bank, and others.

Upon the installation of a new government of national unity in 2005, it was estimated that 300,000 people had lost their lives in the 12-year civil war. Collaterally, GDP had declined by more than a third, and per capita annual income had plummeted to $100. Among other distressing indicators, nearly 60 percent of the country's children suffered from stunted growth due to poor nutrition, according to one relief agency. The IMF called upon the new administration to pursue "good governance" and address the nation's "urgent social needs" in order, among other things, to attract foreign investment.

A poor coffee harvest limited GDP growth to 3.5 percent in 2007. Supporters of the government cited advances in education and health care as evidence of recent progress, although corruption and a small but "persistent" insurgency (see Current issues, below) continued to compromise efforts to combat the growing HIV/AIDS infection rate, spur economic development, and improve the power grid (reportedly, only 1 percent of the population had regular access to electricity).

GDP growth improved to an estimated 4.5 percent in 2008, although annual inflation by the end of the year had risen sharply to 22 percent, mostly due to dramatic hikes in food and fuel prices. In February 2009 the IMF, describing the government's economic efforts as "broadly satisfactory," joined the World Bank in canceling $1.4 billion of Burundi's debt and called upon the government to invest the "savings" in social programs and infrastructure improvements.

GOVERNMENT AND POLITICS

Political background. Established in the 16th century as a feudal monarchy ruled by the Tutsi, Burundi (formerly Urundi) was incorporated into German East Africa in 1895 and came under Belgian administration as a result of World War I. From 1919 to 1962 it formed the southern half of the Belgian-administered League of Nations mandate (later The United Nations Trust Territory) of Ruanda-Urundi. Retaining its monarchical form of government under indigenous Tutsi rulers (*mwami*), Urundi was granted limited self-government in 1961 and achieved full independence as the Kingdom of Burundi on July 1, 1962.

Rivalry between Tutsi factions and between Tutsis and Hutus resulted in the assassination of Prime Minister Pierre NGENDANDUMWE in January 1965 and an abortive Hutu coup the following October. The uprising led to repressive action by government troops under the command of Capt. Michel MICOMBERO. Named prime minister as the result of military intervention in July 1966, Micombero suspended the constitution, dissolved the National Assembly, and on November 28 deposed King NATARE V. In addition to naming himself president of the newly proclaimed Republic of Burundi, Micombero took over the presidency of the Union and National Progress (*Union et Progrès National*—Uprona), the Tutsi-dominated political party that was accorded monopoly status.

Despite antigovernment plots in 1969 and 1971, the Micombero regime was generally able to contain conflict in the immediate post-coup era. In 1972, however, the mysterious death of the former king and another attempted Hutu uprising provoked renewed reprisals by Micombero's Tutsi supporters. At least 100,000 deaths (largely of Hutus) ensued, with countless thousands fleeing to neighboring countries.

On November 1, 1976, Micombero was overthrown in a bloodless coup led by Lt. Col. Jean-Baptiste BAGAZA, who suspended the constitution and announced that a 30-member Supreme Council of the Revolution would assume formal power under the "Second Republic" with himself as head of state. At an Uprona congress in December 1979 the Supreme Council was abolished, effective January 1980, and its functions were transferred to a party Central Committee headed by the president. On October 22, 1982, elections were held for a new National Assembly and for pro forma reconfirmation of Bagaza as chief executive. Following his redesignation as party leader at the Uprona congress of July 25–27, 1984, Bagaza was nominated for a third presidential term (the first by direct election), obtaining a reported 99.6 percent of the vote in a referendum on August 31.

Bagaza's subsequent administration was marked by progressively more stringent measures against the Roman Catholic Church, which traditionally maintained strong links with the Hutu community. Many Tutsis even eventually joined the condemnation of "dictatorial" anticlerical measures such as the expulsion and imprisonment of church leaders and the proscription of weekday masses. Amid growing alienation, Bagaza was ousted in a bloodless revolt on September 3, 1987, while attending a francophone summit in Canada. The leader of the coup, Maj. Pierre BUYOYA, suspended the constitution, dissolved the National Assembly, and named a 31-member Military Committee for National Salvation (*Comité Militaire pour le Salut National*—CMSN) to exercise provisional authority. On September 9 the CMSN designated Buyoya as president of the "Third Republic," and on October 1 Buyoya announced the formation of a new government, pledging that the "military will not remain in power long."

On October 19, 1988, following a renewal of Tutsi-Hutu conflict, President Buyoya named a 23-member cabinet that contained an unprecedented majority of Hutus, including Adrien SIBOMANA as occupant of the newly reestablished post of prime minister. However, the timetable for a return to constitutional rule remained unclear, and the CMSN, composed entirely of Tutsis, remained the dominant decision-making body until mid-1990, when it was replaced by the National Security Council (*Conseil National de Sécurité*—CSN), an 11-member civilian grouping of six Tutsis and five Hutus.

In furtherance of President Buyoya's campaign for ethnic reconciliation, a national charter calling for "unity, respect for human rights and freedom of expression" was endorsed by Uprona in December 1990 and adopted by popular referendum on February 5, 1991. In accordance with charter provisions calling for an end to military rule, Buyoya on March 22 empowered a 35-member constitutional commission to outline the framework of a multiparty system. The commission's report, released on September 10, served as the basis of a pluralist constitution that was approved by an overwhelming majority in a referendum on March 9, 1992, and promulgated four days later.

On November 17, 1992, President Buyoya appointed a national electoral commission charged with overseeing the legislative and presidential balloting scheduled for 1993. The 33-member body included two representatives from each of eight registered political parties, with the balance being drawn from a broad spectrum of public and religious organizations.

In the presidential election of June 1, 1993, the Hutu opposition candidate, Melchior NDADAYE, was a better than three-to-one victor over Buyoya, and in legislative balloting on June 29 Ndadaye's Front for Democracy in Burundi (*Front pour la Démocratie au Burundi*—Frodebu) won 65 of 81 seats. Despite international praise for the electoral process, some 5,000 Tutsis took part in street demonstrations denouncing the "ethnic nature" of the Hutu victories, and on July 3 an abortive coup attempt by troops loyal to Buyoya was reported.

On July 10, 1993, Ndadaye reached out to the previously dominant Tutsis and included seven Uprona members in a new cabinet that was also headed by a Tutsi, Sylvie KINIGI, as prime minister. Pledging continuance of his predecessor's reconciliation program, Ndadaye in September amnestied 5,000 prisoners (earlier he had granted clemency to Bagaza, allowing the former president to return from six years in exile). In early October Ndadaye announced plans to begin the repatriation of the approximately 300,000 Burundians displaced by earlier conflicts.

Optimism engendered by the reconciliation effort was dashed on October 21, 1993, when Ndadaye, the National Assembly president, and a number of senior Hutu government officials were slain during an abortive military coup attempt spearheaded by Tutsi paratroopers. The rebellion ended within two days as senior military personnel, some of whom had been implicated in the plot, sought to disassociate themselves from an ethnic frenzy unleashed by the president's assassination. In addition to a number of senior Tutsi officers from the Burore region, the coup plotters allegedly included Bagaza; the recently appointed army chief-of-staff, Col. Jean BIKOMAGU; and François NGEZE, a former interior minister and vocal critic of the new administration, who on October 21 was named president of the rebels' short-lived National Committee of Public Salvation (an appointment he later claimed was forced on him). Denying involvement in the uprising, Bikomagu on October 24 offered to aid in reestablishing the government in exchange for amnesty. However, the offer was rejected by Prime Minister Kinigi, who said, from her refuge in the French embassy, that she would remain underground until the military had returned to its barracks and an international protective force had been established for the government.

By October 24, 1993, most of the rebel soldiers had fled Bujumbura in the face of a massing of progovernment troops and revenge-minded Ndadaye supporters. On November 2, following the arrest of at least ten of the plotters, including Ngeze, Kinigi emerged from her embassy sanctuary to retake control of the government. Six days later she met with 15 cabinet ministers under the protection of a French special forces unit to discuss ways of ending the tribal bloodbath that had left 10,000 dead and hundreds of thousands exiled in Rwanda, Tanzania, and Zaire.

On January 13, 1994, the National Assembly elected a Hutu moderate, Agriculture Minister Cyprien NTARYAMIRE, to the presidency. However, Ntaryamire and Rwandan President Juvénal Habyarimana were killed in an airplane bombing over Kigali, Rwanda, on April 6, 1994. On April 8 Sylvestre NTIBANTUNGANYA, who had been elected assembly president on December 23, 1993, became Ntaryamire's acting successor.

Amid escalating violence, opposition leaders boycotted talks on the selection of a new president in June 1994. However, on July 13 a power-sharing agreement was concluded, under which Frodebu was to be awarded control of 9 provinces and 74 communes, with opposition groups being given 7 provinces and 48 communes. A follow-up "Convention on Government" was signed on September 10, under which 45 percent of cabinet posts, including the prime ministership and interior ministry, were to be allocated to the Uprona-led opposition, with the defense and justice portfolios reserved for "neutral persons." Subsequently, the National Assembly ratified the convention's nomination of the acting president for a regular term, with swearing-in ceremonies on October 1. Instability nonetheless continued, with the controversial election on December 3 of Frodebu's Jean MINANI as National Assembly speaker being defended by the Uprona prime minister, Anatole KANYENKIKO, who had succeeded Kinigi in February. Opposition to Minani led to his replacement by Léonce NGENDAKUMANA on January 12, 1995, while Kanyenkiko was, in turn, obliged to resign on February 15 after being expelled from Uprona for indiscipline in regard to the Minani affair. With the appointment of the Uprona-nominated Antoine NDUWAYO as Kanyenkiko's successor as prime minister on February 20, the political crisis appeared to ease, although Tanzania reported that some 25,000 refugees had crossed its border with Burundi since the first of the month.

A new cycle of fighting erupted following the murder on March 11, 1995, of a prominent Hutu leader, Ernest KABUSHEMEYE, prompting another wave of refugees into Zaire and Tanzania. Meanwhile, President Ntibantunganya rejected proposals (apparently advanced by U.S. officials) that the problems of Burundi and Rwanda be addressed by the creation of two ethnically based countries, in effect a "Hutuland" and a "Tutsiland." In July the UN announced the formation of a commission of inquiry into the October 1993 coup attempt and urged the feuding political groups to begin peace negotiations, warning that the UN could play only a minor role in ending the conflict.

Following the killing of at least 58 Tutsis at a displaced persons camp in early August 1995, Prime Minister Nduwayo claimed that former Rwandan soldiers and militiamen (both Hutu-dominated) were responsible for at least "two-thirds of the recent violence." Nduwayo's assertion worsened the already incendiary debate within the cabinet over which ethnic group was responsible for the latest round of violence, and on October 12 President Ntibantunganya reshuffled the government, ousting the most vocal combatants and replacing them with less "partisan" ministers. The violence nonetheless continued, and in December three of the ten parties participating in the government withdrew.

With ethnic fighting intensifying, the United States and the European Union (EU) suspended aid payments to Burundi, citing the government's failure to end the violence. President Ntibantunganya and Prime Minister Nduwayo agreed in principle in early July 1996 to the deployment of foreign peacekeeping forces to quell ethnic violence and protect Burundi's infrastructure, borders, and political leaders. That plan was denounced by militants in both the Tutsi and Hutu camps, however, and, following the massacre by Hutu rebels of over 300 Tutsis in a camp on July 20, antigovernment demonstrations broke out in Bujumbura and other cities. After being stoned by Tutsi mourners at funeral services for the massacre victims, President Ntibantunganya sought refuge in the U.S. embassy on July 23. The next day Uprona announced it was withdrawing from the coalition government. On July 25 the military declared that it had taken power, dismissed the government, suspended the constitution and the National Assembly, and appointed former president Buyoya head of state. (Prime Minister Nduwayo accepted his dismissal, but President Ntibantunganya subsequently insisted that he remained the nation's lawful head of state.) On July 31 Maj. Buyoya announced the appointment of Pascal Firmin NDIMIRA, a Hutu member of Uprona, as prime minister, and a new 25-member Uprona-based government was formed on August 2. Despite Maj. Buyoya's reputation as a "moderate" among Tutsi military leaders and the credit he had received for the orderly transfer of power three years earlier, the July 1996 coup was broadly denounced by the United Nations, Western capitals, and, most strongly, by neighboring states, who immediately imposed severe economic sanctions against Burundi. For his part, asserting that the military had taken over only to "stop the bloodshed," Maj. Buyoya called for a three-year transitional period prior to a return to civilian government and pledged to clamp down on military abuses.

On September 12, 1996, in the face of the strong international condemnation of the recent coup, Buyoya declared that the assembly suspension had been lifted and that political party activity could resume. However, less than half of the legislators participated in the reopening of the assembly on October 7, contributing factors including the recent murder of a number of legislators, an opposition boycott, and apathy resulting from the fact that the suspension of the constitution had left the body virtually powerless. In October regional leaders decided to maintain the economic sanctions against Bujumbura despite the regime's announcement that it intended to hold unconditional peace talks with the dominant rebel group—the National Council for the Defense of Democracy (*Conseil National pour la Défense de Démocratie*—CNDD). Moreover, in late 1996 both the UN and Amnesty International charged the regime with responsibility for massacres that had taken place since July.

In March 1997 the government announced that it had arrested eight people (five of whom belonged to former president Bagaza's Party for National Recovery [*Parti pour le Recouvrement National*—Parena]) for their alleged roles in a coup plot against the president as well as bomb attacks in Bujumbura. Despite continued violence, in mid-April regional leaders agreed to loosen sanctions on humanitarian supplies. On June 7 former president Ntibantunganya left the U.S. embassy, declaring his intention to resume his political life and calling for the opening of peace talks. One week later Buyoya asked for international assistance in establishing a genocide tribunal to punish those responsible for the recent ethnic violence. However, the UN Security Council rejected his request, citing continued high levels of instability.

Following intense negotiations on a power-sharing agreement between Buyoya and Hutu remnants in the assembly (led by Speaker Léonce Ngendakumana), Buyoya signed a transitional constitution into law on June 6, 1998. Provisions included enlargement of the assembly, the formal recognition of established political parties, and formation of a transitional government. Consequently, Buyoya was officially sworn in as president on June 11, and the following day he appointed two vice presidents, including Frodebu leader Frederic BAMVUGINYUMVIRA, to assume responsibilities formerly held by the prime minister, whose post was abolished. On June 13 the president appointed a new cabinet, 13 of whose 22 members were Hutus, while the Transitional National Assembly was inaugurated on July 18, new members representing small parties as well as social and professional groups.

Regional leaders meeting in Tanzania in early September 1997 agreed to maintain economic sanctions against the Burundian regime, warning President Buyoya that "additional measures" would be considered unless progress was made toward restoration of civilian government. Buyoya had declined to participate in the summit's proposed peace talks, in part, reportedly, out of conviction that Tanzania was "pro-Hutu." (It was estimated that as many as 300,000 Hutu refugees were encamped inside the Tanzanian border.) In his defense, Buyoya appeared to be attempting to follow a difficult middle course between the militant Hutu guerrilla groups, who had been fighting since 1993 to take over the government, and predominately Tutsi hard-liners in the government and military, who opposed negotiations of any sort with the "rebels." At the same time, Western capitals remained concerned over the Buyoya regime's refusal to permit the resumption of normal political party activity as well as its highly controversial "resettlement" program in which perhaps as many as 600,000 people were confined to "refugee" camps. Although the government argued that the measures were designed to protect people displaced by guerrilla activity, critics argued that Hutus were being placed in the camps so that they could not offer support to the rebels.

Perhaps in part to improve his "battered image" in the West, President Buyoya in March 1998 agreed to participate in talks with representatives of Frodebu, the CNDD, and other factions. A series of peace talks began in June under the leadership of Julius Nyerere, the former Tanzanian president representing the regional nations who had imposed economic sanctions. During the fourth round of negotiations in January 1999, the sanctions were lifted, following earlier calls for their suspension or cessation by the EU and UN Security Council. The power-sharing agreement reached six months earlier between the government and the opposition appeared to have persuaded critics of the regime that it was making progress. However, peace negotiations in Tanzania dragged on through the year, the slow pace of the discussions reflecting intraparty disagreements between peacemakers and hard-liners.

Following Nyerere's death in October 1999, former South African president Nelson Mandela assumed the task of facilitating the negotiations. He announced in May 2000 that an agreement in principle had been reached, and a partial, preliminary agreement was signed on August 28. However, details remained to be settled regarding highly sensitive issues such as the length and composition of a transitional government, the specifics of the new electoral system, and the integration of the nation's security forces. Highly contentious negotiations on these matters dragged on for months, as did efforts by the government to negotiate a cease-fire with the Hutu rebel groups that had rejected the accord—the Forces for the Defense of Democracy (*Forces pour la Défense de Démocratie*—FDD) and the National Forces of Liberation (*Forces Nationales de la Libération*—FNL). Finally, following mediation by the Organization of African Unity (OAU, subsequently the African Union—AU) and further efforts by Mandela, a power-sharing agreement was accepted on July 23, 2001, during a meeting in Arusha of 19 groups (representatives from the government, Transitional National Assembly, and all members of the pro-Hutu Group of Seven and pro-Tutsi Group of Ten—see listings in Political Parties and Groups, below).

On October 28, 2001, the assembly adopted a transitional constitution to implement the Arusha accords, and the following day the assembly confirmed Buyoya as president of the new transitional government and Domitien NDAYIZEYE, secretary general of Frodebu, as vice president. Buyoya was sworn in on November 1 for an 18-month term, after which he was to be replaced, according to the agreement, by Ndayizeye for the remaining 18 months of the transition period. (A Tutsi was scheduled to replace Ndayizeye as vice president following his elevation to president, although Buyoya announced he would not be a candidate for that post.) A new cabinet, comprising 15 political parties, was also installed on November 1, while on November 27 the assembly adopted legislation providing for a new transitional legislature. However, the two main rebel groups (the FDD and FNL) remained adamantly opposed to the accord and, in fact, intensified their military activity. (Other rebel forces had accepted the Arusha provisions for their gradual integration into what would ultimately become ethnically balanced national defense and security forces.) Moreover, even within the political parties that had signed the power-sharing agreement, Tutsi and Hutu hard-liners scoffed at the prospects for a permanent negotiated settlement and the potential for cohesiveness within the coalition government, which contained highly disparate elements. Nevertheless, President Buyoya and Vice President Ndayizeye pledged to "fight the ideology of genocide" and to promote national unity. Meanwhile, South Africa deployed peacekeeping troops in Burundi to protect the hundreds of thousands of Hutu refugees (including numerous prominent politicians) who had been invited to return to Burundi. The UN endorsed the South African initiative, which was soon augmented by forces from other neighboring countries. However, no official UN peacekeeping mission was authorized at that point in view of the lack of a cease-fire agreement from the rebels.

Fighting between government forces and both the FDD and FNL continued into the autumn of 2002, despite several attempts to negotiate peace settlements. However, the declaration of a cease-fire with the FDD in December and subsequent deployment of an AU peacekeeping force began to convince skeptics that a long-term settlement was possible. Under the terms of the transitional constitution, at the end of his 18-month term Buyoya turned the presidency over to Ndayizeye, who was inaugurated on April 30, 2003. That same day, Alphonse-Marie KADEGE of Uprona was appointed vice president.

Renewed fighting in July 2003 between the government and the FNL led the UN to withdraw its nonessential personnel from the country and by September had left 170 dead and created some 50,000 additional internal refugees. In October peace negotiations under the leadership of South African President Thabo Mbeki led to an agreement that granted five cabinet posts to the primary CNDD faction, now known as the CNDD-FDD. Three provincial gubernatorial posts and the vice presidency of the assembly were also accorded to the CNDD-FDD. In return, the CNDD-FDD pledged to begin disarmament. To oversee that process, the AU peacekeeping force was increased to more than 3,000 troops. On November 16 the government and the CNDD-FDD signed a comprehensive peace agreement to implement the Arusha accords, and on November 23 Ndayizeye reshuffled the cabinet to form a government of national unity that included the CNDD-FDD and most other major parties. In December Pierre NKURUNZIZA, the leader of the CNDD-FDD, returned to Burundi for the first time since 1993, and 6,000 CNDD-FDD fighters began demobilization. However, at least one faction of the FNL continued its armed struggle. In May 2004 the UN authorized its own peacekeeping mission (the United Nations Operation in Burundi [*Opération des Nations Unies au Burundi*—ONUB]) to succeed the AU forces and supervise the disarmament of an estimated 40,000 "rebels."

On October 20, 2004, Ndayizeye signed a new draft constitution that had been approved by a special joint session of the legislature. The document called for permanent power sharing between the Tutsis and Hutus through a system of proportional representation (see Constitution and government, below). National legislative elections were subsequently scheduled for July 2005, and Ndayizeye's term was extended until the new elections, at which time a new president would be chosen by the legislature. (Subsequent presidents would be popularly elected.) Ndayizeye announced that he intended to retire from politics at the end of his current term.

On November 10, 2004, Vice President Kadege resigned following continued disagreements with the president over power-sharing arrangements and Kadege's opposition to the new constitution. Frederic NGENZEBUHORO of Uprona replaced Kadege the following day.

In December 2004 President Ndayizeye signed legislation creating a new national army and police force incorporating the former FDD fighters. At that point sporadic, albeit intense, fighting between government forces and the FNL still presented a serious barrier to successful conclusion of the transitional government.

Voters approved the proposed new constitution by a 92 percent margin in a national referendum on February 28, 2005, and in May most elements of the FNL finally agreed to a truce. Consequently, communal elections were held on June 3, with the CNDD-FDD (now a legal party) securing more than 55 percent of votes and more than 1,780 of the 3,325 seats up for election. The CNDD-FDD also dominated the July 4 assembly balloting, and CNDD-FDD leader Nkurunziza was elected president (as the sole candidate) with 91 percent of the votes cast during a joint session of the assembly and the Senate on August 19. In keeping with constitutional requirements, Nkurunziza appointed a Tutsi (Martin NDUWIMANA, from Uprona) as first vice president. Nkurunziza subsequently formed a new national unity government that included members from the CNDD-FDD, Uprona, Frodebu, Parena, and several small parties. However, Frodebu in March 2006 announced its withdrawal from the government (see Frodebu under Political Parties and Groups, below).

President Nkurunziza effectively lost his legislative majority in early 2007 as a result of severe CNDD-FDD fractionalization (see Current issues and CNDD-FDD under Political Parties and Groups for details). He attempted to form a new cabinet in June but could not achieve legislative approval when Uprona, Frodebu, and the CNDD-FDD dissidents refused to participate. After reaching agreement with Frodebu (in late October) and Uprona (in early November), Nkurunziza on November 14 announced a new national unity cabinet that included four Frodebu and two Uprona ministers, although the CNDD-FDD retained control of the major ministries. The new government also included a new first vice president—Dr. Yves SAHINGUVU of Uprona (see Uprona in Political Parties and Groups, below, for background information). The cabinet was reshuffled on January 29, 2009, although the constitutionally prescribed ethnic and party distribution of positions was again carefully followed.

Constitution and government. (For details on the March 1992 constitution and subsequent constitutional developments until 2001, see the 2007 *Handbook*.) Following the signing of the Arusha power-sharing accord in July 2001, the assembly adopted a "Constitution of Transition" on October 28 providing for a three-year transitional government. Power was concentrated in the presidency and vice presidency, with a Tutsi (President Buyoya) to serve as president for 18 months before being replaced for the next 18 months by a Hutu. Provision was also made for a new Transitional Parliament to include a National Assembly and a Senate. Elections were scheduled to be held, under undetermined electoral arrangements, at the communal level by the end of the first 18 months of the transition and at the national level (for a new assembly and senate) by the end of the second 18-month period.

The new constitution approved via national referendum on February 28, 2005, was most noteworthy for its efforts to institutionalize Hutu/Tutsi power sharing. The new basic law provided for the new legislature to elect the next president, but subsequent chief executives will be popularly elected.

The president is elected for a five-year term, renewable once. There are two vice presidents; if the president is a Hutu, then the first vice president must be a Tutsi, and vice versa. The first vice president must also be from a different party than the president. It is mandated by the constitution that maximum cabinet membership be 60 percent for Hutus and 40 percent for Tutsis. In addition, all parties that secure more than 5 percent in an assembly election must be represented in the subsequent cabinet in proportion to the number of seats won. The defense minister must also be from a different ethnic group than the minister responsible for internal security, and no single ethnic group can make up more than 50 percent of military and security forces.

For administrative purposes the country is divided into 17 provinces, each headed by an appointed governor. The provinces are subdivided into 129 communes as well as smaller districts, with elected communal and district councils directing local affairs.

Foreign relations. Internal conflicts have significantly influenced Burundi's relations with its neighbors. During the turmoil of the Micombero era, relations with Rwanda (where the Hutu were dominant), as well as with Tanzania and Zaire, were strained. Under President Bagaza, however, a new spirit of regional cooperation led to the formation in 1977 of a joint Economic Community of the Great Lakes Countries (*Communauté Économique des Pays des Grande Lacs*—CEPGL), within which Burundi, Rwanda, and Zaire agreed to organize a development bank, exploit gas deposits under Lake Kivu, and establish a fishing industry on Lake Tanganyika.

Burundi is also a member, along with Rwanda, Tanzania, and Uganda, of the Organization for the Management and Development of the Kagera River Basin. In February 1984 a revised plan for a 2,000-kilometer rail network linking the four countries was approved, thereby addressing Burundi's concern about its lack of access to reliable export routes. Hydroelectric and communications projects by the organization also signaled greater economic cooperation, as did Burundi's entrance (along with the rest of CEPGL) into the Economic Community of Central African States.

Relations were poor between the first Buyoya government and Libya, where former president Bagaza was reported in early 1989 to have gained asylum. In April 1989 Burundi expelled Libyan diplomats and other Libyan nationals for alleged "destabilizing activities," reportedly in connection with a coup plot uncovered the previous month among Bagaza loyalists.

An August 1991 meeting of Burundian, Rwandan, and Ugandan representatives yielded agreement on efforts to contain ethnic destabilization movements operating near border areas. However, observers reported mounting grassroots tensions stemming from persistent rumors of Tutsi "empire-building" ambitions. Although punctuated by cross-border rebel activities, negotiations continued in 1992 between Burundi and Rwanda on establishing cooperative security arrangements.

The October 1993 presidential assassination and coup attempt in Burundi were immediately and unanimously condemned by international observers, with initial calls for economic and political isolation of the rebels giving way to plans to establish a regional peacekeeping force to bolster the government and stem the ethnic violence. However, with the Tutsi military and Uprona leadership openly hostile to intervention, UN and OAU officials resisted the Kinigi government's call for a large-scale intervention.

International efforts to contain ethnic violence were frustrated throughout 1995 by the intransigence of the combatants as well as by the Tutsi military leadership's adamant opposition to a foreign military presence. Burundi expressed wariness over Tanzanian and Ugandan mediation in the first half of 1996, suggesting that its East African neighbors were interested in expanding their territories. Burundi's relations with its neighboring countries subsequently remained tense, and Burundian troops were sent into the Democratic Republic of the Congo (DRC, formerly Zaire) in 1999 in an attempt to dislodge staging areas of the rebel FDD.

Burundi's troops in the DRC reached 3,000 prior to a withdrawal in January 2002. Meanwhile, continued fighting between the DRC government and its own rebels in the DRC prompted the flight of some 35,000 refugees to Burundi. In addition, more than 300,000 refugees from fighting in Burundi reportedly continued to reside in Tanzania. Progress in the repatriation of refugees was reported in 2004–2005. Moreover, following the installation of the newly elected power-sharing government in Burundi in 2005, Burundi concluded an agreement with Uganda, Rwanda, and the DRC for establishment of a regional intelligence gathering unit.

ONUB (the UN's peacekeeping mission) disbanded on December 31, 2006, although it left behind "neither war nor peace," considering the ongoing stalemate between the government and Palipehutu-FNL rebels (see Current issues, below). ONUB's role was assumed by a new AU peacekeeping force, which once again relied heavily on South African troops, as had ONUB. At the same time, the UN announced that Burundi would be one of the first targets for the international organization's new "peacebuilding" initiative.

Even though Burundi itself remained unsettled, the government announced in March 2007 that it would contribute 1,700 troops to the proposed AU peacekeeping mission in Somalia. Analysts suggested that, in addition to trying to promote regional stability in general, the CNDD-FDD government had a vested interest in preventing an Islamist takeover of Somalian affairs (see Current issues, below, for possibly related developments). The other major regional initiative in 2007 involved Burundi's accession in June to the East African Community (EAC), which became the focus for proposed infrastructure development and other initiatives (such as a planned trade deal with the EU) considered critical by the Burundian government to the nation's economic advancement. On a less positive note, however, violence in Kenya and renewed conflict in the DRC underscored the region's fragile status, as did tension over the proposed return of the estimated 280,000 Burundian refugees in Tanzania. (Although some of those refugees were slated to return to Burundi following the cease-fire there in 2008, a majority, many of whom had been in Tanzania for some 35 years, reportedly opted to be formally integrated into the Tanzanian population.)

Current issues. The CNDD-FDD completed a remarkable transition in 2005 from a former rebel group to the country's dominant political force. Observers attributed the CNDD-FDD's success to appreciation within the Hutu population for the past willingness of the CNDD-FDD to "back up" its political stance "with guns." In contrast, Hutu support for Frodebu had declined as the perception had apparently grown that its "engagement" with Uprona since the mid-1990s had been largely ineffective.

The three-month election cycle of mid-2005 was for the most part conducted peacefully, with only sporadic and isolated violence on the part of holdout FNL rebels being reported. EU and UN observers described the balloting as generally free and fair, prompting optimistic observers to suggest that the national unity government installed under the leadership of the CNDD-FDD had at least a modest chance of preserving the fledgling Hutu/Tutsi peace and addressing the nation's daunting economic and social needs. At the same time, cautious analysts cited several potential barriers to effective governmental action, including the inexperience of the new administration and concern (particularly within the Tutsi community) over the CNDD-FDD's militant background. (New president Pierre Nkurunziza had been sentenced, in absentia, to death by a court in Burundi in 1998 for his rebel activity before being covered by the amnesty provisions of the Arusha accord.) The international community broadly welcomed Burundi's first democratically elected government since 1993, which, among other things, was considered a significant triumph for South Africa's recent wide-ranging diplomatic efforts throughout Central Africa.

Despite the fact that some FNL rebel activity continued in mountainous areas near Bujumbura, the UN in April 2006 announced that ONUB peacekeepers would be withdrawn gradually throughout the rest of the year. (UN officials described the mission as "by and large a success story.") For its part, the new administration announced plans to raise the salaries of civil servants, provide greater aid to farmers (particularly in the famine-threatened north), expand health care (especially to pregnant women and mothers with young children), and modernize the coffee and sugar sectors. President Nkurunziza also pledged to implement anticorruption measures and to intensify the disarmament of former fighters and the civilian population as a whole. However, as of May, it remained unclear when (or if) a South African–style truth and reconciliation commission would be established (as provided for in the Arusha accords) to deal with other lingering effects of the long civil conflict, which had cost the lives of more than 300,000 people.

Its initial popular support notwithstanding, the CNDD-FDD–led government by mid-2006 was the target of intense criticism from the opposition, as well as from important international observers, for a perceived heavy-handed and inefficient governing style that disregarded the "spirit" of the 2005 power-sharing agreement. Further intensifying the administration's authoritarian image was the announcement in August that a diverse group of people, including former president Ndayezeye and former vice president Kadege, had been arrested for participation in an alleged coup plot. Most analysts doubted that the plot was real, some suggesting that the government had manufactured the allegations in order to justify repressive tactics against the opposition. Meanwhile, UN officials accused security forces of human rights abuses (including torture) and the government of incompetent, sometimes corrupt, financial management.

Underscoring the complexity of political affairs as well as friction within the CNDD-FDD, Second Vice President Alice NZOMUKUNDA resigned in September 2006, accusing CNDD-FDD leader Hussein RADJABU of strong-arm interference in the administration and of being largely responsible for a perceived high level of cronyism and corruption. Marina BARAMPAMA, a previously little known member of the CNDD-FDD, succeeded Nzomukunda, although Frodebu and Uprona boycotted the legislative vote on the matter.

In early September 2006 President Nkurunziza signed a cease-fire agreement with Agathon RWASA, the leader of the Palipehutu-FNL rebel holdouts. Although some heralded the accord as the end of the country's 13-year civil war, negotiations were still required concerning the final disarmament of the FNL and its conversion into a political party. Meanwhile, tensions between the government and the opposition reportedly eased because of the acquittal in January of Ndayezeye, Kadege, and most of the other defendants in the alleged coup plot.

Apparent growing friction between President Nkurunziza, an evangelical Christian, and Radjabu, a Muslim who had reportedly engineered the placement of Muslims in an inordinate (relative to the percentage of Muslims in the population) number of party, government, and business leadership positions, came to a head at an extraordinary CNDD-FDD congress in February 2007 at which Radjabu was replaced as party leader. Within days, the government conducted a "purge" of Radjabu's supporters, with Second Vice President Barampama, assembly Speaker Imaculee NAHAYO, several cabinet ministers, and a number of parastatal directors among those who lost their jobs. The United States and France reportedly tacitly endorsed Radjabu's ouster, in part because of his apparent recent "flirtation" with the Islamist Sudanese government. However, the dispute severely split the CNDD-FDD; many of Radjabu's supporters moved into oppositional status in the legislature, and Radjubu was arrested in April. No longer enjoying a legislative majority, Nhurunziza in his June reshuffle initiative appeared to be trying to circumvent constitutional requirements for inclusion of opposition parties by naming ministers from Uprona and Frodebu who did not have the approval of their parties to participate. However, the subsequent boycott of the assembly by Uprona, Frodebu, and the CNDD-FDD dissidents forced Nkurunziza into substantive negotiations with Uprona and Frodebu that produced a tenuous coalition government in November that at least permitted legislative activity to proceed.

Meanwhile, negotiations with the FNL stalled throughout 2007, the FNL having withdrawn in June from the Joint Verification and Monitoring Mechanism set up to oversee implementation of the September 2006 accord. The FNL accused the government of failing to follow through on its promises of jobs for FNL supporters, including integration of FNL fighters into a new national army that would more accurately reflect the Hutu majority. Although Nkurunziza invited the FNL to return to the negotiations in early 2008, significant fighting between the FNL and government forces broke out in April, forcing the evacuation of tens of thousands of civilians. In the face of intense international pressure, the FNL's Rwasa pledged at the end of May to end his participation in the 15-year civil war, with the understanding that the FNL would be accorded legal party status and would be included in new power-sharing arrangements. The agreement was cautiously described in most quarters as offering genuine hope for permanent peace, which would allow the government to focus its energy on pressing issues such as rising food prices, the proposed return of hundreds of thousands of refugees from neighboring countries, and unrest among civil servants. However, progress was slow over the next six months in regard to a final settlement as the government appeared to drag its feet regarding legalization of an FNL political party and most FNL fighters retained their weapons. Friction was also reported late in the year between the CNDD-FDD and other parties on several issues, including the CNDD-FDD's perceived "authoritarian tendencies" and reluctance to authorize the establishment of a new independent election commission.

Under intense pressure from regional leaders, the government and the FNL appeared to resolve most of their outstanding issues at a meeting in early December 2008. Among other things, the government reportedly agreed to release FNL detainees and appoint FNL members to positions of authority in various state institutions. The civil war officially came to an end in April 2009 when Rwasa ceremoniously turned over his rifle and declared that the FNL, which was formally registered as a political party, was now "a part of society." An estimated 3,500 FNL fighters were scheduled for integration into the police or army, while some 5,000 more were given modest financial incentives to demobilize and return to civilian life. Although some analysts warned that "uncontrolled elements of society" remained a threat to stability, most attention subsequently turned to the presidential and legislative elections due in mid-2010.

POLITICAL PARTIES AND GROUPS

Of the 24 political parties that contested Burundi's pre-independence elections in 1961, only the Union for National Progress (Uprona) survived, serving as the political base of the Micombero and Bagaza regimes. On April 16, 1992, a month after the constitutional revival of pluralism, President Buyoya signed a bill guaranteeing that the next election would be conducted on a multiparty basis. In March 1993 the government forwarded a "code of conduct" for signature by all active parties to promote "understanding and dialogue" during the "democratic process." By midyear, 11 parties, including Uprona, had been legally registered. Political party activity was suspended following the coup of July 1996 but was reactivated under the transitional constitution of June 1998. Many of the smaller parties were given seats in the 1998 Transitional National Assembly.

Two main groupings were involved in the negotiations in 1999–2001 of the Arusha accord providing for a new transitional government. Initially, Hutu-oriented parties coalesced in the Group of Six (G-6), which included Frodebu, the CNDD, PP, Frolina, the Liberal

Party (*Parti Libéral*—PL), and the Burundi People's Rally (*Rassemblement du Peuple Burundien*—RPB). The G-6 subsequently became the G-7 with the addition of Palipehutu. Meanwhile, the pro-Tutsi Group of Ten (G-10) included Uprona, Parena, *Inkinzo*, AV-*Intwari*, Abasa, the PRP, PIT, PSD, the Rally for Democracy and Economic and Social Development (*Rassemblement pour la Démocratie et le Développement Économique et Social*—Raddes), and the National Alliance for Rights and Development (*Alliance Nationale pour les Droits et le Développement*—Anadde). All of the G-7 and G-10 parties were offered seats in the new Transitional National Assembly, while 15 of the parties accepted seats in the new cabinet installed on November 1, 2001. (For information on the RPB, Raddes, and Anadde, see the 2008 *Handbook*.)

Government and Government-Supportive Parties:

National Council for the Defense of Democracy–Forces for the Defense of Democracy (*Conseil National pour la Défense de Démocratie–Forces pour la Défense de Démocratie*—CNDD-FDD). The CNDD-FDD is one of the successors to the CNDD that was formed in 1994 in Zaire following the assassination of President Ndadaye and the flight into exile of many Hutu political figures. Leonard Nyangoma, a former member of Frodebu and former cabinet minister who was branded a "warlord" by the Ntibantunganya government, led the CNDD from exile in Kenya. Nyangoma, who charged Frodebu with being terrorized by the "mono-ethnic Tutsi army," called in early 1995 for the deployment of a 5,000-man "international intervention force to protect the country's democratic institutions." If such intervention was not forthcoming, he asserted that the CNDD's armed wing—the Forces for the Defense of Democracy (*Forces pour la Défense de Démocratie*—FDD)—would have "no other choice but to step up popular resistance."

In March 1996 the CNDD issued a list of conditions for a cease-fire, including the release of 5,000 Frodebu political prisoners; the return of government troops to their barracks; and the withdrawal of international arrest warrants for Nyangoma and his second-in-command, Christian SENDEGEYA. Although some observers cited the CNDD's willingness to negotiate as cause for optimism about scheduled peace talks, within weeks the rebels had reversed their stance, vowing to keep fighting until the Tutsis gave "power back to the people." Rebel leader Nyangoma was excluded from peace talks in June, prompting a surge in FDD military activity. In March 1997 the regime blamed CNDD operatives for deadly bomb attacks in Bujumbura, and the following month the government asserted that former Rwandan "Interhamwe" fighters (see article on Rwanda) and Zairean Hutus were supporting the rebels.

In April 1997 the CNDD criticized regional leaders for easing sanctions on the regime in Burundi, and in June the rebels turned down an invitation to attend a peace conference in Switzerland. However, the group subsequently agreed to participate in peace talks sponsored by regional leaders, earning the enmity of Palipehutu (below), with whose forces the FDD clashed repeatedly in late 1997 and early 1998. In March 1998 the CNDD began a purge that ousted at least seven leading figures, including Sendegeya. Relations between the CNDD, which attended the June 1998 peace talks, and the FDD, which was not invited (reportedly at the insistence of the mediation leader, President Nyerere of Tanzania), came to a breaking point in May when CNDD leader Nyangoma sacked Jean-Bosco NDAYIKENGURUKIYE, head of the FDD, as well as Hussein Radjabu, a CNDD party official. However, CNDD spokesman Jerome NDIHO claimed that the party had, in fact, suspended Nyangoma and replaced him with Ndayikengurukiye. Nonetheless, Nyangoma attended the talks as CNDD president, and the CNDD joined the G-7. Observers in Bujumbura saw the split between the political and military wings of the rebel movement as the result of jockeying for positions of power in advance of a possible near-term settlement.

The Nyangoma faction subsequently became increasingly marginalized within the CNDD in favor of supporters of Ndayikengurukiye, who strongly criticized the finalization of the 2001 power-sharing accord with the government. However, it was reported that a faction led by Pierre Nkurunziza and Radjabu had ousted Ndayikengurukiye in September 2001. The anti-Ndayikengurukiye wing was described as "pro-Frodebu" and inclined to pursue further negotiations with the government, and it participated in a regional summit on Burundi's future in Pretoria in October. However, with both factions still claiming legitimacy, fierce fighting was reported in FDD strongholds in the east and south between the FDD and government troops in the last two months of the year following the installation of the new transitional government.

Elements of the FDD entered into negotiations with the government in 2002, with the Ndayikengurukiye faction signing a cease-fire in December and the Nkurunziza faction in October 2003. (By that time the Nkurunziza faction was referencing itself as the CNDD-FDD.) The CNDD-FDD was given four portfolios in the November 2003 cabinet, while one ministry was accorded to the Ndayikengurukiye faction of the CNDD.

In May 2004 Ndayikengurukiye announced that his group would thenceforth be known as *Kaza* (Welcome)-FDD. In early 2005 the interior ministry announced the formal registration of *Kaza*-FDD, the CNDD-FDD, and the CNDD (still under Nyangoma's leadership) as separate parties for the upcoming legislative elections. (See section on Nyangoma's CNDD, below).

The CNDD-FDD dominated the communal elections in June 2005 as well as the National Assembly and Senate balloting in July. Nkurunziza resigned as leader of the CNDD-FDD shortly before he was elected president of the republic in August. Radjabu succeeded him in the CNDD-FDD post. By early 2006, the CNDD-FDD claimed to have made significant strides toward its goal of becoming a truly "national party" by having Tutsis fill a number of leadership posts.

Relations between Nkurunziza and Radjabu subsequently deteriorated, in part due to perceptions that Radjabu (a Muslim) was pursuing the "Islamization" of the party and, by extension, the government. (Among other things, Radjaba had reportedly organized an armed youth wing of the party with 30,000 members.) Radjabu was also strongly criticized by Alice Nzomukunda when she resigned as second vice president of the republic in September (see Current issues, above). Radjabu eventually lost the ensuing power struggle within the CNDD-FDD when Jeremy Ngendakumana, a former ambassador to Kenya, replaced him as party chair at a special congress in early February 2007. However, more than 20 of the CNDD-FDD's 59 members of the assembly remained loyal to Radjabu and boycotted subsequent assembly sessions, thereby costing the party its legislative majority and prompting a political stalemate (see Current issues, above, for additional information). The CNDD-FDD dissidents, many of whom had joined other parties, were dismissed from the assembly in May 2008, while Radjabu was sentenced to 13 years in prison following his conviction on charges of plotting a rebellion and "insulting the president." Meanwhile, an extraordinary CNDD-FDD congress in January had also expelled Nzomukunda from the party.

Leaders: Pierre NKURUNZIZA (President of the Republic), Gabriel NTISEZERANA (Second Vice President of the Republic), Jeremy NGENDAKUMANA (Chair), Gervais RUFYIKIRI (Speaker of the Senate), Evariste NDAYISHIMIYE (Parliamentary Leader), Léonce NDARUBAGIYE (Spokesperson).

Union for National Progress (*Union pour le Progrès National*—Uprona). Founded in 1958 as the *Union et Progrès National*, Uprona was dissolved after the 1976 coup but subsequently reemerged as the country's only authorized party. In December 1979 the party pledged to return the country to civilian rule under President Bagaza's leadership. Following the 1987 coup and designation of Maj. Pierre Buyoya, previously a little-known Uprona Central Committee member, as president of the republic, all Uprona leaders were dismissed, and formal party activity ceased. By early 1988 the party was again functioning, a Buyoya supporter having been selected as its new secretary general. Thereafter, with Tutsis comprising 90 percent of Uprona's membership, party leaders attempted to recruit more Hutus and implement additional "democratization" measures. The March 1992 Uprona congress approved a new Central Committee with a Hutu majority.

Uprona won only 16 of 81 legislative seats at the June 1993 nationwide balloting. Subsequently, party president Nicolas MAYUGI decried Frodebu's "antidemocratic" electoral victories, claiming they were based on "ethnic manipulation." Although observers described Mayugi's sentiments as pervasive in the Tutsi community, seven members of the government named in July, including the prime minister, were Uprona members. Similar concessions were made in the government arrangements of 1994–1995.

In 1995 and the first half of 1996, Uprona militants called for the ousting of President Ntibantunganya and repudiation of the power-sharing arrangements with Frodebu. Uprona also refused to negotiate with representatives from the CNDD, despite otherwise broad consensus that the latter's participation was imperative for any peace initiative.

In addition, Uprona remained steadfastly opposed to foreign military intervention. Thus, in June 1996 Tanzanian President Nyerere labeled Uprona as one of the "main obstacles" to peace. It was therefore not surprising that Uprona was heavily represented in the new government formed following the July coup.

A split occurred in Uprona between those who supported President Buyoya's efforts to reach a negotiated settlement with opposition groups in 1997–1998 and those opposed to any concessions to the "rebels." Uprona President Charles MUKASI, a member of the latter camp, was reportedly briefly detained in late 1997 for conducting a press conference in September 1997 in which he criticized the government for dealing with "genocidal" Hutu rebels. Ironically, Mukasi was one of the few high-ranking Hutus in the predominately Tutsi Uprona. The dispute over how to deal with the rebels came to a head in October 1998 when Mukasi expelled three members from the party, including Luc RUKINGAMA, a cabinet minister. Buyoya immediately reasserted his authority, and the Central Committee suspended Mukasi and replaced him with Rukingama as interim chairman. While divisions remained with the party, the Mukasi wing was subsequently largely marginalized.

New Uprona President Jean-Baptiste MANWANGARI opposed the constitution approved in February 2005 on the grounds that it provided insufficient guarantees for Tutsis. Uprona won only 6.3 percent of the vote in local elections in June 2005 and 7.3 percent in assembly balloting in July, *Africa Confidential* subsequently describing the party as having "quietly accepted its defeat." Manwangari was defeated in his bid for reelection to the Uprona presidency at a congress in January 2006. Uprona subsequently split into two factions, one (led by Uprona President Aloys Rubeka) inclined to participate in the government headed by the CNDD-FDD and the other (led by Bonaventure GASUTWA) firmly entrenched in the opposition camp. The internal dissension came to a head in July 2007 when Uprona's Martin NDUWIMANA was suspended from the party for remaining in the government as first vice president despite Uprona's formal refusal to participate in the recently announced cabinet. Following Uprona's decision to join the national unity cabinet in November (at which time Dr. Yves Sahinguvu replaced Nduwimana as first vice president), the party in May 2008 launched an internal "reunification" drive.

Leaders: Aloys RUBUKA (President of the Party), Maj. Pierre BUYOYA (Former President of the Republic), Dr. Yves SAHINGUVU (First Vice President of the Republic).

Front for Democracy in Burundi (*Front pour la Démocratie au Burundi*—Frodebu). Frodebu was launched in support of a "no" vote at the referendum of March 1992, arguing that the government's failure to convene a national conference meant that there had been no opposition input to the constitutional draft. However, following the vote, the group's leadership announced, "We are ready to play the game."

Party leader Melchior Ndadaye won the presidency of the republic on June 1, 1993, with Frodebu securing 65 of 81 assembly seats on the basis of a 71.4 percent vote share. However, the October 21 assassination of President Ndadaye and a number of other prominent party members eviscerated Frodebu. Furthermore, a number of Frodebu leaders were tainted by their involvement in subsequent revenge attacks on Tutsis.

On December 23, 1993, Sylvestre Ntibantunganya, foreign minister and Ndadaye confidante, was elected party president and president of the National Assembly. Ntibantunganya became acting president of the republic on April 8, 1994, and president five months later.

Despite the emergence of militant anti-Tutsi emotions within Frodebu, a number of prominent leaders, including party president Jean Minani, called in 1995 for continued dialogue with their Tutsi counterparts. However, following the coup of July 1996, some Frodebu leaders urged supporters to join forces with the CNDD in attempting to topple the Buyoya regime.

In early 1997 Minani called on the international community to pressure the UN to send troops into Burundi and to observe the sanctions imposed on the regime in July 1996. In addition, he decried Bujumbura's "villagization" efforts for having created "concentration camps." The following week, party Secretary General Augustin NOJIBWAMI was jailed for "sabotaging the government's efforts to establish peace" after he echoed Minani's statements. In early 1998 Frodebu leaders reaffirmed their support for all-party talks toward a negotiated settlement of the conflict in Burundi, although the party was splitting into differing factions. For example, Minani remained in exile in Tanzania and attended the peace talks as the party's representative, while certain CNDD elements argued that they, not he, represented the genuine Frodebu leadership.

In the wake of the power-sharing agreement of June 1998, Frodebu was authorized to keep the 65 legislative seats in the new Transitional National Assembly that it had obtained in 1993. However, the party had to appoint new legislators to more than 20 of the seats, the incumbents having either fled into exile or fallen victim to the recent violence. Concurrently, Nojibwami took over leadership of the Frodebu faction functioning in Burundi.

In July 1999 reports indicated that Minani had entered into an alliance with former president Bagaza and Parena in opposition to President Buyoya and Uprona, an initiative that was condemned by Nojibwami and others. This split was accommodated within the Arusha negotiations through the presence of the "internal" Nojibwani Frodebu wing in the National Assembly delegation to the talks. Minani led the main "external" Frodebu delegation. Following the installation of the new transitional government on November 1, 2001, Minani, who had recently returned to Burundi after more than five years in exile, was elected president of the new Transitional National Assembly.

After Frodebu's Domitien Ndayizeye became president of the republic in April 2003, Frodebu campaigned in support of the new constitution approved in February 2005. However, Frodebu secured only about 23 percent of the vote in the June 2005 local elections and July assembly poll. Many Frodebu supporters by that time had reportedly defected to the CNDD-FDD. Internal party leadership struggles continued, and late in the year Minani was voted out of the party presidency in favor of Léonce Ngendakumana, although a number of Frodebu stalwarts reportedly remained outside the new president's sphere of influence.

Frodebu joined the national unity government installed in September 2005, although sharp dissatisfaction was voiced because the party had received neither the vice-presidential post nor the number of ministerial positions it believed it deserved based on its standing as the second largest group in the assembly. Tensions culminated in a March 2006 decision by Frodebu to withdraw from the government. When three Frodebu ministers opted to stay in the cabinet, they were expelled from the party.

Frodebu agreed to join the national unity cabinet in November 2007, receiving four ministerial and two vice-ministerial posts, although friction reportedly continued within the party regarding the degree of cooperation with CNDD-FDD initiatives. In June 2008 Minani announced that he and some 12 legislators had formed a new faction called Real Frodebu (Frodebu-*Nyakuri*), which was seen as more closely aligned with the CNDD-FDD. (Ngendakumana had strongly criticized the recent dismissal [requested by the CNDD-FDD] of 22 members of the assembly who had left the CNDD-FDD following an internal dispute within that party.)

Former Burundian president Ndayizeye was reportedly chosen in 2009 as Frodebu's candidate for the 2010 presidential election.

Leaders: Léonce NGENDAKUMANA (President of the Party), Domitien NDAYIZEYE (Former President of the Republic), Jean MINANI (Former President of the Party), Frederic BAMVUGINYUMVIRA (Vice President of the Party), Euphrasie BIGIRIMANA (Secretary General).

Guarantor of Freedom of Speech in Burundi (*Inkinzo y Ijambo Ryabarundi*). Founded in 1993, *Inkinzo* (also referenced then as the Shield of Freedom of Speech) joined the PRP and Raddes in their December 1995 withdrawal from the government. However, *Inkinzo* subsequently participated in the first cabinet led by the CNDD-FDD.

At a March 2009 congress, Tite Bucumi defeated incumbent Alphonse RUGAMBARARA for the leadership of the party, now referenced as the **Pan-Africanist Socialist Movement–*Inkinzo*** (*Mouvement Socialiste Panafricain–Inkinzo*—MSP-*Inkinzo*).

Leader: Tite BUCUMI.

Movement for the Rehabilitation of the Citizen (*Movement pour la Réhabilitation du Citoyen*—MRC). After securing 2 seats in the 2005 assembly elections, the MRC (also referenced as the National Resistance Movement for the Rehabilitation of the Citizen) accepted the public service and social security portfolio in the new cabinet led by the CNDD-FDD.

Leaders: Laurent NZEYIMANA, Col. (Ret.) Epitace BAYAGANAKANDI.

Party for National Recovery (*Parti pour le Recouvrement National*—PRN or Parena). Launched in August 1994 by former head of state Col. Jean-Baptiste Bagaza, Parena was allegedly linked with a number of Tutsi militias. Bagaza, who had dismissed the 1993 elections as an "ethnic referendum," refused to sign the 1994 power-sharing agreement, saying there could be no solution that included Frodebu. He also accused the president's party of planning a Tutsi genocide. In 1995 Bagaza reportedly concurred with calls for the establishment of a "Tutsiland" and a "Hutuland" as separate entities.

On January 18, 1997, the Buyoya regime's security forces placed Bagaza under house arrest, and on March 17 five senior Parena members were imprisoned for their alleged roles in a coup plot against the president. However, Bagaza was subsequently released and permitted to travel to neighboring countries to participate in discussions regarding a possible permanent solution to the instability in Burundi. (The others were convicted in January 2000 of plotting to kill Buyoya, but they were released in August 2000.) Parena was frequently critical of the Arusha negotiations, accusing Buyoya of selling out Tutsi interests. Although it eventually signed the accord, Parena subsequently declined to ratify various implementation measures. In November 2002 the government banned Parena and placed Bagaza under house arrest. However, the ban and arrest were suspended in May 2003. In February 2005 there were reports that a new rebel group, the **Justice and Liberty United Front,** had been formed to support Bagaza. However, Parena accepted a ministerial position in the new coalition government installed in September 2005.

Leaders: Col. Jean-Baptiste BAGAZA, Cyrille BARANCIRA (Secretary General).

African-Burundi Salvation Alliance (*Alliance Burundaise-Africaine pour le Salut*—Abasa). Abasa is a small Tutsi-dominated opposition group that in 1997 called for new national leadership, criticizing the Buyoya regime for lacking a "clear strategy."

Leaders: Terrence NSANZE (Former Permanent Representative to the UN), Serge MUKAMARAKIZA (in exile).

Other Parliamentary Party:

National Council for the Defense of Democracy (*Conseil National pour la Défense de Démocratie*—CNDD). This grouping was reorganized under the CNDD rubric in early 2005 after sustained factionalization within the original CNDD (see CNDD-FDD, above, for details). The CNDD won four seats in the 2005 assembly poll and dominated balloting in local elections in Bururi Province, home of the CNDD leader, Leonard Nyangoma, who filled one of the assembly seats. However, Nyangoma went into exile in 2006 (after his parliamentary immunity was lifted) because of what he claimed was systematic suppression of opposition parties by the CNDD-FDD. Nyangoma returned to Burundi in July 2007 and, following the formation of a national unity cabinet in November, became the de facto leader of the opposition.

Leaders: Leonard NYANGOMA, François BIZIMANA.

Other Parties:

National Forces of Liberation (*Forces Nationales de la Libération*—FNL). Founded in the mid-1990s by Palipehutu military leader Cossan KABURA, the FNL (often referenced at that time as the Palipehutu-FNL) subsequently conducted guerrilla actions against government forces, primarily in and around Bujumbura. The hard-line Palipehutu-FNL appeared to separate from the main Palipehutu grouping when the latter agreed in 1999 to participate in the Arusha peace talks.

In late February 2001 it was reported that Kabura had been "ejected" from the FNL by a faction led by Agathon Rwasa, said by that time to command some 90 percent of the FNL's fighters. Rwasa and his supporters criticized Kabura for failing to convene a national congress to discuss strategy. Apparently to underscore its militancy, the Rwasa faction invaded Bujumbura in early March in an apparent takeover attempt that was eventually repulsed by government forces. Both FNL factions condemned the July power-sharing accord, and more intense FNL attacks were reported late in the year.

In December 2002 dissident members of the FNL formed the **FNL-Icanzo** under the leadership of Alain MUGABARABONA. (In 2007 Mugabarabona was sentenced to 20 years in prison following his conviction on charges relating to the alleged coup plot of 2006 [see Current issues, above]. Mugabarabona claimed that his confession had been elicited through torture and subsequently denied that any plot had been undertaken.) Following the cease-fire between the government and the FDD, the FNL subsequently remained the only major rebel group still fighting the transitional government. The group became increasingly marginalized and lost much of its foreign support following an attack in August of 2004 on a UN refugee camp in Gatumba, Burundi. The government and several neighboring states subsequently designated the FNL a terrorist organization. FNL forces were repulsed in a December 2004 attack but managed to assassinate the governor of Bubanza Province in January 2005.

In May 2005 the government and the FNL reportedly signed a peace deal whereby both sides agreed to cease fighting. Additional agreements to allow the FNL to participate in upcoming elections or future governments remained elusive, however.

In October 2005 reports surfaced that Rwasa had been ousted as chair of "Palipehutu-FNL" in favor of a "pronegotiation" leadership including Jean-Bosco SINADAYIGAYA as chair. In January 2006 Sinadayigaya announced that his faction had ceased hostilities. However, Rwasa's faction continued antigovernment activity in the hills around Bujumbura into May 2006, having reportedly forged an alliance with rebels in the DRC. Rwasa signed a temporary cease-fire agreement in September 2006, but a permanent resolution remained elusive. Outstanding issues included the proposed integration of the estimated 3,000 FNL fighters into the national army and civil service, the future political role of the FNL, and the release of imprisoned FNL supporters.

FNL negotiators disengaged from talks with the government in July 2007, and fighting was reported in September between Rwasa's supporters and FNL dissidents, who accused Rwasa of "insincerity" in pursuing a final agreement and were pursuing demobilization (which included a financial incentive) on their own. The FNL also launched attacks against government forces near Bujumbura in April and May 2008, prompting President Nkurunziza to call for international help in resolving the rebellion. For its part, the FNL accused the government of prolonging the hostilities by "chasing" FNL fighters and trying to "eliminate" them rather than dealing with issues surrounding demobilization.

Regional leaders subsequently reportedly told Rwasa and his fighters that they faced expulsion from Tanzania unless they laid down their arms. Consequently, Rwasa in May 2008 signed yet another tentative peace agreement with the Burundian government and returned to Bujumbura after nearly two decades of guerrilla activity.

In January 2009 Rwasa announced that the Palipehutu-FNL was formally dropping Palipehutu from its name to conform with the constitutional injunction against ethnically based political parties. The FNL was granted formal party status in April (see Current issues, above, for additional information.)

Leaders: Agathon RWASA, Jean-Berchmans NDAYISHIMIYE, Pasteur HABIMANA.

Movement for Security and Democracy (*Mouvement pour la Sécurité and la Démocratie*—MSD). The MSD was formed in December 2007 by Alexis Sinduhije, who had gained prominence since the early 2000s as the operator of a radio station devoted to reconciliation between Hutus and Tutsis, a theme the MSD hoped to pursue for the 2010 legislative elections. However, the government refused to register the MSD, and Sinduhije and nearly 40 of his supporters were arrested in early November 2008 on charges of "conducting an illegal political meeting." Although the other MSD members were released shortly thereafter, Sinduhije remained in jail until his March 2009 acquittal on a charge of insulting the president, the case having prompted widespread criticism from the international community of the government's apparent heavy-handed tactics.

Leader: Alexis SINDUHIJE.

People's Reconciliation Party (*Parti pour la Réconciliation du Peuple*—PRP). The promonarchist PRP was founded in September 1991 on a platform calling for a parliamentary monarchy with a prime minister and an ethnically mixed council of nobles. The group was officially recognized on July 1, 1992, and in November it called for the government to open negotiations with the opposition.

PRP candidate Pierre-Claver Sendegeya finished a distant third in the June 1, 1993, presidential balloting, and the party failed to secure representation in the subsequent legislative elections. Considered an extremist by the government, PRP leader Mathias Hitimana was arrested in August 1994, provoking a series of deadly street clashes by his followers that shut down the capital for three days.

The PRP was awarded a post in the government named in March 1995; however, nine months later it quit the cabinet, and in January 1996 Hitimana was again arrested. In July party militants took part in the anti-Ntibantunganya demonstrations that sought to vilify the president for agreeing to foreign intervention. Although the PRP was given a ministerial post in the transitional cabinet of November 2001, its minister left the government in July 2002. However, the party accepted a new post in 2003.

Déo Niyonzima, the president of the PRP, was among those arrested in mid-2006 in connection with an alleged coup plot (see Current issues, above). However, he was acquitted in January 2007.

Leaders: Déo NIYONZIMA (President), Mathias HITIMANA (Former President), Pierre-Claver SENDEGEYA (1993 presidential candidate), François MBESHERUBUSA, Jean Bosco YAMUREMYE.

Hutu People's Liberation Party (*Parti Libération du Peuple Hutu*—Palipehutu). Palipehutu was formed by Hutu exiles in Rwanda and Tanzania who opposed the long-standing political and economic dominance of Burundi's Tutsis. The government attributed the Hutu-Tutsi conflict of August 1988, as well as the attempted coup of November 1991, to Palipehutu activism, although there was no outside confirmation of either allegation. In 1990 Palipehutu founder Rémy GAHUTU died in a Tanzanian prison. (His successor, Etienne Karatasi, remained exiled in Denmark.)

In 1993 the party was split by the defection of its military leader, Cossan Kabura, who "declared war on the Ndadaye government." He subsequently founded the National Forces of Liberation (FNL, below). In early 1997 *Africa Confidential* reported that Palipehutu and the FNL had agreed to form a military alliance with a group from the DRC styled the **National Council of Kivu Resistance** (*Conseil Nationale de Résistance du Kivu*—CNRK). Led by Arema Bin AMISI, the ethnic Bembe CNRK reportedly opposed the government of Laurent Kabila in the DRC.

In the second half of 1997 Palipehutu leaders accused the CNDD of "collaborating" with the Buyoya regime by agreeing to join peace talks. Severe intra-Hutu fighting was subsequently reported between Palipehutu forces and the CNDD's armed wing, the FDD. In early 2000 it was reported that FNL fighters had clashed in Burundi with Rwandan Hutu guerrilla groups with which the FNL had previously been allied. Palipehutu eventually joined the G-7 grouping at the Arusha talks and was a signatory to the August 28, 2000, accord, although the FNL did not accept the agreement. Palipehutu reportedly joined the national unity government installed in 2003. However, Palipehutu-FNL continued military action against the government (see FNL, below, for details).

Leaders: Etienne KARATASI, Antoine SEZOYA-NGABO.

National Liberation Front (*Front de Libération Nationale*—Frolina). A small movement composed primarily of militant Hutu refugees, Frolina (previously referenced as *Umbumwé* [Solidarity]) was organized in the mid-1980s. It reportedly conducted a guerrilla attack on a Burundi military installation in Mabandal on August 13, 1990. Four days later the group's leader, former Palipehutu member Joseph Karumba, was arrested in Tanzania.

In June 1992 Karumba was linked to militant refugees in Mpanda, Tanzania. In announcing their intent to arrest the group, Tanzanian officials reported that Karumba had recently sought their assistance in "liberating" Burundi. However, Karumba was subsequently granted asylum in Tanzania, from which he conducted Frolina's political affairs while Frolina fighters, referenced as the People's Armed Forces, engaged in sporadic guerrilla action in Burundi through 1998. In signing the Arusha accord of August 2000, Karumba agreed that Frolina forces would eventually be incorporated into the national forces of Burundi, although a militant Frolina wing reportedly remained opposed to that measure and other Arusha "concessions." Frolina named four of its members to the new Transitional National Assembly in late 2001; however, no ministers in the new cabinet were identified as belonging to Frolina. Karumba was among the former rebels who were "demobilized" in mid-2005.

Leader: Joseph KARUMBA.

Other past government parties have included the **Alliance of the Brave** (AV-*Intwari*), a small grouping that joined the transitional legislature and participated in subsequent peace talks; the **Independent Workers' Party** (*Parti Indépendent de Travailleurs*—PIT), which is led by Nicéphore NDIMURUKUNDO and Etienne NTAHONZA and which held portfolios in the cabinets of 1994, 1995, 2001, and 2003; the **People's Party** (*Parti Populaire*—PP), a pro-Frodebu grouping that is led by Shadrack NIYONKURU and Apollinaire BUTOYI and which was allocated one cabinet ministry in 1995, 2001, and 2003; and the **Social Democratic Party** (*Parti Social-Démocrate*—PSD), a pro-Uprona Tutsi grouping (led by Vincent NDIKUMASABO and Godefroy HAKIZIMANA) that had been awarded the civil service ministry in March 1995.

Other political parties and groups include the **Democratic Forum** (*Forum Démocratique*—FODE), formed in 1999 and led by Deogratias BABURIFATO; the **Liberal Alliance for Development** (*Alliance Libérale Pour la Développement—Imboneza*), created in 2002 and led by Joseph NTIDENEREZA; the **New Alliance for Democracy and the Development of Burundi** (*Alliance Nouvelle Pour la Démocratie et le Développement au Burundi*), formed in 2002 by Jean-Paul BURAFUTA; the **Party for Democracy and Reconciliation** (*Parti pour la Démocratie et la Réconciliation*—PDR), formed in 2002 and led by Augustin NZOJIBWAMI; the **Patriots' Council**, formed in early 2009 under the leadership of Anicet NIYONGABO; and the **Union for Peace and Development** (*Union pour la Paix et le Développement*—UPD), established in 2002 and led by Freddy FERUVI.

LEGISLATURE

The new constitution approved in February 2005 codified the bicameral **Parliament** (*Parlement*) consisting of a Senate and a National Assembly elected for five-year terms. (For extensive information on parliamentary developments from 1987–2002, see the 2007 *Handbook.*)

Senate (*Sénat*). The upper house comprises 34 indirectly elected members (1 Hutu and 1 Tutsi from each province as selected by electoral colleges comprised of members of the local councils within each province), all former presidents (currently 4), 3 members of the Twa ethnic group, and enough women to make the number of female senators at least 30 percent of the total. (There are currently 49 members.) The first elections in the provincial electoral colleges took place on July 29, 2005. Of the 34 seats filled in that process, 30 were reportedly secured by the National Council for the Defense of Democracy–Forces for the Defense of Democracy, 3 by the Front for Democracy in Burundi, and 1 by the National Council for the Defense of Democracy.

Speaker: Gervais RUFYIKIRI.

National Assembly (*Assemblée Nationale*). The lower house is comprised of 100 members directly elected by party-list proportional representation, enough additional members (currently 15) to fulfill the constitutional mandates that 60 percent of the regular seats be filled by Hutus and 40 percent by Tutsis and that 30 percent of the regular seats be filled by women, and three members of the Twa ethnic group. In the first balloting of July 4, 2005, the National Council for the Defense of Democracy (CNDD-FDD) won 59 seats; the Front for Democracy in Burundi (Frodebu), 25; the Union for National Progress (Uprona), 10; the National Council for the Defense of Democracy, 4; and the Movement for the Rehabilitation of the Citizen, 2. Of the 15 additional seats subsequently allocated to meet the constitutional mandates, 5 each were given to the CNDD-FDD, Frodebu, and Uprona.

The next election was scheduled for mid-2010.

Speaker: Pie NTAVYOHANYUMA.

CABINET

[as of June 1, 2009]

President	Pierre Nkurunziza (CNDD-FDD)
First Vice President (In Charge of Political and Administrative Affairs)	Dr. Yves Sahinguvu (Uprona)
Second Vice President (In Charge of Social And Economic Affairs)	Gabriel Ntisezerana (CNDD-FDD)
Ministers	
Agriculture and Livestock	Ferdinand Nderagakuru (Frodebu)
Civil Service, Labor, and Social Security	Annonciata Sendazirasa (Frodebu) [f]

Ministry	Minister
Commerce, Industry, and Tourism	Euphrasie Bigirigama (Frodebu) [f]
Communications, Information, Relations with Parliament, and Government Spokesman	Vénérand Bakevyumusaya (Frodebu)
Decentralization and Communal Development	Pierre Mupira (CNDD-FDD)
East African Community Affairs	Hafsa Mossi (CNDD-FDD) [f]
Energy and Mines	Samuel Ndayiragije (CNDD-FDD)
External Relations and International Cooperation	Augustin Nsanze (CNDD-FDD)
Fight Against AIDS	Spéciosa Baransata (Uprona) [f]
Finance, Economy, and Development Cooperation	Clotilde Nizigama (CNDD-FDD) [f]
Higher Education and Scientific Research	Saidi Kibeya (CNDD-FDD)
Human Rights and Gender	Rose Nduwayo (Frodebu) [f]
Interior	Edouard Nduwimana (CNDD-FDD)
Justice, Keeper of the Seals, and Attorney General	Jean Bosco Ndikumana (CNDD-FDD)
National Defense and War Veterans	Lt. Gen. Germain Niyoyankana (ind.)
National Solidarity, Repatriation of Refugees, and Social Reintegration	Immaculée Nahayo (CNDD-FDD) [f]
Office of the President(Good Governance and Privatization)	Martin Nivyabandi (CNDD-FDD)
Planning and Reconstruction	Tabu Abdallah Manirakiza (CNDD-FDD)
Primary and Secondary Education	Ernest Mberamiheto (Frodebu)
Public Health	Dr. Emmanuel Gikoro (Uprona)
Public Works and Equipment	Anatole Kanyenkiko (Frodebu)
Public Security and Police Commissioner	Gen. Alain Guillaume Bunyoni (ind.)
Technical Education, Professional Training, and Literacy	Rose Gahiru (CNDD-FDD) [f]
Transport, Posts, and Telecommunications	Philippe Njoni (Uprona)
Water, Environment, Territorial Management, and Urban Planning	Déogratias Nduwimana
Youth, Sports, and Culture	Jean-Jacques Nyenimigabo (CNDD-FDD)
Secretary General of the Government and Governmental Spokesperson	Philippe Nzobonariba

[f] = female

COMMUNICATIONS

A new media law in 2003 provided for broad journalistic freedom. However, the CNDD-FDD government installed in 2005 has been charged with a wide-ranging campaign of repression and intimidation of print and radio journalists, who have reportedly been subjected to arrest and attack by security forces.

Press. The following are published in Bujumbura: *Le Renouveau du Burundi* (20,000), government daily, in French; *Umbumwé* (20,000), weekly, in Kirundi; *Burundi Chrétien,* weekly publication of the Gitega Archbishopric, in French; *Burundi Réalités*, independent daily; *Ndongozi Yaburundi,* Catholic fortnightly, in Kirundi; and *Arc-en-Ciel*, independent. In June 2004 a new newspaper, *La Tribune du Burundi*, began publication as a monthly.

News agency. The official Agence Burundaise de Presse issues daily bulletins.

Broadcasting and computing. The government facility, *Radio-Télévision Nationale du Burundi* (RTNB), broadcasts in French, Kirundi, and Swahili. *Radio Publique Africaine* (a popular nationwide station) was temporarily shut down by the government in mid-2005 for alleged bias in its election coverage. Another popular radio station is the independent *Bonesha FM.* As of 2008 there were 8.1 Internet users per 1,000 inhabitants.

INTERGOVERNMENTAL REPRESENTATION

Ambassador to the U.S.: Angele NIYUHIRE.

U.S. Ambassador to Burundi: Pamela Jo Howell SLUTZ.

Permanent Representative to the UN: Zacharie GAHUTU.

IGO Memberships (Non-UN): AU, AfDB, BADEA, CEEAC, CEPGL, Comesa, Interpol, NAM, OIF, WCO, WTO.

CAMBODIA

Kingdom of Cambodia
Preahreachanachak Kampuchea

Political Status: Became independent as the Kingdom of Cambodia on November 9, 1953; Khmer Republic proclaimed October 9, 1970; renamed Democratic Kampuchea by constitution of January 5, 1976, following Communist (*Khmer Rouge*) takeover on April 17, 1975; de jure authority contested by the Coalition Government of Democratic Kampuchea (CGDK) and the People's Republic of Kampuchea (PRK, formed January 8, 1979) following the Vietnamese invasion of December 1978; PRK redesignated as State of Cambodia on April 30, 1989; CGDK redesignated as National Government of Cambodia on February 3, 1990, collateral with reversion of Democratic Kampuchea to Cambodia; transitional Supreme National Council formally endorsed by all-party peace agreement signed in Paris, France, on October 23, 1991; interim coalition regime (without *Khmer Rouge* participation) authorized on June 16, 1993, following multiparty legislative election of May 23–28; current constitution ratified on September 21 and promulgated on September 24, 1993.

Area: 69,898 sq. mi. (181,035 sq. km.).

Population: 11,437,656 (1998C); 14,866,000 (2008E).

Major Urban Center (2005E): PHNOM PENH (1,350,000). Following the 1975 Communist takeover, virtually the entire population of the capital, some 1.8 million, was evacuated. In early 1979 substantial reverse migration commenced, with the population again in excess of 1 million by 2003.

Official Language: Khmer; in addition, French is widely spoken.

Monetary Unit: Riel (official rate December 1, 2009: 4,155.00 riels = $1US).

Monarch: King NORODOM SIHAMONI; elected by the Royal Throne Council on October 14, 2004, and crowned on October 29, succeeding NORODOM SIHANOUK, who had announced his wish to abdicate, for reasons of health, on October 6.

Prime Minister: HUN SEN (Cambodian People's Party); former cochair of the Council of Ministers of the Provisional National Government; named second prime minister of government formed on October 23, 1993; named prime minister on November 26, 1998, in succession to First Prime Minister UNG HUOT (formerly Funcinpec Party) under formal coalition agreement of November 23; continued in office as a caretaker following the legislative election of July 27, 2003; renominated as prime minister by the king on July 14, 2004, confirmed by the National Assembly on July 15, and sworn in on July 16 as the head of a renewed coalition government; most recently elected by the National Assembly on September, 25, 2008, following the legislative election on July 27.

THE COUNTRY

The smallest of the French Indochinese states to which independence was restored in 1953, Cambodia is bounded by Thailand on the west and northwest, Laos on the north, and Vietnam on the east and southeast. The southwestern border of the country is an irregular coastline on the Gulf of Thailand. It is a basically homogeneous nation, with Khmers (Cambodians) constituting approximately 85 percent of the total population. Ethnic minorities were estimated in 1970 to include 450,000 Chinese, 400,000 Vietnamese, 80,000 Cham-Malays (Muslims descended from the people of the ancient kingdom of Champa), 50,000 Khmer Loeus (tribals), and 20,000 Thais and Laotians. Many of the Chinese and most of the Cham-Malays and Vietnamese were reported to have been massacred during the period of *Khmer Rouge* rule, from 1975 to 1979.

Social cohesion and stability traditionally derived from a common language (Khmer), a shared sense of national identity, and the pervading influence of Theravada Buddhism, the state religion. Only a handful of Muslims and Christians were said to have survived the 1975–1979 holocaust. Women have long played a major economic role as agricultural laborers and have also been prominent as local traders; they constitute about half of the economically active population. Female participation in government is low, accounting for about 16 percent of the National Assembly elected in 2008.

Cambodia's economy was traditionally based on the agricultural sector (including forestry and fishing), which continues to employ about 60 percent of the active labor force and to account for 30 percent of GDP. The chief food crops are rice (accounting for 80 percent of the cultivated area), cassava, maize, soybeans, and sugarcane. Timber and rubber long accounted for the bulk of export earnings, but since 1997 a rapidly expanding garment industry has been more important, as has tourism. About 15 percent of the workforce is employed in manufacturing, with the industrial sector as a whole contributing about 25 percent of GDP. Total visitor arrivals have nearly doubled since 2004 and in 2007 surpassed 2 million for the first time.

Despite robust economic growth averaging 9 percent a year in 2000–2005, Cambodia has a high incidence of poverty, particularly in rural areas. The Asian Development Bank in 2007 cited a "pressing need" for Cambodia to diversify its economy, although it commended the government for its fiscal prudence and progress in structural reforms. External debt, comprising about a third of Cambodia's GDP, has also been an issue of ongoing concern, inasmuch as Cambodia has not repaid substantial loans from the United States, Russia, or the Paris Club of creditors, among others. In February 2008 the government cited "more pressing concerns" in refusing to repay $339 million in U.S. debt incurred in the 1970s.

GDP growth averaged 10.5 percent annually in 2006–2007 but was projected at about 6.5 percent for 2008, owing to a slowdown in garment exports. Also, inflation was reported to be at a nine-year high of over 15 percent, driven by increasing food and fuel prices; the World Bank described the latter as posing a serious threat to the country's growth. In recent years vast oil reserves have been discovered off the coast of Cambodia. With several international companies having secured drilling rights, including Chinese firms and U.S.-based Chevron, the financial prospects for Cambodia could improve dramatically after 2011.

GOVERNMENT AND POLITICS

Political background. Increasing pressure from Siam (Thailand) and Vietnam had almost extinguished Khmer independence prior to the establishment of a French protectorate at the request of King ANG DUONG in 1863. In the early 1940s Japan, in furtherance of its "Greater East Asia Co-prosperity Sphere," seized de facto control of Cambodia. A Thai claim to the western portion of the region had been resisted by the French, but Japan permitted Thailand to annex the provinces of Battambang and Siem Reap, with the French retaining nominal control in the rest of the country. After the surrender of Japan in World War II, Cambodia was recognized as an autonomous kingdom within the French Union, and the two northwestern provinces were returned by Thailand. In 1949 Cambodia signed an accord with France that brought it into the French Union as an Associated State.

Political feuds within the governing Democratic Party having hampered negotiations with the French, King NORODOM SIHANOUK dissolved the National Assembly in January 1953 and personally negotiated his country's full independence, which was formally announced on November 9. Independence was reinforced by the Geneva Agreement of 1954, which called for the withdrawal from Cambodia of all foreign troops, including *Vietminh* elements that had entered from North Vietnam as a "liberation" force. To enhance his status as national leader, Sihanouk abdicated in 1955 in favor of his father, NORODOM SURAMARIT. Reverting to the title of prince, Sihanouk organized his own mass political movement, the People's Socialist Community (*Sangkum Reastr Niyum*), which dominated the government for the next decade.

Opposed only by the People's Party (*Kanakpak Pracheachon*), a pro-Communist formation, the *Sangkum* captured all 82 National Assembly seats in an election held in September 1966. Unlike in the past, however, the candidates were not handpicked by Sihanouk, and the conservative tendencies of the resultant government, headed by Lt. Gen. LON NOL, prompted Sihanouk to set up a countergovernment of moderates and leftists to act as an extraparliamentary opposition. Subsequent

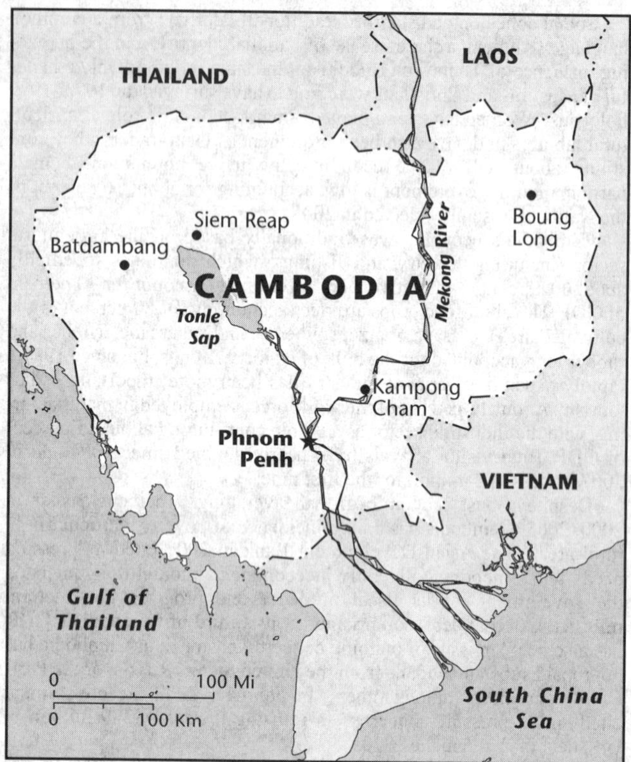

rivalry between the conservative and radical groups, coupled with an April 1967 revolt in Battambang Province in which Communists played a leading role, led Sihanouk to assume special powers as head of a provisional government in May. The new cabinet resigned in January 1968, and Sihanouk appointed another headed by PENN NOUTH. Penn Nouth resigned in July 1969, and Gen. Lon Nol returned to the premiership. In March 1970 Prince Sihanouk was deposed as head of state, and on October 9 the monarchy was abolished and Cambodia was proclaimed the Khmer Republic. An election initially scheduled for the same year was postponed because of a military confrontation with North Vietnam.

Under a new constitution adopted on May 4, 1972, the Lon Nol government allowed political parties to organize and then held a presidential election in June. The final tally gave Lon Nol 55 percent of the vote. Opposition parties then boycotted the September legislative election, and all seats in the Senate and National Assembly fell to the progovernment Social-Republican Party.

During 1974 a four-year war between government forces and insurgent communists, the *Khmers Rouges* ("Red Khmers"),gained in intensity. At midyear Lon Nol offered to engage in peace negotiations with the Communist-affiliated National United Front of Cambodia (*Front Uni National du Cambodge*—FUNC), nominally headed by Prince Sihanouk, who rejected the offer in a statement issued from exile in Beijing. Following *Khmer Rouge* advances to the vicinity of the capital in early 1975, Prime Minister LONG BORET presented the president with a request, signed by a number of military and civilian leaders, that he leave the country. On April 10 Lon Nol flew to Indonesia, and the president of the Senate, Maj. Gen. SAUKHAM KHOY, was named interim president of the republic. Two days later, U.S. embassy personnel evacuated Phnom Penh. Upon Saukham Khoy's departure with the Americans, a temporary Supreme Committee of the Republic surrendered to the FUNC on April 17. The Communist-controlled government that followed included Prince Sihanouk, who was reinstated as head of state, and Penn Nouth, who returned as prime minister.

In December 1975 the National United Front of Kampuchea (FUNK, formerly the FUNC) approved a new constitution for what was to be known as Democratic Kampuchea, effective from January 5, 1976. An election of delegates to a new People's Representative Assembly was held in March, and in April Prince Sihanouk resigned as head of state, receiving a life pension and the honorary title of "Great Patriot." At its opening session on April 11 the assembly designated KHIEU SAMPHAN as chair of the State Presidium and POL POT as prime minister. During its ensuing period of rule, the Pol Pot regime launched a massive effort at social change, in the course of which most urban dwellers were forced to relocate to rural areas under conditions of such brutality that upward of 2 million are estimated to have perished.

The traditional hostility between the Khmer and Vietnamese peoples reached a climax in late 1978 with an expansion of many months of border conflict into a full-scale invasion by the Vietnamese, supported by a small force of dissident Khmers calling themselves the Kampuchean National United Front for National Salvation (KNUFNS). On January 7, 1979, Phnom Penh fell to the invaders, who proclaimed a People's Republic of Kampuchea (PRK) the following day and installed HENG SAMRIN, a former assistant chief of the Kampuchean General Staff, as president of a People's Revolutionary Council. Remnants of the defending forces withdrew to the west, where guerrilla-type operations against the Vietnamese-supported regime were maintained by *Khmer Rouge* and right-wing *Khmer Serei* ("Free Cambodian") forces, in alliance with a smaller unit claiming allegiance to Prince Sihanouk.

In June 1982, after more than 18 months of negotiations, the three anti-Vietnamese groups concluded an agreement in Kuala Lumpur, Malaysia, on a Coalition Government of Democratic Kampuchea (CGDK). Under the agreement, Prince Sihanouk would serve as president; Khieu Samphan as vice president in charge of foreign affairs; and SON SANN, the leader of the *Khmer Serei*'s Khmer People's National Liberation Front (KPNLF), as prime minister. In December 1984 the chair of the PRK Council of Ministers, CHAN SI, died, and he was succeeded in January 1985 by Vice Chair and Foreign Minister HUN SEN, a former *Khmer Rouge* official who had defected to the Vietnamese in 1977.

In January 1988 Prince Sihanouk formally resigned as nominal leader of the three-party coalition after having engaged in two rounds of talks in France with the PRK's Hun Sen. He withdrew the resignation a month later but resigned again in early July, two weeks before a meeting in Bogor, Indonesia (the first so-called "Jakarta Informal Meeting"—JIM), that brought together, for the first time, representatives of all four Cambodian factions as well as those of Vietnam, Laos, and the members of the Association of Southeast Asian Nations (ASEAN). Sihanouk met again with Hun Sen in France in November and resumed the CGDK presidency in February 1989, immediately prior to a second round of all-party discussions in Jakarta (JIM-II).

An additional meeting between Sihanouk and Hun Sen in Jakarta in May 1989 followed an announcement by the PRK premier that his government was changing the country's official name to State of Cambodia (SOC). Collaterally, the regime invited Sihanouk to return as SOC head of state, with new elections to follow. Further talks in Paris between Hun Sen, Prince Sihanouk, *Khmer Rouge* leader Khieu Samphan, and the KPLNF's Son Sann proved unproductive, however, as did a July 30–August 30 Paris International Conference on Cambodia (PICC), chaired by France and Indonesia. Vietnam nonetheless announced the withdrawal of its troops from Cambodia on September 20, honoring a pledge made the previous May.

In mid-January 1990 the UN Security Council's five permanent members (P-5) reiterated an earlier appeal for an effective UN presence in the strife-torn country. A week later Prince Sihanouk again resigned as president of the CGDK to show the world that he was not "an accomplice of the *Khmers Rouges.*" On February 3, in an effort to dissociate the resistance movement from the earlier Democratic Kampuchean regime, he announced that the CGDK would henceforth be known as the National Government of Cambodia (NGC).

On June 6, 1990, during a meeting in Tokyo, Sihanouk and Phnom Penh representatives signed an accord that called for the establishment of a Supreme National Council (SNC) of rebel and government members to pave the way for a cease-fire by the end of July. However, the *Khmer Rouge* guerrillas refused to participate unless they were granted representation equal to that of Phnom Penh.

During an informal meeting in Jakarta on September 9 and 10, 1990, the four parties approved a P-5 "framework document" that provided for assignment of most SNC powers to the UN pending the election of a new Cambodian government. A 12-member SNC thereupon convened in Bangkok, Thailand, and on December 21–22, meeting in Paris, it accepted "most of the fundamental points" of a November P-5 document that provided for a UN Transitional Authority in Cambodia (UNTAC) charged with overseeing a cease-fire, nationwide balloting, and the drafting of a new constitution. In January 1991, however, hardline elements of the SOC effectively repudiated the agreement.

Nevertheless, on May 1, 1991, the first cease-fire in the history of the 12-year struggle took effect. Subsequently, during an SNC meeting in Pattaya, Thailand, in June, Prince Sihanouk won agreement on a permanent truce and acceptance of the council as a supergovernment superior to both the SOC and NGC. In mid-July, during what was described as an informal meeting in Beijing, Sihanouk resigned as NGC president and was named SNC chair. Immediately thereafter a P-5 delegation met in the Chinese capital with representatives of the PICC cochairs to discuss implementation of UNTAC, and on August 23 a 12-member UN truce-monitoring team arrived in Cambodia.

SNC negotiations in August and September 1991 resolved the most contentious remaining issues, and a formal peace agreement was signed in Paris on October 23. On November 19 Sihanouk announced a "treaty of cooperation" between the Hun Sen regime and his own political formation, known since 1989 as the United National Front for an Independent, Neutral, Peaceful, and Cooperative Cambodia (*Front Uni National pour un Cambodge Indépendant, Neutre, Pacifique et Coopératif*—Funcinpec). However, the November 19 alliance, which had been widely construed as an attempt to limit *Khmer Rouge* influence, was abruptly terminated on December 5, reportedly at Chinese insistence.

The *Khmers Rouges* boycotted the election of a constituent National Assembly held May 23–28, 1993, at which the Funcinpec Party (FP), as Funcinpec had been renamed, won a plurality of 58 seats to 51 for the SOC's Cambodian People's Party (CPP). On June 16 the FP and the CPP agreed that Hun Sen and Prince NORODOM RANARIDDH, Sihanouk's eldest son and FP chair, would share powers equally as cochairs of the Council of Ministers, with Sihanouk as head of state. The two leading formations also agreed that each would hold 45 percent of cabinet posts, with 10 percent allocated to Son Sann's Buddhist Liberal Democratic Party (BLDP, successor to the KPNLF), which had run a distant third in the legislative balloting.

Cambodia's new constitution was approved on September 21, 1993, and promulgated three days later, at which time Sihanouk was recrowned king. On October 23 a new royal government was formed, with Prince Ranariddh as first prime minister and Hun Sen as second prime minister.

A major government offensive on remaining *Khmer Rouge* strongholds in the first half of 1996 yielded increasing numbers of defectors from the movement as well as a split in which a group led by IENG SARY opted to abandon the military struggle and to negotiate with the government. The fracturing of the *Khmers Rouges* eventually served to intensify the power struggle between Second Prime Minister Hun Sen and First Prime Minister Prince Ranariddh, both camps reportedly seeking alliances with *Khmer Rouge* factions. In February 1997 Ranariddh rankled Hun Sen further by announcing the formation of a National United Front (NUF) electoral alliance that included opposition leader SAM RAINSY, then of the Khmer Nation Party (KNP). In a further complication, *Khmer Rouge* leader Khieu Samphan subsequently indicated that his supporters might back the alliance. These developments contributed to intermittent fighting between FP and CPP loyalists.

In April 1997 Hun Sen announced the defection of several legislators from the FP, which had split into pro- and anti-Ranariddh factions. He also accused the prince of collaboration with the *Khmers Rouges*. By June the government was rent virtually in half, as were the *Khmers Rouges:* Pol Pot apparently ordered the execution of long-standing *Khmer Rouge* military leader SON SEN for negotiating with the government, while several days later *Khmer Rouge* radio announced that Pol Pot himself had been "arrested." The *Khmers Rouges* subsequently convicted Pol Pot of "treason" and sentenced him to house arrest.

With the threat of *Khmer Rouge* and KNP support for Prince Ranariddh growing steadily, Hun Sen's supporters went on the offensive. Civil war broke out near Phnom Penh in July 1997, and Prince Ranariddh left the country. The National Assembly on August 6 confirmed Hun Sen's choice of Foreign Minister UNG HUOT, a leader of the anti-Ranariddh FP camp, to replace Ranariddh as first prime minister. At the same time, the legislature stripped Ranariddh of his immunity and charged him with treason for conspiring with the *Khmers Rouges* and with illegally importing weapons. Nevertheless, in September the assembly refused to approve a new cabinet devoid of all FP members. After initially resisting any compromise, Hun Sen in February 1998 accepted a Japanese-brokered agreement under which Ranariddh briefly returned to Cambodia from Thailand on March 30, having received a prearranged pardon from King Sihanouk related to his convictions earlier in the month on the arms smuggling and treason charges.

Meanwhile, government operations against the *Khmers Rouges* continued in the north, with reports surfacing in March 1998 that defecting troops and government forces had driven hard-line commander TA MOK (UNG CHOEUN) from his base in Anlong Veng. Accompanying Ta Mok were Khieu Samphan and former second-in-command NUON CHEA as well as Pol Pot, who died on April 15, reportedly of a heart attack, although subsequent accounts gave the cause of death as everything from suicide to execution. By the end of May, Ta Mok's final stronghold, Ta Tum, had fallen, and on June 15 five more senior *Khmer Rouge* officials defected, amid frequent reports that the handful of remaining guerrilla leaders were negotiating terms of surrender.

In the run-up to the July 26, 1998, legislative balloting, the opposition repeatedly accused the CPP of campaign violations that ranged from scare tactics to murder, leading Sam Rainsy, now the head of his own Sam Rainsy Party (SRP), to threaten an election boycott. In the end, however, 39 parties contested the election, in which the CPP received 41.4 percent of the votes, followed by the FP with 31.7 percent and the SRP with 14.3 percent. While the formula for allocating the assembly's 122 seats awarded the CPP a majority of 64, compared to 43 for the FP and 15 for the SRP, the distribution left Hun Sen far short of the two-thirds needed to form a new government. Neither Ranariddh nor Rainsy accepted the results, which led to public demonstrations that drew up to 20,000 participants and provoked reprisals by CPP supporters.

With King Sihanouk presiding, Hen Sen, Prince Ranariddh, and Sam Rainsy met in Siem Reap on September 22, 1998. On November 14 Ranariddh concluded a coalition agreement with Hun Sen that had been brokered by King Sihanouk. The pact, formally signed on November 23, provided for Hun Sen to serve as sole prime minister, Ranariddh to assume the presidency of the National Assembly, and CPP chief CHEA SIM, theretofore presiding officer of the assembly, to become chair of a newly created, largely advisory Senate. The CPP and the FP agreed to control 12 and 11 ministries, respectively, while continuing to share the defense and interior portfolios. On November 30 the National Assembly approved the new cabinet.

Early December 1998 witnessed the defection of additional *Khmer Rouge* troops near the Thai border, the number being variously estimated at between 1,000 and 5,000. On December 24–25 Khieu Samphan and Nuon Chea surrendered to the government. They soon relocated to Pailin, in the northwest, where their former colleague, Ieng Sary, supported by 25,000 or more former *Khmers Rouges*, had established a semiautonomous enclave. By mid-2001 the only *Khmer Rouge* leaders awaiting trial for the 1975–1979 reign of terror were Ta Mok, who had been captured on March 6 (he died in 2006), bringing the insurgency to an end, and KANG KEK IEU (a.k.a. DUCH), once the chief of national security but now a Christian missionary, who freely admitted his part in torture and murder (see Current issues, below).

In the National Assembly election of July 27, 2003, the CPP won 73 of 123 seats, 9 fewer than the two-thirds needed to form a government on its own. Initially, both Funcinpec and the SRP, the only other parties to win representation, refused to join any coalition headed by Hun Sen, who in turn refused to step aside as prime minister. His refusal produced an 11-month impasse, during which the existing CPP-Funcinpec government continued on as a caretaker. On June 2, 2004, Hun Sen and Prince Ranariddh announced that they had resolved remaining differences on a 73-point governmental platform and would again share power. The resultant accord, formally signed on June 30, gave the CPP 60 percent of the cabinet posts and did not include the SRP.

On July 8, 2004, the new National Assembly convened for the first time and quickly passed constitutional amendments enabling the prime minister and assembly president to be elected by a single show of hands rather than, as previously, by separate secret ballots. The Senate concurred, but King Sihanouk, who had been in North Korea since April, refused to sign the measure and instead asked that Chea Sim, the acting head of state, "please sign or not sign . . . in accordance with his opinion." On July 13, however, Chea Sim left the country for Thailand, fueling speculation of a split in the CPP, and the bill was ultimately signed into law by Senate deputy chair NHIEK BUN CHHAY of Funcinpec. The next day King Sihanouk nominated Hun Sen as prime minister and asked him to form a cabinet, which the National Assembly approved 96–0 on July 15. (The SRP boycotted the vote.)

Writing from Beijing on October 6, 2004, King Sihanouk, citing his age (81) and health concerns, expressed his desire to abdicate, and on October 14 the Royal Throne Council endorsed his preferred successor, Prince NORODOM SIHAMONI. The new king was crowned on October 29.

On March 2, 2006, the National Assembly passed a constitutional amendment requiring that a new government be backed by a simple majority of lower house members rather than by a two-thirds majority. Although Hun Sen stated after the vote that the CPP did not intend to force Funcinpec from Cambodia's governing coalition, he quickly dismissed the Funcinpec coministers of defense and interior. On March 3 Prince Ranariddh resigned as president of the National Assembly.

In regularly scheduled direct elections for the National Assembly on July 27, 2008, the CPP won a commanding 90 of the legislature's 123 seats; the SRP, with 26 seats, was the only other party in double digits as Funcinpec, damaged by Prince Ranariddh's departure and subsequent formation of the Norodom Ranariddh Party (NRP), won only 2. On September 24 the National Assembly, despite a boycott by opposition members, voted to reelect Hun Sen as prime minister. He immediately formed a new Council of Ministers that, except for one position, exclusively consisted of CPP members.

Constitution and government. Under the 1993 basic law, Cambodia's head of state is again a monarch who enjoys considerable latitude, including the power to dissolve the legislature during a national emergency. Selection of the monarch is the responsibility of the Royal Throne Council, which can choose from among any of several royal lines. The prime minister, chosen from the leading parliamentary party, is to be appointed by the monarch upon recommendation by the president of the National Assembly. For more than a decade, the government was required to win a two-thirds majority vote of the National Assembly before taking office, but in March 2006, with the backing of the opposition, the lower house passed a constitutional amendment to reduce the requirement to a vote of one-half plus one.

The November 1998 CPP-FP pact included provision for establishing a Senate as the upper house of a bicameral Parliament, and in March 1999 the constitution was amended to that effect by the National Assembly, which is directly elected for a five-year term. Although the initial Senate comprised 61 appointees, since January 2006 it has been indirectly elected, except for 2 appointees named by the monarch and 2 chosen by the National Assembly. The Senate's role is largely advisory; principally, it may recommend changes to legislation passed by the lower chamber, which, however, is under no obligation to enact them. The president of the Senate serves as acting head of state when the king is abroad.

The nine-member Constitutional Council is empowered to resolve election disputes as well as to interpret the constitution and legislation. The independent judiciary is headed by a Supreme Court. In 2004 the National Assembly approved a law establishing an Extraordinary Chambers in the Courts of Cambodia (ECCC) to handle prosecution of *Khmer Rouge* leaders accused of war crimes between 1975 and 1979. The ECCC's trial chamber has three Cambodian and two international judges; the Supreme Court Chamber has four Cambodian and three international judges. Trial Chamber decisions require concurrence by at least four judges; Supreme Court Chamber decisions, five. The first trial began in 2009 (see Current issues, below).

Local administration encompasses 24 provinces and municipalities, the former subdivided into districts (*srok*) and communes (*khum*), and the latter into sectors (*khan*) and urban communes (*sangkat*). Local council elections were held for the first time in February 2002. Indirect voting (by communal councilors) for provincial, municipal, and district councils were first conducted in May 2009.

Foreign relations. The neighboring country most directly affected by the quarter-century of strife in Cambodia—and the one most deeply opposed to recognition of the Vietnamese-backed Heng Samrin government in 1979—was Thailand, whose eastern region provided sanctuary for some 250,000 Khmer refugees. It was not until June 2000 that Thai and Cambodian officials signed a memorandum of understanding regarding demarcation of land boundaries. The two governments also agreed to work jointly toward elimination of smuggling, drug-trafficking, and illegal entry.

Thai-Cambodian tensions flared up in January 2003 following comments allegedly made by a Thai TV personality regarding Thai ownership of the world historical site at Angkor Wat. Anti-Thai riots in Phnom Penh on January 29 led Thailand to close the border. Hun Sen apologized and offered restitution, but the border was not fully reopened until March. Full diplomatic relations were restored in late April. In February 2006 the two countries announced that they intended to complete their land border demarcation before the end of the year, with the maritime demarcation to follow in 2007, but the process was slowed by the September 2006 coup in Thailand. The most recent border clash, in October 2008, resulted in the deaths of four soldiers near the Hindu temple of Preah Vihear, an 11th-century site that was awarded to Cambodia by the International Court of Justice in 1962. The disputed area, about 4.6 square kilometers, has become a focus of attention for the Thai-Cambodia Joint Commission on Demarcation of the Land Boundary.

Indonesia was instrumental in bringing together Cambodia's warring factions in mid-1988 and provided venues for a number of subsequent all-party meetings. In July 1989 it joined with France in cosponsoring the PICC, and both countries, in addition to Thailand and the five permanent UN Security Council members, were key players in the events leading to the peace accord of October 1991. Most UNTAC units withdrew in November 1993, at which time, in the first action of its kind, the UN General Assembly established a human rights center in Phnom Penh to serve as a local watchdog agency and to train government officials in drafting laws on human and civil rights.

The collapse of the Soviet Union and the attendant loss to Phnom Penh and its Vietnamese backers of both financial and political aid contributed significantly to the domestic events of 1993. At the same time, the United States, recognizing that what it termed its "neutral" stance in the Cambodian matter had primarily benefited guerrilla forces, began supporting the new coalition government's military efforts to eliminate the remaining *Khmer Rouge* strongholds.

Cambodia's relations with other countries were dramatically affected by the political turmoil in 1997–1998. Following Prince Ranariddh's ouster, the UN refused to allow the Hun Sen/Ung Huot government to occupy the Cambodian seat in the General Assembly, while many Western countries suspended foreign aid. Japan, however, refused U.S. pressure to cut off aid and signaled its growing interest in Cambodian affairs by brokering the cease-fire of January 1998 between Prince Ranariddh and Hun Sen.

Following formation of the November 1998 coalition government, Cambodia was permitted to reclaim its UN General Assembly seat, and in April 1999 the country was formally admitted to ASEAN. The formation of a coalition government also reopened the pockets of Western donors, who had agreed in January on a $470 million aid package. In May 2000 a meeting of aid agencies and donor countries concluded with pledges totaling $548 million, in return for which the government agreed to reduce the size of the military, improve fiscal control, attack illegal logging, continue its efforts to reduce poverty, and reform the judiciary.

In October 2004 Cambodia became a member of the World Trade Organization (WTO). Cambodia signed a bilateral Trade and Investment Framework Agreement (TIFA) with its largest trading partner, the United States, in 2006, followed in 2007 by the first visit to the kingdom by a U.S. trade representative. Relations with Washington warmed as Cambodia hosted two U.S. Navy vessels for the first time in 30 years and cooperated in a U.S. Peace Corps program. In another significant development in relations in 2007, the United States offered to assist with antiterrorism training in Cambodia.

Cambodia's relations with China have been well-established in recent years, with the Chinese government providing millions in development loans and heavily investing in the kingdom's infrastructure, specific crops for Chinese consumption, steel mills, and military patrol boats to counter piracy. Prime Minister Hun Sen has praised China for its assistance, which he said has been offered without the criticism of lack of good governance that has accompanied Western aid. In February 2008 Cambodian and Chinese developers initiated a special economic zone in Sihanoukville, said to be the largest of its kind in the kingdom.

Current issues. With the apparent demise of Funcinpec as a political force, in the 2008 National Assembly election the only viable option for opponents of Hun Sen's continued rule was the SRP, which nevertheless managed only a slight improvement over its 2003 performance at the polls. Despite governmental corruption and lack of transparency, plus concerns about authoritarian rule, the voters gave the CPP more than three-fourths of the seats in the lower house. The CPP's leading role was confirmed by the country's first nationwide indirect elections for district, municipal, and provincial councils, held May 17, 2009. With only communal-level councilors voting, the CPP won 76 percent of the vote, compared to 21 percent for the SRP and 4 percent for an alliance of Funcinpec and the NRP.

The much-delayed first formal indictment by the ECCC against a *Khmer Rouge* figure was issued on August 13, 2008, the target being Kang Kek Ieu, now 67 and the youngest of the five confirmed defendants. Age and ill health may be a significant factor in other ECCC proceedings. Nuon Chea, now 83, was arrested in September 2007 and has suffered at least one stroke. Arrested in November 2007 were Khieu Samphan, 78, following his hospitalization, also for a stroke; Ieng Sary, now 85; and his wife, IENG THIRITH, 77. In September 2009 the ECCC drew the wrath of Prime Minister Hun Sen when it agreed to consider investigating five other potential defendants. Hun Sen, who has been accused of exerting political pressure on the Cambodian jurists, blamed unnamed foreign governments of trying to stir up trouble in Cambodia.

Kang Kek Ieu's trial for war crimes, crimes against humanity, torture, and murder began on March 30, 2009, even while the ECCC continued to appeal to international donors for sufficient funds to continue its operations through at least 2010. Testimony in his trial concluded in mid-September, with closing arguments expected in November.

In an unrelated trial, three former *Khmer Rouge* guerrillas were convicted in October 2008 of the 1996 kidnapping and murder of a British mine-clearing expert and his Cambodian interpreter. Six months earlier, a U.S. court had convicted CHHUN YASITH of involvement in a November 2000 attack on Cambodian government buildings by a group called the Cambodian Freedom Fighters. The failed coup attempt led to at least eight deaths.

POLITICAL PARTIES

No current party claims a *Khmer Rouge* heritage, although various leaders of the Cambodian People's Party (CPP), including Prime Minister Hun Sen, were at one time *Khmers Rouges.* From a historical perspective, the Democratic National United Movement (DNUM), formed in 1996 by *Khmer Rouge* defector Ieng Sary, would appear to have been the last successor to a series of *Khmer Rouge* parties: the Pol Pot wing of the Communist Party of Kampuchea (PCK; see under CPP), which ruled the country from 1975 to 1979 but was declared dissolved in December 1981; the Party of Democratic Kampuchea—PDK (*Pheakki Kampuchea Prachea Thipatai*), which claimed in mid-1985 to have adopted a "new ideology of democratic socialism"; and the Cambodian National Unity Party—CNUP (*Kanakpak Samakki Cheat Kampuchea*), which was launched in 1992. The CNUP was ostensibly formed to contest the 1993 National Assembly elections, although it ended up boycotting them. Subsequent abortive efforts to bring the CNUP into the political structure were followed in early 1996 by a renewed government offensive against *Khmer Rouge* strongholds. A major split in the CNUP/*Khmer Rouge* hierarchy occurred in August when Ieng Sary, a former Democratic Kampuchea deputy premier (and brother-in-law of Pol Pot), entered into talks with the government, reportedly with the backing of military commanders controlling about half the *Khmer Rouge* forces.

Having received a pardon from King Sihanouk, Ieng Sary set up the DNUM in Pailin, his base. Technically not a political party, it did not compete in the 1998 national election. The DNUM is no longer active.

Of Cambodia's 57 registered parties, only 11 were declared eligible to contest the July 27, 2008, National Assembly elections. Under the election law, parties had to present at least 41 candidates to qualify.

Governing Coalition:

Cambodian People's Party—CPP (*Kanakpak Pracheachon Kampuchea*). The CPP was launched as a non-Communist successor to the Kampuchean People's Revolutionary Party (KPRP) during an extraordinary party congress in Phnom Penh held October 17–18, 1991.

The KPRP had been founded in early 1951, when the Indo-Chinese Communist Party, led by Ho Chi Minh, was divided into separate entities for Cambodia, Laos, and Vietnam. Following the 1954 Geneva Agreement, it encompassed three factions: the *Khmer Vietminh*, controlled largely by the North Vietnamese; an underground force that served as the ideological core of the *Khmers Rouges;* and adherents of the legal People's Party (*Kanakpak Pracheachon*). At its Second Congress, held secretly in Phnom Penh in 1960, the organization changed its name to the Communist Party of Kampuchea (*Parti Communiste du Kampuchea*—PCK/*Kanakpak Kumunist Kampuchea*) but continued to be divided, largely between supporters of the North Vietnamese and a Maoist contingent led by Pol Pot (then known as Saloth Sar). In 1962 the incumbent PCK general secretary was assassinated, allegedly on order of Pol Pot, who assumed the office the following year.

The two factions were nominally reunited during 1970–1975, although most pro-Vietnamese went into exile in the wake of a purge that commenced in 1974. Following the overthrow of the *Khmer Rouge* government in 1979, the Hanoi-supported exiles staged a "reorganization Congress" at which PEN SOVAN was elected secretary general (he also served briefly as chair of the PRK Council of Ministers in 1981), and the KPRP label was readopted to distinguish the Phnom Penh group from the *Khmer Rouge* faction that continued to be led by Pol Pot until its formal dissolution on December 6, 1981. Two days earlier, the KPRP Central Committee, following an apparent power struggle, had elected Heng Samrin as its secretary general. Later that month, a congress of the Kampuchean National United Front for National Salvation (KNUFNS), a mass organization established in 1978 by Khmer opponents of the Democratic Kampuchean regime, recognized the KPRP as its "leading nucleus." At the same congress the front changed its name to the Kampuchean United Front for National Construction and Defense (KUFNCD). Another change, to the United Front for the Construction and Defense of the Kampuchean Fatherland (UFCDKF), occurred in 1989. The most recent renaming, to the **Solidarity Front for Development of the Cambodian Motherland** (SFDCM), occurred at the Front's fifth congress, held in May 2006.

In addition to abandoning Marxism-Leninism, the CPP at its 1991 founding congress supported the adoption of a multiparty system, endorsed a free-market economy, called for the designation of Buddhism as the state religion, and announced a number of structural and leadership changes. The former KPRP Politburo and Secretariat were merged into a single CPP Standing Committee; Heng Samrin, theretofore KPRP general secretary, was named CPP honorary president; and Chea Sim and Hun Sen, the second- and third-ranked members of the KPRP Politburo, were designated chair and vice chair, respectively, of the CPP Central Committee. The party was runner-up in the balloting of May 1993, winning 51 assembly seats on a vote share of 38.2 percent.

Amid charges of campaign and voting irregularities, in the July 1998 election the CPP took 41 percent of the vote and 64 seats, making it the leading legislative party. It retained that standing in the July 2003 election, winning 47 percent of the vote and 73 seats—a majority, but shy of the two-thirds needed to govern on its own. A year later, following the conclusion of protracted coalition negotiations with the Funcinpec Party, the CPP's two main factions—the hard-liners led by Chea Sim and the more moderate faction of Hun Sen—apparently collided over the issue of cabinet-level appointments, which may have been a factor in Chea Sim's departure for Thailand, ostensibly for regular medical treatment. (Some reports said he was under armed guard.)

In October 2007 the party nominated Hun Sen as its candidate for prime minister in 2008. In the run-up to the midyear election, several members of Funcinpec left what was described as an "ailing" party to join the CPP (see Funcinpec, below). In February 2008 Hun Sen reaffirmed that his party's alliance with Funcinpec would continue if the CPP were to win the upcoming election.

In June 2008 the CPP won 58.1 percent of the vote and a commanding 90 seats, after which Hun Sen was reelected prime minister.

Leaders: HENG SAMRIN (President of the National Assembly, Chair of the SFDCM National Council, and Honorary Chair of the CPP), CHEA SIM (Chair of the CPP Central Committee and President of the Senate), HUN SEN (Prime Minister and Vice Chair, CPP Central Committee), SAY CHHUM (Chair of the Permanent Committee).

Funcinpec Party (FP). Funcinpec, the acronym for *Front Uni National pour un Cambodge Indépendant, Neutre, Pacifique et Coopératif* (United National Front for an Independent, Neutral, Peaceful, and Cooperative Cambodia), was proclaimed in 1989 as the political counterpart of the National Army of Independent Cambodia, formerly the Sihanoukist National Army (*Armée Nationale Sihanoukiste*—ANS). At a congress held February 27–28, 1992, the group was redesignated as the Funcinpec Party, with Prince Norodom Ranariddh, who had theretofore served as general secretary, being named chair. The FP secured an unexpected plurality of 58 National Assembly seats in May 1993 on a vote share of 45.5 percent. In June Prince Ranariddh was named cochair of the interim government's Council of Ministers and then, in October, first prime minister under the new constitution.

The FP was split in 1997 between those who supported Prince Ranariddh (and his courting of *Khmer Rouge* elements as potential electoral allies) and those more in consonance with the policies of Hun Sen's CPP. A number of FP legislators defected to the CPP parliamentary camp in April, establishing a dissident faction under the leadership of TOAN CHHAY, who then formed the unsuccessful National Union

Party (*Kanakpak Ruop Ruom Cheat*) to contest the 1998 election. Following the ouster of Prince Ranariddh from the government as the result of the midyear civil war, anti-Ranariddh FP dissident Ung Huot was named first prime minister; he subsequently campaigned under the banner of the Populism Party (*Reastr Niyum Party*—RNP), while former Funcinpec secretary general LOY SIM CHHEANG formed the New Society Party (*Sangkum Thmei Party*—STP). Neither the RNP nor the STP won any seats at the election. (Ung Huot ultimately returned to the FP; the STP became moribund after the death of its leader.)

Prior to the July 1998 election, Funcinpec formed a National United Front (NUF) alliance with the Sam Rainsy Party; the Son Sann Party (SSP); and the small Khmer Neutral Party (*Kanakpak Kampuchea Appyeakroet*), which had largely disappeared after an unsuccessful 1993 election campaign but reemerged in 1996. In the 1998 balloting the FP was runner-up to the CPP, claiming 31.7 percent of the vote and 43 seats in the National Assembly. The November 1998 coalition agreement with the CPP specified that the FP would control 11 of 25 ministries and would share the defense and interior portfolios.

In mid-January 1999 the SSP merged with the FP. The SSP had originated in a faction of the Buddhist Liberal Democratic Party (BLDP) that was loyal to the former BLDP president, Son Sann. (Both factions had claimed a legal right to the BLDP name, but before the 1998 election they agreed to adopt alternate designations: the SSP and the Buddhist Liberal Party.) Despite participation in the NUF alliance, the SSP won no seats at the July 1998 election. With Son Sann having retired from politics, SSP leadership passed to his son, SON SOUBERT, who was subsequently named to the Constitutional Court and therefore resigned from his party post. The party's de facto leader, KEM SOKHA, negotiated the merger with the FP.

At the FP national congress held March 19–21, 2000, Prince Ranariddh urged the party to readmit former members who wished to rejoin, particularly the RNP contingent. In May and June 2002, however, Funcinpec saw two new eponymous parties formed by departing leaders Prince NORODOM CHAKRAPONG and Hang Dara.

In the July 2003 general election the FP lost 17 seats, and its vote share fell to 21 percent. A month later it formed an Alliance of Democrats with the SRP (below) as part of their joint effort to deny the CPP's Hun Sen another term as prime minister. After protracted negotiations, Ranariddh signed a new coalition agreement with the CPP in late June 2004.

On March 3, 2006, a day after Hun Sen had dismissed the Funcinpec coministers of defense and interior, Ranariddh resigned as National Assembly president, "for the purpose of strengthening and moving forward the Funcinpec Party." Within days, he announced a party reorganization that included naming former party dissident Prince Norodom Chakrapong (who had led the eponymous Norodom Chakrapong Soul Khmer Party at the time of the 2003 election) as secretary general and Ung Huot as one of four new deputy secretaries general. On October 18, however, Ranariddh lost control of the party when an extraordinary congress chose the country's ambassador to Germany, Keo Puth Rasmey, as his successor. A week later, the National Assembly confirmed Keo as a deputy prime minister. Ranariddh's ouster was attributed to corruption: he allegedly had kept $3.6 million for himself from the sale of party headquarters. He subsequently was sentenced to 18 months in jail, but from exile in 2007 he claimed that the charge was politically motivated. Ranariddh earlier had refused the title of historic president and established the Norodom Ranariddh Party (NRP, below).

In October 2007 the party nominated as its 2008 candidate for prime minister Princess NORODOM ARUN RASMEY, the youngest daughter of Norodom Sihanouk, wife of party president Keo Puth Rasmey, and Cambodia's ambassador to Malaysia. Early in 2008 several party members defected to the CPP, including Women's Affairs Minister ING KANTHA PHAVY, Religions and Cults Minister KHUN HAING, Secretary of State for Finance CHEA PENG CHHEANG, and Secretary of State for Civil Aviation MAO HAS VANNAL, reportedly due to their lack of confidence in the FP leadership.

In the 2008 National Assembly election Funcinpec won only 5.1 percent of the vote and two seats. Nevertheless, it was retained in the government by Prime Minister Hun Sen, who offered it one cabinet-level position and a number of junior appointments.

Leaders: KEO PUTH RASMEY (President), NHIEK BUN CHHAY (Deputy Prime Minister and Secretary General of the Party).

Parliamentary Opposition:

Sam Rainsy Party—SRP (*Pak Sam Rainsy*). In March 1998 the faction of the Khmer Nation Party (KNP) led by labor activist and former finance minister Sam Rainsy changed its name to the SRP, following the government's earlier decision to officially recognize the KNP faction led by KONG MONI. Rainsy had established the KNP in 1995, having been expelled from the FP in May and the National Assembly in June after complaining of corruption in the awarding of government contracts. (Kong Moni's faction, renamed the Khmer Angkor Party in 1998, had no electoral success.)

In the July 1998 election the SRP won 14.3 percent of the vote and 15 seats in the National Assembly. Rainsy later accepted the CPP-FP coalition pact but challenged creation of the new Senate on constitutional and budgetary grounds. In 2003 the SRP won 24 legislative seats, only 2 less than the FP. Although the SRP strongly opposed Hun Sen's continuation as prime minister, in 2004 it considered joining the CPP and the FP in a three-way coalition government. That possibility ended, however, when the CPP and the FP agreed to constitutional amendments that would permit the election of the prime minister and National Assembly president by a single show of hands. From Thailand, where he and all the other SRP legislators were ensconced during the July 15 confirmation vote, Rainsy declared the process unconstitutional and the resultant government illegal.

In February 2005 Rainsy fled to France after the National Assembly revoked his parliamentary immunity, leaving him open to criminal lawsuits alleging defamation. He had accused Hun Sen of ordering a grenade attack at a 1997 party rally that killed 16 people. He had also accused Prince Ranariddh of accepting bribes to cement Funcinpec's alliance with the CPP. Convicted in absentia in December and sentenced to 18 months in prison, Rainsy was pardoned by the king in early February 2006 after offering apologies. Another SRP legislator, CHEAM CHANNY, was also pardoned. In August 2005 a military court had sentenced Cheam to seven years in prison for involvement in "an illegal rebel group"—an opposition committee formed to examine the government's defense-related decisions. On February 10 Rainsy returned to Cambodia, and on February 28 the National Assembly reinstated him, Cheam Channy, and a third SRP legislator, CHEA POCH, who had also fled into exile a year earlier to avoid defamation charges.

In 2007 the party nominated Sam Rainsy as its candidate for prime minister in the 2008 elections. The party also submitted draft legislation that would limit the prime minister to one term, but the proposal was rejected by the CPP and did not advance.

After having lost more than 85 percent of its seats in the April 2007 local council elections, many SRP members began defecting to the CPP, including the editor of the party's newspaper. In February 2008 Sam Rainsy rejected the NRP's proposal for a merger of the two weakened parties. By March, some 12,000 SRP members reportedly had been accepted into the CPP; at least one defector joined Funcinpec. Also in March, a member of the SRP and two others were arrested for allegedly intimidating party members who sought to defect. The SRP claimed the arrests were orchestrated by the CPP.

In the 2008 National Assembly election the SRP won 21.9 percent of the vote and 26 seats. In January 2009 the SRP and the Human Rights Party (below) announced formation of a **Democratic Movement for Change.** The parties' leaders stated that they intended to run jointly in the next national election.

In February 2009 Sam Rainsy once again briefly lost his parliamentary immunity for allegedly defaming CPP leaders. His immunity was restored in March, after he had agreed to pay a fine of 10 million riels ($2,450).

Leaders: SAM RAINSY (President), ENG CHHAY EANG (Secretary General), MU SOCHUA (Deputy Secretary General).

Human Rights Party (HRP). Formation of the HRP was announced in July 2007 by Kem Sokha, a human rights campaigner and former member of the Buddhist Liberal Party (see Funcinpec, above). A leading critic of the CPP, Sokha had been jailed for several weeks in 2006 for defaming the prime minister.

In 2008 the HRP won 6.6 percent of the vote and three seats in the National Assembly.

Leader: Kem SOKHA.

Norodom Ranariddh Party (NRP). Following Prince Ranariddh's ouster from the leadership of the FP in October 2006, he announced his intention to form the NRP. In mid-November, however, having accused the Interior Ministry of delaying his new party's registration, he was elected president of the small Khmer Front Party—KFP (*Ronakse Chuncheat Khmer*), which, led by SUTH DINA, had won less than 0.75 percent of the vote at the 2003 legislative election. The KFP then revised its bylaws and changed its name to the NRP, which quickly established itself as a royalist challenger to the FP.

Ranariddh was convicted on a corruption charge in 2006 (see Funcinpec, above) and was living in exile as of 2007. He was nominated as his party's candidate for prime minister in the 2008 elections but faced an 18-month jail term in Cambodia, and it was not clear when or if he would return. Meanwhile, retired King Sihanouk urged Ranariddh to quit politics and accept a job in the royal palace. In February 2008 Ranariddh called for a merger of the NRP and the SRP, but the latter rejected the proposal.

In the 2008 National Assembly election the NRP won 5.6 percent of the vote (slightly better than Funcinpec) and two seats. The following October, shortly after returning from exile in Malaysia, Ranariddh resigned from the party and, having been pardoned by the king, accepted an appointment as president of the Supreme Privy Advisory Council. He also stated that his name should be removed from the party.

With Ranariddh's departure, a leadership dispute broke out involving his successor as NRP president, Chhim Seak Leang, and Suth Dina, who had been serving as party spokesman. Dina, who wanted to rename the party as the Khmer National Front, was ousted in late January 2009.

Leaders: CHHIM SEAK LEANG (President), YOU HOCKRY (Secretary General).

Other Parties:

Six additional parties contested the 2008 National Assembly election. The **Khmer Democratic Party** (*Kanakpak Pracheathipatei Khmer*), led by UK PHOURIK, had claimed 1.8 percent of the 2003 vote but in 2008 won only 0.5 percent. The **Hang Dara Democratic Movement Party** (*Hang Dara Cholana Pracheathipatei*), an FP splinter led by HANG DARA, won 0.4 percent, slightly better than it had in 2003. The **Khmer Anti-Poverty Party,** founded in 2007 by DARAN KRAVANH, finished last, with under 0.2 percent of the vote. The **Khmer Republican Party,** established in 2006 and led by LON RITH, son of Lon Nol, won 0.2 percent. The **League for Democracy Party,** established in 2006 by KHEM VEASNA, won 1.2 percent. The **Society of Justice Party** (*Sangkum Yutethor*), established in 2006 by BAN SOPHAL, won 0.2 percent. The Election Commission ruled that the **United People of Cambodia Party** led by SARSATH OEURN, could not compete after declaring several of its proposed candidates ineligible because they were not registered voters, leaving the party with fewer than the minimum number of candidates.

LEGISLATURE

Constitutional amendments passed by the National Assembly in March 1998 reestablished a bicameral **Parliament** (*Sepiacheat*) by creating an upper house, the Senate.

Senate (*Pritsepia*). As constituted on March 25, 1999, the upper house comprised 61 appointed senators: 59 named by parties, in proportion to representation in the lower house, and 2 named by the king. All were to serve five-year terms. In January 2003 the government announced that the first senatorial election, slated for 2004, would be shelved for budgetary reasons, and the Senate term was later extended twice. Senators now serve six-year terms.

The indirect election of January 22, 2006, for 57 seats produced the following seat distribution: Cambodian People's Party, 45; Funcinpec Party, 10; Sam Rainsy Party, 2. Members were elected from eight constituencies (with varying numbers of seats) by 11,382 eligible electors: the 123 members of the National Assembly plus the representatives who had been elected to 1,621 local councils in 2002. The king and the National Assembly each appointed 2 additional members.

President: CHEA SIM.

National Assembly (*Radhsphea Ney Preah Recheanachakr*). The 123 members of the National Assembly were most recently elected to five-year terms on July 27, 2008. The Cambodian People's Party won 90 seats; the Sam Rainsy Party, 26; the Human Rights Party, 3; the Funcinpec Party, 2; and the Norodom Ranariddh Party, 2.

President: HENG SAMRIN.

CABINET

[as of October 1, 2009]

Prime Minister	Hun Sen
Deputy Prime Ministers	Sar Kheng
	Bin Chhin
	Hor Namhong
	Keat Chhon
	Ke Kimyan
	Men Samon [f]
	Nhiek Bun Chhay (FP)
	Sok An
	Gen. Tea Banh
	Yim Chhayly
Senior Ministers	
Commerce	Cham Prasidh
Environment	Mok Mareth
Land Management, Urban Planning, and Construction	Im Chhunlim
Planning	Chhay Than
Special Envoys	Serei Kosal
Ministers	
Agriculture, Forestry, and Fisheries	Chan Sarun
Culture and Fine Arts	Him Chhem
Economy and Finance	Keat Chhon
Education, Youth, and Sports	Im Sethy
Foreign Affairs and International Cooperation	Hor Namhong
Health	Mom Bunheng
Industry, Mines, and Energy	Suy Sem
Information	Khieu Kanharith
Interior	Sar Kheng
Justice	Ang Vong Vathna
Labor and Vocational Training	Vorng Soth
National Defense	Gen. Tea Banh
Office of the Council of Ministers	Sok An
Parliamentary Affairs and Inspection	Som Kimsuor [f]
Post and Telecommunication	So Khun
Public Works and Transport	Tram Iv Tek
Religions and Cults	Min Khin
Royal Palace	Kong Sam Ol
Rural Development	Chea Sophara
Social Affairs, Veterans, and Youth Rehabilitation	Ith Sam Heng
Tourism	Thong Khon
Water Resources and Meteorology	Lim Kean Hor
Women's Affairs	Ing Kantha Phavy [f]

[f] = female

Note: Except as indicated, all cabinet members belong to the CPP.

COMMUNICATIONS

Although the Cambodian constitution grants freedom of expression, press, and publication, "no one shall exercise this right to infringe upon the rights of others, to affect the good traditions of the society, or violate public law and order and national security." In practice, the government has often acted to restrict publication of information it considers false or defamatory.

In 2008 the watchdog group Reporters Without Borders began expressing concern about freedom of the press in the run-up to the July elections. (Also, the group noted that three journalists reportedly had received death threats for their coverage of logging issues.) Although opposition parties were allowed airtime on state-run media, news broadcasts focused almost exclusively on positive aspects of the CPP-led government's performance. Private television stations basically ignored the opposition.

Press. The newspapers with the largest circulation are Phnom Penh's *Rasmei Kampuchea* (Light of Cambodia), pro-CPP daily; *Kampuchea Thmey,* progovernment daily; and *Kaoh Santepheap,* progovernment daily. Other newspapers are *Cambodia Daily,* in Khmer and English; *Cambodia Times*, weekly in English; *Moneaksekar Khmer,* pro-SRP, *Phnom Penh Post*, independent fortnightly, in English; *Pracheachon* (The People), semiweekly CPP organ; and *Samleng Yuveakchon Khmer,* NRP daily. Reliable circulation figures are not available for most publications.

News agencies. A Cambodian News Agency (*Sapordamean Kampuchea/Agence Kampuchea Presse*—AKP) was established in 1978. Several foreign services, including the Associated Press and Reuters, maintain Phnom Penh offices.

Broadcasting and computing. The government-controlled National Radio of Cambodia (*Vithyu Cheat Kampuchea*) and National Television of Cambodia (TVK) dominate broadcasting, although private radio and television stations also transmit. The Voice of America and Radio Free Asia are also received. In April 2008 the country's first satellite television service was established as a joint venture of TVK and the Cambodian DTV Network (CDN).

As of 2008 there were 5.1 Internet users per 1,000 inhabitants.

INTERGOVERNMENTAL REPRESENTATION

Ambassador to the U.S.: Hem HENG.

U.S. Ambassador to Cambodia: Carol Ann RODLEY.

Permanent Representative to the UN: Kosal SEA.

IGO Memberships (Non-UN): ADB, ASEAN, CP, Interpol, IOM, NAM, OIF, PCA, WCO, WTO.

CAMEROON

Republic of Cameroon
République du Cameroun

Note: Prime Minister Ephraim Inoni (Democratic Rally of the Cameroon People) was dismissed by President Paul Biya on June 30, 2009. The president appointed Philémon Yungi Yang as prime minister on the same day and extensively reshuffled the cabinet.

Political Status: Independence proclaimed 1960; federation established 1961; one-party unitary republic declared June 2, 1972; multiparty system introduced under legislation approved December 6, 1990.

Area: 183,568 sq. mi. (475,442 sq. km.).

Population: 10,493,655 (1987C); 18,931,000 (2008E).

Major Urban Centers (2005E): YAOUNDÉ; (1,525,000), Douala (875,000).

Official Languages: French, English.

Monetary Unit: CFA Franc (official rate December 1, 2009: 434.59 francs = $1US). The CFA franc, previously pegged to the French franc, is now permanently pegged to the euro at 655.957 CFA francs = 1 euro.

President: Paul BIYA (Democratic Rally of the Cameroon People); served as prime minister 1975–1982; installed as president on November 6, 1982, to complete the term of Ahmadou Babatoura AHIDJO, who had resigned on November 4; reelected without opposition on January 14, 1984, and April 24, 1988; reelected for a five-year term in multicandidate balloting on October 11, 1992, for a seven-year term on October 12, 1997; reelected for another seven-year term on October 11, 2004.

Prime Minister: (*See headnote.*) Ephraim INONI (Democratic Rally of the Cameroon People); appointed by the president on December 8, 2004, to replace Peter Mafany MUSONGE; reappointed by the president on September 7, 2007.

THE COUNTRY

Situated just north of the equator on the Gulf of Guinea and rising from a coastal plain to a high interior plateau, Cameroon is the product of a merger in 1961 between the former French and British Cameroon trust territories. Its more than 100 ethnic groups speak 24 major languages and represent a diversity of Christian (53 percent), traditional African (25 percent), and Muslim (22 percent) religious beliefs. Reflecting its dual colonial heritage (the source of lingering political cleavage), Cameroon is the only country in Africa in which both French and English are official languages. In 1996 women were reported to constitute 38 percent of the official labor force.

Cameroon's economy has long been primarily rural, and despite the discovery of major oil deposits in 1973, agriculture has provided a large share of the country's export earnings. Coffee, cocoa, and timber are among the most important agricultural products, but bananas, cotton, rubber, and palm oil also are produced commercially. Oil production has declined since 1985, but the government has adopted laws meant to encourage investors. Industrial development has focused on aluminum smelting from both domestic and imported bauxite. More recent initiatives have been aimed at hydroelectric expansion, the resolution of long-standing transportation problems, and the development of medium-sized farms to halt the exodus of rural youth to urban areas. The economy faltered during the mid-1980s and early 1990s under the influence of depressed oil and other commodity prices, sustained capital flight, rising external debt, and widespread corruption and inefficiency in state-run enterprises. The government, which initially shunned involvement with the International Monetary Fund (IMF), since 1988 has negotiated agreements with it and other international lenders in a context of budget austerity and a commitment to privatization.

Following the devaluation of the CFA franc in 1994, Cameroon's inflation rate rose to 25.8 percent in 1995. However, from 1996 to 1998 the country enjoyed average real GDP growth of approximately 5 percent annually, according to the IMF, as overall world economic activity increased and inflationary pressures eased. Still, analysts urged the government to continue efforts to increase transparency in the public sector, warning that corrupt official practices were endangering economic progress. To that end, in late 1999 the IMF asked the government to set up a system whereby oil revenues would be directly deposited in a monitorable state budget. In addition, the IMF counseled Yaoundé to continue its efforts to raise the "non-oil revenue-to-GDP ratio." While the IMF and the World Bank subsequently praised the government's efforts regarding structural reforms and anticorruption measures, concerns were raised over the pace of privatization and poverty reduction. In 2000 the World Bank granted Cameroon $2 billion in a multiyear debt reduction program; however, the program was suspended in 2004 due to perceived financial mismanagement by the government and a slowdown in the pace of reforms.

While oil production decreased from 164,000 barrels per day in the 1990s to 85,000 in 2002, GDP growth nonetheless averaged 4.3 percent annually from 2001 to 2006 as the non-oil sector expanded. Inflation has remained low. The opening of the Chad-Cameroon pipeline in 2003 further supported the overall improvement in the economy. In 2006 Cameroon was approved for debt relief of $1.3 billion by the IMF and World Bank, and in an agreement with significant long-term economic implications, the country gained sovereignty over the oil-rich Bakassi Peninsula (see Foreign relations, below). GDP growth remained steady at 4 percent in 2007, but dipped to a more modest 2.3 percent annually in 2009–2010, due to declining oil prices and exports and the global economic recession.The IMF noted that reform of the public sector would continue to be "key to improving the business environment" in Cameroon.

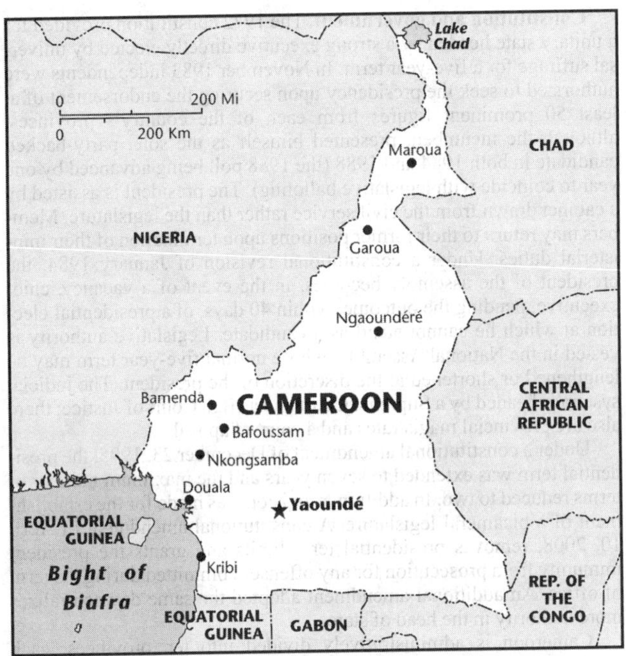

GOVERNMENT AND POLITICS

Political background. A German protectorate before World War I, Cameroon was divided at the close of that conflict into French and British mandates, which became United Nations trust territories after World War II. French Cameroons, comprising the eastern four-fifths of the territory, achieved autonomous status within the French Community in 1957 and, under the leadership of Ahmadou Babatoura AHIDJO, became the independent Republic of Cameroon on January 1, 1960. The disposition of British Cameroons was settled in February 1961 by a UN-sponsored plebiscite in which the northern and southern sections voted to merge with Nigeria and the former French territory, respectively. On October 1, 1961, the Federal Republic of Cameroon was formed, with Ahidjo as president and John Ngu FONCHA, prime minister of the former British region, as vice president.

The federal structure was designed to meet the challenge posed by Cameroon's racial, tribal, religious, and political diversity. It provided for separate regional governments and political organizations, joined at the federal level. A transition to unitary government began with the 1965–1966 merger of the regional political parties to form the Cameroon National Union (UNC) under the leadership of President Ahidjo and was completed on June 2, 1972, following a referendum on May 20 that indicated overwhelming support for the adoption of a new constitution. Subsequently, President Ahidjo faced no organized opposition, and on April 5, 1980, he was reelected to a fifth successive term. However, in an unanticipated move on November 4, 1982, Ahidjo announced his retirement in favor of his longtime associate, Prime Minister Paul BIYA. Immediately following his installation as president, Biya, a southerner, named a northern Muslim, Maigari Bello BOUBA, to head a new government designed to retain the somewhat tenuous regional and cultural balance that had been established by the former head of state. Bouba was dismissed in August 1983, following a coup attempt that allegedly involved Ahidjo, then resident in France. (Ahidjo died in Senegal on November 30, 1989.)

President Biya was unopposed for reelection on January 14, 1984, and immediately following his inauguration on January 21 the National Assembly voted to abolish the post of prime minister and to abandon "United Republic of Cameroon" as the country's official name in favor of the pre-merger "Republic of Cameroon." The following April Biya survived a coup attempt by elements of the presidential guard. While reportedly dealing harshly with the rebels, the administration nevertheless initiated steps toward democratization. Elections for local and regional bodies within the government party, which had been renamed the Democratic Rally of the Cameroon People (RDPC), also referenced in English as the Cameroon People's Democratic Movement (CPDM) in 1985, were held in 1986, followed by local government elections in 1987 that, for the first time, featured competitive balloting, albeit within an RDPC/CPDM framework. Alternative candidates also were presented for National Assembly balloting on April 24, 1988; however, each of the two lists was restricted to ruling party nominees, with opponents attacking the "snail's pace" of liberalization, continued repression of dissent, and barriers to any genuine political challenge to Biya, who was unopposed in the presidential poll.

In emulation of trends elsewhere in Africa and beyond, democratization advocates intensified their pressure in late 1989 and early 1990. Initially, the government responded harshly: 11 opposition leaders were arrested in February 1990, and a massive prodemocracy demonstration in the western town of Bamenda was violently broken up by security forces, leaving at least six people dead. However, in the wake of growing domestic and international criticism, President Biya announced in June that a multiparty system would be introduced and other reforms implemented. Consequently, on December 6 the National Assembly enacted legislation restricting the government's authority to deny legal status to opposition groups, and the formal recognition of new parties began in early 1991. On the other hand, Biya's refusal to call a national conference (similar to those convened in other regional countries) to determine the nation's political future provoked continued antigovernment demonstrations.

In an effort to force the government's hand regarding a national conference, opposition parties in June 1991 launched a *villes mortes* ("dead cities") campaign during which shops were closed on weekdays to undercut tax revenue. In response, the government put seven provinces under military administration and temporarily banned several of the parties responsible for the general strike. However, faced with ongoing unrest, Biya announced in October that new legislative elections would be moved up by a year to early 1992. He also convened a meeting of government and opposition leaders that in November established a ten-member committee to oversee constitutional reform. In addition, the government promised to release detainees from earlier protests in return for discontinuation of the *villes mortes* campaign.

In the March 1, 1992, assembly balloting the RDPC/CPDM won 88 seats, enough to ensure its continued government control in coalition with the small Movement for the Defense of the Republic (MDR). However, the results were tainted somewhat by the refusal of some groups, most importantly the anglophone Social Democratic Front (SDF) and a faction of the Cameroonian People's Union (UPC), to participate in the election. Boycott leaders insisted that a ban on coalition or independent candidates favored the government formation and that the early balloting made it impossible for fledgling opposition parties to organize effectively. On April 9 President Biya announced the appointment of Simon ACHIDI ACHU, an anglophone, as prime minister. However, Achidi Achu's designation failed to stem ongoing ethnic and political violence, while the regime's efforts to quell the unrest were described as "repressive."

In September 1992 Biya announced that presidential elections scheduled for March 1993 would be advanced to October 11 and, following a widely criticized run-up to the poll, Biya subsequently claimed a narrow victory over SDF leader John FRU NDI and four other candidates. On October 15 the Supreme Court rejected a petition by Fru Ndi and the third-placed Maigari Bello Bouba, now leader of the National Union for Democracy and Progress (UNDP), to annul the balloting on the basis of prepoll and election day irregularities. The polling process was also denounced by international observers, who charged that inspectors were denied access to some balloting sites. On October 23 the official election results confirmed Biya's victory, with 39.98 percent of the vote, over Fru Ndi (35.97 percent) and Bouba (19.22 percent). Subsequently, nationwide antigovernment rioting was reported, the most serious incidents occurring in Bamenda in Fru Ndi's home province. Six days later Fru Ndi was placed under house arrest as violent street protests continued despite the declaration of a state of emergency in Bamenda.

On November 25, 1992, Biya reappointed Achidi Achu, and two days later a new government, including a number of opposition members, was named. Further efforts by the regime to ease postelection tensions included the release of Fru Ndi in early December, termination of the state of emergency in Bamenda on December 29, and the freeing of some 175 political prisoners in January 1993. However, renewed violence was reported in March as the opposition increased pressure on Yaoundé to hold a national conference.

In November 1994 President Biya announced that a "debate" on the constitution, in addition to scheduling of municipal elections, would be forthcoming; however, he refused to agree to a sovereign conference and gave no date for the local balloting, which had already been postponed several times. In early April 1995 Biya pledged that elections would be held by the end of the year, and on April 24, 64 new local districts were created by presidential decree. In November, buoyed by the IMF's endorsement of his administration's 1995–1996 economic and financial reform plan, the president ordered that local elections be held in January 1996.

Propelled by a candidate list nearly twice the size of its closest competitor, the RDPC/CPDM captured 57 percent of the posts in municipal balloting on January 21, 1996. The SDF followed with 27 percent, while the UNDP and Cameroonian Democratic Union (UDC) garnered the remainder. The administration's decision to place presidential appointees in 20 municipalities that the opposition claimed to have captured in the local balloting drew immediate condemnation and calls for civil disobedience from opposition leaders. In March at least five people were killed when antigovernment demonstrators clashed with security forces. Subsequent antigovernment initiatives were undermined, however, by the opposition's intraparty factionalization and their mutual distrust. On September 19 the president announced that he had appointed businessman Peter Mafany MUSONGE to replace Achidi Achu as prime minister. The new government formed the following day was generally described as being of the "technocrat" variety.

In the run-up to the May 17, 1997, legislative elections, the opposition criticized the administration's allegedly fraudulent handling of electoral preparations. Subsequently, both domestic and international observers charged that the ruling party's capture of 109 seats had been severely tarnished by blatant irregularities and the violent intimidation of opposition candidates and supporters. In second-round polling in early August the RDPC/CPDM captured all of the undecided seats (raising its total to 116), and at mid-month the Supreme Court dismissed opposition appeals for fresh elections. Meanwhile, the administration rejected widespread calls for it to establish an independent electoral commission prior to presidential balloting and refused to meet with opposition leaders, whose preelection demands also included a shortening of the presidential term from seven to five years, equal distribution of state campaign funds, and access to the state-run media. In September the leading opposition legislative parties (the SDF, UNDP, and UDC) announced that they would not take part in the presidential elections and called on voters to observe another *villes mortes* boycott to undermine the polling.

At balloting on October 12, 1997, Biya easily recaptured the presidency, reportedly securing 92 percent of the vote; meanwhile, the nearest of the six minor party candidates to compete garnered less than 3 percent. However, administration claims that 84 percent of eligible voters had participated in the polling were disputed by the opposition, which labeled the elections a "farce" and asserted that a boycott by over 80 percent of the electorate had made them the "victors." On December 7 Biya reappointed Musonge as prime minister; three UNDP representatives, including former prime minister Bouba, were included in the reshuffled government announced the same day. Reshuffles were announced on March 18, 2000, and April 27, 2001. The most recent cabinet included members from the RDPC/CPDM, the UNDP, the UPC, and independents.

Municipal elections originally scheduled for January 2001 were postponed first to January 2002 and then to June 30. Although the government gave technical reasons for the postponements, opposition parties claimed that the government was stalling the operation of the democratic process. In any event, the RDPC/CPDM dominated the local balloting as well as the National Assembly poll conducted the same day. President Biya also was easily reelected on October 11, 2004, securing a reported 70.8 percent of the vote against 15 rivals. On December 8 Biya appointed Ephraim INONI to head a new cabinet that included members of the RDPC, UNDP, UPC, and the MDR. (The SDF and UDC reportedly declined cabinet representation.) President Biya reshuffled the cabinet on September 22, 2006, retaining Ephraim Inoni as prime minister and maintaining the dominance of the RPDC/CPDM.

In the July 22, 2007, assembly elections, the RDPC/CPDM increased its significant majority by four seats. Despite claims of vote-rigging and fraud by a number of political parties that petitioned the Supreme Court, the court upheld the results in all but five districts. (Elections were repeated in those districts on September 30, with the RDPC/CPDM securing most of the seats.) The cabinet was reshuffled on September 7, 2007, the vast majority of posts still held by the RPDC/CPDM, and Prime Minister Ephraim Inoni retained his post. (*See headnote.*)

Constitution and government. The 1972 constitution provided for a unitary state headed by a strong executive directly elected by universal suffrage for a five-year term. In November 1983 independents were authorized to seek the presidency upon securing the endorsement of at least 50 prominent figures from each of the country's provinces, although the incumbent presented himself as the sole, party-backed candidate in both 1984 and 1988 (the 1988 poll being advanced by one year to coincide with legislative balloting). The president is assisted by a cabinet drawn from the civil service rather than the legislature. Members may return to their former positions upon termination of their ministerial duties. Under a constitutional revision of January 1984, the president of the assembly becomes, in the event of a vacancy, chief executive, pending the outcome, within 40 days, of a presidential election at which he cannot stand as a candidate. Legislative authority is vested in the National Assembly, whose normal five-year term may be lengthened or shortened at the discretion of the president. The judicial system is headed by a Supreme Court and a High Court of Justice; there also are provincial magistrates and a court of appeal.

Under a constitutional amendment of December 23, 1995, the presidential term was extended to seven years and the maximum number of terms reduced to two. In addition, provision was made for the establishment of a bicameral legislature. A constitutional amendment of April 10, 2008, removes presidential term limits and grants the president immunity from prosecution for any offenses committed during his term of office. An additional amendment adopted the same day centralizes more authority in the head of state.

Cameroon is administratively divided into ten provinces, each headed by a provincial governor appointed by the president. The provinces are subdivided into regions and local districts, the latter totaling 340 (307 rural, 22 urban, and 11 special regime districts) following the creation of 64 new jurisdictions in April 1995. On November 12, 2008, President Biya replaced the provinces with regions, each headed by a governor appointed by the president..

Foreign relations. Cameroon maintains relations with a variety of nations. Ties with France remain especially strong, with Yaoundé becoming a full participant in francophone affairs during the May 1989 summit in Dakar, Senegal.

Dominating foreign policy concerns for many years was the civil war in neighboring Chad, which resulted in an influx of some 100,000 refugees into the country's northern provinces. Thus the Ahidjo government took part in several regional efforts to mediate the dispute prior to the ouster of the Libyan-backed Queddei regime in Chad in mid-1982; later Cameroon served as a staging ground for France's support of the Habré government.

Relations with other neighboring states have been uneven. Border incidents with Nigeria, resulting in a seven-month suspension of diplomatic relations in May 1981, continued into early 1987, with Lagos threatening "to take military reprisals" against alleged incursions by Cameroonian *gendarmes* into Borno State. However, relations improved thereafter.

In October 1992 the Biya regime's alleged manipulation of presidential balloting drew widespread criticism from Western observers, including the European Community, Germany, and the United States, with the latter two announcing the suspension of aid payments in mid-November. On the other hand, Paris's continued support of the regime drew outcries from Cameroonian opposition leaders.

In late 1993 conflict again erupted with Nigeria in the form of an alleged Cameroonian troop raid into Nigeria's Cross River State and the reported dispatch of Nigerian soldiers to two islands off the Bakassi Peninsula that were claimed by Cameroon. Underlying the dispute was the presence of substantial oil reserves along an ill-defined border between the two countries. In 1994 Cameroon filed a suit in the International Court of Justice (ICJ). The conflict reignited in September with a Nigerian attack that left ten Cameroonian soldiers dead. In October Nigeria claimed to have indisputable proof of its claim to the Bakassi region in that a 1913 agreement transferring the area to German Kameroun had never been ratified because of the outbreak of World War I. Two months later the Organization of African Unity (OAU, subsequently the African Union—AU) formally agreed to mediate the dispute.

On November 1, 1995, Cameroon was officially granted membership in the Commonwealth. Although a full participant in francophone affairs, Yaoundé had campaigned for membership as part of an effort to appease secessionist leaders in the former British Cameroons region.

The border conflict remained unresolved, with skirmishes reported between Cameroonian and Nigerian forces in the late 1990s, and the two countries trading charges that the other was attempting to influence the ICJ's decision. At a June 1999 summit, Biya and his Nigerian counterpart, Gen. Abdulsalam Abubakar, reportedly held "breakthrough" talks regarding the Bakassi region. However, in early 2000 the Nigerian military was placed on "maximum alert" following Lagos's discovery that France was constructing a military base near the peninsula in Cameroon. Furthermore, Nigerian officials accused Cameroonian forces of regularly firing on its forces. Although minor skirmishes continued in 2000 and 2001, the Nigerian Cross River state opened its Cameroonian border in June 2000.

In 2002 the ICJ ruled in favor of Cameroon in its boundary dispute with Nigeria, but Lagos initially refused to accept the decision. However, after UN-brokered mediation talks in Geneva in August 2003, the two countries agreed to settle the dispute, and a three-year demarcation project was initiated. By December 2003 Nigeria had turned control of 32 villages over to Cameroon, while Cameroon had turned one village over to Nigeria. In January 2004 the two countries agreed to reopen diplomatic ties and to establish joint patrols in the region until final demarcation was completed. In July a second round of territorial exchange occurred. However, Nigeria failed to meet the next round of transfer requirements on September 15, leading to renewed UN efforts to finalize a settlement. In June 2006 President Biya and Nigerian president Olusegun Obasanjo signed an agreement that called for Nigeria to withdraw all of its troops from the Bakassi Peninsula within two months and for Cameroon to assume full authority over the region in two years. While thousands of Nigerians protested turning over what they referred to as their ancestral land, some 3,000 Nigerian troops withdrew by the August deadline. By October the border situation was reported to be "calm" with steady progress being made on demarcation.

Tensions resumed in the region in November 2007 when gunmen killed 21 Cameroonian soldiers, with a Cameroon separatist group claiming responsibility (see Regional Groups in Political Parties, below). The Nigerian senate subsequently declared the Bakassi agreement with Cameroon unconstitutional and thus "illegal," but the federal government declined to reopen the issue. Attacks occurred again in mid-2008, when two soldiers were among 12 people killed, and rebels, under the rubric Niger Delta Defense and Security Council (NDDSC), threatened more fighting if Cameroon did not renegotiate its claim to the territory. Though Nigeria formally handed over control of the Bakassi Peninsula to Cameroon on August 14, another major attack occurred several months later when pirates in the Gulf of Guinea exchanged gunfire with Cameroonian soldiers. The NDDSC, which claimed responsibility, took 10 hotstages and threatened to kill them unless their demand for autonomy was met. The group finally released the hostages in November in a prisoner exchange with Cameroon.The piracy prompted the United States and France to consider military aid to Cameroon, despite allegations of corruption in the armed forces.

Relations with neighboring Equatorial Guinea were strained in late 2008 following the kidnapping of a former colonel in the Equatorial Guinean army (and a nephew of Equatorial Guinea's president, Gen. Teodoro Obiang Nguema Mbasogo), who had been granted refugee status in Cameroon in 2003. Two Cameroonian police officers reportedly received $30,000 in the plot. Allegations of involvement by Cameroonian officials remained unresolved. Meanwhile, the Equatorial Guinea embassy denied claims that it was involved in the abduction.

In addition to strengthening economic relations with China in 2009, Cameroon embraced the Chinese government's donation in March of a malaria research center in Yaoundé, the first of 14 it planned to open throughout Africa.

Current issues. Attention in mid-2000 centered on continued secessionist unrest in the North-West and South-West provinces (see the Southern Cameroon National Council under Regional Groups, below) and the controversial pipeline to carry oil from southern Chad to the Cameroonian port of Kribi. Cameroon was expected to receive $500 million from Chad for leasing the pipeline over 25 years, but some observers feared the revenue would be misused by the allegedly corrupt government.

Accusations of fraud and other irregularities surrounded the June 30, 2002, local and national elections in which the RDPC/CPDM was credited with resounding victories. (Reruns were ordered for some 17 assembly seats.) The SDF launched a two-month boycott of legislative activity to protest the perceived heavy-handedness of the administration, which in 2003 presented what it called reform of the electoral oversight body to meet opposition demands. However, even international observers criticized some aspects of the October 2004 presidential poll. Meanwhile, Biya's subsequent appointment of Ephraim Inoni as the new prime minister in December was seen as an attempt to "promote national unity." Inoni, a career civil servant who had represented Cameroon in its contentious negotiations with Nigeria (see Foreign relations, above), was expected to be popular among the English-speaking population. In addition, the expanded cabinet reportedly included some 17 Muslims.

Corruption continued to be at the forefront of the country's problems. In 2006 the government reported finding some 45,000 "ghost workers" on its payroll, and 73 civil servants were accused of embezzling. On another front, tensions flared between ethnic groups around the country, with reports of 55 killed in five incidents within a year.

Although the government proposed legislation in June 2006 that would delineate details for the formation of the second chamber, or a senate, no further action was reported. In December the government created a new electoral commission, Elections Cameroon (ELECAM), to replace in 18 months the controversial National Electoral Observatory (NEO), which opposition leaders charged was controlled by President Biya and contributed to fraud in the balloting of 2002. However, the opposition immediately leveled some of the same criticism on ELECAM, whose members were appointed by the president. Subsequently, the assembly elections in July 2007 were organized by the minister of territorial administration and decentralization, who is a member of the RDPC/CPDM. That and the lack of international observers evoked sharp criticism from the opposition following the RDPC/CPDM's landslide victory. Though 45 parties reportedly fielded candidates, the RDPC/CPDM was the only one to have candidates on the ballot in all ten provinces, easily securing the two-thirds majority needed to amend the constitution to extend Biya's mandate.

Following protests in February 2008 in Douala over rising fuel and food prices and the proposed constitutional amendments, demonstrations spread to Yaoundé, resulting in the deaths of at least 40 people through early March as police attempted to break up the crowds of thousands who blocked roads and ransacked cars. The widespread demonstrations came in the wake of another deadly rally protesting the government's closing of a private television station (see Communications, below) and a televised speech by President Biya in which he vowed to use "all legal means" to restore order. Within days, police were patrolling the streets and the violence subsided. In light of the angry response, the European Union recommended that the proposed constitutional revisions be open to public debate. However, in April parliament approved the controversial amendment removing restrictions on the number of presidential terms, thus allowing Biya to stand for reelection in 2011, among other revisions (see Constitution and government, above). Described as a setback to democracy, the term-limits revision drew sustained criticism from not only the opposition, but also the MDR, which had been generally supportive of the government. Fifteen SDF members of parliament boycotted the vote. Subsequently, Cameroonians in Switzerland called for freezing President Biya's Swiss bank accounts because of his "manipulation" of the constitution "to remain president for life."

The arrests of numerous senior government officials allegedly involved in corruption scandals in 2008 were seen by observers as paving the way for Biya's reelection in 2011, "based on his anti-corruption crusades." Meanwhile, the president also increased government salaries by 15 percent, ordered price cuts for food staples, and reduced fuel costs. However, in 2009 it was unclear whether the aging president, reportedly ailing, would, in fact, stand for reelection. With no apparent successor and the president spending more and more time out of the country, observers speculated about a potential power vacuum.

After a delay of two years, President Biya finally nominated members of ELECAM—all connected to the governing party—in December 2008. The swearing in of the members on January 29, 2009, seemingly served to energize the opposition, which decried the commission's lack of independent civil society, or opposition members. Even one governing RDPC/CPDM member of parliament said the appointments were "inconsistent with the law," according to published reports. Subsequently, the SDF challenged the move by filing a petition with the Supreme Court. The ELECAM appointments also drew criticism from the European Union. ELECAM members, responding to the criticism, pledged to conduct free, fair, and transparent elections.

On a more positive note, Pope Benedict, on his first trrip to Africa as pope in March 2009, visited Cameroon, where his message of hope and renewed faith was cheered by an audience of thousands, including the president and his wife.

POLITICAL PARTIES

Cameroon had only one legal party (the Cameroon National Union [UNC], later the Democratic Rally of the Cameroon People [RDPC]/ Cameroon People's Democratic Movement [CPDM], below) from 1966 until early 1991 despite the fact that the 1972 constitution guaranteed the right of political parties to organize and participate in elections. In June 1990 President Biya announced that the government, which had theretofore refused to legalize opposition parties, would no longer stand in the way of a multiparty system. In December the National Assembly passed new legislation covering the registration of parties, and as of November 2000, nearly 170 parties had been legalized.

Prior to the 2004 presidential balloting, nine opposition parties (including the SDF, UDC, UPC, MDP, and MLDC, below) formed a National Coalition for Reconciliation and Reconstruction (NCRR) with the goal of coalescing behind a single candidate. However, the SDF (the leading party in the coalition) subsequently withdrew following a dispute over the selection of the NCRR standard-bearer. The NCRR candidate, Adamon Ndam Njoua of the UDC, finished third in the balloting with 4.4 percent of the vote.

Government and Government-Supportive Parties:

Democratic Rally of the Cameroon People (*Rassemblement Démocratique du Peuple Camerounais*—RDPC). Formerly the Cameroon National Union (*Union Nationale Camerounaise*—UNC), the RDPC was until early 1991 the only officially recognized party. The RDPC is also referenced in English as the Cameroon People's Democratic Movement (CPDM). The UNC was formed in 1966 by merger of the Cameroon Union (*Union Camerounaise*); the former majority party of East (French) Cameroons; and of several former West (British) Cameroons parties, including the governing Kamerun National Democratic Party (KNDP), the Kamerun United National Congress (KUNC), and the Kamerun People's Party (KPP). The present name was adopted, over significant anglophone resistance, at a 1985 congress that also established a National Council as the party's second-highest body. The latter, at its first meeting held November 24–26, 1988, urged that Cameroon maintain its nonaligned foreign policy, called for the imposition of stiff anti-embezzlement measures, and asked citizens to accept the "necessary compromise between freedom and order."

At the party congress in June 1990, President Biya called for a loosening of subversion laws and told party members to expect political "competition," the way for which was cleared by the National Assembly's approval of a pluralism law in December. The RDPC/CPDM won 88 seats in the March 1992 legislative elections, subsequently forming a coalition with the MDR (below) to create a working majority in the assembly. At an extraordinary RDPC/CPDM congress on October 7, 1995, Biya secured a new five-year term as party president.

Beginning with the resignation of Ayissi NVODO in October 1996, the RDPC/CPDM and Biya were stung by the defection of three prominent party statesmen and their declarations of presidential candidacy. Following Nvodo in that regard were Albert NDZONGANG and the minister of health and Biya's personal physician, Titus EDZOA, who accused the administration of "permanent attempts to humiliate him." Edzoa was subsequently arrested on fraud charges, and in mid-1997 Nvodo, who had been ill, died. On the other hand, the party's success in legislative balloting in May was attributable, in part, to its recruitment of prominent UNDP and SDF leaders. In addition, observers credited the party's legislative gains to the adoption of a preelection primary process and the support of Prime Minister Musonge's ethnic Sawa constituency in the South-West and Littoral provinces.

The government named in December 1997 reflected, in part, a shift of power within the RDPC/CPDM from those sympathetic to Edzoa, who had been sentenced to 15 years in prison in October, and more senior members to a youthful cadre with "technocratic" tendencies in line with the prime minister's. In April 2001 and September 2006 Biya reshuffled the cabinet, both times strengthening control over his faction-ridden party. In July 2006 Biya was reelected to another five-year term as president of the party.

Following the party's resounding success in the 2007 assembly elections, its leaders began to press for the constitutional revision that would lift presidential term limits, paving the way for Biya's reelection and fulfillment of his modernization program for Cameroon. Meanwhile, rifts reportedly developed in the party with those who wanted to leave Biya's name out of the constitutional revision process so as not to link his tenure to the amendment. Observers said the party's desire to have Biya as "president for life" could result in the opposition's rallying greater support against the proposed revision. In February 2008 Biya called for an extraordinary congress to delineate strategies for organizing grassroots support for the proposed amendment, which subsequently was adopted by parliament and promulgated in April. The party's dominance in the legislature also enabled Biya to follow up with a decree that further enhanced his executive power over government agencies.

Leaders: Paul BIYA (President of the Republic and of the Party), Ephraim INONI (Former Prime Minister), Grégoire OWONA (Deputy Secretary General), René Emmanuel SADI (Secretary General).

National Union for Democracy and Progress (*Union Nationale pour la Démocratie et le Progrès*—UNDP). Seen primarily as a vehicle for supporters of former president Ahidjo, the UNDP was formed in 1991 under the leadership of Samuel Eboua. In early 1992, however, it was reported that Eboua had been "squeezed out" of his position by former prime minister Maigari Bello Bouba, who had recently returned from exile. After a last-minute reversal of a proposed electoral boycott, the UNDP won 68 seats in the March legislative balloting, running most strongly in the predominately Muslim northern provinces. Bouba was subsequently described as the "strongman of the opposition."

In the immediate aftermath of the October 1992 presidential election the UNDP leader, who had finished third, joined SDF leader Fru Ndi in petitioning the Supreme Court to annul the controversial poll. Nevertheless, in late November two party members, Hamadou MOUSTAPHA and Issa Tchiroma BAKARY, accepted cabinet ministries, and in early 1993 Fru Ndi denounced Bouba for negotiating with President Biya on the formation of a unity government.

On November 8, 1994, the UNDP announced a boycott of the National Assembly, pending the release of 30 party activists who had been arrested in July. While the walkout was abandoned four weeks later, the UNDP Central Committee confirmed in late December that Moustapha and Bakary had been expelled from the party (the latter proclaiming the formation of a rival UNDP). Although advancing the second-highest number of candidates (180) in the 1996 local elections, the UNDP finished third in the balloting. Highlighting the UNDP's electoral showing was the victory of former president Ahidjo's son, Mohamed AHIDJO, who had returned from exile two years earlier. Subsequently, the party was buffeted by a power struggle between Bouba and the virulently anti-Biya Mohamed Ahidjo.

Still reeling from the loss of Moustapha and Bakary in 1994, the UNDP fared poorly in legislative balloting in May 1997, its representation dropping to 13 seats. Having reached an impasse in its dialogue with the administration concerning a possible unity government, the UNDP helped spearhead a boycott of the October presidential elections, after which Bouba disputed the government's claims to a high voter turnout. Nevertheless, in December Bouba announced that he had accepted a cabinet post, asserting that Biya was seeking to incorporate opposition leaders in his government and admitting that his appointment was part of an apparent presidential effort to isolate Fru Ndi. Bouba remained in the cabinet following the March 2000 reshuffling, although substantial criticism was reported at the UNDP congress in June over his decision to stay in the government despite what delegates charged was a distinct lack of progress regarding the political liberalization promised by the Biya administration in the 1997 compact. (The dissent to Bouba became more apparent with the resignation of UNDP vice president Nicole OKALA in July.) The congress formally criticized the government's human rights record and demanded broad changes in the electoral code and establishment of an independent election commission prior to the 2002 balloting.

In the 2007 assembly elections, the UNDP increased its number of seats by five, though the party was among those leveling fraud charges against the government after the results were announced. Bouba, nevertheless, retained his post following a cabinet reshuffle in September. Though some "militant" members of the party wanted to speak out against President Biya's appointments to the electoral commission in 2009 (see Current issues, above), Bouba refrained from making any public statement on the matter.

Leaders: Maigari Bello BOUBA, Youmegne Manuel PAPIN, Peter Kuma KOMBAIN, Pierre Flambeau NGAYAP (Secretary General).

Cameroon People's Union (*Union des Populations Camerounaises*—UPC). The Marxist–Leninist UPC was formed in 1948 and, although outlawed in 1955, continued to operate clandestinely in

Cameroon, its membership fragmenting into pro-Soviet and Maoist factions in the 1960s. Sporadic UPC guerrilla activity presented no serious challenge to the Ahidjo regime, and by 1971 most UPC adherents had been forced into exile. Headquartered in Paris, the UPC subsequently served as the most prominent of the groups opposing Cameroon's one-party regime, claiming thousands of "militants" in both France and Cameroon.

In October 1990 UPC secretary general Ngouo WOUNGLY-MASSAGA, having been accused by colleagues of "anti-social behavior and embezzlement," broke with the party and returned to Cameroon, where he eventually organized the People's Solidarity Party (*Parti de la Solidarité du Peuple*—PSP). Upon legalization of the UPC in 1991 most former exiles returned, including Ndeh Ntumazah, the "last surviving founder of the UPC," who reportedly enjoyed a "larger-than-life" reputation in Cameroon despite his 20-year absence. The party subsequently split regarding the March 1992 legislative elections, Ntumazah leading a partial boycott of the balloting despite Secretary General Augustin Frederick Kodock's decision that the UPC should participate. Presenting candidates in about half of the 180 districts, the UPC won 18 seats, thereby becoming the third-leading parliamentary party.

In May 1992 the party was a founding member of the National Convention of the Cameroonian Opposition (see under PDC, below), and in September Henri Hogbe Nlend was described as a UPC presidential candidate. However, there were no reports of his having garnered any votes or of the UPC having taken part in the elections. In February 1995 Woungly-Massaga returned to the UPC, which absorbed his PSP.

Intraparty tension mounted following the UPC's poor showing in the January 1996 municipal elections, in which it won only 3 of 336 contests, and in April the party announced a number of dismissals and reportedly sought closer ties with the RDPC/CPDM. In May the UPC's parliamentary leader, Charles Oma BETOW, and three other senior leaders announced the removal of Secretary General Kodock, labeling his party management "disastrous." Kodock argued that his detractors had met illegally, thus invalidating their motion. Kodock was named minister of state for agriculture in the government announced on September 20, a UPC conference earlier in the month reportedly revealing at least four factions in the grouping.

At legislative balloting in May 1997 Kodock's "pro-Biya" wing forwarded 35 candidates, while Ntumazah and his followers supported an additional 17; subsequently, the group's representation plummeted from 16 posts to 1 as Kodock alone secured a seat. In presidential polling in October the party once again forwarded Henri Hogbe Nlend, who secured only 2.8 percent of the vote. In December Nlend was named minister of scientific and technical research in the new cabinet. In 2001 the UPC was reportedly split into two factions, out of which Kodock's became increasingly "anti-Biya," while Nlend's wing represented the "pro-Biya" orientation.

In the 2002 legislative elections the national election board treated the two factions as a single party, although candidates identified themselves as UPC (N) for the Nlend supporters and UPC (K) for the Kodock supporters. Kodock accepted a cabinet post after the balloting and continued to serve in the reshuffled cabinet after the presidential elections in 2004. The UPC (N) participated in the anti-Biya presidential electoral coalition in 2004. In 2006 Kodock reiterated his support for Biya, but in September 2007 he was dismissed from his cabinet post in the wake of allegations of embezzlement within his ministry. He then denounced Biya for "assassination of democracy" by dropping the UPC from his cabinet (though ultimately another UPC member received a cabinet post.)

Efforts to reconcile party factions were under way in 2008. In 2009 Kodock reiterated the party's pledge to try to bring about change in the country.

Leaders: Henri Hogbe NLEND (1997 presidential candidate and UPC [N] Leader), Augustin Frederick KODOCK (UPC [K]) Secretary General).

Movement for the Defense of the Republic (*Mouvement pour la Défense de la République*—MDR). The northern-based MDR, supported primarily by the small Kirdi ethnic group, was organized shortly before the March 1992 legislative balloting in an apparent effort to dilute the electoral strength of the UNDP (above), the region's dominant party. Six of the MDR's 32 candidates won assembly seats, enough to make the party a crucial element in formation of the subsequent government. Five MDR members were appointed to the cabinet in April, including party leader Dakolé Daïssala, who had been placed in detention following the 1984 coup attempt. Although never formally charged or tried, Daïssala had remained in jail until 1991, when he began what was viewed as an extraordinary ascent to governmental prominence.

At legislative balloting in May 1997 the MDR managed to recapture only one of its legislative posts. Subsequently, the party was not included in the government named in December. The MDR failed to gain any seats in the 2002 elections, but Daïssala joined the government in 2004 as minister of transport. He was dismissed in the cabinet reshuffle of September 2007, reportedly as a result of alleged ineptitude and also in part because President Biya considered him to be "politically baseless" since the MDR did not win any seats in the 2007 assembly.

Leader: Dakolé DAÏSSALA (President).

Opposition Parties:

Social Democratic Front (SDF). The SDF was launched in early 1990 in the English-speaking town of Bamenda in western Cameroon. Shortly thereafter a number of its leaders were arrested for belonging to an illegal organization, and an SDF rally in May was broken up by security forces, leaving several people dead. However, following the government's endorsement of political liberalization in June, the SDF detainees were released, and the party (legalized in 1991) became one of the most active opposition groups. Although it would probably have secured substantial representation, particularly in the anglophone western provinces, the SDF boycotted the March 1992 legislative election on grounds that there was insufficient time for opposition parties to organize effectively and that the electoral code favored the RDPC/CPDM.

Party president John Fru Ndi's strong showing in the October 1992 presidential balloting was heralded by the SDF as evidence that its appeal was not limited to the anglophone community. Hence, the party continued to distance itself from the Cameroon Anglophone Movement, the self-described "socio-cultural association" headquartered in Buea in the South-West province, which advocated a return to the 1972-style federal government system. In November the SDF rejected calls for a unity government headed by Biya, insisting that his handling of the presidential balloting and Fru Ndi's arrest proved that he could not be trusted. Instead it called for a two-year transitional program to be highlighted by the establishment of a new electoral code and the convening of a constitutional conference to draw up a new basic charter.

In May 1994 Secretary General Siga ASSANGA was dismissed by the party's disciplinary council for making approaches to the government on possible SDF participation in a government of national unity. Five months later Fru Ndi spearheaded the launching of the Allies' Front for Change (FAC, below), prior to yielding the office under a revolving presidency system to Samuel Eboua (then of the UNDP) in January 1995.

In early 1995 the SDF experienced a deep crisis that resulted in the departure or exclusion from its executive committee of a dozen influential members. One of those excluded, party treasurer Jean DJOKOU, accused Fru Ndi of "secret management and swindling the party finances," while others complained of the lack of attention to francophones within the party, most of whom strongly supported a unitary state.

During the run-up to balloting in January 1996 the SDF suspended its membership in the FAC and issued a list of 105 candidates. In the January 21 polling the party secured victories primarily in large towns and "traditional fiefdoms." Subsequently, the party's performance in legislative balloting in May 1997 (43 seats captured) fell shy of analysts' predictions. Thereafter, SDF militants took to the streets to protest the government's alleged fraudulent administration of the polling, and on June 12 a number of party members were arrested. Nevertheless, on June 17 Fru Ndi called on the party's legislators to assume their seats. Fru Ndi's "statesman-like" decision to distance himself and the SDF from violent dissention had its roots, according to some analysts, in his ambitions for the presidential elections scheduled for October. Subsequently, Fru Ndi and other senior SDF members traveled to African and Western capitals to gain allies in their efforts to pressure the recalcitrant Biya administration into addressing the opposition's preelectoral demands. While such visits reportedly improved Fru Ndi's standing with the international community, Biya's stance remained unchanged. Consequently, on September 12 in Paris Fru Ndi announced the SDF's decision to boycott the presidential polling.

The SDF's (then) secretary general, Tazoacha ASONGANY, led the party's negotiating team in talks with the government, which opened in December 1997. The talks collapsed in early 1998, and in mid-February the SDF formed a "common front" with the UDC (below). In July the SDF suffered its most traumatic infighting since 1995, as 10 of the party's 43 legislators resigned from the party to protest Fru Ndi's leadership, which they reportedly characterized as "authoritarian." Subsequently, Fru Ndi ousted SDF vice chair Souleimane MAHAMAD after Mahamad convened an extraordinary party congress that served as an anti–Fru Ndi forum. In lopsided balloting at the SDF's annual congress in April 1999, Fru Ndi retained the party's top post.

The SDF protested that the 2002 legislative elections were flawed because of government interference, and Fru Ndi launched a boycott of the assembly and municipal councils. However, in July Fru Ndi announced an end to the boycott, prompting a group of SDF dissidents to form a new party (see AFP, below).

The SDF was instrumental in the formation of the anti-Biya electoral coalition, the NCRR, in April 2004. However, Fru Ndi withdrew the SDF from the NCRR in September after a dispute over the manner in which the coalition's presidential candidate would be chosen. Fru Ndi instead ran as the SDF's candidate and received 17.4 percent of the vote.

Rifts in the party developed in late 2005 after Asonganyi criticized party leadership for being ineffectual as a catalyst for change in Cameroon. Asonganyi was subsequently suspended, prompting protest by some members, who walked out. He was then replaced as secretary general by Michael NDOBEGANG. Asonganyi was dismissed from the party in early 2006 after the party found him guilty of six "charges," including questioning or criticizing party policies, ideals, and hierarchy. Shortly thereafter, Ndobegang resigned over Asonganyi's expulsion. In May 2006, with tensions again on the rise and reports of some 300 members having defected to the RDPC/CPDM, the SDF split into two factions, with Fru Ndi elected chair of one and Ben MUNA chosen as leader of the rival wing at separate congresses. Precipitating the dispute was Muna's challenge to Fru Ndi's party leadership and an attempt by Fru Ndi to amend the party constitution in a way critics said was meant to enhance his control. In November, however, the high court confirmed Fru Ndi as the legitimate SDF chair. Muna subsequently joined the AFP.

Following assembly elections in 2007, Fru Ndi led the way in the opposition's claims of fraud and "gross irregularities," unsuccessfully petitioning the Supreme Court to have the elections annulled. The SDF lost six seats in the balloting, its only stronghold being in Fru Ndi's North-West region.

In early 2008 two people were killed when police broke up an SDF demonstration against the government's ban on a private television station. The SDF also was vocal in its continuing opposition to the 2008 constitutional amendment that lifted presidential term limits, Fru Ndi supporting revision only if it were done through a constitutional conference. In August Fru Ndi's murder trial got under way on charges that he beat to death Gregoire DIBOULE, secretary of the Muna faction, in 2006. Fru Ndi, for his part, said the charges were politically motivated and meant to keep him from standing in the 2011 presidential election. Meanwhile, another SDF militant, Pierre Roger LAMBO, was on trial for allegedly inciting violence during the February 2008 protests.

In the wake of its protests against the Biya-appointed members of the electoral commission in 2008, the SDF said it would try to prevent any election from taking place. Fru Ndi called the appointment of RDPC/CPDM members "an electoral coup d'état" by Biya.

In 2009 two SDF members of parliament reportedly defected to the RDPC/CPDM. About the same time, a member of the RDPC/CPDM defected to the SDF.

Leaders: John FRU NDI (Chair), Pierre KWEMO, Bernard TABALI, Elizabeth TAMANJONG (Secretary General).

Cameroonian Democratic Union (*Union Démocratique du Cameroun*—UDC). The UDC was formed in 1991 under the leadership of Adamou Ndam Njoya, who held several senior posts in the Ahidjo administration. Although the party boycotted the March 1992 legislative election, Ndam Njoya subsequently competed in the October 1992 presidential elections, gaining 3.62 percent of the vote.

In 1997 Ndam Njoya was a leading advocate of the opposition's boycott of the October presidential polling, although the party had secured five seats in the May legislative balloting. Following the 2002 elections the UDC became the third-largest party in the assembly with five seats. Ndam Njoya helped form the anti-Biya coalition in the 2004 presidential election and was the coalition's candidate for the presidency. He placed third with 4.4 percent of the vote. In late 2006, Njoya claimed the government tried to assassinate him during a reported military operation at his residence in which one person was killed.

The UDC lost one seat in the 2007 assembly elections, the party leader subsequently alleging that President Biya was leading the country into "civil war" in the wake of violent incidents in several regions. In 2009 Njoya denounced Biya's electoral commission appointments, saying the move turned over the electoral process to the governing party "on a platter of gold."

Leaders: Adamou NDAM NJOYA, Theophile Yimgaing MOYO.

Progressive Movement (*Mouvement Progressif*—MP). The opposition MP, led by Jean-Jacques Ekindi, was formed in 1991 after Ekindi split from the CPDM. Following a government crackdown on protest marches in August 2004, in advance of the October presidential elections, Ekindi was placed under house arrest. He was among 16 registered presidential candidates, winning just 0.27 percent of the vote. Subsequently, Ekindi challenged the results of the election, claiming voterigging.

In 2007, Ekindi was elected to a seat in the assembly.

Leader: Jean-Jacques EKINDI (President of the Party and 2004 presidential candidate).

Other Parties and Groups:

Movement for the Liberation and Development of Cameroon (*Mouvement pour la Libération et le Développement du Cameroun*—MLDC). The MLDC was formed by dissident members of the Movement for the Liberation of Cameroonian Youth (*Mouvement pour la Libération de la Jeunesse Camerounaise*—MLJC) in 2002. Led by Dieudonné TINA, the MLJC secured one seat in legislative balloting in May 1997 and none in the 2002 balloting. A subsequent leadership dispute led members to leave the party and establish a new political group. The MLDC participated in the anti-Biya electoral coalition in 2004.

Leaders: Marcel YONDO, Jean PAHAI.

Alliance of Progressive Forces (*Alliance des Forces Progressistes*—AFP). Created in 2002, the AFP was formed by former members of the SDF who opposed Fru Ndi's leadership and willingness to compromise with President Biya. The party's 2004 presidential candidate reportedly was rejected by the high court. One of the party's founders, Évariste Fopoussi Fotso, returned to the party in 2005 after having resigned in 2002.

In 2008 party leader Ben Muna, formerly of the SDF, spoke out against the constitutional amendment backed by President Biya and his governing party. Further, the AFP claimed that Biya's appointments to the electoral commission were unconstitutional.

Leaders: Ben MUNA, (Chair), Saidou MAIDADI (Secretary General).

Social Movement for the New Democracy (*Mouvement Social pour la Nouvelle Démocratie*—MSND). The MSND, said to have support among the urban middle class, was formed in 1991 by Yondo Black, a former president of the Cameroon Bar Association who had been active in the prodemocracy movement for several years, at times in conjunction with the organizers of the SDF. Black had been arrested in February 1990 for his activities and sentenced to three years' imprisonment for "subversion" but was released in August. Black received 0.36 percent of the vote in the 2004 presidential election.

Leader: Yondo Mandengue BLACK (2004 presidential candidate).

Allies' Front for Change (*Front des Alliés pour le Changement*—FAC). The FAC was launched in October 1994 under the guidance of SDF leader John Fru Ndi, although he and his party withdrew from the grouping to campaign independently for the 1996 municipal elections. The FAC was initially reportedly composed of 15 parties; however, only the 3 parties immediately below were subsequently identified as members.

The status of the front was further clouded in October 1997 when the MDP's Samuel Eboua campaigned for the presidency under his party's banner (below).

Leaders: Njoh LITUMBE (PLD), Victorin Hameni BIELEU (UFDC), Samuel EBOUA (MDP).

Liberal Democratic Party (*Parti Libéral Démocrate*—PLD). The PLD was formed in 1991 under the leadership of Njoh Litumbe, who subsequently visited the United States as a spokesperson for the opposition groups in Cameroon. Dormant for many years, the group called in 2005 for President Biya to negotiate with the SCNC (below).

Leader: Njoh LITUMBE.

Union of Democratic Forces of Cameroon (*Union des Forces Démocratiques du Cameroun*—UFDC). The UFDC was considered one of the more important groups to boycott the March 1992 legislative election, its leader, Victorin Hameni Bieleu, having served as president of an opposition coordinating committee in 1991. On November 3, 1992, Bieleu was arrested for his involvement in antigovernment protests. Bieleu ran for the presidency in 2004 but received less than 1 percent of the vote.

Leader: Victorin Hameni BIELEU.

Movement for Democracy and Progress (*Mouvement pour la Démocratie et le Progrès*—MDP). The MDP was headed by former UNDP leader Samuel Eboua, who was elected to a FAC leadership post in 1996. Eboua's 1997 presidential campaign yielded just 2.4 percent of the vote in October balloting. Eboua, who had been a state minister in the 1970s and 1980s, died in 2000 after a lengthy illness. In 2008 the party made an appearance at an anniversary celebration in Matomb.

Social Liberal Congress (SLC). The SLC, based in Buea in southern Cameroon, was founded in 2000 by George Dobgima Nyamndi, formerly of the UDC and the LDA. Nyamndi, who promoted electoral and education reforms, secured 0.18 percent of the vote in the 2004 presidential election.

Leader: George Dobgima NYAMNDI (2004 presidential candidate).

Cameroonian Party of Democrats (*Parti des Démocrates Camerounais*—PDC). The PDC is Cameroon's member of the Christian Democratic International. One of its leaders, Louis-Tobie Mbida, was instrumental in launching an antigovernment coalition, the **National Convention of the Cameroonian Opposition** (*Convention Nationale de l'Opposition Camerounaise*—CNOC), in early 1992.

Leaders: Louis-Tobie MBIDA (President), Gaston BIKELE EKAMI (Secretary General).

Action for Meritocracy and Equal Opportunity (AMEC). In presidential balloting in October 1997 the anglophone AMEC's candidate, Joachim Tabi Owono, secured less than 1 percent of the vote. In 2007 the party fielded candidates in the legislative elections but did not win any seats. In 2008 the AMEC was among the parties challenging the legality of the constitutional amendments adopted by parliament. The Supreme Court rejected the claims.

Leader: Joachim Tabi OWONO (President of the Party and 1997 presidential candidate).

Other parties that contested the 2002 legislative or the 2004 presidential elections included the **Alliance for Development and Democracy** (*Alliance pour la Démocratie et le Développement*—ADD), led by 2004 presidential candidate Garga Haman ADJI; the **Justice and Development Party** (JDP), which promotes the rights of English-speaking Cameroonians under the leadership of publisher Boniface FORBIN, who was the JDP's 2004 presidential candidate; and the **African Movement for New Independence and Democracy** (*Mouvement Africain pour la Nouvelle Indépendance et la Démocratie*—MANIDEM), led by Anicet EKANE and comprised of former members of the UPC.

(For a list of some 40 other small parties and groups, see the 1999 edition of the *Handbook.*)

Regional Groups:

Southern Cameroon National Council (SCNC). The leading vehicle for expression of secessionist sentiment in the former British Cameroons region, the SCNC originally served as the elected executive organ of the Southern Cameroon People's Conference (SCPC), an umbrella organization for a number of professional and trade associations, political parties, youth groups, and other grassroots bodies opposed to the domination of francophone influence in the country. The SCPC was the successor to the All Anglophone Conference (AAC), which first met in 1993 in an effort to persuade the nation's francophone leadership to return to the federal structure of the 1960s in which the anglophone region enjoyed broad autonomy. The SCPC rubric was subsequently adopted in part because the term *anglophone* was deemed too "colonial" and "limiting" and in part to reflect the region's shift in favor of independence based on a perceived lack of interest in dialogue regarding autonomy on the part of the Biya administration. Most observers subsequently referred to the SCNC when discussing affairs in the Southern Cameroons, prompting the SCPC, for the sake of clarity, to formally adopt the SCNC name.

In August 1995 an SCNC delegation petitioned the UN to mediate between the secessionists and Yaoundé, warning that lack of intervention would result in "another Somalia." Two months later the council released a proposed timetable for independence, and the Cameroonians responded by arresting a number of SCNC adherents. SCNC founding chair Sam Ekontang ELAD resigned in late 1996, ostensibly due to illness, and he was succeeded by former Cameroonian diplomat Henry Fossung.

In late March 1997 more than 200 SCNC supporters were arrested, many in connection with what the government said was an attack on the headquarters of security forces in Bamenda in which several people were reportedly killed. The crackdown apparently suppressed SCNC activity for more than a year as Fossung reportedly returned to his outlying village to maintain a low profile. In April 1998 a group led by SCNC treasurer Arnold Yongbang attempted to revive the organization, electing Esoka NDOKI MUKETE, the "charismatic" provincial chair of the SDF, as the new SCNC chair. However, that decision was challenged as "undemocratic" by Fossung and others, including the influential SCNC–North America (SCNC-NA), and the council remained factionalized and, consequently, ineffective.

In October 1999 a military tribunal in Yaoundé sentenced nine SCNC members to prison for their roles in the alleged 1997 attack, prompting renewed turmoil in the North-West and South-West provinces (which the SCNC prefers to reference as the Northern and Southern zones). Shortly thereafter, the SCNC again petitioned the UN for recognition, and in December it was reported that SCNC militants, under the leadership of Ndoki Mukete (who had been forced to resign his SDF post because that party does not endorse independence for the anglophone region), planned to declare independence by the end of the year. However, Fossung continued to oppose such a unilateral declaration, and the Cameroonian government indicated it would react harshly to any independence announcement. Consequently, Ndoki Mukete was reported to be "traveling abroad" on December 30 when SCNC militants took over the radio station in Buea to declare the establishment of the Federal Republic of the Southern Cameroons. Ndoki Mukete was subsequently described as having left the SCNC, the effective leadership mantle falling to Frederick Ebong Alobwede, who had read the independence declaration and been arrested with a number of supporters shortly thereafter following a series of pro-independence demonstrations.

An SCNC meeting in late January 2000 again attempted to resolve the leadership dispute, Fossung continuing to describe himself as chair and disavowing the recent declaration. In February the Northern and Southern zones each elected their own executive bodies, and those groups then elected a new SCNC executive body, with Ebong as chair, thereby "president" of the newly announced republic. The council remained formally committed to nonviolence, although that philosophy was expected to be reconsidered at a "constituent assembly" scheduled for late September in which a constitution secretly adopted in 1996 also was scheduled for review. (The constitution reportedly calls for a federal structure for the Southern Cameroons based on 13 essentially tribal-based provinces.) Meanwhile, the Biya administration maintained its hard line toward the SCNC. In October 2001 violent clashes between police and SCNC demonstrators on the 40th anniversary of unification left three dead and dozens injured. In July 2001 Ebong announced the formation of his "cabinet," and the SCNC boycotted the 2002 legislative elections and the 2004 presidential polling.

In late 2005 several party members, including Henry Fossung, the chair of one of the factions, were arrested after illegal demonstrations. Party official Chief Ayamba Ette Otun was released but soon rearrested for his role in launching Radio Free Southern Cameroons (see Broadcasting and computing, below), which aired programs highly critical of the administration. In early 2006 one of the detainees died, his supporters alleging his death was the result of torture. In April 65 people were arrested during a meeting at the residence of one of the members.

In November 2007 a faction referred to as the Southern Cameroon Peoples Organization (SCAPO), also known as the Ambazonians, led by Kevin Ngwang GUMNE, claimed responsibility for the killing of 21 Cameroonian soldiers in the Bakassi region, declaring that region and other areas of the country as the independent Republic of Ambazonia.

In February 2008 some 20 SCNC members were arrested and 10 jailed following the group's preparations for a Youth Day celebration. A year later party leaders Ayamba Ette Otun and Nfor Nfor, along with 22 other activists, were arrested at the residence of party secretary general James Sabum. After the court adjourned the case until April 6, 2009, the group returned to Sabum's home, whereupon soldiers arrived and allegedly attacked and beat some of them. Meanwhile, the new "president" of the so-called Southern Cameroons Restoration Government said that a proposed constitution had been written and would be circulated via the Internet for debate and discussion.

The SCNC gained new hope for its push for autonomy under the auspices of Libya's leader, Col. Muammar Abu Minyar al-QADHAFI. As president of the AU, Qadhafi invited SCNC leaders to Addis Ababa, Ethiopia, in February 2009 in connection with the SCNC's request to the African Commission for Human and People's Rights for a ruling on the SCNC's independence. Seen as another boost to the SCNC cause was the AU's deletion from the agenda of an item that had been pressed by the Biya administration regarding the Bakassi Peninsula. SCNC officials claimed it was because of them that the item was removed from the agenda, according to *Africa News*. The published report said such a move might cause Biya some concern since he was aware of Qadhafi's "track record as far as liberation movements are concerned." (Qadhafi had helped other "outlaw" groups such as the Irish Republican Army and the Palestine Liberation Organization.)

Leaders: Henry FOSSUNG (Chair of the SCAPO/Ambazonia faction), Augustine NDANGAM (Deputy Chair of the SCAPOAmbazonia faction), Chief AYAMBA Ette Otun (SCNC Chair), Frederick EBONG Alobwede (National Chair of the SCNC and President of the Federal Republic of the Southern Cameroons), Nfor NFOR (Vice Chair of the SCNC), Hitler MBINGLO (Chair of the Northern Zone), James SABUM (Secretary General).

South West Elite Association (SWELA). The reactivation of SWELA was announced in March 2000, apparently at the urging of Prime Minister Musonge in the hope of countering the secessionist movement in South-West province led by the SCNC. SWELA leaders subsequently voiced support for a "united Cameroon." In July 2006 Enow Orock was elected to a two-year term as the party's new leader.

Leader: Enow OROCK (Secretary General).

Guerrilla Group:

National Liberation Front of Cameroon (*Fronte de la Libération Nationale du Cameroun*—FLNC). The anti-Biya FLNC is led by Mbara Guerandi, who reportedly fled from Cameroon in 1984 following his indictment for participating in an alleged coup attempt. In late 1997 it was reported that Guerandi, now based in Burkina Faso, had reached agreement with antigovernment rebels in Chad to coordinate guerrilla activities.

Leader: Mbara GUERANDI (in exile in Burkina Faso).

LEGISLATURE

The **National Assembly** (*Assemblée Nationale*) currently consists of 180 members elected for five-year terms. In the April 1988 election voters in most districts were permitted to choose between two lists (in the case of single-member constituencies, between two candidates) presented by the Cameroon People's Democratic Movement. Multiparty balloting was introduced in the March 1, 1992, election, which was brought forward one year in response to pressure from the nation's burgeoning prodemocracy movement. However, no independent or coalition candidates were permitted, contributing to the decision by some opposition groups to boycott the poll. The number of parties participating in legislative balloting increased from 32 in 1992 to 40 in 1997, and the number of parties securing seats rose from 4 to 7, respectively.

Following the most recent legislative elections on July 22, 2007, and in subsequent by-elections on September 30 for 17 assembly seats that were annulled by the Supreme Court because of irregularities, the Democratic Rally of the Cameroon People won 153 seats; the Social Democratic Front, 16; the National Union for Democracy and Progress, 6; the Cameroonian Democratic Union, 4; and the Progressive Movement, 1.

President: Djibril Cayavé YEGUIE.

CABINET

[as of March 1, 2009]
(*see headnote*)

Prime Minister	Ephraim Inoni (RDPC/CPDM)
Deputy Prime Ministers	Ali Amadou (RDPC/CPDM)
	Jean Nkuete (RDPC/CPDM)
Ministers of State	
Posts and Telecommunications	Maigari Bello Bouba (UNDP)
Secretary General of the Presidency	Laurent Esso (RDPC/CPDM)
Territorial Administration and Decentralization	Marafa Hamidou Yaya (RDPC/CPDM)
Ministers	
Agriculture and Rural Development	Jean Nkuete (RDPC/CPDM)
Civil Service and Administrative Reform	Emmanuel Bondé (RDPC/CPDM)
Communication	Jean Pierre Biyidi Bi Essam
Culture	Ama Tutu Muna [f]
Economy, Planning, and Regional Development	Louis-Paul Motaze (UPC)
Employment and Professional Training	Zacharie Perevet (RDPC/CPDM)
Environment	Pierre Hélé (RDPC/CPDM)
Finance	Lazare Essimi Menye
Foreign Affairs	Henri Eyebe Ayissi
Forests and Wild Animals	Elvis Ngolle Ngolle (RDPC/CPDM)
Higher Education	Jacques Fame Ndongo (RDPC/CPDM)
Justice	Ali Amadou (RDPC/CPDM)
Labor and Social Insurance	Robert Nkili (RDPC/CPDM)
Lands	Pascal Anon Abidime
Livestock, Fisheries, and Animal Industries	Aboubakari Sarki (RDPC/CPDM)
Mines, Industry, and Technological Development	Badel Ndanga Ndinga
National Education	Haman Adama (RDPC/CPDM) [f]
Public Health	André Mama Fouda
Public Works	Bernard Messengue Avom (ind.)
Scientific and Technical Research	Madeleine Tchuenté (ind.) [f]
Secondary Education	Louis Bapes Bapes (RDPC/CPDM)
Small and Medium Enterprises	Laurent Etoundi Ngoa (RDPC/CPDM)
Social Affairs	Cathérine Bakang Mbock (RDPC/CPDM) [f]
Sport	Augustin Edjoa (RDPC/CPDM)
Tourism	Baba Amadou (RDPC/CPDM)
Trade	Luc Magloire Mbarga Atangana (ind.)
Transport	Gounoko Haounaye
Urban Development and Housing	Clobert Tchatat (RDPC/CPDM)
Water and Power	Jean-Bernard Sindeu (RDPC/CPDM)
Women and the Family	Suzanne Mbomback (ind.) [f]
Youth	Adoum Garoua (RDPC/CPDM)

[f] = female

COMMUNICATIONS

Prior censorship has long been practiced in Cameroon, and journalists have occasionally been detained for publishing "sensationalist" or "tendentious" material. Although President Biya announced in June 1990 that restrictions on the press would be loosened in consonance with the government's political liberalization program, the censorship law was retained, and several newspapers were suspended in 1991 for publishing articles criticizing the administration. In September 1992 the newspaper *Le Messager* was one of several publications temporarily suspended by the government; the editor was imprisoned for nine months in 1998 for printing a "false story" about President Biya. In

October 2001 the opposition publication *La Nouvelle Expression* reportedly came under scrutiny for stories on the secessionist movement. On the eve of the 2004 presidential elections, several media outlets, including *Mutations*, and more than a dozen radio and television stations were suspended. The suspensions were lifted after the election.

In February 2008 at least two people were killed when police and demonstrators clashed during a rally called to protest the closing of a private television station, Equinoxe TV, for its broadcasts critical of the government, and radio station Magic FM, for allegedly not paying its licensing fees. The bans were lifted in July. Meanwhile, state-owned CRTV in 2008 reportedly warned journalists not to broadcast any anti-government statements by the opposition Social Democratic Front, prompting opposition parties to demand that the communications minister be fired. The watchdog group Reporters Without Borders expressed concern at the media crackdown, including the government's prevention of independent newspapers from publishing and the pressuring of private media to be "responsible." Following a raid on a private radio station in Douala in late February, only state-approved media were distributed, according to Reporters Without Borders.

Press. The principal newspapers are *Le Tribune du Cameroun*/*Cameroon Tribune* (Yaoundé), government daily in French (66,000) and English (20,000); *Cameroon Post* (50,000), weekly in English; *La Gazette* (Douala, 35,000), twice weekly in French; *Le Messager* (34,000), independent fortnightly in French; *Le Combattant* (21,000), independent weekly in French; *Cameroon Outlook* (Victoria, 20,000), thrice weekly in English; *Politiks* (10,000), independent daily in French; *Mutations*, biweekly independent; *La Révélation; L'Action;* two dailies, *The Post* and *The Herald*, both in English; and *La Nouvelle Expression*, thrice weekly in French.

News agencies. The former *Agence Camerounaise de Presse* (ACAP) was replaced in 1978 by the *Société de Presse et d'Edition du Cameroun* (Sopecam), which, under the Ministry of Information, is responsible for the dissemination of foreign news within Cameroon and also for publication of *Le Tribune du Cameroun.* The principal foreign agency is *Agence France-Presse*.

Broadcasting and computing. The *Office de Radiodiffusion–Télévision Camerounaise* (CRTV) is a government facility operating under the control of the Ministry of Culture. Programming is in French, English, and more than two dozen local languages, with 24-hour programming launched in 2005. Dozens of private radio stations, including Magic FM in Yaounde and Radio Siantou, have opened since 2000. An opposition radio station, Radio Free Southern Cameroons, began broadcasting in English an hour a week in late 2005 under the aegis of the SCNC (see Political Parties, above). Also in late 2005, a radio station operated by the Seventh-Day Adventist church began broadcasting. As of 2008 there were 38 Internet users per 1,000 inhabitants.

INTERGOVERNMENTAL REPRESENTATION

Ambassador to the U.S.: Joseph FOE-ATANGANA.

U.S. Ambassador to Cameroon: Janet E. GARVEY.

Permanent Representative to the UN: Michel Tommo MONTHE.

IGO Memberships (Non-UN): AfDB, AU, BADEA, BDEAC, CEEAC, CEMAC, CWTH, IDB, Interpol, IOM, NAM, OIC, OIF, PCA, WCO, WTO.

CANADA

Note: On December 30, 2009, Governor General Michaëlle Jean suspended Parliament (until March 3, 2010) at the request of Prime Minister Stephen Harper. The prorogation effectively halted an inquiry that had threatened the government into allegations that Canadian troops had handed off detainees in Afghanistan to harsh treatment by Afghan authorities.

Political Status: Granted Dominion status under the British North America Act of 1867; recognized as autonomous state within the Commonwealth in 1931; constitution "patriated" as of April 17, 1982.

Area: 3,855,081 sq. mi. (9,984,670 sq. km.), including inland water.

Population: 31,612,897 (2006C); 33,334,000 (2008E). The 2006 figure is unadjusted for underenumeration (the unadjusted number in 2001 rose by 3.1 percent after adjustment). The 2008 figure is extrapolated from government estimates, including adjustments for underenumeration.

Major Urban Centers (urban areas, 2006C): OTTAWA (1,130,761), Toronto (5,113,149), Montreal (3,635,571), Vancouver (2,116,581), Calgary (1,079,310), Edmonton (1,034,945), Quebec (715,515), Winnipeg (694,668), Hamilton (692,911).

Official Languages: English, French.

Monetary Unit: Canadian Dollar (market rate December 1, 2009: 1.04 dollars = $1US).

Sovereign: Queen ELIZABETH II.

Governor General: Michaëlle JEAN; appointed by Queen Elizabeth II on the advice of the prime minister and installed for a five-year term on September 27, 2005, succeeding Adrienne CLARKSON.

Prime Minister: Stephen HARPER (Conservative Party of Canada); asked by the governor general on January 24, 2006, to form a new government following the general elections of January 23, and inaugurated with new government on February 6 in succession to Paul MARTIN (Liberal Party of Canada); returned to office for a second term following early elections on October 14, 2008.

THE COUNTRY

Canada, the largest country in the Western Hemisphere and the second largest in the world (after Russia), extends from the Atlantic to the Pacific and from the Arctic to a southern limit near Detroit, Michigan. Because of its northerly location, severe climate, and unfavorable geographic conditions, only one-third of its total area has been developed, and more than two-thirds of its people inhabit a 100-mile-wide strip of territory along the U.S. border. Colonized by both English and French settlers, it retained throughout a long period of British rule a cultural and linguistic duality that continues as one of its most serious internal problems. Of the more than 6.7 million Canadians who claim French as their mother tongue, approximately 86 percent are concentrated in the province of Quebec, where demands for political and economic equality (or even separation from the rest of Canada) persist. A major step toward linguistic equality was taken in 1969 with the enactment of an official-languages bill that provided for bilingual districts throughout the country. Nevertheless, Quebec enacted legislation establishing French as its sole official language in 1977, although a series of court rulings from 1984 to 1988 voided some provisions of the act.

In early 1987 the *Inuit*, an Eskimo people accounting for about 17,000 of the sparse overall population of 51,000, won tentative agreement to the formation of their own territory (Nunavut) in the larger, eastern portion of the vast Northwest Territories; the smaller western region is home to a more varied population that includes Western Arctic (*Inuvialuit*) Eskimos, Yukon Indians, Athapaskan-speaking *Déné* Indians, and *Métis* (mixed Indian and European), but with a narrow white majority. The creation of Nunavut was eventually approved in 1992 (see Constitution and government, below), and the new territory was formally founded on April 1, 1999.

Women constitute approximately 47 percent of the Canadian labor force, concentrated largely in the service sector (particularly health care and social assistance), sales, and teaching. Women currently occupy 7 of 28 cabinet positions, 35 of 102 occupied Senate seats, and 22 percent of the seats in the House of Commons. As of mid-2009, 3 of 13 provincial lieutenant governors and territorial commissioners and 1 of 3 territorial premiers, but no provincial premiers, were women.

For many decades the economy relied on foreign investment capital, primarily from the United States, to finance development, and industry still has a high proportion of foreign ownership. However, the country's resultant prominence among the world's manufacturing and trading nations has more recently permitted Canada, in turn, to become a major investor abroad, with investment outflow exceeding inflow. The economy's health continues to depend highly on trade, especially with the United States, which absorbed 83 percent of Canadian exports in 2003. Having concluded a free trade agreement in 1988, Canada and

the United States subsequently joined Mexico in the North American Free Trade Agreement (NAFTA), which entered into force in 1994. (Notably, imports from the United States slid from 77 percent of total imports in 1998 to 63 percent in 2008.)

The once-dominant agricultural sector (including fishing and forestry) now employs only 3 percent of the workforce while contributing about 2.2 percent of GDP. Nevertheless, Canada's farms and ranches continue to produce vast quantities of wheat and beef, substantial portions of which are available for export. In addition, Canada ranks first among world exporters of wood pulp, paper, and fish. Industry as a whole, including mining, constitutes about 30 percent of GDP and employs about 22 percent of the labor force. In addition to processed foods, paper, and wood products, leading manufactures include automobiles and auto parts (roughly one-fourth of the country's exports), fabricated metals, and electrical and electronic products. Mineral wealth also plays an important role. Possessing significant petroleum reserves, Canada is additionally a major source of cobalt, copper, gold, iron ore, lead, molybdenum, nickel, platinum, silver, uranium, and zinc. Mineral products make up about 15 percent of exports.

Following a slow recovery from the international recession of the early 1990s, Canada saw its GDP rise at an average annual rate of 3.3 percent from 1994 to 1997, easily outpacing the average for the Group of Seven (G-7) leading industrial states. Despite adverse world commodity prices and the negative effect of an Asian financial crisis, GDP rose 3.1 percent in 1998. At the same time, unemployment continued its decline from more than 11 percent in 1993 to 8.3 percent, while core consumer price inflation stood at 1.2 percent. Aided by the buoyant U.S. economy, GDP growth reached more than 5 percent in 2000, marking the country's longest uninterrupted expansion in more than three decades. While growth slipped in 2001 and 2003, it ran at or above 2.5 percent annually through 2007. With unemployment falling below 6 percent (the lowest level in 33 years) and core inflation declining in the second half of 2007, the International Monetary Fund (IMF) commended Canada's impressive macroeconomic performance since the mid-1990s. However, GDP grew by only 0.5 percent in 2008, while unemployment rose to 8.4 percent. The government consequently announced a stimulus program that was endorsed by the IMF, which praised the strong regulatory structure built into the plan. The Fund also cited the risk-averse nature of the country's banking system, in counterpoint to systems in the United States and elsewhere. Nevertheless, GDP was expected to decline by 2.5 percent in 2009 under the influence of the global recession.

GOVERNMENT AND POLITICS

Political background. United under British rule in 1763 following France's defeat in the Seven Years' War, Canada began its movement toward independence in 1867 when the British North America Act established a federal union of the four provinces of Quebec, Ontario, Nova Scotia, and New Brunswick. The provinces reached their present total of ten with the addition of Newfoundland in 1949.

Under the 1867 act, executive authority was vested in the British Crown but was exercised by an appointed governor general; legislative power was entrusted to a bicameral Parliament consisting of a Senate and a House of Commons. Canada's growing capacity to manage its affairs won formal recognition in the British Statute of Westminster of 1931, which conferred autonomous status within the Commonwealth.

With a political system and institutional structure closely modeled on British precedents, the country was for all practical purposes governed for more than a century by alignments equivalent to today's Liberal and Conservative parties. Liberal governments, headed successively by W. L. MacKenzie KING and Louis ST. LAURENT, were in office from 1935 to 1957, when the Conservatives (named Progressive Conservative Party [PCP] in the 1940s and the Conservative Party of Canada [CPC] in 2003 following the PCP's merger with the Canadian Alliance) returned to power under John DIEFENBAKER, prime minister from 1957 to 1963. Lester B. PEARSON, leader of the Liberal Party, headed minority governments from 1963 until his retirement in 1968, when he was succeeded by Pierre Elliott TRUDEAU. The new prime minister secured a majority for the Liberals in the election of June 1968 and was returned to power with a reduced majority in October 1972. Contrary to preelection forecasts, the Trudeau government won decisive control of the House of Commons in July 1974.

In May 1979 the 16-year Liberal reign ended when the PCP won 136 of 282 seats in the newly expanded House. Although his party remained 6 seats shy of an absolute majority, the PCP's Charles Joseph CLARK was sworn in as prime minister in June, Trudeau becoming leader of the opposition. In December, however, the Clark government experienced a stunning parliamentary defeat in an effort to enact a series of stringent budgetary measures, necessitating a dissolution of the House and the calling of a new election for February 1980. Given an evident resurgence of Liberal popularity, Trudeau agreed to withdraw his November 1979 resignation as party leader and returned to office in March as head of a new Liberal government that commanded a majority of 6 seats in the Commons.

As a French Canadian, Trudeau deployed his political weight against the proindependence Quebec Party (*Parti Québécois*—PQ), which had come to power in the province in 1976, thereby helping to defeat the PQ government's "sovereignty-association" plan in a Quebec referendum in May 1980. However, continued economic difficulties, combined with accusations of political patronage, began to erode the Trudeau administration's popularity. In February 1984 Trudeau again resigned the leadership of his party; he was replaced at a party convention in June by John Napier TURNER, who had served as finance minister from 1972 to 1975. Heartened by polls indicating that the transfer of power had aided his party's popularity, newly installed Prime Minister Turner called a general election for September, but the balloting produced a decisive reversal: the PCP won 211 of 284 House seats, and PCP leader Brian MULRONEY took office as prime minister.

During the ensuing four years the Mulroney administration encountered widespread resistance to its fiscal and defense policies, was embarrassed by a series of scandals involving cabinet officials, and encountered strong opposition to the Meech Lake constitutional reform proposals (see Constitution and government, below). Nonetheless, in an early general election in November 1988, the PCP retained control of the Commons by capturing 170 of 295 seats.

The future of the country's de facto two-party system was challenged by a devastating Liberal loss to the New Democratic Party (NDP) in Ontario provincial elections on September 6, 1990, followed by a third-place Liberal finish behind the NDP in Manitoba five days later. The NDP further asserted itself in October 1991 by toppling a Social Credit (Socred) administration in Saskatchewan and a Conservative government in British Columbia.

His party's standing in the opinion polls having plummeted to an unprecedented low, Mulroney resigned as prime minister and PCP leader on June 23, 1993, in favor of Kim CAMPBELL, who proved unable to reverse the anti-Conservative tide. On October 25 the PCP suffered the most punishing blow to any ruling party in Canadian history, with its parliamentary representation plunging from 153 to 2. Installed as prime minister on November 4, Liberal leader Jean CHRÉTIEN faced major challenges from both the separatist Quebec Bloc (*Bloc Québécois*—BQ), led by Lucien BOUCHARD, and the western populist Reform Party, the former becoming the official opposition.

A renewed threat to the Canadian federation resulted from provincial elections in Quebec on September 12, 1994, when the PQ, after nine years in opposition, defeated the incumbent Liberals by a decisive seat margin of 77 to 47. A PQ government committed to taking Quebec to independence was installed on September 27 under the premiership of Jacques PARIZEAU. In December 1994 Parizeau introduced detailed independence proposals and launched a "consultation" process aimed at securing referendum endorsement of Quebec's "sovereignty" by the end of 1995. The Chrétien federal government, initially relaxed about the referendum initiative, became more concerned when the small proautonomy Democratic Action of Quebec (*Action Démocratique du Québec*—ADQ), potentially commanding the swing vote in Quebec, endorsed the proposal. When the highly able Bouchard took over the leadership of the PQ's campaign from Parizeau, the Chrétien administration launched a major drive against separation. The effort succeeded by the barest of margins: in a turnout of 93 percent on October 30, 1995, 2,308,028 votes (49.4 percent) were cast in favor of the proposition and 2,361,526 (50.6 percent) against. In January 1996 Parizeau was succeeded as provincial premier and PQ leader by Bouchard, who recommitted the PQ to the goal of independence for Quebec but declared that his more immediate aim was the province's economic revival.

In a daring move, Prime Minister Chrétien announced on April 27, 1997, that new elections would be held in June (17 months earlier than required), following the shortest campaign in Canadian history. Chrétien's decision was apparently influenced by the Liberals' large lead in public opinion polls and a desire to solidify the government's toughened position against unilateral separation by Quebec. The June 2 balloting kept the Liberal Party in power, albeit with Canada's smallest-ever majority, 155 seats out of 301 total. Having won 60 seats, the Reform Party replaced the BQ (38 seats) as the official opposition. In general, Canada's electorate fragmented along regional lines, and only the small NDP (21 seats) could claim a national representation (a seat in three different regions).

In the Quebec provincial election of November 1998, Premier Bouchard was reelected, although the PQ's support softened as the Liberals edged the secessionists by 1 percent in the popular vote. During his campaign Bouchard said he would not seek another referendum on independence until "winning conditions" were clearly in place. Three months earlier, on August 20, the Supreme Court had ruled that Quebec could secede, but only with the agreement of the federal government and the other provinces on such questions as settlement of national debt and continued use of a common currency. Despite strong objections from the BQ, in March 2000 the House of Commons passed a controversial "clarity" provision that outlined procedures for secession. Passed into law by the Senate in July, the bill authorized the House to determine whether the wording of future independence referendums is sufficiently clear.

On October 22, 2000, five days after a cabinet reshuffle, Prime Minister Chrétien called a federal election for November 27, 19 months before the expiration of his mandate. Buoyed by Canada's healthy economy, the Liberals won 172 seats in the House of Commons, while the new Canadian Alliance—in large part a right-wing successor to the Reform Party—won 66 seats. The BQ, the NDP, and the PCP all saw their federal representation decline in the election that again confirmed the country's regional divide.

In June 2002 Chrétien sacked Paul MARTIN (Chrétien's chief Liberal rival) after nine years as finance minister, apparently because Chrétien believed Martin had begun his campaign to be the next prime minister too early. However, Martin was subsequently elected as the new Liberal leader (see Political Parties, below, for details), and on December 12, 2003, he succeeded Chrétien as prime minister, appointing a new cabinet on the same day.

Faced with a rapidly developing financial scandal, Martin called early elections for June 28, 2004, at which the Liberals were able to secure only a plurality of 135 of the 308 seats in the House of Commons. Martin formed a new minority government on July 20. However, the ongoing scandal and the Liberals' weak parliamentary position continued to plague the Martin government (see Current issues, below). On November 24, 2005, Conservative Party leader Stephen HARPER introduced a no-confidence motion, which passed 171–133 on November 28. The following day Martin asked Governor General Michaëlle JEAN to dissolve Parliament and call new elections. In the election on January 23, 2006, the Conservatives secured a plurality of 124 seats, compared to 103 seats for the Liberals. Consequently, Harper was sworn in as the head of the minority Conservative government on February 6. The cabinet was reshuffled in January and August 2007 and in May and June 2008.

With apprehension over his government's prospects for securing opposition party support for policy proposals, Harper called for an early election on October 14, 2008. Although the Conservatives improved to a plurality of 143 seats, the subsequent government (named October 30 and again led by Harper) remained in minority status, prompting a series of complicated political maneuvers (see Current issues, below, for details).

Constitution and government. From 1867 until 1982 the British North America Act served as Canada's basic law. A lengthy effort by Prime Minister Trudeau to "patriate" a purely Canadian constitution generated considerable controversy in the provinces and met with mixed judicial construction, which led to a September 1981 determination by the Supreme Court that the government's effort was legal but that it offended "the federal principle" by proceeding without overall provincial consent. Trudeau responded by convening a meeting with the provincial premiers in early November, at the conclusion of which all but Quebec's René LÉVESQUE agreed to a compromise that included an amending formula and permission for the provinces to nullify bill-of-rights provisions within their boundaries, should they so wish. On this basis, the Canada Bill (the Constitution Act 1982) was approved by the British Parliament in March 1982 and formally signed by Queen Elizabeth II in a ceremony in Ottawa on April 17. The document did not, however, secure final Canadian parliamentary approval until June 22, 1988, after the Mulroney administration (in the Meech Lake Accord of April–June 1987) had agreed to recognize Quebec as a "distinct society." The concession, which required the approval of all ten provinces, was bitterly opposed by a number of prominent Canadians, including former prime minister Trudeau, who had long been committed to a bilingual country of politically equal provinces and who argued that the distinct-society clause would open the door to Quebec's eventual departure from the federation. The latter prospect was by no means precluded when the deadline for approval of the accord expired on June 22, 1990, after cancellation by Newfoundland of a scheduled ratification vote.

In June 1991 a Citizens' Forum on Canada's Future that had been established by Ottawa in late 1990 submitted a report urging recognition of Quebec as a unique entity within the federal system, the introduction of self-government for aboriginal peoples, and restructuring or abolition of the Canadian Senate. Mulroney responded to the proposals in late September by placing before the House of Commons a document entitled "Shaping Canada's Future Together" that again would recognize Quebec as a "distinct society," while transferring a number of federal functions, particularly in the area of culture, to provincial administrations. The document also called for granting indigenous inhabitants self-government within ten years, removing a number of restrictions on trade between the provinces and territories, and establishing an elective Senate.

Following a series of national "consultations" on the Mulroney proposals, political agreement on a new reform plan was achieved at a conference of federal, provincial, territorial, and native leaders in Charlottetown, Prince Edward Island, held August 18–23, 1992. However, on October 26 voters decisively rejected the accord in a nationwide referendum (only the third in Canada's history), opposition being strongest in Quebec, where radical separatists regarded its provisions as insufficient, and in the western provinces, where the concessions to Quebec were seen as overly generous (see Current issues, below, for subsequent developments).

Meanwhile, on December 16, 1991, the government had announced formal agreement with *Inuit* representatives on formation of the Nunavut ("Our Land" in Inuktitut, the *Inuit* language) territory, subject to approval by voters in the existing Northwest Territories (NWT), from which the new entity would be detached. Under the accord, the *Inuit* would be granted self-government (not independence, as some had demanded) and a share in mining and oil proceeds from lands that would remain largely under federal ownership. In addition, a wildlife management board would be established to regulate hunting and trapping, while a fund of approximately US $653 million would be set up to assist in implementation of the homeland by 1999. The agreement was ratified on May 4, 1992, by a NWT majority of 54 percent (90 percent in the east) and on November 3–5 by 69 percent of about 8,000 participants in an *Inuit* referendum. The autonomous territory of Nunavut was founded on April 1, 1999.

Under the present constitution, the British monarch, as sovereign, is represented by a governor general, now a Canadian citizen appointed on the advice of the prime minister. The locus of power is the elected House of Commons, in which the leader of the majority party is automatically designated by the governor general to form a cabinet and thus become prime minister. The House may be dissolved and a new election called in the event of a legislative defeat or no-confidence vote. The Senate, appointed by the governor general (on the advice of the prime minister) along both geographic and party lines, also must approve all legislation but tends largely to limit itself to being a secondary, restraining influence. It is prohibited from introducing financial legislation.

Provincial governments operate along comparable lines. Each of the provinces has its own constitution; a lieutenant governor appointed by the governor general; a Legislative Assembly whose principal leader is the provincial premier; and its own judicial system, with a right of appeal to the Supreme Court of Canada. Municipalities are governed by elected officials and are subject to provincial rather than federal authority. The Yukon is governed by a premier and a popularly elected Council. The Northwest Territories are governed by a premier and a popularly elected Legislative Assembly. Nunavut is governed by a premier and a 19-member popularly elected legislature. (The legislative bodies elect the premiers in the territories.)

Province and Capital	*Area (sq. mi.)*	*Population (2008E)*
Alberta (Edmonton)	255,540	3,575,000
British Columbia (Victoria)	364,762	4,450,000
Manitoba (Winnipeg)	250,114	1,196,000
New Brunswick (Fredericton)	28,150	751,000
Newfoundland and Labrador (St. John's)	156,452	502,000
Nova Scotia (Halifax)	21,345	934,000
Ontario (Toronto)	415,596	12,922,000
Prince Edward Island (Charlottetown)	2,185	139,000
Quebec (Quebec)	595,388	7,750,000
Saskatchewan (Regina)	251,365	1,009,000
Territory and Capital		
Northwest Territories (Yellowknife)	519,732	44,000
Yukon Territory (Whitehorse)	186,271	31,000
Nunavut (Iqaluit)	808,181	31,000

Foreign relations. Canadian foreign policy in recent decades has reflected the varied influence of historic ties to Great Britain, geographical proximity to the United States, and a growing national strength and self-awareness that made the country one of the most active and influential "middle powers" of the post–World War II period. Staunch affiliation with the Western democratic bloc and an active role in the North Atlantic Treaty Organization (NATO) and other Western organizations have been accompanied by support for international conciliation and extensive participation in UN peacekeeping ventures and other constructive international activities.

While maintaining important joint defense arrangements with the United States, Canada has shown independence of U.S. views on a variety of international issues. In addition, anti-U.S. sentiment has been voiced in connection with extensive U.S. ownership and control of Canadian economic enterprises and pervasive U.S. influence on Canadian intellectual and cultural life. Thus, a general review of Canada's international commitments begun in the late 1960s resulted in diversification of the nation's international relationships. In line with this trend, Canada reduced the number of troops committed to NATO, and Prime Minister Trudeau made state visits to the Soviet Union and the People's Republic of China. In the face of a substantially reduced threat from Eastern Europe, the NATO commitment was further curtailed in September 1991, while the Mulroney government's pledge in February 1992 that for budgetary reasons all Canadian combat troops would be withdrawn from Europe by late 1994 was in fact accomplished by late 1993.

While disputes with the United States over fishing rights and delimitation of maritime boundaries in the Gulf of Maine were largely resolved following a decision of the International Court of Justice in October 1984, the effects of U.S.-produced acid rain on Canadian forests remained an area of contention between the two countries. However, immediately before the third annual U.S.-Canadian summit in April 1987, President Ronald Reagan announced that his government would spend \$2.5 billion over five years on demonstration projects aimed at cleaner coal burning, while President George H.W. Bush in early 1989 promised that he would seek prompt approval of additional clean air legislation. In another area of contention with Washington, the Canadians hailed the conclusion in early 1988 of an agreement on Arctic cooperation, although the pact did not include U.S. recognition that waters adjacent to the Arctic archipelago are subject to Canadian sovereignty. In September 1996 Ottawa hosted the inauguration of the eight-nation Arctic Council, established on Canada's initiative to promote cooperation among states with Arctic territories (see article on Arctic Council).

While France has been careful not to become overtly involved in the Quebec separatist issue since a controversial visit to the province by President Charles de Gaulle in 1967, a maritime controversy erupted between Ottawa and Paris following Canada's declaration of a 200-mile economic zone in 1977. France responded by claiming a similar zone around the French islands of St. Pierre and Miquelon, which are located only a few miles off the coast of Newfoundland. Eventually, the two parties agreed to submit the dispute to binding arbitration, the outcome of which in June 1992 limited France to a 12-mile zone around the two islands, save for a 10.5-mile-wide corridor running south for 200 miles to international waters. In December 1994 the two sides concluded a ten-year agreement on allowable catch quotas in the area.

On January 1, 1990, Canada became the 33rd member of the Organization of American States (OAS). It had held observer status with the hemispheric body since 1972 but had been reluctant to become a full member of a grouping perceived as being dominated by the United States.

Despite its historic sensitivity over trade with the United States, Canada participated in extension of the 1988 U.S.-Canadian free trade agreement to include Mexico. Initialed on August 12, 1992, and subsequently ratified by all three parties, the North American Free Trade Agreement (NAFTA) entered into force on January 1, 1994. It was the first such accord to link two industrialized powers with a developing state.

Relations in general with the United States remained strong even when Canada's trade and cultural ties with Cuba became a source of friction after the U.S. Congress in March 1996 passed the Helms-Burton Act, which strengthened the U.S. embargo of the island. More recently, Canada's relations with Cuba have cooled over Havana's human rights record.

Canada's long-standing sensitivity to cultural domination by imports of American songs, films, magazines, and other products resurfaced in 1998 as members of the Organization for Economic Cooperation and Development (OECD) reached an impasse in April on the Multilateral Agreement on Investment (MAI), which is intended to encourage direct, cross-border investments. Canada, differing with the United States, wanted cultural industries excluded. Ottawa and Washington also were divided over whether NAFTA provisions exempt culture and therefore permit the Canadians to restrict U.S. media.

From April 20 to April 22, 2001, Quebec City hosted the third Summit of the Americas, which was attended by the heads of state and government from 34 hemispheric countries. Approximately 30,000 protesters, most of them opposing globalization, threatened to disrupt the meeting, leading to tight security and several hundred arrests.

Following the September 11, 2001, attacks in the United States, Ottawa concluded a number of agreements with Washington providing for increased cooperation in the areas of intelligence and security, designed, among other things, to monitor border crossings more effectively. Canada also adopted stronger domestic antiterrorism legislation. (In October 2006 the courts struck down four provisions of the law, including its definition of terrorism. In February 2007, Parliament allowed the controversial provisions for holding suspects without charges and compelling testimony to expire.) Despite these new accords, relations between Canada and the United States subsequently grew colder, if not more contentious. Facing declining public support for going to war in Iraq and considerable opposition within his Liberal Party, Prime Minister Jean Chrétien declared in March 2003 that, in the absence of UN authorization, Canada would not participate in the invasion of Iraq. Members of the U.S. and Canadian administrations subsequently traded criticisms, including the comment by one of Chrétien's cabinet members referring to President George W. Bush as a "moron." Expectations of improved relations were raised when Paul Martin became prime minister in December 2003, but tensions continued over defense and trade issues.

During a visit by President Bush in November 2004, Martin's administration continued to press for the end of the ongoing U.S. ban on Canadian beef imports because of mad cow concerns raised in 2003 and the 27 percent tariff that the Bush administration imposed on Canadian softwood lumber imports in 2001. In February 2005 Martin declared that Canada would not participate in the development of the U.S.-led missile defense program.

By the end of 2004 Canada's economic relations with China had deepened as Chinese energy companies discussed ambitious deals for petroleum development in the province of Alberta. China's rapidly growing energy needs had already driven world petroleum prices higher and were beginning to cause increased competition over Canadian supplies, one of the largest sources of petroleum imports for the United States.

In the period following the September 11 attacks on the United States, Canada created a human security program as a central component of its foreign policy, covering five areas: protecting civilians, peace support operations, conflict prevention, governance and accountability, and public safety. Specific projects have ranged from a concerted effort to promote acceptance of the Rome Statute of the International Criminal Court, to peacekeeping duties in Afghanistan, to reform and reconstruction efforts in Haiti after the departure of Jean Bertrand Aristide in February 2004.

Following the installation of the Harper administration in February 2006, expectations rose for a closer Canadian relationship with the United States. Among other things, Harper, widely perceived as a strong supporter of President Bush, promised a legislative vote on whether Canada would become involved in the proposed NATO missile defense plan.

Concurrently, Harper announced that an agreement had been reached on softwood lumber trade, and in May 2006 the House of Commons voted to extend Canada's mission in Afghanistan until 2009. Harper also aligned himself with U.S. foreign policy by defending Israel during its conflict in the summer of 2006 with Hezbollah in Lebanon. On the other hand, Harper subsequently announced that Canada would not participate in the U.S. missile defense program.

In 2008 the government (with the support of the Liberals) announced that Canadian forces would remain in Afghanistan until 2011, with the stipulation that 1,000 troops from other nations would be assigned to Afghanistan's turbulent Kandahar Province. New U.S. president Barack Obama in early 2009 thanked Canada for the sacrifices it had made in Afghanistan, offered no objection to the 2011 withdrawal plan, and pledged to commit more U.S. troops to Kandahar. At their meeting in early February, Obama and Prime Minister Harper also found common ground on trade issues, including side agreements on features of NAFTA that had been criticized by Obama during his primary campaign. On less positive notes, Harper criticized the "Buy American" provisions in Obama's stimulus package, while Canada continued to reject U.S. and European claims that the Arctic's Northwest Passage constituted international waters. (Canada had earlier reaffirmed its sovereignty stance by imposing stricter registration requirements on ships seeking to use the passage.)

Current issues. One perplexing and difficult current issue for Canada remains national unity, in particular the will of a provincial population versus the constitutional integrity of Canada. Few countries in the world allow unfettered departure of a part of national territory, and none without the approval of some central authority. The continuing question of Quebec sovereignty, which never disappears from the headlines, took an unexpected turn in January 2001 with a surprise resignation announcement by Quebec premier Lucien Bouchard, who acknowledged his failure to make progress on the issue. According to reports, Bouchard had also grown weary of fending off party militants, who insisted, for example, on instituting stiffer French-language laws and scheduling another independence referendum. His successor, Bernard LANDRY, although a somewhat more ardent champion of separation, could hardly ignore a May 2000 opinion poll that registered only 43 percent support for independence among Quebec's residents. (In November 2006 Prime Minister Harper, facing a proposed motion from the BQ that would have declared Quebec a "nation," offered his own motion recognizing Quebec as a "nation within a united Canada." Harper's motion, which had prompted the resignation of Minister for Intergovernmental Affairs Michael CHONG [who opposed Harper's language and described Canada as "undivided" and "one nation"], was approved by the House of Commons on November 27 by a 266–16 vote.)

In recent years Canada has taken historic steps to grant self-government to native peoples. April 1, 1999, marked the division of the Northwest Territory and the founding of Nunavut, a territory considerably bigger than Alaska (or western Europe) that is now governed to a large extent by the *Inuit*. Earlier, in November 1998, after 20 years of negotiations, the *Nisga'a* Indians ratified a treaty giving them 745 square miles of British Columbia, the first comprehensive land settlement made by the province in the 20th century. With dozens of other Indian bands also pressing their case in the province, in April 1999 the *Nisga'a* agreement received the approval of the provincial assembly. In December the House of Commons passed the agreement despite opposition from the Reform Party, which argued that the precedent would endanger Canada's constitutional integrity. Passage through the Senate followed in April 2000, with the treaty then receiving royal assent from the governor general and entering into force on May 11. It remained subject to a number of lawsuits, however, including some brought by other native bands. On March 10, 2001, the *Nuu-chah-nulth* Tribal Council, representing about 7,000 Indians in 12 bands, also signed a treaty agreement with federal and provincial officials. The agreement, which awaits approval by the individual bands and the federal and provincial legislatures, includes provisions on self-rule and shared control of old-growth forests and other natural resources contained in about 260 square miles of Vancouver and Meares islands. Federal and Quebec provincial government officials have also signed an agreement-in-principle that would grant semiautonomous status to *Inuit* communities in northern Quebec as of 2009. The agreement anticipates the establishment of a regional government and legislature with policy authority over education, health, and transportation. (Prime Minister Harper took another step toward reconciling Canada with its past treatment of indigenous peoples in 2008 when he addressed parliament and apologized for the century-long practice, discontinued only in the 1990s, of removing aboriginal children from their homes for all but a few months a year. The program had been designed to eliminate traditional beliefs and languages—to assimilate the children, as some described it, or to "kill the Indian in the child," as a director of one of the schools once characterized the apparent goal.)

In 2000 Jean Chrétien became the first prime minister to win three consecutive parliamentary majorities since Mackenzie King in 1945. He undoubtedly benefited from Canada's strong economy, which enabled him to cut income and other taxes in 2000 while keeping the federal budget in surplus, thereby exploiting what had traditionally been Conservative issues. He also benefited from the Alliance's inability to attract more Progressive Conservatives into the new party, which continued the right-wing split, and from divisions in Quebec over how and when to pursue greater regional autonomy. Chrétien's success was made more remarkable by the fact that, earlier in the year, he had overcome calls from within his party asking him to step down in favor of a younger leader.

After assuming the premiership in December 2003, Paul Martin had only a brief honeymoon before a financial scandal roiled the government. (A February 2004 audit accused the federal government of blatant misuse of about $190 million in various promotional activities.) The Liberals clearly suffered from a loss of popular support as a result of the scandal in the June 2004 balloting for the House of Commons. At the same time, most observers described the performance of the new Conservative Party of Canada (CPC) as worse than had been expected. Stephen Harper, the leader of the CPC, had pledged to increase military spending and reduce taxes, earning him criticism as a "right-winger" from the Liberals and the NDP.

A December 2004 Supreme Court ruling that the government could expand marriage rights to gays and lesbians caused splits within both major parties. Meanwhile, Canada had continued toward decriminalization of marijuana use, a trend that had contributed to tension with the United States. The flow of an estimated $7 billion worth of marijuana into the United States had, among other things, prompted the governors of U.S. states adjoining Canada to call for greater U.S. federal border enforcement, also an issue in regard to illegal immigration and the potential entrance of terrorists into the United States.

Prime Minister Martin announced in April 2005 that he would ask for dissolution of Parliament within a year, a timetable that was initially accepted by the NDP, on whom the Liberals were relying for support. However, the minority Liberal government remained fragile, even though the opposition parties offered no coherent policies on which they might form a majority administration. Underscoring the administration's tenuous status, its budget legislation passed in May only because of a tie-breaking vote by the Speaker.

The Gormery Commission (charged with investigating the "sponsorship" scandal uncovered in 2004) issued its first report in early

November 2005. The commission exonerated Martin but found fault with the administration of former prime minister Chrétien for ignoring procedural safeguards that might have prevented the abuses. Although Martin avoided being directly criticized, the report reportedly raised concerns within the NDP about the Liberals and provided Harper with a context for the no-confidence motion that brought down the government in late November. (The motion, which was supported by all members of the opposition parties, was the first successful no-confidence motion conducted outside of a substantive policy issue.)

In their successful campaign for the January 2006 elections, the Conservatives proposed five major initiatives: a reduction in the goods and service tax, tougher criminal penalties, stricter accountability for politicians and civil servants, a child care subsidy, and a maximum waiting time for surgery. Initial aspects of the tax reduction, child care, and accountability legislation were approved by the House of Commons in June, and pilot projects regarding waiting times for surgery were subsequently launched, some in association with provincial governments. Meanwhile, various proposals for stricter criminal laws remained under consideration. However, Harper's proposal to ban same-sex marriage was defeated in December by a vote of 175–123, and Harper announced he would not revisit the issue.

Controversy continued in the second half of 2006 regarding environmental issues, as the Harper administration declared the goals and timetables in the global Kyoto Protocol to be unrealistic. The government prepared an alternative plan, which was broadly derided at the Group of Eight (G-8) meeting in Germany in 2007. Meanwhile, in April 2007 Environmental Minister John BAIRD announced that Canada would not be able to meet its Kyoto goals until at least 13 years after the proposed target date. Harper's minority government proved its staying power in October 2007 when, after presenting its agenda, it survived three no-confidence motions, all the major opposition parties agreeing that they did not want a snap election.

Attention in the first half of 2008 focused on the controversy over Canada's troop commitment in Afghanistan. Harper was ultimately able to broker an agreement with the Liberals to continue Canada's combat role through 2011 under the condition that NATO deploy additional troops in the Kandahar region, where Canadian troops have been suffering mounting casualties. However, the prime minister subsequently failed to identify "common ground" with the Liberals regarding other proposed legislative initiatives. With Canada appearing on the brink of recession after GDP grew by only 0.1 percent in the second quarter under the influence of a decline of exports (particularly to the United States), Harper met with Liberal leader Stéphane DION to discuss possible points of agreement for the upcoming parliamentary session. However, the meeting ended prematurely (without agreement), prompting Harper to describe the House of Commons as "dysfunctional" and Dion to declare that an early election was inevitable. On September 7 the governor general granted Harper's request to dissolve the government; new elections were scheduled for October 14. At that point, it was apparent that Harper hoped that the Conservatives would be able to secure a legislative majority before the worst effects of the economic downturn took hold, while Dion hoped the Liberals could unseat the Conservatives as the governing party.

Unfortunately for the Liberals, their 2008 campaign's emphasis on a carbon tax to address environmental concerns proved ill-timed in face of the nation's economic distress. In addition, the Conservative's questioning of Dion's leadership abilities appeared to strike a chord with the electorate. However, the Conservatives plurality of 143 seats still left it short of a majority, and Harper's new minority government (installed on October 30), quickly foundered. In late November Finance Minister James FLAHERTY presented plans to Parliament calling for spending cuts, the suspension until 2011 of the right of civil servants to strike, and, crucially, the elimination of government subsidies in support of political parties. Although all three proposals were unacceptable to the opposition, the proposed elimination of the subsidies was particularly upsetting since the opposition parties relied heavily on them for funding. Consequently, the Liberals and the NDP in early December announced plans to topple the government (by defeating the government's economic plan in what would have amounted to a no-confidence vote) and install a ruling Liberal-NDP coalition that, with the pledged support of the BQ, would enjoy majority legislative control. Harper responded to the plan by making several concessions in his economic proposals, including the restoration of the party subsidies. He also suggested that a government defeat in the House of Commons would prompt him to ask for new elections. However, the opposition continued to pursue the no-confidence motion, and Harper asked the governor general to suspend Parliament temporarily. The prorogation request was granted on December 4, with the Parliament being scheduled to reconvene on January 26, 2009.

One immediate effect of Harper's maneuver was Dion's resignation as Liberal leader and his replacement as interim leader by Michael IGNATIEFF, a reluctant supporter of the Liberal-NDP coalition concept who was also wary of relying on BQ support to run a government. Although it therefore appeared that his government would survive when Parliament reassembled, Harper moved quickly to improve his chances even further by filling 18 senate vacancies. (The move ran counter to Harper's long-stated intention to reform the Senate by having senators earn their positions through elections, but the risk of the opposition taking control of government and appointing senators to vacancies that Harper had been reluctant to fill until reforms were in place had him reprioritize his plans.)

Shortly after Parliament reconvened in late January 2009, Ignatieff announced the Liberals would support the government's new economic plan, thereby ending the immediate political standoff and assuring the continuance of the Harper administration. Among other things, the revamped economic legislation provided for significant stimulus spending (the first deficit spending since 1996) and retained the party subsidies. Although the Liberals characterized their support for the revised plan as a matter of principle, analysts also perceived a degree of pragmatism in the decision, since it was uncertain if a no-confidence vote would have prompted the governor general to approve a Liberal-NDP government or call a new election. Subsequently, however, the Liberals once again grew uneasy with Harper's policies and introduced two nonconfidence motions in August, which failed because the NDP refused to join the effort to topple the government, apparently in exchange for legislation increasing unemployment insurance.

POLITICAL PARTIES

Canada's traditional two-party system diversified in the 1930s, and the process gathered pace in the 1980s. The Liberals were the only party to win more than 20 percent of the national vote in 1993 (when the Quebec Bloc [BQ] first appeared and the political right split between the Reform Party and Progressive Conservatives) and again in 1997 (when the split on the right was maintained and the BQ retained influence). However, in the 2000 election the right began to coalesce once again, and the 2004 and 2006 elections featured the return of a two-party dominant national political scene, centered on the Liberals and Conservatives.

Provincial elections since 2001 have witnessed considerable turnover of the governing parties. The Liberals won British Columbia from the NDP in 2001 and held their majority in 2005 and 2009. Moreover, the Liberals won the critical province of Ontario from the PCP in 2003 and retained control in 2007. The Liberals also took control of New Brunswick in 2006 and Prince Edward Island in 2007. On the other hand, the PCP won Newfoundland and Labrador from the Liberals in 2003 and recorded a landslide victory there in 2007. In Quebec the Liberal Party of Quebec took over from the *Parti Québécois* in 2003. In 2007 the Liberals retained control of Quebec, but only through a minority government, as the ADQ surged into status as official opposition in the province. The Liberals again finished first in Quebec, this time with a majority of seats, in a December 2008 snap election, which also saw the PQ return to status as the official opposition party, with the ADQ finishing a distant third with only 7 seats. The PCP fell from majority to minority control in Nova Scotia in 2003, maintained its position in 2006, but finished third in the 2009 balloting, at which the NDP surged to a 60 percent majority. However, the PCP continued its majority control in Alberta in 2008. The NDP won slim majority control in Saskatchewan in 2003, ending the existing Liberal-NDP coalition formed in 1999, but in 2008 the Saskatchewan Party won 38 of the 58 assembly seats. In 2007 the NDP maintained its sizable majority in Manitoba. The resurgent Yukon Party pushed the Liberals out of power in the Yukon Territory in 2002 and retained its majority status in 2006. Meanwhile, the Assembly of the Northwest Territories consists entirely of independent members (candidates do not contest elections under party labels), and there are no political parties in Nunavut.

Government Party:

Conservative Party of Canada (CPC). The CPC is the result of the 2003 merger of Canada's two leading conservative parties—the

Canadian Reform Conservative Alliance (Canadian Alliance) and the Progressive Conservative Party (PCP).

The Canadian Alliance traced its origins to a September 1998 convention called to discuss formation of a "national, broad-based, democratic conservative movement." The effort was spearheaded by Preston MANNING and other leaders of the Reform Party of Canada, who hoped to convince other conservatives, particularly those in the PCP, to participate. Following up on the initial meeting, a United Alternative Convention convened in February 1999, with a number of United Alternative Action Committees then being established in the fall to draft a platform and a constitution for the new organization. A second convention was held in January 2000, at which time the organization's name and founding documents were approved. Party tenets include lowering and simplifying taxes; paying down the national debt; making balanced federal budgets mandatory; increasing defense spending; downsizing government; furthering free and open trade; eliminating public funding of multiculturalism; and reemphasizing the role of the provinces in setting social policy with regard to health, education, housing, and related areas. On March 27, 2000, the Canadian Alliance became the official opposition party in the House of Commons, about 92 percent of the Reform Party's membership having voted in favor of merging into the new formation.

A right-wing populist group, the Reform Party had been launched in Alberta in 1988 but subsequently attracted broad western support. The party strongly opposed the Charlottetown agreement in the October 1992 referendum and also opposed new federal proposals for constitutional accommodation with Quebec after the October 1995 independence referendum. It finished third in federal representation following the 1993 vote and in March 1996 sought, without notable success, to extend its power base by presenting candidates in a series of federal by-elections in the eastern provinces. In the federal election of June 1997 the party won 60 seats and thereby became the official opposition party.

After formation of the Canadian Alliance, Manning was soon challenged for the leadership by Stockwell DAY, a conservative populist and Alberta's treasurer. Day, an opponent of abortion and gay rights, secured the leadership position in second-round balloting in July 2000. In the November 2000 House of Commons election the Canadian Alliance won 25.5 percent of the national vote and 66 seats, all but 6 of them in Alberta, British Columbia, and Saskatchewan, and thereby retained its status as the official opposition. In May 2001 dissatisfaction with Day's leadership reportedly led a number of members to leave the party. Day resigned in December in preparation for another leadership election in 2002, John REYNOLDS succeeding him on an interim basis. In balloting on March 20, 2002, economist Stephen Harper defeated Day and two minor candidates for the alliance's leadership post. Harper won a by-election for a House of Commons seat from Calgary on May 13 (neither the Liberal Party or the PCP offered an opponent), thereby gaining access to the position of leader of the opposition.

The PCP was more nationalistic in outlook and traditionally less willing to compromise with the Quebec separatists than the Liberals. It also placed greater emphasis on Canada's British and Commonwealth attachments while actively promoting programs of social welfare and assistance to farmers. Following the replacement of Charles Joseph Clark by Brian Mulroney as party leader in June 1983, the PCP climbed steadily in the polls before winning decisive control at the federal level in September 1984. Although losing 41 seats in November 1988, the PCP became the first party to win a second consecutive term since 1953 and claimed that securing representation in nine of the ten provinces was a sign of "national unity." However, by the end of 1990 Prime Minister Mulroney's rating in the public opinion polls had fallen to a low of 12 percent. The voters' rejection of the Charlottetown constitutional reform agreement in October 1992 caused further problems for Mulroney, who announced on February 24, 1993, that he would not lead the PCP in the forthcoming general election. His successor, Kim Campbell, served as prime minister for only 134 days before the party's crushing defeat on October 25, only 2 seats being retained. On December 13 Campbell stepped down as party leader in favor of Jean J. CHAREST.

The PCP launched a comeback by scoring a stunning victory on June 8, 1995, in provincial balloting in Ontario, Canada's most populous province, where the party had been in opposition since 1985 (most recently to the NDP). Standing on a populist, antiwelfare ticket, new provincial PCP leader Mike HARRIS, a former golf professional and ski instructor, led the party to an overall majority of 82 seats out of 130 on a 45 percent popular vote share.

Charest quit as party leader in March 1998 and was succeeded by Joe Clark, former federal prime minister, who rejected efforts by the Reform Party to bring the PCP into what became the Canadian Alliance. Meanwhile, the party continued to fare well at the provincial level. In Ontario the PCP and Harris were returned to office in June 1999 despite Liberal gains. The PCP also assumed control of the New Brunswick and Nova Scotia governments in 1999 but lost Manitoba to the NDP.

Having suffered several parliamentary defections to the Liberals and the Alliance in 1999 and 2000, the PCP saw its representation in the House decline to 12 in November 2000, down from the 20 seats won in 1997. Clark announced in August 2002 that he would resign as PCP leader by mid-2003, thereby setting the stage for renewed efforts to merge the PCP with the Canadian Alliance. In the run-up to new elections for the PCP leadership, and amid speculation of a merger with the alliance, leadership hopeful David ORCHARD agreed to support rival Peter MACKAY on the condition that he would not pursue merger talks. Nonetheless, after winning, Mackay agreed to merge with the Canadian Alliance in October 2003 and became deputy leader of the CPC.

The CPC represented an attempt to "unite the Right" around a Conservative platform that advocated strong national defense, personal tax reduction, retirement savings accounts, support for ranchers in western provinces, and opposition to gun registration and gay marriage. Other less traditionally Conservative policy positions included support for a massive infusion of funds into the national health care system and a pledge not to legislate on abortion.

Stephen Harper resigned his Canadian Alliance post as leader of the opposition on January 12, 2004, to run for leader of the CPC. On March 20, 2004, he easily defeated two other leadership candidates on the first ballot. In the June 2004 election, the CPC gained 27 seats for a total of 99 seats, but its 29.6 percent of the vote was 8.1 percentage points below the combined totals received by the Canadian Alliance and the PCP in November 2000. Nevertheless, the CPC's second-place finish gave it the position of official opposition in the House of Commons. In the January 2006 balloting the CPC won 36.3 percent of the vote and 124 of 308 seats and formed a minority government under the premiership of Harper. The CPC's success was attributed to Harper's ability to quell doubts about his earlier strongly conservative positions on social matters, a moderated perception of the party in general, and the late December 2005 official announcement of alleged financial misdeeds by the Liberals' finance ministry. Campaigning on the theme that the Liberals were ill-suited to handle the nation's deteriorating financial system, the CPC improved its seat total to 143 in the October 2008 early elections, although Harper's hope of forming a majority government was foiled.

Leaders: Stephen HARPER (Prime Minister), Guy LAUZON (Caucus Chair), Jay HILL (Government House Leader), Gordon O'CONNOR (Whip), Don PLETT (President), Michael D. DONISON (Executive Director).

Opposition Parties:

Liberal Party of Canada. Historically dedicated to free trade and gradual social reform, the Liberal Party is sometimes regarded as the "natural party of Canada" because it has formed the government for most of the past century. Recently, it has promoted federal-provincial cooperation and an international outlook favoring an effective UN, cooperation with the United States and Western Europe, and a substantial foreign economic aid program. The Liberal Party was in power in all but two years from 1963 to 1984, mostly under the premiership of Pierre Trudeau. Shortly after Trudeau retired in June 1984, the new Liberal leader and prime minister, John TURNER, called a September election that produced the Liberals' worst defeat in history, as they won just 28 percent of the vote and 40 seats. Subsequent battling over his ability to return the party to power forced Turner to fend off three ouster attempts. Despite the turmoil, Turner was credited with leading an effective albeit losing campaign in November 1988 that yielded a doubling of Liberal parliamentary representation. In February 1990 Turner resigned as opposition leader, with Jean Chrétien, a former Trudeau aide, being elected his successor on June 23 and steering the party to victory in October 1993. The Liberals won again, with a smaller majority of 155 seats (22 less than in 1993), in June 1997. In the November 2000 election the party won 40.9 percent of the vote and 172 seats, making Chrétien the first prime minister since 1945 to win parliamentary majorities in three consecutive elections. Nevertheless the party entered a period of turmoil when increasing competition for party leadership from Finance Minister Paul Martin caused Chrétien to sack him from the cabinet in June 2002. Martin's dismissal apparently involved his perceived unofficial campaign to succeed Chrétien, the prime minister having directed that no campaigning or fund-raising be conducted until a party convention scheduled for February 2003.

In August 2002 Chrétien announced that he would not seek another term as prime minister, and a party convention in November 2003 overwhelmingly elected Martin as the new party leader. Chrétien then moved his retirement (scheduled for February 2004) up to December 12, 2003, on which date he was succeeded by Martin as prime minister.

Martin led the party in the June 28, 2004, election when it lost its majority status but won a plurality of votes and seats. It subsequently formed a minority government. In May 2005 the Liberals barely survived a budget battle that could have turned into a vote of no confidence only to lose a similar vote six months later. The January 2006 election saw the Liberals' vote fall by 6.5 points, to 30.2 percent, and its seats reduced to 103. Following the defeat, Martin resigned as leader on February 1. Bill GRAHAM replaced him as interim leader of the party and leader of the opposition.

Michael Ignatieff, a well-known academic who had lived in the United Kingdom and the United States for several decades until 2005, was considered the early favorite among eight candidates in December 2006 balloting for the party leader's post. Although he led the first two ballots, Ignatieff lost the fourth and final ballot to Stéphane Dion. Dion subsequently became a foil for the Conservatives, whose campaign for the October 2008 election focused on his on-air fumbling of questions on what he would do about the upheaval in financial markets, his proposed environmental tax policies, his difficulties in expressing himself clearly and forcefully in English (his second language), and his perceived lack of overall leadership abilities.

The Liberals' seat total fell to 77 in the October 2008 balloting, and Dion shortly thereafter announced he would resign his leadership post in May 2009. However, the subsequent short-lived attempt by the Liberals, NDP, and BQ to form a new government (see Current issues, above, for details) proposed that Dion be installed as prime minister. When the proposed no-confidence motion against the Harper government was forestalled by the prorogation of Parliament in early December 2008, Dion, under heavy pressure from all quarters of the party, announced he would step down as party leader as soon as a replacement was selected. Ignatieff, who had earlier signaled his reluctance to join forces in government with the NDP, was named interim party leader on December 10. A party convention in May 2009 affirmed Ignatieff's permanent position, no challenger having surfaced.

Leaders: Michael IGNATIEFF (Leader of the Official Opposition), Ralph GOODALE (House Leader), Anthony ROTA (Caucus Chair), Rodger CUZNER (Whip), Don FERGUSON (President), Rocco ROSSI (National Director).

Quebec Bloc (*Bloc Québécois*—BQ). The BQ is a francophone grouping organized by former Liberal environment minister Lucien Bouchard and six defectors from other parties after the collapse of the Meech Lake Accord in mid-1990. Although presenting candidates only in Quebec Province, it became the second-ranked federal party in October 1993, Bouchard thereby becoming leader of the opposition. Operating as the Ottawa representative of Quebec separatism, the BQ backed the provincial Quebec Party (PQ, below) in its declared aim of independence for Quebec following the September 1994 balloting, subject to the creation of a two-state institutional framework covering political and economic relations.

Bouchard's popular standing increased by late 1994 as he led the separatist movement in the national capital. A year later, after the failure of the sovereignty referendum in 1995 and the subsequent resignation of Quebec's premier Jacques Parizeau, Bouchard left federal politics to become premier of Quebec and leader of the PQ. The BQ was the third-ranked party, with 44 seats, after the 1997 federal election and retained that position in November 2000 despite dropping to 38 seats in the House of Commons, based on a provincial vote share of 39.9 percent. In the 2004 elections the BQ retained its third-place ranking, but it increased its seat total to 54 in the House of Commons. In 2006 its seat total fell slightly, to 51, again making it the third-largest parliamentary party. The October 2008 balloting led to a further slight decline, but its 49 seats maintained the BQ as the third largest parliamentary party. While it pledged to support the planned November 2008 vote of no-confidence and thereafter support a proposed Liberal-NDP government, it declared it would not join a federal government as a matter of party principle.

Leaders: Gilles DUCEPPE (Leader), Pierre PAQUETTE (House Leader), Michel GUIMOND (Whip), Louis PLAMONDON (Caucus Leader), Gilbert GARDNER (General Director).

New Democratic Party (NDP). A democratic socialist grouping founded in 1961 by merger of the Cooperative Commonwealth Federation and the Canadian Labour Congress, the NDP favors domestic control of resources, a planned economy, broadened social benefits, and an internationalist foreign policy. Traditionally strong in the midwest prairie provinces, the NDP long played the role of third party in relation to the Liberals and Progressive Conservatives, its lower house representation rising to 43 in the election of November 1988. Its highly respected leader, John Edward BROADBENT, retired in 1989 and was succeeded by Audrey McLAUGHLIN (the first woman to lead a significant North American party).

In September 1990 the party won a spectacular victory by defeating the incumbent Liberal administration of Ontario. It scored equally impressive victories in October 1991 by ousting a Social Credit administration in British Columbia and the Conservative government in Saskatchewan (an NDP stronghold), although in October 1992 it lost control of Yukon Territory. Its momentum was more decisively reversed a year later when its representation in the House of Commons plunged from 43 members to 9. In September 1995 McLaughlin was succeeded as NDP federal leader by Alexa McDONOUGH. In the 1997 federal election the NDP recovered somewhat, winning 21 seats, but its total fell again, to 13, in November 2000, when it captured only 8.5 percent of the national vote. McDonough announced in June 2002 that she would retire from her NDP leadership post at the convention scheduled for late in the year. In the June 2004 federal election, the NDP recovered somewhat by securing 19 seats in the House of Commons under the leadership of Jack Layton. In January 2006 the party rebounded further, having its best results since 1988, winning 17.5 percent of the vote and 29 seats.

Layton approached the October 2008 election as if he were a serious contender for prime minister. The NDP won 37 seats on 18.1 percent of the vote, its highest seat and vote percentage totals in 20 years. The NDP indicated it would support Liberal leader Stéphane Dion for prime minister in the unsuccessful effort in late 2008 to form a Liberal/NDP government.

Leaders: Jack LAYTON (Federal Leader), Anne McGRATH (President), Libby DAVIES (House Leader), Yvon GODIN (Whip), Jean CROWDER (Caucus Chair).

Other Parties:

The parties that participated unsuccessfully in the October 2008 election were the **Animal Alliance Environment Voters Party** (AAEV), led by Liz WHITE (527 votes); the **Canadian Action Party**, which, led by Constance FOGAL, took 0.02 percent of the 2008 vote; the **Christian Heritage Party of Canada,** led by Ronald O. GRAY (0.19 percent); the **Communist Party of Canada,** which dates from 1921 and is led by Miguel FIGUEROA (0.03 percent); the **First Peoples National Party** (FPNP), which, under interim leader Barbara WARDLAW, advocates aboriginal rights (0.01 percent); the **Green Party of Canada,** led by Elizabeth MAY (6.78 percent); the **Libertarian Party of Canada,** led by Dennis YOUNG (0.05 percent); the **Marijuana Party,** led by Blair T. LONGLEY (0.02 percent); the **Marxist-Leninist Party of Canada,** led by Anna DI CARLO (0.06 percent); the **Neorhino Party** (neorhino.ca), led by François GOULD (0.02 percent); the **Newfoundland and Labrador First Party** (NLFP), active at the federal and provincial levels and led by Jordan LESTER (0.01 percent); **People's Political Power** (PPP) led by Roger POISSON (186 votes); the **Progressive Canadian Party** (PC), currently led by Sinclair M. STEVENS (0.04 percent); the **Western Block Party** (WBP, 195 votes)), led by Douglas H. CHRISTIE, who also heads the separatist organization **Western Canada Concept Party**; and the **Work Less Party** (WLP) led by Jessica MASON-PAULL (423 votes).

Perhaps of greatest historical significance is the **Social Credit Party** (Socred), which controlled Alberta from its founding in 1935 until 1971 and which governed British Columbia from 1975 until 1991. It has not been represented at the federal level since 1980.

Regional Parties:

Quebec Party (*Parti Québécois*—PQ). The PQ was founded in 1968 by the journalist René LEVESQUE. Running on a platform of French separatism, it won control of the provincial assembly from the Liberals in the election of November 1976, Lévesque becoming premier. In a referendum held in May 1980, however, it failed to obtain a mandate to enter into "sovereignty-association" talks with the federal government. In April 1981 it increased its majority in the 122-member assembly to 80. In 1985 the party was weakened by the defection of a militant group to form the Democratic Rally for Independence (*Rassemblement Démocratique pour l'Indépendance*—RDI).

In October 1985 Pierre-Marc JOHNSON was sworn in as provincial premier in succession to Lévesque, who was in poor health and whose influence had waned because of divisiveness over the sovereignty issue. However, neither Johnson's conciliatory posture on federalism nor an emerging conservatism on economic issues averted a crushing defeat in provincial balloting in December, when the PQ obtained only 23 seats to the Liberals' 99.

Lévesque died in November 1987. Ten days later, amid a resurgence of proindependence sentiment, Johnson stepped down as party president. His successor, Jacques Parizeau, promised a return to the PQ's separatist origins, and in provincial elections on September 12, 1994, the PQ won a commanding majority of 77 of the 125 legislative seats. On being inducted as premier, Parizeau pledged that a referendum on the independence question would be held in 1995. The vote on October 30 yielded a margin of less than 1 percent against separation and the resignation of Parizeau as PQ leader and Quebec premier. He was succeeded in January 1996 by Lucien Bouchard, theretofore leader of the federal BQ.

The PQ won 75 seats in the provincial election of November 30, 1998, although observers attributed the victory more to the moderate Bouchard's successes in the economic sphere than to his gradualist approach toward the sovereignty issue. At a party convention in May 2000, 91 percent of the delegates endorsed his leadership. In January 2001, however, a series of developments, including continuing pressure from adamant separatists (many of whom want more stringent French-language laws and less attention to minority rights), led Bouchard to announce his surprise resignation from party and government offices, effective upon designation of a successor. In February Quebec finance minister Bernard Landry assumed the party leadership, promising to reinvigorate the separatist cause upon becoming premier in early March. Despite Landry's pledge, the PQ lost control of the provincial government to the rival Liberal Party of Quebec (*Parti Libéral du Quebec*—PLQ) in the 2003 balloting, securing only 45 of 125 seats.

Landry announced in late summer 2004 that he would stay on as leader. However, after a vote on his leadership in June 2005 fell short of the endorsement he was seeking, he was replaced on an interim basis by Louise HAREL and then, in the November leadership election, by Andre BOISCLAIR. Harel stayed on as leader of the opposition in Quebec, because Boisclair did not hold an assembly seat.

The PQ's electoral fortunes declined further in the March 2007 provincial balloting, at which it finished third with only 36 seats on a vote share of 28.3 percent and lost its position as official opposition in the province to the ADQ (see below). (The PLQ led all parties with 48 seats to retain control of the provincial government.) Boisclair announced his resignation in May, and he was succeeded in late June by Pauline Marois, the only announced candidate for the post. When Premier Jean Charest (PLQ) called a snap election for December 8, 2008, the PQ electoral fortunes rebounded, as it won 35 percent of the vote and 51 seats. These increases came mostly at the expense of the ADQ, allowing the PQ to regain its position as the official opposition party in the province.

Leaders: Pauline MAROIS (Leader), Jonathan VALOIS (President).

Democratic Action of Quebec (*Action Démocratique du Québec*—ADQ). The ADQ's founding congress took place in March 1994. The party was launched by former Liberals who wanted Quebec to remain within a Canadian confederation but with substantially greater autonomy. It won 6.5 percent of the vote and 1 seat (taken by its leader) in the September 1994 provincial election, thereafter increasing its opinion poll support to around 15 percent. Its endorsement of the June 1995 PQ-BQ pact on postindependence economic and political links with Canada was accordingly seen as boosting the prospects of a "yes" vote in the planned referendum. By negotiating both sovereignty and "association" (with Canada) as part of the tripartite agreement among the ADQ, the PQ, and the BQ, leader Mario DUMONT led the partners to accept a role for Canada in the social and economic development of an independent Quebec. In the provincial election of November 1998, the ADQ almost doubled its share of the popular vote, gaining 11.8 percent, although it still won only 1 seat. In the 2003 provincial elections the ADQ secured 4 seats on an 18.2 percent vote share, and it continued to gain strength in the 2007 provincial balloting, at which it finished second with 41 seats on a 30.8 percent vote share and became the official opposition to the PLQ's minority provincial government.

In the October 2008 federal elections most ADQ leaders endorsed the Conservatives. When Quebec Premier Charest called a snap provincial election for December, the ADQ was caught unaware, leading to its vote support dropping to 16.4 percent (good for only seven seats). Dumont subsequently announced he would resign as leader; Sylvie Roy became interim leader in February, 2009, and was expected to hold that position until the leadership election results were announced a year later.

Leaders: Sylvie ROY (Leader), Mario CHARPENTIER (President).

Saskatchewan Party (SP). The SP was established in August 1997 and held a leadership election in April 1998 that was won by a former Reform Party MP, Elwin HERMANSON. Contesting the provincial election of September 1999 on a platform that called for lower taxes, better health care, and improved highways, the SP finished a surprising second, capturing 26 of the 58 seats in the Legislative Assembly. In the November 2003 provincial balloting the SP improved to 28 seats on a 39 percent vote share. In the November 7, 2007, provincial balloting the SP won 38 seats on a vote share of 51 percent, the first absolute vote majority in the province since the NDP won 51 percent in 1991.

Leaders: Brad WALL (Premier of Saskatchewan), Gary MESCHISHNICK (President).

Yukon Party (YP). A newly formed group, the YP won a plurality in Yukon territorial elections on October 19, 1992, thus ousting the NDP from the territorial government. Holding 7 of the 17 seats, it subsequently formed a minority administration under John OSTASHEK. In the 1996 election the party retreated to 3 seats as the NDP surged, while in April 2000 the YP captured only 1 seat in the territorial legislature as the Liberal Party won control. When early elections were called in 2002, voters, reportedly angry at having to vote after only two years, gave the YP an overwhelming victory with 12 of the 18 legislative seats. Resignations reduced the YP majority to 10 seats as of May 2006. The YP retained its 10-seat majority in the October 2006 territorial elections, followed by the Yukon Liberal Party (5 seats) and the Yukon New Democratic Party (3 seats).

Leaders: Denis FENTIE (Premier and Party Leader), Dan MACDONALD (President).

Dozens of additional provincial parties exist—more than 30 are officially registered in British Columbia, for example, counting regional branches of national parties—but none currently hold seats in any provincial or territorial legislature.

LEGISLATURE

Influenced by British precedent (although without its own peerage), Canada's bicameral **Parliament** consists of an appointed Senate and an elected House of Commons.

Senate. The upper house consists of individuals appointed to serve until 75 years of age by the governor general and selected, on the advice of the prime minister, along party and geographic lines. Its current and normal size is 105 senators, although under a controversial constitutional provision successfully invoked for the first time by Prime Minister Mulroney in 1990, it can, with the queen's assent, be increased to no more than 112. Senate reforms remain under consideration. Among other things, Prime Minister Harper has promised to recommend the appointment of senators who have been chosen by unofficial popular referendums in the provinces. In the first action in that regard, Harper in 2007 successfully recommended the appointment of an Albertan who had won a plurality of votes in an election in Alberta in 2004 and had since then been known as a "senator in waiting." In a September 2007 speech Harper argued that the Senate must be reformed or "vanish."

As of June 1, 2009, the distribution of seats was as follows: the Liberal Party of Canada, 56; the Conservative Party of Canada, 38; the Progressive Conservative Party, 3; independents, 4; unaffiliated, 1; vacant, 3.

Speaker: Noël KINSELLA.

House of Commons. The lower house currently consists of 308 members elected for five-year terms (subject to dissolution) by universal suffrage on the basis of direct representation. In the election of October 14, 2008, the Conservative Party of Canada won 143 seats, the Liberal Party of Canada, 77; the Quebec Bloc, 49; the New Democratic Party, 37; and independents, 2.

Speaker: Peter Andrew Stewart MILLIKEN.

CABINET

[as of June 1, 2009]

Prime Minister	Stephen Harper
Ministers	
Agriculture and Agri-Food	Gary Ritz
Asia-Pacific Gateway	Stockwell Day
Atlantic Gateway	Peter Gordon MacKay
Canadian Heritage and Official Languages	James Moore
Canadian Wheat Board	Gary Ritz
Citizenship, Immigration, and Multiculturalism	Jason Kenney
Environment	Jim Prentice
Finance	James Michael Flaherty
Fisheries and Oceans	Gail Shea [f]
Foreign Affairs	Lawrence Cannon
Health	Leona Aglukkaq [f]
Human Resources and Skills Development	Diane Finley [f]
Indian Affairs and Northern Development and Federal Interlocutor for Métis and Non-Status Indians	Charles Strahl
Industry	Tony Clement
Intergovernmental Affairs	Josée Verner [f]
International Cooperation	Beverley Oda [f]
International Trade	Stockwell Day
Justice and Attorney General	Robert Douglas Nicholson
La Francophonie	Josée Verner [f]
Labor	Rona Ambrose [f]
National Defense	Peter Gordon McKay
National Revenue	Jean-Pierre Blackburn
Natural Resources	Lisa Raitt [f]
Public Safety	Peter Van Loan
Public Works and Government Services	Christian Paradis
Transport, Infrastructure, and Communities	John Baird
Veterans Affairs	Gregory Francis Thompson
Government Leader in the House	Jay Hill
Government Leader in the Senate	Marjory LeBreton [f]
President, Queen's Privy Council for Canada	Josée Verner [f]
President, Treasury Board	Vic Toews

[f] = female

Note: All of the above are members of the Conservative Party of Canada.

COMMUNICATIONS

News media are free from censorship or other direct government control.

Press. Until the start of *The National Post* in October 1998, there were no national press organs; of the roughly 1,200 newspapers, about 100 are dailies, most of them owned by ten publishing chains. The following are English-language dailies, unless otherwise noted, with circulation numbers as of January 1, 2008: *Toronto Star* (Toronto, 634,886 daily, 465,803 Saturday); *Globe and Mail* (Toronto, 410,285 morning, 337,387 Saturday); *Le Journal de Montréal* (Montreal, 274,522 morning, 319,899 Saturday), in French; *National Post* (Toronto, 206,003 morning, 217,115 Saturday); *Toronto Sun* (Toronto, 194,042 morning, 311,689 Sunday); *La Presse* (Montreal, 217,797 morning, 277,624 Saturday), in French; *Vancouver Sun* (Vancouver, 171,782 morning, 204,791 Saturday); *The Province* (Vancouver, 146,473 morning, 173,016 Sunday); *The Gazette* (Montreal, 139,146 morning, 150,078 Saturday), the oldest Canadian newspaper, founded 1788; *Ottawa Citizen* (Ottawa, 131,419 morning, 139,615 Saturday); *Edmonton Journal* (Edmonton, 124,822 morning and 132,089 Saturday); *Winnipeg Free Press* (Winnipeg, 126,569 evening, 162,399 Saturday); *Calgary Herald* (Calgary, 123,793 morning, 126,529 Saturday); *The Spectator* (Hamilton, 108,304 morning, 117,172 Saturday); *London Free Press* (London, 81,660 morning, 97,766 Saturday); *Financial Post* (Toronto, 90,000 morning); *Le Soleil* (Quebec, 83,793 morning, 108,164 Saturday), in French; *Windsor Star* (Windsor, 68,022 morning, 74,913 Saturday), *Edmonton Sun* (Edmonton, 68,342 morning, 87,464 Sunday).

News agencies. In January 1985 the Canadian Press, a cooperative of more than 100 daily newspapers, became Canada's only wire service after buying out its only competitor, United Press Canada. Numerous foreign agencies maintain offices in the leading cities.

Broadcasting and computing. Radio and television broadcasting is supervised by the Canadian Radio-Television and Telecommunications Commission (CRTC), which was formed by the 1968 Broadcasting Act. The publicly owned Canadian Broadcasting Corporation/Société Radio Canada (CBC/SRC) provides domestic radio and television service in English, French, Déné, and Inuktitut. Most major television stations not associated with the CBC are affiliated with the CTV Television Network, Ltd., although there are several other smaller services, some emphasizing French-language and/or educational programming. As of 2008 there were 754.3 Internet users per 1,000 inhabitants.

INTERGOVERNMENTAL REPRESENTATION

Ambassador to the U.S.: Gary Albert DOER.

U.S. Ambassador to Canada: David C. JACOBSON.

Permanent Representative to the UN: John McNEE.

IGO Memberships (Non-UN): AC, ADB, AfDB, APEC, BIS, CDB, CP, CWTH, EBRD, G-7/G-8, G-10, G-20, IADB, IEA, Interpol, IOM, NATO, OAS, OECD, OIF, OSCE, PCA, WCO, WTO.

CAPE VERDE

Republic of Cape Verde
República de Cabo Verde

Political Status: Former Portuguese dependency; became independent July 5, 1975; present constitution adopted September 25, 1992.

Area: 1,557 sq. mi. (4,033 sq. km.).

Population: 436,863 (2000C); 503,000 (2008E).

Major Urban Centers (2005E): CIDADE DE PRAIA (São Tiago, 129,000), Mindelo (67,000).

Official Language: Portuguese.

Monetary Unit: Cape Verde Escudo (official rate December 1, 2009: 73.95 escudos = $1US). When Portugal adopted the euro as its official

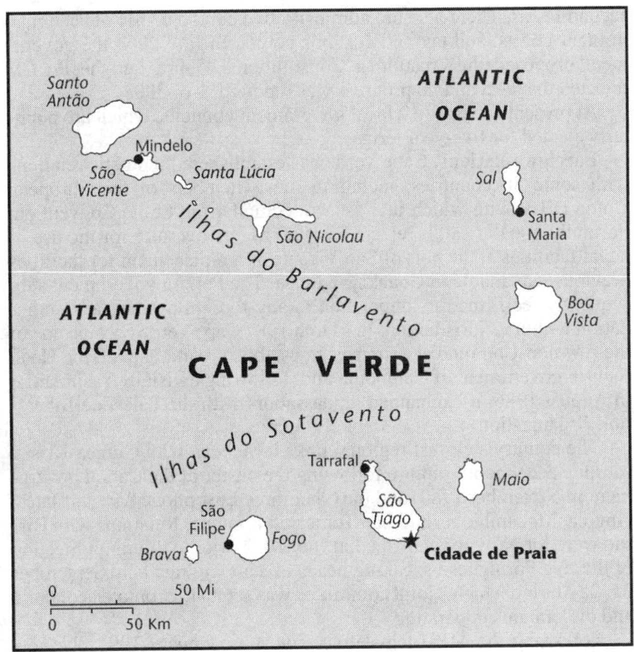

currency in 2002, the Cape Verde escudo, which had been pegged to the Portuguese escudo since 1998, was pegged to the euro at the rate of 110.265 Cape Verde escudos = 1 euro.

President: Gen. (Ret.) Pedro Verona Rodrigues PIRES (African Party for the Independence of Cape Verde); elected by popular vote on February 25, 2001, and inaugurated on March 22 for a five-year term, succeeding António Mascarenhas MONTEIRO (nonparty, backed by Movement for Democracy); reelected to another five-year term on February 12, 2006, and inaugurated on March 6.

Prime Minister: José Maria Pereira NEVES (African Party for the Independence of Cape Verde); appointed by the president on February 1, 2001, and sworn in (along with the new cabinet) on the same day in succession to António Gualberto DO ROSARIO (Movement for Democracy) following legislative election of January 14; reappointed by the president and sworn in on March 8, 2006, following legislative election of January 22.

THE COUNTRY

Cape Verde embraces ten islands and five islets situated in the Atlantic Ocean some 400 miles west of Senegal. The islands are divided into a northern windward group (Santo Antão, São Vicente, Santa Lúcia, São Nicolau, Sal, and Boa Vista) and a southern leeward group (Brava, Fogo, São Tiago, and Maio). About 60 percent of the population is composed of *mestiços* (of mixed Portuguese and African extraction), who predominate on all of the islands except São Tiago, where black Africans outnumber them; Europeans constitute less than 2 percent of the total. Most Cape Verdeans are Roman Catholics and speak a Creole version of Portuguese that varies from one island to another. Partly because of religious influence, women have traditionally been counted as less than 25 percent of the labor force, despite evidence of greater participation as unpaid agricultural laborers; female representation in party and government affairs has been increasing slowly, and the current government contains six women.

The islands' economy has historically depended on São Vicente's importance as a refueling and resting stop for shipping between Europe and Latin America. The airfield on Sal has long served a similar function for aircraft. Corn is the major subsistence crop, but persistent drought since the late 1960s has forced the importation of it and other foods. The Monteiro administration's World Bank–supported efforts both to privatize state-run enterprises and attract foreign investment were underlined in 1995 by the sale of 40 percent of the telecommunications facility to Portuguese investors. In June 1997 efforts to rehabilitate the island's infrastructure were boosted by a loan from the African Development Fund of $4.9 million for road projects.

Cape Verde in 1998 adopted a structural reform program prescribed by the International Monetary Fund (IMF) in an effort to restore financial stability in the wake of a dismal economic performance in the first half of the decade. Debt reduction and private sector growth topped the government's goals. GDP grew in real terms by 8.6 percent in 1999, and 6.8 percent in 2000, in part due to increased tourism and greater export of manufactured goods. On the negative side, unemployment increased, and by 2002 some 36 percent of the population was reportedly living in poverty. The IMF, World Bank, and African Development Bank subsequently provided significant additional assistance to support the government's economic restructuring. After a slide in GDP to 4.5 percent in 2004, largely because of the drought's effect on agriculture, the economy rebounded in 2005, with recorded annual GDP growth of 5.5 percent and continued low inflation. GDP growth soared to 11 percent in 2006, dipping to 7 percent in 2008. The unemployment rate declined to single digits, and poverty rates dropped as well. However, as a result of a decline in tourism and construction due largely to the global economic crisis, annual growth for 2009 and 2010 slowed to an average of 4.5 percent. The government planned to provide fiscal stimulus to offset some of the anticipated losses.

GOVERNMENT AND POLITICS

Political background. Cape Verde was uninhabited when the Portuguese first occupied and began settling the islands in the mid-15th century; a Portuguese governor was appointed as early as 1462. During the 1970s several independence movements emerged, the most important being the mainland-based African Party for the Independence of Guinea-Bissau and Cape Verde (*Partido Africano da Independência do Guiné-Bissau e Cabo Verde*—PAIGC), which urged the union of Cape Verde and Guinea-Bissau, and the Democratic Union of Cape Verde (*União Democratica de Cabo Verde*—UDCV), which was led by João Baptista MONTEIRO and rejected the idea of a merger.

An agreement signed with Portuguese authorities on December 30, 1974, provided for a transitional government prior to independence on July 5, 1975. A 56-member National People's Assembly was elected on June 30, 1975, but only the PAIGC participated; the results indicated that about 92 percent of the voters favored the PAIGC proposal of ultimate union with Guinea-Bissau. Upon independence, the assembly elected Aristides PEREIRA, the secretary general of the PAIGC, as president of Cape Verde. On July 15 Maj. Pedro PIRES, who had negotiated the independence agreements for both Cape Verde and Guinea-Bissau, was named prime minister of Cape Verde. However, the question of eventual unification with Guinea-Bissau remained unresolved, both governments promising to hold referendums on the issue. In January 1977 a Unity Council composed of six members from each of the national assemblies was formed, although in December the two governments asserted that it was necessary to move cautiously, with initial emphasis to be placed on establishing "a common strategy of development." Both countries continued to be ruled through the PAIGC, President Pereira serving as its secretary general and President Luis Cabral of Guinea-Bissau as his deputy.

On September 7, 1980, the assembly adopted Cape Verde's first constitution with the expectation that a collateral document under preparation in Guinea-Bissau would be virtually identical in all key aspects. On November 14, however, the mainland government was overthrown, and on February 12, 1981, the Cape Verdean assembly voted to expunge all references to unification from the country's basic law. Although formal reconciliation between the two governments was announced in mid-1982, the parties agreed that there would be no immediate resumption of unification efforts. Meanwhile, the offshore component of the ruling party had dropped the reference to Guinea in its title.

In keeping with currents elsewhere on the continent, the National Council of the African Party for the Independence of Cape Verde (PAICV, as the PAIGC had been restyled in 1981) announced in April 1990 that the president would henceforth be popularly elected and that other parties would be permitted to advance candidates for the assembly. On July 26 Pereira stepped down as PAICV party leader, declaring that the head of state should be "above party politics."

In the country's first multiparty balloting on January 13, 1991, the recently formed Movement for Democracy (*Movimento para Democracia*—MPD) won 56 legislative seats on the strength of a 68 percent vote share, compared to the PAICV's 23 seats. Prime Minister Pires announced his resignation on January 15, and on January 28 he was succeeded by the MPD's Carlos Alberto Wahnon de Carvalho VEIGA, who formed an MPD-dominated interim government pending the presidential poll. Continuing the PAICV's decline, President Pereira was defeated in the February 17 balloting by António Mascarenhas MONTEIRO, who had the support of the MPD, by a vote of 74 to 26 percent. Following Monteiro's inauguration on March 22, a permanent Veiga government was installed on April 4.

In legislative balloting on December 17, 1995, the MPD once again secured an absolute majority, capturing a reported 60 percent of the vote, the clear-cut legislative triumph being described by observers as validation of both the government's economic policies and Prime Minister Veiga, who had vowed to resign if faced with the political "instability" of having to form a coalition government. In addition, the PAICV's failure to increase its legislative representation reportedly convinced former prime minister Pires to shelve plans for a presidential campaign. President Monteiro was reelected unopposed in the presidential balloting of February 18, 1996.

On July 29, 2000, Prime Minister Veiga, who had become increasingly at odds with President Monteiro on several issues, including economic policy, announced he would no longer serve as prime minister in order to prepare for a campaign to succeed Monteiro (limited to two terms by the constitution) in the 2001 elections. Veiga argued that his decision meant that Deputy Prime Minister António Gualberto DO ROSARIO should be elevated to the premiership at least on an interim basis. However, the PAICV labeled the maneuvering unconstitutional, and President Monteiro also criticized the action as undermining his authority to appoint the prime minister. (It was not clear if Veiga was officially resigning or merely "suspending" his prime ministerial responsibilities.) An institutional crisis was finally averted when Veiga subsequently submitted a formal resignation letter. On October 6 President Monteiro invited do Rosario to form a new government that, as constituted on October 9, comprised all but one of the incumbent ministers.

In legislative balloting on January 14, 2001, the PAICV won 47 percent of the vote and 40 seats. On January 26 President Monteiro invited PAICV leader José Maria Pereira NEVES to form a new government, which was sworn in on February 1. Subsequently, former prime minister Pires of the PAICV was elected after two rounds of presidential balloting on February 11 and February 25, defeating Veiga and two independent candidates. Pires again defeated Veiga in the presidential balloting of February 12, 2006, securing 50.92 percent of the vote versus Veiga's 49.02 percent, following the PAICV's winning 41 seats in legislative balloting on January 22. Neves was reappointed to head another PAICV government and was sworn in along with the new (mostly PAICV) government on March 8. The cabinet was reshuffled on June 27, 2008.

Constitution and government. The constitution of September 7, 1980, declared Cape Verde to be a "sovereign, democratic, unitary, anticolonialist, and anti-imperialist republic" under single-party auspices. Legislative authority was vested in the National People's Assembly, which elected the president of the republic for a five-year term. The prime minister was nominated by the assembly and responsible to it. The basic law was amended in February 1981 to revoke provisions designed to facilitate union with Guinea-Bissau, thus overriding, inter alia, a 1976 judiciary protocol calling for the merger of legal procedures and personnel. The likelihood of a merger was virtually eliminated by adoption of the mainland constitution of May 1984, which emulated its Cape Verdean counterpart by lack of reference to the sister state.

On September 28, 1990, the National People's Assembly approved constitutional and electoral law revisions, forwarded in early 1990 by the PAICV National Council, which deleted references to the party as the "ruling force of society and of state," authorized balloting on the basis of direct universal suffrage, and sanctioned the participation of opposition candidates in multiparty elections that were subsequently held in January and February 1991.

A new constitution that came into force in September 1992 provided for direct presidential election to a five-year term, with provision for a run-off if no candidate secures a majority in the first round. Legislative authority is vested in a popularly elected national assembly of between 66 and 72 deputies. The assembly's normal term is also five years, although the president may, in certain circumstances, dissolve it. The prime minister continues to be nominated by and responsible to the assembly, although appointed by the president. On the prime minister's recommendation the president appoints the Council of Ministers, whose members must be assembly deputies. The court system features a Supreme Court of Justice, beneath which are courts of first and second resort. There also are administrative courts, courts of accounts, military courts, and tax and customs courts. In July 2004 the government proposed the creation a Constitutional Court, but the PAICV rejected the idea, and no progress was reported as of 2008.

At present there are 17 local government councils, which are popularly elected for five-year terms.

Foreign relations. Cape Verde has established diplomatic relations with some 50 countries, including most members of the European Union (EU), with which it is associated under the Lomé Convention. Formally nonaligned, it rejected a 1980 Soviet overture for the use of naval facilities at the port of São Vicente as a replacement for facilities previously available in Conakry, Guinea. The Pereira government subsequently reaffirmed its opposition to any foreign military accommodation within its jurisdiction. In March 1984 Cape Verde became one of the few non-Communist countries to establish relations with the Heng Samrin government of Cambodia and, following a visit by Yasir Arafat in August 1986, it exchanged ambassadors with the Palestine Liberation Organization.

The country's closest regional links have been with Guinea-Bissau (despite a 20-month rupture following the ouster of the Cabral government in November 1980) and the other three Lusophone African states: Angola, Mozambique, and Sao Tome and Principe. Relations with Bissau were formally reestablished in July 1982 prior to a summit meeting of the five Portuguese-speaking heads of state in Praia held September 21–22, during which a joint committee was set up to promote economic and diplomatic cooperation.

Following the MPD legislative victory in January 1991, the new prime minister, Carlos Veiga, declared that no major foreign policy changes were contemplated, although he moved quickly to strengthen relations with anti-Marxist groups in Guinea-Bissau, Angola, and Mozambique.

In August 1998 international attention focused on Praia as the recently launched Community of Portuguese Speaking Countries (CPLP), under Monteiro's leadership, and the Economic Community of West African States (ECOWAS) forged a cease-fire agreement between the combatants in Guinea-Bissau.

The government established diplomatic and trade relations with China in 2001, while in 2002 it launched a broad initiative to gain preferential trade relations with the EU. Subsequently, a seaborder agreement with Mauritania in December 2003 offered the hope for additional oil and mineral exploitation.

In 2007 the EU approved a "special partnership" agreement with Cape Verde, aimed at strengthening the relationship between the entities. In 2009 Cape Verde announced plans to negotiate its own economic partnership with the EU, abandoning a similar agreement established through ECOWAS. The government's decision was due largely to Cape Verde's preference for access to European markets versus the West African market. Also in 2009, bilateral relations with Cuba were strengthened following a visit to Cape Verde by Vice President José Ramón MACHADO Ventura.

Current issues. The MPD lost control over five key municipalities in local balloting in February 2000. In addition, a degree of discord developed within the MPD in midyear as President Monteiro described the recent privatization of the national fuel company as having lacked transparency, a charge that was sharply rejected by Prime Minister Veiga. The friction intensified later in the year as the result of the controversy surrounding Veiga's relinquishing of his prime ministerial duties (see Political background, above). Also contributing to declining MPD popularity was rising unemployment, linked, in the minds of some voters, to the government's recent structural adjustment efforts and additional promarket emphasis. Consequently, most observers were not surprised by the January 2001 legislative victory by the PAICV, led by José Neves, a symbol of the "new generation" in Cape Verdean political affairs. At the same time, the presidential campaign pitted the warhorses of the two dominant parties against one another in an extremely close poll. The National Electoral Commission initially declared former prime minister Pires the victor in the second round by 17 votes, a margin that was reduced to 12 following Supreme Court rulings on challenges from both sides. Despite contending that the balloting had been marred by fraud, Veiga accepted the final verdict and successfully urged his supporters to remain calm in the face of the exasperating defeat. Among other things, Pires's victory precluded the need for a PAICV/MPD "cohabitation" government, which the PAICV argued would have been a severe hindrance to its economic plans. Despite its center-left orientation, the Neves government presented a development plan in early 2002 calling for intensified cooperation with the private sector, particularly in regard to promoting tourism and otherwise attracting foreign investment, goals that reportedly also influenced a March 1 cabinet expansion.

Drought contributed to famine conditions prior to heavy rains in 2003, while locusts reportedly plagued some 30 percent of the arable land. For its part, the government pledged to promote economic growth by constructing a new international airport, improving roads and other infrastructure, and supporting small businesses. However, it was not clear how much enthusiasm the population retained for the PAICV administration. In 2004 the MPD won control of 9 of 17 municipal councils in local balloting, but that proved to be of little help in maintaining any momentum for the party, as it secured only 29 of 72 seats in the legislative election of January 22, 2006. Further, party leader Veiga again lost to rival Pires in the presidential balloting of February 2006, the Supreme Court having dismissed claims of fraud by Veiga and his MPD supporters.With increasing political stability in the country, attention turned to developing tourism and other efforts to further bolster the economy. On a positive note, Cape Verde became a member of the World Trade Organization (WTO) in December 2007.

An increase in drug trafficking and money laundering in recent years led to parliament's unanimous approval in 2009 of a draft law requiring stricter inspection of offshore banks and more rigorous rules regarding the reporting of suspicious financial activity.

POLITICAL PARTIES

Although a number of parties existed prior to independence, the only party that was recognized for 15 years thereafter was the African Party for the Independence of Guinea-Bissau and Cape Verde (PAIGC). The reference to Guinea-Bissau was dropped and the party restyled the African Party for the Independence of Cape Verde (PAICV), insofar as the islands' branch was concerned, on January 20, 1981, in reaction to the mainland coup of the previous November.

Government Party:

African Party for the Independence of Cape Verde (*Partido Africano da Independência de Cabo Verde*—PAICV). The PAIGV's predecessor, the PAIGC was formed in 1956 by Amílcar Cabral and others to resist Portuguese rule in both Cape Verde and Guinea-Bissau. Initially headquartered in Conakry, Guinea, the PAIGC began military operations in Guinea-Bissau in 1963 and was instrumental in negotiating independence for that country. Following the assassination of Cabral on January 20, 1973, his brother Luís, and Aristides Maria Pereira assumed control of the movement, Luís Cabral serving as president of Guinea-Bissau until being overthrown in the 1980 coup.

In February1990 the National Council endorsed constitutional changes that would permit the introduction of a multiparty system, and in April the council recommended that further reforms be adopted in preparation for legislative and presidential elections. In August Maj. Pedro Pires was elected PAICV secretary general, replacing Pereira, who was defeated for reelection as president of the republic on February 17, 1991, and promptly announced his retirement from politics.

At a party congress on August 29, 1993, Pires was appointed to the newly created post of party president to exercise "moral authority." Aristides Lima, the party's parliamentary leader, was subsequently elected to the vacated general secretary position. Pires won reelection to the PAICV's top post at a party congress in September 1997, staving off a challenge by newcomer José Neves.

Apparently bolstered by his party's success in local balloting in February 2000, Pires announced in March that he was stepping down from his PAICV post to prepare for presidential balloting scheduled for 2001. A June PAICV congress elected Neves to succeed Pires over PAICV vice president Felisberto Viera. In the legislative elections in January 2001, the PAICV won 47 percent of the vote, and Pires secured 46 percent of the votes in the first round of presidential voting in February and was elected in a stunningly close race in the second round with 49.43 percent of the vote. In local elections in March 2004, the PAICV suffered a major defeat by losing control of the council on Sal Island, the country's major tourist destination. In response to the losses, Neves reshuffled the cabinet in April. Pires was reelected in 2006, and the PAICV won a majority of seats in the 2006 assembly elections.

Leaders: Pedro Verona Rodrigues PIRES (President of the Republic), José Maria Pereira NEVES (Prime Minister and President of the Party), Manuel Inocencio SOUSA (Vice President of the Party), Rui SEMEDO (National Secretary), Aristides Raimundo LIMA (Secretary General and Speaker of the National Assembly), António DUARTE, Basílio Mosso RAMOS (Secretary General).

Opposition Parties:

Movement for Democracy (*Movimento para Democracia*—MPD). Then a Lisbon-based opposition grouping, the MPD issued a "manifesto" in early 1990 calling for dismantling of the PAICV regime, thereby prompting the ruling party to schedule multiparty elections. In June the MPD held its first official meeting in Praia, and in September it met with the PAICV to discuss a timetable for the balloting that culminated in MPD legislative and presidential victories of January and February 1991.

The MPD retained legislative control in 1995, although its seat total dropped from 56 to 50. In addition, President António Monteiro, an independent who enjoyed the support of the MPD, was reelected unopposed to a second term as president of the republic in February 1996. However, in the wake of estrangement between Monteiro and the MPD's Carlos Veiga, prime minister from March 1991 to October 2000 (see Political background and Current issues, above, for details), the party secured only 39 percent of the vote in the January 2001 legislative poll, losing control to the PAICV. Meanwhile, Veiga finished second in the first round of presidential balloting in February with 45 percent of the vote before losing an exceedingly close race in the second round. (He finally was credited with only 17 fewer votes than his PAICV opponent.) Following the MPD's gaining control of 9 municipal councils, up from 6, in March 2004,. the elections confirmed the leadership of Agostinho Lopes, who had been subject to increasing dissatisfaction after the 2001 national elections. However, in 2006 the MPD's power showed signs of decline as Veiga again lost a presidential bid and the party won only 29 seats in the legislative election. Jorge Santos was elected party president in late 2006.

Leaders: Jorge SANTOS (President), Agostinho LOPES, Carlos Alberto Wahnon de Carvalho VEIGA (Former Prime Minister, Former Chair of the Party, and 2001 and 2006 presidential candidate), Fernando Elísio FREIRE.

Cape Verdean Independent and Democratic Union (*União Caboverdeana Independente e Democrática*—UCID). The UCID is a right-wing group long active among the 500,000 Cape Verdean emigrants in Portugal and elsewhere. In mid-1990 the UCID, whose local influence appeared to be limited to one or two islands, signed a cooperation agreement with the MPD.

In legislative balloting in December 1995, the UCID received 5 percent of the vote, the third-largest tally, but failed to secure representation. The UCID was one of the components, with the Democratic Convergence Party (PCD) and the Labor and Solidarity Party (PTS), in the Democratic Alliance for Change (*Aliança Democrática para a Mudança*—ADM), which fielded candidates in the 2001 legislative election. (The ADM won 6 percent of the vote and two assembly seats [one each for the PCD and the PTS] in 2001.) There was no reference to the ADM in the 2006 elections; the UCID placed a distant third in legislative balloting with 2.64 percent of the vote. The UCID promised to fight for political ethics in parliament.

Leaders: Antonio Mascarenhas MONTEIRO (President of the Party and Former President of the Republic), Celso CELESTINO.

Other Parties:

Democratic Socialist Party (*Partido Socialista Democrático*—PSD). Launched in 1992, the PSD was legalized on July 14, 1995. The party's platform calls for greater governmental support for development programs and the elimination of "injustices." The PSD secured less than 1 percent of the vote in the 1995, 2001, and 2006 legislative balloting.

Leader: João ALEM.

Democratic Renewal Party (*Partido da Renovação Democrática*—PRD). Established in July 2000, the PRD is an offshoot from the MPD. The party won 3.2 percent of the vote in the 2001 legislative balloting but failed to secure any seats. In 2003 the PRD joined with the PCD in discussions on a new coalition ahead of the 2006 legislative elections. The PRD won less than 1 percent of the vote in balloting on January 22, 2006.

Leader: Simao MONTEIRO.

Democratic Convergence Party (*Partido da Convergência Democrática*—PCD). The PCD was launched in 1994 by Dr. Enrico Correira Monteiro, a dissident MPD legislator, whose reelection to the assembly in 1995 was the group's sole electoral victory. In 2003 the PCD began efforts to create a new electoral coalition with the PRD to oppose the MPD and PAICV ahead of the 2006 legislative elections. There was no reference to the PCD in the 2006 elections, however.

Leader: Dr. Enrico Correira MONTEIRO.

Labor and Solidarity Party (*Partido de Trabalho e da Solidariedade*—PTS). This grouping is a "socialist-oriented" party that was launched by the mayor of São Vicente, Onésimo SILVEIRA, in May 1998. In a confusing series of events following the formation of the ADM, Silveira announced his plans to run for president in 2001 as an independent before withdrawing from the race several days prior to the balloting. (He had previously been listed as the successful ADM/PTS candidate in the January 2001 assembly poll.) In 2006 Silveira was reported to be a member of the PAICV.

LEGISLATURE

The unicameral **National People's Assembly** (*Assembleia Nacional Popular*) became a 79-member bipartisan body in the election of January 14, 1991; in 1995 the membership was reduced to 72. The normal term is five years, although the body is subject to presidential dissolution. Following the most recent balloting on January 22, 2006, the African Party for the Independence of Cape Verde won 41 seats; Movement for Democracy, 29; and Cape Verdean Independent and Democratic Union, 2.

Speaker: Aristides Raimundo LIMA.

CABINET

[as of September 1, 2009]

Prime Minister	José Maria Pereira Neves
Ministers	
Culture	Manuel Monteiro da Veiga
Decentralization, Housing, and Regional Development	Sara Maria Duarte Lopes [f]
Defense and State Reform	Maria Cristina Lopes Almeida Fontes Lima [f]
Economy, Growth, and Competitiveness	Fátima Maria Carvalho Fialho [f]
Education and Higher Education	Vera Valentina Benrós de Melo Duarte Lobo de Pina [f]
Environment, Rural Development and Maritime Resources	José Maria Veiga
Finance and Public Administration	Cristina Duarte [f]
Foreign Affairs, Cooperation, and Communities	José Brito
Internal Administration	Livio Fernandes Lopes
Justice	Marisa Helena do Nascimento Morais [f]
Labor, Family, and Solidarity	Maria Madalena Brito Neves [f]
Presidency of the Ministers' Council and Parliamentary Affairs	Janira Isabel Fonseca Hopffer Almada [f]
Youth and Sports	Sidónio Fontes Lima Monteiro
Secretaries of State	
Economy	Humberto Brito
Education	Octávio Ramos Tavares
Foreign Affairs	Jorge Borges
Public Administration	Romeu Modesto
Ministers of State	
Health	Basilio Ramos
Infrastructure, Transport, and the Sea	Manuel Inocéncio Sousa

[f] = female

COMMUNICATIONS

The Cape Verdean press has been described by the *Financial Times* as "relatively free," though much of the media is state-owned. According to the watchdog group Reporters Without Borders, there have been no obstacles to privately owned media.

Press. The following are published in Praia, unless otherwise noted: *Jornal Horizonte* (Horizon Journal), weekly; *Novo Jornal Cabo Verde* (5,000), government-supported biweekly; *Expresso das Ilhas*, online weekly founded by the MPD; *A Semana* (5,000), PAICV weekly; *Boletim Informativo* (1,500), published weekly by the Ministry of Foreign Affairs; *Boletim Oficial*, government weekly; *Terra Nova*, published monthly by the Catholic Church; *Unidade e Luta*, PAICV organ.

News agency. The domestic facility is Inforpress, the official government news agency, headquartered in Praia; several foreign bureaus also maintain offices in the capital.

Broadcasting and computing. The government-controlled *Radio Nacional de Cabo Verde* broadcasts over two stations located in Praia and Mindelo, and a number of private radio stations reportedly had started by early 2006; *Radio Nova* is a Catholic station in São Vicente; limited television service, launched in 1985 by *Televisão Nacional de Cabo Verde*, transmits from Praia to about 2,000 receivers. As of 2008 there were 206.1 Internet users per 1,000 inhabitants.

INTERGOVERNMENTAL REPRESENTATION

Ambassador to the U.S.: Maria de Fatima LIMA DE VEIGA.

U.S. Ambassador to Cape Verde: Marianne M. MYLES.

Permanent Representative to the UN: Antonio Pedro Monteiro LIMA.

IGO Memberships (Non-UN): AfDB, AU, BADEA, CILSS, CPLP, ECOWAS, Interpol, IOM, NAM, OIF, WCO, WTO.

CENTRAL AFRICAN REPUBLIC

Central African Republic
République Centrafricaine

Political Status: Became independent August 13, 1960; one-party military regime established January 1, 1966; Central African Empire proclaimed December 4, 1976; republic reestablished September 21, 1979; military rule reimposed September 1, 1981; constitution of November 21, 1986, amended on August 30, 1992, to provide for multiparty system; present constitution adopted January 7, 1995, following acceptance in referendum of December 28, 1994; civilian government suspended following military coup on March 15, 2003; new constitution adopted by national referendum on December 5, 2004, providing for a return to civilian government via national elections that were held March–May 2005.

Area: 240,534 sq. mi. (622,984 sq. km.).

Population: 2,463,616 (1988C); 4,171,000 (2007E).

Major Urban Center (2005E): BANGUI (783,000).

Official Language: French. The national language is Sango.

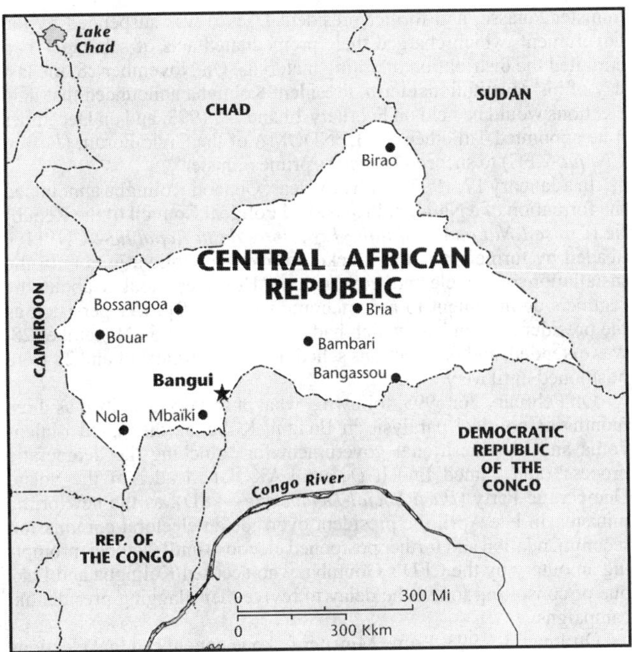

Monetary Unit: CFA Franc (official rate December 1, 2009: 434.59 francs = $1US). The CFA franc, previously pegged to the French franc, is now permanently pegged to the euro at 655.957 CFA francs = 1 euro.

President: Gen. François BOZIZÉ Yangouvonda (nonparty); declared himself president on March 16, 2003, following the overthrow of Ange-Félix PATASSÉ (Central African People's Liberation Movement); popularly elected in two-round balloting on March 13 and May 8, 2005, and inaugurated for a five-year term on June 11.

Prime Minister: Faustin-Archange TOUADERA (nonparty); appointed by the president on January 22, 2008, to succeed Elie DOTÉ (nonparty), who resigned along with his government on January 18, 2008, pending a no-confidence vote against him in parliament; reappointed on January 19, 2009, following the president's dissolution of the government the previous day; named a new government on January 19.

THE COUNTRY

The Central African Republic (CAR) is a landlocked, well-watered plateau country in the heart of Africa. Its inhabitants are of varied ethnic, linguistic, and religious affiliations. In addition to French and many tribal dialects, Sango is used as a lingua franca. A majority of the population is Christian, and there also are sizable animist and Muslim sectors.

About four-fifths of the inhabitants are employed in farming and animal husbandry, primarily at a subsistence level. Leading exports include diamonds, coffee, timber, and cotton. Most of the small industrial sector is engaged in food processing, while uranium resources have been developed with French and Swiss partners. Economic diversification, long impeded by a lack of adequate transportation facilities, was further constrained by the personal aggrandizement in 1976–1979 of self-styled Emperor Bokassa, a virtually empty national treasury at the time of his ouster in September 1979 only partially mitigated by marginal increases in commodity exports in ensuing years. France is the country's main source of imports, chief market for exports, and principal aid donor.

Recent development programs have focused on trade promotion, privatization of state-run operations, encouragement of small- and medium-sized enterprises, civil service reductions, and efforts to combat widespread tax and customs fraud. In the mid-1990s political turmoil significantly diverted attention from economic development; however, following the restoration of stability in the CAR, the republic recorded real GDP growth of 5.1 percent in 1997 and 3 percent in 1998. In July 2000 the International Monetary Fund (IMF) noted that, despite ongoing social and political problems, the government had made progress in restructuring the banking system, although the proposed privatization of the petroleum sector still lagged behind other reforms. Real GDP grew by 3.4 percent in 1999 and 4.1 percent in 2000, although aid agencies reported that two-thirds of the population continued to live in poverty and had little access to health care or basic services such as electricity, running water, or sanitation systems. Financial affairs were further complicated by the arrest of more than 20 government officials in 2002 on charges of embezzling some $3 million in government funds, prompting the IMF and World Bank to temporarily suspend some aid programs. International financial institutions also reacted negatively at first to the coup of March 2003, although aid was resumed in 2004 after the new administration implemented initiatives designed to fight corruption and increase government revenue.

Real GDP averaged only 1.6 percent in 2004-2005. While the IMF commended the country's peaceful transition to an elected government in 2005, it was highly critical of the government's management of public resources and security, citing widespread corruption. However, in early 2006 the IMF's increased confidence in the newly elected government was evidenced by its approval of $10.2 million in emergency assistance to help stabilize the economy. GDP growth increased to 4.1 percent in 2006, the highest in a decade, and at year's end, the republic qualified for $54.5 million in aid over three years under the IMF's poverty reduction program. In addition, the World Bank approved $6.8 million to help the government provide such basic services as water, health care, and education. Annual GDP growth remained at about 4 percent in 2007, and the IMF commended the government for its efforts to enhance the management of public spending and the collection of domestic revenues. Following the progress made in poverty reduction and in peace talks in 2008 (see Current issues, below), full donor aid was restored, allowing the government to pay civil service salary arrears. Recovery in the agriculture sector further bolstered the economy, with annual average GDP of 5 percent forecast for 2009-2010.

GOVERNMENT AND POLITICS

Political background. Formerly known as Ubangi-Shari in French Equatorial Africa, the Central African Republic achieved independence on August 13, 1960, after two years of self-government under Barthélemy BOGANDA, founder of the Social Evolution Movement of Black Africa (*Mouvement de l'Évolution Sociale de l'Afrique Noir*—MESAN), and his nephew David DACKO, the republic's first president. As leader of MESAN, President Dacko rapidly established a political monopoly, dissolving the principal opposition party in December 1960 and banning all others in 1962. Dacko was ousted on January 1, 1966, in a military coup led by Col. Jean-Bédel BOKASSA, who declared himself president. Bokassa abrogated the constitution, dissolved the assembly, assumed power to rule by decree, took over the leadership of MESAN, and became chief of staff and commander in chief of the armed forces.

Following his assumption of power, Bokassa survived a number of coup attempts, often relying on French military intervention. Designated president for life by MESAN in 1972, he assumed the additional office of prime minister in April 1976 but relinquished it to Ange-Félix PATASSÉ the following September, when a new Council of the Central African Revolution (*Conseil de la Révolution Centrafricaine*—CRC) was established. In the context of widespread government and party changes, Bokassa further enhanced his image as one of Africa's most unpredictable leaders by appointing former president Dacko to be his personal adviser.

On October 18, during a state visit by Libyan leader Muammar al-Qadhafi, Bokassa revealed that he had been converted to Islam and would henceforth be known as Salah al-Din Ahmad Bokassa. On December 4 he announced that the republic had been replaced by a parliamentary monarchy and that he had assumed the title of Emperor Bokassa I. On December 7 the emperor abolished the CRC, and the next day he abandoned his Muslim name because of its incompatibility with the imperial designation.

In the wake of a lavish coronation ceremony in Bangui on December 4, 1977, the Bokassa regime became increasingly brutal and corrupt. In mid-1979 Amnesty International reported that scores of schoolchildren had been tortured and killed after protesting against compulsory school uniforms manufactured by the Bokassa family. In August an African judicial commission confirmed the report, the emperor responding with a series of arrests and executions of those who had testified before the commission.

On the night of September 20–21, 1979, while on a visit to Libya, the emperor was deposed, with French military assistance, by former president Dacko. While several prominent members of the Bokassa regime were arrested, the "government of national safety" that was announced on September 24 drew widespread criticism for including a number of individuals who had held high-ranking posts in the previous administration. (Bokassa lived in exile until he returned in 1987 to face trial on charges of murder, torture, and cannibalism. Following conviction on the murder charge he was imprisoned until his sentence was commuted in 1993. Prolonged ill health precluded any subsequent extensive political activity on his part, and Bokassa died in November 1996.)

In a presidential election on March 15, 1981, Dacko was credited with 50.23 percent of the votes cast, as contrasted with 38.11 percent for his closest competitor, former prime minister Patassé. Alleged balloting irregularities triggered widespread violence in the capital prior to Dacko's inauguration and the naming of Simon Narcisse BOZANGA as prime minister on April 4. In mid-July opposition parties were temporarily banned after a bomb explosion at a Bangui theater, and on July 21 the army, led by Gen. André-Dieudonné KOLINGBA, was asked to restore order. On September 1, it was announced that Dacko, known to be in failing health, had resigned in favor of a Military Committee for National Recovery (*Comité Militaire pour le Redressement National*—CMRN), headed by General Kolingba, which suspended the constitution, proscribed political party activity, and issued a stern injunction against public disorder.

Patassé and a number of senior army officers were charged with an attempted coup against the Kolingba regime on March 3, 1982, after which the former prime minister took refuge in the French Embassy in Bangui. He was flown out of the country a month later.

Internal security merged with regional concerns in late 1984 after an opposition group led by Alphonse MBAIKOUA, who had reportedly been involved in the alleged 1982 coup attempt, joined with Chadian *codo* rebels in launching border insurgency operations. The following April the CAR and Chad began a joint counterinsurgency campaign that failed to curb the rebels, most of whom sought temporary refuge in Cameroon.

In keeping with promises to launch a gradual return to civilian rule, Kolingba dissolved the CMRN in September 1985 and placed himself, in the dual role of president and prime minister, at the head of a cabinet numerically dominated by civilians, although military men remained in the most powerful positions. At a referendum on November 21, 1986, a reported 91 percent of the electorate approved a new constitution, under which General Kolingba continued in office for a six-year term. The constitution also designated a Central African Democratic Rally (*Rassemblement Démocratique Centrafricain*—RDC) as the nucleus of a one-party state, General Kolingba having asserted that a multiparty system would invite "division and hatred as well as tribalism and regionalism."

Balloting for a new National Assembly was held in July 1987, although voter turnout was less than 50 percent, apparently because of opposition appeals for a boycott. In May 1988, in what the government described as the final stage of its democratization program, more than 3,000 candidates, all nominated by the RDC, contested 1,085 local elective offices.

On March 15, 1991, General Kolingba divested himself of the prime ministerial office, transferring its functions to his presidential coordinator, Edouard FRANCK. In late April, pressured by international aid donors and encountering increased social unrest, Kolingba abandoned his opposition to pluralism. On May 18 the regime offered to accelerate political reform in exchange for an end to civil strife, and on June 7 a national commission was established to revise the constitution and prepare for the introduction of multipartyism. In July the government announced that political parties were free to apply for legal status. Subsequently, a broad-based committee was named to prepare for the convening of a national conference on February 19, 1992. However, during an early 1992 visit to the United States, President Kolingba referred to the projected talks as a "great national debate" that "cannot be a sovereign national conference."

Because of its lack of plenary power, the conference that convened on August 1, 1992, was boycotted by most opposition groups and was accompanied by street demonstrations and antigovernment strikes. On August 30 the National Assembly adopted a number of conference recommendations, including party registration guidelines, and on September 7 Kolingba announced plans for presidential and legislative elections on October 25. Polling (with Kolingba apparently running next-to-last behind Dr. Abel GOUMBA Guéne of the Concertation of Democratic Forces [*Concertation des Forces Démocratiques*—CFD], former prime minister Patassé, and former president Dacko) was suspended by the government, which charged that "premeditated acts of sabotage" had curtailed the distribution of voting materials. On November 28, the last day of his constitutional term, President Kolingba announced that new elections would be held on February 14 and 28, 1993, and on December 4 he appointed Timothée MALENDOMA of the Civic Forum (*Forum Civique*—FC) to succeed Franck as prime minister.

In a January 17, 1993, radio broadcast General Kolingba announced the formation of a National Provisional Political Council of the Republic (*Conseil National Politique Provisoire de la République*—CNPPR), headed by former president Dacko, to oversee public affairs until the installation of an elected government. However, doubts about the regime's commitment to a democratic transfer of power persisted as the president's mandate, which had officially ended on November 28, was extended, and the elections scheduled for February 14 and 28 were postponed until May.

On February 26, 1993, following what observers described as three months of political paralysis in Bangui, Kolingba dismissed Malendoma and his transitional government for "blocking the democratic process" and named Enoch Dérant LAKOUÉ, leader of the Social Democratic Party (*Parti Social-Démocrate*—PSD), as the new prime minister. In late April the president overrode an electoral commission recommendation and further postponed elections until October, prompting an outcry by the CFD's Goumba, who accused Kolingba and Lakoué of conspiring to use the delay to revive their flagging presidential campaigns.

On June 11, 1993, Prime Minister Lakoué announced that elections would be brought forward to August. The policy reversal came only six days after the French minister of cooperation, Michel Roussin, reportedly told Kolingba that continued aid was directly linked to the speed of reform. At the August 22 poll eight candidates, including Africa's first female contender, Ruth ROLLAND, vied for the presidency, while 496 candidates contested 85 legislative seats. Although the election was conducted in the presence of international observers, Kolingba, faced with unofficial tallies showing that he had finished in fourth place, attempted to halt release of the official results; however, he was obliged to reverse himself upon domestic and international condemnation of what Goumba described as the "last convulsion of his regime."

In second-round presidential balloting on September 19, first-round plurality winner Patassé defeated Goumba 53.49 to 46.51 percent. In concurrent rounds of legislative balloting, Patassé's Central African People's Liberation Movement (*Mouvement de Libération du Peuple Centrafricaine*—MLPC) won 34 seats, followed by the CFD, whose members collectively won 17. Meanwhile, on September 1 Kolingba had released thousands of convicted criminals, the most prominent of whom was former emperor Bokassa.

On October 25, 1993, Patassé named an MLPC colleague, Jean-Luc MANDABA, as prime minister. Five days later Mandaba announced the formation of a coalition government that drew from the MLPC, the Liberal Democratic Party (*Parti Liberal-Démocratic*—PLD), the CFD-affiliated Alliance for Democracy and Progress (*Alliance pour la Démocratic et le Progrès*—ADP), supporters of former president Dacko, and members of the outgoing Kolingba administration.

Prime Minister Mandaba was forced to resign on April 11, 1995, upon the filing of a nonconfidence motion signed by a majority of National Assembly members, who charged him with corruption, maladministration, and a lack of communication between the executive and legislative branches. President Patassé promptly named as his successor Gabriel KOYAMBOUNOU, a senior civil servant who announced that combating financial irregularities would be one of his principal objectives.

In early April 1996 a newly formed opposition umbrella group, the Democratic Council of the Opposition Parties (*Conseil Démocratique des Partis de l'Opposition*—CODEPO), organized an anti-Patassé rally in Bangui. An even more serious challenge developed on April 18 when several hundred soldiers, angered over payment arrears, left their barracks in the Kasai suburb of Bangui and took control of important locations in the capital. The rebels went back to their barracks several days later, after French troops were deployed in support of the government, but they returned to the streets on May 18. The rebellion finally ended on May 26 after French forces, supported by helicopter gunships, engaged the mutinous soldiers in fierce street battles. Patassé, describing the nation as "shattered" by the near civil war, replaced Koyambounu on June 6 with Jean-Paul NGOUPANDÉ, a former ambassador to France. Thereafter, in a further attempt to stabilize the political situation, Patassé's MLPC and the major opposition parties signed a pact under which, among other things, the authority of the prime minister was to be extended so as to dilute presidential control. Moreover, on June 19 Ngoupande announced the formation of what was optimistically described as a "government of national unity."

On November 16, 1996, another mutiny erupted in Kasai, and by early December the rebellious soldiers, who were demanding the president's resignation, were reportedly in control of several sections of the capital. In late December, amid reports that over a third of the city's population had fled as the fighting took on a "tribal character," the government and rebels appeared to agree to a cease-fire; however, it was subsequently reported that Capt. Anicet SAULET, the leader of the mutineers, had been detained by his own forces for having signed the accord. In early January 1997 French and government troops forced the rebels from a number of their strongholds in an offensive sparked by the assassination of two French troops on January 4.

On January 25, 1997, in Bangui, Patassé and Saulet signed a peace accord that had been brokered by a group comprising representatives of Burkina Faso, Chad, Gabon, and Mali. The agreement included provisions for a general amnesty for the mutinous soldiers, the reintegration of the rebels into their old units, and the deployment of a regional peacekeeping force styled the Inter-African Mission to Monitor the Bangui Accords (*Mission Internationale du Suivi des Accords de Bangui*—MISAB). On January 30 Patassé appointed Foreign Minister Michel GBEZERA-BRIA to replace Prime Minister Ngoupandé, and on February 18 a new 28-member cabinet, the Government of Action for the Defense of Democracy (*Gouvernement pour l'Action et la Défense de la Démocratie*—GADD), was installed. Although the MLPC retained all the key posts, the GADD included representatives from ten parties, including nine members from four "opposition" groups. On March 15 the National Assembly voted to extend amnesty to those remaining rebels who agreed to be disarmed by the peacekeepers within 15 days; however, clashes broke out later in the month when a number of the rebels resisted the peacekeeping forces.

On May 5, 1997, the nine opposition cabinet ministers announced the "suspension" of their postings and called for nationwide strikes to protest the deaths two days earlier of three alleged mutinous soldiers being held in police custody. Amid mounting tension, on May 20 the rebels' two cabinet representatives (they had been appointed in April as part of the Bangui agreement) also quit the government. Subsequently, more than 100 people, primarily civilians, were killed in Bangui and the Kasai camp during clashes between rebel and government troops, the latter again supported by French troops, before another cease-fire was signed on July 2.

MISAB, which had the endorsement of the UN Security Council, began disarming the army mutineers in mid-July, and in late August the government released the last of more than 110 detainees connected to the "revolt." Consequently, the nine cabinet members who had walked out in May formally rejoined the government of September 1. Tension continued at a somewhat reduced level into 1998, prompting the convening of a national conference in late February. On March 3 the conference's participants, including the opposition parties coalesced under the banner of the influential Group of 11 (G-11), signed a reconciliation pact aimed at improving interparty relations and reducing the lawlessness gripping the country.

A new UN peacekeeping force took over MISAB and French responsibilities on April 15, 1998, with a mandate that included assisting in preparations for legislative elections. In early August the polling was postponed amid opposition criticism of the government's organization of the balloting, and in October the UN force's mandate was extended as the peacekeepers began preparations for the elections that had been rescheduled for November/December.

Approximately 30 parties forwarded candidates for the 109 seats (enlarged from 85) available at first-round legislative balloting on November 22, 1998, the MLPC emerging with a small lead after that round. However, opposition groups signed an electoral pact under the banner of the Union of Forces Supporting Peace and Change (*Union des Forces Acquises à la Paix et au Changement*—UFAPC), whereby they agreed to back the leading opposition candidates in the undecided contests. As a result, following second-round balloting on December 13, the UFAPC-affiliated parties controlled 55 seats (led by the RDC with 20) and the MLPC 47. However, the small PLD (2 seats) and five independents subsequently confirmed their allegiance to the MLPC, and Patassé supporters were ultimately able to gain legislative control when, under highly controversial circumstances, a legislator-elect from the PSD defected to the MLPC. (The opposition charged the MLPC with "hijacking" the results of the election through bribery but lost its legal challenge when the Constitutional Court ruled that legislators represented their electorates and not their parties, thereby deeming the defection to have been legal.) Most opposition legislators boycotted the convening of the new assembly in early January 1999, and ten opposition cabinet members resigned from the government in protest against the MLPC's actions. On January 4 Patassé named Finance and Budget Minister Anicet Georges DOLOGUÉLÉ to replace Gbezera-Bria as prime minister. However, the UFAPC rejected Patassé's authority in the matter, arguing that it should have control over the appointment as holder of the true legislative majority.

On January 15, 1999, Prime Minister Dologuélé announced a new cabinet comprising eight ministers from the MLPC, four from the PLD, four from the opposition Movement for Democracy and Development (*Mouvement pour la Démocratie et la Développement*—MDD), one from the MLPC-allied National Convention (*Convention National*—CN), and eight independents. However, three of the MDD members resigned several days later, party leaders reiterating their support for the UFAPC.

The opposition ended its assembly boycott in early March 1999, apparently in part due to the government's agreement to let UFAPC members sit on a new election commission charged with overseeing the upcoming presidential poll. On September 19, Patassé secured another six-year term by winning 51.6 percent of the vote in the first-round balloting, defeating nine other candidates, including Kolingba, Dacko, and Goumba. Dologuélé was subsequently reappointed to head another MLPC-led government, the UFAPC having declined overtures to join the cabinet. In January 2000 the administration issued several decrees designed to restructure the armed forces so as to reduce the likelihood of a repeat of the 1996–1997 mutinies. Among other things, the size and authority of the powerful presidential guard were to be reduced. Subsequently, the UN peacekeepers formally withdrew on February 15, while Paris announced an increase in aid to Bangui for military training. The Patassé/Dologuélé administration announced that its new top priority was to attract international economic assistance. However, the image-building campaign stalled in April when a series of scandals involving alleged money-laundering and other corrupt practices precipitated a cabinet reshuffle amid opposition complaints that economic reforms contained in the 1997 peace accord were being ignored.

Because of increasing economic difficulties, the government was unable to pay the salaries of state employees and military personnel for most of 2000. The government's handling of the situation cost Dologuélé his post, as he was replaced by the president in April 2001 by the MLPC's Martin Ziguélé. On April 6 Ziguélé announced a new cabinet that included the MLPC, the PLD, the CN, the African Development Party (*Parti Africain du Développement*—PAD), the Democratic Union for Renewal/Fini Kodro (*Union Démocratique pour le Renouveau/Fini Kodro*—UDR/FK), one independent, and others.

In May 2001 the government managed to suppress a coup attempt reportedly masterminded by the former president and de facto leader of the RDC, André-Dieudonné Kolingba, who nevertheless remained at large. (It was subsequently reported that Kolingba had traveled to Uganda and then, in September 2002, to France. By that time he had been sentenced in absentia to death for his role in the coup attempt. Sentences in absentia also were handed down against more than 500 other participants.) Human rights activists voiced concern over the alleged acts of retaliation against Kolingba's Yakoma ethnic group. Reportedly, more than 200 people were killed and 50,000 displaced in the fighting following the coup attempt. Some cabinet members, as well as Gen. François BOZIZÉ, the chief of staff and close associate of Patassé, were also implicated in the conspiracy. Following a reshuffle in August that replaced those ministers allegedly supportive of the coup, Patassé dismissed Bozizé in late October. Government troops subsequently fought Bozizé loyalists who offered armed resistance to an effort to arrest the general. After Bozizé fled to Chad in November, the situation got increasingly "internationalized" (see Foreign relations, below), as many neighboring countries worked to arrange negotiations among Patassé, Kolingba, and Bozizé. In what some saw as a possible sign of compromise, the Central African Republic's courts dropped legal proceedings against Bozizé in December. However, sporadic skirmishes broke out along the Chadian border in the first half of 2002, the CAR government accusing Chad of supporting rebellious CAR soldiers. The Organization of African Unity (OAU, subsequently the African Union—AU), called upon the UN to send peacekeepers to the CAR, but no such action ensued. Among other things, Western capitals objected to the continued presence in the CAR of Libyan troops and tanks, which had rushed to Patassé's aid in May 2001. For his part,

Bozizé in September 2002 announced his intentions of ousting Patassé by force.

In October 2002 government forces supported by Libyan troops turned back pro-Bozizé rebels who were advancing on Bangui. However, after the Libyan troops withdrew in January 2003 in favor of a 350-member peacekeeping force from the Central African Economic and Monetary Community (*Communauté Économique et Monétaire de l'Afrique Centrale*—CEMAC), Bozizé's forces entered Bangui on March 15 while Patassé was out of the country on a diplomatic mission. The following day Bozizé declared himself president, suspended the constitution, and disbanded the National Assembly. On March 23 Bozizé appointed what was termed a government of national unity (comprising five major parties) under the leadership of Abel Goumba of the Patriotic Front for Progress. At the end of May, Bozizé established a 98-member National Transitional Council (*Conseil National de Transition*—CNT) to oversee the planned return to civilian government under a revised constitution within 18–30 months. Goumba was dismissed in favor of Célestin-Leroy GAOMBALET on December 12.

The revised constitution was approved by a reported 90.4 percent of voters in a national referendum on December 5, 2004. In accordance with the provisions of the new constitution, the first parliamentary and presidential elections were held in two rounds of balloting on March 13 and May 8, 2005. Bozizé lacked a majority with 43 percent of the vote in the first round, with MLPC leader Ziguélé receiving 24 percent, and the RDC-backed Kolingba, 16 percent. In the two-way runoff, Bozizé, with the support of some of the other presidential candidates who had received only a small percentage of votes, defeated Ziguélé with 64.6 percent of the vote. Ziguélé called for the election to be invalidated, claiming soldiers intimidated voters, but the constitutional court dismissed the allegations as unfounded. Meanwhile, a coalition of business groups and small political parties that had formed under the name National Convergence (*Kwa na Kwa*—KNK) to support Bozizé won 42 legislative seats, while the former ruling party (the MLPC) won only 11 seats, and independents won 34.

A new government, composed largely of members of the KNK, was sworn in on June 19. The cabinet reshuffle on January 31, 2006, included a number of other groups in addition to the dominant KNK. The cabinet was reshuffled again on September 2.

On January 18, 2008, Prime Minister Elie Doté and his government resigned as parliament was considering a no-confidence vote against Doté in the wake of a weeks-long civil service strike. On January 22 the president appointed Faustin-Archange TOUADERA, a math professor, as prime minister. Touadera named a new cabinet on January 28 that included five women and President Bozizé as defense minister.

Following national reconciliation talks that began in early 2008, parliament in October approved an amnesty, paving the way for a final round of peace talks. The talks culminated in a peace accord negotiated December 8-20, 2008, among the government, former president Patassé, political parties, rebel and opposition groups, and civil societies. Subsequently, President Bozizé dissolved the Touadera government on January 18, 2009, and the following day he reappointed the prime minister and named a new "consensus" government that included one representative from each of the two main rebel groups—the Popular Army for the Restoration of the Republic and Democracy (*Armée Populaire pour la Restauration de la Republique et la Démocratie*—APRD) and the Union of Democratic Forces for the Rally (*Union des Forces Démocratique pour le Rassemblement*—UFDR)—and at least five political parties.

Constitution and government. The imperial constitution of December 1976 was abrogated upon Bokassa's ouster, the country reverting to republican status. A successor constitution, approved by referendum on February 1, 1981, provided for a multiparty system and a directly elected president with authority to nominate the prime minister and cabinet. The new basic law was itself suspended on September 1, 1981, both executive and legislative functions being assumed by a Military Committee for National Recovery, which was dissolved on September 21, 1985. The constitution approved in November 1986 was a revised version of the 1981 document, one of the most important modifications being confirmation of the RDC as the country's sole political party. The 1986 basic law also provided for a congress consisting of an elected National Assembly and a nominated Economic and Regional Council.

In June 1991 General Kolingba appointed a national commission to draft constitutional amendments providing for political pluralism, and in July the government announced that parties could apply for legal status. Other amendments approved at the "grand national debate" of August 1992 included creation of a semipresidential regime with executive authority vested in a prime minister and stricter separation of executive, legislative, and judicial powers. The basic law that was ratified in a referendum in December 1994 retained those provisions while expanding the permissible mandate of the head of state to two six-year terms and specifying that the prime minister will implement policies proposed by the president, who is to "embody and symbolize national unity." In addition, the new charter (formally adopted on January 14, 1995) expanded the judicial system by adding a Constitutional Court to the existing Supreme Court and High Court of Justice and provided for an eventual substantial devolution of state power to directly elected regional assemblies.

The constitution was suspended following the coup of March 2003, although the 1995 basic law served as a model in many areas for the new constitution that was approved by national referendum on December 5, 2004, and entered into effect on December 27. The new constitution reduced the presidential term from six to five years (renewable once), while the prime minister (to be appointed by a majority within the new 105-member National Assembly) was given expanded powers.

Foreign relations. As a member of the French Community, the country has retained close ties with France throughout its changes of name and regime. A defense pact between the two states permits French intervention in times of "invasion" or outbreaks of "anarchy," and French troops, in the context of what was termed "Operation Barracuda," were prominently involved in the ouster of Bokassa. By contrast, in what appeared to be a deliberate policy shift by the Mitterrand government, some 1,100 French troops remained in their barracks during General Kolingba's assumption of power and, despite debate over alleged French involvement in the Patassé coup attempt, the French head of state declared his support for the regime in October 1982. French troops remained permanently stationed at the Bouar military base and were instrumental in propping up the Patassé administration during the army revolt of April–May 1996.

The civil war in neighboring Chad long preoccupied the CAR leadership, partly because of the influx of refugees into the country's northern region. In addition, trepidation about foreign intrusion not only from Chad but also from throughout Central Africa prompted the CAR in 1980 to sever diplomatic ties with Libya and the Soviet Union, both of which had been accused of fomenting internal unrest. Relations with the former, although subsequently restored, remained tenuous, with two Libyan diplomats declared *persona non grata* in April 1986. Formal ties were reestablished with the Soviet Union in 1988 and with Israel in January 1989. In July 1991 China severed diplomatic relations with the CAR after the Kolingba regime reestablished links with Taiwan.

In the run-up to the August 1993 balloting, Abel Goumba emerged as France's "consensus candidate" while his primary competitor, Ange-Felix Patassé, was reportedly viewed with trepidation by Paris because of commercial links to Washington and other Western capitals. On August 28 Paris condemned Kolingba's efforts to stall the release of election results, suspended all aid payments, and stated that French troops and materials were no longer at the president's disposal.

Tension with the CAR's "new" neighbor, the Democratic Republic of the Congo (DRC), developed in 1997, and in February 1998 fighting was reported along their shared border. However, in May the two signed a defense pact, and thereafter CAR troops were reported to be assisting the forces of DRC President Kabila. The CAR was subsequently described as trying to maintain a neutral position in regard to the intertwined conflicts that produced what one reporter called a "ring of fire" in the region into mid-2000.

Relations between the CAR and the DRC soured, with the increasingly close ties between President Patassé and the DRC rebels, most prominently the forces loyal to Jean-Pierre Bemba (see article on the DRC). Patassé employed Bemba's troops and Libyan military detachments to suppress the coup attempt in May 2001. The CAR's relations with Chad also became strained in late 2001 after Gen. François Bozizé, who was accused by Patassé of having been involved with the coup attempt, fled to Chad in November. In December Patassé and Chadian president Idriss Déby met in Libreville, Gabon, for talks under the auspices of CEMAC, which deployed an ultimately ineffective peacekeeping force to the CAR after Bozizé's successful coup in 2003. In the years following the coup, the peacekeeping forces spread out beyond the capital to the troubled northern and eastern regions as violence increased. In early 2006, CAR leaders met with the leaders of six other African countries in their continuing efforts to defuse the escalating tensions at the border of Chad and Sudan. For its part, the CAR extended its relations with Sudan by signing an agreement with the latter and the United Nations High Commissioner for Refugees (UNHCR) providing for the return of the first group of 10,000 Sudanese refugees who had lived in the CAR for 16 years. Tensions reignited in 2006 when the CAR dismissed its ambassador in Sudan over alleged ongoing contact with Patassé, and government officials accused Patassé loyalists of training rebels in Sudan. (For more developments in the region, see Current issues, below.)

In 2007 the government signed economic cooperation agreements with Egypt and China to assist in developing the republic's oil and mineral resources.

Adding to the CAR's cross-border conflicts, in 2008 the Lord's Resistance Army (LRA), a Ugandan rebel group, targeted villages in southeast CAR, abducting civilians and looting. In response to the attacks, the government sent troops to its border with the Republic of the Congo in January 2009.

Current issues. The March 2003 coup was initially condemned by regional powers and the broader international community. However, General Bozizé quickly muted much of the criticism by pledging a quick return to civilian government and initiating a campaign to combat the corruption that had been widely perceived as systemic in the Patassé administration. Moreover, mass demonstrations in Bangui appeared to support the coup leaders, and most political parties (including Patassé's MLPC) soon expressed a desire to look to the future rather than dwell on the events leading to the takeover. Also well received were the appointments of leaders from a broad spectrum of political and civic groups to the transitional national government led by "opposition" leader Abel Goumba as well as to the CNT. The new government won additional domestic support when it paid public salaries for the first time in two years and launched a series of economic reforms. Those measures prompted a quick resumption of aid from France and the EU, assisted by Bozizé's generally pro-Western policies and rhetoric.

In June 2003 the government launched a program to disarm and demobilize 5,700 fighters, including soldiers loyal to either Bozizé or Patassé. In early 2004 the government reached a compromise with former rebels who had been blamed for numerous clashes with troops in the capital. The Chadian government provided mediators for the talks with the rebels, many of whom were former Chadians who helped bring Bozizé to power.

The December 2004 constitutional referendum appeared to put a final plan in place for the return to civilian government. However, a sour note was struck, in the opinion of many observers, by Bozizé's subsequent announcement that he would be a candidate for president. (After seizing power in 2003 the general insisted he had no political ambitions and would not seek elected office.) National elections were held successfully in March and May 2005 with high voter turnout. Despite hopes for peace following the elections, violence escalated in the northern regions, forcing thousands to flee to Chad in early 2006. The government for years had attributed the violence to local bandits, but in March Bozizé for the first time blamed rebels linked to Patassé. The attacks escalated at year's end between rebel fighters and government troops backed by French forces. Rebel groups took control of three northern towns in November, and fighting continued into early 2007, ultimately forcing nearly all the inhabitants of at least one northern town to flee.

Reconciliation was achieved on February 2, 2007, when the Patassé-backed rebels and the government signed an agreement mediated by Libya to end the fighting and to permit the rebels to join government security forces (see Rebel Groups, under Political Parties and Groups, below). The accord provided the first step toward ensuring that peacekeeping troops would be sent to the region, the UN Security Council having postponed a deployment to the CAR's border with Chad and Sudan until reconciliation occurred. In February it was reported that the leaders of the CAR, Chad, and Sudan met at a summit and repeated a previous pledge not to back rebels that were attacking each other's territory. Meanwhile, the United Nations Children's Fund (UNICEF) reported that the CAR was facing a "mounting humanitarian disaster" as a result of the border conflicts. In late 2007 the UN decided to employ an EU peacekeeping force in Chad and the CAR.

A protracted strike by civil service workers that began in January 2008 was the backdrop for upheaval in the government, as parliament convened to consider a vote of no confidence against Prime Minister Doté. The strike, precipitated by six months of payment arrears, crippled government administration and prompted the closure of public schools as students protested against both the civil service workers and the government. After Doté's exit several weeks into the strike, President Bozizé named another independent prime minister, 51-year-old Faustin-Archange Touadera, who subsequently named a new cabinet, replacing most of the ministers of the former government who had resigned along with Doté. As public discontent continued, the president began negotiations with the unions in February. Meanwhile, an announcement was made that the EU's joint military force, EUFOR, would be deployed in Chad and the Central African Republic to protect Sudanese refugees and other internally displaced people in the region. Also in February, the CAR reopened its borders with the DRC and Sudan. Ultimately, four rebel groups—the APRD, UFDR, the Democratic Front of the Central African People (*Front Démocratique du Peuple Centrafricaine*—FDPC), and the Movement of Central African Liberators for Justice (*Mouvement des Libérateurs Centrafricains pour la Justice*—MLJC)—agreed to peace overtures by the government, paving the way for an inclusive national dialogue. However, the process was threatened months later when three of the groups balked at the provisions of an amnesty bill being debated in the National Assembly and withdrew from the peace process. Subsequently, rebels and government troops clashed in several northern towns, the rebels' weapons reported to have been supplied by Libya. At the end of September parliament passed a law granting amnesty affecting actions of both the government and rebels dating from the overthrow of Patassé in March 2003 to the date the law was promulgated, October 13, 2008. It also called for an immediate cease-fire and the disarming of all groups involved, and it specifically granted amnesty to Patassé and the leaders of the APRD and FDPC. Excluded from the law were acts of genocide, crimes against humanity, and other war crimes, which prompted criticism by rebel groups who wanted a more general amnesty. Meanwhile, violence continued in the north, albeit sporadically, resulting in the death of 12 government soldiers. Nevertheless, the government pressed on with the peace process, which culminated in talks in Gabon facilitated by the former president of Burundi, Pierre Buyoya, and for which former president Patassé returned after five years in exile in Togo. The 12-day inclusive peace talks in December produced Patassé's stunning declaration that he would recognize Bozizé, the man who had ousted him from power, as well as producing a formal peace agreement and plans for a unity government, municipal elections in 2009, and presidential and legislative elections in 2010.

In January 2009, following the reappointment of Touadera as prime minister, a new unity government included one member each from the APRD and the UFDR, as well as members of several other parties retained from the previous government. Whether the former rebel groups were legalized as political parties remained unclear. It had been reported that the UFDR was granted political party status under a 2007 accord with the government and that the APRD had established a political wing, styled the New Alliance for Progress (*Nouvelle Alliance Pour le Progrès*—NAP), but the groups continued to be referenced as rebel organizations. Meanwhile, some cracks in the unity structure began to appear, as in early 2009 the FDPC and the MLJC threatened to again take up arms, claiming that the government had failed to adhere to the terms of the December accord, and clashes between new rebel groups and government forces intensified from January to March. Further, an association of army officers in March called for Bozizé's ouster. The new government, for its part, followed through with its efforts toward peace and stability as outlined in the accord by establishing a committee to oversee disarmament, demobilization, and reintegration. Meanwhile, the UN approved deployment of 5,000 peacekeepers to replace EU troops in the northern CAR-Chad border area.

POLITICAL PARTIES AND GROUPS

The 1980 constitution called for the establishment of a multiparty system, but General Kolingba banned political parties in the wake of the 1981 coup and did not include their legalization in his promise of future civilian rule since to do so would invite "weakening and paralysis of the state and make it prey to individualistic demands." In late 1983 the three main opposition parties (FPP, MLPC, and MCLN, below) formed a coalition styled the Central African Revolutionary Party (*Parti Révolutionnaire Centrafricain*—PRC), which the RPRC (see below, under Central African Movement for National Liberation) subsequently joined. In 1986 the FPP and MLPC also formed a United Front (*Front Uni*) that sought restoration of the 1981 constitution. No opposition grouping was accorded legal status upon formation of the regime-supportive RDC in 1986.

In September 1990 the government arrested 25 members of the opposition Coordination Committee for the Convocation of a National Conference (*Comité de Coordination pour la Convocation de la Conférence Nationale*—CCCCN), including its chair, Aristedes SOKAMBI. In late October, during an extraordinary congress in Berberati, the RDC voted against the introduction of a multiparty system. However, in April 1991 President Kolingba reversed the Berberati decision, declaring that "Henceforth, all kinds of thought . . . can be expressed freely within the framework of parties of their choice." Three months later the regime officially overturned its ban on political party formations. Subsequently, a number of somewhat shifting opposition coalitions emerged.

Following the formation of an MLPC-led "unity" government in June 1996, 11 opposition parties, most of whom were theretofore aligned under the banner of the Democratic Council of the Opposition Parties (*Conseil Démocratique des Partis de l'Opposition*—CODEPO), formed the **Group of Eleven** (G-11), under the leadership of former CODEPO president Dr. Abel GOUMBA Guéne. Four G-11 members (the ADP, FPP, PSD, and RDC) were awarded a total of nine cabinet posts in February 1997. On May 5, 1997, the G-11 cabinet members announced that they had "suspended" their participation in the government and called for national strikes to protest the death three days earlier of three alleged rebel soldiers. However, they returned to their portfolios in September.

Throughout most of 1998 the G-11 coordinated the activities of the main opposition groups; however, during the run-up to legislative balloting the G-11 appeared to have been superseded by the **Union of Forces Committed to Peace and Change** (*Union des Forces Acquises Ã la Paix et au Changement*—UFAPC), which comprised a number of parties (including the RDC, PSD, FPP, MDD, FODEM, and FC), labor unions, and human rights organizations. (See Political background, above, for details regarding the UFAPC and the legislative balloting and subsequent cabinet formation.) The UFAPC, also routinely referenced as the UFAP, proved unable to coalesce behind a single candidate for the first round of presidential balloting in September 1999, although an accord was reported if a second round had been required. Despite apparent objections from some components, the UFAPC rejected overtures from President Patassé to join the new cabinet in early November, and the grouping was subsequently described as in disarray following the withdrawal of the PSD and FPP and was reduced to limited membership as of late 1999.

Following the March 2003 coup, a government of national unity was formed with members from the FPP, RDC, FODEM, PSD, MDD, and the PUN. The MLPC and the MDI-PS were subsequently added to the cabinet.

After General Bozizé in 2004 announced his intention to seek the presidency in 2005, a coalition called the National Convergence (see below) was formed to support his candidacy, although Bozizé ran as an independent. A coalition of groups opposed to Bozizé, styled the Union of the Active Forces of the Nation (*Union des Forces d'Active de la Nation*—UFVN), was unsuccessful in its bid to have the 2005 legislative elections declared invalid due to alleged fraud. Coordinated by Henri POUZÈRE, the UFVN was said to include under its umbrella the APRD, FDPC, MLPC, RDC, and UFDR.

Government Parties:

National Convergence (*Kwa na Kwa*—KNK). This coalition of business groups and small political parties was formed in 2004 to support Gen. François Bozizé's presidential bid in 2005. The KNK also entered candidates in the 2005 legislative balloting and secured by far the most seats (42). The KNK retained positions in the new unity government named in 2009.

Leader: Jean-Eudes TÉYA.

Central African Democratic Rally (*Rassemblement Démocratique Centrafricain*—RDC). The RDC was launched in May 1986 as the country's sole legal party, General Kolingba declaring that the formation would represent "all the various tendencies of the whole nation" but would deny representation to those who "seek to impose a totalitarian doctrine." At an extraordinary party congress on August 17, 1991, one month after the official endorsement of multipartyism, President Kolingba resigned as party president, saying he wanted to operate "above politics." Kolingba nonetheless ran as the RDC's 1993 presidential candidate, failing to make the second-round ballot because of a fourth-place finish on the first.

In mid-1995 party militants organized antigovernment demonstrations to protest the imprisonment of party leader and *Le Rassemblement* editor Mathias Gonevo Reapogo, who had been convicted of publishing an "insulting" article about President Patassé. Furthermore, the RDC leadership denounced the administration for its "policy of exclusion as well as arbitrary arrests." However, following the aborted army mutiny of April–May 1996, the RDC (unlike most other opposition groupings) signed the national unity agreement and was given four ministries in the government announced on June 19. The RDC cabinet members resigned in early 1999. (The RDC, whose strongest support comes from the south, finished second in the 1998 legislative poll with 20 seats. Kolingba also finished second in the 1999 presidential balloting with 19.4 percent of the vote.) The party remained part of the UFAPC (see above) as of late 1999. The RDC and Kolingba were reportedly involved with the failed coup attempt in May 2001. Subsequently, numerous party officials and members were arrested, although Kolingba remained at large. The RDC's activities were suspended for three months in June, with the government threatening to shut down the party permanently in late 2001. In late 2004, however, Kolingba announced his intention to return to the CAR and run for the presidency in 2005. He received 16.36 percent of the vote, while his party won 8 assembly seats. Days after the balloting, Kolingba's camp claimed that a shooting incident outside his residence between his guards and soldiers had been an assassination attempt, but the government dismissed the matter as "confusion" in communications between the two sides. Subsequently, one of Kolingba's sons was named to the new cabinet announced in early 2006.

In 2009 the RPC was reported to be among several parties in the grouping known as the UFVN (see Political Parties and Groups, above) that opposed the reappointment of Prime Minister Touadera. Meanwhile, Kolingba was named to serve on a committee, along with President Bozizé, to implement provisions of the 2008 peace accords.

Leaders: André-Dieudonné KOLINGBA (Former President of the Republic, de facto Leader of the Party, and 2005 presidential candidate), Louis-Pierre GAMBA (Deputy President), Honoré NZASSIWE, Mathias Gonevo REAPOGO (imprisoned), Daniel LAGANDI (Secretary General).

Movement for Democracy and Development (*Mouvement pour la Démocratie et le Développement*—MDD). The MDD was launched in January 1994 by former president David Dacko. MDD members were given four posts in the Dologuélé cabinet announced on January 15, 1999. However, party leaders, denying any interest in participating in an MLPC-led government, pressured three of the appointees to quit several days later. (The fourth member, who remained in government reportedly against the wishes of the grass roots, was not reappointed in the new cabinet formed in April 2001.) Dacko, who had won 20 percent of the presidential vote in 1993, finished third with 11.2 percent in 1999, his strength being the greatest in the capital region in the South. Dacko died in 2003.

There was no reference to the MDD in the 2005 election, although leader Auguste Boukanga reportedly ran as a presidential candidate under the banner of the Union for Renewal and Development (see below). In the new government installed in 2009, the MDD retained one cabinet position.

Leaders: Auguste BOUKANGA, Ambroise ZAWA.

National Unity Party (*Parti de l'Unité Nationale*—PUN). Led by former prime minister Jean-Paul Ngoupandé, the PUN won three seats in the late 1998 legislative balloting. Following the 1999 presidential balloting, in which Ngoupandé won 3.1 percent of the vote, a PUN member was named to the new cabinet, albeit reportedly without the endorsement of the party leadership, and was not reappointed in the new cabinet formed in April 2001. In the 2005 presidential balloting, Ngoupandé won 5.08 percent of the vote in the first round and backed Bozizé in the second round. Subsequently, he was appointed to the cabinet as one of the ministers of state, but justice minister Lea Koyassoum Doumta, the party's secretary general, was dismissed. Subsequently, Ngoupandé was replaced in a cabinet reshuffle of September 2, 2006, and the party was no longer represented in the government until the formation of a new cabinet of January 28, 2008, and the appointment of Gaston MACKOUZANGBA. He was retained in the new government named in 2009.

Leaders: Jean-Paul NGOUPANDÉ (Former Prime Minister and 2005 presidential candidate), Lea Koyassoum DOUMTA (Secretary General).

National Party for a New Central Africa (*Partie Nationale pour la Nouvelle Afrique Centrale*—PNCN). Little has been reported about this hitherto unreferenced party, a member of which was appointed to the cabinet in 2008. Cyriaque Gonda, who was named minister of communication and national reconciliation, was deputy speaker of parliament in 2005 and was a spokesperson for President Bozizé in 2006 and 2007. Gonda was named a minister of state in the 2009 cabinet.

Leader: Cyriaque GONDA (Chair).

Former Rebel Groups That Joined the Government in 2009:

Union of Democratic Forces for the Rally (*Union des Forces Démocratique pour le Rassemblement*—UFDR). The UFDR, also referenced as the Union of Democratic Forces for Unity, formed in October 2006, demanding that Bozizé step down or share power. The group, dominated by the Muslim Gula ethnic group, claimed responsibility for numerous attacks in northern regions of the Central African Republic, particularly in the town of Birao, that resulted in the deaths of at least 20 soldiers and civilians in late 2006 (and forced nearly all of the town's residents to flee by early 2007). After numerous clashes with government forces, the UFDR agreed to reconciliation. A peace accord was signed in February 2007 by Abdoulaye Miskine, leader of the UFDR faction referenced as the FDPC (below); Andre Ringui Le Gaillard, associated with the APRD (below); and the CAR. Meanwhile, UFDR leader Michel Djotodia, who lived in exile in Benin, was arrested by Benin authorities. The CAR, in the aftermath of the February accord, asked Benin to release Djotodia and another rebel faction leader, Abacar Sabone. Meanwhile, fighting was reported in the northeast, particularly in Birao, between the UFDR and government forces in March 2007. A renewed peace accord was signed on April 13, granting amnesty to rebels and establishing a cease-fire.

Djotodia and Sabone were still imprisoned as of December 2007, and a rival, Zacharia Damane, was the titular head of the party. Damane was reported to have signed a separate peace deal with the government in April 2007 and was subsequently named a presidential adviser. Miskine reportedly refused an offer of the post of presidential adviser in August on the grounds that the government had not implemented the peace agreement. According to the *Africa Research Bulletin,* the group allegedly has bases in the Darfur region of Sudan.

In December 2008 the UFDR participated in extensive peace talks with the government and other groups, and signed on to a peace accord designed to end years of guerrilla warfare. Subsequently, a member of the group was named to a ministry in the new unity government installed in January 2009. In February Djotodia and Sabone were released from prison in Benin, both men saying they wanted to return to the CAR and participate in the national reconciliation effort. Sabone headed the splinter rebel group MLCJ (see Rebel Groups, below).

Leaders: Zacharia DAMANE, Michel DJOTODIA, Djarnib GREBAYE.

Popular Army for the Restoration of the Republic and Democracy (*Armée Populaire pour la Restauration de la Republique et la Démocratie*—APRD). The APRD, formed in April 2006 with reported ties to Patassé, was allegedly responsible for burning homes and seizing several northern towns in early 2007. The group, led by Jean-Jacques Demafouth, a former defense minister who lives in exile in France, claimed that little has been done on behalf of people in the northwest region; its armed members reportedly include Chadians, Nigerians, and Cameroonians. In December 2007 the APRD did not participate in preparations for a national dialogue for reconciliation among political groups that was being organized by President Bozizé. According to *Africa Research Bulletin*, the APRD had earlier in the year established ties with Lord's Resistance Army (LRA) rebels in Uganda in 2007.

However, in February 2008 the APRD agreed to participate under certain conditions, including the return of former president Patassé and other political exiles. Subsequently, Demafouth said he hoped the peace agreement he signed in May would improve the lives of the people who had suffered for so long in northwestern CAR. In August, when the group was allowed to form a political party, it established a political wing, also headed by Demafouth, called the New Alliance for Progress (*Nouvelle Alliance pour le Progrès*—NAP). In December the APRD signed on to the inclusive peace accord, and was subsequently given a cabinet post in the unity government formed in 2009.

Leaders: Jacques DEMAFOUTH, Bedaya NDJADDER, Laurent NDIGNOUE, Henri Tchebo WAFIO.

Opposition Parties:

Central African People's Liberation Movement (*Mouvement de Libération du Peuple Centrafricaine*—MLPC). The MLPC was organized in Paris in mid-1979 by Ange-Félix Patassé, who had served as prime minister from September 1976 to July 1978 and was runner-up to Dacko in the presidential balloting of March 1981. At an extraordinary congress held September 14–18, 1983, Patassé was accorded a vote of no confidence and replaced with a nine-member directorate as part of a move from "nationalism" to "democratic socialism." In July 1986 it was announced that the MLPC had joined forces with the FPP (see below) to present a united front against the Kolingba government, with subsequent news stories again referring to Patassé, then living in Togo, as the MLPC's leader. The party was granted legal status in September 1991.

In early 1993 Patassé, who had reportedly been running second when presidential balloting was suspended in October 1992, accepted an appointment to the CNPPR, despite allegations that Kolingba was using the council to co-opt the most prominent opposition figures. In March, on the other hand, the party refused to enter the Lakoué government.

Patassé was elected president of the republic in 1993, while MLPC candidates secured a plurality of 34 legislative seats. The MLPC, whose strength was concentrated in the north, advanced to 47 legislative seats in 1998. Following his appointment as prime minister in January 1999, former MLPC stalwart Anicet Georges Dologuélé reportedly asserted that he wanted to be regarded as an independent. Patassé replaced him as the prime minister on April 1, 2001, with his close associate and leading party member, Martin Ziguélé, who then formed another MLPC-dominated cabinet on April 6. Following his ouster in March 2003, Patassé went into exile in Togo. The MLPC subsequently endorsed General Bozizé's schedule for a return to civilian government. After Patassé's proposed candidacy was rejected by the transitional constitutional court, Ziguélé was named as the MLPC standard-bearer for the 2005 elections but he ultimately lost to Bozizé in the second round of presidential balloting.

One member of the MLPC was named to the cabinet in early 2006, although Patassé clearly remained at odds with the government. In April the Bozizé administration asked the International Criminal Court at The Hague to investigate alleged war crimes on Patassé's part during the 2002–2003 turmoil. In August 2006 Patassé was tried in the CAR and found guilty of fraud in connection with misuse of public funds during his term in office. He was sentenced to 20 years' imprisonment. A month earlier Patassé had been suspended from the party and replaced as president by Ziguélé.

In 2009 the MLPC was critical of the peace process steered by President Bozizé and denounced the reappointment of Prime Minister Touadera. Ahead of the 2010 presidential elections, Ziguélé urged the opposition to unite to defeat Bozizé.

Leaders: Martin ZIGUÉLÉ (President of the Party and Former Prime Minister; 2005 presidential candidate), Luc Apollinaire DONDON (Vice President of the Party), Francis Albert OUKANGA (Secretary General).

Alliance for Democracy and Progress (*Alliance pour la Démocratie et le Progrès*—ADP). A founding member of the CFD (see Political background, above), the ADP applied for legal status in late 1991. In October 1992 (then) party leader Jean-Claude CONJUGO was killed by government forces during a union-organized demonstration. However, the party was one of five groups represented in the government named on October 30, 1993, thereby breaking with the CFD. One of the party's leaders, Olivier Gabirault, ran for president in 2005, finishing last with less than 1 percent of the vote.

Leaders: Jacques MBOITEDAS, Olivier GABIRAULT (2005 presidential candidate), Tchapka BREDE (National Secretary).

Patriotic Front for Progress (*Front Patriotique pour le Progrès*—FPP). Launched initially by Abel Goumba Guéne as the Congo-based Ubangi Patriotic Front–Labor Party (*Front Patriotique Oubanguien–Parti Travailliste*—FPO-PT), the FPP repudiated the Dacko government in 1981, called for the withdrawal of French troops, and forged links with the French Socialist Party and other European socialist groups. Linkage with the MLPC was announced in 1986, the two groups calling for a boycott of the 1987 legislative balloting and the creation of a multiparty system as envisioned by the 1981 constitution. Between September 1990 and March 1991 Goumba was imprisoned for his involvement with the CCCCN. Leader of the core party of the opposition's Concertation of Democratic Forces (*Concertation des Forces Démocratiques*—CFD), Goumba was reported to be outpolling his four competitors at the abortive presidential balloting of October 1992 but fell to second place in 1993 and fourth place in 1999 (with 6.6 percent of the vote).

Goumba was appointed prime minister in the transitional government named following the March 2003 coup, but he was replaced in that post in December and named "honorary vice president." After receiving less than 3 percent of the vote in the first round of the 2005 presidential balloting, Goumba claimed widespread fraud. He was subsequently dismissed as honorary vice president on March 16. The official government explanation for his removal was that the new constitution did not provide for a vice president, but observers said his refusal to join those backing Bozizé cost him the post. However, in mid-2005, Goumba was appointed as "mediator of the republic" to improve relations between citizens and the government. The party won two seats in the 2005 legislative elections. In 2006 rifts were reported, as an unspecified splinter group held a separate congress.

Leaders: Dr. Abel GOUMBA Guéne (President and 2005 presidential candidate), Patrice ENDJIMOUNGOU (Secretary General).

Social Democratic Party (*Parti Social-Démocrate*—PSD). For the October 1992 balloting the PSD offered as a presidential candidate its leader, Enoch Dérant Lakoué, who was reportedly running in last place when the poll was aborted. In February 1993 Lakoué accepted appointment as Prime Minister Malendoma's successor.

During the first half of 1993 the PSD suffered numerous defections, while Lakoué's own popularity continued to plummet. Thus, by the June 11 opening of a party congress, the PSD was, according to *Africa Confidential*, "run almost entirely by [Lakoué] family and friends."

At legislative balloting in 1998 the PSD captured six seats; however, one successful candidate, Dieudonné KOUDOUFARA, immediately defected to the MLPC, giving that party and its allies a disputed one-vote legislative majority. Two other PSD legislators reportedly followed Koudoufara's example in March 1999. Lakoué finished seventh in the 1999 presidential balloting with only 1.3 percent of the vote. The cabinet announced in November 1999 included a PSD member, but he was not reappointed in the new cabinet formed in April 2001. In 2005, the party won four seats in the assembly.

Leader: Enoch Dérant LAKOUÉ (Former Prime Minister).

Löndö Association. (*Levons-nous*). This human rights group won one assembly seat in 2005 balloting.

Other Parties That Participated in the 2005 Elections:

Union for Renewal and Development (*Union pour la Renaissance et le Développement*—URD). The URD, founded in 2002, reportedly supported Bozizé initially but backed MDD leader Auguste Boukanga, who ran under the URD flag as its 2005 presidential candidate.

Democratic Forum for Modernity (*Forum Démocratique pour la Modernité*—FODEM). FODEM was launched in the summer of 1997 by Agriculture Minister Charles Massi, who had recently been held hostage by rebellious soldiers and reportedly had been persuaded of the merits of their case. Massi was dismissed from the government in December, ostensibly because of his dealings in the diamond sector.

FODEM was officially recognized in May 1998, and in September Massi was cleared of the charges that had led to his removal from government in 1997. Massi won 1.3 percent of the vote in the 1999 presidential balloting and 3.2 percent in the 2005 presidential elections. He backed Bozizé in the 2005 runoff and was appointed a minister of state in 2006.

In May 2008 Massi was suspended from the party due to his links with the rebel group CPJP (see Rebel Groups, below.)

Leader: Nicaide SALLE (Secretary General).

Other Parties:

Movement for Democracy, Independence, and Social Progress (*Mouvement pour la Démocratie, l'Indépendance, et le Progrès Social*—MDI-PS). Formed in 1991 in an effort to develop a national party that would avoid the regional and ethnic group influences that were dominating other groupings, the MDI-PS was one of the few remaining members of the UFAPC as of late 1999. In 2000 the party demanded that President Patassé step down. Party leader Daniel Boysembe was appointed to a cabinet post in the 2004 transitional government.

Leader: Daniel NDITIFEI BOYSEMBE (Secretary General and Former Finance Minister).

Liberal Democratic Party (*Parti Liberal-Démocratic*—PLD). The PLD was launched prior to the 1993 legislative balloting, at which it won seven seats. The party was given four portfolios in the January 1999 cabinet, having won two seats in the late 1998 balloting as part of the "presidential majority" supportive of the MLPC. Former leader Nestor KOMBO-NAGUEMON reportedly committed suicide in 2004.

National Convention (*Convention National*—CN). Founded in October 1991 by David Galiambo, the CN won three seats in the 1993 National Assembly poll. It was represented in the cabinet from 1999 to 2003.

Leader: David GALIAMBO.

Civic Forum (*Forum Civique*—FC). Theretofore in opposition, the Civic Forum was suspended by the CFD in August 1992 for continuing its participation in the "grand national debate." On December 4 FC leader Gen. Timothée Malendoma was appointed prime minister by President Kolingba. However, scarcely more than two months later, on February 26, 1993, he was dismissed for "blocking the democratic process." As of late 1999 the FC was one of the few parties that remained part of the UFAPC (see above). In 2003 the party supported a national dialogue to bring about peace between the government and rebel forces.

Leader: Gen. (Ret.) Timothée MALENDOMA (Former Prime Minister).

Democratic Movement for the Renaissance and Evolution of Central Africa (*Mouvement Démocratique pour la Renaissance et l'Evolution en Centrafrique*—MDREC). In mid-1992, MDREC party leader Joseph Bendounga, a prodemocracy advocate, was arrested and sentenced to six months' imprisonment for criticizing the president. The group secured one legislative seat in 1993. Bendounga, the mayor of Bangui, supported incumbent President Patassé in the 1999 presidential poll. Through 2001 the MDREC remained supportive of the MLPC and Patassé. The party named Bendounga as its candidate for the 2005 presidential election, but his name did not appear in the list of results.

Leaders: Joseph BENDOUNGA, Léon SEBOU (Secretary General).

Social Evolution Movement of Black Africa (*Mouvement de l'Évolution Sociale de l'Afrique Noire*—MESAN). The present MESAN is a faction-torn remnant of the group founded in 1949 and once headed by former president Dacko. The party won one assembly seat in 1993 balloting, and a MESAN member was appointed minister of communication in June 1996.

In 2006 MESAN leader Dieudonne Stanislas Mbangot was among three ministers removed from the cabinet for alleged financial irregularities.

Leader: Dieudonne Stanislas MBANGOT (Chair).

People's Union for the Republic (*Union du Peuple pour le République*—UPR). The UPR secured one seat in the 1998 legislative poll. In 2000 the UPR was among a group of opposition parties that called for President Patassé's resignation.

Leader: Pierre-Sammy MACKFOY.

Central African Republican Party (*Parti Républicain Centrafricain*—PR). Also a former member of the CFD, the PR participated in the Malendoma government with its leader, Ruth Rolland, who had previously denounced the regime for tribalism and the misappropriation of public funds, accepting the Social and Women's Affairs portfolio. Subsequently, Rolland became the first African woman to present herself as a presidential candidate, although finishing last in 1993 with a mere 1 percent vote share. Rolland died in June 1995.

Central African Movement for National Liberation (*Mouvement Centrafricaine pour la Libération Nationale*—MCLN). The pro-Libyan MCLN, organized in Paris by Dr. Rodolphe Idi Lala, a former member of the FPP, claimed responsibility for the July 1981 theater bombing in Bangui, in the wake of which it was outlawed. Idi Lala, who was condemned to death in absentia by a military court in May 1982, was challenged as leader in late 1983 by elements within the party that declared the bombing "off target"; at the time of its entry into the Central African Revolutionary Party (*Parti Revolutionnaire Centrafricain*—PRC), its leadership included former members of the Kolingba government who had been involved in the 1982 coup attempt. These individuals, especially Gen. Alphonse Mbaikoua, were subsequently involved in guerrilla action in the north, with the assistance of Chadian insurgents.

In late 1987 *Africa Confidential* reported that about 50 MCLN members were in prison in Bangui and described Gen. François Bozizé, then reportedly an MCLN leader operating from Libya, as a "constant headache" to Kolingba. In January 1988 Idi Lala was reported to have been arrested in Benin, and in October 1989 Bangui confirmed that Bozizé had been in detention in the Central African Republic since August, when Benin had agreed to "extradite" him, reportedly for a $3 million fee. In October 1991 Bozizé was acquitted of charges stemming from the 1982 coup attempt, and he was subsequently identified as leader of the Popular Rally for the Reconstruction of Central Africa (*Rassemblement Populaire pour la Reconstruction de la Centrafrique*—RPRC). Bozizé secured 1.5 percent of the presidential vote in 1993 as a technically independent candidate, having recently returned from nine years in exile. He was subsequently named chief of staff of the armed forces under President Patassé. Bozizé was dismissed in October 2001 by Patassé for allegedly having been involved in the attempted coup d'état in May. He left the country in November but returned to lead a successful overthrow of the Patassé government in March 2003.

The cabinet formed in April 2001 also included members from two small, previously unreferenced groups—the **African Development Party** (*Parti Africain du Développement*—PAD) and the **Democratic Union for Renewal/Fini Kodro** (*Union Démocratique pour le Renouveau/Fini Kodro*—UDR/FK). In 2008 Laurent Ngon BABA, a former PAD cabinet minister, retained a cabinet post but was listed as a member of the KNK.

Other Group:

Patriotic Front for the Liberation of Central Africa (*Front Patriotique pour La Libération du Centrafrique*—FPLC). The formation of the FPLC was announced in Brazzaville, Congo, in June 1996 by exiled former CAR soldiers who had supported the army rebellion in April and May and opposed French intervention on behalf of the CAR government. The FPLC leaders promised "armed resistance" to both the Patassé administration and "French occupation."

In 2006 the International Criminal Court issued an arrest warrant for Thomas LUBANGA, said to be the leader of the military wing of the FPLC, for allegedly recruiting child soldiers.

Leaders: Lt. Jean Bertrand BIAMBA, Maj. Leopold ADETO, Dr. Jean Paul MANDAKOUZOU.

Rebel Groups:

Democratic Front for the Central African People (*Front Démocratique du Peuple Centraficaines*—FDPC). A former faction within the UFDR, the FDPC is headed by Abdoulaye Miskine, a former Chadian and body guard for former President Patassé. In 2003 Miskine was charged with war crimes by the International Criminal Court, and in 2005 he joined the armed resistance against the Bozizé government. The FDPC faction split off from the UFDR in 2007, when Miskine signed a peace accord with the government. Throughout most of 2008 the FDPC balked at participating in further accords, however, and FDPC rebels were blamed in attacks that took place in November near the border with Chad. Subsequently, Miskine signed on to the inclusive peace accord that evolved from a December meeting between the government and opposition and rebel groups.

FDPC rebels again took up arms and attacked in a northern town in February 2009, reports saying they were displeased with the government's efforts toward disarmament, demobilization, and reintegration.

Leaders: Abdoulaye MISKINE, Ringui Le GAILLARD.

Movement of Central Africa Liberators for Justice (*Mouvement des Libérateurs de l'Afrique Centrale pour la Justice*—MLCJ). Once part of an alliance formed by the UFDR in 2006, the MLCJ in December 2008 signed the peace accord with the government and other opposition and rebel groups. Subsequently, in actions similar to those of the FDPC, the MLCJ accused the government of failing to adhere to terms of the accord, including a cease fire, and in February 2009 the group launched attacks in northern CAR.

Leader: Abacar SABONE.

Forces for the Unification of the Central African Republic (*Forces pour l'Unification de la République Centraficaine*—FIRCA). A splinter from the UFDR over the latter's signing a peace accord with the Bozizé government in April 2007, FIRCA was reported to have seized control of a northern village near Sudan in October 2008.

Leader: Oumar SOBIAN.

Convention of Patriots for Peace and Justice (*Convention des Parties pour la Paix et de la Justice*—CPJP). Established in January 2009, the CPJP called for the end of the inclusive government established on January 19. Its fighters were reported to have clashed with government soldiers in northern CAR in February. The CPJP leader, Charles Massi, is a former minister and former leader of FODEM, which expelled him in 2008 because of his ties to the rebel group.

Leader: Charles MASSI (2005 presidential candidate).

LEGISLATURE

The 1986 constitution provided for a bicameral Congress (*Congrès*) encompassing a largely advisory Economic and Regional Council composed of nominated members and an elective National Assembly with a five-year mandate.

The assembly was suspended following the March 2003 coup, and self-declared President Bozizé on March 30 established a 98-member National Transitional Council (*Conseil National de Transition*—CNT). The members were chosen by the president to represent the military, clergy, trade unions, political parties, human rights groups, and other sectors. The December 2004 constitutional revision provided for the creation of a new 105-member National Assembly. Following two rounds of balloting on March 13 and May 8, 2005, the distribution was as follows: the pro-Bozizé National Convergence coalition, 42 seats; the Central African People's Liberation Movement, 11; the Central African Democratic Rally, 8; the Social Democratic Party, 4; the Patriotic Front for Progress, 2; the Alliance for Democratic Progress, 2; the Löndö Association, 1; independents, 34; and undeclared, 1.

Speaker: Célestin-Leroy GAOMBALET.

CABINET

[as of September 1, 2009]

Prime Minister	Faustin-Archange Touadera (ind.)
Ministers	
Civil Service, Labor, and Social Security	Gaston Mackouzangba (PUN)
Environment and Ecology	François Naoyama (APRD)
Equipment and Integration	Cyriaque Samba Panza
Family and Social Affairs	Bernadette Sayo [f]
Finance and Budget	Albert Bessé
Foreign Affairs, Regional Integration, and Francophone Affairs	Gen. Antoine Gambi
Habitat and Housing	Djollo Djidou (UFDR)
Justice and Keeper of the Seals	Laurent Ngon Baba (KNK)
National Defense, Veterans, and Military Affairs	Gen. François Bozizé
National Education, Higher Education and Research	Ambroise Zawa (MDD)
National Security and Public Order	Gen. Jules Ouandé
Posts and Telecommunications, In Charge of New Technologies	Thierry Savonarole Maleyombo
Promotion of Small and Medium-Size Enterprises	Moïse Kotaye
Public Health and AIDS Prevention	André Nalke-Dorogo
Reconstruction of Public Buildings, Town Planning, and Housing	Faustin Ntelnoumbi
Rural Development and Agriculture	Fidèle Ngouandjika (KNK)
Secretary General of the Government and Relations with Parliament	Désiré Zanga-Kolingba (RDC)
Territorial Administration and Decentralization	Élie Wefio
Tourism and Handicrafts	Solange Pagonéndji Ndackala (ind.) [f]

Trade and Industry	Béatrice Emilie Epaye [f]
Water, Forestry, Fisheries, and the Environment	Emmanuel Bizot
Youth, Sports, Arts, and Culture	Aurélien Simplice Zingas (RDC)
Ministers Delegate	
Defense, Veterans, War Victims, and Restructuring of the Army	Gen. François Bozizé
Economy, Planning, and Internal Cooperation	Raymond Adouma
Energy and Water	Jean Chrysostome Mekondongo
Finance and Budget, and Mobilization of Financial Resources	Hassan Abdallah Kadi
Foreign Affairs, Regional Integration, and Francophone Affairs	Ambroisine Kpongo [f]
National Education and the Elimination of Illiteracy; and Primary and Secondary Education	Djibrine Sall
Rural Development in Charge of Livestock and Animal Health	Youssoufa Yerima Mandjo
Ministers of State	
Communication, Good Citizenship, Dialogue, and National Reconciliation	Cyriaque Gonda (PNCN)
Mines, Energy, and Water	Lt. Col. Sylvain Ndoutingaï (KNK)
Planning, Economy, and International Cooperation	Sylvain Maliko (KNK)
Transport and Civilian Aviation	Col. Parfait-Anicet Mbay (KNK)

[f] = female

COMMUNICATIONS

In May 2000 journalists in the CAR conducted a one-day strike to protest what they perceived as the government's efforts to "gag" the press, criticizing in particular the recent arrest of several editors and reporters for publishing anti-Patassé stories. In December 2004 the CNT decriminalized a range of press offenses including "defamation" and the publication of "false material," thereby overturning a restrictive 1998 press law that had been used in July 2004 to charge the editor of *Le Citoyen* with slander. This move, unusual in the region, prompted the watchdog group Reporters Without Borders to say, "If proof were needed that decriminalizing press offenses were beneficial to democracy, this country provided it."

In 2007, however, the president of a private press group was sentenced to two months in prison for publishing statements critical of the government. The charges against him were related to an article critical of the Chadian government published in a private weekly. In January 2008 a reporter for the weekly *Les Collines de l'Oubangui* was sentenced to six months in prison following his conviction on charges of inciting revolt and defamation. Within a month, however, the reporter was pardoned by President Bozizé. *Le Citoyen* was suspended for a month in 2009 for allegedly referring to members of parliament as "sickly and mangy dogs," according to the international Committee to Protect Journalists.

Press. The following are published in Bangui: *E Le Songo* (2,000), daily tabloid in Sango; *Renouveau Centrafricaine* (1,000), weekly in French; *Journal Officiel de la République Centrafricaine,* fortnightly in French; *Terre Africaine*, weekly in French; *Le Rassemblement,* RDC organ; *Le Démocrate,* independent daily; *The Courier; Le Citoyen,* independent; and *Le Centafriqu'Un* and *Les Collines de l'Oubangui,* private weeklies.

News agency. The official facility is *Agence Centrafricaine de Presse* (ACAP).

Broadcasting and computing. The government-controlled *Radiodiffusion-Télévision Centrafrique* broadcasts in French and Sango. As of 2008 there were 4.4 Internet users per 1,000 inhabitants.

INTERGOVERNMENTAL REPRESENTATION

Ambassador to the U.S.: Stanislas MOUSSA-KEMBE.

U.S. Ambassador to the Central African Republic: Frederick B. COOK.

Permanent Representative to the UN: Fernand POUKRÉ-KONO.

IGO Memberships (Non-UN): AfDB, AU, BADEA, BDEAC, CEEAC, CEMAC, Interpol, NAM, OIF, WCO, WTO.

CHAD

Republic of Chad
République du Tchad

Political Status: Independent since August 11, 1960; military regime instituted in 1975, giving way to widespread insurgency and ouster of Transitional Government of National Unity in 1982; one-party system established by presidential decree in 1984; constitution of December 10, 1989, suspended on December 3, 1990, following military coup; interim national charter announced February 28, 1991; transitional national charter adopted by Sovereign National Conference effective April 9, 1993; present constitution approved by national referendum on March 31, 1996, and revised by national referendum on June 6, 2005.

Area: 495,752 sq. mi. (1,284,000 sq. km.).

Population: 6,279,931 (1993C); 11,103,000 (2008E). The 1993 figure includes an adjustment of 1.4 percent for underenumeration.

Major Urban Center (2005E): N'DJAMENA (864,000).

Official Languages: French and Arabic. In addition, some 25 indigenous languages are spoken.

Monetary Unit: CFA Franc (official rate December 1, 2009: 434.59 francs = $1US). The CFA franc, previously pegged to the French franc, is now permanently pegged to the euro at 655.957 CFA francs = 1 euro.

President: Col. Idriss DÉBY Itno (Patriotic Salvation Movement); self-appointed as president on December 4, 1990, following overthrow of the government of Hissène HABRÉ on December 2; confirmed by national charter adopted February 28, 1991; reconfirmed by the Sovereign National Conference on April 6, 1993; popularly elected to a five-year term in two-stage multiparty balloting on June 2 and July 3, 1996, and sworn in on August 8; reelected on May 20, 2001, and sworn in for another five-year term on August 8; reelected for another five-year term on May 3, 2006.

Prime Minister: Youssouf Saleh ABBAS (nonparty); appointed by the president on April 16, 2008, to succeed Delwa Kassiré KOUMAKOYE (National Assembly for Democracy and Progress), who had been dismissed the same day; formed new government on April 23, 2008.

THE COUNTRY

Landlocked Chad, the largest in area and population among the countries of former French Equatorial Africa, extends from the borders of the equatorial forest in the south to the Sahara in the north. Its unevenly distributed population is characterized by overlapping ethnic, religious, and regional cleavages. The primarily black population in the south is largely animist or Christian, while the north is overwhelmingly Sudanic and Muslim. Of the country's 12 major ethnic groups, the largest are the Saras in the south and Arabs in the center, north, and east. However, the

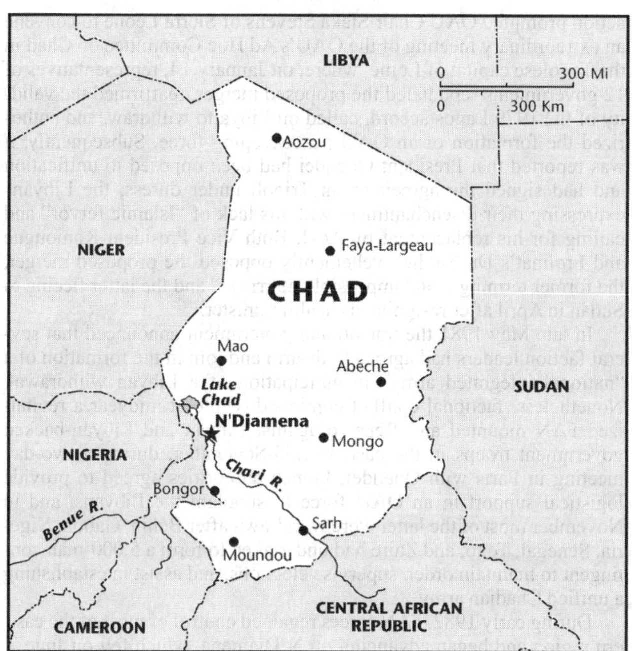

Zaghawa clan (an estimated 5 percent of the population) has dominated political affairs since the installation of the Déby regime in 1990. French is an official language, but Chadian Arabic has recognized status in the school system, and the major black ethnic groups have their own languages. Women constitute roughly 21 percent of the official labor force and more than 65 percent of unpaid family workers. Female participation in government and politics, traditionally close to nonexistent, has increased slightly in recent years. The government also has recently introduced new legislation designed to protect certain rights of women, reportedly generating criticism from conservative elements of the population.

Until significant oil production began recently (see below), the economy was almost exclusively agricultural, nearly one-half of the gross national product being derived from subsistence farming, livestock raising, and fishing. Cotton, grown primarily on the rich farmland in the south, accounted for more than 70 percent of export earnings, with cotton-ginning being the most important industry. Uranium and other mineral deposits are believed to be located in the northern Aozou Strip, long the source of a territorial dispute with Libya (see Foreign relations, below), while gold and diamonds also are mined.

Despite aid from such sources as the UN Development Programme, the World Bank, and the African Development Fund, widespread civil war through much of the 1970s, 1980s, and early 1990s precluded measurable economic development. In the mid-1990s the government began to privatize many state-run enterprises and to adopt other measures designed to promote free-market activity, earning support from the International Monetary Fund (IMF) for its efforts. However, the IMF urged Chadian leaders to move beyond "crisis management" and "fiscal stabilization" to long-term policies designed to combat poverty.

Chad remains one of the poorest nations in the world, with a per capita annual income of less than $300. An estimated 80 percent of the population lives below the poverty level, nearly one-third of that number existing in near-starvation conditions. Meanwhile, the illiteracy rate is estimated at 75 percent. Chad is also widely considered to be one of the world's most corrupt nations, with a "culture of clans and warlordism" dominating much of everyday existence and contributing to insurgencies that have compromised development efforts.

Prospects for economic advancement are focused almost exclusively on exploitation of the southern oil fields, which are estimated to contain at least 900 million barrels of oil. A 665-mile pipeline to carry the oil through Cameroon to the Atlantic Ocean was opened in October 2003, a consortium led by the Exxon Mobil Corporation having earmarked more than $4 billion for the extraction and piping processes. Significant financing was also provided by the World Bank, which was given control of an escrow fund containing Chad's portion of the oil revenue. As part of the arrangements with the World Bank, the Chadian government agreed to direct two-thirds of that revenue toward improving living standards and to deposit 10 percent into a special fund to be reserved for use after the oil reserves were exhausted.

GDP grew by more than 30 percent in 2004 under the influence of the oil program and significantly increased foreign investment. However, growth declined to 13 percent in 2005 as the result of internal unrest and political discord that also prompted a serious dispute between the government and the World Bank (see Current issues, below). Ongoing instability slowed growth to only 1.3 percent in 2006, although inflation dropped to 8 percent from 20 percent in 2005.

A dispute over taxes led two major foreign oil companies to halt production in August 2006, but an agreement was reached in October that permitted resumption. (Critics accused the government of "extorting funds" from the companies.) Subsequently, government resources were severely strained by the outbreak of rebel activity along the eastern border with Sudan. Growth remained low at 1.7 percent in 2007 as the government reportedly continued to direct oil revenues toward its security forces in the face of ongoing rebel activity. GDP contracted by 0.5 percent in 2008 in the aftermath of a rebel incursion in February, while inflation rose to more than 11 percent, primarily as a result of rapidly increasing food prices.

In September 2008 the World Bank announced it was withdrawing from the Chad-Cameroon pipeline project because the Chadian government had failed to allocate oil revenues to social programs and development projects as originally promised. At that point, Chad was exporting approximately 170,000 barrels of oil per day, worth $8-10 million and providing an estimated three-quarters of the government's revenue.

GOVERNMENT AND POLITICS

Political background. Brought under French control in 1900, Chad became part of French Equatorial Africa in 1910 and served as an important Allied base in World War II. It was designated an autonomous member state of the French Community in 1959, achieving full independence under the presidency of François (subsequently N'Garta) TOMBALBAYE one year later. Tombalbaye, a southerner and leader of the majority Chad Progressive Party (*Parti Progressiste Tchadien*—PPT), secured the elimination of other parties prior to the adoption of a new constitution in 1962.

The northern (Saharan) territories—historically focal points of resistance and virtually impossible to govern—remained under French military administration until 1965, when disagreements led Chad to request the withdrawal of French troops. Dissatisfaction with Tombalbaye's policies generated progressively more violent opposition and the formation in 1966 of the Chad National Liberation Front (*Front de Libération National Tchadien*—Frolinat), led by Aibrahim ABATCHA until his death in 1969, and then by Dr. Abba SIDDICK. French troops returned in 1968 at the president's request, but, despite their presence and reconciliation efforts by Tombalbaye, the disturbances continued, culminating in an attempted coup by Frolinat in 1971 (allegedly with Libyan backing). In a further effort to consolidate his regime, Tombalbaye created the National Movement for Cultural and Social Revolution (*Mouvement National pour la Révolution Culturelle et Sociale*—MNRCS) in 1973 to replace the PPT.

On April 13, 1975, Tombalbaye was fatally wounded in an uprising by army and police units. Two days later, Brig. Gen. Félix MALLOUM, who had been in detention since 1973 for plotting against the government, was designated chair of a ruling Supreme Military Council. The new regime, which banned the MNRCS, was immediately endorsed by a number of former opposition groups, although Frolinat remained aloof.

Following a major encounter between Libyan and Frolinat forces in the Tibesti Mountains in June 1976, Frolinat military leader Hissène HABRÉ attempted to negotiate a settlement with the Malloum regime but was rebuffed. In September Habré lost control of the main wing of Frolinat to Goukhouni OUEDDEI, who elected to cooperate with the Libyans, and in early 1978 Frolinat launched a major offensive against government forces in Faya-Largeau, about 500 miles northeast of the capital. Subsequently, on February 5, the government announced that it had concluded a cease-fire agreement with a rebel group, the Armed Forces of the North (*Forces Armées du Nord*—FAN), that was loyal to Habré. A truce also was reached with Oueddei's People's Armed Forces (*Forces Armées du Peuple*—FAP), the largest Frolinat faction, in late

March. However, the FAP resumed military operations in April, its advance being repulsed only with major French assistance to the Chadian government. As of midyear the northern two-thirds of the country remained in the effective control of one or the other of the competing Frolinat factions.

On August 29, 1978, President Malloum announced the appointment of Habré as prime minister under a "basic charter of national reconciliation" pending the adoption of a permanent constitution. However, a serious rift developed between Malloum and Habré later in the year, and an abortive coup on February 12, 1979, by forces loyal to Habré was followed by a month of bloody, but inconclusive, confrontation between the rival factions. On March 16 a four-party agreement was concluded in Kano, Nigeria, involving Malloum, Habré, Oueddei, and Aboubakar Mahamat ABDERAMAN, leader of the Popular Movement of Chadian Liberation (*Mouvement Populaire de la Libération Tchadienne*—MPLT). Under the Kano accord, Oueddei on March 23 became president of an eight-member Provisional State Council, which was composed of two representatives from each of the factions and was to serve until a new government could be constituted. French troops were to be withdrawn under a truce guaranteed by Cameroon, the Central African Empire, Libya, Niger, Nigeria, and Sudan. At a second Kano conference on April 3–11, however, the pact broke down, primarily because agreement could not be reached with five other rebel groups, one of which, the "New Volcano," headed by the Revolutionary Democratic Council (*Conseil Démocratique Revolutionaire*—CDR) of Ahmat ACYL, had apparently become a leading beneficiary of Libyan support in the north. Meanwhile, former Malloum supporter Lt. Col. Wadal Abdelkader KAMOUGUÉ, commander of the Chadian Armed Forces (*Forces Armées Tchadiennes*—FAT), had launched a secessionist uprising in the south, also with Libyan backing.

On April 29, 1979, a second provisional government was announced under Lol Mahamat CHOUA of the MPLT, with Gen. Djibril Negue DJOGO, former army commander under President Malloum, as his deputy. However, the Choua government was repudiated by the six "guarantor" states during a meeting in Lagos, Nigeria, held May 26–27, no Chadian representatives being present. In early June fighting erupted in N'Djamena between Frolinat and MPLT contingents, while other altercations occurred in the east, south, and north (where an invasion by a 2,500-man Libyan force, launched on June 26, met stiff resistance). In another effort to end the turmoil, a fourth conference convened August 20–21 in Lagos, attended by representatives of 11 Chadian groups and 9 external states (the original 6, plus Benin, Côte d'Ivoire, and Senegal). The August meeting resulted in the designation of Oueddei and Kamougué as president and vice president, respectively, of a Transitional Government of National Unity (*Gouvernement d'Union National de Transition*—GUNT), whose full membership, announced on November 10, included 12 northerners and 10 southerners.

Although the August 1979 Lagos accord had called for demilitarization of N'Djamena by February 5, 1980, fighting resumed in the capital on March 21, 1980, between Defense Minister Habré's FAN and President Oueddei's FAP, the latter subsequently being reinforced by Kamougué's FAT and elements of the post-Lagos Front for Joint Action, of which Ahmat Acyl was a leader. The coalescence of all other major forces against the FAN occurred primarily because of the perception that Habré, contrary to the intent of the Lagos agreement, had sought to expand his sphere of influence. While the FAN, clearly the best organized of the military units, continued to maintain control of at least half the city, the Organization of African Unity (OAU, subsequently the African Union—AU) and such regional leaders as Togo's President Eyadéma arranged several short-lived cease-fires in late March and April.

Moving into a vacuum created by the removal of the last French military contingent on May 17, 1980, Libya on June 15 concluded a military defense treaty with the Oueddei government. By early November, 3,000–4,000 Libyan troops had moved into northern Chad and also had established a staging area within 40 miles of N'Djamena. Habré's position in the capital subsequently came under attack by Libyan aircraft, and fighting in the countryside spread as the government attempted to sever the FAN's link to its main base at Abéché, near the Sudanese border. An assault against FAN-controlled sectors of the capital was launched by government and Libyan forces on December 6, after Habré had rejected an OAU-sponsored cease-fire. Five days later the FAN withdrew from the city, some elements retreating toward Abéché and others crossing into Cameroon.

On January 6, 1981, the governments of Chad and Libya announced a decision to achieve "full unity" between their two countries. The action prompted OAU Chair Siaka Stevens of Sierra Leone to convene an extraordinary meeting of the OAU's Ad Hoc Committee on Chad in the Togolese capital of Lomé, where, on January 14, representatives of 12 governments repudiated the proposed merger, reaffirmed the validity of the 1979 Lagos accord, called on Libya to withdraw, and authorized the formation of an OAU peacekeeping force. Subsequently, it was reported that President Oueddei had been opposed to unification and had signed the agreement in Tripoli under duress, the Libyans expressing their disenchantment with his lack of "Islamic fervor" and calling for his replacement by Acyl. Both Vice President Kamougué and Frolinat's Dr. Siddick vehemently opposed the proposed merger, the former terming it an "impossible marriage" and the latter fleeing to Sudan in April after resigning as health minister.

In late May 1981 the transitional government announced that several faction leaders had agreed to disarm and join in the formation of a "national integrated army" in anticipation of a Libyan withdrawal. Nonetheless, factional conflict continued, while at midyear a revitalized FAN mounted an offensive against Libyan and Libyan-backed government troops in the east. In mid-September, during a two-day meeting in Paris with Oueddei, French authorities agreed to provide logistical support to an OAU force to supplant the Libyans, and in November most of the latter were withdrawn after Benin, Gabon, Nigeria, Senegal, Togo, and Zaire had undertaken to form a 5,000-man contingent to maintain order, supervise elections, and assist in establishing a unified Chadian army.

During early 1982, FAN forces regained control of most of the eastern region and began advancing on N'Djamena, which fell on June 7. GUNT president Oueddei fled to Cameroon before establishing himself at the northern settlement of Bardai on the border of the Libyan-controlled Aozou Strip. Upon entering the capital, the Council of the Commander in Chief of the FAN (*Conseil du Commandement en Chef des FAN*—CCFAN) assumed political control, and on June 19 it named Habré to head a 30-member Council of State. Earlier, on June 11, OAU Chair Daniel arap Moi had ordered the withdrawal of the OAU force, which, at maximum strength, had comprised only 3,000 troops, two-thirds from Nigeria. During the ensuing months, the FAN, with assistance from FAT units, succeeded in gaining control of the south.

On September 29, 1982, the CCFAN promulgated a Fundamental Act (*Acte Fondamental*), based on the August 1978 charter (which had been effectively abrogated in 1979), to "govern Chad until the adoption of a new constitution." In accordance with the new act, Habré was sworn in as president of the republic on October 21. Following his investiture, the new chief executive dissolved the Council of State in favor of a 31-member government that included Dr. Siddick; DJIDINGAR Dono Ngardoum, who had served briefly as prime minister under Oueddei in May; and Capt. Routouane YOMA, a former aide of Colonel Kamougué. As stipulated in the Fundamental Act, Habré also announced the formation of a 30-member National Consultative Council (*Conseil National Consultatif*—CNC) to serve as the state's "highest advisory organ." Two months later N'Djamena announced that the FAN and FAT would be consolidated as the Chadian National Armed Forces (*Forces Armées Nationales Tchadiennes*—FANT).

After the declaration in Algiers in October 1982 of a "National Peace Government" by 8 of the 11 signatories of the 1979 Lagos accord, Oueddei forces regrouped in Bardai with renewed support from Tripoli. By May 1983 GUNT units were advancing south, and, with the aid of 2,000 troops and several MIG fighters supplied by Libya, they captured the "northern capital" of Faya-Largeau on June 24. Habré immediately called for international assistance and received aid from Egypt, Sudan, and the United States, with France avoiding direct involvement despite a 1976 defense agreement. FANT troops recaptured Faya-Largeau on June 30, only to lose it again on August 10, while France, under mounting pressure from the United States and a number of francophone African countries, began deploying troops along a defensive "red line" just north of Abéché on August 14. The French—who eventually numbered some 3,000, in addition to 2,000 Zairean troops—imposed a tenuous cease-fire for the remainder of the year while calling for a negotiated solution between the two factions. While Habré continued to urge France to aid him in a full-scale offensive against Oueddei, the Mitterrand government refused, at one point urging "a federation of Chad" as a means of ending the conflict. Meanwhile, in the wake of renewed fighting, the "red line" was moved 60 miles north.

In April 1984 Libyan leader Muammar al-Qadhafi proposed a mutual withdrawal of "Libyan support elements" and French forces, with talks thereupon initiated between France and Libya that yielded an accord on September 17. The French pullout was completed by the end of the year; Libya, however, was reported to have withdrawn less than half of its forces from the north by that time, and the political-military stalemate continued. Meanwhile, the Habré regime had attempted to consolidate its power with the June formation of the National Union for Independence and Revolution (*Union Nationale pour l'Indépendence et la Révolution*—UNIR), the first legally recognized political party in Chad since the 1975 banning of the MNRCS.

In a statement issued in Tripoli on October 15, 1985, Oueddei was declared dismissed as FAP leader. The GUNT president repudiated the action and on November 5 announced the release of Acheikh ibn OUMAR, leader of the GUNT-affiliated CDR, who reportedly had been arrested a year earlier. On November 11 the Habré administration responded by concluding a "reconciliation agreement" with a breakaway faction of the CDR, the Committee for Action and Concord (*Comité d'Action et de Concord*—CAC).

In February 1986 GUNT forces mounted an offensive against FANT troops at the center of the "red line," but by early March they had been repulsed, reportedly with heavy losses. On June 19 FAT leader Kamougué announced his resignation as the GUNT vice president, while in August Oumar declared that the CDR had "suspended collaboration" with the GUNT but would "maintain solidarity with all anti-Habré factions." Clashes between CDR and GUNT units followed, the latter offering to open peace talks with N'Djamena. However, the Habré government insisted that the GUNT would first have to repudiate the Libyan intervention. Subsequently, during a meeting of GUNT factions in Cotonou, Benin, in mid-November, Oueddei was "expelled" from the grouping, with Oumar being named its president. In late December, as FANT forces were reported to be moving north, fighting broke out between FAP units loyal to Oueddei and what Libyan sources characterized as Oumar's "legitimate" GUNT.

On March 22, 1987, in what was seen as a major turning point in the lengthy Chadian conflict, FANT troops captured the Libyan air facility in Ouadi Doum, 100 miles northeast of Faya-Largeau. Deprived of air cover, the Libyans withdrew from Faya-Largeau, their most important military base in northern Chad, abandoning an estimated $1 billion worth of sophisticated weaponry. On August 8 Chadian government troops captured the town of Aozou, administrative capital of the northern strip; however, it was retaken by Libyan forces three weeks later. Chad thereupon entered southern Libya in an unsuccessful effort to deprive Libyan forces of air support in the continued struggle for the disputed territory. Subsequent international and regional criticism of the Chadian "invasion" led Habré to accept a September 11 cease-fire negotiated by OAU chair Kenneth Kaunda of Zambia; however, by late November the government reported FANT clashes with Libyan troops crossing into eastern Chad from Sudan.

In early 1988 Habré charged that Libya was still violating Chadian air space and backing antigovernment rebels despite Qadhafi's pledge of support for OAU peace-treaty negotiations. Nonetheless, Chad and Libya agreed in mid-October to restore diplomatic relations and "resolve peacefully their territorial dispute" by presenting their respective Aozou strip claims to a special OAU committee (see Foreign relations, below, for subsequent developments).

In April 1989 Habré survived a coup attempt that allegedly involved a number of senior government officials, including former FANT commander Idriss DÉBY, who subsequently mounted a series of cross-border attacks from sanctuary in Sudan. Eight months later, Chadian voters approved a constitution to replace the Fundamental Act. One of its provisions extended Habré's incumbency for another seven years; others formalized the UNIR's supremacy and authorized an elected National Assembly, balloting for which was conducted in June 1990.

In November 1990 a variety of antigovernmental forces, allied under Déby's leadership in the Patriotic Salvation Movement (*Mouvement Patriotique du Salut*—MPS), mounted a decisive offensive against FANT troops in eastern Chad. The rebels captured Abéché on November 30, reportedly prompting large-scale desertion by government troops. With France having announced that it would not intervene in what was characterized as an "internal Chadian power struggle," the MPS was left with a virtually unimpeded path to N'Djamena; consequently, Habré and other government leaders fled to Cameroon. (Habré was indicted in February 2000 in Senegal and charged with torture during his term in power. In June, however, the court ruled that Senegal did not have jurisdiction over the case, a decision that was heavily criticized as being politically motivated; human rights groups, which had filed the initial complaint against Habré, appealed to a higher Senegalese court. In March 2001 the appeals court upheld the lower court's ruling, President Wade of Senegal stating that he was prepared to send Habré to a third country to face trial. However, Habré remained in Senegal, although there had been attempts to extradite him to Belgium by victims of the regime who were Belgian citizens. In January 2006 the AU heads of state voted not to order the extradition of Habré to Belgium [Senegal had asked for the vote]. However, in July an AU panel declared that Habré should be tried in Senegal on genocide charges. Although a commission was subsequently established in Senegal to gather evidence in the case, little progress toward prosecution had been achieved by mid-2009. By that time the Belgian government had asked the International Court of Justice to force Senegal to either try Habré or extradite him to Belgium. For its part, the Senegalese government indicated that the expected cost of the trial was proving to be a barrier. Meanwhile, a magistrate's court in Chad had sentenced Habré to death in absentia.)

On December 3, 1990, one day after having occupied the capital, Déby suspended the constitution and dissolved the assembly. On December 4 he announced that a provisional Council of State had assumed power with himself as president and a fellow commander, Maldoum BADA ABBAS, as vice president. On February 28, 1991, an interim National Charter was adopted, and on March 5 the Council of State was dissolved in favor of a new Council of Ministers and an appointed Provisional Council of the Republic. The vice presidency was abandoned upon formation of the new government, Bada Abbas being named minister of state for the interior and former National Assembly president Jean Bawoyeu ALINGUÉ being appointed to the revived post of prime minister.

The overthrow of the Habré regime generated minimal international concern or domestic protest, in part because of reports that the deposed government had engaged in widespread human rights abuses. For his part, President Déby pledged to work toward implementation of a multiparty democracy in which "fundamental rights" would be guaranteed. However, the new regime also insisted that "security issues" took precedence over political liberalization.

In response to opposition demands for the convening of a Sovereign National Conference (*Conférence Nationale Souveraine*—CNS) to chart the nation's political future, Déby tentatively scheduled such a body for May 1992. Meanwhile, the Council of Ministers adopted guidelines for registering parties.

The regime faced a serious challenge in late 1991 when Habré loyalists, organized as the Movement for Development and Democracy (*Mouvement pour le Développement et la Démocratie*—MDD), launched an invasion from the Lake Chad border region. The campaign enjoyed some initial success, and, as the rebels advanced on N'Djamena in early January 1992, French paratroopers reinforced the brigade of 1,110 French soldiers permanently stationed near the capital. In addition to its symbolic significance, the French reinforcement permitted the release of additional Chadian troops to confront the rebels, and within days the government reported that the MDD forces were in full retreat. In the wake of the insurgency, security forces arrested a number of prominent opposition leaders and launched what was perceived as a reprisal campaign against suspected MDD supporters, former officials in the Habré administration, and members of the fledgling Rally for Democracy and Progress (*Rassemblement pour la Démocratie et le Progrès*—RDP). Shortly thereafter, in response to pressure from Paris, the government announced an amnesty for those recently detained as well as those implicated in an alleged October 1991 coup attempt. Reaffirming its commitment to democratization, the regime began legalizing opposition parties, including the RDP, in March. However, the CNS opening scheduled for May was postponed indefinitely because of ongoing security concerns, the government having reported another coup attempt in April.

On May 19, 1992, the National Charter was modified to strengthen the authority of the prime minister, and the following day Alingué was replaced by Joseph YODEYMAN. On May 22 a new Council of Ministers was announced that included representatives of newly organized parties, although a number of them subsequently resigned from the "coalition" government as the result of policy disputes. Following a minor reshuffle in October, the government announced that the CNS would convene on January 15, 1993, with a mandate to appoint a new prime minister, select a "transitional" legislature, and draw up constitutional revisions that would lead, following a national referendum on the proposals, to multiparty presidential and legislative balloting. Significantly, the CNS was not empowered to replace Déby, who was viewed as having the best chance to maintain a semblance of stability in an increasingly divided society. Thus, Déby remained as president and commander in chief of the armed forces under the transitional national charter adopted at the conclusion of the CNS on April 6, 1993. Quasi-legislative authority was extended to a Higher Transitional Council (*Conseil Supérieur de Transition*—CST), whose members were elected by the CNS. In addition, broad responsibility for economic and social policies was conferred on the prime minister, Dr. Fidèle MOUNGAR, a southerner named by the CNS to form the first transitional government. The CNS, supported by some 40 political parties (recognized and unrecognized), several rebel movements, and numerous trade and professional associations, approved a transitional period of up to 12 months pending the drafting of a permanent constitution and the holding of national elections. However, the CST was authorized to extend the charter's authority for an additional year, if necessary.

Despite the prime minister's expression of confidence that he and the president could work together, friction between the two leaders quickly surfaced, Déby being particularly critical of the new government's "amateurish" economic program. The dispute culminated with the CST forcing Dr. Moungar's resignation via a nonconfidence motion on October 28. After three rounds of voting, the CST on November 6 elected Delwa Kassiré KOUMAKOYE, the outgoing justice minister, to succeed Dr. Moungar. A new cabinet was named one week later, followed by a minor reshuffle in January 1994 in which MPS dominance was maintained despite the continued presence of ministers from anti-Déby parties. Subsequently, on April 4, the CST voted to extend the transitional period for 12 more months in view of the nation's seeming inability to reverse political fragmentation, with a major cabinet reshuffle following on May 17.

The CST approved a new electoral code and a draft constitution in January 1995; however, the subsequent registration of voters was strongly criticized by opposition leaders, who claimed the process was skewed in favor of the MPS. Acknowledging that the validity of the new voter lists was questionable, the CST postponed a constitutional referendum indefinitely, and in early April it extended the transitional period for another 12 months. Collaterally, the CST dismissed Prime Minister Koumakoye on April 8 for failing to "create the proper conditions" for elections, replacing him with Djimasta KOIBLA, who suspended his activity within the Union for Democracy and the Republic (*Union pour la Démocratie et la République*—UDR) upon assuming national office.

The extension of the nation's transitional political status in 1995 was controversial, opponents noting that a National Reconciliation Committee appointed in 1994 had negotiated peace accords with several rebel groups and thereby reduced security concerns. Consequently, with the Déby regime reportedly facing international pressure to proceed with democratization, the constitutional referendum was finally conducted on March 31, 1996. The new basic law (see Constitution and government, below) was approved by 63.5 percent of the voters in what officials reported to be a 69 percent turnout. (Not surprisingly, the "no" vote was heaviest in the south, where sentiment had long preferred a federal structure that would accord substantial autonomy to the region.) As approved by the referendum, Déby remained in office pending new presidential balloting, while the CST continued to operate until the election of a new legislature. In addition, although the cabinet submitted an essentially pro forma resignation on April 18, Déby reappointed Koibla the next day to head an interim government that included all but one of the incumbent ministers.

Fifteen candidates contested the first round of presidential balloting on June 2, 1996, Déby being credited with 43.9 percent of the votes. His closest rival was former southern military leader and GUNT vice president Kamougué, running under the banner of the Union for Renewal and Democracy (*Union pour le Renouveau et la Démocratie*—URD), who secured 12.4 percent of the votes. Déby was subsequently elected to a five-year term on July 3 in the second-round balloting, defeating Kamougué 69.1 percent to 30.9 percent. Déby again named Prime Minister Koibla to head the significantly revamped government announced on August 12.

Although opposition parties charged that "massive fraud" had occurred in the first round of the presidential election in June 1996, international observers reportedly expressed satisfaction with the conduct of the balloting. The vote shares garnered by President Déby and Colonel Kamougué appeared to reflect the long-standing cultural, religious, and ethnic divide between southern Chad and the rest of the country. Meanwhile, Western capitals (most importantly Paris) signaled their support for President Déby as Chad's best hope for ongoing stability, despite concern over his administration's human rights record and its ties with Sudan and collateral support for the Islamic fundamentalist movement.

Elections to the new National Assembly were held on January 5 and February 23, 1997, with MPS candidates ultimately securing 65 of 125 seats following a redistribution ordered by the national electoral commission upon appeal by the governing party (which was initially credited with only 55 seats). Election monitors described the balloting as "relatively free and fair." On the other hand, there was widespread domestic and international condemnation of the allegedly progovernment bias of the national electoral commission, especially regarding perceived irregularities in the initial tallies. However, Western leaders appeared willing to overlook such heavy-handed tactics, perhaps out of appreciation for the relative stability of the Déby regime in a region of recent intense political and military turbulence. For its part, the government continued to pursue cease-fire agreements with various rebel groups, as observers warned that tribal influences remained the most serious threat to the regime and the fledgling democratic process.

On May 16, 1997, President Déby appointed Nassour OUAÏDOU Guelendouksia to succeed Koibla as prime minister, a number of incumbents retaining their posts in the new cabinet announced on May 21. Ouaïdou also headed the reshuffled cabinet appointed on January 1, 1998. However, on December 13, 1999, in the wake of economic turbulence, President Déby appointed a "technocrat," Negoum YAMASSOUM, as prime minister. Yamassoum's new cabinet, announced December 14, included ministers from the MPS, URD, and the National Union for Development and Renewal (*Union National pour le Développement et le Renouvellement*—UNDR).

President Déby was reelected to another term with 68 percent of the vote in controversial balloting on May 20, 2001. The opposition objected to de facto control by the MPS over the electoral commission as well as perceived bias in the votes registration process. (The European Union [EU] "regretted" the many shortcomings in the poll and expressed concern about the restriction of political liberties by the government.) Following his inauguration on August 8, Déby reappointed Yamassoum as prime minister.

The MPS maintained its dominance in the April 21, 2002, National Assembly balloting (postponed from 2001 on the grounds that the government lacked sufficient funds to conduct the poll), the opposition charging that the balloting was fraudulent. On June 11 President Déby appointed Haroun KABADI as prime minister. Kabadi was succeeded by Moussa FAKI on June 24, 2003, and Pascal YOADIMNADJI on February 3, 2005.

A national referendum was held on June 6, 2005, on constitutional changes proposed by the assembly, the most contentious being elimination of the two-term presidential limit, which thereby permitted Déby to seek another term. Most opposition parties, many of which had served in Déby governments, strongly condemned the revisions and urged a boycott of the referendum. However, the government announced that 58 percent of voters participated in the referendum and that the changes were approved by a 66 percent "yes" vote. Subsequently, Déby reshuffled the cabinet on August 7; the most significant change involved his consolidation of control of the armed forces through the transfer of the defense ministry to the office of the president. Following the outbreak late in the year of renewed rebel activity (some on the part of military deserters incensed over the constitutional changes), the assembly in January 2006 voted 129–0 (with opposition legislators boycotting the vote) to postpone the assembly elections scheduled for April 2006 until at least April 2007, citing security and budget concerns.

In controversial balloting on May 3, 2006, Déby was reelected to another five-year presidential term, officially securing 77.5 percent of the votes against only four other candidates. (Nearly all opposition parties had called for a boycott of the election in view of the recent failed rebel takeover attempt.)

Prime Minister Yoadimnadji died on February 22, 2007, and five days later Déby reappointed former prime minister Koumakoye to the position. A major cabinet reshuffle in March was most notable for the inclusion of several former rebels—including Mahamat NOUR Abdelkerim of the United Front for Change (*Front Uni pour le Changement*—FUC). However, Nour was dismissed from the cabinet in December 2007 (see FUC under Political Parties and Groups for details).

After his government nearly fell to a rebel offensive in January–February 2008 (see Current issues, below), President Déby dismissed Prime Minister Koumakoye on April 16 and immediately named Youssouf Saleh ABBAS, theretofore Déby's diplomatic adviser, to the post. Five days later Abbas announced a new cabinet, which, although still dominated by the MPS, included four members of the opposition's Coordination of Parties for the Defense of the Constitution (*Coordination des Partis pour la Défense de la Constitution*—CPDC). Several subsequent reshuffles did not significantly alter the makeup of the cabinet.

Constitution and government. A 17-member Constitutional Committee, established in December 1993, drafted a new basic law in 1994 calling for establishment of a bicameral legislature and a strong presidential system based on the French model. The changes were endorsed by the Higher Transitional Council in January 1995, but the national referendum was postponed until March 31, 1996, when the proposed constitution was endorsed by 63.5 percent of the voters.

The new basic law provided for direct popular election (in two-round balloting, if necessary) of the president for a maximum of two five-year terms. The prime minister is appointed by the president, although he is also held "responsible" to the legislature. The constitution also authorized the creation of a Constitutional Council and a Supreme Court, both of which were installed in April 1999.

Although the 1996 constitution provided for a new Senate, that body was never constituted, and a constitutional revision approved by national referendum on June 6, 2005, eliminated references to the Senate in favor of an advisory body called the Economic, Social, and Cultural Council, whose members were to be appointed by the president, subject to approval by the assembly. However, no appointments had been made as of mid-2008. In a more controversial area (see Current issues, below), the amendments also permitted President Déby to seek a third term and removed an age restriction of 70 for the president.

In early 2000 the government doubled the number of prefectures (previously 14) and subprefectures, which are administered by government appointees. The cited reason was to promote decentralization of government functions. However, critics claimed that the reforms also had the effect of further cementing the ruling party's hold on power.

Foreign relations. Chad's internal unrest was exacerbated for many years by conflict with Libya over delineation of their common border. The dispute was intensified in 1975 by Libya's annexation of an area of some 27,000 square miles in northern Chad (the Aozou Strip) that was said to contain substantial iron ore and uranium deposits. (For information regarding developments in this matter from 1977 to 1994, see the 2007 *Handbook.*) In February 1994 the International Court of Justice (ICJ) ruled in favor of Chad by a vote of 16–1. After initially appearing to hesitate in the matter, Libya formally accepted the ICJ ruling in April, and the withdrawal of Libyan troops from the territory was completed by the end of May. Shortly thereafter President Déby met with Libya's Colonel Qadhafi in Tripoli to sign a treaty of friendship and cooperation. In February 2006 the two countries signed a declaration calling for full normalization of relations.

Relations with France have been complicated since the mid-1970s, when French involvement in the Chadian civil war was intensified by rebel kidnapping of a French national. In March 1976 a new cooperation pact was concluded, France agreeing to come to Chad's defense in the event of external, but not domestic, attack. Despite this assertion, French forces aided government troops throughout the late 1970s in stemming rebel, most notably Frolinat, offensives. By contrast, a French decision not to intervene in the fighting that broke out in November 1990 was considered critical to the success of the MPS campaign. Not surprisingly, the new Chadian president in early 1991 invited the approximately 1,100 French troops to remain in the country for security purposes, and their presence was considered a psychological factor in the Déby regime's ability to withstand several subsequent overthrow attempts.

Chadian affairs also were of particular interest to a number of other Western nations in the 1980s, especially in relation to the Habré government's dispute with Libya. Thus, U.S. surveillance photographs and anti-aircraft weapons were allegedly used by Habré forces during the 1987 struggle in southern Libya. However, concern over developments in Chad subsequently waned, the U.S. protest over the events of late 1990 being relatively moderate, despite apparent Libyan support for the victorious rebel forces.

In September 1998 Chad sent more than 2,000 troops to support the Kabila regime in the civil war in the Democratic Republic of the Congo (DRC, formerly Zaire). In April 1999 the Déby administration announced that the soldiers (some 200 of whom had been killed) would be withdrawn soon, as regional mediators attempted to broker a settlement to that intractable dispute, which had drawn in some half-dozen of the DRC's neighbors (see article on the DRC for details). Meanwhile, troops from Nigeria and Niger continued to assist in flushing out Chadian rebels in the Lake Chad region. (Fighting had broken out between Nigerian and Chadian troops in April 1998 over possession of an island in the lake; however, the conflict had settled down quickly, the two countries agreeing to leave formal demarcation of the boundary to the Lake Chad Basin Commission.) Chad's relations with Sudan and Libya also continued to improve, some observers suggesting that the Déby regime was hoping to dilute the country's long-standing dependence on French support or at least increase its negotiating leverage with Paris. However, in 2002 President Jacques Chirac became the first French head of state to visit Chad.

Tension intensified with the Central African Republic (CAR) in 2001 when Chad provided refuge for Gen. François Bozizé, one of the main protagonists in the CAR's infighting (see article on the CAR for details). However, relations improved when Bozizé assumed control in the CAR, and Chad sent troops to help maintain order in the CAR following the takeover.

In 2002 Chad joined Algeria, Mauritania, and Niger in signing the "Pan Sahel Initiative" with the United States under which U.S. forces were to be deployed to the region to help combat terrorism, drug trafficking, and arms smuggling. As part of that project, Chadian and U.S. troops reportedly broke up an Algerian rebel operation in Chad in 2004.

The intense fighting that broke out in the Darfur region of Sudan in early 2003 had major repercussions for Chad. Some 200,000 refugees from the non-Arab population of Darfur fled across the border into Chad, populated by many of the same ethnic groups as those in Darfur (including President Déby's Zaghawa group). Sudan subsequently accused Chad of permitting Sudanese rebels to operate out of Chad, while Chad made similar accusations about Chadian rebels in Sudan. President Déby was prominent in subsequent efforts to mediate a settlement to the Darfur violence.

In August 2006 Chad broke off ties with Taiwan and restored relations with China, apparently seeking increased investment from China and also hoping that Chinese influence might help resolve the crisis in Darfur. (See Current issues, below, for details on subsequent developments in the related issues of Darfur, rebel attacks on N'Djamena, and the influence of France, the United States, and Libya in Chadian affairs.)

Current issues. Criticism of President Déby's "increasingly autocratic rule" intensified in May 2004 when the assembly proposed an amendment to the constitution to permit him to run for a third term. The opposition parties called for a boycott of the June constitutional referendum on the matter and described the government's official results of the voting as "imaginary." More threatening to the regime was the desertion of members of the presidential guard and other military forces in October and the collateral organization of well-armed rebel groups along both sides of the Sudanese border. In addition, the government reported that it had thwarted an attempted coup in November on the part of soldiers at two bases. In response, Déby launched a "sweeping purge" of the military and formed a new security force under his direct command amid other manifestations of popular discontent prompted, in part, by the widespread perception that two years of windfall oil revenues had been mismanaged.

In late December 2005 the assembly approved new legislation permitting the administration to allocate additional oil revenue toward the general budget, which critics argued Déby would use almost exclusively to purchase armaments. The World Bank, which had been charged with allocating the oil revenues, decried the change as a violation of a prior agreement (see The Country, above, for details) and in January 2006 suspended the disbursement of $125 million in accumulated revenues. The Bank also halted its own lending program to Chad. The Déby administration responded with a threat to halt oil production altogether if the Bank did not reverse its course, sending a shiver through the world's oil markets.

Opposition parties strongly criticized the assembly's decision in January 2006 to postpone the upcoming April elections for a year, arguing that the government was simply trying to maintain its control of the legislature prior to the presidential balloting scheduled for May. Further mass military defections to the newly formed United Front for Change (FUC) were reported in February, and more than 100 soldiers were arrested in March in relation to an alleged attempt to shoot down Déby's plane. The unrest culminated in a rapid incursion by FUC forces from the Sudanese border that reached the outskirts of N'Djamena on April 13 before encountering significant resistance. The rebels were finally repulsed at the steps of the assembly building. More than 300 people were killed in the fighting, which also severely damaged eastern portions of N'Djamena. Déby accused the Sudanese government of backing the FUC, announcing that a "state of hostility" existed between Chad and Sudan. (Most analysts agreed with Déby's assertions, suggesting that Sudan, which had supported Deby's takeover in 1990, was now convinced that the Chadian government was providing assistance to the largely Zaghawa rebel groups fighting the *Janjaweed* militias in Darfur [see article on Sudan for details].)

Significantly, France sent an additional 150 troops to its garrison in Chad during the April 2006 FUC incursion, and a French jet fired warning shots over the rebel forces in an apparent indication that France would not tolerate any attacks on French citizens. Although the French forces did not assist government troops in repulsing the rebels, their presence underscored the widespread perception that France preferred that Déby remain in power. Other Western countries also appeared to consider Déby the most likely leader to prevent Chad from descending further into ethnic/regional/political fragmentation that might threaten oil flows or lead to installation of a "pro-Sudan" administration. Consequently, Western criticism was moderate concerning the May presidential election, which Chadian opposition parties characterized as Déby simply "installing himself for life." (Déby's only opponents were "three cronies" and one candidate from a minor opposition party.) Realpolitik also appeared to play a role in the World Bank's decision to resume lending to Chad in May and to agree to begin releasing oil revenue gradually upon the anticipated adoption of more transparent accounting practices by the Chadian administration. The accord also permitted the government to close the fund that had been established for the "post-oil" years and, apparently, to direct additional resources to security matters.

Rebels operating out of Sudan launched a series of attacks in eastern Chad in September 2006. (The coalition of rebel forces included the FUC and the Union of Forces for Democracy and Development [*Union des Forces pour la Démocratie et le Développement*—UFDD], which, under the leadership of Mahamat NOURI, reportedly enjoyed support from the Sudanese government.) UFDD attacks continued in November, prompting the government to declare a state of emergency in the east to, among other things, deal with an estimated 50,000 internal refugees. Reports subsequently surfaced that the Sudanese government had insisted that the rebel groups coalesce under the command of the UFDD's Nouri in order to continue to receive financial and other support. As an apparent consequence, the FUC's Nour Abdelkerim, fearful of being marginalized under the new rebel structure, launched negotiations with the Chadian government that produced a peace agreement in late December providing for a general amnesty for FUC fighters. Additionally, Nour Abdelkerim joined the cabinet as minister of national defense as part of the March 2007 reshuffle.

After initially deeming eastern Chad too dangerous to deploy peacekeepers, the UN Security Council in the spring of 2007 approved plans for an 11,000-member force. However, the Déby administration refused permission for a UN advance team to deploy, announcing it no longer believed a peacekeeping mission was necessary.

Although the Chadian government accused Sudan of launching airstrikes along the border in March 2007, the presidents of the two countries in May signed an accord in Saudi Arabia in which each pledged not to support rebel groups against the other, subject to the scrutiny of international monitors at the border. Subsequently, under Libyan mediation, the Chadian government and the major rebel groups in the east launched peace negotiations in June.

France and the UN began airlifting aid to the estimated 350,000 refugees in eastern Chad in June 2007, and the EU in July reached agreement in principle on a military force to protect the refugees and facilitate the disbursement of humanitarian supplies. Meanwhile, after six months of talks, the MPS in August concluded an agreement with the opposition CPDC under which a new independent elections commission would be established to oversee preparations for new assembly elections by the end of 2009. On an additional potentially positive note, the UFDD and the three other main rebel groups in the east agreed to a cease-fire in late October. However, most of the rebels resumed antigovernment military action a month later. The nation's turmoil also intensified in December when President Déby dismissed Defense Minister Nour and ordered government forces to move against remaining FUC fighters. Among other things, the turbulence delayed the deployment of the European Force Chad/CAR (EUFOR Chad/CAR), authorized by the EU eventually to comprise 4,300 troops (more than one-half from France). However, deployment of the United Nations Mission in the Central African Republic and Chad (*Mission des Nations Unies en République Centrafricaine et au Tchad*—MINURCAT) continued. (MINURCAT had been established by the UN Security Council in September to assist refugees and police forces.)

In late January 2008 the UFDD and the other eastern rebels launched an offensive that reached N'Djamena in several days. By February 2 the 3,000 well-armed rebels had surrounded the presidential palace and appeared poised to oust Déby. However, French forces protected the capital's airport from a rebel takeover, permitting government helicopters to attack the rebels, who were forced to withdraw after three days of fierce fighting that left more than 700 people dead and 10,000 displaced. (France had initially adopted a neutral stance in regard to the conflict but became "pro-Déby" after the UN Security Council condemned the rebel incursion and called upon member states to support the government. An AU summit also condemned the rebel initiative, as did the United States, with whom Déby had been cooperating recently regarding the U.S. antiterror campaign.)

President Déby in mid-February 2008 announced a state of emergency under which strong press restrictions were adopted and a number of opposition leaders were arrested. He also described the rebels as "Sudanese mercenaries," although in March he concluded another nonaggression accord with Sudan's President al-Bashir. Faced with an international backlash against his crackdown on the opposition, Déby subsequently called for new dialogue toward implementation of the August 2007 political accord, culminating in the appointment in April of a new prime minister and "unity" government that included members of the CPDC. However, the rebels in the east vowed to continue their anti-Déby campaign, describing him as a "corrupt and autocratic ruler" who had "plundered" recent oil revenues. The rebels also urged EUFOR Chad/CAR, which had become operational in March, not to intervene on the side of the government in the event of future warfare.

Rebel activity intensified in June 2008 on the part of the newly formed National Alliance (see below), and although the government subsequently claimed a "decisive victory," attacks were also reported later in the year. Meanwhile, international aid groups warned of a growing humanitarian crisis among the refugees in eastern Chad.

In January 2009 the UN Security Council extended the mandate of MINURCAT until at least March 2010 and expanded the mission's force level to 5,200 so that a new military component could provide follow-up to EUFOR Chad/CAR, whose mandate was set to expire in March. Underscoring the growing complexities facing many UN operations throughout the world, MINURCAT troops were called upon, among other things, to protect civilians from both rebel and government forces, facilitate humanitarian aid, and shield UN workers from attack or abuse. At that point it was estimated that there were approximately 290,000 refugees from Darfur in eastern Chad, 50,000 refugees from the CAR in southern Chad, and 180,000 internally displaced Chadians.

Chadian government troops in May 2009 repulsed another rebel offensive that had been launched by the recently formed Union of Resistance Forces, which most analysts described as enjoying Sudanese backing. Tensions with Sudan became even more inflamed when Chadian warplanes crossed the border to attack rebel bases in Sudan. One consequence of the ongoing conflict was the postponement of legislative elections until at least 2010, although reports surfaced that the EU was distressed by the delay and the overall lack of progress toward "good governance" on the part of the Déby administration.

POLITICAL PARTIES AND GROUPS

Prior to the collapse of the Habré regime and the suspension of the constitution on December 3, 1990, by Idriss Déby, single-party government control had been exercised by the National Union for Independence and Revolution (*Union Nationale pour l'Indépendence et la Révolution*—UNIR). President Déby, governing in the name of the Patriotic Salvation Movement (MPS, see below), declared himself to be a supporter of multipartyism, and on October 1, 1991, the Council of Ministers authorized the legalization of parties provided they "shun intolerance, tribalism, regionalism, religious discrimination, and recourse to violence." The first parties were recognized in March 1992.

Parties and Groups Represented in the Cabinet:

Patriotic Salvation Movement (*Mouvement Patriotique du Salut*—MPS). The MPS was formed in Libya in March 1990 by a number of groups opposed to the regime of President Hisséne Habré. The movement was headed by Idriss Déby, a former Chadian military leader and presidential adviser, who had participated in an April 1989 coup attempt. (For a list of groups that participated in the launching of the MPS, see the 2007 *Handbook*.)

The MPS endorsed a prodemocracy platform, while "preaching neither capitalism nor socialism." After ousting the Habré government in late 1990, it gained the allegiance of a number of other groups. Déby subsequently governed in the name of the MPS, remaining as president of the republic and commander-in-chief of the armed forces. An extraordinary MPS congress held April 10–11, 1996, "unanimously" selected Déby as the party's presidential nominee, the MPS leader later receiving the endorsement of a number of minor parties grouped as the Republican Front during his successful campaign. The MPS initially was credited with winning 55 seats in the assembly elections of early 1997 but was subsequently given additional seats following a controversial review by the national electoral commission. Its final total was placed at 65, which gave the MPS a working majority in the 125-member legislature. The MPS was credited with 108 seats in an expanded 155-member assembly in the 2002 balloting.

Leaders: Idriss DÉBY Itno (President of the Republic and Chair of the Party), Idriss Ndélé Moussa YAMINI (Parliamentary Leader), Mahamet HISSENE (Secretary General).

Coordination of Parties for the Defense of the Constitution (*Coordination des Partis pour la Défense de la Constitution*—CPDC). In 2004 some 20–30 opposition parties (including a number formerly aligned with the MPS) formed the CPDC to protest, among other things, the MPS plan to revise the constitution to permit another presidential term for Déby. The CPDC also demanded revision of the electoral code, appointment of a truly independent election commission, and the use of international election observers at future balloting. Having failed to affect the plans of the MPS, the CPDC (whose components were considered to be in agreement on the constitutional issues "but little else") called for a boycott of the 2005 national referendum and the 2006 presidential election. Following the rebel attack on N'Djamena in April 2006, CPDC spokesperson Ibni Oumar Mahamat Saleh said the CPDC was neither prorebel nor progovernment, although it opposed violent overthrow of the administration. Rebel leaders insisted that CPDC representatives be included in the peace talks launched in June 2007 (see Current issues, above), but the government rejected that request. However, the government and the CPDC concluded an agreement in August 2007 under which new legislative elections were tentatively scheduled for December 2009 under the auspices of a new independent election commission.

Following the rebel attack on N'Djamena in January–February 2008, several CPDC leaders were temporarily detained by security forces, and Saleh's whereabouts subsequently remained unknown. However, in April four representatives from CPDC parties were named to the new cabinet, CPDC leaders urging President Déby to enter into peace negotiations with the rebels. As of late 2008 it was widely assumed (although not officially confirmed) that Saleh had died while in the custody of Chadian security forces. Although members of some CPDC components subsequently continued to serve in the cabinet, other members strongly criticized the government for perceived repressive policies.

Union for Renewal and Democracy (*Union pour le Renouveau et la Démocratie*—URD). The URD was legalized in May 1992 under the leadership of Lt. Col. Wadal Abdelkader Kamougué, a former commander of the forces of the Chadian Armed Forces (*Forces Armées Tchadiennes*—FAT) in southern Chad who had served as a GUNT vice president (see Political background, above) and was subsequently a member of the Provisional Council of the Republic.

Kamougué was the runner-up to President Déby in the first round of the June 1996 presidential election, earning a reported 12.4 percent of the votes. Although the URD leader alleged major irregularities had occurred in that balloting, he ultimately agreed to stand against Déby in the second round, in which he was credited with 30.9 percent of the votes. Kamougué's strong performance in the 1996 race established the URD as the nation's leading opposition force, particularly in view of its strong southern support. The URD finished second to the MPS in the 1997 legislative balloting with 29 seats. Kamougué was elected president of the new assembly, and the URD subsequently participated in MPS-led cabinets. In the 2001 presidential election Kamougué received 6 percent of the vote. The URD, which won 3 seats in the 2002 assembly poll, subsequently moved into the opposition camp to protest various constitutional changes engineered by the MPS. Kamougué was named minister of national defense as one of the CPDC members of the new cabinet named in April 2008.

Leaders: Gen. Wadal Abdelkader KAMOUGUÉ (1996 and 2001 presidential candidate and Former President of the National Assembly), Sangde NGARNOUDJIBE (Secretary General).

National Union for Development and Renewal (*Union National pour le Développement et le Renouvellement*—UNDR). The UNDR is led by Saleh Kebzabo, who was a minister of public works and transportation in the Moungar government and ran third in the first round of the June 1996 presidential election with 8.6 percent of the vote. He subsequently announced the UNDR's alliance with the MPS and threw his support to President Déby for the second round, thereby earning appointment to the cabinet formed in August. The party won 15 seats in the 1997 legislative poll, reportedly participating in an electoral alliance with the MPS. News reports surrounding subsequent political activity described the UNDR as primarily representing the interests of Muslims in the southwest of Chad.

Kebzabo was named minister of mines, energy, and oil in January 1998, but he and two UNDR secretaries of state left the government four months later. However, Kebzabo and four UNDR colleagues were named ministers in the December 1999 cabinet reshuffle. Kebzabo ran for president in 2001, receiving 7 percent of the vote. The UNDR won 6 seats in the 2002 assembly poll and was subsequently referenced as being firmly in the opposition camp.

Kebzabo was reportedly targeted for arrest following the rebel offensive of early 2008 but fled the country. He subsequently returned after a security guarantee from the government, and served as the primary spokesperson for the CPDC into mid-2009, arguing that dialogue with President Déby had broken down and that little progress had been achieved in implementing the August 2007 accord on electoral reform. Meanwhile, the UNDR announced that it hoped to present common candidates with the other CPDC parties in the next legislative election..

Leader: Saleh KEBZABO (President, Parliamentary Leader, and 2001 presidential candidate).

National Alliance for Development (*Alliance Nationale pour le Développement*—AND). Nabia NDALI, a member of the AND, was named minister of civil service and labor in the May 1992 cabinet. However, he resigned two months later following a dispute between AND leaders and Prime Minister Yodeyman, who was initially described as "close" to the AND but was subsequently reported to have been formally expelled from the group.

The AND was initially reported to have won no seats in the 1997 assembly balloting but, following a review by the national electoral commission, it was subsequently awarded two. AND President Salibou Garba was a member of the cabinet from May 1994 to April 2002, although he was subsequently referenced as a leader of the opposition's CPDC.

Garba, who reportedly narrowly avoided arrest following the rebel offensive in early 2008, reportedly objected to the inclusion of CPDC members in the April 2008 cabinet, arguing that President Déby was trying to "divide" the CPDC.

Leader: Salibou GARBA (President).

Rally for Democracy and Progress (*Rassemblement pour la Démocratie et le Progrès*—RDP). The RDP held its organizational congress in December 1991, its leadership including the mayor of N'Djamena, Lol Mahamat Choua, who had been proposed as president of an eventually aborted provisional national government in 1979. A number of RDP members were reportedly among those killed or arrested by Chadian security forces during the crackdown that followed the coup attempt of January 1992. (It was believed that the RDP was subjected to reprisal because of the support it enjoyed among the Kanem ethnic group, centered in the Lake Chad area, where the rebels had apparently received popular assistance.) Nevertheless, the RDP in early March was one of the first political parties to be legalized and was considered one of the leading components of the opposition coalition prior to the designation of Choua as chair of the Higher Transitional Council (CST) in April 1993.

In October 1994 Choua was replaced as CST chair, the RDP leader subsequently accusing the Déby regime of human rights violations, including the harassment of many RDP members. Choua was credited with 5.9 percent of the vote in the first round of the

1996 presidential election. In a surprise development, Choua supported President Déby in the 2001 presidential election.

The RDP secured 14 seats in the 2002 assembly balloting and subsequently served in the cabinet until November 2003, when it withdrew from the government to protest Déby's announced plans to seek a third term. Choua subsequently served as a prominent figure in the anti-Déby CPDC, and he was briefly detained by security forces following the rebel attack on N'Djamena in early 2008.

Leaders: Lol Mahamat CHOUA (Parliamentary Leader and Former Chair of the Higher Transitional Council), Chetti Ali ABBAS.

Union for Democracy and the Republic (*Union pour la Démocratie et la République*—UDR). The UDR was launched by Jean Bawoyeu Alingué in March 1992 and formally recognized a month later. Although Alingué was replaced as prime minister in May, the new cabinet included Djimasta Koibla, another UDR member. However, after being named prime minister in April 1995, Koibla was subsequently described as having taken a leave of absence from the party. Meanwhile, the UDR moved into a position as one of the main opposition parties, Alingué receiving 8.3 percent of the vote in the first round of the 1996 presidential election. He also was one of the main critics of the government's involvement in the Democratic Republic of the Congo in 1998 and 1999. Alingué ran for president again in 2001, receiving only 2 percent of the ballots cast. The UDR boycotted the 2002 legislative elections, and Alingué subsequently remained a vocal critic of the government and proponent of the formation of opposition coalitions. However, he was named justice minister in the cabinet named in April 2008.

Leader: Dr. Jean Bawoyey ALINGUÉ (President of the Party and 2001 presidential candidate).

Party for Freedom and Development (*Parti pour la Liberté et le Développement*—PLD). Formed in late 1993 to promote the "rehabilitation" of Chad, the PLD captured three seats in the 1997 legislative elections. The PLD's candidate, Ibni Oumar Mahamat Saleh, secured 3 percent of the vote in the 2001 presidential election. The PLD boycotted the 2002 legislative elections. Saleh subsequently was described as the leader of the CPDC. Following the rebel offensive against N'Djamena in January–February 2008 Saleh was reportedly arrested by security forces. Although CPDC members joined the cabinet named in April, Saleh's whereabouts subsequently remained unknown, and his followers announced they would not support the new government.

Leaders: Ibni Oumar Mahamat SALEH (2001 presidential candidate), Paul SARADORI.

Rally of Nationalists for the Development of Chad/Redemption (*Rassemblement des Nationalistes pour le Développement du Chad/le Réveil*—RNDT). After the RNDT won a seat in the 2002 assembly balloting, its leader, Albert Pahimi Padacke, was named agriculture minister in 2005 and was a presidential candidate in 2006, securing 5.4 percent of the vote. He subsequently served as justice minister and was named minister of posts and information and communications technologies in April 2008.

Leader: Albert Pahimi PADACKE.

Other Legislative Parties:

Front of Action Forces for the Republic (*Front des Forces d'Action pour la République*—FFAR). Described as a "separatist" grouping, the FFAR won one seat in the 1997 legislative balloting. Its legislator, Ngarledjy Yorongar, subsequently became a prominent critic of government policy regarding the development of oil fields in southern Chad. He received a surprising 14 percent of the vote while finishing second in the 2001 presidential election. The FFAR was also credited with winning 10 seats in the 2002 assembly poll.

Although Yorongar called for a boycott of the 2005 constitutional referendum and the 2006 presidential poll, he and the FFAR did not participate in the CPDC. Yorongar also described the August 2007 electoral agreement between the CPDC and the government as a "waste of time." He was briefly detained by security forces following the rebel offensive of early 2008 and reportedly left the country briefly for France in March.

Leaders: Yorongar LEMOHIBAN, Ngarledjy YORONGAR (Parliamentary Leader and 2001 presidential candidate).

National Assembly for Democracy and Progress (*Rassemblement National pour la Démocratie et le Progrès*—RNDP). Formed in the spring of 1992, the RNDP (also regularly referenced as VIVA-RNDP) was subsequently described as a prominent exponent of the formation of opposition coalitions; its leader, Delwa Kassiré Koumakoye, served as spokesperson for a number of such groups. Koumakoye was named justice minister in the reshuffled transitional government announced in June 1993 and was elected prime minister in November. Following his dismissal in April 1995, Koumakoye charged that he had been made a scapegoat by President Déby and the Higher Transitional Council, whom he described as bearing true responsibility for the delay in national elections.

In March 1996 Koumakoye was sentenced to three months in prison for the illegal possession of weapons, the RNDP leader accusing the Déby regime of manufacturing the charge in order to thwart his presidential ambitions. The following September it was announced that Koumakoye had been named spokesperson for a new opposition alliance called the Democratic Opposition Convention, which claimed the allegiance of more than 20 parties. The RNDP was initially credited with having secured four seats in the 1997 legislative poll, but all were given to other parties following the review by the national electoral commission. Koumakoye won 2 percent of the votes in the 2001 presidential poll.

The RNDP served in various cabinets following the 2002 assembly balloting, at which it won five seats. Koumakoye, by then considered to be aligned with Déby, was one of five candidates in the 2006 presidential election; he finished second with 8.8 percent of the vote. Following the death of Prime Minister Pascal Yoadimnadji in February 2007, Koumakoye was again appointed as prime minister. However, he was dismissed in April 2008 after his relations with Déby had again become strained.

Leader: Delwa Kassiré KOUMAKOYE (Former Prime Minister, President of the Party, and 2001 and 2006 presidential candidate).

National Union (*Union National*—UN). The UN was established in early 1992 by Abdoulaye Lamana, a former Chadian ambassador to Belgium. Its members reportedly included a number of former Frolinat adherents, notably Mahamat Djarma, former deputy to Frolinat leader Goukhouni Oueddei. An April 1996 party congress selected Lamana as its presidential nominee, the UN chair finishing well down the list among the 15 candidates in the first round of balloting. According to initial reports, the party won two seats in the 1997 legislative balloting, but they were taken away following the postelection review by the national electoral commission. Lamana was named minister of mines, energy, and oil in May 1998 but was not included in the reshuffled cabinet announced in December 1999. In 2005 Lamana was reportedly serving as chair of the government-appointed committee established to oversee the allocation of oil revenues.

Leaders: Abdoulaye LAMANA (Chair), Mahamat DJARMA.

Other minor parties that gained a single seat in the National Assembly in the 2002 election included **Action for the Renewal of Chad** (*Action pour le Renouvellement du Tchad*—ART), led by Oumar BOUCHAR; the **Chadian Social Democratic Party** (*Parti Social-Démocrate du Tchad*—PSDT), a southern grouping led by businessman Niabe ROMAIN; the **Convention for Democracy and Federalism** (*Convention pour la Démocratie et le Fédéralisme*—CDF), led by Ali GOLHOR; the **Party for Democracy and Integral Independence** (*Parti pour la Démocratie et l'Indépendance Intégrale*—PDI); the **People's Movement for Democracy in Chad** (*Mouvement Populaire pour la Démocratie au Tchad*—MPDT) whose leader, Mahamat ABDOULAYE, was appointed to the cabinet in 2005 and was a presidential candidate in 2006; and the **Rally for the Republic–LINGUA** (*Rassemblement pour la République*–LINGUA—RPR-LINGUA), led by Mersile Atti MAHAMAT.

Other Parties:

Action for Unity and Socialism (*Action pour l'Unité et le Socialisme*—Actus). Actus is a former GUNT tendency that in March 1990 announced it was regrouping with the **Revolutionary Movement of the Chadian People** (*Mouvement Révolutionnaire du Peuple Tchadien*—MRPT), another GUNT faction led by Bire TITINAN, to form a joint **Rally for Democratic Action and Progress** (*Rassemblement pour l'Action Démocratique et le Progrès*—RADP). However, Actus leader Dr. Fidèle Moungar was appointed to the May 1992 cabinet under his own formation's rubric, not that of the RADP. Dr. Moungar was subsequently named to form a transitional government in April 1993, although he was forced to resign as prime minister in October following passage of a nonconfidence motion by the Higher Transitional Council. The Actus leader was disqualified from running for president in 1996 by the Chadian Court of Appeal on the grounds that he did not meet the nation's residency requirements. Actus was at first reported to have won four seats in the 1997 legislative poll, but that number was ultimately halved by the national electoral commission.

Some reports credited Actus with winning one seat in the 2002 assembly poll. Moungar has reportedly been living in exile recently.

Leader: Dr. Fidèle MOUNGAR (Former Prime Minister).

National Convention for Social Democracy (*Convention National pour la Démocratie Sociale*—CNDS). The leader of the CNDS, former Habré minister Adoum Moussa SEIF, won 4.9 percent of the vote in the first round of the 1996 presidential election, and the party won one seat in the 1997 legislative balloting. In 1998, however, Seif was described in news reports as heading a rebel group in the Lake Chad region, the Armed Resistance Against Anti-Democratic Forces. The rump CNDS, under the leadership of Adoum Daye Zere, supported President Déby in his 2001 reelection campaign. Some reports credited the CNDS with winning one seat in the 2002 assembly poll.

Leaders: Adoum Daye ZERE, Assane Amath PATCHA.

Also active have been the **New African Socialist** (*Socialiste Africain Rénové*—SAR), which fielded a candidate, Ibrahim KOULAMALLAH, in the 2006 presidential election; the **Rally for Progress and Social Justice** (*Rassemblement pour le Progrès et la Justice Sociale*—RPJS), registered in January 1996 and the first Chadian party to be led by a woman (Leopoldine Adoun NDARADOUNRY); the **Rally of Chadian Nationalists** (*Rassemblement des Nationalistes Tchadiennes*—RNT); and the **Socialist Movement for Democracy in Chad** (*Mouvement Socialiste pour la Démocratie au Tchad*—MSDT), led by Albert Mbainaido DJOMIA.

Other Groups:

Union of Forces for Democracy and Development (*Union des Forces pour la Démocratie et le Développement*—UFDD). The UFDD, based in eastern Chad and perceived to be supported by Sudan, was formed in mid-2006 under the leadership of Mahamat Nouri, a northerner who had been considered the second in command (as leader of the UNIR) during the Habré regime but had also served as a cabinet minister and diplomat in the Déby administration. The UFDD was prominent (along with the FUC, CDR, and SCUD) in the rebel coalition that invaded eastern Chad from Sudan in September 2006 (see Current issues, above, for additional information). The UFDD, whose members come mainly from the Goran ethnic group, in December announced military cooperation with the RFC and CNT and continued antigovernment activity throughout the first half of 2007, the UFDD at that point being considered the leading rebel organization in view of the FUC's Mahamat Nour Abdelkerim having joined the Déby cabinet.

In October 2007 the UFDD joined the RFC, CNT, and UFDD Fundamental (see below) in signing a Libyan-brokered cease-fire agreement that called for a permanent peace settlement under which the rebels would be integrated into the national army. However, a month later Nouri accused Déby of reneging on the agreement, and fighting broke out again between government forces and the UFDD, RFC, UFDD Fundamental, and other rebel groups, who in late January 2008 launched an offensive against the capital that almost deposed Déby (see Current issues, above, for details). Following their retreat, the UFDD, UFDD Fundamental, RFC, and other small groups announced the formation of a **National Alliance** (*Alliance Nationale*—AN) to continue the anti-Déby campaign under the "single leadership" of Nouri. (Some members of the component groups reportedly objected to Sudan's apparent insistence that the post be given to Nouri, and news reports subsequently referred to Ali GADAYE as the leader of the AN.) The AN, urging French or other foreign troops not to "prop up" the Déby government, vowed further efforts to take over the capital unless all-inclusive negotiations toward a unity government were launched. A new AN offensive was reported in mid-June.

Leaders: Mahamat NOURI, Hassane BOULMAYU, Abakar TOLLIMI (Secretary General).

Union of Forces for Democracy and Development Fundamental (*Union des Forces pour la Démocratie et le Développement Fondamentelle*—UFDD Fundamental). The Arab-led UFDD Fundamental broke from the UFDD in 2007 in a leadership dispute with UFDD leader Mahamat Nouri. However, the UFDD Fundamental joined the UFDD and other rebel groups in the attack on N'Djamena in early 2008.

Leaders: Abdelwahid Aboud MAKAYE, Acheickh ibn OUMAR.

Rally of Forces for Change (*Rassemblement des Forces pour le Changement*—RFC). A new rebel faction, the RFC was organized in December 2006 by brothers Tom and Timan Erdimi, relatives of President Déby who stopped supporting the president after the controversial constitutional revision in 2004 to permit Déby to run for another term. The Erdimis had previously participated in the Platform for Change, Unity, and Democracy (*Socle pour le Changement, l'Unité, et la Démocratie*—SCUD), which had been formed in October 2005 by some 300 former members of the Presidential Guard and other government forces. The SCUD, which reportedly attracted members of President Déby's Zaghawa clan, subsequently engaged government troops in eastern Chad but did not participate in the failed April 2006 attack on N'Djamena by the FUC. Major rebel activity for the rest of 2006 was conducted by an umbrella group called the Rally of Democratic Forces (*Rassemblement des Forces Démocratiques*—RAFD), which included the SCUD and the CNT. The RFC appeared to serve as a partial successor to the RAFD in 2007. (See UFDD, above, for information on the RFC's participation in subsequent antigovernment activity.)

In January 2009 the RFC served as a core founder (along with the UFDD and UFCD) of the **Union of Resistance Forces** (*Union des Forces du Résistance*—UFR), an umbrella for some eight rebel groups dedicated to the overthrow of President Déby. Timan Erdimi was named chair of the grouping, whose estimated 2,000 fighters launched an unsuccessful offensive against government forces in May 2009.

Leaders: Tom ERDIMI, Timan ERDIMI.

Union of Forces for Change and Democracy (*Union des Forces pour le Changement et la Démocratie*—UFCD). The UFCD was formed in March 2008 by UFDD and RFC dissidents who opposed the designation (apparently at Sudan's insistence) of the UFDD's Mahamat Nouri as the leader of the new National Alliance of rebel groups. However, a degree of reconciliation with the National Alliance was subsequently reported.

Leaders: Adouma HASSABALLAH, Karim Bory ISSA.

Chadian National Concord (*Concorde Nationale Tchadienne*—CNT). The largely Arab CNT was one of the most active rebel groups in eastern Chad in 2006, often in alliance with the RAFD. The CNT joined other rebel groups in signing a much-heralded peace agreement with the government in October 2007. However, when the other three signatories resumed antigovernment activity a month later, CNT leader Hassan Al Djinedi, other CNT officials, and their followers remained supportive of the government and the cease-fire. Al Djinedi was named a secretary of state in a February 2008 cabinet reshuffle, although some CNT members continued their rebel activity, having announced the "expulsion" of Al Djinedi and his supporters.

Leaders: Hassan Al DJINEDI, Ismail MOUSSA (leader of militant faction).

United Front for Change (*Front Uni pour le Changement*—FUC). The FUC was formed in December 2005 by the **Rally for Democracy and Liberty** (*Rassemblement pour la Démocratie et la Liberté*—RDL) and a number of other groups, some of which comprised deserters from the Chadian army as well as Chadian exiles in Sudan opposed to the recent constitutional changes and the "dictatorial rule" of President Déby. The RDL had been formed earlier in the year in the Darfur region of Sudan and had launched an unsuccessful attack on the Chadian city of Adré near the Sudanese border on December 18. The RDL was led by Mahamat Nour Abdelkerim, who had branched out of the National Alliance of Resistance (*Alliance Nationale de la Résistance*—ANR), which had been formed in the mid-1990s by five rebel groups and had grown to include eight antigovernment groups operating in the eastern part of the country. The ANR signed a peace agreement with the government in January 2003 with a long-term plan to transition to a formal political party, and Col. Mahamat GARFA (an ANR founder) joined the MPS-led cabinet later in the year. However, one faction of the ANR refused to accept the cease-fire and continued fighting under the leadership of Nour Abdelkerim, who was instrumental in the organization of the FUC, which demanded the convening of a national forum to address the country's political future, the installation of a transitional government, and new elections. (Nour Abdelkerim is a member of the Tama ethnic group, which reportedly led to leadership tension within the FUC, a predominantly Zaghawa grouping.) The FUC, also referenced as the United Front for Democratic Change, attempted a military takeover of the government in April 2006, the Déby government alleging that the Sudanese government was supporting the FUC (see Current issues, above, for additional information). On December 24, 2006, Nour Abdelkerim signed a peace agreement with the government, and he was appointed minister of defense in March 2007. Among other things, the recent accord called for the integration of FUC fighters (estimated at 6,000) into the national army. However, reports indicated that disaffected members of the FUC had established a rival rebel grouping, still called the FUC, but with a new leadership, led by Abderman KOULAMALLAH.

Nour Abdelkerim was dismissed as defense minister in December 2007, in part, apparently, because he had been reluctant to direct FUC fighters to join the government's battle against the UFDD and other rebel groups. President Déby had also ordered government forces to forcibly disarm the FUC, which led to FUC/government fighting. It was subsequently reported that a number of Nour Abdelkerim's Tama supporters had been arrested, while Nour Abdelkerim, apparently in poor health, took refuge in the Libyan embassy. Some FUC fighters reportedly joined the rebel offensive against N'Djamena in early 2008, and Nour Abdelkerim was subsequently sentenced to death in absentia by a Chadian magistrate's court.

Leaders: Mahamat NOUR Abdelkerim, Col. Regis BECHIR.

United Front for Democracy and Peace (*Front Uni pour la Démocratie et la Paix*—FUDP). Formed in 2005 by dissidents from the MDJT as well as members of rebel groups based in Benin seeking a negotiated peace settlement, the FUDP subsequently was joined by a number of other parties and rebel groups, including the MDD.

Movement for Development and Democracy (*Mouvement pour le Développement et la Démocratie*—MDD). The MDD was formed in 1991 as the political arm of pro-Habré rebel forces, which in late December launched an attempted overthrow of the Déby regime from the western border, where they had been camped since Habré's ouster a year earlier. Although the government at first estimated the MDD strength at more than 3,000, it was subsequently reported that only about 500 had participated in the attempted coup.

Despite the highly publicized announcement of several peace agreements during 1992, fighting continued between government troops and MDD followers, who sometimes referred to themselves as the Western Armed Forces (*Forces Armées Occidentales*—FAO). In early 1993 the MDD was reportedly split into a pro-Habré faction known as the National Armed Forces of Chad (*Forces Armées Nationales Tchadiennes*—FANT), led by Mahamat Saleh FADIL, and an anti-Habré faction loyal to Goukhouni Guët (reportedly in prison). Members of the latter faction were reportedly invited to the Sovereign National Conference that began in January, but the FANT, described by *Africa Confidential* as "much feared in N'Djamena by both government and opposition," remained outside the national reconciliation process.

In January 1994 the MDD announced an alliance with another guerrilla group, the **National Union for Democracy and Socialism** (*Union National pour la Démocratie et le Socialisme*—UNDS) and called upon other anti-Déby rebels to join them in united military activity. A year later, however, the MDD was described as still split into two factions "fighting each other, not Déby." Meanwhile, Habré remained in exile in Senegal, the general amnesty of December 1994 having specifically excluded him.

The apparent reunification of the MDD factions was reported in April 1995, and an extraordinary congress in August elected a new 16-member executive bureau headed by Mahamat Seïd Moussa MEDELLA. Subsequently, in November, an agreement was announced between the government and the MDD calling for the cessation of hostilities, exchange of prisoners, and the integration of MDD guerrillas into the national army. Some MDD fighters subsequently remained in conflict with government forces, however, and factionalization on that issue surfaced within the grouping again in 1998. The MDD joined the FUDP in 2003. By that time there were two main factions of the MDD: one led by Ibrahim Malla Mahamet, the other led by Issa Faki Mahamet.

Leaders: Goukhouni GUËT (in detention), Aboubarkaye HAROUN (Representative in Paris), Ibrahim Malla MAHAMET (Chair of the Executive Bureau).

Chad National Liberation Front (*Front de Libération National Tchadien*—Frolinat). Frolinat was established in 1966 by northerners opposed to the administration of President Tombalbaye, a southerner. The organization eventually suffered such severe factionalization that Frolinat became little more than a generic name for various groups originally based in the north, including splinters loyal to subsequent Chadian presidents Goukhouni Oueddei and Hissène Habré.

Following Habré's capture of N'Djamena in 1982, most of the factions opposed to his Frolinat/FAN coalesced under a reconstituted GUNT. During 1983 and 1984, dissent among GUNT factions over the extent of Libyan involvement led to reported dissolution of the coalition, although pronouncements continued to be issued in its name. During a meeting in Sebha, Libya, on August 7, 1984, most of the pro-Libyan military components of GUNT joined in forming the National Council of Liberation (*Conseil National de la Libération*—CNL), which was succeeded by a more inclusive Supreme Revolutionary Council (*Conseil Suprême de la Révolution*—CSR) a year later. By 1986, however, anti-Libyan sentiment appeared to have gained the ascendancy, with Oueddei being removed as CSR chair (and president of GUNT) in November. Thereafter, the CSR declined in importance, many of its component groups having announced their dissolution and acceptance of integration into the UNIR. Although Oueddei announced a cabinet reshuffle in May 1988 in an attempt to consolidate his position among remaining GUNT factions, he was described in mid-1990 as "essentially marginalized" as an antigovernment influence.

Continuing to position himself as the leader of Frolinat, Oueddei made a highly publicized return from exile to meet with President Déby in May 1991 and suggested that cooperation with the new regime was possible if opposition political parties were permitted. Subsequently, however, Oueddei returned to Algiers and, following the abortive October coup, was reportedly informed that he was again not welcome in his homeland. During an interview in mid-1992 Oueddei described Frolinat as "still an armed liberation movement" but one that was "currently not fighting" and dedicated, for the time being, to "resolving problems through dialogue." Oueddei, described as remaining widely respected by the public and considered a potential mediator among Chad's many ethnic and political adversaries, participated in the Sovereign National Conference in early 1993. Although he was reported in 1995 to be still harboring presidential ambitions, there was little evidence of his influence in the nation's 1996 democratization process. In December 1998 Oueddei issued a statement in Algiers calling for an "uprising" against the Déby government, and in early 1999 Frolinat announced its support for the Toubou rebels in northern Chad.

Oueddei, who has lived primarily in Algeria and Libya since leaving Chad in the early 1990s, in late 2005 said that he supported the rebels in eastern Chad who were attempting to overthrow the Déby regime. However, in mid-2007 he offered to serve as a mediator between the remaining rebels and the government, and in mid-2008 he called for a "national dialogue" among all Chadian groups.

Leaders: Goukhouni OUEDDEI (Former President of the Republic), Mahmoud Ali MAHMOUD.

Movement for Democracy and Justice in Chad (*Mouvement pour la Démocratie et la Justice en Tchad*—MDJT). Led then by Youssef TOGOIMI, a former minister in the Déby administration, the MDJT launched guerrilla activity against government troops in late 1998 in northern Chad and by April 1999 was claiming control of substantial territory. It was still active in mid-2001, although there was little independently verifiable information on the breadth and scope of its activities. The government was sufficiently concerned about the MDJT to periodically issue communiqués minimizing the extent of the rebellion. The grouping reportedly drew its support from the Toubou ethnic group, described as a "traditional warrior community" in the Tibesti mountain region along the border with Niger.

In 2002 Togoimi was killed by a land mine, and one faction of the MDJT left the group to participate in the formation of the FUDP (see above). The government subsequently was reported to have negotiated a cease-fire with a number of local MDJT commanders, and a broader accord was brokered in January 2003, many MDJT elements reportedly accepting amnesty for an end to attacks. In August 2005 the government signed a final agreement with the MDJT that provided for the eventual integration of remaining MDJT fighters into the national army. At an extraordinary congress in November 2006, MDJT members still opposed to conciliation with the government reportedly voted to disband the MDJT and merge with Frolinat. However, it was reported in late 2008 that a rump MDJT had aligned with the recently formed National Alliance rebel grouping.

Other rebel groups that were active in 2007 included the **Movement for Peace, Reconstruction, and Development** (*Mouvement pour la Paix, la Reconstruction, et le Développement*—MPRD), which is led by Djibrine DASSERT and operates from the Central African Republic; and the **Union of Democratic Forces for the Assembly** (*Union des Forces Démocratiques pour le Rassemblement*—UFDR), a coalition of smaller rebel groups in the northern areas of Chad, led by Michel DETODIA.

LEGISLATURE

As provided for in the constitution approved by national referendum in December 1989, a 123-member unicameral **National Assembly** (*Assemblée Nationale*) was elected by direct universal suffrage for a five-year term on July 8, 1990. However, the assembly was dissolved on December 3 upon the overthrow of the Habré regime. Subsequently, President Déby appointed a Provisional Council of the Republic (*Conseil Provisoire de la Républic*) to serve as an interim consultative body, which in turn was replaced by a 57-member Higher Transitional Council (*Conseil Supérieur de Transition*—CST) elected by the CNS in April 1993. The national constitutional referendum in March 1996 authorized the CST to continue to function pending the installation of the new bicameral legislature. Elections (for a four-year term) to the new 125-member National Assembly were held on January 5 and February 23, 1997. In February 2001 the assembly extended its mandate until at least April 2002.

Following the election to an expanded 155-member assembly on April 21, 2002, and subsequent by-election for 3 seats, it was reported that the Patriotic Salvation Movement held 108 seats; the Rally for Democracy and Progress, 14; the Front of Action Forces for the Republic, 10; the National Union for Development and Renewal, 6; the National Assembly for Democracy and Progress, 5; the Union for Renewal and Democracy, 3; and Action for the Renewal of Chad, the Chadian Social Democratic Party, the Convention for Democracy and Federalism, the National Alliance for Development, the National Rally for Democracy in Chad/Redemption, the National Union, the Party for Democracy and Integral Independence, the People's Movement for Democracy in Chad, and the Rally for the Republic–LINGUA, 1 each. (Reports varied slightly regarding these results.) In January 2006 the assembly voted to postpone new elections (scheduled for April 2006) until at least April 2007. New balloting was subsequently again postponed due to security problems in the east and the government's related imposition of a state of emergency. The next elections were most recently postponed until December 2010, although some analysts suggested the balloting might eventually be delayed again to coincide with the 2011 presidential poll .

President: Nassour Guélendouksia OUAÏDOU.

CABINET

[as of June 15, 2009]

Prime Minister	Youssouf Saleh Abbas
Ministers	
Agriculture	Naïmbaye Lossimian Mbaïlaou (CPDC)
Civil Service and Labor	Fatimé Tchombi (MPS) [f]
Commerce and Industry	Mahamat Ali Hassan
Communication and Government Spokesman	Mahamat Hissene (MPS)
Culture, Youth, and Sports	Djibert Younous
Economy and Planning	Qusmane Matar Breme (MPS)
Environment and Lake Resources	Ali Souleymane Dabye
Finance and Budget	Gata Ngoulou
Foreign Relations	Moussa Faki Mahamat (MPS)
Higher Education, Scientific Research, and Professional Formations	Ahmad Taboye
Human Rights and Promotion of Liberties	Abdraman Djasnabaille
General Control of the State and Moralization	Ahmadaye Alhassan
Infrastructure and Transportation	Adoum Younousmi (MPS)
Interior and Public Safety	Ahmat Mahamat Bachir (MPS)
Justice and Guardian of the Seals	Jean Bawoyeu Alingué (CPDC)
Livestock and Animal Resources	Moctar Moussa
Micro-Finance and the Fight Against AIDS	Mahamat Mamadou Addy
Mines and Energy	Ahmat Mahamat Karambal
Minister Delegate to the Prime Minister (Decentralization)	Emmanuel Nadinger (CPDC)
National Defense	Gen. Wadal Abdelkader Kamougué (CPDC)
National Education	Abderamane Koko
Oil and Engery	Mahamat Nasser Hassane
Posts and Information and Communications Technologies	Albert Pahimi Padacke (RNDT)
Public Health	Dr. Ngombaye Djaïbe
Social Action, National Solidarity, and Family	Ngarmbatina Carmel Soukate (MPS) [f]
Territorial Development, Urban Planning, and Housing	Hamid Mahamat Dahalob (CPDC)
Tourist Development and Handicrafts	Ahmat Barkai Animi
Water	Taher Sougoudi
Secretary General to the Government	Limane Mahamat

[f] = female

COMMUNICATIONS

The Ministry of Information controls most media. Journalists from *L'Observateur* and *Le Temps* were arrested in the first half of 2005 for articles critical of the administration, prompting strong protest from domestic and international journalism organizations. As part of a temporary state of emergency declared following rebel attacks in the fall of 2006, the government imposed new restrictions on the print media and ordered private radio stations not to broadcast information on security topics. Several arrests of journalists and closures of media outlets were subsequently reported. Reporters Without Borders in 2008 describe the relationship between the government and the private media as one of "mutual distrust." The government also decreed new press restrictions following the attempted rebel takeover in February 2008.

Press. Only a few, mostly low-circulation papers are published, with little readership outside N'Djamena. They include *Info-Tchad*, daily bulletin of the official news agency, ATP; *Al-Watan*, government weekly; *N'Djamena-Hebdo* (10,000), independent weekly; *L'Observateur* (10,000), independent weekly; *Le Temps*, independent weekly, *Le Progrès*, a privately owned but progovernment daily; and *Al Wihda*, an opposition weekly.

News agencies. The domestic agency is *Agence Tchadienne de Presse* (ATP). *Agence France-Presse* and Reuters also maintain offices in N'Djamena.

Broadcasting and computing. *Radiodiffusion Nationale Tchadienne* (RNT) broadcasts in French, Arabic, and local languages, while an independent radio station, *Radio Liberté*, began operations in June 2000. However, in October 2002 the station was suspended following critical reports about the president; it resumed broadcasting in December 2003. In April 2006, the government announced that private media companies could provide broadcasts of election coverage, subject to monitoring by the High Commission for Communication. *Télé-Chad* transmits from N'Djamena. As of 2008 there were 11.9 Internet users per 1,000 inhabitants.

INTERGOVERNMENTAL REPRESENTATION

Ambassador to the U.S.: Bechir Mahamoud ADAM.

U.S. Ambassador to Chad: Louis John NIGRO, Jr.

Permanent Representative to the UN: Ahmad ALLAM-MI.

IGO Memberships (Non-UN): AfDB, AU, BADEA, BDEAC, CEEAC, CEMAC, CILSS, IDB, Interpol, NAM, OAU, OIC, OIF, WCO, WTO.

CHILE

Republic of Chile
República de Chile

Political Status: Independent republic since 1818; present constitution approved September 11, 1980 (in effect from March 11, 1981), partially superseding military regime instituted in 1973; fully effective as of March 11, 1990.

Area: 292,256 sq. mi. (756,945 sq. km.).

Population: 15,116,435 (2002C); 16,765,000 (2008E). The 2002 figure lacks an adjustment for underenumeration.

Major Urban Centers (2005E): SANTIAGO (4,771,000), Puente Alto (602,000), Antofagasta (306,000), Viña del Mar (288,000), Valparaíso (260,000), Concepción (215,000).

Official Language: Spanish.

Monetary Unit: Peso (market rate December 1, 2009: 498.55 pesos = \$1US).

President: Michelle BACHELET (Socialist Party of Chile); elected in runoff balloting on January 15, 2006, and inaugurated on March 11 for a four-year term, succeeding Ricardo LAGOS Escobar (Party for Democracy).

THE COUNTRY

Occupying a narrow strip along about 2,700 miles of South America's west coast, the Chilean national territory also includes Easter Island, the Juan Fernández Islands, and other smaller Pacific territories. The population is predominantly mestizo (mixed Spanish and Indian) but also includes German, Italian, and other foreign groups. Roman Catholicism, which was disestablished in 1925, is the religion of 85 percent of the people. Women constitute about 33 percent of the paid labor force, a majority in domestic service, with the rest concentrated in agriculture, education, and health care. Save during the Allende regime of 1970–1973, when women were prominent both in government and in the opposition, female political representation was minimal until 1999, when women were awarded nearly one-third of ministerial appointments.

Chile, the fifth-largest economy in Latin America, is the world's leading copper producer, the commodity accounting for more than two-fifths of export earnings and a third of all government revenue, although reserves are expected to be exhausted within 20 years. Other commercially mined minerals include gold, silver, coal, and iron. In addition, there are extensive nitrate deposits in the north and some oil reserves in the south. Since World War II, the country has suffered from lagging agricultural production, with a reliance on food imports contributing to record balance-of-payment deficits in the early 1980s. From 1985 to 1997 the economy grew at an average rate of 6.4 percent a year, with deceleration thereafter to –1.1 percent in 1999 before a gradual rise to 6 percent in 2004 and 2005. Inflation, which had crested at 505 percent in 1974, declined to 2.3 percent in 1999, and then nearly doubled to 4.5 percent in 2000 before falling again to an average of 2.3 percent from 2001 to 2005.

According to the International Monetary Fund (IMF), annual GDP growth averaged 4.7 percent in 2006–2007. As unemployment reached nearly 8 percent, the government in 2007 announced tax cuts and other stimulus measures designed to promote small- and medium-sized businesses. Even with those measures, GDP growth declined to 3.2 percent in 2008. As a result of the global recession and falling copper prices, the country's economy was expected to stagnate in 2009 with 0.1 percent growth. Further, Chile's unemployment rate was forecast to reach 10.3 percent. Meanwhile, exports declined by more than 40 percent, and the price of copper dropped by 56 percent year on year due to a decline in global demand.

GOVERNMENT AND POLITICS

Political background. After winning its independence from Spain from 1810 to 1818 under the leadership of Bernardo O'HIGGINS, Chile experienced a period of alternating centralized and federal constitutions. The political struggles between conservative and liberal elements culminated in the civil war of 1829–1830, the conservatives emerging victorious. Conflicts with Peru and Bolivia from 1836 to 1839 and 1879 to 1884 (the War of the Pacific) resulted in Chile's territorial expansion at the expense of both.

Liberal elements prevailed in the presidential balloting following World War I. The election of Arturo ALESSANDRI Palma in 1920 was a victory for the middle classes, but the reforms he advocated were never implemented because of parliamentary intransigence. Left-right antagonism after World War II occasioned widespread fears for the future of the democratic regime, but the election in 1964 of Eduardo FREI Montalva initially appeared to open the way to fundamental economic and social reforms. The failure of the Frei regime to accomplish these goals led to the election of Salvador ALLENDE Gossens in 1970, Chile thus becoming the first republic in North or South America to choose an avowedly Marxist president by constitutional means. Allende immediately began to implement his openly revolutionary "Popular Unity" program, which included the nationalization of Chile's principal foreign-owned enterprises, a far-reaching redistribution of social benefits, and the pursuit of a more independent foreign policy. Despite the very real benefits that began to accrue to the lower classes as a result of these and other policies, Allende gradually alienated the middle class, a sizable portion of the legislature, the judiciary, and finally the military. He died (subsequent evidence indicating suicide) during a right-wing coup on September 11, 1973, which resulted initially in rule by a four-man junta. On June 26, 1974, Maj. Gen. Augusto José Ramón PINOCHET Ugarte was designated head of state, the other junta members assuming subordinate roles.

Proclaimed president on December 17, 1974, Pinochet governed on the basis of unwavering army support, despite widespread domestic and foreign criticism centering on human rights abuses, including the "disappearance," arbitrary arrest and detention, torture, and exiling of opponents. Citing the need for harsh measures to combat communism, the Pinochet regime typically operated under either a state of siege or a somewhat less restrictive state of emergency.

In a national referendum on January 4, 1978, Chileans were reported, by a 3-to-1 majority, to have endorsed the policies of the Pinochet government. However, the significance of the poll was lessened by the inability of opposition groups to mount an effective antireferendum campaign.

On September 11, 1980, the electorate, by a 2-to-1 margin, approved a new constitution designed over a nine-year period that commenced March 11, 1981, to serve as the framework for "slow and gradual evolution" toward a democratic order. At a plebiscite of October 5, 1988, 54.7 percent of the participants rejected a further eight-year term for General Pinochet. As a result, he continued in office only until March 11, 1990, when Patricio AYLWIN Azócar, a Christian Democrat who had led a Coalition of Parties for Democracy (*Concertatión de los Partidos por la Democracia*—CPD) to a 53.8 percent vote share at presidential balloting on December 14, 1989, was sworn in as his successor.

In the general election of December 11, 1993, Eduardo FREI Ruiz-Tagle (Frei Montalva's son) secured a remarkable 58 percent majority in a field of seven presidential contenders. The CPD was equally successful, retaining its majorities of elected senate and chamber members. However, the coalition failed to gain control of the upper house because of unelected senators named to eight-year terms by the Pinochet administration in 1989.

The legislative balance was essentially unchanged after the election of December 11, 1997, with rightist forces continuing to control the Senate and the Chamber limited to passage of a nonbinding motion "rejecting and repudiating" Pinochet's scheduled congressional seating, which, preferring to remain as army commander, he subsequently deferred until March 1998. In a related action the Communist Party of Chile filed an unsuccessful suit in the Court of Appeals attempting to block Pinochet's move to the Senate for having engaged in "genocide, kidnapping, and illegal burying of bodies" during his tenure as president. (Pinochet subsequently secured to the title of senator-for-life, a position granted by the 1980 constitution to any president serving more than six years. This position afforded him immunity from prosecution in his own country. While visiting England for medical treatment in

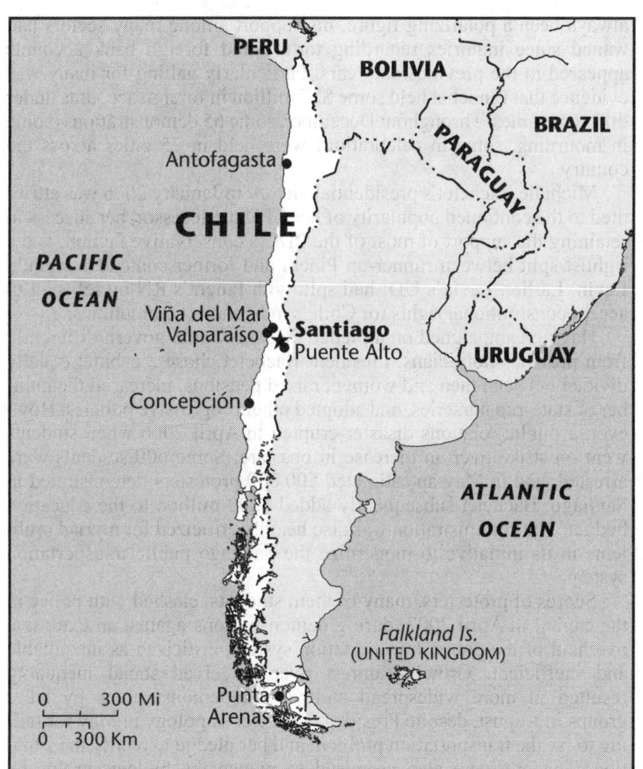

1998, however, he was arrested on a warrant issued by a Spanish court. He was placed under house arrest until 2000, when he was allowed to return to Chile.)

In the first round of presidential balloting on December 12, 1999, CPD candidate Ricardo LAGOS bested his right-wing opponent, Joaquín LAVÍN Infante, by less than 1 percentage point, necessitating the first runoff in Chilean history. Despite a marginally improved victory in the second round on January 16, Lagos, a former Socialist, faced formidable opposition from the Senate controlled by a right-leaning majority.

At the time of Pinochet's return to Chile in 2000, more than 100 actions had been filed against him, most on behalf of the more than 3,000 people who had died or disappeared during his tenure. A major hurdle to legal action was Pinochet's senatorial immunity, thus prompting the Chilean prosecutor to request that the immunity be abolished. In May, contrary to most expectations, the Chilean Court of Appeals complied. Then, in a complicated scenario, the appeals court suspended proceedings against Pinochet in July 2001 on the grounds that he was suffering from "moderate dementia."

Meanwhile, in the legislative election of December 16, 2001, the CPD retained its lower house majority by a greatly reduced margin, while the right-wing Independent Democratic Union (*Union Demócrata Independiente*—UDI) supplanted National Renovation (*Renovación Nacional*—RN) as the dominant component of the opposition alliance.

The decision to suspend the Pinochet trial for medical reasons was upheld by the Supreme Court on July 1, 2002, which appeared to void further prosecution by ruling that the former president's dementia was irreversible. On July 4 Pinochet resigned as senator-for-life. Subsequently, in May 2004 the appeals court removed Pinochet's immunity from prosecution, and on December 13 Pinochet was indicted on charges of kidnapping and murder, an action that was upheld by the Supreme Court on January 4, 2005. Further legal proceedings culminated in a Supreme Court ruling on December 26 that Pinochet was mentally fit to stand trial.

Except for the elimination of nonelective senators, the legislative distribution was relatively unchanged after the election of December 11, 2005. The CPD displayed marginal improvement in the Chamber of Deputies, winning 65 of 120 seats, while retention of its existing 20 seats yielded a majority in the now wholly elective Senate. In the presidential race on December 11, 2005, and runoff balloting on January 15, 2006, Michelle BACHELET of the CPD's Socialist component outpolled her competitors but failed to win an absolute majority. In runoff balloting on January 15, however, she defeated Sebastián PIÑERA Echenique of the right-wing Alliance for Chile 53.5 percent to 46.5 percent to become the country's first elected woman president.

The cabinet was reshuffled on March 27, 2007, January 8, 2008, and March 12, 2009.

Constitution and government. The basic law drafted by the former Council of State and adopted by popular vote in September 1980 provided for a directly elected president serving a nonrenewable eight-year term, in the course of which he or she would be permitted one legislative dissolution. It also called for a bicameral National Congress encompassing a Senate of 26 elected and 9 designated members (exclusive of former presidents) and a 120-member Chamber of Deputies sitting eight and four years, respectively, subject to dissolution. In an unusual electoral requirement, political lists or coalitions must double their rivals' votes to secure both parliamentary seats in any district.

At a plebiscite on July 30, 1989, the term of the next president (but not those of the president's successors) was reduced to four years, and the number of directly elected senators was increased to 38; in addition, the congressional majority needed for constitutional amendment was reduced from three-quarters to two-thirds, and the ban on Marxist parties was replaced by a clause calling for "true and responsible political pluralism." By constitutional amendment in January 1994 Congress approved a new presidential term of six years. In November 2004 the presidential term was again reduced, to four years, with simultaneous presidential and congressional elections. The 2004 changes also eliminated life-time seats (thus ensuring that all future senators would be popularly elected) and restored the president's authority to remove military commanders. The double-your-rival provision was retained, but failing approval in the Senate was a provision calling for the Congress to elect a presidential successor should the incumbent die or become incompetent.

In 1975 the country's 25 historic provinces were grouped into 12 regions plus the metropolitan region of Santiago, each headed by a governor (*governador*), and were further subdivided into 40 new provinces and more than 300 municipalities, headed by intendents (*intendentes*) and mayors (*alcaldes*), respectively.

Foreign relations. Chile has traditionally adhered to a pro-Western foreign policy, save for the Allende era, when contacts with Communist states were strengthened, including the establishment of diplomatic relations with Cuba. Concomitantly, Chilean relations with the United States cooled, primarily as a result of the nationalization of U.S. business interests. Following the 1973 coup, U.S. relations improved, diplomatic ties with Cuba were severed, and links with other Communist-bloc nations were curtailed. However, the assassination in Washington, D.C., on September 21, 1976, of Orlando LETELIER del Solar, a prominent government official under the Allende regime, became a festering bilateral issue. In May 1979 the Chilean Supreme Court refused a U.S. Justice Department request for the extradition of three army officers who had been charged in the case, including the former chief of the Chilean secret police, and Washington moved to curtail diplomatic, economic, and military relations with Santiago after the Court-ordered closure of investigations into possible criminal charges against the three in Chile. A Chilean court reopened the case in mid-1991, only weeks before expiration of a statute of limitations, and indictments were subsequently handed down for two of the three men (the third having confessed his involvement after voluntarily surrendering to U.S. authorities in 1987). In January 1992 an international tribunal awarded noncontestable damages of $1.2 million to the Letelier family, plus damages of $815,000 to the family of an aide who had also been killed, while the two officers indicted in Santiago—Gens. Manuel CONTRERAS Sepúlveda and Pedro ESPINOZA Bravo—were found guilty and sentenced to prison terms of seven and six years, respectively, in November 1993. In June 1994 Chile's Supreme Court ruled that a 1978 amnesty law did not apply to the convicted Letelier killers, and on May 30, 1995, the Court upheld the convictions.

In March 1978 Bolivia severed diplomatic relations with Chile because of its alleged inflexibility in negotiations in regard to Bolivia's long-sought outlet to the Pacific (see Bolivia: Foreign relations). Further inflaming tensions were two Bolivian military incursions into Chile in May 2004 and Peru's claim in October 2005 to about 70,000 square miles of ocean controlled by Chile under treaties concluded in 1952 and 1954, which Lima insisted referenced only fishing rights. (In 2008 Peru sued Chile in the International Court of Justice over the unresolved water rights. Resolution of the legal issues was expected to take at least seven years.) A lengthy dispute with Argentina over the ownership of three islands in the Beagle Channel north of Cape Horn was technically resolved in May 1977, when a panel of international arbitrators awarded all three islands to Chile. However, the award was repudiated by Argentina, as it permitted Chile to extend its territorial limits into the Atlantic, thereby strengthening its claims to contested territory in the Antarctic. Mediation initiated by Pope John Paul II in 1981 yielded an agreement in 1984 under which Chile still received the islands but claimed only Pacific Ocean territory, conceding all Atlantic rights to Argentina.

In August 1991, Presidents Aylwin of Chile and Carlos Menem of Argentina reached accord on all but one of 23 other boundary disputes that had long plagued relations between their countries, but it was not until June 1999 that ratifications were completed on the Continental Glacier Treaty that resolved the last remaining border controversy. At the conclusion of the 1991 state visit to Argentina (the first by a Chilean president in 38 years), Aylwin and Menem also signed a number of accords dealing with investment and transportation, including access to Pacific port facilities for Argentine exporters.

During the Summit of the Americas in Miami, Florida, in December 1994, Chile was invited to become the fourth nation to join the North American Free Trade Agreement (NAFTA). The action came six months after Santiago had announced that Chile intended to join Mercosur, Latin America's biggest trading bloc, as an associate member, an agreement that was signed on June 25, 1996. Five months later, Chile responded to the effective U.S. obstruction of Chilean membership in NAFTA—the Clinton administration had failed to persuade the U.S. Congress to pursue "fast track" approval—by concluding a bilateral free-trade agreement with NAFTA member Canada, complementing an earlier commercial accord with Mexico. It was not until late 2002 that the pact with the United States was finalized.

Tension with Britain arose in October 1998 over the arrest of General Pinochet at a London medical clinic on a Spanish warrant alleging "crimes of genocide and terrorism" against Spanish nationals during his presidency. On October 28 the British High Court quashed the warrant on the grounds that Pinochet was entitled to sovereign immunity while serving as head of state. The decision was reversed by the House of Lords on November 25, and on December 9 Chile recalled its ambassador to London. In March 1999 a panel of law lords upheld the legality of Pinochet's detention, although it ruled that 27 of the 30 charges filed by the Spanish prosecutor were invalid because they involved events before 1988, the year the International Convention Against Torture was implemented in the United Kingdom. After 16 months of house arrest, Pinochet was released on grounds of mental and physical infirmity, and on March 3, 2000, he returned to Santiago to face a variety of domestic charges (see Political background, above).

A recent destabilizing regional factor has been the foreign policy of Venezuelan president Hugo Chávez and its polarizing effect within the CPD government. In 2006, when Venezuela and Guatemala competed for a seat on the UN Security Council, President Bachelet initially indicated solidarity with Chávez. However, her foreign minister, Christian Democrat Alejandro FOXLEY Rioseco, was very much against the Venezuelan leader. Over time, the Chilean government became less sympathetic to Chávez's "Bolivarianism" and more firm in its defense of market-based, social-democratic policies, as evident from Bachelet's meeting with Mexican president Felipe Calderón in 2007. While there was sympathy within the more left-leaning parties in the CPD for Chávez's anti-imperialist rhetoric, if not his policies, Chile, along with Brazil, remained uncomfortable with subordinating its foreign policy agenda to Chávez's or turning Mercosur into a larger platform for Chávez.

On May 23, 2008, Chile joined the Union of South American Nations (Unasur) as a founding member. While the union still only existed on paper in 2009, Chilean president Michelle Bachelet was picked to serve as Unasur's first president pro tempore.

In April 2009 Chilean and Bolivian officials said they were nearing a deal to compensate Bolivia for the use of Silala River water by Chilean companies. Chile was expected to pay for using 50 percent of the river's water, which is needed by the country's mining companies. Officials said the deal, scheduled to be completed in May, would eliminate a long-standing area of conflict and would also clear the way to confront larger water resource issues between the two nations.

Current issues. General Pinochet died on December 10, 2006, and his legacy became the dominant topic of discussion. Though he had always been a polarizing figure, his support among many sectors had waned since inquiries regarding torture and foreign bank accounts appeared in the previous six years. Particularly galling for many was evidence that Pinochet held some $27 million in foreign accounts under different names. Throughout December, some 65 demonstrations (some in mourning, some in celebration) were held in 25 cities across the country

Michelle Bachelet's presidential victory in January 2006 was attributed to the continued popularity of her CPD predecessor, her success in retaining the support of most of the PDC's conservative faction, and a rightist split between runner-up Piñera and former contender Joaquín Lavín. Earlier, Lavín's UDI had split with Piñera's RN by refusing to accept constitutional rights for Chile's indigenous communities.

Having campaigned on a pledge that she would govern differently from previous politicians, President Bachelet chose a cabinet equally divided between men and women, raised pensions, increased the number of state-run nurseries, and adopted other progressive policies. However, a public relations disaster erupted in April 2006 when students went on strike over an increase in bus fare. Some 600 students were arrested, and in May an estimated 500,000 protesters demonstrated in Santiago. Bachelet subsequently added $200 million to the education budget. The administration was also heavily criticized for myriad problems in its initiative to modernize the Santiago public transportation system.

Scores of protesters, many of them students, clashed with police in the capital in April 2007, during demonstrations against an extensive overhaul of the public transportation system, criticized as inequitable and inefficient. Growing unrest over perceived social inequality resulted in more widespread and violent demonstrations by labor groups in August, despite President Bachelet's apology in May for failing to fix the transportation problem and her pledge to rectify the situation. The president also promised to reduce the budget surplus by spending more money on education, and in November she signed into law a consensus bill on education reform.

Meanwhile, rifts in the CPD began to undermine the governing coalition's control, as the coalition lost its majority in the lower Chamber of Deputies in 2008 for the first time since Chile's return to democracy. After a PDC member was expelled in late 2007 for voting against the government on the transportation issue, five PDC members resigned in protest in January 2008, leaving the governing coalition with only 57 of 120 seats. President Bachelet subsequently reshuffled the cabinet on January 8, maintaining a balance among the four parties in the coalition. Observers said the cabinet reorganization was not expected to herald major changes in government policy.

In early 2008, violence erupted in the Araucania region, where indigenous Mapuche residents had set fire several times to equipment owned by logging and agribusiness firms. The Mapuche claimed that the land being used for commercial purposes belonged to them. Clashes with police followed, killing at least one Mapuche activist. Meanwhile, a nonindigenous woman prisoner staged a 111-day hunger strike on behalf of the Mapuche cause, bringing international attention to the claims of disenfranchisement by the Mapuche. The upheaval prompted President Bachelet to create a special commission for indigenous affairs. She also offered prison benefits as a concession to the activist, who then ended her hunger strike for a brief period, reportedly resuming it in early March. The president continued to face public opposition throughout 2008, with AC presidential candidate Sebastián Piñera favored to succeed her in the 2009 balloting.

The Bachelet administration effectively checked public anger over Chile's financial problems in 2009 by instituting more than $4 billion in stimulus spending, and analysts predicted that the fundamental strength of Chile's economy would allow it to absorb the shocks of the downturn without serious threat to its stability. President Bachelet, according to an April poll, maintained a high approval rating despite the country's spiraling unemployment rate. Her popularity reached the highest level—62 percent—since her election,. But worsening economic conditions prompted street protests, some violent, throughout the country, including one demonstration that drew 12,000 people in Santiago in April. Trade union demands included social security increases and a state-administered pension system. Meanwhile, attention in 2009 turned to the presidential election scheduled for December. While Sebastián PIÑERA Echenique, the center-right Alliance for Chile nominee, was widely held to be the leading contender (the constitution prevents Bachelet from seeking a second consecutive term), an unexpected late surge in June opinion polls supporting independent leftist candidate Marco Antonio ENRIQUEZ-OMINAMI Gumucio stirred speculation about the election's outcome. Enriquez-Ominami, a former Socialist Party member who split off for his presidential run, was seen by many voters as a more engaging and popular figure than his former CPD colleague and CPD nominee Eduardo FREI Ruiz-Tagle. Enriquez-Ominami's rapid assent called into question the outlook on Frei's election chances and also pulled Piñera back to the center from a more conservative position, observers said.

POLITICAL PARTIES AND GROUPS

Chile's traditional multiparty system ran the gamut from extreme right to extreme left, and parties have historically played an important role in the nation's political life. In the wake of the 1973 coup, however, the military government, declaring party politics to be inappropriate, outlawed those groups that had supported the Allende government and forced the remainder into indefinite recess. In 1977, following the alleged discovery of a subversive plot by the Christian Democrats, Chile formally dissolved all existing parties and confiscated their assets. In the early 1980s, as opposition to the Pinochet regime crystallized, the traditional formations resurfaced, most of them, although still illegal, being tolerated by the government within unstated but generally understood limits. A number of somewhat fluctuating coalitions followed, and in March 1987 legislation was approved that permitted the reregistration of most groups, save those of the far left.

A large number of parties contested the post-Pinochet balloting of December 11, 1989, the principal contenders on the right being the PRN and UDI (below), both of which supported the presidential candidacy of Hernán BÜCHI Buc against the centrist Coalition of Parties for Democracy (CPD), then a 17-member grouping that endorsed Patricio Aylwin AZÓCAR (for more detailed coverage of pre-1990 alignments, see the 1992 *Handbook*, pp. 147–149).

By 1993 the CPD had become the somewhat less inclusive formation referenced below, while the PRN and UDI had joined with the smaller UCCP in the right-wing Union for Progress of Chile (UPC), subsequently the Alliance for Chile (AC). As of 2007 the party system appeared to be moving back to its pre-Pinochet structure with a wide range of ideologies supported by political groups.

Five electoral coalitions formed or continued their electoral agreements in advance of the 2009 legislative and presidential elections: the Coalition of Parties for Democracy (*Concertación de los Partidos por la Democracia*—CPD), which included the Christian Democratic Party, the Socialist Party, the Party for Democracy, and the Social Democratic Radical Party; the Alliance for Chile (*Alianza por Chile*—AC), consisting of the National Renovation party and the Independent Democratic Union; the Coalition for Change (*Coalición por el Cambio*—CC)., formed by the Chile First Party and the Christian Humanist Movement; the Together We Can Do More for Chile (*Juntos Podemos Más*—JPM) coalition, comprised of the Communist Party of Chile and the Humanist Party; and the Progressive Left Pole (*Polo Progresista de Izquierda*—PPI), containing the Social Movement Party, the Social and Democratic Force, and the Generation 80 Movement.

Governing Coalition:

Coalition of Parties for Democracy (*Concertación de los Partidos por la Democracia*—CPD). The CPD had its origins in the anti-Pinochet *Multipartidaria*, which was formed in early 1983 and months later became the Democratic Alliance (*Alianza Democrática*—AD). In 1987 the Christian Democratic core of the AD endorsed "single-party" opposition to the regime that would include right-centrist and moderate-leftist formations, while excluding groups advocating the use of violence. The result was the formation of the CPD, which successfully supported Aylwin Azócar's bid for the presidency in 1989 and was equally successful in backing the 1993 candidacy of Frei Ruiz-Tagle.

The Democratic Left Participation (*Participación Democrática de Izquierda*—PDI), a coalition member formed in 1991 by a group of former Communist Party of Chile human rights activists, was dissolved in November 1994, after having failed to gain the required minimum vote share of 5 percent in the 1993 election. PDI leader Fanny POLLAROLLO joined the Socialist Party of Chile, while PDI secretary general Antonio LEAL joined the Party for Democracy.

The CPD won 70 Chamber seats in 1993 and a similar number in 1997, fell to 62 in 2001, and recovered marginally in 2005.

Michelle Bachelet, the former defense minister and Socialist Party member, won the presidency in 2006 with 53.49 percent of votes in a run-off election against Alliance for Chile candidate Sebastián Piñera. . Bachelet maintained soaring popularity throughout her term, mainly due to the popular belief that she had competently navigated the country through the global economic downturn. Term limits prevented her from running again in 2009. Former president Frei Ruiz-Tagle was widely expected to be the coalition's presidential candidate for the December 2009 elections. Meanwhile in April, the CPD met with the JPM coalition to negotiate forming an electoral alliance in an effort to defeat the favored AC in the December elections. The negotiations followed the defections of several leftist CPD members over their disillusionment with what they perceived to be the coalition's drift to the center.

Leaders: Michelle BACHELET (President of the Republic), Ricardo LAGOS Escobar and Eduardo FREI Ruiz-Tagle (former President of the Republic).

Christian Democratic Party (*Partido Demócrata Cristiano*—PDC). Founded in 1957, the PDC is currently Chile's third-strongest party, although long divided into right-, center-, and left-wing factions. It obtained 39 lower house seats in 1997, 24 in 2001, and 20 in 2005.

The PDC reportedly considered leaving the CPD in late 2006 to protest apparent corruption in government ministries. In 2007 party rifts developed, and in January 2008, five PDC deputies resigned their chamber posts in protest over the party's dismissal in December 2007 of Sen. Adolfo ZALDIVAR, who had refused to support financing for the administration's transportation initiative. Zaldivar also had clashed with other party leaders, most notably Soledad ALVEAR, who replaced him as party president. With chamber representation reduced to 57 seats following the resignations, coupled with resignations from the PPD (below), the CPD was seen as losing significant political influence.

On April 5, 2009, the PDC's Frei Ruiz-Tagle, a senator and Chile's former president, defeated PRSD senator José Antonio GÓMEZ to secure the CPD nod to represent the coalition in the December presidential elections. Frei Ruiz-Tagle's platform focused on continuing the programs begun in the Bachelet administration and enhancing social protections. But the nation's slowing economy and protests over public education and transportation issues found Frei Ruiz-Tagle's falling behind in polls in the run-up to the election.

Leaders: Juan Carlos LATORRE Carmona (President of the Party), Francisco Renán FUENTEALBA (First Vice President), Eduardo FREI Ruiz-Tagle (Former President of the Republic, President of the Senate and 2009 presidential candidate), Patricio AYLWIN Azócar (Former President of the Republic), Andrés ZALDIVAR Larraín (Former President of the Senate), Jaime MULET Martínez, Moisés VALENZUELA Martínez (National Secretary).

Socialist Party of Chile (*Partido Socialista de Chile*—PS or PSCh). Founded in 1933, the PSCh was long split into a number of factions that reunited in late 1989 under the presidency of Clodomiro ALMEYDA Medina, with Jorge ARRATE MacNiven as general secretary. Subsequently, Arrate succeeded Almeyda as president, and yielded the position in November 1991 to Ricardo NUÑEZ. Almeyda died on September 25, 1997.

In the run-up to the 2001 congressional poll, the PSCh split with the PDC in asserting that it would support Communist candidates in two constituencies; however, it subsequently reversed itself and agreed to support CPD nominees. In recent years, the party has been described as becoming more centrist.

PS dissident Marco Antonio Enriquez-Ominami Gumucio was nominated as the PS candidate in the 2009 presidential election.

Leaders: Michelle BACHELET (President of the Republic), Camilo ESCALONA Medina (President of the Party), Isabel Allende BUSSIi (First Vice President), Marcelo SCHILLING Rodriguez (Secretary General).

Party for Democracy (*Partido por la Democracia*—PPD). The PPD was organized in 1987 by a group of Socialist Party dissidents under Ricardo Lagos Escobar, who was succeeded as president by Eric SCHNAKE in mid-1990. The PPD and the PSCh formed a subpact for the June 1992 municipal poll, and both endorsed Lagos Escobar for the presidency in 1993.

The PPD was rattled in 2006 by a corruption scandal involving allegations dating back to the Lagos administration. Several prominent leaders subsequently left the party, including former PPD president Jorge SCHAULSOHN, who said there was an "ideology of corruption" within the CPD. The dissidents launched a splinter centrist group, **Chile First** (*Chile Primero*), in advance of the 2009 presidential election to promote education and combat poverty (see below).

Leaders: Pepe Auth STEWART (President of the Party), Ricardo LAGOS Escobar (Former President of the Republic), Guido GIRARDI Lavín (Vice President), Alejandro BAHAMONDES Saavedra (Secretary General).

Social Democratic Radical Party (*Partido Radical Social Demócrata*—PRSD). The oldest of Chile's extant parties, the Radical Party (*Partido Radical*—PR) was founded in 1863, but appeared, according to the *Latin American Weekly Report*, to be "headed for extinction" as the result of its extremely poor showing in the 1993 balloting. In an effort to revamp its image, the party adopted its present name in 1994. It increased its chamber representation from two seats to four in 1997, to six in 2001, and to seven in 2005.

Leaders: José Antonio GÓMEZ (President), Fernando Meza MONCADA (First Vice President), Ernesto VELASCO Rodriguez (Secretary General).

Opposition Groups:

Alliance for Chile (*Alianza por Chile*—AC). A coalition of Chile's leading center-rightist groups, the Alliance was launched before the 1997 election as the Union for Chile (*Unión por Chile*) in emulation of its 1993 predecessor, the Union for the Progress of Chile (*Unión por el Progreso de Chile*—UPC). It adopted its present name in 1999. The coalition, in all of its incarnations, has not won a presidential election since democracy was reinstated after the end of Pinochet's dictatorship in 1990.

In 2006, AC candidate Sebastián Piñera came in second place in a run-off election for president with 46.51 percent of the vote against CPD winner Michelle Bachelet. After local elections in 2008, the AC for the first time held more mayors seats than center-left groups, signaling improving conditions for their more conservative message.

The center-right alliance consolidated power in both houses of congress on March 18, 2009, for the first time since 1990 after the CPD expelled a coalition party, which left it without a majority in either legislative body. UDI and alliance member Rodrigo ÁLVAREZ was elected chamber of deputies president a week after UDI senator Jovino NOVOA was appointed senate president. Rifts in the alliance began to appear, though, in the run-up to the 2009 elections. The alliance's presidential campaign suffered a significant setback when UDI senator Pablo LONGUEIRA resigned as head of RN presidential candidate Sebastián PIÑERA Echenique's election team. The shuffling of legislative candidates between the alliance's constituent parties prompted the withdrawal.

Leader: Sebastián PIÑERA Echenique.

National Renovation (*Renovación Nacional*—RN). The RN, then most commonly referenced as the National Renovation Party (PRN or Parena), was formed in 1987 by merger of the Movement for National Union (*Movimiento de Unión Nacional*—MUN), led by Andrés Allamand Zavala; the National Labor Front (*Frente Nacional del Trabajo*—FNT), led by Sergio Onofre JARPA Reyes; and the UDI (see below), with whom it split over the 1988 plebiscite. Jarpa withdrew as a presidential candidate in August 1989, and the coalition subsequently joined the UDI in supporting the candidacy of Hernán Büchi.

The RN's long-standing support of the military eroded in late 1992 when two of its leaders, Evelyn MATTHEI and Sebastián Piñera, were forced to withdraw as presidential hopefuls in the wake of a wiretapping incident involving the army's telecommunications battalion. Piñera subsequently ran in 1993 as an independent, and in 1999 as the candidate of the alliance. Recently the RN has been perceived as separating itself from the legacy of General Pinochet and adopting a more centrist position.

In 2005, Piñera, one of the wealthiest men in Chile, lost his presidential bid by a narrow margin in a runoff election with Michelle Bachelet.

The RN gained some popular support in the October 2008 local elections, when the party won a significant number of mayoral and council races. In 2009 Piñera declared his intention to run in the December presidential election.

Leaders: Carlos LARRAIN Pena (President), Sebastián PIÑERA Echenique (1999, 2005, and 2009 presidential candidate), Andrés ALLAMAND Zavala, Cristian MONCKEBERG Bruner (Vice President), Baldo PROKURICA (Vice President), Lily PÉREZ San Martín (Secretary General).

Independent Democratic Union (*Unión Demócrata Independiente*—UDI). The UDI joined in the formation of Parena but withdrew following the expulsion in April 1988 of its founder, Jaime GUZMAN Errázuriz, from the coalition leadership. Previously a legal adviser to General Pinochet, Guzman organized a "*UDI pour el Sí*" campaign on Pinochet's behalf in October 1988. He was assassinated, with the Manuel Rodriguez Patriotic Front (FPMR) claiming responsibility, on April 1, 1991.

The UDI won pluralities of 33 chamber and 9 senate seats in the 2005 election, making it the single party holding the most legislative seats. The conspicuous absence of the UDI's Jaoquín Lavín from Pinochet's funeral in 2006, and his earlier offer to assist President Bachelet with the student strike, appeared to reveal an effort by Lávin to move from the right toward the center, possibly with the goal of appealing to Christian Democrats, according to observers.

Leaders: Juan Antonio COLOMA Correa (President), Carlos VILLARROEL (Vice President), Jovino NOVOA Vasquez, Joaquín LAVÍN Infante (1999 and 2005 presidential candidate), Victor PÉREZ (Secretary General), Rodrigo ALVAREZ (Chamber of Deputies President).

Other Parties:

Coalition for Change (*Coalición por el Cambio*—CC). The two centrist groups, Chile First and MHC, launched the CC in April 2009. The two groups agreed to focus their joint campaign on eliminating inequality and pressing the upcoming election's presidential front-runner, Sebastian Piñera, to do the same during his presumed administration.

Chile First (*Chile Primero*). *Chile Primero* is a splinter centrist group launched in 2007 by PPD dissidents, including Sen. Fernando Flores, in advance of the 2009 presidential election. The party planned to present its own candidate for president, criticizing the approach of the leading parties as populist, ineffective, and overly encumbered by Chile's history. Its manifesto emphasized the need to pragmatically address income inequality, access to technology, and Chile's global competitiveness. It focused specifically on disenfranchised young voters.

Leaders: Alberto PRECHT (President), Eduardo BASTÍAS (Secretary General), Juan Carlos SCHMIDT (First Vice President).

Christian Humanist Movement (*Movimiento Humanista Cristiano*—MHC). Formed in 2007, the MHC claims a broad-based, non-ideological, and non-denominational approach to politics. The MHC's major objectives were to improve the economy and to provide for the welfare of all Chileans.

Leaders: Roberto MAYORGA (President), Gerardo Garcia HUIDOBRO (Vice President), Carlos PEREZ (Secretary General)

Wallmapuwen. *Wallmapuwen* was launched in February 2006 to represent the indigenous Mapuche people located largely in the Araucanía region of southern Chile. The group supports Mapuche autonomy and calls itself democratic, progressive, and pluralistic.

Leaders: Pedro Gustavo QUILAQUEO, Pedro MARIMÁN, Claudio CURIHUENTRO.

Together We Can Do More for Chile (*Juntos Podemos Más*—JPM). The JPM is a coalition of left-wing groups that came together in 2003 to present a single front against the country's two major coalitions. The group's platform states as goals the right to work, redistribution of income, dissolution of the North American Free Trade Agreement (NAFTA), and sovereignty over the country's wealth and copper resources. In the 2005 legislative elections, the JPM failed to gain representation in either legislative body.

Leader: Tomás René HIRSCH Goldschmidt (2005 presidential candidate).

Communist Party of Chile (*Partido Comunista de Chile*—PCC or PCCh). Founded in 1922 and a participant in the Allende government of 1970–1973, the PCCh was proscribed during the Pinochet era. In January 1990 the party renounced its policy of "armed popular rebellion" and secured legal recognition the following October. Ten months later its president at the time, Volodia TEITELBOIM, declared that Marxism-Leninism was a "narrow formula" and that the dictatorship of the proletariat was "reductionist."

In 1991 the PCCh was the core party in formation of the Movement of the Allendist Democratic Left (*Movimiento de Izquierda Democrática Allendista*—MIDA). MIDA leader Andrés Pascal ALLENDE, a nephew of the former president, had led the Movement of the Revolutionary Left (*Movimiento de Izquierda Revolucionaria*—MIR), a quasi-guerrilla organization formed by PCCh elements in the 1960s, before returning secretly from exile in August 1986. MIDA secured a vote share of 6.6 percent in the June 1992 municipal balloting, with its presidential candidate securing only 4.7 percent in 1993.

The PCCh ran on its own in 1997, winning 4 Senate seats. The party secured no congressional representation thereafter. Its former president and 1999 candidate for president of the republic, Gladys MARIN Millie, died in March 2005.

Leader: Guillermo TEILLIER del Valle (President).

Groupings affiliated with the PCCh following the demise of the MIDA included the **Chilean Christian Left Party** (*Partido Izquierda Cristiana de Chile*); the **Socialist Alternative Party** (*Partido Alternativa Socialista*); and the **New Popular Alliance Party** (*Partido Nueva Alianza Popular*).

Humanist Party (*Partido Humanista*—PH). Formerly a member of the CPD, the PH joined with the Greens (below) in a Humanist-Green Alliance (*Alianz Humanista-Verde*—AHV) for the 1993 presidential campaign in support of Crístián REITZE. It campaigned as an ally of the PCCh in 2005 but secured no congressional representation.

Leaders: Maril Olmos CABRERA (President), Fernando Lira HAQUIN (First Vice President), Tomás René HIRSCH Goldschmidt (2005 presidential candidate), Susana Rodriguez CORDOVA (Secretary General).

The Greens (*Los Verdes*). The Greens joined their former PH partner in the AHV for the 1993 campaign. They have no current representation. The party reportedly renewed itself as the **Ecology Party** (*Partido Ecologista*) in January 2008, with environmentalist Sara Larrain as party president. The party's stated goal was to be a "distinct alternative."*Leaders:* Sara LARRAIN (President of the Party and 1999 presidential candidate), Manuel BAQUEDANO, Isabel LINCOLAO.

Progressive Left Pole (*Polo Progresista de Izquierda*—PPI). The left-wing PPI coalition was formed on March 23, 2009, by former PS member, Senator Alejandro NAVARRO, who announced his intention to run for president in the December elections. Navarro renounced his membership in the CPD coalition due to what he said were inert policies that did not address the problems of a majority of the population. He also distanced PPI from JPM, the other leftist coalition, because of political differences with Teillier de Valle, the PCC leader.

Leader: Alejandro NAVARRO Brain (2009 presidential candidate).

Social Movement (*Movimiento Amplio Social*—MAS). The MAS was established on March 11, 2008, as a left-wing and progressive alternative to the two parties that have dominated Chile's politics. It focused on improving the living conditions and prosperity of Chileans. The group called for more home rule and decentralization of power away from the two major parties, which it said had become divorced from the country's workers.

Leaders: Felipe HAZBUN Marin (President), Fernando ZAMORANO Fernandez (Vice President), Francisco BUCAT Oviedo (Secretary General).

Social and Democratic Force (*Fuerza Social y Democrática*—FSD) Founded in April 2001 with a manifesto for change, the FSD was allied with MAS in 2008 and subsequently was absorbed into the PPI coalition. The group called for reform of the education, health-care, and social security systems to better support Chile's lower and middle classes. It also called for more resources to support small-business.

Leaders: Jorge Pavez Urrutia, Gustavo Méndez Araya, Darío Vásquez Salazar (National Coordinators).

Generation 80 Movement (*Movimiento Generación 80*—G80). The G80 is a left-wing conglomerate, formed in 2005, and includes as members those who pushed for political change after the tyranny of the 1980s. The group views the implementation of reforms following the 1980 constitution to be incomplete and uneven. The G80 also identifies itself as prodemocratic and anti-capitalist. Though the G80 had been initially aligned with the JPM, the group split over what the G80 believed were too many concessions to the right, and realigned with PPI in April 2009. The G80 considers itself to be the heir to the legacy of former president Salvador Allende.

Leaders: Vólker GUTIÉRREZ, Alejandro TORO (Coordinators).

LEGISLATURE

The bicameral **National Congress** (*Congreso Nacional*) established under the 1980 constitution encompasses a Senate and a Chamber of Deputies, elected for terms of eight and four years, respectively, subject to a one-time presidential right of dissolution.

Senate (*Senado*). The upper house currently consists of 38 directly elected members, with half of the members renewed every four years. The alliance/party distribution of seats following the December 11, 2005, election was as follows: Coalition of Parties for Democracy, 20 (Socialist Party of Chile, 8; Christian Democratic Party, 7; Party for Democracy, 3; Social Democratic Radical Party, 2); Alliance for Chile, 17 (Independent Democratic Union, 9; National Renovation Party, 8); independent, 1.

President: Jovino NOVOA Vásquez.

Chamber of Deputies (*Cámara de Diputados*). The lower house consists of 120 directly elected members. In the most recent election on December 11, 2005, the Coalition of Parties for Democracy won 65 seats (Party for Democracy, 21; Christian Democratic Party, 20; Socialist Party of Chile, 15; Social Democratic Radical Party, 7; allied independents, 2); the Alliance for Chile, 54 (Independent Democratic Union, 33; National Renovation Party, 19; allied independents, 2); independent, 1.

President: Rodrigo ALVAREZ Zenteno.

CABINET

[as of June 1, 2009]

President	Michelle Bachelet (PS) [f]
Ministers	
Agriculture	Marigen Hornkohl Venegas [f]
Culture and the Arts	Paulina Urrutia Fernandez (ind.) [f]
Defense	Francisco Vidal Salinas
Economy	Hugo Lavados Montes
Education	Mónica Jiménez [f]
Energy	Marcelo Tokman Ramos
Environment	Ana Lya Uriarte Rodriguez [f]
Finance	Andrés Velasco Brañes (ind.)
Foreign Relations	Mariano Fernandez Amunatequi (PDC)
Health	Alvaro Erazo Latorre (PS)
Housing and Urban Development	Patricia Poblete Bennett (PDC) [f]
Interior	Edmundo Perez Yoma (PDC)
Justice	Carlos Maldonado Curti
Labor and Social Welfare	Claudia Serrano Madrid [f]
Mining	Santiago Gonzalez Larrain
National Assets	Romy Schmidt Crnosija (PPD) [f]
Planning and Cooperation	Paula Quintana [f]
Presidency	José Antonio Viera-Gallo Quesney (PS)
Public Works	Sergio Bitar Chacra
Transport and Communications	René Cortázar Sanz
Secretary General of Government	Carolina Toha Morales [f]
Women's Affairs	Laura Albornoz Pollmann (PDC) [f]

[f] = female

COMMUNICATIONS

Until 1973 the Chilean news media enjoyed freedom of expression and were among the most active on the South American continent. Subsequently, policies adopted by the military junta severely depleted the ranks of both press and broadcasting facilities while sharply curtailing the freedom of those that remained. Most press restrictions were lifted before the December 1989 balloting, but press offenses have not been decriminalized. According to the watchdog group Reporters Without Borders, five journalists were stoned and beaten by police and three others were arrested during a demonstration in May 2007.

Press. The following are published in Santiago: *La Tercera* (200,000); *Las Ultimas Noticias* (150,000 daily, 130,000 Sunday); *El Mercurio* (120,000 daily, 280,000 Sunday), the world's oldest Spanish-language paper (founded 1827), conservative; *La Nación* (45,000), financial; *La Segunda* (40,000); *Qué Pasa?* (30,000), weekly; *Diario Oficial* (10,000). *El Siglo*, a Communist Party fortnightly, claimed a clandestine circulation of 25,000 until September 4, 1989, when it resumed legal publication.

News agencies. The domestic facility is *Orbe Servicios Informativos;* a number of foreign bureaus, including ANSA, AP, Reuters, TASS, and UPI, maintain offices in Santiago.

Broadcasting and computing. *Radio Nacional de Chile* is a government-operated network; the owners of more than 300 private stations are members of the *Asociación de Radiodifusores de Chile* (ARCHI). *Televisión Nacionale de Chile* has more than 150 outlets; there also are a number of private facilities. Four of the country's universities offer noncommercial television programming. As of 2008 there were 324.7 Internet users per 1,000 inhabitants.

INTERGOVERNMENTAL REPRESENTATION

Ambassador to the U.S.: Jose GONI.

U.S. Ambassador to Chile: Paul E. SIMONS.

Permanent Representative to the UN: Heraldo MUÑOZ.

IGO Memberships (Non-UN): ALADI, APEC, BIS, CAN, IADB, Interpol, IOM, Mercosur, NAM, OAS, OPANAL, PCA, SELA, WCO, WTO.

CHINA

Zhongguo (Chung-hua)

Note: As of January 1, 1979, the People's Republic of China officially adopted a system known as *Pinyin* for rendering Chinese names into languages utilizing the Roman alphabet. The system was not concurrently adopted in Taiwan, where the Wade-Giles form of transliteration, introduced by the British in the 19th century, was, for the most part, retained. For Taiwan, the complexities of the issue surfaced in October 2000, when its education minister recommended the adoption of *Pinyin* (more specifically, the *Hanyu* version in use on the mainland); however, others preferred a recent variant known as *Tongyong*, which was designed to accommodate island dialects and was adopted for street names by the Taipei city government in 1997. In August 2002 *Tongyong Pinyin* was adopted as Taiwan's official romanization system. In the material that follows, personal and place names—such as Mao Zedong (Mao Tse-tung) and Beijing (Peking)—are rendered in *Hanyu* or *Tongyong Pinyin*, as appropriate, with occasional parenthetical reference to Wade-Giles or other English equivalents for purposes of clarification. For Taiwan and the Special Administrative Regions of Hong Kong and Macao, some anomalies will be evident, particularly for individuals who have adopted English given names.

Political Status: Politically divided since 1949; mainland under (Communist) People's Republic of China; Taiwan under (Nationalist) Republic of China

Area: 3,705,805 sq. mi. (9,598,045 sq. km.), including Taiwan.

Population: 1,355,105,000 (2008E), mainland (including Hong Kong and Macao) plus Taiwan.

THE COUNTRY

The most populous and one of the largest countries in the world, China dominates the entire East Asian landmass but since 1949 has been divided between two governments. The Communist-ruled People's Republic of China (PRC) controls the Chinese mainland, including Manchuria, Inner Mongolia, Sinkiang (Chinese Turkestan), Tibet, Hong Kong, and Macao. The anti-Communist government of the Republic of China on Taiwan (Nationalist China) administers the island province of Taiwan and some smaller islands, including Kinmen (Quemoy), Matsu, and the Pescadores.

Climatically and geographically, the vast and varied expanse of mainland China ranges from tropical to far-northern temperate, from desert to extremely wet-humid, from river plains to high mountains. Population density varies from fewer than 1 to more than 200 per square kilometer. Of the mainland population, 93 percent is ethnically Han Chinese, but there are 18 minority groups totaling over 1 million, including Manchus, Mongols, Tibetans, and Uygurs (Uighurs). In 1998 45 percent of the labor force was female, with approximately 90 percent of adult women employed full time outside the home; female representation in the party and government averages about 20 percent.

With the majority of the population still living in the countryside, agriculture remains a major occupation, employing some 40 percent of the labor force in 2007, although agriculture currently contributes only 11 percent of GDP. In comparison, industry accounts for 49 percent and services for 40 percent of GDP. Over the last two decades China's "socialist market economic system" has expanded at an annual average of 9.6 percent, and since 2003 it has grown by 10 percent or better annually (11.9 percent in 2007), making China one of the fastest-growing economies in the world. Much of the growth has been linked to the export of chemicals, capital goods, and electronics. The electronics sector, in particular, has benefited from China's success in supplanting other Asian countries as a final assembly point for goods.

Taiwan, a semitropical island 100 miles off China's southeastern coast, has small plains suitable for agriculture in the west and towering mountains along its east-central spine. About 98 percent of the population is ethnically Chinese; the remainder comes from 13 aboriginal tribes of Malayo-Polynesian stock. The Chinese may be divided into three groups: numerically predominant Amoy Fukienese, whose ancestors arrived before the Japanese occupation of Taiwan in 1895; a minority of Hakkas, whose ancestors likewise arrived before 1895; and "mainlanders," who arrived after 1945 from various parts of China. Population density, at more than 1,500 persons per square mile, is exceeded only by Singapore and Bangladesh among independent eastern Asian jurisdictions.

The major occupations in Taiwan are commerce and other services, with the service sector as a whole contributing 72 percent of GDP according to the government. Light and high-tech manufacturing leads the industrial sector, which constitutes 28 percent of GDP and employs 37 percent of the workforce. Taiwan's leading export is electronics. The economy's traditional mainstays, farming and fishing, now account for only 5 percent of employment and less than 2 percent of GDP. The government reported GDP growth of 6.2 percent in 2004, 4.2 percent in 2005, 4.9 percent in 2006, and 5.7 in 2007. In the second half of 2008, however, the economy fell into recession, with the GDP down 8.4 percent in the fourth quarter as the global economic crisis took hold. The standard of living is one of the highest in East Asia, with per capita gross national income of about $30,000 in 2007, as compared with the mainland's $5,370 (in terms of purchasing power parity). As of 2005 women constituted about 42 percent of the workforce; female representation in government has increased in recent years, with women holding about 30 percent of the seats in the current Legislative Branch

POLITICAL HISTORY

China's history as a political entity is less ancient than its cultural tradition but extends back to at least 221 B.C., when northern China was unified under the Ch'in dynasty. In succeeding centuries of alternating unity and disunity, the domain of Chinese culture spread southward until it covered what is today considered China proper.

After the fall of the Manchu dynasty in 1912, a republic was established under the leadership of Sun Yat-sen, who abdicated the presidency in favor of the northerner Yuan Shih-kai but subsequently formed a rival regime in the south following Yuan's attempt to establish a new dynasty. During the Northern Expedition of 1926–1928 (an attempt by the southern government, after Sun's death, to reunify China), Chiang Kai-shek defeated his rivals, gained control of the Nationalist Party (*Chung-kuo Kuo-min Tang* or Kuomintang—KMT), and expelled the Communists from participation in its activities. With the capture of Beijing (Peking) in June 1928, the Kuomintang regime gained international recognition as the government of China. Many warlord regimes continued to exist, however, while the Communists set up local governments in Jiangxi Province (Kiangsi) and later, after the Long March of 1934–1935, in Yan'an, Shaanxi Province (Yenan, Shensi). In a display of Chinese unity following the Japanese invasion of July 1937, most groups, including the Communists, accepted the leadership of the central government.

Communist strength increased during World War II, and the failure of postwar negotiations on establishing a coalition government was followed by full-scale civil war, in which the Communists rapidly won control of the entire mainland. In December 1949 the Nationalists moved their capital to Taipei on the island of Taiwan, whence they continued to claim legal authority over the whole of China. The Communists established their own government, the People's Republic of China (PRC), in Beijing on October 1, 1949, and have since maintained a parallel claim to sovereignty over all of China, including Taiwan.

While both governments sought diplomatic recognition from as many states as possible, a decisive breakthrough for the PRC occurred on October 25, 1971, when the UN General Assembly voted to recognize its delegation as comprising "the only legitimate representatives of China" to the world body. This action also encouraged increased acceptance of the PRC by individual governments, an overwhelming majority of which now recognize the PRC.

In 1980 the PRC succeeded Taiwan as Chinese member of the International Monetary Fund (IMF) and World Bank group, and in 1984 the PRC joined the International Atomic Energy Agency. In 1986 it acceded to membership in the Asian Development Bank (ADB), which had agreed to change Taiwan's membership title from "Republic of China" to "Taipei, China."

In 1989 Taipei began inching toward direct, but limited, relations with the mainland. In May a delegation led by Taiwan's finance minister attended an ADB meeting in Beijing; subsequently, Taiwan participated in the PRC-hosted 1990 Asian Games, although Beijing succeeded in blocking Taipei's bid to act as host for the 1998 Games. In an unprecedented gesture that entailed implicit recognition of the PRC, Taiwan's president Lee Teng-hui called at his 1990 inaugural for the establishment of "full academic, cultural, economic, trade, scientific and technological exchanges between the two countries." The offer was contingent, however, on Beijing's promoting democracy and a free economy, abandoning its goal of conquering Taiwan, and not interfering with Taipei's foreign affairs, all of which were characterized by Beijing as "impossible preconditions."

In February 1991 Taiwan's recently established National Unification Council (NUC) drafted "Guidelines for National Unification," which proposed incremental steps toward reuniting Taiwan and the mainland. Two months later an extraordinary session of the National Assembly approved constitutional measures permitting Lee to terminate the "Period of National Mobilization for the Suppression of the Communist Rebellion." From April 28 to May 5, 1991, members of the private, but officially recognized, Straits Exchange Foundation (SEF) of Taiwan held a series of meetings with the Chinese State Council's Taiwan Affairs Office in the first such officially approved contact. The SEF acted on the basis of a mandate from Taipei's Mainland Affairs Council (MAC) to seek resolution of "cross-strait" disputes in such areas as trade, travel, piracy, and illegal immigration. In a somewhat reciprocal action in mid-August, two mainland journalists were permitted to attend the trial of a group of Chinese fishermen arrested a month earlier in Taiwanese waters, while the arrival one week later of two Chinese Red Cross representatives to meet with the fishermen constituted the first visit to Taiwan by officials of the PRC.

By 1992 the MAC was overseeing substantial fiscal penetration of the mainland, with cumulative Taiwanese investment in the PRC estimated at $5 billion by the end of the year. Meanwhile, reformers within Taiwan's governing KMT were increasingly urging abandonment of the "one China" policy in favor of a "divided nation" model, under which China would be redefined as a country with two political systems.

In April 1993 a Taiwanese group led by the chair of the SEF met unofficially in Singapore with a group headed by the mainland's nongovernmental Association for Relations Across the Taiwan Strait (ARATS). In June 1997, through the offices of the two organizations, the PRC and Taiwan reached agreement on the repatriation of airplane hijackers and other illegal entrants. A month earlier Beijing had extradited a Taiwanese hijacker, while Taiwan in mid-July reciprocated by repatriating two hijackers to the PRC.

During 1998 relations with the PRC eased further. In July the ARATS deputy secretary general visited Taiwan as a guest of the SEF, and two months later the SEF vice chair paid an official visit to China. The SEF chair made a similar visit in October, during which a four-part agreement was concluded between SEF and ARATS representatives on both political and economic issues.

In 2000 the PRC bitterly opposed Chen Shui-bian's quest for Taiwan's presidency because his Democratic Progressive Party supported independence. In the wake of his March election, however, Chen adopted what became known as his "four no's plus one" policy, giving assurances that Taiwan would not declare independence, alter its official name, amend the constitution in a way that could be interpreted as acknowledging the existence of two states, or hold a referendum on the independence question. He also stated that the NUC and its "Guidelines for National Unification" would remain in place. Furthermore, late in 2000 Chen's administration announced its intention to complete work on a "three links" plan for direct trade, transport, and postal services between the two regimes. As a step toward that goal, in January 2001 three ships completed the first direct transit between the mainland and nearby Kinmen and Matsu since 1949, thereby opening what was dubbed the "mini-three-links."

In September 2003 Taiwan's Legislative Branch amended the island's Statute Governing Relations Between People of the Taiwan Area and the Mainland Area by giving the MAC and SEF authority to sanction links to the mainland by local government bodies and private groups. On January 29, 2005, shortly before the Chinese New Year holiday, a charter jet left Beijing airport for a nonstop flight to Taipei, restoring after 56 years direct, albeit strictly limited, civil aviation links.

In March 2005 the PRC passed an antisecession law amid continued assertions by the PRC leadership that the use of force would "become unavoidable" if Taiwan openly defied the "one China" principle. Although the law caused a furor in Taiwan, on April 26, 2005, the KMT chair, Lien Chan, began an eight-day visit to the PRC. The first KMT chair to travel to the mainland since 1949, he signed a joint communiqué with PRC president Hu Jintao calling for an end to the "hostile situation," establishment of economic links, and discussion of the island's international status.

In early 2006 President Chen clearly hardened his public stance toward reunification, suggesting, for example, that UN membership might be sought for "Taiwan" instead of the "Republic of China" and that a new constitution should be drafted. In addition, on February 27 Chen announced that the NUC would "cease to function," a decision widely criticized by Taiwan's opposition parties, the United States, and the PRC's Hu Jintao, who described the move as a "dangerous step" and a "grave provocation," even though the council had not met since 2000. Chen further indicated his intention to abandon the Guidelines for National Unification. A year later, Chen further roiled relations with Beijing. In a March 4, 2007, speech he outlined "four wants and one without": independence for Taiwan, a change in the jurisdiction's official designation, a new constitution, and new economic development, all without reference to left/right politics.

In January 2008 the MAC complained that Beijing, in an effort to influence the outcome of Taiwan's March 22 presidential election, had "set up obstacles" to concluding arrangements for passenger and cargo flights. Meanwhile, KMT presidential candidate Ma Ying-jeou had pledged to resume SEF-ARATS negotiations, which had been stalled under President Chen, and to press for establishment by mid-2008 of weekend charter flights to the mainland. In a controversial move following his election victory, Ma named a proindependence politician to head the MAC, but he also pledged not to pursue de jure independence during his term in office.

The thaw that accompanied Ma's election was immediately evident. In the highest-level meeting of executives since 1949, on April 13, 2008, Vice President-elect Vincent Siew met informally with PRC president Hu Jintao on the sidelines of a regional forum in Hainan,

China. On May 27–31, 2008, the KMT chair, Wu Poh-hsiung, visited the mainland, where he conferred with the Chinese Communist Party general secretary (and PRC president), Hu Jintao, the first such meeting in 60 years. Less than a month later, on June 12–14, the first formal SEF-ARATS session in 9 years concluded with an agreement to set up liaison offices and to establish direct weekend charter flights between Taiwan and the mainland. The first such flights took place on July 4. On November 3–7 Chen Yunlin, the ARATS chair, made the most senior official visit to Taiwan in 60 years, during which the number of weekly roundtrip flights was expanded to 108 (connecting 8 cities on Taiwan with 21 mainland cities), approval was given for 60 direct cargo flights per month, and the opening of 11 Taiwanese ports and 63 PRC ports (expanded to 68 in May 2009) to handle freight shipments, and improved postal links were authorized. These "three direct links" were officially inaugurated on December 15. In April 2009 Chen and the chair of the SEF, Chiang Ping-king, signed additional economic agreements, in part to make it easier for PRC companies to invest in Taiwan.

On May 18, 2009, Wu and Hu met for a second time. Shortly before, Jia Qinglin, the chair of the Chinese People's Political Consultative Conference (CPPCC), an umbrella grouping of various mainland political, social, cultural, and other groups, called for broad-based exchanges and cooperation between the PRC and Taiwan.

PEOPLE'S REPUBLIC OF CHINA

Zhongguo Renmin Gongheguo
(Chung-hua Jen-min Kung-ho Kuo)

Political Status: Communist People's Republic established October 1, 1949; government controls mainland China, Hong Kong (since 1997), and Macao (since 1999); present constitution adopted December 4, 1982.

Area: 3,692,213 sq. mi. (9,562,842 sq. km.), excluding Taiwan.

Population: 1,242,612,226 (2000C, excluding Taiwan, Hong Kong, and Macao); 1,332,042,000 (2008E, excluding Taiwan).

Major Urban Centers (urban areas, 2005E): BEIJING (Peking, 12,100,000), Shanghai (18,150,000), Guangzhou (Canton, 9,550,000), Wuhan (9,100,000), Tianjin (Tientsin, 6,350,000), Shenyang (4,550,000), Nanjing (Nanking, 3,500,000), Harbin (3,400,000), Dalian (Dairen, 2,900,000). Most of these figures are substantially less than previous estimates.

Official Language: Northern (Mandarin) Chinese (*putunghua* is the officially promoted Beijing dialect).

Monetary Unit: Yuan (official rate December 1, 2009: 6.82 yuan = $1US). The overall currency is known as renminbi (people's currency). China shifted from a state-set, dual-rate exchange system to a single exchange system pegged to the U.S. dollar on January 1, 1994. On July 21, 2005, the government announced it would permit the yuan to fluctuate within a narrow band against a basket of foreign currencies.

President of the People's Republic and General Secretary of the Chinese Communist Party: HU Jintao; named to succeed JIANG Zemin as general secretary on November 15, 2002; elected president for a five-year term by the National People's Congress on March 15, 2003, succeeding Jiang Zemin; reelected March 15, 2008.

Vice President: XI Jinping; elected by the National People's Congress on March 15, 2008, for a term concurrent with that of the president, succeeding ZENG Qinghong, who had reached the mandatory retirement age.

Premier of the State Council: WEN Jiabao; elected to a five-year term by the National People's Congress on March 16, 2003, succeeding ZHU Rongji; reelected March 16, 2008.

GOVERNMENT AND POLITICS

Political background. Following its establishment in 1949, the government of the People's Republic of China (PRC) devoted major attention to the consolidation of its rule in China and outlying territories and to socialization of the Chinese economy. Within China proper, Communist rule was firmly established by the early 1950s. Xizang (Tibet), over which China historically claimed suzerainty, was brought under military and political control in 1950–1951 and then, after a nationalist revolt and the flight of the DALAI LAMA (TENZIN Gyalso) to India in 1959, was incorporated as an autonomous region of the PRC in 1965. In contrast, occupation of Taiwan was prevented by the protective role assumed by the United States in 1950, although the offshore islands of Kinmen (Quemoy) and Matsu were sporadically shelled in subsequent years as an ostensible prelude to the "liberation" of Taiwan itself.

The internal policy and economic planning of the PRC, originally modeled on Soviet experience and supported by Soviet technical aid and loans, began to deviate markedly from Soviet models with the proclamation in 1958 of the "Great Leap Forward," a new system of economic development based on organization of the peasant population into rural communes and the use of labor-intensive, as opposed to capital-intensive, methods of production. The failure of the Great Leap Forward was followed by a period of pragmatic recovery from 1961 to 1965 that coincided with growing ideological differences between the Chinese and Soviet Communist parties.

Apparently believing that the revolutionary ardor of the Chinese Communist Party (CCP) had succumbed to bureaucratization, Chairman MAO Zedong (MAO Tse-tung) launched the "Great Proletarian Cultural Revolution" in 1965–1966 to reassert the primacy of Marxist-Leninist doctrine against "revisionist" tendencies imputed to leading elements within the CCP. A period of internal turmoil and civil strife from 1966 to 1968 found Mao, Defense Minister LIN Biao (LIN Piao), and others denouncing the influence of PRC Chair LIU Shaoqi (LIU Shao-ch'i), whose ouster was announced in October 1968, and other alleged revisionists, some of whom—including former CCP secretary general DENG Xiaoping (TENG Hsiao-p'ing)—were subsequently "rehabilitated." After causing vast internal turbulence that reached a peak in 1967, the Cultural Revolution diminished in intensity during 1968 and early 1969 amid indications that one of its main results had been an increase in the power of the military.

At the CCP's Ninth Congress, held in April 1969, Lin Biao was hailed as the "close comrade in arms and successor" of Chairman Mao. Two years later, however, Lin disappeared from public view and was subsequently branded as an inveterate anti-Maoist who had been largely responsible for the excesses of the Cultural Revolution. He was later reported to have perished in a plane crash in Mongolia in September 1971 while en route to the Soviet Union after failing in an attempt to seize power. In early 1974 "counter-revolutionary revisionism" of the Lin variety was indirectly, but vigorously, attacked by means of a campaign directed against China's ancient sage Confucius, with some arguing that the true target was Premier ZHOU Enlai (CHOU En-lai). By the end of the year, however, increasing numbers of senior officials had reappeared, including many military men who had been purged during the Cultural Revolution.

A subsequent period of relative quiescence was shattered by the deaths of Premier Zhou on January 8, 1976, and of Chairman Mao on September 9. Shortly after Zhou's death, Vice Premier HUA Guofeng (HUA Kuo-feng) was named acting premier. The appointment came as a surprise to foreign observers, who had anticipated the elevation of the rehabilitated Deng Xiaoping. As first vice premier, Deng had performed many of Zhou's functions during the latter's long illness, but in April, following demonstrations in Beijing and elsewhere in support of Deng, it was announced that he had again been dismissed from all government and party posts and that Hua had been confirmed as premier. A widespread propaganda campaign was subsequently launched against Deng and other "unrepentant capitalist-roaders."

Mao's death precipitated a renewed power struggle that resulted in a victory for the "moderate," or "pragmatic," faction within the Political Bureau (Politburo) over the "radical" faction composed of Vice Premier ZHANG Chunqiao (CHANG Ch'un-ch'iao); JIANG Qing (CHIANG

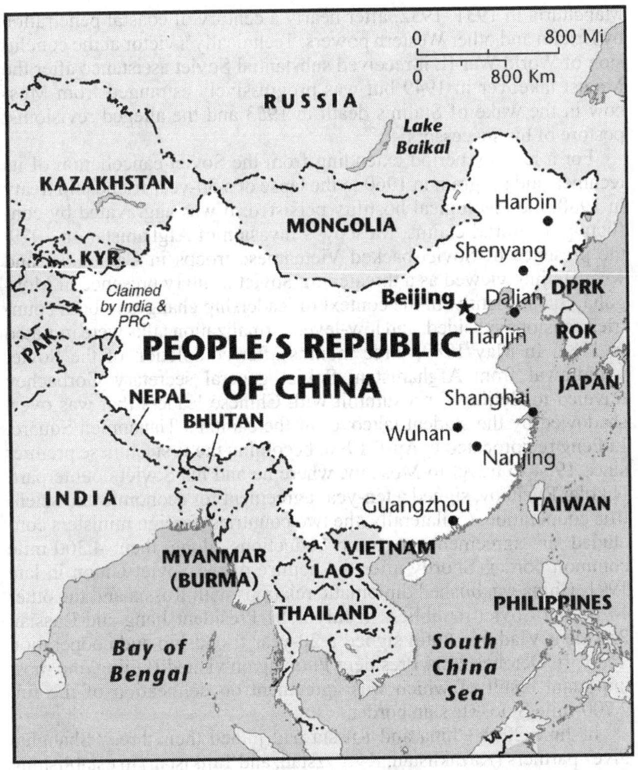

Ch'ing), Mao's widow; WANG Hongwen (WANG Hung-wen); and YAO Wenyuan (YAO Wen-yüan), who had called for a return to the principles of the Cultural Revolution. Stigmatized as the "Gang of Four," the radicals were arrested in October 1976, a day before Hua's designation as chair of the CCP Central Committee. Having been indicted on charges that included plotting to overthrow the government. all four, plus six associates of Lin Biao, were convicted in January 1981, with Jiang and Zhang receiving deferred death sentences. (The ailing Jiang was released to house arrest in 1984 and committed suicide in 1991; Zhang, released in 1998 for medical reasons, died in April 2005.)

In July 1977 Deng Xiaoping, for the second time, was rehabilitated and restored to his former posts of CCP deputy chair, vice premier of the State Council, and chief of staff of the armed forces. Though the Fifth National People's Congress (NPC), which met in Beijing in February–March 1978, reconfirmed Hua as premier and named CCP Deputy Chair YE Jianying (YEH Chien-ying) as NPC chair—a post vacant since the 1976 death of Marshal ZHU De (CHU Teh)—most observers considered Deng to be at least as powerful as Hua.

Subsequently, the PRC began a sweeping reform in agricultural policy that, as implemented in 1979–1980, progressively nullified the Maoist commune system by permitting a return in many areas to farming on a family basis. Some land was later converted to cash- and industrial-crop production, while additional acreage was taken out of agriculture entirely for the construction of local workshops and plants. Collaterally, the state farms were transformed into integrated enterprises operating on the basis of long-term, low-interest loans rather than state subsidies.

During a February 1980 plenum of the CCP Central Committee, the party Secretariat, which had been abolished during the Cultural Revolution, was reinstated with HU Yaobang (HU Yao-pang), a Deng ally, named general secretary, while Liu Shaoqi was posthumously rehabilitated as "a great Marxist and proletarian revolutionary." The trend continued in an August–September session of the NPC, which at its conclusion accepted Hua's resignation as premier of the State Council and named Vice Premier ZHAO Ziyang (CHAO Tzu-yang) as his successor. In an apparent effort to ease the transition, Deng also resigned as vice premier, while Hua retained titular status as party chair. Hua subsequently retired from public view after yielding the CCP chairmanship to Hu at a Central Committee plenum held in June 1981. The post of general secretary was left vacant. Hua was also removed as chair of the party's Military Commission, with Deng being named his successor.

The 12th CCP Congress, which met in September 1982, adopted a new party constitution that abolished the posts of chair and vice chair while reinstating that of general secretary, to which former chair Hu was again named. The restructuring of the upper CCP echelon was accompanied by a program of widespread personnel "rectification" at the provincial and municipal levels in late 1982 and early 1983. The following October, a three-year consolidation campaign was announced to eliminate vestiges of "leftist factionalism" among party cadres. One year later, the party's Central Committee unanimously approved an unprecedented program for "Reform of the Economic Structure" that urged reliance "on the world's advanced methods of management, including those of developed capitalist countries."

The "rectification" campaign continued into 1985, with General Secretary Hu Yaobang announcing in April that some 70 percent of the leaders in 107 party and State Council departments, as well as in 29 regional, provincial, and municipal governments, were to be replaced. The most dramatic implementation of the policy came in September, when an extraordinary National CCP Conference of Party Delegates (less amenable to local influence than a congress) was convened for the first time since 1955 and proceeded to abolish "de facto lifelong tenure" by retiring nearly one-fifth of the Central Committee; the latter body then met to accept the resignation of approximately 40 percent of the ruling Politburo. Although further consolidating the position of Deng Xiaoping, the shake-up at the senior level fell short of purging all those with misgivings about his policies, including Hua Guofeng.

Earlier, in December 1982, the NPC had approved a new PRC constitution that reinstated the post of head of state (abolished under the 1975 constitution), with the incumbent to bear the title of president rather than that of chair. Following elections to the Sixth NPC in March–April 1983, LI Xiannian (LI Hsien-nien) was named to fill the new position, with a prominent Inner Mongolian leader, General ULANHU (ULANFU), being named vice president,. In the course of an extensive government reorganization at the opening session of the Seventh NPC in March–April 1988, the two leaders were replaced by YANG Shangkun and WANG Zhen, respectively.

Political relaxation had reached its peak during 1986. Early in the year, General Secretary Hu endorsed open criticism of party pronouncements and subsequently revived a short-lived 1957 appeal by Chairman Mao to "Let a hundred flowers bloom." In December student demonstrations broke out in at least a dozen cities, including Beijing, calling for the election of more genuinely representative people's congresses. The situation generated bitter resentment among conservatives, and in January 1987 Hu was forced to resign as party leader. Named as his successor, on an acting basis, was Zhao, who stepped down as premier coincident with confirmation of his status as CCP general secretary in November. LI Peng was designated to fill Zhao's vacated post.

The death of Hu Yaobang in April 1989, in the course of an attempted political comeback, prompted student demonstrations in Beijing that precipitated a split within the government and party leadership. By mid-May the protest had led to student occupation of Tiananmen Square, which proved an embarrassment to the government by severely disrupting a visit by Soviet general secretary Mikhail Gorbachev (the first such event in three decades). Immediately after the Soviet leader's departure, martial law was declared in the capital, although it was not until the early morning of June 4, with hard-liners having assumed control of the CCP Politburo, that the military was ordered to disburse the demonstrators in an action that reportedly resulted in several thousand deaths. On June 24 General Secretary Zhao Ziyang was formally purged and replaced by the Shanghai party chief, JIANG Zemin. On November 9 Deng Xiaoping turned over his last party post, the chair of the Central Military Commission, to Jiang, albeit with no indication that his status as China's most powerful political figure was in jeopardy.

The most important domestic event of 1992, the 14th CCP Congress, held in October, saw an unusually large number of Politburo and Central Committee members replaced. Subsequently, at the first session of the Eighth NPC in March 1993, General Secretary Jiang was named to succeed Yang Shangkun as PRC president. Li Peng was reconfirmed as premier, although he received an unprecedented 330 negative ballots. Jiang's elevation meant that he held the three key posts of PRC president, party general secretary, and chair of the CCP Central Military Commission—a consolidation unequaled since Hua Guofeng had held them in the immediate post-Mao era.

Deng Xiaoping, who had not appeared in public since early 1994, died in February 1997. No major policy changes ensued, in large part because the succession issue had long been settled with the accession of Jiang Zemin at the head of a third generation of leaders. In the other major event of the year, Hong Kong returned to Chinese sovereignty on July 1 (see Special Administrative Regions, below). Jiang was reelected PRC president by the first session of the Ninth NPC in March 1998, while ZHU Rongji was named to succeed the outgoing premier, Li Peng, who was elected NPC chair.

Sweeping leadership changes marked the first session of the Tenth NPC, held March 5–18, 2003. HU Jintao, who had been named CCP secretary general in November 2002, was designated state president. On March 17 a new State Council was announced, only a handful of whose members were carryovers from the previous body. The second session of the Tenth NPC, held March 5–14, 2004, approved a number of constitutional amendments, including formal guarantees of private property and human rights. Six months later, on September 19, a CCP Central Committee plenum relieved former president Jiang as chair of the Central Military Commission, Hu Jintao thereby becoming, like his predecessor, holder of the three most powerful positions in state and party.

Hu was reelected to a second presidential term on March 15, 2008, at the first session of the newly elected 11th NPC. The following day, Wen was returned as premier, heading a restructured cabinet that included five new "superministries": Environmental Protection, Housing and Urban-Rural Construction, Human Resources and Social Security, Industry and Information, and Transport.

Constitution and government. The constitution adopted by the First NPC on September 20, 1954, defined the PRC, without reference to the Communist Party, as "a people's democratic state led by the working class and based on the alliance of workers and peasants"; by contrast, both the 1975 and 1978 constitutions identified the PRC as "a socialist state of the dictatorship of the proletariat" and specifically recognized the CCP as "the core of leadership of the whole Chinese people."

Article One of the most recent (1982) constitution defines the PRC as "a socialist state under the people's democratic dictatorship led by the working class and based on the alliance of workers and peasants." The document defines minority rights, mandates equal pay for equal work, and specifies that deputies may be recalled at all legislative levels. Enumerated responsibilities include observing "labor discipline," paying taxes, and exercising family planning. Rights to a defense and to a public trial are retained, save in cases "involving special circumstances as prescribed by law."

The National People's Congress, "the highest organ of state power," convenes once a year. Deputies are elected by lower-level legislative bodies and by units of the armed forces for five-year terms. Among the NPC's functions are constitutional amendment and the election of most leading government officials, including the president and vice president of the PRC, whose terms are concurrent with that of the legislature; state councilors (including the premier and vice premiers); and ministers. Judicial authority is exercised by a hierarchy of people's courts under the supervision of the Supreme People's Court. A Supreme People's Procuratorate supervises a parallel hierarchy of people's procuratorates, with both the courts and the procuratorates accountable to legislative bodies at relevant levels. The principal regional and local organs are provincial and municipal people's congresses (elected for five-year terms); prefecture, city, and county congresses (elected for three-year terms); and town congresses (elected for two-year terms).

In 1999 the NPC approved two constitutional amendments, one of which declared private enterprise to be "an important component of the socialist economy"—a marked change from the 1954 specification that capitalists be "used, restricted, and taught," and even from the language of a 1978 amendment, which had required the private economy to be "guided, supervised, and managed" as a "supplement" to the socialist economy. The impact of a surging economy and China's heightened presence on the world stage was reflected in 2003 amendments concerning property rights and human rights, although a loophole was attached to the former by confining its scope to "legal private property" as defined, presumably, by the regime.

Administratively, the PRC is divided into 22 provinces (excluding Taiwan); the 5 autonomous regions of Guangxi Zhuang, Nei Monggol (Inner Mongolia), Ningxia Hui, Xinjiang Uygur (Sinkiang Uighur), and Xizang (Tibet); 2 special administrative regions, namely Hong Kong and Macao; and the 4 centrally governed municipalities of Beijing (Peking), Chongqing (Chungking), Shanghai (Shanghai), and Tianjin (Tientsin).

Foreign relations. Historically a regional hegemon periodically weakened by dynastic and other internal difficulties, China suffered its most extensive modern occupation following the Japanese invasion of Manchuria in 1931–1932, after nearly a century of coastal penetration by Britain and other Western powers. Technically a victor at the conclusion of World War II, it received substantial Soviet assistance after the Maoist takeover in 1949 but was progressively estranged from Moscow in the wake of Stalin's death in 1953 and the alleged revisionist posture of his successors.

For a lengthy period extending from the Soviet cancellation of its technical aid program in 1960 to the lapse of a 30-year friendship treaty in 1980, the ideological hostility persisted. It was aggravated by conflicting territorial claims, Moscow's invasion of Afghanistan in 1979, the presence of Soviet-backed Vietnamese troops in Cambodia, and what Beijing viewed as a threatening Soviet military presence in Mongolia. Subsequently, in the context of leadership changes in both countries, tensions subsided, and low-level normalization talks were initiated in 1982. In May 1989, three months after completion of the Soviet withdrawal from Afghanistan, Soviet general secretary Gorbachev traveled to Beijing for a summit with Chinese leaders that was overshadowed by the student takeover of the capital's Tiananmen Square. Li Peng reciprocated in April 1990, becoming the first Chinese premier since 1964 to travel to Moscow, where he and his Soviet counterpart, Nikolai Ryzhkov, signed a ten-year agreement for economic and scientific cooperation. Collaterally, the two countries' foreign ministers concluded an agreement on troop reductions along their 4,300-mile common border. Shortly after the demise of the Soviet Union in late 1991, China established diplomatic relations with Russia and the other 14 former Soviet republics. In July 2001 President Jiang and Russian President Vladimir Putin signed a 20-year friendship and cooperation treaty. In October 2004 President Putin again visited Beijing, the most important result of which was agreement on delineation of the full 2,700-mile Sino-Russian border.

In June 2001 China and Russia had joined their three "Shanghai Five" partners (Kazakhstan, Kyrgyzstan, and Tajikistan) in establishing a new Shanghai Cooperation Organization (SCO). The original Shanghai forum had emerged from a 1994 meeting in Shanghai directed toward resolving border disputes and addressing security issues in Central Asia. It had subsequently developed a more encompassing posture toward regional stability, a principal focus being mutual opposition to Islamic militancy. Joining the Shanghai Five as a founding member of the SCO was Uzbekistan. The eighth SCO summit took place in August 2008 in Dushanbe, Tajikistan.

An ally of Hanoi during the Vietnam War, China denounced Vietnam as Moscow's "Asian Cuba" in mid-1978 and continued its support for Kampuchea (Cambodia) in the border dispute that culminated in the Vietnamese invasion of its western neighbor at the end of the year. A Chinese incursion into northern Vietnam in February 1979, triggered by the Vietnamese action in Cambodia but rooted in a series of border disputes going back to the mid-19th century, proved to be an embarrassment for the comparatively inexperienced Chinese military. Although Chinese forces registered local successes, serious personnel and equipment shortcomings were evident in engagements against the battle-hardened Vietnamese militia. The Chinese withdrew in mid-March, claiming that they had succeeded in their objective of "teaching Hanoi a lesson." Sporadic border clashes continued thereafter, some of the more serious occurring in April through June 1984 and in 1985. In 1991, upon completion of a peace agreement that ended 13 years of conflict in Cambodia, China and Vietnam began normalizing relations.

In 1994 long-smoldering tension over the Spratly Islands erupted, with Beijing denouncing Vietnam for violating its "indisputable sovereignty" over the islands, which are also claimed by Brunei, Malaysia, Philippines, and Taiwan. Three months later it expressed its "grave concern" over Hanoi's oil-prospecting in the region, which drew a countercharge from Vietnam of "systematic and unacceptable" intrusion by Chinese fishermen into its exclusive economic zone in the Gulf of Tonkin. Concurrently, it was reported that China had moved to create an air and naval rapid response force to defend its claims in the South China Sea. Relations fluctuated for several years thereafter, but the two neighbors signed a land border agreement on December 30, 1999, and in 2000 pledged to resolve the sea disputes. In December 2000 the two settled the Tonkin issue, but the conflicting claims in the South China Sea remain open. In February 2007 Chinese, Vietnamese, and Philippine oil companies agreed to conduct joint seismic studies in a wide area that includes the Spratlys.

For more than a quarter century, relations with India were strained by a territorial dispute that resulted in full-scale fighting between the two countries in October 1962. China occupied some 14,500 square miles of territory adjacent to Kashmir in the west and also claimed some 36,000 square miles bordering Bhutan in the east, south of the so-called McMahon Line drawn by the British in 1915.

The first direct negotiations on the issue were held in Beijing in 1981. Periodic discussions thereafter culminated in a visit to Beijing by Indian prime minister Rajiv Gandhi in December 1988—the first such meeting in 34 years—during which it was agreed that a joint working group of technical experts would be established to facilitate settlement "through peaceful and friendly consultation." In September 1993, during a visit to Beijing by Indian prime minister P.V. Narasimha Rao, the two governments agreed on a mutual reduction of troops deployed along the border and pledged to observe the de facto line of control, pending conclusive settlement of the dispute. Renewed border talks began in March 1999. In 2003 India acknowledged Chinese sovereignty over Tibet, while China indicated de facto recognition of India's sovereignty over Sikkim. In April 2005, following meetings between Premier Wen Jiabao and Indian prime minister Manmohan Singh, the two countries announced plans for a "strategic and cooperative partnership for peace and prosperity." They also set out an 11-point framework for settling the border issue. In July 2006 the Nathu Lu pass, a trade route between Tibet and Sikkim, was opened for the first time in 44 years.

Japan, long China's leading trading partner, recognized the PRC as the "sole legal government of China" in 1972, and in 1978 the two signed a treaty of peace and friendship, culminating six years of intermittent talks. In November 1998 President Jiang became the first Chinese head of state to visit Japan. While the event was considered a breakthrough in Sino-Japanese relations, Jiang was unable to secure concessions from Tokyo in regard to Taiwan or to obtain a long-sought formal apology for the suffering inflicted by Japan's occupation of China from 1937 to 1945. Since then, relations have remained cool, in part because U.S.-Japanese security guidelines have implications regarding the defense of Taiwan. In October 2006 the new Japanese prime minister, Shinzo Abe, made his first overseas visit a trip to Beijing, where he met with President Hu Jintao, who described the occasion as a "turning point" in relations. Premier Wen Jiabao then visited Japan in April 2007, as did newly reelected President Hu in May 2008.

A lengthy process of rapprochement between China and South Korea concluded in August 1992 with the normalization of diplomatic relations. While the reaction from North Korea was muted, Taiwan, which immediately severed relations with Seoul, branded the action as a "violation of international justice." More recently, Seoul has acknowledged China's importance in regional affairs, particularly its influence with North Korea. Since the opening in August 2003 of six-party talks (also involving Japan, Russia, South Korea, and the United States) on Pyongyang's nuclear ambitions, Beijing has played a crucial role in repeatedly bringing the Kim Jong Il regime back to the bargaining table.

Beginning in the early 1970s, relations with the West improved dramatically, highlighted initially by U.S. president Richard Nixon's visit to China in February 1972, at which time a joint communiqué included acknowledgment that "all Chinese on either side of the Taiwan Strait maintain that Taiwan is part of China." The United States and the PRC established de facto diplomatic relations in 1973 by agreeing to set up liaison offices in each other's capitals and subsequently completed the exchange, on a de jure basis, on January 1, 1979.

In 1993 the United States imposed a number of economic sanctions against China, claiming that it had breached the 1968 UN Treaty on the Non-Proliferation of Nuclear Weapons, which China had ratified in 1992, by selling missile technology to Pakistan. The action came two months after Washington had agreed to a one-year renewal of China's most-favored-nation (MFN) trading status, despite continued criticism of Beijing's human rights record. That record was believed to be at least partially responsible for a late September decision by the International Olympic Committee to reject China's bid to host the 2000 Summer Games, although it was subsequently named host for the 2008 Games. In May 1994 Beijing agreed to cease jamming Voice of America broadcasts and to end the export to the United States of prison-made products. In return, U.S. president Bill Clinton again renewed China's MFN status, implicitly severing its linkage to the human rights issue. A new trade issue promptly surfaced over U.S. charges of intellectual copyright infringement. The trade dispute was momentarily resolved during "last-ditch" talks in February 1995.

Other highly divisive Sino-U.S. issues provided the backdrop to a meeting between President Jiang and President Clinton in October 1995. The issues included Beijing's recent incarceration of a number of human rights activists, U.S. complaints of Chinese arms shipments to Iran and Pakistan, Chinese anger over an unofficial visit by Taiwan's president Lee Teng-hui to the United States, and restrictions placed on delegates to official and unofficial women's conferences in China. In early 1996 trade issues again loomed large, although a partial defusing allowed President Clinton to announce another one-year renewal of China's MFN status in May, while at the same time reiterating U.S. reservations about China's eligibility for membership in the World Trade Organization (WTO). In October 1997 President Clinton welcomed his Chinese counterpart to a White House summit by calling for a "new era" in Sino-U.S. relations.

In mid-1998 Clinton paid the first presidential visit to China since the 1989 Tiananmen massacre. In April 1999 Premier Zhu Rongji reciprocated with a nine-day visit to the United States, but he was unable to secure Washington's backing on WTO entry, reportedly because of continued U.S. congressional opposition in the wake of charges—which ultimately proved to be unfounded—that Beijing had stolen highly classified military information from the nuclear weapons laboratory in Los Alamos, New Mexico. It was not until September 19, 2000, that the way was paved for WTO accession by U.S. Senate approval of a landmark bill that granted China permanent trading status. (Formal WTO admission came in December 2001.) Since then, the most persistent principal conflict between Washington and Beijing has involved a massive trade imbalance (see Current issues, below).

Relations with the United Kingdom long centered on the status of Hong Kong. In September 1984 the two governments issued a joint declaration on the future of the crown colony, as a consequence of which China, under the slogan "one country and two systems," regained full sovereignty over Hong Kong on July 1, 1997, when the 99-year lease of the New Territories expired. China agreed to maintain the enclave as a capitalist "Special Administrative Region" for at least 50 years thereafter. The agreement on Hong Kong was followed in 1987 by a joint Sino-Portuguese declaration on the future of Macao, which reverted to Chinese sovereignty on December 20, 1999.

In April 1998 representatives of China and the European Union (EU) met in London for the first in a projected annual series of talks, with the participants pledging greater mutual cooperation in trade and other economic relations. Nevertheless, with the WTO's quota system for textiles exports having expired on January 1, 2005, Chinese textile exports to the EU (and the United States) jumped by more than 50 percent in the first five months of the year, aggravating an already heated argument over market penetration versus protectionism. In June the EU and China reached agreement on limiting imports of certain types of clothing for three years, but it took until September to correct deficiencies in the agreement. The EU agreement expired at the end of 2007.

Politically, the EU aggravated Beijing in October 2008 when it awarded its Sakharov Prize for Freedom of Thought to Chinese dissident HU Jia, who was recognized for his commitment to human rights, environmental causes, and the HIV/AIDS crisis. In March 2008 the Chinese courts had sentenced Hu to three and a half years in prison for subversion.

Recently, international human rights activists and many governments have urged China to exert more pressure on Sudan to end the humanitarian crisis in Darfur. Beijing, the leading market for Sudanese oil and the principal arms supplier to the government, has blocked UN Security Council action against Khartoum.

Current issues. The 17th CCP Congress, held October 15–21, 2007, was expected to provide insight into who might succeed Hu Jintao and Win Jiabao in 2012. Most analysts focused on the elevation of Shanghai party chief XI Jinping, 54, and Liaoning Province chief LI Keqiang, 52, to the nine-member Politburo Standing Committee. The two, a decade younger than any of the other Standing Committee members, represent the fifth generation of party leadership. The subsequent election, in March 2008, of Xi as PRC vice president and Li as a vice premier confirmed their status.

Beijing viewed the August 8–24, 2008, Summer Olympic games in Beijing as an opportunity to confirm China's rightful place on the international stage, but activists around the world used the passage of the symbolic Olympic torch around the world as an occasion to highlight the government's human rights failings, especially after rioting in Tibet in March drew renewed attention to the status of that autonomous region. What apparently began on March 10 as a demonstration in the Tibetan capital, Lhasa, marking the 49th anniversary of a failed uprising, quickly escalated into rioting by Tibetans, who reportedly targeted non-Tibetan Chinese migrants and Muslims. The Chinese authorities responded with force, but tight restrictions on media access made it impossible to confirm the number of deaths and injuries, or the amount of damage. During the next several weeks protests and rioting were also reported outside the region, in localities with large Tibetan communities.

The onset of the disturbances coincided with the opening of the 11th NPC, prompting newly reelected President Hu to accuse followers of the Tibetan spiritual leader and head of the government-in-exile in Dharamshala, India, the Dalai Lama, of masterminding and orchestrating the rioting not only to press for Tibetan independence but also to undermine the Olympics. The Dalai Lama, a Nobel Peace Prize winner, rejected all such accusations, asserting that while he sought "meaningful cultural autonomy"—a "middle way"—for Tibet, he viewed independence as "out of the question" and that, furthermore, he supported the Beijing Olympics. On May 4 representatives of the Dalai Lama and the PRC government met in Shenzhen, with both sides agreeing to resume formal talks. (Nevertheless, marking the 50th anniversary of the uprising, the Dalai Lama on March 10, 2009, accused China of having unleashed "untold suffering and destruction" on Tibet.)

On May 12, 2008, domestic and international attention was diverted to southwestern China, where the most devastating earthquake in 30 years, 7.9 on the Richter scale, struck Sichuan Province. In a departure from previous practice, Prime Minister Wen rushed to the stricken area and was seen via live television feeds coordinating rescue and relief efforts. Confirmed deaths totaled 69,000, with another 18,000 missing. An estimated 5 million were left homeless. Particularly disturbing for many in the affected areas was the disproportionate death toll among children—5,300 according to the government, although estimates by others ran as high as 10,000—many of whom had been killed when their schools collapsed. Although the government rejected claims that local officials had been bribed to ignore shoddy work by construction companies, it immediately began an inspection of the country's 390,000 schools. A year later government authorities reported that all damaged factories and shops had reopened and that housing reconstruction would be completed by September 2010.

Alongside Tibet, the most restive area of China involves Xinjiang Uygur Autonomous Region, where a Muslim separatist movement has long opposed the central government (see the discussion of Dissident and Separatist Groups, below). Before the September 11, 2001, al-Qaida attacks on the United States and the consequent invasion of Afghanistan by U.S.-led forces, an indeterminate number of Uygurs had received weapons and other forms of military training in the Afghanistan-Pakistan border region, In the aftermath of the U.S. invasion, a number of Uygurs were detained by or handed over to U.S. forces. Classified as "enemy combatants," approximately two dozen were ultimately shipped to the U.S. detention facility in Guantánamo Bay, Cuba. Although they were subsequently cleared for release or transfer by the George W. Bush administration, most continued to languish in the detention camp because of opposition to their entry into the United States and the failure of other governments—the notable exception being Albania—to accept them. At the same time, China demanded their return, which would guarantee their prosecution for terrorism and possible execution. In October 2008 a U.S. judge ordered the release of the remaining 17, but the Bush administration successfully appealed. As a consequence, the problem carried over to the new Obama administration. In late May 2009 the U.S. Department of Justice stated that the Uygurs would be released to any country that would admit them. As of early October, only two governments had stepped forward: Bermuda, which accepted 4 of the Uygurs in June, and Palau, which in September had agreed to accept 6. The other 7 detainees reportedly rejected relocation to Palau because they feared its relative proximity to China.

Broader human rights issues continued to command domestic and international attention. The 20th anniversary of the Tiananmen Square crackdown of June 1989 was marked by heightened security measures, the arrest of dissidents, and tight media restrictions. In January the government had released the last individual imprisoned as a consequence of the protests, but efforts to promote political reform continued to be met harshly. A leading dissident, LIU Xiaobo, who had joined more than 300 others in drafting a reform manifesto in December 2008, was subsequently charged with "inciting to subvert state power."

The financial crisis and recession that threatened to strangle the world economy in the final quarter of 2008 dramatically altered Beijing's economic outlook. Less than a year earlier, the government, concerned that the economy was overheating due to double-digit growth, was contemplating efforts to hold expansion closer to the 7.5 percent annual target of the 11th Five-Year Plan (2006–2010). Rising inflation, which had averaged 4.8 percent in 2007, was a related concern. By December 2008, however, the government faced rising unemployment as overseas markets retracted, deflation had replaced inflation as a potential threat, the central bank had introduced the largest interest rate cut in a decade, and Beijing had hurriedly introduced a $586 billion economic stimulus package, emphasizing infrastructure projects. Addressing the second session of the 11th NPC in March 2009, Premier Wen Jiabao noted the "unprecedented difficulties" facing the economy but reassured the legislators that China could still achieve 8 percent growth in 2009. The most significant additional initiatives proposed at that time concentrated on social measures, including increased funding for education, healthcare, and low-income housing.

In other economic matters, at the end of the 2009 NPC session the premier told the assembled press that he was "definitely a little bit worried" about the continued creditworthiness of the United States, given that China holds some $2 trillion in U.S. debt, half of it in government securities. A week later, the governor of China's central bank went so far as to propose that the special drawing right (SDR) of the International Monetary Fund (IMF) replace the U.S. dollar as a global currency.

In 2008 the PRC's record trade surplus of $296 billion (up from $178 billion in 2006 and $262 billion in 2007) gave further credence to an international charge that the value of the yuan was still being artificially manipulated despite China's decision in July 2005 to permit its narrow fluctuation against a basket of foreign currencies. That theme was reiterated in January 2009 by Timothy Geithner, at the time U.S. president Barack Obama's nominee for secretary of the treasury, and also echoed by the IMF's Dominique Strauss-Kahn, who labeled the yuan as "significantly undervalued." Meanwhile, the U.S. trade deficit with China had reached a record $266.3 billion in 2008 (including reexports from Hong Kong) although in November and December both the U.S. deficit and the Chinese surplus were already turning downward. By mid-2009 it was clear that 2009 would not be yet another record-breaking year.

Since 2007 Chinese industry has repeatedly come under fire for having shipped a host of substandard products around the world, including contaminated pet food, toothpaste, fish, and toys. In the most publicized case of official corruption, in July ZHENG Xiaoyu, former head of the PRC's State Food and Drug Administration, was executed after having been convicted of taking bribes from pharmaceutical companies seeking regulatory approvals. In 2008 the agency was placed directly under the Ministry of Health. At the same time, the State Environmental Protection Administration was upgraded to a "superministry" in recognition of the need for greater attention to environmental considerations, including pollution and access to clean water. The biggest scandal of 2008 concerned the deliberate adulteration of infant formula and milk with the chemical melamine, which resulted in falsely high protein readings. Over 300,000 Chinese may have been sickened by the tainted products. Dozens of individuals were tried for the contamination, and in January 2009 two of those convicted received death sentences.

POLITICAL PARTIES AND GROUPS

Although established essentially as a one-party Communist state, the PRC has preserved some of the characteristics of a "United Front" regime by permitting the continued existence of eight small minority parties, some of whose leaders hold high government office along with Communists and nonparty personnel. In addition, the **Chinese People's Political Consultative Conference** (CPPCC), which originally included representatives of all bodies adopting the 1949 constitution, reemerged in 1978, its last previous meeting having been held in 1965. Among the groups represented were political parties; minority nationalities; the All-China Federation of Trade Unions, the All-China Women's Federation, and the Communist Youth League, all three of which had been denounced during the Cultural Revolution; religious groups; and an assortment of other social, scientific, artistic, and cultural interests. The current chair of the CPPCC is JIA Qinglin, a member of the Communist Party Politburo.

Leading Party:

Chinese Communist Party—CCP (*Zhongguo Gongchan Dang*). The CCP, founded in 1921 in Shanghai, exerted unquestioned political dominance from 1949 until it was weakened as a result of the Cultural

Revolution and the disruptive activities of Red Guard forces in the mid-1960s. However, reconstruction of the party organization, begun in late 1969, was largely completed by late 1973, with the revolutionary committees created during the Cultural Revolution being made subordinate to party committees. The CCP's resurgence was formalized in 1975, when, for the first time, it was constitutionally recognized as the "vanguard" of state and society; by contrast, in the 1982 constitution the party is mentioned only in the preamble, where, at several points, its leadership role is acknowledged.

The party's highest organ is the National Party Congress, whose Central Committee elects a Political Bureau (Politburo) as well as other top figures. In theory, party congresses are elected every five years and hold annual sessions; however, the 8th Congress held only two sessions (in 1956 and 1958), while the 9th Congress did not convene until 1969. The 12th Congress, which met in September 1982, adopted a new party constitution, under which the posts of CCP chair and vice chair were abolished.

The ongoing process of internal reform was further advanced at the 13th Congress, held October 25–November 1, 1987, when most of the remaining "founding generation" CCP leaders retired, including Deng Xiaoping, who continued, however, as chair of the party's Central Military Commission until November 1989.

The 14th Congress was held in Beijing October 12–18, 1992, with 1,989 indirectly elected and 41 "specially invited" delegates representing a claimed 52 million party members. A new Central Committee of 189 full and 130 alternate members (new members constituting nearly half of the total) was elected. In addition, a new Politburo of 7 Standing Committee and 19 other members (including 2 alternates) was named. More than half of the appointments were new, and most of those were economic reformers, while the military lost all of its representatives save one.

The party's 15th Congress, held September 12–18, 1997, in Beijing, concluded by removing almost all members older than 70 from its Central Committee, while increasing the size of the body to 193 full and 151 alternate members. The sixth plenary session, held September 24–26, 2001, focused on party-building, including improved leadership, governance, and anticorruption efforts in the context of "Marxism-Leninism, Mao Zedong Thought, and Deng Xiaoping Theory."

The 16th Congress, initially scheduled for September 2002, was postponed until November 8–14, reportedly because of a power struggle over the composition of the new generation of leaders. At the congress, a new Central Committee of 198 full and 158 alternate members was named, which designated a 9-member Standing Committee, headed by Hu Jintao, and 15 other Politburo members. The fifth plenary session, held October 8–11, 2005, approved the 11th Five-Year Plan (2006–2010), which was submitted to the National People's Congress in March 2006.

The party's 17th Congress met October 15–21, 2007. Changes in the membership of the Central Committee and the Politburo generally represented the rise of a new fifth generation of leaders without, however, displacing key figures in the current hierarchy, except for those who had reached the mandatory retirement age of 68, such as Vice President ZENG Qinghong. More than 2,200 delegates attended the session, which elected 204 full members of the Central Committee (from 221 candidates) and an additional 167 alternates. Of the full and alternate members, 49 percent were new. The Central Committee expanded the Politburo to 25 members.

General Secretary: HU Jintao (PRC President and Chair, Central Military Commission).

Other Members of Politburo Standing Committee: HE Guoqiang (Secretary, Central Commission for Discipline Inspection), JIA Qinglin (Chair, Chinese People's Political Consultative Conference), LI Changchun, LI Keqiang (Vice Premier), WEN Jiabao (Premier), WU Bangguo (Chair, National People's Congress Standing Committee), XI Jinping (PRC Vice President), ZHOU Yongkang (Secretary, Central Committee Political and Legislative Affairs Committee).

Other Members of Politburo: BO Xilai (Party Secretary, Chongqing), GUO Boxiong (Vice Chair, Central Military Commission), HUI Liangyu (Vice Premier), LI Yuanchao (Director, Central Committee Organization Department), LIU Qi (Party Secretary, Beijing), LIU Yandong (State Councilor), LIU Yunshan (Director, Central Committee's Publicity Department), WANG Gang (Vice Chair, Chinese People's Political Consultative Conference), WANG Qishan (Vice Premier), WANG Lequan (Party Secretary, Xinjiang Uygur Autonomous Region), WANG Yang (Party Secretary, Guangdong Province), WANG Zhaoguo (Vice Chair, Standing Committee of the National People's Congress), XU Caihou (Vice Chair, Central Military Commission), YU Zhengsheng (Party Secretary, Shanghai), ZHANG Dejiang (Vice Premier), ZHANG Gaoli (Party Secretary, Tianjin).

Secretariat: HE Yong, LI Yuanchao, LING Jihua, LIU Yunshan, WANG Huning, XI Jinping.

Regime-Supportive Minority Parties:

While expected "to work under the leadership of the Communist Party," in 1979 the following groups, largely middle-class and/or intellectual, were permitted to recruit new members and to hold national congresses for the first time in two decades: the **China Association for Promoting Democracy** (*Zhongguo Minzhu Cujin Hui*), a Shanghai cultural and educational group founded in 1945; the **China Democratic League** (*Zhongguo Minzhu Tongmeng*), founded in 1941 by a group of intellectuals opposed to Chiang Kai-shek's Nationalist Party (*Chung-kuo Kuo-min Tang* or Kuomintang—KMT); the **China Democratic National Construction Association** (*Zhongguo Minzhu Jianguo Hui*), a business-oriented group founded in 1945; the **China Party for Public Interests** (*Zhongguo Zhi Gong Dang*), an outgrowth of a 19th-century secret society organized by overseas Chinese; the **Chinese Peasants and Workers' Democratic Party** (*Zhongguo Nong Gong Minzhu Dang*), founded in 1947 as an outgrowth of a prewar movement that had joined forces with the CCP in 1935; the **Revolutionary Committee of the Kuomintang** (*Zhongguo Guomin Dang Geming Weiyuanhui*), founded in 1948 by a group of Hong Kong–based KMT dissidents opposed to Chiang Kai-shek's leadership; the **September 3, 1945 (V-J Day) Society** (*Jiu San Xuehui*); and the **Taiwan Democratic Self-Government League** (*Taiwan Minzhu Zizhi Tongmen*), founded in 1947 by a group of pro-PRC Taiwanese.

Dissident and Separatist Groups:

During 1998 a number of dissidents sought to organize legal parties, notably WANG Youcai, QIN Yongmin, and XU Wenli on behalf of the China Democratic Party (CDP). In November Wang, Qin, and Xu were arrested for "subversion of the state process" and sentenced to 11, 12, and 13 years imprisonment, respectively. The sentencing of 15 other CDP leaders during the ensuing year virtually destroyed the party. (Xu and Wang were released for medical reasons in December 2002 and March 2004, respectively, and left for the United States.) In early 1999 the regime also cracked down on the China Labor Party, although in March it released two leaders, LI Li and WANG Ce, of the China Democratic United Front–Liberal Democratic Party after four months' incarceration. In August 2008 the government released HU Shigen, cofounder of the China Freedom and Democracy Party, from prison after he had served 16 years of a 20-year sentence.

A clandestine **East Turkestan Islamic Movement** (ETIM) operates primarily in Xinjiang Uygur Autonomous Region, where elements of the Uygur minority have long sought separation. Small-scale antigovernment attacks appear to have become more frequent in recent years, but foreign journalists have had only restricted access to the region and incidents are not uniformly reported. In 2003 the Chinese government branded the ETIM (also known as the Turkistan Islamic Party) and three other groups—the **East Turkestan Information Center,** the **East Turkestan Liberation Organization,** and the **World Uygur Youth Congress**—as terrorist organizations. In January 2007 police reported destroying a camp in southern Xinjiang run by the ETIM, killing 18 and arresting 17 others. In July 2008 the ETIM claimed responsibility for bus bombings that took two lives in Kunming, and in the most deadly recent attack, was allegedly behind an August 4 attack in Kashgar that killed 17 police. Less than a week later, 12 were reported killed in Kuqa.

LEGISLATURE

National People's Congress—NPC (*Quanguo Renmin Daibiao Dahui*). A unicameral body indirectly elected for a five-year term, the NPC holds one session annually, although the Second Congress (1959–1963) did not meet in 1961 and the Third Congress met only once. No subsequent election was held until 1974, after which the Fourth Congress convened in complete secrecy in Beijing in January 1975.

Meetings became regularized with the 5th Congress, elected at a series of municipal and provincial congresses held between November 1977 and February 1978. A total of 2,987 newly elected deputies from 34 electoral units plus the People's Liberation Army were authorized to attend the first session of the 11th Congress, which was held in Beijing on March 5–18, 2008. The second session met on March 5–13, 2009.

Chair of the Standing Committee: WU Bangguo.

CABINET

[as of October 1, 2009]

Premier	Wen Jiabao
Vice Premiers	Hui Liangyu
	Li Keqiang
	Wang Qishan
	Zhang Dejiang
State Councilors	Dai Bingguo
	Liang Guanglie
	Liu Yandong [f]
	Ma Kai
	Meng Jianzhu
Senior Ministers	
Environmental Protection	Zhou Shengxian
Housing and Urban-Rural Construction	Jiang Weixin
Human Resources and Social Security	Yin Weimin
Industry and Information	Li Yizhong
Transport	Li Shenglin
Ministers	
Agriculture	Sun Zhengcai
Civil Affairs	Li Xueju
Commerce	Chen Deming
Culture	Cai Wu
Education	Zhou Ji
Finance	Xie Xuren
Foreign Affairs	Yang Jiechi
Health	Chen Zhu
Justice	Wu Aiying [f]
Land and Natural Resources	Xu Shaoshi
National Defense	Liang Guanglie
Public Security	Meng Jianzhu
Railways	Liu Zhijun
Science and Technology	Wan Gang
State Commission for Ethnic Affairs	Yang Jing
State Commission for National Development and Reform	Zhang Ping
State Commission for Population and Family Planning	Li Bin
State Security	Geng Huichang
Supervision	Ma Wen
Water Resources	Chen Lei
Auditor General	Liu Jiayi
Chair, Central Military Commission	Hu Jintao
Governor, People's Bank of China	Zhou Xiaochuan
Secretary General, State Council	Ma Kai

[f] = female

Note: All members of the cabinet belong to the CCP except the unaffiliated minister of health and the minister of science and technology, who is a member of the China Party for Public Interests.

COMMUNICATIONS

Mainland media are under rigid government control, and numerous journalists have been jailed for failing to follow government prescripts. In Hong Kong, however, media have retained considerable editorial independence since reversion.

Chinese citizens have limited access to foreign news sources. In August 2005 the Ministry of Culture announced that it would not permit additional foreign-owned satellite television channels and would tighten controls on the 31 current operators to help protect what the government termed "national cultural identity." In advancing China's successful bid to host the 2008 Olympic Games in Beijing, the government had agreed to permit foreign journalists greater freedom, but as the event drew closer, journalists continued to complain that they had insufficient access.

In addition, the government routinely monitors and blocks access to independent Internet sites. In September 2005 the international group Reporters Without Borders asserted that the Hong Kong–based branch of Internet giant Yahoo! had supplied damaging information about a journalist who had been sentenced to ten years in prison for revealing state secrets. In early 2006 another major Internet company, Google, admitted that it had censored its Chinese-language search engine to produce results deemed acceptable by the government. In November 2007 Yahoo! concluded an out-of-court settlement with the families of two "cyberdissidents" who had been sentenced to ten-year prison terms.

At the beginning of June 2009 Beijing, preparing for the 20th anniversary of the Tiananmen Square crackdown, blocked access to a number of Internet services, including Twitter, photo-sharing site Flickr, and other blogging and social networking sites. Foreign media reports marking the anniversary were also censored. The government has undertaken a broad campaign to install Internet filtering software on all personal computers as part of an effort to create a so-called Great Fire Wall between computer users and pornographic and politically sensitive Internet sites. Access to social network and messaging sites is also being restricted.

Press. There are some 2,100 newspapers published in China by the government or the CCP. Reported circulation estimates for the following selection (dailies published in Beijing, unless otherwise noted) vary widely: *Sichuan Ribao* (Chengdu, 8,000,000); *Cankao Xiaoxi* (Reference News, 2,600,000); *Renmin Ribao* (People's Daily, 2,500,000), official CCP Central Committee organ; *Guangzhou Ribao* (Guangzhou Daily, 1,600,000); *Jingji Ribao* (Economic Daily, 1,500,000); *Wenhui Bao* (Wenhui Daily, Shanghai, 1,300,000); *Yangcheng Wanbao* (Yangcheng Evening News, Guangzhou, 1,300,000); *Beijing Wanbao* (Beijing Evening News, 1,000,000); *Gongren Ribao* (Workers' Daily, 1,000,000); *Jiefang Junbao* (Liberation Army Daily, Shanghai, 1,000,000); *Jiefang Ribao* (Liberation Daily, 1,000,000); *Nongmin Ribao* (Farmer's Daily, 1,000,000 nationwide); *Xin Min Wanbao* (Xinmin Evening News, Shanghai, 1,000,000); *Zhongguo Qingnian Bao* (China Youth News, 1,000,000); *Beijing Ribao* (Beijing Daily, 900,000), organ of Beijing CCP Municipal Committee; *Nanfang Ribao* (South China Daily, Guangdong Province, 750,000). *China Daily* (200,000) began publication in 1981 and remains China's only English-language daily; a New York edition was launched in 1983 and a London edition in 1986.

News agencies. The leading official facility is *Xinhua She* (New China News Agency—NCNA), which is attached to the State Council and has offices around the world; a number of other agencies service PRC-sponsored papers abroad. Some two dozen foreign agencies maintain offices in Beijing.

Broadcasting and computing. China National Radio (CNR) provides service in *putunghua* and various local dialects via more than 1,200 broadcast outlets, while China Central Television (CCTV) operates through approximately 200 television stations (excluding relays). There are many additional provincial and municipal stations. A few foreign stations are available in Guangdong, but broadcasting a foreign-made program requires government consent.

As of 2008 there were 222.8 Internet users per 1,000 inhabitants.

INTERGOVERNMENTAL REPRESENTATION

Ambassador to the U.S.: ZHOU Wenzhong.

U.S. Ambassador to China: Jon M. HUNTSMAN, Jr.

Permanent Representative to the UN: ZHANG Yesui.

IGO Memberships (Non-UN): ADB, AfDB, APEC, BIS, CDB, G-20, IADB, Interpol, PCA, WCO, WTO.

SPECIAL ADMINISTRATIVE REGIONS

Hong Kong. The former Crown Colony of Hong Kong, situated on China's southeastern coast, consists of Hong Kong Island and Kowloon Peninsula, both ceded by China to Great Britain "in perpetuity" in the mid-19th century, as well as the mainland area of the New Territories, leased for 99 years in 1898. Its total area is 423 square miles (1,095 sq. km.), the New Territories alone occupying 365 square miles. The inhabitants, concentrated on Hong Kong Island and Kowloon, total some 6,896,000 (a 2007 by-census figure that may involve some underenumeration). The population is 98 percent Chinese, nearly one-quarter from the PRC. The capital is Victoria, on Hong Kong Island.

The economy was formerly based on exported industrial products, especially cotton textiles, but the services sector now accounts for 91 percent of GDP, in the wake of Hong Kong's emergence as one of the world's premier banking and financial centers. In 2003 hundreds of Hong Kong residents were afflicted with a previously unknown viral illness, termed severe acute respiratory syndrome (SARS) by the World Health Organization. The disease caused a drastic decline in tourism, weakening a struggling economy and contributing to a record unemployment rate of 8.6 percent at midyear. Thereafter, extraordinary growth on the mainland, an upswing in business, and improving trade spurred a recovery that continued into 2004, when GDP grew by 8.6 percent. Growth for 2005–2007 remained high, averaging about 6.8 percent, while per capita income in 2007 stood at $44,050 (in terms of purchasing power parity), more than eight times that of the mainland. As a consequence of international financial turmoil and a slowdown in trade, growth for 2008 was projected at 3.7 percent.

Responding to mounting indications of uneasiness on the part of the business community, in October 1982 British and Chinese diplomats had begun discussing a transition to full Chinese sovereignty. The talks culminated in the signature on December 19, 1984, in Beijing of a "Sino-British Joint Declaration of the Question of Hong Kong," which took effect in May 1985. Under the slogan "one country and two systems," China would regain title to the entire area on July 1, 1997, when the lease of the New Territories expired, but agreed to maintain the enclave as a capitalist "Special Administrative Region" for at least 50 years thereafter. In the wake of the June 1989 Tiananmen Square massacre in Beijing, concern mounted in Hong Kong regarding the 1997 reversion, with London coming under criticism for its unwillingness to permit the emigration to Britain of the 3.5 million Chinese—approximately 60 percent of Hong Kong's residents—who were entitled to restricted "British National Overseas" passports.

On April 4, 1990, the PRC's National People's Congress (NPC) approved a postreversion "mini-constitution" that included a complicated formula for Legislative Council (LegCo) representation: one-third of its members were to be elected at the first postreversion balloting, with the proportion rising to two-fifths in 1999 and to one-half in 2003. The law made no reference to the future status of a Bill of Rights that had been approved by the colony's Executive Council a month earlier.

In late April 1990 the UK House of Commons approved a bill permitting the issuance of British passports to some 300,000 Hong Kong Chinese. The documents would be awarded on the basis of a point system that limited admission to select categories, such as leading businesspersons, civil servants, and educators. To the surprise of British authorities, fewer than 60,000 applied for passports prior to the expiration date for "first tranche" requests at the end of February 1991.

In September 1991 the United Democrats of Hong Kong (UDHK), led by Martin LEE Chu-ming, joined other prodemocracy groups in winning 16 of 18 contested LegCo seats in the colony's first direct election in 150 years of British rule. The following March, the Chinese government responded by naming a 44-member panel of advisers to assist in the forthcoming transition; all of the panel's local members were representatives of pro-Beijing groups.

In April 1992 UK prime minister John Major announced that Chris Patten, the Conservative Party chair, would replace Sir David Wilson as governor of Hong Kong at midyear. The new governor quickly became embroiled in an acrimonious dispute with Beijing over plans for reform of Hong Kong's system in the period before its reversion to China, which claimed that his plan breached signed Sino-UK agreements. Patten, backed by liberal members of LegCo, published his proposals in March 1993. At the same time, Beijing continued to create alternative bodies to handle the transfer, including a Preparatory Committee (PC) for the Hong Kong Special Administrative Region (HKSAR). Amid growing strains in UK-Chinese relations, the director of the Hong Kong and Macao Affairs Office of the Chinese State Council, LU Ping, visited the colony in May but refused to meet with Patten.

In 1994 Hong Kong prepared for its first fully democratic elections. In April the UDHK announced a merger with the prounification Meeting Point group to form the **Democratic Party** (DP), which advocated autonomy for Hong Kong following the reversion to Chinese sovereignty. Also launched in April, the business-oriented Hong Kong Progressive Alliance (HKPA), with Ambrose LAU Hon-chuen as its spokesperson, favored close relations with China. In addition, the **Association for Democracy and People's Livelihood** (ADPL), led by Frederick FUNG Kin-kee, attracted considerable support in the run-up to the election, which took place in September for a total of 346 seats on 18 district boards. Independents won 167 seats; the DP, 75; the ADPL, 29; four pro-Chinese parties, a total of 68; and other parties, 7. The prodemocracy DP and ADPL also polled strongly in elections to urban and regional councils held in March 1995.

Two months earlier, new strains had developed over China's demand for access to the personal files of Hong Kong civil servants, and in May Lu Ping again visited the colony without meeting Patten. Tensions eased somewhat with the signature in June of an accord on maintaining elements of an independent legal system after reversion. Prodemocracy parties fiercely criticized concessions made to the PRC, but LegCo passed the agreement by a two-to-one margin in July. Earlier in the month, the Hong Kong chief secretary, Anson CHAN (CHAN Fang On-sang), confirmed that she had paid an unprecedented visit to Beijing for talks with Chinese leaders.

Elections to the 60-seat LegCo in September 1995 gave the DP 12 of the 20 directly elected seats plus 7 indirectly elected seats, although China had indicated that no DP members would be permitted to serve in the future legislature of the HKSAR. The **Liberal Party** (LP), a business group favoring accommodation with Beijing, won 10; the strongly pro-Chinese **Democratic Alliance for the Betterment of Hong Kong** (DAB), 6; and the ADPL, 4, with independents claiming most of the balance.

In December 1995 China published the names of the 150 members of the PC, including 94 Hong Kong residents but no DP supporters. At its first meeting, held in January 1996 in Beijing, the PC formally replaced the Preliminary Working Committee that had hitherto represented China's interests. Tasks assumed by the PC included establishing a 400-member selection committee to appoint a chief executive for the HKSAR, and in March it voted 149 to 1 to constitute a Provisional Legislative Council (PLC) that would replace the existing LegCo until formation of a new LegCo after reversion; the sole dissenting member was Fung of the ADPL.

In the course of a visit to Hong Kong in March 1996, Prime Minister Major protested against Beijing's decision to abolish LegCo, its refusal to deal with Governor Patten, and its disregard for the Bill of Rights. The UK prime minister also announced that some 2.4 million Hong Kong Chinese would be given limited rights to enter Britain, but not the guaranteed residence rights demanded by the DP.

Shipping magnate TUNG Chee-hwa (generally known as "C.H.") resigned from the Executive Council in June 1996 while remaining vice chair of the PC. He was regarded as China's favored candidate for the position of HKSAR chief executive. The first round of balloting by the selection committee in November (when Foreign Minister Qian made his first visit to Hong Kong) was contested by 8 candidates, after China had rejected 23 other nominees. Anson Chan had announced her decision not to run, in light of Tung's declared wish to retain her as chief secretary. Tung won 206 votes in the first round and was formally designated chief executive after securing 320 votes in a runoff in December against former chief justice Sir TI-LIANG Yang and Peter WOO. In late December the PC went on to nominate the 60 members of the PLC, thereby generating a series of DP-led demonstrations as well as strong protests from Patten, who nevertheless pledged to cooperate with Tung in the transition period.

At midnight on June 30, 1997, in a colorful ceremony attended by Britain's Prince Charles, Chinese President Jiang Zemin, and UK Prime Minister Tony Blair, Hong Kong was returned to Chinese sovereignty. Immediately thereafter Chief Executive Tung formally named an administrative team that included Anson Chan as chief secretary and, somewhat surprisingly, Sir Donald Tsang (Tsang Yam-kuen), the incumbent financial secretary, who had earlier expressed opposition to Tung's economic policies. Most of the remaining members of the Executive Council were newcomers.

In April 1998 approximately 5 percent of Hong Kong's 2.6 million voters, representing professional, labor, and religious groups, were permitted to vote for 588 members of an 800-seat Election Committee that was, in turn, to name 10 members of the first postreversion LegCo. Another 30 LegCo members were to be selected by professional and business groups. In the LegCo election in May, prodemocracy candidates won 14 of the 20 directly elected seats but constituted a minority because pro-China groups dominated the remaining 40 seats. The DP once again led the prodemocracy forces, taking 9 directly elective seats, while a new party, **The Frontier,** led by Emily LAU Wai-hing, took 3; Christine LOH Kung-wai's Citizens' Party, 1; and an independent, 1. The DAB, led by TSANG Yok-sing, won 5 seats in the direct balloting. The LP won only 1; its leader, Allen LEE Peng-fei, was among the defeated.

By May 2000 Tung's popularity had fallen to 18 percent and the DP was also losing support, apparently because of widespread frustration with the convoluted electoral system. Among other difficulties, controversy had erupted over whether the Election Committee, for which balloting was held on July 9, was authorized to choose the chief executive in addition to its functions regarding LegCo.

The turnout was only 43.6 percent in the election of September 10, 2000, after which the prodemocracy DP held only 12 of 60 seats on a declining vote share, while the pro-Beijing DAB total rose to 11. The overall balance of power on the LegCo remained with the pro-Beijing forces following the election, which also saw the LP, the HKPA, the Frontier, and the **New Century Forum,** led by MA Fung-kwok, winning seats.

Although denying that she was reacting to pressure from Beijing, the enclave's popular civil rights advocate, Anson Chan, resigned as chief secretary on January 12, 2001. Financial Secretary Tsang was named as her successor on February 15, amid speculation that Chan might challenge Tung's reelection bid in early 2002.

Passage of the Chief Executive Election Bill by the LegCo on July 11, 2001, generated considerable controversy and precipitated a walkout by opponents, principally because of a provision permitting Beijing to remove a chief executive considered "incapable of serving." Opposition deputies, including Martin Lee, branded the provision as a fundamental betrayal of Hong Kong's autonomy.

The voting for chief executive on February 28, 2002, was conducted by a committee containing a minority of pro-Beijing appointees, with three-fourths of the 800 delegates representing various functional and other constituency groups. The result was a fait accompli, however, since Tung, who retained solid support from President Jiang, had collected more than 700 nominating signatures, thereby preventing any prospective opponent from obtaining the minimum 100 signatures needed for consideration. On June 24 Tung announced the formation of a new Executive Council, which was approved by a 36–21 LegCo vote despite strenuous opposition from prodemocracy forces.

In November 2003 prodemocracy parties won 144 of 206 relatively meaningless district council seats, but they failed to gain an expected majority of LegCo seats in the September 12, 2004, election, in which 30 seats were directly elected from geographic constituencies and the other 30 chosen by functional groups. Prodemocracy advocates came away with 25 seats, but the DP, led by Martin Lee and YEUNG Sum, saw its total drop to 9. The Frontier and the ADPL each won 1 seat, with most of the remaining prodemocracy seats being claimed by unaffiliated candidates. The DAB and the resurgent LP, the latter now led by James TIEN Pei-chun, won 12 and 10 seats, respectively, to lead the pro-Beijing contingent, which won an overwhelming majority of functional constituency seats and thereby ended up with 35 seats overall. (In February 2005 the DAB absorbed the HKPA.)

A new centrist organization of barristers, the Article 45 Concern Group, led by Alan LEONG Kah-kit, won 4 prodemocracy seats in the September 2004 election on a platform that called for direct election of the chief executive (as advocated in Article 45 of Hong Kong's Basic Law) in 2007 and LegCo in 2008. Leong's group had originally been formed as the Article 23 Concern Group, which had mounted a successful campaign against adoption of a stringent national security law despite its being mandated by Article 23 of the Basic Law.

After weathering numerous demonstrations, triggered in part by Beijing's assertion in April 2004 that it would not tolerate a direct election in 2007, Chief Executive Tung resigned on March 10, 2005, citing health reasons, and was succeeded on an interim basis by his deputy, Donald Tsang. Having declared himself a candidate to fill the two-year balance of Tung's term, Tsang resigned on May 25 and was replaced by the financial secretary, Henry Tang Ying-yan. The DP's LEE Wing-tat also declared his candidacy, but Tsang was confirmed on June 16 after obtaining over 700 signatures of support from members of the Election Committee. He was sworn in on June 24 in Beijing.

In October 2005 the Tsang administration revealed plans to double the Election Committee to 1,600 members and to add ten seats to LegCo, five of them directly elected. A month later, in an apparent effort to mollify prodemocracy advocates, who had rejected the electoral reform as inadequate, Tsang revived and expanded a Commission on Strategic Development, one of whose committees would develop "a road map for universal suffrage." Nevertheless, on December 21 the LegCo failed to approve the proposed electoral reforms, which received 34 votes, 6 short of the two-thirds needed for referral to the PRC's NPC. Earlier in December, crowds numbering as many as 250,000 (63,000, according to the police) demonstrated in favor of a timetable for full democracy.

In March 2006 the Article 45 Concern Group announced formation of a new **Civic Party** (CP), led by Leong and Audrey EU. Leong subsequently indicated his intention to run for chief executive as the candidate of the CP and DP. (Martin Lee and Anson Chan both declined to run.) Although Leong secured sufficient supporting signatures to contest the March 25, 2007, election, Tsang won another term easily, by a 649–123 vote of the 796-member Election Committee. Leong, who had not expected to win, stated that he intended to run again in 2012 and would continue to advocate universal suffrage and full democracy.

Earlier, in August 2006, LegCo voted 32–0 in favor of granting police wide powers to conduct covert surveillance, including wiretapping, bugging homes and businesses, and monitoring e-mail. Prodemocracy legislators boycotted the vote after failing to add a prohibition against political surveillance.

On December 29, 2007, the Standing Committee of the NPC stated that it would actively consider electing Hong Kong's chief executive by universal suffrage in 2017, but not in 2012. It also ruled out direct election of the full LegCo until at least 2020.

The district council elections of November 18, 2007, were marked by a surge in support for the DAB, which nearly doubled its 2003 representation, to 115 seats. The DP, in contrast, saw its representation drop from 95 to 59 seats. The CP won 8; the **League of Social Democrats** (LSD), a prodemocracy party formed in October 2006 and led by Raymond WONG Yuk-man, 6; and the LP, 1.

In the LegCo election of September 7, 2008, the pro-Beijing faction retained a majority by virtue of its strength among functional constituencies, among which it won 24 of 30 seats. Overall, the DAB, now led by TAM Yiu-chung, won a leading 13 seats for the pro-Beijing faction, followed by the LP, 7; the Alliance, a functional constituency group led by Abraham SHEK Lai-him, 3; the Hong Kong Federation of Trade Unions, 1; and individuals, 10. Among the prodemocracy parties, the DP won 8; the CP, 5; the LSD, 3; the ADPL, 2; the **Civic Act-Up,** 1; the Frontier, 1; the Hong Kong Confederation of Trade Unions, 1; and others, 2. Three seats were won by independents. The prodemocracy group's 23 total seats were sufficient to deny the pro-Beijing faction, with 34 seats, a controlling two-thirds majority.

The relatively poor electoral performance of the LP led James Tien, who had lost his LegCo seat, to resign as chair, leaving acting chair Miriam LAU Kin-yee in charge. At the same time, three of the LP's recently elected legislators announced their resignations from the party. In other party developments after the 2008 election, the Alliance changed its name to the **Professional Forum,** and the Frontier announced in November that it would cooperate with the DP while retaining its separate identity.

Chief Executive: Sir Donald TSANG (TSANG Yam-kuen).
Secretary for Finance: Henry TANG Ying-yan.
Secretary for Security: Ambrose LEE Siu-kwong.

Macao. Established in 1557 as the first European enclave on the China coast, Macao comprises a peninsula and two small islets in the mouth of the Canton River, about 40 miles west of Hong Kong. Its area of 6 square miles (15.5 sq. km.) contains some 517,000 inhabitants (a 2007 by-census figure that may involve some underenumeration). The population is predominantly Chinese, with a Portuguese minority of 2,000–3,000. Its economy shrank by 4.6 percent in 1998 and by 2.9 percent in 1999, but increased substantially thereafter as the former Portuguese colony became an Asian center of casino gambling. Recently, growth has exceeded even the mainland's accelerated pace, reaching 16.5 percent in 2006 and then 25.3 percent in 2007. For 2008, however, despite rapid expansion in the first quarter, average GDP growth for the year fell to 13.2 percent, reflecting a steady rate decline in the second and third quarters and a downturn of 7.6 percent in the fourth as Macao felt the impact of the international financial crisis.

In 1974 Western diplomats in Beijing reported that the governor of Macao, Col. José Eduardo Martinho García Leandro, had been directed to communicate to Chinese representatives the Lisbon government's willingness to withdraw from the enclave. China had no desire, however, to alter the status of the territory, which was flourishing, partly because of legalized casino gambling—the source of nearly half of its revenue—and partly because of its status as an entrepôt for trade with China. (It had long been alleged that the port also exported opium into the international market.) The trade relationship had been enhanced by creation of a Special Economic Zone in the nearby province of Zhuhai.

The establishment of diplomatic relations between Portugal and the PRC in February 1979 did not alter the status of Macao, Portuguese prime minister Carlos Mota Pinto declaring that it would remain "Chinese territory under Portuguese administration." Following conclusion of the agreement on Hong Kong's future in December 1984, China changed course, however, and initiated discussions on Macao's status.

In May 1985, following the designation of Joaquim Pinto Machado as Macao's latest governor, Portuguese president António Eanes announced that Sino-Portuguese talks on reversion would begin in 1986. On May 26, 1987, the two countries initialed an agreement for the return of the territory to Chinese sovereignty on December 20, 1999, under a plan similar to the "one country and two systems" approach approved for Hong Kong. China agreed to grant Macao 50 years of noninterference with its capitalist economy, and residents holding or entitled to hold Portuguese passports were given the right to continue doing so after reversion.

In January 1993 the ninth and final session of the Macao Special Administrative Region (MSAR) Basic Law Drafting Committee, meeting in Beijing, approved the text of the document that would serve as the MSAR constitution following reversion. In late March the text was approved by the Chinese legislature. In the last assembly balloting before the reversion to Chinese rule, a record 64.4 percent turnout in September 1996 delivered a majority for pro-Chinese groupings.

A Chinese-appointed MSAR Preparatory Committee was launched in Beijing in May 1998. Charged with defining the procedure for the election of Macao's first postreversion government, the committee consisted of 100 members, 40 of whom were from China. In its fourth plenary session held in November, the group authorized its chair, Chinese vice premier Qian Qichen, and his vice chairs to designate candidates for a 200-member Nominating Committee, which, following election by the Preparatory Committee, would be responsible for electing members of the new government. In December Beijing announced a new nationality law for the enclave: upon reversion, all residents of Chinese descent would become Chinese citizens, while those of mixed Chinese and Portuguese descent would be allowed to choose either Chinese or Portuguese allegiance.

Immediately following its formation in April 1999, the Chinese Nominating Committee winnowed the list of potential chief executives from nine to two, with HO Hau Wah (Edmund HO), a banker, appearing to hold a decided preelection advantage over AU Chong Kit (Stanley AU), another banker. On May 15 the committee elected Ho by a landslide of 163 votes to 34. The territory's inhabitants looked to the widely popular Ho to reverse a languishing economy and take decisive action against long-standing violence by underworld groups, known as triads. Because of the turmoil, which had severely damaged the economy by inhibiting tourism, Chinese troops were widely applauded by Macanese at reversion in December 1999.

In its first postreversion parliamentary election, held September 23, 2001, Macao saw the 10 popularly elected seats filled by 4 pro-Beijing, 4 probusiness, and 2 prodemocracy representatives, including NG Nuok Cheong, leader of the **New Democratic Macao Association** (*Associação de Novo Macau Democrático*—ANMD). An additional 10 Legislative Assembly members were indirectly elected by four interest groups: labor; employers; professionals; and welfare, cultural, educational, and sports constituencies. The final 7 assembly members were subsequently appointed by Chief Executive Ho.

The election of September 25, 2005, saw 58 percent of Macao's voters turn out to fill 12 seats on the 29-seat Legislative Assembly. A dozen associations offered candidates, with 8 of them winning at least 1 seat, including 2 each by the ANMD, the **Union for Development** (*União para o Desenvolvimento*—UD), the **United Citizens' Association of Macao** (*Associaçãdos Cidadão Unidos de Macau*—ACUM), and the **Union for Promoting Progress** (*União Promotora para o Progresso*—UPP). As in the past, interest groups indirectly elected 10 members, and Chief Executive Ho appointed the balance.

In March 2007 the troubled Macao-based Banco Delta Asia (BDA) returned to the headlines when the U.S. Treasury Department ruled, in confirmation of allegations made in 2005, that the bank had aided North Korea in laundering money. In the context of ongoing six-party talks in Beijing aimed at ending North Korea's nuclear weapons program, the United States agreed to the transfer to Pyongyang of $25 million frozen in a BDA account, although it took until June to complete the transaction.

On January 30, 2008, former secretary of transport and public works AO Man-long was sentenced to 27 years in prison for having accepted some $100 million in bribes from companies seeking approvals for casino and hotel projects. Ao was the highest-ranking public official to face corruption charges since the reversion to China in 1999.

In May 2009 the government announced the names of the 300 members of the Chief Executive Election Committee (254 representatives of socioeconomic sectors, the 12 Macanese deputies to the National People's Congress, 16 representatives from Macao's Legislative Assembly, 12 members of the Chinese People's Political Consultative Conference, and 6 religious representatives). With Edmund Ho ineligible for a third term, the front-runner for the July 26 contest was generally regarded to be Fernando Chui Sai-on, who resigned his post as secretary for social affairs and culture to stand for election. Other expected candidates were Prosecutor General HO Chio-meng and Secretary for Economy and Finance Francis TAM Pak-yuen, but in the end Chui proved to be the only candidate. Declared the winner on July 26, he won the approval of the PRC's cabinet on August 10.

Sixteen groups contested the 12 directly elected Legislative Assembly seats at polling held September 20, 2009. An unusual number of potentially spoiled ballots delayed the release of final results, although prodemocracy advocates claimed that they had won three seats.

Chief Executive: CHUI Sai-on (Fernando CHUI Sai-on).

CHINA: TAIWAN

Republic of China
Chung-hua Min-kuo

Note: In view of the Republic of China's decision to abandon its claim that it constituted the sole legitimate representative of all of China, the Taipei Economic and Cultural Office in New York has indicated that the designation Republic of China on Taiwan (*Tsai Taiwan te Chung-hua Min-kuo*) is acceptable for informal usage.

Political Status: Chinese province; controlled by the government of the Republic of China (established 1912), whose authority since 1949 has been limited to the island of Taiwan (Formosa), Penghu (the Pescadores), and certain offshore islands, including Kinmen (Quemoy) and Matsu; present constitution adopted December 25, 1946, effective from December 25, 1947.

Area: 13,592 sq. mi. (35,203 sq. km.).

Population: 22,300,929 (2000C); 23,063,000 (2008E).

Major Urban Centers (2005E): TAIPEI (2,619,000), Kaohsiung (1,522,000), Taichung (1,039,000), Tainan (761,000), Keelung (394,000).

Official Language: Mandarin Chinese.

Monetary Unit: New Taiwan Dollar (market rate December 1, 2009: 32.19 dollars = $1US).

President: MA Ying-jeou (Nationalist Party); elected March 22, 2008, and sworn in May 20 for a four-year term, succeeding CHEN Shui-bian (Democratic Progressive Party).

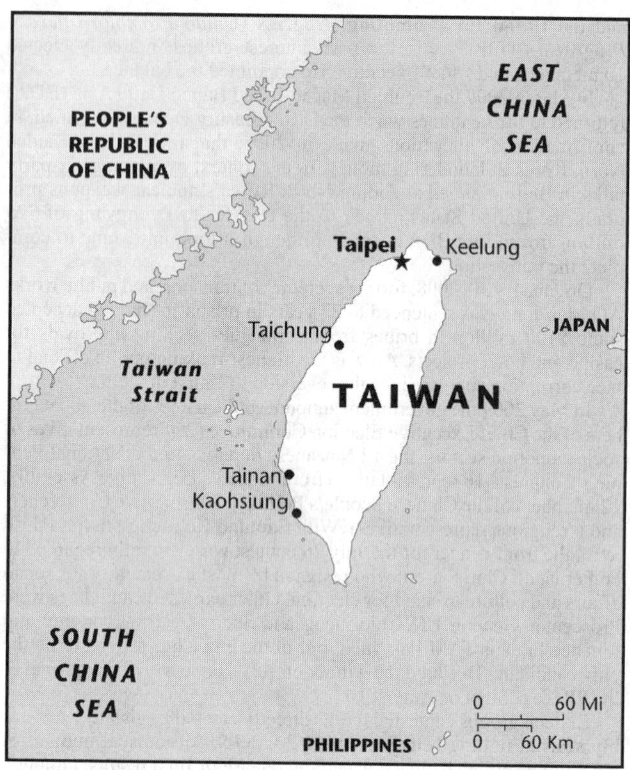

Vice President: Vincent SIEW (Nationalist Party); elected March 22, 2008, and sworn in May 20 for a term concurrent with that of the president, succeeding LU Hsiu-lien (Annette LU, Democratic Progressive Party).

President of Executive Branch (Premier): WU Den-yih (Nationalist Party); designated by the president on September 7, 2009, upon the announcement by Premier LIU Chao-shiuan (Nationalist Party) that he would step down in three days; sworn in at the head of a revamped cabinet on September 10.

GOVERNMENT AND POLITICS

Political background. Following its move to Taiwan in 1949, the Chinese Nationalist regime continued to insist that it represented all of China and vowed to return eventually to the mainland. The danger of Communist conquest, which appeared very real in 1949–1950, was averted primarily by the decision of U.S. president Harry S Truman to interpose the protection of the American Seventh Fleet upon the outbreak of the Korean War in 1950. Thereafter, the Nationalist government continued under the domination of the Nationalist Party, or Kuomintang (*Chung-kuo Kuo-min Tang*—KMT), led by CHIANG Kai-shek until his death in 1975.

As part of a major reorganization in 1969, the post of vice premier was awarded to President Chiang's son, CHIANG Ching-kuo, who was subsequently named premier in 1972. The younger Chiang was selected by the National Assembly in 1978 to succeed C.K. YEN as president. Vice President LEE Teng-hui, an islander who had served earlier as governor of Taiwan, succeeded to the presidency following Chiang's death in 1988 and was then elected to the post in 1990.

In 1991, a year after Lee's implicit recognition of the People's Republic of China (PRC) on the mainland (see the People's Republic of China article for details), the National Assembly rescinded the "Temporary Provisions" that, since 1948, had conferred emergency powers on the president and frozen the tenure of mainland-elected deliberative officials. In addition, a number of constitutional amendments were promulgated, including a stipulation that all mainland parliamentarians would be obliged to retire prior to the election of a new National Assembly. In May 1991 the Legislative Branch repealed the Statute of Punishment for Sedition that for more than four decades had served as the principal weapon against the KMT's opponents. Nevertheless, the KMT secured a resounding victory in the December 1991 National Assembly election, winning 254 of 325 seats, while its principal competitor, the Democratic Progressive Party (DPP), won 66.

The KMT suffered a serious reversal in the election for a new 161-member Legislative Branch in December 1992. While it retained control with nearly 60 percent of the seats, KMT candidates garnered only 53 percent of the vote. In January 1993, after losing a tumultuous intraparty struggle with liberal opponents, the conservative HAU Pei-tsun, who had served as premier since June 1990, signaled his wish to resign, and in February the ethnic Taiwanese provincial governor, LIEN Chan, was approved by the KMT's Central Standing Committee as his successor.

At the Legislative Branch election of December 1995, the KMT retained a narrow majority (85 of 164 seats), although its vote share was a worst-ever 46 percent. Earlier, in July 1994, the National Assembly, over the objections of the DPP, had passed constitutional reforms that included direct presidential elections. In the first such presidential balloting, held in March 1996, Lee secured a second term by winning 54 percent of the vote. In simultaneous election of a third National Assembly, the KMT won 183 of the 334 seats with 55 percent of the votes, while the DPP advanced to 99 seats and 30 percent.

Lien Chan had resigned as premier in January 1996 to pursue the vice presidency as Lee's running mate, but he had then been sworn in as head of a caretaker government at the end of February. Despite some resistance in the new National Assembly, in June Vice President Lien was reappointed premier.

In the months that followed, President Lee encountered rising popular discontent over the issue of corruption, efforts to downsize provincial government, and a deterioration in law and order. Undaunted, Lee moved ahead in 1997 with a series of reform proposals that had been broached at a National Development Conference in December 1996. In the end, a consensus was reached on a number of key elements in the Lee agenda, but only after the prounification New Party (NP) had withdrawn from the deliberations to protest a "tacit coalition" between the KMT and the DPP.

Under the package as approved by the National Assembly in July 1997, the president would have sole discretion in the selection of a premier, while the legislature, with the support of one-third of its members, would be able to propose a no-confidence motion. It was also agreed that the number of Legislative Branch members would be increased from 164 to 225 and that elections for Taiwan's provincial governor and legislators would be suspended upon expiration of the incumbents' terms in late 1998, pending the adoption of legislation to reduce the scale of the provincial administration. In late July Vice President Lien announced that he intended to resign as premier, and on September 1 Vincent SIEW, former head of the Mainland Affairs Council (MAC), was installed as his successor.

At the large-city mayoral and county magistrate elections in November 1997, the KMT was, for the first time, outpolled by the DPP, 43 to 42 percent, raising what some Taiwanese considered to be the once-unthinkable prospect that the DPP might become Taiwan's next ruling party. In elections in January 1998, however, the KMT rebounded to win 59 percent of the contests for county and city councilors, small-city mayors, and township chiefs, and in December it again won a majority in Legislative Branch balloting.

In a stunning development, in the presidential poll of March 18, 2000, the KMT's nominee, Lien Chan, finished third, with 23 percent of the vote, behind the DPP's CHEN Shui-bian (39 percent) and James SOONG (37 percent), a KMT dissident who ran as an independent. Shortly after the election, the DPP and KMT agreed to abolish the National Assembly; however, the move was superseded on April 24 by the assembly's own decision to transfer significant powers to the Legislative Branch (see Constitution and government, below).

At his inauguration on May 20, 2000, President Chen distanced himself somewhat from the position of his own party. He declared, in what became known as his "four no's plus one" policy, that, in the absence of aggressive action by the PRC, Taiwan would not declare independence, alter its official name, amend the constitution to suggest the existence of two Chinas, or hold an independence referendum. He added that his predecessor's National Unification Council (NUC) and its phased "Guidelines for National Unification," drafted in 1991, would remain in place. Earlier, on May 1, he had announced a cabinet headed by his KMT predecessor's defense minister, Gen. TANG Fei, but Tang resigned five months later, ostensibly for health reasons, although most analysts considered the precipitating factor to be his opposition to a presidential decision terminating work on the country's fourth nuclear power plant. On October 4 Chen's former campaign manager, Vice Premier CHANG Chun-hsiung, stepped in as Tang's successor.

At the general election of December 1, 2001, the KMT lost its legislative majority for the first time, capturing only 68 seats in the 225-member Legislative Branch. It nevertheless retained control of the legislature by virtue of the 46 seats won by James Soong's new People First Party (PFP), the KMT's principal partner in an informal "pan-blue" alliance (a reference to the KMT's party color) that also included the NP. The DPP achieved a plurality of 87 seats, while its allies, the Taiwan Solidarity Union (TSU) and the small Taiwan Independence Party (TAIP), won 13 and none, respectively, as part of the DPP-led "pan-green" alliance (a reference to the DPP's color). Although President Chen had proposed during the election campaign that the leading parties establish a "National Stabilization Alliance," both the KMT and the PFP dismissed the idea after the polling.

As mandated by the constitution, Premier Chang and the entire cabinet resigned on January 21, 2002, prior to the opening of the new legislative session. President Chen immediately named YU Shyi-kun, a former vice premier, as Chang's replacement, and a substantially new cabinet, which included four KMT members despite the objections of their party, assumed office on February 1. In the meantime, the township, county, and provincial elections of January 26, 2002, had confirmed the KMT's relative strength at the local level.

The presidential election of March 20, 2004, concluded with President Chen and his "pan-green" running mate, Vice President LU Hsiu-lien (Annette LU), also of the DPP, winning 50.1 percent of the vote, but the "pan-blue" ticket (49.9 percent) of the KMT's Lien and the PFP's Soong immediately challenged the results. In the end, the Supreme Court dismissed KMT allegations of electoral fraud and other irregularities, including that Chen and Lu had staged a March 19 assassination attempt in which they were both slightly wounded by gunfire. Chen's razor-thin success at the polls did not, however, carry over to the Legislative Branch election of December 11, after which the KMT and its allies continued to hold a slim majority, 114 seats, compared to 101 for the DPP and the TSU. On January 25, 2005, President Chen named the mayor of Kaohsiung, Frank Chang-ting HSIEH, to succeed Premier Yu, who, along with the rest of the cabinet, had resigned the previous day. Most of the departing ministers were, however, reappointed on January 31.

With the backing of both the DPP and the KMT, on August 23, 2004, the Legislative Branch had approved a constitutional reform package that included halving its own membership, to 113 seats, and abolishing the National Assembly. Following an ad hoc election on May 14, 2005, to fill its 300 seats, a final National Assembly convened and on June 7 voted 249–48 in favor of the constitutional amendments, which the president promulgated on June 10.

Premier Hsieh resigned on January 17, 2006, following DPP losses in the local elections of December 2005, and was replaced by SU Tseng-chang (DPP). Sworn in on January 25, Premier Su conducted an immediate cabinet shuffle. Meanwhile, President Chen was arguing for further constitutional reform. He also announced that he intended to abolish the NUC and abandon the "Guidelines for National Unification," a proposal attacked by the opposition and viewed by Washington as potentially destabilizing. On February 27 Chen confirmed that the NUC would "cease to function"—a considered change in language that Washington had reportedly encouraged but that failed to placate Beijing. Under increasing pressure to resign over corruption allegations, charges of mismanagement, and dissatisfaction with his hard-line stance toward cross-strait relations, Chen stated on May 31 that he would transfer many of his powers to Prime Minister Su, retaining authority only in defense matters and foreign policy, and that he would disengage from party politics.

Premier Su resigned on May 12, 2007, less than a week after he was defeated by former premier Hsieh in an intraparty contest for the DPP's 2008 presidential nomination. On May 14 President Chen returned Chang Chun-hsiung to the premiership. A reshuffled cabinet took office under Chang on May 21.

As opinion polls had predicted, the election on January 12, 2008, to a downsized Legislative Branch concluded with a resounding victory for the KMT, which, with its allies, won 85 of 113 seats and 55.9 percent of the party-list vote. The DPP took 27 seats and 40.7 percent of the proportional vote. Two months later, on March 22, the KMT's MA Ying-jeou defeated the DPP's Frank HSIEH for the presidency, winning 58.5 percent of the vote. He was sworn in on May 20, as was a new cabinet headed by former vice premier and university president LIU Chao-shiuan.

On September 7, 2009, accepting responsibility for the government's inadequate initial response to a deadly typhoon that struck Taiwan on August 7–8, Premier Liu announced that he and his cabinet would resign on September 10. President Ma, who had already issued his own apology for the government's failure, immediately named WU Den-yih, the KMT secretary general, as Liu's replacement. Premier Wu and members of a substantially new cabinet were sworn in on September 10. Additional changes to the Executive Branch were made later in the month.

On September 11, 2009, former president Chen was convicted of embezzlement, accepting bribes, and other offenses during his terms in office. He and his wife, WU Shu-chen, who was also convicted on corruption charges, received life sentences.

Constitution and government. The government of the Republic of China (ROC), launched in 1912 under the leadership of SUN Yat-sen, drew on both Western and traditional Chinese elements in a constitution promulgated January 1, 1947, effective from December 25, 1947. At the apex of the complex system was the 3,045-member National Assembly, which was popularly elected on an all-China basis for a six-year term. The term was extended, however, following the government's exodus to Taiwan, and for more than four decades its surviving members periodically reconvened either as an electoral college to select the president and vice president (as in March 1990) or as a constituent body (as in April 1991). Although downsized to fewer than 350 members in a December 1991 election, it continued to hold powers of recall and impeachment, of constitutional amendment, and of nomination to three of the government's five specialized branches, or *yuans* (Judicial, Examination, and Control).

An election for a third, 334-member National Assembly took place in March 1996, but an election scheduled for March 2000 was canceled, after which the assembly was reduced, by constitutional amendment, to a nonstanding body of 300 members empowered to consider a limited range of matters—constitutional amendments, presidential or vice presidential impeachment, national boundaries—referred to it by the Legislative Branch.

Following passage of a constitutional reform bill by the Legislative Branch on August 23, 2004, an ad hoc National Assembly election was called for May 14, 2005. Voter turnout was only 23 percent. On June 7 this final National Assembly passed the reform package, which included its abolition as an institution. Upon promulgation of the reforms by the president on June 10, the National Assembly's impeachment powers were transferred to the Judicial Branch. Constitutional amendments and boundary changes now require not only approval by at least three-fourths of a Legislative Branch quorum but also concurrence by at least half of those eligible to vote in a referendum.

The president, elected for a once-renewable four-year term since 1996, can declare war and peace and issue emergency decrees that must, however, secure legislative confirmation within ten days. The president also has wide powers of appointment, acts as mediator in disputes between two or more *yuans,* and may dissolve the Legislative Branch if it passes a vote of no confidence in the government. The president's authority with regard to cross-strait relations is also extensive. A cabinet-level Mainland Affairs Council (MAC) oversees cross-strait policy implementation. With the imprimatur of the MAC, a private Straits Exchange Foundation (SEF) has served as a semiofficial vehicle for contact with the mainland government (see the Peoples' Republic of China article for details).

The president of the Executive Branch (premier) is appointed by the state president but is subject to a legislative nonconfidence vote. The Legislative Branch, currently a 113-member body popularly elected for a four-year term, enacts laws but cannot increase the budget. Its powers include initiating impeachment of the president or vice president, which requires a two-thirds vote of the full membership for the charges to be forwarded to the Judicial Branch.

The 15-member Court of Grand Justices sits at the apex of the Judicial Branch. Nominated by the president and confirmed by the legislature, the grand justices serve terms of four or eight years. Their duties include constitutional interpretation and administrative oversight of the entire court system. When considering impeachment questions, they sit as the Constitutional Court. Also within the Judicial Branch are district courts, high courts, and the Supreme Court.

The Examination Branch deals with personnel, legal, and other matters affecting civil servants. Its 21 members are presidentially appointed, subject to Legislative Branch confirmation.

The Control Branch, comprising 29 members serving six-year terms, is responsible for auditing and general administrative surveillance and can impeach or censure public officials. Filled by presidential nomination, subject to legislative confirmation, it did not function from January 31, 2005, and the end of Chen's term because of opposition objections to his nominees. Newly elected President Ma presented a new slate of nominees in June 2008, and 25 members took office on August 1. (Four nominees were rejected by the legislature, and it was mid-November before the balance of the *yuan* membership was filled.)

The territorial jurisdiction of the ROC currently extends to one Chinese province (Taiwan) and part of a second (Fujian's offshore islands). The province of Taiwan is currently subdivided into 16 counties and 5 cities. Taipei and Kaohsiung are defined as special municipalities.

On December 31, 1998, the Legislative Branch formally declared the uninhabited Tiaoyutai Islands northeast of Taiwan and the Spratly Islands in the South China Sea to be within Taiwan's territorial jurisdiction. The former are also claimed by both China and Japan, while the latter have long been subject to rival claims by Brunei, China, Malaysia, the Philippines, and Vietnam.

Foreign relations. The most important factor in the foreign policy of the Taiwan government has been the existence on the mainland of the Communist regime, which was awarded the Chinese seat at the United Nations (UN) on October 25, 1971. Reflecting its diminished political status, the ROC is today recognized by none of the major powers, though its trade relations are extensive. Relations with the United States, once extremely close, cooled after President Richard Nixon's visit to the mainland in February 1972. The communiqué issued at the conclusion of the Nixon visit acknowledged "that all Chinese on either side of the Taiwan Strait maintain that there is but one China" and advocated "a peaceful settlement of the Taiwan question by the Chinese themselves."

Concurrent with the announcement in December 1978 that the United States and the PRC would establish diplomatic relations on January 1, 1979, Washington issued a statement saying that both diplomatic relations and, upon expiration of a required one-year's notice, the Mutual Defense Treaty with the ROC would be terminated. Although all U.S. military personnel were withdrawn from Taiwan, arms shipments have been permitted in the interest of maintaining a balance of power with the mainland.

In contrast with its earlier practice of shunning relations with states or intergovernmental organizations linked to Beijing, more recently Taipei has adopted "pragmatic diplomacy," aimed particularly at ministates capable of being wooed by development assistance. On such a basis it broadened its international contacts, including diplomatic relations with 31 countries as of early 1996. The diplomatic network shrank marginally thereafter, most significantly by the severance of relations with South Africa. As of June 2009, the Holy See plus 22 countries in Africa, the Pacific, Latin America, and the Caribbean maintained full diplomatic relations with Taiwan. In May 2008 the outgoing foreign minister, a vice premier, and a deputy defense minister resigned in connection with the loss of some $30 million to two private individuals who had been hired as part of an effort to establish diplomatic ties with Papua New Guinea.

For years the government has sought to secure ROC readmission to the United Nations, but the UN General Committee has repeatedly refused to act, citing a lack of consensus in the matter. In 2007, for the first time, the government applied for admission as "Taiwan" but was again rebuffed. Two referenda held on March 22, 2007, in conjunction with the presidential election, asked the Taiwanese voters if they wished to pursue readmission to the UN under the name Taiwan or the Republic of China. Although both received a majority of "yes" votes, neither achieved the necessary threshold for passage (50 percent of registered voters).

Washington has not actively supported Taiwan's UN bid, but during the 1990s it moved to enhance the ROC's official presence in the United States by allowing what had been known as the Coordinating Council for North American Affairs to restyle itself in a number of locations as the Taipei Economic and Cultural Office. In addition, in December 1994 President Bill Clinton permitted U.S. Transportation Secretary Federico Peña to become the first American cabinet official to visit Taiwan in more than 15 years. The action, which caused Beijing "strong displeasure," heightened pressure from Taipei for a long-sought visit by President Lee to the United States, and in early May 1995 the U.S. Senate and House of Representatives, by votes of 97–1 and 360–0, respectively, approved resolutions calling upon President Clinton to permit Lee to enter the country in a "private capacity." After some hesitation, the White House agreed, and in June, in what Beijing termed a "wanton wound inflicted upon China," the Taiwanese leader arrived to attend an alumni reunion at Cornell University. The mainland regime responded by suspending all contacts with Taiwan; further protests were issued by Beijing following issuance of a visa to Vice President Li Yuan-zu for a 1996 stopover in Los Angeles while en route to Guatemala. A similar courtesy was extended to Vice President Lien Chan in 1998 and President Chen in 2001, although denied to the outspoken Vice President Annette Lu in September 2000.

On November 11, 2001, the World Trade Organization endorsed membership for "Chinese Taipei," which became the organization's 144th member on January 1, 2002, under the listing of "Separate Customs Territory of Taiwan, Penghu, Kinmen, and Matsu."

Current issues. Even before his inauguration on May 20, 2008, President Ma moved toward thawing relations with Beijing. On April 14 Vice President–elect (and former premier) Vincent Siew, heading a delegation of the Cross-Straits Common Market Foundation, met Chinese President Hu Jintao, and it was subsequently announced that the KMT chair, WU Poh-hsiung, had accepted an invitation from the Chinese Community Party to visit the mainland in late May, thereby becoming the first head of a Taiwanese ruling party to do so. In his inaugural address Ma pledged to liberalize travel connections to the mainland by midyear and urged his mainland counterparts to "face reality, pioneer a new future, shelve controversies, and pursue a win-win solution." In the preceding week, the prospect for closer relations had also been indirectly enhanced by Taiwan's many expressions of support and offers of assistance as Beijing marshaled efforts to recover from the devastating earthquake that had struck Sichuan Province on May 12.

The new president's overall tone differed markedly from that of his predecessor, who in March 2007 had drawn criticism from the opposition and from the United States for a speech in which he outlined "four wants and one without": independence for Taiwan, a change in the jurisdiction's official designation, a new constitution, and new economic development, all without reference to "leftist or rightist policy lines." Taiwan's overriding issue, he asserted, involved "national identity and whether to unify with China or secure Taiwan's formal independence." In contrast, President Ma appeared ready to set aside resolution of that issue, indicating both that there would be no declaration of independence during his tenure and that reunification was "unlikely in our lifetime." Instead, the government would follow a middle course some described as "one China, two interpretations."

With former president Chen having lost his presidential immunity, the Supreme Prosecutor's Office quickly announced that it would investigate corruption allegations that had already seen his wife, Wu Shu-chen, and several presidential aides indicted for misuse of a discretionary state affairs fund controlled by the president. In a televised address in November 2006 Chen had admitted lying and falsifying receipts but claimed that the subterfuge had been necessary to conceal confidential diplomatic efforts on Taiwan's behalf. At least initially, many Taiwanese appeared ready to accept Chen's explanation, but the DPP was further damaged in September 2007, when Vice President Lu and former premier Yu Shyi-kun were among those also charged with misappropriating funds from expense accounts.

In March 2009 the DPP accused the judiciary of bias, given that no KMT politicians had yet been charged with misuse of expense accounts. In the decades since the KMT introduced the accounts, informal understandings have largely determined how the funds have been used. Although intended for work-related expenses, officials have long used part of the funds as personal allowances, without repercussion. Many observers expect that those days are now over, but it remains unclear how many present and former officeholders face prosecution for their handling of similar accounts.

Meanwhile, former president Chen found himself facing additional corruption charges. In November,2008 he was arrested and held for suspicion of forgery and money-laundering, and a month later he and a dozen other individuals, including close relatives, were indicted for embezzlement and taking bribes. The convictions announced in September 2009 were widely expected, but the life sentences imposed on Chen and his wife, who had entered a guilty plea on money-laundering and forgery charges early in the year, were seen by many as too severe and tainted by political considerations. A son, a daughter, and their spouses have also been convicted of corruption, and the former president is still facing a second trial on other charges.

The resignation of Premier Liu and his cabinet in September 2009 was in response to a public outcry over the government's lack of disaster preparedness and its slow response to Typhoon Morakot, the worst storm to strike the island in half a century and, in terms of rainfall, by far the heaviest ever recorded there. Over 700 people were killed or declared missing, as flooding and severe mudslides caused more than $3 billion in damage.

POLITICAL PARTIES

Prior to 1986, two non-KMT (*tang-wai*) political groups were occasionally successful in Taiwanese elections, although their representatives were obliged to run as independents since opposition parties were not allowed to compete for public office. In a major concession to opposition sentiment, the government in May 1986 permitted an umbrella Tangwai Public Policy Association to open offices in Taipei and elsewhere; four months later, two new dissident groups were formed, one of which, the Democratic Progressive Party (DPP), was permitted to participate in the December 1986 election, even though it did not achieve legal status until 1989. By August 1993 some 74 parties were reported to have been formed, but only the KMT, the DPP, and the New Party (NP) had significant standing.

In the run-up to the December 2001 legislative election, two informal alliances began to be commonly labeled, with reference to the dominant parties' respective colors, as the "pan-blue" camp (the KMT, the People First Party [PFP], and the NP) and the "pan-green" camp (the DPP, the Taiwan Solidarity Union, and the now-defunct Taiwan Independence Party). Neither alliance subsequently evolved formal structures, although the KMT and PFP offered a combined ticket for the 2004 presidential/vice presidential election, and they, along with the NP, coordinated their candidate lists for the December 2004 Legislative Branch election. The camps split, however, over the constitutional amendments passed by the National Assembly in June 2005. The two largest parties, the KMT and DPP, supported the package, whereas the other four parties voted in opposition.

As of 2006 the number of registered parties stood at 118, although only a dozen presented candidates for the 2008 Legislative Branch election.

Governing "Pan-Blue" Alliance:

Nationalist Party (*Chung-kuo Kuo-min Tang* or Kuomintang—KMT). Founded in 1912 by the Republic of China's first president, Sun Yat-sen, the KMT dominated Taiwanese politics until March 2000 at all levels of government. The KMT traditionally resembled a communist party in structure, with a National Congress, a Central Committee, party cells, and so on. In November 1976, at its first congress since 1969, the party elected Premier Chiang Ching-kuo to succeed his father, Chiang Kai-shek, as chair. In 1984, as the result of a party "rejuvenation" campaign, it was reported that 70 percent of an estimated 2 million party members were native Taiwanese.

Contrary to expectations that newly legalized groups might undercut the party's longtime political dominance, the KMT secured a landslide victory in the National Assembly election of December 1991, giving it substantially more than the three-quarters majority needed for unilateral constitutional revision. It was less successful at the Legislative Branch poll of December 1992 but still won 96 of 161 seats. Subsequently, many younger and reform-minded members formed an alternative New KMT Alliance within the party. Most withdrew to launch the New Party (NP, below) in August 1993. In the same month, at its 14th congress, the previously "revolutionary democratic" KMT redefined itself as a "democratic party" and provided for election of its chair by secret ballot.

In December 1995 Judicial Branch President LIN Yang-kang and former premier HAU Pei-tsun were ousted from the KMT for campaigning on behalf of NP candidates in that month's Legislative Branch poll, which left the KMT with a bare three-seat majority. Subsequently, the two ran for president and vice president, respectively, on an independent ticket.

The KMT won only 45 percent of the seats in local council balloting in June 1998; however, it recovered to win 57 percent (123 of 225 seats) at the Legislative Branch poll in December. It ran third in the presidential contest of March 2000, winning only 23 percent of the vote and surrendering the Taiwanese presidency for the first time. President Lee Teng-hui, assuming responsibility for the defeat of the KMT's candidate, Lien Chan, transferred the party chair to Lien on a temporary basis.

In late 2000 the KMT announced that it would hold its first direct election for party chair in early 2001. The March 24 election of Lien Chan ended up being uncontested, however, as his only announced opponent, TUAN Hong-chun, failed to collect the necessary 100,000 nominating signatures. In September 2001 the KMT formally expelled former president Lee, who had emerged as a supporter of the new Taiwan Solidarity Union (TSU, below).

Leading up to the December 2001 Legislative Branch election, the similar stances of the KMT, NP, and PFP in favor of eventual reunification with the mainland produced the informal "pan-blue" alliance (a reference to the KMT's party color). In the election the KMT lost considerable support to the PFP and the TSU, contributing to the first loss of its majority in the Legislative Branch. Four members of the KMT, including Minister of National Defense TANG Yian-min, were named to the new DPP-led cabinet in January 2002, which led to the suspension of their party rights.

In December 2004 the party gained 11 Legislative Branch seats over its 2001 tally, for a total of 79—sufficient, in coalition with its "pan-blue" allies, the PFP and NP, to control the body. Largely as a result of subsequent defections from the PFP, by the end of 2006 the KMT's legislative delegation had risen to 89, surpassing that of the DPP.

In late April 2005 Lien Chan had become the first KMT chair to visit the PRC. With Lien having decided to step down as chair, in a leadership election in July 2005 Deputy Chair WANG Chin-ping garnered only 28 percent of the vote in losing to Taipei's mayor, Ma Ying-jeou. At the party's 12th congress, held in July 2006, it adopted reforms that included a collective leadership and abolition of internal factions.

In February 2007, immediately after being indicted for corruption involving some $330,000 in expenditures from a special discretionary allowance fund during his years as mayor, Ma resigned the chair. He indicated, however, that he would seek the KMT's nomination for president in 2008, as did Legislative Branch president Wang Jin-pyng, representing the indigenous Taiwanese wing of the party. On May 2 Ma received the party's nod for the 2008 presidential race and later named former premier Vincent Siew as his running mate. In August a district court acquitted Ma of the corruption allegations, and the decision was affirmed by the Supreme Court in April 2008.

In January 2007 the KMT and its principal ally, the PFP, had agreed to field joint candidates in the next Legislative Branch election. The possibility of bringing the Non-Partisan Solidarity Union (NPSU, below) into the alliance was also raised, although, in the end, the KMT instead endorsed the three successful NPSU candidates. In contrast, the NP directed its incumbents to join the KMT and ran only a slate of party-list candidates. The "pan-blue" alliance won 85 seats, including 8 for the PFP. In the March presidential contest, Ma won handily, garnering 58.5 percent of the vote.

Upon the resignation of Premier Liu Chao-shuian in September 2009, President Ma selected as his successor the KMT's secretary general, Wu Den-yih. Wu's replacement, Chan Chuen-po, had been serving as secretary general of the Presidential Office.

Leaders: MA Ying-jeou (President of the Republic), WU Poh-hsiung (Chair), LIEN Chan (Honorary Chair), Vincent SIEW (Vice President of the Republic), WU Den-yih (Premier), WANG Jin-pyng (President, Legislative Branch), CHAN Chuen-po (Secretary General).

People First Party (PFP). The PFP is a prounification formation launched by KMT dissident James Soong following the 2000 presidential election, in which he placed second with a 36.8 percent vote share. The PFP performed well in the December 2001 Legislative Branch election, winning 46 seats, primarily at the expense of the KMT and NP.

Prior to the December 2004 legislative election the PFP and its "pan-blue" partners, the KMT and the NP, agreed to coordinate their campaigns to avoid vote-splitting. Largely as a consequence, the PFP lost 12 seats and the KMT gained 11 more than in 2001, which created considerable resentment within the PFP. Although the KMT and PFP both supported the successful constitutional reform package that was approved by the National Assembly in June 2005, subsequent defections to the KMT further soured PFP hard-liners.

Talks in December 2005 with the KMT leadership were widely expected to lead to a long-anticipated merger, but differences could not be resolved. In February 2006 Soong announced that the PFP would "walk its own path" in future relations with the KMT. Following a third-place finish, with only 4 percent of the vote, in the December 2006 contest for mayor of Taipei, Soong announced his intention to retire from politics, although he did not immediately resign as party chair.

For the January 2008 Legislative Branch election the PFP again ran in conjunction with the KMT. It won 6 constituency seats (5 under the KMT banner plus 1 aboriginal seat) and 3 proportional seats from a joint KMT-PFP list.

Leaders: James SOONG Chu-yu (Chair), CHIN Chin-sheng (Secretary General).

New Party—NP (*Hsin Tang*). The prounification NP was formally launched in August 1993 by a group of KMT dissidents theretofore associated with the New KMT Alliance. Seeking support from second-generation mainlanders, the new formation advocated more energetic reform than the KMT leadership but opposed the DPP's policy of Taiwanese independence. The NP placed a distant third in the urban and provincial balloting of November 1993, winning only 3.1 percent of the vote. A week prior to the election it reportedly absorbed the Chinese Social Democratic Party (CSDP), formed in 1991 by a group of DPP dissidents, although the CSDP chair, JU Gau-jeng, did not pledge to withdraw the party's registration until 1994, when he was campaigning for the Taiwan governorship under the NP banner.

Proportionally, the NP was the most impressive contestant in December 1995, tripling its Legislative Branch representation from 7 to 21. It did not, however, present a 1996 presidential candidate; its leader, WANG Chien-shien, withdrew from the race after the legislative poll in an effort to consolidate a "third force" in Taiwanese politics. Its Legislative Branch representation fell to 11 in 1998.

With much of the NP leadership supporting independent presidential contender James Soong, the party's official nominee, LI Ao, won only 0.1 percent of the 2000 presidential vote. Further injured by defections to Soong's PFP, the party secured only 1 Legislative Branch seat in 2001. For the 2004 election most of the party's legislative candidates ran under the banner of its principal "pan-blue" ally, the KMT, although the NP again won 1 seat under its own name. In 2005 it parted ways with the KMT on the issue of constitutional reform, which it opposed.

Prior to the December 2006 municipal elections, the NP chair, Yok Mu-ming, speculated that the NP might disband if it failed to carry all 4 of the seats it was contesting in the 52-seat Taipei city council. It won the seats, however, after which Yok pledged to work toward "pan-blue" unity. In an unusual move, the NP directed its sitting legislators to join the KMT prior to the January 2008 Legislative Branch election, in which its constituency candidates ran as KMT members. Two, Alex FEI and LAI Shih-bao, won seats. In the party-list contest the NP won just under 4 percent of the vote and thus no additional seats.

In September 2008 the party cleared Yok of allegations that he had received financial aid from the PRC for the purchase of real estate in China.

Leader: YOK Mu-ming (Chair).

"Pan-Blue" Ally:

Non-Partisan Solidarity Union (NPSU). The centrist NPSU was established in June 2004 by ten independent members of the Legislative Branch, led by former interior minister CHANG Po-ya. Advocating a "middle way" between the "pan-blue" and "pan-green" camps, the party won 6 seats in the December 2004 Legislative Branch election.

Following the December 2006 municipal elections the NPSU proposed setting up a joint think tank with the PFP and increasing their cooperation in legislative matters. Although not a member of the "pan-blue" alliance, in January 2008 its three successful constituency candidates ran with KMT endorsement. The NPSU won only 0.7 percent of the party-list vote.

Leader: LIN Pin-kuan (Chair).

"Pan-Green" Alliance:

Democratic Progressive Party—DPP (*Min-chu Chin-pu Tang*). Despite the ban on organization of new parties, a group of dissidents, advocating trade, tourism, and communications links with the mainland, met in Taipei in September 1986 to form the DPP (sometimes rendered as Democratic Progress Party). Although unrecognized, the group won 11 National Assembly and 12 Legislative Branch seats in December 1986.

Delegates to the party's second annual congress in 1987 approved a resolution stating that "the people have the freedom to advocate Taiwan independence"; however, its leaders agreed to abandon the position during a meeting with KMT representatives in February 1988, and the party was legalized in April 1989. As a former political prisoner, DPP Chair HUANG Hsin-chieh continued to be barred from election to public office in the December 1989 balloting, in which the party nearly doubled its representation, to 21 legislative seats.

In 1990 HUANG Hwa, the leader of a New County Alliance faction, was given a ten-year prison term for "preparing to commit sedition" by an attempted revival of the campaign for Taiwanese independence. In 1991 another prominent DPP member, LIN Cheng-chieh, resigned from the party over advocacy of island separatism by the New Tide, a faction with views similar to those of the New County Alliance. Separatism prevailed, however, at the DPP's fifth national congress, in October 1991, which issued a draft manifesto pledging to "build a Taiwanese republic with independent sovereignty." At that time the DPP elected as its new chair HSU Hsin-liang, founder of the banned opposition magazine *Formosa.* Although sentenced to a ten-year prison term upon his clandestine return from exile in 1989, he had received a presidential amnesty in 1990. Hsu resigned in favor of SHIH Ming-teh following the mayoral and county executive elections of 1993, in which the number of DPP officeholders dropped from seven to six.

In gubernatorial and municipal elections in 1994, the DPP's most notable accomplishment was winning the Taipei mayoralty. It then won 25 percent of the Legislative Branch seats in 1995 and 31 percent in 1998. Having captured the presidency in March 2000 on a 39.3 vote share, the DPP went on to claim a plurality of 87 Legislative Branch seats in the December 2001 election. Nevertheless, the DPP and its allies in the "pan-green" camp (so named for the DPP's party color) fell short of a majority.

President Chen Shui-bian and his running mate, Annette Lu, won reelection by a minuscule 0.2 percent margin in March 2004. Although the DPP hoped to win an outright majority in the December Legislative Branch election, its total declined by 2 seats. In view of the outcome, Chen resigned as chair of the party, which in January 2005 elected Su Tseng-chang as his replacement. The following December, the party suffered a major defeat in local elections, winning only 42 percent of the vote to the KMT's 51 percent, prompting Su to step down as party chair. In mid-January 2006 a Chen ally, former premier Yu Shyi-kun, won election as Su's successor despite dissatisfaction within the party over Chen's leadership. One of the leading critics, former chair LIN Yihsiung, resigned his membership on January 24, a day before Su was sworn in as premier in succession to Frank Hsieh. Former chairs Hsu Hsin-liang and Shih Ming-teh had already departed, and in August 2006 the latter launched a public movement to oust President Chen.

Former premier Hsieh finished second in the December 2006 race for mayor of Taipei, surpassing expectations with 41 percent of the vote. In general, the party did better than expected in the local elections, given President Chen's difficulties. It elected the first female mayor of Kaohsiung and gained an additional legislative seat on both the Taipei and Kaohsiung city councils.

In 2007, four party leaders—Hsieh, Premier Su, Vice President Lu, and DPP Chair Yu—sought the party's 2008 presidential nomination. On May 7 Hsieh unexpectedly took 45 percent of the intraparty vote, after which Su (33 percent) and the other candidates withdrew. Five days later Su resigned as premier, although he later agreed to be Hsieh's running mate.

In September 2007 Vice President Lu and DPP Chair Yu were among several DPP members charged with corruption involving alleged misappropriations from expense accounts. All proclaimed their innocence, although Yu resigned his party post. President Chen later announced that he would accede to the chair, but he resigned the position following the party's defeat in the January 2008 Legislative Branch election, in which the DPP won only 27 seats, 14 of them on the basis of 40.7 percent of the party-list vote. Presidential candidate Hsieh thereupon assumed the party presidency but stepped aside after his March defeat.

On May 18, 2008, the DPP elected its first female chair, former vice premier Tsai Ing-wen, who, with 57 percent of the vote, defeated proindependence traditionalist KOO Kuan-min despite the latter's late endorsement by TRONG Chai, the third candidate for the top party post. Difficulties facing the new chair included the party's dismal standing in opinion polls—18 percent approval, following revelations of the failed effort by the Chen government to entice diplomatic recognition from the government of Papua New Guinea; the continuing influence of various party factions, which had been ostensibly dissolved in 2006; and a significant financial debt.

In December 2008 Chen Shui-bian became the first former president to be indicted for corruption, and thus, in September 2009, the first to be convicted.. Meanwhile, the pretrial phase continued in the cases against former vice president Lu and former premier Yu.

Leaders: TSAI Ing-wen (Chair), KER Chien-ming (Legislative Whip), Frank HSIEH (2008 presidential candidate), SU Tseng-chang (2008 vice-presidential candidate), LU Hsiu-lien (Annette LU, Former Vice President of the Republic), CHEN Shu (Mayor of Kaohsiung), WANG Tuoh (Secretary General).

Taiwan Solidarity Union (TSU). Formation of the TSU was announced in July 2001 by former KMT leader and interior minister HUANG Chu-wen. Declaring Taiwan to be a sovereign state, the TSU attracted defectors from both the KMT and the DPP, its most senior supporter being former president Lee Teng-hui. (Lee, having accused the KMT of aligning with Beijing, was subsequently expelled by the KMT, but he never officially joined the TSU.) The TSU finished fourth, with 13 seats, in the December 2001 election, a ranking that was retained with 12 seats in 2004.

Huang resigned after the party's disappointing performance in the 2004 election. His successor, SU Chin-Chiang, likewise resigned following the December 2006 municipal elections. Huang Kun-fei, who was named chair in January 2007, has stated his intention to transform the TSU into a center-left party oriented toward meeting the needs of the Taiwanese people. In October–November 2007 four of the TSU's Legislative Branch members joined the DPP, and in the January 2008 legislative election the TSU lost its remaining seats. It won only 3.5 percent of the party-list vote.

In May 2008 Huang asked all TSU members to reregister and announced that the party would put aside the independence issue and focus its attention on serving the "medium- and low-echelon sectors of society."

Leaders: HUANG Kun-fei (HUANG Kun-hui, Chair), LIN Chih-chia (Secretary General).

Taiwan Constitution Association (TCA). Organized in 2007, the TCA was not a factor in the 2008 legislative election. It ran candidates in only a handful of constituencies, and its three party-list candidates attracted only 0.3 percent of the vote.

Leader: WU Ying-siang.

Other Parties:

Green Party Taiwan (GPT). The GPT dates from 1996, when it was organized by members of the Taiwan Environmental Protection Union to contest the March National Assembly election, in which the GPT's KAO Ming-ting unexpectedly won a seat. The party's platform is based on such traditional green party concerns as ecological balance, opposition to nuclear power, antimilitarism, and social equality. It won 1 seat in the Legislative Branch poll in December 2001 but lost it in 2004. In 2008 the party won only 0.6 percent of the party-list vote. It ran in conjunction with the small **Raging Citizens Act Now!** alliance, led by WANG Fang-ping.

Leaders: CHANG Hong-lin and CHUNG Bau-Ju (Cochairs), Calvin WEN, PAN Han-shen (Secretary General).

In addition, a number of small parties ran unsuccessfully in the 2008 Legislative Branch election. They were the **Citizens' Party** (0.5 percent of the party-list vote), the **Hakka Party** (0.4 percent), the **Home Party** (0.8 percent), the **Taiwan Farmers' Party** (0.6 percent), and the **Third Society Party** (0.5 percent).

LEGISLATURE

Under the unusual post–World War II constitutional system of the ROC, parliamentary functions were performed by the National Assembly (*Kuo-min Ta-hui*), the Legislative Branch, and even the Control Branch before its 1992 transformation into a more supervisory agency. The National Assembly, whose powers included selecting the president (until 1996) and approving constitutional amendments, was abolished in June 2005 (see the discussion in the Constitution and government section, above).

Legislative Branch (*Li-fa Yuan*). The unicameral Legislative Branch, the formal lawmaking organ of the ROC, first convened in 1948. Its 760 members were popularly elected on a regional and occupational basis for three-year terms. On December 19, 1992, in the first balloting for a full house since 1948 (all mainland members had retired by late 1991), a total of 125 directly elected and 36 proportionally allocated seats were filled.

In the election held December 11, 2004, a total of 168 members were directly elected from multimember constituencies, 41 by proportional representation, 8 from aboriginal constituencies, and 8 by party appointment from overseas Chinese. Constitutional reforms ratified by the National Assembly in May 2005 halved the Legislative Branch to 113 members, effective from the next election, which was held on January 12, 2008. Under a new single constituency, two ballot electoral system, 73 members were directly elected from redrawn single-member constituencies, 6 seats were filled by aboriginal communities, and 34 at-large and overseas expatriate seats were proportionally allocated to political parties that won at least 5 percent of the votes on a separate ballot. In addition, the legislative term was lengthened from three to four years.

Results were as follows for the "pan-blue" coalition: Nationalist Party (KMT), 81 (61 constituency seats and 20 party-list seats, including 5 constituency seats and 3 party-list seats won by PFP members who ran under the KMT banner, and 2 constituency seats won by candidates who were endorsed by the New Party); Non-Partisan Solidarity Union, 3 constituency seats won with the endorsement of the KMT; PFP, 1 aboriginal constituency seat. The Democratic Progressive Party won all 27 "pan-green" seats (13 constituency, 14 party-list). The final constituency seat was won by an independent.

President: WANG Jin-pyng.

CABINET

The cabinet is known as the Executive Branch Council (*Hsing-cheng Yuan Hu-yi*). The premier is currently chosen by the president (subject to a legislative nonconfidence vote), whereas the vice premier and other cabinet members are appointed by the president upon recommendation of the premier. Cabinet officials are chosen individually; the cabinet is not responsible collectively.

[as of October 5, 2009]

President, Executive Branch (Premier)	Wu Den-yih
Vice President, Executive Branch (Vice Premier)	Eric Li-Luan Chu
Ministers	
Economic Affairs	Shih Yen-shiang
Education	Wu Ching-ji
Finance	Li Sush-der
Foreign Affairs	Timoth Chin-tien Yang
Health	Yaung Chih-liang
Interior	Jiang Yi-huah
Justice	Wang Ching-feng [f]
National Defense	Kao Hua-chu
Transportation and Communications	Mao Chi-kuo
Ministers Without Portfolio	Chang Jin-fu
	Fan Liang-shiow
	James Cherng-tay Hsueh
	Liang Chi-yuan
	Tsai Hsung-hsiung
	Ovid J. L. Tzeng
Commission Ministers	
Central Election	Chang Masa
Fair Trade (Acting)	Wu Shiow-ming
Consumer Protection	Eric Li-luan Chu
Financial Supervisory	Sean C. Chen
Mongolian and Tibetan Affairs	Kao Su-po
National Communications	Bonnie Peng [f]
National Youth	Wang Yu-ting [f]
Overseas Compatriot Affairs	Wu Ying-yih [f]

Public Construction	Fan Liang-shiow
Research, Development, and Evaluation	Chu Chin-peng
Veterans' Affairs	Tseng Chin-ling

Council Ministers

Agriculture	Chen Wu-hsiung
Atomic Energy	Tsai Chuen-horng
Aviation Safety	Wu Jing-shown
Cultural Affairs	Huang Pi-twan [f]
Economic Planning and Development	Tsai Hsung-hsiung
Hakka Affairs	Huang Yu-cheng
Indigenous Peoples	Sun Ta-chuan
Labor Affairs	Wang Ju-hsuan [f]
Mainland Affairs	Lai Shin-yuan [f]
National Science	Lee Lou-chuang
Sports	Tai Hsia-ling [f]

Other Ministers

Coast Guard Administration	Wang Jin-wang
Directorate General of Budget, Accounting, and Statistics	Shih Su-mei [f]
Environmental Protection Administration	Stephen Shu-hung Shen
Chief, Government Information Office	Su Jun-pin
Director, National Palace Museum	Chou Kung-shin [f]
Chair, Central Personnel Administration	Wu Tai-cheng
Governor, Central Bank	Perng Fai-nan
Secretary General, Executive Branch	Lin Join-sane

[f] = female

COMMUNICATIONS

Until 1988 long-standing restrictions limited the number of newspapers to 31, nearly half of which were owned either by the government or by the KMT. Individuals with close ties to the KMT controlled several of the others. In 1998 the government began accepting applications for new papers for the first time since 1951, although it continued to be illegal for journalists to "advocate communism" or to support independence for the island. In recent years, however, neither proscription has been enforced, and press freedom is largely unchallenged. Newspapers now number in the hundreds.

Press. The following dailies are published in Taipei, unless otherwise indicated: *Tzu-yu Shih-pao* (Liberty Times, 1,300,000); *Chung-kuo Shih-pao* (China Times, 1,000,000); *Lieh-ho Pao* (United Daily News, 1,000,000); *Apple Daily* (600,000), tabloid launched in 2003, reputedly Taiwan's most widely read newspaper; *Chung-hua Jih-pao* (China Daily News, Taipei and Tainan, 600,000), KMT organ; *Chung-yang Jih-pao* (Central Daily News, 600,000), KMT organ; *Taiwan Hsin-sheng Pao* (Taiwan New Life Daily, 460,000); *Taiwan Jih-pao* (Taiwan Daily News, 250,000); *China Post* (140,000), in English; *China News* (100,000), in English; *Taiwan Hsin-wen Pao* (Daily News, Kaohsiung, 100,000); *Chung-kuo Wan-pao* (China Evening News, Kaohsiung, 60,000).

News agencies. There were some 1,200 registered news agencies as of December 2004, most of them small and specialized. The oldest and largest domestic facility is the publicly owned, independent Central News Agency—CNA (*Chung-yang Tung-hsun She*). *Agence France-Presse,* AP, and Reuters are among the organizations maintaining bureaus or stringers in Taipei.

Broadcasting and computing. Most broadcasting facilities are commercial, although all are government supervised. There are about 170 domestic radio stations; additional stations broadcast to the mainland and overseas. The newest of Taiwan's five terrestrial television channels, the Public Television Service, began operations in 1998. Many cable and satellite systems also provide television.

As of 2008 there were 657.3 Internet users per 1,000 inhabitants.

INTERGOVERNMENTAL REPRESENTATION

A founding member of the United Nations, the Republic of China lost its right of representation in that body's major organs on October 25, 1971. The United States terminated formal diplomatic relations on January 1, 1979. Informal relations continue to be maintained through the American Institute in Taiwan and its Nationalist Chinese counterpart in Washington (and other U.S. cities), the Taipei Economic and Cultural Office.

IGO Membership (Non-UN): ADB (listed as "Taipei, China"), APEC, BCIE, WTO (listed as "Separate Customs Territory of Taiwan, Penghu, Kinmen, and Matsu").

COLOMBIA

Republic of Colombia
República de Colombia

Political Status: Independent Gran Colombia proclaimed 1819; separate state of New Granada established 1831; republican constitution adopted 1886; bipartisan National Front regime instituted in 1958 but substantially terminated in 1974; current constitution promulgated July 5, 1991.

Area: 439,734 sq. mi. (1,138,914 sq. km.).

Population: 42,888,592,000 (2005C); 44,453,000 (2008E). The 2005 figure includes an adjustment for underenumeration.

Major Urban Centers (urban areas, 2005E): SANTAFÉ DE BOGOTÁ (formerly Bogotá, 8,350,000), Medellín (3,450,000), Cali (2,700,000), Barranquilla (1,925,000), Cartagena (1,075,000).

Official Language: Spanish.

Monetary Unit: Peso (principal rate December 1, 2009: 1,995.31 pesos = $1US).

President: Álvaro URIBE Vélez (Independent); elected May 26, 2002, and inaugurated August 7 for a four-year term, succeeding Andrés PASTRANA Arango (Conservative Party); reelected May 28, 2006, and inaugurated August 7 for a second four-year term.

Vice President: Francisco SANTOS Calderón (Independent); elected May 26, 2002, and inaugurated August 7 for a term concurrent with that of the president; reelected May 28, 2006, and inaugurated August 7 for a term concurrent with that of the president.

THE COUNTRY

Situated at the base of the Isthmus of Panama, with frontage on both the Caribbean and the Pacific, Colombia is divided geographically into three main regions defined by ranges of the Andes Mountains: a flat coastal area, a highland area, and an area of sparsely settled eastern plains drained by tributaries of the Orinoco and Amazon rivers. In terms of population, Colombia is more diverse than most other Latin American countries. About 75 percent of Colombians are of mixed blood, including both mestizos and people who claim dual European and African heritage. Groups claiming a single ethnicity (Spanish, Indian, or African) are quite small. Spanish is the language of most people, except for isolated Indian tribes. More than 80 percent of the population identifies itself as Roman Catholic, while the remainder are Protestants and evangelical Christians. Women constitute approximately 40 percent of the official labor force, with a substantial additional proportion engaged in unpaid agricultural labor; in the urban sector, women are concentrated in domestic service and informal trading. Overall, female participation in government is minor, although three women held cabinet posts as of mid-2009.

Colombia's economy is diverse and includes large manufacturing, agriculture, and mineral sectors, as well as sizable public and

private-service sectors. Petroleum and petroleum products rank first among official exports. Coffee, cut flowers, and bananas are the most important agricultural exports, while efforts to develop agricultural alternatives—cotton, palm oil, and sugar, in particular—have been partially successful. Compared to some of its Latin American neighbors, Colombia has a reputation for prudent economic management, with a tradition of modest debt and independent monetary policy. The country did not record a single year of negative GDP growth between the 1930s depression and the late 1990s, when a severe economic crisis, caused chiefly by a worsening armed conflict, brought a contraction of the economy. The country's debt increased during the 1990s, as a new constitution added a number of social obligations without an accompanying increase in tax revenue. Meanwhile, tax revenue increased significantly during the 2000s. However, broad disparities in income remained an issue; in 2007 the United Nations Development Program (UNDP) reported that the wealthiest 10 percent of the country earned 46.9 percent of the national income, compared with 2.5 percent for the poorest 20 percent.

Economic recovery was recorded in the mid-2000s, as annual GDP growth reached 7.5 percent in 2007, with corollary declines in inflation and unemployment. Inflation, which had been in double digits in 2000, slowed to 5.5 percent in 2007, while the unemployment rate over the same period fell from 20 percent to 11.2 percent. Annual growth contracted in 2008 to 2.5 percent, owing in large part to the global economic crisis. The government forecast annual growth to decline to between 0.5 percent and 1.5 percent in 2009. However, the International Monetary Fund (IMF) and the central bank of Colombia projected zero growth for 2009.

GOVERNMENT AND POLITICS

Political background. Colombia gained its independence from Spain in 1819 as part of the Republic of Gran Colombia, which also included what is now Ecuador, Panama, and Venezuela. In 1830 Ecuador and Venezuela separated. The remaining territory, New Granada, was designated the Granadan Confederation in 1858, the United States of Colombia under a federal constitution promulgated in 1863, and the Republic of Colombia under a unitary constitution adopted in 1886. Panamanian independence, proclaimed in 1903, was not recognized by Bogotá until 1909.

The critical 19th-century issues of centralism versus federalism and the role of the Catholic Church gave rise to the Liberal (*Partido Liberal Colombiano*—PL) and Conservative (*Partido Conservador Colombiano*—PC) parties, which remain critical, if no longer exclusive, determinants of Colombian politics. Relative calm extended from 1903 to the early 1940s, when domestic instability emerged, culminating in a decade (1948–1958) of internal violence (*la Violencia*) that may have taken as many as 300,000 lives. This period included a coup d'état in 1953 that yielded a four-year dictatorship under Gen. Gustavo ROJAS Pinilla. To avert a resumption of full-scale interparty warfare after the fall of Rojas, the two major parties agreed in the so-called Pact of Sitges, concluded in July 1957, to establish a National Front (*Frente Nacional*) under which they would participate equally in government, to the exclusion of other parties. The National Front lasted until 1974, with Conservative Misael PASTRANA Borrero in 1970 the last president to have won under this framework. The 1970 elections were also noteworthy for allegations of electoral fraud from supporters of former dictator Rojas, who ran as a third-party candidate. (The subsequent guerrilla movement known as M-19 [see Political parties, below] took its name from the date of the disputed election—April 19.)

Electoral competition for the presidency resumed, in 1974, with Alfonso LÓPEZ Michelsen representing the Liberals and Álvaro GÓMEZ Hurtado representing the Conservatives. López captured 56 percent of the vote, Liberals and Conservatives together securing 90 percent of the legislative seats. The presidential election of June 4, 1978, was much closer with the Liberal candidate, Dr. Julio César TURBAY Ayala, defeating his Conservative opponent, Dr. Belisario BETANCUR Cuartas, by a paper-thin margin.

In a March 1982 legislative election the Liberals captured a majority of lower house seats; however, an intraparty dispute between orthodox and New Liberalism (*Nuevo Liberalismo*—NL) factions resulted in the nomination of ex-president López by the former and of Dr. Luis Carlos GALÁN Sarmiento by the latter for the presidential balloting on May 30. As a result of the Liberal split, Betancur, who had been renominated by the Conservatives, emerged as the victor with 46.8 percent of the valid votes and was inaugurated as the new chief executive on August 7.

The Liberal cleavage proved less costly in the legislative balloting of March 7, 1986, the mainstream group securing a majority in both houses. As a result, Galán, who had been renominated by the NL, withdrew from the presidential election of May 25, in which Virgilio BARCO Vargas decisively defeated the Conservatives' 1974 nominee, Gómez.

Galán, an unswerving critic of the Medellín and Cali drug cartels, the powerful and violent organizations that controlled much of the world's cocaine trade,, resurfaced in 1989 as the Liberals' leading presidential candidate but was assassinated on August 18. His equally outspoken successor, César GAVIRIA Trujillo, easily defeated Gómez (now running as a candidate of his party, the National Salvation Movement [MSN]) in the May 1990 presidential election, with the official Conservative, Rodrigo LLOREDA Caicedo running fourth behind Antonio NAVARRO Wolff, who had become the candidate of the recently legalized April 19 Movement (M-19, see Other Parties and Non-Rebel Groups, below) following the assassination of Carlos PIZARRO León-Gómez on April 26.

While M-19 secured only one seat in the legislative poll of March 11, 1990, it captured second place (only five seats behind the Liberals) in Constituent Assembly balloting on December 9, suggesting that the traditional bipartisan era might have run its course. Subsequently, after six months of debate a new constitution (see below) was adopted. Meanwhile, the drug problem, increasingly involving the Revolutionary Armed Forces of Colombian (FARC) and National Liberation Army (ELN) guerrilla groups (see below), who began to fund their operations with cocaine proceeds, drained government resources.

The Liberals retained control in legislative and gubernatorial balloting on October 27, 1991, winning majorities in both houses of Congress and capturing 15 of 27 governorships, while leftist parties suffered a major defeat in the legislative poll of March 13, 1994, the voters, in effect, endorsing a return to the historic dominance of Liberals and Conservatives. Subsequently, the narrow victory of the Liberal candidate, Ernesto SAMPER Pizano, in the second-round presidential balloting on June 19, accompanied by a remarkably low voter turnout of only 35 percent, was attributed to the basic similarity of the leading parties' programs.

On December 2, 1993, the head of the Medellín drug cartel, Pablo ESCOBAR, who had escaped from confinement in mid-1992 after having surrendered to authorities a year earlier, was killed by security forces. President Gaviria immediately proclaimed the "dismemberment" of the Medellín group, while indicating that the drug problem would remain, until destruction of the more sophisticated cartel in the southwestern city of Cali. The latter effort yielded significant results during the first half of 1995, with the arrests of several top Cali cartel figures. However, four months earlier the ruling Colombian Liberal Party (*Partido Liberal Colombiano*—PL) had been plunged into crisis over alleged links of nine of its legislators to the cartel. On July 27 Santiago MEDINA, President Samper's 1994 campaign treasurer, was arrested on charges of having accepted contributions from the Cali drug lords. Accused by Medina of involvement in the affair was Defense Minister Fernando BOTERO Zea, who resigned on August 8 and was arrested a week later amid allegations that Samper himself was aware of the funding source.

By 1996 public opinion, which had initially supported the president against his accusers, appeared to have turned decisively against him. Nonetheless, Samper, benefiting in part from an upsurge in anti-U.S. sentiment over the drug issue—Washington had revoked the president's U.S. visa—succeeded in rallying a majority of the lower house to his side in late May, thus averting a threat of impeachment.

By 1998 guerrilla strength, particularly that of the FARC, had risen, by army estimates, to control two-fifths of the country's municipalities. The rapidly growing force alarmed U.S. and Colombian observers with a string of overwhelming victories against outmatched Colombian forces in remote rural zones.

In the 1998 presidential election the Liberals were badly split between pro- and anti-Samper factions, many of the latter supporting the PC nominee, Andrés PASTRANA Arango, who defeated his Liberal opponent, Horacio SERPA Uribe, by half a million votes in the second-round balloting on June 21. The Liberals, however, retained decisive legislative majorities (56 percent of seats in the Senate and 60 percent in the Chamber of Representatives).

Pastrana won election in large part because voters viewed him as more likely to be able to negotiate a peace accord with guerrilla groups. He launched peace talks with the FARC in late 1998, but negotiations faltered quickly, and the talks' credibility subsequently eroded. Along with a badly slumping economy, the failure of the FARC talks, which ultimately failed in February 2002, fundamentally undermined Pastrana's presidency.

Despite the introduction of an ambitious "Plan Colombia," designed to defeat the drug traffickers with the massive infusion of $1.3 billion in primarily military aid from the United States, President Pastrana's popularity plummeted to a low of 20 percent by September 2000. On October 29, in municipal balloting that was termed a "punishment vote" against the administration, Conservatives won only 2 of 30 gubernatorial races and an equal number of mayoralties in departmental capitals.

In the presidential election of May 26, 2002, independent Álvaro URIBE Vélez, a longtime Liberal running with Conservative support, easily defeated the PL's official candidate, Serpa. A hard-liner and outspoken opponent of Pastrana's peace effort, Uribe benefited from his predecessor's inability to conclude a successful negotiation. Earlier, on March 10, both of the traditional parties were outpolled in legislative balloting by an unprecedented aggregate of minor candidates, most of whom declared their support for the new chief executive. Uribe's efforts to end both rightist and leftist insurgencies (including the passage of a "justice and peace" law in 2005 establishing the conditions for demobilizing the country's insurgents), yielded unusually high approval ratings during the ensuing three years, paving the way for a reelection bid in May 2006.

In 2006 the two leading left-of-center parties announced that they would merge to form an Alternative Democratic Pole (*Polo Democrático Alternativo*—PDA, see under Political parties, below) to contest the legislative and presidential elections. In the legislative elections on March 12, 2006, the opposition PL won a plurality of 36 seats, but the majority of seats once more was won by an aggregate of parties allied with the president. In first-round presidential balloting on May 28, Uribe was reelected with 62 percent of the vote (with 45 percent voter turnout), well above the 50 percent threshold to avoid a runoff. Sen. Carlos GAVIRIA Díaz of the PDA placed second with 22 percent, while PL candidate Horacio Serpa Uribe was third with 11.8 percent. Four candidates received 1 percent or less: former Bogotá Mayor Antanas MOCKUS (Indigenous Social Alliance Movement—*Movimiento Alianza Social Indígena*); Enrique PAREJO (Democratic National Reconstruction Movement—*Movimiento Reconstrucción Democrática Nacional*) ; Alvaro LEYVA (National Reconciliation Movement—*Movimiento Nacional de Reconciliación*); and Carlos Arturo RINCÓN (Communal and Communitarian Movement—*Movimiento Comunal y Comunitario de Colombia*).

Small-party opposition and pro-Uribe candidates continued to perform well in October 28, 2007 municipal and departmental elections. The Liberals won 9 and Conservatives 3 of the country's 32 departments. Together, the two parties accounted for about 40 percent of the mayors in Colombia's 1,100 municipalities. Candidates from pro-Uribe parties or movements took all but 2 of the remaining 20 governorships, with the PDA winning only 1. Left-of-center parties and movements, including the PDA in Bogotá, won the mayorships of Colombia's three largest cities (Bogotá, Medellín, and Cali).

Constitution and government. The 1886 constitution, one of the world's oldest, had been extensively revised before its replacement in 1991. The most notable amendment had been that of 1957, which instituted the *Frente Nacional,* under which the presidency alternated between Liberals and Conservatives, with equal numbers of offices held by members of the two parties. The parity rule also applied to the legislative and judicial branches until 1974, when a new president and all legislative bodies were elected on a nonrestrictive basis.

Most notable among the 1991 reforms were changes affecting Congress and the judiciary. The Senate was reduced from 114 seats to 102 (including 2 for indigenous communities), with senators elected nationally rather than by department. The Chamber of Representatives was reduced from 199 members to 161, each department or territory electing at least 2 representatives, with additional seats allotted on a population basis. In addition, up to 5 special seats could be assigned to minority groups or citizens living abroad.

The earlier Napoleonic judicial system was supplanted by an essentially adversarial U.S. system. An office of general prosecutor (*fiscalía general*) was established to investigate and charge offenders; an inspector-general (*procuraduría*) investigates and metes out administrative sanctions for offenses committed by state representatives; in addition, a people's defender (*defensor del pueblo*) must oversee the *fiscalía* and ensure the protection of human rights, while a judicial council (*consejo superior de la judicatura*) reviews the professional qualifications of the judiciary. Finally, a *corte constitucional* interprets the constitution, leaving to the Supreme Court the sole responsibility of serving as the highest court of appeal.

In October 2003 a referendum on a number of constitutional reforms sought by President Uribe (including a further reduction in the number of legislative seats) failed because the electoral turnout fell short of a mandated 25 percent. In December 2004, however, Congress gave formal approval to an amendment permitting presidential reelection, which was affirmed by the Constitutional Court in late 2005 (procedural issues had been raised).

Another constitutional amendment promulgated in 2003 and implemented for the first time in the 2006 elections, requires political parties to offer only one list of candidates per office. The new rules raised to 2 percent in legislative elections the threshold required for a party to maintain its legal status (exempting indigenous and Afro-Colombian parties).

Colombia is divided into 32 departments plus the Federal District of Santafé de Bogotá. Before 1991 there were 23 departments and 9 national territories, but the 1991 constitutional reforms converted the territories into departments. Since 1991 the governors of the departments have been popularly elected. (The president had appointed the governors under the 1886 constitution.) Reform in 1988 allowed for the popular election of mayors (akin to county administrators in all but large urban areas).

Foreign relations. Apart from cooperation with the United States in attempts to limit the drug trade, Colombia's activity on the international scene has recently centered on regional affairs. Relations with Nicaragua, already strained because of deportations of Colombian migrant workers, were further exacerbated in late 1979 by Managua's decision to revive a series of long-standing claims to the Caribbean islands of San Andrés and Providencia, both acquired by Colombia under a 1928 treaty, and the uninhabited cays of Quita Sueño, Roncador, Serrana, and Serranilla, which were assigned to Colombia under a 1972 agreement with the United States. In February 1980 Nicaragua formally denounced the 1928 accord as having been concluded under U.S. military occupation, while arguing that the cays were located on its continental shelf and thus constituted part of its national territory. On December 13, 2007, the International Court of Justice (ICJ) ruled in Colombia's favor in the case of San Andrés, Providencia, and Santa

Catalina islands, citing Nicaragua's failure to mount a challenge in the first 50 years after the 1928 treaty. The ICJ also determined that it could adjudicate any future disputes over the three cays and the two countries' maritime border.

Since 1979 relations with Venezuela, the country's northeastern neighbor, have been strained because of a dispute involving the maritime boundary through the Gulf of Venezuela. Tensions over contraband trade and containment of cross-border guerrilla activity intensified in February 1995 as the result of a National Liberation Army (*Ejército de Liberación Nacional*—ELN) guerrilla raid that resulted in the death of eight Venezuelan marines. President Samper then proposed that a joint force be created to patrol the area while rejecting Venezuela's claim to a right of "hot pursuit" of intruders. In November, following an incursion of Venezuelan troops into Colombia, the two countries announced the appointment of a bilateral commission to delineate the border more accurately as a means of preventing the recurrence of such incidents.

A serious row with Venezuela erupted in late 2004 with the kidnapping in Caracas of the FARC "foreign minister" Rodrigo GRANDA (a.k.a. Ricardo GONZALEZ), who was transported to the border and handed over to Colombian agents. In mid-January 2005, after Venezuela had threatened to break relations, Colombia admitted that it had paid bounty hunters for the abduction. Relations with Venezuela remain strained, including the withdrawal of Venezuela from the Andean Community (CAN—see separate entry) over, among other things, a free trade pact negotiated between Colombia and the United States.

Relations improved in mid-2007 when Venezuelan president Hugo Chávez visited President Uribe in Bogotá on August 31, 2007, to accept Uribe's unusual offer to allow Chávez to mediate negotiations with the FARC for a release of hostages. After Uribe abruptly terminated Chávez's involvement on November 22, 2007 (see Current Issues, below), relations between the two countries deteriorated sharply. The two leaders have regularly exchanged hostile rhetoric, with Chávez calling Uribe a "lackey of the empire" in early 2008, while Uribe had called Chávez a "legitimizer of terrorism." In mid-2008 the bilateral relationship had grown even more tense, as captured guerrilla computers indicated that the Venezuelan government may have begun providing material support to the FARC (see Current issues, below).

Colombia's relations with Ecuador have also deteriorated, as disagreements with the left-of-center government of Rafael Correa arose regarding aerial herbicide fumigation of coca plants in border zones, border security cooperation, and, most crucially, the March 1, 2008, Colombian incursion into Ecuadorian territory that killed a top FARC leader (see Current issues, below). Both countries withdrew their ambassadors. (In 2009 reports of the FARC's funding of Correa's 2006 presidential campaign, later denied by both Correa and the FARC, fueled further tensions between the two countries.)

In June 2008 relations with Nicaragua were strained following the granting of asylum in Nicaragua to three Colombian citizens who survived the Colombian Army's March raid on a FARC guerrilla camp in Ecuador. Nicaraguan President Daniel Ortega accused President Uribe of "state terrorism" and wanting to "murder" the three citizens. The Colombian government denounced Nicaragua before the Organization of American States (OAS) for "supporting terrorism."

In 2008 tensions between Colombia and Venezuela presented what was widely perceived as a major security concern in the hemisphere. However, in June President Chávez surprised observers by calling on the FARC and ELN to release all of their kidnap victims and disband. Uribe and Chávez held friendly meetings in January and April 2009, during which they discussed infrastructure projects and economic cooperation. Security and defense cooperation remained nonexistent in the border zone, however, and Colombian defense officials alleged that key FARC leaders were operating freely on the Venezuelan side of the border.

Relations with the United States have long been shaped by the drug issue. On balance, Colombian administrations have been cooperative with Washington on this subject, with the Uribe administration being the most cooperative to date. If Uribe is the high point of U.S.-Colombian relations, then the Samper administration (1994–1998) was the low point. In mid-1996 Washington announced the cancellation of Samper's U.S. visa as the result of accusation of linkages between Samper and the Cali cartel; four months earlier the administration of U.S. president Bill Clinton had "decertified" Colombia for insufficient anti-drug efforts, an action that was repeated in February 1997, despite ongoing cooperation between the two countries' military establishments. The United States continued to be displeased by the Colombian Congress's final vote in November 1997 on revocation of its ban on extradition; while the change was approved, it was made nonretroactive, thus precluding the extradition of Cali cartel kingpins for trial in U.S. courts (after several years in Colombian prisons, however, the Cali cartel's senior leaders were extradited to the United States in 2004). Extraditions—the first in nearly a decade—were resumed in late 1999 as the U.S. Congress moved to approve a $1.36 billion anti-drug package. Under the Uribe administration extradition of drug traffickers has resumed. On August 30, 2000, Clinton strongly endorsed President Pastrana's commitment to coca eradication in a one-day visit to Cartagena. On November 22, 2004, and March 11, 2007, President George W. Bush also visited Colombia, where he praised Uribe's anti-insurgent efforts and indicated that he would ask the U.S. Congress to augment the more than $5.4 billion spent from 2000 to 2007 and to approve a bilateral free-trade agreement signed in November 2006 (the United States is Colombia's largest trading partner). The trade pact has not been embraced by the U.S. Congress, despite an intense lobbying effort that included two visits to Washington by President Uribe in 2007. Democratic congressional leaders, along with labor and human rights groups, opposed the pact, citing the large number of Colombian labor union members killed with impunity. The U.S. congressional leadership resisted calling a vote to ratify the agreement. When the Bush administration sought to force a vote by introducing the agreement in the U.S. House of Representatives in April 2008, the House Democratic leadership employed an unusual legislative maneuver to postpone consideration of the agreement indefinitely. (As of mid-2009, the agreement's future remained uncertain.)

The Bush administration's support for President Uribe was further underscored by Bush's awarding Uribe the Medal of Freedom, the highest U.S. civilian honor, in January 2009. Subsequently, Uribe's relations with U.S. president Barack Obama have cooled but have remained cordial in the wake of the Obama administration's reversals on key issues: it refrained from promoting the free-trade agreement in Congress; proposed a 5 percent cut in military aid to Colombia; and was more vocal about human rights concerns than the Bush administration. However, Colombia remains the world's seventh-largest recipient of U.S. government aid. During a two-day visit to Washington in June 2009 to promote the free-trade agreement, President Uribe engaged in talks about bilateral and regional issues with President Obama. In July, negotiations to allow the United States to increase its number of troops in Colombia in an expanded anti-drug effort angered President Hugo Chávez, who subsequently withdrew Venezuela's ambassador from Bogotá following accusations by Colombia that Venezuela had assisted the FARC. The proposed troop increase also angered other states in the region, analysts describing Colombia as becoming "increasingly isolated" from its neighbors.

Current issues. Recent years have witnessed a three-cornered struggle among government, far-right paramilitary groups, and left-wing armed forces, all having largely abandoned ideology in a contest over control of the drug trade.

Following his inauguration on August 7, 2002, President Uribe moved energetically to counter the insurgencies that had plagued his predecessors (see the 2007 *Handbook*), adopting what he called a "democratic security" strategy of increased troop deployments, defense spending, and integration of the population in intelligence-gathering. Uribe also offered to negotiate with any armed group that first declared a cease-fire, an offer that was only accepted by the rightist paramilitaries. In December the main components of the paramilitary umbrella organization, the United Self-Defense Groups of Colombia (*Autodefensas Unidas de Colombia*—AUC, see Rebel and Clandestine Groups, below) agreed to demobilize, although the process was not complete until mid-2006.

The paramilitaries' demobilization took place within the framework of a 2005 law, known as the "Justice and Peace" law, which granted light (maximum eight-year) prison terms in exchange for a commitment to tell the truth about past crimes, compensate victims, and help dismantle the paramilitaries' powerful drug trafficking and political networks. A 2006 Constitutional Court decision strengthened the law's provisions, addressing some of the arguments of the law's critics that the law failed to provide the legal tools necessary to dismantle the paramilitary warlords' sources of wealth and political control. The Uribe government held that paramilitary leaders who cooperated with Justice and Peace investigators would not be extradited to the United States to face drug-trafficking charges.

President Uribe's campaign against left-wing guerrillas has registered several notable successes, bringing violence down to levels not seen since the early 1990s. Abductions have decreased by about three-quarters and murders by about 40 percent since 2002. While nearly all of this progress has occurred in cities and along main roads, these areas encompass about 75 percent of Colombia's population and most of its economic activity. Increased security in these areas has thus spurred robust economic growth and maintained President Uribe's approval rating in the 70 to 80 percent range, the highest of any Latin American leader.

The March 2006 legislative elections gave the pro-Uribe parties a majority of seats in the Congress, a strong signal that Uribe would win reelection. In peaceful first-round balloting on May 28, 2006, Uribe won convincingly—the first time an incumbent Colombian president had been reelected in more than a century.

The most significant challenge during Uribe's second term has been the "para-politics" scandal, in which scores of politicians have faced accusations of collusion, among other things, with paramilitary groups responsible for drug-related killings and other crimes. (As of mid-2009 the scandal had affected 67 members of the Congress that was seated in 2006, as well as several governors, mayors, and a former presidential intelligence chief, nearly all of them political supporters of President Uribe.) While there had been accusations in the past of collusion between mainstream politicians and paramilitaries, information collected from a computer owned by former paramilitary leader Rodrigo TOVAR Pupo (a.k.a. "Jorge 40," leader of the Northern Bloc paramilitary group) and the public confessions of paramilitary leaders as part of the Justice and Peace investigation led to dramatic evidence of electoral manipulation and intimidation in Colombian departments where the right-wing paramilitaries, with their drug trafficking and death squad activities apparent to all Colombians, have long operated freely. Among the first to be arrested, in 2007 was Jorge NOGUERA, the former head of the secret police, who was alleged to have supplied the AUC with the names of trade union leaders and human rights activists, who were later killed by paramilitaries. Noguera was charged with aggravated homicide. Other prominent politicians in detention included Sen. Álvaro ARAÚJO Castro and his father, former senator Álvaro ARAÚJO Noguera—the brother and father respectively of Foreign Minister Maria Consuelo ARAÚJO, who resigned in March 2007. That same month, a leaked U.S. Central Intelligence Agency (CIA) report also implicated Gen. Mario MONTOYA, the commander of the Colombian army, alleging extensive collaboration between Montoya and AUC leaders in operations against the FARC.

Meanwhile, the FARC, though weakened, has remained a security threat, especially in the southern jungle lowlands. In mid-2007, the guerrillas held 57 hostages with the aim of using them to secure the release of captured FARC militants. The hostages included 33 soldiers and police, former senator Ingrid BETANCOURT, a dual citizen of France and Colombia, 3 U.S. citizens employed by a Defense Department contractor, and 12 deputies from the Valle departmental legislature. The guerrillas demanded the demilitarization of two municipalities east of Cali to create a "security zone" for hostage negotiations, a condition rejected by President Uribe. In June the FARC killed 11 of the Valle deputies, prompting public protests by 1 million Colombians across the country in July. In August President Uribe accepted Venezuelan president Hugo Chávez's offer to mediate talks between the government and the FARC, and Uribe further extended the invitation to include renewed negotiations with the ELN in Cuba over a ceasefire. Chávez's participation brought a new dynamic to the peace process, according to analysts, because he was respected by the leaders of both the FARC and the ELN, and his high profile in the region put pressure on the FARC to show some flexibility regarding conditions for a prisoner exchange. Venezuelan efforts at mediation failed to yield quick results, and Chávez's participation in a phone conversation with the chief of Colombia's army resulted in President Uribe's dismissal of Chávez as mediator.

In December 2007 the FARC announced that, in an "act of sympathy" for Chávez, the group would release three hostages. In February 2008 four Colombian politicians were released. Meanwhile, President Chávez caused an uproar in Colombia when he made a speech calling on the nations of the world to offer political recognition to the FARC and ELN and to remove the groups from their lists of terrorist organizations. The remarks spurred a massive demonstration on February 4 by some 10 million Colombians protesting against the FARC and its tactics. In March government forces killed a FARC leader about a mile inside Ecuadorian territory, the incident provoking a major diplomatic crisis over Ecuadorian sovereignty. Subsequently, Ecuador withdrew its ambassador, and Venezuelan president Chávez ordered the deployment of troops to the Colombian border. Ultimately, negotiations were brokered by several neighboring states at a previously scheduled March 6 summit of the region's leaders in the Dominican Republic. Despite public declarations that the crisis was over, tensions between Colombia and its neighbors remained strained over Colombia's allegations that Venezuela and Ecuador had provided the guerrillas with weapons and equipment.

In April 2008 President Uribe's cousin and longtime political collaborator, the senator for Antioquia, Mario URIBE, was arrested in connection with the para-politics scandal. As criminal evidence mounted against paramilitary leaders and speculation pointed to an increasing number of politicians potentially involved in the scandal—the government extradited 14 AUC officials to the United States to face drug charges in May. Two more people were extradited in the next 12 months, along with all captured leaders of the defunct North Valle cartel that had dominated cocaine transshipments during the late 1990s and early 2000s. Victims' groups, meanwhile, expressed concern that the paramilitary leaders, once in U.S. custody, would no longer be required to reveal the names of people who aided the group, the truth about those they had killed, the locations of bodies, or the land and other assets they took by force. Violence by the FARC continued to escalate, though the group had declined in size (but still claimed an estimated 8,000–10,000 members). Attacks on military and civilian targets occurred at least once daily in many regions of the country, and the guerrillas held 47 hostages, including three Americans. In a crackdown on July 2, the army carried out "*Operación Jaque*" (Operation Check), in which soldiers posing as humanitarian workers rescued 14 hostages, including the three Americans and Íngrid Betancourt. Following the attack the guerrillas retreated to more remote areas, including border zones, and began to rely more heavily on landmines, improvised explosive devices, and sneak attacks on small military targets.

The military came under severe criticism in September and October 2008 when it was alleged that members of the army had been killing civilians, then presenting their bodies as those of members of armed groups killed in combat in order to reap rewards for high "body counts. The so-called false positives scandal underscored long-standing allegations by human rights groups in Colombia, amid claims that 535 civilians had been killed in this manner in 2007 and the first half of 2008. Subsequently, media reports said that more than a dozen young men who had disappeared in the poor suburb of Soacha had been buried as combatants hundreds of miles away. The scandal forced the resignation of army chief Gen. Montoya and prompted increased criticism of the president, whose demands that the military produce more results were seen as creating a climate for such abuse.

Meanwhile, the Uribe administration was accused in other scandals. In November 2008 several pyramid schemes were uncovered that not only caused widespread economic hardship, but also generated anger toward the president for what was described as his heavy-handed crackdown on the schemes and because of alleged links between the schemes and members of the administration. Among the claims was that the most notorious of these enterprises, DMG, had made financial contributions to the president's reelection campaign. In February 2009 the secret police were accused of surveillance of opposition politicians, reporters, human rights defenders, and Supreme Court justices, specifically those justices investigating para-politics cases.

In February 2009 FARC guerrillas released their two remaining civilian hostages, along with four police officers and soldiers, to a citizens' group, Colombians for Peace, which had been negotiating with guerrilla leaders. As of mid-2009 the FARC was still holding 22 military and police personnel—some for as long as 12 years—and was pressuring for a prisoner exchange. Meanwhile, with the exception of a failed offensive south of Bogotá in March, the guerrillas appeared to be increasing their operations.

Despite a mounting list of scandals, including accusations in April 2009 that the president's two sons had benefited improperly from a business deal involving tax-free zones, President Uribe's popularity stood at 70 percent in mid-year polls. For the second time in four years the president pressed Congress for a constitutional amendment that would allow him to seek a third term, though some of the president's key supporters voiced misgivings, including Germán VARGAS Lleras of the progovernment Radical Change (*Partido Cambio Radical*—CR) party. Observers indicated that Congress was likely to approve such an amendment, and subsequently, cabinet ministers began resigning to meet the legal requirement that they leave government 12 months before elections if they planned to run for office, fueling speculation that the president would face several challengers. Among the potential candidates in the 2010 presidential election were Agriculture Minister Andrés Felipe ARIAS and Defense Minister Juan Manuel SANTOS, both of whom resigned in 2009.

POLITICAL PARTIES

The Liberal and Conservative parties have traditionally dominated Colombian politics and from 1958 to 1974 shared power under the National Front system, with the leading minority group remaining entitled to representation in the executive branch until adoption of the 1991 constitution. The Conservatives have been waning since the early 1990s and the Liberals, once thought to be a permanent majority party, have seen their electoral fortunes diminish in recent cycles and have become part of the opposition countering the various parties and factions of the "*uribistas*" that support the Uribe government.

Social Party of National Unity (*Partido Social de Unidad Nacional*—PSUN) or, as more commonly referenced, the Party of the U (*Partido de la U*). PSUN is a new pro-Uribe party formed of former members of the PL and miscellaneous small parties. Its most prominent founder, journalist and former government minister Juan Manuel SANTOS, was named in 2006 to the post of defense minister, which he held until May 2009.

The party's 2006 legislative results changed the balance of power in Congress as the PSUN candidates won 30 seats in the Chamber on a national vote share of 16.7 percent (making the party the second-largest voting bloc in the lower house and the largest bloc of votes supporting the Uribe government) and won a plurality in the Senate (20 seats and 17.5 percent of the vote), thus disrupting the balance of power among the traditional rivals, the PL and the PC.

In early to mid-2008 PSUN leaders initiated a petition drive to try to change Colombia's constitution to allow President Uribe to run for a third consecutive term. In early 2009 President Uribe's high commissioner for peace, Luis Carlos Restrepo Ramírez, left office after more than six years to become party president in an effort to rally the pro-Uribe legislative bloc to push the reelection provision through Congress.

Leader: Luis Carlos RESTREPO Ramírez (Party President).

Colombian Conservative Party (*Partido Conservador Colom biano*—PC). A traditional party formerly based in the agrarian aristocracy, the *Partido Conservador* was long divided between National Front conservatives and an independent faction composed of followers of the late president Laureano Gómez. The split continued until November 1981, when the more moderate *ospina-pastranistas,* led by Dr. Misael Pastrana Borrero (president, 1970–1974), concluded an agreement with the rightist *alvaristas,* led by Dr. Álvaro Gómez Hurtado (an unsuccessful 1974 candidate who was later murdered in 1995). In 1986 Gómez Hurtado was the Conservative nominee but was decisively beaten by the PL's Barco, in part because of the association with his dictatorial father, Laureano, during the period of *la Violencia*.

For the 1990 campaign the party was again split, the official candidate, Rodrigo LLOREDA Caicedo, being outpaced by Gómez Hurtado, who, as candidate of a dissident **National Salvation Movement** (*Movimiento de Salvación Nacional*—MSN), was decisively defeated by the PL's Gaviria Trujillo in the May balloting. (From 1987 to 1992 the party operated under the name Social Conservative Party [*Partido Social Conservador*—PSC], although it then reverted back to the PC rubric.) In 1994 Andrés Pastrana Arango (running as an independent with PC endorsement) lost to the PL's Samper Pizano by a mere 0.8 percent of the second-round vote. Before accepting the PC nomination, Pastrana Arango, a former mayor of Bogotá, headed a dissident conservative group, the **New Democratic Force** (*Nueva Fuerza Democrática*—NFD), which secured eight Senate seats in 1991 (only one less than the mainline PC) but only one upper house seat in 1998. Pastrana defeated the PL's Horacio Serpa Uribe in second-round presidential balloting on June 21, 1998. For the 2002 campaign a largely disoriented PC endorsed the former Liberal and current president, Álvaro Uribe (after its candidate withdrew from the contest). Carlos HOLGUIN Sardi resigned as PC president following his party's poor showing in the March legislative poll.

In the March 2006 legislative elections the PC secured 29 seats in the Chamber and 18 seats in the Senate. Shortly afterward, President Uribe named Holguín to the post of interior minister. The party supported Uribe in the May 2006 presidential election, rather than fielding its own candidate.

Leaders: Efraín José CEPEDA Sarabia (President), Alirio VILLAMIZAR (Vice President), Benjamín HIGUITA Rivera (Secretary General).

Colombian Liberal Party (*Partido Liberal Colombiano*—PL). A traditional party that tends to reflect the interests of the more commercialized and industrialized sector of the electorate, the PL (not abbreviated as PLC) has endorsed moderately paced economic and social reform and has observer status in the Socialist International.

At a party convention in September 1981, former chief executive López Michelsen was designated Liberal candidate for the presidency in 1982, leading his archrival, Lleras Restrepo, and another former president, Alfonso Lleras Camargo, to support an independent center-left campaign launched by Dr. Luis Carlos GALÁN Sarmiento of the then newly organized **New Liberalism** (*Nuevo Liberalismo*—NL). Galán drew enough Liberal votes from López Michelsen to throw the May presidential election to the Conservative candidate, Belisario Betancur.

For the 1986 campaign the mainstream leadership, including the still-influential Lleras Camargo, joined in supporting the former mayor of Bogotá, Virgilio Barco Vargas, a political centrist, whose capture of the presidency on May 25 was preceded by a PL victory in the legislative poll of March 9.

Having fared poorly in the 1986 legislative balloting, the NL reentered the parent party in mid-1988 to bolster support for President Virgilio Barco. Galán Sarmiento, who had emerged as the leading Liberal candidate for the presidency in 1990, was assassinated on August 18, 1989. Subsequently, in an unprecedented primary poll conducted in conjunction with legislative and municipal balloting on March 11, 1990, César Gaviria Trujillo was formally selected as the new PL nominee and went on to defeat his closest competitor, Conservative dissident Gómez Hurtado, by a near two-to-one margin.

The PL's presidential candidate in 1994, Ernesto Samper Pizano, was from the *Nuevo Liberalismo,* while his running mate was drawn from the party's right wing. Although outpolling the Conservatives by a more than two-to-one margin in first-round balloting on March 8, 1998, the PL's Horacio Serpa Uribe lost the presidency to the independent (and PC-endorsed) candidate Andrés Pastrana in second-round balloting on June 21. Returning as his party's nominee in 2002, Serpa Uribe ran second to Álvaro Uribe Vélez, a former PL conservative who ran as an independent.

In 2006 Serpa was again the PL presidential nominee, placing third behind President Uribe and the PDA candidate, Carlos Gaviria Díaz. Serpa polled less than 12 percent in the election—widely described as the worst showing by a Liberal candidate in the modern era. The PL won a plurality in the legislative elections, with 35 seats in the Chamber. It tied with longtime rival PC for the second-largest bloc of Senate seats (18). In the para-politics scandals that surfaced after the elections, Juan Manuel López, a Liberal senator from Córdoba, was identified as one of the politicians who had signed the "Pact of Ralito," a declaration of common political purpose, with leaders of the AUC.

César Gaviria was reelected party director in May 2007. The party has been divided between those who support President Uribe and those who publicly oppose his administration.

Leaders: César GAVIRIA Trujillo (Director and Former President of the Republic), Horacio SERPA Uribe (1998, 2002, and 2006 presidential candidate), Jose Noe RIOS Muñoz (Secretary General).

Radical Change (*Partido Cambio Radical*—CR). Founded in 1998 by a group primarily made up of dissident Liberals, the center-right party supported Uribe in the 2002 election and in 2006 became one of several medium-sized parties to form a pro-Uribe legislative bloc.

The CR's electoral strength has been concentrated around Bogotá and the departments of Antioquia, Cundinamarca, Valle, Boyacá, and Tolima.

The CR secured 20 Chamber seats and 15 seats in the Senate in the 2006 legislative elections.

In March 2009 Germán Vargas Lleras, a presidential aspirant, split with President Uribe over the issue of another presidential term for the incumbent. The party did not require its members to adopt Vargas's position, and as of mid-2009, most had not.

Leaders: Germán VARGAS Lleras (President), Federico ECHAVARRÍA Olarte (Supervisor), Antonio ÁLVAREZ Lleras (General Secretary).

Citizens' Convergence Party (*Partido Convergencia Ciudadana*—CC). Formed in 1997 by Luis Alberto Gil Castillo (former teacher's union leader and M-19 member) and Jairo Céspedes Camacho, this rightist party's strength lies in the Santander department, where it was founded. In the 2006 legislative elections the CC won 8 seats in the Chamber and 7 in the Senate. It is one of a handful of pro-Uribe parties whose membership has been disproportionately implicated in the para-politics scandal.

Leaders: Samuel ARRIETA Buelvas (President), Fabio Tadeo BUSTOS (Vice President), Ricardo FLÓREZ (General Secretary).

Wings–Team Colombia Movement (*Movimiento Alas–Equipo Colombia*—MAEC). The MAEC was formed in anticipation of the 2006 elections by the merger of *Partido ALAS* and the *Movimiento Equipo Colombia*, the latter having first contested national elections in 2002. The Christian social democracy party emphasizes divinity, human rights, social unity and the sanctity of the family unit, and a mixed-market economy with concern for fair and sustainable socio-economic development. It has been strongest in Colombia's north, particularly the department of Cesar, where Alvaro Araújo, one of the senators jailed for alleged collusion with paramilitaries, was one of the party's most prominent members. The MAEC is another of the pro-Uribe parties whose members have been significantly exposed in the para-politics scandal.

In the 2006 legislative elections the MAEC won 8 seats in the Chamber and 5 seats in the Senate.

Leader: Javier PINILLA Palacio (Secretary General).

Democratic Colombia (*Colombia Democrática*—CD). The CD is the party associated most closely with Mario Uribe, President Álvaro Uribe's cousin. It won 3 Senate seats and 2 Chamber seats in 2006. All three senators have chosen to step down in favor of alternates as they faced para-politics accusations.

Leader: Mario URIBE Escobar (National Director).

Living Colombia Movement (*Movimiento Colombia Viva*—CV). The CV, a small right-of-center party, was created by a coalition of legislators from Colombia's Caribbean coastal region and protestant evangelical leaders. It won two Senate seats in 2006 and no seats in the Chamber. The CV was criticized during that campaign for accepting candidates expelled from other parties on suspicion of paramilitary ties. The party has had difficulty keeping its two Senate seats, as the replacements of those forced to resign by para-politics scandals were also forced to resign.

Leadership remained unclear after the February 2007 arrest of party president Sen. Dieb MALOOF.

Alternative Democratic Pole (*Polo Democrático Alternativo*—PDA). The left-of-center PDA was launched in late 2005 by merger of the *Independent Democratic Pole* (*Polo Democrático Independiente*—PDI) and the **Democratic Alternative** (*Alternativa Democrática*—AD) and contains elements of a number of far-left parties like the **Communist Party of Colombia** (*Partido Comunista de Colombia*—PCC) and the **Independent and Revolutionary Labor Movement** (*Movimiento Obrero Independente y Revolucionario*—MOIR).

With a significant representation of demobilized M-19 members, the PDI had been formed in July 2003 by former labor leader Luis Eduardo ("Lucho") GARZON, who argued that President Uribe's policy of "democratic security" had emphasized security to the detriment of democracy, and in 2004 was elected as the first leftist mayor of Bogotá. The AD had been organized in November 2003 by a group of minor left-wing parties equally opposed to the president's policies.

In 2006 PDA flagbearer Carlos Gaviria Díaz lost to President Uribe, having secured only 22 percent of the vote in the presidential run-off balloting. The party won 10 Senate seats and 8 Chamber seats in the legislative elections.

As the para-politics scandal reached its zenith in March and April of 2007, PDA senator (and former M-19 member, see Other Parties and Non-Rebel groups, below) Gustavo Petro criticized President Uribe, claiming that Uribe was linked to the paramilitaries in his activities as governor and later as president. Petro also drew attention when he criticized the PDA leadership in July for not being more openly critical of the FARC, especially in the wake of the deaths of the 11 provincial deputies held hostage by the FARC. Petro's remarks drew the ire of the party's leadership, who met to consider sanctioning Petro and abstained from any public defense of his remarks.

In the October 2007 municipal and gubernatorial elections the party maintained control of the mayorship of Bogotá with the victory of Polo candidate Samuel MORENO by devoting much of its resources to that race. Its only other significant victory was in the Nariño department, where former M-19 leader Antonio NAVARRO Wolff was elected as the party's only governor. In mid-2009 opinion polls showed Moreno to be the city's least popular mayor since the early 1990s.

As of mid-2009 the PDA was in danger of fragmentation, as more moderate and electorally successful members like Garzón feuded with more leftist members, who generally led more effective political operations. Garzón officially abandoned the party in May, though other moderate members like Petro and Navarro chose to remain.

The two chief contenders for flagbearer of the party in 2010 were Petro and Gaviria Díaz.

Leaders: Carlos GAVIRIA Díaz (President), Gustavo PETRO, Carlos BULA Camacho (General Secretary).

Smaller parties that received less than 3 percent of the vote but nonetheless gained legislative representation in 2006 included: the **Afro-Colombian Social Alliance** (*Movimiento Alianza Social Afrocolombiana*—ASA), led by Josefina VILLARREAL Sanchez; **Afrounincca; For the Country of Our Dreams** (*Por el Pais que Soñamos*—PePqS), led by Enrique PEÑALOSA Londoño; the **Green Party Center Option** (*Partido Verde Opción Centro*—OC), led by Héctor Elías PINEDA Salazar; the **Liberal Opening Movement** (*Movimiento Apertura Liberal*), led by Miguel Ángel FLÓREZ Rivera; the **Huila and New Liberalism** (*Huila Nueva y Liberalism*—HNL), a regional party from Huila department; the **Indigenous Authorities of Colombia Movement** (*Movimiento Autoridades Indígenas de Colombia*—AICO), led by Yesid BRIÑEZ Poloche; the **Indigenous Social Aliance** (*Movimiento Alianza Social Indígena*—MASI), led by Marco AVIRAMA; the **Mira Movement** (*Movimiento MIRA*—MM) an evangelical Christian party led by Alexandra MORENO Piraquive; the **National Afro-Colombian Movement** (*Movimiento Nacional Afrocolombiano "Afro"*), led by Marcel Leonardo ECHEVERRY; the **National Salvation Movement** (*Movimiento de Salvación Nacional*), led by Eduardo JARAMILLO Hoyos; the **People's Participation Movement** (*Movimiento de Participación Popular*), led by Gustavo CASTELLANOS Pulido; the **Progressive National Movement** (*Movimiento Nacional Progresista*), led by Guillermo RODRÍGUEZ DAZA; the **Regional Integration Movement** (*Movimiento de Integración Regional*—IR), led by Dorky JAY Julio; the **Renovation Movement Labor Action**; the **Social Action Party** (*Partido de Acción Social*—PAS), led by Alfonso ANGARITA Baracaldo; and the **United People's Movement** (*Movimiento Popular Unido*—MPU), led by José Eliecer ARMERO Riascos.

Another 45 parties and political movements participated in the 2006 legislative elections but failed to gain the percentage of the vote necessary to maintain their legal status. These included the remnants of **Anapo**, the "Let Moreno Play" movement led by high-profile pro-Uribe senator (and later ambassador to South Africa) Carlos MORENO de Caro, and several parties with locally focused, single-candidate or evangelical Christian platforms

Other Parties and Non-Rebel Groups:

Democratic Alliance/April 19 Movement (*Alianza Democrática/ Movimiento 19 de Abril*—AD/M-19). Initially a self-proclaimed armed branch of the **National Popular Alliance** (*Alianza Nacional Popular*—Anapo) that shocked the military establishment by a daring raid on an army arsenal north of the capital in January 1979, M-19 was subsequently responsible for the two-month occupation of the Dominican Embassy in Bogotá in early 1980 and the 27-hour seizure of the Palace of Justice in the capital in November 1985, during which more than 100 people were killed. In early 1990 M-19 agreed to lay down its arms and joined with several small groups in forming a Nationalist Action for Peace (*Acción Nacionalista por la Paz*—ANP) that succeeded in outpolling the UP (see below) in the legislative and municipal balloting of March 11. Pizarro was assassinated on April 26 and was succeeded as M-19 leader by Antonio Navarro Wolff, who ran a surprising third in the presidential election of May 27 as the candidate of a 13-member leftist coalition styled the Democratic Convergence (*Convergencia Democrática*—CD). Following the May election the Navarro Wolff grouping operated as AD/M-19, which more than doubled its vote share to nearly 27 percent in the December Constituent Assembly election before slipping to 10 percent in October 1991. It declined further to a meager 3.8 percent in the first-round presidential balloting of May 30,

1994, with Navarro Wolff subsequently joining the PDI (see under PDA, above). Navarro Wolff was elected governor of Nariño department in 2007.

As an electoral group, the AD/M-19 is moribund, with its more significant members (e.g., Navarro and Sen. Gustavo Petro) now affiliated with the PDA (see above).

Patriotic Union (*Unión Patriótica*—UP). The UP was formed in May 1985 as the reputed political arm of the Revolutionary Armed Forces of Colombia (FARC, see below). Advancing a program that included political and trade union freedom, agrarian reform, and opposition to U.S. interference in Latin America, the UP won 1 Senate and 10 Chamber seats in March 1986. A number of UP leaders were subsequently murdered (reportedly by paramilitary police units), including the organization's president, Jaime PARDO Leal, on October 11, 1987. The UP performed poorly in the March 1990 balloting, partly because of competition from the recently launched ANP and partly because of a lengthy "dirty war" against it that cost the lives of more than 1,000 of its members in 1989 alone. Before the 1990 presidential poll, its candidate, Bernardo JARAMILLO Ossa, was assassinated, reportedly by order of the Medellín cartel. In 1994, after deaths of its members had risen to more than 2,300, the party declined to advance a presidential candidate, its principal leader (recently returned from exile in Switzerland) declaring simply that "he would be killed." Manuel CEPEDA Vargas, the last UP member to hold a seat in the Senate, was assassinated in August 1994. The group participated in the 1998 balloting but secured no representation. UP president Aida ABELLA has spent more than a decade in exile after receiving death threats.

Rebel and Clandestine Groups:

In 1985 the two groups immediately following (ELN and FARC) joined with M-19, **Hope, Peace and Liberty** (*Esperanza, Paz y Libertad*—EPL), the **Quintín Lame Commando** (*Comando Quintín Lame*) and **Free Homeland** (*Patria Libre*) formations operating in Cauca and Sucre departments, respectively, and the **Workers' Revolutionary Party** (*Partido Revolucionario de los Trabajadores*—PRT) in forming a National Guerrilla Coordination (*Coordinadora Guerrillera Nacional*—CGN). The name was changed to **National Guerrilla Coordination Simón Bolívar** (*Coordinadora Nacional Guerrillera Simón Bolívar*—CNGSB). Quintín Lame and the PRT laid down their weapons in 1991, with the CNGSB becoming defunct after a breakdown in talks on demobilizing the remaining rebel units. The EPL was dealt a near fatal blow when the faction led by Oscar William Calvo that operated in the Antioquia, Caldas, and Risaralda departments surrendered to government forces in July 2006. By 2008 the FARC and ELN no longer coordinated their efforts but were instead rivals. (For recent demobilization developments, see Current issues, above.)

National Liberation Army (*Ejército de Liberación Nacional*—ELN). Once the largest and most militant of the insurgent organizations, the Cuban-line ELN was founded by radical students and priests in 1964. Less involved in the drug trade, it has supported itself by pioneering the practice of kidnapping for ransom, as well as extortion, particularly of businesses in the energy sector. It has mounted more than 400 attacks on the country's oil pipelines, causing losses estimated at more than $1 billion.

A "moderate" breakaway group, the **Socialist Renovation Current** (*Corriente de Renovación Socialista*—CRS), agreed to sign a final peace agreement in April 1994. Longtime ELN leader Gregorio Manuel PEREZ Martínez, a priest born and raised in Spain, died on February 14, 1998. It is now commanded by a five-member Central Command led by Nicolás RODRIGUEZ Bautista, alias "Gabino."

Peace talks with ELN representatives and the Pastrana government were opened at an undisclosed northern location in late December 1999 but proved unproductive and were ultimately called off in May 2002.

ELN leader and spokesperson Gerardo Bermudez, known as Francisco Galán, was released conditionally from prison in January 2007 after serving 15 years of a 30-year sentence. Galán's release was intended to further progress in peace talks between the government and the ELN in Havana, Cuba (see Current issues, above). As of mid-2008, these talks are at a standstill, with ELN leaders refusing to respond to the government after President Uribe's November 2007 termination of Venezuelan president Hugo Chávez's mediating role. Bermudez announced his departure from the ELN in early 2008.

The ELN's top command structure has been weakened by the government's military campaigns, and ELN forces have been on the short end of armed confrontations with the FARC in Arauca and Nariño departments over oil profits and drug smuggling routes. So far the ELN has refused to demobilize under the terms of the justice and peace law, however, and has reiterated the demand for a constituent assembly for formulating social and economic reforms as a precondition. The group has refused a government demand that an ELN cease-fire include the guerrillas' concentration in specific zones, which the ELN views as tantamount to surrender.

One small splinter group of the ELN known as the *Ejército Revolucionario del Pueblo*—ERP, operating in Bolívar department, demobilized in April 2007.

In 2008 ELN activity diminished, and 18 rebels and 45 breakaway group members surrendered to the government. Violence increased in 2009, particularly in the departments of Arauca, Bolívar, and Nariño, owing largely to the group's increased involvement in drug trafficking. In July the government seized explosives from ELN rebels in the department of Boyaca, preventing an attack on Colombian Independence Day.

Leaders: José Nicolás RODRIGUEZ Bautista (a.k.a. Gabino, Political Commander), Antonio GARCIA (Military Commander), Pablo BELTRAN, Juan Carlos CUELLAR, Oscar SANTOS.

Revolutionary Armed Forces of Colombia (*Fuerzas Armadas Revolucionarias de Colombia*—FARC). Founded in 1964 by radicalized peasants, the FARC was long a Moscow-line guerrilla group affiliated with the now moribund **Communist Party of Colombia** (*Partido Comunista de Colombia*—PCC). In late 1983 it indicated a willingness to conclude a cease-fire agreement, which was formalized in March 1984. The agreement was renewed on March 2, 1986, in return for which the Betancur government guaranteed (without conspicuous fulfillment) the safety of electoral candidates advanced by the FARC's alleged political wing, the Patriotic Union (see above). Inconclusive peace talks with the government were resumed in late 1989, with the group formally joining the CNGSB a year later, shortly after the death of its cofounder, Luis Alberto MORANTES (a.k.a. Jacobo Arenas). FARC's urban wing is known as the **Bolivarian Militias** (*Milicias Bolivarianas*), which have been significantly weakened by the Uribe government's urban-focused security policies.

In July 1998 President-elect Pastrana held an unprecedented jungle meeting with FARC commander Manuel MARULANDA Vélez, after which Pastrana declared that he would comply with the rebels' demands for withdrawal of government forces from five southern municipalities as a precondition for peace talks that would commence subsequent to his August inauguration. On January 7, 1999, Pastrana participated in a ceremonial launching of the talks in San Vincente del Caguán. Although Marulanda failed to appear because of alleged threats against his life, Pastrana insisted that his absence would not derail the peace process. However, the FARC withdrew from the peace negotiations temporarily later in the month in the wake of increased activity by the AUC. The FARC would go on to suspend the talks on numerous occasions. The demilitarized zone was extended eleven times between 1999 and 2002, while the negotiators failed to move from procedural issues to more substantive topics. After the FARC hijacked an aircraft and kidnapped a senator on February 20, 2002, President Pastrana declared the FARC peace talks over.

Fueled by proceeds from its drug trade, the FARC grew rapidly during the 1990s, reaching approximately 18,000 members by the early 2000s. The guerrilla group, which is unpopular in Colombia because of its human rights record, has suffered reversals during the years of the Uribe presidency. Its membership is now about 12,000, and it has lost at least eight senior leaders since 2007. It nonetheless remains a formidable and well-funded force with a presence in the vast majority of Colombia's departments.

In May 2008 it was reported that the FARC's paramount leader and cofounder, Pedro Antonio MARIN (a.k.a. Manuel MARULANDA), had died. He was replaced by FARC Secretariat member Guillermo León Saenz Vargas (a.k.a. Alfonso CANO).

In June 2009, in what was reported as "a heavy blow" to FARC, the military killed three associates of a key FARC commander, Jorge Torres Victoria (a.k.a. Pablo Catatumbo, who allegedly controlled cocaine distribution policies. The U.S. State Department was reported to be offering a $2.5 million reward for the capture of Torres.

Leaders: Guillermo León SAENZ, Vargas Jorge BRICENO Suárez (a.k.a. Mono JOJOY), Luciano Martín ARANGO (a.k.a. Iván MARQUEZ), Rodrigo Londoño ECHEVERRI (a.k.a. Timoleón JIMENEZ or Timochenko), Milton de Jesús TONCEL (a.k.a. Joaquín GOMEZ), Jaime Alberto PARRA (a.k.a. Mauricio JARAMILLO or "The Doctor"), and Jorge TORRES Victoria.

The most prominent right-wing paramilitary grouping has long been the **United Self-Defense Groups of Colombia** (*Autodefensas Unidas de Colombia*—AUC), which was organized in 1996 to coordinate the activity of about 20 smaller organizations. Many of these groups had been founded by drug traffickers, large landowners, businessmen, conservative politicians, and military factions as counterinsurgent militias, with the goal of reducing the influence of guerrillas and leftist political activists.

Until 2003, the leader of the AUC was Carlos CASTAÑO, who had earlier formed the Cordoba and Uraba Self-Defense Union (*Autodefensas Unidas de Córdoba y Urabá*—ACCU) following the death of his father, a wealthy landowner, reportedly at the hands of leftist guerrillas. At its zenith in the late 1990s and early 2000s, the AUC was responsible for the majority of human rights abuses in Colombia, and Colombia's security forces faced widespread accusations of collusion with the rightist militias.

In mid-2001 the AUC claimed that 5,000 new recruits had joined its ranks, bringing their total to 13,000. During the early 2000s, the group became more divided over the question of drug trafficking, an important source of its income. Castaño, who opposed the increasing influence of drug lords in the group, was later murdered by his own men in 2004.

In 2002 the AUC entered into peace talks with the Colombian government; beginning in November 2003, 27 of the AUC's component blocs—32,000 people in all—participated in demobilization ceremonies, turning in about 15,000 weapons.

Reports from the Organization of American States Mission to Support the Peace Process in Colombia (OAS-MAPP) and nongovernmental analysts have raised concerns regarding the success of the demobilization of the AUC and other right-wing paramilitary groups. They have warned that some within the junior leadership have refused to participate in the demobilization process and were still heavily involved in drug trafficking. Moreover, demobilized members who soured on the peace process were joining the holdouts and resuming paramilitary activities.

In May 2008 14 of the AUC's leaders were extradited to the United States, where they were to face narcotrafficking charges. The state of the groups' leadership, and its dominion over criminal activity in Colombia, remained unclear. By mid-2009 estimates of new groups, at least partly led by former mid-level AUC leaders, reportedly claimed between 4,000 and 10,000 members. Some of the most commonly named paramilitary groups were the **Black Eagles**; ***Rastrojos***; **New Generation**; **Office of Envigado**; and ***Cuchillos***. Many were engaged principally in drug trafficking and claimed to do drug business with guerrillas, rather than identifying themselves as counterinsurgency groups. A former paramilitary believed to have been a principal sponsor of some of the new groups, Daniel RENDÓN Herrera (or "Don Mario,") was arrested in April 2009.

LEGISLATURE

The Colombian **Congress** (*Congreso*) is a bicameral legislature consisting of a Senate and a Chamber of Representatives, each elected for a four-year term. From 1958 to 1974 both houses were theoretically divided equally between Liberals and Conservatives, although members of other groups could run as nominal candidates of one of the two major parties and thus gain representation. At each of the seven regular elections before 2002, the Liberals obtained majorities in both houses. The election of March 10, 2002, was highly fractionalized, although support for President Uribe was subsequently credited as overwhelming in both the Senate and Chamber.

Since 2006 numerous lawmakers have resigned from Congress, most of them forced to do so to confront allegations related to the parapolitics scandals. The party of any legislator who resigns remains in control of the seat, with the party naming as replacement the runner-up candidate on the party list. (Some seats have been occupied by as many as five lawmakers since 2006.) Congress subsequently failed to pass a measure that would have left empty for the duration of the term any seat that had been occupied by a legislator who resigned. Pro-Uribe parties opposed the measure after it became evident that, with their congressional representation reduced, they might lack the votes necessary to reform the constitution to extend the president's term.

Senate (*Senado de la República*). The upper house is presently composed of 102 members, including 2 elected to represent indigenous communities.

In the most recent election of March 12, 2006, the seat distribution was as follows: the Social Party of National Unity, 20; Colombian Conservative Party, 18; Colombian Liberal Party, 18; Radical Change, 15; Alternative Democratic Pole, 10; Citizens' Convergence, 7; Wings-Team Colombia Movement, 5; Democratic Colombia, 3; Mira Movement, 2; Living Colombia Movement, 2; Indigenous Authorities of Colombia Movement, 1; and Indigenous Social Alliance, 1.

President: Javier CÁCERES Leal.

Chamber of Representatives (*Cámara de Representantes*). The lower house has 166 members, with each department being entitled to at least 2 representatives and 5 seats being set aside for special representation (2 for blacks, 1 for indigenous persons, 1 for Colombians living abroad, and 1 for political minorities).

In the most recent election of March 12, 2006, the seat distribution was as follows: the Colombian Liberal Party, 35; Social Party of National Unity, 30; Colombian Conservative Party, 29; Radical Change, 20; Alternative Democratic Pole, 8; Citizens' Convergence, 8; Wings-Team Colombia Movement, 8; Liberal Opening Movement, 5; Regional Integration Movement, 4; Democratic Colombia, 2; Huila and New Liberalism, 2; National Afro-Colombian Movement, 2; United People's Movement; 2; For the Country of Our Dreams, 2; Mira Movement,1; National Salvation Movement, 1; People's Participation Movement, 1; Progressive National Movement, 1; Renovation Movement Labor Action, 1; Social Action Party, 1; Green Party Center Option, 1; Afro-Colombian Social Aliance, 1; and Afrounincca, 1.

President: Edgar GÓMEZ Román.

CABINET

[as of August 1, 2009]

President	Álvaro Uribe Vélez
Vice President	Francisco Santos Calderón
Ministers	
Agriculture and Rural Development	Andrés Fernández Acosta
Communications	María del Rosario Guerra de la Espriella [f]
Culture	Paula Marcela Moreno [f]
Education	Cecilia María Vélez White [f]
Environment, Housing, and Territorial Development	Carlos Rufino Costa Posada
Finance and Public Credit	Óscar Iván Zuluaga
Foreign Affairs	Jaime Bermúdez Merizalde
Foreign Trade, Industry, and Tourism	Luis Guillermo Plata Páez
Interior and Justice	Fabio Valencia Cossio
Mines and Energy	Hernán Martínez Torres
National Defense	Gabriel Silva Luján
Social Protection	Diego Palacio Betancourt
Transport	Andrés Uriel Gallego Henao

[f] = female

COMMUNICATIONS

The press in Colombia is privately owned and enjoys complete freedom, though one of the world's highest rates of unpunished murders and threats against journalists ensures that a fair amount of self-censorship occurs. President Uribe and other top officials have been criticized for referring to some independent reporters as "terrorists" or FARC supporters. Rebel groups, meanwhile, have continued to target journalists whose investigations were deemed too aggressive or whose editorial positions were deemed too critical of the groups. In March 2009 the government was found to be responsible for the death of an *El Tiempo* reporter, who was killed by a soldier in Arauca, where he was investigating alleged corruption in the mayor's office and the military. The soldier who shot him was sentenced to 20 years in prison; the government was ordered to pay the journalist's family $380,000 in damages. The watchdog Committee to Protect Journalists said 16 of 20 cases in which journalists were killed in the past decade remain unresolved. In July another watchdog group, Reporters Without Borders, reported that an arrest had been made in the April slaying of a radio journalist. Police reported that a paramilitary group had paid the suspect about $7,000 to kill the journalist, who had frequently reported on corruption cases.

Press. The following are dailies published in Bogotá, unless otherwise noted: *El Tiempo* (270,000 daily, 550,000 Sunday), *El Colombiano* (Medellín, 90,000); *El Heraldo* (Barranquilla, 70,000); *El Nuevo Siglo* (68,000); *El País* (Cali, 60,000 daily, 110,000 Sunday); *La Patria* (Manizales, 22,000). Most newspapers function as the organs of political parties or factions.

Colombia's oldest daily, *El Espectador,* which was launched in 1887, was converted into a Sunday weekly in August 2001 but returned to daily status in May 2008.

News agencies. The domestic facility is the National News Agency "Colprensa" (*Agencia Nacional de Noticias "Colprensa"*); in addition, a number of foreign agencies maintain bureaus in Bogotá.

Broadcasting and computing. The 11 major radio networks, of which only *Radiodifusora Nacional* is publicly owned, service more than 500 stations. The country's three national television channels are controlled by the *Instituto Nacional de Radio y Televisión,* although broadcasting time is distributed among private production companies. There are also six regional channels; cable service for Bogotá was introduced in 1985. As of 2008 there were 385 Internet users per 1,000 inhabitants.

INTERGOVERNMENTAL REPRESENTATION

Ambassador to the U.S.: Maria Carolina Barco ISAKSON.

U.S. Ambassador to Colombia: William R. BROWNFIELD.

Permanent Representative to the UN: Claudia BLUM.

IGO Memberships (Non-UN): ACS, ALADI, BCIE, CAN, CDB, IADB, Interpol, IOM, Mercosur, NAM, OAS, OPANAL, PCA, SELA, WCO, WTO.

COMORO ISLANDS

Union of the Comoros
Union des Comores (French)

Note: Supporters of President Ahmed Sambi reportedly won 19 of the 24 directly elected seats in balloting for the Assembly of the Union on December 6 and 20, 2009.

Political Status: Former French dependency; proclaimed independent July 6, 1975; Federal Islamic Republic of the Comoros proclaimed in constitution approved by national referendum on October 1, 1978; constitution of October 20, 1996, suspended following military coup of April 30, 1999; new constitution providing for the Union of the Comoros adopted by national referendum on December 23, 2001.

Area: 718 sq. mi. (1,860 sq. km.), excluding the island of Mahoré (Mayotte), which voted in 1976 to retain its affiliation with France as a "Territorial Collectivity," subsequently became classified as a French "Overseas Collectivity" and in 2009 voted to extend its relationship further by becoming an "Overseas Department."

Population: 576,660 (2003C), excluding residents of Mahoré; 921,000 (2008E).

Major Urban Centers (2005E): MORONI (Ngazidja [Grande Comore], 43,000), Mutsamudu (Nzwani [Anjouan], 24,000), Fomboni (Mwali [Mohéli], 13,000).

Official Languages: Arabic, French. (A majority of the population speaks Comorian, a mixture of Arabic and Swahili.)

Monetary Unit: Comoros Franc (official rate December 1, 2009: 325.94 francs = $1US). Previously pegged to the French franc, the Comoros franc is now permanently pegged to the euro at 491.968 francs = 1 euro.

President of the Union: Ahmed Abdallah Mohamed SAMBI (Nzwani); elected in Union-wide runoff election on May 14, 2006, and inaugurated for a four-year term on May 26 in succession to Col. Assoumani AZALI (Ngazidja). (President Sambi's term was extended until 2011 by controversial constitutional revision in May 2009.)

Vice Presidents of the Union: Ikililou DHOININE (Mwali) and Idi NADHOIM (Ngazidja); elected on May 14, 2006, and inaugurated on May 26 for a term concurrent with that of the president, succeeding Rachid Ben MASSOUNDI (Mwali) and Mohamed Caabi El YACHROUTU (Nzwani).

President (Governor) of Mwali (Mohéli): Mohamed Ali SAÏD; directly elected in runoff balloting on June 24, 2007, and inaugurated for a five-year term on July 1 in succession to Mohamed Saïd FAZUL. (Term shortened by one year in 2009.)

President (Governor) of Ngazidja (Grande Comore): Mohamed ABDOULOIHABI; directly elected in runoff balloting on June 24, 2007, and inaugurated for a five-year term on June 30 in succession to Abdou Soule ELBAK. (Term shortened by one year in 2009.)

President (Governor) of Nzwani (Anjouan): Moussa TOYBOU; directly elected in runoff balloting on June 29, 2008, and inaugurated for a five-year term (shortened by two years in 2009) on July 5. (Col. Mohamed BACAR, who had controversially declared himself reelected as president in June 2007, had been deposed by Union military forces [supported by soldiers from the African Union] on March 25, 2008. Lailizamane Abdou CHEIKH, theretofore the president of the appeals court on Nzwani, had served as interim president [as appointed by Union President Sambi] prior to Toybou's inauguration.)

THE COUNTRY

Located in the Indian Ocean between Madagascar and the eastern coast of Africa, the Union of the Comoros consists of three main islands: Mwali (Mohéli); Ngazidja (Grande Comore), site of the capital, Moroni; and Nzwani (Anjouan). A fourth component of the archipelago, Mahoré (Mayotte), is claimed as national territory but remains under French administration (see France: Related Territories). The indigenous inhabitants in the Comoros derive from a mixture of Arab, Malagasy, and African strains. Islam is the state religion (as codified in the May 2009 constitutional revision); most Muslims are Sunnis.

Volcanic in origin, the islands are mountainous, with a climate that is tropical during the rainy season and more temperate during the dry season. There are no significant mineral resources, and soil conditions are poor on the more populous islands of Nzwani and Ngazidja. Economically, the islands have long suffered from an overemphasis on the production of a few export crops, such as vanilla, cloves, olives, and perfume essences—the latter shipped primarily to France—and an insufficient cultivation of food, particularly rice, needed for local consumption. Most of the population is engaged in subsistence agriculture, and manufacturing is practically nonexistent. The government remains highly dependent on foreign assistance to cover administrative and developmental expenses as well as trade deficits. Annual per capita income is currently estimated at approximately $1,150, and more than half of the people live below the poverty line. Remittances

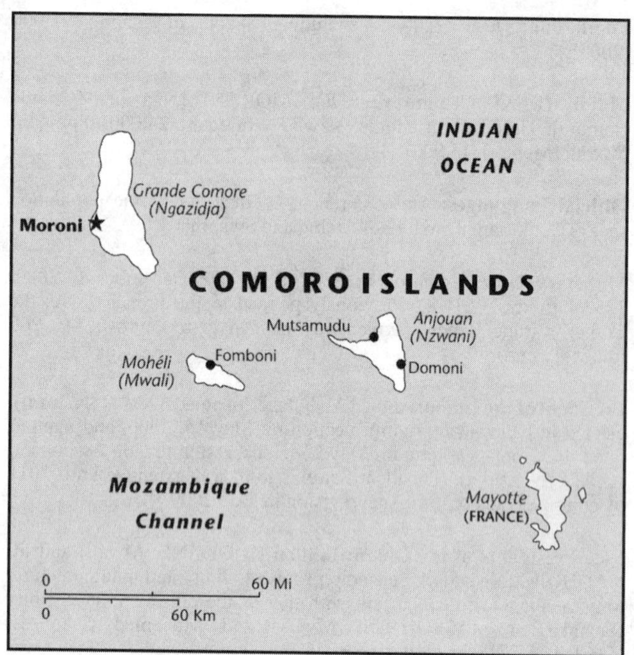

from Comorans living abroad (particularly on Mayotte) contribute significantly to the economy.

Development has been severely hampered since independence in 1975 by some 20 coups or coup attempts, sustained interisland conflict, and widespread corruption. Per-capita annual income declined in the 1990s, while real GDP growth was marginal throughout most of the decade before falling by 1.1 percent in 2000 in the wake of severe political uncertainty following a bloodless military coup in April 1999. The turmoil also depressed tourism, impeded government economic plans, and precipitated a sharp decline in donor support. However, the international community pledged substantial aid in 2002 in response to negotiations that had led to the establishment of the Union of the Comoros (see Political background, below), which proponents hoped would, among other things, resolve separatist pressures on Nzwani. The World Bank and the European Union (EU) coordinated the "Friends of Comoros" to support the transition. However, the International Monetary Fund (IMF) rejected a request from the Comoros for additional assistance, citing continued power-sharing contention between the island governments and the Union government. GDP growth averaged only 2.5 percent annually in 2001–2006 and fell to approximately 0.5 percent in 2007, the IMF citing the small size of local markets, high transportation costs, and continued interisland tensions as factors in the deterioration.

After nearly a year of political conflict between the Union government and the self-proclaimed government on Nzwani ended with a Union military victory in March 2008, the Union government, IMF, and development banks expressed hope that focus could return to negotiations regarding badly needed debt cancellation or rescheduling. The Union government also pledged to combat deep-rooted poverty and other social problems, a glimmer of hope possibly being presented by the recent issuance of oil exploration contracts and pledges from foreign investors to revamp a number of resorts. However, growth remained stagnant in 2008 (despite a modest increase in tourism), while rising food and fuel prices pushed inflation to more than 6 percent. The IMF in 2009 described the government's fiscal efforts as "broadly satisfactory" and indicated that current negotiations regarding additional structural reform were expected to lead to additional support from the Fund and other lenders, particularly for debt relief and poverty reduction.

GOVERNMENT AND POLITICS

Political background. Ruled for centuries by Arab sultans and first visited by Europeans in the 16th century, the Comoro archipelago came under French rule in the 19th century. Mayotte became a French protectorate in 1843, while Anjouan, Grande Comore, and Mohéli were added in 1886. In 1912 the islands were joined administratively with Madagascar, from which they were governed until after World War II. Because of the lengthy period of indirect rule, the Comoros suffered comparative neglect, as contrasted with the nearby island of Réunion, which became an overseas French department in 1946.

In the wake of a 1968 student strike that was suppressed by French police and troops, France agreed to permit the formation of legal political parties in the archipelago. In December 1972, 34 of the 39 seats in the Comoran Chamber of Deputies were claimed by a coalition of proindependence parties: the Democratic Rally of the Comoran People, led by Prince Saïd Mohamed JAFFAR; the Party for the Evolution of the Comoros, which was linked to the Tanzanian-based National Liberation Movement of the Comoros; and the Democratic Union of the Comoros, led by Ahmed ABDALLAH Abderemane. The other five seats were won by the anti-independence Popular Movement of Mahoré, headed by Marcel HENRY. As a result of the election, the chamber named Abdallah president of the government, succeeding Prince Saïd IBRAHIM, who had served as coleader with Ali SOILIH of the People's Party (*Umma-Mranda*), which had campaigned for a more gradual movement toward independence. The new government immediately began negotiations with France, and an agreement was reached in July 1973 providing for a five-year transition period during which France would retain responsibility for defense, foreign affairs, and currency. The only unresolved issue was the status of Mayotte, whose inhabitants remained strongly opposed to separation from France.

In a Comoran referendum held December 22, 1974, 95 percent of participating voters favored independence, despite a negative vote from Mayotte, where 25 percent of the registered electorate abstained. On July 6, 1975, a unilateral declaration of independence was approved by the territorial Chamber of Deputies, which designated Abdallah as head of state and prime minister. The action was timed to preempt the passage of legislation by the French National Assembly calling for an island-by-island referendum on a Comoran constitution—a procedure designed to allow Mayotte to remain under French jurisdiction. Having announced his intention to sever economic as well as political ties with France, the increasingly dictatorial Abdallah (who was visiting Anjouan at the time) was ousted on August 3 in a coup led by Ali Soilih and supported by a National United Front of several parties. On August 10 governmental power was vested in a 12-member National Executive Council headed by Prince Jaffar, who was appointed president and prime minister. In September, following an armed invasion of Anjouan by forces under Soilih, Abdallah surrendered. He was subsequently exiled.

At a joint meeting of the National Executive Council and the National Council of the Revolution on January 2, 1976, Soilih was named to replace Jaffar as head of state, and the National Council of the Revolution was redesignated as the National Institutional Council. The presidency was also divorced from the premiership, and on January 6 Abdellahi MOHAMED was named to the latter post.

As president, Soilih encountered substantial resistance in attempting to mount a Chinese-style program designed to "abolish feudalism." During a month-long *"Période Noire"* in 1977, he dismissed civil servants, temporarily dismantled the regular governmental machinery, and vested the "people's power" in a 16-member National People's Committee of recent secondary-school graduates. The "revolution" also included establishment of people's committees at island, district, and local levels, despite numerous skirmishes between people's militia forces and Islamic traditionalists. Between April 1976 and January 1978, at least three unsuccessful countercoups against the regime were mounted.

During the night of May 12–13, 1978, President Soilih was ousted by a group of about 50 mercenaries under the command of Col. Bob DENARD (the alias of Gilbert BOURGEAUD), a Frenchman previously involved in rebellions elsewhere in Africa and southern Arabia. The successful coup resulted in the return of Ahmed Abdallah, who joined Mohamed AHMED as copresidents of a Political-Military Directorate that also included Denard. It was subsequently reported that Soilih had been killed on May 29 in an attempt to escape from house arrest. An exclusive "political directorate" was announced on July 22 in view of the "calm" that had resulted from a decision to return to traditional Islamic principles.

Copresident Ahmed resigned on October 3, 1978, following the approval by referendum two days earlier of a new constitution that had proclaimed the establishment of the Federal Islamic Republic of the Comoros. Abdallah was thus enabled to stand as the sole candidate in presidential balloting held October 22. Following a legislative election that concluded on December 15, Salim Ben ALI was designated prime minister, a post he continued to hold until he was dismissed by the president on January 25, 1982. Ali's successor, Foreign Minister Ali MROUDJAE, was appointed on February 8, with the rest of the cabinet being named a week later. President Abdallah was unopposed in his bid for reelection to a second six-year term on September 30, 1984.

Amid evidence of serious dissent within the government, President Abdallah, following his reelection in 1984, secured a number of constitutional amendments that abolished the position of prime minister and reduced the powers of the Federal Assembly. These actions prompted a coup attempt by junior members of the presidential guard on March 8, 1985, while the chief executive was on a private visit to Paris. Subsequently, the Democratic Front, a Paris-based opposition group, was charged with complicity in the revolt. Many of the domestic supporters of the coup attempt were sentenced to life imprisonment in early November, although some were granted presidential amnesty at the end of the year.

At legislative balloting on March 22, 1987 (denounced as manifestly fraudulent by regime opponents), the entire slate of 42 candidates presented by President Abdallah was declared elected. Ostensibly open to any citizen wishing to compete as an independent, polls on two of the islands (Anjouan and Mohéli) involved only presidential nominees. By contrast, opposition candidates were advanced in 20 constituencies on Grande Comore. In November the president survived another coup attempt with the assistance of Colonel Denard who, although officially retired, had remained in control of the country's small security force.

On November 4, 1989, an ostensible 92 percent of the participants in a national referendum approved a constitutional amendment permitting Abdallah to seek a third term. However, on November 27 Abdallah was assassinated in a reported clash between the Presidential Guard and forces loyal to a former army commander, Ahmed MOHAMED. (Subsequent evidence suggested that Abdallah had been killed by his own troops on the order of Colonel Denard.) Abdallah was succeeded on an interim basis by the president of the Supreme Court, Saïd Mohamed DJOHAR, who was elected to a regular six-year term on March 4 and 11, 1990, in the country's first contested presidential balloting since independence. Three months earlier, Denard, who denied complicity in the Abdallah assassination, was deported (in the company of some 30 other mercenaries) to South Africa, with the Presidential Guard being supplanted by a contingent of French paratroopers. The latter were credited with thwarting a coup attempt by four mercenaries allegedly linked to Mohamed TAKI Abdoulkarim, the runner-up in the March presidential poll, on the weekend of August 18–19.

On August 3, 1991, the new president of the Supreme Court, Ibrahim Ahmed HALIDI, failed in an attempt to oust President Djohar by judicial impeachment and was arrested, along with a number of colleagues. Ten days later, amid mounting social unrest, public demonstrations were banned, and on August 27 a major cabinet shakeup was announced, from which the president's own party, the Comoran Union for Progress (*Union Comorienne pour le Progrès*—UCP/*Udzima*), dissociated itself.

In October 1991 five domestic participants in an Opposition Union accepted an invitation from the exiled Mohamed Taki to meet in Paris to discuss the formation of an interim government of national union and the scheduling of a National Conference. Subsequently, Taki and his associates met with Djohar in Paris, and on November 25 Taki and Djohar returned together to Moroni. Halidi and the other detainees from the failed impeachment effort in August were released on December 2, and on December 17 President Djohar announced his willingness to enter into a pact of reconciliation with his opponents, on condition that they not challenge the legitimacy of his incumbency or attempt to destabilize the regime. On December 31, upon endorsement of the pact by all of the recognized parties, Djohar dissolved the existing government. On January 6, 1992, he appointed a broadly based nine-member successor, with Taki described somewhat vaguely as "coordinator of government action."

A long-sought National Conference, encompassing nearly two dozen parties, met January 24–April 8, 1992, and approved the draft of a new constitution. On May 8 President Djohar announced the formation of a new cabinet headed by Taki, and the new constitution was endorsed by a 74 percent majority in a national referendum on June 7. Although Taki's cabinet had been scheduled to serve until the next election, the president dismissed the government on July 4 following Taki's designation of a former mercenary as the country's international investment adviser. A new transitional administration was named with no ministerial head.

On September 26, 1992, while President Djohar was visiting Paris, a group of some 30 officers from the Defense Forces mounted a coup attempt, which was put down the following day. Additional clashes occurred on October 13 and 21, with the president, at opposition insistence, announcing a third postponement of the next legislative poll to November 8. In first-round balloting that had been further deferred until November 22, only 4 of 42 seats were filled outright. A second round on November 29 was scarcely more conclusive, with none of the 22 participating groups winning a majority of seats.

The vacant post of prime minister was filled on January 1, 1993, with the appointment of Ibrahim Abderemane HALIDI (not related to Ibrahim Ahmed Halidi), who announced the appointment of a 12-member cabinet five days later. A period of extreme instability ensued. On February 25 the president ordered an extensive cabinet reshuffle, and on May 19 Prime Minister Halidi was himself ousted by a parliamentary vote of no confidence for his "manifest inability to rally support" and the "inability of the government to cope with social problems." On May 25 the president called upon Saïd Ali MOHAMED to form a new government, which, however, drew support from only 13 of the 42 legislators. Thus, to forestall another no-confidence vote, the president on June 18 dissolved the assembly. Despite a declaration of support for Mohamed at the time of dissolution, President Djohar dismissed Mohamed the following day, naming a former adviser, Ahmed Ben Cheikh ATTOUMANE, as the new prime minister.

Although the constitution called for legislative balloting within 40 days of the assembly's dissolution, a series of postponements delayed the poll until mid-December 1993. In the wake of the first cancellation, the president issued a decree ousting Electoral Commission members deemed hostile to the administration. A second decree established new constituency boundaries and revoked a requirement that ministers resign before standing for election. Both were branded as unconstitutional, and in early November, President Djohar, in a concession to the opposition, removed the incumbent chair of the Electoral Commission.

Despite the blatant gerrymandering and other irregularities, all four individuals elected in first-round legislative balloting on December 12, 1993, were from the opposition, with the second round on December 20 characterized in one report as a "veritable masquerade." Thus, after the opposition had appeared to have swept the entire island of Anjouan, the voting was declared "null and void." The interior ministry then pronounced that government candidates had triumphed on Anjouan, while on Mohéli the secretary general of the presidency, whose candidacy had been formally invalidated in the first round, was permitted to contest the second. Understandably, the opposition called for cancellation of the second-round results, failing which it announced that it would participate in no further electoral activity and would take up no seats in the Federal Assembly.

On January 2, 1994, President Djohar named Mohamed Abdou MADI, secretary general of the recently launched Rally for Democracy and Renewal (*Rassemblement pour la Démocratie et le Renouveau*—RDR), to head a new government of regime supporters. In the wake of a scandal following attempted privatization of the national air carrier, *Air Comores*, coupled with a prolonged strike by schoolteachers and hospital workers, Prime Minister Madi was dismissed on October 13 and replaced by a relatively obscure education official, Halifa HOUMADI. In the ninth government change in 40 months, Houmadi was himself replaced on April 29, 1995, by former finance minister Mohamed Caabi El YACHROUTU.

The last four months of 1995 were marked by a degree of instability that was remarkable even by Comoran standards. On the night of September 27–28, Colonel Denard reappeared as the leader of some 30 mercenaries who, with local support, seized President Djohar and established a "military committee of transition" headed by a little-known army captain, Ayouba COMBO. Meanwhile, Prime Minister Yachroutu, who had sought refuge in the French embassy, called on France to intervene. On October 3 Combo announced that he was withdrawing in favor of Mohamed Taki Abdoulkarim and Prince Saïd Ali KEMAL as civilian joint presidents. The next day 900 French troops landed and quickly rounded up the mercenaries. (Paris courts in 2006 and 2007 found Denard and others guilty of various charges in connection with the 1995 coup attempt, although all received suspended sentences, fueling speculation that some French intelligence sectors may have been aware of Denard's plans in advance. Denard died in October 2007.) The French troops did not, however, reinstate the 80-year-old Djohar, who was flown to the nearby French island of

Réunion, with Yachroutu proclaiming himself "interim president in accordance with the constitution." Yachroutu thereupon named a new Government of National Unity, which Djohar repudiated from Réunion by announcing a rival government headed by former prime minister Saïd Ali Mohamed.

On December 3, 1995, a somewhat diverse group of Comoran political leaders assembled in Paris in an effort to persuade Yachroutu to cancel a snap presidential election that he had scheduled for January 21, 1996. Yachroutu responded by calling for two-stage balloting on January 28 and February 7, arguing that although the dates fell within the month-long Muslim feast of Ramadan, postponement would mean loss of Comoran consideration in the current cycle of World Bank/IMF structural-adjustment programming. Subsequently, however, he relented and postponed the voting to March 6 and 16. He also agreed to send representatives to a conference sponsored by the Organization of African Unity (OAU, subsequently the African Union—AU) in Madagascar concerning Djohar's status. The gathering yielded agreement on January 23, 1996, that Djohar would return to Moroni as president but would cease to have any executive authority forthwith and would accept a new electoral code that effectively barred him from seeking reelection by specifying an obligatory 40–70 age range for a presidential candidate. With some 50 French troops remaining on station to guarantee order, presidential balloting accordingly went ahead on March 6 and 16, with 15 candidates contesting the first round. Of these, Mohamed Taki Abdulkarim of the National Union for Democracy in the Comoros (*Union National pour la Démocratie aux Comores*—UNDC) headed the first round with 21.3 percent of the vote. He secured a 64.3 percent second-round victory over Abbas DJOUSSOUF, leader of the Movement for Democracy and Progress, standing as candidate of the Forum for National Recovery (*Forum pour le Redressement National*—FRN).

Sworn in on March 25, 1996, President Taki assigned the premiership to Tadjidine Ben Saïd MASSONDE (UCP/*Udzima*), who named a government on March 28 that included several of the candidates eliminated in the recent first round of presidential balloting. On April 11 President Taki dissolved the assembly and announced that new balloting would take place on October 6 (notwithstanding the constitutional requirement of elections within 40 days of dissolution), adding that a referendum on a new constitution would be held before the end of June (later rescheduled to October). In August, Taki formally proposed the establishment of a single "presidential" party, with opposition forces grouped into two parties. Among the critics of the proposal were two government parties, both of whom subsequently lost their cabinet postings. On October 6 the propresidential National Rally for Development (*Rassemblement National pour le Développement*—RND) was formed, Taki confidante Ali Bazi SELIM being named to head the group.

On October 20, 1996, 85 percent of those voting in a national referendum approved a new constitution that increased presidential powers and restricted political party formations. The new charter had been championed by Taki and the RND, but its controversial amendments had elicited opposition condemnation and calls for a boycott of the referendum. Thereafter, relations between the administration and opposition continued to deteriorate, and on November 10, 1996, the opposition announced that it would boycott the upcoming legislative elections after the government refused to establish an independent electoral commission. Consequently, in balloting on December 1 and 8, RND candidates faced little competition, capturing an overwhelming majority of the assembly seats being contested, with the remaining seats being secured by the Islamic National Front for Justice (*Front National pour la Justice*—FNJ) and an independent candidate. On December 27 Ahmed ABDOU, a former assistant to ex-president Abdallah, was named prime minister, replacing Massonde, who had resigned on December 11.

Antigovernment strikes and violent demonstrations erupted in early 1997, sparked by the Taki administration's failure to fulfill an earlier pledge to pay civil-servant salary arrears. On Anjouan, where the government's increasing inability to provide basic services had already fueled simmering secessionist emotions, the unrest quickly gained intensity. In mid-March deadly clashes erupted between strikers and government security forces following the arrest of Abdou ZAKARIA, the leader of the Democratic Front Party (*Parti du Front Démocratique*—PFD). Subsequently, amid reports that the demonstrators were in open rebellion, the government dismissed the Anjouan governor.

Following the arrest of secessionist leader Abdallah IBRAHIM and the banning of antigovernment parties in late July 1997, full-scale rioting broke out in the Anjouan capital of Mutsamudu. Thereafter, separatist militants affiliated with the Anjouan People's Movement (*Mouvement du Peuple d'Anjouan*—MPA) gained control over key island facilities. On August 3 the MPA declared independence from the Comoros government and announced its intention to petition France for a return to overseas territory status. On August 5 the MPA named Ibrahim, who had been released from detention, president of the breakaway state and head of a 12-member cabinet. Meanwhile, separatists on Mohéli also declared their independence. For its part, France rebuffed the entreaties from the secessionists and urged them to respect Comoros' "territorial integrity." Subsequently, under pressure from the OAU, which had also refused to recognize the declaration of independence, the MPA agreed to participate in reconciliation talks with the Taki administration in Ethiopia in September.

On September 3, 1997, seaborne government forces attempting to regain control of Anjouan suffered heavy casualties while being repelled by separatist fighters, who also took dozens of the "invaders" captive. The government's ill-fated offensive, which it had at first declared a success, drew sharp OAU criticism, and reconciliation talks were indefinitely postponed. On September 8 Ibrahim announced the creation of the "State of Anjouan" and declared that he would rule by decree. Meanwhile, amid rumors in Moroni of an impending military coup, President Taki dissolved the Abdou government and assumed absolute power on September 9. On September 13 Taki formed a State Transition Committee, an advisory body that included three representatives from Anjouan and two from Mohéli.

On October 26, 1997, secessionist officials in Anjouan organized a referendum on independence that reportedly received a 99 percent affirmative vote. Two days later Ibrahim was formally appointed head of the provisional government of Nzwani (the island's traditional name having been readopted by the secessionists) and was charged with drafting a constitution and preparing for elections. Such efforts were delayed, however, when in mid-November Ibrahim's provisional government again succumbed to OAU pressure and agreed to attend talks with the Taki administration in Ethiopia in December. On December 7 Taki appointed Nourdine BOURHANE, a former cabinet official with ties to Nzwani, to head a government that included a number of members of the State Transition Committee.

From December 10 to 14, 1997, representatives of the Taki government and secessionist representatives from Nzwani and Mwali met in Ethiopia for OAU-sponsored "reconciliation" talks, which failed to yield any major breakthroughs. In mid-February 1998 fighting erupted in Nzwani between Ibrahim's forces and a dissident faction led by Mohamed Abdou MADI, who, Ibrahim claimed, had the backing of the OAU. Unable to dislodge Ibrahim, Madi was forced to flee, and a number of his fighters were arrested.

At a constitutional referendum on February 25, 1998, voters in Nzwani reportedly approved a basic document that called for the revocation of all Comoran laws. Thereafter, despite OAU calls for the secessionists to delay further provocations, Ibrahim named CHAMASSI Ben Saïd Omar as prime minister of Nzwani in March. However, Ibrahim and his new prime minister subsequently clashed, and in July Chamassi and his supporters reportedly attempted to oust Ibrahim. Fighting among the various factions on Nzwani, including Madi's reorganized militants, continued through the end of 1998.

Following violent antigovernment rioting by civil servants in Moroni in mid-May 1998, Taki dismissed the Bourhane government on May 29. The following day he named a cabinet that did not include a prime minister.

On November 5, 1998, President Taki died of a heart attack. The following day former prime minister Tadjidine Ben Saïd Massonde assumed the presidency as constitutionally mandated because of his position as president of the High Council of the Republic (the country's constitutional court). On November 22 Massonde named the FRN's Abbas Djoussouf to head an interim government. Djoussouf's appointment and subsequent formation of an FRN-dominated (with six ministers) cabinet was denounced by the RND, whose governmental representation had fallen to four posts. Meanwhile, Massonde called for a loosening of economic sanctions against the secessionists on Nzwani and appealed to their leaders to participate in an internationally sponsored, interisland conference. However, plans for the meeting were derailed by the outbreak of fierce fighting on Nzwani in December 1998. Subsequently, Massonde announced that presidential elections would be postponed until the secessionist crisis was resolved, and in February 1999 the High Court approved the extension of his mandate.

At an OAU-mediated conference in Madagascar on April 19–25, 1999, representatives from Ngazidja, Nzwani, and Mwali tentatively reached agreement on a pact that would have granted the latter two increased autonomy within the republic (to be restyled the Union of Comoran Islands). General elections consequently were scheduled for April 2000. The delegation from Nzwani departed, however, without signing the accord, and violent demonstrations subsequently erupted on Ngazidja, where protesters reportedly chanted anti-Nzwani slogans and attacked people who had been born on Nzwani. On April 30, Armed Forces Chief of Staff Col. Assoumani AZALI announced that, in an effort to stem the unrest, the military had assumed control of the country, ousted the president and government, and suspended the constitution, legislature, and judiciary.

Among Colonel Azali's first acts upon seizing power was to announce his intention to honor the 1999 Madagascar accord, including its provisions for presidential and legislative elections in 2000. Nevertheless, the coup was widely condemned by the international community, with the criticism from the OAU and France being among the more strident.

Facing continued international isolation, on December 7, 1999, Colonel Azali announced the appointment of Bianrifi TARMIDI as prime minister to head a new government, which Azali hoped would be viewed more positively because of the inclusion of several political parties. Meanwhile, events continued to percolate on Nzwani, where yet another referendum on January 23, 2000, endorsed independence by a reported vote of 95 percent. In response, the OAU on February 1 imposed economic sanctions on the separatists.

In April 2000 several demonstrations protested the passing without action on the one-year deadline for Azali's promised withdrawal from power. Also to protest the delay, Hachim Saïd HACHIM resigned his post as chair of the National Salvation Coordination (*Coordination de Salut National*—CSN), a grouping of former party figures and civic leaders that had been formed to support Azali. For his part, Azali claimed he had been unable to act as expected due to the intransigence of the leaders of Nzwani. However, in August, Azali and Lt. Col. Saïd ABEID Abdéréman reached agreement on a preliminary plan for a new federal entity that would provide each island with substantially expanded autonomy. Although the OAU lambasted the accord as contrary to the guidelines established in Madagascar in 1999, the agreement appeared to represent the best hope for a negotiated settlement to date, despite the at times violent opposition of hard-line separatists on Nzwani.

On May 6, 2000, Colonel Azali was sworn in as president, and he appointed a cabinet-like state council with six ministers from Ngazidja, four from Mwali, and two from Nzwani, promising to turn over the reins of authority to a civilian government within one year. He also introduced a new "constitutional charter" authorizing himself to rule by decree (in conjunction with a "state committee") while negotiations continued toward the adoption of a new constitution. Meanwhile, Abeid, the former French officer who had "elbowed out" Ibrahim for dominance on Nzwani, announced the formation of a government on that island and indicated that Nzwani would not adhere to the Madagascar agreement, prompting the OAU to threaten sanctions and even military intervention.

On November 29, 2000, President Azali named Hamada Madi BOLERO, one of his chief negotiators with Nzwani, to replace Prime Minister Tamadi. Bolero formed a new government on December 10, although he was unable to persuade opposition parties to join.

On February 17, 2001, a potentially historic agreement was reached in Fomboni, the capital of Mwali, by members of the military junta, the former separatists on Nzwani (led by Colonel Abeid), delegates from Mwali, and representatives from political parties and civic organizations. Although Colonel Abeid was overthrown in a bloodless coup in Nzwani in August, his successor, Maj. Mohamed BACAR, quickly signaled his support for the proposed new federal system. A national referendum on a new constitution establishing a Union of the Comoros was held on December 23, voters responding with a reported 76 percent "yes" vote.

On January 17, 2002, President Azali nominated Prime Minister Bolero to head a new transitional government (installed on January 20) to prepare for presidential elections for the Union as well as for each island. Azali on January 21 resigned as president, as he was constitutionally required to do to compete in the upcoming balloting for the presidency of the Union. The primary was held March 17 on Ngazidja, with Azali finishing first with 39.8 percent of the vote, followed by Mahamoud MRADABI with 15.7 percent. Also on March 17, voters on Mwali and Nzwani approved the requisite new local constitutions. However, the constitutional referendum on Ngazidja failed, prompting a rerun (this time successful) on April 9.

Although the top three finishers in the March 17, 2002, primary on Ngazidja were authorized to compete in the Union-wide balloting for president of the Union on April 14, Azali ultimately ran unopposed when the other two candidates boycotted the poll to protest what they considered to be "anomalies" in the first round and ongoing questions about the integrity of electoral rolls. The national election commission ruled the results of April 14 to be void in view of the boycott, but the commission was dissolved for "incompetence" on April 23 by the follow-up committee charged with overseeing implementation of the 2001 Fomboni Agreement. A special commission was subsequently established to review the matter, and Azali's victory was confirmed on May 8. Azali was sworn in as president of the Union on May 26, and on June 5 he announced his Union cabinet, which comprised his two vice presidents and only three other members. Meanwhile, separate balloting on each of the islands had resulted in Bacar's election as president of Nzwani, the selection of Mohamed Saïd FAZUL as president of Mwali, and a presidential victory on Ngazidja for Abdou Soule ELBAK, an outspoken critic of Azali.

Elections for the proposed island and Union assemblies were postponed indefinitely in March 2003 in the wake of ongoing conflict over power-sharing issues and an apparent coup plot against Azali emanating from Ngazidja. However, at a meeting sponsored by the AU in Pretoria, South Africa, in August, representatives of the island and Union governments appeared to settle several contentious issues, including how tax revenues would be shared. The accord also provided for each island to have its own police force, while the army would remain under Union control. Azali and the three island presidents ratified the agreement on December 20 and established a national committee to oversee its implementation.

Balloting for the three island assemblies was held on March 14 and 21, 2004. The Azali, pro-Union camp fared poorly in the face of coordinated opposition efforts. Pro-Bacar candidates won 20 of 25 seats on Nzwani, pro-Elbak candidates won 14 of 20 seats on Ngazidja, and pro-Fazul candidates won 9 of 10 seats on Mwali. The opposition (now formally coalesced as the Camp of the Autonomous Islands [*Camp des Îles Autonomes*—CdIA]) also dominated the April 18 and 25 balloting for the Assembly of the Union, securing 12 directly elected seats compared to 6 for the pro-Azali Convention for the Renewal of the Comoros (*Convention pour le Renouveau des Comores*—CRC). Because of its control of the island assemblies, the CdIA also gained all 15 of the indirectly elected seats in the Assembly of the Union.

On July 13, 2004, President Azali formed a new Union cabinet in which CRC members held a majority of the portfolios. However, the "opposition" was given three seats—one from Nzwani, one from Mwali, and one from the Islands Fraternity and Unity Party. Elbak declined an invitation to appoint a cabinet member from Ngazidja, citing Azali's perceived foot-dragging in devolving power to the islands. Azali announced another cabinet reshuffle in early July 2005.

In primary balloting on Nzwani for the president of the Union on April 16, 2006, moderate Islamist leader Ahmed Abdallah Mohamed SAMBI of the FNJ led 13 candidates with 23.7 percent of the vote, followed by two "secular" rivals—Mohamed DJAANFARI (a retired French air force officer) with 13.1 percent and former prime minister Ibrahim Halidi (who had Azali's endorsement) with 10.4 percent. In the nationwide runoff balloting among the three on May 14, Sambi was declared the winner with 58 percent of the vote. He formed a new cabinet on May 27.

In balloting on June 10 and 24, 2007, Mohamed ABDOULOIHABI, a judge described as "close" to Sambi, was elected president of Ngazidja and Mohamed Ali SAÏD, a strong opponent of outgoing president Fazul, was elected president of Mwali. However, the presidential election on Nzwani generated intense turmoil, with Mohamed Bacar declaring himself reelected as president of the island in balloting conducted on June 10 against the orders of the Union government (see Current issues, below, for details). Following nine months of acrimonious efforts to resolve the dispute, Union soldiers supported by AU troops seized control of Nzwani on March 25, 2008, and Bacar fled to Mayotte. Union Vice President Ikililou DHOININE was temporarily placed in charge of governmental affairs on Nzwani by President Sambi, but Sambi on March 31 named Lailizamine Abdou CHEIKH as Nzwani's interim president pending new elections. In second-round balloting on June 29, Sambi's preferred candidate, Moussa TOYBOU (a civil engineer described as new to politics), was elected president of

Nzwani with 52.4 percent of the vote versus 47.6 percent for Mohamed Djaanfari, who had led the first-round balloting.

President Sambi reduced the size of his cabinet (as requested by the IMF in connection with its assistance program) in a December 2008 reshuffle, while the government was revamped again in June 2009 following the controversial constitutional revision that had, among other things, extended Sambi's term until 2011 and prompted the postponement of new balloting for the Assembly of the Union until December. *(See headnote.)*

Constitution and government. The 1996 constitution was suspended by the military junta that assumed power on April 30, 1999, and all state institutions were dissolved. On May 6, 1999, Col. Assoumani Azali, the leader of the junta, proclaimed a new "constitutional charter" with himself as president and head of a State Committee empowered to govern pending the return to civilian government. A progovernment "national congress" in Moroni on August 7, 2000, adopted a "national charter" that extended the authority of the president (as chosen by the military) even further. Among other things, the new document called for the president to appoint a prime minister and envisioned the eventual establishment of a vaguely defined "legislative council."

Following extensive and difficult negotiations among government officials, opposition parties, and representatives of Mwali and Nzwani, a national referendum on December 23, 2001, approved a new federal structure for the renamed Union of the Comoros. (The complete official name of the country had previously been the Federal Islamic Republic of the Comoros.) Autonomy was granted to the three island components of the Union to a much greater degree than in previous constitutions, especially in regard to finances. Meanwhile, the Union government was given responsibility for religion, currency, external relations, defense, nationality issues, and national symbols. New constitutions were also subsequently adopted by referendums on each island, although the division of authority between the island governments and the Union government was insufficiently delineated to prevent the immediate outbreak of confusion, especially on Ngazidja (see Current issues, below).

Under the 2001 constitution the president of the Union served a four-year term, with the office rotating among the islands each term. Two vice presidents, one from each of the islands not holding the presidency, also serve. The president and vice presidents constitute a Council of the Union. A primary election is held on the island scheduled to assume the presidency (Ngazidja was chosen as first in the rotation, to be followed in order by Nzwani and Mwali). The top three vote-getters in the primary earn a place on the ballot in subsequent Union-wide balloting. Each presidential candidate must select two vice-presidential running mates, one from each of the islands that the presidential candidate does not represent, prior to the Union-wide poll. The president is authorized to appoint a prime minister and cabinet, although the new basic law required that all the islands be represented in the federal government. Legislative power was vested in an elected Assembly of the Union (see Legislature, below, for details). The new constitutions for the islands also provided for direct election of their presidents and island assemblies.

Several major constitutional revisions were approved in a controversial referendum on May 17, 2009 (see Current issues, below, for additional information). The presidential term of office was extended from four to five years (ostensibly to permit simultaneous Union and island voting in 2011), while island presidencies were reclassified as governorships. In an additional effort to strengthen the authority of the Union president, he was empowered to dissolve the Assembly of the Union if the legislators were deemed to be "an impediment to national development."

The Union's other prominent institution is the High Council, which serves as a constitutional court and is responsible for validating election results as well as ruling on questions regarding the division of authority between the federal and island governments. Members of the High Council are appointed for six-year terms by the president and vice presidents of the Union, the president of the Assembly of the Union, and the presidents of the island governments. The judiciary is headed by a Supreme Court.

Foreign relations. Following the declaration of independence in July 1975, Comoran foreign relations were dominated by the Mayotte (Mahoré) issue. On November 21, French military personnel resisted an "invasion" by Ali Soilih and an unarmed contingent that attempted to counter the Mahori "secession." At the end of the year, France recognized the sovereignty of the other three islands, but referendums held on Mayotte in February and April 1976 demonstrated a clear preference for designation as a French department. On December 16 the French Senate ratified a measure according the island special standing as a *collectivité territoriale*, with that status being extended on December 6, 1979, for another five years. In October 1981 President Abdallah pressed for French withdrawal during a Paris meeting with President Mitterrand, who, he noted, had in 1975 opposed detachment of Mayotte from the rest of the archipelago. Abdallah repeated the argument during a visit to France in June 1984, the French government responding that a further referendum on the issue would be deferred because the inhabitants of Mayotte were not sufficiently "well informed" on the options open to them. The decision was endorsed by the French National Assembly in a bill approved on December 19, and no subsequent referendum has been held.

On January 20, 1995, a mass demonstration was mounted outside the French embassy in Moroni to protest a decision by French Prime Minister Edouard Balladur to reimpose a requirement that citizens of the Comoros obtain entry visas for travel to Mayotte. Thereafter, Mohamed Taki contested the March 1996 presidential election on a public platform of Islamic traditionalism and moderate nationalism, depicting his main rival as the candidate preferred by the French government. However, once in office Taki confirmed that the existing defense agreement with France not only would be maintained but also would be expanded to cover the external defense of the Comoros and to allow a French military presence on the islands.

In early 1997 French financial aid was suspended pending Moroni's restarting discussions with the IMF and World Bank on the establishment of a structural adjustment program. In 1998 international attention focused on the crisis on Nzwani, France in March rejecting the secessionists' call for the reestablishment of links as "unrealistic." Meanwhile, the OAU, whose mediation efforts were rebuffed by the separatists, also adopted an increasingly hard-line stance against the breakaway movement. (In early December the OAU urged its members to comply with Moroni's call for military intervention to end the violence.)

The OAU and most of the rest of the international community strongly criticized the coup of April 1999, while the OAU continued to pressure the separatists on Nzwani into early 2001 (see Political background, above, for further information). However, most capitals and the OAU/AU ultimately endorsed the political settlement subsequently reached regarding the new constitutional structure for the Comoros. France restored full ties with the Comoros in September 2002 and signed several economic agreements in 2005.

In 2006 and 2007 Iran agreed to assist the Sambi government on several fronts, including security matters, agricultural development, and the payment of salary arrears to civil servants. Concurrently, conservative Pakistanis reportedly established religious schools on several islands, although most analysts agreed that the Comoran population in general did not embrace the highly doctrinaire Islamic schools. Subsequently, Sambi was described as having made the Comoros an "enthusiastic member" of the Arab League.

Tension continued in 2007–2008 between the Comoros and France over the question of illegal immigration from the Comoros to Mayotte. Meanwhile, China's initiative to expand its influence throughout Africa extended to Comoros in the form of financing for a new airport at Moroni and several commercial agreements.

The Sambi administration condemned the March 2009 referendum on Mayotte (in which 95 percent of the voters endorsed the island's eventual upgrade in status to a French Overseas Department) as an "unfriendly act" on the part of France and said it would not recognize the results. In a similar vein, Iranian president Mahmoud Ahmadinejad, who visited the Comoros in February, to, among other things, underscore cooperative efforts in defence, trade, and other sectors, criticized France's "colonialist aims" in Mayotte. (For additional information on events in Mayotte, see France: Related Territories.)

Current issues. Not surprisingly, considering the chaos of recent years, the balloting for president of the Union of the Comoros in the spring of 2002 was highly controversial and, in the opinion of major opposition parties, a "fiasco" that undercut the legitimacy of President Azali's victory. Following Azali's appointment of his new cabinet in June, it also quickly became clear that the Union was facing a potentially fatal institutional crisis involving the failure of the Union and island constitutions to fully delineate the separation of power between the federal and island authorities. Conflict was most apparent on Ngazidja, where that island's president, Abdou Soule Elbak, attempted to make appointments and even occupy office space that Azali considered within the purview of the federal administration.

The contentious island and Union legislative elections in 2004 did little to settle the simmering power-sharing issues, particularly with the anti-Azali, "anti-Union" CdIA winning control of all of the legislatures. Tension also intensified when the pro-Azali camp introduced legislation that would have permitted Azali to run for president of the Union again in 2006. (According to the rotating mechanism codified in the constitution, the next Union president was scheduled to be elected from Nzwani.) Although the proposed revision was withdrawn in the face of public protests, political uncertainty continued to pose a threat to the April 2006 primary election on Nzwani, prompting the AU to send a contingent of peacekeepers and police officers to help ensure peaceful balloting. (Local forces were confined to their barracks.) Surprising those analysts who predicted that the Comoros was not yet ready for a peaceful transfer of power, the April primary and May nationwide balloting proceeded in a generally orderly fashion, the AU characterizing the voting as "free, transparent, and credible." New president Sambi presented himself as a political newcomer devoted to combating corruption, by, among other things, developing an independent judiciary and investigating the perceived widespread "embezzlement" of government funds in recent years. Some observers suggested that Sambi, a Muslim theologian educated in Iran, might promote the installation of an Islamic regime, but he declared that Comorans were currently opposed to such a change and that he would accept public opinion on the matter. A successful businessman, Sambi pledged that his administration's activities would involve "more economics and less politics."

Facing criticism over his perceived foot-dragging regarding power-sharing, President Sambi in September 2006 signed legislation designed to broadly define arrangements between the Union and island governments in regard to the judiciary, security, health care, and the ownership of public companies. However, negotiations on the implementing legislation broke down in December, and island authorities grew increasingly critical of Sambi, who argued that it was "absurd" for a country as small as the Comoro Islands to have four presidents, four legislatures, and four "armies." The latter element proved particularly troublesome in February and May 2007 when Union soldiers clashed with island armed forces on Nzwani, whose president, Mohamed Bacar, argued that each island required extensive armaments to preserve its "security." In light of the turmoil, the Union government, supported by the AU, ordered Bacar to postpone the upcoming presidential elections in Nzwani. However, Bacar snubbed his nose at the directive and declared himself reelected to a second term in balloting conducted on June 10. President Sambi and select AU officials initially suggested that an AU military force might be sent to Nzwani to disarm Bacar's army. However, the AU, noting the "constitutional complexities" of the Comoros and perhaps cognizant of the formidable nature of Bacar's forces, subsequently called for new elections on Nzwani as offering the best hope for a resolution of the impasse. When Bacar refused to schedule new elections, the AU in mid-October imposed economic sanctions on Nzwani and a travel ban on the island's leaders in the hope of convincing Bacar to change his mind.

Mediation efforts aimed at presenting Bacar with an "honorable exit" were declared a failure in February 2008 by the AU, which endorsed military action to settle the conflict. (South Africa strongly objected to the AU's decision, arguing that Bacar had indicated a willingness to conduct new presidential elections.) On March 25 about 400 Union troops and 600 AU forces (primarily from Tanzania and Sudan) launched a campaign that took control of Nzwani within hours in the face of minimal resistance that generated few casualties. (The public on Nzwani was generally perceived as unperturbed by the changeover.) Although France (like the United States) had supported the anti-Bacar initiative and provided logistical support to the Union forces, anti-French riots broke out in Moroni and elsewhere after Bacar fled to Mayotte and then to the French island of Réunion, where a court denied an extradition request from the Comoros. The Union government at midyear also faced public demonstrations against rising food prices, and some analysts suggested that President Sambi would pursue further strengthening of the authority of the Union government in order to facilitate economic development. At the same time, however, concern was voiced in several quarters over Sambi's perceived "authoritarianism," while Mohamed Djaanfari, who narrowly lost the special presidential election in June in Nzwani to Sambi's preferred candidate, alleged that the balloting had been "rigged." (Djaanferi had been supported by the presidents of Ngazidja and Mwali.)

In April 2009 President Sambi announced that a Union-wide referendum would be held in May on a number of proposed constitutional revisions designed to strengthen the authority of the Union president and to harmonize Union and island election schedules. Opposition leaders strongly criticized the short notice of the proposal and called for a boycott of the vote, arguing that Sambi was primarily concerned with remaining in power by extending his term for at least one year (until 2011). The presidents of Ngazidja and Mwali also joined in the protest, expressing concern over the proposed downgrading of their offices from presidencies to governorships and the reduction of their current terms to permit simultaneous Union and island balloting in 2011.

The government reported a 51.8 percent turnout and a 94 percent "yes" vote in the May 17, 2009, referendum on Sambi's proposed constitutional changes, although the opposition (supported by some independent analysts) argued that turnout had been only 15–20 percent. Most Western capitals appeared "cautious" in their reaction to the rapid political developments, although there appeared to be broad agreement that simplification of some kind was needed in the Comoros' complex system of governance. For his part, Sambi within a week of the vote declared its provisions to have become law, despite clear evidence that enforcement could prove difficult, if not impossible. Upon installing a new cabinet in June, the president said he was stressing "competence," not regional or "insular" preferences in his administration, which he instructed to focus on energy and water issues. Sambi also announced that significant foreign investment had been pledged recently for the modernization and expansion of seaports and airports.

POLITICAL PARTIES

In 1979 the Federal Assembly effectively voided an endorsement of pluralism in the 1978 constitution by calling for the establishment of a single-party system, which prevailed until the resanctioning of multiparty activity in December 1989. Under the Djohar presidency, Comoran parties were mostly aligned into progovernment and opposition camps.

The October 1996 constitution included a number of restrictive regulations for political party activity that the Taki administration had been advocating since assuming power the previous March. However, the December 2001 constitution permitted parties to operate without hindrance, provided they respect "national sovereignty, democracy, and territorial integrity."

Some 20 political parties, led by, among others, Houmed Msaidir of the CRC (below), announced plans in late May 2009 to formulate a manifesto based on their opposition to the recent constitutional referendum and the government's decision to delay national legislative balloting. The fledgling bloc also indicated it would attempt to back joint candidates in upcoming election.

National Front for Justice (*Front National pour la Justice*—FNJ). The FNJ is a moderate Islamic party that was founded by Ahmed Abdallah Mohamed Sambi (nicknamed "Ayatollah" because of his theological training in Iran). In December 1996 legislative balloting the FNJ captured its first-ever seats, including one by Sambi.

FNJ members were not immediately linked to the unrest on Anjouan in 1997, and at midyear the group issued a statement saying that it was not a separatist body. However, the FNJ expressed sympathy for critics of government "negligence" and called for establishment of a "proper federal state."

The FNJ eventually joined the government following the coup of April 1999 but withdrew in October 2001 to protest the decision to remove "Islamic" from the name of the country in the constitution being readied for a national referendum in December. Sambi, a prominent businessman in addition to being a popular cleric, was elected president of the Union in 2006, running formally as an independent.

Mohamed ABDOULOIHABI, elected president of Ngazidja in 2007 with 57 percent of the vote in the second round of balloting, was identified in some reports as the candidate of a pro-Sambi **Union Presidential Movement**. In the June 2008 balloting for the president of Nzwani, Sambi actively supported the candidacy of Moussa Toybou, although the FNJ's Bastoine SOULAIMANE was also a candidate.

President Sambi's current formal relationship to the FNJ is unclear. In 2009 several sources referenced a **Movement of Citizens for Justice and Progress** (led by former prime minister Ahmed Abdou) as "Sambi's party."

Leaders: Ahmed ABOUBACAR, Soidiki M'BAPANOZA, Ahmed RACHID.

Convention for the Renewal of the Comoros (*Convention pour le Renouveau des Comores*—CRC). The CRC was launched in September 2002 by members of the Movement for Socialism and Democracy (*Mouvement pour le Socialisme et la Démocratie*—MSD), which had been formed in July 2000 by Abdou SOEFOU after he and his supporters were expelled from the FDC (below) for supporting President Azali following the April 1999 coup. The CRC was described as an extension of the National Salvation Coordination that had been formed following the coup. The CRC was established to provide Azali with a party prior to the elections for island and Union assemblies.

The CRC fractionalized in its efforts to present a candidate for the 2006 Union presidential elections. One group, led by former prime minister Mohamed Abdou Madi (who had sought the CRC nomination), reportedly backed Union Vice President Mohamed Caabi El Yachroutu, while Soefou and Azali supported Ibrahim Halidi of the MPC (below). El Yachroutu secured 9.56 percent of the vote in the presidential primary. Soefou was replaced as the CRC secretary general in early 2007 in the wake of a financial scandal. CRC Secretary General Houmed Msaidie won 7.2 percent of the vote in the June 2007 presidential balloting on Ngazidja.

Leaders: Col. Assoumani AZALI (Former President of the Union of the Comoros), Houmed MSAIDIE (Secretary General).

Movement for the Comoros (*Mouvement pour les Comores*—MPC). Formed in 1997 by Saïd Hilali, an adviser to President Mohamed Taki Abdoulkarim, the MPC stressed "national unity" under a federal government. Ibrahim Halidi, the MPC's secretary general, finished third in the Union's April 2006 presidential primary, having secured the endorsement of President Azali's faction of the CRC as well as the Chuma and Djawabu parties (see below). Among other things, Halidi, who had served briefly as prime minister in 1993, promised greater "friendship" with France if elected.

Leaders: Ibrahim Abderemane HALIDI (Secretary General and 2006 candidate for president of the Union), Saïd HILALI.

Rally for a Development Initiative with an Enlightened Youth (*Rassemblement pour une Initiative de Développement avec une Jeunesse Avertie*—RIDJA). Launched in April 2005 by Saïd Larifou, a prominent lawyer who had led antigovernment protests in 2003, RIDJA was a vocal opponent of efforts to rewrite the constitution to permit President Azali to run for another term. The RIDJA candidate, Chadhouli Abdou, finished seventh in the Union's 2006 presidential primary with 3.12 percent of the vote. Larifou finished second in the second round of presidential balloting in Ngazidja in 2007 with 43 percent of the vote.

Larifou urged a boycott of the May 2009 constitutional referendum and subsequently accused the government of using threats and intimidation to influence the voting and of releasing "false results."

Leaders: Saïd LARIFOU (Chair), Chadhouli ABDOU (2006 candidate for president of the Union), Abdou SOIMADOU.

Djawabu Party. This grouping promotes the policies espoused by the administration of former president Soilih (see Political background, above). Its candidate, Youssouf Saïd Soilih, won 6.7 percent of the vote in the 2002 primary for president of the Union. In 2006 the party supported Ibrahim Halidi of the MPC in his campaign for president of the Union. Saïd won only 1.8 percent of the vote in the first round of presidential balloting in Ngazidja in June 2007.

Leader: Youssouf SAÏD Soilih.

Camp of the Autonomous Islands (*Camp des Îles Autonomes*—CdIA). Launched by the five parties below and other smaller groups, the CdIA campaigned for the island and assembly elections in 2004 on a platform calling for greater autonomy for the islands and support for the three island presidents. On the island of Ngazidja, the coalition was commonly referenced as Autonomy (*Mdjidjengo*).

The CdIA dominated the 2004 balloting for the Assembly of the Union, capturing 12 of the 18 directly elected seats and all of the 15 indirectly elected seats. However, references to the CdIA subsequently declined significantly, suggesting that its mission had been purely electoral. Components of the CdIA endorsed various candidates in the April 2006 primary election for president of the Union, although the three island presidents endorsed Ahmed Abdallah Mohamed Sambi in the May final balloting.

Movement for Democracy and Progress (*Mouvement pour la Démocratie et le Progrès*—MDP). The MDP, also styled the Popular Democratic Movement (*Mouvement Démocratique Populaire*), is a Moroni-based formation that campaigned in favor of the 1992 constitution. It later became the leading element of an anti-Djohar alliance called the Forum for National Recovery (*Forum pour le Redressement National*—FRN), of which MDP leader Abbas Djoussouf was the principal spokesperson.

The FRN was launched in January 1994 by opposition parties that had presented joint lists in the December 1993 elections. President Djohar's eventual agreement to a transfer of power served to relax FRN discipline, in that a majority of its components put up candidates for the March 1996 presidential contest in their own right. Following the 1996 election, parties that had supported the failed candidacy of Djoussouf reorganized under the FRN rubric. In October the group was bolstered by the addition of Chuma (below) and the Forces for Republican Action (*Forces pour l'Action Républicaine*—FAR), which had rejected President Taki's call for the establishment of a single presidential party. Subsequently, the FRN organized boycotts of both the October 20 constitutional referendum and the December legislative balloting.

On January 18, 1997, Djoussouf and the FDC's Mustapha Saïd Cheikh were detained and questioned about their roles in the unrest that had erupted at the beginning of the year. On March 1 senior French government officials met with FRN leaders in an effort to persuade them to establish a dialogue with the Taki administration. However, the opposition's relations with the government subsequently worsened when security officials accused the FRN of financing student disturbances in Moroni. Ironically, observers cited the FRN's financial difficulties as the main reason the group failed to secure a more prominent negotiating role in the late 1997 reconciliation talks.

Djoussouf was appointed prime minister in November 1998, and he subsequently formed an FRN-dominated cabinet. Not surprisingly, he strongly protested the April 1999 coup, announcing the withdrawal of the MDP from the FRN when it appeared that some FRN components had acquiesced to the government of self-proclaimed President Azali. Djoussouf subsequently became the dominant figure in the opposition camp as it participated in negotiations on the creation of a new federal structure. He signed the Fomboni Agreement of February 2001 in that capacity and urged his supporters to vote "yes" in the December constitutional referendum. Djoussouf finished fourth in the 2002 primary election for president of the Union by securing 7.9 percent of the vote, analysts suggesting he probably would have made the top three and thereby qualified for the runoff if the FRN had been preserved.

Leaders: Abbas DJOUSSOUF (1996 and 2002 presidential candidate), Ali Bacar CASSIM, Fouad Mohamed AHMED.

Democratic Front of the Comoros (*Front Démocratique des Comores*—FDC). The FDC was formerly an exile group led, within the Comoros, by its secretary general, Mustapha Saïd Cheikh, who was imprisoned for complicity in the 1985 coup attempt until President Abdallah's assassination. The front was one of the opposition groups invited to participate in the Djohar administration of August 1990. Subsequently, it campaigned in favor of the 1992 constitution and was a leading component of the FRN. Some FDC members supported the government of President Azali following the April 1999 coup and were expelled from the party.

Cheikh won 3.4 percent of the vote in the 2002 primary election for president of the Union and subsequently served as a major founding member of the CdIA.

Leaders: Mustapha Saïd CHEIKH, Ahmed Saïd ALI, Abdou MHOUMADI (2002 candidate for president of Ngazidja), Abdallah HALIFA (Secretary General).

Islands' Fraternity and Unity Party (*Chama cha Upvamodja na Mugnagna wa Massiwa*—Chuma). Chuma, a "patriotic alliance to fight the antidemocratic regime of Ahmed Abdallah," was formed in the 1980s by the Paris-based National Committee for Public Salvation (*Comité National de Salut Public*—CNSP), an exile group led by Prince Saïd Ali Kemal, and two other exile groups—the Comoran National United Front (*Front National Uni des Komores*—FNUK) and the Union of Comorans (*Union des Komoriens*—Unikom). Kemal headed the economy and trade ministry in the first Djohar administration.

Chuma did not immediately adhere to the FRN, since Kemal was abroad at the time of the FRN's creation. Having stood unsuccessfully in the March 1996 presidential election, Kemal was appointed to the first post-Djohar government, but he was dismissed in August for opposing President Taki's proposal for a merger of government parties. Subsequently, Chuma announced that it was aligning with the FRN.

Kemal urged his supporters to vote "no" in the constitutional referendum of December 2001, arguing that the proposed federal structure would lead to the "Balkanization" of the Comoros. Kemal finished third in the primary election on Ngazidja for president of the Union in March 2002 with 10.8 percent of the vote; he called for a boycott of the runoff in April. Chuma supported Ibrahim Halidi of the MPC in the 2006 balloting for president of the Union, Kemal serving as one of Halidi's vice-presidential running mates. Kemal won 3.6 percent of the vote in the June 2007 presidential balloting on Ngazidja.

Leader: Prince Saïd Ali KEMAL (1996 and 2002 presidential candidate).

National Rally for Development (*Rassemblement National pour le Développement*—RND). The RND was officially launched on October 6, 1996, as a merger of the National Union for Democracy in the Comoros (*Union National pour la Démocratie aux Comores*—UNDC) and a number of former FRN parties under the leadership of a confidante of Mohamed Taki, Ali Bazi SELIM. The formation of a single "presidential" party was first proposed by newly elected President Taki in August 1996 on the grounds that almost all of the eliminated first-round candidates had supported his candidacy in the runoff balloting.

Subsequent intraparty competition for the RND's 26 elected Central Committee seats was described as "fierce," and the results—14 seats for Selim's supporters and 12 for a "youth wing" led by Abdoul Hamid AFFRETANE—underlined reports of deep divisions in the fledgling grouping. Additional seats were set aside for the general secretaries of the parties joining the RND as well as for what was described as the Comoran "diaspora." Thereafter, despite the RND's electoral success in December 1996 legislative balloting, observers reported that its members' support for Taki remained their only commonality.

In November 1998 the RND denounced the appointment of the FRN's Djoussouf to the top government post. Subsequently, the RND's cabinet representation fell to four posts, and in early 1999 two former RND members were appointed to the government (see Maecha Bora Party, below).

One faction of the RND reportedly backed the new administration of President Azali after the coup of 1999, while another, led by Omar TAMOU, lobbied for the reinstatement of former interim president Massonde. Mtara MAECHA, the former foreign minister who secured 7.86 percent of the vote in the 2002 primary election on Ngazidja for president of the Union, was identified as the candidate of the RND's "revival wing." Maecha reportedly supported Ahmed Abdallah Mohamed Sambi in the May 2006 balloting for president of the Union. Subsequently, Kamar EZAMANE Mohamed was regularly referenced as the secretary general of the UNDC, while Vice President Idi Nadhorm was identified as a member of the UNDC executive body. Ezamane ran for the presidency of Ngazidja in 2007 as the candidate of the UNDC, finishing fourth with 8.4 percent of the vote, while Maecha ran for the post as the candidate of the RND-Revival, finishing ninth in the first round of balloting with 4.1 percent of the vote.

Comoran Party for Democracy and Progress (*Parti Comorien pour la Démocratie et le Progrès*—PCDP). The PCDP is led by Ali Mroudjae, who was an *Udzima* leader prior to President Abdallah's assassination and subsequently held the production and industry portfolio under Djohar. The party joined *Udzima* in moving into opposition in November 1991. Mroudjae secured 4.2 percent of the vote in the 2002 primary election for president of the Union. Abdou Soule Elbak, the president of Ngazidja until 2007, is a former deputy in the PCDP and until recently was still referenced regularly as a member of the party. Meanwhile, several members of the PCDP served in Elbak's cabinet on Ngazidja.

Adinane was the candidate of the PCDP in the 2006 primary for Union president, but he received less than 3 percent of the vote and did not qualify for the general election.

Elbak failed in his bid to be reelected president of Ngazidja in 2007 when he finished third in the first round of balloting with 13 percent of the vote. In April 2008 it was reported that Elbak had founded the **Social Democratic Party of Comoros** (*Parti Social-Démocratique des Comoros—PSDC-Dudja*) to pursue "national reconciliation."

Leaders: Loufti ADINANE (Chair), Ali MROUDJAE (Secretary General).

Maecha Bora Party. Maecha Bora is led by two RND dissidents, Issoufi Saïd Ali and 1996 presidential candidate Ali Ben Ali, who were named to the Djoussouf government in early 1999.

Leaders: Issoufi Saïd ALI, Ali Ben ALI (1996 presidential candidate).

Comoran Popular Front (*Front Populaire Comorien*—FPC). Also known as the *Front Populaire Mohélien* (FPM), the FPC was awarded the education portfolio in the government of May 1992 and campaigned for the new constitution; it later joined the FRN.

Mohamed Hassanali, leader of the FPC, was the leading vote-getter in the first round of balloting for president of Mwali in 2002 with 26.2 percent of the vote; however, he was defeated in the runoff.

Leaders: Mohamed HASSANALI, Abdou MOUSTAKIM (Secretary General).

Comoran Union for Progress (*Union Comorienne pour le Progrès*—UCP/*Udzima*). Launched as a regime-supportive group in 1982 by President Abdallah, *Udzima* was the sole legal party until 1989. *Udzima* presented Saïd Mohamed Djohar, interim president following Abdallah's assassination in November 1989, as its official candidate in the presidential balloting of March 1990. However, *Udzima* withdrew its support from Djohar in November 1991 and moved into opposition to protest the formation of a coalition administration three months earlier. It did not participate in the 1992 balloting after its principal leaders had been either imprisoned or driven into hiding because of alleged complicity in the September coup attempt.

A member of the opposition FRN beginning in January 1994, *Udzima* experienced internal divisions after President Djohar had agreed to a transfer of power, with the result that two candidates (Omar Tamou and Mtara Maecha) from *Udzima* stood in the March 1996 presidential election. Although both were eliminated in the first round, the *Udzima* leader, Tadjidine Ben Saïd Massonde, was appointed prime minister by the successful UNDC candidate. Massonde resigned as prime minister in December 1996, but he was named, due to his position as president of the High Council of the Republic, as interim president of the Republic following President Taki's death in November 1998. Confusion subsequently surrounded *Udzima*'s membership, as news reports referenced Massonde, Tamou, and Maecha as being members of the RND in 1999. In early 2002, Tamou, former *Udzima* secretary general, returned to the Comoros after two years in France.

Republican Party of the Comoros (*Parti Républicain des Comores*—PRC). The PRC was formed in the second half of the 1990s by Mohamed Saïd Abdallah Mchangama, then president of the Federal Assembly, and Hamada Madi Bolero, who served as PRC secretary general until rallying to the cause of President Azali following the coup of April 1999. Mchangama, the son-in-law of former president Djohar, had been instrumental in the launching of the Rally for Democracy and Renewal (*Rassemblement pour la Démocratie et le Renouveau*—RDR) in December 1993 by merger of the Dialogue Proposition Action (*Mwangaza*), led by Mchangama, and dissidents from other parties. Personal rivalries had resulted in three prominent RDR members, including Mchangama, contesting the March 1996 presidential election, all being eliminated in the first round.

Mchangama called for dialogue with the Azali administration following the coup of April 1999, but the PRC was described as a member of the opposition in early 2001. Mchangama won 3.5 percent of the vote in the first round of presidential balloting on Ngazidja in 2007.

Leader: Mohamed Saïd Abdallah MCHANGAMA.

Other parties include the **Rally for Change** (*Rassemblement pour le Changement*), led by Mohamed ZEINA and described as being close to the center-right Rally for the Republic in France; ***Shawiri***, based in Moroni and led by Col. Mahamoud MRADABI; ***Shawiri-Unafasiya*** (SU), formed in 2003 by former members of *Shawiri* and led by Hadji Ben SAID; the **Revolutionary Left of the Comoros** (*Gauche Révolutionnaire des Comores*—GRC), a socialist party established in 2003; the **Social Action Movement for Democracy and Alternation**, whose candidate, Abdou DJABIR, finished third in the first-round presidential balloting on Mwali in 2007; the **Party for the Evolution of the**

Comoros (*Parti pour l'Évolution des Comores*—PEC), led by Fabmi Said IBRAHIM; and the **Party for National Salvation** (*Parti pour le Salut National*—PSN) and the **Rally for Development and Democracy** (*Rassemblement pour le Développement et la Démocratie*—RDD), which in 2006 decided to cooperate as the PSN/RDD under the leadership of Saïd Ahmed MOUHYIDDINE (president) and Antoy ABDOU (secretary general). Abdou was replaced as general secretary of the Union government after he and the PSN/RDD supported (against the wishes of President Sambi) Mohamed Djaanfari in the June 2008 presidential balloting on Nzwani.

Separatist and Other Groups:

Anjouan People's Movement (*Mouvement du Peuple d'Anjouan*—MPA). The MPA emerged as the most prominent of the secessionist groups in Anjouan after the arrest of its leader, Abdallah IBRAHIM (a well-known businessman), on July 22, 1997, served as a rallying cry for antipresidential and separatist militants. Ibrahim was released days later, and on August 5 he was named president of the "State of Anjouan" (name later changed to Nzwani). The MPA lobbied against the Union constitution of December 2001. In February 2002 it named Col. Mohamed Bacar, then the military ruler of Nzwani, as MPA honorary chair. Following Bacar's election to the presidency of Nzwani in March, some elements of the MPA joined the island government, and two MPA members were appointed to the nine-member Nzwani cabinet. Bacar emerged as the most vocal proponent of greater autonomy for the islands. However, other members of the MPA remained staunch secessionists and denounced Bacar for even his limited cooperation with the Union government. Abdullah Mohamed was subsequently identified as the leader of the hard-line secessionist wing of the party. In 2005 he and other members of the MPA were arrested for antigovernment activity, and there have been few reports of MPA activity since those developments.

Leader: Abdullah MOHAMED.

Organization for the Independence of Anjouan (*Organization pour l'Indépendance d'Anjouan*—OPIA). Theretofore a propresidential grouping, the OPIA in late 1996 grew critical of the Taki administration and was subsequently linked to the growing number of antigovernment demonstrations in Anjouan. In mid-1997 leadership of the OPIA reportedly shifted from former armed forces chief of staff Col. Ahmed Mohamed HAZI to Mohamed Ahmed Abdou. Critics of Abdou, who has also been identified as a spokesperson for the **Coordination Committee of Anjouan,** accused him of placing his personal ambitions ahead of the movement's. The OPIA steadfastly maintained its separatist stance into mid-2002, although subsequent references to OPIA activity have been very limited.

Leader: Mohamed Ahmed ABDOU.

LEGISLATURE

The 1992 constitution provided for a bicameral legislature. However, the Senate, which was to have 15 members (5 from each island) indirectly elected to six-year terms, was never named and was abolished by the 1996 basic charter. Prior to the April 1999 coup, legislative authority was vested in a Federal Assembly (*Assemblée Fédérale*), which comprised 43 members directly elected for four-year terms (subject to dissolution).

Under the December 2001 constitution, an **Assembly of the Union** (*Assemblée de l'Union*) was established as well as assemblies for each of the three islands that comprise the Union. Until 2009, the Assembly of the Union comprised 33 members—18 directly elected (9 from Ngazidja, 7 from Nzwani, and 2 from Mwali) and 15 indirectly elected by the three island assemblies (5 each)—who serve five-year terms. In the direct balloting on April 18 and 25, 2004, the Camp of the Autonomous Islands (CdIA) secured 12 seats, and the propresidential Convention for the Renewal of the Comoros, 6. All 15 indirectly elected seats were filled by the CdIA, anti-Azali coalitions having earlier won heavy majorities in all three island assemblies.

Elections due in April 2009 were postponed by the government pending the May 2009 constitutional referendum, after which the elections (for 24 directly elected members and 9 indirectly elected members) were scheduled for December. *(See headnote.)*

Speaker: Saïd Dhoifir BOUNOU.

CABINET

[as of July 1, 2009]

President	Ahmed Abdallah Mohamed Sambi (Nzwani)
Vice Presidents	Ikililou Dhoinine (Mwali)
	Idi Nadhoim (Ngazidja)
Ministers	
Agriculture, Fishing, and Environment	Mikidar Houmadi
Civil Service, Administration Reform, and Human Rights	Fouad Ben Mohadji
Economy, Foreign Commerce, Labor, and Relations with Parliament	Hassane Ahmed El Barwane
Foreign Affairs and Cooperation	Ahmed Ben Saïd Jaffar
Health, Solidarity, and Promotion of Gender Equality	Hodhoaer Inzouddine
Interior and Information	Bourhane Hamidou
Justice, Prison Administration, and Islamic Affairs	Miftah Ali Bamba
National Education, Research, Arts and Culture, and Government Spokesperson	Kamaliddine Affraitane
Posts and Telecommunications	Ahmed Abdou
Territorial Development, Infrastructure, Town Planning, and Housing	Mohamed Larif Oukacha
Transportation, Tourism, and Investments	Idi Nadhoim

COMMUNICATIONS

The constitution of 2001 provided for freedom of the press, and, for the most part, that principle has been upheld by the government. However, the editor of *L'Archipel* was detained by the government for three days in March 2006 following the publication of an article critical of security officials. The arrest prompted an outcry from international media watchdogs. There have also been several other reports of the harassment of journalists, and some journalistic watchdog organizations in 2009 reported a decline in press freedom.

Press. The nation's print media includes two weeklies, the state-owned *Al Watwan* (1,500) and the independent *L'Archipel*. A new daily, *Le Matin des Comores,* was introduced in March 2002, and another independent daily, *La Gazette des Comores*, has been widely quoted in other news reports recently. There is also a monthly, *La Tribune de Moroni*, and another daily, *Le Canal*.

News agency. The domestic facility is the privately owned *Agence Comorienne de Presse* (HZK-Presse), located in Moroni.

Broadcasting and computing. The state broadcasting company is the *Office de la Radio et de la Télévision des Comores.* Although a number of new private radio and television stations were launched between 1995 and 2005, the Union and island governments continued to censor private stations, one station being suspended in 2005 after broadcasting programs critical of the government. As of 2008 there were 34.8 Internet users per 1,000 inhabitants.

INTERGOVERNMENTAL REPRESENTATION

Ambassador to the U.S. and Permanent Representative to the UN: Mohamed TOIHIRI.

U.S. Ambassador to the Comoros: R. Niels MARQUARDT (resident in Madagascar).

IGO Memberships (Non-UN): AfDB, AMF, AU, BADEA, Comesa, IDB, Interpol, IOC, LAS, NAM, OIC, OIF, WCO.

DEMOCRATIC REPUBLIC OF THE CONGO

République Démocratique du Congo

Political Status: Independent republic established June 30, 1960; one-party constitution of February 1978 modified in June 1990 to accommodate multiparty system; all government institutions dissolved on May 17, 1997, following rebel takeover of the capital, and executive, legislative, and judicial authority assumed the same day by a self-appointed president backed by the military; interim constitution providing for a transitional national government approved April 2, 2003, by various groups participating in the Inter-Congolese National Dialogue; new constitution endorsed by national referendum on December 18, 2005, and promulgated on February 18, 2006, providing for new national elections later in the year.

Area: 905,562 sq. mi. (2,345,409 sq. km.).

Population: 29,916,800 (1984C); 63,846,000 (2008E).

Major Urban Centers (2005E): KINSHASA (7,000,000), Mbuji-Mayi (1,300,000), Lubumbashi (1,275,000).

Official Languages: French. Kikongo, Lingala, Swahili, and Tshiluba are classified as "national languages."

Monetary Unit: Congolese Franc (market rate December 1, 2009: 909.27 francs = $1US).

President: Joseph KABILA (nonparty); appointed by the Legislative and Constituent Assembly–Transitional Parliament on January 24, 2001, and inaugurated on January 26 to succeed his father, Laurent Désiré KABILA (Alliance of Democratic Forces for the Liberation of Congo-Zaire), who had died on January 18 of injuries suffered in an assassination attempt two days earlier; inaugurated as interim president on April 7, 2003, in accordance with a peace agreement signed on April 2; popularly elected in second-round balloting on October 29, 2006, and inaugurated for a five-year term on December 6.

Vice President: Abdoulaye YERODIA Ndombasi (People's Party for Reconciliation and Development); elected concurrently with the president on October 29, 2006, and inaugurated for a five-year term on December 6 in succession to a team of transitional vice presidents comprising himself, Jean-Pierre BEMBA (Movement for the Liberation of the Congo), Azarias RUBERWA Manywa (Congolese Rally for Democracy), and Arthur Z'ahidi NGOMA (Forces of the Future).

Prime Minister: Adolphe MUZITO (Unified Lumumbist Party); appointed by the president on October 10, 2008, to succeed Antoine GIZENGA (Unified Lumumbist Party), who had submitted his resignation on September 25; announced new cabinet on October 20, 2008 (approved by Parliament on November 22).

THE COUNTRY

Known prior to independence as the Belgian Congo and variously thereafter as the Federal Republic of the Congo, the Democratic Republic of the Congo (for the first time), Congo-Kinshasa, and Zaire, the Democratic Republic of the Congo (DRC) is situated largely within the hydrographic unit of the Congo River basin, in west-central Africa. The second-largest of the sub-Saharan states, the equatorial country is an ethnic mosaic of some 200 different groups. Bantu tribes (Bakongo, Baluba, and others) represent the largest element in the population, about half of which is Christian. Among the rural population, women are responsible for most subsistence agriculture, with men being the primary cash-crop producers; in urban areas women constitute more than a third of wage earners, many of whom also engage in petty trade on the black market to supplement family income.

The DRC has major economic potential based on its vast mineral resources, agricultural productivity sufficient for both local consumption and export, and a system of inland waterways that provides access to the interior and is the foundation for almost half of the total hydroelectric potential of Africa. Mineral extraction dominates the economy: cobalt, copper, diamonds, tin, manganese, zinc, silver, cadmium, gold, and tungsten are among the commercially exploited reserves. In addition, offshore oil began flowing in late 1975. Important agricultural products include coffee, rubber, palm oil, cocoa, and tea. Despite these assets, per capita income is one of the lowest in Africa, and the economy has for many years hovered on the brink of disaster. Consequently, infant mortality is high, and primary and secondary education is poor. In addition, universities, once among the continent's finest, are currently neglected, while the country (nearly the size of Western Europe) remains largely devoid of roads outside the major cities.

The International Monetary Fund (IMF) and World Bank provided assistance in the early 1990s in response to government austerity measures and liberalization of the investment code. However, in June 1994 the IMF suspended Zaire's voting rights and called on the Mobutu administration to take steps to eliminate its debt arrears. Corruption subsequently continued to hamper economic adjustment efforts and to drain foreign reserves. At the time of the rebel takeover of Kinshasa in May 1997, the economy was in collapse, and the new government immediately announced its intention to focus on rebuilding and expanding the country's infrastructure. Despite barriers such as the DRC's $14 billion external debt, Western investors reportedly expressed eagerness to participate in development, the new administration having proclaimed its intention to incorporate free-market practices in its economic system despite President Laurent Kabila's former Marxist orientation. However, in early 1998 the IMF suspended its loan program after Kabila reneged on a pledge to resume debt repayments. Subsequently, economic issues were relegated to the background when civil war broke out in August (see Political background, below). Real annual per capita GDP fell significantly over the next three years, reaching a low of $85 by the end of 2000 (down from $224 in 1990). The alarming situation was also marked by hyperinflation (more than 550 percent in 2000), an estimated 2 million internally displaced persons, and some 350,000 refugees from other countries.

Increased exports of oil and minerals (primarily diamonds) helped foster GDP growth of 3 percent in 2002 and 5 percent in 2003. The IMF and World Bank approved a reduction of some 80 percent of the DRC's external debt in 2003, and continued economic improvement was expected in the wake of the partial conclusion of the five-year civil war in 2003 and the installation of a transitional national unity government. However, overall economic and humanitarian aid remained minimal as the international community diverted its attention from what the UN called one of the world's "worst human crises." An estimated 3–4 million people had died as a result of the recent civil war, mostly from conflict-related disease, starvation, and lack of medicine. In addition, one-fifth of the country's children were dying by the age of five, contributing to "1,200 unnecessary deaths per day," while 1.6 million people remained internally displaced, mostly in the "lawless" east.

GDP grew by nearly 7 percent in 2004, and more debt relief was subsequently promised by the government's commercial creditors. The IMF and World Bank also pledged an additional $2.4 billion in aid, provided the administration addressed corruption in the state-owned oil company and systemic graft throughout other sectors. The IMF additionally chided the government for spending too much on security concerns and too little on poverty-reducing programs; IMF lending was suspended in March 2006.

Presidential and legislative elections in 2006 offered hope that political conditions would stabilize and therefore permit the necessary emphasis on economic development. Consequently, the World Bank in May 2007 agreed to provide additional support for the transition. On a more negative note, however, an inquiry was launched in early 2007 into the perceived lack of transparency in mining deals concluded with several Western companies in 2005. For its part, the government announced in June that it would review mining contracts awarded from 1998 to 2003, indicating that it would attempt to renegotiate the contracts so that the DRC would have greater ownership of the assets under review.

In what was considered a highly significant initiative, China in September 2007 announced plans to invest $5–10 billion to rehabilitate mines and related infrastructure in the DRC. Resource-hungry China

was also reportedly considering a reduction in the DRC's debt in return for preferred access to copper and cobalt mines.

GDP growth exceeded 6 percent in 2007, although the IMF criticized the government for an overly expansionary budget and called for additional reforms to improve the management of public finances, promote additional privatization, and strengthen the judiciary. Meanwhile, conditions remained extremely difficult for many citizens, particularly in the conflict-riddled east.

Although GDP grew by 6 percent in 2008, conditions deteriorated sharply in the final quarter of the year as the result of the global economic crisis. The mining sector was particularly hard hit due to a collapse in prices and a collateral decline in foreign investment. With unemployment soaring and annual inflation climbing to 50 percent in April 2009, the IMF predicted growth of only 2.7 percent for 2009. Consequently, the Fund approved $195 million in emergency lending to help offset the recent shocks and indicated that significant debt relief might be in the offing, provided changes were made in the controversial Sino-Congolese "mines for infrastructure" plan. (The IMF and other creditors demanded that Chinese aid become more concessionary so as not to add to the DRC's external debt.)

GOVERNMENT AND POLITICS

Political background. The priority given to economic rather than political development during Belgium's 75-year rule of the Belgian Congo contributed to an explosive power vacuum when independence was abruptly granted in June 1960. UN intervention, nominally at the request of the central government headed by President Joseph KASAVUBU, helped check the centrifugal effects of factionalism and tribalism and preserved the territorial integrity of the country during the troubled early years, which witnessed the removal and death of its first prime minister, Patrice LUMUMBA, and the gradual collapse of separatist regimes established by Albert KALONJI in Kasai, Moïse TSHOMBE in Katanga (now Shaba Region), and Antoine GIZENGA in Stanleyville (now Kisangani). The withdrawal of UN peacekeeping forces in 1964 did not mark the end of political struggle, however, with Tshombe, who was appointed interim prime minister in July, and Kasavubu subsequently vying for power of what became (for the first time) the Democratic Republic of the Congo in August. On November 24, 1965, the commander of the army, Maj. Gen. Joseph D. MOBUTU, who had previously held control of the government from September 1960 to February 1961, dissolved the civilian regime and proclaimed himself president of the "Second Republic."

During 1966 and 1967 President Mobutu put down two major challenges to his authority by white mercenaries and Katangan troops associated with the separatist activities of former prime minister Tshombe. (Tshombe died in captivity in Algeria in June 1969.) Other plots were reported in 1971, one of them involving former associates of Mobutu, who in 1970 had been directly elected (albeit as the sole candidate) to the presidency following establishment of the Popular Movement of the Revolution (*Mouvement Populaire de la Révolution*—MPR). Shortly thereafter, in an effort to reduce tension and solidify national unity, Mobutu embarked upon a policy of "authenticity," which included the general adoption of African names. The country was officially redesignated the Republic of Zaire in October 1971.

The country's Shaba Region was the scene of attempted invasions in March 1977 and May 1978 by rebel forces of the Congolese National Liberation Front (*Front de la Libération Nationale Congolaise*—FLNC) directed by a former Katangan police commander, Nathaniel MBUMBA. The first attack, repulsed with the aid of some 1,500 Moroccan troops airlifted to Zaire by France, was said to have failed because of Mbumba's inability to enlist the aid of other groups opposed to the Mobutu regime, particularly the Popular Revolutionary Party (*Parti de la Révolution Populaire*—PRP) in eastern Zaire, led by Laurent Désiré KABILA. Government forces were initially assisted in 1978 by French and Belgian paratroopers, whose presence was defended as necessary to ensure the orderly evacuation of Europeans, and later by a seven-nation African security force that was not withdrawn until July–August 1979.

The 1977 Shaba invasion was followed by a series of government reforms that included the naming in July of MPINGA Kasenda to the newly created post of first state commissioner (equivalent to prime minister) and the holding of direct elections in October to urban councils, to the National Legislative Council (*Conseil Législatif National*—CLN), and for 18 seats on the MPR Political Bureau. Having been reconfirmed by referendum as MPR president, Mobutu was invested for a second seven-year term as head of state on December 5.

In March 1979 the National Executive Council (cabinet) was reorganized, with André BO-BOLIKO Lok'onga being named to replace Mpinga, who became permanent secretary of the MPR. Jean NGUZA Karl-I-Bond was designated first state commissioner on August 27, and Bo-Boliko assumed the new position of party executive secretary. In April 1981 Nguza resigned while on a trip to Belgium, declaring that he would have been imprisoned had the announcement been made prior to his scheduled departure; N'SINGA Udjuu Ongwakebi Untube was named as his successor. N'singa was in turn replaced by Joseph Léon KENGO wa Dondo in a major government reorganization on November 5, 1982, following a single-party (but multiple-candidate) election to the CLN on September 18–19.

Again presenting himself as the sole candidate, President Mobutu was reelected for a third seven-year term on July 27, 1984. Fifteen months later, on October 31, 1986, he announced that the post of first state commissioner had been abolished. However, the office was restored in the course of a major ministerial reshuffling in January 1987, with former finance minister MABI Mulumba being designated its incumbent. Mabi was in turn succeeded on March 7, 1988, by SAMBWA Pida Nbagui. In the fourth cabinet reshuffling of the year, Sambwa was removed on November 26, and Kengo wa Dondo returned to the post he had held in 1982–1986.

On April 24, 1990, bowing to rising demands for social and political change, Mobutu announced an end to Zaire's one-party system, calling for the constitution to be revised to permit the formation of trade unions and at least two additional parties. One day later he named the secretary general of the Economic Community of Central African States, Vincent de Paul LUNDA Bululu, to succeed Kengo wa Dondo as head of a substantially restructured "transitional" government that was installed on May 4.

The euphoria generated by the prospect of a liberalized "Third Republic" quickly dissipated with continued repression of opposition activity and a presidential declaration that the launching of the limited multiparty system would not take place for at least two years. The result was a bloody confrontation at the University of Lubumbashi on May 11, 1990, during which more than 50 student protesters were reported to have been killed. The legislature responded in late June by altering the constitution to accommodate the regime's April promises and reduce Mobutu's powers. Domestic and international impatience with the government's economic and human rights policies nonetheless continued, and in late November the basic law was further amended in favor of "full" multiparty democracy. On December 31 the president pledged that both presidential and legislative elections, in addition to a referendum on yet another new constitution, would be held in 1991.

On March 3, 1991, most of the more than five dozen political parties issued a demand that the government call a National Conference to consider more extensive constitutional revision. The government acquiesced to the request, but on May 2 the National Conference was postponed following the massacre of 42 opposition supporters by security forces. Subsequently, on July 22, the regime announced that Étienne TSHISEKEDI wa Malumba, leader of the opposition Sacred Union (*Union Sacrée*) coalition, had agreed to become prime minister, and on July 25 MULUMBA Lukoji, who had been named on March 15 to succeed Lunda, was dismissed. However, under pressure from Sacred Union members, Tshisekedi denied that he had accepted the government's offer, and on July 27 Mulumba was returned to office.

The National Conference finally convened on August 7, 1991, but it was suspended a week later after opposition delegates had walked out, protesting that they had been harassed by the police and that the meeting had been illegally packed with regime supporters. The conference reconvened on September 16 after Mobutu agreed to grant it sovereign powers but was again suspended after a near-riotous first day. On September 29 Mobutu accepted a proposed reduction of presidential powers and formation of a cabinet dominated by the opposition. However, the next day Tshisekedi was elected prime minister, triggering a power struggle between the heads of state and government that prevented a scheduled resumption of the National Conference on October 2. On October 14 Tshisekedi secured acceptance of his cabinet nominees, but seven days later he was dismissed by Mobutu. Tshisekedi immediately challenged the legality of the action, and the Sacred Union refused the president's invitation to nominate a successor. Mobutu responded on October 23 by naming Bernadin MUNGUL Diaka, the leader of a small Sacred Union affiliate, to head a new government. Encountering an increasingly violence-prone public, the president on November 22 agreed to a Senegalese-mediated accord with the Sacred Union that stipulated that the next prime minister would be a mutual choice that would "of necessity, come from the ranks of the opposition." Thereupon, former prime minister Jean Nguza Karl-I-Bond, nominally an opposition leader but an opponent of Tshisekedi, presented himself as a candidate for the position and was immediately expelled from the Sacred Union. Apparently hoping to exploit the opposition's disarray, Mobutu disregarded the accord of three days before and designated Nguza as prime minister on November 25.

Mobutu's third seven-year term as president expired on December 4, 1991, but he refused to step down, insisting that he would remain in office until elections could be scheduled. On December 11 the National Conference reconvened, naming Laurent MONSENGWO Pasinya, the archbishop of Kisangani and an outspoken critic of Mobutu, as its president the following day.

On January 14, 1992, Prime Minister Nguza ordered suspension of the National Conference on the grounds that some of its decisions were "provoking a political crisis," and in early February he called for the convening of a smaller "national round table" to draft a new constitution and set a timetable for elections. However, the conference resumed on April 6, and 11 days later it disregarded a government order by asserting its sovereign status. On June 21 President Mobutu again suspended the conference after it had begun debate on the choice of a new prime minister, insisting that such an appointment was a presidential prerogative. That objection notwithstanding, a "global comprehensive policy on transition" was reached on July 30, whereby Mobutu would remain in office for the duration of the interregnum, with former prime minister Tshisekedi being redesignated as head of government.

On August 29, 1992, Tshisekedi named a 21-member cabinet, which, unlike his previous short-lived administration, included no Mobutu associates or MPR members. On September 4 the ban on political demonstrations was lifted, and on September 19 the National Conference revealed details of a draft multiparty, parliamentary-style constitution that it promised to present for a referendum prior to general elections. Meanwhile, Mobutu announced that the MPR would "take no part in the government of national union" and that he too would be presenting a draft constitution. On October 5 Mobutu, supported by the 20,000-strong Special Presidential Division (*Division Spéciale Présidentielle*—DSP), reconvened the CLN for constitutional debate, ignoring the National Conference's August dissolution of the CLN. However, with both Tshisekedi and National Conference president Monsengwo urging a boycott of the "rebellious" legislature, the proceedings were poorly attended and were quickly halted.

On December 1, 1992, Mobutu ordered the dissolution of the Tshisekedi government and the National Conference. Thereafter, faced with the prime minister's refusal to step aside, the president ordered DSP troops to be deployed throughout the capital and released new 5-million zaïre notes, which he insisted were necessary to pay the army. Meanwhile, on December 6, the National Conference concluded its sitting, electing Monsengwo as head of a transitional legislature (the High Council of the Republic [*Haut Conseil de la République*—HCR]) and demanding that Mobutu abandon his efforts to dissolve the transitional government.

On January 7, 1993, Mobutu declared that he would ignore the HCR's "ultimatum" that he recognize the Tshisekedi government, describing the HCR as having been established "according to antidemocratic procedures." Consequently, the HCR authorized the government to seek foreign intervention to force Mobutu to comply with its dictates and, after accusing Mobutu of "high treason" for "blocking the functioning of the country's institutions at every level," declared its intent to begin impeachment proceedings. On January 20 Tshisekedi announced that he would include MPR members in a "reconciliation" cabinet, and the Sacred Union, announcing a unilateral truce, suspended its demonstrations in support of Mobutu's ouster. However, a new crisis erupted on January 28, when DSP troops attacked anti-Mobutu forces in the capital. On January 29 Belgium and France dispatched troops to protect their citizens, but within days more than 45 people were reported killed, including the French ambassador. On February 3 Belgium, France, and the United States issued a joint statement blaming Mobutu for the breakdown in public order and threatening to isolate the president unless he transferred his executive powers to the prime minister. Mobutu responded two days later by announcing the dismissal of Tshisekedi because of his "inability" to form a national unity government. The president also initiated legal proceedings against Tshisekedi for offenses against state security. On February 9 the HCR, while reportedly chastising Tshisekedi for failing to form a government more acceptable to the president, rejected the dismissal order.

The HCR's efforts to initiate a dialogue between Mobutu and Tshisekedi collapsed on February 24, 1993, when soldiers surrounded the HCR building and demanded that the council recognize the new zaïre note. The siege ended on February 26 following Western diplomatic intervention, and on March 5 Mobutu met with Monsengwo. Although the two failed to reach agreement, Mobutu on March 9 inaugurated a "conclave of the last chance," which, he claimed, had HCR support. On March 17 the conclave, which was ultimately boycotted by the HCR, named former Sacred Union spokesperson Faustin BIRINDWA as prime minister. Birindwa, who had been expelled from the Sacred Union on March 1 for "political truancy," was confirmed by Mobutu on March 29 at the opening of an extraordinary session of the CLN, which had been charged by the president with adopting a "Harmonized Constitutional Text" drafted by the mid-March conference.

On April 2, 1993, Mobutu, in an effort to bolster both his and the CLN's legitimacy, promulgated constitutional amendments establishing the CLN as a transitional institution equal in status to the HCR and confirming the president's right to appoint the prime minister. Concurrently, Birindwa announced a government highlighted by the appointment of Nguza as deputy prime minister for defense. On April 5 Sacred Union activists organized a general strike to protest Birindwa's action, and on April 9 Tshisekedi, who had rejected Birindwa's right to name a cabinet, presented his own reshuffled government, which was approved by the HCR on April 13. On May 7 the Birindwa government released an election timetable calling for a constitutional referendum on July 30, to be followed three months later by elections to choose among the competing governmental institutions. The HCR promptly disputed Birindwa's legal right to call a referendum and urged the opposition to boycott any such proceedings.

In mid-July 1993 the Mobutu regime announced that it had dispatched presidential guardsmen to Kasia, Kivu, and Shaba provinces to help quell ethnic violence that had reportedly claimed more than 3,000 lives. By August the number of casualties had reportedly doubled, eliciting charges by foreign observers that the president's forces were exacerbating the situation in an effort to slow the democratization process. Thereafter, negotiations in September between the regime-supportive Political Forces of the Conclave (*Forces Politiques du Conclave*—FPC) and the Sacred Union of Radical Opposition (*Union Sacrée de l'Opposition Radicale*—USOR), a successor to the Sacred Union, yielded a draft Constitutional Act of the Transition. However, efforts to finalize the accord stalled through the remainder of the year as the FPC continued to reject the USOR's demand that Tshisekedi's prime ministerial status be recognized, arguing that the National Conference's authority had been superseded by the HCR. Meanwhile, at a December 14 rally attended by former prime minister Nguza, Shaba governor

Gabriel KUNGUA Kumwanza declared the province's "total autonomy" from Zaire and reversion to its former name of Katanga.

On January 4, 1994, Mobutu issued an ultimatum to the deadlocked FPC and USOR leaderships, ordering them to implement the September 1993 agreement by January 12. Consequently, the two sides agreed on January 11 to the formation of a national unity government that included members from both Birindwa's and Tshisekedi's cabinets, thus prompting Mobutu's January 14 dismissal of Birindwa and dissolution of the CLN and HCR. In addition, Mobutu directed the newly organized High Council of the Republic–Parliament of Transition (*Haut Conseil de la République–Parlement de Transition*—HCR-PT) to deliberate on the prime ministerial candidacies of Tshisekedi and Mulumba Lukoji, who was backed by moderate opposition parties. However, on January 17 Tshisekedi rejected Mobutu's right to dissolve the original HCR and called for a "dead city" general strike on January 19 (the date the new legislature was scheduled to convene).

On January 23, 1994, the HCR-PT held its inaugural meeting, and two days later it appointed Monsengwo as its president. Thereafter, on April 8, the HCR-PT endorsed a second transitional constitution act, inaugurating a 15-month transitional period to culminate in general elections. Following the HCR-PT's acceptance of the credentials of seven prime ministerial candidates (including Tshisekedi) on May 2, Tshisekedi's followers announced their intention to boycott the proceedings and rebuked their USOR coalition partners for nominating candidates to compete against Tshisekedi. Two weeks later, the split within the USOR was formalized when the Tshisekedi faction ousted a number of parties aligned with former prime minister Kengo wa Dondo's Union for the Republic and Democracy (*Union pour la République et la Démocratie*—URD). On May 13 the HCR-PT appointed a commission to define the criteria for choosing a prime minister, and on June 11 it ratified a list of seven individuals that did not include Tshisekedi because "he had not made a proper application to be a candidate." On June 14 the HCR-PT restored Kengo wa Dondo as prime minister, and on July 6 Kengo wa Dondo named a new government. For his part, Tshisekedi insisted that he remained Zaire's legitimate prime minister.

In August 1994 Kengo wa Dondo announced the formation of two electoral preparation commissions and pledged to adhere to a transitional schedule calling for prompt elections. Two months later the USOR rejoined the HCR-PT, and on November 16 Kengo wa Dondo reshuffled his cabinet to allow USOR members to assume posts that had been set aside for them in July. Subsequently, already strained relations between Kengo wa Dondo and Mobutu further deteriorated when Mobutu refused to endorse Kengo wa Dondo's nominee to head the Central Bank of Zaire. Meanwhile, Kengo wa Dondo in mid-December announced in mid-December that long overdue presidential and parliamentary elections, as well as a constitutional referendum, would be held in July 1995; however, in May 1995 the balloting was again postponed.

FPC interim president Mandungu BULA Nyati orchestrated a legislative alliance between his party and the USOR that on June 30, 1995, provided overwhelming support for a two-year extension of the political transition period and, on July 2, successfully forwarded a motion calling for the resignation of HCR-PT president Monsengwo. Thereafter, amid reports that the alliance was planning to force his ouster, Prime Minister Kengo wa Dondo invited the "whole spectrum of the political class" to hold a dialogue and reportedly sought opposition participation in the reshuffled government he named on July 23. However, his entreaties were rebuffed by the USOR, which described the new cabinet as "illegal."

In February 1996 Kengo wa Dondo ousted 23 cabinet ministers, including all remaining opposition sympathizers, and filled their slots with his supporters, thereby rejecting the FPC's call for a new division of cabinet portfolios. Underscoring the level of factionalization in Kinshasa, the prime minister's allies boycotted the inauguration of the National Elections Commission (*Commission des Élections Nationales*—CEN) on April 3, claiming that they had been excluded from leadership positions. Meanwhile, the CEN was charged with preparing for a constitutional referendum in December 1996, presidential and legislative elections in May 1997, and local balloting in June and July 1997.

In May 1996 fighting broke out between indigenous Banyamulenge Tutsis and Rwandan Hutu refugees in the eastern region of South Kivu. Tension had been escalating there since an estimated 700,000–1,000,000 Hutus had fled Rwanda to Zaire in 1994 following the takeover of Kigali by Tutsi military forces. Among the refugees were members of *Interahamwe*, the Hutu militia that had been implicated in the massacre of hundreds of thousands of Tutsis and Hutu "collaborators" in Rwanda in April 1994 (see article on Rwanda). The Hutu militants subsequently gained control of the camps in Zaire, providing a degree of security for the Hutu refugees, who feared reprisals from Tutsis on both sides of the border for the recent "genocide" in Rwanda. Conflict quickly developed between the refugees and the Banyamulenge Tutsis, who numbered an estimated 400,000 in eastern Zaire, where their ancestors had migrated 200 years earlier and where they had achieved a high level of unofficial governmental autonomy. For their parts, the Rwandan government accused the *Interahamwe* of cross-border attacks in western Rwanda, while the Zairean government claimed that Banyamulenge militants were being armed and trained in Rwanda.

On October 8, 1996, amid escalating hostilities in the region, the deputy governor of Kivu, citing a 1981 law stripping the Tutsis of their Zairean citizenship, ordered them to leave the country within a week or risk annihilation. Although the governor was immediately suspended for his comments, thousands of Tutsis fled the area. At the same time, the Banyamulenge fighters, now reportedly numbering 3,000, launched an offensive that resulted in the quick rout of the Hutu fighters from the refugee camps and the retreat of the Zairean troops.

On October 29, 1996, Kinshasa declared a state of emergency in North and South Kivu as theretofore sporadic firefights between Rwandan and Zairean regular forces escalated into intense cross-border shelling. Collaterally, Kinshasa accused the Rwandan and Ugandan governments of attempting to take advantage of the absence of President Mobutu, who continued to convalesce in France from the effects of cancer surgery in August. Meanwhile, the Tutsi rebels, now widely identified as associated with the Alliance of Democratic Forces for the Liberation of Congo-Zaire (*Alliance des Forces Démocratiques pour la Libération du Congo-Zaire*—AFDL) and led by longtime anti-Mobutu guerrilla Laurent Kabila, continued to gain territory along Zaire's eastern border. Their numbers having grown with the addition of militants from dissident ethnic groups, the AFDL fighters reportedly faced little resistance from fleeing Hutus and Zairean troops (many of whom were accused of pillaging the towns they were assigned to protect).

Earlier, in Kinshasa on October 6, 1996, the HCR-PT had adopted a draft constitution that it pledged to present for a referendum in December. The proposed charter was immediately denounced by the USOR's Tshisekedi, who argued that the constitution produced by the 1991–1992 National Conference should be presented unaltered for referendum.

Faced with continued AFDL advances, the HCR-PT on November 1, 1996, called for the expulsion of all Tutsis from Zaire. On November 2 the AFDL captured the city of Goma, and on November 4 Kabila announced a unilateral cease-fire to allow international aid groups to facilitate the repatriation of refugees, the bulk of whom (700,000) were reportedly massed near Mugunga. Amid international demands for the deployment of a military intervention force to stave off a humanitarian disaster, the AFDL on November 11 agreed to open a corridor for aid to reach the refugees and subsequently drove off the remaining Hutu militiamen in the area. Consequently, from November 15 to 19 more than 400,000 Hutu refugees, apparently convinced that it was now safer in Rwanda than in Zaire, flowed across the border, thus effectively dampening international support for the UN's military deployment plans.

On November 21, 1996, the AFDL declared an end to its cease-fire, and over the next several days it announced the appointment of its own officials to administrative positions in the Kivu regions. By early December the rebels had encircled Kisangani, Zaire's fifth-largest city, and reportedly controlled five large towns and a wide swath of territory. On December 17 a visibly ailing Mobutu returned to Kinshasa, and the following day he appointed a new chief of staff, Gen. Mahele Lioko BOKUNGU, and charged him with ending the rebellion. Mobutu met with a broad spectrum of political leaders on December 19 in an attempt to establish a government of national unity to confront the AFDL advance. However, Tshisekedi and his Union for Democracy and Social Progress (*Union pour la Démocratie et le Progrès Social*—UDPS) boycotted the meeting, effectively dooming its chances for success. Consequently, following a week of reportedly intense debate within the presidential circle, Mobutu on December 24 reappointed Kengo wa Dondo as prime minister.

The AFDL drive across Zaire proceeded quickly in early 1997, forcing a tide of Hutu refugees ahead of it, as demoralized Zairean troops offered little effective resistance to the rebels, who were substantially supported by Rwandan forces. (France, the last nation to drop a strong pro-Mobutu stance, described the AFDL as an "invading army.") On

March 23 Prime Minister Kengo wa Dondo resigned, although he accepted caretaker status pending establishment of a new government. In what appeared to be a desperate final effort at a political settlement that would preclude a humiliating surrender, Mobutu on April 2 appointed longtime foe Tshisekedi as prime minister. A new cabinet, which included six spots reserved for the AFDL, was announced the following day. However, conflict between security forces and UDPS supporters subsequently broke out in Kinshasa, and Mobutu abruptly dismissed Tshisekedi on April 9, replacing him with Gen. Likulia BOLONGO, former defense minister, who named a cabinet dominated by the military on April 11.

With the international community calling for a negotiated settlement and establishment of a transitional government to avoid widespread bloodletting as the AFDL neared Kinshasa, Mobutu agreed to meet with Kabila and South African president Nelson Mandela on a boat moored off the Zairean coast on May 4. However, although Mobutu reportedly expressed a willingness to relinquish power to a transitional government, final arrangements for his departure were never settled. Mobutu ultimately fled Kinshasa for Togo (and eventually Morocco, where he died on September 7) at the last moment on May 16. Following a brief but murderous rampage by Mobutu loyalists against "traitors" in Kinshasa, AFDL forces entered the capital on May 17. Kabila, still located in the east, immediately declared himself president of the renamed Democratic Republic of the Congo (DRC) and ordered all governmental institutions dissolved.

Kabila arrived in Kinshasa on May 20, 1997, and, after conferring with leaders of various political groupings, made the first appointments to his new cabinet on May 22. However, to the great dismay of long-standing Mobutu opponents, the new regime announced there would be no role for Tshisekedi, whose supporters immediately organized a protest demonstration. In view of the unrest, Kabila on May 26 ordered the suspension of all political party activity and banned mass gatherings of any sort. Surrounded by the presidents of Angola, Burundi, Rwanda, Uganda, and Zambia, Kabila took the presidential oath of office on May 29, having promised a referendum on a new constitution by the end of 1998 and new legislative and presidential elections by April 1999.

After 32 years of Mobutu's dictatorial rule, the populace in May 1997 initially appeared, for the most part, to welcome the AFDL forces as "liberators." Regional leaders also strongly endorsed the regime of President Kabila, reflecting their long-standing complaint that Mobutu had permitted their opponents to conduct rebel activity against them from Zaire. The support from Western capitals was somewhat more cautious, particularly as reports surfaced of the alleged massacre of Hutus by the AFDL during its march across the country. Concern on that front deepened throughout the year and into early 1998 as the administration appeared to stonewall a UN investigation. In addition, widespread domestic disenchantment was reported by early 1998, particularly in regard to the stifling of political party activity and the dismissive treatment accorded to the UDPS and former prime minister Tshisekedi, described as the most popular political figure in the country. Ethnic tensions also continued to simmer, as evidenced by anti-AFDL rebel activity in several regions and reported growing concern over the heavy Tutsi influence at all levels of the AFDL administration. Kabila argued that "outsiders" did not appreciate the difficulties facing the DRC and that it was appropriate for his government to concentrate on reconstruction and the restoration of order while proceeding at a moderate pace toward general elections.

In April 1998 the UN withdrew its investigators, asserting that the Kabila government had purposely blocked their inquiry. Meanwhile, relations deteriorated between the president and the Rwandan-backed Banyamulenge Tutsis who had guided him to power; furthermore, increasing ethnic unrest was reported in the provinces bordering Rwanda and Uganda. In late July Kabila demanded that Rwanda withdraw all of its remaining forces (he had reportedly become convinced that Kigali was preparing to overthrow his government). On August 2 government soldiers stationed in the east were attacked by Banyamulenge rebel forces supported by Rwandan troops. Within days the rebels had opened a second front within striking distance of Kinshasa, and, at a mid-August summit in Goma, the anti-Kabila forces—now bolstered by the addition of "Mobutists" and other former Kabila supporters—formed the Congolese Rally for Democracy (*Rassemblement Congolais pour la Démocratie*—RCD). Meanwhile, the rebel forces continued to capture large swaths of territory and appeared prepared to launch a full-scale attack on Kinshasa. However, in late August Zimbabwean and Angolan troops fighting on behalf of Kabila launched a counteroffensive against the RCD, and soon thereafter Kabila's defenders (now including Namibia and Chad) had fought the rebels to a standstill.

Fierce clashes were reported throughout the end of 1998 and in early 1999, and concern grew among regional and international observers that the fighting would spread beyond the DRC's borders. Peacemaking efforts were stymied, however, by Kabila's refusal to negotiate with the RCD, which he had described as a front for Rwandan and Ugandan invasion forces.

A cease-fire agreement was signed in July 1999 at a meeting in Lusaka, Zambia, of the six countries then involved in the fighting in the DRC (Angola, Namibia, and Zimbabwe on the government's side; and Rwanda and Uganda in support of differing RCD factions and increasingly in conflict with one another) as well as Jean-Pierre BEMBA, the "Mobutist" leader of an increasingly important rebel force backed by Uganda called the Movement for the Liberation of the Congo (*Mouvement pour la Libération du Congo*—MLC). The Lusaka accord envisioned the withdrawal of all foreign troops from the DRC, the disarming of local militias under the supervision of a Joint Military Commission, and the eventual deployment of UN peacekeepers. The ruptured RCD (see Political Parties and Groups, below) signed the agreement in August, but renewed fighting quickly broke out between the RCD factions, both of which had repudiated the agreement by the end of the year. (Among other things, the RCD infighting served as a surrogate for the conflict between the forces from Uganda and Rwanda, each of whom was viewed in many quarters as participating in the exploitation of the DRC's mineral wealth.) Nevertheless, in November the UN Security Council authorized the creation of the UN Organizational Mission in the Democratic Republic of the Congo (*Mission de l'Organisation des Nations Unies en République Démocratique du Congo*—MONUC) to assist in monitoring any eventual peace settlement. (In February 2001 the Security Council authorized up to 5,000 personnel for MONUC.)

President Kabila was shot by one of his bodyguards on January 16, 2001, and he was declared dead from the wounds two days later. (The motive for the attack and any possible related conspiracy remained unclear, the assailant having been shot to death immediately after the attack.) On January 24 Kabila's son, Maj. Gen. Joseph KABILA, theretofore his father's chief of staff, was selected by the transitional legislature (installed by Laurent Kabila in August 2000 [see Legislature, below]) to succeed his father. Joseph Kabila immediately called for an intensification of talks toward national reconciliation, and in February another tentative UN-brokered accord was reached. The following month the first MONUC forces arrived in the DRC, but the proposed withdrawal of other foreign troops was delayed, in large part due to Rwanda's insistence that the Hutu militias be disarmed as a precondition to withdrawal. In April, Kabila appointed a new cabinet from which antinegotiation ministers were purged. Fighting, often intense, among RCD factions and between government forces and the rebels continued throughout 2001 and into early 2002 as peace talks inched toward a settlement.

In July 2002 the DRC and Rwanda finally reached a conclusive agreement providing for the withdrawal of the 20,000 Rwandan troops in the DRC starting in mid-September. Two months later a similar accord was struck with Uganda, setting the stage for intensification of talks (known as the Inter-Congolese National Dialogue) involving the government, domestic opposition parties, and rebel groups. Under the weight of heavy international pressure, a potentially historic accord was signed in mid-December in Pretoria, South Africa, by Kabila, the RCD factions, the MLC, and representatives of opposition parties and civil society. The accord provided for a cease-fire and installation of a transitional government pending new national elections within 30 months. Power in the interim government was to be shared, with Kabila, as president, being assisted by four vice presidents and a transitional legislature, whose members would be selected, on a carefully allocated basis, by the signatories.

The warring factions approved a new interim constitution providing for the installation of Kabila's national unity government in April 2003. Integral to the composition of the cabinet was the inclusion of the four vice presidents representing various constituencies (see Vice President, above). More than half of the cabinet members represented either opposition or rebel groups. In late June most of the former combatants agreed in principle to their integration into a unified national army in which power sharing was to be carefully delineated. That initiative began in August, with Kabila appointing several former rebel commanders to prominent military positions. Rebel groups, civil organizations, and opposition parties were also represented prominently in Kabila's appointments in May 2004 to new provisional governments for the country's ten regions and capital district.

On May 5, 2005, the transitional legislature approved the draft of a new constitution (see Constitution and government, below, for details) for consideration via national referendum, which on December 18 endorsed the new basic law with an 84 percent "yes" vote. President Kabila signed the new constitution into effect on February 18, 2006, setting the stage for national elections of a permanent civilian government.

In the first round of presidential balloting on July 30, 2006, President Kabila, running as an independent but supported by the People's Party for Reconciliation and Development (*Parti du Peuple pour la Réconciliation et le Développement*—PPRD) and some 30 other parties in the Alliance for a Presidential Majority (*Alliance pour la Majorité Présidentielle*—AMP), was credited with 45 percent of the vote. Second place (20 percent of the vote) went to Vice President Jean-Pierre Bemba, the candidate of the MLC and some 23 other parties aligned in the Rally of Congolese Nationalists (*Regroupement des Nationalistes Congolais*—RENACO). The announcement of the first-round results (characterized as fraudulent by Bemba and other candidates) triggered violent demonstrations in Kinshasa. Meanwhile, results from the July 30 voting for the 500-seat National Assembly indicated that the AMP and its allies had secured more than 300 seats, followed by RENACO, with approximately 100 seats, and the Unified Lumumbist Party (*Parti Lumumbiste Unifée*—PALU), with 34 seats.

Kabila was credited with 58 percent of the vote in the runoff presidential balloting against Bemba on October 29, 2006. Bemba immediately challenged the results as fraudulent, but the courts (supported by reports from international observers describing the balloting as generally free and fair) upheld the tally, and Kabila was inaugurated on December 6. On December 31 Kabila announced the appointment of Antoine Gizenga, the aged secretary general of PALU, as prime minister. Following Senate elections on January 19, 2007 (in which the AMP secured a majority of seats), Gizenga formed a new multiparty cabinet on February 5. The size of the cabinet was reduced significantly in a reshuffle the following November.

Prime Minister Gizenga announced his resignation as prime minister on September 25, 2008, citing his advanced age and ill health as obstacles to the government's prospects for resolving the nation's economic crisis and the recent intensification of rebel activity in the east. President Kabila subsequently named PALU's Adolphe MUZITO, theretofore the budget minister, to head a new cabinet, which was approved by the Parliament on November 2.

Constitution and government. A constitution drafted under President Mobutu's direction and approved by popular referendum in 1967 established a strong presidential system, certain features of which were drastically modified by amendments enacted in August 1974. (For lengthy information on constitutional changes and various proposals for revision from 1974 to 1997, see the 2007 *Handbook*.)

President Laurent Kabila appointed a constitutional commission in September 1997 to produce a new draft basic law by the end of March 1998. The commission was expected to endorse a strong presidential system based on the U.S. model. On March 30, 1998, the commission reportedly adopted a draft basic charter that included provisions for the creation of an elective vice-presidential post, the establishment of an enhanced judiciary system topped by a Supreme Court, and the dissolution of the prime minister's post. Subsequently, President Kabila issued a decree authorizing the formation of a 300-member Legislative and Constituent Assembly, which upon inauguration was to be charged with preparing for a constitutional referendum and legislative elections. Although the assembly was inaugurated in August 2000, no action was taken on the proposed constitution prior to Kabila's death in January 2001, after which the nature of the country's next constitutional arrangements was a primary focus of discussions between the government and rebel forces regarding a permanent peace settlement.

An interim constitution providing for a transitional government was adopted in April 2004 by most of the participants in the Inter-Congolese National Dialogue. The bicameral transitional legislature established by that accord (see Legislature, below, for details) subsequently (in May 2005) approved a draft of a new permanent constitution that was endorsed by national referendum in December. The new basic law provided for a "semipresidential" system in which the prime minister has greater authority than in the past. The president's term was set at five years, renewable once. The minimum age for presidential candidates was reduced to 30, a measure clearly inserted to permit current President Joseph Kabila (34) to run for the office. Presidential balloting is conducted by direct vote under a two-round (if necessary) majoritarian system. The president was mandated to appoint the prime ministerial candidate selected by the majority party (or coalition of parties needed to make a majority) in the National Assembly, the lower house of the new Parliament (see Legislature, below, for details on the Parliament).

The new constitution permitted the current transitional government to remain in place until new national elections were held. Other important aspects included provisions to protect freedom of religion, expression, and political pluralism and to strengthen the judiciary. Citizenship was extended to members of all ethnic groups that were residing in the country at the time of independence.

The new constitution also called for significant devolution of governmental authority to the provinces, the number of which were to be extended from 10 to 26 (including the capital "province" of Kinshasa). Provincial authority was to be shared by presidentially appointed governors and directly elected provincial assemblies. Provinces were to be further subdivided into communes and cities. The provinces were slated to receive 40 percent of all government revenues, but the new decentralization law (covering revenue distribution as well as final codification of provincial powers) remained under debate in the Parliament as of early 2009, reportedly causing consternation among local officials. Judicial authority at the national level was invested in a Supreme Court, a Constitutional Court, a Court of Cassation, and a High Military Court.

Foreign relations. The DRC has generally pursued a moderate line in foreign policy while avoiding involvement in non-African issues. Relations with Belgium, its former colonial ruler, were periodically strained following independence, partly because vocal anti-Mobutu factions were based in Brussels. However, Belgium remained a major aid donor. Development efforts following independence led to enhanced economic ties with Japan, the United States, and Western European countries, especially France, which Kinshasa in 1986 called its new European "fountainhead."

Relations with former French territories in central Africa have fluctuated. The Union of Central African States was formed with Chad in 1968, and more than 3,000 Zairean troops were sent to Chad in support of President Habré in 1983. In addition, Burundi and Rwanda joined Zaire in establishing the Economic Community of the Great Lakes Countries, the object being an eventual common market. Relations with Zambia remained cordial despite a Zairean claim (resolved in 1987) to part of that country's northern Kaputa and Lake Mweru districts. In the west, border incidents involving the Republic of the Congo periodically erupted in the 1980s, while in the east, Zairean troops were given permission by Kampala in July 1987 to cross into Ugandan territory to engage rebels associated with the Congolese National Movement (see Political Parties and Groups, below).

A lengthy cold war between Zaire and Angola was formally terminated as the result of a visit by Angolan President Neto to Zaire in August 1978 and a reciprocal visit by President Mobutu to Angola the following October. The latter concluded with the signing of a cooperation agreement between the two governments and a mutual pledge to proceed with the establishment of a commission under the Organization of African Unity (OAU, subsequently the African Union—AU) to guard against rebel violations from either side of the 1,250-mile common border. By 1987, however, it had become apparent that the United States was deeply involved in covert activities in the vicinity of the Belgian-built air base at Kamina in southern Zaire, with plans to remodel the facility for delivery of supplies to the Angolan rebel forces led by Jonas Savimbi. Such collusion notwithstanding, President Mobutu joined in April with the heads of state of Angola, Mozambique, and Zambia in concluding, in Luanda, a declaration of intent to reopen the Benguela railroad, which had effectively been closed by Angolan guerrilla operations since 1976.

In May 1982 Kinshasa announced that it was resuming diplomatic relations with Israel, reversing a rupture that had prevailed since the 1973 Arab–Israeli war. In response, a number of Arab governments severed relations with Zaire, while regional leaders expressed concern at the Israeli "reentry" into Africa. In November, Israel's defense minister, Ariel Sharon, flew to Zaire to conclude arrangements for the supply of arms and the training of Zairean forces, particularly a "presidential battalion" under Mobutu's direct command. Further military-aid commitments were secured by Mobutu during a May 1985 visit to Israel, the regional backlash being tempered in 1986 by Zaire's resumption of participation in the OAU after a two-year hiatus occasioned by the OAU's admission of the Saharan Arab Democratic Republic.

In January 1989 President Mobutu, who had been strongly criticized in the Belgian press for financial aggrandizement, announced that he was abrogating agreements defining his country's postcolonial relations with Belgium. In addition, he said Zaire would halt payments on its more than $1 billion Belgian debt and explore alternatives to shipping its minerals to Belgium for refining. However, the dispute was settled, and relations were normalized at midyear.

In May 1990 Mobutu, labeling Brussels the "capital of subversion," rejected appeals from Belgium and the European Community (EC, subsequently the European Union—EU) for an international inquiry into the slayings at Lubumbashi University. Consequently, on May 24 Belgium halted aid payments, and, following Kinshasa's decision to sever diplomatic links on June 22, Belgium withdrew a debt-cancellation pledge. In August the U.S. Lawyers' Commission for Human Rights released a report describing Zaire's human rights record as a "systematic pattern of abuses." Subsequently, on November 5 the U.S. Congress voted to suspend military aid and redirect humanitarian aid through nongovernmental agencies.

On September 24, 1991, France and Belgium ordered their troops to Zaire to protect foreign nationals threatened by widespread rioting and looting. One month later France and Belgium announced their disengagement from Kinshasa and called for regional intervention. Mobutu responded by vowing to stay in power and accusing international forces of "wanting my head at any price." In November, U.S. officials described Mobutu as having "lost the legitimacy to govern" and called for the regime to begin sharing power with the opposition.

In June 1992 the government announced that it was seizing the assets of all foreign oil companies as a means of alleviating chronic fuel shortages. While officials insisted that the measure was only temporary and promised reimbursement, the companies argued that the action was equivalent to confiscation, given Zaire's lack of currency reserves.

The appointment of the Tshisekedi government in August 1992 paved the way for an end in October to a ten-month-old aid embargo by the EC, although the EC stated its intention to continue to withhold funding until it received guarantees that it would be channeled to the appropriate recipients. Subsequently, in early December 1992 Prime Minister Tshisekedi's Western supporters criticized President Mobutu's attempts to dissolve the government, with Belgium reportedly preparing for a possible military role. The likelihood of such intervention increased dramatically in mid-January 1993 after the HCR had granted the government authorization to seek foreign assistance in ousting the president. Thereafter, following the outbreak of widespread military rioting in Kinshasa, Belgian and French troops were deployed in Kinshasa to protect their citizens.

On February 3, 1993, Belgium, France, and the United States issued a joint statement that described Mobutu as the architect of Zaire's ruin, called for the president's resignation, and threatened "total political and economic isolation" of his regime if he refused to capitulate. In late February, Western diplomats continued to pressure Mobutu, warning him that he would be held personally responsible for the lives of the HCR members then being held captive in Kinshasa. The siege ended the following day.

Following the establishment of the Birindwa government in early April 1993, Mobutu's relations with Zaire's three largest donors deteriorated even further. On April 7 the EC, which followed the lead of several of its members in repudiating the legal status of the new regime, reaffirmed its support for the Tshisekedi government, announced an embargo on arms sales to Zaire, and imposed visa restrictions on Mobutu and his allies. The Birindwa government responded by denouncing the "interference" in its internal affairs, expelling two Belgian diplomats, and, while rebuffing a CLN call to sever ties with the Europeans, warning against further Western action.

In February 1994 Amnesty International accused the regime of continued complicity in human rights violations, charging the Mobutu-controlled military with responsibility for "indiscriminate executions." Moreover, international observers reporting on the plight of Rwandan refugees encamped along the Zairean border in mid-1994 accused Zairean troops of attacking refugees and confiscating their property. However, the Mobutu regime's support for French peacekeeping efforts in Rwanda was apparently rewarded with an easing of international pressure on Mobutu's domestic policies, and in mid-1994 France, Belgium, and the United States recognized the Kengo wa Dondo government.

In early September 1994 Zaire announced that the approximately 1.2 million Rwandan refugees in Zaire would have to leave by the end of the month. Although observers described the demand as unrealistic, it provoked renewed dialogue on the refugees' plight, and on October 24, Rwanda, Zaire, and the United Nations High Commission for Refugees (UNHCR) signed an agreement designed to facilitate their repatriation. However, during the first half of 1995 no further diplomatic progress was reported and conditions in the approximately 40 camps continued to deteriorate. On August 18, 1995, Zaire again ordered the expulsion of the refugees, citing rumors that both Rwanda and Burundi were preparing to attack the camps to suppress rebel groups. Within five days, 15,000 people were forcibly repatriated, while more than 100,000 others fled into the countryside. Pressured by the international community to end the expulsions, Kinshasa halted the program on September 7 and signed an accord with the UNHCR that, echoing the events of 1994, provided for the repatriation of the refugees by December.

In February 1996 Zairean troops, under UNHCR supervision, began sealing off the camps (in an effort to isolate them from the local communities) and urging the refugees to return home. The program was quickly abandoned, however, when the troops, demanding payment of salary arrears, left their posts.

Reportedly concerned about who would actually benefit from a militarily backed humanitarian aid program, as well as fearing involvement in a Somalia-like imbroglio, a number of regional and international capitals, including Washington, reacted warily toward a French- and Spanish-led call for foreign intervention in eastern Zaire in 1996. However, faced with the onset of what aid agencies predicted would ultimately be mass starvation, Canada, South Africa, and the United Kingdom had agreed by November to participate. Further bolstered by a U.S. commitment of 1,000 troops on November 13, the UN-sponsored, Canadian-led multinational force of 15,000 troops began deployment preparations on November 14. The efforts were suspended, however, following the subsequent mass repatriation of hundreds of thousands of refugees to Rwanda between on November 15–19. Consequently, despite continued French lobbying for the dispatch of a military force, wide support for the plan dissipated, and at a meeting of the representatives of 29 countries and 6 aid agencies in Stuttgart, Germany, the operation was officially abandoned on November 22.

The DRC's foreign relations from 1998 to 2001 turned on the roles its neighbors played on both sides of the civil war that erupted in August 1998. Officially supporting the Kabila government with troops were Zimbabwe, Angola, Namibia, and Chad. In addition, Equatorial Guinea, Eritrea, Gabon, and Sudan expressed their sympathies with the DRC government but adopted far smaller roles in the dispute than did the aforementioned countries. On the side of the rebels, Rwanda and Uganda provided such large amounts of personnel and supplies that the Kabila administration accused them of invading DRC territory. To a lesser extent the insurgents were aided by Angolan rebels and supporters in Burundi. Noting the number of countries directly involved in the fighting, a Western official in late 1998 warned that the region was on the brink of the first "African world war."

Uganda withdrew its forces from the DRC by May 2003, and the two countries in 2004 agreed to cooperate in suppressing rebel groups on both sides of their border. However, relations with Rwanda remained strained, the DRC charging that Rwanda was still "stoking discontent" as of 2005.

In December 2005 the International Court of Justice (ICJ) ruled in favor of the DRC in regard to the case the DRC had filed charging Uganda with an "illegal incursion" into the DRC during the 1998–2003 conflict and the "plunder" of the DRC's natural resources. Uganda was ordered by the ICJ to pay reparations to the DRC, although a final amount was not determined. (The DRC was reportedly seeking $6–10 billion.) A similar DRC case was filed against Rwanda, but Rwanda refused to accept ICJ jurisdiction.

Tension resurfaced at the border with Uganda in mid-2007 over islands on Lake Albert, a major base for oil operations in the region. Uganda protested the DRC's establishment of a military presence on one of the islands, but the two countries subsequently agreed to form a joint commission to demarcate the border. (Little progress was reported in that context by mid-2009, while additional border questions had arisen in regard to Uganda's northwest frontier with the DRC, where significant oil deposits had recently been discovered.)

In the wake of extensive fighting in eastern DRC, the DRC and Rwanda in November 2007 announced an agreement to cooperate in disarming militias formed by Hutu rebels in the region. In addition, in April 2008 the DRC, Rwanda, Uganda, and Burundi signed an accord pledging not to harbor each other's dissidents. Meanwhile, the DRC's relations with Belgium deteriorated after a Belgian official criticized the human rights situation in the DRC, perceived ongoing corruption, and the DRC's growing ties with China (whose financial support did not come with the good-governance addendums favored by the EU and Belgium.)

Ugandan and Rwandan forces were invited into the DRC in late 2008 and early 2009, respectively, as part of controversial new anti-rebel campaigns (see Current issues, below, for details). Rwanda reestablished diplomatic relations with the DRC in the spring, while the DRC established a joint commission with Angola to negotiate a settlement in regard to their poorly demarcated border, a recent source of friction.

Current issues. An estimated 3–4 million people may have died in the 1998–2003 civil war, which also destabilized the entire region. In early 2005 the UN reported that sporadic but intense fighting in resource-rich areas of the country was still leading to the deaths of thousands of people per month. Although most major rebel groups had been integrated into the national army, small ethnic militias (often under the direction of local warlords) continued to terrorize the population. President Kabila was described in 2005 as "lurching from crisis to crisis," having reportedly survived several coup attempts in 2004. In January 2005 the government announced that the new national elections tentatively scheduled for June 2005 would not be held until June 2006, prompting massive public protests (led in large part by the UDPS). The government defended its decision on the grounds that all militias needed to be disarmed before voting could take place. Difficulties in registering some 26 million prospective voters and implementing electoral procedures were also cited in the delay.

Despite charges of widespread corruption, continued conflict in the east, and ongoing miserable conditions for the average citizen, the transitional government survived for the rest of 2005, buoyed in part by the constitutional referendum in December. Government officials reported a turnout of 60 percent for the referendum vote, which EU observers described as free and fair. Few analysts challenged the official tally of an 84 percent "yes" vote, most major parties and factions (with the notable exception of the UDPS) having supported the new basic law as representing at least a chance for the country to put its seemingly interminable chaos behind it.

The force strength of MONUC (already the largest and most expensive such UN deployment) was increased to more than 17,000 peacekeepers and military police to preserve order during the 2006 elections. The EU also provided 2,000 troops to assist in electoral oversight. Considering the number of candidates (33 for the presidency and more than 9,700 for the National Assembly) and the problems associated with conducting a poll in a country the size of Europe with few paved roads, one UN official described the successful conclusion of the July 2006 balloting as a "small miracle." Many observers had anticipated a first-round presidential victory for Kabila, who appeared to enjoy the support of most Western capitals, particularly after the UDPS's Etienne Tshisekedi announced he would not be a candidate and called for a boycott of the balloting. However, vice president and former rebel leader Jean-Pierre Bemba ran a strong campaign, based on his promise to bring economic competence to the national government.

Following the July 2006 legislative poll, the AMP reportedly refused to appoint pro-Bemba deputies to any committee chairs, which opposition parties criticized as contrary to Kabila's pledge for "national reconciliation." Supporters of the Kabila and Bemba camps clashed in Kinshasa in late August, prompting intervention by UN and EU troops. In a possibly related initiative, Kabila announced a cabinet reshuffle in early October in which he appointed a close ally as interior minister. Kabila's subsequent triumph in the second round of presidential balloting was in part attributed to support from the third- and fourth-place finishers in the first round. The AMP and its allies also dominated the January 19, 2007, Senate elections and the gubernatorial balloting on January 27. The administration hoped that the installation of a multiparty cabinet in February would signal a peaceful conclusion of the four-year transitional period. However, fighting again broke out in March when security forces apparently attempted to disarm some of Bemba's militia. More than 60 people died, and the government issued an arrest warrant for Bemba, who took refuge in the South African embassy before leaving the country. Significantly, France signaled its support for the Kabila administration as it attempted, as one analyst put it, to "build a nation from the bottom up."

Security conditions in the east deteriorated sharply in the fall of 2007 when the National Congress for the Defense of the People (*Congrès National pour la Défense du Peuple*—CNDP) announced it was "going to war" with the DRC army and Hutu militias to protect the Tutsi population. (See section on the CNDP, under Political Parties and Groups, below, for additional information.) The government negotiated a cease-fire with the CNDP and some 20 other small rebel groups in January 2008, but multifaceted unrest (fueled by the illegal trade in diamonds) still simmered as of mid-year, contributing to a continued humanitarian crisis that was marked by widespread dislocations and attacks on civilians. The security situation was complicated by the presence in the east of factions of the Democratic Forces for the Liberation of Rwanda (*Forces Démocratiques pour la Libération du Rwanda*—FDLR), which had not signed the earlier cease-fire. (See Political Parties in the article on Rwanda for information on the FDLR, which had been formed by Hutus who had fled to the DRC in the 1990s.)

Periodic violations of the January 2008 cease-fire with the CNDP continued throughout the summer, and the accord collapsed completely in late August and early September when supporters of the CNDP's Laurent NKUNDA launched an intensive campaign against government troops in North Kivu. The fighting displaced more than 250,000 civilians, who also reportedly faced assaults by soldiers on both sides of the conflict as MONUC peacekeeping forces proved ineffective.

In late 2008 the DRC government accused the Rwandan government of backing the CNDP, a charge that was at least partially validated by a subsequent UN report. Facing intense international pressure, Rwanda in early 2009 agreed to send some 2,000 troops into the DRC for a joint campaign against the FDLR. At the same time dramatic changes within the CNDP significantly altered that group's status (see CNDP under Political Parties and Groups, below, for details). (It was widely assumed that a secret deal had been negotiated under which Rwanda had agreed to undercut the CNDP in return for the DRC's genuine cooperation against the FDLR). President Kabila was criticized in some domestic quarters for "inviting foreign forces" into the DRC in connection with the anti-FDLR campaign, and Rwanda withdrew its troops in March. Although the FDLR reportedly suffered heavy losses, its "eradication" had not been accomplished by midyear, and refugee humanitarian issues remained substantial. DRC forces also continued to battle remnants of the Lord's Resistance Army (LRA) who had crossed over the border from Uganda, despite an anti-LRA campaign in the region involving some 3,000 Ugandan troops earlier in the year.

POLITICAL PARTIES AND GROUPS

All existing parties were outlawed in 1965. For the greater part of the next quarter century the only legal grouping was the Popular Movement of the Revolution (MPR). Established under General Mobutu's auspices in April 1967, the MPR progressively integrated itself with the governmental infrastructure. The formation in 1980 by a number of parliamentarians of the opposition Union for Democracy and Social Progress (UDPS) was countered by the MPR, which effectively co-opted most of the UDPS domestic leadership and severely repressed the remainder.

In April 1990 the president announced that the MPR, the UDPS, and one other party would be granted legal status during a "transitional period" culminating in a multiparty election in December 1991. Thereupon, more than 60 groups presented themselves for the remaining legal party position. However, in the face of manifest dissatisfaction with the pace and breadth of his reform program, President Mobutu reversed himself in October and lifted the numeric restriction. As a result, 28 parties were registered by January 1991, the applications of 94 others having been rejected as "incomplete." An additional 38 parties were registered by mid-February, a majority of which were reportedly sympathetic to the MPR, and by March 30 a total of 58 parties had accepted the government's terms for the National Conference scheduled to convene on April 29. Meanwhile, however, leaders of the Sacred Union (*Union Sacrée*), an opposition coalition that included the influential UDPS, UFERI, and the PDSC (see below), announced plans to boycott the conference, refused to recognize the recently named transitional government, and called for President Mobutu's resignation. Thereafter, while the 159 parties registered for the May 3–19 National Conference preparatory committee were described as largely proregime, Mobutu's continued reluctance to enact reforms had begun to alienate many groups, and by midyear the Sacred Union was credited with a membership of approximately 150 parties. The Sacred Union adopted the rubric of the Sacred Union of the Radical Opposition (*Union Sacrée de l'Opposition Radicale*—USOR) in 1993. (For an extensive history of the USOR, defunct as of 1998, see the 1999 *Handbook*.)

Governmental authority was taken over in May 1997 by the Alliance of Democratic Forces for the Liberation of Congo-Zaire (*Alliance des Forces Démocratiques pour la Libération du Congo-Zaire*—AFDL), a predominantly Tutsi grouping of three rebel factions and the ADP (see RCD, below) that had been formed in November 1996 under the leadership of Laurent Kabila, a non-Tutsi "Lumumbist" who had been linked to anti-Mobutu militant groups since the 1960s. (For more information on the AFDL, which was dissolved by Kabila in 1999, see the 2005–2006 *Handbook*.) The AFDL immediately suspended all political party activity indefinitely, but President Kabila in late January 1999 lifted the ban on the formation of new political parties without, however, addressing the status of the previously existing parties. Moreover, the requirements for registering new parties demanded organizational and financial resources beyond most prospective groupings, while restrictions (such as a ban on any parties with connections to international organizations) also served to preclude participation.

Joseph Kabila ordered the barriers to party activity lifted in May 2001, and more than 150 parties had reportedly registered by the end of the year. However, in many cases, it was impossible to determine if the new parties were in fact positioned to genuinely affect domestic affairs.

During the negotiations for the Pretoria Accord of 2002, 15 of the largest opposition political parties formed an alliance called the Opposition General Assembly (OGA) to coordinate strategy and priorities. As a result of the discussions, one of the four vice-presidential posts was designated for Arthur Z'ahidi NGOMA (Forces of the Future), the president of the OGA. Ngoma's appointment was opposed by some opposition parties, while other groups later became dissatisfied with his performance and called for his resignation. The result was a fracturing of the OGA.

In March 2004 Kabila signed a new law designed to grant parties access to media and provide them with state grants. The law also barred parties from involvement in fighting or military actions against the government. By 2005 more than 400 parties had reportedly registered with the Central Election Commission, with some 213 reportedly presenting candidates for the legislative balloting in 2006.

Parties supporting the presidential candidacy of Kabila (officially an independent) formed an Alliance of the Presidential Majority (*Alliance pour la Majorité Présidentielle*—AMP) in June 2006. Core components included the PPRD, UDEMO, PALU, MSR, CCU, PDC, UNAFEC, and more than 20 other small parties. Meanwhile, a number of small parties joined with the MLC to support the presidential candidacy of the MLC's Jean-Pierre Bemba in a coalition called the Rally of Congolese Nationalists (*Regroupement des Nationalistes Congolais*—RENACO). For the second round of presidential balloting, the pro-Bemba parties formed a new coalition called the Union for the Nation (*Union pour la Nation*—UpN).

Government and Government-Supportive Parties:

People's Party for Reconciliation and Development (*Parti du Peuple pour la Réconciliation et le Développement*—PPRD). Formed in March 2002, the PPRD, composed mainly of former regime supporters and members of the government, was seen primarily as a political vehicle for President Joseph Kabila. Kabila initially asserted that he was not formally a member of the party, and even though press reports routinely referenced him as the PPRD presidential candidate in 2006, Kabila officially ran as an independent in order to be the candidate of "all the Congolese people." However, recent reports have routinely referenced the PPRD as "Kabila's party," and the president appeared to solidify his control in March 2009 when he orchestrated the resignation of the PPRD's Vital KAMERHE as speaker of the assembly. Kamerhe, who had criticized Kabila's recent antirebel compact with Rwanda, was succeeded by Kabila loyalist Evariste Boshab.

Leader: Evariste BOSHAB (Secretary General and President of the National Assembly).

Unified Lumumbist Party (*Parti Lumumbiste Unifiée*—PALU). Another party claiming adherence to its namesake's teachings, PALU is headed by Antoine Gizenga, the former leader of one of the three separatist regimes that emerged in Zaire following Belgium's withdrawal in 1960. On July 29, 1995, at least ten party members were killed during a clash with government security forces outside the parliamentary building.

Gizenga finished third in the first round of presidential balloting in July 2006 with 13 percent of the vote and subsequently endorsed President Kabila in the second round. As the new prime minister, Gizenga formed a government of national unity in February 2007. Following Gizenga's resignation in September 2008, he was succeeded as prime minister by PALU stalwart Adolphe Muzito.

Leaders: Antoine GIZENGA (Former Prime Minister and 2006 presidential candidate), Adolphe MUZITO (Prime Minister), Rémy MAYELE (Secretary).

Other parties that participated in the launching of the AMP included the **Social Movement for Renewal** (*Mouvement Social pour le Renouveau*—MSR); the **Convention of United Congolese** (*Convention des Congolais Unis*—CCU); the **Christian Democratic Party** (*Parti Démocrate Chrétien*—PDC); and the **Union of the Federalist Nationalists of the Congo** (*Union des Nationalistes Fédéralistes du Congo*—UNAFEC). Following the first round of presidential balloting, the **Union of Mobutuist Democrats** (*Union des Démocrates Mobuistes*—UDEMO), whose candidate (François Joseph Nzanga MOBUTU, a son of former president Mobutu) had finished fourth with 4.8 percent of the vote, announced its support for President Kabila in the second round.

Other Parties and Groups:

Union for Democracy and Social Progress (*Union pour la Démocratie et le Progrès Social*—UDPS). The UDPS was the outgrowth of an effort in late 1980 to establish an opposition party within Zaire dedicated to the end of President Mobutu's "arbitrary rule." Subsequently, the government arrested, sentenced, and eventually amnestied a number of its members. The leadership was thrown into disarray in late 1987 when UDPS President Frédéric KIBASSA Maliba and several other prominent party members joined the Central Committee of the MPR (see below) following a meeting with President Mobutu in which an agreement was reportedly reached to permit the UDPS to operate as a "tendency" within the governing formation. However, other leaders, including Secretary General Etienne Tshisekedi wa Malumba, vowed to remain in opposition and press for creation of a multiparty system, accusing government security forces of continuing to imprison and torture UDPS adherents.

During a visit to the United States in November 1990, Tshisekedi declared, "The people of Zaire are demanding that he [Mobutu] must go," and, following the UDPS's official registration on January 16, 1991, he announced his presidential candidacy. Thereafter, the party stated that it would boycott any national conference not granted sovereign status and would refuse to join in a transitional government as long as Mobutu remained president.

On September 30, 1991, Tshisekedi agreed to be named prime minister, but two weeks later, following a struggle with Mobutu for executive authority, he was dismissed. Refusing to accept the validity of the president's action, Tshisekedi on November 1 chaired the first meeting of a parallel cabinet. On August 14, 1992, the National Conference voted to return Tshisekedi to the post of prime minister, which he retained until his controversial ouster on December 1.

Tshisekedi served as prime minister for one week in April 1997 as Mobutu desperately attempted to find a political solution to his impending ouster by the AFDL. The UDPS supporters were subsequently described as welcoming to the AFDL and new president Laurent Kabila. However, the relationship deteriorated quickly when Kabila declined to name Tshisekedi to his new government. The UDPS leader was detained in June 1997, and in February 1998 he was sent to his home village under house arrest for violating the ban on party activity. In July, Tshisekedi was returned to Kinshasa and released.

Following Kabila's death in early 2001, Tshisekedi proved to be one of the few old-time party leaders able to retain significant influence. Among other things, he participated in peace and reconciliation negotiations in conjunction with rebel groups and other opposition figures. Nonetheless, the UDPS refused to participate in the 2003 transitional government, and in 2005 it organized a series of demonstrations and rallies to protest the postponement of elections.

Under Tshisekedi's direction (called "dictatorial" by some party dissidents), the UDPS called for a boycott of the December 2005 constitutional referendum. Although Tshisekedi in early 2006 appeared ready to rejoin the political process in preparation for a presidential bid, he ultimately called for a boycott of the presidential and legislative balloting to protest the government's refusal to conduct new voter registration. (Some UDPS dissidents registered for the assembly poll, prompting their expulsion from the party.) Tshisekedi had been considered President Kabila's potentially most serious rival, while the UDPS, which claimed support of some 30 percent of the electorate, had been expected to perform well (and perhaps lead) the legislative election.

The UDPS officially declined to endorse either candidate in the second round of presidential balloting in September 2006, although some local party cadres reportedly supported the MLC's Jean-Pierre Bemba. The UDPS also refused to participate in the February 2007 national unity government. Although some reports subsequently continued to describe Tshisekedi as the "noninstitutional" leader of the opposition, others suggested that the UDPS leader may have "missed the bus" as far as the country's political future was concerned.

Leaders: Etienne TSHISEKEDI wa Malumba (President of the Party), Rémy MASSAMBA Makiesse (Secretary General).

Congolese Rally for Democracy (*Rassemblement Congolais pour la Démocratie*—RCD). The RCD was formed in mid-August 1998 in Goma by the leaders of the predominantly Banyamulenge Tutsi rebels who had launched a military offensive against the government of Laurent Kabila on August 2. Ernest WAMBA dia Wamba, a theretofore largely unknown academic, emerged from the Goma meeting as the leader of the anti-Kabila forces. In addition, the RCD's leadership committee included Arthur Z'ahidi Ngoma, the prominent founder of the anti-Mobutu and subsequently anti-Kabila Forces of the Future, as well as two former Kabila government ministers, Bizima KARABA and Déogratias BUGERA. Bugera had been the leader and founder of the People's Democratic Alliance (*Alliance Démocratique des Peuples*—ADP), a military grouping of Tutsis that had been described as the dominant component of the AFDL as it marched across Zaire to seize the capital in May 1997 but had been ordered out of Kinshasa by the president in late July 1998.

In early 1999 RCD dissidents led by Bugera broke away from the group and formed the Reformers' Movement (*Mouvement des Réformateurs*—MR), and in February Ngoma formed the Union of Congolese for Peace, which he asserted would seek a peaceful solution to the country's crisis. Further intraparty friction was reported in March between Wamba dia Wamba, who allegedly sought a "political" end to the civil war, and a promilitary faction led by Alexis TAMBWE and former prime minister Vincent de Paul Lunda Bululu. Meanwhile, a hard-liner, Emile ILUNGA, assumed command of the RCD's military operations amid reports that Wamba dia Wamba was losing control of the group. In May, Ilunga replaced Wamba dia Wamba as president of the RCD, and the group split into two warring factions, Ilunga's being backed by Rwanda and Wamba dia Wamba's by Uganda. In October the latter faction adopted the rubric **RCD–Liberation Movement** (*RCD—Mouvement de la Libération*—RCD-LM). Ilunga was succeeded as president of the main RCD faction (now referenced as RCD-Goma) in October 2000 by Adolphe Onusumba Yemba. Meanwhile, yet another faction (**RCD–National** [RCD-N]) had broken off in June 2000 under the leadership of Roger Lumbala Tshitenge. In May 2001 Antipas Mbusa Nyamwisi forcefully took control of the RCD-LM from Wamba dia Wamba.

The RCD groups participated in the Inter-Congolese National Dialogue and were signatories to the Pretoria Accord. Under the terms of the agreement, RCD-Goma secretary general Azarias Ruberwa Manywa was appointed one of four vice presidents of the republic in July 2003. The RCD factions agreed to disarm, and a portion of their troops were integrated into the national security forces. In addition, the RCD factions received seats in both the Senate and National Assembly and posts in the transitional cabinet. However, the RCD-Goma briefly suspended participation in the transitional government in 2004 to protest the massacre of Tutsis in neighboring Burundi and what it viewed as the failure of the DRC government to take stronger action to protect refugees.

For the 2006 presidential election Ruberwa was listed as the official candidate of the RCD, although press reports continued to reference him as the candidate of RCD-Goma, while Lumbala ran as a candidate of the RCD-N and Nyamwisi as the candidate of the **Forces of Renewal** (*Forces du Renouveau*—FR).

Ruberwa finished 6th in the first round of presidential balloting in July 2006 with 1.7 percent of the vote, while Nyamwisi finished 11th with 0.6 percent and Lumbala 17th with 0.45 percent. (Shortly before the election, Nyamwisi had announced his support for President Kabila, and Nyamwisi joined the cabinets installed in February and November 2007 as a representative of the FR.)

Leaders: Antipas Mbusa NYAMWISI (RCD-LM and FR), Adolphe ONUSUMBA Yemba (RCD-Goma), Roger LUMBALA Tshitenge (RCD-N), Azarias RUBERWA Manywa (Vice President of the Republic and Secretary General of RCD-Goma).

Movement for the Liberation of the Congo (*Mouvement pour la Libération du Congo*—MLC). The MLC was launched in Equateur Province in November 1998 by Jean-Pierre Bemba, a "Mobutist" who was allegedly funded by Ugandan sources. Subsequently, bolstered by a series of military successes against government forces, the MLC agreed to coordinate its actions with the RCD, which was backed by Rwanda. That alliance proved short-lived, however, in view of the conflict that soon developed between Uganda and Rwanda.

Like the other major rebel groups, the MLC participated in the Inter-Congolese National Dialogue and signed the Pretoria Accord. MLC fighters were subsequently integrated into the national security forces, and the party became a member of the transitional government. MLC leader Bemba was sworn in as one of four vice presidents for the DRC on July 17, 2003, and the MLC was given equal representation with the RCD-Goma and the opposition alliance in the cabinet and the transitional legislature.

After finishing second in the 2006 presidential election, Bemba was accused by the government in early 2007 of fostering antigovernment "rebellion." He left the country for Portugal after a warrant for his arrest was issued in the DRC in March 2007. Bemba was arrested in May 2008 in Belgium on a warrant issued by the International Criminal Court (ICC) in The Hague, Netherlands, accusing him of war crimes in connection with MLC activity in the Central African Republic (CAR) in 2002–2003. (The MLC had intervened in the CAR in support of President Patassé, who was ultimately overthrown.) Bemba, a DRC senator who had recently been "elected" as the unofficial leader of the opposition, was arraigned at the ICC in July, and his assets were subsequently seized in Portugal. Meanwhile, friction was reported between MLC hard-liners and those party members inclined to cooperate with the new national unity government. (Bemba's case remained in initial procedural status as of mid-2009).

Leaders: Jean-Pierre BEMBA (2006 presidential candidate; currently under arrest in Netherlands), Moise MUSANGANA, Delly SESANGA, François MUAMBA (Secretary General).

Alliance for the Renaissance of Congo (*Alliance pour la Renaissance du Congo*—ARC). The ARC was formed in April 2006 by National Assembly President Olivier Kamitatu, who had recently left the MLC along with a number of others opposed to MLC leader Jean-Pierre Bemba. The ARC presented some 200 candidates in the 2006 assembly poll while supporting the FR's Antipas Mbusa Nyamwasi for president. In 2009 the ARC was regularly referenced as a participant in the pro-Kabila AMP.

Leader: Olivier KAMITATU (Former President of the National Assembly).

Federalist Christian Democracy. This party is led by Pierre Pay-Pay wa Syakassighe, a former central bank governor who, as the candidate of the 18-party **Coalition of Congolese Democrats** (*Coalition des Démocrates Congolais*—CODECO), finished seventh in the first round of presidential balloting in July 2006 with 1.6 percent of the votes. He endorsed Joseph Kabila in the second round, and CODECO joined the AMP, thereby earning participation in the 2007 national unity cabinet.

Leader: Pierre Pay-Pay wa SYAKASSIGHE (2006 presidential candidate).

Popular Movement for Renewal (*Mouvement Populaire Renouveau*—MPR). Founded in 1967 as the principal vehicle of the Mobutu regime and known until August 1990 as the Popular Movement of the Revolution (*Mouvement Populaire de la Révolution*), the MPR was long committed to a program of indigenous nationalism, or "authenticity." Prior to political liberalization in 1990 each Zairean was legally assumed to be a member of the party at birth.

The 1988 MPR Congress reaffirmed support for the country's single-party system. However, in May 1990 President Mobutu, after signaling the introduction of a multiparty system, stepped down as MPR chair, stating that he would henceforth serve "above parties"; he resumed the post in April 1991. During Mobutu's absence the party split into factions led by N'SINGA Udjuu Ongwakebei (the new chair) and Felix Vunduawe te Pemako, who termed the restructured entity "illegitimate" and presented himself as leader of a "group to renew the People's Revolution."

Faced with vigorous Western opposition to Mobutu's continuance in office, the party at an April 1993 general meeting called on the Birindwa government to sever diplomatic relations with Belgium, France, and the United States, all of which were accused of "stirring up hatred, division, and destruction" and engaging in "neo-colonialism, imperialism . . . and terrorism against Zaire."

Mobutu died of prostate cancer in September 1997, only months after his ouster from Kinshasa by the AFDL. Subsequently, the MPR (with the term "Revolution" once again being used routinely in its references rather than "Renewal") split into two factions, one led by Vunduawe and a second led by Catherine Nzuzi wa Mbombo. Nzuzi was subsequently jailed for 20 months before being released by Joseph Kabila. She was appointed minister for solidarity and humanitarian affairs in the 2003 transitional government, and she received 0.38 percent of the vote in the first round of presidential balloting in July 2006.

Leaders: Felix VUNDUAWE te Pemako, Catherine NZUZI wa Mbombo (2006 presidential candidate).

Innovating Forces of the Sacred Union (*Forces Innovatrices de la Union Sacrée*—FONUS). FONUS is led by Joseph Olenghankoy, a hard-line USOR member who was arrested in 1994 for declaring the government guilty of "unconstitutional" behavior and in 1998 for engaging in illegal party activity. Olenghankoy was appointed minister of transport and communication in the 2003 transitional government. He received 0.6 percent of the vote in the first round of presidential balloting in July 2006.

Leader: Joseph OLENGHANKOY (2006 presidential candidate).

Democratic and Social Christian Party (*Parti Démocrate et Social Chrétien*—PDSC). The PDSC applied for legal status in mid-1990 in a bid to secure what was then expected to be the third and final party slot. The party was ultimately recognized in early 1991, and by midyear it had emerged as one of the most influential groups in the Sacred Union.

The PDSC was one of the "moderate" USOR parties that, aligned under the banner of the Union for the Republic and Democracy (*Union pour la République et la Démocratie*—URD), advocated better relations with the Mobutu regime and a more democratic process within the USOR. (Other groups in the URD included the UDI, below; the **Nationalist Common Front** [*Front Commun Nationaliste*—FCN], led by Gerard KAMANDA wa Kamanda [a former minister in the Mobutu and Tshisekedi governments and the FCN presidential candidate in 2006] and MANDUNGU-BULA Nyati; and the **Planters' Solidarity Party** [*Parti du Solidarité du Planteurs*—PSP], led by Pierre LUMBI Okongo, a former external relations minister.) The URD was expelled from the USOR in May 1994 after, in the climax of a long-running feud, it nominated three candidates for the prime minister's post despite the USOR's official designation of Etienne Tshisekedi as the sole USOR candidate. There has been little reference to PDSC activity since 2002.

Leaders: André BO-BOLIKO Lok'onga, Tuyaba LEWULA (Secretary General).

Union of Federalists and Independent Republicans (*Union des Fédéralistes et Républicains Indépendants*—UFERI). UFERI was created by the 1990 merger of the National Federation of Committed Democrats (*Fédération Nationale des Démocrates Commettres*—Fenadec) and the Independent Republicans' Party (*Parti des Républicains Indépendants*—PRI), which had been launched in April by state commissioner of foreign affairs Jean Nguza Karl-I-Bond. At the time of the merger, Nguza described the new grouping, which he was subsequently named to head, as a "serious adversary to the MPR." The party was officially registered in January 1991 and soon thereafter was described as one of the most prominent groups in the Sacred Union coalition. In September UFERI asserted that it would join only in a government formed by a sovereign national conference, and in October UFERI agreed to support the Sacred Union's efforts to reinstate Etienne Tshisekedi as prime minister. Nevertheless, on November 21 Nguza, dismissing coalition criticism, agreed to assume the prime minister's post, from which he was ultimately obliged to resign on August 17, 1992.

Subsequently, Nguza warned that UFERI's Katangan supporters would not accept Tshisekedi's appointment, and violent clashes between the two groups were reported. Furthermore, the "ethnic cleansing" of Kasais from Shaba (formerly Katanga) Province, which by mid-1993 had reportedly resulted in thousands of deaths and dislocations, was allegedly sanctioned by Mobutu and executed by Nguza's supporters. In April 1993 Nguza was named deputy prime minister for defense in the Birindwa government. In mid-1996 UFERI leaders denounced the Kengo wa Dondo government for its "anti-democratic behavior" after the party was banned from organizing political activities in Katanga. Nguza died of a heart attack in July 2003, and there has subsequently been little reference to UFERI activity.

Leader: Gabriel KYUNGU wa Kumwanza.

Congolese National Movement (*Mouvement National Congolais*—MNC). From the 1970s to the 1990s, the MNC was an exile group with at least two discernible factions, the Congolese National Movement–Lumumba (*Mouvement National Congolais–Lumumba*—MNC-L), whose military wing operated as the Lumumba Patriotic Army (*Armíe Patriotique Lumumba*—APL), and the Reformed Congolese National Movement (*Mouvement National Congolais Rénové*—MNCR). The MNC became visible in 1978 when its president was detained by Belgian authorities and expelled to France, with similar action taken against its secretary general in 1984 after the group claimed responsibility for a series of March bombings in Kinshasa. In 1985 the MNC emerged as the most active of the external groups; in April it issued a statement calling Mobutu "an element of instability in central Africa" and listing those allegedly killed by government troops during disturbances in eastern provinces in late 1984. In September 1985 leaders of both the MNC-L and the MNCR joined with the Swiss-based Congolese Democratic and Socialist Party (*Parti Démocratique et Socialiste Congolaise*), led by Allah FIOR Muyinda, in inviting other opposition groups to participate in a joint working commission to oversee "activities [to be launched] over the whole country in coming days." MNCR leader Paul-Roger MOKEDE was named president of the exile provisional government at a meeting in Switzerland in September 1987 but rejected the designation on the grounds that Zaire could not "afford the luxury" of a parallel regime.

In September 1994 a group identifying itself as the MNC-L was reportedly "formed" in Kinshasa by "nationalists" and Lumumbists under the leadership of Pascal TABU, Mbalo MEKA, and Otoko OKITASOMBO. The older, or original, MNC faction became known as the MNC–*Lumumba Originel* or Original Lumumba (MNC-LO).

In early 1998 François Lumumba, eldest son of the former prime minister, charged that the regime of Laurent Kabila was denying freedom of expression to him and other family members. Lumumba emerged as leader of the MNC-L. He was briefly detained by the government in 2000.

Leader: François Tolenga LUMUMBA (MNC-L).

Mai-Mai Ingilima. The Mai-Mai was an ethnic Bahunde militia whose members were described as "armed mystics" for their belief, among others, that the grass headgear they wore in battle possessed the power to turn their enemies' bullets into water (*mai-mai* is the Swahili word for water). Credited with disarming Hutu fighters and Zairean soldiers at the start of the 1996 rebellion, the Mai-Mai was expected to coordinate their actions with the AFDL as the fighting moved into northern Zaire. However, in December 1996 the Mai-Mai was accused of attempting to assassinate AFDL commander Andre Ngandu KISSASSE, who allegedly wanted the Mai-Mai to disarm and report for training. In early 1997 further clashes between the rebel groups were reported, and later in the year the Mai-Mai grouping was described as fully confrontational with the national army of the new Kabila regime in pursuit of regional autonomy for South Kivu. Thereafter, beginning in August 1998, the Mai-Mai was described as alternately cooperating with and clashing with elements of the RCD, in addition to continuing its antigovernment military activities. The Mai-Mai became formally allied with the Kabila government during the Inter-Congolese National Dialogue that culminated in the Pretoria Accord, and the Mai-Mai was subsequently given cabinet posts and seats in the transitional government. However, some Mai-Mai forces later turned hostile to the government under the leadership of a warlord identified as GÉDÉON and assumed control of regions of Katanga. After his forces were accused of attacks on civilians, Gédéon surrendered to MONUC in April 2006. The group presented candidates in the 2006 assembly balloting under the banner of the **Mai-Mai Movement** (*Mouvement Maï-Maï*—MMM).

Fighting was subsequently reported between members of the CNDP (below) and a Mai-Mai offshoot called the **Congolese Resistance**

Patriots (*Patriotes Résistants du Congo*—Pareco), described as a "progovernment civil defense" grouping under the leadership of Sendugu MUSEVENI. Pareco was also believed to have aligned itself informally with the FDLR in eastern DRC, but in February 2009, following the DRC/Rwanda initiative against the FDLR, it was reported that Pareco for the most part had agreed to integrate into the DRC's military, while Pareco sought legal party status under Museveni's leadership. Subsequently, a faction called **The Alliance of Patriots for a Free and Sovereign Congo** (*Alliance des Patriotes pour un Congo Libre et Souverain*—APCLS) reportedly remained in conflict with the government.

Union of Congolese Patriots (*Union des Patriotes Congolais*—UPC). The UPC was formed as an antigovernment militia by members of the Hema ethnic group in the Ituri region. Although the UPC was reportedly subsequently registered as a political party, its leader, Thomas LUBANGA, was turned over to the new International Criminal Court (ICC) in March 2006 to face charges of war crimes and human rights abuses. By that time, some remnants of the UPC had reportedly helped launch the MRC (see below). ICC judges ordered Lubanga released in July 2008 on the grounds that evidence had been mishandled by prosecutors, although Lubanga remained in custody pending an appeal of that decision. The case against Lubanga was reinstated in early 2009.

Congolese Revolutionary Movement (*Mouvement Révolutionnaire Congolais*—MRC). The MRC was reportedly formed in Uganda in the second half of 2005 by Congolese rebels who had not accepted the peace process and integration into the proposed national army. MRC participants reportedly included remnants of the UPC (see above), the **Patriotic Resistance Front of Ituri** (*Front de Résistance Patriotique en Ituri*—FRPI), the **Front for National Integration**, the **People's Army of Congo**, and the RCD. Government forces launched an offensive against the MRC in eastern DRC in March 2006.

National Congress for the Defense of the People (*Congrès National pour la Défense du Peuple*—CNDP). The CNDP was formed in late 2006 by rebel leader Gen. Laurent Nkunda, a Congolese Tutsi whose followers had aligned with Rwanda in the rebellion against the government of Laurent Kabila in the late 1990s. Nkunda described the CNDP as a "political-military movement" intended to protect the interests of Tutsis, who reportedly felt "marginalized" by the DRC government and threatened by Hutu rebels who had coalesced in eastern DRC as the Democratic Forces for the Liberation of Rwanda (*Forces Démocratiques pour la Libération du Rwanda*—FDLR). Fighting was reported later in the year between the CNDP and FDLR, with the CNDP accusing MONUC and the DRC government of "siding" with the FDLR.

In January 2007 Nkunda agreed to discuss a peace agreement with the government on the assumption that CNDP fighters would eventually be integrated into the national army and that the government would agree to protect the rights of Tutsis. However, in September Nkunda announced his forces would resume antigovernment military activity and intensify its anti-FDLR campaign. Heavy fighting throughout the rest of the year left as many as 500,000 people displaced in the conflict zone. Having achieved significant military success (despite the tacit endorsement by the United States and other western nations of the government's anti-CNDP initiative), Nkunda in January 2008 joined a number of other rebel leaders in signing a cease-fire agreement with the government providing for a buffer zone to be monitored by MONUC, amnesty for the "insurrectionists," and integration of rebel troops into the national army. However, the accord subsequently collapsed, the CNDP having been charged with numerous violations of the cease-fire as well as human rights abuses.

After a UN report in late 2008 catalogued the CNDP's Rwandan ties, the Rwanda government in early 2009 appeared to sever any relationship with Nkunda and other CNDP militants, apparently in return for the DRC's cooperation in an anti-FDLR campaign (see Current issues, above, for additional information). Bosco Ntaganda, theretofore the CNDP's chief of staff and, like Nkunda, wanted on war crimes charges by the ICC, announced that he had assumed leadership of the CNDP. In a dramatic reversal of fortune, the Rwandan authorities arrested Nkunda in late January in Rwanda, where he remained under house arrest while Ntaganda announced a cease-fire with the DRC. The CNDP subsequently indicated it would seek legal party status in the DRC under the leadership of Désiré Kamandji.

Leaders: Gen. Laurent NKUNDA, (under house arrest in Rwanda), Bosco NTAGANDA, Désiré KAMANDJI, Bertrand BISIMWA.

Bundu Dia Kongo (BDK). The BDK is a political-religious movement dedicated to the restoration of the former Kingdom of Kongo in the DRC's southwestern province of Bas-Congo and surrounding regions, both inside and outside the DRC. Significant fighting was reported in March 2008 between BDK fighters and government security forces.

Leader: Ne Mwanda NSEMI.

Other groups include the **Congolese People's Movement for the Republic** (*Mouvement Populaire Congolais pour le République*—MPCR), led by Jean-Claude VUEMBA; the **Congolese Socialist Party,** led by Christian BADIBANGI; the **Forces of the Future** (*Forces du Futur*—FDF), led by Arthur Z'ahidi NGOMA, who had been jailed from November 1997 to June 1998 and subsequently became an RCD leader before going into exile in France (see RCD, above) and then returning to serve as vice president of the republic from 2003 to 2006 (Ngoma ran for president in 2006 as the candidate of a party called **Camp of the Fatherland** [*Camp de la Patrie*]); the **Movement for Solidarity, Democracy, and Development** (*Mouvement pour la Solidarité, la Démocratie, et le Développement*—MSDD), whose leader, Christophe LUTUNDULA Apala, chaired the legislative committee that investigated alleged corruption in the issuance of government contracts during the 1998–2003 civil war; the **National Convention for Political Action**; the **Union of Republicans** (*Union des Républicains*), whose leader, Norbert LUYEYE, was arrested in May 2009 for criticizing the presence of Ugandan and Rwandan troops on DRC territory; the **Peasant Reconciliation and Development Party**, formed in April 2009 by a Mai-Mai faction led by Bita ZEBEDE; and the **Congolese Democratic Party**, whose leader, Gabriel MOKIA, was sentenced to ten months in prison in April 2009 on a charge of "undermining the authority of the state" in connection with his criticism of government military policy.

Other parties that won representation in the assembly in the 2006 balloting included the **Convention of the Christian Democrats** (*Convention des Démocrates Chrétiens*—CDC), whose presidential candidate, Florentin Mokonda BONZA, won 0.29 percent of the vote in 2006 and whose president is Gilbert KIAKWAMA; **Christian Democracy** (*Démocratie Chrétienne*—DC), which presented Eugene Ndougala DIOMI as its 2006 presidential candidate; the **Rally of Socialist Forces** (*Rassemblement des Forces Sociales et Fédéralistes*—RSF), whose presidential candidate, Vincent de Paul LUNDA Bululu (former prime minister), placed eighth in the first round of the 2006 poll with 1.4 percent of the vote; the **Convention for the Republic and Democracy** (*Convention pour la République et la Démocratie*—CRD), whose leader, Christophe N'KODIA Pwango Mboso, secured 0.47 percent of the vote in the first round of the 2006 presidential poll; the **Alliance of Congolese Democrats** (*Alliance des Démocrates Congolais*—ADECO), whose 2006 presidential candidate was Jonas Kadiata Nzemba MUKAMBA; and the **Union for the Defense of the Republic** (*Union pour la Défense de la République*—UDR), whose 2006 presidential candidate was Wivine N'Landu KAVIDI.

Other parties that participated in the 2006 elections included the **Socialist Liberal Union** (*Union Socialiste Libérale*—USL), whose presidential candidate, Bernard Emmanuel SUILA, placed 12th in the polling; the **Rally for a New Society** (*Rassemblement pour une Nouvelle Société*—RNS), whose leader, Alafuele KALALA Mbuyi, received less than 1 percent of the vote in the presidential poll; the **Movement of Democrats** (*Mouvement des Démocrates*—MD), whose candidate, Justine Kasa-Vubu M'POYO, was 18th in the first round of the presidential balloting with 0.44 percent of the vote; the **Renewal for Development and Democracy** (*Renouveau pour le Développement et la Démocratie*—RDD), whose candidate, Osee Ndjoko MUYIMA, was 31st in the presidential election; the **Politial Coalition of Christians** (*Coalition Politique des Chrétiens*—CPC), whose presidential candidate was Jacob Souga NIEMBA; the **Party for Peace in the Congo** (*Parti pour la Paix au Congo*—CONGO-PAX), whose presidential candidate was Marie Thérese Mpolo Nene NLANDU; and the **African Congress of Democrats** (*Congrés Africain des Démocrates*—CAD, whose presidential candidate was Harsan Uba THASSINDA.

Other rebel groups include the **Nationalist and Integrationist Front** (*Front Nationaliste Integrationiste*—FNI), an ethnic Lendu separatist group active in Ituri that was suspected of being responsible for attacks against MONUC forces and whose military leader, Etiene LONA, surrendered to the UN in March 2005 (another former FNI leader, Mathieu Ngudjolo CHUI, was arrested in February 2008 on an

ICC warrant accusing him of war crimes in relation to ethnic fighting in Ituri in 2002–2003, although he and other FNI fighters had been integrated into the DRC's national army); the **Congolese Patriots Union–Kisembo** (UPC-Kisembo), a breakaway faction of the UPC, led by Floribert Kisembo BAHEMUKA; the **Patriotic Resistance Force in Ituri**, (*Force de Résistance Patriotique en Ituri*—FRPI), a Lendu group linked to the FNI and led by Germain KATANGA, who was transferred to the control of the ICC in 2008 after being charged with war crimes; the **Popular Front for Justice in the** Congo (*Front Congolais pour la Justice au* Congo—FCJC), an FRPI offshoot formed in October 2008 and subsequently reported to be conducting operations against government forces in the northeast; and the **Front for the Liberation of Eastern Congo,** a group composed of former members of the RCD. In addition, the **Rwanda Democratic Liberation Front,** a Rwandan Hutu group, remained active in 2006 in South Kivu, conducting raids into Rwanda and attacks on DRC government installations and security forces.

LEGISLATURE

On August 21, 2000, a new Legislative and Constituent Assembly–Transitional Parliament was inaugurated. President Laurent Kabila directly appointed 60 of the 300 members, while the remaining members were selected in consultation with a presidentially appointed commission. (For information on quasi-legislative development from 1992 to 2000, see the 2007 *Handbook*.)

The December 2002 Pretoria Accord provided for the establishment of a bicameral legislature through an interim constitution. The representatives from both chambers were appointed from the major political parties, civic groups, and rebel factions. Both chambers of the transitional Parliament were inaugurated on August 23, 2003.

The constitution promulgated in February 2006 provided for a new bicameral **Parliament** comprising a Senate and a National Assembly.

Senate (*Sénat*). The interim Senate appointed through negotiations following the Pretoria Accord of 2002 consisted of 120 members. Each of the 5 major political groups received 22 positions, including propresidential parties (led by the People's Party for Reconstruction and Development [PPRD]); the opposition alliance; the Congolese Rally for Democracy (RCD-Goma); the Movement for the Liberation of Congo (MLC); and civic groups. In addition, the Mai-Mai received 4 seats; the RCD-Liberation Movement, 4; and the RCD-National, 2.

The current Senate comprises 108 members elected indirectly by the provincial assemblies for five-year terms, as well as all former elected presidents of the republic, who serve as senators for life. Direct elections for the nation's 11 provincial assemblies were held on October 29, 2006, and those assemblies selected the members of the Senate on January 19, 2007, resulting in the following distribution of elected seats: the PPRD, 22; the MLC, 13; the RCD, 8; the Christian Democrat Party, 8; the Forces for Renewal, 6; the Convention of Christian Democrats, 1; the RCD-National, 1; the Democratic Social Christian Party, 1; the National Alliance Party for Unity, 1; the Union of Mobutuist Democrats, 1; the Democratic Convention for Development, 1; the Social Front of Independent Republicans, 1; the Coalition of Congolese Democrats, 1; the Alliance of Congolese Democrats, 1; the National Union of Christian Democrats, 1; the Rally of Social and Federalist Forces, 1; the Rally for Economic and Social Development, 1; the Federalist Christian Democracy, 1; the National Union of Federalist Democrats, 1; others, 4; and independents, 25.

President: Joseph Léon KENGO wa Dondo.

National Assembly (*Assemblée Nationale*). The interim National Assembly comprised 500 deputies appointed from the major political groups in the DRC. The five main groups each received 94 seats, including propresidential parties (led by the People's Party for Reconstruction and Development [PPRD]); the opposition alliance; the Congolese Rally for Democracy (RCD-Goma); the Movement for the Liberation of Congo (MLC); and civic groups. The RCD–Liberation Movement was given 15 seats; the Mai-Mai, 10; and the RCD-National, 5.

The current assembly comprises 500 deputies—69 elected by one-round plurality voting in single-member constituencies and 431 elected by proportional representation in 109 multimember constituencies. In the first elections to the new assembly on July 30, 2006, the PPRD won 111 seats; the MLC, 64; the Unified Lumumbist Party, 34; the Social Movement for Renewal, 27; the Forces for Renewal, 26; the Congolese Rally for Democracy, 15; the Coalition of Congolese Democrats, 10; the Union of Mobutuist Democrats, 9; the Camp of the Fatherland, 8; the Federalist Christian Democracy–Convention of Federalists for Democracy, 8; the Christian Democrat Party, 8; the Union of Federalist Nationalists of the Congo, 7; the Alliance of Congolese Democrats, 4; the Rally of Congolese Democrats and Nationalists, 4; the Convention of United Congolese, 4; the National Alliance Party for Unity, 3; the Party of Nationalists for Development, 3; the Democratic Convention for Development, 3; the National Union of Federalist Democrats, 3; the Union of Congolese Patriots, 3; the Convention for the Republic and Democracy, 3; the Alliance of the Builders of the Congo, 3; the Union for the Republican Majority, 2; the Renaissance Electoral Platform, 2; the Renewing Forces for Union and Solidarity, 2; the Rally of the Social and Federalist Forces, 2; Solidarity for National Development, 2; the Alliance of Believing Congolese Nationalists, 2; the Democratic and Social Christian Party, 2; the Party of the Revolution of the People, 2; the National Union of Christian Democrats, 2; the Congolese Party for Good Governance, 2; the Movement for Democracy and Development, 2; the Alliance for the Renewal of the Congo, 2; Christian Democracy, 1; the National Convention for the Republic and Progress, 1; the Action Movement for the Resurrection of the Congo/Labor Party, 1; the Union of Liberal Christian Democrats, 1; the Front of Christian Democrats, 1; the Solidarity Movement for Democracy and Development, 1; the Congolese Union for Change, 1; the National Party of the People, 1; the Union of Congolese Nationalist Patriots, 1; Republican Generations, 1; the Congolese Party for the Well-Being of the People, 1; the Front for Social Integration, 1; the Social Front of Independent Republicans, 1; the Union for the Defense of the Republic, 1; the National Convention of Political Action, 1; the Progressive Lumumbist Movement, 1; the Mai-Mai Movement, 1; the Conscience and Will of the People, 1; the Front of Social Democrats for Development, 1; the Self-Defense Movement for Integrity and the Maintenance of Independent Authority, 1; the Political Organization of Kasavubists and Allies, 1; the Party of National Unity, 1; the Popular Movement of the Revolution, 1; the Rally for Economic and Social Development, 1; the Christian Union for Renewal and Justice, 1; the Action Rally for Reconstruction and National Edification, 1; the Rally of Congolese Ecologists (The Greens), 1; the Movement of the Congolese People for the Republic, 1; the Alliance of Congolese Nationalists, 1; the Rally of Christians for the Congo, 1; the Christian Convention for Democracy, 1; and independents, 63.

Speaker: Evariste BOSHAB.

CABINET

[as of July 1, 2009]

Prime Minister	Adolphe Muzito (PALU)
Deputy Prime Ministers	
Reconstruction	Emile Bongeli (PPRD)
Security and Defense	Mutombo Bakafwa Nsenda (PALU)
Social Affairs	François Joseph Mobutu (Udemo)
Ministers	
Agriculture	Norbert Basengezi
Budget	Michael Lokola Elamba (PALU)
Civil Service	Michel Botoro Bodias
Communications and Media	Lambert Mende Omalanga
Culture and Arts	Esdras Kambale
Decentralization and Land-Use Planning	Antipas Mbusa Nyamwisi
Energy	Laurent Muzangisa
Environment, Conservation of Nature, and Tourism	José Endundu Bononge
Finance	Athanese Matendu Kyelu
Foreign Affairs	Alexis Thambwe Mwamba
Gender, Family, and Children	Marie-Ange Lukiana Mufwankol (PPRD) [f]
Higher Education	Léonard Mashako Mamba
Human Rights	Upio Karura

Hydrocarbons	René Isekemanga Nkeka
Industry	Simon Mboso Kiamputu
Infrastructure, Public Works, and Reconstruction	Pierre Lumbi Okongo (MSR)
Interior	Célestin Mbuyu
International and Regional Cooperation	Raymond Tshibanda Ntngamulongo
Justice	Luzolo Bambi Lesa
Labor and Social Security	Ferdinand Kambere
Land Affairs	Kisimba Ngoy Maje [f]
Mines	Martin Kabwelulu Labilo
National Defense and Veterans	Charles Mwando Nsimba
National Economy and Commerce	André Philippe Futa
Planning	Olivier Kamitatu Etsu
Post, Telephones, and Telecommunications	Louise Munga [f]
Primary, Secondary, and Professional Education	Macair Mwangu Famba
Public Health	August Mopipi Mukulumanya
Relations with Parliament	Adolphe Lumanu
Rural Development	Taty Azili
Scientific Research	Joseph Bitibiyo Afata
Small- and Medium-Sized Enterprises	Claude Batibuhe Nyamugabo
Social Affairs, Humanitarian Action, and National Solidarity	Barthélémy Botswali Lengomo
State Assets	Jeannine Mabunda Lioko [f]
Transport	Mathieu Pita
Urban Development and Housing	Générose Loshiku Muya [f]
Youth and Sports	Patrick Sulubika

[f] = female

COMMUNICATIONS

Newspapers were increasingly subject to government control under the Mobutu regime, and a "restructuring" of the press reduced the number of papers being issued. Strict control was also reported under the administration of Laurent Désiré Kabila.

Opposition parties have recently accused state media of favoring the PPRD over other parties, and journalists have been arrested for reporting on demonstrations. In addition, the state media regulatory agency has suspended licenses of broadcast media for "biased reporting" of antigovernment activities. In late 2005 journalism watchdog organizations reported that press freedom was "deteriorating," while opposition groups decried the perceived "total control" of the state-run media by supporters of President Kabila and the AMP during the 2006–2007 elections. Critics also charged the government with subsequently "targeting" media owned by failed presidential candidate Jean-Pierre Bemba. Meanwhile, Reporters Without Borders described the media as "highly politicized" and reported that journalists faced a bewildering array of legal restrictions.

Press. The following are dailies published in Kinshasa, unless otherwise noted: *Le Potentiel* (8,000); *L'Avenir; Le Phare* (4,000), close to the UDPS; *La Référence; Le Forum; La Dépêche* (Lubumbashi); *Salongo*; *Le Journal* (three times per week); *L'Alerte,* independent, *Le Soft,* independent; *Le Nouvel Observateur*, progovernment; *L'Hebdo de l'Est*, independent weekly.

News agencies. The domestic facility is the Congolese Press Agency (*Agence Congolaise de Presse*—ACP). *Agence France-Presse, Xinhua,* and Pan-African News Agency also maintain bureaus in Kinshasa.

Broadcasting and computing. Radio broadcasting is provided by the government over the national station, *La Voix du Congo,* and regional stations. Television is provided by the government-operated, commercial Television Congolaise. There are also several private radio and television stations broadcasting from Kinshasa. MONUC temporarily sponsors a radio station called *Radio Okapi.* However, television and radio broadcasts from Kinshasa do not reach some parts of the country, including the volatile eastern region. As of 2008 there were 4.5 Internet users per 1,000 inhabitants.

INTERGOVERNMENTAL REPRESENTATION

Ambassador to the U.S.: Faida MITIFU.

U.S. Ambassador to the Democratic Republic of the Congo: William John GARVELINK.

Permanent Representative to the UN: Atoki ILEKA.

IGO Memberships (Non-UN): AfDB, AU, BADEA, CEEAC, CEPGL, Comesa, Interpol, IOM, NAM, OIF, PCA, SADC, WCO, WTO.

REPUBLIC OF THE CONGO

République du Congo

Note: President Gen. Denis Sassou-Nguesso (Congolese Labor Party)) abolished the post of prime minister during a cabinet reshuffle on September 15, 2009.

Political Status: Independent since August 15, 1960; one-party People's Republic proclaimed December 31, 1969; multiparty system authorized as of January 1, 1991; constitution approved in referendum of March 15, 1992, suspended in October 1997 following overthrow of the government; current constitution adopted by referendum of January 20, 2002.

Area: 132,046 sq. mi. (342,000 sq. km.).

Population: 2,591,271 (1996C); 4,436,000 (2008E).

Major Urban Center (2005E): BRAZZAVILLE (1,275,000).

Official Language: French.

Monetary Unit: CFA Franc (official rate December 1, 2009: 434.59 francs = $1US). The CFA franc, previously pegged to the French franc, is now permanently pegged to the euro at 655.957 CFA francs = 1 euro.

President: Gen. Denis SASSOU-NGUESSO (Congolese Labor Party); sworn in on October 25, 1997, following the military overthrow of the government of Pascal LISSOUBA (Pan-African Union for Social Democracy) on October 23; elected for a seven-year term on March 10, 2002, and inaugurated on August 10; reelected for another seven-year term on July 12, 2009.

Prime Minister: (*See headnote.*) Isidore MVOUBA (Congolese Labor Party); appointed by the president on January 7, 2005. (The position of prime minister is not mandated in the current constitution and was abolished by President Sassou-Nguesso on November 3, 1997, when Bernard KOLÉLAS [Congolese Movement for Democracy and Integral Development] held the position. The post was restored with the appointment of Mvouba.)

THE COUNTRY

The Republic of the Congo is a narrow 800-mile-long strip of heavily forested territory extending inland from the Atlantic along the Congo and Ubangi rivers. It is bordered on the west by Gabon, on the north by Cameroon and the Central African Republic, and on the east and south by the Democratic Republic of the Congo (formerly Zaire). The members of the country's multitribal society belong mainly to the Bakongo, Matéké, Mbochi, and Vili tribal groups and include numerous pygmies, who are thought to be among the first inhabitants of the area. Linguistically, the tribes speak related Bantu languages; French, although the official language, is

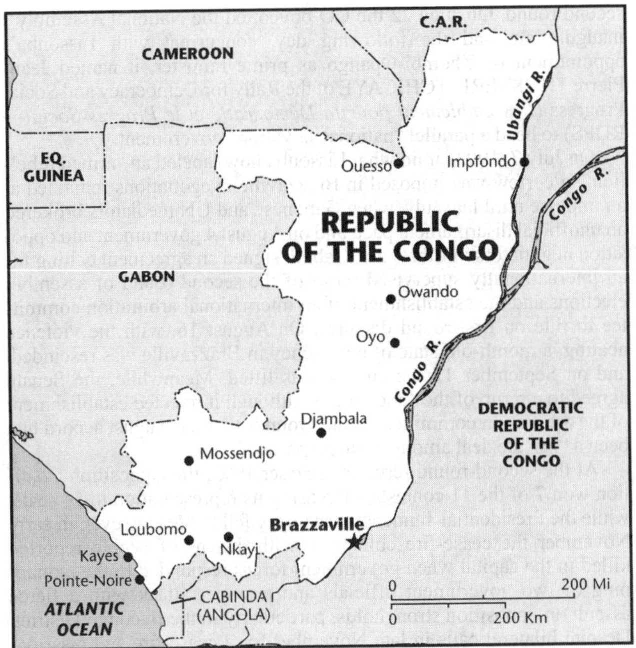

not in widespread use. There is, however, a lingua franca, Monokutuba, which is widely employed in commerce. In recent decades there has been substantial rural-to-urban migration, with close to 50 percent of the population now living in or near Brazzaville or Pointe Noir. Partly because of its level of urbanization, the Republic of the Congo has a literacy rate estimated at 70–85 percent, one of the highest in black Africa. About half of the population adheres to traditional religious beliefs, while Roman Catholics, Protestants, and Muslims comprise the remainder.

Although the country possesses exploitable deposits of manganese, copper, lead-zinc, and gold, its leading resources are oil and timber, with the first accounting for more than 88 percent of export earnings in 2003. The economy was severely compromised following the five-month civil war of mid-1997, which, among other things, heavily damaged the capital and reduced GDP growth from about 6.3 percent in 1996 to a negative rate in 1997.

The International Monetary Fund (IMF) and the World Bank suspended aid to the Republic of the Congo in 2000 because of the perceived failure of the government to enact economic reforms. Partial aid was restored in 2004, although the government by that time faced heavy international criticism on an important regional issue—diamond exporting (see Current issues, below). Meanwhile, the Republic of the Congo remained one of the poorest countries in the world, although increased revenue from high oil prices had at least permitted the government to pay off arrears in civil service salaries.

High oil prices, along with increased stability since the end of the civil war, helped bolster the economy in 2005–2006, with average GDP growth of about 6 percent recorded. However, a debt relief agreement with the IMF and the World Bank in early 2006 failed to come to fruition in October due to the government's reported failure to provide greater transparency in state finances, particularly in regard to oil revenues. The IMF was particularly concerned by a British court's confirmation that Sassou-Nguesso's government had channeled oil revenues into secret accounts. On a more positive note, the IMF reported "robust growth" in the country's non-oil sector, reflecting greater economic diversity.

A temporary setback in oil production, caused by an accident at an oil platform, contributed to a decline in overall economic activity in 2007, according to the IMF, but robustness resumed in 2008 in both the oil and non-oil sectors, with annual GDP growth of 8.5 percent. Fund managers also commended the government for its social reforms, a number of which had helped offset the impact of high food and fuel prices early in the year. In December the IMF approved $12.5 million in poverty reduction aid over three years, which fund managers in 2009 said "had put the Congolese authorities in a good position to address the challenges posed by the difficult global (financial) environment." The sharp decline in oil prices during the recession and sluggish growth in the non-oil sector led to a contraction of the economy of about 1.5 percent in 2009.

GOVERNMENT AND POLITICS

Political background. Occupied by France in the 1880s, the former colony of Middle Congo became the autonomous Republic of the Congo in 1958 and attained full independence within the French Community on August 15, 1960. The country's first president, Fulbert YOULOU, established a strong centralized administration but resigned in 1963 in the face of numerous strikes and labor demonstrations. His successor, Alphonse MASSAMBA-DÉBAT, was installed by the military and subsequently reelected for a five-year term. Under Massamba-Débat the regime embraced a Marxist-type doctrine of "scientific socialism," and the political system was reorganized on a one-party basis. In 1968, however, Massamba-Débat was stripped of authority as a result of differences with both left-wing and military elements. A military coup led by Capt. Marien NGOUABI on August 3 was followed by the establishment of a National Council of the Revolution to direct the government.

Formally designated as head of state in January 1969, Ngouabi proclaimed a "people's republic" the following December, while a constitution adopted in January 1970 legitimized a single political party, the Congolese Labor Party (*Parti Congolais du Travail*—PCT). Three years later, a new basic law established the post of prime minister and created a National Assembly to replace the one dissolved in 1968.

President Ngouabi was assassinated on March 18, 1977, and the PCT immediately transferred its powers to an 11-member Military Committee headed by Jacques-Joachim YHOMBI-OPANGO, which reinstituted rule by decree. Former president Massamba-Débat, who was accused of having plotted the assassination, was executed on March 25. On April 3 it was announced that Maj. Denis SASSOU-NGUESSO had been named first vice president of the Military Committee and that Maj. Louis-Sylvain GOMA, who retained his post as prime minister, had been named second vice president.

Responding to pressure from the Central Committee of the PCT after having made disparaging remarks about the condition of the country's economy, General Yhombi-Opango, as well as the Military Committee, resigned on February 5, 1979. The Central Committee thereupon established a ruling Provisional Committee and named Sassou-Nguesso as interim president. At a March congress the party confirmed Sassou-Nguesso as president, while on July 8 the voters approved a new constitution and elected a People's National Assembly in addition to district, regional, and local councils. On July 30, 1984, the president was elected for a second term, and on August 11, as part of a reshuffling aimed at "strengthening the revolutionary process," he named Ange-Edouard POUNGUI to succeed Goma as prime minister.

In July 1987, 20 military officers linked to a group of Paris-based exiles were arrested on charges of plotting a coup. Thereafter, an alleged co-conspirator, Lt. Pierre ANGA, who charged that Sassou-Nguesso had participated in the murder of former president Ngouabi, led a rebellion in the north. Reports of attacks by rebel forces continued until July 4, 1988, when the killing of Anga by government troops ended the uprising.

On July 30, 1989, Sassou-Nguesso was reelected for a third term at the fourth PCT party congress. However, continued debate over the foundering economy led to an extraordinary congress in August at which a moderate technocrat, Alphonse POATY-SOUCHLATY, was named to succeed Poungui as prime minister.

During the ensuing year, pressure mounted for abandonment of the PCT's claim to political exclusivity. In October 1990, confronted with a general strike that had brought the country to a standstill and acting on a party decision reached three months earlier, General Sassou-Nguesso announced that a multiparty system would be introduced on January 1, 1991, followed by the convening of an all-party National Conference to chart the nation's political future. On January 14 he appointed a "transitional" government headed by former prime minister Goma, Poaty-Souchlaty having resigned on December 3 in protest over the president's call for the introduction of pluralism.

The National Conference, which encompassed representatives of 30 parties and 141 associations, convened for a three-month sitting on February 25, 1991, eventually approving the draft of a new democratic constitution; dropping "People's" from the country's name; transferring most presidential powers to the prime minister; scheduling a constitutional referendum for November; and calling for multiparty local, legislative, and presidential elections during the first half of 1992. On June 8, two days before its conclusion, the conference elected André MILONGO prime minister. Four days later, Milongo named a 25-member cabinet, which on September 15 was reduced to 15 ministers amid charges that members of the opposition coalition Forces of Change (*Forces de Changement*—FDC) were overrepresented.

After a series of postponements, the March 15, 1992, referendum on the new basic law was credited with securing 96 percent approval. Meanwhile, the Milongo government had barely survived a January 19 army mutiny triggered by allegations that transfers of senior officers had been politically motivated. Municipal elections, originally scheduled for March, were eventually held on May 3, while two-stage legislative balloting that was to have been held in April and May was also delayed, with numerous complaints of irregularities at the first stage on June 24.

At second-stage assembly balloting on July 24, 1992, the Pan-African Union for Social Democracy (*Union PanAfricaine pour la Démocratie Sociale*—UPADS) emerged as the clear winner, as it did in a senate poll two days later, albeit without securing a majority in either body. In first-round presidential balloting on August 2, the UPADS nominee, Pascal LISSOUBA, led a field of 17 candidates but secured only 35.9 percent of the vote, thus necessitating a second round against Bernard KOLÉLAS of the Congolese Movement for Democracy and Integral Development (*Mouvement Congolais pour la Démocratie et le Développement Intégral*—MCDDI), who had garnered 22.9 percent. Among those eliminated in the first round were Sassou-Nguesso and Milongo, with vote shares of 16 and 10 percent, respectively. On August 11 the UPADS and PCT announced a coalition, with the outgoing president urging his followers to support the UPADS leader. Thus reinforced, Lissouba outdistanced Kolélas in the second round on August 16 by a margin of 61.3 to 38.7 percent. In the wake of his victory, Lissouba promised a broadly representative government and indicated that he would petition the National Assembly to pardon Sassou-Nguesso and other top officials for crimes committed while in office. On September 1 Lissouba named Maurice-Stéphane BONGHO-NOUARRA of the National Alliance for Democracy (*Alliance Nationale pour la Démocratie*—AND) as prime minister. Six days later Bongho-Nouarra announced a cabinet that included a number of opposition leaders, although Kolélas declined to join them.

In late September 1992 the UPADS-PCT pact dissolved over the choice of a National Assembly president. Shortly thereafter, the PCT concluded an Opposition Coalition (*Coalition de l'Opposition*—CO) with Kolélas's recently formed Union for Democratic Renewal (*Union pour le Renouveau Démocratique*—URD), itself a seven-party antigovernment alliance that included the MCDDI. The CO moved quickly to assert itself and on October 31 successfully moved a no-confidence vote against the government. On November 11 the coalition called for a campaign of civil disobedience and strikes in an effort to force Lissouba to name a CO member as prime minister. On November 14 Bongho-Nouarra resigned, praising President Lissouba for attempting to "pull Congo out of the abyss." Subsequent negotiations between Lissouba and Kolélas led to an impasse, and on November 17 the president, accusing the coalition of "despicable and premeditated acts," dissolved the National Assembly and scheduled a new election for December 30. A wave of civil unrest promptly paralyzed the capital's commercial sector, and by the end of November opposition legislators and security forces were described as in "open confrontation." On December 2 the military occupied Brazzaville, dispersed demonstrators, ordered the government and opposition to form a unity government headed by a compromise prime minister, and suspended election preparations. Four days later, Lissouba appointed Claude-Antoine DACOSTA, an agronomist and former World Bank representative, as prime minister. The government named by Dacosta on December 25 included 12 members from the CO and 9 with links to the president.

At rescheduled assembly balloting on May 2 and June 6, 1993, President Lissouba's 60-party Presidential Tendency (*Tendance Présidentielle*) was credited with winning 69 of 125 seats. However, insisting that the first round had been "tarnished by monstrous irregularities," the opposition demanded a rerun in 12 constituencies and boycotted the second-round balloting. Furthermore, on June 8 Kolélas called for a campaign of civil disobedience to force new elections, thus igniting widespread violence. Subsequent negotiations to stem the unrest failed, as the Opposition Coalition rejected Lissouba's offer to rerun the second round. On June 22 the CO boycotted the National Assembly's inauguration, and the following day, concurrent with Lissouba's appointment of Yhombi-Opango as prime minister, it named Jean-Pierre THYSTERE-TCHICAYE of the Rally for Democracy and Social Progress (*Rassemblement pour la Démocratie et le Progrès Social*—RDPS) to head a parallel "national salvation" government.

On July 7, 1993, amid what Lissouba now labeled an "armed rebellion," a curfew was imposed in Brazzaville. Negotiations remained at an impasse until late July, when Gabonese and UN mediators brokered an unofficial disarmament pact, and on August 4 government and opposition negotiators in Libreville, Gabon, signed an agreement calling for an internationally supervised rerun of the second round of assembly elections and the establishment of an international arbitration committee to rule on first-round disputes. On August 16, with the violence abating, a month-old state of emergency in Brazzaville was rescinded, and on September 17 the curfew was lifted. Meanwhile, the Senate agreed to a rerun of the June voting, although it rejected establishment of the arbitration committee on the grounds that the August accord had been a "private deal among political parties."

At the second-round rerun in October 1993, the Opposition Coalition won 7 of the 11 contests, increasing its representation to 56 seats, while the Presidential Tendency's majority fell to 65. However, in early November the cease-fire collapsed, with dozens of people reported killed in the capital when government forces responded to the kidnapping of two government officials and a sniper attack with a fierce assault on opposition strongholds, particularly in the Bacongo District. Despite bilateral calls in late November for a cease-fire and disarmament, fighting continued throughout 1994.

On January 23, 1995, CO unity was shattered by a URD agreement to participate in a restructured Yhombi-Opango government, a move that was flatly rejected by the PCT. Another coalition member, the National Union for Democracy and Progress (*Union Nationale pour la Démocratie et Progrés*—UNDP), echoed the PCT's sentiments, declaring that it would take no part in the government's "chaotic management of the country" and accusing President Lissouba of "a divide-and-rule strategy."

Regional divisions remained at the fore in 1995 as the Lissouba administration sought to end the northerners' dominance of the 25,000-member military as well as to disarm and integrate the numerous militias that were organized during the 1993 civil unrest and continued to cause widespread instability. In August Lissouba declared that the military would be restructured to reflect a "tribal and regional equilibrium"; however, the military leadership and opposition strenuously objected to the plan, particularly efforts to integrate Lissouba loyalists. In September government troops attempting to disarm militiamen loyal to Sassou-Nguesso met fierce resistance in Brazzaville. Consequently, on November 3 Lissouba proposed assimilating all militiamen into the armed forces. Nevertheless, two days later, National Defense Minister (and former prime minister) Maurice-Stéphane Bongho-Nouarra rejected an administration attempt to absorb 250 militiamen with alleged presidential loyalties, saying that he wanted to depoliticize the recruitment process.

On December 24, 1995, the leaders of the Congo's major propresidential and opposition tendencies signed a peace pact that included provisions for the disarmament and subsequent integration of the former combatants into the national army. However, efforts to implement the accord were dealt a setback on February 14, 1996, when more than 100 recently integrated former militiamen with ties to the UPADS led a violent mutiny in Mpila that left 5 people dead and 40 injured. The rebellion ended on February 19 after negotiations between the government and rebellious troops yielded another integration agreement favoring the latter. Consequently, the opposition United Democratic Forces (*Forces Démocratiques Unies*—FDU) boycotted the peace process for a month, denouncing the government's willingness to "reward" the mutineers and calling for equal representation in the armed forces.

On August 23, 1996, Prime Minister Yhombi-Opango resigned. (He subsequently went into exile in 1997.) His replacement, David Charles GANAO, leader of the Union of Democratic Forces (*Union des Forces Démocratiques*—UFD), on September 2 organized a new government that was nearly evenly split between old and new ministers.

Preparations for presidential elections (scheduled for July 27, 1997) had begun in earnest on May 4, 1996, when the National Census Commission (*Commission Nationale pour le Recensement*—CNR) was inaugurated. However, the CNR was immediately immersed in controversy when the opposition sharply criticized the appointment of President Lissouba as the commission's chair, arguing that it undermined the government's pledge to "ensure transparency" during the electoral run-up. Lissouba subsequently resigned as CNR chair; however, the appointment of Prime Minister Yhombi-Opango as his successor proved equally unsatisfying to the opposition, which called for establishment of an independent commission. In July MCDDI leader Kolélas announced his presidential candidacy, joining a field that already included Lissouba and Gen. Jean-Marie Michel MOKOKO of the Movement for Congolese Reconciliation (*Mouvement pour la Réconciliation Congolaise*—MRC).

Tensions between supporters of Sassou-Nguesso and Lissouba, the two leading presidential candidates, increased as the election approached. In May 1997 Sassou-Nguesso survived an assassination attempt while campaigning, and on June 5 the army surrounded his home, claiming it was part of an effort to disarm private militias. The showdown quickly escalated into civil war, and by mid-July about 4,000 were dead. President Lissouba successfully petitioned the Constitutional Court to postpone the election and extend the expiration date of his mandate, as of July 22. The action enraged Sassou-Nguesso's forces, and fighting spread north despite mediation efforts by the United Nations (UN) and the Organization of African Unity (OAU, subsequently the African Union—AU).

Lissouba appointed Kolélas, then mayor of Brazzaville, as prime minister on September 9, 1997, replacing Ganao, who had resigned on the same day. Kolélas formed a new unity government on September 13, but allies of Sassou-Nguesso declined the posts reserved for them. Kolélas was backed by a 40-party movement, the Republican Space for the Defense of Democracy and National Unity (*Espace Républicain pour la Défense de la Démocratie et Unité Nationale*—ERDDUN), though apparently it was identified too closely with Lissouba forces to have credibility with the rebels.

With the participation of a variety of mercenaries and regular troops from neighboring countries, the civil war continued into mid-October, with Sassou-Nguesso triumphantly entering the destroyed capital on October 23 and being sworn in as president two days later. On November 3 Sassou-Nguesso named a new, broadly representative transitional government but abolished the position of prime minister and initially reserved the defense portfolio for himself.

On January 5–14, 1998, the government hosted the National Forum for Reconciliation, Unity, Democracy, and the Reconstruction of the Congo, which was attended by more than 1,400 participants, most of them, however, from within parties or other organizations identified with the FDU. The forum endorsed a "flexible" three-year transition to democracy during which a new constitution would be drafted and a national constitutional referendum held. New presidential and legislative elections would follow. The forum elected a 75-member National Transition Council to oversee the process, but it also accused the ousted president, Lissouba, and his allies of a planned "genocide" and urged that they be brought before the appropriate judicial venue. Meanwhile, Lissouba and Kolélas proclaimed a government in exile, with the former prime minister calling for a campaign of civil disobedience in opposition to the Sassou-Nguesso regime.

Throughout 1998, militias loyal to Lissouba and Kolélas—the so-called Cocoyes (in the south) and Ninjas (in the central Pool region), respectively—continued to battle the Cobra militias, which supported Sassou-Nguesso, forcing tens of thousands of civilians to flee and causing thousands of deaths. In December a major battle for control of Brazzaville erupted, and it was not until mid-1999 that victories by the army and Cobra forces made the eventual outcome a near-certainty. In August Sassou-Nguesso offered amnesty to opposition militiamen who surrendered their arms, and on November 16 a peace plan, including the amnesty and a cessation of hostilities, was accepted by most of the opposition forces. Lissouba and Kolélas, still abroad, rejected the agreement. In late December, President Omar Bongo of Gabon, who had assumed the role of mediator between the interim government and the opposition militias, oversaw the signing of a second peace agreement, and by early 2000 the conflict appeared to have reached a conclusion. The 1990s had witnessed an estimated 20,000 deaths due to civil strife, with some 800,000 made homeless. On May 4, 2000, Kolélas and his nephew, former minister of the interior Col. Philippe BIKINKITA, having been tried in absentia, were sentenced to death for crimes committed against prisoners in 1997. Kolélas subsequently went into exile.

Although some areas of the country remained under militia control, in January 2001 the government announced that a "non-exclusive national dialogue" on a draft constitution, the peace plan, and national reconstruction would be held. Local sessions were conducted throughout the country in March and were followed by a convention in Brazzaville April 11–14. Although some representatives of former governments participated, Lissouba and Kolélas continued their opposition. The convention concluded by adopting the constitutional draft, which was approved in final form by the National Transition Council in September. The new basic law, which retained a strong presidency and a bicameral parliament, was endorsed by 84 percent of the voters in a public referendum on January 20, 2002, though much of the opposition leadership urged a boycott. A month earlier Lissouba had been convicted in absentia of treason and misappropriation of funds and sentenced to 30 years in prison.

Sassou-Nguesso, facing no significant opponent following the withdrawal of former prime minister Milongo from the race, was elected to a seven-year term in presidential balloting on March 10, 2002, with 89.4 percent of the vote. He was sworn in on August 14. In two-stage balloting for the new 137-seat National Assembly on May 26 and June 20, the president's PCT and the allied FDU won 83 seats, while indirect elections for the 66-seat Senate on July 11 produced an even greater majority for the government.

The PCT and FDU reportedly secured more than two-thirds of the seats in local balloting on June 30, 2002, a number of opposition parties having boycotted those elections to protest perceived mismanagement in the recent presidential poll. Consequently, the new Council of Ministers appointed on August 18 did not include any members of the opposition.

On January 7, 2005, President Sassou-Nguesso appointed Isidore MVOUBA of the PCT to what the president called the "honorary" post of prime minister and reshuffled the cabinet. In a partial senate election on October 2, 2005, the PCT won 23 of 30 contested seats, with 6 of the remaining seats reportedly going to members of government coalition parties and 1 to an independent.

In March 2007, ahead of National Assembly elections scheduled for June and July, President Sassou-Nguesso reshuffled the cabinet, and in a notable political move he offered former CNR rebel leader Frédéric BITSANGOU a nonministerial government position. (The CNR had registered as a political party in January 2007.) Another historically significant event occurred following Kolélas's return from exile (see Current issues, below), when the MCDDI agreed in April 2007 to an electoral alliance with the PCT for the 2007 legislative elections and the 2009 presidential poll. (Fighting in the Pool region, where the MCDDI has significant support, had restricted the MCDDI's participation in the 2002 assembly elections to only 8 of 24 areas in the region.) The unprecedented alliance with the PCT was seen as enhancing prospects for both parties for a "comfortable and stable majority" in the isolated Pool region. The two parties agreed to "rule together," according to the pact.

In balloting that the opposition claimed was marred by irregularities—charges that postponed second-round balloting by several weeks—the PCT and its allies reportedly secured 124 of the 137 National Assembly seats in the elections held on June 24 and August 5, 2007. While independents were recorded as having won 37 seats, most of those candidates were said to be aligned with the PCT. Eight of the independents elected were said to be affiliated with the Pole Young Republicans (PJR), a political association established by the president's son, Christel Denis SASSOU-NGUESSO. Meanwhile, Bitsangou's status in his new-found government position was unclear as of October 2007, following an outburst of violence in which at least two rebels were killed when former Ninjas traveled to the capital in advance of a ceremony in which Bitsangou was to have formally accepted his post.

The president reshuffled the cabinet on December 31, 2007. While the PCT retained its dominance in government posts, the cabinet also included two members of the MCDDI and at least one member each from five small parties (see Political Parties and Groups, below.) In addition, at least one independent minister was reportedly affiliated with the PJR.

In advance of the 2009 presidential election, a coaliton of opposition parties and groups, spearheaded by UPADS, asked President Sassou-Nguesso to conduct a census and to engage in talks before revising the voter registry. Following a national forum to discuss the electoral process (which the opposition boycotted), President Sassou-Nguesso announced in May that elections would be held on July 12. He did not declare his candidacy until June 6. A ruling by the Constitutional Court on June 19 disqualified four candidates, leaving Mathias DZON of the Alliance for the Republic and Democracy (*Alliance pour la République et Démocratie*—ARD) as the main opposition candidate among the 12 challengers on the ballot. Two days ahead of the poll, six candidates, all running as independents though some represented opposition parties, called for the election to be delayed on the grounds that the voter lists were bloated and fraught with errors.

President Sassou-Nguesso, as expected, was reelected on July 12, 2009, with 78.61 percent of the vote, the opposition again claiming massive irregularities. His closest challenger, Joseph Kignoumbi Kia MBOUNGO of UPADS, who ran as an independent, received 7.46 percent of the vote. Dzon was fourth with 2.3 percent of the vote and subsequently sought to have the results voided on the grounds of fraud (see Current issues, below). However, on July 25 the Constitutional Court confirmed the results. (*See headnote.*)

Constitution and government. The 1979 constitution established the Congolese Labor Party (PCT) as the sole legal party, with the chair of its Central Committee serving as president of the republic. Under a constitutional revision adopted at the third PCT congress in July 1984, the president was named chief of government as well as head of state, with authority to name the prime minister and members of the Council of Ministers.

The 1979 document was abrogated and a number of existing national institutions dissolved by the National Conference in May 1991. President Sassou-Nguesso remained in office pending the election of a successor, while a 153-member Higher Council of the Republic (*Conseil Supérieur de la République*—CSR) was appointed to oversee the implementation of conference decisions.

The constitution endorsed by the CSR on December 22, 1991, and approved by popular referendum on May 3, 1992, provided for a president elected for a once-renewable five-year term. The head of state, authorized to rule by decree in social and economic matters, appointed a prime minister capable of commanding a legislative majority. The bicameral parliament consisted of an indirectly elected Senate sitting for a six-year term and a directly elected National Assembly with a five-year mandate, subject to dissolution. A Supreme Court headed the judicial system, with a High Court of Justice empowered to rule on crimes and misdemeanors, with which the president, members of parliament, and other government officials could be charged. A Constitutional Court interpreted the constitutionality of laws, treaties, and international agreements.

The 1992 constitution was suspended by the new Sassou-Nguesso regime following its military takeover in October 1997. During the subsequent transitional period, the republic was governed by Sassou-Nguesso as self-appointed president with the assistance of a National Transitional Council (see Legislature, below). In November 1998 the regime established a 26-member committee to rewrite the constitution, and in November 2000 the government approved a draft document that was then discussed in March and April 2001 as a key element in a "non-exclusive national dialogue." With the participation of many opposition groups (but not those closest to Bernard Kolélas and Pascal Lissouba), the draft was approved on April 14, and a final version was endorsed by referendum on January 20, 2002.

The current constitution retains a bicameral parliament and provides for a directly elected president, serving a once-renewable seven-year term, who functions as both head of state and head of government. The president has sole power to appoint and dismiss government ministers, but he does not have the power to dismiss parliament. Nor does the legislature have the power to remove the president. Members of parliament forfeit their seats if they switch parties during the legislative term.

The judicial branch is headed by a Supreme Court. There are also Courts of Appeal, a Court of Accounts and Budgetary Discipline, and a Constitutional Court. Local administration is based on ten regions (subdivided into 76 districts and 5 municipalities) and the capital district, each with an elected Regional Council.

Foreign relations. The People's Republic of the Congo withdrew from the French Community in November 1973 but remained economically linked to Paris. In June 1977 it was announced that diplomatic ties with the United States would be resumed after a 12-year lapse, although the U.S. embassy was not reopened until November 1978, and ambassadors were not exchanged until May 1979.

For many years Brazzaville maintained close relations with Communist nations, including the People's Republic of China, Cuba, and the Soviet Union, signing a 20-year Treaty of Friendship with the USSR in May 1981. While the Congo remained on relatively good terms with its other neighbors, recurrent border incidents strained relations with Zaire (now the Democratic Republic of the Congo) despite the conclusion of a number of cooperation agreements, the most notable being the economic and social "twinning" of the countries' capital cities in February 1988. Subsequent reports of mutual deportations and a mass exodus of Zaireans from the Congo were downplayed by Brazzaville and Kinshasa as an exaggeration of the international press.

As an active member of the then OAU, the Republic of the Congo hosted a number of meetings aimed at resolving the civil war in Chad, although it tacitly endorsed the claims of Chadian leader Hissein Habré by serving as a staging area in 1983 for Habré-supportive French troops. In 1986 President Sassou-Nguesso was selected the OAU's chief mediator in the Chadian negotiations. In early 1987 he embarked on a nine-nation European tour to emphasize the gravity of the economic situation facing sub-Saharan Africa and the need for effective sanctions against South Africa. Further enhancing the country's image as regional mediator was the choice of Brazzaville for international peace talks on the Angola-Namibia issue in 1988 and 1989. Because of his key role in the Namibian negotiations Sassou-Nguesso in mid-February 1990 was the first African leader to be welcomed to Washington, by U.S. President George H.W. Bush.

In early 1989 Brazzaville became the first francophone African capital to negotiate a debt swap, trading shares in agriculture, timber, and transport industries to a U.S.-based lender in return for debt reductions. Another financial "first" for the government was the signing of a comprehensive investment agreement with the United Kingdom in May 1989. Later Sassou-Nguesso met with Cameroon's Paul Biya and Gabon's Omar Bongo as part of an ongoing effort by the three to create a joint bargaining unit to negotiate with external creditors.

The 1997 overthrow of the Lissouba government reportedly involved a number of foreign powers. President Lissouba claimed that the Sassou-Nguesso forces included a coalition of Rwandan Hutu militiamen and elements of the defeated army of Zaire's Mobutu Sese Seko, though Lissouba's own fighters also were reported to include former Mobutu forces. The participation of the former Zairean elements on the rebel side was apparently enough to induce the new neighboring Kabila regime of the Democratic Republic of the Congo, whose capital of Kinshasa had been shelled from Brazzaville, to send troops in support of Lissouba, even though he had been one of Africa's last supporters of Mobutu. Meanwhile, the apparent entry into the fray by Angola on the side of the insurgents helped turn the tide with tanks and air power. Lissouba had reportedly hired mercenaries from the National Union for the Total Independence of Angola (UNITA), the rebel group whose participation gave Angola another reason to support Sassou-Nguesso. The Angolans were also keen to eliminate the separatist movement in Cabinda, an oil-rich Angolan province bordering the Republic of the Congo, where the separatists were suspected of having bases.

The insurrection of 1997, starting just three weeks after the Kabila victory in the neighboring Democratic Republic of the Congo, disturbed Western diplomats and African democrats, who suggested that both conflicts, ostensibly civil wars, were actually regional wars in which African armies crossed their borders to enforce political change in a neighboring country. In October the U.S. State Department protested Angola's involvement in the Republic of the Congo and threatened to cut off aid.

Following the outbreak of a rebellion in the Pool region of the Republic of the Congo in 2002 (see Current issues, below), Angola sent troops to assist the Congolese forces in dealing with the insurrection. (Angola, the Democratic Republic of the Congo, and the Republic of the Congo had signed an agreement in 1999 to cooperate regarding border and refugee issues.) The Republic of the Congo was chosen over Sudan to head the AU in 2006 as a result of opposition to the situation in Darfur, where the AU had peacekeepers.

In 2009 relations between Brazzaville and the Democratic Republic of the Congo were strengthened by an agreement for a road and railway bridge to link the two capital cities by 2014.

Current issues. As was expected, the exiled opposition questioned the legitimacy of Sassou-Nguesso's overwhelming election victory in March 2002. Nevertheless, even if the president could not fairly claim nearly 90 percent support nationwide, the Congolese voters were presented with no realistic alternative to his continued presidency. Since returning to power in 1997 Sassou-Nguesso had effectively marginalized his two principal opponents, Lissouba and Kolélas, whose refusals to participate in any of the recent government-sponsored reconciliation initiatives had injured their standing among the internal opposition. Moreover, neither the former president nor the former prime minister, facing arrest if they returned from exile, could meet the constitutional requirement of a two-year residency before seeking the presidency. Prior to the May–June 2002 National Assembly election, the leaders of the principal domestic opposition parties formed the latest in a series of multiparty coalitions, the Convention for Democracy and Salvation (*Convention pour la Démocratie et le Salut*—Codesa), but their inability to present a unified electoral option left Sassou-Nguesso's political forces in full control of the national government.

Reconciling long-standing differences within the country's diverse population remained Sassou-Nguesso's principal challenge. Despite incentives for the country's many militia groups to surrender their weapons, some remained heavily armed and capable of offering resistance. The most serious violence occurred in the Pool region, where National Assembly elections and local balloting were postponed in mid-2002. Leading the rebellion was the CNR, which called for greater autonomy for the region, from which an estimated 10,000 people were displaced. Following the signing of a cease-fire agreement in March 2003, the European Union (EU) pledged financial aid in support of demobilization of the CNR's so-called Ninjas, and some 2,300 rebels subsequently were reported to have laid down their arms.

In July 2004 the Republic of the Congo was excluded from the UN-sponsored Kimberley process, under which an international commission was authorized to certify that diamond sales in the region were not funding armed conflict. The oversight group alleged that the republic was being used to smuggle diamonds out of the Democratic Republic of the Congo. (It was estimated that diamond exports from the Republic of the Congo exceeded actual production in the country by as much as 100 times.)

In October 2005, some opposition parties boycotted the partial Senate elections based on what they claimed was the government's pretense of a democratic system. Later that month, Kolélas was allowed to return to Brazzaville to bury his wife, prompting renewed clashes between Ninja rebels loyal to Kolélas and government troops in the city's southern districts. Subsequently, Sassou-Nguesso, backed by a unanimous vote in the National Assembly, granted Kolélas amnesty. In December Kolélas apologized to the Congolese people for his role in the civil war and indicated his interest in reconciliation.

The stunning announcement in April 2007 of Kolélas's MCDDI and the PCT joining in an electoral alliance for the 2007 National Assembly elections, scheduled for June and July, was noted by observers as something that would have been "unthinkable" a few years earlier. Among the reasons cited for the reconciliation was a recent trip Kolélas made to the grave of Sassou-Nguesso's brother, near the president's northern hometown of Oyo. The two parties' pact was further enhanced by a reaffirmation of peace the government had reached with the CNR, which had officially shed its rebel-group status by registering as a political party in January.

In June 2007, amid what was described as "chaotic" circumstances, and with most of the opposition parties boycotting the elections, the PCT was credited with winning 23 of the 44 assembly seats decided in first-round balloting. Immediately thereafter, the director in charge of electoral affairs was suspended in connection with alleged irregularities, and all protests and demonstrations were banned in advance of second-round voting, postponed until August 5. The PCT and its numerous small allied parties secured a landslide victory. The main opposition party, UADS, won only 11 seats, prompting most of the opposition parties to rally in protest after the results were announced. Notably, the CRN participated in elections for the first time, though it did not win any seats. In October, the Constitutional Court voided election results in four constituencies because of fraud; the ruling affected four independent candidates allied to the opposition.

Following reports of a gun battle in September 2007 involving former rebels and government forces, CNR leader Frédéric Bitsangou, who was scheduled to return to Brazzaville to take up his government post, remained outside of the capital, and calm was subsequently restored. Bitsangou was again invited to accept his new office "without conditions" in October. It was unclear exactly when Bitsangou officially took up his post. In early 2008 the government's armed forces began to destroy all ordnance abandoned during the civil war, and in February 2009 the government launched a scheme in the Pool region to buy back thousands of weapons.

President Sassou-Nguesso's daughter, Edith, the wife of President Omar Bongo of Gabon and a longtime symbol of the close ties between the two countries, died in March 2009. (Bongo himself died in June.) In May a French court ruled that a lawsuit brought by a nongovernmental organization against Sassou-Nguesso, Omar Bongo, and President Teodoro Obiang of Equatorial Guinea was admissible. The ruling cleared the way for investigations into allegations, denied by all three leaders, that they and their families had used stolen money to buy numerous upscale properties in France and a fleet of luxury cars.

Most of the attention in 2009, however, was focused on the forthcoming presidential election—the second since the end of the civil war. Some 20 opposition parties and groups comprising the FUPO coaliton, led by former National Assembly president Guy-Romain KINFOUSSIA of the Union for Democracy and the Republic–Mwinda (*Union pour la Démocratie et la République*—UDR-Mwinda), protested the government's revision of the voter registry, which the coalition said contained the names of dead and fictious people. The FUPO also called for an independent electoral panel composed of members of the judiciary, claiming that the sitting commission was biased in favor of Sassou-Nguesso and his allies. In April the FUPO boycotted the government-sponsored "Republican Dialogue," a national forum for civic and political groups to prepare for the election; a subsequent rally planned by the opposition was banned by the government. On May 11 it was announced that the president had signed a decree setting July 12 as the election date. Though it was widely understood that Sassou-Nguesso would seek reelection, he did not announce his candidacy until June 6. Meanwhile, other coalitions had been forged ahead of the election, notable among them the Rally for the Presidential Majority (*Rassemblement pour la Majorité Présidentielle*—RMP). In that electoral alliance, former prime minister Jacques-Joachim Yhombi-Opango of the opposition Rally for Democracy and Development (*Rassemblement pour la Démocratie et le Développement*—RDD) agreed to present a single candidate (Sassou-Nguesso) and to join the government if Sassou-Nguesso were reelected. The opposition ARD, meanwhile, encompassed 14 small parties, including the Patriotic Union for National Reconstruction (*Union Partriotique pour la Réconstruction Nationale*—UPRN), whose leader, Mathias Dzon, received the bid as the ARD's presidential candidate. On June 19 the Constitutional Court disqualified four candidates, three of them for not having met the residency requirement, including former prime minister Ange-Edouard Pongui of UPADS. Christophe MOUKOUÉKÉ, described as a UPADS dissident, was rejected on the grounds that, at 70, he exceeded the age limit. The UPADS criticized the court's rejection of Pongui, claiming it was politically motivated since the chief of the court was a longtime ally of President Sassou-Nguesso. Meanwhile, observers said the court's action left Dzon as the most viable opposition candidate in a field of 12 challengers, most of whom dropped their affiliation and were listed as independents. Two days before the poll, the FUPO and six opposition candidates—including Dzon—called for a boycott, claiming the electoral lists contained the names of ineligible voters and "ghost lists" of people who did not exist. (*Africa Confidential* reported that independent observers believed the lists contained 458,000 ghost voters.) Supporting their claims was the Congolese Observatory for Human Rights (OCDH), which called the electoral lists "grotesque."

With the lack of unity for a single opposition challenger, and as a result of Sassou-Nguesso having broadened his political base to include some former leftists, including Yhombi-Opango of the RDD, observers said the president was assured of reelection. Following the announcement of provisional results on July 15, delayed for one day by the government, the president was credited with 78.61 percent of the vote, while his closest challenger, Joseph Kignoumbi Kia Mboungo of UPADS, who ran as an independent, received a vote share of only 7.46 percent. Nicéphore Anntoine FYLLA of the Liberal Republican Party finished third, with 6.98 percent. Dzon, who received 2.3 percent, and the five other candidates who had boycotted the balloting, disputed the government report of 66.42 percent turnout, claiming that less than 10 percent of voters had participated. Dzon appealed to the Constitutional Court to void the election, but on July 25, 2009, the court confirmed the results.The OCDH reported that the poll was marked by fraud and irregularities and that the government's official rate of participation was "exaggerated." However, international monitors, including those from the AU and the Economic Community of Central African States (CEEAC), found the election to be free and transparent. The president's spokesman subsequently said that Sassou-Nguesso was committed in his second term to peace and reconciliation and to "rebuilding the state and cleaning up the public finances."

POLITICAL PARTIES

The Republic of the Congo became a one-party state in 1963 when the National Revolutionary Movement (*Mouvement National Révolutionnaire*—MNR) supplanted the two parties that had been politically dominant under the preceding administration: the Democratic Union for the Defense of African Interests (*Union Démocratique pour la*

Défense des Intérêts Africains—UDDIA) and the African Socialist Movement (*Mouvement Socialiste Africain*—MSA). The MNR was in turn replaced by the Congolese Labor Party (PCT) in 1969, coincident with the declaration of the People's Republic. On July 4, 1990, the PCT agreed to abandon its monopoly of power, and nearly two dozen opposition groupings were legalized as of January 1, 1991. Thereafter, estimates of the number of parties ranged to upward of 100.

Following Denis Sassou-Nguesso's return to power in 1997, an already complex political party system, in which personal, tribal, and regional loyalties typically overpowered ideology, became further entangled. (See the 1999 *Handbook* for more detailed information about the period preceding the 1999 civil conflict.) In 2002 a reported 141 parties and alliances presented candidates for at least one of the 137 National Assembly seats. At that time the principal formations were Sassou-Nguesso's PCT and the allied United Democratic Forces; the opposition Convention for Democracy and Salvation (Codesa), a new multiparty alliance led by former prime minister André Milongo of the Union for Democracy and the Republic (UDR); the Pan-African Union for Social Democracy (UPADS), led from exile by former president Pascal Lissouba; and the Congolese Movement for Democracy and Integral Development (MCDDI), led from exile by former prime minister Bernard Kolélas.

In advance of the 2007 National Assembly elections, a grouping of seven small parties, formerly members of the United Democratic Forces (FDU) coalition (launched in 1994), aligned themselves as the New Democratic Forces (FDN), led by Léon Alfred OPIMBA and Jean-Marie TASSOU. The FDN included some 15 parties and groups, including the National Union for Democracy and Progress (UNDP), led by Pierre NZE, and the Union for National Renewal (URN), led by Gabriel BOKILO.

In early 2007 the PCT was reported to have retained its association with the FDU, though that association eventually dissolved after PCT hard-liners rejected a proposal by President Sassou-Nguesso that the PCT and the FDU merge. The URN subsequently withdrew after Gabriel Bokilo failed to secure the FDN presidency.

The FDN won three seats in the legislature in August 2007. In advance of the 2009 presidential election, the FDN joined the Rally for the Presidential Majority (RMP), which included the PCT, the MCDDI, and the Union of Democratic Forces (UFD). Subsequently, the heretofore opposition Rally for Democracy and Development (RDD) joined the RMP in an electoral alliance with the PCT, pledging its support to Sassou-Nguesso. Meanwhile, a coalition of 20 parties, the United Front of Opposition Parties (FUPO) led by led by Guy-Romain Kinfoussia of the UDR-Mwinda, called for a boycott of the balloting. Another oppositon grouping, the Alliance for the Republic and Democracy (ARD), named former finance minister Mathias Dzon as its candidate. Dzon, along with several other candidates, boycotted the election, but his name remained on the ballot and he received 2.3 percent of the vote.

Government and Government-Supportive Parties:

Rally for the Presidential Majority: Ahead of the 2009 presidential election, the PCT, as part of the larger RMP coalition, brought the opposition RDD on board in an electoral alliance following assurances that the RDD would back the PCT's Sassou-Nguesso and that the RDD would participate in the new government. The FDN (above), the MCDDI, and the Union of Democratic Forces (UFD) were also part of the broader coalition.

Leaders: Michel NGAKALA (Vice President), Isidore MVOUBA (Prime Minister and Secretary General).

Congolese Labor Party (*Parti Congolais du Travail*—PCT). The PCT monopolized Congolese political life from its launching in 1969 until its agreement in 1990 to allow the formation of opposition groups. In mid-1992 the PCT finished third in the National Assembly election (19 seats) and fifth in the senate poll (5 seats). On August 2 the party's fall from power was seemingly completed by Sassou-Nguesso's inability to proceed beyond the first round of presidential balloting; however, it allied itself with the UPADS for the second round and was included in the government named on September 1. The alliance broke down shortly thereafter, with the PCT entering into a new coalition with Bernard Kolélas's Union for Democratic Renewal (*Union pour la Renouveau Démocratique*—URD), a seven-party alliance that included the MCDDI and the RDPS (see below).

Although generally listed as a member of the FDU (see below), the PCT ran in its own right in the May–June 2002 National Assembly election, winning 53 seats. PCT candidates won 15 lower-house seats in 1993. In the October 2, 2005, partial Senate elections, the PCT won most of the 30 contested seats, with 21 going to the party's "new direction" wing and 2 to an unidentified dissident faction.

Meanwhile, the PCT formed an alliance with the MCDDI meant to increase stability and governance in the southern Pool region (the PCT already having strong ties in the north linked to President Sassou-Nguesso's ethnic group). The alliance with the MCDDI was also seen as helping to ensure security in the southern area, which had been a stronghold of former militants of the CNR. Subsequently, in balloting that the opposition charged was marred by irregularities, the PCT and its allies won an overwhelming majority of seats in the 2007 legislative elections.

Ambroise Noumazalaye, who had been president of the Senate and secretary general of the PCT, died in 2007.

In the run-up to the 2009 elections, the PCT expanded the progovernment coalition to include the opposition RDD. Sassou-Nguesso, as widely expected, was reelected for a seven-year term.

Leaders: Gen. Denis SASSOU-NGUESSO (President of the Republic), Isidore MVOUBA (Interim Secretary General).

Congolese Movement for Democracy and Integral Development (*Mouvement Congolais pour la Démocratie et le Développement Intégral*—MCDDI). A right-of-center group and former member of the Forces of Change (*Forces de Changement*—FDC) coalition, the MCDDI was formed in 1989 by Bernard Kolélas, who had served as an adviser to former prime minister Milongo. In 1990 Kolélas was a leader of the opposition movement that successfully campaigned for multipartyism. In the first local and municipal elections in 1992, the party ran second, while Kolélas was runner-up in the subsequent presidential poll, with 38.7 percent of the vote. The MCDDI and the RDPS (below) were the principal members of the Union for Democratic Renewal (*Union pour la Renouveau Démocratique*—URD) alliance that was launched in mid-1992 and shortly thereafter formed the Opposition Coalition with the PCT.

In legislative balloting in 1993, the MCDDI secured 28 seats, half of the opposition's total. Meanwhile, Kolélas's leadership role in what the Lissouba administration labeled an "armed rebellion," made him a target for progovernment forces, and in October his residence in Brazzaville was hit by artillery fire. In a demonstration of antigovernment sentiment, Kolélas was elected mayor of Brazzaville in July 1994.

Kolélas maintained an opposition stance against the Lissouba government as well as a complex relationship with Sassou-Nguesso, ostensibly an ally but also a rival when the two were 1997 presidential candidates. However, during the four-month insurrection of 1997, Kolélas attempted to mediate between the Lissouba government and the Sassou-Nguesso rebels before joining the government as prime minister in September. He fled the country when the government fell in October, and the party effectively split into two wings, one remaining loyal to Kolélas and the other, headed by Michel Mampouya, supporting the new interim regime. Mampouya himself accepted a cabinet post and assumed party leadership. In the 2002 legislative election, Kolélas called for a boycott, but Mampouya, despite contending that "there is only one MCDDI," headed a slate of unsuccessful candidates.

In late 2005 Kolélas was pardoned by the government and allowed to return from exile to bury his wife in Brazzaville. A subsequent reconciliation with the Sassou-Nguesso administration ensued, a move which led in early 2006 to the resignation of several MCDDI members, including Mampouya, who subsequently established a new group, the PSV (below). Observers widely believed that Kolélas's pardon paved the way for his renewed alliance with the Sassou Nguesso government.

In advance of the 2007 legislative balloting, the MCDDI and the PCT joined in an agreement called the Bedrock of National Unity to ensure peaceful elections in the war-torn Pool region and joined in an electoral alliance, the RMP, for the assembly elections, as well as for the 2009 presidential elections. With the divisive episode of the party apparently over, the president named two members of the MCDDI to his reshuffled cabinet in December 2007.

Leaders: Bernard KOLÉLAS (President), Jacques MAHOUKA.

Rally for Democracy and Development (*Rassemblement pour la Démocratie et le Développement*—RDD). Led by former prime minister Jacques-Joachim Yhombi-Opango, who returned from exile, the RPP, under his leadership, pledged to support President Sasso-Nguesso in advance of the 2009 presidential election, abandoning the opposition ANR coalition (below).

Leader: Jacques-Joachim YHOMBI-OPANGO (Former Prime Minister).

Union of Democratic Forces (*Union des Forces Démocratiques*—UFD). Although close to President Lissouba, the UFD's leader, David Charles Ganao, was reportedly backed by the opposition to succeed André Milongo as National Assembly president because of his reputation for nonpartisanship. Ganao was replaced as prime minister in September 1997 when President Lissouba appointed the MCDDI's Bernard Kolélas in an effort to settle the civil war. In January 1998 the UFD broke with the opposition, urging its members to support the reconciliation and reconstruction efforts of the Sassou-Nguesso government, and in February Sebastien EBAO was elected chair. At the time Ganao was in exile, but by November 2001 he had resumed control of the party and, in a turnaround, concluded an electoral pact with Sassou-Nguesso's PCT. The party won one seat in the 2007 National Assembly elections.

Leader: David Charles GANAO (Former Prime Minister).

National Resistance Council (*Conseil National de Résistance*—CNR). Having emerged from militia groups loyal to former president Lissouba, the CNR's "combat wing" (known as "Ninjas") was led by Frédéric Bitsangou (alias Pastor Ntoumi). By 2002 the CNR had reportedly broken with Lissouba in pursuit of greater autonomy for the Pool region. Although some factions (including the MNLC, see above) broke from the CNR to form legal parties, the Ninjas launched attacks on government and security sites that forced the postponement of assembly balloting in Pool in 2002. The CNR and the government signed a cease-fire in March 2003 that called for the exchange of prisoners, demobilization of CNR fighters and their integration into national security forces, and a general amnesty. Nevertheless, some Ninja groups continued to conduct operations against government forces and international aid workers. Bitsangou subsequently called for CNR's inclusion in a proposed new government of national unity, but President Sassou-Nguesso refused. In 2005 Bitsangou reportedly began to disarm the rebels, and subsequently the CNR announced that it hoped to participate as a political party in future elections in Pool.

The CNR registered as a political party in January 2007 and subsequently entered an agreement with the government to reaffirm the peace accord of 2003 and the reinstitution of a cease-fire. President Sassou-Nguesso's offer in May of a government position to CNR leader Frédéric Bitsangou drew criticism from some party members, as the president had changed the position offered to Bitsangou, from head of humanitarian affairs to general delegate to the office of the president in charge of promoting peace and postwar reconstruction. After security issues marred Bitsangou's trip to Brazzaville to formally accept the position, the president called on him in October 2007 to return to the capital and to take up his new post "without conditions."

The CNR contested the 2007 legislative elections but did not win any seats. Bitsangou was reported by *Africa Confidential* to be "inactive but wary of the regime" in the run-up to the 2009 presidential election.

Leaders: Frédéric BITSANGOU, Ane Philippe BIBI.

Among the small parties whose members were represented in the cabinet following the 2007 National Assembly elections (in which they won seats) were the **Action and Renewal Movement** (*Action et Mouvement de Renouvellement*—MAR), founded by Jean-Bâptiste TATI-LOUTARD, who died in 2009; the **Citizens' Rally** (*Le Rassemblement des Citoyens*—RC), led by Claude Alphonse NTSILOU; the **Union for Progress** (*Union pour le Progrès*—UP), led by Jean-Martín MBEMBA; the **Take Action for Congo** (*Agir pour le Congo*—APC), led by Henri OSSEBI; and the **Club 2002–Party for the Unity of the Republic** (*Partie pour l'Unité de la République*—PUR).

Other Legislative Parties:

Rally for Democracy and Social Progress (*Rassemblement pour la Démocratie et le Progrès Social*—RDPS). Despite dissident withdrawals, the RDPS secured both upper- and lower-house representation in the 1992 legislative balloting. The party's leader, Jean-Pierre Thystere-Tchicaye, a former PCT member, was eliminated from presidential contention after capturing only 5.8 percent of the first-round vote. In legislative balloting in 1993 the RDPS secured ten seats. Thystere-Tchicaye was named prime minister of a short-lived parallel government named by the Opposition Coalition, and then in mid-1994 was elected mayor of the country's second-largest city, Pointe-Noire.

In late 1996, in anticipation of the scheduled 1997 presidential election, the RDPS joined the Union for the Republic (*Union pour la République*—UR) of Benjamin BOUNKOULOU and the Movement for Democracy and Solidarity (*Mouvement pour la Démocratie et la Solidarité*—MDS) of Paul KAYA in forming a coalition called the Movement for Unity and Reconstruction (*Mouvement pour l'Unité et la Réconstruction*—MUR). After the civil war of 1997 the party was reportedly divided over the extent to which it should cooperate with the government. In 2002 the party's cofounder and former secretary general, Jean-Félix Demba TELO, ran for president as an independent, finishing fourth with 1.7 percent of the vote.

In 2001 the RDPS concluded a cooperation agreement with the PCT. In August 2002 Thystere-Tchicaye was selected to serve as speaker of the new lower house. The RDPS won two seats in the 2007 National Assembly elections.

Leader: Jean-Pierre THYSTERE-TCHICAYE (President of the Party and Speaker of the National Assembly

Six other small parties that won seats in the 2007 legislative elections as allies of the PCT were the following: the **Movement for Solidarity and Development** (*Mouvement de Solidaire et le Développement*—MSD), established in March 2007 by René Serge Blanchard OBA and Jean François OBEME; the **Youth Movement** (*Mouvement de la Jeunesse*—JEM), led by François KAMBO; the **Life Party** (*La Vie*), led by Benedict BATI; the **Movement for Democracy and Progress** (*Mouvement pour la Démocratie et le Progrès*—MDP), led by Jean-Claude IBOVI; **Patriotic Union for Democracy and Progress** (*Union Patriotique pour la Démocratie et le Progrès*—UPDP), led by Ngongarad-Auguste Celestine NKOUA; and the **Union for the Republic** (*Union pour la République*—UR), led by Benjamin BOUNKOULOU.

Other Parties and Groups:

Alliance for the Republic and Democracy: Formed in October 2008 in advance of the 2009 presidential election, the Alliance for the Republic and Democracy (*Alliance pour la République et Démocratie*—ARD) was composed of 14 parties and groups.

The ARD's 2009 presidential candidate, Mathias Dzon of the **Patriotic Union for National Reconstruction** (*Union Partriotique pour la Réconstruction Nationale*—UPRN), had participated in the PCT government in the early 1990s and then went into exile in 1996 until Sassou-Nguesso was returned to power in 1997. Dzon later served as finance minister in the PCT government but ultimately was dismissed amid allegations of corruption. The UPRN, of which Dzon remained chair, joined the opposition ARD in 2007.

Minor parties included in the ARD were: the UPRN, led by André GANFINA; **Congolese Social Democratic Party** (CSDP), led by Clement MIERASSA, who ran as an independent in the 2009 presidential election; **Movement for the General Construction of the Congo** (MGCC), led by Jean Michel BOKAMBA-YANGOUM; **Rally for the Democracy and the Republic** (RDR), led by Raymond Damase NGOLLO; **Citizens Convergence** (CC), led by Bonaventure MBAYA; **Republican Convention** (CR), led by Hervé MALONGA; **Republican Movement of the Congo** (MRC), led by Gérard BOUKAMBOU; **Green Movement of the Congo** (VMC), led by Christophe NGOKAKA; **Social Party for the Republic and Democracy** (PSDR), led by Gabriel NGOULOU; **People's Congress** (PC), led by Eugene DKAMONA; **National Convention for Alternance in 2009** (CNA), led by Aurélien MIANISSA; **Rally for the Congo** (Rapco), led by Ebate-Stanislas MONGO; **National Convention for Democracy and Development** (CNDD), led by André NGALIBAKI; and a group known by the initials **MJDAC**, led by Eustache BOMBOKO.

United Front of Opposition Parties: The FUPO coalition, formed by Guy-Romain Kinfoussia in advance of the 2009 presidential election, was composed of 20 parties, most significantly the UPADS and the UDR-Mwinda.The FUPO challenged nearly every step in the electoral process, beginning with the government's decision to suspend revision of the voter lists, which the coalition said were flawed. Further, the FUPO called for replacing the national elections commission with an independent panel; boycotted the government-sponsored national forum to prepare for the election; and finally, called for a boycott of the July 12 balloting. At least two parties in the coalition fielded presidential candidates, who ran as independents (see below).

Leaders: Guy-Romain KINFOUSSIA (MDR-Mwinda), Pascal TSATY-MABIALA (UPADS).

Pan-African Union for Social Democracy (*Union PanAfricaine pour la Démocratie Sociale*—UPADS). Previously a member of the National Alliance for Democracy (*Alliance Nationale pour la Démocratie*—AND), a coalition of 40-plus parties that objected to the 1991 Milongo government, the UPADS ran alone in the 1992 municipal, legislative, and presidential elections. The party's preelectoral prospects were bolstered by attracting numerous dissidents from the RDPS (above) and the UNDP, which had been a leading component of the prodemocracy movement (and which later helped form the FDU). In legislative polling at midyear the UPADS secured a plurality of seats in both houses. Following the first presidential round in August, the party concluded a pact with the PCT that ensured the second-round victory of the UPADS candidate Pascal Lissouba. The alliance, upon which a legislative majority had been forged, was dissolved soon after Lissouba's inauguration.

The UPADS was the key player in the Presidential Tendency (*Tendance Présidentielle*), formed prior to the National Assembly balloting of June 1993 by a large number of pro-Lissouba parties (including many that would establish Codesa in 2002). The formation controlled a majority of seats following the second-round repolling in October. The UPADS retained its legislative plurality in 1993 but was weakened on January 27, 1995, by the withdrawal of 12 of its MPs, who complained of being marginalized and subsequently formed a new grouping, the Union for the Republic (UR).

At a UPADS congress on December 30, 1995, Lissouba was reelected to the party's top post. In addition, a 220-member National Council was formed in an apparent attempt by party leaders to appease its largest internal tendency, the "Reforming Democrats Group," which complained of the lack of partywide deliberations. In the midst of the 1997 civil war the UPADS was a principal member of the 40-party self-described peace movement called the **Republican Space for the Defense of Democracy and National Unity** (*Espace Républicain pour la Défense de la Démocratie et de l'Unité Nationale*—ERDDUN).

Following the overthrow of President Lissouba, the UPADS split into two wings, one headed by Lissouba from abroad and the other led by Martin Mberi, a member of the National Council who became a minister in the new government of Sassou-Nguesso. In 2001 Mberi left and formed the CNRS (see below), but the UPADS remained divided over strategy. It presented a slate of candidates for the 2002 National Assembly election and won three seats, although Lissouba had urged his supporters to boycott the balloting. In March the UPADS presidential candidate, Joseph Kignoumbi Kia MBOUNGOU, finished second with 2.8 percent of the vote.

In 2006 the government and UPADS remained at odds over what the government described as an "inadequate" apology from the party on behalf of Lissouba, whom authorities insist must acknowledge responsibility for his role in the country's civil war.

The UPADS was the only major opposition party contesting the 2007 National Assembly; it won 11 seats and subsequently claimed the polling was rigged.

The party's candidate for the July 2009 presidential election, former prime minister Ange-Edouard Pongui, whose wife is a cousin of Saasou-Nguesso, was disqualified in June by the Constitutional Court on the grounds that he had not continuously lived in the country for at least two years. Joseph Kignoumbi Kia Mboungou, who ran as an independent, finished a distant second behind Sassou-Nguesso.

Leaders: Pascal LISSOUBA (in exile), Joseph Kignoumbi Kia MBOUNGOU (President and 2009 presidential candidate), Alphonse Ongagou DATCHOU, Ange-Edouard PONGUI (Former Prime Minister), Pascal TSATY-MABIALA (Secretary General).

Union for Democracy and the Republic–Mwinda (*Union pour la Démocratie et la République*—UDR-Mwinda). This offshoot of the UDR (below) was originally established by André Milongo and affiliated with Codesa. The party won 1 seat in the 2007 legislative elections. Following Milongo's death in July 2007, Dominica Basseyla was named acting president. The UDR-Mwinda briefly participated, along with the RDD and UPADS, in a coaliton known as the Alliance for the New Republic (ANR), but abandoned that grouping in 2008. Following his election as chair in 2008, Guy-Romain Kinfoussia formed the FUPO opposition coalition in advance of the 2009 presidential election. Kinfoussia, who had called for a boycott of the election, ran as an independent and finished sixth with 0.9 percent of the vote.

Leaders: Guy-Romain KINFOUSSIA (Former National Assembly President and 2009 presidential candidate), Dominica BASSEYLA.

Pole Young Republicans (PJR). This grouping was formed in 2005 by Christel Denis Sassou-Nguesso, the president's son, and Bernard Caesar Serges Bouya in support of the Sassou-Nguesso administration. In the 2007 National Assembly elections, eight candidates of the PJR were elected as independents because the PJR's status as a political association prevented it from fielding its own candidates. One of the independent cabinet members, Minister of Industrial Development Emile MABONZO, was reportedly affiliated with the PJR.

In August 2007 a London court dismissed a case brought by Christel Denis Sassou-Nguesso in which he attempted to have documents linking him to alleged corruption removed from the Web site of a watchdog group. Christel Sassou-Nguesso, who is in charge of marketing for the state-owned oil company, was reported to have spent as much as $35,000 in oil money on private purchases.

Leaders: Christel Denis SASSOU-NGUESSO (Chair), Bernard Caesar Serges BOUYA (Vice Chair), Frédéric Privat NDEKÉ (Secretary General).

Convention for Democracy and Salvation (*Convention pour la Démocratie et le Salut*—Codesa). Formation of Codesa was announced in late March 2002 by a dozen parties. (See the 2003 edition of the *Handbook* for details.) An anti-PCT/FDU coalition, Codesa was the latest in a series of unwieldy opposition formations in which individual parties have historically failed to coalesce, thereby diminishing their effectiveness as an electoral force. The UDR won six seats in the 2002 assembly balloting, while the rest of Codesa was credited with two seats. Codesa was factionalized over the question of whether to participate in subsequent local and regional elections. Most of the major Codesa components, including the UDR (see below), ultimately boycotted that balloting.

One of the party's vice presidents, Anselme Mackoumbou-Nkouka, was initially an independent candidate for president in 2002 but withdrew before the balloting in protest over the lack of electoral reforms. The party boycotted the partial senate elections of 2005.

Leaders: Anselme MACKOUMBOU-NKOUKA and Saturnin OKABE (Vice Presidents); Hervé Ambroise MALONGA.

Union for Democracy and the Republic (*Union pour la Démocratie et la République*—UDR). Launched following a split in the MCDDI (see above) and subsequently characterized as "close to the Presidential Tendency," the UDR secured six assembly seats in the first two rounds of balloting in May and June 1993; however, as a result of the second-round rerun in October, its representation dropped to two seats. Its leader, André Milongo, ran for president in 1992 but was eliminated in the first round, securing only 10.2 percent of the vote. In July 1993 Milongo's selection as assembly president drew sharp criticism from the Opposition Coalition.

In 2002 Milongo withdrew from the presidential election shortly before the March balloting, which he characterized as a "masquerade." In the subsequent National Assembly election the UDR won six seats to lead the opposition. Milongo had also established the UDR-Mwinda (above), which participated in the 2007 National Assembly elections.

In April 2006 the ousted leader of the MCDDI, Michel MAMPOUYA, announced a new party, referenced as the **Party of the Safeguard of Values** (*Parti de la Sauvegarde des Valeurs*—PSV), meant to appeal to the people of the Pool region and Brazzaville. Other parties include the **Liberal Republican Party**, whose 2009 presidential candidate, Nicéphore Antoine Fylla, placed third and the **Congolese People's**

Party, whose 2009 presidential canidate, Marcel GUITOUKOULOU, was disqualified before the election. Guitoukoulou was also referenced as chair of the opposition **People's Congress and Sympathizers/Citizens Consensus.**

(See earlier editions of the *Handbook* for details on additional smaller parties, many of which have participated since the early 1990s in various alliances of shifting membership.)

LEGISLATURE

The former 133-member People's National Assembly (*Assemblée Nationale Populaire*) was dissolved by the 1991 National Conference, with assignment of its functions going to an appointed but broadly representative Higher Council of the Republic (*Conseil Supérieur de la République*—CSR), a 153-member body charged with implementing National Conference decisions.

The constitution endorsed by the CSR in December 1991 and approved by popular referendum in May 1992 provided for a bicameral Parliament (*Parlement*) composed of a Senate and National Assembly. Following the civil war of mid-1997, the parliament was replaced by the National Transitional Council (*Conseil National de la Transition*—CNT), whose 75 members were elected in mid-January 1998 at a reconciliation forum attended by more than 1,400 delegates. The CNT candidate lists were put forward by political and legal commissions as well as the government. The forum recommended that the CNT exercise quasi-legislative authority pending the proposed election of a new bicameral assembly following a constitutional referendum. The constitution approved by referendum in January 2002 restored a bicameral system, with the **Parliament** comprising a Senate and a National Assembly.

Senate (*Sénat*). The upper house is a 66-member body—6 senators from each region and from the capital—indirectly elected by local and regional councils for a six-year term. Initial balloting was held on July 11, 2002, in all regions except Pool, where violence had forced cancellation of voting. In the future, one-third of the membership is to be renewed every two years. Of the 60 seats filled on July 11, 2002, the Congolese Labor Party (PCT) reportedly won 44 seats; the United Democratic Forces, 12; the Convention for Democracy and Salvation, 1; others (civic organizations and independents), 3. In partial elections held on October 2, 2005, for 30 seats, the PCT won 23, with 6 going to government coalition parties and 1 independent.

Following partial elections on August 5, 2008, 42 seats were filled, 33 by members of the Rally for the Presidential Majority (comprised of the PCT and the Rally for Democracy and Development), and the body was expanded to 72 to include members from the new department of Pointe-Noire. Also, for the first time, elections were held in the Poole region. Two members of the the Pan-African Union for Social Democracy and seven independents also won seats.

President: André Obami ITOU.

National Assembly (*Assemblée Nationale*). The lower house has 137 members directly elected for five-year terms. Balloting is conducted in two rounds, with a majority needed for election. In the most recent balloting of June 24 and August 5, 2007, the seat distribution was reported to be the following: the Congolese Labor Party won 46 seats; the Congolese Movement for Democracy and Integral Development, 11; the Pan-African Union for Social Democracy, 11; the Movement for Solidarity and Development, 5; the Action and Renewal Movement, 5; the Take Action for Congo, 3; the Club 2002-Party for Unity and the Republic, 3; the New Democratic Forces, 2; the Rally for Democracy and Social Progress, 2; the Union for the Republic, 2; the Patriotic Union for Democracy and Progress, 2; the Union for Progress, 2; the Union of Democratic Forces, 1; the Movement for Democracy and Progress, 1; the Youth Movement, 1; the Citizens' Rally, 1; the Life Party, 1; the Union for Democracy and the Republic–Mwinda, 1; independents, 37. Balloting in two remote constituencies was held on August 19 and 20, 2007. Independents won both seats (reflected in the listed results.)

Subsequently, the government listed the members of the Congolese Labor Party as holding 47 seats; the Movement for Solidarity and Development, 3; the New Democratic Forces, 3; and the other parties the same number of seats as listed above.

Speaker: Justin KOUMBA.

CABINET

[as of August 1, 2009] (*see headnote*)

President	Denis Sassou-Nguesso
Prime Minister	Isidore Mvouba
Ministers	
Agriculture, Livestock, and Fisheries	Rigobert Maboundou (PCT)
Commerce, Consumption, and Supplies	Jeanne Dambendzet (PCT) [f]
Communications, in Charge of Relations with Parliament; Government Spokesman	Alain Akouala-Atipault
Construction, Town Planning, Housing, and Land Reforms	Claude Alphonse Ntsilou (RC)
Coordinator for Government Action and Privatization	Isidore Mvouba (PCT)
Culture and Arts	Jean-Claude Gakosso (PCT)
Energy and Water	Bruno Jean-Richard Itoua (PCT)
Equipment and Public Works	Brig. Gen. Florent Ntsiba
Finance, Economy, and Budget	Pacifique Issobeika
Fisheries, in Charge of Aquaculture	Guy Brice Parfait Kolélas (MCDDI)
Foreign Affairs and Francophone Affairs	Basile Ikouébé (PCT)
Forestry and Environment	Henri Djombo (PCT)
Health, Social Affairs, and Family Affairs	Emilienne Raoul [f]
Higher Education	Henri Ossebi (APC)
Industrial Development and Promotion of the Private Sector	Emile Mabonzo (Ind.)
Labor, Employment, and Social Security	Gilbert Ondongo
Land Reform and Preservation of Public Property	Lamyr Nguelet (Ind.)
Maritime Transport and Merchant Marine	Martin Parfait Aimé Coussoud-Mavoungou
Mines, Mineral Industries, and Geology	Pierre Oba (PCT)
Posts and Telecommunications	Thierry Moungala (PCT)
Presidency, in charge of Development Cooperation	Justin Ballay Megot
Presidency, in charge of Humanitarian Action and Solidarity	Charles Zacharie Bowao
Presidency, in charge of National Defense and Veterans Affairs	Jacques-Yvon Ndolou
Primary and Secondary Education	Rosalie Kama [f]
Promotion of Women and the Integration of Women in Development	Jeanne-Françoise Lekomba Loumeto [f]
Scientific Research and Technical Innovation	Hellot Mampouya (MCDDI)
Security and Public Order	Gen. Paul Mbot
Small and Medium Enterprises and Handicrafts	Yvonne-Adelaide Moundele Ngollo (Club 2002–PUR) [f]
Sports and Youth	Serge Michel Odzoki (PCT)
Technical Education and Vocational Training	Pierre Michel Nguimbi (PCT)
Territorial Administration and Decentralization	Raymond Mboulou (PCT)
Tourism and the Environment	André Okombi-Salissa (PCT)
Transport and Civil Aviation	Emile Ouosso (MAR)
Ministers of State	
Civil Service and Administrative Reform	Jean-Martín Mbemba (UP)
Hydrocarbons	Vacant
Justice and Human Rights	Aimé Emmanuel Yoka (PCT)
Planning, Territorial Management, and Economic Integration	Pierre Moussa (PCT)

[f] = female

COMMUNICATIONS

Legislation passed in 2001 outlawed censorship and assured freedom of information, although libeling senior authorities or inciting ethnic conflict are among those offenses punishable by fines. In September 2005 *Radio Moka,* a community station based in Impfondo, was suspended indefinitely by the government on allegations of "lack of impartiality" in news coverage. In 2006 the editor of a weekly newspaper, *Thalassa*, was arrested and jailed briefly on defamation charges. He was fined and ordered to suspend publication for six months.

Newspapers in the Republic of the Congo are privately owned.

The watchdog Reporters Without Borders has described the Republic of the Congo as among several African countries that "ensure a satisfactory degree of press freedom despite episodes of violence and harassment." However, journalists covering the controversial July 2009 presidential election were allegedly harassed, the watchdog Committee to Protect Journallists reported.

Press. Mweti (7,000) is a French-language daily published in Brazzaville. Other newspapers include Aujourd'hui, L'Eveil de Pointe-Noire, the Journal de Brazzaville, Le Choc, L'Observateur, L'Humanitaire, Le Tam Tam, Les Echos du Congo, and La Semaine Africaine, the latter published by the Catholic church, and the weekly Thalassa.

News agencies. The official news agency is *Agence Congolaise d'Information;* the *Agence d'Information d'Afrique Centrale* is also located in the capital. Resident foreign bureaus include *Agence France-Presse,* the Pan-African News Agency, and Reuters.

Broadcasting and computing. Broadcasting is dominated by the state-owned *Radiodiffusion-Télévision Nationale Congolaise* (RTNC), which offers programming in French, English, Portuguese, and a variety of indigenous languages. In April 1997 the government established a new official radio station, Radio Brazzaville. Other radio stations include the state-run Radio Congo, the private *Radio Liberté*, and a community station in Brazzaville, Canal FM. Television service is limited. As of 2008 there were 42.9 Internet users per 1,000 inhabitants.

INTERGOVERNMENTAL REPRESENTATION

Ambassador to the U.S.: Serge MOMBOULI.

U.S. Ambassador to the Republic of the Congo: Alan W. EASTHAM, Jr.

Permanent Representative to the UN: Raymond Serge BALÉ.

IGO Memberships (Non-UN): AfDB, AU, BADEA, BDEAC, CEEAC, CEMAC, Interpol, IOM, NAM, OIF, WCO, WTO.

COSTA RICA

Republic of Costa Rica
República de Costa Rica

Political Status: Part of the Captaincy General of Guatemala that declared independence from Spain in September 1821; member of the United Provinces of Central America that was launched in 1824; autonomy reestablished in 1839; republic declared in 1848; democratic constitutional system instituted in 1899.

Area: 19,575 sq. mi. (50,700 sq. km.).

Population: 3,925,331 (2000C); 4,401,000 (2008E).

Major Urban Centers (2005E): SAN JOSÉ (344,000), Limón (62,000), Alajuela (49,000), San Francisco (46,000).

Principal Language: Spanish (there is no "official" language).

Monetary Unit: Colón (market rate December 1, 2009: 558.01 colónes = $1US).

President: Oscar ARIAS Sánchez (National Liberation Party); elected on February 5, 2006, and inaugurated for a four-year term on May 8, succeeding Abel PACHECO de la Espriella (Social Christian Unity Party).

First Vice President: Vacant, following resignation of Laura CHINCHILLA (National Liberation Party) on October 8, 2008.

Second Vice President: Vacant, following resignation of Kevin CASAS Zamora (National Liberation Party) on September 22, 2007.

THE COUNTRY

One of the smallest of the Central American countries, Costa Rica lies directly north of Panama and combines tropical lowland, high tableland, and rugged mountainous terrain. Its people, known as *Costarricenses,* are overwhelmingly of European (predominantly Spanish) descent. This unusual homogeneity is broken only by mestizo and African minorities, which are concentrated in the provinces of Guanacaste and Limón, respectively. More than 90 percent of the population adheres to Roman Catholicism, the state religion, but other faiths are permitted. The country's literacy rate, which was 96.2 in 2005, is among the highest in Central America. Women constituted 40.7 percent of the nonagricultural, paid workforce in 2006. They are employed mainly in administrative positions, human resources, and customer services. In 2006 women earned about 87.5 percent of what men earned, up from 79.7 percent in 1994 but down from 91.2 percent in 2005. Additionally, 22 members of the current legislature are women.

In 1948 Costa Rica embarked on the establishment of what became one of the world's most progressive welfare states, providing a universal program of health care and education for its citizens that contrasted with less generous systems elsewhere in Latin America. Substantial economic growth, yielding one of the region's highest standards of living, continued through most of the 1970s before giving way to depressed prices for coffee, beef, bananas, and sugar exports, accompanied by increased oil import costs. By the early 1980s the country was experiencing deep recession, marked by high inflation, unemployment, budget deficits, and trade imbalances. Bankruptcy was averted by means of aid from the United States, the World Bank, and the International Monetary Fund (IMF), although several IMF agreements were compromised by Costa Rica's inability to meet fund conditions. By the mid 1990s, the proportion of families living in poverty had risen to an estimated 30 to 38 percent, with nearly one-quarter of workers engaged in the "informal sector."

GDP growth was less than 1.0 percent in 1996, but by 1999 it was the highest in Latin America, at 8.3 percent. A rapid reversal occurred in 2000, when GDP expanded by just 1.4 percent, largely attributed to higher prices for imported petroleum and lower earnings from exports. Improvement thereafter culminated in annual average GDP growth of 5.1 percent in 2003–2005. Robust growth of 8.7 percent in 2006 and 6.8 percent in 2007 was recorded, along with a record low for the poverty level (16.7 percent of the population) in 2007. As economic growth slowed to 2.9 percent in 2008, poverty increased, despite the lowest unemployment rate (4.8 percent) since 1994. Meanwhile, surging food and fuel prices, as well as rapid credit expansion, pushed the 2008 inflation rate to a record high 13.9 percent, driving up the cost of living and compounding poverty. In 2009, with little or no annual economic growth forecast, the IMF approved $735 million in stand-by funds to support Costa Rica's efforts to cope with the adverse global economic environment. The IMF cited the government's strategies for strengthening fiscal and monetary policies and noted that the country's banking system was generally strong.

GOVERNMENT AND POLITICS

Political background. Costa Rica declared its independence from Spain in 1821 but accepted inclusion in the Mexican Empire of 1822–1823. It was a member of the United Provinces of Central America from 1824 to 1839, when its autonomy was reestablished. A republic was formally declared in 1848 during a period characterized by alternating political conflict and rule by the leading families, who monopolized the indirect electoral system. In 1897 Costa Rica joined

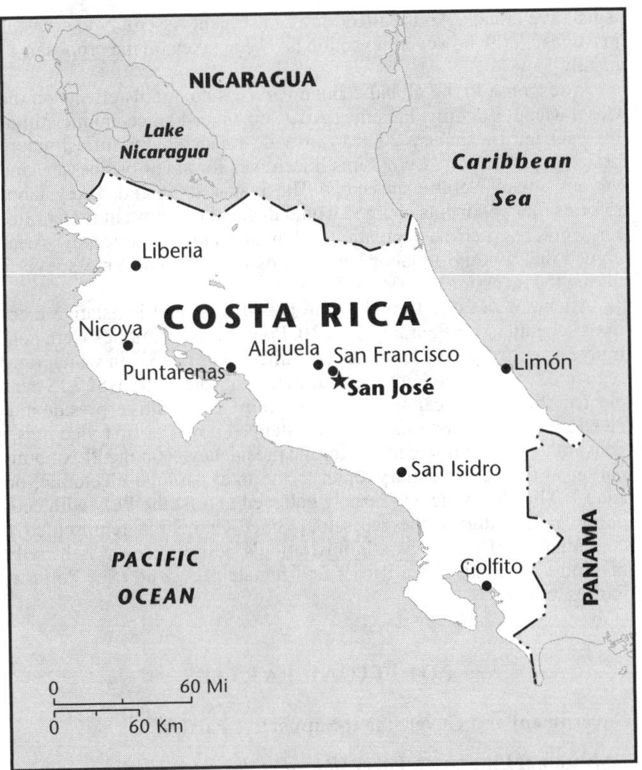

El Salvador, Honduras, and Nicaragua in the Greater Republic of Central America, but the federation was dissolved in 1898. A year later, President Bernardo SOTO sponsored what is considered to be Costa Rica's first free election, inaugurating a democratic process that has survived with only two major interruptions, one in 1917 and the other in 1948. Since the uprising led by José FIGUERES Ferrer, following annulment of the 1948 election by President Teodoro PICADO, transfer of power has been accomplished by constitutional means, further securing Costa Rica's reputation as what has been called "perhaps the most passionately democratic country in Latin America."

In the election of February 6, 1994, Figueres Ferrer's son, José María FIGUERES Olsen of the National Liberation Party (*Partido Liberación Nacional*—PLN) defeated Miguel Angel RODRÍGUEZ of the Social Christian Unity Party (*Partido Unidad Social Cristiana*—PUSC). However, in a close race with the PLN's José Miguel CORRALES, Rodríguez was elected president in balloting on February 1, 1998. In concurrent legislative balloting the PUSC reversed the tables on the PLN (the leading party in the previous assembly) by securing 27 of the 57 seats.

Four years later, the PUSC lost 8 of its seats in the legislative balloting on February 3, 2002, although it retained a 2-seat plurality over the PLN. The PUSC's presidential candidate in that year—Abel PACHECO—led a field of 13 in the concurrent first round of presidential balloting, with Rolando ARAYA Monge finishing second with 31 percent. Pacheco won the second round over Araya by 58 to 42 percent. These 2002 elections marked the end of the two-party system in Costa Rica, as neither of the two historically dominant political parties—the PUSC and the PLN—won a majority of seats in the legislature. The new Citizens' Action Party (PAC), a faction that split from the PLN, won 13 seats. (See Political Parties, below.)

In 2003 the Supreme Court validated presidential reelection, overturning a 2000 ruling that the court lacked constitutional authority in the matter. The action generated intense debate, with the opposition PAC insisting that an issue of such importance should be decided by elected, rather than by nonelected, officials.

Although PLN candidate Oscar ARIAS Sánchez garnered only a thin margin of 40.9 percent over the PAC candidate in the 2006 election, he subsequently achieved sufficient legislative support for his new government (installed on May 8) by reaching accommodation with the centrist Libertarian Movement Party (*Partido Movimiento Libertario*—PML), which held 6 legislative seats.

In September 2007. Second Vice President Kevin CASAS Zamora resigned in the wake of a scandal surrounding the upcoming referendum on implementing the Central American Free Trade Agreement (CAFTA), an effort headed by Alfredo VOLIO, who resigned his ministerial post to undertake the task. In October 2008 First Vice President Laura CHINCHILLA resigned in order to run for president. That same year, two other ministers resigned, one having been accused of corruption. Another minister accused of corruption resigned in 2009.

Constitution and government. The 1949 constitution provides for three independent branches of government: legislative, executive, and judicial. The legislative branch enjoys genuinely coequal power, including the ability to override presidential vetoes. The president serves as chief executive and is assisted by two elected vice presidents in addition to a cabinet selected by the president. By Latin American standards the president's powers are limited, and a 1969 constitutional amendment prohibited the reelection of all previous incumbents. However, in an unexpected and controversial ruling in April 2003, the Supreme Court declared the amendment invalid.

The judicial branch is independent of the president, its members being elected for eight-year terms by the legislature. The judicial structure encompasses the Supreme Court of Justice, which may rule on the constitutionality of legislation; four courts of appeal; and numerous local courts distributed among the judicial districts. One unique feature of the Costa Rican governmental system is the Supreme Electoral Tribunal (*Tribunal Supremo de Elecciones*), an independent body of three magistrates and three alternate magistrates elected by the Supreme Court of Justice for staggered six-year terms. The Tribunal oversees the entire electoral process, including the interpretation of electoral statutes, the certification of parties, and the adjudication of alleged electoral irregularities.

For administrative purposes the country is divided into 7 provinces and 81 *municipios,* the former administered by governors appointed by the president. The latter are governed by councils that have both voting and nonvoting members and by executive officials appointed by the president. The executive officers may veto council acts, but all such vetoes are subject to judicial review.

Costa Rica is one of only a handful of countries that constitutionally prohibit the raising of a national army, except under strictly limited circumstances of public necessity. The proscription has, however, yielded a proliferation of legally sanctioned armed groups, including private auxiliary police units and separate police forces for virtually every government ministry, most of which are beyond the control of the ministry of public security.

Foreign relations. A founding member of the United Nations (UN) and of the Organization of American States (OAS), Costa Rica has typically been aligned with the liberal, democratic wing in Latin American politics and has opposed dictatorships of both the right and the left. In May 1981 it broke relations with Cuba after a protest regarding the treatment of Cuban political prisoners had elicited an "insulting" response by Cuba's representative to the UN. The principal external concern for the remainder of the decade was the Nicaraguan *sandinista-contra* conflict and the associated U.S. involvement in regional affairs. Although formally neutral on the issue, Costa Rica strongly criticized Nicaragua's post-Somoza Marxist orientation, while accepting more than $730 million in economic aid from the United States. In early 1987 President Arias introduced a peace plan that served as the basis of intensive effort to negotiate an end to fighting in Nicaragua, El Salvador, and Guatemala. The initiative earned him the 1987 Nobel Peace Prize, while his reputation was further enhanced by brokering the *sandinista-contra* cease-fire in March 1988.

In early 1991 President Rafael Angel CALDERÓN Fournier concluded a free trade agreement with Venezuelan President Carlos Pérez and subsequently became the first Central American chief executive to negotiate a similar agreement with Mexico, which he hoped would pave the way to membership in the North American Free Trade Agreement (NAFTA). However, when the latter accord came into effect on January 1, 1995, there was concern that Costa Rica would be adversely affected by the recent devaluation of the Mexican peso. Meanwhile, Costa Rica had failed to ratify the Central American Parliament treaty, arguing that the institution would be a threat to its sovereignty and insisting that its neighbors had made insufficient progress in the implementation of domestic democratic processes. In June 1995, on the other hand, Costa Rica formally ratified the December 1991 Tegucigalpa Protocol establishing the Central American Integration System as a means of promoting regional economic integration. In March 2004 it also signed the CAFTA pact with the United States (see Current issues, below, for subsequent developments).

In a move that some viewed as an attempt to reduce unemployment among Costa Ricans, the government in late 1993 launched a campaign to deport an estimated 2,000 undocumented Nicaraguans. The action, which came in the wake of two highly publicized kidnappings by Nicaraguans, exacerbated a long-standing dispute over navigation rights and demarcation of the border along the San Juan River. While an 1858 treaty had granted Nicaragua sovereignty over the river, it guaranteed both parties "free navigation" for commercial purposes, which Nicaragua interpreted to exclude tourism. A further problem stemmed from Costa Rica's issuance in 1979 of land deeds to *campesino* settlers on a tract of land south of the river that later proved to be Nicaraguan territory. On June 26, 1995, despite a long-standing Costa Rican offer of relocation to its side of the border, the settlers proclaimed the independence of the "Republic of Airrecú" (a word meaning "friendship" in the local Maleku language), thereby provoking the dispatch of Nicaraguan troops to evict them. In July 1998 the two countries concluded an agreement to make the treaties governing navigation on the San Juan "more functional," including a provision that army vessels could accompany Nicaraguan police patrols along the river. The agreement was, however, rescinded by Nicaragua less than a month later.

During the 1980s thousands of Nicaraguans fled domestic insurrection to the relative safety of Costa Rica. Subsequent underemployment in Nicaragua served to maintain the flow, with 300,000 to 500,000 migrants estimated to have crossed the border by 1996. In October 1999 about 160,000 of the migrants were reported to have availed themselves of an amnesty declared by Costa Rica after Hurricane Mitch had devastated their homeland, although Nicaragua continued to insist that they were being mistreated. Tension over the river dispute was partially abated by an agreement in mid-2000 that restored Costa Rica's right to armed patrols as long as Nicaragua received prior notification of their movements.

The river controversy appeared to be further abated in September 2002 by an agreement on bilateral talks over a three-year period. However, soon thereafter Nicaraguan President Enrique Bolaños ordered the interdiction of Costa Rican police boats "under any circumstances," and in September 2005, after Costa Rica had submitted the dispute to the International Court of Justice (ICJ), he announced that henceforth all vessels navigating the river would be obliged to fly the Nicaraguan flag. Costa Rica responded by suggesting in May 2006 that police officers patrol the border, raising concerns in Nicaragua. (A ruling by the ICJ was expected by the end of 2009.)

In March 2009 Costa Rica and Cuba agreed to reestablish diplomatic relations.

On June 28, 2009, Honduran president Manuel Zelaya was ousted in a coup. He sought refuge in Costa Rica, and President Arias agreed to mediate talks in July between Zelaya and Roberto Micheletti, the interim head of the new government.

Current issues. The primary goal of the Arias administration was to implement CAFTA, the issue having been a prominent element of his campaign platform. While he attracted the opposition of unionists and students for his support of CAFTA, Arias pledged to maintain the PLN's social-democratic thrust, despite opening up state monopolies. Arias initially anticipated that CAFTA ratification would be achieved by a vote in the assembly. However, in April 2007 the Supreme Electoral Tribunal ruled that the opposition had the right to seek a national referendum on the matter. Arias subsequently announced he would welcome such a vote and Production Minister, Alfredo Volio resigned his post to lead the proreferendum effort. Popular approval seemed uncertain following reports in September of a memo written by Second Vice-President Kevin Casas recommending that the government use a "campaign of fear" to convince Costa Ricans to vote for CAFTA. Casas was also accused of pressuring mayors by threatening to cut off municipal funds if they did not support the referendum. Casas subsequently resigned, and the referendum was narrowly approved by 51.6 percent of voters on October 7. Twelve new laws, called "enabling legislation," were passed by the assembly near the end of 2008, and CAFTA was implemented on January 1, 2009.

Corruption scandals marred the Arias administration. In 2008 the housing minister resigned over allegations that his office misused $1.5 million in public funds, and in 2009 the minister of environment, energy, and telecommunications resigned after PAC activists accused him of assigning a mineral mining contract to a family member's company.

In December 2008 the presidency minister, Rodrigo ARIAS Sánchez, proposed modernizing the 1949 constitution by giving presidential decrees increased weight over legislation, placing restrictions on the assembly's ability to amend legislation proposed by the executive, and limiting the president to two terms. The PAC accused the PLN of attempting to strengthen the executive branch at the expense of the legislative branch. Arias called for a Constituent Assembly to convene in August 2009; however, no action had been taken on the proposals as of July 1.

In response to the global economic recession and its effects on the Costa Rican economy, President Arias announced an economic stimulus package in January 2009 to provide financing for infrastructure projects, public works programs, incentives for small businesses, and various social welfare measures. The plan also included key labor reforms that opponents charged would dismantle important protections for workers, such as regulations of hours and overtime pay. Arias argued that modifying labor laws was essential to avoid mass layoffs during the recession.

Attention in 2009 turned to the presidential and legislative elections scheduled for February 7, 2010. Presidential primaries were held midyear, with the PAC's first-ever primary on May 31, in which only registered party members were allowed to vote. Ottón SOLÍS was elected the party's candidate for the third consecutive presidential election. Laura Chinchilla, who had stepped down as first vice president and justice minister to run for the presidency, won the PLN nomination in the party primary, open to the total national electorate, on June 7. The electorate was largely believed to trust the PLN with economic policy during the recession. Since Chinchilla represented a continuation of the Arias administration's policies, she was heavily favored to become Costa Rica's first female president. (See Political Parties, below.)

POLITICAL PARTIES

Government and Government-Supportive Parties:

National Liberation Party (*Partido Liberación Nacional*—PLN). Founded by former president José Figueres Ferrer in the aftermath of the 1948 revolution, the PLN has traditionally been the largest and best organized of the Costa Rican parties and is a classic example of the democratic left in Latin America. Affiliated with the Socialist International, it has consistently favored progressive programs.

In July 1976 President Figueres precipitated a crisis within the party leadership by calling for revocation of the constitutional requirement that a president may not serve more than one term, thereby contributing to the defeat of Luis Alberto Monge as PLN presidential candidate in 1978. Subsequently, the cultivation of a network of predominantly regional and local support, coupled with a "return to the land" (*volver a la tierre*) campaign slogan, enabled Monge to secure a decisive victory in 1982. Although Oscar Arias Sánchez won a primary election over the more conservative Carlos Manuel CASTILLO in early 1985 (subsequently serving as president from 1986 to 1990), disagreement between their supporters, largely abated during the 1986 campaign, continued in the assembly. Castillo was the party's nominee to succeed Arias in 1990 but fell short by obtaining only 48 percent of the vote. Longtime party leader Figueres Ferrer died on June 8, 1990.

The PLN's José María Figueres captured the presidency in 1994, but the party failed to retain either that office or a legislative plurality in 1998 or 2002. The membership of the party's 2002 presidential candidate, Rolando Araya Monge, was suspended for six months in March 2003 for dubious electoral financing.

Arias's second-term effort succeeded by a narrow margin. By seeking a second term in 2006, Arias appeared to flaunt the constitution but also, as a neoliberal, generated ideological controversy within the PLN. A number of displeased high-ranking members left the party, including its secretary general, Luis Guillermo SOLÍS, and former president Luis Alberto MONGE. In the December 2006 local elections, the PLN won control of nearly three-fourths of the municipalities, including the mayorship of San José.

The main objective of the Arias administration was to shepherd CAFTA through the implementation process (see Current issues, above). In November 2007 President Arias signed the CAFTA treaty and appealed to the opposition to help pass the 13 needed reforms. When Security Minister Fernando BERROCAL resigned in March 2008, some speculated that President Arias forced the resignation to avoid antagonizing the left, which could block implementation of CAFTA.

In 2009 former vice president and minister of justice Laura Chinchilla reportedly received Arias's backing to succeed him as president. She defeated former San Juan mayor Johnny ARAYA to secure the party's nomination in the presidential primary on June 7, 2009.

Leaders: Oscar ARIAS Sánchez (President of the Republic), Francisco Antonio PACHECO Fernández (President of the Party), Laura

CHINCHILLA (2010 presidential candidate), Antonio CALDERÓN Castro (Secretary General).

Libertarian Movement Party (*Partido Movimiento Libertario—PML*). Launched in early 1995, the PML is a right-of-center group that opposes state interventionism and policies that constrain individual liberties and advocates privatization of all state monopolies. The PML sharply improved its legislative representation from one seat to seven seats in February 2002, winning 9.3 percent of the vote, although its candidate took only 1.7 percent in the first round of presidential balloting. The party fell to six legislative seats in 2006, its leader placing third in the presidential poll. The PML subsequently agreed to support the PLN government in the legislature in return for the PLN's pledge to pursue reforms designed to promote business competitiveness and to make it easier for people in border regions and marginal urban areas to gain property rights. In June 2008, the party announced a reorganized executive committee in preparation for the 2010 elections. On July 9, 2009, the PML National Assembly nominated Otto Guevara as the party's 2010 presidential candidate.

Leaders: Otto GUEVARA Guth (President and 2002, 2006, and 2010 presidential candidate), Patricia PEREZ (Secretary General).

Other Legislative Parties:

Citizens' Action Party (*Partido Acción Ciudadana—PAC*). Launched in early 2001 by, among others, PLN defector Ottón Solís Fallas and Epsy Cambell BARR, the PAC ran in the 2002 election on a populist platform promising to combat corruption and help farmers and traditional industries that had been weakened by recent market reforms. Solís finished a surprisingly strong third in the first round of presidential balloting in February 2002 with 26 percent of the vote, while the PAC garnered 13 seats in concurrent legislative balloting. A year later, six PAC members withdrew to form the Patriotic Bloc (*Bloque Patriotico—BP*).

In his 2006 campaign for the presidency, Solís lost to the PLN's Arias by 1.1 percent of the vote. The PAC won 17 seats in the concurrent legislative election.

Solis won the PAC's presidential primary on May 31, 2009, defeating Barr.

Leaders: Alberto Cañas ESCALANTE (President), Ottón SOLÍS Fallas (2002, 2006, and 2010 presidential candidate), Margarita Bolaños ARQUINE (Secretary General).

Social Christian Unity Party (*Partido Unidad Social Cristiana—PUSC*). The party is a loose alliance of the essentially conservative parties, including the **Calderonist Republican Party** (*Partido Republicano Calderonista—PRC*), formed in 1976; the **Christian Democratic Party** (*Partido Demócrata Cristiano—PDC*), formed in 1962; the **Popular Union Party** (*Partido Unión Popular—PUP*); and the former Democratic Renovation Party (see National Union Party, below). The PUSC campaigned before the 1978 election as the *Partido Unidad Opositora* (PUO) and as the *Coalición Unidad* in 1978, adopting its present name in December 1983. Partly because of conflict within the PLN leadership, the party won the presidency in 1978 but was defeated in both 1982 and 1986. The PUSC returned to power with a 52 percent presidential mandate in 1990 before losing a close race in May 1994. It regained the presidency in 1998 and retained it in 2002. In the 2006 presidential election, PUSC candidate Ricardo Toledo came in fourth, and the party won five parliamentary seats in concurrent balloting, amid allegations of corruption against the administration of retiring president Abel Pacheco. In addition, corruption charges were filed against former presidents Miguel Angel Rodriguez, and Rafael Angel Calderon Fournier. (For more information on the PDC, the PDC, and the PUP, see the 2008 *Handbook*.)

Despite being on trial for corruption, in April 2009 Calderon announced that he would run for the presidency. He was the sole PUSC candidate.

Leaders: Luis Fishman ZONZINSKI (President of the Party), Rafael Angel CALDERÓN Fournier (Former President of the Republic and 2010 presidential candidate), Ricardo TOLEDO (2006 presidential candidate), Xinia CARVAJAL Salazar (Secretary General).

National Union Party (*Partido Unión Nacional—PUN*). The PUN was formed in April 1985 by the leader of the previously PUSC-affiliated Democratic Renovation Party (*Partido Renovación Democrática—PRD*), Oscar AGUILAR Bulgarelli, who opposed Rafael Calderón's "absolute and antidemocratic control" of the PUSC coalition, including an alleged effort to change its posture from social democratic to liberal. The PUN won one legislative seat in the 2006 parliamentary election and 1.6 percent of the presidential vote.

Leaders: Arturo ACOSTA Mora (President), José Manuel ECHANDI Meza (2006 presidential candidate), Ricardo Rojas Hernán ZAMORA Rojas (Secretary General).

Accessibility Without Exclusion Party (*Partido Accesibilidad Sin Exclusión—PASE*). This San José–based party was formed in 2005 as a voice against the free trade agreement and against discrimination toward the disabled, senior citizens, and their families. The new party won one seat in the 2006 assembly poll; they did not run a presidential candidate that year.

Leaders: Oscar Andrés LÓPEZ Arias (President), Victor Emilio GRANADOS Calvo (Secretary).

Broad Front (*Frente Amplio*). This progressive group, which promotes "more participative and direct forms of democracy," is a provincial party based in San José with a platform advocating sustainability, equal rights, feminism, and human rights. It won one seat in the 2006 assembly elections. In 2009 the party announced its intention to nominate a presidential candidate and legislative candidates in all provinces in the 2010 elections..

Leaders: José MERINO del Río (President), Sonia SOLÍS Umana (Secretary).

National Restoration Party (*Partido Restauración Nacional—PRN*). A San José–based provincial party based on a platform of "Christian ethics," the PRN won one seat in the 2006 assembly poll with 2 percent of the vote; it did not field a presidential candidate that year.

Leaders: Carlos Luis AVENDAÑO Calvo (President), César Alexander ZUÑIGA Ramírez (Secretary General).

Other Parties that Contested the 2006 Legislative and/or Presidential Elections:

Costa Rican Renewal Party (*Partido Renovación Costarricense—PRC*). A small conservative party, the PRC won no seats in the 2006 legislative poll; its presidential candidate, Bolivar Serrano Hidalgo, secured less than 1 percent of the vote.

Leaders: Justo OROZCO Alvarez (President and 2002 presidential candidate), Bolivar SERRANO Hidalgo (2006 presidential candidate), Jimmy SOTO Solano (Secretary).

Homeland First Party (*Partido Patria Primero—PPP*). The PPP was launched before the 2006 elections, in which its presidential candidate captured 1.1 percent of the vote, and the party won 1.6 percent of the legislative vote.

Leaders: Juan José VARGAS Fallas (President and 2006 presidential candidate), Wilberth HERNÁNDEZ Vargas (Secretary).

National Integration Party (*Partido Integración Nacional—PIN*). The PIN was launched in 1996 but won no representation in 2002 or 2006. Its presidential candidate won 0.3 percent of the vote.

Leaders: Dr. Walter MUÑOZ Céspedes (President and 2006 presidential candidate), Marlyn BENDAÑA Valverde (Secretary General).

National Democratic Alliance (*Alianza Democrática Nacionalista—ADN*). The ADN's presidential candidate in 2006 captured 0.2 percent of the vote.

Leaders: José Miguel VILLALOBOS Umaña (President of the Party and 2006 presidential candidate), Emilia María RODRÍGUEZ Arias (Secretary General).

Democratic Force Party (*Partido Fuerza Democrática—PFD*). The PFD was launched before the 1994 election as the *Fuerza Democrática* (FD), a leftist coalition that included the **Costa Rican People's Party** (*Partido del Pueblo Costarricense—PPC*), the **Workers' Party** (*Partido de los Trabajadores—PT*), the **Ecological Humanist Movement** (*Movimiento Humanista Ecologista—MHE*), the **Progress Party** (*Partido del Progreso—PP*), and the subsequently dissolved Costa Rican Socialist Party (*Partido Socialista Costarricense—PSC*). (For more information on the now-absorbed PPC and PT parties, see the 2008 *Handbook*.)

The PFD candidate for president in 2006 secured less than 0.2 percent of the vote.

Leaders: Marco NUÑEZ González (President), Vladimir DE LA CRUZ de Lemos (Secretary General and 1994 and 2006 presidential candidate).

National Rescue Party (*Partido Rescate Nacional*—PRN). Organized in 1996, the PRN placed 12th in the 2006 presidential balloting with less than 0.2 percent of the vote.

Leaders: Fabio Enrique DELGADO Hernández (President), Alvaro Eduardo MONTERO Mejia (2006 presidential candidate), Alejandro LÓPEZ Martínez (Secretary General).

Popular Vanguard Party (*Partido Vanguardia Popular*—PVP). Founded in 1931 as the Costa Rican Communist Party (*Partido Comunista Costarricense*—PCC), the PVP adopted its present name in 1943 and regained legal status in 1975, following the lifting of a long-standing proscription of nondemocratic political organizations. During the 1978 and 1982 campaigns, it participated in a People United (*Pueblo Unido*—PU) coalition that included the PSC and PT (see above). In 1983 a struggle erupted between the essentially moderate old guard leadership and a younger hard-line group. In 1985 the PPC and its allies were permitted to register under the PU label. As a result, the PVP formed a coalition for the 1986 campaign styled the Popular Alliance (*Alianza Popular*—AP), with the former PU standard bearer, Dr. Rodrigo GUTIÉRREZ Sáenz, as its presidential candidate, securing one legislative seat. In 1995 the PVP, while retaining its separate identity, joined with a group of independents to form the **People's United Party** (*Partido Pueblo Unido*—PPU). Manuel MORA Valverde, the founder of the PPC and a leader of the 1948 civil war, died in 1994. Running under the banner of the **Coalition of the United Left** (*Coalición Izquierda Unida*—IU), an alliance of the PVP and the Revolutionary Party of Workers (*Partido Revolutionario de los Trabajadores*), the PVP won 0.4 percent of the legislative vote in 2006. Its presidential candidate won 0.1 percent of the vote.

Leaders: Trino BARRANTES Araya (President), Humberto Elías VARGAS Carbonell (2006 presidential candidate and Secretary General).

Union for Change (*Unión Para el Cambio*—UPC). The UPC is a small formation launched before the 2006 election. Its presidential candidate secured 2.4 percent of the vote in 2006.

Leaders: Antonio ÁLVAREZ Desanti (President and 2006 presidential candidate), Roberto Javier GALLARDO Nuñez (Secretary).

Patriotic Union Party (*Partido Unión Patriótica*—PUP). The PUP candidate for president in 2006 received 0.1 percent of the vote, while the party secured 0.5 percent of the legislative vote.

Leaders: José Miguel CORRALES Bolaños (President), José Humberto ARCE Salas (Vice President and 2006 presidential candidate), Rafael Angel Granados VARELA Granados (Secretary General).

Provincial parties that contested the 2006 elections unsuccessfully included the **Agricultural Force Party of the Cartagonians** (*Partido Fuerza Agraria de los Cartagineses*—PFAC) of Cartago, led by Alicia SOLANO Bravo; the **Agricultural Labor Action Party** (*Partido Acción Laborista Agrícola*—PALA) of Alajuela, led by Eliécer RODRÍGUEZ Vásquez; the **Patriotic Alliance Party** (*Partido Alianza Patriótica*—PAP) of Alajuela, led by Esli Antonio VEGA Alvarado; the **Authentic Heredian Party** (*Partido Autentica Herediano*) of Heredia, led by José Francisco SALAS Ramos; the **Cartagen Agricultural Union Party** (*Partido Unión Agricola Cartaginesa*—PUAC) of Cartago, led by Juan Guillermo BRENES Castillo; the **Green Ecologist Party** (*Partido Verde Ecologista*) of Cartago, led by Rodrigo José ARIAS Gutiérrez; the **Independent Guanacaste Party** (*Partido Guanacaste Independiente*—PGI) of Guanacaste, led by José Angel JARA Chavarría; the **Movement of Workers and Peasants** (*Movimiento de Trabajadores y Campesinos*—MTC) of Limón, led by Orlando BARRANTES Cartín; the **New Feminist League** (*Nueva Liga Feminista*) of San José, led by Ana Felicia TORRES Redondo; and the **Provincial Integration Party "Three"** (*Partido Integración Provincial "Tres"*—PIP3) of Cartago, led by Isabel Cristina ARIAS Calderón.

LEGISLATURE

The **Legislative Assembly** (*Asamblea Legislativa*) is a unicameral body whose 57 members, representing the provinces in proportion to population, are elected under a proportional representation system for four-year terms by direct popular vote and may not be immediately reelected. In the most recent election of February 5, 2006, the National Liberation Party won 25 seats; the Citizens' Action Party (PAC), 17; the Libertarian Movement Party (PML), 6; the Social Christian Unity Party, 5; the Accessibility Without Exclusion Party, 1; the Broad Front, 1; the National Restoration Party, 1; and the National Union Party (PUN), 1. Subsequently, one member of the PAC, one member of the PML, and the lone member of the PUN declared themselves independents.

President: Francisco Antonio PACHECO Fernández.

CABINET

[Party affiliations for cabinet members are unavailable.]

[as of July 1, 2009]

President	Oscar Arias Sánchez
First Vice President	vacant
Second Vice President	vacant
Ministers	
Agriculture and Livestock	Javier Flores Galarza
Communications	Mayi Antillon [f]
Culture and Youth	María Elena Carballo [f]
Economy, Trade, and Industry	Marco Vargas Díaz
Environment, Energy, and Telecommunications	Jorge Rodriguez (acting)
Finance	Guillermo Zúñiga
Foreign Affairs and Worship	Bruno Stagno Ugarte
Foreign Trade	Marco Vinicio Ruiz
Health	Dr. María Luisa Ávila Agüero [f]
Housing and Human Settlements	Clara Silvia Zomer Rezler [f]
Justice	Viviana Martín Salazar [f]
Labor	Francisco Morales Hernández
Planning and Economic Policy	Roberto Gallardo Núñez
Presidency	Rodrigo Arias Sánchez
Presidential Adviser for Competitiveness and Regulatory Improvement	Jorge Woodbridge
Public Education	Leonardo Garnier
Public Security	Janina del Vecchio [f]
Public Works and Transport	Karla González Carvajal [f]
Science and Technology	Eugenia M. Flores Vindas [f]
Tourism	Carlos Ricardo Benavides

[f] = female

COMMUNICATIONS

All news media are free of censorship, subject to limitations such as the abuse of public officials. The country's defamation laws place some limits on freedom of expression.

Press. The following are Spanish dailies published in San José: *La Nación* (125,000), conservative; *Diario Extra* (120,000), independent; *La República* (60,000), independent; *La Prensa Libre* (50,000), independent; *The Tico Times* (15,000), independent English weekly.

News agencies. The regional *Agencia Centroamericana de Noticias* (ACAN) serves in lieu of a domestic facility. *Agence France-Presse, Deutsche Presse-Agentur, Prensa Latina,* and TASS maintain offices in San José.

Broadcasting and computing. Broadcasting is supervised by the government's *Departamento Control Nacional de Radio-Televisión.* Television and radio stations are commercial, except for several offering religious or cultural programming. The *Sistema de Radio y TV Cultural* (SINART) network was organized by the government in 1978 to transmit news and cultural programs, while U.S.-based Cable Network News (CNN) is available by subscription. As of 2008 there were 323.1 Internet users per 1,000 inhabitants.

INTERGOVERNMENTAL REPRESENTATION

Ambassador to the U.S.: Luis Diego ESCLANTE.

U.S. Ambassador to Costa Rica: (Vacant).

Permanent Representative to the UN: Jorge URBINA.

IGO Memberships (Non-UN): ACS, BCIE, IADB, Interpol, IOM, OAS, OPANAL, PCA, SELA, SICA, WCO, WTO.

CÔTE D'IVOIRE

République de Côte d'Ivoire

Note: In November 1985 the United Nations responded affirmatively to a request from the Ivorian government that *Côte d'Ivoire* be recognized as the sole official version of what had previously been rendered in English as Ivory Coast and in Spanish as *Costa de Marfil.*

Political Status: Independent since August 7, 1960; present constitution adopted October 31, 1960; under de facto one-party regime prior to legalization of opposition parties on May 30, 1990; constitution suspended and governmental authority assumed by the military following a bloodless coup on December 24, 1999; new constitution providing for a return to civilian government approved by national referendum on June 23–24, 2000.

Area: 124,503 sq. mi. (322,463 sq. km.).

Population: 15,366,672 (1998C); 21,160,000 (2008E).

Major Urban Center (2005E): Abidjan (4,100,000). In March 1983 the interior city of YAMOUSSOUKRO (484,000, 2005E) was designated as the nation's capital. However, as of mid-2009 most government offices remained in Abidjan (the former capital), and most foreign governments were also still maintaining their embassies there.

Official Language: French.

Monetary Unit: CFA Franc (official rate December 1, 2009: 434.59 francs = $1US). The CFA franc, previously pegged to the French franc, is now permanently pegged to the euro at 655.957 CFA francs = 1 euro.

President: Laurent GBAGBO (Ivorian Popular Front); elected on October 20, 2000, and inaugurated for a five-year term on October 27 to succeed Gen. Robert GUEÏ, who had come to power via a coup on December 24, 1999; term extended for one year following UN Security Council Resolution 1633 (October 21, 2005); term extended by UN Security Council Resolution 1721 (November 1, 2006).

Prime Minister: Guillaume Kigbafori SORO (New Forces); appointed by the president on March 29, 2007, and sworn in on April 4 to succeed Charles Konan BANNY (nonparty) following peace agreement of March 4; formed multiparty government on April 7, 2007.

THE COUNTRY

A land of forests and savannas, with a hot, humid climate, Côte d'Ivoire is the richest and potentially the most nearly self-sufficient state of former French West Africa. A substantial percentage of the population consists of migrant workers, mostly from Burkina Faso, Ghana, and Mali. There traditionally has also been a sizable non-African expatriate community consisting primarily of Lebanese and French. A majority of the population is either Muslim (40 percent) or Christian (30 percent), with the balance adhering to traditional religious practices. Women constitute approximately 33 percent of the adult labor force, primarily in agriculture; female representation in government is minimal, although there have been several women in recent cabinets.

The economy experienced rapid growth following completion in 1950 of the Vridi Canal, which transformed Abidjan into a deepwater port. An impressive average real growth rate of 7.5 percent was reported for 1960–1980, but a variety of factors led to a severe five-year recession thereafter. Although agriculture now accounts for only one-fourth of total GDP, Côte d'Ivoire is the world's leading producer of cocoa. (Cocoa accounted for 20 percent of GDP and 40 percent of exports in 2006, although the quality of Ivorian cocoa had reportedly declined as the result of the recent civil war.) Côte d'Ivoire is also one of Africa's primary exporters of coffee, bananas, and tropical woods. Despite a UN embargo, diamonds continue to be smuggled out of the country. Meanwhile, the government has recently signed contracts with several foreign companies to develop new gold mines, the first of which was scheduled to begin production in 2010.

The country's image as a model African economy was tarnished in the 1980s by debts attributed to extensive government borrowing in the 1970s. In the first half of the 1990s, sagging cocoa and coffee prices, the decimation of lumber-producing forests, and the government's inability to make debt payments prompted economic reform and diversification efforts. Such measures enabled Côte d'Ivoire to rebound quickly from the inflationary effects of the 1994 CFA franc devaluation, and between 1995 and 1998 the country experienced average real GDP annual growth of more than 6 percent. However, Côte d'Ivoire's fiscal situation remained fragile. The International Monetary Fund (IMF) and the World Bank cited poor economic management and a multitude of perceived governance problems as contributing to the country's difficulties. (The IMF temporarily suspended aid in 1999 because of perceived corruption within the administration.) In light of the political uncertainty that followed a military coup in December 1999, the economy shrunk by 2.5 percent in 2000 and 1.5 percent in 2001.

The resumption of civil war in 2002 (see Political background and Current issues, below) strained the economy even further, GDP declining by 3.8 percent in 2003. The IMF and World Bank suspended some aid and debt-reduction programs because of the strife, which also compromised major trade routes through the north of the country to neighboring states and prompted a sharp decline in foreign investment. GDP fell by 2.3 percent in 2004, but a UN-sponsored peace initiative in 2005 offered hope for economic recovery. Also encouraging was the opening of new oil fields in the Baobab region in 2005. The country's oil production reached 80,000 barrels per day, and the transitional government signed additional exploration agreements with several foreign companies.

The government launched a broad campaign in August 2006 to meet the conditions necessary for the resumption of IMF and World Bank lending. GDP growth of 1.8 percent was reported for 2006, while a peace agreement in March 2007 (see Current issues, below) appeared to set the stage for full focus on much-needed economic development. (The recent civil war had left more than 3,000 people dead and more than 700,000 displaced.) The IMF quickly approved emergency support for the new transitional government's economic program. On a less positive note, rising food prices contributed to a jump in inflation and several protest demonstrations in 2008. Pessimists also pointed to a lag in implementation of many of the peace accord's elements as cause for concern, along with perceived systemic corruption in the banking, oil, and cocoa sectors.

GDP grew by 2.3 percent in 2008 (up from 1.6 percent in 2007), although inflation rose to 9 percent for the year. Following up emergency credits in 2008 to help offset the effects of higher food prices, the IMF in March 2009 approved $565 million in new lending to support the government's economic program. The Fund and the World Bank shortly thereafter announced that Côte d'Ivoire had qualified for $3 billion in debt relief from the Paris Club and was eligible for similar relief from commercial banks. The debt arrangements were contingent upon the government's intensification of structural reforms and poverty-reduction efforts. (Some estimates placed the poverty rate at more than 60 percent of the population.)

GOVERNMENT AND POLITICS

Political background. Established as a French protectorate in 1842, Côte d'Ivoire became part of the Federation of French West Africa in 1904, an autonomous republic within the French Community in 1958, and a fully independent member of the French Community in August 1960, although its membership was abandoned with the adoption of its present constitution two months later. Its dominant political figure since the 1940s was Félix HOUPHOUËT-BOIGNY, who in 1944 organized the *Syndicat Agricole Africain,* an African farmers' union, and was one of the founders of the African Democratic Rally (*Rassemblement Démocratique Africain*—RDA), an international

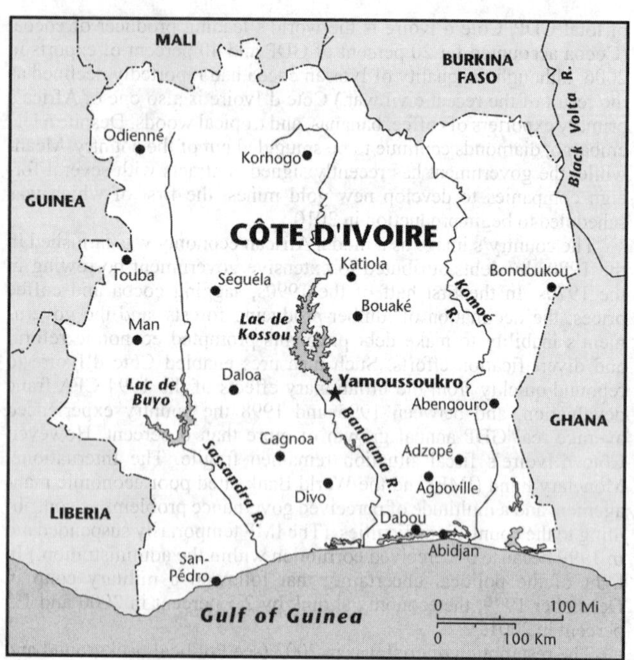

political party with branches in numerous French African territories. As leader of the RDA's Ivorian branch—the Democratic Party of the Ivory Coast (*Parti Démocratique de la Côte d'Ivoire*—PDCI)—Houphouët-Boigny served in the French National Assembly from 1946 to 1959, became prime minister of the autonomous republic in 1959, and served as president from 1960 (until his death in 1993).

The postcolonial era was relatively stable by African standards, although there were periodic student demonstrations and university closings. Another source of tension was the presence of many foreign workers, with whom indigenous Ivorians sporadically clashed in competition for jobs.

The election of an enlarged National Assembly on November 9 and 23, 1980, marked the first time since independence that nominees were not confined to a single PDCI list. Although all 649 officeseekers were party members, incumbents captured only 26 of 147 seats, while a similar infusion of new representatives occurred at municipal balloting later in the month.

On May 30, 1990, the government was compelled by increasingly strident protests to authorize opposition party activity. On October 28 Houphouët-Boigny won a seventh term in office, capturing a reported 82 percent of the vote, while Laurent GBAGBO, leader of the opposition Ivorian Popular Front (*Front Populaire Ivoirien*—FPI), was credited with the remainder. On November 7, one day after the National Assembly approved creation of the post, the highly regarded governor of the Central Bank of West African States (*Banque Centrale des États de l' Afrique de l'Ouest*—BCEAO), Alassane OUATTARA, was appointed prime minister.

On December 7, 1993, Houphouët-Boigny died in his Yamoussoukro palace of complications stemming from an operation earlier in the year. On the same day, Prime Minister Ouattara held a cabinet meeting in the presidential offices. However, National Assembly president Henri Konan BÉDIÉ announced that evening that he had assumed presidential power in accord with a 1990 constitutional amendment. Two days later Ouattara resigned, apparently unwilling to cooperate with Bédié, his PDCI rival. On December 9 the Supreme Court confirmed Bédié's succession, and the following day the president appointed Daniel Kablan DUNCAN as prime minister. On December 15 Duncan, a former economy minister described as a "technocrat" dedicated to economic reform, named a 24-member interim cabinet.

In preparation for presidential and legislative elections scheduled for late 1995, the PDCI-dominated National Assembly voted overwhelmingly in late 1994 to adopt a new electoral code that the opposition had strongly criticized as biased in favor of the government. The run-up to the 1995 poll was marked by violent protests against the code, its new provisions (requiring parents and grandparents of presidential candidates to have been of Ivorian birth) having thwarted the aspirations of Ouattara, Bédié's main challenger and the consensus leader of the new opposition Republican Front (*Front Républicain*—FR). Moreover, the government refused to appoint an independent electoral commission. Although the government in September banned all demonstrations for three months, the FR continued its antigovernment marches, and on October 2 at least 5 people were killed when government forces attempted to disperse protestors. Meanwhile, the field of presidential contestants (which had numbered 11) continued to dwindle as candidates announced their intention to observe the FR's call for an electoral boycott. Consequently, at presidential balloting on October 22, President Bédié easily won reelection, capturing 96.25 percent of the tally while his sole adversary, Francis WODIÉ of the Ivorian Workers' Party (*Parti Ivoirien des Travailleurs*—PIT), secured a meager 3.75 percent. Although the government claimed a 62 percent voter participation rate, the opposition reported much lower figures.

Following a meeting with President Bédié in early November 1995, the FR announced its intention to participate in the upcoming legislative balloting. However, the FR proved unable to agree on a joint list of candidates; consequently, at assembly balloting on November 26 the PDCI retained all 148 of its seats while the FPI and the Rally of Republicans (*Rassemblement des Républicains*—RDR) managed only small gains.

In May 1996 the government confirmed rumors that a coup attempt led by senior military officers had been thwarted prior to the 1995 assembly balloting. (The administration had previously maintained that the clashes were between government security forces and opposition militants.) On August 10 the administration removed Minister of Sports Gen. Robert GUEÏ, who was the army chief of staff in 1995 and had subsequently been linked by junior military officials to the "conception and preparation" of the coup plot (a charge he denied). Moreover, between November 1996 and January 1997 the government dismissed eight senior officers, including Gueï, from the armed forces and penalized at least four others for their alleged roles in the 1995 coup attempt.

On June 30, 1998, the PDCI-dominated assembly approved constitutional amendments that dramatically increased the scope of the chief executive's powers and, two years after it was first proposed, provided for the establishment of an upper legislative body, or Senate (see Constitution and government, below). Opposition legislators (including those from the FPI) boycotted the assembly vote, asserting that the PDCI had ignored their legislative recommendations, including a call for the amendments to be submitted to a national referendum. Subsequently, antigovernment demonstrations erupted in Abidjan in September. However, the ruling party and the FPI began discussions that yielded a "good governance," prodemocracy pact on December 24. Four days later the National Assembly took action on a key element of the agreement, adopting a draft law that authorized the government to grant amnesty to opposition activists jailed during the 1995 unrest. Electoral reform was the focus of the accord's other major directives, most notably the financing of presidential election campaigns and the establishment of a national electoral commission. Meanwhile, although the agreement elicited nearly universal acclaim from Ivorian political leaders, the praise was tempered by opposition demands that the government begin negotiations with all of the major parties. Subsequently, in March 1999, the PDCI launched talks with the RDR on establishing the conditions necessary for elections in 2000 and the drafting of a "consensus constitution." However, the discussions quickly stalled, and attention in Abidjan turned toward the potential for an electoral confrontation between Bédié and Alassane Ouattara, the latter having reportedly announced his intention to relinquish his position as IMF deputy secretary general to mount a presidential campaign as the RDR's standard-bearer.

Growing dissatisfaction with President Bédié's autocratic rule contributed to his overthrow in a bloodless military coup on December 24, 1999. General Gueï, the dominant figure in the junta, assumed the presidency of a transitional National Committee of Public Salvation (*Comité National de Salut Public*—CNSP), promising he would cede power within a year to a democratically elected president. In January 2000 membership in the CNSP was expanded to include the PDCI, FPI, and RDR, although ultimate control remained in the hands of the military. Gueï subsequently appeared to be maneuvering to consolidate his power in anticipation of a possible run for the presidency, despite his previous pledge that he would not be a candidate. The question of candidate eligibility was significant in the preparation of the new draft constitution, which originally required that a person needed only one parent of Ivorian nationality to be a legal candidate, a provision that would have permitted Ouattara to run. However, at Gueï's insistence, the draft basic law was redrawn to require that both parents of a presidential candidate had to be Ivorian citizens. In early October, the Supreme Court, headed by Gueï's former legal adviser, confirmed that Ouattara's candidacy was invalid, as was that of Emile Constant BOMBET, the potential candidate of the RDR.

The new constitution was approved in a national referendum July 23–24, 2000 (see Constitution and government, below, for details). Gueï and the FPI's Laurent Gbagbo were the primary contenders in the October 22 presidential balloting, a boycott by the PDCI and RDR having reduced the rest of the field to several candidates from minor parties. Voter turnout was low (only 35 percent), in large part due to the boycott. When initial results suggested a Gbagbo victory, Gueï attempted to dismiss the Independent Electoral Commission and declare himself victor. However, massive street demonstrations erupted to protest Gueï's actions, and he was forced to abdicate power and accept the legitimacy of the victory by Gbagbo, who was sworn in as president on October 27. One day later Gbagbo named Pascal Affi N'GUESSAN of the FPI to head a new cabinet that was dominated by the FPI but also included members of the PDCI and PIT.

New assembly balloting was held on December 10, 2000, the RDR boycotting the poll because Ouattara was again declared ineligible to be a candidate. The FPI scored considerable gains, securing 96 seats to 77 for the PDCI. (Elections were not held for 28 northern seats due to violence related to the RDR boycott.)

The PDCI significantly improved its legislative standing in the January 14, 2001, balloting for 26 of the 28 seats that had not been filled the previous December, winning 17 of the contests. However, the FPI subsequently established a more comfortable plurality by negotiating a cooperation agreement with independent legislators who in February formed the new, pro–Gueï Union for Democracy and Peace in Côte d'Ivoire (*Union pour la Démocratie et la Paix de la Côte d'Ivoire*—UDPCI). On January 24 a new cabinet, again led by N'Guessan, was appointed, with the FPI, PDCI, and PIT accepting portfolios. Municipal elections in March 2001 were most noteworthy for the success of the RDR, which, among other things, shed some of its reputation as a "one man" or "one region" party by gaining control of local councils throughout the country.

Under heavy international pressure, President Gbagbo convened a Forum for National Reconciliation in October 2001, which upon its conclusion in January 2002 had heard from Gbagbo, Bédié, Gueï, and Ouattara. The "big four" attended negotiations together in late January to review the forum's proposals, which, among other things, called for Ouattara to be issued a nationality certificate. Based on the success of those talks, the RDR joined the new government named on August 5.

In the wake of efforts to resolve a bitter civil war that broke out in September 2002 (see Current issues), Gbagbo in January 2003 appointed Seydou DIARRA, a well-respected independent, as prime minister. After intense negotiations, it was announced that a new cabinet would be formed comprising ten members from the FPI, eight from the PDCI, seven from the RDR, seven from the Patriotic Movement of Côte d'Ivoire (*Mouvement Patriotique de la Côte d'Ivoire*—MPCI), one from the Movement for Justice and Peace (*Mouvement pour la Justice et la Paix*—MJP), one from the Ivorian Popular Movement for the Greater West (*Mouvement Popular Ivoirien du Grand Ouest*—MPIGO), and additional ministers from small established parties. (The MJP and MPIGO were former rebel groups. See Current issues, below, for details.) However, the unity cabinet essentially collapsed before it began work when antigovernment protests (asserting that Gbagbo had reneged on his pledge regarding the prime minister's authority) were met with violent suppression. Fighting resumed in several areas, and even international observers were unable to pinpoint which side was to blame.

Following the postponement of national elections scheduled for October 2005, independent Charles Konan BANNY was named to head a new transitional government (installed on December 28) that comprised representatives of the FPI, PDCI, MPCI, PIT, RDR, UDPCI, and the New Forces (*Forces Nouvelles*—FN), a former rebel grouping. Banny and his cabinet resigned on September 6, 2006, in the wake of a toxic waste scandal (see Current issues, below), but the president reappointed Banny on September 16 to head a reshuffled cabinet. Following the signing of a peace agreement in March 2007, former rebel leader Guillaume SORO of the FN was named prime minister in April to head yet another national unity cabinet comprising members of the FPI, FN, PDCI, RDR, and other minor parties.

Constitution and government. The 1960 constitution provided the framework for a one-party presidential system based on the preeminent position of President Houphouët-Boigny and the PDCI. Although other parties were not proscribed, no challenge to the PDCI was permitted until May 1990 when the government authorized the registration of opposition groups, in May 1990. (For constitutional developments from 1990 through 1998, see the 2007 *Handbook*.)

The military junta that assumed power in a bloodless coup on December 24, 1999, immediately suspended the constitution. However, a new basic law was presented for a national referendum July 23–24, 2000, with 87 percent of the voters, according to official reports, approving the document. Much of the language in the 1960 constitution was retained in the 2000 version. A strong presidential system was confirmed; among other things the president retained the authority to appoint the prime minister and, in consultation with the prime minister, the Council of Ministers. The president's term was reduced to five years, renewable once. The post is selected through direct universal suffrage in two-round (if necessary) majoritarian balloting. Restrictions were also placed on presidential candidates regarding their parentage and formal nationality, again prompting substantial controversy (see Political background, above). (The National Assembly in December 2004 passed legislation to allow citizens with only one Ivorian parent to run for office, although President Gbagbo insisted a national referendum would be required for the change to be implemented.) The National Assembly remained the sole legislative body, a proposed Senate, which had never been established, being formally abolished. For the first time, the new constitution included detailed protection for human rights. Other noteworthy provisions included one granting civil and penal immunity for people involved in the 1999 coup.

The judiciary is headed by a Constitutional Council comprising three members appointed by the president and three appointed by the president of the assembly. There are also a High Court of Justice (whose members are elected by the assembly), a Court of Cassation, and local appeals courts. In addition, the new constitution created the post of a presidentially appointed mediator of the republic to serve as a national ombudsman.

The country is divided for administrative purposes into 58 departments, each headed by a prefect appointed by the central government, but with an elected council. Municipalities (numbering nearly 200) have elected councillors and mayors.

Foreign relations. In line with its generally pro-French orientation, Côte d'Ivoire has adhered to a moderate policy in African affairs and a broadly pro-Western posture in general. Relations with neighboring states were periodically strained in the 1980s, particularly in the wake of growing xenophobic sentiment in Côte d'Ivoire, especially among the mainly Christian population in the south. Although ties with neighboring Burkina Faso had previously been weakened because of that country's links with Libya and Ghana, Burkinabè leader Capt. Blaise Compaoré, who led the 1987 overthrow of Col. Thomas Sankara's government, long enjoyed close personal relations with Houphouët-Boigny. Relations with the Central African Republic (CAR), cool upon the provision of sanctuary by Côte d'Ivoire to the CAR's former emperor Bokassa, improved once the ex-sovereign departed for Paris in late 1983. Relations with Israel, which had been broken off in 1973, were reestablished in December 1985.

In the early 1990s, France, the country's leading financial donor and cultural influence, appeared to lose interest in maintaining a high profile in its former protectorate. Among other things, France stunned Côte d'Ivoire in 1990 by refusing Houphouët-Boigny's request for troops to help quell an uprising of military conscripts.

Burdened by the presence of 200,000 refugees along its western border, Côte d'Ivoire continued diplomatic efforts to resolve the Liberian crisis through the first half of the 1990s. In September 1996 Abidjan, citing the need to stem attacks on its nationals as well as foreign refugees, established a military "operational zone" along its border with Liberia. In April 1997 the Bédié government and the United Nations Office of the High Commissioner for Refugees (UNHCR) reached agreement on a plan to repatriate the approximately 200,000 Liberians still living in Côte d'Ivoire. (By the end of 2006, the number of such refugees had reportedly declined to 26,000.)

The Organization of African Unity (OAU, subsequently the African Union—AU) and the Economic Community of West African States (ECOWAS) did not agree with General Gueï's successful efforts to bar the presidential candidacy of Alassane Ouattara in the summer of 2000, and they subsequently exerted considerable diplomatic pressure to undermine Gueï's legitimacy. The international community, particularly the European Union (EU), also strongly urged all of the key political figures in Côte d'Ivoire to participate fully in the reconciliation process so as to permit resumption of aid.

Current issues. More than 300 people died in violence that erupted following the October 2000 presidential election, much of it centered on conflict between the RDR and security forces as well as between the predominantly Muslim northern supporters of the RDR and the mainly Christian southern supporters of the FPI. Continued political tension and unrest in the military were reflected in an unsuccessful military coup attempt in early January 2001. Fighting was also reported in the west between Ivorians and migrant workers from Burkina Faso who generally supported the RDR.

Hope was widespread in August 2002 that a return to stability was in the offing in view of the RDR's decision to join the cabinet. However, in mid-September a group of soldiers about to be demobilized launched antigovernment attacks that soon left more than half of the country in the hands of the new MPCI. France sent additional troops to augment its 500-member permanent garrison in case a quick evacuation was required but declined to assist the government militarily, calling the conflict a domestic issue. For its part, the Gbagbo administration blamed the insurrection on supporters of General Gueï, who was killed under murky circumstances in a seemingly nonmilitary situation on the first day of fighting.

With the predominantly Muslim MPCI holding significant portions of the northern and central regions, the government in late September 2002 reportedly instituted harsh countermeasures that led the RDR to withdraw its support for the administration. Meanwhile, two new rebel groups—the MJP and the MPIGO—had emerged in the west. With the conflict having developed into a full-blown civil war, France deployed some 2,500 troops to Côte d'Ivoire to try to maintain order, while regional leaders initiated mediation efforts. In January 2003 an agreement was reached under the auspices of ECOWAS under which Gbagbo was to remain president while allowing security authority to be assumed by a new prime minister. For their part, the rebel groups agreed to end hostilities, with both sides being guaranteed amnesty for any human rights violations. ECOWAS peacekeepers joined French forces in an effort to patrol the cease-fire line.

The appointment of Seydou Diarra as prime minister in January 2003 appeared to be a promising development, since he was widely respected by opposition groups as well as the international community. However, the proposed new national unity government collapsed (see Political background, above), and Diarra's subsequent willingness to negotiate with the rebels reportedly contributed to friction between him and President Gbagbo.

In June 2003 the UN Security Council authorized the creation of UN peacekeeping for Côte d'Ivoire (the UN operation for Côte d'Ivoire [*Opération des Nations Unies pour Côte d'Ivoire*—ONUCI]), but fighting continued, the three rebel groups coalescing in August under the banner of the FN. Meanwhile, progovernment demonstrations for the most part appeared to be conducted by the Coordination of Young Patriots (*Coordination des Jeunes Patriotes*—CJP), which was strongly criticized for alleged responsibility for a campaign of violence against opposition leaders and foreigners. The CJP was banned in September, but its hallmark attacks continued. For his part, Guillaume Soro, the leader of the FN, announced his forces would not lay down their arms until Gbagbo surrendered his security power. In response, the UN imposed an arms embargo on the country in November 2004. However, subsequent reports indicated that the government and rebel groups were able to violate the embargo easily.

By the end of 2004 some 250,000 Ivorians had fled the civil war to neighboring countries, and 600,000 people had been displaced internally. In addition, tensions had grown between the government and French peacekeepers, French forces having "destroyed" the Ivorian air force after a government attack on a rebel base had accidentally left nine French soldiers dead.

President Gbagbo and FN leader Soro met at a summit in April 2005 sponsored by South African President Mbeki and reached yet another tentative peace agreement. The rebels began to disarm in late June, while rebel and government forces started to withdraw from conflict zones. The cease-fire continued throughout the summer, despite ethnic clashes in cocoa-producing areas that left more than 100 dead in June. (Gbagbo deployed special police and security forces in Abidjan in the wake of that turmoil.)

In July 2005 the assembly endorsed legislation required by the recent peace agreement that provided for public financing of political campaigns, a new voter registration campaign, reform of citizenship laws, and establishment of a new election commission in preparation for the presidential and legislative elections scheduled for October. However, the FN temporarily withdrew from the peace process in September, claiming that South African officials were exhibiting a bias toward the Gbagbo administration. Consequently, upon the recommendation of UN Secretary General Kofi Annan that the elections be postponed, the UN Security Council on October 21 endorsed the extension of Gbagbo's presidential mandate for up to 12 months. The UN also called upon Gbagbo to appoint a new prime minister with enhanced powers to lead a new transitional government.

The AU and ECOWAS endorsed the UN's decision, but the FN rejected the action and demanded that Soro be named as the nation's new prime minister. Collaterally, FN forces "remobilized," and President Gbagbo created new elite security forces to deal with the potential resumption of fighting. However, in November 2005 the FN returned to negotiations, which, after 16 other candidates were rejected, led to the appointment of Charles Banny, a governor of the Bank of West African States, to the premiership.

Prime Minister Banny, an independent described as "pro-French," soon clashed with President Gbagbo over the extent of Banny's authority. Consequently, the UN established an International Working Group (IWG) to assist the new transitional government. In one of its first decisions, the IWG in January 2006 announced that it would not endorse the proposed extension of the mandate of the current assembly (a primary source of support for Gbagbo). The president's supporters subsequently launched a series of protests that included the occupation of UN headquarters in Abidjan and attacks on foreign businesses. In response, the UN threatened to impose travel restrictions and financial sanctions on any Ivorian leaders perceived as encouraging the unrest, and general calm returned. On January 27 Gbagbo announced that the mandate of the assembly had in fact been extended for up to one year. The IWG described the extension as a violation of the spirit of the peace agreements but took no formal action. A number of parties boycotted the subsequent assembly activity.

Another round of peace talks was held by the main factions in February 2006, with tentative agreement being reached for new national elections in October. Collaterally, the UN bolstered its peacekeeping mission by transferring troops to it from the successful UN initiative in Liberia. Voter registration began in May, along with an intensified campaign to disarm former rebel groups and progovernment militias.

In August 2006 a Greek freighter leased by a European energy firm unloaded a cargo of toxic waste in Côte d'Ivoire in an apparent attempt to avoid the high costs of processing the material in Europe. The toxins reportedly killed ten people in Côte d'Ivoire and caused health problems for thousands of others, prompting widespread protest demonstrations. Government corruption was suspected in the matter because of the unusual speed with which the ship was granted a license to unload its cargo. Included in the cabinet installed in September were a new minister of environment, water, and forests, and five other new ministers. (In February 2007 the energy firm agreed to pay the government $200 million to settle the incident.)

By mid-2006 some 2,000 fighters from rebel and progovernment militias had reportedly still not been disarmed or integrated into the security forces, prompting the UN to extend the mandate of its peacekeeping forces. In addition, opponents and supporters of the government continued to clash in many areas of the country. On November 1, the UN Security Council (with the support of the AU and ECOWAS) extended President Gbagbo's term for another year, accepting his argument that new elections could not be held in light of continuing government/rebel conflict and organizational problems in arranging elections. However, the resolution also demanded the strengthening of the powers of the prime minister and the dilution of presidential authority. Among other things, the prime minister was granted the power to schedule and organize future elections, and the president was stripped of the ability to postpone balloting any further. The prime minister was also given authority over the security forces.

Another round of violence began in November 2006 when some 200 militia fighters abducted UN personnel in the town of Duejoue, in the west of the country, following clashes between pro- and antigovernment militias. In mid-December Gbagbo called for a new peace dialogue that he suggested could include a general amnesty for rebel fighters. Talks began in mid-January 2007 under the mediation efforts of Burkina Faso's President Blaise Campaoré, and a comprehensive peace agreement was signed on March 4 between Gbagbo and Soro in Burkina Faso. The accord called for disarmament of rebel forces (estimated at more than 40,000), the integration of some of them into a new national army, the phased withdrawal of ONUCI peacekeeping forces, and comprehensive identification of voters in advance of new national elections. (A major impetus for the rebellion had been that many northerners [as many as 3 million] had been denied Ivorian nationality papers, costing them, among other things, their voting rights.) The settlement also paved the way for Soro (Gbagbo's former archenemy) to replace Banny as prime minister in April as head of a new unity government. (Banny objected to his ouster and led a protest rally in Yamoussoukro against the new accord.)

The March 2007 peace accord called for elections to be held within ten months, but that schedule, clearly optimistic to begin with, was soon compromised by continuing security issues, underscored by a rocket attack on Prime Minister Soro's airplane in late June just after it had landed at the airport in Bouake, where the FN was headquartered. (Soro was unhurt, but four others were killed.) In September the government announced that elections would be postponed until at least October 2008, primarily because of delays in the massive proposed voter identification process. Independent analysts in early 2008 also cited a lack of progress regarding disarmament of the FN fighters and the proposed creation of a new integrated army, although the dearth of fighting had permitted the dismantling of peacekeeping checkpoints in the buffer zone that had been established in 2002 between the north and south. (FN officials reportedly continued to exercise de facto authority in much of the north even though government representatives had returned to many official posts.) Meanwhile, opposition parties alleged that they were being marginalized in the reunification initiative and strongly criticized the government for its perceived failure in battling corruption, crime, and high food prices. Because of the delays in the implementation of the peace accord and the other domestic problems, Côte d'Ivoire remained high on the list of potential "failed states." However, the government in April announced that new presidential elections would be held on November 30, with legislative balloting to follow soon after. Officials from ONUCI (currently comprising nearly 8,000 troops) welcomed the new electoral schedule, but they warned that both sides of the conflict continued to purchase arms through diamond sales prohibited by the UN embargo. In early November the government announced that the elections were again being postponed due to delays in voter identification and other procedural matters.

In December 2008 President Gbagbo and Prime Minister Soro signed another accord, which provided for some 5,000–9,000 former rebels to be integrated in national forces and authorized a "demobilization allowance" for the others. Under continued heavy pressure from the UN, the government in May 2009 announced that the first round of presidential balloting would be held on November 29. However, with many major political players benefiting from the status quo, the elections were subsequently delayed until March 2010.

POLITICAL PARTIES AND GROUPS

On May 30, 1990, Côte d'Ivoire ceased to be a one-party state with the legalization of 9 opposition groups. By the first-round legislative balloting of November 25 the number of recognized parties exceeded two dozen, while in May 1991 the government legalized 14 more, some of which were alleged to be PDCI fronts created to dilute opposition cohesiveness. By July 1993 40 of the reported 82 active political parties had been recognized. The July 2002 constitution provided for unrestricted party activity "within the law."

In advance of presidential elections scheduled for October 2005, opposition groups formed a loose electoral coalition known (in homage to former president Houphouët-Boigny) as the **Rally of Houphouëtistas for Democracy and Peace** (*Rassemblement des Houphouëtistas pour la Démocratie et la Paix*—RHDP). The group subsequently became commonly known as the G7 after the FN agreed to work with the coalition. (G7 referred to the fact that it contained seven groups—the FN, PDCI, RDR, UDPCI, MFA, and two minor parties.) In July 2005 the RDR's Alassane Ouattara and the PDCI's Henri Bédié held discussions in Paris aimed at agreement on a single opposition candidate to challenge President Gbagbo in the planned presidential elections. Alphonse Djédjé Mady (the secretary general of the PDCI) was appointed as the nominal leader and spokesperson for the G7. After the presidential elections were postponed, the G7 organized mass protests against Gbagbo in Abidjan in November 2005. The G7 supported the proposed appointment of the FN's Guillaume Soro as prime minister in December 2005 but endorsed Charles Banny after his appointment to the post. The G7 also organized mass protests and a boycott of the assembly after it was announced that the mandate of the current assembly would be extended. The parties and groups within the G7 continued to operate as independent entities and use the coalition only as a coordinating body. The G7 endorsed the accession of the FN's Soro to the prime minister's post in April 2007, although friction was subsequently reported within the group over strategy for the upcoming presidential and legislative elections.

Reports on opposition activity in 2008 and the first half of 2009 for the most part referenced the RHDP (comprising the PDCI, RDR, UDPCI, and MFA) rather than the G7. Initial assessments suggested that the RHDP components would present separate candidates for the November 2009 presidential election.

Parties and Groups Represented in the Cabinet as of Mid-2009:

Ivorian Popular Front (*Front Populaire Ivoirien*—FPI). The FPI was founded by history professor Laurent Gbagbo, who, upon his return to Côte d'Ivoire in September 1988, was granted a state pardon for previous dissident activity. At its founding congress in November 1989, the FPI adopted a platform calling for a mixed economy with a private sector emphasis. Legalized in May 1990, and becoming thereafter the unofficial leader of a coalition that included the PIT and USD, the party called for President Houphouët-Boigny's resignation, the appointment of a transitional government, and freedom of association. It endorsed Gbagbo's bid to succeed the incumbent chief executive at its first legal congress in September. Angered at apparent electoral irregularities and claiming fraudulent tallying, FPI supporters clashed with government forces during and after the October 28 presidential balloting, with 120 reportedly being arrested. In mid-1991 the FPI refused to join in an opposition call for a national conference, insisting instead that Houphouët-Boigny's government resign.

Reportedly believing that the FPI would be offered the premiership in a transitional government, Gbagbo publicly backed Henri Konan Bédié of the PDCI in the months prior to Houphouët-Boigny's death in December 1993. However, when it became apparent that Bédié would not extend such an offer, Gbagbo broke off negotiations with the ruling party.

In February 1994 Gbagbo called for the establishment of a transitional government, the creation of a West African currency, the holding of "clean" elections, and repeal of the constitutional amendment detailing presidential succession procedures. In July 1995 Gbagbo called the government's electoral code "legalized fraud," and he subsequently withdrew from the presidential campaign.

After Gbagbo was elected president of the republic in October 2000, he appointed the FPI's Pascal Affi N'Guessan to head a new FPI-dominated cabinet. N'Guessan, who had managed Gbagbo's presidential campaign, succeeded Gbagbo as FPI leader in mid-2001.

Following the renewed civil war in 2002, a number of propresidential groups affiliated with the FPI emerged. Foremost among them was the Coordination of Young Patriots (*Coordination des Jeunes Patriotes*—CJP), led by a close Gbagbo ally, Charles Blé GOUDÉ. The CJP organized a number of demonstrations in support of the president, but it was banned in September 2003 for the alleged use of violence and intimidation.

The FPI filled 7 seats (the most of any party) in the new transitional government installed in December and retained a plurality of 11 posts in the April 2007 cabinet.

Leaders: Laurent GBAGBO (President of the Republic), Pascal Affi N'GUESSAN (President of the Party and Former Prime Minister), Sylvain Miaka OURETTA (Secretary General).

Democratic Party of Côte d'Ivoire (*Parti Démocratique de la Côte d'Ivoire*—PDCI). Established in 1946 as a section of the African Democratic Rally (*Rassemblement Démocratique Africain*—RDA), the PDCI (often referenced as the PDCI-RDA) was the country's only authorized party for the ensuing 44 years, although other parties were never formally banned. Although the PDCI reportedly divided into fractious "old and new guards" in response to the country's mounting socioeconomic problems, the party's 1990 congress endorsed President Houphouët-Boigny's bid for a seventh term, proposed the naming of a prime minister, and revived the office of party secretary general.

Divisions within the party were underscored in mid-1992 when Djény KOBINA, a spokesperson for the party's so-called progressive wing, called for the release of opposition leaders detained in February. Prime Minister Alassane Ouattara announced in early 1993 that he would seek the party's 1995 presidential nomination, thus highlighting the widening gulf between his northern, Muslim followers and the southern, predominantly Catholic supporters of the National Assembly president and presidential "heir apparent," Henri Konan Bédié. In the wake of Houphouët-Boigny's death and Bédié's subsequent succession, there were reports that Ouattara was planning to launch his own party and that the old-line "barons of *houphouëtisme*" had aligned with him and were demanding an extraordinary PDCI congress to reconsider succession policy. Nonetheless, Bédié was unanimously elected party chair in April 1994.

In June 1994 Kobina's wing, including a number of senior party officials, broke from the party to form the RDR (see below), with a loss to the PDCI of nine assembly seats. Subsequently, Ouattara, who had accepted an IMF post in May, disavowed his PDCI membership. (He joined the RDR in 1995.)

Discouraged by the party's primary system, a number of PDCI legislative aspirants reportedly opted to compete as independents in the general elections in 1995; however, there was no indication of their having secured seats. Delegates to the 1996 PDCI congress reportedly approved the establishment of a "high leadership," which included an executive branch and five commissions (political, economic, human resources, security, and environmental affairs). Furthermore, a 400-member deliberative body that had been created in 1990 was expanded into a 1,500-member parliament led by a "council of old ones" and charged with aiding the party president in charting "major political directions." In addition, Bédié and Laurent Dona-Fologo were reelected as party president and general secretary, respectively.

Following the overthrow of the PDCI government by the coup of December 1999, Bédié fled to Paris, from where he attempted to retain control of the party. Although disagreement existed regarding the extent to which the PDCI should cooperate with the coup leaders, several party members joined the transitional government of Gen. Robert Gueï, who subsequently tried to secure the PDCI nomination for president of the republic. However, the party rejected Gueï's plan, nominating instead former interior minister Emile Constant BOMBET, whose candidacy was ultimately ruled invalid by the Supreme Court. The PDCI accepted three posts in the new cabinet appointed in October 2000 and has participated in all subsequent cabinets.

Bédié returned from France in October 2001 and was reelected as PDCI president at the April 2002 party congress. In 2003 the PDCI temporarily suspended participation in the government along with other parties. However, its ministers rejoined the cabinet in August 2004.

Bédié returned in September 2005 from one year of self-imposed exile to participate in the presidential election then scheduled for October. After those elections were postponed, Bédié was active in negotiations regarding the installation of a new transitional cabinet in which the PDCI was accorded four seats. In March 2006 a PDCI congress selected Bédié as the party's candidate in the presidential poll originally scheduled for October. The PDCI was given five ministries in the new cabinet installed in April 2007. Bédié subsequently campaigned to be the single opposition candidate in the presidential poll most recently rescheduled for November 2009, announcing that his age (76) would force this campaign to be his last.

Leaders: Henri Konan BÉDIÉ (President of the Party and Former President of the Republic), Laurent DONA-FOLOGO (Former Secretary General), Alphonse Djédjé MADY (Secretary General).

Ivorian Workers' Party (*Parti Ivoirien des Travailleurs*—PIT). The PIT was formally recognized in May 1990, although a PIT rally three months later was dispersed by government forces. The party captured one seat in the November legislative balloting. Three PIT leaders were among those given prison terms in March 1992 for alleged involvement in the February rioting.

At presidential balloting in 1995 PIT leader Francis Wodié captured less than 4 percent of the vote. Wodié's candidacy had been sharply criticized by his opposition colleagues, who cited the PIT leader's own advocacy of a boycott in 1990. In August 1998 Wodié was appointed to the Bédié government, while party members also held posts in 2000 in the transitional governments of Gen. Gueï. Wodié secured 5.7 percent of the vote in the October 2000 presidential balloting, and the PIT participated in all of the subsequent FPI-led cabinets, including the 2005 transitional government and the April 2007 national unity government. As of mid-2009 it appeared that the PIT would support President Gbagbo's reelection effort.

Leader: Francis WODIÉ (General Secretary and 2000 presidential candidate).

Rally of Republicans (*Rassemblement des Républicains*—RDR). The essentially centrist RDR was launched in June 1994 by ex-PDCI members, led by Djény Kobina and a number of ministers from the government of former prime minister Alassane Ouattara who had operated within the parent formation for the previous three years as a "reform" wing loyal to Ouattara. Kobina announced that the new grouping controlled 30 National Assembly seats and had a membership of 1.5 million. Initially, the RDR could claim only to have "excellent relations" with Ouattara, whose willingness to campaign under the RDR's banner was considered necessary to the party's electoral viability. However, in January 1995 Kobina announced that Ouattara had joined the party.

In July 1995 the RDR officially endorsed Ouattara as its presidential candidate; however, the government refused to rescind the electoral code, and on August 2 Ouattara, who was ineligible under the new provisions, abandoned his campaign plans, citing his respect for Ivorian laws, even those he considered "aberrant." Thereafter, on November 22 the constitutional court rejected Kobina's appeal of the nullification of his legislative candidacy, both of his parents reportedly being Ghanaian.

Meanwhile, the RDR had earlier helped to launch the Republican Front (*Front Républicain*—FR), an electoral alliance that also included the FPI and the UFD (see ADS, below). Although the FR called for a boycott of the October 1995 presidential elections, the PIT's Wodié participated in the balloting, securing 3.75 percent of the vote. After a meeting with President Bédié in early November, the FR agreed to participate in the upcoming legislative elections. However, staggered by legal problems and unable to agree on a joint candidate list, coalition members fared poorly at assembly balloting. Flagging coalition cohesiveness was underscored by the decision by the RDR and the FPI to forward competing candidates in more than 100 municipal electoral races in February 1996.

Djény Kobina died in October 1998, and he was succeeded as RDR secretary general by Henriette Dagbi Diabaté, who reportedly became the first woman to hold such a powerful post in an Ivorian political party. Thereafter, in the wake of the signing of the government-FPI accord, the RDR urged the Bédié administration to begin separate negotiations with each of the prominent opposition parties.

In early 1999 Ouattara confirmed that he would be the RDR's standard-bearer at the 2000 presidential elections. A number of party leaders were detained late in the year, prompting violent antigovernment demonstrations in RDR strongholds.

The RDR initially welcomed the December 1999 coup, since General Gueï was widely viewed as supportive of Ouattara, who returned from exile on December 29. A number of RDR members were appointed to Gueï's transitional cabinet, but relations between the RDR and military leaders subsequently deteriorated as Gueï began to retreat from his pledge not to run for president. Several RDR officials were detained in the wake of an aborted coup in early July 2000, while Ouattara's subsequent exclusion from the presidential campaign (see Political background, above) signaled a final rupture with Gueï. Following Gueï's failed attempt to manipulate the presidential balloting in October, RDR supporters fought with security forces as well as partisans of the FPI. The RDR's "outside" status continued into December, Ouattara being ruled ineligible to compete in the legislative balloting, which the RDR boycotted. However, some RDR members ignored the boycott and campaigned for assembly seats under the rubric of the **RDR–Movement of Moderate Activists and Candidates** (*RDR–Mouvement des Militants et Candidates Modérés*—RDR-MMCM).

Secretary General Diabaté was briefly detained by the government following the unsuccessful coup attempt in January 2001, and a number of RDR members remained imprisoned throughout the summer in connection with the violence that had erupted in late 2000. Despite the government pressure, the RDR performed very well in the March 2001 local elections, securing victories in the south, west, and center of the country as well as the traditional RDR strongholds among the northern Muslim population.

Following the outbreak of civil war in 2002, Ouattara went into exile, from where he reportedly became the opposition's leading presidential candidate. However, President Gbagbo continued to consider Ouattara ineligible to run due to his failure to meet residency and citizenship requirements, despite a National Assembly ruling to the contrary in December 2004. In December 2005 Gbagbo issued a decree allowing Ouattara to campaign in future presidential elections, and Ouattara returned from exile in January 2006. The RDR, which had received five seats in the December 2005 transitional government, was also given five portfolios in the April 2007 cabinet. Ouattara, still considered the most popular northern politician, was expected to be a candidate in the presidential balloting scheduled for November 2009.

Leaders: Alassane Dramane OUATTARA (Former Prime Minister), Amadou Gon COULIBALY (Deputy Secretary General), Henriette Dagbi DIABATÉ (Secretary General).

New Forces (*Forces Nouvelles*—FN). The FN was launched in August 2003 by the three main rebel groups opposing the Gbagbo government, including the **Patriotic Movement of the Côte d'Ivoire** (*Mouvement Patriotique de la Côte d'Ivoire*—MPCI), the predominately Muslim northern grouping that had initiated the 2002 civil war. The other FN components were the **Movement for Justice and Peace** (*Mouvement pour la Justice et la Paix*—MJP) and the **Ivorian Popular Movement for the Greater West** (*Mouvement Populaire Ivoirien du Grand Ouest*—MPIGO), both based in western regions of the country and formed after the 2002 strife had commenced. In April 2003 the leader of the MPIGO, Félix DOH, was killed by government forces.

Under the Marcoussis Accords of January 2003, the three FN components were allocated posts in the cabinet of March 2003. However, the FN representatives did not take their seats until August 2004.

In 2005 friction was reported within MPIGO over the apparent efforts by Roger BANCHI (one of MPIGO's leaders and a cabinet minister) to forge closer relations with President Gbagbo. (Banchi left the cabinet in July, officially for personal reasons.) After the FN's efforts to have Guillaume Soro (the FN secretary general) named prime minister failed in October, the FN was given six posts (including Soro as minister of state for reconstruction and reintegration) in the new transitional cabinet installed in December. However, the status of the MJP and MPIGO within the FN at that point was unclear, some reports indicating that the MJP and MPIGO had left the ranks of the umbrella organization.

Following Soro's appointment as prime minister, the FN was accorded seven portfolios in the new national unity government installed in April 2007. Soro was too young (37) to be a candidate in the November 2009 presidential poll, and it was not clear if the FN would endorse a first-round candidate. Meanwhile, Soro announced that his MPCI, not the FN overall, planned to seek official party status for upcoming legislative elections.

Leaders: Guillaume SORO (Prime Minister), Sidiki KONATE (Secretary General), Louis-André Dakoury TABLEY (Deputy Secretary General), Alain LOBOGNAN.

Union for Democracy and Peace in Côte d'Ivoire (*Union pour la Démocratie et la Paix de la Côte d'Ivoire*—UDPCI). The UDPCI was launched in February 2001 by former members of the PDCI who had left that party to support Gen. Robert Gueï in the 2000 presidential campaign. (As many as 14 of the successful "independent" candidates in the December 2000 assembly balloting were subsequently identified as belonging to the PDCI dissident group; most were believed to have participated in the formation of the UDPCI.) General Gueï was elected president of the UDPCI in May 2002. On September 19, 2002, Gueï was killed when fighting erupted between government forces and rebels. The UDPCI joined the national unity government in 2002 and also participated in the 2005 transitional government and the April 2007 government.

Leaders: Albert MABRI TOIKEUSSE (President), Paul Akoto YAO, Alasane SALIF N'DIAYE (Secretary General).

Democratic Citizen's Union (*Union Démocratique Citoyenne*—UDCY). Launched in January 2000, the UDCY criticized the PDCI for failing to make the "necessary changes" to promote national "reconciliation and reconstruction." UDCY Chair Theodore Mel Eg, mayor of the Cocody District in Abidjan, was credited with 1.5 percent of the vote in the October 2000 presidential balloting, while the party secured one seat in the December legislative poll. The UDCY was given one cabinet post in 2003, and Eg was appointed minister of culture and Francophone affairs in the 2005 transitional government and minister of urban development and sanitation in the April 2007 cabinet.

Leader: Theodore MEL EG (Chair).

Other Parties and Groups:

Movement of Forces for the Future (*Mouvement des Forces pour l'Avenir*—MFA). The MFA, formed in 1995, was credited with one seat in the December 2000 legislative balloting, although little other information concerning the grouping was available. In 2003 the MFA joined the national unity government, and it remained in the 2005 and 2007 transitional governments. However, MFA leader Kobenan Anaky announced in March 2009 that the party was leaving the cabinet to protest lack of electoral progress.

Leader: Kobenan ANAKY (Secretary General).

Alliance for Democracy and Socialism (*Alliance pour la Démocratie et le Socialisme*—ADS). The launching of the left-wing ADS was announced in mid-2000 by the PPS, Renaissance, the **Party for the Protection of the Environment** (*Parti pour la Protection de l'Environnement*—PPE), and the **Party for National Reconstruction and Democracy** (*Parti pour la Reconstruction National et la Démocratie*—PRND). However, there were few subsequent reports of ADS activity.

Party for Social Progress (*Parti pour le Progrès Social*—PPS). The predominantly ethnic Djoula PPS is led by Bamba Morifére, reportedly one of the wealthiest opposition politicians. During the run-up to legislative balloting in November 1995 Morifére was jailed for alleged financial fraud and subsequently given a four-month suspended sentence, a verdict the FPI's Gbagbo decried as "shameful."

The PPS had been one of the members of the Union of Democratic Forces (*Union des Forces Démocratiques*—UFD), an opposition grouping launched in December 1992. Other UFD members had included the PIT, the UND, the **Social Democratic Movement** (*Mouvement Démocratique et Social*—MDS), and the **African Party for the Ivorian Renaissance** (*Parti Africain pour la Renaissance Ivoirienne*—PARI). PPS leader Morifére had served as president of the UFD. His proposed candidacy (presumably under the ADS rubric) for the 2000 presidential election was rejected by the Supreme Court.

Leader: Bamba MORIFÉRE.

Renaissance. Initially known as FPI-Renaissance, this grouping was formed in 1996 under the leadership of Don Mello Ahoua, who claimed that his faction would remain within the FPI but would work independently to promote "democracy" within the larger body. However, in July 1997, following an alleged shooting attack on Ahoua's car and threats to faction members, the group withdrew from the FPI.

Leader: Don Mello AHOUA (Coordinator).

Union of Social Democrats (*Union des Sociaux-Démocrates*—USD). The USD describes itself as a "compromise between capitalism and socialism." Longtime leader Bernard ZADI-ZAOUROU resigned as USD general secretary in July 2000. The presidential candidacy of his successor, Jerome Climanlo Coulibaly, was subsequently rejected by the Supreme Court. Following the outbreak of civil war in 2002, Coulibaly emerged as a major opposition figure to the Gbagbo regime.

Leader: Jerome Climanlo COULIBALY (General Secretary).

Republican Party of Côte d'Ivoire (*Parti Républicain de la Côte d'Ivoire*—PRCI). The PRCI is a right-wing grouping organized in 1987. In September 1995 party leader Robert Gbai-Tagro withdrew from the presidential race, citing electoral code shortcomings as his reason. In January 2000 Gbai-Tagro announced his support for General Gueï, leader of the recent coup.

Leader: Robert GBAI-TAGRO.

National Union for Democracy (*Union National pour la Démocratie*—UND). In December 1994 the UND was credited with one assembly seat.

Leader: Amadou KONE.

Other recently formed groups and parties include the **Coalition of Republican Forces of Côte d'Ivoire** (*Coalition des Forces Républicaines de Côte d'Ivoire*—COFREPCI), formed in 2005 by former army chief of staff Mathias DOUÉ as an opposition group to Gbagbo's regime (rebels reportedly linked to Doué allegedly attacked Ivorian border towns from Ghana in early 2007, prompting a temporary closure of the main border crossing); the **National Union of Ivorians for Renewal** (*Union Nationale des Ivoiriens du Renouveau*—UNIR), established in June 2006 under the leadership of Claude SAHI and Ibrahim COULIBALY, disaffected members of the FN; the **New Democratic Alliance of Côte d'Ivoire for Justice, Development, and Peace,** formed in October 2005 by Charles Blé Goudé, who had been a ranking member of the FPI and the mayor of Saioua; and the

Republican Union for Democracy (*Union for Républicaine pour la Démocratie*—URD), formed in May 2006 by former communications minister Danielle Akissi BON-CLAVERIE. (For a list of small parties from the 1990s, some of which may still be active, see the 1999 and 2000–2002 *Handbooks*.)

Conflict was reported in 2007–2008 between supporters of the UNIR's Coulibaly and members of the FN, who accused Coulibaly of attempting to sabotage the recent peace accord between the FN and the government. Coulibaly, reportedly one of the leaders of the failed 2002 antigovernment military initiative, had been one of the founders of the FN but had disengaged from that grouping after having apparently been marginalized by the FN's Guillaume Soro. Although Benin in early 2008 announced a decision to expel Coulibaly, reports subsequently surfaced that he remained at large in that country. In 2009 a French court sentenced Coulibaly in absentia to four years in prison on a charge that he had recruited mercenaries on French soil for his anti-Gbagbo activities.

LEGISLATURE

The **National Assembly** (*Assemblée Nationale*) is a unicameral body with 225 members (raised from 147 to 175 in 1985 and to 225 in 2000) serving five-year terms. The assembly was suspended following the December 1999 coup, but balloting for a new legislature was held on December 10, 2000, with the Ivorian Popular Front winning 96 seats; the Democratic Party of Côte d'Ivoire (PDCI), 77; the Ivorian Workers' Party, 4; the Rally of Republicans/Movement of Moderate Activists and Candidates (RDR-MMCM), 1; the Democratic Union of Côte d'Ivoire, 1; the Movement of Forces of the Future, 1; and independents, 17. Balloting was not held at that time for 28 seats in northern constituencies because of unrest affiliated with an election boycott by the main faction of the RDR. Balloting for 26 of the outstanding seats was conducted on January 14, 2001, with the PDCI winning 17 to increase its total to 94, the RDR-MMCM winning 4 to increase its total to 5, and independents winning 5 to increase the total number of independents to 22. The mandate of the current assembly was extended for up to one year by a controversial presidential decree in late January 2006 and again in November 2006. Under the peace accord signed in March 2007, new legislative balloting was to be held in early 2008, although the date was subsequently postponed until at least March 2010.

President: Mamadou KOULIBALY.

CABINET

[as of July 1, 2009]

Prime Minister	Guillaume Kigbafori Soro (FN-MPCI)
Minister of State	
Development and Planning	Paul-Antoine Bohoun Bouabre (FPI)
Ministers	
African Integration	Amadou Kone (FN)
Agriculture	Amadou Gon Coulibaly (RDR)
Commerce	Youssouf Soumahoro (FN)
Communications	Ibraham Sy Savane (FN)
Culture and Francophonie	Komoe Augustin Kouame (ind.)
Defense	Michel Amani N'Guessan (FPI)
Economic Infrastructure	Patrick Achi (PDCI)
Environment, Water Resources, and Forests	Aka Daniel Ahizi (PIT)
Family, Women, and Children	Jeanne Peuhmon Adjoua (RDR) [f]
Fight Against AIDS	Dr. Christine Adjobi Nebout (FPI) [f]
Finance and Economy	Charles Diby Koffi (ind.)
Fishery Resources and Livestock	Alphonse Douati (FPI)
Foreign Affairs	Youssouf Bakayoko (PDCI)
Handicrafts and Tourism	Sidiki Konate (FN)
Health and Public Hygiene	Dr. Rémi Allah Kouadio (PDCI)
Higher Education and Scientific Research	Ibraham Bacango Cisse (RDR)
Industry and Promotion of the Private Sector	Marie Tehoua (PDCI) [f]
Interior	Désiré Tagro (FPI)
Justice and Guardian of the Seals	Mamadou Kone (FN-MPCI)
Labor and Civil Service	Hubert Oulaye (FPI)
Mining and Energy	Léon Emmanuel Monnet (FPI)
National Education	Gilbert Bleu-Laine (ind.)
National Reconciliation and Relations with Institutions	Sébastian Danon Djedje (FPI)
Reconstruction and Integration	(Vacant)
Solidarity and War Victims	Louis-André Dacoury-Tabley (FN)
Technical Education and Professional Training	Moussa Dosso (FN)
Telecommunications and New Technologies	Hamed Bakayoko (RDR)
Transport	Albert Mabri Toikeuse (UDPCI)
Urban Development and Sanitation	Théodore Mel Eg (UDCY)
Urban Planning, Housing, and Construction	Marcel Amon-Tanoh (RDR)
Youth, Civil Education, and Sport	Dagobert Banzio (PDCI)

[f] = female

COMMUNICATIONS

Côte d'Ivoire has long been known for its "pluralistic" press, although there were numerous reports of the intimidation of journalists in 2006 on the part of the "Young Patriots" aligned with President Gbagbo. Although Reporters Without Borders consequently described Côte d'Ivoire as one of "Africa's most dangerous countries for both local and foreign media," conditions eased significantly following the peace accord of March 2007. Nevertheless, critics expressed concern over the influence being exercised by President Gbagbo on the state-run media in advance of the presidential elections scheduled for late 2009.

Press. The following are published in Abidjan, unless otherwise noted: *Notre Voie*, FPI newspaper; *Fraternité-Matin* (80,000), state-owned daily; *Ivoir Soir* (50,000), PDCI organ launched in 1987 to concentrate on social and cultural events as a complement to *Fraternité-Matin; Le Patriote,* RDR organ; *La Voix d'Afrique,* monthly regional magazine; *Le Populaire Nouvelle Formule*, independent daily; *Le Jour Plus* (16,000), independent daily described as close to the opposition; *Le National*, "fiercely nationalist" daily supportive of former president Henri Konan Bédié; *Le Libéral; L'Inter,* independent daily; *Soir Info*, independent daily; *Le Nouveau Reveil*, pro-PDCI; *Tassouma,* close to the RDR; *Le Qoutidient,* pro-FPI daily; *L'Intelligent d'Abidjan,* independent daily; and *Le Temps,* described as close to the FPI.

News agencies. The domestic agency is *Agence Ivoirienne de Presse* (AIP). *Agence France-Presse,* the Associated Press, and Reuters maintain offices in Abidjan.

Broadcasting and computing. The government-operated Ivorian Radio and Television (*Radiotélévision Ivoirienne*) transmitted to approximately 736,000 television receivers in 2003. As of 2008 there were 32.1 Internet users per 1,000 inhabitants.

INTERGOVERNMENTAL REPRESENTATION

Ambassador to the U.S.: Charles KOFFI.

U.S. Ambassador to Côte d'Ivoire: Wanda L. NESBITT.

Permanent Representative to the UN: Ilahiri A. DJÉDJÉ.

IGO Memberships (Non-UN): AfDB, AU, BADEA, BOAD, CENT, ECOWAS, IDB, Interpol, IOM, NAM, OIC, OIF, UEMOA, WCO, WTO.

CROATIA

Republic of Croatia
Republika Hrvatska

Political Status: Former constituent republic of the Socialist Federal Republic of Yugoslavia; constitution proclaiming Croatian sovereignty promulgated December 21, 1990; independence declared June 25, 1991; dissociation from Yugoslavia approved by the Croatian Assembly effective October 8, 1991.

Area: 21,829 sq. mi. (56,538 sq. km.).

Population: 4,437,460 (2001C); 4,451,000 (2008E).

Major Urban Centers (2005E): ZAGREB (687,000), Split (185,000), Rijeka (134,000).

Official Language: Croatian.

Monetary Unit: Kuna (market rate December 1, 2009: 4.84 kune = $1US).

President: Stjepan MESIĆ (Croatian National Party); elected in runoff balloting on February 7, 2000, and inaugurated on February 18 for a five-year term to succeed Vlatko PAVLETIĆ (Croatian Democratic Union), the chair of the House of Representatives who had been serving as acting president since November 26, 1999; reelected in runoff balloting on January 16, 2005, and inaugurated for a second five-year term on February 18.

Prime Minister: Ivo SANADER (Croatian Democratic Union); appointed by the president on December 9, 2003, to form a new government following legislative elections on November 23 and inaugurated on December 23 in succession to Ivica RAČAN (Social Democratic Party of Croatia); reappointed by the president on December 15, 2007, following legislative balloting on November 25 and sworn into office on January 12, 2008.

THE COUNTRY

With a long western coastline on the Adriatic Sea, Croatia half encircles Bosnia and Herzegovina in an arc that extends north and eastward to the province of Vojvodina in Serbia; it also borders Hungary in the northeast and Slovenia in the northwest. At independence in 1991, Croats comprised 78 percent of the population, which also included a 12 percent ethnic Serb component, concentrated south of the capital, Zagreb, and along the western Bosnian border; however, an exodus from these areas in the 1995 hostilities reduced the Serb population to an estimated 2–3 percent. Forests covering more than a third of the country have supported a major timber industry, while agricultural activity in the eastern Pannonian plain is devoted to the growing of wheat, maize, and potatoes, in addition to the raising of cattle, sheep, pigs, and poultry. Extensive mineral resources, including hydrocarbons, bauxite, iron ore, and copper, helped make Croatia the most industrialized component of the former Yugoslav federation, with a GDP per capita substantially higher than that of Yugoslavia as a whole. However, the onset of regional conflict in the early 1990s resulted in the loss of about 30 percent of Croatian territory to the Serbs, inflicted substantial damage on Croatia's economy, and decimated the important tourist industry. National output declined by 50 percent in 1992, during which the annual inflation rate peaked at 662 percent. A partial recovery in 1993–1994 was offset by the high cost of supporting hundreds of thousands of refugees from strife-torn areas of former Yugoslavia. Croatia's recovery of most of its territory and the Dayton Accords of late 1995 stimulated the economy, which, despite continued high unemployment, subsequently exhibited relatively strong growth and low inflation. Also supporting that progress were structural reforms pursued by the government beginning in 1993, including the privatization of state-run enterprises, reduction of tariffs, rehabilitation of the banking sector, and revision of the pension system. GDP growth averaged about 6 percent annually from 1995 to 1998, with unemployment running at about 17 percent at the end of that period.

Real GDP declined by 0.4 percent in 1999, in part because of regional economic disruption arising from the conflict in Kosovo. In addition, by that time it had become apparent that enthusiasm for free-market reform within the administration of longtime President Franjo TUDJMAN had been for the most part rhetorical rather than grounded in deeply held convictions. Critics charged the government with retaining too much control of industry and generally mismanaging an economy noted for widespread corruption, an emphasis on political patronage, and a lack of transparency. The new government installed in early 2000 immediately pledged to promote foreign investment, accelerate privatization, and pursue membership in the European Union (EU) and the North Atlantic Treaty Organization (NATO). GDP growth averaged 4 percent between 2001 and 2004, while inflation declined to 2.1 percent at the end of 2004.

Economic restructuring slowed prior to the 2003 legislative elections, many market reforms having proven unpopular with some citizens. However, the new government installed in late 2003 pledged to further privatize state-run enterprises (notably in the banking and energy sectors) in pursuit of assistance from the International Monetary Fund (IMF) and proposed membership in the EU by 2009 (see Current issues, below).

Foreign investment in Croatia subsequently expanded significantly, reaching an estimated $3.8 billion in 2006, and $5.56 billion in 2007. Foreign banks also invested heavily in the Croatian financial sector, and 90 percent of private banks were foreign-owned by 2006. GDP growth of 5.6 percent was reported for 2007, with inflation measuring 2.2 percent and unemployment 11.8 percent. Meanwhile, the government's deficit was reduced to 2.6 percent of GDP. The improving economy allowed the government to increase spending on a variety of social programs, including a 25 percent rise in direct assistance payments to individuals and families. The government also continued its privatization program as three major state-owned metal plants were sold. Tourism has become an increasingly important part of the Croatian economy, generating $10.8 billion in 2007. That year, more than 10 million foreign tourists visited the country, rising to 11.3 million in 2008.

The global economic crisis contributed to a slowdown in Croatia's economy. GDP growth in 2008 slowed to 2.4 percent and unemployment rose to 13.7 percent, compared with the overall EU rate of 8.2 percent. Nonetheless, inflation remained low at 2.6 percent, and the deficit continued to shrink to 1.4 percent following government spending cuts of 4 percent (see Current issues, below). Per capita income in 2008 was $15,500, placing Croatia ahead of EU members from the region such as Bulgaria, Latvia, Lithuania, Poland, and Romania.

GOVERNMENT AND POLITICS

Political background. The greater part of historic Croatia was joined with Hungary in a personal union under the Hungarian monarch from the early 12th century until after World War I, except for a period of Ottoman Turkish rule from 1526 to the early 18th century. By the 19th century Serbo-Croat had evolved as the common language of Croats and Serbs (the two main South Slav groups), although the Catholic Croats use the Latin alphabet and the Orthodox Serbs use Cyrillic script. In December 1918 the country became part of the Kingdom of the Serbs, Croats, and Slovenes, which was officially renamed Yugoslavia in October 1929. When the Germans invaded Yugoslavia in April 1941, an "Independent State of Croatia" was proclaimed by the *Ustaše* movement, a fascist grouping whose brutality (including the massacre of tens of thousands of Serbs) induced much of the population to support the Communist-inspired partisan forces led by Josip Broz TITO. In November 1945 Croatia became one of the six constituent republics of the Federal People's Republic of Yugoslavia under the one-party rule of what became the League of Communists of Yugoslavia.

On April 22 and May 6–7, 1990, in the first multiparty balloting since World War II, the right-wing Croatian Democratic Union (*Hrvatska Demokratska Zajednica*—HDZ) won 208 of 349 seats in the constituent republic's tricameral legislature, which on May 30 named HDZ leader Franjo Tudjman state president and his associate, Stjepan MESIĆ, president of the Executive Council (prime minister). On July 22 the word "Socialist" was deleted from the constituent republic's official name, and the Executive Council was redesignated as the

government. Three days later Serb leaders in Croatia issued a statement proclaiming their community's right to sovereignty and autonomy. The action was followed on October 1 by the Serbs' proclamation of three "autonomous regions" encompassing districts within Croatia where they were in a majority. Subsequently, on December 21, the assembly, in an action boycotted by Serb deputies, approved a new constitution that formally asserted the republic's sovereignty, including the right to secede from the Yugoslav federation.

On February 8, 1991, in response to a directive from the collective state Presidency of Yugoslavia that all "unauthorized" military units surrender their arms to federal authorities within ten days, Croatia and Slovenia concluded a mutual defense pact. Three weeks later, Croatia's Serb enclaves announced the formation of a "Serbian Autonomous Region of Krajina," which promptly declared its intention to secede from Croatia and subsequently, on joining with adjacent Serb areas of Bosnia and Herzegovina, assumed the name "Republic of Serbian Krajina" (RSK).

In a May 19, 1991, referendum, 83.6 percent of Croatia's registered electorate voted for dissociation from Yugoslavia, and on June 25 the republic joined Slovenia in declaring independence. The Croatian government shortly thereafter accepted a three-month moratorium on the dissociation process, as urged by the European Community (EC, subsequently the EU) in an effort to prevent a military conflict. (Due to the presence of a significant Serbian population in Croatia, Serbian leaders had indicated a much stronger inclination to resist Croatia's secession, as opposed to Slovenia's.) As part of the EC-brokered negotiations, Mesić was named president of the Yugoslavian Collective State Presidency on July 1, although the appointment ultimately proved to be essentially meaningless. The long-feared civil conflict immediately erupted, with the Serb-dominated Yugoslav National Army (*Yugoslavenska Narodna Armija*—JNA), openly allied with local Serb insurgents, winning control of nearly one-third of Croatia by early September. The Croatian government refused to extend the July dissociation moratorium beyond its three-month deadline and announced formal separation from Yugoslavia effective October 8. (Although Mesić remained in his federal post until he declared that "Yugoslavia no longer exists" and resigned on December 5, the Croatian legislature, upon approving the resignation, backdated it to October 8.) The fierce Serb-Croat conflict subsided following the declaration of a cease-fire on January 3, 1992, and the acceptance by both sides of a UN Security Council resolution of January 8 that provided for the deployment of a peacekeeping force in sensitive areas. Accordingly, advance units of the UN Protection Force (UNPROFOR) arrived on March 9.

On August 2, 1992, Croatia's first elections since independence involved balloting for both the House of Representatives and the presidency. The HDZ maintained its substantial overall majority in the legislative contest, and President Tudjman received a decisive 57 percent popular mandate to serve another term, with Hrvoje ŠARINIĆ taking office as prime minister on September 8. Subsequently, in polling for the new upper House of Counties in February 1993, the HDZ was again the victor, gaining majorities or pluralities in 20 of the 21 constituencies. The Šarinić government resigned on March 29, 1993, and was succeeded on April 3 by another HDZ-dominated administration, headed by Nikica VALENTIĆ.

In 1993–1994 the opposition parties, as well as some HDZ members, claimed that the government had authoritarian tendencies and that a distinct "cult of personality" was emerging around President Tudjman. As a result, the government's parliamentary majority was reduced in April 1994 by the withdrawal of some 18 liberal HDZ deputies to form the Croatian Independent Democrats (*Hrvatski Nezavisni Demokrati*—HND), with the attendant acrimony provoking an opposition boycott of parliament until September.

Croatia's overriding priority in 1995 remained the recovery of the third of Croatia's territory that had come under Serb control in the 1991–1992 fighting. Croatia launched a major military offensive on April 30, and its forces quickly overran Serb positions in western Slavonia. Serb forces in the RSK retaliated by shelling Zagreb on May 2–3, killing civilians and strengthening Croatia's post-1994 alliance with the Bosnian Muslim-Croat Federation. In a new offensive in late July and early August, Croatian forces overran Serb positions in western Krajina, capturing the capital, Knin, on August 4 and prompting the mass flight of ethnic Serbs from the area. As a result of the Croatian advances, the only part of Croatia still under Serb control in late 1995 was eastern Slavonia, on the border with Serbia proper (see Foreign relations, below, for subsequent developments regarding eastern Slavonia).

Buoyed by military success, the Tudjman government was confirmed in power in lower house elections on October 29, 1995, although the ruling HDZ failed to achieve its target of a two-thirds majority, which is required for constitutional amendments. A new HDZ government appointed on November 7 was headed by Zlatko MATEŠA, a close associate of the president. The HDZ consolidated its strength in the upper house balloting of April 13–15, 1997, securing 40 of 63 elective seats, while Tudjman was reelected to another five-year term by receiving 61 percent of the votes in the presidential election of June 15.

Early in 1998 the nation was rocked by a series of protests over a new 22 percent value-added tax. By the end of the year, the HDZ had been further weakened by a succession struggle between party moderates and hard-liners, with several of President Tudjman's leading advisers quitting the government over allegations that party right-wingers were using the intelligence service to spy on and smear the moderates.

Tudjman's deteriorating health in late 1999 prompted a constitutional crisis because no process had been put in place to deal with such a situation. On November 24 the legislature approved new legislation that permitted the Constitutional Court on November 26 to declare Tudjman "temporarily incapacitated"; presidential authority therefore devolved on an acting basis to Vlatko PAVLETIĆ, the chair of the House of Representatives and a longtime close associate of Tudjman's. Tudjman died on December 10, prompting new elections.

A coalition of four parties led by the Social Democratic Party of Croatia (*Socijaldemokratska Partija Hrvatshe*—SDP) and the Croatian Social-Liberal Party (*Hrvatska Socijalno-Liberalna Stranka*—HSLS) surprised most observers by winning a substantial plurality of 71 seats in the balloting for the House of Representatives on January 3, 2000, while the HDZ's representation fell to 46 seats. The SDP's Ivica RAČAN was inaugurated as prime minister on January 27 to lead a reformist government that included the HSLS as well as four smaller parties (the Croatian Peasant Party [*Hrvatska Selijačka Stranka*—HSS], the Croatian National Party [*Hrvatska Narodna Stranka*—HNS], the Istrian Democratic Assembly [*Istarki Demokratski Sabor*—IDS], and the Liberal Party [*Liberalna Stranka*—LS]) that had won 24 house seats as an electoral coalition.

In retrospect, at least, the collapse of the HDZ following the death of President Tudjman in late 1999 should not have been considered a surprise. The economy was in the midst of a recession, unemployment was high, and the administration was perceived as riddled with corruption. In addition, Tudjman's decade of autocratic rule had kept Croatia largely outside the reformist movement so prevalent in many of the other former communist states. In particular, Western capitals criticized Tudjman's record on minority rights, the slow pace of democratic reform, and his lack of enthusiasm for full implementation of the provisions in the Dayton Accords, particularly the return of Serbian refugees to Croatia and the extradition of Croatian military leaders as requested by the UN International Criminal Tribunal for the Former Yugoslavia (ICTY).

Although many analysts expected the SDP/HSLS coalition to dominate the first round of presidential balloting on January 24, 2000, its candidate, Dražen BUDIŠA of the HSLS, finished second to Stjepan Mesić, the candidate of the HNS/HSS/IDS/LS coalition. Mesić outdistanced Budiša by 56 percent to 44 percent in the runoff on February 7.

Despite its remarkable achievement in ousting the HDZ from power in 2000, the new coalition government subsequently experienced internal conflict on a regular basis. In June 2001 the IDS left the government because of the refusal by the other coalition members to support its request that Italian be made an official language in Istria, the peninsula near the head of the Adriatic Sea with many ties to Italy. A number of HSLS ministers also quit the cabinet in July to protest the government's decision to extradite several generals to the ICTY for possible prosecution regarding war crimes in the 1991–1995 fighting. The HSLS finally left the coalition completely in early July 2002 because of its opposition to the government's recent agreement with Slovenia over the operation of the Krsko nuclear power plant, located in Slovenia but paid for in part by Croatia during communist rule. (The HSLS opposed the provision that forced Croatia to handle radioactive waste from the plant.) Prime Minister Račan and his government resigned on July 5, but Račan retained the prime ministership in a new government (comprising the SDP, HSS, HNS, LS, and several HSLS dissidents) that was approved by the House of Representatives on July 30.

The HDZ regained a plurality in the November 23, 2003, balloting for the House of Representatives and managed to form a minority government that included a minister from the Democratic Center (*Demokratski Centar*—DC) and was supported in the legislature by the HSLS, HSS, and several independent deputies. Ivo SANADER of the HDZ was named prime minister.

Thirteen candidates vied for the presidency in elections in 2005, with most center-left parties supporting incumbent President Mesić. In the first round of balloting on January 2, 2005, Mesić received 48.9 percent of the vote, followed by Jadranka KOSOR, the vice president of the HDZ, with 20.3 percent of the vote. Mesić was reelected for a second five-year term by securing 65.9 percent of the vote in the runoff balloting.

In February 2005 a minor cabinet reorganization merged the ministries of foreign affairs and European integration and replaced two ministers with the prime minister. In February 2006 tensions between the prime minister and the justice minister, Vesna ŠKARE-OŽBOLT, the leader of the DC, led to her forced resignation. The DC subsequently withdrew its support for the government.

In legislative elections on November 25, 2007, the HDZ won the majority of seats in the assembly and formed a coalition government with the HSLS, the HSS, and the Independent Democratic Serbian Party (*Samostaina Demokratska Srpska Stranka*—SDSS). In addition, the government had the support of the Croatian Pensioners' Party (*Hrvatska Stranka Umirovljenika*—HSU) and four independent deputies, giving it 82 votes in the 153-member chamber. Sanader was again appointed prime minister. Sanader's government included two new ministries, regional development and tourism, and the number of deputy prime ministers was expanded from two to four.

In October 2008 in response to perceived government inaction against organized crime, the opposition SDP sponsored a no-confidence vote against the Sanader government. The motion failed on a vote of 75 opposed and 53 in favor. Sanader replaced the interior minister and the minister of justice in an effort to improve law enforcement efforts (see Current issues, below).

Constitution and government. The 1990 constitution defined the Republic of Croatia as a unitary (and indivisible), democratic, and social state, in which power "comes from and belongs to the people as a community of free and equal citizens." The highest values of the republic were stated to be freedom, equal rights, national equality, peace, social justice, respect for human rights, inviolability of ownership, respect for legal order, care for the environment, and a democratic multiparty system of government. Legislative power was vested in a bicameral assembly, both houses of which were directly elected and sat for four-year terms. The "supreme head of the executive power" was the president, who was directly elected for a five-year term and who, subject to parliamentary confirmation, appointed the prime minister and, on the proposal of the latter, other members of the government.

Significant changes to the constitution were approved by the House of Representatives on November 9, 2000, primarily to reduce the power of the president. According to those revisions, the prime minister and the cabinet are now appointed by the legislature, although the president remains commander in chief of the military. Another important change was made in March 2001 when the House of Representatives (by then controlled by reformist parties) voted to abolish the upper house (the House of Counties), which was still dominated by the HDZ.

The ordinary court system is headed by a Supreme Court, whose judges are appointed and relieved of duty by a 15-member Judicial Council of the Republic elected by the House of Representatives. There is also provision for a Constitutional Court, whose members are elected by the House of Representatives for eight-year terms. The main local self-government units are 21 counties (*Zupanije*) and more than 500 towns and other small municipalities.

On December 12, 1997, the legislature approved a constitutional amendment proposed by President Tudjman forbidding Croatia from joining a union with any Yugoslav or Balkan state.

Foreign relations. Germany unilaterally recognized Croatia on December 23, 1991, with the EC following with recognition of both Croatia and Slovenia on January 15, 1992. Croatia and Slovenia established diplomatic relations with each other on February 17, 1992. On that same date, Russia accorded diplomatic recognition to Croatia. The United States followed suit on April 7. On May 22 Croatia joined Slovenia and Bosnia and Herzegovina in gaining admission to the UN. The mandate of the UNPROFOR forces deployed in Croatia from March 1992 was regularly renewed thereafter, although with increasing reluctance on Croatia's part.

Admitted to the Conference on Security and Cooperation in Europe (CSCE, subsequently the Organization for Security and Cooperation in Europe—OSCE) in March 1992 and to the IMF in January 1993, Croatia also developed its regional links, becoming a member of the Central European Initiative (CEI), originally formed in 1989. The government thereafter declared its aim of accession to the EU and to other Western bodies, while seeking Western support for recognition of Croatia's former borders.

In January 1993 Croatia launched an offensive to recover territory lost in 1991 to what had became the Serb-controlled RSK. However, despite some strategic successes on the part of the Croatian thrust, the RSK remained viable, and sporadic fighting continued, although not on the scale of the escalating conflict in Bosnia and Herzegovina. In May 1993 the Tudjman government signed the Vance-Owen peace plan for Bosnia and Herzegovina, albeit clearly without any expectation that it would be implemented in the form proposed. In June, Tudjman and Serbian President Slobodan Milošević reportedly reaffirmed their aim of bringing about the eventual partition of Bosnia and Herzegovina between Croatia and Serbia on the basis of an "orderly" transfer of population. In 1994, however, advocates of a resumption of the earlier Croat-Muslim alliance gained the ascendancy in Croatia. The result was the signing on March 18 of a U.S.-brokered agreement between Bosnian Croats and Muslims providing for a federal structure in the neighboring republic (see article on Bosnia and Herzegovina), accompanied by a preliminary accord envisaging the creation of a confederation between the new Bosnian federation and Croatia, with each remaining sovereign entities.

In October 1994 Croatia welcomed the creation of the so-called Zagreb Four (Z-4) mini-contact group (the UN, EU, United States, and Russia), which was charged with resolving the Croat-Serb deadlock. Speedy progress seemed to be made by the Z-4 under a December agreement reestablishing essential services between Croatia and the RSK and reopening major roads; however, the accord was suspended by the RSK in February 1995 after Croatia had given formal notice of terminating the UNPROFOR mandate. In the same month Croatia rejected a Z-4 peace plan as "unacceptable" in its "structure, basic provisions, title, and preamble." On March 6 the military commanders of Croatia, the Bosnian government, and the Bosnian Croats concluded a formal alliance in response to a military pact between Croatian Serb and Bosnian Serb forces announced on February 20. A week later President Tudjman bowed to U.S. and German pressure by agreeing to the renewal of the UNPROFOR mandate from March 31, on condition that most UN forces would be stationed on Croatia's international borders.

In the wake of Croatian military successes in 1995 and the restoration of government control over most of Croatia, President Tudjman was a key participant in the Dayton Accords talks that yielded a Bosnian peace agreement in November, and he was a signatory of the accord in Paris in December. On November 30 the UN Security Council voted to withdraw UN troops from Croatia by mid-January 1996. In a state of the nation address on January 15, Tudjman reported that, in what he called the "homeland war" of 1991–1995, Croatia proper had suffered some 13,500 deaths and nearly 40,000 people injured, as well as material damage estimated at $27 billion.

Although the status of Serb-held eastern Slavonia did not feature in the accords, Croatia's endorsement of the agreement was predicated on an international understanding that the area would be restored to Croatian rule. An agreement signed by Croatia and local Serb leaders on November 12, 1995, provided for the reintegration of eastern Slavonia into Croatia within two years, during which a UN-sponsored transitional administration would exercise authority. In January 1996 the UN Security Council approved the deployment of a 5,000-strong peacekeeping force (the UN Transitional Administration for Eastern Slavonia, Baranja, and Western Sirmium—UNTAES) to supervise the demilitarization of the area. The deployment began in May as the Serbs of the region elected a new leadership that appeared to be reconciled to the eventual restoration of Croatian rule. (Croatia formally reassumed authority over Slavonia on January 15, 1998, following the expiration of the UNTAES mandate. A small UN support group was collaterally assigned to remain in the region to monitor relations between the Croatian police and returning displaced persons.) The progress made on the Slavonian front in 1996 enabled Croatia, following talks between Presidents Tudjman and Milošević near Athens on August 7, to sign a formal accord with the Federal Republic of Yugoslavia on August 23 providing for the establishment of full diplomatic relations between the two countries. Collaterally, Croatia increased pressure on the Bosnian Croats to accept federation with the Bosnian Muslims, to which end Presidents Tudjman and Izetbegović of Bosnia, conferring in Geneva on August 14, reached agreement on detailed steps to inject substance into a federation structure theretofore existing only on paper. Croatia joined the Council of Europe on October 16, 1996, after the government issued assurances on a 21-point program on democracy and human rights previously negotiated with the council. After years of negotiations, Croatia tentatively accepted two agreements with Bosnia and Herzegovina on November 22, 1998. The Ploce-Neum accord gave Bosnia, which had very limited sea access, the right to use Croatia's large-vessel port of Ploce, while the Croatians gained transit rights through Bosnia's Neum region without border formalities. A second treaty called for a "special relationship" between Croatia and the Muslim-Croat Federation of Bosnia and Herzegovina.

Although Croatia continued to express an interest in joining the EU and NATO during the latter years of the Tudjman administration, Croatia satisfied neither group that it was committed to key prerequisites for inclusion, including press freedom, fair elections, civilian control of the military, and full implementation of the Dayton peace agreements (particularly the return of Serb refugees). As a result, NATO took no immediate action on Croatia's application to join the Partnership for Peace program. However, Croatia voiced support for NATO air strikes against Serbia in March 1999, and Foreign Minister Mate GRANIĆ claimed on April 1 that he had obtained a security guarantee from NATO in the event that the conflict in Kosovo spread.

Following Tudjman's death in late 1999 and the subsequent installation in early 2000 of a reformist government, Croatia's relations with the West improved with remarkable speed. In May membership in NATO's Partnership for Peace program was approved, in December Croatia joined the World Trade Organization, and in October 2001 Croatia signed an association agreement with the EU.

In April 2002 Croatia negotiated an agreement to delineate the border between Croatia and Montenegro, and President Mesić and the president of Serbia and Montenegro in 2003 exchanged mutual apologies for atrocities committed during the civil war. (As of 2006 more than 85,000 Croatian Serbs remained in Serbia, and in an effort to promote return, the Croatian government announced a plan to build more than 9,000 apartments for returning refugees.)

President Mesić was outspoken in his opposition to the U.S./UK-led invasion of Iraq in early 2003, and Croatia rebuffed a request to contribute troops to that initiative. However, relations with Washington improved following the installation of the HDZ government in late 2003, and Croatia subsequently agreed to permit the United States to use Croatian airspace and waters in future military action. Croatia also deployed 150 troops to train Afghan security forces in 2003.

On May 2, 2003, Croatia signed an Adriatic Charter along with the United States, Albania, and Macedonia. Among other things, Croatia, Albania, and Macedonia agreed to work together to pursue NATO membership, while the United States pledged to promote the candidacy of all three for simultaneous membership. In May 2006 U.S. Vice President Dick Cheney made a visit to Croatia. Croatia concurrently began upgrading its military transport aircraft so they could further support missions in Afghanistan and other out-of-area operations. Croatia and Italy announced an agreement in 2006 that would allow Italians to own land in Croatia. (Italians had been forbidden from purchasing property in Croatia because of continuing disputes over property rights in Istria, which had been transferred to Yugoslavia from Italy at the end of World War II.) Also in 2006 Croatia announced plans to build a new gas and oil pipeline system that would allow the export of energy resources to neighboring states such as Hungary and Serbia.

In March 2007 Croatia signed a trade agreement with the People's Republic of China designed to remove barriers to Chinese investment in the country and to open Chinese markets to Croatian goods. (Croatia had imported about $1 billion in products from China in 2006 but had exported only $17 million.) Also, in 2007, Croatia joined the International Whaling Commission (IWC). Meanwhile, as of 2007 Croatia had contributed troops to ten UN peacekeeping missions, including operations in Ethiopia, Eritrea, Haiti, Cyprus, Georgia, Kashmir, and Sierra Leone. Croatia also increased its deployment in Afghanistan to 300 soldiers in 2008.

In March 2008 Croatia offered diplomatic recognition to Kosovo. Recognition was strongly opposed by the Serb community in Croatia (see Current issues). Also, Serb protesters in Belgrade, Serbia, subsequently damaged the Croatian embassy on February 21. Croatia was invited to join NATO at the alliance's April summit in Bucharest, Romania.

Russian shipments of natural gas were cut off to Croatia in January 2009 during a dispute between Russia and Ukraine. The incident prompted Croatia, which imports 40 percent of its natural gas from Russia, to launch a broad effort to reduce energy imports. In April Croatia and Albania signed an agreement to develop a joint nuclear power plant as part of that initiative.

Membership in NATO enjoyed broad public and political support, and had the unanimous endorsement of both government and opposition parties. Croatia formally joined NATO on April 1, 2009. Negotiations over Croatian entry into the EU were delayed over a lingering boundary dispute with Slovenia over maritime rights and the land border in and around the Bay of Piran. The Sanader government had sought to conclude talks with the EU and gain membership by the end of 2009, but the disagreement threatened to delay entry until 2010 or 2011.

Current issues. In 2000 President Mesić, described, in sharp contrast to longtime president Tudjman, as "unpretentious" and "mild-mannered," immediately reversed his predecessor's positions on many issues that had been perceived as retrograde; he also pledged to eliminate covert support to Croatians in Bosnia and Herzegovina who were opposed to the current political structures in that country. Prime Minister Račan strongly endorsed the reformist agenda, vowing to pursue Croatia's eventual full membership in the EU and NATO with vigor. The international community responded keenly to the government's new directions. However, some initiatives provoked conflict within the coalition government and certain sectors of the population. For example, mass protest demonstrations were staged in 2001 in connection with the extradition of several generals to The Hague for prosecution by the ICTY. The return of the HDZ to government control in late 2003 was not seen as a surprise, considering the fragmentation of the SDP-led coalition and its perceived failure to invigorate the economy. New prime minister Sanader promised economic, military, and judicial reforms, primarily aimed at entry into the EU. In 2004 the EU authorized the start of formal accession negotiations, in part because of Croatia's apparent willingness to cooperate more enthusiastically with the ICTY. Croatia indicated it hoped to gain EU membership by 2007, but progress stalled in April 2005 when the UN accused the Croatian government of poor faith in extraditing alleged war criminals to the ICTY. (The government argued that it had been unable to locate Ante GOTOVINA, one of the most prominent suspected war criminals. However, the ICTY alleged Gotovina was being shielded by supporters that included Croatian officials.)

In the May 2005 local elections, the far-right Croatian Party of Rights (*Hrvatska Stranka Prava*—HSP) saw its representation triple in consonance with growing popular antipathy toward the ICTY. Sanader subsequently strongly criticized the ICTY for expanding the list of Croatians it hoped to bring to trial. In October the ICTY's chief prosecutor issued a positive report on Croatia's cooperation with the tribunal, and as a result accession negotiations recommenced. Croatia's prospects for EU membership subsequently brightened considerably in December 2005, when Gotovina was arrested by Spanish authorities in the Canary Islands, partially as a result of intelligence provided by the Croatian government. Since the arrest and transfer of Gotovina to The Hague in late 2005, Croatia has continued to cooperate fully with the ICTY and was certified to be in full compliance, clearing the way for continued EU negotiations. In 2006 the EU granted Croatia €245 million to aid in preparations to join the organization, and formal accession talks were launched on June 12 in Luxembourg. In October 2006 Branimir GLAVAS, a member of the House of Representatives (see the Croatian Democratic Assembly of Slavonia and Baranja under Political Parties, below) and former military officer was stripped of his immunity and arrested on charges related to the massacre of ethnic Serbs in 1991. Glavas was the Croat with the highest profile to date to be tried for crimes against humanity by the national judiciary.

In March 2007 Prime Minister Sanader rebuffed opposition efforts to force a referendum on NATO membership, arguing that the constitution did not require such a vote. Meanwhile, the country continued to make progress in satisfying the requirements for EU membership, and a new target date of 2009 was set for its accession. In the November House elections, no political party gained an absolute majority. Both the HDZ and the SPD endeavored to form a coalition government, but the president reappointed Sanader once the HDZ reached an agreement with the HSLS, the HSS, and the SDSS. In the legislative balloting, Nazif MEMEDI, a member of the Roma ethnic minority, was elected to the House for the first time. Despite his ongoing trial, Glavas was also elected to the legislature.

Croatia's recognition of Kosovo independence in March 2008 led to protests by ethnic Serbs in the country. In addition, SDSS Deputy Prime Minister Slobodan UZELAC attempted to resign in protest; however, his resignation was not accepted by Sanader. In October 2008 the high-profile murder of two journalists by organized crime figures (see Communications, below) prompted a range of government efforts to reduce crime, including the replacement of the interior and justice ministers. The government created a new, specialized police unit that concentrated specifically on organized crime. Despite the rise in organized crime, overall crime rates continued to decline in Croatia. The worldwide economic crisis that began in 2008 prompted the government to cut spending and reduce wages for most public-sector employees by 6 percent. GDP was expected to decline by 3.5 percent in 2009, while unemployment rose to 15 percent by April 2009. In April the government announced that it would not seek assistance from the IMF or other international bodies and predicted a return to economic growth in 2010.

POLITICAL PARTIES

For four and a half decades after World War II, the only authorized political party in Yugoslavia was the Communist Party, which was redesignated in 1952 as the League of Communists of Yugoslavia (*Savez Komunista Jugoslavija*—SKJ). In 1989 noncommunist groups began to emerge in the republics, and in early 1990 the SKJ approved the introduction of a multiparty system, thereby effectively triggering its own demise.

Government and Government-Supportive Parties:

Croatian Democratic Union (*Hrvatska Demokratska Zajednica*—HDZ). Founded in June 1989, the right-wing HDZ won a decisive majority of seats in the 1990 elections in each of the three assembly chambers in the Croatian constituent republic within Federal Yugoslavia. After leading Croatia to independence in 1991, the HDZ won a further overall parliamentary majority in the 1992 balloting, when the party's leader was popularly returned as head of state with 56.7 percent of the vote. Having previously headed a coalition government, the HDZ was the sole ruling party until, after winning a majority in upper house balloting in February 1993, it accepted the small Croatian Peasant Party (see below) as a ministerial partner. In September 1994 ideological conflict flared when extreme rightist Vladimir ŠEKS resigned as deputy prime minister but was speedily elected chair of the party's parliamentary group. Strengthened by Croatian military advances against the Serbs, the HDZ retained a comfortable lower house majority on a 45.2 percent vote share in October 1995. In the upper house elections of April 1997, the HDZ won 40 of 63 elected seats, while President Tudjman in June won a landslide victory in the presidential balloting. He was also unanimously reelected as party president in February 1998. Tudjman appeared to side with party hard-liners in a succession struggle leading to the resignation of two top presidential advisers in October 1998. The hard-liners, who reportedly shared with Tudjman a desire to carve Croatian territory from Bosnia and Herzegovina, were led by Ivić PAŠALIĆ, the president's special adviser for domestic affairs, who many observers believed was the likely successor to the president.

Following Tudjman's death in late 1999, Pašalić lost the HDZ leadership election to Mate Granić, who finished a disappointing third in the first round of the 2000 presidential poll with 22.4 percent of the vote. The party's fortunes also slid significantly in the January 2000 legislative balloting as it secured only 24 percent of the vote and 46 seats. Granić subsequently left the HDZ (along with three other HDZ legislators) to form the Democratic Center. Meanwhile, Ivo Sanader was selected as the new HDZ president in 2000, Pašalić being expelled from the party in July 2002 for characterizing Sanader's reelection as "illegal." (Pašalić subsequently formed the Croatian Bloc–Movement for a Modern Croatia.)

HDZ Vice President Jadranka Kosor placed second in the first round of presidential voting in 2005 and was defeated in the runoff balloting by the incumbent president. The HDZ expelled three legislators from the party in 2005 for advocating greater regional autonomy.

The HDZ won 43.1 percent of the vote in the 2007 legislative elections and 66 seats in the House, and Sanader formed a new HDZ-led government in January 2008. The following May Sanader was reelected HDZ leader for the fourth time, and in June Ivan Jarnjak was unanimously reelected as secretary general of the party for a second four-year term.

Leaders: Ivo SANADER (Prime Minister and Chair), Jadranka KOSOR (Deputy Prime Minister, Deputy Chair, and 2005 presidential candidate), Luka BEBIĆ (Speaker of the House of Representatives and Parliamentary Leader), Ivan JARNJAK (Secretary General and Deputy Speaker of the Parliament).

Croatian Peasant Party (*Hrvatska Seljačka Stranka*—HSS). Originally founded in 1904 as the Croatian Popular Peasant Party and influential in the interwar period, the HSS was relaunched in November 1989 as a party committed to pacifism, localism, and economic privatization. It won 3 lower house seats in August 1992 and 5 upper house seats in February 1993, thereafter accepting ministerial representation in coalition with the dominant HDZ. It switched to opposition status for the October 1995 election, winning 10 seats as a member of the Joint List Bloc (*Zajednica Lista*—ZL), which also included the HNS, HKDU, IDS, and SBHS. The ZL took second place on an 18.3 percent vote share, which yielded a total of 18 seats (10 for the HSS, 4 for the IDS, 2 for the HNS, and 1 each for the HKDU and SBHS). However, the ZL did not present candidates for the April 1997 House of Counties balloting, its members variously running their own candidates, collaborating with other Bloc components, or even aligning with parties outside the Bloc. The HSS presented a number of joint candidates with the HSLS in that balloting.

The HSS contested the 2000 legislative balloting in coalition with the IDS, HNS, and LS, the coalition securing 16 percent of the vote and 24 seats (16 for the HSS). The so-called Opposition Four also presented the successful 2000 presidential candidate—Stjepan Mesić of the HNS. In the 2003 legislative elections, the HSS ran outside of its previous coalition, winning 9 seats (just over half of its previous representation). The HSS subsequently supported the HDZ-led government, although it did not receive any cabinet posts. The HSS supported President Mesić in the 2005 presidential election.

In March 2007 the HSS signed a coalition agreement with the HSLS and the Primorian-Goranian Union (*Primorsko-Goranski Savez*—PGS) to cooperate ahead of the legislative elections scheduled for November. In the balloting, the HSS secured 6 seats. It joined the subsequent HDZ-led coalition government.

In 2008 party leader Josip Friščič was elected as a deputy speaker in Parliament. The HSS finalized a series of joint electoral agreements with its coalition partners ahead of local balloting planned for May 2009.

Leaders: Josip FRIŠČIĆ (Chair), Josip M. TOBAR (Honorary Chair), Stjepan RADIĆ (Honorary President), Ivan STANČER (Vice President), Stanko GRČIĆ (General Secretary).

Croatian Social-Liberal Party (*Hrvatska Socijalno-Liberalna Stranka*—HSLS). Founded in May 1989, the HSLS was characterized as a traditional European liberal grouping. Having performed modestly in the 1990 election, it became the second-strongest and main opposition party in August 1992, winning 14 lower house seats and, for its leader, a creditable 21.9 percent of the presidential vote. Securing 16 seats in the 1993 upper house balloting, the HSLS took part in an opposition boycott of Parliament in mid-1994. In the 1995 lower house balloting the HSLS took 11.6 percent of the vote, confirming its status as the single strongest opposition party. However, in April 1997 balloting for the House of Counties, the HSLS slipped from 16 to 6 seats of its own, although it had supported successful candidates from the HSS in some districts. In the June presidential race, HSLS candidate Vlado GOTOVAĆ, who was beaten up by an army officer at a rally and couldn't finish the campaign, came in third in the three-man race despite having the backing of a number of other opposition parties. The HSLS's showing in the 1997 elections apparently indicated it was declining in strength relative to the SDP, and divisions within the HSLS came to a head at the party's congress in November when a deadlock between Gotovać and his longtime rival Dražen Budiša prevented the election of a party president. Aside from the leadership issue, the party was also divided over whether to cooperate with the HDZ. On December 6, following his defeat by Budiša in the party's presidential election, Gotovać and his leading supporters resigned from the party to form a new grouping called the Liberal Party (see below).

Budiša, also endorsed by the SDP, finished second in the first round of presidential balloting in 2000 with 27.7 percent of the vote and lost the runoff with 44 percent. Meanwhile, the HSLS, now described as a "mildly nationalistic, socially conservative" party, won 24 seats in the 2000 elections to the House of Representatives as part of a coalition with the SDP, PGS, and SBHS. Although the HSLS joined the government following that balloting, Budiša's relationship with Prime Minister Račan of the SDP proved conflictual, and the HSLS officially left the cabinet in July 2002, although some HSLS members kept their posts and left the party. The HSLS ran with the Democratic Center in an electoral coalition in the 2003 elections.

The HSLS began merger negotiations with the smaller **Liberal Party** (*Liberalna Stranka*—LS) in 2005. The LS had been launched in January 1998 by defectors from the HSLS, including HSLS founders such as Vlado Gotovać, its presidential candidate in 1997, and a number of HSLS legislators. The LS saw itself as a guardian of the democratic principles on which the HSLS was founded, including staunch opposition to the HDZ. The LS was part of the "Opposition Four" coalition with the HSS, HNS, and IDS in the 2000 legislative balloting. Gotovać died in late 2000.

The LS participated in an electoral alliance for the 2003 legislative elections with the SDP, IDS, and Libra; the LS secured 2 of the alliance's 43 seats. After supporting President Mesić in the 2005 presidential polling, the LS was formally absorbed by the HSLS in 2006, and former LS President Zlatko KRAMARIĆ became a vice president of the expanded HSLS. Opponents of the merger, led by Ante TEŠIJA, split from the LS and formed the **Dalmatian Liberal Party** (*Dalmatinska Liberalna Stranka*—DLS). In 2006 Durda Adlešić was reelected president of the HSLS with 80 percent of the vote at a party congress.

In March 2007 the HSLS joined the HSS and the PGS in an electoral coalition to contest the November House of Representatives elections. The HSLS won two seats in the balloting and joined the HDZ-led government. The HSLS pledged to continues its coalition with the HSS and the PGS in local elections in May 2009.

Leaders: Durda ADLEŠIĆ (Deputy Prime Minister and President); Zlatko KRAMARIĆ (Deputy President); Dražen BREGLEC, Ivan CEHOK, Želimir JANJIĆ, Zlatko KRAMARIĆ, Hrvoje VOJKOVIĆ, Stanko ZRILIĆ (Vice Presidents).

Independent Democratic Serbian Party (*Samostaina Demokratska Srpska Stranka*—SDSS). Based in Vukovar, a major town in Slavonia, the SDSS was founded as the Independent Serbian Party in October 1995; the party adopted its current name in March 1997 in time for Serbs to contest the local elections in April. It quickly merged with the Party of Serbs (*Stranka Srpski*—SS) led by Milorad Pupovac. (The SS, advocating democratic and liberal principles, had been launched in 1993 and included the *Prosveta* ["Enlightenment"] movement.) The SDSS initially was formed to represent ethnic Serbs in Slavonia, but the merged party aimed to address the concerns of the 120,000 Serbs throughout Croatia. However, in its first outing, the party limited itself to contests for local and county assemblies and did not seek representation in the upper house in Zagreb. Ethnic Croatian parties won 16 of the 27 districts in eastern Slavonia, with 11 going to the SDSS. Following the April elections to the House of Counties, President Tudjman appointed SDSS party leader Vojislav Stanimirović and another ethnic Serbian leader, Jovan BAMBURAC, to the upper house, accounting for two of the five appointments the president made to that body. To the surprise of some analysts, the SDSS was unsuccessful in the 2000 balloting for the House of Representatives. However, in the 2003 legislative election, the SDSS gained the 3 seats reserved for the Serb minority. In exchange for support on key issues, the HDZ-led government agreed to advocate on behalf of SDSS priorities, including refugee return and increased minority rights. In the 2007 House elections the SDSS secured 3 seats and joined the HDZ governing coalition. The SDSS opposed the 2008 recognition of Kosovo by Croatia and threatened to leave the coalition; however, negotiations kept the party in the government.

Leaders: Vojislav STANIMIROVIĆ, Milorad PUPOVAC (President), Slobodan UZELAC (Deputy Prime Minister).

Croatian Pensioners' Party (*Hrvatska Stranka Umirovljenika*—HSU). The HSU was a center-left party that was formed in 1991 to promote pensioners' rights. In the 2003 assembly elections the HSU won three seats and the party supported the HDZ-led coalition government. In 2007 the party won 4.1 percent of the vote and one seat and subsequently supported the new HDZ-led government. In 2008 Silvano Hrelja was elected to replace Vladimir Jordan as party leader. Ahead of the 2009 local elections, the HSU signed a coalition agreement with the SDP (see below).

Leader: Silvano HRELJA.

Other Parliamentary Parties:

Social Democratic Party of Croatia (*Socijaldemokratska Partija Hrvatske*—SDP). Founded in 1937 as the Communist Party of Croatia and redesignated in 1952 as the League of Communists of Croatia (*Savez Komunista Hrvatske*—SKH), the SDP was runner-up to the HDZ in the 1990 balloting, winning 75 of 349 legislative seats outright, in addition to 16 captured in joint lists with other parties. Then called the Party of Democratic Changes (*Stranka Demokratskih Promjena*—SDP) to signify its rejection of communism, it slumped to only 11 seats (out of 138) in the 1992 election. The party changed its name again in April 1993 when it became the Social Democratic Party of Croatia, angering another leftist party of the same name (*Socijaldemokratska Stranka Hrvatske*—SDSH), with which it would merge a year later. (The SDSH, launched in December 1989, had won 1 seat in 1990 and was a member of the ruling coalition until August 1992, when its leader, Antun VUJIĆ, finished last of eight presidential candidates.)

The sole successful SDP candidate in the 1993 upper house polling was returned by virtue of an alliance with the HSLS. The united SDP performed better in the October 1995 lower house election, winning 8.9 percent of the vote. In the April 1997 upper house elections the SDP showed further strength (in frequent alliance with the HNS), and in the June presidential campaign SDP candidate Zdravko TOMAC ran second (21 percent) in the three-way race. The SDP's gains in both races indicated to some observers that it had displaced the HSLS as the strongest opposition party.

The SDP participated in an electoral coalition in the 2000 legislative elections with the HSLS, PGS, and SBHS. The coalition secured 47 percent of the vote and 71 seats; SDP leader Ivica Račan subsequently formed a coalition government. However, the joint SDP/HSLS presidential candidate, Dražen Budiša of the HSLS, finished second in the 2000 presidential poll.

In the 2003 legislative elections the SDP formed a new coalition with the LS, IDS, and Libra (see under HNS below). The SDP developed a broader coalition in 2005 to support the candidacy of President Mesić.

In April 2007 Račan's health rapidly declined, and he resigned as SPD leader. Zeljka ANTUNOVIĆ became interim president, but she announced that she would not campaign to be prime minister or president, thereby opening a leadership race for the party ahead of the November 2007 legislative elections. Zoran MILANOVIĆ was elected SDP president at a party congress on June 2 to fill the remainder of Račan's term. In the 2007 legislative balloting the SPD placed second with 31.2 percent of the vote and 56 seats in the House. Milanović was reelected party leader on May 11, 2008. In 2009 the SDP joined the HSU in an electoral coalition for local balloting.

Leaders: Zoran MILANOVIĆ (President); Zlatko KOMADINA, Milanka OPAČIĆ (Vice Presidents).

Croatian National Party–Liberal Democrats (*Hrvatska Narodna Stranka–Liberalni Demokrati*—HNS). Formed in January 1991, the

Croatian National Party (HNS) was also very widely known as the Croatian People's Party. The party secured lower house representation by the co-option of five deputies elected in 1990 under other party labels. It was an antitraditionalist grouping committed to political pluralism and a free-market economy. The party won six seats in the 1992 legislative election, with its leader securing 6 percent of the presidential vote. It slipped to two seats in 1995 and ran joint candidates with the SDP in the 1997 House of Counties balloting.

The HNS participated in the 2000 legislative elections in a coalition with the HSS, IDS, and LS, gaining 2 of the coalition's 24 seats. Despite its modest status in the realm of Croatian parties, the HNS served as the springboard for the successful presidential campaign in 2000 of Stjepan Mesić, a founding member of the HDZ who had broken from President Tudjman in 1994 and joined the HNS in 1997. Mesić won 41.1 percent of the vote in the first round of the presidential poll and 56.0 percent in the runoff.

In the 2003 elections the HNS joined a coalition with the SBHS and the PGS. In 2005 Mesić was reelected president with support from an SDP-led coalition. In February 2005 a party convention voted to merge the HNS with the Party of Liberal Democrats (*Stranka Liberalni Demokrati*—Libra) and adopt the expanded party name, while apparently retaining the HNS abbreviation. Libra had been formed in 2002 by former members of the HSLS when the HSLS left the SDP-led coalition government over the handling of the Krsko nuclear power plant issue with Slovenia. Libra deputies continued to support the government after the departure of the HSLS. Libra sought to appeal to younger, more educated urban voters with a centrist, economically liberal platform. In the 2003 House of Representatives elections Libra joined the SDP-led electoral coalition and secured three seats. Libra also participated in the SDP-led coalition that supported President Mesić in the 2005 presidential election before merging with the HNS. Libra President Jozo Radoš became a vice president of the expanded HNS in 2005.

In the 2007 House elections the HNS secured six seats. In April 2008 Radimir Čačić was reelected as party president.

Leaders: Stjepan MESIĆ (President of the Republic); Radimir ČAČIĆ (President); Savka DABČEVIĆ-KUČAR (Honorary President); Mladen BELIICZA, Jozo RADOŠ (Vice Presidents).

Istrian Democratic Assembly (*Istarski Demokratski Sabor*—IDS). Founded in February 1990, the IDS represents ethnic Italians and other minorities in Istria, advocating the creation of a "trans-border region" encompassing Croatian, Slovenian, and Italian areas. In the 1992 lower house balloting it formed a regional front with **Dalmatian Action** (*Dalmatinska Akcija*—DA), led by Mira LJUBIĆ-LORGER, and the Rijeka Democratic Alliance (see PGS, below), which won six seats, of which the IDS took four. In the 1993 upper house election the IDS took 66 percent of the vote in Istria, winning one elective seat and being allocated two more by presidential prerogative. In 1995 the IDS tally as part of the ZL was four seats. The party won two seats in the April 1997 elections for the House of Counties. In August the IDS called a meeting of several opposition parties to agitate for changes in electoral law that would reduce the power of the presidency and make referendums mandatory for all key issues.

The IDS won four seats in the 2000 balloting for the House of Representatives in coalition with the HSS, HNS, and LS. The IDS joined the January 2000 cabinet formed by the SDP's Ivica Račan but left the government in June 2001. The IDS again campaigned with the SDP coalition in the 2003 House election, and it also joined the SDP-led coalition that supported President Mesić in his 2005 reelection campaign. In the November 2007 legislative polling the IDS won three seats in the House.

Leaders: Ivan JAKOVČIĆ (President), Tedi CHIAVALON (Secretary General); Damir KAJIN, Nevija POROPAT, Giovanni SPONZA, Valter DRANDIĆ (Vice Presidents).

Croatian Party of Rights (*Hrvatska Stranka Prava*—HSP). A far-right formation established in 1990, the HSP is descended from a prewar nationalist party of the same name. Discord among party leaders during 1991 led a faction to form the **Croatian Democratic Party of Rights** (*Hrvatska Demokratska Stranka Prava*—HDSP) in June 1992. The HSP went on to win five seats in the August 1992 lower house election, its (then) president, Dobroslav PARAGA, taking 5.4 percent of the vote in the national presidential contest. Thereafter, the party came under pressure from the authorities, which in October asked the Constitutional Court to ban the HSP and instituted legal proceedings against three leading members. The HSP's military wing, called the Croatian Defense Association (*Hrvatska Obrambeni Savez*—HOS), was heavily involved in interethnic conflict; from mid-1993 steps were taken by the authorities to integrate the HOS into the official security forces. Paraga was ousted from the party leadership in September 1993, subsequently forming the breakaway HSP-1861. The HSP narrowly surmounted the 5 percent threshold in the October 1995 legislative balloting, securing four seats.

The HSP contested the 2000 legislative balloting in coalition with the HKDU, securing four of the five seats won by the coalition. Meanwhile, Anto Dapić, president of the HSP, won 1.8 percent of the votes in the first round of the 2000 presidential poll. In the 2003 House of Representatives elections the HSP formed a coalition with the Democratic Party of Zargorje (ZDS) and the Medimurian Party (MS). Only the HSP secured representation with eight seats. Slaven Letica was the HSP candidate in the 2005 presidential polling. He placed fifth with 7.59 percent of the vote.

In August 2005 it was announced that the HSP would absorb the Croatian Democratic Republican Party (*Hrvatska Demokratska Republikanska Stranka*—HDRS). The HDRS had been launched in October 2000 via merger of Croatian Spring (*Hrvatska Proljeća*—HP) and two other small opposition parties. In the 2003 elections the HDRS had received less than 1 percent of the vote.

In March 2007 the HSP announced it would contest the November legislative elections without any coalition partners. In the balloting the HSP won one seat in the House. In January 2009 HSP national board member Ante TANFARA and about 20 other local leaders from Sibenik left the party and joined the HDZ. The defectors asserted that the HSP had become too conservative.

Leaders: Anto DAPIĆ (President), Slaven LETICA (2005 presidential candidate).

Croatian Democratic Assembly of Slavonia and Baranja (*Hrvatski Demokratski Savez Slavonije i Baranje*—HDSSB). The HDSSB is a right-wing political party that was formed in May 2006 in Osijek under the leadership of Branimir Glavas, an independent member of the House of Representatives, and Kresimir Bubalo, the county prefect of Osijek-Baranja. Two other deputies in the House of Representatives joined the new party, and Glavas became the leader of the parliamentary faction. He was subsequently stripped of his parliamentary immunity and arrested in June 2006 following charges that he participated in crimes against humanity against ethnic Serbs in 1991. In the 2007 balloting, despite his trial, Glavas was elected to the House along with two other members of the HDSSB. The Glavas trial was suspended following his election, but the House again voted to strip his immunity in January 2008 and the trial resumed in November.

Leaders: Vladimir ŠIŠLJAGIĆ (President), Ines TESKARA, Kresimir BUBALO, Boro GRUBIŠIĆ, Damir JURIĆ (Vice Presidents), Dinko DURIĆ (Secretary General).

Party of Democratic Action of Croatia (*Stranka Demokratske Akcije Hrvatske*—SDAH). The SDAH was formed in 1990 to represent the interests of the Bosniak ethnic community in Croatia. The SDAH secured one seat in the House in the legislative elections in 2003 and 2007. Semso Tanković, the sole SDAH member of Parliament, was elected party leader in 2001 and 2005.

Leaders: Semso TANKOVIĆ (President), Mirsad SREBRENIKOVIĆ (Secretary General).

Other Parties and Groups:

Democratic Center (*Demokratski Centar*—DC). The DC was founded in March 2000 by former foreign minister Mate Granić and several HDZ legislators. The new party advocated Croatia's accession to the EU and NATO and other efforts to improve "international integration." In the 2003 House of Representatives elections the DC joined the HSLS in a coalition. However, the DC subsequently joined the HDZ-led coalition government, although party leader Vesna Škare-Ožbolt was forced to resign her cabinet post in February 2006 following repeated disagreements with the prime minister and charges that she leaked confidential government materials. The DC subsequently withdrew from the government. The DC campaigned with the ZS, but neither party gained enough votes to secure representation in the House.

Leaders: Vesna ŠKARE-OŽBOLT (Chair), Joško MORIĆ.

Primorian-Goranian Union (*Primorsko-Goranski Savez*—PGS). Also known as the Alliance of Croatian Coast and Mountains Department, this party was initially established in March 1990 as the Rijeka Democratic Alliance (*Riječki Demokratski Savez*). The party changed its name in 1996 to reflect its activities beyond the Rijeka region. Its platform advocates respect for all ethnic groups, a free-market economy, and civil liberties. The PGS ran in coalition with the SDP and the HNS for the House of Counties in 1997; by virtue of the success of SDP candidates in some of those races, the PGS was referenced as a parliamentary party, although no PGS members were legislators in their own right. In the 2000 balloting for the House of Representatives the PGS secured two seats as part of an electoral coalition with the SDP, HSLS, and SBHS. The PGS campaigned in a coalition with the HNS and the SBHS in the 2003 legislative elections. In the 2005 presidential election the PGS joined the pro-Mesić coalition. In March 2007 the PGS signed a coalition agreement with the HSS and the HSLS for the November 2007 legislative elections; however, unlike its coalition partners, it failed to gain representation in the House.

Leader: Nikola IVANIŠ (President).

Croatian Christian Democratic Union (*Hrvatska Kršćanska Demokratska Unija*—HKDU). The HKDU was formed in December 1992 by the **Croatian Christian Democratic Party** (*Hrvatska Kršćanska Demokratska Stranka*—HKDS), led by Ivan CESAR, and a majority faction of the Croatian Democratic Party of Rights (HDSP), led by Marko Veselica, both constituents dating from 1989. (Veselica had spent 11 years in jail during communist rule.) The HKDS had participated in the ruling coalition from 1990 but lost its two lower house seats in August 1992, Cesar placing seventh in the concurrent presidential poll. As part of the ZL, the HKDU won one seat in the 1995 lower house balloting. The HKDU secured one seat in the 2000 balloting for the House of Representatives, which it contested in coalition with the HSP. The HKDU failed to gain representation in the House in the 2003 legislative elections. Anto KOVAČEVIĆ, the party's candidate in the 2005 presidential balloting, received less than 1 percent of the vote. The party did not win any seats in the 2007 legislative balloting.

Leaders: Petar ĆURLIN (President), Marko VESELICA (Honorary President).

Serbian People's Party (*Srpska Narodna Stranka*—SNS). Founded in May 1991, the SNS (also known as the Serbian National Party) is an ethnic party that advocates a market economy, civil rights, and membership in the EU. Although much of Croatia's ethnic Serb population was not under Zagreb's jurisdiction at the time of the August 1992 election, the SNS returned three deputies on a platform of opposition to the Serb separatism represented by the self-proclaimed Republic of Serbian Krajina. Following Zagreb's recovery of Krajina in 1995 and the resultant exodus of many ethnic Serbs, the SNS won only two seats in the October election. Its representation fell to one in the 2000 balloting for the House of Representatives. The SNS did not secure any seats in the 2003 and 2007 House elections as the SDSS emerged as the dominant Serb party. In 2009 the SNS led an unsuccessful effort to force a national referendum on Croatian membership in NATO.

Leaders: Zmago JELINCIĆ (President), Josip MANOLIĆ (Honorary President).

Croatian Independent Democrats (*Hrvatski Nezavisni Demokrati*—HND). Led by the (then) presiding officers of Croatia's parliament, the HND was formed on April 30, 1994, by some 18 left-of-center dissident deputies of the ruling HDZ (including former president of the government Stjepan Mesić), who charged President Tudjman with authoritarianism and an ill-advised policy of waging war with Bosnia's Muslims. Both party leaders were replaced in their parliamentary posts by HDZ regulars. The HND failed to surmount the 5 percent barrier in the October 1995 lower house balloting but won one constituency seat. A dispute divided the party leadership in October 1996, and Mesić subsequently joined the HNS. In 2002 it was reported that one disaffected HDZ legislator had left that party and joined the HND. The HND did not gain any seats in the 2003 House of Representatives elections, HND leader Josip Manolić having urged party members to support the HDZ in the balloting. It was subsequently reported that many HND members had joined the HDZ.

Leaders: Josip MANOLIĆ (President), Marija DUIĆ (Secretary General).

Croatian Party of Slavonia and Baranja (*Slavonsko-Baranjska Hrvatska Stranka*—SBHS). Founded in December 1992, the SBHS aimed to represent ethnic Croats in what had been Serb-majority Croatian territory occupied by Serb forces in the 1991–1995 conflict. It won one lower house seat in 1995 as a member of the Joint List Bloc. It retained that seat in the 2000 House of Representatives elections in which it participated in a coalition with the SDP, HSLS, and PGS. The SBHS joined the HNS-led coalition, along with the PGS, for the 2003 legislative balloting but failed to gain any seats, nor did it receive any seats in the 2007 balloting.

Leaders: Damir JURIĆ (President), Zdenko MARUS (Secretary General).

Other parties include the **Croatian Democratic Peasant Party** (*Hrvatska Demokratska Seljačka Stranka*—HDSS), led by Ivan MARTAN, which gained one seat in the 2003 House elections but none in 2007; the **Croatian Bloc–Movement for a Modern Croatia** (*Hrvatski Blok–Pokret za Modernu Hrvatsku*), formed in 2002 and led by 2005 presidential candidate Ivić PAŠALIĆ; the **Croatian Liberation Movement** (*Hrvatski Oslobodilački Pokret*—HOP), led by Ivan CURIĆ and Slavko GRUBIŠIĆ; the **Croatian Popular Party** (*Hrvatska Pučka Stranka*—HPS), whose leader, Tomislav MERČEP, won 0.9 percent of the vote in the first round of the 2000 presidential election and 0.1 percent in 2005; the **Croatian Pure Party of Rights** (*Hrvatska Čista Stranka Prava*—HCSP), led by Luka PODRUG; the **Croatian Republicans** (*Hrvatski Republikanci*—HR), led by Tomislav BOGDANIĆ; the **Croatian Republican Party** (*Hrvatska Republikanska Stranka*—HRS), led by Borko JURIN; the **Croatian Republican Union** (*Hrvatska Republikanska Zajednica*—HRZ), an outgrowth of the HRS, led by Mario M. OSTOJIĆ; the **Democratic Party of Zagorje** (*Zagorska Demokratska Stranka*—ZDS), led by Stanko BELINA; the **Medimurian Party** (*Medimurska Stranka*—MS), which campaigned in a coalition with the HSP and ZDS in 2003; the **Movement for Human Rights/Party of Ecologically Conscious Citizens** (*Pokret za Ljudska Prava/Stranka Ekološki Sujesnih Gradana*—POL/SESG), led by Rikard MORITZ; the **New Alternative Party,** led by Aljoša BABIĆ; **New Croatia** (*Nova Hrvatska*—NH), whose candidate, Ante PRKAČIN, won 0.30 percent of the vote in the first round of the 2000 presidential balloting and 0.28 percent in 2005; the **Socialist Workers Party of Croatia** (*Socijalistička Radnička Partija Hrvatske*—SRPH), a leftist, anti-NATO grouping formed in October 1997 under the leadership of Stipe ŠUVAR; the **Croatian Citizen Peasant Party** (*Hrvatska Gradansko Seljačka Stranka*—HGSS), led by Stjepan VUJANIĆ; **Croatian Dalmatian Home** (*Hrvatski Dalmatinski Dom*—HDD), a right-wing regional grouping formed in May 1996 and led by Goran SLADOLJEV, which is active in Split-Dalmatia; **Croatian Peasant Labor Party** (*Hrvatska Seljačko Radnička Stranka*—HSRS), led by Josip DENT; the **Gypsy Party of Croatia** (*Stranka Roma Hrvatske*—SRH), led by Stevo DURDEVIĆ; and the **Istrian Independent Party** (*Istarska Nezavisna Stranka*—INS), led by Franko ŠTURMAN.

Other minor parties are the **Albanian Christian Democratic Party of Croatia** (*Albanska Demokršćanska Stranka Hrvatske*—ADMSH), led by Mikel MARKAJ; **Central European Action** (*Srednjoeuropska Akcija*—SEA), led by Damir MILIĆ; the **Christian Social Union** (*Kršćanska Socijalna Unija*—KSU), formed in 1999 under the leadership of Nikša SENTIĆ; the **Citizen Party of Sisak** (*Sisačka Gradanska Stranka*—SGS), led by Božidar PINTARIĆ; the **Croatian Defense Order** (*Hrvatski Obranbeni Red*—HOR), led by Branimir PETENER; the **Croatian Democratic Republican Party** (*Hrvatska Demokratska Republikanska Stranka*—HDRS), founded in 2000 under the leadership of Joško KOVAĆ; the **Croatian Ecological Alliance** (*Hrvatski Ekološki Savez*—HES), led by Zlatko SVIBEN; the **Croatian Homeland Party** (*Hrvatska Domovinska Stranka*—HDMS); **Dalmatian Action** (*Dalmatinska Akcija*—DA), led by Mira LJUBIĆ-LORGER; the **Democratic Party of Pensioners** (*Demokratska Stranka Umirovljenika*—DSU), founded in 2001 under the leadership of Zlatko MAVRLJA; the **Freedom Party of Croatia** (*Slobodarska Stranka Hrvatske*), formed in 2001 under the leadership of Boris BABIĆ; the **Green Left of Croatia** (*Zelena Ljevica Hrvatske*—ZEL), led by Zvjezdana CIKOTA (President); the **Green Party** (*Zelena Stranka*—ZS), led by Zoran PIŠL; the **Island's Democratic Party** (*Otočna Demokratska Stranka*—ODS), led by Tomislav OROVIĆ; the **Italian Democratic Union** (*Talijanska Demokratska Zajednica–Unione Democratica Italiana*—TDZ-UDI), led by Tulio PERSI; **Only Croatia-Movement for Croatia** (*Jedino Hrvatska–Pokret za Hrvatsku*), formed by Milovan Sibl; the **Party of Croatian State Rights** (*Stranka Hrvatkog Dravnog Prava*—SHDP), led by Nikola BIĆANIĆ; the **Party of Danubian's Serbs** (*Partija Podunavskih Srba*—PPS), led by Radivoj LESKOVAC; the **People's Assembly of Rab** (*Rapski Pučki Sabor*—RPS), led by Milijenko MATIJEVIĆ; the **Serbian Democratic Party of Baranja** (*Srpska Demokratska Baranjska Stranka*—SDBS), led by Ljubomir MIJATOVIĆ; the **South Croatian Party** (*Južnohrvatska Stranka*—JHS), formed in 2001 under the leadership of Srečko KLJUNAK; and the **Dalmatian Liberal Party** (*Dalmatinska Liberalna Stranka*—DLS), established in 2005 and led by Ante TEŠIJA.

In November 2006 five small parties led by the SRPH formed an electoral coalition to contest the 2007 legislative elections. This new left-of-center grouping, called the United Left, also included the **Social Democratic Action of Croatia** (*Akcija Socijaldemokrata Hrvatske*—ASH), the **Adriatic Social Democratic Party of Croatia** (*Jadranska Socijaldemokratska Stranka Hrvatske–Jadranski Socijaldemokrati*—JSD), the **Croatian Workers' Party**, and the **New Alternative Party–Green Movement** (*Stranka Nove Alternative–Pokret Zelenih*—SNA).

LEGISLATURE

Under the 1990 constitution, the Croatian **Assembly** (*Sabor*) consisted of an upper House of Counties (*Županijski Dom*) and a lower House of Representatives, both popularly elected for four-year terms. The new bicameral structure was implemented by elections to the House of Representatives in August 1992 and, following the passage of legislation establishing the country's 21 counties, to the House of Counties in February 1993. The House of Counties was abolished (effective upon the expiration of its current term in May 2001) by a vote in the House of Representatives in March 2001.

House of Representatives (*Zastupnički Dom*). The present House comprises 140 members elected from ten regular constituencies (14 seats each) under a proportional system that requires a party to receive 5 percent of the vote in any constituency to gain representation from that constituency. An additional 5 members are elected (on a plurality basis) to represent ethnic minorities (1 each for Serbian, Hungarian, and Italian minorities; 1 shared by the Czech and Slovak minorities; and 1 shared by the Austrian, German, Ruthenian, Ukrainian, and Jewish minorities), while up to 15 are elected on a proportional basis by Croatians living abroad. (The number of seats from the diaspora is determined at each election via comparison of voter turnout relative to previous turnouts.)

The most recent balloting, held November 25, 2007, resulted in the election of 153 members (including 5 representing Croatians living abroad). The seat distribution was as follows: Croatian Democratic Union (HDZ), 66; Social Democratic Party of Croatia (SDP), 56; Croatian National Party (HNS), 6; Croatian Peasant Party (HSS), 6; Croatian Democratic Assembly of Slavonia and Baranja (HDSSB), 3; Istrian Democratic Assembly (IDS), 3; Independent Democratic Serbian Party (SDSS), 3; Croatian Social-Liberal Party (HSLS), 2; Croatian Party of Rights (HSP), 1; Croatian Pensioners' Party (HSU), 1; Party of Democratic Action of Croatia (SDAH), 1; independents, 5.

Speaker: Luka BEBIĆ.

CABINET

[as of May 1, 2009]

Prime Minister	Ivo Sanader (HDZ)
Deputy Prime Ministers	Jadranka Kosor (HDZ) [f]
	Damir Polenčec (HDZ)
	Durda Adlešič (HSLS) [f]
	Slobodan Uzelac (SDSS)
Ministers	
Agriculture, Forestry, and Water Management	Božidar Pankretić (HSS)
Culture	Božo Biškupić (HDZ)
Defense	Branko Vukelić (HDZ)
Economy, Labor, and Enterprise	Damir Polenčec (HDZ)
Environmental Protection, Physical Planning, and Construction	Marina Matulović Dropulić (HDZ) [f]
Family, Veterans' Affairs, and Intergenerational Solidarity	Jadranka Kosar (HDZ) [f]
Finance	Ivan Šuker (HDZ)
Foreign Affairs and European Integration	Gordon Jandroković (HDZ)
Health and Social Welfare	Darko Milinović (HDZ)
Interior	Tomislav Karamarko (HDZ)
Justice	Ivan Šimonovič (HDZ)
Maritime Affairs, Tourism, Transport, and Development	Božidar Kalmeta (HDZ)
Regional Development, Forestry and Water Management	Petar Čobankovič (HDZ)
Regional Development, Reconstruction and Return of Refugees	Slobodan Uzelac (SDSS)
Science, Education, and Sports	Dragan Primorac (HDZ)
Tourism	Damir Bajs (HSLS)

[f] = female

COMMUNICATIONS

Government control of the media was heavy under the Tudjman administration, a situation that was attracting ever-increasing international and domestic criticism prior to Tudjman's death in late 1999. Restrictions were subsequently relieved substantially as part of the new government's efforts to present a reformist image to Western capitals. In 2006 the government eliminated imprisonment as a punishment for libel, a sentence that had been used to intimidate the press. In June 2008 a prominent Croatian journalist was attacked and badly beaten after a series of reports on organized crime. On October 23, 2008, a car bomb killed Ivo PUKANIC, owner of the NCL Media Group, and Niko FRANJIC, marketing direct of the weekly *National*. An investigation revealed that the attack had been carried out by organized crime figures. In its 2008 annual report, Reporters Without Borders ranked Croatia 44 out of 173 countries in freedom of the press.

Press. The following are dailies published in Serbo-Croat: *Večernji List* (Evening Paper, Zagreb, 300,000); *Slobodna Dalmacija* (Free Dalmatia, Split, 110,000); *Jutarnji List* (Zagreb, 100,000); *Novi List* (New Paper, Rijeka, 60,000); *Vjesnik* (Courier, Zagreb, 50,000), formerly progovernment, now independent; *Novi Vjesnik* (New Courier, Zagreb, 45,000); *Glas Slavonije* (Slavonia News, Osijek, 25,000); *Glas Istre* (Istrian News, Pula, 18,000). Weeklies include *Nacional* (Zagreb, 80,000); *Globus* (Zagreb, 180,000); *Feral Tribune* (Split, 50,000), satirical.

News agency. The official government body since 1990 has been the HINA News Agency.

Broadcasting and computing. Croatian Radio-Television (*Hrvatska RadioTelevizija*) broadcasts in Serbo-Croat over three nationwide radio stations and three television channels. Croatian television was controlled by the government until 2000 and was criticized internationally for biased reporting and favoritism in its election coverage. In October 1997, for example, the OSCE called on two stations to broadcast public apologies for having "failed to meet even minimally acceptable standards" of fairness. After a long dispute with the government and a demonstration by 100,000 supporters in November 1996, independent Radio 101 received a five-year license in November 1997. Also in November 1997 Radio Vukovar resumed broadcasting in the eastern Slavonian city for the first time since its fall to a Serbian assault six years earlier. The first license for a nationwide private station (Nova TV) was issued in July 2000. As of 2008 there were 506 Internet users per 1,000 inhabitants.

INTERGOVERNMENTAL REPRESENTATION

Ambassador to the U.S.: Kolinda GRABAR-KITAROVIC.

U.S. Ambassador to Croatia: James B. FOLEY.

Permanent Representative to the UN: Ranko VILOVIĆ.

IGO Memberships (Non-UN): BIS, CEI, CEUR, EBRD, Eurocontrol, IADB, Interpol, IOM, IWC, NATO, OSCE, PCA, WCO, WTO.

CUBA

Republic of Cuba
República de Cuba

Political Status: Independent republic founded in 1902; under Marxist-inspired regime established January 1, 1959; designated a Communist system in December 1961; present constitution adopted February 16, 1976.

Area: 42,803 sq. mi. (110,860 sq. km.).

Population: 11,177,743 (2002C); 11,308,000 (2008E).

Major Urban Centers (2005E): HAVANA (2,244,000), Santiago de Cuba (434,000), Camagüey (311,000), Holguín (285,000), Santa Clara (216,000), Guantánamo (215,000).

Official Language: Spanish.

Monetary Unit: Peso (official rate December 1, 2009: 1 peso = $1.00US [a 10 percent Cuban tax is also added when converting directly from dollars to pesos]). There are two pesos used in Cuba. One, the "regular" peso, is used for state salaries and government goods and services. The "convertible peso" is used by visiting foreigners and by Cubans for most goods and services. It had been pegged at 1.00 convertible peso = $1US for many years until the government announced two revaluations in the first half of 2005 (2008 exchange rate quoted above). The regular peso in 2008 continued to trade at approximately 24 regular pesos = 1 convertible peso. Meanwhile, the dollar, which had been permitted to circulate since 1993, had ceased being accepted as legal tender as of November 8, 2004, by order of President Fidel Castro.

President of the Council of State and of the Council of Ministers, and Second Secretary of the Communist Party of Cuba: Gen. Raúl CASTRO Ruz; elected February 24, 2008; designated first vice president of the Council of State and of the Council of Ministers by the National Assembly on December 2, 1976; reappointed in 1981, 1986, 1993, 1998, and on March 16, 2003; named acting president on July 31, 2006, following incapacitation of President Fidel CASTRO Ruz.

Vice Presidents of the Council of State: José Ramón MACHADO Ventura (First Vice President), Juan ALMEIDA Bosque, Corps Gen. Abelardo COLOMÉ Ibarra, Juan Esteban LAZO Hernández, Gen. Julio CASAS Reguiero. Almeida has served since 1976; Colomé and Lazo were appointed on March 15, 1993, to replace Osmany CIENFUEGOS Gorriarán, Carlos Rafael RODRIGUEZ Rodríguez, and Pedro MIRET Prieto. Carlos LAGE Dávila was forced out of the Council of State on March 2, 2009. Ventura and the remaining incumbent vice presidents were reappointed on February 24, 2008.

THE COUNTRY

The largest of the Caribbean island nations, Cuba lies at the western end of the Greater Antilles, directly south of Florida. Its varied terrain, with abundant fertile land and a semitropical climate, led to early specialization in the production of sugar as well as tobacco, coffee, and other crops. Its demographic composition is a mixture of Caucasian and African ethnic groups. A plurality of the population is Roman Catholic (50.5 percent in Cuba, 72 percent in Havana) though the church's mainstream religion is increasingly being challenged by *santería*, a hybrid religion characterized by components of Catholicism and African animism. In addition, there are more than 50 registered Protestant denominations, nearly half of which are joined in a largely regime-supportive Ecumenical Council of Cuba (*Consejo Ecuménico de Cuba*), and a notable Jewish community. Women constitute nearly 40 percent of the labor force and provide close to half of the country's administrators.

The Cuban economy faced great difficulty following the 1959 Communist revolution. Production lagged, dependence on foreign assistance (mainly from the Soviet Union) increased, and real per capita income declined. Despite sporadic attempts at industrialization, the Castro regime emphasized agricultural development, and sugar remained the principal export. The nearly three decades of economic adversity was followed by a degree of recovery in 1988–1989, generating expectations that renegotiation of the country's $6.4 billion external debt might be imminent; however, political developments within the Soviet Union and Eastern European "socialist camp" in 1989–1990 resulted in the effective loss of Cuba's leading trade partners and a need to place the domestic economy on a near-wartime footing, including an expansion of rationing to include virtually all consumer goods. In May 1991, following a five-month suspension in food shipments from the Soviet Union, it was agreed that such shipments would thenceforth be made only on a barter basis; concurrently, it was announced that as of 1992 hard currency valuation would be required for Soviet oil. As a result, the government mounted a drive to achieve self-sufficiency in food production, coupled with an effort to augment foreign reserves by enhancing tourism and the export of pharmaceuticals. The opening of farmers' markets on October 1, 1994, led to a substantial decline in domestic prices and in the black market rate for U.S. dollars. By December 1 the government had opened markets for consumer goods at deregulated prices.

After suffering a contraction of 40 percent from 1989–1994, the GDP grew, according to government figures, by an average of 4.7 percent annually during the next five years and expanded by 5.6 percent in 2000, before declining to 2.6 percent growth in 2003. Meanwhile, unemployment, although showing signs of recent improvement, was officially reported to be 32 percent in late 2003. Much of the difficulty stems from a long-standing U.S. trade embargo, which has left Cuban citizens facing what one *New York Times* reporter described as an "unending scramble to make ends meet."

Arguing that wages alone did not indicate "true purchasing power," Cuba in 2005 adopted a new measure of economic growth that included free services to its citizens. The result was a surge in reported GDP, which precluded meaningful comparison with other developing economies. Economic growth rates of 5.5 percent and 7.3 percent were recorded in 2006 and 2007, respectively. Robust growth was interrupted in 2008, however, owing in large part to the damage of three successive hurricanes, Gustav being the most devastating in 50 years. The hurricanes caused more than $5 billion in damage, and annual economic growth subsequently contracted to 4.3 percent. The economy was expected to contract significantly in 2009, perhaps to about 1 percent annual growth, due to the global economic downturn, a collateral ballooning trade deficit, low productivity, and lack of diversification,

GOVERNMENT AND POLITICS

Political background. Liberated from Spanish rule as a result of the Spanish-American War of 1898, Cuba was established as an independent republic on May 20, 1902, but remained subject to U.S. tutelage until abrogation of the so-called Platt Amendment in 1934. Subsequent political development was severely limited by the antidemocratic influence of Fulgencio BATISTA, who ruled the country directly or indirectly from 1933 to 1944 and maintained a repressive dictatorship from 1952 to 1959. On January 1, 1959, a revolutionary movement, *Movimiento 26 de Julio,* under Fidel CASTRO Ruz, who had commenced guerrilla operations in 1956, overthrew Batista's regime, which had been weakened by army and middle-class disaffection.

After a brief period of moderation, the Castro government embarked on increasingly radical internal policies, which gradually developed into a full-scale social revolution purportedly based on the adaptation of Marxist-Leninist ideas to Latin American conditions. Relations with the United States deteriorated rapidly as the result of Castro's strident anti-Americanism, leading to the October 1960 expropriation of all U.S. business interests. The United States responded by severing diplomatic relations, imposing a trade embargo, and supporting an ill-fated invasion by anti-Castro Cuban exiles at the Bay of Pigs in April 1961.

Coincident with the decline in U.S.-Cuban relations, Castro cultivated increasingly close ties with Communist countries, particularly the Soviet Union, whose emplacement of offensive missiles in Cuba precipitated the Cuban Missile Crisis of October 1962. Thereafter, the Castro government consolidated its internal authority, aided in part by

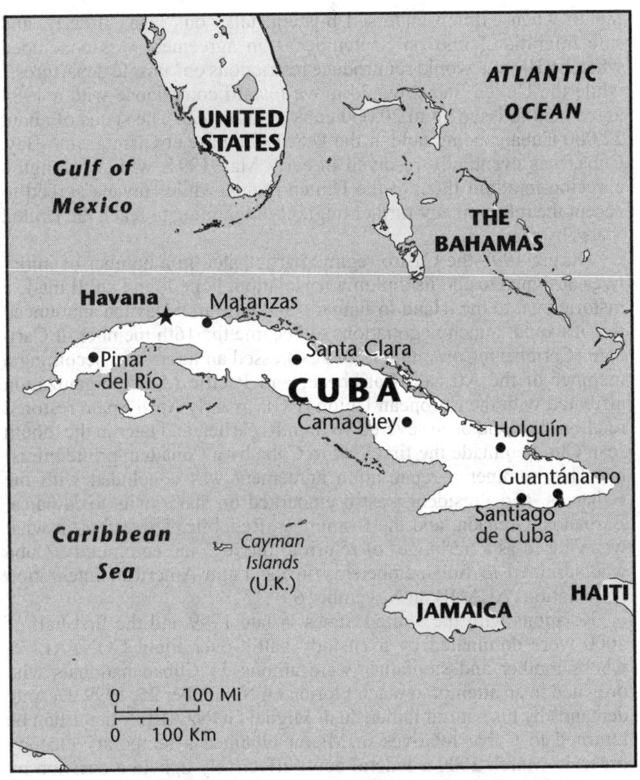

the departure of thousands of disaffected Cubans, most of whom settled in the United States.

In the fifth general election on April 30 and May 7, 1989, 14,246 delegates were elected to local municipal bodies, with subsequent indirect election to provincial and national assemblies. Thereafter, a party Central Committee meeting in January 1990 decided that the responsibilities of the municipal and provincial assemblies would be strengthened and that the National Assembly would be converted from a largely ceremonial body into a genuine parliament. Thus, on February 24, 1993, the National Assembly was for the first time directly "elected" when candidates approved by the Communist Party of Cuba (PCC) faced a "yes or no" decision from the voters. The sole anti-regime option (exercised by 11.6 percent of the participants) was to vote against the solitary candidate in each race.

Heightened isolation and economic distress, brought about by the end of Soviet subsidies, prompted a series of major policy reforms in 1993. The government legalized the possession and spending of U.S. dollars and other convertible currencies, lifted restrictions on exile visitations and on self-employment in 117 occupations, including taxi drivers and sellers of farm products. In late October the new self-employed sector was declared subject to progressive taxation, based on income as part of a new revenue system designed to "re-establish order" in the state's finances. One indicator of such a need was a sharp decline in the sugar harvest (an estimated 4.2 million tons, as contrasted with 7.0 million tons in 1992).

The second election to the National Assembly was held on January 11, 1998, with the 601 candidates approved by the PCC again facing a "yes or no" decision from the voters. All of the candidates received the required 50 percent endorsement in what was officially reported as a 98 percent turnout. (President Castro hailed the election as a "vote of unity" by his country.) On February 24 the new assembly reappointed Castro to another five-year term as president of the Council of State. All six incumbent vice presidents were also reappointed (including Castro's brother, then First Vice President Raúl CASTRO Ruz, who had reportedly been exercising growing governmental influence), and some new members were included in the Council.

Subsequent direct elections of assembly deputies were held on January 19, 2003 with results identical to those of 1998, except that the number of members had been increased to 609. Following the poll, President Castro and all six incumbent vice presidents were again reappointed.

On July 31, 2006, President Castro was hospitalized for an undisclosed but obviously serious internal illness, and he ceded power, on a provisional basis, to his brother Raúl. In legislative balloting on January 20, 2008, Fidel Castro was reelected, despite an 18-month hiatus from public politics. On February 19, five days before the Council of State met to elect a new president, Fidel Castro announced that he would not consider another term. On February 24, Gen. Raúl CASTRO Ruz was unanimously elected president of the Council of State, and president of the Council of Ministers. The change in the presidency brought about only minor changes in the cabinet. A major cabinet reshuffle occurred on March 3, 2009, further distinguishing the presidencies of the Castro brothers (see Current issues, below).

Constitution and government. A revised basic law, which had been under preparation for nearly a decade, was approved at the first PCC congress in December 1975, adopted by popular referendum on February 16, 1976, and declared in effect eight days later, on the anniversary of the commencement of the 1898 war of Cuban independence. It provided for an indirectly elected National Assembly, which, under a 1991 amendment, was changed to a directly elected body. The assembly designates a Council of State from among its membership. The Council of State appoints a Council of Ministers in consultation with its president, who serves as head of state and, in his role of president of the Council of Ministers, as chief of government. The judiciary consists of a People's Supreme Court in addition to intermediate and local courts. Members of the judiciary, as well as of the state council and cabinet, are subject to legislative recall.

Under the 1976 constitution, Cuba's 6 traditional provinces were abandoned in favor of a 14-province structure, with provincial assemblies designed to encourage greater popular involvement in government. Members of the provincial assemblies are drawn from 169 popularly elected municipal assemblies, an earlier provision for intraprovincial regional assemblies having been dropped following a "popular power" experiment in Matanzas Province in June 1975. Members of the municipal and provincial assemblies serve for terms of two-and-one-half years, while the National Assembly sits for five years. According to Cuban electoral law one deputy is elected to the assembly for every 20,000 inhabitants and each municipality is guaranteed at least two deputies regardless of size. Thus, with population growth the size of the assembly increases.

In mid-1991 the existing terms of both the national and subnational assemblies were extended, with municipal elections being held on December 20, 1992, and provincial and national assembly balloting taking place on February 24, 1993.

The 1991 adoption of direct and secret balloting did not authorize opposition formations, and "the final objective of building a Communist society" was reaffirmed. However, in calling for socialist ownership of the means of production, the wording was revised to "basic means of production," while (then) National Assembly president Juan ESCALONA Reguera subsequently declared that retention of the one-party system was necessary because of the U.S. economic blockade. In other changes, all references to the Soviet Union were deleted, the state's religious orientation was characterized as laical rather than atheistic, and the sanctioning of "mixed enterprises" opened the door to joint ventures with foreign investors. In September 1995 investment rules were further relaxed to permit 100 percent foreign ownership, equality of opportunity for émigré investors, and free remittance abroad of profits and capital. In 2002 the constitution was amended to state that socialism, the political system, and the revolutionary society established by the constitution are "irrevocable and Cuba will never return to capitalism."

Foreign relations. Partly because of its attempt to promote Castro-type revolutions throughout Latin America, Cuba was for a number of years ostracized by most other Latin American governments. It was excluded from participation in the Organization of American States (OAS) in 1962, and the OAS imposed diplomatic and commercial sanctions in 1964. However, following the 1967 death in Bolivia of the Argentine-born revolutionary Ernesto ("Ché") GUEVARA, the Castro regime scaled down its support of external guerrilla activity. Subsequently, Havana served as a conduit for the flow of military and other assistance to the *sandinista* government of Nicaragua as early as 1967. By 1974 a number of OAS states had moved to reestablish relations. In July 1975 the OAS itself, while not formally lifting the sanctions, adopted a resolution stating that its members would henceforth be "free to normalize" relations with Havana.

Although Cuba no longer stands out as a self-proclaimed nemesis of other Latin American governments, its foreign relations were long shaped by an ingrained hostility toward the United States and other established governments in the Americas, and by a corresponding affinity for revolutionary movements around the world. In March 1969 it became the first country to accord formal recognition to the National Liberation Front of South Vietnam and during 1975 initiated a major program of military assistance to the Soviet-backed regime in Angola. As host of the Sixth Conference of Heads of State of the Nonaligned Movement in September 1979, it sought, with some success, to identify the "socialist camp" as the "natural ally" of the third world movement.

During 1981 Havana's international posture was dominated by an increasing emigration of Cuban citizens after President Castro had indicated that Cuban exiles in the United States would be permitted to pick up anyone who wished to leave from the port of Mariel. Subsequently, more than 114,000 Cubans departed by boat for Florida in what came to be known as the Mariel Boatlift.

In 1982 Cuba was placed on the U.S. "State Sponsors of Terrorism" list and in the wake of the Grenada crisis in October 1983, Cuban relations with the United States and the region at large fell to their lowest ebb in years, Cuba being placed in a state of national alert. Although there were indications of a thaw in 1984, with formal talks on the status of the Mariel refugees leading to a December 1984 immigration agreement, the accord was suspended by Havana in May 1985 after Radio Martí, an "alternative" radio station directed at Cuba, had commenced transmissions from Florida. Five years later, following the U.S. launching of a companion TV Martí, the Cuban government initiated 24-hour jamming of the broadcasts. Today radio broadcasts from Havana on the same frequency effectively block Radio Martí signals while TV Martí reaches the island via prohibited satellite dishes.

A major foreign policy development in 1988 stemmed from a series of U.S.-mediated discussions among Cuban, Angolan, and South African representatives that commenced in London in May and concluded at UN headquarters in New York on December 22 with the signing of an accord for the withdrawal of an estimated 40,000–50,000 Cuban troops from Angola, coupled with South African acceptance of a 1978 Security Council resolution demanding UN-supervised elections for an independent Namibia. Under the agreement, which followed the departure of South African forces from Angola in September, Cuba pledged to withdraw its troops during a 30-month period. A similar pullout from Ethiopia (where nearly 15,000 Cubans had been deployed at the height of the Ogaden war) was completed in September 1989.

In September 1991 Havana, reeling from the withdrawal of Soviet economic support (the Soviet Union would dissolve officially on December 31, 1991), reacted angrily to Moscow's unilateral declaration that it would soon remove all of its military personnel from the island. Havana termed the announcement, made without reference to the presence of U.S. troops at Guantánamo Bay, an "unconditional concession" that provided the United States with a "green light to go ahead with its aggressive plans against Cuba." Nonetheless, the two governments agreed in September 1992 that the former Soviet military brigade that had been on the island since the 1962 missile crisis would be withdrawn by mid-1993. Earlier, in mid-August, a foreign office spokesperson indicated that Cuba was prepared to accede to the 1967 Tlatelolco Treaty prohibiting nuclear weapons in Latin America (see OPANAL, under Intergovernmental Organizations), a pledge that was fulfilled in March 1995.

In October 1992 U.S. President George H. W. Bush signed the Cuban Democracy Act (popularly known as the "Torricelli Law"), which tightened the U.S. economic embargo by making it illegal for overseas subsidiaries of U.S. firms to trade with Cuba. In an unusually strong response, the UN General Assembly voted 59 to 3, with 92 abstentions, to support repeal of the measure, reflecting a steady erosion of the U.S. position. A similar vote in November 1995 yielded a drastically enhanced majority of 117–3–38, while the 16th such poll in 2007 was 184–4, with the Marshall Islands and Palau joining the United States and Israel in opposition. In actions reflecting Washington's lack of political consensus, President Bill Clinton in October 1995 eased a number of constraints, including certain impediments to travel and communication, despite the approval, only days before, of a congressional bill to tighten the embargo.

Earlier, a crisis had arisen over Cuban boat people. Castro, in evident frustration with U.S. intransigence over the embargo, announced in August 1994 that Cubans would no longer be prevented from leaving. More than 13,000 promptly did so (more than the total for the preceding decade). President Clinton reacted by declaring that Cubans arriving in Florida would be accorded the same treatment as Haitians in being denied automatic refugee status. The crisis eased late in the month when Clinton endorsed bilateral talks on "legal, orderly, and safe migration," and on September 9 an agreement was concluded whereby Havana would reintroduce restrictions on "unsafe departures," while the United States would move toward compliance with a 1984 agreement to issue up to 20,000 entry visas a year. The status of about 22,000 Cubans being held at the U.S. naval base at Guantánamo Bay, Cuba, was eventually resolved in early May 1995, with Washington agreeing to admit them to the United States, while Havana agreed to accept the return of any further migrants attempting to reach the United States by sea.

During 1998 the Castro regime participated in a number of initiatives designed to end its diplomatic isolation. Pope John Paul II made a historic visit to the island in January, and in March Havana announced that it would launch negotiations to become the 16th member of Caricom (Caribbean Community) and expressed an interest in becoming a member of the African, Caribbean, and Pacific (ACP) organization affiliated with the European Union (EU). In early April Spain restored relations that had been severed 16 months earlier, and later in the month Jean Chrétien made the first visit to Cuba by a Canadian prime minister. That summer a repatriation agreement was concluded with the Bahamas, and President Castro embarked on state visits to Jamaica, Barbados, Grenada, and the Dominican Republic. Thereafter, in what was viewed as a harbinger of return to the regional community, Cuba was admitted to full membership in the Latin American Integration Association (ALADI) on November 6.

Relations with the United States in late 1999 and the first half of 2000 were dominated by a custody battle over Elián GONZALEZ, whose mother and stepfather were among 11 Cuban nationals who drowned in an attempt to reach Florida on November 25, 1999. Despite demands by his natural father, Juan Miguel GONZALEZ, that Elián be returned to Cuba, relatives in Miami obtained a temporary custody order. In March 2000 a federal court effectively upheld a decision by the U.S. Immigration and Naturalization Service (INS) to send the boy back to Cuba, and on April 6 Juan Miguel arrived to claim his son. The two were reunited after INS agents had forcibly seized Elián in the early morning of April 22 and remained secluded thereafter in Washington, D.C., until June 28, when the U.S. Supreme Court refused to preclude their embarking for Havana.

On April 12, 2000, President Castro called for abolition of the International Monetary Fund (IMF) in an attack on the global capitalistic system during a Group of 77 summit in Havana. Cuba withdrew its ACP application, 15 days later, after the EU had voted with the United States in favor of a UN resolution that criticized Cuba's record on human rights.

Russian President Vladimir Putin visited Havana in December 2000, the first such visit by a Russian leader since the collapse of the Soviet Union. The trip was described as an effort to "mend the ravaged relations" between the two countries, and several cooperation agreements were signed. Diplomatically, little reference was made to the estimated $20 billion Soviet-era debt still owed by Cuba, although several partially completed projects envisioned by the earlier lending were reportedly scrapped.

At U.S. insistence, Cuba was excluded from the Summit of the Americas held in Quebec, Canada, in April 2001, which endorsed establishment of the Free Trade Agreement of the Americas (FTAA), in which Cuba was also not permitted to participate. When former U.S. president Jimmy Carter traveled to Cuba in May 2002, the U.S. administration of President George W. Bush criticized Carter for his suggestion that Washington consider ending the embargo. Among other things, Carter met with Cuban dissident Oswaldo PAYA, who had attracted international attention by submitting a petition to the National Assembly calling for a national referendum on the extension of political freedom.

Relations with the United States deteriorated in 2003, even though U.S. food sales to Cuba surged and, despite retention of the embargo for most commodities, the United States by early 2004 had become Cuba's seventh-largest trading partner. In June 2004 the Bush administration announced a series of measures drastically increasing restrictions on travel to the island. Under the new rules, Cuban Americans could visit only once every three years, instead of once a year, and more stringent limits were imposed on the amount of cash and baggage that could be carried.

By contrast, a number of U.S. congressional delegations have traveled to Cuba, the largest a ten-member bipartisan group headed by Rep. Jeff FLAKE that visited Havana on December 15–17, 2006. Upon his return, Flake asserted that Castro's illness was an opportunity for the two countries to become reengaged, while warning that in the event of the Cuban leader's death, "the chaos that many [have] predicted isn't going to happen."

In a slap at the United States, Cuba in early 2006 won a seat on the recently launched UN Human Rights Council, formed as successor to the discredited UN Commission on Human Rights, which in April 2004, by a margin of one vote, had approved a motion censuring Cuba for human rights abuses.

While Raúl Castro reportedly has not left the island since taking power in July 2006, an increasing number of foreign dignitaries have visited from China, Jamaica, Vietnam, Uruguay, Venezuela, and Brazil, including Brazilian president Luiz Ignacio "Lula" da SILVA. At the same time an increasing number of Cuban officials are traveling abroad on official delegations. On June 19, 2008, the EU defied the United States and voted to conditionally lift sanctions on Cuba. (While that move was meant to encourage reforms, according to news reports, Cuban police arrested several dissidents within hours after the announcement.)

Relations with the United States have remained rocky at best. In 2008 the U.S. Congress voted to increase United States Agency for International Development (USAID) funding for democracy promotion in Cuba to $45.7 million for fiscal year 2009, five times the previous funding levels. Tensions between the United States and Cuba heightened in May 2008 after Cuba accused top U.S. embassy officials in Havana of passing money to dissidents on the island. The United States, for its part, said the money was for humanitarian purposes. Following the inauguration of U.S. president Barack Obama in 2009, a shift in U.S. policy began to occur, most notably the easing of some travel restrictions between the two countries (see Current issues, below).

In June 2009 an American couple was charged with spying in U.S. federal court for allegedly having turned over government secrets to Cuban agents over the past 30 years by "using a shortwave radio, by swapping carts at a grocery store, and in at least one face-to-face meeting with former Cuban leader Fidel Castro in Cuba," according to news reports.

Current issues. Despite being publicly absent for a year and a half, Fidel Castro was reelected to the assembly following the January 20, 2008 poll. On February 19, just four days before the Council of State was to announce its choice for president, he published a letter in the state-owned newspaper withdrawing himself from consideration for the presidency, leaving the council open to nominate his brother Raúl.

Beginning in February 2008, Raúl Castro announced a series of minor reforms aimed at enhancing an individual's ability to make and spend money. Shortly after taking office Raúl signed two international human rights treaties that his brother had refused to sign; including one that guarantees numerous political rights denied under the regime of Fidel Castro. The new administration also encouraged unprecedented debate and moved to address some of the public's concerns, such as the substandard transportation system. However, much of the economic and political progress was derailed by the three hurricanes that struck the island in 2008, which posed the first major challenge to the administration of. Raúl Castro.

Soon after Raúl Castro's ascension to power, international attention turned to the possibility of political reform, but such speculation was rebuffed by Raúl. He, subsequently bolstered the communist system by placing loyalists in key cabinet positions in 2009, removing ten members, including Vice President Carlos LAGE Dávila and Foreign Minister Felipe PEREZ Roque. Their dismissal, along with that of another PCC official, all of whom had extensive international contacts and was deemed by observers to be reformers, was regarded as a move to purge the government of *Fidelistas* loyal to the hard-line of Fidel rather than the militaristic and seemingly reformist ways of Raul. Days later, however, Fidel stated his support for the changes and claimed that he had, indeed, been consulted.

On a positive note, remittances and travel from Cuban-Americans living in the United States increased dramatically in 2009 after U.S. president Obama eased travel restrictions for Americans with family members in Cuba and promised to review U.S. policy toward the country, In response, Raúl Castro agreed that the two leaders should meet, stating that everything—including human rights and democracy—was open for discussion. An open rift between the Castro brothers developed shortly thereafter, when Fidel reinterpreted his brother's message to exclude certain topics from the diplomatic agenda. Officials of the two countries began meeting informally in Washington in April.

In June 2009 the Organization of American State's (OAS) voted to lift the ban on Cuba's membership imposed in 1962. Before full reintegration into the regional organization would be permitted, however, Cuba was required to comply with various stipulations for a democratic government and respect for human rights. Cuba, for its part, had not been advocating its return to the OAS. The government issued a statement expressing its appreciation, but reiterated its accusations that the OAS played a role in U.S. hostility toward Cuba over many decades.

Meanwhile, the government reasserted that whatever steps were taken toward economic liberation should not be interpreted as political reform. The crackdown on dissidents continued, when in May police disrupted a meeting of about 30 dissidents, 17 of whom were briefly detained for allegedly maintaining connections to the U.S. embassy and planning a protest on the U.S. Independence Day, July 4. Among those arrested were three of the president's most vocal critics, including Martha Beatriz ROQUE Cabello (see Dissident Groups under Political Parties and Groups, below). In June police carried out a series of raids in Havana, arresting several homosexuals and prostitutes.

POLITICAL PARTIES AND GROUPS

Communist Party of Cuba (*Partido Comunista Cubano*—PCC). The country's only authorized political party, the PCC, is a direct descendant of the Rebel Army and the 26th of July Movement (*Movimiento 26 de Julio*), which constituted Fidel Castro's personal political following during the anti-Batista period. The organizational revolution began in 1961 with the formation of the Integrated Revolutionary Organizations (*Organizaciones Revolucionarias Integradas*—ORI), which included the Popular Socialist Party (*Partido Socialista Popular*—PSP), the 26th of July Movement, and the Revolutionary Directorate (*Directorio Revolucionario*—DR). The ORI was transformed into the United Party of the Cuban Socialist Revolution (*Partido Unido de la Revolución Socialista Cubana*—PURSC) in 1963, the latter being redesignated as the PCC in 1965. The first PCC congress was held December 17–22, 1975, and the second December 17–20, 1980. The third congress, which held its first session February 4–7, 1986, reconvened November 30–December 2, primarily to discuss a campaign aimed at the "rectification of mistakes and negative tendencies." The rectification campaign received added emphasis at an extraordinary plenum on February 16, 1990, during which the Central Committee reiterated its commitment to one-party Marxism-Leninism, "adapted to Cuban mentality, history and traditions."

During its fourth congress, held in Santiago de Cuba October 10–14, 1991, the PCC endorsed direct election to the National Assembly, dropped a requirement that only atheists could become party members, abolished the party Secretariat and the appointment of alternates to other party organs, and approved a substantially restructured Politburo from which five existing members were excluded. In July 1994 numerous changes in provincial leaders were announced as part of a revamping of political cadres. The party's fifth congress was held in Havana October 8–10, 1997.

At a Plenary Party Meeting on July 1, 2006, a new 12-member Executive Committee was launched, seemingly as a resuscitation of the former Secretariat. In addition, seven additions to the Central Committee were announced, including Francisco SOBERÓN Valdés, president of the National Bank, and six provincial first secretaries. Raúl Castro announced that the next Plenary Party Meeting would be held in late 2009 to evaluate the future of party policies.

First Secretary: Dr. Fidel CASTRO Ruz.

Acting General Secretary, Second Secretary: Gen. Raúl CASTRO Ruz (President, Council of State and Council of Ministers).

Other Members of Politburo: Ricardo ALARCON de Quesada (President, National Assembly), Juan ALMEIDA Bosque (Vice President, Council of State), José Ramón BALAGUER Cabrera (Minister of Public Health), Concepción CAMPA Huergo (Director, Finlay Institute), Miguel Mario Diaz CANEL Bermúdez (First Secretary, Villa Clara Provincial Committee), Lt. Gen. Julio CASAS Regueiro (First Deputy Minister, Revolutionary Armed Forces), Gen. Leopoldo CINTRA Frías (Chief, Western Army), Gen. Abelardo COLOMÉ Ibarra (Vice President, State Council; Interior Minister), Misael ENAMORADO Dager (First Secretary, Las Tunas Provincial Committee), Gen. Ramon ESPINOSA Martín (Chief, Eastern Army), Estebán LAZO Hernández (Vice President, State Council), José Ramón MACHADO Ventura (First Vice President, Council of State), Abel Enrique PRIETO Jiménez (Culture Minister), Lt. Gen. Ulises ROSALES del Toro

(Sugar Minister), Pedro ROSS Leal (Ambassador to Angola), Pedro SAEZ Montejo (First Secretary, Havana City Provincial Committee), Jorge Luis SIERRA Cruz (Transportation Minister), Yadira GARCIA Vera (Basic Industry Minister), Ramiro Valdés Menéndez (Information and Communications Minister), Salvador Antonio Valdés Mesa (Secretary General, Confederation of Cuban Workers), Alvaro López Miera (Vice-Minister and Chief of the General Staff, Revolutionary Armed Forces).

Dissident Groups:

There are numerous dissident groups that tend to fluctuate, in part as their leaders are jailed or released. Many have appealed, without success, for official recognition. As of early 2007 about 365 such groups had joined an **Assembly to Promote the Civil Society in Cuba** (*Asamblea para Promover la Sociedad Civil en Cuba*), led by Martha Beatriz Roque Cabello. The most visible dissident group is ***Las Damas de Blanco*** (The Ladies in White), also led by Roque.

LEGISLATURE

A unicameral **National Assembly of People's Power** (*Asamblea Nacional del Poder Popular*) was convened, with a five-year term, on December 2, 1976, following elections (the first since 1958) to municipal assemblies, which in turn had elected delegates to both provincial and national legislative bodies. A similar procedure was used to elect assemblies that convened in December 1981 and December 1986. In July 1991 the assembly voted to extend its existing mandate by one year to consider reform proposals within the one-party context.

The second direct election to the nationwide body was held on January 11, 1998, coincident with replenishment of the provincial assemblies. All 601 candidates approved by the Communist Party of Cuba received the 50 percent favorable vote required for election. (The assembly had been enlarged from 589 to 601 members for the balloting; however, when the new body convened, its membership was reported to be 595.) In the most recent balloting on January 20, 2008, an increased total of 614 members were elected to the assembly.

President: Ricardo ALARCON de Quesada.

CABINET

[as of June 11, 2009]

President, Council of State and Council of Ministers	Raúl Castro Ruz
First Vice President, Council of Ministers	José Ramón Machado Ventura
Vice Presidents, Council of Ministers Executive Committee	José Ramon Fernández Alvarez
	Gen. Pedro Miret Prieto
	Marino Alberto Murillo Jorge
	Osmany Cienfuegos Gorriarán
	Ricardo Cabrisas Ruiz
	Ulises Rosales Toro
	Ramiro Valdés Menéndez
	José Luis Sierra Cruz
Ministers	
Agriculture	Ulises Rosales del Toro
Auditing and Control	Gladys Maria Bejarano Portera [f]
Basic Industry	Yadirá García Vera [f]
Construction	Fidel Fernando Figueroa de la Paz
Culture	Abel Enrique Prieto Jiménez
Domestic Trade	Jacinto Angulo Prado
Economy and Planning	Marino Alberto Murillo Jorge
Education	Ena Elsa Velázquez Cobiella [f]
Finance and Prices	Lina Olinda Pedraza Rodriguez [f]
Food and Fishing	Maria del Carmen Concepción Gonzalez [f]
Foreign Relations	Bruno Eduardo Rodriguez Parrilla
Foreign Trade	Rodrigo Malmierca Díaz
Higher Education	Juan Vela Valdes
Information and Communications	Ramiro Valdés Menéndez
Interior	Gen. Abelardo Colomé Ibarra
Iron, Steel, and Engineering Industry	Salvador Pardo Cruz
Justice	María Ester Reus González [f]
Labor and Social Security	Margarita Marlene Gonzalez Fernandez [f]
Light Industry	José Silvano Hernández Bernárdez
Public Health	José Ramón Balaguer Cabrera
Revolutionary Armed Forces	Julio Casas Regueiro
Science, Technology, and Environment	Jose Miguel Miyar Barruecos
Sugar Industry	Luis Manuel Ávila González
Tourism	Col. Manuel Marrero Cruz
Transportation	Jorge Luis Sierra Cruz
President, Central Bank of Cuba	Ernesto Medina Villaveirán

[f] = female

Note: All cabinet members are members of the PCC.

COMMUNICATIONS

The press is censored and all channels of communication are under state control.

Slight advances in freedom of the press were seen in 2008 in the *Juventud Rebelde*, which published dissenting op-ed pieces for a brief period. However, that same year Cuban authorities denied dissident blogger Yoani Sánchez permission to travel to Spain to accept an award for digital journalism, further deflating any prospects for major political reform. Since March 2008 Fidel Castro has published "Reflections," or op-ed style articles, in *Granma*, commenting on political issues in Cuba and throughout the world. On several occasions Fidel has used his reflections to show either his support for or disapproval of his brother (and current Cuban leader) Raúl Castro's policies. Some 23 dissident journalists remained in detention in 2009, after having been arrested years earlier.

"The Cuban government continues to restrict nearly all avenues of political dissent, strictly limiting freedom of expression, association, assembly, movement, and the press," the international Human Rights Watch reported in 2009.

Press. The following newspapers are published in Havana, unless otherwise noted: *Granma,* official PCC organ, morning and weekly editions; *Juventud Rebelde,* organ of the Communist Youth; *Los Trabajadores,* labor-oriented; *Tribuna de la Habana; Adelante* (Camagüey); *Sierra Maestra* (Santiago de Cuba); *Vanguardia* (Santa Clara). Circulation figures are currently unknown because of the introduction of restrictions in the availability of newsprint to all papers (including party organs) in late 1990. In addition, it was announced in February 1991 that *Granma* would thenceforth be issued only from Tuesday to Saturday, while *Juventud Rebelde* and *Los Trabajadores* would appear only on Sunday and Monday, respectively.

News agencies. The domestic facilities are the government-controlled *Prensa Latina* and *Agencia de Información Nacional* (AIN). A large number of foreign agencies maintain offices in Havana.

Broadcasting and computing. Broadcasting is controlled by the Ministry of Communications and the *Instituto Cubano de Radio y Televisión.* There are five national radio networks (classical music, instrumental music, general entertainment, music and sports, and 24-hour news) in addition to short-wave service provided by *Radio Habana, Cuba;* about 50 TV stations operate throughout the country. As of 2008 there were 129.4 Internet users per 1,000 inhabitants.

In March 1994 an independent panel established by the U.S. Congress recommended changes in television broadcasts to Cuba, including conversion of TV Martí transmissions from VHF (confined to predawn hours because of a requirement under international law not to interfere with local programming) to UHF (thus affording prime-time programming because Cuba did not use the latter channels).

INTERGOVERNMENTAL REPRESENTATION

There are, at present, no diplomatic relations between Cuba and the United States. On September 1, 1977, however, a U.S. interest section was established in the Swiss Embassy in Havana; concurrently, a Cuban interest section was established in the Czech Embassy in Washington, D.C., which moved to the Swiss Embassy after the post–Communist Czech government announced in early 1990 that it no longer wished to serve as Havana's "protecting power" in the United States.

Permanent Representative to the UN: Pedro Núñez MOSQUERA.

IGO Memberships (Non-UN): ACS, ALADI, Grupo del Rio, Interpol, NAM, OAS, OPANAL, PCA, SELA, WCO, WTO.

CYPRUS

Republic of Cyprus
Kypriaki Dimokratia (Greek)
Kıbrıs Cumhuriyeti (Turkish)

Political Status: Independent republic established August 16, 1960; member of the Commonwealth since March 13, 1961; under ethnic Greek majority regime until coup led by Greek army officers and subsequent Turkish invasion on July 20, 1974; Turkish Federated State proclaimed February 13, 1975, in Turkish-controlled (northern) sector; permanent constitutional status under negotiation (currently suspended) despite proclamation of independent Turkish Republic of Northern Cyprus (TRNC) on November 15, 1983.

Area: 3,572 sq. mi. (9,251 sq. km.), embracing approximately 2,172 sq. mi. (5,625 sq. km.) in Greek-controlled (southern) sector and 1,400 sq. mi. (3,626 sq. km.) in Turkish-controlled (northern) sector.

Population: 819,000 (2008E), not including the Turkish-occupied region, from which Nicosia in 2001 excluded some 115,000 recent settlers in arriving at a figure of 87,900.

Major Urban Centers (Urban Areas, 2005E): NICOSIA/LEFKOSÍA (224,000, excluding Turkish sector), Limassol/Lemesós (175,000), Larnaca/Lárnax (77,000), Paphos/Néa Páfos (54,000). In 1995, city names were changed by the government as part of a campaign to standardize them in accordance with their Greek pronunciation; however, both names are accorded official status.

Official Languages: Greek, Turkish.

Monetary Unit: Euro (market rate December 1, 2009: 1 euro = $1.51US). In the wake of its accession to the European Union in May 2004, Cyprus on January 1, 2008, adopted the euro to replace the Cyprus pound as its official currency.

President: Dimitrios (Dimitris) CHRISTOFIAS (Progressive Party of the Working People); elected in second-round popular balloting on February 24, 2008, and inaugurated for a five-year term on February 29, succeeding Tassos PAPADOPOULOS (Democratic Party); formed new government on February 29, 2008.

Vice President: Vacant. Rauf R. DENKTAŞ, then president of the Turkish Republic of Northern Cyprus (see article on Cyprus: Turkish Sector), was elected vice president by vote of the Turkish Community in February 1973, but there has been no subsequent vice-presidential balloting.

THE COUNTRY

Settled by Greeks and Phoenicians in antiquity, the island of Cyprus formed a part of the Roman and the Byzantine Empires. It was conquered by the Crusaders in 1191 and the Ottoman Empire in 1571, placed under British administration in 1878, and annexed by Britain in 1914. Cyprus has been independent since 1960 (although de facto partitioned since 1974). The largest island in the eastern Mediterranean, it supports diverse and often antagonistic ethnic groups and traditions. About 78 percent of the population speaks Greek and belongs to the Orthodox Church, while about 18 percent is Turkish-speaking Muslim; adherents of other religions account for approximately 4 percent.

Although Cyprus was historically an agricultural country, the Greek Cypriot rural sector presently employs only about 13 percent of the total labor force and contributes a small and decreasing percent of GDP (the corresponding Turkish Cypriot figures being 25 and 12 percent, respectively). Nonetheless, vegetables, fruits, nuts, and wine rank with clothing and footwear as leading exports. Following the de facto partition of the island into Greek and Turkish sectors in 1974, rebuilding in the south emphasized manufacturing of nondurable consumer goods, while the more severely damaged north has relied on its citrus groves, mines, and tourist facilities as well as on direct budgetary assistance from Turkey (estimated at around 20 percent of budgeted expenditure in recent years). Whereas 70 percent of predivision productive resources had been located in the north (including 80 percent of the island's citrus groves and 60 percent of tourist installations), the postdivision southern economy rapidly outdistanced that of the north, achieving consistently high annual growth rates and virtually full employment. In addition to developing tourism and agriculture, Greek Cyprus diversified into financial, shipping, and other services, becoming a major offshore banking center and suffering only a temporary downturn as a result of the 1990–1991 Gulf crisis.

The economy performed well in the first half of the 1990s, growth averaging more than 4 percent annually and unemployment remaining negligible. However, disturbances along the dividing line between the Greek Cypriot and Turkish Cypriot territories in 1996 led to a decline in tourism, the collateral slowdown in economic growth being exacerbated by the effect of drought in 1996–1997 on agricultural production. Subsequently, the economic focus was on efforts to harmonize policies in areas such as taxation, customs, and government spending with those of the European Union (EU), with which Cyprus began conducting formal accession negotiations in 1998. With one of the strongest economies among the EU candidate states, Cyprus completed 24 of 29 chapters in the EU accession process by late 2001. However, some economic slowdown was noted, mainly due to the global recession and declining tourism.

GDP grew by 4.1 percent in 2001, 2.1 percent in 2002, and 1.9 percent in 2003. To join the EU, the government initiated broad reforms in the banking sector and agreed to raise taxes on its offshore financial companies. Accession to the EU on May 1, 2004, was seen as providing substantial opportunities for economic growth, although the unresolved political division of the island continued to be a significant complication. In 2004 GDP grew by 3.5 percent, with inflation (2.5 percent) and unemployment (3.4 percent) remaining well below European averages. In addition, by that time per capita annual income had reportedly reached about 80 percent of EU norms. Government priorities included deficit reduction (in part through pension reform and wage constraint for public sector workers) and overall labor market reform.

In 2007 the International Monetary Fund (IMF) reported that Cyprus's economy continued to recover from its "weak performance" of four years ago, citing low inflation (2.5 percent), a significant deficit reduction, and a higher standard of living. Growth in housing and tourism helped boost annual GDP growth to 3.8 percent. Similar annual growth was recorded in 2008, owing in large part to gains in the manufacturing, electricity, gas, and water sectors.

In the wake of the global financial crisis, tourism was expected to decline significantly in 2009, adversely affecting Cyprus's economy, with annual growth of about 0.3 percent forecast, though growth was stronger, at 2 percent, in the first quarter.

The northern economy (for which reliable figures are scarce) appears to have made only limited progress since 1974, being hard hit by the collapse in 1990 of the Polly Peck International fruit-packaging and tourism conglomerate (which had accounted for a third of the Turkish Republic of Northern Cyprus's [TRNC] GDP and 60 percent of its exports) and by external rulings banning imports from the TRNC as an unrecognized entity. The TRNC announced a five-year plan for economic development in 1997, although progress appeared to continue to depend on a resolution of the political statement on the island. Meanwhile, aid from Turkey remained the major support for the TRNC,

which, by using the Turkish lira as its unit of currency, has been forced to deal with rapid inflation, unlike the Greek Cypriot sector.

GOVERNMENT AND POLITICS

Political background. The conflict between Greek and Turkish Cypriot aspirations shaped the political evolution of Cyprus both before and after the achievement of formal independence on August 16, 1960. Many Greek Cypriots had long agitated for *enosis,* or the union of Cyprus with Greece; most Turkish Cypriots, backed by the Turkish government, consistently rejected such demands, opposed the termination of British rule in 1960, and advocated division of the island into Greek and Turkish sectors. Increased communal and anti-British violence after 1955 culminated in the Zurich and London compromise agreements of 1959–1960, which provided for an independent Cyprus guaranteed by Greece, Turkey, and Britain and instituted stringent constitutional safeguards for the protection of the Turkish community. These agreements expressly prohibited either union with Greece or partition of the island between Greece and Turkey.

The government of Archbishop MAKARIOS proposed numerous constitutional changes in November 1963, including revision of articles considered inviolable by the Turkish Cypriots. The proposals led to the outbreak of communal conflict, the withdrawal of Turkish Cypriots from the government, Turkish air raids and invasion threats, and, in 1964, the establishment of the UN Force in Cyprus (UNFICYP), whose mandate was thereafter regularly extended for six-month periods by the Security Council. Most Turkish Cypriots were forced to move to UNFICYP-protected enclaves. Further conflict broke out in 1967, nearly precipitating war between Greece and Turkey.

Following the 1967 violence, Turkish Cypriots moved to implement an administration for their segment of the island. This organization, known as the Turkish Cypriot Provisional Administration, constituted a de facto government in the Turkish communities. The Turkish Cypriot withdrawal also meant that from 1967 until the Turkish military intervention in July 1974 the prime conflicts were between the Makarios regime and radicals in the Greek community (led, until his death in January 1974, by Gen. Georgios GRIVAS).

On July 15, 1974, the Greek Cypriot National Guard, commanded by Greek army officers, launched a coup against the Makarios government and installed a Greek Cypriot newspaper publisher and former terrorist, Nikos Georgiades SAMPSON, as president following the archbishop's flight from the island. Five days later, Turkish troops were dispatched to northern Cyprus, bringing some 1,400 square miles (39 percent of the total area) under their control before agreeing to a cease-fire. On July 23 the Sampson government resigned and the more moderate presiding officer of the Cypriot House of Representatives, Glafcos CLERIDES, was sworn in as acting president. On the same day, the military government of Greece fell, and on July 25 representatives of Britain, Greece, and Turkey met in Geneva in an effort to resolve the Cyprus conflict. An agreement consolidating the cease-fire was concluded on July 30, but the broader issues were unresolved when the talks collapsed on August 14 and the Turkish invasion was resumed, before a final cease-fire was proclaimed on August 16. Upon his return to Cyprus and resumption of the presidency on December 7, Makarios rejected Turkish demands for geographical partition of the island, although he had earlier indicated a willingness to give the Turks increased administrative responsibilities in their own communities.

On February 13, 1975, Turkish leaders in the occupied northern sector proclaimed a Turkish Federated State of Cyprus (see map) with Rauf DENKTAŞ, the nominal vice president of the republic, as president. Although the action was immediately denounced by both President Makarios and Greek Prime Minister Karamanlis, the formation of a Turkish Cypriot Legislative Assembly was announced on February 24.

Extensive negotiations between Greek and Turkish representatives were held in Vienna in April 1977, following a meeting between Makarios and Denktaş in February. Although it was revealed that the more recent Greek proposals embraced the establishment of a bicommunal federal state, the Makarios government insisted that only 20 percent of the island's area be reserved for Turkish administration, while the Turks countered with demands that would entail judicial parity and a presidency to rotate between Greek and Turkish chief executives.

Archbishop Makarios died on August 3, 1977, and was succeeded, as acting president, by Spyros KYPRIANOU, who was elected on August 31 to fill the remaining six months of the Makarios term. Following the kidnapping of Kyprianou's son on December 14 by right-wing extremists, Clerides withdrew as a contender for the presidency, and Kyprianou became the only candidate at the close of nominations on January 26, 1978. As a result, the election scheduled for February 5 was canceled, Kyprianou being installed for a five-year term on March 1. In April 1982 the two government parties, the Democratic Party (*Dimokratiko Komma*—DIKO) and the (Communist) Progressive Party of the Working People (*Anorthotiko Komma Ergazomenou Laou*—AKEL), agreed to support Kyprianou for reelection in February 1983.

In a three-way race that involved Clerides and Vassos LYSSARIDES, the leader of the United Democratic Union of Cyprus–Socialist Party (*Ethniki Dimokratiki Enosi Kyprou–Sosialistiko Komma*—EDEK-SK), who technically withdrew on January 4, Kyprianou won reelection on February 13, 1983, securing 57 percent of the vote. On November 15, the Turkish Cypriot Legislative Assembly unanimously approved the declaration of an independent TRNC.

President Kyprianou and Turkish Cypriot leader Denktaş met at UN headquarters January 17–20, 1985, for their first direct negotiations in five years. Prior to the meeting, the two had endorsed a draft proposal to establish a federal republic that entailed substantial territorial concessions by the Turkish Cypriots and the removal of foreign troops from the island. Although UN Secretary General Javier Pérez de Cuéllar declared that the gap had "never been so narrow" between the two sides, the talks collapsed after Kyprianou reportedly characterized the plan as no more than an "agenda." Subsequently, the government's coalition partner, AKEL, joined with the opposition Democratic Rally (*Dimokratikos Synagermos*—DISY) in blaming Kyprianou for the breakdown in the talks and calling for his resignation as president.

At the conclusion of a bitter debate on the president's negotiating posture, the House of Representatives voted unanimously on November 1, 1985, to dissolve itself, paving the way for an early legislative election. In the balloting on December 8, Kyprianou's DIKO gained marginally (though remaining a minority grouping), while the opposition failed to secure the two-thirds majority necessary to enact a constitutional revision that would require the chief executive to conform to the wishes of the House.

Deprived of the backing of AKEL, Kyprianou placed third in first-round presidential balloting on February 14, 1988. In a runoff election one week later, Georgios VASSILIOU, a millionaire businessman running with AKEL endorsement, defeated Clerides by securing a 51.5 percent majority.

On August 24, 1988, presidents Vassiliou and Denktaş met in Geneva for the first summit talks between the two communities in over three years, with formal negotiations being resumed in September. By June 1989 deadlock had again been reached, an acceptance in principle by both sides of the UN-proposed concept of a bicommunal, bizonal federation under one sovereignty being negated by fundamental differences on implementation. More positively, in May 1989 both sides began the withdrawal of forces from 24 military posts along the central Nicosia/Lefkosía sector dividing the island.

A new round of UN-sponsored talks in February 1990 ended prematurely the following month when a demand by Denktaş for a "right of self-determination" was construed by Vassiliou as a demand for separate sovereignty. Relations were further exacerbated by the Greek Cypriot government's application in July for entry into the European Community (EC, subsequently the EU). Benefiting from association with Vassiliou's high negotiating profile, AKEL registered the biggest advance in legislative balloting on May 19, 1991, but DISY retained a narrow plurality as DIKO representation plummeted.

In 1992 the UN suggested a demarcation of Greek and Turkish sectors under a federal structure that would entail the transfer of about 25 percent of TRNC territory to Greek Cypriot administration. The plan was described as "totally unacceptable" by Denktaş, who warded off growing criticism from TRNC hard-liners by reiterating his self-determination/sovereignty demand for Turkish Cypriots. Also divided were the Greek Cypriots, with AKEL and DISY broadly supporting Vassiliou's acceptance of the UN plan, whereas DIKO and the EDEK-SK complained that the president was accepting effective partition. Because of the continuing deadlock, the UN Security Council in November proposed so-called confidence-building measures as the basis for an overall settlement, including troop reductions, small transfers of TRNC territory to UN administration, and the reopening of Nicosia international airport (closed since 1974). However, differences on these proposals proved to be as intractable as those on the fundamental issues.

Veteran DISY leader Clerides emerged as the surprise victor in Greek Cypriot presidential balloting on February 7 and 14, 1993, when Vassiliou (again backed by AKEL) was narrowly defeated in the runoff contest (50.3 to 49.7 percent). During the campaign the DISY leader's previous support for the Vassiliou line had mutated into forceful criticism, thus enabling DIKO and the EDEK-SK (whose joint candidate was eliminated in the first round) to swing behind Clerides in the second round. A new government appointed by Clerides on February 25 contained six DISY and five DIKO ministers.

Hopes that Clerides would break the deadlock in the Cyprus negotiations were quickly disappointed. On the other hand, because of continuing economic progress in Greek Cyprus, the administration went into legislative balloting on May 26, 1996, in a buoyant mood. DISY retained its narrow plurality of 20 seats, DIKO lost 1 of its 11, and AKEL managed only a 1-seat advance, to 19; the remaining seats went to the EDEK-SK, 5; and the new Free Democrats Movement (*Kinima ton Eleftheron Dimokraton*—KED), 2.

The DISY-DIKO coalition collapsed when the DIKO central committee decided to break from the government on November 4, 1997, after Clerides revealed his intention to seek reelection in the February 1998 elections. The five DIKO cabinet members who consequently resigned were replaced by nonparty ministers. There were seven candidates in the February 1998 presidential balloting: President Clerides; Georgios IACOVOU, an independent backed by AKEL and DIKO; Georgios Vassiliou, former president and the leader of the KED; Nikos ROLANDIS, leader of the Liberal Party (KP); Vassos LYSSARIDES, president of EDEK-SK; Nikolaos KOUTSOU of New Horizons (NO); and independent candidate Alexis GALANOS, who had broken from DIKO over its endorsement of Iacovou.

Iacovou led Clerides by a very slight margin in the first-round balloting (40.61 to 40.06 percent) on February 8, with Lyssarides finishing third with 10.59 percent. The EDEK-SK took no position regarding the runoff, but the other first-round contenders endorsed Clerides, who secured a 50.8 to 49.2 percent victory in the second round on February 15 at which a 94 percent turnout was reported. On February 28 Clerides announced a new "national unity" government comprising, in addition to DISY, the KP, EDEK-SK, United Democrats, and several DIKO "rebels." Among other things, the multiparty cabinet was reportedly designed to present a unified stance regarding EU membership and proposed reunification talks. However, the EDEK-SK resigned from the government in late 1998 as the result of a dispute regarding the proposed deployment of Russian missiles on the island (see Current issues, below).

In legislative balloting on May 27, 2001, AKEL secured a plurality of 20 seats, followed by DISY with 19. In presidential elections on February 16, 2003, Tassos PAPADOPOULOS of DIKO, campaigning on domestic political issues, won a first-round election with 51.5 percent of the vote. His new coalition cabinet was sworn in on March 1, 2003.

On July 14, 2003, after the breakdown of negotiations between the Greek and Turkish Cypriots over reunification, the Greek Cypriot House of Representatives unanimously approved EU entry. Greek Cypriots rejected the UN-brokered peace plan in a referendum on April 24, 2004, which meant that the Republic of Cyprus joined the EU on May 1, 2004 without a resolution of its political problem (see Current issues, below).

In the parliamentary elections of May 21, 2006, DIKO received 17.9 percent of the vote, up from 14.8 percent in 2001, while support for both AKEL and DISY declined somewhat. The president reshuffled the cabinet on June 8, with members of DIKO, AKEL, and KISOS (as the EDEK-SK had been renamed) predominating.

In the first round of presidential balloting on February 24, 2008, Ioannis Kassoulides won 33.51 percent of the vote and Dimitrios (Dimitris) CHRISTOFIAS, 33.29 percent. Papadopoulos, who received the fewest votes with 31.79 percent, was disqualified from the second round. DIKO and KISOS subsequently endorsed Christofias in exchange for a place in the incoming coalition government. In the second poll on February 24, 2008, Christofias won 53.37 percent of the vote to Kassoulides's 46.63 percent, marking the first time an AKEL candidate was elected. Christofias formed a new government that included members of AKEL, DIKO, and KISOS (formerly EDEK) on February 29, 2008

Constitution and government. The constitution of 1960, based on the Zürich and London agreements, provided for a carefully balanced system designed to protect both Greek Cypriot and Turkish Cypriot interests. A Greek president and a Turkish vice president, both elected for five-year terms, were to name a cabinet composed of representatives of both groups in specified proportions. Legislative authority was entrusted to a unicameral House of Representatives, with 35 Greek and 15 Turkish members to be elected by their respective communities. In addition, Greek and Turkish Communal Chambers were established to deal with internal community affairs. Collateral arrangements were made for judicial institutions, the army, and the police. Following the original outbreak of hostilities in 1963 and the consequent withdrawal of the Turkish Cypriots from the government, there were a number of changes, including merger of the police and gendarmerie, establishment of a National Guard, abolition of the Greek Communal Chamber, amendment of the electoral law, and modification of the judicial structure.

Subsequent to withdrawal, the Turkish community practiced a form of self-government under the Turkish Cypriot Provisional Administration, an extraconstitutional entity not recognized by the government. It formed a Turkish Cypriot Provisional Assembly composed of the 15 Turkish members of the national legislature and the 15 representatives to the Turkish Cypriot Communal Chamber. In early 1975 the Provisional Administration was reorganized as a Turkish Federated State in the northern sector of the island, followed by a unilateral declaration of independence in November 1983 (see article on Cyprus: Turkish Sector). From the December 1985 election the national membership of the House of Representatives was increased to 80 seats, although only the 56 Greek Cypriot seats were filled in that and subsequent contests.

Prior to the invasion by mainland Turkish forces, the island was divided into six administrative districts, each headed by an official appointed by the central government. Municipalities were governed by elected mayors.

Foreign relations. Following independence in 1960, Cyprus became a member of the UN and a number of other intergovernmental organizations. Cyprus joined the Non-Aligned Movement, and on several occasions Archbishop Makarios made diplomatic overtures toward third world countries, although even prior to the 1974 conflict, internal problems made it difficult for him to follow up on such initiatives. As a result of the events of 1974, the domestic situation became in large measure a function of relations with Greece and Turkey, two uneasy NATO partners whose range of disagreement has by no means been confined to Cyprus. Britain, because of its treaty responsibilities in the area and its sovereign bases on the island, has long played a major role in attempting to mediate the Cyprus dispute, while the United States, prior to the George H. W. Bush presidency, played a less active role. The intercommunal talks, held intermittently since 1975, were initiated at the request of the UN Security Council, which has assumed the principal responsibility for truce supervision through the UNFICYP.

In October 1987 the government concluded an agreement with the EC to establish a full customs union over a 15-year period commencing January 1, 1988; in July 1990 it submitted a formal application for full membership. In October 1993 the Council of Ministers of the EU called on the Brussels Commission to begin "substantive discussions" with Cyprus to prepare for accession negotiations. The result was agreement by the EU's Corfu summit in June 1994 that Cyprus would be included in the next round of enlargement negotiations due to begin in 1996 or 1997. Uncertainties remained, however, as to linkage between EU accession and resolution of the basic Cyprus question, especially in light of vehement opposition by both the TRNC and Turkey to the Greek Cypriots' unilateral pursuit of membership. (Formal negotiations regarding the accession of Cyprus to the EU were launched in March 1998, and Cyprus joined in 2004.)

Turkish Cypriot hostility to Greek Cypriot EU aspirations was compounded when the European Court of Justice ruled on July 5, 1994, that all EU imports from Cyprus would require authorization from the Greek Cypriot government, thus in effect banning direct trade between the EU and the Turkish sector. President Denktaş informed the UN Security Council on July 26 that resumption of the peace talks was contingent on cancellation of the court's ruling, while TRNC Assembly resolutions of late August called for defense and foreign policy coordination with Turkey and rejected a federal Cyprus solution as required by the UN, urging instead "political equality and sovereignty" for the Turkish sector.

Pursuant to an agreement of November 16, 1993, placing Cyprus within the "unified Greek defense space," joint Greek–Greek Cypriot military exercises were held for the first time in October 1994. Seven months later, President Clerides headed a visit to Athens by the Greek Cypriot National Council (consisting of the main party leaders) for a "unity" meeting with Greek government ministers. Concurrently, closer relations were established between the Greek Cypriot government and Russia, which in March 1995 informed Turkey of its firm commitment to a federal solution to the Cyprus problem in accordance with UN resolutions.

In 2007 Cyprus and Turkey were engaged in a dispute over oil and gas exploration rights in the Mediterranean granted to Egypt and Lebanon. Turkey had warned the latter countries that any agreements with Greek Cyprus also required discussion with the Turkish north. Egypt subsequently halted its agreement with Cyprus; Lebanon did not succumb to pressure from Turkey.

Current issues. Amid persistent deadlock in intercommunal negotiations, the Greek Cypriot took some comfort from the specific condemnations of Turkish Cypriot intractability that issued regularly from the UN secretary general and Security Council beginning in 1992. President Clerides subsequently adopted a tougher stance by categorically ruling out any formal talks on a "confederation" and insisting that further discussions be based on the UN-endorsed concept of a bicommunal federation preserving a single sovereignty.

While continuing to attach importance to U.S. and British mediation, the Greek Cypriot government gave increasing priority to the "EU route" to a settlement, believing that its application for full EU membership could yield a breakthrough in the deadlock. Under this scenario, the Turkish Cypriot would perceive the potential benefits of EU membership to the beleaguered northern economy and would accordingly be brought to accept a federal "one sovereignty" settlement as the Greek Cypriot application progressed. Besides, the EU would form an ideal anchor for the successful implementation of any settlement. However, such hopes were dashed in August 1996 when Greek Cypriot antipartition demonstrators clashed with Turkish soldiers and civilians after penetrating the UN buffer zone. Two protesters were killed by Turkish forces, causing outrage in the Republic of Cyprus and Greece. An international mediation effort to ease the tension between the two communities was subsequently launched by France, Germany, and the UK.

In response to a UN draft agreement for the establishment of a federal Cyprus in 1997, President Denktaş restated his demand that Cyprus suspend its application for EU membership before talks proceeded. The prospects for future rapprochement remained slim, as Denktaş met with the Turkish foreign affairs minister, İsmail Cem, and announced that a joint committee would be formed to implement "partial integration" between the TRNC and Turkey. In December the EU summit in Luxembourg included Cyprus among the six countries for whom formal membership negotiations would begin in the spring of 1998 (Turkey being pointedly excluded from the list), and the TRNC subsequently suspended all bicommunal activities. The Greek Cypriot government invited the TRNC to appoint representatives to the Cypriot team being established to negotiate with the EU; however, the Denktaş administration rejected the overture, reportedly out of concern (in part, at least) that it would be in a "subservient" position under such arrangements.

Tension between the Greek Cypriot government and the TRNC escalated sharply in late December 1998 when Clerides announced the impending deployment of Russian S-300 anti-aircraft missiles on Greek Cypriot soil. Turkey quickly threatened possible military intervention, and the EU said it would suspend accession talks with Cyprus if the plan was pursued. Consequently, Clerides agreed to have the missiles deployed instead on the Greek island of Crete, with Greece maintaining "operational control" of the weapons. Subsequently, the administration called upon the international community to bring greater pressure on Ankara and the TRNC to return to the bargaining table. Although both Washington and the UN pledged to intensify their mediation efforts, little hope for compromise appeared following nationalists' significant gains in April 1999 balloting in Turkey and no sentiment for a "unitary state" having surfaced in the TRNC.

Apparently in consonance with Greek-Turkish rapprochement (see articles on Turkey and Greece), the tension between Greek and Turkish Cypriots eased considerably after a major earthquake hit western Turkey in mid-August 1999, the Greek Cypriot government sending monetary and humanitarian aid to Turkey. However, the improved relations failed to produce any breakthrough in a series of UN proximity talks conducted through 2000. In what some saw as a compromise step, Denktaş in 2001 backed away from his insistence of Cypriot recognition of the TRNC as a precondition to resuming talks and proposed a "partnership republic" instead of confederation.

For most of 2002 periodic negotiations between the Greek and Turkish sides failed to produce tangible results. However, a report published in October by the European Commission announced that Cyprus, among others, had fulfilled the political criteria for admission to the EU and was expected to sign an accession treaty in the spring of 2003 in anticipation of membership in 2004. Consequently, international pressure intensified for resolution of the Turkish/Cypriot dispute. (Although the EU made it clear that Cyprus's accession was not contingent on a political settlement and that the EU was prepared, if necessary, to admit only the "Greek" part of Cyprus, it was clear that the preference was strong for the island's entry as a "unified entity.") In an effort to solve the deadlock, UN Secretary General Kofi Annan launched a comprehensive plan in early November, proposing a reunification plan in which the two component states would have equal status and substantial autonomy.

Central to Annan's plan was the return of property from the Turkish Cypriots to the Greek Cypriots and compensation for property losses in both communities. Annan's proposal envisioned a reduction of the TRNC from 36 percent of the island to 28.5 percent. The plan would displace 42,000 Turkish Cypriots and allow 85,000 Greek Cypriots to return to their former homes.

With the February 2003 presidential election of Tassos Papadopoulos, there was concern about a potential hardening of Greek Cypriot positions. Yet Papadopoulos declared his commitment to the UN plan. While the partial reopening of the "Green Line" on April 23 helped defuse tension and allowed refugees from both sides to visit their homes, little progress was realized through the talks.

In early 2004 Papadopoulos agreed to authorize UN Secretary General Kofi Annan to arbitration on unresolved issues within the revised UN reunification plan and present it to a national referendum. A few days before the referendum, Papadopoulos surprisingly made a strong appeal against the plan, demanding more concessions from the TRNC, particularly in regard to property reparations. Consequently, the plan was defeated by Greek Cypriots by a three-to-one margin on April 24, and, as a result, only the Greek Cypriot sector joined the EU on May 1. (Sixty-five percent of voters in the TRNC had supported the plan forwarded by UN Secretary General Annan.)

The UN-controlled border between the TRNC and the south opened to some trade and travel in 2004, although the TRNC government charged that the Greek Cypriot government was limiting trade from the north by its administrative requirements. Although bitterness continued on both sides, new reunification talks were launched in mid-2005, Papadopoulos arguing that the island was "too small" to remain divided. (See article on Cyprus: Turkish Sector for additional information on the reunification issue.)

In the May 2006 parliamentary elections, the mood of the voters reflected their rejection of the UN reunification plan as presented in 2004. Papadopoulos's DIKO gained a small increase in vote share compared to 2001 results, while parties, most notably DISY, that had backed the UN plan for reunification did not fare well. The elections included one Turkish Cypriot candidate, and for the first time since

1963, Turkish Cypriots living in the Greek-controlled part of the island were allowed to vote.

Meanwhile, Turkey's consideration for admission into the EU continued to influence politics and government activity in both Cyprus and the TRNC (see article on Turkey for details on its negotiations with the EU). In July 2006, under a "set of principles" mediated by the UN, Greek Cypriot and TRNC officials traded lists of bicommunal issues for discussion, the new effort coming on the heels of a meeting between presidents Papadopoulos and Talat in Nicosia several days earlier. In the TRNC, friction within the ruling coalition over reunification led to the collapse of the government in September and the establishment of a new coalition government (see article on Cyprus: Turkish Sector for details).

Bilateral north/south talks continued in 2007, consideration of the UN reunification plan having stalled. Goodwill gestures were advanced, including a meeting in Cyprus between the religious leaders of the Turkish and Greek Cypriot communities to try to promote reconciliation, the removal by Turkish Cypriots of a controversial footbridge erected in 2005 and the opening of a roadblock dividing Nicosia/Lefkosía at Ledra Street (Lokmacı Kapısı) by the Greek Cypriot government.

Despite expectations that AKEL would again support the candidacy of President Papadopoulos in the February 2008 presidential elections, AKEL leader Dimitrios (Dimitris) Christofias announced in July 2007 his decision to run for president. His candidacy was also supported by EDI. While the incumbent president Papadopoulos was supported by DIKO, KISOS, EVROKO, and the Green Party, DISY supported the candidacy of the former foreign minister and member of the European Parliament Ioannis KASSOULIDES and was joined by European Democracy (*Evropaiki Dimokratia*—EVRODI). In the first round of the presidential elections on February 24, 2008, Kassoulides secured 33.5 percent of votes and Christofias, 33.3 percent. Papadopoulos was disqualified from the second round after taking the lowest share, 31.8 percent. Following the results of the first round, DIKO and KISOS announced their support for Christofias in order to join the incoming government. In the second round on February 24, 2008, Christofias took 53.4 percent of the vote, while Kassoulides won 46.6 percent. The election of Christofias to the presidency marked a milestone in the history of the Republic of Cyprus, as this was the first time a leader of Cyprus's Communist Party, AKEL, was elected. The fact that AKEL has historically been the Greek Cypriot political party with the closest links with Turkish Cypriots raised hopes about the resolution of the Cyprus question under the Christofias administration. This seemed confirmed when, following protracted negotiations, the Nicosia/Lefkosía footbridge was removed and the Ledra Street roadblock crossing was reopened on April 3, 2008, through the first weeks of the Christofias administration, raising hopes for a breakthrough in ensuing negotiation.

Intercommunal negotiations were launched again on September 3, 2008, following a four-year hiatus, amid optimism fueled by what was viewed as Christofias's and Talat's moderate approach. Yet significant differences during negotiations made it unlikely that a breakthrough was imminent. Some of the thorniest issues, such as the constitution, were discussed, while others, including territorial arrangements, were not. The negotiations were expected to draw increasing international attention as Turkey's EU accession process was scheduled for review by the European Council late in the year, and the expiration of a deadline neared for Turkey to lift its embargo on Cypriot vessels and aircraft. Because of the embargo, Cyprus blocked the opening of some of the issues in EU-Turkey accession negotiations. Meanwhile, relations between AKEL and the junior coalition members were at times strained because of DIKO's and KISOS's opposition to Christofias's alleged willingness to make concessions to the Turkish Cypriots in the course of intercommunal negotiations. That same month, the escape of the notorious criminal Antonios KITTAS from a private hospital caused a major domestic political crisis, as details about his extremely lax treatment by prison authorities at the hospital were leaked. The minister of justice and public order, Kypros CHRYSOSTOMIDES, resigned, along with the leadership of the police. Kittas was subsequently rearrested in January 2009.

In 2009 attention turned to the controversial property issue in Cyprus when the European Court of Justice (ECJ) issued a ruling regarding a British couple who had bought and developed land in the town of Lapithos/Lapta. They were sued by the displaced owner of the property, who had not exercised effective control over it since 1974. In April the ECJ supported the earlier ruling of a Cypriot court that the British couple demolish their home, return the land, and pay damages, and further ruled that the order must be recognized and enforced by the EU even though the land in question is in the north of the island. This ruling strengthened Greek Cypriot positions on the property issues and was seen as the potential harbinger of similar cases.

Meanwhile, the global financial crisis inevitably developed as one of the top domestic issues. Yet despite the expected sharp fall in tourism, one of the country's major revenue sources, the Cypriot economy was deemed to be among the best-prepared in the Euro-zone to weather the crisis, due to its low indebtedness and unemployment.

POLITICAL PARTIES

Throughout the 14 years preceding the Turkish intervention, the Cypriot party system was divided along communal lines. As a result of population displacement, the Greek parties now function exclusively in the south, while the Turkish parties function in the north. All are headquartered within the divided city of Nicosia. The Greek parties are listed below (see article on Cyprus: Turkish Sector for Turkish parties).

Government Parties:

Progressive Party of the Working People (*Anorthotiko Komma Ergazomenou Laou*—AKEL). Organized in 1941 as the Communist Party of Cyprus, AKEL dominates the Greek Cypriot labor movement and claims a membership of about 15,000. Its support for President Kyprianou, withdrawn for a period in 1980 because of the latter's handling of "the national issue," was renewed in September when the government agreed to a renewal of intercommunal talks; it was again withdrawn as a result of the breakdown in talks at UN headquarters in January 1985. The party won 12 legislative seats in 1981 and 15 in 1985; it endorsed the candidacy of Georgios Vassiliou in 1988.

In January 1990 a number of dissidents, including 4 of the Politburo's 15 members, were dismissed or resigned in a controversy over democratic reforms that led to the creation of ADISOK (see below, under the EDE) by 5 of the party's (then) 15 parliamentarians. None was reelected in May 1991 balloting, in which AKEL representation increased to 18 seats. A further advance, to 19 seats (and 33 percent of the vote), was registered in May 1996. AKEL supported independent Georgios Iacovou in the February 1998 presidential poll. The party got a surprising victory in the May 2001 balloting with 34.7 percent of the vote and became the largest party in the legislature with 20 seats. AKEL, having supported DIKO candidate Papadopoulos in the 2003 presidential elections, received four posts in the new Council of Ministers.

In general, the party has supported a federal solution to the divided island, backing an independent, demilitarized Cyprus and rapprochement with Turkish Cypriots. However, it urged a "no" vote in the 2004 referendum on the proposed UN plan for reunification. AKEL's share of the vote dropped to 31.1 percent in the May 2006 parliamentary elections, resulting in a loss of two seats. Despite initial expectations that AKEL would support the re-election of President Papadopoulos, Secretary General Dimitrios (Dimitris) Christofias announced his own candidacy. On February 23, 2008, Christofias was elected president, thus becoming the first communist political leader to reach the highest office of the republic.

Leader: Dimitrios (Dimitris) CHRISTOFIAS (Secretary General and President of the Republic).

Democratic Party (*Dimokratiko Komma*—DIKO). The Democratic Party is a center-right grouping organized in 1976 as the Democratic Front to support President Makarios's policy of "long-term struggle" against the Turkish occupation of northern Cyprus. The leading component of the government alliance in the House of Representatives after the 1976 election, at which it won 21 seats, its representation fell to 8 seats in 1981. In December 1985 it obtained 16 seats (28 percent) in an enlarged House of 56 members, after its former coalition partner, AKEL, had supported a censure motion against then President Kyprianou. DIKO absorbed the Center Union (*Enosi Kentrou*—EK), a minor formation led by former chief intercommunal negotiator Tassos Papadopoulos, in February 1989. It won 11 legislative seats in 1991 and endorsed Clerides for the presidency in 1993, then slipped to 10 seats (on a 16.5 percent vote share) in May 1996.

The run-up to the February 1998 presidential election produced a serious split in DIKO, whose leadership formally endorsed (along with AKEL) the candidacy of independent Georgios Iacovou. Many DIKO members reportedly objected to that endorsement, and DIKO Vice President Alexis GALANOS presented himself as a candidate, securing 4 percent of the vote in the first round of balloting. Galanos (and, apparently, many of his backers) supported Clerides in the second round, and several DIKO "rebels" were appointed as independents to the new coalition government, with Galanos being named a presidential adviser. Galanos, a former president of the House of Representatives, was subsequently identified as the leader of a new Eurodemocratic Renewal Party.

DIKO's vote share fell to 14.8 percent in the May 2001 balloting and the party's legislative representation slipped to nine seats.

Kyprianou, former president of the republic and a founder of DIKO, stepped down as president of the party in 2000 due to ill health; he died in March 2002. Kyprianou was replaced by Tassos Papadopoulos, who adroitly gained the support of AKEL and the Social Democrats' Movement (KISOS) in the February 2003 presidential election with a campaign that emphasized the need for more concessions from the TRNC in negotiations for a permanent peace plan. He won the election with 51.5 percent of the vote.

DIKO urged a "no" vote in the 2004 referendum on the proposed UN reunification plan. It garnered a vote share of 17.9 percent in the May 2006 parliamentary balloting. In October 2006 Papadopoulos stepped down from DIKO presidency and was replaced by Marios KAROGIAN. Following the failure of Papadopoulos to reach the second round in the February 2008 presidential elections, DIKO supported the candidacy of Dimitrios (Dimitris) Christofias in the second round. Following Christofias' election, DIKO President Marios Karogian was elected president of the House of Representatives in accordance with the terms of the pre-second round agreement between DIKO and AKEL. Papadopoulos died in December 2008.

Following the formation of Christofias's coalition government, two factions formed within the party: those aligned with Karogian favored closer cooperation with AKEL and compromise in order to achieve a breakthrough in intercommunal negotiations, and those led by the elder son of the late Tassos Papadopoulos, Nikolaos (Nikolas) Papadopoulos, who opposed any deviations from the stance that had been supported by the Papadopoulos administration.

Leaders: Marios Karogian (President of the House of Representatives and Party President), Georgios KOLOKASIDES (Deputy President), Kyriakos KENEVEZOS (Secretary General).

Social Democrats' Movement (*Kinima Sosial-dimokraton*—KISOS). This grouping was formerly known as the Unified Democratic Union of Cyprus–Socialist Party (*Ethniki Dimokratiki Enosi Kyprou–Sosialistiko Komma*—EDEK-SK), a moderately left-of-center grouping that supported a unified and independent Cyprus. The EDEK-SK had concluded an electoral alliance with the Democratic Front and AKEL in 1976 but campaigned separately in 1981, its three representatives refusing to support the government after the new House convened. Its chair (and founder of the EDEK-SK), Vassos Lyssarides, campaigned for the presidency in 1983 as leader of a National Salvation Front; although announcing his withdrawal prior to the actual balloting as a means of reducing "polarization" within the Greek Cypriot community, he was nonetheless credited with obtaining a third place 9.5 percent vote share. The party obtained six legislative seats in 1985. Lyssarides ran fourth in the first round of the 1988 presidential poll, after which EDEK-SK threw its support to Georgios Vassiliou. The party improved to seven seats in the 1991 House election but fell back to five in May 1996 (on a 10 percent vote share). Lyssarides secured 10.6 percent of the votes in the first round of the February 1998 presidential balloting. Although the EDEK-SK did not endorse President Clerides in the second round (encouraging members to vote for the candidate of their choice), the party was given the defense and education portfolios in the subsequent coalition government. However, the EDEK-SK withdrew from the government following Clerides's decision to cancel the proposed deployment of Russian missiles on the island in December.

The party adopted its current name in 1999. In the 2001 legislative balloting, the party's vote share fell to 6.5 percent. KISOS supported DIKO candidate Tassos Papadopoulos in the 2003 presidential elections and received two posts in the new coalition government. The party, while backing a federal solution to reunification, urged a "no" vote in the 2004 referendum on the proposed UN reunification plan.

In the May 2006 parliamentary elections, KISOS's vote share was 8.9 percent, and it increased its number of seats to five. In the February 2008 presidential elections KISOS supported the candidacy of President Tassos Papadopoulos. When he was disqualified from the second round, KISOS shifted its support towards the AKEL candidate Dimitrios (Dimitris) Christofias. Christofias's election secured KISOS's participation in the new government. Yet major differences persisted regarding the resolution of the Cyprus question, as KISOS was thought to oppose any compromise solution close to the failed Annan Plan; that is, any solution with a clear bizonal, bicommunal character.

Leaders: Yiannakis OMIROU (President), Kyriakos MAVRONICOLAS (Deputy President), Vassos LYSSARIDES (Honorary President), Antonis KOUTALIANOS (General Secretary).

Opposition Parties:

Democratic Rally (*Dimokratikos Synagermos*—DISY). The Democratic Rally was organized in May 1976 by Glafcos Clerides following his resignation as negotiator for the Greek Cypriots in the intercommunal talks in Vienna. The Rally has long favored a strongly pro-Western orientation as a means of maintaining sufficient pressure on the Turks to resolve the communal dispute. It secured 24.1 percent of the vote in 1976 but won no legislative seats. Its fortunes were dramatically reversed in the 1981 balloting, at which it obtained 12 seats, with 7 more being added in 1985. The party absorbed the small New Democratic Alignment (*Nea Dimokratiki Parataxi*—NEDIPA), led by Alekos MIHAILIDES, prior to the 1988 presidential balloting, at which Clerides was defeated in the second round. The party won a plurality of 19 seats at the legislative election of May 1991, with an additional seat going to its coalition partner, the Liberal Party (*Komma Phileleftheron*—KP).

Glafcos Clerides withdrew from the party presidency upon being elected president of the republic in February 1993, following which he appointed a government of DISY and the Democratic Party. A DISY-Liberal alliance won 20 seats in the May 1996 election, with a vote share of 34 percent, all seats going to DISY candidates. In February 1998 the KP officially merged with DISY. The KP had been organized in 1986 by Nikos ROLANDIS (formerly a close associate of President Kyprianou), who supported Georgios Vassiliou in 1988. It secured one legislative seat as an electoral partner of DISY in 1991 but failed to retain it in 1996. Rolandis won less than 1 percent of the vote in the first round of the 1998 presidential balloting and, after throwing his support behind Clerides in the second round, was subsequently named to the February 1998 cabinet. In the first round of the February 2003 presidential elections, Clerides received 38.8 percent of the vote. The party supported the UN reunification proposal in advance of the 2004 referendum, in which Cypriot voters overwhelmingly rejected the UN plan. In 2005 dissidents opposed to the party's support of the UN reunification plan left to form a new party, EVROKO (see below), with disaffected members of other groups. This caused a serious crisis that questioned the cohesion of the party given its traditional right-wing political affiliation and the nationalist leanings of a large part of its electoral base, which was disaffected by the party's position in the 2004 referendum.

In the May 2006 parliamentary election, DISY secured 30.34 percent of the vote and lost 1 of its 19 seats. In the February 2008 presidential elections, DISY nominated Ioannis KASSOULIDES, former foreign minister of the Clerides administration and member of the European Parliament. In his electoral campaign, Kassoulides advocated a "European Cyprus," fully integrated into European institutions. In the first round of the elections, he surprisingly won the plurality of votes, leaving AKEL candidate Christofias second and disqualifying the incumbent president Papadopoulos. While the alliance between Christofias and Papadopoulos secured a rather comfortable victory for Christofias in the second round, Kassoulides's performance attested to the resilience of DISY, which recovered from the 2004 crisis to secure a central role in Cypriot politics. Following the formation of the AKEL-DIKO-KISOS government alliance, DISY remained the chief opposition party in parliament. Its criticism focused on issues of domestic politics, while the party appeared ready to endorse a compromise plan aimed at breaking the decade-long deadlock over the Cyprus question. Yet the perennial animosity between the DISY and AKEL cadres seemed to hinder the cooperation needed to turn public opinion in favor of a compromise solution regarding Cyprus.

Leaders: Nikolaos (Nikos) ANASTASIADES (President), Averof NEOPHYTOU (Deputy President), Eleni VRAHIMI (Secretary General).

European Party (*Evropaiko Komma*—EVROKO). The European Party was founded in July 2005 by dissidents from DISY who had opposed DISY's stance on the 2004 referendum, in partnership with the New Horizons party. In advance of the 2006 parliamentary elections, EVROKO also formed an alliance with the Fighting Democratic Movement. EVROKO garnered 5.75 percent of the vote and three seats, all credited to EVROKO. In the February 2008 presidential elections, EVROKO supported the candidacy of President Papadopoulos, while in the second round it abstained from endorsing a candidate.

Despite the opposition of its founding members to the UN plan of 2004, EVROKO states that it favors a reunification plan based on the resolution of EU issues with Turkey. In the view of the party leadership, this would be a "truly European" solution, which would respect the fundamental European freedoms for all Cypriot citizens and throughout the island.

Leader: Dimitrios SILLOURIS.

New Horizons (*Neoi Orizontes*—NO). NO was launched in early 1996 backed by the church and advocating that Cyprus should be a unitary rather than a federal state. It failed to win representation in the May 1996 election. Party leader Nikolaos (Nikos) Koutsou won less than 1 percent of the vote in the first round of the 1998 presidential balloting. The NO received 3 percent of the vote in the May 2001 balloting, winning a single seat. In the 2003 presidential election Koutsou received 2.1 percent of the vote. In 2005 the party merged with dissident DISY members to form EVROKO.

Leaders: Nikolaos (Nikos) KOUTSOU (Chair and 1998 and 2003 presidential candidate), Stelios AMERIKANOS (Secretary General).

Fighting Democratic Movement (*Agonistiko Dimokratiko Kinima*—ADIK). ADIK is a breakaway formation from DIKO that was launched in 1999. It won a single seat, held by ADIK president Dinos Michailides, with 2.16 percent of the vote in the May 2001 balloting. ADIK formed an electoral alliance with EVROKO prior to the 2006 parliamentary elections. However, Michailides, running on the EVROKO ticket, failed to win reelection. There were reports that ADIK was committed to retaining a separate identity despite its agreement with EVROKO. Election results show ADIK receiving 0.23 percent of the vote, raising questions about the official relationship between EVROKO and ADIK. In the February 2008 presidential elections, ADIK supported the candidacy of President Papadopoulos and abstained from endorsing a candidate in the second round.

Leaders: Dinos MICHAILIDES (President), Yiannis PAPADOPOULOS (Secretary General).

Ecological Environmental Movement–Cyprus Green Party (*Kinima Oikologon Perivallontiston*). The Cyprus Green Party was established as a political party in February 1996 but failed to make much impact in the May 1996 election, winning only 1 percent of the vote. The party managed to gain legislative representation for the first time in the May 2001 balloting. It received 1.98 percent of the vote and won a single seat. The party retained its seat with 1.95 percent of the vote in the May 2006 elections. In 2007 the Green Party made a joint announcement with the Turkish Cypriot **New Cyprus Party,** calling for military withdrawal from Nicosia as a first step toward demilitarization of the entire island. The party opposed any division of the island based on geography, ethnicity, or religion. In the February 2008 presidential elections, the party supported the candidacy of President Papadopoulos, while in the second round it endorsed the Christofias candidacy.

Leaders: Savvas PHILIPPOU (Deputy General Secretary), Georgios PERDIKIS (General Secretary).

Other Parties that Contested the 2006 Legislative Elections:

United Democrats (*Enomenoi Dimokrates*—EDI). The leftist EDI was formed in 1996 by members of the Free Democrats Movement (*Kinima ton Eleftheron Dimokraton*—KED) and the Democratic Socialist Reform Movement (*Ananeotiko Dimokratiko Sosialistiko Kinima*—ADISOK). The center-left KED had been launched in April 1993 by former president Georgios Vassiliou following his unexpected failure to win a second term in February. He pledged that the new group would "promote the admission of Cyprus into Europe." The party won two seats on a 3.6 percent vote share in the May 1996 election.

The ADISOK had been launched in early 1990 by a number of AKEL dissidents favoring settlement of the Cyprus issue on the basis of UN resolutions. It failed to retain legislative representation in the 1991 and 1996 elections.

Vassiliou, who won just 3 percent of the vote in the first round of the February 1998 presidential balloting, supported President Clerides in the second round. Vassiliou was subsequently named as the government's chief EU negotiator, while the EDI was also given a ministry in Clerides's new coalition government. The EDI won a single legislative seat in 2001.

The EDI, which supported the UN reunification proposal put forth in the 2004 referendum, subsequently lost its legislative seat in the May 2006 elections, securing only 1.6 percent of the vote. Party president Michalis PAPAPETROU subsequently resigned.

In 2007 former cabinet minister Costas Themistocleous announced his bid for the presidency in the 2008 elections, saying he favored changes to the UN plan for reunification that would impose a deadline on negotiations. If further talks failed, Themistocleous said, he would call for a new referendum on the issue. Despite Themistocleous' candidacy, the EDI ultimately decided to endorse the Christofias candidacy in the February 2008 presidential elections, to reduce the reelection chances of President Papadopoulos.

Leaders: Michalis PAPAPETROU (President), Praxoula Antoniadou KYRIAKOU (First Vice President), Petros EVLOGIMENOS (Second Vice President), Nicolas SHIANIS (Secretary General).

European Democracy (*Evropaiki Dimokratia*—EVRODI). The European Democracy party was founded by DISY dissident Prodromos Prodromou after the 2004 referendum on the UN plan for reunification of Cyprus, which Prodromou had opposed. European Democracy had been considering participating in the formation of EVROKO, but it ultimately ran on its own in the 2006 parliamentary elections, receiving less than 1 percent of the vote. In the February 2008 presidential elections, the party supported the Kassoulides candidacy.

Leader: Prodromos PRODROMOU (President).

Other minor parties that contested the 2006 parliamentary elections were the **Free Citizens' Movement,** led by Timis EYTHIMIOU, and the **Hunters' Political Movement,** led by Michalis PAFITANIS.

LEGISLATURE

The Cypriot **House of Representatives** (*Vouli Antiprosópon/Temsilciler Meclisi*) is a unicameral body formerly encompassing 35 Greek and 15 Turkish members, although Turkish participation ceased in December 1963. By contrast, the balloting of December 8, 1985, was for an enlarged House of 56 Greek members. At the most recent election of May 21, 2006, the seat distribution was as follows: the Progressive Party of the Working People, 18; the Democratic Rally, 18; the Democratic Party, 11; the Social Democrats' Movement, 5; the European Party, 3; and the Ecological Environmental Movement–Cyprus Green Party, 1. There are also 24 seats nominally reserved for Turkish Cypriots.

President: Marios KAROGIAN.

CABINET

[as of June 1, 2009]

President	Dimitrios (Dimitris) Christofias (AKEL)
Deputy Minister to the President	Titos Christophides (AKEL)
Ministers	
Agriculture, Natural Resources, and Environment	Michalis Poliniki Charalambides (EDEK)
Commerce, Industry, and Tourism	Antonis Paschalides (DIKO)
Communications and Works	Nikolaos (Nikos) Nikolaides (KISOS)
Defense	Costas Papacostas (AKEL)
Education and Culture	Andreas Demetriou (AKEL)
Finance	Charilaos Stavrakis (ind.)
Foreign Affairs	Markos Kyprianou (DIKO)
Government Spokesperson	Stephanos Stephanou (AKEL)
Health	Christos Patsalides (DIKO)
Interior	Neoklis Sylikiotes (AKEL)
Justice and Public Order	Loukas Louka (AKEL)
Labor and Social Insurance	Sotiroula Charalambous (AKEL) [f]

[f] = female

COMMUNICATIONS

The material that follows encompasses Greek-sector media only; for Turkish media, see article on Cyprus: Turkish Sector.

Freedom of the press is protected under the constitution of Cyprus, and the media in the republic are independent. One significant issue, according to Reporters Without Borders, was the hindrance of the free flow of information between northern and southern sectors of the island. The example cited was the refusal of the Greek Cypriot government in 2006 to allow journalists from the Turkish Republic of Northern Cyprus to report on a sports event in the south.

Press. The following newspapers are published daily in Nicosia in Greek, unless otherwise noted (circulation figures are daily averages for 2004): *Phileleftheros* (Liberal, 25,000), independent; *Simerini* (Today, 6,500), right-wing; *Apogevmatini* (Afternoon, 8,000), independent; *Haravghi* (Dawn, 9,000), AKEL organ; *Alithia* (Truth, 11,000), right-wing; *Agon* (Struggle, 5,000), right-wing; *Politis* (Citizen, 4,500); *Cyprus Mail* (3,600), independent, in English; *Machi* (Battle, 3,000), right-wing.

News agencies. A Greek-sector Cyprus News Agency (*Kypriakon Praktoreion Eidiseon*—KPE) was established in 1976; numerous foreign bureaus maintain offices in Nicosia.

Broadcasting and computing. Prior to the 1974 conflict, broadcasting was controlled by the semigovernmental Cyprus Broadcasting Corporation (*Radiofonikon Idryma Kyprou*—RIK) and the government-owned *Radyo Bayrak* (RB) and *Radyo Bayrak Televizyon* (RBT). At present, radio service in the Greek sector is provided by the RIK, in addition to 3 private island-wide and 24 local stations. The RIK maintains television service from its station on Mount Olympus (Troodos), while the RB and the RBT stations broadcast from the Turkish sector. The Greek channel ET-1 is rebroadcast on Cyprus, while radio service is also provided by the BBC East Mediterranean Relay and by the British Forces Broadcasting Service, Cyprus. As of 2008 there were 387.8 Internet users per 1,000 inhabitants.

INTERGOVERNMENTAL REPRESENTATION

Ambassador to the U.S.: Andreas S. KAKOURIS.

U.S. Ambassador to Cyprus: Frank C. URBANCIC, Jr.

Permanent Representative to the UN: Minas A. HADJIMICHAEL.

IGO Memberships (Non-UN): CEUR, CWTH, EIB, EU, Eurocontrol, Interpol, IOM, OSCE, PCA, WCO, WTO.

CYPRUS: TURKISH SECTOR

Turkish Republic of Northern Cyprus
Kuzey Kıbrıs Türk Cumhuriyeti

Political Status: Autonomous federal state proclaimed February 13, 1975; independent republic (thus far recognized only by Turkey) declared November 15, 1983; TRNC constitution approved by referendum of May 6, 1985.

Area: Approximately 1,400 sq. mi. (3,626 sq. km.).

Population: 256,644 (2006C); 279,000 (2008E), on the basis of Turkish Cypriot claims, which include nonindigenous settlers (more than half of the total). The latter figure has not been adjusted to accord with the 2006 census. The 2006 result has been challenged by Greek Cypriots, who base their estimates on the known Turkish population in 1974, augmented by natural increases plus an adjustment for emigration.

Major Urban Centers (2005E): LEFKOŞA (Turkish-occupied portion of Nicosia, 42,200), Gazi Mağusa (Famagusta, 37,100).

Principal Language: Turkish.

Monetary Unit: Turkish Lira (renamed Turkish Lira on January 1, 2009) market rate December 1, 2009: 1.50 liras = $1US). Use of the Cyprus pound as an alternative unit of exchange was terminated on May 16, 1983.

President: Mehmet Ali TALAT (Republican Turkish Party); elected in first round of popular balloting on April 17, 2005, and inaugurated April 24 for a five-year term in succession to Rauf R. DENKTAŞ (nonparty).

Prime Minister: Derviş EROĞLU (National Unity Party); succeeded Ferdi Sabit SOYER (Republican Turkish Party) following early assembly elections on April 19, 2009; formed new government on May 4.

GOVERNMENT AND POLITICS

Political background. The Turkish Cypriots withdrew from participation in the government of the Republic of Cyprus in January 1964 in the wake of communal violence precipitated by Archbishop MAKARIOS's announcement of proposed constitutional changes in November 1963. In 1967 a Turkish Cypriot Provisional Administration was established to provide governmental services in the Turkish areas, its representatives subsequently engaging in sporadic constitutional discussions with members of the Greek Cypriot administration. Meanwhile, an uneasy peace between the two communities was maintained by a UN peacekeeping force that had been dispatched in 1964, while most Turkish Cypriots were forced under Greek Cypriot pressure to move to UN-protected enclaves. The constitutional talks, which ran until 1974, failed to bridge the gap between Greek insistence on a unitary form of government and Turkish demands for a bicommunal federation.

A Turkish Federated State of Cyprus was established on February 13, 1975, following the Greek army coup of July 15, 1974, and the subsequent Turkish occupation of northern Cyprus. Rauf DENKTAŞ, nominal vice president of the Republic of Cyprus and leader of the National Unity Party (*Ulusal Birlik Partisi*—UBP), was designated president of the Federated State, retaining the office as the result of a presidential election on June 20, 1976, in which he defeated the Republican Turkish Party (*Cumhuriyetçi Türk Partisi*—CTP) nominee, Ahmet Mithat BERBEROĞLU, by a majority of nearly four to one. He was reelected for a five-year term in June 1981, remaining in office upon proclamation of the Turkish Republic of Northern Cyprus (TRNC) in November 1983.

Intercommunal discussions prior to the death of Archbishop Makarios on August 3, 1977, yielded apparent Greek Cypriot abandonment of the unitary government condition but left the two sides far apart on other issues, including Greek Cypriot efforts to secure a reduction of approximately 50 percent in the size of the Turkish Cypriot sector, in accordance to the population size of the Turkish Cypriot community, and Turkish Cypriot demands for virtual parity in such federal institutions as the presidency (to be effected on the basis of communal rotation) and the higher judiciary. In the meantime, an intensive settlement project was launched. Thousands of Turkish citizens were invited to settle on the properties of Greek Cypriots who were displaced during the events of 1974, in an apparent attempt to tilt the demographic balance on the island in favor of Turkish Cypriots.

Prior to the breakdown in discussions between Denktaş and the president of the Republic of Cyprus and Greek Cypriot leader Spyros KYPRIANOU at UN headquarters in January 1985, the Turkish Cypriots had agreed to make significant concessions, particularly with regard to power sharing and territorial demarcation of the projected federal units. Specifically, they had abandoned their earlier demand (revived in 1991) for presidential rotation and had agreed on a reduction of the area to be placed under Turkish local administration to approximately 29 percent of the island. However, the two sides were unable to agree on a specific timetable for Turkish troop withdrawal, the identification of Turkish Cypriot-held areas to be returned to Greek Cypriot control, or a mechanism for external guarantees that the pact would be observed. In announcing on January 25 that presidential and legislative elections would be held in June, President Denktaş insisted that neither the balloting nor the adoption of the TRNC constitution should be construed as efforts to "close the door to a federal solution."

The constitution was approved by 70 percent of those participating in a referendum on May 5, 1985, with the leftist CTP actively campaigning for a "no" vote. At the presidential poll on June 9, Denktaş was accorded a like margin, while the UBP fell two seats short of a majority at the legislative balloting of June 23. On July 30 a coalition government involving the UBP and the Communal Liberation Party (*Toplumcu Kurtuluş Partisi*—TKP), with Derviş EROĞLU as prime minister, was confirmed by the assembly.

The Eroğlu government fell on August 11, 1986, after the TKP had refused to endorse a proposal to expand the scope of trade and investment in the sector. However, the prime minister was able to form a new administration on September 2 that included the center-right New Dawn Party (*Yeni Doğus Partisi*—YDP) as the UBP's coalition partner.

President Denktaş drew 67.5 percent of the vote in securing reelection to his fourth five-year term on April 22, 1990. Subsequently, a rift developed between Denktaş and Eroğlu over the conduct of negotiations with the south, the prime minister advocating a harder line on concessions to the Greek Cypriots than did the president. As a result, a group of dissidents withdrew from the UBP in July 1992 to form the Democratic Party (*Demokrat Parti*—DP), to which Denktaş transferred his allegiance in late October, thereby provoking a power struggle with UBP leader Eroğlu, who became highly critical of the president's "unacceptable concessions" in negotiations with the Greek Cypriots.

Denktaş eventually gained the upper hand by calling an early assembly election on December 12, 1993, in which the UBP, although retaining a narrow plurality, lost ground, while the DP and the CTP both registered gains. The outcome was the formation on January 1, 1994, of a center-left DP-CTP coalition headed by DP leader Hakki ATUN, which supported the Denktaş line in the intercommunal talks.

In the run-up to the 1995 presidential balloting, Atun resigned as prime minister on February 24 after the CTP had opposed President Denktaş's preelection offer to distribute to TRNC citizens the title deeds of Greek Cypriot property in the north. In the presidential contest on April 15 and 22, Denktaş for the first time failed to win an outright majority in the first round (taking only 40.4 percent of the vote), although he scored a comfortable 62.5 to 37.5 percent victory over Eroğlu in the second. Protracted interparty negotiations were needed to produce, on June 3, a new DP-CTP administration headed by Atun. The coalition again collapsed in November, following the resignation of the CTP deputy premier, Ösker ÖZGÜR, but it was reestablished the following month with Mehmet Ali TALAT of the CTP as Atun's deputy. The DP-CTP coalition government resigned on July 4, 1996, and the UBP's Eroğlu was again given, on August 1, 1996, the job of forming a new government. A UBP-DP coalition cabinet headed by Eroğlu was approved by the president on August 16, 1996.

In the legislative balloting of December 6, 1998, the UBP improved from 17 to 24 seats. On December 30 President Denktaş approved Eroğlu to head a new UBP-TKP coalition government, the DP having fallen into dispute with the UBP over economic policies and cabinet representation. The legislature approved the new cabinet on January 12, 1999, by a strict party-line vote of 31–18. Denktaş won 43.6 percent of the vote in the first round of presidential balloting on April 15, 2000, while UBP candidate Eroğlu received 30.1 percent; the TKP's Mustafa AKINCI, 11.7 percent; the CTP's Mehmet Ali Talat, 10 percent; and Arif Hasan TAHSIN of the Patriotic Unity Movement (*Yurtsever Birlik Hareketi*—YBH), 2.6 percent. Three other minor candidates each received less than 1 percent of the vote. The second round of balloting, scheduled for April 22, was canceled when Eroğlu withdrew on April 19 after the TKP decided to back neither of the candidates for the second round. Denktaş was sworn in on April 24.

After a series of disagreements between the coalition partners (mainly regarding the direction to be taken in foreign relations), the UBP-TKP government resigned on May 25, 2001. President Denktaş asked Eroğlu to form a new government, and a UBP-DP coalition was appointed on June 7.

The CTP returned to a plurality (19 seats) in the December 14, 2003, assembly balloting, and Talat formed a CTP-DP coalition government on January 13, 2004. However, only two days after the TRNC population had endorsed a UN plan for reunification (see Current issues, below), the coalition became a minority government when two DP legislators quit the party to protest the administration's pro-unification stance. After numerous attempts by Talat and the UBP's Eroğlu to form coalition governments failed, new assembly elections were held on February 20, 2005. The CTP increased its seat total to 24, and Talat was able to form a more secure CTP-DP coalition cabinet on March 16.

Talat secured 55.6 percent of the vote in the first round of presidential balloting on April 17, 2005, with Eroğlu finishing second with 22.7 percent. Talat resigned as prime minister on April 20 and was inaugurated as president on April 24. The following day, Ferdi Sabit SOYER, a close ally of Talat and CTP stalwart, formed another CTP-DP coalition government. The government collapsed in September 2006 over differences between the coalition partners. A new coalition government, again headed by Soyer, was established in October between the CTP and the newly formed Freedom and Reform Party (*Özgürlük ve Reform Partisi*—ÖRP), headed by former UBP leader Turgay AVCI. The new government enjoyed good relations with the Greek Cypriot government led by the Justice and Development Party (*Adalet ve Kalkınma Partisi*—AKP) and maintained a moderate stance on the Cyprus issue. Talat and Christofias have held several informal meetings, while expert committees representing both parties have met regularly since April to prepare the start of direct negotiations. Public foreign debt dropped from 14.9 percent of GDP in 2006 to 14.6 in 2007 and was projected to fall to 14 percent in 2008.

In the wake of rising popular discontent, the CTP-BG called for early parliamentary elections on April 19, 2009. The mandate turned out to be a clear defeat for the CTP-BG, as the right-wing nationalist opposition, the National Unity Party (*Ulusal Birlik Partisi*—UBP), won 44 percent of the vote and 26 seats, while the CTP-BG won 29 percent of the vote and 15 seats. UBP chair Derviş Eroğlu was named prime minister and formed a new, single-party government on May 4.

Constitution and government. The constitution of the TRNC provides for a presidential-parliamentary system headed by a popularly elected chief executive, who cannot lead a party or be subject to its decisions. The president appoints a prime minister, who (unlike other ministers) must be a member of the legislature and whose government is subject to legislative recall. Like the president, the 50-member Assembly of the Republic is elected for a five-year term (subject to dissolution) and its presiding officer, who is chosen at the beginning of the first and fourth year of each term, becomes acting head of state in the event of presidential death, incapacity, or resignation. The members of the Supreme Court, composed of a president and seven additional judges, also form a Constitutional Court (five members) and a Court of Appeal and High Administrative Court (three members each). Lesser courts and local administrative units are established by legislative action.

Current issues. The European Council meeting held in late 1997 decided that Cyprus would be included in the first group of applicants to join the expanded European Union (EU), while determining that "political and economic conditions" required for the membership of Turkey were not satisfied. The EU also expressed a desire to see action taken on the Cyprus government's wish to include the Turkish Cypriots in the negotiating delegation. However, President Denktaş of the TRNC indicated his unwillingness to proceed with negotiations unless further international recognition of the TRNC was forthcoming, and new discussions were not launched as expected. In August Denktaş attempted to counter the UN push for reunification by formally proposing a confederation of "equal states," with the UN continuing to patrol the border. That proposal was quickly rejected by most of the international community, despite Denktaş's assessment that "Turks and Greeks on Cyprus are like oil and water. They can no longer be mixed."

Meanwhile, the question of Greek Cypriot properties in the TRNC entered the political agenda as a result of appeals of Greek Cypriot refugees against Turkey at the European Court of Human Rights (ECHR). In its July 1998 verdict on the *Loizidou v. Turkey* case the ECHR confirmed the property rights of the applicant over her house in Kyrenia (Girne) and declared that Turkey, not the TRNC, had violated her property rights and was liable for compensation. The significance of this decision lay not only in the recognition of Greek Cypriot property rights in the TRNC, but also in the refusal to recognize the TRNC as the case defendant.

Approximately 1,400 displaced Greek Cypriots followed the Loizidou example and appealed to the European Court of Human Rights, demanding confirmation of their property rights as well as compensation. In the 2006 *Xenides-Arestis v. Turkey* case, the court, while confirming the property rights of displaced Greek Cypriots, indicated that Turkey should offer redress for the applicants' losses. Pending implementation of general measures, the court adjourned its consideration of all relevant individual applications. This provided Turkey and the TRNC with an opportunity to organize an "Immovable Properties Compensation Commission" as an "effective domestic remedy" to keep Greek Cypriots from directly appealing to the European Court by granting them legal recourse in Cyprus.

The TRNC's strong economic dependence on Turkey, which includes direct financial aid, rendered its economy vulnerable between 1999 and 2001 to turmoil in the Turkish economy, which was brought on in part by corruption or inefficient public regulatory mechanisms, with the resultant economic turmoil generating popular protest.

Tension between the TRNC government and opposition parties and groups became more severe with Denktaş's decision to withdraw from the talks with the Greek Cypriot side in late 2000. However, observers noted some easing after Denktaş decided to resume dialogue in 2002. Attention subsequently focused almost exclusively on the plan forwarded by UN Secretary General Kofi Annan under which the island would be reunified in a loose federation with the Greek Cypriot and Turkish Cypriot constituent states retaining broad autonomy in most domestic areas. (For complete details on the Annan plan, see Current issues in article on Cyprus.) A critical point was reached in December 2002, when the Copenhagen European Council was to make a decision on the accession of the Republic of Cyprus. On the eve of the decision, the president of the Republic of Cyprus, Glafkos CLERIDES, declared his intention to sign the Annan Plan, if the Turkish Cypriot side was willing to do the same. Denktaş's refusal to sign the plan attested to the intransigence of the Turkish Cypriot side and facilitated the European Council's decision to approve Cyprus's EU membership without resolving the Cyprus issue. Denktaş later tried to defuse mounting domestic and international pressure by showing his commitment to a resolution. A major symbolic move was the opening on April 23, 2003, of the "Green Line" dividing the island. This allowed refugees from both sides to visit their homes for the first time in 29 years. However, the decoupling of Cyprus's EU accession from the resolution, combined with a change of government in the Republic of Cyprus in February 2003, reduced the incentive for Greek Cypriots to endorse the Annan Plan. Having secured EU membership without committing to the UN plan, the new Papadopoulos administration saw EU membership as an opportunity to gain more concessions against Turkish Cypriots.

With the encouragement of new prime minister Talat of the CTP (which had led all parties in the December 2003 assembly balloting), the voters in the TRNC endorsed the UN reunification plan by a 65 percent "yes" vote in a national referendum on April 24, 2004, despite Denktaş's opposition. The plan, however, was rejected by a three-to-one margin by the Greek Cypriot community. Consequently, the TRNC was excluded when Cyprus acceded to the EU with nine other new members on May 1. The EU immediately pledged substantial economic assistance to the TRNC as a reward for the "yes" vote regarding reunification. However, in October Cyprus vetoed an EU plan to establish trade relations with the TRNC. The government of Cyprus indicated that too much assistance to the TRNC might embolden Turkish Cypriots still hoping for additional recognition for the TRNC. The EU membership thus provided Greek Cypriots with additional leverage, as their veto power effectively meant that any EU initiatives in favor of Turkish Cypriots had to meet Greek Cypriot approval first.

The early legislative elections of February 2005 in the TRNC were widely viewed as a strong endorsement of reunification, the Turkish Cypriots clearly having suffered political and economic isolation since Cyprus's accession to the EU. Following Talat's election in April to succeed President Denktaş (who, at age 81, had decided to retire), those favoring unification again saw reason for hope. Negotiations, again centered on the Annan plan, subsequently resumed in an atmosphere that led one observer to conclude that nearly "everyone seems to want reunification." Included on that list were Russia (which had been unconvinced in early 2004), the United States (which sent economic development missions to the TRNC), Greece, and Turkey (for whom the stakes were arguably higher than for the others). Turkey, hoping to begin its own EU accession process, keenly desired an end to the island's split in view of the fact that the perpetuation of the conflict could pose an additional obstacle to its own EU membership. In July, Turkey signed a protocol that would (upon approval by the Turkish legislature) extend its long-term customs union with the EU to the ten new EU members, including Cyprus. However, Turkey insisted its decision did not constitute recognition of the Republic of Cyprus. (Turkey was the only country to recognize the TRNC and the only European country yet to recognize the Republic of Cyprus.)

Despite continued heavy international pressure, no substantive negotiations toward reunification were conducted throughout the remainder of 2005. Further exacerbating the situation, Cyprus forced the EU to withhold $140 million in aid earmarked for the TRNC. On a more positive note, the TRNC assembly in December ratified legislation permitting Greek Cypriots to seek the return of property seized in the north following the 1974 partitioning of the island. (The commission established to adjudicate the property returns [or reparations] was described as fully operational as of May 2006.)

UK Foreign Secretary Jack Straw met with TRNC President Talat in the TRNC in January 2006, prompting strong criticism from Greek Cypriot leaders who accused some EU members of attempting to "legitimize" the northern government. In return, Straw described the current Greek Cypriot stance as "not conducive" to reunification. Complex EU issues subsequently continued to dominate TRNC affairs. Just a day after formally authorizing the start of EU accession talks with Turkey, the EU in February announced it would release $165 million to the TRNC for infrastructure development. Although the Republic of Cyprus accepted that decision, it continued to block the proposed easing of EU trade sanctions against the TRNC. For its part, Turkey pressed for a comprehensive settlement of the island's status rather than a "piecemeal" approach. As a result, even discussions on minor "technical" issues, such as immigration and environmental protection remained stalled in May 2006.

The legislative elections in the south in May 2006 (see article on Cyprus for details) indicated growing popular support for President Papadopoulos's negative stance toward the UN reunification plan. Collaterally, TRNC President Talat acknowledged that Turkish Cypriots had become "greatly disheartened and pessimistic" over the lack of progress in talks with the Greek Cypriots and the ongoing economic "isolation" of the north. Nevertheless, Talat said his government had not yet reached the point of pursuing additional international recognition of the TRNC as an independent entity, preferring instead to retain its support for the UN plan. On July 8, Presidents Talat and Papadopoulos agreed to a "set of principles" mediated by the UN that recommitted both sides to discussions on the UN plan by, among other things, establishing the "right atmosphere" for such talks. By the end of the month both sides had submitted issues for discussion, but the effort was short-lived. A subsequent plan by Finland to host an emergency summit in November was canceled, the reason reported as "no progress would be forthcoming." Meanwhile, the EU, citing Turkey's lack of progress toward normalizing relations with Cyprus, halted the opening of relevant chapters in accession negotiations with Turkey until the latter agreed to open its ports and airports for use by Cyprus. Reunification was at the core of the dispute between the CTP and the DP that resulted in the collapse of the government in September and the establishment of a new coalition that received official approval in October. The CTP allied itself with the new ÖRP, which had been formed by dissident deputies from the DP and the UBP.

While progress on reunification had stalled in early 2007, the leading Muslim cleric from the TRNC for the first time crossed the demarcation line into Cyprus to meet with the head of the Greek Orthodox Church in an effort to promote the resumption of talks. During the February 2008 presidential elections in the Republic of Cyprus, the incumbent president Papadopoulos was defeated by the AKEL president Dimitrios (Dimitris) CHRISTOFIAS. As Papadopoulos was perceived as a "hard-liner" who had already recommended the rejection of the Annan Plan in the April, 23, 2004, referendum, it was hoped that Christofias's election provided a new opportunity to resolve the Cyprus question. This position was reinforced by the historic links of AKEL with the Turkish Cypriot community of the island and the personal links between Talat and Christofias. A few days after the opening of the Ledra Street (*Lokmacı Kapısı*) roadblock, Talat crossed the checkpoint on April, 11, 2008, and visited Greek Cypriot shops along Ledra Street. His unexpected move had a positive effect on Greek Cypriot public opinion and improved the outlook for reconciliation.

The launch of intercommunal negotiations on September 3, 2008, for the first time since 2004 produced short-lived optimism over the possibility of a resolution, given the moderate stance of both Talat and Christofias. However, negotiations proceeded at a slow pace with no deadlines for the drafting of a comprehensive solution, and the issue of Turkey's EU accession negotiations became another stumbling block. The international trade and transport embargo against the TRNC further complicated matters, though it was to come under review in late 2008 by the European Council.

A key property rights issue was the focus of attention in April 2009 when the European Court of Justice (ECJ) ruling regarding a case involving British property owners strengthened Greek Cypriot positions on the divisive Cyprus property issue and raised concerns about the viability of the TRNC vacation real estate sector (see Political Handbook article on Cyprus for details.)

Relations between Nicosia and Ankara have always been a key parameter of TRNC politics, with cordial relations having been maintained between President Talat and the AKP government in Turkey. Their common agenda included the promotion of EU-Turkey relations and the incorporation of Turkish Cypriots in the European Union through a compromise solution of the Cyprus issue based on the UN initiatives. However, following the investigation and subsequent trials in the so-called Ergenekon conspiracy in Turkey in 2008, significant repercussions were felt in the TRNC. (Ergenekon was a clandestine terrorist organizations accused of plotting to overthrow the Turkish government; see the article on Turkey for details.) Subsequently, speculation arose about the connections of former TRNC President Rauf Denktaş and UBP leader and Prime Minister Derviş Eroğlu to the Ergenekon plot, given their close ties to the key defendants in the case. (In 2009 Denktaş and Eroğlu were under investigation for their possible involvement in the case.)

Economic dependence on Turkey continued, as Turkey contributed $800 million to the TRNC budget in 2008. Promised administrative and economic reform did not materialize, however. An oversized public sector increasingly controlled by the CTP-BG government became one of the major obstacles to any domestic reform. A government plan to tighten spending in the public sector met with the fierce opposition of civil servant unions and was eventually withdrawn. This and the fact that intercommunal negotiations were expected to reach a critical point in 2009 prompted the CTP-BG to call for early parliamentary elections in April in an effort to strengthen the standing of the TRNC in its talks with Cyprus. During the campaign, UBP leader Eroğlu called for a strong mandate for a single-party UBP government, arguing that "now it is time for national unity." Meanwhile, CTP leader, Prime Minister Ferdi Sabit Soyer, warned that the UBP campaign claims distorted the reality about the state of the TRNC economy and could threaten the TRNC's integration in the European Union.

Shortly before the April 19, 2009, election Soyer requested that Denktaş and Eroğlu be investigated based on the material uncovered by the Ergenekon investigation in Turkey. Yet no major development took place prior to the elections, which resulted in a majority victory for UBP, which won 26 seats to the CTP's 15, and Eroğlu being named prime minister. Having won a majority of seats, the UBP did not have to form a coalition government. Subsequently, Eroğlu said that "the continuation of Cyprus talks was one of the main policies of UBP" and added that his government would support President Talat to that end and act in unity with Turkey on any progress achieved at the negotiations.

The 2009 parliamentary election highlighted growing Turkish Cypriot discontent with the pro-solution forces in the TRNC, owing largely to the lack of any significant change regarding the trade and transport embargo against the TRNC, combined with the rise of anti-EU sentiment and nationalism in Turkey. While President Talat remained chief negotiator for the Turkish Cypriots, his political clout had been weakened by his "cohabitation" with Eroğlu, according to observers. In addition, the UBP's clear victory in the poll did not bode well for the prospects of Talat's candidacy in the TRNC presidential elections scheduled for 2010, observers said.

POLITICAL PARTIES

Most of the Turkish Cypriot parties share a common outlook regarding the present division of the island. Differences have surfaced, however, as to the degree of firmness to be displayed in negotiations with the Greek community.

Government Parties:

National Unity Party (*Ulusal Birlik Partisi*—UBP). The right-wing UBP was established in 1975 as an outgrowth of the former National Solidarity (*Ulusal Dayanışma*) movement. Originally committed to the establishment of a bicommunal federal state, it captured three-quarters of the seats in the Turkish Cypriot Legislative Assembly at the 1976 election but was reduced to a plurality of 18 seats in 1981 and survived a confidence vote in the assembly on September 11, only because the motion failed to obtain an absolute majority. The UBP's former leader, Rauf Denktaş, was precluded by the constitution from serving as president of the party or from submitting to party discipline while president of the republic; nevertheless, he was instrumental in launching the breakaway DP in 1992 after clashing with party leader Derviş Eroğlu, who moved to an increasingly pro-partition stance. The UBP retained its plurality in the 1993 balloting but remained in opposition. Eroğlu took Denktaş to the second round in the 1995 presidential election, winning 37.5 percent of the vote. Staying in the opposition until a DP-CTP coalition government came to an end on July 4, 1996, the UBP rose to power as a member of a coalition government with the DP on August 16, 1996. The UBP increased its vote share to over 40 percent in the 1998 legislative balloting, Eroğlu subsequently forming a coalition with the TKP. Eroğlu ran as presidential candidate for the UBP on April 15, 2000, and won 30.1 percent of the vote at the first round. He withdrew from the race on April 19 prior to the scheduled second round between himself and Denktaş. The UBP-TKP coalition broke down in May 2001, and Eroğlu formed a new government with the DP in June. However, he was obliged to resign as prime minister following the December 2003 legislative balloting, in which the UBP was outpolled by the CTP 35 percent to 33 percent. The UBP secured 19 seats on a vote share of 31.7 percent in the February 2005 assembly balloting, while Eroğlu finished second in the first round of presidential balloting in April with 22.7 percent of the vote. Citing the need for "fresh blood" in the party's leadership, Eroğlu resigned as UBP chair in late 2005. He was succeeded in February 2006 by Hüseyin Özgürgün. Three UBP deputies resigned in September 2006 to establish, with a former DP deputy, the ÖRP, which became the junior partner in a new coalition government with the CTP.

Following an election at the UBP Congress on December, 16, 2006, Özgürgün was replaced by Tahsin ERTUĞRULOĞLU. The party has maintained a hard-line stance regarding the resolution of the Cyprus question and accused the Talat administration of being willing to compromise Turkish Cypriot sovereignty in favor of a solution of the Cyprus question. Despite this stance, official talks with a Greek Cypriot political party were held for the first time on May 27, 2007, when a delegation from the opposition Democratic Rally (*Dimokratikos Synagermos*—DISY), led by DISY president Nikolaos (Nikos) ANASTASIADES, visited the UBP headquarters. In fall 2008, Ertuğruloğlu was replaced by Eroğlu, which gave the party a more centrist profile. In the election campaign, Eroğlu attempted to shed his nationalist profile by insisting he would derail bi-communal negotiations if elected.

The UBP gained government control following the April 19, 2009, parliamentary elections, in which it won 44 percent of the vote and 26 seats, overturning the authority of the CTP (below), which had won 25 seats in the previous election and only 15 in 2009.

Leaders: Derviş EROĞLU (Prime Minister and Chair), Nazım ÇAVUŞOĞLU (Secretary General).

Republican Turkish Party–United Forces (*Cumhuriyetçi Türk Partisi–Birleşik Güçler*—CTP-BG). A Marxist formation at the time, the CTP campaigned against the 1985 constitution because of its repressive and militaristic content. For the 1990 election (at which it lost 5 of 12 seats won in 1985) the CTP joined with the TKP and YDP (see DP, below) in a coalition styled the Democratic Struggle Party (*Demokratik Mücadele Partisi*—DMP). It made a comeback to 13 seats in the 1993 balloting, entering a coalition with the DP that effectively collapsed in February 1995 on the issue of Greek Cypriot property rights but was later reconstituted in May. Two further coalition collapses and reconstitutions in 1995 led to the ouster of Ösker ÖZGÜR as CTP leader in January 1996. A DP-CTP coalition government under the leadership of Hakki ATUN resigned on July 4, 1996, and the CTP became the main opposition party. However, it was supplanted in that regard by the DP following the 1998 legislative balloting, in which CTP representation fell from 13 to 6 seats on a vote share of 13.4 percent. In part, the electoral decline was attributed to the CTP's stance that negotiations should be resumed with Greek Cypriot officials regarding a settlement of the political stalemate on the island. Chair Mehmet Ali Talat ran as the party's presidential candidate on April 15, 2000, and received 10 percent of the vote.

The CTP competed in the 2003 assembly elections under the rubric of the CTP–United Forces (*CTP–Birleşik Güçler*—CTP-BG) to reflect its attempt to broaden its base through extended cooperation with nongovernmental organizations and independent voters on an anti-Denktaş, pro-EU platform. The CTP-BG secured a plurality of 19 seats in the 2003 balloting on a vote share of 35 percent.

Talat subsequently formed a coalition government with the DP, which continued in office following the February 2005 assembly balloting in which the CTP-BG's vote share grew to 44 percent (good for 24 seats). The coalition collapsed in September 2006 following a dispute with the DP over the CTP's demand for a reallocation of ministries based on the additional two seats the CTP gained in assembly by-elections in June, and, more significantly, over reunification. Prime Minister Soyer criticized the DP for its hard-line positions in negotiations with Greek Cypriots, despite pressure from the EU, and for its increasing nationalism. The CTP subsequently formed a coalition with the newly formed ÖRP, the alliance being granted official approval by the president and, in October, by the assembly. However, the party appeared to have subsequently returned to the CTP-BG designation by 2008 in an effort to promote the appearance of a broader leftist grouping that extended beyond the party. The close historic links of the CTP with AKEL improved the outlook for relations when AKEL candidate Christofias was elected president of the Republic of Cyprus in February 2008. On June 30, the CTP became a consultative member of Socialist International. However, a decision on granting full membership was postponed due to the objection of the Greek Cypriot Movement of Social Democrats (EDEK).

Meanwhile, on July 9, 2008, the CTP-BG parliamentary group backed Mehmet Ali Talat's proposed solution on the Cyprus based on a single sovereignty–single citizenship basis. In the run-up to the 2009 elections, the party stressed that its primary focus would be to open the gates of the European Union. Yet lack of any progress in resolving the Cyprus issue, ending the economic embargo, and resolving long-standing economic and social problems led to the weakening of the party's popular appeal. In the April parliamentary elections, the party won 15 seats, down from 25 in the previous election, losing its stronghold to the UBP (below).

Leaders: Mehmet Ali TALAT (President of the TRNC), Ferdi Sabit SOYER (Former Prime Minister and Chair), Ömer KALYONCU (Secretary General).

Other Legislative Parties:

Freedom and Reform Party (*Özgürlük ve Reform Partisi*—ÖRP). The ÖRP was formed in September 2006 by Turgay Avcı, former secretary general of the UBP. He was joined by two other UBP deputies and one from the DP to promote a "reformist, democratic, and transparent" government. The four defectors blamed their parties for not working in harmony with Turkey. Observers said the ÖRP would help move the TRNC government toward averting "a major crisis" in Turkey's bid for EU membership (see article on Cyprus for details). The new party became a junior partner in coalition with the CTP in September 2006, the alliance vowing to pursue political equality for the TRNC and a bizonal solution to reunification. Avcı said he left the UBP because he wanted a party that would promote policies similar to those of Turkey.

In 2006 the ÖRP was given four cabinet ministries, including foreign affairs, when the new coalition government was formed. Strong tension has characterized the relations between the UBP and the ÖRP ever since, with former UBP chair Derviş EROĞLU at the center of many disagreements. The party was also accused of developing ties with Turkey's incumbent AKP. Despite tension and polarization, however, the party won two seats in the April 19, 2009, parliamentary elections.

Leaders: Turgay AVCI (Chair), Erdoğan SANLIDAĞ, Mustafa GÖKMEN.

Democrat Party (*Demokrat Parti*—DP). The DP was formed in 1992 by a group of pro-Denktaş UBP dissidents who advocated a more conciliatory posture in the intercommunal talks than the party mainstream. The DP was runner-up in the 1993 legislative balloting, thereupon entering into a majority coalition with the CTP (see above). In 1993 the party accepted the **New Dawn Party** (*Yeni Doğus Partisi*—YDP), led by Ali Özkan ALTINIŞIK, into its ranks. The DP-CTP coalition government ended on July 4, 1996, and the UBP's Derviş Eroğlu formed a new coalition government with the DP as a partner on August 16, 1996. However, the DP moved into opposition status following the December 1998 legislative poll, at which it secured 22.6 percent of the vote. Meanwhile, in September 1998 the DP had reportedly accepted the Free Democratic Party (*Hür Demokrat Parti*—HDP) into its ranks. The HDP, led by İsmet KOTAK and Özel TAHSİN, was one of several parties launched following the 1990 election. Prior to the 1993 election the HDP had joined with two smaller groups, the Homeland Party (*Anavatan Partisi*—AP) and the Nationalist Justice Party (*Milliyetçi Adalet Partisi*—MAP), led by Zorlu TÖRE, in a coalition styled the National Struggle Party (*Milli Mücadele Partisi*—MMP). The DP extended support to Rauf Denktaş in the 2000 presidential election. The DP became the junior partner in the new coalition government announced with the UBP in June 2001. Following the December 2003 balloting, the DP joined an unsteady CTP-led coalition. Two of the seven DP legislators resigned from the party in April 2004 to protest the government's pro-unification stance, forcing early elections in February 2005, at which the DP gained six seats on a 13.5 percent vote share. Mustafa Arabacıoğlu won 13.2 percent of the vote in the first round of the April 2005 presidential poll.

The rift between the DP and the CTP increased, primarily over reunification of the island, resulting in the resignation from the party of another DP deputy in 2006. DP leader Denktaş maintained that the reunification issue could not be resolved until the TRNC is recognized. He also blamed Turkey for allegedly influencing the DP and UBP deputies' decision to resign, a move he said was designed ultimately to further Turkey's bid to join the EU. Following the collapse of its coalition government with the CTP and the party's subsequent move into opposition status, the DP called for early elections, boycotted the initial meeting of the assembly under the new government, and held demonstrations. The DP then became increasingly alienated from Turkey's AKP government, due to its alleged support for the coalition government of the CTP-BG and the ÖRP. In domestic policy, Denktaş supported a "third-way" program that allegedly bridged social and ideological divisions to promote social justice and development. In the 2009 legislative campaign, Denktaş stressed the critical state of the Cyprus issue and focused on economic issues. In the April 19 elections, the party won five seats.

Leaders: Serdar DENKTAŞ (Chair and Former Deputy Prime Minister), Mustafa ARABACIOĞLU (2005 presidential candidate), Ertuğrul HASIPOGLU (Secretary General).

Communal Democracy Party (*Toplumcu Demokrasi Partisi*—TDP). The TDP was formed in November 2007 by the merger of the two parties below, the **Peace and Democracy Movement** (*Bariş ve Demokrasi Hareketi*—BDH) and the **Communal Liberation Party** (*Toplumcu Kurtuluş Partisi*—TKP). In the April 19, 2009, parliamentary elections, the party won two seats.

Leader: Mehmet ÇAKICI.

Peace and Democracy Movement (*Bariş ve Demokrasi Hareketi*—BDH). The BDH is a coalition of leftist parties that joined together to improve their electoral opportunities prior to the 2003 legislative elections. The grouping was formed under the leadership of Mustafa Akıncı, formerly the party leader of TKP, which provided the core of the BDH. Other constitutive parties of the BDH included the **Socialist Party of Cypress** (*Kıbrıs Sosyalist Partisi*—KSP) and the **United Cyprus Party** (*Birleşik Kıbrıs Partisi*—BKP). The BDH won six seats in the 2003 assembly balloting but only one in the 2005 poll (on a 5.8 percent vote share).

Following the poor electoral showing in 2005, some core components reportedly left the BDH, although the BDH continued its institutional existence under the leadership of Akıncı. The BDH, along with one independent deputy, cast the only two votes against the new CTP-ÖRP coalition in the October 5 assembly session. The BDH merged with the TKP in November 2007 to form the Communal Democracy Party (*Toplumcu Demokrasi Partisi*—TDP), led by Mehmet ÇAKICI.

Leaders: Mustafa AKINCI (Chair), Mehmet ÇAKICI (Secretary General).

Communal Liberation Party (*Toplumcu Kurtuluş Partisi*—TKP). Also known as the Socialist Salvation Party, the TKP is a left-of-center grouping organized in 1976. The six assembly seats won by the party in 1976 were doubled in 1981, two of which (for an enlarged chamber) were lost in 1985. The TKP joined the Eroğlu government in July 1985 but withdrew in August 1986.

In 1989 the TKP absorbed the Progressive People's Party (*Atılımcı Halk Partisi*—AHP), which itself had resulted from the merger in early 1986 of the Democratic People's Party (*Demokratik Halk Partisi*—DHP) and the Communal Endeavor Party (*Toplumsal Atılım Partisi*—TAP). The DHP, which advocated the establishment of an independent, nonaligned, and biregional Cypriot state, was organized in 1979 by former prime ministers Nejat KONUK and Osman ÖREK, both of whom had left the UBP because of dissension within the party. The TAP was a centrist party formed in 1984.

The TKP's legislative representation fell from ten seats to seven in 1990 and to five in 1993. It rebounded to seven seats (on a vote share of 15.4 percent) in December 1998 and became the junior partner in the subsequent coalition government with the UBP. Chair Mustafa Akıncı ran as the TKP's presidential candidate on April 15, 2000, and received 11.7 percent of the vote. The TKP subsequently decided to encourage its voters to vote for their candidate of choice for the second round, a move that caused the UBP's Eroğlu to withdraw from the race. Following the breakdown of the coalition government with the UBP in May 2001, the TKP joined the opposition. Chair Akıncı subsequently stepped down as the party leader, and the post was assumed by the former secretary general, Hüseyin Angolemli.

Given the party's poor results in the 2006 municipal and parliamentary by-elections, and its affinity for the BDH, the twentieth congress of the TKP approved the party's merger with the latter in November 2007, forming the new Communal Democracy Party (*Toplumcu Demokrasi Partisi*-TDP) under Mehmet Çakıcı.

Leaders: Hüseyin ANGOLEMLİ (Chair), Güngör GÜNKAN.

Other Parties that Participated in the 2009 Legislative Elections:

United Cyprus Party (*Birleşik Kıbrıs Partisi*—BKP). The BKP, which was founded by İzzet İZCAN in 2002 and had joined the BDH coalition in previous elections, fielded candidates independently in the April, 19, 2009, parliamentary elections. It was supported by the liberal newspaper *Afrika.* The party did not win any seats in 2009.

Leader: İzzet İZCAN (Chair).

Politics for the People Party (*Halk İçin Siyaset Partisi*—HİS). The Islamist, nationalist, and populist party was founded by Ahmet YÖNLÜER in 2007 and failed to win any seats in the 2009 parliamentary elections.

Leader: Ahmet YÖNLÜER (Chair).

Other Parties:

New Party (*Yeni Parti*—YP). The YP was founded in 2004 by Nuri Çevikel, a former member of parliament who had resigned from the CTB-BG. Çevikel was a settler from Turkey, and the party reportedly was established to focus on the issues of other settlers. Çevikel has been known for his views opposing Denktaş and the UBP.

Leader: Nuri ÇEVIKEL.

Nationalist Justice Party (*Milliyetçi Adalet Partisi*—MAP). The far-right-wing MAP supports unification with Turkey and extension of Turkish citizenship to northern Cypriots. In 1993 the party joined with the HDP and AP to form MMP. The MAP backed President Denktaş in the 2000 presidential election.

The party gained one seat in the assembly after a former DP parliamentarian, Kenan AKIN, defected to the MAP in December 2000. The MAP, which had opposed the UN reunification proposal in the 2004 referendum, ultimately ran on its own in the 2005 parliamentary elections.

Leader: Zorlu TÖRE (Chair).

Nationalist Peace Party (*Milliyetçi Bariş Partisi*—MBP). The MBP was formed as the result of a merger between the MAP and the center-right **Renewal Progress Party** (*Yenilikci Atilim Partisi*—YAP). In the 2003 legislative elections, the MBP received 3.23 percent of the vote. Its cochairs are Ali Riza GÖRGÜN and former UBP member and former president of the legislature, Ertuğrul HASIPOĞLU.

Leaders: Ali Riza GÖRGÜN (Cochair), Ertuğrul HASIPOĞLU (Cochair).

Solution and EU Party (*Çözüm ye AB Partisi*—ÇABP). Established as a pro-unification grouping in 2003, the ÇABP secured 2 percent of the vote in the December 2003 legislative poll. It was headed by Ali EREL, a former president of the Turkish Cypriot Chamber of Commerce. Despite its poor electoral performance the party has spearheaded efforts for the resumption of negotiations aiming to resolve the Cyprus question on the basis of the Annan Plan.

Leader: Ali EREL (President).

Patriotic Unity Movement (*Yurtsever Birlik Hareketi*—YBH). The left-wing YBH was formed as a result of a merger of the **New Cyprus Party** (*Yeni Kıbrıs Partisi*—YKP) and some former members of the CTP (see above) in 1998. The YKP had been founded in 1989 by Alpay Durduran, the TKP/AHP 1985 presidential candidate. In 1998 Durduran urged Turkish Cypriot leaders to return to the bargaining table with their Greek Cypriot counterparts.

The YBH favors the unification of the island and equal treatment for all Cypriots, Greek and Turkish. In 2003 the YBH filed suit with the European Court of Human Rights to challenge the electoral process of the TRNC. The party presented Arif Hasan TAHSİN as its candidate in the first round of presidential balloting in 1999.

In 2006 it was reported that the YKP had reemerged as a separate party with Rasih KESKINER as secretary general. The party held its ninth general congress in May 2007, inviting leftist political parties from Turkey, Greece, and the Republic of Cyprus.

Leader: Alpay DURDURAN (Chair).

Reports on the 1998 legislative balloting indicated that a **National Resistance Party** (*Ulusal Direniş Partisi*—UDİP) had received 4.5 percent of the vote, and the recently formed **Our Party** (*Bizim Parti*—BP), led by Okyay SADIKOĞLU, had received 1.2 percent. The BP, described in 1998 as the first Islamist grouping to participate in a TRNC election, supported President Denktaş in his reelection bid.

On August 25, 2000, Arif Salih KIRDAĞ formed the **Freedom and Justice Party** (*Özgürlük ve Adaleţ Partisi*—ÖAP) to "safeguard bank victims' rights." In December a new centrist formation, the **New Democracy Party** (*Yeni Demokrasi Partisi*), was founded by Eşref DÜŞENKALKAR. In January 2001 the **Liberal Party** (*Liberal Parti*—LP) was launched by Kemal BOLAYIR and Ünal Aki AKİF. In 2004 the **Free Thought Party** was reportedly launched under the leadership of Salih COSAR; the party's initial membership reportedly included two defecting DP legislators, although one subsequently returned to the DP fold.

For information on **National Revival Party** (*Ulusal Diriliş Partisi*—UDP), see the 2008 *Handbook*.

LEGISLATURE

A Turkish Cypriot Legislative Assembly, formerly the Legislative Assembly of the Autonomous Turkish Cypriot Administration, was organized in February 1975. Styled the **Assembly of the Republic** (*Cumhuriyet Meclisi*) under the 1985 constitution, it currently consists of 50 members who are elected for five-year terms on a proportional basis in which parties must surpass a 5 percent threshold to gain representation. Following the election of December 14, 2003, the Republican Turkish Party (CTP) held 19 seats; the National Unity Party (UBP), 18; the Democratic Party (DP), 7; and the Peace and Democracy Movement (BDH), 6.

In the most recent elections on April 19, 2009, the seat distribution was as follows: the UBP, 26 seats; CTP, 15; DP, 5; Communal Liberation Party, 2; and Freedom and Reform Party, 2.

President: Hasan BOZER.

CABINET

[as of June 1, 2009]

Prime Minister	Derviş Eroğlu
Ministers	
Agriculture and Natural Resources	Nazım Çavuşoğlu
Economy and Energy	Sunat Atun
Finance	Ersin Tatar
Foreign Affairs	Hüseyin Özgürgün
Health	Ahmet Kaşif
Interior and Local Administration	İlkay Kamil
Labor and Social Security	Türkal Tokel
National Education, Youth, and Sport	Kemal Dürüst
Public Works and Transportation	Hasan Taçoy
Tourism, Environment, and Culture	Hamza Ersan Saner

COMMUNICATIONS

The constitution of the TRNC guarantees freedom of the press, save for legislative restrictions intended to safeguard public order, national security, public morals, or the proper functioning of the judiciary. According to the International Press Institute (IPI), however, in 2006 "freedom of the press and the right to free expression continue to be violated." Numerous cases have been brought against the editor of the newspaper *Afrika,* cases that would result in more than 2,000 years of imprisonment if the government were successful in all of its prosecutions, according to the IPI. Reports of journalists being harassed, threatened, and arrested reportedly prompted Greek Cypriot journalists to boycott all events in the north for a two-week period in August.

Press. The following are published in Nicosia in Turkish: privately owned *Kıbrıs* (Cyprus), "populist" monthly; *Birlik* (Unity), center-right daily (affiliated with the UBP); *Halkın Sesi* (Voice of the People), daily; *Avrupa* (Europe), independent leftist; *Yeni Düzen* (New Order), CTP organ; *Ortam* (Situation), TKP organ; *Yeni Demokrat* (New Democrat), DP organ; *Vatan* (Homeland), and "anti-establishment" *Afrika*. In addition, a number of mainland Turkish papers circulate, of which the leaders are *Sabah* (Morning), *Milliyet* (Nation), and *Hürriyet* (Liberty).

News agency. The Turkish-sector facilities are Turkish Agency Cyprus (*Türk Ajansı Kıbrıs*—TAK) and the Northern Cyprus News Agency (*Kuzey Kıbrıs Haber Ajansı*).

Broadcasting. Broadcasting in the Turkish sector had been controlled by *Radyo Bayrak* and *Bayrak Radyo Televizyon* (BRT). Currently there are several privately owned stations, including GENÇ-TV, Kanal T, and Kıbrıs. In addition, there is the island-wide public Cyprus Broadcasting Corporation. There were approximately 306,000 radio and 77,400 television receivers in the sector in 1999. In addition to *Radio Bayrak* and the BRT, there are two private radio stations, *First FM* and *Kıbrıs FM*.

INTERGOVERNMENTAL REPRESENTATION

The Turkish Federated State maintained no missions abroad, except for a representative in New York who was recognized by the UN as official spokesperson for the Turkish Cypriot community; it did, however, participate in an Islamic Conference meeting on economic cooperation in Ankara, Turkey, held November 4–6, 1980. The present Turkish Republic of Northern Cyprus has proclaimed itself independent but has been recognized as such only by Turkey, with whom it exchanged ambassadors on April 17, 1985.

IGO Memberships (Non-UN): ECO, OIC.

CZECH REPUBLIC

Česká Republika

Political Status: Independent Czechoslovak Republic proclaimed in 1918; People's Republic of Czechoslovakia established June 9, 1948; redesignated Czechoslovak Socialist Republic on July 11, 1960; renamed Czech and Slovak Federative Republic on April 21, 1990; present Czech Republic proclaimed upon separation of the constituent components of the federation on January 1, 1993.

Area: 30,450 sq. mi. (78,864 sq. km.).

Population: 10,230,060 (2001C); 10,359,000 (2008E).

Major Urban Centers (2005E): PRAGUE (1,165,000), Brno (368,000), Ostrava (312,000), Plzeň (163,000).

Official Language: Czech.

Monetary Unit: Koruna (official rate December 1, 2009: 17.19 koruny = $1US).

President: Václav KLAUS (Independent); elected by the parliament in the third round of balloting on February 28, 2003, and sworn in for a five-year term on March 7 to replace Václav HAVEL (nominated by ruling coalition headed by the Civic Democratic Party); reelected in the third round of balloting on February 15, 2008, and sworn in for a second five-year term on March 7.

Prime Minister: Jan FISCHER (Independent); appointed by the president on April 9, 2009, to succeed Mirek TOPOLÁNEK (Civic Democratic Party), who had tendered his resignation after losing a vote of confidence in the Chamber of Deputies on March 24; formed new government sworn in on May 8, which won confidence vote in the Chamber of Deputies on June 7.

THE COUNTRY

Situated at the geographical heart of Europe, the Czech Republic consists of about 60 percent of the area of the former Czechoslovak federation. It is bounded by Slovakia on the east, Austria on the south, Germany on the west, and Poland on the north. Incorporating the old Czech "crown lands" of Bohemia and Moravia (plus part of Silesia), the country has a population that is 90.4 percent Czech; small ethnic minorities include Slovaks, Poles, Germans, Roma (Gypsies), and Hungarians (Magyars). The 2001 census did not list "Moravian" as an ethnic category, although 373,294 respondents identified themselves as such. The inhabitants are to a large extent nominally Roman Catholic but encompass a sizable Protestant minority.

Contending with the upland nature of much of the terrain and moderate soil quality, agriculture nonetheless features an extensive dairy sector, as well as traditional strength in the cultivation of grains, potatoes, and hops. The Czech industrial sector, centered in Ostrava and Prague, includes the Škoda automobile manufacturer (part of the German Volkswagen group) and producers of steel, armaments, heavy machinery, glass, and footwear. Export of electrical and electronic goods has grown significantly in recent years, with record annual trade surpluses in 2006 and 2007, led by exports of automobiles, computers, and advanced technologies. Tourism is another important source of foreign currency.

In postwar Eastern Europe, Czechoslovakia ranked second only to the German Democratic Republic in per capita income, although Slovakia had long been less affluent than Bohemia and Moravia. From 1990 the post-Communist government's economic reform efforts focused on removal of restrictions on private enterprise, including the sale of government-owned businesses, modernization of the country's industrial base, and encouragement of foreign investment. These changes accentuated the economic differences between the Czech and Slovak republics, in that progress toward a market economy was much more rapid in the former than in the latter. The economic divergence fueled pressure for political separation, leading to the "velvet divorce" agreements of late 1992 and final separation on January 1, 1993.

By the end of 1995 some 90 percent of state enterprises, with a total capital value of around $35 billion, had been privatized. However, the Czech Republic experienced recession in 1997–1998, undermining the country's ability to meet the economic criteria for proposed accession to the European Union (EU). Prospects improved markedly in 2000, with the government moving forward rapidly on additional reforms, including banking sector privatization.

The world economic contraction that began in late 2008 put the Czech economy into recession in 2009. GDP, which averaged 6 percent in 2005 and 2006, accelerated to 6.5 percent in 2007 before slowing to 3.1 percent in 2008 as the economy began its slide into recession. Projections for 2009 forecast negative growth of as much as 4 or 5 percent but with a return to modest growth in 2010. Inflation climbed from 1.9 percent in 2005 to 2.5 percent in 2006 and 2.8 percent in 2007; prices rose more than 6 percent in 2008 but fell sharply in the last quarter of 2008 and averaged under 2 percent in the first half of 2009. Unemployment hovered near 8 percent in 2005 and 2006 and then fell to 6.6 percent in 2007, fell again to 6 percent in 2008, and then reversed direction and rose steadily in 2009 to stand at 8.5 percent by August as the recession sparked layoffs.

A broad range of economic reforms, some of which contributed to political discord, were required by the EU for membership. Additional

controversial reforms have also been proposed for the country's expected adoption of the euro and incorporation into the Eurozone. As a sign of progress, in 2008 the Czech Republic escaped EU disciplinary proceedings by reducing its public finance deficit below the required 3 percent of GDP in 2006 (2.7 percent) and 2007 (1.6 percent). The improved budget performance was the result of public sector spending reforms and robust economic growth. This momentum was lost in the crisis conditions of 2009, however, as the government approved deficits between 4.5 and 5 percent for the near term as part of its recovery plan, exceeding the EU limit.

GOVERNMENT AND POLITICS

Political background. From its establishment in 1918 until its dismemberment following the Munich agreement of 1938, Czechoslovakia was the most politically mature and democratically governed of the new states of Eastern Europe. Due mainly to the preponderant role of Soviet military forces in the liberation of the country at the close of World War II, the Communists gained a leading position in the postwar cabinet and assumed full control in February 1948.

The trial and execution of top Communist leaders such as Vladimír CLEMENTIS and Rudolf SLÁNSKÝ during the Stalinist purges in the early 1950s exemplified the country's posture as a docile Soviet satellite under the leadership of Antonín NOVOTNÝ, first secretary of the Communist Party and (from 1957) president of the republic. By 1967 growing unrest among intellectuals and students had produced revolutionary ferment, which led in early 1968 to Novotný's ouster and his replacement by Alexander DUBČEK as party first secretary and by Gen. Ludvík SVOBODA as president. Dubček, a prominent Slovak Communist, rapidly emerged as the leader of a popular movement for far-reaching political and economic change.

A reformist cabinet headed by Oldřich ČERNÍK took office in April 1968 with a program that included strict observance of legality, broader political discussion, fewer economic and cultural restrictions, and increased Slovak autonomy under new constitutional arrangements designed in part to provide for redress of economic disadvantages. Widely hailed within Czechoslovakia, the so-called Prague Spring was sharply criticized by the Soviet Union, which, on August 20–21, 1968, invaded and occupied the country in concert with the other Warsaw Pact nations except Romania.

The period after the 1968 invasion was characterized by the progressive entrenchment of more conservative elements within the government and the party and by a series of pacts that specified Czechoslovakia's "international commitments," set limits on internal reforms, and allowed the stationing of Soviet troops on Czech soil. For a time, the pre-August leadership was left in power, but Dubček was replaced by Gustáv HUSÁK as party leader in 1969, removed from his position in the Presidium, and expelled from the party in 1970. Černík retained his post as chair of the government until 1970, when he was also expelled from the party. The actions against the "Prague Spring" leaders were paralleled by widespread purges of other reformers during 1969–1971, some 500,000 party members ultimately being affected. President Svoboda, although reelected by the Federal Assembly to a second five-year term in 1973, was replaced on May 29, 1975, by Husák, who retained his party posts. Husák was unanimously reelected president in 1980 and 1985.

The policies of reconstruction (*perestroika*) advanced in the Soviet Union following Mikhail Gorbachev's assumption of power in 1985 proved particularly difficult for the Czech leadership to emulate, since it appeared the government was being called upon to implement reforms that it had been charged with eradicating after 1968. Thus, the designation in mid-December 1987 of Miloš JAKEŠ to succeed Husák as party leader seemed to represent a compromise between hard-line conservatives and Gorbachev-oriented liberals. Over the course of 1988, numerous members of Charter 77 (formed by prominent playwright Václav HAVEL and other dissidents to monitor compliance with both domestically and internationally mandated human rights obligations) were arrested, as were hundreds of Roman Catholics. There were notable dissident protests in August 1988 on the 20th anniversary of the Soviet-led invasion and again in October on the 70th anniversary of the country's independence.

As elsewhere in Eastern Europe, the edifice of Communist power crumbled quickly in Czechoslovakia in late 1989. On November 20, one day after formation of the opposition Civic Forum under Havel's leadership, 250,000 antiregime demonstrators marched in Prague, and government leaders held initial discussions with Forum representatives the next day. On November 22 Dubček returned to the limelight with an address before an enthusiastic rally in Bratislava, and on November 24 Karel URBÁNEK was named to succeed Jakeš as party general secretary. In the course of a nationwide strike on November 28 (preceded by a three-day rally of 500,000 in Prague), the government agreed to power sharing, but an offer on December 3 to allocate a minority of portfolios to non-Communist ministers was rejected by opposition leaders. Two days later the regime accepted loss of its monopoly status, and on December 10 President Husák resigned after swearing in the first non-Communist-dominated government in 41 years, under the premiership of Marián ČALFA. On December 29 the assembly unanimously elected Havel as the new head of state.

The Civic Forum and its Slovak counterpart, Public Against Violence, won a substantial majority of federal legislative seats in nationwide balloting on June 8 and 9, 1990, with Čalfa (who had resigned from the Communist Party on January 18) forming a new government on June 27 and Havel being elected to a regular two-year term as president on July 5. However, during 1991 the anti-Communist coalition, its major objective achieved, crumbled into less inclusive party formations. In November negotiations between federal and republican leaders over the country's future political status collapsed, with the Federal Assembly becoming deadlocked over the issue of a referendum on separate Czech and Slovak states. With the legislature's presidium having called an election for June, a contest between Czech Finance Minister Václav KLAUS and former Slovak prime minister Vladimír MEČIAR emerged. Klaus favored a right-of-center liberal economic policy with rapid privatization; Mečiar preferred a slower transition to capitalism for the eastern republic, where unemployment, at 12 percent, was three times that of the Czech lands. The two retained firm control of their respective regions in federal and national balloting on June 5–6, after which Mečiar returned to the post of Slovak prime minister, with Klaus choosing to serve as prime minister of a Czech, rather than a federal, administration.

In postelection constitutional talks, the Czech side argued that there should be either a properly functioning federation with a strong central administration or a speedy separation. When the Slovak side rejected Prague's concept of a continued federation, Klaus moved quickly for a formal dissolution, which was endorsed by the two governments by late August 1992. Since majority public opinion in both republics opposed separation, the left-wing opposition parties mounted determined rearguard resistance to the governmental plan, which on October 1 failed to obtain the required three-fifths majority in the federal parliament. Amid growing constitutional confusion, Klaus and Mečiar on October 6 drew up virtually identical separation blueprints, to come into effect on January 1, 1993. On November 25 the plan secured the backing of 183 of the 300 federal deputies—3 more than the required minimum—during a historic vote in which several opposition members broke party discipline by voting in favor. Concurrently, a proposal by the left-wing parties that the separation issue should be submitted to a popular referendum was rebuffed.

Following the official birth of the new state on January 1, 1993, Klaus remained as the Czech Republic's prime minister, heading an ongoing coalition of his own Civic Democratic Party (*Občanská Demokratická Strana*—ODS), the Civic Democratic Alliance (*Občanská Demokratická Aliance*—ODA), and the Christian and Democratic Union–Czech People's Party (*Křest'anská a Demokratická Unie–Česká Strana Lidová*—KDU-ČSL). On January 26 the Czech Parliament endorsed the government's unopposed nomination of Havel as president for a five-year term. Other constitutional institutions were subsequently put in place, including a Constitutional Court. Legislation adopted in July 1993 declared the former Communist regime to have been illegal and lifted the statute of limitations on politically motivated crimes committed during the Communist era.

In October 1994 the government was shaken by the disclosure of alleged corruption in the much-vaunted privatization program. Klaus strove to calm public fears, but the left-wing opposition parties were boosted in their claim that overly hasty privatization was mainly benefiting profiteers and criminals. Nevertheless, the ODS took some 30 percent of the vote, well ahead of the other parties, in the November local elections.

Relative political stability and economic progress in 1995 appeared to confirm the Czech Republic as being the ex-Communist state closest to achieving Western European standards, although a substantial gap remained to be closed. In the campaign for legislative elections on May 31–June 1, 1996, the ruling coalition parties stressed the need for continuity, while the left-wing parties called for political change amid widespread public disquiet about the negative social consequences of rapid transition to a market economy. The results yielded an unexpected setback for the government, which was reduced to minority status (99 seats) in the new Chamber of Deputies, while the Czech Social Democratic Party (*Česká Strana Sociáln Demokratická*—ČSSD) quadrupled its support; the Communists also gained ground, although the left fell well short of an aggregate majority. The outcome was the formation on July 4 of a minority center-right coalition of the ODS, ODA, and KDU-ČSL under the continued premiership of Klaus, who also received a conditional promise of external support from the ČSSD. The ČSSD continued its electoral advance in November in the nation's first Senate balloting, securing 25 seats to the ODS's 32.

In the wake of an ODS campaign financing scandal and mounting evidence that the Czech economic "miracle" had been somewhat illusory, Klaus, under pressure from Havel, ODS dissidents, and his coalition partners, submitted his resignation on November 30, 1997, although he agreed to stay on in a caretaker capacity. On December 17 Havel invited Josef TOŠOVSKÝ, governor of the central bank, to form a government, which, as approved on January 2, 1998, included anti-Klaus representatives from the ODS, members of the ODA and the KDU-ČSL, and a number of unaffiliated "technocrats." Subsequently, on January 20, Havel was reelected to a second five-year term, albeit by only one vote in the second round of parliamentary balloting. Eight days later the government won a confidence motion by a vote of 123–71, thanks in part to the support of the ČSSD, which had agreed only upon the condition that early elections be held in the summer.

The ČSSD won a plurality of 74 seats in the legislative balloting of June 19–20, 1998, followed by the ODS with 63 seats. However, neither Miloš ZEMAN, the prime minister-designate of the ČSSD, nor the ODS's Klaus was able to form a majority coalition government following the balloting. Zeman was ultimately appointed on July 17 as a result of an "opposition contract" under which the ODS agreed to support the ČSSD in crucial legislative votes, if necessary, while remaining outside the government. On the following day he announced a ČSSD cabinet, in which many ministries went to former members of the Communist Party. President Havel formally appointed the new cabinet on July 22, and it received a 73–39 vote of confidence in the Chamber of Deputies on August 19, the ODS deputies, as agreed, not participating in the vote. The 24 deputies from the Communist Party of Bohemia and Moravia (*Komunistická Strana Čech a Moravy*—KSČM) also abstained.

The ČSSD won a plurality of 70 seats at the June 14–15, 2002, balloting for the Chamber of Deputies. On July 15 Vladimír ŠPIDLA of the ČSSD was sworn in to head a new cabinet comprising the ČSSD, the KDU-ČSL, and the Freedom Union–Democratic Union (*Unie Svobody Demokratická Unie*—US-DEU). Upon his installation as prime minister, Špidla made it clear that EU accession was the top priority. To that end, the government initiated bank reforms, introduced new tax measures, and reduced public spending in order to bring the deficit down to EU standards. However, those initiatives caused a split within the ČSSD (whose left-wingers accused Špidla of caving in to the demands of the rightist elements of the KDU-ČSL and the US-DEU) and discord within sections of the population adversely affected by the cutbacks.

It took three rounds of contentious balloting to choose a new president in 2003, after incumbent President Václav Havel announced his intention to resign at the end of his term. As a result, following Havel's resignation on February 2, the duties of the president were temporarily divided between the prime minister and the speaker of the Chamber of Deputies. Finally, on February 28, Václav Klaus of the ODS was declared the victor over Jan SOKOL of the ČSSD.

President Klaus remained a vocal opponent of the Czech Republic's accession to the EU, but a national referendum on July 13–14, 2003, endorsed membership by a 77 percent "yes" vote. Consequently, the Czech Republic joined the EU with nine other new members on May 1, 2004. However, the cutbacks and other reforms required by the EU appeared to erode support for Prime Minister Špidla, who resigned on June 30 in the wake of the fifth-place performance by the ČSSD in the recent balloting for the European Parliament in June 2004 (the ČSSD won only 8.8 percent of the vote, compared to 30 percent for the ODS and 20 percent for the KSČM). He was succeeded by former deputy prime minister and interior minister Stanislav GROSS, who also assumed leadership of the ČSSD. Gross's new government (also comprising the ČSSD, KDU-ČSL, and US-DEU) won approval by a vote of 101–98 in the Chamber of Deputies on August 24. Gross raised public sector wages while also indicating his administration would attempt to improve the economic climate for the business community.

The KDU-ČSL members resigned from the cabinet in late March 2005 as the result of questions raised concerning Prime Minister Gross's financial affairs in his private property dealings. Gross resigned on April 25, and he was succeeded by the ČSSD's Jiří PAROUBEK, who immediately announced a cabinet comprising the same three parties and many of the ministers who had belonged to the previous government. Paroubek pledged to lower income taxes but also reduce the budget deficit, which to many observers sounded like a standard (but probably unattainable) campaign platform in advance of the legislative elections scheduled for June 2006. Paroubek also promised to push for Czech ratification of the proposed EU Constitution but was unable to secure enough support in parliament.

In a close election that divided the electorate almost evenly between the left and center-right, the ODS won a plurality of 81 seats in the legislative balloting of June 2–3, 2006, followed by the ČSSD with 74 seats. Neither party secured enough seats to form a majority government without including the other or the communist KSČM (with 26 seats) in a coalition. The close split between the two major parties led to a political stalemate over the next seven months and raised the prospect of early elections.

On August 16, 2006, President Klaus accepted the resignation of Prime Minister Paroubek's government and appointed ODS leader Mirek TOPOLÁNEK as prime minister. Topolánek's efforts to form a coalition government with the KDU-ČSL and the Green Party (*Strana Zelených*—SZ) fell apart on August 22. A subsequent bid to form an ODS minority government was nixed by the ČSSD. A ČSSD gambit to form a coalition government with the KDU-ČSL and the KSČM failed in late August.

On September 4, 2006, Topolánek formed a minority government comprising nine members of the ODS and six independents. The new government was rejected on October 3 in a 99–96 vote of no confidence in the Chamber of Deputies; the entire cabinet subsequently resigned on October 11. President Klaus reappointed Topolánek as prime minister on November 8 with instructions to form a majority government. After his negotiations with the ČSSD, KDU-ČSL, and SZ failed to yield an agreement into early December, Topolánek assembled a coalition with the KDU-ČSL and SZ later in the month. However, with the three parties controlling only 100 seats in the 200-seat chamber, the coalition's ability to secure a vote of confidence depended on tacit support from opposition deputies. The new government, with nine ODS, five KDU-ČSL, and four SZ ministers, was appointed by the president on January 10, 2007; it won approval from the Chamber of Deputies (by a 100–97 vote) on January 19, 2007, when two ČSSD deputies were deliberately absent from the vote of confidence and another deputy abstained. Soon after the vote of confidence, the new culture minister resigned to protest alleged pressure from Prime Minister Topolánek to appoint a deputy minister who had been instrumental in lobbying the renegade ČSSD deputies. In early February KDU-ČSL Chair and Deputy Prime Minister Jiří ČUNEK was accused of accepting a half-million-koruna bribe five years earlier while he was mayor of Vsetin, and he faced the prospect of prosecution despite his public denial of any wrongdoing. The opposition parties called for his immediate dismissal from the cabinet in February. Topolánek refused to seek Čunek's resignation, preferring to await action from the KDU-ČSL to remove Čunek, more concrete official charges, or a finding of guilt. But Green Party Chair and Deputy Prime Minister Martin BURSÍK called directly for Čunek's departure from the government. The KDU-ČSL refused to remove Čunek, however, and threatened to leave the coalition if Čunek were dismissed.

SZ Education Minister Dana KUCHTOVÁ resigned in October 2007 for failure to secure eligible EU funds in support of research and development for Czech educational programs. The SZ's Ondřej LIŠKA, was appointed to the post by President Klaus on December 4. Deputy Prime Minister Jiří Čunek was forced to resign from the cabinet on November 7, in the wake of renewed corruption charges. President Klaus reinstated Čunek to his previous cabinet positions on April 2, 2008, after Čunek was acquitted.

In the third round of presidential balloting on February 15, 2008, President Václav Klaus was reelected, defeating challenger Jan ŠVEJNAR in a joint session of parliament by a vote of 141–111. Several rounds of balloting the previous week had failed to yield the required majority in each chamber for one candidate. Klaus was sworn in for a second five-year term on March 7, 2008. Švejnar, a university professor in the United States but a Czech citizen and former economic adviser to President Havel, agreed to run against Klaus with the support of the ČSSD and the SZ. He did not have the backing of the KSČM, however, whose votes were necessary to unseat Klaus. The first round of the election was held on February 8, 2008, in a joint session of parliament and by public ballot (the ODS had moved for a secret ballot, but that measure was defeated). After two inconclusive rounds in which Klaus prevailed in the Senate poll, but Švejnar won the Chamber of Deputies poll, a third round was scheduled for the following day, when the ballots of both houses would be pooled. The February 9 round proved inconclusive as Klaus fell 1 vote short of the 140 votes needed for victory (KSČM MPs declined to vote for either candidate). A new election was scheduled for the following week. On February 15 the election once again had two inconclusive rounds. In the third round Klaus prevailed with 141 votes to 111 for Švejnar.

After a poor showing for the coalition parties in the October 2008 Senate balloting, Topolánek announced a reshuffling of the cabinet in January 2009. President Klaus appointed four new ministers on January 23 as replacements at the ministries of health, transport, minorities and human rights, and the legislative council. Among those dismissed was Jiří Čunek; leader of the KDU-ČSL. Vlasta PARKANOVÁ, minister of defense and KDU-ČSL deputy chair, was named the new deputy prime minister.

Prime Minister Topolánek's mandate was always razor thin, and after surviving four no-confidence votes in the midst of numerous cabinet-level scandals and public relations fiascos throughout 2007 and 2008, the ODS-led government finally lost its mandate following passage of a no-confidence vote sponsored by the ČSSD on March 24, 2009. Two ODS and two SZ deputies broke party ranks to vote with the ČSSD and KSČM deputies to pass the motion with 101 votes. The cabinet submitted its resignation immediately thereafter but was not dismissed until a new interim government of nonpartisan experts and civil servants, negotiated by the coalition parties with the opposition ČSSD, was appointed by President Klaus on May 8; the interim cabinet was under the leadership of Jan FISCHER, head of the Czech Statistical Office, who Klaus named prime minister on April 9. The interim government won a vote of confidence from the Chamber of Deputies on June 7.

Constitution and government. Adopted by the then Czech National Council on December 16, 1992, the constitution of the Czech Republic came into effect on January 1, 1993, upon the dissolution of the Czechoslovak federation. It defines the Czech Republic as a unitary state with legislative power vested in a bicameral parliament, in which three-fifths majorities are required for the passage of constitutional amendments. Considerable executive authority is exercised by the president, who is elected for a five-year term by parliament. The president appoints the prime minister and, in consultation with the prime minister, the Council of Ministers. A new Council of Ministers must pass a vote of confidence in the Chamber of Deputies within one month of the council's appointment.

The National Council decided that much Czechoslovak federal law would continue to apply in the Czech Republic; however, in cases of conflict between Czech and federal law, the former would apply. Following the deletion from the Czechoslovak Constitution in December 1989 of the guarantee of Communist power, a systematic revision of legal codes was initiated to reestablish "fundamental legal norms," including the appointment of judges for life. A revision of the criminal law included abolition of the death penalty and provision of a full guarantee of judicial review, while a law on judicial rehabilitation facilitated the quashing of almost all of the political trials of the Communist era. Commercial and civil law revisions established the supremacy of the courts in making decisions relating to rights. In July 2000 parliament passed electoral revisions that, for purposes of decentralization, established 14 regional assemblies.

Both houses of the Czech Parliament have debated measures that would allow for the direct election of the president, particularly in view of the difficulties associated with the past three presidential elections. (Opinion polls consistently show that public sentiment is in favor of direct elections.) On June 4, 2003, the government approved legislation for popular presidential elections in which the winning candidate would have to receive a majority of the vote in the first round of balloting or face a run-off election. When that legislation did not pass, and another contentious election in February 2008 left all sides bruised from the encounter, new calls for direct election of the president were put forward in parliament. Since a change in the manner of election entails a constitutional amendment, these bills must be approved by three-fifths majorities in both houses of parliament; neither house has yet been able to achieve the needed votes.

On June 15, 2009, President Klaus signed into law a special constitutional bill limiting the term of the sitting parliament and paving the way for early elections in early October 2009. On September 10 the Constitutional Court overturned the law. Soon thereafter both chambers of parliament passed a new amendment providing for the Chamber of Deputies to dissolve before the end of term by a three-fifths vote of the Chamber. The amendment was promulgated by President Klaus on September 13.

Foreign relations. The collapse of Communist rule in late 1989 led to a transformation of Czechoslovakia's external relations, establishing new parameters that were subsequently inherited by the independent Czech Republic. On December 14 the newly installed non-Communist foreign minister, Jiří DIENSTBIER, declared that the 1968 agreement under which Soviet troops were stationed in Czechoslovakia was invalid because it had been concluded under duress. Subsequently, during a visit by President Havel to Moscow on February 26–27, 1990, the Soviets agreed to withdraw most of their forces by May, with the remainder to leave by July 1991 (a pledge that was honored, amid considerable Czech fanfare, on June 25, 1991).

In September 1990 the Federative Republic signaled its return to the international financial community by rejoining the International Monetary Fund (IMF) and the World Bank; a founding member of both institutions, it had withdrawn from membership in 1954 after a dispute with the IMF over consultation on exchange restrictions. On January 21, 1991, Czechoslovakia joined with Hungary and Poland in withdrawing from participation in the Warsaw Pact (disbanded soon thereafter), while in June of that year the (Soviet-bloc) Council for Mutual Economic Assistance (Comecon) was formally dissolved after the failure of half-hearted proposals for a successor body. (See *Political Handbook of the World 1991* for articles on both groupings.) Meanwhile, Czechoslovakia had been admitted to the Council of Europe on February 21 and had publicly set membership of the European Community (EC, subsequently the EU) and the North Atlantic Treaty Organization (NATO) as key objectives. On December 16, 1991, an EC-Czechoslovak association agreement was signed.

The goal of eventual EC membership was the joint aim of the "Visegrád" cooperation bloc formed on February 15, 1991, by Czechoslovakia, Hungary, and Poland. Czechoslovakia also participated in the Central European Initiative (CEI) created on January 28, 1992, and on March 18 became the first former Communist state to ratify the European Convention of Human Rights. President Havel signed a ten-year friendship treaty with the Russian Federation in Moscow on April 1, as well as a collateral agreement with the Commonwealth of Independent States (CIS), settling outstanding issues related to the withdrawal of Soviet troops.

On December 21, 1992, the Visegrád countries concluded a Central European Free Trade Agreement (CEFTA), to which the Czech and Slovak republics were deemed to have acceded at their attainment of separate sovereignty on January 1, 1993. (See Poland, Foreign relations, for additional information about CEFTA.) In May 1999 the four Visegrád states held their first summit since 1994 in renewed furtherance of regional cooperation.

On January 19, 1993, the UN General Assembly admitted the Czech and Slovak republics to membership, dividing between them the seats on various subsidiary organs that had been held by Czechoslovakia. The Czech Republic also became a member of the Conference on (later Organization for) Security and Cooperation in Europe (CSCE/OSCE), the European Bank for Reconstruction and Development (EBRD), and the Council of Europe. After some delay, revised association agreements were signed by the EC with the Czech Republic and Slovakia on October 4, 1993. Meanwhile, President Havel had signed a further friendship and cooperation treaty with Russia during a visit by President Boris Yeltsin in August. The treaty was finally ratified by parliament in September 1995.

A priority for the new Czech Republic was to normalize its relations with Slovakia. A temporary currency union between the two countries quickly broke down, while the notional existence of a customs union did not prevent a dramatic slump in bilateral trade in 1993. Progress was made in 1994 in implementing some 30 bilateral treaties and agreements, covering such matters as the division of federal property, debt settlement, and border arrangements. However, disputes persisted, notably over outstanding Slovak debts and the Czech rejection of a Slovak proposal for joint citizenship for the 300,000 Slovaks in the Czech Republic. At prime ministerial meetings on November 24, 1999, and May 22, 2000, the two republics resolved their remaining property and debt disputes.

It became clear in 1994 that neither NATO nor the EU envisaged the speedy accession of the former Communist states. In the case of NATO, the Czech government welcomed, though without great enthusiasm, the alternative Partnership for Peace program (becoming a signatory in March), while instituting major army reforms designed to bring about compatibility with NATO norms and to reduce the Czech military complement from 85,000 to 65,000. In July 1997 NATO invited the Czech Republic, Hungary, and Poland (but, notably, not Slovakia) to join the alliance, and formal entry occurred on March 12, 1999.

The Czech Republic joined with the other Visegrád states in a continuing effort to promote NATO expansion to other Central and East European states. The Czech Republic in particular sought the inclusion of Slovakia in NATO as a means to secure the state's eastern borders and to enhance Slovakia's democratic prospects. At NATO's 2002 Prague summit, seven states from the region, including Slovakia, were invited to join the alliance (formal accession occurred in March 2004).

On January 23, 1996, the Czech Republic formally applied for EU membership despite domestic opposition from the unreconstructed left and the ultra-nationalist right. In December 1997 the EU included the Czech Republic in the so-called first wave of potential new members (see EU article for details), and entry negotiations began in the spring of 1998 in anticipation of accession within five years.

Prague's quest for EU membership had been complicated by the issue of the property of the Sudeten Germans expelled from Czechoslovakia immediately after World War II. German government officials had warned that the Czechs would have to negotiate on this issue, whereas Prague insisted that it would accept liability only for property confiscated after the Communist takeover in 1948. In January 1994 the Czech government adopted a draft law providing for the restitution of certain Jewish properties expropriated after 1938; however, a preamble defined this measure as exceptional and as not providing a precedent for claims in respect to the Sudeten Germans. In March 1995, moreover, the Constitutional Court upheld the legality of the 1945 expulsion of the ethnic Germans and the confiscation of their property. The issue was prominent during the 1996 Czech election campaign, after the German finance minister, Theo Waigel, had on May 25 called on the Prague government to apologize for the postwar treatment of the Sudeten Germans. His remark drew a public rebuke from Prime Minister Klaus and a request from the Czech foreign minister that German politicians stop "lecturing" Czechs about events surrounding World War II. Czech parliamentary debate on the issue was capped on March 5, 1997, when the Senate followed the lower chamber in approving (54 votes to 25) the Czech-German declaration already ratified by Germany. In that document Germany expressed its regret for its occupation of Czech territory, while Prague took a similar stance regarding excessive brutality in expelling ethnic Germans. Both sides agreed not to strain their relationship by pursuing further legal or political claims arising from the war.

At the EU Copenhagen summit in December 2002, the Czech Republic was one of ten states invited to join the EU. In a referendum held on June 13–14, 2003, Czechs approved EU entry on a vote of 77.3 percent in favor and 22.7 against. Differences between the government and the president were evident during the referendum's campaign, as Klaus declined to publicly campaign in support of accession. The Czech Republic joined the EU on May 1, 2004. President Klaus continued to challenge integration with the EU in February 2005 when he asked the Constitutional Court to rule whether the EU Constitution is in harmony with the Czech Constitution, to which the court responded that the case had no standing since the EU Constitution had not yet been adopted or submitted to Klaus for signing. Throughout 2005 the EU repeatedly warned the Czech Republic that it lagged far behind in adopting directives related to a wide range of economic activity, even initiating proceedings in some cases.

The Czech Republic achieved another milestone in EU integration when it joined the Schengen zone in December 2007; the Schengen treaty provided for the elimination of border controls for citizens of signatory countries, allowing Czech citizens unrestricted travel within the zone without the need for passports or identification cards. (Tensions arose in 2008, however, when Czech motorists complained about excessive police stops by Austrian and German police beyond the border crossings.)

Belgium, Denmark, and France indicated in 2008 that they intended to open their labor markets to Czech citizens by 2009. In addition, the Czech Republic joined the European Space Agency on June 25, 2008. Currency integration remained the major obstacle to full integration, however, as Czech public deficits remained above the thresholds set for entering the Eurozone. Even as the deficits came in line with EU criteria in 2008, the Czech government put off setting a target date for adoption of the euro. Some additional areas of diplomatic friction remained. After receiving a lower carbon emission quota than it requested in 2007, the Czech government sued the European Commission for the first time, citing its projected growth rate as its reason for requesting an emission quota that exceeded Czech yearly emissions. Czech and international human rights organizations criticized the government in 2007 for not ratifying the International Criminal Court (ICC) treaty (the Czech Republic was the last EU holdout). In July 2008 the Czech Senate voted to acknowledge the ICC treaty, moving a step closer to ratification. The Czech government pushed for EU enlargement in 2008–2009 to include the Balkan states, despite the preference of Germany, France, and others for ratification of the Lisbon Treaty before accepting new members.

U.S. President George W. Bush visited President Klaus in Prague (before the June 2007 G8 summit in Germany) to advance the ongoing U.S. effort to secure a radar facility in the Czech Republic as part of a proposed U.S. antimissile defense system. (Washington announced that the system was designed to detect attacks from the Middle East, with the missile interceptor site to be located in Poland.) Bush pledged in return to eliminate visa requirements for Czech citizens visiting the United States. The Russian government had previously reacted negatively to the initiative, calling it a threat to Russian security and countering with threats to target the antimissile facilities with Russian weapons. The controversy surrounding the radar base dominated discussions between Russian President Putin and President Klaus in April on the first official state visit to Russia by a Czech head of state. During the June 2007 G8 summit, President Putin proposed that a Russian radar base in Azerbaijan be used jointly with the United States to detect missile attacks, instead of building the radar facility in the Czech Republic. Negotiations continued with the United States until the Czech government announced that a final agreement had been reached in early April 2008. The parties signed the treaty on July 8, 2008, pending ratification by the legislatures of the two governments. Several days later, amid protests and veiled threats of military countermeasures from its defense ministry, the Russian government announced that oil supplies to the Czech Republic would be reduced by several hundred thousand tons in July. The decline was attributed to technical difficulties, not retaliation for the radar agreement. Tensions between Russia and the Czech Republic over the radar base continued into 2009. In September 2009 U.S. President Barack Obama cancelled the plans to build the radar base, citing a reassessment of the missile capability of Iran, the principal potential threat the defense shield was intended to deter.

A recent regional dispute involved the start up in October 2000 of the Temelin nuclear power plant. Austria, in particular, objected to completion of the facility, and in September environmentalists blocked border crossings with Austria and Germany in protest. In December the Austrian and Czech governments reached a measure of accommodation, agreeing to a new EU-supervised environmental impact study (the Melk agreement). However, tension over the plant resurfaced in 2001, with Austria threatening to block the Czech Republic's proposed accession to the EU unless safety issues were resolved. Late in the year Prime Minister Zeman announced that some $27 million would be spent to alleviate the concerns. The controversy flared up again in early March 2007 after Prime Minister Topolánek met in late February in Prague with his Austrian counterpart, Chancellor Alfred Gusenbauer, to discuss Austrian concerns over the plant's safety and management within the terms of the Melk agreement. The two leaders agreed to establish a joint Czech-Austrian commission to oversee operation of the facility. A leak of radioactive water from the facility occurred on the same day as the bilateral meeting; news of the incident was not made public for several days. Reports of the incident sparked new protests from Austrian antinuclear demonstrators at the Czech border and complaints from Gusenbauer over Czech reluctance to share information. A second, smaller leak occurred during a test one week later. Subsequently, the Austrian government announced preliminary plans to file an international lawsuit to enforce the December 2000 Melk agreement or close the plant. In May 2007 the Austrian foreign ministry sent a diplomatic note on the issue to Prague. Continued antinuclear protests by Austrian activists at the Czech border disrupted travel and increased the pressure on the Austrian government to pursue the lawsuit. In response, a Czech ultranationalist party staged a counterprotest at the Austrian border. The Czech government complained that the border protests were disrupting travel and commerce in violation of EU rules.

Prime Minister Topolánek opened a new opportunity to resolve another minor regional dispute in a January 2007 visit to Warsaw, Poland, when he signaled a willingness to settle a disputed border between the two countries. At issue were 368 hectares of farmland across seven municipalities in Silesia. A final settlement agreement, however, was not expected before 2010.

About 500 Czech troops served in the NATO-led Kosovo Force (KFOR) after that operation began in 1999, and a much smaller contingent has served in Bosnia and Herzegovina. After the Kosovars declared independence from Serbia in 2008 the Czech government, despite internal divisions over the move, recognized Kosovo and opened an embassy.

The Špidla administration declined a request to contribute troops to the U.S./UK-led invasion of Iraq in 2003, although the subsequent governments provided a small contingent of support staff to assist coalition efforts in that country. Czech troops have been participating in the NATO Multinational Force in Afghanistan since March 2005. In April 2007 a Czech military hospital was set up in Afghanistan to support NATO troops. An additional 63 troops from a biological and chemical warfare unit were authorized in June 2008. The total Czech deployment to Afghanistan was approximately 480 by September 2009.

The Czech Republic sought election to the UN Security Council for the 2008–2009 term, but pulled out of the voting after failing to secure enough votes in the first ballot (Croatia subsequently was selected for the seat).

The Czech ambassador to Pakistan was killed in a terrorist bomb attack on a hotel in Islamabad on September 20, 2008.

In January 2009 the Czech Republic assumed the rotating presidency of the EU for the customary six-month term. The collapse of the governing coalition halfway into the EU presidency and the refusal of President Klaus to sign the Lisbon Treaty (see Current issues, below) undermined the effectiveness of the Czech EU presidency and its initiatives.

In August 2009 the Czech Republic and Liechtenstein established formal diplomatic relations, overcoming a rift concerning confiscation of property following World War II. Bhutan and the Marshall Islands are the only remaining nations without formal diplomatic relations with the Czech Republic.

Current issues. In 2007 President Klaus and Prime Minister Topolánek steered the coalition government away from adoption of the text of the EU Constitution rejected by French and Dutch voters in 2005. They argued instead for a renegotiated, stripped-down constitutional text, a position that prevailed at the June 2007 EU summit in Lisbon, where member states agreed to draw up a new "reform treaty" to replace the original text. The Lisbon Treaty had to be ratified by the Czech Parliament. After the first reading in parliament ODS deputies moved to refer questions of whether the reform treaty was consistent with the Czech constitutional regime to the Czech Constitutional Court. The SZ and ČSSD MPs, however, pushed for approval without further delay. The court ruled in late November 2008 that the provisions under question did not violate the Czech constitution. The Chamber of Deputies ratified the treaty on February 18, 2009, and the Senate followed suit several months later. Nonetheless, President Klaus refused to sign it, asserting that the treaty was in conflict with the Czech constitution and that it was unnecessary to promulgate the treaty unless Irish voters, who had previously voted it down in a referendum, ratified it with new protocols in place addressing Irish objections.

After surviving the confidence vote in January 2007, Prime Minister Topolánek's three-party coalition government had little or no margin for error since it could only count on 100 votes, 1 vote short of a majority in the Chamber of Deputies. Popular support for the new ODS-led government in early 2007 gave Topolánek some leverage over his chief political rivals. This popular advantage gradually diminished as controversial government proposals, including the U.S. radar base treaty and unpopular health reforms, combined with numerous political scandals eroded trust within the coalition government and shifted public sentiment toward the ČSSD. Topolánek compounded his precarious strategic situation with several high-profile personal gaffes, coarse treatment of political opponents, and highly publicized points of disagreement with President Klaus.

Despite the political tightrope inspired by its razor-thin electoral mandate, Topolánek's government undertook several major policy initiatives. The first was the announcement in February 2007 that the Czech Republic would permit the United States to station an antimissile radar base on Czech soil. Bilateral talks on the issue had begun under the Paroubek government, but after the plan became public in 2007 the ČSSD repudiated that stance and came out against the base. Both the ČSSD and KSČM called for a national referendum on the issue (opinion polls consistently showed a large majority of the public was against the base). Within the coalition government, SZ cabinet members initially pledged support, but only if the facility was brought under NATO's auspices, a condition the government eventually met in negotiations with the United States and NATO. In return for hosting the base, the United States promised to ease U.S. visa requirements for Czechs, to extend financial aid for the Czech military, and to establish stronger security measures to protect against terrorist attacks. The visa issue was resolved via a bilateral agreement in 2008, despite EU objections that the bilateral agreement was outside of EU-sanctioned auspices. In early April 2008 the terms for the radar base and a Status of Forces Agreement were finalized between the two governments. U.S. Secretary of State Condoleezza Rice traveled to Prague to sign the radar base agreement on July 8, 2008. Before the final treaty was ratified in either country the United States cancelled the plan to build the radar base in September 2009, after a review of the missile capability of and the perceived threats from the Middle East, especially from Iran.

A second major initiative of the ODS-led government was a fiscal reform plan designed to address persistent public sector deficits. The deficits made it difficult to reach the EU convergence criteria, thereby blocking ascension into the Eurozone and delaying adoption of the euro. Left unchecked, demographic trends threatened to send public pension and health care costs spiraling upward after 2009. In April 2007 the cabinet released a package of spending cuts and tax reforms. On the spending side, the measures provided for the eliminantion of the indexing of welfare payments, the introduction of new health care fees, incentives for shorter parental leave, and the abolition of sick benefits for the first three days of illness, all introduced in 2008. The tax measures included introduction of a flat personal income tax of 15 percent, a raise in the value-added tax (VAT) rate, and a gradual decrease in the corporate tax, paired with the introduction of new taxes on less efficient sources of energy (the energy taxes were in response to EU environmental policy mandates). Despite the opposition's charges that the plan was regressive in its impact, giving tax breaks to the wealthy while raising taxes for middle- and lower-income Czechs, the most serious political challenge to the reform proposals came from within the ODS parliamentary group. The need for strict party discipline to pass the reform package gave hard-line ODS deputies leverage to press successfully for even greater tax reductions on personal income and corporations. The financial reforms went into effect despite protests from labor and opposition leaders as well as press reports that a large percentage of Czech families lost child and welfare benefits.

The ČSSD challenged the finance reform legislation in the Constitutional Court, claiming that the measures had been adopted contrary to the procedural requirements of the constitution, and that various provisions of the reform law violated the Charter of Fundamental Rights and Freedoms. The Constitutional Court ruled on January 31, 2008, that the passage of the reforms did not violate the fundamental law, but in a later ruling issued in April the court overturned the unpaid sick leave provision because it failed to protect an employee's right to security during illness. In a third ruling issued in May, the court upheld the fees instituted for physician visits and hospital stays. The fees proved popular with Czech physicians, as they reduced the heavy demand for office visits and cut down on abuse of the health care system. But popular opposition to the health care fees and to new government proposals for reform, including measures aimed at charging tuition for university and raising the retirement age, grew over the course of 2008. Responding to the pressure to scale back, the government agreed to exempt children younger than six years old from the medical fees, but declined to exempt older children and pensioners, despite support for these exemptions from the KDU-ČSL and SZ ministers. Nonetheless, the opposition to the reforms culminated in a massive one-day work stoppage on June 24 during which more than 1 million Czechs joined strikes or slowdowns, including many workers from the transport and health care sectors.

The parliament passed antidiscrimination legislation in April 2008 that guaranteed equal access to health care, social welfare, and educational benefits without regard to race, ethnic origin, religion, age, gender, or sexual orientation. The Czech Republic was the last holdout in adopting the measures mandated by the EU's European Commission. Consistent with his euroskepticism, President Klaus vetoed the legislation on May 16 claiming it was "unnecessary, counterproductive, and of poor quality." The Chamber of Deputies overturned the veto in June 2009 with 118 votes.

The interim government led by Prime Minister Jan Fischer made passage of an economic stimulus priorities package, privatization of several state-owned enterprises (including the national airline), and spending on transportation infrastructure and education its top priorities. President Klaus vetoed the stimulus measure, however. The Chamber of Deputies overturned the veto in September with 101 votes.

After the fall of the ODS-led government the expectation among all legislative parties was for elections to be held in early October, based on an amendment to the Constitution passed in June and signed by President Klaus (see Constitution and government, above). An objection brought to the Constitutional Court by an independent deputy who sought to halt a premature expiration of his mandate was upheld by the court in September. Parliament immediately passed a new amendment providing for the early dissolution of the Chamber of Deputies by a three-fifths vote of that chamber as well as an amendment to the election law speeding up the permissible scheduling of polls in order to bring early elections in November. The ČSSD, however, in a turnabout, refused to support the vote to dissolve the Chamber of Deputies, and the KSČM announced it would abstain from any votes on dissolution. New elections are not likely before the expiration of the mandate in June 2010.

An alarming, growing trend of anti-Roma marches, protests, and acts of violence inspired by far-right ultranationalist movements (and right-wing political parties allegedly affiliated with these groups) gripped the Czech Republic throughout 2008 and 2009. The marches sparked violent clashes between the far-right protestors and riot police, as well as the protestors and counter-protestors. In response to the rise in racist rhetoric and a series of violent attacks on Romany families, Czech Roma advocates called for emigration of Romany to Canada to escape the persecution. An attempt by the ODS-led government in early 2009 to ban far-right parties was struck down by the administrative courts for lack of evidence of direct links to the ultranationalist groups. The interim government renewed the effort to suppress groups associated with racist appeals after a much-publicized near-fatal arson attack in April 2009 on a Romany family in Moravia. In June the government cracked down on selected far-right groups with a series of police raids and by August had arrested four suspects in the arson case with ties to such groups. Soon thereafter the interim government sought once more to ban the Workers' Party for its alleged links to these organizations.

POLITICAL PARTIES AND GROUPS

From 1948 to 1989 Czechoslovakia was under effective one-party rule, although the National Front of the Czechoslovak Socialist Republic (*Národní Fronta*—ČSR), controlled by the Communist Party (*Komunistická Strana Československa*—KSČ), included four minor parties in addition to trade-union, farmer, and other groups. Termed by its most visible leader, Václav Havel, as a "temporary organization" to assist in the transition to democratic rule, the Civic Forum (*Občanské Fórum*—OF) was formally launched by a number of anti-Communist human rights groups on November 19, 1989; nine days later, in conjunction with its Slovak counterpart, it negotiated the settlement under which the KSČ agreed to give up its monopoly of power. Having won the June 1990 general election, the OF in February 1991 split into two wings, a majority of its leadership later voting to establish the Civic Democratic Party (ODS), while others participated in the launching of the Civic Movement (see under ČSNS, below).

During 1992, specifically Czech and Slovak parties became far more influential than those attempting to maintain federal constituencies, thus setting the stage for the breakup of the federal system at the end of 1992. On the establishment of the independent Czech Republic on January 1, 1993, the parties that had claimed a federal identity ceased to do so.

Twenty-six parties or groups and more than 5,000 candidates contested the 2006 legislative elections (18 parties put forward candidates in each of the regions). However, with voter turnout at 64.5 percent, only five parties surpassed the 5 percent threshold for securing seats in the lower house. All but one of the other parties failed to secure 1 percent of the vote.

Less than 15 percent of those participating in a 2007 opinion poll expressed trust in political parties, ranking parties lower in that regard than other institutions such as the media, military, police, and churches. In a 2008 poll, 51 percent expressed dissatisfaction with the operation of democracy in the country, while 49 percent indicated that democracy was the best system. The size of the dissatisfied group grew by 6 percent from the previous year, while those satisfied remained stable.

Two hundred candidates registered to contest the October 2008 Senate elections, in which 27 of 81 seats were up for election, but only the ODS, ČSSD, and KSČM fielded a candidate in each of the districts. The ČSSD sweep in the Senate and regional elections set off a chain reaction of events that substantially altered the leadership structure and strength of the coalition parties, eventually bringing down the ODS-led coalition government, triggering early parliamentary elections, and driving party factions to split and form new parties to contest the elections. The opposition ČSSD and KSČM were largely untouched by the turmoil.

Government Parties:

Civic Democratic Party (*Občanská Demokratická Strana*—ODS). The ODS resulted from the inability of the Civic Forum leadership in early 1991 to transform the somewhat diffuse movement into a formal party. Intensely anti-Communist, the ODS quickly built a strong organization and concluded an electoral alliance with the Christian Democratic Party (*Křest'ansko-Demokratická Strana*—KDS), which had originated in the mid-1980s as an unofficial ecumenical Christian group calling for political pluralism and had been registered as a party in December 1989 under the leadership of Václav BENDA, a leading dissident in the Communist era. In the June 1992 election the ODS/KDS became the leading formation both at the federal level and in the Czech National Council, ODS leader Václav Klaus heading the Czech regional administration. Upon formal separation from Slovakia on January 1, 1993, the Czech coalition headed by the ODS became the government of the independent Czech Republic, with Klaus continuing as prime minister.

In November 1995 the ODS formally merged with the KDS under the ODS rubric, although five of the ten KDS deputies preferred to join the KDU-ČSL. The ODS lost ground in the spring 1996 balloting for the Chamber of Deputies, falling to 68 seats, but Klaus was able to form a minority coalition. However, allegations of irregularities regarding campaign finances intensified in 1997, contributing to the collapse of the Klaus government in late November. Klaus was reelected chair at the ODS Congress in December, and he finally decided that the party would not participate in the "transitional" government led by Josef Tošovský. Many party dissidents, reportedly upset with Klaus's autocratic style and the alleged financial improprieties, objected to the chair's directive, and four ODS members accepted positions in the January 1998 government. Anti-Klaus legislators subsequently resigned from the ODS to form the new Freedom Union (see US-DEU, below), and several cabinet members reportedly also left the party. Klaus was unable to forge a coalition government following the June 1998 legislative balloting (at which the ODS secured 63 seats, second to the ČSSD) and subsequently endorsed an "opposition contract" that permitted installation of a ČSSD minority government.

Following the November 2000 partial Senate election, the ODS held 22 seats in the upper house, second to the Quad Coalition (see KDU-ČSL, below). In regional assembly contests, the party won control of six and tied the Quad Coalition in a seventh. In the June 2002 Chamber of Deputies elections, the ODS won 58 seats and continued as the leading opposition party. Klaus resigned as party leader on November 2, 2002, to run for the presidency and was replaced at a party conference by Mirek Topolánek on December 15. After three contentious rounds of balloting in parliament, Klaus was elected president on February 28, 2003. The ODS dominated the balloting in 2004 for the country's 13 regional councils (established in 2000) with 36 percent of the vote.

In the run-up to the 2006 legislative elections, Topolánek's platform emphasized tax reform, with implementation of a 15 percent flat tax rate for the VAT, personal income, and corporate income taxes. He also promised increased anticorruption measures.

The ODS won a plurality in the June 2006 Chamber of Deputies election with 81 seats on a 35.4 percent vote share. Topolánek's subsequent struggle to form a majority government generated tension between him and President Klaus, and the latter questioned publicly whether the government appointed in January 2007 would survive long.

In March 2007 Topolánek announced that Czech conservative MEPs (the ODS had nine European Parliament seats in 2007) would form an alliance with British conservatives to create a new parliamentary group starting in 2009. News reports in the same month detailed that the ODS was cooperating with the KSČM in 65 municipal governments despite a ban against cooperation with the communists at the local level issued by the ODS leadership in November 2006.

President Klaus announced in February 2007 that he would seek a second presidential term. Despite initial concerns about Klaus's earlier public statements deriding the survival chances of the Topolánek premiership, by May the ODS parliamentary members had closed ranks and voted unanimously in their caucuses to support his candidacy. At a national party congress held in Prague in November, the ODS MPs reaffirmed their unanimous support for Klaus. Party Leader Topolánek addressed the congress to defend the ODS-led government's performance and appeal for an end to infighting. He also emphasized that there should be no cooperation with communist parties, even in local government coalitions.

At an ODS national conference in April 2008 Topolánek again defended the party's record in government, claiming that the ODS ministers had defended the party's policy program but had to moderate some goals to accommodate coalition partners. Topolánek publicly criticized ODM Deputy Vlastimil TLUSTÝ in early June 2008, suggesting that Tlustý was no longer welcome in the party after obstructing the finance reforms in August 2007 and derailing legislation on restitution to the Catholic Church in 2008.

Tlustý was back in the news in September when he collaborated with investigative journalists to expose the activities of fellow ODS delegate Jan MORAVA, who allegedly sought sensitive information that could be used to compel MPs in the coalition parties (including Tlustý and SZ MP Olga ZUBOVÁ) to vote with the government. Morava resigned from his seat in parliament on September 8. Another ODS deputy closely allied with Tlustý, Juraj RANINEC, resigned from the party (he remained an MP) the following week in protest over the party's response to the scandal. A third deputy, Jan SCHWIPPEL, followed suit in quitting the ODS but remaining in parliament as an unreliable vote for the government. The internal dissention and resignations weakened the tenuous ODS position in the Chamber of Deputies, making it more difficult for the ODS-led government to survive future no-confidence motions.

The ODS won only three races in the October 2008 Senate elections and was soundly defeated by the opposition parties in many of the regional elections, a disastrous showing for Topolánek in his bid to maintain control of the government and lead the national party. Pavel BEM, mayor of Prague and a rival for the ODS leadership, called for an extraordinary party congress and signaled his willingness to unseat Topolánek as party leader. The embattled Topolánek responded to the mounting internal criticism by saying he would resign if new leadership emerged that could forge consensus in the party ranks, but Bem in his view was not that leader. At the party congress in December Topolánek was able to consolidate support from the regional party bosses and beat back Bem's challenge, securing reelection with 284 votes over 162 for Bem. Meanwhile, President Klaus announced that he was leaving the party due to its ideological move toward the center.

Despite his resilience in retaining leadership of the party, Topolánek's ability to maintain discipline within the ODS parliamentary group and the reeling coalition partners was fatally compromised by the chain of events in 2008. The opposition parties brought down the government with a no-confidence measure in late March 2009.

In the European Parliament elections in June 2009 the ODS rebounded somewhat as it won nine seats with a 31 percent vote share. Shortly thereafter, the ODS formed a new right-wing faction in the European Parliament with the British Conservative Party and the Polish Law and Justice Party.

Leaders: Mirek TOPOLÁNEK (Leader of the Party and Former Prime Minister); David VODRÁŽKA (Deputy Leader); Petr NEČAS; Ivan LANGER, Petr GANDALOVIČ, Petr BENDL (Vice Chairs).

Christian and Democratic Union–Czech People's Party (*Křest'anská a Demokratická Unie–Česká Strana Lidová*—KDU-ČSL). The KDU-ČSL is descended from the Czechoslovak People's Party that had been founded in 1918, banned in 1938, and revived in 1945 as a component of the Communist-dominated National Front. From late 1989 the People's Party had sought to reestablish its independence, joining the broad-based coalition government appointed in December. The party contested the election of June 1990 in an alliance that won 19 seats in the Czech National Council. Included in the post-election Czech coalition government, the alliance suffered defections in late 1991, and in April 1992 it was officially redesignated as the KDU-ČSL, which in the June 1992 election won 15 seats in the Czech National Council. The party became a member of the ODS-led Czech coalition government that took the republic to independence in January 1993, after which it no longer advocated autonomy for Moravia, from which it had long drawn the bulk of its support.

In late 1995 the KDU-ČSL was strengthened by the adhesion of five deputies of the KDS (see ODS, above), who rejected the latter's decision to merge with the dominant ODS; however, the party fell back to 18 seats in the 1996 Chamber balloting.

The KDU-ČSL increased its representation to 20 in the 1998 balloting for the Chamber of Deputies. Josef LUX, chair of the party, subsequently resigned his post and withdrew from political life in September due to illness.

The KDU-ČSL was a founding member of the center-right Quad Coalition that was formed prior to the November 1998 Senate and municipal elections. (Other members included the US, ODA, and the DEU. See the 2007 *Handbook* for additional information.) Jan Kasal was elected KDU-ČSL chair in May 1999, with Kasal then being succeeded by Cyril Svoboda at a May 2001 party conference. In the elections for the Chamber of Deputies in 2002, the KDU-ČSL won 21 seats.

At a party conference on November 8, 2003, Miroslav Kalousek defeated incumbent party leader Svoboda by a vote of 164 to 131 to become the chair of the KDU-ČSL. Kalousek positioned the party for the 2006 elections with assurances that the KDU-ČSL would work to hold the line on taxes and prevent any communist influence in the government.

In the June 2006 Chamber of Deputies election, the KDU-ČSL won only 13 seats on a 7.2 percent vote share. Following the election, the KDU-ČSL engaged in unsuccessful negotiations first with the ODS and SZ and then the ČSSD and the KSČM to form a government, before finally entering into the coalition agreement with the ODS and SZ in late December 2006. The poor election performance and failed negotiations with the ČSSD and the KSČM proved costly to Kalousek; he resigned as chair in late August after the KDU-ČSL senior leadership balked at joining any coalition involving the communist KSČM. Jan Kasal took over on an interim basis until Jiří Čunek, a senator, was selected chair at a party congress in December 2006. Čunek brought the party into coalition with the ODS and Green Party and was named deputy prime minister in the new cabinet, one of the five cabinets posts for the KDU-ČSL.

Corruption allegations surfaced against Čunek in early 2007, creating more tension within the party. Čunek was accused by a former aide of accepting a bribe from a real estate developer while mayor of Vsetin, the town where he rose to national prominence after evicting Roma rent squatters. As the investigation got under way, Čunek issued a public denial and received the full support of the party presidium in mid-February, but some party members expressed frustration that the case was hurting the party's public image and standing in the coalition government. The party's national committee issued a one-line statement of support for Čunek on March 6, but several KDU-ČSL senators issued a public statement asking Čunek to step down until the investigation was completed. Political observers noted that with only 7 percent of the vote in the 2006 election and declining public support in the wake of the allegations, the KDU-ČSL was in danger of slipping below the 5 percent threshold in future elections. Nevertheless, the party's official position was that Čunek would remain chair and that any move to remove him from the cabinet would threaten the KDU-ČSL's support for the government. The charges against Čunek were dropped in August, but a new corruption investigation prompted him to resign from the cabinet on November 1. He was reinstated to his previous cabinet positions by President Klaus on April 2, 2008, after he was cleared by the investigation and a subsequent audit of his finances.

The KDU-ČSL national committee recommended that its deputies and senators support the reelection of President Klaus over challenger Jan Švejnar in the February 2008 presidential election.

At a party conference in Pardubice in April Čunek's leadership mandate was reaffirmed, as only 5 of 300 delegates voted for a proposal to elect a new party chair. Čunek's address to the conference blamed disunity within the party for its decline in popular support and apologized for the ordeal party members experienced because of his investigations on bribery charges. The party also chose its list of 15 candidates for the European parliamentary elections in 2009.

The KDU-ČSL generally has supported the ODS-led coalition positions on the U.S. radar base agreement; in regard to the health finance reforms, it advocated a position that the reforms should be tempered by elimination of fees for children and the elderly. It took a more cautious approach to the question of recognition of Kosovo's independence from Serbia and was against proposals for direct election of the president if the powers of the office were thereby expanded. The KDU-ČSL platform has included efforts to restrict abortion, a position at odds with the coalition partners and counter to the weight of public opinion.

The KDU-ČSL did not win any additional seats in the October 2008 Senate election. Party leader Čunek was dismissed from the cabinet in January. In the European Parliament elections in June 2009 the KDU-ČSL held on to its two seats with 7.6 percent of the vote.

At the May 30 party conference Cyril Svoboda returned to leadership of the party. Soon thereafter, many members left the KDU-ČSL to join a new party, **TOP 09**, formed by former KDU-ČSL leader Miroslav Kalousek along with four other deputies. Jiří STODŮLKA, the party's general secretary, resigned in September after public disclosure by the media that Stodůlka was implicated in an influence peddling investigation.

Leaders: Cyril SVOBODA (Chair), Michaela ŠOJDROVÁ (Deputy Chair), Jan KASAL, Rostislav SLAVOTINEK, Petr PITHART.

Green Party (*Strana Zelených*—SZ). Originally founded in 1989 and prominent in the "Velvet Revolution," the SZ failed to win representation in the 1990 election. For the 1992 poll it joined the broader Liberal Social Union but reverted to independent status in November 1993. The party was barred from the 1996 legislative elections for failing to put up the required deposit. The SZ received 2.36 percent of the vote in the 2002 legislative elections for the Chamber of Deputies, below the minimum threshold for securing representation.

Martin Bursík was elected party chair in autumn 2005. He led the party into the 2006 elections with a message that it was the party most concerned with the environment, human rights, and the rights of women and minorities and would help eliminate the perceived corruption and vote-trading of the last decade. The election proved to be a breakthrough for the SZ as it finally transcended the 5 percent threshold for securing seats in the lower house with a 6.3 percent vote share, good for six seats. In the postelection cabinet negotiations, the SZ, despite its small block of seats, was the most sought after partner for the two major parties because of the SZ's growing public profile. Bursík took the party into a coalition government with the ODS and the KDU-ČSL and secured four cabinet posts for the party. However, Karel SCHWARZENBERG, Bursík's designee for foreign minister, was not an SZ member. The Schwarzenberg nomination sparked a controversy within the party, with 50 members delivering a signed statement to Bursík complaining about the lack of communication between the chair and party members over the appointment. The dissidents also raised concerns about Schwarzenberg's support for the U.S.-Czech bilateral negotiation on a proposed radar base (see Foreign relations, above). Bursík downplayed the dispute, maintaining that the SZ supported the radar base only on the condition that it be under NATO's control. At the party's national congress in mid-February 2007, this position was moderated somewhat, with the party pledging not to seek a national referendum on the base and to advocate for debate over the base issue at the level of the European Parliament and NATO.

The Green Party went on record in opposition to the reelection of President Klaus in 2008 because of the president's persistent denials of the importance of global climate change. The Greens instead endorsed the candidacy of Jan Švejnar, in league with the ČSSD. After the messy election process and aftermath, Bursík announced in late May that the Greens had drafted a proposal for a referendum to authorize direct election of the president.

Dissension within the party grew in the wake of the forced resignation of Education Minister and SZ party Deputy Chair Dana Kuchtová from the cabinet in October 2007. Dissatisfaction began with an internal struggle over naming a successor to Kuchtová. After two months of wrangling Bursík finally nominated Ondřej Liška instead of the candidate recommended by the party's national council, prompting the resignation of the council's chair. In the wake of Bursík's compromise positions within the government in the first half of 2008, especially on support for the U.S. radar treaty, the left-of-center elements within the party, including Kuchtová, charged that Bursík was ruling from the top down and was too concerned with preserving the coalition at the expense of faithfulness to the party's platform. An April 2008 national party conference in Prague reaffirmed that the Greens would remain in the government, even after KDU-ČSL leader and Deputy Prime Minister Jiří Čunek was reinstated, something the Greens had previously opposed. By July Bursík announced an extraordinary party congress to convene in September to reaffirm his mandate (and remove Kuchtová as deputy leader) or select new leadership. Moreover, he proposed new party rules to be promulgated at the meeting designed to strengthen the hand of party leaders and weaken the power of the party's national council. The meeting was also expected to clarify the party's position on ratifying the U.S. radar agreement and the Lisbon Treaty. Kuchtová announced on July 23 that she would run against Bursík for party leader in the SZ congress. In August the national council proposed that the congress be held after the October 2008 Senate and local elections, but Bursík prevailed and the congress was scheduled for September.

At the party congress, held in Teplice on September 6–7, Bursík defeated Kuchtová in the race for party leader 227 votes to 109; Kuchtová also lost the post of deputy party leader to Ondřej Liška. Bursík's new party rules were not considered but his opponents on the SZ national council were dismissed. Several unhappy SZ deputies demanded soon thereafter more open discussion within the party of issues and positions that were at odds with the coalition government's programs and proposals as the price for continued support of the government.

The turmoil within SZ ranks led to a disastrous result for the party in the October 2008 Senate elections, having won no new seats. Following the defeat, Olga Zubová, head of the SZ national council, resigned from that post. During a party congress in Pardubice in late November 2008, Zubová and Věra JAKUBKOVÁ both announced that they were leaving the SZ deputies group but for the time being would support the coalition government.

With the collapse of the coalition government in March 2009, the SZ's infighting boiled over. A faction of the party split off and formed a rival Green party, the **Democratic Green Party,** in anticipation of the new parliamentary elections, despite the dismal electoral support the party received in the 2008 Senate election and the June 2009 European Parliament election, in which the SZ only won 2 percent of the vote. After the miserable European parliamentary poll results Bursík resigned as leader and was replaced by Deputy Chair Liška as acting leader.

Leaders: Ondřej LIŠKA (Acting Chair); Martin ANDER, Kateřina JACQUES (Deputy Chairs); Ladislav VRCHOVSKÝ; Zuzana DRHOVÁ; Džamila Stehlíková; Přemysl RABAS.

Opposition Parties:

Czech Social Democratic Party (*Česká Strana Sociálne Demokratická*—ČSSD). First organized in 1878, the ČSSD was the plurality party in Czechoslovakia's first parliamentary election in 1920 but went underground in 1939. In 1948 it was forced to merge with the KSČ, resurfacing as a separate party in late 1989. It won no seats at the 1990 federal election, after which its Czech and Slovak wings became, in effect, separate parties. In the June 1992 election the ČSSD won 16 seats in the Czech National Council. It mounted strong opposition to the proposed "velvet divorce" between Czechs and Slovaks, arguing in favor of a "confederal union," but eventually accepted the inevitability of the separation. At its first postindependence congress in February 1993, the party formally renamed itself the "Czech" SSD and said it would seek to provide a left-wing alternative to the neoconservatism of the ruling coalition.

Benefiting from public unease over the social consequences of economic transition, the ČSSD achieved a major advance in the 1996 Chamber election, to 61 seats and 26.4 percent of the vote. It opted to give qualified external support to a further center-right coalition, the immediate reward being the election of the ČSSD Chair Miloš Zeman as president of the new Chamber of Deputies. At its congress of March 1997 the party reelected Zeman as chair and endorsed his call for confrontation with the coalition government. The ČSSD supported the transitional government of Josef Tošovský in the January 1998 parliamentary confidence vote with the provision that early elections would be called. The party won a plurality of 74 seats in the June 1998 legislative balloting (on the strength of 32.3 percent of the vote), leading to the installation of a minority ČSSD government led by Zeman, with external ODS support. Objecting to the continuing pact with the ODS, Petra BUZKOVÁ resigned as deputy chair in January 2000.

The ČSSD fared poorly in 13 regional assembly elections in November 2000, winning control of none and capturing only 15 percent of the vote. At simultaneous balloting for 27 Senate seats, the party won just 1, for a loss of 8, leaving it far behind the Quad Coalition and the ODS.

In the 2002 Chamber of Deputies elections, the ČSSD won 70 seats, making it the largest party in the lower house. Vladimír Špidla replaced Zeman as prime minister and chair of the party. Špidla formed a coalition government with the KDU-ČSL and US-DEU. In the October 25–26, 2002, Senate elections, the ČSSD won just 7 seats, bringing its representation in the upper house down to 11 from 15 (compared with 26 for the ODS). In 2003 dissidents within the ČSSD refused to support Špidla's presidential candidate, Jan Sokol, which contributed to the victory by Václav Klaus of the ODS. In response, Špidla forced the leader of the dissidents, Trade and Industry Minister Jiří RUSNOK, to resign. In EU elections in June 2004, the ČSSD came in fifth and won only 2 seats. Špidla resigned on June 26, 2004, and was replaced by Stanislav Gross as prime minister and party leader. Gross stepped down from the premiership in April 2005 in the wake of a crisis over his financial affairs. He resigned as party chair on September 24, 2005. Deputy chair Jiří Paroubek was appointed prime minister on April 25, 2005, and elected chair at a party conference on May 13, 2006.

In the run-up to the 2006 legislative balloting, Prime Minister Paroubek steered the party toward themes of "Security and Prosperity," with promises to reduce unemployment, reform the health care system along the German model, increase public assistance, raise the average annual salary, increase monthly pensions, reduce (modestly) the corporate income tax rate, and increase investment in pubic infrastructure, research, and development. He painted a gloomy picture of an ODS election victory, warning that it could mean the "collapse of the welfare state" given the scale of the ODS financial reform and tax reduction proposals. The ČSSD won 74 seats with a 32.3 percent vote share, an increase of 4 seats over the previous election, but, due to the ODS's gains, the ČSSD fell back to the second largest party in the lower house. After losing the plurality in the chamber, Paroubek offered his resignation as prime minister. However, with no clear majority coalition government in waiting immediately after the election, President Klaus refused to accept Paroubek's resignation. Unable to form a rival coalition government after the failure of the ODS's first attempt in August 2006, Paroubek's standing in the party was further undermined by tepid results in the October 2006 Senate elections (ČSSD candidates won 6 seats) and the actions of two members of the party's parliamentary delegation, Miloš MELČÁK and Michal POHANKA, who broke ranks and deliberately were absent from the vote of confidence for the ODS-led coalition government in January 2007. Pohanka resigned from the party immediately thereafter. Paroubek moved in February to expel Melčák from the party, bringing the ČSSD lower house delegation down to 72 seats. Soon thereafter Paroubek appealed to both former members to continue to support the ČSSD party line in future votes in parliament.

Soon thereafter the party faced a major embarrassment over unpaid legal fees and penalties owed to Zdenek ALTNER, the lawyer who successfully defended the party from 1997 to 2000 in its battle to establish ownership of the Prague party headquarters. Altner claimed his contract, signed with then ČSSD Chair Miloš Zeman, entitled him to over 19 billion koruna for his services plus outstanding interest and penalties. Observers speculated that the dispute might drive the party into bankruptcy or force it to reorganize. Zeman subsequently announced his resignation from the ČSSD in the face of a legal proceeding initiated against him by the party over the matter. Paroubek repeatedly sought an out-of-court settlement with Altner, but the lawyer refused to make a deal and initiated proceedings to have the party declared bankrupt, which the trial court dismissed. The party countered with a libel lawsuit against Altner in July.

Paroubek emerged from the March 2007 party conference with his leadership position intact, but his support among the delegates was the lowest of all the ČSSD leaders selected, with only 60 percent of the votes. Political observers speculated that Deputy Chair Bohuslav Sobotka was the most likely replacement should Paroubek's support in the party collapse with future missteps.

In a 2007 by-election the party picked up 1 additional seat in the Senate for a total of 13.

The party expelled Deputy Evžen SNÍTILÝ in February 2008 after he broke ranks with the party and voted for the reelection of President Klaus instead of voting for Jan Švejnar, the candidate endorsed by the ČSSD. Snítilý, however, refused to resign his seat in parliament. Petr Wolf announced he was leaving the party deputies group in late June, charging that party leader Paroubek had pressured him to vote for the challenger Jan Švejnar in the presidential election and to pledge to vote against the radar base agreement by threatening to publicly release sensitive information about Wolf if he failed to comply.

Paroubek called a two-day party conference in late May to set the party's policy agenda for the October 2008 Senate elections. The ČSSD, with a sizable and consistent lead over the ODS in public opinion polls throughout 2008, emphasized discipline among its members behind its positions against the ratification of the radar base treaty with the United States, for elimination of the new medical fees, against university tuition fees, and for the reinstatement of child benefits. Meanwhile, former party chair, prime minister, and presidential candidate Miloš Zeman announced that he would consider a presidential bid if parliament changed the rules to permit direct election of the president. In July his supporters officially registered the Friends of Miloš Zeman Civic Association with the Interior Ministry.

In the October 2008 Senate election the ČSSD won an overwhelming majority of the races, securing 23 of the 27 seats. However, in the European Parliament elections in June 2009 the ČSSD won 7 seats, 2 fewer seats than rival ODS, a disappointing result after soundly defeating the ODS in the Senate and regional elections the previous year. Moreover, ČSSD leaders, especially Paroubek, were targeted by egg-throwing protestors at the election rallies. The protests over the party's role in bringing down the ODS-led government prompted the ČSSD to ask the interim government for extra police protection.

Internal leadership of the ČSSD remained relatively stable in 2009. Party Chair Paroubek won reelection at a party conference in 2009. The party did not choose a female vice party chair, however, despite rules requiring at least one woman in the post.

Leaders: Jiří PAROUBEK (Chair and Former Prime Minister); Stanislav GROSS (Former Prime Minister); Bohuslav SOBOTKA (Deputy Chair), Roman ONDERKA, Zdeněk ŠKROMACH, Milan URBAN, Lubomír ZAORÁLEK (Vice Chairs); Petr VÍCHA; Michal HAŠEK; Alena GAJDŮŠKOVÁ.

Communist Party of Bohemia and Moravia (*Komunistická Strana Čech a Moravy*—KSČM). Established under its present name in March 1990, the KSČM is descended from the Communist Party of Czechoslovakia (KSČ) founded in 1921 by the pro-Bolshevik wing of the ČSSD. The KSČ was the only East European Communist Party to retain legal status in the 1930s, until it was banned in the aftermath of the 1938 Munich agreement. Its leaders returned from Moscow at the end of World War II as the dominant element of a Soviet-sponsored National Front and effectively seized sole power in 1948. In March 1990, as non-Communists took over leading government posts, the Czech component of the KSČ relaunched itself as the KSČM, with a socialist rather than a Marxist-Leninist orientation. At the June 1990 multiparty election, the Communists took second place in the Czech National Council, winning 32 of the 200 seats. They then went into opposition for the first time since 1945, amid a continuing exodus of party members.

In mid-1991 the KSČ was officially dissolved, but both the KSČM and its Slovak counterpart remained "Czechoslovak" in orientation. In the June 1992 election the KSČM-led Left Bloc won 35 of the 200 Czech National Council seats and subsequently resisted dissolution of the federation. Following the creation of the independent Czech Republic in January 1993, the party experienced much internal strife, including the resignation of Jiří Svoboda as leader over the rejection of his proposal to drop "Communist" from the party's title. He was replaced in June 1993 by the conservative Miroslav GREBENÍČEK, whose election precipitated the formation of the two breakaway factions that later reorganized as the SDS (see below). The secessions meant that the KSČM had lost a majority of its ten deputies elected in 1992; however, it recovered strongly in the 1996 balloting, winning 22 seats, whereas the various breakaway groups failed to obtain representation. The KSČM fared even better in the 1998 balloting for the Chamber of Deputies, winning 24 seats on the strength of 11 percent of the vote. Following the November 2000 Senate election, it held 3 seats (a loss of 1) in the upper house.

In balloting for the Chamber of Deputies in June 2002, the KSČM won 41 seats. It joined the conservative ODS as the opposition to the coalition government. In the 2004 elections for the European Parliament, the party exceeded analysts' expectations, apparently because of growing popular discontent with the coalition government. The KSČM received the second-largest number of votes with 20.3 percent of the total vote and won 6 seats. Considered one of the "least reformed" communist parties among the countries recently admitted to the EU, the KSČM in 2005 campaigned against the proposed new EU Constitution. The party took an important modernizing step when on September 20, 2005, hard-line leader Miroslav Grebeníček stepped down as chair. Vojtech Filip was elected chair on October 1, defeating rival Vaclav EXNER for the post.

Filip led the party into the 2006 elections with public assurances that the KSČM would not seek to nationalize Czech industries or assets or engage in a "bloody" class war. However, he pledged that the party would seek withdrawal from NATO, increased security for workers, and expanded public housing with 50,000 new apartments every year. The KSČM won 26 seats with a 12.8 percent vote share, a step back from its 2002 showing, but it remained the third largest party in the lower house. It subsequently joined the ČSSD in opposition to the ODS-led coalition government. After the October 2006 Senate election the KSČM had 2 seats in the Senate. In a 2007 Senate by-election the party picked up 1 additional seat.

Filip made controversial remarks at a February 2007 KSČM central committee meeting during which he inquired whether the party's members were ready "to initiate and take the lead in possible revolutionary processes" and called for a return to a Leninist ideology. His remarks prompted a police investigation and condemnation from anticommunist political opponents.

Political observers contended that the party was facing a potential membership crisis: While it remains the largest mass membership party in the Czech Republic with more than 75,000 members, the party's declining percentage of the national vote and its average member age of over 70 years indicate that the KSČM is failing to attract younger Czech voters dissatisfied with aspects of capitalism and globalization. In this regard, the party has lost ground to the ČSSD and the Green Party.

KSČM Deputy Josef Vondruška was charged with abuse of office in 2008 for the mistreatment of political prisoners during the 1980s at the Minkovice jail. The Chamber of Deputies had voted in late 2007 to remove his immunity to prosecution.

The KSČM leadership created controversy once again in late February by announcing that it embraced the ideals of the party circa 1948, the time of the Communist putsch, which the party defended as a constitutionally sound revolution. The Communist leaders acknowledged, however, that this era contained "inadequacies and tragic deformations."

The KSČM held a party congress on May 17, 2008, in Hradec Králové where Vojtěch Filip was reelected as party leader. Filip was challenged by three candidates for the leadership but won handily with 176 of 275 total votes.

The KSČM won one Senate race in the October 2008 election, maintaining a total of three seats in that chamber. In the elections for the European Parliament in June 2009 the KSČM won 14 percent of the vote and four seats.

The KSČM continues to face efforts by the other parties to have the party declared unconstitutional on the grounds that it has not renounced violence as a means to achieve its political aims.

An investigative news report published in September alleged that two KSČM vice party chairs were implicated in an influence-peddling scheme. Party leader Filip called for the resignation of Jiří Dolejš and Čeněk Milota soon thereafter.

Leaders: Vojtěch FILIP (Chair); Jana BYSTŘICKÁ, Jiří DOLEJŠ, Leo LUZAR, Jiří MAŠTÁLKA, Čeněk MILOTA, Vera ŽEŽULKOVÁ (Vice Chairs); Pavel KOVARČÍK; Zdenék LEVÝ; Otakar ZMÍTKO.

Other Parties that Contested the 2006 Elections:

Freedom Union–Democratic Union (*Unie Svobody–Demokratická Unie*—US-DEU). The US-DEU had its origins in the dissension in the ODS over the leadership of Václav Klaus and his handling of a campaign finance scandal as nearly half of the ODS's 69 deputies reportedly left the party to form the Freedom Union (*Unie Svobody*—US) on January 17, 1998. Defections of ODS cabinet members to the US were also subsequently reported. The US won 19 seats on a vote share of 8.6 percent in the June balloting for the Chamber of Deputies.

Party Chair Jan RUML resigned in December 1999, with his successor being elected in February 2000. In late 2001 the US and the Democratic Union (*Demokratická Unie*—DEU) announced that the two groups would be merged, the new party to be known as the US-DEU. (A right-wing formation founded in June 1994, the DEU had won one Senate seat in 1996 but none in 2000. The merged US-DEU won ten seats in the 2002 balloting for the Chamber of Deputies).

On December 6, 2003, DEU leader Ratibor MAJZLIK led 300 supporters in a mass defection after failing to oust the US-DEU leadership at a party conference. In June 2004 other defectors from the DEU formed a new political party, the **Democratic Union of the Czech Republic,** or DEU-CR. The new party was led by Jan DORANT.

In June 2004 Pavel NEMEC became US-DEU chair when Petr MAREŠ resigned following the party's poor performance in the European Parliament elections (the party failed to win any seats). Němec announced a new party name, the **New Freedom Union** (*Nová Unie Svobody*—NUS), in April 2006 before the June legislative elections. The name change was seen as an effort to recast the party as a libertarian party of freedom and protest, with a platform that advocated legalization of some drugs and euthanasia, drastic reduction of income taxes, and public provision of universal Internet access. Despite the image makeover, another poor performance in the elections (the NUS secured only 0.3 percent of the vote) led to the resignation of Nemec as party chair.

By 2007 the party had returned to its US-DEU designation and selected new leadership, with Jan Černý as the new chair. One senator remained in office who had run on the US-DEU list until the October 2008 Senate election, and another senator remained who had been elected on a coalition list of the US-DEU and the ODA.

Leaders: Jan ČERNÝ (Chair); Petr HŮLA (First Vice Chair); Lenka ČERNÁ, Petr NOVOTNÝ, Jan POLECHA (Vice Chairs); Pavel FAJT (General Secretary).

Association of Independent Candidates and European Democrats (*Sdružení Nezávislých a Evropští Demokraé*—SNK–ED). The merger of the SNK and the ED was formalized on December 12, 2005. Formed prior to the 2002 elections and led by former ODS leader Josef ZIELENIEC and Igor PETROV, the Association of Independents (SNK) was a center-right party that, unlike the ODS, was highly supportive of European integration. The party sought to appeal to young conservatives who were dissatisfied with the more nationalistic ODS. In the 2002 elections for the Chamber of Deputies, the SNK received 2.8 percent of the vote. However, it won two seats in the 2002 Senate elections. The SNK formed a coalition with the European Democrats (ED) in 2004, having substantial success in the June 2004 balloting for the European Parliament (three seats on an 11 percent vote share).

The SNK-ED received only 2.1 percent of the vote in the June 2006 legislative elections, below the 5 percent threshold for securing a seat. In 2007 three senators were affiliated with the SNK-ED.

New party leaders were selected at a party conference on May 12, 2007, with Helmut Dohnálek as the new chair.

Sen. Josef NOVOTNÝ made allegations following the 2008 presidential election that an ODS senator offered him a 2-million-koruna bribe to vote for the reelection of President Klaus. No charges were drawn up by investigators, however, since there was no tangible evidence to corroborate the allegation.

Leaders: Helmut DOHNÁLEK (Chair), Markéta REEDOVÁ (First Deputy Chair), Josef MARTINIC (Deputy Chair).

Czech National Social Party (*Česká Strana Národně Sociální—ČSNS*). The ČSNS adopted its current name in September 1997, having previously been called the Free Democrats–Liberal National Social Party (*Svobodní Demokraté–Liberálni Národně Sociální Strana*—SD-LNSS). The centrist SD-LNSS was formed as a merger of the SD and LNSS in late 1995, although most LNSS deputies rejected the union and later launched a separate, short-lived parliamentary group, the Civic National Movement (*Občanské Národní Hnutí*—ONH). The SD component, dating as such from 1993 and led by Jiří Dienstbier, grew out of the Civic Movement (OH) wing of the Civic Forum (OF) launched in 1991 but was unrepresented in the 1992–1996 parliament. The LNSS was descended from the National Socialist Party (founded in 1897), which played a dominant role in the interwar period and was a member of the postwar Communist-led National Front, becoming the Czechoslovak Socialist Party (*Československá Strana Socialistická*—ČSS) in 1948. Unsuccessful in the 1990 election, the ČSS in 1991 merged with the former Agrarian Party (*Zemědělská Strana*—KS) and the Green Party (SZ, see above) to form a Liberal Social Union (*Liberálně Sociální Unie*—LSU) that won 16 Czech National Council seats in 1992 but thereafter suffered dissension and broke up. Most of the old ČSS component opted in June 1993 to form the centrist-inclined LNSS.

Dienstbier, a prominent dissident during the Communist era and subsequently Czechoslovakia's foreign minister, later left the SD-LNSS. In November 2000 he competed unsuccessfully as a ČSSD senatorial candidate. A year earlier the ČSNS had indirectly achieved lower house representation when Marie MACHATÁ, who had been elected from the Freedom Union, joined the party. (She technically sat as an independent.) In the 2002 lower house elections, the ČSNS received only 0.81 percent of the vote; by 2006 its share had fallen to 0.02 percent.

Leaders: Jaroslav ROVNÝ (Chair), Viktor TRKAL (Deputy Chair).

The Moravians (*Moravané*).The Moravians were formed by the December 17, 2005, merger of the Moravian Democratic Party (*Moravská Demokratická Strana*—MDS) and the Movement for an Independent Moravia and Silesia–Moravian National Union (*Hnutí Samosprávné Moravy a Slezska–Moravské Národní Sjednocení*—HSMS-MNS). The MDS was formed in April 1997 by merger of the Moravian National Party (*Moravská Národní Strana*—MNS) and the Bohemian-Moravian Center Union (*Českomoravská Unie Středu*—ČMUS). The ČMUS was derived from the Movement for Self-Governing Democracy–Association for Moravia and Silesia (*Hnutí za Samosprávnou Demokracii–Společnost pro Moravu a Slezsko*—HSD-SMS), founded in 1990 in support of a demand that the historic province of Moravia-Silesia should have status equivalent to Bohemia and Slovakia. In the 1990 election the HSD-SMS took third place in the Czech National Council, winning 22 seats, 8 of which were lost in 1992. Thereafter, strains developed between moderates and a radical faction favoring extraparliamentary action. The proparliamentary Bohemian-Moravian Center Party (*Českomoravská Strana Středu*—ČMSS) was announced in January 1994, the new title indicating the party's intention to extend its activities to Bohemia. Later in the year it joined other centrist groups, including the Liberal Social Union (*Liberálně Sociální Unie*—LSU), the Farmers' Party (*Zemědělské Strany*—ZS), and the Christian Social Union (*Křest'ansko Sociální Unie*—KSU), in a loose alliance, the ČMUS. Formal merger occurred in February 1996. For the 1998 election the party cooperated with the HSMS-MNS.

Ivan DŘÍMAL, the former MNS leader, was reelected MDS chair in April 2000. In elections for the Chamber of Deputies in 2002, the MDS received just 0.27 percent of the vote. With the long-term goal of self-rule for Moravia and Silesia, the Moravians hoped for a better showing in the June 2006 election for the Chamber of Deputies but received only 0.23 percent of the vote.

Leaders: Pavel DOHNAL (Chair), Pavel HÁLA (First Deputy Chair), Milan TRNKA (Deputy Chair).

Independent Democrats (*Nezávislí Demokraté*—ND, or NEZ/DEM). The NEZ/DEM was founded on June 23, 2005, by former ČSSD member of parliament Jana VOLFOVÁ with the help of Vladimír Železný, at that time leader of the Independents (*Nezávislí*). The Independents (the NEZ) had been founded in 1995 by Železný, a former Nova TV general director, as a center-right, euroskeptic party. In the 2002 senatorial elections, the NEZ won two seats. In the 2004 EU parliamentary elections, the NEZ received 8.2 percent of the vote and gained two seats. Bowing to the fact that Železný's name was better known than that of the ND, the party was renamed Independent Democrats (Chair V. Železný), with the chair's name becoming a formal component of the party name. (The Independents [the NE] carried on as a separate entity under the leadership of Frankisek ZWYRTEK.) The NEZ/DEM then merged with the Party for a Secure Life (*Strana za Životní Jistoty*—SŽJ), which focused on senior citizens and other economically vulnerable groups, under the name Independent Democrats. (See *Political Handbook of the World 2005–2006* for history of the SŽJ.)

Party leader Železný formed a Czech branch of the eurosceptic European parliamentary grouping Libertas.eu in January 2009 with two former ODS MPs, Vlastimil Tlustý and Jan Schwippel, to contest the EP elections in June. The new party, **Libertas.cz** failed to win any seats.

Leaders: Vladimír ŽELEZNÝ (Chair); Petr HUDLÍK, Vladimír LITWAN, Naděžda MARTÁKOVÁ (Deputy Chairs).

Other minor parties (*strana*) and movements (*hnutí*) that contested the 2002 or 2006 legislative elections or the 2004 elections for the European Parliament included (all of the parties in the list below received less than 1 percent of the vote in the various elections): **Balbín's Poetic Party** (*Balbínova Poetická Strana*—BPS), founded in 2002 and led by Jiří HRDINA; the **Common Sense Party** (*Strana Zdravého Rozumu*—SZR), founded in 2002 and led by Petr HANNIG; the **Czech Crown** (*Koruna Česká*—KČ), a monarchist party for Bohemia, Moravia, and Silesia led by Václav SRB; the **Czech Movement for National Unity** (*České Hnutí za Národní Jednotu*—ČHNJ), led by Pavel SVOBODA; the **Czech Right** (*Česká Pravice*—CP), a conservative party registered in January 1994 and led by Michal SIMKANIČ; **Helax-Ostrava Is Having Fun** (*Helax-Ostrava se baví*—HOB), formed in 2002 and led by Gabriela ZIMERMANOVÁ; the **Humanist Party** (*Humanistická Strana*—H.S.) registered in 1996 and led by Jan TAMÁŠ; the **Liberals.cz** (*Liberállové.cz*), formerly the Liberal Reform Party—LiRA, which in 2007 had one affiliated candidate in the Senate and was led by Milan HAMERSKÝ; the **Movement of Independents for a Harmonic Development of Community and Town** (*Hnutí Nezávislých Za Harmonický Rozvoj Obcí a Měst*—HNHRM), which in 2008 had one affiliated candidate in the Senate; the **National Party** (*Národní Strana*—NS), an ultranationalist party, currently led by Petra EDELMANNOVÁ, that was registered in 2002 and drew increasing media attention with a series of protests targeting foreigners and ethnic minorities, including Sudeten Germans, Jews, and Roma, and formed a paramilitary corps called the National Guard; the **Republicans** (*Republikáni*), a right-wing, euroskeptic party founded on March 4, 2002, by former members of the SPR-RSČ (see *Political Handbook of the World 2008* for history of the SPR-RSČ) and led by Jan VIK; the **Republicans of Miroslav Sládek** (*Republikáni Miroslava Sládka*—RMS), a far-right party formed in 2002 by Miroslav SLÁDEK and former members of the SPR-RSČ which was suspended for one year by the Czech Supreme Court in February 2008 for failure to submit annual financial reports for several previous years; the **Right Bloc** (*Pravý Blok*—PB) led by Petr CIBULKA; the **Romany Civic Initiative** (*Romská Občanská Iniciativa*—ROI), a party promoting the interests of Roma led by Štefan LIČARTOVSKÝ; the **Party of Democratic Socialism** (*Strana Demokratického Socialismu*—SDS), made up of disaffected former members of the KSČM and now led by Jiří HUDEČEK; and the **Party for an Open Society** (*Strana pro Otevřenou Společnost*—SOS), led by Pavel RYTÍŘ.

In addition, several small parties joined in a coalition list led by Radoslav ŠTĚDROŇ called the **Coalition for the Czech Republic** (*Koalice pro Českou Republiku*—Koal ČR) to contest the 2006 Chamber of Deputies election. The Koal ČR, which failed to win more than 0.15 percent of the vote, included seven parties: the **Club of Committed Non-Party Members** (*Klub Angažovaných Nestraníků*—KAN), a liberal party that formed in 1968 during the Prague Spring and is currently led by Pavel HOLBA; **Democratic Union of the Czech Republic** (*Demokratická Unie České Republiky*—DEUČK) led by Jan DORANT; the **Independent Initiative** (*Nezávislá Iniciativa*—NEI), a sexual-freedom party formerly known as the Independent Erotic Initiative, led by Richard KNOT; **Masaryk's Democratic Party** (*Masarykova Demokratická Strana*—MDS), led by Otomar VENZHÖFER; the **Party of Businessmen and Entrepreneurs** (*Strana Drobných Živnostníků a Podnikatelů*—SDŽP), a party of small business formed in 2004 and led by Miloslav KOPECKÝ; the **Movement in Support of**

Volunteers (*Hnutí na Podporu Dobrovolných Hasičů a dalších Dobrovolníků*—HNPD), led by Jan SZOTKOWSKI; and the **Work Party** (*Strana Práce*—SP), led by Radoslav Štědroň.

A number of new minor parties or groups emerged to contest the 2006 elections, including the feminist **Equality of Prospects Party** (*Strana Rovnost Šancí*—SRŠ), founded in 2005 and led by Zdenka ULMANNOVÁ; **Folklore as Well as Society** (*Folklor i Společnost*—FiS), led by Miroslav LEJSEK; the far-right **Law and Justice Party** (*Právo a Spravedlnost*—PaS), formed on January 28, 2006, by the merger of National Unification, the Workers' Party, the Democratic Party of Social Justice, and the Agrarian Party, and led by Petr VALEŠ; and **4 Visions** (*4 VIZE*), registered in 2006 and led by Zdeněk MACURA. (The far-right **Workers' Party** [*Delnická Strana*—DS], led by Tomáše VANDASE, was targeted in 2008 and 2009 in the government's crackdown on anti-Roma activities and acts of violence by far-right nationalists.) A new Roma party, the **Romany Social Democratic Party** (*Romská Demokratická Sociální Strana*—RDSS), was established in April 2005 in support of the integration of Romany minorities into mainstream society, led by Miroslav TANCOŠ. The **Czech-Roma Civic Movement** (*Česko-romské občanské sdružení*) represents another Roma faction, a rival to RDSS.

Other Parties or Groups:

Civic Democratic Alliance (*Občanská Demokratická Aliance*—ODA). The right-wing ODA was launched in December 1989, and it contested the June 1990 multiparty election as part of the victorious Civic Forum, participating in both the federal and Czech republican governments. It contested the June 1992 election in its own right, winning 14 of the 200 Czech National Council seats on a 5.9 percent vote share. As a member of the subsequent Czech coalition government headed by the ODS, it supported the creation of a separate Czech Republic. Its promarket line is similar to that of the ODS, the main difference being its greater emphasis on regional self-government. The party lost 1 of its 14 Chamber seats in the 1996 election.

Chair Jan KALVODA, the target of reports that he falsely claimed to have a doctorate, resigned from government positions and did not seek reelection at the party congress in March 1997, when the ODA elected Michael ŽANTOVSKÝ to succeed him. However, Žantovský, a spokesperson for President Havel, could not reconcile rival party factions; he stepped down in November and was replaced by Deputy Premier Jiří SKALICKÝ. The friction evidently could not be contained, as a number of right-wing members left to form the Conservative Consensus Party (SKS). In mid-February 1998 Skalický resigned as chair of the ODA in a fight involving a campaign finance scandal, and several other prominent ODA members (including cabinet ministers) reportedly also left the party. The ODA chose not to contest the election for the Chamber of Deputies in June 1998, party leaders calling upon ODA supporters to vote for candidates from the ODS or US. The ODA was dropped from the Quad Coalition in early 2002 after it failed to make arrangements to pay off its substantial debt from previous campaigns.

In the 2002 elections for the Chamber of Deputies, the ODA received less than 1 percent of the vote, leaving the party with one seat in the Senate as its sole representation in parliament. The ODA did not put forward any candidates for the 2006 Chamber of Deputies or Senate elections.

At a national conference in December 2007 the party decided to disband effective December 31 of that same year. The lone remaining ODA senator, Karel Schwarzenberg, served as an SZ representative in the Topolánek cabinet and announced that he would join the newly formed TOP 09 party to stand in the October 2009 elections.

Leaders: Jiřina NOVÁKOVÁ (Chair); Jaromír Mário CÍSAŘ, Petr BAŠÍK (Vice Chairs).

Communist Party of Czechoslovakia (*Komunistická Strana Československa*—KSČ). Its name indicating a rejection of the dissolution of Czechoslovakia, the KSČ was founded in March 1995 as the Party of Czechoslovak Communists (*Strana Československých Komunistů*—SČK) by Miroslav Štěpán, a former head of the Prague Communist Party who had been expelled from the KSČM. Štěpán formed the SČK after his release from a 30-month jail term for having ordered the breakup of prodemocracy demonstrations in the late 1980s. In April 1996 the SČK was barred from the forthcoming legislative balloting on the ground that it had failed to pay the required deposits for its candidates. The SČK was renamed the KSČ at a congress in December 1999, at which time it asserted that the KSČM "abuses" the term "Communist Party." It did not contest the 2002 or 2006 elections to the Chamber of Deputies.

The current KSČ central committee, with 13 members and the General Secretary, was selected in December 2002.

Leader: Miroslav ŠTĚPÁN (General Secretary).

Path of Change (*Cesta Změny*). Path of Change is a centrist party founded in 2001 by Jiří Lobkowicz. The party supports continued free-market reforms and is pro-European integration; however, it accuses the established parties of cronyism and corruption. The Path of Change also strongly supports the direct election of the president. Soon after its formation, a leadership struggle led Monika PAJEROVÁ, one of the student leaders of the Velvet Revolution, to leave the group and establish a rival party, Hope. In the 2002 elections for the Chamber of Deputies, the Path of Change received less than 1 percent of the vote. It was able to gain one seat in the October 2002 Senate elections. Path of Change offered no candidates for the 2006 Chamber of Deputies balloting.

Leaders: Jiří LOBKOWICZ (Chair), Helena FRANKENBERGEROVÁ (First Deputy Chair), Zdeněk VERNER (Deputy Chair).

TOP 09. This new party, whose initials stand for "tradition, responsibility, and prosperity" (*Tradice Odpovědnosti Prosperita*), was formed in mid-2009 after the fall of the coalition government and its replacement by an interim government. Most of the new party's leadership split from the KDU-ČSL to join TOP 09 after Cyril Svoboda regained leadership of the KDU-ČSL, most notably TOP 09 founder Miroslav Kalousek. The party soon attracted other disaffected KDU-ČSL leaders and former ministers, including former defense minister Vlasta Parkanová. Karel Schwarzenberg, the former foreign minister, joined TOP 09 and was immediately designated to head the new party's ticket for the autumn 2009 legislative elections, given his stature as the most popular former member of the Topolánek cabinet.

The party's ideological orientation is center-right, with a platform that emphasizes social conservatism, fiscal responsibility, andChristian values. Soon after forming, the party worked out an alliance with the **Movement for Mayors and Independents.**

An influence-peddling scandal ensnared MP Ladislav ŠUSTR in September 2009. Šustr, one of the KDU-ČSL deputies who joined TOP 09 in 2009, was alleged by an investigative news report to have agreed to alter lottery legislation in exchange for a large contribution to party coffers. He resigned immediately from parliament and claimed he acted without knowledge of the party.

Leaders: Karel SCHWARZENBERG (Chair), Miroslav KALOUSEK (Vice Chair), Vlasta PARKANOVÁ, Jaromír DRÁBEK, Pavol LUKŠA, Josef MALÝ.

In 2007 several minor parties were organized, including the **Republican Party of Bohemia, Moravia, and Silesia** (*Republikánská Strana Čech, Moravy a Slezska*—RSČMS) and the **Party for Dignified Life** (*Strana Důstojného Života*—SDŽ), led by former ČSSD deputy and then Independent Democrats founder Jana VOLFOVÁ. Additional parties that formed in 2008 and early 2009 included the **European Democratic Party** (*Evropská Demokratická Strana*—EDS), a pro-European party founded in November 2008 to promote Czech development and European integration, led by Jana HYBÁŠKOVÁ; the **Party of Free Citizens** (*Strana Svobodných Občanů*—SSO), a eurosceptic party opposed to ratification of the Lisbon Treaty, led by Petr MACH; the **Czech Pirate Party** (*Česká Pirátská Strana*—ČPS), an Internet-oriented party inspired by its Swedish counterpart and concerned with reform of copyright and patent law as well as privacy rights, led by Kamil HORKÝ.

LEGISLATURE

The **Parliament of the Czech Republic** (*Parlament České Republiky*) consists, under the 1992 constitution, of a Senate and a Chamber of Deputies. To achieve the transition to separate statehood on January 1, 1993, the composition of the lower house was decreed to be identical to that of the previous Czech National Council (*Česká Národní Rada*) elected in June 1992. The parliament operated as a single-chamber legislature until an entirely new Senate was elected in 1996.

Senate (*Senát*). Under legislation enacted in September 1995, the 81 members of the upper house are elected on a majoritarian basis for a six-year term from single-member constituencies, with one-third of the seats normally being renewed every two years. All 81 seats were filled in the first election held November 15–16 and November 22–23, 1996.

The most recent balloting for 27 seats was held October 17–18 and October 24–25, 2009, with the seats being distributed as follows: Civic Democratic Party, 35 (3 seats won in 2009); Czech Social Democratic Party, 29 (23); Christian and Democratic Union–Czech People's Party, 7 (0); Communist Party of Bohemia and Moravia, 3 (1); Association of Independent Candidates and European Democrats, 2 (0); Civic Democratic Alliance, 1 (0); Greens, 1 (0); independents, 3 (0). Some senators have declared themselves independents or joined new parties since the resignation of the government in March 2009. Two by-elections held in April 2007 had previously yielded 1 seat for the Czech Social Democratic Party and 1 seat for the Communist Party of Bohemia and Moravia, and 2 fewer seats for independents.

President: Přemysl SOBOTKA.

Chamber of Deputies (*Poslanecká Snemovna*). The lower house consists of 200 deputies directly elected for a four-year term by universal suffrage of those ages 18 and older. The thresholds for representation are 5 percent of the national vote for single parties, 7 percent for alliances of two or three parties, and 10 percent for alliances of four or more parties. In early 1998 the Chamber of Deputies approved a constitutional amendment cutting its current term in half to permit new elections in June. A similar measure was enacted in September 2009 to permit the chamber to prematurely end its mandate by a three-fifths vote for dissolution.

Under controversial electoral reform legislation passed in July 2000, with effect from 2002 the thresholds for representation were raised to 5 percent for single parties, 10 percent for two-party alliances, 15 percent for three-party alliances, and 20 percent for alliances of four or more parties. The reforms also increased the number of electoral districts from 8 to 35.

At the most recent election of June 2–3, 2006, the seats in the Chamber were distributed as follows: the Civic Democratic Party, 81; Czech Social Democratic Party, 74; Communist Party of Bohemia and Moravia, 26; Christian and Democratic Union–Czech People's Party, 13; the Green Party, 6. The Czech Social Democratic Party expelled two members from the party in February 2007. A third member was expelled in February 2008 for voting against the party line in the 2008 presidential election, and a fourth left in June, reducing the party bloc of seats to 70 (see Political Parties and Groups, above).

The next scheduled elections are in June 2010.

President: Miloslav VLČEK.

CABINET

[as of August 1, 2008]

Prime Minister	Jan Fischer
Deputy Prime Ministers	Jan Kohout Martin Barták
Deputy Premier for European Affairs	Štefan Füle
Ministers	
Agriculture	Jakub Šebesta
Culture	Václav Riedlbauch
Defense	Martin Barták
Education, Youth, and Sport	Miroslava Kopicová [f]
Environment	Ladislav Miko
Finance	Eduard Janota
Foreign Affairs	Jan Kohout (ind.)
Health	Dana Jurásková
Industry and Trade Information Technology	Vladimír Tošovský
Interior	Martin Pecina
Justice	Daniela Kovářová [f]
Labor and Social Affairs	Petr Šimerka
Regional Development	Rostislav Vondruška
Transport and Communication	Gustáv Slamečka
Without Portfolio (Responsible for Minority Issues and Human Rights)	Michael Kocáb
Without Portfolio (Head of Government Legislative Council)	Daniela Kovářová [f]

[f] = female

COMMUNICATIONS

Press. The following dailies are published in Czech in Prague, unless otherwise noted: *Blesk* (Lightning, 420,000), Swiss-owned independent tabloid; *Mladá Fronta Dnes* (Youth Front Today, 350,000), former organ of the Socialist Union of Youth, now independently owned by the MAFRA publishing company; *Právo* (Justice, 350,000), former KSČM organ (called *Rudé Právo* until September 1995), now independently owned by the Borgis company; *Slovo* (Free Word, 230,000); *Hospodářské Noviny* (Economic News, 130,000), business paper owned by the Economia company; *Večerník Praha* (Evening Prague, 130,000); *Svoboda* (Freedom, Ostrava, 100,000); *Lidové Noviny* (People's News, 68,320), independent, owned by the MAFRA publishing company; *Haló Noviny* (Hello News), KSČM organ, now owned by Futura company.

News agencies. The state-owned domestic service is the Czech News Agency (*Česká Tisková Kancelář*—ČTK, or Četeka). Numerous foreign agencies also maintain bureaus in Prague.

Broadcasting and computing. The former federal broadcasting structures ended on January 1, 1993, when the state-funded Czech Radio (*Český Rozhlas*) and Czech Television (*Česká Televize*) assumed full responsibility within the Czech Republic. The strict government control of the Communist era had ended in 1991, when the supervision of broadcasting was transferred to independent authorities approved by the respective parliaments. In March 1991 the republics were authorized to license independent radio and television stations, with the first independent television outlet, TV Nova, being launched in Prague in 1994. Another privately owned network, TV Premiéra (now known as Prima TV), began broadcasting in 1997. As of 2008 there were four nationwide broadcast stations and more than 20 regional stations. There are presently seven nationwide radio stations and 76 regional stations. Six major Internet service providers operate in the Czech Republic.

As of 2008 there were 584.1 Internet users per 1,000 inhabitants.

INTERGOVERNMENTAL REPRESENTATION

Ambassador to the U.S.: Petr KOLÁŘ.

U.S. Ambassador to the Czech Republic: (Vacant).

Permanent Representative to the UN: Martin PALOUŠ.

IGO Memberships (Non-UN): BIS, CEI, CERN, CEUR, EIB, ESA, EU, Eurocontrol, IEA, Interpol, IOM, NATO, OECD, OSCE, PCA, WCO, WEU, WTO.

DENMARK

Kingdom of Denmark
Kongeriget Danmark

Political Status: Constitutional monarchy since 1849; under unicameral parliamentary system established in 1953.

Area: 16,629 sq. mi. (43,069 sq. km.).

Population: 5,349,212 (2001C); 5,475,000 (2008E). Area and population figures are for mainland Denmark; for Greenland and the Faroe Islands, see Related Territories, below.

Major Urban Center (2005E): COPENHAGEN (502,000; metropolitan area, 2,050,000).

Official Language: Danish.

Monetary Unit: Krone (market rate December 1, 2009: 4.93 kroner = $1US).

Sovereign: Queen MARGRETHE II; proclaimed queen on January 15, 1972, following the death of her father, King FREDERIK IX, on January 14.

Heir to the Throne: Crown Prince FREDERIK, elder son of the queen.

Prime Minister: Lars Løkke RASMUSSEN (Liberal Party); formed coalition government on April 5, 2009, succeeding Anders Fogh RASMUSSEN (Liberal Party), who had resigned the same day to become secretary general of the North Atlantic Treaty Organization.

THE COUNTRY

Encompassing a low-lying peninsula and adjacent islands strategically situated at the mouth of the Baltic, Denmark has a largely homogeneous population, although a degree of controversy has emerged in regard to the entry of increasing numbers of asylum seekers and the families of immigrant workers. A vast majority (95 percent) of the inhabitants belong to the state-supported Evangelical Lutheran Church. Approximately 48 percent of the wage labor force is female, with 40 percent of working women concentrated in "female intensive" service and textile manufacturing jobs. In government, 8 of 19 cabinet ministers are women, holding portfolios of 10 of 22 ministries. Women occupy 68 of the 179 seats in the unicameral parliament, with significantly less representation at the local level.

About three-quarters of Denmark's terrain is devoted to agriculture, and most of the agricultural output is exported (chiefly meat, dairy products, and eggs). However, industrialization was substantial after World War II, with manufactures (principally machinery and electrical equipment, processed foods and beverages, chemicals and pharmaceuticals, textiles, clothing, and ships) accounting for about 70 percent of total exports by 1990. Although a member of the European Community/European Union (EC/EU) since 1973, Denmark voted by referendum in September 2000 not to join the EU's Economic and Monetary Union (EMU), thus rejecting use of the euro as currency.

After healthy GDP growth during the mid- and late 1990s, the economy slowed from 2001 through 2003. However, it rebounded in 2004–2006 when tax reductions contributed to an increase in disposable income. GDP grew by 3.9 percent in 2006, but growth slowed in 2007 as interest rates increased and the housing market sagged. The end of 2007 and beginning of 2008 produced two consecutive quarters of GDP contraction, although a technical contraction was averted due to a modest growth rate of 0.5 percent in the second quarter of 2008. Growth was estimated at approximately zero for all of 2008, and it appeared that the economy would be in recession in 2009 and remain weak in 2010, despite the fact that Denmark had initially been shielded from the worst aspects of the upheaval in global financial markets. At the same time, unemployment was expected to remain low (approximately 4 percent) due to the ongoing labor shortage.

GOVERNMENT AND POLITICS

Political background. The oldest monarchy in Europe, Denmark has lived under constitutional rule since 1849 and has long served as a model of political democracy. Its multiparty system, reflecting the use of proportional representation, has resulted since World War II in a succession of coalition governments, most of minority status. The Social Democratic Party (*Socialdemokratiet*—SD) maintained its prewar position as the strongest single party, heading coalition governments in 1947–1950, 1953–1968, and 1971–1973, latterly under the premiership of Anker JØRGENSEN. After two years of a nonsocialist minority government under Poul HARTLING of the Liberal Party (*Venstre*), Jørgensen returned following the 1975 election, heading a series of minority coalitions until 1982, when he was succeeded by Poul SCHLÜTER of the Conservative People's Party (*Konservative Folkeparti*—KF) as head of another minority government that included the Liberals, Center Democrats (*Centrum-Demokraterne*—CD), and the Christian People's Party (*Kristeligt Folkeparti*—KrF).

The first Conservative prime minister since 1901, Schlüter faced heavy opposition to his proposed austerity measures. For the first time since 1929, the budget failed, and he was forced to call an early election on January 10, 1984, which yielded a decrease in class-alliance voting, with Danes supporting the traditional Conservative outlook on economic issues, including lowered interest rates. As a result, Schlüter remained in office as head of the existing four-party government.

On April 14, 1988, the opposition SD secured legislative approval of a resolution requiring that vessels from the North Atlantic Treaty Organization (NATO) be formally "reminded" of Denmark's 31-year-old ban on nuclear weapons. Prime Minister Schlüter responded by calling a snap election for May 10, at which the socialist bloc suffered a marginal loss, while the stridently anti-immigrant Progressive Party (*Fremskridtspartiet*—FP), unacceptable as a government coalition partner, increased its parliamentary seats from 9 to 16. Since the anti-NATO forces retained a narrow majority, the prime minister submitted his resignation on May 11 but continued in government while negotiations over government composition took place. A fourth Schlüter cabinet, comprising the Conservatives, the Liberals, and the Radical Liberal Party (*Det Radikale Venstre*—RV), was announced on June 3.

In a referendum on June 2, 1992, Danish voters by a 50.7 to 49.3 percent majority rejected the Maastricht Treaty of the previous December that provided for a common European currency and pledged EC members to seek common foreign and security policies. While both EC and Danish leaders were surprised by the outcome, it reflected a widely held view that increased European integration would lead to a loss of Danish national identity. The rejection came despite a number of safeguards that had been built into the treaty, including optional adherence to the common currency.

Unwilling to accept the electorate's decision on the Maastricht Treaty, the government on October 27, 1992, secured a "national compromise" agreement among seven of the eight parliamentary parties (the exception being the FP) setting out terms of joint support for the treaty in a second referendum. Its main stipulations were that Denmark would be able to opt out of the proposed single European currency, defense policy coordination, cooperation on legal and police matters such as immigration control, and EU citizenship arrangements. These requirements were largely accepted by the EC heads of government meeting in Edinburgh (Scotland) on December 11–12.

Having headed five minority center-right governments since 1982, Schlüter resigned in January 1993 after a judicial report found that he had misled parliament in 1989 over government policy on the admission of the relatives of Tamil refugees from Sri Lanka already in Denmark (the so-called "Tamilgate" scandal). The SD leader, Poul Nyrup RASMUSSEN, thereupon formed Denmark's first majority government since 1971, securing the agreement of the RV, CD, and KrF for a center-left coalition that commanded a one-seat majority in parliament. The new administration promptly called a further referendum on the Maastricht Treaty on May 18, 1993. This time the Danish version of the instrument, including the opt-outs agreed upon in Edinburgh, received endorsement by 56.8 percent of those voting.

Despite government efforts to combat unemployment and to reform tax policies, economic progress was slow, and the coalition parties performed poorly in local elections in November 1993. Rasmussen

encountered further difficulty in February 1994, when the newly appointed social affairs minister, Bente JUNCKER, was obliged to resign over a leak of controversial and unsubstantiated information about a political opponent. She subsequently left the Center Democrats to sit as an independent in the *Folketing* (Parliament), where the government was thus reduced to technical minority status with 89 of the 179 seats.

The ruling coalition suffered an overall reversal in the June 1994 European Parliament balloting, in which two specifically anti-European lists obtained over a quarter of the votes cast. The same pattern was apparent in national balloting on September 21, although government losses were less than some had predicted. While the KrF failed to surmount the 2 percent barrier, the SD remained the largest party, with 34.6 percent. The opposition Liberals made significant gains, overtaking the Conservatives as the second leading party, but that advance was partially offset by entry of the Red-Green Unity List into the *Folketing.* The outcome was the appointment on September 26 of a minority center-left coalition, headed by Rasmussen and consisting of his SD, the RV, and the CD. Although the government as formed commanded only 76 seats (including one of the two Greenland deputies) in the 179-member *Folketing*, it could rely on the external support of the Socialist People's Party (*Socialistisk Folkeparti*—SF) and the Red-Green Unity List on most issues. Its position was nevertheless precarious, faced by a center-right opposition with a seat total of 83.

The Rasmussen administration in 1995 set as its main priority the reduction of unemployment, which was still about 11 percent in a country that had enjoyed full employment for most of the postwar period. However, the government's scope for concrete policy action continued to be circumscribed by an equal commitment to preserving the parity of the krone within the unofficial narrow band of the EU's exchange rate mechanism. Meanwhile, the center-right opposition contended that the government was shirking necessary pruning of Denmark's generous welfare provision and of the extensive rights and benefits accorded to Danish labor.

The government's position became even more tenuous in mid-December 1996 when the two CD cabinet members resigned their posts after the CD had unsuccessfully opposed the terms on which the 1997 budget secured parliamentary endorsement. Meanwhile, Denmark's relations with its self-governing dependencies, the Faroe Islands and Greenland, remained strained as the result of economic problems in the former and security issues in the latter. (Opinion polls showed significantly increased support for greater autonomy in both territories.)

The SD maintained its front-runner status in the November 1997 municipal elections, although its percentage of the vote dropped slightly as the far-right, flatly "anti-immigration" Danish People's Party (*Dansk Folkeparti*—DFp) made a strong electoral debut with nearly 7 percent support and 13 seats. In February 1998 Rasmussen announced that legislative elections would be held on March 11, some six months early, in part at least to prepare for the upcoming national referendum on the EU's recent Amsterdam Treaty (see article on EU for details). Surprising many observers, the SD and its coalition allies once again managed to secure a narrow 90-seat majority in the *Folketing* with the support of two deputies from the Faroes and Greenland. Rasmussen reshuffled his cabinet on March 23, although incumbents were reappointed to most major portfolios. Subsequently, in a referendum on May 28, the Danish voters endorsed the Amsterdam Treaty by a 55–45 percent vote, although on September 28, 2000, in a major reversal for the government, they rejected participation in the EU's euro zone by 53–47 percent.

In what proved to be a disastrous political miscalculation, Prime Minister Nyrup Rasmussen called an early election on October 31, 2001, expecting to ride a recent surge in popularity to another term. Instead, voters on November 20 awarded a plurality of 56 seats to the center-right Liberal Party, and on November 27 Liberal leader Anders Fogh RASMUSSEN announced formation of a minority government in coalition with the KF, which had won 16 seats. Eighteen seats short of a majority in the 179-seat *Folketing*, Fogh Rasmussen was forced to rely on external support from the DFp, which held 22 legislative seats.

In elections held on February 8, 2005, Danish voters sent a mixed message to the government. Both the ruling Liberal Party and the largest opposition party (the SD) declined slightly in representation, while the smaller, right-wing parties gained. Following the election, Prime Minister Rasmussen became the first Liberal leader to win a second consecutive term of office and again formed a minority government in coalition with the KF, again relying on the DFp for legislative support. He appointed a new cabinet on February 18. Rasmussen (with the pledged legislative support of the DFp and a legislator from the Faroe Islands) formed another Liberal-KF government on November 23, 2007, following snap elections on November 13, in which the Liberals had secured a plurality of 46 seats.

Prime Minister Rasmussen resigned on April 5, 2009, after accepting appointment as the secretary general of NATO. He was succeeded the same day by the Liberal Party's Lars Løkke RASMUSSEN (no relation), who formed a government with the same coalition partner and supporters as the previous administration.

Constitution and government. The constitution adopted in 1953 abolished the upper house of parliament while leaving intact the main outlines of the Danish political system. Executive power, nominally vested in the monarch, is actually exercised by a cabinet responsible to the *Folketing*, a legislative body that includes representatives from the Faroe Islands and Greenland. The judicial system is headed by a 15-member Supreme Court and encompasses two high courts, local courts, specialized courts for labor and maritime affairs, and an ombudsman who is appointed by the *Folketing*. Judges are appointed by the Crown on the advice of the minister of justice.

Under a major reform enacted in 1970, the former 25 regional districts were reduced to 14 counties (*amtskommuner*), each governed by an elected council (*amtsiåd*) and mayor (*amtsborgmester*). The counties in turn are divided into 277 local administrative units, each featuring an elected communal council (*kommunalbestyrelse*) and mayor (*borgmester*).

In 2002 the government appointed a commission to propose ways to reorganize and reduce the number of counties and municipalities. Following intermunicipal negotiations in 2004 and adoption of a plan in 2005, on January 1, 2007, the preexisting 14 counties were reduced and reorganized into 5 regions and the 270 municipalities were reduced to 98. Councils of 41 members, elected every four years, govern the regions. Regional governments' principal responsibility is delivery of hospital and health services. The regions have no power to tax; their revenues come from municipal subsidies and the central government. The city of Copenhagen is governed by a city council (*borger repræsentation*) and an executive consisting of a head mayor (*overborgmester*), two deputy council chairs (*næstformand*), and six deputy mayors (*borgmestie*).

Foreign relations. Danish foreign policy, independent but thoroughly Western in outlook, emphasizes support for the United Nations, the economic integration of Europe, and regional cooperation through the Nordic Council and other Scandinavian programs. Formerly a member of the European Free Trade Association (EFTA), Denmark was admitted to the EC on January 1, 1973; dissatisfaction with fishing agreements led to the withdrawal of newly autonomous Greenland from the EC in 1982, followed by sporadic conflict with individual community members, particularly the United Kingdom, over North Sea fishing rights. Although committed to collective security, the Danish government long resisted pressure by NATO to increase its defense appropriations in real terms; indeed, responding to widespread popular agitation, the Social Democrats and their allies were able, in May 1984, to force legislation making Denmark the first NATO member to withdraw completely from missile deployment. Danish voters in February 1986 endorsed (by popular referendum) continued participation in the EC; however, leftist opposition parties in the *Folketing* succeeded in enacting measures to further reduce effective involvement in NATO, including, in April 1988, the passage of legislation reiterating a longstanding (but unenforced) ban on visits by nuclear-equipped vessels. While the EC issue dominated Danish foreign (and domestic) policy in 1992–1993, the government continued to attach importance to Nordic and other regional cooperation. In March 1992 it became a founding member of the ten-nation Council of the Baltic Sea States, while in May it was an enthusiastic signatory of the European Economic Area (EEA) treaty between the EC and most EFTA countries.

The 2003 invasion of Iraq was a contentious issue in Denmark as it was in much of Europe. The *Folketing* voted in March 2003 to send troops to Iraq, with 93 of the *Folketing*'s 179 members voting for the measure. Denmark contributed a warship, a submarine, and 160 troops to the 2003 attack on Iraq. After the downfall of the Saddam Hussein regime, a 460-member Danish peacekeeping force was sent to Iraq, and in 2005 Denmark had approximately 500 troops stationed there. Despite deep divisions within parliament and the public over the decision to participate in the invasion, the issue of the subsequent occupation of Iraq was not particularly contentious in Denmark (see Current issues, below).

On August 6, 2004, Denmark and Greenland signed a pact with the United States allowing the latter to upgrade its early-warning radar facility in Thule. The science minister made a controversial announcement in October that Demark was going to map the seabed north of Greenland to explore a geological case for claiming the international territory of the North Pole—a vast source of oil and natural gas—for Denmark.

Denmark's relationship with many Muslim countries was seriously damaged when the *Jyllands-Posten*, the country's largest-circulation newspaper, published political cartoons of caricatures of the Prophet Mohammed on September 30, 2005. Many Muslims were offended by publication of the cartoons because depictions of the Prophet Mohammed are forbidden under Islamic religious law. The following month, Prime Minister Rasmussen declined to meet with ten ambassadors from Muslim countries where the cartoons prompted large-scale protests, saying that he neither possessed nor wanted the power to limit freedom of the press. The reappearance of the caricatures in publications in 2006 provoked violent protests by Muslims throughout the world, resulting in a reported 285 deaths, with observers attributing much of the violence to Islamic extremists. Subsequently, Iran, Libya, and Syria withdrew their ambassadors from Denmark, and radical Islamists declared a *fatwa* (religious edict) against the Danes serving in Iraq. As a further consequence, Muslim countries boycotted Danish goods, severely affecting dairy sales in particular. (Trade with the Middle East reportedly was reduced by half between February and June 2006.) Ultimately, Danish-Muslim relations began to stabilize, with Denmark reopening its embassies in Muslim countries by midyear, and Muslim countries ending their boycott. In May, a court dismissed a lawsuit against the *Jyllands-Posten* by Muslim groups seeking compensation for alleged defamation.

In August 2007 Russia planted a flag on the North Pole seabed while a Danish expedition was collecting evidence on whether the Pole is geologically linked to Greenland. Prime Minister Rasmussen responded to the Russian action by saying the North Pole is shared property for the world, but his science minister said he believed it belonged to Denmark. At stake are natural resources, including as much as a quarter of the world's energy reserves, and the power to regulate navigable sea routes if the polar ice continues to melt. Denmark subsequently committed itself to negotiations, which were launched in May 2008 by the five nations with claims to the Arctic region.

Current issues. Danish attention in 2002 turned to immigration, an issue brought increasingly to the forefront due to concerns about international terrorism and the growing demands on the country's welfare system. In June the legislature approved a new law tightening restrictions on asylum seekers and reducing welfare benefits for immigrants. In 2004 immigration laws were amended (on the recommendation of the DFp) to restrict the entry of Muslim clerics, or *imams*. Despite criticism by the United Nations High Commissioner for Refugees (UNHCR) and by the Council of Europe's human rights commissioner, polls indicated public support for further limits on immigration, the issue becoming a major one in the legislative elections of February 2005, which saw an increase in support for the DFp. Rasmussen, who called the elections nine months early, had the advantages of a strong economy and the absence of major divisive issues in the country, observers noted.

As the one-year anniversary of the publication of caricatures of the Prophet Mohammed approached in September 2006 (see Foreign relations, above), authorities arrested nine Muslims suspected of plotting a terrorist attack in Denmark. Tensions increased a month later after far-right groups invited more potentially offensive cartoons, provoking outrage in the Muslim community. (One of the Danish Muslim leaders thought to have stirred much of the anger behind the violent protests, Ahmed Abu LABAN, died in early 2007.)

In mid-2006, with broad backing by political parties, the government laid out wide-ranging plans for reforming the welfare system, effective in 2017, an agenda that prompted large public protests in Copenhagen. Under the agreement reached by conservative, liberal, and opposition parties, the retirement age would be raised by two years, and the early retirement age would be pushed back by two years. Hailed by the IMF as a plan that would "safeguard pension and health-care costs" over the long term (through 2027), the proposal also included provisions to improve integration of immigrants in an effort to boost the country's labor supply.

Although Denmark was among the first countries to send military support to Iraq in 2003 and later increased that support, in February 2007 the government announced it would withdraw its troops because the Iraqi security capability had improved. All combat troops had been withdrawn by December, leaving only a small contingent in Baghdad to guard Danish diplomats.

The Rasmussen government drew praise in the summer of 2007 not only for its handling of the cartoon controversy but also for Denmark's recent robust economic performance, which included 15 consecutive quarters of growth. In addition, unemployment was at its lowest level in three decades, taxes had been reduced, and the budget surplus equaled 3 percent of GDP. Nevertheless, difficult issues remained, including an anticipated rise in interest rates, an expected housing slump, public sector wage negotiations required by the end of the year, additional tax cuts scheduled for 2008, and the proposed relaxation of anti-immigration policies to combat the labor shortage. Further complicating matters was the upcoming decision on the EU's proposed Reform Treaty, possibly accompanied by a national referendum on Denmark's potential opt-out status. Consequently, Rasmussen decided that a fresh mandate was needed for his government and called for snap elections in November, 15 months earlier than required. Among other things, the Liberals reportedly hoped that electoral success might permit them to form a coalition government with the KF that would no longer rely so heavily on support from the DFp, which opposed new tax cuts, offered only tepid support for the EU, and stood as a major obstacle to immigration reform.

The Social Democrats, the major opposition party, staked out few areas of policy disagreement with the government except for the party's opposition to more tax cuts. Both sides favored a parliamentary vote rather than a referendum on the EU Reform Treaty and endorsed some form of relaxation of immigration restrictions. Meanwhile, the recently launched New Alliance (*Ny Alliance*—NA) pledged to reclaim the political center for the Danish people. (See section on the Liberal Alliance [*Liberal Alliance*—LA], below, for additional information.) However, the NA failed to meet expectations that it would win enough seats to become a pivotal party, and the Liberals eked out a one-seat plurality over the Social Democrats. Despite the Liberals' earlier hopes, Rasmussen once again was forced to depend on support from the DFp to secure a 90-seat minimal legislative majority for his new Liberals-KF government. The continued reliance on the DFp gave rise to speculation that the government was unlikely to survive a full four-year term. The government scored an early success regarding pay increases for some public sector workers, but tens of thousands of nurses and case workers went on strike in the spring of 2008, claiming that proposed wage hikes fell short of what was promised during the campaign. Subsequently, the thorny EU issues were put on hold in Denmark by the Irish referendum defeat of the proposed treaty in June 2008.

In February 2009 the government announced a stimulus package that included increased spending and plans to cut the top marginal income tax from 63 to 55 percent. In addition, in light of the slumping economy (which, among other things, had forced interest rate hikes to stave off speculative attacks on the Danish krone), public and governmental support reportedly grew for the eventual adoption of the euro.

The April 2009 appointment of Prime Minister Rasmussen as NATO's secretary general generated a degree of controversy. Although France, Germany, and the United Kingdom endorsed the proposed appointment immediately, the United States did not commit its support until a G-20 meeting in early April, apparently in deference to concerns from Turkey over Rasmussen's ability to work effectively with Muslims. (The Turkish misgivings focused on Rasmussen's refusal to apologize for the 2005 cartoon episode, as well as the fact that the Danish government had allowed the Kurdistan Workers' Party to operate a television news network from Denmark.) However, Turkey eventually agreed to the NATO appointment.

New prime minister Lars Løkke Rasmussen and the Liberal Party appeared to face an uncertain political future. Polls showed an approval rating for Rasmussen of only 16 percent, more than 20 points behind his leading rival, Hell THORNING-SCHMIDT of the Social Democrats. However, with that sizable personal polling advantage and other polls throughout the spring forecasting that the Social Democrats would win a 25 to 28 percent vote in the June 2009 balloting for the EU Parliament, the Social Democrats' 21 percent of the vote to the Liberals' 20 percent revealed just how uncertain the political future is on both sides of the political divide. Danish voters showed strong interest in the EU elections, with their highest-ever EU election turnout of 60 percent. Voters also made two Euro-skeptic parties, the Danish People's Party and the Socialist People's Party, the notable winners. Each gained one seat by doubling its vote share compared to 2004. The results left the thirteen-member Danish delegation with five Euroskeptic members.

POLITICAL PARTIES

Government and Government-Supportive Parties:

Liberal Party (*Venstre*—V). Founded in 1870 as the Agrarian Party but currently representing some trade and industrial groups as well as farmers, the Liberal Party (commonly referenced in Danish as *Venstre* [Left] rather than *Liberale Parti*) stands for individualism as opposed to socialism in industry and business, reduction of taxation through governmental economy, relaxation of economic restrictions, and adequate defense. Its parliamentary representation rose from 22 in 1988 to 29 in 1990, while the party was the main victor in the September 1994 national election, winning 23.3 percent of the vote and 42 seats, although it remained in opposition.

In the 2001 election the Liberals won 31 percent of the national vote and a plurality of 56 seats, permitting the party chair, Anders Fogh Rasmussen, to forge a center-right minority government on November 27. In the general election in February 2005, the Liberal Party won 29 percent of the vote and 52 seats in parliament, 4 fewer than it had won in the previous election. Nevertheless, the party's showing was strong enough to allow party leader and Prime Minister Rasmussen to win a second term at the head of a minority coalition government with the KF (see below). The Liberals won a 26.2 percent vote plurality and 46 seats in the November 2007 elections. Following brief negotiations, a third Rasmussen government (again comprising the Liberals and the KF, with pledged support from the DFp and a Faroe Islands member) took office on November 23. When Rasmussen was named secretary general of NATO in April 2009, Lars Løkke Rasmussen, the former vice chair of the party, was named acting party leader.

Leaders: Lars Løkke RASMUSSEN (Prime Minister and Acting Chair), Anders Fogh RASMUSSEN (Former Prime Minister), Jens Skipper RASMUSSEN (Secretary General).

Conservative People's Party (*Konservative Folkeparti*—KF). Founded in 1916 as an outgrowth of an earlier Conservative grouping (*Højre*), the KF mainly represents financial, industrial, and business groups. It supports adequate defense, protection of private property, sound fiscal policy, and lower taxation. Under the leadership of Poul Schlüter, the party recovered from a low of 5.5 percent of the vote in 1975 to 14.5 percent in 1981, enabling Schlüter in 1982 to form a center-right coalition, which remained in office for more than a decade. A further surge to 23.4 percent in 1984 was followed by a decline to 16 percent in 1990 and the resignation of Schlüter in January 1993.

The KF has not recovered from its decline in popularity in the early 1990s. In the 1998 general elections, the party lost 11 seats, winning a total of only 16, a loss attributed in part to support being drawn off by the emergence of the right-wing Danish People's Party. Nevertheless, since 2001 the party has been able to sustain a high profile in government as the junior partner in the coalition government led by the Liberal Party. In the 2005 general election, the KF marginally improved its representation, winning 10.3 percent of the vote. The KF maintained its 18 seats in the 2007 elections on a vote share of 10.4 percent and returned as the junior partner in the coalition government.

Leader: Lene ESPERSON (Chair).

Danish People's Party (*Dansk Folkeparti*—DFp). The DFp was launched in October 1995 by dissident deputies of the right-wing Progress Party (FP, see below), including former FP leader Pia Kjærsgaard. While espousing similar policies, the DFp is regarded as being to the right of the parent party. The nationalistic DFp, openly anti-immigrant, did very well in the November 1997 municipal elections and was one of the biggest winners in the March 1998 national election, more than tripling the parliamentary representation won by the FP by winning 13 seats compared to the FP's 4. Its vote share rose to 12 percent in the November 2001 general election, in which it won 22 seats, making it the third-largest political party in Denmark. The party retained that position in the February 2005 general election, winning 24 seats. It remained the third largest party in parliament following the 2007 elections, winning 13.9 percent of the vote and 25 seats. While the DFp disagrees with the ruling Liberal Party over the latter's support for increasing integration within the EU, it has officially supported recent governments.

Leaders: Pia KJÆRSGAARD (Chair), Peter SKAARUP (Deputy Chair).

Opposition Parties:

Social Democratic Party (*Socialdemokratiet*—SD). Founded in 1871, the SD mainly represents industrial labor and advocates economic planning, full employment, extensive social security benefits, and environmental planning. The SD has been the ruling party of Denmark for most of the past 75 years. Most recently, the SD led the ruling government coalition from 1993 until 2001. In 2003 the SD, along with the RV (see below), refused to support the government's bid to send soldiers to Iraq following the U.S. invasion.

In the 2005 elections the SD won 47 seats in the *Folketing*, a loss of 5 seats from the previous elections. On April 12, 2005, Helle Thorning-Schmidt was elected leader of the SD, becoming the first woman to head the party. In the 2007 legislative balloting the party won 45 seats, 2 fewer than in 2005 and 1 shy of the Liberals' plurality, and 25.5 percent of the vote.

Leaders: Helle THORNING-SCHMIDT (Party Leader), Nicolai WAMMEN (Vice Chair), Nick HAEKKERUP (Vice Chair), Lars MIDTIDY (Secretary).

Socialist People's Party (*Socialistisk Folkeparti*—SF). The SF was formed in 1958 by former Communist Party chair Aksel LARSEN, who had disagreed with Moscow over the suppression of the 1956 Hungarian Revolution. Subsequently, the party advocated left-wing socialism independent of the Soviet Union, unilateral disarmament, and opposition to NATO, Danish membership in the EC, and Nordic cooperation. It has often acted as an unofficial left wing of the SD, concentrating on influencing the platform and voting patterns of the larger party. Traditionally anti-EU, the party was split at its August 1997 congress when parliamentary leader Steen GADE resigned in order to campaign for ratification of the EU's Amsterdam Treaty. In the February 2005 elections the SF attracted 6 percent of the vote and 11 seats. The SF more than doubled its vote to 13.0 percent in the 2007 balloting and won 23 seats, thereby becoming the fourth largest party in parliament.

Leaders: Villy SØVNDAL (Chair), Jakob NØRHØJ (Deputy Chair), Ole SOHN (Parliamentary Leader), Turid LEIRVOLL (Secretary).

Radical Liberal Party (*Det Radikale Venstre*—RV). Also characterized in English as a "Social Liberal" grouping, the RV was founded in 1905; it represents mainly small landowners and urban intellectual and professional elements. In domestic affairs, the party advocates strengthening of private enterprise in a social-liberal context; in foreign affairs, it is pacifist in outlook and has recently strengthened its formerly lukewarm pro-European stand. With a record of often joining or endorsing SD-led governments, it nevertheless supported the

Schlüter KF-led coalition in 1982. Following the September 1987 election, (then) parliamentary leader Niels Helveg PETERSEN rebuffed Anker Jørgensen's appeal to realign with the Social Democratic and Socialist People's parties, thereby precluding the establishment of a new Socialist administration. The RV was awarded five cabinet posts in the 1988 Schlüter government, but withdrew from formal participation in 1990.

The party has attracted liberal voter support in the wake of the victory by the center-right parties in the 2001 elections. The RV increased its seats in the February 2005 election, bringing its total to 17. In 2007 internal division over the party's close ties to the Social Democrats led Danish parliamentarian Naser Khader and EU parliamentarian Anders Samuelsen to leave the RV and form the New Alliance (see below). The RV won only 5.1 percent of the vote and 9 seats in the 2007 legislative poll.

Leaders: Margrethe VESTAGER (Chair and Parliamentary Leader), Søren BALD (President).

Liberal Alliance (*Liberal Alliance*—LA). This party was known until August 2008 as the New Alliance (*Ny Alliance*—NA), which was founded in May 2007 by Naser KHADER, a former RV member of the Danish parliament; Anders Samuelsen, a former RV member of the European Parliament; and Gitte SEEBERG, a former KF member of the Danish parliament. The NA announced its intention to offer a middle-ground party with an emphasis on liberal market policies (including calls for tax reductions beyond those proposed by the Liberal Party), reformed and relaxed immigration policies, greener energy, pro-EU stands, and increased foreign aid. Syrian-born Khader rose in Danish public prominence as a well-received voice of moderation in the wake of the cartoon controversy (see Foreign relations, above), and early polls indicated the NA could capture as many as 15 seats in a parliamentary election. However, in the wake of a less than deft campaign leading up to the November 2007 balloting, the party won only 5 seats on 2.8 percent share of the vote. (Analysts attributed the poor showing to mixed policy signals and the party's refusal to announce whether it would support a new Rasmussen-led government.) In February 2008 two members resigned from the party, including Seeberg, who left to sit in parliament as an independent. In July Seeberg stood down from parliament altogether and was replaced by an appointed NA member. In January 2009 Khader also left the party, leaving it with only two members in parliament.

Leader: Anders SAMUELSEN (Chair).

Red-Green Unity List (*Enhedslisten-De Rød-Grønne*). The Red-Green formation was launched in 1989 as a coalition of three left-wing/environmentalist groups: the VS and DKP (see below) and the Trotskyist **Socialist Workers' Party** (*Socialistisk Arbejderparti*—SAP), the last led by Søren SONDERGAARD. The Maoist **Communist Workers' Party of Denmark** (*Danmarks Kommunistisk Arbejderparti*—DKA) joined the coalition in 1991. Strongly opposed to EU membership and the Maastricht process, the Unity List achieved a breakthrough in the September 1994 general election, winning 3.1 percent of the vote and 6 seats. Officially, the party has no chair, but rather is directed by a 21-person collective leadership. The Unity List lost one of its 6 seats in the March 1998 elections with a vote share of 2.7 percent. It lost another in 2001, when its vote share totaled 2.4 percent. The party did significantly better in the February 2005 election, attracting 3.4 percent of the vote and increasing its seats in parliament to 6. In the November 2007 legislative elections party support dropped to 2.2 percent, good for 4 seats.

Civil Center (*Borgerligt Centrum*—BC). The BC was founded in January 2009 by Simon Emil Ammitzbøll, a parliamentarian who had left the RV two months earlier. The party emphasized three issues: an increased focus on personal responsibility, a moderate immigration policy for skilled immigrants, and a restructuring of the welfare state through greater attention to health care and education and a reduction in the length of time for eligibility for unemployment benefits. Few commentators expected the party to surmount the required 2 percent threshold to gain parliamentary seats if it contests the next election.

Leader: Simon Emil AMMITZBØLL.

Other Party that Contested the 2007 Elections:

Christian Democrats (*Kristelig Demokraterne*—KD). The KD was originally formed as the Christian People's Party (*Kristeligt Folkeparti*—KrF) in 1970 in opposition to abortion and liberalization of pornography regulations. The party achieved representation in the *Folketing* for the first time in 1973 and placed two representatives in the center-left coalition formed in January 1993. The KrF vote slipped to 1.1 percent in the June 1994 European elections (insufficient for representation) and took only 1.8 percent in the September national balloting, thereby exiting from both the *Folketing* and the government. The KrF returned to the *Folketing* following the March 1998 election, in which it won four seats on a vote share of 2.4 percent. It retained all four in 2001.

The KrF changed its name to Christian Democrats in October 2003 in an attempt to enhance its public image, prompting the resignation of party chair Jann SJURSEN. He was replaced by Marianne KARLSMORE. The KD won only 1.7 percent of the vote in the 2005 general election, which was not enough to win any seats in parliament. Karlsmore resigned in 2005 after the party's poor showing in the elections. In the 2007 balloting the CD vote share sank to 0.9 percent, below the 2 percent threshold needed for parliamentary representation.

Leaders: Bjarne Hartung KIRKEGAARD (President), Mogens NØRGÅRD (Vice President).

Other Parties:

Progress Party (*Fremskridspartiet*—FP). The right-wing FP was formed in 1972 by Mogens GLISTRUP, who was convicted in February 1978 of tax evasion and sentenced in 1983 to a three-year prison term. The party advocated gradual dissolution of the income tax and abolition of the diplomatic service and the military. The second largest parliamentary group after the 1973 balloting, it had slipped to eighth place by 1984, with one of its six representatives subsequently joining the Conservatives and another becoming an independent. In an unexpected recovery, it won 9 seats in 1987, but the FP was unable to join in what would have been a six-party Schlüter majority because of a Radical Liberal refusal to ally itself with a party viewed not only as extremist, but also as racist because of a strong anti-immigrant posture. The FP registered the largest single-party gain in the 1988 balloting, winning 16 seats, 4 of which were lost in 1990. The FP vote slumped to 2.9 percent in the June 1994 European Parliament balloting but recovered to 6.4 percent in the September national poll. Internal divisions in 1995 resulted in the ouster of Pia Kjærsgaard as FP leader, after which she and three supporters withdrew to form the DFp (above). The party lost 7 of its 11 seats in the 1998 elections and won no seats in 2001 with only 0.6 percent of the vote. The FP did not contest the 2005 or 2007 parliamentary elections.

Leaders: Ove JENSEN (President), Niels HØJLAND (Vice President), Ernst SIMONSEN (Secretary).

Left Socialist Party (*Venstresocialisterne*—VS). The VS split from the SF in 1967 and achieved representation in the legislature for the first time in 1968–1971. In 1984 the party's "revolutionary" wing, informally known as the "Leninist" faction, broke with the leadership over its unwillingness to organize cadres along traditional communist lines. Two members defected to the SF in July 1986. Subsequently, the party was weakened by growing factionalization, with the "Red Realists" favoring cooperation with the SF and the "Left Oppositionists" following a rigid Marxist-Leninist line. The VS has maintained a distinct identity within the Red-Green Unity List. The party has no titular chair, the principal leadership being regarded as collective.

In 2006 Danish authorities arrested several VS members and charged them with supporting Palestinian and Colombian terrorist organizations, but in December 2007 a Copenhagen court found all of them innocent of the charges because the supported organizations were not, in the court's opinion, terror groups.

Leaders: Karen NYGARD, Henrik FORCHAMMER, Albert JENSEN, and Michael SCHOELARDT (Spokespersons).

Communist Party of Denmark (*Danmarks Kommunistiske Parti*—DKP). The DKP was formed in 1919, achieved parliamentary representation in 1932, and participated in the immediate postwar coalition government. The party was greatly weakened by the 1956 Hungarian revolt and the schism that subsequently led to the formation of the Socialist People's Party. Its representation in the *Folketing* following the 1973 election was its first since 1956. However, it lost all of its 7 legislative seats in the 1979 balloting. As a member of the Red-Green Unity List coalition, the DKP remains a loose network of militants rather than a full-fledged party. In 1990 a Marxist-Leninist faction of the group opposed to participation in the Unity List formed the **Communist Forum** (*Kommunistisk Forum*), which became the **Communist Party in Denmark** (*Kommunistisk Parti i Danmark*—KPiD) in November 1993 under the leadership of Betty Frydensbjerg CARLSSON. After a period of collective leadership, Henrik Stamer Hedin subsequently became chair.

Leader: Henrik Stamer HEDIN (Chair)

Center Democrats (*Centrum-Demokraterne*—CD). The CD grouping was formed in November 1973 by the dissident Social Democrat Erhard JAKOBSEN to protest "leftist" tendencies in the government and plans for increased taxation, in the belief that traditional "left" and "right" political distinctions were no longer appropriate in contemporary Denmark. The party scored an electoral breakthrough in the 1973 balloting (14 seats) and was involved in the center-right coalition government in 1982–1988. It also joined the SD-led government in 1993 before resigning over policy differences in December 1996. Campaigning in the March 1998 election on a platform of protecting welfare programs and accommodating refugees and immigrants, the CD added 3 seats to the 5 it had won in 1994. In 2001 it won only 1.8 percent of the votes and no seats. In 2005 the party garnered only 1 percent of the vote, and again failed to win a seat in parliament. The CD did not contest the 2007 national elections, and in February 2008 a party conference decided to dissolve the party.

Danish political movements that contested the 1994, 1999, and 2004 European Parliament elections included the **June Movement** (*Juni Bevægelsen*), led by Hanne DAHL and named after the month of the 1992 initial rejection of the Maastricht Treaty. The **People's Movement against the European Union** (*Folkesbevægelsen mod EU*) took 10.3 percent of the vote and 2 seats (against 18.9 percent and 4 seats in 1989) in the 1994 European Parliament balloting and 1 seat in 1999 and 2004.

LEGISLATURE

The ***Folketinget*** (also frequently rendered as *Folketing*) is a unicameral legislature whose members are elected every four years (subject to dissolution) by universal suffrage under a modified proportional representation system. Of its present membership of 179, 135 are elected in 17 metropolitan districts, with 40 additional seats being divided among those parties that have secured at least 2 percent of the vote but whose district representation does not accord with their overall strength. In addition, the Faroe Islands and Greenland are allotted two representatives each.

In the most recent election, November 13, 2007, the Liberal Party won 46 seats; the Social Democratic Party, 45; the Danish People's Party, 25; the Socialist People's Party, 23; the Conservative People's Party, 18; the Radical Liberal Party, 9; the New Alliance, 5; and the Red-Green Unity List, 4. The Faroe Islands are represented by Union and Republic party members; Greenland's members come from the Eskimo Brotherhood and Forward parties (see Related Territories, below).

President: Thor PEDERSEN.

CABINET

[as of May 1, 2009]

Prime Minister	Lars Løkke Rasmussen (V)
Ministers	
Climate and Energy	Connie Hedegaard (KF) [f]
Culture	Carina Christensen (KF) [f]
Defense	Søren Gade Jensen (V)
Development Cooperation	Ulla Tørnaes (V) [f]
Ecclesiastical Affairs	Birthe Rønn Hornbech (V) [f]
Economic Affairs and Business Affairs	Lene Espersen (KF) [f]
Education	Bertel Haarder (V)
Employment	Inger Støjberg (V) [f]
Environment	Troels Lund Poulsen (V)
Equal Rights	Inger Støjberg (V) [f]
Finance	Claus Hjort Frederiksen (V)
Food, Agriculture, and Fisheries	Eva Kjer Hansen (V) [f]
Foreign Affairs	Per Stig Møller (KF)
Health and Prevention	Jakob Axel Nielsen (KF)
Interior and Social Affairs	Karen Elleman (V) [f]
Justice	Brian Mikkelsen (KF)
Nordic Cooperation	Bertel Haarder (V)
Refugees, Immigration, and Integration Affairs	Birthe Rønn Hornbech (V) [f]
Science, Technology, and Innovation	Helge Sander (V)
Taxation	Kristian Jensen (V)
Transport	Lars Barfoed (KF)

[f] = female

COMMUNICATIONS

Freedom of the press is constitutionally guaranteed, and newspapers and magazines are privately published. International attention focused on Denmark in 2005 following the publication of political cartoons depicting caricatures of the Prophet Mohammed by *Jyllands-Posten*. The cartoons offended many Muslims and prompted violent protests by Muslims around the world. Subsequently, in its annual report on global press freedom, Reporters Without Borders noted that democratic countries did not defend Denmark, even though its embassies were attacked and its journalists threatened. In 2007 the editor responsible for publishing the cartoons received an award from Denmark's Free Press Society.

Press. Many newspapers reflect political party viewpoints, although most are not directly owned by a party. The following newspapers are published in Copenhagen, unless otherwise noted: *Ekstra Bladet* (159,500 weekdays, 192,900 Sunday), independent Radical Liberal; *BT* (149,910 weekdays, 190,053 Sunday), independent Conservative; *Politiken* (153,000 weekdays, 205,000 Sunday), independent Radical Liberal; *Morgenavisen Jyllands-Posten* (Viby, 172,000 weekdays, 269,000 Sunday), independent; *Berlingske Tidende* (160,000 weekdays, 195,000 Sunday), independent Conservative; *Erhvervs-Bladet* (110,000 daily); *Jydske Vestkysten* (Esbjerg, 94,234 weekdays, 106,157 Sunday); *Ålborg Stiftstidende* (Ålborg, 72,000 weekdays, 92,000 Sunday), independent; *Fyens Stiftsti-dende* (Odense, 66,000 weekdays, 98,000 Sunday), independent; *Århus Stiftstidende* (Århus, 72,743 weekdays, 93,772 Sunday), independent; *Det Fri Aktuelt* (42,262 daily), Social Democratic; *Borsen* (42,700 daily).

News agencies. The domestic agency, owned by the Danish newspapers, is *Ritzaus Bureau;* numerous foreign bureaus also maintain offices in Copenhagen.

Broadcasting and computing. Radio and television stations have traditionally been controlled by the government-owned, noncommercial *Danmarks Radio* (now *DR Radio*). The monopoly was terminated by the *Folketing* in 1986, which sanctioned the immediate establishment of independent local radio broadcasting, with a nationwide commercial television channel commencing operation in late 1988, followed by a satellite television station in 1991. As of 2008 there were 838.9 Internet users per 1,000 inhabitants.

INTERGOVERNMENTAL REPRESENTATION

Ambassador to the U.S.: Friis Arne PETERSEN.

U.S. Ambassador to Denmark: Laurie Susan FULTON.

Permanent Representative to the UN: Carsten STAUR.

IGO Memberships (Non-UN): AC, ADB, AfDB, BIS, CBSS, CERN, CEUR, EBRD, EIB, ESA, EU, Eurocontrol, IADB, IEA, Interpol, IOM, NATO, NC, NIB, OECD, OSCE, PCA, WCO, WTO.

RELATED TERRITORIES

Faroe Islands (*Faerøerne*, or *Føroyar*). The Faroe Islands (numbering 18) in the North Atlantic have been under Danish administration since 1380. Their area is 540 square miles (1,399 sq. km.), the population is 48,000 (2006E), and the capital is Tórshavn (population 16,900

[2001E]). The principal language is Faroese, with most inhabitants also Danish-speaking. Fishing and sheep raising are the most important ingredients of the islands' economy, which in 1992–1993 entered an unprecedented crisis due to the disappearance of fish stocks as well as the collapse of a 1980s investment boom and resultant heavy indebtedness.

The islands, which send two representatives to the *Folketing*, constitute a self-governing territory within the Danish state. A local legislature (*Løgting*) with between 27 and 33 members (currently 33) elects an administrative body (*Landsstýri*) headed by a chair (*løgmadur*). The Crown is represented by a high commissioner (*ríkisumbodsmadur*). The islands have been represented on the Nordic Council since 1969.

The principal political groups are the **Union Party** (*Sambandsflokkurin*), which urges the retention of close links to metropolitan Denmark; the **Social Democratic Party** (*Javnarflokkurin*); the conservative-liberal **People's Party** (*Fólkaflokkurin*); the left-wing **Republic** (*Tjóðveldi*), which advocates secession from Denmark (the party changed its name in 2007 from the Republican Party [*Tjøðveldisflokkurin]*); the **Home Rule Party** (*Sjálvstýrisflokkurin*); the **Progressive and Fisheries Party** [and] **Christian People's Party** (*Framburs–Fiskivinnuflokkurin Kristeligt Folkeparti*); the **Labor Front** (*Verkmannafylkingin*), founded in 1994 by dissident Social Democrats and trade unionists; and the **Center Party** (*Miflokkurin*).

In elections on July 7, 1994, all of the above parties won representation in the islands' 32-member legislature. The leading formation was the Union Party (eight seats), whose leader was sworn in on September 15 as prime minister of a center-left coalition that also included the Social Democrats, the Labor Front, and the Home Rule Party. The previous coalition had consisted of the Social Democratic, Republican, and Home Rule parties.

In the national election of September 21, 1994, the two Faroe Islands' seats in the Danish *Folketing* were won by candidates of the Union and People's parties. In 1996 the Social Democratic Party was replaced in the government coalition by the People's Party, while the Social Democratic Party and the People's Party each secured one seat in the March 1998 Danish *Folketing* balloting.

In the legislative elections of April 30, 1998, the dominant issue was the islanders' growing demand for sovereignty, which was embraced in varying degrees by candidates across the political spectrum. Anti-Copenhagen sentiment was inflamed by continuing controversy over the Faroese government's 1993 purchase of a failing Danish-owned bank, one of only two on the islands, whose condition the Faroese alleged had been misrepresented by the Danes. The Republican Party led the 1998 balloting, winning 8 seats with a vote share of 23.8 percent, followed closely by the Social Democratic Party and the People's Party. Anfinn KALLSBERG, leader of the People's Party, subsequently formed an 18-seat coalition government consisting of his own party, the Republicans, and the Home Rule Party. In August the new government said it would seek independence while remaining under the Danish monarchy and monetary system, hoping to submit independence to a referendum.

Meanwhile, after two decades of talks, the failure of island and British negotiators to settle a boundary dispute over a potentially large oil and gas field on the ocean floor, in the so-called White Zone in the North Atlantic, prevented the Faroese from going forward with exploration of the site. Finally, in May 1999 representatives from the Faroe Islands, Denmark, and the United Kingdom reached a settlement of the dispute over the maritime border. The islands were granted sovereignty over some 40 square miles of the area in question, further fueling the drive for independence in view of the potential new oil wealth. However, the Danish government in March 2000 hardened its stance on the independence question, announcing that Danish subsidies (estimated at $110 million per year) would cease 4 years after independence rather than being phased out over 15–20 years as proposed by Faroese leaders. In February 2001 the Faroese government announced May 26 as the date for a referendum on the issue of full sovereignty by 2012, but in March the vote was called off because of declining support in the face of Copenhagen's firm position on the subsidies.

In January 2003 government officials from the Faroe Islands and Denmark began talks aimed at transferring responsibility in several policy areas to the Faroese government. On June 26, 2003, the talks culminated in the signing of an agreement that transferred authority over the Faroese judicial system, police, and civil law. Responsibility for security for the Faroe Islands remains with Denmark. In December 2003 the governing coalition collapsed when the Republican Party withdrew its support as the result of charges of an accounting scandal involving the administration of Prime Minister Anfinn Kallsberg (People's Party). On January 20, 2004, parliamentary elections resulted in the anti-independence Union Party winning 23.7 percent of the vote. While this was the highest percentage won by any party, it was down 2.3 percent from the Union Party's showing in the 2002 elections. On February 3, 2004, the Union Party, the Social Democratic Party, and the People's Party formed a new coalition government with Social Democrat Jóannes EIDESGAARD as prime minister. In the January 2008 balloting the Republic party won vote and seat pluralities. On February 5 Prime Minister Eidesgaard formed a new three-party center-left government of the Social Democratic, Republic, and People's parties. That coalition subsequently broke up and was replaced on September 26 by a right-of-center coalition comprising the Union, People's, and Social Democratic parties, headed by Union Party leader Kaj Leo Johannesen.

High Commissioner: Dan KNUDSEN.

Prime Minister: Kaj Leo JOHANNESEN (Union Party).

Greenland (*Grønland,* or *Kalaallit Nunaat*). Encompassing 840,000 square miles (2,175,600 sq. km.), including an extensive ice cover, Greenland is the second-largest island in the world, after Australia. The population, which is largely Eskimo, totals approximately 59,000 (2005E), with residents of the capital, Nuuk (Godthåb), accounting for some 15,200. The indigenous language is Greenlandic. Fishing, mining, and seal hunting are the major economic activities. A number of oil concessions were awarded to international consortia in 1975, but most were subsequently abandoned.

Although under Danish control since the 14th century, the island was originally colonized by Norsemen and only through an apparent oversight was not detached from Denmark along with Norway at the Congress of Vienna in 1815. It became an integral part of the Danish state in 1953 and was granted internal autonomy, effective May 1, 1979, on the basis of a referendum held January 17. The island continues to elect two representatives to the Danish *Folketing.* After achieving autonomy, the island government sought compensation from the United States for the 1953 relocation of indigenous villagers during the construction of U.S. airbases in the northwest. Also persistently controversial was the crash in 1968 of an American B-52 bomber near the Thule base and the eventual disclosure that it had been carrying nuclear weapons, in breach of the Danish ban on nuclear weapons on its territory.

In a preautonomy general election held April 4, 1979, the socialist **Forward** (*Siumut*) party obtained 13 of 21 seats in the new parliament (*Landsting*), and *Siumut* leader Jonathan MOTZFELDT subsequently formed a five-member executive (*Landsstyre*). Other participating groups included the **Solidarity** (*Atássut*) party, led by Lars CHEMNITZ, which obtained the remaining 8 seats, and the proindependence **Eskimo Brotherhood** (*Inuit A taqatigiit*—IA).

In the balloting of April 1983 for an enlarged *Landsting*, the *Siumut* and *Atássut* parties won 12 seats each, Motzfeldt again forming a government with the support of two IA representatives. A further election on June 6, 1984, necessitated by a nonconfidence vote two months earlier, yielded a formal coalition of the *Siumut* and IA parties, which had obtained 11 and 3 seats, respectively. However, a disagreement ensued regarding the prime minister's alleged "passivity" over the projected installation of new radar equipment at the U.S. airbase in Thule, forcing another early election on May 26, 1987, the results of which were *Siumut* and *Atássut*, 11 seats each; *Inuit Ataqatigiit*, 4; and a new political party, *Issittup Partiia* (Polar Party), representing the business community and fishing industry, 1. On June 9 Motzfeldt succeeded in forming a new administration based on the previous coalition.

The "Thule affair" returned to prominence in January 1995, when the metropolitan government announced a parliamentary inquiry into the 1968 crash, amid continuing demands from Greenlanders for compensation for its alleged consequences, including a high local incidence of cancer. Controversy intensified in July when the Danish foreign minister disclosed that as early as 1957 the U.S. government had informed the then prime minister that nuclear weapons were present in Greenland and that he had raised no objection. (In May 2003 Greenland and Denmark signed an agreement stipulating that in exchange for Greenland's support for modernization of the U.S. radar station in Thule, Greenland would be consulted on all foreign affairs matters relating to the island.)

In September 1997 former prime minister Motzfeldt returned to the premiership when Lars Emil JOHANSEN, a strong proponent of the exploitation of Greenland's mineral and oil wealth, moved into the business sector. In the Danish *Folketing* balloting of March 11, 1998, *Siumut* and *Atássut* each won 1 seat, with the *Siumut* deputy becoming allied with the government coalition. In the *Landsting* election of February 16, 1999, *Siumut* won 11 seats, *Atássut,* 8; the IA, 7; and independents, 5. Among the major issues were calls for more autonomy from Denmark, proposed adoption of the euro should Denmark join the EU's Economic and Monetary Union, and oil exploration. Following the election, *Siumut* and the IA formed a new coalition government under the leadership of Motzfeldt, *Atássut* returning to opposition.

In September 1999 Danish Prime Minister Rasmussen formally apologized to Greenland's indigenous population for the forced relocation of villagers in 1953 in connection with the construction of U.S. bases.

While autonomy remained an ongoing issue in the country's politics, domestic issues were highlighted in the December 3, 2002, parliamentary elections. The new Democratic Party (*Demokratüt*), which stressed issues of improving Inuit education and relieving the housing shortage, received 15.6 percent of the vote and won 5 seats in the *Landsting*. The biggest winner of the election was the ruling Forward Party (*Siumut*), which secured 10 seats and formed a new coalition government under Prime Minister Hans Enoksen. The left-wing Eskimo Brotherhood Party (*Inuit Ataqatigüt*) won 8 seats, and the proindependence Solidarity Party (*Atussut*) won 7 seats. A month later the coalition collapsed after a political disagreement, and on January 17, 2003, the Forward Party formed a new coalition with just the Solidarity Party.

In September 2003 the Forward Party again formed a new government in coalition with the proindependence Eskimo Brotherhood Party after a rift with the Solidarity Party over a budgetary issue. In the most recent election of November 22, 2005—called a year early by the prime minister after the coalition parties failed to reach agreement on a budget—the Forward Party retained 10 seats, the Eskimo Brotherhood and the Democratic parties won 7 each, and the Solidarity Party secured 6. A new left-right coalition government was formed under Prime Minister Enoksen, including all but the Democratic Party. Observers reported that social matters, not independence, were the overriding issues of the election.

In 2006 Greenland, Denmark, and the EU signed an agreement in which the EU would pay millions in subsidies to Greenland in exchange for control over policies regarding climate change and scientific research, prompted by reports of the significant retreat of Greenland's ice sheet, revealing huge mineral resources. The Eskimo Brotherhood Party withdrew from government in May 2007 in a dispute over prawn fishing regulations. Also in 2007 the EU and Greenland signed a new fisheries agreement meant to support the latter's policies in the wake of declining fish populations. Spurred by the prospects of oil revenue, Prime Minister Enoksen proposed a November 2008 referendum to expand the scope of Greenland's self-governance.

On November 25, 2008, 75 percent of those voting in a referendum endorsed the proposed expansion of the island's autonomy, which supporters hoped would lead to full independence from Denmark by 2020. The home-rule government in Greenland was scheduled to begin in June 2009 to assume greater responsibility for police affairs, the justice system, immigration, the coast guard, and other policy areas, although Denmark was to retain control over most security and foreign policies. Collaterally, Greenland was also scheduled to begin to receive much of the income from oil, gas, and gemstone deposits, whose value was expected to increase dramatically in coming years. Prime Minister Enoksen called for early parliamentary elections to be held on June 2, 2009, in advance of the devolution of power, scheduled to begin on June 21.

With financial scandals swirling around Enoksen's government, and with doubts about his party's ability to govern with the newfound autonomy, the Forward Party in June 2009 lost its place in government for the first time since home rule was granted to Greenland in 1979. The Eskimo Brotherhood ran far ahead of Forward, receiving 44 percent of the vote to Forward's 27 percent. With 14 seats, 2 short of an outright majority, the Eskimo Brotherhood announced on June 7 that it would form a government with the centrist Democrats (*Demokraatit*) and the single center-right independent candidate elected under the party label of the Association of Candidates (*Kattusseqatigiit*). The three-party coalition assumed office June 12 under the leadership of Prime Minister Kuupik Kleist. After joining the Queen in a June 21 weekend celebration of Greenlandic self-rule, Kleist announced that his government would turn its attention inward to deal with Greenland's social ills of alcoholism, domestic violence, and child abuse.

High Commissioner: Søren Hald MØLLER.
Prime Minister: Kuupik KLEIST (*Inuit Ataqatigiit*)

DJIBOUTI

Republic of Djibouti
République de Djibouti (French)
Jumhuriyah Djibouti (Arabic)

Political Status: Former French dependency; proclaimed independent June 27, 1977; new constitution with provisions for limited multiparty elections in effect as of September 1992; limit on the number of parties lifted in September 2002.

Area: 8,958 sq. mi. (23,200 sq. km.).

Population: 847,000 (2008E), including nonnationals. There has been no census since 1960–1961.

Major Urban Center (2005E): DJIBOUTI (599,000).

Official Languages: French and Arabic.

Monetary Unit: Djibouti Franc (official rate December 1, 2009: 162.50 francs = $1US).

President: Ismail Omar GUELLEH (Popular Rally for Progress); elected on April 9, 1999, and inaugurated for a six-year term on May 8 in succession to Hassan GOULED Aptidon (Popular Rally for Progress); reelected (as the sole candidate) to another six-year term on April 8, 2005.

Prime Minister: Dileïta Mohamed DILEÏTA (Popular Rally for Progress); appointed by the president on March 4, 2001, and sworn in on March 7 to succeed Barkat GOURAD Hamadou (Popular Rally for Progress), who had announced his resignation on February 6; reappointed on May 21, 2005; reappointed on March 26, 2008.

THE COUNTRY

Formerly known as French Somaliland and subsequently as the French Territory of the Afars and the Issas, the Republic of Djibouti is strategically located in East Africa just south of the Bab el Mandeb, a narrow strait that links the Gulf of Aden to the Red Sea. Djibouti, the capital, was declared a free port by the French in 1949 and has long been an important communications link between Africa, the Arabian peninsula, and the Far East. The largest single population group (40 percent) is the ethnically Somalian Issa tribe, which is concentrated in the vicinity of the capital, while the Afar tribe (35 percent) is essentially nomadic and ethnically linked to the Ethiopians. The remaining 25 percent consists largely of Yemeni Arabs and Somalis.

Serviced by a number of international airlines and heavily dependent on commerce, Djibouti also provides Ethiopia with its only railroad link to the sea. The country is largely barren, with less than 1 percent of its land under cultivation, few known natural resources, and little industry; consequently, the government relies extensively on aid from France and other Western donors, several Arab countries, and various multilateral organizations. Real GDP declined by around 3 percent a year in the first half of the 1990s, before stabilizing in 1996, as structural adjustment measures negotiated with the International Monetary Fund (IMF) in April began to bring a measure of credibility to government finances. Meanwhile, it was estimated that about 40 percent of the potential work- force was unemployed. In 1998 and early 1999 Djibouti's economic agenda was dominated by continued negotiations with the IMF and France, the latter's decision to reduce its military presence having sparked concern in Djibouti about potential financial repercussions. In October the IMF approved a new three-year loan to support the government's reform program, encouraging privatization of state-run enterprises, market liberalization, and change in labor regulations. The IMF also called for greater attention to poverty-reducing efforts and other social programs. IMF disbursements were suspended for six months in 2000–2001, the fund demanding that

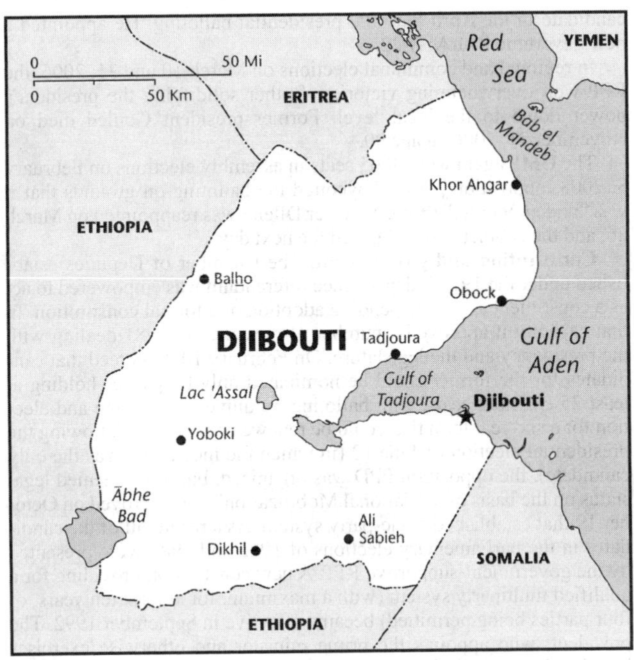

greater attention be paid to the "inefficiency of public expenditures" and a lack of transparency in government finances. Real GDP growth of 1 percent and inflation of 2.4 percent were reported for 2000. Subsequently, the administration was forced to grapple with social unrest triggered by two oil price increases, budgetary pressures associated with Djibouti's hosting of the Somalia National Peace Conference, and the need to demobilize the soldiers who had been recruited to deal with hostilities in northern Afar regions in the 1990s but were no longer needed in view of the recent formal peace accord.

Pervasive poverty and high unemployment remained priorities addressed by a 2004 review. The government pledged to improve revenue collection and adopt free-trade-zone legislation, among other things. In late 2005 the economy was bolstered by a funding agreement with the World Bank for $17 million to support the education and energy sectors. In accordance with the country's first self-monitored program with the IMF, plans were under way for reforms in taxes, banking, and public administration. While annual GDP growth averaged 3.3 percent in 2005–2006, increasing to an average of 5.4 percent annually in 2007-2008, the World Trade Organization issued a report emphasizing the need for greater economic diversification. In a significant boost to the economy, Djibouti undertook a major expansion of the port of Doraleh with financial backing from the United Arab Emirates. Described as one of the largest and most modern terminals in Africa, the port opened in early 2009. Despite robust activity in construction, foreign investment, and maritime services, GDP growth slowed to 4.4 percent in 2009. However, monetary authorities commended the government for helping to generate more revenue by instituting a value-added tax and revising regulations regarding free trade zones. The IMF also noted that "fiscal transparency has been strengthened" through the publication of monthly reports on finances. Meanwhile, GDP growth for 2010 was forecast to hold steady at about 4 percent.

GOVERNMENT AND POLITICS

Political background. The area known as French Somaliland was formally demarcated by agreement with Emperor Menelik II of Ethiopia in 1897 following a half-century of French penetration that included a series of treaties with indigenous chiefs between 1862 and 1885. Internal autonomy was granted in 1956, and in 1958 the voters of Somaliland elected to enter the French Community as an Overseas Territory. Pro-independence demonstrations during a visit by President de Gaulle in August 1966 led to a referendum on March 19, 1967, in which a majority of the predominantly Afar voters opted for continued association with France. Somali protest riots were severely repressed, and the name of the dependency was changed to Territory of the Afars and the Issas to eliminate exclusive identification with the Somali ethnic group.

On December 31, 1975, a UN General Assembly resolution called on France to withdraw from the territory, and during 1976 extensive discussions were held in Paris between leading tribal representatives and the French government. In the course of the talks, France tacitly agreed that the Afar president of the local Government Council, Ali AREF Bourhan of the National Union for Independence, no longer represented a majority of the population; consequently, Paris approved a new nationality law governing eligibility for a second referendum on independence. Aref subsequently resigned, and on July 29 a new ten-member council, composed of six Issas and four Afars, was formed.

On May 8, 1977, 98.8 percent of the electorate voted for independence while simultaneously approving a single list of 65 candidates for a Chamber of Deputies. Following the passage of relevant legislation by the French parliament, the territory became independent as the Republic of Djibouti on June 27. Three days earlier, Issa leader Hassan GOULED Aptidon of the African People's League for Independence had been unanimously elected president of the republic by the chamber. On July 12 President Gouled named Afar leader Ahmed DINI Ahmed to head a 15-member Council of Ministers.

On December 17, 1977, Dini and four other Afar cabinet members resigned amid charges of "tribal repression," the duties of prime minister being assumed by the president until the designation of a new government headed by Abdallah MOHAMED Kamil on February 5, 1978. Mohamed Kamil was in turn succeeded by Barkat GOURAD Hamadou on September 30, 1978. Gourad, an Afar advocate of "detribalization," formed subsequent governments on July 7, 1981 (following the reelection of President Gouled on June 12); on June 5, 1982 (after a legislative election on May 21); and on November 23, 1987 (after balloting on April 24).

Although all of the cabinets formed since independence had ostensibly been designed to strike a careful balance in tribal representation and all three prime ministers named by President Gouled were Afars, charges of Issa domination persisted, and most members of the opposition Djibouti People's Party (*Parti Populaire Djiboutien*—PPD) formed in August 1981 were from the ethnic minority. The regime's immediate response was to arrest PPD leader Moussa Ahmed IDRISS and the party's entire 12-member executive committee. However, all were released by January 1982, after the enactment of legislation establishing Gouled's Popular Rally for Progress (*Rassemblement Populaire pour le Progrès*—RPP) as the sole authorized party.

Despite a constitutional limit of presidential tenure to two terms, Gouled was permitted to run again in 1987 on the ground that he had initially been appointed by the Chamber of Deputies rather than having been popularly elected. As sole candidate, the incumbent was reported to have secured 90 percent of the vote in the April 24 poll.

In 1990 the regime's reported backing of the rebels in Somalia sparked internal conflicts between the Issa majority and Afar/Gadabursi kinsmen of Somalian leader Siad Barre; as a consequence, the government on January 9, 1991, arrested 68 people for alleged involvement in a "vast plot" to incite "civil war" between the Afar and Issa communities. While most were soon released, the detention of seven "ringleaders," including former chief minister Ali Aref Bourhan, was confirmed by the interior ministry on January 17; three days later it was announced that "about 20" individuals had been formally charged with attempting to overthrow the government. At midyear, ethnic clashes were reported between Issas and Oromos, and in October Afar rebel forces, having coalesced as the Front for the Restoration of Unity and Democracy (*Front pour la Restauration de l'Unité et de la Démocratie*—FRUD), launched attacks on government installations.

In response to the fighting, France urged Djibouti to institute "rapid" liberalization of its political system, and on November 27, 1990, the government revealed plans for a referendum "to consult" the population "on changes to be made in the political domain." On December 19 it announced that the referendum would be held in May 1992, but only if rebel activity had ceased. Eleven days later an RPP spokesman reported that legislative elections to be held immediately after the referendum would be open to candidates from "several parties." Meanwhile, the slaying by government forces of 40 Afars and the wounding of 50 others in a Djibouti slum severely eroded what support remained for the regime. Thereafter, 14 parliamentarians led by Mohamed AHMED Issa ("Cheiko") formed a parliamentary opposition group, and in January 1992 the health and public service ministers resigned, with the former decrying the regime's "war logic." Concurrently, a French spokesman insisted that the escalating civil war was an "internal matter" not covered by a defense agreement concluded between the two countries in 1977. Nonetheless, a French military contingent was deployed in February to implement a cease-fire between government and FRUD units. Subsequently, a committee formed by President Gouled presented a preliminary draft of a new constitution, which was not acceptable to the rebels, however, because it would retain a strong presidency.

On June 20–24, 1992, representatives of most of the leading opposition groups (under the banner of the United Opposition Front of Djibouti [*Front Uni de l'Opposition Djiboutienne*—FUOD] under Political Parties and Groups, see below) met in Paris to forge a common front against the Gouled regime. The session concluded with a demand for a "transitional government led by a prime minister from the ranks of the opposition," who would be charged with initiating a democratic transitional process that would include the drafting of a multiparty constitution.

In a national referendum on September 4, 1992, a reported 97 percent of the voters approved the draft constitution presented by the administration, providing for, among other things, multiparty activity, although a separate vote also endorsed a proposal to limit the number of legal parties to four. Subsequently, FRUD and other opposition members of FUOD boycotted the legislative balloting of December 18 (at which the RPP was awarded all of the seats) as well as the presidential election of May 7, 1993, at which President Gouled defeated four other candidates by a wide margin in securing reelection to a fourth term.

In mid-1994 a split developed within FRUD between supporters of its newly designated president Ali MOHAMED Daoud, who favored peace talks with the government, and his recently ousted predecessor, former prime minister Dini, who, along with most of the FUOD leadership, supported continued resistance. The peace talks, which reportedly had commenced as secret negotiations between Prime Minister Gourad and the "New FRUD" secretary general, Ougoureh KIFLE Ahmed, eventually yielded a reconciliation agreement on December 26 that in a cabinet reshuffle of June 8, 1995, provided the Kifle faction with two ministerial portfolios.

The December 1994 accord yielded greatly reduced hostilities in 1995, although by early 1996 dissension within the government had become intense, with the justice minister and RPP secretary general, Moumin BAHDON Farah, leading those who contended that the agreement had not brought real peace and stability to Djibouti. The dominance of the pro-accord camp was demonstrated on March 27 when Bahdon was dismissed from the government, together with Ahmed BOULALEH Barre, the defense minister. Bahdon and his allies subsequently launched a new opposition group, Group for the Democracy of the Republic. Collaterally, the episode showed that in the bitter contest between possible successors to an increasingly infirm Gouled, ascendancy had been gained by the president's nephew and *chef de cabinet*, Ismail Omar GUELLEH.

In assembly elections on December 19, 1997, the RPP—"New FRUD" electoral coalition captured all 65 seats (54 by the RPP and 11 by "New FRUD"), garnering a reported 78.55 percent of the vote tally compared to 19.19 percent for the Party of Democratic Renewal and 2.25 percent for the National Democratic Party. On December 28 President Gouled reappointed Gourad as head of a reshuffled government.

In February 1999 President Gouled announced that he would not seek reelection in balloting scheduled for the following April, and the RPP promptly chose Guelleh as its presidential candidate. Guelleh captured 74.09 percent of the vote on April 9, 1999, easily outdistancing his sole competitor, Moussa Ahmed Idriss. Despite gaining the endorsement of the newly formed Unified Djiboutian Opposition (see Political Parties, below), Idriss garnered just 25.78 percent of the vote. Prime Minister Gourad was reappointed on May 10, and a reshuffled cabinet was formed two days later.

After 22 years in office, Prime Minister Gourad announced his resignation in February 2001; he was succeeded on May 7 by Dileïta Mohamed DILEÏTA, a former chief of the presidential staff. In the wake of a comprehensive agreement between the administration and FRUD, several FRUD members were included in the new cabinet installed on July 4. In addition, in September 2002 President Guelleh announced the establishment of a full multiparty system. The ruling Union for a Presidential Majority (*Union pour la Majorité Présidentielle*—UMP) still won all 65 seats in balloting for the Chamber of Deputies on January 10, 2003. Also undercutting the administration's stated goal of broader governmental participation, Guelleh was the only candidate in the April 8, 2005, presidential balloting. He appointed a new government on May 22.

In regional and communal elections on March 10 and 31, 2006, the RPP won overwhelming victories, further solidifying the president's power down to the local level. Former president Gouled died on November 21, 2006, at age 90.

The UMP again won all 65 seats in assembly elections on February 8, 2008; opposition parties boycotted the balloting on grounds that it was "undemocratic." Prime Minister Dileïta was reappointed on March 26, and the cabinet was reshuffled the next day.

Constitution and government. The Chamber of Deputies established under the 1977 independence referendum was empowered to act as a constituent assembly pending adoption of a formal constitution. In that capacity it approved a number of measures in 1981 dealing with the presidency and the legislature. On February 10 it decreed that candidates for the former could be nominated only by parties holding at least 25 chamber seats, with balloting by universal suffrage and election for a six-year term that could be renewed only once. Following the presidential election of June 12 (in which the incumbent was the only candidate), the opposition PPD was organized, but it was denied legal status on the basis of a "National Mobilization" law approved on October 19 that established a one-party system. As a result, all of the candidates in the parliamentary elections of 1982 and 1987 were presented by the government-supportive RPP. A new constitution providing for a qualified multiparty system (with a maximum, for at least ten years, of four parties being permitted) became effective in September 1992. The president, who appoints the prime minister and otherwise exercises broad authority, is limited to two six-year terms. In September 2002 the government eliminated all restrictions on party registration.

The colonial judicial structure, based on both French and local law, was technically abolished at independence, although a successor system based on Muslim precepts remains imperfectly formulated. For administrative purposes the republic is divided into five districts, one of which encompasses the capital. Local elections to regional assemblies, envisioned under recent decentralization plans negotiated by the government with groups such as FRUD, were held in March 2006.

Foreign relations. Djibouti's small size and its mixed population of Ethiopian-oriented Afars and Somali-oriented Issas make it highly vulnerable in a context of historic friction between its two neighbors. Despite bilateral accords in 1986 and 1987, Somalia has long regarded Djibouti as a "land to be redeemed," while the nearly 500-mile railroad between the port of Djibouti and Addis Ababa was viewed by Ethiopia as vital to its export-import trade during the lengthy revolt in its Red Sea province of Eritrea. The country's security depends in part on a French garrison, which was of crucial importance during the prolonged Soviet military presence in Ethiopia and South Yemen.

In January 1986 President Gouled hosted a six-nation conference to set up an Intergovernmental Authority on Drought and Development in East Africa (IGADD, subsequently the Intergovernmental Authority on Development—IGAD), which marked the first meeting between the Ethiopian head of state, Lt. Col. Haile-Mariam, and President Siad Barre of Somalia since the two countries went to war in 1977. The other states participating in the conference as IGADD members were Kenya, Sudan, and Uganda. Subsequently, peace talks between the 1977 combatants, mediated by Djibouti, were held in Addis Ababa in May, with Gouled reaffirming his country's role in the peace negotiations during a state visit to Ethiopia in September. A second IGADD summit was held in March 1988, with the Djibouti president being elected to a second term as the authority's chair.

The repatriation of some 50,000 Ethiopians who had fled to Djibouti during the Ogadan conflict began in 1983 but was subsequently halted because of the drought; it was resumed in December 1986 amid charges that the "voluntary" program would in fact expose the refugees to potential mistreatment. By 1987 it was estimated that fewer than 20,000 expatriates remained, with Djibouti insisting that they too would have to leave since resources were lacking for their assimilation.

The early 1990 intensification of the Somalian civil war, coupled with Djibouti's continued tacit support of the Somalian National Movement (SNM), an Issa rebel group, resulted in a deterioration of relations between Djibouti and Mogadishu and mutual border militarization. Midyear diplomatic efforts, including a heads of state meeting in May, were inconclusive, and in October Somalian claims of military intrusion yielded closure of the maritime border while igniting ethnic hostilities in Djibouti. Meanwhile, observers described Djibouti's dependence on French security forces and aid (renewed for ten years in July) as motivation for publicly siding with allied forces in the Gulf crisis, despite a number of Djibouti-Baghdad military and economic agreements.

The outbreak of ethnic violence in 1991 severely strained Djiboutian- French relations. In October Paris, which had deployed troops in March to disarm Ethiopian soldiers fleeing into Djibouti, dismissed the government's claims that Ethiopian Afars were seeking to establish a "greater Afaria" and ordered its troops to remain in their barracks. Concurrently, France pressed the Gouled regime to accelerate political liberalization and enter into cease-fire negotiations with the rebels. In November France rejected Djibouti's request for supplies and labeled the regime's international efforts to solicit weapons as "intolerable." Following the government's violent suppression of Afar slum dwellers in Djibouti in December, Paris warned Djibouti that it would suspend economic aid unless there was immediate "democratization," and in February 1992 France intervened to enforce a standoff between government and rebel forces that continued for the remainder of the year. Relations with Paris improved in the wake of the December 1994 peace accord that the government signed with a FRUD faction, with French defense minister Charles Dillon confirming, during a visit to Djibouti in January 1996, that France would maintain its military presence in the republic. On the other hand, as French economic aid continued its precipitous decline (from $77 million in 1977 to $21 million in 1996), a number of Djiboutian economic planners rallied behind efforts to broaden ties with other countries in the region.

An unresolved territorial dispute flared up in mid-April 1996 when Djiboutian and Eritrean forces clashed in a northern border area claimed by Eritrea on the strength of a 1935 colonial-era map. In June the Organization of African Unity (OAU, subsequently the African Union—AU) authorized Djibouti, Burkina Faso, and Zimbabwe to mediate the border dispute; however, in November Eritrea severed relations with Djibouti, accusing the Gouled administration of supporting Ethiopia's military campaign. (In early 1999 the OAU named a new negotiating team after the delegates from Burkina Faso and Zimbabwe refused to enter Eritrea without their banned Djiboutian colleagues [see separate articles on Eritrea and Ethiopia for more details].) Normal relations were reestablished with Eritrea following the conclusion of the conflict, in part assisted by the two countries' similar stances regarding events in Somalia.

In late 2001 and early 2002 Djibouti was frequently referenced as having achieved a higher international profile due to its potentially strategic geographic location in regard to the West's war on terrorism. Among other things, President Guelleh agreed to allow the United States to establish a military base in Djibouti, while also endorsing an ongoing French military presence. At the same time, the Guelleh regime, cognizant of the status of Islam as the nation's majority religion, evinced a strongly pro-Arab and pro-Palestinian posture in regard to the turmoil in the Middle East. In September 2003 Djibouti expelled some 80,000 illegal immigrants, mostly Ethiopians and Somalis. It was subsequently reported that U.S. concerns over possible attacks on Western interests had led the government of Djibouti to detain several hundred suspects. In 2006 Djibouti opposed an AU decision to send peacekeeping troops to Somalia, and denied accusations by the UN that it was supplying weapons to Somali Islamists. At the AU summit in early 2007, following renewed fighting in Somalia, Djibouti agreed to the proposed AU peacekeeping mission, which was to be replaced by a UN peacekeeping force within six months (see Current issues, below).

With piracy becoming a growing threat to coastal countries in East Africa, in 2009 nine countries in the Indian Ocean and Red Sea regions, including Djibouti, announced plans to cooperate on combating the threat. The resulting Djibouti Code of Conduct allows for the countries that are party to the agreement to send troops into other signatory countries' territorial waters to pursue pirates.

Also in 2009, Iran and Djibouti signed a memorandum of understanding regarding bilateral cooperation following a visit to Djibouti by Iranian president Mahmoud Ahmadinejad.

Current issues. The first months of President Guelleh's administration were marked by the same heavy-handed tactics for which its successor was noted. Domestic and international critics charged the new government with the illegal detention and abuse of "New-FRUD" sympathizers and other human rights abuses, while a crackdown on the opposition press (see Communications, below) and seemingly unnecessarily harsh treatment of Moussa Ahmed Idriss of the ODU (see introduction to Political Parties and Groups, below) were also condemned. However, the government's image shed some of its tarnish in February 2000 when a cease-fire was signed with FRUD militants on May 12 (see FRUD, below, for details).

In December 2000 it was reported that a group of police officers had taken over several government buildings as part of a coup attempt after their commander had been demoted by the president. However, the mini-revolt was put down within eight hours and was not considered an influence in the subsequent resignation of longtime Prime Minister Gourad, whose health reportedly had recently declined significantly. New Prime Minister Dileïta, an Afar (in the power-sharing tradition that has held since independence), did not name a new cabinet immediately as negotiations continued with FRUD on a permanent political settlement. Under the accord, the government pledged to help rebuild areas damaged by the earlier insurgency and agreed to intensify decentralization efforts. Although some FRUD demands (such as greater Afar representation in the civil service and establishment of an independent judiciary) were not fully addressed, the front was sufficiently satisfied to agree to join the new "national unity" government and to start preparing for formal party status. Despite the lifting of the restrictions on the number of parties in 2002, the opposition alleged fraud and other irregularities in the January 2003 legislative elections. (Opposition leader Ahmed Dini Ahmed bitterly criticized the electoral structure, which denied antigovernment parties any seats, though they had won 37 percent of the vote.) On a more positive note, new electoral rules not only permitted but required female candidates for the first time. In fact, ten seats in the Chamber of Deputies were set aside for women.

The opposition parties boycotted the April 2005 presidential balloting, citing what they perceived as a continued lack of transparency in the electoral process. President Guelleh nevertheless ran an "active campaign" in order to boost voter turnout.

In late 2005 clashes were reported between Afar rebels and government troops, precluding a full reconciliation in the wake of Guelleh's election. Following regional and communal balloting in March 2006, the FRUD's hopes for decentralization were shattered after the party's losses to Guelleh's RPP in every area, and the government reportedly continued military operations to disrupt arms supplies to rebels in the north.

Drought was a major concern in 2006 in the Horn of Africa, prompting U.S. president George W. Bush to pledge some $92 million to the countries facing starvation, including Djibouti. The UN made additional appeals in 2007 for millions of dollars more for its world food program to help alleviate the situation for 53,000 people in Djibouti alone who were affected by the severe drought. On a more positive note, water drilling projects were under way early in the year with the help of the U.S. military command in the Horn of Africa and financial support from a United Arab Emirates foundation.

Attention in early 2007 focused on the fighting in Somalia (see article on Somalia for details), the government being supported in its defense by Ethiopian troops and, in part, by the United States, which conducted air strikes in January from its base in Djibouti. Although President Guelleh denounced the air strikes against suspected Islamic militants in Somalia and denied the attacks were launched from the base in Djibouti, he continued to support counterterrorism measures in the republic.

In early 2008 an unresolved case from more than a decade earlier continued to strain Djibouti's relationship with France. The case involved the mysterious shooting death of a French judge in Djibouti in 1995. The judge by various accounts had been investigating arms smuggling or money-laundering allegedly involving major political figures in Djibouti. Although the case was initially ruled a suicide, further evidence indicated it was a homicide, and allegations followed against government officials in France and Djibouti, including justice minister Moumin Bahdon Farah, who was said to have ordered the French judge to conduct the investigation. When France refused to turn over information it had gathered in the case, Djibouti appealed to the International Court of Justice, but the court ultimately ruled that France was not obliged to share the investigative information with Djibouti.

Tensions heightened between Djibouti and Eritrea again in May 2008, when Djibouti claimed that Eritrea had invaded its territory with the aim of taking over a town and an island strategically located at the mouth of the Red Sea, close to Yemen, for purposes that included blocking Ethiopia's main maritime route, as well as blocking a plan for the world's largest suspension bridge between Djibouti and Yemen. Subsequently, Eritrean troops withdrew from the border region, but fighting erupted in June between Eritrean and Djiboutian forces, with more than 70 killed and wounded on both sides in a battle that resulted in thousands of troops amassed along both sides of the border. In addition, Eritrea was reported to have 4,000 troops inside Djibouti. Meanwhile,

Djibouti, for its part, was reported to be disappointed by France's failure to mount an "energetic" defense. Diplomatic efforts to resolve the situation were unsuccessful, as Djibouti expelled the Eritrean ambassador in June. Meanwhile, Eritrea's refusal to support a UN investigation into the border clashes drew a rebuke by the UN in September. By October, Djibouti was warning that Eritrea's occupation of Djibouti territory could lead to war if the dispute was not resolved soon.

On January 14, 2009, the UN Security Council adopted a resolution urging the two countries to come to a peaceful resolution and demanding that Eritrea withdraw its forces by February 18. Eritrea immediately rejected the resolution, calling it "ill-considered, unbalanced, and unnecessary." Given Djibouti's high profile in the region, with U.S. and French forces stationed there—in a significant anti-terrorism effort—and as the center of the European Union's anti-piracy mission in the Horn of Africa, the UN Security Council appeared "likely" to revisit the issue, according to its March report. Further complicating the matter, however, was the lack of any official border demarcation between the two countries. By mid-2009 the Security Council was considering sanctions against Eritrea.

POLITICAL PARTIES AND GROUPS

Negotiations with the French that culminated in the referendum of May 8, 1977, were conducted by a United Patriotic Front representing five of the territory's major political groups. In preparing a list of candidates for the assembly election that accompanied the referendum, the Front acted under the name of the Popular Independence Rally (*Rassemblement Populaire pour l'Indépendance*—RPI). Its successor, the Popular Rally for Progress (RPP), was the only participant in the presidential election of June 1981 and continued as the country's only legal political party until the legislative balloting of December 1992.

In July 1997 former justice minister Moumin Bahdon Farah announced in Paris that the Group for the Democracy of the Republic (GDR) had formed a coalition with the United Opposition Front of Djibouti (FUOD) and a faction of the Party of Democratic Renewal (PRD) led by Kaireh ALLALEH Hared to campaign, according to the *Indian Ocean Newsletter*, for "the installation of a democratic legal framework" in anticipation of legislative elections in late 1997. However, a strong opposition challenge failed to materialize as, in addition to the PRD, both the Front for the Restoration of Unity and Democracy (FRUD) and the National Democratic Party (PND) suffered from factionalization.

In anticipation of upcoming presidential elections, by early 1999 a number of opposition leaders declared their intention to campaign for the chief executive's post, including Abbate Ebo Adou of the Action for Revision of Order in Djibouti (ARDD), the PND's Aden Robleh Awaleh, and the PRD's Abidillahi Hamareiteh. However, in February the aforementioned withdrew from the race as their parties, under the reported direction of the GDR's Bahdon, formed an electoral alliance, subsequently styled the **Unified Djiboutian Opposition** (*Opposition Djiboutienne Unifiée*—ODU), which then chose Moussa Ahmed IDRISS, a former independence fighter who had only recently resigned from the RPP, as its standard-bearer. Following his defeat in the 1999 presidential polling, Idriss was arrested in September for "attacking the morale of the armed forces" by publishing an article critical of the government in *Le Temps*. Idriss and 19 of his supporters were found guilty and sentenced to four months' imprisonment; however, Idriss was later released and granted amnesty. Subsequently he was invited to resume his role as a member of the Chamber of Deputies.

According to a separate measure approved in connection with the September 1992 constitutional referendum, a maximum of only four legal parties was established for a ten-year period. However, on September 4, 2002, President Guelleh announced the introduction of a full multiparty system. Eight parties participated in the 2003 legislative elections, four each in progovernment and opposition electoral blocs. In the 2008 legislative elections, only the UMP fielded candidates. The Union for a Democratic Alternative (*Union pour l'Alternance Démocratique*—UAD, below) boycotted the balloting, claiming it was undemocratic.

Government-Supportive Parties:

Union for a Presidential Majority (*Union pour la Majorité Présidentielle*—UMP). Formed as an electoral bloc prior to the 2003 legislative elections by the RPP, FRUD, PND, and PPSD, the UMP secured all 65 seats in that balloting with a reported 62 percent of the vote. The four groups also backed Guelleh in the 2005 presidential election. In the 2008 legislative balloting, the UMP, this time including the four groups and the UPR, again won all 65 seats.

Leaders: Ismail Omar GUELLEH (RPP), Ali Mohamed DAOUD (FRUD), Aden ROBLEH Awaleh (PND), Moumin BAHDON Farah (PPSD).

Popular Rally for Progress (*Rassemblement Populaire pour le Progrès*—RPP). The RPP was launched on March 4, 1979, its leading component being the socialist African People's League for Independence (*Ligue Populaire Africaine pour l'Indépendance*—LPAI). Long the principal spokesman for the Issa majority, the LPAI was not represented in the Afar-dominated preindependence Chamber of Deputies, although two of its members held ministerial posts.

The RPP was the first political group to be legalized under the "pluralist" constitution of 1992 and was credited with a clean sweep of chamber seats in December. In February 1994 it was reported that President Gouled would step down as RPP chair at a party congress scheduled for early March; however, in an apparent effort to avoid a conflict between potential successors, he accepted reelection at the congress that finally convened on May 26. In September 1996, Gouled announced his intention to serve out his presidential term (despite his failing health) and also to retain the party leadership until 1999.

In September 1996 the party announced the composition of its reshuffled Executive Committee, highlighted by the appointment as third deputy chair of Ismail Omar Guelleh, the apparent front-runner in the party's bitter contest to succeed the increasingly infirm Gouled. At a party congress in 1997, Gouled was reelected chair, while party delegates also elected a 125-member Central Committee and adopted a resolution confirming its alliance with the "New FRUD." Guelleh, who had succeeded Gouled as president of the republic in 1999, was also elected as the new RPP chair in March 2000, Gouled having retired from party activity.

The party won a majority in all five regional and three communal area elections in March 2006. Subsequently, tensions developed with FRUD, which had hoped to gain more power on the local level.

Leaders: Ismail Omar GUELLEH (President of the Republic and President of the Party), Dileïta Mohamed DILEÏTA (Prime Minister and Vice President of the Party), Idriss ARNAOUD Ali (Secretary General of the Party and Speaker of the Chamber of Deputies).

Front for the Restoration of Unity and Democracy (*Front pour la Restauration de l'Unité et de la Démocratie*—FRUD). The Afar-dominated FRUD was organized in Balho in northern Djibouti in August 1991 by nominal merger of the three groups below on a platform calling for the overthrow of President Gouled's "tribal dictatorship" and the installation of a democratic multiparty system. Responsibilities for political and military operations were assigned to a 17-member executive committee.

In September 1991 leaders of FRUD and the MNDID (see under PND, below) met in Ethiopia, and one month later their combined forces clashed with government troops in Djibouti's southern Yokobi region. Front officials denied government claims that their forces were Ethiopian Afars, although admitting that they had been trained across the border. Meanwhile, a second rebel summit, this time including the Democratic Union for Djiboutian Justice and Equality, was held in Somaliland.

The FRUD representative in the capital, Abbate Ebo Adou of the AROD (below), was arrested in December 1991 but was released following French intervention in February 1992. Two months later a small armed Gadabursi movement, the **Front of Democratic Forces** (*Front des Forces Démocratiques*—FFD), led by Mahmoud ABAR Derane and Omar CHARDIE Bouni, was reported to have linked up with FRUD. The following August, during a congress in an area "liberated" by FRUD, the incumbent president, Mohamed ADOYTA Yusuf, was named first vice president, while former Prime Minister Ahmed DINI Ahmed, theretofore resident in Yemen, was named FRUD president.

Meanwhile, FRUD had been instrumental in the June 1992 formation in Paris of the United Opposition Front of Djibouti (*Front

Uni de l'Opposition Djiboutienne—FUOD), an alliance of Afar and antiregime Issa groups. (See 2000–2002 *Handbook* for additional information on FUOD.)

A rather confused FRUD leadership picture emerged during the first half of 1994. On February 22 it was reported that Dini had been ousted and a new executive committee appointed with Ougoureh Kifle Ahmed as its secretary general. Subsequently, Kifle was said to have been engaged in a series of peace talks with the government that were opposed by supporters of Dini. At a "reconciliation" meeting of FRUD factions on June 21–25, Ali Mohamed Daoud (a.k.a. Jean Marie) was formally designated as the successor to Dini, who, from residence in Ethiopia, continued to reject the posture of political conciliation displayed by the current leadership. By late July the latter itself appeared to back away from continued peace talks by issuing a series of demands calling for ethnic balance in the government and armed forces. Meanwhile, FUOD had refused to recognize the new FRUD leadership, continuing to support the FRUD-Dini group, which, during a September congress "in the northern part of the country," named a rival seven-member executive committee sworn "to pursue the armed struggle against the Gouled regime."

In December 1994 the "New FRUD" leadership concluded an agreement with the government (from which the group's deputy secretary general, Ibrahim Chehem Daoud, dissociated himself) that called for an end to armed resistance and integration of FRUD units into the regular military, an alliance with the RPP that would include cabinet portfolios for two FRUD faction members, and the reform of electoral lists prior to the next election. In accordance with the agreement, the legalization of FRUD as the fourth political party permitted under Djibouti's constitution was announced by the interior minister on March 9, 1996, although the split between the legalized "New FRUD" and the FRUD-Dini faction remained unresolved at that stage.

Ending over 19 years in exile, FRUD-Dini Vice President Adoyta Yusuf returned to Djibouti in November 1996, along with some 15 supporters. Their return was facilitated by high-level negotiations between the Djiboutian prime minister and his Ethiopian counterpart and sparked speculation that Adoyta would join the Gouled cabinet. In March 1997 the FRUD's longtime European representative, Ismael Ibrahim Houmed, also returned from exile.

The "New FRUD" held its first congress on April 15–16, 1997, officials revealing that they had signed a secret political platform with the ruling party in December 1994 that included provisions for both higher profile joint governmental activities and the preparation of a shared list of candidates for the legislative balloting scheduled for December 1997. Furthermore, party delegates elected a multiethnic, 21-member Executive Committee and a 153-member National Committee. The former's composition underlined the party's pledge to include non-Afars in leadership positions.

Meanwhile, the "New FRUD's" tightened alliance with the government widened the chasm between it and the FRUD-Dini faction, which, according to the *Indian Ocean Newsletter*, continued to enjoy support from the grassroots groups that viewed the "New FRUD" with "little esteem." Underscoring the reportedly widespread antipathy felt toward the "New FRUD," demonstrators on May 1, 1997, disrupted the group's attempt to open an office in a predominantly Afar neighborhood in the capital. Following the FRUD-Dini's alleged attack on government forces in September, the Gouled administration authorized a military offensive against the rebel militants and urged its allies abroad to deny asylum to the FRUD-Dini's exiled leadership. Consequently, a number of FRUD-Dini faction leaders were extradited to Djibouti, while others were reported to have been forced to leave their safe havens. On November 10–12 the FRUD-Dini organized a congress within Djibouti's borders where delegates reelected Dini chair and elected a 13-member political bureau. Furthermore, the faction asserted that, while it was committed to further warfare, it remained open to establishing a dialogue with the government.

On November 26, 1997, FUOD president Ahmed Issa died. He was succeeded by Mahdi Ibrahim Ahmed, who in November 1998 called for an interim government, including the main opposition parties prior to the 1999 presidential balloting. However, there were few subsequent reports of FUOD activity, attention focusing on government negotiations with the remaining FRUD antigovernment forces.

In March 1998 FRUD-Dini and PRD delegates appealed to IGAD ministers meeting in Djibouti to intervene in the strife, claiming that foreign mercenaries were assisting government forces in the latest outbreak of fighting. The militants' entreaties were shelved by IGAD, and skirmishes were reported throughout the year and into 1999.

In November 1999 Dini suggested a Ramadan cease-fire and negotiations toward a peace settlement, and, following a series of secret meetings in France, an accord was signed on February 7, 2000, in Paris providing for an immediate cessation of hostilities, reciprocal prisoner releases, the eventual reintegration of the militants into their former jobs, and further discussions regarding the proposed devolution of political authority to the regions (primarily in the north of the country) involved in the rebel activity. Dini returned to Djibouti in late March from his long exile in France, and a FRUD-Dini congress on April 5–6 endorsed the Paris accord and reaffirmed its confidence in Dini's leadership, although the faction's fighters were to remain armed pending negotiation of a comprehensive peace settlement. Meanwhile, it was unclear how the recent agreement would ultimately affect the seven-year FRUD factionalization.

A final agreement was reached in May 2001 for, among other things, the demobilization of FRUD forces, which subsequently proceeded smoothly, facilitated by a September amnesty bill. FRUD also contributed several ministers to the July 2001 "postwar cabinet." However, friction continued within FRUD, particularly when Dini announced plans to launch a party called FRUD-National, which would seek countrywide membership that would include a significant non-Afar segment. Reports indicated that some FRUD continued to object to Dini's perceived efforts to place his personal imprint on the movement, while the so-called "Armed-FRUD" still remained skeptical of the peace process in general.

FRUD formalized its relationship with the RPP with the launching of the UMP prior to the 2003 legislative poll, while Dini established his own opposition party (see ARD, below). By that time there did not appear to be an armed FRUD rump of any consequence, though in late 2005 battles between Afar rebels and government troops were reported in the northern area of the country.

Following the RPP's overwhelming victory in local elections in 2006, disputes within FRUD over criticism of the election led to the ouster of at least one local FRUD party leader. In 2008 FRUD secretary general Ougoureh Kifleh Ahmed was reelected to the Chamber of Deputies on the UMP candidate list. (He was elected in 1997 and 2003, and he also held several cabinet posts.)

Leaders: Ali Mohamed DAOUD (President), Ougoureh KIFLEH Ahmed (Secretary General).

Action for Revision of Order in Djibouti (*Action pour la Révision de l'Ordre à Djibouti*—AROD). The most prominent of the FRUD partners, AROD was launched on March 11, 1991, by Abbate Ebo Adou and Mohamed Adoyta Yusuf, theretofore leader of the Union of Democratic Movements (*Union des Mouvements Démocratiques*—UMD). The UMD had been organized in Belgium in February 1990 by the merger of the MNDID (see under PND, below) and Adoyta's Democratic Front for the Liberation of Djibouti (*Front Démocratique pour la Libération de Djibouti*—FDLD), itself a product of the June 1979 consolidation of two Afar groups—the National Union for Independence (*Union Nationale pour l'Indépendance*—UNI) and the Ethiopian-based Popular Movement for the Liberation of Djibouti (*Mouvement Populaire pour la Libération de Djibouti*—MPLD).

Relations with an intellectual faction, the **Alliance of Forces for Democracy** (*Alliance des Forces pour la Démocratie*—AFD), which joined AROD soon after the AFD's launching by Ali MOHAMED Ali ("Coubba") in Djibouti in 1989, were reportedly subsequently strained by AFD disagreements with the FRUD leadership.

In July 1998 Ebo Adou reportedly began efforts to position himself for a presidential campaign as a joint FRUD/PRD candidate. However, Ebo's alleged self-promotion reportedly angered a number of prominent FRUD leaders, and he was expelled from the coalition in December. No recent activity has been reported for the AROD.

Leaders: Mohamed ADOYTA Yusuf (President), Iwad HASSAN (Spokesperson).

National Democratic Party (*Parti National Démocratique—PND*). The PND was reported to have been launched in Paris in late 1992 by Aden Robleh Awaleh, theretofore leader of the Djiboutian National Movement for the Installation of Democracy (*Mouvement National Djiboutien pour l'Instauration de la Démocratie—MNDID*). A former Gouled cabinet member and vice president of the RPP, Robleh had formed the MNDID in early 1986 after fleeing Djibouti in the face of government allegations that he had been a "silent partner" in a bombing. He accused the government of harassing him out of fear that he might become a presidential contender and called on other antigovernment exiles to join the MNDID and create unified opposition to the "tyranny" of President Gouled. The party's initial communiqué called for promulgation of a constitution that would terminate the single-party system and usher in a "true liberal democracy." Robleh, who traveled widely during 1986–1987 in search of support for the MNDID, established his headquarters in Paris, with a reported branch in Addis Ababa. Some "personal rivalries" were reported within the MNDID in 1989, hindering efforts to form a common anti-Gouled front with other opposition groups. Subsequently, although the MNDID was not officially linked to FRUD, the two groups held a September summit in Ethiopia, and one month later MNDID forces were identified as part of the FRUD-led rebel unit that clashed with government troops.

In September 1993 Robleh met in Paris with the PRD's Djame, the two leaders subsequently reiterating the opposition's 1992 appeal for a transitional government of national unity. Nonetheless, Robleh joined his PRD counterpart in endorsing the December 1994 accord between "New FRUD" and the government.

In April 1996 a Paris judge issued an international arrest warrant against Robleh and his wife in connection with a French inquiry into a September 1990 grenade attack on a cafe in Djibouti, in which a six-year-old French child was killed and 15 people (mostly French nationals) were injured. Suspected by French investigators of having been the brains behind the attack, the PND leader reportedly fled Paris to seek refuge in Morocco.

In May 1997 Robleh's decision to suspend party spokesperson Farah ALI Wabert exacerbated an already growing chasm between the chair and his opponents on both the Political Bureau and National Council. Subsequently, all of the Political Bureau members, with the exception of Mahdi AHMED Abdillahi, who was also wanted for the 1990 attack, endorsed a letter urging Robleh to resign by August 31, 1997. According to the *Indian Ocean Newsletter*, Robleh's detractors were critical of his unwillingness to cooperate with other opposition groupings and claimed that the legal travails that have dogged him since 1996 hampered his ability to run the party. A Paris court sentenced five defendants in absentia to life imprisonment for the 1990 attack. However, the case against Robleh was deferred, and he was briefly considered as the potential PND candidate for president in 1999 until the party joined the ODU. A number of PND members were reportedly arrested in late 1999 for what the government termed an illegal street demonstration. In April 2001 Robleh was given a six-year suspended sentence after being convicted of complicity in the 1990 attack. By 2003 the PND agreed to participate in the electoral bloc under the UMP, and in 2005 Robleh announced the party's endorsement of President Guelleh's reelection bid. In 2007 Robleh was reelected president of the party, and in 2008 he was reelected to parliament on the UMP list, having been seated for the first time in 2003. In 2008 he was a representative in the Pan-African Parliament.

Leaders: Aden ROBLEH Awaleh (President of the Party and 1993 presidential candidate), Moussa HUSSEIN, Abdallah DABALEH.

People's Social Democratic Party (*Parti Populaire Social Démocrate—PPSD*). The PPSD was launched in 2002 under the leadership of Moumin Bahdon Farah, who had been dismissed as justice minister in March 1996 and had subsequently helped to establish the Group for the Democracy of the Republic (*Groupement pour la Démocratie de la République—GDR*) to oppose President Gouled. (For additional information on the GDR, see the 2000–2002 *Handbook*.) Bahdon stayed on as the leader of the PPSD, and the party backed Guelleh in the 2005 presidential election.

In 2008 accusations were levied against Bahdon concerning his alleged involvement in the case of a French judge who was apparently murdered (see Current issues, above.) Bahdon denied any role in the matter.

Leader: Moumin BAHDON Farah.

Union of Reformed Partisans (*Union des Partisans Reformés—UPR*). The launching of the UPR was announced in early 2005 under the leadership of Ibrahim Chehem Daoud, a former FRUD leader. The UPR endorsed President Guelleh in the 2005 presidential balloting. In 2008 the UPR joined the UMP electoral bloc for the assembly elections.

Leaders: Ibrahim CHEHEM Daoud, Adou Ali ADOU (Secretary General).

Other Parties:

Union for a Democratic Alternative (*Union pour l'Alternance Démocratique—UAD*). Formed prior to the 2003 legislative elections, the UAD won 37 percent of the vote, but no seats, prompting UAD leaders to appeal (unsuccessfully) for cancellation of the results based on allegations of fraud. The UAD boycotted the April 2005 presidential election, arguing that the electoral process lacked transparency and that the opposition was being denied fair access to the media. The UAD also boycotted the 2008 legislative elections, with the grouping claiming shortly before the balloting that the leaders of its component parties were under house arrest.

Leaders: Ismael Guedi HARED (President of the Party; formerly head of UDJ), Ahmad Youssouf HAMED (ARD), Souleiman Farah LODON (MRDD), Mohamed Daoud CHEHEM (PDD).

Republican Alliance for Democracy (*Alliance Republicaine pour la Démocratie—ARD*). The ARD was registered in 2002 under the leadership of former FRUD leader Dini, who subsequently became the most prominent spokesman for the UAD. Dini's death in September 2004 reportedly left both the ARD and the URD at sea in regard to leadership. In 2006 a new executive committee was formed to reactivate the party, and although some called for a return to militancy, a majority of party members favored less radical means of promoting democratic reforms. Leaders called the governments' attempts at a multiparty democracy "a facade."

Leaders: Ahmad Youssouf HOUMED (Chair), Adan Mohamed ABDOU, Faradda WITTI, and Ali Mahamadé HOUMED (Vice Chairs), Kassim Ali DINI (Secretary General).

Movement for Democratic Renewal and Development (*Mouvement pour le Renouveau Démocratique et le Développement—MRDD*). Legalized in 1992, the MRDD is an offshoot of the Party of Democratic Renewal (PRD), which had been formed in 1992 and served as a leading opposition grouping. (See 2000–2002 *Handbook* for additional information on the PRD.) MRDD leader Daher Ahmed FARAH is editor of the opposition weekly *Le Renouveau*, which has been the object of repeated closures by the government.

Leaders: Daher Ahmed FAHER, Souleiman Farah LODON.

Union for Democracy and Justice (*Union pour la Démocratie et la Justice—UDJ*). The UDJ was established in 2002 under the leadership of Ismail Guedi Hared, a former cabinet director for President Gouled. UDJ Secretary General Farah Ali WABERI resigned from his post in March 2005 to protest the UAD's decision to boycott the upcoming presidential election.

Djibouti Development Party (*Parti Djiboutien pour le Développement—PDD*). The PDD served as a founding component of the UAD, but PDD leader Mohamed Daoud Chehem angered the other UAD parties in early 2005 by flirting with a possible presidential candidacy (subsequently abandoned).

Leaders: Mohamed Daoud CHEHEM, Bouha Daoud AHMED (Secretary General).

LEGISLATURE

The **Chamber of Deputies** (*Chambre des Députés*) is a unicameral body of 65 members elected for five-year terms. Prior to 1992 there was no alternative to a single list presented by the Popular Rally for Progress (RPP). Under the system of limited pluralism approved in September 1992 a total of four parties was permitted to compete for chamber seats. However, the limit on the number of parties was eliminated in 2002.

In the most recent balloting on February 8, 2008, the Union for a Presidential Majority captured all 65 seats.

President: Idriss ARNAOUD Ali.

CABINET

[as of September 1, 2009]

Prime Minister	Dileïta Mohamed Dileïta
Ministers	
Agriculture, Livestock, and Marine Affairs	Abdoulkader Kamil Mohamed
Commerce and Industry	Rifki Abdoulkader Bamakhrama
Communication, Culture, Posts and Telecommunications	Ali Abdi Farah
Employment, Insertion, and Professional Training	Moussa Ahmed Hassan
Energy and Natural Resources	Moussa Bouh Odowa
Equipment and Transportation	Ali Hassan Bahdon
Finance, National Economy, and Privatization	Ali Farah Assoweh
Foreign Affairs and International Cooperation	Mahamoud Ali Youssouf
Housing, Urban Planning, Environment, and Relations with Parliament	Elmi Obsieh Waiss
Interior and Decentralization	Yacin Elmi Bouh
Justice, Muslim and Penal Affairs, and Human Rights	Mohamed Barkat Abdillahi
Muslim Affairs and Endowment	Hamoud Abdi Soultan
National Defense	Ougoureh Kifleh Ahmed
National Education	Abdi Ibrahim Absieh
Presidential Affairs and Investment Promotion	Osman Ahmad Moussa
Promotion of Women, Families, and Social Affairs	Nimo Boulhan Houssein [f]
Public Health	Abdallah Abdillahi Miguil
Youth, Sports, Leisure, and Tourism	Hasna Barkat Daoud [f]
Delegate Minister	
Attached to the Minister of Foreign Affairs (International Cooperation)	Ahmed Ali Silay
Secretary of State	
Prime Minister's Office, in charge of National Solidarity	Mohamed Ahmed Awaleh

[f] = female

COMMUNICATIONS

Le Temps, an opposition monthly associated with 1999 UMO presidential candidate Moussa Ahmed Idriss, was banned in September 1999, and one of its editors was sentenced to six months in prison for "disseminating false news." Shortly thereafter two French journalists were expelled for articles deemed by the government to have "tarnished" the country's "image." Another opposition weekly, *Le Renouveau*, published by the Movement for Democratic Renewal and Development (MRDD), also closed temporarily in October when its editor was jailed. In 2003 *Le Renouveau*'s managing editor was arrested and detained several times. In early 2007 international watchdog groups urged the government to drop its libel case against *Le Renouveau* and stop harassing the staff. Authorities allegedly arrested and briefly detained relatives of the managing editor, took equipment so the newspaper could not be published, and charged the managing editor's brother with libel. The newspaper was shut down completely in 2007, prompting sharp criticism from the watchdog group Reporters Without Borders.

As of 2008, Djibouti was one of the few countries in Africa that had no privately published newspapers.

Press. The government-owned *La Nation de Djibouti* (4,000) is published twice a month in Arabic and French, while *Carrefour Africain* (500), a Roman Catholic publication, is also issued twice monthly. *La République* is published by the PND.

News agencies. The domestic facility is *Agence Djiboutienne d'Information*. In addition, *Agence France-Presse* maintains an office in Djibouti.

Broadcasting and computing. *Radiodiffusion-Télévision de Djibouti* transmits in French, Afar, Somali, and Arabic. As of 2008 there were 22.6 Internet users per 1,000 inhabitants.

INTERGOVERNMENTAL REPRESENTATION

Ambassador to the U.S. and Permanent Representative to the UN: Roble OLHAYE.

U.S. Ambassador to Djibouti: James Christopher SWAN.

IGO Memberships (Non-UN): AfDB, AFESD, AMF, AU, Comesa, IDB, IGAD, Interpol, LAS, NAM, OIC, OIF, WCO, WTO.

DOMINICA

Commonwealth of Dominica

Note: In early elections to the House of Assembly on December 18, 2009, the Dominica Labour Party (DLP) won 18 seats and the United Workers' Party won 3 seats. Prime Minister Roosevelt Skerrit of the DLP subsequently formed a new DLP cabinet.

Political Status: Former British dependency; joined West Indies Associated States in 1967; independent member of the Commonwealth since November 3, 1978.

Area: 290.5 sq. mi. (752.4 sq. km.).

Population: 71,727 (2001C); 70,700 (2008E).

Major Urban Center (2005E): ROSEAU (14,000).

Official Language: English (a French patois is widely spoken).

Monetary Unit: East Caribbean Dollar (official rate December 1, 2009: 2.70 EC dollars = $1US).

President: Nicholas LIVERPOOL; elected by the House of Assembly on October 2, 2003, and inaugurated for a five-year term on October 6, succeeding Vernon SHAW; inaugurated for a second five-year term on October 2, 2008.

Prime Minister: *(See headnote.)* Roosevelt SKERRIT (Dominica Labour Party); sworn in January 8, 2004, succeeding Pierre CHARLES (Dominica Labour Party), who died on January 6; remained in office following election of May 5, 2005.

THE COUNTRY

The largest of the West Indies Associated States as constituted in 1967, Dominica is located between Guadeloupe and Martinique in the Windward Islands of the eastern Caribbean. Claimed by both France and Great Britain until coming under the latter's exclusive control in 1805, the island continues to reflect a pronounced French influence. Most of its inhabitants are descendants of West African slaves who were brought as plantation laborers in the 17th and 18th centuries, although a few hundred members of the Carib Indian tribe, which once controlled the entire Caribbean and gave the area its name, remain. Roman Catholicism is the dominant religion, but there are also long-established Anglican and Methodist communities.

One of the poorest and least developed of third world countries, Dominica was devastated by hurricanes in 1979 and 1980, which virtually destroyed the economy. Particularly hard hit was banana production, which typically accounts for about 70 percent of the country's exports. An increase in tourist arrivals, some inflow of foreign capital in support of labor-intensive export industry, and improved

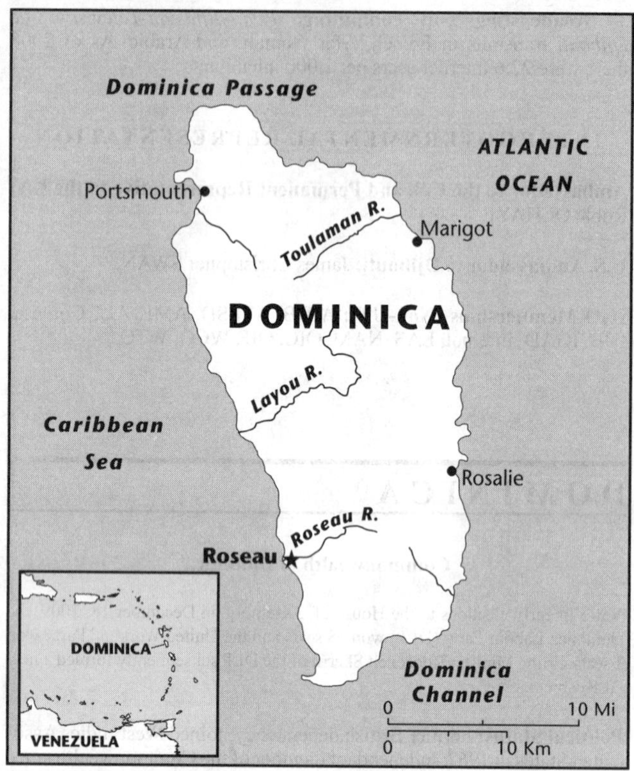

banana output subsequently yielded a measure of economic recovery, although sustained development has been hindered by poor infrastructure, including an inadequate road system, and the ravages of further major hurricanes (notably Hugo in September 1989 and Luis in September 1995).

Real GDP growth in 1994 was reported to be 2.1 percent, as contrasted with 6.6 percent in 1990, while unemployment was approximately 23 percent. The growth rate fluctuated thereafter, despite good showings by tourism and nonbanana agriculture, because of hurricane-induced banana losses, registering an estimated 3.5 percent in 1998 but dropping to 0.3 percent in 1999. It declined further to –5.2 percent in 2002 but revived thereafter, reaching 4.1 percent in 2006. In 2007 the economy, after displaying a remarkable recovery from its weather-induced problems, was pummeled again in late August by Hurricane Dean, which inflicted widespread damage on both agriculture and infrastructure and slowed growth to a little over 1 percent, with inflation surging from 1.6 percent in 2006 to 6.7 percent in 2008.

GOVERNMENT AND POLITICS

Political background. An object of contention between Britain and France in the 18th century, Dominica was administered after 1833 as part of the British Leeward Islands. In 1940 it was incorporated into the Windward Islands, which also included Grenada, St. Lucia, and St. Vincent. It participated in the Federation of the West Indies from 1958 to 1962 and became one of the six internally self-governing West Indies Associated States in March 1967.

The West Indies Act of 1966 stipulated that the islands' external dependency on Britain was completely voluntary and could be terminated by either party at any time. Thus, having failed to agree on a plan for regional unity, the Associated States declared in December 1975 that each would separately seek full independence. The details of an independence constitution for Dominica were discussed at a London conference in May 1977, and in July 1978 both houses of Parliament approved an Order in Council terminating the association as of November 3. Pending a new election, the existing premier, Patrick Roland JOHN, was designated prime minister, while the incumbent governor, Sir Louis COOLS-LARTIQUE, continued as interim chief of state.

Following government rejection of an opposition nominee for president, the Speaker of the House, Fred E. DEGAZON, was elected to the largely ceremonial post by the legislature and was sworn in December 22, 1978. Subsequently, in the wake of an extended general strike and a series of opposition demonstrations in Roseau, President Degazon retired to Britain, his successor, Sir Cools-Lartique, also being forced to resign only 24 hours after his return to office on June 15, 1979. On June 21 Prime Minister John was obliged to step down after a number of his legislative supporters had moved into opposition, the interim president, Jenner ARMOUR, designating former agriculture minister Oliver James SERAPHINE as his successor. In the legislative balloting on July 21, 1980, both Seraphine and John were denied reelection, and Mary Eugenia CHARLES of the victorious Dominica Freedom Party (DFP) was asked by President Aurelius MARIE (who had succeeded Armour in late February) to form a new government. Charles was the region's first female prime minister.

There were two attempts by supporters of former prime minister John to overthrow the government in 1981, the second of which included an effort to free him from a jail term that had been imposed under a state of emergency. Following his acquittal and release from prison in June 1982, John moved to reunify the opposition Democratic Labour Party (DLP), from which Seraphine had withdrawn in 1979. The effort succeeded in mid-1983, Seraphine being designated DLP leader and John his deputy. In early 1985 opposition forces further closed ranks as the DLP absorbed the United Democratic Labour Party (UDLP) and the Dominica Liberation Movement Alliance (DLMA), although the enlarged group failed to oust the DFP in the parliamentary election of July 1. Subsequently, John was convicted on retrial of the 1981 conspiracy charge and sentenced in October to 12 years in prison; he was released on May 29, 1990, after having served only four and one-half years of his sentence and in late 1991 was appointed general secretary of the National Workers' Union.

Prime Minister Charles remained in office following the May 1990 election, in which the DFP retained a bare one-seat majority of Assembly seats. While continuing as prime minister, Charles stepped down as party leader on August 14, 1993, in favor of Brian ALLEYNE. However, Alleyne proved unable to prevent a one-seat victory on June 12, 1995, by the United Workers' Party (UWP), whose leader, Edison JAMES, was named to form a new government. Since the DFP and DLP had each won five seats, Alleyne accepted appointment as leader of the opposition with the understanding that he would withdraw after one year in favor of the DLP's Roosevelt (Rosie) DOUGLAS; however, the change was mandated only a month after the election when a DFP victor was declared ineligible for parliamentary service (although subsequently reinstated).

In August 1996 Alleyne resigned his parliamentary seat to accept a judicial appointment in Grenada, the DFP again being reduced to third-party status by losing the ensuing by-election.

The DLP won 10 of 21 elective Assembly seats in the election of January 31, 2000, Douglas being named prime minister as head of a coalition with the DFP on February 3. Following Douglas's death on October 1, the deputy DLP leader, Pierre CHARLES, was sworn in as his successor. No major government changes were made at that time, although a downsized and reshuffled cabinet was announced in June 2001. Charles died on January 6, 2004, and was succeeded two days later by Roosevelt SKERRIT, who, at age 31, became the world's youngest head of government and remained in office following the election of May 5, 2005. Subsequently, September 6 marked the death of the "Iron Lady of the Caribbean," Dame Mary Eugenia Charles.

Constitution and government. Under the constitution that became effective at independence, the Commonwealth of Dominica is a "sovereign democratic republic" based on a respect for the principles of social justice. The head of state is a president who is elected for a five-year term by the legislature after joint nomination by the prime minister and the leader of the opposition, or by secret ballot in the event of disagreement between the two. The president may not hold office for more than two terms. Parliament consists of the president and a House of Assembly, which includes one representative from each electoral constituency (as defined by an Electoral Boundaries Commission) and nine senators who, according to the wishes of the legislature, may be either elected or appointed (five on the advice of the prime minister and four on the advice of the leader of the opposition). The term of the House is five years, subject to dissolution. The president appoints as prime minister the elected member who commands a majority in the House; in addition, he may remove the prime minister from office if, following a no-confidence vote, the latter does not resign or request a dissolution. Provision is made for a Public Service Commission to make appointments to and exercise disciplinary control over the public service, as well as for a Police Service Commission and a Public Service Board of Appeal. The court system embraces the Supreme Court of the West Indies Associated States (redesignated, in respect of Dominica, as the Eastern Caribbean Supreme Court), courts of summary jurisdiction, and district courts (the latter dealing with minor criminal offenses and civil cases involving sums of not more than $EC500). In late 2004 Parliament approved legislation for Dominica's participation in the Trinidad-based Caribbean Court of Justice (CCJ), replacing the London-based Privy Council as the country's final court of appeal; as of early 2009, however, formal accession had not taken place, Prime Minister Skerrit endorsing the rationale for the CCJ but wishing to "take the correct steps" in effecting the change.

Partially elected local government bodies function in the principal towns and villages, with Roseau and Portsmouth controlled by town councils consisting of both elected and nominated members.

Foreign relations. Although Dominica was admitted to the Commonwealth at independence and to the United Nations shortly thereafter, its diplomatic ties are extremely limited. It maintains only token representation in the United States, most official contacts with Washington being maintained through the U.S. ambassador to Barbados, who is also accredited to Roseau. Regional memberships include the Organization of American States (OAS) and various Caribbean groupings, including the Organization of Eastern Caribbean States (OECS).

Closely allied with the United States, upon which it relied heavily for foreign aid, Dominica joined the multinational force that participated in the U.S.-led invasion of Grenada in October 1983 (see article on Grenada), and endorsed the U.S. bombing of Libya in April 1986. However, formal diplomatic ties were established between Dominica and Libya in early 2001, prompting Tripoli to promise significant development aid. Dominica also signed several social and economic cooperation agreements with Cuba in 2001. More importantly, it switched relations with Taiwan to the People's Republic of China in early 2004, after China had offered a $12 million aid package.

Prime Minister Charles supported an effort by St. Vincent's James Mitchell to persuade the seven OECS members to form a unitary government. Given no discernable progress in the matter, Dominica joined with its Windward Island neighbors to launch a four-member grouping. During the third meeting of a Regional Constituent Assembly in Roseau, Dominica, in September 1991, agreement was reached on a federal system with a common legislature and executive. However, no further action on the less inclusive structure has yet taken place.

A long-standing dispute centered on the status of tiny Bird Island (Isla de Aves), 70 miles west of Dominica but controlled by Venezuela, some 350 miles to the south. In 2001 Dominica asked its Caribbean neighbors for support in pursuing its claim to the island, which falls within competing maritime economic zones. The action was sharply rebuffed by Venezuela, which in 2005 established a naval base on the island. In June 2006 Prime Minister Skerrit conceded that the international community recognized Venezuelan sovereignty over the island and announced that a bipartisan commission would be established to delineate the maritime boundary.

The Bird Island issue notwithstanding, Prime Minister Skerrit in early 2008 took Dominica into the controversial Bolivarian Alternative for the Americas (ALBA), a Venezuelan-led trade organization had had been launched in response to the U.S.-backed Free Trade Area of the Americas (FTAA).

Current issues. In September 2006, two months after Skerrit's reversal on Bird Island, Venezuela agreed to provide Dominica with up to 1,000 barrels of fuel oil per day under low-interest financing and to join a feasibility study on the construction of a small-scale refinery to supply oil to other Caribbean countries.

Joining ALBA in 2008 was condemned by the opposition UWP after Venezuelan president Hugo Chávez had called on ALBA members, which also included Bolivia, Cuba, and Nicaragua, to form an "anti-imperialist" military alliance to protect the region from potential attacks by the United States. Undeterred, Prime Minister Skerrit defended participating in the trade grouping as of benefit to Dominica, while declaring that Dominica would not become a member of the proposed military alliance.

Earlier, President Liverpool had broached a number of constitutional reforms, not acted upon by mid-2009, that included direct election of the president to serve for a five-year term as both head of state and head of government.

POLITICAL PARTIES

The Dominican party system has been in a state of considerable flux since independence. In early 1979 a number of parliamentary members of the original Dominica Labour Party (DLP) withdrew under the leadership of Oliver Seraphine to form the Democratic Labour Party (subsequently the Dominica Democratic Labour Party—DDLP), while the cabinet named by Seraphine on June 21 drew on a recently organized Committee of National Salvation (CNS)—an alliance of former opposition groups that included the Dominica Freedom Party (DFP), headed by Mary Eugenia Charles. The CNS was, however, divided between a left-wing faction, representing trade-union interests, and the traditionally conservative DFP. Another component of the CNS, the National Alliance Party (NAP), had recently been formed by Michael A. DOUGLAS, who subsequently became finance minister in the Seraphine government.

The 1980 election was contested by a rump of the DLP, led by Patrick John; the DDLP; the DFP; and a recently organized Dominica Liberation Movement Alliance (DLMA). The principal contenders in 1985 were the DFP and the Labour Party of Dominica (LPD), with the recently formed United Workers' Party (UWP) becoming a serious contender in 1990 and securing a legislative majority in 1995. In 2000 the DLP won a plurality and formed a coalition government with the DFP as its junior partner.

Government Party:

Dominica Labour Party (DLP). The present DLP was formed in early 1985 by merger of the preexisting Dominica Labour Party (DLP), the United Dominica Labour Party (UDLP), and the Dominica Liberation Movement Alliance (DLMA). The dominant party after the 1975 election, the DLP was weakened by the defection of Oliver Seraphine and others in 1979 as well as by a variety of charges against party leader Patrick John, including an allegation that, as prime minister, he had attempted to secure South African backing for a number of developmental projects. The DLP won no seats in the 1980 election, and John was subsequently charged with attempting to overthrow the government.

After leaving the DLP, Seraphine launched the Democratic Labour Party, restyled the Dominica Democratic Labour Party (DDLP) before the 1980 election, in which it secured two Assembly seats without, however, returning its leader. In late 1981 the opposition parliamentarian, Michael Douglas, who claimed to have been designated DDLP leader at a meeting in September, was expelled from the party and organized the UDLP, while Seraphine brought the DDLP back into the DLP in mid-1983.

A self-proclaimed "new left" grouping, the DLMA was organized by Atherton MARTIN following his dismissal from the Seraphine government in October 1979, allegedly for advocating closer links to Cuba. In January 1984 an investigation was launched into the activities of the group's general secretary, William REVIERE, following the discovery, during the Grenada invasion, of letters from him requesting aid from Eastern-bloc countries.

In a contest for the DLP leadership, Douglas defeated Seraphine at a merger conference by a vote of 12–3, Seraphine and Henry Dyer, former minister of communications and works in the Charles government, being elected deputy leaders. Concurrently, John was named DLP general secretary, a post that he was obliged to vacate, along with his Assembly seat, when he was reimprisoned in October. (John resigned from the party in September 1987 in a move that was interpreted as aimed at securing his freedom.)

Despite a dispute as to who would stand in a by-election to replace John, Douglas was reelected party leader at an August 1986 DLP convention; in March 1992 he was reported to be terminally ill with inoperable cancer and on November 29 the annual party convention elected his brother, Rosie Douglas, as his successor.

In June 1995 the DLP won five House seats on a third-place vote share of 29.6 percent. Its leader succeeded Brian Alleyne as leader of the opposition when a DFP seat was vacated in July 1995. He became prime minister following the election of January 31, 2000. Douglas died on October 1, 2000, and was succeeded by his (then) deputy party leader, Pierre Charles. Pierre Charles died on January 6, 2004, and was succeeded by Roosevelt Skerrit.

Leaders: Roosevelt SKERRIT (Prime Minister and Party Leader), Ambrose GEORGE (Deputy Leader), Peter ST. JEAN (Party President).

Opposition Party:

United Workers' Party (UWP). The UWP was launched in July 1988 by the former general manager of the Dominica Banana Marketing Corporation to "promote sound and orderly development" in the face of an "erosion of basic democratic rights" and a "state of fear in the nation." The party won six House seats in the 1990 election, supplanting the DLP as the principal opposition grouping. In 1995 it secured a narrow majority of 11 seats on a second-place vote share of 34.4 percent; its margin was strengthened by the acquisition of an additional seat in a by-election in August 1996. It returned to opposition after winning only nine Assembly seats in January 2000, one of which was lost in 2005.

Earl WILLIAMS resigned as party leader and leader of the opposition on July 30, 2008, following allegations of financial irregularities in the purchase of Dominican land for a U.S.-based investor.

Leader: Ron GREEN (Leader of the Opposition and President of the Party).

Other Parties:

Dominica Freedom Party (DFP). A right-of-center grouping long associated with propertied interests in Roseau, the DFP won 17 of 21 elective House of Assembly seats in 1980, 15 in 1985, and a bare majority of 11 in 1990. In August 1993 the party elected Foreign Affairs Minister Brian ALLEYNE to succeed Dame Eugenia Charles as DFP leader after the prime minister's retirement before the next election. The DFP won a plurality of 35.8 percent of the votes in the balloting of June 12, 1995, but captured only 5 of 21 house seats, one of which was briefly vacated in July 1995 by the High Court, which ruled that the incumbent was a public service employee.

In April 1996 Charles SAVARIN, Dominica's former ambassador to the European Union, was elected party leader, in succession to Alleyne, who had resigned for "personal and professional reasons."

The DFP won two legislative seats in January 2000, thereafter joining the DLP in a government coalition. It secured no parliamentary representation in the May 2005 poll, although Savirin served briefly as foreign minister in the Skerrit administration. The appointment was criticized by most of his colleagues, who elected businessman Michael ASTAPHAN to succeed him as party leader in August 2007. Subsequently, Astaphan was succeeded by hotelier Judith Pestaina.

Leader: Judith PESTAINA.

Also active are the **Dominica Progressive Party** (DPP), led by Leonard (Pappy) BAPTISTE; **A Righteous Kingdom Party** (ARKP), launched in early 2005 by Hermina VALENTINE as Dominica's first Christian party; and the **People's Democratic Movement**, formed by William Pava RIVIERE in mid-2006.

LEGISLATURE

Parliament consists of the president, ex officio, and a **House of Assembly** that sits for a five-year term and encompasses 21 elected representatives and 9 senators who, at the discretion of the House, may be either appointed or elected, in addition to the speaker and the attorney general. Following the election of May 5, 2005, the Dominica Labour Party held 13 representative seats; and the United Workers' Party, 8. The next election was scheduled for December 2009. *(See headnote.)*

Speaker: Alix BOYD-KNIGHT.

CABINET

[as of June 1, 2009] *(See headnote)*

Prime Minister	Roosevelt Skerrit (DLP)
Ministers	
Agriculture, Fisheries, and Forestry	Matthew Walter (DLP)
Caribbean Affairs	Kelly Graneau (DLP)
Community Development, Culture, Gender Affairs, and Information	Loreen Bannis-Roberts [f]
Economic Development and Urban Renewal	Julius Timothy (DLP)
Education, Sports and Youth Affairs, and Human Resource Development	Sonia Williams [f]
Finance and Economic Planning	Roosevelt Skerrit (DLP)
Foreign Affairs, Immigration, and Labour	Vince Henderson (DLP)
Health and Environment	John Fabien (DFP)
Housing, Lands, and Telecommunications	Reginald Austrie (DLP)
Legal Affairs	Ian Douglas (DLP)
National Security	Roosevelt Skerrit (DLP)
Prime Minister's Office	Rayburn Blackmore (DLP)
Public Utilities, Energy, Ports, and Public Service	Charles Savarin (DFP)
Public Works and Infrastructural Development	Rayburn Blackmore (DLP)
Social Security	Roosevelt Skerrit (DLP)
Tourism	Ian Douglas (DLP)
Trade, Industry, Consumer Affairs, Private Sector Relations, Caricom, OECS, and Diaspora Affairs	Sen. Collin McIntyre
Attorney General	Francine Baron-Royer [f]

[f] = female

COMMUNICATIONS

Press. The following are published in Roseau: *New Chronicle* (3,000), independent weekly; *The Tropical Star* (3,000), weekly; *Official Gazette* (550), weekly.

Broadcasting and computing. The government-operated Dominica Broadcasting Corporation (DBC) provides radio service in English and French patois; two independent subscription services, Marpin Television and Video One, offer cable programs from the United States. As of 2008 there were 411.6 Internet users per 1,000 inhabitants.

INTERGOVERNMENTAL REPRESENTATION

Ambassador to the U.S.: (Vacant).

U.S. Ambassador to Dominica: (Vacant).

Permanent Representative to the UN: Crispin S. GREGOIRE.

IGO Memberships (Non-UN): ACS, Caricom, CDB, CWTH, Interpol, NAM, OAS, OECS, OIF, OPANAL, WTO.

DOMINICAN REPUBLIC

República Dominicana

Political Status: Independent republic established in 1844; under constitutional regime reestablished July 1, 1966.

Area: 18,816 sq. mi. (48,734 sq. km.).

Population: 8,562,541 (2002C); 9,531,000 (2008E).

Major Urban Centers (2005E): SANTO DOMINGO (1,922,000), Santiago de los Caballeros (526,000).

Official Language: Spanish.

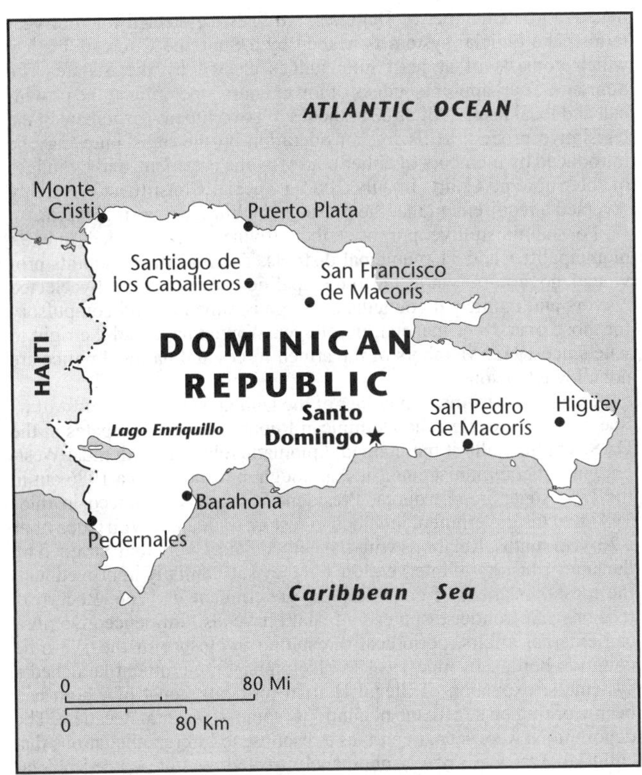

Monetary Unit: Peso (market rate December 1, 2009: 35.97 pesos = $1US).

President: Leonel Antonio FERNÁNDEZ Reyna (Dominican Liberation Party); served as president 1996–2000; reelected on May 16, 2004, and inaugurated on August 16 for a four-year term, succeeding Rafael Hipólito MEJÍA Domingues (Dominican Revolutionary Party); reelected on May 16, 2008, and inaugurated for a third term on August 16.

Vice President: Rafael ALBUQUERQUE De Castro (Dominican Liberation Party); elected on May 16, 2004, and inaugurated with the president on August 16, for a term concurrent with that of the president, succeeding Milagros ORTIZ Bosch (Dominican Revolutionary Party); reelected on May 16, 2008, and sworn in on August 16.

THE COUNTRY

The Dominican Republic occupies the eastern two-thirds of the Caribbean island of Hispaniola, which it shares with Haiti. The terrain is varied, including mountains, fertile plains, and some desert. About 70 percent of the population is biracial, claiming Spanish and Amerindian or African ancestors, with small minorities (about 15 percent each) of pure Spanish and African origin. The cultural tradition is distinctly Spanish, with 98 percent of the people professing allegiance to the Roman Catholic Church.

According to 2004 World Bank data, women comprised 35 percent of the labor force. Female representation in government has long been virtually nonexistent, although President Fernández named two women to cabinet posts during his first term and three in his second and third.

The Dominican Republic's economy is primarily agricultural, the leading cash crops being sugar, coffee, cocoa, and tobacco. The agricultural sector employs nearly 50 percent of the labor force and accounts for nearly half of the country's foreign exchange earnings. Manufacturing is largely oriented toward agricultural processing, but deposits of gold, silver, ferronickel, and bauxite contribute significantly to export earnings. In the 1980s spiraling foreign indebtedness and plummeting commodity prices severely crippled the economy, with austerity measures further inhibiting the capacity of most individuals to meet basic food and shelter needs. During the period unemployment was consistently in excess of 20 percent, with inflation soaring to more than 60 percent in 1989. Partially offsetting a decline in world commodity prices was a surge in tourism, which gave rise to an increasingly active service sector. As a result, economic growth rose to 8.3 percent in 1999 (one of the world's highest such increases), with inflation dropping to less than 6.0 percent. By 2003, however, the country again faced economic crisis, with mounting public debt, surging inflation, and economic contraction of –1.0 percent. Thereafter, a series of comprehensive macroeconomic policies by President Fernández generated another resurgence, with 2005 showing a 9.3 percent increase in GDP, a decline in inflation to 7.4 percent, and a reduction in unemployment to 17 percent. Further growth of 10.7 percent in 2006, with inflation at 6.1 percent, was termed "extraordinary" by a U.S. investment analyst. By the middle of 2007, unemployment had declined again from its 2004 peak to 15.6 percent, but the end of 2007 saw inflation surge to 8.88 percent due to increasing oil prices and agricultural and infrastructure damage from two tropical storms. Unemployment remained relatively unchanged, at an estimated 15.4 percent in 2008. The International Monetary Fund (IMF) reported GDP growth of 5.3 percent in 2008 but forecast a contraction to 3 percent in 2009 due to the global economic downturn. On a positive note, the IMF in 2009 commended Dominican Republic authorities' efforts to limit public expenditures, progress in structural reforms, and "enhanced targeting of assistance to the poorest."

GOVERNMENT AND POLITICS

Political background. Since winning its independence from Spain in 1821 and from Haiti in 1844, the Dominican Republic has been plagued by recurrent domestic conflict and foreign intervention. Administered by a U.S. military governor from 1916 to 1924, the country entered into a 30-year period of control by Gen. Rafael Leonidas TRUJILLO Molina in 1930. Trujillo ruled personally from 1930 to 1947 and indirectly thereafter until his assassination in 1961, his death giving rise to renewed political turmoil. An election in December 1962 led to the inauguration of Juan BOSCH Gaviño, a left-of-center democrat, as president in February 1963. Bosch was overthrown in September 1963 by a military coup led by (then) Col. Elías WESSIN y Wessin. Subsequently, the military installed a civilian triumvirate that ruled until April 1965, when civil war erupted. U.S. military forces—later incorporated into an Inter-American Peace Force sponsored by the Organization of American States (OAS)—intervened on April 28, 1965, and imposed a truce while arrangements were made to establish a provisional government and prepare for new elections. Dr. Joaquín BALAGUER Ricardo, a moderate who had been president at the time of Trujillo's assassination, defeated Bosch in an election held in June 1966. Emphasizing material development and political restraint, Balaguer was reelected in 1970 and successfully dealt with an attempted coup in 1971. In 1974 he was virtually unopposed for election to a fourth term, all of his principal opponents having withdrawn in anticipation of election irregularities. After the election Silvestre Antonio GUZMAN Fernández, speaking on behalf of the opposition coalition, demanded annulment of the results; however, he agreed not to press the demand after securing Balaguer's assurance that he would not seek further reelection in 1978. Despite his pledge, Balaguer contested the 1978 election but lost to Guzmán Fernández by a three-to-two majority. The inauguration of the new president on August 16 was the first occasion in Dominican history that an elected incumbent had yielded power to an elected successor.

In late 1981 four-time former chief executive Balaguer surprised many observers by announcing that he would seek to regain the presidency in 1982, despite his age at 74 and failing eyesight. The announcement came in the wake of mounting economic problems and a significant weakening of President Guzmán's influence within the ruling Dominican Revolutionary Party (PRD). At midyear, Guzmán declared that he would not seek reelection and formally endorsed Vice President Jacobo MAJLUTA Azar as his successor. However, at a PRD convention in November Majluta was decisively rejected in favor of Guzmán's archrival, Salvador JORGE Blanco, who had been defeated for the 1978 nomination and whom Guzmán had succeeded in ousting from the party presidency in late 1979.

In the May 1982 election, Jorge Blanco defeated Balaguer by a 10 percent margin, while the PRD retained its majority in both houses of Congress. On July 4 President Guzmán died of an apparently self-inflicted gunshot wound, being succeeded on an acting basis by Majluta Azar until Jorge Blanco's inauguration on August 16.

In the vote on May 16, 1986, Balaguer was elected to a fifth term, narrowly defeating Majluta after the PRD had succumbed to severe internal friction attributed primarily to a left-wing faction led by José Francisco PEÑA Gómez.

Announcement of the 1990 presidential outcome was delayed for nearly a month, with Balaguer being credited in mid-June with a 14,000-vote victory over former president Juan Bosch. The paper-thin victory was equaled in the Senate, with Balaguer's Social Christian Reformist Party (PRSC) retaining control by a margin of only one seat; in contrast, the opposition secured an overwhelming majority in the Chamber of Deputies.

Balaguer was initially declared the winner of the May 1994 presidential race by fewer than 30,000 votes. However, only three weeks before the August 16 constitutional deadline for swearing in a new president the Santo Domingo electoral board responded to numerous complaints by voiding the results (40 percent of the total) at the capital. On August 2 the Junta Electoral Central (JCE) ignored a report by its electoral committee in overruling the Santo Domingo body. However, the action drew intense opposition, including a threat of military intervention, and on August 10 Balaguer concluded a "Pact for Democracy" ("*Pacto por la Democracia*") with José Peña Gómez, who had succeeded Majluta as PRD leader, to foreshorten the presidential term to 18 months, with new balloting on November 16, 1995. While Bosch's Dominican Liberation Party (PLD) also supported the accord, it subsequently reversed itself and joined with the PRSC in endorsing a two-year term. On August 14 a constitutional amendment to such effect was hurriedly approved by Congress, along with amendments banning future presidents from serving consecutive terms, reforming the JCE, creating a National Judiciary Council to ensure the independence of the judiciary, and establishing dual citizenship for Dominicans living outside the country. The PRD responded to revision of the August 10 agreement by withdrawing from the congressional session and boycotting Balaguer's inauguration of his seventh term.

At first-round presidential balloting on May 16, 1996, the PRD's Peña Gómez was accorded a 45.9 percent plurality, substantially outdistancing the PLD's Leonel FERNÁNDEZ Reyna (38.9 percent) and Vice President Jacinto PEYNADO Garrigoza of the PRSC (15.0 percent). Before the second round on June 30, President Balaguer joined with the leaders of a number of small right-wing groups in endorsing Fernández, who won a narrow (51.3 to 48.8 percent) victory over Peña Gómez and was installed as Balaguer's successor on August 16.

Despite the death of Peña Gómez on May 10, 1998, the PRD won a sweeping legislative victory (83 seats in an enlarged 149-seat body) on May 16, while gaining control of about 90 percent of the island's 115 municipalities. By contrast, President Fernández's PLD won only 49 seats.

In the May 2000 presidential election, the PRD's Hipólito MEJÍA received a near majority of 49.86 percent and was declared the winner when his opponents withdrew from runoff contention. In congressional balloting on May 16, 2002, the PRD lost its lower house majority, although it retained a plurality and increased its Senate representation.

Seeking reelection in 2004, President Mejía faced opposition within his party. In addition, his administration was buffeted by numerous problems, including rampant inflation, a breakdown in electrical-generating capacity, and the collapse of the nation's second largest bank. The result was a landslide victory for the PLD's Leonel Fernández, who avoided a runoff by securing 57.1 percent of the first-round vote.

For the first two years of his restored mandate, Fernández faced a legislature dominated by the PRD. However, on May 16, 2006, Mejía's party suffered a massive defeat, with the PLD securing overwhelming majorities in both houses of Congress (see Legislature, below). The PLD's winning record extended to the May 16, 2008, presidential elections, when incumbent president Fernández secured 54 percent of the vote and a third term in office. He named a new government after his inauguration on August 16.

Constitution and government. The constitution of November 28, 1966, unchanged in its structural components by a 1991 successor, established a unitary republic consisting of 26 (later 32) provinces and a National District. Executive power is exercised by the president, who is elected (together with the vice president) by direct vote for a four-year term, save for the truncated two-year mandate imposed in 1994. Members of the bicameral Congress of the Republic, consisting of a Senate and a Chamber of Deputies, are likewise elected for four-year terms. The judicial system is headed by a Supreme Court of Justice, which consists of at least nine judges elected by the Senate. The Supreme Court appoints judges of lower courts operating at the provincial and local levels. All three branches of government participate in the legislative process. Bills for consideration by the legislature may be introduced by members of either house, by the president, and by judges of the Supreme Court. In July 2002 a Special Constituent Assembly reversed a requirement that the president be limited to a single term.

For administrative purposes the provinces are divided into 95 municipalities and 31 municipal districts. The president appoints provincial governors, while the municipalities are governed by elected mayors and municipal councils. Suffrage is universal and compulsory for those over 18 or married, if younger. Women have had the right to vote since 1942. Members of the armed forces and national police are not allowed to vote.

Foreign relations. A member of the United Nations and most of its Specialized Agencies, the Dominican Republic also participates in the OAS. Traditionally it maintained diplomatic relations with most Western but not communist countries, although in response to a 1986 cut in the U.S. sugar import quota, President Balaguer announced in mid-1987 that his government intended to restore trade links with Cuba after a 26-year hiatus. Relations with the United States were long strained by the latter's history of intervention, but they substantially improved with the reestablishment of constitutional government in 1966. Recurring tensions and frontier disputes with Haiti have also influenced Dominican external affairs, periodically resulting in closure of the 193-mile common border. In June 1991 the Dominican government launched a systematic expulsion of illegal Haitian residents, most of whom had been working on sugarcane plantations (some for several decades). The deportations were seen, in part, as a response to foreign allegations that child laborers were being inhumanely treated on state-owned plantations. The expulsions escalated in early 1997, about 15,000 Haitians being deported in late January and the first half of February. Shortly thereafter, at a summit of the Caribbean Community and Common Market (Caricom) on February 20–21, President Fernández reached an agreement with Haitian President Préval to halt large-scale repatriations while securing acknowledgment of his country's right to expel illegal immigrants. However, a new wave of expulsions in November 1999 further exacerbated relations between the two countries. Tensions again eased in February 2002 during a visit by Haitian President Jean-Bertrand Aristide that yielded an agreement to provide jobs for Haitians at the countries' common border. The cyclical pattern resumed in mid-2005 with the recall of the Haitian ambassador after the lynching of three Haitians in Santo Domingo. The Fernández administration responded by deporting 1,000 illegal residents on August 15 and shortly thereafter 1,000 more of the estimated 1 million Haitians said to be living in the country. In November 2006 the government reiterated a long-standing contention that it did not mistreat Haitians but indicated that it would continue to deport illegal immigrants and, in a position that had drawn international criticism, would refuse to grant citizenship to Haitian offspring born within its borders. In September 2007 the government activated the Specialized Frontier Security Corps (Cesfront) to patrol the 193-mile border the Dominican Republic shares with Haiti. The group, which was expected to expand to 2,000 members in 2008, was given the mandate to control cross-border movement of immigrants, drugs, and other contraband.

Although not a member of Caricom, the Dominican Republic concluded a free trade agreement with the organization. A similar pact with the United States was proposed in mid-2002 by President Mejía, and in early 2004 his administration conducted negotiations for accession to the trade pact between the United States and the recently launched Central American Free Trade Agreement (CAFTA). The CAFTA-DR accord provided for immediate elimination of 80 percent of intragroup tariffs, with the remaining tariffs to be phased out over a ten-year period. However, for a number of technical reasons, the agreement, signed on Au-gust 5, 2006, did not come into effect until March 1, 2007. CAFTA was expected to at least partially offset the Dominican Republic's competitive losses to China in the garment industry by giving the country preferential access to U.S. markets.

In a separate indication of strengthening ties between Central America and the Caribbean nation, President Fernández at the end of July 2007 signed an accord with Belize to increase cooperation between the two countries. The Dominican Republic also entered into negotiations to sign bilateral free trade agreements with Mexico and Haiti, the latter offering the possibility of formalizing over $700 million in unregulated commerce between the two neighbors.

On September 7, 2005, the Dominican Republic joined Petrocaribe, a regional initiative by Venezuela to provide preferential financing of oil to Caribbean and Central American countries. Under the deal, the Dominican Republic is required to provide a fraction of the money for oil purchases up front and can pay for petroleum purchases with agricultural products.

Santo Domingo was host to the 2008 meeting of the Rio Group, an international organization of Latin American and Caribbean countries. The event, beginning March 6, nominally focused on energy, environment, and development issues, though a recent incursion by Columbia into Ecuador, and subsequent reconciliation at the summit, overshadowed the talks.

Tensions between the Dominican Republic and Haiti again began to fray in November 2008, following an attack on a Dominican and resulting in violent reprisals on Haitians in the country. The Fernández administration deported 500 Haitians in an attempt to quell the violence.

Current issues. Upon returning to office in 2004, President Fernández promised to mount a "democratic revolution" that would involve both political and economic reforms. Backed by widespread popular support and a substantial congressional majority, he sought to revise the electoral cycle to align presidential and legislative balloting. Meanwhile, continued economic growth provided an opportunity for the Fernández administration to comply with the mandate of the International Monetary Fund (IMF) to reduce the nation's debt: The government in 2007 raised taxes for the third consecutive year. Not surprisingly, the opposition insisted that the government should first attempt to curtail its "wasteful spending," but the president insisted that CAFTA-DR, while a boon to the business sector, would bring in less customs income, necessitating the new levies. By the end of the first half of 2007, the government reported a fiscal surplus along with higher government spending, both the result of efforts to decrease tax evasion.

Public approval of the center-right Fernández administration gave his PLD party majorities in both houses of the legislature during the 2006 elections. Voters showed their support for the president's measures to improve and stabilize the country's economy. The main opposition party, PRD, was hampered by a lingering public perception of the group's mismanagement of the economy and corruption during the Mejía administration (see below). In a move that many party members found unnecessary, the PRD formed an electoral alliance with the PRSC, another major opposition group, and several smaller parties. The move failed, as the PLD won 96 seats in the Chamber of Deputies and 22 of 32 senate seats. Twenty major and minor parties vied for votes during the election, according to the country's electoral commission.

Voter support continued through 2008 and carried Fernández into a third, and second consecutive, term. Fernández secured 53.8 percent of the popular vote, while his center-left PRD rival, Miguel VARGAS, won 40.5 percent. The conservative PRSC placed a distant third with 4.59 percent. Seven smaller parties also participated in the election.

On July 18, 2008, President Fernández announced a set of measures to address inflated fuel and food prices. The provisions included a 15 percent wage increase for some government workers; an increase in the minimum wage, government pensions, and propane subsidies; and the shelving of new infrastructure construction projects. But those measures were not enough to offset growing social unrest as the country experienced power blackouts and began to feel the effects of the global economic downturn. Declining exports and tourism, suspended mining operations, and reduced revenues from Dominicans working abroad combined to trigger scattered protests in 2009. The occasionally violent street demonstrations, which were organized by a group called Alternative Social Forum, were directed at the slow pace of government infrastructure improvements that had been promised by President Fernández during the 2008 campaign.

In January 2009 congress began debating a major constitutional reform package being championed by President Fernández. The proposed amendments included measures to replace the current two-term maximum for presidents with an allowance for former presidents to run again after a four-year hiatus from office; an increase in the number of seats in both houses of congress; judiciary reform; investment in education, science, and technology; environmental protection; and independent government oversight. On April 21 180 of 201 members of a constitutional reform assembly approved proposed amendments to the constitution. Additional amendments proposed shutting down human trafficking operations, adopting stronger stances against abortion and gay marriage, and modernizing the military and police. President Fernández pushed all of the changes. Further committee reviews were required before the changes could be adopted into law.

Meanwhile, in an effort to address some of the country's most pressing needs, the president in 2009 readied plans for $400 million in road improvements; pledged to increase spending for education, health care, and energy; and initiated the Caribbean's first subway. In March public calls for anti-corruption measures grew more pronounced after it was announced that some 500 military personnel and 31 generals had been removed because of connections to drug-trafficking operations and other irregularities.

POLITICAL PARTIES

The shifting political groupings that have appeared in the Dominican Republic since the fall of Trujillo reflect diverse ideological viewpoints as well as the influence of specific personalities. Party divisions and splinter groups are common with a total of 20 parties and coalitions registered for the May 2006 legislative election.

In 2006 several parties joined electoral coalitions: The Progressive Bloc (*Bloque Progresista)* alliance, led by the Dominican Liberation Party (*Partido de la Liberación Dominicana*—PLD), won a majority in both houses of congress. Other alliance members included the Institutional Social Democratic Bloc (*Bloque Institucional Social Démocrata—BIS)*, the Alliance for Democracy (*Alianza por la Democracia*—APD), the Christian Democratic Union (*Unión Demócrata Cristiana*—UDC), the Dominican Workers Party (*Partido de los Trabajadores Dominicanos—PTD)*, and the Liberal Party (*Partido Liberal de República Dominicana*—PLRD). The bloc's main challenger, the Grand National Alliance (*Gran Alianza Nacional)*, was led by the **Dominican Revolutionary Party** (*Partido Revolucionario Dominicano*—PRD), and included the **Social Christian Reformist Party** (*Partido Reformista Social Cristiano*—PRSC), the **Quisqueyan Democratic Party** (*Partido Quisqueyano Demócrata*—PQD), the **National Party of Civil Veterans** (*Partido Nacional de Veteranos Civiles*—PNVC), the **Dominican Social Alliance** (*Alianza Social Dominicana*—ASD), the **Popular Democratic Party** (*Partido Demócrata Popular*—PDP), and the **Christian Popular Party** (*Partido Popular Cristiano*—PPC).

Presidential Party:

Dominican Liberation Party (*Partido de la Liberación Dominicana*—PLD). A breakaway faction of the PRD (see below), the PLD was organized as a separate party under PRD founder Juan BOSCH Gaviño during the 1974 campaign. Bosch ran unsuccessfully as PLD presidential candidate in both 1978 and 1982, securing 9.8 percent of the vote on the latter occasion. Subsequently, he was highly critical of the Blanco regime's economic policies as well as its often harsh anti-protest tactics. Although popular opinion polls showed Bosch running second to Balaguer in late 1985, the PLD nominee placed third, with 18.4 percent of the vote, in the 1986 presidential balloting; in an extremely close contest, he ran second to Balaguer in 1990.

In March 1991 Bosch stepped down as PLD leader and withdrew from party membership to protest deep-rooted animosity between right- and left-wing factions; he reversed himself two weeks later in response to appeals from his colleagues.

In April 1992 the PLD experienced a severe crisis when 47 of its left-wing members, including one senator and ten members of the Chamber of Deputies, resigned in protest at the expulsion of a popular trade unionist, who had criticized the party's position on a proposed new labor code. The intraparty split had first emerged at a PLD congress in February 1991, when a right-wing group under Chamber president Jorge Botello had won control of the governing Political Committee. In May a number of additional persons were expelled from the party, including its former vice-presidential candidate, José Francisco Hernández Castillo, the mayor of San Pedro de Macorís, Manuel Rodríguez Roblés, and three deputies, all of whom, characterized by Juan Bosch as "rotten mangos," subsequently participated in organization of the APD (below).

Bosch, with the support of the right-wing **Progressive National Force** (*Fuerza Nacional Progresista*—FNP), headed by Marino Vinicio (Vincho) CASTILLO, ran a distant third in the presidential balloting of May 16, 1994, and on June 19 announced his resignation as PLD president. He died on November 1, 2001, at the age of 92.

Although the PLD held only 12 of 120 lower house seats, its candidate, Leonel Fernández Reyna, secured a narrow victory in second-round presidential balloting on June 30, 1996, with the support of former president Balaguer. It ran second to the PRD in the 1998 legislative and 2000 presidential polls. It continued as runner-up to the PRD in the 2002 Chamber elections, while losing three of its four Senate seats. Fernández Reyna was elected to a second presidential term in 2004, and the PLD won majorities in both legislative houses in 2006, illustrating growing support for the president during the midterm election. Fernández Reyna took 71.5 percent of the votes during the primary on May 6, 2007, besting former presidential secretary Danilo MEDINA before securing a third presidential term in 2008 with 53.83 percent of the vote.

PLD wins in 2006 and 2008 came after widespread problems and reports of corruption from the then-ruling PRD. Voters' desire for change and a strategy for addressing the economic downturn placed their confidence in the PLD platforms highlighting constitutional, judicial, and economic reforms along with a belt-tightening austerity program advocated by Fernández Reyna.

Leaders: Leonel FERNÁNDEZ Reyna (President of the Republic and President of the Party), Dr. Rafael ALBUQUERQUE (Vice President of the Republic), Reinaldo PARED Pérez (Secretary General).

Other Legislative Parties:

Dominican Revolutionary Party (*Partido Revolucionario Dominicano*—PRD). Founded as a left-democratic grouping by former president Juan Bosch Gaviño in 1939, the PRD has rejected both communism and Castroism but has been critical of U.S. "imperialism" and "neocolonialism." A member of the Socialist International since 1966, the party boycotted both the 1970 and 1974 elections but won the presidency and a majority in the Chamber of Deputies under the relatively conservative leadership of Antonio Guzmán Fernández in 1978, repeating the performance under Salvador Jorge Blanco in 1982. A three-way split within the PRD in the run-up to the 1986 election raised two distinct possibilities: that former vice president Majluta Azar might compete as the nominee of his right-wing *La Estructura* faction, and that Blanco supporters, unhappy with the president's endorsement of left-leaning José Peña Gómez, would rally for reelection of the incumbent. In July 1985 Majluta registered *La Estructura* as a separate party, but in January 1986 was named the PRD candidate with Peña Gómez succeeding him as party president. Majluta attributed his defeat in the May balloting to Peña Gómez, many of whose followers were reported to have supported Juan Bosch of the PLD. Lacking a congressional majority after the election, President Balaguer named a number of PRD/*La Estructura* members to the cabinet formed in late August. In 1990 Majluta and his associates ran separately (see PRI, below).

In July 1993 the PRD nominated Peña Gómez as its 1994 presidential candidate; supporters of President Balaguer then launched an intense personal attack against Peña Gómez, who was black and of Haitian extraction.

For the 1994 campaign, the PRD concluded pacts with a number of minor parties, including the **Democratic Assembly** (*Concertación Democrática*—CD); the **Democratic Unity** (*Unidad Democrática*—UD); and the PTD (under PRSC, see below). However, the UD, which was awarded three upper and seven lower house seats, refused to support the PRD's postelectoral boycott, thus substantially reducing the effectiveness of the action.

In August 1995 the PRD concluded a 1996 electoral pact with three parties that had formerly supported the PRSC: the PQD (see below), the **Institutional Democratic Party** (*Partido Democrático Institucional*—PDI), and the **National Party of Civil Veterans** (*Partido Nacional de Veteranos Civiles*—PNVC). PRD candidate Peña Gómez led the first-round presidential poll on May 16, 1996, with 45.8 percent of the vote but was defeated in the June 30 runoff after the PRSC's Balaguer had endorsed the PLD's Fernández. Gravely ill, Peña Gómez announced his retirement from politics in April 1997 and died on May 10, 1998.

Having won control of both houses of Congress in May 1998, the PRD completed its sweep with the election of Hipólito Mejía as president two years later. However, in 2002 it lost its majority in the Chamber, securing instead a plurality of 73. In 2004 the party was divided as to whether President Mejía should run for reelection; he was, however, nominated and overwhelmingly defeated by former president Fernández Reyna in the balloting of May 16. In the 2006 legislative poll, the PRD ran a poor second to the resurgent PLD, falling from 29 seats to 6 in the Senate and from 73 to 60 in an enlarged Chamber of Deputies. PRD presidential candidate Miguel VARGAS received 40.48 percent of the popular vote during the 2008 elections, 13 percent less than the winning PLD incumbent, but far ahead of the other contesting parties.

Leaders: Ramón ALBURQUERQUE (President), Hipólito MEJÍA Domingues and Salvador JORGE Blanco (Former Presidents of the Republic); Miguel VARGAS Maldonado (2008 presidential candidate); Dr. José Joaquín Puello (2008 vice-presidential candidate), Rafael SUBERVI Bonilla (2004 vice-presidential candidate), Orlando Jorge MERA (Secretary General).

Social Christian Reformist Party (*Partido Reformista Social Cristiano*—PRSC). Created in 1963 by Joaquín BALAGUER, the PRSC stresses a policy of economic austerity, national reconstruction, and political consensus. Drawing heavily on peasant and middle-class support, it won the elections of 1966, 1970, and 1974, but lost in 1978 after its leader had withdrawn a pledge not to become a candidate for another term. It lost again in 1982, Balaguer being defeated in the presidential election by a 37 to 47 percent margin; however, public recollection of a strong economy under Balaguer gave the ex-president a narrow victory over his PRD opponent in May 1986; his margin of victory was even narrower (0.7 percent) in winning a sixth term in May 1990, while the PRSC lost its former plurality in the Chamber of Deputies. Balaguer resigned as PRSC party president in February 1991, citing the time-consuming nature of government leadership; he won a seventh presidential term in 1994, which was shortened to two years. In 1996 he offered only lukewarm first-round support to his party's presidential nominee and backed the PLD's Leonel Fernández in the second round. He ran for an unprecedented eighth term in the balloting of January 2000, gaining third place on a 24.6 percent vote share. The 95-year-old former president died on July 14, 2002.

In the 2008 presidential election, the party's candidate, Amable ARISTY Castro, placed a distant third with 4.59 percent of the vote. PRSC president Federico ANTÚN Batlle subsequently indicated that he would resign in September as a result of the party's poor showing.

Leaders: Federico ANTÚN Batlle (President of the Party), Ramon Rogelio GENAO (Vice President of Party), Amable ARISTY Castro (2008 presidential candidate).

Other Parties:

Independent Revolutionary Party (*Partido Revolucionario Independiente*—PRI). The PRI was launched before the 1990 election by Jacobo MAJLUTA Azar, the leader of the PRD's *La Estructura* faction, after he had been defeated for control of the party by José Peña Gómez. Before his death on March 2, 1996, Majluta committed the PRI, which had no congressional representation but voting strength of about 100,000, to the support of the PRD's Peña Gómez in the 1996 presidential race. In December 2001 President Mejía accepted the honorary presidency of the PRI, and the party secured congressional representation in May 2002 by running candidates under the PRD banner. The party garnered 0.22 percent of the vote in the 2006 legislative elections.

In the 2008 presidential election, PRI candidate Trajano Santana, who had campaigned for public investment in higher education, won 0.04 percent of the vote.

In March 2008 the party expelled several high-ranking members, including the vice president and secretary general, for supporting the candidacy of incumbent president Leonel Fernández.

Leaders: Trajano SANTANA (2004 and 2008 presidential candidate), Victor Diaz ALBA (Secretary).

Alliance for Democracy (*Alianza por la Democracia*—APD). Launched in mid-1992 by a group of left-wing PLD dissidents, the APD indicated a willingness to join in a broad front in 1994 to prevent the reelection of President Balaguer. However, in April 1993 it split into two factions led, on the one hand, by Sen. Max Puig and former PLD vice-presidential candidate José Francisco Hernández, and, on the other, by economist Vicente Bengoa and union leader Nelsida Marmolejos. The latter group, which sought to forge an alliance with the PRD, was suspended for six months by an "emergency secretariat" organized by the Puig/Hernández faction. The party seeks broad alliances as a bridge to increasing public participation. The APD received 1.55 percent of the vote in the 2006 legislative elections.

Leaders: José Francisco HERNÁNDEZ Castillo (former PLD vice-presidential candidate), Sen. Max PUIG (party president), Manuel RODRIGUEZ Roblés, Nelsida MARMOLEJOS (dissident faction), Vicente BENGOA (Secretary General).

Christian Democratic Union (*Unión Demócrata Cristiana—UDC).* The UDC was created on March 12, 1998. It received less than 1 percent of the vote in the 2006 legislative elections. The party organizes in the poorest communities to achieve power.

Leader: Luis Acosta MORETA (President).

Dominican Workers' Party (*Partido de los Trabajadores Dominicanos—PTD).*The PTD is a revolutionary socialist and democratic party that advocates for the universal adoption of democracy, social justice, freedom, and development. The party came into existence on Dec. 21, 1980, as two communist groups merged: the June 14 Red Line and the Proletarian Flag. The party won 0.56 percent of the 2006 legislative election.

Leaders: José González ESPINOSA (President), Esteban Díaz JAQUEZ (First Vice President), Antonio FLORIÁN (Secretary General).

Liberal Party (*Partido Liberal de República Dominicana—*PLRD). An autonomous component of the PRI, the PLE joined the Liberal International in 1986. It endorsed former president Joaquín Balaguer as its candidate for the 2000 race. As part of the Progressive Bloc coalition, it received 0.48 percent of the vote in the 2006 legislative elections.

Leaders: Andrés VAN DER HORST (President), Vinicio Lorenzo ARIAS (Secretary General).

Institutional Social Democratic Bloc (*Bloque Institucional Social Démocrata—BIS).* The BIS splintered from the PRD in the May 2006 legislative elections to support the PLD and President Fernández. It received 2.5 percent of the vote.

Leader: Jose Francisco PEÑA Guaba (President).

Popular Alliance Party (*Partido Alianza Popular*—PAP). Recognized by the Central Election Board in October 2007, the PAP fielded its only candidate during the 2008 presidential election, founder Pedro de Jesus Candelier. The party's platform focused on advancing participatory democracy and the economy by fighting corruption, government abuse, and social inequality. Candelier, former police chief of the country, was dismissed by President Mejía in 2002 in response to high numbers of civilian killings at the hands of the police. He received 0.15 percent of the vote in the 2008 presidential election.

Leader: Pedro de Jesus CANDELIER Tejada (2008 presidential candidate).

Quisqueyan Democratic Party (*Partido Quisqueyano Demócrata*—PQD). A right-wing group, the PQD was formed by Gen. Elías Wessin y Wessin following his departure into exile in the United States after the civil disturbances of 1965; two years earlier, the general had led the military coup that overthrew President Juan Bosch. The PQD supported Wessin y Wessin in the 1970 presidential campaign and participated in the coalition that boycotted the 1974 election. In September 1977 General Wessin announced his candidacy for the 1978 presidential election but subsequently withdrew in favor of MID candidate Francisco Augusto Lora. Wessin ran a distant fourth in the 1982 presidential balloting. In November 1986 he was named interior minister in the Balaguer administration, to which the armed services portfolio was added in June 1988; he continued as armed services minister after a cabinet reshuffle in August 1989, with the PQD being credited with Balaguer's margin of victory in May 1990.

The party received 0.8 percent of the vote in the 2006 legislative elections.

Leaders: Pedro BERGES (President), Dr. Elías WESSIN Chávez (Secretary General).

Movement for Independence, Unity and Change (*Movimiento Independencia, Unidad y Cambio*—MIUCA). A small leftist group associated with the international communist movement, MIUCA received 0.32 percent of the 2006 legislative election vote. The party is led by former attorney general Guillermo MORENO, who stood as the party's nominee in the 2008 presidential elections, winning 0.44 percent of the vote on a platform supporting development, small business, and improved living conditions and jobs for the poor. MIUCA has received greater support in the country's municipal elections.

Leaders: Aulio COLLADO (President), Guillermo MORENO (2008 presidential candidate), Virtudes ALVAREZ (Co-president), Fermin ALVAREZ, Juan Dionisio RODRIGUEZ (Secretary General).

Revolutionary Social Christian Party (*Partido Revolucionario Social Cristiano*—PRSC). A party of the democratic left that rejects both capitalism and communism, the PRSC is patterned after other Christian Democratic parties of Latin America and draws most of its supporters from young professionals as well as from youth and labor. Its youth wing is considerably more radical in its approach than is the party mainstream.

Leaders: Dr. Claudio Isidoro ACOSTA (President), Alfonso Moreno MARTINEZ, Dr. Alfonso LOCKWARD (Secretary General).

Revolutionary Social Democratic Party (*Partido Revolucionario Social Demócrata*—PRSD). The PRSD, a splinter of the PRD led by former PRD president Hatuey De Camps, embraces the tenets of the social democratic movement, which seeks to incorporate elements of socialism and capitalism. The party garnered 1.56 percent of the vote in the 2006 legislative elections.

The party's nominee for the 2008 presidential elections, Eduardo Estrella, running under the banner of The Fourth Way, received 0.47 percent of the vote.

Leaders: Hatuey De CAMPS Jimenez (founder), Eduardo ESTRELLA (2008 presidential candidate).

Joining the PRSC, PLD, PQD, and PCD in presenting presidential candidates in recent elections have been the **Christian Popular Party** (*Partido Popular Cristiano*—PPC), backed by representatives of the Unification Church; the right-wing **National Progressive Force** (*Fuerza Nacional Progresivo*—FNP), led by Dr. Marino VINICIO Castillo; the **New Power Movement** (*Movimiento Nuevo Poder*—MNP), led by Antonio REYNOSO; and the **Dominican Social Alliance** (*Alianza Social Dominicana*—ASD), whose presidential candidate, Carlos RAMON Bencosme, also ran in 2004. Other minor parties and their candidates in 2004 included the **National Solidarity Movement** (*Movimiento Solidaridad*—MSN), led by Ramon Emilio CONCEPCION; the **New Alternative Party** (*Partido Nueva Alternativa*—PNA), led by Ramon María ALMANZAR; and the **Popular Democratic Party** (*Partido Demócrata Popular*—PDP), led by Ramon Nelson DIDIEZ.

For more information on the **Democratic Integration Movement** (*Movimiento de Integración Democrática*—MID), the **Movement of National Conciliation** (*Movimiento de Conciliación Nacional*—MCN), the **Revolutionary Force** (*Fuerza de la Revolución*—FR), and the **Dominican Popular Movement** (*Movimiento Popular Dominicano*—MPD), see the 2008 *Handbook*.

LEGISLATURE

The **Congress of the Republic** (*Congreso de la Republica*) consists of a Senate and a Chamber of Deputies, both directly elected for four-year terms. The next legislative elections were scheduled for 2010.

Senate (*Senado*). The Senate currently consists of 32 members, 1 from each province and the National District. Following the election of May 16, 2006, the Dominican Liberation Party held 22 seats; the Dominican Revolutionary Party, 6; and the Social Christian Reformist Party, 4.

President: Reinaldo PARED Pérez.

Chamber of Deputies (*Cámara de Diputados*). The Chamber presently consists of 178 members elected on the basis of 1 deputy for every 50,000 inhabitants, with at least 2 from each province. As a result of the election of May 16, 2006, the Dominican Liberation Party held 96 seats; the Dominican Revolutionary Party, 60; and the Social Christian Reformist Party, 22.

President: Julio César VALENTÍN.

CABINET

[as of June 1, 2009]

President	Leonel Fernández Reyna
Vice President	Rafael Albuquerque
Secretaries of State	
Administrative Secretary of the Presidency	Luis Manuel Bonetti Veras
Agriculture	Salvador (Chio) Jiménez
Armed Forces	Maj. Gen.Pedro Rafael Pena Antonio
Attorney General	Radhames Jiménez
Culture	José Rafael Lantigua
Economy, Planning and Development	Juan Temistocles Montas Dominguez
Education	Melanio Paredes
Environment and Natural Resources	Jaime David Fernandez Mirabal
Finance	Vicente Bengoa
Foreign Relations	Carlos Morales Troncoso
Higher Education, Science and Technology	Ligia Amada Melo de Cardona [f]
Industry and Commerce	José Ramon Fadul
Interior and Police	Franklin Almeyda
Labor	Max Puig
Presidency	Cesar Pina Toribio
Public Health and Welfare	Bautista Rojas Gómez
Public Works and Communication	Victor Diaz Rúa
Sports, Physical Education and Recreation	Felipe Jay Payano
Tourism	Francisco Javier García
Women's Affairs	Alejandrina German [f]
Youth	Franklin Rodriguez

[f] = female

COMMUNICATIONS

Press freedom in the Dominican Republican is guaranteed by law, and diverse, private media generally operate without restrictions. The watchdog Reporters Without Borders has rated the Dominican Republic as having a "satisfactory situation," though in recent years it has reported an increasing number of attacks on journalists. In 2005 President Fernández banned press coverage of natural disasters without prior government clearance, stating that the measure was necessary to quell public panic. He eventually repealed the decree, claiming it was a misunderstanding. Two journalists were killed in 2007, possibly related to their coverage of drug-trafficking. Reporters Without Borders urged the government to do more to protect journalists.

Press. The following privately owned newspapers are published in Santo Domingo, unless otherwise noted: *Listín Diario* (85,000), moderate independent; *Ultima Hora* (50,000); *El Nacional* (45,000), leftist nationalist; *Hoy*, (40,000); *El Caribe* (30,000), moderate nationalist; *La Noticia* (18,000); *La Información* (Santiago de los Caballeros) (15,000); *Primicias*; *El Nuevo Diario*; and *Diario Libre*.

News agencies. There is no domestic facility; several foreign agencies maintain bureaus in Santo Domingo.

Broadcasting and computers. Broadcasting is supervised by the *Dirección General de Telecomunicaciones*. There are more than 140 radio stations as well as seven commercial television networks, two of which also offer educational programming. As of 2008 there were 215.8 Internet users per 1,000 inhabitants.

INTERGOVERNMENTAL REPRESENTATION

Ambassador to the U.S.: Roberto B. SALADIN.

U.S. Ambassador to the Dominican Republic: (Vacant).

Permanent Representative to the UN: Federico Alberto Cuello CAMILO.

IGO Memberships (Non-UN): ACP, ACS, IADB, IBRD, ICAO, ICC, ICRM, IFRCS, IHO, IMF, Interpol, IOC, IOM, IPU, ISO (correspondent member), ITSO, ITUC, NAM, OAS, OPANAL, PCA, RG, SELA, Union Latina, WCO, WTO.

ECUADOR

Republic of Ecuador
República de Ecuador

Political Status: Gained independence from Spain (as part of Gran Colombia) in 1822; independent republic established in 1830; present constitution approved by a constituent assembly elected November 30, 1997, and in effect from August 10, 1998.

Area: 109,482 sq. mi. (283,561 sq. km.), excluding the region previously in dispute with Peru, but including the Galápagos Islands.

Population: 12,922,474 (2001C), including adjustments for underenumeration; 13,908,000 (2008E).

Major Urban Centers (2005E): QUITO (1,526,000), Guayaquil (2,194,000), Cuenca (315,000), Ambato (166,000).

Official Language: Spanish.

Monetary Unit: U.S. Dollar. The dollar was phased in from January 2000 to March 2001 to replace the sucre as Ecuador's legal tender (market rate December 1, 2009: 25,0000 sucre = $1US).

President: Rafael CORREA Delgado (Country Alliance); reelected in first-round balloting on April 26, 2009, and inaugurated August 10, 2009, for a four-year term, succeeding Alfredo PALACIO Gonzáles (Independent).

Vice President: Lenin MORENO Garcés (Country Alliance); reelected in first-round balloting on April 26, 2009, and inaugurated August 10, 2009, for a term concurrent with that of the president, succeeding Alejandro SERRANO Aguilar.

THE COUNTRY

South America's fourth-smallest republic has four main geographic regions: the Pacific coastal plain (*Costa*), the Andes highlands (*Sierra*), the sparsely populated eastern jungle (*Oriente*), and the Galápagos Islands (*Archipélago de Colón*) in the Pacific. The population is roughly 40 percent Indian, 40 percent mestizo, 10 percent white, and 10 percent black. Although Spanish is the official language, numerous Indian languages are spoken, the most important of which is Quechua. Approximately 90 percent of the population professes Roman Catholicism, but other religions are practiced, including tribal religions among the Indians. According to the World Bank, 27 percent of the labor force is female, primarily in domestic service, market trade, and transient agricultural labor; female participation in government had been quite limited, in 2009 seven out of 28 cabinet members, and 40 of 124 National Assembly members, were women.

Adverse climate, jungle terrain, volcanic activity, and earthquakes limit the country's habitable area and have slowed its economic development. The economy is primarily agricultural, with approximately one-half of the population engaged in farming, mainly on a subsistence level. The most important crops are bananas (of which Ecuador is the world's largest exporter), coffee, and cocoa. Following the lowering of tariff barriers for exports to the United States, cut flowers, broccoli, and mangoes emerged as important cash crops. Hardwoods and balsa are harvested from the forests, while Ecuadorian Pacific waters are a prime tuna-fishing area. Gold, silver, and copper continue to be mined, and production from Amazonian oil fields has placed Ecuador fifth among South American countries in petroleum output (Ecuador has the second largest oil reserves in South America) and second among the continent's suppliers of crude oil to the United States. Other energy resources include natural gas deposits in the Gulf of Guayaquil and considerable hydroelectric potential.

The economy experienced a severe recession during the mid-1980s. Some recovery was registered in 1988, although inflation of nearly 75 percent was recorded by late 1989. The Gulf crisis in August 1990 yielded a surge in oil revenue, with the government disappointing creditors by electing to use the windfall for social programs rather than debt. Overall, annual GDP rose by an average of 2.9 percent during 1991–1998 before declining significantly in 1999 due to the collapse of Ecuador's currency. Further, in mid-1999 a proposed round of austerity measures as preconditions for a $400 million International Monetary Fund (IMF) loan generated strikes and protests that led to the retraction of a government-promised price freeze. As a result, Ecuador became the first country to default formally on a series of so-called U.S. "Brady" bonds by failing to pay $44 million in interest. A month later Ecuador announced that it would also default on $500 million in outstanding Eurobonds.

Following the adoption of the dollar as the medium of exchange in 2000, inflation declined and stable growth resumed due, in large part, to the strength of high worldwide oil prices.

GDP growth of 4.7 percent was recorded in 2005, and 4.1 percent in 2006. Growth slowed to 2.5 percent in 2007, due to disruptions in oil production, but increased to 6.5 percent in 2008. In 2009 the government was projecting GDP growth for the year of 2.3 percent, while the IMF expected a 2.2 percent reduction.

Remittances to family members from some two million Ecuadorians who have emigrated to the United States and Europe (primarily Spain) in recent years have amounted to a significant revenue stream of about $2.5 billion a year.

GOVERNMENT AND POLITICS

Political background. Charismatic individuals rather than political platforms have dominated Ecuador's political life through most of the period since the country's liberation from Spanish rule in 1822 and its establishment as an independent republic in 1830. A historic division between Conservatives and Liberals (now of little practical significance) emerged in the 19th century, the Conservatives being based in the highlands and the Liberals on the coast. More recently, Ecuador has experienced tremendous political instability, with eight chief executives within an 11-year period, politicized high courts, and little popular support for the legislature. The country has just adopted its 19th significant constitutional revision since it became an independent republic.

A bright spot in Ecuadorian political life occurred in 1948 with the election of Galo PLAZA Lasso as president. The first chief executive since 1924 to complete his full term, Plaza created a climate of stability and economic progress, while his successor, José María VELASCO Ibarra, stood out in a lengthy catalog of interrupted presidencies and military juntas. Before his election in 1952 (his only full term), Velasco had served twice as president, in 1934–1935 and in 1944–1947. He was subsequently elected in 1960 and in 1968, but coups ended both terms prematurely. His 1961 successor, Carlos Julio AROSEMENA Monroy, also was ousted by a military junta in July 1963. During his last term in office, Velasco in mid-1970 dissolved the National Congress and assumed dictatorial powers to cope with a financial emergency. He was deposed for a fourth time in February 1972, the stimulus to military intervention being the approach of a presidential election in which Assad BUCARAM Elmhalim, a populist politician, appeared the likely winner. The military leadership, under Gen. Guillermo RODRÍGUEZ Lara, canceled the election, nominally restored the Liberal constitution of 1945, and advanced a "nationalist, military, and revolutionary" program emphasizing the objectives of social justice and popular welfare.

In December 1975 President Rodríguez announced his intention to make way for a return to civilian rule, but his actual departure in January 1976 was precipitated by a government crisis during which the entire cabinet resigned. A three-man junta headed by Vice Adm. Alfredo POVEDA Burbano succeeded Rodríguez, declaring that the 1972 program of the armed forces would be honored and that the nation would be returned to civilian leadership within two years; however, it was not until July 16, 1978, that a presidential election, in which no candidate obtained a majority of votes, was held. In a runoff on April 29, 1979, the center-left candidate, Jaime ROLDÓS Aguilera, defeated his conservative opponent, Sixto DURAN-BALLEN Córdovez, by a more than two-to-one majority and was inaugurated, without incident, on August 10.

Roldós, his minister of defense, and a number of others were killed in a plane crash on May 24, 1981, and the Christian Democratic vice president, Osvaldo HURTADO Larrea, was immediately sworn in to complete the remainder of Roldós's five-year term. On June 2 the late

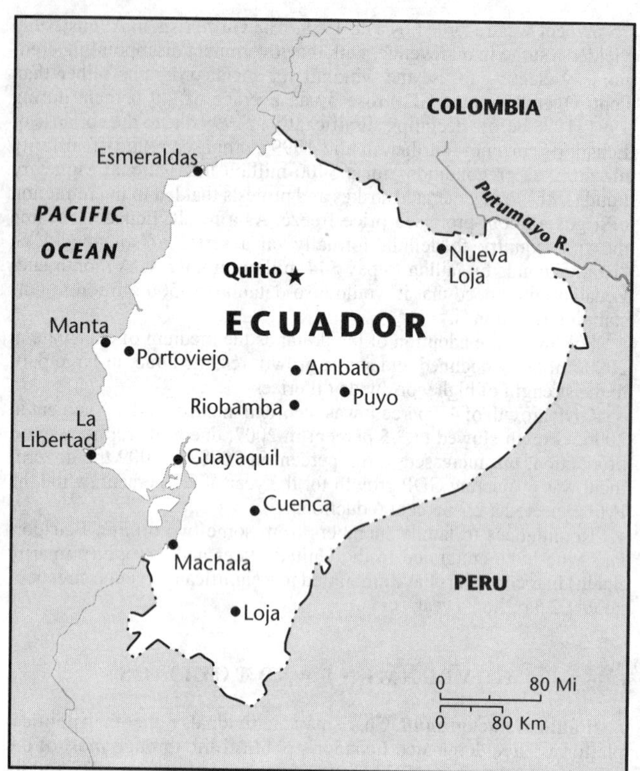

president's brother, León ROLDÓS Aguilera, by a legislative margin of one vote, was elected to the vice presidency.

A dispute between the president and vice president in early 1982, ostensibly over rapprochement with neighboring Peru (see Foreign relations, below), led to the resignation of two *Roldosista* ministers and, amid mounting economic problems, a period of uncertain legislative support for Hurtado, who was constitutionally precluded from reelection in 1984. In the balloting on January 29, with 17 parties competing, the opposition Democratic Left (*Izquierda Democrática*—ID) won 24 of 71 legislative seats, while its presidential candidate, Rodrigo BORJA Cevallos, obtained a slim plurality. However, in a second-round poll on May 6, Borja was narrowly defeated by the nominee of the conservative National Reconstruction Front (*Frente de Reconstrucción Nacional*—FRN), León FEBRES Cordero. Subsequently, a major constitutional struggle erupted between the executive and legislative branches over control of the judiciary, with the president refusing to recognize a new Chamber-appointed Supreme Court. The issue was eventually resolved in December, when the Chamber agreed to the resignation of both judicial panels and the appointment of a new court composed of pro-government and opposition members.

In June 1985 two ID deputies joined five members of the independent Radical Alfarista Front (*Frente Radical Alfarista—FRA*) in shifting their allegiance to the president, thereby, with the support of the Concentration of Popular Forces (*Concentración de Fuerzas Populares*—CFP), providing the government with its first legislative majority since the 1984 election. However, the government was shaken in mid-March 1986 by a brief revolt led by Lt. Gen. Frank VARGAS Pazzos, who had been dismissed as armed forces chief of staff after demanding the discharge and imprisonment of Defense Minister Luis PIÑEIROS Rivera and army commander Gen. Manuel ALBUJA for alleged misuse of public funds.

At midterm legislative balloting in June 1986 (postponed from January to allow for voter recertification), the pro-government parties again lost control of the Chamber by a decisive margin of 27–43, while the referendum on independent candidacies was defeated by an even more impressive 25.2 to 58.8 percent vote. The result was a renewal of friction between the two branches, with the president rejecting a congressional amnesty granted to General Vargas in September.

On January 16, 1987, Febres was kidnapped by dissident paratroopers at Taura air base and held for 11 hours, until agreeing to the release of Vargas. The legislature then approved a nonbinding resolution calling on the president to resign. The chief executive responded by declaring that he intended to remain in office until the expiration of his term in August 1988.

In the general election of January 31, 1988, Social Christian (*Partido Social Cristiano*—PSC) presidential candidate Sixto DURÁN-BALLÉN ran a poor third to the ID's Borja Cevallos and Abdalá BUCARAM Ortiz of the Ecuadorian Roldosist Party (*Partido Roldosista Ecuatoriano*—PRE). Buttressed by a comfortable legislative majority, Borja defeated Bucaram in runoff balloting on May 8 and formed a largely ID administration following his inauguration on August 10.

The president's legislative supporters were reduced to a minority in the biennial election of January 31, 1990, with Averroes BUCARAM Saxida (a cousin of Abdalá) being elected Chamber president. In late October, however, with the creation of a "Political Ethics Bloc" (*Bloque de Etica Política*), the body tilted briefly in favor of Borja, who was thereby able to secure Bucaram's ouster as presiding officer. Subsequently, legislative control again passed to the opposition, which displayed its hostility toward the president by impeaching no less than six of his ministers by mid-1991.

At second-round presidential balloting on July 5, 1992, Durán-Ballén, who had been denied renomination by the PSC, defeated his former party's candidate, Jaime NEBOT Saadi, by sweeping 19 of the country's 21 provinces. The PSC had, however, secured a legislative plurality, with Durán-Ballén's recently organized Republican Unity Party (*Partido Unidad Republicano*—PUR) in third place after the PRE. The most conspicuous loss in the presidential election was the formerly dominant ID, whose candidate attracted a vote share of only 8.2 percent.

In the midterm legislative election of May 1, 1994, the PSC won 22 of the 65 contested seats, while Durán-Ballén's PUR plummeted from 12 seats to 3. The result was an intensification of the long-standing legislative-executive rift, with the Chamber forcing changes in most leading ministries either by impeachment or the threat of impeachment.

In August 1995 Vice President Alberto DAHIK became the center of a corruption scandal. In the wake of imperfectly validated suggestions by the vice president that the government had made payments to members of the legislature and judiciary to ensure favorable treatment of economic reform measures, Dahik himself was accused of illegal use of discretionary funds kept in the personal accounts of two of his secretaries. Among the alleged uses of the funds was a down payment on the purchase of a radio station by former foreign minister Diego PAREDES Delgado, who, along with Dahik's secretaries, went into hiding. In late September President Durán-Ballén urged Dahik to resign. He refused and in early October escaped dismissal by the failure of a legislative vote of impeachment. However, also facing charges by the Supreme Court, he resigned on October 11 and fled to Costa Rica, where he appealed for political asylum. A week later the president secured approval for the naming of former education minister Eduardo PEÑA Triviño as Dahik's successor. The Durán-Ballén administration suffered a further embarrassment when all 11 of its constitutional reform proposals were rejected in a plebiscite on November 26 (see Constitution and government, below).

In the first-round presidential poll of May 19, 1996, the PSC's Jaime Nebot and the PRE's Abdalá Bucaram qualified for runoff balloting with vote shares of 27.4 and 25.5 percent, respectively. In the second round on July 7, the populist Bucaram confounded earlier opinion polls by easily defeating his opponent (54.3 to 45.7 percent) and was sworn in on August 10. However, the PRE held only 19 of 82 legislative seats, leaving Bucaram, like his predecessor, with the difficult task of seeking support from a deeply divided Chamber of Representatives.

Following his inauguration, President Bucaram abandoned most of his populist campaign promises and advanced an economic reform program that included privatization of state-owned enterprises, elimination of guaranteed job security, and devaluation of the Ecuadorian sucre from approximately 3,500 to 4,000 per U.S. dollar. The result was a wave of domestic unrest amid plummeting presidential popularity. On February 6, 1997, the National Chamber of Representatives ousted Bucaram because of "mental incapacity" and designated its presiding officer, Fabián ALARCÓN Rivera, as his successor. Two days later the Chamber yielded to the constitutional claim of Vice President Rosalía ARTEAGA Serrano, electing her interim president. On February 11 Arteaga submitted her resignation, and Alarcón was reinstated as chief executive for an 18-month term, with new elections scheduled for May 1998. Alarcón's incumbency was endorsed by 65 percent of those participating in a May 25 referendum, the voters also approving a call for a constituent assembly that was elected on November 30 with a party distribution not significantly different from that of the National Chamber. The assembly's principal output was a new set of electoral rules that included an increase in the number of legislative seats from 82 to 121 and the abolition of midterm replenishment.

At nationwide election on May 31, 1998, the Popular Democracy (*Democracia Popular*—DP), a restyled Christian Democratic grouping, won a plurality of Chamber seats, while its presidential nominee, Jamil MAHUAD Witt, bested five opponents with a 35 percent vote share. In a second-round contest on June 12, Mahuad secured 51.3 percent of the vote, defeating the *Roldosista* runner-up, Alvaro Fernando NOBOA Pontón.

President Mahuad assumed office in August 1998 amid severe economic problems The new government proposed austerity measures in January 1999 designed to reduce the budget deficit, but it was forced to abandon planned increases in taxes and fuel prices at the insistence of the PSC, on which the DP was relying for a legislative majority.

By August 1999 President Mahuad's popularity had declined from 68 percent to 12 percent, and by January 1, 2000, had plummeted further to an unprecedented 2 percent in the wake of a debt-restructuring effort that generated a new wave of protests. The president responded by declaring a state of emergency and adopting the dollar as the Ecuadorian currency. On the streets, the native *Confederatión de Nacionalidades Indígenas del Ecuador* (Conaie) launched a campaign to oust not only Mahuad but also members of Congress and the Supreme Court in favor of a "patriotic government of national unity." On January 21 Mahuad was overthrown in a coup led by a group of colonels who had joined forces with Conaie leaders. However, Gen. Carlos MENDOZA, who had been installed with Conaie president Antonio VARGAS and former Supreme Court president Carlos SOLORZANO as a ruling triumvirate, promptly mounted a countercoup that endorsed the "constitutional" elevation of Vice President Gustavo NOBOA Benjarano to the post that Mahuad had ostensibly abandoned. Conaie responded by charging the military with betrayal and called for a plebiscite to remove legislative and judicial incumbents, reverse the use of the dollar as the currency, end the U.S. military presence at an airbase in Manta, and secure amnesty for those participating in the January 21 uprising.

On November 24, 2002, Lucio GUTIÉRREZ Borbúa, a retired colonel who had participated in the ouster of Mahuad (an event commemorated in the full title of his small group, the Patriotic Society Party of January 21 [*Partido Sociedad Patriótica 21 de Enero*—PSP]), defeated Alvaro Noboa Pontón, now running as leader of the Institutional Renewal Party of National Action (*Partido Renovador Institucional de Acción Nacional*—PRIAN), in second-round presidential balloting. Nine months later, in the wake of an apparent shift to the right after Gutiérrez had attempted to introduce a number of IMF-mandated economic reforms, his administration was severely weakened by the withdrawal of the Conaie-based New Country–Pachakutik Movement (*Movimiento Nuevo Pais–Pachakutik*—MNPP). The president then entered briefly into an implausible alignment with the two leading legislative parties, the center-right PSC and the center-left ID. The effort soon failed, with both of the erstwhile allies joining an opposition drive for the president's impeachment. By mid-2004 poll results showed 68 percent of the public felt Gutiérrez should resign. However, he persevered by courting the *Roldosistas*. Although having earlier opposed the return of Abdalá Bucaram from exile in Panama, Gutiérrez met with the former president on September 1. Less than three months later, Gutiérrez deflected impeachment by negotiating a "new majority" that included the far-left Democratic Popular Movement (*Movimiento Popular Democrático*—MPD), the right-wing PRIAN, and the PSP, the PRE, and the CFP. Emboldened by an opposition suddenly in disarray, Gutiérrez recalled Congress in early December and pushed through a constitutionally questionable measure that removed all 31 Supreme Court justices. This allowed new appointees who would clear the way for former president Bucaram's return by dismissing the charges against him. On March 31, 2005, the charges were annulled and Bucaram returned on April 2. These maneuvers aroused the public, and a wave of demonstrations in Quito, including an incursion of rioting students into the congressional building, yielded a 60–2 legislative vote on April 20 to remove Gutiérrez in the wake of a spurious finding that he had abandoned his post. Also purged were all 31 members of the Supreme Court.

Vice President Alfredo PALACIO Gonzáles, assuming the presidency after election by Congress on the same day in 2005 that Gutiérrez was removed, encountered an equally intractable legislature. In June 2005 he called for a referendum to establish "more democratic representation" by breaking with party-controlled electoral lists in favor of constituency-specific candidates (single-member districts) but was rebuffed by Congress.

On October 4, 2005, Gutiérrez returned from exile and was arrested on charges of attempting to destabilize the government by not recognizing the legitimacy of Palacio as his successor. Members of the country's third Supreme Court in less than a year were installed on November 30. Gutiérrez was released by judicial order in March 2006 after a high court ruling that Gutiérrez's conspiracy accusations against Palacio were not a violation of law and his actions did not threaten national security.

Palacio's government was plagued by civil unrest in the first half of 2006 (see Current issues, below) and a constant stream of cabinet reshuffling during his tenure in office; at least 55 ministers served from April 2005 until the swearing in of his successor in January 2007.

First-round balloting for president on October 15, 2006, resulted in a runoff from an original list of 13 candidates between Alvaro Noboa Pontón of the PRIAN, a right-of-center populist millionaire, and Rafael CORREA Delgado, leader of a new left-wing bloc, the Country Alliance (*Alianza País*—PAÍS), an economist and former finance minister. Correa was elected in the second round on November 26, having prevailed in a particularly bitter campaign in which Noboa won the first round. Noboa challenged the final results, which gave Correa 57.07 percent of the vote to Noboa's 42.96 percent, and refused to concede, despite validation by the electoral commission and international organizations. Correa was inaugurated on January 15, 2007, and formed a new government, drawn mostly from PAÍS members, the same day. Legislative elections concurrent with the 2006 presidential election gave the PRIAN a plurality in Congress, with nine other parties also holding seats. No PAÍS candidates won seats.

The cabinet was reshuffled in June 2007, when three ministers stepped down to register as candidates for the constituent assembly. In a second reshuffling in July, finance minister Ricardo PATIÑO was reassigned in the wake of a scandal involving alleged manipulation of the bond markets for Ecuadorian debt.

The cabinet was reshuffled in January and July 2008, and again in February 2009, the latter when several ministers resigned to seek election to the National Assembly.

Presidential and legislative elections were held on April 26, 2009, as required by the new constitution approved by referendum in September 2008 (see Constitution and government below). President Correa was reelected with 51.9 percent of the vote, enough to avoid a run-off and well ahead of former president Lucio Gutiérrez of the PSP with 28.2 percent, and the PRIAN's Álvaro Noboa with 11.4 percent. Correa's victory was the first time an Ecuadorian candidate had won in the first round since the restoration of democracy in 1979. The PAIS secured a plurality in concurrent legislative elections, with 45.9 percent of the vote, followed by the PSP with 14.87 percent, the PSC with 13.5 percent, PRIAN with 5.8 percent. Thirteen smaller parties also won representation.

Constitution and government. In a referendum held January 15, 1978, Ecuadorians approved a new constitution that came into force with the retirement of the military junta and the inauguration of Jaime Roldós Aguilera in August 1979. The new basic law provided for a unicameral legislature and a single four-year presidential term, extension of the vote to illiterates (presumed to be about 30 percent of the population), and establishment of a framework of social rights for citizens. The judicial system is headed by a Supreme Court, which is responsible for supervising superior courts. The superior courts in turn supervise lower (provincial and cantonal) courts.

On March 1, 1994, President Durán-Ballén launched a program of constitutional reform by announcing an eight-part plebiscite coincident with the May 1 congressional poll that included provisions for presidential reelection, compulsory voting, creation of an upper legislative chamber, and four-year terms for all representatives. However, the Supreme Electoral Tribunal (*Tribunal Supremo Electoral*—TSE) immediately struck down the proposal as "illegal and impractical." The TSE also rejected a call on June 10 for a July 31 plebiscite on formation of a constituent assembly to consider the changes, with the president insisting that the TSE's action was itself illegal since he had the right to "consult the people" on any matter that he wished. Subsequently, a scaled-down plebiscite was held on August 28, following the August 10 commencement of a new congressional session. An unusually low turnout of voters by a 2–1 majority approved most of the package, including a limitation on congressional power to determine public spending, authorization for nonparty candidates to stand for elective posts, and reelection of elected officials, including the president.

A second set of reform measures was rejected by approximately 56 percent of the participants in a plebiscite on November 26, 1995. Among the proposals were election of all legislators from single-member constituencies for four-year terms, presidential authority to dissolve the legislature, a ban on public service strikes, administrative decentralization to the provinces and municipalities, and partial privatization of the social security system. The constituent assembly elected in 1997 redrafted the constitution; the changes, which went into force on August 10, 1998, provided for a national congress of a size (currently 100) determined by a somewhat complex population-based formula, with members sitting for four-year terms; it also lowered the first-round cutoff for presidential balloting to 45 percent, with the victor serving a four-year term.

In 2007 President Correa launched yet another initiative for reform, calling for a national referendum to establish a constituent assembly to draft a new constitution. Eighty percent of voters approved the ballot measure on April 15. In subsequent elections for delegates to the constituent assembly, the PAÍS won a large majority, and the new assembly was seated on November 29. After missing a May 2008 deadline, the assembly approved 257 articles in the final 30 days leading up to its July 24 deadline. The new draft constitution was approved by 64 percent of voters in a national referendum on September 28, 2008. The new constitution permits two consecutive four-year presidential terms and enhances presidential authority by granting the president greater control over the central bank and in the energy and telecommunications sectors. It gives the president the authority, once per term, to disband Congress and call new elections for obstructing the president's "development plan." Additionally, the new charter sets forth provisions for immediate elections if a president is impeached or if the legislature is dissolved, and it allows for a presidential recall referendum. Further, the new constitution creates a fifth branch of government known as the Council of Citizen Participation and Social Control to appoint the committees that nominate the attorney general, ombudsman, comptroller, and National Electoral Council.

Administratively, the country is divided into 24 provinces including the Galápagos Islands. The provinces are subdivided into municipalities.

Foreign relations. The most enduring foreign-affairs issue for many years was a boundary dispute with Peru that dates to the 16th century and involves a 125,000-square-mile tract of land between the Putumayo and Marañón rivers, both tributaries of the upper Amazon. The dispute resulted in periodic conflict and a number of agreements, including the Rio Protocol of January 1942, which awarded the greater part of the area to Peru and was formally repudiated by Velasco Ibarra in 1960 on the ground that Ecuador had been pressured into acceptance of its terms by the guarantor states (Argentina, Brazil, Chile, and the United States). The frontier established by the Rio Protocol was itself never fully delineated, a 50-mile stretch in the vicinity of the Condor Mountains remaining to be charted along the presumed watershed of the Zamora and Santiago rivers, in an area where a new tributary of the Marañón was subsequently discovered.

In January 1981 Ecuador and Peru engaged in five days of fighting in the Condor region, while representatives of the guarantor states convened in Brasília, Brazil, for negotiations on a cease-fire that was accepted by the combatants on February 2. However, it was not until March 17 that the two sides began to withdraw their forces from the disputed area.

The dispute flared up again in August 1991, when Peruvian border units reportedly discovered Ecuadorian troops clearing woods for raising cattle inside Peruvian territory. Subsequently, Ecuador reiterated its rejection of the Rio Protocol, while the Peruvian popular press headlined the incident as a full-scale invasion by its neighbor.

In October 1993 a suggestion by Foreign Minister Paredes Delgado at the United Nations that Ecuador would seek an accord with Peru not to resort to force over the territorial issue promoted a "clarification" by Quito that it was not proposing a nonaggression pact with its neighbor. Two months earlier President Durán-Ballén had announced that he would repay the compliment of three visits to Ecuador by Peruvian president Alberto Fujimori in 1992 by embarking on the first state visit by an Ecuadorian president to Lima, Peru. However, in the wake of widespread criticism within Ecuador, the trip had not materialized by late January 1995, when troops, tanks, and fighter planes massed on both sides of the border. While Peruvians outside the contested area were reported to be largely indifferent to the latest confrontation, Ecuador charged its neighbor with "launching a massive offensive" and vowed a "fight for the fatherland."

Despite the announcement of a cease-fire on February 1, 1995, renewed fighting erupted the following day, with peace talks in Rio de Janeiro, Brazil, being broken off on February 5. Thereafter, in another about-face, the two sides signed a peace agreement in Brasília on February 17, though fighting did not cease until the end of the month. Under the so-called Itamaraty Declaration, the guarantor states would dispatch a team of observers on a renewable 90-day mission to oversee a gradual and mutual demobilization of the area and initiate talks aimed at resolving the long-standing dispute. It was not until July 25 that the two sides accepted full demilitarization in a further agreement that did not, however, settle the central issue of border demarcation. In a remarkable display of warmth accompanying the July accord, Durán-Ballén congratulated his Peruvian counterpart on his reelection, while Fujimori indicated that he would attend a Rio Group summit in Quito in early September. Although the two did not formally meet on the latter occasion, Fujimori stated that their countries were undergoing a "recovery of mutual trust" and extended an invitation to Durán-Ballén to reinstate his earlier intention to visit Lima.

Tension again flared in late 1995, when Peru learned that Ecuador was about to take delivery of four military aircraft from Israel in a deal approved by the United States, despite its status as a guarantor of the Rio Protocol. A number of border incidents ensued, with Israel declaring on January 1 that it would not proceed with delivery of the planes until peace negotiations had been concluded. An easing of relations, if not a resolution of the dispute, was evidenced by a symbolic embrace between the chairmen of the Ecuadorian and Peruvian joint chiefs of staff in the frontier region on February 11. The two generals subsequently held meetings in Quito on March 1 and in Lima on March 4, while a further series of meetings occurred in Brasília in 1997. Finally, on January 19, 1998, agreement was reached in Rio de Janeiro on a timetable leading to a peace treaty. Under the accord, four commissions dealing with major aspects of the controversy would be established, including one dealing with the thorniest issue: border demarcation.

The lengthy dispute was formally settled with a "global and definitive" accord signed by presidents Mahuad and Fujimori in Brasília on October 26, 1998. While the disputed territory was awarded to Peru, control (but not sovereignty) of the principal town of Tiwintza, in addition to a corridor from the border, was assigned to Ecuador, which was also granted free navigation rights along the Amazon and the right to establish two port facilities within Peruvian territory. Provision was also made for linkup between the two countries' electrical grids and oil pipelines. Resolution of the lengthy controversy appeared to be confirmed by the presence of the two countries' chief executives at a frontier marker ceremony on May 13, 1999.

During a ministerial meeting in Geneva, Switzerland, on September 16, 1992, Ecuador announced its withdrawal from the Organization of the Petroleum Exporting Countries (OPEC) in protest over the high annual membership fee of US$2 million and an inability to gain approval for increasing its production quota. However, it maintained linkage with the group as a nonvoting associate member. (Ecuador rejoined OPEC as a full member in October 2007 for what it claimed were "strategic reasons.")

Regionally, Ecuador and Chile signed a free trade agreement in December 1994 designed to liberalize 90 percent of their bilateral trade by 1997. However, recent relations with Colombia have been mixed.

In September 2005 Ecuador and Colombia became involved in controversy over whether the Colombian guerrilla group, the Colombian Revolutionary Armed Forces (FARC), should be considered a "terrorist" organization, as claimed by Colombia, or an "irregular armed group," as defined by Ecuador. The Palacio administration agreed in January 2006 to let the border area serve as an "anvil" against which the Colombian military could "hammer" the guerrillas, but did not fundamentally alter Ecuador's long-standing policy of nonintervention in Colombia's domestic conflict. Less than two weeks later, however, relations again soured in the wake of an incursion by Colombia in pursuit of rebel forces. Nonetheless, Ecuadorian army units were deployed in February to disrupt FARC activities in the eastern Amazonian provinces, where they found and destroyed several FARC bases and captured several guerrillas. Similar activity by Ecuadorian troops in May demonstrated that despite the noninterference rhetoric, FARC activities were receiving greater attention.

Ecuador's relations with Europe have largely revolved around trade issues (particularly banana exports to the European Union [EU]) and of late on the growing number of Ecuadorian émigrés in the region. In

November 2006 Ecuador renewed its complaints against the EU's import restrictions on its banana exports. Ecuador's suit before the World Trade Organization claimed that the EU banana import tariff introduced in January 2006 was discriminatory and had the effect of reducing its market share vis-à-vis the shares of African and Caribbean former colonies, contrary to a 2001 agreement guaranteeing Ecuador's share of the EU banana trade.

By 2006 Ecuador's relations with Peru had improved, with the two countries finalizing a deal for electricity from Peru to help Ecuador supplement its hydroelectric power generation deficit. Also, Ecuador's military redeployed troops that had been on the border with Peru to the Colombian border, closing down the bases left behind.

Like its Andean neighbors Colombia and Peru, Ecuador pursed negotiations with the United States over a bilateral free trade agreement in 2006. The agreement was meant to codify and extend trade preferences granted to Ecuador under the U.S. Andean Trade Promotion and Drug Eradication Act (ATPDEA), but negotiations subsequently broke down after the passage of a windfall profit tax on oil revenues earned by foreign energy firms and the seizure of a U.S.-based energy firm's Ecuadorian assets (see Current issues, below). The government then announced that it would seek to enhance commercial links with Chile and Mexico and to work out trade agreements with Central American neighbors who have bilateral free trade agreements with the United States. The United States, for its part, claimed that Ecuador acted in violation of the bilateral investment treaty between the two nations. The Correa administration declined to renew the 1999 military base access agreement with the United States that allowed U.S. forces access to the Pacific coast base at the port of Manta, exclusively for counter-narcotics operations. The agreement was set to expire in November 2009; U.S. assets vacated Manta by July. That month, Colombian media revealed that the United States was nearing agreement to station them at bases in Colombia.

Ecuador turned to Venezuela for energy cooperation and assistance after the 2006 cancellation of the Occidental Petroleum contract, signing an agreement to cooperate broadly for the initiation of joint enterprises between the state petroleum companies in May 2006. Ecuador also considered an arrangement to have Venezuela refine a portion of its oil output for domestic use, an arrangement with favorable terms that was expected to save Ecuador hundreds of millions of dollars. Given the tense relations between the United States and Venezuela, however, the Palacio government announced less extensive strategic alliances with Brazilian and Argentine state-owned oil companies, thus avoiding the appearance of being too friendly with Venezuela's president Hugo Chávez. In early 2008, Ecuador and Venezuela announced plans to build a huge oil refinery in the coastal province of Manabí, Ecuador.

Relations with Colombia deteriorated after a March 1, 2008, Colombian Army raid about a mile inside Ecuadorian territory that killed one FARC leader and at least 20 other people, including an Ecuadorian citizen. To protest the breach of Ecuador's sovereignty, President Correa suspended diplomatic relations with Colombia. (Neither country had an ambassador stationed in the other's capital as of mid-2009.)

Relations with Venezuela warmed in 2008, as President Hugo Chávez was the most vocal proponent of Ecuador's position in the regional crisis spurred by Colombia's March 1 raid inside Ecuador. In August, presidents Correa and Chávez signed a series of economic cooperation agreements, including joint oil ventures.

Relations with Brazil grew tense in 2008, largely due to a dispute over Ecuador's expulsion of a Brazilian construction company because of a faulty dam it built in San Francisco, and a collateral request for international arbitration to determine whether Ecuador must repay its $258 million loan for the project.

Tensions over the border situation with Colombia heightened again in November 2008, when the Correa government accused the United States of covert involvement in the March 1 raid. President Correa subsequently denounced the FARC and rejected the Colombian government's claims that it had received no response from Quito after providing the coordinates of FARC encampments detected in Ecuador. In December, the Correa government announced an "Enhanced Registration" program to provide refugee status to 50,000 Colombians fleeing the conflict.

Also in December 2008, Correa and Iranian president Mahmoud Ahmadinejad signed 12 agreements aimed at increased cooperation in the energy, oil, banking, and health sectors.

The FARC insurgency produced new tensions in February 2009, when a former Ecuadorian vice-minister was accused of having frequent contact with the FARC and possibly with Colombian drug traffickers (see Current Issues). Subsequently, Ecuador announced that it would bolster its military and police presence along the border with Colombia. Later that month Ecuador expelled two diplomats from the U.S. embassy in Quito. Relations with the United States warmed somewhat in June 2009, when President Barack Obama commended Ecuadorians' "commitment to democracy" following Correa's election.

Meanwhile, Correa enhanced Ecuador's relations with Venezuela by agreeing to enter the Caracas-influenced Bolivarian Alliance of the Americas (ALBA) after years of reluctance.

In 2009 tensions were reignited when Colombian intelligence officials alleged that top FARC leaders were seeking refuge in Ecuador and may have been given Ecuadorian identity documents. In June Ecuador announced plans to seek an international investigation into the death of an Ecuadorian citizen during the March 1, 2008, raid inside Ecuador. Later that month, a judge in the border province of Sucumbíos issued an arrest warrant for the Colombian defense minister for his alleged role in the raid.

Current issues. During his brief tenure in office, President Alfredo Palacio faced a series of public protests led by oil workers, university students, labor unions, and indigenous groups, over the status of a foreign oil company operating in Ecuador and the government's negotiations over a bilateral free trade agreement with the United States. The unrest began with a violent protest in Napo province in February 2006 that disrupted the flow of oil to pipelines, spurring Palacio to declare a state of emergency and arrest several public officials sympathetic to the protesters (who sought action on promises by the government to fund the construction of local transportation infrastructure projects). Additional protests erupted in March, followed by a general strike organized by the largest labor syndicate in opposition to the free trade negotiations. Soon, larger-scale unrest, coordinated by the indigenous group Conaie, spread more broadly in protest of the trade negotiations and the government's reluctance to cancel a contract with Occidental Petroleum. Tens of thousands of protesters disrupted much of the nation's transportation and commerce as Conaie organized highway barricades in half of the nation's provinces. Palacio appealed for calm, declared a broader state of emergency, and dispatched his ministers to demobilize some of the protests with promises of government investment in local projects. Meanwhile, Palacio vowed to continue negotiations over the trade agreement.

In March Congress passed legislation that imposed a higher tax on foreign oil companies, increasing the windfall profit tax rate from 30 percent to 60 percent. Palacio subsequently moderated his position, announcing that the free trade agreement would be adopted only if it was in the country's best interest. Palacio also proposed a 50 percent windfall profit tax rate, which congress ratified on April 19. The move prompted the United States to halt negotiations on the trade agreement. In May Conaie and other groups again put pressure on the government to cancel the Occidental Petroleum contract (though the company had offered to pay a $20 million penalty and windfall profit taxes), and on May 15 the contract was canceled. The United States then formally suspended negotiations over the free trade agreement, and Occidental filed a lawsuit against Ecuador with the World Bank Group.

In mid-2006 attention turned toward the October presidential and legislative elections. Thirteen candidates registered to run for the presidency, with former vice president León Roldós Aguilera of the new Ethics and Democracy Network (*Red Ética y Democracia*—RED) party emerging as the front-runner in the early months of the campaign. However, by September, Roldós's close ties to the ID/RED alliance's congressional candidates (at a time when public regard for the Congress was low) eroded his support. By early October the new front-runners were two populists: Alvaro Noboa Pontón, of the recently formed center-right PRIAN, and Rafael Correa Delgado, leader of the new far left alliance PAÍS. In the first round of balloting on October 15, Noboa won with 26.8 percent of the vote over Correa's 22.8 percent. Gilmar Gutiérrez, the PSP candidate and brother of former president Lucio Gutiérrez, ran a strong third with 17.4 percent. Roldós placed fourth with 14.8 percent. Each of the remaining candidates received less than 10 percent of the vote. Prior to the second round of presidential balloting in November, Noboa portrayed his runoff opponent, Correa, as a radical, a communist, and a lackey of Venezuelan president Hugo Chávez. Correa, for his part, accused Noboa, a banana magnate, of seeking to run the country for his own personal gain. Noboa advocated a diplomatic distance from Venezuelan president Chávez and Cuba, offering instead to embrace closer ties with the United States and a resurrection of the free trade agreement. Correa's election platform drew on themes from anti-U.S. Andean leftist populism. Correa called for an increase in social spending, the suspension or restructuring of repayment on foreign debt, a renegotiation of investment contracts with foreign oil companies, and nonrenewal of the agreement for the U.S. military base. He opposed the U.S. free trade agreement, suggesting that it would hurt small agricultural producers. Correa's victory in the second round of balloting, with nearly 58 percent of the vote, set up yet another showdown between the executive and legislature. Since PAÍS did not field any legislative candidates, the party had no dedicated support in Congress other than from the small number of seats won by the left-wing MPD and from the MNPP.

Following his inauguration in 2007 Correa issued a decree calling for a national referendum on a constituent assembly to rewrite the constitution. In order to secure congressional approval, Correa reached an accord with the PSP and the PRE to support the referendum. Congress approved the referendum on February 13, and the electoral tribunal set the date for April. However, the tribunal's crafting of the ballot question to grant the constituent assembly plenipotentiary powers, including the power to dissolve the Congress, prompted opposition deputies in Congress to declare the measure unconstitutional. Five deputies filed a lawsuit challenging the referendum; another 52 deputies voted with the original 5 for the removal of the tribunal's president. The tribunal, for its part, ordered the removal of the 57 legislators for one year on grounds of obstruction. Congress was unable to reconvene with the necessary quorum until March 20, when 21 alternates arrived under armed guard. In the interim, some of the dismissed legislators tried to reenter Congress resulting in turmoil, with two legislators wounded by gunfire. The 21 alternate deputies ultimately formed an alliance, styled the *Dignidad Nacional*, which included 9 members of the PRIAN and the PSP, and 3 PSC members who supported conferring plenipotentiary powers on a constituent assembly.

In the national referendum on April 15, 2007, with 80 percent voter approval. A week later the electoral tribunal ruled for the reinstatement of 50 of the dismissed legislators. The next day the Congress, without the expunged legislators, voted to dismiss the tribunal judges. On April 24 an arrest warrant was issued for two dozen of the dismissed legislators, accusing them of sedition. More than a dozen lawmakers briefly fled to Colombia, requesting asylum and seeking international intervention. Ultimately, the crisis abated as Congress continued to operate without the suspended legislators.

Though President Correa had threatened to suspend Ecuador's payments on its foreign debt, the finance ministry paid off all outstanding debt to the IMF in early 2007 and vowed to end dealings with it. However, in February, Correa and his finance minister, Ricardo PATIÑO, began threatening not to make a scheduled interest payment to Ecuador's foreign creditors and bond markets in order to shift priorities to spending on education and antipoverty programs. The government paid the interest on February 14, but warned that it reserved the right to default on future payments and would try to restructure its payment terms. In May a videotape surfaced showing Patiño discussing manipulation of bond markets with representatives from two U.S. securities firms just two days before the interest payment. Ecuadorian legislators alleged that Patiño had deliberately manipulated prices for Ecuadorian government bonds for personal gain and called for his dismissal. In July the president reassigned Patiño to a new department overseeing the coastal provinces.

In mid-2007 attention turned to political maneuvering in anticipation of the constituent assembly election on September 30. The PAÍS won decisively with 69.5 percent of the vote and 80 of the 130 seats. The closest competitor was the PSP, with just under 7.3 percent of the vote and 18 seats. Following the assembly's first meeting on November 29, delegates overwhelmingly voted to declare Congress in recess without pay, effectively dissolving it, until approval of a new constitution in a referendum scheduled for 2008. The constituent assembly then assumed the powers of Congress and began rewriting the country's constitution. Critics blasted the assembly's action, claiming that it was giving too much power to the executive branch, particularly after the attorney general, the banking chief, and other top officials were suspended. In a symbolic gesture, Correa declined to step down. Subsequently, the constituent assembly approved a new draft constitution on July 24. The referendum campaign in August and early September was dominated by accusations of Venezuelan influence, with the Ecuadorian opposition claiming that Correa was seeking to perpetuate himself in power like Hugo Chávez. Meanwhile, Correa claimed that elements in Venezuela's opposition were training their Ecuadorian counterparts in violent tactics. Voters approved the referendum by a margin of 64 percent to 28 percent, with those in Guayaquil, the largest city, registering a large majority of the vote against the new measure. (Guayaquil's mayor, Jaime NEBOT of the PSC, threatened to resign if a majority of the city's voters approved the constitution.) The new constitution enhances the president's authority, including greater fiscal control over provincial authorities, and guarantees that all citizens have access to water, health care, pensions, and free university education. The establishment of foreign military bases and the concentration of large landholdings are prohibited. Supreme Court judges subsequently voiced their opposition, protesting a provision that would reduce their 31-member court to a 21-member national court of justice, subject to oversight by a constitutional court.

In October 2008, an interim legislative commission (known as the "*Congresillo*" or "Little Congress") became the country's temporary legislative body, pending the election and inauguration of a new Congress in mid-2009. Named by the outgoing constituent assembly, the interim Congress was dominated by the PAÍS, with 46 of 76 members. It was empowered to name a provisional 21-member Supreme Court, the directors of the temporary electoral authorities who would oversee the 2009 presidential and legislative elections, and the members of the Council of Citizen Participation and Social Control, a new and powerful fifth branch of government that would make permanent appointments to electoral and oversight institutions. The opposition claimed that PAÍS domination of the interim congress would effectively weaken checks on executive power.

In early 2009 economic difficulties mounted due to the global financial crisis and the related steep drop in oil prices. Further, remittances from Ecuadorians abroad also declined sharply. In an effort to stave off increased unemployment, President Correa imposed a series of import restrictions on many imported goods. Soon domestic attention turned to the upcoming presidential and legislative elections, against the backdrop of the new constitution. Correa's main challengers in the 8-candidate field were former president Lucio Gutiérrez of the PSP, Álvaro Noboa of PRIAN, and Martha Roldós of RED. During the campaign President Correa had to defend against the earlier arrest of José CHAUVÍN, a deputy interior minister under one of Correa's closest political allies. Chauvín was charged with ties to a drug-trafficking network involving Colombia's FARC guerrilla insurgency. Chauvín denied the drug allegations, but acknowledged having met several times with the FARC leader killed by Colombian forces in a March 2008 cross-border raid. Correa's opponents sought to use the Chauvín scandal to tie the president himself to the FARC. Despite the bitter campaign, Correa was reelected on April 26, a notable, if narrow, first-round victory with just under 52 percent of the vote—marking the first time since 1979 that a runoff was not required. Former president Gutiérrez , who finished second, claimed electoral fraud, and though the Organization of American States (OAS) monitors noted problems with the balloting, the election stood as fair. In the concurrent legislative elections, the PAÍS won a plurality.

POLITICAL PARTIES

Historically dominated by the Conservative and Liberal parties and long complicated by pronounced personalist tendencies, the Ecuadorian party system has recently been in a state of considerable flux. Many of the traditional parties have been built around particular candidates or families, consistent with the elite character of the country's political culture for many generations. Party organizations have therefore been weak. Party alliances and coalitions have tended to form to win particular election contests or deal with immediate crises, then dissolve after the elections or crises have receded.

The principal coalitions formed for the 1984 elections were a right-of-center National Reconstruction Front (*Frente de Reconstrucción Nacional*—FRN), which supported the presidential candidacy of Febres Cordero, and a left-of-center Progressive Front (*Frente Progresista*— FP). Both groups subsequently underwent a degree of restructuring, ultimately constituting a minority presidential bloc and a majority opposition bloc after the midterm congressional balloting of June 1986. In the second-round presidential balloting of May 1988, Rodrigo Borja was supported by the ID, DP, CFP, FRA, FADI, and MPD, which had collectively obtained a majority of legislative seats in January. By contrast, Borja's ID lost more than half of its seats in the June 1990 legislative election, giving an opposition grouping led by the PSC and PRE a slim majority that the president was able to reverse in late October by concluding a fragile alliance of deputies ranging from

Communists to Conservatives. By early 1991 the unlikely accord had dissipated, with legislative-executive conflict persisting for the remainder of Borja's term.

Shifts in the balance of legislative power have by no means been confined to electoral outcomes. During Durán-Ballén's first year in office (1992–1993), no fewer than 22 of the Chamber's then 77 representatives were officially reported to have changed their party affiliations. The fluidity was responsible, in part, for the downfall of presidents Bucaram in 1997, Mahuad in 2000, and Gutiérrez in 2005.

Following the 2009 legislative elections, 13 legislators from the PRE and smaller parties formed an alliance called the National Agreement for Decentralization and Equity (*Acuerdo Democrático por la Descentralización y la Equidad*—ADE) in support of President Correa and the PAÍS, thus giving the administration control of 72 of the 124 assembly seats.

Government Party:

Country Alliance (*Alianza País*—PAÍS). The PAÍS is a loose collection of socialist organizations, civil-society groups, indigenous leaders, and left-of-center personalities organized in 2006 largely by Rafael Correa, its presidential candidate. Correa chose not to participate in the presidential primaries sponsored by Conaie (below), instead forming alliances with the PS-FA, PSP, and the MNPP, among others, for support in the second round of balloting.

During his 2006 campaign, Correa had targeted for radical reform what he labeled the "*partidocracia*" of traditional parties that had long controlled the National Congress and brought down or crippled successive presidential administrations. Subsequently, the PAÍS refused to field candidates in the 2006 legislative elections amid corruption allegations among various parties. After winning the election, President Correa successfully steered the PAÍS toward securing a majority of seats in the constituent assembly election in September 2007. Correa rejected an attempt by some advisers to launch a party whose acronym would match his initials, deriding this as another example of the destructive pattern of personalization of politics in Ecuador.

The party was fined close to $1 million by the electoral tribunal in 2007 for concealing campaign spending from the November 2006 presidential runoff, but the tribunal backed away from that decision after Correa claimed that the investigation had not treated the PAÍS and the opposition PRIAN equally with regard to overspending.

Correa's reelection in 2009 did little to bolster the PAÍS, which won only a plurality in concurrent legislative elections.

Leaders: Rafael CORREA Delgado (President of the Republic and Leader of the Alliance), Lenin MORENO Garcés (Vice President of the Republic).

Other Legislative Parties:

Patriotic Society Party of January 21 (*Partido Sociedad Patriótica 21 de Enero*—PSP). Launched in the run-up to the 2002 election, the PSP was joined by the MNPP (below) in supporting the successful candidacy of Lucio Gutiérrez, the PSP's charismatic founder and leader, whose platform emphasized anticorruption measures and support for the poor. After Congress removed Gutiérrez in April 2005, he fled the country, and upon his return in October he was arrested on sedition charges. The case against him was dismissed in March 2006. Two months prior to his release, Gutiérrez was nominated by the PSP as their presidential candidate for the October election. Gutiérrez promised to call a constituent assembly to reform what he described as the dysfunctional political system. However, that the supreme electoral tribunal barred Gutiérrez's candidacy for two years because of an alleged campaign finance violation. Nevertheless, Gutiérrez continued to campaign in defiance of the electoral board ruling. Subsequently, the PSP announced that it would form an alliance with the PRIAN for the presidential election, backing the PRIAN's Alvaro Noboa for president and Gilmar Gutiérrez (the brother of Lucio) for vice president.. By September, however, the parties had gone their separate ways, with Gilmar Gutiérrez registering under the PSP banner. The PSP list won 17.5 percent of the vote in the legislative election, giving it the second largest bloc of seats in the congress. The PSP renewed its loose alliance with the PRIAN for the November 26 presidential runoff, supporting Noboa in exchange for promises that a Noboa government would prosecute perpetrators of the 2005 "coup" against Lucio Gutiérrez.

After its defeat in the presidential elections, the PSP eventually agreed to support a national referendum to create a constituent assembly. Soon thereafter some PSP legislators joined other opposition members in voting to dismiss the electoral tribunal chief in the wake of a dispute over the constituent assembly's authority, and the lawmakers were subsequently dismissed. In the 2007 constituent assembly elections, the PSP won 7.3 percent of the vote, with Gilmar Gutiérrez elected as a delegate.

Lucio Gutiérrez ran again in the April 2009 presidential elections, finishing second with 28.24 percent of the vote. PSP candidates won the second-largest legislative bloc, 19 seats, on a vote share of 14.87 percent.

Leaders: Col. (Ret.) Lucio Edwin GUTIÉRREZ Borbúa (Former President of the Republic and 2009 presidential candidate), Gilmar GUTIÉRREZ Borbúa (National Director and 2006 presidential candidate), Fidel ARAÚJO, Carlos TERÁN (Secretary General).

Social Christian Party (*Partido Social Cristiano*—PSC). A moderately right-of-center party, the PSC was founded in 1951 by former president Camilo PONCE Enríquez. Subsequently, it joined in a coalition with the PCE and the Ecuadorian Nationalist Revolutionary Action (*Acción Revolucionaria Nacionalista Ecuatoriana*—ARNE), a rightist group that was denied electoral registration in 1978 and was later dissolved. Sixto Durán-Ballén, the PSC's 1988 presidential candidate who failed to secure sufficient votes in first-round balloting, eventually embarked on an ultimately successful race for the presidency as the PUR nominee.

The PSC's legislative representation increased from 9 seats in 1988 to a plurality of 16 in 1990; it retained its plurality in 1992 by capturing 21 seats. In 1996 the PSC held 27 seats.

In 2006, the PSC presidential candidate, Cynthia Viteri, won 9.6 percent of the vote in the first round. In concurrent legislative elections the PSC list won 13.5 percent of the vote.

In the 2009 presidential election, the party backed PRIAN candidate Álvaro Noboa. In legislative voting, the PSC finished third with 13.59 percent, gaining 11 seats.

Leaders: Pascual DEL CIOPPO Aragundi (President), Pedro Carlos FALQUEZ Batallas (Vice President), Cynthia VITERI (2006 presidential candidate), Antonio Xavier NEIRA Menendez (2002 presidential candidate), Jaime NEBOT Saadi (1996 presidential candidate), Xavier Eduardo BUITRÓN Carrera (Secretary General).

Institutional Renewal Party of National Action (*Partido Renovador Institucional de Acción Nacional*—PRIAN). The PRIAN, a center-right party, was founded by former *Roldosista* Alvaro Noboa Pontón, reportedly Ecuador's wealthiest man, to support his presidential bid in 2002.

In July 2006 the PRIAN and the PSP formed an alliance to contest the presidential election, with Noboa as the presidential candidate, despite his earlier statements that he would not run. The PRIAN won 24.5 percent of the national vote in concurrent legislative elections of 2006, displacing the PSC (below) as the largest bloc in the chamber.

Despite its opposition to Correa's proposed constituent assembly, the PRIAN fielded candidates for the assembly election in 2007, winning 6.6 percent of the vote, with Noboa elected as a delegate. Jorge Cevallos Macías, president of Congress, was expelled from the party in June, reportedly because he opposed the dismissal of 57 lawmakers ordered by the Supreme Electoral Tribunal, a stance that broke with the party's position.

Noboa ran again in the 2009 presidential elections, finishing third with 11.41 percent of the vote. Meanwhile, PRIAN candidates won 5.8 percent of votes and 7 seats in concurrent legislative elections.

Leaders: Wilson SÁNCHEZ (President), Vicente TAIANO (National Director and 2006 vice presidential candidate), Alvaro NOBOA Pontón (2002, 2006, and 2009 presidential candidate), Sylka SÁNCHEZ, Gloria GALLARDO.

Municipalist Movement for National Integrity (*Movimiento Municipalista por la Integridad Nacional*—MMIN). The MMIN was founded in 2008 by mayors and councilmen from several parts of the country. Its most visible figure has been former Quito mayor Paco Moncayo, a former ID member. The party won 1.84 percent of votes and 5 seats in the 2009 legislative elections.

Leaders: Juan SALAZAR (President), Paco MONCAYO.

Ecuadorian Roldosist Party (*Partido Roldosista Ecuatoriano*—PRE). A populist party founded in 1982, the PRE is closely associated with former president Abdalá Bucaram Ortiz, who remains exiled in Panama. Its party stronghold is in Bucaram's home city of Guayaquil. In 2009 the party won 4.11 percent of votes and 3 legislative seats. The PRE subsequently backed the PAÍS as part of the ADE coalition (above).

Leader: Abdalá BUCARAM Pulley (President, son of former President of the Republic Abdalá Bucaram).

Democratic Popular Movement (*Movimiento Popular Democrático*—MPD). Although initially banned from participation in the 1978 election, the MPD was subsequently registered as a legal party. Drawing much of its support from trade unions and teachers, the MPD, described as a far-left party, won just two seats in 1998 and three seats in 2002.

In 2004 the MPD was part of the "new majority" that helped President Lucio Gutiérrez avoid impeachment and push through a measure that removed all 31 Supreme Court justices. In 2006 the party's presidential candidate, Luis Villacis, won just 1.3 percent of the vote in first-round balloting. Subsequently, the MPD supported Correa.

In the 2009 legislative elections, the MPD won 4 percent of the vote and 5 seats. The party subsequently joined the ADE coalition in support of the PAÍS.

Leaders: Luis VILLACIS (National Party Director and 2006 presidential candidate), Geovanii ATARIHUANA (First Assistant Director), Eduardo MEDINA (Second Assistant Director).

New Country–Pachakutik Movement (*Movimiento de Unidad Plurinacional Pachakutik – Nuevo Pais*—MNPP). The New Country Movement (*Movimiento Nuevo Pais*—MNP) was formed as an antiestablishment grouping that backed TV journalist Freddy Ehlers Zurita, who had entered the 1996 presidential race in February as an independent candidate on an anticorruption, environmentalist platform. Ehlers finished with a third-place 21 percent vote share in the first-round of presidential balloting. Subsequently, he insisted that the *Nuevo País* was the "real winner" because it had led in the 11 highland provinces, and he predicted that the group would prevail over the "old country" parties in 2000.

In 1998 the MNP joined with Pachakutik, the political wing of the 2.5 million strong Conaie, in a coalition styled the MNPP that supported Lucio Gutiérrez for president but went into opposition in August 2003. Most of the MNPP's electoral strength has been based in the Andean highlands and Amazonian provinces, where the 11 indigenous and ethnic groups it represents are concentrated.

In 2006 the party's presidential candidate, Luis Macas, finished a distant sixth in the first-round balloting, with 2.2 percent of the vote. The party secured 3 percent of the vote in concurrent legislative balloting. Its alliance with the PS–FA to contest the constituent assembly elections netted less than 1 percent of the overall vote. The MNPP won 1.37 percent of the vote, and 4 seats, in the 2009 legislative elections.

Leader: Jorge GUAMÁN (National Coordinator).

Democratic Left (*Izquierda Democrática*—ID). The ID, a moderate social democratic party, fielded Rodrigo Borja Cevallos as its presidential candidate in 1978, endorsing Roldós Aguilera in the subsequent runoff, and offering partial support to the Hurtado Larrea government after Roldós's death. It narrowly lost the presidency in the May 1984 runoff after having captured a substantial legislative plurality in January.

In 1988 Borja Cevallos was the front-runner in the first-round of presidential balloting and went on to defeat the PRE's Abdalá Bucaram in a runoff to become president of the republic.

In 1992, Raúl Baca Carbo, ran a distant fourth in the first-round presidential vote.

In 1996 the party's legislative representation plummeted from 8 seats to 4, but it won 17 seats in 1998. In 2002 the party held 16 seats.

The ID joined forces with Leon Roldós's RED party to contest the 2006 presidential elections, throwing its support behind Roldós.

In 2009, the ID again joined with the RED in backing Martha Roldós, who placed fourth. In concurrent legislative balloting, the ID won 1.43 percent of votes and 3 seats.

Leaders: Andrés PÁEZ (President), Agustin Ortiz (Vice President), Rodrigo BORJA Cevallos (Former President of the Republic and 1998 and 2002 presidential candidate), Raúl BACA Carbo (1992 presidential candidate), Luis PARODI Valverde (Former Vice President of the Republic).

National Democratic Concertation Movement (*Movimiento Concertación Nacional Democrática*–MCND). Formed in 2008, the MNCD incorporates three right-of-center groups: the **Citizen Vision** (*Visión Ciudadana*, headed by Mae Montaño); the **Future Now** (*Futuro Ya*, headed by Pablo Lucío Paredes); and the **National Democratic Concertation** (*Concertación Nacional Democrática*, headed by César Montúfar). The grouping won 1.86 percent of legislative votes in 2009 and 1.

Leaders: Mae MONTAÑO, Pablo Lucío PAREDES, César MONTÚFAR.

The minor parties that won legislative seats in 2009 were: **Deeds Are Love Independent Movement** (*Movimiento Independiente Obras son Amores*–MIOSA); **Social Conservative Movement of Carchi** (*Movimiento Social Conservador del Carchi*–MSC); **Regional Autonomous Movement** (*Movimiento Autonómico Regional*–MAR); **Regional Action for Equity / Latin American Popular Alliance** (*Acción Regional por la Equidad / Alianza Popular Latinoamericana*–ARE-APL); **United for Pastaza Independent Movement** (*Movimiento Independiente Unidos por Pastaza*–MIUP); **Amauta Yuyai Independent Political Movement** (*Movimiento Político Independiente Amauta Yuyai*); and **Citizen Conscience** (*Conciencia Ciudadana*).

The MIOSA, MSC, MAR, ARE-APL, and MIUP are members of the ADE coalition (above).

Other Parties that Participated in the 2009 Elections:

Ethics and Democracy Network (*Red Ética y Democracia*—RED). Formed in January 2005 by its leader and former vice president of the republic León Roldós Aguilera, the social democratic party focused on reform of the constitution to create a bicameral legislature with elements of party-list proportional representation and geographic constituencies, greater autonomy for local and regional authorities, eradication of political corruption, and reform of the education system.

RED formed an alliance for the 2006 presidential election with the ID, with Roldós standing as the coalition's presidential candidate. In the legislative elections, the RED won 6 of the 10 seats won by the ID/RED alliance.

In the 2007, constituent assembly elections, the RED, no longer in alliance with the ID, won just over 2 percent of the vote.

In 2009 presidential candidate Martha Roldós finished fourth with 4.33 percent of the vote. In the concurrent legislative elections, the RED won 1.87 percent of the vote.

Leaders: León ROLDÓS Aguilera (President of the Party, Former Vice President of the Republic, and 2006 presidential candidate), Dolores PADILLA (Vice President), Ney BARRIONUEVO (Second Vice President), Carlos AGUINAGA (Secretary General), Martha ROLDÓS (2009 presidential candidate), Eduardo DELGADO (2009 vice-presidential candidate).

Fertile Earth Movement (*Movimiento Tierra Fertil*–MTF). The MTF, a center-left party, fielded presidential candidate Melba Jácome in 2009. Jácome finished sixth with 1.35 percent of the vote. In concurrent legislative elections, the party won 0.88 of the vote.

Leaders: Melba JÁCOME (2009 presidential candidate), Ricardo GUAMBO (2009 vice-presidential candidate).

Christian Democratic Union (*Unión Demócrata Cristiana*—UDC). In late 1977 the Christian Democratic Party (*Partido Demócrata Cristiano*—PDC) joined with the Progressive Conservatives in organizing the Popular Democratic Coalition (*Coalición Popular Democrática*), which, having been denied separate registration by the electoral tribunal, joined with the CFP (below) in supporting the 1978/1979 presidential candidacy of Jaime Roldós Aguilera. In August 1981 the Popular Democratic legislative group (subsequently identified as the *Democrácia Popular*—DP) joined with a number of other members in a government-supportive alliance styled the Democratic Convergence (*Convergencia Democrática*). During the 1984 presidential race, the group (also identified as *Democracia Popular–Unión Demócrata Cristiana*) campaigned under the Popular Democracy label in support of former PCP leader Julio César TRUJILLO. It supported Borja Cevallos in second-round balloting in May 1988.

At a meeting of the party's national junta on July 3, 1989, which was boycotted by those who wanted to maintain an executive (but not legislative) partnership with the ID, a pro-Hurtado faction secured approval of a motion to withdraw from this alliance. In early August, however, the decision was reversed, with the ID agreeing to support the reelection of Christian Democrat Wilfredo Lucero as president of the Congress. The party fared poorly in both the presidential and legislative elections in 1992 and held only 4 Chamber seats after the 1994 balloting. In 1996 the party tripled its Chamber seats to 12.

In 2002 former president Hurtado participated in the formation of a youth-oriented **United Fatherland** (*Patria Solidaria*—PS), becoming that party's presidential candidate.

By 2006, the DP name had disappeared from national election campaigns; the UDC, however, won 8.1 percent of the legislative vote, securing 5 seats in congress. In 2009 the UDC won 0.83 percent of the vote in legislative balloting.

Leaders: Carlos LARREATEGUI (President), Ordóñez DIEGO Guerrero, Jamil MAHUAD Witt and Osvaldo HURTADO Larrea (Former Presidents of the Republic), Wilfredo LUCERO Bolaños, Dario FLORES Rubio (Secretary General).

Thousandfold Victory Movement (*Movimiento Triunfo Mil*–MTM). A small moderate-left party that broke with the PAÍS due to ideological differences, the MTM fielded presidential candidate Carlos Sagñay de la Bastida in 2009. Sagñay finished fifth with 1.57 percent of the vote. In concurrent legislative balloting, the party won 0.34 of the vote.

Leader: Carlos SAGÑAY de la Bastida (2009 presidential candidate).

Social Integration and Transformation Movement (*Movimiento de Integración y Transformación Social*–MITS). A small leftist party, the MITS fielded its leader, Diego DELGADO Jara, in the 2009 presidential election. He finished seventh with 0.63 of the vote. The MITS won 0.33 percent of the vote in concurrent legislative elections.

Leader: Diego DELGADO Jara (2009 presidential candidate).

Independent Just and Solidarity Movement (*Movimiento Independiente Justo y Solidario*–MIJS). The MIJS, a small centrist party, was represented in the 2009 presidential election by Carlos GONZÁLEZ Albornoz, a former congressman. González finished eighth with 0.49 percent of the vote. The MIJS won 0.27 percent of the vote in concurrent legislative balloting.

Leader: Carlos GONZÁLEZ Albornoz (2009 presidential candidate).

Two other parties that participated in the 2009 legislative elections were the **Movement for a National Agreement Party** *(Partido Movimiento de Acuerdo Nacional—MANA),* which won 0.52 percent of the vote, and the **National Movement for Social Concertation** *(Movimiento Nacional por la Concertación Social—MNCS)*, which won 0.20 percent of the vote.

Other Parties and Groups:

Socialist Party–Broad Front (*Partido Socialista–Frente Amplio*—PS-FA). A long-established leftist formation (its founder, Ricardo PAREDES, having broken away to found the Ecuadorian Communist Party in 1931), the PS formed a coalition with the FA that secured three Chamber seats in 2002. For the 2002 presidential campaign, the coalition joined with the DP and the CFP in supporting former vice president León Roldós Aguilera, who finished third on a 15.5 percent vote share.

The FA is a six-party formation whose core group has long been the **Ecuadorian Communist Party** (*Partido Comunista Ecuatoriano*—PCE). The other parties are the **Committee for the People** (*Comité del Pueblo*—CDP), a splinter group of the Maoist **Marxist-Leninist Communist Party** (*Partido Comunista Marxista-Leninista*—PCML); the **Socialist Revolutionary Party** (*Partido Socialista Revolucionario*—PSR), a pro-Cuban group that withdrew from the Socialist Party in 1962; the **Revolutionary Movement of the Christian Left** (*Movimiento Revolucionario de Izquierda Cristiana*—MRIC), supported by a number of left-wing Catholics; the **Movement for Leftist Unity** (*Movimiento por la Unidad de la Izquierda*—MUI); and the **Second Independence Movement** (*Movimiento Segunda Independencia*—MSI). In 1988 the FA supported General Vargas in the first presidential round and Borja Cevallos in the runoff; it supported Gustavo ITURRALDE in 1992.

The PS-FA allied itself with Rafael Correa and the *Alianza País* for the 2006 elections. Like Correa's party, the PS–FA boycotted the legislative elections, instead endorsing Correa for president. PS-FA party leader Guadalupe Larriva was selected by Correa to be his first defense minister, becoming the first woman named to the post. She died in a helicopter crash in January 2007.

The PS-FA formed an alliance with the MNPP to contest the constituent assembly election in September 2007, securing less than 1 percent of the vote.

Leaders: Silvia SALGADO Andrade (President), Gustavo VALLEJO Fierro (Vice President).

Alfarist Radical Front (*Frente Radical Alfarista*—FRA). The FRA was founded by Abdón CALDERÓN Muñoz, a maverick Guayaquil businessman who was assassinated on November 29, 1978. The party's legal recognition was withdrawn in early 1979, after which its supporters were reported to have joined the ID to participate in the congressional election of April 29. Its legal status restored, the FRA made an unexpectedly strong showing in local and provincial elections in December 1980, winning more than 20 percent of the national vote, but by 1998 was reduced to only 3 Chamber seats, all of which were lost in 2002.

FRA leader Fabián Alarcón Rivera, president of the republic from February 1997 to August 1998, was arrested on corruption charges in March 1999, his supporters describing the action as motivated by politics. There has been little party activity reported since 2002.

Leaders: Fabián ALARCON Rivera (President of the Party and Former President of the Republic), César VERDUGA Vélez, Iván CASTRO Patiño.

Concentration of Popular Forces (*Concentración de Fuerzas Populares*—CFP). Formed in 1946 by Carlos Guevara Moreno, the CFP is committed to broad-based socioeconomic change. Its longtime leader, Assad Bucaram, was the front-runner in the abortive 1972 presidential campaign and was considered the leading contender in 1978 until being declared ineligible on the basis of foreign parentage. Bucaram's protégé and nephew-in-law, Jaime Roldós Aguilera, the candidate of a coalition of the CFP and Popular Democrats, obtained a plurality of ballots cast on July 16 and defeated Durán-Ballén in a runoff on April 29, 1979. Following the CFP victory, a pronounced breach emerged between Roldós and his former mentor, most party leaders remaining loyal to Bucaram. In 1980 Roldós formally broke with the CFP, organizing a group called People, Change, and Democracy (*Pueblo, Cambio y Democracia*—PCD). Further defections occurred, and on November 6, 1981, Bucaram died, leaving the rump CFP with no firm leadership. The party's Chamber representation fell from 6 seats in 1988 to 3 in 1990; it plunged further to a single national constituency seat in 1992, which was lost in 1994, regained in 1996, and again lost in 1998. In 2002 it joined with the PS-FA in endorsing the presidential candidacy of León Roldós Aguilera while continuing to lack Chamber representation.

The CFP's 2006 presidential candidate, Jaime Damervil Martinez, secured less than 0.5 percent of the vote in first-round balloting.

Leaders: Averroes BUCARAM Saxida (1992 presidential candidate), Jaime DAMERVIL Martínez (2006 presidential candidate), Galo VAYAS (Director).

Ecuadorian Popular Revolutionary Action (*Acción Popular Revolucionaria Ecuatoriana*—APRE). Formerly styled the Ecuadorian Popular Revolutionary Alliance (*Alianza Popular Revolucionaria Ecuatoriana*), APRE resulted from a rivalry within the Concentration of Popular Forces (below) in the 1950s between a majority faction led by Assad BUCARAM and a leftist minority led by José HANNA Musse. In 1958 Hanna Musse formally broke with the CPF, his new organization being known until 1978 as the National Guevarista Party (*Partido Nacional Guevarista*). APRE supported General Vargas for president in 1988 and 1992, winning one legislative seat on the latter occasion and adding another in 1994, by which time Vargas had become its acknowledged leader.

Leader: Lt. Gen. (Ret.) Frank VARGAS Pazzos (1988, 1992, and 1996 presidential candidate).

Radical Liberal Party (*Partido Liberal Radical Ecuatoriano*—PLRE). The PLRE is the principal heir to the traditional Liberal Party (*Partido Liberal*—PL), which was dominant in Ecuadorian politics for a half-century after 1895, though frequently toppled by military coups, but subsequently split into a number of factions and ceased to exist in 1994. The PLRE lost its only legislative seat in May 1996, and failed to win any in 1998. Its candidate for the 2002 presidential election, Ivonne JUEZ, received 1.8 percent of the vote and the party lost its legal status. *Leaders:* Ivonne Leyla JUEZ Abuchakra (2002 presidential candidate), Blasco Manuel PEÑAHERRERA Padilla (Former Vice President of the Republic), Julio PONCE Arteta (Director), Alejandro LASSO de la Torre (Secretary General).

Ecuadorian Conservative Party (*Partido Conservador Ecuatoriano*—PCE). Formed in 1855, the PCE is Ecuador's oldest political party. It is based on a traditional alliance between church and state and has historical roots in the Andean highlands. In early 1976 the party split into right- and left-wing factions, the latter subsequently organizing as the Progressive Conservative Party (*Partido Conservador Progresista*—PCP), which joined with a number of other parties, including the Christian Democrats (see Christian Democratic Union, above), in a 1978 alliance styled the Popular Democratic Coalition that supported the presidential candidacy of Jaime Roldós Aguilera. By 1986 its Chamber representation had been reduced to a single seat, which it retained in 1988 before recovering to three in 1990 and six in 1992, all of which were retained in 1994. The party fell back to two legislative seats in 1996 (both retained in 1998), even though it had absorbed then president Durán-Ballén's Republican Unity Party (*Partido Unidad Republicano*—PUR) in 1995. (A PSC splinter, the PUR was registered in October 1991 as a 1992 campaign vehicle for Sixto Durán-Ballén, who had run as PSC candidate in 1978 and 1988. Following Durán-Ballén's inauguration, the PUR experienced internal rancor, culminating in mid-1993 with the withdrawal of former president Carlos Julio AROSEMENA, who insisted that the group lacked leadership and direction.)

The party still has some support in the provinces of Carchi and Imbabura, where it cooperates with the PSC.

Leaders: Sixto DURÁN-BALLÉN (Former President of the Republic), Alberto DAHIK Garzoni (Former Vice President, currently in exile).

Ahead of the 2007 constituent assembly election, several new parties emerged, including the **National Honesty Movement** (*Movimiento Honradez Nacional*—MHN), led by Ximena BOHÓRQUEZ, which won 0.7 percent of the vote, and **A New Option** (*Una Nueva Opcion*—UNO), which won 1.1 percent.

Indigenous Organizations:

Confederation of Ecuadorian Indigenous Nationalities (*Confederación de Nacionalidades Indígenas del Ecuador*—Conaie). The confederation serves as an umbrella organization for nearly a dozen indigenous groups. It has advanced claims to most of the Andean province of Pastaza. To reinforce their demands, which included administrative autonomy and control of natural resources, including oil, the Indians mounted a brief insurrection in June 1990 and staged a protest march in Quito in April 1992. They were instrumental in forcing the ouster of President Mahuad in January 2000. With nearly 2.5 million members, the organization has proved a powerful political force.

Antonio VARGAS, the former president of Conaie, hoped to be the 2002 presidential candidate of Conaie and its political arm—the Pachakutik Movement (see under MNPP, above), but he resigned as president of the confederation because of a scandal involving signatures on a referendum petition.

In 2006 Conaie played a major role in organizing and staging the March protests against the free trade agreement negotiations with the United States and against any accommodation for Occidental Petroleum with regard to the alleged breach of its oil production contract with Ecuador. Conaie also appealed to the UN and human rights groups to monitor the situation in Ecuador to safeguard against excessive use of force to stop the protests.

Conaie proposed a single primary in late July for all of the left-of-center parties to select a candidate for the October 2006 elections. Its leader, Luis Macas, secured the nomination under the MNPP banner and won 2.19 percent of the vote.

Leaders: Marlon SANTI (President), Miguel GUATEMAL (Vice President), Luis MACAS.

Federation of Indigenous People, Peasants, and Negroes of Ecuador (*Federación de Pueblos Indígenas, Campesinas y Negros del Ecuador*—Fedepicne). Fedepicne was launched in 1996 by a group of Conaie dissidents. In 2005, former party president Marco MORILLO was identified as a member of the ID.

Leaders: Luis PACHALA (President), Ricardo GUMABO, Pedro GUAMBO.

LEGISLATURE

The current legislature is a unicameral **National Assembly** (*Asamblea Nacional*) of 124 members, popularly elected, serving four-year terms. Following the most recent elections on April 26, 2009, the seat distribution was as follows: Country Alliance 59; Patriotic Society Party of January 21 19; Social Christian Party 11; Institutional Renewal Party of National Action 7; Democratic Popular Movement 5; Municipalist Movement for National Integrity 5; New Country–Pachakutik Movement 4; Ecuadorian Roldosist Party 3; Democratic Left 3; Deeds Are Love Independent Movement 1; Social Conservative Movement of Carchi 1; Regional Autonomous Movement 1; Regional Action for Equity / Latin American Popular Alliance 1; United for Pastaza Independent Movement 1National Democratic Concertation Movement 1; Amauta Yuyai Independent Political Movement 1; and Citizen Conscience 1.

(The number of seats held by parties frequently changes as a result of legislators' shifting alliances.)

President: Fernando CORDERO Cueva.

CABINET

[as of September 1, 2009]

President	Rafael Correa Delgado
Vice President	Lenin Moreno Garcés
Ministers	
Agriculture, Cattle and Fisheries	Walter Poveda Ricaurte
Coastal Affairs	Nicolás Issa Wagner
Coordinating Minister for Economic Policy	Diego Borja Cornejo
Coordinating Minister for Internal and External Security	Miguel Carvajal Aguirre
Coordinating Minister for Natural and Cultural Patrimony	Alexis Rivas
Coordinating Minister for Policy	Ricardo Patiño
Coordinating Minister for Production	Nathalie Cely [f]
Coordinating Minister for Social Development	Jeannette Sánchez Zurita [f]
Coordinating Minister for Strategic Sectors	Galo Borja Pérez
Culture	Ramiro Noriega
Defense	Javier Ponce Cevallos
Economic and Social Inclusion	María de los Ángeles Duarte [f]
Education	Raúl Vallejo Coral
Electricity and Renewable Energy	Alecksey Mosquera
Environment	Marcela Aguiñaga [f]
Finance	María Elsa Viteri Acaiturri [f]
Foreign Relations, Commerce, and Integration	Fander Falconi Benítez
Government, Police and Municipalities	Gustavo Jalkh
Industry and Competitiveness	Xavier Abad Vicuna
Justice and Human Rights	Néstor Arbito Chica
Labor and Employment	Antonio Gagliardo Valarezo
Mines and Petroleum	Germánico Pinto
Public Health	Caroline Chang [f]
Secretary General for National Planning and Development	René Ramírez
Secretary General for the Presidency	Patricia Moncayo de Valdivieso [f]
Secretary General for Public Administration and Communication	Vinicio Alvarado Espinel
Sport	Sandra Vela [f]
Tourism	Verónica Sión [f]
Transportation and Public Works	David Ortiz
Urban Development and Housing	Walter Solís Valarezo

[f] = female

COMMUNICATIONS

Ecuador's Constitution guarantees freedom of speech, and journalists have normally been able to do their work unhindered. However, in recent years, the watchdog group Reporters Without Borders noted that press freedom had deteriorated under the administrations of President Lucio Gutiérrez Borbúa and President Rafael Correa. In 2007 Correa reportedly stopped holding news conferences in response to perceived hostility from journalists. Also in 2007, a journalist received a 60-day prison sentence for criticizing a politician. In July 2008 a privately owned TV station and two private radio stations were seized in the run-up to the constitutional referendum, according to Reporters Without Borders, and in November a newspaper editor was sentenced to 10 months in prison for the crime of "insulting" a judge. In December a journalist was sentenced to six-months in prison for allegedly slandering a former mayor. Further, the former mayor sued the journalist for $1 million while he was still serving his sentence.

In May 2009 President Correa called Ecuador's media "a corrupt instrument of the oligarchy" and the "principal enemy of change."

Press. The following are daily newspapers published in Guayaquil, unless otherwise noted: *El Universo* (143,000), independent Conservative; *El Comercio* (Quito, 100,000), independent Conservative; Ultimas Noticias (Quito, 60,000), evening counterpart of *El Comercio; Hoy* (Quito, 72,000), center-left; *El Telégrafo* (60,000 daily, 55,000 Sunday), liberal; *El Expreso* (60,000), center-right; *El Tiempo* (Quito, 35,000), independent Conservative; *La Razón* (28,000), liberal; and *La Hora*.

News agencies. There is no domestic facility. A number of foreign agencies maintain bureaus in either Quito or Guayaquil.

Broadcasting and computing. Broadcasting is supervised by the nongovernmental *Asociación Ecuatoriana de Radiodifusión* (AER) and the *Instituto Ecuatoriano de Telecomunicaciones* (Ietel). Of the more than 300 radio stations (the most numerous, on a per capita basis, in Latin America), about two dozen are facilities of the religious *La Voz de los Andes*. There are 14 television stations, most of which are commercial. As of 2008 there were 288 Internet users per 1,000 inhabitants.

INTERGOVERNMENTAL REPRESENTATION

Ambassador to the U.S.: Luís Benigno GALLEGOS Chiriboga.

U.S. Ambassador to Ecuador: Heather M. HODGES.

Permanent Representative to the UN: Francisco CARRIÓN-MENA.

IGO Memberships (Non-UN): ALADI, CAN, IADB, Interpol, IOM, Mercosur, NAM, OAS, OPANAL, OPEC, PCA, SELA, WCO, WTO.

EGYPT

Arab Republic of Egypt
Jumhuriyat Misr al-Arabiyah

Political Status: Nominally independent in 1922; republic established in 1953; joined with Syria as the United Arab Republic in 1958 and retained the name after Syria withdrew in 1961; present name adopted September 2, 1971; under limited multiparty system formally adopted by constitutional amendment approved in referendum of May 22, 1980.

Area: 386,659 sq. mi. (1,001,449 sq. km.).

Population: 72,580,653 (2006C); 75,260,000 (2008E), excluding Egyptian nationals living abroad.

Major Urban Centers (2005E): AL-QAHIRA (Cairo, 8,090,000), al-Giza (5,957,000), al-Iskandariyah (Alexandria, 3,990,000), Es-Suweis (Suez, 688,000), Bur Said (Port Said, 562,000).

Official Language: Arabic.

Monetary Unit: Egyptian Pound (market rate December 1, 2009: 5.47 pounds = $1US).

President: Muhammad Husni MUBARAK (National Democratic Party); appointed vice president on April 15, 1975; succeeded to the presidency upon the assassination of Muhammad Ahmad Anwar al-SADAT on October 6, 1981; confirmed by national referendum of October 13 and sworn in for a six-year term on October 14; served additionally as prime minister from October 14, 1981, to January 2, 1982; sworn in for a second presidential term on October 13, 1987, for a third term on October 13, 1993, and for a fourth term on October 5, 1999, following unanimous nomination by the People's Assembly on June 2 and confirmation in national referendum of September 26; elected to a fifth six-year term in limited multicandidate balloting on September 7, 2005, and inaugurated on September 27.

Prime Minister: Ahmed NAZIF; appointed by the president on July 9, 2004, following the resignation the same day of Atef Muhammad OBEID; asked by the president to form a new government, which was sworn in on July 14, 2004; asked by the president after the 2005 legislative elections to form a new government, which was installed on December 31, 2005.

THE COUNTRY

Situated in the northeast corner of Africa at its juncture with Asia, Egypt occupies a quadrangle of desert made habitable only by the waters of the Nile, which bisects the country from south to north. Although the greater part of the national territory has traditionally been regarded as wasteland, Egypt is the most populous country in the Arab world: 90 percent of the people are concentrated in 4 percent of the land area, with population densities in parts of the Nile Valley reaching 6,000 per square mile. (Ambitious projects inaugurated in the late 1990s created massive irrigation canals from Lake Nasser [formed by the Aswan High Dam] in the south and from four new lakes in the northwest [formed after flooding], permitting industrial and agricultural development in the desert. Another major irrigation canal was built eastward from the Nile along the northern coast into the Sinai Peninsula.) Arabic is universally spoken, and more than 80 percent of the ethnically homogeneous people adhere to the Sunni sect of Islam, much of the remainder being Coptic Christian. Women were listed as 29 percent of the paid labor force in 1996, with the majority of rural women engaged in unpaid agricultural labor; urban employed women tend to be concentrated in lower levels of health care and education.

Completion of the Aswan High Dam in 1971 permitted the expansion of tillable acreage and of multiple cropping, while the use of fertilizers and mechanization also increased production of such crops as cotton, wheat, rice, sugarcane, and corn, although Egypt still imports more than 50 percent of its food. Much of the population continues to live near the subsistence level, high rural-to-urban migration having increased the number of urban unemployed. A growing industrial sector, which employs 30 percent of the labor force, has been centered on textiles and agriprocessing, although the return by Israel of Sinai oil fields in 1975 permitted Egypt to become a net exporter of petroleum. Other natural resources include gas, iron ore, phosphates, manganese, zinc, gypsum, and talc.

The reopening of the Suez Canal (closed from the 1967 war until 1975) helped stimulate the gross domestic product, which displayed average annual real growth of 9 percent from mid-1979 to mid-1983. By 1985 economic conditions had sharply deteriorated as the decline in world oil prices not only depressed export income but severely curtailed remittances from Egyptians employed in other oil-producing states; in addition, tourism, another important source of revenue, declined because of regional terrorism and domestic insecurity. Compounding the difficulties were rapid population growth (an increase of approximately 1 million every nine months), an illiteracy rate estimated at nearly 50 percent, a high external debt, and an inefficient, bloated, and often corrupt bureaucracy of some six million civil servants.

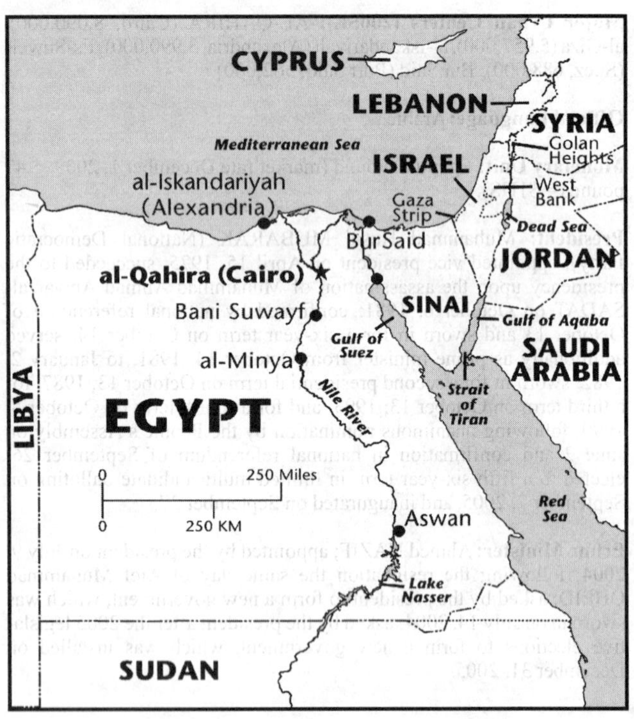

In the early 1990s the government pledged to privatize state-run enterprises, reduce tariffs and price subsidies, devalue the Egyptian pound, and pursue further economic liberalization.

In the early 2000s the International Monetary Fund (IMF) noted Egypt's progress in implementing structural reforms and reducing fuel subsidies, but it cited concerns about widespread poverty, particularly in urban areas. GDP growth averaged 7 percent annually in 2005-2008, driven by private consumption and investment, according to the IMF. However, inflation of 20 percent was recorded in late 2008. Nevertheless, the trade and tourism sectors helped bolster the economy, as did revenues from the Suez Canal. In the wake of the global economic downturn in 2008-2009, Egypt's banking system was reported to be largely unaffected, though the IMF cited "mixed progress" in regard to the government's structural reforms. Monetary authorities took note of Egypt's property tax reforms, instituted in January 2009, but expressed concern over the delay of a value-added tax to generate additional revenue. Though annual GDP growth slowed to 5.5 percent in 2009, the IMF commended authorities for progress in reforms under "difficult circumstances."

GOVERNMENT AND POLITICS

Political background. The modern phase of Egypt's long history began in 1882 with the occupation of what was then an Ottoman province by a British military force, only token authority being retained by the local ruler (*khedive*). After establishing a protectorate in 1914, the United Kingdom granted formal independence to the government of King FUAD in 1922 but continued to exercise gradually dwindling control, which ended with its evacuation of the Suez Canal Zone in 1956. The rule of Fuad's successor, King FAROUK (FARUK), was abruptly terminated as the result of a military coup on July 23, 1952. A group of young officers (the "Free Officers"), nominally headed by Maj. Gen. Muhammad NAGIB, secured Farouk's abdication on June 18, 1953, and went on to establish a republic under Nagib's presidency. Col. Gamal Abdel NASSER (Jamal Abd al-NASIR), who had largely guided these events, replaced Nagib as prime minister and head of state in 1954, becoming president on June 23, 1956.

The institution of military rule signaled the commencement of an internal social and economic revolution, growing pressure for the termination of British and other external influences, and a drive toward greater Arab unity against Israel under Egyptian leadership. Failing to secure Western arms on satisfactory terms, Egypt accepted Soviet military assistance in 1955. In July 1956, following the withdrawal of a Western offer to help finance the High Dam at Aswan, Egypt nationalized the Suez Canal Company and took possession of its properties. Foreign retaliation resulted in the "Suez War" of October–November 1956, in which Israeli, British, and French forces invaded Egyptian territory but subsequently withdrew under pressure from the United States, the Soviet Union, and the United Nations.

On February 1, 1958, Egypt joined with Syria to form the United Arab Republic under Nasser's presidency. Although Syria reasserted its independence in September 1961, Egypt retained the UAR designation until 1971, when it adopted the name Arab Republic of Egypt.

Egypt incurred heavy losses in the six-day Arab-Israeli War of June 1967, which resulted in the closing of the Suez Canal, the occupation by Israel of the Sinai Peninsula, and an increase in Egypt's military and economic dependence on the USSR. Popular discontent resulting from the defeat was instrumental in bringing about a subsequent overhaul of the state machinery and a far-reaching reconstruction of the Arab Socialist Union (ASU), then the nation's only authorized political party.

A major turning point in Egypt's modern history occurred with the death of President Nasser on September 28, 1970, power subsequently being transferred to Vice President Anwar al-SADAT. The new president weathered a government crisis in 1971 that included the dismissal of Vice President Ali SABRI and other political figures accused of plotting his overthrow. A thorough shake-up of the party and government followed, with Sadat's control being affirmed at a July ASU congress and, two months later, by voter approval of a new national constitution as well as a constitution for a projected Federation of Arab Republics involving Egypt, Libya, and Syria. At the same time, the pro-Soviet leanings of some of those involved in the Sabri plot, combined with Moscow's increasing reluctance to comply with Egyptian demands for armaments, generated increasing tension in Soviet-Egyptian relations. These factors, coupled with Sadat's desire to acquire U.S. support in effecting a return of Israeli-held territory, culminated in the expulsion of some 17,000 Soviet personnel in mid-1972.

The apparent unwillingness of U.S. President Nixon in 1972 to engage in diplomatic initiatives during an election year forced Sadat to return to the Soviet fold to prepare for another war with Israel, which broke out in October 1973. After 18 days of fighting, a ceasefire was concluded under UN auspices, with U.S. Secretary of State Henry Kissinger ultimately arranging for peace talks that resulted in the disengagement of Egyptian and Israeli forces east of the Suez Canal. Under an agreement signed on September 4, 1975, Israel withdrew to the Gidi and Mitla passes in the western Sinai and returned the Ras Sudar oil field to Egypt after securing political commitments from Egypt and a pledge of major economic and military support from the United States.

Although he had intimated earlier that he might step down from the presidency in 1976, Sadat accepted designation to a second six-year term on September 16. On October 26, in the first relatively free balloting since the early 1950s, the nation elected a new People's Assembly from candidates presented by three groups within the ASU. Two weeks later, the president declared that the new groups could be termed political parties but indicated that they would remain under the overall supervision of the ASU. The role of the ASU was further reduced in June 1977 by promulgation of a law that permitted the formation of additional parties under carefully circumscribed circumstances, while its vestigial status as an "umbrella" organization was terminated a year later.

On October 2, 1978, Sadat named Mustafa KHALIL to head a new "peace" cabinet that on March 15, 1979, unanimously approved a draft peace treaty with Israel. The People's Assembly ratified the document on April 10 by a 328–15 vote, while in a referendum held nine days later a reported 99.95 percent of those casting ballots voiced approval. At the same time, a series of political and constitutional reforms received overwhelming support from voters. As a result, President Sadat dissolved the assembly two years ahead of schedule and called for a two-stage legislative election on June 7 and 14. Sadat's National Democratic Party (NDP) easily won the multiparty contest—the first such election since the overthrow of the monarchy in 1953—and on June 21 Prime Minister Khalil and a substantially unchanged cabinet were sworn in. On May 12, 1980, however, Khalil resigned, with President Sadat assuming the prime ministership two days later.

By 1981 Egypt was increasingly dependent on the United States for military and foreign policy support, while growing domestic unrest threatened the fragile political liberalization initiated in 1980. In an unprecedented move in early September, the government imprisoned more than a thousand opposition leaders, ranging from Islamic fundamentalists to journalists and Nasserites.

On October 6, 1981, while attending a military review in Cairo, President Sadat was assassinated by a group of Muslim militants affiliated with al-Jihad ("Holy War"). The assembly's nomination of Vice President Muhammad Husni MUBARAK as his successor was confirmed by a national referendum on October 13, the new president naming a cabinet headed by himself as prime minister two days later. On January 2, 1982, Mubarak yielded the latter office to First Deputy Prime Minister Ahmad Fuad MUHI al-DIN.

The NDP retained overwhelming control of the assembly at the March 1984 election, the right-wing New Wafd Party being the only other group to surpass the 8 percent vote share needed to gain direct representation. However, popular discontent erupted later in the year over measures to combat economic deterioration, and numerous opposition leaders, accused of "fomenting unrest," were arrested. Meanwhile, Islamic fundamentalists continued a campaign for the institution of full sharia law that provoked a new wave of arrests in mid-1985.

At his death in June 1984 Muhi al-Din was succeeded as prime minister by Gen. Kamal Hasan ALI. Ali was replaced in September 1985 by Dr. Ali Mahmud LUTFI, who, in turn, yielded office on November 12, 1986, to Dr. Atif Muhammad SIDQI, a lawyer and economist whose appointment appeared to signal a willingness to institute drastic reform measures sought by the IMF and World Bank. Anticipating a resurgence of opposition and facing court challenges to the legality of an assembly that excluded independent members, the president confounded his critics by mounting a referendum in February 1987 on the question of legislative dissolution. The subsequent election of April 6 reconfirmed the NDP's control, and on October 5 Mubarak received public endorsement for a second term.

President Mubarak's swift response to the Iraqi invasion of Kuwait in August 1990 received widespread domestic support, and, at balloting on November 29 to replenish the assembly (whose 1987 election had been declared illegal in May 1990), the ruling NDP won an increased majority. The landslide victory was tarnished, however, by low voter turnout and an election boycott by three leading opposition parties and the proscribed, but prominent, Muslim Brotherhood. On December 13 Dr. Ahmad Fathi SURUR was elected assembly president, assuming the responsibilities left vacant by the assassination of the previous speaker, Dr. Rifaat al-MAHGOUB, on October 12.

Following a May 1991 cabinet reshuffle, Mubarak indicated that measures would be considered to reduce the NDP stranglehold on government activity. However, the state of emergency in effect since 1981 was extended for three more years, Mubarak citing ongoing "subversion" by fundamentalist militants as justification. Subsequently, international human rights organizations charged that the administration was continuing to torture and otherwise abuse its opponents, particularly the fundamentalists, with whom a state of "all-out war" was said to exist by 1992. For their part, the militants, vowing to topple the "corrupt" Mubarak government and establish an Islamic state, intensified their guerrilla campaign against police, soldiers, government officials, and tourists.

On July 21, 1993, the assembly nominated Mubarak for a third term by a vote of 439–7, and the president received a reported 95 percent "yes" vote in the national referendum of October 4, opposition leaders strongly questioning the accuracy of the tally. Although President Mubarak had promised an infusion of "new blood" into his administration, many of the previous cabinet members were reappointed in the reshuffle announced on October 14 by Prime Minister Sidqi.

On June 26, 1995, Mubarak narrowly escaped assassination when a group of alleged fundamentalists opened fire on his motorcade after his arrival in Addis Ababa, Ethiopia, for a summit of the Organization of African Unity (OAU). It was the third attempt on his life in 22 months. In September 1996, three defendants were sentenced to death by an Ethiopian court for their role in the 1995 attack, which President Mubarak blamed on the militant Islamic Group (see Illegal Groups under Political Parties, below).

Despite the regime's rhetorical commitment to broadening the governmental role of lesser parties, the NDP again completely dominated the legislative elections of late 1995, opposition leaders claiming they had been hamstrung by new press restrictions and the ongoing ban (under the long-standing state of emergency) on political demonstrations. On the other hand, the appointment of Kamal Ahmed al-GANZOURI as prime minister on January 3, 1996, launched what was widely perceived as significant economic liberalization.

The level of violence between the government and fundamentalist militants peaked in 1995 when more than 400 were killed from a combination of terrorist attacks and government reprisals against militant strongholds. International human rights organizations criticized the mass detention of political prisoners and "grossly unfair" trials leading, in many cases, to executions.

Sporadic incidents occurred throughout 1996 and into early 1997. In view of continued conflict with fundamentalist militants, the state of emergency was extended in 1997 (and again in 2006), permitting the government to continue to detain "terrorists" without formal charges for lengthy periods and to try defendants in special courts. Meanwhile, local elections in April again failed to reveal any hint of a political challenge to NDP control, nearly half of the ruling party's candidates running unopposed.

In mid-1997 imprisoned fundamentalist leaders reportedly called for a "cease-fire," and Egypt's vital tourist industry continued to revive. However, the government, apparently unconvinced that a truce had been achieved, proceeded with several mass trials and imposed harsh sentences on a number of defendants. Subsequently, militants massacred some 70 tourists at an ancient temple at Luxor in November, again bringing the conflict to the forefront of world attention. By that time, most observers agreed that a split had developed in the militant camp and that the faction committed to violence comprised possibly only several hundred guerrillas. It was also widely believed that there was little popular support for the militants, and only a few serious incidents were reported in 1998. By early 1999 the government had released an estimated 5,000 of the 20,000 people detained since the crackdown had begun, and in March the Islamic Group renounced violent methods.

All political parties having been distinctly "marginalized," President Mubarak faced no challenge to his nomination in June 1999 by the People's Assembly for a fourth term, duly confirmed by an official "yes" vote of 94 percent in a national referendum on September 26. Upon his inauguration, Mubarak announced the appointment of Atef Muhammad OBEID as the new prime minister. Subsequently, the NDP ultimately again won unchallenged control of the assembly in 2002. Some 70 percent of the NDP candidates also ran unopposed in the April 2002 municipal elections.

In June 2004, for the first time in Egypt's history, a member of the opposition leftist National Progressive Unionist Party—NPUP (*al-Hizb al-Watani*) won a seat in the Shura Council, and in October 2004, a third political party was allowed to form (see Constitution and government, below). Prime Minister Obeid resigned along with the entire cabinet in the wake of mounting criticism concerning the economy in 2004. Obeid was succeeded by Ahmed NAZIF, former minister of communications and information technology, a technocrat, who at age 52 was considerably younger than other government leaders.

President Mubarak was elected in controversial multicandidate balloting in September 2005 with 88 percent of the vote, most notably defeating Ayman NUR, formerly jailed leader of the leftist Tomorrow Party (*al-Ghad*), and then-leader of the New Wafd Party—NWP Hizb (*al-Wafd al-Gadid*), Numan GOMAA (see Political Parties and Groups, below). Seven other candidates each received less than 1 percent of the vote. Mubarak retained Prime Minister Nazif and asked him to form a new cabinet, which was sworn in on December 31.

Legislative elections in November and December 2005 resulted in the NDP retaining an overwhelming majority, but significant inroads were made by independents affiliated with the outlawed Muslim Brotherhood, whose representation increased more than five-fold to 88 seats. Runoffs for 12 undecided seats were left vacant because of violence in several districts. The cabinet was reshuffled on August 28, 2006, after the minister of justice resigned. Partial elections to the Consultative Council on June 18, 2007, were dominated by the NDP. The Muslim Brotherhood participated for the first time by backing independent candidates for the council, though none secured a seat. Other independents won 3 seats, and the Nationalist Progressive Unionist Party (NPUP) was the only other party to win representation (1 seat).

In municipal elections on April 8, 2008, the NDP won 92 percent of 52,000 council seats in polling that was boycotted by the Muslim Brotherhood. The elections were the first to be held since a 2005 constitutional amendment requiring presidential candidates to secure the backing of local councilors. On May 26, 2008, the assembly, by a 305-103 vote, approved the government's request to extend emergency law for two more years.

The cabinet was reshuffled on March 11, 2009.

Constitution and government. Under the 1971 constitution, executive power is vested in the president, who is nominated by the People's

Assembly and elected for a six-year term by popular referendum. The president may appoint vice presidents in addition to government ministers and may rule by decree when granted emergency powers by the 454-member assembly, which functions primarily as a policy-approving rather than a policy-initiating body. (Since assuming the presidency in 1981, Mubarak has chosen to rule without a vice president.) In May 1990 the Supreme Constitutional Court invalidated the 1987 assembly elections, claiming the electoral system discriminated against opposition and independent contenders. Consequently, the government abolished electoral laws limiting the number of independent candidates, rejected the "party list" balloting system, and enlarged the number of constituencies.

For only the third time since forming in 1977, Egypt's Political Parties Committee allowed the creation of a new political party, Tomorrow (*al-Ghad*), in February 2004. On June 9, 2005, the assembly approved a draft law to elect the president by direct, secret balloting, replacing the referendum system. This followed adoption of a constitutional amendment in May 2005 to allow Egypt's first multicandidate presidential election. The amendment was approved in a public referendum, albeit marked by huge public demonstrations over what is still perceived as too much government control over potential candidates.

A Consultative Council (*Majlis al-Shura*), formerly the Central Committee of the ASU, is composed of 176 elected and 88 appointed members who serve six-year terms. It serves in an advisory capacity as an "upper house" of the assembly. In addition to the Supreme Constitutional Court, the judicial system includes the Court of Cassation, geographically organized Courts of Appeal, Tribunals of First Instance, and District Tribunals. A Supreme Judicial Council is designed to guarantee the independence of the judiciary. Emergency laws, in effect since 1981, provide the government with broad arrest and detention powers. In addition, special military courts were established in late 1992 for the prosecution of those charged with "terrorist acts" in connection with the conflict between the government and militant Islamic fundamentalists.

For administrative purposes Egypt is divided into 26 governorates, each with a governor appointed by the president, while most functions are shared with regional, town, and village officials. In April 1994 the People's Assembly approved legislation whereby previously elected village mayors would thenceforth be appointed by the Interior Ministry.

Constitutional amendments passed by the assembly on April 30, 1980, and approved by referendum on May 22 included the following: designation of the country as "socialist democratic," rather than "democratic socialist," and designation of the Islamic legal code (sharia) as "the" rather than "a" principal source of law. An amendment adopted in 2005 allowed for multicandidate presidential elections and required candidates to gain the backing of assembly members and municipal councilors. In 2006 President Mubarak proposed 19 constitutional amendments that were approved by parliament and in a public referendum in March 2007 (see Current issues, below).

Foreign relations. As the most populous and most highly industrialized of the Arab states, Egypt has consistently aspired to a leading role in Arab, Islamic, Middle Eastern, African, and world affairs and has been an active participant in the UN, the Arab League, and the Organization of African Unity. For a number of years, its claim to a position of primacy in the Arab world made for somewhat unstable relations with other Arab governments, particularly the conservative regimes of Jordan and Saudi Arabia, although relations with those governments improved as a result of the 1967 and 1973 wars with Israel. Relations with the more radical regimes of Libya and Syria subsequently became strained, largely because of their displeasure with the terms of the U.S.-brokered disengagement. Thus a January 1972 agreement by the three states to establish a loose Federation of Arab Republics was never implemented.

Formally nonaligned, Egypt has gone through a number of distinct phases, including the Western orientation of the colonial period and the monarchy, the anti-Western and increasingly pro-Soviet period initiated in 1955, a period of flexibility dating from the expulsion of Soviet personnel in 1972, and a renewed reliance on the West—particularly the United States—following widespread condemnation of Egyptian-Israeli rapprochement by most Communist and Arab governments.

On November 19, 1977, President Sadat began a precedent-shattering three-day trip to Jerusalem, the highlight of which was an address to the Israeli *Knesset*. While he offered no significant concessions in regard to the occupied territories, was unequivocal in his support of a Palestinian state, and declared that he did not intend to conclude a separate peace with Israel, the trip was hailed as a "historic breakthrough" in Arab-Israeli relations and was followed by an invitation to the principals in the Middle Eastern dispute and their great-power patrons to a December meeting in Egypt to prepare for a resumption of the Geneva peace conference. Israeli Prime Minister Begin responded affirmatively, but all of the Arab invitees declined. Consequently, on December 5 Egypt broke relations with five of its more radical neighbors (Algeria, Iraq, Libya, Syria, and South Yemen).

A dramatic ten-day "summit" convened by U.S. President Carter at Camp David, Maryland, in September 1978 yielded two documents—a "Framework for Peace in the Middle East" and a "Framework for a Peace Treaty between Israel and Egypt"—that were signed by President Sadat and Prime Minister Begin at the White House on September 17. By mid-November details of a peace treaty and three annexes had been agreed upon by Egyptian and Israeli representatives. Signing, however, was deferred beyond the target date of December 17 primarily because of Egyptian insistence on a specific timetable for Israeli withdrawal from the West Bank and Gaza, in addition to last-minute reservations regarding Article 6, which gave the document precedence over treaty commitments to other states. Thus, on March 8, President Carter flew to the Middle East for talks with leaders of both countries, and within six days compromise proposals had been accepted. The completed treaty was signed by Begin and Sadat in Washington on March 26, and on April 25 the 31-year state of war between Egypt and Israel officially came to an end. On May 25 the first Israeli troops withdrew from the Sinai under the terms of the treaty and negotiations on autonomy for the West Bank and Gaza opened in Beersheba, Israel.

The Arab League responded to the Egyptian-Israeli rapprochement by calling for the diplomatic and economic isolation of Egypt. By midyear all league members but Oman, Somalia, and Sudan had severed relations with the Sadat regime, and Cairo's membership had been suspended from a number of Arab groupings, including the league, the Arab Monetary Fund, and the Organization of Arab Petroleum Exporting Countries. Egypt succeeded in weathering the hard-line Arab reaction largely because of increased economic aid from Western countries, including France, West Germany, Japan, and the United States, which alone committed itself to more aid on a real per capita basis than had been extended to Europe under the post–World War II Marshall Plan.

Although Egypt and Israel formally exchanged ambassadors on February 26, 1980, a month after opening their border at El Arish in the Sinai to land traffic, negotiations on the question of Palestinian autonomy were subsequently impeded by continued Jewish settlement on the West Bank, the Israeli annexation of East Jerusalem in July 1980, and the invasion of Lebanon in June 1982. Following the massacre of Palestinian refugees at Sabra and Chatila in September 1982, Cairo recalled its ambassador from Tel Aviv. (Relations at the ambassadorial level were ultimately reestablished in September 1986, despite tension over Israel's bombing of the PLO headquarters in Tunis in October 1985.)

The Soviet intervention in Afghanistan in December 1979 generated concern in Egypt, with the government ordering Moscow in February 1980 to reduce its diplomatic staff in Cairo to seven, while offering military assistance to the Afghan rebels. In 1981, accusing the remaining Soviet embassy staff of aiding Islamic fundamentalist unrest, Cairo broke diplomatic relations and expelled the Soviet ambassador. Relations were resumed in September 1984, as the Mubarak government departed from the aggressively pro-U.S. policy of the later Sadat years, while a three-year trade accord was signed by the two governments in late 1987.

Relations with most of the Arab world also changed during President Mubarak's first term, Egypt's stature among moderate neighbors being enhanced by a virtual freeze in dealings with Israel after the 1982 Lebanon invasion. Although relations with radical Arab states, particularly Libya, remained strained, Egypt's reemergence from the status of Arab pariah allowed it to act as a "silent partner" in negotiations between Jordan and the PLO that generated a 1985 peace plan (see entries on Jordan and the Palestinian Authority). However, the subsequent collapse of the plan left the Mubarak administration in an uncomfortable middle position between its "good friend" King Hussein and the PLO, whose Cairo offices were closed in May 1987 after the passage of an "anti-Egyptian" resolution by the Palestine National Council.

During an Arab League summit in Amman, Jordan, in November 1987, the prohibition against diplomatic ties with Egypt was officially lifted, although the suspension of league membership remained in effect. It was widely believed that the threat of Iranian hegemony in the Gulf was the principal factor in Cairo's rehabilitation. Egypt, which had severed relations with Iran in May 1987 upon discovery of a fundamentalist Muslim network allegedly financed by Tehran, possessed the largest and best-equipped armed force in the region. Following the Amman summit, Egypt authorized reopening of the PLO facility, instituted joint military maneuvers with Jordan, increased the number of military advisers sent to Iraq, and arranged for military cooperation with Kuwait, Saudi Arabia, and the United Arab Emirates.

By January 1989 only three Arab League countries—Libya, Lebanon, and Syria—had not renewed diplomatic relations with Cairo, and Egypt returned to full participation in the organization during its Casablanca, Morocco, summit in May. Meanwhile, a dispute that had marred relations with Israel since the latter's 1982 withdrawal from the bulk of the Sinai was resolved on February 26, when the two countries agreed to reaffirm Egyptian sovereignty over Taba, a beach resort on the northern tip of the Gulf of Aqaba (see Israel map, p. 705).

Lebanon and Syria restored diplomatic relations with Cairo in 1989, and relations with Libya also improved as President Mubarak journeyed to Libya in October to meet with Col. Muammar al-Qadhafi, the first such visit by an Egyptian president since 1972. Meanwhile, Cairo increased pressure on Jerusalem to begin negotiations with the Palestinians in the West Bank and Gaza Strip, forwarding a ten-point plan to speed the onset of elections and lobbying the United States to exercise its diplomatic influence over Israel.

Egyptian-Iraqi relations were rocked in June 1989 by Baghdad's imposition of remittance restrictions on foreign workers, leading to the repatriation of 1 million Egyptians, many of whom complained about Iraqi mistreatment. In what was clearly his boldest foreign relations move, President Mubarak spearheaded the Arab response to Iraq's incursion into Kuwait in August 1990. At an Arab League summit in Cairo on August 10 the Egyptian leader successfully argued for a declaration condemning the invasion and approving Saudi Arabia's request for non-Arab troops to help it defend its borders. Subsequent Egyptian efforts to facilitate an Iraqi withdrawal were rebuffed by Baghdad. Overall, more than 45,000 Egyptian troops were deployed to Saudi Arabia, elements of which played a conspicuous role in the liberation of Kuwait.

In the wake of Iraq's defeat in 1991, policy differences arose between Egypt and its allies. Cairo had long urged that postwar regional security be entrusted to an all-Arab force. By contrast, Gulf Cooperation Council (GCC) members indicated that they looked with favor on a continued U.S. presence in the area. Particularly irksome was a Saudi statement that the monarchy did not welcome the permanent stationing of Egyptian forces on its soil, Cairo subsequently withdrawing all its troops by the end of August. A corollary to the dispute over military policy was increased uncertainty as to the level of economic aid that Egypt could expect from its oil-rich neighbors. For their part, Western creditors quickly rewarded Cairo for its support during the Desert Shield and Desert Storm campaigns. Shortly after the defeat of Iraqi forces, the United States and Gulf Arab states forgave about $14 billion of Egypt's $50 billion external debt, and Paris Club members subsequently agreed to gradually write off another $11 billion. Globally, its prestige was enhanced by the selection of its leading diplomat, former deputy prime minister Boutros BOUTROS-GHALI, as the secretary general of the United Nations effective January 1, 1992.

Egyptian officials reportedly played an important advisory role in the secret talks that led up to the accord between Israel and the PLO in September 1993. In addition, Egypt won the backing of other North African governments for its hard-line antifundamentalist posture. Cairo's relations with Amman improved after a three-year rift caused by Jordan's pro-Iraqi stand during the Gulf crisis. In February 1995 President Mubarak hosted Jordan's King Hussein, Israeli Prime Minister Yitzhak Rabin, and PLO Chair Yasir Arafat in a summit designed to revitalize prospects for implementation of the Israel/PLO peace accord. The summit also reportedly addressed growing tension between Egypt and Israel regarding nuclear weapons. (See the International Atomic Energy Agency, under UN: Related Organizations, for details.)

By mid-1995 tension with Egypt's southern neighbor, Sudan, had intensified because of an intimation by Mubarak that Sudanese officials had played a role in the June 26 assassination attempt in Ethiopia. In June Sudan accused Egypt of provoking a clash in the disputed border region of Halaib, with Mubarak declaring his support for exiled opponents of the fundamentalist Khartoum regime. In 2004, Egypt reluctantly agreed to send military officers as observers to Sudan, but stopped short of getting involved in attempting to resolve the Sudanese civil war.

On March 13, 1996, Egypt hosted the so-called "terrorism summit" of some 27 heads of state and government in the wake of suicide bomb attacks in Israel earlier in the month that appeared to threaten the Middle East peace process. Following the election of Benjamin Netanyahu as Israel's new prime minister in May, President Mubarak became more critical of him over the next six months in the face of what he described as Netanyahu's "lack of action" in implementing the Israeli/PLO peace accord. The Egyptian president intensified his attacks on Netanyahu's policies in 1997, particularly in regard to the expansion of Jewish settlements in the West Bank. In early 1998 Mubarak strongly objected to U.S. plans to take military action against Iraq after Baghdad blocked the activities of UN weapons inspectors. Meanwhile, by that time significant improvement had been registered in relations between Egypt and Sudan, the two countries having apparently agreed to address each other's "security" concerns, i.e., Sudanese support for fundamentalist militants in Egypt and Egyptian support for antiregime activity in Sudan, particularly on the part of southern rebels. Full diplomatic relations were restored between Sudan and Egypt in December 1999, following a visit by Sudan's president, Umar Hassan Ahmad al-Bashir, to Cairo. Relations with Iran were also reported to have improved later in 1998, but in 2005 they were again strained after a security court convicted an Egyptian of plotting to assassinate the president and of spying for Iran.

President Mubarak welcomed the election of Ehud Barak as prime minister of Israel in May 1999 as a "hopeful sign" regarding a peace settlement between Israel and the Palestinians, and Egypt was a prominent mediator in negotiations through mid-2000. However, Egypt recalled its ambassador to Israel in November 2000 in response to the Israeli bombing of the Gaza Strip. Egyptian/Israeli relations cooled even further following the election of hard-liner Ariel Sharon as prime minister of Israel in February 2001. By 2004, however, after Sharon had unveiled his unilateral disengagement plan for the Gaza Strip, in consultation with Egypt and the United States, relations between Egypt and Israel began to thaw. Egypt's role in security arrangements in Gaza were vital to the process and widely seen as enhancing Egypt's role as a power broker in the region. In December 2004, Egypt and Israel conducted their first prisoner exchange, marking a shift in relations and paving the way for a December 12 pact between the two countries on exports. In February 2005, Mubarak again helped mediate between Israel and the Palestinians, adopting a high-profile diplomatic role. Mubarak's diplomatic efforts in the latter part of 2006 focused on negotiations toward a Palestinian unity government to include Hamas and Fatah, subsequently straining Egypt's relations with Israel, which refused to accept Hamas as a legitimate partner in any Palestinian government. In September, Egypt resumed diplomatic ties with Costa Rica and El Salvador after both decided to move their embassies back to Tel Aviv from Jerusalem.

In 2007 Egypt faced an increasing number of applications for visas from Iraqis, as more than 120,000 refugees, mostly Shiites, had arrived in Cairo since the beginning of the Iraq war in 2003. The government repeatedly voiced its concerns to U.S. President George W. Bush that sectarian violence could spread to Egypt, particularly if Iranians were to "infiltrate" and organize attacks in response to a threat to Iran from Israel or the United States. Egypt subsequently implemented stricter entry rules for Iraqis, citing security reasons.

In June 2007 Egypt called a summit with leaders of Israel, Jordan, and the Palestinian Authority to address ways to further isolate Hamas, including an international arrangement to secure the border with Gaza. Border issues involving Egypt's monitoring of the flow of weapons to and from the Gaza Strip flared in 2007 with accusations that Egypt's vigilance was lacking. Tensions increased when Israel sent videotapes to the U.S. government that allegedly showed Egyptian security forces helping Hamas militants smuggle arms across the border. In December the U.S. Congress voted to freeze $100 million in aid to Egypt pending a further assessment of progress against arms smuggling. Events took a dramatic turn in January 2008 when Egypt allowed the border to be breached by tens of thousands of Palestinians seeking food and other emergency supplies in the wake of Israel's blockade of Gaza (the Palestinians being dependent on Israel for water, electricity, and other essentials). The United Nations declared a humanitarian crisis following Israel's closure of all borders with Gaza in response to rocket attacks by militants. Mubarak said he would allow the Palestinians to return to Gaza as long as they were not taking weapons with them. In February President Bush made a brief (three-hour) stop in Egypt during his eight-day Middle East trip, a visit that observers said reflected Egypt's "diminished" significance in the region. Bush praised Egypt's role in maintaining security in the region without mentioning control of the border with Gaza. The Mubarak administration, for its part, stated its preference that the Palestinian Authority president, Mahmoud ABBAS, take charge of the Gaza border issue, and it urged Israel to end its blockade.

In the wake of Israel's intensive ground and bombing attacks in Gaza in response to Hamas' continuing attacks on southern Israel (see article on Israel for details), President Mubarak came under increasing criticism by Arab nations in January 2009 for the government's refusal to open its border with Gaza to allow through humanitarian aid. Egyptian officials were also criticized for their lack of diplomatic pressure on Israel to halt its bombing campaign in Gaza. Meanwhile, President Mubarak and other officials blamed Hamas for breaking the cease-fire. Egypt's foreign minister stated that Hamas had "served Israel the opportunity [to attack] on a golden platter." Meanwhile, there was reportedly a "widespread belief" of Egyptian complicity in the Gaza attacks, stemming from a visit to Cairo by Israel's foreign minister, Tzipi Livni, the day before the attacks started. Egypt also refused to allow international troops to use the Egyptian side of the Gaza border to stage troops as part of any cease-fire agreement between Israel and Hamas. Subsequently, though Egypt had been trying to help mediate a truce between Israel and Hamas, tensions heightened with Israel following remarks by the new foreign minister, Avigdor Liebeman, who rejected the U.S.-backed peace process, launched in Annapolis, Maryland, in 2007, as having "no validity." Newly elected Israeli prime minister Benjamin Netanyahu sought to mend ties with Egypt following Lieberman's remarks. Meanwhile, Egypt rejected an agreement signed by the United States and Israel aimed at preventing arms smuggling into Gaza, claiming that the accord infringed on Egypt's sovereignty. However, in February Egypt turned back an Iranian ship suspected of carrying weapons for Hamas.

In March 2009, Egyptian officials were again the focus of international attention when they welcomed Sudan's President Bashir to Cairo, by all accounts "undeterred" by the arrest warrant issued against Bashir by the International Criminal Court (ICC). (Egypt was not a signatory to the ICC agreement obliging its member states to arrest Bashir if he enters their territory.) On March 28 President Mubarak boycotted the Arab League summit, reportedly because of its differences with Qatar over the countries' stances on the conflict between Israel and Gaza.

Current issues. Under increasing pressure from prodemocracy activists, as well as from the United States, President Mubarak in February 2005 called for a constitutional amendment to allow multi-candidate elections. Unprecedented public demonstrations and calls for Mubarak to step down preceded his historic announcement. The amendment was approved in a referendum in May 2005, but the government still faced vehement criticism for the restrictive conditions it placed on potential candidates; for example, leaders of the recognized parties could run, but independent candidates must get the backing of 250 members of the assembly and local councils. Four opposition parties immediately announced a boycott of the presidential elections scheduled for September 2005. Egyptian authorities had attempted to ban referendum-day protests, but large demonstrations took place nonetheless. The government also arrested members of the opposition Muslim Brotherhood. The ongoing crackdown against Islamists and other opposition groups sparked bold, massive protests, leading to further arrests. The leftist Tomorrow, the one new party granted a permit, saw its leader Ayman NUR jailed for six weeks on charges of forging signatures on his political party application. His June 2005 trial was postponed until after presidential elections, in which he ran a distant second to Mubarak. Nur was sentenced on December 24 to five years in prison. The European Union joined Washington in condemning Nur's conviction, which led to postponement of talks on a free trade agreement with the United States in 2006.

While the 2005 presidential election was trumpeted as a move toward democratization, most observers considered the election to be a very limited step toward reform. Some 19 candidates were disqualified, the government refused to allow international monitors, turnout was extremely low, and laws severely restricting political activity remained in place. Assembly elections a few months later were marked by violence, with at least nine people allegedly killed by government security forces who reportedly blocked some polling stations in opposition strongholds. Hundreds of supporters of Muslim Brotherhood–backed candidates were arrested during the three-stage elections. While the NDP again dominated in the results, candidates allied with the Muslim Brotherhood significantly increased their representation, strengthening the group's position as the major opposition force. In what was regarded as a move to preserve the NDP's power, the government postponed local elections (scheduled for April 2006) for two years, saying the delay was necessary to give the assembly more time to adopt laws that would increase the role of local governments.

Terrorist attacks plagued Egyptian tourist areas in 2005 and 2006. After three bomb explosions in the southern Sinai resort of Dahab on April 24, 2006, killed at least 24 people, Israel closed its border with Egypt for security reasons. Within days, Egyptian authorities arrested 10 people, linking some of them to previous attacks, and in May security forces killed the leader of an obscure group alleged to be behind the Dahab bombing.

Tensions increased in 2006 following parliament's approval in May of a two-year extension to the 1981 emergency law. In a subsequent blow to political reform, the high court dismissed an appeal by Ayman Nur, and, on the same day, another court took disciplinary action against one of two judges (the second was exonerated) who lost their judicial immunity after publicly charging electoral fraud in the 2005 parliamentary elections. Thousands of riot police attempted to disperse massive demonstrations in Cairo following the court ruling, and hundreds were arrested. The protests were backed by the country's 7,000 judges, who demanded they be granted independent oversight of all aspects of elections, as provided for in constitutional amendments of 2000. The judges contended that they were restricted to monitoring polling places, not vote counting. Observers saw the judges' demands as a challenge to the NDP's ability to retain control and, ultimately, to handpick Mubarak's successor. The latter was a topic of considerable speculation, particularly after Mubarak's son, Gamal MUBARAK, gained a more prominent leadership role in the NDP and made a public address in September citing the need for Egypt to develop nuclear power, which the government quickly announced was among its top priorities.

The court cases against the judges, along with the imprisonment of two prominent political opponents (Nur and Talaat SADAT, who was sentenced to a year in prison for accusing the military of involvement in the death of his uncle, the former president), and the arrest and detainment of hundreds of protesters appeared to observers to have weakened the president's popularity, despite the country's substantial economic progress. Meanwhile, the government's increasing repression of the opposition appeared to have strengthened the Muslim Brotherhood, observers said, even as hundreds of the group's members were arrested in 2006 and 2007.

Attention in 2007 turned to controversial constitutional amendments, which were approved by 75.9 percent in a referendum on March 26, 10 days ahead of the scheduled date and only 7 days after parliament approved the president's proposed changes. Official reports recorded voter turnout of 21.7 percent, which observers attributed in part to a boycott by the Muslim Brotherhood and other opposition groups. Human rights organizations claimed turnout was as low as 5 percent and that the vote was rigged. Among the most significant constitutional changes, which went into effect immediately, were provisions granting the government the authority to ban political parties based on religion (which observers said was aimed at the Muslim Brotherhood), entrenching most of the restrictions in effect under the emergency law (including a broadening of police authority to circumvent legal processes to combat terrorism), giving the president the authority to dissolve parliament, and reducing judicial oversight of balloting. Egypt's judges rejected the results and vowed not to supervise future balloting. Opposition and human rights groups were vociferous in their criticism, saying the changes were a major setback to Egyptians' basic freedoms and were designed to consolidate the ruling party's control. Amnesty International called the amendments "the greatest erosion of human rights in 26 years."

In a significant move in 2007 on an issue that had drawn increasing international criticism for its practice throughout Africa, Egypt banned all female circumcisions following the much-publicized death of a 12-year-old girl. On another issue of global concern, Mubarak announced that Egypt would begin accepting bids in 2008 to build its first nuclear reactor, which he said was for civilian purposes. However, the president refused to agree to stricter inspection measures sought by the UN nuclear watchdog agency.

In early 2008 attention turned to the long-delayed local elections, scheduled for April 8 and seen by some as another benchmark for the administration's commitment to democracy. In the run-up to the elections, hundreds of Muslim Brotherhood members were arrested—more than 900 by March—on grounds of belonging to an illegal political group. Nonetheless, the Brotherhood chose to back independent candidates for some of the 52,000 seats on local councils, though the government reportedly blocked 90 percent of the Islamist candidates from registering. Subsequently, it was reported that dozens of candidates backed by the Brotherhood had gone underground in an attempt to avoid arrest before the balloting. The United States harshly criticized the crackdown on the opposition, and in what observers described as an overture to Cairo, whose help the U.S. sought to help resolve the Palestinian-Israeli turmoil, Secretary of State Condoleezza Rice waived the freeze on some of Washington's aid to Egypt (see Foreign relations, above). Nevertheless, a general strike by opposition groups and labor activists was staged the weekend before the elections, followed by demonstrations by thousands of supporters of the Muslim Brotherhood that turned violent when police intervened. On April 7 the Brotherhood announced that it was boycotting the elections, the candidates backed by the group having been allowed to contest only 20 seats. In balloting marked by extremely low turnout, the NDP was reported to have won 92 percent of the seats, after having run unopposed in about 90 percent of the contests. The Muslim Brotherhood called the elections a fraud since most opposition candidates were barred from running, and Brotherhood leaders were contemplating legal action. Only about 2 percent of candidates were from legal opposition groups. Despite harsh criticism from the Bush administration and human rights advocates regarding the conduct of the elections, the NDP described its victory as "resounding and honorable." On April 15, some family members of 40 detained Muslim Brotherhood members were arrested while they awaited a verdict from a military court; 25 of the 40 were subsequently sentenced to up to 10 years in prison on charges that included terrorism and money laundering. Five others, tried in absentia, received 10-year prison terms for terrorism. Brotherhood leader Muhammad Mahdi Akef, for his part, called the government "a bunch of gangsters" following the military tribunal's actions.

In April 2008 President Mubarak proposed a 30 percent pay increase for government workers, reportedly in response to the strikes protesting high food prices and layoffs. In an effort to cover the cost of the pay hikes, the assembly on May 5 approved price increases for fuel, cigarettes, and vehicle licenses. Subsequently, he government issued ration cards to an additional 17 million people and doubled the amount of rice they could receive to offset higher food prices. On May 26 President Mubarak requested a two-year extension of the state of emergency, citing the threat of terrorism. Within hours—in a session significant for its haste and lack of debate—parliament approved the request, thus continuing the state of emergency until June 1, 2010. Opposition groups and human rights organizations immediately criticized the action, claiming that the emergency law was primarily used against the political opposition. Throughout the latter part of 2008 and into early 2009, attention turned to Egypt's actions in connection with the conflict in Gaza between Israel and Hamas. President Mubarak was heavily criticized by his Arab neighbors for refusing to open the border to Gazan refugees, and for not doing more to help resolve the conflict (see Foreign Relations, above). Meanwhile, the government quashed several demonstrations in support of Gaza organized by opposition groups and the Muslim Brotherhood, arresting thousands of Brotherhood members (see Political Parties and Groups, below).

In a surprising political development, prosecutors released Ayman Nur, former leader of the leftist Tomorrow party, on February 19, 2009, after four years' imprisonment. Some observers claimed that his release was connected to Egypt's efforts to improve relations with the United States, rather than the official reason regarding Nur's health. Meanwhile, Nur rejected speculation that he would again seek public office or try to regain leadership of his party. Instead, he said he would help to rebuild the party and focus on two demands: ending emergency law and drafting a new constitution. He called for a nationwide strike if the government did not meet those demands by April 2010. Nur also verbally attacked President Mubarak for not pardoning him earlier, when 1,500 other prisoners were released, in light of his ill health. In April, Nur was allowed to seek medical treatment outside of the country.

POLITICAL PARTIES AND GROUPS

Egypt's old political parties were swept away with the destruction of the monarchy in 1953. Efforts by the Nasser regime centered on the creation of a single mass organization to support the government and its policies. Following unsuccessful experiments with two such organizations, the National Liberation Rally and the National Union, the Arab Socialist Union—ASU (*al-Ittihad al-Ishtiraki al-Arabi*) was established as the country's sole political party in December 1962.

Prior to the legislative election of October 1976 President Sadat authorized the establishment of three "groups" within the ASU—the leftist National Progressive Unionist Assembly (NPUA), the centrist Egyptian Arab Socialist Organization (EASO), and the rightist Free Socialist Organization (FSO)—which presented separate lists of assembly candidates. Following the election, Sadat indicated that it would be appropriate to refer to the groups as distinct parties, though the ASU would "stand above" the new organizations. A law adopted on June 27, 1977, authorized the establishment of additional parties under three conditions: (1) that they be sanctioned by the ASU; (2) that, except for those established in 1976, they include at least 20 members of the People's Assembly; and (3) that they not have been in existence prior to 1953.

On February 4, 1978, the ASU Central Committee modified the impact of the 1977 legislation by permitting the *Wafd*, the majority party under the monarchy, to reenter politics as the New Wafd Party (NWP). Less than four months later, however, representatives of the NWP voted unanimously to disband the party to protest the passage of a sweeping internal security law on June 1. Subsequently, President Sadat announced the formal abolition of the ASU, the conversion of its Central Committee into a Consultative Council (*Majlis al-Shura*) to meet annually on the anniversary of the 1952 revolution, and the establishment of a new centrist group that, on August 15, was named the National Democratic Party (NDP). In an April 1979 political referendum, the voters overwhelmingly approved removal of the first two conditions of the 1977 law, thus clearing the way for the formation of additional parties. In May 1980 a constitutional amendment, also approved by referendum, removed reference to the defunct ASU as the sole source of political activity, thus formally legitimizing the limited multiparty system. In July 1983 the assembly approved a requirement that parties obtain 8 percent of the vote to gain parliamentary representation. One month later, the NWP announced that it was "resuming public activity," a government attempt to force the group to reregister as a new party being overturned by the State Administrative Court the following October.

At the 1984 election only the NDP and the NWP won elective seats, the former outdistancing the latter by a near 6–1 margin. In 1987 the NDP obtained a slightly reduced majority of 77.2 percent, the remaining seats being captured by the NWP and a coalition composed of the Socialist Labor Party (SLP), the Liberal Socialist Party (LSP), and "Islamists" representing the Muslim Brotherhood (see below). Following a Supreme Court decision in May 1990 that overturned the results of the 1987 balloting, the government enacted a number of electoral changes, including reversal of the 8 percent requirement.

In 2002 the administration introduced controversial new regulations that precluded political activity on the part of any group receiving money from overseas that had not been approved by and channeled through the government. Opponents of the regime decried the measure as an attempt to throttle parties that might be funded by foreign prodemocracy organizations. In 2005, ten parties formed an alliance to promote reforms (see Other Legislative Parties, below). Still other parties are summarily banned.

Government Party:

National Democratic Party—NDP (*al-Hizb al-Watani al-Dimuqrati*). The NDP was organized by President Sadat in July 1978 as the principal government party, its name being derived from that of the historic National Party formed at the turn of the century by Mustapha Kamel. In August it was reported that 275 deputies in the People's Assembly had joined the new group, all but 11 having been members of the Egyptian Arab Socialist Party—EASP (*Hizb Misr al-Arabi al-Ishtiraki*), which, as an outgrowth of the EASO, had inherited many of the political functions earlier performed by the ASU. The EASP formally merged with the NDP in October 1978. President Mubarak, who had served as deputy chair under President Sadat, was named NDP chair at a party congress on January 26, 1982.

Two months after his pro forma reelection in October 1993, President Mubarak announced the composition of the new NDP political bureau, most leadership posts being retained by incumbents despite the president's campaign pledge to revitalize both the NDP and the national administration. In November 1998 the NDP nominated Mubarak as its candidate for the 1999 presidential election. Official NDP candidates reportedly won only 27 percent of the seats in the 2000 assembly balloting, although many successful independent candidates joined (or rejoined) the party to give it 388 out of 442 elected seats. Analysts attributed the poor performance of the official NDP candidates to public perception that the party lacked an ideological foundation and existed only to rubber-stamp the administration's agenda.

President Mubarak was reelected as chair of the NDP at the September 2002 congress, while his son, Gamal Mubarak, who has been mentioned as a possible successor to his father, was elevated to a new post as head of the NDP's policy board.

In 2005, the NDP won the two-thirds majority (ultimately reported as 320 seats) needed to amend the constitution, which will determine how Mubarak's successor will be chosen. In 2006 Gamal Mubarak was elevated to the post of assistant secretary general of the party, observers suggesting that he was being "groomed" to succeed his father, despite the elder Mubarak's comments in November indicating his interest in remaining president for as long as he lives.

The party's vice president, Mustafa Khalil, resigned in November 2007 due to health reasons. (Khalil, a former prime minister, died on June 7, 2008, at age 88.) At the party congress that same month, Husni Mubarak was reappointed as party chair despite intensified speculation that Gamal Mubarak would again be promoted. Though the younger Mubarak had received much publicity for his earlier announcement that Egypt would pursue a large-scale nuclear power project—a move some observers thought was designed to assure his ascendancy—his father assumed control over that issue in 2007 (see Current issues, above). However, the party congress resulted in the by-laws being amended to make it easier for Gamal Mubarak to legally succeed his father as Egypt's president. A "supreme body" of 45 leading party members was given the authority to choose the party's next presidential candidate, with each member of the group having the right to run for president after having served on the panel for one year. Among the members was the president's son.

In early 2009 Gamal Mubarak organized two large rallies in support of his father's policies regarding the conflict in Gaza, and made public pronouncements defending him and denouncing "Islamist and leftist forces" who, he claimed, were using the war to stir Egyptians against their government. His pronouncements were described as references to the Muslim Brotherhood, the *Kifaya* movement, and the NADP in particular. Meanwhile, the NWP and NPUP were said to have supported the NDP's position.

Leaders: Muhammad Husni MUBARAK (President of the Republic and Chair of the Party), Zakaria AZMI, Gamal MUBARAK (Assistant Secretary General and Chair of the Policies Committee), Muhammad Safwat al-SHARIF (Secretary General).

Other Legislative Parties:

Prior to the assembly elections of 2005, opposition leaders announced on October 8 they had formed a coalition of ten parties and movements seeking greater representation in the legislative body. Independent candidates allied themselves with movements or groups not officially recognized by the government. The **National Front for Political and Constitutional Change,** led by former prime minister Sidqi, was an apparent partial successor to the **Consensus of National Forces for Reform** (*Tawafuq al-Qiwa al-Wataniyah lil-Islah*), a group of eight opposition parties formed in 2004. Notably excluded from the ten-member 2005 coalition was the Tomorrow Party (*al-Ghad*), reportedly because of dissension within that party. Among those included were **Arab Dignity** (*Karama al-Araybia*), established by disenchanted Nasserists and led by Hamdin SABAHI; **Enough** (*Kifaya*), also referenced as the **Egyptian Movement for Change**, which includes leftists, liberals, and Islamists, co-founded in 2004 by George ISHAQ (arrested in 2009 for allegedly inciting unrest at an opposition rally) and Amin ESKANDAR; the **Labor Party**; the **Center** (*Hizb al-Wasat*), an offshoot of the Muslim Brotherhood, led by Abdul-Ela MADI; the **Popular Campaign for Change**; and three parties already represented in the assembly (the New Wafd Party, the Nasserist Arab Democratic Party, and the National Progressive Unionist Party).

In November 2008 a group referenced as the **Coalition of Democratic Parties** was reported to include the NWP, NPUP, NADP, and Democratic Front. The group denounced what it said were unwarranted attacks on opposition parties by the NDP.

New Wafd Party—NWP (*Hizb al-Wafd al-Gadid*). Formed in February 1978 as a revival of the most powerful party in Egypt prior to 1952, the NWP formally disbanded the following June but reformed in August. In 1980 a "new generation of *Wafd* activists" instigated demonstrations in several cities, prompting the detention of its leader, Fuad SERAGEDDIN, until November 1981. In alliance with a number of Islamic groups, most importantly the proscribed Muslim Brotherhood (below), the NWP won 15 percent of the vote in May 1984, thus becoming the only opposition party with parliamentary representation. In 1987 the NWP won 35 seats (23 less than in 1984), the Brotherhood having entered into a de facto coalition with the SLP and the LSP (below). The NWP boycotted the *Shura* poll in 1989, complaining that electoral procedures remained exclusionary; it also boycotted the 1990 assembly elections, although party members running as independents retained at least 14 seats.

Following the 1995 national balloting, NWP leaders charged that electoral fraud had been the "worst in history." The NWP also boycotted the April 1997 local elections. However, although the NWP had urged a boycott of the 1993 presidential poll, it urged a "yes" vote for President Mubarak in 1999. Serageddin died in August 2000 and was succeeded as party leader by Numan Gomaa, who was a distant third in 2005 presidential balloting. The party won 6 seats in the 2005 assembly elections. It agreed "in principle" with the proposed constitutional amendments but boycotted the Consultative Council elections in 2007.

Following internal strife in early 2006, resulting in the naming of Mahmud Abazah as chair, Gomaa refused to give up control, and in April he was arrested after a highly publicized incident at party headquarters between rival factions that resulted in the death of one member. The assembly's Political Parties Committee subsequently ruled that Mustapha al TAWIL was the legitimate leader of the party, but in May a court determined that Tawil's appointment was illegal. The leadership rift appeared to have been settled in February 2007 after a court overturned the party's ouster of Gomaa as chair. However, despite the court ruling, Abazah continued to be referenced as the party's leader. Gomaa, for his part, reportedly "stayed at home" and made no appearances at party headquarters.

In October 2007 it was reported that Abazah was forming a coalition to push for political and constitutional reforms, including the drafting of a new proposed constitution. The grouping was to include the NPUP, the NADP, and the newly formed Democratic Front Party (below), and was reported to specifically exclude the Muslim Brotherhood. Later that month, Abaza and two journalists affiliated with the party's newspaper (see Communications, below) were sentenced to a month in jail on libel charges; they remained free pending appeals.

In 2008 the president of the assembly rejected a request from Gomaa supporters to remove Abazah as head of the party's parliamentary delegation

Leaders: Mahmud ABAZAH (Chair), Fouad BADRAWY (Vice Chair), Numan GOMAA (2005 presidential candidate), Muhammad SARHAN, Samed EBEID (Assistant Secretary General), Munir Fakhri Abd al-NUR (Secretary General).

Liberal Socialist Party—LSP (*Hizb al-Ahrar al-Ishtiraki*). The Liberal Socialist Party, which was formed in 1976 from the right wing of the ASU, focuses on securing a greater role for private enterprise within the Egyptian economy while protecting the rights of workers and farmers. The party's assembly representation fell from 12 to 3 seats in June 1979 and was eliminated entirely at the 1984 balloting, on the basis of a vote share of less than 1 percent. It obtained 3 elective seats in 1987 as a member of a Socialist Labor Party–led coalition. It subsequently discontinued its alliance with the SLP and Muslim Brotherhood. It boycotted the November 1990 poll, although one of its members reportedly won a seat as an independent. The party won 1 seat in the 2000 and 2005 assembly elections and supported Mubarak in the 2005 presidential election.

Leader: Hilmi SALIM.

National Progressive Unionist Party—NPUP (*Hizb al-Tajammu al-Watani al-Taqaddumi al-Wahdawi*). Although it received formal endorsement as the party of the left in 1976, the NPUP temporarily ceased activity in 1978 following the enactment of restrictive internal security legislation. It contested the June 1979 assembly election on a platform that, alone among those of the four sanctioned parties, opposed the Egyptian-Israeli peace treaty, and it failed to retain its two parliamentary seats. In both 1979 and 1984 the party leadership charged the government with fraud and harassment, although on the latter occasion, President Mubarak included a NPUP member among his assembly nominees. In November 1990 the NPUP resisted opposition appeals for an electoral boycott and captured 6 assembly seats; meanwhile, the party led opposition criticism against U.S. military involvement in the Gulf. The NPUP urged a no vote against Mubarak in the 1993 presidential referendum and called for a boycott of the 1999 poll. The party won 1 seat in the 2005 assembly elections.

Leaders: Rifaat al-SAID (Chair), Hussein Abdul RAZEQ (Deputy Chair), Abu al-Izz al-HARIRI, Muhammad Abd al-Aziz SHABAN.

Tomorrow Party (*al-Ghad*). Officially recognized by the government in October 2004, this leftist party became only the third new party allowed since 1977. Tomorrow seeks constitutional reform to reduce the power of the presidency and an end to the country's emergency law. Espousing a commitment to social justice, the party is made up largely of dissidents from the NWP. Former leader Ayman Nur, jailed for six weeks in 2005 (see Current issues, above), came in a distant second to Mubarak in the September 2005 presidential election. A rift over leadership occurred after the election between Nur's supporters and those led by Musa Mustafa Musa. His splinter group elected him the new party leader on October 1, 2005, though Nur insisted he was still party president. Nur was sentenced to five years in prison in December 2005 following his conviction on charges that he forged documents used to register his party. On December 30, however, the party's general assembly elected Naji al-Ghatrifi to be its new leader, named Nur its honorary leader, and sacked four dissident members. The party won 1 seat in the 2005 assembly elections. Nur remained in prison in 2006 after his appeal was rejected.

In March 2007 Ihab El Kholi was narrowly elected party chair, but in July a court ruling reinstated Musa to the post. Meanwhile, another court rejected an appeal for Nur's release due to health concerns. The rift in the party intensified, with reports of two separate *Al Ghad* parties, one loyal to Musa and the other led by Nur's wife, Gamila ISMAIL. In November, Ismail resigned as deputy chair following claims by Musa that she and El Kholi held their posts illegally. In February 2008 it was reported that Musa was allegedly behind the seizure of Nur's assets, including his house and his wife's law office, and Nur's party offices were turned over to Musa. In November the divisiveness reached its peak when the party's headquarters were set on fire while Ismail and other dissidents were inside electing their own chair (Wael NAWWARA). Seven people were injured and several others were arrested. Subsequently, Musa lodged a complaint over illegal use of the headquarters and expelled Ismail, El Kholi, and other dissidents from the party.

In what was widely regarded as a surprise move by authorities, Nur was released from prison on February 19, 2009, and declared he would not try to return as leader of the party. Instead, he pledged to work within the party to rebuild it and issued two demands for the government to meet by 2010, or else face a general strike in the country. (See Current issues, above.)

Leaders: Musa Mustafa MUSA (Chair), Naji al-GHATRIFI, Ragab Helal HEMEIDA (Secretary General).

Other Parties that Participated in Recent Elections:

Nasserist Arab Democratic Party (NADP). Also referenced simply as the Nasserist Party, the NADP, formed in 1992, won one seat in the 1995 assembly balloting, three in the 2000 poll, and none in the 2005 elections. Its platform called for the government to retain a dominant role in directing the economy and to increase the provision of social services. In 2007 the party boycotted the referendum on proposed constitutional amendments and the elections for the Consultative Council.

Rifts widened in the party in 2007 among the "old guard" who backed the 80-year-old Daoud's leadership, supporters of the party's secretary general, Ahmed Hassan (blamed by many for the party's downfall), and a reformist wing headed by Sameh ASHOUR, who had left the party in 2002. Some of the dissidents joined the Arab Dignity party.

Leaders: Diaeddin DAOUD (Chair), Ahmed HASSAN (Secretary General).

National Party (*Hizb al-Umma*). A small Muslim organization, the National Party has ties to the supporters of Dr. Sadiq al-MAHDI, former prime minister of Sudan. It participated unsuccessfully in the 2000 assembly balloting on a platform that called for the strengthening of the "democratic process."

Leader: Ahmad al-SABAHI Awadallah (Chair and 2005 presidential candidate).

Green Party (*Hizb al-Khudr*). The Green Party, recognized by the Political Parties Tribunal in April 1990, was reported to have emerged in response to a 1986 newspaper column by (then) Vice President Abdel Salam DAOUD that criticized his country's lack of interest in environmental issues. The formation claimed 3,000 members and, while professing no interest in gaining political power, participated unsuccessfully in the 1990 legislative campaign. The party supported President Mubarak in the 2005 presidential campaign.

Leader: Abdul Moneim al-AASAR (Chair).

Other parties that participated in the 2005 elections were the **Democratic Unionist Party** (*Hizb al-Itahadi Democrati*), formerly led by Ibrahim TURK, the party's presidential candidate, who was killed in an automobile accident in 2006; the **Egyptian Arab Socialist Party**, led by Wahid al-UQSURI (presidential candidate who was disqualified a week before the election); the **Generation Party** (*al-Gayl*), founded in 2002 and led by Naji al-SHAHABI; the **National Conciliation Party**, led by Al-Sayyid Rifaat al-AGRUDI (presidential candidate); **Solidarity** (*al-Takaful*), a socialist grouping led by Usama Mohammad SHALTOUT (presidential candidate); the **Egypt 2000 Party** (*Misr*), led by Fawsi Khalil Mohammad GHAZAL (presidential candidate); and the **Social Constitutional Party**, led by Mamduh Mohammad QINAWI (presidential candidate).

Other Parties and Groups:

Muslim Brotherhood (*al-Ikhwan al-Muslimin*). Established in 1928 to promote creation of a pan-Arab Islamic state, the Brotherhood was declared an illegal organization in 1954 when the government accused its leaders, many of whom were executed or imprisoned, of plotting a coup attempt. However, for many years the Mubarak government tolerated some activity on the part of the Brotherhood since it claimed to eschew violence, as a means of undercutting the militant fundamentalist movement. With much of its support coming from the northern middle class, the Brotherhood retains the largest following and greatest financial resources among Egypt's Islamic organizations despite the emergence of more radical groups. It dominates many Egyptian professional associations, collaterally providing a wide range of charitable services in sharp contrast to inefficient government programs.

The Brotherhood secured indirect assembly representation in 1984 and 1987. Although the Brotherhood boycotted the 1990 assembly balloting, joint SLP/Brotherhood candidates contested a number of seats in November 1992 municipal elections. Many Brotherhood adherents were removed from local and national appointive positions in 1992–1993 as a side effect of the government's antifundamentalist campaign. Friction with the government intensified further in early 1995 when a group of Brotherhood members were charged with having links to the militant Islamic Group (below). The government arrested more than 50 members of the group in July on charges of belonging to an illegal organization. Sentences of up to five years in prison were handed down against most of the defendants in early November, essentially precluding effective Brotherhood participation in the legislative balloting later that month. (It was subsequently reported that only one successful assembly candidate could be identified as a Brotherhood adherent.) The Brotherhood urged a boycott of the April 1997 local elections, claiming that many of its supporters and preferred candidates had been subjected to government "intimidation."

In January 1996 a number of former Brotherhood members reportedly launched a **Center Party** (*Hizb al-Wasat*) along with representatives of the Coptic community in an avowed effort to "heal the breaches" within the Egyptian populace. However, the government denied the party's request for recognition and arrested some 13 of its founders with purported Brotherhood ties. In August, seven of the defendants were convicted of antigovernment activity by a military court and sentenced to three years in prison. *Al-Wasat* was again denied legal status in May 1998, the government describing it as insufficiently different from other parties to warrant recognition. (See Other Legislative Parties, above.)

A number of the officially independent candidates in the 2000 assembly balloting were clearly identifiable as belonging to the Brotherhood, and 17 of them were elected, permitting the return of the Brotherhood to the assembly after a ten-year absence. Though Brotherhood leaders subsequently again denied any connection to militant groups, a number of Brotherhood members were arrested in the government crackdown on Islamists in late 2001 and early 2002.

The death of 83-year-old leader Mamoun al-HODAIBI on January 9, 2004, was seen as an opportunity to attract the younger generation, but on January 14 the party selected an "old guard" successor: Muhammad Mahdi Akef, 74. He maintained that the Brotherhood would not change its approach. Akef had been convicted in 1954 of the attempted assassination of President Nasser and served 20 years in prison.

While Akef called for dialogue with the government, in May 2004 security forces arrested 54 members of the Brotherhood and for the first time targeted the organization's funding sources, closing various businesses and the group's Web site. In March 2005, some 84 members were arrested in police raids in the midst of massive demonstrations, said to be the largest in Cairo's history. The Brotherhood ran 120 candidates as independents in the November–December 2005 assembly elections, securing 88 seats in balloting marked by violence, including the death of one Brotherhood supporter. It was widely reported that government security forces blocked some polls and detained scores of group members. Brotherhood leaders said they would use the gains made in representation to push for the abolition of laws that restrict political activity. Arrests of Brotherhood members continued throughout 2006, and the government banned the group's leaders from traveling outside the country and its members from seeking office in trade union and student elections. About 140 student members, as well as some Brotherhood leaders, were arrested in December after a campus protest.

The crackdown on Brotherhood members continued into 2007 and intensified in 2008 in the run-up to the April municipal elections (see Current issues, above), with some 900 reportedly having been arrested by March for belonging to an illegal political organization. More than 1,000 members were arrested in 2009 during pro-Gaza demonstrations in Cairo. Members also took part in a large rally referenced as "The Day of Anger in Egypt" on April 6, 2009, demanding an increased minimum wage and the election of a committee to draft a new constitution. More than 100 members of parliament, most of them Brotherhood members, were arrested at the rally.

Leaders: Muhammad Mahdi AKEF, Mohamed HABIB (Deputy Chair), Mohamed HILAL, Essam el-ERIAN, Mohamed MORSI, Mohamed Khairar al-SHATIR, Mahmoud EZZAT (Secretary General).

The **Young Egypt Party** (*Misr al-Fathah*), founded in 1989 and led by Abdul Hakim Abdul Majid KHALIL and the **Social Justice Party**, formed in 1993 and led by Mohammad Abdul AALA, were suspended in the early 2000s. (The latter was subsequently reinstated.) The **Democratic Peace Party**, led by Ahmed Mohammad Bayoumi al-FADALI, and the Egypt Youth Party, led by Ahmed Abdul HADI, were approved in 2005. Two parties, the **Conservative Party**, led by Mustafa Abd al-AZIZ, and the **Free Public Party**, were approved in 2006. Another new party was approved in 2007: the **Democratic Front Party**, co-founded by Yahya al-GAMAL, a former government minister, and Osama el-Ghazali HARB (party chair), a former member of the NDP. Observers said the establishment of the Democratic Front was approved in an apparent effort to stem criticism that the administration was not moving forward with democratic reforms, the issue that reportedly prompted Harb's resignation from the NDP.

In 2008 a group referenced as the **April 6 Youth Movement** was formed through the online social networking site Facebook by Israa RASHID and Ahmad MAHER in support of industrial workers who were planning to strike on April 6. The founders, who said their group was not a political party, were arrested in May in an apparent attempt to shut down the movement, and Maher was arrested again in July for alleged "incitement against the regime." In 2008 and 2009 the group participated in pro-Gaza demonstrations.

Illegal Groups:

Holy War (*al-Jihad*). A secret organization of militant Muslims who had reportedly split from the Muslim Brotherhood in the second half of the 1970s because of the latter's objection to the use of violence, *al-Jihad* was blamed for attacks against Copts in 1979 and the assassination of President Sadat in 1981. In the first half of the 1980s it appeared to be linked to the Islamic Group (below), but the two organizations emerged with more distinct identities during the mid-1980s. Although some observers described *al-Jihad* as continuing to seek recruits, particularly in the military, its influence appeared to have diminished in the late 1980s as the result of government infiltration of its ranks and growing support for the Islamic Group. However, security officials charged that a revival of the group was attempted in the first half of the 1990s in conjunction with the increasingly violent fundamentalist/government conflict. A number of reported *al-Jihad* supporters were imprisoned in mid-1993 on charges of plotting the overthrow of the government, while, according to authorities, about 30 members were arrested in an April 1994 security sweep. Meanwhile, members of an apparent splinter, variously referenced as New *Jihad* or the Vanguards of Conquest (*Talai al-Fath*), were subsequently given death sentences for complicity in assassination plots against top government officials. Some reports linked that activity to Ayman al-ZAWAHIRI, a former Cairo surgeon who had been imprisoned (and reportedly subjected to extreme torture) for three years following the assassination of President Sadat. Zawahiri was also reportedly linked to the bombing of the Egyptian embassy in Pakistan in 1995.

In 1998, in the wake of the Luxor attack of 1997, Zawahiri and his brother, Mohammad al-ZAWAHIRI, were described as attempting to "reorganize" *al-Jihad* from Afghanistan, where they had reportedly established ties with the al-Qaida network of Osama bin Laden. (Ayman al-Zawahiri had not been seen in Egypt since 1986.) Among other things, Ayman al-Zawahiri endorsed bin Laden's 1998 call for attacks on "Jews and Crusaders" (the latter a reference to Americans and their allies). At that point it appeared that a portion of *al-Jihad*, having been effectively suppressed in Egypt, had shifted away from a goal of overthrowing the Egyptian government to a global anti-Western campaign in concert with al-Qaida (for information on al-Qaida, see article on Afghanistan). However, some members of *al-Jihad* reportedly objected to that new focus and split from Ayman al-Zawahiri.

A number of alleged *al-Jihad* adherents received long prison terms in early 1999, while nine were sentenced to death in absentia, including Ayman al-Zawahiri and Yasser al-SIRRI, a London-based leader. Al-Zawahiri was also indicted in absentia in 1999 in the United States for his alleged role in the planning of the bombings of the U.S. embassies in Kenya and Pakistan in 1998. Following the attacks on the United States in September 2001 that were quickly attributed to al-Qaida, al-Zawahiri, noted for his organizational skills, was described as the number two leader, after bin Laden, in that network. Some reports linked al-Zawahiri to the July 2005 bombings in Sharm El-Sheikh, Egypt, that killed at least 64 people, and in 2006 al-Zawahiri claimed that the Islamic Group (below) had joined *al-Jihad*, which he said was linked to al-Qaida. As of mid-2008, he continued to elude U.S. authorities.

In May 2007 Egypt released 135 prisoners, all said to be members of *al-Jihad*, after they reportedly signed statements renouncing violence. It was also reported at the same time that a guerrilla leader of *al-Jihad*, Abdul-Aziz al-SHERIF, described as a longtime associate of al-Zawahiri, had also prepared a renunciation of extremism from his prison cell. Al-Sherif was also affiliated with the Islamic Group, and known as the man who "crafted al-Qaida's guide to jihad." Such prison dissensions were said to have caused rifts within al-Qaida. (See Islamic Liberation Party, below.)

Islamic Group (*Gamaat i-Islami*). The Islamic Group surfaced in the late 1970s as the student wing of the Muslim Brotherhood, subsequently breaking from that organization and aligning (until the mid-1980s) with *al-Jihad* in seeking overthrow of the government. Having gained adherents among the poor in the Cairo slums and the villages in southern Egypt, it served as a loosely knit, but highly militant, umbrella organization for as many as three dozen smaller organizations. The government accused the group of spearheading attacks on security forces, government officials, and tourists beginning in 1992, and hanged a number of its members who had been convicted of terrorist activity.

Egyptian authorities in the mid-1990s asked the United States to extradite Sheikh Omar ABDEL RAHMAN, the blind theologian who is reputed to be the spiritual leader of the Islamic Group and had been in self-imposed exile in the New York City area since 1990. In April 1994 Sheikh Abdel Rahman was sentenced in absentia by an Egyptian security court to seven years in prison for inciting his followers to violence in 1989. In addition, 25 codefendants received jail terms of various lengths. In January 1996 Sheikh Abdel Rahman was sentenced to life in prison in the United States following his conviction on charges of conspiring to commit a series of bombings in the New York City area, including as mastermind of the 1993 World Trade Center bombing. Eight codefendants were given prison terms of 25 years to life. Meanwhile, Safwat Abd al-Ghani, viewed as the political leader of the Group, was confined to prison in Egypt on a charge of illegal weapons possession. Ghani and other Islamic Group defendants had initially been charged with murder in the 1990 assassination of

Assembly President Rifat al-Mahgoub; however, the charges were dismissed in 1993 following a court ruling that confessions had been extracted from them by torture.

Talaat Yassin HAMMAN, described by Egyptian authorities as the "military commander" of the Islamic Group, was killed by security forces in April 1994. His "intended successor," Ahmad Hassan Abd al-GALIL, also died in a shoot-out with police the following November. It was subsequently reported that Group military activities were being conducted under the leadership of Mustapha HAMZA and Rifai TAHA, apparently based in Afghanistan.

Two members of the group were executed in February 1995 after being convicted of a bombing in which a German tourist was killed, while two others were executed in late March for the attempted killing of Nobel laureate Naguib MAHFOUZ in October 1994. The Egyptian government also accused the Group (and Hamza in particular) of being behind a June 1995 attempt on the life of President Mubarak in Ethiopia.

In mid-1996 reports surfaced that a faction of the Islamic Group had signaled an interest in negotiations with the government. However, that possibility was apparently rejected by the Mubarak administration. Factionalization within the group was also apparent in 1997, particularly in regard to a "cease-fire" ordered by its imprisoned leaders at midyear. Although the militants responsible for the attack at Luxor in November appeared linked to the group, long-standing group leaders disavowed responsibility, suggesting they were no longer in control of at least some "rogue" guerrilla cells. Subsequently, spokesmen for the group emphasized that it had reached "political maturity" and had renounced violence in favor of attempting to establish an Islamic state in Egypt through the political process. Sheikh Abdel Rahman appeared to endorse that shift in late 1998 when he called on his followers to pursue "peaceful means," and the Islamic Group announced in March 1999 that a unilateral cease-fire was in effect. That cease-fire remained in effect through mid-2005. Islamic Group members still committed to violence reportedly subsequently joined the al-Qaida network of Osama bin Laden. In April 2006, it was reported that Egyptian authorities had released 950 members of the organization, including its founder, Najeh Ibrahim, though officials denied having released that number and said those who were released posed no risk to national security. In July 2007 some 130 detained members of the group were reported to have been released by the government after they signed pledges of nonviolence.

Leaders: Najeh IBRAHIM, Safwat Abd al-GHANI, Salah HASHEM, Talaat Fuad QASIM (Spokesman in Europe).

Islamic Liberation Party (*Hizb al-Tahrir al-Islami*). This radical political movement wants to create an Islamic society in Egypt and is on the United States' list of foreign terrorist organizations.

In September 2002 some 51 defendants were given jail sentences in connection with the alleged activity of a clandestine organization known as *al-Waad* (The Pledge). First arrested on charges of belonging to an illegal organization, the defendants were also subsequently accused of planning violent acts in pursuit of the establishment of an Islamic state in Egypt. In early 2005 an Egyptian court upheld a five-year sentence for Mohammed Abdel Fattah, convicted along with 24 others the previous year, but Fattah managed to escape. He and the others were accused of trying to reorganize the party, which has been banned since 1974.

In 2006 a key member of the group, a Briton identified as Majid NAWAZ, was released from Egyptian prison, where he had spent four years on charges of promoting the group's ideology. A year after his release he was reported to have renounced his belief in an Islamic caliphate and to have adopted a more "centrist" position upon his return to England.

Also subject to government crackdowns have been the Islamic fundamentalist **Survivors from Hell** (*al-Najoun Min al-Nar*), charged in 1988 with the attempted murder of two anti-Muslim former government ministers, and **Denouncement and Holy Flight** (*Takfir wa al-Hijra*). (Some 245 members of the latter were reportedly arrested in April 1996.) An obscure Islamic group, **Islamic Pride Brigades of the Land of the Nile**, claimed responsibility for a bombing in the heart of Cairo in April 2005. Nasser el-MALLAHI, the leader of an obscure party operating in the Sinai area, **Monotheism and Struggle** (*Tawhid wal-Jihad*), was killed by security forces in 2006 in connection with the bombings at Dahab. The group was reportedly founded by Khaled MOSSAD, who was killed by Egyptian forces in 2005.

Clandestine left-wing formations against which the government has moved energetically in the past included, most prominently, the **Egyptian Communist Party** (*al-Hizb al-Shuyui al-Misri*). Founded in 1921, the party subsequently experienced numerous cleavages that yielded, among others, the **Egyptian Communist Labor Party** and the Maoist **Revolutionary Current.** In 1990 another splinter, the **People's Socialist Party**, was launched under the leadership of veteran Communist Michel KAMEL, who later died in exile in France.

Two Islamist groupings—the **Reform** (*Islah*) **Party**, formed in 1997 under the leadership of Gamal SULTAN; and the **Islamic Law** (*Sharia*) **Party**—sought permission to participate in the 2000 assembly elections, but their applications were emphatically rejected by the government.

LEGISLATURE

The **People's Assembly** (*Majlis al-Shaab*) is a unicameral legislature elected in two-round balloting for a five-year term. As sanctioned by a popular referendum, President Sadat dissolved the existing assembly (which had two years remaining in its term) on April 21, 1979, and announced expansion of the body from 350 to 392 members, in part to accommodate representatives from the Sinai. Prior to the election of May 27, 1984, the assembly was further expanded to 458 members, including 10 appointed by the president.

On May 19, 1990, the Supreme Constitutional Court voided the results of an assembly poll of April 6, 1987, because of improper restrictions on opposition and independent candidates, and an October 11 referendum approved formal dissolution of the body. A new election, boycotted by most of the leading opposition formations, was held November 29 and December 6, 1990, the assembly having been reduced to 454 members, including the 10 presidential appointees.

Elections to the current assembly were held in November–December 2005. First-round balloting was conducted for three groups of districts on three days (November 9 and 20 and December 1); second-round balloting was held six days after each first round. The government reported that some 5,000 candidates competed for 444 seats. The results for 12 seats were annulled. The government reported the seat distribution for the remaining 432 seats as follows: the National Democratic Party, 265; the New Wafd Party, 6; the National Progressive Unionist Party, 1; the Liberal Socialist Party, 1; the Tomorrow Party, 1; independents 157; and vacant, 1. However, it was widely agreed that 88 of the independent candidates were clearly identified as allied with the Muslim Brotherhood, while many of the remaining independents were considered allied with the NDP. (Most news reports credited the NDP with having secured 320 seats.) Ten parties and groups fielded candidates under a coalition referenced as the National Front for Change.

The government subsequently reported that the National Democratic Party and affiliated independents held a total of 320 seats.

President: Dr. Ahmad Fathi SURUR.

CABINET

[as of October 1, 2009]

Prime Minister	Ahmed Mahmoud Muhammad Nazif
Ministers	
Agriculture	Amin Ahmed Muhammad Othman Abaza
Civil Aviation	Lt. Gen. Ahmad Shafiq
Communications and Information Technology	Tariq Muhammad Kamal
Culture	Faruq Abd al-Aziz Husni
Defense and Military Production	Fld. Mar. Muhammad Hussein Tantawi Sulayman
Economic Development	Othman Muhammad Othman
Education	Youssri Saber Husayn al-Gamal
Electricity and Energy	Hassan Ahmed Younes
Finance	Yussef Boutros-Ghali
Foreign Affairs	Ahmed Ali Abu al-Ghayt
Foreign Trade and Industry	Rashid Muhammad Rashid

Health	Hatem Moustafa Moustafa al-Gabaly
Higher Education	Hani Mafouz Helal
Housing, Utilities, and Urban Communities	Ahmed al-Maghrabi
Information	Anas Ahmed al-Fiqy
Interior	Gen. Habib al-Adli
International Cooperation	Fayza Abu-al-Naga [f]
Investment	Mahmoud Muhiy al-Din
Irrigation and Water Resources	Muhammad Nasreddin Allam
Justice	Mamduh Muri
Local Development	Muhammad Abd al-Salam Mahgoub
Manpower and Immigration	Aisha Abdel Hady Abdel Ghany [f]
Petroleum	Amin Sameh Samir Fahmi
Religious Trusts	Mahmoud Hamdi Zakzuk
Social Solidarity	Ali Moselhi
Tourism	Muhammad Zuhayr Muhammad Wahid Garana
Transport	Muhammad Yunis Mansur Lufti Mansur

Ministers of State

Administrative Development	Ahmed Mahmoud Darwish
Environmental Affairs	Majid George Ghattas
Family and Population	Moshira Mahmoud Khattab [f]
Legal Affairs and Parliamentary Councils	Mufid Muhammad Mahmud Shihab
Military Production	Sayed Abdou Moustafa Meshal
Scientific Research	Hani Mafouz Helal

[f] = female

COMMUNICATIONS

The Supreme Press Council, established under a constitutional amendment in May 1980, oversees newspaper and magazine activity while government boards also direct the state information service, radio, and television. The government retains 51 percent ownership (exercised through the *Shura*) of many major newspapers and consequently exercises substantial editorial control. Although the development of an active and often highly critical opposition press was permitted in the 1980s, significant censorship has been imposed in recent years in conjunction with the conflict between the government and Islamic fundamentalist militants. A new press law was adopted in May 1995 providing for prison sentences and heavy fines for, among other things, "insulting" public officials or state institutions. However, in June 1996 some of the harshest elements of the new code were rescinded after the government was strongly criticized by domestic and international journalists for attempting to "muzzle" the press.

In February 2005, the president announced an end to imprisonment for various publication offenses, yet three months later, three journalists from an independent daily were found guilty of libeling the housing minister and sentenced to a year in jail. In July 2005 the government reshuffled the leadership of the press, appointing new heads to all the major government dailies. In 2006 journalists protested a new law, approved by parliament in July, that allowed the jailing of journalists who investigate allegations of corruption or publish articles critical of the government or of foreign heads of state. In July, the editor of an independent weekly was convicted of libel and sentenced to a year in prison. Later in the year, several Internet columnists critical of the government were arrested. Twelve journalists, including the editor of the New Wafd Party's newspaper, were prosecuted in 2007 on allegations of harming the country's interests, defamation, and breaching national security. An Internet blogger was sentenced to four years in prison for criticizing Islam and the president, and the Web site of another blogger was shut down by the government. Meanwhile, the U.S.-based Committee to Protect Journalists cited "a steady erosion of press freedoms" in Egypt over the past five years.

In February 2009 five journalists were fined $1,800 each for allegedly defying a gag order during the murder trial of a prominent Egyptian businessman, described as a "stalwart" of the governing National Democratic Party—NDP (*al-Hizb al-Watani al-Dimuqrati*). That same month an appeals court overturned jail terms imposed on four journalists in 2007 for "insulting senior members" of the NDP. The guilty verdicts were upheld, but the sentences were reduced from one year in jail to a fine of $3,600 each.

Press. The following are Cairo dailies published in Arabic, unless otherwise noted: *al-Ahram* (1,000,000 daily, 1,200,000 Friday), semi-official with *al-Ahram al-Massai* as an evening daily; *al-Akhbar* (800,000), Saturday edition published as *Akhbar al-Yawm* (1,100,000); *al-Jumhuriyah* (650,000), semi-official; *al-Misaa; Le Journal d'Egypte* (72,000), in French; *Egyptian Gazette* (36,000), in English; *Le Progrès Egyptien* (22,000), in French; *al-Hayat*. Among other newspapers are *al-Dustour*, independent opposition weekly; the independent *Sawt al-Umma*; *al-Usbu*, independent "nationalist" weekly; and *al-Masr al-Yawm*, and the weekly *Karama*. The party organs include the Socialist Labor Party's bi-weekly *al-Shaab* (50,000), which was closed in April 2005; the Socialist Liberal weekly *al-Ahrar*; the National Progressive Unionist weekly *al-Ahali*; the New Wafd's daily *Anwar* al-Hawari; the NDP's weekly *Shabab Beladi*; the Nasserist Arab Democratic Party's al-Arabi; the Tomorrow Party's al-Ghad; the National Party's weekly al-Umma; and the Green Party's weekly al-Khudr.

News agencies. The domestic agency is the Middle East News Agency—MENA (Wakalat al-Anba al-Sharq al-Awsat). In addition, numerous foreign bureaus maintain offices in Cairo.

Broadcasting and computing. The Egyptian Radio and Television Union (ERTU) operates numerous radio stations broadcasting in Arabic and other languages, and some three dozen television stations transmitting in two programs. Commercial radio service is offered by Middle East Radio (*Idhaat al-Sharq al-Awsat*). The satellite television station, Al Jazeera, also operates in Egypt.

The first Egyptian communications satellite was launched by the European Space Agency in 1998; some 80 channels were expected to be broadcast regionally by the satellite, known as "Nilesat," under the control of the ERTU.

In 2007 the *Al-Ghad* party launched its own Web-based radio station. As of 2008 there were 166.5 Internet users per 1,000 inhabitants.

INTERGOVERNMENTAL REPRESENTATION

Ambassador to the U.S.: Sameh SHOUKRY.

U.S. Ambassador to Egypt: Margaret SCOBEY.

Permanent Representative to the UN: Maged Abdelfattah ABDEL-AZIZ.

IGO Memberships (Non-UN): AfDB, AFESD, AMF, AU, BADEA, CAEU, Comesa, IDB, Interpol, IOM, LAS, NAM, OAPEC, OIC, OIF, PCA, WCO, WTO.

EL SALVADOR

Republic of El Salvador
República de El Salvador

Political Status: Part of the Captaincy General of Guatemala that declared independence from Spain in September 1821; member of the United Provinces of Central America that was launched in 1823; status as independent political entity formalized in constitution of 1841; the Republic of El Salvador formally established in constitution of 1859; constitution of 1962 suspended following the military coup of October 15, 1979; provisional government superseded following promulgation of new constitution on December 20, 1983; peace treaty with Farabundo Martí National Liberation Front (FMLN) guerrillas (effective February 1) signed January 16, 1992.

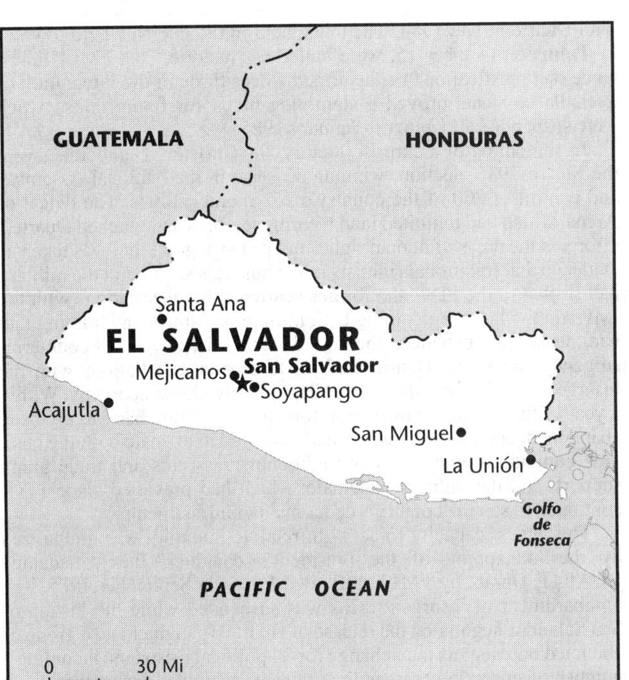

Area: 8,124 sq. mi. (21,041 sq. km.).

Population: 5,118,599 (1992C); 7,222,000 (2008E). The 1992 figure is unadjusted for underenumeration.

Major Urban Centers (2005E): SAN SALVADOR (508,000), Soyapango (295,000), Mejicanos (189,000), San Miguel (183,000), Santa Ana (179,000).

Official Language: Spanish.

Monetary Unit: Effective January 1, 2001, El Salvador adopted the U.S. dollar as its currency.

President: Carlos Mauricio FUNES Cartagena (Farabundo Martí National Liberation Front); popularly elected on March 15, 2009, and inaugurated for a five-year term on June 1, succeeding Elías Antonio ("Tony") SACA González (Nationalist Republican Alliance).

Vice President: Salvador SÁNCHEZ CERÉN (Farabundo Martí National Liberation Front); popularly elected on March 15, 2009, and inaugurated on June 1 for a term concurrent with that of the president, succeeding Ana Vilma ALBANEZ de Escobar (Nationalist Republican Alliance).

THE COUNTRY

The smallest of the Central American countries and the only one whose territory does not touch the Caribbean Sea, El Salvador is oriented geographically and, to some extent, psychologically toward the Pacific and the other isthmus countries. Its population density is the highest in the Americas, while its per capita income is among the lowest. Although there is a small Indian minority, the people are largely of mixed Spanish and Indian descent, with 90 percent classified as mestizo. The Catholic Church is predominant, but Protestant and Jewish faiths are represented. Women constitute approximately 35 percent of the paid labor force, concentrated largely in domestic and human service sectors and in manufacturing; female participation in government is minimal.

Traditionally dependent on agriculture, with coffee as the primary cash crop, El Salvador—before the domestic instability generated by the coup of October 1979—had become the region's leading exporter of manufactured goods. The industrial sector as a whole now accounts for about 30 percent of GDP, while agriculture contributes 10 percent (down from nearly 40 percent in 1980). Most external sales are made to the United States and neighboring Central American nations.

During 1979–1989 all major economic indicators steadily declined, counterinsurgency being described by one analyst as the country's "only growth sector." Most severely affected was agriculture, with production of coffee, cotton, and sugar each falling by approximately 50 percent from 1979 to 1982, and capital flight reported at more than $1 billion through the period. More than half the population remained below the national poverty line, and much of the workforce was under- or unemployed; in addition, despite land-redistribution efforts in the early 1980s, no more than 15 percent of the rural population holds a land title. In mid-1989 the Cristiani administration announced a "National Rescue Plan" that called for government spending cuts, the lifting of price controls, and the privatization of state-run industries (including coffee plantations) in order to reduce budget deficits and external debt arrears. The effort yielded measurable results by 1992 with real GDP growth of 4.6 percent and a halving of inflation to 11.2 percent. Annual growth for the 1990s as a whole averaged 4.7 percent, but by 2001 expansion had slowed to 1.7 percent.

In 2001 El Salvador adopted the U.S. dollar as its currency in an effort to stabilize exchange rates and attract foreign investment. However, growth showed little improvement until 2005, when it increased marginally to 2.8 percent. Annual GDP averaged 3.8 percent in 2006-2007 as a result of sustained economic reforms, according to the International Monetary Fund (IMF), but contracted to 2.5 percent in 2008 due to the global financial crisis, high commodity prices, and what the IMF described as "domestic electoral uncertainty."

In January 2009 the IMF approved $800 million in stand-by funds to bolster the economy in the wake of the global downturn, while noting that Salvadoran authorities did not intend to draw on the funds. Meanwhile, fund managers reported that the banking system remained strong, and they commended the government for seeking congressional approval of a law to strengthen regulation of the financial sector. Annual GDP growth declined to less than 1 percent in 2009, with a marginal increase forecast for 2010.

GOVERNMENT AND POLITICS

Political background. After the colonies comprising the Captaincy General of Guatemala declared their independence from Spain in 1821, a period of conflict ensued with Mexico over perceived Mexican domination efforts. El Salvador subsequently joined Costa Rica, Guatemala, Honduras, and Nicaragua in forming the United Provinces of Central America in 1823. In the wake of the collapse of that star-crossed federation into civil war in 1838, El Salvador formally declared its status as an independent entity in a constitution adopted in 1841. Many constitutional revisions were subsequently enacted during ongoing political turbulence throughout the rest of the 1800s, which also included several abortive attempts to reform a Central American Federation. However, El Salvador enjoyed periods of relative calm during the first three decades of the 20th century and again from 1950 to 1960. Lt. Col. Oscar OSIRIO ruled from 1950 to 1956 and was succeeded by an elected president, Lt. Col. José María LEMUS, but a coup d'état in 1960 overthrew Lemus and inaugurated a period of renewed instability.

A new constitution was promulgated in January 1962 and an election was held the following April, although the opposition did not participate. Col. Julio Adalberto RIVERA, candidate of the recently organized National Conciliation Party (*Partido de Conciliación Nacional*—PCN), was certified as president and served a five-year term. Subsequent PCN victories brought Gen. Fidel SÁNCHEZ Hernández and Col. Arturo Armando MOLINA Barraza to power in 1967 and 1972, respectively, but announcement of the 1972 results provoked an unsuccessful coup by leftist forces, in the wake of which their candidate, José Napoleón DUARTE Fuentes, was exiled.

Following the election of February 20, 1977, the PCN candidate, Gen. Carlos Humberto ROMERO Mena, was declared president-elect with a majority of 67 percent of the votes cast, although the opposition, as in 1972, charged the government with massive electoral irregularities. The PCN won 50 of 54 seats in the legislative election of March 18, 1978, which was boycotted by most of the opposition because of inadequate assurances that the tabulation of results would be impartial.

In the wake of rapidly escalating conflict between right- and left-wing groups, General Romero was ousted on October 15, 1979, in a coup led by Col. Jaime Abdul GUTIÉRREZ and Col. Adolfo Arnoldo MAJANO Ramos, who were joined by three civilians on October 17 in a five-man ruling junta. While appealing to extremist forces to respect "the will of the majority" and aid in the installation of a "true democracy," the junta was actively opposed by leftist elements protesting military rule, and a state of siege, lifted on October 23, was reimposed three days later.

Two of the three civilian members of the junta, as well as all civilian cabinet members, resigned on January 3, 1980, in protest at a "swing to the right" for which the remaining civilian junta member, Mario Antonio ANDINO, was allegedly responsible. Andino himself resigned the following day. Three prominent members of the Christian Democratic Party (*Partido Demócrata Cristiano*—PDC) joined the junta on January 9 after obtaining assurances that rightist influence would be contained and a dialogue initiated with leftist organizations. One of the three, Héctor DADA Hirezi, withdrew on March 3 and was replaced by former PDC presidential candidate José Napoleón Duarte, who had returned from exile after the October coup. The most widely publicized terrorist act of the year was the assassination of the liberal Msgr. Oscar Arnulfo ROMERO y Galdames, archbishop of San Salvador, on March 24. While the junta initially blamed leftist forces for the act, the actual perpetrators were widely assumed to be rightist elements.

Earlier, three major mass organizations, in concert with the Salvadoran Communist Party, had announced the formation of a Revolutionary Coordination of the Masses (*Coordinadora Revolucionaria de las Masas*—CRM) to oppose the PDC-military coalition. In April 1980 the CRM was superseded by the Revolutionary Democratic Front (*Frente Democrático Revolucionario*—FDR), a coalition of 18 leftist and far-leftist groups, including a dissident faction of the PDC. Subsequently, the major guerrilla organizations formed the Farabundo Martí National Liberation Front (*Frente Farabundo Martí para la Liberación National*—FMLN) to serve as the FDR's military affiliate. In the wake of these and other developments, including the apparent complicity of government security forces in the murder of three American nuns and a lay worker on December 2, the junta was reorganized on December 3, with Duarte and the increasingly hard-line Gutiérrez being sworn in as its president and vice president, respectively, on December 22.

Although FMLN activity was widespread by early 1981, President Duarte on March 5 named a three-member commission to update electoral registers for Constituent Assembly balloting in March 1982. By midyear the PDC and four rightist parties had been registered, subsequently being joined by the Nationalist Republican Alliance (*Alianza Republicana Nacionalista*—Arena) of former army major Roberto D'AUBUISSON Arrieta, who was reported to have been implicated in the murder of Archbishop Romero. The FDR, on the other hand, refused to participate, continuing efforts initiated in January to secure external support for its revolutionary program.

In the election of March 28, 1982, the Christian Democrats secured the largest number of seats (24) in the 60-member assembly. However, four right-wing parties collectively constituted a majority and refused to permit Duarte to continue as president. The ensuing interparty negotiations resulted in a deadlock, with the Christian Democrats insisting on representation in the new government proportional to their share of the vote. On April 22 the assembly convened for its first session and elected Major d'Aubuisson as its president by a vote of 35–22. After further negotiations that were reportedly influenced by pressure from the United States, the armed forces presented the assembly with a list of individuals whom it considered acceptable as candidates for provisional chief executive, pending a direct presidential election. One of those listed, the independent, Dr. Alvaro MAGAÑA Borja, was accepted by the assembly on April 29 and sworn in on May 2 together with three vice presidents representing the PDC, the PCN, and Arena. Two days later a tripartite administration was formed.

The move toward democracy generated no reprieve from insurgent activity. Nonetheless, the five parties represented in the Constituent Assembly agreed in August 1983 to establish a multiparty commission to prepare a timetable for new elections. Following promulgation of a revised constitution on December 20, the assembly approved presidential balloting for March 1984 and legislative and municipal elections for March 1985.

The 1984 election was contested by eight candidates, the acknowledged front-runners being d'Aubuisson and Duarte, neither of whom secured a majority. In a runoff on May 6, Duarte emerged the clear winner, with 53.6 percent of the vote, and was inaugurated on June 1.

The FDR-FMLN, refusing to participate in the presidential campaign, stepped up its military activity, although agreeing to peace talks with Duarte in late 1984. The talks, held in the guerrilla-held town of La Palma on October 15, were hailed as "historic," but FMLN insistence on "purification" of the armed forces through the integration of guerrilla elements proved a stumbling block for future talks, which were suspended altogether in January 1985.

In something of a surprise victory, the Christian Democrats swept the March 1985 election, winning 33 seats in the National Assembly and control of 200 of the country's 262 municipalities. The defeat of Arena, which had inhibited land reform measures and blocked Duarte's efforts in the areas of human rights and peace negotiation, was taken as evidence that traditional rightists in the business sector and the military had shifted to the PDC, the former heartened by negotiations with the IMF and the latter welcoming U.S. military aid funds and training that had measurably enhanced the armed forces' firepower and counterinsurgency capability. Duarte pledged to reopen negotiations with the insurgents while rebuilding the collapsed Salvadoran economy. Within a year of the election, however, efforts at negotiation had largely been abandoned; economic measures had managed to alienate both the business community and Duarte's traditional grassroots and trade union support; and the military stalemate, which had prevailed since 1981, continued to sap the country's economy and infrastructure.

The rebels' capacity to act with relative impunity was dramatized by the kidnapping of the president's daughter, Inés Guadalupe DUARTE Durán, by FMLN-affiliated forces in September 1985. The bombardment of insurgent areas was suspended while the bishop of San Salvador negotiated the release of Duarte's daughter and a group of abducted bureaucrats in exchange for 34 political prisoners, including a number of guerrilla commanders, with 98 wounded insurgents given safe passage to Mexico City. The agreement provoked resentment on the part of the armed forces, as well as a widespread perception that only Inés Duarte's abduction had prevented the indefinite detention of the kidnapped officials. Public discontent was further fueled by the government's 1986 economic austerity plan, which included a 100 percent currency devaluation, limited wage concessions, tax increases, and a doubling of gasoline prices. Business leaders charged Duarte with "bowing to the dictates of the IMF," while labor unrest intensified. On February 21 thousands marched in San Salvador to protest sharp increases in the cost of living, which had risen by more than 125 percent since 1980.

Through the mediation of Peruvian President Alan García, the first meeting in more than a year between government and rebel representatives was held in Lima, Peru, in May 1986. However, Duarte's close advisor, Minister of Culture Julio REY Prendes, insisted that the administration had been "deceived" into believing that the opposition leaders would be speaking for their individual parties rather than on behalf of the FMLN, and the talks were quickly suspended.

On the basis of a peace plan advanced by the five Central American presidents in August 1987, discussions with FDR-FMLN representatives resumed in San Salvador in early October. However, the government insisted that the rebels lay down their arms as a precondition for inclusion in the "democratic" process and the talks again foundered. In legislative balloting in March 1988, Arena won a near majority of 30 seats, with the PDC and PCN winning 23 and 7, respectively. Two months later Arena secured an absolute majority as the result of a PCN crossover.

In November 1987, Dr. Guillermo UNGO and Rubén ZAMORA Rivas, leaders, respectively, of the National Revolutionary Movement and the Popular Social Christian Movement, had announced the formation of a leftist Democratic Convergence (*Convergencia Democrática*—CD), with the declared aim of seeking a resolution to the conflict through electoral participation. Since the two also served as president and vice president of the FDR, the action provided a linkage between the legal political process and the insurgency. Following the 1988 legislative elections (for which the CD did not present candidates), it was announced that the new grouping would participate in the 1989 presidential campaign. (For background on the now-defunct CD, see the 2008 *Handbook*.)

In early 1989 the FMLN leadership advanced a plan whereby the rebels would lay down their arms if the government would agree to a number of stipulations, including a six-month delay in the balloting scheduled for March 19. While rejecting the plan as unconstitutional, the government (responding in part to intense U.S. pressure) agreed to participate in formal talks with the insurgents that commenced February 22 in Qaxtepec, Mexico. Four days later President Duarte offered to postpone the first-round voting until April 30, leaving sufficient time for a second round, if necessary, before the June 1 expiration of his five-year term. However, both the rebels and Arena, rejected this proposal, with Arena candidate Alfredo CRISTIANI Burkard securing the presidency on the basis of a 53.8 to 36.6 percent single-round victory over the PDC nominee, Fidel CHÁVEZ Mena.

Protracted negotiations over the next two years, punctuated by a series of rebel offensives, culminated in a meeting in Mexico City (the first to be attended by FMLN field commanders) held April 4–27, 1991, that yielded agreement on a tentative package of constitutional amendments. During further talks in Caracas, Venezuela, in late May the two sides endorsed the formation of a human rights monitoring team, the United Nations Observer Mission in El Salvador, whose initial contingent was deployed on July 26. Two months later, during a New York meeting on September 25, Cristiani and FMLN representatives reached general agreement on a permanent ceasefire to end the bloody 12-year conflict. On January 16, 1992, a treaty (incorporating a formal cessation of hostilities on February 1) was signed in Mexico City. The document provided for UN supervision of the cease-fire while rebel forces disbanded over a nine-month period; purchase by the government of land for distribution to peasants in rebel-held areas; a blanket pardon for all combatants; "purification" of the government's officer corps; absorption of the infamous national guard and treasury police by the regular army; dissolution of the military's intelligence, civil defense, and counterinsurgency units; and the creation of a new civil police force.

Despite setbacks that delayed completion of the peace process by two months, demobilization of both rebel units and the government's notorious Immediate Reaction Infantry Battalions was completed on December 15, 1992, at which time the war was declared at an end and the FMLN legally certified as a political party.

Heading a leftist coalition, Rubén Zamora was defeated in second-round presidential balloting on April 24, 1994, by Arena's Armando CALDERÓN Sol. Subsequently, splits within both Arena and the FMLN led to withdrawals and the formation of new parties by the dissidents (see Political Parties, below).

In the legislative balloting of March 16, 1997, Arena barely outpaced the FMLN, while in local contests leftists captured most of the country's major cities, including the capital, San Salvador. However, the leftist surge subsequently lost momentum, and Arena's Francisco FLORES easily outpolled six challengers to win the presidential poll of March 7, 1999, his nearly 52 percent of the vote precluding the need for runoff balloting. In the legislative election of March 2000, the FMLN captured a slim plurality of seats, but not enough to take control from the allied conservative forces of Arena, the Christian Democrats, and the PCN. The result was the same in March 2003, while Arena retained the presidency with the election of Antonio ("Tony") SACA on March 21, 2004.

The legislative distribution was not radically altered in the triennial balloting of March 12, 2006, although Arena replaced the FMLN as the plurality grouping by a gain of six seats (see Legislature, below).

In December 2006 President Saca reinstated the ministry of public security and justice (previously under the interior ministry) in an effort to improve security.

In parliamentary elections on January 18, 2009, the FMLN won 42 percent of the vote and 35 seats, edging out Arena by just 3 seats. Arena lost two seats, but remained close behind the FMLN with a total of 32 seats in the new assembly. The presidential balloting on March 15, 2009, proved a historical event with the election of the first left-wing president in nearly two decades. The FMLN's Carlos Mauricio FUNES won 51.3 percent of the vote against Arena's Rodrigo AVILA with 48.7 percent. Funes was sworn in on June 1 and subsequently formed a new government that included members of the CD and the PDC.

Constitution and government. The constitution adopted by the Constituent Assembly on December 6, 1983, provides for a president and vice president, both elected by direct popular vote for five-year terms, and for a unicameral National Assembly elected for a three-year term. The judicial system is headed by a Supreme Court, whose 13 members are elected by the assembly. The country's 14 departments are headed by governors appointed by the chief executive.

Foreign relations. El Salvador belongs to the United Nations, the Organization of American States, and their subsidiary bodies. It is an active member of the Organization of Central American States, whose secretariat is located in San Salvador, and of other regional institutions.

In the early 1980s, following allegations of aid to the FMLN by the Sandinist National Liberation Front (*Frente Sandinista de Liberación Nacional*—FSLN), or *sandinista*, regime in Nicaragua, cooperation between El Salvador, Guatemala, and Honduras increased. In October 1983, at the urging of the United States, a revival of the Central American Defense Council (Condeca), originally a four-member group that included Nicaragua, was announced in support of a joint approach to "extra-continental aggression of a Marxist-Leninist character." Although no formal action was undertaken by the truncated council, El Salvador and Honduras cooperated during U.S. military maneuvers in the region in 1983–1984, as well as in attempts to interdict Nicaraguan arms shipments to Salvadoran rebel forces. On November 26, 1989, Cristiani severed diplomatic relations with Managua after a Nicaraguan-registered plane, loaded with Soviet SAM-7 missiles allegedly consigned to the FMLN, crashed in El Salvador. Eleven months later a number of SAM-7 and SAM-14 missiles, reportedly supplied by dissident *sandinistas*, were handed over by the FMLN to Nicaraguan authorities. The action came in the wake of an unprecedented joint appeal by Moscow and Washington for political settlement of the Salvadoran conflict.

During 1987–1988 El Salvador came under increasing criticism for the alleged misuse of U.S. aid funds, the economic and military components of which totaled more than $400 million in 1987 alone. Relations were further complicated by a U.S. district court ruling in April 1988 that a long-standing exodus of Salvadorans to the United States consisted largely of economic (hence illegal) entrants, rather than of political refugees.

In October 1990 the U.S. Senate voted to withhold half of an $85 million military aid appropriation for El Salvador until the Cristiani government "demonstrated good faith" in talks with the FMLN, curbed military assassinations and abductions, and mounted a meaningful inquiry into a number of murders, including those of six Jesuit priests a year earlier. The funds were finally released by U.S. president George H.W. Bush following the killing of two U.S. airmen by rebels in January 1991. In September, 2 of 11 military personnel (a colonel and a lieutenant) were convicted of the Jesuit massacre. While most foreign observers were disappointed at the number of those exonerated (some of whom had confessed to complicity in the affair), others felt that even two convictions represented "an historic achievement."

In September 1992 a long-standing territorial dispute that had provoked a brief war between El Salvador and Honduras in 1969 was resolved by a World Court judgment. In addition to ruling on control of a number of coastal land "pockets" (*bolsones*), two-thirds of which were awarded to Honduras, the court decided that the waters of the Gulf of Fonseca were not international but a closed condominium of El Salvador, Honduras, and Nicaragua, which benefited Honduras by providing it with access to the Pacific Ocean. In September 1995 a Bi-National Commission set up to implement the judgment agreed that residents of the territory could choose either Salvadoran or Honduran nationality. In February 1998 Honduran and Salvadoran representatives signed two treaties on demarcation of their borders, about 70 percent of which remained in dispute. However, approval of the treaties by Honduras was not immediately forthcoming because of opposition objections to their terms. Claiming that the Goascoran River, used to define the border, had changed its course over the past 200 years, El Salvador in late 2002 appealed the 1992 ruling, but the bid was unsuccessful.

In June 1997 President Calderón met with U.S. legislators in Washington to seek relief from tough new U.S. immigration laws under which more than 300,000 undocumented Salvadorans could be subject to deportation. In addition to hardship for the expatriates, El Salvador could have lost up to $1 billion a year in remittances (60 percent of export earnings and 15 percent of the country's GDP). A year later Washington expressed its displeasure over the release of three of five Salvadoran national guardsmen who had received 30-year prison sentences in 1984 for the 1980 rape and murder of three American nuns and a lay worker.

In March 1999 U.S. president Bill Clinton visited El Salvador as part of a tour designed to highlight Washington's financial support to assist Central American recovery from the devastating effects of Hurricane Mitch in late 1998. Clinton also took the opportunity to comment on U.S. support for the government in the 1980s in its campaign against leftist insurgents. He noted that U.S. policy had caused "deep divisions" in U.S. society and pledged that the "mistakes" of the past would not be repeated.

In 1996 El Salvador and Guatemala, with a combined 60 percent of Central America's GDP, agreed to combine their customs agencies. In early 2000 the accord was amplified by the signing of an Investment and Service Trade Treaty, with a free flow in goods and services expected by 2002.

In March 2000 the Flores government came under attack for agreeing to let the United States set up a logistics base for its war on drugs at a military sector of the international airport in Comalapa, 20 miles from the capital. The Legislative Assembly approved the pact on July 7 by a 49–35 vote, despite objections by the FMLN, which insisted that a three-quarters majority was necessary because the issue impinged on the nation's sovereignty.

In December 2004 El Salvador became the first Central American country to ratify the Central American Free Trade Agreement (CAFTA) with the United States. Salvadoran agricultural exports to the United States fell 3.7 percent in 2006, while imports from the United States grew by 17 percent. In April 2006 the presidents of Honduras and El Salvador signed documents marking the end of 26 years of border demarcation dispute and announced they would reactivate the plan to build the joint El Tigre hydroelectric power plant on the Honduras side of the river.

In early September 2005 El Salvador joined the United States, Mexico, Guatemala, and Honduras in a joint operation against the Mara Salvarucha gangs. Nearly 200 individuals were arrested and, in late November of that year, a military deployment was ordered against 10,000 Mara gang members estimated to be active in El Salvador.

In November 2006 the United States approved the Millennium Challenge Account for El Salvador, which would provide $460 million for improvements in transportation, expansion of running water and electricity, formal and informal education, and assistance to agricultural producers. In a possibly related vein, El Salvador has been the only Latin American country to send troops in support of the U.S.-led initiative in Iraq.

El Salvador enjoys normal diplomatic and trade relations with all its neighbors, including Honduras, with whom it continues to differ regarding maritime borders in the Gulf of Fonseca. Both countries have agreed to settle the dispute with the International Court of Justice.

In August 2008 President Saca announced that he would deploy more troops to support the U.S. effort in Iraq. However, after reports of the deaths of Honduran soldiers, El Salvador withdrew its troops in December. Earlier that year the Spanish National Court began investigating a case against former Salvadoran President Cristiani and 14 other government officials in connection with the killing of six Jesuit priests, most of who were born in Spain. Though the Archbishop of San Salvador opposed the reopening of the 1989 case, and the Jesuit order in El Salvador decided not to participate, two human rights groups based in Spain and the United States pressed charges.

Current issues. In the run-up to the separate parliamentary and presidential elections in 2009, attention turned to the government's response to the economic crisis. President Saca attempted to maintain support for the Arena party by appointing a committee of ministers to recommend solutions for dealing with rising food and fuel prices, and by cracking down on violent crime. Some 45 Mara gang members across the country were subsequently arrested.

While the FMLN won the most seats in the January 2009 legislative elections, it failed to gain a majority, paving the way for the Arena party to form minority coalitions to counter the new political heavyweight. Many analysts believed that the parliamentary elections would be a good indicator of the results of upcoming presidential elections based on party strongholds throughout the country. Population figures turned out to be a contentious issue, as the FMLN criticized the electoral commission for not relying on the most recent census before establishing the vote. The FMLN, for its part, argued that heavily populated San Salvador—a strong base of support for the party—should have a larger seat allocation. Subsequently, the FMLN won a narrow three-seat victory over second-place Arena, with three smaller parties winning a total of 17 seats. The FMLN and Arena faced off again in the March presidential election, following an acrimonious campaign season in which the Arena's Rodrigo Avila, the former head of the national police, tried to maintain its hold on the government with veiled references to the country's civil war strife and potential return of socialism. The references alluded to the return of civil unrest if the FMLN's Mauricio Funes, a popular television personality, were elected. Funes, the FMLN's first non-militant candidate, countered the attacks by alleging that Arean was prepared to carry out voter fraud in order to stay in power. Funes further distanced himself from party hardliners and radical leftists by framing himself as a moderate, similar to Brazilian president Lula da Silva. Breaking from the traditional position of the FMLN, Funes also supported the continued use of U.S. dollars in place of the Salvadoran colon. He chose as his running mate veteran FMLN leader Salvador SÁNCHEZ Cerén. Funes won a narrow victory in March, marking the end to Arena's power for the first time in 18 years.

Following his election, Funes turned his attention to the pressing issues of poverty, the economic crisis, and public security. While he had promised not to be "soft" on the Mara gangs, Funes abandoned some of the more aggressive policies of his predecessor, which relied heavily on police and military operations. Meanwhile, Funes announced new youth development programs to address the issues of gang membership and violence. Shortly after Funes's inauguration in June, political tensions heightened as opposition members in Congress blocked the confirmation of five Supreme Court judges and the attorney general, positions traditionally held by Arena members. The president's attempts to change these key officeholders posed an institutional crisis for the country as Arena initially refused to relinquish its authority over them. After weeks of deadlock in the legislature, the FMLN and Arena reached an agreement in which the presidency of the assembly went to Arena ally Ciro Cruz ZEPEDA of the PCN, and Arena's preferred candidate was named to head the Supreme Court. Observers said the appointments bolstered Arena's ability to restrict President Funes's reform agenda.

POLITICAL PARTIES

In 1988 electoral laws were reformed, requiring political parties to obtain citizens' signatures in support of national party recognition, establishing a threshold of 0.5 percent of the national vote to retain party status, and to participate in at least every other election.

The principal contenders in the 1989 presidential and 1991 legislative elections were the right-wing Nationalist Republican Alliance (Arena) and the basically centrist Christian Democrats, with the conservative National Conciliation Party (PCN) running a distant third and the pro-insurgent Democratic Convergence (CD) consigned to fourth place on both occasions, although the vote share for the CD in 1991 exceeded that of the PCN by more than one-third. In 1994 the recently legalized Farabundo Martí National Liberation Front (FMLN) emerged as runner-up to Arena and fell only one seat short of a tie with the latter in 1997.

In the March 1999 presidential election Arena's Francisco Flores defeated the FMLN candidate, resulting in a movement toward a more traditional hard-line posture on the part of the government.

In legislative polls of March 12, 2000, and March 16, 2003, the FMLN won a plurality of seats; Arena, however, retained control by means of right-wing coalitions with the PCN and the Christian Democratic Party (PDC). After retaining the presidency in 2004, Arena in 2006 wrested a legislative plurality legislative from the FMLN by two seats.

Prior to the 2009 elections, the FMLN formed coalitions with the Revolutionary Democratic Front (FDR) and the CD in 34 municipal races. Despite speculation about a potential coalition between Arena and the PCN, both parties fielded their own candidates. Following the election the FDR was deregistered because it failed to gain enough votes to meet the threshold requirement.

Government Parties:

Farabundo Martí National Liberation Front (*Frente Farabundo Martí para la Liberación Nacional*—FMLN). The FMLN was organized in October 1980 as the paramilitary affiliate of the Revolutionary Democratic Front (*Frente Democrático Revolucionario*—FDR, below), an umbrella formation of dissident political groups. Headed by a National Revolutionary Directorate (*Dirección Revolucionaria Nacional*—DRN) composed of representatives of participating armed units, the FMLN was in active rebellion until the late 1991 agreement that led to a formal cessation of hostilities on February 1, 1992. During ensuing months the FMLN engaged in a process of phased disarmament and on December 15 was recognized by the Supreme Electoral Tribunal as a legal political party.

At its first congress on September 6, 1993, the FMLN endorsed Rubén Zamora of the CD (below) as its 1994 presidential candidate. Following the election an internal split emerged between the People's Renewal Expression (*Expresión Renovadora del Pueblo*—ERP) and the National Resistance (*Resistencia Nacional*—RN), on the one hand, and the Salvadoran Communist Party (*Partido Comunista Salvadoreño*—PCS), the Popular Liberation Forces (*Fuerzas Populares de Liberación*—FPL), and the Central American Workers Revolutionary Party (*Partido Revolucionario de los Trabajadores Centroamericanos*—PRTC), on the other. While surfacing as a dispute over the selection of legislative officers, a major factor of the split appeared to be resistance by the tripartite group to the ERP leader's advocacy of a departure from Marxism-Leninism, and in December 1994 both the ERP and RN left the Front, save for a rump RN faction headed by Eugenio CHICA and Marco JIMÉNEZ. In early 1995 the remaining FMLN components agreed to changes designed to yield a unitary organization and by midyear had begun to dissolve their respective party structures to become "currents" or "tendencies" within the revamped larger grouping. In 2004 and 2005, five members of the Legislature split from FMLN to from the Democratic Revolutionary Front (*Frente Democratico Revolucionario*—FDR). However, FDR maintained just one legislative seat in the 2006 elections and failed to win representation in the 2009 elections. (For information on the FDR, see the 2009 *Handbook.)*

The PCS was formerly a pro-Moscow group that was repudiated by most mass and guerrilla organizations for its "revisionist" outlook. In early 1980 it adopted a more militant posture, becoming under its secretary general, Schafik Jorge HANDAL, a de facto component of the FMLN. Following his party's break with the Democratic Nationalist Union (*Unión Demócrata Nacionalista*—UDN), Handal became official coordinator and subsequently coordinator general of the legitimized FMLN.

The FPL was previously the FMLN's largest military component. In May 1993 a scandal erupted as the result of an explosion at a clandestine FPL arsenal in Managua, Nicaragua, of arms that were supposed to have been turned over to the United Nations Observer Mission in El Salvador for destruction. A number of other such caches were subsequently discovered, tarnishing the credentials of the FMLN as a legal party.

The PRTC was a small FMLN component, which advocated a regional, as opposed to state, revolution. One of its leaders, Francisco VELIS, was assassinated in October 1993.

Having gained as much public support as the governing Arena party in the 1997 legislative poll, the FMLN held high hopes of achieving government control in the March 1999 presidential balloting. However, friction between orthodox Marxists and the modernist wing ("renovators") caused sustained difficulty in choosing a candidate. The ultimate selection, Facundo GUARDADO, a former guerrilla leader supported by the "renovators," generated little enthusiasm among the non-FMLN voters and won only 28.9 percent of the vote. Having failed even to force a runoff ballot, Guardado resigned as the FMLN's general coordinator on March 15, with his successor, Fabio Castillo, heading a new leadership in which traditional Marxists held a slim majority.

The FMLN rebounded to win a legislative plurality in March 2000 but was unable to gain control in the face of an Arena-led conservative coalition. Thereafter, the sharp division between the orthodox and reform wings persisted, and in October 2001 it was reported that Guardado had been "expelled," although he announced he would continue to participate in FMLN activity. Hard-liner Salvador Sánchez Cerén was elected as the new general coordinator in November. Subsequently, in early 2002, it was reported that a group of reformist FMLN legislators had left the party's parliamentary bloc, including Héctor SILVA, who stood for president in 2004 as the candidate of a PDC/CDU coalition (see under PDC, below).

Although retaining its legislative plurality of 31 in March 2003, the FMLN, led by Schafik Jorge Handal, was again rebuffed in its bid for the presidency in March 2004.

In March 2005 the party was weakened by the withdrawal of seven of its legislative deputies who joined with other FMLN dissidents to form a new party, the Revolutionary Democratic Front (which was deregistered following the 2009 elections for failure to meet the electoral threshold.) Subsequently, the death of Handal on January 24, 2006, appeared to provide an opening for reconciliation between his supporters and the FDR; however, his hard-line deputy, Sánchez Cerén, was named to head the FMLN legislative bloc, and in the March 12 election the party, while gaining one slot, lost its plurality to Arena.

In the January 2009 legislative elections, the FMLN gained three seats to overcome Arena as the party with the most seats, though the two parties were separated only by a three-seat margin, forcing both to form alliances. The FMLN's greatest victory came in the March presidential election when Mauricio Funes, among the most recognizable media personalities in the country, defeated Arena candidate Rodrigo Avila by a narrow margin. Though Funes was the first FMLN candidate who was not an ex-guerrilla commander, his election led to increased dissension between the Funes camp and party hardliners regarding the president's policies and his moderate cabinet choices.

Leaders: Carlos Mauricio FUNES Cartagena (President of the Republic), Salvador SÁNCHEZ Cerén (Vice President of the Republic), José Luis MERINO (PCS), José MANUEL Melgar (PRTC), Fabio CASTILLO (Former General Coordinator), Medardo GONZÁLEZ (General Coordinator).

Christian Democratic Party (*Partido Demócrata Cristiano*—PDC). An essentially centrist grouping, the PDC was the core component of the National Opposition Union (*Unión Nacional Opositora*—UNO), which won 8 legislative seats in 1972 and 14 in 1974 but boycotted the 1976 and 1978 balloting. Its best-known figure, José Napoleón Duarte, returned from exile following the October 1979 coup, joined the junta on March 3, 1980, and became junta president on December 22. He was succeeded by Provisional President Alvaro Magaña in May 1982 after the PDC had failed to secure a majority at the March Constituent Assembly election. Although Duarte continued as president under the new constitution in May 1984, the PDC did not win legislative control until March 1985; it returned to minority status as a result of the 1988 legislative balloting (an outcome attributed, in part, to intraparty bickering) and lost the presidency in 1989. Duarte died on February 23, 1990, For the 1991 election the party appealed to the left by forming an alliance with two labor-based groups, the **National Union of Peasant Labor** (*Unión Nacional Obrera Campesina*—UNDC) and the **Salvadoran Workers' Central** (*Central de Trabajadores Salvadoreños*—CTS)

Two leading factions, led by Fidel Chávez Mena and Abraham RODRÍGUEZ, competed for the party's presidential nomination in 1994, Chávez Mena (the 1989 nominee) receiving the designation and finishing third in the March first-round balloting. At a party convention in late November the party elected a *fidelista* directorate loyal to Chávez Mena, leading dissident *abrahamistas* (loyalists of Rodríguez) to withdrawal from the party on December 11 to form the Social Christian Reform Party (*Partido Reformista Social Cristiano*—PRSC).

The election of Ronald Umaña, representing a relatively young new guard or new political class as secretary general at the 1995 convention yielded a dispute with long-time old guard leader Julio SAMAYOA, who succeeded in forcing his opponent's expulsion from the party. In March 1996 the electoral tribunal confirmed the dismissal of Umaña and six associates, who promptly challenged the ruling's legality, and in December the tribunal reinstated Umaña.

For some constituencies in the March 1997 balloting, the PDC formed a "Great Center Coalition" with the Democratic Party (*Partido Democrático*—PD), which elected three deputies as compared with seven elected by the PDC outright.

Indicative of internal problems within the PDC was its replacement in January 1998 of Secretary General Ronald Umaña by Horacio TRUJILLO only to have Umaña reinstated in March by the electoral tribunal. Rodolfo Antonio Parker Soto, former legal adviser to the military during the civil war, was the PDC standard-bearer in the March 1999 presidential campaign, during which the PDC attacked what it perceived as widespread corruption in the Arena governments of the 1990s. Parker secured 5.8 percent of the vote, thereby dropping the PDC to fourth place behind the newly formed United Democratic Center (*Centro Democrático Unido*—CDU) in party rankings.

For the 2004 presidential race the PDC joined with the CDU in sponsoring former FMLN leader Héctor Silva Arguello; however, Silva's vote share of 3.9 percent was less than the joint minimum required to maintain the parties' registrations. In 2005 three PDC legislators left the party to help form the new **Popular Social Christian Party** (*Partido Popular Social Cristiano*—PPSC) under the leadership of former PDC secretary general René AUILEZ. Those legislators subsequently joined with members of the newly formed FDR and the CDU to create a bloc of 14 legislators known as the G-14. However, G-14 influence declined substantially following the 2006 assembly poll, when most of its members ran under the CD banner. Meanwhile, the PDC won six assembly seats in 2006, one more than in 2003. In 2009 the party won five seats.

Leaders: Ana Guadalupe MARTÍNEZ (Adjunct Secretary of the Party), Fidel CHAVEZ Mena (1994 presidential candidate), Ronald UMAÑA, Carlos Rolando HERRARTE, Rodolfo Antonio PARKER Soto (1999 presidential candidate and Secretary General).

Democratic Change (*Cambio Democrática*—CD). The center-left CD was founded in 1988 as a coalition of three political parties called the *Convergencia Democrática*. The CD won eight seats in 1989. The CD supported the unsuccessful bid of FMLN candidate Rubén Zamora for president in 1992, and in 1999 the party participated in elections as part of the United Democratic Center (*Centro Democrático Unido*—CDU). In 2005 the CDU became *Cambio Democrática*, The party won one legislative seat in 2009.

Leaders: Héctor Miguel Dada HIREZI, Oscar Catan, Juan Pablo DURÁN Escobar.

Other Legislative Parties:

Nationalist Republican Alliance (*Alianza Republicana Nacionalista*—Arena). The Arena party was launched in 1981 as an outgrowth of the Broad National Front (*Frente Amplio Nacional*—FAN), an extreme right-wing grouping organized a year earlier by ex-army major Roberto d'Aubuisson. D'Aubuisson was arrested briefly in May 1980 as the instigator of an attempted coup against the junta, which he had accused of "leading the country toward communism." Runner-up in the 1982 election with 19 assembly seats, the Alliance formed a conservative bloc with the PCN, which succeeded in scuttling most of the post-coup land-reform program and secured the appointment of a right-wing judiciary. Although remaining second-ranked in the March 1985 balloting, Arena's legislative representation dropped to 13 seats on the basis of a 29 percent vote share. Amid mounting evidence that his leadership and reputation had become a liability to the group, d'Aubuisson formally resigned as secretary general in September, holding thereafter the title of honorary president until his death in February 1991.

Arena secured a 53.8 percent popular vote victory in presidential balloting in March 1989 but slipped to a plurality of 44.3 percent in 1991 that gave it only 39 of 84 legislative seats. The party's legislative representation was unchanged in 1994, although Armando Calderón Sol defeated the FMLN's Rubén Zamora Rivas by a better than two-to-one margin in the second round of the presidential race. In 1997 a number of prominent Arena members defected to the PCN (below), with the party benefiting, in turn, by desertions from the PDC (below). The net result in the March balloting was a 1-seat Arena plurality over the FMLN.

As its 1999 presidential candidate, Arena chose Francisco Guillermo Flores Pérez, a 39-year-old economist who had held several ministerial posts and most recently had served as president of the Legislative Assembly, where he had earned a reputation as a skillful negotiator based on what *Central America Report* described as a "calm and balanced approach to politics" (in contrast to some previous Arena leaders). Flores easily outdistanced six other candidates to win the March 1999 presidential poll with nearly 52 percent of the vote. His successor, Elías Antonio ("Tony") Saca, also won easily in March 2004, with a 57.7 percent vote share.

Theretofore second-ranked, Arena gained plurality status in the 2006 legislative poll with 34 seats. It also won a plurality of municipalities in the 2006 local balloting.

Arena legislators revived civil war tensions in 2007 by proposing legislation to make party founder Roberto d'Aubuisson a "blessed son of the motherland," despite his alleged role in the 1980 slaying of Archbishop Óscar Romero. In February three Arena members (including a son of the late D'Aubuisson) were killed in Guatemala. The motive for the slayings was unclear.

In the January 2009 legislative elections, Arenas lost two seats and thus its overall lead to the FMLN. Meanwhile, the nomination of Rodrigo Ávila, a congressman and former national police chief, as party standard-bearer in the March presidential election caused a rift as some members accused him of campaign fraud. Ávila revised the Arena slogan of "Peace, progress and liberty" to "A more just country, progress with equality" in an effort to move the party to the center to compete more effectively in the elections. Nevertheless, Avila was narrowly defeated by the FMLN's Carlos Mauricio Funes, marking the first time in 18 years that Arena was not the governing party.

Leaders: Elías Antonio ("Tony") SACA (former President of the Republic); Rodrigo ÁVILA (President of the Party and 2009 presidential candidate); Francisco Guillermo FLORES Pérez (Former President of the Republic), Armando CALDERÓN Sol (Former President of the Republic), Alfredo Félix CRISTIANI Burkard (Former President of the Republic); Orlando Cabrera CANDRAY (Executive Director).

National Conciliation Party (*Partido de Conciliación Nacional*—PCN). At the time of its founding in 1961, the PCN enjoyed a fairly broad range of political support and displayed some receptivity to social and economic reform. Over the years, however, it became increasingly conservative, serving the interests of the leading families and the military establishment. Following the declared willingness of its leadership to support peace talks with the rebels in mid-1982, 9 of its 14 assembly members withdrew to form the Salvadoran Authentic Institutional Party (*Partido Auténtico Institucional Salvadoreño*—Paisa). The PCN's Francisco GUERRERO, running as a candidate of moderation, placed third in the March 1984 presidential balloting, and his refusal to back d'Aubuisson in the runoff was considered crucial to Duarte's victory. The party won 12 legislative seats in March 1985, 5 of which were lost in the 1988 poll. Its 1989 presidential candidate, Rafael MORAN Casteñeda, ran third in the March 19 balloting, winning only 4.2 percent of the vote. Its legislative representation rose from 4 to 11 seats in 1997, when it also performed well in mayoralty races. However, PCN Co-Secretary General Rafael Hernán Contreras finished fifth in the March 1999 presidential poll, his 3.8 percent of the vote just barely surpassing the required 3 percent for continued party registration.

The party won 16 legislative seats in 2003 but placed fourth, with 2.7 percent of the vote, in the 2004 presidential race. The party won 11 seats in 2009.

Leaders: Ciro Cruz ZEPEDA Peña (President of the Assembly), Rubén ORELLANA (former President of the Assembly), José Rafael MACHUCA Zelaya (2004 presidential candidate), Tomás CHÉVEZ.

Other Parties that Participated in the 2009 Parliamentary Elections:

Among other parties that failed to win seats were the Social Democratic Party, subsequently dissolved; the National Action Party, the Christian Force, the National Liberal Party, and the United Democratic Center (*Centro Democratico Unido*—UDC). (For information on a number of other parties and groups that were active in the 1990s, see the 2007 *Handbook*.)

LEGISLATURE

Formerly a 60-member body, the Legislative Assembly (*Asamblea Legislativa*) currently consists of 84 legislators, 64 elected from multi-member constituencies and 20 by proportional representation, serving three-year terms.

Following the most recent election on January 18, 2009, the seat distribution was as follows: the Farabundo Martí National Liberation Front, 35; Nationalist Republican Alliance, 32; National Conciliation Party, 11; Christian Democratic Party, 5; and Democratic Change, 1.

President: Ciro Cruz ZEPEDA Peña.

CABINET

[as of September 1, 2009]

President	Carlos Mauricio Funes Cartagena (FMLN)
Vice President	Salvador Sánchez Cerén (FMLN)
Ministers	
Agriculture and Livestock	Manuel Ramón Sevilla Avilés (FMLN)
Defense	David Mungía Victoriano Payés (ind.)
Economy	Héctor Miguel Antonio Dada Hirezi (CD)
Education	Salvador Sánchez Cerén (FMLN)
Environment and Natural Resources	Herman Humberto Rosa Chávez (ind.)
Foreign Affairs	Hugo Roger Martínez Bonilla (FMLN)
Finance	Carlos Cáceres (ind.)
Interior	Humberto Centeno Najarro (FMLN)
Labor and Social Welfare	Victoria Marina Velásquez de Avilés (FMLN) [f]
Public Health and Social Assistance	María Isabel Rodríguez (ind.) [f]

Public Security and Justice	José Manuel Melgar Henríquez (FMLN-PRTC)
Public Works	Gerson Martínez (FMLN)
Tourism	José Napoleón Duarte Durán (PDC)
Secretaries	
Secretary for Social Inclusion	Vanda Guiomar Pignato (FMLN) [f]
Secretary for Strategic Affairs	Hato Hasbún (FMLN)
Technical Secretary	Alexander Segovia (ind.)

[f] = female

COMMUNICATIONS

News media, with the exception of one official journal and certain broadcasting facilities, are nominally free of censorship and government control. Most commercial media are, however, owned by right-wing interests.

Press. The following newspapers are published daily in San Salvador: *El Diario de Hoy* (100,000 daily, 96,000 Sunday), ultraconservative; *La Prensa Gráfica* (98,000 daily, 116,000 Sunday), conservative; *El Mundo* (58,000 daily, 63,000 Sunday); *La Noticia* (30,000); *Diario Latino* (20,000); *Diario Oficial* (2,100), government-owned.

News agencies. There is no domestic facility, the media relying primarily on the government's National Information Center (*Centro de Información Nacional*—CIN) and the regional Central American News Agency (*Agencia Centroamericana de Noticias*—ACAN).

Broadcasting and computing. The former *Administración Nacional de Telecomunicaciones* (Antel) was divested in 1998. Virtually all of the licensed radio stations are now commercial, one exception being the cultural *Radio Nacional de El Salvador*. Of San Salvador's 11 television channels, 2 feature educational programming and are government operated. As of 2008 there were 106 Internet users per 1,000 inhabitants.

INTERGOVERNMENTAL REPRESENTATION

Ambassador to the U.S.: (Vacant).

U.S. Ambassador to El Salvador: (Vacant).

Permanent Representative to the UN: Carmen María GALLARDO DE HERNÁNDEZ.

IGO Memberships (Non-UN): ACS, BCIE, IADB, Interpol, IOM, OAS, OPANAL, PCA, SELA, SICA, WCO, WTO.

EQUATORIAL GUINEA

Republic of Equatorial Guinea
República de Guinea Ecuatorial

Note: In balloting on November 29, 2009, President Teodoro Obiang Nguema Mbasogo was overwhelmingly reelected by securing 95.4 percent of the vote against four other candidates. He was inaugurated for another seven-year term on December 8 and announced a new, enlarged cabinet (again led by Prime Minister Ignacio Milam Tang) in January 2010.

Area: 10,830 sq. mi. (28,051 sq. km.).

Population: 406,151 (1994C); 513,000 (2008E).

Major Urban Centers (2005E): MALABO (Bioko, 90,000), Bata (Río Muni, 70,000).

Official Language: Spanish. (French was adopted as a "commercial" language in September 1997 during a period of friction between Malabo and Madrid. In addition various African dialects are spoken, and pidgin English serves as a commercial lingua franca.)

Monetary Unit: CFA franc (official rate December 1, 2009: 434.59 CFA francs = $1US). The CFA franc, previously pegged to the French franc, is now permanently pegged to the euro at 655.957 CFA francs = 1 euro.

President: *(See headnote.)* Gen. Teodoro OBIANG Nguema Mbasogo (Democratic Party of Equatorial Guinea), assumed power as president of a Supreme Military Council following the ouster of MACIE (formerly Francisco Macías) Nguema Biyogo Ñegue Ndong on August 3, 1979; inaugurated October 12, 1982, following confirmation for a seven-year term by constitutional referendum on August 15; reelected for seven-year terms on June 25, 1989, February 25, 1996, and, in early elections, on December 15, 2002.

Prime Minister: Ignacio Milam TANG (Democratic Party of Equatorial Guinea), appointed by the president on July 8, 2008, following the president's dismissal on July 4 of Ricardo Mangue Obama NFUBE (Democratic Party of Equatorial Guinea); formed a new government on July 14.

THE COUNTRY

The least populous and the only Spanish-speaking African nation, Equatorial Guinea consists of two sharply differing regions: the mainland territory of Río Muni, including Corisco, Elobey Grande, and Elobey Chico islands as well as adjacent islets; and the island of Bioko (known prior to 1973 as Fernando Póo and from 1973 to 1979 as Macías Nguema Biyogo), including Pagalu (known prior to 1973 as Annobón) and adjacent islets in the Gulf of Guinea. Río Muni, whose area is 10,045 square miles (26,017 sq. km.), accounts for more than nine-tenths of the country's territory and about three-quarters of its total population; Bata is the principal urban center. Bioko's area covers 785 square miles (2,034 sq. km.); Malabo is the chief town and the capital of the republic.

The two basic ethnic groups, both Bantu subgroupings, are the Fang, who reportedly account for the majority of the population, and the Bubi, primarily located in Bioko. (Bubi/Fang friction remains an important issue on Bioko, while resentment has also reportedly surfaced among the rest of Fang over the dominance within that group of President Obiang's Mongomo sub-clan.) Other elements include the Kombe and various coastal tribes in Río Muni, and Fernandinos (persons of mixed racial descent) in Bioko. Roman Catholicism is the religion of approximately 80 percent of the population.

Until the discovery of oil in the mid-1990s, the economy was dominated by agriculture, the principal exports being cocoa, coffee, and timber. Industry consisted primarily of small-scale agriprocessing operations, while a small fishing sector also operated. Following the August 1979 coup, substantial aid was tendered by Spain, France, and other international donors to help Equatorial Guinea recover from the economic devastation of the Macie era, during which most skilled workers were killed or fled the country, cocoa production and per capita GNP plummeted, and such essential urban services as power and water were disrupted. In contrast to the Eastern-bloc affiliation of its predecessor, the post-Macie government adopted generally pro-Western, free-market policies. However, economic recovery was initially slow, the adverse effects of high budget and trade deficits, inflation, and a burdensome external debt being only partially offset by improvements resulting from Equatorial Guinea's admission to the franc zone, a monetary union, in 1985. Cocoa and timber prices also declined in the late 1980s, further complicating the situation.

Equatorial Guinea's economic prospects surged dramatically in the mid-1990s when significant oil and gas reserves were discovered off the north coast of Bioko. Pumping began in 1996 and had reached more than 100,000 barrels per day by early 1999; concurrently, GDP grew by nearly 100 percent in both 1997 and 1998. However, there was broad concern over the distribution of the oil wealth, reports indicating that it had been concentrated in the hands of only 5 percent of the population. Members of President Obiang's sub-clan were believed to have benefited the most extensively, and international donors restricted aid over the lack of transparency in the oil sector and perceived widespread corruption in government and business. Meanwhile, it has been estimated that as much as 75 percent of the population remained impoverished, the World Bank and International Monetary Fund (IMF) insisting that income from oil exploitation be redirected toward social services and infrastructure development.

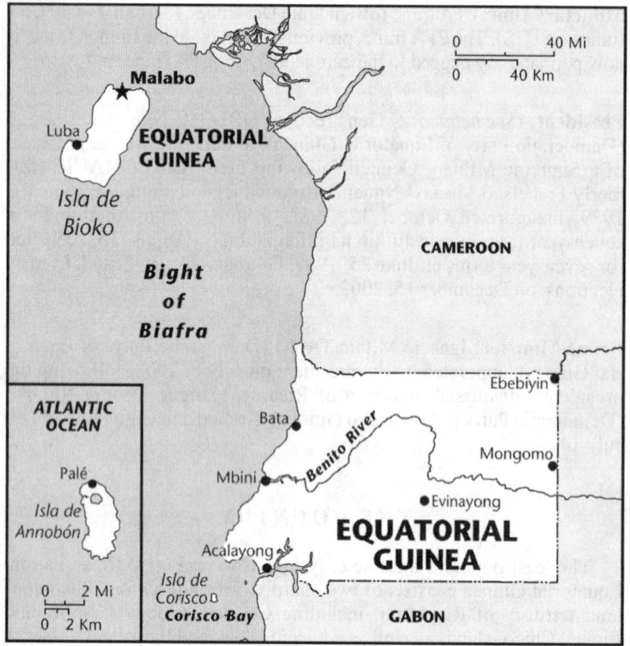

Economic growth averaged 37 percent annually from the mid-1990s to the mid-2000s, buoyed by additional discoveries of oil and potentially lucrative gas deposits. The increased revenue provided the government with regular budget surpluses in the early 2000s, although critics continued to cite perceived corruption and inefficiency, and widespread poverty persisted. Oil production peaked at close to 400,000 barrels per day in 2004 before flattening out in 2005 and declining slightly in 2006, in part due to a cap imposed by the government. Although GDP growth overall slowed to 6.5 percent in 2005 and 1 percent in 2006, the non-oil sector continued to grow at a significant pace, which the IMF cited as an indicator of progress in economic diversification. Annual GDP growth soared to 21.4 percent in 2007, buoyed again by the oil sector. However, monetary officials encouraged the government to begin planning more effectively for the use of oil revenue, rather than using it on an "ad hoc" basis without regard for long-term consequences, and the lack of transparency in the government's management of oil wealth continued to be of concern. Increased production of liquid natural gas helped offset a decline in oil production in 2008, contributing to annual GDP growth of 7.4 percent. An inflation rate of 7.5 percent was attributed, in large part, to higher food and oil prices. A further decline in oil production in 2009 slowed annual growth to 5.2 percent, with a slight contraction forecast for 2010, as no new oil fields were scheduled to come online. The IMF, though, commended authorities for having developed a national economic strategy for the next decade.

GOVERNMENT AND POLITICS

Political background. The former territory of Spanish Guinea, with Spanish sovereignty dating from 1778, was granted provincial status in 1959 and internal autonomy in 1964, achieving full independence under the name of Equatorial Guinea on October 12, 1968. The pre-independence negotiations with Spain had been complicated by differences between the mainland Fang, whose representatives sought the severance of all links with Spain, and the island Bubi, whose spokespeople advocated retention of some ties with Spain and semiautonomous status within a federal system. A compromise constitution and electoral law, submitted for popular approval in a UN-supervised referendum on August 11, 1968, was accepted by 63 percent of the people, the substantial adverse vote reflecting Bubi fears of mainland domination as well as Fang objections to the degree of self-rule accorded the islanders. In presidential balloting a month later, MACÍAS Nguema Biyogo, a mainland Fang associated with the Popular Idea of Equatorial Guinea (*Idea Popular de Guinea Ecuatorial*—IPGE), defeated the head of the pre-independence autonomous government, Bonifacio ONDO Edu of the Movement for the National Unity of Equatorial Guinea (*Movimiento de Union Nacional de Guinea Ecuatorial*—MUNGE).

In 1969 President Macías seized emergency powers during a major international crisis involving tribal rivalries, allegations of continued Spanish colonialism, and conflicting foreign economic interests. Following an unsuccessful coup d'état led by Foreign Minister Atanasio NDONGO Miyone of the National Movement for the Liberation of Equatorial Guinea (*Movimiento Nacional de Liberación de la Guinea Ecuatorial*—Monalige), the president arrested some 200 individuals, most of whom (including Ndongo) were executed. An accompanying panic, aggravated by the extralegal activities of Macías's youth militia, provoked the flight of the country's Spanish population. Subsequently, a highly centralized, single-party state was instituted, Macías's control being formalized by his assuming the presidency for life in July 1972. Along with other Equatorial Guineans, Macías dropped his Christian name (Francisco) on September 26, 1975; in 1976 he also changed his surname from Macías to Macie.

The 11-year rule of Macías/Macie (during which the country became widely known as the "Auschwitz of Africa") was terminated on August 3, 1979, in a coup led by the president's nephew, Lt. Col. Teodoro OBIANG Nguema Mbasogo, who assumed the presidency of a Supreme Military Council that later in the month named Capt. Florencio MAYÉ Elá and Capt. Salvador ELÁ Nseng as first and second vice presidents, respectively. In February 1980 Elá Nseng was succeeded by Capt. Eulogio OYO Riquesa, presiding officer of the military tribunal that had ordered Macie's execution on September 29, 1979, for crimes that included genocide, treason, and embezzlement. The government was further reshuffled in early December 1981, the first vice presidency becoming vacant in the wake of Mayé Elá's assignment to the United Nations and Capt. Cristino SERICHE Bioko succeeding Oyo Riquesa as second vice president.

Concurrent with the adoption, by referendum, of a new constitution on August 15, 1982, Colonel Obiang was confirmed as president for a seven-year term. Subsequently, Captain Seriche was named prime minister, the two vice-presidential roles being eliminated. The first National Assembly election mandated by the new constitution was held on August 28, 1983.

An attempted coup of unclear origin (the third since 1981) failed to unseat Colonel Obiang in July 1986 while he was in France attending Bastille Day celebrations. At first, the government denied a revolt had occurred; a month later, however, Eugenio ABESO Mondu, a former diplomat and a member of the National Assembly, was executed for his alleged involvement, with 12 others, including prominent cabinet members and military officers, being sentenced to jail terms.

In late 1987 President Obiang launched a government formation, the Democratic Party of Equatorial Guinea (*Partido Democrático de Guinea Ecuatorial*—PDGE), as a precursor to political liberalization. However, there was little immediate movement in that direction: as in 1983 a July 1988 legislative poll was strictly pro forma, and Obiang was the only candidate in presidential balloting in June 1989. Although Obiang hailed his reelection as the launching of a democratization process and invited political exiles to return, he rejected suggestions that a multiparty system be introduced, arguing that "political pluralism would send convulsions through the population." However, in 1990 failure to implement political reforms severely constricted foreign aid and investment. As a result, an extraordinary PDGE congress in August endorsed the adoption of a democratic constitution, which was overwhelmingly approved in a referendum of November 17, 1991. On January 23, 1992, the president appointed a new administration, headed by Silvestre SIALE Bileka as prime minister, to serve "as a prelude to the introduction of multiparty politics," and in late May the government legalized the first two of six parties.

Meanwhile, tensions between Obiang and the opposition continued to mount, with the latter accusing the government of killing an opposition activist, Feliciano MOTO, and attempting to intimidate pro-democracy advocates. The regime denied involvement in Moto's death, but in September 1992 the president's brother, National Security Director Armando NGOR Nguema, was linked to the violent breakup of a meeting of the newly formed Joint Opposition Platform (*Plataforma de la Oposición Conjunta*—POC).

Political discord continued into 1993, with Washington in mid-January accusing the Obiang regime of engaging in torture, intimidation, and unlawful imprisonment of its opponents. On March 3 the U.S. ambassador was called home for "consultations" after allegedly being targeted by a government-inspired death threat. A week later the UN Commission for Human Rights announced that it would appoint a special rapporteur to monitor conditions in Equatorial Guinea.

At poorly attended legislative balloting on November 21, 1993, the PDGE, aided by the POC's boycott, dominated the eight-party field, capturing 68 of the 80 seats. Both Spain and the United States denounced the proceedings, while the POC termed the low voter turnout a "slap in the face to the dictatorship" and insisted that absentee voters should be considered its supporters. Undeterred, the government on December 6 imposed a ban on unauthorized opposition demonstrations. Furthermore, the cabinet named two weeks later, again headed by Prime Minister Siale Bileka, included no opposition members.

International and domestic dissatisfaction with the Obiang regime continued to mount in 1994. In January Spain suspended aid payments to Malabo, protesting the president's apparent attempts to derail the democratization process, and in February Amnesty International condemned the government's human rights record. In April the administration urged opposition members to participate in a voter registration drive organized to prepare for municipal elections (then) scheduled for November. However, in August negotiations were suspended with a prominent opposition party, the Progress Party of Equatorial Guinea (*Partido del Progresso de Guinea Ecuatorial*—PPGE), after its leader, Severo MOTO Nsa, had criticized the government, and on October 5 two people were killed in a clash between government troops and demonstrators in Malabo. Subsequently, the government suffered a major setback when House speaker Felipe Ondo OBIANG Alogo and his deputy, Antonio Pascual Oko EBOBO, both prominent PDGE members, resigned on October 25, because of the "very poor management" that had led Equatorial Guinea into a "disastrous social and economic situation."

The nation's first multiparty municipal elections were held on September 17, 1995, the PDGE being credited with victories in 18 of the 27 localities. However, domestic and international observers challenged the government's voting tally, the POC arguing that the opposition had really garnered about 80 percent of the votes.

On January 12, 1996, Obiang decreed that presidential elections would be held on February 25, three months before his term was set to expire. Opposition leaders immediately denounced the president's actions as unconstitutional and designed to preclude effective organization on their part. By late January a number of opposition candidates had emerged, including the PPGE's Moto and three from the POC. However, the subsequent run-up was reportedly marked by gross malfeasance, including harassment of opposition activists and replacement of a UN-compiled electoral list with a government list that excluded voters in regions that had supported the opposition in previous polling. Consequently, most opposition candidates ultimately withdrew and called on their supporters to boycott the election.

At the February 25, 1996, polling President Obiang was credited with 97.85 percent of the votes. However, citing the pre-polling malpractice, apparent election day irregularities, and the dearth of impartial international election monitors, most observers dismissed the election as a sham. On March 29 Obiang appointed Angel Serafin Seriche DOUGAN to succeed Prime Minister Siale Bileka. Several parliamentary parties joined the expanded cabinet announced on April 9, although, not surprisingly, the major opposition groupings declined Obiang's invitation to join in a government of national unity. On January 15, 1998, Dougan and his cabinet resigned in accordance with a presidential mandate that required the prime minister to submit his government for review after two years in office. Two days later, Obiang reappointed Dougan head of a reshuffled government. In mid-January 1998 Prime Minister Dougan's claim to having preserved "national unity" during his first term was challenged in Bioko Island, where ethnic Bubi separatists reportedly attacked government offices. (The Bubi were the dominant group on the island until independence but since then have been surpassed in numbers by the Fang.) Denying a role in the violence, leaders of the Movement for the Self-Determination of the Island of Bioko—MAIB (see Political Parties, below) charged the government with a "veritable genocide" and reaffirmed their desire for self-rule. In March the Obiang administration denied charges by Amnesty International that it was torturing separatist prisoners. Thereafter, a military court sentenced 15 of the separatists to death in June for their alleged roles in the uprising, although the president commuted the death sentences in September following the prison death of a dissident who had reportedly been beaten by security forces. (The president's acts of clemency came amid speculation that his international economic sponsors were reconsidering their support.) Meanwhile, the government had reportedly arrested dozens of opposition activists in an apparent attempt to disrupt their preparations for legislative balloting (scheduled for late 1998, but postponed until early 1999). In balloting on March 7, 1999, the PDGE increased its legislative dominance, capturing 75 of the 80 posts in polling that was reportedly again marked by widespread irregularities. On July 9 Obiang reappointed Dougan prime minister, and on July 22 Dougan announced a streamlined, reshuffled cabinet.

The PDGE reportedly won 230 of 244 seats and control of all 30 municipal councils in the local elections of May 28, 2000. Observers described the balloting as generally free and fair, although its significance was greatly undercut by the fact that three leading independent parties boycotted what they described as just the most recent "electoral farce." Some analysts suggested that Western capitals were ignoring the lack of democratic progress (as well as continued human rights violations) in view of the dramatic surge in oil production.

In light of continued corruption allegations against various government officials, President Obiang reportedly asked Prime Minister Dougan to resign as early as October 2000, although it wasn't until February 23, 2001, that Dougan acquiesced to the pressure. Incoming prime minister Cándido Muatetema RIVAS, a former deputy secretary general of the PDGE, pledged the new government, which included members of several small parties in junior positions, would protect the "economic" and "social" rights of all citizens while maintaining the "stability" that the country has enjoyed for more than two decades. For its part, the "frail" opposition charged that oil proceeds were being diverted to promote a "clan dictatorship," a reference to reports of maneuvering within the president's ethnic group to ensure long-term retention of power.

Amid continuing political turmoil and continued government suppression of the opposition, President Obiang moved the next presidential balloting up from February 2003 to December 15, 2002. Most opposition parties boycotted the election, and Obiang was reelected with 97.1 percent of the vote. Although Obiang had promised to appoint a government of national unity, he reappointed Rivas to head a reshuffled cabinet that was again dominated by the PDGE and included two of Obiang's sons.

The PDGE and its allies (the newly formed Democratic Opposition coalition) won 98 of 100 seats in the April 25, 2004, balloting for the House of People's Representatives. They also secured nearly all of the seats in concurrent municipal elections. Prime Minister Rivas resigned on June 11 and was succeeded three days later by Miguel Abia Biteo BORICO.

Borico and the entire cabinet resigned on August 10, 2006 (see Current issues, below), and President Obiang appointed Ricardo Mangue Obama NFUBE as prime minister on August 14. On August 15 the president appointed two vice prime ministers, both from the PDGE. On August 16 Nfube named a new cabinet, which again was dominated by the PDGE but also included members of the Democratic Opposition coalition.

Following dissolution of the House of People's Representatives on February 29, 2008, President Obiang called for early elections on May 4 to coincide with municipal elections. The PDGE again dominated the legislative balloting, winning 89 seats. The Democratic Opposition, a coalition of eight parties with whom the PDGE had formed an electoral alliance, won ten seats. The PDGE was victorious in the municipal elections as well. On June 8, the president appointed Ignacio Milam TANG, the country's ambassador to Spain, to replace Prime Minister Nfube, whom the president had dismissed on July 4. Following the resignation of the cabinet on the same day, the president referred to the outgoing government as "one of the worst ever," levying blanket accusations of corruption and mismanagement. On July 14 the president appointed a new cabinet, composed entirely of PDGE members. The national security minister was replaced on February 27, 2009.

Constitution and government. The 1982 constitution provided for an elected president serving a seven-year term and for a Council of State, one of whose functions was to screen candidates for presidential nomination. A National Council for Economic and Social Development was linked to the administration in a consultative capacity, while legislative functions were assigned to a unicameral National Assembly, whose members were elected for five-year terms.

The basic law of November 1991 called for a separation of functions between the president and prime minister, while authorizing competing parties. At the same time, it severely limited opposition activity by banning from presidential or parliamentary eligibility all individuals who had not been continuously resident in the country for the preceding two years. In addition, it stipulated that the head of state could "not be impeached, or called as a witness before, during and after his term of office." Subsequent legislation on the formation of political parties specified that no such group could be organized on a tribal, regional, or provincial basis.

In late 1980 the country was divided into 6 provinces (4 mainland and 2 insular) as part of a process of administrative reform, while there are currently 30 elected municipal governments.

Foreign relations. While officially nonaligned, the Macie regime tended to follow the lead of the more radical African states. Diplomatic relations were established with—and aid received from—several Communist regimes, including the Soviet Union, the People's Republic of China, Cuba, and North Korea. Relations with Gabon and Cameroon were strained as a result of territorial disputes, while by 1976 the mistreatment of Nigerian contract workers had led Lagos to repatriate some 25,000 people, most of them laborers on cocoa plantations. By contrast, the Obiang regime has striven for regional cooperation, with a Nigerian consulate opening in Bata in 1982 and a joint defense pact being concluded during a three-day official visit to Lagos by President Obiang in January 1987. Economic agreements were signed with Cameroon and the Central African Republic in 1983, and Obiang was active in the formation of the Central African Economic Community, announced in October 1983. Two months later, Equatorial Guinea became the first non-French-speaking member of the Central African Customs and Economic Union (UDEAC). As the only African country with Spanish as its official language, Equatorial Guinea was also anxious to develop links with Latin America and was accorded permanent observer status with the Organization of American States (OAS).

At the time of Macie's ouster, France was the only Western power maintaining an embassy in Malabo, although Spain had long been purchasing export commodities at above-market prices. Madrid made its first overture to the new regime in December 1979 with a state visit by King Juan Carlos, in the wake of which economic and military assistance was tendered; in 1983, Spain played a leading role in renegotiating the Equatorial Guinea's $45 million foreign debt. Nevertheless, following Equatorial Guinea's admission to the franc zone in 1985, Malabo emphasized rapidly expanding ties with France and francophone West African countries.

Frayed by Spain's criticism of Equatorial Guinea's political and human rights practices, ties between the two countries weakened steadily in 1993. In August the government of Equatorial Guinea charged Madrid with inciting antigovernment violence on Annobon Island. In November Spain formally refused to underwrite the legislative balloting, saying it failed to meet "minimum requirements," and following the expulsion of its consul general in Bata, Madrid recalled its ambassador. Among other Western observers, only France openly supported the electoral process, with the United States and the United Nations refusing to provide poll watchers.

In September 1997 Equatorial Guinea temporarily suspended diplomatic relations with Spain after Madrid refused to repeal the refugee status of PPGE leader Severo Moto Nsa. (For further details about the Moto case, see the PPGE below and the 1998 *Handbook*.)

In mid-1999 Equatorial Guinea filed a complaint against Cameroon with the International Court of Justice after Cameroon had made territorial claims to a section of the Gulf of Guinea that included Bioko Island. Fueling the dispute, as well as an ongoing border disagreement between Equatorial Guinea and Nigeria, were the recent discoveries of offshore oil deposits. In an effort to reduce tensions and increase cooperation in the Gulf region, a Gulf of Guinea Commission was established in November by Equatorial Guinea, Angola, Congo, Gabon, Nigeria, and São Tome e Príncipe. In September 2000, Equatorial Guinea and Nigeria settled their border dispute, each country gaining sovereignty over one of the two major disputed oil fields.

Full economic ties with Spain were restored by 2001, and Madrid in 2003 forgave some $65 million of Equatorial Guinea's external debt. In addition, Spain offered diplomatic support to Equatorial Guinea when Gabonese troops occupied the disputed island of Mbagne. Gabon subsequently offered to withdraw its troops in exchange for an oil-sharing agreement that would cover the island and its surrounding waters, but President Obiang rejected that proposal. Also in 2003, the United States reopened its embassy in Equatorial Guinea as U.S. companies continued to dominate oil exploration and production in the republic.

After Gabon and Equatorial Guinea agreed in 2004 to abide by the decision of a UN mediator appointed to investigate the island dispute, the case was submitted to the International Court of Justice in 2006. In June 2008, UN Secretary General Ban Ki-Moon began mediation to help facilitate a resolution. Meanwhile, China continued its investments on the continent by committing $2 billion to Equatorial Guinea for projects restricted to Chinese companies using Chinese products.

In November 2008 an odd event strained relations with Cameroon, when a nephew of President Obiang was kidnapped in Yaoundé, allegedly by two Cameroonian police officers who received $30,000 for their effort. Cameroon arrested the officers, denied any involvement, and accused the Equatorial Guinean embassy of being involved in the plot. (The president's nephew, a former army colonel, had been granted refugee status in Cameroon in 2003, and in 2005 he was sentenced to 30 years in absentia for his role in a failed coup attempt against President Obiang.) The Equatorial Guinean embassy denied any involvement.

Tensions with Cameroon were strained further in 2009 following the death of a Cameroonian fisherman in Equatorial Guinean waters, the maritime border having become contentious. In January Cameroon released three seafarers from Equatorial Guinea in exchange for three Cameroonian fishermen detained by Equatorial Guinean troops near the southern border.

Current issues. The already strained relations between the regime and the opposition deteriorated even further when the government in March 2002 initiated a major crackdown that included the arrest of numerous party leaders. The government claimed it was responding to an alleged coup conspiracy, although the opposition and some members of the international community accused Obiang of merely trying to clear the way for his reelection.

In the aftermath of Obiang's victory in the December 2002 presidential elections, a new cabinet was formed that included the president's son Teodoro Nguema OBIANG Mangue. Speculation continued that Obiang's son was being prepared as his successor. Meanwhile, international observers widely agreed with Obiang's domestic critics that the presidential poll and the legislative elections of April 2004 were deeply flawed—or even fraudulent and invalid.

In December 2003 a number of senior military officers were arrested on suspicion of plotting a coup, and most were given secret trials beginning in February 2004. In March, 19 others were arrested in a separate alleged coup plot. Finally, in a bizarre series of events that attracted substantial worldwide attention, Zimbabwe detained 70 suspected mercenaries en route to Equatorial Guinea. Simon MANN, a former British special forces officer, was charged with masterminding the plot. The group went on trial in Zimbabwe in July, and many pleaded guilty to minor offenses, including illegal possession of weapons and immigration violations, and received minor sentences. On August 25 Mark THATCHER, son of former British prime minister Margaret THATCHER, was arrested in South Africa and charged with providing $275,000 to support the coup. On January 19, 2005, he pleaded guilty in exchange for a $506,000 fine, a suspended jail sentence, and the opportunity to leave South Africa for the United States. A condition of his release was that Thatcher answer questions about his role for Equatorial Guinean prosecutors. Later that year Malabo lost its claim for civil damages in the case in a British court. Obiang accused a variety of foreign governments, including Spain and the United Kingdom, of being involved in the coup attempt and ordered the forced deportation of several hundred foreign nationals. Obiang also ordered the arrest of a number of opposition figures, and accused exiled members of the opposition of involvement in the attempted overthrow. Most of the mercenaries were released from prison in Zimbabwe in May 2005.

Early in 2006, U.S. Secretary of State Condoleezza Rice drew criticism for meeting with President Obiang in Washington in the wake of State Department accusations of torture and other human rights violations, particularly regarding prisoners. One day earlier Obiang had signed an aid agreement with the United States. In April Equatorial Guinea and the U.S. Agency for International Development (USAID) signed an agreement establishing a social development fund to enhance health, education, and other social services, financed by Equatorial Guinea with USAID oversight of transparency and accountability.

By mid-2006 attention focused on the government upheaval precipitated by the resignation of Prime Minister Borico and the entire cabinet following months of criticism by President Obiang over alleged "corruption and ineptitude." The new prime minister, Ricardo Mangue Obama Nfube, was the first Fang to hold that position since the republic gained independence in 1968. Some observers noted that by placing a fellow Fang at the head of the government, Obiang was further tightening his rule. (Previous prime ministers had been chosen from the Bubi group, in what analysts perceived to be a gesture toward political equity.) Other analysts saw Nfube's appointment as providing protection for marginalized members of Obiang's Fang sub-clan. There followed some speculation that Nfube could be Obiang's likely successor.

In November 2006 the president's son, Teodoro Nguema Obiang Mangue, made international headlines after a company he managed bought a luxury home in the United States valued at $35 million. News reports noted his yearly salary of approximately $5,000 as a cabinet minister. In a similar case before a South African court regarding two Cape Town homes valued at $7 million, the younger Obiang contended that he was earning money by owning companies permitted to bid on government contracts with foreign groups. (In many countries, unlike Equatorial Guinea, ministers are not permitted to conduct such business as a conflict of interest.)

The protracted case of Simon Mann received significant attention following his rearrest in 2007 on a warrant for his deportation issued by Equatorial Guinea. He was extradited from Zimbabwe to Equatorial Guinea on February 1, 2008, to face charges of plotting a coup, with the government in Equatorial Guinea promising a fair trial.

In accordance with his near-authoritarian power, President Obiang dissolved parliament on February 29, 2008, and called for early elections—11 months ahead of schedule—to coincide with municipal elections on May 4, in what was described as a cost-saving measure. With the support of the Democratic Opposition coalition, Obiang's PDGE retained control of the House of the People's Representatives, the CPDS securing only 1 seat (a loss of 1 seat). According to news accounts, the PDGE received 100 percent of the votes in numerous districts and 99 percent in others. The party also won overwhelmingly in the concurrent municipal elections. The president replaced the prime minister in July, making public reference to the former government as "the worst ever." Observers speculated that part of the reason for the appointment of Ignacio Milam Tang and a new, all-PDGE government was related to allegations that one of the ministers in Nfube's cabinet had been involved in the coup attempt linked to Simon Mann, who one day before the prime minister's appointment was sentenced to 34 years in prison for leading the plot.

Accusations of torture continued to be levied against President Obiang, and in mid-2008 Amnesty International called for the unconditional release of all political prisoners. Subsequently, the president released 14 prisoners, most of whom had been held for up to six years and allegedly tortured. In October, a rumor that President Obiang had died was quashed when the president publicly blamed the "exiled opposition" for declaring that he was in an "irreversible coma." The 66-year-old president denied reports of ill health.

An attack on the presidential palace on February 17, 2009, was blamed on rebels from the Niger Delta region of Nigeria. President Obiang was not in residence when gunmen arrived by speedboat and stormed the palace in what was described as a criminal act, not a coup attempt. Subsequently, 16 men were arrested, the Nigerian government denying any involvement. Ten days later President Obiang dismissed the national security minister and banned speedboats from Equatorial Guinean waters. In March the new national security minister addressed another matter of concern when he asked the army and security forces to stop "the plundering violence and other barbaric acts against foreigners." Some analysts speculated that the violence was a result of misinterpretation of remarks by the president calling for the repatriation of all foreigners suspected of breaking the law. It was also reported in March that 12 Nigerians had been killed and 128 imprisoned in Equatorial Guinea, allegedly because they belonged to militant groups.

POLITICAL PARTIES

Political parties were banned in the wake of the 1979 coup. In late 1987 President Obiang announced the formation of a government party (the Democratic Party of Equatorial Guinea—PDGE), as part of what he called a democratization process that might eventually lead to the legalization of other groups. In late 1991 and early 1992 the Obiang regime approved legislation that (albeit with restrictive provisions, including a requirement that applicant groups pay a deposit of approximately $110,000) provided a legal framework for the formation of political parties. In May 1992 two parties, the Liberal Democratic Convention (CLD) and the Popular Union (UP), were registered, and by the end of the year four more had been legalized.

During February 10–March 18, 1993, the government sponsored an assembly of the PDGE and the (then) ten legal opposition parties to discuss ways to improve the "democratization process," including lessened restrictions on party activities and increased access to state funds and media. Nevertheless, charging a lack of government action, most opposition parties declared that they would boycott elections then scheduled for August. Ultimately, eight parties, including the PDGE, took part in the November balloting; however, the three leading members of the Joint Opposition Platform (POC) refused to participate. After suffering from what they perceived as government electoral abuses in the September 1995 municipal elections, many opposition parties boycotted the February 1996 presidential poll. (There have been no references to the POC since the late 1990s.)

For its part, the POC was unable to agree upon a single candidate in the chaotic run-up to the 1996 presidential election and was subsequently reported to have "collapsed in acrimony" over the issue. Two parties previously associated with the POC (the CLD and the Social Democratic Union [UDS, below]) accepted cabinet posts in April 1996.

In October 1997 the two most prominent former POC members, the Progress Party of Equatorial Guinea (PPGE) and the UP, joined with the Union for Democracy and Social Development (UDDS) and the Republican Democratic Force (FDR) to form a new coalition, the **National Liberation Council.** The council's platform was highlighted by a pledge to "bring a change of government . . . at all costs." In December the legislature passed a law forbidding the formation of coalitions prior to legislative balloting (then scheduled for mid-1998, but subsequently postponed until March 1999).

In early 2000 Victorino BOLEKIA Bonay, the leader of the opposition Progressive Democratic **Alliance** (*Alianza Demócratica y Progresiva*—ADP) and former mayor of Malabo, announced that the opposition, including the Convergence for Social Democracy (CPDS) and the UP, would boycott municipal balloting scheduled for May. According to Bolekia, the opposition would only participate if the government agreed to conduct a fair electoral census, invite international observers to oversee the polling, and, in addition to other demands, allow opposition activists freedom of expression and movement.

Various, and at times overlapping, opposition alliances were formed in 2000 and 2001, the most prominent of which was the **Democratic Opposition Front** (*Frente de la Oposicion Demócratica*—FOD) that included the UP, ADP, the CPDS, the PPGE, and the Social Democratic Party (PSD). The FOD was launched in November 2000. In December the **Equatorial Guinea National Resistance** (*Resistencia Nacional Guinea Ecuatorial*—RENAGE) was launched in Barcelona, Spain; it included the UP, the UDDS, the FDR, the MAIB, and the Union of Independent Socialists (UDI). In March 2001 a new opposition alliance was reportedly formed by the UP, the CPDS, the PPGE, the FDR, the UDI, the MAIB, the National Alliance for the Restoration of Democracy (ANRD), the UDDS, the Party of the Democratic Coalition, and the Forum for Democracy in Equatorial Guinea (see below). Although instrumental in the formation of all of the above opposition alliances, the Popular Union (UP) accepted a junior cabinet post in March 2001. However, the UP campaigned against the dominant PDGE in the 2004 elections.

Government and Government-Supportive Parties:

Democratic Party of Equatorial Guinea (*Partido Democrático de Guinea Ecuatorial*—PDGE). The PDGE was launched in October 1987 by President Obiang, who said it would be used to address the country's development problems while promoting national unity and "respect for the constitution and freedoms." Shortly thereafter, the House of Representatives approved a law requiring all public officials and salaried employees to contribute 3 percent of their salaries to the new formation.

During an extraordinary party congress in Bata on August 4–6, 1991, party delegates urged the government to establish short-, medium-, and long-term plans to lead to the legalization of other political groups. The party also adopted resolutions calling for the adoption of a multi-candidature presidential system and the drafting of a law on press rights.

At the PDGE's second national congress on March 20–26, 1995, President Obiang reaffirmed the party's preeminent role in the implementation of public policy and the PDGE has since remained the dominant government party. In legislative elections in 2004 the PDGE and its allies in the Democratic Opposition (see below) received 87.9 percent of the vote and 98 of the 100 seats in the legislature. In local elections, the PDGE and its allies won 237 of 244 posts. In 2008 the party won 89 seats in the assembly elections and also swept the concurrent local elections. Because of its electoral alliance with the Democratic Opposition (below), the PDGE effectively controlled 99 of the 100 legislative seats.

Leaders: Brig. Gen. Teodoro OBIANG Nguema Mbasogo (President of the Republic), Ignacio Milam TANG (Prime Minister), Ricardo Mangue Obama NFUBE (Former Prime Minister), Miguel Abia Biteo BORICO (Former Prime Minister), Alberto Sima NGUEMA (Vice President), Cristina Djombe DJAGANI (Vice President), Severino OBIANG Efong (Deputy Vice President), Evangelina Filomena Oyó EBULE (Deputy Vice President), Santiago NGUA Mfumu (Deputy Secretary General), Filiberto Ntutumu NGUEMA (Secretary General).

Democratic Opposition (Electoral Coalition). Formed in 2004, this coalition of eight pro-presidential parties campaigned with the support of the PDGE in both legislative and local elections. The coalition gained 30 seats in the legislature, and legislators from two of the parties—the Liberal Democratic Convention and the Social Democratic Union—were appointed to posts in the government. The Democratic Opposition also campaigned with the PDGE in the concurrent municipal elections, winning, with the PDGE, 237 of 244 posts.

In 2008 the coalition won 10 assembly seats in an electoral alliance with the PDGE, but no posts in the new government.

Leaders: Alfonse MOKUY (CLD), Carmelo MODÚ Acusé Bindang (UDS).

Liberal Democratic Convention (*Convención Liberal Democrática*—CLD). Also identified as the Liberal Party (*Partido Liberal*—PL), the CLD was legally recognized in May 1992. In November Santos Pascual BIKOMO Nanguande, who had previously been linked to the **People's Alliance** (*Alianza del Pueblo*—AP), was named to serve as CLD chair until the party's first congress. An attempt to hold such a congress in January 1994 was blocked by the government after Bikomo had charged it with election irregularities.

The CLD was credited with winning one legislative seat in November 1993. Although an original member of the POC, the CLD supported President Obiang in the February 1996 presidential balloting, and Bikomo was named information minister in the new April government. Although Bikomo left his post in 1997, the CLD remained a government-supportive party and held junior ministries following the 1999 and 2004 elections. The party held no ministry posts following the July 14, 2008, cabinet reshuffle, when the president named an all-PDGE government.

Leader: Alfonse MOKUY (President).

Social Democratic Union (*Unión Demócrata Social*—UDS). Formerly a Gabon-based grouping affiliated with the ADP and the **Democratic Social Union** (*Unión Social Democrática* —USD), the UDS was officially recognized in October 1992 under the leadership of Carmelo Modú Acusé Bindang. In November it was reported that the UDS leadership had expelled Modú for pursuing "ideals which ran counter to the principles" of the party and had named Angel Miko Alo Nchama as interim chair. However, Modú was subsequently again described as the leader of the UDS, which won 5 legislative seats in November 1993. After supporting President Obiang for reelection, Modú was named minister of state for labor and social security in the April 1996 cabinet and has subsequently held several government posts. The party's former secretary general, Aquilino Nguema Ona NCHAMA, who originally sought political refuge in Gabon, was reportedly living in exile in Spain and was secretary general of the UDDS (see Other Parties and Groups, below).

Leaders: Carmelo MODÚ Acusé Bindang, Angel Miko Alo NCHAMA.

Social Democratic and Popular Convention (*Convención Social Demócrata y Popular*—CSDP). The CSDP is reportedly split into two factions. The first, led by Rafael Obiang, apparently remained aligned with the POC, having boycotted the 1993 parliamentary elections and the 1996 presidential balloting. The second, led by Secundio Oyono Awong, participated in the 1993 legislative campaign, winning 6 seats. The latter also forwarded Oyono Awong as a presidential contender in 1996, several reports describing him as the only opposition candidate not to withdraw from the campaign prior to balloting.

Leaders: Rafael OBIANG, Secundio OYONO Awong (1996 presidential candidate).

Social Democratic Coalition Party (*Partido de Coalición Social Demócrata*—PCSD). The PCSD was officially registered in 1993. In early 1996 party leader Buenaventura Mezui Masumu announced his presidential candidacy; however, he withdrew from the campaign to protest the government's allegedly fraudulent pre-election activities. In the 2004 legislative and municipal elections, the PCSD garnered less than 1 percent of the vote.

Leader: Buenaventura Mezui MASUMU.

Social Democratic Party (*Partido Social Demócrata*—PSD). Formed by Marcellino Mangue MBA and recognized as a party in 1992, the PSD was formerly affiliated with the anti-Obiang group, the Party of the Democratic Coalition (see below). However, it joined the pro-presidential coalition in 2004.

Leader: Benjamín BALINGA (President).

Other members of the Democratic Opposition include the **Progressive Democratic Alliance** (*Alianza Demócrata Progresista*—ADP), led by Victorino Bolekia BONAY, former mayor of Malabo; the **Democratic National Union of Equatorial Guinea** (*Unión Demócráta Nacional*—UDENA), led by José MECHEBA; and the **Liberal Party** (*Partido Liberal*—PL).

Other Legislative Party:

Convergence for Social Democracy (*Convergencia para la Democracia Social*—CPDS). The CPDS was launched in Paris in May 1984, setting as its goal talks with President Obiang designed "to democratically transform all the state institutions, to guarantee fundamental liberties, and to promote a policy of cooperation with neighboring countries and the Western world." The party was legally recognized in February 1993; however, on September 19, two days after he was convicted of murder in a summary military trial, CPDS activist Romualdo Rafael NSOGO was executed. Subsequently, CPDS leaders denounced the regime, accusing it of killing Nsogo in an attempt to intimidate the opposition.

In early 1996 the CPDS presented Anoncio NZE Angue as its presidential candidate, although he withdrew, along with the other POC candidates, to protest the government's tactics prior to the balloting. Nze was reportedly arrested in March for possessing CPDS documents referring to the Obiang administration as "an unreconstructed family dictatorship." At that time *Africa Confidential* referred to the CPDS as the "most radical" opposition group and the least likely to participate in national unity talks with the government.

In early 1998 a CPDS spokesperson reportedly accused the West of refusing to put pressure on the Obiang administration to enact political and social reforms because of Western "economic interests" in the country. In April the group claimed that nearly 50 of its members had been arrested by government security forces.

The CPDS won one seat in legislative polling in March 1999 but its representative subsequently refused to assume the post in protest over the government's alleged electoral malfeasance. On May 9, 2002, Secretary General Plácido Micó Abogo was arrested on charges of conspiracy to assassinate the president. He was pardoned in August 2003.

The CPDS won 2 seats in the 2004 legislative balloting but denounced the results because of alleged voting problems.

In January 2005 Santiago Obama Ndong was elected party president. In May the party's publication, *The Truth* (*La Verdad*), reportedly was shut down by the government, a month after several CPDS activists were arrested following clashes with security forces. The government denied any crackdown on the group, which in the early 2000s was described by observers as the main opposition group in Equatorial Guinea.

In the run-up to the 2008 legislative elections, the party's headquarters were reportedly raided by police. The CPDS won just one seat in the assembly, the party's secretary general subsequently alleging fraud.

Leaders: Santiago Obama NDONG (President), Celestino Bonifacio BACALE (2002 presidential candidate), Pio OBAMA, Juan NZO (Deputy Secretary General), Plácido Micó ABOGO (Secretary General).

Other Parties and Groups:

Popular Union (*Unión Popular*—UP). The UP was legally recognized in May 1992. However, in October party members were detained and beaten by government security forces, and in March 1993 the group reportedly concluded a merger agreement with the PPGE (although there was no confirmation of the accord).

In August 1993 the government announced that a UP activist, Pedro MOTU Mamiaka, had committed suicide while in detention. However, Amnesty International accused security forces of torturing him to death, and the UP described the killing as another demonstration of the government's persecution of dissenters.

The UP presented Andrés Moisés Mba Ada as a candidate in the 1996 presidential campaign, reportedly angering more senior politicians in the POC. In April 1998 the UP claimed that the government had detained 200 of its activists during a nationwide crackdown on opposition members. Furthermore, in August the group charged the government with expelling its members from electoral oversight committees.

The UP won 4 seats in the 1999 legislative balloting, but party leaders ordered the UP legislators to refuse to take their seats as a protest against perceived electoral fraud on the part of the government. However, two of the legislators reportedly disobeyed the orders of the UP leaders, producing a split in the party between those members who support a degree of cooperation with the PDGE and those who insist on substantial reform of the political process prior to such compromise. The former faction seemed to have captured the party's higher positions with the election of Jeremias ONDO Ngomo to replace Mba as the president in October 2000. The UP then reversed its previous decision to boycott the assembly, and Ondo accepted a junior post in the new government formed in March 2001. The UP secretary general, Fabián Nsue Nguema, was subsequently arrested for treason but was pardoned in November 2002. The UP reportedly remained active in various opposition alliances, and it joined the boycott of the 2004 legislative election.

Under pressure by the government in 2007 to elect a new leader, the UP held a party congress in October and chose Faustino Ond Ebang as its president. However, the government subsequently refused to recognize Ebang. In the aftermath of the attack on the presidential palace in February 2009, nine members of the UP, including Ebang's brother and two others who previously were members of the outlawed PPGE, were arrested and detained without charge, according to Amnesty International.

Leaders: Faustino Ond EBANG (President), Jeremias ONDO Ngomo, Andrés Moisés MBA Ada (Former President of the Party), Fabián Nsue NGUEMA (Secretary General).

Socialist Party of Equatorial Guinea (*Partido Socialista de Guinea Ecuatorial*—PSGE). Citing legislative constraints on party activity, the PSGE in January 1992 described President Obiang's multiparty advocacy as an attempt to "deceive" international observers. Subsequently, party leader Tomas Mecheba Fernández called for foreign intervention, "military if necessary," to force the regime to cease its human rights violations. The PSGE later supported cooperation with the PDGE, and Fernández accepted a junior post in the cabinet in 2001. However, the party did not gain seats in the 2004 legislative election and did not participate in the subsequent cabinet.

Leader: Tomas Mecheba FERNÁNDEZ (President).

Democratic Movement for the Liberation of Equatorial Guinea (*Reunión Democrática para la Liberación de Guinea Ecuatorial*—RDLGE). Formed in 1981, the Paris-based RDLGE announced a provisional government-in-exile in March 1983 following the failure of reconciliation talks between its leader and Colonel Obiang in late 1982. The RDLGE was considered a relatively moderate opposition group, the formation of the CPDS apparently representing its response to the creation by more strident groups of the *Junta Coordinadora* (below, under ANRD).

Leader: Manuel Rubén NDONGO.

African Socialist Party of Equatorial Guinea (*Partido Socialista Africano de Guinea Ecuatorial*—PSAGE). Based in Oviedo, Spain, the PSAGE was little known prior to its CPDS alliance with the RDLGE.

Progress Party of Equatorial Guinea (*Partido del Progreso de Guinea Ecuatorial*—PPGE). Also referenced as the People's Party of Equatorial Guinea, the PPGE was formed in Madrid in early 1983 by Severo Moto Nsa, a former secretary of state for information and tourism. Moto and other PPGE leaders returned to Malabo in mid-1988, apparently believing that the government had adopted a conciliatory attitude toward its opponents. However, a PPGE petition for recognition as a legal party was denied, and Moto returned to exile. In September several PPGE members, including Secretary General José Luis Jones, were jailed in connection with an alleged coup plot. Given a lengthy prison sentence shortly after his arrest, Jones received a presidential pardon in January 1989; also departing the country, he condemned the June presidential poll as "clearly not valid."

In August 1991 Moto planned a second termination of exile to campaign for a multiparty system and the holding of free elections, but the government refused to renew his passport until May 1992, when he returned to Malabo. In early September PPGE members were among those detained in another government crackdown on dissident activity. Nonetheless, the party was legalized in October.

In July 1994 the government severed relations with the PPGE after Moto allegedly "defamed" the Obiang regime, and in November the PPGE leader accused Obiang of involvement in the death of his brother, Vincente MOTO. Subsequently, in March 1995, Moto was sentenced to 18 months in prison for allegedly bribing a government official and defaming the head of state. A far more severe sentence of 28 years was imposed on Moto in April by a military tribunal investigating an alleged coup plot. The sentences were condemned by a number of Western governments, and, following the intercession of French President Jacques Chirac, President Obiang granted amnesty to Moto on August 3.

Moto announced his candidacy for president in early 1996; however, like most other opposition candidates, he withdrew prior to the balloting and urged PPGE supporters to boycott the election. Nevertheless, at midyear Moto was reported to have indicated the willingness of the PPGE and some of the other remaining POC component groups to reopen discussions with the Obiang government. In June 1997 the government banned the PPGE after it was revealed that Moto had allegedly been planning to overthrow the Obiang government. The following month the party ousted Moto after he restated his willingness to use violence to topple the government. On August 18 Moto was convicted in absentia of high treason and sentenced to at least 30 years in jail. Concurrently, the government ordered the PPGE to dissolve.

In October 1997 Moto, who was still being identified by observers as the PPGE's leader, surfaced in the Democratic Republic of the Congo as the organizer of a new antigovernment coalition. Subsequently, the PPGE suffered another blow when its first and second deputy leaders reportedly defected to the PDGE in early 1998.

In early 1999 Moto filed suit in Spain against the Obiang government, charging it with engaging in "state terrorism and genocide." Furthermore, Moto announced that his party would boycott legislative polling in March. The government called on Madrid to expel Moto, who had reportedly been residing there for two years. The PPGE also boycotted the 2004 elections, joining with other exile groups to form a government-in-exile in Spain with Moto as its leader.

In late 2005, Spain revoked political asylum for Moto but refused to return him to Equatorial Guinea or any other country that would not guarantee his safety.

In March 2008 eight party members were arrested in Equatorial Guinea, one of whom was reported to have died in custody. Subsequently, Moto was arrested in Spain in April on charges of arms trafficking to Equatorial Guinea. The PPGE was banned from participating in Equatorial Guinea's legislative elections in May. Meanwhile, Moto, who had been arrested in Spain on charges of arms trafficking, was sentenced in absentia to 62 years in prison for his alleged involvement in a 2004 coup attempt .*Leaders:* Severo MOTO Nsá (President, in exile), Armengol ENGONGA (Vice President), José Luis JONES (Secretary General).

Republican Democratic Force (*Fuerza Demócrata Republicana*—FDR). In October 1997 this grouping was reported among the founders of the National Liberation Council. Subsequently, its cofounders, Felipe Ondo Obiang and Guillermo Nguema Ela, were described by party members as having been "abducted"; however, the government then admitted holding the two, and in mid-November they were released without explanation. In March 1998 the two were rearrested and charged with making defamatory comments about the president. They were released in March 2000, at which time they vowed to continue their campaign against the administration. In 2002 exiled resistance leader Daniel Oyono (see UDI, below) accused the government of tossing Nguema's body into the ocean from a plane and of torturing and killing Ondo. In 2003 Amnesty International reported that Ondo was being held by the government and tortured. The government denied reports that security forces had killed Ondo, saying that he had been transferred from one prison to another.

Leaders: Felipe ONDO Obiang, Guillermo NGUEMA Ela, Bonifacio NGUEMA, German Pedro Tomo MANGUE.

Union for Democracy and Social Development (*Unión para la Democracia y el Desarrollo Social*—UDDS). The UDDS was the core component of the Opposition Coordination of Equatorial Guinea

(*Coordinación Oposición de Guinea Ecuatorial*—COGE), launched in March 1992 by several groups, including the PR, the Zaire-based **Movement for the National Unification of Equatorial Guinea** (*Movimiento para la Unificación Nacional de Guinea Ecuatorial*—MUNGE); the **Republican Party of Equatorial Guinea** (*Partido Republicano de Guinea Ecuatorial*—PRGE); the **National Movement for the Reliberation of Equatorial Guinea** (*Movimiento Nacional para la Reliberación de Guinea Ecuatorial*—Monarge); and the PSGE, which subsequently joined the POC.

Led by vociferous regime critic Antonio Sibacha Bueicheku, the UDDS in early 1993 called on the Guinean clergy to publicly denounce the Obiang administration's human rights record and urged the European Community (EC, subsequently the European Union—EU) and France to impose sanctions to stem the "perpetual violations." On May 31 five UDDS members were detained when security forces raided a party meeting. Consequently, in early June the party exhorted opposition members to fight the "last dictatorship." In early 1994 the party applauded Spain's decision to suspend aid to Equatorial Guinea and urged other donors to follow suit. In 2004 the UDDS renewed its request for intervention by the UN, the United States, France, and Spain to help bring about political change.

Leaders: Antonio SIBACHA Bueicheku, Aquilino Nguema Ona NCHAMA (Secretary General).

National Alliance for the Restoration of Democracy (*Alianza Nacional de Restauración Democrática*—ANRD). Founded in 1974, the Swiss-based ANRD announced in August 1979 that it would regard the ouster of Macie as nothing more than a "palace revolution" unless a number of conditions were met, including the trial of all individuals for atrocities under the former dictator and the establishment of a firm date for termination of military rule.

In April 1983 the ANRD was instrumental in the launching of the Coordinating Board of Opposition Democratic Forces (*Junta Coordinadora de las Fuerzas de Oposición Democrática*), formed by a group of Spanish-based exile formations, then including the PPGE, to present a united front against President Obiang, whom it accused of failing to live up to the people's expectations and exhibiting a lack of respect for the law. The *Junta* denounced the August 1983 legislative balloting as a "sham" and called for an economic embargo of the Obiang regime by regional governments. Other participants in the *Junta* included the **Movement for the Liberation and Future of Equatorial Guinea** (*Movimiento de Liberación y Futuro de Guinea Ecuatorial*—Molifuge), the **Liberation Front of Equatorial Guinea** (*Frente de Liberación de Guinea Ecuatorial*—Frelige), and the **Democratic Reform** (*Reforma Democrática*). The ANRD boycotted the 2004 legislative elections.

Leader: Luis Ondo AYANG (Secretary General).

Union of Independent Democrats (*Unión Democrática Independiente*—UDI). Formation of the Revolutionary Command Council of Socialist Guinean Patriots was announced in September 1981 by Daniel Oyono, a former secretary of state for economy and finance, as a union of three internal groups: the Union of Independent Democrats (*Unión de Demócratas Independientes*—UDI), the Revolutionary Movement, and the Socialist Front. In addition to political liberalization, the new formation called for the withdrawal of foreign troops from Equatorial Guinea, a reference to the Moroccan and Spanish troops in the presidential guard. The extent of the council's subsequent activity has been unclear, although in mid-1999 it was reported that the council and Bubi nationalists had agreed to coordinate their activities. The UDI rubric was routinely referenced in news reports in the early 2000s.

Leader: Daniel OYONO.

Four other anti-Obiang groups are the Party of the Democratic Coalition, led by Francisco JONES; the People's Alliance of Equatorial Guinea, led by Miguel Esono EMAN; the Forum for Democracy in Equatorial Guinea; and the National Movement for the Liberation of Equatorial Guinea (*Movimiento Nacional de Liberación de la Guinea Ecuatorial*—Monalige), a continuation of a historic group (see Political background).

In April 2005 it was reported that former prime minister Christino Seriche Malabo BIOKO had joined exiled opposition activists in Spain and founded the **Vanguard for the Defense of Citizens' Rights** in December 2004 to "promote the establishment of a real democratic state" in Equatorial Guinea.

Separatist Groups:

April 1 Bubi Nationalist Group. The Bubi Nationalist coalition was launched in Madrid in April 1983 by a number of groups advocating independence for the island of Bioko (formerly Fernando Póo) where the Bubi people then constituted a majority. The Bubi organizations had been excluded from the *Junta Coordinadora* because of their opposition to its goal of promoting a "national identity." The new Bubi formation subsequently issued a number of calls for an end to alleged human rights abuses against the islanders.

Leader: Bwalalele BOKOKO Itogi (Secretary General).

Movement for the Self-Determination of the Island of Bioko (*Movimiento par la Autodeterminación de la Isla de Bioko*—MAIB). The role of the Movement, established in 1993 in the Bubi nationalist movement, came under increased scrutiny following the arrest of a number of its members in July 1995. In late January 1998 the Movement denied government charges that it had organized deadly attacks on Bioko Island, countering that, following the incidents earlier in the month, the island's residents had been subjected to killing and torture by government forces and that 800 people had been arrested.

In June 1998, 15 Movement members were sentenced to death for their alleged roles in the January uprising. In addition, one of the group's leaders, Martin PUYE, was given a 20-year prison term; however, Puye, who, along with a number of the other Movement defendants, had showed signs of being tortured, died in jail in July. In August the president commuted the remaining death sentences to terms of life imprisonment.

Party activist Weja Chicampo returned from exile in Spain in 2003. In 2004, according to Amnesty International, he was arrested by hooded police officers, beaten, and imprisoned. He was freed by President Obiang in 2005. In February 2006 the group alleged that the government had killed one of its founders, Laesa Atanasio Bita ROPE, who had been sentenced to death in absentia by Equatorial Guinea in 1998. Rope was killed in the Côte d'Ivoire.

Leaders: Anacieto BOKESSA, Weja CHICAMPO, Paco AUDIJE.

LEGISLATURE

The present constitution provides for a unicameral **House of People's Representatives** (*Cámara de Representantes del Pueblo*) to meet for a five-year term. The PDGE-dominated, 41-member legislature elected in July 1988 was dissolved by the president in early July 1993. In balloting on March 7, 1999, for the 80-member House (enlarged to its current size in 1993), the Democratic Party of Equatorial Guinea (PDGE) won 75 seats; the Popular Union (UP), 4; and the Convergence for Social Democracy (CPDS), 1. As of mid-2000 the legislators from the UP and the CPDS had refused to fill their seats as a protest against the government's conduct of the election. However, the UP later reversed its decision. In 2003, the legislature was enlarged to 100 seats in preparation for the 2004 elections.

In the most recent election on May 4, 2008, the PDGE won 89 seats; the Democratic Opposition, 10; and the CPDS, 1.

President: Angel Serafin-Seriche Dougan MALABO.

CABINET

[as of October 1, 2009] *(see headnote)*

Prime Minister	Ignacio Milam Tang
Ministers	
Agriculture and Forests	Teodoro Nguema Obiang Mangue
Defense	Gen. Antonio Mba Nguema
Economy, Trade, and Promotion of Business	Pedro Ondo Nguema
Education, Science, and Sport	Anselmo Ondo Esono
Finance and Budget	Estanislao Don Malavo
Fisheries and Environment	Anastasio Asumu Mum Munoz
Foreign Affairs, International Cooperation, and Francophone Affairs	Pastor Micha Ondo Bile
Health and Social Welfare	Francisco Pascual Eyeque Obama
Information, Culture, and Tourism	Jeronimo Osa Ekoro

Infrastructure and Public Works	Marcelino Oyono Ntutumu
Interior and Local Corporations	Clemente Engonga Nguema Onguene
Justice	Salvador Ondo Ncumu
Labor and Social Security	Mauricio Bokung Asumu
Mines, Industry, and Energy	Marcelino Owono Edu
National Security	Nicholas Obama Nchama
Parliamentary Relations and Judicial Affairs of the Government	Angel Masie Mibuy
Planning, Economic Development, and Public Investment	Jose Ela Oyana
Presidency, in charge of the Civil Cabinet	Braulio Ncogo Abeque
Presidency, in charge of Special Duties	Alejandro Evuna Owono Asangono
Public Sector and Administrative Planning	Salvador Manque Ayingono
Regional Integration	Baltasar Engonga Edjo
Social Affairs and Promotion of Women	Eulalia Envo Bela [f]
Transport, Technology, Posts, and Telecommunications	Enrique Mercader Costa
Secretary General to the Government, in charge of Administrative Coordination	Vicente Ehate Tomy

[f] = female

COMMUNICATIONS

Although the constitution of Equatorial Guinea provides for freedom of thought, ideas, and opinions, the media are severely repressed through censorship, arrests of journalists, and the dearth of a private press. In recent years several people reportedly have been arrested for having access to the opposition publication *La Verdad*. In 2005 *La Verdad* reportedly was seized by the government in the wake of a crackdown on opposition party members. One of the few independent journalists in the country was arrested in connection with an article outlining an attempted military coup in the republic, and the country's only association of journalists was suspended, its members allegedly harassed or threatened. According to the international watchdog Reporters Without Borders, press freedom in Equatorial Guinea "does not exist or is constantly under attack." The republic is described as one of the world's most censored countries.

On January 19, 2009, four broadcast journalists were fired for alleged "lack of enthusiasm" and insubordination for failing to praise the regime's merits, according to the watchdog Reporters Without Borders. "Equatorial Guinea is one of those African countries about which nothing or almost nothing is known because the authorities do everything possible to hide the sad reality," the group reported.

Press. The following are published irregularly in Malabo: *Ebano* (1,000), in Spanish; *Poto Poto* (Bata), in Spanish and Fang; *Unidad de la Guinea Ecuatorial*. In January 1994 the weekly *El Sol* became the first private newspaper to be recognized by the government. Two new independent papers, *Tiempo* and *La Nation*, were reportedly granted operating licenses in 2000. Other publications include *La Opinion* (an independent weekly) and an opposition newsletter, *La Verdad*.

News agency. The only facility currently operating in Malabo is Spain's *Agencia EFE*.

Broadcasting and computing. State-run *Radio Nacional de Guinea Ecuatorial* (RNGE) broadcasts over two stations in Malabo and one in Bata in Spanish and vernacular languages. There are also English-language stations, Radio Africa and Radio East Africa, which offer music and religious programming from Malabo. *Radio Asonga*, the only private radio station in Bata, is owned by the president's son. The state-run *Television Nacional* transmits over one channel in Malabo. As of 2008 there were 18.2 Internet users per 1,000 inhabitants.

INTERGOVERNMENTAL REPRESENTATION

Ambassador to the U.S.: Purificación Angue ONDO.

U.S. Ambassador to Equatorial Guinea: (Vacant).

Permanent Representative to the UN: (Vacant).

IGO Memberships (Non-UN): AfDB, AU, BADEA, BDEAC, CEEAC, CEMAC, Interpol, NAM, OIF.

ERITREA

State of Eritrea

Political Status: Former Italian colony; became part of UN-sponsored Ethiopian–Eritrean Federation in September 1952; annexed as a province of Ethiopia in November 1962; declared independent on May 24, 1993, following secessionist referendum of April 23–25; new constitution approved by the Constitutional Assembly on May 23, 1997, but largely unimplemented as of mid-2009.

Area: 46,774 sq. mi. (121,144 sq. km.).

Population: 2,748,304 (1984C); 5,095,000 (2008E), including nonresidents.

Major Urban Centers (2005E): ASMARA (554,000), Keren (89,000).

Principal Languages: Tigrigna and Arabic.

Monetary Unit: Nakfa (government rate of exchange as of December 1, 2009: 15 nakfa = $1US).

State President and Chair of the Executive Council of the People's Front for Democracy and Justice: ISAIAS Afwerki (People's Front for Democracy and Justice); named secretary general of the Eritrean People's Liberation Front in 1987; named head of Provisional Government of Eritrea following defeat of Ethiopia's Mengistu regime in May 1991; named state president on May 22, 1993; named chair of the Executive Council of the People's Front for Democracy and Justice on February 16, 1994.

THE COUNTRY

With a coastline stretching some 750 miles along the African border of the Red Sea, Eritrea is bordered on the northwest by Sudan, on the south by Ethiopia, and on the southeast by Djibouti. It is home to many ethnic groups (including the Afar, Bilen, Hadareb, Kunama, Nara, Rashida, Saho, Tigray, and Tigrigna); its people are almost equally divided between Christians and Muslims.

The leading agricultural products are cereals, citrus fruits, cotton, and livestock (including camels and goats). Fish are plentiful in the vicinity of the islands off the Red Sea port of Massawa, while mineral resources include copper, gold, iron ore, potash, and nickel. The region's economic infrastructure was severely crippled by a long (1962–1991) war of independence from Ethiopia, the output of most industries being reduced during the conflict to a fraction of capacity. Conditions improved following the end of that war, and although GNP per capita ($115) remained one of the world's lowest, agricultural production had increased four-fold by May 1993. With the installation of a famine early warning system and infrastructural improvements, a return to agricultural self-sufficiency was reported by late 1994. Subsequently, Eritrea's real GDP growth averaged 6.0 percent annually for 1994–1998, although annual inflation averaged 8.2 percent for the same period. Progress came to a halt with the outbreak of a border war with Ethiopia (Eritrea's main export market) in May 1998. By the time hostilities ended (at least temporarily) in 2000, it was estimated that GDP had fallen by 9 percent.

The government launched a five-year, $249 million economic recovery program in 2000, concentrating on agriculture, infrastructure, and support for the private sector. However, the economy subsequently continued to languish, particularly as a final resolution of the conflict with Ethiopia proved elusive and the expense of an army of 200,000 soldiers (one of Africa's largest) siphoned resources away from development programs. GDP grew by only 1.8 percent in 2004, while remittances from the estimated 850,000 Eritreans living abroad declined substantially. Although growth rose to 4.8 percent in 2005, GDP contracted by 1 percent in 2006 and grew by only 1 percent in 2007. In response, the government accepted a World Bank recommendation that

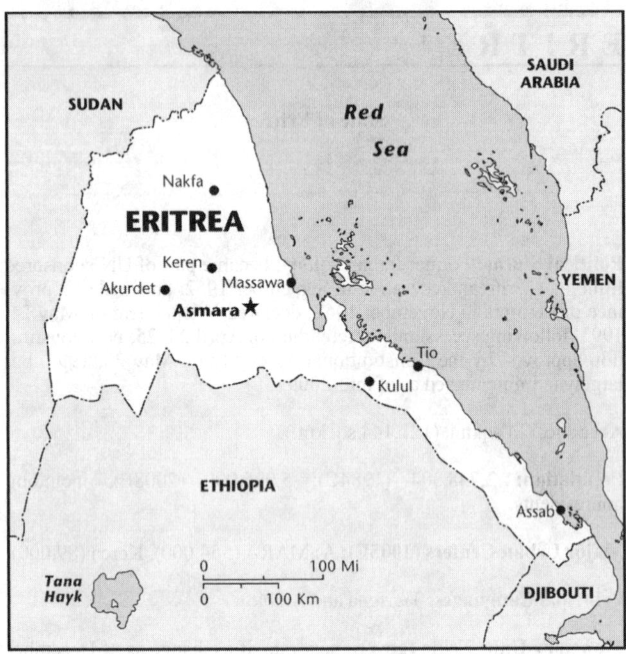

emphasis be given to improving food production through, among other things, the creation of an extensive irrigation system. Meanwhile, in a development of political as well as economic importance, China in 2007 cancelled much of Eritrea's debt and offered additional trade and cooperation accords.

Tension with Ethiopia continued to compromise the Eritrean economy in 2008 as the port of Massawa, which formerly handled goods to and from Ethiopia, was described as a "ghost town" due to Ethiopia's use of the port in Djibouti. Eritrea's limited private industry also suffered from a lack of access to Ethiopian markets. On a brighter note, mining prospects improved significantly in the second half of 2008 when final guidelines were established in regard to the state's participation in joint ventures with foreign companies. A Canadian company was slated to open a gold mine by 2010, oil licenses were issued to a Chinese company, and additional licenses to explore for a broad range of industrial metals were reportedly solicited by companies from India, the United Kingdom, and other countries.

GOVERNMENT AND POLITICS

Political background. After several centuries of intermittent Ethiopian and Ottoman control, the coastal area of what became known as Eritrea was occupied in the 1880s by Italy, which in 1890 proclaimed it a colony and in 1935–1936 used it as a staging area for its conquest of Ethiopia. Administered by Britain in the immediate post–World War II era, the region was declared by the United Nations in 1952 to be an autonomous component of an Ethiopian federation. Ten years later it was annexed by Ethiopia, with Eritreans who opposed the action mounting a guerrilla campaign that lasted until the downfall of the Mengistu regime in May 1991 (see article on Ethiopia for additional information).

On June 15, 1992, the Eritrean People's Liberation Front (EPLF) announced the formation of a Provisional Government of Eritrea (PGE), headed by EPLF secretary general, ISAIAS Afwerki. In a referendum on April 23–25, 1993, 99.8 percent of those participating voted for independence, which was accepted by Ethiopia on May 3 and became effective on May 24, with Isaias assuming the title of president. The EPLF was succeeded by the People's Front for Democracy and Justice (PFDJ) in February 1994.

At independence Eritrea's overriding concern was recovery from decades of economic neglect and military devastation. The damage to its infrastructure during the war of independence had been estimated at more than $2 billion. In addition, the port of Massawa had been all but destroyed by enemy bombardment. The divorce from Ethiopia was nonetheless described by *Africa Confidential* as "pragmatic," with no reparations being sought from Addis Ababa and no indication that a return of Ethiopian assets was being considered.

The new Eritrean state exhibited a decided assertiveness on territorial issues, as evidenced by strained relations with Yemen, Djibouti, and Sudan (see Foreign relations, below). Nevertheless, many international observers expressed surprise in May 1998 when a crisis erupted between Eritrea and Ethiopia over a disputed territory within their ill-defined border region. On May 13 Ethiopia accused Eritrea of having forcibly occupied the Badme Triangle region in "northwest Ethiopia." On the following day, Eritrea claimed that Ethiopian troops had in fact initiated the skirmish on "sovereign Eritrean territory." Subsequently, with both sides claiming to possess colonial Italian maps as evidence of their sovereignty claims, open warfare erupted in the region in late May. Meanwhile, in an attempt to explain the outbreak of fighting, analysts suggested that relations between the two countries had been deteriorating since Eritrea introduced its own currency, the nakfa, in 1997. That decision had been followed by Ethiopia's insistence that all trade between the two must be in hard currency—a move that adversely affected the Eritrean economy and set off a series of tit-for-tat exchanges that increased tension between the two and, arguably, set the stage for the 1998 conflict.

Amid reports of continued fighting, the Organization of African Unity (OAU, subsequently the African Union—AU) and the United Nations spearheaded diplomatic attempts to settle the dispute in the second half of 1998. However, Eritrea rejected cease-fire proposals in both June and November, asserting that the proposals favored Ethiopia. In late January 1999 Eritrea also opposed a troop withdrawal plan backed by the UN and OAU, and within a week full-scale warfare had recommenced, with Ethiopia reported to have launched massive offensives on the Badme front and against the Eritrean port city of Assab. In late February Eritrea acknowledged having lost the Badme territory and agreed to abide by the earlier OAU proposal. Nevertheless, fierce fighting continued through March.

The July 1999 Algiers Summit of the OAU formally endorsed a peace plan that would have returned both sides to their prewar positions and would have established a border demarcation mechanism. However, the proposed deal collapsed in September, in part due to Ethiopian concerns over technical aspects of the plan, particularly regarding the proposed Eritrean withdrawal. The subsequent months saw relatively little fighting, but Ethiopia launched a major offensive in May 2000 that concluded in a June truce after Ethiopian forces had reclaimed all the land previously lost and had advanced deep into Eritrea. In addition to a cease-fire, the combatants also agreed to eventual deployment of international peacekeepers. A final peace accord was signed by Isaias and President Meles of Ethiopia in Algeria on December 12. In April 2001 an independent boundary commission (the Eritrea-Ethiopia Boundary Commission—EEBC) established a 15-mile-wide buffer zone comprised exclusively of territory that belonged to Eritrea prior to the conflict. A UN Mission for Ethiopia and Eritrea (UNMEE)—comprised of some 4,200 peacekeepers from about 40 nations—was charged with monitoring the buffer zone. In March 2003 the border commission clarified its ruling, awarding the disputed town of Badme to Eritrea (see Current issues section for subsequent developments).

Constitution and government. On May 22, 1992, the Provisional Government of Ethiopia issued a proclamation on Eritrea's transitional government structure. It stated that, prior to the adoption of a permanent constitution, the EPLF Central Committee would serve as the country's legislative body. Executive authority was invested in a 28-member Advisory Council (subsequently a 24-member State Council), chaired by the EPLF secretary general. In addition, a judiciary was authorized to function independently of the EPLF Central Committee, the Advisory/State Council, and the secretary general. The new basic law provided for the country's ten provinces to be headed by governors, each of whom was also authorized to serve on the Advisory/State Council.

On May 22, 1993, EPLF Secretary General Isaias was proclaimed president of Eritrea. Concurrently, a transitional National Assembly was established. (By a resolution of the PFDJ congress a year later, the assembly became a 150-member body encompassing the 75 members of the PFDJ's Central Committee, plus a number of indirectly elected members.) In March 1994 the National Assembly approved a resolution to establish a 50-member Constitutional Commission to prepare a draft basic law for the country. The commission issued its recommendations in 1996, and a special 527-member Constitutional Assembly was subsequently elected in direct balloting and charged with preparing a final document. As unanimously approved on May 23, 1997, by the Constitutional Assembly (which subsequently dissolved), the new constitution provided for a directly elected National Assembly, which was authorized to select a president, who was granted strong executive authority. The president's term was set at five years, renewable once. A multiparty system was envisioned, although its final structure was left to the current National Assembly, as were details regarding other electoral matters. No precise timetable was established for the final implementation of the new constitution. Among other things, the 1998–2000 border war with Ethiopia served as an obstacle to implementation, while critics of President Isaias continued as of mid-2009 to accuse him of dragging his feet on the issue.

In May 1995 the National Assembly approved legislation dividing the country into six provinces, each of which would be further divided into regions, subregions, and villages. In early November the legislators decided that 30 percent of the provincial council seats would be reserved for women and gave the provinces nonethnic names (Southern Red Sea Region, Northern Red Sea Region, Anseba Region, Gash Barka Region, South Region, and Central Region).

Regional elections were held on May 20, 2004, but National Assembly elections were repeatedly postponed and remained unscheduled as of mid-2009.

Foreign relations. A number of countries, including the United States, recognized Eritrea on April 27, 1993. All-important recognition by Ethiopia on May 3 paved the way for the proclamation of independence three weeks later. On October 10 Eritrea and Ethiopia concluded an agreement on freedom of cross-border transit for citizens of the two countries. By the end of the year Eritrea had been admitted to the United Nations and most of its affiliated bodies.

In late 1993 Eritrea complained of an attack by an armed Islamic group that had infiltrated from Sudan. A similar outbreak in November 1994 yielded a rupture in diplomatic relations with Khartoum, which the Asmara leadership had privately charged with "Islamic and imperialistic ambitions." Subsequent peace talks in Yemen broke down in late December after Sudan had refused to condemn infiltrators that Eritrea had accused of destabilizing activities. Eight months earlier, at the conclusion of a defense treaty with Ethiopia, a foreign ministry spokesman had declared that "Eritrea, in collaboration with Ethiopia if necessary, will make a short shrift of militant Islam."

On November 11, 1995, a simmering dispute between Eritrea and Yemen over claims to three small islands in the Red Sea erupted into armed confrontation. The three islands, Greater Hanish (Hanish Al Kubra), Lesser Hanish (Hanish Al Suhrah), and Zukar (Jabel Zukar) had been retained by Britain when it withdrew from Aden in 1967 but were handed over to South Yemen three years later. Subsequently, the archipelago came under Yemeni development as a center for tourists, particularly French scuba enthusiasts. The November firefight, occasioned by the presence of Yemeni troops on Greater Hanish, was followed by a more bloody encounter on December 15–17. Thereafter, the two sides agreed to a cease-fire monitored by a four-member committee composed of one representative each from Eritrea and Yemen, plus diplomats from the U.S. embassies in Eritrea and Yemen.

Mediated by the UN and France, subsequent talks yielded the signing of an accord in Paris on May 21, 1996, under which Eritrea and Yemen renounced the use of force and agreed to submit the dispute to binding arbitration by a panel of five judges, with Eritrea and Yemen appointing two each and these four naming the fifth. Nevertheless, the dispute flared up again in early August, when Eritrean troops occupied Lesser Hanish; they withdrew at the end of the month only on the express order of the UN Security Council. (In October 1998 the International Court of Justice [ICJ] ruled largely in Yemen's favor in the dispute, granting it sovereignty of the so-called Zukar-Hanish island groups, while ceding Eritrea control over a smaller island grouping. Moreover, the ICJ asserted that traditional fishing patterns—both Eritrean and Yemeni—should be protected. Both countries promptly agreed to comply with the decision.)

The relationship between Eritrea and Sudan continued to deteriorate in 1996–1997 as the former joined forces with Ethiopia and Uganda to form a regional front to contain militant Islamic fundamentalism (see article on Ethiopia). In late July 1996 Khartoum claimed that its troops had repulsed an incursion by Eritrean forces as tensions mounted along their shared border. Sudanese-Eritrean relations plummeted further in June 1997 when Eritrean officials announced that they had uncovered an alleged Sudanese-backed plot to assassinate President Isaias. Following the tentative conclusion of the Eritrean/Ethiopian war in late 2000, Eritrea concluded a border security agreement with Sudan in July 2001, though it was widely reported that Sudan subsequently continued to support anti-government movements in Eritrea (see Political Groups section). (In 2008 Sudan suspended the activity of all Eritrean opposition groups on Sudanese soil, an apparent show of support for the Eritrean government in its multifaceted conflict with Ethiopia, which, among other things, had allegedly prompted Eritrean assistance for antigovernment Islamists in Somalia. See Current issues, below, for additional information.)

Relations with the United States, European Union, and the UN were described as tenuous in mid-2006 due to what was perceived in the West as President Isaias's "confrontational approach" to UNMEE (see Current issues). Meanwhile, Eritrea reportedly by that time had significantly increased its ties with Pakistan in regard to oil exploration and other "entrepreneurial" activity. Eritrea also continued to provide aid to numerous Ethiopian opposition groups as an expression of its anger over the impasse in final border demarcation.

In April 2007 Eritrea announced it was suspending its membership in the Inter-Governmental Authority on Development (IGAD) in response to what Eritrea perceived as the regional body's support for the recent Ethiopian intervention in Somalia, which Eritrea opposed. In a related vein, the United States and the UN accused Eritrea of supplying arms to Islamist insurgents in Somalia, Washington going so far as to suggest it might place Eritrea on the U.S. list of countries that sponsor terrorism because of the issue. Meanwhile, President Isaias denied his country was providing arms to Somalia's antigovernment Islamists and accused Ethiopia and the United States of "destabilizing" the region with their efforts in Somalia and anti-Eritrean rhetoric.

A long-standing border dispute with Djibouti erupted into small-scale military conflict in June 2008 after Eritrea reportedly sent troops into the disputed Ras Doumenia peninsula on the Red Sea. The United States (which relies on bases in Djibouti for military activity in the region), the AU, Arab League, and IGAD condemned the Eritrean actions, while Eritrea claimed sovereignty over the territory (experts agreed that the border had never been definitively demarcated). A UN team was dispatched to investigate the conflict, which had the potential to impact vital shipping lanes in and out of the Red Sea, and the UN Security Council subsequently expressed "deep concern" over the continuing border tension, although a de facto cease-fire held into mid-2009.

Current issues. The ferocity of the 1998–2000 border war with Ethiopia was very difficult for the international community to comprehend, since the narrow strip of land in question held few natural resources and was generally considered a poor candidate for development. The estimates of the number of Eritrean deaths in the conflict ranged from 20,000 to 50,000, while some 60,000 people were displaced. In addition, the Eritrean government reportedly spent $1 billion on armaments to conduct the campaign against its former Ethiopian allies, thereby dealing a severe blow to an economy already in desperate need of investment. Some analysts attributed Eritrea's intensity in the dispute to a "sense of indomitability" arising from the long war of independence and to a degree of hubris on the part of President Isaias. Although Isaias and his administration continued to maintain that Eritrea had been waging a defensive war and declared "victory" in the final settlement, most observers concluded that Ethiopia had, in fact, achieved military superiority prior to the cease-fire.

President Isaias appeared to retain broad popular support throughout the war, although what one journalist called "quiet questions" were raised over the possibility that the president may have misjudged Eritrean capabilities. Following the war, criticism intensified noticeably, beginning with the issuance in late 2000 of the so-called "Berlin Manifesto" on the part of PFDJ supporters outside the country who argued that constitutional implementation was being unnecessarily delayed and that power remained inordinately concentrated in the president's hands. Subsequently, in May 2001, a number of influential government and party officials also broke ranks with Isaias (see PFDJ under Political Groups, below). Disconcerting many international donors, Isaias responded with a crackdown in September, arresting a number of government and party officials for "disloyalty." He also clamped down on the independent press.

Meanwhile, final border demarcation was left to the EEBC, whose ruling in April 2002 allocated sufficient territory to each side to permit each to claim it was satisfied with the outcome, although overall the decision appeared to favor Ethiopia. In March 2003 the border commission officially awarded the disputed town of Badme to Eritrea, but the Ethiopian government did not announce it accepted the ruling "in principle" until November 2004. Despite the EEBC's decision, border skirmishes continued to flare up, land mines were periodically detonated, and the UN expressed concerns over Eritrea's lack of cooperation with the peacekeeping force patrolling the border. Although his external reputation continued to decline, Isaias still clung to his hard line. Meanwhile, opposition groups continued to coalesce and regroup (see Political Groups, below), some of them backed by the governments of Sudan, Yemen, and Ethiopia.

In October 2005 the Eritrean government banned UNMEE helicopter flights and other activity in the disputed border area to protest Ethiopia's unwillingness to accept the proposed final demarcation and return Badme to Eritrean control. Although the Security Council threatened to impose sanctions on Eritrea for its unilateral action, Isaias continued to maintain that sanctions would be more appropriate if leveled at Ethiopia. (Isaias claimed that Eritrea was the "law-abiding party" in the dispute and that Ethiopia was receiving preferential treatment from the west because of President Meles's assistance in the U.S.-led "war on terror.") The two countries were described as once again "on the brink" in November in view of continued troop and tank buildups and an Eritrean demand (reluctantly accepted by the Security Council) that all western troops be withdrawn from UNMEE. Complicating matters for Eritrea was a report in mid-December by an independent claims commission at the Permanent Court of Arbitration that adjudged that Eritrea had initiated the 1998 war by invading Badme. (The commission collaterally held both sides liable for property damage and abuse of civilians during the conflict.)

Clearly annoyed by Isaias's "belligerence" regarding UNMEE, UN Secretary General Kofi Annan in January 2006 suggested that the peacekeeping mission might be downgraded or even converted into a "defensive force" on the Ethiopian side of the Temporary Security Zone (TSZ). Concurrently, Isaias's critics accused him of focusing on the "false issue" of sovereignty at the expense of attention to the nation's many economic and political problems.

Concerns grew in late 2006 that war might reignite with Ethiopia when Eritrean forces moved into the TSZ, purportedly to help "harvest crops." Tensions subsequently intensified even further when Ethiopian troops (with U.S. backing) entered Somalia in December to assist the transitional Somali government, led by President Abdullahi Yusuf Ahmed, in its battle for control with Islamists led by the Islamic Courts Union (ICU). Although the Yusuf Ahmed administration regained the upper hand in Mogadishu with the Ethiopian support, an ICU guerrilla campaign subsequently continued, most analysts concluding that the insurgents were being armed in large part by Eritrea in what was seen as a Eritrean-Ethiopian "proxy war" in Somalia. In July 2007 Ethiopian President Meles Zenawi announced he was expanding the Ethiopian army to protect against a possible attack by Eritrea, and President Isaias described Ethiopia as a "U.S. mercenary" in the region.

In early 2008 Eritrea blocked fuel supplies to UNMEE forces in the TSZ, forcing the 1,700-strong UN force to relocate to the Ethiopian side of the border. The UN Security Council condemned Eritrea's "hostility" toward the peacekeeping force, as concern remained high that an "unintended" skirmish could reignite a full-scale border war. Ethiopia called for new negotiations, arguing that permanent borders makers were required on the ground before the demarcation issue could be considered settled. (The UN had been able to establish only a "virtual border" electronically.) However, the Isaias administration insisted on Ethiopian withdrawal from Badme before talks could begin, prompting renewed international criticism. Meanwhile, low morale was reported in some segments of the Eritrean army, while ongoing corruption in the business sector, human rights abuses on the part of the government, and the lack of movement toward genuine democratic activity were reportedly fueling a degree of domestic discontent.

In July 2008 the UN Security Council terminated the UNMEE's mandate, accusing Eritrea of "obstruction." The "heavily armed truce" between Eritrea and Ethiopia continued into 2009, with President Isaias maintaining his anti-U.S. rhetoric while concentrating on intensified ties with China, Iran, and Sudan. Following the withdrawal of Ethiopian forces from Somalia early in the year and the subsequent offensive by antigovernment Islamists there, the AU and IGAD asked the Security Council to impose sanctions on Eritrea for its alleged support for the Somali insurgents. The Security Council obliged in December by imposing an arms embargo on Eritrea and providing for penalties against military or political leaders who violate the embargo.

POLITICAL GROUPS

In late 2000 the National Assembly approved statutes providing for eventual formation of political parties, although critics argued that accompanying restrictions represented an effective barrier to genuine multiparty activity. While describing party activity as "acceptable" in theory, the assembly in early 2002 upheld a ban on the legalization of parties, and the PFDJ remained the sole legal party as of mid-2009.

Opposition to the EPLF/PFDJ has primarily involved shifting, often overlapping, and mostly ineffective coalitions, usually led by the ELF (below). In November 1996 it was reported that the ELF had initiated formation of an Eritrean National Alliance (ENA), together with a faction of the EIJM and the **Eritrean Liberation Front–National Council** (ELF-NC). Reportedly established with the assistance of Sudan, the ENA, whose components were described as having "fundamentalist tendencies," called for the ousting of the Isaias government and the installation of a multiparty system. ENA Chair Abdella Idriss of the ELF also called for investigation of alleged human rights violations on the part of the administration. Significantly, the **Eritrean Liberation Front–Revolutionary Council** (ELF-RC), a predominately Muslim but nonfundamentalist and nonmilitary group, declined to join the ENA because of the inclusion of the EIJM faction in the alliance.

In March 1999 the ENA appeared to be superseded by a broader coalition of opposition groups styled the Alliance of Eritrean National Forces (AENF) that included the ELF, ELF-NC, ELF-RC, EISM (see EIJM, below), and a number of small Marxist formations. Despite enjoying the support of Ethiopia, the AENF was described as maintaining a low profile during the Eritrean-Ethiopian war, supporting the 2000 truce while continuing to call for the ouster of the Isaias government.

In late 2002 reports once again began to reference the ENA, described as comprising some 13 parties and groups under the leadership of the ELF's Idriss as president and HIRUY Tedla Bairu of the small, recently formed **Eritrean Cooperative Party** (ECP) as secretary general. Although the revitalized ENA reportedly initially indicated it would not use military force to try to overthrow the government, it was reported in May 2003 that an ENA military wing had been established. By that time, it appeared that the ENA was receiving financial aid from Ethiopia, Sudan, and Yemen. Once again undermining effective opposition cohesion, the ELF-RC refused to participate in the alliance, arguing that Hiruy was under "foreign influence."

In early 2004 four ENA members (the ELF-NC, RSADO, DMLEK, and the **People's Democratic Front for the Liberation of Eritrea** [PDFLE]) joined the EPM in forming an opposition alliance called the Four Plus One. In October additional small parties joined the grouping, which described itself as a means of strengthening the ENA rather than replacing it.

New ENA leaders were reportedly elected in January 2005, Hiruy replacing Idriss as president and Husayn KHALIFA succeeding Hiruy as secretary general. However, the ENA was again apparently superseded in February by the formation in Sudan of the **Eritrean Democratic Alliance** (EDA), which included the ELF, ELF-RC, EDP, EPM, the small **Eritrean Federal Democratic Movement** (EFDM), the "newly emerging" **Eritrean National Salvation Front** (ENSF), and, apparently, the **Eritrean Islamic Islah Movement** (EIIM). The role of the EIIM was controversial, since it supported the use of violence against government forces (EIIM fighters killed a number of Eritrean soldiers in early 2005) while other EDA components (notably the EDP and EPM) opposed the use of such force. Meanwhile, Hiruy and his EPC remained outside the EDA, with Khalifa being referenced as the EDA leader and Abdallah Aden of the EPM as his deputy. Hiruy subsequently criticized the EDA for "monopolizing" financial aid from Ethiopia, Sudan, and Yemen designed to support opposition activity in Eritrea. The EDA was described in early 2006 as "virtually paralyzed" by a lack of effective coordination. In March 2007 it was reported that Ethiopian President Meles Zenawi was supporting the EDA faction that comprised the ENSF, ELF-RC, and the EDP. Subsequently, in August, EDA leaders called for intensification of the antigovernment struggle, describing the country as a "big prison."

The EDA general congress in the spring of 2008 opened its doors to all organizations dedicated to the overthrow of the "despotic" Isaias regime, thereby hoping to put an end to fractionalization within the opposition. At that point the EDA membership reportedly included the DMLEK; EPM; EFDM, led by Bashir ISHAQ; the **Islamic Congress Party** (ICP); EDP; EIIM, led by Khelil AMER; ELF; ELF-RC; the **Eritrean *Nahda* Party**, led by Nur IDRIS; ENSF, led by Abdallah Aden; EPC, led by Taher SHENGEB; the **Eritrean Popular Democratic Front** (EPDF), led by Tewelde GEBRESELASSIE; and RSADO. Several subgroups were formed by EDA components in 2009, although they all voiced continued allegiance to the EDA, described as enjoying Ethiopian support under the leadership of the EPDF"s Gebreselassie.

Government Party:

People's Front for Democracy and Justice (PFDJ). The PFDJ's predecessor—the Eritrean People's Liberation Front (EPLF)—was launched in 1970 as a breakaway faction of the Marxist-oriented ELF (below). The EPLF was an avowedly nonsectarian, left-wing formation supported by both Christians and Muslims in its pursuit of Eritrean independence. With an estimated 100,000 men and women under arms, the EPLF for much of its preindependence existence controlled large areas of the Eritrean countryside, establishing schools, hospitals, a taxation system, and other government services.

After the EPLF revised its ideology to accommodate multipartyism and a "regulated" market economy, in May 1991 the United States for the first time supported the EPLF's call for a self-determination referendum. Immediately after the subsequent Ethiopian defeat, Isaias Afwerki, who had been named secretary general of the EPLF at its 1987 congress, announced that the group was establishing a provisional government in Eritrea until a UN-supervised independence vote could be conducted. At independence on May 24, 1993, Isaias was installed as Eritrean president. At its 1994 congress, the EPLF adopted its present name and elected a 75-member Central Council and a 19-member Executive Council chaired by Isaias.

In the wake of the disastrous 1998–2000 war with Ethiopia, which, among other things, directed attention away from proposed political reform, a group of 15 prominent PFDJ leaders (including members of the Executive Council) published a letter in May 2001 criticizing Isaias's "autocratic" rule and demanding a "legal and democratic transition to a truly constitutional government." Isaias reacted harshly to the challenge, and some of the so-called G-15 were among those arrested in a government crackdown in September 2001. Subsequently, PFDJ dissidents who had escaped arrest by fleeing the country announced the formation of an EPLF-Democratic Party in exile (see EDP, below).

Leaders: ISAIAS Afwerki (President of Eritrea and Chair of PFDJ Executive Council); Yemane GEBREAB, Hagos GEBHREHIWET, Yemane GEBREMESKAL, and Zemeheret YOHANNES (PFDJ Department Heads); Ahmad al-Amin Mohammed SAÏD (Secretary General).

Opposition Groups:

Eritrean Liberation Front (ELF). The predominantly Muslim ELF initiated anti-Ethiopian guerrilla activity in 1961 in pursuit of Eritrean autonomy. Its influence plummeted following the formation of the EPLF, and numerous splinter groups subsequently surfaced. By 1992 the ELF was considered to have become virtually nonexistent within Eritrea. However, in November 1996 it helped to launch the first of several opposition alliances (see above for subsequent developments).

In May 2009 it was reported that the ELF had established the Eritrean Solidarity Front (ESF) with the EIJM, EIIM, and EFDM in pursuit of the "restoration of the rights" of Muslims and other "marginalized" elements of the population.

Leaders: Abdella IDRISS, Hussein KHELIFA.

Eritrean Islamic Jihad Movement (EIJM-*Jihad Islammiya*). An Islamic fundamentalist group, the EIJM upon its formation was largely based in Sudan and was devoted to armed operations within Eritrea.

In August 1993 the military wing of the EIJM announced from Saudi Arabia that it had dismissed its Political Bureau, headed by Sheikh Mohammed ARAFA, for having established contact with the Eritrean government. For his part, Arafa continued to claim leadership of the group. The factions each operated under the EIJM label until 1998 when it was reported that the military wing had restyled itself the **Eritrean People's Congress** (EPC), while Arafa's followers had reorganized under the banner of the **Eritrean Islamic Salvation Movement** (EISM-*Harakat al Khalas al Islammiya*). Despite their differences, both groups agreed to join the AENF in early 1999. In 2003 the U.S. State Department reportedly listed EIJM as an alleged member of al-Qaida.

Eritrean Democratic Party (EDP). The EDP is a successor to the EPLF-Democratic Party that was formed in exile by PFDJ dissidents after the government crackdown of 2001. The founding EDP congress was held in Germany in early 2004, the party committing itself to nonviolent opposition to the Isaias government. The EDP was subsequently described as split into two factions, which apparently prompted party leader Mesfin HAGOS, a former defense minister, to resign his post in mid-2009 when the EDP announced a planned merger with EPM and the **Eritrean People's Party** (EPP, chaired by Woldeyesus AMAR). Earlier, the EPP had announced a merger with the **Eritrean Democratic Resistance Movement of Gash-Setit** (EDRMGS, chaired by Ismail NADA).

Leader: Tesfamichael YOHANES.

Red Sea Afar Democratic Organization (RSADO). The RSADO joined the ENA in 2002 to advocate for the rights of the Afar ethnic group in the southern Red Sea region. In 2004 its chair, Ibrahim HAROUN, survived an assassination attempt, which some critics alleged may have been plotted by the ruling PFDJ.

RSADO attacks on Eritrean military posts were reported in late 2008 and early 2009, the attackers apparently operating out of Ethiopia with the support of the Ethiopian military. In mid-2009 the RDASO announced plans to establish a Democratic Movement of Eritrean Nationalists (DMEN) in conjunction with the DMLEK (below).

Democratic Movement for the Liberation of Eritrean Kunama (DMLEK). This group was a founding member of the ENA. It calls for more autonomy for the Kunama—an ethnic group indigenous to the Gash-Setit areas of western Eritrea.

Leader: Kerneleos UTHMAN.

Eritrean People's Movement (EPM). The EPM was founded in May 2004 to bypass the ELF/EPLF divide. It reportedly had the support of Sudan, Ethiopia, Australia, Europe, and the United States.

Leaders: Adhanom GEBREMARIAN (Former Ambassador to Nigeria), Mekonen HAILI, Abdallah ADEN (Former Ambassador to Sudan), Mohammed IBRAHIM.

In 2003 the **Afar Revolutionary Democratic United Front** (ARDUF), led by Mohamouda GAAZ, was launched with the reported goal of establishing an Afar state within Eritrea, similar to the Afar State in Ethiopia. In December 2004 Gaaz announced his support for a new Eritrean opposition organization, the **Afar Federal Alliance** (AFA), which had been formed by his cousin, Ahmed Saled GAAZ, a veteran of the ELF.

LEGISLATURE

The proclamation by the Provisional Government of Eritrea on May 22, 1992, called for legislative authority to be exercised by the Eritrean People's Liberation Front's Central Committee, which was subsequently augmented by representatives of provincial assemblies to form a transitional **National Assembly** (*Hagerawi Baito*). A resolution by the People's Front for Democracy and Justice (PFDJ) on May 1994 provided for the establishment of a successor body encompassing the 75 members of the PFDJ Central Council, 3 members from each provincial council (currently a total of 18 members following the establishment of six provinces in 1995), and 45 representatives of professional groups, women's organizations, and other social bodies. (The latter were selected by the State Council from lists recommended by the organizations involved.) The 1997 constitution provided for a unicameral legislature of directly elected members. However, elections were subsequently delayed for several reasons, notably the 1998–2000 war with Ethiopia and ongoing failure to finalize border arrangements (see Current issues). In early 2000 the assembly endorsed a new electoral law, declaring, among other things, that 30 percent of the seats in the next assembly election would be reserved for women. As of August 2009, new assembly elections had not been scheduled.

Chair: ISAIAS Afwerki.

STATE COUNCIL

[as of July 1, 2009]

President	Isaias Afwerki
Councillors	
Agriculture	Arefaine Berhe
Commissioner for Eritrean Relief and Refugee Commission	Dragon Hailemelekot
Defense	Gen. Sebhat Ephrem
Education	Semere Russom
Energy and Mines	Ahmad Haji Ali
Finance and Development	Berhane Abrehe
Fisheries	Saleh Meki
Foreign Affairs	Osman Saleh Mohammed
Health	Amna Nurhusein [f]

Information (Acting)	Ali Abdu
Justice	Fawzia Hashim [f]
Labor and Human Welfare	Selma Hassan [f]
Land, Water, and Environment	Tesfai Gebreselassie
National Development	Giorgis Teklemikael
Public Works	Abraha Asfaha
Regional Administration	Woldenkiel Gebremariam
Tourism	Askalu Menkerios [f]
Transportation and Communications	Woldemichael Abraha

[f] = female

COMMUNICATIONS

In September 2001 the government closed down all 12 of the nation's privately owned newspapers and arrested a number of journalists in the wake of growing dissent over the authoritarian rule of the Isaias administration. The crackdown elicited an international outcry, but the government did not ease its hard-line position. Reporters Without Borders in 2007 strongly criticized the government and the PFDJ for an "ultra-nationalist" stance that characterized any criticism from journalists or reformists as a threat to national security and therefore an appropriate target for suppression. The journalism watchdog also reported that some of the journalists arrested in 2001 may have died due to "penal colony conditions" surrounding their detention, while a number of other prominent independent journalists had fled the country. Reporters Without Borders in 2008 placed Eritrea last in the press freedom index (characterizing the state-run media as "Soviet-style instruments of propaganda") and in 2009 asked the European Union to suspend its development aid to Eritrea in light of a new spate of arrests of journalists.

Press. The principal press organ is the state-run Hadas Eritrea (New Eritrea, 25,000), published five times a week in Tigrigna and Arabic. There is also an English-language government-owned weekly (Eritrea Profile) and an English-language Eritrea Daily. Opposition groups and others have recently started several online newspapers, although Internet usage is reportedly heavily scrutinized by the government.

News agency. Daily news updates are provided by the state-run Eritrean News Agency (ENA).

Broadcasting and computing. The Eritrean national radio service is Voice of the Broad Masses (Dimtsi Hafash), broadcasting in Afar, Amharic, Arabic, Kunama, Tigre, and Tigrigna. Eri-TV, broadcasting from Asmara and Assab, can be received in about 90 percent of the country. As of 2008 there were 40.6 Internet users per 1,000 inhabitants.

INTERGOVERNMENTAL REPRESENTATION

Ambassador to the U.S.: Ghirmai GHEBREMARIAM.

U.S. Ambassador to Eritrea: Ronald K. McMULLEN.

Permanent Representative to the UN: Araya DESTA.

IGO Memberships (Non-UN): AfDB, AU, Comesa, IGAD, Interpol, NAM, PCA, WCO.

ESTONIA

Republic of Estonia
Eesti Vabariik

Political Status: Absorption of independent state by the Soviet Union on August 6, 1940, repudiated by Estonian Supreme Council on March 30, 1990; resumption of full sovereignty declared August 20, 1991, and accepted by USSR State Council on September 6; present constitution approved in referendum of June 28, 1992.

Area: 17,462 sq. mi. (45,227 sq. km.).

Population: 1,370,000 (2000C); 1,332,000 (2008E).

Major Urban Centers (2005E): TALLINN (395,000), Tartu (101,000), Narva (68,000).

Official Language: Estonian.

Monetary Unit: Kroon (official rate December 1, 2009: 10.36 krooni = $1US). Pegged at one-eighth of a Deutsche mark, which is now pegged to the euro, the kroon was introduced on June 20, 1992. Estonia's adoption of the euro has been delayed until at least 2012.

President: Toomas Hendrik ILVES (Social Democratic Party); elected by electoral college on September 23, 2006, and sworn in for a five-year term on October 9, succeeding Arnold RÜÜTEL (People's Union of Estonia).

Prime Minister: Andrus ANSIP (Estonian Reform Party); nominated by the president on March 31, 2005, following the resignation of Juhan PARTS (Union for the Republic) and sworn in (along with a new government) on April 13 following parliamentary approval of his nomination on April 12; nominated by the president to form a new government following legislative elections of March 4, 2007, and inaugurated on April 5 following parliamentary approval of his new three-party government on April 4.

THE COUNTRY

The northernmost of the three former Soviet Baltic republics, Estonia is bordered on the north by the Gulf of Finland, on the east by Russia, and on the south by Latvia. During 1979–1989 the number of ethnic Estonians dropped by 3.2 percent and in June 1990 the government established quotas for the admission of "foreign citizens." (In 1998–1999, largely due to Estonia's efforts to be admitted to the European Union [EU], the citizenship requirements were eased.) The 2000 census showed that only 29.2 percent of the population adhered to a specific religious faith, the vast majority of them being Christian, either Lutheran (46.4 percent of religious persons) or Orthodox Christian (43.8 percent). As of 2005, 68.5 percent of the population was Estonian, 25.7 percent Russian, 2.1 percent Ukrainian, 1.2 percent Belarusan, and 0.8 percent Finnish.

The economy is based on services, which contributed 68.4 percent of GDP in 2008, followed by industry (29 percent) and agriculture (2.6 percent). Estonia is a net importer of gas from Russia, although Tallinn is supplied with gas extracted from extensive deposits of oil shale. The country is well endowed with peat, some of which is used for the generation of electricity, and with phosphate, from which superphosphate is refined.

Estonia in June 1992 became the first former Soviet republic to abandon the ruble in favor of its own national currency, the kroon. The immediate impact of the action was to slow the rate of inflation from over 1,000 percent to 90 percent in 1993, although real GDP plunged by 26.3 percent during the year (as contrasted with declines of 12.6 percent in 1991 and 3.6 percent in 1990), in part because of a shortfall in oil and other needed supplies from neighboring Russia.

Under the influence of free-market reforms introduced in 1992 as well as the return of most of the "Baltic gold" held by the Bank of England and other Western depositaries since the Soviet takeover in 1940, signs of recovery began to emerge in mid-1993, and Estonia subsequently became one of the best-performing transition economies. Real GDP growth reached 10.4 percent in 1997, but in 1998 growth slowed to 5.0 percent, in part due to the effects of the Russian financial crisis. Foreign investment reached a new high in 1998, and, for the first time since the government adopted policies designed to reorient the economy toward the EU, a majority of exports went to EU countries (led by Sweden and Finland). Meanwhile, exports to Russia declined to 13 percent of the total.

Although the economy contracted by 0.7 percent in 1999 (primarily due to export shortfalls associated with the regional impact of the Russian crisis), growth averaged more than 8 percent annually over the next six years, earning the government high marks for its fiscal policies from the EU and the International Monetary Fund (IMF). Unemployment also declined steadily from 13.7 percent in 2000 to 7.0 percent in

2006. However, inflation increased from approximately 4 percent in 2006 to 10.4 percent in 2008 in response to rising global food and fuel prices in the first half of the year. The high inflation delayed Estonia's adoption of the euro (the EU mandates that inflation must be below 3 percent for adoption). Following years of consideration, the government in 2009 announced a target date for eurozone entry in 2012. As food and fuel prices fell, inflation was expected to decline to less than 1 percent in 2009 and 2010. Meanwhile, unemployment increased from 4.2 percent in mid-2008 to 9.2 percent in mid-2009 in response to the global economic crisis, which had decimated Estonia's previously booming retail and real estate sectors.

Estonia's economy is based on services, which contributed 68.4 percent of GDP in 2008. Industry and agriculture comprised the balance, providing 29 percent and 2.6 percent, respectively. Estonia is a net importer of gas from Russia, although Tallinn is supplied with gas extracted from extensive deposits of oil shale. The country is well endowed with peat, some of which is used for the generation of electricity, and with phosphate, from which superphosphate is refined.

GOVERNMENT AND POLITICS

Political background. Ruled by the Livonian Knights for the greater part of the 13th to 15th centuries and by Sweden until its defeat by Peter the Great in the Great Northern War of 1700–1721, Estonia was granted local autonomy by Russia in April 1917. A declaration of independence in February 1918 was followed by German occupation, but the country's sovereign status was recognized by the Versailles peace treaty of June 28, 1919, and by the Soviet-Estonian Tartu treaty of February 2, 1920. In September 1921 Estonia was admitted to the League of Nations.

In March 1934, under a new constitution adopted two months earlier, Estonia succumbed to the virtual dictatorship of Konstantin PÄTS. In February 1936 the 1934 instrument was revoked, and Estonia formally returned to a democratic system under a basic law of July 29, 1937, that provided for a presidency (to which Päts was elected in April 1938) and a two-chambered parliament. In October 1939 the country was forced to accept Soviet military bases, and on August 6, 1940, it was incorporated into the USSR under a secret protocol of the German-Soviet nonaggression pact of August 23, 1939. German occupation in 1941–1945 was followed by the restoration of Estonia's status as a Soviet republic.

On November 12, 1989, the Estonian Supreme Soviet unilaterally annulled the 1940 annexation, and in February 1990 it abolished provisions in its constitution that accorded a "leading role" to the Communist Party. On March 30 what had become styled as the Supreme Council called for eventual independence, and on May 8 it repudiated the designation "Estonian Soviet Socialist Republic" in favor of the earlier "Republic of Estonia." In February 1991 ethnic Estonians conducted private balloting for a "Congress of Estonia," and a referendum on March 3 yielded a 77.8 percent vote in favor of independence; a declaration to such effect on August 20 was accepted by the USSR Supreme Soviet on September 6.

At legislative balloting on March 18, 1990, a majority of seats had been won by proindependence groups, notably the Estonian Popular Front (*Eesti Rahvarinne*), whose chair, Edgar SAVISAAR, was named prime minister on April 3. Savisaar's appointment had been preceded on March 29 by the reappointment of Arnold RÜÜTEL as legislative chair (de facto president of the republic).

Savisaar resigned on January 23, 1992, after the government had failed to win enough legislative votes to support a state of emergency for coping with post-Soviet food and energy shortages. On January 30 the Supreme Council approved the formation of a new coalition administration, with Tiit VÄHI as caretaker prime minister. In general elections on September 20, Rüütel won a substantial plurality (42.2 percent) of the votes cast in presidential balloting, although in the legislative returns his Secure Home (*Kindel Kodu*) grouping ran second to the Fatherland ("Pro Patria") National Coalition (*Rahvuslik Koonderakond Ismaa*—RKEI), which supported Lennart MERI. Since neither presidential candidate had secured a majority, the choice was constitutionally assigned to the legislature, where a three-party nationalist alignment on October 5 endorsed Meri by a narrow margin. On October 21 a coalition government of the RKEI, the Moderates, and the Estonian National Independence Party was sworn in under the premiership of the RKEI's Mart LAAR. The goals of the new administration included the reinforcement of Estonian statehood, defense of democracy, economic stabilization, the creation of environmental and social guarantees necessary for the development of a market economy, the restoration of a civil society, and integration into Europe.

Following the appointment of a new economy minister in January 1993, Estonia experienced an economic upturn, during which the government's popularity was also enhanced among ethnic Estonians by the passage in June of nationality legislation effectively defining ethnic Russians as foreigners. President Meri delayed signing the measure to give time for the Council of Europe and the Conference on (later Organization for) Security and Cooperation in Europe (CSCE/OSCE) to examine its content. The law as finally enacted in July incorporated clarifications of the social security rights of ethnic Russians and dropped a requirement that foreigners' residence permits had to be renewed every five years. Local referenda on July 16–17, in which the predominantly ethnic Russian inhabitants of the towns of Narva and Sillamae voted in favor of autonomy, were declared illegal by the Estonian authorities.

On November 15, 1993, the government survived a parliamentary no-confidence motion, but on September 2, 1994, the president of the Bank of Estonia, Siim KALLAS, revealed that in 1992 Prime Minister Laar had secretly ordered the sale of 2 billion rubles to the breakaway Russian republic of Chechnya, in contravention of an agreement with the IMF that the rubles would be transferred to the Russian central bank. On September 26 a no-confidence motion was carried with the support of 60 deputies, and Laar was replaced on October 20 by Andres TARAND, theretofore nonparty environment minister, who was endorsed by the legislature on October 27 and formed a moderately reshuffled government in early November.

Parliamentary elections on March 5, 1995, produced a plurality of 41 seats, for the relatively conservative alliance known as the Coalition Party and Rural Union (*Koonderakonna ja Maarahva Ühendus*—KMÜ), headed by the 1992 caretaker prime minister, Tiit Vähi, who on April 12 formed a new coalition government of the KMÜ and Edgar Savisaar's Estonian Center Party (*Eesti Keskerabond*—EK). Prime Minister Vähi took pains to deny that his government was dominated by ex-Communists and asserted that it would continue the promarket reforms of its predecessors. Six months later, Savisaar was dismissed as interior minister over allegations that he had authorized secret tape recordings of the recent coalition negotiations. When the Center Party backed Savisaar, Vähi tendered the resignation of the whole government and proceeded to form a new majority coalition in which the Estonian Reform Party (*Eesti Reformierakond*—RE), led by Kallas, replaced the Center Party.

Allegations that President Meri's sympathies inclined toward Moscow on bilateral issues underscored contentious presidential balloting in the *Riigikogu* in August 1996. Nominated for a second term by a cross-section of deputies, the incumbent was at first opposed, as in

1992, only by Arnold Rüütel of the Estonian Rural People's Party (*Eesti Maarahva Erakond*—EME). Meri led in three successive ballots of the deputies on August 26, 27, and 28, without obtaining the required two-thirds majority of the full complement of 101 members. In accordance with the constitution, the speaker subsequently transferred the contest to an electoral college of 374 members (the 101 parliamentarians plus 273 local council representatives), whereupon two additional candidates were nominated. They were eliminated in the first electoral college ballot on September 20, with Meri prevailing over Rüütel in the second later the same day by 196 votes to 126. The reelected president pledged to use his further term to press for Estonia's full integration into European structures, particularly the EU and the North Atlantic Treaty Organization (NATO).

In November 1996 Vähi renewed the alliance between his Estonian Coalition Party (*Eesti Koonderakond*—KE) and Savisaar's Center Party, which broke the RE's hold on the Tallinn city council. The RE then withdrew from the government and the ruling coalition, leaving six ministerial posts vacant. The Progress Party (*Arengupartei*—AP), recently formed by a group of Center Party dissidents, rejected Vähi's invitation to join the government. As a consequence, Vähi formed an exclusively KMÜ minority government that President Meri approved on December 1.

On February 25, 1997, Vähi resigned, two weeks after narrowly surviving a no-confidence vote. The KE named Mart SIIMANN, its caucus head, as its candidate for prime minister. However, he was unsuccessful in persuading former partners in the Center Party or the RE to join his new government, which, as formed on March 14, included most of the previous KMÜ ministers. The AP was given one portfolio.

The KE secured only 7 seats in the March 7, 1999, election, as did its former KMÜ partner, the EME. Although a resurgent Center Party led all parties with 28 seats, the Fatherland Union (18 seats), RE (18 seats), and Moderates (17 seats) coalesced to form a center-right government, with Mart Laar returning to the prime minister's post.

With President Meri ineligible for a third term, the 2001 presidential election was again decided by electoral college vote after the Parliament proved unable to give any nominee the necessary two-thirds majority. The governing coalition's initial candidate, former prime minister Andres Tarand of the Moderates, narrowly finished second to the Center Party's Peeter KREITZBURG in the first round of parliamentary balloting on August 27 and then stepped aside, to no avail, for Peeter TULVISTE of the Fatherland Union for the second and third ballots a day later. The electoral college's second ballot on September 21 selected Arnold Rüütel, now of the opposition People's Union of Estonia (*Eestimaa Rakvaliit*—ERL), over the RE's Toomas SAVI by a vote of 186–155.

Due to increasing conflict among the government coalition partners (see Current issues in the article on Estonia in the 2000–2002 *Handbook* for details), Prime Minister Laar on December 19, 2001, announced his intention to resign. He was succeeded by Siim Kallas, former finance minister and current chair of the RE, who formed a new Center Party/ RE cabinet on January 28.

Municipal elections in October 2002 were most notable for the strong performance by the recently launched Union for the Republic (*Res Publica*—RP). Campaigning on an anticorruption and anticrime platform, the RP won nearly one-quarter of the votes in the March 2, 2003, legislative balloting, tying the Center Party for the most seats (28). Declining a coalition offer from the Center Party, the RP subsequently agreed to an RP/RE/ERL government that was inaugurated on April 10 under the leadership of the RP's Juhan PARTS, who at 36 became the youngest prime minister in Europe.

Despite its emphasis on "new politics," the new RP-led center-right coalition government in 2003 did not deviate from plans laid by previous administrations for Estonia's accession to NATO and the EU. The *Riigikogu* in January 2004 also endorsed EU accession, which was formally achieved on May 1. Prime Minister Parts resigned on March 24, 2005, in response to the *Riigikogu*'s adoption of a nonconfidence motion against the administration's justice minister. With the EK replacing the RP in the government coalition, a new three-party government was installed on April 13 under the premiership of the RE's Andrus ANSIP.

Toomas Hendrik ILVES of the Social Democratic Party (*Sotsiaaldemokraatlik Erakond*—SDE) was elected president on September 23, 2006, by the electoral college after three rounds of balloting in Parliament failed to give any candidate the required two-thirds majority vote. Ilves defeated incumbent president Rüütel by a vote of 174–162 in the electoral college.

The RE led all parties in the March 4, 2007, legislative balloting with 31 seats, followed by the EK with 29 and the newly formed Pro Patria and Res Publica Union (*Isamaa ja Res Publica Liit*—IRL). (In May 2006 the governing councils of the RP and the Fatherland Union [*Erakond Ismaaliit*—IL] had agreed to a merger, which in June had led to the launching of the IRL.) Eschewing further cooperation with the EK, which had blocked some of his previous government's proposed economic changes, Ansip formed an RE/IRL/SDE coalition in April.

Constitution and government. In September 1991 the Supreme Council appointed a Constitutional Assembly (*Põhiseaduslik Assamblee*), composed of 60 members drawn equally from itself and the Congress of Estonia, a 495-member body elected in March 1990 by citizens of prewar Estonia and their descendants. The new basic law that emerged from the assembly's deliberations provided for a parliamentary system and a presidency with defined powers. Providing no national voting rights for Russians residing in Estonia unless they qualified for citizenship, the document was approved by a reported 93 percent majority on June 28, 1992. Independent Estonia's first presidential election in September 1992 was by popular vote, with the 101-member *Riigikogu* then choosing from the two top contenders because neither had won an overall majority of the votes cast. However, subsequent presidential elections were to be by parliamentary ballot, with the successful candidate needing a two-thirds majority of all the deputies (i.e., at least 68 votes). If after three ballots no candidate has succeeded, the decision passes to an electoral college in which the deputies are joined by a larger number of local representatives and in which a simple majority vote suffices. The president serves a five-year term and is limited to two terms. (The 1992 election was for a four-year term on a one-time basis.)

The president nominates the prime minister and approves the latter's nominations for the cabinet, all subject to legislative approval. The *Riigikogu* is elected via direct party-list balloting in 11 districts. Most seats are distributed on a proportional basis within each district, although some are allocated as "national compensation mandates" to parties securing at least 5 percent of the national vote.

Administratively, the country is divided into 15 counties (*maakond*), which are subdivided into communes (*vald*), and 6 major towns (the other urban areas being subordinate to the counties). In February 2003 the *Riigikogu*, in the first amendment to the constitution since its adoption, lengthened the term of office for local councils from three to four years.

Foreign relations. Soviet recognition of the independence of the Baltic states on September 6, 1991, paved the way for admission of the three to the CSCE on September 10 and admission to the UN on September 17. Prior to the Soviet action, diplomatic recognition had been extended by a number of governments, including, on September 2, the United States, which had never recognized the 1940 annexations. Estonia was admitted to the IMF in 1992 and to the Council of Europe in 1993.

Regionally, Estonia, Latvia, and Lithuania concluded a Baltic Economic Cooperation Agreement in April 1990, which led on September 24, 1991, to a customs union agreement intended to permit free trade and visa-free travel between their respective jurisdictions. Nevertheless, with each state adopting its own currency and establishing customs posts on its borders, the development of trade among them was slow. Estonia was a founding member of the Council of the Baltic Sea States (see separate article) in 1992, which served as a conduit for Swedish and other Scandinavian involvement in Estonia's quest for modernization.

Postindependence Estonia's key objective of securing the withdrawal of Russian troops from its territory was complicated in 1993 by Moscow's intense criticism of alleged discrimination against ethnic Russians under Estonia's new citizenship law. Western pressure persuaded Moscow to adhere to an August 1994 deadline for withdrawal, subject to Russian retention of the Paldiski communications base for an additional year. Prior to the Russian withdrawal, President Yeltsin on June 26 decreed that the Russian-Estonian border should be based on the Soviet-era line, thus effectively rejecting the Estonian contention that the 1920 border should be restored. In November 1995 Estonia bowed to reality by agreeing in principle to the maintenance of the existing border, but relations with its powerful neighbor remained tense. Tallinn sought to gain international support for its contention that Estonia's 500,000-strong ethnic Russian population was the result of Moscow-directed settlement during the half-century of Soviet rule. In an effort to bring closure to its difficult negotiations with Russia over a border treaty, Estonia had dropped its insistence that the treaty include mention of the 1920 Tartu treaty and had accepted demarcation lines unilaterally set by the Russians. However, in January 1997 the Russians threatened sanctions and said they would not sign the treaty until Estonia stopped alleged human rights violations against its ethnic Russians. (The Council of Europe, which ended its human rights monitoring in Estonia on January 30, praised Tallinn for making rapid progress but noted areas that needed improvement.) In December 1998 Estonia adopted legislation allowing children who had been born in Estonia to ethnic Russians to become Estonian citizens, a measure that was welcomed by the Council of Europe, OSCE, and, to a certain extent, Moscow, although Russia pressed for further liberalization regarding stateless adult ethnic Russians. Subsequently, in March 1999, tentative agreement was reached on demarcation of the Russian-Estonian border that would involve the transfer of only a small amount of territory. Meanwhile, the status of ethnic Russians in Estonia continued to be a contentious issue. Although a significant number of them had achieved Estonian citizenship, it was estimated in 2004 that 120,000 had opted for Russian citizenship because of language and other restrictions, while more than 170,000 remained "stateless." (Noncitizens are ineligible to vote in national elections, although all permanent residents, regardless of citizenship status, can participate in local balloting.) On May 18, 2005, Russia and Estonia signed a treaty clarifying the common land border and the delimitation of the maritime zones in the Gulf of Finland and Gulf of Narva. However, Russia withdrew from the agreement a month later after the *Riigikogu* made references to the Russian occupation while ratifying the treaty in June. Russia had not ratified as of 2009.

Estonia became a signatory of NATO's Partnership for Peace in February 1994, subsequently reiterating its desire for full NATO membership and also for eventual accession to the EU. It made significant progress toward the latter goal on June 13, 1995, when it joined the other two Baltic republics in signing an association agreement with the EU that placed them on the same footing as the other East European applicant states. In December 1997 the EU invited Estonia, but not the other Baltic states, to join the first wave of EU expansion, and formal membership negotiations began in March 1998. Among other things, the EU called upon Estonia to make it easier for ethnic Russians to become citizens.

Although it was not among the three states invited by NATO to join the alliance in April 1999, Estonia was among five others designated as prime candidates for the next accession phase. In what some called a consolation prize for not gaining quick admission to NATO, Estonia joined the other Baltic states in signing the Charter of Partnership with the United States in January 1998. In March 2000 Defense Minister Jüri LUIK presented Estonia's plan for joining NATO, including a proposal to increase defense spending to 2 percent of the GDP by 2002, to conform to NATO standards. A NATO summit in November 2002 formally invited Estonia to accede to the alliance, and Estonia was among seven new members admitted to NATO in April 2004. (The *Riigikogu* had endorsed the NATO initiative in March.)

In June 2003, upon the request of the Iraqi Interim Government, Estonia deployed a light infantry platoon to support troops stationed in Iraq. In addition to contributing troops to such military operations, Estonia subsequently sought to strengthen diplomatic ties with the United States and the EU. (President Ilves, an American-raised career diplomat, recently indicated that he viewed the Western allies as a balance against perceived efforts by Russia to reassert its influence in the Baltics.) The last Estonian troops returned from Iraq in December 2008. Meanwhile, Estonia planned to deploy 140 personnel to provide security for the Afghan elections in August 2009 as part of its cooperation with NATO.

The new RE/IRL/SDE government in Estonia faced a diplomatic dilemma almost immediately upon taking office in 2007 in regard to the Bronze Soldier, a statue then located in central Tallinn in commemoration of Soviet soldiers killed in Estonia during WW II. It had long been a source of conflict, attracting predominantly Russian nationalist displays and generating resentment among ethnic Estonians regarding the Soviet occupation following the war. In late April 2007 the government ordered the statue transferred from the city center to a cemetery in a less prominent location, prompting mass protests by ethnic Russians in May that occasionally turned violent. Many of the protestors reportedly belonged to the Kremlin-sponsored Nashi youth movement. Demonstrators also blockaded the Estonian embassy in Moscow, with no apparent intervention by Russian authorities to ensure the safety of embassy personnel. In addition, Estonian officials claimed that Russia had launched a "cyberspace war" by "attacking" Estonian government websites during the disturbances. A delegation of Russian MPs dispatched shortly after the riots suggested that the "fascist" Estonian government be replaced. Estonia responded by accusing Russia of encouraging unrest by spreading misinformation. The Russian involvement was widely viewed as an unusually direct attempt to pressure Estonia, possibly as the first step in a broader Russian effort to reestablish influence in the region.

Some Estonian officials saw potential for improved relations upon the inauguration of the new Russian president, Dmitry Medvedev, in May 2008. However, such hopes were undercut by Russia's subsequent military confrontation with Georgia in regard to South Ossetia and Abkhazia (see article on Georgia for details). The Baltic states deemed the situation to be a threat to Georgia's integrity, prompting the Estonian *Riigikogu* to post an affirmation of Georgia's sovereignty on its official website. The Russian embassy in Tallinn cancelled a visa granted to former prime minister Laar on April 24, 2009, and potential for rapprochement in the intermediate term seemed unlikely.

Current issues. The 2007 *Riigikogu* poll was widely viewed as a strong mandate for the Reform Party. New prime minister Ansip promised additional tax cuts but at the same time pledged to pursue other policies designed to curb inflation in order to facilitate eventual entry into the eurozone. However, Estonia continued to be separated politically along ethnic lines, and ethnic Russians protested the establishment of a memorial commemorating the Estonian war for independence in central Tallinn, as well as the removal of the Bronze Soldier statue commemorating Soviet WWII veterans (see Foreign relations, above). Nevertheless, the economy overtook historical interpretation as the chief political and policy issue by mid-2008, as a drop in consumption steeply reduced government revenues and heightened social anxiety, causing division within a coalition that, in the aftermath of the May 2007 riots, had been reasonably unified.

The economy remained the preeminent policy consideration in 2009. While Estonia faced the global economic crisis with stronger fundamentals than Latvia, it remained vulnerable, facing a burst real estate bubble, rising unemployment, and deflated consumer confidence in its domestic and foreign markets. The government accordingly announced an interim budget in February 2009 and viewed its passage as a political mandate. Nevertheless, controversy regarding the appropriate strategy for eliminating the budget deficit continued to animate the ruling coalition. It was expected that the deficit could reach 2.9 percent of GDP in 2009, edging close to the 3 percent maximum set by the EU and thereby potentially jeopardizing Estonia's bid to join the eurozone. Additional cuts were implemented in April, with pension contributions being reduced until 2011. Nevertheless, the rising cost of unemployment insurance in response to job losses was expected to exhaust the government fund by 2010. The junior partners in the ruling coalition offered contrasting solutions to the economic crisis: the SDE focused on higher taxes and extended social services, while the IRL emphasized structural reform. Policy differences were exacerbated by a dispute over redundancy payments and unemployment benefits (see Political Parties, SDE, below) resulting in the exit of the SDE from government in May 2009. The move rendered the government a minority coalition and increased the likelihood of early elections.

As parties prepared for the scheduled balloting for European Parliament in 2009, the IRL sought to regain conservative supporters who had switched to the RE, while the SDE continued to emphasize bolstering public finances over tax cuts. The opposition EK remained confident about its support in upcoming polls, although it displayed little desire to lead in the dismal economic climate. Meanwhile, the president blocked plans endorsed by the legislature to change the borders of Tallinn's electoral districts ahead of the local elections scheduled for the fall. European election results showed the EK passing the RE, with 26.07 percent of votes to the ruling party's 15.34 percent. Independents, meanwhile, garnered 25.81 percent of votes, while the IRL and the SDE followed the RE with 12.21 percent and 8.7 percent, respectively. The EU poll reflected the difficulty of leading during a dramatic recession and indicated that the EK represents a credible opposition.

POLITICAL PARTIES

The first opposition parties since World War II began to emerge in 1988, but their impact was little more than that of political pressure groups until 1990. Largely because of a split within the Estonian Communist Party on the independence issue, the legislative distribution of seats was blurred following Estonia's first contemporary multiparty balloting on March 18, 1990. Thus, the principal adversaries were not parties, per se, but two prosecessionist formations and a movement (supported largely by ethnic Russians) opposed to independence, with Communists distributed across all three slates. Following independence in 1991, the earlier broad movements gradually broke up into a large array of smaller parties and groupings, which formed a variety of electoral alliances in 1992 and 1995. In November 1998 the Parliament banned electoral alliances in future balloting in an apparent attempt to reduce the number of small parties, although the use of joint lists was permitted in the March 1999 legislative poll.

Government Parties:

Estonian Reform Party (*Eesti Reformierakond*—RE). The RE was founded in late 1994 by Siim Kallas, who as president of the Bank of Estonia had played a key role in the downfall of the Pro Patria prime minister, Mart Laar, in September, but had then failed to secure legislative endorsement as his successor. Described as "liberal rightist" in orientation, the RE incorporated the Estonian Liberal Democratic Party (*Eesti Liberaaldemokraatlik Partei*—ELDP), which had contested the 1992 election as part of the winning Pro Patria coalition but had withdrawn in June 1994 to protest Prime Minister Laar's leadership style. The RE won 16.2 percent of the vote in the March 1995 legislative poll, after which Kallas resigned from his post at the bank.

Having at first remained in opposition, the RE replaced the Estonian Center Party in the coalition government in October 1995 but withdrew from the government in late 1996. As was the case with the Fatherland Union and the Moderates, the RE was given five cabinet posts in the new government formed after the March 1999 legislative balloting, in which the RE had secured 18 seats on a 15.9 percent vote share. After the collapse of that three-party coalition, the RE in January formed a new government with the Center Party, with Kallas assuming the post of prime minister.

The RE secured 19 seats on a 17.7 percent vote share in the March 2003 *Riigikogu* poll and accepted "junior" status in the subsequent RP/RE/ERL government. The replacement of the RP by the Center Party in the government coalition in April 2005 allowed the RE to name Andrus Ansip to the post of prime minister. The RE garnered 31 seats on a 27.8 percent vote share in the 2007 parliamentary elections, granting it the mandate to form a coalition with the IRL and the SDE. (Ansip became the first prime minister to be "reelected" since independence.)

Despite a rise in its popularity in the aftermath of the Bronze soldier incident in 2007 (see Foreign relations, above, for details), the RE in 2008 looked more vulnerable as the economic slowdown threatened the party's tax cut plan, which it sought to maintain in tandem with a balanced budget. Proposed austerity measures led to more frequent disagreements with its coalition partners in 2009, and polls showed the RE's popularity was declining to the benefit of the opposition EK. The ruling party did not plan to introduce any supplementary budgets in the intermediate term but indicated that more cuts would be necessary in order to avoid a deficit of over 3 percent in 2009.

Tallinn Council member Sergei Ivanov, a prominent ethnic Russian in the RE, left the party in April, arguing that the party was responsible for instigating Russophobia.

Leaders: Andrus ANSIP (Party Chair and Prime Minister); Keit PENTUS (Parliamentary Faction Chair); Rein AIDMA, Peep ARU (Parliamentary Vice Chairs); Kristiina OJULAND (Parliamentary Vice President).

Pro Patria and Res Publica Union (*Isamaa ja Res Publica Liit*—IRL). The IRL was formed in June 2006 by a merger of the RP and the IL in the hopes of improving the right's representation in the 2007 *Riigikogu* elections. However, the IRL secured only 17.9 percent of the vote and 19 seats (compared to 35 in 2003 for the RP and IL combined). Nevertheless, the IRL was subsequently invited to join the new RE-led coalition government. The IRL in 2008 supported various patriotic initiatives commemorating Estonia's struggle for independence and condemning excesses committed under communism, as well as budget cuts. At a party council on February 7, 2009, the chair called for extensive structural reform in order to save the economy from the global economic crisis. In April the IRL claimed the support of 13 percent of voters, tying the party with its fellow junior coalition partner, the SDE. The IRL leadership has suggested merging the Baltic stock markets and cutting welfare payments in order to counter the recession and widening government debt. Both the IRL and the SDE have taken steps to refund the parliamentary pay increase granted in 2008 in light of more recent budget pressures.

Leaders: Mart LAAR (Chair and Former Prime Minister); Margus TSAHKNA (Secretary General); Tõnis LUKAS (Vice Chair and Minister of Education); Ene ERGMA (Vice Chair and Speaker of the Riigikogu); Jaak AAVIKSOO (Vice Chair and Minister of Defense); Andres HERKEL, Urmas REINSALU (Parliamentary Vice Chairs).

Union for the Republic (*Res Publica*—RP). Formed originally by young anti-Soviet activists (including several prominent academics) as a political "club" in 1989, the rightist RP became a formal party in December 2001. Apparently appealing to Estonians dissatisfied with Estonia's center and center-left parties, the RP gained about one-quarter of the vote in the local and regional elections in 2001. Similar results (24.6 percent of the vote nationally) in the 2003 national legislative polls secured 28 seats for the RP, which then formed a coalition government with the RE and ERL under the leadership of the RP's Juhan Parts. When the Parliament passed a no-confidence vote against the justice minister, Parts and the rest of the RP withdrew from the government, to be replaced in the ruling coalition by the Center Party.

Fatherland Union (*Erakond Isamaaliit*—IL) Also referenced as the Pro Patria Union, the IL was launched in December 1995 by merger of the Fatherland ("Pro Patria") National Coalition (*Rahvuslik Koonderakond Isamaa*—RKEI) and the Estonian National Independence Party (*Eesti Rahvusliku Sõltumatuse Partei*—ERSP). Having dominated the previous government, the two parties had contested the March 1995 election in alliance as the Pro Patria/ERSP Bloc (*Isamaa ja ERSP Liit*) but had retained only eight seats on a 7.9 percent vote share and thus went into the opposition.

The RKEI had been formed in early 1992 as an alliance of four Christian democratic and right-of-center parties seeking to make a complete break with the Communist era. In September 1992 the alliance elected a plurality of 29 deputies, who joined the ERSP contingent and others to elect Lennart Meri president the following month. RKEI leader Mart Laar then turned the alliance into a unitary formation and was named to head a coalition government. After failing to sustain coalition unity, he was ousted as prime minister in September 1994.

At its founding in August 1988 the ERSP had been the only organized non-Communist party in the USSR. Although centrist in ideology, it was consistently more anticommunist than other proindependence formations, declining to participate in the 1990 Estonian Supreme Soviet elections and instead organizing the alternative "Congress of Estonia." Following independence in 1991, it was the country's strongest party, but it was eclipsed by the RKEI in the September 1992 balloting. Thereafter, the ERSP became a junior coalition partner in the Laar government.

Mart Laar returned to the prime minister's post in March 1999 as head of the new three-party coalition government installed following legislative balloting, in which the Fatherland Union had finished second with 18 seats on a 16.1 percent vote share. However, his coalition collapsed in late 2001, and the IL moved into opposition following the installation of the new RE/Center Party government.

Laar resigned as chair of the Fatherland Union following the party's poor performance in the October 2002 local elections. Laar was succeeded by Tunne KELAM, deputy speaker of the parliament. The Fatherland Union's electoral slide continued in the March 2003 legislative poll, in which it secured only seven seats on a vote share of 7.3 percent. In the 2004 election to the European Parliament, the first for Estonia, the IL won 10.5 percent of the popular vote and one of the six seats from Estonia.

Opposition Parties:

Estonian Center Party (*Eesti Keskerakond*—EK). Launched in October 1991 as the Estonian People's Center Party (*Eesti Rahva-Keskerakond*—ERKE), the party adopted its current name in April 1993. Founded by Edgar Savisaar, the Center Party is an offshoot of the Estonian Popular Front (*Eesti Rahvarinne*), a broad proindependence movement that coalesced in 1988 but split into various parties after independence. The Center Party used the Front's designation in the 1992 election, winning 15 seats (with 12.2 percent of the vote) and achieving a creditable third place for its presidential candidate, Rein TAAGEPERA. As Front party chair, Savisaar was prime minister from April 1990 to January 1992, having previously been chair of the Soviet-era Estonian Planning Committee.

The Center Party absorbed the Estonian Entrepreneurs' Party (*Eesti Ettevõtjate Erakond*—EEE) prior to the March 1995 balloting, at which it won 14.2 percent of the vote. It took four portfolios in the subsequent coalition, with Savisaar becoming interior minister. In October 1995, however, Savisaar's dismissal over an alleged phone-tapping scandal precipitated his party's exit from the government, with Savisaar himself being replaced as party chair by Andra VEIDEMANN. Having initially declared his retirement from political life, Savisaar made a comeback at the head of anti-Veidemann elements in early 1996, securing reelection as chair in late March. Two months later, the Veidemann group launched the Progress Party (see New Estonia Party, below, under ERL), to which the Center Party lost 7 of its 16 deputies. In July the state prosecutor closed the Savisaar case, having found nothing criminal in the former minister's conduct.

In May 1998 the Center Party absorbed the Estonian Greens (*Eesti Rõhelised*), which had been launched in 1991 as a coalition of several organizations and had secured 1 legislative seat in 1992. The movement drew attention to the huge environmental damage resulting from the Soviet military presence in Estonia, which government experts in 1994 said would cost $4 billion to remedy.

Described as a "canny populist," Savisaar led the EK to a first-place finish in the March 1999 balloting (28 seats and 23.4 percent of the vote) on a platform designed to appeal to segments of the populace wary of free-market economic reforms. Prior to the balloting, the party announced it hoped to form a new government with the EME (see ERL, below), but between them they secured only 35 seats and could find no other suitable coalition partners. The Center Party then remained in opposition to the three-party coalition government formed in March. After the demise of the government in January 2002, the Center Party was admitted to the new cabinet.

Savisaar was reelected mayor of Tallinn in 2002, and the party retained its popularity at the March 2003 legislative poll, leading all parties with 25.4 percent of the vote. However, it was unable to persuade the RE to pursue a coalition government and subsequently returned to opposition status. When the RP dropped out of the government in March 2006, the EK took its place a month later and formed a new government with the remaining governing parties. However, that government's tenure ended following the March 2007 legislative elections, despite a strong showing by the Center Party (29 seats on a 26.1 percent vote share).

Among other things, dropping the EK from the new RE-led coalition in 2007 permitted the government to pursue economic policies previously blocked by the EK. Savisaar has since denied that the EK had any interest in governing with the RE, though the EK was considered to be a desirable alternative partner for the RE if the current coalition failed.

According to a public opinion poll published by the Estonian Market and Opinion Research Centre (Emor) in April 2009, the EK had overtaken the RE as the most popular party in Estonia. The party also enjoyed the support of 61 percent of non-Estonian speakers. However, links with other parties have suffered due to the EK's hesitation to clearly condemn the Russian presence in Georgia and its opposition to the relocation of the Bronze Soldier memorial. The EK also opposed the majority of the *Riigikogu* on electoral law, lobbying the president to overturn the decision to retain Tallinn's existing electoral districts in the fall 2009 balloting for local governments. The party attracted criticism in 2009 for accepting some $100,000 from Slovakian donors.

Leaders: Edgar SAVISAAR (Chair and Mayor of Tallinn); Priit TOOBAL (Secretary General); Vilja SAVISAAR, (Parliamentary Chair); Ain SEPPCIK, Toomas VAREK (Parliamentary Vice Chairs); Jüri RATAS (Vice President of the *Riigikogu*).

Social Democratic Party (*Sotsiaaldemokraatlik Erakond*—SDE). The SDE is the successor (as of 2003) to the Moderates (*Rahvaerakond Mõõdukad*—M), launched in 1990 as an electoral coalition of the Estonian Social Democratic Party (*Eesti Sotsiaaldemokraatlik Partei*—ESDP) and the Estonian Rural Center Party (*Eesti Maa-Keskerakond*—EMKE).

The ESDP had descended from the historic party founded in 1905 and maintained in exile during the Soviet era. Relaunched in Estonia in 1990 as a merger of three social democratic and workers' parties, it became part of the independence movement, its strong anticommunism enabling it to participate in right-oriented postindependence governments. Founded in 1990 to represent the interests of Estonia's farming community, the EMKE differed from other agrarian formations in that it gave full backing to promarket policies.

Mõõdukad won 12 legislative seats in the 1992 election, its campaign including charges on behalf of the EMKE that the rural parties in the Coalition Party and Rural Union (KMÜ; see Estonian Coalition Party, below) alliance were dominated by former communists. *Mõõdukad* subsequently joined the new Pro Patria–led government, although the ESDP sought to preserve a social welfare dimension to the promarket reforms favored by the other members of the coalition. *Mõõdukad* lost half of its representation in the 1995 balloting, despite the endorsement of Prime Minister Andres Tarand. The alliance established a more formal structure in April 1996, with Tarand being elected chair.

The Moderates ran on a joint list for the 1999 legislative poll with the newly formed Estonian People's Party (*Eesti Rahvaerakond*—R); the two groupings formally merged after that balloting, resulting in the party's new Estonian name (*Rahvaerakond Mõõdukad*). The People's Party had been launched in March 1998 by the Estonian Farmers' Party (*Eesti Talurahva Erakond*—ETRE) and the Republican and Conservative People's Party (*Vabariiklaste ja Konservatiivide Rahvaerakond "Parempoolsed"*—VKRE). The latter, by its own choice rendered "Right-Wingers" in English, had left the Pro Patria–led coalition government in June. The VKRE won five seats in the March 1995 election on a 5 percent vote share.

In early April 1998 the People's Party elected Foreign Affairs Minister Toomas Hendrik Ilves as chair and initially agreed to support the KMÜ in the legislature. However, the effort to stabilize the ruling coalition failed, and Ilves resigned from his cabinet post in November, under pressure from rural elements in the KMÜ. However, he returned to the post in the coalition government named in March 1999, the *Mõõdukad*/People's Party joint list having won 17 seats on a 15.2 percent vote share. Collaterally, *Mõõdukad* Chair Tarand was elected to head the nine-member council established by the governing parties to coordinate their activities and legislative initiatives.

At a party congress on May 18, 2001, Tarand stepped down as chair in what proved to be an unsuccessful pursuit of the state presidency. He was succeeded as chair by Ilves. Like the Fatherland Union, the Moderates performed poorly in the 2002 local elections, prompting the resignation of Ilves as party chair. The decline continued in the March 2003 legislative balloting (six seats on a 7 percent vote share), and in early 2004 party delegates approved the adoption of the SDE rubric to reflect the party's policies more accurately. Subsequently, the SDE surprised analysts by securing three seats (including one for Ilves) in the June 2004 voting for Estonia's six seats in the European Parliament. In the October 2005 local elections the SDE won 6.43 percent of all votes cast, an improvement over the 4.39 percent the party won in 2002. Ilves continued the party's upswing in 2006 by gaining the presidency of the republic (see Political background, above). Ilves, an American-raised career diplomat, heightened the SDE's relevance through his election to the post, which is typically imbued with only ceremonial power domestically but holds practical influence in affairs abroad. The SDE secured a 10.6 percent vote share in the 2007 legislative poll and joined the subsequent RE-led coalition government.

The SDE took issue with RE policies for employment contracts in January 2008, and in May the SDE also proposed delaying the income tax cuts proposed in the RE campaign platform due to the lower-than-expected revenues from value-added taxes. Friction with the RE increased as it became apparent that the government would cut social spending in 2009 to respond to the crisis. Jüri Pihl was elected party chair at a congress on March 6, 2009. He called for higher taxes (characterizing the RE ideology as "dead") and cited the need to focus on health, training, and employment. Policy disputes continued, with the SDE ultimately exiting government in May 2009 in response to the government's move to reduce redundancy payments in order to allow more firms to cut costs and avoid bankruptcy. The cuts were to be accompanied by increased unemployment benefits.

Leaders: Jüri PIHL (Chair and Minister of Internal Affairs); Eiki NESTOR (Parliamentary Chair); Indrek SAAR, Katrin SAKS, Peeter KREITZBERG (Vice Chairs); Randel LÄNTS (Secretary General); Toomas Hendrik ILVES (President of the Republic and Former Chair); Ivari PADAR (Minister of Finance and Former Chair).

Estonian Greens (*Erakond Eestimaa Rohelise*—EER). The EER was launched in 2006 after a long respite on the part of the Greens from politics in Tallinn. The Greens began as the Estonian Green Movement in 1988, which then splintered when a political wing, the Estonian Green Party (*Eesti Rohelised*—ER), split off in 1989. The Greens nevertheless won 8 of 105 seats in the first democratic election to the Estonian Supreme Council in 1990. Their chair, Toomas FREY, subsequently became the first Green to be given the environment portfolio.

The ER fared poorly in the first elections following independence, securing 1 seat and a 2.62 vote share in the 1992 parliamentary elections. A merger with the Estonian Royalist Party (*Rojalistlik Partei*—PR) in 1995 afforded no seats in that year's election. In 1998, membership dipped below the 1,000-member threshold required by Estonian electoral law. Green parties did not participate in the 2003 national elections.

Party organization improved in 2006 with a membership drive sponsored by the Green Party Initiative Group (*Rohelise Erakonna Algatusgrupp*). The EER had received over 1,000 membership applications by November and was consequently registered as an official party for the 2007 legislative poll. Campaigning on the platform of "New Energy," which combined green politics with probusiness energy innovations, the EER won six seats on a 7.1 percent vote share. The last party congress was held on June 14, 2008.

Leaders: Valdur LAHTVEE (Chair); Marek STRANDBERG (Vice Chair); Mikk SARV (Spokesperson); Mart JUSSI, Katrin IDLA, Maire FORSEL, Jüri GINTER, Agu KIVIMAGI, Ott KOSTNER, Ahto OJA, Peeter JALAKAS, Ene SAVOLAINEN, Riho RAASSILD (Board Members).

People's Union of Estonia (*Eestimaa Rahvaliit*—ERL). The ERL was established in October 1999 as successor to the Estonian Rural People's Party (*Eesti Maarahva Erakond*—EME). In June 2000 the ERL absorbed the Estonian Rural Union (*Eesti Maaliit*—EM) and the Estonian Pensioners' and Families' Party (*Eesti Pensionäride ja Perede Erakond*—EPPE).

The EME, also often referenced as the Country People's Party, had been founded in September 1994 and helped to rally agrarians to the KMÜ. The EME leader, Arnold Rüütel, was chair of the Estonian Supreme Soviet in the Soviet era but had supported moves to throw off Moscow rule, becoming independent Estonia's first head of state. He won a plurality in the 1992 presidential elections as the Secure Home candidate but lost to the Pro Patria nominee in the decisive legislative balloting.

Although the EME was a prominent member of the KMÜ-led government, it defected from the KMÜ on key votes in 1998 regarding the budget as well as the ban on electoral alliances. It further distanced itself from the Estonian Coalition Party (see KE, below) and the KMÜ in early 1999 when it announced plans to form a postelectoral coalition government with Edgar Savisaar's Center Party. A number of members of the Progress Party, including prominent politician Andra Veidemann, subsequently agreed to run on the EME list, but the party nonetheless managed only 7 seats (7.3 percent of the vote).

The EM was founded in March 1991 and took eight of the KMÜ seats in March 1995. The EM reached an agreement in January 1998 with the opposition Center Party to support each other in the Parliament in order to protect Estonian farmers and their markets. The EM then ran on the KE list in the March 1999 legislative balloting, as did the EPPE.

The EPPE descended from the Estonian Democratic Justice Union/Pensioners' League (*Eesti Demokraatlik Õigusliit/Pensionäride Ühendus*—EDÕL/PÜ), which dated from 1991 but was not represented in the Parliament elected in 1992. The EPPE's immediate predecessor, the Estonian Pensioners' and Families' League (*Eesti Pensionäride ja Perede Liit*—EPPL), won 6 legislative seats in 1995 as part of the KMÜ.

Following the formation of the ERL, the new grouping was reported to have the largest membership among Estonian parties. The ERL's Rüütel won the presidency on September 21, 2001, in a second-round electoral college ballot. The ERL went on to win 13 percent of the vote and 13 seats in the March 2003 legislative balloting, its membership having been bolstered by a proposed merger with the New Estonia Party (*Erakond Uus Eesti*—UE). (See the 2000–2002 *Handbook* for details on the UE.)

The ERL's representation fell to six seats (on a 7.1 percent share of the vote) in the 2007 legislative elections. The decline was partly attributed to the newly reconstituted Greens, whose appeal to traditional values and concern for environmental issues apparently appealed to portions of the ERL's base. The EK and the ERL had agreed to govern together as coalition partners if sufficient seats were secured, but the parties mutually agreed the pact was void in August 2007 following disappointing electoral returns.

The ERL's congress in December criticized the ruling coalition's economic policies as inequitable, citing the need to address the impact of inflation. The party remained active in 2009, submitting a list of candidates for European elections, and denied rumors that it intended to merge with the SDE or any other party.

Leaders: Karel RÜÜTLI (Chair), Mai TREIAL (Vice Chair), Arnold RÜÜTEL (Former President of the Republic) .

Other Parties Contesting the 2007 Legislative Elections:

Estonian Christian Democrats (*Eesti Kristlikud Demokraadid*—EKD). This party was formerly known as the Estonian Christian People's Party (*Eesti Kristlik Rahvapartei*—EKRP). Established in December 1998, the EKRP earned 2.4 percent of the vote in the 1999 legislative poll and 1.1 percent in 2003. Prominent EKD platform proposals included addiction management and limiting pornography and obscenity in public places. The EKD increased its vote share to 1.7 percent in the 2007 elections, the best performance by the parties that failed to win seats. The EKD was also the only nonparliamentary party to receive state funding in 2009, although it was fined in March for violating regulations by accepting funds from private, noncredit institutions. The party countered that the financing regulations favored factions in government. It also opposed the construction of a mosque in Tallinn, which the EKD believed would radicalize moderate Estonian Muslims due to its funding from the UAE.

Leaders: Aldo VINKEL (Chair), Paul RÄSTA (Vice Chair).

United Left Party of Estonia (*Eestimaa Ühendatud Vasakpartei*—EUVP). The EUVP was formed through a merger of the EVP and KK in 2008, with the party agenda for the first year focused on transition and maximizing electoral advantage in the next balloting.

Leaders: Sergei JÜRGENS (KK Chair), Heino RÜÜTEL (EVP Co-Chair).

Estonian Left Party (*Eesti Vasakpartei*—EVP). The EVP is a successor to the Estonian Social Democratic Labor Party (*Eesti Sotsiaal demokraatlik Tööpartei*—ESDTP). Undeterred by the ouster from power of the Estonian Communist Party (*Eestimaa Kommunistlik Partei*—EKP) during the transition to independence, elements of the old party adopted the name of Estonian Democratic Labor Party (*Eesti Demokraatlik Tööpartei*—EDTP) in 1992, asserting that the party now had a democratic socialist orientation. It unsuccessfully contested the 1995 election within the Justice (*Õiglus*) alliance, which also included the Party for Legal Justice (*Õigusliku Tasakaalu Erakond*—ÕTE), led by Peeter TEDRE. The EDTP's subsequent efforts to establish ties with the Estonian Social Democratic Party were rebuffed. The party changed its name to Estonian Social Democratic Labor Party in December 1997. The ESDTP contested the 1999 poll on the joint list of the EÜRP. Running independently in the 2003 balloting, the ESDTP won only 0.42 percent of the vote, and in the 2004 European Parliament balloting only 0.5 percent of the vote. In the 2007 legislative poll, the newly renamed EVP secured 0.1 percent of the vote. In May 2008 the EVP announced plans for a merger with the KK (below).

Leaders: Sirje KINGSEPP (Chair), Malle SALUPERE (Vice Chair).

Constitution Party (*Konstitutsioonierakond*—KK). A successor to the Estonian United People's Russian Party (*Eestimaa Ühendatud Vene Rahvapartei*—EÜVRP), also formerly known as Estonian United— People's Party (*Eestimaa Ühendatud Rahvapartei*—EÜRP), the KK is widely viewed as the most active political faction for minority ethnic Russian concerns. Then considered the strongest of the numerous ethnic Russian parties in Estonia, the EÜRP participated in the March 1995 election in the alliance known as Our Home Is Estonia (*Meie Kodu on Eestimaa*), along with the Russian Party of Estonia (see VEE, below) and the Russian People's Party of Estonia (*Eesti Vene Rahvapartei*—EVRP). *Meie Kodu* strongly opposed the 1993 Estonian citizenship law, which, by limiting the franchise to citizens, prevented the alliance from obtaining a higher vote among the estimated 20–30 percent ethnic Russian component of the populace. The grouping secured 6 seats, the legislators subsequently coalescing as a parliamentary Russian Faction.

The EÜRP contested the March 1999 balloting on a joint list with the ESDTP and the VÜP (see 2006 *Handbook*); the list secured

6 seats. In May 2000 Viktor ANDREJEV, a leader of the EÜRP, signed a cooperation agreement with Yevgenii PRIMAKOV, the leader of the Fatherland/All Russia faction of the Russian Duma. The agreement was denounced by main Estonian parties as a "sign of EÜRP's disloyalty to the country." In 2000 EÜRP leader Sergei IVANOV left to form the VBEE (see VEE, below), and later joined the RE temporarily (see RE, above). The EÜRP legislators voted to approve the new coalition government formed in January 2002.

In mid-2002 the EÜRP called for a merger of all the Russian parties in Estonia, but the party ultimately did not participate in the enlargement of the VEE (see below). Instead, the EÜRP adopted the EÜVRP rubric in December. The EÜVRP secured only 2.24 percent of the vote in the 2003 legislative balloting, marking the first time since independence that no Russian party would be represented in the *Riigikogu.* The party's electoral slide continued in the 2005 local elections, in which it won less than 1 percent (0.69) of all votes cast, much lower than the 4.31 percent it won in the 2002 local elections. The KK in May 2008 announced a merger with the EVP (see EVP, above).

Leader: Sergei JÜRGENS (Chair).

Estonian Independence Party (*Eesti Iseseivuspartei*—EIP). An opponent of Estonia's accession to the EU, the EIP was founded in November 1999 after its predecessor, the Future's Estonia Party (*Tuleviku Eesti Erakond*—TEE), was denied ballot access for failing to meet registration requirements. The EIP won 0.55 percent of the vote in the 2003 legislative balloting and 0.2 percent in 2007. In April 2008 the EIP was reportedly considering a merger with the EDP (subsequently the LEE) and the PK. The alliance remained a possibility in 2009 (see LEE, below).

Leaders: Vello LEITO, Peeter PAEMURRU (Chairs).

Russian Party of Estonia (*Vene Erakond Eestis*—VEE). The VEE was formed in 1994 under Sergei KUZNETSOV and competed in the *Meie Kodu* coalition of ethnic Russian groupings in 1995. In 1996 the VEE absorbed much of the Russian People's Party of Estonia (EVRP), but VEE membership was undercut in 1997 by the formation of the breakaway Russian Unity Party (*Veni Üntsuspartei*—VÜP), which participated in the EÜRP joint list in the 1999 legislative balloting. Running independently in that poll, the VEE failed to gain representation on a 2.0 percent vote share.

In December 2002 the VÜP announced it was merging back into the VEE, along with two other parties—the Russian Baltic Party in Estonia (*Vene Balti Erakond Eestis*—VBEE) and the Unity of Estonia Party. (For more on the VBEE, see 2007 *Handbook.*)

Although the enlarged VEE claimed a bigger constituency than the EÜVRP, it secured only 0.18 percent of the vote in the 2003 legislative elections, and only 0.3 percent of the June 2004 vote for the European Parliament. Subsequently, the VÜP, VBEE, and Unity were occasionally referenced as still maintaining separate identities. In 2007 the VEE secured just 0.2 percent of the vote share, underscoring the fact that the KK remains a more popular organized political medium for ethnic Russians in Estonia. The VEE ruled out a merger with the KK in 2009 when it emerged that the KK would unite with the EVP.

Leaders: Stanislav CHEREPANOV (Chair), Pavel CYRIL (General Secretary).

Other Parties:

Libertas Eesti (*Libertas Eesti Erakond*—LEE). The LEE is the rubric adopted in March 2009 by the Democrats–Estonian Democratic Party (*Demokraadid–Eesti Demokraatlik Partei*—EDP). The EDP was formally established in February 2001 as the successor to the Estonian Blue Party (*Eesti Sinine Erakond*—ESE). The EDP won 1.2 percent of the vote and no seats in the 2004 European Parliament elections. No votes were recorded for the EDP in 2007, implying that party membership had tapered off below the 1,000-member minimum. The EDP was reportedly considering a merger with the PK and EIP in 2008.

The LEE designation was adopted in 2009 to identify the party with the broader European "euroskeptic" movement, Libertas. A possible merger with the PK and EIP was still under consideration in April 2009, predicated on the IRL rejecting unification with the EIP and the PK.

Leaders: Jaan LAAS (Chair), Endel KALJUSMAA (Vice Chair), Märt MEESAK (Secretary).

Farmers' Assembly (*Põllumeeste Kogu*—PK). Founded in 1992, the conservative PK contested the 1995 election as part of the KMÜ. Having formed part of the subsequent government majority, the PK withdrew in February 1996, claiming that ministers were disregarding farmers' interests. It contested the 1999 poll on its own, failing to secure representation.

In mid-2002 it was announced that the PK would merge with the Conservative Club to form a new party called the National Conservative Party–Farmer's Assembly, which later attempted, under the leadership of Mart HELME, to coalesce with the EIP (see above) for the 2003 legislative poll. The proposed merger with the EIP fell through, however, and in October 2006 it was announced that PK planned to merge into the recently formed IRL. The PK reported it had received a proposal for a merger from the LEE (then the EDP) in April 2008, as observers suggested the two parties might join forces with the EIP before the next poll. The merger was still being discussed in 2009 (see LEE, above).

Leader: Tõnu OJAMAA (Chair).

Estonian Coalition Party (*Eesti Koonderakond*—KE). The KE was founded in December 1991, its leader, Tiit Vähi, becoming caretaker prime minister in January 1992. In the September 1992 balloting the party was part of the Secure Home coalition, a broadly conservative grouping that won 17 legislative seats in the 1992 poll on a 13.6 percent vote share and formed the main parliamentary opposition until 1995.

The KE was the dominant component of the Coalition Party and Rural Union (*Koonderakonna ja Maarahva Ühendus*—KMÜ), which was created for the March 1995 legislative election by the KE, EME, EM, EPPL, and PK. Campaigning on a platform promising agricultural subsidies and increased social expenditures, the KMÜ secured a plurality of 41 seats (18 for the KE) and 32.2 percent of the vote. Consequently, Vähi was named prime minister of a KMÜ coalition government, which also initially included the Center Party. When Vähi resigned in February 1997, he was succeeded by Mart SIIMANN, the head of the KE's parliamentary group. However, the governing coalition continued to decline (see Political background, above), and the KE won only 7 seats on a 7.6 percent vote share in the March 1999 poll.

In August 2001 the party chair indicated that the KE was not interested in serving as a "niche party" and would in all likelihood be dissolved at a party congress in November. Meanwhile, the KE's sole remaining member of Parliament, former prime minister Siimann, was spearheading formation of a new political association, **With Reason and Heart**. Indeed, in November the party congress decided to disband the KE, while Siimann reportedly postponed his plans to transform With Reason and Heart into a political party. The KE was formally dissolved in November 2002.

LEGISLATURE

The former Supreme Soviet/Council (Ülemnõukogu) ceased to exist on September 14, 1992, prior to balloting on September 20 for a new unicameral **Parliament** (*Riigikogu*) of 101 members elected by proportional representation for four-year terms. In the most recent election of March 4, 2007, the Estonian Reform Party won 31 seats; the Estonian Center Party, 29; the Pro Patria and Res Publica Union, 19; the Social Democratic Party, 10; the People's Union of Estonia, 6; and the Estonian Greens, 6.

Speaker: Ene ERGMA.

CABINET

[as of July 1, 2009]

Prime Minister	Andrus Ansip (RE)
Ministers	
Agriculture	Helir-Valdor Seeder (IRL)
Culture	Laine Jänes (RE) [f]
Defense	Jaak Aaviksoo (IRL)
Economic Affairs and Communications	Juhan Parts (IRL)
Education and Research	Tõnis Lukas (IRL)
Environment	Jaanus Tamkivi (RE)
Finance	Jürgen Ligi (RE)

Foreign Affairs	Urmas Paet (RE)
Internal Affairs	Marko Pomerants (RE)
Justice	Rein Lang (RE)
Population and Ethnic Affairs	Maret Maripuu (RE) [f]
Regional Affairs	Siim-Valmar Kiisler (IRL)
Social Affairs	Maret Maripuu (RE)

[f] = female

Note: RE = Estonian Reform Party; IRL = Pro Patria and Res Publica Union.

COMMUNICATIONS

Press. Due to economic difficulties, press circulation declined sharply after independence, although most dailies continued to publish. The following are Estonian-language dailies published in Tallinn, unless otherwise noted: *Postimees* (Postman, 59,000), leading Tartu paper; *Rahva Hääl* (Voice of the People, 175,000), government organ; *Eesti Ekspress* (Estonian Express, 40,000), weekly; *Eesti Päevaleht* (Daily, 40,000); *Õhtuleht* (Evening Gazette, 20,000); *Äripäev* (Daily Business, 15,000); *Hommikuleht* (Morning Paper, 14,500); *The Baltic Times* (14,000), English-language weekly; *Estoniya* (Estonia, 11,000), in Russian; *The Baltic Independent* (7,200), English-language weekly.

News agencies. The Estonian Telegraph Agency (*Eesti Teadate Agentuur*—ETA) coordinates its services with Latvian and Lithuanian agencies. The Baltic News Service (BNS) began operations in 1991.

Broadcasting and computing. Estonian Radio (*Eesti Raadio*) broadcasts in Estonian, Russian, Swedish, Finnish, English, Esperanto, Ukrainian, and Belarusan; Estonian Television (*Eesti Televisoon*) and two foreign-owned commercial stations transmit in Estonian and Russian. In August 2001 the cabinet approved combining the state radio and TV operations as the Estonian National Broadcasting Company (*Eesti Rahvusringhaaling*). As of 2008 there were 662.1 Internet users per 1,000 inhabitants.

INTERGOVERNMENTAL REPRESENTATION

Ambassador to the U.S.: Vaino REINHART.

U.S. Ambassador to Estonia: Stanley Davis PHILLIPS.

Permanent Representative to the UN: Tiina INTELMANN.

IGO Memberships (Non-UN): BIS, CBSS, CEUR, EBRD, EIB, EU, IOM, Interpol, NATO, NIB, OSCE, PCA, WCO, WTO.

ETHIOPIA

Federal Democratic Republic of Ethiopia

Political Status: Former monarchy; provisional military government formally established September 12, 1974; Marxist-Leninist one-party system instituted September 6, 1984; communist constitution approved by referendum of February 1, 1987, resulting in redesignation of the country as the People's Democratic Republic of Ethiopia; "state responsibility" assumed by rebel coalition upon surrender of the former regime's military commander and acting president in Addis Ababa on May 27, 1991; national charter and transitional government approved by multiparty National Conference that met on July 1–5, 1991; present constitution promulgated December 8, 1994; Federal Democratic Republic of Ethiopia proclaimed August 22, 1995.

Area: 436,349 sq. mi. (1,130,138 sq. km.).

Population: 53,477,265 (1994C); 79,244,000 (2008E).

Major Urban Centers (2005E): ADDIS ABABA (2,890,000), Dire Dawa (270,000), Nazret (218,000), Gondar (186,000), Dese (161,000), Jimma (151,000), Harer (117,000).

Working Language: Amharic (all Ethiopian languages enjoy equal state recognition).

Monetary Unit: Birr (official rate December 1, 2009: 12.66 birr = $1US).

President: GIRMA Wolde Giorgis (initially elected as an independent but currently a member of the Ethiopian People's Revolutionary Democratic Front [EPRDF]); nominated by the EPRDF and elected by the Parliament on October 8, 2001, to a six-year term, succeeding NEGASO Gidada (Oromo Peoples' Democratic Organization); reelected by Parliament on October 9, 2007, to a second six-year term.

Prime Minister: MELES Zenawi (Tigray People's Liberation Front); elected by the House of Peoples' Representatives on August 23, 1995, succeeding TAMIRAT Layne (Amhara National Democratic Movement); reelected to five-year terms on October 10, 2000, and October 10, 2005.

THE COUNTRY

One of the oldest countries in the world, Ethiopia exhibits an ethnic, linguistic, and cultural diversity that has impaired its political unity and stability in spite of the preponderant position long occupied by the Christian, Amharic- and Tigrinya-speaking inhabitants of the central highlands. Among the more than 70 different ethnic groups, the Amhara and the largely Muslim Oromo (Galla) account for approximately 40 percent of the population each. Amharic, the working language, is spoken by about 60 percent of the people; Galla, Tigrinya, Arabic, Somali, and Tigray are also prominent among the country's 70 languages and over 200 dialects, while English, Italian, and French have traditionally been employed within the educated elite. The Ethiopian Orthodox (Coptic) Church embraces about 40 percent of the population, as does Islam (most Ethiopian Muslims are Sunnis). Christians have long dominated governmental affairs. In 1994 women accounted for 37 percent of the labor force, the vast majority as unpaid agricultural workers. Although females have traditionally influenced decision making among the Amhara and Tigrayan peoples, their representation in the Mengistu government was minimal. There are 116 women in the current House of Peoples' Representatives, up from 42 in the previous membership, while several females have been appointed to recent cabinets.

One of the world's poorest countries in terms of per capita GNP (estimated at $130 in 1994), Ethiopia remains dependent on agriculture, with over 85 percent of its rapidly expanding population (the largest in Africa) engaged in farming and livestock-raising. (Despite free-market reforms initiated in the second half of the 1990s, most land remains owned by the government.) Coffee, the principal crop, accounts for more than 40 percent of export earnings (Ethiopia is the continent's largest coffee grower). Cotton and sugar are also widely harvested. Agricultural success waxes and wanes in response to variable rainfall, and drought and famine have routinely "stalked the land," often generating massive, albeit not always sufficient, international aid shipments. Gold and marble are mined commercially, and deposits of copper, potash, and natural gas are awaiting exploitation. Oil exploration rights have been granted recently, although they reportedly remain highly speculative. Industrial development, primarily concentrated in nondurable consumer goods, was severely hampered by the 1962–1991 civil war in Eritrea and guerrilla activity in other regions. Industry currently accounts for about 13 percent of GDP, compared to 48 percent for agriculture.

The World Bank negotiated forgiveness of some of Ethiopia's commercial debt in the mid-1990s, although nearly $4 billion of additional external debt continued to constrain economic advancement. The International Monetary Fund (IMF) also supported the government's pursuit of structural reforms in the second half of the decade. Although Ethiopia was considered as of early 1998 to be positioned for sustained economic improvement, the 1998–2000 border war with Eritrea (see Political background and Current issues, below) severely eroded the confidence of investors and redirected national funds desperately needed for social services toward the military. The conflict also slowed down the government's privatization campaign and plans to strengthen the financial sector.

Drought contributed to economic contraction in the 2002–2003 fiscal year. Agricultural recovery in 2003–2004 produced growth of 11.6 percent, although Ethiopia ranked 170th out of 177 countries in the UN's Human Development Index. In addition, 45 percent of the population was considered to be living in poverty, and Ethiopia remained one of the world's biggest per capita recipients of emergency assistance (it was estimated that 11 million people depended on humanitarian aid). The economy grew by 10.5 percent in 2004–2005 and 9.6 percent in 2005–2006, according to the IMF, giving Ethiopia a three-year level more than twice the continent's average. However, a significant increase in inflation was subsequently reported (more than 12 percent in 2006).

The IMF announced additional debt relief for Ethiopia in late 2005 and called for increased donor assistance. Russia also cancelled more than $1 billion of Ethiopia's debt, while new lending from China was subsequently reported. However, the United Kingdom and other western donors temporarily suspended some direct aid in the wake of severe political discord that erupted in late 2005 and the subsequent government crackdown on the opposition. Aid distribution was described as returning to normal in late 2007 as the government pursued "reconciliation" with its opponents. Meanwhile, the IMF called upon the government to reinvigorate its privatization program, pursue additional reforms, and direct greater public resources toward infrastructure, health, and education. (Ethiopia's army of more than 180,000 troops, one of Africa's largest, currently consumes the lion's share of expenditures.) In a related vein, Ethiopia continued to seek membership in the World Trade Organization (WTO), while promoting increased exports of flowers, tea, and textiles. However, President Meles indicated that he did not by any means fully accept the "neoliberal," free-market "orthodoxy" of the major international financial institutions, saying that state intervention in the economy for the sake of development remained an important policy component.

GDP continued to grow by more than 11 percent annually into 2008, but the growth rate subsequently declined, in part due to rapidly rising food prices, which also pushed the annual inflation rate to 40 percent at the end of 2008. The IMF approved several special disbursements in 2009 to support government efforts to combat price increases and effects of the global recession.

GOVERNMENT AND POLITICS

Political background. After centuries of medieval isolation, Ethiopia began its history as a modern state with the reign of Emperor MENELIK II (1889–1913), who established a strong central authority and successfully resisted attempts at colonization by Italy and other powers. Emperor HAILE SELASSIE I (Ras TAFARI Makonnen) succeeded to the throne in 1930 on the death of his cousin, the Empress ZAUDITU. Confronted with a full-scale invasion by Fascist Italy in 1935, Haile Selassie appealed in vain for assistance from the League of Nations and remained abroad until Ethiopia's liberation by the British and the liquidation of Italy's East African Empire in 1941. In accordance with a decision of the UN General Assembly, the former Italian colony of Eritrea was joined to Ethiopia in 1952 as an autonomous unit in an Ethiopian-Eritrean federation. Abandonment of the federal structure by formal incorporation of Eritrea into Ethiopia in 1962 fanned widespread separatist sentiment in Eritrea.

Although the post–World War II period witnessed a movement away from absolute monarchy, the pace of liberalization did not meet popular expectations, and in early 1974 an uprising among troops of Ethiopia's Second Army Division gradually escalated into a political revolt. As a result, Prime Minister Tshafe Tezaz AKLILU Habte-Wold resigned on February 28 and was replaced by ENDALKACHEW Makonnen, who also was unable to contain discontent among military, labor, and student groups. By late spring many aristocrats and former government officials had been imprisoned, and on July 22 Endalkachew was forced to resign in favor of Mikael IMRU.

On September 12, 1974, the military announced that the emperor had been deposed and that a Provisional Military Government (PMG) had been formed under Lt. Gen. AMAN Mikael Andom. Initially, the military presented a united front, but rival factions soon emerged. On November 24 approximately 60 officials, including two former prime ministers and Aman Andom, were executed, apparently on the initiative of (then) Maj. MENGISTU Haile-Mariam, strongman of the little-publicized Armed Forces Coordinating Committee, or *Dergue*, as it was popularly known. After November 28 the *Dergue* acted through a Provisional Military Administrative Council (PMAC), whose chair, Brig. Gen. TEFERI Banti, served concurrently as acting head of state and government.

On March 21, 1975, the PMAC decreed formal abolition of the monarchy, while declaring its intention to organize a new national political movement "guided by the aims of Ethiopian socialism." Former emperor Haile Selassie, in detention since his deposition, died in August.

On February 3, 1977, following reports of a power struggle within the *Dergue*, General Teferi and six associates were killed in an armed encounter in the Grand Palace in Addis Ababa. Eight days later, Mengistu and Lt. Col. ATNAFU Abate were named chair and vice chair, respectively, of the PMAC in a proclamation that also modified the *Dergue* structure. However, Colonel Atnafu was executed on November 11 for alleged "counter-revolutionary crimes." Collaterally, antigovernment violence, dubbed the "white terror," flared in Addis Ababa amid indications of growing coordination between several opposition groups, including the Marxist Ethiopian People's Revolutionary Party (EPRP) and the more conservative Ethiopian Democratic Union (EDU). The Mengistu regime responded by mounting an indiscriminate "red terror" in December 1977–February 1978 based in part on the arming of civilians in urban dweller associations (*kebeles*).

The struggle for control in Addis Ababa was accompanied by military challenges on three major fronts. By March 1977 virtually all of northern Eritrea was under the administration of Eritrean rebels, while government forces were being subjected to increased pressure by EDU guerrillas in the northwest. Moreover, in late July the government conceded that the greater part of the eastern region of Ogaden had fallen to insurgents of the Western Somalia Liberation Front (WSLF), who were supported by Somali regular forces. On September 7 Ethiopia severed relations with Somalia because of the "full-scale war" that existed between the two countries. By mid-December, however, a massive influx of Cuban personnel and Soviet equipment had shifted the military balance in Ethiopia's favor, and most of the region was recovered prior to formal Somali withdrawal in March 1978. A renewed offensive was then mounted by government forces in Eritrea, and in late November they recaptured the last two major cities held by the rebels—the strategically important Red Sea port of Massawa and Keren, some 70 miles northwest of Asmara.

Despite the success of the 1978 anti-insurgent campaigns, a major offensive in mid-1979 to wipe out remaining resistance in Eritrea proved ineffectual, with government control remaining limited to the principal towns and connecting corridors. Similar conditions prevailed in the Ogaden, where the WSLF and its ally, the Somali Abo Liberation Front (SALF), continued to launch guerrilla attacks. In response,

Ethiopia was reported to have initiated a "scorched-earth" policy—poisoning water supplies, killing herds of livestock, strafing settled areas—that further aggravated what the UN Office of the High Commissioner for Refugees had earlier described as the world's worst refugee problem.

Following a number of unsuccessful attempts to unite existing Marxist parties, a Commission for Organizing the Party of the Working People of Ethiopia (COPWE) was formed in December 1979 to pave the way for a Soviet-style system of government. On September 10, 1984, the COPWE's work was declared to have been completed, with Colonel Mengistu being designated secretary general of a new Workers' Party of Ethiopia (WPE); however, the PMAC remained in effective control, pending completion of a civilian governing structure.

A commission appointed and chaired by Colonel Mengistu presented the draft of a new constitution in early 1987. A reported 81 percent of voters approved the document at a referendum on February 1, the government announcing three weeks later that the country would thenceforth be styled the People's Democratic Republic of Ethiopia (PDRE).

A unicameral national legislature (*Shengo*), elected on June 14, 1987, convened on September 9, and on the following day it selected Colonel Mengistu as the country's first president. The *Shengo* also named Lt. Col. FISSEHA Desta, theretofore deputy secretary general of the PMAC Standing Committee, as PDRE vice president and elected a 24-member State Council, headed by Mengistu and Fisseha as president and vice president, respectively. The former deputy chair of the PMAC Council of Ministers, Capt. FIKRE-SELASSIE Wogderes, was designated prime minister of an administration whose composition, announced on September 20, was largely unchanged from that of its predecessor.

The new government was greeted by vigorous rebel offensives: the Eritrean People's Liberation Front (EPLF) claimed a succession of victories over government troops beginning in September 1987, while in March 1988 the Tigray People's Liberation Front (TPLF) took advantage of Addis Ababa's setbacks in Eritrea to launch a renewed offensive in its 13-year struggle for autonomy. In April, President Mengistu, buffeted by military reversals and deteriorating troop morale, signed a cease-fire with Somali president Siad Barre, thus freeing Ethiopian troops for redeployment to Eritrea, most of which, despite the recapture of some rebel-held villages, remained under EPLF control.

Conditions worsened substantially for the central government during 1989. A failed military coup in mid-May, during which the defense and industry ministers were killed, provoked a purge of senior officers that yielded the loss of most seasoned commanders. Three months earlier the Ethiopian People's Revolutionary Democratic Front (EPRDF), a base-broadening coalition recently established by the TPLF, had launched another offensive that dealt the government a series of major setbacks. In August Colonel Mengistu felt obliged to augment his army (already one of black Africa's largest at more than 300,000 personnel) by mass mobilization and conscription. A month later Mengistu accepted an overture by former U.S. president Jimmy Carter to open peace talks with the EPLF, subsequently accepting Carter and former Tanzanian president Julius Nyerere as cochairs of the discussions. Meanwhile, preliminary negotiations with the EPRDF were launched in Rome in October, although they were linked by the Tigrayans to "the irrevocable fall of the current regime." In November, with EPRDF forces moving toward the capital, Prime Minister Fikre-Selassie was dismissed for "health reasons" and replaced, on an acting basis, by Deputy Prime Minister HAILU Yimanu. Shortly thereafter, fighting also broke out in the east between government troops and rebel forces of the Oromo Liberation Front (OLF). Faced with continued military adversity, diminished Soviet support, and renewed projections of widespread famine, President Mengistu in March 1990 formally terminated his commitment to Marxism. However, the regime remained on the brink of collapse as EPRDF troops advanced to within 150 miles of Addis Ababa and EPLF forces gained control of all of Eritrea except for several major cities.

In January 1991 the EPRDF and the EPLF, which had been coordinating military operations for two years, devised a "final" battle plan after the TPLF reportedly agreed to a self-determination referendum in Eritrea following the anticipated rebel victory. With the OLF also a participant, the anti-Mengistu alliance launched a decisive offensive in February.

In what was seen as a last-ditch effort to salvage his regime, President Mengistu on April 26, 1991, announced the appointment of former Foreign Minister TESFAYE Dinka, a moderate with ties to the United States and Western Europe, to the vacant position of prime minister and named Lt. Gen. TESFAYE Gebre-Kidan as vice president. However, on May 21, as EPRDF troops encircled Addis Ababa, Colonel Mengistu, under pressure from U.S. officials to prevent further bloodshed, resigned as head of state and fled to Zimbabwe, Vice President Tesfaye becoming acting president. Three days later the EPLF sealed its control of Eritrea by capturing the towns of Asmara and Keren, and, with EPRDF fighters poised to attack the capital, General Tesfaye "effectively surrendered" on May 27. Under an agreement reached at a U.S.-brokered conference in London, the EPRDF took control of Addis Ababa on May 28 with only minimal resistance from hold-out government troops. On the same day TPLF leader MELES Zenawi announced the impending formation of an interim government that would assume responsibility for "the whole country" until Ethiopia's political future could be further defined. Concurrently, however, EPLF leader Isaias Afwerki announced the establishment of a separate provisional government for Eritrea. Although some friction was subsequently reported between the two groups, a multiparty National Conference was launched on July 1 to chart the country's political future. On July 3 the EPRDF and the EPLF (technically attending as an observer) announced an agreement whereby the former would support a referendum in 1993 on Eritrean independence in return for access to the Red Sea port of Assab. At the conclusion of the conference two days later, a National Charter was adopted that offered guarantees of basic human rights, freedom of association, access to mass media, judicial independence, and substantial autonomy for the country's numerous ethnic groups. In addition, an 87-member Council of Representatives was named, which on July 21 formalized Meles Zenawi's status as head of state. Subsequently, on July 29, the acting chief of government, TAMIRAT Layne, was confirmed as prime minister, with a 16-member cabinet being announced on August 10.

At the long awaited referendum in Eritrea on April 23–25, 1993, 99.8 percent of those participating voted for independence, and on May 3 Addis Ababa endorsed the action, which was formalized on May 24. Subsequently, balloting for a 547-member Ethiopian Constituent Assembly was held on June 5, 1994, with the EPRDF winning an overwhelming majority in reporting districts (polling in Dire Dawa and elsewhere in the east and southeast being postponed until August 28 because of unsettled conditions in the largely Somali-dominated region).

While most of the major non-EPRDF groups participated in the 1993 Constituent Assembly poll, all but the largely progovernment Ethiopian National Democratic Party (ENDP) objected to the constitution adopted on December 8, 1994, and declared their intention to boycott the federal and state elections of May 7, 1995. Despite two negotiating sessions between government and opposition delegates, no resolution of the impasse was found. Representatives of the opposition Council of Alternative Forces for Peace and Democracy in Ethiopia (CAFPDE), led by BEYENE Petros, complained of a "stranglehold" by the EPRDF on the police and armed forces, the detention of numerous regime opponents, and a ban on many party activities. For its part, the government, through its chief negotiator, DAWIT Yohannes, called for acceptance of Ethiopia's existing state bodies and denied that it held political prisoners, insisting that those incarcerated encompassed only "warmongers." As a result of the stalemate, the EPRDF and its constituent groups swept the May balloting.

On August 21, 1995, the recently elected House of Peoples' Representatives convened to accept a transfer of power from its military-backed predecessor, and on August 22, after formal proclamation of the Federal Democratic Republic of Ethiopia, the legislature elected NEGASO Gidada to the essentially titular office of federal president. On August 23 the legislators elected former interim president Meles Zenawi to the far more powerful office of prime minister.

The cabinet named by Prime Minister Meles in 1995 did not represent a cross-section of Ethiopian politics; it was, however, carefully balanced along ethnic lines, containing four Amharas, four Oromos, two Gurage, and one representative each from the Afar, Hadiya, Harari, Kembata, Somali, Tigray, and Welayita communities. By mid-1996 the government was reported to be under heavy external pressure to bring nonsecessionist opposition groups into the federal administration. However, the EPRDF resisted the appeals, apparently concentrating instead on what the *Indian Ocean Newsletter* described as efforts "to prove that all its opponents are apprentice terrorists."

In October 1995, after four months of deliberation, the High Court in Addis Ababa ruled that, as a signatory of the international convention on genocide, Ethiopia was competent to try members of the former regime on charges of crimes against humanity. Accordingly, it was announced that a trial would proceed for more than 70 defendants, including, all in absentia, former president Mengistu Haile-Mariam, former prime minister Fikre-Selassie Wogderes, and former vice president Fisseha Desta. The trial, which the *New York Times* called possibly the most extensive of its kind since Nuremberg, proceeded slowly, however. In addition to the initial defendants, more than 1700 former soldiers, police, and "mid-level" administrators were also awaiting trial in 1996. On February 13, 1997, special prosecutors in Addis Ababa brought additional charges against Mengistu and more than 5,000 officials of the *Dergue* regime (3,000 of them in absentia). (In late December 2006 the High Court found Mengistu, Fikre-Selassie, Fisseha, and many of the other *Dergue* officials guilty of genocide. Mengistu, resident in Zimbabwe, was sentenced in absentia to life imprisonment [later changed by the Supreme Court to a sentence of death], although no return to Ethiopia was expected. Analysts criticized the length of the trial, which they argued diminished the pursuit of justice. [Nearly 30 defendants had died since the trial began.])

During March 1997 social discontent surfaced in segments of the Amhara population, resulting from the government's "land reform" projects, which were seen by opponents as a policy to serve the interests of the peasants close to the ruling EPRDF. Attention throughout the rest of the year focused on efforts by the EPRDF to negotiate agreements with Oromo, Somali, and Afar groups that would permit implementation of the delayed regional autonomy plan (see various sections below for further information).

With a swiftness that stunned observers, a border dispute between Ethiopia and Eritrea escalated from what was initially depicted as a minor skirmish in early May 1998 into full-scale fighting by June. Among the many casualties of the war was their joint effort, along with Uganda, to contain Sudan's regional influence, in particular Khartoum's effort to spread militant Islamic fundamentalism. Indeed, in its quest for regional allies, Addis Ababa reportedly toned down its anti-Sudanese rhetoric and opened a dialogue with Khartoum.

The war with Eritrea dominated Ethiopian affairs for the remainder of 1998 through 2000. (See Political background in article on Eritrea for an extensive history of the conflict.) Nearly every segment of Ethiopian society, including the opposition parties, appeared to support the Ethiopian military campaign, and the EPRDF dominated the balloting that began in May 2000 for the House of Peoples' Representatives, while Meles was reelected to a second five-year term as prime minister on October 10, 2000, by acclamation in the House of Peoples' Representatives. On October 8, 2001, GIRMA Wolde Giorgis was selected to succeed President Negaso, who had become embroiled in a dispute with Meles and his supporters over the outcome of the war (see Current issues, below).

New balloting for the House of Peoples' Representatives was held on May 15, 2005, initial results indicating a strong challenge to the EPRDF from two new opposition alliances—the Coalition for Unity and Democracy (CUD) and the United Ethiopian Democratic Forces (UEDF). Both opposition groups charged the government with widespread fraud in the conduct of the poll and the tallying of the votes, and reballoting was ordered by the National Election Board in a number of constituencies. However, the EPRDF was credited with winning all of the seats subject to reballoting, and the final results (released in September) accorded the EPRDF and its allies an even greater majority than originally projected, prompting severe domestic turmoil (see Current issues, below). Meles was reelected by a show of hands in the legislature in a session on October 10 that was boycotted by more than 100 opposition members. The new cabinet that was appointed the following day was substantially reshuffled, although portfolios remained primarily in the hands of EPRDF components.

Although President Girma was initially not expected to run for a second term due to his advanced age (82) and poor health, he was nominated again by the EPRDF and reelected to a second term by Parliament on October 9, 2007.

Constitution and government. An imperial constitution, adopted in 1955, was abrogated when the military assumed power in 1974. The 1987 constitution provided for a communist system of government based on "democratic centralism." In July 1991, two months after the overthrow of the Mengistu regime, a National Conference was convened that approved a transitional government charter providing for an 87-member quasi-legislative body, the Council of Representatives, drawn from the various national "freedom units." The council, intended to serve for a 24-month period, was empowered to designate a chair to serve as head of a transitional government. Subject to council approval, the chair was authorized to appoint a prime minister and other cabinet members. Meanwhile, the council was directed to oversee the drafting of a constitution that would ensure the realization of "a completely democratic system" and to prepare the country for elections to a National Assembly under the new basic law.

The document promulgated in December 1994 provided for a new House of Peoples' Representatives, which serves as "the highest organ of State authority." In addition, representatives of Ethiopia's "nations, nationalities, and peoples" constitute a senate-like House of the Federation, whose functions include that of constitutional interpretation. The president of the republic is nominated by the House of Peoples' Representatives and elected for a once-renewable six-year term by a two-thirds vote of the two houses in joint session. A prime minister, who serves as chair of the Council of Ministers and commander in chief of the armed forces, is elected by the House of Peoples' Representatives from among those sitting as members of the majority party or coalition for a term normally coincident with the legislative mandate. The judiciary includes both Federal and State Supreme Courts, appointed by their respective legislative councils; there is also a federal High Court and a Court of Constitutional Inquiry, whose principal activity is to review disputes for submission to the House of the Federation.

Ethiopia was traditionally divided into 15 provinces, exclusive of the capital. However, in late 1987 legislation was enacted to redraw the internal boundaries in favor of 24 administrative regions, plus (in an apparent effort to placate separatists) five "autonomous regions," four of which (Assab, Dire Dawa, Tigray, and Ogaden) would be coterminous with administrative regions, while Eritrea would contain three administrative regions. The present republic encompasses the following nine states: Afar; Amhara; Beneshangul-Gumuz; Gambela Peoples; Harari People; Oromia; Somalia; Southern Nations, Nationalities, and Peoples; and Tigray. The federal capital, Addis Ababa, is a separate entity, although it also serves as the capital of Oromia. In addition, there is a separate Dire Dawa Administrative Council. (Both cities enjoy the same autonomy as the states; for example, each elects its own representatives to the national legislature.) New states may be created following majority approval by a nationality group and endorsement by a two-thirds vote of the relevant state council. A somewhat unusual guarantee of self-determination includes a right of secession if requested by a two-thirds majority of the group's legislative body, endorsed by a similar state council majority, and approved by a majority vote in a referendum called by the federal government.

Foreign relations. A founding member of both the United Nations and the Organization of African Unity (OAU, subsequently the African Union—AU), Ethiopia under Emperor Haile Selassie was long a leading advocate of regional cooperation and peaceful settlement in Africa. Addis Ababa was the site of the first African summit conference in 1963 and remains the seat of the AU Secretariat and the UN Economic Commission for Africa.

As a result of the emperor's overthrow in 1974, Ethiopia shifted dramatically from a generally pro-Western posture to one of near-exclusive dependence on the Soviet bloc. Moscow guided Addis Ababa in the formation of a Soviet-style ruling party and provided weapons and other assistance to military units (including some 11,000 Cuban troops) during the Ogaden war in 1977–1978. While Russia initially maintained a low profile in regard to the Eritrean secessionist movements (the two most important of which were Marxist-inspired), it gradually increased its support of counterinsurgency efforts. In 1988 the Soviets provided the government with 250,000 tons of grain for relief purposes, thus avoiding repetition of criticism it had received for failing to provide assistance during the 1984 famine. Meanwhile, despite the continued presence of 1,400 Soviet military advisors, Moscow's interest in supporting the Mengistu government's war against the rebels appeared to be waning, and, in September 1989, Cuba announced plans to withdraw all its troops.

Because of ethnic links to Somalia and the presence of virtually equal numbers of Muslims and Christians in Eritrea, most Arab governments (with the exception of Marxist South Yemen) remained neutral or provided material support to the guerrilla movements. Most black African governments, on the other hand, tended to support Addis Ababa, despite an OAU posture of formal neutrality.

During the 1980s, relations with neighboring countries were strained by refugees fleeing Ethiopia because of famine or opposition to the Mengistu regime's resettlement policies. Tensions with Somalia, including sporadic border skirmishes in 1987, centered on the Ogaden region, with Addis Ababa accusing Mogadishu of backing the secession efforts of the Somalian-speaking population. However, in April

1988 Mengistu and Somalia President Siad Barre signed a treaty calling for mutual troop withdrawal, an exchange of POWs, and an end to Somalian funding of the rebels.

Relations with Sudan also fluctuated after the Sudanese coup of April 1985. In mid-1986 Khartoum announced that it had ordered the cessation of Eritrean rebel activity in eastern Sudan, apparently expecting that Addis Ababa would reciprocate by reducing its aid to the Sudanese People's Liberation Army (SPLA). Subsequently, Khartoum denounced continued Ethiopian support of the SPLA as "aggression." In 1988 the continued SPLA insurgency forced more than 300,000 southern Sudanese refugees across Ethiopia's border, many starving to death en route.

Although Ethiopia remained strongly linked to the Soviet Union, anti-American rhetoric became manifestly subdued during an influx of U.S. food aid, valued at more than $430 million, from 1984 through 1986. Following the Ethiopian government's March 1988 expulsion of international aid donors from rebel-held areas, Washington reportedly began channeling food supplies to northern Ethiopian drought areas through Sudanese and rebel organizations. The U.S. policy of limiting its support to humanitarian aid continued into 1989, despite the decision of international creditors to fund Addis Ababa's agricultural reform program. In April 1989 the Mengistu regime indicated a desire to resume full diplomatic relations with Washington (reduced to the chargé level in 1980) but withdrew the overture in the face of a cool U.S. response. Washington reportedly exerted considerable pressure on Colonel Mengistu to resign in May 1991, named an ambassador to the new government in June, and was one of a dozen foreign governments to send a team of observers to the National Conference in July.

The attempted assassination of Egyptian President Mubarak on June 26, 1995 (see article on Egypt), initially led to friction between Cairo and Addis Ababa because of intimations from Egyptian intelligence sources that the attack might have been aided by members of Ethiopia's security forces. Subsequently, Ethiopian-Sudanese relations again plummeted in the wake of charges by Addis Ababa that Khartoum was sheltering several people implicated in the Mubarak affair. In September 1996 an Ethiopian court sentenced three men to death in connection with the assassination attempt, which by then was being attributed to the Islamic Group (see Illegal Groups under Political Parties and Groups in article on Egypt). Ethiopian prosecutors charged that the defendants had received military training in "terrorist" camps in Sudan. Egyptian officials praised the verdict and finally commended the Ethiopian authorities for their handling of the case.

According to many observers, the Ethiopian, Eritrean, and Ugandan governments tried to coordinate efforts in 1996–1997 to control the spread of Islamic fundamentalism in the Horn of Africa, a policy that was also promoted by the United States. The campaign was primarily directed toward isolating Sudan's government, the Ethiopian government providing support to the Sudanese opposition, mainly the SPLA. It also endorsed the Sodere agreement signed in January 1997 by 26 Somalian factions, which was intended to sideline Somalia's self-declared "president" and United Somali Congress—SNA leader, Hussein Mohamed FARAH AIDID (see article on Somalia). In addition, Ethiopia reportedly convinced those factions to assist in the fight with the Islamic Union guerrillas that were operating along the border of Ethiopia and Somalia.

Ethiopia immediately expressed concern over the takeover of the Somalian capital of Mogadishu in mid-2006 by followers of the Islamic Courts Union (ICU), and Ethiopia was subsequently perceived to be playing a covert role in supporting Somalia's Transitional Federal Government (TFG) against the Islamist militants. Finally, with apparent U.S. endorsement, Ethiopian forces invaded Somalia in late December, Meles declaring that an ICU victory in Somalia would endanger Ethiopia's "sovereignty." The Ethiopian campaign, which included the use of warplanes and heavy tanks, quickly turned the tide in favor of the TFG (see article on Somalia for details). U.S. elite troops subsequently used bases in Ethiopia to launch attacks on suspected al-Qaida leaders in several nearby countries. The Bush administration subsequently remained a staunch ally of the Meles regime, although the U.S. House of Representatives (controlled by the Democratic Party) in late 2007 endorsed the Ethiopia Democracy and Accountability Act, which called for a sharp reduction in aid to Ethiopia unless the record was significantly improved in regard to human rights and democratization. (The proposed legislation did not reach a floor vote in the U.S. Senate.)

Current issues. In describing the 1998–2000 border war with Eritrea, the *New York Times* said it was "hard to think of a more pointless and wasteful international conflict." As many as 60,000 Ethiopians lost their lives in the fighting, which, while sporadic, was described at its most intense moments as the "biggest war in the world," although international attention was minimal. Despite the costs, the Ethiopian populace embraced the cause with enthusiasm and wildly celebrated the country's military success and the government's proclamation of "victory." However, the terms of the peace accord (see Current issues in article on Eritrea for details) subsequently proved highly controversial in Ethiopia. Critics both within and outside the EPRDF accused Prime Minister Meles of having "caved in" by accepting a settlement that did not appropriately reflect the Ethiopian military dominance. Among other things, Meles's opponents decried the failure of the government to gain guaranteed access in the agreement to the Eritrean ports of Assab and Massawa. (Ethiopia had become landlocked by Eritrea's independence, and its economy had been severely constrained by the lack of port access since the outbreak of hostilities.) Tension over the matter culminated in an attempt by TPLF hard-liners to remove Meles from his party post in early 2001. Although Meles survived, the rebellion had spread to other components of the EPRDF, and Meles's position remained fragile. Student protests in April contributed to the sense of instability, and the government subsequently launched an extensive crackdown on its opponents, against many of whom it leveled corruption charges. Meanwhile, President Negaso sided with the critics, sealing his political fate in view of Meles's successful counterattack. Girma Wolde Giorgis, Negaso's successor, was not widely known, even though he was a member of the House of Peoples' Representatives. Significantly, however, Girma was a member of the Oromo ethnic group (as was Negaso), his selection apparently reflecting the TPLF's intensifying concern over the growing unease in Oromia and other southern regions regarding TPLF dominance at the national level. Meanwhile, battles were reported in 2002 between Ethiopian forces and fighters from the OLF, Ogaden National Liberation Front (ONLF), and other, smaller secessionist and/or anti-EPRDF groups.

By November 2004 it was clear that final peace talks between Eritrea and Ethiopia had broken down. Among other things, Meles, under heavy domestic pressure, refused to accept the UN's proposed demarcation of the border, particularly the decision that the town of Badme would be Eritrean. Despite the presence of 4,200 UN peacekeepers, Ethiopia deployed its own troops to control Badme.

The turmoil was expected to give the newly reorganized opposition parties an opportunity to present a genuine challenge to the EPRDF in the legislative balloting of May 15, 2005. For the first time, opposition candidates were allowed to "campaign openly" and were granted some access to state-run media. The election was also keenly observed by the west, which hoped the poll would represent an important step in the maturation of Ethiopia's fledgling democratic process and solidify Meles's credentials as one of the new breed of reformist African leaders. However, the election and its aftermath had just the opposite effect. The CUD and UEDF immediately challenged the preliminary results as fraudulent, claiming that they should have been credited with a majority of the seats and that the vote had been rigged. Although at least token reballoting was ordered in some constituencies, Meles quickly signaled a hard-line attitude toward protesters by banning all demonstrations in Addis Ababa and placing the capital police under his direct control. Student demonstrators clashed with police in several cities in June, leaving some 40 people dead, and the antigovernment outcry intensified in September when the government's official final results gave the EPRDF and its allies more than 68 percent of the seats. For their part, EU observers concluded that the election had failed to meet international standards.

Unrest culminated in another deadly conflict between protesters and government forces in early November 2005 during an AU summit in Addis Ababa. The government blamed "stone-throwers" for initiating the battle, while the opposition blamed unnecessarily harsh reactions by security forces to a peaceful demonstration. Nearly 50 people died in the clashes, to which the government responded by detaining thousands of protesters and arresting nearly all of the CUD leadership, prominent members of other opposition parties, and a number of journalists and human rights activists. Those arrested were charged with treason, promoting violence, and attempting to overthrow the government.

Human rights groups expressed outrage over the 2005 crackdown, and the World Bank, EU, and UK suspended aid to Ethiopia in an effort to pressure Meles to adopt a more conciliatory stance. However, the trials of the detainees opened in May 2006, with Meles dismissing accusations about his "dictatorial rule." By that time, the prime minister was also facing growing international pressure regarding Ethiopia's continued refusal to accept the final decisions of the UN commission established to demarcate the border with Eritrea.

Reports surfaced in October 2006 that the Ethiopian commission created to investigate the events of 2005 initially intended to characterize the attacks on civilians as a "massacre." However, after several members of the commission had fled the country, the final report, accepted by the legislature in March 2007, concluded that security forces had taken "necessary measures" to quell the disturbances. In contrast, Amnesty International accused security forces of carrying out a systematic campaign of intimidation, detention, and even torture of its opponents.

In early April 2007 the federal High Court dismissed the controversial charges of attempted genocide and treason against the 2005 defendants and dropped all charges against some of the detainees. However, in June the court found more than 40 defendants guilty of various charges ranging from armed rebellion to "outrage against the constitution" and imposed harsh sentences (including life in prison in some cases). Most of the defendants subsequently signed a carefully crafted "letter of apology" in which they accepted responsibility for "mistakes" that had contributed to the unrest. Shortly thereafter, Prime Minister Meles announced that President Girma had pardoned the defendants and restored their civil rights in the name of "reconciliation." The United States reportedly helped mediate the resolution of the conflict, which had tarnished Meles's image despite his "pro-western" role in Somalia and the "war on terror" in general (see Foreign relations, above). The international community also expressed concern that the proxy war in Somalia might combine with the unresolved border dispute to reignite fighting between Ethiopia and Eritrea (see article on Eritrea for additional information).

Ethiopian forces remained in Somalia (often under attack by antigovernment Islamists) as efforts to achieve a negotiated settlement there produced little progress by mid-2008 (see article on Somalia for details). Among other things, President Meles called for the deployment of a large international peacekeeping force in Somalia that would permit the withdrawal of Ethiopian troops. Meanwhile, the Ethiopian government continued its military buildup in case of a renewed border war with Eritrea, which Ethiopia accused of arming and training Ethiopian rebels, most notably the ONLF, against whom the government had been waging an intense campaign since the spring of 2007 (see ONLF under Political Parties and Groups, below). For its part, the ONLF accused the government of having perpetrated a "reign of terror" against civilians in the Ogaden region. Human rights activists echoed at least some of the charges and warned of a potentially massive humanitarian crisis as the result of the government crackdown. The Meles administration also faced heavy domestic criticism for the alleged intimidation and harassment of opposition candidates in the April 2008 local elections, which were dominated by the EPRDF.

Tensions remained high with Eritrea throughout the rest of 2008 and first half of 2009 as the mandate of UN peacekeepers was terminated in the face of Eritrean "obstruction." Meanwhile, Ethiopian troops withdrew from Somalia in early 2009, prompting a surge by Islamic militants against Somalia's transitional government (see article on Somalia for details).

Having accused the ONLF and other opposition groups of bomb attacks in 2008, the government reported in May 2009 that it had uncovered a coup plot connected to exiled opposition leaders and a number of army officers. However, critics charged that no coup had been planned and that the government was manufacturing threats as part of its efforts to secure support in advance of the 2010 legislative elections. Meles's opponents also described recent legislation constraining the activities of nongovernmental organizations as an attempt to hide ongoing human rights violations.

POLITICAL PARTIES AND GROUPS

Political parties were not permitted under the monarchy, while legal party activity during the period of rule by the Provisional Military Administrative Council did not emerge until the formation of the regime-supportive Workers' Party of Ethiopia (WPE) in 1984. The 1987 constitution reaffirmed the WPE's position as the country's only authorized party, describing it as the "leading force of the state and society" and granting it wide authority, including the right to approve all candidates for the National Assembly. As the Mengistu regime faced accelerating rebel activity and declining Soviet support, the WPE in March 1990 abandoned its Marxist-Leninist ideology, changed its name to the Ethiopian Democratic Unity Party (EDUP), and opened its ranks to former members of opposition groups in an unsuccessful effort to broaden its base of public support. Following the overthrow of the Mengistu government in May 1991, leaders of the interim government announced that the EDUP had been dissolved. More than 70 parties were registered as of 2007, although many of them were operating only at the regional level.

A new opposition coalition—the Forum (*Medrek*) for Democratic Dialogue in Ethiopia—was launched in early 2009 with the goal of presenting joint candidates in the 2010 legislative balloting. Participants included the EDUM, UEDF, UDJ, OFDM, and the **Arena Tigray for Democracy and Sovereignty Party**. Among the *Medrek* leaders were former Ethiopian president Negaso Gidada and former defense minister Siye ABRACHA.

Government Parties:

Ethiopian People's Revolutionary Democratic Front (EPRDF). The EPRDF was launched in May 1988 by the TPLF in an effort to expand its influence beyond Tigray Province, over which it had recently achieved military dominance. Although the TPLF had long subscribed to Marxist-Leninist ideology, an EPRDF congress in early 1991 called for development of a "small-scale" economy in which farmers would lease land from the government and control the sale of their products. While the new platform called for tight government control of foreign trade, it also endorsed an expanded role for private investment in the economy. In another significant policy shift, the congress, while displaying a clear preference for a united Ethiopia, accepted Eritrea's right to self-determination.

Joined in a loose military alliance with the Eritrean People's Liberation Front (see article on Eritrea) and the OLF (below), the EPRDF led the march on Addis Ababa that ousted the Mengistu regime in May 1991. Assuming power in the name of the EPRDF, Meles Zenawi was confirmed as head of state by the National Conference pending the outcome, under a new constitution, of multiparty elections originally scheduled for 1993 but not held until May 1995. The EPRDF won over 90 percent of the seats in that balloting, and Meles was elected prime minister by the House of Peoples' Representatives in August, the office of president (which he had previously held) having been reduced to figurehead status. The EPRDF dominated the 2000 legislative balloting and unanimously reelected Meles as EPRDF chair at a congress on September 1, 2001, the prime minister having survived serious dissension within the TPLF and other EPRDF component groups (see below). The congress also selected a new 140-member council, a 38-member Executive Committee, and an 8-member "Control Commission." Meles was reelected as chair at the September 2006 EPRDF congress, and, in light of the surprising success of the opposition in the 2005 elections, the EPRDF subsequently intensified its organizational efforts for the 2008 municipal balloting, which it dominated.

Meles was reelected as the EPRDF chair at the September 2008 congress. Prior to a September 2009 party meeting he surprisingly announced that he and other long-standing leaders might step down to make room for a "new generation." However, it was subsequently reported that Meles had been endorsed at the meeting for at least one more term as prime minister.

Leaders: MELES Zenawi (Prime Minister of the Republic and Chair of the EPRDF), GIRMA Wolde Giorgis (President of the Republic), ADDISU Legesse (Deputy Prime Minister and Deputy Chair of the EPRDF), SHIFERAW Jarso (Parliamentary Leader).

Tigray People's Liberation Front (TPLF). Formed in 1975 by former students who had been strongly influenced by Marxism-Leninism, the TPLF initially pursued independence or at least substantial autonomy for Tigray Province. However, the front's subsequent goal became the overthrow of the Mengistu regime and establishment of a new central government involving all ethnic groups. Established in 1985, a pro-Albanian Marxist-Leninist League of Tigray (MLLT) gained ideological ascendancy within the TPLF, and MLLT leader Meles Zenawi was elected TPLF chair at a 1989 congress. By that time the TPLF had become one of the country's most active antigovernment groups, its fighters having gained control of Tigray and having pushed south toward Addis Ababa. The TPLF subsequently began to shed its ideological rigidity, reflecting both the growing worldwide disillusionment with communism and a need to broaden the front's philosophical base in preparation for a possible government takeover. Consequently, by the time TPLF soldiers captured Addis Ababa in the name of the EPRDF in May 1991, the front's leaders were describing themselves as supporters of Western-style multiparty democracy and limited private enterprise. However, disagreement was subsequently reported within the TPLF regarding the proposed privatization of state-run enterprises.

Following the tentative conclusion of the border war with Eritrea in 2000, hard-liners in the TPLF reportedly came close to ousting Meles in March 2001. Among other things, the dissidents, who included TEWOLDE Wolde-Mariam, then vice chair of the TPLF, strongly objected to the perceived lack of results in the peace accord as well as the imposition of economic austerity measures requested by the IMF and World Bank. Meles and his "reformist" supporters subsequently launched a purge of many of the critics.

Leaders: MELES Zenawi (Prime Minister of the Republic and Chair of the TPLF), Seyoum MESFIN (Deputy Chair).

Amhara National Democratic Movement (ANDM). The ANDM was initially established in 1980 as the Ethiopian People's Democratic Movement (EPDM) by former members of the EPRP (below) under the guidance of the TPLF. In 1986 a number of pitched battles were reported in Wollo Province between EPDM forces and government troops. Subsequent ideological controversy generated the creation of an Ethiopian Marxist-Leninist Force (EMLF) to serve the same function in the EPDM as the MLLT was serving in the TPLF. The EPDM joined the TPLF in the 1988 formation of the EPRDF and adopted the ANDM rubric at its third congress in January 1994.

In October 1996 it was reported that former prime minister Tamirat Layne had been dismissed as ANDM secretary general during an emergency meeting of the Central Committee for "acting contrary to the principles for which the ANDM has stood during the last 16 years." Tamirat was also subsequently fired from his posts of deputy prime minister and minister of national defense as part of what was widely viewed as an anticorruption campaign. He was sentenced in 1999 to 18 years in prison on corruption charges.

Divisions were reported within the ANDM in 2005–2006, as some members objected to what they perceived as growing anti-Amhara rhetoric on the part of members of the TPLF and OPDO. Factionalization reportedly continued into mid-2009.

Leaders: ADDISU Legesse (Chair and Deputy Prime Minister of the Republic), TEFERA Walwa (Deputy Chair), BEREKET Simeon, HILAWE Yosef, Ayalew GOBEZE, Yoseph RETA.

Oromo Peoples' Democratic Organization (OPDO). The OPDO was formed in April 1990 under the direction of the TPLF, its membership reportedly comprising Oromo prisoners of war captured by the TPLF in sporadic clashes with the OLF (below). The OLF immediately challenged the creation of the OPDO as an "unfriendly and hostile gesture," and the OPDO's existence remained a source of friction between the TPLF and the OLF. During 1992 the OPDO was reported to have been weakened by the desertion of a number of its followers to the OLF.

The OPDO, as expected, dominated the May 2000 elections in the state of Oromia, securing 173 of 178 seats in the House of Peoples' Representatives and 535 of 537 seats on the State Council. As with the TPLF and SEPDF, the OPDO was subsequently riven by dissension generated by hard-liners unhappy with Prime Minister Meles, particularly in regard to the conclusion of the border war with Eritrea. Among the consequences of the fractionalization was the dismissal of Negaso Gidada, then president of the republic, from the OPDO central committee and his eventual departure from the party. The OPDO declined to 110 seats in the 2005 balloting for the House of Peoples' Representatives.

Leaders: Abdullah GEMEDA (President), Girma BIRU, Junedi SADO (President of the State of Oromia).

Southern Ethiopia Peoples' Democratic Front (SEPDF). The SEPDF comprises many small, mostly ethnically based parties. It secured 112 of 123 seats from the state of Southern Nations, Nationalities, and Peoples in the 2000 balloting for the House of Peoples' Representatives. (For a list of component parties that gained representation, see Legislature in the article on Ethiopia in the 2005–2006 *Handbook*.) A number of members of the SEPDF's Central Committee were dismissed in 2002 in the wake of friction attributed to ethnic disputes, as well as disagreement, reflective of similar problems in the OPDO and TPLF over the policies of Prime Minister Meles. At the 2008 EPRDF congress, SEPDF leaders reportedly sought greater funding and additional government posts for SEPDF members.

Leaders: HAILEMARIAM Desalegn (Chair), SHIFERAW Shigute, KASSU Illala.

Somali Peoples' Democratic Party (SPDP). The SPDP was launched in Jijiga in Ethiopia's state of Somalia in June 1998 by the Ethiopian Somali Democratic League (ESDL) and a progovernment faction of the ONLF (below) that had split from its parent grouping regarding the question of independence. (The ESDL, which had been formed in February 1994 by a number of progovernment eastern region groups [see the 2007 *Handbook* for details], and the ONLF faction had formed a victorious coalition in the 1995 elections in the region.)

ESDL leader Abdulmejid HUSSEIN, who had been the target in July 1996 of an assassination attempt that the government blamed on separatist rebels, was named leader of the SPDP at its formation. He was succeeded in 2000 by Mohammad Drir, who had already taken over Hussein's cabinet post.

A pro-EPRDF formation, the SPDP won 19 of the 23 seats from the state of Somalia in the House of Peoples' Representatives and 148 of the 168 Somali State Council seats in 2000. Severe fractionalization was reported within the party in 2002, although the SPDP won all 23 house seats from the state of Somalia in the 2005 poll.

Leaders: Mohammad DRIR (Chair), Abdulrashid Dulene RAFLE (Vice Chair), Sultan Ibrahim (Secretary General).

Other Legislative Parties:

Coalition for Unity and Democracy (CUD). Launched in 2004 as an electoral coalition in advance of the 2005 legislative balloting by the following four groups, the CUD called for constitutional changes to reduce the authority of the executive branch and to promote democratization and human rights. Other campaign promises included intensified land privatization and a switch to proportional legislative balloting. Supported primarily by urban Amharas, the CUD also called for a more highly centralized government in which the ethnically based states would be replaced by a return to the former provincial structure. Under the CUD proposals, the constitution would also no longer include provisions for legal regional secession.

The CUD was the leading opposition force in the May 2005 national and state elections, dominating the balloting in Addis Ababa and other cities. The government ultimately credited the CUD with winning 109 seats in the House of Peoples' Representatives, although the coalition strongly challenged the accuracy of the final results and a number of its successful candidates refused to take their seats in the house. CUD members also declined to accept their council seats in Addis Ababa, and a "caretaker" administration was subsequently appointed for the capital by the federal government.

The question of whether or not to boycott the legislature in 2005 apparently caused significant dissension within the coalition, and undercut efforts by CUD Chair Hailu Shawel to merge the CUD components into a single party. In September the AEUP, RE:MDSJ, and EDL reportedly announced support for the proposed merger and creation of a Coalition for Unity and Democracy Party (CUDP). However, the UEDP-Medhin resisted that initiative, prompting the national election board to refuse recognition of the CUDP on the grounds that the CUDP required full participation of all of its electoral components.

Many of the CUD leaders (including Hailu and CUD legislators who had refused to take their seats in the House of Peoples' Representatives) were arrested in the government crackdown of November 2005, which reportedly scuttled the single-party proposal for good. Following their conviction on various charges in April 2007, Hailu and the other CUD detainees were pardoned in July, although the 14 CUD seats won in Addis Ababa in the 2005 election to the House of Peoples' Representatives were declared vacant by the government. Hailu reportedly dismissed the letter of apology he and others had signed as having been coerced by the government, but he subsequently reportedly denied making such comments. In any event, the CUD was later described as riven with internal disputes, particularly after the government recognized a faction under the name of **CUD/*Kinjit*** (under the leadership of Ayele Chamismo) as the "official" party. Chamismo, described by critics as having been coopted by the government, was elected to the local council in Addis Ababa in April 2008, although the EPRDF was credited with winning the remaining 137 of the council's 138 seats. In addition, the EPRDF won the 14 former CUD seats from Addis Ababa in concurrent by-elections to the House of Peoples' Representatives.

Meanwhile, Hailu continued to urge the United States to withhold aid from the Meles regime, although the Bush administration in Washington displayed a strong preference to dealing with other, less "radical" opposition groups. The CUD consequently appeared unlikely to serve as a significant force in subsequent elections, some former leaders having opted to help form new parties recently.

Leader: Ayele CHAMISMO (leader of the CUD/ *Kinjit*).

All Ethiopian Unity Party (AEUP). This party is an outgrowth of factionalization within the All-Amhara People's Organization (AAPO), which initially supported the EPRDF but went into opposition over the issues of ethnic regionalization. The AAPO's president, Dr. ASRAT Woldeyes, was one of several AAPO leaders sentenced to prison in June 1994 for inciting armed opposition to the government. Asrat remained incarcerated until late 1998. Upon his release, the ailing former physician for Emperor Selassie left the country for medical treatment.

After winning only one seat in the 2000 balloting for the House of Peoples' Representatives, the AAPO suffered internal division. Hailu Shawel, the vice president of AAPO, lost a bid for the AAPO presidency, and he formed his own grouping under the AEUP rubric in consonance with its stated goal of downplaying its Amharic orientation in favor of outreach to "all Ethiopians." By that time a number of former AAPO members reportedly had joined the new EDP (see UEDP-Medhin, below). Hailu subsequently became prominent in the formation of the CUD in 2005, although CUD factionalization prompted him to return to the AEUP as his primary political affiliation following his release from prison in 2007.

Leaders: HAILU Shawel (President), Makonnen BISHAW (Secretary General).

United Ethiopian Democratic Party–Medhin (UEDP-Medhin). The formation of the UEDP was announced in 2003 by several groups, including the Ethiopian Democratic Party (EDP) and the Ethiopian Democratic Action Group. The EDP, a moderate grouping espousing "unity and peace," was launched in December 1999 and secured 2 seats from Addis Ababa in 2000 in the House of Peoples' Representatives. The EDP was subsequently reported to be opposed to the conditions of the peace accord accepted by the Meles government with Eritrea. Founding members of the EDP included Lidetu Ayelaw, a former head of the AAPO youth wing. The relationship of the UEDP with another group with a similar name—the Ethiopian Democratic Union Party (EDUP)—was unclear, although it was reported that the UEDP–Medhin rubric had been adopted prior to the 2005 national balloting as a result of several formal mergers of former single parties.

Lidetu (who had been serving as the group's acting leader) was reportedly elected chair of the UEDP–Medhin in late 2005 after he broke with CUD components on the issue of participation in the legislature. (Lidetu supported the decision by most of the successful UEDP–Medhin candidates to take their seats.) Among other things, Lidetu accused CUD leader Hailu of trying to form a single party of the CUD components that would be dominated by the AEUP. In early 2009 a party congress reportedly readopted the EDP rubric in advance of the 2010 elections, pledging to campaign as a center-right party focused on "individual rights" rather than the rights of ethnic groups.

Leaders: LIDETU Ayelaw (President), Sofia YILMA (Vice President), Mushe SEMU (Secretary General).

Rainbow Ethiopia: Movement for Democracy and Social Justice (RE:MDSJ). Launched by prominent human rights activists in November 2004, the RE:MDSJ called upon the country's myriad opposition parties to coalesce in advance of the May 2005 legislative elections. The party's leader, BERHANU Nega, reportedly declined a government post following the election, and he was among the prominent opposition politicians who were arrested in November 2005. He was pardoned along with other CUD officials following their conviction in 2007 and moved to the United States, where he helped to launch the Movement for Justice, Freedom, and Democracy and the opposition grouping called ***Ginbot*** **7** (May 15, a reference to the May 15, 2005, balloting). In April 2009 the Ethiopian government arrested some 45 people for involvement in what the government described as a plot to assassinate Ethiopian officials. Berhanu, who was charged in absentia, described the allegations as "scurrilous" and said *Ginbot* 7, although dedicated to the ouster of the Meles regime, was committed to the rule of law.

Ethiopian Democratic League (EDL). The EDL was launched in 2002 by opponents of the Meles administration. The new party described itself as open to all Ethiopians, regardless of ethnicity or regionality. Founding members reportedly included Berhanu Nega (a prominent economist) and Mesfin Wolde Mariam (a human rights activist). Both men were arrested in 2002 on charges of having incited disturbances at the University of Addis Ababa the previous year, but they were subsequently released, in part due to heavy international pressure. They were also arrested in the November 2005 government crackdown, Berhanu and Mariam then being referenced as the leaders of the newly formed RE:MDSJ.

Leaders: Chekol GETAHUN, MULENEH Eyuel.

United Ethiopian Democratic Forces (UEDF). Launched in mid-2003 by the following groups and other parties (both within Ethiopia and in the diaspora) opposed to the EPRDF government, the UEDF (comprising mostly southern parties and dominated by Oromos) called for peaceful regime change, land reform, privatization of state-run enterprises, greater press freedom, and greater free-market influence in the economy. With the primary goal of defeating the EPRDF, the UEDF cooperated informally with the CUD in the May 2005 elections, the two groups pledging to forge a coalition government if successful in the balloting. However, opposition to the EPRDF regime appeared to be the only genuine shared position between the UEDF and the CUD, as UEDF officials made it clear they strongly opposed the CUD's plan to redraw regional boundaries and establish a more highly centralized government. Many UEDF supporters also criticized the CUD's proposed land privatization proposal as a pretext for "Amhara land grabs" in the south.

The UEDF was credited with winning 52 seats in the House of Peoples' Representatives in 2005, all but one of the successful candidates reportedly taking their seats despite a CUD call for a boycott of the legislature. UEDF President Beyene Petros and (then) Vice President Merera Gudina supported the decision to participate in the legislature and called for a national dialogue with the EPRDF and other parties toward installation of a national unity government. As a result, hard-line UEDF dissidents meeting in October announced that Beyene and Merera had been relieved of their UEDF leadership posts in favor of the EPRP's Fasika BELETE and Ayalsew DERSIE and that "underground" antigovernment was being considered. However, Beyene rejected the validity of the dissident action and continued to serve as UEDF spokesman, initialing a memorandum of understanding with the EPRDF and the OFDM providing for ongoing negotiations to resolve the nation's political problems in a peaceful manner and with respect for constitutional structures. However, the UEDF accused the government of illegally blocking the candidacies of many UEDF members in the April 2008 local elections. Merera was elected chair and Beyene vice chair at the April 2009 UEDF congress.

Leaders: MERERA Gudina (Chair), BEYENE Petros (Vice Chair).

Council of Alternative Forces for Peace and Democracy in Ethiopia (CAFPDE). An umbrella organization for a number of opposition groupings, the CAFPDE was formed under the leadership of Beyene Petros, also the leader of the SEPDC, the core component of the CAFPDE. In 1994 Beyene described the constitutional revision then underway as "undemocratic" and inappropriately dominated by the TPLF. The CAFPDE declined to participate fully in the 1995 elections on the grounds that insufficient arrangements had been made for foreign observation of the polls.

The CAFPDE participated with other leading groups in forming the Coalition of Ethiopian Opposition Political Organizations (CEOPO) in Paris in September 1998. However, Beyene subsequently withdrew the CAFPDE from the CEOPO and declared the CAFPDE's intention to contest the 2000 legislative elections on its own. As a result, hard-liners within the CAFPDE announced that Beyene had been replaced as chair by KIFLE Tigneh Abate. However, the National Electoral Board ordered Beyene reinstated in January 2000.

The CAFPDE was credited with winning four seats in the House of Peoples' Representatives in the 2000 balloting, while the SEPDC secured two and the **Hadiya National Democratic Organization** (HNDO), a small grouping also led by Beyene, won three. Following the balloting, Beyene strongly criticized the EPRDF for the perceived "intimidation" of members of the CAFPDE and other opposition parties.

In 2006 Beyene announced that the CAFPDE had been renamed the **Ethiopian Social Democratic Party** (ESDP) in an effort to merge the CAFPDE components into a single party. By that time, with the ONC having been factionalized (see below), Beyene and others also described the ESDP as the dominant component of the UEDF.

Leader: BEYENE Petros (Chair).

Southern Ethiopia Peoples' Democratic Coalition (SEPDC). The SEPDC was launched in 1992 by a number of small parties representing some 34 different tribal groups and holding 16 seats in the 87-member Council of Representatives. In March 1993 the SEPDC organizations participated in a "Peace for Ethiopia" conference in Paris that included the OLF and COEDF. In a statement issued at the conclusion of the conference, participants strongly condemned the regime in Addis Ababa for its alleged repressive tendencies, while calling on it to permit nonviolent opposition activity. The Council of Representatives reacted by calling on SEPDC members to repudiate the conference resolutions.

Beyene Petros, the leader of the SEPDC and HNDO, left his post as a vice minister in the transitional government as a result of the events of 1993. He subsequently became chair of the CAFPDE. After having agreed to participate in the 2000 legislative elections, the CAFPDE and the SEPDC boycotted local elections in December 2001 in the state of Southern Nations, Nationalities, and Peoples.

Oromo National Congress (ONC). Formed in 1998 by political science professor Merera Gudina, the ONC pledged to support the rights of the Oromo people, including preservation of the right to self-determination. Although the ONC won only 1 seat in the 2000 elections in the House of Peoples' Representatives, it reportedly secured some 39 of the UEDF's 52 seats in the 2005 poll, dominating balloting in several southern areas. Most of the successful ONC candidates, including Merera, subsequently took their legislative seats, although debate was reported within the ONC on the question. The party was subsequently severely split as dissidents announced in September that they had expelled Merera from the ONC and had withdrawn the ONC from the UEDF. However, Merera dismissed those measures as invalid actions on the part of only a few disgruntled ONC members. The national election board subsequently indicated that it believed the dissident faction had the strongest legal claim to the ONC rubric, and Merera in October announced the formation of the **Oromo People's Congress** (OPC), which was authorized by the government to compete only in elections in Oromia Regional State.

Leader: DEYASA Leta.

Oromo Federalist Democratic Movement (OFDM). After winning 11 seats in the May 2005 balloting for the House of Peoples' Representatives, the recently organized OFDM, which had resisted preelection overtures from the CUD and UEDF, called for a "national dialogue" between the opposition parties and the EPRDF. Among other things, the OFDM urged that no changes be made in the powers or boundaries of the nation's states. OFDM leaders strongly criticized the government's handling of the April 2008 local elections, claiming that potential OFDM candidates had been frightened away from participation due to intimidation by EPRDF supporters.

Leader: Balcha DEMESKA.

Beneshangul-Gumuz Peoples' Democratic Party (BGPDP). Described as a pro-EPRDF party, the BGPDP secured 6 of the 9 seats from the state of Beneshangul-Gumuz in the 2000 balloting for the House of Representatives and 71 of 80 State Council seats.

Leader: Mulualem BESSE.

Afar National Democratic Party (ANDP). The ANDP was formed in August 1999 by the merger of five groups in the state of Afar: the Afar Peoples' Democratic Organization (APDO), the Afar Revolutionary Democratic Union Front (ARDUF), the Afar National Democratic Movement (ANDM), the Afar National Liberation Front (ANLF), and the Afar Liberation Front Party (ALFP).

The APDO, established originally as the Afar Democratic Union, had adopted the APDO rubric in 1992. Having benefited from dissension within the ALF (see below), the APDO was subsequently described as exercising dominant political authority, in alignment with the EPRDF, in the Afar region under the leadership of Ismail ALISERIO.

The ARDUF was formed in 1991 to "liberate Afar territories" of the former autonomous region of Assab from Eritrean domination. The ARDUF subsequently became an anti-EPRDF secessionist movement under the leadership of former WPE first secretary and Assab governor Mohamoda Ahmed GAAS. Sporadic fighting was reported in 1996 between the ARDUF's armed wing, *Ugugumo* (Revolution), and TPLF forces. During 1997, however, the government initiated a policy of dialogue with the ARDUF to reach a reconciliation over the future of the Afar National Regional State. The discussions brought about a division within the ranks of the ARDUF between pro- and anti-agreement factions. The former reportedly formally discontinued its armed struggle in 2002. Meanwhile, hard-liners led by Gaas apparently reached an agreement with the ONLF to coordinate the opposition to the current regime. (The rump ARDUF was described in 2007 as an active rebel group in the northeast of the country.)

The ANDM, a pro-EPRDF formation, was launched in February 1995 by Ahmed Mohamed AHAW, a son of the influential Sultan of Biru in the northwestern Danakil region.

The ANDP secured all of the eight seats from the state of Afar in the 2000 balloting for the House of Peoples' Representatives and all but three of the Afar State Council seats, the grouping being widely perceived as a pro-EPRDF, pro-Meles party.

Gambela Peoples' Democratic Movement (GPDM). The GPDM was formed in 2003 following the dissolution of the Gambela Peoples' Democratic Front (GPDF), which had secured all three of the seats from the state of Gambela in the House of Peoples' Representatives in the 2000 balloting and most of the Gambela State Council seats. Although the GDPF had presented its candidates in 2000 without declaring a cooperative stance with any other parties, it was later described as supportive of the pro-Meles faction of the TPLF and EPRDF.

The GPDF resulted from a merger of the Gambela People's Liberation Party (GPLP)—a party representing the Anyuak ethnic group that, allied with the EPRDF, had won the 1995 elections in Gambela—and the Gambela People's Democratic Unity Party (GPDUP), a Nuer party. However, the GPDF was reportedly later dissolved following the collapse of power-sharing arrangements and the outbreak of sporadic deadly fighting between the Anyuak and the Nuer.

The GPDM secured 3 seats in the 2005 voting for the House of Peoples' Representatives and nearly all of the Gambela State Council seats. It subsequently concluded a cooperation agreement with the EPRDF.

Leader: Ket TUACH.

Other parties securing seats in the 2005 balloting for the House of Peoples' Representatives included: the **Argoba National Democratic Organization** (ANDO); the **Harari National League** (HNL), a pro-EPRDF formation that also won a majority in the Harari State Council in 2005; and the **Shecko Mejenger People's Democratic Unity Organization**. (In 2006 it was reported that ANDO had merged with the **Argoba People's Democratic Movement** [APDM].)

Other Parties and Groups:

Ogaden National Liberation Front (ONLF). The secessionist, ethnically Somali ONLF was organized in January 1986, reportedly by militant members of the Western Somalia Liberation Front (WSLF) opposed to Ethiopian-Somalian talks on the future of the Ogaden that did not involve participation by regional representatives. (For additional information on the WSLF, now disbanded, see the 2007 *Handbook.*) The ONLF reportedly began fighting for independence of the Ogaden/ Somali region in the early 1990s, many supporters calling for creation of a "Greater Somalia" that would include Somalia and the Somali-populated areas of Ethiopia, Djibouti, and Kenya. The Ethiopian government responded to that campaign with a crackdown that included the arrest of a number of ONLF leaders and, reportedly, the killing of others. In September 1996 the Ethiopian army conducted cross-border operations inside Somaliland against ONLF guerrillas.

In June 1998 an ONLF faction that had reportedly been cooperating with the progovernment ESDL since 1995 formed a separate grouping—the SPDP (see above). For their part, ONLF secessionists continued to clash with government troops.

In April 2006 the ONLF claimed responsibility for several attacks on government troops. Approximately 1,000 ONLF fighters were reportedly training in Eritrea at that point. In April 2007 the ONLF claimed responsibility for an attack on a Chinese-owned oil site in the state of Somalia, having previously warned foreign companies to leave the region. The Ethiopian government subsequently launched heavy countermeasures that, among other things, attracted international criticism for the effects on civilians, many of them impoverished nomads. Sporadic but severe fighting between the ONLF and government forces continued for the next year, the Meles regime accusing Eritrea of supporting the ONLF as a way of destabilizing Ethiopia. In May 2008 the ONLF announced it had merged with the Western Somali Democratic Party (WSDP) and called upon all "ethnic Somalis" to join the antiregime "struggle." In September the ONLF called upon the international community to address the "humanitarian crisis" arising from the government offensive. Significant fighting between government troops and ONLF adherents continued throughout 2009.

Leaders: Mohamed Omar OSMAN, Abdirahman MAHDI, Mohamed Ismaïl Omar, Shimber Abdel KADIR, Mohamed HUSSEIN.

Oromo Liberation Front (OLF). Initially centered in the eastern and mid-country regions, the OLF in the late 1980s expanded its activities to the west and south. Although it represented the largest ethnic group in Ethiopia, the OLF was the least powerful militarily of the rebel units that toppled the Mengistu government. Previously committed to the creation of a new country of "Oromia" in what is currently southern Ethiopia, OLF leaders said in June 1991 that they would consider remaining part of a Ethiopian federation that provided for substantial regional autonomy. In mid-July the OLF concluded a "unity" pact with four other Oromo groups: the **Islamic Front for the Liberation of Oromia** (IFLO), the **Oromo Aba Liberation Front** (OALF), the **United Oromo People's Liberation Front** (UOPLF), and the OPDO (above). Earlier the OLF had occasionally allied itself with the EPLF (see under Eritrea entry) in skirmishes with the EPRDF, and it withdrew from the EPRDF-led coalition in June 1992 because of alleged electoral fraud, harassment of its members, and perceived inadequate tribal representation in the government. In the spring of 1994 the OLF and IFLO were reported to have agreed to offer coordinated opposition to the forthcoming draft constitution. In early 1995 a number of skirmishes took place between government troops and OLF militants, and it was subsequently reported that several hundred OLF supporters had been imprisoned as a result of the front's low-level guerrilla campaign.

In mid-1996 the OLF announced that it had signed a cooperation pact with the hard-line faction of the ONLF. The two groups pledged, according to the *Indian Ocean Newsletter*, to coordinate their diplomatic, political, and military activity to secure self-determination referendums for their respective regions. Minor skirmishes between security forces and OLF militants continued throughout 1997 as the front reportedly remained divided between pro- and antidialogue factions. The party engaged in reportedly fruitless discussions with the government in 1997, and at an extraordinary OLF congress in early 1998 the antidialogue faction appeared to have won control of the group's policy-making Executive Committee. The OLF was subsequently described as "reinvigorated," partly as the result of aid from Eritrea. OLF antigovernment military activity in pursuit of independence was reported in mid-2002, although severe factionalization was reported between OLF militants, led by Daoud Ibsa, and moderates inclined to negotiate with the government. The OLF remained "at war with the regime" in early 2005, although Gelasa Dilbo, the OLF chair who had been under house arrest, had been permitted to leave for Kenya in late 2004.

Prime Minister Meles reportedly offered in late 2005 to negotiate with the OLF toward a possible peace settlement, but the OLF continued to support "mobilization" against the EPRDF regime. Meanwhile, the front reportedly remained split between supporters of Gelasa and supporters of Ibsa. The government accused the OLF of having taken part in recent attacks on security forces in the state of Somalia in 2007 and also alleged OLF cooperation with the ONLF in subsequent antigovernment activity. OLF members were reportedly among those arrested in November 2008 for alleged involvement in bomb attacks in Addis Ababa.

Leaders: GELASA Dilbo (Former Chair, in exile), Daoud IBSA, (Chair), Hassan HUSSEIN (Spokesperson), Shigat GELETA (resident in Berlin, Germany), Beyan AROBA.

Arena Tigray for Democracy and Sovereignty Party. Led by Meles critic Gebru Asrat, the former president of Tigray Regional State, this grouping was launched in October 2007 by TPLF dissidents to challenge the TPLF in local balloting in Tigray. In 2008 it was reported that former Ethiopian president Negaso Gidada had agreed to join Arena in establishing a new opposition coalition that was slated to also include the OFDM, UEDF, **Somali Democratic Forces Coalition,** and other groups.

Leader: GEBRU Asrat.

Afar Liberation Front (ALF). Long considered the most important of the Afar groups, the ALF was organized in 1975. Although its leadership was then based in Jeddah, Saudi Arabia, the ALF also operated in Ethiopia's Hararge and Wollo Provinces, where it was supported by followers of Ahmed ALI Mirah, the sultan of Awsa. In July 1991 the sultan returned from 17 years in exile and nominally endorsed Eritrea's right to self-determination, although his nomadic subjects occupied a lengthy portion of the Red Sea coast and had long had as their principal objective an Afar state within an Ethiopian federation. In April 1995 the sultan suspended his son, Hanfareh ALI Mirah, as ALF chair in response to preelectoral dissension within the Front; however, the ALF Executive Committee refused to endorse the action. The leadership of the ALF subsequently remained unclear as some reports suggested that the sultan and at least one of his sons had expressed support for the new Afar party (see ANDP, above), while other sons (including Umar ALI Mirah, Habib ALI Mirah, and Ousman ALI Mirah) continued to oppose the EPRDF. Renewed fighting between ALF hard-liners and Ethiopian forces was reported in mid-2002.

In 2006 it was reported that antigovernment "remnants" from the ALF, ARDUF (including *Uguguma* militants), and the ANLF had launched (with Eritrean support) the **Afar National Democratic Front** (ANDF) under the leadership of Mohamed IBRAHIM.

Oromo People's Liberation Front (OPLF). Characterizing the EPRDF as an "occupying enemy," the OPLF was launched in London in 1992 with the issuance of a program calling for the formation of an independent state of Oromia. The position was reiterated in December 1994 at a meeting in Kenya, with representatives of the UOPLF (under OLF, above) and the **Oromo People's Liberation Organization** (OPLO). However, during a congress in Harar in May 1995 a new central committee was appointed that excluded exiled members of its predecessor and adopted a conciliatory attitude toward the EPRDF in view of a "climate of peace and development" that had allegedly been attained in eastern Ethiopia. Cooperation with the OLF and other Oromo groups was launched in 2000.

Ethiopian Democratic Union Party (EDUP). The conservative Ethiopian Democratic Union (EDU) fought government troops in the northwest in the late 1970s before collapsing as the result of a leadership crisis. With the reported support of conservative Arab governments, the EDU later resurfaced, albeit with minimal impact. Although a participant in the 1991 National Conference, the EDU was also a member of the antigovernment COEDF (below). It adopted the EDUP rubric prior to the 1995 elections. An opponent of the recent peace accord with Eritrea, the EDUP has complained of government harassment of its members. Cooperation with the EDP was under consideration in mid-2002.

Leader: Mengesha SEYOUM.

Coalition of Ethiopian Democratic Forces (COEDF). The COEDF was launched in April 1991 in Washington, D.C., by a number of groups (including the EDU, see EDUP, above) whose "common denominator" appeared to be concern over the implications of a government takeover by the EPRDF. Continued friction between the EPRDF and the COEDF subsequently hindered the latter's efforts to play a substantial role in national negotiations on Ethiopia's political future.

Several of the COEDF leaders listed below were among those arrested upon their arrival in Addis Ababa for a dissident peace conference of December 1993. In July 1996 the COEDF initiated the formation of an opposition alliance, the **Ethiopian Unity Front** (EUF), which brought together the COEDF, the **Beneshangul Peoples' Democratic Movement** (BPDM), and a majority faction within the **Kefagn Patriotic Front** (KPF).

The COEDF was reported to be seriously fragmented as of mid-1999; some members were promoting the CEOPO (see CAFPDE, above), while others were in negotiations with the government. The disintegration of the coalition was further highlighted by a report that even its core component, the EPRP, was reluctant to describe itself as operating under the COEDF banner.

Leaders: ABERA Yemaneab, GENENEW Assefa, GUENET Giram, MESFIN Tefer.

Ethiopian People's Revolutionary Party (EPRP). The EPRP initiated an unsuccessful antigovernment guerrilla campaign in north-central Ethiopia in 1977. Its forces also battled with the TPLF in Tigray Province, its defeat there in 1978 precipitating a sharp split within the party. One faction served as the formative core of the EPDM in alliance with the TPLF while a rump group was relatively quiescent until a series of kidnappings and other guerrilla acts in Gojam Province in early 1987. Although the EPRP was committed to the overthrow of the Mengistu regime, its relations with the EPRDF and the EPLF were strained. Following the rebel victory in May 1991, the EPRP, with an estimated 5,000 fighters controlling parts of Gojam and Gondar Provinces, was described as the "only really organized opposition" to the TPLF-dominated interim government. Like the country's other previously Marxist formations, the EPRP now supports multiparty democracy.

In 2001 the EPRP called for renewed action against the "racist" TPLF-led regime, and there were several reports in 2002 of fighting between the EPRP and government forces. Some reports described the EPRP as a participant in the UEDF in 2005, although the government continued to describe the EPRP as an illegal organization.

Leaders: Col. TADERSE Muleneh, Iyassu ALEMAYEHU (in exile).

Ethiopian People's Democratic Alliance (EPDA). Founded in 1982, the EPDA was an attempt by right-wing opponents of the PMAC to regroup elements of the EDU. The EPDA subsequently comprised an "internal" wing, headquartered in Sudan, and an "external" wing operating in Britain and the United States. The alliance's strongly anticommunist posture reportedly generated $500,000 in annual support from Washington in the late 1980s, but the financing was cut off as the result of changing U.S. policy toward the nominally left-wing rebels.

Other groups reportedly participating in the COEDF included the **All-Ethiopian Socialist Movement** (*Meison*) and the **Tigray People's Democratic Movement** (TPDM). (TPDM fighters reportedly have conducted guerrilla activity recently in concert with other armed groups, including a faction of the EPRP, and TPDM leader FESEKA Hailemariam was reportedly assassinated in early 2008 by Ethiopian intelligence forces.) The ONC (above) was also subsequently referenced as a member as the COEDF.

Islamic Union (*al-Itahad al-Islami*). Operating along the southern part of the border between Ethiopia and Somalia, the Islamic Union conducted guerrilla activity in the early 1990s in support of the establishment of an "Ethiopian Ogaden State." The grouping was accused by the government of several bomb attacks, prompting military countermeasures in the second half of 1996. On July 8, 1996, minister of transport and communication and the chair of the ESDL, Abdulmejid Hussein, was shot and wounded by *Al-Itahad* members. Government forces subsequently conducted territorial and extraterritorial military operations against *Al-Itahad*, the organization losing its last major bases to an Ethiopian assault in July 1997. (See article on Somalia for information on *al-Itahad* activity in that country.)

Tigrayan Alliance for National Democracy (TAND). The TAND surfaced in Washington, D.C., in February 1995 as an exile grouping that reportedly included the **Multi-National Congress Party of Ethiopia** (MNCPE), and the TPDM, as well as former members of the TPLF and EDC.

Other parties winning single seats in the 2000 balloting for the House of Peoples' Representatives were the **Gambela Peoples' Democratic Congress** (GPDC), an anti-EPRDF formation with support within the Nuer ethnic group; the **Sidama Hadicko Peoples' Democratic Organization;** and the **Siltie Peoples' Democratic Party**.

Small formations include the **Tigray Democratic Union** (TDU), an anti-TPLF grouping that launched an armed struggle in 2000 under the leadership of AREGAWE Bereh, one of the founders of the TPLF; the **Sidama Liberation Movement** (SLM), led by Yilma CHAMOLA; the **Oromo National Liberation Party** (ONLP), launched in October 2000 under the leadership of ESAYAS Shegaw to "liberate Oromia from poverty and suffering."

Groups formed in advance of the 2005 legislative poll included the **Afar Liberation Party**; the **All Ethiopian Democratic Party**, launched by former members of the EDUP; the **Dal-Webi Democratic Movement**, which operates in the state of Somalia; and the **Ethiopian Pan-Africanist Party**, led by Abd al-Fatah HULDAR.

In 2006 the government announced several "victories" over fighters from an allegedly Eritrean-backed Amhara group called the **Ethiopian People's Patriotic Front** (EPPF), although some analysts expressed skepticism that the EPPF represented a significant threat. In November 2007 the EPPF participated in the launching of the antiregime **Unity of Ethiopians for Democratic Change** (UEDC), which included other armed groups such as the TPDM, the **Southern Ethiopia People's Front for Justice and Equality,** and the **Beneshangul People's Movement.**

Other recently registered parties include the **Ethiopian Democratic Unity Movement** (EDUM), led by GUESH Gebreselasi; the **Bershan for Unity and Democracy Party,** led by MULATU Tashwe; and **Unity for Democracy and Justice** (UDJ), led by Birtukan MIDEKSA, a former leader of the RE:MDSJ and former vice chair of the CUD. Mideksa, a former judge, was arrested with other opposition leaders in 2005 and released in 2007. However, she was rearrested in early 2009, the reinstatement of her life sentence prompting heavy domestic and international criticism of the government.

LEGISLATURE

The constitution of December 1994 provides for an Ethiopian **Parliament** encompassing a House of the Federation selected by the states and a popularly elected House of Peoples' Representatives. Both bodies have five-year mandates.

House of the Federation (*Yefedershein Mekir Bete*). The upper House currently consists of 108 members (serving five-year terms) who represent Ethiopia's "nations and nationalities," each of which is entitled to at least one member, with an additional representative for each one million of its population (The regional distribution of seats is as follows: Southern Nations, Nationalities, and Peoples, 54; Amhara, 17; Oromia, 16; Tigray, 6; Somalia, 4; Beneshangul-Gumuz, 4; Gambela Peoples, 4; Afar, 2; Harari People, 1.) Members are designated by state councils, which may elect them directly or provide for their popular election. The House of the Federation was most recently replenished in October 2005 following the State Council elections of May–August.

Speaker: DEGEFE Bula.

House of Peoples' Representatives (*Yehizb Tewokayoch Mekir Bete*). The House of Peoples' Representatives consists of no more than 550 members (minority nationalities being accorded at least 20 seats) directly elected for a five-year term from single-member districts by a plurality of votes cast. The most recent balloting in eight states and the administrative regions of Addis Ababa and Dire Dawa was held on May 15, 2005. (The balloting in the state of Somalia was deferred due to security concerns and administrative difficulties in providing electoral access to the nomadic population.) The preliminary election results were strongly challenged by opposition parties, and reballoting was held in 31 constituencies on August 21. The elections in the state of Somalia were held on August 15.

The government released final results in September 2005 for a total of 546 contested seats. However, some opposition legislators (mostly from the Coalition for Unity and Democracy) declined to take their seats when the house convened in October in a protest over what they perceived as government malfeasance during the balloting. Most opposition parties continued to argue that they had been defrauded out of a number of seats. Following is the distribution of 526 seats as reported by the government, which announced that those elected for the remaining 20 seats had declined to be seated: Ethiopian People's Revolutionary Democratic Front, 327 (EPRDF: Oromo Peoples' Democratic Organization, 110; Southern Ethiopian Peoples' Democratic Movement, 92; Amhara National Democratic Movement, 87; Tigray People's Liberation Front, 38); Coalition for Unity and Democracy, 89 (CUD: All Ethiopian Unity Party, 43; United Ethiopian Democratic Party–Medhin, 36; Rainbow Ethiopia: Movement for Democracy and Social Justice, 8; Ethiopian Democratic League, 2); United Ethiopian Democratic Forces, 52; Somali Peoples' Democratic Party, 24; Oromo Federalist Democratic Movement, 11; Benshangul-Gumuz Peoples' Democratic Unity Front, 8; Afar National Democratic Party, 8; Gambela Peoples' Democratic Movement, 3; Argoba National Democratic

Organization, 1; Harari National League, 1; Shecko Mejenger Peoples' Democratic Unity Organization, 1; independent, 1. New balloting for unclaimed seats was held in April 2008, with the EPRDF reportedly winning all 14 Addis Ababa seats that had been won by the CUD in 2005.

Speaker: TESHOME Toga Chanaka.

CABINET

[as of September 1, 2009]

Prime Minister	Meles Zenawi
Deputy Prime Minister	Addisu Legesse
Ministers	
Adviser to the Deputy Prime Minister	Mesfin Abebe
Cabinet Office	Berhanu Adelo
Communication Affairs Office	Bereket Simon
Culture and Tourism	Mahmud Dirir
Economic Adviser to the Prime Minister	Newayekiristos Gebrab
Defense	Siraj Fergesa
Economic Development and Finance	Sufian Ahmed
Education	Demeke Mekonnen
Federal Affairs	Shiferaw Teklemariam
Foreign Affairs	Seyoum Mesfin
Government Whip	Hailemariam Desalegn
Health	Dr. Tewodros Adhanon Gebreyesus
Justice	Berhan Hailu
Mines and Energy	Alemayehu Tegenu
National Security Adviser to the Prime Minister	Mulugeta Alemseged
Public Organization and Participation Adviser to the Prime Minister	Abay Tsehaye
Public Works	Arkebe Oqubay Mitiku
Rural Development and Agriculture	Tefera Deribew
Science and Technology	Junedin Sado
Special Advisers to the Prime Minister	Shiferaw Jarso Mukhtar Kedir
Trade and Industry	Girma Biru
Transport and Communications	Diriba Kuma
Water Resources	Asefaw Digamo
Women's Affairs	Muferiat Kamil [f]

[f] = female

COMMUNICATIONS

The media were strictly controlled by the Mengistu government and presented the official version of international and domestic events to a small circle of governmental officials, teachers, army officers, and other members of the educated elite. Increased press freedom was promised in the wake of Mengistu's ouster. However, the successor regime's actual policy subsequently remained less than tolerant, and Ethiopian journalists accused the EPRDF of a campaign of "harassment and intimidation" that included arrests of reporters and closure of a number of newspapers. The government proposed a controversial new press law in late 2003 that would have limited the number of newspapers, but protests prevented its official adoption. However, in April 2005 it was reported that many of the measures perceived to be repressive had been "discreetly" introduced, apparently forcing some journalists into exile. In addition, more than 20 journalists were among those arrested in the government crackdown of late 2005. A number of them were subsequently released or pardoned in mid-2007 after signing the controversial letter of "apology" (see Current issues), although international journalistic watchdogs continued to express concern over the status of several detainees and the poor state of press freedom overall.

Press. Except as noted, the following are dailies published in Addis Ababa: *Addis Admas* (31,000), independent weekly in Amharic; *Addis Nagar* (20,000), independent weekly in Amharic; *Addis Zemen* (18,000), government-owned, in Amharic; *Ethiopian Herald* (9,900), government-controlled, in English; the *Daily Monitor* (1,800), in English; the *Reporter* (11,000), biweekly in Amharic; *Al-Alem* (1,000), weekly in Arabic; *Fortune* (7,000), independent weekly; *The Reporter* (2,700), weekly in English; *Awramba Times*, weekly; and *Lisane Hezeb*, opposition weekly. Other opposition papers include *Hadar, Asqual, Menilik*, *Ethiopian Review*, and *Satenaw*.

News agencies. The domestic facility is the Ethiopian News Agency (*Itiopia Zena Agelgilot*—Izea); a number of foreign bureaus maintain offices in Addis Ababa.

Broadcasting and computing. Radio Ethiopia broadcasts locally and internationally in Amharic, English, Arabic, and a number of other languages. The EPRDF controls its own station—*Radio Fana.* Two privately owned stations have been licensed by the Ethiopian Broadcasting Agency, and the first began broadcasting in 2006. Ethiopian Television (*Itiopia Television*) has been broadcasting under government auspices since 1964; the single channel broadcasts mostly in English and Amharic. As of 2008 there were 4.5 Internet users per 1,000 inhabitants.

INTERGOVERNMENTAL REPRESENTATION

Ambassador to the U.S.: Samuel ASSEFA Lemma.

U.S. Ambassador to Ethiopia: (Vacant).

Permanent Representative to the UN: (Vacant).

IGO Memberships (Non-UN): AfDB, AU, BADEA, Comesa, IGAD, Interpol, NAM, PCA, WCO.

FIJI

Republic of the Fiji Islands
Matanitu Tu-Vaka-i-koya ko Viti (Fijian)
Fiji Ripablik (Hindustani)

Note: On September 1, 2009, the Commonwealth suspended Fiji from membership, citing the government's failures to negotiate with the opposition and to schedule a legislative election for 2010. Acting President Epeli Nailatikau, having won cabinet endorsement in late October 2009, was sworn in as president on November 5.

Political Status: Voluntarily assumed the status of a British dependency in 1874; became an independent member of the Commonwealth on October 10, 1970; republic declared on October 15, 1987; current constitution promulgated on July 25, 1997, with effect from July 27, 1998; constitution abrogated by presidential decree on April 10, 2009.

Area: 7,055 sq. mi. (18,272 sq. km.).

Population: 828,900 (2007C); 833,000 (2008C). The 2007 figure is provisional.

Major Urban Center: SUVA, 74,481 (centre), 173,137 (urban area) (2007C).

Official Languages: English, Fijian (*Na Vosa Vakaviti*), and Hindustani (Fijian Hindi).

Monetary Unit: Fiji Dollar (official rate December 1, 2009: 1.90 dollars = $1US).

President (Acting; *see headnote*): Ratu Epeli NAILATIKAU; appointed vice president on April 17, 2009, by President Josefa ILOILO; became Acting President upon Iloilo's retirement, effective July 30, 2009.

Vice President: (Vacant).

Interim Prime Minister: Commodore. Frank Vorege BAINIMARAMA (Josaia Voreqe BAINIMARAMA); sworn in January 5, 2007, succeeding Jona Baravilalala SENILAGAKALI, who had been designated by Bainimarama on December 5, 2006, to replace ousted Prime Minister Laisenia QARASE (United Fiji Party); reappointed by President Iloilo on April 10, 2009, for a further five years.

THE COUNTRY

Situated in the South Pacific east of Australia and north of New Zealand, Fiji consists of a group of some 330 islands, many of them mountainous and only about one-third inhabited, together with 500 islets spread over an area of 250,000 square miles of ocean. Viti Levu, the largest island, accommodates close to 80 percent of the population and is the site of Suva, the capital, and of the airport in Nadi, an important hub for air routes throughout the South Pacific islands. Native Fijians (mainly Melanesians, save for Polynesians in the far northern island of Rotuma) became a minority of Fiji's mixed population in consequence of the introduction of numerous Indian indentured laborers following the establishment of British rule in 1874. In the 1976 census Fijians constituted about 44 percent of the population; Indo-Fijians, 50 percent; other Pacific Islanders, 2 percent; Europeans and part-Europeans, 3 percent; and Chinese, 1 percent. By contrast, the percentages of ethnic Fijians and Indo-Fijians in the 1996 census were 51 and 44, respectively, largely as the result of Indian emigration following military coups in 1987. Virtually all ethnic Fijians are Christian, approximately 85 percent being Methodist and 12 percent Roman Catholic. The Indo-Fijian population is predominantly Hindu, with a Muslim minority. In 2006 women constituted 35 percent of the official labor force, although a higher proportion of women are thought to be engaged in nonmonetary subsistence activities such as agricultural cultivation and processing.

Traditionally, Fiji's economy was based on agriculture. Although that sector now accounts for approximately 16 percent of GDP, it employs over 60 percent of the workforce. Sugar remains the country's most important export, despite declining production because of lack of capital investment in new technology and disputes between Fijian landowners and Indo-Fijian leaseholders over tenure and rentals. Fish, coconuts, and ginger also are significant sectoral exports. Industry, led by food processing and garment production, contributes about one-fourth of GDP and employs one-third of the labor force. Gold mining is the most important extractive industry. Within the services sector, tourism is a major source of income, accounting for one-fifth of GDP; Fiji hosted 585,031 visitors in 2008. At that time Fiji's main export markets were the United States, the United Kingdom, Australia, Samoa, Tonga, and New Zealand; its main sources of imports were Singapore, Australia, New Zealand, and China.

After a decline of 7 percent in the year following the 1987 military coups, real GDP rose by an average of 6.2 percent during 1987–1990, with per capita income over the period increasing by nearly 40 percent (from F$1,800 to F$2,500). However, the economy stagnated thereafter, in part because of a decline in virtually all export sectors, accompanied by disappointing returns from a value-added tax (VAT). After a contraction of 0.9 percent in 1997, the economy grew at a rate of 1.5 percent in 1998 and 9.2 percent, in 1999, due largely to a revival in sugar production. In 2000, however, political turmoil led to a 28 percent drop in tourist arrivals and contributed to a 2.8 percent downturn for the year. The return of political stability and the recovery of tourism raised the GDP growth rate to 2.7 percent in 2001 and on to a peak of 4.9 percent in 2004.

The December 2006 coup precipitated a flight of capital and skilled people and a 14 percent contraction of tourism earnings. The economy was further depressed when the European Union (EU), the United States, Australia, and New Zealand partially suspended aid programs, banned travel to their countries by members of the military-led government, and cautioned their citizens against unnecessary travel to Fiji because of possible civil disorder. Foreign investment sagged, remittances declined by 20 percent, and inflation rose to 4.6 percent. The government reduced expenditures by 14.2 percent during 2007, which slowed public works and raised unemployment. Overall the economy shrank by 6.6 percent in calendar year 2007, the current account balance remained negative at 19.6 percent of GDP, and total public debt rose to 50.3 percent of GDP. Population subsisting below the poverty line, mainly in rural areas and proliferating urban squatter settlements, was estimated at 25 percent.

Despite a modest rebound of 1.2 percent growth in 2008, the Asian Development Bank forecast that the GDP would shrink by 0.5 percent in 2009 as a result of floods, a reduction of tourism earnings and remittances, and sagging international commodity prices and demand. In April 2009 the interim prime minister dismissed the governor of the Reserve Bank of Fiji, ordered the devaluation of the Fiji dollar by 20 percent to attract tourists, and decreed the retirement of civil servants aged 55 and over to reduce government expenditure.

GOVERNMENT AND POLITICS

Political background. Discovered by the Dutch explorer Abel Tasman in 1643 and visited by Captain James Cook in 1774, Fiji became a British possession in 1874, when it was unconditionally ceded to the United Kingdom by the Fijian paramount chief to ensure internal peace. The beginnings of modern Fijian administration came with implementation of the Fijian Affairs Ordinance in 1945, which laid the foundations for local government. A ministerial system was introduced in 1966 under a British constitutional order providing for a Legislative Council elected in such a way as to ensure robust Fijian representation. Indian insistence on the introduction of the "one man, one vote" principle delayed further constitutional progress until early 1970, when Indian leaders agreed to postpone their demands until after independence. Following compromises negotiated in May at a constitutional conference in London, Fiji became independent on October 10, 1970.

The Alliance Party (AP), with Ratu Sir Kamisese K.T. MARA at its head, dominated postindependence governments until 1977. It unexpectedly lost its parliamentary majority in the election of April 1977, but the opposition National Federation Party (NFP) was unable to form a government, and Mara continued to serve as caretaker prime minister

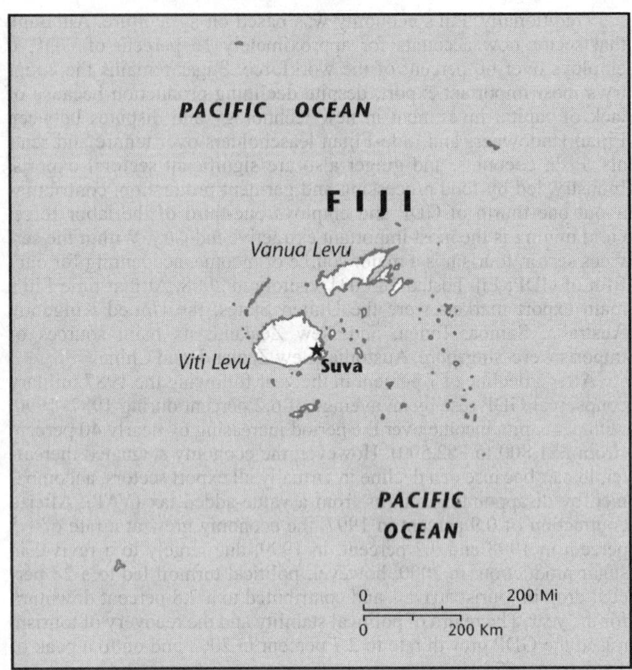

until his party recovered its majority in the September 1977 election. Mara and the AP narrowly retained power in the election of July 1982.

Prior to the next election in 1987 the NFP formed a coalition with the Fiji Labour Party (FLP), which had been launched in mid-1985 with Indian and trade-union backing. Prime Minister Mara called for an early election on April 4–11, at which the AP won only 24 of 52 legislative seats. On April 14 the NFP-FLP coalition (a majority of whose representatives were Indo-Fijians) formed a government headed by the FLP's ethnic Fijian leader, Dr. Timoci BAVADRA. Ethnic Fijians, who were demanding constitutional changes that would preclude alleged Indo-Fijian political domination, staged demonstrations. On May 14 an army unit led by (then) Lt. Col. Sitiveni RABUKA stormed the Parliament building and arrested Bavadra and his fellow ministers. Declaring that he had assumed control pending elections under a new constitution, Rabuka announced the appointment of a 17-member interim ruling council composed largely of former AP officials, including Ratu Mara as foreign minister.

On September 25, 1987, in the wake of inconclusive constitutional discussions and mounting racial clashes, Rabuka, now promoted to colonel, mounted a second coup, formally abrogated the 1970 constitution, and replaced the existing civilian administration with a military council. On October 7 Rabuka (now a general) proclaimed the establishment of a republic and announced the appointment of a largely nonmilitary government of 23 members. On December 5 former governor general Sir Penaia GANILAU was designated president of Fiji, stating that his principal objective was to effect "a return to parliamentary democracy and the reestablishment of links with Her Majesty the Queen." Subsequently, he swore in a new cabinet that included Ratu Mara as prime minister and General Rabuka as home minister.

The country returned to full civilian rule on January 5, 1990, when Rabuka and two other serving army officers resigned their cabinet portfolios. But in July 1991 General Rabuka regained the home affairs portfolio and was named codeputy prime minister after resigning his army commission. He subsequently assumed the presidency of the reorganized Fijian Political Party (*Soqosoqot ni Vakavulewa ni Taukei*—SVT). In the election of May 23 and 30, 1992, 30 of the 37 Fijian seats in the new House of Representatives were won by the SVT, and on June 2 Rabuka became prime minister. His cabinet included 15 SVT members, 2 members of the General Voters' Party (GVP), 1 Fijian independent, and the MP from Rotuma.

During the 1992 election campaign differences had surfaced between Rabuka and his principal SVT rival, Deputy Prime Minister Josevata KAMIKAMICA, whom former prime minister Mara had favored as his successor, and a party split threatened to bring down the government. However, Rabuka supporters successfully courted FLP leader Mahendra Pal CHAUDHRY and his Indo-Fiji MPs. Consequently, Rabuka, the champion of Fijian nationalism, in December formed a new "government of national unity" with the backing of the FLP, a party to which he had long been opposed, thereby alienating right-wing elements within both the SVT and the broader ethnic Fiji community.

Political unrest mounted in the wake of a cabinet shake-up in October 1993, and on November 29 the House of Representatives rejected the government's 1994 budget bill. Rabuka thereupon called for a legislative dissolution. At the ensuing election of February 18–24 the SVT gained an additional seat, while 6 Indian seats shifted from the FLP to the NFP, permitting Rabuka to form a new government on February 28.

In mid-1994, responding to international criticism of the racially biased 1990 constitution of 1990, which systematically over-represented ethnic Fijians in parliament at the expense of the Indo-Fijians, Prime Minister Rabuka announced the appointment of a constitutional review commission headed by former New Zealand governor general Sir Paul Reeves. The Constitutional Amendment Bill approved by President Mara on July 25, 1997, mollified most critics by substantially increasing Indo-Fijian representation in parliament and permitting a non-Fijian to become prime minister. As a consequence, many ethnic Fijians who had endorsed the 1990 constitution felt betrayed by its successor, which guaranteed them only 23 of 71 lower house seats.

In the House of Representatives balloting on May 5–15, 1999, a People's Coalition, encompassing the FLP, the Fijian Association Party (FAP), and the Party of National Unity (PANU), won 51 seats, while the government coalition of the SVT and the United General Party (UGP) secured only 10. On May 19 the FLP's Mahendra Chaudhry was sworn in as the nation's first ethnic Indo-Fijian prime minister. He appointed a multiracial cabinet in which ethnic Indo-Fijians held 11 of 17 full ministerial posts.

A year later, on May 19, 2000, feeding on ethnic Fijian resentment at growing Indo-Fijian influence, a group of gunmen led by George SPEIGHT, a failed Suva businessman, stormed the Parliament building, took hostage Prime Minister Chaudhry, many cabinet members, and a number of MPs, and declared himself prime minister. But on May 29 Commodore Frank Vorege BAINIMARAMA, commander in chief of the armed forces, declared martial law and announced that President Mara had resigned. On July 10 the military signed the so-called Maunikou Accord with Speight for the election of a new president by tribal leaders in return for release of the hostage parliamentarians. On July 13 the last hostages, including Chaudhry, were released, and Vice President Josefa ILOILO was named interim president. On July 26–27 Speight and 350 of his followers were taken into custody following a violent confrontation with the military that resulted in injury and loss of life. On August 11 Speight was charged with treason; he was convicted in February 2002 and sentenced to life imprisonment.

An interim government was sworn in on July 28, 2000, with Laisenia QARASE, a banker supported by Bainimarama, as prime minister. However, on November 15 a High Court justice ruled that the 1997 constitution remained in effect, that Mara remained president, that the current interim government was illegitimate, and that the legislature should be called into session. This decision was unanimously supported by the Court of Appeal on March 1, 2001, and on March 7 Chaudhry, now restored as prime minister, asked the interim president, Iloilo, to recall Parliament for the purpose of formally dissolving itself and calling new elections. But Iloilo, on the advice of the Great Council of Chiefs, on March 8 rejected the Court's decision and supported retention of Qarase as prime minister until new elections could be held. Iloilo, confirmed as president by the Great Council, on March 13 dismissed Chaudhry and called for a new election.

In the balloting of August 25–September 1, 2001, Prime Minister Qarase's recently established United Fiji Party (*Soqosoqo Duavata ni Lewenivanua*—SDL) captured a plurality of 32 seats, while Chaudhry's FLP took 27. To form a governing coalition, Qarase turned to George Speight's Conservative Alliance (*Matanitu Vanua*—MV), which had won 6 seats in the 71-member lower house. Despite a constitutional requirement that all parties receiving at least 8 seats be offered cabinet positions, Qarase refused to include the FLP, asserting that the SDL and the FLP were incompatible. Sworn in on September 10, two days later Qarase presented a new cabinet that included only one Indo-Fijian.

Chaudhry challenged the constitutionality of these moves in court and won in the Court of Appeal and then on July 18, 2003, in the Supreme Court. But Chaudhry rejected the 14 minor posts offered by Qarase and on November 24 Chaudhry announced that the FLP would no longer seek a role in the cabinet and would instead lead the official parliamentary opposition.

In November 2004 Attorney General Qoriniasi BALE ordered the release, on grounds of poor health, of former vice president Jope SENILOLI from prison after serving only a tenth of his sentence for illegally taking an oath of office administered by the 2000 coup leaders. The military viewed this decision as tantamount to endorsement of the 2000 coup, during which several soldiers were murdered. Subsequently, tension between the Qarase administration and the military heightened, with Commodore Bainimarama announcing in late January 2006 that he no longer recognized the authority of Home Affairs Minister Josefa VOSANIBOLA and that the military questioned the legitimacy of the civilian government.

A general election called for May 6–13, 2006, produced a victory for Qarase's SDL party, which attracted 44.6 percent of the vote and won 36 seats, an outright majority in the House of Representatives. The opposition FLP attracted 39.2 percent of votes and won 31 seats. The United People's Party, contesting the "European" seats, gained 0.8 percent of votes and was awarded 2 seats in the House. Independents won 4.9 percent of the vote and 2 seats. Ten other parties contested the election but won no seats. Qarase, designated prime minister by President Iloilo, named a new cabinet.

In October 2006 Bainimarama called the Qarase government "corrupt and unjust" and insisted that it withdraw a legislative initiative, the Reconstruction, Tolerance, and Unity (RTU) bill, under which the 2000 plotters could seek amnesty. The commissioner of police indicated he would be investigating Bainimarama for possible sedition during the 2000 coup. In November, Qarase agreed to suspend the RTU and to replace the commissioner of police, who was an Australian citizen on secondment to the Fiji government, with a Fijian appointee. But Bainimarama remained unsatisfied and called for Qarase's resignation. The standoff ended when Bainimarama spearheaded Fiji's fourth coup on December 5, 2006, and deposed the civilian government. Bainimarama assumed the role of acting president. Iloilo initially called the coup "clearly outside the constitution" and "contrary to the rule of law and democracy." However, he was persuaded by the military leaders to dissolve Parliament, name Bainimarama as interim prime minister, and legitimize the installation of an interim government of military officers and cooperative civilians, in return for which he was reinstated as president on January 5, 2007.

In the wake of a Court of Appeal ruling denying the legitimacy of the government, President Iloilo, again backed by the military, on April 10, 2009, dismissed all of Fiji's judges, declared the constitution abrogated and a state of emergency in force, and appointed Bainimarama interim prime minister for a further five years. Bainimarama reshuffled his cabinet on April 11, 2009. Six days later, Iloilo named Epeli NAILATIKAU as vice president, filling a post that had been vacant since the 2006 coup. When Iloilo, 88, retired on July 30, Nailatikau became acting president.

Constitution and government. Fiji's 1970 constitution established Fiji as a fully sovereign and independent state with a titular head, the British monarch, represented locally by a governor general. Executive authority was vested in a prime minister and cabinet appointed by the governor general and responsible to a bicameral Parliament consisting of an appointed Senate and an elected House of Representatives. A complex electoral system was devised to ensure strong representation for the Fijian community, encompassing both communal and national electoral rolls. The judicial system included a Fiji Court of Appeal, a Supreme Court (the superior court of record), magistrates' courts, and provincial and district courts. A High Court above the courts of first instance and below the Court of Appeal was added in 1990. Judicial appointments were assigned to the governor general, with provision for an ombudsman to investigate complaints against government officials.

Following independence, Fiji was partitioned into four administrative divisions (Northern, Southern, Eastern, and Western), each headed by a divisional commissioner assisted by district officers. Divisions and lower-level districts are headed by appointed commissioners and officers, respectively. Urban areas include cities and towns, each of which elects a governing council. There also are local rural authorities responsible primarily for matters of public health. Native Fijian affairs are governed through a separate overlapping system based on the village (*koro*) and extending up to the provincial level. Each of 14 communal provinces has a partially elected provincial council and an executive head (*roko tui*). Executives are named by the Fijian Affairs Board, which oversees administration of ethnic Fijian matters. At the apex of the provincial councils, a Great Council of Chiefs (*Bose Levu Vakaturaga*) was empowered to advise the government on Fijian affairs. A National Land Trust Board was given administrative responsibility over four-fifths of the nation's land, which could not be alienated, on behalf of village groups. Indians were restricted to leasing holdings for up to 10 years (later expanded to 30 years), a situation that, along with the system of representation, remained the object of persistent Indian dissatisfaction.

The 1970 constitution was abrogated after the second coup of September 1987. Its successor, promulgated on July 25, 1990, was also complex. A president, named for a five-year term by the Great Council of Chiefs, and expected always to be an ethnic Fijian, was endowed with executive authority, as well as with capacity to initiate legislation under emergency conditions. A Presidential Council was to provide advice on matters of national importance. The administration was headed by a prime minister who selected cabinet associates from members of Parliament. The legislature remained bicameral, with a nonelective, Fijian-dominated Senate authorized to amend, alter, or repeal any measure affecting the customs, land, and tradition of the indigenous population. Sitting for a five-year term, the House of Representatives contained 70 members, 37 of whom were required to be Fijian. Of the remaining 33 members, only 27 were elected from Indo-Fijian constituencies, 5 from those of other ethnic groups, and 1 from Rotuma, confirming the constitutionally subordinate status of the non-Fijians to the ethnic Fijians. A High Court was added to the judicial hierarchy and assigned constitutional review functions to be shared with the Supreme Court. Provision also was made for the establishment of indigenous courts, while a Native Land Commission was assigned ultimate jurisdiction in any dispute relating to customary land rights and usage. Finally, the 1990 constitution called for Judicial, Police, and Public Sector commissions mandated to ensure that no less than 50 percent of all appointments were reserved for Fijians and Rotumans. Administration of divisions, districts, cities, towns, and villages, and the functions of the Fijian Affairs Board, remained the same as before 1970.

The manifestly discriminatory constitution of 1990 was superseded in 1997 by a constitution that provided for continued Fijian predominance in the Senate but opened the door to possible Indo-Fijian control of the House through the election of 25 members on a nonracial basis (see Legislature, below). The ensuing designation of Mahendra Chaudhry as prime minister in 1999 served as a catalyst for the coup led by George Speight, whose short-lived government in May 2000 abrogated the 1997 constitution. But on November 15 the High Court ruled that the 1997 Constitution remained in force, and that decision was confirmed by the Court of Appeal on March 1, 2001.

The 1997 constitution remained nominally in force after the December 5, 2006 coup, but its civil liberties provisions were violated when the interim government delayed the holding of an election to return Fiji to civilian rule, curbed political party activity, intimidated the media, and packed the human rights commission with political appointees. Interim prime minister Bainimarama in October 2007 hinted that he wished to abolish the racial electoral roles but by early 2009 had not initiated any legislative steps to that end, mainly because the House of Representatives elected in 2006 was never allowed to convene. Meanwhile, he joined with the Catholic bishop of Fiji to appoint a National Council for Building a Better Fiji and promote the drafting of a "People's Charter." Critics alleged that the council and charter would be used to undermine the constitution, sidestep the Parliament, and legitimize Bainimarama's populist rule. On February 1, 2009, Bainimarama dissolved Fiji's 12 municipal councils and appointed town clerks and special administrators to replace the 12 mayors, explaining this was done to combat corruption at the local level.

On May 5, 2009, the Court of Appeal, overturning a prior judgment by the High Court on a case brought by deposed prime minister Qarase, ruled that the December 2006 seizure of power was illegal and the interim government was illegitimate. President Iloilo responded by dismissing first the judges of the Court of Appeal, then the entire judiciary, abrogating the constitution, declaring a state of emergency, and reappointing Commodore Bainimarama as interim prime minister for five years.

Foreign relations. Fiji is a member of the United Nations (UN) and of many of its associated agencies as well as of several regional organizations, including the Pacific Community. It was a founding member of the 16-member Pacific Islands Forum (formerly South Pacific Forum), and Suva is the site of its Secretariat. Since June 1978 Fiji has been a major contributor to UN peacekeeping forces, from which it earned a substantial but undisclosed amount of foreign exchange for the government. In December 2004, Fiji dispatched a company of 134 troops to Iraq to assist the UN in peacekeeping and in protecting key personnel, and in April 2005 it sent a further 90. In 2009 Fijian soldiers and police engaged by the United Nations for peacekeeping and security work in the Middle East numbered approximately 2,000, and they remitted home an estimated F$20 million a year.

Upon independence Fiji joined the Commonwealth. But in October 1987, in response to criticism from London, the leaders of the military coup declared Fiji a republic. This prompted the Commonwealth Heads of Government Meeting in Vancouver, Canada, to declare that Fiji's membership in the Commonwealth had "lapsed." The joint statement went on to say that Fiji's status might be reconsidered should "the circumstances warrant." As readmission required the unanimous endorsement of the members, and because India was reluctant to give its assent under constitutional arrangements perpetuating political subordination of Indians, it took the adoption of a new constitution in 1997 before India agreed to Fiji's readmission in August 1997 (effective October 1). Fiji's status was again jeopardized by the May 2000 coup, which resulted in suspension from participation in meetings of the Commonwealth. The action came after the United States had resumed its aid program, India had reopened its Suva embassy, and Fiji was preparing to host the representatives of more than 70 African, Caribbean, and Pacific countries for the signing of a successor to the EU-sponsored Lomé Convention that was to have been known as the Suva Convention. As a consequence of the coup, the meeting was moved to Cotonou, Benin, where the Cotonou Agreement was concluded on June 23, 2000. Full participation in the Commonwealth was restored following the August–September 2001 democratic election.

Fiji was again suspended from Commonwealth meetings in the wake of the 2006 coup pending consultations on the return to democracy. Fiji's coup was strongly condemned also by the UN Security Council and the European Commission. Numerous foreign governments, including Australia, New Zealand, the United States, and member states of the EU, ceased diplomatic and military contacts, suspended aid, curtailed migrant work permits, and imposed travel bans on the Bainimarama regime. Nevertheless, the EU on November 29, 2007, signed an interim Economic Partnership Agreement that allowed sugar and other eligible Fiji exports preferential duty-free entry into the European market, replacing the longstanding sugar agreements negotiated under the Lomé and Cotonou auspices. At the same time the EU made it clear that US$203 million in aid to modernize the ailing sugar industry was at risk if constitutional government was not restored, and in May 2009 the European Commissioner for Development Louis Michel cancelled an allocation for Fiji sugar industry reform worth US$33.4 million.

The Pacific Islands Forum in March 2007 established a Forum-Fiji Joint Working Group, which at a Forum foreign ministers' meeting in Auckland in March 2008 affirmed the necessity of Fiji's return to democracy via an election to be held in the first quarter of 2009. Australia, New Zealand, and the United States pledged to provide technical assistance to Fiji to facilitate the election but kept sanctions in place pending an election schedule, as did the European Union. In July the Commonwealth Secretariat sent New Zealand's former governor-general Sir Paul Reeves to Suva to mediate between the interim government and the civilian political leaders. Also in July a European Union delegation and a group of South Pacific foreign ministers visited Suva to encourage progress toward an election. These initiatives failed to change the interim government's policies. In August Bainimarama left the country to attend the Beijing Olympics at the invitation of the government of China, and in early 2009 the China Development Bank reportedly negotiated a loan of US$60 million for hydroelectric development, bringing the total of China's loan and aid commitments since the December 2006 coup to nearly US$200 million.

In January 2009 the Pacific Islands Forum leaders gave the interim government until May 1 to produce a plan for fresh elections, and upon expiry of that deadline the Forum suspended Fiji's leaders from all Forum meetings and eligibility for Forum aid and technical assistance. The unconstitutional actions of April 10 by President Iloilo stimulated Australia, New Zealand, Great Britain, the United States, the Commonwealth Secretariat, the Commission of the European Union, and the UN Security Council to condemn the interim government and foreshadow further sanctions if steps were not take to restore constitutional government. International lawyers' groups, such as the International Bar Association and the Commonwealth Lawyers Association, issued similar condemnations. Fiji was formally suspended from the Commonwealth on September 1.

In May UN under secretary general for political affairs Lynn Pascoe announced that the UN would not recruit Fiji soldiers for new peacekeeping duties, although current contracts would be allowed to run their course. Meanwhile Bainimarama visited Indonesia in the latest in a series of visits to Asian capitals including Beijing, where he sought diplomatic acceptance, loans, and aid to offset the deterioration of relations with Fiji's traditional partners, such as Australia and New Zealand.

Current issues. Race relations, and therefore politics, in Fiji are directly related to questions of land tenure and the rights of landlords. Under the Native Land Trust Act, a 12-member Native Land Trust Board (NLTB) administers indigenous land holdings, which now amount to about 88 percent of the country's territory. Another 3 percent is classified as state land, which is held in trust for the people, while only 9 percent (freehold land) can be bought and sold without restriction. Although ethnic Fijians "own" the land administered by the NLTB, they cannot alienate it, nor can they easily appeal to the courts if they object to NLTB decisions.

In 1966 Fiji passed the Agricultural Landlords and Tenants Act (ALTA), which set forth basic guidelines for leasing and tenancy and established 30-year leases as the standard. Those leases began expiring in 1997 and many landlords, unable to secure higher rent from the ALTA, refused to renew the leases and began evicting Indo-Fijians, who grew virtually all of the country's sugar cane.

In 2001 the NLTB, with its close ties to the traditional chiefs and the ethnic Fijian political parties, took over administration of ALTA. Although the NLTB has argued the advantages of setting rents at values that are closer to market rates, many indigenous landlords also have had their differences with the NLTB, which siphons off 15 percent of rent payments for operating expenses, holds another 10 percent in trust, and distributes 22.5 percent to the traditional hierarchy. Meanwhile, tenants still have no way to obtain their own land, are not guaranteed compensation for any improvements they make to leased land (even for erecting housing), and have no right to automatic lease renewal. Because of the uncertainty of tenure, the sugar industry has suffered, with considerable acreage lying fallow.

The issue took a new turn in February 2008 when the NLTB released a commissioned report by economist Dr. KRISHNAMURTHI recommending "de-reservation" of native lands as a means of reviving the sugar industry and stimulating rural enterprise. This proposal precipitated widespread criticism by ethnic Fijian leaders, including former prime minister Sitivini Rabuka, but cautious approval by the FLP and the Indo-Fijian minister of finance, Mahendra Chaudhry.

In March 2007, under pressure from EU representatives and at the urging of Pacific Islands Forum leaders, Bainimarama lifted the state of emergency that had been imposed at the time of the coup and pledged to conduct an election leading to return to constitutional civilian government by the end of March 2009. But the government was slow to undertake necessary measures, such as the appointment and staffing of an electoral boundaries commission and appropriation of funds for the administration of the election. Policies governing the registration and permissible activities of candidates such as Qarase and political parties such as the SDL remained ambiguous. A supervisor of elections, lawyer Felicity Heffernan from New Zealand, was appointed in May 2008.

However, doubt regarding Bainimarama's commitment to restoring constitutionalism was raised by such episodes as the imposition of a temporary state of emergency in September 2007, the arrest and beating of 16 alleged antigovernment conspirators in November 2007, the sacking of the chief justice and the chief of police, the summary expulsion of New Zealand diplomats Michael Green in June 2007 and Caroline McDonald in December 2008, the blacklisting of two Australian editors of the *Fiji Times* and New Zealand journalists Michael Field and Barbara Dreaver, Bainimarama's appointment of himself as chair of the Great Council of Chiefs (which chooses the president) in February 2008, and his withdrawal in June from the Forum-Fiji Joint Working Group consultations regarding election preparations. In July Bainimarama announced that no election would take place until electoral reforms were completed, possibly in 2010, and on July 1, 2009 he extended that timeframe to a new constitution by 2013 and elections by 2014. Meanwhile, Bainimarama initiated and appointed a National Council for Building a Better Fiji and directed the drafting of a "People's Charter for a Better Fiji." After a series of managed public consultations, the People's Charter, described as a "supplement to the Constitution," was completed on December 5, 2008 and approved and promulgated by President Iloilo on December 19.

Protest in Suva against Bainimarama's April 10-11, 2009, power seizure was muted, confined to a few members of the legal profession and the Nationalist *Vanua Tako Lavo* (NVTLP). party. Outlying centers remained quiet, no violence erupted, and no curfew was imposed. Reports of intimidation of opposition figures, lawyers, and journalists by anonymous threats, temporary detention, assault, and fire-bombing of homes circulated but no perpetrators were apprehended. On June 22 the Interim Government renewed the Public Emergency Regulations which legalized censorship of the media and the banning of public meetings, and in July banned the annual conference of the Methodist Church and temporarily detained six Methodist leaders.

POLITICAL PARTIES

Political party activity was first suspended in October 1987, although most groups remained active in preparation for parliamentary elections, which were ultimately held under the 1990 constitution in May 1992. The most conspicuous casualty was the Alliance Party (AP), a multiracial grouping formed in 1968 by the Fijian Association, the Indian Alliance, and the General Electors' Association. Under Ratu Sir Kamisese K.T. Mara, the AP led the country to independence but by 1990 had become effectively dormant.

Formal party activity was again temporarily suspended in the wake of the May 2000 coup, with considerable realignment then occurring in preparation for the August–September 2001 general election. In early 2005, looking toward the general election scheduled for 2006, Prime Minister Qarase stepped up efforts to unite the major ethnic Fijian parties. In late February Qarase's United Fiji Party (SDL) and its junior coalition partner, the Conservative Alliance (MV), announced that they would cooperate in nominating candidates and subsequently served as the basis of a short-lived Grand Coalition Initiative Group (GCIG). In the election of May 2006, only 3 of 13 contesting parties won seats.

The coup of December 5, 2006, and imposition by the military of a state of emergency again halted political party activity. After the lifting of the state of emergency in March 2007 the SDL was virtually banned and its leader, Qarase, confined to his home island distant from Suva for several months. A meeting between Qarase and Bainimarama in May 2008 was reportedly cordial but produced no liberalization of the interim government's policies. Other parties remained nominally free, but their leaders remained wary of attracting threats and reprisals from the military authorities. An early exception was the Fiji Labor Party (FLP), which supported the interim government and whose leaders were rewarded by appointment to government bodies. In late 2008 six minor parties formed the People's Movement for Political Reform and supported the People's Charter, the President's Forum, and other political initiatives sponsored by Commodore Bainimarama; they were the Conservative Alliance (MV), the Fijian Political Party (SVT), the General Voters Party (GVP), the Justice and Freedom Party (JFP), the National Alliance Party of Fiji (NAPF), and the Party of National Unity (PANU).

Parties Winning Seats in Parliament in 2006:

United Fiji Party (*Soqosoqo Duavata ni Lewenivanua*—SDL). The SDL was established in May 2001 by Laisenia Qarase, at that time the caretaker prime minister, in preparation for the upcoming national election. The new party attracted members from the principal indigenous formations, including the Fijian Political Party (SVT, below), the Fijian Association Party (FAP, below), and the Christian Democratic Alliance (*Veitokani ni Lewenivanua Vakarisito*—VLV). A predominantly Methodist party that had been formed in 1998, the VLV won three parliamentary seats in 1999 and ran under the SDL banner in 2001, but it became dormant after that and was deregistered in February 2004.

The SDL emerged from the August–September 2001 balloting with a plurality of 32 seats in the House of Representatives. Having negotiated a coalition arrangement with George Speight's Conservative Alliance Party (MV, below), Qarase formed a new government that also included a representative of the New Labour Unity Party (NLUP).

In 2005 the SDL and three other Fiji nationalist parties formed the so-called Grand Coalition Initiative Group (GCIG), which was committed to the maintenance of a Fiji-dominated government. Only the SDL won seats and its coalition partners remained politically without substantial influence. The SDL party won a majority of 36 seats in May 2006 and formed a government. The interim government from December 2006 banned public assemblies by the SDL and intimidated its leaders, particularly Qarase. The SDL remained hostile towards the interim government and although its leaders participated in some of the public meetings on the People's Charter, they were excluded by the interim prime minister from an all-party forum on April 6, 2009.

Leaders: Laisenia QARASE (Former Prime Minister), Ratu Kalokalo LOKI (President), Peceli KINIVUWAI (Party Director).

Fiji Labour Party (FLP). Launched in July 1985 by leaders of the Fiji Trades Union Congress, the FLP presented itself as a "multi-racial political vehicle for all working people," although drawing most of its support from the Indo-Fijian community. It outpolled the NFP (below) in winning 8 Suva city council seats in November 1985 and subsequently gained 3 parliamentary seats held by NFP defectors. For the 1987 campaign the two groups decided to present a joint list.

Partly to neutralize criticism that an Indo-Fijian might become prime minister, an ethnic Fijian, Dr. Timoci Bavadra, was named to head the coalition slate, with the NFP's Harish SHARMA as his deputy. Both were forced from office by the Rabuka coup. Bavadra, in ill health, died on November 3, 1989, and the FLP leadership was assumed by his widow, Adi Kuini SPEED. In August 1991 Adi Kuini Speed stepped down and eventually left the party to join the All National Congress (ANC, under FAP, below).

The FLP backed Rabuka for prime minister in June 1992 after the Fijian Political Party (SVT, below) leader had promised to launch a review of the ethnically biased 1990 constitution; it did not, however, join the de facto ruling coalition and withdrew its support of the Rabuka administration in June 1993.

In August 1998 the FLP formed an electoral alliance called the People's Coalition with the FAP and the PANU (see under PNU, below) that was viewed as presenting a major challenge to the SVT for the 1999 poll. In addition to favoring a multiracial approach to government, the coalition pledged to halt a privatization program that had led to the dismissal of many public sector employees. In the balloting of May 8–15 the FLP obtained a majority of 37 lower house seats, with its leader, Mahendra Chaudhry, serving as prime minister until his ouster after the coup of May 19, 2000.

The FLP went on to finish second in the August–September 2001 election but, not invited to join the SDL-controlled government, it served as leader of the parliamentary opposition.

In the 2006 legislative poll, the FLP (supported in a People's Coalition by the UPP, FAP, and PNU, below) finished second to the SDL, with 31 House seats. However, a deep rift within the party surfaced at midyear over opposition senatorial candidates, with the attorney general ruling that by accepting a number of cabinet appointments the FLP could no longer claim opposition status.

In January 2007, Chaudhry, despite attacks on his leadership from within his party, accepted appointment as finance minister in Bainimarama's interim administration, where he played an active role as civilian spokesperson for the government and defender of current policies, weathering media accusations of tax evasion. He resigned from the government on August 18, 2008, and Commodore Bainimarama assumed his portfolio.

Leaders: Mahendra Pal CHAUDHRY (Former Prime Minister), Jokapeci KOROI (President).

United People's Party (UPP). In an effort to broaden its appeal, the former United General Party (UGP) changed its name in 2003 to the UPP. The UGP, representing "General Electors" (those not belonging to either the ethnic Fijian or Indo-Fijian communities), was formed in September 1998 by merger of the General Voters' Party (GVP) and the smaller General Electors' Party (GEP). At the May 1999 election the UGP won 2 parliamentary seats. In May 2001 President David PICKERING was succeeded by Mick Beddoes, and in June Pickering joined the NFP (below). Beddoes won the party's only seat at the 2001 general election. In 2002–2004, while the FLP's right to join the government remained in the courts, Beddoes served as leader of the opposition in the House.

Running in tandem with the FLP in 2006, the UPP won 2 legislative seats in its own right, with Beddoes being redesignated opposition leader in the wake of the Chaudhry tax evasion controversy. Beddoes was consistently critical of the interim government in 2007 and 2008, and he and his party were not invited to the all-party forum convened by Commodore Bainimarama on April 6, 2009.

Leader: Millis (Mick) BEDDOES (Party Leader).

Other Parties Contesting the 2006 Election:

National Federation Party (NFP). The NFP was formed in 1963 by A.D. PATEL, Siddiq KOYA, and Jai Ram REDDY as a union of two parties: the Federation, a predominantly ethnic Indian party, and the National Democratic Party, a Fijian party. Most of its support came from the Indo-Fijian community because of its advocacy of the "one man, one vote" principle.

In the elections of 1977 and 1982 the NFP remained in opposition but in 1987 in tandem with the FLP, it won cabinet portfolios. However, its ministers were ousted by the coup of May 14. In May 1989 it was announced that the NFP and the FLP had agreed to merge, although their subsequent relationship remained that of a coalition (occasionally referenced as the Coalition Party) under the overall leadership of the FLP's Adi Kuini Speed. The coalition itself became moribund in late 1991 after the NFP had voted not to join the FLP's proposed boycott of the 1992 election.

The party's only successful candidate in the 2001 general election was Prem SINGH, who was named leader of the opposition in the House of Representatives by President Iloilo after the FLP's Mahendra Chaudhry declined that designation. The Supreme Court in August 2002 voided Singh's victory because of electoral irregularities.

At its annual convention in August 2004 the NFP elected a new leadership as part of a restructuring effort. In February 2005 the party's new general secretary noted that in view of the country's shrinking Indo-Fijian population, the NFP should seek to participate in the government rather than remain outside it.

In 2006 the NFP was the third most popular party, attracting 6.2 percent of the popular vote, but it won no seats. It was excluded from an all-party forum called by Commodore Bainimarama on April 6, 2009.

Leaders: Dorsami NAIDU (Leader), Raman SINGH (President), Chandhu LODHIA (Treasurer), Pramod RAE (General Secretary).

National Alliance Party of Fiji (NAPF). Based on the multiracial model of the defunct AP, the NAPF was launched in early 2005 by veteran political leader Ratu Epeli Ganilau, former chair of the Great Council of Chiefs who now serves as minister of foreign affairs in the interim government. Bolstered by a merger with the Justice and Freedom Party in April 2006, the NAPF emerged as the fourth most popular party in the 2006 election, with 22,504 votes, but it won no seats. In 2008 it participated in the six-party People's Movement for Political Reform and supported the interim prime minister's political initiatives.

Leader: Ratu Epeli GANILAU.

Party of National Unity (PANU). The PANU emerged originally in April 1998 to provide greater legislative representation for Viti Levu's northern province of Ba. For the May 1999 balloting the PANU joined the FLP and the Fijian Association Party (FAP, below) to present coalition candidates, winning 4 House seats. In April 2001 PANU leader Ponipate Lesavua joined Sitiveni Rabuka of the Fijian Political Party (SVT, below), the FAP's Adi Kuini Speed (the widow of former prime minister Timoci Bavadra, who had been ousted in the coup of May 1987), FLP leader Tupeni Baba, and Mick Beddoes of the UGP in calling for adherence to the rule of law and a commitment to political multiethnicity. Regarded as one of Fiji's "moderate" parties, the PANU failed to retain any House seats in the subsequent national election.

In 2004 the PANU and another Ba party, the Protector of Fiji (*Bai Rei Viti*—BKV), led by Ratu Tevita MOMOEDONU, merged as the People's National Party (PNP), but the merger quickly disintegrated. Efforts were then made to revive the PANU and the BKV. In the end, in early 2006 the BKV and the remnants of the PNP decided to merge into the restored PANU. Among those drawn to the new formation were key members of the Taukei Movement (below), including Minister of Agriculture Apisai TORA, of the former PANU.

The PANU contested the 2006 legislative poll as an ally of the FLP but won no seats. It was a founder of the People's Movement for Political Reform in 2008 and gave its approval to the interim prime minister's proposed reforms.

Leaders: Tui Ba Ratu Sairusi NAGAGAVORA, Ponipate LESAVUA, Meli BOGILEKA.

Nationalist *Vanua Tako Lavo* Party (NVTLP). A strongly anti-Indian communal organization, the NVTLP is a descendant of the Fijian Nationalist Party (FNP) launched in 1974. The FNP's strenuous campaigning drew many votes from the AP and contributed to the latter's reversal in the election of March–April 1977. The FNP won no seats in 1982 or 1987, many of its candidates losing their deposits.

The FNP was reorganized as the Fijian Nationalist United Front (FNUF) prior to the 1992 balloting. Subsequently, FNUF leader Sakeasi BUTADROKA moved the party into opposition, branding General Rabuka as the "betrayer of the century." In August 1992 Butadroka urged the deportation of all Indo-Fijians to their ethnic homeland. The FNUF won 5 lower house seats in 1992, all of which were lost in 1994 under the banner of the Fijian-Rotuman Nationalist United Front Party. The NVTLP entered the 1999 election campaign opposing the existing constitution and demanding that the primacy of Fijian customary law be restored. It won 2 seats at the balloting of May 8–15. Butadroka died in December 1999.

A number of Nationalists were directly involved or implicated in the May 2000 coup, including the party's president, Iliesa Duvuloco, who was sentenced to 18 months in prison in February 2002, and a vice president, Viliame SAVU, who was convicted twice: in December 2002 for misprision of treason and in August 2004 for taking an illegal oath. Savu won early release on the second charge in January 2005. Following Duvuloco's conviction, the party elected Manasa MOCE as president; Moce died in February 2005 while on trial for taking an illegal oath.

In the 2001 national election the NVTLP failed to win any House seats. In late 2001 Josaia WAQABACA, the party's general secretary, was charged with conspiring to kidnap Prime Minister Qarase, Commodore Bainimarama, and the attorney general, but he was acquitted in March 2002. In 2006 the party attracted fewer than 3,700 votes. The NVTLP was critical of the December 2006 coup and the interim prime minister, who reciprocated by excluding the NVTLP leaders from an all-party meeting he convened on April 6, 2009. On April 27 Duvuloco and five party members were arrested for distributing leaflets urging President Iloilo to resign and the public to resist Bainimarama's decrees.

Leaders: Iliesa DUVULOCO, Saula TELAWA, Samisoni BOLATAGICI.

Fijian Political Party (*Soqosoqo ni Vakavulewa ni Taukei*—SVT). The SVT was launched by the Great Council of Chiefs in mid-1991 to fill the vacuum created by the demise of the Fijian Association, although its appeal was expected to be limited largely to ethnic Fijians. In October Deputy Prime Minister Sitiveni Rabuka won the party presidency, despite not being a chief. The party secured pluralities in the election of May 1992 and February 1994, with Rabuka forming governments that included representatives of the General Voters' Party (GVP) on both occasions. In May 1999, running on a multiracial platform with UGP and the NFP, the SVT placed third in the election, winning 8 lower house seats.

In January 2001 the SVT, the former Christian Democratic Alliance (*Veitokani ni Lewenivanua Vakarisito*—VLV), and the Tu'uakitau Cokanauto faction of the FAP announced an alliance, the Combined Fijian Political Parties (CFPP), subsequently called the Fijian Political Parties Forum (FPPF), to represent indigenous Fijians. But having lost the endorsement of the Great Council of Chiefs, the SVT failed to win any seats in the August–September 2001 House election.

In April 2004 Rabuka again floated the concept of an alliance, this time for a "Fijian Multiracial Alliance." Six months later the SVT called for the release of all those convicted in connection with the May 2000 incidents. In the 2006 election the SVT garnered only 238 votes. It was among six parties that formed the People's Movement for Political Reform to support Commodore Bainimarama's political initiatives in 2008.

Leaders: Ratu Sitiveni RABUKA (Former Prime Minister), Ema DRUAVESI (Secretary General).

National Democratic Party (NDP). The first National Democratic Party was a merger of Apisai Tora's Western Democratic Party with Isikeli NADALO's Fijian National Party formed in the early 1960s. It drew its support mainly from the province of Ba and other western regions. It subsequently merged with the Federation Party to form the National Federation Party. It was revived to contest the general election of 2006. It contested only the Serua Navosa Open Constituency and received only 123 votes. The party is currently inactive.

Justice and Freedom Party (JFP). The JFP was established in 2000 on an Indo-Fijian platform. Its manifesto pledged to give scholarships to Indo-Fijian students, urged Britain to give passports to Indo-Fijians, and advocated dual citizenship for Indo-Fijians living abroad. It won only 0.1 percent of the vote and no seats in the 2001 election. In May 2006 its sole candidate remained on the ballot, winning 18 votes, despite an April announcement of a merger with Ratu Epeli Ganilau's

National Alliance Party of Fiji (NAPF). In 2008 the party joined five other parties in a People's Movement for Political Reform to support the interim prime minister's political initiatives.

None of the following parties attracted more than several dozen votes in 2006: the **Coalition of Independent Nationals** (COIN), formed originally by six independents to contest the 1999 election and led by Prince Vyas Muni LAKSHMAN; the **Party of the Truth** (POTT), led by Nimilote FIFITA; and the **Social Liberal Multi-Cultural Party** (SLMCP), led by Jokentani DELAI.

Other Parties:

Conservative Alliance Party (*Matanitu Vanua*—MV, or CAMV). Formation of the CAMV was announced in April 2001, and the party was formally launched in mid-June by supporters of coup leader George Speight. It won 6 seats in the August–September 2001 election (including 1 by the incarcerated Speight) and then entered into a coalition government with the plurality SDL.

A former party president and deputy speaker of the House of Representatives, Rakuita VAKALALABURE, was convicted in August 2004 of taking an illegal oath and was sentenced to a six-year prison term. Naiqama LALABALAVU, a northern paramount chief as well as minister of lands and mineral resources, was sentenced to eight months in jail, for a 2000 offense, in April 2005. His cabinet replacement, Samisoni Tikoinasau (Sam SPEIGHT), was George Speight's brother.

In February 2006 it was reported that the SDL and CAMV had merged, but elements of the CAMV opposed the merger and vowed to keep the CAMV alive. With its nominal leader George Speight serving a life sentence for treason, the party is barely viable. In 2008 it lent its support to the interim government as part of the People's Movement for Political Reform.

Leaders: George SPEIGHT (Ilikimi NAITINI), Ropate SIVO (Secretary General).

Fijian Association Party (FAP). The FAP was launched in 1995 by merger of the former Fijian Association (FA) and the multiracial All National Congress (ANC). The FA had been formed prior to the 1994 election by a group of SVT dissidents led by former finance minister Josevata KAMIKAMICA, whose objection to the 1994 budget had caused the government's defeat in November 1993. The new formation was held to only 5 parliamentary seats in February 1994. The ANC had been organized in 1991 by elements of both the former Alliance Party and its longtime political rival, the NFP.

The FAP joined in the coalition government announced in August 1997 but withdrew from it in November. It contested the May 1999 poll in alliance with the FLP and the PANU. FAP leader Adi Kuini Speed campaigned on the message that conditions for ethnic Fijians had deteriorated under the Rabuka regime.

The FAP placed second in the legislative poll of May 1999, winning 10 seats. In September 1999, while serving as a deputy prime minister in the Chaudhry government, Speed was removed as party leader by Tu'uakitau Cokanauto's faction. The action was thrown out by the High Court, however, and Speed narrowly prevailed in a party election in October. Differences between the two factions persisted, with the Cokanauto faction announcing in April 2000 that it would no longer cooperate with the government and then in March 2001 reiterating its objection to restoration of the 1997 constitution. The FAP failed to win any seats in 2001, which led Speed to resign as party leader. She died in December 2004. The party was still registered in 2006.

Leader: Tu'uakitau COKANAUTO.

Other minor parties include the **Dodonu ni Taukei** (DNT), an FAP breakaway led by Dr. Fereti Seru DEWA; the **Fiji Democratic Party** (FDP), formed in late 2002 by a group of SVP and FAP dissidents, including former foreign minister Felipe BOLE; the **Girmit Heritage Party** (GHP), led by Beni SAMI; the **Voice of the Rotuman** (*Lio 'On Famor Rotuma*—LFR), led by Sakumanu PENE; the **General Voters Party** (GVP), led by Fred CAINE; the New Nationalist Party, led by Saula TELAWA, a splinter of the NVTLP; and the New Labour Unity Party (NLUP).

Taukei Movement (*Soqosoqo I Taukei*). A "movement" rather than a party, the right-extremist *Soqosoqo I Taukei* is one of a number of *taukei* (indigenous) groups formed in the wake of the 1987 military takeover. In June 1990 some 250 of its adherents demonstrated in Suva to demand the deportation of a number of political opponents and the closure of the *Fiji Times* for having resorted to "abusive language," contrary to traditional Fijian values. After a period of decline, the movement was revived in April 2000 under the leadership of Tevita BOLOBOLO and Apisai Tora, former leader of the PANU, and many of its members supported the May 2000 coup. Despite previous ties to the SVT, a number of the Movement's leaders backed formation of the BKV (see under PANU) in 2001. In 2008 it objected to the proposal to dereserve native land.

LEGISLATURE

Under the 1970 Constitution, **Parliament** consisted of an appointed Senate of 22 members serving staggered six-year terms and an elected House of Representatives of 22 Fijian, 22 Indian, and 8 "general" members serving five-year terms, subject to dissolution. Both bodies were suspended in the wake of the May 1987 coup. The 1990 constitution provided for a bicameral legislature that was overtly discriminatory, while its 1997 successor, without restoring ethnic parity, made substantial concessions to Indo-Fijian demands. Under pressure from the leader of the December 2006 coup, President Iloilo dissolved Parliament, and as of May 2009 no steps had been taken by the interim government to reconvene or reconstitute it.

Senate (*Seniti*). The 1990 basic law called for a nonelective upper house of 34 seats, 24 for Fijians nominated by the Great Council of Chiefs, 9 for Indo-Fijians and others, and 1 for inhabitants of Rotuma. Under the 1997 document the chamber's size was reduced to 32, with the president appointing 14 members nominated on a provincial basis, 9 named by the prime minister, 8 designated by the leader of the opposition, and 1 chosen by the Rotuma Council.

The Senate term is concurrent with that of the lower house.

President (at dissolution): Taito WAQAVAKATOGA.

House of Representatives (*Vale*). The 1990 Constitution called for an elective lower house of 70 seats (37 reserved for Melanesians, 27 for Indians, 5 for others, and 1 for the island of Rotuma). In 1997 the size of the House was increased to 71, of which 25 were to be open to all races, with 23 reserved for Melanesians, 19 for Indo-Fijians, 3 for general voters, and 1 for Rotuman Islanders. The House term is five years, subject to early dissolution. At the election of May 6–13, 2006, the Fiji United Party won 36 seats; the Fiji Labour Party, 31; the United People's Party, 2; and independents, 2. Ten other parties contested the election but none won a seat.

Speaker (at dissolution): Ratu Epeli NAILATIKAU.

INTERIM CABINET

[as of October 1, 2009]

Prime Minister	Commodore Frank Vorege Bainimarama
Ministers	
Defense, National Security, Immigration	Brigadier Ratu Epeli Ganilau
Education, National Heritage, Culture and Arts, Youth and Sports, Labour, Industrial Relations and Employment	Filipe Bole
Finance, National Planning, Sugar, Public Service, People's Charter for Change, Information, Provincial Development, Indigenous and Multi-Ethnic Affairs	Commodore Frank Vorege Bainimarama
Foreign Affairs, Civil Aviation, International Cooperation	Ratu Inoke Kubuabola
Health	Neil Sharma
Justice, Electoral Reform, Public Enterprises, Anti-Corruption, Industry, Tourism, Trade, Communication	Aiyaz Sayed-Khaiyum
Lands and Mineral Resources	Netani Sukanaivalu
Local Government, Urban Development, Housing and Environment	Colonel Samuela Saumatua

Primary Industries	Joketani Cokanasiga
Public Utilities, Works, and Transport	Brigadier Timoci Lesi Natuva
Women, Social Welfare and Poverty Alleviation	Jiko Luveni [f]
Attorney General	Aiyaz Sayed-Khaiyum

[f] = female

COMMUNICATIONS

Freedom of speech and of the press is guaranteed under the 1997 constitution, but such freedoms may be limited by law for reasons that include preserving national security, public safety, public order, and public morality, as well as "preventing attacks on the dignity of individuals, groups, or communities or respected offices or institutions in a manner likely to promote ill will between the races or communities or the oppression of, or discrimination against, any person or persons."

After December 2006 the interim government allegedly threatened and harassed journalists critical of its policies. In September 2007 a one-month state of emergency temporarily curtailed press activity. On February 25, 2008, *Fiji Sun* editor Russell Hunter, an Australian citizen, was declared a prohibited immigrant and summarily deported after his paper ran stories about alleged tax evasion by Finance Minister Chaudhry. On May 1 *Fiji Times* Australian publisher Evan Hannah was similarly deported. In July Bainimarama announced his government's intention to consolidate and strengthen existing media laws and create a new tribunal with power to hear complaints and impose fines on media breaking the law, and in December veteran Television New Zealand presenter Barbara Dreaver was unexpectedly denied entry at Nadi airport and sent back to Auckland without explanation.

Following its consolidation of power on April 10, 2009, the interim government dispatched Ministry of Information officials to the newsrooms of the main broadcast stations and newspapers, warning journalists not to disseminate "negative' reports about the government on pain of closure. Most media refused to promulgate any political news, and newspapers published blank pages, in protest. One Australian and two New Zealand journalists were deported and three local journalists were temporarily detained. The Fiji Media Council (Suva), the Pacific Island News Association-PACNEWS (Suva), the International Federation of Journalists (Brussels), Reporters without Borders (Paris), and the Committee to Protect Journalists (New York) decried these actions as censorship and stifling legitimate political reporting. Internet blogs such as Fiji Uncensored and Coup Four And A Half sprang up to fill the vacuum of political news from Fiji

Press. The first three of the following papers are owned by the international media tycoon Rupert Murdoch; all are published in Suva: *The Fiji Times* (30,000), founded in 1869, in English; *Nai Lalakai* (20,000), Fijian weekly; *Shanti Dut* (10,000), Hindustani weekly; *Fiji Daily Post*, public-private joint ownership, daily, in English; *Fiji Sun*, daily.

Broadcasting and computing. The Fiji Broadcasting Commission operates several FM and AM radio stations broadcasting in English, Fijian, and Hindustani to approximately 520,000 receivers; in addition, the privately held Communications (Fiji) Ltd. currently broadcasts in English, Fijian, and Hindustani from separate FM outlets. In 1994 domestic television transmissions were launched by Fiji Television Limited; two companies currently provide subscription services. As of 2008 there were 122 Internet users per 1,000 inhabitants.

INTERGOVERNMENTAL REPRESENTATION

Ambassador to the U.S.: Winston THOMPSON.

U.S. Ambassador to Fiji: C. Steven McGANN.

Permanent Representative to the UN: Bernado VUNIBOBO.

IGO Memberships (Non-UN): ADB, CP, CWTH, Interpol, PC, PCA, PIF, WCO, WTO.

FINLAND

Republic of Finland
Suomen Tasavalta (Finnish)
Republiken Finland (Swedish)

Political Status: Independent since December 6, 1917; republic established July 17, 1919, under presidential-parliamentary system.

Area: 130,119 sq. mi. (337,009 sq. km.).

Population: 5,181,115 (2000C); 5,330,000 (2008E).

Major Urban Centers (2005E): HELSINKI (551,000), Espoo (239,000), Tampere (208,000), Turku (178,000).

Official Languages: Finnish, Swedish.

Monetary Unit: Euro (market rate December 1, 2009: 1 euro = $1.51US).

President: Tarja HALONEN (Finnish Social Democratic Party); reelected in second-round balloting on February 29, 2006, and inaugurated for a six-year term on March 1, 2006.

Prime Minister: Matti VANHANEN (Finnish Center); designated by the president on June 24, 2003, following the legislative election earlier that day; sworn in on June 24, 2003, as part of a three-party coalition government replacing Anneli JÄÄTTEENMÄKI (Finnish Center), who had resigned on June 18, 2003; reappointed by the president following legislative elections on March 18, 2007, and sworn in on April 19 as the leader of a four-party coalition government.

THE COUNTRY

A land of rivers, lakes, and extensive forests, Finland is, except for Norway, the northernmost country of Europe. More than 93 percent of the population is Finnish-speaking and belongs to the Evangelical Lutheran Church. The once-dominant Swedish minority, now numbering about 7 percent of the total, has shown occasional discontent but enjoys linguistic equality; there also is a small Lapp minority in the north. Women constitute approximately 48 percent of the labor force, concentrated in textile manufacture, clerical work, human services, and the public sector (with women holding 70 percent of all public sector jobs). Female participation in elective bodies is currently around 40 percent. Notably, the new cabinet installed in 2007 included 12 women, or 60 percent total, the highest percentage in the world at the time. In addition, there were 84 women elected to the Finnish Parliament, the largest number ever in legislative balloting in the country.

Finland underwent a tumultuous economic transformation in the 1980s and 1990s that ultimately modernized and diversified what was previously an agriculturally based economy. Once having prided itself on its ability to "live on its forest," Finland now devotes less than 8 percent of its labor force to agriculture and forestry. Finland's traditional leading exports of wood, paper, pulp, and other forestry-related products remain important sources of revenue, but during the 1990s they were supplanted as the leading merchandise earners by consumer electronics, especially cellular phones produced by Nokia, the largest private employer in Finland. In particular, Nokia dominated the global cellular phone market in the 1990s and not only helped lift the country out of a recession in 1993 but sparked six years of unprecedented nationwide growth. Finland was a founding member of the European Union's (EU) Economic and Monetary Union on January 1, 1999.

Finland has enjoyed steady growth since the mid-1990s, with GDP rising on average approximately 4 percent per year. Growth peaked in 2000 at 6 percent, and annual GDP growth remained between 1 and 2 percent during 2001–2004. Despite a labor dispute in the paper industry, overall growth remained strong in 2005 at 3.2 percent, and the GDP

grew at 3.8 percent in 2006 and 4.3 percent in 2007. In contrast, unemployment has remained high, hovering between 8 and 9 percent during 2000–2006. Inflation in 2006 was 2.2 percent and 2.5 percent in 2007, while unemployment declined to an average of 7.2 percent in the early months of 2007. Finland's trade surplus rose to $11.5 billion in 2007. Although corporate taxes were reduced from 29 percent to 22 percent in 2005, the government has enjoyed regular budget surpluses, with the 2007 surplus equal to 5.3 percent of GDP. The global financial crisis caused an economic contraction in Finland in 2008–2009 (see Current issues below). GDP growth slowed to 0.9 percent in 2008 and the government surplus fell to 4.2 percent of GDP as the result of reduced tax revenues. After six months of negative economic growth, Finland officially entered a recession in March 2009, with GDP expected to decline by 3–5 percent during the year. Meanwhile unemployment rose from 6.4 percent in 2008 to 7.6 percent by March 2009.

GOVERNMENT AND POLITICS

Political background. The achievement of Finnish independence followed some eight centuries of foreign domination, first by Sweden (until 1809) and subsequently, by virtue of Finland's status as a Grand Duchy, within the prerevolutionary Russian Empire. The nation's formal declaration of independence dates from December 6, 1917, and its republican constitution from July 17, 1919, although peace with Soviet Russia was not formally established until October 14, 1920. Soviet territorial claims led to renewed conflict during World War II, when Finnish troops distinguished themselves both in the so-called Winter War of 1939–1940 and again in the "Continuation War" of 1941–1944. Under the peace treaty signed in Paris in 1947, Finland ceded some 12 percent of its territory to the Soviet Union (the Petsamo and Salla areas in the northeast and the Karelian Isthmus in the southeast) and assumed reparations obligations that totaled an estimated $570 million upon their completion in 1952. A Treaty of Friendship, Cooperation, and Mutual Assistance with the Soviet Union, concluded under Soviet pressure in 1948 and renewed in 1955, 1970, and 1983, precluded the adoption of an anti-Soviet foreign policy.

Finnish politics from World War II to the late 1980s was marked by the juxtaposition of a remarkably stable presidency under J. K. PAASIKIVI (1946–1956), Urho K. KEKKONEN (1956–1981), and Mauno KOIVISTO (1981–1994) and a volatile parliamentary system that yielded a sequence of short-lived coalition governments based on shifting alliances. Most were center-left administrations in which the Finnish Social Democratic Party (*Suomen Sosiaalidemokraattinen Puolue*—SSDP) played a pivotal role, especially under the premierships of Kalevi SORSA between 1972 and 1987. A significant change occurred in the election of March 15–16, 1987, in which the conservative National Coalition (*Kansallinen Kokoomus*—Kok) gained 9 seats, drawing to within 3 of the plurality Social Democrats. On April 30, for the first time in 20 years, a Kok leader, Harri HOLKERI, became prime minister, heading a four-party coalition that included the SSDP, the Swedish People's Party (*Ruotsalainen Kansanpuolue/Svenska Folkpartiet*—RKP/SFP), and the Finnish Rural Party (*Suomen Maaseudun Puolue*—SMP), the last eventually withdrawing in August 1990. In second-round electoral college balloting on February 15, 1988, President Koivisto (SSDP) easily won election to a second six-year term.

In the face of mounting economic adversity that included surging unemployment, high interest rates, and a drastically weakened GDP, both the Kok and the SSDP fared poorly at the parliamentary poll of March 17, 1991, with the opposition Finnish Center (*Suomen Keskusta–Finlands Centern*—Kesk), led by Esko AHO, emerging as the core of a new center-right coalition that included the Kok, the RKP/SFP, and the Finnish Christian Union (*Suomen Kristillinen Liitto*—SKL). The balloting produced a record number of legislative turnovers, approximately two-thirds of the incumbents being denied reelection.

Following the 1991 election, Prime Minister Aho announced a drastic stabilization program to alleviate the country's worst recession since World War II. In November, with the economy continuing to worsen, the markka was devalued by 12.3 percent, while labor agreed to a wage freeze until 1993. In an effort to avoid further devaluation, the government in April 1992 announced public sector cuts equivalent to approximately 2 percent of GDP. Another devaluation, in the form of a decision to let the markka float vis-à-vis other European currencies, was nonetheless ordered in September.

Unexpectedly selected as the SSDP candidate in preference to former premier Sorsa, career diplomat Martti AHTISAARI was the comfortable victor in presidential elections held in two rounds on January 16 and February 6, 1994. In the runoff balloting, he took 53.9 percent of the vote, against 46.1 percent for Defense Minister Elisabeth REHN of the RKP/SFP.

Having agreed with Brussels in March 1994 on terms for entry into the European Union (EU, formerly the European Community—EC), Finland became the first of the three Scandinavian aspirants to conduct a referendum on the issue. Most of the political establishment favored entry, and Prime Minister Aho had deflected opposition from the farming constituency of his own Kesk party by appointing a vocal EU critic, Heikki HAAVISTO, as foreign minister in charge of the entry negotiations. The decision of the small anti-EU SKL in June to leave the coalition proved to be only a minor setback. Held on October 16, the referendum yielded a 53 to 47 percent margin in favor of entry, the majority "yes" vote of urban southern areas outweighing the mainly "no" verdict of the rural north.

With EU entry safely accomplished on January 1, 1995, the Aho government faced a general election amid continuing economic adversity, a modest upturn in 1994 not having reduced unemployment appreciably (unemployment peaked at 22 percent). The result of the balloting on March 19 was a swing to the left, the Social Democrats achieving their highest postwar vote share and the Left-Wing Alliance (*Vasemmistoliitto*—Vas) also gaining ground. A month later SSDP leader Paavo LIPPONEN formed an ideologically diverse ("rainbow") coalition government that included the RKP/SFP, Kok, the Vas, and the Green League.

The electoral swing to the left in 1995 was attributed to public disenchantment with the harsh economic consequences of the previous government's free-market, deregulatory policies, which were seen as having accentuated the damaging effects of international economic recession. It also appeared that Finnish voters sought to balance the new international course represented by EU membership with familiar welfare state policies at the domestic level. There was nevertheless consensus within the new coalition that the austerity program instituted by the previous government should be continued, albeit with greater emphasis on job creation.

The SSDP retained its plurality in the legislative balloting of March 21, 1999, although its seat total declined from 63 to 51. The Kok finished second with 48 seats, followed by the Kesk, whose total jumped from 39 in 1995 to 46. After several weeks of negotiations, the five parties of the previous coalition agreed to form a new government, which was installed on April 15 under Lipponen's continued leadership.

Foreign Minister Tarja HALONEN of the SSDP led seven candidates in first-round presidential balloting on January 16, 2000, with

40 percent of the vote. She defeated Aho, 51.6 to 48.4 percent, in the runoff poll on February 6 and was inaugurated as Finland's first female president on March 1.

The recent trend of close elections continued on March 16, 2003, as the Kesk captured 55 seats; the Kesk formed a three-party coalition government on April 15 with the former ruling SSDP (53 seats) and the RKP/SFP (8 seats) headed by the Kesk's Anneli JÄÄTTEENMÄKI. With the appointment of Jäätteenmäki, Finland became the only country in Europe with both a female president and prime minister. However, Jäätteenmäki resigned on June 18 following a major dispute over the possible leaking of secret documents (see Current issues, below). She was succeeded on June 24 by Matti VANHANEN of the Kesk.

President Halonen won reelection in January 2006, narrowly defeating Sauli NIINISTÖ, 51.8 to 48.2 percent, in the second round of balloting. The election largely focused on the future direction of Finland's relationship with Europe, the North Atlantic Treaty Organization (NATO), and the effects of globalization (see Foreign relations, below).

The Kesk narrowly retained a plurality in the March 18, 2007, legislative election, securing 51 seats, compared to 50 for Kok and 45 for the SSDP. In view of the better than expected showing by the conservative parties, the SSDP was dropped from the four-party (Kesk, Kok, RKP/SFP, and Green League) coalition installed under Vanhanen's continued premiership on April 19.

In municipal elections in September 2008 that were marred by a controversy over e-voting (see Current issues below), the Kok secured the highest number of votes, followed by the SDP, and the Kesk which both saw their vote totals decline from the 2004 local elections. The True Finn Party (*Perussuomalaiset*—PS), which placed fifth in the polling, gained the largest percentage of votes with an increase of 4.5 percent from the previous balloting.

Constitution and government. The constitution of 1919 provided for a parliamentary system in combination with a strong presidency, which in practice has tended to grow even stronger because of the characteristic division of the legislature (*Eduskunta/Riksdagen*) among a large number of competing parties. The president is directly elected (since 1994) for a six-year term in two rounds of voting if no candidate obtains an absolute majority in the first. The head of state is directly responsible for foreign affairs and, until recently, shared domestic responsibilities with the prime minister and the cabinet. The *Eduskunta,* a unicameral body of 200 members, is elected by proportional representation for a four-year term, subject to dissolution by the president. The judicial system includes a Supreme Court, a Supreme Administrative Court, courts of appeal, and district and municipal courts.

Administratively, Finland is divided into 12 provinces (*läänit*), which are subdivided into 415 municipalities and rural communes. The 11 mainland provinces are headed by presidentially appointed governors, while the Swedish-speaking island province of Åland enjoys domestic autonomy (see Related Territory, below).

After decades of piecemeal reform of constitutional law, the *Eduskunta* on February 12, 1999, endorsed the text of a new constitution and, following the elections of March, the new basic law also was formally approved by the new legislature. The new constitution, which entered into force on March 1, 2000, strengthened the powers of Parliament at the expense of the presidency by, among other things, limiting the president's authority in domestic matters (for example, subsequent prime minister-designates were named by the Parliament, not the president).

Foreign relations. Proximity to the Soviet Union and recognition of that country's security interests were decisive factors in the shaping of post–World War II Finnish foreign policy, although Helsinki followed a course of strict neutrality and abstention from participation in military alliances. The desire "to remain outside the conflicting interests of the Great Powers," formally recorded in the Soviet-Finnish treaty of 1948, did not preclude active and independent participation in such multilateral organizations as the United Nations (UN), the Nordic Council, and eventually the Organization for Economic Cooperation and Development. Finland also was a leading proponent of the Conference on (later Organization for) Security and Cooperation in Europe (CSCE/OSCE), in recognition of which the landmark CSCE Final Act of 1975 was concluded in Helsinki.

Joining the European Free Trade Association (EFTA) at its inception in 1960 as an associate member, Finland, on a similar basis, became in 1973 the first free-market economy to be linked to the Soviet bloc's Council for Mutual Economic Assistance. In 1985 it became a full member of EFTA. Despite continuing ties to its eastern neighbor, trade with the Soviet Union declined sharply after 1988, with the country moving to adopt EC industrial standards to protect its access to the EC's impending unified market. On January 20, 1992, the 1948 treaty was formally superseded by a new Russo-Finnish mutual cooperation pact, and on March 18 Finland applied for EC membership. As a prelude to EC entry, Finland became a signatory on May 2 of the European Economic Area treaty between the EC and EFTA countries. Earlier in March it had become a founding member of the Council of the Baltic Sea States.

Negotiations on EC/EU membership opened formally in February 1993 and were successfully completed in March 1994, entry being duly accomplished January 1, 1995, following final parliamentary approval on November 18. In April 1994 Finland became linked to NATO by joining the alliance's Partnership for Peace program. Approximately one-third of the Finns favored joining NATO, and the issue became central during the 2006 presidential election.

In response to the ongoing crisis in Iraq, Finland has joined the International Reconstruction Fund Facility for Iraq and pledged $6.2 million for reconstruction. Finnish firms also have won reconstruction contracts. However, the government has rejected U.S. requests for Finnish peacekeeping forces to be deployed to Iraq.

A key factor in the Finnish vote to enter the EU was a belief that membership would afford protection against a revival of Russian imperialism. Much discussion had been generated by the strong showing of Vladimir Zhirinovsky's ultra-nationalist Liberal Democrats in the 1993 Russian election and of Zhirinovsky's declared aim of restoring Finland to the Russian empire. The subsequent course of Moscow's external policy provided little reassurance for the Finns. Indeed, President Boris Yeltsin of Russia reopened old wounds when he was in Helsinki for a summit with U.S. president Bill Clinton in March 1997. Yeltsin said Russia was opposed to any attempt by Finland to join NATO. His remark and the summit itself renewed discussion of Finland's balancing act on the political continuum between East and West. Notwithstanding its participation with NATO and the EU, Finland sought to maintain friendly relations with Moscow by signing six economic and military cooperation accords with Russia during a visit to Helsinki by Prime Minister Viktor Chernomyrdin in May 1996. Relations with Russia subsequently continued to improve as President Halonen and Russian president Vladimir Putin forged a strong working relationship; this yielded agreements in 2006 on immigration along their common border and a Russian pledge to pay off its outstanding debt, originating back in the Soviet era.

Finland assumed the six-month rotating EU presidency on July 1, 2006. Its presidency was marked by efforts to prevent a weakening of the proposed EU Constitution, which the Finnish legislature ratified in December.

Finland's foreign policy continued to encompass multiple regions in 2007. In September, Finland and Vietnam signed an accord, in which the Finnish government agreed to provide $26.7 million in technical and logistical support for integration of minority groups in Vietnam. Finland hosted peace talks between rival Iraqi groups in an attempt to end sectarian violence in the same month.

Finland agreed to contribute troops to the EU-led peacekeeping operation in the Central African Republic in January 2008. On March 7, Finland recognized Kosovo's independence, attracting opposition from Serbia's ally Russia, which rejected international recognition for the breakaway Serbian province. The parliament also approved the participation of Finnish troops in NATO's rapid reaction force in March. Finland had about 100 peacekeepers deployed in Afghanistan as part of the NATO-led International Security Assistance Force as of mid-2008.

In May 2008 two Finnish reporters were detained in China, but released nine hours later. The government formally protested the arrests. The Parliament approved the EU's Lisbon Treaty on a vote of 151 in favor and 27 opposed in June. Finland also announced support for Turkish membership in the EU. In October former president Ahtisaari received a Nobel Peace Prize for his role in mediating conflicts around the globe.

Current issues. The 2003 Iraq War played an important role in Finnish domestic and foreign policy. In early 2003 President Halonen and Prime Minister Lipponen called for Iraqi compliance with the UN Security Council resolutions. However, they asserted that UN weapons inspectors had not found any clear evidence justifying an attack against Iraq. In addition, Finland's foreign minister maintained that without an additional Security Council mandate, any preemptive war against Iraq would be "illegal and should not be allowed." However, during the March 2003 elections Kesk leader Anneli Jäätteenmäki allegedly leaked foreign ministry documents to the news media that seemed to indicate that Prime Minister Lipponen would ultimately support the U.S. coalition against Iraq. The issue appeared to resonate with the

Finnish electorate, which, by a 79 percent majority, did not favor any kind of military action against Iraq, and the Kesk was rewarded with a narrow legislative victory. However, Jäätteenmäki resigned as prime minister after only two months in office when coalition partner SSDP withdrew its support for her because of the leaked documents issue. (Jäätteenmäki apologized for the release of the papers but denied they were secret. In March 2004 she was acquitted on all charges related to the matter.) The scandal reportedly raised issues about the Finnish public's trust in government—previously ranked by Transparency International as one of the world's least corrupt—as well as the future direction of Finland's foreign policy.

In 2006 Finland began construction of the first nuclear power plant in the Baltic region since the Chernobyl accident in 1986. Currently under construction on Eurajoki, the reactor is scheduled to come online in 2009. With limited domestic energy resources, Finland derives about two-thirds of its energy from foreign sources, and nuclear energy offers an avenue to avoid increased levels of dependence on Russian fossil fuels.

In 2008 the new center-right coalition government quickly announced an ambitious job creation program that called for tax cuts of $3.5 billion, centered on a reduction of the VAT (value added tax) from 17 percent to 12 percent. At the same time, increases in taxes on alcohol, tobacco, and fuel were announced, and a nationwide smoking ban in public places was enacted. The ruling coalition also began a multiyear program to increase the pay of health and social workers, along with other increases in spending on social services. The government also continued its privatization program, selling its shares in the Kemira fertilizer company for $890 million. By 2008, the government still had investments of more than $38 billion in 19 Finnish firms that employed approximately 200,000 people.

On November 7, 2007, Pekka-Eric Auvinen, a student, shot and killed eight students and school officials, injuring an additional dozen before shooting himself at the Jokela High School. Finland had the highest rate of gun ownership in Western Europe, but the incident led the government to drop objections to an EU plan to raise the minimum age of gun ownership to 18 years (it was previously 15 with adult supervision). Another school shooting occurred on September 23, 2008 in Kauhajoki. A hospitality college student, Matti Juhanni Saari, killed nine students and an instructor, before shooting himself. The government proposed new restrictions to prevent people with mental disabilities from obtaining guns.

Foreign Minister Ikkla KANERVA was forced to resign in April 2008 after it was discovered that he had sent about 200 text messages to an erotic dancer. Although Kanerva did not break any laws, the incident limited his credibility in diplomatic negotiations. In municipal balloting in October, an e-voting pilot program had numerous problems, resulting in the loss of approximately 2 percent of the votes. In April 2009 the Finnish Supreme Court annulled the results of the districts that used e-voting machines and ordered a new round of balloting.

In February 2009 the government announced a €2 billion stimulus program, equal to 1.7 percent of GDP, in an effort to counter the nation's recession. Additional spending was directed to construction projects and worker retraining.

POLITICAL PARTIES

Finland's multiparty system, based on proportional representation, prevents any single party from gaining a parliamentary majority. Although still used for assessment of broad electoral trends, the traditional classification of parties as "socialist" and "nonsocialist" became less relevant in the 1980s, as policy differences eroded and coalitions were formed across what remained of the right-left ideological divide.

Government Parties:

Finnish Center (*Suomen Keskusta–Finlands Centern*—Kesk). The group that was formed in 1906 as the Agrarian Union (*Maalaisliitto*) and renamed the Center Party (*Keskustapuolue*) in 1965 has traditionally represented rural interests, particularly those of the small farmers. Because of major population shifts within the country, it now draws additional support from urban areas. The party surged from 40 parliamentary seats in 1987 to a plurality of 55 in 1991, with the 37-year-old Esko Aho becoming the youngest prime minister in Finnish history, but also, amid economic recession, the most unpopular by 1994. The party slumped to 44 seats in the 1995 balloting, after which it went into the opposition. It secured 48 seats in 1999.

Aho also served as the Kesk standard-bearer in the 2000 presidential campaign, finishing second with 34.4 percent in the first-round voting and nearly defeating the SSDP's Tarja Halonen in the second round on the strength of a last-minute popularity surge based in part on his opposition to EU sanctions against Austria. The Kesk continued to gain strength and earned 55 seats in the 2003 elections.

Prime Minister Vanhanen opted to run for the January 2006 presidential elections and finished third in the first round of voting with 18.6 percent of the vote. He has continued to aggressively integrate Finland into the European and global economy while adopting a more moderate position on social issues. For instance, Vanhanen met with Muslim leaders and expressed disappointment that cartoons depicting the Prophet Mohammed had been posted on the Web site of Suomen Sisu, a Finnish right-wing nationalist group.

In the March 2007 elections, the Kesk lost 4 seats but remained the largest single party in the legislature with 51. In the 2008 municipal balloting, Kesk won 20.1 percent of the vote, a decrease of 2.7 percent from the previous local elections.

Leaders: Matti VANHANEN (Prime Minister and Chair), Mauri PEKKARINEN (Minister of Economic Affairs), Timo KALLI (Chair of the Parliamentary Group), Jarmo KORHONEN (Secretary General), Markus OJAKOSKI, Mari Johanna KIVINIEMI (Deputy Group Chair).

National Coalition Party (*Kansallinen Kokoomus*—KK or Kok). A conservative party formed in 1918, the Kok is the prime representative for private enterprise and the business community as well as for landowners. In the March 1979 general election, it displaced the SKDL (see Vas, below) as the second-largest parliamentary party. Retaining this position in 1983 and 1987, the Kok's success in the latter election enabled it to return to government (after 21 years in the opposition) as head of a coalition government. The party dropped to third place in 1991, when its representation plummeted from 53 to 40 seats and it became a junior coalition partner. It continued in this status following a marginal decline to 17.9 percent in the 1995 balloting. However, in 1999 the Kok made the biggest gain of any of the 13 parties by picking up 7 additional seats. Riitta UOSUKAINEN, speaker of the Parliament, gained 12.8 percent of the vote in the first round of the 2000 presidential balloting.

In the March 2003 parliamentary elections the Kok won 40 seats, a drop from the 45 seats it held after the 1999 election. The Kok has placed Finland's role in the EU as the centerpiece of its platform. It favors enlargement of the EU while simultaneously calling for clarifying and strengthening the rules that govern that institution. Sauli Niinistö continued these themes in his unsuccessful 2006 presidential bid. Embracing globalization and free trade, Niinistö called for a greater role for Finland in both European and transatlantic affairs.

In the 2007 legislative elections the Kok secured 50 seats and became the second largest party in parliament. Niinistö was subsequently elected speaker of Parliament. The Kok placed first in the 2008 municipal balloting and won 23.5 percent of the vote and elected 2,021 councilors.

Leaders: Jyrki KATAINEN (Chair and Deputy Prime Minister); Sampsa KATAJA, Eija-Riitta KORHOLA, Henna VIRKKUNEN (Vice Chairs); Paula RISIKKO (Minister of Health and Social Services and Vice Chair); Sauli NIINISTÖ (Speaker of the Parliament and 2006 presidential candidate); Pekka RAVI (Chair of Parliamentary Group); Harri JASKARI (Secretary General).

Green League (*Vihreä Liitto*—VL or Vihr). The Vihr was launched in 1988 as an unstructured alliance of several mainstream environmental organizations, including the **Green Parliamentary Group** (*Vihreä Eduskuntaryhmä*), which had won 2 seats in 1983, 4 in 1987, and 10 in 1991. The Vihr fell back to 9 seats on a 6.5 vote share in 1995 (but nevertheless entered government for the first time) before rebounding to 11 seats in 1999. Heidi HAUTALA, a member of Parliament, served as the Vihr presidential candidate in 2000, collecting 3.3 percent of the first-round votes. Vihr earned its best ever result in the March 2003 parliamentary elections, increasing its number of seats from 11 to 14. The current party leadership was elected at a party conference on May 22, 2005.

In the 2007 legislative balloting the Vihr gained 15 seats and subsequently joined the Kesk-led coalition government. Vihr gained 370 seats on municipal councils in the 2008 local elections.

Leaders: Tarja CRONBERG (Minister of Labor and Party Chair); Tuija BRAX (Minister of Justice); Sulevi RIUKULEHTO; Anni SINNEMÄKI (Chair of Parliamentary Group); Ville NIINISTÖ, Janne LÄNSIPURO (Deputy Chairs); Ari HEIKKINEN (Secretary).

Swedish People's Party (*Ruotsalainen Kansanpuolue/Svenska Folkpartiet*—RKP/SFP). Liberal in outlook, the SFP has represented the political and social interests of the Swedish-speaking population since 1906. Consistently taking 5–6 percent of the overall vote and with strong indirect support in the predominantly Swedish Åland Islands (see Related Territory), it has participated in a variety of postwar coalitions. In the 1994 presidential balloting its candidate, Elisabeth Rehn, was the surprise runner-up in the first round but lost in the runoff to Ahtisaari. The RKP/SFP won 12 seats in the 1995 and 1999 legislative polls, while Rehn declined to 7.9 percent of the vote in the first-round presidential balloting in 2000. The RKP/SFP suffered a serious setback in the March 2003 parliamentary elections by retaining only 7 of its 10 seats. In June 2006 Stefan Wallin was elected party chair. In the 2007 elections the party secured 9 seats and reentered the governing coalition after securing the support of the lone representative of the Åland Islands, a member of the independent voters' bloc, the **Bourgeois Alliance** (*Borgerlig Allians*).

In the 2008 municipal balloting, the RKP/SFP secured 510 seats, maintaining majorities in ethnically Swedish areas.

Leaders: Stefan WALLIN (Minister of Culture and Sport and Chair); Monica SIRÉN-AURA, Christel LILJESSTRÖM, Nils TORVALDS (Deputy Chairs); Ulla-Maj WIDEROOS (Parliamentary Group Leader); Ulla ACHRÉN (Secretary General).

Other Parliamentary Parties:

Finnish Social Democratic Party (*Suomen Sosiaalidemokraattinen Puolue*—SSDP). The SSDP was formed in 1899 as the Finnish Labor Party. It is supported mainly by skilled laborers and lower-class, white-collar workers, with additional support from small farmers and professionals. It has been the largest party in the legislature following virtually every election since 1907, one of the most conspicuous exceptions being in 1991 when, running second to the Center Party, its parliamentary representation dropped from 56 to 48 seats. Having been in office continuously since 1966, the party went into opposition in 1991. Paavo Lipponen led the party to a major victory (in Finnish terms) in the 1995 elections, the SSDP vote share increasing by over six points to 28.3 percent. However, the SSDP declined to 51 seats on a vote share of 22.9 percent in 1999.

After Martti Ahtisaari decided not to run in the May 1999 primary for the party's 2000 presidential nomination, the SSDP elected Foreign Minister Tarja Halonen as its candidate. As is the custom for Finnish presidents, Halonen resigned from the party following her election in order to serve in a nonpartisan capacity. In the March 2003 parliamentary elections the SSDP held onto its 53 seats but was unable to maintain its majority position in the coalition government. Lipponen stepped down as prime minister and assumed the role of the speaker of Parliament.

President Halonen stood for reelection in January 2006 and won after the second round of voting in a surprisingly close election against the Kok's Sauli Niinistö. Reaffirming the party's center-left position, Halonen defended the role of the welfare state in protecting citizens' rights and needs in a globalized world. Support from the labor unions played a critical role in her victory. Party Chair Paavo LIPPON announced in March 2006 that he would resign his position after holding the post for more than 12 years. In June 2006 former party secretary Eero Heinaluoma was elected chair.

The SSDP suffered its worst electoral defeat since 1962 in the 2007 legislative balloting, falling to the third largest parliamentary group, and became part of the opposition. In June 2008 a party conference elected Jutta Urpilainen chair of the SSDP. Support for the SSDP also declined in the October municipal elections where its vote share declined by 2.9 percent, compared with the 2004 local polling.

Leaders: Jutta URPILAINEN (Chair), Ari KORHOREN (General Secretary), Tarja FILATOV (Chair of the Parliamentary Group), Ilkka KANTOLA, Maria GUZENINA-RICHARDSON, Pia VIITANEN (Vice Chair).

Left-Wing Alliance (*Vasemmistoliitto*—VL or Vas). Vas was launched in April 1990 during a congress in Helsinki of representatives of the leading communist and left-socialist groups. Following the congress, the Finnish Communist Party (*Suomen Kommunistinen Puolue*—SKP) and its electoral affiliate, the Finnish People's Democratic League (*Suomen Kansan Demokraattinen Liitto*—SKDL), voted to disband. (The SKP reorganized in 1994; see SKP, below.)

The SKDL front had been created in 1944 by the pro-Soviet SKP (founded in 1918) and had established a sizable electoral constituency, winning a narrow plurality in 1958 and participating in various center-left coalitions until 1982. Meanwhile, in 1969 the SKP had split into majority revisionist and minority Stalinist wings, the latter being formally ousted in 1984. In 1986 the SKP launched its own Democratic Alternative front, which achieved little more than to weaken the SKDL. The alliance and adoption of a left-socialist and anti-EC/EU platform at the 1990 congress alleviated most of these old rifts, with Vas advancing to 11.2 percent of the vote in 1995 and joining a coalition government headed by the Social Democrats. Vas won 20 seats in the 1999 poll, down 2 from 1995.

Vas gained an additional seat in the 2003 parliamentary elections to reach a total of 19 seats. Reacting against the economic pressures associated with globalization and the free movement of capital, Vas has defined its role as a defender of Finnish labor and agriculture.

In May 2006 Vas elected Martti Korhonen party chair. Korhonen immediately announced his intention to make "progressive tax reform" and the expansion of social welfare programs for the poor the centerpieces of the party's message for the 2007 election. The Vas secured 17 seats in the 2007 election. In local elections the following year, Vas secured 833 council seats.

Leaders: Martti KORHONEN (Chair), Annika LAPINTIE (Parliamentary Leader), Esko SEPPANEN (Member of European Parliament), Ralf SUND (Secretary and Party Election Coordinator), Pekka RISTELÄ (Secretary for International Affairs).

Christian Democrats in Finland (*Suomen Kristillisdemokraatit*—KD). The KD adopted its present name at a May 2001 party conference, having previously been called the Finnish Christian Union (*Suomen Kristillinen Liitto*—SKL). The SKL was formed in 1958 to advance Christian ideals in public life. It won 8 legislative seats in 1991 and joined a Center-headed coalition before withdrawing in 1994 because of its opposition to EU accession. It lost 1 of its seats on a 3 percent vote share in 1995 and won 10 seats in 1999. Emphasizing the need to reform the Finnish economy to be more socially and ecologically responsible, the KD suffered a setback in the March 2003 parliamentary elections, losing 3 of its 7 seats. For the 2007 poll the KD emphasized increased employment, the enhancement of family life, and guaranteed access for all of the population to basic public services, and won 7 seats. In the 2008 balloting, the KD gained 351 seats on municipal councils.

Leaders: Paivi RÄSÄNEN (Chair), Marjo ANTTOORA, Peter ÖSTMAN, Asmo MAANSELKÄ (Vice Chair), Annika KOKKLO (Secretary General), Sari ESSAYAH (Secretary), Bjarne KALLIS (Parliamentary Leader).

True Finn Party (*Perussuomalaiset*—PS). Formerly known as the Finnish Rural Party (*Suomen Maaseudun Puolue*—SMP), the PS has roots that extend back to a small Poujadist faction—a conservative reactionary movement seeking to protect small business—that broke from the Agrarian Union in 1956. As a protest group representing farmers and merchants, the SMP made substantial gains in the 1983 election, winning 17 seats and subsequently joining the government coalition; its representation fell to 9 seats in 1987, and it was awarded only one cabinet post as a member of the Holkeri coalition. It withdrew from the coalition in August 1990, slipped to 7 seats in 1991, and, having opposed EU membership, retained only 1 seat in 1995 (with a 1.3 percent vote share). The renamed grouping won 1 seat in 1999 with a vote share of 1 percent. During the March 2003 election, the PS adopted a platform that mixed socialism with a hard-line, right-wing populist stance that emphasized low taxes, encouraged small businesses, and advocated relief for personal debt. Its resurgence as an alternative party has been in part credited to the charismatic personality of its new leader, Timo Soini.

The party gained 2 additional seats in the 2007 legislative elections to bring its representation to 5. It also increased its representation in the 2008 local elections, securing 443 council seats, up from 106 in 2004.

Leaders: Timo SOINI (Chair and 2003 presidential candidate), Raimo VISTBACKA (Vice Chair), Hannu PURHO (Public Relations Officer), Raimo VISTBACKA (Parliamentary Leader), Tony HALME (Member of Parliament).

Other Parties Contesting the 2007 Legislative Election:

Liberals (*Liberaalit*). This grouping was launched as the Liberal People's Party (*Liberaalinen Kansanpuole*—LKP) in 1965 as a merger of the former Finnish People's Party and the Liberal Union. Having participated in most governments from 1966, the LKP contested the 1979 election in alliance with the Kesk and in 1982 voted to merge with that party while retaining its own identity. The LKP formally reestablished its independence in 1986, although many of its former supporters remained in the Kesk, and the LKP won no legislative seats in 1987, 1991, or 1995. It participated (unsuccessfully) in an electoral alliance with the NSP in 1999. In 2001 the LKP changed its name to the Liberals. The Liberals received less than 0.2 percent of the vote in 2007 and did not gain any seats in the 2008 council elections.

Leaders: Ilkka INNAMAA (Chair), Toni HEINONEN, Janne VAHALA (Deputy Chair).

Communist Party of Finland (*Suomen Kommunistinen Puolue*—SKP). A descendant of the original SKP (see Vas, above), the current SKP emerged at a congress in 1994 held by communists wishing to maintain a separate identity outside Vas. The reforged grouping opposed many policies of the subsequent rainbow government coalition and formally registered as a party in February 1997. The SKP secured only 0.8 percent of the vote in the 1999 legislative poll and also failed to capture any seats in the March 2003 and March 2007 parliamentary elections. The SKP did gain 9 council seats in the 2008 local elections.

Leaders: Yrgö HAKANEN (Chair), Riita TYNJÄ (Vice Chair), Arto VIITANIEMI (General Secretary).

Communist Workers' Party (*Kommunistinen Työväenpuolue*—KTP). The KTP was launched in May 1988 by a group of former Democratic Alternative Stalinists. The party contested the 1991, 1995, 1999, and 2003 elections under the rubric "For Peace and Socialism," winning less than 0.1 percent of the vote in 2003 and in 2007. It did not secure any seats in the 2008 municipal elections.

Leaders: Hannu HARJU (Chair), Heikki MÄNNIKKÖ (General Secretary).

Other parties contesting the 2007 election were: the **Senior Citizen Party** (*Suomen Senioripuolue*—SSP); led by Esko REPO, with 0.6 percent of the vote in 2007 and two council seats in the 2008 balloting; the **Independence Party** (*Itsenäisyyspuolue*—IP); led by Antti PESONEN, which secured 0.2 percent of the vote in 2007 and two council seats in 2008; the **Finnish Worker's Party** (*Suomen Työväenpuolue*—STP); led by Juhani TANSKI, and which received 0.1 percent of the vote in 2007, but no seats in 2008; **For the Poor** (0.1 percent); the **Finnish Patriotic Movement** (*Suomen Isänmaallinen Kansanliike*—SIK); less than 0.1 percent; and the **Finnish People's Blue-Whites** (*Suomen Kansan Sinivalkoiset*—SKS); led by Olavi MÄENPÄÄ, 0.1 percent.

In September 2007, the **Finnish Islamic Party** (*Soumen Islamilainen Poulue*—SIP) was founded by Abdullah TAMMI. The party sought to implement Islamic law and force Finland to withdraw its troops from Afghanistan.

LEGISLATURE

The **Parliament** (*Eduskunta/Riksdagen*) is a unicameral body of 200 members elected by universal suffrage on the basis of proportional representation in 15 districts. Its term is four years, although the president may dissolve the legislature and order a new election at any time. Following the election of March 18, 2007, the seat distribution was as follows: Finnish Center, 51; National Coalition Party, 50; Finnish Social Democratic Party, 45; Left-Wing Alliance, 17; Green League, 15; Swedish Peoples Party, 10 (Swedish Peoples Party, 9, and the Bourgeois Alliance, 1); Christian Democrats in Finland, 7; and the True Finn Party, 5.

Speaker: Sauli NIINISTÖ.

CABINET

[as of May 1, 2009]

Prime Minister	Matti Vanhanen (Kesk)
Deputy Prime Minister	Jyrki Katainen (Kok)
Ministers	
Agriculture and Forestry	Sirkka-Liisa Anttila (Kesk) [f]
Communications	Suvi Lindén (Kok) [f]
Culture and Sport	Stefan Wallin (RKP/SFP)
Defense	Jyri Häkämies (Kok)
Economic Affairs	Mauri Pekkarinen (Kesk)
Education	Henna Virkkunen (Kok) [f]
Environment	Paula Lehtornaki (Kesk) [f]
Finance	Jyrki Katainen (Kok)
Foreign Affairs	Alexander Stubb (Kok)
Foreign Trade and Development	Paavo Väyrynen (Kesk)
Health and Social Services	Paula Risikko (Kok) [f]
Housing	Jan Vapaavuori (Kok)
Interior	Anne Holmlund (Kok) [f]
Justice	Tuija Brax (Vihr) [f]
Labor	Tarja Cronberg (Vihr) [f]
Migration and European Affairs	Astrid Thors (RKP/SFP) [f]
Public Administration and Local Government	Mari Kiviniemi (Kesk) [f]
Social Affairs and Health	Liisa Hyssälä (Kesk) [f]
Transport	Anu Vehviläinen (Kesk) [f]

[f] = female

COMMUNICATIONS

Finland enjoys complete freedom of the press; broadcasting is largely over government-controlled facilities. In 2008, Reporters Without Borders had Finland tied with Ireland and Estonia for fourth place in press freedom.

Press. Newspapers are privately owned, some by political parties or their affiliates; many others are controlled by or support a particular party. The following are dailies published in Helsinki in Finnish, unless otherwise indicated: *Helsingin Sanomat* (446,000), independent; *Ilta-Sanomat* (218,000), independent; *Aamulehti* (Tampere, 135,500), National Coalition; *Turun Sanomat* (Turku, 115,000), independent; *Iltalehti* (135,000), independent; *Kaleva* (Oulu, 85,000), independent; *Maaseudun Tulevaisuus* (84,000, triweekly); *Kauppalehti* (85,000), independent; *Keskisuomalainen* (Jyväskylä, 77,000), independent; *Savon Sanomat* (Kuopio, 67,000), Center Party; *Hufvudstadsbladet* (52,500 daily, 61,000 Sunday), in Swedish, independent; *Demari* (17,000), organ of the Finnish Social Democratic Party.

News agencies. The Finnish News Agency (*Oy Suomen Tietotoimisto*—STT/*Finska Notisbyrån Ab*—FNB) is a major independent facility covering the entire country; most leading international news agencies also maintain offices in Helsinki.

Broadcasting and computing. Broadcasting is largely controlled by the state-owned Finnish Broadcasting Company (*Oy Yleisradio Ab*), which offers radio programming in both Finnish and Swedish and services two television channels; there is one commercial television channel, MTV 3, in addition to the offerings of local television outlets. As of 2008 there were 826.2 Internet users per 1,000 inhabitants.

INTERGOVERNMENTAL REPRESENTATION

Ambassador to the U.S.: Pekka LINTU.

U.S. Ambassador to Finland: Bruce J. ORECK.

Permanent Representative to the UN: Jarmo VIINANEN.

IGO Memberships (Non-UN): AC, ADB, AfDB, BIS, CBSS, CERN, CEUR, EBRD, EIB, ESA, EU, Eurocontrol, IADB, IEA, Interpol, IOM, NC, NIB, OECD, OSCE, PCA, WCO, WTO.

RELATED TERRITORY

Åland Islands (*Ahvenanmaa*). Lying in the Gulf of Bothnia between Finland and Sweden, the Ålands encompass more than 6,500 islands, fewer than 10 percent of which are populated. The total land area is 599 square miles (1,552 sq. km.), inclusive of inland water. The capital is Mariehamn (*Maarianhamina*) on Åland Island. The inhabitants, an overwhelming majority of whom are Swedish-speaking, were estimated to total 27,150 in 2007.

The islands were under Swedish rule until 1809, when Finland was ceded to Russia and they became part of the Finnish Grand Duchy. When Finland declared its independence in 1917, the islanders expressed a desire for reversion to Sweden but were obliged to settle for internal autonomy, a status that was confirmed by a League of Nations decision in 1921.

While constitutionally one of Finland's 12 provinces, the islands were granted expanded autonomy in 1951 and again in 1991 (effective January 1, 1993). Provisions included enhanced legislative and fiscal authority, in addition to a recognition of regional citizenship, the right to tax alcohol sales, and full control of postal services. In 1988 the principle of majoritarian parliamentary government was introduced, supplanting a system whereby any party electing at least 5 deputies to the 30-member legislature (*Lagting*) could secure representation in the Executive Council (*Landskapsstyrelse*). The leading political groups are the **Center Party** (*Åländsk Center*), the **Moderate Party** (*Frisinnad Samverkan*), the **Åland Social Democratic Party** (*Ålands Socialdemokrater*), the **Liberal Party of Åland** (*Liberalerna på Åland*), the independent **Nonaligned Rally** (*Obunden Samling*), the **Free-Thinking Cooperation Party** (*Frisinnad Samverkan*), the **List for Åland's Future** (*Ålands Framtid*), and the **Greens of Åland** (*Gröna på Åland*), the first three of which formed a coalition government after the election of October 20, 1991. In the October 1995 election the Social Democrats ran fourth (4 seats) and were not included in the coalition of the Center (9 seats) and Moderate (6 seats) parties, which invited an independent to join with them in forming a new government.

In the election of October 17, 1999, the Center and Liberal parties each won 9 seats, while the Moderates dropped to 4 and the Social Democrats to 3. A **Progress Group** (*Ålands Framstegsgrupp*) won 1, with the remaining seats being taken by the Nonaligned Rally. Once again the Center and Moderate parties, joined by the Independents, formed a governing coalition. The islands' single representative in the Finnish Parliament had consistently been returned by the **Åland Coalition** (*ÅlAAländsk Samling*), grouping all the main local parties. Elisabeth NAUCLÉR was elected in 2007 as the islands' representative. She was a member of the independent coalition **Bourgeois Alliance** (*Borgerlig Allians*) who followed tradition and supported the Swedish Peoples Party grouping in the Finnish Parliament.

In the October 21, 2007, elections, the Liberal Party of Åland won 10 seats; the Center Party, 8; the Nonaligned Rally, 4; the Social Democrats, 3; the Free-Thinking Cooperation Party, 3; and the List for Åland's Future, 2. Following the elections, Viveka Eriksson, the leader of the Liberal Party, became the first female head of government for the islands. Her predecessor, Roger Nordlund, was elected speaker of the *Lagting*. The next elections were scheduled for October 2011.

In a separate referendum on EU accession, held on November 20, 1994, the Åland islanders followed the rest of Finland (and Sweden) by voting in favor, but by a much larger margin of 73.7 to 26.3 percent. Thanks to the islands' special tax-free status, negotiated by Helsinki when Finland joined the EU in 1995, tourism is thriving, and Mariehamn has become a center for Baltic Sea ferry services.

During negotiations over ratification of the EU's Lisbon Treaty in 2008, the islands received concessions from the Finnish government and the EU on several issues, including recognition of Åland's autonomy in language and separate participation of the islands in several EU bodies. The concessions required changes to the formal 1991 act on autonomy which were presented to both the Åland and Finnish Parliaments in April 2009.

Leaders: Viveka ERIKSSON (Chair [*Landtråd*] of the *Landskapsstryrelse* and Prime Minister), Roger NORDLUND (Speaker [Talman] of the *Lagting*).

FRANCE

French Republic
République Française

Political Status: Republic under mixed parliamentary-presidential system established by constitution adopted by referendum of September 28, 1958, and instituted on October 4.

Area: 211,207 sq. mi. (547,026 sq. km.).

Population: 58,518,395 (1999C); 62,254,000 (2008E). Area and population figures are for metropolitan France (including Corsica); for overseas departments and other dependent jurisdictions, see Related Territories, below.

Major Urban Centers (2005E): PARIS (2,147,000), Marseilles (797,000), Lyons (473,000), Toulouse (435,000), Nice (338,000), Nantes (277,000), Strasbourg (275,000), Montpellier (249,000), Bordeaux (233,000), Rennes (210,000), Le Havre (186,000), Saint-Étienne (176,000).

Official Language: French.

Monetary Unit: Euro (market rate December 1, 2009: 1 euro = $1.51US).

President: Nicolas SARKOZY (Union for a Popular Movement); elected for a five-year term in runoff balloting on April 22, 2007, and inaugurated May 16, succeeding Jacques CHIRAC (Union for a Popular Movement).

Premier: François FILLON (Union for a Popular Movement); appointed by the president on May 17, 2007, succeeding Dominique de VILLEPIN (Union for a Popular Movement); tendered pro forma resignation on June 18, 2007, following the legislative election of June 10 and 17, and immediately reappointed by the president.

THE COUNTRY

The largest country of Western Europe in area and once the seat of a world empire extending onto five continents, France today is largely concentrated within its historical boundaries, maintaining its traditional role as the cultural center of the French-speaking world but retaining only a few vestigial political footholds in the Pacific and Indian Oceans and the Americas. While 94.4 percent of the population of metropolitan France, which includes the island of Corsica, are citizens, immigration has become a major political issue, the principal foreign ethnic groups being of North African (Arab), Portuguese, Turkish, Italian, Spanish, and German origins. French is the near-universal language, although German has co-official status in Alsace schools, and Alemannic, Basque, Breton, Corsican, and other languages and dialects are spoken to some extent in outlying regions. The Roman Catholic Church, officially separated from the state in 1905, is predominant, but there are substantial Protestant and Jewish minorities as well as a growing Muslim population, and freedom of worship is strictly maintained. Women constituted 47 percent of the labor force in 2007, concentrated in health and social work, wholesale and retail trade, public administration, other services, and manufacturing; female representation in the national legislature has risen in recent years, reaching more than 18 percent in the National Assembly elected in 2007.

In addition to large domestic reserves of iron ore, bauxite, natural gas, and hydroelectric power, France leads Western European countries in the production and export of agricultural products; it also is an important exporter of chemicals, iron and steel products, automobiles, machinery, precision tools, aircraft, ships, textiles, wines, perfumes, and *haute couture*. The industrial sector contributes 21 percent of GDP and 23 percent of employment, with the service sector accounting for most of the balance. Agriculture accounts for only 2 percent of GDP and 3 percent of employment.

Post–World War II economic planning, associated particularly with the name of Jean MONNET, contributed to the strengthening and expansion of an economy that had been traditionally characterized by fractionalization of industry and inefficient production techniques. The key turning point was France's participation in the European Community (EC, subsequently the European Union—EU), which began with formation of the European Coal and Steel Community in 1951.

GDP growth averaged 1.7 percent annually in 2000–2007 and was forecast at 1.6 percent in 2008, but by the end of that year France was feeling the effects of the global financial crisis and economic slowdown. For 2009 the economy was expected to contract by about 3 percent, with a modest recovery occurring in 2010.

GOVERNMENT AND POLITICS

Political background. For most of the century after its Revolution of 1789, France alternated between monarchical and republican forms

of government, the last monarch being NAPOLEON III (Louis Napoleon), who was deposed in 1870. Overall, the republican tradition has given rise to five distinct regimes: the First Republic during the French Revolution; the Second Republic after the Revolution of 1848; the Third Republic from 1870 to 1940; the Fourth Republic, proclaimed in October 1946 but destined to founder in the 1950s on dissension occasioned by the revolt in Algeria; and the Fifth Republic, established in 1958 by Gen. Charles DE GAULLE, who had headed the first postwar government.

Reentering public life at a moment of threatened civil war, de Gaulle agreed in May 1958 to accept investiture as premier on the condition that he be granted decree powers for six months and a mandate to draft a new constitution. Following adoption of the constitution by referendum and his designation by an electoral college, de Gaulle took office on January 8, 1959, as president of the Fifth Republic, naming as premier Michel DEBRÉ. De Gaulle's initially ambiguous policy for Algeria eventually crystallized into a declaration of support for Algerian self-determination, leading in 1962 to the recognition of Algerian independence.

Debré's resignation in April 1962 marked the end of the decolonization phase of the Fifth Republic and was followed by the induction as premier of Georges POMPIDOU, who was confirmed in office by a November 1962 election that gave the Gaullists a majority in the National Assembly.

Under a 1962 constitutional amendment calling for direct election of the president, de Gaulle won a second term in 1965 in a runoff against François MITTERRAND, leader of the newly formed Federation of the Democratic and Socialist Left (*Fédération de la Gauche Démocrate et Socialiste*—FGDS). In the 1967 National Assembly election, reflecting a further decline in the president's popularity, the Gaullists lost their majority and required the support of the Independent Republicans (*Républicans Indépendants*—RI), led by Valéry GISCARD D'ESTAING.

The Fifth Republic was shaken in May–June 1968 by a period of national crisis that began with student demonstrations and led to a nationwide general strike and an overt bid for power by leftist political leaders. After a period of indecision, de Gaulle dissolved the National Assembly and called for a new election, which yielded an unexpectedly strong Gaullist victory. Maurice COUVE DE MURVILLE succeeded Pompidou as premier. Following popular rejection of regional devolution and other constitutional proposals in a referendum held in April 1969, de Gaulle resigned, and the president of the Senate, Alain POHER, succeeded him on an interim basis. (De Gaulle died in November 1970.)

Former premier Pompidou, the Gaullist candidate for president, defeated Poher—a centrist accorded reluctant support by the left—in a June 1969 runoff. Pompidou then appointed Jacques CHABAN-DELMAS, president of the National Assembly, as premier in a cabinet that included former prime minister Debré as minister of defense and Giscard d'Estaing as minister of economy and finance. The revelation that Chaban-Delmas had utilized tax loopholes to personal advantage contributed to his resignation and replacement in July 1972 by Pierre MESSMER. Despite a loss of some 100 seats, the Gaullists succeeded in retaining a majority in the 1973 legislative election.

President Pompidou's death in April 1974 led to what was essentially a three-way presidential race among François Mitterrand, joint candidate of the Socialist Party (*Parti Socialiste*—PS), the French Communist Party (*Parti Communiste Français*—PCF), and other left-wing parties; Giscard d'Estaing for the center-right Independent Republicans; and Chaban-Delmas for the Gaullists. In the end, Giscard d'Estaing narrowly defeated Mitterrand in the May runoff. Although he was the first non-Gaullist president of the Fifth Republic, Giscard d'Estaing appointed a Gaullist, Jacques CHIRAC, as premier.

In August 1976 Premier Chirac resigned, charging that the president would not grant him sufficient authority to deal with the nation's problems; he was immediately replaced by the politically independent Raymond BARRE, an economist. Chirac then proceeded to reorganize the Gaullist party into the new Rally for the Republic (*Rassemblement pour la République*—RPR). The legislative election of March 1978 saw the "government majority," comprising the RPR and a new Giscardian coalition, the Union for French Democracy (*Union pour la Démocratie Française*—UDF), obtain a substantially larger margin of victory than in 1973.

Seeking reelection in 1981, President Giscard d'Estaing narrowly led a field of ten candidates (including Chirac for the RPR) in the first round, but he was defeated by Mitterrand in the May runoff. A month later, the Socialists secured a commanding legislative majority, after which Pierre MAUROY, who had succeeded Barre as premier in May, announced a new Socialist-led multiparty government.

Confronted by an increasingly critical left, Mauroy resigned in 1984 and was succeeded in July by Laurent FABIUS. During 1985 the prospect of "cohabitation" between a Socialist president and a rightist government loomed as former premier Chirac forged a conservative alliance between the RPR and the UDF. While the Socialists remained the largest single party in the National Assembly after the election of March 1986, the RPR/UDF grouping drew within a few seats of a majority and, with Chirac's redesignation as premier, *"la république à deux têtes"* became a reality. The delicate balance persisted until the 1988 presidential election, in which Mitterrand was the principal candidate of the left, while the rightist vote was split between Chirac, former premier Barre of the UDF, and Jean-Marie LE PEN of the far-right National Front (*Front National*—FN). Mitterrand obtained a plurality of 34.1 percent in first-round balloting and a 54.3 percent majority in the May runoff against Chirac.

Following Mitterrand's reelection, the Socialists and their allies registered substantial gains at an early legislative poll in June 1988 but fell short of an overall majority. Michel ROCARD, who had been named to head a minority administration in May, managed to form a new government with the support of a number of centrists and independents. Faced with dwindling legislative support, Rocard resigned in May 1991 and was succeeded by the country's first female premier, Edith CRESSON. Cresson's approval rating soon fell, however, and after an unprecedented Socialist drubbing in regional elections in March 1992, she was replaced by her finance minister, Pierre BÉRÉGOVOY.

In 1992 the Bérégovoy government convinced a narrow majority of voters to support the EC's Maastricht Treaty (see Foreign relations, below) but was beset by a series of scandals and pervasive public fears over third world immigration—fears that both the FN and the "respectable" conservative parties sought to articulate. In the 1993 legislative election, the RPR/UDF achieved greater gains than had been expected and emerged from the second round with 80 percent of the 577 assembly seats. The PS and its allies retained only 70 of their 282 seats. Bracing himself for a further period of "cohabitation," Mitterrand accepted the RPR's nomination of Edouard BALLADUR, a former finance minister, as the new premier.

The first round of the 1995 presidential election gave the Socialist Lionel JOSPIN a surprise lead with 23.3 percent, but the crucial outcome was Chirac's second-place showing (20.8 percent) over Balladur (18.6 percent). In the May runoff Chirac took 52.6 percent of the vote against Jospin. After a speedy transfer of power from the terminally ill Mitterrand, Chirac named Alain JUPPÉ, his campaign manager and the incumbent foreign minister, to head a new RPR/UDF government.

The Juppé government quickly ran into problems, beginning with the disclosure in June 1995 that luxury Paris apartments owned by the city had been allocated to senior Gaullists (including Chirac and Juppé) at strikingly low rents. By-election and Senate election reversals for the center-right parties in September, combined with plummeting opinion poll ratings, impelled Juppé to resign in November so that he could form a slimmer and reshaped government. It was immediately faced, however, with widespread action by public sector workers protesting against government economic policy.

In a surprising decision, President Chirac in April 1997 announced that parliamentary elections would be held ten months earlier than required. The first round was a disaster for the government, as the RPR/UDF secured only 30 percent of the vote. Consequently, Prime Minister Juppé announced that he would resign regardless of the second-round results. Chirac's personal appeal for support from the electorate had little effect, and the PS and its allies ended up with 274 seats, while the RPR fell to 134 and the UDF to 108. With support from the Communists, who had won 38 seats, Jospin was sworn in as prime minister and named a multiparty cabinet. The Socialist surge continued in the March 1998 regional elections, although several UDF incumbents retained regional presidencies thanks to the controversial backing of the FN.

In the first round of presidential voting on April 21, 2002, President Chirac emerged as the front-runner, with a lackluster 19.8 percent of the vote in a field of 16 candidates, but the second-place finish of the FN's Le Pen (16.9 percent) sent shockwaves through the political system and generated considerable international criticism. Undercut by a splintering among left and green parties, which had eight candidates on the ballot, and humiliated by his 16.2 percent showing, Premier Jospin immediately announced that he would retire from politics. The mainstream left, facing no viable alternative, joined with the center-right in rallying around Chirac, and in the runoff balloting on May 5 the incumbent received 82.2 percent of the vote. Buoyed by his success, Chirac then authorized formation of a new electoral coalition, the Union for the Presidential Majority (*Union pour la Majorité Présidentielle*—UMP), at the opening of the legislative campaign later in May.

With the RPR, much of the UDF, and most of the Liberal Democracy (*Démocratie Libérale*—DL) as its principal components, the UMP swept the National Assembly election of June 9 and 16, 2002, claiming 355 seats, to 140 for the PS, 21 for the PCF, and none for the FN. On June 17 President Chirac appointed as premier Liberal Democrat Jean-Pierre RAFFARIN, who had been serving as interim premier since May 6. Premier Raffarin's cabinet encompassed ministers from a number of center-right parties, chiefly the RPR, as well as independents. In November 2002 the UMP was reorganized as a unitary party, the Union for a Popular Movement (*Union pour un Mouvement Populaire*—UMP).

In regional elections on March 21 and 28, 2004, the UMP was resoundingly defeated by a PS/PCF/Greens coalition, which won 20 of 21 mainland regional councils. In response, Premier Raffarin, who had promoted an unpopular reform agenda aimed at tightening pensions and other social benefits, offered his resignation, but Chirac instead named Raffarin to head a reshuffled cabinet that was announced on March 31. Less than three months later the government suffered another major defeat, this time in the elections for the European Parliament. Whereas the left again made significant advances, the UMP's share of the vote dropped to 16.6 percent.

On February 28, 2005, paving the way for a national referendum on an EU constitution, a joint session of the Senate and National Assembly amended the French constitution to make it compatible with the proposed EU document. Despite Parliament's 730–66 vote (with 96 abstentions) in favor of the changes, nearly 55 percent of the voters rejected the May 29 referendum, dealing another blow to Chirac. Two days later Premier Raffarin tendered his resignation, with Chirac thereupon naming the minister of the interior, Dominique de VILLEPIN, as Raffarin's successor. A streamlined cabinet, announced on June 2, was most notable for the appointment of the UMP's president, Nicolas SARKOZY, as minister of state, a position second to premier.

On October 28, 2005, in the Paris suburb of Clichy-sous-Bois, young Muslims, mainly of North African and sub-Saharan descent, initiated a wave of violent rioting triggered by the deaths of two youths during a police chase. Over the next several days the disturbances expanded into other Parisian suburbs, long notorious for high unemployment, decrepit "council estate" housing, crime, and conflicts with police. The disturbances drew international attention to the status of the growing Muslim community in France, which, numbering 5–10 million according to various estimates, had faced major social barriers to integration, including widespread discrimination in housing and employment. By November 8 the riots had spread to some 300 communities, prompting Prime Minister de Villepin to declare a state of emergency. By mid-November the "popular revolt" (to quote a police intelligence agency report) had significantly diminished in intensity, although the state of emergency was not lifted until January 4, 2006. More than 250 schools and 200 other public buildings had been burned or attacked and 10,000 vehicles destroyed. Arrests totaled 4,800.

Firmly supported by the UMP, Sarkozy entered the 2007 presidential campaign in the lead against the Socialist Ségolène ROYAL. The first round of voting on April 8 concluded with Sarkozy (31.2 percent of the vote) and Royal (25.9 percent) finishing ahead of the UMP's François BAYROU (18.6 percent), the FN's Le Pen (10.4 percent), and eight other candidates. Bayrou refused to endorse either Sarkozy or Royal in the second round, while Le Pen called upon his supporters to boycott the April 22 contest. In the end, Sarkozy won 53.1 percent to Royal's 46.9 percent. The day after his May 16 inauguration Sarkozy named the UMP's François FILLON as prime minister, after which he focused his energies on winning the National Assembly election scheduled for June 3 and 17. After the first round some analysts predicted that the UMP might collect as many as 400–500 seats, but in the end Sarkozy had to settle for a reduced majority of 313 seats—36 fewer than the UMP had held before the election.

Constitution and government. The constitution of the Fifth Republic, accepted by a national referendum on September 28, 1958, retained many traditional features of France's governmental structure while significantly enhancing the powers of the presidency in a mixed presidential-parliamentary system. The president, originally chosen by an electoral college but now directly elected in accordance with a 1962 constitutional amendment, holds powers expanded not only by the terms of the constitution itself but also by President de Gaulle's broad interpretation of executive prerogative. In addition to having the power to dissolve the National Assembly with the advice (but not necessarily the concurrence) of the premier, the president may hold national referenda on some issues and is granted full legislative and executive powers in times of emergency. A partial check on the president's authority is the existence of a Constitutional Council, which supervises elections, passes on the constitutionality of organic laws, and must be consulted on the use of emergency powers.

The broad scope of presidential authority has curtailed the powers of the premier and the Council of Ministers, whose members are named by the president (upon the recommendation of the premier) and over whose meetings the president is entitled to preside. The cabinet has, however, been strengthened vis-à-vis the National Assembly, in that there are limits to the conditions under which the government can be defeated, although the government's ability to push through legislation without assembly debate was limited by passage in July 2008 of a major constitutional reform package. Described as encompassing the most significant changes ever made to the 1958 document, the package amended 47 of the 89 articles and added 9 new ones. Among other changes, presidents were limited to two terms in office, the assembly was given veto power over some presidential appointments, and troop deployments of more than four months now required legislative assent. In addition, a new article provided for an office of "Defender of Rights" (ombudsperson). The assembly must still give priority to bills presented by the government "during two weeks of sittings out of four" (with additional priority for finance and social security bills as well as bills concerning states of emergency), and the government may still open debate on a bill and propose amendments.

The legislative capacity of the once all-powerful National Assembly remains circumscribed. It can pass specific legislation in such fixed areas as civil rights and liberties, liability to taxation, the penal code, amnesty, declarations of war, electoral procedure, and the nationalization of industries; however, it can only determine "general principles" in the areas of national defense, local government, education, property and commercial rights, labor, trade unions, and social security. Unspecified areas remain within the jurisdiction of the executive, and no provision is made for the National Assembly to object to a government decree on the ground that it is within a parliamentary mandate. The assembly has, however, played a more assertive role recently, making greater use of its powers of parliamentary oversight to investigate the conduct of foreign policy and to judge the conduct of government ministers.

The Senate, most of whose members are indirectly elected by an electoral college, was reduced under the Fifth Republic to a distinctly subordinate status, with little power other than to delay the passing of legislation by the National Assembly. The 1958 constitution further provided that if the presidency of the republic becomes vacant, the president of the Senate will become president ad interim, pending a new election. A separate consultative body, the Economic and Social Council, represents the country's major professional interests and advises on proposed economic and social legislation.

The higher judiciary consists of courts of assize (*cours d'assises*), which handle major criminal cases; courts of appeal (*cours d'appel*), for appeals from lower courts; and the Court of Cassation (*Cour de Cassation*), which judges the interpretation of law and the procedural rules of the other courts. Courts of instance (*tribunaux d'instance*) function locally.

In 1999 both houses of the legislature approved an amendment "favoring equal access to women and men to elected positions," the most direct consequence being a requirement that political parties nominate men and women in equal proportion for public office, effective with the 2001 local elections (in towns of 3,500 or more). Another 1999 amendment authorized the "transfer of competencies" needed to establish the EU's economic and monetary union and, under the 1997 Treaty of Amsterdam, to establish rules governing immigration, border controls, and free movement of persons. Additionally, a July 1999 amendment recognized, in accordance with a 1998 treaty, the jurisdiction of the UN-sponsored International Criminal Court. In September 2000 French voters approved a referendum reducing the presidential term from seven to five years, effective with the 2002 election. A February 2006 joint session of Parliament passed a constitutional amendment permitting either chamber, by a two-thirds vote, to begin presidential impeachment proceedings for dereliction of duty.

The territory of metropolitan France (outside Paris) is divided into 22 regions and 96 departments (*départements*), the latter subdivided into more than 340 arrondissements, 4,000 cantons, and some 37,000 communes. In addition, there are 4 overseas regions and 4 coterminous departments—French Guiana, Guadeloupe, Martinique, and Réunion—as well as a number of other overseas jurisdictions (see Related Territories, below). The administrative structure is identical in all metropolitan regions and departments. Each department is headed by a commissioner of the republic (*commissaire de la république*), the traditional title of prefect (*préfet*) technically having been abandoned with the enactment of decentralization legislation in 1982, although continuing in general use. While the commissioner continues to be appointed by and responsible to the central government, some of the commissioner's traditional administrative and financial functions have been transferred to locally elected departmental assemblies (*conseils généraux*) and regional assemblies (*conseils régionaux*). The smallest political unit, the commune, has a popularly elected municipal council (*conseil municipal*) headed by a mayor.

In December 1999 negotiations opened between the central government and Corsican representatives on autonomy for Corsica. The resultant Matignon Accords, which were approved in July 2000 by the Corsican Assembly, called for devolving administrative and a degree of legislative authority in such areas as finance, tourism, culture, the environment, and education, as well as the teaching of the Corsican language. Most politicians on the right, including Chirac, objected to what they regarded as a weakening of the republic, but in December 2001 a significantly amended autonomy bill won final parliamentary approval. In January 2002, however, the Constitutional Council declared key elements of the plan unconstitutional. In March 2003 the French legislature approved constitutional amendments designed to permit decentralization not only in Corsica but also throughout France's regions and in many of its overseas dependencies. On July 6 Corsican voters narrowly rejected, 51 percent to 49 percent, a referendum on administrative devolution for the island. A number of overseas dependencies have, however, accepted devolution.

Foreign relations. French foreign policy as developed under President de Gaulle was dominated by the objective of restoring France's former leading role in international affairs and its independence of action. This was particularly evident in de Gaulle's strenuous effort to establish an independent nuclear force and his collateral refusal to sign treaties banning nuclear testing and proliferation. Within the Europe of "the Six" (the founding members of the EC: Belgium, France, the Federal Republic of Germany, Italy, Luxembourg, and the Netherlands), France accepted the economic provisions of the Treaty of Rome but resisted all attempts at political integration on a supranational basis, twice vetoing British membership in the EC. Within the Atlantic community, France accepted the provisions of the North Atlantic Treaty but withdrew its own military forces from North Atlantic Treaty Organization (NATO) control in 1966—France would not be fully represented again at a meeting of NATO defense ministers until 1994 and did not rejoin the military command structure until 2009—and refused the use of its territory for Allied military activities. Denouncing the United States for alleged "hegemonic" tendencies in international political, economic, and financial affairs, de Gaulle sought to restrict U.S. capital investment in France, assailed the "privileged" positions of the dollar and pound as international reserve currencies, and reduced French cooperation in international monetary arrangements. In world politics, France under de Gaulle's leadership tended to minimize the significance of the United Nations (UN) and its agencies (although remaining a member of the Security Council) and initiated a variety of foreign policy ventures of a more or less personal character, among them a close alignment with the Federal Republic of Germany, recognition of Communist China in 1964, intermittent attempts to establish closer relations with the Soviet Union, persistent criticism of U.S. actions in Vietnam, condemnation of Israeli policy during and after the 1967 Arab-Israeli conflict, and cultivation of French-speaking Canadian separatist elements.

The most pronounced foreign policy change under President Pompidou was the adoption of a more flexible attitude toward British admission to the EC, which led to the community's enlargement in 1973. President Giscard d'Estaing introduced a more positive posture of cooperation with the United States and other Western powers, based in part on a close personal relationship with West German Chancellor Helmut Schmidt.

The international standing of President Mitterrand, who was viewed at the outset of his incumbency as a consummate statesman, was undercut by the sinking, at the hands of French agents, of the antinuclear Greenpeace vessel *Rainbow Warrior* in Auckland harbor, New Zealand, in July 1985. The Socialist-led government was not without its successes, however, including its strong support for the EC's Maastricht Treaty on political and economic union, which the French electorate endorsed in September 1992 by a narrow majority (51 percent).

French forces participated in the U.S.-led multinational expedition that liberated Kuwait from Iraqi occupation in 1991 and also contributed significantly to the unsuccessful U.S.-led UN effort in 1992–1993 to prevent Somalia's descent into anarchy. Non-UN French forces were rapidly deployed in June 1994 to contain the carnage in Rwanda but were withdrawn in late August.

France shared responsibility for the failure of the EC and other European structures to make an effective response to the escalating conflict in former Yugoslavia in 1992, later becoming a member of the Contact Group (with Britain, Germany, Russia, and the United States) charged with expediting a Bosnian settlement. French troops continue to be deployed as peacekeepers in the region.

Newly installed President Chirac generated intense controversy in June 1995 by announcing the resumption of French nuclear testing at Mururoa Atoll in the South Pacific, where a moratorium on testing had been declared in April 1992 and had been followed by France's signing of the UN Treaty on Non-Proliferation of Nuclear Weapons. Spokespersons explained that a limited testing program would yield the data for future computer simulation of nuclear explosions, thereby permitting France to ban future tests. In October France sought to defuse regional criticism by announcing that in 1996 it would join with the United States and Britain in signing the 1985 South Pacific Nuclear Free Zone Treaty. Following the sixth test in the series in January 1996, President Chirac announced that he had decided to end French nuclear tests "permanently," and in September France signed the UN-sponsored Comprehensive Nuclear Test Ban Treaty, which it ratified in 1998.

Although relations between Paris and London were strengthened in the early years of Chirac's presidency, the cornerstone of French external policy remained the alliance with Germany and the determination of the two governments to be the joint driving force of a new phase of EU integration, starting with the move to a single currency by the end of the century. Meanwhile, French reintegration into NATO's military command structure stalled over French demands for the appointment of a European, presumably French, commander of NATO's southern command. Despite this dispute, France actively supported NATO's policy toward Serbia, both by committing ground troops to a peacekeeping force based in Macedonia and by participating in the NATO air strikes against Yugoslavia during the Kosovo crisis in March–June 1999. At the same time, France supported establishment of a separate European military capability and subsequently committed significant personnel to the new EU-backed rapid reaction force.

From 1970 the principal vehicle for cooperation with other French-speaking nations was the Agency for Cultural and Technical Cooperation (*Agence de Coopération Culturelle et Technique*—ACCT). The ACCT was succeeded in 1998 by the International Organization of the Francophonie (*Organisation Internationale de la Francophonie*—OIF), which in 2009 had 53 full and 3 associate members. The first in an ongoing series of francophone summits convened in Paris in 1986, and periodic Franco-African summit conferences also are held.

French forces were traditionally deployed in French-speaking Africa to assist with the quashing of army insurrections or in other moments of crisis. Upon taking office in 1997, Premier Jospin announced a reevaluation of French policy in Africa to counter what he called the "paternalistic" approach of previous governments. Changes subsequently included a reduction in the number of French troops stationed in Africa, resistance to further unilateral military intervention on that continent, and a reallocation of development assistance to emphasize democratic progress, economic realism, and humanitarian, as opposed to strategic, considerations. In January 2008 France agreed to provide the majority of some 4,300 military personnel being sent by the EU to support the UN Security Council's UN Mission in the Central African Republic and Chad.

Since the September 11, 2001, attacks on the United States, France has been at the forefront of European efforts to halt terrorism and break up underground terrorist cells. Dozens of suspected terrorists, the majority of them North African, have been arrested and put on trial; many radical Muslim clerics have been deported; and new antiterrorism measures have been enacted. Although France was widely praised by the U.S. George W. Bush administration for its antiterrorism efforts, relations with Washington took a sharp downturn beginning in late 2002, when Paris emerged as perhaps the most vocal critic of U.S. efforts to marshal international support in the UN Security Council for military action against the Saddam Hussein regime in Iraq. France's sharp opposition to the U.S.-led invasion of Iraq in March 2003 provoked a period of anti-French sentiment in the United States. Subsequently, Washington and Paris appeared to be making a concerted effort to repair relations, with Presidents Bush and Chirac meeting in Brussels, Belgium, in early 2005, during a European visit by the American executive. During the 2007 presidential campaign Nicolas Sarkozy explicitly called for a renewal of close ties.

Current issues. During President Sarkozy's first year in office, he moved forward with an aggressive agenda, including job-creation and infrastructure schemes targeting youth and deprived suburbs. At the same time, he set his sights on reining in the most generous public sector pension plans. He also began to pursue institutional reforms, outlining in December 2007 nearly 100 steps intended to streamline government administration and increase competitiveness. Formal commissions made hundreds of other recommendations for constitutional, administrative, and economic reforms.

Perhaps influenced by opposition to some of his economic policies and what many voters perceived as Sarkozy's arrogance, as well as his luxurious lifestyle, the UMP and its allies suffered significant losses in the March 9 and 16, 2008, local council elections, winning only 45 percent of the first-round vote, as compared to 48 percent for the PS, the Greens, and other parties on the left. Although Sarkozy and Premier Fillon responded to the disappointing results by repeating their commitment to reform, it was soon apparent that Sarkozy was taking steps to tone down his image. In a major test of his leadership, on July 2 a rare joint "congress" of the Senate and National Assembly approved by the narrowest of margins constitutional reforms that some described as the most significant changes ever made to the 1958 constitution (see the Constitution and government section, above). The 539–357 vote was only 1 more than the necessary three-fifths majority.

Among other developments in 2008, the government obtained passage of a bill eliminating the mandatory 35-hour work week, called for cutting the number of active military personnel by 17 percent while increasing funding for hardware upgrades, and reaffirmed its decision to rejoin NATO's joint military command. The administration also continued to support NATO military action in Afghanistan despite an August ambush by Taliban forces that left 10 French soldiers dead and another 21 wounded. In September the PS withdrew its support for the mission.

The results of the September 21, 2008, partial Senate election mirrored the results of the previous spring's local elections. In the contest for 114 senatorial seats (12 of them newly created), the PS and its allies gained 20 seats, while the UMP and its allies lost 8. Less than a year later, however, voting for the EU's European Parliament (EP) in June 2009 produced the opposite results, with the PS losing more than half the seats it had previously held and the UMP, allied with the small New Centre (*Nouveau Centre*—NC), gaining 4 even though EP restructuring reduced the French delegation from 78 to 72 seats. The gain for the UMP matched a conservative trend in many other EU countries, where Eurosceptic and anti-immigrant sentiment may have trumped the ongoing international recession as political issues.

The UMP may have benefited from Sarkozy's quick response to the accelerating international financial crisis. In early October 2008 the government confirmed that the economy was in recession, the GDP having dropped by 0.3 percent in the second quarter of the year and by another 0.1 percent in the third. Within days €360 billion ($486 billion) had been proposed to support bank lending and recapitalization, coupled with a "strategic investment fund" to aid French companies at risk of falling to foreign "predators." In early December the government added a €26 billion ($33 billion) stimulus package, amounting to 1.3 percent of GDP, and in February 2009 it offered a range of targeted measures, including preferred loans to auto manufacturers Renault and Peugeot-Citroën, restrictions on bonuses for financial professionals, tax cuts for low-income families, increased unemployment insurance, and additional welfare payments. In March the government predicted that for 2009 as a whole, the GDP would decline by 1.5 percent, but in May that was revised downward to 3.0 percent.

Immediately following the EP election, Sarkozy initiated a major cabinet reshuffle, necessitated in part by the pending departure of two ministers who had won EP seats. Notable cabinet changes included the appointment of the former RPR president and departing interior minister, Michèle ALLIOT-MARIE, as minister of justice and minister of state, and the designation of Frédéric MITTERRAND, a political independent and nephew of the late Socialist president, as minister of culture and communication. Sarkozy also brought in a senator from François Bayrou's new centrist party, the Democratic Movement (*Mouvement Démocrate*—MoDem), as the minister for rural affairs, and the mayor of Nice, former motorcycle racer Christian ESTROSI, as minister of industry.

During the 2007 campaign Sarkozy had vowed to introduce measures designed to restrict immigration and to require such measures as French language and culture tests for prospective immigrants. Of particular concern has been the growth of the Muslim community, which has been estimated to number 5–10 million and which has faced major social barriers to integration, including widespread discrimination in housing and employment. Muslims have also been perceived as challenging the secular state, which led in 2004 to the banning of headscarves as well as other religious symbols (large crucifixes, yarmulkes, and so forth) in state schools and colleges. In December 2008 the European Court of Human Rights ruled that France had not violated the rights of two Muslim schoolgirls by prohibiting their wearing of headscarves while attending classes. In June 2009 Sarkozy continued his cultural campaign, telling Parliament that the wearing of burqas was "not welcome" in France. He described the Muslim head-to-toe covering as a "sign of subservience" for women, who were rendered "prisoners behind netting." His comment came in the context of Parliament's considering launching an inquiry into whether wearing burqas undermines women's rights and French secularism.

Having lost his immunity from investigation and prosecution upon leaving office, in November 2007 Jacques Chirac became the first former head of state to be formally placed under investigation for criminal acts. The possible offenses concerned a jobs scandal when he was mayor of Paris in 1977–1995. A judicial investigation concluded in April 2009, but as of June prosecutors had not announced whether they would proceed against the 77-year-old former president. Meanwhile, former premier de Villepin faced trial for his involvement in the "Clearstream Affair," named after a Luxembourg-based bank, Clearstream International. In 2004 an anonymous accusation had surfaced that various businessmen, intelligence agents, and politicians, including Nicolas Sarkozy, held secret bank accounts as part of a complex web of corruption centering around defense contracts. The corruption allegations were quickly discredited, but a subsequent investigation into the attempted smear uncovered the apparent source of the plot, a former associate of former premier de Villepin. Although de Villepin was not implicated in the original bogus accusation, he was charged with being an "accessory to criminal libel." De Villepin denied the accusations. His trial opened on September 21, 2009.

POLITICAL PARTIES

Although the particulars have changed almost beyond recognition since World War II, the current French party system nevertheless displays, in its broad structure, many similarities with that prevailing more than half a century ago. The left continues to be dominated by the Socialists and Communists, save that the former, since a relaunch in the early 1970s, has far outstripped the latter as an electoral force. An array of small formations still compete in the political center, largely grouped from 1978 until 2002 under the umbrella of the Union for French Democracy (UDF; see under Democratic Movement, below). De Gaulle's political heirs, campaigning from 1976 until 2002 as the Rally for the Republic (RPR) and now as the Union for a Popular Movement (UMP), are the main force on the conservative right; however, there remains a substantial populist far-right constituency, now most prominently represented by the National Front (FN). The only significant new phenomenon of the last half-century has been the "green" movement.

Government Parties:

Union for a Popular Movement (*Union pour un Mouvement Populaire*—UMP). The present UMP was established as a unitary party at a congress on November 17, 2002. It had been launched in May 2002 as the Union for the Presidential Majority (*Union pour la Majorité Présidentielle*—UMP), a center-right electoral alliance that included, principally, the Rally for the Republic and elements of both the Liberal Democracy (DL) and the Union for French Democracy (but not the Democratic Force faction of UDF leader François Bayrou). It won a majority of 355 seats at the June 2002 National Assembly election. Former premier Alain Juppé was selected to head the UMP on an interim basis.

The Rally for the Republic (*Rassemblement pour la République*—RPR) had been established in 1976 as successor to the Union of Democrats for the Republic (*Union des Démocrates pour la République*—UDR), itself heir to various formations descended from the Union for the New Republic (*Union pour la Nouvelle République*—UNR), launched by de Gaulle in 1947. The RPR was organized as the personal vehicle of Jacques Chirac in his political rivalry with President Giscard d'Estaing, which had resulted in Chirac's resignation as premier in August 1976. In the election of March 1978 the RPR emerged as the largest single party in the National Assembly.

Chirac placed third in first-round presidential balloting in 1981, and two months later the RPR ran second to the Socialists in the National Assembly election. In 1985 the RPR concluded an alliance with the UDF, after which the two groups' 286-seat plurality enabled Chirac to form a government in "cohabitation" with the Socialist president, François Mitterrand. The alliance was unsuccessful, however, in 1988.

Despite Chirac's having lost to Mitterrand in the second round of the 1988 presidential race, the RPR's capture of an assembly plurality in 1993 provided a springboard for Chirac's third run for the presidency in 1995. Even though the RPR prime minister, Edouard Balladur, also chose to stand, Chirac finished second in the first round and won a second-round victory. In October the postelection premier, Alain Juppé, was installed as RPR president in succession to Chirac.

Splits in the RPR continued through the 1997 legislative elections, one issue being whether to co-opt or to repudiate the anti-immigrant stand of the increasingly popular FN. After the disappointing first round of voting in May 1997, Juppé announced his resignation as premier, and later in the summer he was replaced as party leader by longtime rival Philippe SÉGUIN, described as a "partially recanted" former opponent of greater European integration.

In May 1998 Séguin accepted the RPR's alignment with the UDF and the DL in The Alliance, an unsuccessful effort to provide cohesion for the center-right parties. Subsequently, a segment of the RPR led by Charles Pasqua (see Rally for France, below) broke from the party's leadership to join with the Movement for France (MPF, below) and contest the upcoming election for the European Parliament on a platform opposing further European integration. In April 1999 Séguin stepped down from the RPR presidency, claiming he had been undermined by Chirac and his supporters. Nicolas Sarkozy, theretofore secretary general of the RPR, was subsequently named interim president, but he resigned after the party fell to third place, behind the Socialists and Pasqua's list, the Rally for France and the Independence of Europe (*Rassemblement pour la France et l'Indépendance de l'Europe*—RPF-IE), at the European Parliament elections in June. Meanwhile, President Chirac's standing was being undercut by continuing accusations of illegal fund-raising while he was mayor of Paris. Both the electoral setback and the ongoing scandal may have contributed to the rejection of Chirac's candidate, Jean-Paul DELEVOY, at the party presidential contest in December. The winner, Michèle Alliot-Marie, became the first woman to head the RPR.

Following his massive reelection victory against the FN's Jean-Marie Le Pen in May 2002, Chirac used his revived standing to organize the Union for a Presidential Majority and then to lead it to a sweeping victory at the June National Assembly elections. In preparation for conversion of the alliance to a unitary party, the RPR voted to dissolve in September 2002. The new formation also incorporated the LD and attracted much of the UDF and many members of Pasqua's RPF-IE. In October 2002 the Radical Party (PR, below) voted to associate with the UMP while retaining its separate identity.

The Liberal Democracy (*Démocratie Libérale*—DL), originally the Republican Party (*Parti Républican*), was organized in 1977 by merger of the former National Federation of Independent Republicans (*Fédération Nationale des Républicains Indépendants*—FNRI) and several smaller groups supportive of President Giscard d'Estaing. The FNRI, founded by Giscard d'Estaing in 1966, was made up primarily of independents originally affiliated with the National Center of Independents and Peasants (CNIP, below). In 1974 Giscard d'Estaing formally severed his affiliation with the FNRI in his search for a new "presidential majority."

The Republican Party changed its name to the DL following the 1997 legislative election, at which the center-right parties lost control of the National Assembly. In May 1998 DL leader Alain MADELIN, described as one of the country's "most vociferous" advocates of a free-market economy, announced that the DL was withdrawing from the UDF but would participate in The Alliance with the UDF and RPR. In the first round of the 2002 presidential election Madelin finished tenth, with 3.9 percent of the vote. Most DL National Assembly candidates agreed to run on the UMP list in June 2002, although two were elected on a separate DL list. Madelin—reluctantly, according to some observers—later led the DL into the unified UMP party.

During its November 2002 founding congress, at which it presented its guiding values as liberty, responsibility, solidarity, the nation, and Europe, the UMP elected Alain Juppé as chair and Philippe DOUSTE-BLAZY as secretary general. Juppé, who was convicted in January 2004 of misusing public funds in 1988–1995 while an aide to Chirac and secretary general of the RPR, received an 18-month suspended sentence and was banned from public office for ten years (reduced to one year, on appeal). In July he resigned as UMP chair, with Nicolas Sarkozy then being elected as his replacement in November. (Juppé was elected mayor of Bordeaux in October 2006 and then named to the initial François Fillon cabinet in May 2007, but he lost the latter position after failing to win a National Assembly seat in June.) The UMP suffered significant losses at the regional elections of March 2004, at which it won only 1 of 22 mainland regional councils, and in the June balloting for the European Parliament, taking only 17 of 77 seats on a 16.6 percent vote share. A spate of government ministers lost in the March balloting, as did Valéry Giscard d'Estaing.

Although President Chirac did not announce that he would not seek a third term until March 11, 2007, Nicolas Sarkozy had received the party's endorsement in January. Late in 2005 Sarkozy had convinced the PS Political Bureau to hold a primary to select a presidential candidate—a change in party rules that was clearly intended to enhance his prospects—but by late 2006 the other prospective candidates, chiefly Prime Minister Villepin, had withdrawn from consideration. In the April 2007 election Sarkozy finished first in the initial round, with 31.2 percent of the vote, and won the presidency with 53.1 percent in the runoff. In mid-May, when Sarkozy resigned the party presidency, Jean-Claude Gaudin assumed the post on an acting basis. In June the UMP, in pursuit of a "presidential majority," won 313 National Assembly seats, considerably less than in 2002.

Acknowledging Sarkozy's continuing preeminence within the party, in July 2007 the UMP decided not to name a permanent replacement but instead to introduce a collective leadership under Gaudin, former secretary general Pierre Méhaignerie, former prime minister Raffarin, and Secretary General Patrick Devedjian. In December 2008 Xavier Bertrand replaced Devedjian, who had been offered a cabinet post.

In June 2009 the UMP and the New Center (NC, below) combined forces in the European Parliament election, winning a leading 29 seats.

Leaders: Nicolas SARKOZY (President of the Republic); François FILLON (Premier); Jean-Claude GAUDIN (President of the Majority

Committee); Pierre MÉHAIGNERIE; Jean-Pierre RAFFARIN (First Vice President of the National Council); Michèle ALLIOT-MARIE, Jean-Louis BORLOO, and Brice HORTEFEUX (Vice Presidents of the National Council); Bernard ACCOYER (President of the National Assembly); Jean François COPÉ (National Assembly Leader); Patrick DEVEDJIAN (Minister Responsible for the Economic Stimulus Plan); Xavier BERTRAND (Secretary General).

Forum of Social Republicans (*Forum des Républicains Sociaux*—FRS). The FRS was organized by Christine Boutin, a socially conservative UDF dissident who won 1.2 percent of the 2002 presidential vote. In June 2002 she was elected to the National Assembly on the UMP list. The FRS subsequently became an associate party of the UMP. The FRS held three assembly seats after the 2007 election.

Leaders: Christine BOUTIN (President), Jean-Frédéric POISSON and Vincent YOU (Vice Presidents), Jean-Louis ICHARD (Secretary General).

National Center of Independents and Peasants (*Centre National des Indépendants et Paysans*—CNIP). Dating back to the 1940s and a significant force through the 1950s, the CNIP has long supported the free-enterprise system, the North Atlantic alliance, and European integration. Although not directly linked to either the RPR or the UDF, it was allied with the center-right coalition in the 1981 and 1986 legislative elections. Continuance of the relationship in 1993 was precluded by the CNIP's de facto support of the FN's anti-immigrant position, although it retained a presence in Parliament, under the "Various Right" label. At present, the CNIP, with two seats in the National Assembly and one in the Senate, is an associate party of the UMP; members are permitted to hold joint enrollment.

Leaders: Annick de ROSCOÄT (President), Bernard BEAUDET (Secretary General).

New Center (*Nouveau Centre*—NC). The NC was formed in late May 2007 by members of the UDF, including 18 members of the National Assembly, who objected to François Bayrou's decision to establish the Democratic Movement (MoDem, below) as successor to the UDF. Whereas Bayrou sought independence from the UMP, the NC supported the newly elected president, Nicolas Sarkozy, and participated in the government of the new prime minister, François Fillon. At the June National Assembly election the NC, running in tandem with the UMP in pursuit of a *majorité présidentielle,* won 22 seats. The NC was also initially known as the European Social Liberal Party (*Parti Social Libéral Européen*—PSLE), the name of its National Assembly grouping.

The party's founding congress was held May 16–17, 2008, at which time Hervé Morin won the presidency with 87 percent support, versus 13 percent for Mireille BENEDETTI.

Leaders: Hervé MORIN (Minister of Defense and President of the Party), Jean-Christophe LAGARDE (Executive President), François SAUVADET (National Assembly Leader), Valérie LÉTARD (Secretary of State for Solidarity), André SANTINI (Secretary of State for the Civil Service), Yvan LACHAUD (Secretary General).

Radical Party (*Parti Radical*—PR). Founded in 1901, the Radical Party was the leading party of the prewar Third Republic and a participant in many Fourth Republic governments. Technically called the Radical and Radical Socialist Republican Party (*Parti Républicain Radical et Radical-Socialiste*—RRRS) but also known as the *Parti Valoisien* from a Rue de Valois address in Paris, the Radicals maintained their traditional anticlerical posture but were more conservative than the Socialists in economic and social matters.

The Radical majority's refusal to join the Union of the Left with the Socialists and Communists caused the exit of a left-wing faction in 1972 to form the Left Radical Movement (see Left Radical Party, below). Radicals held ministerial office under the presidency of Giscard d'Estaing (1974–1981), during which the party sought to forge greater center-left unity. In July 1977 the Movement of Social Liberals (*Mouvement des Sociaux Libéraux*—MSL), which had been organized in February 1977 by Olivier STIRN (a former Gaullist secretary of state), announced its incorporation into the Radical Party. (Stirn relaunched the MSL as a separate group in 1981, but it dissolved in 1984.)

In 1978 the Radicals became founding members of the UDF. Almost eliminated from the National Assembly in the 1981 Socialist landslide, the PR recovered somewhat in the 1986 elections and held office in the subsequent "cohabitation" government. However, the party fell back to three seats in 1988 and again went into opposition. It returned to office following the center-right assembly landslide of March 1993. Since 2002 it has been aligned with the UMP while maintaining its separate identity.

Leaders: Jean-Louis BORLOO (President of the Party and Minister of State), André ROSSINOT (Honorary President), François LOOS (Former President), Serge LEPELTIER (First Vice President), Laurent HÉNART (Secretary General).

Before the end of 2007, two new movements took shape, both representing the Sarkozy-supportive left. **The Progressives** (*Les Progressistes*), describing itself as social democratic, was established by a defector from the Socialist Party, Éric BESSON, who served as secretary of state for forward planning, assessment of public policies, and development of the digital economy; was subsequently named an assistant secretary general of the UMP; and is now minister for immigration, integration, national identity, and mutually supportive development. Other central figures in the movement included Marc d'HÉRÉ, president of the European and Social Initiative (*Initiative Européenne at Sociale*—IES), and Emmanuel DUPUY, president of the Union of Radical Republicans (*Union des Républicains Radicaux*—URR). Defining itself as social-liberal, the **Modern Left** (*Gauche Moderne*—GM) was formed by Jean-Marie BOCKEL, mayor of Mulhouse and secretary of state for defense and veterans in the Fillon government.

Other Parliamentary Parties:

Socialist Party (*Parti Socialiste*—PS). Originally established in 1905 and known for many years as the French Section of the Workers' International (*Section Française de l'Internationale Ouvrière*—SFIO), the French Socialist Party headed the 1936–1938 Popular Front government of Léon BLUM as well as several postwar coalitions, party leader Guy MOLLET being prime minister of the Fourth Republic's longest-lasting administration in 1956–1957. The advent of the Fifth Republic in 1958 accelerated the party's electoral decline, and in 1965 it joined the broader Federation of the Democratic and Socialist Left (*Fédération de la Gauche Démocrate et Socialiste*—FGDS) chaired by François Mitterrand, leader of the small Convention of Republican Institutions (*Convention des Institutions Républicains*—CIR). Unlike Mollet, Mitterrand had opposed de Gaulle's return to power in 1958. Backed by the FGDS and the Communists, Mitterrand secured 44.8 percent of the second-round vote in the 1965 presidential election, while the FGDS made major gains in the 1967 National Assembly election. Proposals to convert the FGDS into a unitary party foundered in the wake of the 1968 political crisis, and Mitterrand refused to back the 1969 Socialist presidential candidate, Gaston DEFFERRE, who won only 5 percent of the vote.

After further false starts and bickering between the factions, in 1971 a "congress of socialist unity" elected Mitterrand as leader of the new Socialist Party, which embarked upon a strategy of left-wing union. Major gains in the 1973 legislative election were followed by a narrow second-round defeat for Mitterrand, as presidential candidate of the combined left, in 1974. In a 1981 rematch against Giscard d'Estaing, Mitterrand was victorious, and the PS then swept the National Assembly election in June. Despite a Socialist defeat in the 1986 assembly election, Mitterrand won a second term by defeating Jacques Chirac in May 1988, and a month later the PS secured a sufficient plurality to regain control of the National Assembly.

Following a massive defeat in the 1993 legislative elections, the PS chose former prime minister Michel Rocard as first secretary, but he was forced to step down when the Socialists fared poorly in the June election for the European Parliament.

Straitened financial circumstances and the implication of various PS officials in corruption cases added to the Socialists' problems in the run-up to the 1995 presidential election. Their candidate, a former PS leader and education minister, Lionel Jospin, defied most expectations, taking the lead in the first round and winning 47.4 percent in the second. In June Jospin replaced Henri EMMANUELLI as PS first secretary, promising to carry out a thorough reform of party structures and policies. In the 1997 legislative elections, Jospin led the PS to a plurality of 241 seats in the National Assembly.

In the 2002 presidential race a divided left contributed to Jospin's third-place finish, with 16.2 percent of the vote. Humiliated, Jospin announced his retirement from active politics. In the June parliamentary election the PS won only 140 seats, and several months later former first secretary Emmanuelli launched a "New World" caucus within the PS in an effort to redirect the party toward its socialist roots and away from the social liberalism of the party's new first secretary, François Hollande. In May 2003, however, the party reelected Hollande as leader.

In the March 2004 local elections the PS made major gains, heading a coalition with the Communists and Greens that won 20 of 21 mainland regional legislatures, up from 8. The PS also won 28.9 percent of the vote in the June 2004 elections to the European Parliament, capturing 31 of 77 seats, compared to 17 for the UMP. In 2005 the party nevertheless remained divided over the proposed EU constitution: Hollande's majority supported further European integration, but a vocal minority, led by longtime party stalwart Laurent Fabius, objected that it did not meet socialist standards. Following the May 2005 rejection of the proposed constitution by the voters, Fabius and his supporters were ousted from the party leadership.

At a party congress in November 2005, Hollande's "modernizers" and the "traditionalists" attempted to heal the rift that had split the party into half a dozen factions. Among other things, the party agreed to unite behind a platform that called for an increase in the minimum wage, opposition to the controversial new youth labor legislation, and reversal of the government's decision to sell a minority stake in the principal state-owned electrical utility company. In other decisions, Laurent Fabius was restored to the party's executive, and the selection of a 2007 presidential candidate was deferred until November 2006.

In September 2006 Lionel Jospin withdrew from the contest for the presidential nomination. In November Ségolène Royal, a former minister of family affairs, won 61 percent of the vote in a party primary, easily defeating former finance minister Dominique STRAUSS-KAHN (21 percent) and Fabius (19 percent). Initially regarded as the front-runner in the race, Royal fell behind early in 2007 and never regained the lead. She won 25.9 percent of the first-round vote and then lost to Nicolas Sarkozy in the runoff, with 46.9 percent. In the June National Assembly election the PS somewhat unexpectedly improved on its 2002 performance, winning 186 seats.

In late May 2007 Bernard KOUCHNER, long a prominent figure on the left and cofounder of the international aid organization Doctors Without Borders (*Medecins sans Frontieres*), was expelled from the party for agreeing to serve as minister of foreign affairs in the Fillon cabinet. Four months later, Strauss-Kahn was named to head the International Monetary Fund.

In March 2008 François Hollande announced that he would not seek reelection as first secretary at the party congress on November 14–16. Leading contenders for the post were Ségolène Royal, who had considerable grassroots support; the more moderate mayor of Paris, Bertrand DELANOË; the mayor of Lille, Martine Aubry, who was backed by Fabius and other "elephants" in the party's old guard; and Benoît HAMON, a member of the European Parliament. After the first round of voting Royal held the lead, but in the second round Aubry defeated her by the narrowest of margins—0.08 percent—after Hamon threw his support to Aubry. Nevertheless, Royal indicated that she intended to seek the party's backing for another presidential run in 2012.

In the June 2009 European Parliament election the Socialist list suffered a serious setback, attracting only 16.5 percent of the vote and winning only 14 seats, 17 fewer than in 2004.

Leaders: Martine AUBRY (First Secretary); Ségolène ROYAL (2007 presidential candidate); David ASSOULINE, Harlem DÉSIR, and Arnaud MONTEBOURG (National Secretaries); François LAMY (Political Counselor); Jean-Marc AYRAULT (National Assembly Leader).

French Communist Party (*Parti Communiste Français*—PCF). An offshoot of the SFIO (see the PS, above), the PCF assumed a separate identity in 1920. It was the largest party of the Fourth Republic, but the single-member constituency system introduced by the Fifth Republic limited its parliamentary representation, despite participation in left-wing electoral and policy alliances. The party nonetheless remained a powerful force in local government and dominated the largest French labor organization, the *Confédération Générale du Travail* (CGT). Although opposing NATO and European integration and favoring closer relations with the East, the PCF publicly rejected the Soviet intervention in Czechoslovakia in 1968. In 1976 it formally abandoned the theory of the "dictatorship of the proletariat," although it did not embrace revisionist "Eurocommunism" until much later and remained in essence a pro-Soviet party until the demise of the USSR.

Following its formal break with the Socialists in 1984, the PCF experienced a major rupture between "traditionalists" and "renovators." In 1988 the latter offered their own presidential candidate, who won 2.1 percent of the first-round vote, while the mainstream nominee, André LAJONIE, slumped to a postwar low of 6.8 percent. Expelled from the PCF, the "renovators" formed a New Left (*Nouvelle Gauche*—NG) party, which later became part of the Red and Green Alternatives (see under The Alternatives, below). In 1993 the PCF retained 23 of 26 legislative seats. The PCF leader, Georges MARCHAIS, who doggedly resisted internal pressure for a "French perestroika," stepped down after 21 years at the party's helm in 1994. His successor, Robert HUE, was assigned the title "national secretary" as part of a decision to abandon the traditional commitment to "democratic centralism." Hue took 8.6 percent of the first-round vote in the 1995 presidential balloting, after which the PCF backed Lionel Jospin of the PS in the second round. In the 1997 legislative elections, the PCF used its opposition to "Europe at any cost" to increase its legislative presence to 38 seats. Although strongly opposed to French participation in the Economic and Monetary Union (EMU), the PCF nevertheless joined the new PS-led government.

At the 31st PCF congress, held in October 2001, Hue was named to the new post of party president and also named as the PCF's 2002 presidential candidate. He finished eleventh out of 16, with 3.4 percent of the first-round vote. Earlier, in November 2001, he had been acquitted of charges related to illegal fundraising. In the National Assembly election of June 2002, the PCF won only 21 seats.

In November 2002 Hue announced his intention to step down as president, and he was succeeded in April 2003 by Marie-George Buffet. In the 2004 regional elections the PCF joined the PS and the Greens in a successful electoral coalition, but efforts to unite the left in the run-up to the 2007 presidential election failed. With some Communists apparently having supported the PS's Royal, Buffet managed to win only 1.9 percent of the vote in the first round. PCF representation then dropped to 15 seats in the June National Assembly election, below the 20 seats needed to form its own parliamentary caucus. As a result, the PCF delegation formed the core of the Democratic and Republican Left group.

For the June 2009 European Parliament election the PCF formed a **Left Front–Overseas Alliance** (*Front de Gauche–Alliances des Outres Mers*) that also included the Left Party and the Unitarian Left (both below) as well as a group of parties from overseas territories. The coalition won a total of five seats.

Leaders: Marie-George BUFFET (National Secretary), François AUGUSTE (President of the National Executive Council), Jean-Claude SANDRIER (National Assembly Leader), Pierre LAURENT (Coordinator).

Left Radical Party (*Parti Radical de Gauche*—PRG). A splinter from the Radical Party, the PRG was organized as the Left Radical Movement (*Mouvement des Radicaux de Gauche*—MRG) prior to participating in the 1973 election as part of the Left Union (*Union de la Gauche*—UG). Its parliamentary strength rose from 10 seats to 14 in the 1981 election, after it had entered the government. It secured only 2 assembly seats in 1986 but 9 in 1988, after which it joined the Rocard government. The MRG shared in the defeat of the left in the March 1993 legislative balloting. It was temporarily strengthened by the addition of controversial business tycoon Bernard TAPIE; however, Tapie was later sentenced to prison for bribery and fraud.

The MRG was relaunched under new leadership in 1996, when it absorbed the small Reunite (*Réunir*) group led by Bernard Kouchner (a former Socialist minister who subsequently rejoined the PS). With the aim of sharpening its image, the party also adopted the new single-word name "Radical"—much to the chagrin of the main Radical Party, which in March secured a court ruling that the MRG title should be restored. Reorganized as the Radical Socialist Party (*Parti Radicale Socialiste*—PRS), the party took part in the 1997 elections under a withholding agreement with the PS. The PRS was given one ministerial position and two subministerial positions in the subsequent Socialist government. The courts again forced the party to choose another name, resulting in adoption of the present designation at a congress in 1998.

In the 2002 presidential balloting the PRG's Christiane TAUBIRA, from French Guiana, finished 13th, with 2.3 percent of the vote. In the June 2002 National Assembly election the PRG won seven seats. Jean-Michel Baylet was reelected party president in December 2004.

In 2007 the PRG supported the Socialist Ségolène Royal for president. (Bernard Tapie broke ranks and backed Nicolas Sarkozy.) It then won seven National Assembly seats.

Leader: Jean-Michel BAYLET (President).

The Greens (*Les Verts*). The Greens, which organized as a unified environmental party in 1984, began as an outgrowth of an Ecology Today (*Aujourd'hui l'Écologie*) movement that had offered candidates in the 1981 National Assembly election. The Greens declined to present candidates for the 1988 election on the grounds that only a return to proportional representation would assure them an equitable number of seats. At municipal balloting in 1989 they ran much more strongly than expected, winning between 8 and 24 percent of the vote in some localities.

Les Verts secured no assembly seats on a minuscule vote share in 1993, despite a noncompetition agreement with the Ecology Generation (below). Partly because of its poor showing, the party, in a decisive move to the left, then elected Dominique VOYNET to succeed 1988 presidential candidate Antoine Waechter, who in 1994 set up the Independent Ecological Movement (below). As the *Les Verts* candidate, Voynet ran eighth of nine contenders in the first round of the 1995 presidential balloting, taking 3.3 percent of the vote. For the 1997 legislative election the Greens cooperated in some districts with the Socialists or the PRS (now the PRG). Having won seven seats, they entered the Socialist Jospin government.

In October 2001 the Greens abandoned their initial 2002 presidential candidate, Alain LIPIETZ, a former Maoist who had previously supported Corsican and Basque separatists. In his place the party nominated Noël MAMÈRE, who ran seventh, with 5.3 percent of the vote, in the first round. *Les Verts* saw its National Assembly representation decline to three seats in June 2002. In January 2003 Voynet was replaced by Gilles LEMAIRE, who was then succeeded by Yann WEHRLING two years later. In December 2006 the party elected a 15-person collegiate executive for a two-year term.

Voynet received the party's endorsement for president in 2007 but won only 1.6 percent of the first-round vote. In June the Greens won four National Assembly seats. Two years later, in the June 2009 election for the European Parliament, the Greens led formation of the **Europe Écologie** alliance, which tied the PS for second place, with 14 of France's 72 seats. Those elected on the list included antiglobalization campaigner José Bové (see Small Farmers' Confederation, below) and Daniel COHN-BENDIT, a Franco-German environmental activist who was a leader of the 1968 student demonstrations and who had previously been elected to the European Parliament from Germany.

Leaders: Cécile DUFLOT (National Secretary), Jean-Marc BRULÉ and Mickaël MARIE (Assistant National Secretaries), Jean-Louis ROUMÉGAS and Djamila SONZOGNI (Spokespersons).

Democratic Movement (*Mouvement Démocrate*—MoDem or MD). The MoDem held its founding conference on December 2, 2007, at which time it absorbed what remained of the Union for French Democracy (*Union pour la Démocratie Française*—UDF). Founder François Bayrou stated that a key purpose of the new party would be to overcome the left-right divide in French politics.

The UDF had been established in 1978 by a number of right-centrist parties, including the Radical Party (PR, above), plus several smaller groups in the governing coalition (for details, see the 2007 or earlier editions of the *Political Handbook*). It supported Valéry Giscard d'Estaing in the 1981 presidential campaign, albeit unofficially as the incumbent voiced a desire to stand as a "citizen candidate" unidentified with any specific grouping. Collaterally, it became possible for individuals to become "direct affiliates" of the UDF without holding membership in one of its constituent groups. In line with a 1985 accord with the RPR, the UDF was awarded five senior cabinet posts in the government formed after the 1986 election. Having abandoned its pact with the RPR, the UDF became the third-ranked legislative grouping in the wake of the 1988 National Assembly election. Giscard d'Estaing remained the dominant UDF personality into the 1990s.

For the 1993 legislative election the RPR and UDF candidates were grouped in the Union for France (*Union pour la France*—UPF). In the 1995 presidential race most UDF support went to Edouard Balladur in the first round but swung behind the victorious Jacques Chirac in the second. The UDF held important posts in the subsequent RPR-led government, while Giscard d'Estaing was invited to give "elder statesman" advice to President Chirac. Giscard d'Estaing stood down as UDF leader in 1996 and attempted to confer the succession on Alain Madelin. However, delegates at a UDF conference preferred former defense minister and Republican President François LÉOTARD.

After dropping from 213 seats in the 1993 legislative poll to 198 in 1997, the UDF also was shaken (as was the RPR) by a poor performance in the 1998 regional elections. Prompting an immediate crisis within the UDF, five UDF incumbent presidents of regional councils accepted the support of the extreme-right FN to retain their posts. Two resigned shortly thereafter, and the UDF eventually expelled the other three.

Among those who attacked Léotard for reacting too slowly and failing to make a "clean break" with the FN was François Bayrou of the Democratic Force (*Force Démocrate*—FD), which had been launched in 1995 within the UDF as a merger of the Center of Social Democrats (*Centre des Démocrates Sociaux*—CDS) and the Social Democratic Party (*Parti Social-Démocrate*—PSD). Bayrou suggested that the UDF be abolished in favor of a new, single center-right party. For his part, Léotard called for a UDF general congress to determine the union's future and to establish policies on the FN and other issues that were splintering the opposition. In May Léotard endorsed the creation of The Alliance among the UDF, RPR, and DL (see the UMP discussion, above), but shortly thereafter he resigned the UDF presidency because of an official investigation into alleged financial irregularities. He was succeeded in September by Bayrou, who continued to lobby for the remaining UDF components to merge. The resultant "New" (*Nouvelle*) UDF was established in 1999, although the leading constituent parties retained de facto identities. (Léotard subsequently left politics.)

Bayrou finished fourth (with 6.8 percent of the first-round vote) in the 2002 presidential election. Although some of the UDF joined Chirac's new UMP prior to the June 2002 National Assembly election, Bayrou's supporters, clustered in the FD faction, ran independently under the UDF label, winning 29 seats, for third place.

Attacking what he termed the "perpetual war" between the UMP and the Socialists, Bayrou again sought the presidency in 2007, winning 18.6 percent of the vote, for third place, in the first round. He then declined to endorse either the UMP's Sarkozy or the Socialist Royal in the runoff, which contributed to a rupture in the party. Bayrou's announcement on May 10 that he was forming a new Democratic Movement prior to the June National Assembly election then led to the defection of 22 out of 29 UMP legislators, 18 of whom formed the UMP-aligned New Center (NC, above). In the subsequent legislative election MoDem won only three seats.

At the same time, three members of the European Parliament (EP) who had been elected under the UDF banner but who objected to formation of MoDem reorganized within the EP as the Civic Alliance for Democracy in Europe (*Alliance Citoyenne pour la Démocratie en Europe*—ACDE). The three, Jean-Marie CAVADA, Claire GIBAULT, and Janelly FOURTOU, subsequently adopted the name Democratic Future (*Avenir Démocrate*—AD). In June 2009 Cavada, running on the UMP list as a member of the New Center, retained his seat.

In June 2009 MoDem won six European Parliament seats. Later in the month MoDem's treasurer, Sen. Michel MERCIER, accepted an appointment as minister of rural affairs and territorial management in the Sarkozy government.

Leader: François BAYROU (President).

Left Party (*Parti de Gauche*—PG). The PG, announced in November 2008 by former members of the PS, held its founding congress in early 2009. The decision to leave the Socialists came when the 2008 PS congress failed to back a policy motion that advocated a harder leftist line. Initially, the PG claimed two senators and two National Assembly deputies.

In June 2009 the PG ran on the Communist-led Left Front list for the European Parliament, with Mélenchon winning a seat.

Leaders: Jean-Luc MÉLENCHON (President of the National Bureau), François DELAPIERRE (General Delegate), Marc DOLEZ (Member of the National Assembly).

Stand Up for the Republic (*Debout la République*—DLR). The DLR began as a faction of the UMP. Gaullist, conservative, and nationalist, the party held its founding congress in November 2008 under Nicolas Dupont-Aignan, who had failed to qualify for the 2007 presidential race. The party, fearing a loss of French sovereignty, opposed reintegration into NATO's military command structure. It currently has two members in the National Assembly. In June 2009 it attracted under 2 percent of the vote and won no seats in the election for the European Parliament.

Leaders: Nicolas DUPONT-AIGNAN, François-Xavier VILLAIN.

Movement for France (*Mouvement pour la France*—MPF). The MPF was launched in 1994 as the successor to The Other Europe (*L'Autre Europe*), which had been established before the June European Parliament election, principally by French-British financier Sir

James GOLDSMITH. Opposed to EC/EU economic and monetary integration, the MPF also attacked the 1993 world trade liberalization agreement. In the 1995 presidential balloting, MPF leader Philippe de Villiers (formerly of the UDF) finished seventh out of nine first-round candidates, taking 4.7 percent of the vote.

To contest the 1999 European Parliament election the MPF formed an alliance with Charles Pasqua's Gaullist Rally for France (RPF, below), which he had formed after breaking from the RPR in 1998. The success of the resultant Rally for France and the Independence of Europe (RPF-IE) list led to the establishment of a unified party late in 1999. In less than a year, however, Pasqua and de Villiers parted company, leading de Villiers to revive the MPF. In September 2005 he announced that he intended to seek the presidency in 2007, but he won only 2.2 percent of the vote in the first round. The party, which won one National Assembly seat in June 2007, has decried the "Islamization" of France and has opposed Turkey's admission to the EU as well as the EU's Lisbon Treaty. De Villiers, a member of the European Parliament, retained his seat in June 2009, running on the **Libertas France** list along with members of the **Hunting, Fishing, Nature, Traditions** (*Chasse, Pêche, Nature, Traditions*—CPNT). The CPNT is rural-oriented and anti-EU. Its leader, Frédéric NIHOUS, won 1.2 percent of the presidential vote in 2007, compared to the 4.2 percent won in 2002 by his predecessor, Jean SAINT-JOSSE.

Leaders: Philippe DE VILLIERS (President), Patrick LOUIS (Secretary General).

Rally for France (*Rassemblement pour la France*—RPF). The RPF was formed by Charles Pasqua, a former minister of the interior, following his break from the RPR in 1998. Gaullist and nationalist in orientation, the party has consistently opposed further EU integration.

In 1999 the RPF joined with the Movement for France (MPF, above) to contest the European Parliament election as the Rally for France and the Independence of Europe (*Rassemblement pour la France et l'Indépendance de l'Europe*—RPF-IE), which finished second to the Socialists. The subsequent unification of the RPF and MPF parties as the RPF-IE lasted less than a year, however, after which Pasqua's party retained the RPF-IE name.

In 2002 Pasqua intended to run for president of the republic, but he failed to obtain the requisite number of signatures to appear on the ballot. At the June National Assembly election the RPF-IE was credited with winning two seats, although several successful candidates on the UMP list also had RPF-IE affiliations. In 2004 Pasqua was reelected to the Senate on the UMP list.

Although never convicted, Pasqua has been investigated for a number of alleged illegalities, including unlawful party funding and sale of arms to Angola. He also was implicated in a kickback scandal involving the Iraqi oil-for-food program in the 1990s—a charge that he vehemently denied.

Leader: Charles PASQUA.

Numerous additional minor parties offered candidates for the 2007 National Assembly election. Candidates categorized as Diverse Left (*Divers Gauche*) won 15 seats; Diverse Right (*Divers Droit*), 9; Diverse, 1; and Regionalist, 1. Those grouped as Extreme Left, Extreme Right, and Ecologist won none.

Other Right and Far-Right Parties:

National Front (*Front National*—FN). The FN, an extreme right-wing formation organized in 1972 on an anti-immigration program, startled observers in 1984 by winning 10 of the 81 French seats in the European Parliament. It made a scarcely less impressive showing in 1986 by winning 35 assembly seats, while its leader, Jean-Marie Le Pen, secured 14.4 percent of the vote in the first round of the 1988 presidential election. It lost all but one of its National Assembly seats two months later, primarily because the election was conducted under majoritarian rather than proportional representation. Its sole deputy was expelled from the party in October 1988, after which the FN was without lower house representation until a by-election victory in December 1989. That seat was lost in 1993. In the 1995 presidential poll, Le Pen took a first-round share of 15 percent. In the municipal elections in June the FN won control of three large southern towns, where it pledged to give preference to French citizens in the allocation of housing and welfare.

With its policies remaining the focus of countrywide debate, the FN secured nearly 15 percent of the vote in the first round of the 1997 legislative poll. In the second round it chose not to withdraw its third-place candidates, having calculated that this would aid a Socialist victory and thus, in the long term, benefit the FN.

In December 1997, for a second time, Le Pen was convicted under antiracism laws for dismissing Nazi gas chambers as a "detail in history" and was fined some $50,000. In April 1998 Le Pen was found guilty of assaulting a female Socialist candidate during the 1997 legislative election campaign. The sentence included the suspension of civil rights for two years, which was reduced to one year on appeal.

Internal conflicts came to a head in December 1998 when deputy leader Bruno Mégret and several of his supporters were expelled from the FN for advocating alliances with parties of the moderate right. Mégret and his supporters declared their expulsion illegal and organized an extraordinary party congress in January 1999 to elect a new leadership. The schism led to the coexistence of two parties, each claiming to be "the" FN, but in May the courts ruled that Mégret's group had usurped the FN designation, which led to the new party's selecting National Republican Movement (MNR, below) instead.

Although the FN/MNR bifurcation initially appeared to split the far-right vote, Le Pen subsequently took advantage of rising anti-immigrant, anticrime, and "French first" sentiment (as well as a divided left) to pull off an unexpected second-place finish—16.9 percent of the vote—in the April 2002 first-round vote for the presidency. However, Le Pen's success had the adverse consequence of drawing all his opponents together in support of President Chirac's reelection, and in the second-round voting in June Le Pen could manage only 17.8 percent of the vote.

In the June 2002 National Assembly election the FN won 11 percent of the vote but no seats. In the March 2004 regional elections the FN won 14.7 percent of the vote in the first round, passing the threshold of 10 percent to contest the second round in most regions. Le Pen, however, was refused a place on the ballot in a southern region because he failed to meet requirements.

Le Pen again sought the presidency in 2007, but this time he finished fourth in the first round, with 10.4 percent of the vote. He then called on his supporters to boycott the second round. In the June 2007 National Assembly election the FN won only 4.3 percent of the vote and no seats.

Subsequently, Le Pen continued to run afoul of the authorities. In February 2008 he was fined and given a suspended sentence for describing the German occupation during World War II as relatively benign, and in March he was fined for incitement because of anti-Muslim comments.

In June 2009 the FN lost four of the seven seats it had held in the European Parliament.

Leaders: Jean-Marie LE PEN (President), Marine LE PEN and Bruno GOLLNISCH (Executive Vice Presidents), Louis ALIOT (Secretary General).

National Republican Movement (*Mouvement National Républicain*—MNR). The MNR was established in 1999 by Bruno Mégret, a former deputy leader of Le Pen's National Front who had been expelled in December 1998 because of his support for forming alliances with center-right parties. In January 1999 Mégret's dissident FN faction elected him leader of the "National Front–National Movement," but in May the courts ruled that the party could not use the National Front designation, which led to adoption of the current name. At the first round of the 2002 presidential race Mégret won 2.3 percent of the vote.

In January 2004 Mégret was convicted of illegal party financing, fined, and given a one-year suspended sentence. In November 2005 the party's National Council decided to begin planning to ensure Mégret a place on the ballot for the 2007 presidential election, but in December 2006, in a "personal and political reconciliation," Mégret threw his support to Le Pen. The party opposed the proposed EU constitution and has fought against "Islamization." In the 2007 National Assembly election, campaigning under the banner of the **MNR–Alliance Patriotique,** the party failed to win any seats.

In May 2008 Mégret announced his intention to retire, but four months later he reasserted control and ousted Secretary General Nicolas BAY and his assistant, Jacques GAILLARD, the two of whom urged their supporters to join them in the already-established **National Convergences** (*Convergences Nationales*—CN). Mégret assumed no formal leadership title, while former vice president Annick Martin became secretary general.

Leaders: Bruno MÉGRET, Annick MARTIN (Secretary General).

New Popular Right (*Nouvelle Droite Populaire*—NDP). Established in April 2008, the NDP was formed by former members of the FN who wished to separate their far-right agenda from Jean-Marie Le Pen's strident political persona. Like the FN and the other far-right parties, the NDP opposes "Islamization," immigration, "ultraliberal globalization," and further EU integration. It champions a return to "family values," decentralization, and fidelity to Hellenic, Celtic, and Christian roots.

Party founders were Robert Spieler and Jean-François TOUZÉ, the latter of whom was dismissed from the party in September 2008 for what were described by his opponents as "liberal" and "pro-American" views. He immediately announced formation of another far-right organization, the **New Republican Right** (*Nouvelle Droite Républicaine*—NDR).

Leader: Robert SPIELER (General Delegate).

Liberal Alternative (*Alternatif Libérale*—AL). The AL was established in 2006 by Édouard FILLIAS and Sabine Herold of the Dear Liberty (*Liberté Chérie*) association. It has espoused a free-market, antiunion, libertarian agenda. In 2007 Fillias failed to qualify for the presidential ballot and the party failed to win any National Assembly seats. Herold has reportedly welcomed comparisons with Margaret Thatcher, the former British prime minister.

Leaders: Sabine HEROLD (President), Louis-Marie BACHELOT (Secretary General).

Other Parties of the Left:

The Alternatives (*Les Alternatifs*). The Alternatives was launched as the Red and Green Alternatives (*L'Alternatives Rouge et Verte*—ARV) in 1989 by merger of the Unified Socialist Party (*Parti Socialist Unifié*—PSU), which dated from 1960, and the New Left (*Nouvelle Gauche*—NG), which had been organized by Pierre JUQUIN following his expulsion from the PCF in 1987. Initially a self-proclaimed anarcho-syndicalist group, the ARV also described itself as "feminist, ecologist, and internationalist."

The ARV adopted its current name in 1998, when new statutes described the organization as a political movement dedicated to creating a postcapitalist society based on human liberation, social justice, and harmony with nature. In 2002 it supported President Chirac's reelection in the second round ("for the first and last time") and in June ran candidates unsuccessfully for various National Assembly seats. In 2007 it supported antiglobalization advocate José BOVÉ for president and ran, unsuccessfully, as part of the alternative left movement in the subsequent National Assembly election.

At its congress in November 2008 the Alternatives reaffirmed a commitment to "construction of a new alternative left political force." In 2009 it chose not to present a list for the European Parliament election but recommended that its members consider supporting candidates offered by the Left Front and the New Anticapitalist Party (NPA, below).

Leaders: Jean-Jacques BOISLAROUSSIE and Rachel LAFONTAINE (Spokespersons).

Cap 21—Citizen Action and Participation for the 21st Century (*Citoyenneté Action et Participation pour le 21ème Siècle*). Corinne Lepage, a former minister of the environment opposed to some of the more leftist policies of the Greens, established CAP 21 as a political forum in 1996 and then transformed it into a political movement in 2000. She won 1.9 percent of the presidential vote in 2002 but threw her support to François Bayrou in 2007. More recently, she has been linked to Bayrou's MoDem.

Leader: Corinne LEPAGE.

Ecology Generation (*Génération Écologie*—GE). The GE was formed in 1990 by Brice LALONDE, a former presidential candidate and subsequently environment minister. "*Les Bleus*" has had no success in national elections, and in 2002 Lalonde failed to obtain the necessary number of signatures to appear on the presidential ballot. Another party president, France Gamerre, tried to run in 2007 but also failed to obtain sufficient signatures. For the 2007 National Assembly election the GE concluded an accord with three like-minded organizations: the **Independent Ecological Movement** (*Mouvement Écologiste Indépendant*—MEI), led by former Green presidential candidate Antoine WAECHTER; Albert LEPEYRE's **Clover–New Ecologists** (*Le Trèfle–Les Nouveaux Écologistes*); and Jacques LE BOUCHER's **Man-Animal-Nature Movement** (*Mouvement Homme-Animaux-Nature*—MHAN).

In 2008 France Gamerre chose not to seek a third term as party president and was succeeded by former vice president Jean-Noël Debroise. For the 2009 European Parliament election the GE and the MEI joined with **France in Action** (*La France en Action*) to offer a joint list, the **Independent Ecologist Alliance** (*Alliance Écologiste Indépendante*—AEI), which was unsuccessful.

Leaders: Jean-Noël DEBROISE (President), Monique BACCELLI (Vice President), Jean Luc LEGAREZ (Secretary General).

Independent Workers' Party (*Parti Ouvrier Indépendant*—POI). The POI was established in mid-2008, upon dissolution of its predecessor, the Workers' Party (*Parti des Travailleurs*—PT). The PT had been established in 1991 as successor to the Trotskyist Internationalist Communist Party (*Parti Communiste Internationaliste*—PCI). Its 2007 presidential candidate, Gérard Schivardi, finished last (as Daniel Gluckstein had in 2002), with only 0.3 percent of the vote.

Leaders: Daniel GLUCKSTEIN, Gérard SCHIVARDI.

New Anticapitalist Party (*Nouveau Parti Anticapitalist*—NPA). The NPA is successor to the Trotskyist Revolutionary Communist League (*Ligue Communiste Révolutionnaire*—LCR), which was founded in 1973 by Alain KRIVINE. In 2007 the LCR's presidential candidate, Olivier Besancenot, won 4.1 percent of the national vote, for fifth place; he had finished eighth in 2002. In 2008 Basancenot announced that he intended to form the NPA as a democratic socialist party that could unite various leftists. The founding congress was held in February 2009.

For the June 2009 European Parliament elections the NPA ran its own list, which was unsuccessful. A breakaway faction, which wanted to join the Left Front list led by the PCF, organized in March 2009 as the Unitarian Left (GU, below).

Leader: Olivier BESANCENOT (Spokesperson).

Republican and Citizen Movement (*Mouvement Républicain et Citoyens*—MRC). The MRC traces its origins to the Citizen's Movement (*Mouvement des Citoyens*—MdC), which was founded in 1993, primarily by former PS adherents who favored a "weaker" EU and who opposed the proposed single EU currency. In 1997 the MdC won seven National Assembly seats and joined the subsequent PS-led government.

In August 2000 the MdC president, Jean-Pierre Chevènement, resigned as interior minister because of his objections to the proposed Corsican autonomy plan. Running for president in 2002 on a platform that combined leftist economics, law and order, and French independence, he finished sixth, with 5.3 percent of the first-round vote. In the June National Assembly election, running on a Republican Pole list (*Pôle Républicain*—PR), the party failed to win any seats. It subsequently reorganized as the MRC. In November 2006 Chevènement announced his intention to again seek the presidency, but a month later he withdrew to support the PS's Royal. More recently, he expressed an interest in trying to unite the left in a single party.

Leaders: Jean-Pierre CHEVÈNEMENT (Honorary President), Georges SARRE (First Secretary).

Unitarian Left (*Gauche Unitaire*—GU). The far-left GU was established in March 2009 by members of the New Anticapitalist Party (NPA, above) who, unlike the leaders of the parent party, wanted to compete in the June European Parliament election on the Communist-led Left Front list.

Leader: Christian PICQUET.

Workers' Struggle (*Lutte Ouvrière*—LO). The LO is a small Trotskyite party whose leader, Arlette Laguiller, has entered six presidential races since 1974, "not at all to be elected" but to "make heard the workers' voice amid the . . . hypocritical declarations" of the leading candidates, including those of the Socialist and Communist parties. In the 2002 presidential contest Laguiller attracted 5.7 percent of the vote in the first round, her best performance to date. In the 2004 regional elections, the LO teamed up with the rival Revolutionary Communist League (LCR, below) in an effort to attract left-wing voters. In 2007 Laguiller won 1.3 percent of the vote in the first round of the presidential election. In June 2009 the LO ran an unsuccessful list for the European Parliament.

Leader: Arlette LAGUILLER.

Other National Political Organizations:

At present, the most visible French antiglobalization crusader is José Bové, a founder of the **Small Farmers' Confederation** (*Confédération Paysanne*), who first came to widespread attention by wrecking a McDonald's restaurant in Millau in 1997. More recently, he has been arrested on several occasions for destroying fields of genetically modified crops. In 2007 he won 1.3 percent of the first-round presidential vote.

Regional Parties and Groups:

Parties and groups seeking Corsican autonomy or separation have long been active, but they have drawn increased international attention as proposals for greater Corsican autonomy have made their way through Parliament. Closest to the political mainstream, the Corsican Nation (*Corsica Nazione*—CN) alliance, led by Jean-Guy TALAMONI, competed with some success against branches of national parties in regional elections. The largest and most prominent of the militant organizations was the Corsican National Liberation Front (*Front de Libération Nationale de la Corse/Fronte di Liberazione Naziunale di a Corsica*—FLNC), which was established in 1976 but which in 1990 split into two organizations: the FLNC–Historic Wing (FLNC–*Canal Historique*—FLNC-CH), which is now called the **Corsican National Liberation Front–Union of Combatants** (FLNC–*Union des Combatants*—FLNC-UC), and the FLNC–*Canal Habituel*, which dissolved in 1997.

The history of the FLNC has been marked by bombings, other terrorist activities, and interfactional feuding, interspersed with periodic cease-fires. An FLNC-CH splinter, the **Armata Corsa**, was established in 1999 by François SANTONI, a former secretary general of *A Cuncolta Indipendentista* (ACI), the legal wing of the banned FLNC-CH; Santoni was murdered in August 2001. In May 2001 the ACI announced that three additional groups—*Corsica Viva*, *Associu per a Suvranita*, and *U Cullettivu Naziounale*—were joining it in formation of Independence (*Indipendenza*). In August 2003 the *Resistenza Corsa*, which had claimed responsibility for a series of bombings earlier in the year, announced that it was merging with the FLNC-UC. One of the more recent FLNC splinters, the **Corsican National Liberation Front–October 22** (FLNC *du 22 Octobre*) opposed a cease-fire that the FLNC-UC had declared in November 2003 in an effort to establish an alliance to contest the March 2004 regional elections. In May 2007 14 alleged members of another splinter, the **Corsican National Liberation Front of the Unnamed** (FLNC *des Anonymes*), were sentenced to lengthy prison terms for a series of bombings in 2001–2002. Those convicted included Antoine MANCINI, the group's head.

In February 2004 the CN and *Indipendenza* were among the groups organizing a National Union (*Unione Naziunale*—UN) list headed by Jean-Guy Talamoni and another moderate nationalist, Edmond SIMÉONI. With the support of the FLNC-UC, the list won 17 percent of the second-round vote in the March elections. In November the CN and *Indipendenza* merged as the **Independent Corsican Nation** (Corsica Nazione Indipendente—CNI).

Six months later, the FLNC-UC ended its cease-fire to protest the trial of 22 nationalists, one of whom, Charles PIERI, was reputedly the FLNC-UC commander. In May 2005 Pieri was convicted and sentenced to ten years in prison for involvement in illegal fund-raising. Nineteen codefendants also were convicted, but two were acquitted, including Talamoni. Since then, the FLNC and the FLNC–October 22 have claimed responsibility for hundreds of bombings. In 2004 **Clandestini Corsi** claimed to be targeting North African immigrants, whom it accused of involvement in drug trafficking. In August 2006 a previously unknown group, **Clandestini Ribelli** (Clandestine Rebels), claimed responsibility for attacking a regional government building. In May 2008 a new **Corsican National Liberation Front 1976** (FLNC 1976) claimed responsibility for some two dozen recent attacks.

In February 2008 the CNI announced that it would contest upcoming local elections independent of the other UN participants, the **National Call** (*A Chjama Naziunale*—CAN) and the **Party of the Corsican Nation** (*Partitu di a Nazione Corsa*—PNC), which was established in December 2002 by merger of several groups that rejected the use of violence. The PNC and CAN subsequently identified their coalition as the **Unione Nationale—PNC–A Chjama**, led by Siméoni. In February 2009 the CNI, still led by Talamoni, joined three other smaller separatist groups, most prominently **Renovation** (*Rinnovu*), under one banner, the **Corsica Libera.**

There are a number of additional regional organizations of varying degrees of militancy. The **Union of the Alsatian People** (*Union du Peuple Alsacien/Elsass Volksunion*—UPA/EVU) has campaigned for regional autonomy and restoration of links to German-speaking Lorraine. In May 2005 the **Alsatian Corps** (*Elsass Korps*), a neo-Nazi group, was banned. The **Breton Democratic Union** (*Union Démocratique Breton*—UDB), a socialist-oriented group, seeks autonomy for Brittany by nonviolent means. Other regional groups include the federalist **Party for the Organization of a Free Brittany** (*Parti pour l'Organisation d'une Bretagne Libre*—POBL); the separatist **Liberation Front of Brittany–Breton Republican Army** (*Front Libération de la Bretagne–Armée Républicain Breton*—FLB-ARB); and the French Basque **Those of the North** (*Iparretarrak*), which was outlawed in July 1987 following the conviction of its leader, Philippe BIDART, for murder. Bidart was freed in 2007.

LEGISLATURE

The bicameral **Parliament** (*Parlement*) consists of an indirectly chosen Senate and a directly elected National Assembly.

Senate (*Sénat*). The French Senate, which under the Fifth Republic has been reduced to a limiting and delaying role, currently consists of 343 members. The 312 senators from metropolitan France (including Corsica) are designated by an electoral college that is dominated by municipal council members but also includes National Assembly deputies and regional and departmental council members. Nineteen senators are indirectly elected by the overseas jurisdictions, and 12 are named by the Higher Council of French Abroad (*Conseil Supérieur des Français à l'Étranger*) to represent French nationals overseas.

Under a 2003 reform, the number of senators was increased from 321 to 331 in 2004 and to the present number of 343 in September 2008; 5 more are to be added in 2011, thus bringing the total membership to 348. (Metropolitan and overseas departments will be represented by 326, other overseas territories by 10, and French citizens abroad by 12.) In addition, the senatorial term was shortened from nine years (selected by thirds every three years) to six years (to be selected by halves every three years).

The September 21, 2008, election for 114 seats produced the following results: Socialist Party, 44; Union for a Popular Movement, 41; Diverse Left, 9; Diverse Right, 8; Left Radical Party, 5; French Communist Party, 3; Presidential Majority, 3 (2 affiliated with the Centrist Union group and 1 with the Union for a Popular Movement); Regionalist, 1 (sitting with the Socialist group). As of September 2009 the distribution of seats by senatorial grouping was as follows: Union for a Popular Movement and allies, 151; Socialists and allies, 115; Centrist Union (mainly former members of the Union for French Democracy), 29; Communist, Republican, Citizen, and Left Party (mainly members of the French Communist Party), 24; Democratic and European Social Rally, 17; unattached, 7.

President: Gérard LARCHER.

National Assembly (*Assemblée Nationale*). The French Assembly presently consists of 577 deputies elected by two-round, majoritarian voting in single-member districts for five-year terms (subject to dissolution). Candidates receiving a majority of the vote in the first round are declared elected; in all other districts, those who receive 12.5 percent of the vote in the first round may proceed to the second, in which a plurality is sufficient for election.

At the most recent election of June 10 and 17, 2007, 110 candidates won in the first round, with the final results from both rounds producing the following distribution: Union for a Popular Movement (UMP), 313 seats; Socialist Party, 186; New Center, 22; French Communist Party, 15; Diverse Left, 15; Diverse Right, 9; Left Radical Party, 7; Greens, 4; Union for French Democracy/Democratic Movement, 3; Movement for France, 1; Regionalist, 1; Diverse, 1.

As of September 2009 the National Assembly listed the members as belonging to the following political groups (*groupes politiques*), each of which must have at least 20 members: UMP, 310 plus 7 allies; Socialist, Radical, Citizen, and Diverse Left, 186 plus 18 allies; Democratic and Republican Left, 25; New Center, 21 plus 2 allies; unaffiliated, 8.

President: Bernard ACCOYER.

CABINET

[as of September 15, 2009]

Prime Minister	François Fillon
Ministers of State	Michèle Alliot-Marie [f]
	Jean-Louis Borloo (PR)
Ministers	
Budget, Public Accounts, Civil Service, and State Reform	Éric Woerth
Culture and Communication	Frédéric Mitterrand (ind.)
Defense	Hervé Morin (NC)
Ecology, Energy, Sustainable Development and the Sea, and Green Technologies and Climate Negotiations	Jean-Louis Borloo (PR)
Economy, Industry, and Employment	Christine Lagarde [f]
Food, Agriculture, and Fisheries	Bruno Le Maire (ind.)
Foreign and European Affairs	Bernard Kouchner (ind.)
Health and Sports	Roselyne Bachelot-Narquin [f]
Higher Education and Research	Valérie Pécresse [f]
Immigration, Integration, National Identity, and Mutually Supportive Development	Éric Besson
Industry	Christian Estrosi
Interior, Overseas France, and the Territorial Collectivities	Brice Hortefeux
Justice and Human Rights, Keeper of the Seals	Michèle Alliot-Marie [f]
Labor, Social Relations, the Family, Solidarity, and Urban Affairs	Xavier Darcos
National Education	Luc Chatel
Relations with Parliament	Henri de Raincourt
Rural Affairs and Territorial Management	Michel Mercier (MoDem)
Youth	Martin Hirsch (ind.)
Minister Responsible for the Economic Stimulus Plan	Patrick Devedjian
Government Spokesperson	Luc Chatel
High Commissioner on Active Solidarity against Poverty	Martin Hirsch (ind.)

[f] = female

Note: Unless otherwise noted, ministers are members of the UMP.

COMMUNICATIONS

France's traditional freedom of the press has been maintained under the Fifth Republic. A long-standing restriction that offensive criticism may not be directed against the head of state and that the private lives of politicians may not be reported is now largely ignored. The circumstances surrounding the dissolution of President Sarkozy's second marriage in 2007 and his February 2008 remarriage attracted massive media coverage and commentary.

Press. The following newspapers are published daily in Paris, unless otherwise noted: *Ouest-France* (Rennes, national circulation, 785,000 daily, 250,000 Sunday); *Le Monde* (370,000), independent evening paper with international readership and weekly edition in English, left-of-center; *Le Parisien* (365,000), popular morning independent; *Le Figaro* (340,000), founded 1826, leading morning independent and standard-bearer of the bourgeoisie; *Sud-Ouest* (Bordeaux, 330,000); *La Voix du Nord* (Lille, 320,000); *Le Journal du Dimanche* (300,000 Sunday); *Le Dauphiné Libéré* (Grenoble, 260,000); *Le Progrès* (Lyon, 260,000); *International Herald Tribune* (245,000), American; *La Nouvelle République du Centre-Ouest* (Tours, 245,000); *La Dépêche du Midi* (Toulouse, 220,000); *La Montagne* (Clermont-Ferrand, 215,000); *Les Dernières Nouvelles d'Alsace* (Strasbourg, 210,000); *L'Est Républicain* (Nancy, 210,000); *Le Télégramme* (Morlaix, 200,000); *Le Provence* (Marseilles, 170,000), largest south-eastern daily, socialist; *Midi-Libre* (Montpellier, 165,000); *Libération* (160,000), left-oriented independent; *Nice-Matin* (Nice, 160,000); *Le Républicain Lorrain* (Metz, 160,000); *Aujourd'hui en France* (150,000), published nationally by *Le Parisien*; *Les Echos* (120,000), financial and economic; *L'Union* (Reims, 120,000); *L'Alsace* (Mulhouse, 115,000); *Le Courrier de l'Ouest* (Angers, 100,000), *La Croix* (90,000), Catholic; *L'Humanité* (120,000), communist.

News agencies. The principal French news agency is the semiofficial French Press Agency (*Agence France-Presse*—AFP), founded in 1835, which operates in most countries and many overseas territories in French, English, and Spanish; other agencies include *Agence Parisienne de Presse* (ACP). The leading foreign news agencies maintain bureaus in France's principal cities.

Broadcasting and computing. Until 1972 the government-owned French Radio and Television Organization (*Office de Radiodiffusion et Télévision Française*—ORTF) held a monopoly of both domestic and international services. Since 1974, when the ORTF was dismantled, the regulatory function has passed through a series of bodies and now resides in an independent Higher Audiovisual Council (*Conseil Supérieur de l'Audiovisuel*—CSA). At present there is a mix of public service (partially state administered) and commercial broadcast outlets, including *France 24*, a global French-language satellite news service that began broadcasts in December 2006.

As of 2008 there were 682.1 Internet users per 1,000 inhabitants. In May 2009 the French Parliament passed a strict antipiracy bill that provides for disconnecting from the Internet repeat offenders who have illegally downloaded music and films.

INTERGOVERNMENTAL REPRESENTATION

Ambassador to the U.S.: Pierre VIMONT.

U.S. Ambassador to France: Charles H. RIVKIN.

Permanent Representative to the UN: Gérard ARAUD.

IGO Memberships (Non-UN): ACS, ADB, AfDB, BDEAC, BIS, BOAD, CERN, CEUR, EBRD, EIB, ESA, EU, Eurocontrol, G-7/G-8 G-10, G-20, IADB, IEA, Interpol, IOC, IOM, NATO, OECD, OIF, OSCE, PC, PCA, WCO, WEU, WTO.

RELATED TERRITORIES

The former French overseas empire entered a state of constitutional and political transformation after World War II, as a majority of its component territories achieved independence and most of the others modified their links to the home country. The initial step in the process was the establishment in 1946 of the French Union (*Union Française*) as a single political entity designed to encompass all French-ruled territories. As defined by the constitution of the Fourth Republic, the French Union consisted of two elements: (1) the "French Republic," comprising metropolitan France and the overseas departments and territories, and (2) all those "associated territories and states" that chose to join. Vietnam, Laos, and Cambodia became associated states under this provision; Tunisia and Morocco declined to do so. The arrangement proved ineffective, however, in stemming the tide of nationalism, which led within a decade to the independence of the Indochinese states, Tunisia, and Morocco; the onset of the war of independence in Algeria; and growing pressure for independence in other French African territories.

In a further attempt to accommodate these pressures, the constitution of the Fifth Republic as adopted in 1958 established the more flexible framework of the French Community (*Communauté Française*), the primary purpose of which was to satisfy the demand for self-government in the African colonies while stopping short of full independence. Still composed of the "French Republic" on the one hand and a group of "Member States" on the other, the community was headed by the president of the French Republic and endowed with its own Executive Council, Senate, and Court of Arbitration. Initially, 12 French African territories accepted the status of self-governing member states, with only Guinea opting for complete independence. In response to the political evolution of other member states, the French constitution was amended in 1960 to permit continued membership in the community even after independence, but no previously dependent territory elected to participate. The community's Senate was abolished in 1961, at which time the organization became essentially moribund.

As a consequence of constitutional changes instituted in March 2003 and legislation passed in July 2003 and February 2007, the present French Republic encompasses, in addition to mainland France and Corsica, four overseas departments, six overseas collectivities, and two overseas collectivities sui generis, each of whose history and present status is discussed below. In March 2009 voters in Mayotte, an overseas collectivity, overwhelmingly supported becoming France's fifth overseas department, which is expected to occur in 2011.

Overseas Departments:

The overseas departments (*départements d'outre-mer*—DOM) all have similar political institutions. Like the metropolitan departments, their chief administrative officers are commissioners of the republic or prefects, appointed by the French Ministry of the Interior. Unlike the metropolitan departments, which are grouped into regions, each overseas department is geographically coterminous with an overseas region (*région d'outre-mer*—ROM). Each overseas department elects a General Council (*Conseil Général*) to which many of the earlier day-to-day prefectural powers, particularly in financial affairs, were transferred in 1982. General councilors are elected to represent individual districts (cantons). Voters also elect, from party lists, a Regional Council (*Conseil Régional*) to which enhanced policy and planning powers in economic, social, and cultural affairs were accorded in 1983. In addition, there are directly elected mayors and municipal councils for the various townships (communes).

French Guiana (*Guyane*). Situated on the east coast of South America between northern Brazil and Suriname, French Guiana became a French possession in 1816, after two centuries of strife involving, at various times, most of the Western European sea powers. It was ruled as a colony until 1946, when it became a department. From 1852 to 1947 it was utilized as a penal colony, including, most notoriously, Devil's Island (*Île du Diable*, one of the Salut group), where political prisoners were incarcerated. In 1968 a major rocket-launch facility was established in Kourou, from which the European Space Agency has launched satellites and space probes since 1983. The economy is heavily dependent on French subsidies and on the European Space Center, which contributes about one-quarter of the department's GDP. Fishing, agricultural production (principally legumes, sugarcane, fruit, and rice), and tourism also contribute to the economy. Among the largely undeveloped natural resources are significant gold deposits.

The department covers an area of 35,135 square miles (91,000 sq. km.). Of its population (2007E) of 212,000, some 90 percent inhabit the coastal region and are mainly Creoles, interspersed with Chinese, Lebanese, Brazilians, Haitians, Surinamese, and others, while the 10 percent living in the interior are largely Indian and *Noir Marrons* (descendants of fugitive slaves). The capital, Cayenne, had an estimated population of 57,100 in 2005. The department elects two deputies to the French National Assembly and, from September 2008, two senators instead of one to the Senate. Local government is based on 2 districts, comprising 19 cantons and 22 communes.

The two main parties are the local branch of the Gaullist Union for a Popular Movement (UMP) and the **Guianese Socialist Party** (*Parti Socialiste Guyanais*—PSG), an affiliate of the French Socialist Party whose longtime advocacy of internal self-rule was recently augmented by a demand for autonomy as a "necessary and preparatory stage" for full independence. Three candidates of the proindependence **Movement for Decolonization and Social Emancipation** (*Mouvement pour la Décolonisation et l'Émancipation Sociale*—MDES) were elected to the Regional Council in March 1998, although the PSG maintained a plurality and retained the presidency of the council. The PSG secured only 5 of 19 seats in the subsequent election for the General Council, with left-winger André LECANTE of the **Guianese Democratic Action** (*Action Démocratique Guyanaise*—ADG) being elected as that council's president. He was succeeded in March 2001 by Joseph HO-TEN-YOU, who had been elected as a *Divers Gauche* (Diverse Left) candidate.

Pressure from government and political leaders within the department for increased autonomy led to a meeting in Paris in December 2000 between recently installed Secretary of State for Overseas Departments and Territories Christian Paul and leaders of the PSG, the RPR (the predecessor of the UMP), the **Guiana Democratic Forces** (*Forces Démocratiques Guyanaises*—FDG) of Sen. Georges OTHILY, and the leftist **Walwari** movement (but not the MDES, which had refused an invitation). In November 2001 the French government endorsed a series of locally drafted autonomy proposals, which included greater legislative and administrative control.

In an unprecedented development, longtime Guianese politician Christiane TAUBIRA, founder of *Walwari*, ran for the French presidency in 2002 as the nominee of the PRG. She won 2.3 percent of the national vote in the first round. At the June National Assembly election French Guiana's two seats were filled by Taubira, who was running for reelection with the endorsement of the Socialist Party as well as the PRG and *Walwari*, and another incumbent, Léon BERTRAND, now of the UMP. Bertrand was subsequently named head of tourism in the Raffarin administration and was succeeded in the assembly by Juliana RIMANE (UMP).

In the Regional Council election on March 21 and 28, 2004, the PSG, headed by Council President Antoine Karam, won 17 seats, with the UMP and an FDG-*Walwari* joint list splitting the other 14 seats. The outcome of balloting for half the General Council was less definitive, with *Divers Gauche* holding a plurality. Following the election, Pierre DÉSERT (*Divers Gauche*) was named president of the General Council.

In October 2006 the French government suspended authorization for development of an open-cast gold mine near Cayenne. Opponents of the facility had convinced Paris that pollution from the mine would cause significant harm to an adjacent nature preserve. Exploitation of the department's gold reserves remains a contentious issue, however, especially in the south, where "informal gold mining" is largely conducted by miners—perhaps as many as 15,000—who have illegally crossed the border. Moreover, their activities have created significant pollution problems along thousands of miles of rivers. Illegal immigration from Suriname and Guyana also remains a significant issue, as does smuggling.

In February 2007 France established by decree the French Guiana Amazonian Park. Encompassing some 3.4 million hectares in the south, the new national park includes 2 million hectares of primary rainforest.

The June 2007 National Assembly election concluded with Taubira having won reelection but with Léon Bertrand losing to the PSG's Chantel BERTHELOT. The local elections of March 9 and 16, 2008, saw a number of incumbent members of the General Council defeated, although the left won sufficient support to retain the leadership. The department's two *Divers Gauche* senators, Jean-Étienne ANTOINETTE and Georges PATIENT, were elected in September 2008.

Prefect: Daniel FEREY.

President of the General Council: Alain TIEN-LIONG (Diverse Left).

President of the Regional Council: Antoine KARAM (PSG).

Guadeloupe. Situated in the Lesser Antilles southeast of Puerto Rico, Guadeloupe encompasses the main islands of Basse-Terre and adjacent Grande-Terre as well as a number of smaller islands, including Marie-Galante, La Désirade, Les Saintes (Terre-de-Haut and Terre-de-Bas), and the uninhabited Îles de la Petite Terre. (The island of Saint Barthelemy and the northern half of Saint Martin were separated from Guadeloupe in 2007—see separate write-ups, below.) Guadeloupe was first occupied by the French in 1635, was annexed as a colonial possession in 1815, and became a French department in 1946. It has an area of 630 square miles (1,632 sq. km.) and a population (2007E) of 471,000, of whom approximately 12,000 are residents of the capital, Basse-Terre. The largest town is Les Abymes (63,000E). Guadeloupians are predominantly black and mulatto, with a few native-born Caucasians and many metropolitan French. The department's economy is based principally on tourism and the export of bananas, sugar, and rum. High unemployment remains a perpetual problem. The department elects four deputies to the French National Assembly and three senators to the Senate. Local administration is based on 2 districts, divided into 40 cantons and 32 communes.

Long-simmering aspirations on the part of leftist organizations erupted in a series of bombings in the 1980s but gave way, by the 1990s, to calls for greater autonomy. At present, the leading parties are branches of PS and the UMP, plus the **Guadeloupian Democratic Progressive Party** (*Parti Progressiste Démocratique Guadeloupéen*—PPDG), which was formed in the early 1990s by dissidents from the **Communist Party of Guadeloupe** (*Parti Communiste Guadeloupéen*—PCG).

Center-right parties secured a majority in the Regional Council election in March 1998, Lucette MICHAUX-CHEVRY of the RPR (the predecessor of the UMP) being reelected as council president despite reportedly being the target of a corruption investigation that she described as "politically motivated." The left continued to control the General Council. In January 1999 the department's treasurer resigned, describing Guadeloupe as riddled with corruption and stuck in an economic and political "coma."

In March 2001 Jacques Gillot of the **United Guadeloupe, Socialism and Realities** (*Guadeloupe Unie, Socialisme et Réalités*—GUSR), a PS offshoot, defeated the incumbent, Marcellin LUBETH of the PPDG, for the presidency of the General Council. In the 2002 National Assembly election the new Union for the Presidential Majority (precursor of the current UMP) won 2 seats; the PS, 1; and *Divers Droite*, 1.

In the second round of Regional Council balloting on March 28, 2004, the UMP-led rightist list headed by Guadeloupe's "Iron Lady," Michaux-Chevry, was handily defeated by a **La Guadeloupe pour Tour** list that brought together the PS, PPDG, GUSR, and other leftists. Led by Victorin Lurel of the PS, the left won 29 of 41 seats, ousting Michaux-Chevry after 12 years in power. At the same time, the left easily retained control of the General Council.

The March 2004 election was viewed as confirmation of a December 7, 2003, referendum in which opponents of decentralization, led by the left, defeated a UMP-backed proposal to replace the Regional and General Councils with one assembly. The 73 percent "no" vote, which came despite support from both existing councils, appeared to reflect fear that greater autonomy would ultimately lead to reduced funding from Paris.

In December 2005 Minister of State Nicolas Sarkozy postponed a scheduled trip to Guadeloupe and Martinique in response to protests over a recent French law requiring public schools to teach the "positive" aspects of French colonial rule. The visit was to have focused on illegal immigration and drug-trafficking.

In the June 2007 election for the National Assembly two seats were won by *Divers Gauche* candidates (Eric JALTON and Jeanny MARC), one by the UMP's Gabrielle LOUIS-CARABIN, and one by the PS's Victorin Lurel. (Lurel was elected from the fourth district, which at the time still included St. Barth and St. Martin. Accordingly, he will continue to represent both new overseas collectivities until the next National Assembly election.) The department's senators are Lucette Michaux-Chevry (UMP), Jacques Gillot (GUSR), and Daniel MARSIN of the **Socialist Renewal** (*Renouveau Socialiste/Divers Gauche*).

At the March 2008 communal elections the left reinforced its General Council majority, while the 79-year-old Michaux-Chevry narrowly won election as mayor of Basse-Terre, a post she had held in the past.

On March 4, 2009, the government and labor representatives reached an agreement preparing the way for ending a 44-day general strike that had crippled the island economy. On February 16–18, several weeks into what had been a peaceful strike to that point, rioting broke out, costing the life of union leader Jacques BINO. In late February groups representing employers agreed to give low-wage earners an additional $250 a month, but the strike continued until the concession won the support of the French government, which also agreed to lower prices on some basic goods.

Prefect: Nicolas DESFORGES.

President of the General Council: Jacques GILLOT (GUSR).

President of the Regional Council: Victorin LUREL (PS).

Martinique. Occupied by the French in 1635, the Lesser Antilles island of Martinique was annexed as a colonial possession in 1790 and became a department in 1946. It has an area of 425 square miles (1,100 sq. km.). Its population of 406,000 (2007E) is predominantly black, with a small number of native-born Caucasians and many metropolitan French. The capital, Fort-de-France, had an estimated population of 92,000 in 2005. The economy, based largely on sugarcane, bananas, and rum, is, like that of the other overseas departments, heavily dependent on direct and indirect subsidies from the French government. Martinique is represented in the French Parliament by four deputies and two senators. Local administration encompasses 4 districts, divided into 45 cantons and 34 communes.

The leading parties include the PS-affiliated **Socialist Federation of Martinique** (*Fédération Socialiste de la Martinique*—FSM) and the UMP, successor to the RPR. There also is a **Martinique Communist Party** (*Parti Communiste Martiniquais*—PCM). In local politics, however, the most successful parties have recently been the separatist **Martinique Independence Movement** (*Mouvement Indépendantiste Martiniquais*—MIM) and the proautonomy **Martinique Progressive Party** (*Parti Progressiste Martiniquais*—PPM).

The RPR retained 2 seats in the 1997 French National Assembly vote, while the PPM incumbent also was reelected. The fourth seat was won by Alfred Marie-Jeanne, a leader of the MIM and mayor of Rivière-Pilote. Marie-Jeanne also was elected president of the Regional Council following the March 1998 election, in which the MIM led all parties by winning 13 of the 41 seats. He was subsequently described as the first proindependence leader of a French regional body.

In the March 2001 local elections, the PPM kept its control of most municipalities, and the PPM's Claude Lise was reelected to lead the General Council. In the 2002 National Assembly election the FSM/PS gained a representative, Louis-Joseph MANSCOUR, while Alfred ALMONT of the new Union for the Presidential Majority (predecessor of the current UMP) held his RPR district. The other two seats were won by the MIM's Marie-Jeanne and Pierre-Jean SAMOT (*Divers Gauche*) of the new, leftist **Build Martinique** (*Bâtir le Pays Martinique*—BPM). In March 2003, however, the Constitutional Council ruled that Samot had improperly received campaign funds from his unregistered party, forcing a by-election that was won by the BPM's Philippe EDMOND-MARIETTE.

A December 7, 2003, referendum on replacing the Regional Council and General Council with a single body was narrowly defeated. The election of March 21 and 28, 2004, saw the proindependence **Martinique Patriots** (*Patriotes Martiniquais*) list, led by the MIM and the **National Council of Popular Committees** (*Conseil National des Comités Populaires*—CNCP), win 28 of the Regional Council's 41 seats. The leftist **Martinique Convergences** (*Convergences Martiniquaises*), a list headed by the PPM, won 9 seats, while the **Martinique Forces of Progress** (*Forces Martiniquaises de Progrès*—FMP), which in 1998 replaced the departmental UDF affiliate, claimed 4 seats. Balloting for 23 of the General Council's 45 seats saw the left increase its majority by 2.

The June 2007 National Assembly election saw three incumbents returned, but Edmond-Mariette lost in the second round to the PPM's Serge LETCHIMY. At the March 2008 communal elections the left easily retained control of the General Council despite a split in the PPM that saw the departure of Claude Lise to form the **Martinique Democratic Rally** (*Rassemblement Démocratique Martiniquais*—RDM). The department is currently represented in the Senate by Lise and Serge LARCHER (*Divers Gauche*).

Mirroring developments in nearby Guadeloupe, workers in Martinique began a general strike in early February 2009 to protest low wages and the rising cost of living. A March 11 agreement brought an end to the 38-day strike, which succeeded in winning a wage increase of $250 a month for low-wage earners. The Sarkozy government also agreed to an aid package for small and medium-sized businesses and to assist the tourism industry, which was suffering the effects of the ongoing international recession.

Prefect: Ange MANCINI.

President of the General Council: Claude LISE (RDM).

President of the Regional Council: Alfred MARIE-JEANNE (MIM).

Reunion (*Réunion*). The island of Reunion, located in the Indian Ocean about 600 miles east of Madagascar, has been a French possession since 1642, although it did not assume its present name on a permanent basis until 1848. It has been an overseas department since 1946. The island has an area of 970 square miles (2,510 sq. km.). Its population of 799,000 (2007E), located mainly on the coast, is composed of Creoles, Caucasians, Malabar Indians, blacks, Malays, Vietnamese, and Chinese. The capital, Saint-Denis, had an estimated population of 207,000 in 2005. The economy is based primarily on sugarcane cultivation, tourism, and public sector employment. Reunion elects five members of the French National Assembly and three senators, with a fourth to be added in 2011. Local administration is based on 24 communes and 49 cantons.

Currently active parties include the local branches of the PS, the UMP, the PRG, and MoDem. Other organizations include the **Reunion Communist Party** (*Parti Communiste Réunionnais*—PCR); the **Reunion Greens** (*Les Verts Réunion*); and **Free-DOM** (for *Free Département d'Outre-Mer*), which was formed in the early 1990s by the Socialist mayor of Saint Denis, Camille SUDRE. Sudre had previously been best known as the president of *Radio Free–DOM* and its affiliate, *Télé Free–DOM,* a pirate facility whose transmitters had been confiscated in 1991 but were recovered following his election as president of the Regional Council in 1992.

In the late 1990s a proposal to divide Reunion into two departments generated considerable controversy, with President Chirac being the most prominent French official to voice support for the idea. In 2000, however, both the Senate and the National Assembly voted down any such division. The issue appeared to play a significant part in the March 2001 local elections, at which the center-right parties made gains. The National Assembly election of June 2002 saw President Chirac's new Union for the Presidential Majority win three seats and the PCR/PS win two.

At the regional election of March 21 and 28, 2004, the sitting Regional Council president, Paul Vergès of the PCR, headed a victorious **Alliance** list that included Free-DOM as well as the PCR among its seven constituent groups. The Alliance claimed 27 Regional Council seats, while the UMP won 11 and a PS-Greens alliance took the remaining 7. In contrast, following balloting for 25 of the General Council's 49 seats, the rightist UMP continued to hold a majority, although with a reduced total of 25 seats. The PCR and the PS, despite gaining 2 seats each, remained in the single digits.

In February 2006 an epidemic of the mosquito-borne viral disease chikungunya ("that which bends up") fever reached its peak on Reunion. In the end, one-third of the population were infected and over 150 individuals died. During the crisis France provided $110 million in emergency health and economic aid and deployed 500 military personnel to help health officials spray mosquito breeding areas. The disease, which is characterized by high fever, rashes, and arthritis-like symptoms, has no known cure and no vaccine. Some Reunion officials criticized Paris for not responding faster when the disease first broke out in 2005.

At the June 2007 National Assembly election only one incumbent, the UMP's Bertho AUDIFAX, lost his seat, which was won by the PS's Jean-Claude FRUTEAU. René-Paul VICTORIA (UMP) and Huguette BELLO (PCR) won reelection, while the two open seats were won by Patrick LEBRETON (PS) and Didier ROBERT (UMP), the latter having easily defeated President Vergès in a runoff. The department's senators are Anne-Marie PAYET, who was elected as a member of the UDF; Gélita HOREAU, who joined the Communist, Republican, and Citizen group in the Senate; and Jean-Paul VIRAPOULLE (UMP).

At the March 2008 communal elections the left, for the first time in three decades, won more communes than the right—12 versus 11, with MoDem taking 1. In the General Council, half of which was up for replenishment, the right continued to hold a majority, 25 seats (down from 31), with the left holding 21 and MoDem 3. Despite considerable sentiment on the right in favor of electing a member of the *Divers Droit* as council president, the incumbent, Nassimah Dindar (UMP), cobbled together a left-right coalition and retained her office by a 30–19 vote over Jean-Louis LAGOURGUE, mayor of Sainte-Marie.

Also during March 2008, Reunion drew international attention following the flight of Col. Mohammed Bacar from the Comoran island of Anjouan, where his rebellious administration had been deposed by Comoran and African Union troops. Having initially fled to Mayotte, Bacar and some two dozen supporters were charged with weapons possession and with illegally entering French waters. They were transferred to Reunion, where on March 30 a court, citing technical shortcomings, annulled the proceedings and put the group under house arrest. In mid-May France denied Bacar's request for asylum but also ruled that sending him back to the Comoros would violate his human rights. On June 5 Bacar and 21 supporters were given suspended sentences for importing arms, and on July 18 Bacar and 3 others were expelled to Benin. On July 20 another 10 allies escaped jail on Anjouan and fled to Mayotte.

Prefect: Pierre-Henri MACCIONI.

President of the General Council: Nassimah DINDAR (UMP)

President of the Regional Council: Paul VERGÈS (PCR).

Overseas Collectivities:

Through the years, various amendments and statutes have defined and redefined the six jurisdictions discussed below. These changes have often been accompanied by revisions in legislative structures. The status overseas collectivity (*collectivité d'outre-mer*) was established by the constitutional reform of March 2003. Legislation passed in February 2007 raised Saint Barthelemy and Saint Martin from communes, within the overseas department of Guadeloupe, to separate overseas collectivities.

French Polynesia (*Polynésie Française*). Scattered over a wide expanse of the South Pacific, the 35 islands and 83 atolls of French Polynesia—comprising the Austral (Tubuai) Islands, the Gambier Islands, the Marquesas Archipelago, the Society Archipelago, and the Tuamotu Archipelago—have a combined area of 1,622 square miles (4,200 sq. km.) and a population of 259,000 (2007E), of whom approximately 28,000 are settled in the territorial capital, Papeete, on the island of Tahiti. A French protectorate from 1843, in 1880 Tahiti was annexed under a treaty signed by King POMARE V. The colony gradually expanded and was renamed French Oceania in 1903. Designated as an overseas territory in 1946, French Polynesia assumed its present name in 1957.

In November 1995 the Territorial Assembly adopted an accord providing for greater autonomy in such areas as transportation, communications, the offshore economic zone, and fishing rights. France retained responsibility for defense and security as well as judicial oversight in the accord, which was approved by the French National Assembly in December and entered into effect in April 1996.

In March 2003, as specified by French constitutional revisions, French Polynesia was reclassified from overseas territory to overseas collectivity, with the provision that additional autonomy could be granted by legislative action. A statute to that effect was passed by the Senate in December 2003 and the National Assembly in January 2004, with the Constitutional Council approving the Autonomy Act for French Polynesia on February 27.

Although a 2004 organic act labeled French Polynesia an overseas country (*pays d'outre-mer*), the Constitutional Council ruled that the designation was without legal or constitutional basis. Thus, French Polynesia remains an overseas collectivity, although the term "overseas country" continues to be used in a descriptive, rather than legal, sense.

Under the 2004 autonomy act local executive responsibilities are vested in a Council of Ministers headed by a president responsible to the Assembly of French Polynesia, which is directly elected for a five-year term. The territory is represented in the French Parliament by two National Assembly deputies and, from September 2008, two senators instead of one. The economy relies heavily on tourism, with additional earnings coming from the harvesting of black pearls, the sale of commercial fishing licenses, and the export of coconut products.

In the 1996 Territorial Assembly election the **Tahoera'a Huira'atira**—TH (People's Front), previously a local section of the metropolitan RPR and now associated with the UMP, secured a slim majority of 22 seats (out of 41). The proindependence **Tavini Huira'atira/Front de Libération de la Polynésie**—FLP (People's Servant/Liberation Front of Polynesia) finished second, with 10 seats, on the strength of its appeal to opponents of the renewed nuclear testing conducted from September 1995 to January 1996, which had been met with international protests and serious violence in Papeete. France began dismantling the Mururoa nuclear test site in 1997, and the project was completed in mid-1998. Serious questions remained, however, over the environmental impact of the testing, the possible exposure of the population to radiation, and the apparent widespread use of underage workers at the site.

In the context of continuing discussions on greater autonomy, the election of May 6, 2001, for an expanded, 49-seat Territorial Assembly again produced a majority for the TH list, which won 28 seats. The separatist *Tavini Huira'atira* won 11 seats; the *Fe'tia Api* (New Star) list of Boris LÉONTIEFF, 7; and others, 3. As a result, the TH's Gaston FLOSSE was elected to a fifth term as president of the government, despite a conviction in 1999 for accepting bribes (on behalf of his party, he asserted) from an illegal gambling operation. Upon appeal, in mid-2001 a Paris court ruled in his favor.

In the French National Assembly election of June 2002 two TH/UMP candidates were elected: Papeete Mayor Michel BUILLARD won reelection and was joined by Béatrice VERNAUDON, who easily defeated the incumbent, Émile VERNAUDON of the *Ai'a Api* (New Land). *Tavini Huira'atira,* led by Oscar Temaru, boycotted the balloting.

An election for the new, 57-member Assembly of French Polynesia was held on May 23, 2004, but a near-stalemate resulted. Flosse's UMP-allied TH won 28 seats and Temaru's newly organized coalition, the **Union for Democracy** (*Union pour la Démocratie*—UPD), won 27, including 24 seats in the Windward Islands of Tahiti and Moorea. The balance of power was thus held by Nicole BOUTEAU of the **This Country Is Yours** (*No Oe E Te Nunaa*) party and *Fe'tia Api*'s Philip SCHYLE, who had become party president as a consequence of Boris Léontieff's death in a 2002 plane crash. Elected president by the legislature on June 15, Temaru indicated his intention to move French Polynesia toward a goal of independence within 20 years.

Temaru's hold on the office proved tenuous, however, as differences within the governing coalition over cabinet portfolios contributed to the departure of dissidents in September. As a consequence, Temaru lost a no-confidence motion 29–0 on October 10, and on October 23 the assembly named Flosse to assume the presidency once again. The issue of whether to conduct a new legislative election, as advocated by Temaru, was complicated on November 15 by a Council of State ruling that electioneering violations justified nullifying the May election results for the 37 Windward Islands seats.

By-elections in the 37 constituencies were held on February 13, 2005, with the UPD, now encompassing seven parties, winning 25 seats, which thereby gave the UPD and Flosse's TH a 27–27 split in the Assembly. In the meantime, Bouteau and Schyle had joined forces in the **Alliance for a New Democracy** (*Alliance pour la Démocratie Nouvelle*—ADN), which held 3 seats. Shortly thereafter Flosse lost a no-confidence motion and then stepped aside as his party's presidential candidate. Temaru, by a vote of 29–26, was reelected president on March 3, defeating the TH's new candidate, Gaston TONG SANG.

By the end of 2005 Flosse's TH had seen its legislative caucus drop to 21 members. Former party leader Jean-Christophe BOUISSOU, following a dispute with Flosse, had announced formation of the **Rautahi** (Unity) party, while several other TH members had become independents. During the same period, Oscar Temaru was repeatedly criticized by the opposition for proindependence statements. In late March 2006 Temaru presented the visiting French minister of overseas territories, François BAROIN, with a plan for devolution, the *Tahiti Nui* (Greater Tahiti) Accords, modeled on New Caledonia's Nouméa Accord. In April Temaru fended off an attempt by "autonomist" (anti-independence) opponents, led by Flosse, Émile Vernaudon, Bouissou, and maverick legislator Hiro TEFAARERE, to take control of the assembly and unseat him. Several cabinet resignations and defections to the opposition were overcome by Temaru's recruitment of defectors from the other side of the aisle and by a cabinet reshuffle.

In January 2006 President Temaru disbanded the Polynesia Intervention Group (*Groupement d'Intervention de la Polynesie*—GIP), a 1,300-person quasi-security force that had been established in the mid-1990s by Flosse to assist in national and regional disaster relief but had since taken on additional land and maritime responsibilities. Several times during 2005 some 300 GIP militants had blockaded the port of Papeete and its industrial zone over a disputed employment contract.

On December 13, 2006, having lost the support of several cabinet members and legislators whom he had recruited in April, Temaru lost a censure motion, by a vote of 29–0, that was boycotted by the UPD. On December 26 the TH's Tong Sang, backed by Vernaudon's *Ai'a Api* and Bouissou's *Rautahi,* was elected president. However, the TH-led coalition's hold on the government remained tenuous, as further evidenced in April 2007 when Flosse's son-in-law, Edouard FRITCH, was elected assembly speaker over the UPD's candidate, former speaker Antony GÉROS, by only a 28–27 vote.

Although President Tong Sang pledged to restore cordial relations with France and to refocus the government's attention to economic development, tensions with Paris continued to exist not only over the autonomy/independence divide but also over endemic corruption and cultural matters. In 2006 France refused to permit use of indigenous languages in assembly debates, and French courts refused to acknowledge any legal role for a restored Indigenous Land Tribunal. Efforts by traditionalists to create a formal customary institution, comparable to one in New Caledonia, have also been rebuffed.

In the June 2007 National Assembly election Michel Buillard won reelection, defeating Oscar Temaru, and the TH's Bruno SANDRAS won the other seat. The collectivity is represented in the Senate by Gaston Flosse and the UPD's Richard TUHEIAVA.

On September 14, 2007, Temaru reassumed the presidency, two weeks after he and Flosse had engineered the ouster of Tong Sang, who subsequently established his own party, the **Polynesia, Our Home** (*O Porinetia, To Tatou Ai'a*—OPTTA). The French secretary of state for overseas territories, Christian Estrosi, responding to Polynesia's seeming inability to establish a stable government, then convinced the French Parliament to reform the collectivity's electoral system. Among other changes, to be elected in a first round of voting Assembly candidates would have to achieve 50 percent of the vote. In all other constituencies, only those candidates winning at least 12.5 percent could advance to a second round. Despite the objections of many Polynesians, including Temaru, who accused Paris of interfering in internal Polynesian affairs, the Council of State approved the reform package in December, thereby permitting an early Assembly election.

At the first round of polling on January 27, 2008, only three candidates won Assembly seats outright. Tong Sang's OPTTA led all parties with 36.5 percent of the vote, followed by Temaru's UPD (32.8 percent) and Flosse's TH (21.8 percent). The second round, held February 10, concluded with Tong Sang's OPTTA-led **Our Home** (*To Tatou Ai'a*—TTA) coalition winning 27 seats, to 20 for the UPD and 10 for the TH. On February 23, defying expectations, Temaru's and Flosse's Assembly forces again joined and defeated Tong Sang's bid for the presidency, with Flosse collecting a bare majority of 29 votes to 27 for Tong Sang. Less than two months later, however, on April 16, Tong Sang, having attracted two defectors to his cause, led a successful no-confidence motion against Flosse and, under the previous year's reforms, immediately took over the presidency, portending further conflict with Temaru, who had been elected Assembly speaker in March, and providing further evidence that the reforms had not achieved their desired goal.

On February 9, 2009, facing a no-confidence vote engineered by Assembly Speaker Temaru, his UPD, the TH, and *Rautahi,* Tong Sang resigned as president. Two days later, Tong Sang faced former president Temaru, Edouard Fritch, and an independent, Sandra LEVY-AGAMI, in yet another presidential election. Temaru, with 24 votes, and Tong Sang, with 20, proceeded to a runoff, from which Temaru emerged with a 37–20 victory. Only two months later, however, Gaston Flosse announced that the TH was ready to join the opposition, in part because of a government proposal to adopt an income tax. President Temaru thereupon formed a surprising alliance with Tong Sang's TTA, cementing his hold on the presidency. A new cabinet announced on April 17 included, in addition to the UPD and the TTA, two members of an Assembly group led by Jean-Christophe Bouissou, and two TH defectors.

On February 17, 2009, former president Flosse was convicted of having illegally used public funds for a postelection celebration in 2004. In addition to receiving a one-year suspended sentence and a fine of $21,000, Flosse was barred from public office for a year.

High Commissioner: Adolphe COLRAT.

President of the Government: Oscar TEMARU (UPD).

Speaker of the Assembly: Philip SCHYLE (TTA).

Mayotte (*Mahoré*). Encompassing Grande-Terre, one of the four principal islands of the Comoros archipelago northwest of Madagascar, as well as the much smaller Petite-Terre and some 30 islets, Mayotte (known locally as Mahoré) was initially settled by Africans and later colonized by Arabs. From the 15th century it was visited by European ships traveling to and from the East Indies. In the aftermath of a devastating period of internal strife that began in the late 1700s, Mayotte was ceded to France in 1841 by a Malagasy sultan.

Mayotte has an area of 145 square miles (375 sq. km.) and a population of 195,000 (2007E). The chief towns are Dzaoudzi (the administrative center, on Petite-Terre), Mamoudzou, and Koungou, with populations (2005E) of 12,800, 55,500, and 19,700, respectively. Although French is the official language, most citizens speak Shimaoré, a Comoran dialect. Economic activity, centered in Mamoudzou on Grande-Terre, was traditionally based on agriculture, the principal export products being vanilla and ylang-ylang, but since 2000 fishing and aquaculture have moved to the fore. The territory is administered by a prefect and an elected General Council of 19 members; it is represented in the French Parliament by one deputy and two senators.

In two referenda held in 1976, the largely Christian residents rejected inclusion in the new Muslim-dominated Republic of the Comoros in favor of French department status. The following December Mayotte was made a territorial collectivity (*collectivité territoriale*) of France, a category construed as being midway between an overseas department and an overseas territory. In 1979 this status was extended by the French National Assembly for another five years, at the conclusion of which a third referendum was to have been held; however, in 1984 the assembly adopted a bill that indefinitely postponed a final decision. The UN General Assembly on several occasions voted in support of Comoran sovereignty over the island, while the Organization of African Unity (OAU, predecessor of the African Union—AU) demanded that France end its "illegal occupation."

Visiting Mayotte in 1994, Prime Minister Balladur announced that a referendum on the island's status would be held by 2000. Shortly thereafter, the introduction of visa requirements for incoming Comoran nationals, intended to curb illegal immigration, provoked protest demonstrations in the Comoros, where the government's hostility to French rule over Mayotte was undiminished by the desire of many Comorans to emigrate to French-ruled territory. Mayotte's economy continued to perform well, particularly relative to the Comoros, where a sense of "deprivation" vis-à-vis the more prosperous Mayotte was considered a contributing factor to the secessionist movement on Anjouan (see article on Comoro Islands).

Negotiations between officials from Mayotte and the French government in 1998 led to a tentative agreement that Mayotte would initially become a "departmental collectivity" (*collectivité départemental*). It was reportedly understood that an "evolutionary process" would subsequently lead to full-fledged departmental status for the island. French officials remained cautious, however, about the implications of any formal settlement that lacked UN and OAU endorsement of French sovereignty over Mayotte.

Over the objections of Mayotte's Senate and National Assembly representatives, Marcel HENRY and Henry JEAN-BAPTISTE, who renewed their call for full overseas departmental status for the island, the General Council and 16 out of 17 communes ultimately approved the *collectivité départemental* proposal, which was formally signed in Paris on January 27, 2000. In a referendum on July 2 nearly three-fourths of the voters supported the plan, although the precise procedures and dates remained to be worked out for the gradual transfer, over a ten-year period, of selected powers from the prefect to the General Council.

Council elections in March 2001 gave the RPR's local branch, the *Fédération de Mayotte du Rassemblement pour la Republic* (FMRPR), 5 seats; the **Mahoran Popular Movement** (*Mouvement Populaire Mahorais*—MPM), which had called for full departmental status, 4; the local branch of the Citizens' Movement (MdC), 2; the PS, 1; Marcel Henry and Henry Jean-Baptiste's new **Mahoran Departmentalist Movement** (*Mouvement Départementaliste Mahorais*—MDM), 1; and independent center or right-wing candidates, 6. In the French National Assembly election in June 2002, Mayotte's seat was won by Mansour KAMARDINE of the FMRPR and the new Union for the Presidential Majority (UMP, subsequently the Union for a Popular Movement).

Although France had passed legislation formally conferring departmental collectivity status on Mayotte, that status was formally changed to overseas collectivity under the 2003 constitutional amendments.

In the General Council election of March 21 and 28, 2004, the allied UMP and MPM won 9 seats and 1 seat, respectively, while the allied MDM and Republican and Citizen Movement (MRC, successor to the MdC) won 6 and 2 seats, respectively. A left-leaning independent won the other seat. In the French senatorial election of September 2004 Mayotte for the first time elected two senators, the victors being Soubahaddine IBRAHIM of the UMP and Adrien GIRAUD, who ran as a *Divers Droite* candidate and then chose to sit with the Centrist Union–UDF contingent in the Senate.

In February 2005 the first deputy president of the General Council, Bacar Ali BOTO, resigned from the coalition of President Saïd Ali OILI and shortly thereafter joined the opposition UMP, depriving Oili of his one-seat majority. The split resulted from differences over Oili's tight control of the budget and expenditures.

In the June 2007 National Assembly election Abdoulatifou ALY of the MDM defeated Kamardine's reelection bid. He then chose to sit with the New Center group but later moved to François Bayrou's MoDem. Following the March 2008 local elections, the UMP's Ahmed Douchina was elected president of the General Council on the strength of an alliance with the MDM and the PS.

On March 29, 2009, voters in Mayotte overwhelmingly endorsed changing the collectivity to a department. The vote in favor of departmental status was reported to be in excess of 99 percent, which did not dissuade the African Union and the government of the Comoros from denouncing the referendum. The change in status is expected to take until 2011.

Prefect: Vincent BOUVIER.

President of the General Council: Ahmed Attoumani DOUCHINA (UMP).

Saint Barthelemy (*Saint-Barthélemy*). Lying east of the Virgin Islands in the Leeward Islands of the Lesser Antilles, with St. Martin to the northwest and St. Kitts and Nevis to the South, St. Barth (also St. Bart, St. Barts, St. Barths) came under French control in 1648, was sold to Sweden in 1784, and was sold back to France in 1878, at which time it was administratively linked to Guadeloupe. On February 21, 2007, President Chirac signed into law legislation converting the island from a commune of the Department of Guadeloupe to a separate overseas collectivity. The relevant laws entered into effect upon publication in the official register on February 22, but Saint Barthelemy was not fully established as a collectivity until its first Territorial Council convened on July 15. The process of amicable separation from Guadeloupe had been put in motion by passage of a referendum on December 7, 2003, in which 96 percent of those voting approved becoming a collectivity.

St. Barth is France's smallest overseas collectivity, with an area of 9 square miles (24 sq. km.) and a population of 6,850 (2006E). The seat of government and largest town is Gustavia (named after a Swedish king). The vast majority of the population is Caucasian, and although French is the official language, English is also widely spoken. With no natural resources to exploit and virtually no arable land, the economy depends heavily on high-end tourism.

The government of St. Barth combines aspects of a commune, a department, and a region. The representative of the French government is a deputy prefect (*préfet délégué*). The Territorial Council comprises 19 members serving five-year terms. The council elects from its membership a president and a six-member Executive Council. In the new collectivity's first election, held July 1, 2007, the **St. Barth First** (*St.-Barth d'Abord*) list, headed by Bruno MAGRAS (UMP), the communal mayor, won an easy victory, taking 72 percent of the vote and 16 council seats. The other 3 seats were split among the other three competing lists: **Together for Saint Barthelemy** (*Ensemble pour Saint-Barthélemy*), headed by Benoît CHAUVIN (MoDem and Cap 21); **All United for Saint Barthelemy** (*Tous Unis pour Saint-Barthélemy*), led by Karine MIOT; and **Action-Balance-Transparency** (*Action-Equilibre-Transparence*), led by Maxime DESOUCHES. Magras was elected president by the council when it convened on July 15.

Pending election of its own National Assembly deputy at the next French general election (no later than 2012), St. Barth will continue to be represented by Guadeloupe's Victorin Lurel (PS), whose district included St. Barth at the time of the June 2007 election. The island's first senator, Michel MAGRAS (UMP), was elected in September 2008.

Deputy Prefect: Dominique LACROIX.

President of the Territorial Council: Bruno MAGRAS (UMP).

Saint Martin (*Saint-Martin*). Lying east of the Virgin Islands in the Leeward Islands of the Lesser Antilles, with Anguilla to the north and Saint Barthelemy to the southeast, the island of St. Martin is divided roughly in half, with the French overseas collectivity of *Saint-Martin* in the north and the Dutch dependency *Sint Maarten* in the south. First claimed by Spain following the early voyages of Christopher Columbus (who, despite legend, neither named nor made explicit reference to the island), Saint Martin was partitioned by the Dutch and French in 1648, although up until 1815, as a consequence of various European wars, the French sector repeatedly fell under Dutch or English control. During this period the island's economy was based on the extraction of salt from salt ponds and the cultivation of cotton, tobacco, and, from the late 1700s, sugarcane, which led to the importation of African slaves far in excess of the Caucasian population. Emancipation came in 1848, after which sugar declined in importance.

From 1946 the French half of the island comprised two communes in the Department of Guadeloupe. Seventy-six percent of St. Martin's voters approved establishment of a separate overseas collectivity in a referendum held on December 7, 2003. On February 21, 2007, President Chirac signed the necessary legislation, which accorded the same collectivity status to nearby Saint Barthelemy, effective February 22. However, St. Martin was not fully established as a collectivity until its first Territorial Council convened on July 15, 2007.

The overseas collectivity of St. Martin encompasses about 20 square miles (53 sq. km.) and has a population of 29,600 (2007E). The administrative center and largest community is Marigot. The population is primarily of African, British, Dutch, French, and Creole ancestry. French is the official language, but English is spoken universally. Today, the economy largely depends on tourism, followed by trade and offshore financial services.

Representing the French government is a deputy prefect. Local legislative responsibility is held by the Territorial Council, which comprises 23 members serving five-year terms. The council elects from its membership a president and an Executive Council. Five lists competed in the collectivity's first election, held July 1 and 8, 2007: the **Union for Progress** (*Union pour le Progrès*—UPP), led by Louis CONSTANT-FLEMING (UMP), which won 40 percent of the first-round vote; **Togetherness, Responsibility, Success** (*Rassemblement, Responsabilité, Réussite*—RRR), led by Alain RICHARDSON (32 percent); **Succeed Saint-Martin** (*Réussir Saint-Martin*—RSM), led by Jean-Luc HAMLET (11 percent); **Alliance for the Overseas Collectivity of Saint Martin** (*Alliance pour le COM de Saint-Martin*), headed by Dominique RIBOUD (9 percent); and the **Democratic Alliance for Saint Martin** (*Alliance Démocratique pour le Saint-Martin*), led by Wendel COCKS (8 percent). The first three proceeded to the second round, in which the UPP won 16 seats, the RRR won 6, and the RSM won 1.

Constant-Fleming was elected president when the Territorial Council convened on July 15, 2007, but he resigned a year later after being sanctioned by the State Council for one year because of a campaign violation. His acting successor, Marthe OGOUNDÉLÉ-TESSI, served until the election of Frantz Gumbs (UMP) on August 7. Gumbs was himself forced to step down on April 10, 2009, following a ruling that an improperly printed ballot had been used at the time of his election, but on May 5 he was again elected president by the council. In the interim, Vice President Daniel GIBBS had served as acting executive.

Until the next French general election (no later than 2012), St. Martin will be represented in the National Assembly by Guadeloupe's Victorin Lurel (PS), whose district included St. Martin at the time of the June 2007 election. St. Martin elected its first senator, Louis Constant-Fleming, in September 2008.

Deputy Prefect: Dominique LACROIX.

President of the Territorial Council: Frantz GUMBS (UMP).

Saint Pierre and Miquelon (*Saint-Pierre et Miquelon*). Located off Newfoundland in the North Atlantic, St. Pierre and Miquelon consists of eight small islands covering 93 square miles (242 sq. km.). Historically rich in fish, the surrounding waters were regularly visited by Basque fishermen well before the advent of British and French territorial claims, which were not definitely resolved, in France's favor, until 1814. The population in 2007 was 6,250, of whom almost 90 percent lived in the capital, St. Pierre. Formerly an overseas territory, the islands were raised to the status of an overseas department in 1976 following a referendum; by 1982, however, popular sentiment clearly favored the status of a territorial collectivity, which came into effect in 1985.

The most serious subsequent issue was a dispute between France and Canada involving a French claim to a 200-mile maritime economic zone—Canada acknowledged only the traditional 12-mile limit—and a collateral controversy centered on fishing quotas. In 1992 an international arbitration tribunal awarded the islands an exclusive economic zone of 3,600 square miles (8,700 sq. km.), or about one-fifth of what France had sought. More recently, severe overfishing of cod and the consequent closure of fishing grounds has had a dramatic effect on the economy. Tourism and fish farming are among the industries now being promoted.

An overseas collectivity since 2003, St. Pierre and Miquelon has an elected General Council, in addition to elected municipal councils, and is represented in the French Parliament by one deputy and one senator.

Elections to the General Council in 1994 ended the long local dominance of the Socialist Party, with UDF-affiliated lists winning 15 of the 19 seats. The local election of March 2000 saw the Socialists return to power, with the combined St. Pierre and Miquelon 2000/Future Miquelon (*St. Pierre et Miquelon 2000/Avenir Miquelon*—SPM 2000/AM) list winning 12 of the 19 seats. The UDF/RPR list, **Archipelago Tomorrow** (*Archipel Demain*—AD), won 5 seats, with the other 2 captured by the **Cape in the Future** (*Cap sur l'Avenir)* list, which was affiliated with the local branch of the PRG.

In the local election held March 19 and 26, 2006, the center-right AD swept the polls, taking 67 percent of the valid votes and 13 of 15 General Council seats in St. Pierre and, through its AD Miquelon affiliate, 61 percent of the votes and 3 of Miquelon's 4 seats. In St. Pierre the *Cap sur l'Avenir* won 2 seats; in Miquelon the **SPM Together** (*SPM Ensemble*) won 1 seat.

In the June 2007 National Assembly election Gérard GRIGNON (UMP), who had served as the territory's deputy since 1986, was defeated by Annick GIRARDIN (Left Radical), who then chose to sit as an ally of the assembly's Socialist, Radical, and Citizen group. The collectivity is represented in the French Senate by Denis DETCHEVERRY (UMP).

St. Pierre and Miquelon made international news in April 2008 when fishermen confronted the crew of the environmentalist ship the *Farley Mowat* in the St. Pierre harbor and forced it to sea. The captain of the ship had angered the fishermen by commenting that while the recent deaths of three seal hunters whose boat had capsized was tragic, the slaughter of seals was "an even greater tragedy."

Prefect: Jean-Pierre BERÇOT.

President of the General Council: Stéphane ARTANO (AD).

Wallis and Futuna Islands (*Wallis et Futuna*). The inhabitants of Wallis and Futuna, French protectorates from 1888, voted in 1959 to exchange their status for that of a French overseas territory. An overseas collectivity since 2003, Wallis and Futuna covers 106 square miles (274 sq. km.) in the South Pacific just west of Samoa, with a population of 15,400 (2007E), excluding some 20,000 Wallisians residing in New Caledonia and Vanuatu. The capital, Mata'utu, has a population of approximately 1,200. The economy relies heavily on French aid, public sector jobs, and remittances sent home from New Caledonia.

The islands are governed by a chief administrator and an elected Territorial Assembly and are represented in the French Parliament by one deputy and one senator. There is also a six-member Territorial Council encompassing the kings of the islands' three traditional kingdoms plus three members appointed by the chief administrator. Monarchical powers are limited to traditional matters and customary law, but the kings remain influential.

Local elections in March 2002 saw 134 candidates contest the 20 Territorial Assembly seats, with members of the RPR and other center-right candidates winning 13 seats to 7 for candidates supportive of the PS and the **Popular Union for Wallis and Futuna** (*Union Populaire pour Wallis et Futuna*—UPWF). In the June National Assembly election Victor BRIAL narrowly won reelection as a candidate of the new Union for the Presidential Majority (predecessor of the current UMP), but the Constitutional Court subsequently ordered a new election because of ballot irregularities. In March 2003 Brial won a repeat victory.

A political crisis was precipitated in 2005 when a grandson of Tomasi KULIMOETOKE, the traditional king of Wallis, sought refuge in the royal palace to avoid serving an 18-month prison sentence for vehicular homicide. Although the grandson surrendered in June and was taken to New Caledonia to serve his sentence, what began as a conflict between customary law and the French penal code had blossomed into a governmental impasse between traditionalists, who continued to support the administration of Prime Minister Kapeliele FAUPALA, and a reformist group led by the UPWF and the **Alliance of Wallis and Futuna** (*Alliance de Wallis et Futuna*—AWF), with tacit backing from Futuna's two royal clans. On May 22 the reformists announced a rival administration, headed by Kolovisi (Clovis) LOGOLOGOFOLAU, that was subsequently recognized by the chief administrator, Xavier de Furst. In September, when the reformists moved forward in an effort to depose the 86-year-old Kulimoetoke, who had ruled on Wallis since 1959, the king's supporters blockaded roads and shut down the airport to prevent the coronation of a new king. A special envoy from New Caledonia, Louis Lefranc, was called in to mediate the conflict, and on September 26 he reaffirmed French recognition of King Kulimoetoke. As a consequence, Logologofolau and a number of his supporters fled to New Caledonia. Early in the year, the AFW's Apeleto (Albert) LIKUVALU had been elected president of the Territorial Assembly, but on November 23 he was replaced by Ermenigilde SIMETE, who had center-right backing.

In March 2006 the two kings of Futuna, Soane Patita MAITUKU and Visesio MOELIKU, met in Paris with President Chirac, who gave his support to their request for Futuna to be made a subprefecture, which would accord the island a greater degree of administrative independence from Wallis. The kings also pressed for improved air and sea links. In February 2007 the French government and island representatives reached agreement on a $50 million developmental aid package for 2007–2011 that focused on needed infrastructure, health, and education.

The local election of April 1, 2007, concluded with center-right candidate lists in the majority, and on April 11 Pesamino TAPUTAI (UMP) was elected president of the Territorial Assembly by a 12–8 vote. Only a month later, on May 7, King Kulimoetoke died after a long illness, but the selection of a successor was postponed for a six-month mourning period. In the June election for the National Assembly Victor Brial was upset by Albert Likuvalu, who ran with the support of the PS. In December, however, Brial was elected president of the Territorial Assembly. The collectivity is represented in the Senate by Robert LAUFOAULU (UMP).

On July 25, 2008, Kapiliele Faupala was crowned king of Wallis. In February 2008 the chiefly clans of Futuna had removed King Maituku from office, reportedly over opposition to his style of management. The coronation of his successor, Petelo VIKENA, took place on November 6.

Chief Administrator: Philippe PAOLANTONI.

President of the Territorial Assembly: Victor BRIAL (UMP).

Overseas Collectivities Sui Generis:

As recently as 2002 there were three overseas territories (*territoires d'outre-mer*—TOM): French Polynesia, Wallis and Futuna, and the French Southern and Antarctic Lands (TAAF). The constitutional amendments of March 2003 eliminated the category from the French constitution, although the TAAF remained an overseas territory by dint of legislation passed in 1955.

The classification "overseas country" (*pays d'outre-mer*) was established to recognize New Caledonia's unique constitutional status under 1998's Nouméa Accord between Paris and what was then the overseas territory of New Caledonia.

The February 2007 legislation categorized both the TAAF and New Caledonia as collectivities sui generis (*collectivités sui generis*)—that is, as unique collectivities. Both nevertheless continue to be referenced, for descriptive rather than legal purposes, as a territory and an overseas country, respectively.

French Southern and Antarctic Lands (*Terres Australes et Antarctiques Françaises*—TAAF). The Southern and Antarctic Lands comprise the Antarctic continent between 136 and 142 degrees east longitude and south of 60 degrees south latitude (Adélie Land) plus four additional districts: the islands of Saint Paul and Amsterdam; the Kerguélen Archipelago; the Crozet Archipelago; and, since February 2007, the Scattered Islands (*Îles Éparses*) in the Indian Ocean. The Scattered Islands are Tromelin Island, situated off the northeast coast of Madagascar, and several islands located in the Mozambique Channel between Madagascar and the west coast of Africa: Bassas da India, Europa Island, Juan da Nova Island, and the Glorioso Islands.

The TAAF embraces some 170,000 square miles (440,000 sq. km.), with a fluctuating population of scientific personnel numbering about 150 in the winter and 300 in the summer, with most based in the Kerguélen Archipelago, located in the southern Indian Ocean, and Adélie Land. In January 2001 the seat of administration was moved from Paris to St. Pierre, Reunion. A Consultative Council that assists the territory's administrator meets at least twice yearly. The legal status of the Antarctic portion of the territory remains in suspense under the Antarctic Treaty of 1959 (see Antarctica in main alphabetical listing).

Chief Administrator: Rollon MOUCHEL-BLAISOT.

New Caledonia (*Nouvelle-Calédonie*). Covering 7,375 square miles (19,000 sq. km.) in the Pacific Ocean east of Queensland, Australia, New Caledonia includes, in addition to the main island of Grande Terre, the Loyalty Islands (*Îles Loyauté*) to the east, the Belep Islands (*Îles Bélep*) to the north, and a number of smaller islands. European contact dates from 1774, with the arrival of English explorer James Cook. France took possession in 1853, but a number of revolts by the indigenous Kanak population followed. After serving as a major base for U.S. Pacific forces in World War II, in 1946 New Caledonia was made an overseas territory.

New Caledonia has a population of 248,000 (2007E), of whom about 95,000 reside in Nouméa, the capital. The largest ethnic group is Melanesian (45 percent), followed by those of European origin (34 percent). Local government is based on 33 communes. New Caledonia is presently represented in the French Parliament by two deputies and one senator, although a second senator is to be added in 2011. An important mining center, the territory possesses some of the world's largest nickel reserves; the metal accounts for 90 percent of export earnings.

A long-term economic development plan, which included a proviso that the territory could not become independent for at least 19 years, was approved by the Territorial Assembly in 1979. In an assembly election the following July that was widely interpreted as a referendum on the issue, the Independence Front (*Front Indépendantiste*—FI), encompassing a group of parties demanding the severance of all links to France, obtained a little over one-third of the vote. Subsequently, the FI succeeded in concluding a legislative coalition with the autonomist Federation for a New Caledonian Society (*Fédération pour une Nouvelle Société Calédonienne*—FNSC), which had theretofore been allied with the anti-independence Rally for Caledonia in the Republic (*Rassemblement pour la Calédonie dans la République*—RPCR). In June 1982 the new de facto majority ousted the RPCR-led government and installed an FI-led "government of reform and development" headed by Jean-Marie TJIBAOU. The change in government without an intervening election precipitated widespread demonstrations by right-wing elements, who invaded the Territorial Assembly chamber in July, injuring three FI deputies. Following a restoration of order, the high commissioner announced that a new constitution for New Caledonia, to be promulgated by mid-1983, would give the territory increased internal autonomy.

Under the proposed statute of autonomy, as presented by the French government in March 1983, substantial powers would be transferred from the French high commissioner to a new territorial government headed by a president, who would be elected by the Territorial Assembly and empowered to name his own ministers. At the conclusion of an all-party conference near Paris in mid-July, the FI and the FNSC accepted the French offer on the basis of an anticipated vote on self-determination that would be confined to Melanesians and other New Caledonians with at least one parent born in the territory. The RPCR, dominated by planters, declared its opposition to any reform that excluded persons other than French military and civil service personnel from the franchise.

In 1984 the French National Assembly approved the autonomy statute, without, however, calling for electoral reform. As a result, the FI position hardened into a demand that the vote be confined exclusively to Melanesians. Subsequently, the FI joined with a number of other proindependence groups in forming the **Kanak Socialist National Liberation Front** (*Front de Libération Nationale Kanak Socialiste*—FLNKS). The FLNKS boycotted the November legislative election, at which the RPCR won 34 of 42 seats. One week later, amid mounting acts of terrorism and the deaths of a number of separatists, the FLNKS announced the formation of a provisional Kanaki government under Tjibaou's presidency.

During 1985 a number of new proposals for resolving the controversy were advanced, including a plan advocated by French Premier Fabius whereby four regional councils would be established. The members would sit collectively as a Territorial Congress, replacing the existing Territorial Assembly. The Fabius plan was immediately condemned as "iniquitous" by the RPCR, but it was tentatively accepted by the FLNKS as strengthening the movement toward independence. The plan was subsequently approved by the French National Assembly, and elections for the regional bodies were conducted in September. The RPCR, which reluctantly agreed to participate, secured 25 of 46 seats in the congress despite winning a majority only in the heavily populated but largely non-Melanesian Nouméa region.

Following the Socialist defeat in the 1986 French National Assembly election, the situation changed dramatically. Criticizing the regional council arrangement as "badly conceived, badly organized, and badly prepared," Bernard Pons, the new minister for overseas departments and territories, advanced a plan under which the councils would be limited to responsibility for local public works and cultural matters. After extensive debate, the proposal to return effective political and economic authority to the high commissioner received parliamentary approval. As a consequence, in August the South Pacific Forum, supported by the FLNKS, recommended that New Caledonia be restored to the UN's list of non-self-governing territories. Despite intense pressure by France, which indicated that it would ignore such action, the UN General Assembly voted overwhelming to do so in December.

In the face of an FLNKS boycott, an independence referendum conducted in September 1987 yielded a 98 percent vote in favor of remaining within the republic. A month later, Pons introduced a new autonomy statute that by means of boundary redefinition left the FLNKS dominant in two, rather than three, of the four regions. In April 1988 the RPCR won 35 of 48 seats in the new Territorial Congress.

Following the Socialists' return to power in 1988, the Rocard government concluded an agreement with pro- and anti-independence forces on a plan whereby the French government, through its high commissioner, would administer the territory for a year, in the course of which New Caledonia would be divided into three new autonomous regions, one (in the south) dominated by settlers and two (in the north and in the Loyalty Islands) by Kanaks. The arrangement, to commence in 1989, would remain in effect for a ten-year period, near the end of which a territory-wide referendum on independence would be held. The "Matignon Accord" ultimately received the FLNKS's backing and was approved by both territorial and mainland voters in November.

Hard-line separatists subsequently branded the 1988 pact as a sell-out to the colonists, and in May 1989 FLNKS leader Tjibaou and his deputy, Yeiwene YEIWENE, were assassinated during a tribal ceremony on the island of Ouvéa. Despite the bloodshed, elections to provincial assemblies for the three regions were conducted, as scheduled, in June 1989, with the RPCR winning in the south and the FLNKS ahead elsewhere. A week later, the restructured Territorial Congress, with limited powers and an RPCR majority, elected its president.

Although he headed one of the FLNKS's relatively hard-line components, Tjibaou's successor, Paul NÉAOUTYINE, called in early 1990 for the coalition to redirect its immediate energies to economic development. He also indicated that as part of its effort to bring all proindependence groups into a single organization, the FLNKS would not rule out talks with the extremist **United Kanak Liberation Front** (*Front Uni de Libération Kanak*—FULK), which had rejected the 1988 accord and whose leader, Yann Céléné UREGEI, had left New Caledonia in the wake of the Tjibaou assassination. Earlier, Nidoïsh NAISSELINE, leader of the equally radical **Kanak Socialist Liberation** (*Libération Kanak Socialiste*—LKS), had announced that the LKS would join the FULK in a front with a structure paralleling that of the FLNKS.

In the 1995 provincial election the RPCR retained a majority in the Territorial Congress and the FLNKS again took second place. Under the new leadership of Rock WAMYTAN of the **Caledonian Union** (*Union Calédonienne*—UC), in February 1996 the FLNKS agreed that a consensus proposal on the territory's future, rather than the stark options of independence or continued French territorial status, should be put to a referendum in 1998. The FLNKS withdrew from discussions with the French government several months later, however, partly because Paris had removed full independence from the list of possible outcomes. Negotiations resumed sporadically later in the year, but no progress was achieved as attention focused on a major dispute over the proposed opening of a new nickel smelter in the north. Some FLNKS elements viewed as "blackmail" French insistence that the facility could be opened only after resolution of the autonomy issue. As a result of the conflict, the FLNKS boycotted the 1997 French National Assembly election, at which the two RPCR incumbents were reelected, and blockaded nickel operations in the south for much of the year. Some FLNKS members questioned its tactics, however, which resulted in formation of the **Federation of Independence Coordination Committees** (*Fédération des Comités de Coordination des Indépendantistes*—FCCI).

On April 21, 1998, representatives of the FLNKS and RPCR concluded an agreement with French officials providing for a period of "shared sovereignty" during which power would gradually devolve to the island. A final referendum on the question of independence would be held in 15–20 years. The "Nouméa Accord" was formally signed on May 5 during a ceremony in the capital attended by French Prime Minister Jospin, and the French Parliament endorsed the pact on July 6. A referendum in New Caledonia on November 8 produced a 72 percent "yes" vote, despite opposition from the local branch of the National Front (FN) and other right-wing parties. The French National Assembly approved the required implementing legislation in December, followed by the Senate in February 1999.

In elections for three new provincial assemblies in May 1999, the RPCR secured a majority in South Province, while proindependence alliances won majorities in North Province and the Loyalty Islands. The provincial assemblies subsequently chose from among their memberships the new 54-member Congress of New Caledonia, in which the RPCR held 24 seats; the FLNKS, 12; two FLNKS constituent groups, the **National Union for Independence** (*Union Nationale pour l'Indépendance*—UNI) and the **Kanak Liberation Party** (*Parti de Libération Kanak*—Palika), 6; the FCCI, 4; the local branch of the FN, headed by Guy GEORGE, 4; Didier LEROUX's **Alliance for Caledonia** (*Alliance pour la Calédonie*—APLC), 3; and the LKS, 1. With the RPCR and the FCCI having formed an alliance, the RPCR's Jean LÈQUES emerged as president of the proportionally balanced government. Although the FLNKS took control of four ministries, to seven for the RPCR/FCCI, the FLNKS's Wamytan was bypassed for vice president in favor of the FCCI's Léopold JORÉDIÉ.

Disagreements over the power-sharing arrangement persisted, however, which contributed to President Lèques's decision to step down following the March 2001 provincial elections. On April 3 the Congress elected the RPCR's Pierre FROGIER to head a new government in which the FLNKS's Déwé GORODEY assumed the vice presidency. With the UC and Palika in conflict over leadership of the FLNKS, Wamytan subsequently lost the Front's presidency.

In the National Assembly election in June 2002 the two incumbents were returned under the banner of President Chirac's new UMP. In runoff balloting Pierre Frogier defeated the FLNKS's Paul Néaoutyine, and Jacques LAFLEUR of the RPCR defeated the APLC's Didier Leroux.

Meanwhile, the government was increasingly beset by internal policy disputes, which ultimately led to its dissolution and reorganization in November 2002, again under the leadership of Frogier. In the new Council of Ministers the RPCR-FCCI coalition remained dominant, holding seven of the ten ministerial posts, to two for the FLNKS and one for the UC.

The May 9, 2004, assembly elections saw a new proautonomy party, the **Future Together** (*Avenir Ensemble*—AE), unseat the RPCR in the south, winning 19 seats to 16 for the RPCR and then forming a provincial government with the support of the FN, which had won the remaining 4 seats. (None of the proindependence parties had met the 5 percent threshold needed for representation under the proportional distribution system.) In Northern Province the proindependence parties continued to dominate, led by the UNI and the UC, while in the Loyalty Islands the assembly's 14 seats were split among six parties. In the resultant Congress the AE and RPCR each held 16 seats, followed by the UNI-FLNKS, 8; the UC, 7; the FN, 4; the LKS, 1; the **Renewed Caledonian Union** (*Union Calédonienne Renouvea*—UCR), 1; and the **Union of Cooperating Committees for Independence** (*Union des Comités de Coopération pour l'Indépendance*—UCCI), 1.

Under the Nouméa Accord, parties with at least six congressional seats are entitled to participate in the power-sharing government, which resulted in a virtual three-way tie among the RPCR (four ministries), the proautonomy AE (four), and the proindependence parties (three). On June 10, 2004, the new government elected the AE's Marie-Noëlle THÉMEREAU to serve as its president, but within hours three RPCR ministers had resigned, forcing dissolution of the government. On June 29 Thémereau won sufficient votes to resume the presidency, with the FLNKS's Gorodey again being named vice president.

The first half of 2006 was marked by differences over construction of facilities at a nickel mine in the south that has been called the biggest industrial project in the South Pacific. Kanak indigenous groups sought to stop the project, which, they asserted, did not adequately address environmental concerns and had been improperly licensed. They received some support from French courts. Meanwhile, ownership of the Goro mine passed in October from a Canadian to a Brazilian company. Another $2 billion venture in the north also changed hands in 2006, from Canadian to Swiss ownership.

On February 17, 2007, in keeping with a commitment in the Nouméa Accord to prevent an influx of Europeans from diluting the indigenous vote, the French Parliament temporarily froze the New Caledonian electoral roll. As a consequence, only those resident in 1998 were to be permitted to vote in the local elections in 2009 through 2014. The measure, which affected some 7,000 French nationals, was strongly opposed by the RPCR and other anti-independence parties. It is expected that after 2014 a minimum residency requirement will be instituted.

In the June 2007 National Assembly election the RPCR/UMP claimed both seats. In runoff balloting, incumbent Pierre Frogier defeated Charles PIDJOT (FLNKS), and Gaël YANNO won against Charles WASHETINE (FLNKS). Losing candidates included incumbent Jacques Lafleur, who, after 29 years in office, failed to make it to the second round. He had been ousted as RPCR leader in August 2006 and consequently set up a new party, the **Rally for Caledonia** (*Rassemblement pour la Calédonie*—RPC). In both districts the AE candidates finished third in the first round, which left analysts questioning the durability of the AE government.

On July 24, 2007, President Thémereau responded to her party's poor performance in the June elections by announcing her resignation. On July 31 Congress elected Pierre Frogier speaker, which paved the way for his predecessor, the AE's Harold Martin, to the assume the presidency on August 7. Two months later, New Caledonia's high commissioner, Michel MATHIEU, resigned, reportedly because of a dispute with Paris over labor policy.

The elections for the three provincial assemblies on May 10, 2009, concluded with anti-independence parties holding a decided overall advantage among the 76 seats. As a consequence, the pro-French contingents in the 54-seat Congress were reported to control 31–34 seats, led by The Rally–UMP (the renamed RPCR/UMP); the **Caledonia Together** (*Calédonie Ensemble*—CE), a new party formed by Philippe Gomès upon his departure from the AE; a coalition of the AE and Sen. Simon LOUECKHOTE's **The Movement for Diversity** (*La Mouvement de la Diversité*—LMD); and the RPC. Successful proindependence parties and coalitions, led by the UNI (Palika and the UCR), also included the UC, the FLNKS, the **Labor Party** (*Parti Travailliste*—PI), and the LKS.

Despite the recent divisions in their camp, the principal anti-independence parties, with encouragement from Paris, hammered out a "stability pact" that saw Gomès, the outgoing president of the Southern Province assembly, elected president of the collectivity on June 5. His predecessor, Harold Martin, was named president of the Congress, while Pierre Frogier took over as Southern Province assembly president. Election of a vice president took until June 15, when the Congress chose Pierre NGAIOHNI of the FLNKS.

High Commissioner: Yves DASSONVILLE.
President of the Government: Philippe GOMÈS (CE).
President of the Congress: Harold MARTIN (AE).

Insular Possession:

Clipperton Island (*Île Clipperton*). Uninhabited Clipperton Island is located in the North Pacific, roughly 800 miles southwest of Mexico. A coral atoll with an area of about 3.5 square miles (9 sq. km.), Clipperton was named after the sea captain who claimed it for Great Britain in 1705. The French claim dates from 1708, when the island was given the competing name Passion Island (*Île de Passion*). Occupied by Mexico in 1897, Clipperton was ultimately awarded to France in 1931 and was then administered, from 1936 until early 2007, by the high commissioner of French Polynesia. Legislation passed in February 2007 assigned the minister for Overseas France direct responsibility.

GABON

Gabonese Republic
République Gabonaise

Note: President El Hadj Omar Bongo Ondimba died on June 8, 2009. Bongo's son Ali Ben Bongo Ondimba was elected in disputed presidential balloting on August 30. Following a recount that began on September 29, the Constitutional Court ruled on October 12 that Bongo was the winner. He was sworn in on October 16 and formed a new, smaller government on October 17.

Political Status: Independent since August 17, 1960; present constitution, providing for "semi-presidential" regime, adopted March 14, 1991.

Area: 103,346 sq. mi. (267,667 sq. km.).

Population: 1,269,000 (2003C); 1,351,000 (2008E).

Major Urban Center (2005E): LIBREVILLE (metropolitan area, 659,000).

Official Language: French.

Monetary Unit: CFA Franc (official rate December 1, 2009: 434.59 francs = $1US). The CFA franc, previously pegged to the French franc, is now permanently pegged to the euro at 655.957 CFA francs = 1 euro.

President: (*See headnote.*) El Hadj Omar (formerly Albert-Bernard) BONGO Ondimba; elected vice president on March 19, 1967; succeeded to the presidency on December 2, 1967, upon the death of Léon MBA; reelected in 1973, 1979, 1986, 1993, and for a seven-year term, on December 6, 1998, and on November 27, 2005.

Vice President: Didjob DIVUNGUI DI NDINGE (Democratic and Republican Alliance); appointed by the president on May 28, 1997; reappointed by the president on January 19, 2006.

Prime Minister: Jean Eyéghe NDONG (Gabonese Democratic Party), appointed by the president on January 20, 2006, to replace Jean-François NTOUTOUME EMANE; reappointed on January 24, 2007, following legislative elections of December 17 and 24, 2006; formed a new government on January 25, 2007.

THE COUNTRY

A tropical, heavily forested country on the west coast of Central Africa, Gabon is inhabited by a sparse population whose largest components, among more than 40 distinct ethnic groups, are the Fang and Eshira tribes. A sizable European (predominantly French) community also is resident. Indigenous Gabonese speak a variety of Bantu languages, with Fang predominating in the north. About 60 percent of the population is Christian (largely Roman Catholic), with most of the rest adhering to traditional beliefs; there also is a small Muslim minority. Women constitute over half of salaried workers in the health and trading sectors, although female representation in party and government bodies is minimal.

Abundant natural resources that include oil, high-grade iron ore, manganese, uranium, and timber provided Gabon with a per capita GNP of over $4,200 in the early 1980s. Oil output accounted for about three-fourths of Gabon's export earnings until 1986. By 1988 the economic impact of recession in the oil industry was dramatically underscored by a drop in per capita GNP to $2,620 (still one of the highest among black African states), with subsequent recovery to about $4,950 in 1993.

Real GDP growth averaged 3.3 percent annually in 1996–1998 before a severe recession hit in 1999, triggered by an 11 percent decline in oil production. GDP fell 9.6 percent in 1999, and the government inaugurated a structural-adjustment program sponsored by the International Monetary Fund (IMF) in an effort to reduce public spending, diversify the economy, promote good governance, and address the severe external-debt problem.

Since 2003 the economy has rebounded, aided by higher oil prices, external-debt rescheduling, and an increase in non-oil revenues. GDP growth was 1.5 percent in 2004, while inflation declined to 0.5 percent, reflecting wage moderation and the monetary discipline imposed by the fixed-exchange regime. The IMF subsequently approved $47 million in assistance to Gabon's economic program. Government corruption reportedly was on the rise, however, and Transparency International cited Gabon as among the most corrupt African nations.

Annual GDP growth averaged 3.4 percent in 2005–2006, the losses in oil revenue offset by similar growth in the non-oil sector, particularly timber and minerals. In 2006 the IMF noted the country's efforts toward developing a poverty-reduction strategy and increasing government transparency. Referencing Gabon's "inevitable exhaustion" of its oil reserves, the IMF encouraged officials to improve management of public funds and to lower debt. GDP growth of 5.6 percent was recorded in 2007 due in part to "brisk activity" in the mining, forestry, and food-processing industries, according to the IMF. As a result of its economic recovery and significant progress in structural reforms and transparency, Gabon was able to negotiate early repayment of its $2.3 million debt to the Paris Club of creditors between December 2007 and January 2008. Annual GDP growth contracted to 4.2 percent in 2008, in part due to a correction from the "unusually high" growth the previous year. Oil production declined but activity in the non-oil sector remained robust, according to the IMF. The fund commended Gabon for its progress in oil-revenue administration, including a reduction in oil subsidies in 2009, and for structural reforms "essential to improving the business climate." GDP growth slowed to 3.9 percent in 2009, in part due to a decline in oil prices, but growth was projected to rebound to 4.3 percent in 2010.

GOVERNMENT AND POLITICS

Political background. Colonized by France in the latter half of the 19th century and subsequently administered as a part of French Equatorial Africa, Gabon achieved full independence within the French Community on August 17, 1960. Its longtime political leader, President Léon MBA, ruled in a conservative yet pragmatic style and supported close political and economic relations with France. However, Mba's attempts to establish a one-party state based on his Gabon Democratic Bloc (*Bloc Démocratique Gabonais*—BDG) were resisted for several years by the Gabonese Democratic and Social Union (*Union Démocratique et Sociale Gabonais*—UDSG), led by Jean-Hilaire AUBAME. Only after an attempted coup by Aubame's army supporters had been thwarted by French military intervention in February 1964 and Mba's party had gained a majority in legislative elections two months later was the UDSG formally outlawed.

Mba was reelected to a seven-year presidential term in March 1967, but he died the following November and was succeeded by Vice President Albert-Bernard (subsequently El Hadj Omar) BONGO Ondimba. Officially declaring Gabon a one-party state in March 1968, Bongo announced a "renovation" policy that included conversion of the former ruling party into a new, nationwide political grouping, the Gabonese Democratic Party (*Parti Démocratique Gabonais*—PDG). The incumbent was the sole candidate for reelection to a fourth term on November 9, 1986, having survived a coup attempt by military officers in 1985.

Pressured by a deteriorating economy and mounting protests against his regime, President Bongo announced in early March 1990 that a national conference would be called to discuss the launching of an inclusive political organization that would pave the way for eventual adoption of a multiparty system. However, the conference ended its month-long deliberations on April 21 with a call for the immediate introduction of democratic pluralism. The president responded by granting legal status to all of the participating organizations. Moreover, on April 29 he announced that longtime Prime Minister Léon MEBIAME would be succeeded by Casimir OYE MBA as head of a government that would include a number of opposition leaders.

First-round legislative balloting was held on September 23, 1990, the results of which were annulled in 32 of 120 constituencies because of alleged improprieties. At the conclusion of second-round balloting on October 21 and 28, 62 seats were declared to have been won by the PDG (including 3 seats by pro-PDG independents). Subsequently, the PDG tally was augmented by 4 seats, with 7 opposition parties being credited with a total of 54.

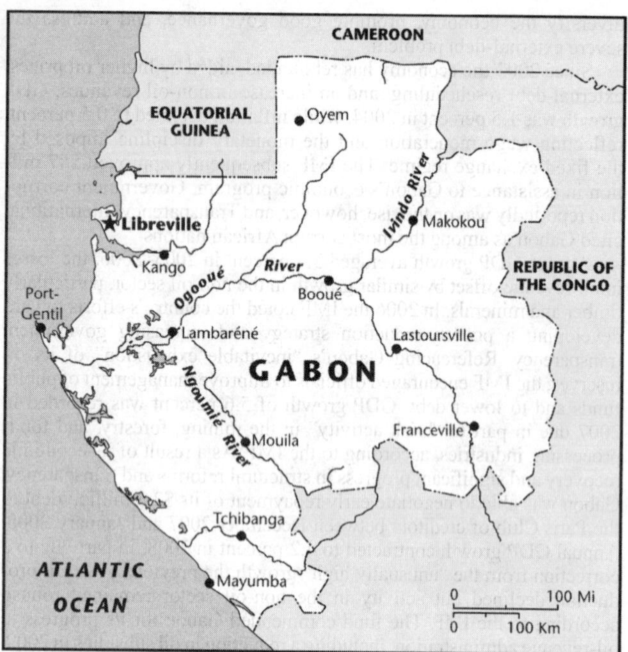

In May 1991 six of the seven opposition parties with legislative representation announced a boycott of parliamentary proceedings, called for a dissolution of the government, and demanded that the Bongo regime comply with the dictates of the 1990 national conference and the constitution adopted on March 14 (see Constitution and government, below). On June 7, two days after an opposition-led general strike, President Bongo announced the resignation of Oye Mba's government and called on the opposition, now united in the Coordination of Democratic Opposition (*Coordination de l'Opposition Démocratique*—COD), to join a "government of national consensus." On June 15 the opposition rejected his offer; three days later Oye Mba was reappointed, and a new government was named that included a limited number of opposition figures.

In July 1992 the PDG-dominated National Assembly rejected an unprecedented no-confidence motion by a vote of 72 to 45. The motion, filed by the opposition to protest the government's rescheduling of local elections, closely followed assembly approval of a new electoral code, which opposition leaders described as "antidemocratic." Despite their drawing together in mid-1993 to form the Committee for Free and Democratic Elections, opposition groups failed to unite behind a single slate, and at balloting on December 5 President Bongo was credited with winning reelection over 13 competitors by a narrow 51.18 percent majority. The result was immediately challenged by runner-up Paul MBA-ABESSOLE of the National Rally of Woodcutters (*Rassemblement National des Bûcherons*—RNB), who accused Bongo of "high treason against the nation by an electoral coup d'état," declared himself president, and announced the formation of a parallel "government of combat" headed by his party's secretary general, Pierre-André KOMBILA Koumba. On December 12 Mba-Abessole announced the formation of the High Council of the Republic (*Haut Conseil de la République*—HCR), which included a majority of the opposition presidential candidates, to serve as an advisory body for his parallel government. On December 14 Bongo, promising a multiparty government of "broad consensus," termed the formation of the alternative body an "anticonstitutional act," and postelectoral unrest quickly subsided as the regime deployed heavily armed regular and paramilitary forces. Meanwhile, legislative balloting originally scheduled for December 26 was postponed until March 1994.

In January 1994 consumer prices skyrocketed, and widespread disturbances were reported after France halved the value of the CFA franc. On February 15 Mba-Abessole urged his supporters to "disobey all government directives" and threatened to expel party members who took part in Bongo's proposed unity government. One week later, nine people were killed when government troops supported by tanks destroyed the RNB's radio station and attacked Mba-Abessole's residence as a "punitive measure" for his having incited "hatred, violence, and intolerance." In addition, elections were rescheduled for August 1994.

On March 11, 1994, Prime Minister Oye Mba resigned, stating that the country had entered a "new political phase"; however, Bongo reappointed him two days later, and on March 25 Oye Mba named a new government, which included no opposition members. On April 8 Libreville lifted the state of alert and curfew that had been imposed almost without interruption since December 9, 1993.

On September 27, 1994, following three weeks of internationally supervised negotiations in Paris, government and opposition representatives signed an agreement calling for the establishment of a transitional coalition government and an independent electoral commission empowered to oversee an electoral timetable providing for local and legislative elections in 12 and 18 months, respectively. Consequently, on October 11 Oye Mba again resigned, and two days later the president named a PDG confidant, Paulin OBAME-NGUEMA, as interim prime minister. Although Obame-Nguema's appointment was generally well received, the RNB continued to urge its members to refuse to participate in a Bongo-affiliated government and denounced the 27-member cabinet named by Obame-Nguema, which included 6 opposition members, for failing to reflect the opposition's legislative strength.

On February 3, 1995, the Constitutional Court, acting at the opposition's urging, ruled that the mandate of the current assembly could continue for the duration of the transition period defined by the 1994 accord. Three days later, opposition deputies ended their legislative boycott, and on April 21 President Bongo agreed to submit a package of constitutional reforms to voters, who provided an overwhelmingly positive response at balloting on June 25. The Bongo administration, however, proved reluctant to implement the Paris Accord, and in February 1996 the opposition called on France to pressure the government to adhere to the transitional schedule. Thereafter, in May, Bongo agreed to organize an electoral commission to schedule and oversee local and, subsequently, national legislative elections.

Local polling, originally scheduled for July 1996, was delayed until October 20 by organizational problems that remained largely unresolved as of election day. Consequently, there were widespread reports of incomplete electoral lists and ballot-box shortages, as well as a voter turnout rate as low as 10–15 percent in some areas. Such problems were so severe in Libreville that balloting there was suspended and completed in late November. Opposition leaders claimed that the disorganization was part of a "deliberate" government attempt to undermine the electoral system. Meanwhile, opposition candidates, led by the RNB, captured a clear majority of the contests.

The opposition fared far less well at National Assembly elections conducted on December 15 and 29, 1996, and January 12, 1997, as the governing PDG scored a decisive victory, securing 82 of the 120 assembly seats. At subsequent balloting on January 26 and February 9, 1997, to fill the Senate for the first time, the governing party again secured a substantial majority. Meanwhile, on January 27 President Bongo reappointed Obame-Nguema, who announced a cabinet the following day.

On March 20, 1997, the National Assembly approved draft constitutional amendments that included provisions for the creation of a vice-presidential post and lengthening of the presidential term to seven years (following the next election). Following Senate approval of the amendments in April, the president named Didjob DIVUNGUI DI NDINGE, leader of the Democratic and Republican Alliance (*Alliance Démocratique et Républicaine*—ADERE), as his vice president on May 28.

In mid-April 1998 the government announced the formation of the National Democracy Council (*Conseil pour la Démocratie Nationale*—CND), a consultative body comprising the former and current leaders of a broad spectrum of governmental and opposition groups, and charged it with assisting in the organization of presidential elections then tentatively scheduled for late 1998. In October the government announced that the first round of balloting would be held on December 6, with a second round, if necessary, on December 20. The Bongo administration rebuffed subsequent opposition requests for additional preparation time, and in early November the HCR and other leading opposition groups withdrew from the national electoral commission to protest what they described as a perfunctory revision of an already suspect voter-registration list. Meanwhile, intraparty factionalization undermined the ability of prominent opposition groups to coalesce behind a competitive challenger to the incumbent.

On December 6, 1998, President Bongo won a seven-year term at polling that his opponents charged was tainted by "massive fraud." Bongo's 66.6 percent vote share dwarfed the returns of six other presidential aspirants, with his nearest competitors, the HCR's Pierre MAMBOUNDOU and the RNB's Paul Mba-Abessole, capturing 16.6 and

13.4 percent, respectively. On January 24, 1999, Bongo named Jean-François NTOUTOUME EMANE to succeed Obame-Nguema, who had resigned two days earlier, and on January 25 a new government was named.

The PDG retained its legislative stranglehold in assembly balloting in December 2001, securing 88 seats. On January 27, 2002, President Bongo reappointed Prime Minister Ntoutoume Emane; notably, however, the new cabinet announced the same day included three members of the RNB (including Mba-Abessole) and the leader of another opposition grouping, the Social Democratic Party (*Parti Social-Démocratique*—PSD).

In local elections in 2002, the PDG achieved an overwhelming victory, albeit with voter participation estimated at less than 20 percent in some areas. In Senate elections held in 2003, the PDG won 60 of the chamber's 91 seats, followed by the Rally for Gabon (*Rassemblement pour le Gabon*—RPG), which took 8 seats.

On November 27, 2005, President Bongo won another seven-year term at balloting that was again challenged as fraudulent by his opponents. Bongo garnered 79 percent of the vote, easily defeating four challengers, most notably Pierre Mamboundou, whose affiliation was listed as the Union of Gabonese People (*Union du Peuple Gabonais*—UPG), 13.6 percent; and Zacharie MYBOTO, an independent affiliated with the newly formed Gabonese Union for Democracy and Development (*Union Gabonaise de la Démocratie et du Développement*—UGDD), 6.6 percent. Two other candidates each received less than 1 percent of the vote: Augustin Moussavou KING of the Gabonese Socialist Party (*Parti Socialiste Gabonaise*—PSG) and Christian-Serge MAROGA of the Rally of the Democrats (RDD). Turnout was recorded at 63.6 percent, with security forces voting on November 25 in a move decreed by Bongo to maintain order at civilian polling on November 27. Bongo was sworn in on January 19, 2006, retaining Vice President Divungui Di Ndinge and appointing a new prime minister, Jean Eyéghe NDONG, on January 20. A new government was installed on January 21.

Following another overwhelming victory by the PDG in National Assembly elections of December 17 and 24, 2006, Ndong was reappointed on January 24, 2007, and a new government, dominated by the PDG but including members of at least four other parties, was named on January 25. Following polling on June 10, 2007, in 20 constituencies where the courts had annulled the 2006 results because of irregularities, the PDG won in 11 constituencies, retaining its 82 seats, while independents reportedly added 1 seat. Allies of the PDG were reported to have won 6 seats and others, 2 seats. A major reshuffle of the cabinet took place on December 27, 2007; additional cabinet changes were made on February 4, 2008, after the minister of foreign affairs was named chair of the African Union Commission. The PDG retained its stronghold in local elections on April 27, 2008, winning 1,100 of 1,990 municipal and departmental seats. On October 7 the cabinet was reshuffled.

The PDG dominated a reshuffled cabinet appointed on January 14, 2009, though the government did include two members of the opposition UGDD and two other parties. The UGDD officially rejected participation in the government and dismissed the two party members who had accepted posts. In Senate elections on January 18, the PDG won 75 of the enlarged chamber's 102 seats, followed by independents with 9 seats, and the RPG with 6. (*See headnote.*)

Constitution and government. Until 1991, when a qualified multiparty system was introduced, popular election was pro forma because of a requirement that all candidates be approved by the PDG. Constitutional amendments approved by the legislature on April 18, 1997, provided for a lengthening of the presidential term from five to seven years; in addition, the amended basic charter empowered the president to name both a vice president (appointees to the newly created post are not eligible to succeed the chief executive) and a prime minister, who must enjoy the confidence of the legislature. The head of the government is the prime minister, who is appointed by the president. The prime minister, in consultation with the president, appoints the Council of Ministers. In 2003 the National Assembly voted to revoke the constitutional limit on the number of terms to which the president may be reelected. This effectively guaranteed Bongo the presidency for life.

Members of the bicameral legislature, which comprises a Senate (created in March 1994 and filled in April 1997) and a National Assembly, are directly elected for six-year and five-year terms, respectively. There is an appointed Economic and Social Council, whose advice on relevant policy issues must be given legislative consideration. The judiciary includes a Supreme Court (divided into judicial, administrative, and accounting chambers) and Courts of Appeal, as well as a Constitutional Court and an extraordinary High Court of Justice to hear impeachment cases.

For administrative purposes Gabon is divided into 9 provinces and subdivided into 37 departments, all headed by presidentially appointed executives. Libreville and Port-Gentil are governed by elected mayors and Municipal Councils, while four smaller municipalities have partly elected and partly appointed administrations.

Foreign relations. Following his accession to power in 1967, President Bongo sought to lessen the country's traditional dependence on France by cultivating more diversified international support. Regionally, Gabon withdrew in 1976 from membership in the Common African and Mauritian Organization, while diplomatic relations with Benin, broken in 1978 after Gabon's alleged involvement in a mercenary attack in Cotonou in 1977 and the expulsion in 1978 of 6,000 Beninese workers, were restored in February 1989. Relations with neighboring Equatorial Guinea suffered until the overthrow of the Macie regime in August 1979, by which time as many as 80,000 Equatorial Guinean refugees had fled to Gabon. Relations with Cameroon deteriorated in May 1981 with the expulsion of nearly 10,000 Cameroonians in the wake of violent demonstrations in Libreville and Port-Gentil. Subsequently, an overt campaign against immigrant workers further strained ties between Gabon and its neighbors. Libreville nonetheless continued to participate in the Economic Community of Central African States, hosting its third summit meeting in August 1987. During the same month, a presidential visit to the United States served to strengthen relations between the two countries, with Bongo pledging to protect American investments of more than $200 million and Washington agreeing to debt restructuring of some $8 million owed by Gabon for military purchases. Earlier, following a meeting with the Palestine Liberation Organization's Yasir Arafat in Tunisia, the regime reiterated its opposition to "apartheid, Zionism, and neocolonialism."

In 1988, despite President Bongo's stated intent, Gabon continued to be heavily dependent on French support, with annual aid hovering at $360 million. In February the government granted the European Economic Community fishing rights to Gabonese territorial waters; thereafter, cooperation agreements were negotiated with the Congo in June and Morocco in October. Meanwhile, the regime's battle with Libreville's large illegal population continued: 3,500 foreigners were arrested in July following Bongo's warning that tougher measures would be used to stop "clandestine immigration."

In late 1992, following two years of negotiations, Gabon and South Africa, which had long been trading partners, established full diplomatic relations. Meanwhile, Libreville's crackdown on illegal immigrants was underscored by the deportation of 7,000 Nigerians.

Angered at Paris's "silence" over French press reports critical of President Bongo, Libreville recalled its ambassador on April 21, 1995. However, relations were quickly restored as Paris reasserted its support for Bongo who, in turn, called for an end to anti-French demonstrations in Libreville.

In the late 1990s President Bongo returned to the role of regional mediator, assuming a prominent position in efforts to reduce tensions in the Republic of the Congo and Côte d'Ivoire. In November 1999 Libreville hosted a summit of the heads of state and foreign ministers of seven Gulf of Guinea nations (Angola, Cameroon, Democratic Republic of the Congo, Republic of the Congo, Equatorial Guinea, Nigeria, and Sao Tome and Principe) that yielded agreement to form a cooperative commission.

In 2003 relations with Equatorial Guinea became tense following Gabon's occupation of the uninhabited islands of Mbagne, Cocotiers, and Congas in the potentially oil-rich Corisco Bay, north of Libreville. In 2004 both countries agreed to negotiations under the auspices of the UN, but a summit scheduled for October was canceled after it was reported that Gabon intended to "sell" the islands, thus trying to stake its claim to legitimate ownership. (The case was submitted to the International Court of Justice in 2006, but there still was no resolution in 2009.)

French support declined in 2005 along with Gabon's oil supply, leaving Bongo to look increasingly to China, which previously had agreed to import large quantities of Gabonese oil and had funded and built Gabon's parliamentary complex. China subsequently loaned Gabon $3 billion to tap iron ore reserves in Belinga. A controversial iron-ore project backed by Chinese financing in 2009 reportedly was suspended because of an outcry over the ultimate destruction of the storied Kongou Falls. Meanwhile, relations with France continued to deteriorate in 2009, as in March the PDG accused France of having conducted "a vast campaign to destabilize Gabon," largely based on legal actions in France regarding corruption allegations against President Bongo and other Gabonese officials (see Current issues, below). Further, the government, through the PDG, made what was described as an appeal for a "thorough" reexamination of cooperative agreements with France.

Current issues. A number of opposition parties boycotted the first-round of assembly elections on December 3, 2001, accusing the administration of having "inflated" electoral rolls in favor of the PDG and its allies. The voting also was marred by sporadic violence and a repeat of the widespread irregularities that had been routinely noted in previous elections. Consequently, other opposition parties urged a boycott of the second-round on December 23, which was conducted peacefully, thanks to heavy security measures, but suffered from low turnout. The subsequent inclusion of the RNB and PSD in the new cabinet was billed by President Bongo as the inaugural of an "open government," with observers noting that the PDG's hegemony had become a significant concern for international donors.

Bongo is Africa's longest-serving president. Although the Paris Accord of 1994 required him to share power with the opposition, he has managed to neutralize his opponents with cabinet positions and state largesse. Many nominal political opponents allegedly are financially supported by Bongo. The 2005 presidential election, while free of violence, saw 9 of 13 candidates disqualified by the elections commission. Another candidate, Pastor Ernest TOMO, withdrew a month prior to balloting and threw his support to Bongo, to whom he is related through marriage. The only international monitors allowed during polling were "some avowedly pro-Bongo French senators," according to *Africa Confidential*. Opponents' claims of vote-rigging were dismissed by a constitutional court in January 2006. Large-scale looting was reported in Libreville in the months following the election, with the opposition claiming five people were killed. The government said one person died.

The PDG retained an overwhelming majority after the December 2006 legislative elections, despite a rift in the party between those who supported the president's son and likely successor, and others who backed cabinet minister Paul TOUNGUI, a top Bongo loyalist. The election also brought into focus a growing division within the RNB/RPG. Although the RPG was referenced as the main faction, winning more seats than the RNB/Kombila, party stalwart Mba-Abessole was not reelected (but he did retain a cabinet position). Mba-Abessole heretofore had been seen by observers as the likely presidential challenger to Bongo.

Bongo announced in 2006 that he would seek another term in the 2012 presidential election, effectively halting discussion about his successor. Some opposition parties, meanwhile, reportedly suggested that the ruling PDG be replaced by a coalition styled as the *Union pour la Majorité Présidentielle Gabonaise* (UMPG), intended to more evenly distribute power among the smaller parties and the PDG. The latter, not surprisingly, opposed the idea. However, midyear talks between the opposition and majority parties resulted in their members being seated on the newly created electoral commission. While the opposition balked at the provision allowing the president veto power over any of the commission's decisions, they were appeased by other provisions allowing access to state-run media, a review of voter-registration lists, public financing of legally registered parties, and limits on campaign spending.

Corruption charges against President Bongo were in the public spotlight in 2007 when he was found guilty in a French court of accepting a bribe to free a French citizen from jail in 1996. Bongo was ordered to pay a fine of nearly $720,000. Subsequently, allegations surfaced that Bongo and his father-in-law, Denis SASSOU-NGUESSO, president of the Republic of the Congo, had embezzled money to buy property in France. Though no prosecutorial action was taken, reportedly due to lack of assistance from Libreville and Brazzaville, relations with France were strained. Tensions heightened in 2008 after France expelled three Gabonese students and Gabon, in turn, deported a French citizen. Meanwhile, a wave of anti-French comments were reported in Gabon's progovernment newspaper.

Following allegations in January 2008 of misuse of public funds by 22 nongovernmental organizations (NGO), all of which had criticized the government's spending practices at the expense of social welfare and infrastructure improvements, the government suspended all of the NGOs for "political meddling." The suspensions were lifted shortly thereafter, following intervention by another NGO that promotes transparency in governance. In October several NGOs filed a complaint with a national commission in connection with allegations against a Libreville prosecutor, who is also President Bongo's nephew. They claimed that the prosecutor received hundreds of thousands of dollars from "third parties" while he was in the public service.

Despite a call by President Bongo in late 2008 for a broad-based government that he said would be better equipped to handle any consequences of the global financial crisis, the cabinet that was sworn in on January 15, 2009, was again dominated by the PDG. Subsequently, the president's overtures to the UGDD, by including two of its members in the government, were officially rebuffed by the opposition party.

In March 2009, in the midst of a months-long strike by public health workers demanding better wages and working conditions, the president's 45-year-old wife, Dr. Edith Lucie BONGO, died after a long illness. She was the daughter of Denis Sassou-Nguesso, president of the Republic of the Congo, and instrumental in the close relationship between the two countries' leaders, both of whom were similarly accused of corruption by French activists. Some observers said that his wife's death delayed President Bongo's response to the health workers' strike and a concurrent strike by teachers, and that the aging president had been handing over more responsibility to his son, defense minister Ali Ben BONGO Ondimba. Meanwhile, corruption charges continued to be the focus of sustained attention in 2009, as a French court froze nine of President Bongo's bank accounts, containing a total of about $5 million, and ordered him to pay nearly $1.5 million he had received in exchange for securing the release of an imprisoned Frenchman; an anti-corruption activist sought $103,000 in damages after having been prohibited from leaving the country to attend a conference in the United States; and the Principality of Monaco, under scrutiny for banking "secrecy," authorized an investigation into several bank accounts in the name of Edith Bongo (a fleet of limousines given to her by her husband allegedly were bought with public funds). Subsequently, President Bongo appealed the French ruling that resulted in his bank accounts being frozen, saying that he had already set aside the money he was ordered to repay. (*See headnote.*)

POLITICAL PARTIES

Officially declared a one-party state in March 1968, Gabon, in practice, had been under one-party government since the banning of the former opposition group, the Gabonese Democratic and Social Union (*Union Démocratique et Sociale Gabonais*—UDSG), in 1964. Twenty-six years later, in February 1990, President Bongo announced that the ruling Gabonese Democratic Party (*Parti Démocratique Gabonaise*—PDG) would be dissolved in favor of a Gabonese Social Democratic Rally (*Rassemblement Social-Démocrate Gabonais*—RSDG), which would pave the way for a multiparty system. In early March he retreated somewhat by announcing that the PDG would continue as a unit within the RSDG. However, delegates to a national political conference in late April rejected the RSDG as a vehicle for phasing in pluralism over a three- to five-year period; Bongo responded by granting legal status (initially for one year) to all of the 13 opposition groups participating in the conference, 7 of which obtained parliamentary representation late in the year. In May 1991, 6 of the 7 parties announced a boycott of parliamentary proceedings and called for dissolution of the coalition government. Meanwhile, a short-lived Coordination of Democratic Opposition (*Coordination de l'Opposition Démocratique*—COD) had been launched by 9 opposition groups, 3 of which merged in early 1992 to form the African Forum for Reconstruction (FAR).

On June 30, 1993, members of Gabon's major opposition parties, meeting in the United States, agreed to form the Committee for Free and Democratic Elections, dedicated to establishing a "democratic state." Following presidential balloting on December 5, the committee was supplanted by the High Council of the Republic (*Haut Conseil de la Republique*—HCR), which had been organized by Paul Mba-Abessole, leader of the National Rally of Woodcutters (*Rassemblement National des Bûcherons*—RNB) and runner-up in the controversial elections, to function as an advisory body for his "administration." The HCR, which reportedly included a majority of the opposition presidential candidates and parties, named Mba-Abessole and PGP leader Pierre-Louis AGONDJO-OKAWE president and vice president, respectively. On January 27, 1994, the HCR was restyled the High Council of Resistance (*Haut Conseil de Résistance*—HCR) and announced that it would no longer refer to Mba-Abessole as the president of the republic, although it vowed to continue to resist the Bongo regime.

At an HCR meeting in December 1997, party delegates elected a new executive bureau headed by Pierre Mamboundou of the Union of Gabonese People (UPG). Furthermore, four HCR members (the FAR, the Movement for People's Social Emancipation [*Mouvement pour l'Emancipation Sociale du Peuple*—MESP], the RNB, and the UPG) signed a new cooperation accord on which they reportedly expected to base their 1998 presidential campaign. In May 1998 the HCR chose Mamboundou as its standard-bearer for the presidential elections due in December; however, in subsequent months the viability of the movement was cast in doubt by reports that it had been reduced to only four or five parties, including the RNB, which had decided to field its own presidential candidate. In November the HCR withdrew from the national electoral commission, declaring that the commission's "hasty" revision of the electoral list had set the stage for "massive fraud" at the presidential balloting.

Of Gabon's 35 registered political parties, most belong to the presidential majority in what Bongo euphemistically calls "convivial democracy." Bongo and his family have a strong grip on the military, and, until recently, he enjoyed the support of the French. (*See headnote.*)

Government and Government-Supportive Parties:

Gabonese Democratic Party (*Parti Démocratique Gabonais*—PDG). Officially established by President Bongo in 1968, the PDG succeeded the earlier Gabon Democratic Bloc (*Bloc Démocratique Gabonais*—BDG) of President Mba. The PDG's most powerful body is its Political Bureau, although the party congress is technically the highest organ. There also is an advisory Central Committee, which oversees a variety of lesser bodies. In September 1986 the Third PDG Congress expanded the Central Committee from 253 to 297 members and the Political Bureau from 27 to 44 members to give "young militants" more access to leadership roles. In 1988 party membership was approximately 300,000. On May 17, 1990, amid increasing political turmoil and criticism of the regime's reform efforts, Bongo resigned as party chair, citing a desire to serve above "partisan preoccupations."

In early 1993 (then) National Assembly President Jules BOURDÈS-OGOULIGUENDE joined Alexandre Sambat in resigning from the PDG to run as an independent presidential candidate. On October 19 President Bongo officially declared his candidacy for reelection, and on November 4 the PDG organized a "New Alliance for Democracy and Change" electoral pact that included the **Association for Socialism in Gabon** (*Association pour le Socialisme au Gabon*—APSG) and the **People's Unity Party** (*Parti de l'Unité du Peuple*—PUP), led by Louis-Gaston MAYILA, both of which had gained legislative representation in 1990, as well as the previously FAR-affiliated **Gabonese Socialist Union** (*Union Socialiste Gabonais*—USG). The PUP won 1 seat in the assembly balloting of 2001.

In 2006 reports surfaced of a rift in the PDG between a faction led by state minister Paul Toungui and his wife (President Bongo's daughter), Pascaline BONGO, and those supporting Ali Ben Bongo Ondimba, the president's son and likely successor. The party retained an overwhelming majority of seats (82) in the 2006 National Assembly elections. In June 2007 the PDG secured its legislative standing by retaining its total of 82 seats following partial elections in 20 constituencies where the 2006 results had been annulled by the courts due to irregularities. The PDG reportedly won in 11 of the 20 constituencies. The party further underscored its authority with overwhelming victories in the 2008 local elections and the 2009 Senate elections.

Party secretary general Simplice Guedet MANZELA lost his post of 10 years when Faustin Boukoubi was elected at a party congress in September 2008.

Leaders: Jacques ADIAHENOT, Ali Ben BONGO Ondimba, Jean Eyéghe NDONG (Prime Minister of the Republic), Georgette KOKO (Vice President of the Party), Angèle ONDO (Spokesperson), Faustin BOUKOUBI (Secretary General).

Circle of Liberal Reformers (*Cercle des Libéraux Réformateurs*—CLR). The CLR was formed in late 1992 by former minister of security Jean-Boniface Assélé, the brother of President Bongo's former wife, who was expelled from the PDG along with two other founders of the new group. The party won representation in the assembly in 2001. In 2006 the party won two seats in the assembly, and Assélé retained his cabinet position.

Leader: Gen. Jean-Boniface ASSÉLÉ.

Democratic and Republican Alliance (*Alliance Démocratique et Républicaine*—ADERE). At balloting in 1996 and early 1997 the ADERE won a number of town council and Senate seats after reportedly forming alliances with local PDG chapters. Furthermore, in May 1997 President Bongo named a senior ADERE leader, Didjob Divungui Di Ndinge, vice president of the republic.

Leader: Didjob DIVUNGUI DI NDINGE (Vice President of the Republic).

Movement of Friends of Bongo (*Mouvement des Amis de Bongo*—MAB). A self-described "apolitical grouping" founded by President Bongo's associates in November 1994, the MAB is not a "PDG offshoot" according to its leaders, who claimed that the group was launched to combat "tribalism, nepotism, disinformation, incrimination, and all forms of corruption." Party leader Georges RAWIRI, who had been president of the Senate, died in 2006.

National Union of Blacksmiths. This group was formed in early 1999 by Thierry A'Agendieu KOMBILA, who had been vice president of the pro-Bongo Union for Development and Liberty (*Union pour le Développement et la Liberté*—UDL) until it disintegrated in December 1998.

National Rally of Woodcutters/Rally for Gabon (*Rassemblement National des Bûcherons/Rassemblement pour le Gabon*—RNB/RPG). Formerly the National Rectification Movement–Woodcutters (*Mouvement de Redressement National–Bûcherons*/Morena–*Bûcherons*), the party adopted the RNB rubric in February 1991 in an effort to more clearly distinguish itself from its parent.

A southern grouping whose claimed membership of over 3,000 (mostly from the Fang ethnic group) supported nonviolent change, the Woodcutters on June 22–24, 1990, mounted the first opposition congress since the multiparty system was legalized. At the 1990–1991 legislative balloting the group became the leading opposition party, securing more than twice as many seats as Morena–*Originels*. Despite its success, the formation accused the government of electoral fraud and intimated that it would refuse to participate in assembly proceedings. In 1991 the Woodcutters joined an opposition call for dissolution of the National Assembly and the mounting of internationally supervised elections.

In mid-1992 *West Africa* reported that strained relations between the RNB and the Gabonese Progress Party (PGP, below) threatened the COD coalition. The enmity reportedly stemmed from the PGP's charge that the RNB's boycott of the later rounds of the 1990 election caused the opposition's defeat, as well as PGP bitterness at the RNB's failure to consult other parties prior to calling a general strike in February 1992. Meanwhile, Fr. Paul Mba-Abessole, the RNB's leader, labeled PGP President Pierre-Louis Agondjo-Okawe a "dangerous Marxist." (Mba-Abessole, who was dismissed by Morena in 1990, returned to Libreville that year at Bongo's invitation, after 13 years in exile.)

In June 1993 the party's secretary general, Pierre-André Kombila Koumba, was named chair of the opposition Committee for Free and Democratic Elections. Five months later, during the run-up to presidential balloting, the Woodcutters and the **National Convention for Change** (*Convention Nationale pour le Change*—CNC) issued a joint statement accusing the Bongo regime of electoral fraud.

In February 1994 RNB members and the party's radio station, *Radio Liberté*, were attacked by government forces deployed to quell antigovernment unrest in Libreville, with RNB leaders subsequently claiming that a number of its members had been detained. The attack on the RNB facilities coincided with the launching of a union-led general strike, which the RNB had publicly supported. Thereafter, the RNB was the most prominent of the opposition parties opposed to any cooperation with the Bongo regime.

At local balloting in October and November 1996, the RNB reportedly secured 62 of 98 contested posts; however, the party fared poorly at subsequent assembly balloting, falling 8 seats short of its 1990 totals. On January 19, 1997, the RNB-dominated Libreville municipal council elected Mba-Abessole as mayor.

In January 1998 the RNB newspaper, *Le Bûcheron*, was suspended by the government for two separate three-month periods for publishing articles "insulting" to the president. In addition, Kombila Koumba, the paper's editor, was fined and given a suspended sentence. In June Mba-Abessole announced that Kombila Koumba had been removed from his party post because of alleged "indiscipline"; however, Kombila Koumba rejected Mba-Abessole's authority to oust him and, at a mid-July congress of his supporters, Kombila Koumba was pronounced RNB president. Subsequently, both Mba-Abessole and Kombila Koumba announced their intention to campaign for the presidency under the splintered RNB banner. Furthermore, in October the Constitutional Court approved the campaign application of another RNB stalwart, Alain ENGOUNG-NZE, thus leaving the party with three presidential contenders. At balloting in December Mba-Abessole finished a distant third with 13 percent of the vote while Kombila Koumba and Engoung-Nze finished near the bottom of the seven-candidate field.

In October 2000 the party reportedly adopted a new name (the Rally for Gabon [RPG]), but subsequent news stories referenced the grouping as the RNB/RPG. Several months earlier, the RNB also had reportedly announced the formation of a Front of Parties for Change (*Front des Parties pour le Changement*—FPC) with three smaller parties—the Congress for Democracy and Justice, the Rally of Republican Democrats, and the Republican Union for Democracy and Progress.

Following the December 2001 legislative balloting, Mba-Abessole, who had recently adopted a stance favoring "convivial democracy," accepted an invitation from President Bongo for the RNB/RPG to participate in an "opening up" of the government, although some party members remained hostile to the initiative. Mba-Abessole and two other RNB/RPG members were included in the new cabinet installed in January 2002. Mba-Abessole, a deputy prime minister, supported Bongo in the 2005 presidential election, although a year earlier he had accused the government of being the leading violator of human rights in the country. By the 2006 legislative elections, references were made strictly to the RPG as the main faction, which won 8 seats, and the **RNB/Kombila,** which in 2006 retained the single seat it had won in 2001. Although Mba-Abessole lost his seat, he was retained in the cabinet as a deputy prime minister. Kombila Koumba also was appointed to the cabinet in 2006 and has since retained his post. In the 2008 Senate elections the RPG won 6 seats.

Leaders: Paul MBA-ABESSOLE (1993 and 1998 presidential candidate and Mayor of Libreville), Pierre-André KOMBILA Koumba (leader of dissident faction and 1998 presidential candidate), Vincent Moulengui BOUKOSSO.

Social Democratic Party (*Parti Social-Démocrate*—PSD). The PSD became a member of the COD following its formation in 1991. During its first congress in Libreville, on April 21, 1992, party president Pierre Claver Maganga-Moussavou was chosen as its 1993 standard-bearer, but he secured a vote share of under 4 percent.

In October 1996 Maganga-Moussavou was ousted from the Obame-Nguema cabinet after he led a vociferous protest against the government's rescheduling of elections. Subsequently, the party reportedly dismissed another PSD leader, Senturel Ngoma MANDOUNGOU, when he assumed Maganga-Moussavou's vacant post.

In November 1998 the PSD withdrew from the national electoral commission to protest its administration of the voter registration lists. Subsequently, at polling in December, Maganga-Moussavou once again secured less than 4 percent of the vote. The PSD leader joined the PDG-led cabinet of January 2002 as the minister of state for agriculture, livestock, and rural development. In June 2004 the group joined the parties making up the ruling coalition, and Maganga-Moussavou was named to the cabinet in September.

Leader: Pierre-Claver MAGANGA-MOUSSAVOU (President of the Party and 1993 and 1998 presidential candidate).

Gabonese Party of Independent Centrists (*Parti Gabonais du Centre Indépendant*—PGCI). The PGCI is led by Jean-Pierre Lemboumba, one of President Bongo's closest advisers. In 2002 the party signed on to be included in the "presidential majority."

Leaders: Jerôme OKINDA, Jean-Pierre LEMBOUMBA (Secretary General).

Other Parties that Participated in Recent Elections:

Gabonese Union for Democracy and Development (*Union Gabonaise de la Démocratie et du Développement*—UGDD). Formed in France on April 30, 2005, by Zacharie Myboto, the party had not been legalized by the November presidential election, forcing Myboto to run as an independent. A defector from the PDG, he formerly was a minister of public works and an administrative secretary of the party. In September 2005 President Bongo said he would seize his opponents' passports to prevent them from "insulting" him abroad. However, observers commented that Bongo wouldn't arrest Myboto, who is popular in Gabon, for fear of "annoying" international donors.

Gabon officially recognized the party in April 2006, and the party subsequently won four seats in the December assembly elections. In the 2008 local elections, the UGDD won 160 seats, a distant second to the PDG.

In January 2009 the UGDD rejected the government's overtures for a unity government, though two UGDD members were named to cabinet posts. Minister Sylvestre Ratanga and minister-delegate Paul Boundoukou-LATHA subsequently were told by party leader Myboto that they no longer represented the UGDD. The party won three seats in the subsequent 2009 Senate elections.

Leader: Zacharie MYBOTO (President of the Party and 2005 presidential candidate), Sylvestre RATANGA (Secretary General).

African Forum for Reconstruction (*Forum Africain pour la Réconstruction*—FAR). Also referenced as the Action Forum for Renewal (*Forum d'Action pour le Renouveau*), FAR was launched in early 1992 by merger of the National Rectification Movement–Originals (*Mouvement de Redressement National*—Morena–*Originels*), which had secured 7 legislative seats in 1990–1991, and two smaller formations, the Gabonese Socialist Union (*Union Socialiste Gabonais*—USG), which had secured 3 seats, and the extralegislative Gabonese Socialist Party (*Parti Socialiste Gabonais*—PSG). The party's platform advocates the establishment of a "state of law and social justice" and a market economy, tempered by the "interests of the State."

Organized in 1981, Morena operated clandestinely within Gabon for the ensuing nine years, during which time, with support from the French Socialist Party, it formed a self-proclaimed government-in-exile in Paris. In 1981–1982 its domestic leaders were repeatedly arrested for distributing leaflets calling for a multiparty system. Many were sentenced to long prison terms, but by 1986 all had been released under a general amnesty that had been urged by French President François Mitterrand. By early 1990 the party had given rise to a number of dissident factions, the most important of which was Morena–*Bûcherons* (above) as distinguished from the essentially northern, ethnic Fang parent group led by Noël Ngwa-Nguema. At a Morena party congress on August 30, 1991, Executive Secretary Jean-Pierre Zongue-Nguema called for a revival of the COD and denounced the "duplicity" of opposition colleagues who had joined the Bongo government.

At presidential balloting in December 1993, party leader León Mbou-Yembit captured a bare 1.83 percent of the vote while Adrien NGUEMA Ondo, running under the National Rectification Movement–Unionist (*Mouvement de Redressement National*—Morena–*Unioniste*) banner, secured less than 1 percent.

In August 1998 the Forum's Morena wing reportedly split into two camps, which subsequently held separate congresses in Libreville and Lambarene under the leadership of Jean Clement BOUTAMBA and Felix Martin Ze MEMINI, respectively.

In the 2005 presidential election, Augustin Moussavou King ran as a candidate affiliated with the PSG, coming in a distant fourth.

Leaders: León MBOU-YEMBIT, Pierre ZONGUE-NGUEMA (COD Chair and Former Morena–*Originel* Leader), Noël NGWA-NGUEMA (Former Morena–*Originel* Executive Secretary), Vincent ESSOLOMONGEU (Secretary General).

Gabonese Progress Party (*Parti Gabonais du Progrès*—PGP). The president of the recently organized PGP, Pierre-Louis Agondjo-Okawe, called in April 1990 for dissolution of the transitional government on the grounds that it was inadequately representative of the Gabonese people. In May the death of party secretary general Joseph Rendjambe was a catalyst for renewed unrest throughout the country. Second runner-up in the 1990 legislative poll, the PGP is composed primarily of members of the Myéné ethnic group.

In July 1998 the party announced that Benoit Mouity-Nzamba would be its standard-bearer at presidential balloting in December; however, there were no further reports regarding his candidacy.

In February 2000 the PGP reportedly accused the government of "organizing electoral fraud" and called on the president to convene talks on electoral and "institutional" reforms. The party won three seats in the 2001 assembly elections. Party leader Agondjo-Okawe died on August 27, 2005. Following Seraphim Ndaot Rembogo's succession to party leadership, some sources referenced the PGP/Ndaot as winning two seats in the 2006 assembly elections. The government reported the results as the PGP winning two seats.

Leaders: Seraphim NDAOT Rembogo, Benoit MOUITY-NZAMBA, Anselme NZOGHE (Secretary General).

Union of the Gabonese People (*Union du Peuple Gabonais—*UPG). In July 1989 the UPG, which is supported largely by the southern Bapounou ethnic group, was reported to have circulated leaflets critical of President Bongo in Paris; the following October, three of its members were arrested in Gabon for alleged involvement in a coup plot. In February 1990 party founder Pierre Mamboundou was expelled from France to Senegal, despite his denial of complicity in the attempted coup.

On July 14, 1992, UPG activists demonstrated in Libreville, calling for Mamboundou's amnesty. On November 2, 1993, the UPG leader was allowed to return from Senegal; however, his bid to stand as a presidential candidate in the December elections was rejected. Subsequently, on November 8–9 UPG demonstrators rioted in Libreville in a futile attempt to force the government to overturn the ban.

Mamboundou's preeminent role within the UPG was diminished on September 25, 1995, when party members elected his former coleader and recent nemesis, Sebastien Mamboundou MOUYAMA, chair. In August 1996 it was reported that Mouyama had launched a new political party called the **Alternative Movement** (*Mouvement Alternatif*—MA). However, Mamboundou ran as the UPG and HCR's presidential candidate in 1998, and he was routinely referenced as the UPG leader in the 2001 legislative campaign, calling for a boycott of the second round of balloting in view of what he termed the "indescribable disorder" of the first round. The legal status of the new group and its relationship with the UPG was not immediately clear.

Defying a ban on demonstrations, members of the UPG participated in a mass protest near Libreville in November 2005 over alleged irregularities in organizing the upcoming elections, and seven party members were arrested.

In March 2006 government authorities raided the UPG offices to "recover arms" following a demonstration by party members, some allegedly armed, in which a protester was killed by government security forces. The party denied there were weapons at its headquarters. Mamboundou, for his part, sought refuge in the South African embassy in Libreville. A month later tensions apparently eased after Mamboundou left the embassy and met with President Bongo.

The party won eight seats in the 2006 legislative elections and 90 members were elected in local balloting in 2008, third after the PDG and the UGDD. Mamboundou returned to Gabon in January 2009, and the party won two seats in the Senate elections on January 18.

Leaders: Pierre MAMBOUNDOU (2005 presidential candidate), Richard MOULOMBA (Secretary General).

Rally of the Democrats (*Rassemblement des Démocrates*—RDD). Founded in 1993 by Christian-Serge Maroga, who defected from UPG, the party was legalized in 1997. Maroga received less than 1 percent of the vote in the 2005 presidential election.

Leader: Christian-Serge MAROGA (2005 presidential candidate).

Minor parties include the **Circle for Renovation and Progress** (*Cercle pour le Renouveau et le Progrès*—CRP); the **Congress for Democracy and Justice** (*Congrès pour la Démocratie et la Justice*—CDJ), which won one seat in the 2001 and 2006 assembly elections, led by Jules Bourdès-Ogouliguende, former president of the National Assembly, and Marc Saturnin Nan NGUEMA, a Fang who was formerly a secretary general of OPEC and a 1993 presidential candidate; he was arrested in December 2004 on trumped-up weapons charges; the **Federation of Gabonese Ecologists** (*Fédération des Écologistes Gabonaises*—FEG), an environmental group led by Alain DICKSON that has been highly critical of the dearth of environmentalists in the government; **Gabon of the Future** (*Gabon Avenir*), which was launched in 1999 under the leadership of Sylvestre OYOUOMI; the **Mebiame Group** (*Groupe Mébiame*—GM); the **Movement for People's Social Emancipation** (*Mouvement pour l'Emancipation Sociale du Peuple*—MESP), led by Victor MOUANGA MBADINGA; the **National Front** (*Front National*—FN), led by Martin EFAYONG; and the **Renaissance of the Gabonese Democratic Bloc,** led by Antoine Meyo MENDOUTOUME; the **Union for Democracy and Social Integration,** led by Nzebi Herve Patrick OPIANGAH, who was jailed in early 2005 after participating in a demonstration demanding legalization of the **African Development Movement**, led by Pierre-Claver ZENG EBOME. A new party, the **Rally of Republican Democrats** (*Rassemblement des Démocrates Républicains*—RDR), won one seat in the 2006 assembly elections.

In 2006 Bongo Must Go (*Bongo Doit Partir*—BDP), described as a radical group based in the United States, joined with a group called *Mamba*, which claimed to have carried out "sabotage" attacks in Libreville in December 2005. The leaders of the BDP were Daniel MENGARA, a Fang who in 2008 called for an armed rebellion, and Serge BESAC.

LEGISLATURE

In March 1994 the (then) unicameral National Assembly adopted a draft constitutional reform bill that provided for a Senate, or upper legislative house. Elections to fill the body were held for the first time in January–February 1997.

Senate (*Sénat*). Created by a constitutional amendment in 1994, the Senate originally was a 91-member body. Senators are indirectly elected for a six-year term by members of municipal councils and departmental assemblies. First-ever balloting to fill the body was held on January 26 and February 9, 1997. The chamber was enlarged to 102 seats in the most recent balloting on January 18, 2009, in which the seat distribution was as follows: the Gabonese Democratic Party, 75; independents, 9; Rally for Gabon, 6; Gabonese Union for Democracy and Development, 3; Circle of Liberal Reformers, 2; Union of the Gabonese People, 2; Gabonese Party of Independent Centrists, 2; Social Democratic Party, 2; and Democratic and Republican Alliance, 1.

President: Rose Francine ROGOMBÉ.

National Assembly (*Assemblée Nationale*). The sole legislative organ prior to 1997, the National Assembly is a 120-seat body whose members are elected for five-year terms. Following the most recent balloting on December 17 and December 24, 2006 (balloting was delayed in seven districts until the latter date), the allocation of seats was as follows: the Gabonese Democratic Party, 82; the Rally for Gabon, 8; the Union of the Gabonese People, 8; the Gabonese Union for Democracy and Development, 4; the Democratic and Republican Alliance, 3; the Circle of Liberal Reformers, 2; the Social Democratic Party, 2; the Gabonese Progress Party, 2; the African Development Movement, 1; the Rally of Republican Democrats, 1; the African Forum for Reconstruction, 1; the Congress for Democracy and Justice, 1; the National Rally of Woodcutters/Kombila, 1; and independents, 4.

Polling was held anew on June 10, 2007, in 20 constituencies in which the 2006 results had been rejected by the courts due to irregularities. Unofficial reports credited the Gabonese Democratic Party with retaining its 82-seat total following the balloting.

President: Guy NDZOUBA-NDAMA.

CABINET

[as of April 1, 2009] (*see headnote*)

Prime Minister	Jean Eyéghe Ndong (PDG)
Deputy Prime Minister	Georgette Koko (PDG) [f]
	Paul Mba-Abessole (RNB/RPG)
	Honorine Dossou Naki (PDG) [f]
Ministers of State	
Foreign Affairs, Cooperation, Francophone Affairs, and Regional Integration	Paul Toungui (PDG)
Gas and Oil	Casimir Oyé Mba (PDG)
Labor, Employment, and Social Security	François Engongah Owono (PDG)
Ministers	
Agriculture, Livestock, and Food Security	Paul Biyoghe Mba (PDG)
Civil Service and State Modernization	Alain-Mensah Zoguelet (PDG)
Commerce and Industrial Development	Patrice Tonda
Communications, Posts, Telecommunications, and Information Technology	Laure Olga Gondjout [f]

Culture, Arts, National Education, and Human Rights	Paul Mba-Abessole (RNB/RPG)
Decentralization and Urban Policy	Richard-Auguste Onouviet (PDG)
Defense	Ali Ben Bongo Ondimba (PDG)
Economy, Finance, Budget, and Privatization	Blaise Louembé
Energy	Frank Emmanuel Issoze-Ngondet
Environment, Sustainable Development, and Protection of Nature	Georgette Koko (PDG) [f]
Family Affairs, Promotion of Women, And Protection of Women and Orphans	Angélique Ngoma (PDG) [f]
Forests, Water, and Fishing	Emile Doumba (PDG)
Government Spokesperson	René Ndemezo Obiang (PDG)
Higher Education and Scientific Research	Fabien Owono Ngoua
Housing and Urban Affairs	Josué Mbadinga
Interior, Civil Security, and Immigration	André Mba Obame (PDG)
Justice and Keeper of the Seals	Pierrette Djouassa [f]
Merchant Navy and Ports	Jacques Adiahenot (PDG)
National Education	Michel Menga (PDG)
Public Health and Hygiene	Gen. Idriss Ngari (PDG)
Public Service Development and Statistical Development	Anaclet Bissiélou
Public Works, Infrastructure, and Construction	Gen. Flavien Nzengui-Nzoundou
Regional Planning and Urban Policy	Pierre-Claver Maganga Moussavou (PSD)
Relations with Parliament and Constitutional Institutions	Martin Mabala (PDG)
Small and Medium-Sized Enterprises and the Fight Against Poverty	Vincent Essone Mengue
Social Affairs	Denise Mekamne [f]
State Controls and Inspections and the Fight against Corruption	Honorine Dossou Naki (PDG) [f]
Technical Education, Vocational Training, And Youth Employment	Pierre-André Kombila Koumba (RNB/RPG)
Tourism and National Parks	Yolande Bike [f]
Transport and Civil Aviation	Sylvestre Ratanga (UGDD)
Youth, Sports, and Leisure	René Ndemezo Obiang (PDG)

[f] = female

COMMUNICATIONS

Most news media are owned and operated by the government. In late 1999 four private radio and television stations were suspended by the National Council of Communication for broadcasting illegally. The few privately owned publications in the country generally have been allowed freedom of expression, according to the watchdog Reporters Without Borders, though there appeared to be increasing crackdowns against media outlets that exposed alleged government misdeeds. A journalist was arrested in 2007 for criticizing the president, and in 2008 one private newspaper was banned for reprinting an article about President Bongo's personal wealth, and two other private newspapers were suspended. In January 2009 five journalists faced fines of about $400 each and jail sentences of up to five years for allegedly trying to incite rebellion after they published a document highly critical of President Bongo. Two of the journalists were provisionally released a few days after their arrest. In February police arrested two European journalists, accusing them of posing as tourists in order to obtain information for a story about France's foreign minister.

Press. The following are published in Libreville: *L'Union* (35,000), government daily; *Gabon-Matin* (18,000), published daily by the *Agence Gabonaise de Presse; La Relance,* weekly PDG organ; *Gabon d'Aujourd'hui,* published weekly by the Ministry of Communications; *Le Journal*, private bimonthly; and *La Lowe*, *Le Temps* and *Le Temoin*, all private weeklies.

News agencies. The domestic facility is the *Agence Gabonaise de Presse* (AGP). The private *Gabonews* also operates in Gabon.

Broadcasting and computing. The government-controlled *Radiodiffusion-Télévision Gabonaise* broadcasts national and regional radio programs in French and local languages, plus educational television programming from Libreville and Port-Gentil. There also are two private channels, *Télé-Africa,* which broadcasts in French, and *Télédiffusion du Gabon*. Africa No1 is a pan-African broadcaster based in Gaton. As of 2008 there were 62.1 Internet users per 1,000 inhabitants.

INTERGOVERNMENTAL REPRESENTATION

Ambassador to the U.S.: Carlos BOUNGOU.

U.S. Ambassador to Gabon: Eunice S. REDDICK.

Permanent Representative to the UN: Emmanuel ISSOZENGO-NDET.

IGO Memberships (Non-UN): AfDB, AU, BADEA, BDEAC, CEEAC, CEMAC, IDB, Interpol, IOM, NAM, OIC, OIF, WCO, WTO.

GAMBIA

Republic of The Gambia

Political Status: Became independent member of the Commonwealth on February 18, 1965; republican regime instituted April 24, 1970; Gambian-Senegalese Confederation of Senegambia, formed with effect from February 1, 1982, dissolved as of September 30, 1989; most recent constitution approved by national referendum on August 8, 1996.

Area: 4,361 sq. mi. (11,295 sq. km.).

Population: 1,364,507 (2003C); 1,710,000 (2008E). The 2003 figure appears to reflect substantial underenumeration.

Major Urban Center (2005E): BANJUL (metropolitan area, 568,000).

Official Language: English.

Monetary Unit: Dalasi (market rate December 1, 2009: 26.90 dalasis = $1US).

President: Yahya JAMMEH (Alliance for Patriotic Reorientation and Construction); installed as chair of the Armed Forces Provisional Ruling Council following military coup that overthrew the government of Alhaji Sir Dawda Kairaba JAWARA Sanyang (People's Progressive Party) on July 22, 1994; popularly elected to a five-year presidential term on September 26, 1996; reelected on October 18, 2001, and sworn in for a second five-year term on December 21; reelected for another five-year term on September 22, 2006, and inaugurated on December 15.

Vice President: Aisatou NJIE-SAIDY (Alliance for Patriotic Reorientation and Construction); appointed by the president on March 21, 1997, to fill previously vacant post; reappointed December 21, 2001; reappointed by the president on October 19, 2006, and sworn in with the cabinet on October 27.

THE COUNTRY

Situated on the bulge of West Africa and surrounded on three sides by Senegal, Gambia is a narrow strip of territory (varying from 6 to 10 miles wide) that borders the Gambia River to a point about 200 miles

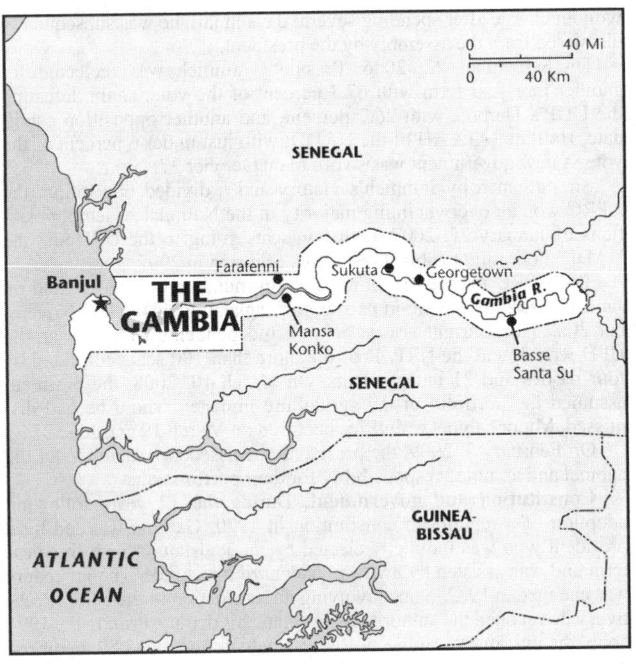

from the Atlantic. The population is overwhelmingly African, the main ethnic groups being Mandingo (40 percent), Fula (13 percent), Wolof (12 percent), and Jola and Serahuli (7 percent each); in addition, there are small groups of Europeans, Lebanese, Syrians, and Mauritanians. Tribal languages are widely spoken, although English is the official and commercial language. Islam is the religion of 80 percent of the people.

The economy has traditionally been based on peanuts, which are cultivated on almost all suitable land and which, including derivatives, typically account for upward of 80 percent of export earnings. Industry is largely limited to peanut-oil refining and handicrafts; unofficially, smuggling into Senegal has long been important. In the early 1990s the government implemented an economic recovery program sponsored by the International Monetary Fund (IMF), which emphasized agricultural development, reductions in external borrowing, promotion of the private sector, and government austerity; those measures were credited with stimulating an improvement in GDP and a decline in inflation. Nonetheless, a slump in the agriculture sector yielded virtually no real economic growth in 1993–1994. Western aid was severely curtailed following the military coup of 1994, the Jammeh regime turning to new donors such as Libya and Taiwan to finance an ambitious infrastructure program. Thereafter, the government adopted another IMF-prescribed structural adjustment program with an emphasis on economic and financial reform. Such efforts were rewarded in 1998 with a real GDP growth rate of over 5 percent and single-digit inflation. Meanwhile, the fund urged the government to continue to increase its support for the private sector. In early 2000 Gambia called on the international investment community to assist African countries in their privatization efforts, asserting that state assets were being treated as "scrap" and sold off at extremely low prices.

Gambia experienced a severe economic downturn in 2002, partly due to a collapse in the peanut harvest. As a result, GDP declined by 3.2 percent, inflation rose to 13 percent, and the government's deficit ballooned to 8.1 percent of GDP. In addition, the currency lost 60 percent of its value against the euro and 45 percent of its value against the dollar. Meanwhile, unemployment approached 50 percent. Adding to the crisis was the rise in world oil prices and one of the world's fastest-growing populations. In response to these economic shocks, the government created the National Emergency Fiscal Committee and implemented programs designed to spur growth. The economy rebounded in 2003 with real GDP growth of 7 percent, although inflation remained high.

In 2004–2005 GDP growth averaged 5 percent annually, with inflation declining to less than 3 percent in 2005. In January 2006 the president announced a 10 percent salary increase for all government workers, an expenditure that was not accounted for in the recently approved budget. The IMF encouraged better management of public resources. Later in the year Jammeh was criticized for authorizing expenditures (amounting to 10 percent of the country's annual budget) associated with Gambia's hosting of the African Union (AU) summit in July (see Current issues, below). Meanwhile, with unemployment and poverty "at record highs," according to the IMF, fund managers urged widespread reforms. On a more positive note, growth in construction, tourism, and telecommunications helped boost annual GDP growth to 6 percent in 2006. Also, potentially significant oil deposits were discovered offshore, raising the possibility of dramatic revenue enhancement in the next decade.

In 2007 the U.S.-based Millennium Challenge Corporation had suspended aid to Gambia as a consequence of perceived government repression and corruption. However, in December the IMF and the World Bank announced that Gambia was eligible for $140 million in debt relief. The economy continued to expand at a robust rate, with average GDP growth of 6.6 percent in 2007-2008. In February 2008 the Paris Club creditors agreed to write off $11.5 million in Gambian debt.

In February 2009 the African Development Bank (AfDB) pledged $6 million in poverty-reduction funds to help with the increased cost of food imports. Annual GDP growth was expected to slow to 4.7 percent in 2009-2010 due in large part to declining tourism revenue in the wake of the global financial crisis.

GOVERNMENT AND POLITICS

Political background. Under British influence since 1588, Gambia was not definitively established as a separate colony until 1888. It acquired the typical features of British colonial rule, achieved internal self-government in 1963, and became fully independent within the Commonwealth on February 18, 1965. Initially a parliamentary regime (with the British monarch serving as head of state), Gambia changed to a republican form of government following a referendum in 1970.

For nearly three decades after independence, leadership was exercised by the People's Progressive Party (PPP), headed by President Dawda K. JAWARA, although opposition candidates secured approximately 30 percent of the popular vote in the elections of 1972, 1977, and 1982. At the May 1979 PPP Congress—the first in 16 years—President Jawara rebuffed demands by some delegates that a one-party system be instituted, commenting that such a change could occur only through the ballot box. However, on November 1, 1980, amid allegations of a widespread antigovernment conspiracy, two opposition movements described by the president as "terrorist organizations" were banned, despite protests from the legal opposition parties.

A more serious threat to the Jawara regime developed in July 1981 when the capital was taken over by elements of Gambia's paramilitary Field Force and the Socialist and Revolutionary Labor Party, a Marxist-Leninist group led by Kukoi Samba SANYANG. The uprising was quelled with the aid of Senegalese troops dispatched under the terms of a 1965 mutual defense and security treaty. Subsequently, President Jawara and Senegalese President Diouf announced plans for a partial merger of their respective states in the form of a Senegambian Confederation, which came into effect on February 1, 1982.

The confederation, which critics branded as the equivalent of annexation by Senegal, was a major issue in the May 1982 presidential election, the first to be conducted by direct vote. However, with the government branding several members of the demonstrably divided opposition as participants in the 1981 coup attempt, Jawara secured a 73 percent majority. The president subsequently appeared to defuse the confederation issue by resisting immediate monetary union with Senegal, a proposal viewed with skepticism by many Gambians.

While President Jawara was returned to office at the general election of March 11, 1987, with a reduced majority of 59 percent, the PPP increased its representation in the 36-member House of Representatives from 28 to 31, most observers attributing the latter success to an economic upturn. Subsequently, amid widespread concern about Gambia becoming "Senegal's eleventh region," the administration evinced little interest in pursuing genuine Senegambian integration, and the confederation was dissolved with the consent of both countries as of September 30, 1989.

After declaring his intention to retire at a PPP congress in December 1991, Jawara reversed himself and stood for a fifth consecutive five-year term in April 1992, reportedly to avoid further electoral slippage that might result in defeat for the ruling party. The outcome was a marginal decline of 5 elected House seats on a vote share virtually identical to that of 1985.

The Jawara government was overthrown on July 22, 1994, in a bloodless coup by junior army officers, who installed Lt. Yahya JAMMEH as chair of a five-member Armed Forces Provisional Ruling Council (AFPRC). Three days later the council named a 15-member government composed almost equally of military and civilian members.

Antagonism toward the Jammeh government subsequently emerged from several quarters. In mid-August tension between the AFPRC and older military officials, who complained of being shunted aside, was underscored by the arrest of two high-ranking officers. Collaterally, friction continued between the AFPRC and members of Jawara's former government. Finally, on October 10, the European Union (EU) and the United Kingdom suspended economic and military assistance following Jammeh's dismissal of Finance Minister Bakary Bunja DARBO, the sole holdover from the previous administration.

In an attempt to mollify his critics, Jammeh in late 1994 announced a four-year transitional timetable that included plans for the drafting of a new constitution, an investigation into government corruption, a crackdown on crime, and a presidential election in November 1998. However, the four-year time frame drew widespread criticism, and in early February 1995 the AFPRC reduced it to two. Meanwhile, as the result of alleged participation in a coup attempt on January 27, two close associates of Jammeh on the AFPRC, Vice Chair Sana SABALLY and Interior Minister Sadibu HYDARA, were arrested and replaced by Capt. Edward SINGHATEY and Capt. Lamin BAJO, respectively. (In late December it was reported that Sabally had been given a nine-year sentence and that Hydara had died in prison.)

On April 10, 1995, the regime named a constitutional commission and charged it with drafting a document that would provide a legal framework for the holding of multiparty elections. However, in October the defection of AFPRC spokesman Capt. Ebou JALLOW, amid charges that he had attempted to overthrow the regime, underscored the internal turmoil that had plagued the AFPRC and Jammeh's cabinet throughout 1995.

The draft constitution was released by the AFPRC in March 1996 and approved (according to government figures) by 70.4 percent of the voters in a national referendum on August 8, 1996, despite opposition charges that the new basic law had been carefully written to ensure that the Jammeh regime would continue in power. Jammeh subsequently announced that presidential elections would be held in September (months earlier than anticipated), with national legislative balloting to follow before the end of the year.

In voting on September 26, 1996, Jammeh was elected to a five-year presidential term as the candidate of the newly formed Alliance for Patriotic Reorientation and Construction (APRC). Official results credited him with 55.76 percent of the votes, his closest pursuer among the three other candidates being Ousainu DARBOE of the United Democratic Party (UDP) with 35.34 percent.

On November 8, 1996, the government announced that legislative elections, due on December 11, would be postponed until January 1997. The decision came after weeks of UDP-orchestrated antigovernment demonstrations. Subsequently, at balloting on January 2, 1997, President Jammeh's APRC captured 33 of the 45 contested seats (the president is empowered to name 4 additional legislators), giving the party the two-thirds majority necessary to pass legislation and make constitutional changes unimpeded. With 7 seats, Darboe's UDP finished a distant second.

Rebuffed in his attempt to name Edward Singhatey as vice president (the 27-year-old Singhatey failed a constitutional requirement that the deputy chief executive be at least 30 years old), Jammeh appointed a new 13-member cabinet on March 7, 1997, which did not include a vice president but placed Singhatey in the powerful post of minister to the president. However, following opposition criticism that the constitution mandated the appointment of a vice president, the president named Aisatou NJIE-SAIDY (his minister of health, social welfare, and women's affairs) to the post on March 21. Njie-Saidy thereby became the first female vice president in western Africa. The transformation from military to civilian rule was completed on April 17 when Jammeh replaced the last four military governors with civilians.

President Jammeh was reelected to a second term with 53 percent of the vote on October 18, 2001, the UDP's Darboe again proving to be his nearest competitor among four opposition candidates. The APRC dominated the January 2002 assembly balloting as the result of a boycott by the major opposition grouping and subsequently dominated local and regional elections in April because of the continuing boycott (see Current issues, below).

In assembly by-elections on September 29, 2005, to replace 4 ousted members, 3 seats went to a newly formed opposition coalition, the National Alliance for Democracy and Development (NADD), and 1 seat was secured by the APRC. Assembly speaker Sherif Mustapha DIBBA, who was arrested in connection with an alleged March 21 coup attempt, was replaced in April. Although Dibba was released without charge after spending several days in jail, he was subsequently dismissed from the assembly by the president.

On September 22, 2006, President Jammeh was reelected for another five-year term with 67.3 percent of the vote, again defeating the UDP's Darboe, with 26.7 percent, and another opposition candidate, Halifah SALLAH of the NADD, with just under 6 percent of the vote. A new government was sworn in on October 27.

Strengthened by Jammeh's victory and a divided opposition, the APRC won an overwhelming majority in the National Assembly elections of January 25, 2007, with few seats going to the UPD and the NADD. Four minor cabinet reshuffles occurred in 2007.

The APRC retained its dominance in municipal elections held on January 24, 2008, owing in part to new legislation adopted in November 2007 (see Current issues, below). Independents won 8 seats, the UPD won 3, and the NRP, 1, of the more than 100 seats contested by four parties and 21 independents. On March 10, 2008, the president assumed the portfolio of the agriculture minister, whom he had dismissed. Minor cabinet reshuffles occurred on March 19 and June 27.

On February 7, 2009, the president dismissed two members of the cabinet and assumed responsibility for their portfolios.

Constitution and government. During the 12 years following adoption of a republican constitution in 1970, Gambia was led by a president who was indirectly elected by the legislature for a five-year term and was assisted by a vice president of his choice. The procedure was changed in 1982 to one involving direct election of the chief executive, who retained the authority to designate his deputy. Prior to the 1994 coup, the unicameral House of Representatives contained 50 members, of whom 36 were directly elected for five-year terms (save for presidential dissolution following a vote of nonconfidence); 5 seats were held by chiefs elected by the Assembly of Chiefs, while the remainder were held by 8 nonvoting nominated members and the attorney general. The 1996 constitution provided for a directly elected president with broad powers (including the authority to appoint the cabinet) and a National Assembly of elected legislators and presidential appointees. The assembly may order the resignation of the head of state or cabinet ministers by a two-thirds vote. The judicial system is headed by a Supreme Court and includes a Court of Appeal, magistrates' courts, customary tribunals, and Muslim courts.

At the local level the country is divided into districts administered by chiefs in association with village headmen and advisers. The districts are grouped into seven regions, which are governed by centrally appointed commissioners and area councils thus far containing a majority of elected members, with district chiefs serving ex officio. Banjul has heretofore been provided with an elected city council.

Foreign relations. While adhering to a formal policy of nonalignment, Gambia has long maintained close relations with the United Kingdom, its principal aid donor, and the African Commonwealth states. By far the most important foreign policy question, however, has turned on relations with Senegal. In 1967 the two countries signed a treaty of association providing for a joint ministerial committee and secretariat, while other agreements provided for cooperation in such areas as defense, foreign affairs, and development of the Gambia River basin. In early 1976 a number of new accords were concluded that, coupled with the need for Senegalese military assistance in 1980 and 1981, paved the way for establishment of the Confederation of Senegambia in February 1982. However, few of its goals had been seriously addressed at the time of the confederation's dissolution in 1989.

Relations deteriorated in the wake of the breakup with Senegal in 1989, with Banjul accusing Dakar of economic harassment (largely in connection with Senegalese attempts to limit the clandestine flow of re-export goods). However, a meeting between Presidents Jawara and Diouf in December 1989 proved beneficial, the Jawara administration reportedly attempting to stabilize relations so as not to jeopardize Gambia's recent economic improvement. Ties were further strengthened by the conclusion of a treaty of friendship and cooperation on January 8, 1991, that provided for annual political summits and the establishment of joint commissions to help implement summit agreements.

In September 1993 Senegal closed its borders with Gambia, voicing renewed frustration with illegal commerce. In November the two countries agreed to the establishment of a technical committee charged with creating a mechanism to alleviate the problem, which had plagued the former confederates since their 1989 split.

Regional relations were at the forefront of Gambia's foreign policy agenda in late 1999 and early 2000. In December 1999 President Jammeh played a leading role in facilitating the signing of a cease-fire pact by the Senegalese government and Casamance rebels, and in April

2000 Gambia and four other West African nations agreed to share a common currency by the end of 2002. However, the deadline was later advanced to the end of 2009. (The other prospective participants are Ghana, Guinea, Nigeria, and Sierre Leone.) Gambia also participated in the regional peacekeeping mission in Liberia by contributing 150 troops. These forces subsequently became part of the UN mission in Liberia.

In November 2000 the Commonwealth Ministerial Action Group visited Gambia, signaling a relative easing of relations that had reportedly been lukewarm since 1995, although Gambia continued to be criticized for its human rights record.

Relations between Gambia and Senegal remained tense in the early 2000s amid repeated claims that the Jammeh government provided aid to antigovernment forces in Senegal. Subsequently, a 100 percent increase in duties on vehicles traveling through Gambia and a doubling of the cost of ferries between northern and southern Senegal temporarily led to the closing of the border between the two countries, to the detriment of both countries' economies. Negotiations brokered by Nigeria in late 2005 resulted in Senegal's agreeing to remove its border blockade following Gambia's partial removal of the ferry charges and an apology by Jammeh.

Renewed fighting along the border between Senegalese government forces and antigovernment rebels in late 2006 led to an influx of 10,000 refugees into Gambia, with reports that some rebel fighters had also entered the republic. President Jammeh, for his part, refused to respond to inquiries from Senegal as to the whereabouts of the rebels. Despite the death of a key rebel leader in Paris in January 2007, heavy fighting between Senegalese rebels and Senegalese forces reignited in March. Intermittent clashes reportedly forced at least 1,000 refugees to flee to Gambia by May. At least nine Senegalese rebels had been charged by the end of the year with conspiracy to commit acts of terrorism against Senegal from Gambian soil. In early 2008 the two countries reaffirmed their commitment to military cooperation aimed at peacekeeping in the region.

Current issues. In September 1999 the Gambian *Daily Observer* reported that an assassination attempt had targeted President Jammeh, who had recently moved his government to his hometown (ostensibly because of renovation work being performed in Banjul). The government dismissed the story, and an *Observer* editor and reporter were arrested. However, following reports of violent clashes between rival groups of presidential guardsmen in Banjul in January 2000, Jammeh claimed that forces loyal to him had killed one guardsman and wounded a second, both facing arrest for allegedly plotting a coup. (Among the alleged targets of the dissidents were Jammeh and his government as well as all army officers above the rank of lieutenant.) In April the already tense capital was rocked by antigovernment demonstrations and rioting that erupted after security forces killed a student. At least 12 people died during the unrest. A commission of inquiry subsequently resulted in amnesty for both security forces involved in the shootings and the leaders of student groups.

The 2001 presidential campaign was marred by several violent incidents, but the balloting proceeded smoothly. Although international observers generally accepted the poll as free and fair, albeit with several significant criticisms, the UDP accused the government of electoral fraud. In late December the UDP and several of its coalition partners announced they would boycott the legislative election scheduled for January 17, 2002, on the grounds that the electoral commission was favoring the Jammeh administration by, among other things, permitting cross-district voting. The major opposition parties also boycotted the municipal and regional elections of April 2002, thereby again ensuring APRC dominance, as the APRC won 99 of 113 constituencies. Four assembly members were expelled in mid-2005 following their launch of the opposition coalition NADD. (The constitution states that elected representatives lose their seats if they change to a party other than the one they were affiliated with when elected.)

Gambia's former army chief, Ndure CHAM, and numerous others were arrested after an alleged coup attempt in March 2006 while the president was on a visit to Mauritania. Following the wide-ranging arrests, some political observers referred to the episode as a "political ruse" in advance of presidential elections (then) scheduled for October. Cham subsequently escaped and reportedly fled to Senegal; other escapees were reportedly killed. One month after the foiled plot, thousands staged a prodemocracy, anticoup demonstration.

Banjul was reported to have spent about $20 million on infrastructure improvements and other preparations for the African Union (AU) summit in July 2006, with observers commenting on Jammeh's efforts as "a prelude to his election campaign." In August Jammeh called for elections to be held a month early, in September, leaving little time for opposition groups to organize their campaigns. Meanwhile, the opposition coalition split when the UDP's Darboe and the NRP's Bah left the NADD to form their own alliance, Darboe withdrawing after he failed to win the coalition's presidential nomination. Subsequently, the UDP and the NRP agreed to form an alliance with the Gambia Party for Democracy and Progress (GPDP), backing Darboe for the presidency (the electoral commission had rejected GPDP leader Henry GOMEZ's candidacy). In addition, the PDOIS's Halifa Sallah also contested the election, backed by the People's Progressive Party (PPP).

In the run-up to the 2006 presidential election, it was reported that Jammeh registered thousands of refugees as Gambian voters, replaced several electoral commission officials with his loyalists, promised improvements to communities that voted for him, and denied opposition groups access to the airwaves. Reporters Without Borders criticized restricted press freedom and public access to information as "so catastrophic that it alone suffices to disqualify these elections." Jammeh's reelection, however, was "far from the landslide he claimed," according to *Africa Confidential*, which cited the 59 percent voter turnout as the lowest since 1965. Nevertheless, observers pointed to the splintered opposition as more of a factor in the president's victory than citizens' support for his "strong-arm" rule. (The two opposition candidates received less than one-third of the vote.) While the elections raised no public concerns by international observers, the opposition rejected the results. Three of the assembly leaders expelled in 2005 were returned to their seats in 2006 by-elections. The fourth, opposition leader Hamat Bah, was accused of vote-rigging and did not gain a seat (nor was he elected in the 2007 assembly balloting).

The ruling party's grip was further enhanced by the APRC's securing 42 of 48 seats in the January 2007 assembly elections, with voter turnout of only about 40 percent recorded. In April, ten army officers convicted of treason in connection with the March 2006 coup attempt were sentenced to prison terms ranging from ten years to life, and four civilians were awaiting trial on similar charges. In a bizarre claim that made international headlines, President Jammeh announced that he had discovered a cure for AIDS. Health officials discounted the claim, and the UN envoy to Gambia was forced to leave the country after she urged patients to continue with their normal treatment. In 2008 President Jammeh announced his ability to cure strokes and skin cancer.

The municipal elections of January 24, 2008, were challenged by the UDP and NRP (see Political Parties, below), which asked the Supreme Court to overturn legislation approved by the National Assembly in November 2007. Under the Local Government Act revisions, which the opposition contended were unconstitutional, the president was granted the authority to fire mayors and dissolve municipal councils at his discretion, in effect giving him control over all local and municipal affairs. The court rejected the parties' request for an injunction against the local elections, in which the APRC won an overwhelming number of council posts and two key mayoral seats.

Gambia's human rights record drew international condemnation in December 2008, following the sentencing of a Christian missionary couple to a year in prison with hard labor for sending out emails criticizing the government. They were reported to be the first foreigners jailed for sedition in Gambia. Amnesty International, in a 2008 report, stated that "fear rules" in the country, as opponents of President Jammeh were routinely subjected to rights violations, including torture. Meanwhile, Jammeh earlier had issued an ultimatum for all homosexuals, drug dealers, and criminals to leave the country immediately or else face serious consequences. In 2009 hundreds of Gambians fled to Senegal following the government's crackdown on people accused of being witches. Up to 1,000 villagers were reportedly rounded up by government forces and taken to secret detention centers (including a farm belonging to President Jammeh), where they were allegedly drugged and abused. Hundreds were released in April, observers citing pressure from Amnesty International as the reason. NADD leader Halifah Sallah was arrested for having written about the government actions.

POLITICAL PARTIES

Prior to the 1994 coup, Gambia was one of the few African states to have consistently sanctioned a multiparty system, despite the predominant position held since independence by the ruling People's Progressive Party (PPP). Following the coup, all party activity was proscribed until August 14, 1996, when, in the wake of the recent approval of a new constitution, the government announced that the ban had been lifted. However, the regime's opponents described the new "preconditions" for party registration as "onerous" and accused President Jammeh of lacking commitment to genuine democratization. Such fears appeared justified when Jammeh announced shortly thereafter that the three main parties from the pre-coup era (the PPP, NCP, and GPP) had been banned. Under intense regional and other international pressure, Jammeh lifted the ban in July 2001 to permit full-party participation in the upcoming presidential election.

Five opposition parties formed a coalition called the National Alliance for Democracy and Development (NADD) on January 17, 2005, in Banjul to present a candidate to challenge Jammeh in the 2006 presidential election.

Government and Government-Supportive Parties:

Alliance for Patriotic Reorientation and Construction (APRC). Founded on August 26, 1996, as a vehicle for Col. Yahya Jammeh's presidential campaign, the APRC was a successor to the July 22 Movement (named in reference to the date of Jammeh's takeover in 1994), which had been launched in mid-1995. (Among other things, its leaders had committed the movement to "national unity," apparently in the hope of bridging the nation's ethnic divisions. The bulk of the support for the Jammeh regime at that point was described as emanating from the Jola ethnic group, which constitutes less than 10 percent of the population.) APRC founders announced they would pursue economic development based on free-market principles and cooperation with neighboring countries. Jammeh resigned his military position (as required by the constitution) shortly before the September 1996 presidential balloting.

In late 1999 Phoday MAKALO, theretofore the APRC's secretary general, reportedly fled the country amid allegations that he had embezzled party funds. The party underscored its ruling power with definitive victories in the 2006 assembly by-elections and presidential election and in the 2007 assembly balloting.

Leaders: Yahya JAMMEH (President of the Republic), Aisatou NJIE-SAIDY (Vice President of the Republic), Musa BITTAYE, Manlafi JARJU (Secretary General).

National Convention Party (NCP). The NCP was organized in late 1975 by Sherif Mustapha Dibba, former vice president of the Republic and cofounder of the PPP. Although jailed in August 1981 on charges of involvement in the July coup attempt, Dibba challenged Jawara for the presidency in 1982, securing 28 percent of the vote. The 5 legislative seats won by the NCP in 1977 were reduced to 3 in 1982. A month after the election, Dibba was released from confinement, the charges against him having been vacated by a Banjul court. The party won 5 House seats in 1987 and 6 in 1992, Dibba running second to Jawara in the presidential balloting on both occasions. The NCP was banned from participating in 1996 elections but regained legal status in July 2001. Dibba won 3.7 percent of the vote in the October presidential poll. Despite his previous criticism of President Jammeh and the APRC, Dibba announced an "alliance" between the NCP and the APRC prior to the legislative balloting of January 2002. Dibba was subsequently nominated by the president to the assembly, of which he was then elected speaker, thereby eliciting criticism from a number of other NCP stalwarts who wished to remain in strict opposition to the APRC. He was removed as speaker in 2006, following allegations that he had been involved in a plot to overthrow the government. Though Dibba denied any involvement, the president dismissed him from the assembly. After Dibba's removal, the status of the party was unclear, although in September an announcement from the party urged NCP members to support Jammeh in the upcoming presidential election. The party did not present candidates in the 2007 assembly elections. Dibba died of a heart attack in June 2008.

Other Parties that Participated in the 2007 Assembly Elections:

National Alliance for Democracy and Development (NADD). Upon its launch on January 17, 2005, the NADD comprised the two groups below and the NDAM, the NRP, and the UDP. The UDP and the NRP dropped out of the alliance in February 2006 and March 2006, respectively, but a Supreme Court justice ruled on January 16, 2008, that the UDP and the NRP were, in fact, still part of the NADD. The ruling came about as a result of a suit filed by the UDP and the NRP in which they sought to halt municipal elections by having amendments to the Local Government Act declared null and void (see Current issues, above). The justice ruled that the UDP and the NRP were not legal entities, since both still belonged to the NADD by virtue of the fact that only the NRP's Hamat Bah and the UDP's Ousainu Darboe, not the parties as a whole, had left the alliance. In February the full court dismissed the UDP/NRP application for review, saying that it did not have the authority to review the ruling of a single judge of the Supreme Court.

The NADD's candidate, Halifa Sallah, finished a distant third in the 2006 presidential election.

In the 2007 assembly elections the NADD, now comprising the PDOIS, the PPP, and the NDAM, was credited with winning one seat. In April the NDAM withdrew from the coalition, and it was reported that the NADD was "on the verge of disintegration."

Halifah Sallah was arrested in March 2009 for writing about the government's crackdown on witches (see Current issues, above), and charged with spying and sedition. The government withdrew the charges several days later "in the interest of peace and justice."

Leaders: Halifah SALLAH (Chair and 2006 presidential candidate), Jallow SONKO.

People's Democratic Organization for Independence and Socialism (PDOIS). The leftist PDOIS was formed at a 1986 congress to approve a lengthy manifesto that accused the PPP of compromising the country's sovereignty by agreeing to the establishment of Senegambia on the basis of an "unequal relationship." Party leader Sidia Jatta, who also had contested the 1992 election, secured a reported 2.87 percent of the vote in the 1996 presidential balloting and 3.2 percent in the 2001 presidential elections. The PDOIS was one of two opposition parties to participate in the 2002 legislative elections, winning two seats. In 2005 the party joined the NADD.

In 2009 Jatta was briefly suspended from parliament after he and another legislator walked out in protest when the speaker interrupted them as they spoke out against the government's alleged abduction of Gambians accused of being witches.

Leaders: Halifah SALLAH, Sidia JATTA (1992, 1996, and 2001 presidential candidate), Samuel SARR.

People's Progressive Party (PPP). The moderately socialist PPP, which merged with the Congress Party (CP) in 1967, governed the country from independence until the 1994 coup. It sponsored adoption of the republican constitution in 1970 and long favored increased economic and cultural links with Senegal as well as maintenance of the Commonwealth association.

PPP Secretary General Dawda Jawara was reelected president of the republic in 1992, defeating four principal rivals with a 58.4 percent vote share. Following the July 1994 coup Jawara was granted political asylum by Senegal.

In November 1994 a number of PPP members were arrested for their alleged involvement in a failed coup plot. Among those arrested were a former cabinet minister, Mamadou Cadi CHAM, and the parliamentary vice president, Dembo JATTA. In June 1995 President Jammeh granted amnesty to the alleged conspirators; however, six months later at least 35 PPP activists were jailed and similarly charged. In 1996 the AFPRC formally charged Jawara with embezzlement, and his assets were seized.

In mid-1996 Jawara, in an announcement issued in London, strongly criticized the new constitution drafted by the Jammeh regime, describing the document as "tailor-made" to elect Jammeh and designed to "confuse" matters in regard to basic individual rights. As with the NCP and the GPP, the PPP was banned from participating in the 1996 elections by the Jammeh government. After the ban was lifted in July 2001 the PPP teamed with the GPP and the UDP in launching an opposition coalition, which supported the UDP's Ousainu Darboe in the October 2001 presidential election. Jawara returned to Gambia in mid-2002 in response to the government's offer of amnesty. He resigned as leader of the PPP in December 2002 and was replaced by Omar Jallow. The PPP joined the NADD in 2005, and months later Jallow was one of three opposition leaders arrested on security charges, which were later dropped.

Leaders: Yaya CEESAY (President), Omar JALLOW (Secretary General).

United Democratic Party (UDP). Launched in August 1996 after the snap presidential election was announced, the UDP was described as having the support of the three parties (the PPP, NCP, and GPP) that had been banned by the Jammeh regime. UDP presidential candidate Ousainu Darboe, a prominent lawyer, ran second to Jammeh in the September 26 balloting, securing a reported 35.34 percent of the votes.

In May 1998 nine UDP members, including party leader Lamin Waa JAWARA, were detained by government security forces. Darboe and a group of UDP members were arrested in June 2000 in connection with an alleged confrontation with APRC militiamen. Darboe was released on bail and served as the presidential candidate of a UDP/PPP/GPP coalition, securing 32.7 percent of the vote in the October 2001 election. (The criminal case against Darboe and the other UDP members was ultimately dismissed.)

The UDP/PPP/GPP coalition boycotted the January 2002 assembly elections. In November 2002 Jawara accused Darboe of misappropriating funds, and Jawara was subsequently expelled from the UDP. He then formed a new political party, the NDAM. In 2005 the UDP joined the NADD in an effort to unseat Jammeh. In the run-up to the 2006 presidential election, however, the UDP dropped out of the NADD and backed its own leader, Darboe, for the presidency. Darboe also gained backing from the NRP and the GPDP in a coalition referenced as the **Alliance for Regime Change**, but the additional support did little to bolster his showing in the polls. The UDP and the NRP participated in an electoral alliance in the 2007 assembly balloting, with the alliance's four successful candidates coming from the UDP. Following the municipal elections in January 2008, in which the UDP won 3 seats, 7 party members were arrested during a confrontation with APRC supporters. The charges were dismissed a week later.

In 2009 a high-ranking UDP member was reported to have defected to the APRC, inspired by President Jammeh's leadership.

Leaders: Yaya JALLOW (Deputy Secretary General), Ousainu DARBOE (Secretary General, and 1996, 2001, and 2006 presidential candidate).

National Reconciliation Party (NRP). Formed quickly in August 1996, the NRP presented Hamat Bah as its candidate in the September 1996 presidential election, the well-known hotel owner garnering 5.52 percent of the votes. Bah ran again in 2001, securing 7.7 percent of the vote. The NRP won 1 seat in the 2002 assembly elections.

In 2005 the party joined the NADD. In March 2006 some 2,500 NRP members reportedly defected to the APRC at a massive rally in Sankuba. The NRP subsequently split from the NADD and teamed up with the UDP and the GPDP under the name Alliance for Regime Change prior to presidential balloting in September, backing UDP candidate Darboe. The NRP and the UDP formed an electoral alliance in the 2007 assembly elections. The alliance's four successful candidates were from the UDP. In the 2008 municipal elections, 1 seat was credited to the NRP.

Leader: Hamat BAH (1996 and 2001 presidential candidate).

Gambia Party for Democracy and Progress (GPDP). The GPDP was formed as an opposition party in 2004 by Henry Gomez, who was based in Germany. The party's platform focused on contributing to the development of Gambia, and in that respect supported the efforts of Jammeh. (Gomez was quoted as saying that being in the opposition did not mean being hostile to the government.) Prior to the 2006 presidential election, Gomez's candidacy was rejected by the electoral commission because of his failure to meet residency requirements. The GPDP then threw its support behind the UDP's Darboe, and along with the NRP referenced the coalition as the Alliance for Regime Change.

The GPDP did not present any of its own candidates in the 2007 assembly elections, Gomez saying the party wanted to concentrate on the next presidential elections. However, the GPDP appeared to support the UDP/NRP assembly candidates as a continuation of the earlier three-party alliance. Two years in advance of the next presidential election, Gomez in 2009 wrote a letter to President Jammeh seeking a political alliance, commending Jammeh for his "visionary and purposeful moves."

Leader: Henry GOMEZ (Secretary General).

National Democratic Action Movement (NDAM). Formed by Lamin Waa Jawara after he was expelled from the UDP in 2002, the NDAM emerged as one of the leading opposition parties in spite of its short existence. Jawara was arrested in 2004 on charges of sedition and served six months in prison. The sentence reportedly increased his popularity among the opposition. In 2005 the NDAM joined the NADD, but it withdrew in April 2007, saying it was time to "go it alone."

In November 2007 party leader Jawara was named by the president to head a local council, a move observers saw as a test of the new legislation granting the president authority over local affairs (see Current issues, above). For his part, Jawara said he did not consult with the party before accepting the president's offer. Subsequently, in May 2008 Jawara was reported to have defected to the APRC during a political rally, declaring that he shared Jammeh's ideology and wanted to promote unity. Jawara said he had a change of heart after his council appointment.

Leaders: Ousainou MBENGA (Deputy Secretary General), Lamin Waa JAWARA (Secretary General),.

Other Party:

Gambia People's Party (GPP). The GPP was launched in early 1985 by former vice president Hassan Musa Camara and a number of other defectors from the PPP to oppose President Jawara at the 1987 general election. As the balloting approached, it was felt by many that the GPP had overtaken the NCP as the principal opposition grouping; however, Camara obtained only 13 percent of the presidential vote, with the GPP securing no legislative representation. Camara again finished third in 1992, while the GPP returned to the House of Representatives with 2 seats. Banned from participating in the 1996 elections (together with the PPP and the NCP), the GPP supported the UDP's candidate in the December 2001 presidential balloting. Camara died in 2007.

LEGISLATURE

Prior to its dissolution following the 1994 coup the unicameral House of Representatives contained 50 members, 36 of whom were directly elected by universal adult suffrage, plus 5 indirectly elected chiefs, 8 nominated members, and the attorney general (ex officio). The 1996 constitution provided for a 49-member **National Assembly,** 45 elected by popular vote in single-member constituencies and 4 appointed by the president. (The size of the assembly was increased to 53 [48 elected, 5 appointed] for the January 17, 2002, election in view of the recent population increase.) The term of the assembly is five years, unless it is dissolved earlier by the president.

All three parties represented in the legislature elected in 1992 (the People's Progressive Party, the National Convention Party, and the Gambia People's Party) were banned from participating in the January 2, 1997, balloting.

In the most recent elections, of January 25, 2007, the Alliance for Patriotic Reorientation and Construction won 42 of the 48 elected seats; the United Democratic Party, 4; the National Alliance for Democracy and Development, 1; and an independent, 1. The president's 5 appointed members were reportedly from the APRC and included 2 people who eventually became speaker and deputy speaker.

Speaker: Fatoumata JAHUMPA-CEESAY.

CABINET

[as of April 1, 2009]

President	Yahya Jammeh
Vice President	Aisatou Njie-Saidy [f]
Secretaries of State	
Agriculture	Yahya Jammeh
Communications and Information Technology	Yahya Jammeh
Defense	Yahya Jammeh
Education	Fatou Faye [f]
Finance and Economic Affairs	Musa Bala-Gaye
Fisheries, Water Resources, and National Assembly Affairs	Yankouba Touray
Foreign Affairs	Omar Touray
Forestry and the Environment	Momodou Kotu Cham
Health and Social Welfare	Dr. Mariatou Jallow [f]
Higher Education and Research	Yahya Jammeh
Interior	Ousman Sonko
Justice and Attorney General	Marie Saine Firdaus [f]
Local Government, Lands, and Religious Affairs	Ismaila K. Sambou
Petroleum, Energy, and Mineral Resources	Ousman Jammeh

Public Works, Construction, and Infrastructure	Lamin Bojang
Tourism and Culture	Nancy Seedy Njie [f]
Trade, Industry, and Employment	Abdou Kolley
Women and Social Affairs	Aisatou Njie-Saidy [f]
Youth and Sports	Sheriff Gomez

[f] = female

COMMUNICATIONS

The news media operated freely prior to the July 1994 coup, although the principal newspaper and national radio station were government owned. However, the Jammeh regime has applied constraints on the press in general and strongly attacked specific antigovernment reporting. Opponents of the administration also contend that the new Gambian constitution was written to permit "muzzling" of the media, and in November 1999 Reporters Without Borders described Gambia as one of a number of Commonwealth countries "flouting" press freedom.

In 2003 a state-run media agency, the National Media Commission, was created and given wide powers, including the authority to arrest journalists and sentence them for up to six months. Additional press laws in 2004 and 2005 also were widely condemned as repressive. The administration continued to draw strong criticism in 2006, with one international group of journalists adding Jammeh to its list of "press freedom predators." The general manager and editor of the *Independent* were released on bail in April after having been detained for three weeks. In May the government threatened to shut down the weekly newspaper of the People's Democratic Organization for Independence and Socialism, *Foroyaa*, which also published online, and arrested three journalists who were working for the publication. In October 2007 two researchers for Amnesty International and a journalist for *Foroyaa* were accused of spying but were cleared of the charges a few days later.

In 2008 the watchdog group Reporters Without Borders described Gambia as having an "absolute intolerance of any kind of criticism." A U.S.-based Gambian journalist faced trial in March on sedition charges in connection with an article she wrote for a Gambian Web site in 2005, and the government banned Radio France International for its allegedly "erroneous reporting." Another journalist who worked for the progovernment *Daily Observer* was asked to resign after being elected to the leadership of the Gambian Press Union. In 2009 the editor of the independent daily *The Point* was allegedly accused by the government of being Senegalese and holding fraudulent identity documents, and in a separate action the government charged him with "dissemination of false news."

Press. The following are English-language publications issued in Banjul: *The Gambia Daily*, state-owned; *The Gambia Weekly* (500), published by the Government Information Office; *The Gambia Times* (1,500), PPP fortnightly; *The Nation*, fortnightly; *The Daily Observer*, registered in 1992; *The Point* (4,000), private daily,; *The Worker*, thrice-weekly organ of the Gambia Labour Congress; *The Gambia Onward*, thrice-weekly; *Foroyaa* (Freedom), weekly; and the *Newswatch*. *Newsmonth*, an independent weekly, commenced publication in April 1993. A private daily introduced in 1999, *The Independent*, has accused the government of systematic harassment.

News agency. The domestic facility is the Gambia News Agency (Gamna).

Broadcasting and computing. Radio broadcasting is provided by the government-owned Radio Gambia, which relays BBC news and carries programs in English and local languages; Radio 1, a private, nonprofit FM outlet; and Radio Syd, a commercial station. The nation's first television station began broadcasting in January 1996, service having previously been available only via transmissions from Senegal. As of 2008 there were 68.8 Internet users per 1,000 inhabitants.

INTERGOVERNMENTAL REPRESENTATION

Ambassador to the U.S.: Neneh MACDOUALL-GAYE.

U.S. Ambassador to Gambia: Barry Leon WELLS.

Permanent Representative to the UN: Susan WAFFA-OGOO.

IGO Memberships (Non-UN): AfDB, AU, BADEA, CILSS, CWTH, ECOWAS, IDB, Interpol, IOM, NAM, OIC, WCO, WTO.

GEORGIA

Sakartvelo

Political Status: Formerly the Georgian Soviet Socialist Republic, a constituent republic of the Union of Soviet Socialist Republics (USSR); renamed Republic of Georgia on November 14, 1990; declared independence on April 9, 1991; renamed Georgia under new constitution promulgated on October 17, 1995. (The autonomous republics of Abkhazia and South Ossetia have unilaterally declared their independence and have defied Georgia's political and military efforts to integrate them into the national structure. However, their independent status had not been recognized by any other country until they were recognized by Russia on August 26, 2008, following the Russian-Georgian military conflict earlier in the month. As of September 2009 Nicaragua was the only other country to have joined Russia in recognizing the independence of Abkhazia and South Ossetia.)

Area: 26,900 sq. mi. (69,700 sq. km.).

Population: 4,371,535 (2002C); 4,386,000 (2008E). While the 2002 figure excludes the population of South Ossetia (included in the 2008 estimate), an overall decline of nearly 1 million since the 1989 census of 5,443,350 is attributed largely to the emigration of working-age people and has been termed a "demographic catastrophe" by local immigration authorities.

Major Urban Center (2005E): TBILISI (1,037,000).

Official Language: Georgian (Abkhazian is recognized in Abkhazia).

Monetary Unit: Lari (official rate December 1, 2009: 1.67 lari = $1US).

President: Mikhail SAAKASHVILI (United National Movement); popularly elected on January 4, 2004, and sworn in for a five-year term on January 25 succeeding Nino BURDJANADZE, who had been declared interim president on November 23, 2003, by opposition leaders participating in the ouster of Eduard Amvrosiyevich (Georgi) SHEVARDNADZE (Citizens' Union of Georgia); reelected in the first round of early elections on January 5, 2008, and inaugurated for a second five-year term on January 20. (Burdjanadze, then the chair of the parliament, served as acting president of Georgia from November 25, 2007 [when President Saakashvili resigned his post in order to campaign for the upcoming election], until January 20, 2008.)

Prime Minister: Nika GILAURI (United National Movement); appointed by the president on January 30, 2009, and approved, along with his new cabinet, by parliament on February 6 to succeed Grigol MGALOBLISHVILI (United National Movement), who had announced his resignation on January 30. (Mgaloblishvili had succeeded Vladimir ["Lado"] GURGENIDZE [United National Movement] on November 1, 2008.)

THE COUNTRY

Located in western Caucasia, Georgia is bordered on the north and northeast by Russia, on the southeast by Azerbaijan, on the south by Armenia and Turkey, and on the west by the Black Sea. It includes three Muslim-dominated areas: the autonomous republic of Abkhazia (estimated population of 200,000) on the northwestern border with Russia, the autonomous republic of Ajaria on the southwestern border with Turkey, and the autonomous region of South Ossetia (estimated population of 50,000–70,000) on the north-central border with Russia. (Abkhazia and South Ossetia have been the source of conflict with the central government throughout most of the 1990s and 2000s; see Political background and Current issues, below.) According to the government, approximately 84 percent of the population is Georgian, 7 percent Azerbaijani, 6 percent Armenian, and 1.5 percent ethnic Russian. An estimated 70 percent of the population adheres to Orthodox Christianity, which has also played an increasingly important political

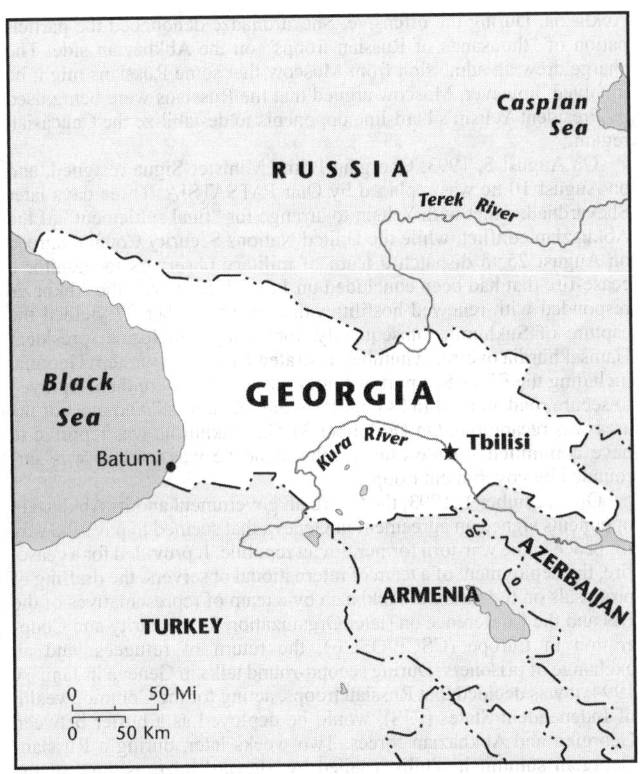

role in recent years as a voice of nationalist sentiment and, in the opinion of some critics, as a source of intolerance toward religious minorities. Approximately 15 percent of the population is Muslim.

The country's terrain is largely mountainous, with a subtropical region adjacent to the Black Sea that supports the production of tea, tobacco, grapes (Georgian wines are highly prized in Russia), and citrus fruits. Mineral resources include manganese, coal, oil, and peat. There also is abundant hydroelectric capacity. Industrial output includes iron and steel, chemicals, machine tools, plastics, and paper.

Georgia's combination of fertile land, scenic coastline, and broad cultural background provided what one journalist described at independence as "all the ingredients for a rich and prosperous nation." However, domestic turmoil and political transition yielded an economic decline of more than 60 percent in 1990–1994 (including large drops in industrial production and agricultural output), accompanied by hyperinflation of around 10,000 percent in 1993 and 7,400 percent in 1994. Remedial action recommended by the International Monetary Fund (IMF) began to produce results in 1995, notably a fall in the inflation rate to 65 percent and output contraction of only 5 percent. Robust annual GDP growth (11 percent) was recorded in 1996 and 1997.

In 1998 the IMF complimented the Georgian government for its reform of the banking sector and its privatization campaign, particularly in regard to the sale of land and agricultural enterprises. However, the IMF said "daunting challenges" remained to be addressed and encouraged the administration to reduce spending and increase tax revenues. As was the case for many former Soviet republics, however, such directives conflicted, at least in the short term, with the administration's efforts to combat pervasive (and persistent) poverty.

Double-digit growth also was anticipated for 1998, but conditions were severely compromised by the Russian financial crisis of that year. Consequently, GDP growth of only 2.9 percent, 3 percent, and 1.9 percent was achieved in 1998, 1999, and 2000, respectively, with inflation registering 10.7 percent, 10.9 percent, and 4.6 percent for the same years.

The economy was described in 2001 as having "hit rock bottom," with more than half of the population living below the poverty line in a country that had been one of the most prosperous republics in the USSR. Problems included widespread corruption, an "old-style" (i.e., Soviet) mentality among government leaders, faltering legal reform, and the plight of an estimated 260,000 refugees of Georgian ethnicity who had fled the civil war in Abkhazia in 1992–1993. However, significant assistance continued to arrive from Western capitals, particularly Washington, which had provided more than $1 billion since independence in an effort to shift Georgia away from Russian influence. On the other hand, private foreign investors remained generally wary, although great attention was given to the proposed construction of an oil pipeline from Azerbaijan through Georgia to a port in Turkey (see article on Azerbaijan for details). Transit fees from the pipeline were expected to have an immediate positive impact on the stalled Georgian economy. (The pipeline was opened in mid-2006.)

Georgia remained one of the poorest of the former Soviet republics in the early 2000s, and the economy continued to suffer from the civil strife that preceded the ouster of the president in 2003. Problems included the failure of the tax collection system and widespread corruption of public officials.

The new government installed in 2004 implemented broad structural reforms designed to revive the economy through, among other things, the extensive privatization of state-run enterprises and the introduction of a simplified tax system. The administration also launched an anticorruption drive with the goal of reducing the role of the "gray" economy (estimated at that point to be responsible for 80 percent of economic activity). GDP grew by 9.3 percent in 2004 and 7.7 percent in 2005, and by 2006 the government was broadly praised for having fostered the return of basic services to the population, increased tax collections fourfold, and reduced bureaucratic inefficiencies. In fact, the World Bank described Georgia as one of the top economic reformers among transition nations. However, despite such progress, foreign investors remained wary of the "frozen conflicts" in Abkhazia and South Ossetia, which also were seen as hindering Georgia's goals for accession to the European Union (EU) and the North Atlantic Treaty Organization (NATO). The IMF also continued to call for judicial reform, particularly in regard to the protection of property rights, while domestic critics charged the government with antidemocratic tendencies.

Tensions with Russia contributed to gas shortages in 2006, which forced Georgia (with little gas or oil of its own) to seek alternative sources such as Azerbaijan and, at least temporarily, Iran. Growth of 8 percent was achieved in 2006, but inflation late in the year grew to nearly 20 percent, prompting the IMF to warn of a looming crisis. Among other things, the IMF criticized the government for spending too much on defense (a priority for Georgia in view of its pro-Western stance, conflict with Russia, and lack of resolution of affairs in Abkhazia and South Ossetia). Real GDP growth expanded to 12 percent in 2007, in part due to the continued influx of foreign investment. However, inflation also remained high (more than 11 percent) under the influence of rising global food and energy prices. Growth declined to only 2 percent for 2008, primarily as the result of the war with Russia in early August in South Ossetia (see Current issues, below). Contraction was predicted for 2009 in view of the lingering effects of that conflict and the global economic crisis in general. Consequently, the IMF authorized several special disbursements to support government efforts to reform the tax system, reorient spending from the military to the social sphere, and improve the nation's antiquated roads. Attention also focused on another proposed line to pipe natural gas from eastern Turkey across Georgia to EU countries.

GOVERNMENT AND POLITICS

Political background. Absorbed by Russia in the early 19th century, Georgia proclaimed its independence in May 1918, with Soviet recognition being extended two years later. However, in February 1921, after having been overrun by the Red Army, Georgia was proclaimed a Soviet republic. In 1922 it entered the USSR as a component of the Transcaucasian Federated Soviet Republic, and in 1936 it became a separate union republic.

In balloting in October–November 1990 for the Georgian Supreme Soviet, a proindependence Round Table–Free Georgia coalition secured a parliamentary majority, and on December 8 the Georgian Communist Party withdrew from the Communist Party of the Soviet Union, announcing that it would seek Georgia's secession from the USSR. In January 1991 the Georgian Supreme Soviet voted to establish a 20,000-member National Guard, and on April 9 it declared the country's independence. Five days later, the Supreme Soviet named its chair, Zviad GAMSAKHURDIA, to the new post of executive president of the republic. On May 26 Gamsakhurdia retained the post by winning 87 percent of the vote in Georgia's first direct presidential poll, although opponents criticized his "dictatorial" tendencies. On August 18, immediately prior to the attempted Moscow coup, Prime Minister Tengiz SIGUA resigned, with Gamsakhurdia assuming personal control of the foreign, interior, and justice ministries, as well as of the republican

security force. On September 16 the leader of the opposition National Democratic Party (NDP), Georgi CHANTURIA, was arrested as he tried to leave the country. Other arrests followed, and on September 24 Gamsakhurdia declared a state of emergency. Violence nonetheless intensified, culminating in full-scale armed conflict in late December.

On January 2, 1992, after meeting with opposition party leaders, rebel commanders Dzhaba IOSELIANI and Tengiz KITOVANI announced the deposition of the president (who subsequently fled to Armenia) and the establishment of a ruling Military Council. On March 6 Eduard SHEVARDNADZE, who had served for 13 years as first secretary of the Georgian Communist Party before being named Soviet foreign minister, returned to Georgia. On March 10 he was named chair of a State Council, whose 50 members included virtually all of the anti-Gamsakhurdia leadership, including Tengiz Sigua, who was reappointed to his former position as nominal head of government. In national elections on October 11, Shevardnadze received a 95 percent popular mandate as head of state, while simultaneous legislative balloting yielded seats for over 30 parties and alliances, none gaining a decisive advantage.

In addition to the struggle for control of Georgia's central administration, the republic was racked by ethnic strife in the early 1990s. In September 1990 the Supreme Soviet of the autonomous *oblast* (region) of South Ossetia, in a move branded as invalid by the Georgian Supreme Soviet, proclaimed itself a full republic (within the USSR) independent of Tbilisi. In January 1991 USSR President Mikhail Gorbachev issued a decree annulling the region's act of secession, and in March President Gamsakhurdia and Russian President Boris Yeltsin agreed to establish a joint Georgian-Russian militia to disarm Georgian and Ossetian paramilitary groups, which had become engaged in what was termed a "mini–civil war." The conflict nonetheless continued, with Yeltsin rejecting appeals for South Ossetia's inclusion within the Russian Federation on the basis of union with North Ossetia. A referendum on January 19, 1992, in which an overwhelming majority of South Ossetians voted for integration with its Russian counterpart, was rejected by Georgia's new Military Council as "a blatant attempt to violate the territorial integrity of a sovereign state."

During the first half of 1992, intermittent fighting continued between government and pro-Gamsakhurdia forces, particularly in western Georgia, where the former president's supporters were entrenched. Tbilisi's problems were compounded on July 23, when Abkhazia's Supreme Soviet proclaimed the republic's "state sovereignty," an action that the Georgian State Council immediately branded as null and void. Although the area's inhabitants were only 18 percent Abkhaz (as contrasted with 46 percent Georgian), the conflict continued. A cease-fire in early September failed to halt an intensification of the struggle during early 1993, with rebel forces being repulsed during a three-day effort in mid-March to capture Sukhumi, the government-occupied capital of Abkhazia. During the offensive, Shevardnadze denounced the participation of "thousands of Russian troops" on the Abkhazian side. The charge drew an admission from Moscow that some Russians might be involved; however, Moscow argued that the Russians were being used by President Yeltsin's hard-line opponents to destabilize the Caucasian region.

On August 5, 1993, Georgian Prime Minister Sigua resigned, and on August 10 he was replaced by Otar PATSATSIA. Three days later Shevardnadze met with Yeltsin to arrange for "final settlement" of the Abkhazian conflict, while the United Nations Security Council agreed on August 25 to dispatch a team of military observers to monitor a cease-fire that had been concluded on July 27. However, the Abkhazis responded with renewed hostilities that on September 27 yielded the capture of Sukhumi. Subsequently, forces loyal to former president Gamsakhurdia overran a number of strategic towns in western Georgia, including the Black Sea port of Poti. Russian units were then deployed to secure road and rail links cut off by the "Zviadists," and most of the area was recaptured. On December 31 Gamsakhurdia was reported to have committed suicide after a rebel band he was leading was surrounded by government troops.

On December 1, 1993, the Georgian government and its Abkhazian opponents signed an agreement in Geneva that seemed to pave the way for peace in the war-torn former Soviet republic. It provided for a cease-fire, the deployment of a team of international observers, the drafting of proposals on the future of Abkhazia by a team of representatives of the UN and the Conference on (later Organization for) Security and Cooperation in Europe (CSCE/OSCE), the return of refugees, and an exchange of prisoners. During second-round talks in Geneva in January 1994, it was decided that Russian troops, acting for the Commonwealth of Independent States (CIS), would be deployed as a buffer between Georgian and Abkhazian forces. Two weeks later, during a Russian-Georgian summit in Tbilisi (hailed by Shevardnadze as "one of the major events in 200 years of history between our two peoples"), a memorandum was signed authorizing the establishment of three Russian military bases within Georgia.

Georgian and Abkhazian officials concluded a further agreement in Moscow on April 4, 1994, that reaffirmed the December 1993 accord, while asserting, in principle, that Abkhazia should be granted the status of an autonomous republic within Georgia. However, the basic conflict of aspirations was again evident in November when the Abkhazian legislature adopted a new constitution enshrining the republic's self-declared sovereignty and elected its chair, Vladislav ARDZINBA, as president, drawing protests from the United States, the UN, and Russia, all of which continued to recognize Georgian sovereignty over the region.

Earlier, in November 1993, President Shevardnadze had sought to broaden his political base by launching the Citizens' Union of Georgia (CUG), while in May 1994 a declaration of "national unity and accord" was signed by 34 parties and groups, including the opposition NDP. Nevertheless, the president continued to face fierce nationalist opposition to his policy of rapprochement with Moscow and acceptance of Abkhazian autonomy. One casualty of the deadly hostilities was NDP leader Chanturia, who was assassinated in Tbilisi on December 3.

In January 1995 government forces successfully resisted an advance by members of the National Liberation Front (NLF) intended to "liberate" Abkhazia, with Tengiz Kitovani being arrested for leading the attempt. In May the government made another effort to confront the NLF-associated *Mkhedrioni* paramilitaries, now led by Dzhaba Ioseliani.

The unremitting violence of Georgian politics was highlighted by a bomb attack on Shevardnadze on August 29, 1995, while he was en route to sign a new presidential constitution approved by the legislature five days earlier. He escaped with minor injuries, and the constitution was duly promulgated on October 17 amid a security crackdown and the dismissal of the security minister, Igor GIORGADZE, who was named as one of bombing's three instigators, all of whom were believed to have fled to Russia. The complete disbandment of the *Mkhedrioni* was announced on October 1, with Ioseliani being arrested on November 15 and charged with complicity in the assassination attempt. (Ioseliani was sentenced in November 1998 to 11 years in prison following his conviction on charges related to the attack, as well as a count of armed robbery.)

The breakaway Abkhazian parliament categorically rejected the definition of Abkhazia as part of Georgia in the new Georgian constitution of August 1995, and the separatists boycotted the Georgian parliamentary balloting of November. However, despite the continuing instability, presidential and parliamentary elections went ahead peacefully, and to all appearances fairly, on November 5, 1995, followed by a second legislative round on November 19 and further balloting for unfilled seats on December 3. Standing as candidate of both his own CUG and the Socialist Party of Georgia (SPG), Shevardnadze easily won the presidential contest against five other candidates, obtaining 76.8 percent of the popular vote. The legislative elections yielded a substantial plurality for the CUG, with the seats won by allied parties ensuring a commanding pro-Shevardnadze majority. A new government appointed on December 11 included Nikoloz LEKISHVILI (former mayor of Tbilisi) as minister of state, the next highest political post after the president. Meanwhile, having denounced the inclusion in the new Georgian Parliament of the 12 Abkhazian deputies elected in 1992, Abkhazia conducted elections to its own 35-member People's Assembly in November 1996, the Georgian government and legislature condemning the balloting as illegal. (The Georgian administration announced that it had polled the ethnic Georgian refugees from Abkhazia and that over 99 percent of them were opposed to the separatist initiative.)

Brokered by Moscow and the OSCE, a security and confidence-building accord was initialed by Georgian and South Ossetian representatives on April 17, 1996, yielding direct talks in September between Shevardnadze and the chair of the South Ossetian legislature, Ludvig CHIBIROV. However, tension rose again when the South Ossetians held a direct presidential election on November 10 (returning Chibirov on a separatist platform), despite the Georgian government's dismissal of the exercise as illegal.

Negotiations with Abkhazia stalled in 1997, despite mediation efforts by Russia, the UN, and Western powers. Shevardnadze and Abkhaz President Ardzinba signed a nonaggression pact on August 15 but could agree on little else. Tbilisi favored replacing the CIS force with an international one organized by the UN, but Abkhazia would not consent.

On the other hand, Georgia appeared to reach an agreement with South Ossetia in March 1997, preserving Georgia's territorial integrity while giving "special powers of self-determination" to the separatist region. A joint commission for economic reconstruction of South Ossetia also was established. However, in December, South Ossetia canceled further negotiations, and a final settlement remained in doubt.

President Shevardnadze was the target of a second assassination attempt on February 9, 1998, when a band of attackers opened fire on his motorcade. They were subsequently reportedly identified as former members of the private army of the late President Gamsakhurdia. Shevardnadze renewed his demand that Moscow extradite former security minister Igor Giorgadze, who was suspected of being a ringleader in the 1995 assassination attempt. The president also speculated that "powerful interests" opposed to the transit of Caspian Basin oil across Georgia may have been involved in the attack.

Tension intensified in Abkhazia in mid-May 1998, as heavy fighting broke out when Abkhazian forces entered the "security zone" along the border with Georgia proper and met resistance from Georgian troops. (Some observers suggested the Abkhazian initiative had been fueled by the region's negative response to a recent CIS proposal that autonomy within a confederal Georgia was Abkhazia's appropriate ultimate political status, not independence.) Some 35,000 ethnic Georgians reportedly fled from Abkhazia and the security zone to escape the fighting. Although a cease-fire was announced at the end of May, sporadic clashes were reported throughout the rest of the year. Meanwhile, many members had resigned from the Georgian cabinet in July and August, ostensibly to permit a restructuring of ministries. The reshuffling of the cabinet was completed by September, the most noteworthy change being the appointment of Vazha LORTKIPANIDZE as minister of state. Municipal balloting held in November was described by the OSCE as generally free and fair, the CUG suffering some slippage but for the most part retaining dominance.

The Georgian government faced another serious threat in October 1998 when several hundred soldiers (reportedly Gamsakhurdia loyalists) revolted at an army base in the town of Senaki. The soldiers seized tanks and advanced on Kutaisi, the country's second-largest city, before being crushed by government troops. Shevardnadze again attributed the unrest to opponents of the trans-Georgia oil pipeline from Azerbaijan.

Discussions toward economic cooperation were reportedly launched with officials from South Ossetia in January 1999, although relations were strained by that region's plan to conduct new legislative balloting in May. Meanwhile, little progress was apparent regarding the Abkhazia stalemate, although a plan was announced in March for repatriating the refugees from the 1998 unrest. Collaterally, the mandates of the CIS and UN missions were extended to at least the middle of the year. On the domestic front, the Shevardnadze administration, perhaps with an eye on the legislative elections scheduled for the fall, announced several anticorruption measures during the first half of 1999, including plans to forcibly dismiss judges (many of whom had been appointed during Communist rule) and replace them with jurists selected through competitive examination.

Legislative balloting was conducted in South Ossetia in May 1999, although the Georgian government denounced the balloting as contrary to the national constitution; the OSCE also refused to recognize the poll's legitimacy. Subsequently, on October 3, Abkhazian President Ardzinba was reelected without opposition in Abkhazia's first-ever popular vote, securing a reported 99 percent of the votes. On the same day, a reported 97 percent of those participating in a referendum in Abkhazia endorsed the 1994 Abkhazian constitution and its declaration of the region's status as an independent republic. The Georgian government challenged the legality of the voting in Abkhazia, noting that, among other things, ethnic Georgians who had fled Abkhazia during the civil war had been excluded from the balloting. Underlining the apparent stalemate in negotiations toward a compromise settlement, the Abkhazian legislature subsequently approved another declaration of sovereignty.

In balloting for the Georgian Parliament in October–November 1999, the CUG retained a solid majority, although a strong challenge was posed by the Revival for Georgia bloc, led by Aslan ABASHIDZE, the chair of the Ajarian Supreme Council and longtime "strongman" of Ajaria. (Opposition parties claimed there had been significant irregularities in the poll, and international observers, while not as harsh, did not fully endorse the balloting.) Abashidze also was expected to be the main challenger to Shevardnadze in the Georgian presidential balloting of April 9, 2000, but the Ajarian leader withdrew shortly before polling day. Abashidze's sudden withdrawal led some analysts to suggest a deal had been struck. In fact, shortly after Shevardnadze was reelected with 79 percent of the vote, the parliament revised the constitution to recognize the "Republic of Ajaria" as an official autonomous region. Moreover, in June, when the Supreme Council of Ajaria adopted a new constitution, flag, and anthem, Shevardnadze announced that those initiatives did not violate the Georgian constitution, in contrast to the administration's consistent rejection of constitutional moves on the part of separatists in Abkhazia and South Ossetia. Meanwhile, Shevardnadze appointed a new cabinet that included Gia ARSENISHVILI in the post of minister of state, whose responsibilities had been expanded in late 1999 to approach those of a prime minister.

Despite the appearance of support surrounding Shevardnadze's presidential victory in 2000, his administration was already besieged on many fronts, and conditions subsequently deteriorated even further as a number of government officials became ensnarled in budget and other financial scandals. Critics also charged that the administration was displaying an inability or unwillingness to protect basic human rights or to extend democratic reforms.

Following a series of protest demonstrations, Shevardnadze reshuffled the cabinet in late 2001, naming Avtandil JORBENADZE as the new minister of state. However, many CUG legislators subsequently left the party to form new opposition groupings, which, along with independents, dominated the June 2002 local elections.

In balloting that was sanctioned by the Georgian government, on November 4, 2001, Abashidze was elected unopposed as president ("Head of the Republic") in Ajaria, voters there also electing a new bicameral legislature (comprising a 35-member Council of the Republic and a 10-member Senate). Subsequently, in unsanctioned first-round presidential balloting in South Ossetia on November 18, President Chibirov finished third among six candidates in controversial balloting. The runoff, held on December 6, was won by businessman Eduard KOKOITY over Stanislav KOCHIYEV, speaker of the South Ossetian legislature and leader of the local Communist Party. The Georgian government and most international organizations deemed the South Ossetian balloting illegal, adopting a similar stance toward the legislative elections held in Abkhazia on March 2, 2002.

National legislative balloting was held on November 2, 2003, in the wake of severe political turbulence and opposition to Shevardnadze's rule (see Current issues, below). Preliminary results indicated a victory for progovernment candidates, but international observers cited widespread irregularities, including apparent falsification of results. Thousands of protesters demonstrated in Tbilisi and other cities, while several Western capitals argued that the Georgian opposition had been denied its rightful victory. Subsequently, some 30,000 demonstrators under the leadership of Mikhail SAAKASHVILI, a former cabinet minister who had quit the CUG in 2001 to protest perceived rampant corruption in government, marched on the parliament building on November 22 to prevent the legislature from convening. When troops declined to intervene, Shevardnadze was evacuated from the building, and he declared a nationwide state of emergency. However, reportedly heeding Russian advice, Shevardnadze resigned the next day (apparently in return for immunity from prosecution), and Nino BURDJANADZE, the chair of the parliament, assumed presidential authority pending new national elections.

In presidential balloting on January 4, 2004, Saakashvili won 97 percent of the vote, and he was inaugurated on January 25. Upon Saakashvili's recommendation, the parliament on February 17 approved a new cabinet headed by Zurab ZHVANIA in the reintroduced post of prime minister. Subsequently, new elections were held on March 28, 2004, to fill the 150 proportional seats in the parliament, with Saakashvili's National Movement–Democrats (NMD) reportedly winning 68 percent of the vote and more than 130 seats.

In March 2004 Ajarian leader Abashidze agreed to hold new legislative elections, but he was forced to step down in April and leave for Moscow after Tbilisi emboldened the local population and police to rise against him. (Saakashvili immediately announced the imposition of his own presidential authority in the region.) Saakashvili's Victorious Ajaria Party won an overwhelming majority in June balloting for the Ajarian legislature, and Levan VARSHALOMIDZE, an ally of the president, was named to head the council of ministers in Ajaria. Meanwhile, the Georgian Parliament adopted several constitutional amendments reducing the level of autonomy for Ajaria.

New, unsanctioned presidential balloting was held on October 3, 2004, in Abkhazia, with Abkhazian Prime Minister Raul KHAJIMBA (supported by Russia) and former prime minister Seregey BAGAPSH as the main contenders to succeed ailing President Ardzinba. Bagapsh was initially announced as the winner, but disorder broke out over the results, prompting a series of takeovers of government buildings by supporters of the two camps. Following the threat of a Russian intervention, Bagapsh and Khajimba agreed to run in new elections on a joint ticket, with Bagapsh as the presidential candidate and Khajimba as the vice-presidential candidate. The "unity" ticket secured more than 90 percent of the vote in reballoting on January 20, 2005, and the two were inaugurated on February 12. Aleksandr ANKUAB was subsequently named prime minister.

Georgian Prime Minister Zhvania died on February 3, 2005, in what was ultimately ruled an accident involving a faulty gas heater. He was succeeded on February 17 by Zurab NOGHAIDELI.

In July 2006 the central government reasserted its control over portions of the Kodori Gorge (which straddles Abkhazia) that had previously been held by militias loyal to a local strongman. Consequently, Georgians who previously had been expelled from Abkhazia established an Abkhazian "government-in-exile" in the region.

On November 12, 2006, Kokoity was reelected as president of South Ossetia with 96 percent of the vote against three rivals. In addition, a concurrent referendum yielded a reported 99 percent "yes" vote regarding independence. However, as expected, the Saakashvili administration described the votes as "illegal" and symptomatic of Russian "provocation." Subsequently, in April 2007, Saakashvili established a "provisional administration" under the presidential leadership of former South Ossetian prime minister Dmitry SANAKOYEV to govern the areas of South Ossetia inhabited by ethnic Georgians. (Sanakoyev, who had previously fought for the region's independence from Georgia, said he had been persuaded by the Rose Revolution to pursue accommodation with the central government.)

In the March 4 and 18, 2007, elections to the People's Assembly in Abkhazia, most of the successful candidates were reportedly supporters of President Bagapsh. The federal government again denounced the poll.

In the wake of mass protest demonstrations (see Current issues, below), on November 7, 2007, President Saakashvili declared a state of emergency, arguing that Russia was fomenting a coup plot. The state of emergency was lifted on November 16 after Saakashvili had accepted the demand from opposition parties that snap presidential elections be held. On the same day, Saakashvili appointed Vladimir GURGENIDZE, a prominent banker, to succeed Prime Minister Noghaideli, who had resigned, ostensibly for health reasons. Saakashvili resigned as president on November 25 to campaign for the presidential poll. Nino Burdjanadze (the chair of parliament) served as acting president until Saakashvili was reinaugurated on January 20, 2008, following his first-round victory in balloting on January 5, in which he was credited with 53.5 percent of the vote. A new cabinet, again headed by Gurgenidze, was approved by parliament on January 31, although opposition parties boycotted the session to protest what they characterized as the fraudulent nature of the presidential election results. The opposition also derided the accuracy of the official results from the May 21 early legislative balloting, in which Saakashvili's United National Movement (UNM) was credited with winning 119 of the 150 seats.

On October 27, 2008, President Saakashvili announced the appointment of Grigol MGALOBLISHVILI to succeed Prime Minister Gurgenidze, and a reshuffled cabinet was approved by parliament on November 1. However, Mgaloblishvili in turn resigned on January 30, 2009, and was succeeded by Nika GILAURI.

The regional parliaments of South Ossetia and Abkhazia endorsed independence for their regions following the Georgian-Russian military conflict of mid-2008. Aslanbek BULATSOV, a former official from North Ossetia, was named prime minister of South Ossetia in October, while parties supportive of President Kokoity dominated the elections (again denounced as illegal by the Georgian government and most of the international community) to the South Ossetian legislature on May 31, 2009. Kokoity dismissed the government in early August amid criticism of economic conditions and the perceived ineffective (if not corrupt) disbursement of financial assistance from Russia. On August 5 Kokoity announced the appointment of Vadim BROVTSEV, the director of a construction company, as the new prime minister. President Bagapsh was elected to a second term in Abkhazia on December 13, 2009, by securing 59.4 percent of the vote in first-round balloting that was again deemed illegitimate by the Georgian government.

Constitution and government. The constitution given legislative approval on August 24, 1995, and promulgated on October 17 defines Georgia as a democratic state with freedom of speech, thought, conscience, and faith being guaranteed. The president, who serves as head of state, commander in chief, and chief executive, is elected for a once-renewable five-year term by universal adult suffrage. The president also appoints and presides over the council of ministers. The position of prime minister was reintroduced on February 11, 2004. Legislative authority is vested in a parliament, which is to have two chambers when conditions permit but is currently unicameral (see Legislature, below). In 1997 parliament approved a law giving the president the right to appoint the mayors of the six largest cities. A National Security Council (inaugurated in January 1996) has a consultative role in defense and security matters.

The country's territory is defined as being established by the Act on the Restoration of the State Independence of Georgia of April 9, 1991. Thus the Soviet-era autonomous republics of Abkhazia and Ajaria and the autonomous region of South Ossetia (each containing a substantial Muslim population) are officially regarded as being under Georgian sovereignty, despite the fact that separatist governments assumed control in all three regions in the early 1990s. Ajaria's autonomous status was codified in June 2002 (see Political background, above), while South Ossetia and Abkhazia declared their independence in 2008 following the military conflict between Georgia and Russia.

Judicial power is exercised by independent courts, normally sitting in public. Final authority resides in the Supreme Court, whose members are elected by parliament on the president's recommendation. A Constitutional Court of nine members serving ten-year terms oversees the constitutionality of legislative and executive acts. Numerous proposed amendments to the basic law were being considered by a recently appointed 70-member commission in the fall of 2009.

Foreign relations. In part because of the civil strife that was then raging, Georgia did not become a member of the CIS at the latter's launching on December 21, 1991. In April 1992 State Council Chair Shevardnadze asserted that Georgian public opinion strongly opposed entry into the CIS, adding, "I don't believe the Commonwealth can survive." However, Georgia sent observers to CIS meetings and, reversing itself, agreed in October 1993 to join the group, with ratification by the Georgian legislature on March 1, 1994.

Georgia joined the IMF on May 5, 1992. It did not, however, become a member of the UN until July 31, when it became the last former Soviet republic to gain admission to that world body.

The United States recognized Georgia's independence on December 25, 1991, but, because of the conditions in Georgia, did not establish full diplomatic relations until March 24, 1992, one day after recognition by the European Community (EC, later the European Union—EU). Coincident with the U.S. action, Georgia was admitted to the CSCE. On April 15 it became a member of the North Atlantic Cooperation Council (NACC), linking NATO to its former adversaries in Eastern Europe. In March 1994 Georgia became a signatory of NATO's Partnership for Peace initiative, having the previous month signed a friendship and cooperation treaty with Russia.

With Georgia's concurrence, the UN Security Council gave its approval in July 1994 to the deployment of Russian peacekeeping forces in Abkhazia (having in May ruled out sending any more than a handful of UN observers to the region). In March 1995 President Shevardnadze initialed a further agreement with Moscow providing for Russia's retention of four military bases in Georgia in exchange for economic assistance. The accord was confirmed when the Russian prime minister visited Tbilisi in September, and in January 1996 the Georgian Parliament ratified the 1994 friendship treaty with Russia.

The government's strategy of alignment with Russia to secure Moscow's backing for the resolution of Georgia's internal conflicts remained controversial in Tbilisi. Shevardnadze justified the granting of military base rights to Russia by pointing out that Moscow had reciprocated by upholding the territorial integrity of Georgia within its Soviet-era borders, meaning that Russia had formally agreed that Abkhazia and South Ossetia were sovereign Georgian territory. Nevertheless, the nationalist parties opposed ratification of the 1994 friendship treaty with Russia and repeatedly called for the withdrawal of all Russian forces from Abkhazia, claiming that the Russian troops were protecting the separatist regime in Sukhumi and preventing the return of ethnic Georgian refugees.

In April 1996 Georgia joined with Armenia and Azerbaijan in signing partnership and cooperation accords with the EU. Collaterally, Georgia sought to improve its relations with neighboring states, although strains with Turkey remained. In April 1997 Georgia hosted a regional conference regarding the possible revival of the historic "Silk Road," which once connected China to Europe via Central Asia, the Transcaucus region, and Turkey. The proposed transportation and telecommunications corridor presented significant political concerns because, among other things, it bypassed Russia. U.S. and EU financing was subsequently pledged for the project, which included eight other countries in addition to Georgia.

Georgia joined the Council of Europe in February 1999, the Shevardnadze administration describing the accession as indicative of the country's movement toward "European political and economic standards." At the same time, the government continued to question its ties with the CIS, which it called ineffective as far as economic and security issues were concerned.

The presence of Russian troops on the four military bases leased from Georgia continued to be an irritant for nationalists, who lobbied for a complete withdrawal. Meanwhile, the parliament threatened to annul the leasing agreement unless Russia supported Georgia's efforts to reassert control over Abkhazia. Georgia also sought backing among CIS states to tighten economic sanctions on the separatist region, Shevardnadze declaring in January 1997 that Georgia would not remain in Russia's "sphere of influence" unless Russia helped Georgia restore its sovereignty over Abkhazia and South Ossetia. The president also indicated that Georgia saw more advantage in joining the EU rather than NATO but did not rule out the possible political involvement of NATO in resolving the Abkhazian conflict. He called on the CIS either to broaden the mandate of its Russian peacekeeping force to more effectively protect Georgians displaced by the conflict in Abkhaz or to comply with the parliament's resolution calling for withdrawal of the force. At its summit in March 1997, the CIS agreed to a broader mandate that would extend the peacekeepers across a wider area to facilitate the return of 200,000 refugees displaced by fighting in 1993, but the CIS failed to implement the redeployment, apparently due to Russian opposition.

Despite the discomfort of Russia, an informal but growing Azerbaijan-Georgia-Ukraine alliance, the "Union of Three," continued to take form in 1997. The alignment, created in late 1996 as an alternative to reliance on the CIS, was Western-oriented and interested in military cooperation independent of Russia. One of its goals was to export Azerbaijan's Caspian oil to Europe via Georgia and the Black Sea, completely bypassing Russia. Moldova declared that it shared strategic interests with the Union of Three in a quadrilateral communiqué issued in November 1997, necessitating the coining of a new abbreviation, GUAM (for Georgia, Ukraine, Azerbaijan, Moldova). (The abbreviation was updated to GUUAM in April 1999 with the addition of Uzbekistan to the grouping; however, Uzbekistan announced in mid-2002 that it was suspending its participation because of the grouping's lack of effectiveness.)

In the early years of the 21st century, Georgia drew closer to the West and away from the Russian orbit. Meanwhile, Georgia continued to accuse Russia of fueling separatist sentiment in South Ossetia and Abkhazia, while Russia alleged that Georgia was preventing effective action against Chechen rebels operating out of the Pankisi Gorge in the mountainous border region between Georgia and the secessionist-minded Russian region of Chechnya. Adding another layer of nuance to the matter was the presence of U.S. special forces, who had arrived earlier in the year to help train Georgian forces in antiterrorism tactics. (Washington believed that members of al-Qaida or other terrorist networks may have also found a safe haven among Muslim refugees from Chechnya in the border area.) Although Russia might have been expected to welcome the U.S. assistance as a means of undercutting the strength of the Chechen rebels, Moscow in fact was reportedly concerned, in private at least, that Washington was attempting to gain inroads into the Russian "sphere of influence" in the Caucasus.

U.S. influence was felt directly in the ouster of President Shevardnadze in 2003 and the installation of the U.S.-educated Mikhail Saakashvili as president after the "Rose Revolution." The United States also continued to maintain troops on Georgian soil and to provide substantial economic aid to Georgia.

For Russia, influence in Georgia remained a vital national security interest, in part because Georgia has two ports that offer access to the Black Sea. Among other things, Russia granted Russian passports to the residents of Abkhazia and South Ossetia, in effect conferring Russian citizenship upon them. Other ongoing points of contention between Russia and Georgia were the Russian military bases maintained in Georgia by treaty rights and Russia's control over Georgia's supplies of oil and gas.

In 2005 the Georgian Parliament issued a national security report that listed the country's foreign policy priorities as strategic cooperation with the United States, Ukraine, Azerbaijan, and Turkey and partnership with Russia. During a visit to Tbilisi in May 2005, U.S. President George W. Bush called upon "all nations" to respect Georgia's "sovereignty," a remark widely construed as critical of Russian support for the breakaway republics. Bush also told the cheering crowd of 100,000 that Georgia was a "beacon of liberty for the region and the world." In a possibly related matter, Russia later in the month announced that it would close its two remaining military bases in Georgia by the end of 2008.

Georgia arrested four Russians on espionage charges in September 2006, provoking a sharp Russian response. Although Western pressure influenced the release of the detainees to Russia in only a week, Russia severed transportation and rail links with Georgia, imposed a partial trade embargo, and deported a small number of the estimated 500,000 Georgians living and working in Russia. Subsequently, Russia imposed a massive increase in the price of its gas exports to Georgia, forcing the Saakashvili administration to make emergency arrangements with non-Russian suppliers. Saakashvili also asked the EU to denounce Russia for attempting "to extend its sphere of influence" through manipulation of its oil and gas reserves. With relations still at a low point with Russia, Georgia in February 2007 launched "intensified dialogue" about NATO membership and in April committed additional troops to the U.S.-led forces in Iraq as evidence of its "worthiness" as a Western ally.

The April 2008 NATO summit rejected President Bush's request that a Membership Action Plan be signed immediately for Georgia. However, the alliance was sufficiently positive about Georgia's prospects for eventual membership to anger Russia, which called NATO expansion "provocative." NATO and the EU condemned the Russian military initiative in Georgia (and subsequent recognition of South Ossetia and Abkhazia as independent nations) in August (see Current issues, below) but seemed limited to rhetorical responses. As of mid-2009 it was widely conceded that Georgia had little hope for NATO membership soon, although the EU included Georgia in the Eastern Partnership launched to promote closer relations with former Soviet states without the promise of eventual EU membership. Meanwhile, Georgia announced its withdrawal from the CIS.

Current issues. Opposition to President Shevardnadze's rule intensified in early 2003 as student-based protest organizations and the principal opposition parties conducted large-scale antigovernment demonstrations. The peaceful overthrow of Shevardnadze in November became known as the "Rose Revolution," a reference to the fact that oppositionists had carried roses during their demonstrations as a symbol of their commitment to nonviolence. In his inaugural address in January 2004, President Saakashvili pledged to root out corruption and restore the central government's control over Ajaria, Abkhazia, and South Ossetia. Meanwhile, the members of the cabinet appointed in February averaged 35 years of age and were mostly Western-educated.

Despite his hopes regarding the three breakaway republics, Saakashvili achieved progress in 2004 only with Ajaria (see Political background, above, for details). Georgia mounted a massive show of military forces along the border with South Ossetia in September, but the deployment backfired when the assault was repulsed by South Ossetian fighters. In December 2005 the president appeared to signal a shift to a less confrontational approach by proposing a settlement plan calling for "demilitarization" of the conflict and the eventual granting of broad autonomy to South Ossetia, albeit still under Georgian sovereignty. Saakashvili also reportedly reached out to the separatist leaders in Abkhazia, suggesting that peace negotiations could lead to a mutually acceptable refinement of a 2000 UN plan that would accord significant autonomy to Abkhazia. Russia initially appeared to support the broad plans for both separatist regions but backed away from that stance in early 2006, apparently in part in response to a row with Georgia in January over gas supplies. (The unexplained bombing of a Russian gas pipeline in North Ossetia had severely compromised deliveries to Georgia, causing widespread heating-fuel shortages.) Tensions in the "cold war" between Georgia and Russia subsequently continued to escalate, the Saakashvili administration accusing Russia of engaging in a "creeping annexation" of South Ossetia and Abkhazia. Exacerbating the hostility was Saakashvili's reassertion of Georgia's goal of joining NATO (anathema to Russia). Meanwhile, on the domestic front, Saakashvili continued to receive praise for his handling of the economy, although opposition parties charged him with having violated the spirit of the Rose Revolution by overconsolidating his authority and "packing" governmental bodies with his supporters.

In September 2006 the government arrested some 29 people in connection with an alleged coup plot. The detainees were described as supporters of former security minister Igor Giorgadze, who had been residing in Russia since being charged with complicity in the 1995 assassination attempt against President Shevardnadze. (Twelve of those arrested were convicted in August 2007 and sentenced to eight years in prison.) Additional friction developed with Russia when Georgia arrested four Russians on espionage charges in September (see Foreign relations, above). Despite (or perhaps because of) the growing conflict with Russia, Saakashvili's United National Movement (UNM) dominated the October 2006 municipal elections, which international observers described as generally free and fair. However, opposition parties objected that the local balloting had been held two months earlier than originally planned. They also strongly criticized the constitutional changes approved by the parliament in December that extended the legislative term and shortened the president's term so that simultaneous balloting could be held in October 2008. The opposition claimed that the measures were meant to help the UNM extend its control, but by the fall of 2007 reports were circulating that Saakashvili's popularity had declined in the wake of rising inflation, ongoing widespread poverty despite overall economic growth, and the strange developments surrounding former defense minister Irakli OKRUASHVILI (see For a United Georgia under Political Parties, below). For his part, Saakashvili blamed the nation's political turmoil on pro-Russian forces led by media tycoon Badri PATARKATSISHVILI. Saakashvili also called upon Russia to become more involved in facilitating a "soft" resolution in Abkhazia and South Ossetia.

Energized by the arrest of Okruashvili, opposition forces began mobilizing large-scale demonstrations in Tbilisi that reached critical mass in early November 2007 when police cracked down on the protesters and Saakashvili imposed a ten-day state of emergency that reportedly caused concern among his Western allies. Saakashvili's gamble on early presidential elections in January 2008 appeared to pay off, albeit just barely considering his less-than-impressive majority (53.5 percent). Runner-up Levan GACHECHILADZE (credited with 25.7 percent of the vote) described the balloting as "rigged," and new demonstrations were held in support of a recount. International observers cited irregularities in the conduct of the poll but suggested that the flaws probably did not affect the outcome.

In a nonbinding referendum held concurrently with the January 2008 presidential balloting, a reported 72.5 percent of those voting endorsed Georgia's controversial proposed membership in NATO. In another concurrent referendum, 69.9 percent of the voters indicated that they wanted to have legislative balloting moved up to the spring. In that regard, the opposition demanded several reforms, including the establishment of a new Central Election Commission with opposition members and additional (if not complete) proportional representation for the new parliament. Some of the proposals were included in amendments approved by parliament in March, although critics argued that retention of 75 seats from single-member constituencies favored the UNM. Observers described electoral conditions for the May poll as improved over the January balloting, but the opposition again accused the government of gross violations, and most opposition legislators boycotted subsequent sessions of the parliament.

The May 2008 legislative poll was conducted with a background of growing tension between Georgia and Russia, particularly in regard to Abkhazia, where a series of incidents had prompted Russia to lift trade restrictions on the separatist enclave. At the same time, the Abkhazian legislature appealed to the international community for recognition as an independent nation, citing as a precedent the recent recognition of Kosovo's independence by the United States and other Western nations. The South Ossetian legislature issued a similar request, and sporadic firefights were reported in early August between South Ossetian fighters and Georgian forces in Georgian villages in the enclave. (Each side accused the other of provoking the turmoil.)

Upon the orders of President Saakashvili, who had campaigned on a platform calling for the return of Georgia's "territorial integrity," Georgian forces shelled the South Ossetian capital of Tskhinvali during the night of August 7–8, 2008. Georgian troops entered the city the next day and overpowered the South Ossetian fighters. However, Russia responded dramatically by sending its own forces into South Ossetia and quickly routing the Georgian army. Significantly, the Russian army subsequently moved deep into Georgia proper before a tentative cease-fire was negotiated under EU mediation. Concurrently, Russian forces easily took control of Abkhazia. Late in the month Russia formally recognized the independence of both enclaves and pledged to keep its forces deployed there for protective purposes. Hundreds of civilians died in the conflict (some as the result of suspected ethnic cleansing on the part of both South Ossetians and Georgians in South Ossetia), while many cities and villages in South Ossetia were reduced to rubble. Although most of its troops withdrew from Georgia proper in the fall, Russia kept an estimated 10,000 soldiers in South Ossetia and Abkhazia and in what it called "zones of responsibility" outside the borders of those regions. Meanwhile, domestic discontent with President Saakashvili's handling of the conflict grew, although the president denied that it had contributed to Prime Minister Gurgenidze's resignation, which was attributed to a "joint consensual decision" made prior to the war. In addition to remaining vigilant regarding "external aggression," new prime minister Mgaloblishvili, an investment banker and theretofore ambassador to Turkey, pledged to pursue financial stability in the wake of sharp economic contraction resulting from war expenses, a collateral decline in tourism, and the effects of the global recession.

More than 10,000 protesters called for Saakashvili's resignation and early elections during a demonstration in Tbilisi in November 2008, and reports surfaced of friction between the president and the prime minister. However, Mgaloblishvili's resignation in January 2009 was attributed to his ill health. Nika Gilauri (33), theretofore finance minister and a deputy prime minister, became the fifth person to serve as premier since Saakashvili became president. The administrative changes did little to quell calls for Saakashvili's resignation, and mass demonstrations supported by most opposition parties were launched in April. For his part, the president blamed Russia for the unrest and pledged to serve out the remainder of his term while nurturing a "new wave of democracy" featuring, among other things, electoral and judicial reform. Although Saakashvili also promised to pursue the return of South Ossetia and Abkhazia to Georgian sovereignty, there appeared to be no likelihood of success in that regard as Russia began building army and naval bases in the enclaves and signed border protection agreements with the de facto governments of both regions. Sentiment in South Ossetia clearly favored eventual absorption into Russia, although Moscow remained formally opposed to that option. Meanwhile, Abkhazian leaders firmly ruled out unification with Russia or reintegration with Georgia.

POLITICAL PARTIES

The formerly dominant Georgian Communist Party (GCP) was dissolved following the abortive Moscow coup of August 1991, with its deputies being expelled from the Georgia Supreme Soviet in mid-September. The secessionist Round Table–Free Georgia coalition that had supported President Gamsakhurdia became largely moribund following his ouster in January 1992.

Legislative elections in October 1992 gave representation to more than 30 parties or alliances, none gaining a meaningful number of seats. Most were as much military as political groupings, being commonly based on clan or regional loyalties. In November 1993 President Shevardnadze launched a new progovernment grouping called the Citizens' Union of Georgia (CUG); however, the revival in June 1994 of the GCP (as the United Communist Party of Georgia) showed that old allegiances remained powerful. A total of 32 parties and alliances presented candidates in the 1999 parliamentary poll.

Nearly 50 parties reportedly participated in the 2003 and 2004 legislative elections, many of them in newly organized (and often unstable) blocs or coalitions that sometimes lacked clearly formulated ideologies or agendas. Following the ouster of the Shevardnadze regime in 2003, many of the old parties lost their relevance. Meanwhile, most new groupings were perceived as still attempting to define themselves and establish viable political goals.

Several blocs were credited with securing legislative seats in the 2003–2004 elections. One of the most important was the **Right Opposition, Industrialists, and News** bloc, an alliance that included the New Rights Party, the Georgian Liberal Party, Industry Will Save Georgia, and other groupings. The well-financed bloc supported private enterprise and included some of the country's most successful business leaders. However, it also suffered at the polls because of its image as a "party of oligarchs." Industry Will Save Georgia reportedly subsequently left the bloc, whose parliamentary faction later was referenced as the Political Union–New Rights, News.

In April 2003 supporters of President Shevardnadze launched the **For a New Georgia** bloc, which included, among others, the CUG, the SSP, the Christian Democratic Union, the NDP, and the Party for the Liberation of Abkhazia. The bloc was reportedly the top performer in the November 2003 legislative balloting. However, following the ouster of Shevardnadze, the bloc factionalized, and it did not present candidates in the 2004 presidential or legislative polls. (For a complete history of the CUG as well as information on other defunct or diminished parties and groups, see the 2007 *Handbook*.)

Three blocs and nine individual parties were permitted to present candidates in the May 2008 legislative poll, the Central Election Commission having rejected the application of nearly 40 other groups for insufficient signatures (30,000 signatures are required for registration). Meanwhile, analysts continued to describe the Georgian party system as "immature," with many groupings focused on leaders rather than ideology.

Government Party:

United National Movement (UNM). Also currently referenced as the National Movement Party or simply as the National Movement, the center-right, nationalist UNM was founded in 2001 in support of governmental and economic reform, closer ties with the EU and the United States, and restoration of Georgian control over Abkhazia and South Ossetia. The UNM platform also called for raising pensions, enhancing social services for the poor, fighting corruption, and increasing state revenues by curtailing the power of the oligarchs.

The UNM was led at its formation by Mikhail Saakashvili, a former cabinet minister who quit the CUG in late 2001 to protest what he considered to be acceptance on the part of the government of widespread corruption. Campaigning with the motto of "Georgia Without Shevardnadze," Saakashvili led a National Movement–Democratic Front to notable success in the June 2002 local elections.

In 2003 the UNM joined with the United Democrats, the Union of National Security, and the youth movement *Kmara* ("Enough") to form the United People's Alliance, which played a central role in the forced resignation of President Shevardnadze. (Candidates for the November 2003 legislative balloting were presented through a **Saakashvili–National Movement** bloc that reportedly also included the Republican Party of Georgia and others.) The alliance subsequently presented Saakashvili as the dominant presidential candidate in the January 2004 balloting, and the UNM served as the core component of the National Movement–Democrats (NMD) that was credited with winning 133 of 150 seats in the new balloting for proportional composure of the legislature. Other components of the NMD included the United Democrats, a centrist grouping formed in June 2002 by former CUG leader and former speaker of the parliament Zurab Zhvania. (The United Democrats in 2002 claimed the allegiance of some 25 legislators. Subsequently, Zhvania formed an electoral alliance with Nino Burdjanadze [chair of the parliament] called the Burdjanadze–Democrats Bloc, which won a number of seats in the November 2003 legislative poll. Several other groups reportedly participated in the 2003 bloc, including the Union of Georgian Traditionalists and the Christian-Conservative Party of Georgia.) Zhvania, an ally of Saakashvili in the Rose Revolution, was named prime minister in February 2004.

The formation of the NMD in early 2004 was described variously as a "merger" or "amalgamation" of the UNM and the United Democrats. However, a degree of tension was subsequently reported between the UNM and the United Democrats, particularly following the death in 2005 of Zhvania. Consequently, references to the NMD subsequently declined, with the UNM being regularly described as the nation's ruling party and many members of the United Democrats (including Burdjanadze) having apparently been absorbed into the UNM.

The UNM reportedly secured approximately two-thirds of the vote in the October 2006 municipal elections, while Saakashvili was elected to a second presidential term in January 2008 on a platform that called for restoration of Georgia's "territorial integrity," NATO membership for Georgia, closer ties with the EU, and the expansion of social welfare programs. Similar themes were stressed by the UNM for the May legislative balloting, at which its candidates (minus Burdjanadze, who withdrew from the UNM proportional list to protest the perceived low placement of her supporters on the list) were presented under the rubric of the UNM–For a Victorious Georgia, which secured 119 of 150 seats on a vote share of 59.2 percent. Burdjanadze subsequently launched a new anti-Saakashvili party (see Democratic Movement–United Georgia, below).

Leaders: Mikhail SAAKASHVILI (President of the Republic), David BAKRADZE (Chair of the Parliament), David KIRKITADZE (Secretary General).

Other Legislative Parties and Blocs:

United Opposition (National Council/New Rights). As structured for the May 2008 legislative balloting, the United Opposition (also referenced as the Joint Opposition) comprised the following five parties plus **We Ourselves** (also referenced as "On Our Own"), a party devoted to the issues of displaced Georgians from Abkhazia and led by Paata DAVITAIA; the *Kartule Dasi* movement, led by Jondi BAGHATURIA; the **National Forum**, led by Kakha SHARTAVA and Irakli MELASHVILI; and **Freedom** (*Tavisuplea*, led by Konstantine GAMSAKHURDIA, the eldest son of former president Gamsakhurdia). The grouping was an outgrowth of the United National Council that was formed in September 2007 to oppose the Saakashvili administration. The council called for the president's resignation, establishment of a purely parliamentary system, greater judicial independence, Georgia's integration into NATO and the EU, and early elections in the spring of 2008. At that time the council included the RPG and the GLP but did not include the New Rights Party. The National Council, whose coordinator was Konstantine Gunrsadze of For a United Georgia, was described as the governing body of the United Opposition (or the United Public Movement), which presented independent Levan Gachechiladze as the primary challenger to Saakashvili in the January 2008 presidential poll. (The grouping had been reduced to nine members by that time, following the exit of the GLP.) Gachechiladze, a prominent businessman who had once served as Saakashvili's campaign manager, accused the president of "authoritarianism" and denounced the official poll results (which credited Gachechiladze with 26.7 percent of the vote) as fraudulent. The RPG ran on its own in the May 2008 legislative elections, analysts suggesting that some RPG members considered the United Opposition's approach to be too radical. It also appeared that the members of the United Opposition lacked significant mutual interests other than the ouster of Saakashvili. Using the rubric United Opposition (National Council/National Rights) after the New Rights Party became affiliated, the coalition was credited with winning 17 seats in the legislative poll on a vote share of 17.7 percent. However, some of the bloc's deputies subsequently declined to take their seats to protest the actions of the administration.

In September 2008 Gachechiladze signed an opposition manifesto in support of the Public Forum for Liberty and Justice, an informal grouping launched by Sozar SUBARI, the Georgian human rights ombudsman who had become highly critical of the government. In July 2009 Gachechiladze announced he was forming a new party called **Defend Georgia.**

Leaders: Levan GACHECHILADZE (2008 presidential candidate), Davit GAMKRELIDZE.

For a United Georgia. This party was formed in September 2007 by supporters of Irakli Okruashvili, a former ally of Mikhail Saakashvili in the Rose Revolution who had been dismissed from the cabinet in November 2006. Okruashvili in September 2007 accused Saakashvili of plotting to kill opponents and charged the administration in general with widespread corruption, prompting large-scale antigovernment demonstrations. In a bizarre series of events, Okruashvili himself was arrested on corruption charges and subsequently reportedly acknowledged that he could not produce evidence for his accusations against Saakashvili. Okruashvili was released on bail and announced his retirement from politics, but he later said that his retraction had been coerced. Meanwhile, his initial arrest had prompted widespread protest demonstrations, and For a United Georgia (also referenced as the Movement for a United Georgia) served as a core component of the new anti-Saakashvili opposition coalition.

Okruashvili was arrested on an Interpol warrant in December 2007 in Germany but was later granted asylum in France. In March 2008 a Georgian court sentenced him in absentia to a prison term following his conviction on extortion charges.

Leaders: Irakli OKRUASHVILI (in exile), Konstantine GUNRSADZE, Giorgi TORTLADZE, Eka BESELIA (Secretary General).

New Rights Party. Formed in October 2000 as the "New Faction" by dissident CUG legislators, this grouping adopted its current name in June 2001 and scored significant victories in the June 2002 local elections. For the 2003 legislative balloting, the New Rights Party formed the **New Right** bloc with the GLP, the Conservative Party of Georgia, and others. It participated in the 2004 legislative poll as part of the Right Opposition, Industrialists, and News bloc, which won 17 proportional seats.

Although the New Right bloc gained legislative representation in 2004 (in part based on cooperation with the NMD), a number of legislators from the bloc supported the drive in early 2006 by opposition parties to force the resignation of President Saakashvili. The party's chair, Davit Gamkrelidze, won 4.0 percent of the vote in the January 2008 presidential poll, the party's support in the business sector having earned Gamkrelidze the endorsement of Industry Will Save Georgia and the NDP. However, the New Rights Party joined the United Opposition for the May legislative balloting, reportedly securing 5 of the bloc's 17 legislative seats. (The party's legislators subsequently declined to take their seats.)

In September 2008 Gamkrelidze called for President Saakashvili's resignation in view of the "catastrophic consequences" of the recent war with Russia.

Leaders: Davit GAMKRELIDZE (Chair), Kakha KATSITADZE.

Conservative Party of Georgia. This grouping was formed in 1995 as a successor to the Liberal-Conservative Party, which had been founded by former members of the Georgian Conservative Monarchists' Party (GCMP). (The GCMP had been launched in late 1989 in support of the Georgian monarchy, for which there was not an obvious claimant.) The Conservative Party secured representation in the 2004 legislative poll as part of the New Right bloc. In early 2006 the party was among the opposition groups that organized public demonstrations calling for the resignation of President Saakashvili. At that point, several of the party's legislators were participating in an opposition parliamentary faction called the Democratic Front that also included the Republican Party of Georgia and Industry Will Save Georgia. In April 2006 the front, led by Davit ZURABISHVILI, announced a boycott of parliament pending action on the front's demands for representation on the national election commission, the direct election of the mayor of Tbilisi (currently appointed by the president), and other reforms. The Conservatives participated in the 2006 local elections in alliance with the RPG. In 2008 and 2009 the party called for a campaign of civil disobedience to prompt the resignation of President Saakashvili.

Leaders: Koba DAVITASHVILI and Zviad DZIDZIGURI (Cochairs); Kakha KUKAVA (Secretary General).

Georgia's Way. This party is led by Salome Zourabichvili, a French citizen who received Georgian citizenship in 2004. A former French diplomat, Zourabichvili served as Georgian minister of foreign affairs until being dismissed in the fall of 2005. With Georgia's Way by then firmly in the opposition camp, Zourabichvili in 2007 announced plans to run for president in 2008. However, the party subsequently joined the United Opposition and supported Levan Gachechiladze in the presidential poll.

Leader: Salome ZURABISHVILI.

People's Party. Formed by former members of the NDP, the People's Party contested the 1999 legislative elections in a coalition with two other small groupings—the **Popular Union** and the **Party of Independence and Unity of Georgia.** The People's Party formed an alliance with the KTK (below) for the June 2002 local elections.

Leaders: Koba DAVITASHVILI, Mamuka GIORGADZE.

Georgian Labor Party (GLP). The GLP is a successor to the Union for a Law-Governed State (ULGS), founded in August 1995 and also rendered in English as the State Justice Union. The ULGS, an ideologically centrist grouping, won one legislative seat in 1995, while the GLP (founded in 1997) secured two seats in 1999 in single-member constituencies despite just barely missing the 7 percent threshold for proportional representation with 6.85 percent of the vote. The GLP also performed well in the June 2002 local elections and won seats in the 2003 and 2004 national legislative polls.

One of the few Georgian parties with a clear ideology, the left-wing GLP enjoys strong support in Tbilisi. At its founding, the GLP was considered "pro-Russian," but its stance has shifted in recent years to one that favors eventual membership for Georgia in NATO. The GLP was among the parties calling for the resignation of Prime Minister Saakashvili in the first half of 2006. The GLP was credited with approximately 10 percent of the vote in the 2006 municipal elections.

The GLP was initially described as one of the founders of the opposition coalition formed in late 2007, but GLP leader Shalva Natelashvili was presented as a single-party candidate in the January 2008 presidential poll, securing 6.5 percent of the vote. Having strongly criticized the administration for recent economic reforms perceived by the party as having failed to assist the poor, the GLP won six seats in the May legislative balloting on a vote share of 7.4 percent. However, the GLP subsequently announced a boycott of the legislature to protest what it described as flawed electoral results.

Leaders: Shalva NATELASHVILI (Chair), Giorgi GUGAVA (Secretary).

Christian Democratic Movement. Founded in early 2008 by Giorgi Targanadze, a popular ex-television anchor from *Imedi TV* (the focus of a recent government crackdown), this grouping described itself as a member of the "moderate opposition." Among other things, its campaign platform called for the Georgian Orthodox Church to be established as the state religion. The party won six seats in the May legislative poll on a vote share of 8.7 percent. Among the parties reportedly participating in the movement were **Forward Georgia**, which had been launched under the leadership of Irakli BATIASHVILI in the wake of the Rose Revolution to provide opposition to the Saakashvili administration; the **Green Party**; and the **Party of the Future**, led by Gia MAISASHVILI, who had won 0.8 percent of the vote in the January 2008 presidential poll.

Leaders: Giorgi TARGANADZE, Levan VEPHKHVADZE (Parliamentary Leader).

Republican Party of Georgia (RPG). Launched in 1990, the RPG participated in the October 1992 legislative elections as a member of the "October 11 Bloc" and later was a founding member of the URP (see PFG, below), which it subsequently left. The RPG participated in the 1999 legislative elections in an electoral alliance called the National Democratic Alliance–The Third Way, which also included the NDP and the Party of National Industry and Economic Revival (recently formed under the leadership of Besik JUGELI, a former NDP legislator).

The RPG was allied with the Saakashvili–National Movement bloc for the 2003 legislative elections and joined the "parliamentary majority" in support of President Saakashvili in 2004. However, a number of RPG legislators subsequently split with the government following conflict between the RPG and the UNM over elections in Ajaria, and the RPG became one of the leading opposition parties calling for Saakashvili's resignation. The RPG aligned with the Conservative Party of

Georgia for the 2006 municipal elections, the coalition securing more than 12 percent of the votes. Although the party participated in the formation of the opposition coalition in late 2007 and supported Levan Gachechiladze in the January 2008 presidential poll, it quit the United Opposition prior to the May 2008 legislative balloting, reportedly in an effort to serve as a more moderate anti-Saakashvili force than some of its former coalition partners. The RPG secured two seats in the legislative elections on a vote share of 3.8 percent.

Leaders: Davit USUPASHVILI, Ivliane KHAINDRAVA, Davit BERDZENISHVILI, Tinatin KHIDASHELI, Temur NERGADZE, Levan BERDZENISHVILI.

Other Parties and Blocs that Participated in the 2008 Legislative Elections:

Georgian Politics. Formed in early 2008 by, among others, several former members of the Georgian Supreme Council, Georgian Politics called for economic cooperation with Abkhazia and opposed Georgia's proposed NATO membership. The party secured 0.5 percent of the May legislative vote.

Leader: Gocha PIPIA.

Rightist Alliance. This electoral bloc (also referenced as the Rightist Alliance–Topadze Industrialists) was formed for the May 2008 legislative poll by the following groups and Unity (see UCPG, below). The coalition won 0.9 percent of the vote in the legislative balloting.

Leader: Giorgi TOPADZE.

Industry Will Save Georgia. The Industry bloc was formed as an electoral alliance for the 1999 legislative balloting by the following two groups and a number of smaller parties, including the center-right Political Union "Sporting Georgia," formed in 1998 under the leadership of economist Roman RURUA; the **Movement for the Georgian State,** a center-right grouping formed in 1998 under the leadership of Irakli BATIASHVILI; and the **National Movement "Georgia First of All,"** a right-wing grouping led by Guram SHARADZE. The bloc won 7.8 percent of the proportional vote in the 1999 legislative balloting. It was described in mid-2006 as controlling seven seats in the parliament.

Industry Will Survive Georgia. Launched in 1999, this nationalist, protectionist grouping was described as comprising "well-heeled business leaders" (including Gogi Topadze, a "beer magnate") opposed to the sale of government assets to foreign investors. It also objected to many of the economic strictures recommended by the IMF.

Leaders: Gogi TOPADZE (Chair), Zurab TKEMALADZE.

Union of Reformers and Agrarians (URA). The URA is a successor to the Reformers' Union of Georgia (RUG), a "liberal-centrist" grouping founded in 1993 in support of closer relations with Russia as well as market reforms designed to facilitate the emergence of a middle class. The RUG had competed in the 1995 legislative balloting as a member of the bloc Reformers' Union of Georgia–National Concord (*Sakartvelos Reformaforta Kavshiri–Erovnuli Tankhmoba*), which won two parliamentary seats. Other members of that 1995 bloc were the **Georgian Citizens' Political Association** (GCPA), launched in August 1995 as a centrist-traditionalist grouping in favor of "unification of national mentality," and the **Sportsmen's Union of Georgia** (SUG), launched in 1994 in support of "consolidation of the nation" and close ties with other CIS countries. (The SUG participated independently in the May 2008 legislative poll, securing 0.2 percent of the vote under the leadership of Valery GIORGOBIANI.)

Leader: Bakur GULUA (Chair).

National Democratic Party (NDP). Claiming to be the heir of a pre-Soviet party of the same name, the NDP was organized in 1988 as a secessionist grouping with a "Christian outlook." It favored restoration of the monarchy as a means of national unification. Allied with the smaller and more secularist **Democratic Party** (DP), it won 32.6 percent of the vote in the 1990 republican election, while in the October 1992 legislative balloting the NDP took 12 seats and the DP, 10.

Having initially supported Shevardnadze's assumption of power in 1992, the NDP subsequently became critical of his policy of rapprochement with Moscow and opposed Georgia's CIS membership. In December 1994, NDP leader Georgi Chanturia was assassinated in Tbilisi in an attack that also seriously injured his wife, Irina SARISHVILI-CHANTURIA, who took over the party leadership despite having one of three bullets that struck her lodged close to her heart.

The former DP chair, Kartlos GHARIBASHVILI, took only 0.5 percent of the vote in the November 1995 presidential election; however, in the legislative balloting the NDP came in second place, with 8 percent of the proportional vote and 34 seats in total. In January 1996, NDP deputies unsuccessfully opposed ratification of the 1994 friendship treaty with Russia, claiming that it contained unacceptable "military union" provisions.

Following the NDP's participation in the For a New Georgia bloc in the November 2003 legislative poll, Irina Sarishvili-Chanturia resigned as NDP leader to form a new grouping, referenced as the **Hope Party** for the January 2008 presidential balloting in which Sarishvili-Chanturia was credited with 0.2 percent of the vote.

Leader: Bachuki KARDAVA.

Traditionalists, Our Georgia, and Women's Party. An electoral bloc established by the following groups in early 2008, this coalition won 0.4 percent of the vote in the May balloting.

Union of Georgian Traditionalists (*Kartvel Traditsionalista Kavshiri*—KTK). Also known as the Traditionalist Party, the conservative KTK won seven seats in the Supreme Council in 1992. Its 4.2 percent share of the vote in 1995 was insufficient for proportional seats in the Georgian Parliament, but it elected two deputies in the constituency contests. The KTK and several other opposition parties unsuccessfully demanded in September 1997 that the Central Election Commission schedule a referendum on how mayors are elected. They also opposed a 1997 law giving the president the right to appoint the mayors of the six largest cities, saying it was passed to ensure a victory by the CUG in the parliamentary elections.

Eleven of the successful candidates from the Revival of Georgia bloc in the 1999 legislative balloting subsequently joined the KTK parliamentary faction. (For detailed information on the Revival of Georgia bloc [led by Aslan Abashidze, the dominant figure in Ajarian affairs at the time], see the 2008 *Handbook*.) The KTK participated in the June 2002 local elections in an electoral alliance with the People's Party (see above). Following the Rose Revolution, it was reported that the KTK had merged into the NDP.

Our Georgia. This party was established in early 2008, mainly by supporters of the late Badri Patarkatsishvili, who had finished third in the January 2008 presidential poll with 7.1 percent of the vote.

Leader: Gocha JOJUA.

Women's Party. This party was established in early 2008 by legislator Guguli Magradze, a recent defector from the UNM.

Leader: Guguli MAGRADZE.

Other parties presenting candidates in the May 2008 legislative elections included the **Radical-Democratic National Party** (0.2 percent of the vote), led by Shalva KUPRASKI; the **Christian-Democratic Alliance** (0.9 percent), led by Giorgi KOBAKHIDZE; and **Our Country** (0.1 percent), led by Tamaz GUGUNISHVILI.

Other Parties:

Democratic Movement–United Georgia. Formed by Nino Burdjanadze, the former chair of the Georgian parliament who split with President Saakashvili in 2008 (see UNM, above), this new party was one of the most influential opposition groups calling for Saakashvili's resignation in 2009.

Leader: Nino BURDJANADZE.

Our Georgia–Free Democrats. Launched in July 2009, this moderate opposition party is led by Irakli Alasania, who stepped down as Georgia's ambassador to the UN in late 2008 and became a critic of the Saakashvili administration, particularly in regard to the midsummer war with Russia. In February 2009 Alasania was named one of the leaders of the informal Alliance for Georgia, which also reportedly included the New Rights Party and the RPG. Upon the formation of Our Georgia–Free Democrats, Alasania said the new party did not mean the end of cooperation with the Alliance for Georgia. Alasania, considered a rising star in Georgian politics due to what one analyst described as his "smooth diplomatic touch," called on the United States to press for political reform in Georgia.

Leaders: Irakli ALASANIA, Zurab ABASHIDZE.

United Communist Party of Georgia—UCPG (*Sakartvelos Komunisturi Partia*). The UCPG was launched in June 1994 in an attempt to unite the various factions that claimed descent from the Soviet-era Georgian Communist Party (GCP). The old GCP had been somewhat less tainted by corruption and abuse of power than its counterparts elsewhere; it was nevertheless dissolved in August 1991 as Georgia moved to independence and its leaders shifted their support to other parties. Prior to the launching of the UCPG, communist support was channeled into the Communist Workers' Party (CWP) and the Alliance of Communists of Georgia (ACG). Despite formation of the UCPG, communist unity was not an important feature of the 1995 elections. In the presidential contest, the UCPG leader, Maj. Gen. Panteleimon Giorgadze, ran fourth with only 0.5 percent, being heavily outpolled by former GCP first secretary Dzhumber PATIASHVILI, who finished second with 19.5 percent of the vote. The UCPG, which had taken a conservative/nationalist line on Abkhazian separatism and favored close alignment with Moscow, contested the 1995 parliamentary election as part of a United Communist Party–Social Democrats bloc that failed to cross the 5 percent proportional barrier and obtained no seats in the single-mandate constituencies.

In 1997 the UCPG played a leading role in the formation of the National-Patriotic Movement for Georgia's Salvation, a bloc of 12 parties favoring close integration with Russia and open to all "patriotic" forces that shared a commitment to socialism. For the 1999 legislative elections, the UCPG participated in the **United Communist Party (Stalin) and Workers' Union** that also included the **Citizens' Political Union "Union of Georgian Workers"** (a recently formed leftist grouping) and the **Workers' Union of Georgia,** led by Vakhtung GABUNIA.

Patiashvili was elected to the legislature in 1999 as a candidate of the Revival of Georgia bloc; he and a number of the bloc's other successful candidates subsequently formed a "Unified Georgia" faction in the parliament. Patiashvili finished second in the 2000 presidential balloting with 17 percent of the vote. In September 2001 he announced the formation of a new grouping called **Unity** (*Ertoba*) in conjunction with Aleksandre CHACHIA.

The UCPG leader is the father of Igor Giorgadze, former chief of the Georgian Security Service, who officials have claimed was a key figure in the attempt to assassinate Shevardnadze in 1995. The government demanded in July 1997 that Moscow extradite the alleged conspirator, but Maj. Gen. Panteleimon Giorgadze said his son was not in Moscow.

Igor Giorgadze, who claimed the charges against him were "utterly groundless," helped launch the **Party of Justice** (registered in 2004 in Georgia) from exile. After having reportedly spent time in some eight countries over the past 11 years, he announced from Moscow in 2006 that he was not seeking Russian citizenship or permanent asylum in Russia but rather intended to attempt to regain political influence in Georgia through the Party of Justice. Subsequently, UCPG leaders claimed that the Georgian government was withholding pension payments from party adherents.

Leader: Maj. Gen. Panteleimon GIORGADZE.

Popular Front of Georgia (PFG). The PFG is a center-right successor to the United Republican Party (URP), which had been launched in 1995 as a merger of the Georgian Public Front (GPF), led by Nodar Natadze; the Charter 1991 Party; and the RPG. (Those three parties had formed the core of the "October 11 Bloc" that had won 27 seats in the October 1992 legislative elections.) The URP failed to achieve the 5 percent proportional minimum in the 1995 legislative poll but won 1 constituency seat. Shortly thereafter, the RPG and Charter 1991 left the URP. Subsequently, the URP supported opposition calls for the removal of Russian troops from Georgian territory, and in November 1997 Natadze called for Georgia's withdrawal from the CIS and denounced the confederation model for settling the disputes in Abkhazia and South Ossetia. The URP adopted the PFG rubric in 1999, and it competed in the 1999 legislative balloting in coalition with the **Ilia Chavchavadze Society,** which had won 7 seats in the 1992 legislative balloting and is currently led by Tamas CKHEIDZE.

Leader: Nodar NATADZE.

Christian-Conservative Party of Georgia. Launched in 1997, this right-wing grouping was an outgrowth of the Movement of National Survival–Resistance Front, which had been prominent in public protests in 1992–1993. The party participated in the 1999 legislative balloting as a member of the Round Table–Free Georgian Bloc that also included the **Helsinki Union of Georgia–National Revival,** led by Tengiz KIKACHEISHVILI; the rightist, monarchist **Royal League of Georgia,** led by David PAVLENISHVILI; and several other small right-wing parties.

Leader: Temur ZHORZHOLIANI.

All-Georgian Union of Revival (*Sruliad Sakartvelos Aghordzinebis Kavshiri*—SSAK). Based in the predominantly Muslim autonomous republic of Ajaria, the SSAK was founded in 1992 as the All-Georgian Union for the Revival of Ajaria, which became the leading party in the autonomous republic and participated in the 1992 legislative poll as part of the *Mshvidoba* (Peace) bloc. In 1995 it came in third place in the national legislative balloting with 6.8 percent of the proportional vote, winning 32 seats in all. In the September 1996 parliamentary elections in Ajaria, the SSAK won an overwhelming majority in a coalition with the CUG. In local elections in November 1998, the SSAK won almost all seats in local councils in Ajaria, its leader, Aslan Abashidze, becoming known as the "strongman" of the Ajarian government. Thirteen of the 57 successful candidates from the Revival of Georgia bloc in the 1999 legislative balloting subsequently joined the SSAK faction in parliament.

Socialist Party of Georgia (*Sakartvelos Sotsialisturi Partia*—SSP). The SSP was founded in 1995 on a democratic, left-wing program, aligning itself with the CUG and endorsing Shevardnadze's presidential candidacy in November. It failed to cross the 5 percent threshold in the 1995 parliamentary elections (taking 3.8 percent) but won four constituency seats thanks to its alliance with the CUG.

Twelve of the successful candidates from the Revival of Georgia bloc in the 1999 legislative balloting subsequently joined the SSP faction in parliament, the SSP having previously moved firmly into an anti-CUG stance. The SSP was one of the leading parties in the June 2002 local elections. It participated in the pro-Shevardnadze For a New Georgia bloc in the November 2003 legislative elections. Following Shevardnadze's ouster, Vakhtang RCHEULISHVILI resigned as the SSP chair.

Leader: Irakli MINDELI (Chair).

Other parties and blocs that competed in 1999 and/or 2003–2004 included the **Citizens' Political Union of Lecturers,** a centrist grouping led by author Nugzar TSERETELI; the **Communist Party of Georgia** (CPG), led by Ivane TSIKLAURI; the centrist **Democratic Center of Georgia,** led by Zurab MURVANIDZE; the center-left **Georgian League of Intellectuals,** led by Irakli LOMTADZE; the **Georgian National State Political Union,** led by Lasha LAMIDZE; the **Georgian Social Democratic Party,** led by Jemal KAKHNIASHVILI; the **Georgian Social Realistic Party,** led by Guram BEROZASHVILI; the **Merab Kostava Society,** a rightist grouping led by Vaja ADAMIA; the **National Ideology Party of Georgia,** a right-wing grouping led by Zurab GAGNIDZE; the **National Independence Party,** led by Irakli TSERETELI; the **Nationalist Party,** led by Zaza VASHKAMADZE; the **Party of Economic and Social Victims of Georgia,** formed in 1999 under the leadership of Malkhaz CISKARISHVILI; the nationalistic **Political Movement "Fate of Georgia,"** led by Temur MDINARADZE; the **Popular Democratic Party,** led by Guram USITASHVILI; **Strong Regions–Strong Georgia,** led by businessman Merab SAMADASHVILI; the conservative **Union of Nationalists of Georgia,** led by Gaioz MAMALADZE; and the **Union of Social Justice of Georgia,** a leftist grouping led by Archil IOSELIANI.

Other recently formed parties include **For the Future of Georgia**, an Ajaria-based grouping led by Nino KVIRIKADZE; the **Movement for a Just Georgia,** a grouping led by former prime minister Zurab Noghaideli that temporarily joined the April 2009 protests calling for the resignation of President Saakashvili but later withdrew because of its objections to the aggressive tactics favored by other parties, and the **People's Forum**, an opposition party led by Akaki ASATIANI, a former leader of the KTK and a former chair of parliament.

Parties supporting South Ossetian president Eduard Kokoity in the 2009 elections for the South Ossetian legislature included the **Republican Party "Unity"**; the **Communist Party,** led by Stanislav KOCHIV (speaker of the legislature); and the formally recognized branch of the **People's Party.** The primary opposition party was the **Republican Socialist Party "Fatherland"**, which, under the leadership of Vyacheslav GOBOZOV, accused Kokoity of using governmental authority to repress dissent. (An unrecognized grouping led by Roland KELEKHSAYEV also claimed the People's Party rubric in announcing cooperation with Fatherland in an anti-Kokoity Civic Forum.)

In Abkhazia, President Sergei Bagapsh announced he would run for reelection in the late 2009 poll as the candidate of **Unified Abkhazia,** a previously informal vehicle for his supporters that was officially recognized as a political party in early 2009. Bagapsh was expected to face a challenge from Beslan BUTBA, a wealthy businessman and former parliamentarian who recently launched the **Economic Development Party of Abkhazia.** Yakub LAKOBA, the leader of the **People's Party of Abkhazia,** announced a cooperation agreement with Butba for the presidential balloting, which Bagapsh won.

LEGISLATURE

The 1995 constitution specifies that when territorial and political conditions permit, the **Georgian Parliament** (*Sakartvelos Parlamenti*) will consist of two chambers, namely a Council of the Republic elected by proportional representation and a Senate composed of deputies elected in the country's territorial units. In the interim, the legislature consists of a single chamber, currently comprising, under revisions approved in March 2008, 150 members (75 elected in single-number constituencies and 75 elected from party lists in one nationwide constituency) serving five-year terms. First-round candidates in the single-member constituencies must receive more than 30 percent of the vote to be elected; if no candidate reaches that level, a runoff is held between the top two vote-getters. The threshold for gaining representation in the proportional poll is 5 percent (reduced prior to the 2008 balloting from 7 percent).

Elections were most recently held on May 2, 2008, after a national referendum on January 5, 2008, approved moving them up from the scheduled time of October. The balloting resulted in the following distribution of seats: United National Movement, 119 (71 in single-member constituencies and 48 from the proportional balloting); the United Opposition (National Council/New Rights), 17 (6, 11); the Christian Democratic Movement, 6 (0, 6); the Georgian Labor Party, 6 (0, 6); and the Republican Party of Georgia, 2 (2, 0).

Chair: David BAKRADZE.

CABINET

[as of September 1, 2009]

Prime Minister	Nika Gilauri
First Deputy Prime Minister	Davit Tkeshelashvili
Deputy Prime Minister	Giorgi Baramidze
State Ministers	
Diaspora Issues	Iulon Gagoshidze
European and Euro-Atlantic Integration	Giorgi Baramidze
Reintegration Issues	Temur Iakobashvili
Ministers	
Agriculture	Baku Kvezereli
Corrections and Legal Assistance	Dimitri Shashkin
Culture, Monument Protection, and Sports	Nikoloz Rurua
Defense	Bacho Akhalaia
Economic Development	Zurab Pololikashvili
Education and Science	Nika Gvaramia
Energy	Aleksandre Khetaguri
Environmental Protection and Natural Resources	Giorgi Khachidze
Finance	Kakha Baindurashvili
Foreign Affairs	Grigol Vashadze
Internal Affairs	Ivane Merabishvili
Justice	Zurab Adeishvili
Labor, Health, and Social Affairs	Aleksandre Kvitashvili
Refugees and Resettlement	Koba Subeliani
Regional Development and Infrastructure	Davit Tkeshelashvili

COMMUNICATIONS

The Shevardnadze government reportedly sought the reinstatement of legislation providing for heavy penalties against journalists deemed guilty of libeling officials, an initiative that watchdog groups described as an effort to thwart investigations into corruption. Nevertheless, the media under Shevardnadze's administration were considered "relatively free" in comparison to some other post-Soviet countries, and the Georgian independent television station *Rustavi 2* was perceived as playing a significant role in support of the Rose Revolution that ousted Shevardnadze. Although the Saakashvili administration was elected on a reformist platform, it was described by critics in 2006 as having exerted "subtle pressure" on media owners in an alleged effort to curtail press freedom, despite parliament's adoption in 2004 of a Law on Freedom of Speech and Expression. In addition, a number of newspapers have been closed since 2004, and. the government shut down the popular *Imedi TV* station during the protest demonstrations in the fall of 2007 (see Broadcasting and computing, below). The media were given only "fair" marks for their coverage of the May 2008 legislative elections in light of the perceived favoritism toward incumbents on the part of some outlets. Journalistic self-censorship was also apparent during the August military conflict with Russia.

Press. There are approximately 200 independent newspapers in circulation, many of them subject to the influence of their financial patrons in politics and business. The independent daily with the highest circulation reportedly is *Alia*. The following are published in Tbilisi in Georgian, unless noted otherwise: *Rezonansi* (10,000), daily; *Akhali Taoba* (New Generation); *Dilis Gazeti* (Morning Newspaper), independent; *Georgian Times* (2,000), opposition paper in English; *Shvidi Dghe* (Seven Days, 3,000); and *Georgian Messenger*, daily in English. Other publications (also published in Tbilisi in Georgian unless noted otherwise) include *Akhalgazrda Iverieli* (Young Iberian); *Eri* (Nation), weekly; *Mamuli* (Native Land); *Rustaveli Society,* fortnightly; *Respublika* (Republic, 40,000), independent weekly; *Sakartvelo* (Georgia), government daily; *Mteli Kvira*, independent weekly; *Kviris Palitra,* independent weekly; and *Tavisupali Sakartvelo* (Free Georgia), former Round Table–Free Georgia organ.

News agency. The domestic facility is the Georgian Information Agency (Sakinform), headquartered in Tbilisi.

Broadcasting and computing. The state-owned Georgian Public Broadcaster transmits in Georgian and a number of regional languages. There are several independent television stations that provide nationwide coverage, including *Rustavi 2*, which the government attempted to shut down in October 2001, thereby precipitating significant protest demonstrations. More recently the station has been described as being at least informally controlled by the government. Another influential station is *Imedi TV*, which was previously co-owned by Rupert Murdoch's News Corporation and Badri Patarkatsishvili, a strong critic of the Saakashvili administration. After being closed during the 2007 protests, the station was permitted to resume broadcasting in December but subsequently ceased broadcasting on its own accord pending the return of "normal" political conditions. Following Patarkatsishvili's death in January 2008, the station reopened in September under completely new ownership that was considered "friendly" to the government. A local channel (*Kavkazia*) in Tbilisi was considered a significant platform for opposition parties in late 2007 and the first half of 2008.

As of 2008 there were 237.8 Internet users per 1,000 inhabitants.

INTERGOVERNMENTAL REPRESENTATION

Ambassador to the U.S.: Batu KUTELIA.

U.S. Ambassador to Georgia: John R. BASS.

Permanent Representative to the UN: Alexander LOMAIA.

IGO Memberships (Non-UN): BSEC, CEUR, EBRD, Interpol, IOM, OSCE, WCO, WTO.

GERMANY

Federal Republic of Germany
Bundesrepublik Deutschland

Note: Following Federal Assembly elections on September 27, 2009, the seat distribution was as follows: Christian Democratic Union / Christian Social Union (CDU/CSU), 239; Social Democratic Party, 146; Free Democratic Party (FDP), 93; the Left, 76; and Alliance '90/The Greens, 68. Chancellor Angela Merkel (CDU/CSU) was reelected by the Federal Assembly on October 28, 2009.

Political Status: Divided into British, French, Soviet, and U.S. occupation zones in July 1945; Federal Republic of Germany under democratic parliamentary regime established in Western zones on May 23, 1949; German Democratic Republic established under Communist auspices in Soviet zone on October 7, 1949; unified as the Federal Republic of Germany on October 3, 1990.

Area: 137,854 sq. mi. (357,041 sq. km.).

Population: 82,360,000 (2008E).

Major Urban Centers (2007E): BERLIN (3,416,255), Hamburg (1,770,629), Munich (1,311,573), Cologne (995,397), Frankfurt am Main (659,021), Stuttgart (597,176), Düsseldorf (581,122), Bremen (547,769), Hannover (518,069), Leipzig (510,512), Dresden (507,513), Nürnberg (503,110), Bonn (316,416). Parliament voted in June 1991 to relocate the capital from Bonn to Berlin; the actual transfer occurred during 1999–2000. A 1994 Berlin-Bonn law defined the former capital as a "federal city," and many government and international offices continue to operate there.

Official Language: German.

Monetary Unit: Euro (market rate December 1, 2009: 1 euro = $1.51US).

Federal President: Horst KÖHLER (Christian Democratic Union); elected by the Federal Convention on May 23, 2004, and sworn in on July 1 for a five-year term; reelected for a second five-year term on May 23, 2009, succeeding Johannes RAU (Social Democratic Party).

Federal Chancellor: (*See headnote.*) Angela MERKEL (Christian Democratic Union); elected by the Federal Assembly and sworn in on November 22, 2005, to succeed Gerhard SCHRÖDER (Social Democratic Party) following legislative elections of September 18.

THE COUNTRY

Germany's commanding position in Central Europe and its industrious population have made it a significant factor in modern European and world affairs, despite the political fragmentation that has characterized much of its history. Flat and low-lying in the north and increasingly mountainous to the south, the country combines abundant agricultural land with rich deposits of coal and other minerals and a strategic position astride the main European river systems. A small group of Danish speakers is located in the northwest, and a vaguely Polish group of Sorbian speakers inhabits the southeast of the former German Democratic Republic (GDR, or East Germany); otherwise, the indigenous population is remarkably homogeneous. On the other hand, large numbers of Turkish and other foreign workers who entered the Federal Republic of Germany (FRG, or West Germany) after World War II have more recently been joined by a flood of asylum seekers and other immigrants. (Germany's once substantial Jewish population was virtually destroyed during the Nazi period in 1933–1945 and presently numbers only about 100,000, mostly immigrants from the former Soviet Union.) Protestantism, chiefly Evangelical Lutheranism, is the declared religion of about 38 percent of the population, with Roman Catholics numbering about 34 percent. Women made up 46 percent of the labor force in 2006 but remained greatly underrepresented in federal and state governmental and legislative bodies.

Although highly industrialized prior to World War II, the German economy exhibited major regional variations that, coupled with quite dissimilar postwar military occupation policies in the east and the west, yielded divergent patterns of reconstruction and development. West Germany—with a greater resource base than East Germany, substantial financial assistance from the Western allies, and a strong commitment to free enterprise—recovered rapidly. Its industry expanded greatly, and by the 1960s the country had become the strongest economic power in Western Europe. Communist East Germany recovered more slowly, although it eventually experienced a surge in development that by 1990 had placed it among the top dozen nations in industrial output and second only to the Union of Soviet Socialist Republics (USSR) in Eastern Europe.

Political reunification on October 3, 1990, was preceded by the entry into force on July 1 of a State Treaty establishing an economic, monetary, and social union of the two Germanies. The principal objectives of the treaty were transition from a socialist to a market economy in the east, replacement of the East German currency by the West German deutsche mark, and economic integration. Particular attention was given to largely obsolete capital stock, severe environmental pollution, and uncertainties about property rights in the former Communist territory. However, compounded by international recession, the economic problems surrounding reunification proved to be much greater than anticipated.

The resilience of Germany's newly united economy was tested in 1993, when GDP fell by 2 percent, the most severe decline since 1945. Growth of more than 2 percent in the following years did not halt the rise in unemployment, which reached 9.5 percent in 1997.

A brief uptick in the economy in the late 1990s was extended through 2000, when annual GDP growth of 3 percent was recorded. However, Germany's economic stagnation resumed thereafter, with annual GDP declining by 0.1 percent in 2003 as unemployment reached a postwar high of 10.7 percent. The government passed a variety of free-market reforms in December, including an $11 billion tax cut package, cuts to unemployment benefits, and a relaxation of employee layoff rules for small businesses, although it was forced to compromise with leftist elements in the cabinet and legislature on deeper economic reforms. GDP increased annually by slightly more than 1 percent in 2004 and 2005, and unemployment soared to 12.6 percent, its highest level since 1933. The unemployment was particularly severe in the east, where more than 20 percent of workers were jobless. The "grand coalition" government installed in 2005 pledged to address structural weaknesses in the labor market, promote job creation, and reduce spending. Labor reforms introduced in 2005, known as Hartz IV and representing the largest overhaul to Germany's welfare system in decades, aimed to cut the number of long-term jobless but sparked massive protests over cuts to unemployment benefits.

Also in 2005, Germany's deficit was higher than the European Union (EU) standard (no more than 3 percent of GDP) for the fifth year in a row. However, the deficit dropped below the EU benchmark in 2006 as GDP grew by 2.5 percent. Annual GDP growth expanded to 2.5 percent in 2007, owing in large part to a significant increase in revenues from exports. Meanwhile, the inflation rate increased by 2.2 percent because of rising food and energy costs and continued to climb into the first quarter of 2008. In mid-2008 the economy began to contract as a result of the global economic recession; some German banks were heavily invested in the collapsing U.S. housing market. By October, Germany had experienced consecutive quarterly declines in GDP growth, meeting the official definition of an economic recession. The economy still felt the effects of the global downturn in 2009, as demand for exports slowed and unemployment neared 9 percent. Meanwhile, the International Monetary Fund forecast a contraction in annual GDP growth of 6 percent in 2009, though industrial production and the trade surplus had improved by midyear.

GOVERNMENT AND POLITICS

Political background. Germany's history as a modern nation dates from the Franco-Prussian War of 1870–1871 and the proclamation in 1871 of the German Empire, the result of efforts by Otto von BISMARCK and others to convert a loose confederation of German-speaking territories into a single political entity led by the Prussian House of Hohenzollern. Defeated by a coalition of powers in World War I, the German Empire disintegrated and was replaced in 1919 by

the Weimar Republic, whose chronic economic and political instability paved the way for the rise of the National Socialist (Nazi) Party and the installation of Adolf HITLER as chancellor in 1933. Under a totalitarian ideology imposed on Germany after World War I that stressed nationalism, anti-Communism, anti-Semitism, and removal of the disabled, Hitler converted the Weimar Republic into an authoritarian one-party state—the so-called Third Reich—and embarked upon a policy of aggressive expansionism that led to the outbreak of World War II in 1939 and, ultimately, to defeat of the Nazi regime by the Allies in 1945.

Following Germany's unconditional surrender on May 8, 1945, the country was divided into zones of military occupation assigned to forces of the United States, Britain, France, and the Soviet Union, whose governments assumed all powers of administration pending the reestablishment of a German governmental authority. Berlin, likewise divided into sectors, was made a separate area under joint quadripartite control with a view to its becoming the seat of the eventual central German government. Elsewhere, the territories east of the Oder and Neisse rivers were placed under Polish administration; East Prussia was divided into Soviet and Polish spheres; and the Saar was attached economically to France.

At the Potsdam Conference in July–August 1945, the American, British, and Soviet leaders agreed to treat Germany as a single economic unit and to ensure parallel political development in the four occupation zones, but the emergence of sharp differences between the Soviet Union and its wartime allies soon interfered. Among other things, Soviet occupation policies prevented implementation of the single economic unit plan, forcing the Western powers to adopt joint measures for their zones only. Protesting a proposed currency reform by its Western counterparts, the Soviet Union in June 1948 instituted a blockade of the land and water routes to Berlin that was maintained until May 1949, prompting Britain and the United States, with French ground support, to resort to a large-scale airlift to supply the city's western sectors.

Having failed to agree with the Soviet Union on measures for the whole of Germany, the three Western powers resolved to merge their zones of occupation as a step toward establishing a democratic state in western Germany. A draft constitution for the West German federal state was approved by a specially elected parliamentary assembly on May 8, 1949, and the Federal Republic of Germany (FRG), with its capital in Bonn, was proclaimed on May 23. The Soviet Union protested these actions and on October 7 announced the establishment in its occupation zone of the German Democratic Republic (GDR), with East Berlin as its capital. An anti-Communist workers' uprising in East Germany in 1953 was ruthlessly suppressed by GDR and Soviet forces.

In West Germany the occupation structure was gradually converted into a contractual relationship based on the equality of the parties involved. Under the London and Paris agreements of 1954, the FRG gained sovereignty on May 5, 1955, when it was admitted to the North Atlantic Treaty Organization (NATO) and the Western European Union (WEU), while on January 1, 1957, the Saar was returned as the result of a plebiscite held in 1955. The Soviet-backed GDR had meanwhile also been declared fully sovereign and was accorded formal recognition by Communist, but not Western, governments. Although Berlin remained technically under four-power control, East Berlin was incorporated into the GDR as its capital, while West Berlin, without being granted parliamentary voting rights, was accorded a status similar to that of a *Länd* (state) of the FRG. The FRG-GDR border served as the focal point for much of the Cold War confrontation of the 1950s and 1960s, with intermittent crises triggered by Soviet/East German interruptions or threats of interruption of land access to West Berlin. This tension, accompanied by accelerating immigration from the East to the West via the open borders inside Berlin, induced the eastern authorities in August 1961 to build the Berlin Wall.

During the eight years following proclamation of the FRG in 1949, the Christian Democratic Union—CDU (*Christlich Demokratische Union Deutschlands*) under Chancellor Konrad ADENAUER maintained coalition governments with the Free Democratic Party (*Freie Demokratische Partei*—FDP) and other minor groups, thereby excluding the Social Democratic Party (*Sozialdemokratische Partei Deutschlands*—SPD) from power. In 1957 the CDU and its Bavarian affiliate, the Christian Social Union (*Christlich-Soziale Union*—CSU), won a clear majority of legislative seats, but in 1961 and again in 1965 they were forced to renew their pact with the FDP. In 1966 disagreements over financial policy led the FDP to withdraw from the coalition, and Ludwig ERHARD, who had succeeded Adenauer as chancellor three years earlier, was obliged to resign. On December 1 a CDU-CSU/SPD "grand coalition" government was inaugurated, with Kurt-Georg KIESINGER of the CDU as chancellor.

As a result of the election of September 1969, Willy BRANDT, SPD leader as well as vice chancellor and foreign minister of the CDU-CSU/SPD government, became chancellor at the head of an SPD/FDP coalition. Although the coalition was renewed after the November 1972 balloting, widespread labor unrest early in 1974 attested to the increasing inability of the Brandt administration to cope with domestic economic difficulties, including a record postwar inflation rate of more than 7.5 percent; however, it was the revelation that one of the chancellor's personal political aides was an East German espionage agent that prompted Brandt's resignation on May 6 and his replacement shortly thereafter by former finance minister Helmut SCHMIDT. Former FDP foreign minister Walter SCHEEL, who had served briefly as interim chancellor following Brandt's resignation, was elected federal president on May 15 and was sworn in on July 1, succeeding the SPD's Gustav HEINEMANN.

In a close election on October 3, 1976, the SPD/FDP coalition emerged with a substantially reduced majority of 253 out of 496 seats in the *Bundestag* (Federal Assembly), and on December 15 Schmidt was reconfirmed as chancellor. However, growing Christian Democratic strength at the state level gave the CDU-CSU an overall majority in the Federal Convention, which is responsible for electing the president; as a result, *Bundestag* president Karl CARSTENS, the CDU candidate, was elected on May 23, 1979, to succeed President Scheel, who had decided not to seek a second term after being denied all-party support.

Chancellor Schmidt remained in office following the *Bundestag* election of October 5, 1980, in which the SPD gained 4 seats and the FDP gained 14. The CDU-CSU, led in the campaign by Franz-Josef STRAUSS, minister-president of Bavaria and CSU chair, lost 17 seats.

An extensive reorganization of the Schmidt cabinet in April 1982 pointed up increasing disagreement within the SPD/FDP coalition on matters of defense and economic policy. On September 17 all four FDP ministers resigned, precipitating a "constructive vote of no confidence" on October 1 that resulted in the appointment of Dr. Helmut KOHL as head of a CDU-CSU/FDP government. Subsequently, in mid-December, Kohl called for a nonconstructive confidence vote that was deliberately lost by CDU abstentions, thus permitting the chancellor to call an early election. In the balloting on March 6, 1983, the three-party coalition won 278 of 498 lower house seats, allowing Kohl to form a new government on March 29.

The governing coalition's mandate was renewed in balloting on January 25, 1987, although the CDU-CSU share of the vote (44.3 percent) was the lowest since the founding of the West German state in 1949. The SPD did marginally better than opinion polls had predicted, drawing 37 percent, compared with 38.2 percent in 1983. Gaining strength at the expense of the major parties were the FDP, which was awarded an additional ministry (for a total of four) in the government formed on March 11, and the Greens, whose parliamentary representation increased from 27 to 42.

In October 1989, in response to political upheavals elsewhere in Eastern Europe, antiregime demonstrations took place in East Berlin and quickly spread to other major cities. In an attempt to quell the growing unrest, East German authorities abolished the restriction on foreign travel for GDR citizens on November 9 and immediately began dismantling sections of the infamous Berlin Wall that had long divided the city. Subsequently, as the Communist regime faced imminent collapse (for details, see the 1990 *Handbook*), appeals for reunification resurfaced. On February 6, 1990, Kohl announced his readiness "to open immediate negotiations on economic and monetary union." A positive GDR response resulted in agreement on a common monetary system by the German finance ministers in mid-May, effective July 1. On the same day, all border restrictions between East Germany and West Germany were eliminated.

The crucial succeeding stages toward reunification were (1) Chancellor Kohl's agreement with Soviet leader Mikhail Gorbachev on July 15–16, 1990, that unified Germany could be a member of NATO; (2) agreement at the "two-plus-four" (the two Germanies plus the four wartime Allies) forum in Paris on July 17 that international legality should be bestowed on Germany by a "treaty of settlement" rather than a peace treaty; (3) the East German parliament's resolution on August 23 that the five newly restored eastern *Bundesländer* (or *Länder,* federal states)—Brandenburg, Mecklenburg–West Pomerania, Saxony, Saxony-Anhalt, and Thuringia—should accede to the Federal Republic; (4) the signing in Berlin on August 31 of a formal unification treaty between East Germany and West Germany; and (5) the signing in Moscow on September 12 by the two-plus-four states of the Treaty on the Final Settlement with Respect to Germany, formally terminating the wartime victors' responsibilities for Germany and Berlin.

On October 1, 1990, the four World War II Allies formally suspended their occupation rights, and in a jubilant midnight ceremony in Berlin on October 2–3 the two Germanies were united. On October 4, 144 members of East Germany's disbanded legislature (*Volkskammer*) joined West German legislators in the inaugural session of an expanded *Bundestag* at Berlin's *Reichstag* building, while 4 ministers from the former GDR, including its only non-Communist minister-president, Lothar DE MAIZIÈRE, entered the Kohl government as ministers without portfolio. At elections held October 14 in the re-created eastern *Länder,* the CDU won control in all but one parliament (Brandenburg, where it ran second to the SPD).

On December 2, 1990, at the first free all-German election in 58 years, Kohl's CDU-CSU/FDP coalition captured 398 of 662 *Bundestag* seats with 54.8 percent share of the vote, while the opposition SPD secured 239 seats on a vote share of 33.5 percent. On January 17, 1991, Kohl was formally reinvested as chancellor to head a new government containing 11 CDU, 4 CSU, and 5 FDP ministers.

The unexpected pace of German unification strongly influenced the policy agenda of the now-enlarged Federal Republic, particularly in regard to its ongoing commitments to the West and the European Community (EC, subsequently the EU). Among other acute problems, the government faced a need for near-total economic conversion in the east, a wave of immigration coupled with mounting antiforeigner feeling, and a variety of political and legal entanglements involving secret police activities in the former GDR and human rights violations committed under the cloak of East German legality.

Because of the involvement of West German expertise and capital, the process of converting the long centrally planned East Germany to a "social market economy" moved forward more quickly and with less short-term difficulty than in neighboring ex-Communist countries. Most leaders conceded, however, that the challenges far exceeded pre-unification expectations. The conversion process was spearheaded by the Trust Agency (*Treuhandanstalt*), responsible for privatizing nearly 8,000 state-owned firms and large agricultural enterprises. After a slow start, the number of sales reached 500 per month by early 1992, although returns were substantially less than anticipated, in part because of the obsolescence of most East German industry, chronic environmental pollution, and the legal uncertainty of deeds subject to claim from pre-Communist owners.

Economic problems resulting from unification heightened popular disquiet over immigration levels, as reflected in substantial electoral gains for the extreme right in successive state and local elections in 1991–1992 and in widening antiforeigner violence. Particular concern arose over open asylum for political refugees, of whom a record number of 438,000 lodged applications in 1992, partly as a result of the population exodus from former Yugoslavia. The government responded to the racial violence by banning a number of extremist groups and by decreeing harsher sentences for those convicted of such activity. It also responded to public concern by securing an amendment to the law on asylum (in May 1993) that allowed authorities to refuse entry to those deemed to be economic migrants. However, the government in mid-June indicated that it would ease restrictions on the attainment of citizenship by aliens, while maintaining the "blood principle" of 1913 that conferred the right to nationality on those of ethnic German ancestry irrespective of place of birth or current location. (In January 1999 reform of the citizen law granted automatic citizenship to German-born children of long-term residents and allowed immigrants to seek naturalization following eight years of residence.)

Alarmed by the spiraling costs of unification, the Kohl government on January 19, 1993, led a drive for a "solidarity pact" designed to finance the estimated $60 billion annual cost of the subsidies required by the eastern region through increased taxation and expenditure cuts. While initially rejected by the SPD for being socially unjust, federal/state negotiations resulted in formal signature of the pact on March 13.

The coalition's standing, already damaged by economic recession, was further impaired in 1993 by a series of ministerial resignations for alleged misconduct. In addition, Kohl's credibility suffered when his controversial nominee for the federal presidency was forced to withdraw because of media reaction to his intensely right-wing views. Subsequently, another CDU nominee, Constitutional Court president Roman HERZOG, was elected to the presidency on May 23, 1994, by a slim 53 percent majority of Federal Convention votes.

State and partial local balloting in the early months of 1994 yielded no clear pattern of voter sympathies, much attention thereby being focused on the all-Germany European Parliament poll on June 12. The results showed that the CDU-CSU had overcome a Europe-wide swing against incumbent parties by increasing its seat total from 32 to 47 in a German contingent that increased from 81 to 99. The European results proved to be a portent, in that the Kohl coalition retained a narrow majority in the federal elections held on October 16. The crucial outcome was the FDP's unexpected surmounting of the 5 percent barrier, its 6.9 percent giving it 47 seats, enough to provide a 10-seat majority for another CDU-CSU/FDP coalition.

The new *Bundestag* duly reelected Kohl as chancellor on November 15, 1994, by 338 votes to 333. Two days later the fifth Kohl government, again a coalition of the CDU-CSU and the FDP, was sworn in, with much the same personnel as its predecessor but with the FDP contingent reduced from five to three ministers. Mixed state election results in 1995 were followed in March 1996 by state contests that strengthened the coalition parties overall, especially the FDP.

The Kohl forces suffered a string of defeats in the 1998 state elections, which included a surprising 13 percent showing in Saxony-Anhalt by the German People's Union (*Deutsche Volksunion*—DVU), which became the first extreme-right party to win seats in an eastern state legislature. The state elections foreshadowed the results of the September 27 *Bundestag* contest in which the SPD, running its reelected premier of Lower Saxony, Gerhard SCHRÖDER, defeated Kohl's CDU-CSU, 40.9 percent to 35.1 percent. Kohl thus became the first incumbent chancellor to be turned out in postwar Germany, and Schröder became the first Social Democratic chancellor in 18 years. Schröder took office on October 27 as the leader of a center-left ("red-green") coalition government with the environmentally oriented Greens (*Die Grünen*), who had won 47 seats with a 6.7 percent vote share.

On May 23, 1999, the SPD's Johannes RAU, former minister-president of North Rhine–Westphalia, was elected federal president in a second round of balloting by the Federal Convention. Sworn in on July 1, Rau became the first president from the SPD since 1974.

Facing polls that showed severe erosion in support for the administration in advance of the September 23, 2002, balloting for the *Bundestag,* Chancellor Schröder launched a highly vocal campaign against U.S. policy toward Iraq that appeared to resonate with the electorate. Consequently, the SPD and Alliance '90/The Greens combined for 206 seats, enough for the two parties to maintain their governing coalition. Later in the year, Schröder announced that priorities for his second term would include a number of potentially unpopular fiscal reforms, known as Agenda 2010, including new limits on unemployment compensation and pensions, more-flexible labor laws, and an increase in the percentage payment required from individuals for health care. The cuts in social spending prompted wide-scale protests in late 2003 and appeared to contribute to a series of disappointing SPD performances in state elections. By early 2004 public opinion had again turned against the SPD, and Horst KÖHLER of the CDU was elected president of the republic in the first round of balloting in the Federal Convention.

With the SPD's popularity continuing to decline, Chancellor Schröder deliberately lost a no-confidence vote on July 1, 2005, and asked for early elections. President Köhler dissolved the *Bundestag* on July 21. In new balloting on September 18, the SPD led all parties with 222 seats, although the governing SPD/Greens coalition failed to secure a majority. Meanwhile, the CDU-CSU combined for 225 seats, although the conservatives too were unable to put together a working legislative majority with their longtime ally, the FDP. (Both the CDU and the SPD rejected forming a coalition with the Left, a new alliance that had won 54 seats [see Political Parties, below].) Consequently, after six weeks of intense negotiation it became clear that a CDU-CSU/SPD "grand coalition" represented the only hope for even short-term stability. Angela MERKEL of the CDU was sworn in on November 22 as chancellor and head of a government that included eight ministers from the SPD, six (including Merkel) from the CDU, and two from the CSU.

In November 2007 the SPD's nominee for vice chancellor and labor affairs minister, Franz MÜNTEFERING, resigned, reportedly for family reasons, though he had become a vocal critic of the coalition's free market policies. Müntefering was replaced by foreign affairs minister Frank-Walter STEINMEIER at the vice chancellery and Olaf SCHOLZ at the Labor Ministry.

Further cabinet changes occurred following the September 2008 Bavarian state election, in which the CSU lost its majority. The CSU's Horst SEEHOFER, who had resigned as agriculture minister to become party chair in an effort to revamp the party, became prime minister of Bavaria. He made several minor changes to the cabinet in 2008 and early 2009.

In May 2009 German president Köhler was reelected to a second term by the Federal Convention with 613 votes, defeating the SPD's Gesine SCHWAN, who received 503 votes, and Left Party candidate Peter SODANN, with 91 votes.

In European parliamentary elections on June 7, 2009, the CDU received 30.7 percent of the vote, followed by the SPD with 20.8 percent, and the Alliance '90/The Greens, 12 percent. The FDP, the Left, and the CSU also won seats.

Constitution and government. Germany, under the Basic Law (*Grundgesetz*) of May 23, 1949, is a federal republic in which areas of authority are both shared and divided between the component states (*Länder*) and the federal government (*Bundesregierung*). Responsibility in such areas as economic, social, and health policy is held jointly, with the federal government establishing general guidelines, the states assuming administration, and both typically providing funds. Each state (*Land*) has its own parliament elected by universal suffrage, with authority to legislate in all matters—including education, police, and broadcasting—not expressly reserved to the federal government. The latter is responsible for foreign affairs, defense, and such matters as citizenship, migration, customs, posts, and telecommunications.

The major federal components are the head of state, or federal president (*Bundespräsident*); a cabinet headed by a chancellor (*Bundeskanzler*); and a bicameral parliament consisting of the Federal Council (*Bundesrat*) and the Federal Assembly (*Bundestag*). *Bundesrat* members are appointed and recalled by the state governments; their role is limited to those areas of policy that fall under joint federal-state responsibility, although they have veto powers where specified state interests are involved. The *Bundestag,* elected by universal suffrage under a mixed direct and proportional-representation system, is the major legislative organ. It elects the chancellor by an absolute majority but cannot remove the chancellor except by electing a successor. The president, whose functions are mainly ceremonial, is elected by a special Federal Convention (*Bundesversammlung*) consisting of the members of the *Bundestag* and an equal number of members chosen by the state legislatures. Ministers are appointed by the president on the advice of the chancellor.

The judiciary is headed by the Constitutional Court (*Bundesverfassungsgericht*), with the two houses of parliament each electing half its judges, and also includes a Supreme Federal Court (*Bundesgerichtshof*) as well as federal administrative, financial, labor, and social courts. While the constitution guarantees the maintenance of human rights and civil liberties, certain limitations in time of emergency were detailed in a controversial set of amendments adopted in 1968. In addition, the Constitutional Court is authorized to outlaw political parties whose aims or activities are found to endanger "the basic libertarian democratic order" or its institutional structure.

The Federal Republic of Germany currently encompasses 16 *Länder,* 10 from the former West Germany and 6 (†; identified in the table below) from the former East Germany. (The government proposed reducing the number of states to 8 in the mid-1990s, but that plan ran into difficulty at its first electoral test in May 1996 when Brandenburg voted against merger with Berlin.)

State and Capital	*Area (sq. mi.)*	*Population (2008E)*
Baden-Württemberg (Stuttgart)	13,803	10,756,000
Bavaria (Munich)	27,238	12,529,000
Berlin (Berlin)†	341	3,420,000
Brandenburg (Potsdam)†	15,044	2,534,000
Bremen (Bremen)	156	668,000
Hamburg (Hamburg)	291	1,769,000
Hesse (Wiesbaden)	8,151	6,057,000
Lower Saxony (Hannover)	18,311	7,972,000
Mecklenburg–West Pomerania (Schwerin)†	6,080	1,680,000
North Rhine–Westphalia (Düsseldorf)	13,149	18,003,000
Rhineland-Palatinate (Mainz)	7,658	4,044,000
Saarland (Saarbrücken)	992	1,038,000
Saxony (Dresden)†	6,839	4,224,000
Saxony-Anhalt (Magdeburg)†	7,837	2,410,000
Schleswig-Holstein (Kiel)	6,053	2,836,000
Thuringia (Erfurt)†	5,872	2,285,000

A 32-member commission was appointed in 2003 to propose revision of the constitution to redistribute certain authority from the states to the federal level in order to provide greater efficiency in, among other areas, implementing economic policy and providing social services. Part of the proposal was that the *Bundesrat* (controlled by the states) would accept reduced veto authority over federal legislation. Negotiations in the commission collapsed in December 2004 over the question of reducing regional control of education. However, general agreement was reached in early 2006 on legislation regarding "federalism reform," prompted in part by the recent installation of a "grand coalition" government. Under the accord, the number of laws subject to veto by the *Bundesrat* would be reduced from 60 percent of the total to approximately 35 percent. In return for the dilution of power at the national level, the states were to be given greater authority over education, the penal system, and the civil service. The constitutional amendments were approved by the parliament during June–July, and a schedule for their gradual implementation was established. Significantly, however, the amendments did not address the contentious issues of revising the formula for distribution of tax revenues between the states and the national government or the proposed merger of small states to make them more "competitive" with the larger states.

Federalism reform was successful in updating Germany's antiterrorism laws, giving federal law enforcement "preventative power" in averting terrorism, and in handing the federal government sole authority to enact environmental law.

Foreign relations. The post–World War II division of Germany and the anti-Soviet and anti-Communist outlook of most West Germans resulted in very close relations between the Federal Republic and the Western Allies, whose support was long deemed essential both to the survival of the FRG and to the eventual reunification of Germany on a democratic basis. The FRG became a key member of NATO, the EC, and the WEU as well as of the Organization for Economic Cooperation and Development (OECD), the Council of Europe, and other multilateral bodies aimed at closer political and economic cooperation. Participation by the GDR in multilateral organizations was for more than two decades limited primarily to the Soviet-backed Council for Mutual Economic Assistance and the Warsaw Treaty Organization.

In August 1970 FRG chancellor Willy Brandt signed a nonaggression treaty with the Soviet Union. The following December he concluded a treaty with Poland by which the Federal Republic gave de facto recognition to Polish acquisition of nearly one-quarter of Germany's pre–World War II territory.

The "two Germanies" concept acquired legal standing with the negotiation in November 1972 of the Basic Treaty (*Grundvertrag*) normalizing relations between the FRG and the GDR. While the agreement stopped short of a mutual extension of full diplomatic recognition, it affirmed the "inviolability" of the existing border and provided for the exchange of "permanent representative missions" by the two governments, thus seeming to rule out the possibility of German reunification. On September 5, 1974, following ratification of the Basic Treaty, both Germanies were admitted to the United Nations.

A treaty voiding the 1938 Munich Agreement was negotiated with Czechoslovakia in June 1973 and ratified a year later. The initiation of this program of postwar "reconciliation" earned a Nobel Peace Prize for Brandt in 1971. (The territorial implications of the treaty were reaffirmed by the Final Act of the 1975 Helsinki Conference on Security and Cooperation in Europe [CSCE] and by a treaty between Poland and newly unified Germany on November 14, 1990.)

Formal unification on October 3, 1990, was made possible by a series of "two-plus-four" talks that began on February 13 and concluded on September 12 with the signing of a Treaty on the Final Settlement with Respect to Germany (see Political background, above). The document was, in actuality, a long-delayed World War II peace treaty, under which the wartime Allies terminated "their rights and responsibilities relating to Berlin and to Germany as a whole," with corresponding "quadripartite agreements, decisions, and practices" and "all related Four Power institutions" being dissolved. For their part, the German signatories agreed to assert no territorial claims against other states; to forswear aggressive war; to renounce the manufacture or possession of nuclear, biological, and chemical weapons; to station only non-NATO forces in the east until completion of Soviet troop withdrawals by the end of 1994; and to reduce their overall armed forces from 577,000 (including East German units) to 370,000 by 1995. Collaterally, West Germany on September 13 signed a Treaty on Good-Neighborliness, Partnership, and Cooperation with the USSR, which was later accepted by Russia and the other Soviet successor states.

Because of the constitutional ban on deployment of German forces outside the NATO area, Germany did not participate in the 1991 Gulf war, although it sent air force units to Turkey (a NATO member) and made a substantial financial contribution to the U.S.-led effort. In November 1991 Bonn issued a ban on arms shipments to Turkey in the wake of charges that German weapons had been used against minority Kurds.

Preunification predictions that the newly enlarged Germany would play a larger and more independent role in world affairs materialized in the early 1990s. Thus, Germany led the world in direct monetary assistance to the Russian Federation. More controversially, Germany used its new diplomatic leverage to insist on speedy EC recognition of the secessionist Yugoslav republics of Slovenia and Croatia (and later Bosnia and Herzegovina), overriding the more cautious approach of Britain and France. When the former Yugoslavia descended into bloody ethnic conflict in 1992, the government authorized a German warship and three reconnaissance aircraft to join a sanctions-monitoring UN/WEU force in the Adriatic, although the German opposition claimed that the deployment was illegal.

Seeking to ground German unification in an EC framework, the Kohl government was firmly committed to the EC's Maastricht Treaty on political and economic union. Ratification of the treaty was completed by the *Bundestag* in December 1992, subject to a Constitutional Court ruling that any future steps toward European union required specific German parliamentary approval. Germany also signed an agreement with France on May 22, 1992, providing for the creation by 1995 of a joint Franco-German army corps, envisaged as the nucleus of a future European military force (see WEU article).

Responding to international criticism of Germany's nonparticipation in the 1991 Gulf war, the government in January 1993 introduced draft constitutional amendments that would enable German troops to be deployed in UN-approved peacekeeping and humanitarian operations. The immediate urgency of the issue lay in whether German air force personnel could participate in implementing the Security Council's decision of March 31, 1993, to enforce a "no-fly" zone over Bosnia and Herzegovina. In an interim ruling on April 8, the Constitutional Court upheld a majority cabinet decision that German crews could participate in UN-approved NATO enforcement actions. On April 21 cabinet approval was given to the dispatch of 1,600 German troops to participate in the UN operation in Somalia. In a definitive ruling on July 12, 1994, the Constitutional Court decreed that German forces could participate in collective defense or security operations outside the NATO area, provided *Bundestag* approval was given in each case.

In the wake of visits to Germany by Russian president Boris Yeltsin and U.S. president Bill Clinton in May and July 1994, respectively, Russian troops completed their withdrawal from Berlin on August 31, with the last Allied troops leaving the city on September 8. Finally cleared of Russian troops, Germany stepped up its diplomatic initiatives in Eastern Europe, supporting the quest of its immediate eastern neighbors to join the EU. In the case of the Czech Republic, however, the question of the ethnic Germans expelled from the Sudetenland at the end of World War II remained problematic, despite the signing of a Czech-German declaration of reconciliation in 1997. Germany insisted that a resolution of the compensation issue should precede the Czech Republic's EU admission. (See the article on the Czech Republic for further information.)

The Franco-German axis remained strong in the EU, the two countries committing to speedy economic and monetary union in the EU, even if only an "inner core" were ready to participate at the outset. Germany also worked closely with France on evolving plans for a European wing of NATO—empowered to act independently of the United States—that contributed to increasing readiness in 1995 to deploy German forces in foreign theaters. Following the allocation of German warplanes and 1,300 troops to the European "rapid reaction force" sent to Bosnia in June, parliamentary approval was given in December for a 4,000-strong German contribution to the Implementation Force (IFOR) set up under the Dayton peace agreement for Bosnia.

In October 1998 Chancellor-elect Gerhard Schröder visited Paris to assure the French that Germany remained committed to EU monetary union and strong economic ties with its leading trading partner. Despite preelection promises by Schröder that his government would maintain continuity in foreign policy, the new "red-green" coalition soon raised concern within NATO in November when Bonn tentatively suggested that the alliance renounce its first-strike nuclear policy.

Both the government and the opposition supported EU expansion in 2004, although Germany joined France in backing provisions in the proposed EU constitution that would preserve the influence of the larger states. (See article on the EU for additional information.) In May 2005 both houses of the German legislature approved the proposed new EU constitution.

Meanwhile, Germany's relations with the United States were severely compromised by Schröder's strong opposition to Washington's Iraq policies. Among the consequences was an announcement by the United States that 35,000 of the 75,000 U.S. troops in Germany would be deployed to other countries.

In January 2006 Chancellor Angela Merkel visited Washington and promised a "new chapter" in U.S.-German relations. She also initially endorsed Schröder's concept of a "strategic relationship" with Russia, reportedly concluding that business interests trumped German concerns over the perceived "autocratic drift" in Russia. Following her appointment to the rotating presidency of the EU in January 2007, Merkel earned praise for facilitating the apparent revival of the EU's constitutional reform process and for promoting improved EU-U.S. economic relations.

Germany contributed naval and air forces to the UN peacekeeping force in Lebanon in 2006 after the Israeli-Hezbollah war and increased its troops in the NATO-led mission in Afghanistan by 500 (bringing its total commitment to approximately 3,500 troops) in March 2007. In October the *Bundestag* extended the Afghanistan mission for another 12 months and capped German personnel there at 3,500. The parliamentary vote also limited the operation to the safer northern areas of the country and to the capital of Kabul, provoking a diplomatic spat with U.S.-led allies over which country would be responsible for the more dangerous operations in Afghanistan. The German government remained opposed to the U.S.-led war in Iraq, but Merkel cooperated with the United States on counterterrorism initiatives, including intelligence sharing and adopting a tougher policy on Iran's nuclear ambitions

Germany's diplomatic relationship with China soured in September 2007, when Merkel met with the Dalai Lama in Berlin, a move Chinese authorities said violated Germany's commitment to the "one China" policy.

In March 2008 Merkel became the first German chancellor to address the Israeli Knesset, declaring that Germany would be "a loyal partner and friend" to Israel and characterizing Iran's threats against Israel as tantamount to threats against Germany. In late 2008 Merkel's relationships with other European leaders were marked by tension, as some viewed her as taking an isolationist approach to the global financial crisis. Dubbed "Madam No" for her refusal to embrace a massive EU stimulus package, Merkel later accepted a spending package and other measures.

U.S. presidential candidate Barack Obama's high-profile speech at the Brandenburg Gate in July 2008 was seen as boding well for improved relations with Germany. However, after Obama's election, friction between the two administrations arose over his support for a bailout of the U.S. auto industry, which Merkel saw as giving American automakers a competitive advantage. Additionally, a rift occurred in June 2009 over Germany's refusal to accept nine prisoners of the Chinese ethnic Uigher minority from the U.S. detention center at Guantánamo Bay, Cuba, citing a lack of information on whether they were a security risk. In August, Germany strengthened support for Georgia to eventually join NATO and called for a halt to all military action following Russian attacks against it in what was widely regarded as a violation of Georgia's sovereignty. Relations with Poland were strained in February 2009, when the German League of Expellees' nominated Erika STEINBACH, regarded as a revanchist, to the board of a new museum commemorating the postwar expulsion of millions of ethnic Germans from European territories. Her nomination was subsequently revoked.

Current issues. In the wake of the terrorist attacks against the United States in September 2001, Germany passed new domestic antiterrorism legislation and quickly launched a crackdown on radical Islamic groups. Germany also authorized troops for the U.S.-led military campaign in Afghanistan against al-Qaida and the Taliban, despite opposition to the deployment from the governing coalition's junior partner, Alliance '90/The Greens, that almost brought about the collapse of the government.

Continued economic doldrums appeared to drain popular support for the administration as elections loomed in September 2002, prompting Chancellor Schröder to campaign for reelection on a platform that strongly urged the United States not to invade Iraq. Germany also supported France's successful efforts in the UN Security Council to block a resolution that would have authorized force against Iraq. The hard stance on Iraq allowed the SPD and Alliance '90/The Greens to form another coalition government, following the 2002 poll, albeit with a reduced legislative majority.

The November 2005 federal elections brought Merkel to power as Germany's first female chancellor, who, at 51, was the youngest person to hold that position since the end of World War II. A physicist, she was also the first chancellor to have been born in the former East Germany. The *Bundestag* elected Merkel on the first ballot with 397 votes, well above the simple majority required but below the combined 448 seats of the new coalition. Observers said many SPD deputies did not support Merkel because they regarded the coalition's program as too politically conservative.

However, Merkel soon appeared to drop some of her bold proposals for economic liberalization, including a flat income tax rate of 25 percent and "decentralizing" wage negotiations by allowing companies to strike their own wage deals. Instead, Merkel pleased coalition partners by pledging to address the country's economic problems through a series of "small steps." During its first year of governing, the coalition took up proposed changes to health care, the minimum wage, and social welfare programs, among other policies. Conservative leaders from the states had begun in mid-2006 to press for reforms that had been promised to the business sector during the 2005 election campaign. In that regard, the government raised the retirement age from 65 to 67, lowered and simplified corporate taxes, and launched negotiations on pension and health care reform. In addition, the administration implemented massive hikes in the VAT and other taxes that greatly improved prospects for an eventual balanced budget.

In July 2006 the government renewed for five years the antiterrorist measures adopted in 2001 in the wake of a failed suicide bomber attack by radical Lebanese Islamists on a train in northern Germany. In October a restructuring of the military was approved to facilitate the use of German forces in multilateral foreign missions and to permit domestic deployment of armed forces during a national crisis. Meanwhile, German police continued their crackdown on ultra-right-wing groups, particularly those with extreme anti-immigrant stances.

By 2007 the economy had improved dramatically, with unemployment down by more than 1 million workers and German industry having reasserted itself as an important component of EU growth. Paradoxically, however, by the fall of 2007 the German population was reported to have lost its enthusiasm for the reforms that had apparently underpinned the recovery, expressing renewed support for greater "social justice" spending by the government and other left-oriented policies.

Growing concerns over terrorism led to the arrest of a number of Muslims charged with ties to radical Islamic groups abroad. In September 2007 officials claimed to have averted massive bomb attacks on the Frankfurt international airport and the U.S. air base at Ramstein, leading to the arrest of four suspects, dubbed the "Sauerland cell," whose members were said to have radical Islamic backgrounds.

Interior Minister Wolfgang SCHÄUBLE referred to the arrests to underpin arguments for a controversial expansion in government surveillance measures and the collection of biometric data for passports. Concerns over privacy infringement and ongoing sensitivity concerning Germany's past wartime abuses in the collection of information on citizens led to debate over the legality of some of the country's national security measures.

In response, the Interior Ministry issued repeated warnings about Germany's vulnerability to attacks from radical Islamists. In December Schäuble disclosed that an internal government report had come to a "worrying conclusion that a radical Islamic potential has developed in Germany." Further, in January 2008 a federal administrative court ruled that the "strategic telephone monitoring" instituted after the September 11 attacks in the United States was legal. However, in February the Constitutional Court ruled that data stored on personal computers is protected by the right of privacy, and secret searches via the Internet are permitted in exceptional cases with judicial approval. (In December, the *Bundesrat* approved a surveillance measure that requires judicial approval of secret police searches of computers via the Internet, even when investigators see an urgent need to act.)

As Germany dealt with the issue of potential terrorism, the government struggled with how to define the rights of Muslims, who make up some 2.7 million residents, primarily of Turkish descent. Political activity by Muslim groups has increased as immigration and citizenship laws have tightened. Disputes over wearing headscarves and building mosques have been particularly heated. In August 2008 the city council of Cologne approved a controversial plan for construction of a grand mosque, despite opposition from residents worried about an "Islamization" of the city.

In an effort to crackdown on potential tax evaders, federal prosecutors in 2008 began investigating hundreds of wealthy Germans who had opened bank accounts in the neighboring tax haven of Liechtenstein. The investigations added to the public's growing resentment over income disparity following a series of corporate corruption scandals.

As Germany's worst recession in six decades began to take hold in late October 2008, the government approved a series of measures to bolster the financial system. All personal bank deposits were guaranteed by the government, and $862 billion was approved to shore up banks, resulting in several of them becoming partially owned by the state. Meanwhile, the SPD gained support from the CDU for measures that would limit executive salaries and benefits. (The CDU had previously backed only voluntary limits on "excessive pay.") Ultimately, the government approved a measure aimed at banks that had received a government bailout, requiring them to impose a salary cap of $650,000. In November another two-year fiscal stimulus package of $22 billion was approved in an effort to further mitigate the effects of the recession. All of the measures prompted intense debate between the moderate and conservative wings of the CDU-CSU, and Merkel was seen as straddling both camps, initially dismissing a second stimulus package on the grounds that doing so could result in higher inflation and become a "senseless race to spend billions." After heavy lobbying by France and the United Kingdom, which believed that the stimulus package fell short of what was needed, Merkel agreed to an additional $86 billion in January 2009, saying that "extraordinary measures" were required.

The additional money was allocated to improve schools, roads, social benefits, and incentives to trade in old cars for newer, environmentally friendlier ones. Another $175 billion was approved for the creation of a "Germany fund" to provide companies an alternative to banks for loans and credit guarantees.

In February 2009 Michael Glos resigned as minister of economics, reportedly in protest of what he believed to be Merkel's straying from her conservative base. He was replaced by Karl-Theodor zu GUTTENBERG, who took a strict stance against government bailouts, particularly the rescue of the German carmaker Opel from the bankruptcy of its U.S. parent company, General Motors, on the grounds that companies should be held responsible for their poor business decisions. Meanwhile, in an effort to mitigate concerns over ballooning public debt, the states and federal government struck a deal to cap public borrowing and eliminate public debt increases by 2020. While domestic concerns were focused primarily on the economic downturn, the popular president, Horst Köhler, was reelected in May 2009 by a single vote, or 614 total, in first-round Federal Assembly balloting, thereby sparing the CDU a serious political blow ahead of September parliamentary elections. In another setback for the SPD, the party's vote share plunged to a record low 20.8 percent in the June European parliamentary election. Federal Assembly elections were held on September 27, 2009. (*See headnote.*)

POLITICAL PARTIES

Following unification in 1990, the established West German parties extended their operations into the former GDR, with considerable success, although the Party of Democratic Socialism (PDS)—successor to the former ruling (Communist) Socialist Unity Party of Germany (SED)—retained significant support in the eastern *Länder*. In federal and state elections, meeting the threshold of obtaining 5 percent of the vote made it difficult for minor parties to achieve legislative representation. Of the 22 parties that contested the October 1994 *Bundestag* election, only 6 were awarded seats, and 1 of those, the PDS, on an ancillary provision.

Under Germany's federal system, power at the state level provides opposition parties with an important counterbalance to the central government. As of May 2008 the CDU and SPD jointly governed Brandenburg, Mecklenberg–West Pomerania, Saxony, Saxony-Anhalt, and Schleswig-Holstein. (The SPD had a legislative plurality in Brandenburg and Mecklenberg–West Pomerania, while the CDU had a plurality in Saxony, Saxony-Anhalt, and Schleswig-Holstein.) A CDU/FDP coalition governed in Baden-Württemberg, Lower Saxony, and North Rhine–Westphalia. (The CDU held a legislative plurality in all of those states.) An SPD/Left coalition governed in Berlin, where the SPD secured a legislative plurality in the September 2006 election.

The CSU held a majority of the legislative seats and governed alone in Bavaria, while its federal partner, the CDU, held legislative majorities and governed alone in Saarland and Thuringia. The SPD retained a majority of seats in Rhineland-Palatinate in the March 2006 election and decided to govern alone. A coalition of the SPD and Alliance '90/The Greens governed in Bremen, where the SPD had secured a legislative plurality in the May 2007 election. The CDU lost its plurality in Hesse and Hamburg in state elections in early 2008, resulting in a set of unusual governing arrangements. In Hesse, the SPD gained parity with the CDU and, while neither party could form ruling coalitions, the CDU maintained a temporary status as "caretaker minority" until a follow-up election in January 2009 established a CDU-FDP coalition firmly in power. Additionally, after losing seats in Hamburg, the CDU and Alliance '90/The Greens formed their first-ever governing coalition. The need for new combinations of political partners has been attributed to the increasing fragmentation of Germany's political parties with the emergence of the Left as a fifth force in German politics.

Germany has dozens of other parties in addition to those discussed below, but none has a national following of electoral significance. (See earlier editions of the *Handbook* for information on additional parties.)

Governing Parties:

Christian Democratic Union (*Christlich Demokratische Union Deutschlands*—CDU). Founded in 1945 as a middle-of-the-road grouping with a generally conservative policy and broad political appeal, the CDU espoused united action by Catholics and Protestants to sustain German life on a Christian basis, while guaranteeing private property and freedom of the individual. Dominated from 1949 to 1963 by Chancellor Konrad Adenauer, the CDU and its Bavarian affiliate, the CSU (below), continued as the strongest party alignment within the Federal Republic until 1969, when it was forced into opposition. With a list headed by CSU chair Franz-Josef Strauss, who had threatened to sever the CDU-CSU bond if denied coalition endorsement in opposing incumbent chancellor Helmut Schmidt, the CDU suffered a loss of 16 of its 190 *Bundestag* seats in the October 1980 election. However, following a transfer of support by the FDP to the CDU on October 1, 1982, Schmidt was obliged to step down as federal chancellor in favor of the CDU's Helmut Kohl, who continued as the head of coalition administrations following the *Bundestag* election of March 6, 1983, and January 25, 1987. After a poor showing in the European Parliament election in June 1989, he regained much of his popularity by waging a vigorous campaign for German unification, which was formally consummated on October 3, 1990.

In the October 1994 federal balloting, the CDU won 34.2 percent of the vote and 244 seats, enabling it to continue the governing coalition with the CSU and the FDP. In late 1997 the CDU nominated Kohl for the September 1998 election, but the aging chancellor could not overcome an early lead by his younger and more telegenic opponent, Gerhard Schröder, who capitalized on high unemployment and a desire for change. The CDU-CSU vote share dropped from 41.4 to 35.1 percent (28.4 percent for the CDU), a loss of 49 seats that toppled the ruling coalition. Kohl even failed to win his home seat, returning to the *Bundestag* only because of his position at the top of the party list. The first postwar chancellor to lose as an incumbent, Kohl subsequently resigned as party chair, and in early November Kohl's handpicked successor, Wolfgang Schäuble, secured the position of CDU chair.

Both Kohl and Schäuble subsequently fell victim to a major party financing scandal. In late 1999 the Bonn public prosecutor announced a criminal investigation into a decade or more of secret donations and bank accounts controlled by Kohl, who had already admitted receiving millions of undeclared deutsche marks during his tenure as party chair. Schäuble announced his resignation as party chair and parliamentary leader on February 16, 2000, having acknowledged receiving undeclared contributions from an arms dealer in 1994. On April 10 a party congress elected Angela Merkel as chair, making her the first woman and the first East German to head the CDU.

In February 2001 Kohl agreed to pay a fine of more than $140,000 in connection with the financing scandal, thereby avoiding probable criminal charges but not a parliamentary inquiry. By that time the party had already been fined approximately $23 million, pending appeal. Financial scandals in the party continued that year, during which the CDU mayor of Berlin was voted out of office on a no-confidence motion. Additionally, more than two dozen CDU members were accused of accepting bribes in connection with a German refinery during a Swiss investigation into France's Elf Aquitaine oil company.

Merkel vied for the party's endorsement as candidate for chancellor in the 2002 national election, but she eventually withdrew from the race when it became clear that support had grown for Edmund Stoiber of the CSU to serve as the joint CDU-CSU candidate. The CDU's Horst Köhler was elected president of the republic on the first ballot in May 2004 as the joint candidate of the CDU, CSU, and FDP. In June 2004 the CDU-CSU alliance continued its electoral recovery by winning the European Parliament elections with 44.5 percent of the vote and 49 of Germany's 99 seats.

In May 2005 Merkel was nominated without opposition as the CDU-CSU candidate in the upcoming early elections. Although the CDU fell from 190 seats in the 2002 *Bundestag* balloting to 179 in the 2005 poll, it managed to secure a small plurality (in conjunction with the CSU) that subsequently propelled Merkel to the chancellorship.

Although Merkel has enjoyed strong popular support since taking office, the CDU was seen struggling to maintain its stronghold in a number of *Länder* as voting trended toward the left. Seeking to secure the position as the political mainstream, the party adopted a new program at its December 2007 conference, defining itself as "the people's party of the center," and agreed to relax some of its economic reforms in favor of extending social benefits. Nevertheless, in early 2008 state elections, the CDU lost its plurality in Hesse and Hamburg and lost substantial ground in Lower Saxony. The losses were seen as major setbacks for the conservatives and for Merkel's authority ahead of national elections in 2009.

In July 2008 the CDU disclosed that its membership had fallen by some 15,000 since mid-2007 to 530,755, though for the first time in history it had surpassed that of the Social Democrats, which saw a steep decline in membership. Significant rifts appeared within the CDU concerning the bailout of failing German firms, the size of the EU and German stimulus packages, and the viability of tax cuts as a means to jump start consumer spending. Merkel made tax cuts a central part of her campaign, but the position was rejected by prominent CDU figures, notably Interior Minister Wolfgang Schaüble, because of the enormous strain it would place on the federal budget. Merkel later played down the prospect of tax relief before 2012.

Leaders: Angela MERKEL (Chancellor and Party Chair), Horst KÖHLER (President of the Republic), Volker KAUDER (Parliamentary Leader), Norbert LAMMERT (President of the *Bundestag*), Peter

MÜLLER (President of the *Bundesrat*), Ronald POFALLA (General Secretary).

Christian Social Union (*Christlich-Soziale Union*—CSU). The Bavarian affiliate of the CDU, which by mutual agreement is unopposed by the CDU in Bavaria and does not present candidates elsewhere, espouses policies similar to its federal partner but tends to be more conservative. Party chair Franz-Josef Strauss became minister-president of Bavaria following the state election of October 15, 1978, and was the unsuccessful CDU-CSU candidate for chancellor in the 1980 national election.

The CSU's *Bundestag* representation of 53 after the March 1983 election was reduced to 51 by the withdrawal of two deputies to form the Republicans (below) the following November. The party lost an additional 2 seats in the balloting of February 1987 but recovered to 51 in December 1990 and retained 50 in 1994 (with a slightly increased national vote share of 7.3 percent). Thereafter, CSU leaders began to distance the party from the CDU's support for EU economic and monetary union, particularly the movement toward a single currency.

The CSU's vote share dropped to 6.7 percent in the September 1998 election, costing the party 3 seats and helping turn out of power the CDU-CSU coalition. Following that electoral setback, in January 1999 Edmund Stoiber, the minister-president of Bavaria, succeeded Theodor WAIGEL as party head. In January 2002 Stoiber, who had won praise for his handling of economic affairs in Bavaria, was selected as the CDU-CSU candidate for chancellor in the 2002 balloting and public leader of the coalition. Stoiber led the CSU to victory in Bavarian state elections in September 21, 2003, with 124 of 180 seats. However, two years later in the 2005 national elections its seat total in the *Bundestag* fell from 58 to 46.

Following several disagreements with the CDU and reported friction with some CSU members, Stoiber resigned as chair of the CSU and minister-president of Bavaria at a CSU congress in September 2007. He was succeeded as minister-president of Bavaria by Günther BECKSTEIN, the hard-line Bavarian interior minister noted for his support for stricter security laws and regulations on noncitizens. Meanwhile, Erwin HUBER, theretofore Bavaria's economy minister and a Stoiber supporter, was elected CSU chair by a 58 percent vote in the congress against several other rivals. The separation of the two posts formerly held by Stoiber was credited with facilitating a "fairly bloodless leadership succession" within the party. A new party platform adopted in late September emphasized the need for climate protection and the duty of immigrants to integrate into German culture as well as the demand that the *Bundeswehr* be deployed on missions only with "clear guidelines" and limited scope.

By early 2008 the dual leadership structure faced difficulties maintaining the party's historic lead in Bavaria. The CSU suffered heavy losses in the March 2008 election in the two major Bavarian cities of Munich and Nuremberg, a portend to September state elections in which the party lost its overall majority, held since 1962, with only 43 percent of the vote. In the Bavarian legislature, the CSU's loss amounted to one-quarter of its seats, while advances were made by Alliance '90/The Greens and the FDP, the latter regaining representation for the first time since 1990 with 8 percent of the vote. The CSU's defeat resulted in a major shake-up in leadership as Huber and Beckstein ceded their posts to deputy chair and agriculture minister Horst Seehofer.

One of Seehofer's most significant early decisions was securing the appointment in early February 2009 of Guttenberg to Merkel's cabinet as economics minister. The 37-year-old "Baron from Bavaria" proceeded to strike a hard stance against propping up flailing German firms, a move that resonated with a public deeply angered by corporate abuses that became apparent during the economic recession. Among Guttenberg's more daring political acts was a public offer to resign his cabinet seat after Merkel proceeded with a deal to save the carmaker Opel from the bankruptcy of its parent company, General Motors, though he did not do so.

Leaders: Horst SEEHOFER (Chair and Minister-President of Bavaria), Edmund STOIBER (Former Chair of the Party, Former Minister-President of Bavaria, and 2002 CDU-CSU candidate for chancellor), Karl-Theodor zu GUTTENBERG (General Secretary).

Social Democratic Party of Germany (*Sozialdemokratische Partei Deutschlands*—SPD). Founded in the 19th century and reestablished in 1945, the SPD discarded its original Marxist outlook in 1959 and embraced the concept of the "social market." With a powerful base in the larger cities and the more industrialized states, the SPD subsequently stressed a strong central government and social welfare programs and was an early advocate of normalized relations with Eastern Europe. It was the principal opposition party before participating in a coalition with the CDU-CSU from 1966 to 1969. After the election of October 1969 the SPD's Willy Brandt formed a governing coalition with the FDP. Brandt was replaced as chancellor in May 1974 by Helmut Schmidt, following an espionage scandal. The coalition continued until October 1982, when the FDP transferred its support to the CDU, thus forcing the SPD into opposition.

Brandt resigned as SPD chair at a stormy leadership meeting in March 1987 after his colleagues had refused to endorse his choice for party spokesperson. Parliamentary leader Hans-Jochen VOGEL was designated as his successor, but the party's relatively poor showing at the 1990 election led Vogel to resign on December 4. He was succeeded by the minister-president of Schleswig-Holstein, Björn ENGHOLM.

Damaged by the revival of an old political scandal, Engholm resigned as chair on May 3, 1993, and was succeeded on June 13 by Rudolf SCHARPING (then minister-president of Rhineland-Palatinate), who led the SPD to its fourth successive federal election defeat in October 1994. However, concurrent SPD advances at the state level gave it a majority in the *Bundesrat,* although the party lost ground in North Rhine–Westphalia and Bremen in May 1995 and in October suffered a major defeat in Berlin (once an SPD stronghold).

Scharping was ousted as SPD chair in November 1995 and was replaced by the more left-wing Oskar LAFONTAINE, the Saarland premier(and 1990 SPD candidate for chancellor). Lafontaine advocated cooperation with the Greens and the ex-Communist PDS but expressed doubts about the plan for a single European currency and questioned the automatic granting of citizenship to ethnic Germans from Eastern Europe. The first electoral test of such policies, in three state elections in March 1996, yielded a lower SPD vote in each case.

In March 1998 the party selected Gerhard Schröder, the premier of Lower Saxony, to be its 1998 candidate for chancellor on the strength of his reelection victory in the state elections. Claiming to represent the "new center," Schröder led the SPD to a 40.9 percent vote share at the September *Bundestag* election, moving the party from 252 to 298 seats. Acknowledging its growing support in the east, the party nominated Wolfgang THIERSE to be president of the lower house, making him the first person from the former East Germany to fill that post.

Belying reports that he controlled the party, Lafontaine quit his SPD leadership post in March 1999 after Schröder appeared to wrest control of the party's agenda during a struggle over economic policymaking. In April, Schröder formalized his victory, winning the party chair at a special SPD congress.

Although there was growing discontent with the party leadership because of Schröder's reform efforts, the SPD won the 2002 legislative elections, and Schröder formed another coalition government with the Greens. In September 2003 SPD member Johannes Rau announced that he would not seek reelection as president of Germany. The SPD and the Greens choose Gesine SCHWAN, the first female candidate to run for the office. Schwan was defeated by the CDU-CSU/FDP candidate, Horst Köhler, in the May presidential poll. In February 2004 Schröder announced his resignation as party leader, and Franz Müntefering was elected chair at a party congress in March. Schröder's subsequent efforts to move the party to the center, epitomized by Agenda 2010, led a group of dissidents to leave the party and form a new left-wing group (see WASG below). In May 2005 Lafontaine resigned from the SPD to become the PDS/WASG standard-bearer, claiming the SPD was pursuing "antisocialist policies."

The SPD fell from 251 seats in the 2002 *Bundestag* balloting to 222 seats in the 2005 poll (at which it secured 34.3 percent of the party-list votes). An SPD congress in mid-November elected Matthias PLATZECK, the minister-president of Brandenburg, as the new SPD chair to succeed Müntefering, who had resigned in a dispute with other leaders concerning a new secretary general. However, Platzeck resigned for health reasons in April 2006 and was succeeded by Kurt BECK, the minister-president of Rhineland-Palatinate. By that time, concern was reportedly being voiced within the SPD over its declining membership, perceived secondary status in the government coalition, and the threat of the increasing popularity of the Left. In the fall of 2007 Beck, apparently securing dominance over the centrist Müntefering camp, won the party's endorsement for a leftward shift that would promote the expansion of social programs and government-funded benefits and was dubbed as a return to the party's traditional social democratic roots. However, by moving further left, the SPD signaled a lack of conciliation with its CDU coalition partner, assuring further difficulty in co-governance, and opened the way for the CDU to take the stage as the political center going into the 2009 national election.

The results of state elections in early 2008 resulted in further political discord within the party. Though the SPD gained enough seats to reach parity with the CDU in Hesse, an attempt by SPD leaders to form a ruling coalition with the Left was abandoned after fierce opposition from centrist elements in the party. The SPD had forsworn any cooperation with the Left in western states, and its apparent attempt to break its promise brought heavy criticism upon Beck, who had set his sites on being the candidate for the chancellorship in 2009, and to SPD frontrunner for minister-president of Hesse, Andrea Ypsilanti, who had been forced to renounce her bid. The nationwide debate over the SPD's flirtation with the Left eventually led to Beck's ouster as party chair in September 2008. Criticized as a lackluster campaigner, Beck was replaced by party stalwart Frank-Walter Steinmeier in October as the chancellor candidate. Müntefering returned to his post as party chair.

In November 2008 Ypsilanti made another attempt to secure the leadership post from the CDU in the Hessian parliament. Again she failed, this time because of four SPD delegates who refused to support her. Müntefering criticized the four delegates for making their feelings known so late, while reiterating that the SPD would not cooperate with the Left at the federal level. In the run-up to the 2009 federal elections, Steinmeier sought to bring a disunited party together by framing the recession as a result of "rule of the free market radicals." In April the SPD launched a platform calling for higher taxes for top wage earners, the introduction of a minimum wage, free day care for children, the reintroduction of a stock exchange turnover tax, and a ban on the far-right NPD. However, the platform seemingly had little resonance with the public. In June the SPD garnered 20.8 percent of the vote in the European parliamentary elections, its worst-ever return in a national election.

Leaders: Franz MÜNTEFERING (Chair), Frank-Walter STEINMEIER (Vice Chancellor), Gerhard SCHRÖDER (Former Chancellor), Hubertus HEIL (General Secretary).

Opposition Parties:

The Left (*Die Linke*). This electoral alliance was quickly formed by the two groups below after Chancellor Gerhard Schröder in May 2005 called for early elections. Showing strength mainly in the ex-Communist eastern states, the alliance secured 54 seats in the September *Bundestag* balloting on a "hard-left" platform with populist undertones. Both the CDU and SPD quickly ruled out coalition talks with PDS and WASG leaders, who in 2006 announced plans for an official formal merger. The merger was approved by both parties in March 2007, and the new party was formally launched on June 16 under the leadership of PDS chair Lothar Bisky and Oskar Lafontaine, the former finance minister under Schröder who resigned from the SPD in 1999 in protest of the government's move toward neoliberal policies, subsequently joining the WASG. The Left, its membership bolstered by disaffected SPD members, subsequently rose to 11 percent support in public opinion polls as it called for a lower retirement age, increased unemployment benefits, and expansion of other social programs. State elections in early 2008 demonstrated the further popularity of the nascent party in western states, as it entered state legislatures in Hamburg, Hesse, and Lower Saxony for the first time. In 2008 it claimed the third-largest political party membership in Germany and was particularly strong among the working class.

The quick rise of the Left has been attributed to a combination of nostalgia for the former East German Communist regime and dismay over SPD and Alliance '90/The Greens compromises with conservatives on economic policies and the rollback of social welfare programs. Once dismissed by the major political parties, the Left has been courted by the SPD as a coalition partner in several states. However, SPD leaders have rejected overtures by the Left to align at the federal level. In an indication of the tenuous political position held by the Left, a new member of the Lower Saxony state legislature, Christel WEGNER, was expelled from the party in February 2008 for advocating a return of the former East German security service, the *Stasi*, to deal with "reactionary forces."

In March 2008 the head of the Federal Office for the Protection of the Constitution claimed that the Left has "strong contacts with left-wing extremist organizations in Germany and abroad" and indicated that surveillance of the party would continue.

In advance of the 2009 federal elections, the Left reported having 76,000 members. The party nominated actor and director Peter Sodann as its 2009 presidential candidate; he received 91 delegate votes, the least of three candidates. Also in May, the party adopted a platform to sharply define itself as the leftmost leaning party, advocating the nationalization of banks, a ban on layoffs at profitable firms, and an end to stock options and hedge funds.

Lafontaine's long-standing critique of inadequate government control over financial markets began to look prescient as German firms buckled under the 2008–2009 economic recession. He called for a Bretton Woods–style system of controls on foreign exchange, international capital flows, and financial products. However, Lafontaine drew scorn for stating, on different occasions, that workers should kidnap their bosses, that Germany is not a "real democracy," and that Merkel's involvement in the Free German Youth in the communist GDR proved she "belonged to the party's reserve of fighters."

Leaders: Lothar BISKY (Co-chair and Former Chair of the PDS), Oskar LAFONTAINE (Co-chair and WASG candidate for chancellor in 2005), Gregor GYSI (Parliamentary Leader).

Alliance '90/The Greens (*Bündnis '90/Die Grünen*). Constituted as a national "antiparty party" during a congress held January 12–14, 1980, in Karlsrühe, *Die Grünen* was an amalgamation of several ecology-oriented groups formed in the late 1970s. Internal divisiveness contributed to a poor showing in the October 1980 federal election, when the party won only 1.5 percent of the vote. At the 1983 balloting, however, it won 27 *Bundestag* seats on the basis of a 5.6 percent vote share, and by late 1987 it had secured representation in 8 of the 11 western state parliaments.

In 1985, following serious electoral losses in Saarland and North Rhine–Westphalia, a split emerged between the fundamentalist (*Fundi*) wing of the party, which rejected participation in coalition governments, and the realist (*Realo*) faction, composed largely of *Bundestag* members. During what was described as a "chaotic" congress in Nuremberg in September 1986, the *Realos* consolidated their hold over the group, which came close to overtaking the Free Democrats in the federal balloting of January 1987, winning 8.3 percent of the vote and 42 *Bundestag* seats.

In late 1989 a Green Party (*Grüne Partei*) was launched in East Germany, and joined with the Independent Women's League (*Unabhängige Frauenbund*) in offering a Greens list at the March 1990 *Volkskammer* poll. Not having endorsed unification, the group was unwilling to join forces with its western counterpart for the all-German balloting in December, entering instead into the anti-unification Alliance '90 coalition, which was able to win eight *Bundestag* seats by meeting the minimum 5 percent vote-share requirement in the former GDR, even though its percentage in the whole of Germany was only 1.2. By contrast, the original Greens, with a 3.9 percent share, were unable to secure the necessary 5 percent in the West.

At parallel congresses in Hannover on January 16–17, 1993, the western Greens and Alliance '90 decided to unite under the official name Alliance '90, while styling themselves informally as the "Greens." The merger was formalized during a congress in Leipzig on May 14. At their Mannheim congress in February 1994, the Greens opted in principle for a "red-green" coalition with the SPD after the October federal elections.

The Greens made a further advance in the October 1994 federal balloting, to 7.3 percent and 49 seats. The new parliamentary arithmetic precluded a coalition with the SPD, but the Greens' presence was acknowledged by the election of a party deputy as one of the *Bundestag*'s four vice presidents. A party congress in December 1995 endorsed the Greens' opposition to any external German military role, although 38 percent of the delegates favored participation in UN peacekeeping missions. The Greens subsequently registered gains in state elections, as a result of which "red-green" coalitions governed five states by the end of 1997. At their convention in February 1998, party leaders said their task was to make clear that the Greens' agenda was not limited to environmental policy and that the party was the best hope for comprehensive change.

In the September 1998 federal elections, the Greens dropped from 7.3 to 6.7 percent of the vote, losing 2 of their 49 seats. Nonetheless, the party was a viable coalition partner for the SPD, and the inclusion of three Green ministers in the new Schröder regime gave the party its first positions of power in the federal government. While the Greens were generally in agreement with the SPD on economic matters, they took a harder line on environmental issues and succeeded in winning a coalition agreement to oppose NATO's first-strike nuclear policy, complicating Schröder's effort to reassure allies that Bonn remained a reliable partner.

On the heels of a setback in Hesse state elections, the Greens convened a conference in March 1999 that reportedly focused on "philosophical" issues and ended with a pledge to move the group's platform back toward its "roots."

In early 2001 Vice Chancellor Joschka FISCHER of the Greens came under attack for his role as a far-left activist in the 1970s, which included participation in violent street demonstrations and association with various members of such militant organizations as the Baader-Meinhof gang, which later became the Red Army Faction. Despite calls from the CDU and other conservative elements for his resignation, Fischer retained the support of Chancellor Schröder, and in January 2002 he was formally designated as leader of the Greens, a new post in the party, which had previously preferred a collective leadership.

The Greens declined slightly from 55 seats in the 2002 *Bundestag* balloting to 51 in the 2005 poll, at which it received 8.1 percent of the party-list vote. Fischer subsequently stepped down as the party leader after the Greens went into opposition. Following two years without representation in any state administration, the Greens joined the SPD in a coalition government in Bremen in June 2007. The party had mixed results in the early 2008 state elections and formed a coalition government with the CDU for the first time in Hamburg, long an SPD stronghold. The unusual alliance signaled the Greens' willingness to compromise for political ends as it backed away from its long-standing opposition to a deepening of the Elbe River in exchange for the cancellation of a new coal-fired power plant in the city.

In November 2008 ethnic Turk Cem Özdemir was elected co-chair of the party, becoming the first member of an ethnic minority to lead a major German political party. He succeeded Reinhard BÜTIKOFER, who had announced in March that he would not seek reelection. Özdemir was previously the first ethnic Turk to be elected to the *Bundestag*, but was forced to resign in 2002 for using "air miles" accumulated from official trips for personal travel. Subsequently, he was elected to the European Parliament in 2004.

In response to the economic recession, the Greens' 2009 federal election platform included the so-called Green New Deal to create one million jobs in Germany over the next four years through investment in combating climate change, education, and health care. The Greens had their best performance ever in the European Parliament elections in June, garnering 12 percent of the vote.

Leaders: Claudia ROTH (Co-chair), Cem ÖZDEMIR (Co-chair); Joschka FISCHER (Former Vice Chancellor and Former Leader of the Party); Renate KÜNASTE, Fritz KUHN.

Free Democratic Party (*Freie Demokratische Partei*—FDP). A moderately rightist party that inherited the tradition of economic liberalism, the FDP stands for free enterprise without state interference but advocates a program of social reform. In the 1980 parliamentary election it won 53 seats (14 more than in 1976), in part because of the defection of Christian Democratic voters dissatisfied with their candidate, Franz-Josef Strauss. The FDP's representation fell to 34 in 1983 but rose to 46 in 1987 and went up to 79 members in 1990, before falling back to 47 in October 1994.

The FDP had formed a governing coalition with the SPD following the elections of 1972, 1976, and 1980 but shifted its support to the CDU in October 1982 after a dispute over the size of the 1983 budget deficit, thereby causing the fall of Helmut Schmidt's government. FDP leader Hans-Dietrich GENSCHER retained his positions as vice chancellor and foreign minister under the successor government of Helmut Kohl, but he resigned on May 18, 1992.

The failure of the party to win representation in a series of state elections from 1992 to 1994 generated much criticism of new leader Klaus KINKEL. He obtained a reprieve when the FDP unexpectedly retained a 47-seat *Bundestag* presence in October 1994 (with a 6.9 percent share of the vote); however, further electoral failures in Bremen and North Rhine–Westphalia in May 1995 obliged Kinkel to vacate the leadership while remaining foreign minister. Named at a special party congress in June, his successor, longtime Hesse leader Wolfgang GERHARDT, distanced himself somewhat from Chancellor Kohl by calling for relaxed citizenship laws, termination of the arms embargo against Bosnian Muslims, and an end to the "solidarity" tax that was financing economic recovery in the former East Germany; with an eye toward the challenge posed by the rise of the Greens, he also called for a greater focus on environmental issues. In January 1996 the FDP staged a relaunch on a more right-wing economic platform, quickly winning representation in three state elections in March and confirming its new orientation at a party congress in Karlsrühe in June.

In the *Bundestag* elections of September 1998 the FDP lost 4 seats, with a vote share of 6.2 percent. In early January 2001 Gerhardt resigned the party chair, with the FDP secretary general, Guido Westerwelle, being formally elected as his successor on May 4 at a party congress. In May 2002 Westerwelle was named as the FDP's first solo candidate for chancellor, having announced in January that the FDP would compete independently in the upcoming federal elections, thereby severing the party's alliance with the CDU. In the 2002 election the FDP won 7.4 percent of the vote and 47 seats. The FDP improved to 61 seats (its best performance since 1990) in the 2005 *Bundestag* poll, at which it secured 9.8 percent of the proportional votes.

The party made minor improvements in seats in the early 2008 state elections, and in January 2009 it entered its fifth state government alliance in Hesse. In May Westerwelle was reelected party chair by an overwhelming 96 percent. The party emerged stronger from the European Parliament elections in June 2009 with 11 percent of the vote, up from 6.1 percent in 2004.

In the run-up to the 2009 federal election the FDP campaigned for more tax cuts to jump start the economy and an end to state bailouts of German firms.

Leaders: Guido WESTERWELLE (Chair and 2002, 2005, and 2009 candidate for chancellor); Hans-Jürgen BEERFELTZ (Chief Executive Officer), Dirk NIEBEL (Secretary General).

Other Parties that Participated in Recent Elections:

Party of Democratic Socialism (*Partei der Demokratischen Sozialismus*—PDS). Pressure exerted by Soviet occupation authorities led in April 1946 to the formation of the Socialist Unity Party of Germany (*Sozialistische Einheitspartei Deutschlands*—SED) by merger of the preexisting Communist and Social Democratic parties. The SED controlled all East German organizations, except the churches, for the more than four decades of Communist rule, using the familiar instrument of a National Front organization.

Longtime party leader Erich HONEKER resigned on October 18, 1989, and was replaced as general secretary by Egon KRENZ. On November 11, in the face of rapidly escalating opposition to the dominance of the SED, all of the party's 22 Politburo incumbents, save Krenz, quit and were replaced by a substantially smaller body of 11 members. On December 3 Krenz also resigned. Six days later, during an emergency congress, the party abandoned Marxism and renamed itself the Socialist Unity Party of Germany–Party of Democratic Socialism (SED-PDS) under a new chair, Gregor GYSI. It formally dropped the SED component of the name at an election congress in late February 1990.

In the all-German balloting of December 1990, the PDS, campaigning jointly with a Left List (*Linke List*), won 17 *Bundestag* seats, with almost all of its combined 2.4 percent vote share coming from the former GDR. The party gained further ground in the October federal elections when it won 30 *Bundestag* seats. A PDS congress in January 1995 endorsed a more moderate "left-wing democratic" program. In the September 1998 federal elections, the PDS won more than 5 percent of the vote nationwide for the first time, with most of its support from the east, thereby increasing its representation to 36 seats.

In November the PDS formed its first formal governing coalition since reunification when it joined the SPD in a state government in Mecklenburg–West Pomerania, with the PDS getting three posts in the eight-member cabinet On October 14, 2000, Gabrielle ZIMMER succeeded Lothar Bisky as chair, reflecting an effort by the party's reform wing to move toward the political center. The party subsequently indicated that it would be prepared to enter the federal government in partnership with the SPD after the 2002 election, a possibility that the SPD immediately rejected. Following the election, party disputes continued over Zimmer's leadership. On June 28, 2003, a special party congress again elected Bisky as chair, to succeed Zimmer. In state elections in Brandenburg in September 2004, the PDS had its best electoral success since reunification with 28.3 percent of the vote. The PDS gained seven seats in the 2004 European Parliament elections.

The PDS, which had secured only 2 seats in the 2002 *Bundestag* balloting, was "rejuvenated" by its electoral alliance with the smaller WASG in 2005, gaining a combined 54 seats. The spring 2007 merger between the PDS and WASG into the Left ended the tenure of the PDS as an autonomous party; members of parliament elected as PDS are listed with the Left faction, and the PDS has adopted the newer party's platform.

Electoral Alternative for Labor and Social Justice (*Wahlalternative Arbeit und Soziale Gerechtigkeit*—WASG). Comprising mostly disaffected members of the SPD and trade unionists led by former foreign minister Oskar Lafontaine, the WASG was launched as a formal party in early 2005. The leaders of the new group accused the SPD leadership, particularly Gerhard Schröder, of having moved to the right in the interest of the business sector. The WASG merger with the larger PDS in the spring of 2007 into the Left effectively ended the WASG as an independent political party.

The Republicans (*Die Republikaner*). The Republicans party was launched in November 1983 by two former Bavarian CSU deputies who objected to Franz-Josef Strauss's "one-man" leadership, particularly in regard to East-West relations. The manifestly ultra-rightist group was self-described as a "conservative-liberal people's party" that favored a reunited Germany, environmental protection, and lower business taxes. Although the party claimed a nationwide membership of only 8,500, its West Berlin section obtained 11 legislative seats on the basis of a 7.5 percent vote share in January 1989.

As reunification became a leading German concern, the party's appeal ebbed. It obtained only 2 percent of the vote at state elections in North Rhine–Westphalia and Lower Saxony in early 1990, and in late May its increasingly controversial chair, former Waffen SS officer Franz SCHÖNHUBER, was obliged to resign, although he recovered the post at a party congress in July. The party made a comeback in the Baden-Württemberg state election in April 1992, winning 11 percent of the vote and 15 seats; in May 1993, moreover, it secured *Bundestag* representation by the defection from the CDU of Rudolf KRAUSE. Prior to the October 1994 *Bundestag* election Schönhuber was again deposed as leader, officially because of an unauthorized meeting with the leader of the DVU (below) but also because of his negative media image. In 2006 state protection authorities delisted the Republicans as a right-wing extremist group, although its positions on issues such as immigration, where it stated there is "no place for Islam in Germany," were still considered far right. The Republicans also called for an end to Germany's participation in the EU.

The party received only 1.9 percent of the *Bundestag* proportional vote in 1994, 1.8 percent in 1998, 0.6 percent in 2002, and 0.6 percent in 2005 as it struggled for votes against the more popular NPD and DVU. In the 2009 European Parliament elections, the Republicans fielded Uschi WINKELSETT as a candidate and won 1.3 percent of the vote.

Leader: Rolf SCHLIERER (Federal Chair).

National Democratic Party (*Nationaldemokratische Partei Deutschlands*—NPD). Formed in 1964 by a number of right-wing groups, the NPD was subsequently accused of neo-Nazi tendencies but avoided exhibiting clear-cut grounds for legal prohibition. Unrepresented in the state parliaments or in the *Bundestag,* its appeal at the federal level slipped to a record low 0.2 percent of the popular vote in 1980 and recovered only marginally thereafter. In April 1995 NPD leader Günter DECKERT received a prison sentence for incitement to racial hatred and other offenses. On May Day in 1998 the party organized a demonstration in Leipzig by 6,000 neo-Nazis, one of the largest such gatherings in years, to protest high unemployment and demand the expulsion of immigrants. At the subsequent federal election, the party took 0.3 percent of the vote.

On December 8, 2000, the *Bundestag* approved a government effort to ban the NPD as "anti-Semitic, racist, xenophobic, and violence-supporting." The proposal had already been backed by 14 of 16 state interior ministers and by the *Bundesrat,* although some elements of the CDU as well as the FDP opposed a ban as counterproductive. On March 18, 2003, the Constitutional Court, which had banned only two parties in the previous 50 years, rejected a ban on the party because some members of the party who had given evidence were police informers. In 2004 state elections, the NPD gained 9.4 percent of the vote in Saxony in its greatest electoral showing to date.

In February 2005 the NPD held what was called the biggest far-right rally in Germany since World War II. The party reportedly contested the 2005 *Bundestag* elections in alliance with the DVU (below), securing 1.6 percent of the proportional vote. In December 2005 it was reported that 3 of the 12 NPD state legislators in Saxony had resigned from the party to protest the NPD's "Nazi-style" ideology.

In the 2006 state elections in Mecklenburg–West Pomerania, the NPD secured 7.3 percent of the vote and six seats in the legislature. It also retained its one seat in the May 2007 balloting in Bremen.

In recent years, the NPD has been beset by a series of criminal indictments, funding problems, and renewed political efforts to ban the party. In the wake of a spate of attacks by right-wing youth on individuals of foreign descent in 2007, SPD regional leaders began pushing again for a ban, while several German banks closed accounts belonging to the NPD because they wanted no part in the party's financial dealings.

The party's financial situation worsened when government prosecutors in December 2007 began investigating the group for fraud for allegedly cheating the government out of political matching funds. Police later arrested the NPD treasurer on embezzlement charges.

Another high-profile right-wing attack in December 2008, this time against a police officer in Bavaria, fueled more support for a ban on the NPD. Chancellor Merkel announced that the government was looking for ways to outlaw the party, but would be careful in doing so to avoid a second failure in the courts.

Short of a ban, German officials explored ways to curb the NPD's strength by blocking more than $1 million in public financing. One proposal that gained attention in late 2008 was a constitutional amendment to prevent political parties from receiving state aid if they were deemed to be "agitating against the principles of the constitution."

In May 2009 the party was fined $1.7 million for accounting irregularities and ordered to return more than $1 million in public money. NPD chair Udo Voigt said the party was suffering an "existential crisis" due to lack of funds.

Voigt and two senior party members were also convicted of inciting racial hatred because of pamphlets they had distributed before the 2006 World Cup that impugned a German football player of Nigerian descent.

Despite these problems, the NPD has become the largest and most prominent far-right political party in Germany, with some 7,000 members. It sought to broaden its appeal among women through ties to new right-wing women's organizations. As of the results of municipal elections in June 2009, the NPD claimed more than 100 seats on regional and city councils. The party's success at the local level has been part of a strategy to make itself appear "mainstream."

Nonetheless, Germany's Office for the Protection of the Constitution has described the NPD as racist, revisionist, and inspired by Nazi ideology.

Leaders: Udo VOIGT (Chair), Holger APFEL, Sascha ROSSMÜLLER (Deputy Chair), Peter MARX (Secretary General).

German People's Union (*Deutsche Volksunion*—DVU). Launched in 1987 by wealthy publisher Gerhard Frey, the DVU was a far-right grouping that, with links to the NPD but claiming not to be neo-Nazi, assumed a strongly anti-immigrant posture, arguing that most Germans wished their country to be "racially pure." It won 6 city council seats in Bremen in September 1991 and 6 of Schleswig-Holstein's 89 assembly seats in April 1992. The DVU backed the Republicans in the October 1994 federal elections in the wake of reports that the two groups might set aside a long-standing rivalry and, in the words of the Republicans' Franz Schönhuber (with apparent reference to the constraints of the 5 percent rule), "build a relationship that will prevent us from blocking our own electoral progress." The DVU's exit from the Bremen legislature in May 1995 (with only 2.5 percent of the vote) was followed by a similar failure in Schleswig-Holstein in October (with 4.3 percent). The party shocked the political establishment in the spring 1998 state elections when it received nearly 13 percent of the vote in Saxony-Anhalt, the first time East Germans elected extreme right-wing candidates to a state legislature and one of the strongest showings of a far-right party since the end of World War II. The party spent more money than all its opponents combined to win a victory viewed by some analysts primarily as a protest vote. In the subsequent federal elections in September, the party received 1.2 percent nationwide. The DVU joined the NPD in an unsuccessful electoral alliance for the 2005 *Bundestag* balloting. Although the DVU was once the largest right-wing party in Germany, its membership had dipped to 7,000 by 2009.

In January 2009 Frey retired as chair. As the chief donor, his departure left the party's future income in question. Frey was replaced by Matthias Faust, who joined the DVU in 2007 and ran a high-profile campaign for the Hamburg parliament in 2008.

The DVU and NPD joined forces, fielding Frank RENNICKE as a presidential candidate in 2009 and winning four delegate votes. In the June municipal elections, the DVU won 1.6 percent of the vote in Brandenburg, a slight gain compared to its 2004 results.

Leader: Matthias FAUST.

Law-and-Order Offensive Party (*Partei Rechtsstaatlicher Offensive*—PRO). Sometimes translated into English as the Legal Offensive Party, the right-wing PRO was organized in 2000 by jurist Ronald SCHILL, who had earned a reputation as "Judge Merciless" for handing down severe sentences in criminal cases. Schill had argued for voluntary castration of convicted sexual offenders, restoration of the death penalty, removal of the right to asylum from the German constitution, and the imposition of minimum ten-year sentences for serious crimes.

The PRO is based in Hamburg, where it won a surprising 19.4 percent of the vote in the September 2001 election and was thus largely responsible for the defeat of the SPD-Greens coalition government. The PRO subsequently joined with the CDU and the FDP in forming a new administration in Hamburg. However, in December 2003 the coalition factionalized because of political differences between the PRO and the CDU/FDP. In the 2002 national legislative election, the PRO received 0.7 percent of the vote. At a party congress on February 23, Mario Mettbach was elected party chair, and PRO founder Schill was expelled from the party. Schill then formed an alternative faction, the Pro-Deutsche Mark/Schill Party (Pro-DM/Schill) with the restoration of the deutsche mark as its main priority. The PRO dissolved in September 2007 after poor election results and an exodus by its remaining leaders to the DVU and NPD.

Leader: Mario METTBACH (Chair).

The Greys (*Die Grauen*). Formerly a pensioners' group within the Greens, the Greys (also referenced as the Grey Panthers) organized as a separate party in mid-1989 to represent the interests of older citizens. It won 0.8 percent of the federal proportional vote in 1990, 0.5 percent in 1994, 0.3 percent in 1998, 0.2 percent in 2002, and 0.4 percent in 2005. While never a large party, the Greys in recent years has faced difficulties in maintaining a political presence due to its aging membership. The party's long-standing chair, Trude Unruh, resigned in September 2007 during a criminal investigation into party finances. In November state funding of the party was terminated. The party was later charged with fraud for allegedly inventing donations to increase its share of state financing and was ordered to pay back $7.6 million in state finances and a fine of $5 million. Unruh was replaced by Norbert RAEDER, who briefly held the chair until the party officially dissolved in January 2008 due to insolvency.

Other minor parties that obtained at least 0.1 percent of the vote in the September 2005 federal elections were the **Animal Protection Party** (*Tierschutzpartei*—TP); the **Bavaria Party** (*Bayern Partei*), which advocates independence for Bavaria; the **Civil Rights Movement Solidarity** (*Bürgerrechtsbewegung Solidarität—BüSo*); the **Ecological Democratic Party** (*Ökologisch-Demokratische Partei*—ÖDP); the **Family Party of Germany** (*Famlienpartei Deutschlands*—FPD); the **Feminist Party** (*Feministische Partei*), which also is identified as **Women** (*Die Frauen*); the **Marxist-Leninist Party of Germany** (*Marxistisch-Leninistische Partei Deutschlands*—MLPD); and the **Party of Bible-Believing Christians** (*Partei der Bibeltreuen Christen*—PBC).

Other Parties:

German Communist Party (*Deutsche Kommunistische Partei*—DKP). West Germany's former Communist Party, led by Max REIMANN, was banned as unconstitutional in 1956; Reimann returned from exile in East Germany in 1969. Meanwhile, plans to establish a new Communist party consistent with the principles of the Basic Law had been announced in September 1968 by a 31-member "federal committee" headed by Kurt BACHMANN. At its inaugural congress in April 1969, the new party claimed 22,000 members, elected Bachmann as chair, and announced its intention to seek a common front with the SPD in the 1969 *Bundestag* election (an offer that was promptly rejected by the SPD). Subsequently, it received financial support from the East German SED, with which it cooperated in a series of "alternative" postwar anniversary celebrations in 1985. This support ended with the changes in East Germany in late 1989, forcing the DKP to curtail its activities. The party's longtime chair, Herbert MIES, resigned in October 1989 and was replaced by a four-member council at the tenth congress in March 1990. In the 2002 national legislative election, the DKP received only 394 votes. The DKP has reportedly worked closely with the Left in recent years by sharing party platforms and, in the case of the 2005 *Bundestag* balloting, candidate lists.

Leaders: Heinz STEHR, Nina HAGER, Günter POHL.

South Schleswig Voters' Union (*Südschleswigscher Wählerverband*—SSW/*Sydslesvigk Vaelgerforening*—SSV). Founded in 1948 with the approval of the British occupation authorities, the SSV represented the interests of ethnic Danes in northern Schleswig-Holstein. Exempted from the 5 percent threshold rule, it consistently obtained representation in the state legislature, increasing from one to two seats in March 1996 on a 2.5 percent vote share and then to three in 2000 with 4.1 percent of the vote. It fell back to two seats in 2005 with 3.6 percent of the vote. The party also has representation in a number of local and regional councils.

Leaders: Flemming MEYER, Rüdiger SCHULZE, Anke SPOORENDONK, Lars HARMS.

Democratic Party of Germany (*Demokratische Partei Deutschlands*—DPD). The DPD was founded in October 1995 to represent the interests of foreigners in Germany and to oppose racism, being based in the 2-million-strong Turkish community. The DPD's prospects for electoral progress are limited by the fact that most non-German immigrants do not have citizenship and are therefore not entitled to vote.

Leader: Sedat SEZGIN (Chair).

Extremist Groups:

Although terrorist activity receded in the 1980s, armed groups on the right and the left remained active in postunification Germany. Neo-Nazi groups, whose overall membership was estimated in early 1985 at 22,000, were particularly active in the early 1990s, mounting attacks on foreign residents and Jews. (By the late 1990s the extremists' numbers were reported to have climbed to more than 50,000.) They included the **Free Workers' Party** (*Frei Arbeiterspartei*—FAP), reputedly the largest neo-Nazi group at the time of its banning in February 1995; the much smaller, Hamburg-based **National List** (*Nationale Liste*—NL), which also was banned in February 1995; the **German League for People and Homeland** (*Deutsche Liga für Volk und Heimat*—DLVH); the **National Socialist Action Front/National Action** (*Aktionsfront Nationaler Sozialisten/Nationale Aktion*—ANS/NA); various "military sport groups" (*Wehrsportgruppen*), including the *Wehrsportgruppe Hoffman* led by Odfried HEPP and allegedly supported by the Palestine Liberation Organization; and the **Viking Youth** (*Wiking Jugend*—WJ), banned in October 1994. In January 2004 Bavaria banned the far-right **Franconian Action Front** (*Aktionsfront Fränkische*—FAF). The federal government banned another neo-Nazi organization, the **Blood and Honor Group**, in 2000, and in 2008 banned two groups for Holocaust denial, the Collegium Humanum, based in Vlotho, and the Association for the Rehabilitation of People Persecuted for Denying the Holocaust.

A surge in violent, right-wing activity in late 2008 and 2009, including the wounding of a Bavarian police officer in a stabbing incident, prompted renewed efforts to find and prosecute members. Of particular concern was an Interior Ministry report in March 2009 that found that among 15-year-old boys, 1 in 20 were members of a right-wing group; the rate was significantly higher, 1 in 8 boys, in the former East Germany. In response, authorities banned the **Patriotic German Youth** (*Heimattreue Deutsche Jugend*—HDJ).

There were a reported 180 far-right groups in Germany in 2009 with a combined 31,000 members.

On the left in the 1970s, the **Red Army Faction** (RAF), an outgrowth of the Baader-Meinhof group, emerged with an estimated strength of about 500. Following the emplacement of Pershing missiles in 1984, the RAF declared an "anti-imperialist war" and claimed responsibility for more than 20 bombings in 1985, mainly at U.S. military and diplomatic installations, which left four dead; the group also claimed credit for the assassination of the arms manufacturer Ernst ZIMMERMAN in February 1985. In April 1992 the RAF announced that it would cease its attacks on public officials if the government released several of its long-incarcerated members. In an apparent response, former RAF activist Günter SONNENBERG was released in mid-May after serving 15 years of a life sentence. In September 1995, however, an RAF member was sentenced to life imprisonment for involvement in terrorist actions in 1977 and 1982. In April 1998 the RAF announced that it had formally disbanded. In May the government pardoned Helmut

POHL, an RAF member who had urged the group to disband in 1996; he had been convicted for the 1981 bombing of a U.S. Air Force base. In February 2007 former RAF member Brigitte MOHNHAUPT was pardoned after being imprisoned for 24 years. In March 2009 RAF co-founder Horst MAHLER was sentenced to five years on top of a six-year sentence for denying the Holocaust.

In August 1998 the government outlawed the **Revolutionary People's Liberation Party/Front** as well as the **Turkish People's Liberation Party/Front**, splinters of **Dev-Sol** (*Devrimce Sol*), a leftist Turkish group founded in Turkey in 1978 on a platform advocating the creation of a "communist society." (Dev-Sol had been originally banned in Germany in 1983.) The government claimed the outlawed groups were extremists who financed their activities through blackmail and violence. The Marxist Turkish group DHKP-C, also banned that year, became active again in late 2002, recruiting new members from poor areas of Germany's big cities. Five suspected members were charged with belonging to a terrorist organization in late 2007. Renewed violence by members of the Kurdish Workers Party (PKK) in 2007 was attributed to Turkish military operations along the border of northern Iraq. In 2008 the head of the German intelligence agency said up to 700 members of radical Islamic groups were under surveillance. In June 2009 Turkish and German authorities discussed restricting the flow of capital to the PKK and extraditing two PKK members from Germany to Turkey.

LEGISLATURE

The bicameral parliament consists of an indirectly chosen upper chamber, the *Bundesrat,* or Federal Council, and an elective lower chamber, the *Bundestag,* or Federal Assembly.

Federal Council (*Bundesrat*). The upper chamber currently consists of 69 members appointed by the state governments, each of whose three to six votes (depending on population) are cast *en bloc*. Lengths of term vary according to state election dates. The presidency rotates annually among heads of the state delegations, usually state minister-presidents. As of April 9, 2008, the seat distribution was as follows: the Christian Democratic Union (CDU), 39; Social Democratic Party (SPD), 18; Christian Social Union (CSU), 6; Free Democratic Party (FDP), 4; the Left, 1; and Alliance '90/The Greens, 1.

President: Peter MÜLLER.

Federal Assembly (*Bundestag*). The lower chamber, which currently has 622 members, is the world's largest democratically elected legislative body. The president can dissolve the assembly, prompting a federal election, upon a chamber vote of no confidence in the chancellor. Deputies are chosen for four-year terms by popular vote under a complicated electoral system combining direct and proportional representation. Following the Federal Assembly elections on September 18, 2005, for 613 seats, the seat distribution was as follows: SPD, 222 seats (145 constituency and 77 party list); CDU, 179 (105, 74); the Left, 54 (3, 51); Alliance '90/The Greens, 51 (1, 50); FDP, 61 (0, 61); and CSU, 46 (44, 2). The CDU won one outstanding seat on October 2. (*See headnote.*)

President: Norbert LAMMERT.

CABINET

[as of August 1, 2009] (*see headnote*)

Chancellor	Angela Merkel (CDU)
Vice Chancellor	Frank-Walter Steinmeier (SPD)
Head, Federal Chancellery	Thomas de Maizière (CDU)
Ministers	
Consumer Protection, Food, and Agriculture	Ilse Aigner (CSU) [f]
Defense	Franz Josef Jung (CDU)
Economic Cooperation and Development	Heidemarie Wieczorek-Zeul (SPD) [f]
Economics and Technology	Karl-Theodor zu Guttenberg (CSU)
Education and Research	Annette Schavan (CDU) [f]
Environment, Nature Conservation, and Nuclear Safety	Sigmar Gabriel (SPD)
Family Affairs, Senior Citizens, Women, and Youth	Ursula von der Leyer (CDU) [f]
Finance	Peer Steinbrük (SPD)
Foreign Affairs	Frank-Walter Steinmeier (SPD)
Health	Ulla Schmidt (SPD) [f]
Interior	Wolfgang Schaüble (CDU)
Justice	Brigitte Zypries (SPD) [f]
Labor and Social Affairs	Olaf Scholz (SPD)
Transport, Building, and Urban Development	Wolfgang Tiefensee (SPD)

[f] = female

COMMUNICATIONS

Freedom of speech and press is constitutionally guaranteed except to anyone who misuses it in order to destroy the democratic system.

Press. Newspapers are numerous and widely read, and many of the principal dailies have national as well as local readerships. There are some very large publishing concerns, notably the Axel Springer group, which is Europe's largest publishing conglomerate. In the eastern *Länder,* most papers were transferred from party to private control in 1990. The circulation figures for the following newspapers are approximate: *Bild-Zeitung* (Hamburg and seven other cities, 5,674,000), sensationalist Springer tabloid; *Westdeutsche Allgemeine Zeitung* (Essen, 1,313,000); *Hannoversche Allgemeine Zeitung* (Hannover, 250,000); *Freie Presse* (Chemnitz, 502,000), former PDS organ; *Mitteldeutsche Zeitung* (Halle, 414,000), formerly *Freiheit*; *Sächsische Zeitung* (Dresden, 416,000); *Thüringer Allgemeine* (Erfurt, 589,000), formerly *Das Volk*; *Rheinische Post* (Düsseldorf, 443,000); *Süddeutsche Zeitung* (Munich, 400,000), center-left; *Express* (Cologne, 468,000); *Frankfurter Allgemeine Zeitung* (Frankfurt-am-Main, 471,000); *Leipziger Volkszeitung* (Leipzig, 380,000), former PDS organ; *Augsburger Allgemeine* (Augsburg, 375,000); *Südwest Presse* (Ulm, 378,000); *Nürnberger Nachrichten* (Nürnberg, 350,000); *Magdeburger Volksstimme* (Magdeburg, 321,000), former PDS organ; *BZ* (Berlin, 370,000), Springer group; *Hamburger Abendblatt* (Hamburg, 329,000), Springer group; *Neue Osnabrücker Zeitung* (Osnabrück, 322,000); *Kölner Stadt Anzeiger* (Cologne, 305,000); *Hessische/Niedersächsische Allgemeine* (Kassel, 325,000); *Berliner Zeitung* (Berlin, 246,000), independent; *Die Rheinpfalz* (Ludwigshafen, 258,000); *Rhein-Zeitung* (Koblenz, 259,000); *Abendzeitung/8-Uhr-Blatt* (Munich, 256,000); *Ruhr-Nachrichten* (Dortmund, 243,000); *Berliner Morgenpost* (Berlin, 178,000), Springer group.

News agencies. There are two principal facilities: the German Press Agency (*Deutsche Presse-Agentur*—DPA), which supplies newspapers and broadcasting stations throughout the Federal Republic while also transmitting news overseas in German, English, French, Spanish, and Arabic, and the DPP News Agency (*Deutscher Depeschendienst Nachrichtenagentur*), which was launched in 1946 as the official East German agency, was reorganized in 1990, and adopted its current name in 1999 upon becoming an independent agency.

Broadcasting and computing. Terrestrial noncable broadcasting networks are independent, nonprofit, public corporations chartered by the governments of the *Länder*. The coordinating body is the Association of Public Law Broadcasting Organizations of the Federal Republic of Germany (*Arbeitsgemeinschaft der öffentlich-rechtlichen Rundfunkanstalten der Bundesrepublik Deutschland*—ARD). There are three national terrestrial television channels, the first provided by ARD affiliates, the second by *Zweites Deutsches Fernsehen* (ZDF), and the third (a cultural and educational service) by several of the regional authorities. There also are numerous cable and satellite channels, more than 50 percent of German households (the highest number in Europe) being wired for cable television. In early 1994 a new state-supported cultural service, *Deutschland Radio,* was launched to promote a sense of community between eastern and western Germans. Non-German broadcasters include the American Forces Network, the British Forces Broadcasting Service, Radio Free Europe, Radio Liberty, the Voice of America, and the state-funded international broadcaster *Deutsche Welle.* In July 1994 U.S. president Clinton announced the relocation of Radio Free Europe and Radio Liberty from Munich to the Czech capital, Prague. As of 2008 there were 753.3 Internet users per 1,000 inhabitants.

INTERGOVERNMENTAL REPRESENTATION

Ambassador to the U.S.: Klaus SCHARIOTH.

U.S. Ambassador to Germany: Philip D. MURPHY.

Permanent Representative to the UN: Hans Peter WITTIG.

IGO Memberships (Non-UN): ADB, AfDB, BDEAC, BIS, BOAD, CBSS, CERN, CEUR, EBRD, EIB, ESA, EU, Eurocontrol, G-8, G-10, G-20, IADB, IEA, Interpol, IOM, NATO, OECD, OSCE, PCA, WCO, WEU, WTO.

GHANA

Republic of Ghana

Political Status: Independent member of the Commonwealth since March 6, 1957; under military control 1966–1969 and 1972–1979; Third Republic overthrown by military coup of December 31, 1981; constitution of Fourth Republic, approved in referendum of April 28, 1992, formally launched on January 7, 1993.

Area: 92,099 sq. mi. (238,537 sq. km.).

Population: 18,912,079 (2000C); 23,954,000 (2008E).

Major Urban Center (2005E): ACCRA (1,963,000).

Official Language: English.

Monetary Unit: New Cedi (market rate December 1, 2009: 1.43 cedi = $1US).

President: John Evans Atta MILLS (National Democratic Congress); elected for a four-year term in runoff balloting on December 28, 2008, and January 2, 2009, and sworn in on January 7 in succession to John Agyekum KUFUOR (New Patriotic Party).

Vice President: John Dramani MAHAMA (National Democratic Congress); elected with the president in runoff balloting on December 28, 2008, and January 2, 2009, and sworn in on January 7 for a term concurrent with that of the president to succeed Alhaji Aliu MAHAMA (New Patriotic Party).

THE COUNTRY

Located on the west coast of Africa just north of the equator, Ghana's terrain includes a tropical rain forest running north about 170 miles from the Gulf of Guinea and a grassy savanna belt that is drained by the Volta River. While the official language of the country is English, the inhabitants are divided among more than 50 linguistic and ethnic groups, the most important being the Akans (including Fanti), Ashanti, Ga, Ewe, and Mossi-Dagomba. About 40 percent of the population is Christian, and 12 percent Muslim, with most of the rest following traditional religions. Over 40 percent of households are headed by women, who dominate the trading sector and comprise nearly 50 percent of agricultural labor; a smaller proportion of salaried women is concentrated in the service sector.

Agriculture employs nearly 60 percent of the population and accounts for about 39 percent of GDP, in large part owing to cocoa production. Other important export commodities include timber, jewelry, and coffee. Manufacturing centers on food processing and the production of vehicles and textiles. Mining accounts for more than one-half of foreign exchange; in addition to gold, there are important deposits of diamonds, bauxite, and manganese.

According to the World Bank, per capita GNP declined by an average of 2 percent annually from 1980 to 1987. A subsequent return to modest economic growth largely resulted from the government's enactment of IMF-sponsored reform programs, including privatization of a number of government-controlled enterprises. However, the economy flagged in the mid-1990s, weighed down by rising debt payments. Although annual economic growth of over 4 percent was achieved from 1996 to 1999, per capita annual income remained at less than $500.

In early 2000 the World Bank refused to forward an anticipated loan, insisting that Ghana's financial practices were not sufficiently transparent. The decision underscored widespread international and domestic concern over apparently pervasive corruption, despite Ghana's image as a model for free-market orientation and democratization in Africa. Battered by tumbling cocoa and gold prices, the economy grew by only 1 percent in 2000, with inflation running at more than 30 percent annually.

By 2005 GDP growth was more than 5 percent, although inflation was close to 15 percent. The IMF noted progress in structural reforms and private-sector investment. However, poverty was unabated, particularly in the north. Annual GDP growth increased to just over 6 percent in 2006–2007, with inflation declining to about 10 percent. The IMF, the World Bank, and the African Development Bank canceled $3.2 billion of Ghana's debt to allow resources to be used for poverty-reduction efforts. Meanwhile, the World Bank approved a $75 million loan for what was described as a model gold-producing project, predicted to generate between $300 million and $700 million for the country over the next 20 years. In 2007 it was reported that gold, for the first time, had surpassed cocoa as the largest source of foreign revenue, each commodity bringing in more than $1 billion, as a result of rising international gold prices and a bumper cocoa harvest. Annual growth averaged 5.3 percent in 2008-2009, the IMF noting that Ghana had made "remarkable success" in developing its financial sector (which, only a year earlier, fund managers had said required urgent agent). As inflation rose to a five-year high of 20.3 percent in February 2009 due chiefly to rising food prices and the global economic downturn, the cedi lost one-third of its value against the U.S. dollar, and Ghana was reported to be facing a financial crisis (see Current issues, below). Meanwhile, the IMF and the World Bank pledged about $1 billion through 2011 to help bolster the country's economy.

GOVERNMENT AND POLITICS

Political background. The first West African territory to achieve independence in the postwar era, Ghana was established on March 6, 1957, through consolidation of the former British colony of the Gold Coast and the former UN Trust Territory of British Togoland. The drive to independence was associated primarily with the names of J. B. DANQUAH and Kwame N. NKRUMAH. The latter became prime minister of the Gold Coast in 1952, prime minister of independent Ghana in 1957, and the country's first elected president when republican status within the Commonwealth was proclaimed on July 1, 1960. Subsequently, Nkrumah consolidated his own power and that of his Convention People's Party (CPP), establishing a one-party dictatorship that neighboring states increasingly viewed with apprehension.

In 1966 the military ousted Nkrumah in response to increasing resentment of his repressive policies and financial mismanagement, which had decimated the country's reserves and generated an intolerably large national debt. An eight-man National Liberation Council (NLC) headed by Lt. Gen. Joseph A. ANKRAH ran the government. Promising an eventual return to civilian rule, the NLC carried out a far-reaching purge of Nkrumah adherents and sponsored the drafting of a new constitution. The NLC era was marked, however, by a series of alleged plots and corruption charges, with Ankrah resigning as head of state in April 1969 after admitting to solicitation of funds from foreign companies for campaign purposes. He was replaced by Brig. Akwasi Amankwa AFRIFA, who implemented plans for a return to civilian government.

Partial civilian control returned following a National Assembly election in August 1969 that designated Kofi A. BUSIA as prime minister. A three-man presidential commission, made up of members of the NLC, exercised presidential power until August 31, 1970, when Edward AKUFO-ADDO was inaugurated as head of state. The Busia administration was unable to deal with economic problems generated by a large external debt and a drastic currency devaluation, and in January 1972 the military, under (then) Col. Ignatius Kutu ACHEAMPONG, again seized control. The National Redemption Council (NRC), which was

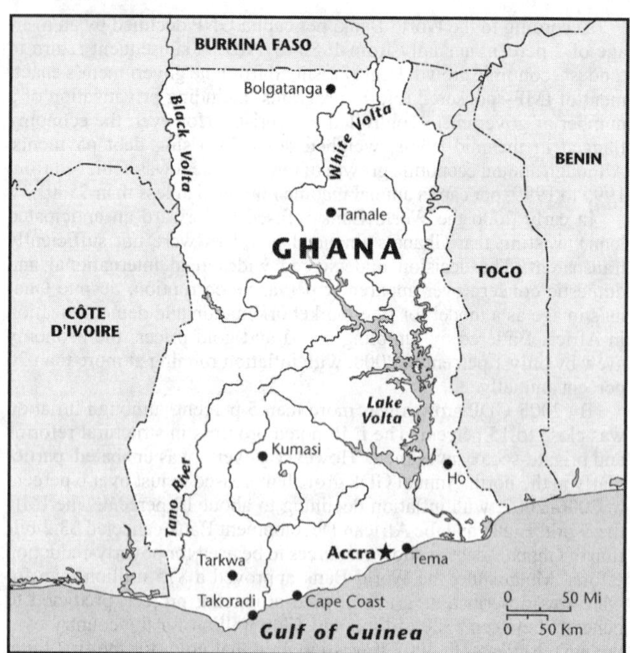

formed to head the government, immediately suspended the constitution, banned political parties, abolished the Supreme Court, and dissolved the National Assembly. In 1975 the NRC was superseded by the Supreme Military Council (SMC).

In the wake of accusations that "governmental activity had become a one-man show," General Acheampong was forced to resign as head of state on July 5, 1978, and he was immediately succeeded by his deputy, (then) Lt. Gen. Frederick W. K. AKUFFO. Promising a return to civilian rule by mid-1979, Akuffo quickly reconstituted a Constitution Drafting Commission, which subsequently presented its recommendations to an appointed, but broadly representative, Constituent Assembly that convened in mid-December.

In the wake of badly received efforts to secure constitutional immunity from future prosecution for existing government officials, Akuffo was ousted on June 4, 1979, by a group of junior military officers. The next day, an Armed Forces Revolutionary Council (AFRC) was established under Flt. Lt. Jerry John RAWLINGS, who had been undergoing court-martial for leading an unsuccessful coup on May 15. Having dissolved the SMC and the Constituent Assembly, the AFRC launched a "house cleaning" campaign, during which former presidents Acheampong, Afrifa, and Akuffo, in addition to a number of other high-ranking military and civilian officials, were accused of corruption and executed. Although the AFRC postponed promulgation of a new constitution until autumn, it did not interfere with scheduled presidential and legislative balloting on June 18. In a runoff presidential poll on July 9, Dr. Hilla LIMANN of the People's National Party, which had won a bare majority in the new National Assembly, defeated Victor OWUSU of the Popular Front Party; Limann was inaugurated on September 24.

The Limann government proved unable to halt further deterioration of the nation's economy and, in the wake of renewed allegations of widespread corruption, was overthrown on December 31, 1981, by army and air force supporters of Lieutenant Rawlings, who was returned to power as head of a Provisional National Defense Council (PNDC). Three weeks later a 17-member cabinet was appointed that included a number of prominent individuals known for their "spotless integrity." Despite a number of subsequent coup attempts (two in 1985 alone), a combination of firmness toward opponents and radical state-policy changes, including reorganization of the judicial and administrative structures, enabled the flight lieutenant to become Ghana's longest post-independence ruler, while district elections in late 1988 and early 1989 were viewed as heralding a return to civilian government.

In January 1991 President Rawlings instructed the National Commission for Democracy (NCD), which had recently sponsored a series of debates on the creation of regional and national assemblies, to draw on its findings, together with the content of past constitutions, in assembling a new national charter. Four months later the regime officially endorsed the NCD's plans for installation of a multiparty system and authorized a nine-member, ad hoc Committee of Experts to draft a constitution. On August 26 the document was submitted to a 258-member consultative assembly, Rawlings announcing that a referendum on the new basic law would be followed by presidential and legislative elections on November 3 and December 8, respectively.

On April 28, 1992, the new constitution, which included provisions for a National Assembly, was approved by 90 percent of the voters, and on May 17 the ban on political parties was lifted. Nevertheless, nine days later the High Court upheld the decision by the Interim National Electoral Commission (INEC) to continue a political-parties law proscribing 21 parties outlawed in 1981 (see Political Parties, below). On September 14 Rawlings resigned from the air force to campaign for the presidency as a candidate for the National Democratic Congress (NDC), the political-party successor to the PNDC.

At presidential balloting on November 3, 1992, Rawlings led the five-candidate field with 58.3 percent of the vote. Although international observers described the polling as "fair," attributing irregularities to deficient "organization and training," the four opposition contenders alleged widespread fraud, including NDC ballot stuffing. On November 13 the opposition announced it would boycott parliamentary balloting until a new electoral register was created (a demand rejected by the administration). Consequently, only 29 percent of eligible voters took part in the legislative poll of December 29 for the 200 assembly seats, with pro-Rawlings candidates securing all but 2.

In 1995 Dr. Kwesi BOTCHWEY, who had championed Ghana's adoption of an IMF-prescribed economic reform program as well as a rescinded value-added tax, resigned as finance minister. Meanwhile, the withdrawal of Vice President Kow Nkensen ARKAAH's National Convention Party (NCP) from the presidential coalition in May reflected ruptured relations between Arkaah and Rawlings.

At presidential balloting on December 7, 1996, Rawlings and his vice-presidential running mate, John Evans ATTA MILLS, defeated by a vote of 57.2–39.8 percent their main rivals, a Great Alliance ticket headed by the New Patriotic Party's (NPP) John KUFUOR, with Arkaah in the vice-presidential slot. At concurrent legislative balloting the NDC retained a nearly 2 to 1 legislative majority, capturing 133 seats to the Great Alliance's 65. Subsequently, in January 1997 the Great Alliance disbanded acrimoniously.

President Rawlings's efforts to name a new government in early 1997 were complicated by difficulties in satisfying the various factions within the NDC as well as by the opposition's insistence that all prospective cabinet members, even incumbents, were subject to assembly approval. As a result, the full cabinet was not completed until midyear, after the opposition had apparently relented on the approval question.

Rawlings being constitutionally prevented from seeking a third term, the NPP's Kufuor led seven candidates in the first round of presidential balloting on December 7, 2000, with 48 percent of the vote and defeated the NDC's Atta Mills by 6 percent in the second round 3 weeks later. Meanwhile, the NPP had also secured a legislative majority in assembly balloting on December 7, setting the stage for installation of an NPP-led cabinet early in 2001.

Kufuor's majority of 52.5 percent of the vote in the presidential balloting of December 7, 2004, secured his second-term victory in the first round of balloting over the NDC's Atta Mills, who received 44.6 percent. The NPP also fared well in the concurrent assembly elections, winning 128 seats in the newly enlarged body of 230 seats. A new government was sworn in on February 1. The cabinet was reshuffled on April 28, 2006, with additional changes made on May 13. The cabinet was reshuffled on July 11, after eight ministers resigned on July 6 to begin campaigning for the presidential election in December 2008. Political party rules require ministers to resign when they apply to be nominated. The cabinet was again reshuffled on January 12, 2008; the energy minister was dismissed in March, and a minor reshuffle took place in May.

As Kufuor's maximum two terms came to an end, a field of eight candidates, including one independent, contested the 2008 presidential elections. After the first-round on December 7, the NPP's Nana Dankwa AKUFO-ADDO garnered 49.1 percent of the vote, while the NDC's John Evans Atta Mills secured 47.9 percent, neither candidate receiving the required 50 percent to clinch the nomination. The results of a subsequent runoff on December 28 were too close to call, leading the electoral commission to schedule one more round of balloting in a single constituency where voting had been postponed due to alleged irregularities. After Atta Mills received 50.2 percent in the runoff in the Tain constituency on January 2, 2009, the electoral commission certified the victory on January 3. Atta Mills and his running mate, John

Dramani MAHAMA, a former communications minister, were sworn in on January 7. The president named a new cabinet, dominated by the NDC and technocrats, which was vetted and approved by parliament in stages from January to mid-February, with most of the 23 ministers seated by February 13.

The NDC was also victorious in concurrent legislative elections on December 7, 2008, becoming the largest party with 114 seats, followed by the previously dominant NPP with 107. On January 7, 2009, Joyce BAMFORD-ADDO became the first woman to be elected speaker of Ghana's National Assembly.

Constitution and government. On August 26, 1991, a consultative assembly of 258 members (117 drawn from district assemblies, 119 representing "identifiable" groups, and 22 governmentally appointed) began deliberations on a new constitution, a draft of which had been published by the government two weeks earlier. The document, which drew from Ghana's previous four constitutions as well as French basic law, was a multiparty instrument featuring a directly elected president; a presidentially appointed vice president; a military–civilian Security Council chaired by the president; a nonpartisan Council of State; a unicameral, directly elected legislative body; and a special committee on human rights and administrative justice.

The new constitution was approved by referendum on April 28, 1992, and on June 10 the PNDC was disbanded, although its ministerial personnel remained in office until March 22, 1993, despite the formal proclamation of Ghana's Fourth Republic on January 7.

Foreign relations. External relations since independence have been pragmatic rather than ideological, the government unilaterally renouncing certain portions of the foreign debt and further disturbing creditor nations by taking partial control of selected foreign enterprises.

Relations with neighboring Togo have been strained since the incorporation of British Togoland into Ghana at the time of independence. In 1977 Ghana accused Togo of smuggling operations aimed at "sabotaging" the Ghanaian economy, while Togo vehemently denied accusations that it was training Ghanaian nationals to carry out acts of subversion in the former British territory. The border between the two countries was periodically closed, Accra repeatedly charging Togolese officials with spreading "vicious lies" about the Rawlings regime and "providing a sanctuary" for its opponents. In a February 1988 effort to interdict commodity smuggling (Togo, without mining, was being credited with multimillion-dollar gold export earnings), Rawlings declared a state of emergency in a number of Ghanaian towns along the Togolese border. The estrangement was substantially alleviated by an October 1991 treaty that resulted in the reopening of border crossings. However, in March 1993 Togolese President Eyadéma accused Ghana of involvement in an attack on his compound, and in early January 1994 the two countries were reportedly "close to war" after Lomé charged Accra with supporting, at least tacitly, a second attack in Togo. On January 7 the Rawlings administration claimed it had no interest in "getting involved in Togo's internal affairs" and urged the Eyadéma government to stop blaming Ghana "whenever there is an armed attack or political crisis." The tension heightened on January 12 when Togolese troops killed 12 Ghanaians at a border post and Togolese naval officers imprisoned 7 Ghanaian fishermen.

In April 1994 Lomé blamed Accra for the "presence of bombs in Togo," thus igniting yet another round of acrimonious exchanges. On a more positive note, Accra appointed an ambassador to Togo in November, and on December 26 the border between the two countries was reopened. In July 1995 Rawlings and Eyadéma signed a cooperation agreement after which Togo appointed an ambassador to Ghana for the first time in over a decade.

Relations with other regional states have been mixed since the 1981 Ghanaian coup. The PNDC moved quickly to reestablish links with Libya (severed by President Limann in November 1980 because of the Qadhafi regime's presumed support of Rawlings), thereby clearing the way for shipments of badly needed Libyan oil. In April 1987 an agreement was signed with Iran for the delivery of 10,000 barrels of crude per day. Concurrently, a number of joint ventures were proposed in agriculture and shipping.

The 1987 overthrow of Burkina Faso's Thomas Sankara by Blaise Compaoré dealt a political and personal blow to Rawlings, who had hoped to form a political union with his northern neighbor by the end of the decade; instead, he encountered in the new Burkinabé president an ally of the Côte d'Ivoire's Houphouët-Boigny, with whom relations were strained. In April 1988, on the other hand, Rawlings and Nigeria's (then) president Gen. Ibrahim Babangida sought to ease tensions stemming from Nigeria's expulsion of Ghanaian workers in 1983 and 1985. In January 1989 the rapprochement yielded a trade agreement that removed all trade and travel barriers between the two countries.

Relations with Côte d'Ivoire worsened further in November 1993, when Ivorians seeking revenge for a murderous attack on supporters of their soccer team in Ghana killed 23 Ghanaian nationals and injured more than 100 others in Abidjan. Although Ivorian authorities established security areas for the Ghanaians, over 9,000 had reportedly fled the country by mid-month. In early 1997, on the other hand, Ivorian president Henri Konan Bédié made the first official visit to Ghana by an Ivorian head of state in nearly four decades. During his stay Bédié proposed broader economic and social ties between the two nations. Tensions heightened somewhat in 2005 after Ghanaian arms smugglers were arrested in the Ivorian town of Tantama. Meanwhile, Ghana indicated enhanced relations with Senegal by opening a new embassy in Dakar. In 2006 Ghana deployed 120 peacekeeping troops to Côte d'Ivoire under the mandate of the United Nations. UN concern was further focused on reports of illegal diamond smuggling into Ghana from Côte d'Ivoire, in violation of UN sanctions and of the Kimberley Process. The UN criticized Ghana for allegedly failing to respond to its own evaluators' reports of suspicious activity.

In 2007 Kufuor was elected president of the African Union (AU). Shortly thereafter, Ghana sent a battalion to help support the AU mission in Somalia. Meanwhile, Ghana signed a 10-year development agreement with Britain, a longtime aid donor.

Hundreds of Liberian refugees were expelled from Ghana and returned to Monrovia in March 2008, despite the refugees' pleas and protests, amid a dispute between the two countries over how to handle the more than 40,000 refugees still in Ghana following the Liberian civil war that began in 1989.

Following the election of President Barack Obama in 2008, the U.S. ambassador described relations with Ghana as "cordial" and suggested that bilateral relations would continue.

Current issues. With the economy in decline in 2000, support for the NDC eroded, contributing to what one observer described as classic "fin de régime" mismanagement on the part of the Rawlings administration. Most analysts attributed the presidential and legislative victories of the NPP in December largely to a general feeling that it was "time for a change," since there were few significant policy differences between the two leading parties. In addition, it was widely acknowledged that candidate Atta Mills lacked the charisma that had carried the previous NDC standard-bearer to electoral success in the 1990s. For his part, Rawlings left office with relative equanimity, calming fears that a peaceful transfer of power from one party to another via free elections, a rare occurrence in the region, might be jeopardized. Meanwhile, new president John Kufuor pledged to intensify free-market economic policies while combating corruption. He also called for "unification," seemingly a reference to the country's potentially unstable ethnic, political, and religious mixes. In that regard, Kufuor established a truth and reconciliation commission to investigate, among other things, the bloodletting that followed the 1979 and 1981 coups. However, that initiative resulted not in harmony but rather in severe NPP/NDC friction as the NDC refused to cooperate with the investigation, claiming it was being "demonized" by the NPP.

Following Kufuor's reelection in 2004 in a race that saw a turnout of about 85 percent and brought praise to Ghana as a stable if struggling democratic nation, the president continued his anticorruption campaign. In a meeting with U.S. President Bush in 2005, Kufuor was commended for his efforts to promote democracy.

Human rights abuses and corruption were the focus of the UN's newly launched African Peer Review Mechanism (APRM) in 2005, with Ghana among the first countries to be reviewed. The initial draft report was "unexpectedly critical," according to *Africa Confidential,* and proposed more funding for government oversight efforts. In early 2006, based on Accra's progress toward policies leading to political stability and economic growth, the UN praised Ghana for its progress. Meanwhile, early in the year, significant tribal conflicts flared in the north, observers warning that continued ethnic conflict could undermine political stability.

Another cause for concern in 2006 was a new law, referenced as the Representation of the People Amendment (ROPA), endorsed by President Kufuor. Five minority parties that opposed the law staged demonstrations in which 9 people were arrested and 20 injured. The law grants some 3 million Ghanaians living abroad the opportunity to vote, clearly benefiting the NPP, according to observers. Supporters contended that since those abroad account for a significant source of foreign revenue, they should have a voice in how the country is run. Opponents, on the other hand, claimed overseas voting without proper monitoring could easily be used to rig elections. The NDC, for its part, threatened to boycott the 2008 elections if Ghanians living abroad are allowed to vote. Nana Dankwa AKUFO-ADDO, the NPP's standard bearer in the 2008 elections, has been described as the leading advocate of ROPA. NPP insiders reportedly saw the demand for allowing Ghanaian ex-patriots to vote as a measure meant to shore up the party, which had become increasingly unpopular since Kufuor barely obtained a majority in 2004. The government had been slow to end the energy crisis, health workers went on strike over pay, and President Kufuor was heavily criticized for spending millions in public money on the AU summit, a new presidential complex, and events to mark the 50th anniversary of independence in 2007. (Most Ghanians abroad were disenfranchised in 2008, the electoral commission citing financial constraints that prevented implementation of registration.)

In November 2007 tensions heightened in a 10-year-old chieftaincy conflict in the Volta region, resulting in violence that left five people dead. Two royal families have been fighting over who should succeed the reigning chief since his death a decade ago. One man reportedly died in police custody and the others died during gunfights with police, raising questions about the extent to which the government should be involved in chieftaincy issues. The constitution bans such involvement, but government officials have said they are compelled to maintain order.

In the run-up to the 2008 presidential elections, the NPP's choice of Akufo-Addo as its presidential candidate over Alan KYEREMATEN, who was favored by President Kufuor, created a party rift that ultimately led to the dismissal of national security minister Francis POKU on January 12, 2008. No official reason was given for the dismissal, but it reportedly was linked to Poku's refusal to arrest leaders of a rally organized largely by the NDC to protest economic disparities. Some observers speculated that Poku's firing had more to do with his refusal to back Kyerematen by securing funds for his campaign. News reports subsequently said Poku had been placed under house arrest and later left the country.

Meanwhile, government officials began talks in early 2008 with oil companies and civil societies to determine how to use revenues from recently discovered offshore oil reserves to best serve the needs of the country. Later in the year, however, the government's announcement that it planned to sell 70 percent of its stake in the state-owned telecommunications company to a British firm for $900 million drew the ire of many, including opposition parties, as the money was earmarked for the government's $130 million deficit at a time when the NPP was "struggling to find the money to pay contractors," according to *Africa Confidential*. Meanwhile, the country's economic troubles were viewed as potentially damaging to the NPP's chances for an upcoming electoral success, as many of the administration's critics said it had not reacted quickly enough to offset the global economic downturn and the resultant price increases. Further, in the days leading up to the December elections, Kufuor approved a civil-service pay raise of between 16 percent and 34 percent and a severance package for himself that included $400,000 in cash, two houses, and six cars, which was passed in a closed session of parliament.

Meanwhile, long-simmering tensions between NDC and NPP supporters in northern Ghana erupted in violence prior to the 2008 general elections, leaving 3 people dead and 12 wounded, with each side accusing the other of looting and stockpiling weapons. However, aside from that episode, there was a marked absence of turmoil surrounding the elections, observers attributing the 69.5 percent turnout to improved security at polling places and a surge in interest by younger voters. Though the NDC edged out both parliamentary and presidential victories in the general elections, the results proved far less than a solid mandate for President Atta Mills, whose margin of victory was less than 50,000 votes, and whose party secured just seven more legislative seats than the NPP. Observers saw little hope for cooperation between the two leading parties, let alone a unity government, citing a "sour political climate" in which many NPP loyalists felt "cheated" after the close elections. Meanwhile, the new president came under attack from his former mentor Rawlings, who publicly criticized him for "mediocre" cabinet appointments and for being "too slow" to prosecute NPP leaders for corruption. (Observers noted that Atta Mills's choice of John Mahama as his running mate, rather than a candidate favored by Rawlings, had been intended, in part, to distance himself from Rawlings in order to counter a commonly held view that Rawlings was likely to direct the new president.) Thus, Atta Mills at once was forced to face "harsh political and economic facts," according to *Africa Confidential*, despite his pledge to unify the country. In addition to the political divisions, the economy was described in dire terms by the World Bank in 2009, and even the newly appointed trade minister declared that Ghana was "broke," which some analysts said was the NDC's way of pointing blame at the NPP's previous failures and explaining why the new administration was unable to follow through on some of its campaign promises, such as cutting gas prices. Nevertheless, Atta Mills began to move forward with plans to stabilize the declining currency, reduce the spiraling budget deficits, and reign in inflation. But in April, the administration raised the minimum wage by 18 percent, despite a provision in the budget of a month earlier that provided for only a 12 percent increase. Meanwhile, Atta Mills ordered a review of Kufuor's severance package and security officers seized some of the former president's property thought to have been state-owned (though some of it was not). He also began tackling alleged corruption, firing some under suspicion from various ministries and the Central Bank (most notably, Mahamudu BAWUMIA, the NPP vice presidential candidate), as well as overhauling public-sector management boards. As Ghana began to deal with an upcoming oil boom, international agencies applauded Atta Mills's announcement that all current and future contracts with oil companies would be made public, described as a "significant move in a sector known more for its secrecy than its openness." Transparency and public input regarding the billions anticipated in oil revenues, as well as the president's broad agenda for reform, were hailed by Oxfam, in particular, as "an important step in the right direction."

POLITICAL PARTIES

Political parties, traditionally based more on tribal affiliation than on ideology, were banned in 1972. The proscription was lifted in early 1979, with 6 groups formally contesting the June election. Following the coup of December 31, 1982, parties were again outlawed until May 17, 1992, when the ban was rescinded in accordance with the multiparty constitution approved on April 28. The new dispensation did not, however, reverse an earlier ruling banning 21 opposition parties, including the All People's Party (APP), Convention People's Party (CPP), National Alliance Party (NAP), Popular Front Party (PFP), Progress Party (PP), and Unity Party (UP). Future parties were also prohibited from using any of the symbols, names, or slogans of the proscribed parties. The Coordinating Committee of Democratic Forces of Ghana (CCDFG), an 11-party, mainly "Nkrumahist" coalition formed in August 1991, strongly objected to the new party provisions and asked the High Court to overturn them. However, the court sided with the ruling Provisional National Defense Council (PNDC).

Four new opposition parties (the New Patriotic Party [NPP], National Independence Party [NIP], People's Heritage Party [PHP], and People's National Convention [PNC]) presented candidates in the November 1992 presidential election. However, the opposition parties boycotted the December legislative elections, charging electoral fraud in presidential balloting on behalf of the National Democratic Congress (NDC), which had been formed to support the presidential campaign of PNDC Chair Jerry Rawlings.

In January 1993 the CCDFG was effectively superseded as the major opposition grouping by the new Inter-Party Coordinating Committee (ICC), which agreed to accept the "present institutional arrangements" but rejected the recent election results, calling for a new round of voting. However, the ICC was weakened somewhat the following August when the NPP (one of the strongest of the new groupings) decided to recognize the disputed election tallies.

Coordinated opposition activity next surfaced in early 1995, under the banner of the Alliance for Change. The NPP-dominated alliance subsequently organized antigovernment demonstrations that forced the Rawlings administration to rescind the recently imposed value-added tax, the coalition's success encouraging it to announce its intention to present an electoral front in 1996. After drawn-out negotiations, which prompted the withdrawal of some components of the Alliance for Change, a new Great Alliance was announced in August 1996 by the NPP and the PCP. Despite being roiled by debate over the choice of legislative candidates until just prior to election day, alliance-affiliated candidates captured over 60 legislative seats in December balloting. Nevertheless, the coalition subsequently collapsed as the NPP and PCP blamed each other for the opposition's failure to secure greater gains.

In the run-up to the 2008 presidential elections, the four legislative parties (the NPP, PNC, CPP, and NDC) signed an agreement that was proposed to be the basis for a law outlining procedures for the orderly transition of power. However, no formal coalitions were formed, and only a few minor parties (including the newly formed Reformed Patriotic Democrats [RPD], below) endorsed the NDC's candidate in the presidential runoff balloting.

Government and Government-Supportive Parties:

National Democratic Congress (NDC). The NDC was formed on June 10, 1992, as a coalition of pro-Rawlings and pro-PNDC political and social clubs, including the New Nation Club and the Development Union. A number of factions emerged within the NDC from 1995 to 1996, including the December 31 Women's Movement (led by the president's wife, Nana Konadu RAWLINGS), which advocated sponsoring female candidates in 30 percent of the constituencies in the upcoming legislative elections. Despite concern over how the party would be able to accommodate its various strains, Jerry Rawlings was selected by acclamation as the NDC presidential nominee at the party's third annual national conference on September 6, 1996. Rawlings, who had been involved in a widely publicized conflict with Vice President Kow Nkensen Arkaah, subsequently selected little-known law professor John Evans Atta Mills as his 1996 running mate.

At the NDC's congress in December 1998, party delegates named Rawlings the NDC "Leader for Life" and, consequently, the president of the party's newly designated decision-making body. Rawlings's ascension to the supreme party post was denounced by members of the NDC Reform Group, who had become increasingly combative following Rawlings's selection of Atta Mills as his would-be successor. In March 1999 the Reform Group announced it intended to form a separate party to compete in the 2000 elections (see National Reform Party, below).

A rift between those loyal to Rawlings and those who supported Chair Obed Yao ASAMOAH surfaced in late 2005, Rawlings blaming Asamoah for the NDC losing in the 2004 elections. Following the party's election of pro-Rawlings candidate Kwabena Adjei to the chairmanship at its December 2005 congress, Asamoah resigned in 2006 and formed a new party (see Democratic Freedom Party, below). Meanwhile, Adjei left the party to become a member of the NPP, and later formed the RPD (below).

In 2007 the NDC staged a two-week parliamentary boycott in protest of the jailing of one of its assembly members on charges of financial irregularities. Subsequently, the party tapped Atta Mills over three other contenders as its 2008 presidential candidate, a move some observers said was meant to demonstrate the party's independence from Rawlings's control. Rawlings had declined to openly support any of the potential NDC candidates. In the run-up to the 2008 elections, several smaller parties were reported to have rejected an electoral alliance with the NDC.

In April 2008 Atta Mills chose as his running mate John Mahama, a 50-year-old former communications minister, in the midst of the ongoing feud between Mills's backers and those loyal to Rawlings and his wife, Nana Konadu Rawlings. Mrs. Rawlings favored another candidate who she thought would challenge the NPP's base in the Ashanti Region. Following a campaign that emphasized the NPP's lack of success in fighting corruption and restoring a battered economy, Atta Mills eked out a narrow victory over the NPP's Akufo-Addo in December 2008, the contest ultimately determined by the results in a single constituency in January 2009. Atta Mills's victory was due, in part, to the RPD's support in the runoff balloting, which split off votes from the NPP. Meanwhile, in the legislative elections the NDC overcame the NPP, albeit by just seven seats, restoring the party to power for the first time since the 1990s, though requiring it to form coalitions in order to achieve a strong majority.

In 2009, Foreign Affairs Minister Alhaji Muhammed Mumuni, under pressure to resign in the wake of a monetary fraud case against him, refused to step down until a court ruled in the matter. President Atta Mills, who had considered replacing the minister, postponed action pending a court decision. Meanwhile, barely 100 days into the new administration, Rawlings was publicly critical of Atta Mills' performance, raising what observers said were fears that someone other than the new president might end up directing the government.

Leaders: John Evans ATTA MILLS (President of the Republic), John Dramani MAHAMA (Vice President of the Republic), Flt. Lt. (Ret.) Jerry John RAWLINGS (Former President of the Republic), Alhaji Muhammed MUMUNI (2004 vice presidential candidate), Haruna IDDRISU, Johnson Asiedu NKETIA (General Secretary).

Convention People's Party (CPP). The CPP considers itself the legitimate successor to the party of the same name formed by former president Nkrumah during the independence campaign. The revived grouping was launched in 1999 under the name Convention Party (due to a legal dispute over the use of the original rubric) as a result of a merger agreement between the People's Convention Party (PCP) and the National Convention Party (NCP).

The PCP had been formed in December 1993 as an apparent successor to the Nkrumahist ICC by the National Independence Party (NIP), the People's Heritage Party (PHP), and the People's Party for Democracy and Development (PPDD). (For further information on the NIP, PHP, and PPDD, see the 1999 *Handbook.*) A faction of the PNC (below) also participated in the launching. (Organizers had reportedly rejected a demand from PNC leader Dr. Hilla Limann that he be named the new party's leader; consequently, only dissident PNC members joined the PCP.)

In early 1996 somewhat confusing reports indicated that the CPP rubric had been revived following a "merger" of the PCP and the NCP, the latter having split from the ruling Progressive Alliance the previous year. However, subsequent news stories routinely still referenced the PCP, and at least a portion of the NCP appeared to remain independent.

In the wake of its disappointing performance (five seats) at December 1996 balloting, the PCP blamed the NPP for the opposition's failure to secure greater representation.

In January 1996 Vice President Kow Nkensen Arkaah participated in the announcement of the "merger" of the NCP and the PCP in a revived CPP. However, other NCP leaders subsequently denounced that coalition, arguing that Arkaah was no longer the leader of their party nor its presidential candidate. Some influential party members later also criticized the Great Alliance formed in August by the NPP and the PCP.

Ending an eight-year legal battle on the issue, the CP was officially permitted to resume use of the CPP rubric in mid-2000. It campaigned for the December elections on a center-left platform that called for increased social spending and deceleration of the pace of economic reform. CPP candidate George HAGAN secured 1.78 percent of the vote in the first round of presidential balloting, the party throwing its support behind the NPP's John Kufuor in the second. The CPP accepted a cabinet post in January 2001, although the party subsequently emphasized that it disagreed with the NPP on many important issues. In the 2004 presidential election, party chair George Aggudey secured just 1 percent of the vote.

In mid-2005 the party reportedly was engaged in unity discussions with the PNC in a move toward gaining political dominance, particularly as more youthful members defected to the CPP from the NPP and the NCP. Three CPP assembly members were dismissed by the party late in the year because they supported the ROPA (see Current issues, above), contrary to the party's position. In 2007 party member Kwaku Emmanuel OSAFO declared his candidacy for the 2008 presidential election. He was endorsed by a group within the party referenced as the Patriots, who vowed to restore Nkrumah's seven-year development plan. Detractors said the so-called Patriots were causing a split in the party with their plans to restructure it.

At the party's congress on December 16–17, 2007, the CPP overwhelmingly elected former minister of public sector reform Paa Kwesi Nduom as its standard-bearer for the 2008 elections. Though Nduom had created a rift in the party when he campaigned for the NPP in 2001, he enjoyed great popular support and political stature. He was reported to have the backing of two key Nkrumahists, both wealthy businessmen who observers note could bring private sector support to the socialist-leaning party. At the same congress, Ladi Nylander, a supporter of Nduom, was elected party chair. Nduom, who subsequently chose Abu SAKARA as his running mate, secured 1.34 percent of the vote in the 2008 presidential balloting, a far distant third in the field of eight candidates. The party, which remained neutral during the presidential runoff, won 1 seat in the concurrent legislative elections.

CPP member Kwabena DUFFUOR, a former central bank governor, stirred controversy when he was named finance minister in 2009, in the wake of 40 percent inflation during his tenure that led to the NPP government firing him in 2000.

Leaders: Ladi NYLANDER (Chair), Paa Kwesi NDUOM (2008 presidential candidate), Abu SAKARA (2008 vice presidential candidate), George AGGUDEY (2004 presidential candidate), Samia NKRUMAH Ivor Kobbina GREENSTREET (Secretary General).

Reformed Patriotic Democrats (RPD). Considered a breakaway group from the NPP, the RPD was subsequently reported to have close ties with the NDC. The party was formed in October 2007 by Kwabena Adjei, a former NDC chair who more recently had been a member of the NPP. The party has its stronghold in the Ashanti Region (which likely helped bolster the NDC in the 2008 presidential runoff election) and among its members were dissident youthful supporters of Ekwow SPIO-GARBRAH, who lost his bid to be NDC flagbearer in 2008. Adjei said the party would focus on the youth of Ghana, with emphasis on "human capacity" and creating jobs, among other things. Following the party's certification in March 2008, its strategy was described by observers as an effort to split the votes between the two main contenders, force a runoff, and then enter into a "serious pact" with the winning party. (The RPD rejected a request in July by the NPP to refrain from contesting the presidential elections.)

Adjei, the party's 2008 presidential candidate, with Rosemond Abraham as his running mate, secured only 0.08 percent of the vote, coming in last among the eight candidates. Subsequently, the RPD strengthened its ties to the NDC by supporting John Evans Atta Mills in the presidential runoff.

Leaders: Kwabena ADJEI (2008 presidential candidate), Rosemond ABRAHAM (2008 vice presidential candidate), Hagan BROWN Jr. (National Chair), John BEDIAKO (Vice Chair), Francis KYEI (Secretary General).

Other Legislative Parties:

New Patriotic Party (NPP). The center-right NPP was launched in June 1992, its founders including former members of the old Progress Party, which had governed Ghana from 1969 to 1972 under Prime Minister Kofi Busia. The NPP's platform advocated the protection of human rights, the strengthening of democratic principles, and the holding of "free and fair elections." At the same time, the new grouping was widely viewed as devoted to the interests of the business class.

In 1994 the NPP sought to forge ties with other opposition groups, agreeing in November to back a single candidate in the next presidential election. Collaterally, it broke off negotiations with the NDC (below), stating that the government was uninterested in maintaining a dialogue. Meanwhile, the party experienced internal debate over its own presidential candidates. At midyear the decision was postponed until 1995 as leaders sought to placate the party's influential Young Executives Forum wing, which had funded Albert Abu BOAHEN's candidacy in 1992 but reportedly sought a new standard-bearer.

At the NPP congress in 1996, delegates chose John Kufuor as the party's presidential candidate. Kufuor declared his intent to forge a coalition with the PCP (see CPP, below), which was achieved in August with the establishment of the Great Alliance. The new alliance selected Kufuor as its common presidential candidate and thereby the main threat to the Rawlings campaign.

After a number of postponements that NPP officials attributed to poor regional organization, the party convened its fourth congress in 1998. At balloting for leadership posts, Secretary General Agyenim BOATENG was ousted in favor of 39-year-old Dan BOTWE, whose victory highlighted what observers described as a youth movement within the party. At further intraparty balloting in October, Kufuor outpolled five other NPP would-be presidential candidates and secured the party's backing for another national campaign in 2000. In part, the NPP's success in the 2000 legislative balloting (100 seats versus 60 in 1996) was attributed to its "clean sweep" in areas dominated by the Ashanti ethnic group. Meanwhile, Kufuor secured 48.2 percent of the vote in the first round of the presidential election before winning the post with 56.9 percent in the second round.

In 2005 a rift developed over allegations attributed to party chair Haruna ESSEKU concerning contributors' kickbacks to the president. Esseku denied he had made such allegations, which some observers claimed were made up to keep him from retaining chairmanship of the party. The president also denied the allegations. Subsequently, Peter Mac Manu was elected party chair at the December congress.

As President Kufuor's second term drew to a close, the party's attention turned to naming a possible successor. However, infighting marked the run-up to the NPP congress in December 2007, when it selected Akufo-Addo as its presidential candidate over Alan Kyerematen, who was favored by Kufuor. In light of large sums of money having been spent on the campaigns of many of the 17 candidates vying for the party's nod, Kyerematen became widely known by the nickname "Alan Cash." Kyerematen ultimately conceded to avoid a runoff "for the sake of unity." Another rift occurred in late 2007 when Kwabena Adjei, a key political figure in the Ashanti Region, and a number of youthful followers formed the Reformed Patriotic Democrats (RPD, above). Adjei had shifted alliances a few times, having been a member of the NDC prior to 2007.

Further tension, albeit short-lived, ensued in April 2008 when Kyerematen abruptly left the party, citing harassment of his supporters following the party's selection of Akufo-Addo as its standard-bearer. Two weeks later, however, President Kufuor persuaded him to return to the fold.

In the run-up to the 2008 general elections, the NDC alleged vote-rigging by the NPP via "bloated" voter-registration rolls, and following an investigation by the electoral commission, some discrepancies were found. Although violent clashes occurred between NPP and NDC supporters in northern Ghana in August, the subsequent elections were reported to be peaceful. However, the NPP lost its dominant status as Akufo-Addo was defeated in presidential balloting by a slim margin, along with running mate Mahamudu Bawumia, and ultimately in a January 2009 single-constituency runoff, which the NPP sought unsuccessfully to delay. The NPP also finished second in the legislative elections, albeit by just seven seats, but suffered a net loss of 20 seats from the 2004 balloting.

Meanwhile, in April 2009 Kyerematen was reported to have already put his name in contention for flagbearer of the NPP in 2012.

Leaders: John Agyekum KUFUOR (Former President of the Republic), Alhaji Aliu MAHAMA (Former Vice President of the Republic), Peter MAC MANU (Chair), Stephen NTIM, Nana Dankwa AKUFO-ADDO (2008 presidential candidate), Mahamudu BAWUMIA (2008 vice presidential candidate), Alhaji A. MUSAH, Ambrose DERY, Nana Ohene NTOW (Secretary General).

People's National Convention (PNC). The PNC was launched on May 30, 1992, by former president Dr. Hilla Limann, who finished third in the November presidential balloting. In late 1993 the party was divided by Limann's initial antipathy toward opposition party unity talks and subsequently by his reported insistence that he be named the leader of any group that emerged therefrom. In October *West Africa* reported that among the PNC members opposing Limann was his close aide, Dr. Ivan ADDAE-MENSAH, who accused the former president of unconstitutional party activities, and by November a number of the PNC's constituent parties had reportedly broken off to join the PCP. In December Limann announced that despite the party schism he would continue to fend off merger efforts and "serve as a watchdog of the constitution."

Criticizing Rawlings's performance as leaving "much to be desired," Limann asserted in April 1994 that he "could prove equal to the task of leading Ghana again." However, at a party congress in 1996 Limann agreed to step aside to allow delegates "to inject fresh blood into the party." Subsequently, Edward Mahama was named the PNC's 1996 presidential candidate by acclamation, the PNC deciding to "go it alone" rather than participate in the Great Alliance formed by the NPP and the PCP. At balloting on December 7, Mahama secured just 3 percent of the presidential tally and the party won 1 legislative seat.

On January 23, 1998, former president Limann died. At the PNC's congress in September, Mahama was elected chair and chosen to represent the party at 2000 presidential polling, at which he secured 2.92 percent of the vote in the first round. (The PNC supported the NPP's John Kufuor in the second round.) During the 2000 presidential and legislative campaigns, the PNC claimed to be the legitimate successor to Kwame Nkrumah's original CPP, although it had lost a legal battle to use the CPP's rubric. The PNC's platform was described as "populist," albeit with a noticeable capitalistic bent. In 2004 Mahama again ran for the presidency as the PNC's candidate, with the backing of the EGLE (below) in what was called the Grand Coalition, but received only 1.9 percent of the vote. In concurrent assembly balloting, the PNC contested the election with the EGLE and the GCPP (below) under the mantle of the Grand Coalition, the PNC being credited with winning four seats.

In 2006 the party was engaged in unity discussions with the CPP, similar talks having been unsuccessful in the past. Also in 2006 First Vice Chair John NDEBUGRE was suspended because of his support for ROPA (see Current issues, above), in opposition to the party's position on the new law. Ndebugre subsequently resigned and was replaced by Alhaji Ahmed Ramadan.

The party again chose Edward Mahama to be its presidential candidate in the 2008 elections. During his campaign, Mahama in January 2008 called for the formation of a coalition government to include the NPP and the NDC to curb the animosity that he said was detrimental to democracy in Ghana. Meanwhile, a tentative electoral alliance with the CPP collapsed due to "mistrust," the PNC subsequently contesting the elections on its own. Mahama, who had chosen Petra Amegashie as his running mate, secured 0.87 percent of the vote, fourth among the eight candidates. The party, which won two seats in concurrent legislative balloting, remained neutral during the presidential runoff election.

Leaders: Dr. Edward MAHAMA (Chair and 1996, 2000, 2004, and 2008 presidential candidate), Petra AMEGASHIE (2008 vice presidential candidate), Alhaji Ahmed RAMADAN (National Chair), Bernard MONARH (General Secretary).

Other Parties that Participated in the 2008 Legislative Elections:

Democratic Freedom Party (DFP). Founded in 2006 by former NDC chair Obed Yao Asamoah, the DFP was launched as an alternative opposition group after Asamoah lost his fight for control of the NDC to a pro-Rawlings faction. Asamoah, a longtime foreign minister and attorney general, said he hoped to attract those disillusioned with all of the main parties.

In 2008 the party chose Emmanuel Ansah-Antwi over the interim national chair, Alhaji Issaka as its presidential candidate, longtime party leader Obed Yao Asamoah having ruled out contesting the election himself. Ansah-Antwi, with Patience Amesimeku as his running mate, won just 0.33 percent of the vote, placing fifth among the eight candidates.

Leaders: Kwaku BAAH (Chair), Obed Yao ASAMOAH, Emmanuel ANSAH-ANTWI (2008 presidential candidate), Patience AMESIMEKU (2008 vice presidential candidate), Alhaji ISSAKA, John AMEKA (Deputy Secretary General), Bede A. ZIEDENG (Secretary General).

Democratic People's Party (DPP). Founded in 1992 after the ban on political parties was rescinded, the DPP is a small party with a Nkruhmaist orientation. Party founder and leader Thomas Ward-Brew, often described as a maverick, missed the filing deadline for the 2004 presidential election. In 2007 the DPP brought a suit against a Dutch-based organization for allegedly illegally funding four political parties in Ghana. Ward-Brew was again nominated to be the party's flagbearer in the 2008 presidential election, choosing Peter Dwamena, a retired banker, as his running mate. Ward-Brew secured just 0.10 percent of the vote, finishing seventh among the eight candidates. While the DPP officially remained neutral during the presidential runoff, a group of DPP members from the northern region allegedly accepted money from the NPP and led the public to believe the party was supporting the NPP. Four of the accused DPP members were subsequently expelled from the party in 2009.

Leaders: Thomas WARD-BREW (Chair and 2008 presidential candidate), Peter DWAMENA (2008 vice presidential candidate), Mohammed Salisu SULEMANA (Secretary General).

New Vision Party (NVP). Founded in June 2008 by the Rev. Daniel Yaw Nkansah, the party endorsed democratic socialist principles, though some observers viewed it as more of a religious-based group. "Prophet Nkansah," as he was known, pledged to help the poor by providing free access to health care and free education up to the senior high school level, and he invited members of all religions to join the party and help unseat "wicked politicians." Though five candidates from the party contested the 2008 legislative elections, none was elected.

Leaders: Rev. Daniel Yaw NKANSAH, Aaron KING, Prince GAMBRAH (Regional Chair), Zurkanain ADAMS (Vice Chair), Samuel DUODU (Regional Secretary).

Other Parties that Participated in Recent Elections:

Every Ghanaian Living Everywhere Party (EGLE). The (then) Eagle Club was formed in 1991, allegedly as a political affiliate of the PNDC. However, in mid-1992 the renamed EGLE party declined to offer a blanket endorsement for all PNDC–NDC legislative candidates, positioning itself only as a pro-Rawlings grouping. EGLE did not put forth its own presidential candidate for the 2004 election, and instead joined in a Grand Coalition with the PNC and the GCPP (below) to support the PNC's Edward Mahama. The coalition also contested the concurrent assembly elections, with only the PNC credited as having won seats.

Party leader Nana Yaa OFORI-ATTA died in May 2007.

The party supported the NDC's Atta Mills in the 2008 presidential election.

Leaders: Alhasan Alhaji BENE (National Chair), Alhaji Rahman JAMATUTU (Vice Chair), Henry GIDI, Sam Pee YALLEY (General Secretary).

Great Consolidated Popular Party (GCPP). Formed in 1996, the GCPP, having lost its bid to be designated as the legitimate successor to the original CPP, presented its chair, Daniel Lartey, as a presidential candidate in 2000. He won only 1.04 percent of the vote in the first round and endorsed the NPP's John Kufuor in the second round. The GCPP did not put forth a candidate for president in 2004, but it supported the PNC's Mahama as part of the Grand Coalition with the PNC and the EGLE. In concurrent assembly elections, the GCPP also was represented in the Grand Coalition.

Though the party nominated Lartey to contest the 2008 presidential elections, his candidacy was rejected by the electoral commission, which said the GCPP had not complied with rules regarding regional party congresses. Though the GCPP threw its support behind the NDC in the presidential runoff, Lartey subsequently vowed to unseat Atta Mills in 2012, when Lartey would be 86 years old.

Leaders: John THOMPSON (Chair), Daniel LARTEY (2000 presidential candidate), Adams ALI (Secretary General).

Other Parties and Groups:

United Ghana Movement (UGM). The UGM was launched in Accra in mid-1996 under the interim chairmanship of Dr. Charles Wereko-Brobby, a former Rawlings cabinet minister and prominent leader of the NPP who had expressed concern that an effective anti-Rawlings front would not be established by the NPP and CPP. After those two groups did in fact agree to a coalition in August, speculation arose that the UGM might be dismantled. However, it was subsequently reported that the movement had proceeded with its request for formal recognition. Earlier, Wereko-Brobby, a leader of the "professional, middle-class" component of the Alliance for Change, had announced his intention to support the proposed (eventually aborted) presidential candidacy of Kwiame PIANIM.

The UGM was granted formal recognition in January 1997, and Wereko-Brobby subsequently vowed to organize supporters in each of Ghana's voting districts to contest the presidential and legislative elections in 2000. However, Wereko-Brobby won only 0.34 percent of the vote in the first round of the presidential poll. In recent years the party has been listed as "in hibernation."

In 2007 it was reported that the party had dissolved.

Leaders: Dr. Charles WEREKO-BROBBY (Chair and 2000 presidential candidate), Eric K. DYTENYA (General Secretary).

National Reform Party (NRP). Originally organized to function as a reform-minded faction within the NDC, the NRP formally registered as an independent party in June 1999 with the intent of forwarding a candidate at the 2000 presidential elections. The reform faction's decision to break with the NDC was reportedly precipitated by alleged attempts by the Rawlings camp to "undemocratically" control the party, in particular the president's pledge to back the presidential candidacy of Vice President Atta Mills.

Augustus Tanoh, a lawyer and businessman and former Rawlings ally, secured 1.21 percent of the vote in the first round of presidential balloting in December 2000. The NRP subsequently supported the NPP's John Kufuor in the second round, although party leaders resisted overtures to join the new cabinet, denying that Cecilia BANNERMAN, the new minister for manpower development and employment, was an official member of the NRP as claimed by the administration.

The party did not field a candidate in the 2008 presidential election. Meanwhile, Secretary General Kyeretwie Opoku was reported to be joining Atta Mills's NDC campaign.

Leaders: Augustus Obuadum "Goosie" TANOH (Chair and 2000 presidential candidate), Peter KPORDUGBE, Kyeretwie OPOKU (General Secretary).

United Renaissance Party (URP). The URP was established in June 2006 by Charles Kofi Wayo, an outspoken NPP and then PNC dissident, as a reformist party with the goal of unseating the NPP in the 2008 elections. The URP leaders vowed to fight alleged government corruption, maldistribution of wealth, and the slow pace of development. Wayo, described as a maverick, said if he was elected he would change the constitution to allow for military ouster of the government if it did not live up to its mandatory "performance contract" within six months.

The party, which has also been referenced as the United Republican Party, was reported to have formed a loose alliance with the NDC in advance of the 2008 elections.

Leaders: Charles Kofi WAYO (Chair), Rev. Sampson SADJIE, Alhaji Alhassan SAEED (Secretary General).

Ghana National Party (GNP). Described as a social democratic party and as the "diaspora party," its founders living in the United States and Europe, the GNP was registered as an official party in 2007 with the intent of fielding candidates in the 2008 presidential and legislative elections. Poverty, unemployment, and perceived government corruption were among the GNP's greatest concerns, with party leaders pledging, if elected, to include all tribes in the government. Party chair K. Ofori Ampofo moved to Ghana upon the party's certification.

It was reported in 2008 that the GNP had formed a loose alliance with the NDC in advance of the presidential elections.

Leaders: Kobina AMO-AIDOO (Chair), K. Ofori AMPOFO (Executive Chair and Cofounder), Eric SARPONG, Maat OPOKU, Michel BOWMAN-AMUAH, Dr. Kwaku Abiam DANSO, Simon DEWOTOR (Secretary General).

United Love Party (ULP). Publicity on this group appeared in February 2008, when its leader, Ramon Osei AKOTO, announced its formation to support his bid for the presidency. Akoto was unsuccessful in getting nominated as an independent prior to the 2004 presidential election and subsequently joined the NDC. However, he later became an outspoken critic of the NPP and the NDC, and as ULP leader made wide-ranging pledges, including free utilities and uninterrupted electricity under his government, the creation of 5 million high-paying jobs within four years, and greater emphasis on the fight against malaria.

Leaders: Ramon Osei AKOTO (Chair), Robert ARMANU, Ken AMOAH (Secretary General).

Ghana Democratic Republican Party (GDRP). Founded in 1992 in the United States and described as an "idealistic" party, the GDRP was linked to billionaire Kofi AMOAH. He proposed bringing the principles of democratic governance, personal freedom, and the enhancement of the private sector back to Ghana. No recent activity by the party has been reported.

LEGISLATURE

The unicameral **National Assembly** elected in June 1979 was dissolved following the coup of December 31, 1981. The new constitution, approved in April 1992, provided for the establishment of a directly elected body of 200 members, each to serve a four-year term.

In 2004, based on census figures from 2000, the assembly was expanded to 230 seats.

In the most recent election, on December 7, 2008, in which 1,060 candidates vied for 230 seats, the seat distribution was as follows: the National Democratic Congress, 114; the New Patriotic Party, 107; independents, 4; the People's National Convention 2; and the Convention People's Party, 1. Two seats were undecided as of April 2009.

Speaker: Joyce BAMFORD-ADDO.

CABINET

[as of April 1, 2009]

President	John Evans Atta Mills
Vice President	John Dramani Mahama
Ministers	
Communications	Haruna Iddrisu
Culture and Chieftancy Affairs	Alex Asum-Ahensah
Defense	Maj. Gen. Joseph Smith
Education	Alex Tettey-Enyo
Employment and Social Welfare	Stephen Amanor Kwao
Energy	Oteng Adjei
Environment, Science, and Technology	Sherry Aryittey [f]
Finance and Economic Planning	Kwabena Duffuor
Food and Agriculture	Kwwesi Ahwol
Foreign Affairs and Regional Integration,	Alhaji Muhammed Mumuni
Health	Dr. George Sippah Yankey
Information	Zita Okai Kwei [f]
Interior	Cletus Avoka
Justice and Attorney General	Betty Mould-Iddrisu [f]
Lands, and Natural Resources	Collins Dauda
Local Government and Rural Development	Joseph Yieleh Chireh
Roads and Highways	Joe Gidisu
Tourism	Juliana Azumah-Mensah [f]
Trade and Industry	Hannah Tetteh [f]
Transport	Mike Hammah
Women's and Children's Affairs	Akusa Sena Danusa [f]
Works and Housing, Water Resources	Albert A. Abongo
Youth and Sports	Muntaka Mubarak
Ministers of State	
Office of the President	Azong Alhassan
	Hajia Rafatu Halutie Dubie Alhassan [f]
	Abdul Rashid Pelpuo
	Amadu Seidu
	Lokpalimor Kwadwo Tawiah
Regional Ministers	
Ashanti	Kofi Opoku Manu
Brong Ahafo	Nyamekye Marfo
Central	Ama Benyiwa-Doe
Eastern	Samuel Ampofo
Greater Accra	Nii Amah Ashitey
Northern	Steven Sumani Nayina
Upper East	Mark Woyongo
Upper West	Mahmud Khalid
Volta	Joseph Amenowode
Western	Paul Evans Aidoo

[f] = female

COMMUNICATIONS

Under the 1979 constitution, state-owned media were required to "afford equal opportunities and facilities for the representation of opposing or differing views," and the Ghanaian press was one of the freest and most outspoken in Western Africa. However, following the 1981 coup, radio and television and the leading newspapers were perceived as little more than propaganda organs. The climate gradually improved and by 2006 Reporters Without Borders significantly increased Ghana's press-freedom ranking (to fourth in Africa), noting that while Ghanaian media faces economic obstacles, "it is no longer threatened by the authorities."

Press. The following are published in English in Accra, unless otherwise indicated: *Ghanaian Voice* (100,000), bi-weekly; *The Pioneer* (Kumari, 100,000), daily; *The Mirror* (90,000), government-owned weekly; *Ghanaian Chronicle* (60,000), independent, three times a week; *Ghanaian Times* (50,000), government-owned daily; *Daily Graphic* (40,000), government-owned daily, *Daily Guide*, private; *Echo* (40,000), weekly; *Weekly Spectator*, government-owned weekly; the *Ghanaian Observer*, private tri-weekly; *Ghana Palaver*, weekly; the *Independent* and the *Sunday Herald*, both weekly.

News agencies. The domestic facility is the official Ghana News Agency (GNA). AFP, AP, *Xinhua*, UPI, DPA, and ITAR-TASS maintain offices in Accra.

Broadcasting and computing. In 1995 and 1996, the government ended the monopoly of the statutory Ghana Broadcasting Corporation by issuing radio and television licenses to more than three dozen private firms. TV3, dating to 1997, is one of the leading private networks. As of 2008 there were 42.7 Internet users per 1,000 inhabitants.

INTERGOVERNMENTAL REPRESENTATION

Ambassador to the U.S.: (Vacant).

U.S. Ambassador to Ghana: Donald Gene TEITELBAUM.

Permanent Representative to the UN: Leslie Kojo CHRISTIAN.

IGO Memberships (Non-UN): AfDB, AU, BADEA, CWTH, ECOWAS, Interpol, IOM, NAM, WCO, WTO.

GREECE

Hellenic Republic
Elliniki Dimokratia

Political Status: Gained independence from the Ottoman Empire in 1830; military rule imposed following coup of April 21, 1967; civilian control reinstituted July 23, 1974; present republican constitution promulgated June 11, 1975.

Area: 50,944 sq. mi. (131,944 sq. km.).

Population: 10,964,020 (2001C); 11,256,000 (2008E).

Major Urban Centers (2007E): ATHENS (720,979, urban area, 3,799,134), Thessaloniki (Salonika, 363,987, urban area, 966,725), Patras (164,741), Iraklion (140,357), Larissa (130,946).

Official Language: Greek.

Monetary Unit: Euro (market rate December 1, 2009: 1 euro = $1.51US).

President: Karolos PAPOULIAS (Panhellenic Socialist Movement); elected by Parliament on February 8, 2005, and sworn in on March 12 for a five-year term, succeeding Konstantinos (Kostis) STEPHANOPOULOS (Democratic Renewal), who was constitutionally precluded from a third term.

Prime Minister: Konstantinos (Kostas) KARAMANLIS (New Democracy); appointed by the president following parliamentary elections of March 7, 2004, and sworn in with a new government on March 10 to succeed Konstantinos (Kostas) SIMITIS (Panhellenic Socialist Movement); reappointed following parliamentary elections of September 16, 2007, and sworn in with a new government on September 19.

THE COUNTRY

Occupying the southern tip of the Balkan Peninsula and including some 3,700 islands in the Ionian and Aegean seas, the Hellenic Republic is peopled overwhelmingly by Greeks but also includes small minority groups of Turks, Pomaks, Roma, and others. Since the early 1990s hundreds of thousands of immigrants from Albania, other Balkan and East European countries, the Middle East, and South Asia have settled in Greece and significantly changed the country's social fabric. More than 95 percent of the people speak modern (*dimotiki*) Greek, a more classical form (*katharevoussa*) no longer being employed in either government or university circles. The majority of the population belongs to the Eastern Orthodox Church, whose status is regulated by Article 3 of the Constitution. (Ecclesiastical decisions are subject to appeal at the Supreme Administrative Court and clergy salaries are paid by the state.) In 1996 women constituted 37 percent of the paid workforce, with three-fifths of those classed as "economically active" in rural areas performing unpaid agricultural family labor; urban women are concentrated in the clerical and service sectors. Female representation in government at all levels is low in comparison to that of most other members of the European Union (EU).

Traditionally based on agriculture, with important contributions from shipping and tourism, the Greek economy in the 1970s witnessed substantial increases in the industrial sector, notably in chemical, metallurgical, plastics, and textile production. This expansion was accompanied by severe inflationary pressures, the consumer price index rising by an average of approximately 20 percent annually from 1980 to 1991, and unemployment at around 10 percent of the labor force. After the end of the Cold War, many Greek firms expanded their operations into southeastern Europe. These investments in neighboring states account today for a considerable percentage of Greece's GNP.

Greece's budget deficit and public debt in 1997 remained well above the criteria set by the Maastricht Treaty for admission to the EU's proposed Economic and Monetary Union (EMU) and collateral use of the new euro currency; the Greek inflation rate of 5.4 percent was also too high to qualify. Consequently, when the European Commission announced its recommendations in early 1998 on the matter, Greece was the only 1 of the 12 EU members interested in the EMU not to be invited to participate in its launching in January 1999. However, Greek leaders pledged to pursue further economic improvement to permit EMU membership as soon as possible. In anticipation of that eventuality, the Greek drachma became part of the EU's Exchange Rate Mechanism in March 1998.

Economic growth in 1998 exceeded the EU average, while the budget deficit was trimmed under the strict economic reforms implemented by the Konstantinos (Kostas) SIMITIS administration, which had also spurred stock market optimism. The International Monetary Fund (IMF) and other global financial institutions praised the government's policies, although they cautioned that additional measures were necessary, including further privatization of inefficient state-run enterprises and moderation in regard to wage increases in order to reduce inflation, which at about 4 percent in 1998 was still outside the Maastricht criteria.

Inflation fell to about 3 percent in 2000, with the budget deficit having declined to only 1.5 percent of GDP, sufficient to permit Greece's formal entry into the EMU and adoption of the euro effective January 1, 2001. At the same time, however, high public debt and unemployment (12 percent) remained problematic, while international financial experts urged the government to work to simplify the tax system, improve public services, and combat corruption within the state sector. Nevertheless, by the end of 2001 the country was enjoying what one journalist called an "unprecedented gloss of prosperity" that had encouraged foreign investors seeking access to emerging markets in nearby countries.

The nation's economic growth subsequently slowed as public spending increased, especially in connection with the government's preparation for the 2004 summer Olympics and the decision of the Konstantinos (Kostas) KARAMANLIS government to alter the accounting standards followed by the Simitis government. The deficit increased to 6 percent of GDP, prompting disciplinary action by the European Commission. Meanwhile, Greece's debt-to-GDP ratio expanded to 105 percent, making it one of the highest in the euro zone. Indeed, in November 2004, Greece's credit rating with Standard & Poor's was lowered to Single A, with the credit agency citing the government's lack of a clear plan to reduce its debt burden. (On January 14, 2009, the rate was further cut to A-minus by Standard & Poor's, which cited the country's weakening finances in the wake of the global economic downturn. This development further increased the borrowing costs of the Greek government.)

In March 2005 the administration announced broad tax increases in order to enhance revenue, and fiscal improvement was quickly noted. Consequently, the EU told Greece that sanctions could be avoided if the deficit target (3 percent of GDP) could be reached by the end of 2006. Greece's budget situation improved markedly throughout 2005, with the deficit in 2006 falling to 2.4 percent, thanks to stronger than expected growth and spending curbs. GDP expanded by 4.3 percent in 2006 up from 3.7 percent in 2005, with inflation at 3.2 percent, and unemployment at 8.6 percent. On May 16, 2007, the European Commission recommended ending disciplinary action. Concern about the budget deficit was heightened by a 2007 inflation rate of 4.9 percent, which was brought on by soaring energy prices. Economic growth expanded by 4 percent in 2007 but was slowed to 2.4 percent in 2008 and was forecast to contract by 1 to 2 percent in 2009, due to the global financial crisis. Unlike other European states, Greece was not able to

implement a comprehensive stimulus program due to its heavy indebtedness, which was projected to exceed 100 percent of the GDP in 2009.

GOVERNMENT AND POLITICS

Political background. Conquered by the Ottomans in the later Middle Ages, Greece emerged as an independent kingdom in 1830 after a protracted war of liberation conducted with help from Great Britain, France, and Russia. Its subsequent history has been marked by championship of Greek nationalist aspirations throughout the Eastern Mediterranean and recurrent internal upheavals, reflecting, in part, a continuing struggle between royalists and republicans. The monarchy, abolished in 1924, was restored in 1935 and sponsored the dictatorship of Gen. Ioannis (John) METAXAS (1936–1941) before the royal family took refuge abroad upon Greece's occupation by the Axis powers in April 1941. The resumption of the monarchy in 1946 took place in the midst of conflict between Communist and anti-Communist forces that had erupted in 1944 and was finally terminated when the Communists were defeated with British and subsequent U.S. military assistance in August 1949. A succession of conservative governments held office until 1964, when the Center Union, a center-left coalition led by Georgios (George) PAPANDREOU, achieved a parliamentary majority. Disagreements with the young King Konstantinos (CONSTANTINE) on military and other issues led to the resignation of Papandreou in 1965, initiating a series of crises that culminated in a coup d'état and the establishment of a military junta on April 21, 1967. An unsuccessful attempt by the king to mobilize support against the junta the following December yielded the appointment of a regent, the flight of the king to Rome, and a reorganization of the government whereby (then) Col. Georgios (George) PAPADOPOULOS, a junta member, became prime minister.

In May 1973 elements of the Greek navy attempted a countercoup in order to restore the king, but the plot failed, resulting in formal deposition of the monarch and the proclamation of a republic on June 1. Papadopoulos's formation of a civilian cabinet and the scheduling of an election for early 1974 resulted in his ouster on November 25 by a conservative military group under the leadership of Brig. Gen. Dimitrios IOANNIDIS. However, following the abortive junta-supported Cyprus coup of July 15, 1974, and the Turkish invasion of the island on July 20, the new regime was forced on July 24 to call on Konstantinos Karamanlis to form a caretaker government in advance of a return to civilian rule. Karamanlis was confirmed as prime minister following a parliamentary election on November 17, and Michael STASSINOPOULOS was designated provisional president a month later. Stassinopoulos was succeeded as president by Konstantinos TSATSOS on June 19, 1975. On November 28, 1977, eight days after an early election in which his New Democracy (ND) party retained control of the legislature by a reduced majority, Karamanlis formed a new government. He resigned as prime minister on May 6, 1980, following his parliamentary designation as president the day before, and he was succeeded on May 9 by Georgios RALLIS.

At the general election of October 18, 1981, the Panhellenic Socialist Movement (PASOK) swept to victory with a margin of 22 seats on a vote share of 48.1 percent, and Dr. Andreas PAPANDREOU (son of the pre-coup premier) formed Greece's first socialist administration three days later. Despite ongoing complaints that the PASOK leadership had failed to make good on its election promises, the government was given a vote of confidence at the European Parliament election in June 1984, winning 41.6 percent of the vote and capturing 10 of the 24 available seats.

President Karamanlis resigned on March 10, 1985, after Papandreou had withdrawn an earlier pledge to support his reelection. In a legislative poll on March 29, the PASOK nominee, Christos SARTZETAKIS, was elected to a regular five-year term as head of state. Subsequently, PASOK remained in power, with a reduced legislative margin of 11 seats on a vote share of 45.8 percent, as the result of an early general election on June 2.

Damaged by a series of scandals, PASOK was defeated at legislative balloting on June 18, 1989, by the ND, which itself fell six seats short of a majority. Two weeks of intense negotiations followed, with the ND and the Communist-led Progressive Left Coalition agreeing on July 1 to form an anti-PASOK administration on condition that its mandate be for only three months and limited to "restoring democratic institutions and cleansing Greek political life." On September 20 Papandreou, his parliamentary immunity having been lifted, was ordered to stand trial on charges of having authorized illegal wiretaps while in office; eight days later the former prime minister and four associates were also indicted for a variety of offenses, which included bribery and the receipt of stolen funds.

On October 11, 1989, the president of the Supreme Court, Ioannis GRIVAS, was asked to form an essentially nonpartisan caretaker administration, which was sworn in the following day. At the year's second parliamentary poll on November 5, the ND registered a net gain of only three seats (three short of a majority), with PASOK gaining an equal number. In consequence, the three main parties agreed on November 21 to form a coalition government under a former governor of the Bank of Greece, Xenophon ZOLOTAS.

Despite an announcement on January 26, 1990, that another legislative election would be held on April 8, the all-party Zolotas government collapsed on February 12 because of continuing disagreement among the coalition partners over economic policy, and it was succeeded by a caretaker administration. At the ensuing poll the ND fell one seat short of a majority, but, with the support of the sole Democratic Renewal (DIANA) member, it was able to secure the installation of a government headed by Konstantinos (Constantine) MITSOTAKIS on April 11. Meanwhile, with the ND abstaining, Parliament had been unable to elect a new state president in three rounds of balloting on February 19, February 25, and March 3. The impasse was broken on May 4 by the new Parliament, which returned former president Karamanlis to office.

On January 17, 1992, PASOK leader Papandreou was acquitted of the corruption charges against him. Despite poor health, previous scandals, and a much-publicized divorce from his second wife, he led his party on October 10, 1993, to decisive victory at an early election necessitated by a series of ND parliamentary defections. These defections were made in reaction to the intention of Prime Minister Mitsotakis to support a compromise solution in Greece's name dispute with the Former Yugoslav Republic of Macedonia (FYROM). The defectors led by former foreign minister Antonios SAMARAS formed a new political party, the now-defunct Political Spring (*Politiki Anixi*—POLAN), which won ten seats in the 1993 elections. Samaras won an MP seat on the ND ballot in the 2007 parliamentary elections.

In September 1994 the Greek Parliament voted, without the participation of ND deputies, to indict three former ND ministers, including former prime minister Mitsotakis, on financial corruption charges. However, arguing that a trial would be politically divisive, Papandreou in mid-January 1995 induced Parliament to drop the charges against Mitsotakis.

In parliamentary balloting for a new president, center-right politician Konstantinos (Kostis) STEPHANOPOULOS was elected on the third ballot on March 8, 1995, with 181 votes to 109 for an ND nominee. The votes for the successful candidate, amounting to one more than the required three-fifths majority, came from PASOK and the small POLAN grouping.

Growing divisions within PASOK were highlighted by the resignation in September 1995 of the commerce, industry, energy, and technology minister, Konstantinos (Kostas) Simitis, because of opposition to his modernization policies in the PASOK executive. When the elderly prime minister fell seriously ill in November, a full-scale succession struggle ensued, with the influence of Papandreou's wife, Dimitra (Mimi) LIANI, proving to be a controversial factor. The recently appointed interior minister, Apostolos-Athanassios (Akis) TSOCHATZOPOULOS, became acting prime minister and appeared to be well placed in the leadership battle. However, following Papandreou's resignation on January 15, 1996, balloting of PASOK deputies on January 18 resulted in a narrow second-round victory for Simitis, who was sworn in as prime minister four days later.

Arguing that he needed a full-term mandate to deal with the challenges facing the country (and encouraged by high public-approval ratings of his initial performance), Simitis called an early general election on September 22, 1996. The outcome was a reduced but still comfortable majority of 162 seats (out of 300) for PASOK, with the added bonus that the main opposition ND slipped to 108 seats, while three small left-wing parties polled strongly to win the remaining 30 seats among them. A further PASOK administration sworn in on September 25 contained a number of personnel changes designed to strengthen Simitis's position, although Tsochatzopoulos, a former general secretary of PASOK and leader of its populist wing, remained in the government, moving to the influential defense portfolio.

The elevation of Konstantinos Simitis to the premiership in January 1996 was seen as bringing to an end the Papandreou era of left-leaning populism in the ruling PASOK and marking Greece's effective Europeanization. A commercial lawyer by profession, Simitis declared a commitment to the modernization of party and government structures, pursuit of a social democratic program, and closer integration within the EU (on which the previous prime minister had always been equivocal).

On the domestic front, the government continued in 1997 and early 1998 to face serious protests over its economic austerity measures. Although the 1997 budget (announced in late 1996) had prompted a large-scale demonstration by farmers and a series of strikes by public- and private-sector workers, Prime Minister Simitis subsequently unveiled yet another tight budget for 1998. Civil servants again went on strike in February 1998 to protest cuts in benefits as well as measures designed to facilitate the privatization of state-run enterprises. Despite continued opposition from workers and other segments of the population supportive of increased spending (such as pensioners and students), the government held fast to its austerity approach in the 1999 budget, Simitis declaring EMU accession on January 1, 2001, to be his top priority.

PASOK infighting and opposition to the government's stringent economic approach contributed to a decline in the ruling party's fortunes in the October 1998 local elections. Consequently, Simitis reshuffled the cabinet in late October, and in November he called for a legislative vote of confidence, which he won by a vote of 163–136, PASOK legislators having been threatened with expulsion from the party if they failed to support the government. The cabinet also took on a new look on February 18, 1999, after the ministers of foreign affairs, the interior, and public order resigned following the politically charged events surrounding the arrest of Kurdish militant Abdullah Öcalan (see Current issues, below).

Simitis called for early elections on April 9, 2000, which produced a surprisingly slim victory of only 1 percent (43.79 percent to 42.73 percent) by PASOK over the ND, which was led by political newcomer Konstantinos (Kostas) KARAMANLIS, the nephew of former prime minister and president Karamanlis. However, due to Greece's complicated proportional-representation system (designed to preclude the need for coalition governments), PASOK secured 158 legislative seats, a sufficient majority to permit Simitis to form a new government on April 13.

Meanwhile, the April 2000 elections were described as "bland" and devoid of major policy differences between the two leading parties. Prime Minister Simitis had called the early balloting in the hope of receiving solid endorsement of his economic reforms, which had prepared the country for entry into the EMU. Instead, PASOK eked out its third consecutive term in office (a record for modern Greece) by only 1 percent of the vote, prompting Konstantinos Karamanlis to call the results a "victory" for his ND, despite his narrow failure to capture the prime ministership. Among other things, Simitis and PASOK appeared to have suffered some loss of support because of declining social services (necessitated by budget austerity). Following elections, Simitis quickly promised "a new cycle of change" that would return social welfare to the forefront of his government's agenda. At the same time, however, the realities of EMU accession (implemented on January 1, 2001) demanded continued conservative structural reforms, including revision of liberal labor and pension regulations. Vehement opposition to austerity measures continued to plague the administration in 2002. Three months of public-sector strike action disrupted tourism and hampered government services in the spring in response to the proposed refinancing of the state pension fund.

While the Simitis government enjoyed some successes in 2003, particularly in regard to the apprehension of terrorists, social reform initiatives and construction projects required for hosting the Olympics progressed slowly in 2003–2004. The 2004 legislative elections were held early (in March) in part to avoid conflict with the summer games. In the wake of growing discontent over several issues, primarily related to public-sector wages and halting preparations for the Olympic Games, Prime Minister Simitis resigned on February 10, 2004, although he returned to the premiership three days later in a caretaker capacity pending early elections on March 7. Ten years of socialist government under PASOK ended with the legislative balloting, in which PASOK won only 40.5 percent of the votes and 117 seats and quickly conceded defeat to the ND, whose leader, Konstantinos Karamanlis, was named prime minister. He was sworn in on March 10 and formed a new government the same day. Prime Minister Karamanlis also assumed the culture portfolio in order to direct Olympic Games affairs, gaining widespread praise when the August games were held without major problems. However, Greece exceeded recommended EU budget deficit limits while hosting the games, requiring increased fiscal discipline in order to avoid EU sanctions. Karamanlis addressed the issue, winning a vote of confidence (165–135) in parliament on June 13, 2005, for his plan to change labor laws and pension benefits in an attempt to rein in deficit spending. The measures, however, did not prevent a series of strikes that plagued the country's economy in 2005–2006.

In an unprecedented vote by 279 of its 300 members, parliament on February 8, 2005, elected Karolos PAPOULIAS, a former foreign minister, as the country's next president, the first to come from the center-left. Papoulias not only received the endorsement of PASOK, of which he is a founding member, but also that of the ND, which nominated him. He was inaugurated for a five-year term on March 12. The cabinet was reshuffled on February 15, 2006.

The ND and Karamanlis narrowly retained control in the snap legislative poll of September 16, 2007, failing to receive the larger mandate desired by the prime minister. Meanwhile, PASOK's seats decreased to 102, while the Communist Party of Greece (*Kommounistiko Komma Elladas*—KKE) and the Coalition of the Radical Left (*Synaspismos Rizospastikis Aristeras*—SYRIZA) both nearly doubled their number of seats (see Legislature, below). Further, for the first time, parliament was represented by five parties, as the ultraright Popular Orthodox Rally (*Laikos Orthodoxos Synagermos*—LAOS) won 10 seats. Karamanlis formed a new government on September 19, 2007.

The cabinet was reshuffled on January 8, 2009. In the EU elections of June 7, 2009, PASOK scored a clear victory for the first time in nine years. The elections were marked by record abstention rates and the increased popularity of the far-right party LAOS.

Constitution and government. The possibility of a return to monarchy was decisively rejected at a plebiscite on December 8, 1974, the Greek people, by a two-to-one margin, expressing their preference for an "uncrowned democracy." The republican constitution adopted in June 1975 provided for a parliamentary system with a strong presidency. Under the new basic law (branded as "Gaullist" by political opponents of Prime Minister Karamanlis), the president had the power to name and dismiss cabinet members (including the prime minister), to dissolve Parliament, to veto legislation, to call for referenda, and to proclaim a state of emergency. These powers were lost by a constitutional amendment that secured final parliamentary approval on March 6, 1986. The action restored full executive power to the prime minister, assuming retention of a legislative majority. The unicameral Parliament, whose normal term is four years, elects the president by a complex procedure that requires a two-thirds majority on a first or second ballot, three-fifths on a third or fourth ballot (a legislative dissolution and election being required prior to the fourth), an absolute majority on a fifth ballot, or a relative majority between the two leading contenders on a sixth. A requirement that the head of state be elected by secret ballot was rescinded by a second amendment, also effective in March

1986. The judicial system is headed by the Supreme Court and includes magistrates' courts, courts of the first instance, and justices of the peace.

Traditionally administered on the basis of its historic provinces, Greece is currently divided into 51 prefectures (plus the self-governing monastic community of Mount Athos), with Athens further divided into four subprefectures. In January 1987 the government approved a plan to divide the country into 13 new administrative regions to facilitate planning and coordinate regional development. In 1997 a major local government reform, the Kapodistrias Plan (*Schedio Kapodistria*), mandated the merger of most of the existing 5,757 communities into 1,033 municipalities, inspiring widespread local resistance.

Foreign relations. Greece has historically displayed a Western orientation, and throughout most of the post–World War II era has been heavily dependent on Western economic and military support. The repressiveness of the 1967–1974 military regime was, however, a matter of concern to many European nations, and their economic and political sanctions were instrumental in Greece's withdrawal from the Council of Europe in 1969. Relations with the United States remained close, primarily because Greece, a member of the North Atlantic Treaty Organization (NATO) since 1952, continued to provide a base for the U.S. Sixth Fleet, but the return to democratic rule was accompanied by increased evidence of anti-American feeling.

The most important issue in Greek foreign affairs is its relationship with Turkey, particularly in regard to the Cyprus question, which has been a source of friction since the mid-1950s. The Greek-inspired coup and subsequent Turkish invasion of Cyprus in July 1974 not only exacerbated tension between the two countries, but also served to bring down the military regime of General Ioannidis and precipitated Greek withdrawal from the military flank of NATO. The return of civilian government, on the other hand, brought a renewal of cooperation with Western Europe. Greece announced in September 1974 that it was rejoining the Council of Europe and subsequently applied for full, as distinguished from associate, membership in the European Economic Community (EEC), with preliminary agreement being reached in Brussels in December 1978 and entry achieved on January 1, 1981.

Greece returned to the NATO military command structure after a six-year lapse, in October 1980. The action was accepted by Turkey's recently installed military regime, although a lengthy dispute between the two countries over the delineation of territorial waters, continental shelf, and air space in the Aegean Sea remained unresolved.

Prior to the 1981 electoral campaign, PASOK had urged withdrawal from NATO and the EEC, in addition to cancellation of the agreement with the United States regarding military bases. During the campaign these positions were modified, Papandreou calling only for "renegotiation" of the terms of membership in the two international organizations.

Although continuing his criticism of the U.S. military presence, the prime minister signed an agreement on September 9, 1983, permitting U.S. military bases to continue operation until the end of 1988. In early 1986 Papandreou again reiterated his intention to "rid the country of foreign bases," and in September he declared, without indicating a timetable, "our decision to remove . . . nuclear weapons from our country is final and irrevocable." Nonetheless, on May 30, 1990, a new eight-year cooperation agreement was announced that ensured continued operation of two of four U.S. facilities in return for about $350 million a year in military aid. Symptomatically, Parliament approved the agreement in late July by a straight party, one-vote margin.

Meanwhile, controversy with Turkey continued, with tension again escalating as the result of a confrontation between Greek and Turkish fighter planes over the Greek Aegean islands during Turkish military maneuvers in early 1989. The Aegean controversy turns on Turkish refusal to recognize territorial waters and airspace wider than six miles, on the grounds that to do otherwise would convert the area into a "Greek lake," denying Greece's demarcation of the Athens Flight Information Region (FIR).

In early 1992 there was virtually unanimous Greek opposition to former Yugoslavia's southernmost republic proclaiming its independence as "Macedonia," a name that historically had embraced parts of modern Greece, Bulgaria, and Albania, as well as Yugoslavia. As a result of Greek pressure, most Western nations, including the United States, refused for 15 months to recognize the new state, pending resolution of the highly charged dispute. It was not until April 7, 1993, that the two neighbors agreed to open discussion on the issue, with United Nations membership being granted the following day to "The Former Yugoslav Republic of Macedonia" (referenced as FYROM).

In a substantial hardening of Athens's position following the October 1993 election, the incoming Papandreou government closed Macedonia's principal trade route through the port of Thessaloniki on February 17, 1994. The action was taken after six of Greece's EU partners (followed by the United States) had extended diplomatic recognition to FYROM, thus complicating Greece's assumption of the EU presidency on January 1. In a highly unusual action against one of its members, the EU challenged the Greek embargo in a suit filed with the European Court of Justice (ECJ) on April 13. The Greek government was unabashed, reasserting that it would "never recognize a state bearing the name of Macedonia or one of its derivatives." It accordingly welcomed a decision by the ECJ on June 29 denying the commission's application for an interim injunction ordering the lifting of the blockade. Subsequent UN and U.S. mediation yielded the signature of an "interim accord" in New York on September 13, under which Macedonia agreed to modify its national flag to meet Greek concerns and to affirm that it had no territorial claim on Greece. The thorniest issue, that of the name "Macedonia," was referred to further talks; nevertheless, Greece felt able to lift the trade embargo on October 14.

Meanwhile, relations with Turkey were further undermined by the territorial-waters dispute, which erupted anew in September 1994. Greece declared that it would formally extend its jurisdiction to 12 nautical miles upon entry into force of the UN Convention on the Law of the Sea (UNCLOS) on November 16. Turkey immediately warned that the move would be considered an "act of aggression," and on October 30 Athens announced that it would defer the introduction of what it continued to view as a "sovereign right." It further angered Ankara by reiterating its right to the extension when ratifying the convention in June 1995, although it made no move to apply it.

The Turkish government also disputed Greek sovereignty over an unidentified number of islets in the Aegean in 1996, with both countries deploying warships in the area. U.S. diplomatic intervention defused the immediate crisis, with the result that both the Greek and the Turkish governments were assailed by right-wing opposition leaders for giving in to U.S. pressure. In a previous escalation in February, Turkey had recalled its ambassador from Athens after Greece had blocked an EU aid grant to Turkey, thereby again demonstrating its opposition to the EU-Turkey customs union effective since the beginning of 1996.

Hope for a reduction in Greek-Turkish tension developed in July 1997 when the two countries signed an agreement during the NATO Madrid summit in which they pledged not to use force against one another and to respect each other's sovereignty. However, Cyprus conducted war games in mid-October, inviting Greek participation for the first time. Subsequently, Turkish armed forces held military exercises in the self-declared Turkish Republic of Northern Cyprus in early November, further straining relations. Turkey also continued to berate Greece for its perceived role in blocking Turkey's proposed EU membership (see article on the EU) and for allegedly supporting the outlawed Kurdistan Workers Party (PKK, see article on Turkey).

Simitis continued to foster improved ties with Turkey in the second half of 1998, as evidenced by his role in convincing the Cyprus government to deploy Russian-made missiles on the Greek island of Crete rather than in Cyprus (see article on Cyprus). However, a full-scale diplomatic crisis erupted between Athens and Ankara in February 1999 following the arrest of PKK leader Abdullah Öcalan in Nairobi, Kenya, minutes after he had left the home of the Greek ambassador. It was subsequently revealed that Öcalan had been smuggled into Greece by pro-Kurdish factions, apparently without the knowledge of the government, which nevertheless then had assumed responsibility for Öcalan's protection and transfer to a safe haven; South Africa was reportedly Öcalan's final destination. Öcalan's arrest was a disaster for the Greek government on several fronts. Ankara strongly denounced Athens's actions, suggesting that Greece should be declared an "outlaw state" for "supporting terrorists." At the same time, Greek embassies and foreign missions became targets for militant Kurdish protesters, who accused Greece of having conspired in the arrest. Some domestic critics accused the government of incompetence for being unaware of Öcalan's entry into Greece. Meanwhile, the government's failure to protect Öcalan once it had accepted that responsibility was perceived as a significant blow to national pride.

Relations between Greece and Turkey improved unexpectedly in the aftermath of an earthquake that hit western Turkey in August 1999. Greece contributed to rescue efforts and extended other aid, gestures that were reciprocated by Turkey when an earthquake struck Athens in

September. Underscoring the rapprochement, Greece finally lifted its veto on EU financial aid earmarked for Turkey and, in December, withdrew its opposition to Turkey's eventual EU accession, contingent on resolution of the Cyprus and Aegean questions.

In the early 1990s, Greece refused to recognize the name adopted by Macedonia, citing the lack of distinction between that name and the territory of ancient Greek Macedonia. Instead, Greece used the provisional name—Former Yugoslavian Republic of Macedonia (FYROM)—referred to by the UN and states that do not recognize the constitutional name of the Republic of Macedonia. Former U.S. undersecretary of state Matthew Nimetz was appointed to mediate the dispute, which escalated after Greece blocked FYROM's accession to NATO in 2008, and Macedonia subsequently referred Greece to the International Court of Justice (ICJ), accusing the country of violating a 1995 pact between the two countries.

Greece's relations with its NATO and EU partners were seriously tested over the former's bombardment of Yugoslavia, which started in late March 1999. With an overwhelming majority of its citizens against the bombing, the Greek government decided not to let its troops join the campaign but to provide logistical support for the NATO force stationed in neighboring Macedonia—a decision highly criticized by the domestic opposition. U.S. president Bill Clinton visited Greece in November 1999 amid fierce protests largely due to widespread anti-Western feelings, further fueled by the NATO action in Yugoslavia. During the visit Greece initially withdrew from a proposed antiterrorism pact with the United States; however, the accord eventually went into effect in September 2000.

Despite diplomatic tension in its relations with traditional allies, Greece's progress toward normalization of relations with Turkey continued through 2000 when a number of cooperation agreements were signed. In November agreement was reached on a procedure for the readmission by Turkey of approximately 700,000 illegal immigrants who had entered Greece from Turkish territory. In March 2002 Greece and Turkey signed an agreement for a 285-kilometer natural gas pipeline through which Turkey would supply Greece with 500,000 cubic meters of gas each day. Finally, it was widely agreed that improved Greek-Turkish relations contributed to the decision in December by Greek and Turkish Cypriots to resume talks after a four-year hiatus. In November 2007 Karamanlis became the first Greek prime minister in almost 50 years to make an official visit to Istanbul. Bilateral talks focused on economic relations.

In another policy shift, Greece differed with Washington's agenda, opposing the U.S.-led invasion of Iraq in March 2003. Opposition to the war led to widespread antiwar protests during that year. Nonetheless, the PASOK government granted the United States overflight and basing privileges during the conflict and did not join fellow NATO members France, Germany, Belgium, and Luxembourg in attempting to block the U.S. alliance's military assistance to Turkey on the eve of the invasion.

Greece's relations with the other members of the EU were strained in 2004 when an EU investigation determined that the country had provided misleading data upon joining the euro currency system in 2001, when deficit spending had been above the 3 percent limit stipulated by the EU. The Karamanlis government blamed the previous PASOK-led government for the false reporting.

In April 2005 Greece became the sixth country to ratify the EU constitutional treaty, with legislators from both the governing ND party and the leading opposition, PASOK, supporting the treaty. On June 11, 2008, Greece became the 18th country to ratify the now-defunct EU Lisbon Treaty (see 2009 Ireland entry). The ratification was supported by the ND and PASOK, although PASOK stated that a referendum should be held. Smaller parties voted against ratification.

Increased cooperation with Russia became a priority under the Karamanlis government, and two major pipeline projects were announced. In March 2007 Russia, Greece, and Bulgaria signed an agreement for the construction of an oil pipeline from the Bulgarian port of Burgas to the Greek port of Alexandroúpolis. A second agreement signed in April 2008 provided for a Russian natural gas pipeline, connecting the Greek portion of the pipeline to another section in Italy. The increased Greek-Russian cooperation was met with concern by American and European partners, who worried that the ventures strengthened Russian leverage in a market already dominated by the energy giant.

In January 2009 a series of Turkish military aircraft flights over Greek islets in the Eastern Aegean raised concerns about the prospects for rapprochement between the two countries.

Current issues. A series of corruption scandals rocked the Karamanlis administration in early 2007, when it was alleged that the government had orchestrated the investment of state-controlled pension funds in expensive, high-risk bonds. The pension funds reportedly were "duped" by the overpriced bond sales, whose proceeds, in part, were kicked back to fund managers. The scandal damaged the reputation of Karamanlis, who had pledged to eliminate corruption, and threatened to affect the ND's standing in opinion polls. To renew the ND mandate while it was still enjoying relatively high popular support, Karamanlis in August called for early elections to be held in September. In late August catastrophic forest fires broke out in the Peloponnese region, killing 65 people in one of the worst natural disasters in Greece in decades. Analysts predicted that the ND would pay a heavy toll in the upcoming parliamentary elections as a result of the government's perceived poor handling of the aftermath. While the ND won the most seats in the September 16 balloting, its winning margin was small (41.8 percent compared to 38.1 percent for PASOK). PASOK, for its part, experienced its worst electoral performance since 1977, losing 15 seats compared to the previous election. (It appeared that the populace had placed at least part of the blame for the widespread destruction from the fires on the policies of previous PASOK administrations.) The ND lost 13 seats but was able to garner a narrow majority of 152 seats.

In late 2007 a number of scandals further diminished Prime Minister Karamanlis's standing. On December 15 the minister of employment and social protection, Vassilis MANGINAS, was forced to resign amid revelations that he had built a villa in a nonresidential zone on the outskirts of Athens and had employed three illegal immigrants as domestic servants. On December 20 the secretary general of the ministry of culture, and a close associate of the prime minister, Christos ZACHOPOULOS, attempted suicide following allegations of corruption in a highly publicized scandal involving his secretary and presumed mistress. Meanwhile, newspapers reported alleged corruption and mismanagement in the ministry of culture, resulting in the implication of an ND member of parliament, Kostas KOUKODIMOS, who subsequently resigned. The government was then left with a single-seat majority of 151. (Koukodimos returned to parliament on July 24, 2008, when the court case against him was suspended.) However, the Zachopoulos scandal was widely seen as having severely undermined the credibility of the government, as well as of the mass media, and reinforced popular public discontent with the government and political parties.

The situation further deteriorated in 2008 when yet another scandal erupted. Following a criminal investigation in Germany, a former executive of German business giant Siemens testified that the company had paid as much as $140 million in bribes to Greek leaders prior to 2004. While some of this money went to ministers and party officials, some went into the party coffers of the ND and PASOK. The testimony was corroborated by Theodoros TSOUKATOS, a former PASOK member of parliament and party administrator in the Simitis era, who admitted that he had accepted a bribe from Siemens to pay PASOK campaign expenses in 2000. A short time later the minister of culture and cousin of Prime Minister Karamanlis, Michalis LIAPIS, was heavily criticized for having taken part in a Siemens junket to attend a Greek soccer game in Germany. At this point, public discontent with both political parties reached unprecedented levels, and for the first time, Greeks debated whether ND or PASOK would be able to solve the country's chronic problems or whether the country needed new political parties.

Meanwhile, constitutional reform also commanded attention in 2008, the process having been debated for several years concerning proposals put forth by both the ND and PASOK. Prime Minister Karamanlis, who had proposed a series of amendments in 2006, was stymied in 2007 by a PASOK boycott. Finally, in May 2008, parliament approved 3 of the ND's 38 proposed changes. The amendments removed the restriction on members of parliament from engaging in another occupation while holding a legislative seat;,expanded parliament's right to amend and monitor the budget, and provided "special legislative care" for the insular and mountainous regions of the country.

In church developments, Archbishop Christodoulos, the head of the Greek Orthodox Autocephalous Church, died in January 2008. Christodoulos, who had enjoyed great popularity, often claimed a distinct political role for himself, using anti-Western, populist, and nationalistic rhetoric in his sermons. He was succeeded in February by Archbishop Ieronymos, who preferred to keep a low profile and avoided engaging the Orthodox Church in party politics.

The killing of teenager Alexandros (Alexis) GRIGOROPOULOS on December 6, 2008, following a skirmish with police in Athens' restive neighborhood of Exarchia sparked a series of street riots, the fiercest in more than 30 years. For several days public buildings, shops, and cars were set ablaze by hooded youngsters, and demonstrations spread to other cities while the government instructed the police not to take decisive action against them in an effort to prevent further casualties. The riots underscored Greece's deep social rifts, as well as rising frustration among youths over the lack of jobs and the corruption in government.

Meanwhile, the ND suffered another lapse as the merchant marine minister, Georgios (Giorgos) VOULGARAKIS, resigned in the wake of allegations linking him to the Vatopedi land scandal in September 2008. Voulgarakis's wife was the agent for the wealthy medieval monastery in the Mount Athos peninsula and reportedly handled the land swap, which ultimately was said to have involved several deputy ministers and a cost to taxpayers of $136 million. The scandal also resulted in the resignation of Theodoros ROUSSOPOULOS, state minister and government spokesman (who denied the allegations), as public anger mounted over corruption. (In June 2009 Roussopoulos announced that he would not seek election in the next parliamentary elections, citing a "witch-hunt" against him.)

As the numerous scandals exacted a heavy toll on the popularity and public image of Karamanlis, the embattled prime minister tried to mitigate some of the damage by reshuffling the cabinet in January 2009. He replaced the minister of economy and finance who had often undertaken the burden of announcing unpopular spending cuts and tight budgets, as well as the ministers of culture and education. In April parliament was asked to decide whether further action should be brought against former minister and ND delegate Aristotelis PAVLIDIS, who was accused in a bribery case by shipowner Fotios MANOUSSIS. Manoussis claimed that Pavlidis had demanded payment in exchange for the awarding of state contracts to Manoussis's ferry company. However, lawmakers voted against removing Pavlidis's parliamentary immunity, thus relieving him of facing further action.

Also in 2009, three suspects in the Siemens bribery case were jailed pending trial, another suffered a stroke, and two others were reported to have fled to Germany. Meanwhile, the wife and daughters of one of the suspects were also implicated on allegations that they shared bank accounts. The entire case was described by one media outlet as having produced "uncommon levels of outrage" among the public. Attention also turned to immigration, as authorities continued to arrest increasing numbers of illegal immigrants, mainly from Turkey. In June the government announced it would tighten its immigration policies.

POLITICAL PARTIES

Government Party:

New Democracy (*Nea Dimokratia*—ND). Formed in 1974 as a vehicle for Konstantinos Karamanlis, New Democracy was, under Karamanlis, a broadly based pragmatic party committed to parliamentary democracy, social justice, an independent foreign policy, and free enterprise. Georgios (George) Rallis, generally viewed as a moderate rightist, was elected party leader on May 8, 1980, and was designated prime minister the next day, following Karamanlis's election as president of the republic. In the wake of the ND's defeat at the 1981 election, Rallis lost an intraparty vote of confidence, and, in a move interpreted as reflecting the ascendancy of right-wing influence within the parliamentary group, he was succeeded in December by the leader of the party's conservative bloc, Evangelos AVEROFF-TOSSITSAS. The latter resigned as leader of the opposition in August 1984, following the ND's poor showing at the European Parliament balloting in June, the moderates rallying to elect Konstantinos Mitsotakis as his successor over Konstantinos Stephanopoulos. Stephanopoulos, in turn, withdrew with a number of his center-right supporters to form the Democratic Renewal (*Dimokratiki Ananeosi*—DIANA) in September 1985 after Mitsotakis's August re-designation as ND leader, despite the party's legislative loss to PASOK two months earlier. (DIANA was dissolved in June 1994, following its inability to win European Parliament representation.)

The party secured a plurality of 145 seats at the legislative balloting of June 18, 1989, following which it agreed to an unlikely (albeit interim) governing alliance with the Progressive Left Coalition (below, under Coalition of the Left, Movements and Ecology) to ensure parliamentary action that would permit the lodging of indictments against former prime minister Papandreou. After the ensuing election of November 5, at which it again fell short of a majority, it joined in a three-way coalition that included PASOK to govern until new balloting on April 8, 1990, at which it won exactly half of the seats. With DIANA's external support, Mitsotakis on April 11 was able to form a new single-party administration, which survived until the early election of October 10, 1993. As a result of the ND defeat, Mitsotakis on October 26 announced his resignation as party leader, and Miltiadis EVERT defeated Ioannis VARVITSIOTIS in a race for the succession.

The party was second to PASOK in the June 1994 European Parliament balloting, winning 9 of 25 seats, and in a high-profile local victory won the Athens mayoralty in October. In the September 1996 balloting the ND slipped to 38.1 percent of the vote and 108 seats, therefore remaining in opposition. Evert resigned as ND leader in the wake of the poll but later decided to contest the resultant leadership election, thereby aggravating a long-running internal feud that was not resolved by his reelection as leader by the ND caucus in October. Ranged against Evert was former prime minister Mitsotakis, who backed the candidacy of his daughter, former ND culture minister Dora Bakoyannis, as well as the candidacies of Stephanos MANOS (former finance minister) and Georgios SOUFLIAS (former education minister). Souflias received the backing of the other two contenders in the unsuccessful bid to prevent Evert from regaining the leadership, following which the party stepped back from the brink of an open split by referring the leadership issue to a full party congress in 1997.

Konstantinos (Kostas) Karamanlis, a nephew of former president Karamanlis (who died in April 1998), was elected as the new president of the party during the fourth congress on March 21, 1997, Evert losing in the first round. Intraparty friction continued in 1998 and 1999, contributing, among other things, to the defection of Manos. However, Manos and the Liberals agreed to support Karamanlis in the April 2000 legislative balloting in which the ND came within one percentage point of assuming governmental control.

In local elections on October 20, 2002, Dora Bakoyannis, the wife of Pavlos BAKOYANNIS, a prominent party member assassinated in 1989 by the terrorist November 17 Revolutionary Organization, was elected the first female mayor of Athens with 61 percent of the vote. The ND won other local races as well, demonstrating the growing decline of voter support for PASOK. In the March 7, 2004, elections, the ND wrested control of government from the long-governing PASOK, winning 165 seats and the prime ministership for Karamanlis.

Eleftherios Zagoritis replaced Evangelos MEIMARAKIS as party secretary in 2006 when Meimarakis accepted the post as defense minister.

The party is informally split into two major factions: the Karamanlis supporters, who claim to be the continuation of the pre-1967 right, and the Mitsotakis supporters, who represent the pre-1967 center, which joined ND after 1974. The Mitsotakis faction has opted for full support of Karamanlis but could reassert itself if Karamanlis declared his intention to withdraw from politics or suffered a serious electoral defeat.

Following the line of Prime Minister Karamanlis, the party has carefully avoided raising thorny political issues, such as acceleration of the privatization program, despite rhetoric in favor of reform. This has secured high levels of public opinion support, which only wavered after the August 2007 fires. Despite clumsy attempts to fault previous PASOK governments for "foreign sabotage," the party was able to survive the crisis with minor losses in the 2007 elections.

Despite mounting public discontent, the party has maintained a clear lead over PASOK in all opinion polls held since the parliamentary elections, possibly because PASOK's loss of public regard has equaled or surpassed that of New Democracy. However, public opinion of New Democracy has further deteriorated, due to recurrent incidents of corruption, which have led Greeks to question the sustainability of the two-party system that has characterized Greek politics since the 1970s.

In the EU elections of June 7, 2009, the ND won 32.29 percent of the vote and eight seats, second to PASOK. This defeat raised questions about the party's ability to maintain its lead in the next parliamentary elections in 2011.

Leaders: Konstantinos (Kostas) KARAMANLIS (President of the Party and Prime Minister), Konstantinos MITSOTAKIS (Former Prime Minister and Honorary President of the Party), Eleftherios (Lefteris) ZAGORITIS (Party Secretary).

Opposition Parties:

Panhellenic Socialist Movement (*Panellinio Sosialistiko Kinima*—PASOK). Founded in 1974 by Andreas Papandreou, PASOK endorsed republicanism and socialization of the economy. In foreign affairs it committed to the dissolution of European military alliances, abolition of U.S. military installations in Greece, and renegotiation of Greek membership in the EEC. In 1975, in the first of a series of internal crises, the party was weakened by the withdrawal of members who disagreed with Papandreou over a lack of intraparty democratic procedure. However, most of the dissidents rejoined PASOK prior to the 1977 election, at which it won 93 parliamentary seats. The 1981 balloting yielded a PASOK majority, permitting Papandreou to form the country's first socialist government.

On March 9, 1985, PASOK announced that it would not support the reelection of President Karamanlis, offering as its candidate Christos Sartzetakis, who was elected to a five-year term by the legislature in procedurally controversial balloting on March 29. In early parliamentary balloting on June 2, the party secured a somewhat diminished majority that permitted Papandreou to continue as prime minister.

PASOK suffered major reverses at local balloting in October 1986 and was runner-up to the ND at the parliamentary elections of June and November 1989, with its leader not a formal participant in the temporary tripartite alliance formed after the latter poll. The party experienced a further, albeit marginal, decline in April 1990 but rebounded at the municipal balloting in October, both alone and in coalition with the Communists. The depth of continuing fissures within PASOK was illustrated at its second congress held September 20–23, when Akis Tsochatzopoulos, Papandreou's choice for election to the newly created post of general secretary of the Central Committee, was approved by a bare majority of one vote. By contrast, Papandreou himself was unanimously reelected party leader and eventually returned as prime minister in October 1993. Subsequently, Papandreou was reelected leader by voice vote at the 1994 congress, with Tsochatzopoulos being reconfirmed by the Central Committee.

Growing divisions within PASOK intensified when Papandreou fell seriously ill in November 1995, the succession struggle being complicated by the political ambitions of his wife, Dimitra Liani. Following Papandreou's resignation in January 1996, four candidates stood for the PASOK parliamentary leadership (and thus the premiership), the victor in balloting of PASOK deputies being the reformist Konstantinos Simitis, who defeated establishment candidate Tsochatzopoulos 86 votes to 75 in the second round. Papandreou died on June 23 and was succeeded as PASOK president by Simitis, who on June 30 again defeated Tsochatzopoulos in balloting at a special party congress, winning 53.5 percent of delegates' votes. He went on to lead PASOK to a further election victory in September, a reduced vote share of 41.2 percent yielding an overall majority of 162 seats.

Simitis was reelected as PASOK leader at a March 1999 congress, although populist influence reportedly grew in the new 180-member Central Committee. Of particular concern to the populist wing were the government's tight economic policies, seen as constituting a threat to organized labor and other traditional PASOK constituencies. After PASOK narrowly won the April 2000 legislative balloting, Simitis was reelected as party leader during an October 2001 congress at which he rebuffed a challenge from the leader of the populist wing, Akis Tsochatzopoulos, who was subsequently replaced as Greece's minister of national defense.

By 2003 polls showed growing support for PASOK's main political rival, the ND. In response, Simitis resigned as leader of the party and was replaced by Foreign Minister Georgios (Giorgos) Papandreou. Papandreou faced voter discontent with corruption, the government's management of the economy and the stock exchange crisis, and the preparations for the 2004 Olympics. In legislative elections in March 2004, PASOK received 40.55 percent of the vote, thereby losing governmental control to the ND for the first time in a decade.

Papandreou's election as party leader shortly before the 2004 elections brought a popular, liberal politician to the PASOK leadership. However, Papandreou soon came under pressure from the conservative leftist faction within his party, which firmly opposed his reform agenda. He then moderated his positions, disappointing the reformist segment of Greek society without maintaining PASOK's appeal to more leftist voters. This ambivalence contributed to PASOK's decreased representation in parliament in the 2007 elections, in which the party lost 15 seats compared to its 2004 showing.

Papandreou was elected president of Socialist International, the worldwide organization of socialist parties, on January 31, 2006.

In direct balloting for party leadership on November 11, 2007, Papandreou secured reelection, winning significantly with 56 percent of the vote, while Venizelos collected 38 percent and the third candidate, Konstantinos (Kostas) SKANDALIDIS, secured 6 percent. Despite Papandreou's easy victory, opinion polls showed that the party was persistently failing to capitalize on rising discontent with the government, while the party continued to lose voters to more-leftist parties.

A major party crisis occurred on June 12, 2008, when, following Ireland's rejection of the Lisbon Treaty (see 2009 Ireland entry), former prime minister Simitis opposed Papandreou's proposal that a similar referendum be held in Greece. Papandreou refrained from expelling Simitis from the party but did expel him from PASOK's parliamentary group. This unprecedented move against a former prime minister and party president manifested the deep internal divide that plagued PASOK. In the EU elections of June 7, 2009, PASOK won 36.64 percent of the vote and eight seats. This was PASOK's first victory under George Papandreou, the victory solidifying his position in the party's leadership and demonstrating the party's potential to win back a majority in the next parliamentary elections.

Leaders: Georgios PAPANDREOU (Party Leader), Konstantinos SIMITIS (Former Party Leader), Nikolaos (Nikos) ATHANASAKIS (General Secretary).

Communist Party of Greece (*Kommounistiko Komma Elladas*—KKE). The KKE is Greece's historic communist grouping, from which the more moderate wing, KKEs (see under Coalition of the Radical Left, above), split in 1968. KKE became the fourth-largest party in Parliament at the 1977 election but experienced numerous membership defections during 1980 in reaction to leadership support of the Soviet intervention in Afghanistan. It recovered to become the only group other than PASOK and New Democracy to secure parliamentary representation in 1981.

Following the 1984 election for the European Parliament, the KKE distanced itself from PASOK, seeking to attract voters from the latter's left wing and hoping to increase its leverage in the next Parliament should PASOK fail to secure a majority. The KKE's continued unwillingness to support PASOK in second-round balloting contributed to the governing party's poor showing in the 1986 municipal elections.

During the latter half of 1989 the KKE experienced renewed internal dissonance. A dispute with the party's youth organization resulted in the dismissal of the latter's entire Central Committee in late September, while a number of trade union affiliate members withdrew to form an anti–Coalition "Militant Initiative" in mid-October. Additional defections followed, including the resignation of eight Central Committee members in late November in protest of the formation of an ecumenical administration.

During the party's 1991 congress "conservatives" won control of the Central Committee over reformists, 60–51, and proceeded to confound earlier expectations by electing Aleka Papariga, a hard-liner, as general secretary. Although the chances of a realignment within *Synaspismos* appeared to have been improved by the selection of a KKE reformist to succeed Florakis as Coalition president on March 18, Papariga announced in mid-June that she was taking the KKE out of the alliance. Subsequently, seven reformers, including Coalition leader Damanaki, were suspended from the party's Central Committee.

The KKE won 9 parliamentary seats in a vote share of 4.5 percent in October 1993 and 2 European Parliament seats in June 1994. It improved further to 5.6 percent (and 11 seats) in the September 1996 general election. After organizing many of the antigovernment protests and orchestrating anti-West sentiments during and after the NATO bombing of Yugoslavia (see Foreign relations, above), the KKE won 5.5 percent of the vote at the general election in April 2000, thereby retaining its 11 seats. In the 2004 elections the KKE received 5.9 percent of the vote and 12 seats in the Parliament. Harilaos Florakis, the party's general secretary from 1972 to 1989 and honorary president, died in March 2005.

To widen its electoral appeal, the party has increasingly imbued its antiglobalization, anti-U.S. rhetoric with nationalism. As chair, Papariga has forged an alliance with nationalist media personalities, such as Liana KANELLI, who was elected to parliament on the KKE ticket in 2004 and 2007. This move paradoxically increased the appeal of KKE within the ranks of rightist, hard-line religious voters, who shared similar views. The party also firmly opposed all reform programs and eschewed any offers of cooperation from more moderate leftist parties.

In the September 2007 elections, however, the party increased its number of seats to 22, subsequently furthering its anti-EU, anti-U.S. stance by criticizing PASOK and SYRIZA for their alleged half-hearted opposition to government policies and support of EU and U.S. positions. In the 2009 EU elections, the KKE garnered 8.35 percent of the vote and 2 seats. This performance appeared to confirm the electoral strength of the party as well as its leading position on the Greek left, which was briefly challenged by SYRIZA.

Leader: Aleka PAPARIGA (General Secretary).

Popular Orthodox Rally (*Laikos Orthodoxos Synagermos*—LAOS). The LAOS party was formed in 2000 by ND dissident Georgios Karatzaferis as a far-right, anti-immigrant party that emphasized populism and the cultural "superiority" of the Greek Orthodox religion. In the 2004 elections LAOS received just 2.19 percent and failed to win a seat in parliament. Subsequently, however, the party won one seat in the 2004 European parliamentary elections. LAOS's showing improved significantly during the snap election of 2007, when the party received 3.8 percent of the vote and ten seats.

In an effort to appeal to a wider faction of New Democracy's voters, Karatzaferis repeatedly claimed that contrary to the records of some of the most prominent members, LAOS was not a far-right party. This remained a major obstacle to the party's attempt to move from the fringe of Greece's political spectrum.

In 2009 LAOS focused on the issue of illegal immigration. In the EU elections in June, LAOS received 7.15 percent of the vote and two seats, a significant increase over previous EU elections.

Leaders: Georgios KARATZAFERIS (President), Othon FLORATOS (Director General).

Coalition of the Radical Left (*Synaspismos Rizospastikis Aristeras*—SYRIZA). SYRIZA was formed in January 2004 by *Synaspismos*/SYN, independent activists, and several small leftist groups, including the **Renewing Communist Ecological Left** (*Ananeotiki Kommounistiki Oikologiki Aristera*—AKOA), the **Internationalist Workers Left** (*Diethnis Ergatiki Aristera*—DEA), the **Movement for the Unity of Action of the Left** (*Kinima gia tin Enotita Drasis tis Aristeras*—KEDA), and **Active Citizens** (*Energoi Polites*). The coalition secured 3.3 percent of the vote and six seats (all held by members of *Synaspismos*/SYN) in the March 2004 elections. Alexandros (Alekos) Alavanos was subsequently elected president of *Synaspismos*/SYN, thereby becoming the leader of SYRIZA.

Despite persistent efforts to establish communication and cooperation with the KKE (below), SYRIZA met with KKE's rejection, while SYRIZA rebuffed attempts by PASOK to establish political cooperation. However, a number of other parties, including DIKKI (below), joined SYRIZA prior to the September 2007 elections, at which SYRIZA, benefiting from public discontent with PASOK, significantly increased its electoral support by winning 5.04 percent of votes and 14 seats. This trend continued through late 2007 and early 2008, as SYRIZA capitalized on PASOK's recurrent crisis as well as the popularity of new *Synaspismos*/SYN president Alexis Tsipras. At one point, opinion polls suggested that SYRIZA might be able to challenge PASOK's supremacy on the left of the Greek political spectrum. However, while SYRIZA succeeded in collecting much of the protest vote against the two big political parties, it failed to produce a comprehensive political program. The December 2008 riots proved to be the turning point for SYRIZA's high ambitions. Its tolerant stance against the rioters alienated a large share of SYRIZA's potential voters.

In the 2009 EU elections SYRIZA won 4.7 percent of the vote and one seat, disappointing party leaders who had fostered hopes at one time of challenging PASOK's leading political position in the left-of-center. The poor result sparked a feud among radicals and moderates with the party, which was further complicated by deteriorating relations between party leader Tsipras and parliamentary leader Alavanos.

Leaders: Alexios (Alexis) TSIPRAS (Leader), Alexandros (Alekos) ALAVANOS (Parliamentary Leader).

Coalition of the Left, Movements and Ecology (*Synaspismos tis Aristeras ton Kinimaton Kai tis Oikologias*—SYN). Also referenced as SYN, *Synaspismos* is a successor to the Progressive Left Coalition (*Synaspismos tis Aristeras kai tis Proodou*), which was formed prior to the June 1989 balloting as an alliance of the KKE (below) and the Greek Left (*Elliniki Aristera*—EAR), plus a number of minor leftist formations. The action served to mitigate a deep rupture that had existed in Greek Communist ranks since 1968. While the drive to promote a broad alliance (*symparataxis*) of the "forces of the Left" had been initiated in early 1988 by the KKE's Harilaos FLORAKIS, the Coalition's eventual leaning was closer to that of the EAR. The new formation won 28 parliamentary seats in June 1989, 7 of which were lost the following November. Its representation was unchanged after the April 1990 balloting, two of its deputies having run as PASOK-Coalition candidates. The KKE formally regrouped as a separate party in June 1991, although nearly half of its parliamentary members opted to leave the party and stay within the Coalition.

The Greek Left had been formally launched in 1987 during an April 21–26 constituent congress of the majority faction of the Communist Party of Greece–Interior (*Kommounistiko Komma Elladas–Esoterikou*—KKEs). The action implemented a decision of the KKEs's fourth national conference in May 1986 to reorganize as a more broadly based party of the left, thereby rejecting an appeal by its (then) secretary, Ioannis (Yannis) BANIAS, that a long-standing specific identification with Marxism-Leninism be retained. The KKEs had been founded in 1968 as the result of a split in the KKE, although the two formations joined with the United Democratic Left (*Eniaea Dimokratiki Aristera*—EDA) to contest the 1974 election as members of a United Left coalition. Ultimately emerging as Greece's principal "Eurocommunist" group, the KKEs participated in the 1977 election as a member of the Alliance of Progressive and Left-Wing Forces (*Symmachia Proodeftikon kai Aristeron Dinameon*), winning one of the Alliance's two seats. Unsuccessful in 1981, it regained a single seat in 1985 and subsequently increased its representation under its new name as a member of *Synaspismos*. The EAR dissolved itself in June 1992, being merged into *Synaspismos,* which became a single party.

Following the 1993 election, at which the Coalition fell marginally short of the 3 percent threshold needed for parliamentary representation, Maria DAMANAKI resigned as president, with a party congress electing Nikolaos (Nikos) KONSTANTOPOULOS as her successor. Subsequently, the group recovered to win two seats at the June 1994 European Parliament poll and ten seats in the September 1996 general election (on a vote share of 5.1 percent). The Coalition secured only 3.2 percent of the vote (six seats) in the 2000 legislative balloting.

At a party conference in June 2003 *Synaspismos* formally changed its name from the Progressive Left Coalition to the Coalition of the Left, Movements and Ecology in order to appeal to "Green" voters. However, the party continued to use *Synaspismos*/SYN as its official designation.

Synaspismos became the senior partner to smaller, hitherto unknown leftist groups at the formation of SYRIZA in January 2004. After the March elections, in which SYRIZA had barely managed to surpass the electoral threshold, economist Nikolaos Konstantopoulos resigned as party leader after a decade in the post and was succeeded by Alexandros Alavanos. Alavanos aimed to give the party a more radical image and furthered cooperation with small leftist groups, which vehemently opposed globalization, privatization, and the reform agenda, which the ND and PASOK claimed to support. Special attention was given to educational reform, and SYRIZA spearheaded the opposition against a proposed constitutional amendment banning non-state universities. An unexpectedly high electoral performance in the Athens municipal elections of October 2006 promoted the reputation of Alexios (Alexis) Tsipras, a strong secondary candidate for the mayorship, as a potential party leader. Meanwhile, the center-left faction of the party was informally led by Michael PAPAGIANNAKIS who died after a long illness on May 26, 2009.

Leaders: Alexios (Alexis) TSIPRAS (President), Alexandros (Alekos) ALAVANOS (Former President), Nikolaos (Nikos) HOUNTIS (Secretary).

Democratic Social Movement (*Dimokratiko Kinoniko Kinima*—DIKKI). DIKKI was formed prior to the September 1996 balloting by a faction of PASOK claiming to be the true representative of the party's socialist heritage. It won a creditable 4.4 percent of the vote in its first electoral contest, yielding nine seats. It lost parliamentary representation, however, after winning only 2.7 percent of the vote at the general election in April 2000. In the April 2004 elections DIKKI received 1.79 percent of the vote. After this poor performance the party leader Dimitrios (Dimitris) TSOVOLAS decided to suspend the operation of the party. However, his decision was legally challenged by some party members. A court decision ruled that the party should continue to exist, and a congress appointed a steering committee consisting of Panagiotis Mantas, Ilias Nikolopoulos, and Georgios (Giorgos) Pantzas.

After poor returns in the September 2007 elections, Tsovolas decided to retire from politics and again suspend the operation of the party. His decision was challenged by a number of party officials who appealed to civil courts to gain permission to use the party name and symbols. These officials ultimately forged an electoral alliance with SYRIZA in August 2007. However, the Greek Court of Cassations refused to include the title of DIKKI under the coalition, citing faulty internal procedures. In the EU elections of June 7, 2009 these officials supported the SYRIZA ticket.

Leaders: Dimitrios (Dimitris) TSOVOLAS (Former President); Panagiotis MANTAS, Ilias NIKOLOPOULOS, Georgios (Giorgos) PANTZAS (Steering Committee).

Other Parties:

Ecologists-Greens (*Oikologoi-Prasinoi*). Following a brief rise of Ecologists-Alternatives (*Oikologoi-Enallaktikoi*) in the late 1980s-early 1990s, this party, founded in December 2002, represents the most serious attempt at the establishment of a green party in the Greek political spectrum. Led by a group of prominent environmentalists, among them Michael (Michalis) TREMOPOULOS, who frequently made headlines with his campaigns, the party benefited from growing popular discontent with established political parties.

In the 2007 parliamentary elections the Greens won just 1.05 percent of the vote. In the 2009 EU elections the party won 3.49 percent of the vote and one seat. This was a clear success, although opinion polls had suggested even higher numbers, as the party entered the European Parliament for the first time.

Leaders: Philippos DRAGOUMIS, Eleonora ZOTOU, Orestis KOLOKOURIS, Aekaterini (Katia) LEMBESSI, Eleni (Lenio) MYRIVILI, Nikolaos (Nikos) CHRYSSOGELOS (Members of the Executive Secretariat).

Democratic Renaissance (*Dimokratiki Anagennisi*—DA). The DA was established by Stylianos (Stelios) Papathemelis, a former PASOK minister. The party did not stand in the 2004 election, but Papathemelis announced in spring 2007 that his party would run independently in the upcoming elections. Papathemelis described his party as "national, social, and democratic," opposing the use of "Macedonia" in the FYROM country name. DA platform issues include strengthening national identity and public services, especially education.

Papathemelis had run on the ND list in the first electoral district of Thessaloniki during the 2004 elections but immediately declared himself an independent MP following his swearing-in ceremony. In the 2007 elections he ran on his own party's ticket and failed to be elected. The DA received 0.8 percent of votes during the September parliamentary poll. In the 2009 EU elections the DA ran under the **Panhellenic Macedonian Front** (*Panellinio Makedoniko Metopo*—PAMME) and garnered 1.38 percent of the vote but no seats.

Leader: Stylianos PAPATHEMELIS (Chair).

Other formations and parties that participated unsuccessfully in the 2007 legislative elections the **Centrists' Union** (*Enosi Kentroon*—EK), with 0.29 percent; the **Communist Party of Greece (Marxist-Leninist)** [*Kommounistiko Komma Ellados (Marxistiko-Leninistiko)*—KKE (M-L)], with 0.24 percent; a similarly named rival faction, with whom KKE (M-L) had previously shared a party, the **Marxist-Leninist Communist Party of Greece** (*Marxistiko-Leninistiko Kommounistiko Komma Ellados*—M-L KKE), with 0.11 percent; the **Front of the Radical Left** (*Metopo Rizospastikis Aristeras*), with 0.17 percent; the **Uniate Anticapitalistic Left** (*Enotiki Antikapitalistiki Aristera*), whose name refers to promoting unity among leftist parties, with 0.15 percent; the **Liberal Alliance** (*Fileleftheri Symmaxia*), with 0.11 percent; the **Liberals Party** (*Komma Fileleftheron*), with 0.04 percent; the **Militant Socialist Party of Greece** (*Agonistiko Sosialistiko Komma Ellados*—ASKE), with 0.03 percent; **OAKKE—Organization for the Restructuring of KKE** (*OAKKE—Organosi gia tin Anasyngrotisi tou KKE*), with 0.03 percent; **Dimosthenis Vergis-Greek Ecologists** (*Dimosthenis Vergis-Ellines Oikologoi*), led by Dimosthenis VERGIS, with 0.02 percent; and **Light-Truth-Justice** (*Fos-Alitheia-Dikaiosyni*), with 0.01 percent. Parties receiving no votes included **Democratic World Greece** (*Dimokratiki Pangosmios Ellas*), **Regional Urban Development** (*Perifereiaki Astiki Anaptyxi*), and the **New Party of Salvation-Christian Democracy** (*Neo Komma Sotirias-Christianiki Dimokratia*).

Extremist Groups:

November 17 Revolutionary Organization (*Epanastatiki Organosi 17 Noemvri*—EO17N). The EO17N is a leftist urban guerrilla organization named after the date of the famous Athens Technical University (*Polytechneio*) insurrection, which had been violently crushed by the military junta on November 17, 1973. The grouping surfaced in 1975 and subsequently claimed responsibility for numerous assassinations and violent attacks. Among its victims were CIA Station Chief Richard Welch, former police officer Evangelos MALLIOS, ND MP Pavlos Bakoyannis, and steel magnate Dimitrios (Dimitris) ANGELOPOULOS. In October 1991 the group claimed responsibility for the attempted murder of a press attaché at the Turkish Embassy in Athens. In July 1992 the EO17N unsuccessfully attempted to assassinate the minister of finance, while in July 1994 it claimed responsibility for the assassination of a Turkish diplomat. In February 1996 an unsuccessful attack on the U.S. Embassy in Athens was believed to have been planned by the EO17N. Subsequently, the EO17N claimed responsibility for the assassination in Athens in June 2000 of a British defense attaché, saying the killing was a response to the NATO air attacks in Yugoslavia in 1999. Greek authorities subsequently came under intensified pressure for the lack of arrests in regard to EO17N activities.

In 2003 Greek authorities made a series of arrests and gained convictions of the top leadership of EO17N. Leader Alexandros GIOTOPOULOS and the group's alleged main assassin, Dimitris KOUFONTINAS, both received multiple life sentences during trials in December 2003. In addition, 12 others were convicted of terrorism charges. The sentences of 13 of the defendants were upheld by the Court of Appeals on May 14, 2007. The convictions effectively ended the operational capabilities of EO17N.

Other terrorist groups include the **May 1st Revolutionary Organization,** the **People's Revolutionary Struggle** (*Epanastatikos Laikos Agonas*—ELA), and the **Revolutionary Nucleus** (*Epanastatikos Pyrinas*—EP), all of which allegedly carried out attacks against "capitalist" and "imperialist" targets throughout the 1980s and 1990s. The People's Revolutionary Struggle split into several factions in 1995. One of these groups, the **Revolutionary Struggle** (*Epanastatikos Agonas*), exploded three bombs in Athens on May 5, 2004, to protest the Olympics. On May 13 another bomb exploded outside of a bank, while a second device was found and detonated by police. The police also found and destroyed a bomb near an Olympic site on May 19. Terrorism made an alarming reappearance on January 15, 2007, when an anti-tank missile was fired against the U.S. Embassy in Athens, causing material damages only. The Revolutionary Struggle group took responsibility for the attack. On June 17, 2009, a group identified as the **Revolutionaries Sect** (*Sechta Epanastaton*) was linked to the killing of a police officer in central Athens, raising concerns about a possible renewal of terrorist violence in Greece.

LEGISLATURE

The unicameral **Parliament** (*Vouli*) consists of 300 members elected by direct universal suffrage for four-year terms, subject to dissolution. Since 1926 the procedure for allocating seats, usually a form of proportional representation, has tended to vary from one election to another. At the October 1993 balloting, simple proportional representation based on the Hagenbach-Bischoff quota was used in the first distribution, with the Hare quota employed in the second for all parties securing a minimum national vote share of 3 percent. The introduction of the 3 percent electoral threshold in 1990 precluded the possibility of independent minority candidates being elected in Thrace, in contrast to the 1989–1990 elections. Under the new circumstances, minority candidates usually run on mainstream-party ballots.

Following early elections on September 16, 2007, the seat distribution was as follows: New Democracy, 152 seats; the Panhellenic Socialist Movement, 102; the Communist Party of Greece, 22; the Coalition of the Radical Left, 14; and Popular Orthodox Rally, 10.

Speaker: Dimitrios SIOUFAS.

CABINET

[as of July 1, 2009]

Prime Minister	Konstantinos Karamanlis
Ministers	
Commerce	Konstantinos Hatzidakis
Culture	Antonios Samaras
Development	Konstantinos Hatzidakis
Economy and Finance	Ioannis Papathanassiou
Education and Religious Affairs	Aristovoulos Spiliotopoulos
Employment and Social Protection	Fani Palli-Petralia [f]
Energy	Konstantinos Hatzidakis
Environment, Physical Planning, and Public Works	Georgios Souflias
Foreign Affairs	Theodora Bakoyannis [f]
Health and Social Solidarity	Dimitrios Avramopoulos
Interior, Public Administration, and Decentralization	Prokopios Pavlopoulos
Justice	Nikolaos Dendias
Macedonia and Thrace	Stavros Kalafatis
Mercantile Marine and Island Policy	Anastassios Papaligouras
National Defense	Evangelos Meimarakis
Public Order	Christos Markoyiannakis
Rural Development and Foods	Sotirios Hatzigakis
Tourism	Konstantinos Markopoulos
Transport and Communications	Evripidis Stylianidis

[f] = female

Note: All cabinet ministers are members of the ruling New Democracy Party.

COMMUNICATIONS

The news media operated under severe constraints while the military was in power. Upon the return to civilian rule, censorship was lifted and a number of theretofore banned papers reemerged, although some have since experienced major shifts in circulation. From 1989 to 1992 overall readership dropped by 36 percent, the greatest decline being experienced by Communist and hard-line PASOK organs.

Under the conservative government of Prime Minister Mitsotakis, the media were subjected to legislation banning the "unwarranted" publicizing of terrorist activity, including the publication of terrorist manifestos. However, the controversial measure was rescinded in December 1993.

The Karamanlis government enacted legislation in January 2005 banning individuals with large shareholdings in media from owning shares in companies that bid for public contracts. The European Commission has called on Greece to change the law, indicating that it violates EU directives.

The publication of several free weekly newspapers gave a new flair to the Greek press market. Newspapers such as *LIFO, Athens Voice, FAQ, and City Press* gained high readability rates and reshaped the Greek media market. On June 22, 2009, the ownership of *Eleftheros Typos* announced the suspension of its publication.

Press. The following are published daily in Athens: *Eleftheros Typos* (Free Press, 36,729), center-right; *Ta Nea* (News, 63,110), center-left; *Eleftherotypia* (Press Freedom, 55,233), center-left; *Ethnos* (Nation, 43,226), center-left; *Apogevmatini* (Afternoon, 13,404), center-right; *Kathimerini* (Daily, 61,245), center-right; *Rizospastis* (Radical, 9,153), KKE organ; *Avriani* (Tomorrow, 2,768), populist left; *Espresso* (17,300), apolitical; *Traffic* (8,258), apolitical; *To Vima* (The Podium, 50,944), center-left; *Niki* (Victory, 375), center-left; *Eleftheros* (Free, 6,231), center-right; *Mesimvrini* (Midday, 99), center-right; *Avgi* (Dawn, 2,193), Eurocommunist; *Estia* (Vesta, 3,093), right; *O Logos* (Speech, 326), formerly *Dimokratikos Logos,* center-left; *Eleftheri Ora* (Free Time, 1,657), far-right; *Adesmeftos Typos* (Unaligned Press, 10,989), populist center-right; and *Vradyni* (Evening, 2,545), center-right.

News agencies. The major domestic service is the Athens News Agency—ANA (*Athinaiko Praktorio Edisseon—*APE). Several foreign bureaus maintain offices in Athens.

Broadcasting and computing. In 1987 Hellenic Radio-Television (*Elliniki Radiofonia Tileorassi*—ERT) became a joint stock company by merger of ERT-1 (the original ERT, which had been state-controlled since 1939 as EIR) and ERT-2, the former Information Service of the Armed Forces (*Ypiresia Enimerosseos Enoplon Dynameon*—YENED), which had been turned over to civilian operation in 1982. The restructuring yielded two television channels, ET-1 and ET-2 (to which ET-3, broadcasting from Thessaloniki, was subsequently added). In addition, the private Mega Channel, Antenna, and Sky (unrelated to the British facility of the same name) are representative of a number of commercial channels that were subsequently launched.

Since 1987 for radio and 1989 for television, local non-state-owned stations have been authorized to operate under government licenses issued on advice of the National Radio and Television Council (ESR), a 19-member body representing a variety of political, social, and cultural groups. By early 1993 the ESR had drafted positive recommendations for 1 Greater Athens and 11 national television stations; however, by midyear the government had failed to take action on any private licenses, with the result that approximately 1,500 local radio and some 100 largely local television stations continued to be operated illegally. By 2001 the ESR had begun to issue licenses regularly and to clear the backlog of applications. The ESR also began to fine stations for advertising violations. The two most popular private TV stations are Mega Channel and Antenna, which commenced operations in late 1989 and early 1990, respectively. As of 2008 there were 435 Internet users per 1,000 inhabitants.

INTERGOVERNMENTAL REPRESENTATION

Ambassador to the U.S.: Vassilis KASKARELIS.

U.S. Ambassador to Greece: Daniel V. SPECKHARD.

Permanent Representative to the UN: Anastassis MITSIALIS.

IGO Memberships (Non-UN): BIS, BSEC, CERN, CEUR, EBRD, EIB, ESA, EU, Eurocontrol, Francophonie, IEA, Interpol, IOM, NATO, OECD, OIF, OSCE, PCA, WCO, WEU, WTO.

GRENADA

State of Grenada

Political Status: Independent member of the Commonwealth since February 7, 1974; constitution suspended following coup of March 13, 1979; restored November 9, 1984.

Area: 133 sq. mi. (344 sq. km.).

Population: 100,895 (2001C); 111,000 (2008E).

Major Urban Center (2005E): ST. GEORGE'S (3,600).

Official Language: English.

Monetary Unit: East Caribbean Dollar (official rate December 1, 2009: 2.70 EC dollars = $1US).

Sovereign: Queen ELIZABETH II.

Governor General: Carlyle GLEAN, Sr; sworn in on November 27, 2008, succeeding Sir Daniel WILLIAMS.

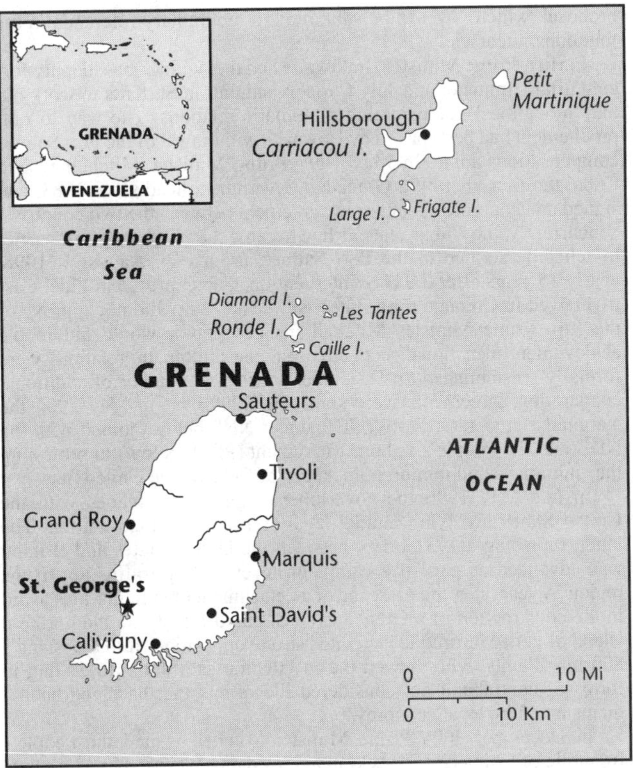

Prime Minister: Tillman THOMAS (National Democratic Congress); sworn in on July 9, 2008, succeeding Dr. Keith C. MITCHELL (New National Party), following legislative election of July 8.

THE COUNTRY

Grenada, located close to St. Kitts-Nevis, encompasses the southernmost of the Caribbean's Windward Islands, about 90 miles north of Trinidad. The country includes the main island of Grenada, the smaller islands of Carriacou and Petit Martinique, and a number of small islets. The population is approximately 75 percent black, the balance being largely mulatto, with a small white minority. English is the official language, while a French patois is in limited use. Roman Catholics predominate, with Anglicans constituting a substantial minority.

Grenada's economy is based on agriculture; bananas, cocoa, nutmeg, and mace are its most important products. Tourism, an important source of foreign exchange, declined substantially in the mid-1970s but subsequently revived. Unemployment has long been a major problem, encompassing upward of 40 percent of the adult population in 1994 before declining to a reported 13 percent in 2008. Structural-reform goals in the early 1990s included liberalization of trade regulations, civil service streamlining, and privatization of state-run enterprises. GDP grew steadily from 3.5 percent in 1996 to 6.0 percent in 1998. Meanwhile, inflation remained low (1.4 percent in 1998), although the International Monetary Fund (IMF) warned that Grenada's "public finances" had deteriorated under the effect of tax cuts, which had contributed to, among other things, a growing budget deficit that threatened to serve as a brake on future economic development. The 1999 and 2000 growth figures were 7.5 and 6.5 percent, respectively; however, the economy was buffeted by a decline in tourism following the September 2001 terrorist attacks in the United States, and real GDP registered –3.3 percent for the year, with marginal improvement in 2002 despite extensive damage from a tropical storm in September. Far more devastating was Hurricane Ivan, which on September 7, 2004, destroyed 90 percent of the country's buildings, with damages estimated in excess of $2 billion and economic contraction of at least 3.5 percent. A marginally less severe hurricane in July 2005 yielded additional destruction estimated at $200 million. Despite these setbacks, annual real growth averaged 5.7 percent, with inflation at 2.9 percent, in 2004–2007. However, GDP growth plummeted to an estimated 0.3 percent in 2008 because of the global recession, which weakened tourism receipts and generated a slowdown in construction.

GOVERNMENT AND POLITICS

Political background. Discovered by Columbus on his third voyage in 1498, Grenada was alternately ruled by the French and British until 1783, when British control was recognized by the Treaty of Versailles. It remained a British colony until 1958, when it joined the abortive Federation of the West Indies. In 1967 Grenada became a member of the West Indies Associated States, Britain retaining responsibility for external relations. Eric M. GAIRY, who had been removed from office by the British in 1962 for malfeasance, was redesignated prime minister upon the assumption of internal autonomy.

On February 7, 1974, Grenada became an autonomous member of the Commonwealth, two years after an election that the British interpreted as a mandate for independence. Many Grenadans, however, were opposed to self-rule under Gairy, whom they compared to Haiti's "Papa Doc" Duvalier. United primarily by their dislike of Gairy, the nation's three opposition parties—the Grenada National Party (GNP), the New Jewel Movement (NJM), and the United People's Party (UPP)—contested the election of December 7, 1976, as a People's Alliance. Although failing to defeat the incumbent prime minister, the Alliance succeeded in reducing the lower house strength of Gairy's Grenada United Labour Party (GULP) to 9 of 15 members.

In the early morning of March 13, 1979, while the prime minister was out of the country, insurgents destroyed the headquarters of the Grenada Defense Force, and a People's Revolutionary Government (PRG) was proclaimed by opposition leader Maurice BISHOP. Joining Bishop in the new government were 11 other members or supporters of the NJM plus two members of the GNP.

In September 1983 disagreement arose between Bishop (who reportedly favored rapprochement with the United States) and Deputy Prime Minister Bernard COARD (who sought a clear-cut alignment with the Soviet bloc), and Bishop was forced to accept an NJM Central Committee decision calling for joint leadership. On October 13 Gen. Hudson AUSTIN, commander of the People's Revolutionary Army (PRA), removed Bishop from office and placed him under house arrest. Six days later, after having momentarily been freed by rioting supporters, Bishop was recaptured and executed, with General Austin being installed as head of a 16-member Revolutionary Military Council (RMC). On October 25, after the governor general, Sir Paul SCOON, had requested the Organization of Eastern Caribbean States (OECS) to intervene and restore order, U.S. military forces, with OECS endorsement and limited personnel support, invaded the island, seizing Austin and others involved in the coup. Subsequently, a provisional administration under Nicholas A. BRATHWAITE was established, which held office until the installation of Herbert A. BLAIZE as prime minister of a new parliamentary regime on December 4, 1984.

In an unusual development, the allegedly "authoritarian" Blaize lost the leadership of the New National Party (NNP) to Dr. Keith MITCHELL at a party convention held January 21–22, 1989. Six months later Blaize dismissed Mitchell from the cabinet and announced the formation of a new grouping, the National Party (NP). Faced with the certainty of an adverse confidence vote, the prime minister prorogued the legislature on August 23. After a long illness, Blaize died on December 19 and was immediately succeeded by his deputy, Ben JONES, who dissolved Parliament in anticipation of an election that was constitutionally mandated by March 1990.

The election of March 13, 1990, yielded a plurality of seven legislative seats for the National Democratic Congress (NDC), whose leader, Brathwaite, formed an administration that moved from minority to majority status with the May 7 defection to the NDC of a GULP representative.

Prime Minister Brathwaite, whose government had encountered criticism over its structural-adjustment policies, resigned as NDC leader in July 1994 and was succeeded in the latter capacity by Agriculture Minister George BRIZAN on September 4. Brathwaite, who had reportedly become disenchanted with party politics, continued as prime minister until February 1, 1995, when Brizan also became head of government. However, despite a nearly five-month run-up, Brizan was unable to lead the NDC to a legislative victory on June 20, being obliged to step down in favor of Mitchell, whose NNP had captured 8 of 15 lower house seats. The NNP won all 15 seats in the election of January 1999 but was reduced to a narrow 1-seat margin in November

2003. In early elections on July 8, 2008, the NDC won 11 house seats, and NDC leader Tillman THOMAS succeeded Mitchell as prime minister.

Constitution and government. Grenada's constitution, originally adopted in February 1967 and modified only slightly on independence, was suspended following the March 1979 coup but restored in November 1984, the legitimacy of laws enacted in the interim being confirmed by Parliament in February 1985. The British monarch is the nominal sovereign and is represented by a governor general. Executive authority is exercised on the monarch's behalf by the prime minister, who represents the majority party in the House of Representatives, the lower house of the bicameral legislature. The House is popularly elected for a five-year term, while the upper chamber, the Senate, consists of 13 members appointed by the governor general: 10 on the advice of the prime minister (3 to represent interest groups) and 3 on the advice of the leader of the opposition. The judicial system includes a Supreme Court composed of a High Court of Justice and a two-tiered Court of Appeal, the upper panel of which hears final appeals from the High Court. There are also eight magistrates' courts of summary jurisdiction.

Grenada is administratively divided into 6 parishes encompassing 52 village councils on the main island, with the minor islands organized as separate administrative entities.

Foreign relations. The United Kingdom and the United States recognized the Bishop government in March 1979, but relations subsequently deteriorated, with Washington condemning St. George's midsummer signing of a two-year technical-assistance pact with Cuba, and London deploring "the unattractive record of the Grenada government over civil liberties and democratic rights." Relations with Washington worsened further in the wake of U.S. and North American Treaty Organization (NATO) naval maneuvers off Puerto Rico in July 1981, Grenada branding the exercises as a rehearsal for invasion of its territory. Nine months later, after Grenada had become the only English-speaking Caribbean state to declare its support for Argentina in the Falkland Islands war, U.S. President Ronald Reagan opened a four-day visit to nearby Barbados by charging that St. George's had joined with Cuba, Nicaragua, and the Soviet Union in an effort to "spread the virus of Marxism" in the area.

Regional reaction to the Bishop regime was initially somewhat mixed, but by mid-1982 all of the other six members of the OECS (Antigua, Dominica, Montserrat, St. Kitts-Nevis, St. Lucia, and St. Vincent) were generally hostile, although the most vocal regional criticism of the PRG came from Prime Minister Tom Adams of Barbados. Bishop's murder provoked even more widespread condemnation, including that of the Cuban government, which announced on October 20, 1983, that "no position claimed as revolutionary . . . can justify savage methods such as the elimination of Maurice Bishop and the outstanding group of honest and moral leaders who died." The ensuing military intervention by U.S. and Caribbean forces, coupled with Reagan's assertion that Grenada had become "a Soviet-Cuban colony being readied for use as a major military bastion to export terror," left little opportunity for an improvement in relations between St. George's and Havana under either the interim administration of Nicholas Brathwaite or the restored parliamentary government of Herbert Blaize. Thus, the last Cuban diplomat remaining in Grenada (a chargé d'affaires) departed in March 1984, with relations between the two countries being further strained during the ensuing year by Havana's attempt to recover $6 million for equipment used to construct an airport at Port Salines that the United States had earlier characterized as a military threat to the region. Subsequently, Grenada participated in the U.S.-backed regional security plan designed to avert future leftist takeovers, Prime Minister Blaize remaining one of the strongest supporters of U.S. Caribbean policy until his death in December 1989.

President Reagan was warmly received during a visit on February 20, 1986, which included a "mini-summit" with other English-speaking Caribbean leaders. Earlier, on October 31, 1985, Queen Elizabeth II was reported to have been given a "subdued welcome" because of Britain's failure to assist in the 1983 intervention and the relatively modest dimensions of its subsequent aid program.

Following an inconclusive response to an appeal by Vincentian prime minister James Mitchell to convert the seven-member OECS into an integrated regime, Grenada joined in 1991 with its Windward Island neighbors to launch a less inclusive four-member grouping. During the third meeting of a regional Constituent Assembly at Roseau, Dominica, in September, agreement was reached on a federal system with a common legislature and executive; however, opposition was voiced to the proposal, which is yet to be submitted to preliminary referenda in the four constituencies.

Earlier, Prime Minister Brathwaite had met with Cuba's deputy foreign affairs minister at a July Caricom summit in St. Kitts to work out the "modalities" for resuming diplomatic relations. The way to rapprochement had been paved by Havana's withdrawal of the Port Salines compensation claim. In May 1997 Prime Minister Mitchell visited Cuba, the first visit by a Grenadan government head since 1983, and signed an economic cooperation agreement between the two countries; concurrently, the Cuban state airline became the first foreign air carrier to schedule service to the Port Salines airport. On August 1, 1998, nearly 15 years after the U.S. intervention, Cuban president Fidel Castro arrived in Grenada for a state visit. While many did not approve of the trip, Prime Minister Mitchell insisted that it would aid in the achievement of national reconciliation, and diplomatic relations were formally reestablished on December 1, 1999. A number of additional cooperation agreements were signed in 2000, and in May 2004 the National Democratic Party (NDP, under NNP below) joined with the NDC and the People's Labour Movement (PLM, below) in protesting the "inhumane and immoral blockade" of Cuba by the United States.

In late May 1996 the government signed two treaties with the United States involving mutual legal assistance and extradition. The latter, replacing a 1931 treaty between the United States and Britain, was advanced as part of a campaign to curb drug trafficking in the region. A year later, the presence of a detachment of U.S. marines to aid in the construction of a Grenadan coast guard facility on the northern island of Petit Martinique generated strong opposition from the island's 800 inhabitants, who viewed the installation as a threat to trading in forms of contraband not considered illegal and that had long been a mainstay of the local economy.

In December 2004 Prime Minister Mitchell visited the People's Republic of China (PRC) seeking aid for damage caused by Hurricane Ivan, and shortly thereafter his administration shifted diplomatic relations from Taiwan to the PRC.

Current issues. In August 2007 New York–based lawyers called for dismissal of a civil lawsuit alleging that Prime Minister Mitchell and his wife had been paid bribes totaling $1 million in a high-yield investment fraud scheme. Collaterally, the U.S. government filed a memorandum in a money-laundering case in Oregon that included a charge that the bribes had, in fact, been paid. However, in December, Washington announced that prosecution "would be incompatible with the United States's foreign policy interests," in addition to the fact that the leader of a foreign government fell "under the doctrine of head-of-state immunity." Undeterred, the Thomas administration confirmed in early 2009 that it would seek evidence from former diplomat Eric RESTEINER, currently serving a U.S. prison sentence, that he had paid Mitchell $500,000 in 2001 for an ambassadorial appointment.

The NDC's sweeping victory over the NNP in the July 2008 legislative election was widely attributed to the desire for change that had resulted in the recent defeat of incumbent governments in several Caribbean nations. The NDC was also helped by the unusually large turnout (80 percent) and support among young voters. Prime Minister Thomas, a lawyer and human rights advocate who had been a political prisoner under the Bishop regime in the early 1980s, pledged greater transparency in government and efforts to cushion the shock of rising food and fuel prices.

POLITICAL PARTIES

Before the 1979 coup, Eric Gairy's Grenada United Labour Party (GULP) had consistently dominated the country's politics, although its majority in the House of Representatives was substantially reduced in the election of December 1976, which the leftist New Jewel Movement (NJM), the centrist United People's Party (UPP), and the conservative Grenada National Party (GNP) contested as a People's Alliance. For the 1984 balloting, only the GULP campaigned under its original name. The recently formed New National Party (NNP) secured an overwhelming majority in 1984, a much slimmer margin in 1995 after a period of ascendancy by the National Democratic Congress (NDC), and total control in 1999.

Government Party:

National Democratic Congress (NDC). The NDC was launched in April 1987 by George BRIZAN and Francis Alexis, who had defected from the NNP and were subsequently joined by a variety of anti-Blaize figures, including leaders of the Grenada Democratic Labour Party (GDLP) and the Democratic Labour Congress (DLC). Launched in March 1985 by (then) opposition leader Marcel PETERS, the GDLP had expressed concern about unemployment, a lack of "Christian values," and Grenada's security in the wake of the U.S. withdrawal. The DLC had been formed in August 1986 by Kenny LALSINGH, a legislative representative who had left the NNP earlier in the year, in a realignment that included the former Christian Democratic Labour Party (CDLP), a centrist formation of ex-UPP members that competed unsuccessfully in the 1984 election. The NDC held its inaugural conference on December 18, 1987.

In January 1989 Brizan stepped down as opposition leader in favor of Nicholas Brathwaite, who had served as head of the 1983–1984 provisional administration, and who became prime minister following the election of March 13, 1990. In March 1991 party chair Kenny Lalsingh resigned as minister of works and communications after being accused of improperly importing transmitting equipment for use by the operator of an unlicensed radio station. In July 1994 Prime Minister Brathwaite resigned as party leader; at the NDC's annual convention on September 4 Brizan was elected his successor, although not replacing Brathwaite as prime minister until February 1, 1995. Four months later the NDC retained only 4 of 15 legislative seats, thereby becoming the opposition party. Brizan was given a one-month suspension from the House of Representatives on August 27, 1997, for criticizing the appointment of Daniel Williams as governor general.

Before the January 1999 legislative vote, Brizan announced that, because of his declining health, Deputy Chair Joan Purcell would serve as the NDC standard-bearer. The party reportedly attempted to negotiate a formal electoral alliance with the GULP, DLP (see under PLM, below), and NP (below); however, agreement could not be reached on seat allocation or leadership. The NDC consequently presented its candidates (including Brizan and Purcell), although informal agreement was reported between the NDC and the GULP/United Labour not to challenge each other's strongest candidates. The party lost all of its seats (on a vote share of 25 percent), and Brizan subsequently announced his retirement from active politics. Tillman Thomas, a former minister of tourism, was elected party leader in October 2000. The NDC won 7 of 15 house seats (on a vote share of 45 percent) in 2003 and became the governing party in 2008 by securing 11 seats on a vote share of 51.2 percent.

Leaders: Tillman THOMAS (Prime Minister and Party Leader), George PRIME (Deputy Leader), Joan PURCELL (President of the Senate), George James McGUIRE (Speaker of the House of Representatives), Peter DAVID (General Secretary).

Opposition Party:

New National Party (NNP). The NNP was launched in August 1984 as an amalgamation of the Grenada National Party (GNP), led by Herbert Blaize; the National Democratic Party (NDP), led by George Brizan and Robert Grant; the Grenada Democratic Movement (GDM), led by Dr. Francis Alexis; and the Christian Democratic Labour Party (CDLP), led by Winston WHYTE. The center-right GNP, founded by Blaize in 1956, had been essentially moribund during its leader's retirement from politics after the 1979 coup. The NDP, organized in early 1984, became the most liberal component of the NNP. The GDM was formed in 1983 by a group of right-wing exiles resident in Barbados and elsewhere, who reportedly benefited from substantial U.S. support. The CDLP (see under NDC, above) withdrew from the coalition in September 1984, after a series of policy disputes with the other groups.

In its 1984 campaign manifesto, the NNP formally endorsed the 1983 military intervention and urged that foreign military and police units not be withdrawn. It dominated the elections of December 3, winning 14 of 15 lower house seats. However, by mid-1985 the coalition was in substantial disarray, GNP elements holding most of the government portfolios. Infighting continued throughout 1986, Brizan and Alexis reportedly mounting an unsuccessful challenge to Blaize's leadership before a December convention at which the GNP faction gained virtually complete control, with Ben Jones, seemingly the prime minister's heir apparent, defeating Brizan for the post of deputy leader. In April 1987 Brizan and Alexis left the government and moved into opposition, leaving the NNP little more than a "reborn GNP," with a diminished legislative majority of 9 seats. A far more critical cleavage was revealed in January 1989 when (theretofore) General Secretary Keith Mitchell, who had previously criticized Blaize for contributing to a "lack of camaraderie" among senior members, defeated the prime minister for the party leadership. Despite the action, Mitchell asserted that because of his "tremendous respect and admiration" for Blaize he would not seek the latter's removal from government office before the next election. Dismissed from the cabinet on July 21, Mitchell joined with Brizan in filing a motion of nonconfidence that failed to be voted upon because of the legislative prorogation of August 23. Mitchell was named prime minister, following the NNP victory of June 20, 1995. The NNP swept all of the 15 parliamentary seats on January 18, 1999, 7 of which were lost on November 27, 2003. The party's vote share fell to 47.8 percent in 2008 when it won only 4 house seats, and Mitchell lost his bid for a fourth consecutive term.

Leaders: Dr. Keith MITCHELL (Leader of the Opposition and Former Prime Minister), Sen. Gregory BOWEN (Deputy Leader), Clarice CHARLES (Secretary General).

Other Parties that Participated in the 2008 Election:

Grenada United Labour Party (GULP). The GULP was founded in 1950 as the personal vehicle of Eric M. Gairy, who headed governments from 1951 to 1957, 1961 to 1962, and 1967 to 1979. Having acquired a reputation for both corruption and repression while in office, Gairy did not present himself for election in 1984, when the GULP secured 36 percent of the popular vote compared to the NNP's 59 percent. The party's only successful candidate, Marcel Peters, after being formally designated leader of the opposition, announced his withdrawal in protest at alleged electoral irregularities, but he later reversed himself and secured the appointment of three associates as opposition senators. In early 1985 Peters formed the GDLP (see under NDC, above) after being expelled from the GULP, which was thus left with no parliamentary representation.

Although Sir Eric had announced in December 1987 that he was retiring from politics, he faced no opposition in reelection as GULP president at the party's annual convention in December 1988. The party was runner-up to the NDC in the March 1990 balloting, winning four legislative seats, Gairy being among those defeated. Following the election, one of GULP's representatives defected to the NDC, while a second defected in the interest of "national unity" after an April 27 fire that destroyed a government complex at St. George's. A third resigned from the party in May 1991, after having been characterized by Gairy as a "recalcitrant schoolboy." The last of the four elected in 1990, Leader of the Opposition Winifred STRACHMAN, was expelled by the party's Executive Council in March 1992 on grounds that included "blatant disloyalty" and a "substandard, negligible and disappointing" performance as an MP. The GULP won two legislative seats in June 1995, with Gairy again among the losers. Sir Eric died after a lengthy illness on August 23, 1997.

After failing to negotiate a more inclusive electoral alliance (see NDC, above), the GULP contested the January 1999 legislative poll jointly with the DLP (see under PLM, below), the ticket being known as GULP/United Labour. However, discord was reported within the GULP over the reemergence of Raphael Fletcher as the party's standard-bearer. Fletcher had been suspended from the GULP in 1988 because of his links to Libya and had subsequently defected to the NNP and served in the Mitchell administration. Fletcher returned to the GULP in late 1998 after his departure from the government and the NNP had triggered early elections. The GULP/United Labour secured only 12 percent of the vote (and no seats), despite the support of Marcelle GAIRY (the daughter of Eric Gairy), who resigned as Grenada's high commissioner to London to participate in the campaign.

For the 2008 legislative poll, the GULP formed a United Labor Platform (ULP) with the PLM, but the electoral alliance was able to secure only 0.8 percent of the vote.

Leaders: Wilfred HAYES (President), Gloria PAYNE-BANFIELD (Party Leader).

People's Labour Movement (PLM). The PLM was initially launched as the Democratic Labour Party (DLP) in December 1995 by four NDC dissidents led by former attorney general Francis Alexis, who had resigned in July from the parent party claiming it was "finished and done with." It competed in the January 1999 legislative poll in alliance with the GULP (above); a similar alliance was formed for the 2008 balloting. However, the party was weakened by a dispute between Alexis and Dr. Terrence MARRYSHOW that led to the latter's resignation as party president.

Leaders: Dr. Francis ALEXIS (Leader), Wayne FRANCIS (Deputy Leader).

Good Ole Democracy (GOD). The GOD offered three candidates in the 1999 election, capturing a minuscule 0.2 percent of the total vote that was, nevertheless, an improvement over its 1995 vote share. It contested only two constituencies, without success, in 2003 and was also unsuccessful in 2008.

Leader: Justin McBURNIE.

Other Parties:

National Party (NP). The NP was organized in July 1989 by Prime Minister Blaize, who had been deposed in January as leader of the NNP. Since the NP did not command a majority of lower house seats, Blaize prorogued the body on August 23, pending an election that was expected to be held late in the year. Immediately following Blaize's death on December 19, the governor general appointed Deputy Prime Minister Ben Jones as his acting successor, despite the party's continued minority status. The NP's legislative representation dropped from five to two in March 1990. In December the party offered its support to the Brathwaite administration, with Jones returning to his former post as external affairs minister; however, on January 5, 1991, Jones resigned after his party had returned to opposition in a dispute over the 1991 budget. The NP won no legislative seats in 1995 and did not present candidates thereafter.

Leaders: Ben JONES (Former Prime Minister), George McGUIRE (Chair), Paul LANDER (Secretary).

Grenada Renaissance Party (GRP). The GRP is a small formation that failed to elect its sole candidate in 2003.

Leader: Martin W. EDWARDS.

United Republican Party (URP). The URP was formed in 1993 by a group of New York–based Grenadans. It contested the 1995 election without success.

Leader: Antonio LANGDON.

Grenada Progressive Party (GPP). The GPP was organized by a former teacher in June 1997 with the avowed aim of appealing to women and young people.

Leader: Prescott WILLIAMS.

LEGISLATURE

The bicameral **Parliament,** embracing an appointed Senate of 13 members and a popularly elected 15-member House of Representatives, was dissolved by the People's Revolutionary Government following the March 1979 coup. It reconvened on December 28, 1984, following a general election on December 3.

Senate. Of the 13 members of the upper house, 10 are nominated by the government and 3 by the leader of the opposition.

President: Joan PURCELL.

House of Representatives. The lower house comprises 15 members elected for a five-year term subject to dissolution. In the most recent election, of July 8, 2008, the National Democratic Congress won 11 seats and the New National Party, 4.

Speaker: George James McGUIRE.

CABINET

[as of June 1, 2009]

Prime Minister	Tillman Thomas
Ministers	
Agriculture, Forestry, and Fisheries	Michael Denis Lett
Carriacou and Petit Martinique Affairs	Sen. George Prime
Education and Human Resources	Sen. Franka Bernadine [f]
Finance, Planning, Economic Development, Energy, and Foreign Trade	Nazim Burke
Foreign Affairs and Tourism	Peter David
Health	Karl Hood
Housing, Lands, and Community Development	Alleyne Walker
Information	Tillman Thomas
Legal Affairs	Tillman Thomas
National Security	Tillman Thomas
Social Services, Ecclesiastical Affairs, and Labor	Glynis Roberts [f]
Without Portfolio	Sen. Pemba Braveboy [f] Sen. Joan Purcell [f]
Works, Physical Development, Public Utilities, and Environment	Joseph Gilbert
Youth Empowerment, Culture, and Sports	Patrick Simmons
Attorney General	Jimmy Bristol
Ministers of State	
Finance, Planning, Economic Development, Energy, and Foreign Trade	Michael Church
Health	Sen. Ann Peters [f]
Housing, Lands, and Community Development	Sen. Glen Noel
Works, Physical Development, Public Utilities, and Environment	Sylvester Quarless
Youth Empowerment, Culture, and Sports	Sen. Arley Gill

[f] = female

COMMUNICATIONS

Press. There are no daily newspapers. The *Grenada Informer* (6,000) is a general-interest weekly; other weeklies include the *Grenadian Voice* (3,000), independent right-wing; the *Grenada Guardian,* a GULP publication; and *Grenada Today*. The *West Indian* is a government-owned biweekly. An opposition *Grenadian Tribune* was launched in June 1987. Strain has been reported in recent years between the media and the Mitchell government, which, among other things, has proposed a code of ethics for journalists.

News agencies. There is no domestic facility; for international news the media rely primarily on the regional Caribbean News Agency (CANA).

Broadcasting and computing. Legislation enacted in October 1990 ended direct government control of the Grenada Broadcasting Corporation (GBC). A statutory board containing private-sector representatives was created to supervise broadcasting and privatize government TV facilities. Full divestiture was achieved in 1997. As of 2008 there were 231.8 Internet users per 1,000 inhabitants.

INTERGOVERNMENTAL REPRESENTATION

Ambassador to the U.S.: Gillian M.S. BRISTOL.

U.S. Ambassador to Grenada: (Vacant).

Permanent Representative to the UN: Dessima M. WILLIAMS.

IGO Memberships (Non-UN): ACS, Caricom, CDB, CWTH, Interpol, NAM, OAS, OECS, OPANAL, SELA, WTO.

GUATEMALA

Republic of Guatemala
República de Guatemala

Political Status: Independent Captaincy General of Guatemala proclaimed 1821; member of United Provinces of Central America, 1824–1838; separate state established 1839; most recent constitution (adopted May 31, 1985, with effect from January 14, 1986) amended by referendum of January 30, 1994.

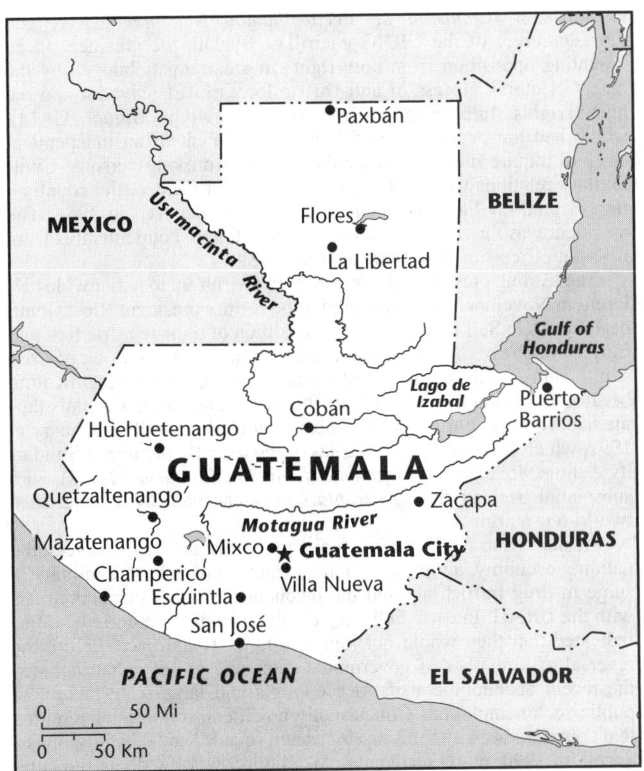

Area: 42,042 sq. mi. (108,889 sq. km.).

Population: 11,237,196 (2002C); 13,687,000 (2008E).

Major Urban Centers (2005E): GUATEMALA CITY (991,000), Mixco (307,000), Villa Nueva (237,901), Quetzaltenango (114,000), Escuintla (72,000).

Official Language: Spanish.

Monetary Unit: Quetzal (market rate December 1, 2009: 8.29 quetzales = $1US). Since May 1, 2001, foreign currencies have been permitted to circulate and may be used in business transactions.

President: Álvaro COLOM Caballeros (National Unity of Hope); elected on November 4, 2007, sworn in for a four-year term and formed new government on January 14, 2008, succeeding Oscar José BERGER Perdomo (Grand National Alliance).

Vice President: Rafael ESPADA (National Unity of Hope); elected on November 4, 2007, and sworn in for a term concurrent with that of the president on January 14, 2008, succeeding Eduardo STEIN Barillas (Grand National Alliance).

THE COUNTRY

The northernmost of the Spanish-speaking Central American countries, Guatemala is also the most populous, with an annual population growth rate close to 3 percent. The population, which is noted for its high proportion (65 percent) of Indians, is concentrated in the southern half of the country. The other major population group, the *ladinos*, is composed of mestizos and assimilated Indians. Although Spanish is the official language, about two dozen Indian languages are spoken, of which the most important are Cakchiquel, Caribe, Chol, Kekchi, Mam, Maya, Pocoman, and Quiché. The dominant religion is Roman Catholicism, although recent inroads by Pentecostal Protestantism have prompted Guatemalan bishops to take a new look at "the discovery of America" and issue calls for a "new evangelism" capable of incorporating indigenous rites and rituals. Women constitute approximately 27 percent of the official labor force, not including subsistence farming and unreported domestic service; employed women are concentrated in sales, clerical jobs, and the service sector and make up 40 percent of professionals. Female participation in government has traditionally been virtually nonexistent. A few women have held ministerial portfolios in recent administrations; in addition, a woman served as president of Congress during the Arzú tenure. In the 2003 election, 15 of 158 seats (9.4 percent) were won by women; in 2007, the number rose to 17 (10.8 percent).

The Guatemalan economy is still largely agricultural, and coffee remains by far the single most important source of foreign revenue; cotton, bananas, and sugar are also exported. Significant progress is currently being registered in manufacturing, which, like commercial farming, is predominantly in the hands of *ladinos* and foreign interests. The latter, including investors from the United States, Europe, and Asia, are deeply involved in the *maquiladora*, virtual sweatshop industries that turn imported materials into finished products (such as textiles) for export.

Severe budgetary difficulties have persisted since the early 1980s, and both poverty and income inequality remain fundamental problems, with up to 60 percent of the population living below the poverty line. Real GDP growth averaged about 4 percent from 1992 to 1997, peaked at 5 percent in 1998, then declined steadily to 1.5 percent in 2004 before rising to an estimated 3.2 percent in 2005, albeit with inflation at 6 percent. GDP remained steady in 2006, echoing the 2005 growth rate of 3.2 percent. In 2007 annual GDP growth increased to 6.3 percent, but dropped to 4 percent in 2008 as the global economic slowdown reduced demand. Inflation reached 9.4 percent in 2008, the highest level since the 1990s, due to high fuel and commodity prices. The impact of the global financial crisis continued to be a concern in early 2009, as the government announced a 3 percent cut in its annual budget as a result of poor tax receipts. It was also reported that remittances from Guatemalans living in the United States-which make up nearly one-tenth of the gross domestic product—fell by more than 10 percent from February 2008 to February 2009. Meanwhile, President Colom announced an $871 million economic stimulus package, much of it dedicated to new construction projects. In April the International Monetary Fund (IMF) approved a $935 million standby loan for Guatemala to help cushion the effects of the financial crisis, as the economy was forecast to contract in 2009.

GOVERNMENT AND POLITICS

Political background. Guatemala, which obtained its liberation from Spanish rule in 1821 and its independence as a nation from the breakup of the United Provinces of Central America in 1839, has existed through much of its national history under a series of prolonged dictatorships, including that of Gen. Jorge UBICO from 1931 to 1944. The deposition of Ubico in 1944 by an alliance of students, liberals, and dissident members of the military known as the "October Revolutionaries" inaugurated a period of reform. Led initially by President Juan José ARÉVALO and then by Jacobo ARBENZ Guzmán, the progressive movement was aborted in 1954 by rightist elements under Col. Carlos CASTILLO Armas. The stated reason for the coup was the elimination of communist influence, Castillo Armas formally dedicating his government to this end until his assassination in 1957. Still another coup, in 1963, overthrew the government of Gen. Miguel YDÍGORAS Fuentes. A new constitution drawn up under Ydígoras's successor, Col. Enrique PERALTA Azurdia, paved the way for the election in 1966 of a civilian president, Julio César MÉNDEZ Montenegro, and the restoration of full constitutional rule with his inauguration on July 1. Méndez was succeeded as president by Col. Carlos ARANA Osorio in an election held March 1, 1970, amid widespread terrorist activity that included the kidnapping of the nation's foreign minister.

The 1974 presidential and legislative balloting presented a confusing spectacle of charges and countercharges. Initially, it appeared that Gen. Efraín RÍOS Montt, the candidate of the National Opposition Front (a coalition of the Christian Democrats and two minor parties) had placed first in the presidential race by a wide margin. Subsequently, however, the government declared that Gen. Kjell Eugenio LAUGERUD García, the candidate of the ruling right-wing coalition, had obtained a plurality of the votes cast. Since neither candidate was officially credited with a majority, the Congress, controlled by the conservatives, was called on to designate the winner, and named General Laugerud.

Similar confusion prevailed in the election of March 5, 1978, evoking numerous allegations of fraud and threats of violence during a five-day period of indecision by the National Electoral Council, which eventually ruled that the center-right candidate, Maj. Gen. Fernando Romeo LUCAS García, had narrowly outpolled his far right-wing opponent, Colonel Peralta Azurdia.

In the election of March 7, 1982, Gen. Angel Aníbal GUEVARA, the candidate of a new center-right grouping styled the Popular Democratic Front, was declared the victor over three opponents representing far-right, centrist, and center-left interests, with no far-left organizations participating. Two days later the defeated candidates joined in a public demonstration protesting the conduct of the election and calling for annulment of the results. The public appeal was rejected by outgoing President Lucas García, and on March 23 a group of military dissidents seized power in a bloodless coup aimed at the restoration of "authentic democracy." On March 24 formal authority was assumed by a three-member junta consisting of General Ríos Montt, Brig. Gen. Horacio Egberto MALDONADO Schaad, and Col. Francisco Luis GORDILLO Martínez. Subsequently, on June 9, Ríos Montt dissolved the junta and assumed sole authority as president and military commander.

Although taking office with strong military and business support, Ríos Montt became increasingly estranged from both by a series of anticorruption and economic reform proposals, while incurring mounting opposition from the Catholic Church because of overt proselytizing by a U.S. Protestant sect to which he belonged. Following a number of apparent coup attempts, he was ousted on August 8, 1983, by a group of senior army officers under Brig. Gen. Oscar MEJÍA Víctores, who promised that an election would be held in 1984 to pave the way for "a return to civilian life."

The balloting of August 1, 1984, in which 17 parties participated, was for a National Constituent Assembly, which drafted a new basic law (adopted on May 31, 1985) modeled largely on its 1965 predecessor. In the subsequent general election of November 3, 1985, the Guatemalan Christian Democratic Party (*Partido Democracia Cristiana Guatemalteca*—PDCG) obtained a slim majority of legislative seats, and in a runoff presidential poll on December 8, its candidate, Marco Vinicio CEREZO Arévalo, defeated the National Center Union (*Union del Cambio Nacionalista*—UCN) candidate, Jorge CARPIO Nicolle, with a margin of 68 to 32 percent of the vote. Assuming office on January 14, 1986, Cerezo Arévalo became the first civilian president of Guatemala since Méndez Montenegro in 1966.

From the early 1960s Guatemala was beset by guerrilla insurgency. Initially, two groups, the Rebel Armed Forces (*Fuerzas Armadas Rebeldes*—FAR) and the 13th of November Movement (M-13), operated in the country's rural northeast. After 1966 counterinsurgency actions drove the guerrillas into the cities, generating urban violence that claimed the lives of many Guatemalans as well as some members of the foreign diplomatic community. In 1976 a new left-wing group, the Guerrilla Army of the Poor (*Ejército Guerrillero de los Pobres*—EGP), claimed credit for a wave of increased terrorism following a devastating earthquake in February. Both left- and right-wing extremism intensified after the 1978 balloting, with the principal left-wing groups forming in January 1981 a unified military command called the Guatemalan National Revolutionary Unity (*Unidad Revolucionaria Nacional Guatemalteca*—URNG). In August 1982 Ríos Montt established the most extensive Civil Self-Defense Patrol (*Patrullas de Autodefensa Civil*—PAC) network in the world, encompassing virtually every adult male in the countryside and eventually constituting a counterguerrilla force of nearly 1 million men. Ríos Montt used the term "scorched earth" to describe his government's counterinsurgency strategy. Thousands of civilians in the countryside were massacred, mostly by the army and civil patrols, with reports of an estimated, 18,000 people killed in 1982. The rebels responded by attempting to establish a "liberated corridor" from Guatemala City to the Mexican border, populated by Indians fleeing army resettlement into "protected" villages. Despite such efforts, vigorous offensive action by the government was reported by late 1983 to have substantially weakened guerrilla operations.

In October 1986 President Cerezo signaled his willingness to enter into peace talks with the country's rebel organizations, including the URNG. However, no formal contacts were made with the insurgents until after the August 1987 Esquipulas II Central American peace accord brokered by Costa Rican president Óscar Arias, whose efforts won him the Nobel Peace Prize. A series of "exploratory talks" began in Madrid, under Spanish government auspices, in October 1987.

Although the ruling Christian Democrats had won a majority of municipal elections in April 1988, military unrest was evidenced by a failed coup in mid-May and the administration was forced to cancel a meeting in Costa Rica between the National Reconciliation Commission (*Comisión de Reconciliación Nacional*—CRN) and representatives of the URNG guerrillas. By fall, the president faced mounting opposition from both right-wing extremists buoyed by the recent electoral success of anti-Duarte forces in El Salvador and the human rights Mutual Support Group (*Grupo de Apoyo Mutuo*—GAM), which had long campaigned for the appointment of an independent body to inquire into the fate of the country's missing persons. Civil-military relations were a frequent challenge for Cerezo, the country's first elected civilian leader since Arbenz was deposed in 1954. The president was the target of two serious, but failed, coup attempts from far-right officers in May 1988 and May 1989.

The leading presidential contenders in the run-up to nationwide balloting in November 1990 appeared to be former president Ríos Montt, heading a "No Sell-Out" (*No-Venta*) coalition of right-wing parties, and Carpio Nicolle of the UCN. In late October, however, the Court of Constitutionality vacated Ríos Montt's final appeal against disqualification because of his involvement in the 1982 coup. Thereafter, Carpio's failure to secure a majority on November 11 forced a runoff on January 6, 1991, which Jorge SERRANO Elías of the recently organized Solidarity Action Movement (*Movimiento de Acción Solidaria*—MAS), with substantial backing from *No-Venta* supporters, won by a better than two-to-one margin.

President Serrano faced four major problems: the fragile state of the nation's economy, an array of human rights abuses by the military, a surge in drug trafficking, and the inconclusive status of negotiations with the URNG. In early February the three leading union federations indicated that they would not join in a new "social pact" before the reversal of a number of government economic policies that included the recent abandonment of price controls and large-scale layoffs of public-sector employees. Concurrently, an official commission reported that there had been 304 killings by "death squads" and 233 "disappearances" in 1990, with Guatemala ranked third, worldwide, in the latter regard. For its part, the United States announced a suspension of military aid in December because of the government's failure to "criticize or exhaustively investigate" those chargeable with human rights abuses, including those responsible for the 1990 death of a U.S. citizen. Earlier, Guatemalan Treasury police revealed that a total of 4,770 kilos of cocaine had been seized in 1990, most of it originating in Colombia, with Guatemala serving not only as a bridge for shipments to the United States but also as a major money-laundering center.

In March and October 1990 the third and fourth rounds of negotiation with URNG representatives were held in Oslo, Norway, and Metepec, Mexico, respectively. The talks proved unproductive because of the Guatemalan military's insistence that it would join in a "dialogue with the subversive delinquents" only after they had laid down their arms. However, the army reversed itself in early 1991, agreeing, for the first time, to participate in a new round of talks launched in Mexico City in late April. The 1991 talks continued in Cuernavaca, Mexico, in June, and in Querétaro, Mexico, in July, where agreement was reached on the need for "a negotiation process [having] as its final objective the search for peace through political means." A further meeting in Mexico City in September yielded a series of rebel demands, including abolition of the PAC units and an end to military conscription; however, no substantive results were reported apart from a number of "approximations" (incremental advances) in regard to human rights issues.

A round of talks that concluded in late February 1992 also failed to yield a breakthrough, despite pressure on both sides stemming from formal settlement in mid-February of the conflict in neighboring El Salvador. In August a compromise was reached on the Civil Self-Defense Patrols, the URNG dropping its demand for their immediate dissolution and the government agreeing not to expand them. In October an agreement (subsequently formalized in a tripartite accord involving the United Nations High Commissioner for Refugees—UNHCR) was concluded on the return of approximately 43,000 Guatemalan refugees, many of whom had spent more than a decade in camps on the Mexican side of the border. By early 1993, however, the parties had become deadlocked over a timetable for implementation of human rights guarantees and the establishment of a truth commission to investigate human rights violations during the lengthy armed conflict.

On May 25, 1993, scarcely more than two weeks after the ruling MAS registered a sweeping victory in municipal balloting, President Serrano attempted to assume near-dictatorial powers that included dissolution of the Congress and dismissal of the Supreme Court. Initially, the action appeared to be supported by the military, but on June 1 the defense minister, Gen. José Domingo GARCÍA Samayoa, responded to widespread popular protests by announcing that both Serrano and Vice

President Gustavo ESPINA Salguero had resigned and that Congress would reconvene to select a successor to the ousted head of state. However, the president of the Supreme Court concurred with Espina's contention that he had remained in office, and the military indicated that on constitutional grounds they would accept him as the new chief executive. A National Consensus Petition (*Instancia Nacional de Consenso*) was then advanced by an unlikely grouping of business, labor, and other leaders, contending that Espína was barred from office because he had supported Serrano's *autogolpe*. The Constitutional Court agreed, and on June 5 the Congress, in a surprising move, selected the country's human rights ombudsman, Ramiro DE LEÓN Carpio, to serve the balance of Serrano's presidential term.

The new chief executive offered the URNG rebels a two-track peace plan that called for the establishment of a representative forum within Guatemala to discuss resolution of the issues that had provoked the conflict, in addition to revival of the talks with rebel leaders in Mexico City. However, the insurgents rejected the overture, as well as a substantially modified plan tendered in early October.

In November 1993, in an effort to purge institutions of unsavory elements, De León proposed a Contract for the Restructuring of the State with Congress, with a referendum encompassing a series of constitutional reforms, including the shortening of congressional and judicial mandates; an increase in the size of the court to 13 members; the review of parliamentary immunity cases by the court, rather than by Congress; increased autonomy for the attorney general and comptroller general; and limitations on the discretionary appointive powers of both president and Congress. The proposals were approved by a 67.9 percent popular majority on January 30, 1994. However, the turnout was only 16.1 percent, meaning that passage involved only 10.9 percent of the electorate. Despite such dubious authorization, the reforms became law on April 8, paving the way for election of a new Congress on August 14.

An agreement with URNG representatives on January 10, 1994, to reopen peace talks led two months later to a Global Human Rights Accord and a timetable for continued negotiations. Subsequently, during a UN-mediated meeting in Oslo the two sides agreed to set up a three-member commission to look into Guatemala's unhappy record of human rights violations and acts of violence.

In the August 1994 balloting for a truncated congressional term (to January 1996), a turnout of scarcely more than 20 percent of the registered voters gave an unexpected plurality to former president Ríos Montt's Guatemalan Republican Front (*Frente Republicano Guatemalteco*—FRG). Initially excluded from the new congressional directorate by a coalition of other rightist groups, among them the second-ranked National Advancement Party (*Partido de Avanzada Nacional*—PAN), the FRG eventually succeeded in forging an alliance with the PDCG and UCN that yielded the designation of Ríos Montt as legislative president on December 2.

During the first half of 1995 the FRG waged a strenuous campaign to overcome Ríos Montt's disqualification as a candidate in the November 12 presidential elections. In mid-February the Constitutional Court, on technical grounds, rejected a series of *ríosmontista* electoral reforms, with the FRG, despite retention of a slim legislative majority, subsequently losing ground on the issue. On August 9, in the wake of a final ruling by electoral authorities, the general's wife, Teresa Sosa DE RÍOS, requested inscription as the FRG candidate for the November poll, but she was also rejected on constitutional grounds a week later. On August 22 the URNG announced a temporary cease-fire to facilitate electoral participation, while declining to endorse any of the contestants.

After failing to win a majority in presidential balloting on November 12, 1995, the PAN's Alvaro Enrique ARZÚ Irigoyen narrowly defeated the FRG's Alfonso PORTILLO Cabrera in a second-round vote on January 7, 1996. Earlier, the PAN had secured outright control of the National Congress by winning 43 of its 80 seats.

Skirmishes with the URNG resumed only two days after Arzú's inauguration on January 14, 1996. Talks with rebel leaders did, however, resume in Oslo on February 6 and in Rome on February 12. Two weeks later the president, in a bold move, traveled to Mexico for a secret meeting with URNG representatives. The action led to a cease-fire on March 20 and formal negotiations that yielded an agreement on socioeconomic and agrarian affairs on May 6. Earlier, the Guatemalan defense minister, Gen. Julio BALCONI Turcios, had declared that the conflict was over, while the president of the government's peace commission, Presidency Secretary Gustavo PORRAS, expressed his confidence that a definitive peace agreement would be signed by mid-September. However, such a target became increasingly problematic because of heightened hard-line activity within the military by a group styling itself Reclaiming the Guatemalan Army (*Recuperando el Ejército Guatemalteco*—PREGULA), which on August 12 issued a document charging 16 civilians and 57 military officers with treason for their support of the peace negotiations. On the other hand, tangible progress in negotiations with the rebels culminated in the signing in Mexico City on September 19 of a UN-mediated agreement, under which the Guatemalan military undertook to reduce its 46,000-strong complement by one-third in 1997 and to concentrate on defending the country's borders rather than on internal security. Another cease-fire on December 4 was followed by a formal peace accord on December 29 that laid out procedures for reincorporating the guerrillas into civilian life and legalizing the URNG, while providing amnesty for a wide range of civil rights violations on both sides of the conflict.

In a May 16, 1999, referendum, an extremely low turnout of voters (18 percent) rejected about 50 constitutional reforms mandated, in large part, by the 1996 accord. As a result, completion of the peace process was substantially imperiled. Earlier, on February 26, an independent Historical Clarification Commission that had been established with UN backing submitted an unexpectedly severe assessment of the 36-year civil war. The commission's report declared that the military had committed "acts of genocide" against the Mayans, including responsibility (together with the PACs) for 85 percent of civilian deaths. It also confirmed earlier reports that the U.S. Central Intelligence Agency had provided both money and training in support of the government effort.

In first-round presidential balloting on November 7, 1999, Alfonso Portillo Cabrera secured 47.8 percent of the vote and went on to defeat the PAN's Oscar BERGER Perdomo by a two-to-one majority in a December 26 runoff. The FRG also won a majority of legislative seats and 147 of 330 municipal contests. Portillo oversaw modest reforms to the security forces, most notably the 2003 dissolution of the Presidential General Staff, a notoriously abusive army intelligence unit whose abolishment was stipulated in the 1996 peace agreement.

At the subsequent balloting of November 9, 2003, Oscar Berger's recently organized Grand National Alliance (*Gran Alianza Nacional*—Gana) won a plurality of 49 legislative seats, while Berger himself led in the presidential race and went on to defeat Álvaro COLOM Caballeros of the center-left National Unity of Hope (*Unidad Nacional de Esperanza*—UNE) in a runoff on December 28.

Guatemalan presidential politics were complex before and after Oscar Berger's inauguration in January 2004. In mid-2003 the Constitutional Court ruled that Ríos Montt could contest the November poll, observing that a ban on persons who had participated in a coup could not be applied retroactively. However, a third-place finish in the first round precluded his involvement in the December runoff. Subsequently, in March 2004 the former president was charged with criminal behavior during disturbances leading up to the court's decision, and he was placed under house arrest to prevent his leaving the country. His legal problems notwithstanding, the FRG leader remained politically influential, and in May one of Gana's constituent parties withdrew from the governing alliance because President Berger had sought Ríos Montt's support for his fiscal-reform program. Meanwhile, Berger's predecessor, Alfonso Portillo, fled the country in the face of charges that he had participated in embezzlement and money laundering.

Following his election, President Berger enjoyed an 89 percent approval rating, but this plummeted to 25 percent, due in large part to soaring crime rates brought on by the *mara* street gangs challenging the drug cartels for control of the drug trade. The police force, which was often subject to corruption, was overwhelmed and failed to prosecute a large proportion of criminals.

The UNE won the largest percentage of the vote (27.08) in the September 9, 2007, legislative election, followed by the Patriotic Party (*Partido Patriota*—PP) with 25 percent. Gana fell to third place with 18.3 percent. In concurrent presidential balloting, the UNE's Álvaro Colom Caballeros defeated 13 other candidates in the first round, including Alejandro GIAMMATTEI of Gana (which declined to support either run-off candidate). Colom secured 52 percent of the vote in run-off balloting on November 4 to defeat the PP's Gen. Otto PÉREZ Molina. Colom formed a new government on January 14, 2008. Minor cabinet reshuffles occurred in March and July 2008, and in January, March, and July 2009.

Constitution and government. The 1985 constitution, as amended in 1993, mandates the direct election for four-year, nonrenewable terms of a president and a vice president, with provision for a runoff between the two leading slates in the absence of a majority. The president is responsible for national defense, security, and naming a cabinet. Legislative power is vested in a unicameral Congress of 158 members serving four-year terms. The 13 members of the Supreme Court are selected by the Congress, with the president of the court supervising the judiciary throughout the country; the Supreme Court head also presides over a separate Constitutional Court. Local administration includes 21 departments and the municipality of Guatemala City, each headed by a governor appointed by the president. In December 1986 Congress approved legislation organizing the departments into eight regions.

Foreign relations. The principal focus of Guatemalan foreign affairs has long been its claim to Belize (formerly British Honduras), which became independent in 1981. Guatemalan intransigence in the matter not only delayed Belizean independence but also adversely affected relations with the United Kingdom, which dispatched military reinforcements to the area in 1975 after receiving reports that Guatemala was massing troops at the border. Despite talks in 1975 and 1976 and a joint commitment in 1977 to a "quick, just, and honorable solution" to the controversy, no agreement was reached. Thus, when the United Kingdom granted independence to Belize in September 1981, the Lucas García government severed all diplomatic ties with London and appealed unsuccessfully to the UN Security Council to intervene. In August 1984, representatives of the three leading groups offering presidential candidates for the forthcoming election met in Washington, D.C., with U.S. officials to formulate a policy that would permit formal recognition of Belize and withdrawal of the British "trip wire" force. While no immediate results were forthcoming, the conciliatory posture was continued by the Cerezo Arévalo administration, and direct discussions were held with Belizean representatives in Miami, Florida, in 1987. Meanwhile, consular relations with the United Kingdom were resumed in August 1986, with full diplomatic ties restored the following January.

In May 1990 tension with Belize again flared after it was revealed that Guatemalan agricultural workers had unknowingly planted crops across the border in Belize's Toledo district. The incident prompted a meeting between President Cerezo and Belizean rime minister George Cadle Price on the Honduran island of Roatán on July 9, although settlement of the lengthy impasse did not occur until the installation of President Serrano in January 1991. In mid-February Serrano asserted that "Belize has the recognition of the international community" and seven months later overruled his foreign minister (who resigned over the issue) by extending diplomatic recognition to the country. Amid continued domestic controversy the Guatemalan Constitutional Court ruled by a narrow margin in November 1992 that the recognition of Belize was valid, subject to approval by a popular referendum.

Belize was not a major issue during the de León Carpio administration. However, Alvaro Arzú revived Guatemala's claim to Belizean territory, while insisting that he was committed to reaching a peaceful settlement. Concurrently, his newly installed foreign minister, Eduardo STEIN, indicated that he was weighing the relative benefits of further negotiations or international arbitration.

In June 1999 a Guatemalan peasant who had apparently strayed across the border was killed by a Belizean military patrol. In October, Belizean authorities arrested four Guatemalans on murder and weapons charges and in February 2000, after another Guatemalan farmer had been killed, Guatemala arrested three Belizean soldiers and a police officer. Insisting that the seizure had occurred on its side of the border, Belize branded the action as a "kidnapping" and withdrew from further talks with its neighbor until the four had been released. A July meeting between Foreign Minister Gabriel ORELLANA Rojas and Belizean prime minister Said Musa led to an agreement on a mechanism for resolving further border and territorial disputes, but incidents involving Guatemalan peasant squatters continued into mid-2001. Agreement was reached in September 2002 on the deployment of Organization of American States (OAS) observers to the disputed area pending the holding of referenda on the issue in the two countries. However, the accord was repudiated by Guatemala in August 2003, and in May 2004 new discussions were launched at OAS headquarters in Washington, D.C., on finding an "equitable and permanent solution" to the long-standing controversy. The talks yielded an agreement in early 2006 to invite a "recognized expert on the Law of the Sea" to help settle maritime aspects of the dispute. (In December 2008 Guatemala and Belize signed an agreement allowing the International Court of Justice (ICJ) to arbitrate Guatemala's territorial claim. The judicial process was to take three to five years

Generally cordial relations with the United States yielded crucial military and other aid that supported relatively successful counter-insurgency efforts during the late 1960s. Subsequently, however, the United States evidenced concern over the diminishing effectiveness of such assistance in a context of increased polarization between right and left. In March 1977 Guatemala repudiated U.S. military support after the Carter administration had announced that human rights considerations would be used in setting allocation levels. Although military and economic assistance was resumed under the Reagan administration, all aid (except for cash sales) was suspended by the U.S. Congress in November 1983 following publication of the Kissinger Commission report on Central America, which attributed thousands of recent civilian deaths to "the brutal behavior of the security forces." The program was again reinstituted in mid-1984, although Guatemalan officials complained that "the most important country in Central America" was receiving a fraction of the aid given to Honduras and El Salvador because of its posture of neutrality in intraregional conflicts. In December 1990 the U.S. Congress imposed a new ban on military assistance and in June 1991 extended it to most categories of economic aid, pending evidence of "progress [in] eliminating human rights violations and in investigating and bringing to trial those responsible for major human rights cases." In May 1993 the United States joined other foreign governments in condemning Serrano's bid for full power and helped set in motion OAS procedures that may have influenced the military's about-face in the matter.

In August 1994, a week before leaving office, Panamanian president Guillermo Endara rejected a request for the extradition of Serrano Elías, on the grounds that the accusations against the former Guatemalan chief executive were political in nature. Endara's decision was upheld by his successor, Ernesto Pérez Balladares, whose September 1 inauguration was boycotted by his Guatemalan counterpart. A third extradition request was rejected by Panama in February 1998.

On September 19, 1994, the UN General Assembly announced the establishment of a Human Rights Verification Mission in Guatemala (MINUGUA). The mission began its work on November 21 with a staff of 200 foreign human rights observers, 60 police officers, and 10 military officers to monitor compliance with the human rights agreement signed by the government and the URNG on March 29. However, high levels of violence continued, prompting MINUGUA to warn in late 2002 of a breakdown of law and order in several regions of the country. Meanwhile, the U.S. government curtailed assistance to an anti-drug police unit that it had helped to establish in 1998, after high-ranking members of the unit were accused of drug trafficking, murder, and kidnapping. The unit was dissolved shortly afterward. As drug trafficking continued, in 2003 the United States "decertified" Guatemala for having "failed demonstrably" to meet its obligations under international counternarcotics agreements.

Despite widespread opposition, Congress approved the Central American Free Trade Agreement (CAFTA) with the United States on March 10, 2005, by a vote of 126–12. CAFTA (implemented on July 1, 2006), eliminated customs tariffs on a number of goods and created clear, enforceable regulations for all aspects of cross-border trade, including investment, government procurement, intellectual property protection, electronic commerce, and the use of sanitation to protect public health.

In late 2005 the government was obliged to cooperate with U.S. authorities in arranging for Adan CASTILLO, the head of its Anti-Narcotics Analysis and Investigation Service (SAIA), the successor to the corrupt police unit, to attend an antidrug training course in Virginia, where he was arrested for complicity in cocaine trafficking. The Berger administration pledged to cooperate with representatives of the U.S. Drug Enforcement Agency in overhauling the SAIA.

Calls to regulate the movement of drugs in the Americas increased in 2007, as did demands for improved regulation of Guatemala's private adoption agents, due to the high number of Guatemalan babies adopted by Americans. While the government attempted to increase the transparency of the process, critics claimed that children were being unlawfully taken from their parents to meet U.S. demand. Meanwhile, the extradition process of former president Alfonso Portillo, who had been in exile in Mexico for more than three years, was suspended in mid-2007 when Mexican courts declared that Guatemala's extradition request was "irregular."

After two years of negotiations, Guatemala signed a bilateral free trade agreement with Panama on February 28, 2008, securing concessions for all Panamanian exports to Guatemala. Exports from other countries were granted access through quotas. Also in 2008 the International Commission Against Impunity in Guatemala (CICIG), a U.S.-backed UN initiative was established to investigate organized crime (see Current issues, below). Its $20 million budget included contributions from 11 countries. President Colom visited Washington in April to discuss a proposed regional antidrug initiative with U.S. president George W. Bush, the two countries agreeing to a collective effort involving more than $4 million in new anti-drug and public security assistance, increased judicial assistance, and additional funding for the CICIG. Subsequently, Guatemala inaugurated a U.S.-supported elite anti-drug unit.

In December 2008 President Colom and El Salvador's president, Elías Antonio Saca, agreed to establish a binational customs union to allow the free transit of goods and services.

In an effort to shore up relations with Cuba, President Colom visited Havana in February 2009, 12 years after the Arzú government had restored relations. Colom presented former leader Fidel Castro with the Order of the Quetzal, the highest honor conferred by the Guatemalan government. The awarding of the honor, a controversial issue in Guatemala, was meant to thank Havana for carrying out medical and literacy programs in Guatemala. Meanwhile, Colóm also apologized publicly in Cuba for Guatemala's role as a staging area for the 1961 Bay of Pigs invasion by U.S.-trained Cuban exiles. In June Guatemala and Cuba signed economic cooperation agreements. Meanwhile, Brazil agreed to loan Guatemala $99 million over 12 years to buy Brazilian aircraft and radar equipment.

Current issues. Politicians, as well as members of the public, were subject to increased violence in the run-up to the September 2007 elections. In February three Salvadoran members of the Central American Parliament (based in Guatemala) and their driver were killed. Four police officers who were arrested in connection with the killings were shot in their cells a few days later, prompting the resignation of the interior minister. Subsequently, two party coordinators for the center-left UNE were killed after leaving a political gathering near the border with El Salvador in April. Meanwhile, Vice President Stein and the Catholic Church had warned in early 2007 that organized crime could affect the upcoming elections. By the end of May, two other political officials had been killed: a mayoral candidate backed by the Encounter for Guatemala (*Encuentro por Guatemala*—EG) and an activist with the FRG. As public outrage mounted, support grew for the reinstatement of the death penalty, promoted by UNE presidential candidate Álvaro Colom, as well as PP presidential candidate Otto PÉREZ Molina. Pérez's slogan, "A strong hand now!" highlighted crime control as the centerpiece of his platform. Colom, for his part, pledged to strengthen the attorney general's office and the National Civil Police to curtail the violence that fueled public disenchantment with traditional parties.

Following the November 2007 balloting, Colom became the first social democrat president elected in over 50 years, as the previous governing alliance had failed to curb corruption, violence, and poverty. Gana's flagbearer, Alejandro Giammattei, was eliminated in the first round, and the party subsequently declined to back either Colom or Otto Pérez, who had strongholds in rural areas and Guatemala City, respectively, in the runoff. Colom defeated Pérez in the runoff, the results fitting the historic voting pattern of Guatemala, which has not returned a ruling party to power since 1986.

Spiraling crime continued to be the main domestic concern for Colom's administration, as 6,292 homicides were recorded in 2008, ranking Guatemala among the most violent countries in the world. Further, Guatemala was estimated to have as many as 12,000 gang members, and 18 armed bands dedicated to kidnapping for ransom. A poll commissioned by the *Prensa Libre* newspaper found that 90 percent of respondents feared being kidnapped, assaulted or extorted, 78 percent were afraid to walk the streets, and 82 percent believed the police were linked to organized crime. Vice President Rafael ESPADA estimated that half of Guatemala's street crime was linked to the drug trade. The PP regularly criticized the Colom government, claiming it was soft on crime and calling for militarization of public security and "states of exception" where constitutional rights would be limited in order to combat criminality. President Colóm accused his opponents of instigating violence in order to increase support for their hard line policies.

In March 2008 Colom formed a panel to declassify military documents connected with the torture, killings, and human rights violations perpetrated during the 36 years of civil war, in the wake of confidential documents that had been leaked to the press a year earlier alleging abuses carried out by Ríos Montt (who won a seat in Congress in 2007). The army resisted the move to declassify its files, arguing that doing so would be unconstitutional. Violence continued unabated, including a shootout involving warring drug gangs in front of a hotel in Zacapa department, in which 11 people were killed. The CICIG encouraged Guatemala's justice system to try the case in the capital, but it was transferred back to Zacapa four times in 2008 because of judges' fear of retribution by the defendants. Additionally, ties to the widespread drug trade were seen as the likely reason for President Colom's firing of several top army officers in July. Months later Colóm cited public security concerns as he announced a plan to increase the size of the armed forces by 2010, a reversal of former president Berger's policy. Colom also requested a significant increase in the defense budget and deployed 1,300 additional troops to the Mexican border for drug interdiction, increasing the total force strength on the border to 2,300. In further efforts to fight crime, Colom appointed a new police chief, Marlene Raquel BLANCO (the first woman to hold the post in Guatemala), and fired the head of the Presidential Security Unit (SAAS) after surveillance equipment was found in the president's residence. Subsequently, the head of the SAAS was arrested; he was replaced by a former guerrilla.

Attention on crime was again brought to the forefront when the CICIG issued its first report in September, stating that 98 percent of crimes committed in Guatemala, and 93 percent of murders, went unpunished. Subsequently, the CICIG recommended that the Supreme Court create special tribunals for high-profile cases. In October former president Portillo returned from Mexico to face corruption charges, including allegations that he stole $15 million earmarked for the Presidential General Staff. Public outcry erupted when Portillo was released on $130,000 bail. Meanwhile, President Colom announced another public security initiative, creating a National Security Council to coordinate internal security strategy. The council's membership included the director of a new Secretariat of Strategic Analysis, which replaced one of the two agencies implicated in the surveillance of the president's residence.

Two more drug-related killings shocked the country in late November 2008. Sixteen passengers traveling from Nicaragua on a bus, which was believed to have cocaine in its cargo hold, died in the crossfire of rival gangs in Zacapa, Another fight in Huehuetenango between a Mexican and a Guatemalan drug gang over the outcome of a horse race resulted in the deaths of 17 people. In December Colom abruptly fired the entire military high command, including those who had been reluctant to declassify military archives about earlier abuses. The crime and corruption issues contributed heavily to a 54 percent disapproval rating for Colom by the end of the year, according to a Vox Latina poll. The decline in Colom's popularity also began to affect his party, as in December 11 UNE deputies defected, leaving the governing party with only 39 of 158 seats. The dissidents formed a new legislative bloc called Renewed Democratic Liberty (LIDER).

In 2009 crime continued to soar, as the U.S. government estimated that 40 percent of the world's cocaine output was transported via Guatemala en route from the Andes to Mexico and the United States. Mexican drug gangs were widely reported to be increasing their presence, the most visible being *Los Zetas*, the armed wing of Mexico's Gulf Cartel, with alleged participation of former Guatemalan Army Special Forces. Some 300 members of *Los Zetas* were reported to be active in Guatemala. In February, progress was made in the request for classified documents, as the military handed over a small cache of documents from its archives regarding past abuses. Subsequently, Colom formed another panel to determine which documents should remain classified, and instituted an arms-control law and penal code reform recommended by the CICIG to strengthen witness protection and make it easier to prosecute extortion. Also in March, the increasingly dangerous climate for human rights defenders—12 were killed in 2008—was highlighted by the kidnapping and beating of the wife of the government's human rights ombudsman.

In another attempt to address the security situation, President Colom in April 2009 signed a National Agreement to Advance Security and Justice, a long-term security-sector reform strategy developed in consultation with religious, academic, and human rights leaders. The document offered a blueprint for reforming the police, controlling the arms trade, improving prisons, and reforming the judiciary and security policy. It also included a two-year extension of the mandate of the CICIG, which had been set to expire in September. Critics of the agreement questioned its lack of focus on immediate crime challenges and the lack of a plan to pay for other reforms. Later in April, five Guatemalan anti-drug agents were killed in a shootout with *Los Zetas* on a road outside Guatemala City. The shootings occurred shortly after President Colom and other top officials, including the police chief and ministers of defense and interior, reported receiving death threats from *Los Zetas*, apparently in retaliation for the February arrest of five members of the group.

Allegations of corruption and the slaying of a well-known lawyer, Rodrigo Rosenberg, presented significant problems for the Colom administration in May 2009. Rosenberg was shot to death while bicycling in Guatemala City. At his funeral the next day, 150 copies of a pre-recorded video were distributed in which Rosenberg claimed he was "murdered by President Colom, with the help of Gustavo Alejos (Colom's private secretary) and Gregorio Valdez (a businessman and major backer of Colom's campaign)." Further, Rosenberg predicted his own demise because one of his clients, businessman Khalil MUSA, had been killed, allegedly for refusing an offer to head one of Guatemala's largest banks, where Musa would have been required to cover up corruption, including money laundering and other illegal activities organized by the president's politically prominent wife, Sandra de Colom. The release of the video prompted massive demonstration in Guatemala City, some in support of the president and others calling for his resignation. The PP and other opposition figures called on Colom to resign and for Vice President Espada to take his place, in order to allow investigations to proceed unhindered. The Colom adminstration blamed Rosenberg's death on organized crime. The divisiveness in the aftermath of the killing helped to derail President Colom's political agenda, as, among other things, efforts to increase taxes to pay for social programs appeared to be stalled. Also, the Social Cohesion Council, which carried out social programs, faced strong challenges because it was headed by Sandra de Colom, who had become a controversial figure as a result of the scandal. In late May, meanwhile, three more UNE legislators left the government's party, joining the newly formed LIDER bloc.

In June police chief Marlene BLANCO, who had been hired a year earlier, was fired by the interior minister. President Colom said that while he did not order the firing himself, he respected the minister's decision. Blanco was replaced by Porfirio PÉREZ Paniagua. On July 25 President Colom received a death threat from *Los Zetas*, according to police, who said that similar threats had been recorded for weeks and included ministers as well.

POLITICAL PARTIES AND GROUPS

Political power in Guatemala has traditionally been personal rather than institutional, with parties developing in response to the needs or ambitions of particular leaders. In a late 2005 survey, a remarkable 84.3 percent of respondents said they sympathized with none of the leaders.

Under current law, parties must maintain a minimum vote share to retain legal status; however, unrecognized groups may, upon petition by a sufficient number of signatories, secure recognition before any given election. In 1995, 14 of 23 participating groups failed to qualify for continued registration. Of the 9 that survived, only incoming President Arzú's PAN, Ríos Montt's FRG, and the left-of-center FDNG were viewed as fully viable formations. The leading parties in 1999 were the FRG and PAN, with the recently formed New Nation Alliance (ANN) a distant third. In 2003 Oscar Berger's Grand National Alliance (Gana) led a field that included Álvaro Colom's National Unity of Hope (UNE), the FRG, PAN, and the ANN.

In January 2009 dissident UNE members of Congress formed a legislative bloc under the rubric **Renewed Democratic Liberty** (*Libertad Democratica Renovada*—LIDER), led by Roberto VILLATE. Members of LIDER said that they do not consistently oppose UNE, but they no longer respond to the government party's leadership.

Government Party:

National Unity of Hope (*Unidad Nacional de la Esperanza*—UNE). The center-left UNE was founded in 2001 by ANN (below) secessionist Álvaro Colom Caballeros, nephew of a leftist Guatemala City mayor killed in 1979. A former vice minister and director of the National Peace Fund, an IMF-supported government entity that made investments in rural areas, Colom first ran for president in 1999 as the candidate of the ANN, a broad leftist coalition that included former guerrilla leaders, among others. He finished third.

The UNE, a more centrist grouping than the ANN, fared well in the 2003 elections, as Colom's message of fighting poverty resonated with rural voters. The party won 30 congressional seats in 2003, with Colom the runner-up in first-round presidential balloting. He lost to the Gana's Oscar Berger in the second round on December 28.

In the run-up to the 2007 presidential election, Colom pledged an improved justice system and increased social expenditures. In the first round of voting, Colom finished first, but fell short of a majority with 28.3 percent of the vote. The UNE also led all parties in the concurrent legislative poll by winning 51 seats and 22.8 percent of the vote. Colom defeated Otto Pérez Molina of the PP in the second round, with 52.8 percent of the vote. Outside of Guatemala City, which he lost in the second round by 19 points, Colom won 57.3 percent of the vote, indicating that the rural poor were an important base of support.

The press reported conflicts within the party, attributed in part to discontent over Colom's cabinet appointments.

Leaders: Álvaro COLOM Caballeros (President of the Republic), Dr. Rafael ESPADA (Vice President of the Republic).

Other Legislative Parties:

Grand National Alliance (*Gran Alianza Nacional*—Gana). Launched in early 2003, Gana is a center-right grouping that presidential aspirant Oscar Berger joined at midyear following his defection from PAN (below). Its founding parties included the **Guatemalan Reform Party** (*Partido Reformador Guatemalteco*—PRG), also known as the **Reform Movement** (*Movimiento Reformador*—MR), and the **Party of National Solidarity** (*Partido Solidaridad Nacional*—PSN), as well as the PP (below). Gana secured a plurality of 49 seats in the November 2003 legislative elections, and Berger won the December presidential runoff to secure political dominance for the group. However, Gana lost 7 of its legislative seats when the PP withdrew in May 2004 to protest an apparent rapprochement between President Berger and former president Ríos Montt.

In the run-up to the 2007 balloting, the **Guatemalan Independent Bloc** (*Bloque Independiente Bancada Guatemala*—BG) was formed by a group of Gana dissidents, including 13 of Gana's 37 legislative deputies, and led by Luis Alberto CONTRERAS Colindres. The splinter group consisted of two factions, one led by Alfredo VILA and the other by Jaime MARTINEZ, which also had the backing of 2007 presidential candidate Alejandro Giammattei. Despite the rift, BG members often voted with Gana.

Gana lost its legislative plurality in the September 2007 balloting, finishing second behind the UNE with 37 seats and 16.5 percent of the vote. Giammattei finished third in the concurrent first round of presidential elections with 17.2 percent of the vote. Several Gana mayors reportedly backed the UNE's Álvaro Colom in the presidential runoff, although the party refrained from formally endorsing either candidate.

Leaders: Oscar José BERGER Perdomo (Former President of the Republic), Eduardo STEIN Barillas (Former Vice President of the Republic), Alejandro GIAMMATTEI (2007 presidential candidate).

Patriotic Party (*Partido Patriota*—PP). Founded in 2001 and initially part of Gana, the PP withdrew from the presidential alliance in May 2004. Its principal founder, Otto Pérez Molina, is a former general known for opposing the military's hardest line and supporting the 1996 peace process. Pérez Molina formed the party shortly after being forced into retirement by the Portillo government in 2000, and moved immediately to the opposition, where he and his new center-right party supported Oscar Berger's successful 2003 candidacy. One of the PP's most prominent members, Rodolfo VIELMAN Castellanos, was killed in March 2006.

As the party's presidential candidate in 2007, Pérez Molina responded to public discontent over violence by promising to expand the police force, reinstate the death penalty, and crack down with an "iron hand, head and heart." He finished second in the first round of voting but lost to the UNE's Álvaro Colom in runoff balloting, securing only 47.2 percent of the vote. Pérez Molina's anti-crime message had made him popular with urban voters but attracted less rural support. The PP won 29 seats in the concurrrent legislative election, finishing third with 15.7 percent of the vote.

Aura Marina SALAZAR Cutzal, an assistant to Pérez, and her bodyguard were shot to death in early October 2007. Pérez Molina blamed organized crime for the killings.

Leader: Otto PÉREZ Molina (Secretary General and 2007 presidential candidate).

Guatemalan Republican Front (*Frente Republicano Guatemalteco*—FRG). A right-wing formation launched in 1988, the FRG participated in Ríos Montt's *No-Venta* coalition for the 1990 campaign. Deregistered thereafter, its legislative members joined the government grouping as an independent bloc that was awarded the leadership of four congressional commissions. In late 1993 the party failed to secure legislative approval for revocation of the constitutional provision banning heads of state who had participated in coups from running for the presidency. It registered a dramatic victory in the 1994 legislative contest, winning 32 seats, with Ríos Montt subsequently being named congressional president.

In 1999 the party won the presidency and a majority of congressional seats. However, by mid-2001 factional differences erupted, with supporters of President Portillo aligned against those loyal to Ríos Montt and Vice President Reyes López. During 2003, allegations of corruption were made against Portillo, and in early 2004 he left the country.

The party won 14 seats in the September 2007 legislative election, finishing fourth with 9.7 percent of the vote. Presidential candidate Luis Rabbé finished fifth in the concurrent first round of presidential balloting with 7.3 percent of the vote.

Leaders: Gen. (Ret.) José Efraín RÍOS Montt (Former President of the Republic, Former President of Congress, and 2003 presidential candidate), Juan Francisco REYES López (Former Vice President of the Republic), Luis RABBÉ (2007 presidential candidate), Zury RÍOS-MONTT de Weller.

Unionist Party (*Partido Unionista*—PU). The PU was organized by former president Alvaro Arzú in the wake of inconsistent support for his policies within the PAN (below). Subsequently eclipsed within the new party by Gustavo PORRAS, a center-left former guerrilla member and government peace negotiator, Arzú eventually regained control. He succeeded in having Guatemala City's center-right mayor, Fritz García-Gallout, named the PU secretary general and standard-bearer for the 2003 presidential campaign. García-Gallout placed fifth in the November poll, with a 3 percent vote share.

In 2007 García-Gallout finished eighth in the first round of presidential balloting with 2.9 percent of the vote. The PU won 7 legislative seats with 6.1 percent of the vote.

Leaders: Alvaro Enrique ARZÚ Irigoyen (Former President of the Republic), Fritz GARCÍA-Gallout (Former Mayor of Guatemala City, 2003 and 2007 presidential candidate, and Secretary General).

Center of Social Action (*Centro de Acción Social*—CASA). The CASA was launched in 2003 to represent the interests of indigenous peoples. In 2007 the CASA won 5 legislative seats with 4.9 percent of the vote, and its presidential candidate, Eduardo Suger, finished fourth in the concurrent first round of presidential balloting with 7.4 percent of the vote.

Leaders: Rigoberto QUEMÉ Chay, Eduardo SUGER (2007 presidential candidate).

Union of Nationalist Change (*Union del Cambio Nacionalista*—UCN). The UCN advocates a constitutional, democratic, and republican regime focused on uniting the country. The party, whose slogan was "better times" (*tiempos mejores*), campaigned for the September 2007 elections on a platform that pledged to advance women's and workers' rights, to fight corruption and to limit social and economic polarization. Presidential candidate Mario Estrada, finished sixth in the first round of the 2007 presidential balloting with 3.2 percent of the vote. The UCN won 5 legislative seats.

Leaders: Mario Amilcar ESTRADA Orellana (2007 presidential candidate), Sydney Shaw ARRIVILLAGA (Secretary General).

Encounter for Guatemala (*Encuentro por Guatemala*—EG). The left-wing EG was organized in 2006 by Nineth Varenca Montenegro Cottom (a member of Congress) and César Montes, who had recently resigned from the New Nation Alliance (*Alianza Nueva Nación*—ANN, below) along with several other legislators. In February 2007 the EG reached an agreement with the indigenous grouping *Winaq* (below) that guaranteed *Winaq* a 50 percent share of the EG's legislative and mayoral candidates for the September election. *Winaq* leader Rigoberta Menchú finished seventh as the EG's candidate in the first round of the 2007 presidential balloting with 3.1 percent of the vote. The EG won four seats in the concurrent legislative elections with 6.2 percent of the vote.

Leaders: César MONTES, Rigoberta MENCHÚ (2007 presidential candidate), Nineth Varenca MONTENEGRO Cottom (General Secretary).

Winaq. An indigenous grouping founded in 2005 by Nobel Peace Prize winner Rigoberta Menchú, *Winaq* gets its name from a Mayan word that means "the wholeness of the human being." Since *Winaq* is not recognized as a party, Menchú represents the EG. A member of the Quiché Maya indigenous nation, Menchú first came to prominence with a 1983 autobiography detailing the violence and discrimination she and her family suffered in Guatemala's conflict, and her own experience as a labor and indigenous-rights organizer. She was awarded the Nobel Prize in 1992

Leader: Rigoberta MENCHÚ.

National Advancement Party (*Partido de Avanzada Nacional*—PAN). The PAN was organized before the 1990 election by the former mayor of Guatemala City, Alvaro Arzú Irigoyen, who placed fourth in the presidential poll and entered the Serrano Elías cabinet as foreign minister. Arzú resigned from his ministerial post in September 1991 after disagreeing with the president over recognition of Belize, thereby shattering the existing governmental coalition. The party was runner-up to the FRG in 1994, winning 24 congressional seats; it secured a legislative majority in 1995, with Arzú winning the presidency in second-round balloting on January 7, 1996. By late 1997 three factions were reported to have emerged within the party: one led by congressional president Arabello Castro and backing Interior Minister Rodolfo MENDOZA for president in 1999, one united behind Guatemala City mayor Oscar Berger, and one loyal to President Arzú. Berger won the party's presidential nomination in early 1999 but was severely beaten by the FRG's Portillo Cabrera in the November runoff.

Dissension within the party led 15 PAN deputies to announce in June 2000 that they intended to sit as independents. At the time, the party was severely split by a leadership struggle between two factions—one loyal to former president Arzú and Rodolfo Mendoza, and the other headed by Oscar Berger and Leonel López, the recently elected secretary general. A principal dispute concerned López's support for an FRG bill that permitted the reelection of Ríos Montt as legislative president.

Berger defeated López for PAN's 2003 presidential nomination; the two then had a falling out, with Berger and nine other legislators leaving the party to join Gana. López thereupon became the PAN standard-bearer, placing fourth in November's first-round balloting.

The party's original 2007 presidential candidate was Francisco ARREDONDO. However, he refused to accept the PAN nominee for vice president, Oscar Rodolfo Castañeda, as his running mate. The party executive ultimately removed Arredondo from the ballot, nominating Castañeda for president. Castañeda finished ninth in the first round of the presidential poll with 2.5 percent of the vote. The PAN won 3 legislative seats with 4.5 percent of the vote.

Leaders: Leonel Eliseo LÓPEZ Rodas (2003 presidential candidate), Oscar Rodolfo CASTAÑEDA (2007 presidential candidate), Rubén Darío MORALES (Secretary General).

Guatemalan National Revolutionary Unity (*Unidad Revolucionaria Nacional Guatemalteca*—URNG). The URNG was formed in January 1981 as a largely exile-based umbrella organization designed to provide various guerrilla groups with a unified military command, which was never fully implemented. Its political wing, led by Raúl MOLINA Mejía, was styled the United Representation of the Guatemalan Opposition (*Representación Unitaria de la Oposición Guatemalteca*—RUOG).

In October 1987 inconclusive "low-level" talks aimed at seeking "peace and democracy" were held with government representatives in Madrid, Spain. A significant increase in URNG activity was reported during late 1989 and early 1990, while another inconclusive round of talks with government representatives was held in Oslo, Norway, during March and April 1990. Seemingly more fruitful discussions were held in Madrid in June, with the URNG and political party representatives agreeing on the need for elections to a constituent assembly in 1991 in which the guerrillas could participate.

After having urged Guatemalans since its formation not to participate in elections, the URNG appealed in May 1995 for a voter turnout in favor of "alternative candidates," without, however, indicating who the candidates in question might be.

A definitive cease-fire was signed by government and URNG representatives in Oslo, Sweden, on December 4, 1996, paving the way for conclusion of a formal peace accord on December 29 (see Political background, above).

The URNG's longtime leader and former secretary general, Ricardo Arnoldo RAMÍREZ de León (a.k.a. Rolando MORÁN), died on

September 4, 1998. On October 19 the URNG formally filed for registration as a legal party. The URNG participated in the 1999 and 2003 balloting as a member of the ANN (below), but that alliance appeared to have splintered by 2007 when the URNG won two seats in the September legislative poll with 3.6 percent of the vote, while Miguel Angel Sandoval finished tenth with 2.1 percent of the vote in the concurrent first round of presidential balloting.

Leaders: Miguel Angel SANDOVAL (2007 presidential candidate), Rodrigo ASTURIAS Amado (2003 presidential candidate), Alba Estela MALDONADO Guevara (Secretary General).

Democratic Union (*Unión Democrática*—UD). Launched before the 1994 election, the UD campaigned vigorously as a party "without a past." However, despite a nationwide campaign that relied heavily on television ads, it secured only one congressional seat in both 1995 and 1999, in coalition, on the latter occasion, with the Greens (*La Organización Verde*—LOV, below). The party won two seats in 2003, while supporting Gana's Berger for the presidency.

The UD secured one legislative seat in the September 2007 elections with 1.4 percent of the vote, while its presidential candidate, Manuel Conde Orellana, received just 0.8 percent in the concurrent first round of presidential balloting, finishing eleventh.

Leaders: Manuel CONDE Orellana (2007 presidential candidate), Gen. Rodolfo Ernesto (Fito) PAIZ Andrade (Secretary General).

Other Parties that Participated in the 2007 Elections:

Authentic Integral Development (*Desarollo Integral Auténtico*—DIA). The DIA was formerly known as the Authentic Comprehensive Development (*Desarollo Inclusivo Auténtico*). The party's 2007 presidential candidate, Héctor Rosales, was shot at while campaigning in August in a rural area close to the town of Cunen. He escaped unhurt and blamed the FRG for the attempt. Rosales won 0.6 percent of the vote in the first round of the presidential poll. In 2007 the party failed to win a legislative seat, with 1.4 percent of the vote, and was stripped of its registration.

Leaders: Héctor ROSALES (2007 presidential candidate), Jorge Luis ORTEGA Torres (Secretary General).

New Nation Alliance (*Alianza Nueva Nación*—ANN). The ANN was formed in February 1999 as a left-of-center electoral alliance of the URNG (above), DIA (below), and a number of smaller groups. Its 2003 presidential candidate, Rigoberto QUEME, withdrew in September after an internal dispute over candidacies, prompting its principal components, the URNG and DIA, to compete separately from the party in the presidential race. The ANN won seven legislative seats in 2003, two less than in 1999.

Presidential candidate Jorge Ismael SOTO García (a.k.a. Pablo Monsanto, a former guerrilla leader), received 0.6 percent of votes in the initial round of the 2007 presidential contest, because the URNG and DIA each presented its own candidate. After ANN failed to win a legislative seat with 1.4 percent of the vote, the party lost its registration.

Leaders: Jorge Ismael SOTO García (2007 presidential candidate), Alfonso BAUER Paiz (Secretary General).

Front for Democracy (*Frente por la Democracia*—EL FRENTE). Founded in January 2006 by dissidents from the FRG and the PDCG, the center-right party did not field a presidential candidate in 2007, and failed to keep its registration after winning 0.9 percent of votes in the concurrent legislative elections.

Leader: Alfonso CABRERA (Secretary General).

Guatemalan Christian Democratic Party (*Partido Democracia Cristiana Guatemalteca*—PDCG). Founded in 1955 as a centrist party of liberal and reformist views, the PDCG secured a majority of 51 congressional seats in 1985, with its longtime leader, Vinicio Cerezo Arévalo, defeating the UCN's Carpio Nicolle in a runoff for the presidency. Its 1990 standard-bearer, Alfonso CABRERA Hidalgo, withdrew from candidacy in late October, ostensibly because of failing health, but was nonetheless credited with a third-place finish. Its congressional representation fell from 28 to 13 seats in 1994.

In April 1995 the PDCG formed an electoral coalition styled the National Alliance (*Alianza Nacional*—AN) with the UCN and Social Democrat Party (*Partido Social Demócrata*—PSD). With the formation of the AN, nine PDCG members of Congress resigned their party memberships and set themselves up as an independent bloc to protest AN's decision to support the presidential candidacy of Andrade DÍAZ Durán. The PDCG's representation dwindled to three congressional seats in 1995 and in 1999 fell to two, both of which were retained in 2003.

After the September 2007 legislative election, in which it failed to win a seat with 0.8 percent of the vote, PDCG lost its registration due to its failure to meet the vote threshold. Meanwhile, its presidential candidate, Vinicio Cerezo Blandón, son of former president Marco Vinicio Cerezo Arévalo, won 0.5 percent of votes in the first round of balloting.

Leaders: Marco Vinicio CEREZO Arévalo (Former President of the Republic), Ana Catalina Reyes SOBERANIS (Former President of the National Congress), Dr. Francisco VILLAGRAN Kramer (Former Vice President of the Republic and Leader of the Right-Wing Faction), René DE LEÓN Schlotter (Leader of the Left-Wing Faction), Vinicio CEREZO Blandón (2007 presidential candidate), Jacobo ARBENZ (2003 presidential candidate).

Other Parties and Groups:

Podemos. The Podemos ("We Can") is a center-right group founded in 2008 by Adela Camacho de Torrebiarte, who had served as interior minister in 2006 and 2007. The party was formed to address the needs of workers, rural residents, and students, among others, according to its founder.

Leaders: Carlos CHAVARRÍA (Assistant Secretary General), Adela CAMACHO de Torrebiarte (Secretary General).

Commitment, Renovation and Order (*Compromiso, Renovación y Orden*—CREO). The CREO is a right-wing political group founded by Roberto González García Durán, a former cabinet minister in the Berger government who broke from Gana in early 2008. As of mid-2009, CREO was in the process of formal registration.

Leader: Roberto GONZÁLEZ García Durán.

The Green Organization (*La Organización Verde*—LOV). The LOV is a coalition of several small groups, including the UD and the Social Democratic Unity (*Unidad Social Demócrata*—USD).

Leaders: Rodolfo ROSALES García Salas (2003 presidential candidate), Marcos Emilio RECINOS Alvarez (Secretary General).

(For information on the **National Liberation Movement** [*Movimiento de Liberación Nacional*—MLN], **Nationalist Authentic Central, Social Democrat Party, New Guatemala Democratic Front,** and a number of other parties and groups that were active in the 1990s, see the 2008 *Handbook*.)

Clandestine Groups:

Anti-Communist Secret Army (*Ejército Secreto Anticomunista*—ESA). A right-wing group presumed to be an outgrowth of the former White Hand (*La Mano Blanca*), the ESA is reportedly linked to the more extreme faction of the MLN. It is known to maintain a "death list" of numerous left-wing activists and has been prominently involved in the escalation of political assassinations that began in late 1978. In early 1980 it threatened to kill 20 leftists for each assassination of a rightist and in mid-1988 issued a communiqué stating it would ensure that communist journalists "either leave the country or die inside of it."

Other extreme right-wing formations include the **Squadron of Death** (*Escuadrón de la Muerte*—EM) and the **Officers of the Mountain** (*Oficiales de la Montaña*—OdeM).

LEGISLATURE

Guatemala's legislative body is a unicameral **Congress of the Republic** (*Congreso de la República*) that currently consists of 158 members elected for four-year terms. In the most recent election of September 9, 2007, the seat distribution was as follows: the National Unity of Hope, 51 seats; Grand National Alliance, 37; the Patriotic Party, 29; the Guatemalan Republican Front, 14; the Unionist Party, 7; the Union of Nationalist Change, 5; Center of Social Action, 5; the Encounter for Guatemala, 4; the National Advancement Party, 3; the Guatemalan National Revolutionary Unity, 2; and the Democratic Union, 1.

President: José Roberto ALEJOS Cámbara.

CABINET

[as of August 1, 2009]

President	Álvaro Colom Caballeros
Vice President	Rafael Espada
Ministers	
Agriculture, Livestock, and Food	Mario Aldana
Communications and Public Works	Luis Alfredo Alejos Olivero
Culture	Jerónimo Lancerio Chingo
Defense	Abraham Valenzuela González
Economy	Rubén Morales
Education	Ana Ordoñez de Molina [f]
Energy and Mines	Carlos Meany
Environment and Natural Resources	Luis Alberto Ferraté
Foreign Affairs	Roger Haroldo Rodas
Interior	Salvador Gándara
Labor and Social Security	Edgar Alfredo Rodriguez
Public Finance	Juan Alberto Fuentes Knight
Public Health and Social Welfare	Celso Cerezo
Chair, Presidential Human Rights Committee	Ruth Del Valle [f]
Head, Peace Secretariat	Orlando Joaquín Blanco Lapola

[f] = female

COMMUNICATIONS

In mid-1991 the *Central America Report* cited an international team of observers to the effect that in Guatemala "freedom of expression is severely restricted by direct violence targeted at journalists and by an ever-present climate of fear and repression." The study indicated that from 1978 to 1985, 47 Guatemalan journalists had been killed and that by 1983 at least 100 had been forced into exile. In August 1991 the Mexican news agency Notimex closed its Guatemala City bureau after its offices had been ransacked, while the British-based Reuters announced the temporary closure of its facility because of a lack of security. Two months earlier *La Epoca*, a left-wing weekly whose premises had been fire-bombed as it commenced publication in early 1988, had been shut down in the wake of another such attack.

In 2008, according to the Center for Informative Reports About Guatemala, 3 reporters were killed, 13 were subject to aggression, and 10 received death threats. A September report from the UN Development Program labeled Guatemala a "country of risk" for journalists. Two more journalists were killed during the first half of 2009. Intimidation reportedly has come principally from organized crime and clandestine groups. Watchdog groups have reported that Guatemalan journalists routinely practice self-censorship, declining to report on sensitive issues, particularly organized crime and corruption.

Press. The following newspapers, all published in Guatemala City, are privately owned Spanish dailies, unless otherwise noted: *Prensa Libre* (110,000); *Siglo Veintiuno* (56,000); *La Hora* (18,000); *Diario de Centroamérica* (15,000); *ElPeriódico* (circulation unknown); *Central America Report*, English-language weekly.

News agencies. The only domestic facility is the independent *Inforpress Centroamericana;* a number of foreign agencies maintain bureaus in Guatemala City.

Broadcasting and computing. Broadcasting is supervised by the government's *Dirección General de Radiodifusión y Televisión Nacional.* Of the approximately 140 radio stations, 5 are government-operated and 6 offer educational programming. There are 6 commercial television stations, in addition to a government educational outlet, a religious station, and a station devoted largely to music and entertainment. As of 2008 there were 143.2 Internet users per 1,000 inhabitants.

INTERGOVERNMENTAL REPRESENTATION

Ambassador to the U.S.: Francisco VILLAGRÁN De León.

U.S. Ambassador to Guatemala: Stephen George McFARLAND.

Permanent Representative to the UN: Gert ROSENTHAL.

IGO Memberships (Non-UN): ACS, BCIE, IADB, Interpol, IOM, NAM, OAS, OPANAL, PCA, SELA, SICA, WCO, WTO.

GUINEA

Republic of Guinea
République de Guinée

Note: President Moussa Dadis Camara suffered a serious head wound in an assassination attempt by a presidential aide on December 3, 2009. Shortly thereafter, Camara sought medical treatment outside the country, and Defense Minister Sékouba Konaté, also a vice president of the National Council for Democracy and Development, was installed as acting president of the republic. Konaté urged negotiations with the opposition, and in January 2010 Jean-Marie Doré of the opposition Union for the Progress of Guinea was appointed prime minister, with the expectation that a new transitional cabinet would be named to oversee national elections and a return to civilian government later in the year. (Camara agreed to remain in exile at least until a civilian government was inaugurated.)

Political Status: Independent republic since October 2, 1958; under one-party presidential regime until military coup of April 3, 1984; multiparty constitution approved by referendum of December 23, 1990, providing for five-year transition to civilian government; constitution suspended following military coup of December 23, 2008.

Area: 94,925 sq. mi. (245,857 sq. km.).

Population: 7,156,406 (1996C); 9,563,000 (2008E). Both figures include refugees from Liberia and Sierra Leone, estimated at 640,000 in 1996.

Major Urban Center (2005E): CONAKRY (1,478,000).

Official Language: French, pending adoption of Soussou or Malinké. (Six other tribal languages are also spoken.)

Monetary Unit: Guinea Franc (market rate December 1, 2009: 5,025.00 francs = $1US).

President: *(See headnote.)* Capt. Moussa Dadis CAMARA; appointed by the National Council for Democracy and Development on December 24, 2008, after military coup following the death of Gen. Lansana CONTÉ (Party of Unity and Progress) on December 22.

Prime Minister: *(See headnote.)* Kabiné KOMARA (nonparty); appointed by the National Council for Democracy and Development on December 30, 2008, replacing Ahmed Tidiane SOUARÉ, who was ousted in the military takeover on December 24; formed new government on January 14, 2009.

THE COUNTRY

Facing the Atlantic on the western bulge of Africa, Guinea presents a highly diversified terrain that ranges from coastal flatlands to the mountainous Foutah Djallon region where the Niger, Gambia, and Senegal rivers originate. The predominantly Muslim population includes over 2 million Fulani (Fulah); over 1.25 million Malinké (Mandingo, who have long been the dominant tribe); over 500,000 Soussou; 350,000 Kissi; and 250,000 Kpelle. While women are responsible for an estimated 48 percent of food production, female participation in government is minimal.

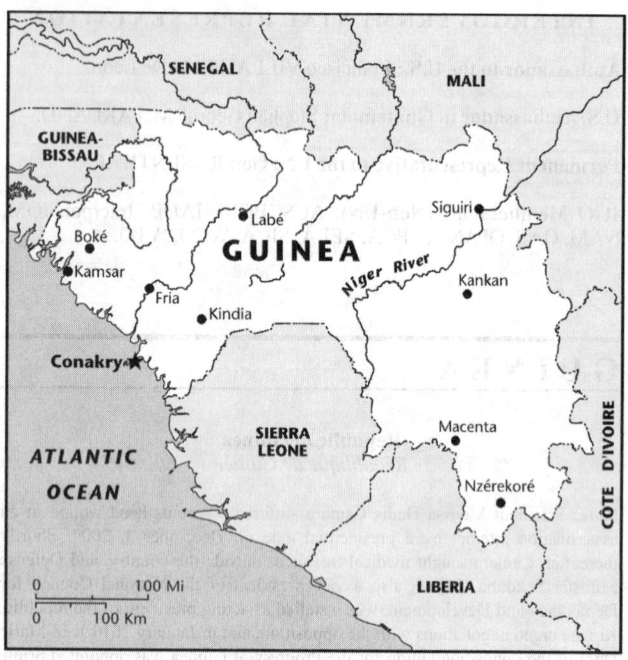

The majority of the population is dependent upon subsistence agriculture. Bananas, coffee, peanuts, palm kernels, and citrus fruits are important cash crops, although much foreign exchange is derived from mining. Guinea is one of the world's largest producers of bauxite, its reserves being exploited largely with the assistance of foreign companies. There are also valuable deposits of iron ore, gold, diamonds, uranium, and oil, in addition to substantial hydroelectric capability. Despite these resources, the GNP per capita was only $480 in 1990, reflecting an economy weakened by a quarter of a century of Marxist-inspired management. Following its takeover of the Sékou Touré government, the CMRN announced a free-market economic policy and a series of economic liberalization measures involving banking and foreign investment. Development aid has since been obtained from a number of regional and European sources, notably France and Belgium.

In late 1996 Guinea launched an economic reform program with the goals of restructuring the banking system, strengthening financial policies, and reducing corruption. In 1997 the International Monetary Fund (IMF) approved a three-year-loan package to support the country's efforts. Subsequently, the IMF reported that increased activity in the agriculture, construction, and trade sectors had spurred real GDP growth to an annual average of 4.7 percent in 1997–1998. In late 1999 Conakry asserted that it had made a "determined" effort to promote private sector development and had implemented strict expenditure controls and monitoring procedures as part of a "rigorous" financial management plan. Furthermore, the government projected a real GDP growth rate of over 5 percent in 2000 despite the continued effects of high petroleum prices. At the same time, the administration continued to call for international aid to help it cope with its large refugee population, made up of Sierra Leoneans and Liberians displaced by fighting in their respective countries.

In May 2001 the IMF approved a three-year arrangement for Guinea to "foster macroeconomic stability, promote growth, improve social services and reduce poverty." The country underwent a dramatic economic slowdown in 2003, with GDP growth declining to 1.2 percent. In addition, inflation rose to 14.8 percent. The economic contraction was the result of a range of factors, including poor harvests and a slump in manufacturing caused by significant problems with public utilities. The most significant negative consequence was a major rise in unemployment, with some estimating it as high as 70 percent. Meanwhile, food and fuel prices doubled. Government reform of its tariff and auditing systems, along with other reforms, led to promises of $800 million in debt relief and up to $82 million in economic aid as part of its arrangement with the IMF. However, delays in addressing structural problems, such as privatizing key industries, led some sources to withhold aid.

In the wake of continuing poor economic performance, the IMF approved a staff-monitored program for Guinea for 2005-2006 in an effort to improve structural reforms, reduce poverty, and bolster economic stability, noting that initial benchmarks had been met. Still, fund advisers cited the need for better monetary control, reform of public utilities, and a flexible exchange rate. Meanwhile, annual GDP growth for 2006 was recorded at 2 percent, partially due to a series of union strikes over rising food and fuel prices that disrupted the lucrative bauxite industry. In early 2007 a general strike virtually shut down the country's economy for several weeks. Inflation rose to about 30 percent annually, and food and fuel prices reportedly tripled. Meanwhile, observers described the economy as "teetering on the verge of collapse," and Transparency International ranked Guinea as the most corrupt country in Africa. After the strikes ended, the government received multimillion-dollar pledges from European donors for infrastructure improvements, the fishing industry, and various reform programs. Also, the IMF approved a three-year poverty-reduction program, and in early 2008 the Paris Club of creditors agreed to cancel $180 million of Guinea's debt and reschedule another $120 million. Protests against high fuel prices resumed late in the year, the government having earlier ended its fuel subsidies. GDP growth, recorded as 2.4 percent in 2009, was expected to increase slightly in 2010, mainly due to increased revenue from tourism. Meanwhile, as a result of the global economic downturn and the unstable political situation in Guinea (see Current issues, below), China held off on investing $5 billion in various projects around the country.

GOVERNMENT AND POLITICS

Political background. Historically part of the regional kingdom of Ghana, Songhai, and Mali, Guinea was incorporated into the French colonial empire in the late nineteenth century. Post–World War II colonial policy led to increasing political activity by indigenous groups, and in 1947 the Democratic Party of Guinea (PDG) was founded. Under the leadership of Ahmed Sékou TOURÉ, the PDG pushed for independence, and, following rejection of membership in the French Community in a referendum held September 28, 1958, Guinea became the first of France's African colonies to achieve complete independence. Since the PDG already held 58 of the 60 seats in the Territorial Assembly, Sékou Touré automatically became president upon establishment of the republic on October 2, 1958. Although the Soviet Union came to Guinea's aid following the abrupt withdrawal of French technical personnel and a collateral crippling of the new nation's fragile economy, Soviet nationals were expelled in 1961 after being charged with involvement in a teachers' strike.

Plots and alleged plots have dominated Guinea's history; at one time or another the United States, Britain, France, West Germany, the Soviet Union, and other countries have been accused of conspiring against the regime. The most dramatic incident occurred in November 1970 when Guinea was invaded by a force composed of Guinean dissidents and elements of the Portuguese army. The action was strongly condemned by the United Nations and resulted in a wave of arrests and executions. In July 1976 Diallo TELLI, the minister of justice and former secretary general of the Organization of African Unity (OAU, subsequently the African Union—AU), was arrested on charges of organizing an "anti-Guinean front" supported financially by France, the Côte d'Ivoire, Senegal, and the United States. Observers viewed Telli's possible complicity in a conspiracy, coupled with evidence of discontent within the people's militia, as indicative of a potentially serious threat to the Touré regime (the severity of which reportedly prompted the flight of nearly one-quarter of Guinea's population to neighboring countries). Subsequently, French sources reported that Telli had been assassinated in prison while awaiting trial.

President Touré was sworn in for the fifth time on May 14, 1982, after an election five days earlier in which he was credited with close to 100 percent of the votes. However, on March 26, 1984, Africa's longest-serving chief executive died while undergoing heart surgery in the United States. Prime Minister Lansana BEAVOGUI immediately assumed office as acting president, but on April 5 a group of junior military officers seized power in a bloodless coup and announced the appointments of Col. Lansana CONTÉ as president of the Republic and Col. Diarra TRAORÉ as prime minister. Despite Touré's legendary status, the military found themselves in control of what had been described as a police state, with widespread corruption permeating both governmental and party bureaucracies and an economy in shambles. While immediate action was taken by the postcoup administration to reduce political repression, the malfunctioning state-controlled economy presented a more intractable challenge.

Following the April 1984 takeover, power struggles were reported between President Conté and the internationally visible Traoré, the former consolidating his power by abolishing the prime minister's post and demoting Traoré to education minister in a December cabinet reshuffle. Subsequently, on July 4, 1985, while President Conté was out of the country, army elements led by Traoré declared the dissolution of the "corrupt" Conté administration and occupied sections of Conakry. The coup attempt was quelled by loyalist forces prior to the president's return on July 5, most of those involved being arrested, pending trial by military courts. Traoré and his co-conspirators were executed shortly after their imprisonment, although there was no official confirmation of their deaths until 1987.

In late 1988 Conté himself criticized the corruption and "transitory" nature of the first four years of his regime. In an effort to counter domestic opposition to his stringent economic programs and inspire the return of Guinean expatriates, he called on men and women "without regard to their abode" to join in the drafting of a bipartisan constitution, which was approved by referendum on December 23, 1990.

On January 9, 1992, in keeping with the spirit of the new basic law, which called for a separation of powers between executive and legislative organs of government, General Conté relinquished the presidency of the quasi-legislative Transitional Committee for National Recovery (CTRN, under Constitution and government, below), while remaining president of the republic. Despite widespread popular protests during the remainder of 1992, the regime rejected appeals for a national conference and countered objections to the pace and breadth of reform by adopting draft laws increasing penalties for the organization of violent demonstrations and banning unauthorized public meetings.

In April 1993 the administration announced plans to hold presidential and legislative elections in the last quarter of the year; however, unrest continued as General Conté rebuffed the opposition's call for an independent electoral commission and all-party talks. In September the government, ignoring the opposition's demand for simultaneous polling, scheduled presidential elections for December 5, with legislative balloting to follow 60 days later. Furthermore, in the wake of violent clashes September 28 and 29 in Conakry, Conté banned all opposition demonstrations until after the elections.

On December 19, 1993, Lansana Conté retained the presidency, leading an 8-candidate field with 51 percent of the vote in polling marred by at least 12 deaths and charges of widespread irregularities. On December 23 the Supreme Court annulled voting results in two opposition districts where second-place finisher Alpha CONDÉ of the Rally of the Guinean People (RPG) had reportedly secured 90 percent of the vote, and on January 4, 1994, the court confirmed the incumbent's victory, ignoring opposition calls for a second round of balloting.

After three postponements, a National Assembly poll was held on June 11, 1995, with 21 of 46 legalized parties participating. Conté's Party of Unity and Progress (PUP) was credited with an absolute majority of 71 of 114 seats and the runner-up RPG with 19, the remainder being distributed across eight other contestants. Most opposition groups challenged the results, although foreign observers indicated that irregularities had been relatively isolated.

On July 5, 1995, the RPG, the Party for Renewal and Progress (PRP), and the Union for the New Republic (UNR), who among them controlled 37 seats, announced their intention to boycott the assembly and joined with nine other opposition parties to form the Coordination of Democratic Opposition (Codem). The new formation was denounced by the government, and Conté refused its entreaties to engage in extraparliamentary negotiations. Subsequently, Codem abandoned the boycott, and the inaugural session of the first democratically elected Guinean Assembly opened on October 5, 1995.

On February 2 and 3, 1996, 50 people were killed and more than 100 others wounded when approximately 2,000 soldiers demonstrating for higher wages and better working conditions rampaged through Conakry, ultimately attacking the presidential palace and taking the president hostage. During his brief captivity Conté reached agreement with the soldiers on amnesty for the mutineers, salary increases, and reform of the armed services; however, following the retreat of the rebellious troops, Conté dismissed reports that their attack on his government had occurred spontaneously and accused opposition activists of helping organize the failed "coup" attempt. Thereafter, despite warnings from the insurgents that the "entire army" would retaliate if any of their comrades were arrested, by June at least 52 people had been detained for their roles in the incident, including Lt. Lamine DIARRA, one of the two alleged masterminds of the rebellion, his alleged co-conspirator, Cmdr. Gbago ZOUMANIGUI, having reportedly fled to Libya. (In August some 40 of the detainees were released after the state prosecutor ruled there was insufficient evidence against them.)

On July 9, 1996, Conté named an economist, Sidya TOURÉ, as Guinea's first prime minister since 1984. Touré's appointment was followed on July 17 by a major cabinet reshuffling that included the departure of interior minister Alseny René GOMEZ, theretofore considered the president's second-in-command. On November 3 Conté, in an apparent attempt to reestablish control of military and security forces, appointed himself to head a newly created national defense ministry. The decision came just one day after government forces allegedly orchestrated an attack against Alpha Condé and his RPG supporters that left over 50 people injured. In early 1997 the president proclaimed executive authority over the national bank.

In February 1998 the newly created State Security Council convened the trial of the military personnel allegedly responsible for the February 1996 uprising. However, in March the court proceedings were overshadowed by deadly clashes between opposition activists and government security forces in Conakry that left at least nine dead and a number of opposition figures imprisoned. In response to the government's subsequent refusal to release the jailed militants, opposition legislators affiliated with Codem boycotted the National Assembly. In September relations between the opposition and government deteriorated further when the government dismissed the opposition's call for the establishment of an independent electoral commission and created an electoral affairs committee, which it charged with preparing for presidential elections in December. In October tensions between the Conté administration and National Assembly President El Hadj Boubacar Biro DIALLO reached a nadir as the latter was suspended from the ruling party for criticizing the government's treatment of the alleged February 1996 insurgents (most of whom had been convicted and sentenced to prison in late September).

At presidential elections on December 14, 1998, President Conté won reelection, capturing 56.12 percent of the vote and easily outdistancing his four competitors. As anticipated, the polling results were immediately challenged by the opposition, whose top two contenders, Mamadou Boye BA of the Union for Progress and Renewal (UPR) and Alpha Condé, had officially secured 24.63 and 16.58 percent, respectively. On March 8, 1999, the president appointed Lamine SIDIMÉ (theretofore head of the Supreme Court) as prime minister, with no official explanation given for the change; on March 12 Conté named a moderately reshuffled government, which was sworn in on April 10.

Twice-postponed municipal elections were held on June 25, 2000, with the PUP winning more than three-quarters of the seats. Subsequently, on November 11, 2001, 98 percent of those voting in a national referendum endorsed a controversial constitutional amendment permitting President Conté to run for a third term in 2003, with the term of office being extended from five to seven years.

The PUP dominated the June 30, 2002, legislative balloting, securing 85 seats; the UPR finished second with 20 seats. Amid severe controversy over electoral procedures and government control of the media, the major opposition parties boycotted the presidential election of December 21, 2003, at which Conté was reelected with an official 95.6 percent of the vote.

In late February 2004 President Conté dismissed Prime Minister Sidimé without explanation, and François Lonseny FALL was appointed on March 1 to head a reshuffled cabinet with a broad mandate to improve economic conditions. However, following a breakdown in relations with Conté, Fall resigned on April 29 and went into exile in the United States. A new prime minister was not appointed until December 9, when Cellou Dalein DIALLO was named to the post.

The PUP swept the postponed municipal elections on December 18, 2005, securing more than three-quarters of the seats. On April 5, 2006, the president ordered a cabinet reshuffle that granted more control to Diallo, but hours later, after a surprise rescinding of the cabinet changes, the prime minister was dismissed for alleged gross misconduct. On May 29 the president reportedly removed all of Diallo's supporters from the cabinet in a major reshuffle that did not include a prime minister.

Following massive strikes in early 2007, the president appointed one of his confidants, Eugène CAMARA, as prime minister on February 9, resulting in further public protests. Camara, who weeks earlier had been appointed by the president as minister of state for presidential affairs, served as prime minister for only three weeks. On February 26 President Conté named Lansana KOUYATÉ as prime minister with enhanced authority, and Camara returned to his ministerial post. On March 28 Kouyaté named a new cabinet, which included only one member of the previous administration. Following three days of rioting by members of the military over salary and other issues, President Conté replaced the minister of defense on May 12 (see Current issues, below). Subsequently, legislative elections scheduled for June 2007 were postponed until December and subsequently delayed again (with the approval of opposition parties) until December 2008. Those elections never took place.

On May 20, 2008, President Conté dismissed Kouyaté, replacing him the same day with Ahmed Tidiane SOUARÉ, an economist and former minister. A new, expanded cabinet, which included four women, several members of Conté's PUP, and one post each for the UPR, UFDG, and UPG, was appointed on June 19.

President Conté, who had been in ill health for years, died at age 74 on December 22, 2008. Hours after his death a group of junior military officers, calling themselves the National Council for Democracy and Development (*Comité National pour le Developpement et la Démocratie*—CNDD), seized power by proclaiming over the airwaves that a coup had taken place. The seated government challenged the claim, but on December 24 the CNDD named its leader, Capt. Moussa Dadis CAMARA, as president, and he immediately dissolved the government, suspended the constitution, and imposed a moratorium on the activities of all political parties and unions. On December 30 the CNDD named a civilian, Kabiné KOMARA, as prime minister, despite calls by supporters of former prime minister Souaré for him to head an interim government and insisting that the speaker of the assembly, Aboubacar SOMPARÉ, be installed as president in accordance with constitutional provisions. Meanwhile, Souaré, Somparé, and other government officials were sent to a military camp for an "informational meeting" and subsequently endorsed the junta. A new, enlarged government composed of technocrats and soldiers (and no members of political parties) was announced on January 14, 2009. Though Camara had pledged that presidential and parliamentary elections would be held in 2010, he later amended the date to 2009, having come under intense pressure from international donors, the AU, and the Economic Community of West African States (ECOWAS). Elections were subsequently postponed to 2010 (see Current issues, below.)

Constitution and government. The 1982 constitution was suspended and the Democratic Party of Guinea dissolved by the Military Committee for National Recovery (*Comité Militaire de Redressement National*—CMRN) in the wake of the April 1984 coup. Subsequently, Guinea was ruled by a president and Council of Ministers named by the CMRN, although the committee itself was dissolved on January 16, 1991, in favor of a Transitional Committee for National Recovery (*Comité Transitoire de Redressement National*—CTRN). The new body, which was to govern the country until the election of an all-civilian administration, included equal numbers of military and civilian personnel.

In a decree issued in May 1984, President Conté ordered that the name "People's Revolutionary Republic of Guinea," adopted in 1978, be dropped in favor of the country's original name, the Republic of Guinea. Subsequently, he announced the formation of a "truly independent judiciary" and revival of the theretofore outlawed legal profession. In August 1985 a Court of State Security was established, with a supreme court judge, two military officers, and two attorneys, to try "crimes against the state."

A 50-member committee, led by Foreign Affairs Minister Maj. Jean TRAORÉ, was appointed in October 1988 to draft a new constitution, which was reportedly approved by 99 percent of the participants in a referendum on December 23, 1990. The new *loi fondamentale* validated replacement of the CMRN by the CTRN, which in turn yielded authority in 1995 to a civilian regime consisting of a president and unicameral legislature, both popularly elected under two-party (subsequently multiparty) auspices, and an independent judiciary. A presidential decree on June 19, 1997, established a consultative Economic and Social Council whose 45 members are appointed by the president upon the recommendation of various civic institutions.

The 1990 constitution was suspended by the president of the transitional CNDD, composed of 26 military officers and 6 civilians, following the coup of December 2008.

The country is administratively organized into four main geographic divisions—Maritime, Middle, Upper, and Forest Guinea—which are subdivided into eight regions—Boké, Faranah, Kankan, Kindia, Labé, Mamou, N'Zérékoré, and Conakry. The Conakry region is subdivided into five "urban communes," while the remaining seven regions are subdivided into a total of 33 prefectures.

Foreign relations. President Touré's brand of militant nationalism and his frequent allegations of externally provoked conspiracy led to strained international relations, including diplomatic ruptures with France (1965–1975), Britain (1967–1968), and Ghana (1966–1973). By January 1978, however, Conakry had moved to ease long-standing tensions with its immediate neighbors. Shortly thereafter, diplomatic relations with Senegal and the Côte d'Ivoire were restored. In October 1980 Guinea acceded to the Mano River Union (MRU), formed seven years earlier to promote economic cooperation between Liberia and Sierra Leone, while in March 1982 Touré called for the unification of Guinea and Mali, arguing that economically the two countries were "two lungs in a single body." In subsequent years Conakry also increased its visibility in the ECOWAS.

In December 1978 French President Giscard d'Estaing visited Guinea, the first Western leader to do so in over two decades. The extremely warm reception he received was viewed as part of a broad effort to scale down assistance from Soviet and other Eastern bloc countries in favor of Western aid and investment. In keeping with the policy shift, President Touré made a number of trips to the United States, Canada, and Western Europe from 1979 to 1983. However, distrust of the "father of African socialism" and an overvalued local currency discouraged large-scale Western involvement. By contrast, in the wake of the 1984 coup, Prime Minister Traoré negotiated a broad aid package with France, while French and other foreign investment increased significantly upon the adoption of monetary and fiscal reforms recommended by the IMF.

Despite Guinean fears of a new "colonialism," raised by the influx of foreign merchants and military advisers into the capital, Conakry continued to pursue external assistance in developing its infrastructure and mineral resources, while concluding resource-development agreements with Morocco, Guinea-Bissau, and Liberia in 1989.

In early 1990 an influx of refugees fleeing the Liberian civil war quickly exhausted the reserves of Guinea's southern border region, and in May, President Conté called for international aid to support refugees claimed to number 200,000. In August, Conakry deployed troops to seal its southern border after a rebel incursion in alleged reprisal for Guinea's participation in ECOWAS activity in Liberia.

In September 1992, after a three-month cease-fire aimed at inducing Liberian and Sierra Leonean rebels to disarm and accept a full amnesty, Guinean and Sierra Leonean troops resumed their joint efforts to repel rebels in eastern and southern Sierra Leone. Meanwhile, the publication of a report claiming that Guinea had trained a Liberian paramilitary force assigned to interim Liberian president Amos Sawyer led to the detainment of its author. In August 1994, 35,000 Liberians were reported to have fled into Guinea, raising the five-year total to approximately 500,000.

In April 1996 Mali recalled its ambassador and criticized the Conté administration after Guinean troops stormed into the Malian embassy in Conakry in search of a leader of the February military uprising. Clashes between Malian and Guinean residents were subsequently reported in April and October near the border.

In April 1997 Belgium closed its consular offices after Conakry refused to release three Belgian nationals it had arrested in March for allegedly plotting to overthrow the government. Meanwhile, observers reported that Guinean security forces had arrested and then released 75 Liberian refugees on similar charges. Increasing incidents of "banditry" and violence along the Guinean-Liberian border were among the topics discussed by President Conté and Liberian President Charles Taylor during a summit in late 1997.

Amid reports that rebels from Sierra Leone had attacked a town in southern Guinea, in early December 1998 Conakry announced that it was closing its borders until after the presidential polling scheduled for December 14. Further Sierra Leonean cross-border activity was reported in early 1999, and in April Liberian troops threatened to enter Guinean territory in pursuit of Liberian antigovernment rebels, whom Monrovia accused Conakry of at least tacitly supporting. In August at least two dozen people died when militants, allegedly operating from a base in Liberia, attacked a town in southern Guinea, and in mid-September Charles Taylor claimed that Guinean forces had killed several hundred Liberians during raids in April and August. Conté subsequently called his Liberian counterpart a "warmonger," although at the same time insisting that no problems existed between the two countries' peoples.

In March 2000 Guinea, Liberia, and Sierra Leone reportedly agreed to the immediate reactivation of the MRU secretariat. (Due to civil wars the body had been dormant since 1990.) However, Guinea and Liberia were subsequently described as still "trading destabilization accusations." (See Current issues, below, and article on Liberia for additional information.)

Economic relations between France and Guinea continued to remain strong through the early 2000s, but Conakry also began to develop stronger security ties with the United States, which had provided military training and equipment to improve Guinea's military capabilities for regional peacekeeping missions. The appointment of Prime Minister

Fall, an English speaker and widely seen as pro-American, as opposed to pro-French, was perceived as a sign of Conté's desire to improve relations with the United States. One manifestation of the increased ties between the two countries was a decrease in Guinean support for Liberian rebel groups, as a result of diplomatic pressure from the United States, and broad support from Conakry for the United Nations peacekeeping mission in Liberia after the departure of Taylor from that country. By mid-2006, a marked decrease in violence at the border with Liberia was reported. In August, Guinea and South Korea agreed to establish bilateral relations.

Relations with regional neighbors and the United States deteriorated quickly in the wake of the 2008 coup by a military junta. Both the AU and ECOWAS suspended Guinea pending democratic elections, and the United States and the European Union (EU) condemned the coup and immediately suspended all aid except for emergency and humanitarian assistance. Nigeria refused to acknowledge the coup leaders, while Senegal urged the international community to recognize the junta.

Current issues. ECOWAS's deployment of troops in Guinean border areas in December 2000 and the completion of a peace accord in Sierra Leone in May 2001 (see article on Sierra Leone) appeared to offer the opportunity for resumption of normal political activity in Guinea. However, the opposition parties strongly objected to the November referendum that permitted a third, extended term for President Conté, calling the initiative a "constitutional coup d'état" designed to make Conté "president for life." (Although the government reported a turnout of 87 percent for the referendum, the opposition, which had called for a boycott, described that figure as outlandishly inflated.) When the opposition announced plans to boycott the new legislative elections, rescheduled for late December after having been delayed twice in 2000, the administration once again postponed the balloting indefinitely. The legislative poll finally took place on June 30, 2002, with most opposition parties boycotting the balloting.

Under heavy international pressure, the government established an interparty commission in 2003 in an effort to convince the opposition to return to full political participation. However, negotiations collapsed in September as the government reportedly refused to relinquish its tight control of the state media. Consequently, another opposition boycott was called for the December presidential election, at which Conté was challenged by only one minor candidate after six others were rejected because of "technical errors" in their candidacy papers. Not surprisingly, international observers described the balloting as neither free nor fair.

The appointment of reformist Prime Minister Fall, described as "pro-American," in March 2004 was seen as part of ongoing efforts to improve relations with the United States. (Under U.S. pressure, Conakry had earlier decreased its support for Liberian rebel groups and endorsed the UN peacekeeping mission in Liberia.) However, Fall left office in less than two months to protest what he perceived as continued political repression and the unwillingness of Conté to pursue economic reform. From exile in the United States, Fall called upon the Guinean opposition parties to coalesce in order to challenge the Conté regime.

A number of public protests broke out in September 2004, and, following his appointment in December, reformist Prime Minister Diallo attempted to relaunch a dialogue with the opposition. In early 2005 he moved to lift a ban on private radio stations, but little progress ensued in his attempts to win over the opposition. Meanwhile, attention focused on the frail health of President Conté, for whom there appeared to be no obvious successor. The government reported an assassination attempt against Conté in January 2005, and reports surfaced about fears of a potential military coup if the president failed to live out his term. Despite calls late in the year by the Republican Front for Democratic Change (*Front de L'Alternance Démocratique*—FRAD) for the president to step down in favor of a government of national unity, observers pointed to ethnic and other differences among the opposition that could render such an alternative unlikely. The government was bolstered by an overwhelming PUP victory in December's municipal elections, postponed from 2004 because of allegations of widespread fraud, which were repeated after the 2005 balloting.

The president's deteriorating health (he was taken to Switzerland in March 2006, reportedly for emergency medical attention) prompted rising concern about the country's uncertain political future. In Conté's absence, a strike to protest low wages shut down the country for five days. As a result, the government reached an accord with unions that provided a 30 percent wage increase for civil service workers and a 10 percent tax cut on state employees' salaries. Further, an unprecedented National Consultation of opposition groups, unions, women's and youth groups, and civil societies resulted in unanimity on the need for a government of national unity to "rescue" the country. However, disarray followed a state radio broadcast on April 5, 2006, announcing extensive cabinet changes that bolstered the influence of Prime Minister Diallo. Within hours it was announced that the changes were rescinded and that Diallo had been dismissed because of alleged serious misconduct. Observers attributed the move to internal power struggles, raising questions about who was really in charge. For his part, Diallo denied claims that he was under house arrest and reiterated his support for Conté. (Subsequently, Diallo sought exile in Senegal, then traveled to the United States and returned to Guinea in April 2007. See Political Parties and Groups, below.) Meanwhile, Conté did not immediately appoint another prime minister but instead named so-called "strongman" and loyalist Elhadji Fodé BANGOURA to the newly created position of minister of state for presidential affairs, in charge of directing government policy. Another strike in June, this time including teachers, ended in violent attacks by government troops, who allegedly killed 21 protesters, some of them children. The strike ended on June 16 when the government reached an agreement with the unions on wage increases, reduced fuel prices, and a fixed price for rice, among other things.

Civil unrest continued to stir, however, rising to the surface on January 10, 2007, with a massive general strike by an alliance comprising numerous unions, civil societies, and political parties. In addition to protesting against the rising cost of living and alleged government corruption, the protesters were angered by reports of the president's alleged intervention that resulted in shortened prison terms for two of his friends convicted of embezzlement. More significantly, however, the unions demanded a new government structure that would put more power in the hands of a "consensus" prime minister, with a collateral reduction in Conté's authority. As the strike continued for weeks, disrupting the transport of bauxite and damaging the economy, government troops clashed with protesters, allegedly killing at least 40 people in Conakry. Conté subsequently acquiesced to some of the unions' demands, including dismissing Bangoura and agreeing to relinquish some of his authority to a new prime minister. On February 9 the president appointed Eugène Camara to fill the post of prime minister, prompting further protests by the unions, which rejected Conté's selection of another close ally. Despite the government's imposition of a state of emergency on February 12, and the president's subsequent vow to extend it beyond 12 days, the unions stood fast in their rejection of Camara. Insisting on a prime minister who was not part of Conté's camp, the unions recommended career diplomat Lansana Kouyaté for the post. On February 23 the parliament, in what the *New York Times* described as "a rare show of dissent," unanimously rejected the president's request for an extension of "the state of siege." Ultimately, the president acceded to the unions' demand and appointed Kouyaté on February 26, giving the prime minister greater authority, and thus ending the strikes that observers said were designed to force Conté to step down. So severe were the potential consequences of the strikes, the *Financial Times* reported, that Guinea had "veered perilously close to becoming the latest in a string of failed and failing states stretching along the African coast." With the appointment of Kouyaté, however, and his naming of a new government comprising technocrats and only one member affiliated with the previous government, order was greatly restored. Meanwhile, human rights groups estimated that at least 120 people had been killed and 1,700 injured by government security forces in January and February. Military unrest flared up in May, with troops engaging in a small riot in Conakry over payment of arrears and salary increases. The turmoil of the past months led to the firing of the defense minister and, subsequently, a joint decision in May by the government and most political parties to postpone legislative balloting from June 2007 to December. (The polls were later postponed to the end of 2008, but were not held.) A coalition of 13 small parties that had been aligned with the PUP reportedly decided to form an opposition alliance in advance of the next legislative elections (see Political Parties and Groups, below). Meanwhile, the PUP named Mamadou SYLLA, a wealthy businessman accused of corruption and a longtime confidant of President Conté, to the post of "honorary chair," thus granting him shared leadership of the party with the ailing president. Observers described the party as being in disarray following the months of public discontent, and the anointing of Sylla fueled further criticism since President Conté personally saw to it that Sylla was released from prison in December 2006, where he had been held in connection with misappropriation of public funds. Even after his release, Sylla remained under investigation. Despite Conté's ill health and the increasing discord, the president said that he would stand for reelection in 2010.

As part of the administration's pledge to hold free and fair elections, a national electoral commission was established in August that included 10 members from the governing coalition and 10 members from opposition parties.

Further turmoil ensued in June 2007, as soldiers were reported to have looted towns and terrorized residents following President Conté's wavering on whether he could find the money for their promised salaries and promotions. Observers noted that the president's promises came at a time when the country's revenues were "at an all-time low" due to the civil unrest that had disrupted the economy. Meanwhile, the assembly authorized the establishment of an independent commission to investigate the earlier violence. Months later, however, international human rights organizations noted that no such investigation had begun, and they issued scathing reports on the alleged brutality of the security forces.

Tensions remained high in 2008 following the president's dismissal in January of one of Prime Minister Kouyaté's popular appointments (the communications minister) without consulting Kouyaté, a move that prompted the unions to call for another national strike. Though the strike was subsequently suspended, the unions became disillusioned with Kouyaté following reports that he had tried to suppress the investigation into the violence the previous year. In addition, the prime minister was said to have spent large sums of money on renovating his home and other unwanted public schemes, costing more than $2 million. The expenditures came at a time when "living conditions for the majority of Guineans remain dire," according to *Africa Research Bulletin*, and the president's recent moves to reassert control "threaten a relapse into chaos." Turmoil resumed briefly following President Conté's dismissal of Kouyaté in May, 15 months after his appointment, the move angering the unions responsible for Kouyaté's selection and soldiers who had been promised arrears. Mobs of soldiers protested with riots and looting, but the violence was quickly quelled when the new prime minister, Ahmed Tidiane Souaré, a technocrat named the same day Kouyaté was dismissed, fulfilled the back-pay promise. In an effort to promote a unity government, Souaré met with representatives of the UFDG and the UPG, and both parties agreed to work with the government. The RPG, for its part, refused to attend the meeting. Subsequently, the UFDG, the UPG, and the UPR were each given one post in the new government named June 19.

Longtime fears of a potential military coup came to fruition in December 2008, following the death of President Conté, when a bloodless coup was staged by junior military officers in a grouping called the CNDD. Moussa Dadis Camara, a 44-year-old junior officer appointed president by the CNDD, broadcast news of the takeover early on December 23, announcing that a transitional "consultative council" of military and civilian personnel would run the country with the dual aims of reviving the economy and fighting corruption. Camara's immediate dissolution of the government and suspension of the constitution and all political parties were challenged by Prime Minister Souaré and by the assembly speaker, Aboubacar Somparé, the latter asking the Supreme Court to name him president as stipulated by the constitution. Camara quickly moved to quash support for such requests, stating that the National Assembly's mandate had ended in 2007 and that a constitutional order of succession would only court disaster in such an unstable country, according to *The New York Times*. Camara subsequently ordered former government officials and key opposition leaders to a military base for a meeting to outline his proposals. Among them were promises to renegotiate and monitor mining contracts and to fight corruption. Souaré and others subsequently made positive pronouncements about the junta. Meanwhile, Conté's funeral in Conakry on December 26 was attended by 20,000 people, including leaders from neighboring countries, but not by Camara. With tensions still simmering, soldiers were sent to search the home of former prime minister and current UFDG leader Cellou Diallo (see UFDG in Political Parties and Groups, below) in an effort to quell suspicions of what the junta reportedly said might be another coup plot. Meanwhile, former prime minister Kouyaté returned to Conakry from Côte d'Ivoire for the first time since his dismissal by President Conté, to attend the funeral and to meet with Camara. (Months later he was reported to have formed a new political party styled the Party for Hope and National Development [PEDN].)

Despite initial confusion and a short-lived curfew after the announcement of Conté's death, the military takeover was reported to be well-received by the public, "weary of years of tyranny," observers reported. Opposition groups were said to have greeted news of the coup "with delight," extending to the naming of the new prime minister, a banker, on December 30 and a new cabinet appointed two weeks later. The transitional government included numerous economists and technocrats who were seen as the appropriate choices to lead the country out of economic and civil crises. Meanwhile, the coup was also popular with more junior members of the military who had been alienated by the Conté government's perceived favoritism to senior officers. Camara, for his part, promised to reform the military by upgrading salaries and promotion structures, among other things.

Among Camara's first announcements was that elections would be held in 2010 (in order to provide enough time to prepare for free and fair balloting), but he later bowed to internal and external pressures and revised the date to sometime in 2009. In the days following the coup, 11 political parties and groups proposed a transition scheme to the junta, including provisions for a national transition council, a transitional period not to exceed 12 months, prohibitions against Camara and other CNDD officials participating in national elections, and the establishment of a special court to resolve constitutional and electoral disputes. In February Camara presented his own transition plan, proposing a process to restore constitutional order, register voters, and lift the suspension of political parties and union activities. He also called for the establishment of a truth and reconciliation committee to review charges against the previous government. Meanwhile, the most vocal public criticism of the junta was directed toward a few appointees in the cabinet who allegedly had been involved in fraud or linked to drug trafficking. Camara, in a follow-up to his anti-corruption promises, quickly ordered the arrests of numerous former government officials, among them Conté's son, Ousmane, and three former ministers in charge of mines, including former prime minister Ahmed Tidiane Souaré. All three ministers were accused of stealing millions of dollars from the mining ministry. Ousmane Conté made a public confession on television to having smuggled cocaine. The junta also investigated numerous business executives in connection with alleged corruption. A fourth former mines minister was arrested in March; the three who had been arrested earlier were released on bail in April after they agreed to repay the stolen money.

While the anti-corruption efforts gained Camara popular support, as did his call for "free, credible, and transparent elections," it was unclear whether Camara would adhere to his original declaration that junta members should not contest the elections, as he later insisted he had the right to run. He also said that those who had been in power under President Conté should not contest the elections, referring to leaders of the PUP, UFR, and UFDG, observers said. Meanwhile, it was reported in April that Camara had agreed to proposals of various groups calling for parliamentary elections on October 11, 2009, and presidential balloting on December 13, with a second round, if necessary, on December 27. However, in August the electoral commission postponed presidential elections to January 31, 2010, to be followed by legislative elections in March. In the interim, more than 150 people were killed on October 2, 2009, during a demonstration calling for a return to a civilian government, and opposition parties subsequently rejected a proposal to form a unity government.

POLITICAL PARTIES AND GROUPS

Prior to the 1984 coup, Guinea was a typical one-party state, according a monopoly position to the Democratic Party of Guinea (*Parti Démocratique de Guinée*—PDG) in all aspects of public life. The Military Committee for National Recovery's initial promise of an introduction of "democracy" was reaffirmed in 1989 by President Conté, and the constitution approved in December 1990 included provisions for two parties, with numerous others being recognized in 1991 and 1992.

During 1993 a number of somewhat transitory opposition coalitions emerged, including Democratic Change (*Changement Démocratique*—CD), a 30-party grouping under whose banner activists clashed with police in Conakry in September. The principal opposition alliances in the run-up to the December presidential balloting were AGUNA (below) and the BPG, while nine of the nearly four dozen recognized parties were reportedly members of a "Presidential Tendency" headed by the PUP (below).

In August 1995 the "Presidential Tendency" splintered because of the failure of the PUP and a number of its erstwhile allies to reach agreement on a new assembly president; subsequently, the defecting parties formed the **Alliance of Democratic Forces** (*Alliance pour les Forces Démocratiques*—AFD), under the leadership of Oumar CAMARA.

Two somewhat overlapping opposition alliances were formed in 2001 to attempt to stop Conté from running for a third term. In July the

UFR, the UFDG, and others formed the **Democratic Change in 2003** (*Alternance Démocratique en 2003*) to oppose the upcoming referendum on amending the constitution. Subsequently, opposition activity focused on the **Movement against the Referendum and for Democratic Change** (*Mouvement Contre le Référendum et pour l'Alternance Démocratique*—Morad), formed by the Codem, UFR, PGP, and four other parties.

In advance of the next legislative elections, postponed until late 2008 (but never held), it was reported that 13 small parties had left the governing coalition of the PUP in May 2007 to form a new coalition referenced as the **National Alliance for Democracy**, organized by the URF's Sidya Touré. Among the minor parties participating were the **National Union for Progress of Guinea**, the **Liberal Party of Guinea**, and the **National Alliance for Progress**.

Political parties were suspended by the military junta in December 2008. Soon after the coup, a group of 11 political parties and groups presented the junta with a plan for transitional governance and called for elections in 2009 (see Current issues, above). Among the political parties were the PDA, UFD, RPG, UFDG, Djama, and UPG. It was reported in March 2009 that former prime minister Lansana Kouyaté had formed a new political party, the PEDN, but little was known about it.

Party of Unity and Progress (*Parti de l'Unité et du Progrès*—PUP). The PUP nominated Gen. Lansana Conté as its presidential candidate in August 1993, subsequently becoming the core component of an informal regime-supportive coalition that included the **Democratic Rally for Development** (*Rassemblement Démocratique pour le Développement*—RDD), led by Georges Koly GUILAVOGUI.

At the PUP's first national congress, held April 4–7, 1997, Conté was named as the party's candidate for upcoming presidential elections, and Aboubacar Somparé's theretofore interim appointment as PUP secretary general was made permanent.

In January 1998, members of the PUP's youth wing launched the **Movement for Lansana Conté's Reelection** (*Mouvement pour la Réélection de Lansana Conté*—MORELAC). In June the presidential supporters formed the **Association of Movements Affiliated to the Party of Unity and Progress**, a coalition of some 200 parties and groups chaired by Karim KANE. The groups were successful in the 2001 referendum to allow Conté to stand for a third term. In early 2005 feuding between Conté loyalists and those supporting the president's unofficial heir apparent, Youth Minister Fode Soumah, was reported. Late in the year, the party made a strong showing in both rural and urban areas in municipal elections. During the strikes in 2006 and 2007, the PUP criticized the unions for moving beyond their social realm with their political goals.

On May 25, 2007, the party unanimously approved Mamadou Sylla as honorary chair of the party, granting him shared leadership with President Conté, who was long reported to be in ill health. Controversy surrounded Sylla (see Current issues, above), provoking trade unions and civil societies in particular, even though Sylla reportedly had helped bring about the appointment of a prime minister by consensus in response to unions' demands earlier in the year. It was subsequently reported that the situation within the PUP was becoming "increasingly volatile" as the president fought off efforts to diminish his authority. Tensions within the party heightened following Conté's death in December 2008, when six members of the party's national political bureau subsequently were dismissed for trying to install Sylla as interim chair until the next party congress.

Leaders: Mamadou SYLLA (Honorary Chair), Sékou KONATE (Secretary General).

Democratic Party of Guinea–African Democratic Rally (*Parti Démocratique de Guinée–Rassemblement Démocratique Africain*—PDG-RDA). The leader of the PDG-RDA (a revival of former President Touré's party) secured less than 1 percent of the vote in the 1993 presidential balloting. In the wake of its poor showing, the party splintered, with dissident members forming the **Democratic Party of Guinea–Renewed** (*Parti Démocratique de Guinée–Renouvellement*—PDG-R). In December 1994 the party suffered yet another mass defection when members claiming continued allegiance to former president Touré withdrew to launch the **Democratic Party of Guinea–Ahmed Sekou Touré** (*Parti Démocratique de Guineé–Ahmed Sekou Touré*—PDG-AST). In the 2002 legislative elections, the PDG-RDA won three seats.

Leader: Ismael Mohammed Gassim GUSHEIN.

Union for National Progress–Party of Unity and Development (*Union pour le Progrès National–Parti pour l'Unité et le Développement*—UPN-PUD). The PUD was one of seven parties that formed a coalition, **Guinean Alliance for National Unity** (*Alliance Guinéene pour l'Unité Nationale*—AGUNA), to support the presidential candidacy of Faciné TOURE. The PUD later merged with the pro-Conté UPN under the leadership of Mamadou Bhoye Barry. The UPN-PUD won one seat in the 2002 legislative elections (the seat was won by Barry). Barry was the sole challenger to Conté in the 2003 presidential election.

Leader: Mamadou Bhoye BARRY.

Union for Progress and Renewal (*Union pour le Progrès et le Renouvellement*—UPR). The UPR was launched in September 1998 as a merger of the Party of Renewal and Progress (*Parti pour le Renouveau et le Progrès*—PRP) and the Union for the New Republic (*Union pour la Nouvelle République*—UNR). While leadership of the new grouping was assumed by Siradiou Diallo, the PRP's secretary general and 1993 presidential candidate, the UNR's Mamadou Boye Ba was named the UPR's presidential candidate. Ba, who had been detained from March to June for his alleged role in the violent clashes in Conakry, finished second at the December balloting with 22 percent of the vote.

The UPR factionalized in 2002, with members who advocated dialogue with Conté and participation in elections remaining in the UPR under Diallo. Those UPR members who supported boycotting the upcoming legislative elections joined the Union of Democratic Forces of Guinea, of which Ba became president. Diallo died on March 14, 2004, of a heart attack, and the UPR elected Ousmane Bah as leader of the party. The UPR reportedly withdrew from the assembly in protest following the municipal elections of December 2005, which the party claimed were "nothing short of electoral robbery." The UPR legislators ultimately returned to parliament, and in 2007 party members participated in talks with Prime Minister Kouyaté regarding postponement of the 2007 legislative elections.

The UPR was represented in the new government named by Prime Minister Souaré in June 2008.

Leader: Ousmane BAH (President).

National Alliance for Progress (*Alliance Nationale pour le Progrès*—ANP). The ANP formed prior to the 1995 legislative elections but remained a minor party for most of its history. However, it was one of the few opposition parties not to boycott the 2002 legislative elections, and it won two seats in the assembly.

Leader: Sagno MOUSSA.

Republican Front for Democratic Change (*Front de L'Alternance Démocratique*—FRAD). The FRAD was originally formed by a coalition of four parties in 2002 and then grew to include seven of the main opposition parties. FRAD emerged from previous anti-Conté groupings, principally the Coordination of the Democratic Opposition (*Coordination de l'Opposition Démocratique*—Codem). The Codem was formed by the RPG, PRP, UNR, and a number of other smaller parties to mount a legislative boycott in response to alleged ballot fraud at the June 1995 poll. In early February 1996 the group supported President Conté's handling of the military unrest in Conakry; however, after the president alleged that opposition activists had been involved in the uprising, Codem parliamentarians boycotted the assembly. Thereafter, intracoalition conflict was reported between the PRP's Siradiou Diallo, who advocated establishing a dialogue with the administration, and the RPG's Alpha Condé, who accused the regime of harassment and the illegal detention of opposition activists.

In late 1996 the Codem announced that it was forming a "resistance militia" in response to violent attacks against its members and to fend off security forces attempting to arrest its supporters. Thereafter, the coalition criticized the Conté administration for reducing the prime minister's powers. Underscoring its increasing hostility toward Conté's policies, the Codem in early 1998 established an Executive Secretariat to coordinate "acts of resistance" against the government. In March a number of opposition leaders, including the UNR's Mamadou Ba, were arrested after violent clashes erupted in Conakry between opposition protesters and government forces. Subsequently, the Codem boycotted legislative proceedings in an effort to persuade the government to release its imprisoned members. (In June, Ba was given a "lenient verdict" and released.)

Codem boycotted the 2001 presidential referendum and announced that it would also boycott the upcoming legislative elections. In 2002 a split emerged in Codem over participation in the presidential elections, leading to the breakup of Codem and the creation of the FRAD by parties that planned to boycott the elections. The main difference between Codem and the FRAD was the absence of the Union for Progress and Renewal (see above). Nonetheless, many of the most prestigious and well-respected opposition figures, including Condé, Ba, Touré, and Boubacar Biro Diallo (then president of the assembly), joined the coalition. The FRAD led the opposition to the presidential election in 2003 and organized a succession of protests and demonstrations against the regime. In response, most of the FRAD's leadership figures, including Condé, Ba, and Touré, have been arrested for brief periods. In 2005 FRAD leaders called on the president to resign to allow for transition to a government of national unity.

Leaders: Mamadou BA (President), Alpha CONDÉ (RPG), Sidya TOURÉ (UFR), Jean-Marie DORÉ (UPG).

Rally of the Guinean People (*Rassemblement Populaire Guinéen*—RPG). In early 1991 Alpha Condé received an enthusiastic welcome from RPG members upon his return from exile. Subsequently, on May 19, government troops violently disrupted the party's attempt to hold an inaugural meeting.

In February 1993 the RPG and the UNR were accused of inciting antigovernment violence in rural communities, and Condé subsequently appealed unsuccessfully for a joint opposition candidate in the December presidential poll, at which he was runner-up with a 19.55 vote share.

In 1994 the RPG adopted a new platform urging "peace, justice, and solidarity," and in April, Condé reiterated the party's desire "to prepare for parliamentary elections in a transparent manner." Nonetheless, RPG activists subsequently accused the government of attempting to assassinate their leader, and in September 1995 at least one person was killed when RPG militants clashed with government security forces in Nzérekoré.

On November 2, 1996, already-confrontational relations between the RPG and the government reached their nadir when government security forces allegedly organized an attack on a motorcade carrying Condé, and an RPG building was attacked by arsonists. Furthermore, on November 19 two prominent RPG leaders, Saliou CISSÉ and Keita BENTOUBA, were arrested. RPG leaders derided the arrests, reportedly describing them as a "dangerous, resounding slip-up," and in late December, Codem officials cited the November incidents as catalysts for their decision to launch a militia.

The Codem's legislative boycott in early 1998 was prompted in part by the ransacking of the RPG's headquarters and the arrest of two RPG parliamentarians. Thereafter, in early December, Alpha Condé returned from self-imposed exile to campaign for the presidency. Despite the large turnouts that greeted his public appearances, the RPG candidate finished a distant third in the polling. Furthermore, on December 15 Condé was arrested as he prepared to enter Côte d'Ivoire, and a number of RPG activists were jailed for their alleged participation in the violent unrest that followed the release of the polling results. Having garnered substantial regional and global interest, the trial of Condé and more than 40 codefendants concluded in September 2000 with Condé being found guilty of sedition. His prison sentence was cut short by a presidential pardon in May 2001. Condé returned to Conakry in 2005 after two years of self-imposed exile in Paris to help organize the party ahead of the December municipal elections (in which the RPG won only a handful of seats). The RPG backed the unions' demands in their 2006–2007 strikes and urged party members to participate in civil disobedience. Numerous party members reportedly were arrested during the protests. In May 2007 the RPG refused to participate in negotiations with the government and other political parties on preparations for the next legislative elections, but the party was planning to participate in the elections.

Following the 2008 coup, Condé called the members of the junta "patriots," but said he would never participate in a government that was not democratically elected.

Leaders: Alpha CONDÉ (Secretary General and 1998 presidential candidate), Ahmed CISSÉ, Ibrahima Kalil KEITA.

Union for the Progress of Guinea (*Union pour le Progrès de Guinée*—UPG). At the December 1993 balloting UPG secretary general Jean-Marie Doré secured less than 1 percent of the vote; nevertheless, Doré emerged as a prominent Codem spokesperson after the UPG secured 2 seats at the 1995 assembly balloting.

At presidential balloting in December 1998 Doré secured just 1.73 percent of the vote. The UPG left Codem in May 1996. Although the UPG took part in the 2002 legislative elections and won three seats, it boycotted the 2003 presidential elections. Doré is one of the main spokespersons for the FRAD. In 2006 the UPG called for President Conté's resignation due to his medical problems.

In 2008 the UPG participated in unity talks with the new prime minister, Ahmed Tidiane Souaré, and accepted a post in the cabinet. Following the 2008 coup, Doré called for a peaceful transition.

Leader: Jean-Marie DORÉ (Secretary General and 1998 presidential candidate).

Union of Democratic Forces of Guinea (*Union des Forces Démocratiques de Guinée*—UFDG). The UFDG was one of the first parties applying for legal status in 1991. Its leader, Amadou Bâ Oury, was arrested on October 27, 1992, for alleged involvement in an attempted assassination of President Conté 11 days earlier, but he was released shortly thereafter in apparent acknowledgment by authorities that false testimony had been given against him.

In May 1996 the Union resurfaced as the leading opponent to the National Assembly's adoption of a law that rehabilitated former president Sékou Touré, calling it a "trivialization" of Touré's crimes. After he left the UPR, Mamadou Ba joined the UFDG and was elected president in October 2002. In 2005, Ba distanced himself from some FRAD members and expressed support for Prime Minister Diallo.

In 2007 Ba backed the choice of Kouyaté for prime minister, along with the unions.

Following former prime minister Diallo's return to Guinea in April 2007, it was reported that Ba had taken over leadership of the party.

In 2008 the party received one post in the government named by Prime Minister Souaré. Following the military coup in December, Diallo's home was raided by soldiers who accused him of providing arms for a plot against the junta. Prime Minister Kabiné Komara met with Diallo the next day to smooth over the incident.

Leaders: Mamadou BA, Cellou DIALLO.

Union of Republican Forces (*Union des Forces Republicains*—UFR). A small grouping formed in 1992, the UFR elected former prime minister Sidya Touré as its president in May 2000. The UFR subsequently was reported to have filed a suit against the government for having prevented its candidates from contesting the June municipal balloting. In 2004 Touré was cleared of charges accusing him of plotting to overthrow the government.

The UFR supported the unions' strikes in 2006–2007.

In 2009 the junta named Touré to a committee formed to review mining agreements as part of the junta's crackdown on corruption.

Leaders: Sidya TOURÉ (President), Bakary ZOUMANIGUI (Secretary General).

The FRAD also includes three minor parties: the **African Democratic Party** (*Parti Démocratique Africain*—PDA), led by Marcel CROS; the **Djama Party** (*Parti Djama*), a moderate Islamist party led by Mohamed Mansour KABA; and the **Union of Democratic Forces** (*Union des Forces Démocratiques*—UFD), led by Mamadou Ba, following the death of Alfa Ibrahim SOW in 2005.

People's Party of Guinea (*Parti Guinéen du Peuple*—PGP). The PGP is an anti-Conté socialist party. At presidential balloting in December 1998 the PGP's candidate, Charles Pascal Tolno, received less than 1 percent of the vote. In 2003 Tolno was rejected as a presidential candidate by the Supreme Court. Jean-Marie Doré, now of the UPG, formerly was affiliated with the PGP.

In 2009 Tolno was alleged to be a drug trafficker during an investigation by the junta into other former government officials and the son of the late President Conté, also accused of drug trafficking.

Leader: Charles Pascal TOLNO (1998 presidential candidate).

Rebel Groups:

In September 2000 the **Guinea Liberation Movement** (*Mouvement pour la Libération de Guinée*—MLG), suspected of working closely with Sierra Leone's **Revolutionary United Front** (RUF, see under Sierra Leone), reportedly infiltrated Guinean territory and engaged in fighting with the government forces. Another rebel group, the **Rally for Democratic Forces of Guinea** (*Rassemblement des Forces Démocratiques de Guinée*—RFDG), claimed responsibility for an attack on a town on the Liberian border.

In August 2001, Nfaly KABA, the leader of the **Union of the Forces for a New Guinea** (*Union des Forces pour une Nouvelle Guinée*—UFNG), vowed war on Guinea if President Conté did not step down. The UFNG's armed wing was reportedly led by former Maj. Gbagbo ZOUMANIGUI, who was involved in the uprising against the president in 1996. In September a new exile opposition movement was formed in Bamako, Mali, under the leadership of Sheikh Mohamed KABA. The movement reportedly adopted the rubric of the **National Alliance of Democratic Patriots** (*Alliance Nationale des Patriotes Démocratiques*—ANPD).

LEGISLATURE

The 210-member People's National Assembly (*Assemblée Nationale Populaire*), elected from a single PDG list for a seven-year term on January 27, 1980, was dissolved in April 1984. Balloting for a successor body, originally scheduled for November 1992, was rescheduled in April 1993 for the last quarter of the year but did not in fact occur until June 11, 1995.

The assembly was dissolved following the military coup of December 24, 2008.

National Assembly (*Assemblée Nationale*). The current assembly is a 114-member body with a five-year mandate. One-third of its deputies are elected by majority vote in single-member districts, two-thirds on a national list vote with proportional representation.

At legislative balloting on June 30, 2002, the Party of Unity and Progress won 85 seats; the Union for Progress and Renewal, 20; the Union for the Progress of Guinea, 3; the Democratic Party of Guinea–African Democratic Rally, 3; the National Alliance for Progress, 2; and the Union for National Progress–Party of Unity and Development, 1. Most major opposition parties boycotted the elections.

President: Aboubacar SOMPARÉ.

CABINET

[as of October 1, 2009] *(See headnote.)*

President	Capt. Moussa Dadis Camara
Prime Minister	Kabiné Komara
Ministers	
Agriculture and Livestock	Abdourahmane Sano
Audits, Transparency, and Good Governance	Joseph Kandouno
Cooperation and African Integration	Abdoul Aziz Bah
Decentralization and Local Development	Naby Diakité
Defense	Gen. Sékouba Konaté
Economy and Finance	Capt. Mamadou Sandé
Environment and Sustainable Development	Papa Koly Kourouma
Fisheries and Aquaculture	Raymond Ounouted
Foreign Affairs and Guineans Abroad	Alexandre Cécé Loua
Health and Public Hygiene	Col. Abdoulaye Cherif Diaby
Higher Education and Scientific Research	Alpha Kabiné Camara
Information and Culture	Justin Morel Jr.
Justice and Keeper of the Seals	Cmdr. Siba Loalamou
Labor, Administrative Reform, and Civil Service	Alpha Diallo
Mines and Energy	Mamoudou Thiam
Planning and Promotion of the Private Sector	Mamadouba Max Bangoura
Presidential Secretary-General	Cmdr. Kélétigui Faro
Presidential Security	Claude Pivi
Pre-University, Technical, Professional, and Civic Education	Kaba Rougui Barry [f]
Promotion of Women and Children	Makoura Sylla [f]
Secretary General in charge of Special Services and the Fight Against Narcotics and Banditry	Capt. Moussa Tiégboro Camara
Secretary General in charge of Public Works and National Reconstruction	Mamadi Kallo
Security and Civil Protection	Gen. Mamadou Ba Toto Camara
State Control	Al Hassan Onipogui
Telecommunications and Information Technology	Col. Mathurin Bangoura
Territorial Administration and Political Affairs	Frédéric Kolié
Territorial Development	Boubacar Barry
Tourism	Leonie Koulibaly [f]
Trade and Industries	Col. Mamadou Korka Diallo
Transport	Mamadi Kaba
Youth and Sports	Col. Fodéba Touré

[f] = female

COMMUNICATIONS

All mass media are owned or controlled by the government. The government in 1992 introduced a National Communication Council (*Conseil Nationale de la Communication*—CNC) as a presidentially appointed regulatory body with the stated aim of "protecting the media from government and special interest encroachment and manipulation." However, the council was subsequently heavily criticized by human rights and media organizations for acting as a government tool to control and censor the media. Since the early 1990s numerous publications have been shut down permanently or temporarily, and journalists have been arrested and incarcerated. "Every year journalists are beaten up or treated as though they were gangsters," Reporters Without Borders stated in its 2006 annual report. During Guinea's 12-day state of emergency in February 2007, there was a "complete news blackout," according to Reporters Without Borders, including blocked Internet access. That same month two journalists attempting to report on aspects of major strikes were allegedly beaten by police in Conakry. In 2008 further violence against journalists occurred during nationwide strikes, and security forces blocked print publications and attacked private radio stations, according to the Committee to Protect Journalists.

Also in 2008 a newspaper editor was arrested after publishing a story that called for the dismissal of Prime Minister Ahmed Tidiane Souaré, according to the Media Foundation for West Africa. The same group reported in 2009 that a freelance cameraman was detained by a member of the military junta for allegedly "working against the interests of the regime."

Press. The press is subject to rigorous government censorship. The following have previously been published in Conakry: *Fonike,* government-owned daily; *Horoya* (Liberty, 20,000), weekly, in French and local languages; *Journal Officiel de Guinée,* fortnightly government organ; and *Le Travailleur de Guinée,* monthly organ of the National Confederation of Guinean Workers. However, in late 1999 a Guinean media observer reported that of 40 independent newspapers once in publication, only the following were still available: *L'Indépendant,* independent weekly; *L'Indépendant Plus,* weekly; *Le Lynx,* satirical weekly; *L'Oeil,* weekly; *La Lance; Le Globe*; and *Le Nouvel Observateur*. *Guinéenews* is an online newspaper. Other newspapers include *La Nouvelle Tribune*, *Le Diplomate*, *L'Enqueteur*, *L'Observateur*, and *Le Populaire*.

News agencies. The official news agency is *Agence Guinéenne de Presse* (AGP), which became operational in July 1986 as part of the UNESCO-supported West African News Agencies Development (WANAD) project. *Xinhua,* APN, and ITAR-TASS are represented in Conakry.

Broadcasting and computing. The government-operated *Radiodiffusion Télévision Guinéenne* operates eight radio transmitting stations, with broadcasts in French, English, Portuguese, Arabic, and local languages. A new radio station, Horizon FM, was approved in August 2008. Several other private radio stations include Radio Nostalgie Guinea, and Liberte FM, Soleil FM, and Familia FM. Television broadcasting was introduced in 1977. As of 2008 there were 9.2 Internet users per 1,000 inhabitants.

INTERGOVERNMENTAL REPRESENTATION

Ambassador to the U.S.: Mory Karamoko KABA.

U.S. Ambassador to Guinea: Patricia Newton MOLLER.

Permanent Representative to the UN: Alpha Ibrahima SOW.

IGO Memberships (Non-UN): AfDB, AU, BADEA, ECOWAS, IDB, Interpol, IOM, MRU, NAM, OIC, OIF, WCO, WTO.

GUINEA-BISSAU

Republic of Guinea-Bissau
República da Guiné-Bissau

Note: Malam Bacai SANHÁ (African Party for the Independence of Guinea and Cape Verde) was elected president in runoff balloting July 26, 2009, with 63.5 percent of the vote. He was sworn in for a five-year term on September 8.

Political Status: Achieved independence from Portugal on September 10, 1974; under rule of Revolutionary Council following coup of November 14, 1980; new constitution of May 16, 1984, amended on May 4, 1991; military control imposed following coup of May 8, 1999; present constitution promulgated July 7, 1999, under direction of military junta.

Area: 13,948 sq. mi. (36,125 sq. km.).

Population: 983,367 (1991C); 1,745,000 (2008E).

Major Urban Center (2005E): BISSAU (247,000).

Official Language: Portuguese (several local languages are also spoken).

Monetary Unit: CFA Franc (official rate December 1, 2009: 434.59 francs = $1US). The CFA franc, previously pegged to the French franc, is now permanently pegged to the euro at 655.957 CFA francs = 1 euro.

Interim President: Raimundo PEREIRA (African Party for the Independence of Guinea and Cape Verde); acceded on March 3, 2009, in accordance with the constitution to succeed João Bernardo VIEIRA (independent), who was assassinated on March 2.

Prime Minister: Carlos GOMES Júnior (African Party for the Independence of Guinea and Cape Verde); appointed by President Vieira on December 25, 2008, to succeed Carlos CORREIA (African Party for the Independence of Guinea and Cape Verde); sworn in with new government on January 7, 2009.

THE COUNTRY

Situated on the west coast of Africa between Senegal on the north and Guinea on the south, the Republic of Guinea-Bissau also includes the Bijagóz Archipelago and the island of Bolama. The population is primarily of African descent (principal tribes include the Balante, Fulani, Mandyako, and Malinké), but there are smaller groups of mulattoes, Portuguese, and Lebanese. The majority continues to follow traditional religious beliefs; however, there is a significant Muslim population and a small Christian minority.

Agriculture employs the vast majority of the population, with peanuts typically producing two-thirds of export earnings. Other important exports are palm products, fish, and cattle, while such crops as cotton, sugar, and tobacco have been introduced in an effort to diversify the country's output; industry is dominated by state enterprises and mixed ventures. The chief mineral resource may be petroleum (the extent of on- and offshore reserves is uncertain, although a number of Western oil companies have signed exploration contracts with the government). Economic development has been hindered by insufficient capital, skilled labor, and transport facilities. Consequently, the country remains one of the poorest in the world.

On May 2, 1997, Guinea-Bissau, citing its desire to "improve its regional trade position," joined the West African Monetary Union (*Union Monetaire Ouest-Africaine*—UMOA), thus abandoning the Guinea peso in favor of the CFA franc. In addition, the government launched comprehensive tax and civil service reform programs. After three years of steady annual increases (1995–1997), GDP declined in real terms by 21 percent in 1998 under the influence of civil war. Positive GDP growth (nearly 8 percent) returned in 1999 while annual inflation dropped to 2.1 compared to 8 percent in 1998. The International Monetary Fund (IMF) approved an emergency post-conflict assistance loan in January 2000 and a three-year debt-reduction arrangement the following December. However, real GDP growth of only 0.2 percent was registered in 2001, and the IMF and other economic observers criticized the government for its handling of the economy.

In 2001 the IMF suspended debt relief to Guinea-Bissau because of the government's unwillingness to enact agreed-upon reforms. Conflict within the country led to a GDP decline of 7 percent in 2002; there was no measurable GDP growth in 2003. That year, donor states suspended aid after the government failed to demobilize ex-soldiers and continue economic restructuring. Following the coup of September 2003 and subsequent legislative elections, donors announced a limited resumption of aid in 2004, including $13 million from the World Bank.

Real GDP growth of about 2 percent was recorded for 2004, with the IMF describing the country's economic situation as "very difficult" following years of political instability, increasing poverty, and little new investment. However, economic activity for 2005-2006 was strong, averaging 3.8 percent annually, owing in part to government efforts toward what the IMF termed "long-overdue" civil service reforms. At the end of the year, international donors pledged $262 million in aid, about half of Guinea-Bissau's goal, based on its sizable debt. Poor economic performance resulted in deterioration of GDP growth to 2.7 percent in 2007, largely due to civil service arrears, according to the IMF. However, the new government installed in April (see Current issues, below) instituted an emergency financial plan, resulting in a significant improvement. Annual GDP growth averaged 3.4 percent in 2008-2009, primarily because of a recovery in the agriculture sector and significant increases in donor revenue, including from the World Bank and the IMF. Similar annual economic growth was forecast for 2010 despite political instability and a cholera outbreak that reportedly affected more than 14,000 people.

GOVERNMENT AND POLITICS

Political background. First discovered by the Portuguese mariner Nuno Tristão in 1446, the territory long known as Portuguese Guinea did not receive a final delimitation of its borders until 1905. Initially, the country was plundered by slave traders, and consequent hostility among the indigenous peoples resulted in uprisings in the early twentieth century. The area was eventually pacified by military means, and in 1952 it was formally designated as an Overseas Province of Portugal.

In 1956 a group of dissatisfied Cape Verdeans under the joint leadership of Amílcar CABRAL, Luís de Almeida CABRAL, Aristides PEREIRA, and Rafael BARBOSA formed the African Party for the Independence of Guinea and Cape Verde (*Partido Africano da Independência da Guiné e Cabo Verde*—PAIGC). Failing to win concessions from the Portuguese, the PAIGC, with assistance from Warsaw Pact nations, initiated an armed struggle in 1963, and by the early 1970s the PAIGC claimed to control two-thirds of the mainland territory. On January 20, 1973, Amílcar Cabral was assassinated in Conakry, Guinea, allegedly by PAIGC dissidents but with the apparent complicity of the Portuguese military. Six months later, Aristides Pereira and Cabral's brother, Luís, were confirmed as party leaders by a PAIGC congress.

A government was formally organized and independence declared on September 23 and 24, 1973. The Portuguese authorities claimed the move was a "propaganda stunt," but the coup in Portugal in April 1974 led to an informal cease-fire and negotiations with the rebel leaders. Although the talks failed to resolve the status of the Cape Verde Islands, an agreement signed August 26, 1974, provided for the independence of Guinea-Bissau as of September 10, 1974, and the removal of all Portuguese troops by October 31.

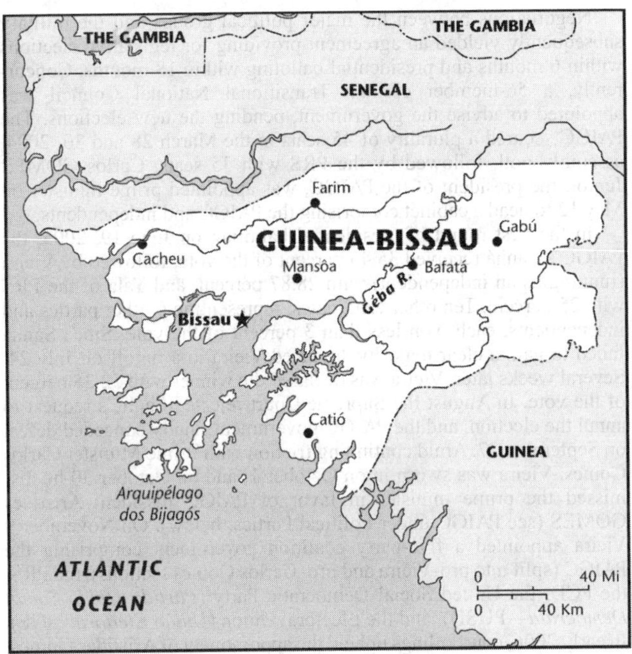

In the first balloting since independence, 15 regional councils were elected during December 1976 and January 1977, the councils in turn selecting delegates to a second National People's Assembly, which convened in March 1977; Cabral was reelected president of the republic and of the 15-member Council of State, while (then) Maj. João Bernardo VIEIRA was designated vice president of the republic and reconfirmed as president of the assembly. Vieira became principal commissioner (prime minister) on September 28, 1978, succeeding Maj. Francisco MENDES, who died on July 7.

The principal political issue of the late 1970s was a projected unification of Cape Verde with Guinea-Bissau, many mainland leaders—including President Cabral and other high officials of the binational PAIGC—being Cape Verdean *mestiços.* On November 10, 1980, an extraordinary session of the National People's Assembly adopted a new constitution that many black Guineans construed as institutionalizing domination by islanders; four days later a coup led by Vieira, a native Guinean, deposed the president. On November 19 the Council of State and the assembly were formally dissolved by a Revolutionary Council that designated Vieira as head of state, and, on the following day, the council announced a provisional cabinet, all but one of whose members had served in the previous administration. Shortly thereafter, President Vieira identified the basic reasons for Cabral's ouster as the country's social and economic difficulties, including severe food shortages; "progressive abandonment of the principle of democratic centralism"; and "corruption of the meaning of unity between Guinea-Bissau and Cape Verde."

At a PAIGC conference in November 1981 it was announced that presidential and legislative elections under a new constitution would be held in early 1982 and that the party would retain its existing name, despite the fact that in the wake of the coup its Cape Verdean wing had formally repudiated the goal of unification with the mainland. In May 1982 President Vieira instituted a purge of reputed left-wingers within the government and the PAIGC. Furthermore, he named Vítor SAÚDE Maria as prime minister, a post that had been vacant since the 1980 takeover. Continued instability persisted for the next two years, culminating in the ouster of Saúde Maria on March 8, 1984, for alleged antistate activity. The return to constitutional rule followed on March 31 with the election of eight regional councils, which, in turn, chose 150 deputies to a new National People's Assembly. The assembly convened on May 14 and two days later approved a new basic law that combined the offices of head of state and chief of government into the presidency of a revived Council of State, to which Vieira was unanimously elected.

A further attempt to overthrow the Vieira regime was reported on November 7, 1985, when security forces arrested some 50 individuals, including the first vice president, Col. Paulo CORREIA, and a number of other prominent military and civilian officials, who were, apparently, opposed to economic austerity moves and upset by a military anticorruption drive. Despite international appeals for clemency, Correia and 5 of his associates were executed in July 1986.

A new National Assembly was designated on June 15, 1989, by and from the regional councils, for which direct single-party balloting had been conducted on June 1. On June 19 General Vieira was reelected to a second term as president of the Council of State, which two days later named its former vice president, Col. Iafai CAMARA, as first vice president, and its former secretary, Dr. Vasco CABRAL, as second vice president. Both of the vice presidencies were abandoned in a government restructuring of December 27, 1991, that marked another restoration of the post of prime minister, to which former agriculture minister Carlos CORREIA was appointed.

In July 1992 the PAIGC agreed to the formation of a national commission with responsibility for facilitating the country's first multiparty balloting. However, the elections, originally scheduled for November and December, were rescheduled in October for March 1993, at which time they were again postponed. In July the Council of State set March 27, 1994, as the new date for simultaneous presidential and legislative balloting, with a further postponement in February 1994 to late May. At the poll that was finally held on July 3, Vieira, who had resigned his commission to qualify as a candidate under a 1991 constitutional revision, was credited with winning 46 percent of valid presidential votes, as contrasted with 21.9 percent for runner-up Kumba YALA of the opposition Social Renewal Party (*Partido para a Renovação Social*—PRS); concurrently, the ruling PAIGC was awarded 64 of 100 parliamentary seats. Vieira went on to secure reelection by defeating Yala, who had been accorded unanimous opposition endorsement, in a runoff on August 7.

On October 25, 1994, Vieira named a senior PAIGC official, Manuel Saturnino da COSTA, to succeed Correia as prime minister. Observers attributed the delay between the election and Costa's appointment to a deep division in the ruling party between its founding members, including Costa, and their younger colleagues, who desired more "pragmatic" economic policy-making. On November 11 Costa named a new government, which included members of both PAIGC tendencies.

On May 27, 1997, President Vieira dismissed Costa in the midst of what the president described as a "serious political crisis." Costa's ouster came as government troops were deployed to quell riots sparked by state workers who were angered at poor working conditions and the government's failure to pay salary arrears. On June 5 Vieira reappointed Carlos Correia as prime minister, and Correia formed a new government the following day. However, Correia's appointment was immediately contested by opposition legislators, who asserted that the president was constitutionally required to consult with the assembly prior to naming a prime minister. Subsequently, a virtual legislative deadlock ensued as opposition legislators refused to consider the government's initiatives while their legal challenge was being considered by the courts. On October 7 the Supreme Court ruled that the administration had erred, and on October 11 the president dismissed Correia; however, following negotiations with legislative leaders, on October 13 Vieira reappointed Correia.

In January 1998 President Vieira dismissed his military chief of staff, Gen. Ansumane MANE, charging him with "dereliction of duty" for allegedly failing to stem the illegal transfer of arms from Guinea-Bissau to Senegalese rebels. Subsequently, in early June, troops directed by General Mane overran the national airport and an army base in Bra as part of a declared effort to remove Vieira from power. Facing minimal resistance from a small contingent of pro-presidential forces, the rebels quickly secured control of a majority of the country. However, bolstered by Senegalese and Guinean troops, Vieira's loyalists fought the rebels to a standstill in Bissau. On August 26 regional mediators in Cape Verde brokered a cease-fire agreement that held until October, when fierce fighting was once again reported. In November the two sides signed a second cease-fire accord in Abuja, Nigeria. The accord included provisions for presidential and legislative balloting in March 1999, as well as the formation of a unity government comprising representatives selected by the president as well as the rebels. In addition, the agreement called for the replacement of the Senegalese and Guinean troops with a regional peacekeeping force supplied by the Economic Community of West African States (ECOWAS). On December 3 Vieira, under strong pressure from the military rebels, named Francisco FADUL, General Mane's aide-de-camp, to replace Correia as prime minister.

In early January 1999 the national balloting envisioned for March was indefinitely postponed as contentious debate continued in Bissau over implementation of the Abuja accord. Fierce fighting was reported in the capital in early February; however, a new cease-fire agreement (based on the Abuja document) was reached on February 4, and ECOWAS troops began arriving en masse soon thereafter. On February 20 Fadul and his nine-member cabinet were sworn in.

Amid reports that troops loyal to the president were seeking to rearm, fresh fighting erupted on May 6, 1999, and the following day General Mane claimed that his forces had overthrown Vieira, who agreed to the unconditional surrender of the government on May 10. (Vieira left the country in June.) On May 14 Mane named the president of the assembly, Malan Bacai SANHÁ, interim president; furthermore, Mane announced that election preparations could continue as scheduled and that he would not be a presidential candidate. In early July the military junta promulgated a new constitution (see Constitution and government, below).

In the first round of presidential balloting on November 28–29, 1999, the PRS's Kumba Yala led a field of 11 presidential aspirants with 34.81 percent of the vote, while interim president Sanhá finished second with 23.34 percent. Meanwhile, at concurrent legislative polling the PRS led a crowded field with 38 seats while the PAIGC's representation fell to 24, which was 4 less than the second-place Guinea-Bissau Resistance–Bah Fatah Movement (*Resistência da Guiné-Bissau–Movimento Bah-Fatah*—RGB-MB).

Having failed to garner the vote share necessary to stave off a second round of balloting, Yala faced off against Sanhá on January 16, 2000. Yala won easily, capturing 72 percent of the vote, and on January 24 he named a PRS leader, Caetano NTCHAMA, prime minister. On February 19 Ntchama was sworn in as the head of a government that included representatives from four political parties and a number of independents, but no members of the PAIGC. However, Ntchama was buffeted by tensions between the PRS and the RGB-MB; in September the RGB-MB ministers were dismissed, but they were reinstated shortly thereafter. In the meantime, conflict between President Yala and the former head of the junta, Ansumane Mane, resurfaced. In November, uneasy with some recent military appointments, Mane announced that he had "reinstated" himself as the chief of staff, and clashes were reported between a few troops following Mane and the majority of the army, which remained loyal to Yala. Some opposition figures, most prominently from the PAIGC, the Union for Change (*União para a Mudança*—UM), and the Democratic Alliance (*Aliança Democrática*—AD), were arrested for allegedly supporting Mane. On November 30, Mane was killed by government troops surrounding his enclave in Quinhamel, north of Bissau.

In January 2001 the RGB-MB left the governing coalition in reaction to an earlier reshuffle the party claimed unfairly favored the PRS. In March, Yala dismissed Ntchama, who was reportedly having medical problems, and named an independent, Faustino Fadut IMBALI, as the new prime minister. Imbali had run in the 1999 presidential elections and had supported Yala in the second round in January 2000. He had also served in Ntchama's government as the deputy prime minister. Imbali formed a government including the PRS, the RGB-MB, the PAIGC, the Guinean Civic Forum (*Foro Civico da Guiné*—FCG), the Social Democratic Party (*Partido Social Democrata*—PSD), the Democratic Convergence Party (*Partido da Convergência Democrática*—PCD), and independents. The PAIGC and the RGB-MB, however, reportedly continued their critical stance toward Yala's presidency and some of Imbali's policies. Yala dismissed Imbali on December 7, 2001, and appointed Alamara NHASSE of the PRS as the new prime minister the following day. Nhasse's new government, formed on December 12, included members from the PRS and the PCD as well as independents.

In the wake of increasing tension between President Yala and Prime Minister Nhasse concerning ministerial and judicial appointments, Yala dismissed Nhasse on November 15, 2002. On November 16 Yala appointed Mario PIRES of the PRS to head a temporary caretaker government. Yala also dissolved the assembly and announced that new legislative elections would be held in early 2003. However, that balloting was postponed several times as the government was perceived as becoming increasingly authoritarian (see Current issues, below).

The military deposed President Yala on September 14, 2003, in a takeover that appeared to have broad domestic support. The army's chief of staff, Gen. Verissimo Correia SEABRA, proclaimed himself interim president and named a military council to conduct governmental affairs pending the appointment of a new civilian government. (Yala was permitted to "resign" as of September 17.) On September 28, Henrique ROSA, a prominent businessman with no formal political ties, was appointed interim president, while Antonio Artur SANHÁ of the PRS was designated head of a caretaker cabinet.

Negotiations between the major political groups and the military subsequently yielded an agreement providing for legislative elections within 6 months and presidential balloting within 18 months. Concurrently, a 56-member civilian Transitional National Council was appointed to advise the government, pending the new elections. The PAIGC secured a plurality of 45 seats in the March 28 and 30, 2004, assembly poll, followed by the PRS with 35 seats. Carlos GOMES Júnior, the president of the PAIGC, was appointed prime minister on May 12 to head a cabinet comprising the PAIGC and independents.

In the first round of presidential balloting on June 19, 2005, the PAIGC's Sanhá received 35.45 percent of the vote, followed by Vieira (running as an independent) with 28.87 percent, and Yala of the PRS with 25 percent. Ten other candidates, representing 6 other parties and independents, each won less than 3 percent of the vote. Since Sanhá failed to gain a clear majority, he faced Vieira in a runoff on July 24. Several weeks later, Vieira was declared the winner with 52.35 percent of the vote. In August the Supreme Court rejected Sanhá's request to annul the election, and the PAIGC government finally conceded defeat on September 27. Amid continuing friction with Prime Minister Carlos Gomes, Vieira was sworn in on October 1, and on October 30 he dismissed the prime minister in favor of PAIGC dissident Aristides GOMES (see PAIGC under Political Parties, below). On November 9 Vieira appointed a five-party coalition government comprising the PAIGC (split into pro-Vieira and pro–Carlos Gomes factions), the PRS, the PCD, the United Social Democratic Party (*Partido Unido Social Democrata*—PUSD), and the Electoral Union (*União Eleitoral*—UE). In early 2006, court rulings upheld the appointment of Aristides Gomes, striking down the PAIGC's argument that it was unconstitutional since Gomes had been suspended from the party (for his support of Vieira) and that the president was obligated to appoint a majority-party member to head the government.

Following a parliamentary no-confidence vote on March 19, 2007, Prime Minister Aristides Gomes announced his resignation on March 29. On April 10 the president appointed a new prime minister, Martinho Ndafa CABI. On April 17 Cabi named a new government comprising members of the PAIGC, the PRS, and the PUSD (and only one minister from the previous government). In what was described as a cost-saving measure, President Vieira announced in July that legislative elections would be postponed from March 2008 to coincide with presidential polling in 2009. (However, in December he revised the date for legislative elections to November 2008.) Following the withdrawal of the PAIGC, again in an opposition stance, from the unity government on July 25, President Vieira dismissed Prime Minister Cabi on August 5, replacing him with former prime minister Carlos Correia. A new government was formed on August 9, dominated by PAIGC supporters of the president but also including members of the PRS, the United Popular Alliance (*Aliança Popular Unida*—APU), and the Republican Party for Independence and Development (*Partido Republicano para a Independência e o Desenvolvimento*—PRID), a PAIGC breakaway party led by Aristides Gomes.

In the parliamentary elections on November 16, 2008, the PAIGC won an overwhelming majority of 67 seats, followed by the PRS with 28, and the PRID with 3. The PRS challenged the results, claiming electoral fraud, but the Supreme Court ultimately upheld the outcome, with the official results announced on November 21. President Vieira survived a coup attempt two days later, leading to the arrest of a nephew of former president Yala (see Current issues, below). On December 25, President Vieira appointed PAIGC leader Carlos Gomes as prime minister. He was installed along with a new, all-PAIGC government on January 7, 2009. Following the assassination of President Vieira on March 2, assembly speaker Raimundo PEREIRA became interim president in accordance with the constitution, pending presidential elections scheduled for June 28. (*See headnote.*)

Constitution and government. The constitution of May 1984 gave the PAIGC the right to define "the bases of state policy in all fields"; for legislative purposes it reestablished the National People's Assembly, members of which were to be designated by eight regional councils. The assembly was, in turn, empowered to elect a 15-member Council of State, whose president was to serve as head of state and commander in chief of the armed forces.

In early 1989 a six-member National Commission, headed by Fidélis Cabral DALMADA, was established by the PAIGC Central Committee to revise the constitution in accordance with recent economic reform and structural adjustment policies. Thereafter, in April 1990, President Vieira promised "freer and more democratic elections," and in August he characterized the democracy movement as "irreversible."

On January 9, 1991, he formally committed himself to political pluralism in a speech that was promptly endorsed by the PAIGC. On May 4 the assembly approved a constitutional amendment voiding the republic's "revolutionary" character and stripping the PAIGC of its status as the "leading force in society." Both president and legislators were henceforth to be popularly elected for five-year terms. Four days later a framework law on political parties won legislative approval, with numerous opposition groups subsequently being recognized in preparation for the country's first contested elections (originally scheduled for late 1992, but not held until mid-1994).

In July 1999 the military junta led by Gen. Ansumane Mane discarded the 1991 basic law in favor of a new constitution that included provisions for presidential term limits (two five-year terms), the abolition of the death penalty, and the establishment of strict residency requirements for government officeholders. In November the junta drafted a new document, a so-called *Magna Carta*, reportedly styled after the basic law imposed in Portugal following its 1974 military coup; however, General Mane withdrew the controversial draft law (which provided for ten years of military rule) following an outcry from Bissau's political leaders. Furthermore, the junta amended the article of the July document that excluded would-be presidential candidates whose parents were foreign-born. In October 2000 President Yala named a State Council to "advise him on decisions such as declaration of war and state of emergency." Some observers suggested that the establishment of the council substantively finalized the transition to civilian rule. (For details of governmental arrangements following the September 2003 coup, see Political background, above.)

Foreign relations. During the struggle for independence, Guinea-Bissau received economic and military assistance from many Communist countries, including the Soviet Union, Cuba, and China. A subsequent deterioration in relations with the USSR because of alleged encroachment upon the country's fishing grounds appeared to have been reversed in early 1978 with a promise of Soviet assistance in modernizing the country's fishing industry. In May 1982, on the other hand, President Vieira replaced two strongly pro-Soviet cabinet ministers with Western-trained "technocrats" and appealed for development aid from non-Communist sources.

In November 1980 Guinea was the first country to recognize Guinea-Bissau's Revolutionary Council; earlier disputes over offshore oil exploration rights had been defused by former Guinean President Sékou Touré's announcement that Guinea would cooperate with other African states in developing on- and offshore resources. Similar controversy with Senegal erupted in early 1984, involving questions about the legality of offshore borders drawn by the French and Portuguese governments before independence. In February 1985 the International Court of Justice (ICJ) offered a settlement of the Bissau-Conakry border question that was accepted by both governments, while in March a meeting between Vieira and Senegalese President Diouf resulted in assignment of the latter dispute to an ad hoc international tribunal. A decision by the tribunal on July 31, 1989, in favor of Senegal, was immediately rejected by Bissau in an appeal to the ICJ.

A meeting with President Pereira of Cape Verde in Mozambique in 1982 yielded an announcement that diplomatic relations would be restored. Despite "reconciliation," the unification sought by Cabral became more and more distant as island influence was purged from the mainland party, with no reference to eventual merger being mentioned in the 1984 Guinea-Bissau constitution. The last vestige of the PAIGC alliances, a joint shipping line, was liquidated on February 29, 1988; both countries cited the nonviolent action as a sign of their "political maturation."

A further border clash with Senegal occurred in April and May 1990, leaving 17 dead and drawing charges by Dakar that Bissau was harboring Casamance separatist guerrillas (see article on Senegal). Tensions eased, however, in the wake of a meeting in the border town of São Domingos on May 29 at which the two countries agreed to a mutual troop withdrawal and termination of aid to each other's insurgent movements. In April 1991 Vieira called for the Casamance rebels to lay down their arms and take advantage of Senegal's multiparty system. Subsequently, in May, Guinea-Bissau was the site of cease-fire talks between Dakar and Casamance representatives. However, in early February 1995 relations between Bissau and Dakar were again strained when Senegal bombed a Guinea-Bissau border village in retaliation for Bissau's alleged support of two recent Casamance rebel attacks against Senegalese military sites. Relations again eased on June 12, when a visit by Senegalese President Abdou Diouf produced a declaration to abandon border hostility and an agreement to share equally in offshore mineral and energy resources.

In early 1996 the Vieira administration agreed to ratify a 1993 maritime joint-exploration pact with Senegal, ignoring its domestic critics' charges that the agreement unfairly favored the neighboring state, and in June, Bissau and Dakar signed a security collaboration accord. (On the basis of such accords Senegal and Guinea dispatched troops to Guinea-Bissau in 1998 in an effort to quell the military uprising.)

In February 1999 the leaders of rebel forces in Guinea-Bissau claimed that French battleships had fired on their positions. Paris denied the charges. Following the military coup in May, ECOWAS peacekeeping forces departed, with both the junta and its regional sponsors agreeing that they were "redundant." On the other hand, a United Nations contingent arrived in Bissau in June in accordance with provisions in the February cease-fire. The UN officials were charged with organizing elections, and in March 2000 their mandate was extended. Among the myriad problems confronting international mediators was the need to smooth relations between Bissau and the Senegalese and Guinean governments, both of whom had sent troops in an ultimately futile attempt to reinforce the Vieira administration. Guinea-Bissau's relations with Senegal were further strained in April, following an attack by Casamance rebels, who had (according to Senegal) infiltrated from Guinea-Bissau's territory. In March 2002 the leader of one of the main rebel factions was arrested and deported to Senegal. The situation subsequently improved, and in September the border was reopened and a joint security commission was formed.

Although the international community initially condemned the overthrow of Yala, Guinea-Bissau's external relations were quickly repaired. Once Rosa assumed office, he made diplomatic visits to a number of neighboring states, and Portugal as well. International aid was resumed soon after the March 2004 elections and included pledges to provide the funds needed to pay the military and civil service until after the June 2005 presidential elections. In addition, the small UN mission charged with monitoring the border between Senegal and Guinea-Bissau had its mandate extended for one year. Conflict at the border reignited in early 2006 (see Current issues, below), with the Casamance rebel leader reportedly refusing to participate in peace talks. In early 2007 Senegalese refugees again fled to Guinea-Bissau following renewed violence in the Casamance region.

In 2008 Guinea-Bissau extradited five suspected al-Qaida members to Mauritania in connection with the killing of French tourists in Mauritania in December 2007. The killings raised concerns that Islamic extremists were broadening their scope of operations to include sub-Saharan West Africa. That same year the United States reopened a diplomatic office in Guinea-Bissau after an absence of 10 years, and the U.S. ambassador in Senegal, who oversees affairs in Guinea-Bissau, said a full embassy would soon be reinstated in the country. Following an attack on President Vieira's residence after the November elections, Senegal deployed troops to its shared border and made a plane available for the Guinea Bissau leader "to evacuate him and his family in case of absolute necessity."

China underscored its relations with Guinea Bissau in 2009 by pledging $48.5 million to help modernize Guinea Bissau's telecommunications network.

Current issues. Political instability has marked Guinea Bissau's recent history, continuing into mid-2002, with President Yala claiming he had survived a coup attempt in May that he attributed to "Gambian influence." Yala's dismissal of Prime Minister Nhasse and dissolution of the assembly in November initiated a period of intensified repression of dissent that included the arrest of a number of prominent opposition figures and the closure of private radio stations that had criticized the administration. Tensions intensified in 2003 when soldiers threatened to mutiny over payment arrears and schools were closed because teachers had not been paid. Consequently, the September 2003 coup elicited little criticism within the populace, particularly after it had become clear that the military intended a quick return to civilian government through new elections. Following the appointment on September 28 of Henrique Rosa as interim president, the administration reopened schools after the World Bank loaned money for teacher salaries.

Most international aid was restored after the May 2004 legislative elections were deemed free and fair by international observers. However, the new government of Prime Minister Carlos Gomes Júnior faced severe problems, including rivalry among heavily armed ethnic groups, reported continued discontent within some sections of the military, and depressed economic conditions. Complicating matters in March 2005 was Yala's announcement that he planned to run as the PRS candidate in the June presidential balloting, despite the fact that he had been "banned" from politics for five years after the 2003 coup. (In May 2005 Yala and Vieira were declared eligible to run after both had initially been barred.) Subsequently, "serious tension" was reported after Yala insisted that he was still president, based on a court ruling that his forced resignation after the coup was invalid. A few days later, Yala briefly occupied presidential headquarters before being removed by government troops. A huge demonstration in support of Yala took place before the June first-round balloting, followed by violent protests in the capital days after his defeat in which three people were killed and five injured in clashes with police. Hundreds of Yala's backers accused the government of vote-rigging and reportedly tried to overrun the National Electoral Commission. Ultimately, Yala supported Vieira in the two-way runoff against the PAIGC's Malam Bacai Sanhá in July, which was conducted fairly, according to international observers. Despite a court challenge by Sanhá, Vieira's victory, with 52 percent of the vote, was upheld. Amid growing friction with his prime minister, Vieira subsequently dismissed Carlos Gomes, replacing him with PAIGC dissident Aristides Gomes. The new coalition government was sworn in on November 10, though controversy continued to surround Vieira's choice of a prime minister (see PAIGC under Political Parties, below), with Vieira's party riven by factionalism. In April 2006 the PUSD, one of ten parties that had backed Vieira in his presidential bid, reportedly withdrew from the government, though the party ultimately rejoined the government.

Also in 2006, the army resumed its offensive against the Casamance rebels, resulting in some 12,000 civilians fleeing the border region, and prompting calls for a cease-fire by the UN. The UN appealed for $3.6 million to help those most vulnerable in northern Guinea-Bissau who were cut off from the rest of the country by landmines, leaving farmers unable to get to the cashew fields in time for the harvest.

Political tensions heightened in early 2007 when former prime minister Carlos Gomes sought refuge in UN offices in Bissau, in the wake of statements he had issued linking the president to the assassination of a former navy chief. The government subsequently lifted Gomes's parliamentary immunity. Riots broke out in the capital in protest of the officer's death, with at least one person killed and several injured. The government, which denied any involvement in the assassination, issued an arrest warrant for Gomes but later dropped it. However, observers pointed to these events and the divisions over Vieira's appointment in 2005 of Aristides Gomes as prime minister (replacing PAIGC favorite Carlos Gomes) as indicators of significant instability and unrest. UN Secretary General Ban Ki-Moon cited "persistent and bitter [political] divisions" that he said threatened to compromise the independence of the judiciary and the legislature in a "very fragile" economic context. Political upheaval culminated in March 2007, when the government lost a no-confidence vote in the assembly in the wake of a "stability pact" by the PAIGC, the PRS, and the PUSD urging a new "government of consensus." The three parties, which held a combined 97 assembly seats, subsequently forced the resignation of Aristides Gomes and used the threat of massive demonstrations to ensure that the president would negotiate with them on the selection of a new prime minister. On April 10 Vieira appointed Martinho Ndafa Cabi, a longtime PAIGC vice president and former cabinet member, a move supported by the three main political parties. Cabi, for his part, pledged to seek a "broad consensus" on political and economic issues and named a new government.

While Vieira's unity government headed into 2008 with international support, Guinea Bissau was nonetheless widely viewed as politically unstable, with the ever-increasing illegal drug trade playing a key role in the country's ongoing power struggles. Meanwhile, the government's postponement of the elections from March until November gained the backing of most of the political parties, following talks with Vieira. By July, however, the political situation had deteriorated significantly, when the PAIGC, again in an opposition stance, pulled out of the consensus government after the prime minister dismissed a number of PAIGC members from senior government posts. Days later the Supreme Court ruled that a law passed in April extending parliament's mandate was unconstitutional, prompting President Vieira to dissolve the assembly and dismiss Prime Minister Cabi. In August the president reappointed former prime minister Carlos Correia, whose new, caretaker government included a majority of Vieira loyalists, among them PAIGC dissidents, just months ahead of the parliamentary elections. Days later, the president suspended the navy commander, Rear Adm. José Americo Bubo NA TCHUTO, accusing him of plotting a coup (Na Tchuto had denied in years past allegations of drug trafficking). Na Tchuto escaped house arrest and fled by boat but was soon rearrested in Gambia. Meanwhile, growing concerns over cocaine trafficking from Latin America prompted observers to cite the "real risk" of Guinea Bissau becoming a narco state. Further, according to *Africa Report,* the country's "political and administrative structures are insufficient to guarantee control of its territory [and] assure minimum public services to counter-balance the army's dominance." The military had reportedly swelled to some 10,000 troops, mainly members of the Balanta tribe, in contrast to the much smaller Papel tribe of which Vieira was a member. Just days after the PAIGC's overwhelming victory in the November poll, in which PRS leader Yala had accused Vieira of being involved in drug trafficking, the president survived a coup attempt when renegade soldiers attacked his palace, killing one guard and wounding others. The president was subsequently assigned a 400-member militia for his protection. On November 25 a nephew of Yala was charged with being the mastermind behind the coup attempt.

Following the appointment in December of PAIGC leader Carlos Gomes as the new prime minister, and just days before a new government was installed in January 2009, the armed forces chief of staff, Gen. Baptista TAGMÉ Na Wai, was shot at by members of the president's militia, who later claimed the attack was accidental. The militia was subsequently disarmed. On March 1, Tagamé, a longtime critic of Vieira, was killed in a bomb explosion at armed forces headquarters in Bissau. News reports said the killing "bore the hallmarks of an attack by drug cartels." Tagamé was also a member of the rival Balante tribe that dominated the military. Political turmoil culminated in the early hours of March 2, when Vieira was killed by army troops while he was asleep in his palace. Analysts said the assassination was to avenge Tagamé's death and was likely also a tribal battle. In the immediate aftermath, the army denied that a coup had taken place, blaming a small group of soldiers instead. In a radio broadcast the same day, the army vowed to uphold "constitution order," allowing for the accession of the president of the national assembly, Raimundo Pereira. Though the constitution also called for new elections to be held within 60 days, presidential balloting was scheduled for June 28. The Community of Portuguese Language Countries (CPLP) immediately sent a diplomatic contingent to help maintain peace, and ECOWAS and other members of the international community called for calm. A state funeral for Vieira, 69, was held on March 10, but no foreign heads of state attended. A short-lived calm was shattered on June 5, when Territorial Minister Baciro DABO, a PAIGC ally of Vieira who was running as an independent in the upcoming presidential election, was killed at his home by military forces. Another Vieira ally, former defense minister Helder PROENÇA, was killed in a separate attack the same day, as was former prime minister Faustino Imbali (who had been severely beaten in April). Imbali, the presidential candidate of the Party for Development, Democracy, and Citizenship (PADEC), had publicly accused the military of corruption. Authorities said Dabo and Proença had been plotting a coup. The killings were immediately condemned by the international community, and the African Union (AU) urged that elections not be postponed. Meanwhile, one of the remaining presidential candidates, Pedro INFANDA of the Guinea-Bissau League for the Protection of Ecology (*Liga da Guiné-Bissau para Protecção Ecologia*—LIPE), withdrew, saying he feared for his life. (Infanda, a lawyer who had represented navy commander Na Tchuto, had been arrested by military officials in March and severely beaten.) Though questions had been raised about whether the presidential poll would proceed as scheduled, interim president Pereira said he had decided to keep the June 28 date after consulting with government and political party officials. Campaigning, which had been briefly suspended after the killings, resumed on June 11. (*See headnote.*)

POLITICAL PARTIES

On May 8, 1991, the National People's Assembly approved the formation of opposition parties, thereby formalizing events set in motion in April 1990. The principal requirements for registration are that each group present to the Supreme Tribunal of Justice a petition signed by 1,000 eligible voters, at least 50 of whom must reside in each of the country's regions and the district of Bissau. By early 1993 more than two dozen parties had been formed, most of which had been legalized.

Government Party:

African Party for the Independence of Guinea and Cape Verde (*Partido Africano da Independência da Guiné e Cabo Verde*—PAIGC).

Formed in 1956 by Amílcar Cabral and others, the PAIGC established external offices in Conakry, Guinea, in 1960 and began armed struggle against the Portuguese authorities in 1963. During its 28 years as the country's only lawful party, the PAIGC was formally committed to the principle of "democratic centralism." Its policymaking and administrative organs include a Central Committee (the Supreme Council of the Struggle), a National Council, a Permanent Committee, and a Secretariat.

Until the coup of November 1980 the party leadership was binational, with Aristides Pereira, president of Cape Verde, serving as secretary general and President Luis Cabral of Guinea-Bissau as deputy secretary. On January 19, 1981, the Cape Verdean branch decided to break with the mainland organization, proclaiming, on the following day, an autonomous African Party for the Independence of Cape Verde (PAICV).

In May 1990 General Vieira instructed the party to begin preparations for the introduction of political pluralism. Accordingly, the Central Committee in July proposed the adoption of "integral multipartyism." At its congress in November 1991 the PAIGC voted to widen intraparty democracy and restructure its executive apparatus by dropping the post of secretary general in favor of a party president and national secretary.

At the party's congress in May 1998, delegates reelected Vieira to the PAIGC presidency and approved the appointment of Paulo Medina to the newly created post of permanent secretary. Despite Vieira's positive account of the meeting, observers asserted that the PAIGC emerged from the congress further factionalized. Thereafter, it was unclear what effect the military uprising of June 1998 would have on the PAIGC, although the vehemently anti-Vieira stance of Francisco Fadul, a long-time party member who was sworn in as prime minister in February 1999, appeared to portend further cleavage.

In the wake of Vieira's removal from office, Manuel Saturnino da Costa was chosen on May 12, 1999, to assume the PAIGC party presidency, and Flavio Provenca was named interim secretary. The party held an extraordinary congress in Bissau September 3–9, with the stated goal of preparing for presidential and legislative polling. Delegates voted to expel Vieira, Carlos CORREIA, and a number of former ministers affiliated with Vieira, and the (then) defense minister and ally of the Mane junta, Francis Benante, was elected as the new PAIGC president.

The PAIGC won 24 seats in the 1999 legislative elections, and its candidate, interim president of the republic Malam Bacai SANHÁ, won 23.34 percent of the votes in the first round in November 1999 presidential elections. He lost in the second round in January 2000, with 28 percent of the vote.

The PAIGC assumed an opposition stance to the PRS-led government formed in February 2000. The party reportedly came under intense scrutiny after allegedly supporting Ansumane Mane's failed bid to reinstate himself as the chief of staff in November. Benante was subsequently arrested and then released for alleged possession of arms, as were other opposition figures. The PAIGC accepted a post in the cabinet announced in March 2001 but remained highly critical of some of the administration's policies. In May the PAIGC voted in the legislature to approve the government's program, but only after amnesty was granted to prisoners from the events of the previous November. The new government appointed in December reportedly did not include any PAIGC members. In 2004 the PAIGC became the largest party in the assembly, receiving 33.88 percent of the vote and 45 seats. Party leader Carlos Gomes became prime minister on May 12, 2004, and subsequently formed a government of PAIGC members and independents. Gomes declared that he would not seek the presidency in 2005 and would instead concentrate on his role as prime minister. Following the election of Vieira in July, friction intensified within the party between those who supported Vieira, including party vice president Aristides Gomes, and those who remained loyal to Carlos Gomes. In September, Aristides Gomes and several other dissident members were suspended, and a month later 14 of the party's 45 legislators resigned, declaring themselves independents. Aristides Gomes joined with some of those dissidents and others from various opposition groups to form the **Forum for the Convergence of Development** (FCD), reportedly in an attempt to create a new majority in the assembly. The continued dissension between Vieira and the Carlos Gomes supporters in the PAIGC resulted in a delay in Vieira's inauguration until October because the pro-Gomes faction refused to recognize his authority. The rift culminated in Vieira's dismissal of the prime minister on October 30, and his appointment on November 2 of Aristides Gomes as the new prime minister. For its part, the PAIGC postponed indefinitely its extraordinary congress scheduled for October, and in November named a new chair, Martinho Ndafa Cabi. Meanwhile, Carlos Gomes's faction of the party continued to contest the appointment of Aristides Gomes, claiming it was unconstitutional, but court rulings in 2006 upheld Vieira's action. The status of Aristides Gomes and his supporters in the PAIGC remained unclear throughout 2007.

The PAIGC, in a "stability pact" with the PRS and the PUSD, was instrumental in the change in government in 2007 through a no-confidence vote in parliament that culminated in the consensus choice of Prime Minister Cabi to replace Aristides Gomes, following negotiations with President Vieira.

In March 2008 Aristides Gomes started a new political party, (see PRID, below), with plans to participate in the legislative elections scheduled for later in the year.

Meanwhile, party veteran Saturnino da Costa, who was given a cabinet post in the government named by Gomes in January 2009, had sought the PAIGC presidential nod for the June 2009 election. However, in April the party named Malam Bacai Sanhá, a member of the Balanta ethnic group, as its presidential candidate over former prime minister Cabi.

Leaders: Martinho Ndafa CABI (Chair and Former Prime Minister), Carlos GOMES Júnior, (Prime Minister),Malam Bacai SANHÁ (2005 and 2009 presidential candidate), Manuel Saturnino da COSTA, Paulo MEDINA. (*See headnote.*)

Other Legislative Parties

Social Renewal Party (*Partido para a Renovação Social*—PRS). The PRS was formed in January 1992 by seven defectors from the FDS (below) led by Kumba Yala, who accused the parent group of secretly collaborating with the PAIGC. Yala was runner-up to Vieira in the 1994 presidential balloting, with the party winning 12 of 100 assembly seats. In November, Yala rejected an offer to join the Costa government. Meanwhile, the PRS reportedly teamed with the Union for Change (UM, below) and the Front of Struggle for the Liberation of Guinea (FLING, below) to form a voting bloc in the assembly.

On November 10, 1995, Yala told a Portuguese daily, *Jornal de Notícias*, that the PAIGC was bereft of both "international credibility" and the "confidence of the people." Calling for early elections, Yala warned that while the PRS was opposed to a civil war, its wide support within the military would allow it to take power in "five or ten minutes."

In January 1998 Yala announced that he would form a parallel government if elections (then scheduled for midyear) were postponed. Thereafter, the PRS joined with other opposition groups demanding Vieira's resignation in early 1999. The PRS won 38 seats in the 1999 legislative elections, and Yala won the presidency in January 2000 with 72 percent of the vote in the second round. In 2003 the party was rife with conflict between those who supported Yala and those who did not. This divide led party president Alamara Nhasse to resign his post and lead a group of defectors to form a new group, the National Reconciliation Party (see below).

In the March 2004 elections, the PRS came in second with 24.76 percent of the vote and 35 seats. After Yala's defeat in the June 2005 presidential election, at least three people were killed during a protest by his supporters, and Sanhá was briefly detained by police.

Rifts in the party resulted in a legal challenge to Yala's presidency in 2007, but a court ruling allowed him to retain his post. In November 2008 President Vieira accused Yala of being behind an attack on the palace, claiming the renegade soldiers involved were linked to the former president. The attack came shortly after the release of official results of the parliamentary elections, in which the PRS won 28 seats, a distant second to the PAIGC.

In 2009, while some in the party backed Baltazar Lopes FERNANDEZ as the party's candidate for president, Yala ultimately won the bid.

Leaders: Kumba YALA (Former President of the Republic and 2005 presidential candidate), Austino DACOSTA, Ibrahima Sori DJALÓ (Vice Chair), Alberto NAMBEIA, Caetano NTCHAMA (Former Prime Minister), Antonio Artur SANHÁ (Former Prime Minister and Secretary General).

Republican Party for Independence and Development (*Partido Republicano para a Independência e o Desenvolvimento*—PRID). PAIGC dissident Aristides Gomes, a Vieira supporter, formed the PRID in March 2008, in advance of the November parliamentary elections, and won one of the three legislative seats his new party captured. Following the assassination of Vieira in 2009, Gomes left the country but subsequently applied to be a presidential candidate in the June election. His bid was rejected by the Supreme Court, which ruled that he was out of the country during the mandated time for candidates to be in residence.

Leader: Aristides GOMES (President and former Prime Minister).

New Democracy Party (*Partido da Nova Democracia*—PND). Little is known about the PND, which emerged in 2008 and won one seat in the November parliamentary elections. It is led by Mamadu Djaló, formerly of the **Party of Renovation and Progress** (*Partido da Renovação e Progresso*—PRP). Djaló had promised that if his party won, he would build a mosque and two schools and help create jobs for youth.

Leader: Mamadu DJALÓ.

Democratic Alliance (*Aliança Democrática*—AD). The AD coalition, of which the PDC (below) was a core component, was credited with winning four seats (including one by the PCD's Victor Mandinga) in the 1999 legislative balloting. In the 2008 legislative elections, the AD was referenced as a party and credited with winning one seat.

Other Parties that Participated in the 2008 Legislative Elections

United Social Democratic Party (*Partido Unido Social Democrata*—PUSD). The PUSD was led by former prime minister Vítor Saúde Maria, who left the PAIGC in 1984 and was a member of the FDS before launching the present formation in June 1991.

In March 1993 Saúde Maria denounced PRD leader da Costa's detainment for alleged involvement in a coup attempt, accusing the government of launching an unprovoked opposition crackdown. Saúde Maria died in October 1999. His replacement as party president, Francisco José Fadul, was chosen at a party congress in late 2000. In the 2004 elections the PUSD became the third-largest parliamentary party with 16.1 percent of the vote and 17 seats. On April 5, 2006, it was reported that the PUSD had withdrawn from the government in a dispute regarding the justice minister, although it subsequently rejoined the government.

Following a dispute with the government for its refusal to dismiss a PUSD cabinet member whom Fadul accused of corruption, Fadul quit the party and started a new party, the PADEC (see below), in 2007. Collaterally, he claimed in a legal challenge that he was the PUSD president.

Social Democratic Party (*Partido Social Democrata*—PSD). Founded by dissident RGB-MB members, the PSD was legalized on August 21, 1995. It won three seats in the legislative elections in 1999 and backed the PRS's Kumba Yala in the second round of the presidential elections in January 2000. Although some PSD members had previously taken part in PRS-led coalition governments, the cabinet installed in December 2001 reportedly did not include any PSD members. In 2002 the party was part of the **Electoral Union** (*União Eleitoral*—UE), along with a few other small leftist and center-left parties. Party leader Joaquim Balde was the spokesman for the National Transition Council, following the coup in 2003.

Leaders: João Seco MANE (President), Joaquim BALDE (1999 presidential candidate), Gaspar FERNANDES (Secretary General).

Guinea-Bissau League for the Protection of Ecology (*Liga da Guiné-Bissau para Protecção Ecologia*—LIPE). The LIPE, also formerly referenced as the LGBPE, applied for legalization in July 1993. The league's president, Bubacar Rachid Djaló, ran in the first round of the presidential elections in November 1999 and backed the PRS's Kumba Yala in the second round in January 2000. Djaló was given a junior cabinet post in the PRS-led government in February but was not reappointed in the new government formed in March 2001.

In 2009 party member Pedro Infanda, who had planned to run as an independent, withdrew as a presidential candidate, stating that he feared for his life (see Current issues, above). Infanda, a lawyer who had represented José Americo Bubo Na Tchuto (see Current issues, above), had been arrested in March and allegedly beaten and tortured by military officials. He said his decision was made in the wake of the killing of another candidate, Territorial Minister Baciro Dabo, in June.

Leader: Bubacar Rachid DJALÓ (President and 1999 presidential candidate).

National Union for Democracy and Progress (*União Nacional para a Democracia e o Progresso*—UNDP). The UNDP was formed in December 1997 by Aboubacar Balde, a former PAIGC official, who was reportedly angered at the ruling party's failure to organize a congress in mid-1997. The party was officially recognized in April 1998 and won one legislative seat in 1999. The UNDP reportedly came under scrutiny after Ansumane Mane's failed bid to reinstall himself as the chief of staff in November 2000. In the 2004 elections, the UNDP received 1.1 percent of the vote. Balde dropped out as a 2005 presidential candidate for financial reasons.

Leader: Aboubacar BALDE (1999 presidential candidate).

National Reconciliation Party (*Partido Nacional do Reconciliation*—PRN). Formed in October 2004 by former PRS leader Alamara Nhasse, the PRN drew a large number of senior PRS figures away from the PRS, including a former defense minister and the former mayor of Bissau.

In 2009 the PRN called on the government of Prime Minister Gomes to step down, blaming it for Guinea Bissau's political turmoil.

Leader: Alamara NHASSE (Former Prime Minister).

Party for Development, Democracy, and Citizenship (*Partido para Democracia, Desenvolvimento e Cidodania*—PADEC). Former prime minister, PAIGC member, and PUSD leader Francisco Fadul formed the PADEC in 2007 after a dispute with the PUSD leadership.

In April 2009, in what human rights organizations described as a government crackdown on critics, party leader Fadul was allegedly beaten at his home by "men in uniform." In May the Supreme Court rejected Fadul's application to be a presidential candidate in the June election, saying he could not run because he had not resigned as head of the court of auditors.

Leader: Francisco FADUL.

Other minor parties that contested the 2008 legislative elections were: the **Guinean Democratic Party** (*Partido Democrático Guinéense*—PDG), led by Manuel CA; **Movement for Democracy in Guinea-Bissau** (*Movimento Democrático Guiné-Bissau*—MDG), led by Silvestre ALVES; the **Socialist Party of Guinea-Bissau** (PS-GB); **Labor Party** (*Partido dos Trabalhadores*—PT); **Democratic Social Party** (*Partido Democrático Social*—PDS); **Alliance of Patriotic Forces** (*Aliança de Forças Patrióticas*—AFP); **Democratic Center** (*Centro Democrático*—CD); **Popular Democratic Party** (*Partido Popular Democrático*—PPD); **Progress Party** (Partido de Progresso—PP); and **Guinean Patriotic Union** (*União Patriótica Guinéens*—UPG), whose 2009 presidential candidate, Francisca Vaz TURPIN, was the only woman to contest the election.

Other Parties and Groups:

Electoral Union (*União Eleitoral*—UE). The UE was formed in 2002 to contest legislative elections by a group of four small leftist and center-left parties. In the 2004 elections the UE gained two seats in the assembly. Other minor parties in the UE include the **Guinean Socialist Party** (*Partido Socialista Guineense*—PSG), led by Cirilo VIEIRA;

Leader: Joaquim BALDE.

United Popular Alliance (*Aliança Popular Unida*—APU). The APU was formed prior to the 2004 legislative elections as an electoral coalition between the ASG (below) and the small **Guinean Popular Party** (*Partido Popular Guineense*—PPG), led by Joao Tatis SA. It won one seat in the 2004 assembly election. In May 2004 the APU signed an agreement with the PAIGC and the UE to "ensure stability." Sa ran last in the field of 13 first-round presidential candidates in 2005.

Socialist Alliance of Guinea-Bissau (*Aliança Socialista da Guiné-Bissau*—ASG). The ASG was launched in May 2000 under the leadership of Fernando Gomes, a human rights advocate. Gomes had run as an independent candidate in the first round of presidential elections in November 1999, receiving 7 percent of the vote. He backed Kumba Yala in the second round. Gomes and the ASG, however, were subsequently among the fiercest critics of the government, especially on the issues of human rights and freedom of the press. Gomes was briefly detained in late May 1999 for having released a communiqué strongly critical of the government. Party president Gomes, who was also the founder of the Guinea-Bissau

Human Rights League, was arrested in 2002, an event Amnesty International said was "politically motivated."

Leader: Fernando GOMES.

United Platform (*Plataforma Unida*—PLATAF). This electoral coalition, led by Helder VAZ and Victor Mandinga, was formed to contest the 2004 legislative elections. Two members of the coalition, the Democratic Front and the Democratic Convergence Party, were also linked in a separate coalition as the Democratic Alliance (see Democratic Convergence Party, below). In 2004, the former leader of the PLATAF, Francisca VAZ Turpin, filed papers to form a new party, the UPG (above).

Democratic Convergence Party (*Partido da Convergência Democrática*—PCD). The PCD first surfaced in the early 1990s under the leadership of a former PAIGC member, Victor Mandinga. The PCD apparently served as the core component of the Democratic Alliance coalition that was credited with winning four seats (including one by Mandinga) in the 1999 legislative balloting. Mandinga supported Ansumane Mane in the events of late 2000, and he was briefly detained by security forces. Mandinga, routinely referenced as leader of the AD, subsequently remained a highly vocal and visible critic of President Yala. Meanwhile, several cabinet ministers installed in March 2001 and December 2001 were referenced as PCD members. In 2005 Mandinga was named minister of finance.

Leader: Victor MANDINGA.

Democratic and Social Front (*Frente Democrática e Social*—FDS). The FDS was launched in early 1990 by former PAIGC president Rafael Barbosa to fight against the "dictatorship" of the existing system. A cofounder of the PAIGC, Barbosa had been accused of collaboration with the Portuguese during the liberation struggle, convicted of treason in 1974, and imprisoned. He was released briefly upon Vieira's seizure of power in 1980 but was again imprisoned after calling for the expulsion of Cape Verdeans from Guinea-Bissau. He was formally amnestied in 1987.

Following a contentious FDS leadership meeting on January 15, 1992, the two-year-old group suffered its third split as seven members left to form the PRS. The FDS won a single seat in the legislature in 1999. In advance of the 2004 assembly election, the FDS formed a coalition with the PUSD, the PRD, and the LGBPE. Longtime party leader Rafael BARBOSA died in January 2007 at age 81.

Front of Struggle for the Liberation of Guinea (*Frente da Luta para a Libertação da Guiné*—FLING). Formerly known as the Front for the Liberation and Independence of Guinea-Bissau (*Frente para a Libertação e Independência da Guiné-Bissau*), FLING claimed to have been organized in 1954 and, as a group opposed to the unification of Cape Verde and the mainland, to have initiated the armed struggle against Portugal. In March 1981 it was announced that it had been dissolved, with its militants accepted into the PAIGC, although remnants of the organization continued to be active, primarily as exiles. It assumed its present name, while retaining the original acronym, in 1991. Its leader, François Mendy Kankoila, returned in 1992 after 40 years in exile. The group applied for legalization in 1992 and won a single seat in 1994.

In June 1996 President Vieira sued Kankoila and suspended him from the National Assembly after Kankoila accused Vieira of orchestrating the disappearance of a FLING member.

Leaders: François Mendy KANKOILA, Catengul MENDES (1999 presidential candidate), José Katengul ENDES.

Other minor parties in the PLATAF include the **Group of Independent Democrats** (*Grupo de Democratas Independentes*—GDI), which was formed by Helder Vaz and dissidents from the RGB-MB; and the **Democratic Front** (*Frente Democrática*—FD), led by Canjura INJAI.

Guinea-Bissau Resistance–Bah Fatah Movement (*Resistência da Guiné-Bissau–Movimento Bah-Fatah*—RGB-MB). Launched in Lisbon, Portugal, in 1986, the RGB-MB was technically precluded from using "Bafata" in its official title because of a legal prohibition of the use of an ethnic, regional, or (in this case) town name for political parties. As a result it substituted "Bah-Fatah" for "Bafata" prior to registration in December 1991. RGB-MB founder Domingos Fernandes Gomes returned after six years in exile on May 18, 1992. The party was runner-up to the PAIGC in the 1994 legislative poll, winning 19 seats. In November, Fernandes refused an invitation to join the Costa government.

In late 1998 the RGB-MB announced that it would not participate in reconciliation talks with President Vieira and called for his resignation. The party had been a vocal critic of Vieira throughout the military uprising, which it had allegedly described as an internecine struggle within the PAIGC.

In the 1999 legislative elections, the RGB-MB won 28 seats and became the second-largest party in the legislature. In the first round of presidential balloting in November 1999 the RGB-MB's candidate was Helder VAZ Lopes, who had become the party chair in September. In the second round in January 2000, Vaz Lopes told his supporters to vote for a candidate of their choice.

The RGB-MB was included in the PRS-led government formed in February 2000. In September all the ministers from the party were dismissed, but they were reinstated shortly thereafter. In January 2001, however, the RGB-MB left the government in reaction to an earlier reshuffle the party claimed unfairly favored their senior partner, the PRS. In March the party was given representation in Faustino Imbali's new government, although it reportedly remained highly critical of Kumba Yala's presidency and of some of Imbali's policies. The government appointed in December reportedly did not include any RGB-MB members. In the 2004 legislative elections, the RGB-MB received only 1.85 percent of the vote and consequently no seats in the assembly. Party leader Domingos Fernandes Gomes announced he would run in the 2005 presidential election, but his name did not appear on the list of candidates. Party leader Salvador Tchongo dropped out the 2005 presidential race, citing financial difficulties and a lack of confidence in the process.

Leaders: Domingos FERNANDES Gomes (1994 presidential candidate), Salvador TCHONGO (President), Mario Ujssumane BALDE (Secretary General).

Union for Change (*União para a Mudança*—UM). The UM was originally organized prior to the 1994 election as a six-party electoral coalition that included the left-of-center Democratic Front (*Frente Democrática*—FD), led by Marcelino BAPTISTA; the United Democratic Movement (*Movimento para a Unidade e a Democracia*—Mude), led by Felintro Vaz MARTINS; the Democratic Party of Progress (*Partido Democrático do Progresso*—PDP); and the Party of Renovation and Development (*Partido da Renovação e Desenvolvimento*—PRD), a grouping of PAIGC dissidents led by João da Costa; as well as the FDS and LGBPE, which did not join their partners in a formal merger in November 1995. The Union secured six seats in 1994 and three in 1999. The party reportedly came under scrutiny after Ansumane Mane's failed bid to reinstate himself as the chief of staff in November 2000 and party president Manuel Rambout Barcelos was arrested. The group's secretary general, Agnello Regala, also was arrested for allegedly supporting Mane. He was released in December. In the 2004 election the UM received only 2 percent of the vote and therefore no seats in the assembly.

Leaders: Manuel Rambout BARCELOS, Amine Michel SAAD (PDP), Agnello REGALA (Secretary General).

Guinean Civic Forum (*Foro Civico da Guiné*—FCG). The FCG's Antonieta Rosa Gomes competed in the 1999 presidential election, and in 2000 she was appointed to the Ntchama government. However, she was dismissed in November 2001. The new government appointed in December 2001 reportedly did not include any FCG members. The FCG received less than 1 percent of the vote in the 2004 elections. Gomes ran for president in 2005 on the FCG ticket in affiliation with the **Social Democracy** (SD) group. She was the only woman to contest the elections.

Leader: Antonieta Rosa GOMES (1999 and 2005 presidential candidate).

Other minor parties include the **Manifest Party of the People** (PMP) and the **Party of National Unity** (*Partido da Unidade Nacional*—PUN), led by Idrissa DJALÓ.

LEGISLATURE

The current **National People's Assembly** (*Assembleia Nacional Popular*) is a directly elected body of 102 members elected for five-year terms. At the most recent balloting of November 16, 2008, for 100 seats, the distribution was as follows: African Party for the Independence of Guinea and Cape Verde, 67; Social Renewal Party, 28; Republican Party for Independence and Development, 3; New Democracy Party 1; and Democratic Alliance, 1.

President: Manuel Serifo NHAMADJO.

CABINET

[as of June 1, 2009]

Prime Minister	Carlos Gomes Júnior
Ministers	
Agriculture and Rural Development	Evarista de Sousa [f]
Civil Service, Labor, and State Modernization	Fernando Gomes
Commerce and Industry	Botche Candé
Defense	Artur Silva
Economy, Planning, and Regional Integration	Helena Nosolini Embalo [f]
Energy and Natural Resources	Antonio Oscar Barbosa
Finance	Mario Vaz
Fisheries	Carlos Mussa Baldé
Foreign Affairs and International Cooperation	Adiato Nandigna [f]
Health	Camilo Simoes Pereira
Infrastructure, Transport, and Communication	José Antonio da Cruz Almeida
Interior	Commandant Lucio Soares
Justice	Mamadu Diallo Pires
National Education, Culture, and Science	Aristides Ocante da Silva
Presidency of the Council of Ministers	Adiato Nandigna [f]
Social Communication and Parliamentary Affairs	Fernando Mendonça
Territorial Administration	Vacant
Tourism and Handicrafts	Lurdes Vaz
War Veterans of National Liberation	Gen. Buota NanBatcha
Women, Family Affairs, Solidarity, and the Fight Against Poverty	Fatima Faty [f]
Youth and Sports	Baciro Dja
Secretaries of State	
Budget and Fiscal Affairs	Gabriela Fernandes [f]
Communications	Lassana Turé
Education	Besna Na Fonta
Energy	Wasna Papai Danfa
Environment and Rural Development	Barros Bacar Banjai
Hospital Administration	Augusto Paulo José da Silva
Territorial Administration	Antonio Inacio Gomes Correia
Transport and Communication	José Carlos Esteves
Treasury	José Carlos Varela Casimiro
Urban Planning	Fernando Dias

[f] = female

COMMUNICATIONS

In October 1991 the National People's Assembly adopted a 55-article law providing for substantially greater freedom of the press than in a previous measure of December 1989. However, in 2002 and 2003 the government closed several private radio stations and fired reporters from the Guinea News Agency because of critical reports on the government. Following the 2003 coup, press restrictions were lifted. In 2006 the government controlled the only television station and one national newspaper, according to the International Press Institute (IPI). One of the biggest problems facing the media in Guinea-Bissau is the lack of money, particularly for state-run media, the IPI reported.

In 2006 supporters of President João Bernardo Vieira accused the independent *Radio Bombolom* of criticizing the president and reportedly forced the station to carry a "retraction." In 2007 the government threatened to shut down *Radio Bombolom* for allegedly broadcasting a program accused of worsening the country's political situation. That same year the International Federation of Journalists (IFJ) called on the government to stop intimidating journalists who were covering drug trafficking in the country. Similar accusations were made in 2008.

Press. The following are published in Bissau: *Nô Pintcha* (6,000), official government daily; *Diario de Bissau*, independent daily; *Banobero*, independent weekly; *Expresso-Bissau*, independent weekly; *Baguerra*, PCD organ; *Voz da Guine* (6,000).

News agency. The domestic facility is the Guinea News Agency (*Agência Noticiosa da Guinea*—ANG).

Broadcasting and computing. Radio programming is offered by the government's *Radiodifusão Nacional da República da Guiné-Bissau* and *Rádio Liberdade*, which after a 16-year silence returned to the airwaves in 1990 to "renew and deepen" democracy; broadcasts are in Portuguese and Creole. Two independent stations were launched in 1995 and 1996. Government-controlled television commenced on an experimental basis in 1989, but it still reaches a quite limited number of receivers. As of 2008 there were 23.5 Internet users per 1,000 inhabitants.

INTERGOVERNMENTAL REPRESENTATION

Ambassador to the U.S.: (Vacant).

U.S. Ambassador to Guinea-Bissau: Marcia Stephens Bloom BERNICAT.

Permanent Representative to the UN: Alfredo Lopes CABRAL.

IGO Memberships (Non-UN): AfDB, AU, BADEA, BOAD, CILSS, CPLP, ECOWAS, IDB, Interpol, IOM, NAM, OIC, OIF, UEMOA, WTO.

GUYANA

Cooperative Republic of Guyana

Political Status: Formerly the colony of British Guiana; independent member of the Commonwealth since May 26, 1966; under republican regime instituted February 23, 1970; present constitution approved February 11, 1980, with effect from October 6.

Area: 83,000 sq. mi. (214,969 sq. km.).

Population: 751,223 (2002C); 754,000 (2008E).

Major Urban Center (metropolitan area, 2003E): GEORGETOWN (231,000).

Official Language: English.

Monetary Unit: Guyana Dollar (market rate December 1, 2009: 203.49 dollars = $1US).

President: Bharrat JAGDEO (People's Progressive Party/Civic); sworn in August 11, 1999, to succeed Samuel A. (Sam) HINDS (People's Progressive Party/ Civic), who had been elevated from Prime Minister to Provisional President upon the resignation of Janet JAGAN (People's Progressive Party) for health reasons on August 1; elected on March 19, 2001, and sworn in for a second term on March 31; reelected on August 28, 2006, and sworn in for a third five-year term on September 2.

Prime Minister: Samuel A. (Sam) HINDS (Civic); sworn in December 19, 1997, succeeding Janet JAGAN (People's Progressive Party); reappointed by the president on August 11, 1999, April 4, 2001, and September 4, 2006.

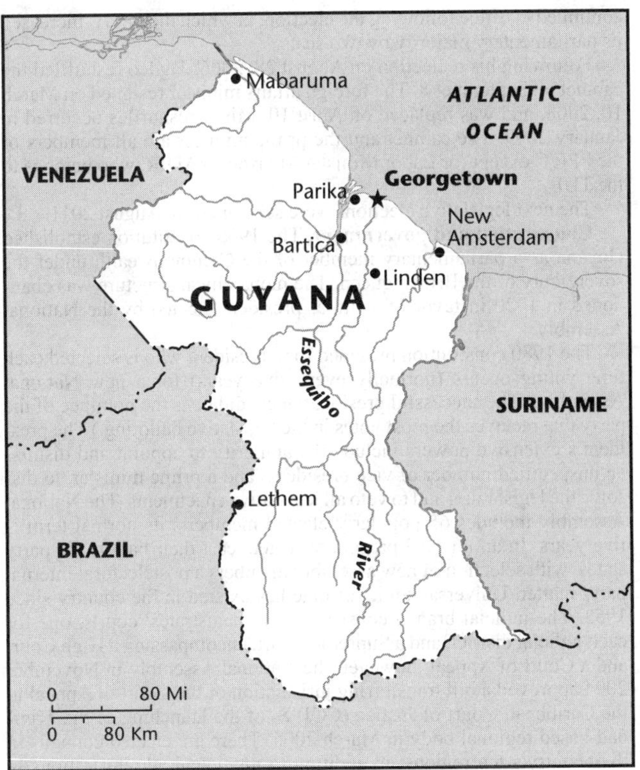

THE COUNTRY

Noted for its dense forests and many rivers, Guyana, whose name is an Amerindian word meaning "land of many waters," is situated on the northern Atlantic coast of South America, with Venezuela and Suriname on the west and east, respectively, and Brazil on the south and southwest. Its inhabitants are concentrated along a narrow coastal belt, the only area suitable for intensive agriculture. Most of their ancestors arrived during the centuries of British colonial rule: African slaves before 1800 and East Indian plantation workers during the nineteenth century. At present about 50 percent of the population is of East Indian origin, mainly engaged in agriculture; 35 percent is African, including most civil servants; 7 percent claim multiple heritages; 7 percent is indigenous Indian; and the remainder is European or Chinese. The principal religions are Christianity (50 percent), Hinduism (30 percent), and Islam (15 percent). In 1997, 33 percent of adult women were in the paid labor force, mainly concentrated in agriculture and cottage industries; female participation in national government was close to 20 percent, with substantially less representation at the local level.

The Guyanese economy is based primarily on agriculture, with sugar and rice being the principal crops, although exploitation of mineral resources, including bauxite, alumina, gold, diamonds, and manganese, has become increasingly important. Bauxite mining and the sugar industry were nationalized in the mid-1970s, and about 80 percent of the country's productive capacity was within the public sector (with cooperatives accounting for another 10 percent) by 1982, when a reversal of the trend began. Since 1975 Guyana has experienced severe economic difficulty, with falling export prices generating large balance-of-payments deficits and shortages of basic commodities creating a vast underground economy supported by widespread smuggling. In 1986 Prime Minister Hoyte attempted to alleviate the situation by launching a "reconstructive" liberalization program that departed significantly from his predecessor's socialist policies. Despite a 70 percent currency devaluation in April 1989 and the removal of most trade restrictions and price controls, lengthy talks with the International Monetary Fund (IMF) failed to yield agreement on standby and structural adjustment facilities until mid-1990, in the wake of another devaluation of 26.7 percent. From 1990 to 2000 GDP growth averaged 4.25 percent per year, according to the IMF. The economy stagnated in the early 2000s but revived in 2006–2007, with annual GDP growth of 5.25 percent. However, unemployment remained in the double digits. In 2008 annual growth fell to 3.2 percent, and higher global food costs resulted in government subsidies and pay raises for civil service employees. In an effort to counter the effects of the global economic recession, the government in 2009 unveiled its largest budget ever, reflecting an 8 percent year-on-year increase. New initiatives in education, health, housing, and water increased spending in those areas by 15.9 percent. The IMF commended Guyanese authorities for their progress in reducing inflation and successfully implementing a value-added tax. In addition, both the IMF and the World Bank acknowledged the government's efforts toward creating a more stable economic environment and alleviating poverty.

GOVERNMENT AND POLITICS

Political background. Guyana's political history during its first decade of independence was largely determined by an unusual ethnic structure resulting from the importation of African slaves and, subsequently, of East Indian laborers to work on the sugar plantations during the centuries of British colonial rule. The resultant cleavage between urbanized Africans and the more numerous rural East Indians was reflected politically in an intense rivalry between the communist-led, East Indian–supported People's Progressive Party (PPP) of Dr. Cheddi B. JAGAN and the African-backed People's National Congress (PNC), led by Linden Forbes BURNHAM, a former PPP leader who broke with Jagan in 1955. Jagan's party, with a numerically larger constituency, came to power in British Guiana under a colonial constitution introduced in 1953 but was removed from office later that year because of British concern over a veer toward communism. Jagan's party again emerged victorious in general elections held in 1957 and 1961 but was defeated in 1964, when the introduction of a new system of proportional representation made possible the formation of a coalition government embracing Burnham's PNC and the small United Force (TUF). In spite of earlier internal disorders, Burnham's administration successfully negotiated with the British for independence and remained in office following the achievement of full Commonwealth status in 1966 and the adoption of a republican form of government in 1970. However, the PNC's continued dominance in 1968 and 1973 generated widespread controversy. Contributing to opposition charges of fraud and withdrawal of the TUF from the governing coalition was a revision of the electoral law to allow Guyanese residing overseas to vote.

The 1970 redesignation of Guyana as a "cooperative republic" attested to the ruling party's increased commitment to socialism. In his "Declaration of Sophia," published on the tenth anniversary of his premiership, Burnham referred to the PNC as a socialist party committed to government land control, the nationalization of foreign business interests, and a domestic economy of three sectors, "public, cooperative, and private," with the cooperative sector predominant. He also called for revision of the nation's constitution to expunge the "beliefs and ideology of our former imperialist masters." Subsequently, in a referendum held July 10, 1978, more than 97 percent of those voting were said to have approved extension of the legislature's term beyond its July 23 expiration date so that the PNC-dominated National Assembly could serve, additionally, as a constituent body to consider a series of drastic changes in the nation's basic law.

World attention focused on Guyana in late 1978 with the bizarre suicide-murder of more than 900 members of the People's Temple commune in Jonestown following an investigation by U.S. representative Leo J. Ryan, whose party was ambushed by cult members as it prepared to enplane at a northwestern airstrip on November 18. Subsequent reports indicated that the Burnham government had been unusually hospitable to a variety of dissident religious sects, including the House of Israel, a 7,000-member group of Black converts to Judaism headed by David HILL (known locally as "Rabbi Washington").

Guyana's new constitution was declared in effect on October 6, 1980, with Burnham assuming the office of executive president and designating Ptolemy A. REID as prime minister. On December 15, in an election branded by an international team of observers as "fraudulent in every possible respect," the PNC was credited with an overwhelming popular mandate, and on January 1, 1981, the government was substantially expanded to include five vice presidents and additional ministers.

In the wake of worsening fiscal conditions, the regime faced mounting internal and external political challenges, culminating in the arrest by Canadian authorities in December 1983 of six persons, including a member of the Toronto-based right-wing Conservative Party of Guyana, who were charged with plotting to assassinate Burnham and other key officials. A number of subsequent leadership changes included the appointment in August 1984 of Vice President Hugh Desmond HOYTE to succeed the reportedly ailing Reid as first vice president and prime minister.

President Burnham died on August 6, 1985, while undergoing surgery in Georgetown, and was succeeded by Hoyte, who was accorded a regular five-year mandate on December 9 in balloting that, as in 1980, yielded allegations of widespread fraud.

Elections that should have been held in late 1990 were postponed to permit the compilation of new electoral rolls, with the National Assembly (due to expire on February 2, 1991) being accorded a series of two-month extensions before formal dissolution on September 28. On November 10 President Hoyte announced that the long-delayed balloting would take place on December 16; on November 22, however, he responded to continued domestic and international criticism of the voter-registration procedure by again postponing the poll. President Hoyte's action was validated by the assembly in December when it reconvened under a state of emergency decree; the parliamentary session was prolonged to September 30, 1992.

In contrast to the two previous elections, a team of 100 foreign observers characterized the balloting on October 5, 1992, as largely fair and impartial. The ongoing 1991 alliance of the PPP and a small social and political party of business owners and professionals—Civic (PPP/C)—won a majority of the popular vote. Dr. Jagan was installed as president four days later, and his party, after lengthy negotiations with TUF and the Working People's Alliance (WPA), secured control of the National Assembly and approval for a government headed by Civic leader Samuel A. (Sam) HINDS.

The PPP/C won 48 of 65 Neighborhood Democratic Councils (NDCs) and three of six municipalities in local government elections on August 8, 1994. The principal loss was in the capital, where 12 of 30 seats were captured by Good and Green for Georgetown (GGG), a new formation led by former prime minister Hamilton Green, who served a one-year term as the city's mayor before defeat in August 1995 and reelection in 1996.

President Jagan suffered a fatal heart attack on March 6, 1997, and was immediately succeeded, for the balance of his term, by Prime Minister Hinds, who also held the post of vice president. On March 17 Hinds appointed his predecessor's wife, Janet JAGAN, as first vice president and prime minister, additionally naming Agriculture Minister Reepu Daman PERSAUD as second vice president.

Mrs. Jagan was named to succeed her husband in the general election of December 15, 1997 (which yielded a largely unchanged distribution of legislative seats), thereafter naming Hinds as first vice president and prime minister, and Bharrat JAGDEO as second vice president. The election generated intense controversy, however, and the PNC did not agree to take up its assembly seats until mid-1998.

Mrs. Jagan resigned for medical reasons on August 1, 1999, and a somewhat complicated scenario ensued. As constitutionally prescribed, Prime Minister Hinds again assumed the presidency on a provisional basis. He then named Jagdeo as first vice president and prime minister and resigned in the latter's favor. Following his installation as president, Jagdeo reappointed Hinds as prime minister, and Hinds proceeded to name a cabinet virtually identical to its predecessor.

In January 2001 a Guyanese Supreme Court judge declared the 1997 election null and void because of the introduction of voter-identification cards. However, in a March 1 clarification the judge ruled that the Jagdeo government was not illegitimate, even though installed under unconstitutional legislation. Shortly thereafter, the issue became moot with the March 19 victory of the PPP/C (characterized by international observers as "basically fair") and the incumbent's reinstallation.

A new election had been anticipated in August 2006. However, in March 2006 the Guyana Election Commission announced that the balloting would be delayed beyond the constitutional deadline of August 4 due to difficulties in assembling a valid electoral list. Regional and general elections were held on August 28. Following the assassination of Agriculture Minister Satyadeow SAWH (see Current issues, below), the new National Assembly was delayed in convening until September 28, over three weeks after the constitutionally required date of September 2 and four months after the May 2 dissolution. The opposition immediately argued that the deferral would require a constitutional amendment, but their claims were dismissed by the chief justice; the PNC and allied Reform party (PNC/R) thereupon indicated that it would appeal the decision to the Caribbean Court of Justice. Jagdeo continued in office following the election, in which the PPP/C increased its parliamentary majority by two seats.

Following his reelection on August 28, 2006, Jagdeo reshuffled the cabinet on September 8. The foreign affairs minister resigned on March 10, 2008, and was replaced on April 10. Minor reshuffles occurred in January 2009. The cabinet and the prime minister are all members of the PPP/C except for Labor Minister Manzoor NADIR, who belongs to the TUF.

The next legislative elections were scheduled for August 2011.

Constitution and government. The 1966 constitution established Guyana as a parliamentary member of the Commonwealth under the sovereignty of the British queen. The monarchical structure was abandoned in 1970 in favor of a titular president elected by the National Assembly.

The 1980 constitution provided for a president who is selected each time voting occurs (normally every five years) for a new National Assembly. (The successful presidential candidate is the nominee of the party that receives the most votes in the legislative balloting.) The president's extensive powers include the authority to appoint and dismiss an unspecified number of vice presidents and a prime minister, to dissolve the legislature, and to veto all legislative enactments. The National Assembly includes 65 popularly elected members; its normal term is five years. In an unusual procedure, voters cast their ballots for party slates, with selection of new assembly members a postelectoral internal party matter. Universal adult suffrage has existed in the country since 1953. The judicial branch consists of ten magistrates' courts, one for each judicial district, and a Supreme Court, encompassing a High Court and a Court of Appeal; however, the National Assembly in November 2004 approved a bill transferring jurisdiction of the Court of Appeal to the Caribbean Court of Justice (CCJ) as of the launching of the Trinidad-based regional body in March 2005. There are elected councils in the country's ten regions, in addition to municipal administrations in Georgetown and four towns, although the balloting of August 1994 was their first replenishment since 1970. Local councilors elect from their membership a National Congress of Local Democratic Organs, which, together with the National Assembly, constitutes a deliberative body known as the Supreme Congress of the People of Guyana.

Constitutional amendments must be approved by the assembly and, if not endorsed by a two-thirds majority, submitted to a popular vote (the legislative extensions of 1991 being technically in the form of constitutional amendments carried by the PNC's [then] overwhelming assembly majority).

Foreign relations. Guyana's major foreign policy problems stem from boundary disputes with both its eastern and western neighbors. The disagreement with Suriname centers on the delineation of a riparian boundary between the two countries: Guyana claims that the boundary follows the Corentyne, while Suriname claims it follows the New River. The dispute with Venezuela is the most serious: Venezuela has long claimed all territory west of the Essequibo River, which amounts to more than half of Guyana's total area (see map). In 1966 the two countries agreed to settle the issue by diplomatic means, while in 1970, after talks had failed, Venezuela agreed to a 12-year moratorium on its claim. The 1970 protocol provided that if the dispute was not resolved by September 18, 1982, it would be referred to an "appropriate international organ" or, failing agreement on such an organ, to the secretary general of the United Nations. In the wake of a series of border incidents that accompanied expiration of the moratorium, Venezuela rejected a Guyanese request to seek a ruling from the International Court of Justice and formally requested the mediation of United Nations Secretary General Javier Pérez de Cuéllar. In March 1983 Venezuela announced that Guyana had acquiesced in the action, but no further progress was reported until February 1985, when the Venezuelan foreign minister indicated that his government was prepared to adopt a conciliatory attitude in furtherance of a "new spirit of friendship and cooperation" between the two countries. Following a November 1989 meeting in Caracas with Venezuelan president Carlos Andrés Pérez, President Hoyte announced that the two governments had agreed to seek the "good offices" of the vice chancellor of the University of the West Indies, Alister McIntyre, in formulating a resolution of the long-standing dispute. Evidence of the changed climate was provided by Guyana's admission to the Organization of American States (OAS) in January 1991, after Venezuela had withdrawn an objection stemming from the boundary issue.

The Essequibo dispute was rekindled in October 1999 after Guyana had awarded offshore oil concessions in waters claimed by Venezuela to three foreign firms. The Guyanese foreign minister pointed out that the contested territory had been awarded to Guyana under an 1899 arbitration award and was "internationally accepted" thereafter. A constituent assembly, then considering changes in the Venezuelan constitution, responded by insisting that it would reject any modifications to the original Captaincy-General of Venezuela that had been "vitiated by nullity." A subsequent agreement to accept a Barbadian diplomat as mediator proved unproductive. Tension increased even further in mid-2000 when a Texas firm, Beal Aerospace, announced plans to erect a $100 million rocket facility in the region claimed by Venezuela, which Caracas argued could serve as a cover for a U.S. military installation. For its part, Georgetown promoted the initiative as the country's biggest development effort to date and extolled its potential in attracting tourists. However, in October, Beal announced it was withdrawing from the project on the grounds that the U.S. National Aeronautics and Space Administration (NASA) had entered the market to build its own technology with taxpayer subsidization and had thus made it impossible for the firm to compete effectively in the rocket-launching business.

The dispute with Suriname was resolved in September 2007 when a UN tribunal ruling gave Guyana rights to 12,800 square miles, almost twice the area awarded to Suriname. The offshore area is thought to hold 15 billion barrels of oil and 42 trillion cubic feet of natural gas. In 2008 Guyana signed two pacts to help alleviate long-standing security and economic problems. On May 19 an anticrime agreement with Suriname dealt with piracy, money laundering, and trafficking in people, drugs, and firearms. On May 23 Guyana joined 11 other South American countries in founding the Union of South American Nations (Unasur) to continue the process of regional integration.

Tensions with Suriname heightened briefly in 2008 when Surinamese authorities seized a Guyanese vessel on the Corentyne River in October. The boat, on a mission to load sugar upriver, was released after a fine was paid for not being captained by a Surinamese citizen.

In February 2009, Norway agreed to pay Guyana hundreds of millions of dollars to slow deforestation. The compensation was meant to encourage Guyana to limit greenhouse gas emissions from deforestation.

In April 2009 the Takutu Bridge was completed between Guyana and Brazil, the final link in the region where Brazil had paved a 60-mile highway between its northern state capital of Boa Vista and the Guyanese town of Lethem to increase trade.

Current issues. On April 22, 2006, Guyana was shocked by the assassination of Agriculture Minister Satyadeow Sawh by a group of masked gunmen, who also murdered Sawh's brother, sister, and a security guard. While the police report indicated that the motive was robbery, President Jagdeo suggested that the perpetrators were attempting to disrupt the election, which was ultimately held on August 28. In an address on the 40th anniversary of independence, May 25, President Jagdeo asserted that the greatest threat to the country came "from the enemy within"—drug lords and armed gangs who had been held responsible for the assassination of Minister Sawh and the theft in February of high-powered weapons from the Guyana Defense Force. Concurrently, a group styling itself the Guyanese Armed Resistance (AGAR) launched guerilla attacks. Violent crimes continued unabated in 2008; by the middle of the year, there had been two gang mass murders in the towns of Lusignan and Bartica. Twenty-three people were killed, including women, children, and several police officers. Gang leader Rondell RAWLINS was suspected in the assassination of Minister Sawh and in the Bartica and Lusignan killings. In January 2008 government soldiers in the village of Buxton fought a battle with armed gunmen; one soldier was killed and two more were wounded.

The issue of internal turmoil was highlighted by the arrest and conviction in New York of Roger KHAN, a Guyanese drug trafficker, whom, opposition leaders insisted, the Hinds administration had given a "shield of protection." Khan had been apprehended on June 26, 2006, and expelled to Trinidad and Tobago, where, on June 29, he was handed over to U.S. law enforcement officials. Criticism of the transaction came from within the PPP/C, former president Janet Jagan joining with others in accusing the Suriname government of playing "stooge to the USA" by allowing Khan's seizure and deportation. As the trial continued in 2008, a confidential source and U.S. prosecutors alleged that Khan had controlled a paramilitary death squad that killed over 200 people in Guyana.

Guyana has been widely recognized as a conduit for South American drugs into the North American and European markets and was plagued by gunrunning and gang violence. Highlighting the country's security problems, PNC/R opposition leader Robert CORBIN in May 2008 claimed drug gangs had infiltrated Guyanese law enforcement and security services. In response to several cases of corruption, the government began polygraph testing for enforcement officials. Several drug enforcement officers, including the agency's chief, were fired because of the results of the tests. Also in May, protests against the government's failure to improve security turned violent when demonstrators attacked the culture ministry and surrounding buildings with Molotov cocktails and gunfire. The government claimed Corbin, who had called for the protests, was inciting acts of political extremism in an attempt to pressure the administration over security concerns.

Attention in 2009 turned to other domestic concerns, as rolling electrical blackouts affected large portions of the country and strikes by air traffic controllers and other civil servants crippled services in key public sectors. A five-day strike by air traffic controllers in February resulted in flight delays and cancellations as the country's sole international airport was forced to shut down night operations. The controllers were protesting pay arrears, which the government disputed. Guyana's airport authority subsequently fired 20 of the controllers, effectively ending the walkout. Parliament subsequently passed laws making it more difficult to strike when critical operations were involved, including those related to health care, telecommunications, and airport and port services.

Further ramifications from the drug trafficking case involving Roger Khan followed the conclusion of his trial in March 2009 in New York, where he faced up to 15 years in prison after pleading guilty to witness tampering, cocaine trafficking, and gun-running. In April the PNCR demanded that the government investigate Khan's activities in Guyana and further claimed that the Jagdeo administration had hindered the Khan probe. Subsequently, parliament began reviewing a new anti-money laundering bill.

On the political front, in an effort to conduct the country's first local elections since 1994, President Jagdeo proposed legislation in May that would reestablish the polls, which had been suspended due to an impasse between the government and the Corbin-led opposition over election reforms. In renewing the effort to hold elections before the end of the year, Jagdeo said the time had come to bring the debate into the public forum. Meanwhile, the elections commission said necessary preparations were in place so that balloting could be conducted in a timely manner.

In June 2009 the health minister, Leslie RAMSAMMY, dismissed opposition calls for his resignation because of alleged links to Roger Khan. The main opposition group, People's National Congress Reform–One Guyana (PNCR-1G), along with the Alliance for Change (AFC), demanded that Ramsammy step down after Khan's U.S. lawyer claimed Ramsammy helped his client buy sophisticated telephone monitoring equipment. The government, for its part, said that Ramsammy had no involvement in the matter.

POLITICAL PARTIES

Government Parties:

People's Progressive Party/Civic (PPP/C). Launched on January 1, 1950, by Dr. Cheddi B. Jagan and his wife, Janet Jagan, the PPP began as an anticolonial party speaking for the lower social classes but subsequently came to represent almost exclusively the large East Indian racial group. It long adhered to a pro-Soviet line, and at a June 1969 Moscow meeting Dr. Jagan formally declared the PPP to be a communist party. While the PPP and other opposition groups charged that the PNC fraudulently manipulated the overseas vote in the 1973 election, Dr. Jagan offered his critical support to the PNC in August 1975. The PPP Central Committee narrowly approved participation in the December 1980 legislative balloting, in which the party was officially credited with winning ten seats. It was awarded eight seats in 1985.

In June 1991 Jagan retreated from his earlier insistence on state ownership by saying that the PPP would "critically examine" enterprises in the public sector and consult with both business and labor "as to the best means of insuring their viability." Dr. Jagan died on March 6, 1997. Under the leadership of his wife, the PPP won a majority of directly elected legislative seats in the balloting of December 15, 1997. Janet Jagan resigned the presidency for medical reasons on August 1, 1999.

Since 1991 the PPP has been allied with the **Civic Party** (PPP/C), a group of local business owners and professionals headed by former interim president and current prime minister Samuel HINDS. Relations between the PPP/C and main opposition party PNC deteriorated over time and culminated in several charges against the opposition. PPP/C leaders claimed that the PNC could not account for $500,000 earmarked for investigation of voter-roll irregularities. PPP/C leaders also charged the PNC with inciting extremism. As the cost of living continued to climb, several protests were staged against the ruling party, including one in April 2008 by sugar workers in the town of New Amsterdam. The PNC staged street protests in the capital.

In 2008 the party and the administration of president Bharrat Jagdeo were implicated in the case of drug trafficker Roger Khan (see Current issues, above). Khan told a U.S. court he had helped Jagdeo's administration fight crime and conduct surveillance. The party denied complicity in the case. In 2009, Khan's lawyer said PPP party member and government health minister Leslie Ramsammy helped his client buy advanced surveillance equipment. The party and the government denied the claim.

Following the death of the former president of the republic and party stalwart Janet Jagan on March 28, 2009, the country observed two days of mourning for the highly popular figure.

Meanwhile, since President Jagdeo is ineligible for reelection in 2011, observers began speculating about a likely successor and the potential for party infighting in the process.

Leaders: Bharrat JAGDEO (President of the Republic), Donald RAMOTAR (General Secretary).

The United Force (TUF). The TUF, a small party founded by Peter D'AGUILAR in the early 1960s, represents conservative business and other interests. It favors racial integration, closer ties to the West, and it draws support from white, Amerindian, and other minority groups.

In 1968 the TUF withdrew from the governing coalition to protest the enfranchisement of overseas voters. The party won two seats in the 1980 legislative elections, which it held until 1992, when it lost one. It held on to one seat in balloting in 1997 and 2001. Party leader Manzoor Nadir became an "opposition" participant in the Hinds government in 2001 and continued in that capacity after the 2006 election.

On February 19, 2008, the TUF signed an agreement with the PPP/C and opposition parties to support the administration in garnering international support to help fight the country's burgeoning crime problem.

In May 2009, in the wake of a five-day strike by air traffic controllers, parliament approved a controversial bill introduced by Nadir, the minister of labor, that limited the ability of workers to strike by requiring that all parties involved in a potential walkout first meet with an arbitration panel appointed by the labor minister.

Leaders: Manzoor NADIR (2001 presidential candidate), Ishmail MUHAMED (Chair).

Principal Opposition Party:

People's National Congress Reform–One Guyana (PNCR-1G). Linden Forbes Burnham created the PNC in 1957 after he broke with PPP leader Cheddi Jagan. Primarily an urban-based party, it represented the African racial bloc, or about one-third of the population, including most of the nation's intellectuals. Initially, it advocated a policy of moderate socialism, anticommunism, and hospitality to private investment, but a swing to the left, culminating in Prime Minister Burnham's 1974 "Declaration of Sophia" (see Political background, above), brought the PNC close to the opposition People's Progressive Party on most domestic issues. In 1987 President Hoyte denied that the party was shifting to the right and insisted that the PNC remain committed to, given local conditions, an innovative form of socialism. The PNC drew heavily on the overseas vote in securing a two-thirds legislative majority in 1973 and was accused of massive fraud in obtaining better than three-quarter majorities in 1980 and 1985. It was runner-up to the PPP/C in 1992, winning 27 assembly seats with 43.6 percent of the vote.

Severe intraparty differences, which had broken out before the 1992 election, continued. Former prime minister Green, Viola BURNHAM (widow of the former president), and 13 other ex-ministers were dropped from the PNC's new parliamentary delegation. In February 1993 Green was expelled from the party following a disciplinary inquiry into misconduct charges. He then filed a High Court writ against Hoyte and other PNC leaders, claiming violation of his constitutional rights and in May announced that he would stand for election as mayor of Georgetown later in the year. Although subsequently identified with a group styled the Forum on Democracy, Green stated that his objective was not to form a new party but "to capture the PNC and bring it back to the people." He captured the Georgetown mayoralty in September 1994 as leader of Good and Green for Georgetown (see GGG, below).

Despite Hoyte's 1987 position, the PNC at its biennial congress in May 1994 adopted a new constitution that omitted reference to it as a "socialist" party, the former prime minister describing the word as a "chameleon term" endorsed by a variety of groups that had "only a ritual jargon in common." Former president Hoyte died on December 22, 2002; Viola Burnham died on October 10, 2003. During the 2001 legislative balloting, the PNC absorbed **Reform** (R), a group comprising a number of prominent business owners and professionals, one of whom, Stanley MING, was slated to be prime minister if the PNC/R had prevailed in the election. When it failed to oust the PPP/C, the party renamed itself the People's National Congress Reform–One Guyana (PNCR-1G) to broaden its appeal to the electorate for the 2006 elections (see 1G, below).

In May 2008 the party organized street protests in the capital against the rising cost of living. That same month it supported the efforts of opposition groups in calling for a probe into possible connections between the PPP/C and drug trafficker Roger Khan. In June PNCR-1G leader Robert Corbin received an anonymous death threat that warned him to stop speaking about the Khan drug-trafficking case in New York (see Current issues, above). President Jagdeo subsequently met with Corbin, who had fiercely criticized the ruling party's response to crime, to discuss security concerns.

In February 2009, members of the party criticized the PPP/C for not responding to the global economic crisis. They claimed that the administration's lack of action would increase the already high unemployment level and shutter key businesses. In May, Corbin left the country to seek medical treatment in New York. While he was out of the country, Richard Van West Charles, a former minister of health, took over the party's helm. Charles, the son-in-law of PNC founder Linden Forbes Burnham, managed to assume leadership even though other party members had backed Aubrey ARMSTRONG. The rift over Charles's accession was another sign of weakening in the party following the ouster of Corbin critic James MCALLISTER, who had attempted to challenge the party leadership. The squabbling led to internal calls for Corbin to step down.

Leaders: Robert Herman Orlando CORBIN (Chair), Dr Richard Van West CHARLES, Winston S. MURRAY, Oscar E. CLARKE (General Secretary).

One Guyana (1G). The One Guyana grouping came together before the country's 2006 elections and was comprised of several smaller parties, including the **National Front Alliance (NFA)**, led by current member of parliament Keith SCOTT. Scott, a former founding member of the **Working People's Alliance**, broke from the WPA to form the **National Democratic Movement**, which was later incorporated into NFA. At the same time the **National Republican Party** (NRP), led by Fiesal Ferose Ali, joined the NFA. The NFA last fielded its own candidates in 2001.

Other Legislative Parties:

Alliance for Change (AFC). In October 2005 Khemraj Ramjattan (a legislator who had been expelled from the PPP/C in 2004 because he accused the PPP/C leadership of corruption) and Raphael Trotman (a PNC legislator) launched the AFC. Former members of the WPA and GAP (below) also reportedly joined the new formation, which argued that the Guyanese were eager to support a racially integrated party after so many years of conflict between the nation's racially divided major parties. The AFC pledged to pursue higher living standards in Guyana based on free-market policies, which led some observers to suggest that it enjoyed support from the United States.

In 2008 the AFC supported opposition groups backing the administration's attempts to garner international help to combat crime. In May Ramjattan joined PNCR-1G leader Robert Corbin and GAP/ROAR (below) in implicating the PPP/C in the case of drug trafficker Roger Khan. The groups called for a probe into the matter.

A court challenge initiated by the AFC in 2008 over a disputed Region 10 parliamentary seat awarded to the PPP/C remained unresolved in 2009. The AFC claimed it should have been awarded the seat.

In early 2009 Ramjattan criticized the expanded government budget, saying the statistics used to create it were not real and that it failed to acknowledge the country's high unemployment rate. He also accused the Jagdeo administration of not having consulted other groups before releasing the spending plan. He recommended shutting down nonessential government ministries to save money. Another party official, Raphael Trotman, joined in the criticism, saying that the budget did not address three key issues that most concerned Guyana's population: poverty, the high cost of living, and unemployment.

Leaders: Khemraj RAMJATTAN (Chair), Raphael TROTMAN.

Guyana Action Party/Rise, Organise, and Rebuild (GAP/ ROAR). GAP and ROAR formed an electoral coalition for the August 28, 2006, elections, centering their joint campaign on reforming Guyana's criminal justice system. The coalition won one l seat.

The GAP/ROAR coalition backed opposition support in 2008 for the administration's attempts to garner international help for the escalating crime problem. GAP/ ROAR also backed calls for a probe into possible connections between the PPP/C and drug trafficker Roger Khan.

Leader: Everall N. FRANKLIN.

Guyana Action Party (GAP). The GAP was launched in January 1989 as the Guyanese Action for Reform and Democracy (Guard). A self-described civic movement that did not seek power as a political party, Guard organized a series of public rallies on behalf of political (particularly electoral) reform in mid-1990. A charge by President Hoyte that the formation was "a political party masquerading as a nonpolitical, apolitical faction" appeared to be substantiated by the issuance of a statement in November that it might take part in a "third slate" involving the now-defunct URP (see 2008 *Handbook*). The situation was further clouded in December, when businessman Sam Hinds resigned as Guard chair to accept designation as PPP shadow prime minister.

While continuing to emphasize the need for reform, Guard announced in August 1991 that it would contest the forthcoming election with Nanda K. GOPAUL, a former trade union official, as its presidential candidate. However, in early 1992 Gopaul emerged as the founder of the **Guyana Labor Party (GLP)**.

Under the GAP rubric, the formation won two legislative seats in 2001 as a partner of the WPA (below).

Leader: Paul HARDY.

Rise, Organise, and Rebuild (ROAR). A small grouping launched in 1999 to promote the rights of the indigenous population, ROAR won one legislative seat in 2001 and in 2006 retained it in coalition with the GAP.

Leader: Ravi DEV.

Other Parties:

Working People's Alliance (WPA). The WPA was organized in late 1976, following the tender of PPP support to the (then) ruling PNC, as a coalition of left-wing groups that included the African Society for Cultural Relations with Independent Africa (ASCRIA), founded by Eusi Kwayana during his affiliation with the PNC. Three of its principal leaders, Dr. Omawale, Dr. Rupert Roopnaraine, and Dr. Walter RODNEY, were indicted on arson charges in July 1979, the last being killed by a bomb explosion in June 1980. The party has been described as having "the appearance of a genuine bridge across the racial barrier in Guyana" in that its membership is drawn from both the African and Indian ethnic communities. It refused to participate in the December 1980 election on the grounds of anticipated irregularities. It won one seat in 1985 and two in 1992.

In January 1994, following a week-long public fast by Walter Rodney's son Shaka, the government announced that a special committee would be appointed to review the files on the 1980 bombing, for which, despite a 1988 ruling of death by "accident or misadventure," the PNC was widely believed to have been responsible. The inquiry led in June 1996 to the issuance of a warrant for the arrest of a former Guyana Defense Force sergeant, Gregory SMITH, who had been living in French Guiana since the 1980 assassination.

A consultative member of the Socialist International, the party contested the 1997 election as the Alliance for Guyana (AG), reverting to its original name for the 2001 campaign, in which it won only two legislative seats in conjunction with the Guyana Action Party (GAP, above).

The social democratic party has recently declined (in part because of the defection of one of its legislators to the AFC in 2005), and it secured no assembly representation in 2006. In 2008 the party condemned the "assault on press freedom and freedom of expression being launched by the PPP/C government" on JFAP leader Chandra Narine Sharma's television station. A statement released by the party in April said the government was limiting the opportunity of the poor to air their grievances through the media.

Leaders: Dr. Rupert ROOPNARAINE (Chair), Dr. Clive THOMAS (1992 presidential candidate), Nigel WESTMAAS, Bonita HARRIS, Eusi KWAYANA.

Justice for All Party (JFAP). Led by Chandra Narine Sharma, a local television station owner, the JFAP claimed that electoral irregularities cost it a seat in the 2001 legislative balloting; it was also unsuccessful in 2006. Sharma, an outspoken critic of President Jagdeo, was ordered to shut his station down for four months beginning April 12, 2008, after the repeated airing of a threat from a caller who wanted to kill the president. Several opposition parties complained about the closure.

Leader: Chandra Narine SHARMA.

Unity Party (UP). Cheddi Jagan Jr. launched the UP on February 13, 2005, after a dispute with the leadership of his parents' PPP. The party's stated goal was to pare down government and help increase private sector growth.

Leader: Cheddi JAGAN Jr.

Good and Green for Guyana (GGG). Former prime minister Hamilton Green, who had been expelled from the PNC in February 1993, formed the GGG as the Good and Green for Georgetown before the 1994 Georgetown municipal campaign. The new party won a plurality of 12 of 30 seats in the September 1994 election with its leader, now Georgetown mayor, signaling a return to national politics under the more inclusive rubric in mid-December. In August 1995 a coalition of PNC and PPP/C councilors succeeded in denying Green election to an additional one year as mayor; however, he was reelected to the post in August 1996.

In early 2009 Hamilton Green fought a proposed effort for local elections that could unseat him.

Leaders: Hamilton GREEN (Mayor of Georgetown), Ramesh KISSOON (Former Deputy Mayor of Georgetown).

Four other parties—the **Guyana National Congress;** the longstanding **National Democratic Front,** led by Joseph BACCHUS; the **Liberal Democrats**; and the **People's Republic Party,** led by Harry DAS—have contested only regionally. For information on the **Guyana Democratic Party**, the **Democratic Labor Movement**, the **People's Democratic Movement**, and the **United Republican Party,** see the 2008 *Handbook*.

LEGISLATURE

National Assembly. The unicameral legislature, which sits for five years, barring dissolution by the president, currently consists of 65 elected members, plus not more than 4 non-elected, non-voting members and 2 parliamentary secretaries appointed by the president. Before 2001, 53 members were directly elected on a proportional basis, 10 were selected by the regional councils (1 by each of the ten councils), and 2 designated by the National Congress of Local Democratic Organs, to which each regional council had elected 2 members. Constitutional amendments in early 2001 provided for direct election of all 65 members, 40 on a proportional basis from national lists and 25 on a "geographic" basis that assigned from 1 to 7 seats to each of the 10 regions.

Following the most recent election on August 28, 2006, the seat distribution was as follows: the People's Progressive Party/Civic, 36 seats; the People's National Congress Reform, 22; the Alliance for Change, 5; The United Force, 1; and a coalition of the Guyana Action Party and Rise, Organise, and Rebuild, 1.

Speaker: Hari Narayen RAMKARRAN.

CABINET

[as of October 1, 2009]

Prime Minister	Samuel A. Hinds (PPP/C)
Ministers	
Agriculture, Forestry, Fisheries, Crops, and Livestock	Robert Montgomery Persaud (PPP/C)
Amerindian Affairs	Pauline Campbell-Sukhai [f] (PPP/C)
Culture, Youth, and Sports	Frank Anthony (PPP/C)
Education	Shaik K. Z. Baksh (PPP/C)
	Desrey Fox (second minister) [f] (PPP/C)
Finance	Ashni Kumar Singh (PPP/C)
	Jennifer Webster (second minister) [f] (PPP/C)
Foreign Affairs	Carolyn Rodrigues-Birkett [f] (PPP/C)
Health	Dr. Leslie Ramsammy (PPP/C)
	Dr. Bheri Ramsaran (second minister) (PPP/C)
Home Affairs	Clement Rohee (PPP/C)
Housing and Water	Irfan Ali (PPP/C)
Human Services and Social Security	Priya Manichand [f] (PPP/C)
Labor	Manzoor Nadir (TUF)
Legal Affairs and Attorney General	Doodnauth Singh (PPP/C)
Local Government and Regional Development	Kellawan Lall (PPP/C)
Presidential Secretariat, Head Public Service	Roger Luncheon (PPP/C)
	Dr. Jennifer Westford [f] (PPP/C)
Tourism, Industry, and Commerce	Manniram Prashad (PPP/C)
Transport and Hydraulics	Robeson Benn (PPP/C)

[f] = female

COMMUNICATIONS

Freedom of the press and freedom of speech are guaranteed in Guyana's constitution, though newspapers have been indirectly censored through government control of newsprint, which was relaxed somewhat in 1986. The media generally operate without interference, and independent media are allowed to criticize the government, according to the monitoring group Freedom House.

Press. The following are published in Georgetown: *New Nation* (26,000), PNC weekly; *Mirror* (25,000), twice-weekly PPP/C organ; *Guyana Chronicle* (23,000 daily, 45,000 Sunday), state-owned; *Stabroek News* (22,000 midweek, 28,000 weekend), independent; the *Catholic Standard* (10,000), weekly; *Dayclean*, WPA weekly. A new daily newspaper, the *Guyana Times*, began publishing on June 5, 2008.

News agencies. The state-owned Guyana News Agency (GNA) was established in 1981, following termination of an agreement with the Barbados-based Caribbean News Agency. A number of foreign agencies maintain bureaus in Georgetown.

Broadcasting and computing. Until recently, radio broadcasting was controlled by the Guyana Broadcasting Corporation (GBC), which was formed from the Guyana Broadcasting Service and Radio Demerara (a local affiliate of Rediffusion, Ltd., London) when the government took over the latter's assets in 1979. In March 2004 the GBC and the Guyana Television and Broadcasting Company (GTV) merged to form a National Communications Network (NCN). More than a dozen television outlets have been operating under government license since 2001; in addition, two private stations relay television programming from the United States. As of 2008 there were 268.5 Internet users per 1,000 inhabitants.

INTERGOVERNMENTAL REPRESENTATION

Ambassador to the U.S.: Bayney Ram KARRAN.

U.S. Ambassador to Guyana: John Melvin JONES.

Permanent Representative to the UN: (Vacant).

IGO Memberships (Non-UN): ACP, ACS, Caricom, CDB, CWTH, IADB, IBRD, ICAO, IMF, Interpol, IOC, ISO, NAM, OAS, OIC, OPANAL, OPCW, PCA, RG, SELA, UNASUR, WCO, WTO.

HAITI

Republic of Haiti
République d'Haïti

Note: Citing a lack of economic improvement, the Senate on October 30, 2009, voted to oust Prime Minister Michèle Pierre-Louis. She was succeeded by Jean-Max Bellerive, theretofore the minister for planning and external cooperation, whose new government, which included a number of incumbents, was inaugurated on November 11. The administration subsequently faced nearly unfathomable challenges when an earthquake on January 12, 2010, devastated Port-au-Prince and other areas, killing as many as 200,000 people and displacing more than 1 million.

Political Status: Independent state proclaimed in 1804; republic established in 1859; military-backed regime installed following coup of September 30, 1991; constitutional government reinstated on November 8, 1994.

Area: 10,714 sq. mi. (27,750 sq. km.).

Population: 7,929,048 (2003C); 10,067,000 (2008E). The 2003 figure does not include an adjustment for undernumeration.

Major Urban Centers (2005E): PORT-AU-PRINCE (1,249,000), Carrefour (446,000), Cap-Haïtien (112,000).

Official Languages: French, Creole.

Monetary Unit: Gourde (market rate December 1, 2009: 39.75 gourdes = $1US).

President: René PRÉVAL (Front for Hope); elected on February 7, 2006, and sworn in on May 14, succeeding acting president Boniface ALEXANDRE (nonparty).

Prime Minister: *(See headnote.)* Michèle Duvivier PIERRE-LOUIS (nonparty); nominated by the president on June 23, 2008, and inaugurated (along with her new cabinet) on September 6 (following approval by the National Assembly) to succeed Jacques-Édouard ALEXIS (Front for Hope), who resigned (as required by the constitution) following a no-confidence vote in the Senate on April 12.

THE COUNTRY

The poorest country, on a per capita basis, in the Western Hemisphere, Haiti occupies the western third of the mountainous Caribbean island of Hispaniola, which it shares with the Dominican Republic. Approximately 95 percent of the population is of predominantly African descent, with the remainder mostly comprising whites and people of mixed black-white background. Roman Catholicism, which coexists with a folk cult based on various voodoo practices, is the official religion, but other faiths are permitted. Women constitute close to 50 percent of the agricultural labor force and 60 percent of the urban workforce, concentrated in domestic service and manufacturing. Female representation under the Duvalier regime was minimal; by contrast, the short-lived Préval government of 1991 included four women of ministerial rank, and there have been two female prime ministers since then.

The economy has been handicapped by political instability, underdeveloped infrastructure, and a paucity of mineral resources. There remain bauxite deposits in the south, but large-scale extraction ceased in 1983. The manufacturing sector has grown, with an emphasis on the assembly and reexport of imported components. However, agriculture remains the country's economic mainstay, drawing two-thirds of the workforce. The agricultural sector has suffered since the 1950s in the face of economic and ecological challenges and today contributes less than 30 percent of GDP. Important crops include sugarcane, cacao, sisal, and coffee, the principal commodity, which accounts for about 30 percent of export earnings. During the exile of President Aristide in 1991–1994, the economy came to a virtual standstill under the weight of trade and financial embargoes. Observers estimate that between 60 and 80 percent of the potential workforce remains outside formal employment, and more than half of primary school–age children are not attending school. Nearly half the population is illiterate, and the maternal mortality rate is considered the highest in the Western Hemisphere. In addition, inequality is extreme: 1 percent of the population controls almost half of the country's wealth. Remittances are the principal source of foreign exchange, equaling almost a quarter of GDP and double the earnings from exports. Two-thirds of the population subsists on less than $1 per day.

Economic growth averaged –5.2 percent annually in 1985–1995, and in 1996 the growth in real GDP reached a decade high of 2.9 percent. This figure remained relatively stable through 1999, before dropping to 0.9 percent in 2000, followed by a further period of political turmoil and GDP contraction (1.1 percent in 2001, 3.8 percent in 2004), with inflation reaching nearly 20 percent.

After several years of better growth, the economy was wracked in early 2008 by a dramatic increase in prices for fuel and imported food (particularly rice), which set off massive protest demonstrations. Later in the year a series of savage hurricanes devastated much of the country's infrastructure and agricultural production. Growth of only 1 percent was projected for 2009 as the effects of the global economic downturn further exacerbated already dreadful conditions. For its part, the government, backed by substantial new aid and debt relief from international lenders and donors, pledged to pursue long-term structural reform to create jobs and increase food production.

GOVERNMENT AND POLITICS

Political background. Since a slaves' revolt that established Haiti in 1804 as the first independent republic in Latin America, the nation's history has been marked by violence, instability, and mutual hostility between blacks and biracial persons. After a period of U.S. military occupation (1915–1934), biracial presidents held office until 1946, when power passed to a black president, Dumarsais ESTIMÉ. His moderate administration was terminated in 1950 by an army coup that paved the way for the regime of another black, Gen. Paul MAGLOIRE, who was himself overthrown in December 1956. Five interim regimes followed before the 1957 election in which François DUVALIER, a country doctor, won the presidency with the support of poor blacks, beating Louis DÉJOIE, the candidate of biracial persons and the urban middle class. Contrary to expectations, the Duvalier administration degenerated into a dictatorship, as recurring threats to the regime fed a prolonged period of repression. In 1961 Duvalier forced an unconstitutional reelection that secured him a second term. In May 1964 he staged another election that made him president for life (official results recorded a 100 percent ballot share for Duvalier).

With many of its opponents in exile, the Duvalier regime maintained a balance of terror using a blend of persuasion, voodoo symbolism, and a personal army of thugs and enforcers, the so-called *Tontons Macoutes* (Creole for "bogeymen"). In early 1971 Duvalier had the constitution amended to allow him to designate a successor; his son, Jean-Claude DUVALIER, was promptly named to the position and assumed the presidency following his father's death on April 21.

The younger Duvalier proved popular internationally. By 1975 U.S. aid to Haiti had risen to over $35 million, up from an average of $3.8 million under his father's rule. With the election in 1976 of Jimmy Carter, a U.S. president with a dedicated interest in human rights, Duvalier appeared to yield somewhat under continuing U.S. pressure to ameliorate the more corrupt and repressive aspects of his family's two decades of rule. In November 1978 he ordered a series of budgetary and ministerial reforms in return for substantially increased U.S. aid.

In the legislative election of February 11, 1979, an independent candidate running on a human rights platform won a clear victory against a government-endorsed opponent, thus becoming the legislature's first member who was not a Duvalier loyalist. In June, in an unprecedented act of public defiance, some 200 intellectuals issued a manifesto protesting the censorship of plays and films. However, the most remarkable development was the appearance at midyear of three new political parties (see Political Parties, below) after publication of a book by Grégoire EUGÈNE, a law professor, which pointed out that such organizations were technically permissible under the Haitian constitution. By the end of the year, however, any stirrings of liberalization appeared to have been beaten back, with the passing of a repressive press law and further *Macoutes* attacks on dissidents.

The first municipal elections in 26 years were held in mid-1983. No opposition candidates presented themselves, several potentials having disappeared before the balloting. In August the national legislature dissolved itself after accepting a new, presidentially drafted constitution. While balloting for a new chamber on February 12, 1984, resulted in the defeat of numerous Duvalierists, foreign observers became convinced that the government, wishing to create the appearance of change,

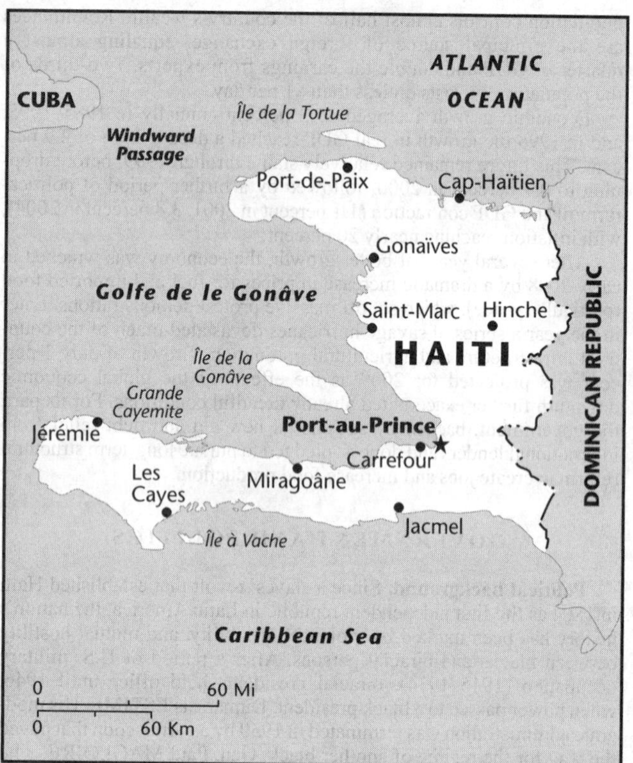

had asked incumbents not to campaign vigorously. Six months later, a regime-supportive Progressive National Party (PNP) was launched under legislation permitting partisan activity by groups agreeing to the life presidency. In November the government announced the discovery of a "communist" plot against the regime, in what was widely perceived as another bid for support from anticommunist donor nations, particularly the United States.

In early 1985, under pressure from the United States and France (another major donor), the government released a number of political prisoners, and in April President Duvalier announced a series of "democratic" reforms. These included the legalization of political parties, increased power for the National Assembly, and provision for a new post of prime minister, to be filled by presidential appointment from the parliamentary majority. However, restrictions on party registration ensured the exclusion of known regime opponents, while the life presidency remained intact.

Riots and demonstrations began to multiply in late 1985, sparked by the killing of several teenagers during an antigovernment protest in Gonaïves. Not yet willing to relax its hold on the country, in December the Duvalier government moved to concentrate power among an inner circle of loyalists. The disturbances intensified, however. On January 8, 1986, schools and universities were closed in the wake of widespread student boycotts, and ten days later police dispersed the first major protest in the capital. With pressure for democratization building internationally as well as domestically, Duvalier on February 7 departed on a U.S. plane to France with an entourage of family and close associates.

Between 1986 and 1991, the army once again moved to the center of Haitian politics, throwing its weight behind a series of six short-lived, nondemocratic governments. The first of these was inaugurated when, immediately upon Duvalier's departure, army chief of staff Gen. Henri NAMPHY assumed power as head of a five-member National Council of Government (*Conseil National du Gouvernement*—CNG) that included two other officers and two civilians. A 19-member provisional government, which initially contained a number of Duvalier loyalists, was announced on February 10. On March 20 the one prominent anti-Duvalierist in the new administration, human rights leader Gérard GOURGUE, resigned from both the CNG and the justice ministry, alleging "resistance" to liberalization. General Namphy responded by excluding Duvalierists from a reconstituted council that included himself, (then) Col. Williams REGALA (the interior and defense minister), and Jacques FRANÇOIS (succeeded as foreign minister in a cabinet reshuffle on March 24 by retired general Jean-Baptiste HILAIRE).

In June 1986, in the face of continued unrest, municipal elections were scheduled for July 1987, to be followed by presidential and legislative balloting in November, and the installation of a new government in February 1988. In September 1986 an election was held for 41 of 61 members of a Constituent Assembly charged with drafting Haiti's 23rd constitution since independence. The new basic law, incorporating a number of safeguards to prevent the return of a Duvalier-type dictatorship, was overwhelmingly approved by a referendum on March 29, 1987.

By mid-1987 the CNG had proven to be unwilling or unable to curb a mounting campaign of terror by disbanded *Macoutes,* and the promised local elections were postponed. Presidential and legislative balloting commenced on the morning of November 29, but within hours that voting was also called off because of widespread violence and voter intimidation. The four principal opposition leaders thereupon withdrew as presidential candidates, and Leslie MANIGAT, a self-proclaimed "democratic centralist" believed to have CNG backing, emerged from the rescheduled poll of January 17, 1988, with a declared majority of 50.3 percent.

On June 17, 1988, President Manigat attempted to remove General Namphy as army commander but was himself overthrown by a military coup two days later. On June 20 Namphy announced the formal deposition of the Manigat administration, declaring that he would thenceforth rule by decree as the country's chief executive. Less than three months thereafter, a revolt by noncommissioned officers of the Presidential Guard, led by Sgt. Joseph HEBREUX, resulted in Namphy's ouster, with power passing to Lt. Gen. Prosper AVRIL on September 18. Subsequently, Avril successfully resisted countercoup efforts by army units on April 2 and 5, 1989, and on September 24 he announced a series of local, national legislative, and presidential elections for 1990.

Following the assassination of a Presidential Guard colonel on January 19, 1990, General Avril declared a nationwide state of siege and instituted a roundup of opposition leaders, some of whom were deported after being brutalized by police. While the emergency decree was rescinded on January 30, popular unrest continued, forcing the general's resignation on March 10. His acting successor, Army Chief of Staff Herard ABRAHAM, promised to remain in office for no more than 72 hours, and on March 13 Supreme Court justice Ertha PASCAL-TROUILLOT was sworn in (also on an acting basis) as the country's first female president and its fifth chief executive since the Duvalier ouster.

Presidential and legislative elections, initially scheduled for September 1990, were deferred due to voter-registration problems until December 16. Fr. Jean-Bertrand ARISTIDE, a radical Catholic priest who had been expelled from his order two years earlier, won a landslide victory with 67 percent of the vote, in what was, given the country's electoral record, an atypically democratic and peaceful process. However, Aristide's somewhat hastily organized coalition, the National Front for Change and Democracy (*Front National pour le Changement et la Démocratie*—FNCD), was able to nominate only 50 candidates for the 110 seats in the two legislative houses. Following his inauguration on February 7, 1991, the new head of state was obliged to settle for his second-choice candidate for prime minister, the politically inexperienced René PRÉVAL, who took office on February 13.

On September 30, 1991, scarcely more than seven months after his installation as Haiti's first democratically elected chief executive, Aristide was ousted and sent into exile in a bloody coup headed (although reportedly not instigated) by the armed forces commander, Brig. Gen. Raoul CÉDRAS. On October 8 a rump group of senators was induced to declare the presidency vacant and approve the installation of Supreme Court president Joseph NERETTE as interim head of state. Nerette, in turn, named Jean-Jacques HONORAT, a former diplomat and government official who had been exiled by the younger Duvalier in 1981, to head a government formed on October 16.

On October 29, 1991, the United States imposed strict economic sanctions, which induced the military-backed regime to enter into negotiations with a mission from the Organization of American States (OAS) aimed at restoring Aristide to office. By late November the talks were at an impasse, with the Haitians demanding an end to the embargo but refusing to reinstate the ousted president. Honorat then challenged the OAS by announcing that new elections would be held in early January, although most of December was spent in an effort to find a prime ministerial candidate who would be acceptable to Aristide, Cédras, and Haitian political and business leaders.

In January 1992 a compromise reached in Caracas, Venezuela, that called for the appointment of René THEODORE, secretary general of the Unified Party of Haitian Communists (*Parti Unifié des Communistes Haïtiens*—PUCH), as prime minister was repudiated by the military leadership. In an understanding reached in Washington, D.C., on February 23 among Aristide, Theodore, and a Haitian parliamentary delegation, Aristide dropped a demand for Cédras's removal and offered immunity from prosecution for all those involved in the coup. Subsequently, however, Aristide withdrew the pledge, while the military-dominated National Assembly refused to endorse the plan after Nerette had characterized it as "unconstitutional."

On May 9, 1992, military, government, and legislative leaders in Port-au-Prince proposed the appointment of a new government and Nerette's resignation "at a suitable moment," with no mention of a successor. Pro-Aristide deputies succeeded in blocking passage of the unilateral scheme, but a more specific version was approved on May 20 that provided for Nerette's departure upon the installation of a new administration, with no presidential replacement until an overall political solution had been reached. Accordingly, Nerette on June 2 named conservative businessperson and former World Bank official Marc Louis BAZIN to head a government that was installed on June 19.

In early July 1992 Aristide demanded a UN presence in Haiti and declared that he would meet with Bazin only after the latter had relinquished office. On the other hand, the head of Aristide's "presidential commission," Rev. Antoine ADRIEN, and Bazin's foreign minister, François BENOIT, met in Washington, D.C., on September 1 with the Haitian regime, agreeing on September 12 to the deployment of 18 human rights observers (3 per department, as contrasted with 18 per department sought by Aristide). However, in mid-December, after being permitted only one brief probe beyond Port-au-Prince, the UN team was charged by the Bazin government as having "no legal basis" to continue its activities. Subsequently, under strong pressure from both the United States and the UN, the government reversed track, and in mid-March the first of several hundred observers arrived under the leadership of UN mediator Dante Caputo.

In mid-April 1993 Caputo left Port-au-Prince after failing to obtain General Cédras's assent to a UN/U.S. plan by which the general would step down in return for an amnesty for his involvement in Aristide's ouster. The regime's intransigence was further reflected by its refusal on May 24 to accept a multilateral military force to supervise Aristide's return to office. On June 15 the Haitian legislature agreed to Aristide's reinstatement as president but set no date for his return and attached conditions (including a general amnesty for his military opponents) that he had long declared unacceptable. Shortly thereafter, the army agreed to "proximity talks" between General Cédras and Aristide, which began on June 27 in New York. Meanwhile, Prime Minister Bazin was obliged to submit his resignation after four of his ministers refused to step down in what appeared to be a failed *autogolpe* (self-coup).

The New York meeting in June 1993 yielded an agreement that provided for Aristide's return to Haiti on October 30, assuming the following sequence of events: (1) a "dialogue" under UN and OAS auspices of Haiti's parties, leading to the annulment of a partial senatorial election that had been conducted, despite an opposition boycott, in January; (2) the naming by Aristide of a prime minister; (3) acceptance of the nominee by the "normalized" Haitian parliament; (4) the lifting of UN and OAS sanctions against Haiti; (5) the modernizing of Haiti's armed forces, with the assistance of a 2,000-member international force (half from the United States); (6) an amnesty for those involved in the 1991 coup; (7) the creation of a new police force under an Aristide-appointed commander; and (8) General Cédras's "early retirement."

On August 3, 1993, it was announced that Robert MALVAL, a wealthy Port-au-Prince businessman, had been asked by President Aristide to become the next prime minister. Malval, characterized as a "profoundly reluctant public figure," was reported to have accepted the job on condition that he play a purely transitional role and be replaced by a permanent successor no later than December 15. On August 25 the Haitian parliament, after extensive wrangling between pro- and anti-Aristide blocs, approved the appointment of Malval, who was sworn in by the exiled president five days later at the Haitian embassy in Washington. However, the military, headed by General Cédras but apparently under the effective control of police chief Michel FRANÇOIS, mounted a concerted effort to block Aristide's return. Perhaps most importantly, it refused to counter a wave of domestic violence by thousands of armed military "attachés" modeled after the *Macoutes*.

On October 15, 1993, U.S. president Bill Clinton dispatched a flotilla of six warships to Haitian waters to enforce an oil and arms embargo ordered by the UN Security Council after a contingent of American and Canadian advisers for a UN peacekeeping force had been prevented from disembarking in Port-au-Prince. The military responded by pressing for completion of the first major highway linking Haiti to the neighboring Dominican Republic.

Prime Minister Malval's formal resignation on December 15, 1993, coincided with the conclusion of a two-week foreign trip, during which he failed in an attempt to mount a national conference to break the country's political stalemate. Although initially supporting the initiative during a meeting with Malval and President Clinton at the White House, Aristide subsequently reversed his position, drawing from Malval the criticism that he possessed "a serious ego problem." Malval went on to characterize the impasse between Cédras and Aristide as involving "a man who refuses to resign and a man who has made a choice to remain abroad as a sort of flag bearer, a mystic symbol."

On January 11, 1994, anti-Aristide upper house members attempted to dismiss the Senate president by lowering the number required for a quorum from 11 to 9. Two days later the Chamber of Deputies employed a less questionable procedure in dismissing its pro-Aristide speaker, Antoine JOSEPH, in favor of Frantz Robert MONDE, a former *Tontons Macoutes* leader.

On February 15, 1994, Aristide rejected a U.S.-backed peace plan that called for the appointment of a broad-based government without setting dates for the exiled president's return or a military stepdown. Another U.S. plan in late March that called for Cédras's removal, but not that of François, was also rejected by Aristide. Washington then called for a global trade embargo of Haiti, which, along with a freeze on the foreign assets of about 600 army officers, was approved by the UN Security Council, effective May 22. Meanwhile, anti-Aristide legislators had on May 11 declared the presidency vacant, thus permitting the 80-year-old president of the Supreme Court, Émile JONASSAINT, to assume the office on a "provisional" basis. On June 24 direct flights to and from the United States were terminated, with all international commercial flights ending on July 30. Finally, on July 30 the Security Council authorized a U.S.-led invasion if Haiti's military attempted to continue in office.

On September 17, 1994, former U.S. president Jimmy Carter, U.S. armed forces chief of staff Gen. Colin Powell, and Senator Sam Nunn flew to Port-au-Prince for a "last best effort" meeting with Cédras and Jonassaint. The talks yielded an agreement signed by Carter and Jonassaint the following day that provided for the "honorable retirement" of "certain military officers of the Haitian armed forces," the approval of a general amnesty by the Haitian parliament, the lifting of economic sanctions "in accordance with United Nations resolutions" (which required President Aristide's return), coordination by U.S. and Haitian military units, and formal approval of the accord by the U.S. and Haitian governments.

On September 19, 1994, an initial contingent of 2,000 U.S. troops landed without incident on Haitian soil. On October 10 General Cédras resigned his command, and he flew to exile in Panama three days later. On October 15 President Aristide received an exuberant welcome on his return to Haiti, and on October 18 he appointed wealthy U.S.-educated businessman Smark MICHEL as prime minister. A new government was named by Michel on November 6 and sworn in November 8 amid pledges to revitalize the economy, in part by privatizing most large industries. Other objectives included "relaunching" the agricultural sector, improving tax collection, creating an autonomous university, and establishing a "truth commission" to investigate human rights abuses during the period of military-backed rule. For his part, President Aristide, bowing to pressure from the Catholic hierarchy, agreed on November 16 to leave the priesthood.

In two-stage balloting for partial Senate replenishment and a new Chamber of Deputies (originally scheduled for June 4 and 25, 1995, but not completed until September 17), President Aristide's Lavalas Political Organization (*Organisation Politique Lavalas*—OPL) gained control of both houses by wide margins.

By mid-1995 Prime Minister Michel was warning of "drastic consequences" if the economic program backed by the IMF should fail. He also reportedly complained of President Aristide's lack of support for one of the plan's crucial components: the privatization of nine state enterprises. Michel resigned on October 16, 1995, and was succeeded by the (then) foreign minister, Claudette WERLEIGH, who was believed to share the president's doubts about divestiture, particularly in view of the anticipated loss of 6,000 jobs.

Despite considerable uncertainty as to his intentions, President Aristide on November 30, 1995, reiterated an earlier pledge that he would not attempt to extend his term to discount his years in exile, and on December 17 the Lavalas candidate, René Préval, secured an overwhelming mandate, albeit on a turnout of substantially less than half of the electorate, as Haiti's next head of state. Although Préval reportedly favored the installation of former Lavalas leader Gérard PIERRE-CHARLES as prime minister, the selection was vetoed by the outgoing president, who preferred retention of the incumbent. It was not until March 6 that Rosny SMARTH, having secured legislative approval, was sworn in as the new head of government.

Subsequently, a rift emerged between the essentially populist Aristide and Prime Minister Smarth, who sought to implement an IMF-approved structural-adjustment program that included substantial privatization. In November 1996 the former president broke with the existing Lavalas organization by forming a competing Lavalas Family movement that applied for registration as a party in early 1997. While Smarth survived a no-confidence vote on March 27, he felt obliged to submit his resignation on June 9 amid a mounting wave of strikes and demonstrations against his policies. On June 25 President Préval named an economist, Ericq PIERRE, as Smarth's successor. However, Pierre failed to secure legislative approval, and on August 20 Smarth announced that he would no longer continue in a "caretaker" capacity. On November 3 Préval nominated another economist, Hervé DENIS, as the next prime minister, but Denis was also rejected by the legislature, on December 23. A third nominee, Jacques-Édouard ALEXIS, was declared eligible by the two houses of Parliament in December 1998, but he fell two votes short of approval by the Chamber of Deputies in early January 1999.

On January 12, 1999, President Préval ruled that the term of office of nearly all members of the National Assembly (as well as those of mayors and many other municipal officers) had expired the previous day under the law governing the 1995 election. He therefore declared the assembly dissolved and announced he would rule by decree, with Alexis serving as prime minister, pending negotiations with various political groups regarding new elections. Discussions with opposition parties yielded an agreement in early March on a transition government, which was sworn in on March 26 under the leadership of Alexis, and establishment of a nine-member Provisional Electoral Council (*Conseil Electoral Provisoire*—CEP) to oversee balloting that the government hoped to conduct before the end of the year.

In June 1999 the CEP set aside the 1997 legislative election results and called for a new poll the following November. The date was subsequently changed to March 21, 2000, then to April 9, and finally to May 21, at which time first-round balloting was conducted for municipal councils, the full Chamber of Deputies, and 19 Senate seats. Opposition parties, many having coalesced under the banner of the Democratic Convergence (*Convergence Démocratique*—CD), charged the government with fraud in counting the votes from the May 21 balloting and called for a boycott of second-round balloting on July 9, arguing that only complete new elections would expunge the irregularities. Meanwhile, on June 17 the CEP president, Léon MANUS, fled the country because of alleged threats over his refusal to certify the May 21 results.

On August 16, 2000, the CEP announced that the Lavalas Family had won 72 of the lower house seats, 18 of the contested Senate seats, and about 80 percent of the municipal seats. The CD-led opposition also boycotted the presidential balloting of November 26, at which Aristide was credited with 92 percent of the vote over six other candidates. Following his inauguration on February 7, 2001, Aristide appointed Jean-Marie CHÉRESTAL, a former finance minister and trade negotiator, to form a new government, which was installed on March 2. However, in light of the continued debilitating impasse with the opposition and rapid economic decline, Chérestal in January 2002 announced his intention to resign as prime minister. He was succeeded on March 14 by Yvon NEPTUNE, theretofore president of the Senate.

During the ensuing two years, the Aristide regime encountered a mounting wave of strikes and mass protests, culminating in an armed uprising that yielded the fall of Haiti's fourth largest city, Goncaïves, to insurgents on February 5, 2004. On February 22, Haiti's second largest city, Cap-Haïtien, also fell. With rebel forces led by Guy PHILIPPE and Louis-Jodel CHAMBLAIN approaching the capital, President Aristide resigned on February 29 and was flown into exile (under duress, he subsequently maintained) on a U.S. aircraft. Concurrently, U.S. president George W. Bush ordered the dispatch of 500 marines to Port-au-Prince, with France announcing that 200 of its troops would be similarly deployed and the UN Security Council authorizing the formation of a multinational interim peacekeeping force.

In the wake of Aristide's departure, his constitutionally designated successor, Supreme Court president Boniface ALEXANDRE, was sworn in as acting head of state on March 8, 2004. On March 9 a U.S.-backed Council of Elders announced that it had appointed as interim prime minister Gérard LATORTUE, who proceeded to name a largely nonpartisan cabinet. On December 9 Latortue stated that he would not contest the presidential balloting originally scheduled for November 2005.

After four postponements, presidential and legislative elections were held on February 7, 2006. Former president René Préval won the presidential balloting, narrowly avoiding a runoff with 51.2 percent of the vote. However, his installation was delayed until May 14 because of inconclusive legislative results that necessitated a runoff poll on April 21 in which a mere 15–20 percent of eligible voters were reported to have participated. Préval took office on May 14, and three days later nominated Alexis to serve again as prime minister, a nomination that was ratified almost unanimously by parliament. Alexis's new cabinet comprised members of five parties.

In the wake of massive protest demonstrations ignited by dramatic price increases on food, fuel, and other basic goods, Prime Minister Alexis lost a censure motion (the equivalent of a nonconfidence vote) by a 16-1 vote in the Senate on April 12, 2008, and was thereby constitutionally required to resign. Following the legislative rejection of President Préval's first two nominees (see Current issues, below), Michèle PIERRE-LOUIS, a nonparty economist, was inaugurated as the country's second female prime minister on September 6; her new cabinet contained members of Préval's Front for Hope (*Fwon Lespwa/ Front de l'Espoir*), Aristide's The Lavalas Family (*La Fanmi Lavalas*), and several smaller parties.

Constitution and government. The 1987 constitution, repudiated by General Namphy in July 1988, was restored by President Pascal-Trouillot in 1990 and remained nominally intact after the 1991 coup. (Haiti returned to constitutional rule in October 2004, but the constitution was not properly enforced until May 2006.) The document provides for a directly elected president, who may serve no more than two nonsequential five-year terms, and a prime minister, who is responsible to a legislature composed of a Senate and Chamber of Deputies. The president negotiates and signs all treaties and presides over the Council of Ministers; the prime minister must come from the legislative majority or, if there is none, be appointed after consultation with the chamber presidents, subject to parliamentary endorsement. Constitutional amendments, which must be supported by a two-thirds majority in each house and approved by a majority of two-thirds of the votes cast in a joint legislative sitting, can come into effect only after the installation of the next elected president. The judiciary encompasses a Supreme Court (*Cour de Cassation*), whose president serves as acting head of state in the event of a vacancy; courts of appeal; courts of first instance; justices of the peace; and special courts as prescribed by law.

The 1987 basic law divided the traditionally monolithic armed forces into distinct military and police components; accorded the universally spoken Creole language official status in addition to French; banned Duvalierists from public office for ten years; authorized an independent commission to supervise elections; asserted the previously nonexistent rights of free education, decent housing, and a fair wage; and eliminated sanctions (theretofore largely ignored) against the practice of voodoo.

Haiti is presently divided into ten departments, each headed by a presidentially appointed prefect and subdivided into *arrondisements* and communes.

Foreign relations. Despite its membership in a number of international bodies, Haiti has avoided close ties with neighboring countries, and before joining the Association of Caribbean States (ACS), founded in 1994, had distanced itself from most moves toward Caribbean economic and political integration. Its historically most sensitive foreign affairs issue, the border relationship with the Dominican Republic, has been periodically aggravated by activities of political exiles from both countries. Relations with the United States, which were briefly suspended in 1963, have fluctuated, the Duvalier government frequently using its votes in international bodies to bargain for increased foreign assistance from Washington.

In early 1983 long-standing litigation regarding the rights of Haitian refugee "boat people" being detained in Florida was resolved by a U.S. landmark decision, which allowed about 1,700 detainees to apply for political asylum while establishing constitutional protection for those remaining incarcerated. In September 1985 Haiti concluded an agreement with the Bahamas that would require all illegal immigrants to register with Bahamian authorities, with only those resident in the islands before December 30, 1980, married to Bahamians, or owning real estate being permitted to remain.

In the wake of President Aristide's ouster in 1991, a new wave of Haitians attempted to flee by boat to the United States. By early 1992 several thousand had been picked up at sea by the U.S. Coast Guard and accorded temporary refuge in Guantánamo Bay, Cuba. By midyear the exodus had largely ended, in the wake of an order by President George H. W. Bush on May 24 that all Haitians intercepted at sea be returned immediately to their homeland without determination of whether they qualified for political asylum. The order was overturned on July 26 by a New York appeals court but upheld by the U.S. Supreme Court on August 1. In early 1993 it was estimated that of more than 40,000 Haitians attempting to reach the United States since the 1991 coup, nearly three-quarters had been returned by the U.S. Coast Guard. By mid-1994 the Clinton administration had demonstrated considerable ambivalence on the matter, initially adhering to the Bush policy of repatriation, then supporting ship-based processing of refugees for possible transfer to third countries. However, a less-than-enthusiastic response to the latter policy, particularly from Panama, led, in early July, to an announcement that the processing facilities in Guantánamo would be reactivated. Thus, despite the ease with which Cubans had thenceforth been able to claim eligibility for asylum in the United States, the number of Haitians that could look forward to such status was held to approximately 5 percent.

The United States, which had favored the conservative Bazin in the 1991 presidential poll, joined the OAS embargo against the military-backed government and was a prime mover in the June 1993 talks that established the original timetable for Aristide's return to office. By the end of September 1994, the U.S. military intervention involved 20,000 troops, with their eventual replacement, a 6,900-member UN Mission in Haiti (UNMIH), being assembled in Puerto Rico. By late December the U.S. contingent had been reduced to approximately 9,000 personnel, of whom only 5,000 remained upon transfer of responsibility for Haitian security to the UNMIH on March 31, 1995. The balance of the U.S. force, apart from about 200 noncombatant personnel, withdrew on January 18, 2000.

The UNMIH mandate was extended for six months from March 1, 1996, albeit only after China (which objected to Haitian relations with Taiwan) had insisted on a reduction to 1,200 troops; however, Canada announced that it would provide an additional 700 personnel at its own expense to bring the total up to the Security Council's target of 1,900. The peacekeeping mission was renewed for an additional five months on July 1 (and renamed the UN Support Mission in Haiti, or UNSMIH), after China had dictated a new cut to 600 (exclusive of 700 from Canada, Pakistan, and Bangladesh, funded jointly by Canada and the United States). In early December the Security Council voted to extend the UNSMIH until May 31, 1997, subject to renewal at that time for two additional months. Although it had been agreed that the mission would not continue past July 31, the mandate was further extended to November 30, with the last UN troops departing during the ensuing month, save for a 300-member police monitoring unit (the United Nations Civilian Police Mission in Haiti/*Mission de Police Civile des Nations Unies en Haïti*—MIPONUH) that was to remain for another year.

In March 1996 President Préval met with his counterpart from the Dominican Republic in the first visit by a Haitian president to the neighboring state in more than six decades. Despite the rapprochement, more than 15,000 Haitians were expelled from the Dominican Republic in late January and early February 1997. In an effort to avert a crisis, the two presidents agreed during a summit of the Caribbean Community and Common Market (Caricom) on February 20–21 to an immediate halt to large-scale repatriation, while acknowledging the right of the Dominican Republic to deport illegal immigrants. Despite the accord, Haitian officials claimed in November that as many as 40,000 Haitians (of an estimated 500,000 without legal status) had been forced to leave the Dominican Republic during the year.

Reciprocating Préval's 1996 visit to the Dominican Republic, Leonel Fernández on June 18–20, 1998, became the first Dominican head of state to visit Haiti since Rafael Trujillo in 1936. A meeting of the two presidents was preceded by a session of a joint Dominican–Haitian commission, which reached agreement in a number of areas without resolving such major issues as migration and trade.

The U.S. military presence in the wake of Aristide's second departure from office in 2004 quickly grew to a 3,600-member force, which on June 1 formally transferred its peacekeeping mandate to a UN Stabilization Mission in Haiti (*Mission des Nations Unies pour la Stabilisation en Haïti*—MINUSTAH), which had 7,413 troops and civilian police deployed as of April 2005. (The mandate for MINUSTAH, focused to a large degree on quelling urban gang warfare, has been extended routinely since 2006, most recently in October 2008 for one year, with the Security Council stating its intention to renew the force for later periods.)

Tension with the Dominican Republic reescalated in mid-2005 with the withdrawal of the Haitian ambassador after the lynching of three Haitians in Santo Domingo. The Dominicans responded by deporting 1,000 illegals on August 15 and, shortly thereafter, 1,000 more of an estimated 1 million Haitians said to be living in the country.

In March 2007 Venezuela and Cuba announced the creation of a $1 billion fund to aid Haiti, while Venezuelan president Chávez, during a visit to Port-au-Prince, promised additional assistance, including an increase in oil shipments from 3,000 to 14,000 barrels per day. Venezuela also provided aid to help Haiti cope with the economic shocks of price increases and hurricanes in 2008, as did the United States and other donors. Among other things, the International Monetary Fund and World Bank in 2009 offered substantial debt relief to Haiti, setting the stage for additional relief from other intergovernmental and commercial lenders. Meanwhile, UN Secretary General Ban Ki Moon named former U.S. president Bill Clinton as his special envoy to Haiti in mid-2009 in support of the government's economic recovery program.

Current Issues. René Préval was accorded a narrow first-round victory in the 2006 presidential race only after the CEF, on somewhat dubious legal ground, eliminated about 85,000 blank ballots from the tabulation. The move drew intense opposition criticism, even though the second-place contender, former president Leslie Manigat, secured only 12.4 percent of the vote. While Préval's *Lespwa* formation won only 22 of 99 lower house seats, the new president was able to secure support from other parties (in return for cabinet posts) for the designation of Prime Minister Alexis and legislative officers.

Préval's return to office left Aristide's status uncertain. The *Fanmi Lavalas* had been divided over support for the former president's one-time protégé, while Préval himself hedged on Aristide's return, stating only that the constitution did not allow for the banishment of any Haitian. For his part, in a videotaped message broadcast on the Internet, Aristide declared that despite voting for "hope" (the name of Préval's party), Haitians had found only "hopelessness."

In a speech at the National Palace in October 2007, President Préval proposed constitutional changes to allow the government greater flexibility to target corruption, promote development, and prepare for the eventual departure of UN peacekeepers. Préval called for parliament to initiate amendments to allow a president to serve for two consecutive terms, as opposed to the nonconsecutive terms currently permitted. He also proposed that future elections be held at five-year intervals and recommended the creation of a constitutional court, as well as the expansion of presidential powers to include the right to dismiss the prime minister, a prerogative currently reserved for parliament. Recognizing that his call for an expansion of presidential authority could raise suspicions about his intentions, Préval reiterated that his tenure would "end on [February] 7, 2011, period." However, Préval's proposals failed to gain sufficient support in the legislature and never reached the floor for a vote.

Hurricanes in August and October 2007 devastated harvests, prompting the start of a food crisis that grew extremely severe in early 2008 as the result of worldwide increases in commodity prices (the country imports most of its fuel and food, including 80 percent of its rice, the primary basic food). Unrest erupted in the southwestern town of Les Cayes in early April 2008 and spread rapidly to other areas, including Port-au-Prince. Several deaths were reported during ten days of rioting and looting, and Prime Minister Alexis was censured by the Senate on April 12 for his administration's perceived ineffectiveness in dealing with the crisis. (Among other things, Alexis had misjudged the extent of popular discontent by initially blaming the demonstrations on drug traffickers.) With the departure of Alexis, the incumbent members of the cabinet remained in place, but in a caretaker capacity, leaving the Préval government unable to take major policy initiatives. Late in the month President Préval nominated Ericq Pierre, the nation's representative to the Inter-American Development Bank, for prime minister, but the Chamber of Deputies rejected Pierre (as had happened in 1997) because he could not produce a birth certificate for one of his grandmothers (prime ministers must be descended from native-born Haitians). Préval's second choice, Robert MANUEL (a former minister of public security and the manager of Préval's 2006 campaign), was also blocked in the Chamber in June, ostensibly on technical grounds, including the fact that Manuel had not lived in Haiti for five consecutive years (as constitutionally required), had only recently registered to vote, and did not own property in Haiti. (Manuel's supporters argued that drug traffickers and other criminals had "paid off" deputies to reject Manuel.) As had been the case with Pierre, much of the opposition to Manuel in the Chamber came from the recently formed Conference of Progressive Parliamentarians (*Concertation des Parlementaires Progressistes*—CPP) in the Chamber, which, reflecting deep divisions with Préval's *Lespwa*, included many *Lespwa* deputies.

On June 23, 2008, Préval nominated a third prime ministerial candidate, Michèle Pierre-Louis. A respected economist and grassroots advocate for Haiti's poor and youth, Pierre-Louis was the director of FOKAL, a nongovernmental organization focused on education and culture and financed by internationalist billionaire George Soros. Her nomination was ratified by the Chamber of Deputies on July 17, with 61 deputies voting in favor, 1 against, and 20 abstaining. On July 31, Pierre-Louis was approved by the Senate by a 12-5 vote.

Pierre-Louis was still expected to face difficulties in forming a cabinet and gaining the necessary approval for her policy goals within the fractious legislature. However, political considerations dwindled when Hurricane Gustav and two other storms killed upwards of a thousand people, inflicted an estimated $1.5 billion in damage, and left more than 1 million people food-deprived and homeless. Préval called for massive international assistance, arguing that Haiti had reached the "tipping point" and could become a "base for terrorism" or a regional "hub for drug trafficking" if total collapse occurred. For her part, Prime Minister Pierre-Louis promised a "cohesive" and "responsible" government, a pledge that critics said was undercut by the CEP's decision not to permit FL candidates to contest the 2009 Senate elections (see FL under Political Parties, below).

POLITICAL PARTIES

All parties were outlawed during the first six years of the François Duvalier dictatorship. In 1963 a regime-supportive National Unity Party (*Parti de l'Unité Nationale*—PUN) was organized with an exclusive mandate to engage in electoral activity. Its Jean-Claudiste successor, the National Progressive Party (*Parti Nationale Progressiste*—PNP), was launched in September 1985. Six years earlier, three unofficial groups had surfaced: the PSCH and PDCH (below), plus a Haitian National Christian Party (*Parti Chrétien National d'Haïti*—PCNH) organized by Rev. René des RAMEAUX; all three were subjected to intermittent repression for the remainder of the Duvalier era.

In March 1987 it was reported that more than 60 new parties had been formed. Two months earlier, a National Congress of Democratic Movements (*Congrès National des Mouvements Démocratiques*—CNMD/Konakom) had been organized in opposition to the Namphy regime by delegates from nearly 300 political groups, trade unions, peasants' and students' organizations, and human rights associations. Subsequently, the CNMD became the core of a loosely organized "Group of 57" that organized a variety of antigovernment protests (including a general strike in Port-au-Prince on June 29) before being amalgamated into a National Front for Concerted Action (*Front National de Concertation*—FNC) in September. The FNC joined the PDCH in boycotting the election of January 1988.

Although a large number of groups participated in the December 1990 balloting, the FNCD (under Alyans, below), Panpra (under PFSDH, below), and the MIDH (below) emerged as the principal formations. By 1995 the PPL (under OPL, below) had become the dominant group, most opposition groups boycotting the legislative balloting of June–August and the December presidential poll; in late 1997, however, the PPL's dominance was challenged by the Lavalas Family (*La Fanmi Lavalas*), a new formation launched by former president Aristide.

Following the disputed first-round elections of May 21, 2000, about 15 opposition parties formed the Democratic Convergence (*Convergence Démocratique*—CD), which became the primary anti-Aristide coalition. United primarily (if not solely) by their "common hatred" of Aristide, the CD parties boycotted the second round of balloting on July 3 as well as the presidential and Senate polls on November 26. Calling the Aristide government "illegitimate," the CD in February 2001 announced that it had named Gérard Gourgue of the FNC (below) as "alternative president." The CD declined an offer to join the government of Prime Minister Neptune in March 2002, demanding instead the installation of a "consensus" administration to oversee new presidential and legislative elections.

About 70 political groups existed before the 2006 elections, of which 10–50 were active in the run-up to the first-round poll on February 7, with numerous changes occurring before the second-round legislative balloting on April 21.

In 2008 a new lower chamber cross-party voting bloc, the Conference of Progressive Parliamentarians (*Concertation des Parlementaires Progressistes*—CPP) was formed to protest the upper house's decision to dismiss Prime Minister Alexis. Bringing together 53 of the 99 deputies, including around 20 dissident *Lespwa* members, the new bloc was seen as a challenge to the authority of President Préval and put an end to his lower house coalition. In June one of the leaders of the new group, Levaillant LOUIS-JEUNE, stated in an interview with Haitian newspaper *Le Nouvelliste* that its goals included the renewal of the country's political class. In the Chamber poll held on May 12, 2008, the 20 CPP members of Préval's party voted against their leader's first chosen prime ministerial candidate, Ericq Pierre, who subsequently alleged that CPP members had wanted him to buy their support. The CPP also opposed Robert Manuel (Préval's second nominee) but endorsed Michèle Pierre-Louis for the premiership.

Legislative Parties:

Front for Hope (*Fwon Lespwa/Front de l'Espoir—Lespwa*). *Lespwa* was launched by René Préval (theretofore a member of Lavalas) in his successful bid for a second presidential term in 2006. Upon completion of the legislative balloting in December, it held a plurality of 22 seats, although the party was fractured (at least temporarily) by the participation of *Lespwa* deputies in the CPP (see above). *Lespwa* won 6 of the 11 contested seats in the 2009 Senate elections, bringing its total to 12, enough to convince some analysts that Préval might be able to cobble together a coalition within the Senate sufficient to endorse his proposed constitutional changes.

Leader: René PRÉVAL (President of the Republic).

Haitian Social-Democratic Fusion Party (*Parti Fusion des Sociaux-Démocrates Haïtiens*—PFSDH or Fusion). Fusion was launched before the 2006 elections by Serge Gilles, who had previously led the Nationalist Revolutionary Progressive Party (*Parti National Progressiste Révolucionnaire*—Panpra) that in 1989 became the first Haitian party to be admitted to the Socialist International. In 2004 Gilles organized the Haitian Socialist Grand Party (*Grand Parti Socialiste Haïtien*—GPSH), which became a component of Fusion.

Fusion was runner-up to *Lespwa* in the 2006 Chamber of Deputies balloting. In 2007–2008 Micha Gaillard, a professor and the former spokesperson for the anti-Aristide coalition CD, emerged as a key voice within Fusion. Gaillard has been a critic of the perceived slow pace of social change in Haiti under President Préval and of the government's response to spiking food costs. In May 2007 Gaillard called a deal signed between the United States and Australia to swap refugees "immoral," insofar as it could spur an increased number of Haitian asylum seekers to head for the U.S. coast under the largely mistaken impression that they might then be resettled in Australia.

Leaders: Victor BENOIT (Chair), Serge GILLES (2006 presidential candidate), Micha GAILLARD (Spokesperson).

Democratic Alliance Party (*Alliance Démocratique*—AD/Alyans). Alyans originated in 2006 as an electoral alliance formed by the Convention for Democratic Unity (*Komite Inite Demokratik*—KID), led by Evans Paul, and the People's Party for Haiti's Rebirth (*Parti Populaire Du Renouveau Haïtien*—PPRH), led by Claude ROUMAIN. The PPRH had been forged in January 2005 as a merger of Roumain's party Generation 2004 and the Haitian Liberal and Social Party.

Paul, who was campaign manager for Jean-Bertrand Aristide in 1990, had formerly been the head of the National Front for Change and Democracy (*Front National pour le Changement et la Démocratie*—FNCD), formed in late 1990 as an alliance of more than a dozen left-of-center groups supporting Aristide. In 1999 he launched the Harmonious Space for Preservation of Democracy (*Espace de Concertation pour la Sauvegarde de la Démocratie*—EC/*Espace*) as an alliance of the FNCD and other groups to contest the legislative balloting conducted on May 21, 2000.

Alyans placed third in the 2006 lower house poll.

Leader: Evans PAUL (Former Mayor of Port-au-Prince).

Organization of the Struggling People (*Organisation du Peuple en Lutte*—OPL). The current OPL is an offshoot of the center-left Lavalas Political Organization (*Organisation Politique Lavalas*—OPL), which emerged after its founding in 1991 as the principal pro-Aristide formation. In 1995 the latter group launched the Lavalas Political Platform (*Plateforme Politique Lavalas*—PPL) as an alliance that also included the PLB (below) and the Movement for the Organization of the Country (*Mouvement d'Organisation du Pays*—MOP), a center-right formation whose leader, Jean MOLIERE, had been the third-ranked presidential candidate in 1988.

In 1996 the original OPL split into two groups—the pro-Aristide FL (below) and the Organization of the Struggling People, which retained the OPL abbreviation and became a "bitter opponent" of Aristide and a leading rival of the FL. The OPL initially joined the Democratic Consultation Group in negotiations with President Préval in February 1999. However, it withdrew from the group following the assassination of OPL senator Jean-Yvon TOUSSAINT in early March, demanding that the crime be solved as a prerequisite to the party's return to discussions with the government. Consequently, the OPL was not represented in the new cabinet installed in late March. The OPL was one of the leading parties in the election scheduled for late 1999, postponed to May 21, 2000.

OPL leader Paul Denis headed an inquiry that in 2005 accused Aristide of misusing $50 million in public money. Denis ran for president unsuccessfully in 2006, and in 2008, after the exit of Prime Minister Alexis, he was suggested as a potential prime ministerial nominee. However, despite Denis's experience as a former senator and as an adviser to President Préval, analysts suggested that his anti-Lavalas credentials rendered him too controversial to secure the position.

When Ericq Pierre received the prime ministerial nomination from Préval, the OPL worked unsuccessfully to form a majority in favor of ratification. Subsequently, the OPL strongly objected to decisions made by the CEP in regard to the 2009 Senate elections.

Leaders: Paul DENIS (2006 presidential candidate), Edgard LEBLANC (Coordinator).

The Lavalas Family (*La Fanmi Lavalas*—FL). The FL was launched by former president Aristide in November 1996. While Aristide denied that the new group was intended as an "instrument of division," it reflected his growing disenchantment with President Préval's economic policies and served as a vehicle for his return to the presidency in November 2000.

Activist and a former priest Gérard JEAN-JUSTE, the FL's initial 2006 presidential candidate, was disqualified by the CEP for not personally submitting his registration by the deadline (which would have been impossible, as he was imprisoned at the time). The party formally boycotted the election, although a portion of its membership endorsed Préval.

On April 30, 2008, four years after the latest ouster of Aristide, 5,000 of his supporters marched in the streets of Port-au-Prince to demand his return from exile. In July speculation resurfaced that Jean-Juste was planning a presidential bid: "I am not a candidate," Jean-Juste was reported as saying, "but if the Lavalas party offered me or asked me to be a candidate, I would consider it."

Reflecting longstanding internal divisions within the FL, two separate FL candidate lists were initially presented for the 2009 Senate elections, prompting the CEP to reject both lists and seek endorsement of a candidate list from Aristide, who called the election a sham and declined to be involved in the process. The competing FL factions subsequently agreed on a single list, which was again rejected by the CEP because of the lack of Aristide's signature on accompanying documents. FL officials noted that such formalities had not surfaced for the 2006 balloting and argued that Aristide had "not been actively making decisions about the party's activities for several years now." The FL, which had been expected to perform well in the Senate balloting, called for a boycott of the elections, while many international observers described the party's exclusion as a setback for democratization.

Leaders: Jean-Bertrand ARISTIDE (Former President of the Republic, in exile), Luis GÉRARD-GILLES (2006 presidential candidate).

National Christian Union for the Reconstruction of Haiti (*Union Nationale Chrétienne pour la Reconstruction d'Haïti*—UNCRH). The UNCRH candidate, Jean Chevannes Jeune, a pastor and civil engineer, placed fourth in the 2006 presidential balloting with a vote share of 5.6 percent.

Leaders: Jean Chavannes JEUNE (2006 presidential candidate), Maryse NARCISSE (Head of Executive Council), Yvon BUISSERETH, Annette AUGUSTE (leader of anti-Narcisse faction).

Mobilization for Haiti's Progress (*Mobilisation pour le Progrès d'Haïti*—MPH). The MPH won four lower house seats in 2006.

Leader: Samir Georges MOURRA.

Rally of Progressive National Democrats (*Rassemblement des Démocrates Nationaux Progressistes*—RDNP). The RDNP was organized by Leslie Manigat while an exile in Venezuela during the 1970s. Strongly anticommunist, Manigat called in mid-1986 for a "solidarity pact" between centrist parties. The lack of an effective response was attributed, in part, to Manigat's reputation as a *noiriste,* hence a threat to the country's powerful biracial elite. He was credited with securing a bare majority of the presidential vote in the highly controversial balloting of January 17, 1988, but was ousted in a coup on June 19. He returned from exile in 1990 but was barred from another presidential bid. In 2002 Manigat was reported to have organized a four-party opposition coalition styled the Patriotic Union (*Union Patriotique*—UP) that was followed in 2004 by a National Democratic Progressive Coalition (*Coalition des Démocrates Nationaux Progressistes*—CDNP).

Manigat placed second in the 2006 presidential race, with 12.4 percent of the vote.

In April 2008 RDNP secretary general and former first lady Myrlande Hyppolite Manigat joined the voices of those involved in the food and fuel price demonstrations, expressing disappointment that the government, and in particular Préval, had not done enough to answer people's concerns.

Leaders: Leslie François MANIGAT (Former President of the Republic and 2006 presidential candidate), Myrlande Hyppolite MANIGAT (Secretary General).

Haiti in Action (*Ayiti an Aksyon*—AAA). The AAA is the rubric recently adopted by the party formerly called Standard-Bearer in Action (*Latibonit an Aksyon/l'Arbonite en Action*—LAAA). The LAAA was formed prior to the 2006 poll, at which it won two senate and four chamber seats. Party leader Youri Latortue was the leading voice among the 16 senators who removed Alexis from office in April 2008. Latortue said that legislators ousted the prime minister because he failed to boost food production, protect people against crime, establish a national security force, and set a timetable for the departure of UN peacekeepers.

Leader: Youri LATORTUE.

Christian Movement for a New Haiti (*Mouvement Chrétien pour une Nouvelle Haïti*—Mochrena). A center-right party formed in 1991 by evangelical Protestant churches (reportedly with financial support from their U.S. counterparts), Mochrena won three seats in the 2000 balloting for the Chamber of Deputies, all of which were retained in 2006. Its 2006 presidential candidate, Luc Mésadieu, placed fifth with a 3.4 percent vote share.

Leaders: Luc MÉSADIEU (2006 presidential candidate), Gilbert N. LEGER.

Cooperative Action to Build Haiti (*Konbit pou Bati Ayiti*—Konba). Konba, which means "fight" or "combat" in Creole, won three lower house seats in 2006.

Leader: Chavannes JEAN-BAPTISTE.

National Reconstruction Front (*Front de la Reconstruction Nationale*—FRN). The FRN was launched in late February 2004 by a group of former rebels led by Guy Philippe, who played a significant role in the ouster of President Aristide. Despite being wanted on drug charges by both U.S. and Haitian authorities, Philippe openly presented himself as a candidate for the 2009 Senate elections; his application was rejected by the CEP.

Leaders: Buteur METAYER (President), Guy PHILIPPE (Secretary General).

Bridge (*Pont*). The Bridge party won two northwest Senate seats in 2006.

Leader: Evallière BEAUPLAN.

Movement for National Reconstruction (*Mouvement pour la Reconstruction Nationale*—MRN). Launched in 1991 by René Théodore, the leader theretofore of the Unified Party of Haitian Communists (*Parti Unifié des Communistes Haïtiens*—PUCH), the MRN was prohibited from participating in the 1995 elections, ostensibly because of a dispute as to whether Théodore or Jacques Rony MODESTIN (also of the MRN) controlled the party name. Subsequently, Théodore, once an Aristide ally, called for annulment of the election results.

The party secured one lower house seat in 2006.

Leaders: René THÉODORE, Jean-Enol BUTEAU.

Heads Together (*Tèt Ansanm*). *Tèt Ansanm* won a lower house seat in 2006, although the Electoral Council rejected the candidacy of its leader on the grounds that he was a U.S. citizen.
Leader: Dumarsais SIMÉUS.

Other groups winning one lower house seat each in 2006 were the **Haitian Democratic and Reform Movement** (*Mouvement Démocratique et Renovateur d'Haïti*—Modereh), led by Dany TOUSSANT and Prince Pierre SONSON; the **Independent Movement for National Reconciliation** (*Mouvement Indépendent pour la Réconciliation Nationale*—MIRN), led by Luc FLEURINORD; the **Justice for Peace and National Development** (*Justice pour la Paix et le Développement National*—JPDN), led by Rigaud DUPLAN; the **Liberal Party of Haiti** (*Parti Liberal Haïtien*—PLH), led by Gehy MICHEL; and the **Union of National and Progressive Haitians** (UNITE), led by Edouard FRANCIQUE.

Other Parties:

Respect (*Respè/Respect*). Respect is a small group launched before the 2006 presidential poll, at which its leader won third place with 8.2 percent of the vote.
Leader: Charles Henri BAKER (2006 presidential candidate).

Open the Gate Party (*Parti Louvri Barye*—PLB). Originally launched as a pro-Aristide party in mid-1992, the PLB won two seats in the 2000 balloting for the Chamber of Deputies. It was subsequently perceived as adopting a middle ground in the nation's political impasse, calling for negotiations between the FL and CD.
Leaders: Renaud BERNARDIN, François PIERRE-LOUIS (Secretary General).

Movement for the Installation of Democracy in Haiti (*Mouvement pour l'Instauration de la Démocratie en Haïti*—MIDH). The MIDH was founded in 1986 by the conservative Marc Louis Bazin, a former World Bank official, who participated in the 1988 boycott. As the 1990 presidential candidate of the National Alliance for Democracy and Progress (*Alliance Nationale pour la Démocratie et la Progrès*—ANDP) that also included Panpra, Bazin was runner-up to Aristide with a 15 percent vote share, while the ANDP ran second to the FNCD in the legislative poll.

Bazin subsequently endorsed the September 1991 coup that resulted in Aristide's ouster, and was named prime minister by Interim President Nerette on June 2, 1992. He resigned from the position on June 8, 1993. The MIDH boycotted the 1995 legislative poll but participated (unsuccessfully) in the 2000 balloting.
Leader: Marc Louis BAZIN (Former Prime Minister).

Patriotic Movement for National Salvage (*Mouvement Patriotique pour le Sauvetage National*—MPSN). The MPSN was formed in 1999 as a coalition of right-wing groups led by the Duvalierist head of the MDN (below). The MPSN participated unsuccessfully in the 2000 legislative balloting, decrying the government's "inappropriate control" of the electoral process.
Leader: Hubert de RONCERAY.

Mobilization for National Development (*Mobilisation pour le Développement National*—MDN). The runner-up to Leslie Manigat in the 1988 presidential balloting and subsequently one of the most outspoken critics of General Avril, MDN leader Hubert de Ronceray was among those expelled from the country in January 1990. He supported Aristide's ouster in 1991, and the MDN became prominent in the opposition following his return in 1994. In August 1996 two leading MDN members were shot dead in Port-au-Prince by unknown assailants. De Ronceray again went into temporary exile in October 1997 following the late August assassination of MDN deputy leader Pastor Antoine LEROY.
Leaders: Hubert de RONCERAY (President), Max CARRÉ (Secretary General).

Haitian Social Christian Party (*Parti Social Chrétien d'Haïti*—PSCH). The PSCH was launched on July 5, 1979, as one of two parties styling themselves the Haitian Christian Democratic Party (see PDCH, below). The party subsequently added the issue date of its manifesto to its name (PDCH–27 Juin), before becoming commonly identified by the Social Christian label. Its leader, Grégoire EUGÈNE, was deported to the United States in December 1980 and prohibited from returning until after the February 1984 election, when he resumed his position as professor of constitutional and international law at Haiti University. For the remainder of the Duvalier era, he and his daughter, Marie, were sporadically subjected to either detention or house arrest. Eugène was credited with running fourth in the 1988 presidential poll. The party is now led by Eugène's son.
Leader: Grégoire EUGÈNE Jr.

Haitian Civic and Political Front (*Front Civico-Politique d'Haïtien*—Fronciph). Fronciph was launched on September 15, 1999, as a right-wing electoral alliance of the PDCH and PAIN (see below) and about 30 other parties and civic organizations, including the **National Cooperative Movement** (*Mouvement Koumbite National*—MKN), led by Volvick Rémy JOSEPH, and the **National Party of Labor** (*Parti National du Travail*—PNT), led by Thomas DESULMÉ.

Haitian Christian Democratic Party (*Parti Démocratique Chrétien d'Haïti*—PDCH). The PDCH was formed on July 5, 1979, by Silvio CLAUDE, who had been arrested and deported to Colombia after standing unsuccessfully for election to the legislature in February. Rearrested on his return to Haiti, he was sentenced in August 1981 to a 15-year prison term for attempting to create "a climate of disorder." Although the sentence was annulled in February 1982, periods of arrest and/or detention continued for the remainder of the Duvalier era. The PDCH refused to participate in the election of January 1988, while its leader placed fourth in the 1990 presidential balloting. A forceful critic of Aristide, Claude was killed in an act of apparent retribution by followers of the ousted president during the 1991 coup. His daughter Marie Denise Claude later became a leading member of the party, although she ran for a Senate seat in 2006 under the Fusion banner.
Leaders: Marie Denise CLAUDE (Leader), Osner FEVRY (Branch Leader).

National Agricultural and Industrial Party (*Parti Agricole et Industriel National*—PAIN). PAIN was formed by Louis Déjoie, the son of a prominent Duvalier opponent, who participated in the 1988 boycott. Déjoie ran third in the 1990 presidential race with a 5 percent vote share. Although PAIN endorsed the overthrow of the Aristide government in 1991, its leader, Louis DÉJOIE II (Déjoie's son) was named Malval's minister of commerce and industry in September 1993. The elder Déjoie died in early 1998.
Leader: Toussaint DESROSIERS (Spokesperson).

National Front for Concerted Action (*Front National de Concertation*—FNC). The FNC was organized in September 1987 through a merger of the "Group of 57" with a number of other moderate left-wing formations. Led by Gérard Gourgue, a prominent lawyer and human rights activist who had resigned as minister of justice in the Namphy administration in March 1986, the party joined the PDCH in boycotting the January 1988 balloting.

On February 6, 2001, the opposition party group, Democratic Convergence (*Convergence Démocratique*—CD), named Gourge the provisional president of their "alternative government," a symbolic gesture to protest what the CD regarded as the flawed process that led to the election of Aristide.
Leader: Gérard GOURGUE.

Other parties and groups include the **Alliance for the Liberation and Advancement of Haiti** (*Alliance pour la Libération et l'Avancement d'Haïti*—ALAH), led by Reynold GEORGES; the **Alternative for Change** (*L'Alternative pour le Changement*—AC), led by Gérard BLOT; the **Alternative for the Development of Haiti Party** (*L'Alternative pour le Développement d'Haïti*—ADH), led by attorney Gerard DALVIUS, the **Citizens Union of Haitians for Development, Democracy, and Education** (*Union des Citoyens Ayisyen pour le Développement, la Démocratie, et L'Education*—UCADDE) whose executive secretary, Jeantel JOSEPH, charged the CEP with inappropriate conduct in declaring the UCADDE candidate the loser in a closely contested Senate race in 2009; **Credo,** a right-wing party led by Prosper AVRIL; **Democratic Action to Build Haiti** (*L'Action Démocratique de Bâtir Haïti*—Adebha), led by René JULIEN; the **Democratic Revolutionary Party of Haiti** (*Parti Révolutionnaire Démocratique d'Haïti*—PRDH), led by François LATORTUE; the **Effort of Solidarity to Build a National and Popular Alternative** (*Effort de Solidarité pour la Construction d'une Alternative Nationale et Populaire*—ESCANP), a party based in the western region of Grand-Anse that cooperates with the influential grassroots group called the Resistance Committee of Grand-Anse (*Komite Reziztans Grand-Anse*—KOREGA); the **Grand Rally for the Evolution of Haiti** (*Grand Rassemblement pour l'Évolution d'Haïti*—GREH), led by Himmler REBU; the anti-FL **Haitian Democrats' Party** (*Parti des Démocrates Haïtiens*—PADEMH), led by Jean-Jacques Clark PARENT; the far-left **Haitian National Popular Party** (*Parti Populaire National Haïtien*—PPNH), a pro-Aristide group formerly led by Bernard SANSARICQ (who narrowly escaped death in a shooting incident with government troops in August 1987) and now led by Ben DUPUY, the editor of the weekly *Haiti Progress;* the **Konbit National Movement** (*Mouvman Konbit Nasyonal*—MKN), led by Volvick Remy JOSEPH; the **Movement for the Advancement, Development, and Innovation of Democracy in Haiti** (*Mouvement pour l'Avancement, le Développement, et l'Innovation de la Démocratie en Haïti*—MADIDH), led by Marc Antoine DESTIN; the **National and Patriotic Movement of November 28** (*Mouvement Nationale et Patriotique du 28 Novembre*—MNP-28), led by former Senate president Déjean BÉLIZAIRE; the anti-FL **National Progressive Democratic Party of Haiti** (*Parti National Démocratique Progressiste d'Haïti*—PNDPH), led by Turneb DELPE; the **National Unity Party** (*Parti de l'Unité Nationale*—PUN), a remnant of the Duvalierist party of the 1960s that has reportedly been gaining new followers recently following Jean-Claude Duvalier's apology (from exile) in 2007 for "wrongs" committed by his administration; the **National Unity Movement** (*Mouvement d'Unité National*—MUN), led by Georges SAATI; the **Organization for the Advancement of Haiti and of Haitians** (*Organisation pour l'Avancement d'Haïti et des Haïtiens*—OLAHH), led by Joel BORGELLA; the extreme-right **Organization for Democracy in Haiti** (*Organisation pour la Démocratie en Haïti*—OPDH), whose leader, Carl DENIS, was arrested in August 1995 for allegedly plotting against the government; the **Papaye Peasants Movement** (*Mouvement Paysan de Papaye*—MPP), described as the nation's largest peasant organization and a member, under the leadership of former Aristide supporter Chavannes JEAN-BAPTISTE, of the CD; the **Party for a Development Alternative** (*Parti pour un Développement Alternatif*—Pada), led by Gerard DALVIUS; the **Party of Haitian Manufacturers, Workers, Merchants and Development Agents** (*Parti des Industriels, Travailleurs, Commercants et Agents du Développement d'Haïti*—PITACH), led by Jean Jacques SYLVAIN; the **Party for the National Evolution of Haiti** (*Parti pour l'Évolution Nationale d'Haïti*—PENH), led by Yves SAINT-LOUIS; the **Party of the Patriotic Camp and of the Haitian Alliance** (*Parti du Camp Patriotique et de l'Alliance Haïtienne*—Paca-Palah), led by Franck François ROMAIN; **Popular Star,** a "people's organization" led by Alexis CLAIRIUS, a supporter of the CD; the **Rally of Christian Democrats** (*Rassemblement des Démocrates Chrétiens*—RDC), led by Eddy VOLEI; the **Social Renovation Party** (*Parti Social Rénovation*—PSR), led by François PIERRE-LOUIS; the **Union for National Reconstruction** (*Union pour la Reconstruction Nationale*—URN), led by neo-Duvalierist Evans NICOLAS, a presidential candidate in 2000; and the **Union of Democratic Patriots** (*Union des Patriotes Démocratiques*—UPD), led by Rockefeller GUERRE.

LEGISLATURE

The present **Legislature** (*Corps Législatif*) or **Parliament** (*Parlement*) is a bicameral body which, when meeting as a whole for such purposes as constitutional amendment, is styled the **National Assembly** (*Assemblée Nationale*). On January 11, 1999, President Préval declared that the terms of most legislators had expired and that the assembly was therefore dissolved. Under arrangements negotiated by Préval with several political parties in March, new legislative elections were expected by the end of the year; however, the first round was not held until May 21, 2000, with a disputed second round held on July 9. The terms of all of the members of the Chamber of Deputies and two-thirds of the members of the Senate elected in 2000 expired on January 11, 2004, and the assembly consequently ceased functioning. New elections were initially scheduled for September 2005, but it was not until February 7, 2006, that presidential and first-round legislative balloting (for all seats in the Senate and Chamber of Deputies) took place. The second legislative round was held April 21.

Senate (*Sénat*). The upper house comprises 30 members (3 senators per department), elected via majoritarian voting for six-year terms, with rotation of one-third of the members every two years. Balloting was erratic in the 1990s due to the nation's political turmoil, and the 1997 election results were set aside by the Provisional Electoral Council (CEP). Consequently, new elections for 19 seats were conducted on May 21 and July 9, 2000. However, most opposition parties boycotted the second-round voting to protest perceived improper calculation of first-round results by the government. The Lavalas Family (FL) was credited with winning 18 of the seats, with 1 going to an independent. The FL was also declared the winner of 8 additional seats contested on November 26, 2000, in a contest boycotted by the major opposition parties. The Senate stopped functioning in January 2004 when the mandates of two-thirds of its members expired, and new balloting was postponed amid the turmoil surrounding the ouster of President Aristide.

First round balloting for all 30 seats (increased from 27) was held on February 7, 2006. Following a second round of balloting on April 21, 2006, coupled with deferred voting for 3 seats on December 3, the Front for Hope (*Lespwa*) held 11 seats; the Haitian Social-Democratic Fusion Party (Fusion), 5; the Organization of the Struggling People (OPL), 4; the Lavalas Family (FL), 3; the Bridge Party, 2; the National Christian Union for the Reconstruction of Haiti, 2; the Standard-Bearer in Action (LAAA), 2; and the Democratic Action Party, 1.

The mandates for ten senators expired on May 11, 2008, elections to fill those seats having been postponed in late 2007 due to turmoil within the CEP and subsequent consideration of proposed electoral law revisions. The balloting for those seats and one other unfilled seat was held on April 19 (first round) and June 21, 2009. (Voting for one other unfilled seat was postponed due to disturbances at polling places.) Of the 11 contested seats, *Lespwa* secured 6; Fusion, 1; OPL, 1; Cooperative Action to Build Haiti, 1; Haiti in Action (as the LAAA had been renamed); 1; and independent, 1.

President: Kelly BASTIEN.

Chamber of Deputies (*Chambre des Députés*). The lower house is currently composed of 99 members, directly elected for four-year terms via majoritarian voting in 99 single-member districts. Following second-round balloting on April 21, 2006, coupled with deferred voting for 11 seats on December 3, the Front for Hope held 22 seats; the Haitian Social-Democratic Fusion Party, 16; the Democratic Alliance Party, 11; the Organization of the Struggling People, 10; the Lavalas Family, 6; the National Christian Union for the Reconstruction of Haiti, 6, the Mobilization for Haiti's Progress, 4; the Rally of Progressive National Democrats, 4; the Standard-Bearer in Action, 4; the Christian Movement for a New Haiti, 3; the Cooperative Action to Build Haiti, 3; the National Reconstruction Front, 2; and the Haitian Democratic and Reform Movement, Heads Together, the Independent Movement for National Reconciliation, the Justice for Peace and National Development, the Liberal Party of Haiti, the Movement for National Reconstruction, and the Union of National and Progressive Haitians, 1 each, with 1 vacancy.

President: Pierre Eric JEAN-JACQUES.

CABINET

[as of September 1, 2009] *(see headnote)*

Prime Minister	Michèle Duvivier Pierre-Louis [f]
Ministers	
Agriculture, Natural Resources, and Rural Development	Joanas Gué
Commerce and Industry	Marie Josée Garnier [f]
Culture and Communications	Olsen Jean Julien
Environment	Jean-Marie Claude Germain
Finance and Economy	Daniel Dorsainvil
Foreign Affairs and Religious Affairs	Alrich Nicolas
Haitians Living Abroad	Charles Manigat
Interior and Territorial Collectives	Paul Antoine Bien-Aimé
Justice and Public Security	Jean Joseph Exumé
National Education and Professional Training	Joël Desrosiers Jean-Pierre
Planning and External Cooperation	Jean-Max Bellerive
Prime Minister's Office in Charge of Relations with Parliament	Joseph Jasmin

Public Health and Population	Alex Larsen
Public Works, Transport, and Communication	Jacques Gabriel
Social Affairs and Labor	Gabrielle Prévillon Baudin [f]
Tourism	Patrick Delatour
Women's Affairs and Women's Rights	Marie Laurence Jocelyn Lassègue [f]
Youth, Sport, and Civil Action	Evans Lescouflair

Secretaries of State

Agricultural Production	Jean-Claude Délicé
Animal Production	Michel Chancy
Finance	Sylvain Lafalaise
Judicial Reform	Daniel Jean
Literacy	Carol Joseph [f]
People with Special Needs	Michel A. Péan
Public Security	Luc Eucher Joseph
Public Works	Frantz Y. Joseph

[f] = female

COMMUNICATIONS

Press. The following are French-language dailies published in Port-au-Prince, unless otherwise noted: *L'Union* (7,000); *Le Nouvelliste* (6,000); *Le Matin* (5,000); *Le Moniteur* (2,000), twice-weekly official gazette; *Le Septentrion* (2,000), weekly.

News agencies. A Haitian Press Agency (*Agence Haïtienne de Press*—AHP), operating in collaboration with *Agence France-Presse,* was launched in 1981.

Broadcasting and computing. The media-rights body Reporters Without Borders observed a dramatic increase in press freedom following the ouster of former president Aristide. Radio remains the main source of information in Haiti, which has more than 250 private radio stations. *Télé Haïti,* a private commercial company, broadcasts over 13 channels in French, Spanish, and English. In addition, the government-owned *Télévision Nationale d'Haïti* offers cultural programming in Creole, French, and Spanish. As of 2008 there were 101.3 Internet users per 1,000 inhabitants.

INTERGOVERNMENTAL REPRESENTATION

Ambassador to the U.S.: Raymond Alcide JOSEPH.

U.S. Ambassador to Haiti: Kenneth H. MERTEN.

Permanent Representative to the UN: Léo MÉRORÈS.

IGO Memberships (Non-UN): ACS, Caricom, CDB, IADB, Interpol, IOM, OAS, OIF, OPANAL, PCA, SELA, WCO, WTO.

HONDURAS

Republic of Honduras
República de Honduras

Note: Ousted President Mel Zelaya returned to Honduras clandestinely on September 21, 2009, and was granted sanctuary in the Brazilian embassy. The two competing political camps in late October reached an agreement designed to resolve the crisis by, among other things, authorizing the National Congress to determine whether Zelaya should be reinstated in the presidency for the remainder of his term. In controversial presidential balloting on November 29, Porfirio Lobo Sosa of the National Party (PN) was elected with 56 percent of the vote, followed by Elvin Santos (who ran as the candidate of the Liberal Party [PL] despite a call for a boycott of the election by Zelaya and his supporters) with 38 percent. Initial reports on the results of the concurrent legislative balloting credited the PN with 71 seats and the PL with 45. On December 2 the congress voted 111 -14 not to restore Zelaya to the presidency. Sosa's inauguration was scheduled for January 27, 2010.

Political Status: Part of the independent Captaincy General of Guatemala, 1821; member of United Provinces of Central America, 1824–1838; separate republic established 1839; present constitution promulgated January 20, 1982, following a decade of military rule.

Area: 43,277 sq. mi. (112,088 sq. km.).

Population: 6,535,344 (2001C); 7,726,000 (2008E). The 2001 figure does not include an adjustment for underenumeration.

Major Urban Centers (2005E): TEGUCIGALPA (857,000), San Pedro Sula (510,000).

Official Language: Spanish.

Monetary Unit: Lempira (market rate December 1, 2009: 18.89 lempiras = $1US).

Provisional President: *(See headnote.)* Roberto MICHELETTI Baín (Liberal Party); appointed by the congress on June 28, 2009, for a six-month term following a bloodless coup the same day that ousted José Manuel (Mel) ZELAYA Rosales (Liberal Party).

First Vice President: Vacant, following the coup on June 28, 2009, that ousted Aristides MEJIA Carranza (Liberal Party).

THE COUNTRY

Honduras, the second largest of the Central American republics, is mountainous, sparsely inhabited, and predominantly rural. Approximately 90 percent of the population is racially mixed; Indians constitute about 7 percent, blacks and whites the remainder. Roman Catholicism is the religion of more than 95 percent of the people, three-quarters of whom are functionally illiterate. Women constitute about 7 percent of the rural labor force, exclusive of unpaid family workers, and 32 percent of the urban workforce, primarily in domestic service; departing from tradition, each of the last six governments has contained at least one female cabinet member.

The nation's economy traditionally depended on agriculture, and coffee, bananas, and shrimp remain important exports. However, industry, with an emphasis on nondurable consumer goods, now accounts for a higher share of GDP (32 percent versus 15–20 percent for agriculture), largely because of the growth during the 1990s of foreign-owned *maquila* companies, which produce garments and other goods for export using materials imported on a virtually duty-free basis. GDP growth during the 1990s averaged 3.2 percent, although the economy contracted by 1.9 percent in 1999 because of severe damage to crops and infrastructure caused by Hurricane Mitch in October 1998. The economy expanded at an annual average of 3.87 percent in 1999–2005, according to the International Monetary Fund (IMF). Growth increased to a robust 6.6 percent in 2006, family remittances (chiefly from some 900,000 Hondurans living in the United States) accounting for more than 25 percent of the country's gross domestic product.

In 2007 annual GDP growth remained stable at 6.3 percent, despite a spiraling unemployment rate of 27.8 percent. Honduras's largely rural and young population, coupled with the prevalence of droughts, hurricanes, and mudslides, has contributed to its cycle of poverty and high unemployment, according to the World Bank. In 2008 annual economic growth contracted to 4 percent and an inflation rate of 11.4 percent was recorded. Despite the growth, Honduras remained one of the least-developed countries in the region, with more than half the population living below the poverty line.

The effects of the global economic downturn resulted in annual GDP growth contracting to 1.5 percent in 2009. Inflation was projected to drop slightly to 9.5 percent, mainly as a result of declining consumer and investment spending, remittances, and tourism. In response to the effects of the global financial crisis, the Honduran government pledged $526 million to stimulate the economy, with 40 percent invested in each of three key sectors: construction, exports, and agriculture. Another 20 percent was targeted for small businesses. The government also announced plans to improve the country's health-care system and to shore up environmental protection efforts.

GOVERNMENT AND POLITICS

Political background. Honduras declared its independence from Spain in 1821 as part of the Captaincy General of Guatemala. After a brief period of absorption by Mexico, the states of the Captaincy General in 1824 organized as the Central American Federation, which broke

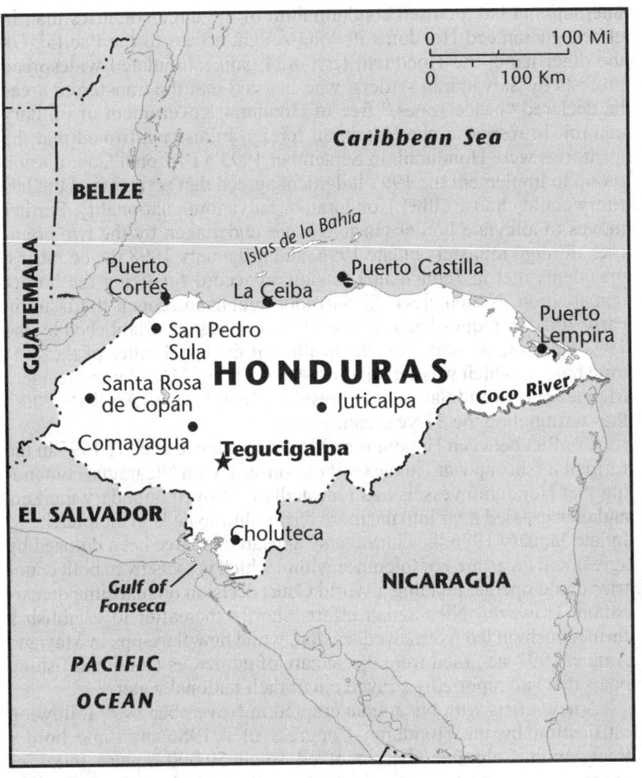

up in 1838. Decades of instability, revolution, and governmental change followed, with Honduras experiencing 67 different heads of state between 1855 and 1932, and U.S. military forces intervening on three occasions between 1912 and 1924. A measure of internal stability, accompanied by a minimum of reform and progress, was achieved between 1932 and 1954 under the presidencies of Tiburcio CARIAS Andino and Juan Manuel GALVEZ. Three years after a military coup in 1954, Ramón VILLEDA Morales was installed as constitutional president and served until his 1963 overthrow in another military action mounted by (then) Col. Oswaldo LÓPEZ Arellano. Subsequently, a Constituent Assembly, with a National Party (*Partido Nacional*—PN) majority, approved a new constitution and designated López Arellano as president.

Immediately before the 1971 election, López Arellano organized the framework for a new government under a Pact of National Unity, which called for the sharing of governmental posts by the two major parties. Although similar to the National Front arrangement in Colombia, the pact was not nearly as successful. After 18 months in office, the administration of President Ramón Ernesto CRUZ was overthrown by the military under former president López Arellano, who served the remainder of Cruz's presidential term. On March 31, 1975, Arellano was replaced as military commander in chief by (then) Col. Juan Alberto MELGAR Castro after a group of dissident junior officers had seized control of the Supreme Council of the Armed Forces, and on April 22 Melgar Castro replaced him as head of state. The new president was in turn ousted on August 7, 1978, by a three-man junta headed by Brig. Gen. Policarpo PAZ García.

On July 25, 1980, the Constituent Assembly that had been elected on April 20 named Paz García to serve as sole executive pending adoption of a new basic law and the popular election of a successor. Dr. Roberto SUAZO Córdova led the Liberal Party (*Partido Liberal*—PL) to a surprisingly conclusive victory in nationwide balloting on November 29, 1981, and assumed office on January 27, 1982, promising "a revolution of work and honesty."

At his inauguration, President Suazo Córdova referenced the Honduran record of 16 constitutions, 126 governments, and 385 armed rebellions in 161 years of independence and declared that "the time had come for rectifications." However, it was obvious that the recent peaceful transition had been achieved by mortgaging the incoming administration to an "iron circle" of military hard-liners headed by Gustavo ALVAREZ Martínez, who was promptly promoted from colonel to general.

On March 31, 1984, General Alvarez was dismissed and sent into exile, following charges of plotting a coup and misappropriating government funds. The latter allegations turned largely on the activities of the Association for the Progress of Honduras (*Asociación para el Progreso de Honduras*—APROH), a right-wing grouping of military and business leaders that, a year earlier, had accepted a $5 million contribution from the intensely anticommunist Unification Church of Sun Myung Moon for the purpose of countering Honduran "subversives." APROH, which was formally outlawed in November 1984, had also advocated direct U.S. military intervention against the Nicaraguan *sandinistas* as a necessary precondition of regional economic development.

In late 1984, amid deepening fissures within the ruling PL, President Suazo Córdova endorsed the former interior minister, Oscar MEJÍA Arellano, as the party's 1985 presidential candidate. However, a majority of the party's congressional delegation backed chamber president Efraín BU Girón, leaving the chief executive with the minority support of only 29 deputies. The split yielded a constitutional crisis in early 1985, with Congress removing five of the nine Supreme Court justices on grounds of corruption and the president responding by ordering the arrest of the new chief justice. In April the old court was reinstalled after the leading parties agreed to an open contest in the forthcoming presidential balloting that would permit any faction of a recognized party to present a presidential candidate; an electoral change approved later in the year declared that the winner would be the leading candidate within the party that secured the most votes. Under the new arrangement, José Simón AZCONA del Hoyo, an anti-*suazocordovista* PL member, was declared president-elect after the election of November 24, despite placing second to the leading PN nominee, Rafael Leonardo CALLEJAS Romero.

Azcona's victory yielded the first transition involving elected civilians in more than half a century. However, because of party fissures, he could look forward to controlling only 46 of 132 legislative seats. As a result, before his inauguration on January 27, 1986, the incoming chief executive concluded a "National Accord" (an echo of the 1971 pact) with the Nationalists that gave the opposition effective control of the judiciary and representation in the cabinet and other influential bodies, thus dimming prospects for major policy changes, including meaningful land reform. Although the accord subsequently deteriorated (see PN under Political Parties, below), PL–PN cooperation at midyear yielded the indefinite suspension of municipal elections scheduled for November, neither party apparently favoring a public test before the presidential and legislative balloting scheduled for 1989.

In the November 1989 election, PN candidate Callejas secured 50.2 percent of the presidential vote, and his party returned to power after 18 years. The new president named two PL members to cabinet posts and appointed a Christian Democrat to oversee agrarian reform as head of the National Institute of Agriculture.

Oswaldo RAMOS Soto secured the PN presidential nomination in 1993 but went on to lose by a wide margin to the PL nominee, Carlos Roberto REINA Idiáquez. The Liberals also won decisively in the legislative balloting, defeating the *nacionalistas* by 71 seats to 55 (a mathematical reversal of the 1989 results).

In the balloting of November 30, 1997, the Liberal presidential nominee Carlos Roberto FLORES Facussé won with nearly 53 percent of the vote. The PL also retained control of the National Congress by a reduced majority of 67 seats. Flores was inaugurated on January 27, 1998, at which time he appointed a cabinet that included only one incumbent minister.

At the president's request, the congress on September 18, 1998, passed a number of constitutional amendments designed to bring the military under civilian control. The administration's efforts to implement the changes, including the abolition of autonomous military spending and designation of the nation's first civilian defense minister, triggered an apparent coup attempt on July 30, 1999.

The PN's Ricardo MADURO Joest defeated the PL's Rafael PINEDA Ponce in the election of November 25, 2001, although the incoming president's party was limited to a plurality (61 of 128 seats) in the National Congress. Widespread crime, which included the reported murder of 820 street children and the assassination of a legislative candidate, was a major issue in the 2001 election. Maduro, whose son had been killed in 1997, pledged "zero tolerance" for criminals during the presidential campaign and maintained a hard line against street gangs after assuming office, reportedly securing a 60 percent reduction in the crime rate.

The 2005 election was reminiscent of 1993. The Liberals, led by Manuel (Mel) ZELAYA, turned back a *nacionalista* effort to retain the presidency, while winning a legislative plurality that was close to being a reversal of the 2001 result (see Political Parties, below). The Zelaya government maintained its predecessor's focus on curbing crime, and subsequently mandated ten two-hour series of government-produced television coverage to counter what he saw as negative or incomplete reporting by the media, particularly in reviewing his policies regarding crime prevention. The initiative was legal under Honduran law but attracted sharp criticism.

Zelaya reshuffled the cabinet on February 1, 2009, after Vice President Elvin Ernesto SANTOS resigned on December 18, 2008, to seek election in the 2009 presidential poll. Former defense minister Arístides MEJIA Carranza was appointed to succeed Santos on January 6, 2009.

In 2009 Zelaya worked to reform the constitution in what his detractors viewed as an attempt to abolish the single-term limit on the office of the presidency. The push eventually turned the congress, the Supreme Court, a significant number of members of Zelaya's own party, and the military against him. On June 28, 2009, soldiers acting on an order by the Supreme Court stormed the presidential palace, detained Zelaya, and exiled him to Costa Rica in the region's first coup in decades. Later that day congress named Roberto MICHELETTI Bain of the PL as provisional president until the next elections, scheduled for November 29. Micheletti reshuffled the cabinet on June 28 (see Current issues, below).

Constitution and government. The current constitution provides for a directly elected president, who may serve for only one term, and a unicameral legislature whose members serve four-year terms concurrent with that of the chief executive. The judiciary includes a Supreme Court and five courts of appeal, each of which designates local justices within its territorial jurisdiction.

Internal administration is based on 18 departments headed by centrally appointed governors. The departments are subdivided into a total of 283 municipalities, each with an elected mayor and municipal assembly (including the capital, which for most of the half century prior to 1985 had been denied local government status).

Foreign relations. A member of the Organization of American States (OAS) and the United Nations, Honduras has long inclined toward a conservative position in inter-American and world affairs (though the country moved to the left under the Zelaya administration, beginning in 2005). It joined in founding the now-inactive Organization of Central American States in 1951 and the Central American Common Market (CACM) in 1960. In 1982 Honduras participated in the U.S.-sponsored formation of a Central American Democratic Community (Condeca), which included Costa Rica, El Salvador, and Guatemala, while excluding Nicaragua; however, the alliance quickly became moribund. In May 1986 Honduras joined with the other four CACM countries in endorsing the creation of a Central American Parliament (*Parlamento Centroamericano*—Parlacen), although neither Costa Rica nor Nicaragua was represented at Parlacen's October 1991 inauguration. In May 1992 the three Parlacen countries announced the formation of a Northern Triangle (*Triángulo Norte*) for trade, which became the Central American Group of Four (*Grupo América Central 4*—AC-4) with the addition of Nicaragua in April 1993. Meanwhile, at a *Triángulo Norte* summit in October 1992 its presidents called for a new effort to establish a regional political grouping in the form of a Central American Federation, with Parlacen as its legislative forum. The projected Federation was advanced as an outgrowth of a Central American Integration System that had been supported by all five regional executives during a December 1991 meeting in Honduras, although subsequently ratified only by Honduras, El Salvador, and Nicaragua.

A series of disagreements with neighboring El Salvador in 1969 led the two countries to an undeclared "soccer war," during which invading Salvadoran forces inflicted hundreds of casualties. The OAS arranged a cease-fire on July 18. Renewed hostilities broke out in July 1976, and it was not until October 30, 1980, that a formal peace treaty was signed in Lima, Peru. Despite the treaty, relations remained tense because of a border controversy and continuing clashes between Salvadoran government forces and guerrilla groups operating from sanctuaries in the ostensibly demilitarized territorial pockets (*bolsones territoriales*).

The boundary dispute centered on claims by Honduras that El Salvador (and, to a lesser extent, Nicaragua) had attempted to block its access to the Pacific Ocean by controlling egress through the Gulf of Fonseca. Unable to come to a resolution, Honduras and El Salvador agreed in 1986 to submit the issue to the International Court of Justice (ICJ), with Nicaragua participating as a limited observer. In a decision handed down in September 1992 the ICJ awarded most of the disputed territory to Honduras, while ruling that the Gulf waters were not international but a closed condominium of the three countries that, in effect, guaranteed Honduras its long-sought access to the Pacific. On the other hand, the Honduran territorial gains stimulated widespread protests by Salvadoran settlers, who insisted that the transferred areas be declared "peace zones," free of Honduran government or military control. In response, the Honduran foreign ministry affirmed that the territories were Honduran. In September 1995 a Bi-Zonal Commission set up to implement the 1992 judgment agreed that residents of the territory could choose either Honduran or Salvadoran nationality. Further moves to alleviate border tensions were undertaken by the two countries' foreign ministers in late 1996, and in January 1998 the countries' presidents met in Tegucigalpa to sign an accord finalizing the border demarcation. Nonetheless, El Salvador sought to reopen the issue in early 2002 by requesting a review of the boundaries established by the 1992 decision. At issue was delineation of the last 4 miles of the 145-mile border, which was settled during a meeting of Honduran president Manuel Zelaya and Salvadoran president Tony Saca on April 18, 2006, thus terminating the 37-year controversy.

Conflict between Honduras and Nicaragua arose in early 1995 in the form of a "shrimp war" in the Gulf of Fonseca, with Nicaragua contending that Honduran vessels had repeatedly destroyed boundary markers and then crossed over into the more fertile shrimp beds in their territory. In late January 1996 the controversy appeared to have been defused by agreement on an area of tolerance within which vessels from both countries could operate pending a World Court decision on maritime demarcation. However, Nicaraguan efforts shortly thereafter to establish a further cushion led to renewed tension, while new flare-ups in May and August 1997 stemmed from the seizure of numerous Honduran fishing boats that had reportedly strayed out of their national waters.

A new crisis with Nicaragua erupted in November 1999 following ratification by the Honduran Congress of a 1986 maritime border treaty with Colombia that involved some 50,000 square miles of coastal waters, portions of which were alleged to have been forcibly ceded to Colombia during the U.S. occupation of Nicaragua in the 1920s. In reprisal, Nicaragua imposed a 35 percent duty on all goods imported from Honduras. In January 2000 the two countries agreed to submit the dispute to another World Court ruling; however, less than a month later peace in the Gulf of Fonseca was again threatened by an exchange between Honduran and Nicaraguan patrol boats, each claiming that it had been attacked by the other. In April 2001, following the intervention of Spanish prime minister José María Aznar, Honduras and Nicaragua, plus El Salvador, agreed to consult more closely and exchange information on military matters in an effort to prevent incidents and maintain the current military balance. But the friction continued into 2002, with periodic seizures of Honduran boats accused of illegally fishing in Nicaraguan waters and Nicaragua authorizing oil prospecting in the region. On November 28, 2006, the Nicaraguan president-elect, Daniel Ortega, offered President Zelaya a partnership agreement including proposals to end the border dispute, reduce poverty, and minimize military presence. The proposal was met with hostility in both countries. (Both countries agreed to a final border demarcation set by the ICJ in October 2007. The ruling gave Honduras 80 percent of the disputed 34,500 square kilometers in the Caribbean Ocean, including sovereign control over the islands of Bobel, Sabana, Port Royal, and Sur.)

In January 2002 outgoing president Flores reestablished relations with Cuba, which had been suspended since 1961. Seemingly prompted by Cuban aid after the 1974 and 1998 hurricanes, the new Maduro administration faced mixed reactions to its rapprochement with the Marxist regime but made no attempt to rescind the action. In October 2007 Zelaya became the first Honduran president to visit Cuba, meeting with its interim leader Raúl Castro.

Despite its rejection of the U.S. position on Cuba and tension caused by warming Honduran relations with Venezuela, Honduras participated in the conclusion of negotiations on establishment of a Central America Free Trade Agreement (CAFTA) in December 2003. Under the U.S.-sponsored initiative, most intraregional trade would, over time, become tariff free. The treaty was formally launched on April 1, 2006.

Honduras continued to cooperate with the United States against the drugs trade. In June 2006, following the creation of a special military unit to support police work, Zelaya asked U.S. president George W. Bush for special forces personnel to counter trafficking in drugs bound for the United States in the country's eastern Mosquitia coast region.

In May 2007 the U.S. government granted an 18-month extension of the Temporary Protected Status (to March 2009), affecting 78,000 Hondurans, 230,000 Salvadorans, and 4,000 Nicaraguans. The status allowed foreign nationals whose homeland conditions are recognized by the U.S. government as being temporarily unsafe to continue residing in the United States but precludes their acquisition of permanent resident status.

On January 15, 2008, Honduras signed an agreement with Venezuela to purchase oil from the state oil company (Petrocaribe) at preferential rates. In October Honduras joined *Alternativa Bolivariana para los Pueblos de Nuestra America* (ALBA), a trade organization begun by Venezuela president Hugo Chávez as an alternative to a U.S. scheme. The increasing ties with Venezuela were in direct contrast to Honduras's declining relationship with the United States.

Current issues. Upon his inauguration in 2006, President Zelaya touted education reform and forest management. Illegal logging remained a problem for agricultural communities, and President Zelaya highlighted the risks posed by deforestation. President Zelaya also proposed a program to protect the rights of Honduran immigrants, not only in the United States but also in Mexico and Guatemala. In December 2007 a fund was initiated to help families of missing, disabled, and deceased emigrants.

The government again addressed pressures on the poor by issuing a decree, effective April 7, 2008, to counter the high cost of fuel. The "No Drive Day" decree prohibited the use of cars one day a week to conserve fuel. A few days later the Supreme Court overruled the policy by nine to six. Zelaya ordered the Congress to investigate on the grounds that the ruling was politically motivated since the nine judges who voted against the measure were affiliated with the opposition PN, while the other six were independent. The PN denied the accusation, but Congress president Roberto Micheletti, a PL member who had been a frequent critic of Zelaya, supported the president's policy and agreed to form a multiparty committee, as requested by the president, to investigate whether political allegiances had influenced the ruling.

Attention was again drawn to corruption in 2008 when, in April, the president of the Prosecutors Association, Víctor FERNÁNDEZ, began a hunger strike and called for the dismissal or suspension of the attorney general and his deputy. He ended his protest a month later when Congress agreed to audit the case files in the attorney general's office. Fernández subsequently formed a new group, the Wide Movement for Dignity and Justice (*Movimiento Amplio por la Dignidad y la Justicia*—MADJ), ahead of municipal elections in November (see Political Parties, below). In July a new law created a special unit in the attorney general's office to investigate all organized crime, removing such efforts from the police. However, violence continued to plague the country and collaterally weakened the governing PL, as homicides increased by 25 percent over the previous year's reported 3,855 cases. Meanwhile, Zelaya made progress in reducing poverty by 9 percent, which some observers attributed to economic changes outside the purview of the presidency.

Attention in November 2008 turned to the primary elections to nominate candidates for the 2009 presidential poll. Violence marred the process, as two members of the PL, including the vice president of congress, were killed earlier in the month, as were two members of the PN. In nationwide primary polling (held by the PL and the PN) in December, the PL's Mauricio VILLEDA, a lawyer and political novice, defeated four other PL aspirants, including Roberto Micheletti, who had widely been regarded as the front-runner. Villeda was standing in for former vice president Elvin Santos, who had resigned to participate but whose bid was blocked by the supreme electoral tribunal. Critics questioned the tribunal's ruling, which cited Santos's periodic work filling in for Zelaya when the president was out of the country as evidence that he was running for reelection while still in office. Villeda, for his part, promised to step aside once the issue was resolved. Subsequently, congress validated Santos's candidacy, and Villeda stepped down and backed Santos. Meanwhile, the PN's Porfirio LOBO easily defeated three other candidates to win his party's nomination. Felicito ÁVILA, the leader of the Christian Democratic Party of Honduras (*Partido Demócrata Cristiano de Honduras*—PDCH), Bernard MARTINEZ of the Innovation and Unity Social Democratic Party (*Partido Innovación y Unidad Social Demócrata*—PINU-SD), and César HAM of the Democratic Unification Party (*Partido Unificación Democrática*—PUD) all received their parties' bid for the 2009 election.

In the run-up to the election, Zelaya's policies continued to come under criticism. In December 2008, in the wake of his administration's failure to secure an agreement between business and labor unions, the president increased the minimum wage by 60 percent, citing his commitment to help the poor. Critics said the higher wage imposed on businesses was untenable, given the country's increasing unemployment rate and the global economic recession. Greater controversy erupted over Zelaya's plan, announced in March 2009, for a nationwide referendum to determine public support to change the nation's constitution. His reasons for desiring changes were vague, but it was believed by some observers that the goal was to rescind the single-term limit on the presidency. The president, for his part, steadfastly denied such claims. Meanwhile, both the PL and the PN opposed the binding referendum, scheduled for June 28, and in the days leading up to the poll, the Supreme Court, following a similar vote by congress, ruled the referendum unconstitutional. Further, the military confiscated ballots to prevent the vote from taking place. On June 25 Zelaya led hundreds on a peaceful protest to an air force base where they attempted to retake the ballots, and he subsequently fired the commander of the armed forces for refusing to order the military to implement the poll. The leaders of the army, navy, and air force resigned their posts in a show of support for the commander. Meanwhile, the Supreme Court ruled that the removal of the commander had been deemed illegal and reinstated him. Ultimately, the electoral tribunal also ruled that the poll was illegal. Nevertheless, Zelaya vowed to hold the referendum as scheduled on June 28. That morning, however, about 100 soldiers stormed the presidential palace in the wake of a secret Supreme Court order two days earlier that Zelaya be arrested, as his actions were illegal. The military removed Zelaya in the first bloodless coup in the country in decades, and immediately put him on a plane to Costa Rica. In accordance with the constitutional order of succession, the president of congress, Roberto Micheletti, was appointed provisional president of the republic. Congress also voted to accept a letter of resignation purportedly written by Zelaya, though he denied producing it. Micheletti, who was installed for a six-month term, immediately named new ministers of defense, finance, labor, and natural resources.

The 2009 coup set off opposing demonstrations in the streets of Honduras on June 29 and prompted widespread condemnation from Zelaya's leftist supporters in Venezuela, Cuba, and Bolivia, as well as from the OAS, the United States, and the United Nations, all of whom refused to recognize the new government. The European Union (EU) and Latin American countries withdrew their ambassadors, as the military was dispatched to patrol the streets and guard government buildings.

A Gallup poll conducted in early July 2009 found that 41 percent of respondents agreed with Zelaya's removal, with 46 percent opposed. Analysts considered the public support for the coup significant, and further described the backing of government agencies, the Catholic Church, and business interests as a victory for Micheletti and the coup leaders. Meanwhile, U.S. and EU financial assistance was put on hold, as was aid from the Inter-American Development Bank, the World Bank, and the Central American Bank for Economic Integration. Venezuela also stopped sending cheap oil. Also, Honduras's membership in the OAS was suspended, after the group's unsuccessful demand that Zelaya be reinstated. Meanwhile, the presidential candidates of both the PL and PN remained quiet in the aftermath of the coup, aiming to positively position themselves in advance of a new election, analysts said.

On July 10, 2009, Costa Rican president Oscar Arias began mediating talks between Zelaya and the de facto government. Proposals put forth by Arias would allow Zelaya to return to the country and finish his term as president; move up new elections to October; grant amnesty for political crimes before and after the coup; and include all major political parties in a government of national unity. Zelaya, under terms of the plan, would have to surrender control of the military and abandon plans for a constitutional referendum. However, the interim government rejected the proposals, prompting Zelaya to threaten to walk away as well. On July 16 Zelaya stationed himself in Nicaragua with hundreds of supporters as the standoff over negotiations continued. Honduran soldiers on the border subsequently blocked a demonstration by about 1,000 Zelaya supporters, and ultimately the protesters returned to Honduras. It was also reported that several of the president's key allies had been detained, PUD deputies had been arrested, and several PL ministers had gone into hiding.

POLITICAL PARTIES

Under the Pact of National Unity concluded before the 1971 election, the country's two major political parties, the National Party (PN) and the Liberal Party (PL), agreed to put up separate candidates for the presidency but to accept equal representation in the Congress, the cabinet, the Supreme Court, and other government organs. The pact became moot upon the resumption of military rule in late 1972 and was not renewed for the election of November 1981, at which the two traditional parties shared 94.2 percent of the vote. In the 1985, 1989, and 1993 balloting, continuance of an essentially two-party system was reaffirmed, the smaller parties collectively being limited to less than 7 percent of the vote on each occasion.

In a move reminiscent of the Pact of National Unity, the PL and PN joined with PINU and the PDCH (below) in organizing the National Council of Convergence (*Consejo Nacional de Convergencia*—Conacon) in September 1995 to promote consensus on social, economic, and political issues. Excluded from the grouping, the Democratic Unification Party (PUD, below) charged that it was launched in an effort to preserve the dominance of the traditional parties.

In the 1997 election the PL won the presidency and a slim majority of legislative seats, in 2001 the PN won the presidency and a plurality of 61 assembly seats, and in 2005 the PL regained the presidency and a plurality of 62 legislative seats.

Manuel Zelaya's PL government was overthrown in a coup on June 28, 2009, after the Supreme Court had voted unanimously that Zelaya had illegally called for a constitutional referendum. Rival PL member and president of Congress, Roberto Micheletti, was named interim president in accordance with the constitutional order of succession.

Government Party:

Liberal Party (*Partido Liberal*—PL). Tracing its political ancestry to 1890, the PL is an urban-based, center-right grouping that has historically favored social reform, democratic political standards, and Central American integration. With the active support of a social-democratic faction, Alipo (below), it secured an impressive victory over the Nationalists in the 1981 balloting, winning the presidency and a clear majority in the National Congress. Following the inauguration of President Suazo Córdova in January 1982, Alipo's influence waned, while the non-*alipista* group split into an "old guard" *rodista* faction (named after former Liberal leader Modesto Rodas Alvarado), composed primarily of traditionally antimilitarist conservatives, and a presidential faction(*suazocordovistas*), encompassing right-wing technocrats with close links to the business community and the armed forces. The latter cleavage resulted in the president's loss of legislative support in early 1985 and the generation of a major constitutional crisis (see Political background, above).

One of four PL candidates, José Azcona del Hoyo, with partial *rodista* and Alipo support, won the presidency in 1985 without the backing of Suazo Córdova, who, with the remaining *rodistas,* supported Oscar Mejía Arellano. In 1987 rightist Carlos Flores Facussé, a strong supporter of U.S. policy, was elected PL president and in 1989 was runner-up to the PN's Rafael Leonardo Callejas for the national presidency, a position that he won in 1997. After losing to the *nacionalistas* in 2001, the PL regained power in the legislature in 2005, but did not gain an overall majority. In concurrent presidential balloting, former minister of the Honduran Social Investment Fund, Manuel Zelaya, a wealthy rancher and logging magnate, was elected by only a 3.7 percent margin. He had campaigned on a platform of government openness and a slogan of "citizen power," which stressed a more responsive government and wider participation in civil society. Under Zelaya, a former three-term congressman, the PL shifted from center-right to center-left as a result of a more socialist agenda. His decision in 2008 to align with President Chávez's ALBA trade organization pulled the country closer to Venezuela, Cuba, Bolivia, and Nicaragua and caused major rifts in the PL, which traditionally had favored closer U.S. ties. The party subsequently was divided between those who supported or opposed the president's move to join ALBA.

PL members subsequently nominated Mauricio Villeda of the "Elvincista movement" (*Movimiento Elvincista*, which backed former vice president Elvin Santos) as its presidential candidate during the 2008 primaries. Villeda was widely accepted as a stand-in for Santos, whose candidacy had temporarily been suspended because of his ties to the Zelaya administration. However, Congress cleared the way for Santos to run in the general election, and Villeda stepped down to back Santos, who became the party's presidential nominee on November 30, defeating Roberto Micheletti.

Meanwhile, Zelaya's push to rewrite the country's constitution provoked much opposition from within his own party, as well as from other branches of government, and was among the factors that ultimately led to his ouster. Following the coup on June 28, 2009, and Zelaya's exile to Costa Rica, one of his fiercest critics, Roberto Micheletti , the president of Congress, was installed as provisional president of the republic, in accordance with the constitutional order of succession.

Leaders: Roberto MICHELETTI Bain (Provisional President of the Republic), Elvin Ernesto SANTOS (2009 presidential candidate and President of the Party), Bill O'Neill Santos BRITO (Secretary General).

Other Legislative Parties:

National Party (*Partido Nacional*—PN). Created in 1923 as an expression of national unity after a particularly chaotic period, the PN is a right-wing party with close ties to the military. While traditionally dominated by rural landowning interests, it has, in recent years, supported programs of internal reform and favors Central American integration. Factionalism within the PN was evidenced in the wake of November 1982 balloting for the party executive, former president Gen. Juan Melgar Castro accusing the *oficialista* faction, led by former president Ricardo Zúñiga, of perpetrating a "worthless farce." In July 1983 two separate PN conventions were held, and three presidential candidates were nominated in 1985. Rafael Leonardo Callejas, supported by most of the party, led all contenders in the 1985 balloting with 43 percent of the total votes. However, the other two PN candidates garnered less than 2 percent each. As a result, under existing electoral procedure, the presidency was awarded to PL, whose nominees had collectively obtained a 51 percent vote share. The PN quickly reached a power-sharing agreement with the PL, but Callejas, after declaring the accord's commitments no longer binding, announced in January 1987 that the PN would move into "more critical" opposition. The PN won the 1989 presidential race with a slight majority of the popular vote but lost in 1993 under the candidacy of former Supreme Court President Oswaldo Ramos Soto. As in the case of the PL, the party contains a number of internal factions.

In the 1997 election, the PN legislative delegation declined by 1, to 54, although César CASTELLANOS narrowly defeated his PL opponent to win the Tegucigalpa mayoralty. Castellanos, considered a potential presidential candidate, was killed in a helicopter crash in late 1998.

In November 2001 PN candidate Ricardo Maduro won the presidency with a 53 percent vote share, although the party failed to secure a legislative majority. During the 2005 presidential elections, Porfirio ("Pepe") Lobo Sosa received 46.2 percent of the vote, finishing second to the PL's Manuel Zelaya. The PN also dropped to second in the legislative balloting in 2005 and has since cooperated intermittently in the passage of PL-sponsored legislation. Capitalizing on public frustration with the ruling party, the PN led thousands in a Tegucigalpa march aimed at pressuring the government to control rising crime rates in April 2007.

PN members of Congress twice abstained from voting on Honduras's accession to two Venezuelan organizations, including the ALBA trade group. The party did not want to appear to be blocking the country from receiving benefits for the poor from the two organizations, but since the PN represents Honduras's conservative and business interests, it sought to ensure that that it was viewed as not having a role in the agreements.

In 2008 party president Lobo received the party's bid as its presidential candidate for the 2009 election. Lobo softened his platform by naming education, social issues, and job creation his top issues, abandoning the tough anti-crime stance he had campaigned on in his failed bid for the presidency in 2005.

Leaders: Porfirio ("Pepe") LOBO Sosa (President of the Party, and 2005 and 2009 presidential candidate), Ricardo MADURO Joest (Former President of the Republic), Ricardo ZÚÑIGA Augustinus (Former President of the Republic), Gen. Juan Alberto MELGAR Castro (Former President of the Republic), Nora GUNERA de Melgar (Former Mayor of Tegucigalpa and 1997 presidential candidate), Rafael Leonardo CALLEJAS Romero (Former President of the Republic).

Democratic Unification Party (*Partido Unificación Democrática*—PUD). The PUD was launched in September 1993 by the merger of four left-wing groups drawn, at least in part, from demobilized elements of the Honduran Revolutionary Movement (*Movimiento Revolucionario Hondureño*—MRH), the Honduran Revolutionary Party (*Partido Revolucionario Hondureño*—PRH), the Morazanista Liberation Party (*Partido Morazanista de Liberación*—PML), the Party for the Transformation of Honduras (*Partido para la Transformación de Honduras*—PTH), and the Patriotic Renovation Party (*Partido Renovación Patriótica*—PRP), which now included the Communist Party of Honduras (*Partido Comunista de Honduras*—PCH), led by Mario SOSA Navarro. In its 1994 legalization of the new formation, the National Congress ruled that the PUD could not engage in electoral activity until 1997. In late 1994 the party called for "the overthrow of [President] Reina and his family" as a means of averting "total disaster." Its founder secured an assembly seat in 1997, while PL defector Filiberto ISAULA captured the mayoralty of La Paz, the stronghold of former PL president Suazo Córdova. It won five assembly seats in 2001, all of which were retained in 2005. Party leader Juan Ángel Almendares Bonilla won 1.5 percent of the vote in the concurrent presidential election.

César Ham, who supported President Zelaya's controversial proposal for a constitutional referendum, received the party's bid as its 2009 presidential candidate. The PUD opposed the 2009 coup that ousted President Zelaya. Immediately following the coup there were unsubstantiated reports, later refuted, that Ham had been killed.

Leaders: César HAM (President and 2009 presidential candidate), Juan Ángel ALMENDARES Bonilla (2005 presidential candidate), Matías FUNES Valladares (1997 and 2001 presidential candidate).

Christian Democratic Party of Honduras (*Partido Demócrata Cristiano de Honduras*—PDCH). The PDCH, a small centrist party with some trade union support, was accorded legal recognition by the Melgar Castro government in December 1977. The action was reversed in November 1978 after complaints by the PN that the PDCH had broken the electoral law by receiving funds from abroad. The party was permitted to contest the 1981 election, at which it ran fourth, with 1.6 percent of the vote. In 1985 it barely secured the 1.5 percent vote share needed to maintain registration; in 1997 it drew only 1.25 percent. Its legislative representation rose from two seats to three in 2001 and to four in 2005. The PDCH 2005 presidential candidate, Juan Ramón Martínez, won 1.4 percent of the vote.

Labor leader Felicito Ávila was nominated as the party's presidential candidate for the 2009 elections. The party opposed the constitutional referendum proposed by President Zelaya in 2009 on the grounds that it was illegal.

Leaders: Lucas AGUILERA (President of the Party), Felicito ÁVILA (2009 presidential candidate), Arturo CORRALES Alvarez (1997 and 2001 presidential candidate).

Innovation and Unity Social Democratic Party (*Partido Innovación y Unidad Social Demócrata*—PINU-SD). Another centrist group, PINU was granted legal status in 1977. It ran third in the 1981 balloting, although securing only 2.5 percent of the vote, and was fourth in 1985 with 1.9 percent. In mid-1986 the party announced that it had become a social democratic formation, although several other groups indicated that they intended to seek formal recognition under the rubric, including one launched the following October as the PSDH. The party increased its legislative representation from two seats to three in 1997 and to four in 2001, only two of which were retained in 2005. PINU-SD's 2005 presidential candidate, Carlos Sosa Coello, received 1 percent of the vote.

The party had adopted the PINU-SD designation as of 2008. As a minority party, it most often has supported the PL in congress.

In February 2009, 46-year-old union leader Bernard Martinez was nominated as the first black presidential candidate in the country's history.

Leaders: Jorge AGUILAR Paredes (President), Rosa Esther LOVO (Vice President), Bernard MARTINEZ, (2009 presidential candidate), Carlos SOSA Coello (2005 presidential candidate), Olban VALLADARES Ordoñéz (1993, 1997, and 2001 presidential candidate).

Other Parties and Groups:

Wide Movement for Dignity and Justice (*Movimiento Amplio por la Dignidad y la Justicia*—MADJ). Founded in late May 2008 with the support of prosecutors, social groups, workers' organizations, and religious figures, the MADJ represents a range of civil society constituencies intent on curbing the widespread corruption plaguing Honduras, particularly at official levels. Led by the president of the Association of Prosecutors, Víctor Fernández, leading party members held a hunger strike against corruption from April 7 to May 14, 2008, based in a "dignity tent" located near the Congress.

Leader: Víctor FERNÁNDEZ.

Popular Liberal Alliance (*Alianza Liberal del Pueblo*—Alipo). Technically a left-of-center tendency within the PL, Alipo has a separate organizational structure but is itself divided into a number of factions, the most important of which are a financial and agro-export-oriented tendency led by Edmond Bogran, and a strongly antimilitary tendency, also known as the Revolutionary Liberal Democratic Movement (*Movimiento Liberal Democrático Revolucionario*—M-Líder), led by former president Carlos Roberto Reina Idiáquez, who committed suicide in August 2003. The status of this group in recent years remains unclear.

Leaders: Edmond BOGRAN, Jorge BUESO Arias, Gustavo GÓMEZ Santos, Jorge Arturo REINA, Victor SIERRA Corea (Secretary General).

Patriotic Action (*Acción Patriótica*—AP). The AP was launched in March 2006 by a group of left-leaning politicians and trade union leaders who felt that the PUD had failed to live up to its early promise to end the "political duopoly" of the PL and PN.

Following the 2009 coup, labor leader Israel Salinas became one of the main supporters of ousted president Manuel Zelaya. Along with other labor leaders, he threatened general strikes and resistance at border crossings in late July.

Leaders: Agapito ROBLEDA (PUD Dissident), Israel SALINAS (President of the United Confederation of Honduran Workers).

Socialist Party Morazánico of Honduras (*Partido Socialista Hondureño Morazánico*—PSHM) José Leonidas Martínez and Santos Eliodoro Briones founded the PSHM, a new leftist grouping, in March 2008. The group was active in the demonstrations against the 2009 coup and strongly supported the reinstatement of President Manuel Zelaya.

Leaders: José Leonidas MARTÍNEZ, Santos Eliodoro BRIONES.

Extremist Groups:

For details on these groups, which have been inactive since the 1990s, see previous editions of the *Handbook*: **the Honduran Revolutionary Movement** (*Movimiento Revolucionario Hondureño*—MRH); the **Cinchonero Popular Liberation Movement** (*Movimiento Popular de Liberación Cinchonero*—MPLC), led by Raúl LÓPEZ; the **Lorenzo Zelaya People's Revolutionary Front** (*Frente Popular Revolucionario–Lorenzo Zelaya*—FPR–LZ), led by Efraín DUARTE; and the **Morazanista Front of Honduran Liberation** (*Frente Morazanista de Liberación Hondureña*—FMLH), led by Gustavo GARCÍA España, Fernando LOPEZ, and Octavio PEREZ (both of the latter names are reportedly aliases).

LEGISLATURE

Under the 1982 constitution the former Congress of Deputies has been replaced by a **National Congress** (*Congreso Nacional*) that consists of 128 members elected on a proportional basis for four-year terms.

In the most recent election of November 27, 2005, the seat distribution was as follows: the Liberal Party, 62 seats; National Party, 55; Democratic Unification Party, 5; Christian Democratic Party of Honduras, 4; and Innovation and Unity Party, 2.

President: José Alfredo SAAVEDRA.

CABINET

[as of August 1, 2009] *(See headnote)*

Provisional President	Roberto Micheletti Baín
First Vice President	Vacant
Ministers	
Agriculture and Livestock	Hector Hernández Amador
Culture, Arts, and Sports	Rodolfo Pastor Fasquelle
Defense	Lionel Sevilla
Education	Marlon Brevé Reyes
Finance	Gabriella Nunez [f]
Foreign Affairs	Carlos López Contreras
Industry and Commerce	Fredis Alonso Cerrato Valladares

Interior and Justice	Victor Orlando Meza Lopez
Labor and Social Security	Nicholas Garcia
National Institute for Women's Affairs (INAM)	Doris Garcia Paredes [f]
Natural Resources and Environment	Valerio Gutierrez López
Presidency	Enrique Flores Lanza
Public Health	Carlos Roberto Aguilar Pineda
Public Works, Transportation and Housing	José Rosario Bonanno Zaldivar
Science and Technology	Desire Rosales [f]
Security	Jorge Alberto Rodas Gamero
Technology and International Cooperation	Karen L. Zelaya [f]
Tourism	Ricardo Martínez
Directors	
Bank for Production and Housing	Julio Quintanilla
Honduran Fund for Social Investment	César Salgado
Honduran Institute for Social Security	Efrain Bu Figueroa
Honduras Telecommunications Company	Jorge Alberto Rosa Zelaya
Institute of Retirements and Pensions for Public Employees	Lucio Izaquirre
Legal Adviser to the Government	Milton Jimenez Puerto
Merchant Marine	Vera Sofia Rubi [f]
National Electric Energy Company	Rixi Moncada [f]
National Institute of Agriculture	Francisco Funez
National Institute for Vocational Training	Sayda Eveth Burgos
National Ports Company	Roberto Babún
President, Central Bank	Edwin Araque Bonilla
President, National Agricultural Development Bank	Jorge Segovia Inestrosa
Private Secretary to the President	Eduardo Enrique Reina

[f] = female

COMMUNICATIONS

The constitution promulgated in 1982 guarantees freedom of the press. However, in September 1993 the legislature gave the government the right to censor all media material, including films and novels, found to "offend [Honduran] culture, morality, family unity, and traditions."

The independent press has faced government pressure since the early 2000s. Though transparency and access to public information laws were adopted in 2008, the Committee for Free Expression, a group of journalists and members of civil societies in Honduras, claimed that public institutions were not abiding by the new law. In 2009 "dangers facing journalists continue to be wedded to the interests of a few powerful businessmen and politicians," according to the World Association of Newspapers. On March 31 unidentified gunmen killed a journalist with *Radio Cadena Voces* (RCV) after he had reported on organized crime.

The government cracked down on the media in the aftermath of the June 28, 2009, coup. Soldiers detained seven foreign reporters, temporarily shut down local television and radio broadcasters, and interrupted the signals of international news organizations. Harassment also reportedly caused a number of journalists to flee the country in fear of their safety.

Press. Except as noted, all newspapers are privately owned and published daily in Tegucigalpa: *La Tribuna* (60,000); *La Prensa* (San Pedro Sula, 60,000); *Tiempo* (San Pedro Sula, 50,000), left-of-center; *El Heraldo* (45,000); *El Nuevo Día* (San Pedro Sula, 20,000); *La Gaceta* (3,000), official government organ; and *Honduras This Week*, a weekly, in English.

News agencies. There is no local facility, most media relying on the regional *Agencia Centroamericana de Noticias* (ACAN) and U.S. news services. In addition, Britain's Reuters, Germany's *Deutsche Presse-Agentur*, and the Spanish *Agencia EFE* maintain offices in Tegucigalpa.

Broadcasting and computing. Broadcasting is under the supervision of the *Empresa Hondureña de Telecomunicaciones* (Hondutel). Many of the more than 280 radio stations are operated by religious groups. Commercial television is dominated by *Telesistema Hondureño* and *Compañía Televisora Hondureña*, both owned by *Emisoras Unidas*. There are several private radio and TV stations. There were approximately 674,000 television receivers in 2003. As of 2008 there were 130.9 Internet users per 1,000 inhabitants.

INTERGOVERNMENTAL REPRESENTATION

Ambassador to the U.S.: (Vacant).

U.S. Ambassador to Honduras: Hugo LLORENS.

Permanent Representative to the UN: Jorge Arturo REINA IDIAQUEZ.

IGO Memberships (Non-UN): ACS, BCIE, IADB, Interpol, IOM, NAM, OAS, OPANAL, PCA, SELA, SICA, WCO, WTO.

HUNGARY

Hungarian Republic
Magyar Köztársaság

Political Status: Independent kingdom created in 1000; republic proclaimed in 1946; Communist People's Republic established August 20, 1949; pre-Communist name revived as one of a number of constitutional changes approved on October 18, 1989.

Area: 35,919 sq. mi. (93,030 sq. km.).

Population: 10,197,119 (2001C); 10,048,000 (2008).

Major Urban Centers (2005E): BUDAPEST (1,700,000), Debrecen (209,000), Miskolc (189,000), Pécs (169,000), Szeged (162,000), Györ (131,000).

Official Language: Hungarian.

Monetary Unit: Forint (official rate December 1, 2009: 180.49 forints = $1US).

President: Laszlo SOLYOM; elected (as the candidate of the Federation of Young Democrats–Hungarian Civic Alliance and several other parties) in third-round balloting by the National Assembly on June 7, 2005, and sworn in for a five-year term on August 5, succeeding Ferenc MÁDL (nonparty).

Prime Minister: Gordon BAJNAI (nonparty); elected as interim premier by the National Assembly on April 14, 2009, following the resignation of Ferenc GYURCSÁNY (Hungarian Socialist Party) on March 21.

THE COUNTRY

Masters for over 1,000 years of the fertile plain extending on either side of the middle Danube, the Hungarians have long regarded their country as the eastern outpost of Western Europe in cultural pattern, religious affiliation, and political structure. More than 90 percent of the present Hungarian population is of Magyar origin; Germans, Roma (Gypsies), Romanians, Slovaks, and Southern Slavs (Croats, Serbs, and Slovenes) are the main ethnic minorities. Despite more than four decades of Communist-mandated antireligious policies from the mid-1940s until

the late 1980s, about two-thirds of the population is classified as Roman Catholic; there are also Protestant, Eastern Orthodox, and Jewish adherents. In 2007 the employment rate for women was 51 percent, although their pay was 11 percent lower, on average, than men's, at a rate below the European Union (EU) average.

Although the Hungarian economy was traditionally dependent on the agricultural sector (largely collectivized following the Communist assumption of power after World War II), agriculture now accounts for only 5 percent of GDP. However, the country remains a net food exporter, with one of the largest agricultural trade surpluses in Eastern Europe. Industry contributed 33 percent of GDP in 1999. In addition to processed foods, leading industrial products, almost all of which require imported raw materials (iron ore, petroleum, copper, and crude fibers), are machinery, transportation equipment, electrical and electronic equipment (including computers), chemicals, and textiles. Bauxite, coal, and natural gas are the chief mineral resources.

Largely because of the collapse of trade with other ex-Communist states, Hungary's GDP fell by 20 percent from 1989 through 1993, and both inflation and unemployment registered in double digits. Growth resumed in 1994 and averaged 4.6 percent annually in 1997–1999 before reaching 5.5 percent in 2000. Meanwhile, unemployment consistently declined, from 11.5 percent in 1993 to about 6.5 percent later in the decade (the lowest rate in Eastern Europe), and consumer-price inflation, which had averaged over 20 percent in 1993–1997, dropped to under 10 percent in 2000. For the 1990s as a whole, Hungary led the region in direct foreign investment, and trade burgeoned, especially with the EU. Led by Germany, EU countries now purchase three-fourths of Hungary's exports and provide two-thirds of its imports.

Hungary was described in a 2000 report from the International Monetary Fund (IMF) as "in the vanguard of the transition economies" seeking EU accession. However, budget deficits began to increase in the early 2000s, prompting the government (under EU pressure) to implement austerity measures. Overall, the EU considered the economic progress of 2002–2003 sufficient to include Hungary among the ten new countries admitted to the EU on May 1, 2004.

Solid growth (4 percent) was achieved in both 2004 and 2005 on the strength of increased exports and rising investment. However, the IMF and the EU warned that the budget deficit and public debt remained unacceptably high. In early 2006, the government announced comprehensive tax increases and budget cuts to reduce the budget deficit (then running at about 10.7 percent of GDP annually). The EU subsequently extended the deadline from 2008 to 2009 for Hungary to meet the EU standard (an annual budget deficit no more than 3 percent of GDP) that is necessary for Hungary's planned adoption of the euro as its official currency. Although the budget initiatives prompted major protest demonstrations, they were endorsed by the IMF.

Despite the government's desire to adopt the euro by 2009, recently revised estimates pushed the date of currency conversion until 2014 or later. While achieving many of its economic targets in the past few years, Hungary trailed Poland, Slovakia, and the Czech Republic. Hungary is known to have the heaviest tax burden in the region, tax evasion is rampant, and the country suffers from a black market that accounts for some 20 percent of GDP.

Growing political resistance to further spending cuts threatened to derail achievement of the economic goals necessary for euro adoption. In March 2008 the European Central Bank issued a report urging Hungary to press ahead with economic reforms, however unpopular, if it expected to join the eurozone and have a competitive market economy.

Forecasts in April 2008 predicted that the budget deficit would be 4 percent of GDP in that year, while annual inflation would reach 5.9 percent. GDP was expected to grow by 2.4 percent. However, as the global economic recession descended in the second half of 2008, Hungary quickly appeared among the hardest hit in Europe, its unprecedented growth collapsing to a GDP uptick of just 0.5 percent in 2008 and a projected decline of 6 percent in 2009. Of particular impact to the economy was the dramatic drop in the value of the forint, which hit an historic low relative to the euro in October. A boom in foreign currency borrowing, especially of low-interest loans in Swiss francs, exposed the country to a high risk of default as the forint tumbled in value. Some 80 percent of the assets in Hungary's banks were foreign owned. Hungary responded by imposing a series of extreme fiscal constraints in order to qualify for loan packages offered by the European Central Bank, IMF, World Bank, and the EU. However, the unpopular measures, which curbed social benefits, led to the resignation of Prime Minister Ferenc GYURCSÁNY in March (see Current issues, below) and prevented Hungary from offering the kind of stimulus packages available in other EU countries.

GOVERNMENT AND POLITICS

Political background. Part of the polyglot Austro-Hungarian Empire, the former Kingdom of Hungary lost two-thirds of its territory (including Transylvania) and the bulk of its non-Magyar population at the end of World War I under the 1920 Treaty of Trianon. A brief but bloody Communist dictatorship under Béla KUN in 1919 was followed by 25 years of right-wing authoritarian government under Adm. Miklós HORTHY, who bore the title of regent. Having regained Northern Transylvania from Romania under the 1940 Vienna Award, Hungary joined Germany in the war against the Soviet Union in June 1941 and was occupied by Soviet forces in late 1944. Under a definitive peace treaty with the Allied Powers signed in February 1947, Hungary reverted to its 1920 borders.

Communists obtained only 17 percent of the vote in a free election held in November 1945, but with Soviet backing they assumed key posts in the coalition government that proclaimed the Hungarian Republic on February 1, 1946. Seizing de facto control in May–June 1947, the Communists proceeded to liquidate most opposition parties and to establish a dictatorship led by Mátyás RÁKOSI. The remaining parties and mass organizations were grouped in a Communist-controlled "front," while the Hungarian People's Republic was formally established in August 1949.

The initial years of the People's Republic were marked by purges and the systematic elimination of domestic opposition, which included the 1949 treason conviction of the Roman Catholic primate, József Cardinal MINDSZENTY. In the post-Stalin era, however, gradual liberalization led to the outbreak in October 1956 of a popular revolutionary movement, the formation of a coalition government under Imre NAGY, and the announcement on November 1 of Hungary's withdrawal from the Warsaw Pact. Massive Soviet military force was employed to crush the revolt, and a pro-Soviet regime headed by János KÁDÁR was installed on November 4. Nagy was hanged in 1958; Cardinal Mindszenty, who had been freed in the 1956 uprising, sought refuge in the U.S. embassy in Budapest, where he remained for 15 years before being allowed to leave the country.

Concerned primarily with consolidating its position, the Kádár government was initially rigid and authoritarian. However, the 1962 congress of the Hungarian Socialist Workers' Party (*Magyar Szocialista Munkáspárt*—MSzMP) marked the beginning of a trend toward pragmatism in domestic policy that was exemplified by the implementation of a program known as the New Economic Mechanism, which allowed for decentralization, more flexible management strategies, incentives for efficiency, and expanded production of consumer goods. At the same time, Hungary strictly adhered to Soviet pronouncements in foreign affairs, as most dramatically demonstrated by the participation of Hungarian troops in the Warsaw Pact invasion of Czechoslovakia in August 1968.

The retreat from Communist domination commenced somewhat earlier in Hungary than elsewhere in Eastern Europe. In May 1988 Kádár was replaced as party general secretary by Károly GRÓSZ, who had been premier since June 1987. Grósz was succeeded as premier in November by Miklós NÉMETH. In early 1989 the National Assembly legalized freedom of assembly and association, and in mid-March 75,000 demonstrators were permitted to assemble in Budapest to demand free elections and the removal of Soviet troops. On May 2, acting on behalf of the Németh government, security forces began dismantling the barbed-wire fence along the border with Austria, and on May 13, five days after Kádár had been forced into retirement from his ceremonial post as party president, talks began with opposition leaders on transition to a multiparty system. On June 16 the martyred Imre Nagy was formally "rehabilitated" by means of a public reburial attended by some 300,000 persons. On October 7 the MSzMP renounced Marxism and renamed itself the Hungarian Socialist Party (*Magyar Szocialista Párt*—MSzP). On October 23 the non-Communist speaker of the National Assembly, Mátyás SZÜRÖS, became acting president of the republic in the wake of legislative action that abolished the Presidential Council, purged the constitution of its Stalinist elements, and paved the way for the first free elections in more than four decades.

At second-stage legislative balloting on April 8, 1990, the recently formed Hungarian Democratic Forum (*Magyar Demokrata Fórum*—MDF) won a substantial plurality of seats, and on May 3 its chair, József ANTALL, was asked to form a center-right government, consisting of the MDF, the Christian Democratic People's Party (*Kereszténydemokrata Néppárt*—KDNP), and the Independent Smallholders' Party (*Független Kisgazda Párt*—FKgP), that was installed on May 23. Earlier, on May 2, the new parliament had named a noted former dissident, Arpád GÖNCZ, to the post of acting state president. A referendum on direct election of the president (favored by 86 percent of those participating) failed on July 29 because of insufficient turnout, and on August 3 the assembly elected Göncz to a regular five-year term.

In 1991–1992 the Antall government secured the passage of legislation providing compensation for property expropriated during the Fascist and Communist eras, as well as for individuals killed, imprisoned, or deported for political reasons between 1939 and 1989. In addition, an amendment was approved in October 1993 allowing the prosecution of certain crimes committed by state authorities during the 1956 Hungarian uprising.

In February 1992 the FKgP withdrew from the ruling coalition because its blueprints for the restoration of land to pre-Communist owners had not become government policy. However, three-quarters of the 44 FKgP parliamentary deputies continued to support the government, initially as the FKgP "Historical Section" (*Történelmi Tagozat*). Antall carried out a controversial ministerial reshuffle in February 1993, but the government was further weakened at midyear when a right-wing MDF faction led by István CSURKA was expelled from the party and formed the Hungarian Justice and Life Party (*Magyar Igazság és Élat Párt*—MIÉP).

The MDF sought to ensure political continuity despite Antall's early death in December 1993 at the age of 61, with succession passed to longtime heir-apparent Péter BOROSS, theretofore the interior minister. However, the change of prime minister did nothing to restore the political fortunes of the MDF, which was overwhelmingly defeated in the May 1994 general election by a resurgent MSzP led by Dr. Gyula HORN. Despite his party's commanding majority, Horn sought to dispel overseas concern about the return to power of Hungary's ex-Communists by forming a coalition with the centrist Alliance of Free Democrats (*Szabad Demokraták Szövetsége*—SzDSz), thus generating the two-thirds majority needed for constitutional amendment.

The Horn government declared its commitment to completing its predecessor's successful privatization program, while giving priority to the investigation of alleged corruption in the disposal of state-owned assets. However, in January 1995 the highly respected László BÉKESI resigned as finance minister, claiming that promarket reform was being resisted by other ministers. In February a new finance minister, Lajos BOKROS, and a special privatization minister were appointed amid government admissions that Hungary's economic difficulties were chronic, largely because of spiraling public debt. The announcement of draconian economic austerity measures in March precipitated the resignation of two more MSzP ministers.

The Horn government also faced deep conflict over its effort to draft a new constitution to replace the much-amended Communist-era text. One area of contention was an FkgP-led effort for direct, popular election of the president, although the party's proposed referendum on the change was struck by the Constitutional Court shortly before the scheduled presidential vote in the National Assembly. On June 19, 1995, the National Assembly handed Arpád Göncz an easy victory to a second five-year term against an independent conservative nominee, Ferenc MÁDL.

In February 1996 Finance Minister Bokros resigned after his colleagues had declined to endorse the next stage of his deficit-reducing plans. However, by early 1998 the MSzP/SzDSz government was being credited with having achieved significant economic progress. In the first round of voting on May 10, the MSzP secured 32.3 percent of the vote, followed by the center-right Federation of Young Democrats–Hungarian Civic Party (*Fiatal Demokraták Szövetsége–Magyar Polgari Párt*—FiDeSz-MPP) with 28.2 percent. Following the second round on May 24, the FiDeSz-MPP emerged with a plurality of 148 seats, with the MSzP winning 134 and the SzDSz claiming only 24. Consequently, the president asked the 35-year-old FiDeSz-MPP leader, Viktor ORBÁN, to form a new government. After rejecting cooperation with the MSzP and the ultranationalist MIÉP, Orbán reached agreement with the MDF (with which the FiDeSz-MPP had presented joint candidates) and the FKgP. Orbán was sworn in on July 6, and the new cabinet took office on July 8.

On June 6, 2000, the National Assembly elected Ferenc Mádl as President Göncz's successor.

Somewhat earlier than expected, and with preparations for accession to the EU in mind, on December 13, 2001, President Mádl announced a National Assembly election for April 2002. Although opinion polls had forecast a repeat victory for Prime Minister Orbán, the opposition Socialists won 42.1 percent of the party-list vote in first-round balloting on April 7, compared to 41.1 percent for the FiDeSz-MPP-MDF. A leftist government composed of the MSzP and the SzDSz took office under former Socialist finance minister Péter Medgyessy on May 27.

In a national referendum on April 12, 2003, voters approved proposed accession to the EU with an 84 percent "yes" vote. (The National Assembly ratified the measure on December 15, and Hungary joined the EU with nine other new members on May 1, 2004.) However, concurrent austerity measures on the part of the government eroded support for Prime Minister Medgyessy, and the government parties fared poorly in the June 2004 European Parliament balloting. Following a dispute between Medgyessy and junior coalition partner SzDSz, Medgyessy announced his resignation on August 25 after apparently having also lost the support of his own party. He was succeeded on September 26 by the MSzP's Ferenc GYURCSÁNY, a wealthy young businessman who had been serving as minister of youth and sports.

On June 7, 2005, Laszlo SOLYOM, who was nominated by the FiDeSz-MPSz (as the FiDeSz-MPP had been renamed [see Political Parties, below]), was elected president in the third round of balloting in the assembly. Solyom was best known for his former post as president of the Constitutional Court.

The governing coalition of the MSzP and SzDSz extended its legislative majority at the assembly balloting of April 9 and 23, 2006. Gyurcsány's government program was approved by a vote of 206–159 in the assembly on June 9, and Gyurcsány on the same day was again sworn in as prime minister to head a reshuffled MSzP/SzDSz cabinet.

Following the public's rejection of major reforms in a March 2008 referendum, Gyurcsány restructured the cabinet. He immediately dismissed health minister Agnes HORVATH and following the SzDSZ's pullout from the coalition he appointed seven new ministers in April and created a new Ministry of National Development and Economy (to replace the former Ministry of Economy and Transport); transportation became a separate ministry. The coalition remained a minority government into 2009, leading the opposition to call for a snap election (see Current issues, below). Facing open hostility from the opposition and from within his own party. Gyurcsány announced his resignation on March 21, 2009, to a party congress by saying that some regarded him as an obstacle to reform. FiDeSz's calls for early elections were backed by the president, who said that a popular vote would be the best way for Hungary to establish a stable government. After rejecting Gyurcsány's nominations for successors, senior figures in the MSzP and SzDSz settled on Gordon BAJNAI, an independent, as a consensus candidate. Bajnai demanded written guarantees from MSzP and SzDSz leaders to approve his fiscal austerity plans as a condition of his nomination. On April 14 the National Assembly passed a "constructive" vote of no confidence in Gyurcsány and formally approved Bajnai as the new prime minister, with 204 in favor and 8 abstentions. FiDeSz-MPSz boycotted the vote. Bajnai, a former economy minister, announced a new cabinet, of which six ministers were politically unaligned. Solyom formally appointed the cabinet on April 20.

Constitution and government. The constitution of 1949 (as amended in 1972) declared Hungary to be a state in which all power belonged to the working people, the bulk of the means of production was publicly owned, and the (Communist) Hungarian Socialist Workers' Party was the "leading force" in state and society. Under the October 1989 revision, Hungary is described as an "independent democratic state" adhering to "the values of both bourgeois democracy and democratic socialism." In addition, civil and human rights are protected; a multiparty parliamentary system is to be maintained; and executive, legislative, and judicial functions are separated. The former 21-member Presidential Council was replaced by an indirectly elected state president who serves as commander in chief of the armed forces and has the capacity to negotiate international agreements. Subsequently, the unicameral National Assembly approved a law on the activity and financing of political parties, prohibited parties from operating in the workplace (thus invalidating the traditional role of Communist party cells), and approved an electoral law based on a mixed system of proportional and direct representation. The judicial system is jointly administered by the Supreme Court, whose president is named by the legislature, and the ministry of justice. Below the Supreme Court are county, district, and municipal courts. A Constitutional Court was also added in 1989 as successor to a Constitutional Law Council established by the assembly five years before.

The country is administratively divided into 19 counties and 23 cities and towns of county status (including Budapest), about 200 other towns, and nearly 3,000 villages. Council members at the local levels are directly elected, while those at the county level are elected by the members of the lower-level councils. Each council elects an executive committee and a president.

Foreign relations. Following the failure of the 1956 revolution, Hungary faithfully followed the Soviet lead in international issues, voting with the Soviet bloc in the United Nations (UN), adhering to the Brezhnev Doctrine of the limited sovereignty of Communist states, and serving as a reliable member of the Warsaw Pact, the Council for Mutual Economic Assistance (CMEA), and other multilateral Communist organs. However, relations with its closest Eastern-bloc neighbors were not always smooth. Disputes over the treatment of ethnic Hungarians in Romania caused tension with Bucharest, while Czechoslovak authorities expressed disapproval of Budapest's efforts, launched in the 1960s, to improve relations with the West.

Communist rule having been brought to an end, the new National Assembly voted unanimously on June 26, 1990, to suspend Hungary's participation in the Warsaw Pact and to withdraw from the alliance by late 1991. The departure of Soviet troops was complicated by acrimonious disputes over financial liabilities, which were, however, largely resolved during reciprocal visits by the Russian and Hungarian presidents in November 1992 and June 1993, respectively.

In November 1990 Hungary became the first East European country to be admitted to the Council of Europe, and the following month it became the first from the region to subscribe to the Social Charter of the European Community (EC, subsequently the EU). The goal of eventual EC membership was a joint aim of the "Visegrád" cooperation bloc formed on February 15, 1991, by Hungary, Poland, and Czechoslovakia (subsequently the Czech Republic and Slovakia). Meanwhile, on December 21, 1992, the Visegrád states signed a Central European Free Trade Agreement (CEFTA; see Foreign relations section in article on Poland for additional information). Hungary is also a member of the Central European Initiative (CEI), originally formed in 1989 as a "Pentagonal" group of Central European states committed to mutual and bilateral economic cooperation within the Conference on (later Organization for) Security and Cooperation in Europe (CSCE/OSCE).

Although Hungary repeatedly stated its acceptance of existing borders, its keen interest in the status of the 32 million ethnic Hungarians in neighboring countries caused regional strains in the post-Communist era. Despite Hungarian attempts to curb the inflow, ethnic Hungarians continued to cross the border from Transylvania in substantial numbers, citing rising Romanian nationalism as the reason. The civil war in former Yugoslavia also resulted in an exodus of ethnic Hungarians, in this case from the Serbian-ruled province of Vojvodina, once part of the Austro-Hungarian Empire. Moreover, Slovakia's move to independence on January 1, 1993, increased concern in Hungary over Slovakia's ethnic Hungarian minority.

Taking a less nationalistic line on ethnic Hungarians in neighboring countries, the Horn government elected in May 1994 sought to improve relations with Romania and Slovakia. In February 1995 Hungary signed the Council of Europe's new Convention on the Protection of National Minorities, and the following month it concluded a friendship and cooperation treaty with Slovakia, which guaranteed the existing border and provided formal protection for minority groups (principally ethnic Hungarians in Slovakia).

A long-negotiated treaty dealing with minority rights and other bilateral issues was signed by the Hungarian and Romanian prime ministers on September 16, 1996, in Timişoara in Romanian Transylvania, where 1.6 million ethnic Hungarians form Europe's largest nonimmigrant ethnic minority. The text represented a compromise, but, inevitably, the treaty was fiercely condemned by the nationalist parties of both countries as a capitulation. Both governments considered finalization of the treaty as an important step toward membership in the EU and the North Atlantic Treaty Organization (NATO).

An agreement between Hungary and the European Free Trade Association (EFTA) entered into force on October 1, 1993, while in December, Hungary applied for membership in the Organization for Economic Cooperation and Development (OECD). In February 1994 Hungary joined NATO's Partnership for Peace program, and in May it was one of nine such countries offered close nonmembership links with the Western European Union (WEU). However, the priority remained closer relations with the EU, to which Hungary on April 1, 1994, submitted an application for full membership following the entry into force of an association agreement two months earlier. In December 1997 the EU issued a formal invitation to Hungary and five other "first-wave" nations to begin discussions in March 1998 regarding membership protocols.

In August 1995 Hungary joined in signing a CEFTA agreement providing for free trade in most industrial products by 1997, this being undertaken as a step toward EU membership for the four CEFTA members. In January 1996 the government committed 400 Hungarian troops to the NATO-commanded International Force (IFOR) charged with implementing the Dayton Accords for Bosnia. Further important integration into Western structures was achieved in March when Hungary enrolled as a full member of the OECD.

In July 1997 NATO invited Hungary, Poland, and the Czech Republic to join the alliance in 1999, but the extreme extraparliamentary parties in Hungary continued to oppose membership. The seven parliamentary parties reportedly agreed to hold a nonbinding referendum on NATO, but the FiDeSz-MPP later called for a binding vote. The cabinet subsequently reversed its position on the referendum and agreed to be bound by the results. Voters approved NATO accession overwhelmingly (85 percent) on November 16, and Hungary quickly submitted its formal membership application. Accession was achieved on March 12, 1999, at a ceremony in the United States, although the timing was poor for the new NATO members in view of the conflict between the alliance and Yugoslavia. The NATO military action was particularly sensitive for Hungary, since the 340,000 ethnic Hungarians resident in Vojvodina were considered possible targets of Serbian reprisals. Budapest dutifully permitted NATO planes access to Hungarian airspace for attacks on Serbia but otherwise was not involved in the campaign.

Hungary supported U.S. policy toward Iraq in 2003 and deployed 350 troops to the U.S./UK-led coalition following the fall of Saddam Hussein. However, Hungary's stance strained relations with France and Germany, and, with more than half of the Hungarian population indicating opposition to the war, the Hungarian troops were withdrawn from Iraq by the end of 2004. Hungary has also contributed to the NATO-led peacekeeping mission in Afghanistan.

Upon his installation as prime minister in 2002, Péter Medgyessy announced that EU membership would be his administration's top priority. His successor, Ferenc Gyurcsány, in 2004 moved to complete agricultural reform demanded by the EU and to pursue the fiscal policies necessary to permit Hungary to adopt the euro by 2010. (The assembly in December 2004 had ratified the proposed new EU constitution by a vote of 322–12.) In 2008 euro adoption was viewed as unlikely before 2016.

In December 2004 Hungary conducted a national referendum on the controversial proposal to offer citizenship to ethnic Hungarians living in other countries. However, the referendum failed because the required 50 percent voter turnout was not achieved.

On December 17, 2007, Hungary became the first EU country to ratify the Lisbon Treaty, the successor to the failed 2005 EU constitution, tallying 325 votes and 14 abstentions in the National Assembly. (The Lisbon treaty was rejected by Ireland, tabling its adoption throughout the rest of Europe. See the Ireland entry in the 2008 *Handbook*.) On December 21 Hungary became one of nine countries in Eastern Europe to join the EU's border-free Schengen zone.

In recent years Hungary has sought to secure a more reliable stream of oil and supplies, given concerns that it was overly dependent upon Russia, which has used its energy reserves as formidable leverage in its foreign policy. Hungary, which receives 80 percent of its gas from Russia, was one of the countries most affected by gas outages in 2006 when Russia cut gas deliveries through a pipeline passing through Ukraine. In February 2008, seemingly contradicting its goal for energy diversification, Hungary signed an agreement with Russia to jointly partner the building of the "South Stream" gas pipeline through Hungary, bypassing Ukraine. Critics said the agreement would deepen Hungary's reliance on Russian gas and that it threatened to disrupt progress on the construction of the EU-backed Nabucco pipeline that would bring gas to Europe from Azerbaijan. Gyurcsány insisted there was nothing to prevent both pipelines from going ahead.

Following a second dispute between Ukraine and Russia in January 2009 that resulted in gas shutoffs to Europe and the Balkans, the Hungarian gas company MOL secured a $277 million loan from the European Bank for Reconstruction and Development to build a new natural gas storage facility in Hungary and advanced the prospects of the Nabucco pipeline by forming a consortium with Austria's OMV gas company to pump from Iraq's Kurdistan region. In June a diplomatic spat erupted with Slovakia over that country's adoption of a language law making it a punishable offense to use minority languages, such as Hungarian, in official communication.

Current issues. In September 2006 a recording was leaked to the media of a supposedly private speech Prime Minister Gyurcsány had made to senior members of the MSzP. Among other things, Gyurcsány admitted in the speech that he had falsely claimed during the legislative campaign that Hungary's budget deficit was only 4.7 percent of GDP, contrary to estimates twice that high from the central bank and international financial institutions. Gyurcsány's acknowledgment that "we lied in the morning, we lied in the evening, and we lied at night" about economic data prompted massive street protests, most notably outside the assembly building. More than 300 people were injured during the demonstrations, and violence also broke out in October during celebrations to commemorate the 50th anniversary of the failed 1956 uprising.

The MSzP suffered major losses in the October 2006 municipal elections, with the opposition FiDeSz-MPSz and KDNP winning majorities on 18 of 19 county councils and 19 of 23 city councils. However, the government survived a no-confidence motion in October by a 207–165 vote in the assembly, and the assembly also endorsed the prime minister's budget plans in December, despite intense opposition from major sectors of the population. Another massive protest demonstration in March 2007 also appeared to threaten a government collapse, but the MSzP and SzDSz announced a new coalition agreement in July that they hoped would keep the government intact.

In an effort to improve accountability, public trust, and the economy, the governing coalition and several opposition parties agreed in August 2007 to establish an independent budget-monitoring office to ensure a predictable budget, tracking changes through political administrations, and to inform the general public about progress in meeting budget targets. Hungary had built up huge budget deficits in 2002 and 2006, resulting in the package of austerity measures that are part of the current euro convergence program.

The National Assembly also approved a major overhaul to the health care system in December 2007, replacing the ailing state-run National Healthcare Insurance Fund Administration with a quasi-private National Health Insurance Center that would provide health care through potentially dozens of health funds. The new system, part of a privatization drive that included the postal, railway, and telecommunications sectors, mandated the government's sale of 49 percent of its shares in its health care system to private industry in an attempt to reduce its public deficit. As part of the provisions, citizens would pay fees for doctor and hospital visits for the first time. However, as part of the agreement that led to the legislation's passage, the FiDeSz-MPSz arranged for these fee provisions, as well as university tuition fees, to be put to a public referendum in March 2008.

By the spring of 2008 the coalition government was beset by internal strife emanating from the growing unpopularity of the economic reforms designed to constrain Hungary's ballooning budget deficit. On March 9, in a highly symbolic referendum organized by the FiDeSz-MPSz, voters overwhelmingly censured core health care reform initiatives considered essential for Hungary's beleaguered economy. The rejection by 80 percent of voters was considered a vote of no confidence in the coalition leadership.

Soon after the vote, Gyurcsány dismissed health minister Agnes HORVATH, prompting further coalition turmoil. The Horvath dismissal was the final blow to a steadily deteriorating relationship between the governing parties over the pace and content of economic reforms. SzDSz announced at the end of March it would pull out of the coalition and remove its three cabinet ministers. In April, Gyurcsány announced a major cabinet reshuffle, appointing several new ministers and creating a new Ministry of National Development and Economy (to replace the former Ministry of Economy and Transport); transportation became a separate ministry.

The MSzP's minority government was tasked with unilaterally discerning how to realize increasingly unpopular economic reform goals while fending off calls by leading opposition party FiDeSz-MPSz to hold early elections. As the economic recession took hold in early autumn, Gyurcsány faced an increasingly complicated political situation. Opposition parties stood against any plan that did not sizably reduce spending, while members of his own party objected to reducing social benefits. In August Gyurcsány announced that he would step down from office if his proposed budget was rejected by parliament. In October Gyurcsány was temporarily bolstered after securing an $8.7 billion loan from the European Central Bank to cover an acute shortage of euros within Hungarian banks, and soon after obtained a $25 billion loan from the IMF, World Bank, and EU. However, both loans were conditioned on Hungary imposing additional spending constraints on its 2009 budget in order to pull the budget deficit to below the EU mandatory cap of 3 percent of GDP. In December Gyurcsány managed to gain just enough votes to pass a tax reform plan (no votes came from the SzDSz) that lowered the capital gains tax and aimed to boost revenue by reducing red tape, corruption, and activities in the black market. Two weeks later the parliament passed a budget proposal that slashed $2 billion in spending.

In February 2009 a revised budget and tax plan was released that included cuts to a host of popular social programs, including a curtailing of disability allowances, pension benefits, and tax exemptions for families. Although Gyurcsány initially received praise from the European Commission for the measures, by early March international support had begun to crumble as well. Faced with their own economic troubles, Western European leaders, led by France and Germany, rejected a second rescue package for Central and Eastern Europe. Additionally, Hungary's call for fast-track membership into the Eurozone as a means to rid itself of the unstable forint was rebuffed. Gyurcsány's resignation brought little immediate change in economic policy. Bajnai entered office in March promising to continue advancing economic austerity measures, including $2.7 billion in spending cuts. In late June the parliament passed a tax reform bill to enter into force in 2010 that shifted the overall tax burden from businesses to individuals as a means to improve investor sentiment and bring down debt. Additionally, the National Assembly passed a revised plan to meet a deficit target of 3.9 percent in 2009 and 3.8 percent in 2010.

POLITICAL PARTIES

As of late 1988 the sole authorized political party was the Hungarian Socialist Workers' Party (*Magyar Szocialista Munkáspárt*—MSzMP), supported by a Communist-controlled umbrella organization, the Patriotic People's Front (*Hazafias Népfront*), which, prior to the emergence of a number of unofficial formations, embraced virtually all organized groups and associations in the country. In January 1989 the National Assembly legalized freedom of assembly and association, and a month later the MSzMP approved the formation of independent parties, some of which had begun organizing on an informal basis as early as the previous September. In May 1989 talks began on transition to a multiparty system, yielding a historic accord on September 19 that sanctioned broad-ranged participation in national elections.

In 1994 some 40 parties (out of well over 100 officially registered) competed for National Assembly seats, with 8 winning representation. In 1998, 26 offered candidates, 6 successfully; in 2002, 4 of 39 won representation; in 2006, 5 of 48.

Government Parties:

Hungarian Socialist Party (*Magyar Szocialista Párt*—MSzP). The origin of the MSzP lies in the June 1948 merger of Hungary's Communist and Social Democratic parties. Known initially as the Hungarian Workers' Party (*Magyar Munkáspárt*—MMP), the merged grouping was reorganized as the Hungarian Socialist Workers' Party (*Magyar Szocialista Munkáspárt*—MSzMP) when János Kádár took over the leadership in the wake of the 1956 revolution. At an extraordinary party congress on October 6–10, 1989, the party renounced Marxism, adopted its current name, and appointed Rezsó NYERS to the newly created post of presidium president. Gyula Horn was, in turn, chosen to succeed Nyers in May 1990. He led the party to a decisive victory in the May 1994 general election.

In the wake of a financial scandal and unpopular austerity measures, a dissident faction within the MSzP, called the Socialist Democratic Group, demanded the replacement of Prime Minister Horn as chair of the party in early 1997. Following the MSzP's decline in the May 1998 legislative poll (which eventually forced the party into opposition), Horn resigned as party leader at the September 1998 MSzP congress. He was succeeded by Lászlo KOVÁCS, former foreign minister and leader of the MSzP's parliamentary group. In October 2000, although refusing to accept a new leadership role, Horn asserted that the party under Kovács had become "too defensive." Miklós Németh, the last premier of the Communist era, also appeared to be assuming an active role in the party, having recently ended a nine-year appointment with the European Bank for Reconstruction and Development (EBRD).

A party congress in June 2001 chose a former nonparty finance minister, Péter Medgyessy, as the MSzP candidate for prime minister in the next national election. The decision paid off at the polls in April 2002, when the MSzP secured 178 seats, sufficient for it to form a governing coalition with the SzDSz.

Voter discontent with economic reforms, electoral losses in the June 2004 EU parliamentary polls, and the dissatisfaction of the Free Democrats all subsequently combined to undermine support for Medgyessy. At an MSzP conference in August 2004, party members voted to replace him with Ferenc Gyurcsány, a millionaire businessman who pledged to pursue a "third way," under which socialism would be "tempered" by free-market policies. Gyurcsány was widely credited with "rescuing" the MSzP from internal strife, and the success of the MSzP/SzDSz coalition in the 2006 assembly poll was attributed to his popularity. Gyurcsány's public standing plummeted following the election (see Current issues), but he was reelected as MSzP chair in February 2007 after threatening to resign as prime minister if he lost his party post.

Gyurcsány has since faced challenges to retain his seat. In October 2007, during anniversary celebrations commemorating the 1956 uprising, a 30,000-strong demonstration turned against Gyurcsány, demanding his resignation. The FiDeSz-led rally accused the prime minister of betraying democracy and of failing to defend Hungary against a resurgent Russia.

Gyurcsány's growing unpopularity had much to do with latent distrust emanating from his 2006 leaked speech. Following the March 2008 referendum the MSzP officials discussed bringing "fresh faces" into the party, while FiDeSz used the moment to demand a "vote of confidence" in Gyurcsány and called for early parliamentary elections, which would likely have led to further MSzP and SzDSz losses. In June the MSzP maintained minority status in the National Assembly and faced difficulties in advancing any new policies. The opposition, led by FiDeSz-MPSz, threatened to block the MSzP legislation as a means to force an early election.

By the time he resigned in March 2009, Gyurcsány's public approval ratings had sunk to 18 percent, though the MSzP as a whole faired only slightly better at 23 percent. Gyurcsány's resignation prompted an ambiguous response within the party. Though increasingly isolated, Gyurcsány offered a degree of stability leading into the 2010 federal elections. He relinquished party leadership on March 28; on April 5 Ildikó Lendvai won party chair with 91 percent of the delegates' votes. After the party posted dismal returns of 17 percent at the EU parliamentary election in June, MSzP leaders reviewed ways to revamp the party and concluded that the past seven years in power had "made the party's voter base unsure, and have exhausted its organizational force" and that the party's goal to modernize the economy while guaranteeing a social net had broken down. Lendvai called on her party to search within its ranks for a new, young candidate it could run for prime minister who would be capable of restoring voter trust. Despite FiDeSz's repeated calls for a snap election, by July it appeared that the MSzP had enough support from the SzDSz to remain in power until the 2010 federal election.

Leaders: Ildikó LENDVAI (Chair), Imre SAZEKERES (Deputy Chair), Katalin SZILI (Speaker of the National Assembly).

Alliance of Free Democrats (*Szabad Demokraták Szövetsége*—SzDSz). Founded in May 1988 as the Network of Free Initiatives (*Szabad Kezdeményezések Hálózata*—SzKH), the SzDSz was reorganized as a political party the following November and held its first general assembly in March 1989. It won 93 legislative seats in 1990, becoming the leading opposition party of the post-Communist era. Factional strife between "pragmatists" and "ideologues" appeared to be healed in November 1992 by the election of Iván PETÓ as party chair.

The party slipped to 69 seats in the May 1994 general election, its first-round voting share being 19.4 percent. Pető subsequently could not contain disagreements over whether the SzDSz should stay in the government coalition, a division that was aggravated by a privatization scandal in October 1996 that implicated both coalition partners. The scandal seriously damaged the party in public opinion polls, with the result that in February 1997 Pető was reelected head of the parliamentary caucus by default as more than ten others declined the leadership role. Pető resigned in April, although he denied any role in the scandal. He was replaced by Interior Minister Gábor KUNCZE, who in November was named the party's candidate for prime minister in 1998. Kuncze resigned as party leader following the May 1998 legislative balloting, at which the SzDSz declined sharply to 24 seats.

A party congress in December 2000 elected the mayor of Budapest, Gábor Demszky, as chair over Gábor Fodor. Demszky stated that his goals included defeating the government in 2002, denying the Socialists a National Assembly majority, and preventing an alliance between the FiDeSz-MPP and the MIÉP. Immediately after the election, the party's parliamentary leader, Gábor Kuncze, resigned his post in view of Demszky's strong criticism of the deputy group. Demszky in turn resigned in June 2001 and was succeeded as chair by Kuncze.

At the 2002 National Assembly election the SzDSz won 20 seats (1 in alliance with the MSzP), all but 3 of them on a proportional basis. A formal coalition agreement with the Socialists was negotiated over the next month, and the government that took office on May 27 included four SzDSz ministers, although cabinet reorganizations later reduced that number to three. The SzDSz was instrumental in forcing the resignation of Prime Minister Medgyessy in 2004 because of fears of potential future electoral losses.

In March 2005 the SzDSz announced that it would henceforth be known as the SzDSz–Hungarian Liberal Party. However, news reports subsequently continued to refer regularly to the original rubric. The SzDSz suffered heavy losses in 2006 municipal elections, apparently in part due to voter discontent with its coalition partner, the MSzP. Kuncze subsequently announced his resignation as party chair, and he was replaced in March 2007 by János Kóka.

However, Kóka barely lasted a year as chair following an internal investigation that confirmed suspicions of fraud during previous party elections that secured his seat. In June 2008 the state party convened, and in a closely contested race replaced Kóka with the more popular and charismatic Gabor FODOR, then the current minister of environment and water management.

Fodor's election was interpreted as increasing the chances of the SzDSz to reform the coalition government with the MSzP, though he preconditioned such a move on Gyurcsány's departure. Fodor promised to widen voter support for the SzDSz, which has suffered heavy losses in recent years because of its role in drafting the painful austerity measures. However, the June 2008 European Parliament election resulted in the SzDSz losing all seats with a mere 2.2 percent of the vote. Taking this as a sign of failed leadership, Fodor and four members of the party leadership offered to resign. On July 12 the SzDSz elected Attila Retkes as the new party chair. Retkes called on Kóka to immediately resign his parliamentary post.

Leaders: Attila RETKES (Chair), Gábor DEMSZKY (Mayor of Budapest), János KÓKA (Parliamentary Leader).

Opposition Parties:

Federation of Young Democrats–Hungarian Civic Alliance (*Fiatal Demokraták Szövetsége–Magyar Polgari Szövetség*—FiDeSz-MPSz). Founded in 1988, the right-wing group then styled simply as the Federation of Young Democrats (FiDeSz) ran fifth in the 1990 parliamentary balloting, winning only 22 of 378 elective seats. Six months later, however, it captured mayoralties in nine of the country's largest cities. Weakened by defections thereafter, the party's national representation declined further to 20 seats in May 1994. A 35-year age limit on membership was abandoned in April 1993, paving the way for merger with the Hungarian Civic Party (*Magyar Polgari Párt*—MPP) and creation of the FiDeSz-MPP. In September 1997 the parliamentary caucus of the party voted to admit 11 members of the KDNP parliamentary group, which had dissolved, making the FiDeSz-MPP the largest opposition group in the parliament.

The FiDeSz-MPP competed for a number of seats in the May 1998 legislative balloting on a joint list with the MDF. In addition, several FiDeSz-MPP candidates came from the MKDSz, an association recently formed by the former KDNP members. The FiDeSz-MPP emerged from the balloting as the leading party (148 seats) and became the senior member of the coalition cabinet subsequently formed with the MDF and the FKgP under the leadership of the FiDeSz-MPP's young chair, Viktor Orbán. At a party congress in January 2000 the posts of prime minister and party chair were separated.

On September 1, 2001, the FiDeSz-MPP concluded an agreement with the MDF establishing an electoral alliance for the 2002 National Assembly balloting. In January 2002, 14 Roma parties and groups also agreed to participate in the pact. Although opinion polls had anticipated an Orbán victory, the FiDeSz-MPP/MDF coalition's 188 seats (164 won by the FiDeSz-MPP) were insufficient to organize a new government after the April election.

In May 2003 the FiDeSz-MPP adopted the FiDeSz-MPSz rubric. In July centrists from the FiDeSz left the party to form a new political entity, the **New Hungary Party**, which pledged to pursue more moderate policies than the FiDeSz. Meanwhile, Orbán signed an agreement on October 2, 2003, with Florian Farkas of the *Lungo Drom Alliance,* a Romany grouping. The agreement called for cooperation between the two parties, and FiDeSz pledged to include at least one Romany candidate on its electoral lists. In May 2004 the FiDeSz-MPSz reached an agreement with the KDNP to run joint candidates in the 2004 EU parliamentary elections and the 2006 legislative elections.

The alliance won 164 seats (141 for the FiDeSz-MPSz) in the 2006 assembly balloting, the poll having been widely perceived as a battle for national supremacy between Prime Minister Gyurcsány and Orbán, who campaigned on a populist platform calling for tax cuts and increased government spending. Orbán offered to resign as leader of the FiDeSz-MPSz after the legislative defeat, but a party congress in May reelected him. Orbán's popularity reportedly increased significantly due to his role in leading antigovernment protests in 2006–2007. Under Orbán, the FiDeSz-MPSz has become the leading opposition party in government. A much publicized poll in late 2007 reported that FiDeSz was twice as popular as the governing MPSz. However, analysts attributed public support largely as a reaction to disenchantment with the ruling coalition and its economic policies.

In late 2007 FiDeSz battled accusations that it was linked to a newly formed right-wing party called the Hungarian Guard (associated with the Movement for a Better Hungary), whose members wear nationalist insignia and are considered anti-Semitic. Orbán insisted that FiDeSz is not anti-Semitic, but he did not condemn the Guard, whose membership is in the hundreds. Political analysts attributed Orbán's ambiguous response to the party's need to court right-wing voters.

In September 2008, a major spy scandal erupted involving accusations that two FiDeSz parliamentary delegates used a security company to infiltrate state agencies and illegally surveyed Socialist politicians. The suspicions were brought by the minister of intelligence and were allegedly based on taped phone conversations.

In the run-up to the EU parliamentary election in June 2009, Orbán prompted outrage in neighboring Slovakia when he said that the election would determine how many deputies would represent ethnic Hungarians in the "Carpathian Basin," a nationalist reference to an historical Hungarian homeland. Nevertheless, FiDeSZ-KDNP won a landslide 56 percent of the vote, amounting to 14 of Hungary's 22 seats and a result that confirmed the FiDeSZ as the probable leading party going into Hungary's 2010 parliamentary election. Orbán was reelected unopposed at a party congress on June 13.

Leaders: Viktor ORBÁN (President and Former Prime Minister), László KÖVÉR (Chair), Tibor NAVRACSICS (Parliamentary Leader).

Christian Democratic People's Party (*Kereszténydemokrata Néppárt*—KDNP). A right-of-center grouping, the KDNP claims to be a revival of the Popular Democratic Party, the leading opposition formation in the immediate post–World War II period. The party won 21 assembly seats in 1990 and 22 in May 1994. In 1997 the Christian Democrats signed a cooperation pact with the FKgP in preparation for the 1998 elections. However, the leadership's subsequent alliance-building efforts went too far for the European Union of Christian Democrats, which expelled the KDNP in July for "unacceptable links" to the extremist MIÉP; dissidents within the KDNP also criticized the party leadership for cooperating with extreme nationalists. The divisiveness culminated in the dissolution of the KDNP's parliamentary caucus in mid-1997, with 11 members deciding to work with the FiDeSz-MPP and forming the MKDSz. The fractured KDNP won no seats in the May 1998 legislative poll, having secured only 2.6 percent of the party-list votes in the first round of balloting.

After failing to secure representation in 2002 in the *Centrum* alliance (see below), the KDNP won 23 seats in the 2006 assembly poll in an alliance with the FiDeSz-MPP. In September 2007 KDNP Chair and Parliamentary Leader Zsolt Semjén caused an uproar by using the opening session of Parliament to issue inflammatory remarks about Jews and SzDSz policies. The KDNP opposed a government bailout of financial institutions and cuts to pensioner incomes in the wake of the 2008–2009 economic crisis.

Leader: Zsolt SEMJÉN (Chair and Parliamentary Leader).

Hungarian Democratic Forum (*Magyar Demokrata Fórum*—MDF). The MDF is a right-of-center nationalist group founded in September 1988 with the avowed purpose of "building a bridge between the state and society." The group claimed 15,000 members at the opening of its first national conference at Budapest in March 1989, when it demanded that Hungary again become "an independent democratic country of European culture." It won 165 of 378 elective seats at the April 1990 election. In January 1993 Prime Minister József Antall survived a challenge to his leadership of the MDF from the party's ultranationalist right, led by István Csurka. In early June, Csurka and three parliamentary colleagues were expelled from the party, and they formed the MIÉP. Antall died on December 12, 1993, and was succeeded, on a temporary basis, by Sándor LEZSÁK, who was named chair of the MDF Executive Committee on February 23, 1994, after yielding the party presidency to Defense Minister Lajos FÜR on February 18. Lezsák withdrew completely from the leadership on June 1, 1994, in view of the MDF's severe decline to 37 legislative seats at the May balloting. On being confirmed as MDF chair in September, Für ruled out a merger with the KDNP "for the time being."

Following Für's decision to stand down, an MDF congress in March 1996 returned Lezsák to the MDF chair, a decision provoking a centrist faction to form the breakaway MDNP (below), leaving the rump MDF with approximately 20 parliamentary deputies. The MDF contested many seats in the May 1998 legislative balloting jointly with the FiDeSz-MPP, emerging with 17 seats and joining its electoral partner in the coalition government named in July.

At a party congress on January 30, 1999, Justice Minister Ibolya Dávid defeated Lezsák for the MDF chair. She was overwhelmingly reelected in January 2001 despite criticism from some members and from coalition partners for her efforts to strengthen cooperation with the MDNP and other groups accepting "moderate, center-right, Christian-Democratic or Christian values."

In April 2002 the MDF won 24 of the National Assembly seats captured by the FiDeSz-MPP/MDF electoral coalition. However, it slipped to 11 seats running on its own in 2006.

In April 2008 the MDF led cross-party discussions on tax cut proposals, securing agreements from the participating parties that tax cuts should be a priority in upcoming years. The MDF advocated an 18 percent flat tax and elimination of the inheritance tax. In late 2008 the MDF was critical of the ruling MSzP for not taking action quickly enough in the unfolding economic crisis, although the two parties reached agreement on several measures that became part of fiscal reform packages.

The party lost faction status in May 2009, after three parliamentary delegates opted out of the party caucus in protest of their leadership's supposed ties to the SzDSz; the three were later formally expelled from the party. The MDF narrowly won one seat in European parliamentary elections in June, taking 5 percent of the vote.

Leaders: Ibolya DÁVID (Chair), Károly HERÉNYI (Parliamentary Leader).

Other Parties:

Hungarian Christian Democratic Federation (*Magyar Kereszténydemokrata Szövetség*—MKDSz). Established in 1997 by former members of the KDNP, the center-right MKDSz is closely allied with the MDF and the FiDeSz-MPP, which included MKDSz members on its candidate list for the 1998 and 2002 elections. The MKDSz participated in the Orbán coalition government, generally in a junior capacity, although a founding member, Péter Harrach, headed the ministry of family protection and social affairs, and another member, Lászlo NÓGRÁDI, briefly served as minister of transport and water management in 2000. Harrach has since joined the KDNP to become its deputy speaker in the National Assembly.

Leaders: Lászlo SURJÁN, János LATORCAI.

Center Party (*Centrum Párt*). The Center Party was formed in November 2001 as an alliance of the KDNP (above), the two parties listed directly below, and the Third Side for Hungary (*Harmadik Oldal Magyarországért Egyesület*—HOM), a nonpartisan civic forum that had been organized the preceding February by Mihály KUPA, at that time an independent in the National Assembly, and István GYENESEI, a county official. In founding the *Centrum*—more formally, the Center of Solidarity for Hungary (*Összefogás Magyarországért Centrum*)—the four organizations agreed to contest the 2002 general election jointly, but the alliance won only 3.9 percent of the party-list vote and no seats. The KDNP left the Center Party to participate in an electoral coalition with the FiDeSz-MPP in 2006, and the rump Center Party also presented (unsuccessfully) its own candidates.

Leaders: Ágnes PÁSZTY (President), János PAPP (Chair of National Committee).

Green Democrats (*Zöld Demokraták*—ZD). The ZD was established as the Green Alternative (*Zöld Alternativa*—ZA) in 1993 by an assortment of ecology-oriented groups, including liberal elements of the increasingly right-wing MZP who had been expelled for their views. The ZA opposed membership in NATO while championing a typical "green" agenda, including environmental protection and opposition to construction of the joint Hungarian-Slovakian dam project on the Danube. The party adopted its present name at a congress in June 2000. In November 2008 the Green Democrats joined their Slovakian counterparts in a demonstration following an incident in which the Hungarian Guard (see **Movement for a Better Hungary**, below) blocked a main road over the river Danube.

Leader: György DROPPA.

Hungarian Democratic People's Party (*Magyar Demokrata Néppárt*—MDNP). The MDNP was founded in March 1996 by Iván SZABÓ after he had been defeated in a contest for the presidency of the MDF by Sándor Lezsák. Formerly the MDF parliamentary leader, Szabó attracted 14 other centrist MDF deputies into the new party. By October 1997 Szabó was so frustrated by lack of party discipline that he announced his resignation as chair, but he withdrew it a few days later. He warned the party against being shaped by the expectations of either the government or the opposition, advocating an alternative to both. The MDNP won no seats in the May 1998 legislative poll, having secured only 1.4 percent of the party-list votes in the first round. The party endorsed FiDeSz-MPP/MDF candidates in the second round. Szabó resigned as MDNP leader shortly after the poll, and it was reported in 2006 that the MDNP had merged back into the MDF.

Independent Smallholders' Party (*Független Kisgazda Párt*—FKgP). Advocating the return of collectivized land to former owners, the FKgP was launched in November 1989 as a revival of the party that dominated Hungary's first postwar election in 1945. The party—formally, the Independent Smallholders', Agrarian Workers' and Civic Party (*Független Kisgazda, Földmunkás és Polgári Párt*)—was subsequently deeply divided over the nature of reparations for property lost during the Communist era. Thus, in December 1989 a number of dissidents led by Imre BOROS withdrew to form the National Smallholders and Bourgeois Party (*Nemzeti Kisgazda és Polgári Párt*—NKgP), most members of which, however, rejoined the parent party in 1991. On February 21, 1992, FKgP leader József Torgyán announced that the party was withdrawing from the government coalition because the MDF had denied it an opportunity to influence policy; the action was accompanied by the expulsion of most of the FKgP's 44 parliamentary deputies, who proceeded to reaffirm their support for the Antall administration. They subsequently announced formation of an FKgP "Historical Section" (*Történelmi Tagozat,* which evolved into the now-defunct United Smallholders' Party [*Egyesült Kisgazda Párt*—EKgP]). In the May 1994 general election the FKgP recovered to win 26 seats.

Following the MDF split in March 1996, the FKgP became the largest opposition party and stepped up its criticism of the Socialist-led government while rebuffing overtures by the nonparliamentary MIÉP for a three-party merger with the KDNP, whose members were described by Torgyán as "disgusting pseudo-liberal worms and vultures." In August Torgyán rejected a proposal by the leader of the nonparliamenary MIÉP for a three-party merger that would have also embraced the KDNP. However, in February 1998 the FKgP reached an agreement with the KDNP for an electoral alliance in the second round of the general elections scheduled for May; the FKgP won 48 seats in that balloting, thereby becoming the third leading party in the assembly. Its subsequent participation in the coalition government led by the free-market–oriented FiDeSz-MPP surprised some observers.

On February 8, 2001, Torgyán resigned as minister of agriculture as a result of a financial scandal that also involved his son, and on February 22 his acting replacement, Imre BOROS, ordered an investigation into Torgyán's financial management of the ministry. Party powers responded, unsuccessfully, in March by demanding Boros's dismissal from the government. With the party clearly divided between Torgyán loyalists and reformers, Torgyán was reelected party leader on May 5, but on the same day the FKgP parliamentary faction, meeting separately, elected Zsolt Lányi as party chair. The latter group attempted to expel Torgyán four days later. A May 17 court decision ordered his reinstatement, but, in a further twist, the National Assembly Procedural Committee on May 28 determined that he should sit as an independent.

In the second half of 2001 the FKgP rupture became a collapse, and at the April 2002 election the party won only 0.8 percent of the party-list vote and no seats.

In July 2001 members of the Lányi group had formed a **Reform Smallholders' Party** (*Reform Kisgazdapárt*—RKgP), which elected Katalin LIEBMANN as chair in September. Lányi himself established the **Hungarian Smallholders' and Civic Party** (*Magyar Kisgazda és Polgári Párt*—MKgPP) in September. Sándor CSEH and a former FKgP parliamentary leader, Attila BÁNK, led another agrarian grouping, the **Smallholders' Party–Party of the Smallholders' Federation** (*Kisgazdapárt a Kisgazda Svövetség Pártja*), into the 2002 national election. None of the smallholder formations elected any parliamentary candidates.

In December 2007 former Smallholder party officials met to discuss forming a new political party in the wake of the upcoming referendum on economic reforms. The Smallholder dissidents were severely critical of the ruling coalition's reform policies.

Leader: József TORGYÁN (Chair).

Hungarian Green Party (*Magyarországi Zöld Párt*—MZP). The MZP was organized in November 1989 and held its founding congress in June 1990. It secured less than 0.5 percent of the vote in 1990, after which its right-wing faction took on an increasingly antifeminist, homophobic, anti-Semitic character. In June 1993 remaining liberal members were expelled. The party has never achieved national representation.

Leader: Zoltán MEDVECZKI (President).

Hungarian Justice and Life Party (*Magyar Igazság és Élet Párt*—MIÉP). The extreme right-wing MIÉP was launched in June 1993 by dissidents of the then-ruling MDF after István Csurka unsuccessfully challenged József Antall for the MDF leadership in January. Conspicuously anti-Semitic, the party stated that Hungary's national revival was being thwarted by a "Jewish-Bolshevik-liberal conspiracy." By late November 1993 the MIÉP boasted 11 assembly deputies, but in the May 1994 balloting it won only 1.6 percent of the first-round vote and no seats. In October 1996 the party attracted tens of thousands of demonstrators to an antigovernment rally in Budapest, while a March 1997 rally against European integration was attended by an estimated 50,000 protesters. The MIÉP's growing influence was also apparent in the May 1998 legislative elections, in which it secured 14 seats—its first ever via the ballot box. The MIÉP was the only parliamentary party in early 1999 to oppose Hungary's accession to NATO.

The party reelected Csurka as chair at a December 2000 conference at which it also encouraged former Hungarian territories toward "a sense of nationhood" and called for formation of a national guard to "expel foreign mafias." Earlier in the year, Csurka had compared Romania's pollution of the Tisza River to genocide.

At the 2002 general election the MIÉP won only 4.4 percent of the list vote, below the threshold for proportional National Assembly seats.

In March 2004 Ernoe ROZGONYI tried to oust Csurka from his leadership position. When this effort failed, Rozgonyi launched a new political party, the **Hungarian National Front** (MNF). The new right-wing party opposed EU membership and Hungarian support for the U.S. intervention in Iraq. The MIÉP contested the 2006 assembly balloting in a **Third Way** coalition with The Movement for a Better Hungary (Jobbik).

Movement for a Better Hungary (*Jobbik Magyarországért Mozgalom*). Popularly known as Jobbik, the party was launched by David KOVACS in 2003 as an outgrowth of the university student organization Right-Wing Youth Community (*Jobboldali Ifjúsági Közösség*—Jobbik). Calling itself a "radical patriotic Christian" party, Jobbik is considered an extreme right-wing party with nationalistic roots. It advocates withdrawal from the EU, greater rights for ethnic Hungarians living in other countries (including dual citizenship), and a crackdown on "Gypsy crime."

The Movement for a Better Hungary was said to be partially responsible for attacks against demonstrators in a gay pride march in Budapest on July 7, 2007. A month later the group formed a uniformed paramilitary arm called the **Hungarian Guard** (*Magyar Gárda*), led by Gabor Vona and former defense minister Lajos FUR. The Guard's charter includes "training to help maintain public order, preserve Hungarian culture, and defend the nation in extraordinary situations." Major political parties condemned the civil defense group, labeling it as "fascist," while the World Jewish Council called for the group to be banned because the Guard's coat of arms is associated with Hungary's pro-Nazi Arrow Cross party. The National Roma Council demanded it be banned along with other paramilitary groups after the Guard marched several times outside Roma villages to protest "Gypsy criminality." Additionally, the World Jewish Council called for the group to be banned because of the Guard's coat of arms is associated with Hungary's pro-Nazi Arrow and Cross party. Following the killings of a Roma man and his young son, a July 2009 appellate court upheld a lower court ruling that banned the group for rejecting equal rights to Romas and inciting resentment against them. The Guard defied the court decision with a mass rally in Budapest.

Jobbik polled third highest in the European Parliament election in June, taking 15 percent of the vote and winning three seats. The results confirmed that Jobbik had emerged as the dominant far-right party in Hungary and could enter the National Assembly following the 2010 federal election.

Leaders: Gabor VONA (President), Robert KISS (Hungarian Guard Chair).

Hungarian Social Democratic Party (*Magyarországi Szociáldemokrata Párt*—MSzDP). Founded in January 1989, the MSzDP was a revival of the party that was forced to merge with Hungary's Communist Party in 1948. During a congress in October 1989, the party split into "historic" and "renewal" wings, but they reunited in October 1993. The MSzDP secured less than 1 percent of the first-round party-list vote in the May 1994 general election. For the 1998 poll it cooperated with the MSzP and, in a few cases, the MP, but it again secured no seats. In 2002 it ran four unsuccessful candidates in conjunction with the MSzP.

However by late 2007 and early 2008 the MSzDP was seeing an uptick in membership, powered primarily by disaffected MSzP members, including a number of lower ranking Budapest officials, critical of the ruling party's move toward neo-liberal economic policies. MSzDP Chair László KAPOLYI, whose representation in parliament is under the MSzP party, sought to stem the tide by tightening the rules required for MSzDP membership. He offered "temporary membership" for the first year, pending the approval of local party units.

The decision may have to do with an MSzDP-MSzP cooperation agreement as well as concern about splitting the liberal vote in the next parliamentary election. The MSzDP promotes an "eco-socialist market economy." Kapolyi has said the party was seeking links with the Centrum Party in advance of EU parliamentary elections. The MszDP grew in 2008 by siphoning members from the MSzP, although Chair László Kapolyi acknowledged at the time that the two parties would likely align during the 2010 federal election.

Leader: László KAPOLYI (Chair).

Workers' Party (*Munkáspárt*—MP). Following the October 1989 party congress of the then-ruling MSzMP, a group of hard-line Communists who were opposed to formation of the MSzP announced the launching of the **János Kádár Society** (*Kádár János Baráti Társaság*) as the "only legal heir" to the parent party. Prior to the 1990 balloting the group reappropriated the MSzMP name, but it succeeded in winning only 3.7 percent of the vote. It adopted its present name in 1992.

Improving on its 1994 performance, in the May 1998 poll the MP received 4.1 percent of the first-round party-list votes, but it again failed to win any seats. Gyula Thürmer was reelected chair at the party's 18th congress in February 1999. In April 2002 the party won 2.8 percent of the party-list vote and then threw its support behind the MSzP in the second round. In 2006 a breakaway faction called the **Worker's Party of Hungary 2006** (*Magyarországi Munkáspárt 2006*—MMP 2006) was created under the leadership of János FRATANOB. The breakaway faction advocated closer cooperation with the ruling MSzP on certain policies and taxing wealthy citizens at an income rate of 50 percent.

One-time vice chair Attila VAJNAI was convicted of wearing a red star symbolizing Communism on his jacket during a demonstration in 2003; he was acquitted by Hungary's Supreme Court in 2009.

Leaders: Gyula THÜRMER (Chair); Karacs LAJOSNÉ, János VAJDA (Vice Chairs).

For more information on the **New Left Party** (*Új Baloldali Párt*), see the 2008 *Handbook*.

Roma Organizations:

Roma, who represent up to 10 percent of the Hungarian population, are the largest ethnic minority and endure abysmal socioeconomic conditions. Recent reports estimate that the Roma suffer 70 percent unemployment, with fewer than 5 percent of children completing high school. In 2007–2008, Hungary hosted the EU's Roma Inclusion Program, a 15-year integration measure spanning nine Eastern European states that seeks to improve social and economic conditions for Roma. Roma organizations, including the Roma Civil Rights Foundation and the National Roma Council, have become increasingly active in 2007 and 2008 because of threats posed by the newly founded paramilitary organization, the Hungarian Guard (see **Movement for a Better Hungary**). In 2009 tensions heightened between Roma and far-right extremists following the sentencing of a Roma family in the 2006 murder of a school teacher. The crime triggered a wave of hostility and killings of Roma. Police doubled the size of a task force investigating anti-Roma attacks. In an EU survey released in April 2009, 90 percent of Roma in Hungary said discrimination due to ethnic origin was widespread. In response, one Roma group announced plans in early 2009 to establish its own "Gypsy Guard" to counter the Hungarian Guard. However, the plan was widely denounced as incendiary by Roma and other party politicians.

A large number of Roma (Gypsy) parties and civic organizations were established in the post-Communist era. Few, however, have more than a local or regional following. The larger groups include the **Lungo Drom Alliance**, led by Flórián FARKAS; the **Hungarian Gypsies' Peace Party**, led by Aladar HORVÁTH, who also chairs the Roma Civil Rights Foundation; the **Hungarian Roma Parliament**; and the **Brotherhood Independent Gypsy Organization** (*Phralipe Független Cigány Szervezet*).

On April 9, 1995, the Roma elected a 53-member National Autonomous Authority of the Romany Minority (*Országos Cigány Kisebbségi Önkormányzat*—OCKÖ; also translated as the National Gypsy Minority Self-Government), the first such officially sanctioned advisory body in Eastern Europe. All of the seats were won by the *Lungo Drom,* as they also were at the election held January 23, 1999.

LEGISLATURE

The Hungarian **National Assembly** (*Országgyülés*) is a unicameral body consisting of 386 elective deputies (including 8 seats reserved for ethnic minority representation), of whom 210 are returned from regional and national lists on a proportional basis and 176 from single-member constituencies on a majoritarian basis. The legislative term is four years. Following two-stage balloting on April 9 and 23, 2006, the party distribution was as follows: the Hungarian Socialist Party (MSzP), 190 (4 of those seats were won in a coalition with the Alliance of Free Democrats); the electoral alliance of the Federation of Young Democrats–Hungarian Civic Party (FiDeSz-MPP) and the Christian Democratic People's Party (KDNP), 164 (FiDeSz-MPP, 141; KDNP, 23); the Alliance of Free Democrats, 20 (2 of those seats were won in a coalition with the FiDeSz-MPP); the Hungarian Democratic Forum, 11; and independents, 1. Subsequent changes within the parties resulted in the following disbursement of seats as of January 2009: the MSzP, 190; FiDeSz-MPP and KDNP, 161; SzDSz, 19; MDF, 10; independents, 5; vacant, 1.

Speaker: Katalin SZILI.

CABINET

[as of July 1, 2009]

Prime Minister	Gordon Bajnai (ind.)
Ministers	
Agriculture and Rural Development	József Gráf (MSzP)
Cultural and Education	István Hiller (MSzP)
Defense	Imre Szekeres (MSzP)
Environmental and Water Management	Imre Szabo (MSzP)
Finance	Peter Oszko (MSzP)
Foreign Affairs	Peter Balazs (MSzP)
Health	Tamas Szekely (ind.)
Justice and Law Enforcement	Tibor Draskovics (MSzP)
Labor and Social Affairs	Laszlo Herczog (sind.)
Local Government and Regions	Zoltan Varga (MSzP)
National Development and Economy	István Varga (ind.)
Prime Minister's Office	Csaba Molnar (MSzP)
Transport, Telecommunications, and Energy	Peter Honig (ind.)
Without Portfolio (In Charge of Social Coordination)	Peter Kiss (MSzP)

COMMUNICATIONS

The formerly pervasive censorship was relaxed in 1988, and in June 1992 a 1974 decree authorizing government supervision of radio and television was declared unconstitutional. The Socialist-led government elected in May 1994 pledged itself to "the legal independence of the national public media from the given government, political powers, and power relations." Subsequently, the Orbán government was widely criticized by the opposition and various international organizations, including the Office of the UN High Commissioner for Human Rights and the EU, for its apparent efforts to control broadcasting and print media. Its actions included naming only progovernment nominees to television and radio boards, the ostensible justification being the failure of the opposition parties to agree on their share of nominees. In its 2008 report on press freedom, the group Reporters Without Borders ranked Hungary 23, along with Namibia and the United Kingdom, out of 173 countries.

Press. The major Budapest papers circulate nationally, but there are also nearly two dozen provincial dailies, all with circulations under 100,000. The following are issued daily in Budapest, unless otherwise noted: *Népszabadság* (People's Freedom, 316,000), former ruling party organ, now German-owned independent; *Metro* (217,000); *Népszava* (Voice of the People, 120,000), organ of the Trades Union Council; *Mai Nap* (Today, 115,000); *Kurír* (Courier, 80,000), founded in 1990; *Magyar Hirlap* (Hungarian Journal, 75,000), British-owned; *Magyar Nemzet* (Hungarian Nation, 70,000), conservative (merged with the right-wing *Napi Magyarorszag* in 2000); *Esti Hirlap* (Evening Journal, 70,000), British-owned.

News agencies. The state-owned Hungarian News Agency (*Magyar Távirati Iroda*—MTI) is the domestic facility; the Associated Press, *Xinhua,* and many of the major European bureaus have offices in Budapest.

Broadcasting and computing. Domestic service is dominated by *Magyar Rádió,* which also transmits abroad in seven languages, and *Magyar Televízió,* which operates two terrestrial channels. In addition, several commercial television (cable and satellite) channels are operational, together with a number of commercial radio stations. In July 1997 two Western-led consortia received television licenses and ended a 40-year state monopoly when they began broadcasting in October. As of 2008 there were 586.6 Internet users per 1,000 inhabitants.

INTERGOVERNMENTAL REPRESENTATION

Ambassador to the U.S.: Bela SZOMBATI.

U.S. Ambassador to Hungary: (Vacant).

Permanent Representative to the UN: (Vacant).

IGO Memberships (Non-UN): BIS, CEI, CERN, CEUR, EBRD, EIB, EU, Eurocontrol, IEA, Interpol, IOM, NATO, OECD, OSCE, PCA, WEU, WCO, WTO.

ICELAND

Republic of Iceland
Lyðveldið Ísland

Political Status: Independent republic established June 17, 1944; under democratic parliamentary system.

Area: 39,768 sq. mi. (103,000 sq. km.).

Population: 275,264 (1998C); 317,000 (2008E).

Major Urban Center (2005E): REYKJAVÍK (114,000).

Official Language: Icelandic.

Monetary Unit: Króna (official rate December 1, 2009: 121.45 krónur = $1US).

President: Dr. Ólafur Ragnar GRÍMSSON (previously People's Alliance); elected on June 29, 1996, and inaugurated on August 1 for a four-year term, succeeding Vigdís FINNBOGADÓTTIR (nonparty); term extended for an additional four years when no potential opponent met the May 19, 2000, deadline for filing the required number of nominating signatures; reelected on June 26, 2004; and term extended for another four years when no opponent met the May 24, 2008, deadline for obtaining the requisite number of nominating signatures; inaugurated for a fourth four-year term on August 1.

Prime Minister: Jóhanna SIGURÐARDÓTTIR (The Alliance) sworn in on February 1, 2009, to succeed Geir HAARDE (Independence Party),who stepped down after his coalition resigned; reappointed as leader of a coalition government on May 10, 2009, following legislative elections of April 25.

THE COUNTRY

The westernmost nation of Europe, Iceland lies in the North Atlantic Ocean just below the Arctic Circle. Although one-eighth of the land surface is glacier, the warm Gulf Stream assures a relatively moderate climate and provides the country's richest resource in the fish that are found in its territorial waters. (It has been estimated that Iceland accounts for 3–5 percent of the world's seafood.) The population is quite homogeneous, the preponderant majority being of Icelandic descent. More than 90 percent of the population adheres to the official Evangelical Lutheran Church, although other faiths are permitted. Approximately 80 percent of adult women work outside the home, mainly in clerical and service sectors. The four-term presidency of Vigdís FINNBOGADÓTTIR (1982–1996) yielded a significant increase in female political representation, with 30 percent of the parliamentary deputies elected in 2003 being women.

Although fishing and fish processing employ only about 9 percent of the labor force, marine products typically account for nearly three-fourths of Iceland's export trade; other leading activities include dairy farming and sheep raising. Recent development efforts have focused on exploiting the country's considerable hydroelectric and geothermal energy supply; thus, aluminum smelting has become an increasingly significant export industry. Foreign investors have been successfully pursued for energy production and smelting, currently estimated to account for about 35 percent of GDP. High-tech industry is also of growing importance. The European Union (EU), led by the United Kingdom, is the principal export market.

Numerous devaluations of the króna beginning in 1981, chronic inflation that peaked at 86 percent in 1983, a foreign debt amounting to nearly half of the GNP, and decline of the fishing industry due to high costs and depleting stocks contributed to economic adversity through the end of the decade. More efficient exploitation of maritime resources and enhanced domestic industrial capacity yielded some improvements in the early 1990s, with inflation falling to 4 percent in 1993. After stagnating in 1992–1993 and again in 1995 the economy expanded by an annual average of nearly 5 percent in 1996–2000 and by 4 percent in 2000. After a brief recession in 2002, growth of more than 4 percent was reported in 2003, while unemployment remained at less than 3 percent. However, the country experienced a series of economic problems in 2006 and Iceland was one of the first countries to experience the effects of the 2008 global economic crisis. The króna declined by 44 percent in 2008 in relation to the euro, and all four major credit firms lowered Iceland's bond rating. In order to stem inflation and protect the currency, the Central Bank increased interest rates several times (see Political background and Current issues, below). The government nationalized the banking industry after the collapse of a number of major financial institutions and a period of dramatic monetary destabilization. The IMF and leading European states intervened and provided a $10 billion loan to stabilize the economy. In 2008 GDP rose by 0.3 percent, but declined by 1.3 percent in the last six months of the year, inflation soared from 4 percent to 17.1 percent, and the unemployment rate climbed from 1.9 percent to 7 percent. Some 80 percent of Iceland's energy needs were fulfilled by renewable energy, mainly geothermal. Iceland has also invested heavily in hydrogen fuel technology. The result has been a 75 percent decline in domestic energy costs.

GOVERNMENT AND POLITICS

Political background. Settled by disaffected Norsemen in the last quarter of the ninth century, Iceland flourished as an independent republic and convened its first parliament (Althing) in 930. However, it came under Norwegian rule in 1262 and in 1381 became (along with other Scandinavian countries) a Danish dominion, stagnating for 500 years under neglect, natural calamities, and rigid colonial controls. The island achieved limited home rule in 1874 under the leadership of Jón SIGURDSSON and in 1918 became an internally self-governing state united with Denmark under a common king. Iceland's strategic position in World War II resulted in British occupation after the fall of Denmark in 1940, with military control being transferred to American forces when the United States entered the war in 1941. Full independence was achieved on June 17, 1944.

Coalition government has dominated Icelandic politics, there having been few single-party governments in the nation's history. A significant change in the postwar era was the defeat of a 12-year centrist coalition of the Independence Party (IP) and the Social Democratic Party in 1971. The election of June 1974 resulted in a coalition involving the IP and the Progressive Party (PP), while that of June 1978 yielded a center-left government of the PP, Social Democratic Party (SDP), and the People's Alliance (PA). The latter government fell in October 1979 and, in the wake of an inconclusive legislative election in December, was replaced by a minority SDP administration that was in turn succeeded in February 1980 by a group of IP deputies led by Gunnar THORODDSEN in coalition with the PA and the PP. On June 29 Vigdís Finnbogadóttir, director of the Reykjavík Theatre since 1972, became the world's first popularly elected female head of state when she defeated three other candidates seeking to succeed Kristján ELDJÁRN, who had declined to seek a fourth term.

In March 1983 Prime Minister Thoroddsen requested dissolution of the Althing and announced that he would not be a candidate for reelection. After another inconclusive poll in April, each of the three major party leaders failed in efforts to form a viable coalition. With the president having threatened to name a nonparty administration, Steingrímur HERMANNSSON of the PP finally succeeded, in May, in organizing a cabinet of his own and IP members.

At the election of April 1987, which was marked by an IP loss of five seats and a doubling (to six) of representation by the feminist Women's Alliance (WA), the coalition fell one seat short of a majority, with the prime minister moving into caretaker status until installation in July of the IP's Thorsteinn PÁLSSON as head of an administration that included PP and SDP representatives. Pálsson resigned in September 1988, with Hermannsson returning as head of a new government that included the SDP and the PA; the coalition's marginal legislative strength was significantly enhanced by addition of the recently organized Citizens' Party in September 1989.

Backed by all of the major parties, President Finnbogadóttir was elected to a third four-year term in June 1988. In the first Icelandic challenge to a sitting head of state, Sigrún THORSTEINSDÓTTIR of the small Humanist Party obtained only 5.3 percent of the popular vote.

At the election of April 20, 1991, Independence parliamentary representation rose from 18 to 26, largely at the expense of the Citizens' Party, all of whose seats were lost. On April 30 Davið ODDSSON, who had succeeded Pálsson as IP leader on March 10, was sworn in as head of a bipartisan administration that included the SDP.

An ongoing austerity program, rising unemployment, and two devaluations of the króna reduced the government's standing in the early 1990s, while the Social Democrats experienced internal divisions that led to a split in September 1994 (see Political Parties, below). A modest economic upturn in 1994 yielded a narrow 32–31 majority for the coalition parties in legislative balloting on April 8, 1995, although the SDP lost many votes to the new Awakening of the Nation list headed by its former deputy chair. Moves to reconstitute the existing coalition proved abortive, the result being a partnership under Oddsson of the IP and PP, which commanded a comfortable majority of 40 seats.

At the opening of the new Althing on October 1, 1995, President Finnbogadóttir announced that she would not seek reelection when her fourth four-year term expired. In popular balloting on June 29, 1996, the former finance minister and former leader of the leftist PA, Ólafur Ragnar GRÍMSSON, defeated four other candidates, winning 40.9 percent of the vote.

In mid-1998 the PA, SDP, and WA agreed to establish an electoral coalition in an effort to unseat Prime Minister Oddsson's government. The resultant Unified Left (The Alliance) failed to make any inroads, however, and Oddsson was returned for a third term in the election of May 8, 1999. A year later, President Grímsson's term was extended for an additional four years when no potential challenger met the nomination deadline. The IP/PP coalition remained in power following the legislative balloting of May 10, 2003, with Oddsson retaining the prime ministership after agreeing to turn the post over to Halldór ÁSGRÍMSSON of the PP part way through his anticipated four-year term. (Ásgrímsson was inaugurated as prime minister on September 15, 2004.) Meanwhile, Grímsson won a third presidential term with 86 percent of the vote on June 26, 2004.

When his party received only 12 percent of the vote in the local elections held on May 27, 2006, Ásgrímsson resigned as prime minister. He was succeeded, on June 15, 2006, by Geir HAARDE, leader of the IP, who immediately announced a cabinet reshuffle.

In the May 2007 legislative elections, the IP again won the majority of seats, and Haarde was reappointed as prime minister to head a new coalition government that included The Alliance instead of the PP. After the election, the ministries of fisheries and agriculture were combined, and the ministry of trade and commerce was divided into two new portfolios.

Presidential balloting scheduled for June 2008 was cancelled when no challengers gathered the required number of nominating signatures by the May deadline. Consequently, Grímsson's tenure was extended for a fourth term in August 2008. A severe economic recession (see Current issues, below) led to tensions within the governing coalition with The Alliance demanding it be given the post of prime minister in exchange for remaining in the government. When Haarde refused, the coalition collapsed and the government resigned on January 26, 2009, after calling new elections. Social Affairs Minister and member of The Alliance Jóhanna SIGURÐARDÓTTIR was appointed to lead an interim minority government that included The Alliance and the Left-Green Alliance (VGF). Sigurðardóttir became the first female and first openly gay prime minister of Iceland. In April 25 balloting for the Althing, The Alliance placed first and formed a coalition government with VGF, which placed third in the voting. Sigurðardóttir was reappointed prime minister. In the election, 27 of the elected members, or 43 percent, were women.

Constitution and government. Iceland's constitution, adopted by referendum in 1944, vests power in a president (whose functions are mainly titular), a prime minister, a legislature, and a judiciary. The president is directly elected for a four-year term. The unicameral legislature (Althing) is currently a 63-member body also elected for four years (subject to dissolution by the president) under a proportional system. The prime minister, who performs most executive functions, is appointed by the president but is responsible to the legislature. Eight district courts occupy the lower level of the judicial system, while the Supreme Court sits at the apex. There are also special labor and impeachment courts.

The number of general electoral districts (*Kjöroemi*) has recently been reduced from eight to six, the latter being employed for the first time in the 2003 elections. The number of independent towns (*Kaupstaðir*) and other municipalities (*sveitarfelög*) was progressively reduced from 204 in 1990 to 104 in 2003 through voluntary consolidation.

Foreign relations. Nordic links and membership in the North Atlantic Treaty Organization (NATO), together with an economic dependence on fishing, are the principal determinants of Icelandic foreign relations. Attempts to extend its territorial waters from 1952 to 1975 embroiled the country in disputes with a number of maritime competitors. The first "cod war" resulted from the proclamation of a 12-mile limit in 1958 and was terminated by agreements with Britain, Ireland, and West Germany in 1961; a second period of hostilities followed the proclamation of a 50-mile limit in 1973 and was ended by a temporary agreement with Britain the same year. In 1975 a third "cod war" erupted following Iceland's extension of the limit to 200 miles despite an adverse ruling in 1974 by the International Court of Justice on the 50-mile limit. The dispute led Iceland to break relations with the United Kingdom for a period of months in 1976, before reaching a compromise. Less volatile confrontations over economic zones, fishing rights, species depletion, and quotas continued to occur with various countries (Norway, Denmark, Russia) over the ensuing two decades. Subsequently, however, Iceland intensified its efforts to settle remaining fishing disputes. Most prominently, in May 1999 it joined Norway and Russia in signing an agreement regulating catches in the Barents Sea.

Traditionally opposed to maintenance of an indigenous military force, the government in 1973 announced its intention to close the U.S.-maintained NATO base at Keflavík in order "to ensure Iceland's security." The decision was reversed in August 1974 by the conservative administration, although the government requested that Icelanders be employed for nonmilitary work previously done by Americans at the base. Relations with Washington were momentarily strained in March 1985 by press reports that Pentagon contingency plans included the movement of nuclear depth charges to the Keflavík base. Shortly thereafter, U.S. officials assured Reykjavík that no such weapons would be deployed without Icelandic approval, while in May the Althing, by unanimous vote, declared the country to be a nuclear-free zone. In January 1994 a new Icelandic-U.S. accord provided for continued U.S. use of the Keflavík base, although with fewer American warplanes stationed there (see Current issues, below, for subsequent developments).

In a move indicative of Scandinavia's historic links to the Baltic states, Iceland on August 26, 1991, became the first country to reestablish diplomatic relations with Estonia, Latvia, and Lithuania. In May 1992 it became a signatory of the European Economic Area (EEA) treaty between the European Free Trade Association (EFTA) and the European Community (EC, later the EU) states, although unlike most other EFTA members it made no effort to join the EC. In November 1992 Iceland became an associate member of the Western European Union (WEU).

The Norwegian electorate's decision in November 1994 not to follow Finland and Sweden into the EU defused the EU debate in Iceland. Those favoring membership had argued that Iceland could not afford to stay out if all four of its Nordic partners were members. However, Norway's negative decision meant that Iceland's chief Nordic competitor in fish exports would have no advantage over Iceland in the vital European market.

An agreement signed in October 1995 provided for Iceland, together with Norway, to accede (as nonvoting members) to the Schengen Accord envisaging the abolition of internal border controls between most EU states. The final details of the arrangement were approved by the EU in November 2000, with effect from March 25, 2001. The agreement enables Denmark, Finland, and Sweden, as EU members, to preserve the 40-year-old Nordic Passport Union with their two non-EU Nordic partners.

In March 1999 whaling reemerged as a foreign policy issue when the Althing voted to rescind a ten-year-old ban. Iceland withdrew from the International Whaling Commission (IWC) in 1992, and it has not signed the UN Convention on International Trade in Endangered Species. Domestic opinion polls indicate 4–1 approval for a return to whaling, and the government has consistently maintained that limited harvesting of certain species will cause no harm and may even increase fish populations. By a very close vote, the IWC readmitted Iceland in October 2002, despite the fact that Reykjavík refused to accept the moratorium on whaling. In August 2003 Iceland permitted the killing of some 38 minke whales for "scientific purposes," prompting international protest and boycotts of the country's increasingly lucrative ecotourism industry. The following year 39 were killed. In March 2006 Greenpeace, which claimed the total had reached 100, announced it would be sending its ship MV *Arctic Sunrise* to Iceland as a part of its ongoing efforts to convince Iceland to give up whaling. Nevertheless, in October Iceland announced that it would resume limited commercial whaling, a decision that prompted a written protest from 25 countries, including the United States and the majority of the EU states.

The Icelandic Crisis Response Unit (ICRU), established in 1997 as a volunteer peacekeeping unit, successfully managed an airport during NATO operations in Kosovo in 2003 and performed a similar function in Kabul, Afghanistan, in 2004–2005. In 2006 the government announced the formation of a new secret service to aid the national police and improve cooperation with the security services of allied nations.

Iceland recognized Kosovo's independence in March 2007. In April Iceland signed separate defense agreements with Denmark and Norway. The accords allowed both countries to undertake military training exercises in Iceland. Later in the month, NATO agreed to take over supervision of Iceland's airspace if the host country covered the cost of facilities. For 2008 Iceland budgeted about $8 million to support multilateral military exercises in Icelandic territory.

The economic downturn of 2008 reignited debate over entry into the EU. The Alliance-led government initiated negotiations over membership and pledged to bring Iceland into the EU by 2011. Meanwhile, a decision by the UK government to use anti-terrorism measures to freeze some Icelandic assets led the government to respond by opposing the deployment of a British air force unit as part of the NATO mission at Keflavik air base.

Current issues. Although the IP/PP governing coalition retained a majority in the May 2003 legislative balloting, the IP suffered a significant loss in vote share and seats, prompting the postelection announcement that Prime Minister Oddsson, Europe's senior head of government, would vacate the post early in favor of the PP's Halldór ÁSGRÍMSSON. Other factors contributing to the September 2004 "transition" reportedly included Oddsson's compromised health and his indecorous dispute with President Grímsson over a proposed new media law (see Communications, below, for details). Among other things, Grímsson's veto of the bill, reportedly the first use of the office's veto power since independence, suggested to some observers that further exercise of presidential authority, strongly encoded in the constitution but rarely exercised, might be in the offing. No formal policy changes accompanied the transfer of the prime ministership. However, analysts noted that Ásgrímsson and the PP were noticeably "more EU-friendly" than Oddsson and the IP, suggesting that eventual EU membership for Iceland might reemerge as a possibility. Also on the international front, Washington in mid-2003 announced plans to withdraw its remaining warplanes from the Keflavík NATO base, declaring their presence in Iceland no longer necessary. However, the Icelandic government and population responded with alarm about being left "without air defenses" and about the possibility the country might eventually need to create its own military forces. Washington subsequently postponed implementation of the decision, in part, apparently, in acknowledgment of the Oddsson government's support for the U.S.-led invasion of Iraq. However, in March 2006 the United States informed Iceland that, in order to redeploy forces to areas of greater need, it had decided to withdraw most of its service members and all of its fighter jets and helicopters from the country by September.

Halldór Ásgrímsson's resignation as prime minister in 2006 was seen as an indication of voters' dissatisfaction with his policy of privatization and his support for Iceland's joining the EU. New prime minister Geir Haarde, most recently the foreign minister but also a widely respected former finance minister, quickly addressed concerns that the nation's "overheated" economy was headed for a difficult adjustment. (Analysts predicted that growth might fall from about 4.5 percent in 2006 to 0–1 percent in 2007.) Among other things, Haarde halted government spending on a number of infrastructure projects and negotiated wage concessions with labor unions. He also announced he would lead the negotiations when Iceland and the United States again take up the question of Iceland's defense.

In September 2006 Iceland and the United States signed a new defense agreement in which Washington pledged that it would continue to defend Iceland even though it would not station forces in the country. The former U.S. military facilities were scheduled to be turned over to Iceland, which estimated that it would cost 5 billion krónur to remove military contaminates.

During the 2007 election campaign, the Left-Green Alliance made the environment a central issue by, among other things, criticizing a variety of industrial projects because of their ecological impact. The Left-Green Alliance was also vocal in its criticism of the Iraq war. The party was rewarded with five new seats, drawing voters away from the centrist PP and the left-of-center Alliance. However, the ruling IP also gained seats by emphasizing economic growth, polls indicating that it too had prospered at the expense of the PP. In the aftermath of the elections, a poll found that the new government had an approval rating of 83 percent—the highest ever recorded for an Icelandic government. In June a smoking ban was instituted in restaurants and public places (about 24 percent of Icelanders smoke cigarettes).

In March 2008 the Central Bank raised interest rates to 15.5 percent, a record high, in response to a spike in inflation, which rose 11.8 percent, its highest level in six years. In an effort to contain inflation and a growing consumer credit crisis, the central banks of Denmark, Norway, and Sweden agreed to provide up to $775 million to commercial banks in Iceland. As a result the króna, which had lost 25.2 percent of its value, gained more than 4 percent against major currencies. In May, Iceland announced that it would continue commercial whaling, setting a quota of 40 minke whales (the quota was 45 whales in 2007). In October, Iceland's leading banks collapsed causing a massive devaluation of the króna and the loss of billions in savings and pension funds. Inflation rose to record levels and the Central Bank raised interest rates to 18 percent. The government responded by nationalizing the banks and adopting a budget that included a $150 billion krónur deficit in order to stabilize the financial sector. It also secured more than $10 billion in loans after agreeing to first compensate foreign investors for losses related to the successive bank failures. Massive protests and demonstrations began in October in response to the government's management of the crisis.

In January 2009 prime minister Haarde called for new elections in the spring. He subsequently announced that he had cancer and would not seek reelection. On January 26, the IP-led government collapsed (see Political background, above) and was replaced by a caretaker coalition led by The Alliance. New Althing elections were held on April 25 and resulted in a coalition government of The Alliance and the VGF, along with two independents. The new government faced severe economic challenges with estimates that GDP would contract by 10 percent in 2009 and unemployment would rise to 10 percent.

POLITICAL PARTIES

Government Parties:

The Alliance (*Samfylkingarinnar*). The Alliance was established as a unified party on May 5, 2000, having originated prior to the May 1999 Althing election as an electoral coalition of three parties: the

People's Alliance—PA (*Althýðubandalagið*), the Social Democratic Party—SDP (*Althýðuflokkurinn*), and the Women's Alliance—WA (*Kvennalistinn*). The three were frequently referred to as the Unified Left.

The PA was launched in 1956 as an electoral front of Communists and a smaller group of disaffected Social Democrats. It traditionally advocated a radical socialist domestic program and a neutralist policy in foreign affairs, including Icelandic withdrawal from NATO. Its parliamentary representation rose from eight to nine in 1991 and remained at that level following the 1995 election. Having been the party chair since 1987, Ólafur Ragnar Grímsson stood down in the fall of 1995 in order to contest the June 1996 presidential election, in which he secured a comfortable victory. By then, the PA had moved to an explicitly democratic socialist orientation. Formation of the Unified Left caused a number of PA Althing members to resign from the party, arguing that it had moved too far to the center in accommodating Social Democrats.

The SDP, which dated from 1916, long advocated state ownership of large enterprises; increased social welfare benefits; and continued support for NATO forces, with eventual replacement by Icelanders when conditions permitted. In the 1987 election the party's legislative strength rose from six seats to ten, all of which were retained in 1991, when it joined in coalition with the IP. Unrest over government austerity measures yielded an unsuccessful challenge to the leadership and the formation of the breakaway Awakening of the Nation-People's Movement (*Thjóðvaki-Hreyfing Fólksins*), which was launched for the 1995 election by former SDP deputy chair and social affairs minister Jóhanna SIGURÐARDÓTTIR. In the 1995 balloting the SDP won only 11.4 percent of the vote and seven seats, while the *Thjóðvaki* won 7.2 percent and four seats. The two groups subsequently reconciled, and Sigurðardóttir became a prominent leader in the Unified Left before the 1999 election.

The WA, which has also been known as the Alliance of the Women's List (*Samtök um Kvennalista*), was organized prior to the 1983 balloting, for which it presented eight candidates, seating three. Said to be the first feminist group in the world to secure such representation, it doubled its seats to six in 1987, one of which was lost in 1991. In 1995 it slipped further to three seats on a 4.9 percent vote share. Its 1996 presidential candidate, Guðrún AGNARSDÓTTIR, finished third, with 26 percent of the vote. Like the PA, the WA lost a number of members who objected to formation of the Unified Left.

In the run-up to the 1999 Althing election, The Alliance called for an expansion of social services and family-oriented government policies (such as longer parental leave) while arguing that Iceland should not consider applying for EU membership for at least four years. It also proposed that the U.S. military presence in Iceland should be reduced but did not challenge continued membership in NATO. Effective unity initially proved elusive for the coalition, particularly in regard to bridging the gap between the centrist SDP and its more strongly leftist partners, and it won only 26.8 percent of the vote and 17 seats.

At its May 2000 inaugural session The Alliance announced that a former SDP leader, Össur SKARPHÉÐINSSON, had been elected chair by vote of the membership; a former PA leader, Margrét FRÍMANNSDÓTTIR, was named deputy chair. The Alliance increased its vote share to 31 percent and its seat total to 20 in the 2003 legislative election. In 2005 Skarphéðinsson was replaced as party leader by Ingibjörg Gísladóttir.

In the May 2007 balloting The Alliance lost two seats, but it subsequently joined the IP-led coalition government. In 2008 the Alliance launched an initiative to end a special provision within the Kyoto Protocol that allowed the country to increase its greenhouse emissions by up to 10 percent per year. The effort led to tension within the governing coalition.

Sigurðardóttir was appointed prime minister and asked to form an interim government following the resignation of the IP-led government in January 2009. In March 2009 **Iceland's Movement–Living Land** (*Íslandshreyfingin–Lifandi Land*) merged with The Alliance. Founded in March 2007 in Reykjavík by environmental activist Omar Ragnarsson, Iceland's Movement campaigned on a green platform stressing stricter environmental regulation. The party campaigned in the 2007 legislative elections, but it received only 3.3 percent of the vote and failed to secure any seats.

Sigurðardóttir was elected party chair of The Alliance at a congress in March 2009 after Gísladóttir declined to seek another term due to health reasons. Sigurðardóttir subsequently led The Alliance to victory in the April Althing elections. The party won 29.8 percent of the vote and secured 20 seats. The Alliance formed a coalition government with the VGF with Sigurðardóttir again as prime minister. After the balloting, party member Ásta R. JÓHANNESDÓTTIR was elected speaker of the Althing.

Leaders: Jóhanna SIGURÐARDÓTTIR (Prime Minister and Chair of the Party), Dagur EGGERTSSON (Vice Chair), Ásta R. JÓHANNESDÓTTIR.(Speaker of the Althing).

Left-Green Alliance (*Vinstrihreyfing-Grœnt Frambod*—VGF). Also referenced as the Red-Green Party and the Left-Green Party, the VGF was formed in 1998 by left-leaning Althing members of the People's Alliance and the Women's Alliance who opposed joining the Unified Left. It won 9.1 percent of the vote and six Althing seats in 1999 and 8.8 percent of the vote and five seats in 2003. The VGF became the third-largest party in the Althing following the May 2007 elections when it won nine seats.

The VGF participated in The Alliance-led interim government following the resignation of the IP-led coalition in January 2009. In the 2009 elections, the VGF won 21.7 percent of the vote and secured 14 seats in the Althing. It again joined in a governing coalition with The Alliance.

Leaders: Steingrímur J. SIGFÚSSON (President), Katrín JAKOBSDÓTTIR (Vice President), Drífa SNÆDAL (Secretary General).

Opposition Parties:

Independence Party—IP (*Sjálfstœðisflokkurinn*). Formed in 1929 by a union of conservative and liberal groups, the IP has traditionally been the strongest party and has participated in most governments since 1944. Although primarily representing commercial and fishing interests, it draws support from all strata of society and is especially strong in the urban areas. It stands for a liberal economic policy, economic stabilization, and the continued presence of NATO forces. A major split occurred in February 1980 when Vice Chair Gunnar THORODDSEN, backed by several Independence MPs, broke with the regular party leadership and formed a coalition government with the Progressive and People's Alliance parties.

The party lost 5 of its 23 seats in the election of April 1987, largely because of the defection of Albert GUMUNDSSON, who had been forced to resign as industry minister in March because of a tax scandal. Party Chair Thorsteinn Pálsson stepped down as prime minister in September 1988 because of a dispute over economic policy. In March 1991 Reykjavík mayor Davíð Oddsson succeeded Pálsson as party chair and formed a government on April 30, following an election in which the party's plurality rose from 18 to 26. The IP lost only 1 seat in the 1995 balloting, winning 37.1 percent of the vote. However, because of losses by its Social Democratic coalition partner, it felt obliged to form a new center-right coalition with the PP.

Oddsson was returned to office in the election of May 1999 (the IP having won 26 Althing seats on an improved vote share of 40.7 percent) and in the May 2003 balloting (the IP having secured 22 seats on a vote share of 33.7 percent). On September 27, 2005, Oddsson stepped down from the government and relinquished his post in the party's leadership to become chair of the Board of Governors of the Icelandic Central Bank. He was replaced the next month by Geir Haarde, who in June 2006 became the new prime minister. Haarde was reappointed prime minister following the May 2007 legislative elections in which the IP increased its representation by 3 seats, to 25. Former communications minister and party member Sturla BÖÒVARSSON was elected president of the parliament following the legislative balloting.

Haarde resigned as prime minister and party chair in 2009. He was replaced by Bjarni BENEDIKTSSON at a party congress in March 2009. In the 2009 legislative balloting, the IP won 16 seats with 23.7 percent of the vote. The IP offered to join a coalition government with The Alliance, but the initiative was rejected, and the IP instead became the main opposition party in the Althing, marking the first time in 18 years that the party had not been part of the government.

Leaders: Bjarni BENEDIKTSSON (Chair), Thorgerður Katrín GUNNARSDÓTTIR (Vice Chair), Kjartan GUNNARSSON (Secretary General).

Progressive Party—PP (*Framsóknarflokkurinn*). Founded in 1916 as a representative of agrarian interests, the Progressive Party has been responsible for many social and economic reforms benefiting agriculture and the fisheries. In the past it expressed qualified support for NATO while advocating the withdrawal of military forces as soon as possible. Although the party placed second in the 1983 balloting, its chair, Steingrímur Hermannsson, succeeded in forming a coalition government in which six of the ten cabinet posts were allocated to the Independence Party. The PP did better than anticipated in the 1987 balloting, retaining 13 of its 14 seats, although Hermannsson was unable to form a new government. The party was awarded four ministries in the Pálsson government of July 8, with Hermannsson returning as head of a three-party coalition in September 1988. The PP went into opposition following the election of April 1991, in which its parliamentary representation was unchanged. It returned to government after the 1995 balloting, in which it advanced to 23.3 percent of the vote.

The PP saw its vote share drop to 18.4 percent in the May 1999 election, giving it 12 seats (a loss of 3), but it remained the junior partner in the governing coalition. The PP retained its 12 seats (on a 17.7 percent vote share) in the 2003 balloting. Under an agreement reached following that election, PP leader Halldór Ásgrímsson was sworn in as head of the ongoing PP/IP coalition government in September 2004. However, he resigned in 2006.

Jón SIGURDSSON resigned as party chair in 2007 after the PP suffered its worst electoral showing in decades, losing five seats to become the fourth-largest party in the Althing. He was immediately replaced by Guðni Ágústsson, who had been vice chair.

In January 2009 at a party congress, the PP reversed its previous opposition to EU membership for Iceland. At the same meeting, Sigmunder Davið GUNNLAUGSSON was elected as the new chair of the PP. In the April Althing elections, the PP secured 14.8 percent of the vote and nine seats.

Leaders: Sigmunder Davið GUNNLAUGSSON (Chair), Halldór ÁSGRÍMSSON (Former Prime Minister and Former Chair of the Party), Sigurdor EYTHORSSON (Secretary General).

Citizens' Movement (*Borgarahreyfingin*). Citizens' Movement grew out of anti-government protests in January 2009. The populist, center-right party advocated economic reforms in response to the 2009 recession. In the April 2009 Althing balloting the Citizens' Movement secured 7.2 percent of the vote and won four seats.

Leader: Þór SAARI.

Other Parties:

Liberal Party (*Frjálslyndi Flokkurinn*). The Liberal Party was formed in 1998 by Sverrir HERMANNSSON, former cabinet minister and former director of the national bank of Iceland. It supports decentralization, a free-market system, a social safety net, tax reduction and simplification, separation of church and state, and continued participation in NATO. In the May 1999 Althing election it exceeded most analysts' expectations, winning two seats on a 4.2 percent vote share. The Liberals continued to improve in the 2003 legislative balloting, securing 7.4 percent of the vote and four seats. The small **New Force** (*Nýtt Afl*) political party merged with the Liberals at the beginning of 2007. In the May 2007 elections the Liberals secured four seats. The party won only 2.2 percent of the vote in the April 2009 elections and failed to gain any seats

Leaders: Guðjón KRISTJÁNSSON (Chair), Magnús HAFSTEINSSON (Vice Chair).

Fighting Union (*Baráttusamtökin*). Formed in March 2007, the party was created to promote the rights and interests of pensioners and senior citizens. Fighting Union formed a coalition with the party **Capital Union** (*Höfudborgarsamtökin*), which had previously competed only in local elections. The coalition was unable to qualify for the 2007 or the 2009 legislative balloting.

Leader: Arndís BJÖRNSDÓTTIR.

Democratic Movement (*Lýðræðishreyfingin*). The Democractic Movement was founded in January 2009. It contested the April 2009 Althing elections but only received 0.6 percent of the vote and, therefore, no seats in the legislature.

Leader: Ástþór MAGNÚSSON.

L-List of Sovereignty Supporters (*L-Listi Fullveldissinna*). The List was formed by organizers of the 2009 anti-government demonstrations. The party qualified for the 2009 legislative polling, but it withdrew its candidates at the beginning of April in response to polling that consistently showed it with less than 1 percent of support among voters.

LEGISLATURE

Iceland's parliament, the **Althing** (*Alingi*), consists of 63 members elected for four-year terms by a proportional system. In the election of April 25, 2009, The Alliance won 20 seats; the Independence Party, 16; the Left-Green Alliance, 14; the Progressive Party, 9; and Citizens' Movement, 4.

President: Ásta JÓHANNESDÓTTIR.

CABINET

[as of June 1, 2009]

Prime Minister	Jóhanna Sigurðardóttir (Alliance) [f]
Ministers	
Agriculture and Fisheries	Jón Bjarnason (VGF)
Business Affairs	Gylfi Magnússon (ind.)
Communications	Kristján Möller (Alliance)
Education, Science, and Culture	Katrín Jakobsdóttir (VGF) [f]
Environment	Svandís Svavarsdóttir (VGF) [f]
Finance	Steingrímur Sigfússon (VGF)
Foreign Affairs	Össur Skarphéðinsson (Alliance)
Health	Ögmundur Jónasson (VGF)
Industry, Energy and Tourism	Katrín Júlíusdóttir (Alliance) [f]
Justice and Ecclesiastical Affairs	Ragna Árnadóttir (ind.) [f]
Social Affairs	Árni Páll Árnason (Alliance)

[f] = female

COMMUNICATIONS

Press. The following are published daily in Reykjavík: *Fréttablaðid* (The Newspaper, 80,000), independent; *Morgunblaðið* (Morning News, 50,000), independent; *DV* (*Dagblaðið-Visir*, 40,000), independent; and *Dagur-Tíminn* (Day-Times, 14,000), Progressive Party organ. *Fréttablaðid* and *DV* are owned by the Northern Lights group, which was recently formed by the Baugur Company, a major retailer in Iceland and the United Kingdom. Northern Lights also owns several major radio and television stations. In 2004 the legislature approved a bill sponsored by the Oddsson administration that would have barred companies from simultaneously owning newspapers and broadcasting stations and also severely limited the percentage of a broadcasting company that could be owned by a company enjoying dominance in another economic sector. However, the bill, which would have forced the breakup of Northern Lights (headed by Jon Asgeir JOHANNESSON, a political opponent of Oddsson's), was vetoed by President Grímsson. Subsequently, further consideration of the matter was postponed until after the 2007 legislative balloting. The 2008 economic crisis prompted the sale of *Fréttablaðid* to the conglomerate that also owned *Morgunblaðið* prompting new concerns about the growing consolidation of the media in Iceland. In 2008 Reporters Without Borders ranked Iceland, Luxembourg and Norway as the countries with the highest degree of freedom of the press.

News agencies. *Agence France-Presse* and United Press International have offices in the capital.

Broadcasting and computing. The Icelandic State Broadcasting Service (*Ríkisútvarpið*) operates numerous radio-transmitting and relay stations; national TV service is also provided through its television division (*Ríkisútvarpið-Sjónvarp*). A number of other radio and television broadcasters transmit less widely. In addition, the U.S. Navy broadcasts from the NATO base at Keflavík. As of 2008 there were 905.6 Internet users per 1,000 inhabitants.

INTERGOVERNMENTAL REPRESENTATION

Ambassador to the U.S.: Hjalmar HANNESSON.

U.S. Ambassador to Iceland: Carol VAN VOORST.

Permanent Representative to the UN: Gunnar PÁLSSON.

IGO Memberships (Non-UN): AC, BIS, CBSS, CEUR, EBRD, EFTA, Interpol, NATO, NC, NIB, OECD, OSCE, PCA, WCO, WEU, WTO.

INDIA

Republic of India
Bharat

Political Status: Independent since August 15, 1947; republican system instituted by constitution of January 26, 1950.

Area: 1,222,559 sq. mi. (3,166,414 sq. km.), excluding approximately 30,160 sq. mi. (78,114 sq. km.) of Jammu and Kashmir presently held by Pakistan and 16,480 sq. mi. (42,685 sq. km.) held by China.

Population: 1,028,610,328 (2001C); 1,161,912,000 (2008E). The 2001 figure excludes three subdistricts of Manipur where administrative and technical difficulties resulted in cancellation of the results.

Major Urban Centers (urban areas, 2005E): NEW DELHI (15,966,000); Mumbai, formerly Bombay (17,893,000); Kolkata, formerly Calcutta (14,213,000); Chennai, formerly Madras (6,877,000); Bengalooru (Bangalore, 6,463,000); Hyderabad (6,096,000); Ahmadabad (5,118,000).

Official Languages: Hindi, English (in addition to other languages that are official at state levels).

Monetary Unit: Rupee (market rate December 1, 2009: 46.31 rupees = $1US).

President: Pratibha Devisingh PATIL (United Progressive Alliance); elected July 21, 2007, by an electoral college and inaugurated July 25 for a five-year term, succeeding A. P. J. Abdul KALAM.

Vice President: Mohammad Hamid ANSARI (United Progressive Alliance); elected by Parliament on August 10, 2007, and inaugurated August 11 for a five-year term, succeeding Bhairon Singh SHEKHAWAT.

Prime Minister: Manmohan SINGH (Indian National Congress); appointed by the president on May 19, 2004, and sworn in on May 22, in succession to Atal Bihari VAJPAYEE (*Bharatiya Janata Party*), who had submitted his resignation on May 13, following the election of April–May; invited to form a new government by the president on May 20, 2009, following the legislative election of April–May 2009, and sworn in as the head of a new Council of Ministers on May 22.

THE COUNTRY

Forming a natural subcontinent between the Arabian Sea and the Bay of Bengal and stretching from the Himalayas in the north to the Indian Ocean in the south, the Republic of India encompasses a mélange of ethnic, linguistic, and socioreligious groups that together constitute a national population second in size only to that of mainland China. India embraces over 1,600 different languages and dialects, most of Indo-European derivation, followed in importance by Dravidian, Austro-Asiatic, and Sino-Tibiti. Although India has the largest Hindu population in the world (about 83 percent of the people), the Muslim component (over 11 percent) makes India the country with the world's fourth-largest Muslim population, after Indonesia, Pakistan, and Bangladesh. Smaller religious groups include Christians, Sikhs, Buddhists, and Jains. All religions enjoy equal status under the constitution, and caste discrimination, although still practiced in rural areas, is outlawed. Despite a rising participation rate, women make up only 28 percent of the active labor force. Under a 1993 constitutional amendment, one-third of local council seats and executive positions are reserved for women. A proposal currently under discussion would extend the one-third reservation to Parliament and the state legislatures. Female representation in the most recently elected lower house of Parliament is under 11 percent.

Agriculture employs about 54 percent of Indian workers and contributes 18 percent of GDP; the principal crops are rice, cotton, and jute (fall harvest); wheat (summer harvest); and oilseeds, sugarcane, coffee, tea, spices, and nuts. Despite employing only 18 percent of the labor force, industry is considerably diversified, producing manufactures ranging from transport equipment (principally two-wheeled vehicles) and diesel engines to aluminum, petroleum products, and televisions as well as such long-established mainstays as cotton textiles and processed foods. Industry as a whole accounts for 29 percent of GDP, compared with 53 percent for services. Leading merchandise exports include mineral products; textiles and garments; gems and jewelry; base metals and related products; chemicals and related products; machinery, appliances, and electrical equipment; and such traditional agricultural commodities as oil cakes, rice, coffee, tea, spices, and cashews.

After independence, economic policy aimed at a "socialist pattern of society," embracing both public and private sectors. Railroads, aviation, armaments, and atomic energy were assigned exclusively to government control, with the state dominating a range of other industries, including iron and steel, shipbuilding, oil, chemicals, certain types of mining, banking, and foreign trade. With the appearance of stagnation and a decline in foreign investment, the government of P. V. Narasimha RAO (1991–1996) attempted a radical overhaul of the Indian economy that included devaluating the rupee, permitting foreign majority control of domestic companies, and reducing constraints on market activity. By 1998 India's economy ranked among the dozen largest in the world; however, about 27 percent of the population—more than 300 million people—remain below the national poverty line, and 44 percent of children under age five are malnourished.

Except for fiscal year (FY) 2002–2003, when GDP growth was only 3.8 percent, economic expansion has been robust, averaging 6.5 percent from April 2001 through March 2005 and registering 9.4 percent in the next year. Growth for FY 2006–2007 held at 9.6 percent but dropped slightly, to 9.0 percent, in the next 12 months. Forecasts for 2008–2009 projected growth at a slower rate of 6.3 percent because of the ongoing international recession

Given the size of the overall economy, the gross economic impact of recent natural disasters has been minimal despite the human toll. On January 26, 2001, a major earthquake centered in the state of Gujarat claimed at least 30,000 lives and left 600,000 or more homeless, while the Indian Ocean tsunami of December 26, 2004, cost some 17,000 Indian lives (including those missing and presumed dead) and displaced another 650,000 in the southern states of Andhra Pradesh, Kerala, and Tamil Nadu, plus the union territories of Puducherry and the severely affected Andaman and Nicobar islands.

GOVERNMENT AND POLITICS

Political background. After a prolonged struggle against British colonial rule, which had been entrenched in 1858, India attained independence within the Commonwealth on August 15, 1947, when Britain put into effect the Indian Independence Act, thereby partitioning the subcontinent into the sovereign states of predominantly Hindu India and Muslim Pakistan. However, the act applied only to former British India, thus setting the stage for confrontation between the two new nations over accession of various princely states and feudatories that had retained nominal independence under the Raj, including Jammu and Kashmir, where a militarized Line of Control (LoC) still separates Indian and Pakistani sectors.

Jawahar Lal NEHRU, leader of the politically dominant Indian National Congress (INC), served as India's first prime minister. A follower of the charismatic advocate of nonviolence Mohandas

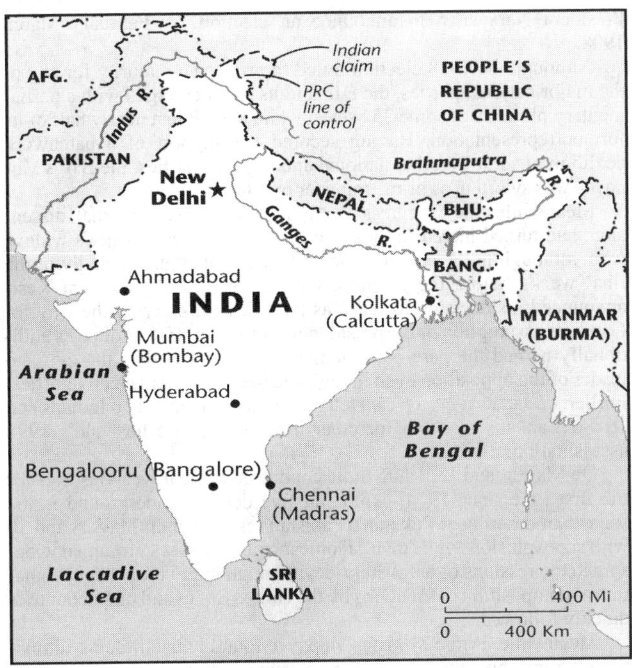

Karamchand GANDHI, who was assassinated in 1948, Nehru enunciated India's basic principles of democracy, secularism, socialism, and nonalignment. Upon his death in 1964 Nehru was succeeded by Lal Bahadur SHASTRI, who died in 1966 and was in turn succeeded by Indira GANDHI, Nehru's daughter.

In 1969 the INC split into Gandhi and conservative factions, the latter subsequently being styled the INC-Organization, or Congress (O), by the Election Commission. With Gandhi's "New Congress" group having swept the parliamentary election of March 1971, she controlled enough seats in the lower house (*Lok Sabha*) to amend the constitution. Between 1971 and 1974 new constitutional amendments were adopted permitting parliamentary restriction of fundamental rights, and legislation was enacted authorizing the use of preventive detention as an antiterrorism measure. In June 1975, however, the High Court of Allahabad ruled in favor of a petition filed by Raj NARAIN, who charged that Gandhi had committed election irregularities in 1971. The ruling disqualified Gandhi from membership in the *Lok Sabha,* but she was granted a 20-day stay to appeal to the Supreme Court.

Opposition party leaders immediately launched a civil disobedience campaign to force Gandhi's resignation, and on June 26, 1975, President Fakhruddin Ali AHMED declared a state of emergency at her request. Nearly 700 opposition leaders were promptly arrested, and press censorship was introduced for the first time since independence. In July Parliament approved the state of emergency, after which a majority of the opposition members withdrew from the lower house in protest. In November the Indian Supreme Court unanimously upheld the prime minister's appeal, and in February 1976 Parliament voted to extend the term of the sitting *Lok Sabha* beyond its five-year mandate.

In January 1977 Gandhi called an election for March. In spite of the short, six-week campaign, a multiparty *Janata* (People's) Front was able to organize behind anticorruption campaigner Jaya Prakash NARAYANAN and Congress (O) leader Moraji R. DESAI. Pledging to end the state of emergency and restore democracy, *Janata* swept the election, Gandhi being among the defeated candidates. Desai was designated prime minister, and the state of emergency was revoked on March 27.

In December 1977 Gandhi resigned from the INC Working Committee and, in January 1978, organized the Indian National Congress–Indira (universally rendered as Congress [I]), which by midyear had become the nation's major opposition party. Gandhi returned to the *Lok Sabha* after winning a November by-election, but in late December she was stripped of her seat and imprisoned for the duration of the parliamentary term by action of the *Janata* majority.

The fragility of the *Janata* coalition was highlighted in mid-1978 by a major leadership dispute between Prime Minister Desai and his home affairs minister, Charan SINGH. Moreover, a series of communal riots in a number of states effectively split the party into Hindu and secular factions and provoked demands by Raj Narain and others that *Janata* adopt the posture of a secular "third force" opposed to both Hindu extremism and Gandhi's "authoritarianism." In mid-July Singh and a number of others resigned to join Narain's recently formed *Janata* Party–Secular (JP-S), thus depriving the government of its majority in the *Lok Sabha* and forcing Desai's resignation as prime minister. Invited by President Neelam Sanjiva REDDY to form a new government, Singh was sworn in on July 28, but he submitted his own resignation three weeks later following the defection of a number of Congress (O) members and an announcement that Congress (I) would not support him in a confidence vote. President Reddy therefore dissolved the *Lok Sabha* on August 22.

In a dramatic reversal of fortune, Gandhi swept back into power in the *Lok Sabha* election of January 1980. However, her administration proved unable to curb mounting domestic violence. A continuing influx of illegal Bengali immigrants generated reprisals in Assam, while riots broke out in Karnataka over a recommendation that Kannada be adopted as the language of instruction. Muslims and Hindus battled sporadically in Uttar Pradesh and Gujarat, and *Harijans* ("Untouchables") were targets for numerous atrocities. Maoists, Naxalites (named after a peasant revolt in the 1960s in Naxalbari, West Bengal), and other extremists continued their frequently violent activities in Manipur, Mizoram, Nagaland, and West Bengal, while demands for autonomy by Sikhs in Punjab led to the storming of Parliament in October 1982 by several thousand individuals as part of a continuing *morcha* ("mass agitation").

The Sikh agitation of the early 1980s was directed by the relatively moderate leader of the *Shiromani Akali Dal* (SAD), Harchand Singh LONGOWAL. During early 1984 Hindu-Sikh violence intensified, fueled in part by supporters loyal to Sikh fundamentalist Jarnail Singh BHINDRANWALE, who operated from sanctuary within the Golden Temple in Amritsar. A series of assassinations, reportedly ordered by Bhindranwale, led to an assault on the Golden Temple by Indian security forces during the night of June 5–6, in the course of which over 1,000 persons, including Bhindranwale, were killed. The action provoked an even deeper Sikh resentment, which reached a climax on October 31 with Gandhi's assassination by two Sikh members of her personal bodyguard.

Mrs. Gandhi's son, Rajiv GANDHI, was immediately sworn in as prime minister, and an election was called at which Congress (I) won an unprecedented 401 of 508 contested seats. In July 1985 the government concluded a peace accord with *Akali Dal.* Sikh extremists responded by assassinating Longowal on August 20, and violence in Punjab and elsewhere persisted through 1986.

In mid-1988 the Gandhi administration lost a critical series of state elections as evidence emerged of extensive corruption, particularly in the placing of arms contracts with Western companies. The government also came under serious challenge from Vishwanath Pratap SINGH, whose anticorruption campaign as defense minister had led to his expulsion from Congress (I) in mid-1987. Singh then played a key role in organizing a seven-party opposition National Front (*Rashtriya Morcha*) within which a three-party *Janata Dal* (People's Party) grouping was formed in October.

Prime Minister Gandhi called an early lower house election for November 1989, at which the National Front and its allies gained a clear-cut majority of seats. On December 2 Singh, although not favored by supporters of *Janata Dal* leader Chandra SHEKHAR, was sworn in as head of a new administration with external support from the right-wing Hindu *Bharatiya Janata* Party (BJP) as well as the two leading leftist formations, the Communist Party of India (CPI) and the Communist Party of India–Marxist (CPI-M).

In September 1990 BJP leader Lal Krishna ADVANI began a religious pilgrimage (*rath yatra*) to the site of an abandoned Muslim mosque in Ayodhya, Uttar Pradesh, where Hindu efforts to construct a temple had led to serious ethnic unrest. On October 23 Prime Minister Singh ordered Advani's arrest, whereupon the BJP withdrew its support. With the National Front government thus weakened, *Janata Dal* split on November 5, 1990, Chandra Shekhar and Deputy Prime Minister Devi LAL forming *Janata Dal*–Socialist (JD-S). Two days later Singh became the first Indian prime minister to be defeated on the floor of the *Lok Sabha,* losing a confidence vote 346–142, and on November 10 Shekhar, with Congress (I) backing, was named as his successor.

Prime Minister Shekhar, whose parliamentary group counted only 54 members, felt obliged to resign on March 6, 1991, in the wake of a rift with Gandhi. On March 13 President Ramaswamy VENKATARAMAN, acceding to a request by the Congress (I) leader, dissolved Parliament. At first-stage legislative balloting on May 20, Congress (I) was the victor in a substantial proportion of completed contests, but on May 21 the election was thrown into chaos by Gandhi's assassination at the hands of Sri Lankan Tamil separatists angered over India's 1987–1990 intervention in support of the Sri Lankan government (see Foreign relations, below). Second- and third-stage polling were immediately postponed, with longtime party stalwart P. V. Narasimha RAO being named Congress (I) president on May 29. Completion of the election on June 15 yielded, as anticipated, less than a legislative majority for the Congress (I) and its allies. Rao nonetheless succeeded in forming a coalition administration and then, through a series of by-election victories and opposition defections, was able to convert his plurality to a majority over the ensuing two years.

During 1994 Prime Minister Rao became increasingly beleaguered by critics of his market-oriented economic policies, and in December he was further weakened by the resignation of his heir apparent, Human Resources Minister Arjun SINGH, who insisted that the administration had turned a deaf ear to the plight of the country's poor.

In March 1995 Congress (I) suffered the latest in a series of state electoral defeats. The losses generated an open revolt within the party, and a dissident rally on May 19 named a longtime rival of the prime minister, Narain Dutt TIWARI, to succeed Rao as party leader. Tiwari and his ally Arjun Singh subsequently formed the All India Indira Congress (AIIC).

Balloting for the 11th *Lok Sabha,* held in several rounds beginning on April 27, 1996, delivered a heavy defeat for Congress (I), which had been sullied earlier in the year by a major corruption scandal and the consequent resignations of ten government ministers. Whereas Congress (I) retained only 140 *Lok Sabha* seats, the fundamentalist BJP won 161. A 14-party center-left alliance, which included *Janata Dal* and which was subsequently redesignated the United Front (UF), secured 177 seats.

Following precedent, President Shankar Dayal SHARMA invited the BJP parliamentary leader, Atal Bihari VAJPAYEE, to form a government. A BJP administration was announced on May 15, 1996, but resigned on May 28 rather than face a confidence vote. The president then turned to the UF, which had selected the Karnataka chief minister, H. D. DEVE GOWDA (*Janata Dal*), as its overall leader. Crucially, Deve Gowda obtained a prompt pledge of support from the Congress (I) leadership. A UF minority government, containing representatives of nine component parties, was sworn in on June 1.

Facing corruption and bribery charges, former prime minister Rao resigned as Congress party president on September 21, 1996. (Although he was convicted in October 2000, the verdict was overturned in March 2002.) He was succeeded two days later, initially in an acting capacity, by the party treasurer, Sitaram KESRI, the first member of a lower caste to head Congress. (By then, having outlasted or reabsorbed most rival Congress formations, the party had largely dropping the appended "I.")

Although the UF and Congress appeared to have few policy differences, on March 30, 1997, the latter announced that it was withdrawing its external support from the government. The UF administration consequently lost a confidence motion on April 11, prompting Deve Gowda to resign. With neither the Congress nor the UF strong enough to form a government on its own, Deve Gowda announced that he would step down as head of the UF, thereby permitting a "face-saving" change of leadership that would facilitate further UF-Congress cooperation. As a result, the highly respected foreign minister, Inder Kumar GUJRAL of the *Janata Dal,* was sworn in as prime minister on April 22. He reappointed most of the incumbent ministers to his new cabinet.

In electoral college voting on July 14, 1997, Vice President Kicheril Raman NARAYANAN, who had the support of all major parties, was elected president, thereby becoming the first head of state with a *Dalit* (formerly "Untouchable" or *Harijan*) heritage.

In August 1997 the public learned that the government-appointed Jain Commission, in the course of its investigation into the 1991 assassination of Rajiv Gandhi, had considered evidence of a possible indirect connection between the Dravidian Progressive Federation (*Dravida Munnetra Kazhagam*—DMK), a member of the UF government, and the suspect Sri Lankan rebels. Consequently, Congress and the UF's *Tamil Maanila* Congress (TMC), which was in competition with the DMK for control of Tamil Nadu, demanded that Gujral oust the DMK. When Gujral refused, Congress withdrew its support from the government, triggering its collapse on November 28. Congress and the BJP both failed in separate efforts to form a new government, prompting President Narayanan to announce an election for February–March 1998.

Although the 1998 election failed to produce a majority for any of the major national parties, the BJP and its allies emerged with a parliamentary plurality of some 252 seats, while the UF lost nearly half of its former representation. Having secured the support of a patchwork coalition of some 20 other national and regional parties, the BJP's Vajpayee was sworn in as prime minister on March 19.

Meanwhile, the Congress Party, facing renewed internal dissension, had turned increasingly toward Sonia GANDHI, Rajiv's widow, who, although not a candidate herself, had campaigned heavily in the final weeks before the election. On March 9, 1998, Sitaram Kesri announced his decision to retire as party leader, clearing the way for Gandhi's assumption of the presidency. On March 16 Gandhi was additionally named the party's parliamentary chair and thus the de facto leader of the opposition even though she had never held elective office. Earlier, on January 28, a New Delhi court had sentenced 10 Indians and 16 Sri Lankans to death for conspiring in her late husband's 1991 assassination.

On May 11 and 13, 1998, India conducted nuclear weapons tests for the first time since 1974, exploding five devices underground in the Rajasthan desert near Pokaran. (Pakistan responded on May 28 and 30 with six explosions of its own.) Domestically, the news prompted widespread expressions of national pride, although international condemnation and imposition of sanctions by the United States and other countries quickly followed.

Meanwhile, Prime Minister Vajpayee found himself facing ultimatums from his own coalition partners, particularly Jayalalitha JAYARAM, the flamboyant leader of the All India Dravidian Progressive Federation (All India *Anna Dravida Munnetra Kazhagam*—AIADMK) and a former chief minister of Tamil Nadu. Vajpayee's rejection of her demands for policy and personnel changes led Jayalalitha (as she is universally known) to withdraw her support, and on April 17, 1999, the government lost a confidence motion 270–269 in the *Lok Sabha*. The prime minister resigned the following day, and after Sonia Gandhi proved unable to forge a Congress-led coalition, President Narayanan dissolved the lower house on April 26.

The ensuing election campaign was marked by considerable political reshuffling, with the BJP announcing in May 1999 the formation of a National Democratic Alliance (NDA) that, by late August, included 24 parties. Significantly, the NDA election manifesto emphasized economic reforms and infrastructural development while omitting Hindu nationalist goals. The most important development of the preelection period, however, was renewed hostilities in the mountainous Kargil area of Kashmir, where Islamic militants and Pakistani troops had crossed the long-established LoC. A negotiated withdrawal was completed late in July, although sporadic artillery exchanges persisted.

At multistage balloting in September–October 1999 the NDA won a clear victory in the *Lok Sabha.* On October 13, with the support of some 18 parties and just over 300 MPs, Prime Minister Vajpayee was sworn in at the head of a massive 70-member cabinet (including ministers of state). Numerous cabinet reshuffles occurred in the following three years, most significantly in September 2001 and July 2002. Two days before the latter reshuffle, Vajpayee had elevated the hard-line minister of home affairs, Lal Krishna Advani, to the post of deputy prime minister.

On February 27, 2002, Muslims burned train cars carrying Hindu activists from the disputed sacred site in Ayodhya. Nearly 60 died in the attack, which generated reprisals by Hindu vigilantes that cost an additional 1,100 Muslim and Hindu lives and forced over 100,000 Muslims to flee their homes. Reports prepared by the United Kingdom and the European Union subsequently alleged that the anti-Muslim riots were not spontaneous, as some officials had claimed, but were instead an organized campaign conducted with the acquiescence—in some cases, the assistance—of government personnel.

On July 15, 2002, A. P. J. Abdul KALAM, a scientist and the architect of India's ballistic missile program, was elected president of India. Although a political novice, the widely popular Kalam, a Muslim, drew support from most of the opposition as well as the NDA. On August 12 Bhairon Singh SHEKHAWAT, a former chief minister of Rajasthan, was elected vice president, his predecessor, Krishan KANT, having died in office on July 27.

Hoping to take advantage of a booming economy, a recent rapprochement with Pakistan, and favorable results from the previous month's state elections, in late January 2004 Prime Minister Vajpayee advised President Kalam to dissolve the *Lok Sabha* and call an early election. Although public opinion polls indicated that Vajpayee would easily lead the NDA to victory, the government's efforts to reduce the deficit, institute major tax reforms, privatize state-run enterprises, and permit foreign investment in a wider variety of industries had apparently contributed to voter perception that the plight of the rural poor was being slighted. In addition, what was widely viewed as an inadequate government response to the communal violence that followed the 2002 train-burning incident had raised questions about the government's commitment to a secular union. As a result, voters confounded expectations, and in staged balloting in April–May Sonia Gandhi's Congress and its allies registered an upset victory, winning 219 seats, versus 185 for the NDA.

On May 13, 2004, Vajpayee submitted his resignation, and on May 19 the president named as India's new prime minister the INC's Manmohan SINGH, a Sikh senator and former finance minister who had been credited with instituting, a decade earlier, reforms that saved India's faltering economy. A day earlier, Gandhi had withdrawn her name from consideration, in part to defuse the divisive issue of her Italian birth. Having obtained the external support of the CPI-M, its Left Front partners, and an assortment of other parties, Singh and a multiparty United Progressive Alliance (UPA) government were sworn in on May 22.

On July 21, 2007, Pratibha PATIL, the UPA candidate and most recently governor of Rajasthan, was elected to serve as president of India. She won 65.8 percent of the vote in defeating Vice President Shekhawat, who had been endorsed by the BJP and most of the other NDA parties. Earlier, a newly formed "third force" United National Progressive Alliance (UNPA) of regional parties had failed to convince President Kalam to seek a second term. On August 10 the UPA's Mohammad Hamid ANSARI won election as vice president, defeating the NDA's candidate, Najma HEPTULLAH, by a 2–1 margin, with the UNPA's Rashid MASOOD a distant third.

On July 8, 2008, the Left Front withdrew its support from Prime Minister Singh over objections to a U.S.-India nuclear power deal involving the transfer of civilian nuclear technology and fuel (see Foreign relations, below). Staking the survival of his minority government on gaining parliamentary approval of the program, Prime Minister Singh managed to attract sufficient backing from the SP, some smaller parties, and independents, which produced on July 22 a 275–256–10 *Lok Sabha* vote in favor of the pact.

The election of April–May 2009 was preceded by several changes in the makeup of the governing UPA and the opposition NDA as well as by the formation of alternative Third Front and Fourth Front alliances, led, in the first case, by the Left Front and the pro-*Dalit Bahujan Samata* Party (BSP) and, in the second, by the Uttar Pradesh–based *Samajwadi* Party (SP). The multistage balloting saw the Congress-led UPA expand its plurality to 262 seats, which, with the external support of the BSP and the SP, enabled Prime Minister Singh to claim another term in office.

Constitution and government. India's frequently amended constitution of January 26, 1950, provides for a republican form of parliamentary government in a secular union (despite Hindu numerical predominance) that currently embraces 28 states and 7 centrally administered territories. Under the Indian constitution, all legislative subjects are divided into three jurisdictions: the union list, comprising subjects on which the union Parliament has exclusive authority; the state list, comprising subjects on which the state assemblies have authority; and the concurrent list, comprising subjects on which both may legislate, with a union ruling predominating in the event of conflict and where state questions assume national importance.

The head of state, a president who serves a five-year term, is chosen, under a weighted voting system, by an electoral college comprising the elected members of both the bicameral Parliament and the state legislatures. The vice president is elected by the members of the full Parliament and serves as ex officio chair of the upper house of the legislature, the Council of States (*Rajya Sabha*). The lower House of the People (*Lok Sabha*), elected for a five-year term (subject to dissolution), is presided over by a speaker elected by its members. The speaker must be a member of Parliament but by convention abandons party affiliation while serving as presiding officer. The prime minister is elected by the parliamentary members of the majority party or coalition of parties and heads a government that is collectively responsible to the legislature.

Each state has a governor, who is appointed by the president for a term of five years, and a popularly elected legislature. The legislatures may be bicameral or unicameral, but all are subject to maximum terms of five years. Administration is carried out by a chief minister heading a cabinet subject to parliamentary responsibility. In the event that constitutional processes in a state are rendered inoperative, the union constitution provides for the institution of direct presidential rule, with the concurrence of both houses of Parliament. The president can also appoint an agent to act as presidential surrogate, while the prime minister can call for new state elections.

The union territories, some of which are former foreign territories or are located in outlying regions, are administered by appointed officials (called lieutenant governors or administrators) responsible to the president. Puducherry and the National Capital Territory of Delhi also have elected assemblies and chief ministers.

In December 2009 the central government approved a proposal that would reestablish a separate state of Telangana, which had been merged with Andhra in 1956 to form Andhra Pradesh. The government's 2009 decision provoked heated opposition, including the mass resignation of over 100 legislators from the Andhra Pradesh state assembly. Statehood was expected to take a year or more to accomplish.

State and Capital	*Area (sq. mi.)*	*Population (2007E)*
Andhra Pradesh (Hyderabad)	106,204	82,539,000
Arunachal Pradesh (Itanagar)	32,333	1,278,000
Assam (Dispur)	30,285	30,044,000
Bihar (Patna)	36,356	98,638,000
Chhattisgarh (Raipur)	52,197	23,327,000
Goa (Panaji)	1,429	1,477,000
Gujarat (Gandhinagar)	75,684	58,252,000
Haryana (Chandigarh)	17,070	23,164,000
Himachal Pradesh (Shimla)	21,495	6,807,000
Jammu and Kashmir (Srinagar)*	39,146	11,970,000
Jharkhand (Ranchi)	30,778	31,105,000
Karnataka (Bengalooru)	74,051	58,811,000
Kerala (Thiruvananthapuram)	15,005	33,908,000
Madhya Pradesh (Bhopal)	119,013	70,402,000
Maharashtra (Mumbai)	118,808	111,457,000
Manipur (Imphal)	8,620	2,884,000
Meghalaya (Shillong)	8,660	2,757,000
Mizoram (Aizawl)	8,139	1,067,000
Nagaland (Kohima)	6,401	2,816,000
Orissa (Bhubaneswar)	60,118	40,631,000
Punjab (Chandigarh)	19,445	27,497,000
Rajasthan (Jaipur)	132,138	89,779,000
Sikkim (Gangtok)	2,740	656,000
Tamil Nadu (Chennai)	50,215	66,663,000
Tripura (Agartala)	4,045	3,528,000
Uttarakhand (Dehradun)	20,650	9,583,000
Uttar Pradesh (Lucknow)	93,022	194,865,000
West Bengal (Kolkata)	34,267	90,027,000
Union Territory and Capital		
Andaman and Nicobar Is. (Port Blair)	3,185	419,000
Chandigarh (Chandigarh)	44	1,025,000
Dadra and Nagar Haveli (Silvassa)	190	409,000
Daman and Diu (Daman)	43	214,000
Lakshadweep (Kavaratti)	12	68,000
Puducherry (Puducherry)	185	1,111,000
National Capital Territory		
New Delhi (Delhi)	573	18,139,000

*Indian-held portion

Foreign relations. India's policies as a member of the Commonwealth, the United Nations, and other multilateral organizations have been governed by a persistent belief in nonalignment, peaceful settlement of international disputes, self-determination for colonial peoples, and comprehensive efforts to ameliorate conditions in the developing nations. Following independence, it avoided participation in regional defense pacts and exclusive alignment with either Western or Communist powers, although it accepted economic and, from 1962, military aid from members of both groups.

India's foreign policy has often focused on Pakistan. The centuries-old rivalry between Hindus and Muslims in the subcontinent was directly responsible for the partition in 1947 and continued to embitter Indo-Pakistani relations thereafter, particularly in regard to the long-standing dispute over Jammu and Kashmir. Fighting over that territory in 1947–1948 resulted in a de facto division into Pakistani- and Indian-held sectors. The Indian portion was subsequently absorbed as a separate state of the Indian Union. That action was strongly protested by Pakistan, and renewed armed conflict between the two countries erupted in 1965. In December 1971, following a political crisis in East Pakistan and the flight of some 10 million Bengali refugees to India, the two nations again went to war. The brief conflict ended with Pakistani acceptance of a cease-fire on the western front and the emergence in the east of the independent state of Bangladesh.

In March 1972 India and Bangladesh concluded a 25-year Treaty of Friendship and Cooperation, and relations remain close despite recent disagreements over boundaries; conflicting claims to newly formed islands in the Bay of Bengal; and the continued presence in Bangladesh of Indian insurgents from Assam, Tripura, and Manipur. (See the Bangladesh article for details.) In December 1996 the two countries concluded a pact on sharing the Ganges River, while an agreement signed on October 1, 2003, covers seven other rivers.

India and Pakistan agreed to resume normal relations in mid-1972, but ambassadors were not exchanged until 1976. In the following decade bilateral sessions focused on such mutual concerns as economic, educational, cultural, and technical cooperation as well as on illegal border crossings, drug-trafficking, smuggling, and terrorism. The Jammu and Kashmir issue continued to poison relations, however, particularly after separatists and Islamic fundamentalists began increasing their attacks in 1989 and Kashmir's most senior Islamic leader, Moulvi Mohammed FAROOQ, was assassinated in 1990.

At least in part to diffuse external criticism of nuclear weapons tests conducted in May 1998, Indian Prime Minister Vajpayee and Pakistani Prime Minister Nawaz Sharif conferred briefly during the July 1998 South Asian Association for Regional Cooperation (SAARC) session in Colombo, Sri Lanka. They met again in September in New York and agreed, among other things, to renew bilateral talks on Kashmir in October.

Of even greater import, on February 20–21, 1999, Vajpayee and Sharif met in Lahore, Pakistan, the first such visit across the border by an Indian leader in a decade and only the third bilateral summit since the 1947 partition. Among the provisos in the resulting "Lahore Declaration" was a commitment by both governments to reduce the possibility of accidental nuclear war. The heightened hostilities in Kashmir in May–July 1999 temporarily halted the peace process, while the coup by the Pakistani military in October 1999 further undermined regional relations. In July 2001 Prime Minister Vajpayee conferred with Pakistan's chief executive, Gen. Pervez Musharraf, in Agra, but the meeting concluded without significant progress.

Meanwhile, the actions of Islamic separatists had led India to charge not only that Pakistan was not taking adequate measures to stop infiltration by terrorists but that its Inter Services Intelligence agency was abetting the attacks. On October 1, 2001, militants carried out an assault on the state assembly building in Srinagar, the summer capital of Jammu and Kashmir, causing nearly 40 deaths. India dispatched additional armed forces to Kashmir, with Pakistan responding in kind. On December 13, terrorists attacked India's Parliament, leaving 14 dead, including the terrorists, and by May 2002, when three gunmen stormed a Kashmiri army base and left nearly three dozen dead, India and Pakistan had a combined million troops or more stationed along the LoC. Diplomatic intervention, led by the United States, ultimately helped defuse the situation, but in Kashmir the familiar pattern of hostilities continued: clashes between Indian forces and separatist guerrillas, shelling by Indian and Pakistani forces across the LoC, bombings, and assassinations.

Speaking in Srinagar on April 18, 2003, Prime Minister Vajpayee called for "open dialogue" with Pakistan, and the gesture quickly led to a mutual upgrading of diplomatic relations. On November 26 the two governments instituted a cease-fire, the first in 14 years, between Pakistani and Indian forces in the disputed border region. The cease-fire was followed by an announcement at the January 2004 SAARC session that the two governments would soon begin a "composite dialogue" and seek a peaceful solution to outstanding bilateral issues. Meeting in New Delhi on April 17, 2005, Manmohan Singh, the new Indian prime minister, and Pakistan's President Musharraf jointly declared that the peace process was "irreversible." In December 2006 Singh described the destinies of the two countries as linked and reiterated the need for peace, security, and friendship, but India temporarily brought a halt to the dialogue following a November 2008 assault on Mumbai by Pakistani-based terrorists who took over 150 lives (see Current issues, below).

In its relations with the People's Republic of China, India initially attempted to maintain a friendly posture; however, border tensions between the world's two most populous nations escalated into military conflict in October 1962. At issue were 14,500 square miles of territory in the Aksai Chin area of eastern Kashmir and some 36,000 square miles of Arunachal Pradesh in the northeast (below the so-called McMahon line, established in 1913–1914), from which China withdrew after the 1962 war. Following a thaw in relations during 1976, ambassadors were exchanged for the first time in nearly 14 years. During a state visit by Prime Minister Rajiv Gandhi to China in December 1988 (the first by an Indian head of government since 1954), "in-depth discussions" on the boundary question were reported. An agreement to reduce troop levels and respect the existing Line of Actual Control (LAC) without prejudice to the rival claims was signed by Chinese Premier Li Peng and Prime Minister Rao in Beijing on September 7, 1993. In April 2005 the two countries agreed to a framework for settling the border issue (see the article on the People's Republic of China for additional information about the border dispute).

Relations between India and the Soviet Union were founded on a general coincidence of views on international political problems, mutual proximity to China, Soviet support for the Indian position on Kashmir, and Soviet economic and military aid. The breakup of the Soviet Union was viewed as having major consequences for India's posture in international affairs, although good relations have continued with the succeeding Russian Federation.

The United States was a strong supporter of Indian independence, and U.S. aid to India for some years thereafter far exceeded that received by any other nation. Politically, relations have fluctuated, the most severe strain occurring in the course of the 1971 conflict between India and Pakistan. Differences also arose over India's explosion of an underground nuclear device in May 1974 and its subsequent refusal to permit international inspection of nuclear facilities. Following the collapse of the Soviet Union in 1991, Washington increased its pressure on New Delhi to sign the Nuclear Non-Proliferation Treaty (NPT) and join with Pakistan and China in limiting nuclear development in East and South Asia. India refused to do so on the grounds that "the treaty in its present form is discriminatory" in that it legitimizes possession of nuclear weapons by a handful of countries. Without referencing the nuclear issue, a U.S.-Indian military accord was concluded in mid-January 1995 that called for joint military exercises, training, defense research, and weapons production.

In February 2000 Prime Minister Vajpayee stated that India would not sign the Comprehensive Nuclear Test Ban Treaty (CTBT) until a national consensus was achieved. Subsequent discussions with Washington proved beneficial, however, and by mid-2001 the U.S. George W. Bush administration appeared willing to forge a closer strategic link. The last of the sanctions that had been imposed after the May 1998 nuclear tests were lifted on September 23, 2001, as the Bush administration marshaled support for an impending assault on the al-Qaida terrorist network and the Taliban regime in Afghanistan.

Despite India's opposition to the U.S.-led invasion of Iraq in 2003 and the American public's concerns about India's role in the outsourcing of U.S. service jobs, relations with the United States continued to strengthen, at least in part because the Bush administration viewed India as a counterweight to China. During a visit by Prime Minister Singh to Washington in July 2005, plans were announced for a new nuclear partnership, although completion of the agreement awaited a return visit by President Bush to India in March 2006. The plan for sharing civilian nuclear technology and fuel requires India to separate its civil and military nuclear programs, permit international monitoring of its civil operations, and refrain from further nuclear tests and the transfer of nuclear technology to third countries. With the Singh government having won a confidence vote in the *Lok Sabha* in July 2008, on August 1 the International Atomic Energy Agency (IAEA), whose approval was required because India remains outside the NPT regime, endorsed the deal, as did the 45-country Nuclear Suppliers Group on September 6. Following passage by both houses of the U.S. Congress, President Bush signed the legislation on October 8.

During 1987 India became directly involved in the ethnic strife engulfing its southern neighbor, Sri Lanka. Sri Lanka's Tamil dissidents had long enjoyed support in the south Indian state of Tamil Nadu, which is predominantly ethnic Tamil. It was not until 1985 that Rajiv Gandhi retreated from the overtly pro-Tamil posture of his recently assassinated mother by declaring that he opposed any attempt by the Tamil minority to establish an autonomous state in Sri Lanka. In late 1986 he proposed the merger of Sri Lanka's largely Tamil Northern and Eastern provinces as a basis of settling the dispute, and in July 1987, during his first official visit to Sri Lanka, he offered military assistance to the Jayawardene government in support of the regionalization plan. Within days, 3,000 Indian troops had been dispatched to the island's Jaffna peninsula to assist in the disarming of the guerrillas. Although some 70,000 Indian troops were deployed by early 1988, the mission proved to be a political liability for both governments, and by March 1990 the Indian troops had been withdrawn. New Delhi made no effort to send them back when the Tamil insurgency in Sri Lanka resumed with even greater ferocity, after which Gandhi himself became a victim.

The Sri Lankan military's impending defeat of the Liberation Tigers of Tamil Eelam (LTTE) insurgency in the second quarter of 2009 generated expressions of concern in New Delhi for the civilians caught in the crossfire, but the Singh government also noted that the LTTE was a "terrorist" organization. Politicians from ethnically Tamil areas were often less circumspect, with former Tamil Nadu chief minister Jayalalitha of the AIADMK calling for Indian intervention to establish a separate Tamil country.

With regard to Nepal, among the more significant recent bilateral developments were the signing in 1996 of the Mahakali Integrated Development Treaty and a subsequent agreement providing Nepal with transit rights across Indian territory to Bangladeshi ports. A continuing dispute involves the Kalapani border area, which Indian troops have occupied since the 1962 Sino-Indian war.

In August 2009 India and the ten-member Association of Southeast Asian Nations (ASEAN) concluded negotiations on establishing a free trade zone. The India-ASEAN pact calls for reduced tariffs in such sectors as chemicals, electronics, machinery, and textiles.

From 1994 India has lobbied extensively for a permanent seat on the UN Security Council, insisting that such action would permit the council to reflect more accurately the distribution of the world's population. The United States, which has actively supported bids by Germany and Japan, characterized the Indian request as "premature," while Pakistan declared its strong opposition, pending resolution of the Kashmir dispute.

Current issues. Upon taking office in 2004 Manmohan Singh's UPA government had quickly announced a broad "Common Minimum Program" that included promoting social harmony; maintaining economic growth of 7–8 percent annually; improving the lives of farmers and other laborers; empowering women; advancing full equality for scheduled castes and tribes; and encouraging entrepreneurs, professionals, and productive enterprises. Singh indicated in October 2006 that priorities during the second half of his term would include banking and insurance reform, investments in infrastructure, and creation of additional special economic zones (SEZs) for industrial development. The most controversial aspect of the SEZ program has entailed land seizures. Numerous clashes have occurred, one of the most violent in Nandigram, West Bengal, in March 2007, when police fired on protesting farmers, contributing to about a dozen deaths and many more injuries.

Despite major defections from the first-term UPA—chiefly, that of the Left Front parties because of their opposition to the Indian-U.S. nuclear technology agreement—Congress pulled together a reconfigured UPA that easily won the April–May 2009 *Lok Sabha* election. Singh thereby became the first prime minister since Nehru to continue in office after completing a full five-year term. Indian voters had expressed concerns about rising commodity prices and inflation, but the government's relative economic success may have been the major factor in their decision to endorse a second term for Singh, an economist who offered stability in the context of the ongoing international recession.

Having quickly risen in the ranks of the world's largest economies, India has collaterally emerged as a key player in international efforts to slow the pace of global warming. Currently ranked fifth among all countries in terms of carbon dioxide emissions, India has rejected efforts to set legally binding targets for emission reductions, but it has introduced plans for massive increases in solar and nuclear energy generation. Shortly before the December 2009 UN Summit on Climate Change in Copenhagen, Denmark, the Singh government also pledged to cut the ratio of pollution to GDP to 20–25% of 2005 levels by 2020. Other efforts to lower emissions are to include introducing mandatory fuel efficiency standards, adopting building codes that mandate greater energy efficiency, and requiring coal-fuel power plants to use cleaner technology.

Another factor in the UPA's 2009 win may have been rejection of the ardent Hindu nationalism represented by some factions of the BJP. In April 2006 Prime Minister Singh had labeled the Maoist insurgency, affecting more than a dozen states, as the biggest threat to national security, but in the year before the election there had been a marked increase in Hindu violence directed against Christians and Muslims, particularly after the murder of Swami Laxmanananda SARASWATI, a leader of the fundamentalist World Council of Hindus (*Vishwa Hindu Parishad*—VHP), in Orissa in August 2008. Although Maoists claimed responsibility, Hindi anger was directed against Christians, prompting violence that Prime Minister Singh labeled a "national disgrace" and that subsequently spread elsewhere, leaving an estimated 16,000 Christians temporarily in refugee centers in just one district of Orissa. At the same time violence in the volatile northeast and elsewhere also escalated, most dramatically in Assam, where, for example, nearly 80 people were killed and some 450 injured on October 30 in a dozen coordinated bombings. The police implicated the extremist *Harkat-ul-Jihad-i-Islami* (HJI) in the bombings, the suggested motive being retaliation for attacks earlier in the month by Bodo tribes people against Muslims, over 80,000 of whom fled to refugee camps. In June 2008 a proposal to transfer 40 hectares of state land in Jammu and Kashmir to a board managing the Hindu shrine of Amarnath led to demands by Muslims that the transfer be halted. During the next two months dozens of people were killed and hundreds injured in the resultant unrest throughout Muslim-dominated Kashmir and Hindu-majority Jammu.

As in the past, Jammu and Kashmir remains the focus of most Islamic militants, who have increasingly been hitting "soft targets," such as the commuter trains and stations in Mumbai that were bombed in a coordinated attack on July 11, 2006, leaving 180 dead and nearly 800 injured. India accused Pakistan's Musharraf government of failing to prevent infiltration by terrorists from such Islamist organizations as *Lashkar-i-Taiba* (LiT), which New Delhi has linked to many other bombings, assaults, and assassinations (see the discussion of Kashmiri separatist and Islamic militant groups in the Political Parties and Groups section).

An audacious attack by 10 Islamic militants on Mumbai on November 26–29, 2009, left 163 people dead and another 300 hurt and jeopardized the India-Pakistan rapprochement. Having landed by inflatable boat at night, the assailants made their way to predetermined targets in a well-planned mission that Prime Minister Singh later described as demonstrating "sophistication and military precision," raising the prospect that "official agencies" of the Pakistani government had been involved in the planning. A previously unknown group calling itself the Deccan Mujaheddin claimed responsibility, but the possibility remained that it was merely a front name for another organization. The attack resulted in the immediate resignation of Home Affairs Minister Shivraj PATIL, the tightening of the Unlawful Activities Prevention Act, and the creation of a National Investigation Agency to pursue terrorists.

All of the assailants, including the lone survivor, Ajmal Amir AMIN (a.k.a. Ajmal KASAB), whose trial began in April 2009, were ultimately shown to have Pakistani addresses, and in February 2009 Islamabad acknowledged that the assault had been at least partially planned there. In July Amin surprised onlookers by changing his plea to guilty, after which he described in detail not only his participation but the training he had received from the LiT. In the same month, Prime Minister Singh and Pakistan's prime minister, Yusuf Gilani, conferred on the sidelines of a Nonaligned Movement meeting in Egypt, at which time they reiterated a common commitment to fighting terrorism.

Looking ahead, there has been widespread speculation as to whether Prime Minister Singh, 78, will serve out a full five-year second term. In addition to noting concerns about Singh's health—he underwent heart bypass surgery in January 2009—many observers believe that at some point Rahul GANDHI, the 39-year-old son of Sonia Gandhi, will ascend to leadership of the INC and then the government. He reportedly turned down a cabinet position in May 2009 in order to focus on party development.

POLITICAL PARTIES AND GROUPS

Although a count during the first general election in 1952 revealed over 100 parties and political groups contesting seats throughout the country, the undivided Indian National Congress dominated the political scene until 1969, when it split into ruling (Gandhi) and opposition factions. The latter, although repudiating the designation, was subsequently styled the Indian National Congress–Organization, or Congress (O), by the Election Commission. The Gandhi Congress easily won the election of 1972. Following the declaration of emergency in June 1975, however, a national *Janata* (People's) Front, comprising Congress (O), the Indian People's Party (*Bharatiya Lok Dal*), the Socialist Party, the Indian People's Union (*Bharatiya Jana Sangh*), and the Congress for Democracy, formed to oppose the Gandhi Congress. In May 1976 the widely respected Jaya Prakash Narayanan announced that the front would be converted into a unified political party in order to present a "democratic national alternative" to Congress rule. In March 1977 the resultant *Janata* Party swept to victory. The Gandhi Congress became increasingly divided after its defeat, and in January 1978 those remaining loyal to Mrs. Gandhi organized separately as the Indian National Congress–Indira (INC-I), or the Congress (I).

Janata split in July 1979, and in 1980 the Congress (I) secured a near two-thirds majority in the lower house. In the wake of Indira Gandhi's assassination, Congress (I) swept nearly 80 percent of contested seats in the *Lok Sabha* election of December 1984. Since 1989, however, broad coalitions have been required to form governments.

The *Janata Dal* (People's Party) formed the core of a seven-party centrist National Front—NF (*Rashtriya Morcha*) alliance that failed to outpoll Congress (I) in November 1989 but was able to form a government with the external support of the two main Communist parties—the Communist Party of India (CPI) and the CPI-Marxist (CPI-M)—and the fundamentalist *Bharatiya Janata* Party (BJP). The BJP's withdrawal of support a year later and a split in *Janata Dal* precipitated the government's fall. Although the NF was broadened to include the Communist and other left-wing parties for the June 1991 election, becoming the NF/Leftist Front (NF/LF), Congress (I) and its allies returned to power.

The April–May 1996 election yielded a major advance for the BJP, but its inability to attract other support enabled an even larger, 14-party NF/LF, subsequently renamed the United Front (UF), to form a minority government under H. D. Deve Gowda of the *Janata Dal.* The ministerial lineup included representatives of nine parties, including *Janata Dal,* Dravidian Progressive Federation (DMK), *Samajwadi* Party (SP), CPI, Assam People's Council (AGP), and the *Telugu Desam* Party (TDP).

While the members of the UF acted in concert in support of its prime ministers, the front was not a permanent political organization with established structures. Dependent on the support of the nonmember Congress, the UF was also caught in its own internal contradictions, and in 1997 the UF's position became untenable. In the election of March 1998 the coalition fell from 177 seats to 97.

The government formed after the 1998 elections was based around the BJP but also included a dozen other parties, among them several mutually antagonistic groups from the southern state of Tamil Nadu. Although not as unwieldy as the preceding UF coalition, the Vajpayee government proved equally susceptible to fracturing and in April 1999 lost a confidence motion by a single vote following the withdrawal of the All India Dravidian Progressive Federation (AIADMK). On May 16 the BJP and a dozen of its allies announced formation of a National Democratic Alliance (NDA) that by the time of the September–October *Lok Sabha* election victory numbered some 24 mostly regional organizations.

Although many of the smaller NDA parties had left the fold since the 1999 balloting, the NDA entered the 2004 election campaign as the odds-on favorite. Most of the BJP's major allies in 1999, including *Shiv Sena* (SS), the *Biju Janata Dal* (BJD), the SAD, and the *Janata Dal* (United), remained in place, and two state governing parties, the TDP of Andhra Pradesh and the AIADMK of Tamil Nadu, had joined. Despite dire predictions of record losses, the Congress had cemented alliances with the main Tamil Nadu opposition parties, including former NDA member DMK; had repaired relations with the leaders of the Nationalist Congress Party (NCP); and had gained the support of a new Andhra Pradesh formation, the *Telangana Rashtra Samithi* (TRS). Congress and its allies prevailed, and with external support from the four-party Left Front alliance and others, they succeeded in forming a minority government.

In April 2006 the SP and the TDP announced their intention to form a new secular "Third Force" of regional parties as a "national alternative" to both UPA/Congress and the NDA/BJP. Among the other parties considered potential Third Force participants were the AIADMK, the AGP of Assam, and the Indian National *Lok Dal* (INLD) of Haryana. On June 6, 2007, those five parties were joined by the *Marumalarchi Dravida Munnetra Kazhagam* (MDMK) of Tamil Nadu, the Jharkhand *Vikas Morcha* (JVM), and a faction of the Kerala Congress (KC) in announcing formation of the grouping, which was soon named the United National Progressive Alliance (UNPA). The ideologically diverse UNPA failed to coalesce into an effective force, however, and numerous realignments occurred in the political landscape in preparation for the next general election.

For the 2009 *Lok Sabha* election the country's 7 "national" parties—the *Bahujan Samaj* Party (BSP), BJP, CPI, CPI-M, INC, NCP, and *Rashtriya Janata Dal* (RJD)—38 "state" parties, and a number of India's 1,000 additional registered parties offered candidates. The main contestants were, once again, the UPA and NDA (both somewhat reconfigured), this time joined by two additional alliances. The Third Front, which was launched in March 2009 and included several of the erstwhile UNPA parties, was led by the four parties of the Left Front and the BSP, while the three-party Fourth Front included the SP and the RJD. Only the UPA parties fared better than they had in 2004, gaining 79 seats, while the NDA parties collectively lost 17; the Third Front parties, 30; and the Fourth Front parties, 37.

In addition to India's myriad political parties, many unregistered or proscribed separatist or militant groups exist. The principal ones are based in Kashmir or the northeast states. The 2004 Unlawful Activities (Prevention) Amendment Ordinance banned 32 groups, including the Maoist Communist Center (MCC), the Jammu and Kashmir Liberation Front (JKLF), the *Hizb-ul-Mujaheddin,* the *Lashkar-i-Taiba,* and many of those discussed under the subhead Principal North and Northeast Militant Organizations.

United Progressive Alliance (UPA):

Indian National Congress (INC). Founded in 1885 and led from 1966 to 1977 by Indira Gandhi, the INC experienced the withdrawal in 1969 of an anti-Gandhi conservative faction that became India's first recognized opposition party, the Indian National Congress–Organization (Congress-O), prior to joining *Janata.* The INC was further weakened by the defection or expulsion of numerous leaders both before and after the 1977 election, at which the party suffered its first defeat. In January 1978 Gandhi's supporters designated the former prime minister as the president of a new national opposition party, the Indian National Congress–Indira (INC-I), or Congress (I). Building from a political base in the traditionally pro-Gandhi south, Congress (I) quickly displaced the rump INC as the principal opposition force. In July 1981 the Election Commission ruled that the Congress (I) was the "real" Congress in that the majority of INC leaders and legislative officeholders at the time of the 1978 division had since become members of Indira Gandhi's party. By late 1982 the anti-Gandhi Congress had, for all practical purposes, disintegrated.

Under the leadership of Indira Gandhi's son Rajiv, Congress (I) easily won the December 1984 *Lok Sabha* election, but in November 1989 its representation plummeted, forcing it into opposition. Following the 1991 poll, however, Congress (I) and its allies held sufficient seats to form a minority government under the premiership of P. V. Narasimha Rao, successor to the assassinated Rajiv.

The Rao government's pursuit of rapid economic liberalization and deregulation, coupled with corruption disclosures and other scandals, contributed to a defeat in the 1996 election. After helping bring about the speedy collapse of the BJP government, the Congress opted to give external support to a minority United Front administration. Rao resigned as party chief in September 1996 and was replaced by the Congress treasurer, Sitaram Kesri—the party's first non-Brahmin leader.

The apparent ability of the late Rajiv Gandhi's Italian-born widow, Sonia Gandhi, to bring support back to the ailing party led to her involvement in the legislative campaign in January 1998. Despite winning only 141 seats, the party emerged as the largest opposition formation. Party President Kesri announced his resignation on March 9, after which Sonia Gandhi was chosen as his replacement and as the party's parliamentary leader, despite holding no elective office.

Meanwhile, Congress had begun welcoming the return of many former dissidents who had formed splinter parties because of opposition to the policies of Mrs. Gandhi or Rao. Among these leaders were Sharad Pawar of the Indian National Congress (Socialist), Madhavrao SCINDIA of the *Madhya Pradesh Vikas* Party (MPVP), Arjun Singh of the All India Indira Congress (AIIC), and Sis Ram OLA of the All India Indira Congress (Secular). With most of the splinter parties no longer functioning, Congress was increasingly being referenced without the appended "I."

In May 1999 Gandhi resigned as INC president when several prominent party leaders, principally Sharad Pawar, proposed a constitutional amendment that would restrict the national presidency, vice presidency, and prime ministership to native-born Indians. Three days later Pawar and two others were expelled by the party, and on May 24 Gandhi withdrew her resignation. Pawar went on to cofound the Nationalist Congress Party (NCP, below), describing the INC leadership as a "virtual cult phenomenon."

At the September–October 1999 *Lok Sabha* election the Congress turned in its worst performance in nearly half a century, winning only 114 seats despite a slight increase in its vote share. On October 17 Gandhi, who had been elected to the lower house in her first contest, was chosen leader of the opposition.

Prior to the 2004 election the Congress picked up additional support through mergers with a number of parties, most prominently the *Tamil Maanila* Congress (TMC) of the late G. K. MOOPANAR, who had left the Congress in April 1996 in opposition to reactivation of an alliance with the Tamil AIADMK (below). Another 1996 splinter, the *Haryana Vikas* Party (HVP), led by former Haryana chief minister Bansi LAL and a son, Surender SINGH, also reunited with the Congress shortly before the election. The *Himachal Vikas* Congress (HVC) of Sukh RAM did likewise. In August 2003 the main body of the *Sikkim Sangram Parishad* (SSP, below), led by former Sikkim chief minister Nar Bahadur BHANDARI, also merged with Congress.

Following its unexpected *Lok Sabha* victory in the election of April–May 2004, when it won 145 seats, Congress elected Sonia Gandhi as its parliamentary leader, paving the way for her designation as prime minister. The BJP and other Hindu parties had already announced, however, their strong objection because of her foreign birth. Despite wide support from most non-NDA parties, on May 18 she withdrew from consideration, asserting that she had never sought to be prime minister. It was also widely believed that her children, having seen their grandmother and father assassinated while in office, had urged her to step aside. In her stead Gandhi put forward Manmohan Singh, a Sikh and respected economist, who thus became the first member of a minority to serve as prime minister.

In March 2006 Gandhi resigned her seat in the *Lok Sabha* to deflect criticism that she had violated a technical provision of a law prohibiting elected politicians from holding salaried positions. Prior to reclaiming her seat in a May by-election, she resigned from her positions in several foundations and other organizations, including as unsalaried chair of the extraconstitutional National Advisory Council, which she had established in May 2004 to direct government policy.

The April–May 2009 general election saw the INC increase its *Lok Sabha* plurality to 206 seats. Prime Minister Singh, who had undergone heart bypass surgery earlier in the year, began a second term on May 22. Many observers believe that before the next general election leadership of the party will pass from Sonia Gandhi to a son, Rahul Gandhi, currently a general secretary.

As of July 2009 the Congress was the governing party in just under half of the states. In September Y.S. Rajashekhar REDDY, the chief minister of Andhra Pradesh, died in a helicopter accident.

Leaders: Sonia GANDHI (President of the Party), Dr. Manmohan SINGH (Prime Minister), A.K. ANTONY (Minister of Defense), Motilal VORA (Treasurer), Arjun SINGH, Ahmed PATEL (Political Secretary), Rahul GANDHI (General Secretary).

All India Trinamul Congress (AITC). The AITC, which is often referenced simply as the **Trinamul Congress,** emerged in September 1997 out of the bitter struggle to wrest control of West Bengal from the CPI-M and its state leader, Jyoti Basu. Formed by Mamata Banerjee, the party won seven seats in the 1998 national election and eight in 1999 as part of the NDA.

In March 2001 Banerjee resigned as minister of railways (for the second time in six months) and pulled her party from the NDA. The timing reflected her desire to ally with Congress and seek the chief ministership of West Bengal. However, the Left Front, led by the CPI-M, easily won the June election, after which Banerjee briefly resigned as AITC leader. In August, having severed its ties to Congress, the party again joined the NDA.

In March 2004 a faction of the Nationalist Congress Party (NCP, below) under Purno Sangma merged with the AITC to form the Nationalist Trinamul Congress (NTC), although the AITC designation was to be retained until after the April–May general election. The party suffered a major setback, however, winning only 2 seats—2 short of the 4 required for registration, under its new name, as a national party. Prior to a February 2006 by-election, Sangma returned to the NCP. Meanwhile, in August 2005 Banerjee distanced her party from the NDA in anticipation of running independently in the April–May 2006 West Bengal assembly election, at which the AITC managed to hold only 30 of the 60 seats it had previously claimed. Despite reaching an agreement with Congress for September 2006 *Lok Sabha* by-elections, the AITC remained aligned with the NDA at the national level.

On December 30, 2006, at the urging of her followers, Banerjee ended a 25-day hunger strike she began as a protest against the forced acquisition of farmland for an automobile factory. Shortly before the 2009 *Lok Sabha* election Banerjee and INC leaders reached a seat-sharing arrangement that brought the AITC into the UPA and resulted in its winning 19 seats, second only to the INC itself among the UPA parties. Banerjee, once again, was then offered the post of railways minister in the new cabinet.

Leaders: Kumari Mamata BANERJEE (Party Leader and Minister of Railways), Pankaj BANERJEE (Chair).

Dravidian Progressive Federation (*Dravida Munnetra Kazhagam*—DMK). The DMK, which dates back to the early years of Indian independence, is an anti-Brahmin regional party dedicated to the promotion of Tamil interests and more autonomy for the states. A major split in 1972 led to formation of the AIADMK (below), which outpaced the DMK in most subsequent Tamil Nadu elections. However, in an unprecedented swing occasioned in part by the alleged corruption of the AIADMK state administration, the DMK in 1996 not only won 17 *Lok Sabha* seats but also returned to power with a landslide majority in the concurrent state election. Allegations related to the DMK's possible indirect involvement in the assassination of Rajiv Gandhi split the informal coalition holding the United Front in power and brought about the elections of 1998, at which the party won only 6 seats.

In preparation for the 1999 *Lok Sabha* election, in mid-May the DMK joined several other Tamil Nadu parties, including the PMK and MDMK (see below), as participants in the NDA. Having carried 12 seats, the DMK agreed to join the Vajpayee cabinet.

In the May 2001 state election the DMK was handily defeated by its nemesis, the AIADMK, and at the end of June party leader M. Karunanidhi was arrested on corruption charges. Mass demonstrations and a governmental crisis followed, and intervention by federal authorities soon led to his release.

The DMK pulled out of the NDA government in December 2003 and then allied itself with Congress. It won 16 *Lok Sabha* seats in the 2004 union election and was awarded several portfolios in the resultant Singh cabinet. As in past elections, for the May 2006 Tamil Nadu assembly balloting the DMK led a multiparty Democratic Progressive Alliance that included Congress as well as the PMK, IUML, CPI-M, and CPI (see below). Reversing its 2001 defeat, the alliance captured 163 of 234 seats in ousting the AIADMK.

In May 2007 the DMK forced its Dayanidhi MARAN to resign from the union cabinet following a disagreement within the party leadership that persisted into 2008. Observers saw the matter as largely a family dispute, since Maran, Karunanidhi, and most of the other leaders are closely related. In the 2009 general election the DMK gained 2 *Lok Sabha* seats, for 18, but initially rejected joining the new Singh government because of dissatisfaction with the cabinet and subcabinet posts it had been offered. In late May, however, the dispute was resolved and the DMK joined the government.

Leaders: Dr. Kalaignar Muthuvel KARUNANIDHI (Chief Minister of Tamil Nadu and President of the Party), M.K. AZHAGIRI, Andimutha RAJA (Minister of Communications and Information Technology).

Nationalist Congress Party (NCP). Formation of the NCP was announced in May 1999 by three Congress members who had been expelled from the parent party for proposing, in a direct affront to Sonia Gandhi, a constitutional amendment requiring that only "natural-born" Indian citizens be permitted to serve as national president, vice president, or prime minister. At its formal launch in June the NCP absorbed what remained of the Indian National Congress (Socialist)—the INC-S or Congress (S)—which traced its origin to the anti-Gandhi Congress of 1977–1978. (The NCP president had served as leader of the INC-S from 1981 until his return to the Congress in 1986.)

The new party won eight seats in the 1999 *Lok Sabha* election. Despite its differences with the parent party, in Maharashtra State the NCP joined the INC and a number of independents in forming a state government under a Democratic Front. In May 2002 the Kerala branch of the NCP reestablished the Congress (S) under Ramachandran KADANNAPPALLY.

The NCP entered the 2004 election campaign allied with Congress and won nine seats. In March a faction led by Purno Sangma had broken away, largely because of opposition to the foreign-born Sonia Gandhi as a prospective prime minister, and joined the AITC (above). Sangma himself returned to the NCP in December 2005. Another faction, based in Chhattisgarh and led by V. C. SHUKLA, also broke away in 2004 and formed the short-lived *Rashtriya Janatantrik Dal*, which then merged with the BJP. In 2006 the NCP absorbed the Kerala-based Democratic Indira Congress–Karunakaran (DIC-K), which had been established in May 2005 by former Congress leader and Kerala chief minister K. KARUNAKARAN and his son, K. MURALEEDHARAN.

In March 2008 Sangma was a prime mover in the Meghalaya Progressive Alliance, a coalition that won sufficient support in the Meghalaya State election to unseat a Congress-led government. In May 2009, however, a Congress-led Meghalaya United Alliance won control of the government after two months of presidential rule. At the union level, the NCP remains within the UPA.

Leaders: Sharad PAWAR (President of the Party and Minister of Consumer Affairs, Food, and Public Distribution); Tariq ANWAR, Purno SANGMA, and Devi Prasad TRIPATHI (General Secretaries).

Jammu and Kashmir National Conference (JKNC). The dominant party in Jammu and Kashmir following independence, the JKNC continued to be led by Sheikh Mohammed ABDULLAH, who was primarily responsible for the 1947 decision to join India, until his death in 1982. From then until the late 1990s, the JKNC, led by the sheikh's son, Farooq Abdullah, was typically allied with Congress, which backed the JKNC in a state election in 1996 (the first since 1987), assisting the party to a decisive overall majority and enabling Farooq Abdullah to resume the post of chief minister. The JKNC then won three seats in the 1998 *Lok Sabha* balloting as a United Front party. In the 1999 election the party picked up an additional seat, after which it joined the NDA government.

In June 2002 Farooq Abdullah turned over the presidency of the party to his son, Omar. In the following September–October state election the JKNC finished with a plurality of seats but lost control of the government to a coalition of the Congress and the Jammu and Kashmir People's Democratic Party (PDP). In July 2003 the JKNC left the NDA, and in the *Lok Sabha* election of 2004 it won two seats while remaining outside both the UPA and the NDA.

The state election of November–December 2008 concluded with the JKNC having won a leading 28 seats, and at the end of December it reestablished ties to the Congress and ousted the PDP from the government. In the 2009 general election it ran within the UPA, winning three seats and joining the Singh government.

Leaders: Omar ABDULLAH (Chief Minister of Jammu and Kashmir and President of the Party), Farooq ABDULLAH (Minister of New and Renewable Energy).

Jharkhand Mukti Morcha (JMM). The JMM (Jharkhand Liberation Front) was organized in 1980 to represent the tribal people of Bihar and Orissa. It was allied with the National Front/Leftist Front in the 1991 national election, winning six *Lok Sabha* seats, but its main faction remained outside the alliance for the 1996 poll, at which its representation was reduced to two members. As an ally of Congress in 1998, the party lost its remaining lower house seats.

In 1999 a factional dispute between Shibu Soren and Suraj MANDAL threatened to split the party, which failed again in its bid for lower house seats. The Soren wing of the party supported Prime Minister Vajpayee's government but broke with the NDA when the alliance backed a BJP candidate for chief minister of the new state of Jharkhand in November 2000. (Mandal, having been expelled from the JMM, went on to form the *Jharkhand Vikas Dal,* which merged with the JD[U] after the 2004 general election.)

In March 2004 the JMM concluded a pact with the Congress, and it then won five *Lok Sabha* seats, after which Soren joined the Singh cabinet. He was forced to resign as minister of coal and mines in late July, however, following issuance of an arrest warrant related to his alleged involvement in a 1975 riot that cost ten lives. He returned to the cabinet in November, resigned in March 2005 in an unsuccessful effort to become chief minister of Jharkhand, again rejoined the Singh cabinet in January 2006, and then resigned once more in November 2006, following his conviction for murdering his secretary. He received a life sentence and was temporarily replaced as party president by his wife, but his conviction was overturned in August 2007.

In August 2008, following the JMM's decision to withdraw its support for the state government, Soren became chief minister of Jharkhand. In January 2009, however, Soren was forced to resign as chief minister of Jharkhand after losing a state by-election. With no party or coalition able to command a majority in the state legislature, president's rule was imposed and then extended for an additional six months in July. In May 2009 Soren was one of two JMM members elected to the *Lok Sabha.* The other, Kameshwar BAITHA, a former Maoist commander, has been under detention since 2005 in Bihar State.

Leaders: Shibu SOREN (President), Rupi SOREN, Sudhir MAHATO (General Secretary).

Indian Union Muslim League (IUML). The IUML (regularly also referenced simply as the Muslim League—ML) is a remnant of the pre-partition Muslim League led by Mohammad Ali JINNAH. It opposes both secularism and Hindu nationalism. It won two lower house seats in 1996, 1998, and 1999, when its successful candidates entered the *Lok Sabha* under the banner of the **Muslim League Kerala State Committee** (MLKSC). In 2004 its general secretary, E. Ahamed, the only winning candidate on the MLKSC list, was named a minister of state in the Ministry of External Affairs. At the time, the IUML was allied with Congress in Kerala's United Democratic Front government, but the coalition lost the 2006 state election. In November 2005 K. T. JALEEL and other dissidents within the IUML organized the CH Secular Forum, which called for closer ties to Left Front parties.

The death of the longtime national president, G.M. BANATWALA, was followed in September 2008 by the election of E. Ahamed as his successor. In the 2009 general election the IUML won two seats.

Leaders: E. AHAMED (Minister of State for Railways and President of the Party), Panakkad Mohammed Ali Shihab THANGAL (Kerala State President), P. K. KUNHALIKUTTY (Kerala General Secretary).

All India Majlis-e-Ittehadul Muslimeen (AIMIM). Based in Hyderabad and aiming to represent India's Muslims, the AIMIM (All India Muslim Federal Assembly) won a *Lok Sabha* seat in a 1994 by-election and expanded to two seats in the 1996 general election. It retained one seat in 1998, 1999, 2004, and 2009.

Longtime leader Sultan Salahuddin OWAISI died in September 2008 and was succeeded as president by a son.

Leaders: Asaduddin OWAISI (President), Akbaruddin OWAISI.

Kerala Congress (KC). Long subject to internal rifts, the KC remains divided into several factions. In the 1999 election the **Kerala Congress (Mani)** and the **Kerala Congress (Joseph),** the latter led by P. J. Joseph, each won one *Lok Sabha* seat. The KC (Joseph) won the party's sole seat in 2004. It later picked up a second seat by absorbing the Indian Federal Democratic Party (IFDP), led by P. C. Thomas, which had originated in 2001 as a loose alliance of *Lok Sabha* independents. In November 2006 a Kerala court threw out Thomas's victory because of a campaign violation, but the Supreme Court stayed the disqualification. Another faction, the **Kerala Congress (Jacob),** merged into the Democratic Indira Congress–Karunakaran (see the NCP, above) in 2005 but was revived following the 2006 Kerala State election. In June 2007 the KC faction under P. C. Thomas joined in forming that year's short-lived UNPA.

In 2009 the only faction to win a *Lok Sabha* seat was the KC (Mani).

Kerala Congress (Mani) Leaders: C.F. THOMAS (Chair), K.M. MANI, Jose K. MANI (Member of the *Lok Sabha*).

Kerala Congress (Joseph) Leaders: P.J. JOSEPH, P.C. THOMAS.

Kerala Congress (Balakrishna Pillai) Leader: R. Balakrishna PILLAI.

Kerala Congress (Jacob) Leader: T.M. JACOB.

Kerala Congress (Secular) Leader: P.C. GEORGE.

Viduthalai Chiruthaigal Katchi (VCK). The VCK (Liberation Panthers Party, *Dalit* Panthers Party) is a small party based in Tamil Nadu. It won two state assembly seats in 2006 and currently participates with the DMK and Congress in the Tamil Nadu government. The VCK won one *Lok Sabha* seat in 2009.

Leader: THIRUMAVALAVAN.

Republican Party of India (RPI). Founded in 1956 by Bhimrao Ramji AMBEDKAR, the Maharashtra-based RPI is dedicated to carrying out the equality clauses of the Indian constitution for its largest constituency, the *Dalits* (from the Hindu for "Oppressed"), formerly called "Untouchables" or *Harijans.* The party's intense factionalism has not helped its cause, although in the 1998 elections three factional leaders were among the four RPI candidates to win *Lok Sabha* seats. With part of the party linked to the Congress and another part favoring the new NCP, all four seats were lost in 1999.

In 2004, running as an ally of Congress, the Ramdas Athawale faction, RPI(A), won one seat in the lower house but was not offered a ministerial portfolio in the Singh cabinet, an "injustice" that led Athawale to question his faction's future loyalty to Congress at the state level. In June 2006 faction leader R. S. GAVAI was named governor of Bihar, where he served for two years before becoming governor of Kerala.

In 2009 the RPI(A) failed to retain its *Lok Sabha* seat.

Leaders: Prakash AMBEDKAR, Ramdas ATHAWALE, Rajendra GAVAI, Jogentra KAWADE, T. M. KAMBLE.

National Democratic Alliance (NDA):

Bharatiya Janata Party (BJP). The BJP (Indian People's Party) was formed in April 1980 by the bulk of *Janata*'s *Jana Sangh* group, which opposed efforts by the *Janata* leadership to ban party officeholders from participation in the activities of the National Volunteer Corps (*Rashtriya Swayamsevak Sangh*—RSS), a secretive paramilitary Hindu communal group that is generally regarded as the BJP's parent organization. By 1982 the BJP was widely viewed as the best-organized non-Communist opposition party.

The BJP experienced a dramatic advance in 1989, winning 88 *Lok Sabha* seats. It supported the National Front government of V. P. Singh until October 1990, when BJP leader L. K. Advani was detained in connection with the Ayodhya temple dispute. The party's legislative representation rose to 119 in 1991 as the leading component of an electoral alliance that included *Shiv Sena* (below). Its anti-Muslim populism then helped it emerge from the April–May 1996 *Lok Sabha* election as the plurality party, with 161 seats, after which it formed a minority government under Atal Bihari Vajpayee. The administration resigned after 13 days, however, rather than face defeat in a confidence vote.

In 1997 the party tried to expand its support through moderating its Hindu nationalist (*Hindutva*) image and forging ties to state and regional parties. In the 1998 election it again emerged as the plurality party, winning 181 seats, with Vajpayee then cobbling together a governing coalition. In 1999 it won 182 seats, and Vajpayee succeeded in forming his third government.

Between then and 2004 the BJP absorbed several smaller parties, including the Manipur State Congress Party (MSCP), the Tamil Nadu–based M. G. R. Dravidian Progressive Federation (*M. G. R. Anna Dravida Munnetra Kazhagam*—MGR ADMK, named after AIADMK founder M. G. Ramachandran), a 1997 offshoot of the AIADMK; and the Chhattisgarh-based *Rashtriya Janatantrik Dal* of former NCP leader V. C. Shukla.

Confounding expectations, the BJP-led NDA fell to Congress and its allies in the 2004 *Lok Sabha* elections, with the BJP winning only 22 percent of the vote and 137 seats. Shortly after the election, L. K. Advani was named leader of the opposition, while former prime minister Vajpayee was awarded the new position of parliamentary party chair. The following October, Advani also took over as BJP president, after the resignation of Venkaiah NAIDU. In May–June 2005 Advani traveled to Pakistan, where he made conciliatory remarks that raised the ire of the party's militant elements. He was further weakened in July when charges of incitement were reinstated against him and seven others in connection with the 1990 Ayodhya mosque incident. (In March 2007 the Supreme Court rejected a petition that could have further delayed the case or led to its dismissal.) Apparently pressured by the RSS and the fundamentalist World Council of Hindus (*Vishwa Hindu Parishad*—VHP), Advani stepped down as party president but remained leader of the opposition.

Late in 2005 several other significant developments occurred, beginning with the expulsion of former secretary general Uma BHARATI, a former chief minister of Madhya Pradesh and a leader of hard-line fundamentalists within the party, for "indiscipline and anti-party activities." Shortly thereafter, she formed a new party, the **Bharatiya Janshakti Party.** Near the end of December RSS figure Sanjay JOSHI resigned as party secretary general for organization after allegations of sexual misconduct surfaced. After being exonerated, Joshi returned to his post in April 2006, but he was again replaced as part of a January 2007 reorganization.

The BJP fell back to 116 seats in the April–May 2009 *Lok Sabha* election., which the *Bharatiya Janshakti* Party did not contest. As of November 2009 BJP chief ministers headed the state governments in Chhattisgarh, Gujarat, Himachal Pradesh, Karnataka, Madhya Pradesh, and Uttarakhand.

Moderate party leader Jaswant SINGH, a key cabinet minister from 1998 to 2004, was expelled by the BJP in August 2009 because of its objections to a recently published book in which he deviated from the party's interpretation of events surrounding the 1947 partition.

Leaders: Rajnath SINGH (President), Lal Krishna ADVANI (Leader of the Opposition), Atal Bihari VAJPAYEE (Former Prime Minister), Arun JAITLEY (Leader in the *Rajya Sabha*), Shivraj Singh CHAUHAN (Chief Minister of Madhya Pradesh), Narendra MODI (Chief Minister of Gujarat), Ananth KUMAR (General Secretary).

Janata Dal (United)—JD(U). *Janata Dal* was created by the merger in 1988 of the *Janata* (People's) grouping, led by Subramanian Swamy; *Lok Dal* (confusingly also meaning "People's Party"); and *Jan Morcha* (People's Front), led by Vishwanath Pratap Singh. *Janata* had been established as a formal merger of several diverse parties following their collective victory in the 1977 elections; *Lok Dal* had been founded in 1979 by a number of dissident *Janata* factions; and *Jan Morcha* had been launched in 1987 by Congress (I) dissidents.

Janata Dal obtained 141 of the 144 seats won by NF candidates in 1989 but only 55 of the 128 NF/LF seats obtained in 1991. The latter election was precipitated by a split in *Janata Dal* that led to the creation of what became the *Samajwadi* Party (below). A further split in 1994 eventually led to formation of the BJP-allied *Samata* Party. The rump *Janata Dal* led the United Front (UF) to a plurality in the 1996 general elections, although its seat tally fell to 45. The party was further reduced by corruption charges against its president, Lalu Prasad Yadav, chief minister of Bihar, whose rebel *Rashtriya Janata Dal* (RJD) substantially eroded the *Janata Dal*'s role in Parliament and in the UF government. In the election of 1998 the party captured only 6 seats.

The party further splintered because of differences between Sharad Yadav and former prime minister H. D. Deve Gowda. With both factions claiming to be the "real *Janata,*" on August 8, 1999, the Election Commission recognized the competing factions as separate entities, with the Deve Gowda branch being called the *Janata Dal* (Secular) and the Yadav branch, *Janata Dal* (United). At the same time, it approved joint use of the arrow symbol by the JD(U), the *Samata* Party, and Ramakrishna HEGDE's *Lok Shakti* (LS), the three having been negotiating a common list for the upcoming election. A week later the JD(U), as expected, joined the NDA, and in the subsequent election the JD(U) list won 21 seats in the *Lok Sabha.*

The *Samata* (Equality) Party had resulted from the *Janata Dal* split in early 1994 that yielded a *Janata Dal* (G); led by George FERNANDES, the new party adopted the *Samata* designation late in the year. Remaining outside the center-left alliance that became the United Front, it won 6 *Lok Sabha* seats in the 1996 balloting, all in the state of Bihar. In 1998 its 12 seats were important to the formation of the BJP-led coalition government.

An anticipated formal merger of the JD(U), the LS, and the *Samata* Party failed to materialize in January 2000 when the *Samata* Party, which had wanted Yadav to step down in favor of Fernandes, rejected unification. The status of the LS and the *Samata* Party was compromised, however, by a decision of the Election Commission that derecognized officeholders of both who had been elected on the JD(U) list. In September 2000 the LS itself was derecognized, and in November former LS leader Ram Vilas Paswan formed the *Lok Janshakti* Party (LJP, below). In March 2001 *Samata* President Jaya JAITLEY, who had replaced Fernandes following the earlier Election Commission ruling, resigned after being videotaped accepting a bribe in a sting operation. Fernandes, although not implicated, resigned as defense minister, but he returned to the post in October.

In December 2003 the long-anticipated merger of the *Samata* Party and the JD(U) was achieved, with Fernandes then becoming JD(U) president. The merger met with objections from a minority of both parties, including former JD(U) parliamentary leader Devendra Prasad YADAV, who instigated formation of a JD(U-Democratic) faction in the *Lok Sabha.* He as well as a number of other dissenters ultimately joined the RJD before the 2004 lower house election, at which the JD(U) won only eight seats.

In the Bihar State elections in October–November 2005 the JD(U) finished first and formed an NDA government with the second-place BJP. In April 2006 Sharad Yadav was elected president of the party over the ailing George Fernandes, who had refused to step aside. In January

2007 Jaya Jaitley and Bhahmanand MANDAL, who had opposed the merger, revived the **Samata Party.** In August, however, a faction led by N. K. SINGH and Shiv KUMAR tried to oust Mandal. The Election Commission declined to recognize either faction.

In 2009 the JD(U) was the only NDA party to show a significant improvement over its 2004 results, gaining 12 *Lok Sabha* seats, for total of 20. George Fernandes, 79, having been denied a party nomination, ran independently but failed to win a seat.

Leaders: Sharad YADAV (President), Nitish KUMAR (Chief Minister of Bihar).

Shiv Sena (SS). Since its formation in 1966 the Maharashtra-based *Shiv Sena* (Army of Shivaji, referencing a 17th-century Hindu king who repulsed the armies of the Muslim Moghul empire) has articulated Hindu nationalism even more forcefully than has the BJP. Led by Bal Thackeray, a former newspaper cartoonist turned populist orator, the movement was prominent in the anti-Muslim violence that led to the destruction of the Ayodhya mosque in December 1992. It won 15 *Lok Sabha* seats in the April–May 1996 election and was represented in the resultant very short-lived government led by the BJP. Closely linked to the BJP, the SS brought its remaining 6 seats into the BJP-led government following the 1998 election. In the 1999 *Lok Sabha* balloting the party returned to its earlier strength, winning 15 seats even though Thackeray had been disenfranchised for six years in July 1999 because of a conviction for inciting communal hatred in a 1987 speech. In the 2004 general election it retained 12 seats.

In early 2003 a dispute between Bal Thackeray's youngest son, Uddhav, and a nephew, Raj THACKERAY, over who would accede to the party leadership concluded with Uddhav's elevation. In December 2005 Raj resigned from the party, and in March 2006 he formed the **Maharashtra Navnirman Sena**—MNS (Maharashtra Reconstruction Army), to which he hoped to attract SS dissidents. In October 2008 he was charged with inciting violence against migrant workers. Earlier in 2008, a former northern party leader, Jai Bhagwan GOYAL, announced that he was forming the **Rashtrawadi Sena** in response to negative comments by Uddhav about northerners living in Maharashtra.

The SS attracted considerable criticism in June 2008 when an editorial in the party newspaper, *Saamana,* called for Hindus to adopt the tactics of Islamist suicide bombers. In the 2009 general election the SS won 11 seats. (The MNS ran 12 candidates without success.)

Leaders: Balashaheb (Bal) THACKERAY, Uddhav THACKERAY (Executive President), Anant GHEETE (Leader in the *Lok Sabha*)

Rashtriya Lok Dal (RLD). The current RLD was established by the September 1998 merger of the preexisting RLD and the *Bharatiya Kisan Kamgar Party* (BKKP). The BKKP had been launched in opposition to the BJP in September 1996 by *Lok Sabha* member Ajit Singh, a former Congress (I) agriculture minister and son of Charan Singh, with the support of Mahendra Singh TIKAIT, a peasant leader in Uttar Pradesh. In the 1999 national election the RLD was allied with the Congress and won two seats. In July 2001 it joined the NDA, although Ajit Singh resigned from the cabinet in May 2003. In the 2004 general election the RLD won three seats. Allied with the *Samajwadi* Party, it added a *Rajya Sabha* seat in 2006.

In the 2009 general election the RLD picked up two *Lok Sabha* seats, for a total of five.

Leader: Ajit SINGH (President).

Shiromani Akali Dal (SAD). Although the Sikh *Shiromani Akali Dal* (Akali Religious Party) contests elections nationally, its influence is confined primarily to Punjab, where it campaigns against excessive federal influence in Sikh affairs. Prior to the June 1984 storming of Amritsar's Golden Temple, leadership of the Sikh agitation had effectively passed from the *Akali Dal* to the more extremist followers of Jarnail Singh Bhindranwale. In July 1985, a year after Bhindranwale's death, the moderate *Akali Dal* leader, Harchand Singh Longowal, concluded a peace agreement with Prime Minister Rajiv Gandhi, but Longowal was assassinated in August.

In 1986 a number of *Akali Dal* leaders, including Parkash Singh Badal, a former chief minister, withdrew to form a separate party, but in 1987 the party reunited under Simranjit Singh Mann, a former police official. Factionalism nevertheless persisted. In 1994–1995 the Sikh religious leadership, led by Manjit SINGH, attempted to unify the party, with half a dozen of the more distinctly nonsecular factions—the most notable exception being the Badal group—adopting an "Amritsar declaration" and briefly appending "Amritsar" to their collective identity. However, Mann, asserting that other party leaders were not abiding by the declaration, subsequently formed a separate party (see SAD [Mann], below).

In 1998–1999 a serious internal feud saw a faction led by Gurcharan Singh TOHRA criticizing the BJP-led central government and President Badal's Punjab administration. In mid-1999 Tohra launched the All India Shiromani Akali Dal (AISAD), which may have contributed to the SAD's losing six of its eight *Lok Sabha* seats in the 1999 election. Three years later, it lost the state poll. Tohra and Badal reconciled in 2003, but Tohra died in March 2004. Less than a month later Jaswant Singh MANN organized a new anti-Badal **All India Shiromani Akali Dal**, one of several minor SAD formations.

At the 2004 general election the SAD won eight seats as a component of the NDA. Shortly afterward a dissident SAD leader, Prem Singh CHANDUMAJRA, announced formation of another anti-Badal offshoot, the *Shiromani Akali Dal* (Longowal), but he rejoined the parent party in January 2007. A month later, in alliance with the BJP, the SAD won the Punjab State election, permitting Badal to reclaim the chief ministership. In 2009 Badal's SAD won only four *Lok Sabha* seats.

Leaders: Parkash Singh BADAL (Chief Minister of Punjab), Sukhbir Singh BADAL (President), Sukhdev Singh DHINDSA (Secretary General).

Telangana Rashtra Samithi (TRS). The TRS was founded in April 2001 by former members of the *Telugu Desam* Party (TDP). They advocated restoration of a separate Telangana State, which had been absorbed by Andhra Pradesh in 1956. In the 2004 general election the party won five seats in the *Lok Sabha.* It joined the UPA government but withdrew in August 2006 over the statehood issue.

In March 2008 the party's 4 remaining *Lok Sabha* members resigned, as did 16 members of the Andhra Pradesh legislature, forcing by-elections at both levels over the statehood issue. The TRS suffered significant defeats, however, returning only 2 of the 4 to the *Lok Sabha* and only 7 to the state legislature. In 2009, having obtained a pledge of support for reestablishing Telangana, the party's president, K. Chandrasekhar Rao, backed the NDA in the national election despite maintaining an alliance with the Third Front's *Telugu Desam* Party (TDP, below) at the state level. The TRS won only 2 seats in the *Lok Sabha* and 10 in the Andhra Pradesh legislature, prompting Rao, not for the first time, to submit his resignation in June. Two days later, however, responding to a unanimous resolution by the party's General Body, he withdrew it.

Leader: K. Chandrasekhar RAO (President).

Assam People's Council (*Asom Gana Parishad*—AGP). The AGP was launched in October 1985 as a coalition (but not a merger) of the All-Assam Students' Union (AASU) and the All-Assam *Gana Sangram Parishad* (AAGSP), which were united by their call for the deportation of (largely Bangladeshi) "aliens" from Assam. It won two *Lok Sabha* seats in 1991 and five in 1996 (and regained a substantial plurality in concurrent state balloting in Assam) but claimed none in 1998 or 1999. In May 2001 it lost the state election to the Congress.

The AGP returned to the *Lok Sabha* in the 2004 election, winning two seats. It remained the leading opposition party in Assam following the 2006 state election, despite a September 2005 split that saw the party's founder, Prafulla Kumar MAHANTA, a former chief minister of Assam, expelled. Mahanta then formed a new Assam People's Council (Progressive), but the party reunited in October 2008. In 2009 the AGP won one *Lok Sabha* seat.

Leader: Chandra Mohan PATOWARI (President).

Indian National Lok Dal (INLD). The INLD was announced by octogenarian politician Devi Lal in October 1996 under the name *Haryana Lok Dal* (HLD). Lal was a leader of the early *Samajwadi* Party but switched to the *Samata* Party before breaking from it to form the HLD, which campaigned as the HLD (*Rashtriya*), or HLD-R, after another political group appropriated the HLD designation. The HLD-R contested the 1998 elections in alliance with the BSP (below) and won four *Lok Sabha* seats, but it subsequently backed the Vajpayee government. In mid-February 1999, however, it withdrew its support to protest subsidy cuts for food grains and fertilizer. By the time the NDA was formed in May 1999, the party was almost uniformly referred to as the INLD, and went on to win five seats in the September–October general election.

In July 1999 Lal's son, Om Prakash Chautala, had returned as chief minister of Haryana following the resignation of Bansi Lal of the now-defunct *Haryana Vikas* Party (HVP; see under INC, above). At a premature state election in February 2000, the INLD won a clear mandate, with the BJP joining the Chautala administration as a junior partner. At the national level, Chautala broke with the BJP shortly before the 2004 general election, at which the INLD won no seats. The INLD lost control of the 90-seat Haryana legislature in the March 2005 state elections, dropping from 47 to 9 seats. In 2009 it failed to win any of the state's 10 *Lok Sabha* seats.

Leaders: Om Prakash CHAUTALA (Former Chief Minister of Haryana and President of the Party), Ajay Singh CHAUTALA (Secretary General).

Left Front (LF):

Communist Party of India–Marxist (CPI-M). Organized in 1964 by "leftist" deserters from the CPI (below) favoring a more radical line, the CPI-M called for small-scale, rural-oriented, labor-intensive development as well as political decentralization. In 1969 some of its more extreme and overtly pro-Chinese members withdrew to form the CPI-ML (below). At its annual conference in January 1992, the CPI-M responded to events in the former Soviet Union by proclaiming itself "the strongest Communist party in the world."

At the party's 16th congress in 1998, it attacked the "multiple threat of communalism and retrograde economic policies" offered by the BJP-led government. In 1998 it retained its 32 seats in the *Lok Sabha* and then added 1 more in 1999. Prior to the latter election the CPI-M and the CPI jointly identified the defeat of the BJP as their primary goal. However, the Revolutionary Socialist Party (RSP) and the Forward Bloc (both below) contended that the left should also disavow any association with the Congress. As a result, the left entered the contest without a unified "Left Front" platform.

In the 2004 general election the CPI-M led a unified Left Front once again, winning 43 *Lok Sabha* seats and subsequently extending external support to the Congress-led government.

At the state level the CPI-M continues to hold an overall majority in Tripura and West Bengal, and in April–May 2006 it led a Left Democratic Front alliance to an upset victory over Congress in Kerala. Party leader Jyoti Basu served as chief minister of West Bengal from 1977 until ill health forced him to step down in November 2000.

In 2009 the CPI(M) lost the majority of its *Lok Sabha* seats, dropping to 16.

Leaders: Jyoti BASU, Basudeb ACHARIA (*Lok Sabha* Leader), V. S. ACHUTHANANDAN (Chief Minister of Kerala), Buddhadev BHATTACHARJEE (Chief Minister of West Bengal), Manik SARKAR (Chief Minister of Tripura), S. Ramachandran PILLAI, Prakash KARAT (General Secretary).

Communist Party of India (CPI). Established in 1925, the CPI was India's largest opposition party, following the new country's first general election in 1952. Although the CPI-M took with it the majority of CPI members when it broke away in 1964, most of the party bureaucracy, legislative representatives, and trade unionists remained in the CPI. In 1980 supporters of former chair S. A. DANGE established the All India Communist Party—from 1989, called the United Communist Party of India—following rejection of Dange's proposal to support the Congress (I).

Throughout the 1990s the party's *Lok Sabha* representation gradually diminished, falling to four in 1999, but in the 2004 general election it won ten seats. It dropped to four again in 2009.

Leaders: Ardhendu Bhushan BARDHAN (General Secretary), Gurudas DASGUPTA (*Lok Sabha* Leader).

All India Forward Bloc (AIFB). Frequently referenced simply as the **Forward Bloc,** the AIFB is a leftist party confined primarily to West Bengal. Its program calls for land reform and nationalization of key sectors of the economy. It won two *Lok Sabha* seats in 1991, three in 1996, and two in 1998 and 1999. The party suffered the loss of one of its most important modern leaders with the death of General Secretary Chita BASU in 1997. In 2009 it won two *Lok Sabha* seats, down from three in 2004.

Leaders: Debabrata BISWAS (General Secretary), N. Vellapan NAIR (Chair), Ashoke GHOSH (West Bengal General Secretary).

Revolutionary Socialist Party (RSP). The RSP is a Marxist-Leninist grouping based in West Bengal, Kerala, and Tripura. It won five *Lok Sabha* seats in 1996, when it was a UF party, but it chose not to join the new UF government.

In May 1999 a rebel faction under the leadership of party veteran Shibhu Baby JOHN held its own convention, where it argued for leftist unity in the effort to prevent the BJP's return to power. The "official" RSP, however, joined the Forward Bloc in advocating a policy of equidistance from both the BJP and the Congress in the forthcoming national election, at which it won three seats, down from five in 1998. It again won three in 2004 but only two in 2009.

Leaders: Abani ROY, T. J. CHANDRACHOODAN (General Secretary).

Other Third Front Parties:

Bahujan Samaj Party (BSP). Representing India's disadvantaged and *Dalits,* the BSP (Party of the Majority) advances no ideological program, save nonsecularism and "power to the majority." It is based in Punjab and in Uttar Pradesh, where it is a principal rival of the SP. The party's founder, Kanshi RAM, died in October 2006.

The party's tally of 11 *Lok Sabha* seats in the 1996 national election dropped to 5 in 1998 before recovering to 14 in 1999. In partnership with the BJP, it regained leadership of the Uttar Pradesh government in May 2002, but the coalition dissolved in August 2003, and Chief Minister Mayawati Kumari stepped down. Five months earlier a scandal had erupted over a videotape that recorded Mayawati asking BSP loyalists to donate to the party money that they had obtained from public projects.

In 2004 the BSP won 18 *Lok Sabha* seats in alliance with Congress. In December 2005 its parliamentary leader, Raja Ram PAL, was one of 11 legislators expelled by the lower house after being caught accepting bribes in a sting operation.

In the April–May 2007 Uttar Pradesh election the BSP won an outright victory, taking a majority in the Legislative Assembly and ousting the SP-led government. Mayawati thereupon returned as chief minister. In June 2008 the BSP withdrew from the UPA, in part over economic policy but also because Congress was allegedly trying to win greater support from the BSP's voter base. Another factor may have been Mayawati's acknowledged ambition to be prime minister. In the 2009 general election the party won 21 *Lok Sabha* seats and then gave external support to the Singh government.

In the latest controversy involving Mayawati, in September 2009 the Supreme Court ordered her government to discontinue using public funds for erecting statues and other monuments honoring BSP figures, including Mayawati herself. The cost of the program was reported to be $425 million.

Leader: Mayawati KUMARI (Chief Minister of Uttar Pradesh and BSP General Secretary).

Biju Janata Dal (BJD). An Orissa party established in 1997, the BJD is led by Naveen Patnaik, the son of a former important state leader, Biju PATNAIK. Naveen, who had taken over his late father's national legislative seat in 1996 while a member of the *Janata Dal,* subsequently left the parent grouping in protest over that party's failure to ally with the BJP. The BJD won nine seats in the March 1998 national balloting, and Patnaik was named minister of mines. In the 1999 election the BJD won ten seats.

Patnaik stepped down as minister of mines to become chief minister of Orissa following a BJD-BJP victory in state balloting in February 2000. Patnaik won a second term as chief minister in the April 2004 state election, while the BJD took 11 *Lok Sabha* seats in simultaneous union balloting. In 2009 the BJD retained its overwhelming majority in the state assembly and, as part of the Third Front, increased its *Lok Sabha* representation to 14 seats.

Leaders: Naveen PATNAIK (Chief Minister of Orissa and President of the Party), Braja Kishore TRIPATHY (Leader in the *Lok Sabha*).

All India Dravidian Progressive Federation (All India *Anna Dravida Munnetra Kazhagam*—AIADMK). The AIADMK is a Tamil party that split from the DMK (above) in 1972. Its founder, former matinee idol Maruthur Gopala RAMACHANDRAN, died in 1987, provoking a succession struggle. In 1991, as an ally of Congress (I), the AIADMK retained the 11 *Lok Sabha* seats won in 1989 and also assumed power in Tamil Nadu under Jayalalitha Jayaram, a former actress. Accused by the opposition of massive financial corruption, Jayalalitha resumed the AIADMK's alliance with the Congress for the 1996 *Lok Sabha* and state elections, but her party was wiped out by the DMK in the former and retained only 4 seats in the latter.

The party won 18 *Lok Sabha* seats in March 1998 and joined the BJP coalition government, from which Jayalalitha repeatedly threatened to withdraw because of her objections to ministerial and military appointments and dismissals. Making good on her threat, she precipitated the confidence vote of April 17, 1999, that brought down the government and led to the September–October election, at which the party, once again allied with Congress, won 10 seats. In February and October 2000 Jayalalitha was sentenced to prison following corruption convictions, but she ultimately prevailed on appeal. Numerous other cases against her have been similarly unsuccessful.

Although herself barred from competing, in the May 2001 state election Jayalalitha once again led her party and its Secular Front alliance to a lopsided victory over the DMK. She then won a by-election in February 2002, permitting her to reclaim the chief ministership.

Prior to the April–May 2004 general election the AIADMK joined the NDA, but it was rejected by the electorate, losing all 33 seats it contested. In early 2006, in preparation for the Tamil Nadu assembly election, the AIADMK forged a Democratic People's Alliance that included the MDMK, the JD(S) (above), splinter groups of the IUML (above) and AIFB (above), and several other small parties. The coalition was routed, however, by a DMK-led alliance. In 2007 Jayalalitha, having parted ways with the NDA, joined in forming the new UNPA, but she soon departed. Having backed the BJP candidate for president, she was expected to seek a renewed alliance with that party before the next general election, but instead the AIADMK aligned itself with the Third Front, returning to the *Lok Sabha* with 9 seats.

Leader: Jayalalitha JAYARAM (Former Chief Minister of Tamil Nadu and General Secretary of the Party).

Telugu Desam Party (TDP). An Andhra Pradesh–based party, *Telugu Desam* (*Telugu* Nation) was reported to have disbanded in March 1992, but a revitalized party, led by former film star Nandmuri Tarak (N. T.) Rama RAO, swept into power in the 1994 state election. Subsequent intraparty divisions ultimately saw the reform-minded Chandrababu Naidu replace Rao as chief minister in September 1995. The leadership of the Rao faction passed, after Rao's death in January 1996, to his widow, Lakshmi PARVATHI.

In the 1996 national election the TDP-Naidu (or TDP-Babu) won 16 lower house seats as a member of the United Front. In 1998 the Parvathi faction, having organized separately as the **NTR Telugu Desam Party,** won no seats, while the Naidu faction slipped from 16 to 12. In March 1999 the TDP leadership voted to leave the United Front, in part because the alliance's central committee had decided to support a Congress Party candidate for speaker of the *Lok Sabha.*

Under Naidu the TDP achieved major gains in 1999, winning 29 *Lok Sabha* seats and extending its support to the NDA government without, however, joining the Council of Ministers. In 2004, as part of the NDA, the TDP saw its *Lok Sabha* representation plummet to 5 seats as the Congress Party successfully exploited a widening gap between the rising fortunes of the state's urban elite and the plight of its rural farmers. In the simultaneous state election the TDP lost all but 45 of its 180 assembly seats.

In 2009 the TDP won 6 seats in the *Lok Sabha* and made a significant recovery in the state assembly election, claiming 105 seats but failing to topple Congress. As in 1999 and 2004, Parvathi's group won no *Lok Sabha* seats.

Leader: N. Chandrababu NAIDU (Former Chief Minister of Andhra Pradesh and President of the Party).

Janata Dal (Secular)—JD(S). The JD(S) name was applied by the Election Commission to the Deve Gowda faction of *Janata Dal* (see JD[U], above) in August 1999. Although the party contested nearly 100 seats in the subsequent national election, it captured only 1, with Deve Gowda himself going down to defeat.

In April 2004 the JD(S) won 3 *Lok Sabha* seats, including 1 contested by Deve Gowda, and placed third in the Karnataka State Assembly. In May, Deve Gowda announced that the JD(S) would form a coalition government with the second-ranked Congress, rather than the plurality BJP, in Karnataka. In January 2006, however, H. D. Kumaraswamy, son of Deve Gowda, led 39 JD(S) members of the Legislative Assembly in a revolt that brought down the Congress-JD(S) government. Realigned with the BJP, Kumaraswamy formed a new administration. Deve Gowda suspended the defectors in February but then, late in the year, welcomed them back into the fold. That outcome precipitated a further split, with Deve Gowda's continuing leadership being opposed by Surendra MOHAN, who formed a breakaway "real" JD(S), the **Janata Dal (Left).**

Following a lengthy political impasse, in November 2007 Kumaraswamy agreed to step down as chief minister and permit the BJP to head the government, as had previously been agreed by the coalition partners. The JD(S) unsuccessfully sought to realign with Congress before the May 2008 state election, at which it suffered significant losses. As part of the Third Front in 2009, it won three *Lok Sabha* seats, including one by Deve Gowda and another by Kumaraswamy.

Leaders: H.D. DEVE GOWDA (Former Prime Minister and Chair of the Party), H.D. KUMARASWAMY (Former Chief Minister of Karnataka), H.D. REVANNA.

Haryana Janhit Congress (HJC). The HJC is a breakaway from the INC. It was formed in 2007 by former Haryana chief minister Bhajan Lal and a son, Kuldeep Bishnoi, after the latter's suspension from the INC for antiparty activity. Another factor in the party's formation was the INC's decision not to name Lal as chief minister following the 2005 state election.

In the 2009 general election Lal won the party's only *Lok Sabha* seat. Two months later, party leader Subhash BATRA announced that he was forming the **Samasat Haryana Janhit Congress** (SHJC) because he objected to the Lal family's domination of the HJC and recent efforts by Lal to draw closer to the BJP.

Leaders: Kuldeep BISHNOI (President), Bhajan LAL .

Marumalarchi Dravida Munnetra Kazhagam (MDMK). The MDMK is a strongly Tamil nationalist grouping, occasionally accused of being too close to Sri Lanka's separatist Liberation Tigers of Tamil Eelam (LTTE) for easy cooperation with national parties. The Jain Commission report on the assassination of Rajiv Gandhi caused the party some difficulties, although its long-standing antipathy to the DMK contributed to its participation in the AIADMK alliance in 1998 and in the subsequent BJP-led government coalition. The party had run five candidates in Tamil Nadu, winning three seats.

In April 1999 the MDMK broke ranks with the AIADMK over the latter's withdrawal of support for the Vajpayee government, which led to a rapprochement with the DMK and the MDMK's participation in the NDA.

As a consequence of urging support for the LTTE, the MDMK's general secretary, Vaiko, was detained by the AIADMK-led Tamil Nadu government from July 2002 until he was released on bail in February 2004. Responding to an imminent NDA-AIADMK pact, the MDMK had left the Vajpayee government in December 2003. It contested the 2004 election with Congress (and the DMK), winning four *Lok Sabha* seats, as it had in 1999.

Somewhat surprisingly, in March 2006 the MDMK aligned with the AIADMK for the May Tamil Nadu assembly election, prompting the DMK to demand the MDMK's removal from the UPA. Subsequently, a dissident faction formed under *Lok Sabha* members L. GANESAN and Ginje RAMACHANDRAN, who objected to the AIADMK alliance and Vaiko's continuing leadership. Both were expelled from the party after backing the government in a July 2008 confidence vote related to the proposed nuclear technology agreement with the United States. In March 2007 Vaiko had broken from the UPA, charging that it had failed to implement most provisions of its program and to address the needs of the common people.

After having initially participated in the UNPA, it joined in forming the Third Front in March 2009 but won only one *Lok Sabha* seat in the April–May national election.

Leaders: VAIKO (V. GOPALASWAMI, Secretary General), A. GANESHAMURTHI (Member of the *Lok Sabha*).

Pattali Makkal Katchi (PMK). Based in the disadvantaged Vanniyar community of northern Tamil Nadu, the PMK (Pattali People's Party) emerged in 1997 as a bitter opponent of the AIADMK, although in the interests of political power it subsequently joined a coalition with its enemy. It won all four seats it contested in the 1998 national election, and five of eight in 1999. In February 2001 it left the NDA, but after a lack of success in the subsequent state elections, it rejoined the alliance in late July. It departed again in January 2004 and joined the DMK and MDMK (below) as allies of Congress for the April–May general election, at which it won six seats.

For the 2006 Tamil Nadu assembly election, the PMK participated in the victorious DMK-led Democratic Progressive Alliance, but in June 2008 it was dismissed from the government. In March 2009, with the national election approaching, it left the UPA and allied with the AIADMK in the Third Front, but it lost all of its *Lok Sabha* seats at the polls.

Leaders: G.K. MANI (President), Dr. S. RAMDOSS (Founder), Anbumani RAMDOSS.

Fourth Front:

Samajwadi Party (SP). The *Samajwadi* (Socialist) Party, based in Uttar Pradesh, held its inaugural convention in October 1992. The new formation was an outgrowth of the *Janata Dal*–Socialist (JD-S), which had been organized by former *Janata Dal* leaders Chandra Shekhar and Devi Lal following their withdrawal from the National Front in November 1990. Shekhar, with Congress (I) support, subsequently served as prime minister until March 1991.

The party won 17 *Lok Sabha* seats in the 1996 election; 20 seats in 1998, second to the CPI-M among UF members; and 26 in 1999, although an attempt by President Mulayam Singh Yadav and the NCP's Sharad Pawar to forge a "Third Force" front in opposition to the NDA and the Congress failed to materialize. After winning 36 seats in the 2004 *Lok Sabha* election, the party backed formation of the Congress-led government in May but remained independent of the Congress in Uttar Pradesh, where it led the state government until ousted by the BSP (below) in the April–May 2007 state election. In August 2007 the SP's Rashid Masood ran as the UNPA's candidate for vice president but finished a distant third in the three-way race.

The largest party in the Fourth Front, the SP finished third overall in the 2009 *Lok Sabha* election, winning 23 seats, but that total was far behind the INC and the BJP and represented a net loss of 13 from 2004. The SP then extended external support to the Singh government.

Leaders: Mulayam Singh YADAV (President of the Party and Former Chief Minister of Uttar Pradesh), Janeshwar MISRA (Vice President), Ram Gopal YADAV (*Rajya Sabha* Leader), Amar SINGH (General Secretary).

Rashtriya Janata Dal (RJD). Formed in 1997 in the state of Bihar, the RJD (National People's Party) emerged from the conflict between the charismatic leader of Bihar state, L. P. Yadav, and his successor as president of the *Janata Dal,* Sharad Yadav. After his indictment on charges stemming from alleged misallocation of $250 million in agricultural support funds, L. P. Yadav was ousted from the *Janata Dal* and formed the RJD. In the March 1998 national balloting the party held its 17 seats in Bihar but failed to move significantly into other states.

In mid-February 1999 L. P. Yadav and his wife, Rabri Devi, the controversial chief minister of Bihar State, were arrested while protesting New Delhi's decision to assume governance of the state in the wake of two massacres of peasants, allegedly at the instigation of private landlords. The central takeover was rescinded in March when the Vajpayee administration could not muster support for the move from a majority of the *Rajya Sabha.*

In the September–October 1999 election the RJD lost all but 7 *Lok Sabha* seats despite an alliance with Congress. In the Bihar State election in February 2000, however, it showed unexpected strength, capturing a plurality of legislative seats. In 2004 the RJD took 21 *Lok Sabha* seats as a Congress ally, but in the February 2005 state election it won only 75 assembly seats and was forced to surrender power. The failure of the BJP and its allies to form a government ultimately led to another state election in October–November 2005, in which the RJD lost another 21 seats and finished third. In the meantime, Yadav had been charged with embezzling agricultural subsidies in 1996, when he was chief minister. As of May 2006 dozens of former government officials and businessmen had been convicted of involvement in "fodder scam." In December 2006 Yadav and his wife were acquitted of having "disproportionate assets" above his known income.

Shortly before the April–May 2009 general election Yadav stated that the SP, RJD, and LJP had united not in opposition to the UPA but to stop communalism. In the election the RJD lost 20 of its 24 seats but gave external support to the new UPA government.

Leaders: Lalu Prasad YADAV (President of the Party), Rabri DEVI (Former Chief Minister of Bihar).

Lok Janshakti Party (LJP). The LJP was formed as the *Janshakti* Party in November 2000 by government minister Ram Vilas Paswan and three other members of the lower house, all formerly of the derecognized *Lok Shakti* (LS; see JD[U], below). The new party was recognized by the Elections Commission under its present name in December 2000.

In April 2002 Paswan resigned as minister of coal and mines and pulled his party out of the governing NDA, citing the government's inability to resolve the ongoing sectarian violence in Gujarat. Allied with Congress in 2004, the LJP won four seats, all from Bihar, and Paswan was again appointed to the cabinet.

In 2005 the LJP did not support the RJD-Congress coalition in the Bihar State elections, prompting the RJD leadership to demand Paswan's ouster from the UPA government. Paswan, a leading advocate for the minority rights of *Dalits,* Muslims, and others, led the LJP into the newly organized Fourth Front for the April–May 2009 general election, but the party failed to retain any *Lok Sabha* seats.

Leader: Ram Vilas PASWAN (President of the Party).

Other Parliamentary Parties:

Assam United Democratic Front (AUDF). The AUDF is a nonsectarian party committed to ending the regional insurgency and promoting the rights and economic betterment of minorities, women, and the disadvantaged. It currently holds ten seats in the Assam legislature, and in 2009 won one *Lok Sabha* seat.

Leaders: Baruddin AJMAL al-Qasimi (President), Hafiz Rashid Ahmad CHOUDHURY (Working President).

Bodoland People's Front (BPF). In February 2003 the Bodo Liberation Tiger Force (BLTF) agreed to end an insurgency in Assam that dated from 1968. The agreement followed a March 2000 cease-fire. On December 6, 2003, a Bodoland Territorial Council (BTC) was established and an amnesty extended to some 2,600 BLTF members who laid down their arms. Former BLTF commander in chief Hagrama Mohilary, now heading the newly formed BPF, was inaugurated as chief executive of the BTC. In 2009 the BPF won its first *Lok Sabha* seat and extended support to the UPA government.

Leaders: Hagrama MOHILARY (a.k.a. Hagrama BASUMATARY), Sansuma Khunggur BWISWMUTHIARY (Member of the *Lok Sabha*).

Jharkhand Vikas Morcha (JVM). The JVM was formed in 2006 by Babulal Marandi, a former Jharkhand chief minister and BJP vice president who had resigned his previous affiliation because of differences over the state government. It participated in the abortive UNPA in 2007 but ran independently for the *Lok Sabha* in 2009, winning one seat.

Leader: Babulal MARANDI.

Mizo National Front (MNF). A leading force in Mizoram State, the MNF won the state's one *Lok Sabha* seat in the election of April–May 2004. In December 2008, however, it lost control of the state government to the INC, which also took away the MNF's *Lok Sabha* seat in 2009. It continues to hold one seat in the upper house.

Leaders: Pu ZORAMTHANGA (Former Chief Minister of Mizoram), Lalhming LIANA (Secretary).

Nagaland People's Front (NPF). In addition to belonging to the governing Democratic Alliance of Nagaland, the NPF claimed the state's only *Lok Sabha* seat in the 2004 election as part of the NDA. In 2009, running independently, it retained the seat, after which it agreed to support the new UPA government.

Leaders: Neiphiu RIO (Chief Minister of Nagaland), C.M. CHANG (Member of the *Lok Sabha*).

Sikkim Democratic Front (SDF). Formed in opposition to the then-ruling *Sikkim Sangram Parishad* (SSP), which had dominated Sikkim politics since 1985, the SDF obtained a commanding majority in the Sikkim State election of December 1994 and went on to win the state's single *Lok Sabha* seat in 1996. It retained the seat in 1998, swept the simultaneous state and national elections in 1999, and held both the *Lok Sabha* seat and the state in 2004. In November 2005, decrying the state government's failure to meet the needs of the people, dissidents led by Chiten Dorjee LEPCHA announced their intention to form a "third force."

In February 2006 the SDF joined the UPA, although it ran independently in May 2009. At that time the SDF won all 32 seats in the state assembly, after which P.K. Chamling was sworn in for a fourth time as chief minister. The SDF retained its one *Lok Sabha* seat at the central level and then extended its external support to the UPA government.

Leader: Pawan Kumar CHAMLING (Chief Minister of Sikkim and President of the Party).

Two other parties, both based in Maharashtra State, won single seats in the 2009 *Lok Sabha* elections: the **Bahujan Vikas Aaghadi,** drawn from the Kunbi community and led by Jadhav Baliram SUKUR, and the **Swabhimani Paksha,** the political arm of the farmer-oriented *Swabhimani Shetkari Sanghatana,* led by Raju SHETTI. Both gave their support to the new UPA government. In addition, the **Swatantra Bharat Paksh,** also based in Maharashtra, was awarded one *Raja Sabha* seat in the June 2004 election; its leader is Sharad JOSHI.

Other Parties:

Autonomous State Demand Committee (ASDC). The ASDC emerged in 1986 seeking greater autonomy for the predominantly tribal Karbi Anglong district of Assam. It won a *Lok Sabha* seat in a 1994 by-election in Assam and retained it in the 1996 and 1998 general elections. In 1999 the party's then-president, Jayanta Rongpi, ran successfully under the banner of the Communist Party of India–Marxist-Leninist (Liberation)—see under CPI-ML, below. Since then, the party has split, more than once, into competing factions. In May 2008 the Assam state government declared that it had evidence of links between ASDC leaders and militant organizations, such as the National Socialist Council of Nagaland (Isaac Muivah) and the *Dima Halam Daogah* (see under the subhead Principal North and Northeast Militant Organizations, below).

Leaders: Holiram TERANG (President), Jotson BEY, Babu RONGPI, Chomang KRO (Secretary General), Daniel TERON (General Secretary, ASDC-Progressive).

Communist Party of India–Marxist-Leninist (CPI-ML). As the result of disagreement over operational strategy for the spread of communism in rural India, an extreme faction within the CPI-M organized the CPI-ML in 1969. Committed to Maoist principles of people's liberation warfare, the party was actively involved in the Naxalite terrorist movement in West Bengal and was banned during the state of emergency. Some members subsequently rejected revolutionary Marxism in favor of parliamentary democracy, but none of the party's many splinters ever secured *Lok Sabha* representation until 1999, when the ASDC's Jayanta Rongpi agreed to run under the banner of the legal **Communist Party of India–Marxist-Leninist (Liberation)** (CPI-ML-L). The party failed to retain the seat in 2004.

In early 2007 the CPI-ML strongly opposed seizures of farmland in West Bengal, where the Left Front government was seeking to establish a special economic zone. In 2009 it objected to the central government's decision to proscribe the CPI-Maoist (below).

Leaders: Dipankar BHATTACHARYA (General Secretary), Jayanta RONGPI, Abhijit MAJUMDER (CPI-ML–Liberation), Indramil BHATTACHARYA (CPI-ML–Provisional Central Committee), Sridhar MUKHERJEE (CPI-ML–New Democracy).

Communist Party of India–Maoist (CPI-Maoist). In 2004 reports surfaced that the Maoist Communist Center (MCC) and the People's War Group (PWG) had merged as the CPI-Maoist. One of the many small communist parties operating in India, the MCC had originated in a Maoist faction that remained aloof from the CPI(ML) upon the latter's formation in 1969. The MCC gained notoriety in connection with the March 1999 killing of Bhumihar caste members in Bihar in revenge for two massacres of peasants, allegedly at the instigation of private landlords. The PWG, which was also known as the Communist Party of India (Marxist-Leninist) People's War following a merger with the CPI-ML–Unity in 1998, dated back to the early 1980s. The merger of the PWG and the MCC in 2004 brought together the two largest Naxalite organizations operating primarily in the northeast. As of 2006 the CPI-Maoist had an estimated 20,000 armed personnel in 13 states.

Since then, several party leaders have surrendered or been arrested, but without a reduction in the level of violence. Having already been banned in Andhra Pradesh, Chhattisgarh, Jharkhand, and Orissa, in June 2009 the party was proscribed across all of India. Maharashtra, Orissa, and West Bengal, in particular, have also been the scene of numerous terrorist attacks by Maoists, who claim to champion the poor and dispossessed. Attacks have most frequently been directed against landowners, corporations, the police, and infrastructure.

In September 2009 authorities arrested Kohad GANDY, reputedly a key member of the CPI-Maoist Politburo.

Desiya Murpokku Dravida Kazhagam (DMDK). The DMDK (National Progressive Dravidian Party) was launched in September 2005 in Tamil Nadu by film star Vijayakant and former AIADMK minister Panruti S. Ramachandran. Advocating "progressive programs and policies," Vijayakant has directly linked himself to the founder of the AIADMK, M. G. Ramachandran, and is widely called "*Karuppu* MGR" (dark-skinned MGR). The DMDK failed to win any seats in the 2009 general election.

Leaders: VIJAYAKANT (President), Panruti S. RAMACHANDRAN (Presidium Chair).

Jammu and Kashmir People's Democratic Party (PDP). Established in 1999, the PDP has called for demilitarization of Jammu and Kashmir. It finished third in the 2002 Jammu and Kashmir State election and went on to join the second-ranked Congress in unseating the Jammu and Kashmir National Conference (JKNC, above) government. In the 2004 national election the PDP won one *Lok Sabha* seat.

In November 2005 the PDP's founder, Mohammed Sayeed, who had served as chief minister of Jammu and Kashmir for three years, was replaced by senior Congress leader Ghulam Nabi AZAD, in accordance with the 2002 coalition pact. The arrangement subsequently collapsed, and in the wake of the 2008 state election, despite gaining 5 assembly seats, for a total of 21, the PDP saw the JKNC and Congress form a new government. In January 2009 the PDP withdrew from the UPA, and it failed to hold its *Lok Sabha* seat in the subsequent general election.

Leaders: Mehbooba MUFTI (President), Mufti Mohammed SAYEED (Former Chief Minister of Jammu and Kashmir).

Janata Party (JP). The present *Janata* Party descends from the *Janata* grouping that Subramanian Swamy led into the *Janata Dal* at its formation in October 1988. A BJP ally, Swami lost his *Lok Sabha* seat in 1999, leaving *Janata* with no MPs. He has been an outspoken critic of the UPA government and supported the BJP in the 2009 general election.

Leader: Dr. Subramanian SWAMY (President).

Shiromani Akali Dal (Mann)—SAD(M). The SAD(M), also frequently referenced as the **Shiromani Akali Dal (Amritsar),** was formed by radical *Akali Dal* faction leader S. S. Mann in the mid-1990s because, he claimed, other leaders had failed to adhere to the 1994 Amritsar declaration (see SAD, above). Mann successfully competed for a *Lok Sabha* seat in 1999. In 2004 and 2009 the party ran a small number of candidates, all unsuccessful.

In a case dating back to 1991, in November 2006 Mann was acquitted of sedition for allegedly advocating establishment of Khalistan, a Sikh homeland.

Leader: Simranjit Singh MANN (President).

The following additional state parties, all unrepresented at the national level, were registered at the time of the 2009 general election: the **Arunachal Congress** (AC), based in Arunachal Pradesh; the **Jammu and Kashmir National Panthers Party** (JKNPP); the **Maharashtrawadi Gomantak** (MAG), Goa's ruling party during most of the 1960s and 1970s; the **Manipur People's Party** (MPP); the **Mizoram People's Conference** (MZPC); the **National People's Party** (NPP) of Manipur; the **Puducherry Munnetra Congress** (PMC); the **Save Goa Front** (SGF); the **United Democratic Party** (UDP) of Meghalaya; the **Uttarakhand Kranti Dal**—UKD (Uttarakhand Revolution Party) of Uttarakhand; and the **Zoram Nationalist Party** (ZNP) of Mizoram.

Kashmiri Separatist and Radical Islamic Groups:

All Parties Hurriyat Conference (APHC). Founded in March 1993 as a coalition of 26 political parties and other groups, the APHC seeks to end the division of the "occupied territories" through peaceful means, including civil disobedience and protests. With offices both in Jammu and Kashmir and in Pakistan, the APHC maintains that it constitutes the sole political representative of the Kashmiri people. As in the past, it did not participate in the most recent Jammu and Kashmir state election, held in November–December 2008, and in the Indian general election of April–May 2009. After describing the state assembly election as a "futile exercise," the APHC adopted a stance of "indifference" toward the national election rather than call for an outright boycott. A statement from the APHC described the election as a "non-issue" that would have no bearing on Kashmir's status.

Among the current APHC participants are Mirwaiz Umar Farooq's **Awami Action Committee;** the **Azad Kashmir People's Party,** a Pakistan People's Party splinter founded and led by Sardar Khalid IBRAHIM; the **Democratic Freedom Party,** founded in 1998 by Shabir Ahmed SHAH; the **Islamic Political Party (Jammu and Kashmir),** led by Muhammad Yousuf NAQASH; the **Ittihad-ul-Muslimeen,** led by Maulana Muhammad Abbas ANSARI; the Muhammad

Yasin MALIK faction of the **Jammu and Kashmir Liberation Front** (JKLF); the **Jammu and Kashmir Liberation Forum,** led by Javaid Ahmad MIR; the **Jammu and Kashmir National Front** (JKNF), led by Nayeem Ahmad KHAN; Abdul Ghani BHAT's **Muslim Conference,** which also includes as prominent leaders Jahangir Gani BHAT and Shabir Ahmad DAR; and the **People's Political Front,** led by Fazal-ul-Haq QURESHI. A major figure in the APHC, Abdul Ghani LONE of the **People's Conference,** was assassinated in May 2002. The conference is currently headed by a son, Bilan Ghani LONE, whose brother, Sajjad LONE, stirred up considerable controversy in 2009 when he became the first separatist in two decades to seek a *Lok Sabha* seat. (The seat was won by a member of the JKNC.) Another APHC participant, the **People's League,** lost its leader on August 11, 2008, when Sheikh Abdul AZIZ was killed by police during a protest march generated by a land dispute near the Hindu shrine of Amarnath. Mukhtar Ahmad WAZA was named as his acting successor.

The JKLF, established in 1977 by Amanullah KHAN, split in 1995 into two organizations, Khan's militant JKLF-A, based in Pakistan, and Malik's moderate JKLF-Y. In June 2005 the two leaders met and resolved to reunite their factions, but both remain active, as do other, smaller factions.

APHC leaders have been detained on numerous occasions. In September 1999 New Delhi arrested 15 APHC leaders under the Jammu and Kashmir Public Safety Act and proceeded to hold them without trial. In April–May 2000 the Indian government released a number of the detainees, including the APHC chair, Syed Ali GILANI (GEELANI) of the *Jamaat-e-Islami*. Shortly afterward, speaking in New Delhi, Gilani repeated that the Kashmir question could be resolved only through tripartite talks involving India, Pakistan, and the Kashmiri people. In July 2000 Abdul Ghani Bhat succeeded Gilani as APHC chair.

In July 2003 the election of Muhammad Abbas Ansari as chair of the Executive Council precipitated a split in the organization, and two months later the more hard-line members, led by Gilani, attempted to replace him with Masrat ALAM. Since then, the organization has remained divided, with the more radical Gilani branch, encompassing about 16 groups, closely identified with the party Gilani formed in 2004, the **Tehrik-e-Hurriyat Jammu and Kashmir** (Jammu and Kashmir Movement for Freedom), as successor to the *Jamaat-e-Islami*.

On January 22, 2004, responding to overtures from New Delhi, a number of moderate APHC leaders, including former chairs Abdul Ghani Bhat and Mirwaiz Umar Farooq, met with representatives of the Indian government and agreed to seek an "honorable and durable solution" through dialogue and step-by-step measures. The delegation met Prime Minister Vajpayee the next day. In July, Ansari resigned as APHC chair in order to facilitate reconciliation, a task undertaken by APHC founder Farooq.

On June 2, 2005, a dozen moderate APHC representatives crossed the LoC into Pakistan's Azad Kashmir for the first time since 1947. Led by Farooq, who addressed the Azad Kashmir Legislative Assembly, the delegation then traveled to Islamabad for meetings with Pakistani officials, including President Musharraf.

In February 2006 Farooq became the first separatist leader to hold a public rally in Hindu-dominated Jammu in over a decade and urged those in attendance to "build bridges" between their various communities. A round table proposed by Indian Prime Minister Singh for later in the month in New Delhi drew a rejection from the APHC moderates, who argued that the talks would not advance the negotiations. Hard-liner Gilani termed the proposed talks a "futile exercise." In contrast, a March 10–12 conference in Islamabad, organized by the Washington-based Pugwash Conferences, was attended not only by various APHC leaders—among them, Yasin Malik, Sajjad Lone, and Abdul Ghani Bhat—but also by civil society leaders, officials from both Azad Kashmir and Indian Kashmir, and "back-channel" diplomats. Moderates and hard-liners alike boycotted a second round table, held May 24–25, in Srinagar.

In December 2006, elaborating a strategy he had previously proposed, Pakistani President Musharraf set forth a four-point plan for Kashmir: greater self-government, demilitarization, opening of the LoC to permit greater freedom of movement within existing borders, and joint supervision by India and Pakistan. The APHC moderates labeled the plan "realistic and bold," and over the next several months even some hard-liners appeared more willing to consider aspects of the plan, particularly demilitarization of Kashmir. Following a January 26, 2007, meeting with Musharraf, Farooq called for an end to violence. On March 16–17 Bhat and Malik were among the Kashmiri leaders who attended an International Kashmir Conference held in Islamabad.

In June 2008 a delegation of moderate APHC leaders—Farooq, Bhat, Bilal Ghani Lone, Sheikh Abdul Aziz, and Qureshi—traveled to Pakistan for an official meeting. By the end of the month, however, the focus of attention had become the Amarnath dispute, which involved a proposal to transfer 40 hectares of state land to a board managing the Hindu shrine. During the next two months dozens of people were killed and hundreds injured in the resultant unrest throughout Muslim-dominated Kashmir and Hindu-majority Jammu. Most prominent APHC leaders, including Umar Farooq and Syed Gilani, were detained or placed under house arrest at various times during this period. Relations with the Manmohan Singh government failed to improve thereafter, with Farooq stating in July 2009 that a dialogue with New Delhi would resume only after the central government revoked "draconian" laws, began to withdraw Indian troops from Kashmir, and released political prisoners. Separatist sentiments had been further inflamed by the alleged rape and murder of two Muslim women by Indian soldiers in late May.

Leader: Mirwaiz Umar FAROOQ (Chair).

United Jihad Council (UJC). A grouping of a dozen or more organizations committed to the separation of Jammu and Kashmir from India, the UJC was established in 1994, allegedly under the auspices of Pakistan's Inter Services Intelligence agency. Participants include the *Hizb-ul-Mujaheddin,* whose chair, Syed Salahuddin, also heads the UJC, and the *Lashkar-i-Taiba* (both discussed separately below). Other member organizations include the **Jamiat-ul-Mujaheddin,** the **al-Umar Mujaheddin** of Mushtaq ZARGAR, and the Pakistan-based **Jaish-e-Muhammad** and **Harkat-ul-Mujaheddin.** Some support Kashmiri independence, but others advocate Kashmir's inclusion in Pakistan.

In March 2007, responding to recent governmental initiatives, Salahuddin called on Kashmiri separatists to reject a "cosmetic solution" to the Kashmir problem and the "continuing futile dialogue" between India and Pakistan. He added that the struggle for self-determination might take "many generations." The UJC subsequently called for a boycott of the 2008 Jammu and Kashmir legislative election and the April–May 2009 national election.

Chair: Syed SALAHUDDIN (a.k.a. Mohammad Yusuf SHAH).

Hizb-ul-Mujaheddin (HuM). Founded in 1990, the HuM is probably the largest of the Islamic militant organizations seeking separation of Jammu and Kashmir from India and establishment of a fundamentalist regime. Unlike many other separatist groups, which typically have bases in the Pakistani territory of Azad Kashmir, the HuM has asserted that it is an exclusively Kashmiri organization, although it has close links to Pakistan's *Jamaat-e-Islami* party. The HuM has claimed responsibility for or been implicated in many of the most widely reported violent incidents in Kashmir in recent years.

On July 24, 2000, the organization's operational chief, Abdul Majid DAR, announced a three-month cease-fire that was rescinded in early August when talks with Indian officials broke down. In May 2002 Dar was expelled for "violating discipline." He was murdered in March 2003, after which his followers announced their separation from the organization's leadership, headed by Syed Salahuddin, whom some opponents accused of ordering the elimination of influential opponents. Dar's successor as operational chief, Saiful ISLAM, died in a gun battle in April 2003, and Islam's successor, Ghulam Rasool DAR, met a similar fate in January 2004. Since then, in an apparent effort to confound authorities, the HuM has tended to identify key field commanders only by aliases.

In January 2009 Mohammad Ahsan DAR, an HuM cofounder and current leader of **Muslim Mujaheddin,** was arrested by Jammu and Kashmir police. Officials indicated that he had recently returned from Pakistan's Azad Kashmir and was engaged in coordinating the activities of various militant organizations.

Leader: Syed SALAHUDDIN.

Indian Mujahideen (IM). A militant Islamic group identifying itself as the IM surfaced with a series of bombings that began in Uttar Pradesh in November 2007. The group also claimed responsibility for bombings in Rajasthan in May 2008, Gujarat in July 2008, and New Delhi in September 2008, resulting in dozens of deaths and hundreds of injuries. Although the IM's origins remains shadowy, speculation has centered on connections to the LiT and the proscribed **Students' Islamic Movement of India** (SIMI) and **Harkat-ul-Jihad-i-Islami** (HJI).

Lashkar-i-Taiba (LiT). The LiT (Army of the Pure) was established between 1990 and 1993 as the military wing of an aboveground religious group, the *Markaz ud-Dawa Wal Irshad,* which was formed in 1986 to organize Pakistani Sunni militants participating in the Afghan revolution. The *Markaz* was officially dissolved in December 2001 and all its assets transferred to the "new" charity **Jamaat-ud-Dawa** (JuD, Party of the Calling) in an effort to avoid proscription.

The LiT, which the United States has labeled a terrorist group, was banned by India in October 2001 and by Pakistan in January 2002. The JuD was placed on a "watch list" but not banned by the Pakistani government in November 2003. Without much credibility, it has denied any connection to the LiT, although Hafiz Mohammed Sayeed continues to be identified in most sources as head of both. Following the terrorist assault on Mumbai in November 2009, the UN Security Council added the JuD to its list of terrorist organizations and Pakistan banned it.

Further complicating matters, the LiT is suspected of using other front names, including **al-Mansurian** and the **Islami Inqilabi Mahaz** (Islamic Revolutionary Group). In its various guises the LiT has claimed responsibility for and been implicated in innumerable bombings, suicide missions, and other attacks within Kashmir and elsewhere. Many of its members have been jailed in India and Pakistan. An LiT commander, Bashir Ahmad KHAN, was killed by Indian forces in April 2004, by which time it was already extending its activities beyond Kashmir to other areas of India. Indian authorities have linked it to the August 2003 Mumbai bombings, which killed over 50 people; the New Delhi bombings of October 2005 (some 60 fatalities); the March 2006 bombing of Hindu shrines in Varanasi (about 15 dead); and the July 11, 2006, coordinated bombings in Mumbai (180 dead). In November 2006 Indian authorities labeled LiT leader Azam CHEEMA as the mastermind behind the July Mumbai attacks. The group's alleged "all-India" coordinator, Abu UMAR, was killed by security personnel in July 2007. India has presented evidence of the LiT's involvement in planning the November 26–28, 2008, Mumbai attack (163 dead, plus 9 of 10 terrorists).

Leaders: Hafiz Mohammed SAYEED, Zaki ur-Rehman LAKHVI, Haji Muhammad ASHRAF, Mahmoud Muhammad Ahmed BAHAZIQ.

For information on other Kashmiri separatist groups, many of which are based in Pakistan's Azad Kashmir, see the article on Pakistan.

Principal North and Northeast Militant Organizations:

In Assam, a **National Democratic Front of Bodoland** (NDFB) denounced a 2003 accord between New Delhi and the Bodo Liberation Tiger Force (BLTF), which led to establishment of a Bodoland Territorial Council. The NDFB remained in militant opposition until announcing a cease-fire that entered into effect in March 2005. More recently, rivalry between the NDFB and the Bodoland People's Front (BPF, above), which descended from the BLTF, has contributed to the emergence of a **Bodo Royal Tiger Force** (BRTF), which reportedly was organized by former members of the BLTF. Another group, the **Bodo People's Progressive Front** (BPPF), led by Rabiram NARZARY, was formed in opposition to the BPF.

The **United Liberation Front of Assam** (ULFA), established in 1979, is led by military commander Paresh BARUA and political chair Arabinda RAJKHOWA. The largest and best-organized of the northeastern separatist organizations, it continues to be responsible for a significant number of terrorist acts against Indian authorities. In the 1990s the ULFA and several other militant organizations began operating from camps set up in nearby Bhutan, but in December 2003, after several years of efforts by the Bhutanese government to negotiate their departure, the Royal Bhutanese Army took to the field against some 30 insurgent bases. The campaign, which extended into early 2004, resulted in the capture of several ULFA leaders and the destruction of its bases, after which the organization reportedly dispersed to the neighboring Indian states of Nagaland, Meghalaya, and Arunachal Pradesh. Additional bases have been reported in Bangladesh, although the Bangladeshi government has denied any support for the organization. Connections have also been reported with outlawed groups in Myanmar. In September 2005 the ULFA's Barua indicated a willingness to begin peace talks, but on September 25, 2006, the Indian army responded to a recent upsurge in violence by ending a cease-fire and resuming military action against the ULFA. As of mid-2009, peace talks had yet to resume. In June 2008 some ULFA leaders declared a unilateral cease-fire, which led to their expulsion from the organization. Other groups forced from Bhutan in 2003–2004 were the NDFB and the **Kamatapur Liberation Organization** (KLO), which has sought creation of a Kamatapur state from districts in Assam and West Bengal.

The **Dima Halam Daogah** (DHD), led by Dilip NUNISA, has sought to create, primarily from part of Assam, a separate state for the Dimasa people. A cease-fire entered into effect at the start of 2003, but it has not been observed by a "Black Widow" faction led by a former DHD president, Jewel GARLOSSA, who was arrested in Bangalore in June 2009. Shortly thereafter, his faction declared a three-month unilateral cease-fire. The **Achik National Volunteers Council** (ANVC), led by Dilash MARAK, has sought to carve an Achik Land from parts of Assam and Meghalaya; it accepted a cease-fire agreement in July 2004, but a competing **Achik National Liberation Front Army** (ANLFA) has since emerged. Another group, the **Adivasi National Liberation Army** (ANLA), led by Mangra ORAN, has been linked to some bombings. Oran was arrested in Jharkhand in December 2008. The Karbi-Anglong district of Assam has also been the focus of a tribal dispute between the **Kuki Revolutionary Army** and the Karbi **United People's Democratic Solidarity.** Many Kukis had fled to Assam from Manipur, where they had been under attack by elements of the **National Socialist Council of Nagaland** (NSCN).

The separatist conflict in Nagaland, dating from 1954, has cost an estimated 200,000 lives, according to separatist sources. The creation of Nagaland State in 1963 failed to halt the insurgency, which sought to establish a "greater Nagaland" that would also include areas of those neighboring states populated in part by Nagas. The principal separatist group, the NSCN, subsequently split into S. S. KHAPLANG (NSCN-K) and Isaac Muivah (NSCN-IM) factions. On January 12, 2003, the leaders of the latter, Isaac SWU and Thuingalend MUIVAH, having met with Prime Minister Vajpayee and other leading government officials, stated that they considered the insurgency at an end, and in a joint statement on January 23 both sides agreed to seek peaceful resolution of their differences. Discussions between the government and the NSCN-K (which has also identified itself as the "Government of the People's Republic of Nagaland"—GPRN) were also ongoing, and in April 2004 the government extended a cease-fire for another year. The following October, peace talks opened in Bangkok, Thailand, with the NSCN-IM. Factional clashes continued, however. In June 2009 a recently formed civil society organization, the Forum for Naga Reconciliation, announced that the NSCN-IM, the NSCN-K, and the **Federal Government of Nagaland** (FGN), led by S. SINGYA, had signed a "Covenant of Reconciliation" in an effort to overcome their differences and present a unified front.

In Manipur, the umbrella organization for the separatist insurgency is the **Manipur People's Liberation Front** (MPLF), which was formed by the **United National Liberation Front** (UNLF), the **People's Revolutionary Party of Kangleipak** (Prepak), and the **People's Liberation Army** (PLA). The UNLF, which was established in 1964 by Areambam Samrendra SINGH, formed a **Manipur People's Army** (MPA) in 1990 in an effort to achieve independence for Manipur. Singh was killed in 2001, and the organization was subsequently led by Rajkumar MEGHEN (a.k.a. Sana YAIMA). The PLA's political wing is the **Revolutionary People's Front of Manipur** (RPFM), which announced in October 2008 that it intended to work in concert with the CPI-Maoist. The **Kangli Tawoi Kanna Lup** (KYKL) and the **Kangleipak Communist Party** (KCP) have also been involved in recent bombings. Other Manipur groups include the **Kuki National Organization** (KNO) and the **United People's Front** (UPF), both of which are umbrella organizations for various Kuki and Zomi rebel groups. In October 2006 the MPLF, the KLO, and the TPDF (below) issued a joint statement pledging their continued commitment to winning "sovereignty and independence for our separate states."

In Meghalaya, the **Hynniewtrep National Liberation Council** (HNLC), led by Cheristerfield THANGKHIEW and Bobby MARWEIN, has claimed to represent the interests of the Khasi tribe. In November 2008 the central government extended a ban on the HNLC (as well as the ULFA and the NDFB) for an additional two years, despite indications from the HNLC that it might be prepared to open negotiations.

In December 2004 the faction of the insurgent **National Liberation Front of Tripura** led by Nayanbasi JAMATIA (NLFT-NB), following up on an April 2004 cease-fire, reached a tripartite peace agreement with the central and state governments, although Jamatia himself had withdrawn from peace negotiations. Since then, however, a number of the NLFT-NB rebels have complained that the government has failed to live up to the agreement, particularly establishment of a rehabilitation fund. At issue in Tripura has not only been independence or autonomy but also the expulsion of Bengali settlers. Another separatist group, the **All Tripura Tiger Force** (ATTF), led by Ranjit DEBBARMA, joined the ULFA and the NDFB in rejecting Prime Minister Vajpayee's April 2004 offer of unconditional peace talks. The ATTF, which is based in Bangladesh, reportedly has a political wing, the **Tripura People's Democratic Front** (TPDF).

Other separatist groups include the **Babbar Khalsa International** (BKI), which is led by Wadhwa SINGH. The BKI is one of several banned groups that have demanded creation of a Sikh state of Khalistan, primarily from Punjab but also encompassing parts of adjoining states. A more moderate Sikh group, **Dal Khalsa,** established in 1978, is currently led by Haracharanjit Singh DHAMI.

In 2006 formation of a **United Gurkha Revolutionary Front** (UGRF), led by Ajay DAHAL, was announced. It has called for creation of a separate Gurkha state in the Darjeeling area of West Bengal.

LEGISLATURE

The union-level **Parliament** (*Sansad*) is a bicameral body consisting of an indirectly elected upper chamber (*Rajya Sabha*) and a directly elected lower chamber (*Lok Sabha*).

Council of States (*Rajya Sabha*). The upper chamber is a permanent body of not more than 250 members, up to 12 of whom may be appointed for six-year terms by the president on the basis of intellectual preeminence; the remainder are chosen for staggered six-year terms (approximately one-third retiring every two years) by the elected members of the state and territorial assemblies, according to quotas allotted to each. As of July 2009 the 231 occupied seats were distributed as follows: Indian National Congress, 67; *Bharatiya Janata* Party, 47; Communist Party of India (Marxist), 15; *Samajwadi* Party, 13; *Bahujan Samaj* Party, 11; All India Dravidian Progressive Federation, 7; *Janata Dal* (United), 6; Communist Party of India, 5; Dravidian Progressive Federation, 4; Nationalist Congress Party, 4; *Rashtriya Janata Dal,* 4; *Shiv Sena,* 4; *Biju Janata Dal,* 3; *Shiromani Akali Dal,* 3; *Telugu Desam* Party, 2; All India *Trinamul* Congress, 2; Assam People's Council, 2; *Janata Dal* (Secular), 2; All India Forward Bloc, Bodoland People's Front, Indian National *Lok Dal,* Indian Union Muslim League, Jammu and Kashmir National Conference, Jharkhand *Mukti Morcha,* Mizo National Front, Nagaland People's Front, *Lok Janshakti, Pattali Makkal Katchi, Rashtriya Lok Dal,* Revolutionary Socialist Party, Sikkim Democratic Front, *Swatantra Bharat Paksh,* 1 each; independents and other, 7; nonparty nominees, 9. Fourteen seats were vacant.

Chair: Mohammad Hamid ANSARI.

House of the People (*Lok Sabha*). Serving a five-year term (subject to earlier dissolution), the lower chamber currently has 545 seats, of which 543 are allocated to directly elected members from the states and union territories, with 2 filled by presidential nomination to represent the Anglo-Indian community. Seventy-nine seats are reserved for members of scheduled castes, and 41 are reserved for members of specified tribes. General elections held in five stages on April 16, 22–23, and 30 and May 7 and 13, 2009, resulted in the following distribution: United Progressive Alliance, 262 (Indian National Congress, 206; All India Trinamul Congress, 19; Dravidian Progressive Federation, 18; Nationalist Congress Party, 9; Jammu and Kashmir National Conference, 3; Jharkhand *Mukti Morcha*, 2; Indian Union Muslim League, 2; Kerala Congress[M], 1; All India *Majlis-e-Ittehadul Muslimeen,* 1; *Viduthalai Chiruthaigal Katchi, 1*); National Democratic Alliance, 159 (*Bharatiya Janata* Party, 116; *Janata Dal* [United], 20; *Shiv Sena,* 11; *Rashtriya Lok Dal,* 5; *Shiromani Akali Dal,* 4; *Telangana Rashtra Samithi,* 2; Assam People's Council, 1); Third Front, 79 (Left Front, 24 [Communist Party of India (Marxist), 16; Communist Party of India, 4; All India Forward Bloc, 2; Revolutionary Socialist Party, 2]; *Bahujan Samaj* Party, 21; *Biju Janata Dal,* 14; All India Dravidian Progressive Federation, 9;*Telugu Desam* Party, 6; Janata *Dal* [Secular], 3; Haryana *Janhit* Congress, 1; *Marumalarchi Dravida Munnetra Kazhagam,* 1); Fourth Front, 27 (*Samajwadi* Party, 23; *Rashtriya Janata Dal,* 4); Assam United Democratic Front, *Bahujan Vikas Aaghadi,* Bodoland Peoples Front, Jharkhand *Vikas Morcha* (*Prajantantrik*), Nagaland People's Front, *Swabhimani Paksha*, Sikkim Democratic Front, 1 each; independents, 8; nominated members, 2; vacancy, 1.

Speaker: Meira KUMAR.

CABINET

[as of December 1, 2009]

Prime Minister	Manmohan Singh (INC)
Ministers	
Agriculture	Sharad Pawar (NCP)
Chemicals and Fertilizers	M.K. Alagiri (DMK))
Commerce and Industry	Anand Sharma (INC)
Communications and Information Technology	Andimutha Raja (DMK)
Consumer Affairs, Food, and Public Distribution	Sharad Pawar (NCP)
Culture	Manmohan Singh (INC)
Defense	A. K. Antony (INC)
Department of Atomic Energy	Manmohan Singh (INC)
Department of Space	Manmohan Singh (INC)
Development of North Eastern Region	Bijoy Krishna Handique (INC)
External Affairs	S.M. Krishna (INC)
Finance	Pranab Mukherjee (INC)
Food Processing Industries	Subodh Kant Sahay (INC)
Heavy Industries and Public Enterprises	Vilasrao Deshmukh (INC)
Home Affairs	Palaniappan Chidambaram (INC)
Housing and Urban Poverty Alleviation	Kumari Selja (INC) [f]
Human Resource Development	Kapil Sibal (INC)
Information and Broadcasting	Ambika Soni (INC) [f]
Labor and Employment	Mallikarjun Kharge (INC)
Law and Justice	M. Veerappa Moily (INC)
Mines	Bijoy Krishna Handique (INC)
New and Renewable Energy	Farooq Abdullah (JKNC)
Overseas Indian Affairs	Vayalar Ravi (INC)
Panchayati Raj	C.P. Joshi (INC)
Parliamentary Affairs	Pawan Kumar Bansal (INC)
Personnel, Public Grievances, and Pensions	Manmohan Singh (INC)
Petroleum and Natural Gas	Murli Deora (INC)
Planning	Manmohan Singh (INC)
Power	Sushil Kumar Shinde (INC)
Railways	Mamata Banerjee (AITC) [f]
Road Transport and Highways	Kamal Nath (INC)
Rural Development	C.P. Joshi (INC)
Shipping	G.K. Vasan (INC)
Social Justice and Empowerment	Mukul Wasnik (INC)
Steel	Virbhadra Singh (INC)
Textiles	Dayanidhi Maran (DMK)
Tourism	Kumari Selja (INC) [f]
Tribal Affairs	Kantilal Bhuria (INC)
Urban Development	S. Jaipal Reddy (INC)
Water Resources	Pawan Kumar Bansal (INC)
Youth Affairs and Sport	M.S. Gill (INC)
Ministers of State (Independent Charge)	
Civil Aviation	Praful Patel (NCP)
Coal	Shriprakash Jaiswal (INC)
Corporate Affairs	Salman Khursheed (INC)
Earth Sciences	Prithviraj Chavan (INC)
Environment and Forests	Jairam Ramesh (INC)
Health and Family Welfare	Ghulam Nabi Azad (INC)
Micro, Small, and Medium Enterprises	Dinsha J. Patel (INC)
Minority Affairs	Salman Khursheed (INC)
Office of the Prime Minister	Prithviraj Chavan (INC)
Science and Technology	Prithviraj Chavan (INC)
Statistics and Program Implementation	Shriprakash Jaiswal (INC)
Women and Child Development	Krishna Tirath (INC) [f]

[f] = female

COMMUNICATIONS

Traditionally among the freest in Asia, Indian news media are protected by the constitution. Nevertheless, state and local officials have sometimes attempted to intimidate publishers and journalists, some of whom have been detained for such alleged violations as "offending religious feelings." Journalists have also come under attack in areas subject to Maoist and separatist insurgencies, especially in the northeast.

Although the public sector remains the only source of radio news broadcasts, a state monopoly on television services ended in 1992.

Press. As of 2006 there were 62,000 newspapers published in 100 languages and dialects. The Hindi press claimed by far the greatest number, 25,000, but the English-language press is dominant at the national level in both political influence and readership. Nearly all of the following dailies publish (sometimes in multiple editions) not only from the listed locations but also from various other cities: *Times of India* (Delhi, 2,540,000), founded 1838, in English; *Malayala Manorama* (Kottayam, 1,810,000), mainly in Malayalam; *Hindustan Times* (New Delhi, 1,330,000), in English; *Gujarat Samachar* (Ahmedabad, 1,320,000), in Gujarati; *Eenadu* (Hyderabad, 1,300,000), in Telugu; *Ananda Bazar Patrika* (Kolkata, 1,260,000), in Bengali; *The Hindu* (Chennai, 1,170,000), founded 1878, in English; *Mathrubhumi* (Kozhikode, 980,000), in Malayalam; *Economic Times* (New Delhi, 330,000), in English; *Ajit* (Jalandhar, 320,000), in Punjabi.

News agencies. India's principal news agencies are the Press Trust of India (PTI) and United News of India (UNI), both of which offer services in English and Hindi; UNI also has an Urdu service. Numerous foreign agencies maintain offices in New Delhi and other principal cities.

Broadcasting and computing. The Ministry of Information and Broadcasting oversees two separately operated facilities: All India Radio (AIR), which remains the country's only radio news source, and *Doordarshan India* (Television India—TVI), which offers more than 20 services. Permitted only since 2000, privately owned FM radio is expanding rapidly. Cable and satellite television services are now widely available. State-run broadcasting is supervised by the autonomous Broadcasting Corporation of India (*Prasar Bharati*).

As of 2008 there were 43.8 Internet users per 1,000 inhabitants.

INTERGOVERNMENTAL REPRESENTATION

Ambassador to the U.S.: Meera SHANKAR.

U.S. Ambassador to India: Timothy J. ROEMER.

Permanent Representative to the UN: Hardeep Singh PURI.

IGO Memberships (Non-UN): ADB, AfDB, BIS, CWTH, G-20, Interpol, IOM, IOR-ARC, NAM, PCA, SAARC, WCO, WTO.

INDONESIA

Republic of Indonesia
Republik Indonesia

Political Status: Independent republic established August 17, 1945; original constitution reinstated by presidential decree in 1959; under modified military regime from March 12, 1966, until democratic multiparty system reinvigorated following change of government on May 21, 1998.

Area: 735,354 sq. mi. (1,904,569 sq. km.).

Population: 206,264,595 (2000C); 234,423,000 (2008E). Both figures exclude East Timor, which became the independent country of Timor-Leste in 2002.

Major Urban Centers (2005E): JAKARTA (8,455,000), Surabaya (2,675,000), Bandung (2,179,000), Medan (2,009,000), Palembang (1,648,000), Tangerang (1,590,000), Semarang (1,524,000), Ujung Pandang (formerly Makassar, 1,190,000), Malang (789,000), Padang (762,000), Yogyakarta (390,000).

Official Language: Bahasa Indonesia (a form of Malay).

Monetary Unit: Rupiah (market rate December 1, 2009: 9,445.00 rupiahs = $1US).

President: Susilo Bambang YUDHOYONO (Democratic Party); elected in runoff balloting on September 20, 2004, and inaugurated on October 20 for a five-year term, succeeding Megawati SUKARNOPUTRI (Indonesian Democratic Party of Struggle); reelected on July 8, 2009, and sworn in on October 20.

Vice President: BOEDIONO (BUDIYONO, nonparty); elected July 8, 2009, and sworn in October 20 for a term concurrent with that of the president, succeeding Muhammad Jusuf KALLA (Golkar Party).

THE COUNTRY

The most populous country of Southeast Asia and fourth in the world, Indonesia is an archipelago of over 13,500 islands that fringes the equator for a distance of 3,000 miles from the Asian mainland to Australia. Java, Sumatra, and Borneo (whose territory Indonesia shares with Malaysia and Brunei) are the principal islands and contain most of the population, which is predominantly of Malay descent but includes a significant Melanesian component in the east and some 3.5–4 million ethnic Chinese. The country embraces the world's largest Muslim population in addition to small minorities of Christians (9 percent), Hindus (2 percent), and Buddhists (1 percent). Overall, a total of more than 500 languages and dialects are in use. Women make up 37 percent of the active labor force, with the majority engaged in agriculture, retail occupations, manufacturing, and hospitality industries. Islamic strictures and, until 1999, the predominance of the military in government have restrained female participation in politics; women held about 17 percent of the 550 seats in the People's Representation Council elected in 2009.

Agriculture employs about 41 percent of the workforce but contributes only 14 percent of GDP. Indonesia nevertheless remains one of the world's principal exporters of rubber and palm oil, with coffee, tea, and spices ranking among other significant sectoral exports. As the leading oil producer in the Far East, the country benefited from high oil prices for several decades but also promoted diversification into agribusiness and manufacturing. Such manufactured goods as garments and other textiles, transportation equipment, electrical appliances, and food products have become major sources of export earnings, as has liquefied natural gas. Indonesia is also a leading producer of tin. In 2007 industry as a whole accounted for about 47 percent of GDP, compared with 40 percent for the service sector, and 19 percent of employment. In May 2008 Indonesia announced that it would withdraw from the Organization of Petroleum Exporting Countries (OPEC) at the end of the year since it was now a net importer of oil.

After more than a decade of rapid economic expansion, the second half of 1997 saw a precipitous decline in the value of the rupiah, mirroring the descent of the Thai baht and other regional currencies and triggering an economic tailspin in 1998: GDP contracted by 13 percent, while inflation, which had averaged 8.5 percent annually in 1990–1997, soared to nearly 75 percent. At the same time, the country was beset by its worst drought in half a century. Efforts to stabilize the economy in 1998–1999 included proposals to reform the banking and energy industries, speed up privatization and foreign participation, restructure corporate debt, and offer greater fiscal autonomy to the provinces.

GDP growth averaged 4 percent in 2000–2003 and then turned upward, to 5 percent, in 2004. The Indian Ocean tsunami disaster of December 26, 2004, which cost an estimated 220,000 lives in Indonesia alone, did not have a major impact on the overall economy in 2005—even though the Asian Development Bank put the total cost at $4.7 billion—because the worst-hit area, Aceh, contributes only a small fraction of GDP. Growth for 2005–2006 averaged 5.6 percent. It climbed to 6.3 percent in 2007, while consumer price inflation, after peaking at 13.1 percent in 2006, dropped to 6.4 percent.

GOVERNMENT AND POLITICS

Political background. Colonized by the Portuguese in the 16th century and conquered by the Dutch in the 17th century, the territory formerly known as the Netherlands East Indies was occupied by the Japanese in World War II. Upon Japanese withdrawal, Indonesian nationalists took control, proclaiming the independent Republic of Indonesia in August 1945. After four additional years of war and negotiation, the Netherlands government recognized the new state on December 27, 1949, and relinquished claim to all its possessions in the East Indies except West New Guinea (Irian Jaya). A Netherlands-Indonesian Union under the Dutch Crown was established by the 1949 agreements but was dissolved in 1956, and in 1963 an agreement sponsored by the United Nations brought Irian Jaya (subsequently renamed Papua, currently encompassing the provinces of Papua and West Papua) came under Indonesian control. In December 1975 Indonesian troops occupied the Portuguese Overseas Territory of East Timor, and on July 17, 1976, the government formally incorporated the region into Indonesia, an action that neither Portugal nor the United Nations recognized. Following a quarter century of strife, including allegations of genocide and other human rights abuses by Indonesia, the annexed territory became independent as the Democratic Republic of Timor-Leste on May 20, 2002.

SUKARNO, one of the leaders of the nationalist struggle, served as constitutional president from 1949 until the late 1950s, when he responded to a series of antigovernment rebellions by proclaiming martial law and, in 1959, imposing a so-called "guided democracy" under which he exercised quasi-dictatorial powers. The Indonesian Communist Party (*Partai Komunis Indonesia*—PKI) assumed an increasingly prominent role and by 1965 had embarked, with Sukarno's acquiescence, on the establishment of a "Fifth Armed Force." The campaign to arm its supporters was actively resisted by the army, and on October 1, 1965, the PKI attempted to purge the army leadership. In retaliation, the military and the Indonesian masses assaulted their perceived opponents by the thousands in rural areas, killing numerous Chinese and virtually eradicating what had been the world's third largest Communist party. In succeeding months President Sukarno attempted to restore order, but public confidence in his leadership had seriously eroded. In March 1966 he was forced to transfer key political and military powers to Gen. SUHARTO, who had achieved prominence by turning back the attempted Communist takeover.

In March 1967 the People's Consultative Assembly (*Majelis Permusyawaratan Rakyat*—MPR) removed Sukarno from office, and he retired to private life until his death in June 1970. Suharto, who had proclaimed a "New Order" as acting president, was elected by the MPR in 1968 for a five-year term as chief executive. Although curbing many of the excesses of his predecessor, Suharto faced widespread discontent over steadily rising prices, domination of important sectors of the economy by foreign (particularly Japanese) capital, and a structure of political representation that permitted an overwhelming majority of the MPR to be drawn from the military and from Golkar, the government-supportive coalition of functional groups.

In 1984 legislation was introduced requiring all political, social, and religious organizations to adopt the five-point *Pancasila* state philosophy of belief in a supreme being, humanitarianism, national unity, consensus democracy, and social justice. The initiative encountered strong opposition, notably from Muslim groups, but by mid-1985 all political groupings had accepted *Pancasila.* A decade of relative stability ensued. At the nationwide election of June 9, 1992, Golkar retained overwhelming control of the largely elective People's Representation Council (*Dewan Perwakilan Rakyat*—DPR), and on March 10, 1993, the MPR unanimously elected President Suharto to a sixth five-year term.

Having made significant gains in the 1992 election, the Indonesian Democratic Party (*Partai Demokrasi Indonesia*—PDI) became the focus of an increasingly vigorous political opposition, which was led from December 1993 by Sukarno's eldest daughter, Megawati SUKARNOPUTRI (familiarly identified as Megawati). The authorities responded by promoting a takeover of the PDI by progovernment elements, which culminated in Megawati's ouster at a PDI congress in June 1996. Condemning the congress as illegally convened and conducted, she and her supporters refused to vacate the party's Jakarta headquarters, the storming of which by the security forces in late July triggered Indonesia's worst civil disorder since 1984.

The May 1997 election for the DPR produced an even more dominant position for Golkar, which won 325 of the 425 elective seats after a campaign that saw an estimated 300 people die during widespread rioting and violence. The only significant opposition came from the United Development Party (*Partai Persatuan Pembangunan*—PPP), which won 89 seats. The PDI took only 11 seats after Megawati encouraged her supporters to vote for the PPP in the wake of the split within the PDI.

On March 10, 1998, the MPR elected President Suharto for a seventh term. It also confirmed Suharto's choice of Bacharuddin Jusuf HABIBIE, a longtime associate, as successor to Vice President Try SUTRISNO. By then, however, the financial crisis that had spread in the second half of 1997 from Thailand throughout East Asia had given new impetus to antigovernment protesters. Peaceful demonstrations on university campuses began demanding far-reaching *reformasi*—the Indonesian term for political reform that was to become a rallying cry in the turmoil ahead. On March 9 the MPR gave Suharto unspecified special powers to maintain social order, and three days later Gen. WIRANTO, the new armed forces commander, warned of a military crackdown if the protests began to threaten national security.

On May 4, 1998, the government announced a deep cut in subsidies for fuel, electricity, and transportation that had been agreed to the previous year as part of a $43 billion economic assistance package put together by the International Monetary Fund (IMF). Widespread outrage at the price increases began degenerating into looting and rioting as civic, religious, ex-military, and political leaders began taking up the call for reform and urging the president to resign. Among the most outspoken critics was Amien RAIS of *Muhammadiyah,* the country's second largest Muslim organization, with some 28 million members.

On May 12, 1998, six students died in Jakarta in street protests, triggering a wave of looting, burning, raping, and other violence directed largely by the urban poor against ethnic Chinese, who had long been prominent in Indonesian business and whom many Indonesians blamed for the country's economic plight. Nearly 1,200 deaths occurred May 12–15, with thousands of businesses and buildings in Jakarta destroyed. On May 21, having lost support within Golkar and the military leadership, Suharto resigned. Vice President Habibie immediately took the oath of office as president.

The following day, pledging a "total reformation of the political, economic, and legal systems," President Habibie presented a new *Kabinet Reformasi* that nevertheless included many holdover ministers. On May 25 he began a series of political prisoner releases and announced that new national elections would be held following an overhaul of the election laws, a process expected to take about a year. In late May a ban on labor unions and restrictions on political party formation were lifted, and dozens of new parties began emerging. Most restrictions on the media were also ended.

In late June 1998 Habibie replaced 41 appointed MPR members accused of "KKN"—an Indonesian acronym for collusion, corruption, and nepotism—and announced a National Action Plan on Human Rights. These and other measures gained the new government cautious support from a number of opposition leaders, including Abdurrahman WAHID of the 30-million-member Council of Scholars (*Nahdlatul Ulama*—NU), the country's largest Muslim organization.

On October 28, 1998, some 8,000 demonstrators challenged the legitimacy of an upcoming special session of the MPR that was to begin work on electoral reform legislation. The activists also demanded Habibie's resignation, formation of a transitional government, prosecution of Suharto for political and economic offenses, and an end to military representation in the legislature. When the MPR session convened on November 10, the student reform movement anticipated receiving support for their cause from a meeting of opposition leaders Megawati, Rais, Wahid, and Sri Sultan HAMENGKU BUWONO X, head of the former royal family of Yogyakarta and recently named governor of the region. However, the four political leaders rejected the idea of a transitional government and instead indicated that they would back measures leading to orderly elections in 1999 and a six-year withdrawal of the military from the political process.

On November 13, 1998, with crowds outside the adjourned legislature having swelled to an estimated 20,000, troops opened fire when unarmed protesters tried to break through barricades, precipitating another wave of civil disorder that left 16 dead. Although the protesters immediately dubbed the day "Black Friday," the disturbances did not reach the proportion of the May rioting, which, according to a government fact-finding report, had been partly instigated by armed forces units. On December 3 the government announced that elections for the DPR would be held on June 7, 1999, with a reconstituted MPR then to convene later in the year to elect a new president. In April 1999 the police force was formally separated from the military; the MPR repealed the 1963 Subversion Law, which under Sukarno and Suharto had been invoked to imprison dissidents; and the DPR passed a law on regional autonomy designed to permit the provinces greater control over their economic and political affairs.

Forty-eight parties contested the June 1999 DPR election, the principal contenders being Megawati's newly registered PDI-Struggle (PDI-*Perjuangan,* or PDI-P); President Habibie's Golkar; Wahid's NU offshoot, the National Awakening Party (*Partai Kebangkitan Bangsa*—PKB); and Rais's National Mandate Party (*Partai Amanat Nasional*—PAN). The intricacies of the complex proportional electoral system delayed final determination of seat assignments until September, when the PDI-P was credited with 153 seats and second-ranked Golkar with 120.

On October 14, 1999, the MPR rejected President Habibie's "accountability" speech, in which he sought to justify his administration's policies but also apologized for its shortcomings. The rejection effectively ended Habibie's political career and contributed to expectations that Megawati would claim the presidency; however, many of the country's new Islamic parties objected to the prospect of a woman chief executive. The decision of the PKB's Wahid, an erstwhile Megawati supporter, to accept the nomination offered by the PAN and a group of other "Central Axis" Muslim parties led to his election by the MPR on October 20 by a 373–313 margin over the PDI-P chair. The following day, with the backing of President Wahid, Megawati was elected vice president over Hamzah HAZ of the PPP, 396–284, thereby quelling a spate of rioting by her disappointed supporters.

The "Cabinet of National Unity" announced by President Wahid on October 26 constituted an ethnic, religious, and regional cross-section, with all of the leading parties represented. Within months of taking office, however, the patched-together coalition government was being disparaged for inexperience and inefficiency. Moreover, although widely respected, Wahid soon began drawing criticism for erratic decision making and for failing to propose effective initiatives for resolving separatist and sectarian conflicts.

In northwest Sumatra secessionist sentiment had resurged in Aceh, where the Free Aceh Movement (*Gerakan Aceh Merdeka*—GAM) repeatedly clashed with security forces. In August 1998 the military had begun withdrawing nonlocal troops from Aceh, with Gen. Wiranto apologizing for human rights abuses inflicted by the military during nearly a decade of suppressive efforts. On May 12, 2000, meeting in Geneva, representatives of the two sides agreed to a limited "humanitarian pause," but security sweeps, ambushes, and other incidents continued. On April 12, 2001, the central government announced that law and order would be reestablished, ending the cease-fire.

Elsewhere, communal strife between Christians and Muslims in Maluku (the Moluccan Islands), in the east, had cost several thousand lives by 2000. A large segment of the Muslim population had long perceived itself as economically victimized by the Christians, many of them ethnic Chinese. On January 15 the Indonesian Council of Ulemas, the country's highest Islamic authority, called for a holy war (*jihad*) against Christians, and in succeeding months several thousand well-trained Muslim fighters from other provinces, the "Holy Warriors" (*Laskar Jihad*), landed in Maluku despite President Wahid's directive that authorities stop them. In late June, Wahid declared a state of civil emergency in the region, by which time similar sectarian outbreaks had occurred elsewhere, including on nearby Sulawesi.

In Kalimantan, a dispute between native Dayaks and immigrant Madurese repeatedly flared up. In predominantly Melanesian West Papua (now officially Papua; see Annexed Territory, below), separatists threatened to declare independence. Most dramatically, an August 30, 1999, proindependence vote in East Timor had precipitated a wave of unprecedented violence by pro-Jakarta militias that was not contained until a UN peacekeeping force began arriving on September 20. On October 19 the MPR endorsed the referendum results, thereby rescinding East Timor's 1976 annexation and paving the way for the former territory's full independence as Timor-Leste after a period of administration by the UN. In early 2000 a report by the Indonesian Commission to Investigate Human Rights Violations in East Timor called for the government to explore the possible prosecution of 33 individuals, including Wiranto and several other generals, in connection with human rights violations in East Timor. On May 16 Wiranto tendered his resignation as coordinating minister for politics and security.

Having apologized to the MPR for the failings of his administration in a speech on August 7, 2000, Wahid announced two days later that he would assign day-to-day "technical" presidential tasks to Vice President Megawati and would reorganize the cabinet. The changes, announced on August 23, included the naming of two new coordinating ministers, one assigned to oversee economic and financial matters and the other to supervise political, social, and security affairs.

On February 1, 2001, the DPR formally censured Wahid 393–4 for his handling of a $2 million donation from the Sultan of Brunei and for an effort by an associate to scam millions from the State Logistics Agency (Bulog). Dissatisfied with his response, which included an assertion that the move against him was unconstitutional, the DPR approved a second censure motion on April 30, and then on May 30 voted 365–4 to convene the MPR to consider impeachment. Cabinet changes in June failed to reduce the momentum against Wahid, even though the attorney general had cleared him of any involvement in "Brunei-gate" and "Bulog-gate." In July the beleaguered president issued a decree dissolving the DPR, but the Supreme Court ruled the move illegal, and the MPR responded by convening earlier than planned. On July 23 it voted 591–0 to remove Wahid and then quickly elected Megawati as his successor. Two days later Wahid agreed to leave the presidential palace, although he continued to insist that he was the rightful president.

The Megawati cabinet, which took the oath of office on August 10, was equally divided between representatives of supportive political parties and nonaffiliated technical experts. Shortly after assuming office President Megawati had backed special autonomy provisions for Aceh, where the conflict had cost an estimated 12,000 lives in the past decade, but the exiled GAM leadership, based in Sweden and headed by Hasan di TIRO, continued to reject any such arrangements. A December 2002 cease-fire and tentative peace accord gradually disintegrated, and at a May 2003 negotiating session in Tokyo the GAM once again refused anything short of independence. In response, President Megawati quickly instituted martial law, ordered a resumption of military action, and in June decreed that all journalists obtain presidential permission before reporting from Aceh. Martial law was downgraded a year later to a state of civil emergency, but much of the province remained restive.

In Maluku, in February 2002 the leaders of the Christian and Muslim communities signed an agreement to end the sectarian fighting that by that time had claimed 5,000 lives and had displaced hundreds of thousands. Although numerous violent incidents were subsequently reported, the peace agreement held relatively intact beyond midyear, and in October it was reported that *Laskar Jihad* had decided to disband. (*Laskar Jihad* had also been active in the sectarian conflict in Sulawesi, where about 1,000 people had died before a peace agreement was signed in December 2001.) In the same month more than a dozen members of the

Christian Maluku Sovereignty Front (*Front Kedaulatan Maluku*—FKM) were convicted of charges related to raising the banned flag of the South Maluku Republic, which had been proclaimed in 1950. Subsequent flag-raising episodes likewise resulted in clashes with security forces, arrests, and additional prosecutions of FKM members for subversion.

On April 5, 2004, Indonesia elected the 550 members of a restructured DPR; the new Regional Representatives Council (*Dewan Perwakilan Daerah*—DPD), which had been established as an upper house of the MPR by a 2002 constitutional amendment; and local legislators—a total of more than 15,200 offices contested by nearly 450,000 candidates. As had been predicted by opinion polls, Golkar won a plurality, 127 seats, in the DPR, followed by Megawati's PDI-P with 109. Somewhat unexpectedly, 58 seats were won by the recently organized Democratic Party (PD), headed by Megawati's former coordinating minister for political and security affairs, Lt. Gen. (Ret.) Susilo Bambang YUDHOYONO.

Encumbered by a perceived lack of progress in eliminating corruption and resolving regional conflicts, President Megawati was defeated in Indonesia's first direct presidential election. In first-round voting on July 5, 2004, she finished second to Yudhoyono, who at the September 24 runoff took 60.9 percent of the vote against the incumbent's 39.1 percent. Inaugurated on October 20, President Yudhoyono formed a new "United Indonesia Cabinet" (*Kabinet Indonesia Bersatu*) that included representatives of his own PD, Golkar, the PKB, the PPP, the recently organized Prosperous Justice Party (*Partai Keadilan Sejahtera*—PKS), the PAN, and the Crescent Star Party (*Partai Bulan Bintang*—PBB).

On December 26, 2004, the largest earthquake in 40 years (9.3 on the Richter scale) occurred off the coast of Sumatra and generated a tsunami that devastated Aceh Province. A June 2005 report put the toll at 220,000 dead or missing (170,000 in Aceh) and 475,000 displaced in Indonesia alone. A political consequence of the tsunami disaster was increased international attention brought to bear on the secessionist conflict in Aceh, where the calamity spurred both sides to return to the negotiating table in 2005. Talks held in January, February, April, and May in Helsinki, mediated by former Finnish president Martti Ahtisaari's Crisis Management Initiative team, made significant strides toward an agreement on "special autonomy" for Aceh. In May, President Yudhoyono lifted the state of civil emergency in the province, and on July 16, at the end of a fifth round of talks, the participants announced a peace agreement that was signed on August 15. By late December the GAM had disarmed and Jakarta had removed a significant proportion of nonlocal troops and security personnel from Aceh.

On July 11, 2006, the DPR unanimously passed the Aceh autonomy legislation, which granted the province 70 percent of revenues from its oil and natural gas resources, extra reconstruction allocations from the national budget, special permission to form local political parties (only national parties are permitted elsewhere), and permission to implement Islamic law (Sharia) for Muslims. A gubernatorial election held December 11 was won by Irwandi YUSUF, a former GAM leader who technically ran as an independent.

The DPR election of April 9, 2009, concluded with President Yudhoyono's PD winning a plurality of 148 seats, followed by Golkar's 106 and the PDI-P's 95. The leaders of all three parties then contested the July 9 presidential election, with Yudhoyono easily securing a second term and avoiding a runoff against second-place finisher Megawati by taking 60.2 percent of the vote. The Golkar candidate, incumbent Vice President Jusuf KALLA, finished a distant third. Immediately after his inauguration on October 20, the president named a new cabinet that included the PD, Golkar, the PAN, the PKS, the PKB, and the PPP. Independents received a number of key posts, including the ministers of defense, finance, foreign affairs, home affairs, and trade.

Constitution and government. In the wake of unsuccessful efforts to draft a permanent constitution in 1950 and 1956, the government in 1959 readopted by decree the provisional constitution of 1945, which allocated most powers to the president under a strong executive system. The five guiding principles (*Pancasila*) identified in the preamble are monotheism, humanitarianism, national unity, democracy by consensus, and social justice.

The president, who is now limited to two five-year terms, remains the commander in chief; "may declare war, make peace and conclude treaties," with legislative concurrence; and may declare a state of emergency under conditions set by the legislature. Since 2004 the president and vice president have been directly elected on a single ticket; if no ticket receives a majority of the votes cast as well as at least 20 percent of the votes in half of the country's 33 provinces , the two leading tickets compete in runoff balloting.

Prior to constitutional reforms passed in 2001 and 2002, the People's Consultative Assembly (MPR) was considered the highest state organ, with sole competence to interpret the constitution and to elect the president and vice president. It included all members of the ordinary legislature, the People's Representation Council (DPR), in addition to regional delegates and representatives of the military and assorted functional groups. Effective from the 2004 general election, the MPR became a bicameral legislature, the new upper house being the indirectly elected Regional Representatives Council (DPD).

The DPD, whose membership may total no more than one-third that of the DPR, has limited authority but can propose legislation on regional autonomy, regional boundaries, the allocation of resources between the central government and the regions, and management of natural resources. The DPD may choose to oversee implementation of related laws and may also advise the lower house, the DPR, on such matters as taxation, the budget, religion, and education. The DPR continues to carry out regular legislative functions and may impeach the president by a two-thirds vote of the entire membership. Dismissal of the president would then require investigation, trial, and concurrence by the Constitutional Court, after which two-thirds of those voting in the MPR would also have to give their assent. The MPR also oversees the inauguration of the president and vice president and is empowered to consider constitutional amendments.

At the apex of the judicial system is the Supreme Court, whose members are proposed by the Judicial Commission of the DPR and appointed by the president. There are also lower public courts, religious courts, military tribunals, and state administrative courts. In addition, a 2002 constitutional change authorized creation of a nine-member Constitutional Court (the president, the DPR, and the Supreme Court each nominate three judges), which, in addition to its role in the presidential dismissal process, has authority to review the constitutionality of legislative acts, to resolve disputes between state organs, to review contested election results, and to consider the dissolution of political parties.

Indonesia is presently divided into 33 provinces, including 2 special regions (Papua and Yogyakarta), 1 special capital district (Jakarta), and since 2006 Nanggroe Aceh Darussalam (formerly the special region of Aceh). In late 2004 a court ruling on the 2003 three-way division of Papua Province let stand the completed separation of the westernmost area of the province as West Irian Jaya but prevented further division because of a conflict with a 2001 law on special autonomy for Papua. In April 2005 the Constitutional Court affirmed the decision. In 2007 West Irian Jaya was officially renamed West Papua.

Each province has an elected legislature (*Dewan Perwakilan Rakyat Daerah*) and, under the post-Suharto reforms, an elected governor; government at the regency (*kabupaten*) and municipal (*kotamadya*) levels includes elected legislatures and elected executives (*bupati* and *walikota,* respectively).

Foreign relations. Following independence, Indonesia initially sought to play a prominent role in Asian affairs while avoiding involvement in conflicts between major powers. In the early 1960s, however, President Sukarno, asserting that a basic world conflict existed between the "old established forces" and the "new emerging forces," attempted to project Indonesia as the spearhead of the latter. While officially nonaligned in foreign policy, his regime formed close ties with the Soviet Union and the People's Republic of China; obtained the surrender of West New Guinea (Irian Jaya) by the Netherlands; and instituted a policy of "confrontation," supported by guerrilla incursions, against the new state of Malaysia. Most of these policies were reversed under Suharto, with Indonesia, although still formally nonaligned, moving markedly closer to the West.

The three-year "confrontation" with Malaysia was terminated in 1966, after which diplomatic relations were established with Malaysia and Singapore. In addition, Indonesia took the lead in forming the Association of Southeast Asian Nations (ASEAN) as an instrument of regional cooperation. Membership in the United Nations and many of its related agencies resumed in 1966, Indonesia having withdrawn in 1965 because of international opposition to its annexation of West New Guinea. Formal diplomatic ties to China, having been suspended in October 1967, were restored in August 1990. Relations suffered as a consequence of attacks against Chinese in the upheaval leading to Suharto's resignation, but in May 1999 President Habibie issued a decree outlawing ethnic discrimination and ended a ban against using or teaching Mandarin Chinese.

Developments in East Timor attracted periodic Australian criticism for more than two decades, even though Canberra, under both Liberal and Labor administrations, recognized Indonesian sovereignty in the territory. In December 1995 Indonesia and Australia signed a security cooperation agreement providing for mutual notification in case of emergency, and in 1997 the two neighbor states completed a treaty establishing mutual maritime boundaries, ending some three decades of debate and tension over the issue. In January 1999 the Australian government, in a significant policy change, stated that it would support an "act of self-determination" for East Timor following a period of autonomy. The about-face left Jakarta with no major ally supporting its hardline stance against self-determination. Shortly thereafter, the Habibie government indicated for the first time that it might accept East Timor's independence.

Australia's prominence in condemning Jakarta's inaction against the postreferendum paramilitary violence of September 1999 in East Timor, followed by its leading role in the resultant UN peacekeeping force, led to a dramatic chilling of relations. Under President Wahid relations initially improved, but Jakarta's failure to discourage a flow of boats carrying asylum-seekers (most of them from Afghanistan and the Middle East) to Australia's outer territories in 2001–2002 drew sharp criticism from the government of Prime Minister John Howard. Relations were further complicated by the threat of terrorism and Jakarta's unwillingness to acknowledge the presence of the *Jemaah Islamiah* (JI) terrorist organization until an October 12, 2002, bombing of a Bali tourist resort claimed 202 lives, 88 of them Australian.

In January 2005 President Yudhoyono warmly acknowledged Australia's unprecedented pledge of A$1 billion in aid following the previous December's earthquake and tsunami disaster, and in April the two countries signed a framework partnership agreement that included among its provisions closer military cooperation. In March 2006, however, Indonesia protested Australia's decision to grant temporary admission to more than 40 proindependence Papuans who were seeking asylum after having entered Australian waters in January. Relations were largely repaired in November, when the two countries' foreign ministers signed a ten-point security agreement that included pledges to respect each other's sovereignty and unity and not to support separatist movements.

Relations with the United States strengthened during the 1980s, primarily because the Ronald Reagan administration regarded Indonesia as an important anticommunist presence in the region. However, a December 1991 massacre in Dili in East Timor led the U.S. Congress to cut off direct military funding. In October 1996, during a U.S. presidential election campaign, allegations surfaced in Washington that an Indonesian business conglomerate had illegally donated some $250,000 to the Democratic Party. Subsequent U.S. congressional criticism of alleged human rights violations in Indonesia further disturbed relations. Following Suharto's resignation, the Bill Clinton administration voiced its support for the Habibie government and, later, the Wahid presidency, although the East Timor turbulence had prompted Washington to temporarily suspend military assistance.

U.S. President George W. Bush described Indonesia as a key ally in the "war on terrorism" despite massive demonstrations in October–November 2001 to protest the U.S.-led campaign in Afghanistan. Widespread opposition also greeted the 2003 U.S.-led invasion of Iraq. During a visit by President Yudhoyono to Washington in May 2005, the Bush administration announced that it was relaxing restrictions on the sale of nonlethal military equipment to Indonesia. Restoration of full military links, including weapons sales and training, was announced by Washington in November 2005.

In August 2004 appeals court decisions overturned the convictions of four high-ranking officers for abuses in East Timor in 1999. In November the conviction of the former civilian governor of East Timor, Abílio SOARES, was also overturned, and he was released. This meant that of the 18 individuals who had been tried for related crimes, only 1 civilian, militia leader Eurico GUTTERES, still faced serving a full sentence. On April 7, 2008, however, the Supreme Court also overturned his conviction, and he was released after having served two years of a ten-year sentence. In January 2005 Timor-Leste and Indonesia had agreed to establish a Commission of Truth and Friendship to examine remaining human rights cases but without prosecutorial authority. The final session of the commission met September 24–27, 2007, in Dili.

In September 2007, during a visit to Indonesia by Vladimir Putin, the Russian president and President Yudhoyono signed nine agreements, including, most significantly, a deal for the purchase of Russian weaponry. Other agreements covered a range of topics, from combating terrorism to protecting the environment.

At the end of 2008 Indonesia withdrew from OPEC because it had become a net oil importer. It has, however, joined the recently established Gas Exporting Countries Forum. It also participated in the G-20, which brings together the world's major industrialized countries and the principal emerging economies.

Current issues. The first Yudhoyono administration's most notable achievement may have been bringing the separatist conflict in Aceh to a conclusion, even though the agreement was attacked by nationalists for granting too much authority to the province and by secularists for permitting the introduction of Islamic law. Yudhoyono also waged a largely successful campaign against the JI, despite coordinated bombings at the Marriott and Ritz-Carlton hotels in Jakarta on July 17, 2009. The attack killed 7 people (plus the bombers) and injured another 50, but it also underscored that no other attacks on a comparable scale had occurred for several years.

The July bombings were allegedly masterminded by NOORDIN Mohammed Top, who was regarded by police and antiterrorist agencies as Southeast Asia's most wanted criminal. Originally associated with the JI, he was more recently identified as the head of the *Tanzim Qaedat al-Jihad* (Organization for the Basis of Jihad), a JI offshoot formed in 2006 when the majority faction of the JI reportedly rejected further attacks targeting civilians. Top was killed by security personnel on September 17.

The government has also had some success in confronting endemic graft and corruption. Critics of Indonesia's Corruption Eradication Commission (*Komisi Pemberantasan Korupsi*—KPK) have accused it of being too timid in its pursuit of major cases and less than impartial in focusing attention on members of previous administrations, but it has successfully prosecuted dozens of cases. Nevertheless, it remains controversial, and calls to reduce or end its wiretapping and prosecutorial powers were embraced by almost all of the party factions in the 2004–2009 DPR.

On March 28, 2008, former president Suharto, who had died on January 27, was posthumously acquitted of having embezzled government funds in a civil suit involving a family charitable foundation. The suit had sought some $1.1 billion in damages. Although the court ruled in Suharto's favor, the charity was ordered to repay $100 million to the government. Other suits against Suharto's estate and family remained pending. His youngest son, Hutomo "Tommy" MANDALA PUTRA, who had previously been convicted of corruption in a land deal and of conspiracy in the murder of a Supreme Court judge, was acquitted of a final corruption charge in February 2009. He subsequently began a campaign to assume the leadership of Golkar.

The president's handling of the economy in response to the international financial crisis of 2008–2009 may also have contributed to the Democratic Party's success at the polls in April 2009 and to his own first-round reelection victory three months later. Government actions included infusing funds into the economy to stimulate consumer spending, to fund labor-intensive infrastructure projects, and to stabilize the stock market and banks. As a consequence, Indonesia avoided falling into a recession, with projected growth for 2009 estimated at 4.0–4.5 percent, among the best rates in Asia.

Recent changes in electoral laws also affected the outcomes of the 2009 legislative and presidential elections. A minimum threshold of 2.5 percent of the national vote was required for political parties to be awarded DPR seats. As a consequence, the number of successful parties dropped to 9, down from 16 in 2004. Two of the winning parties—the Great Indonesia Movement Party (*Partai Gerakan Indonesia Raya*—Gerinda) and the People's Conscience Party (*Partai Hati Nurani Rakyat*—Hanura)—were contesting their first election, with 9 parties that had previously held as many as 14 seats being eliminated. In a further change from 2004, a presidential election law passed in 2008 mandated that only parties or coalitions that won 25 percent of the DPR seats or 20 percent of the national vote could nominate presidential candidates. This meant that only the DP, which had narrowly achieved both thresholds, could have nominated a candidate on its own. In the end, the DP paired with the Prosperous Justice Party (*Partai Keadilan Sejahtera*—PKS), the PAN, the PPP, the PKB, and a host of nonparliamentary parties to back the ticket of President Yudhoyono and a new contender for vice president, the governor of the central bank, BOEDIONO. The PDI-P again nominated Megawati Sukarnoputri, with Gerinda's Prabowo SUBIANTO, a controversial former commander of the army special forces, as her running mate. The third ticket encompassed the sitting vice president, Golkar's Jusuf Kalla, at the top and Hanura's Gen. Wiranto. Yudhoyono took 60.8 percent of the vote, while Megawati won 26.8 percent and Kalla finished third, with 12.4 percent.

Following the April 2009 DPR election, the Central Election Commission (*Komisi Pemilihan Umum*—KPU) grappled for five months after the April DPR election with challenges to how legislative seats should be filled under the country's complicated regulations for awarding proportional seats. At one point, the KPU was presented with competing rulings from the Supreme Court and the Constitutional Court, and it wasn't until September that the matter was largely settled.

On February 18–19, 2009, the recently installed U.S. Secretary of State, Hillary Clinton, included a stop in Indonesia during her first official visit to the Far East. Her visit to the largely Muslim country was seen as reinforcing the new Barack Obama administration's effort to strengthen ties to moderate Islam. Obama's November 2008 election had generated a mostly favorable response in Indonesia, where he had spent part of his boyhood, despite continuing widespread objections to U.S. policy in Iraq and Afghanistan.

POLITICAL PARTIES

Prior to May 1998 the government was supported by a coalition of social groups familiarly called Golkar, with only two other parties—the United Development Party (PPP) and the Indonesian Democratic Party (PDI), both dating from 1973—being allowed to contest elections. Subsequent efforts to promote democracy and reform included formation of three groups in 1991: a 45-member Democracy Forum, one of whose leaders was Abdurrahman Wahid of the Council of Scholars (*Nahdlatul Ulama*—NU); the more radical League for the Restoration of Democracy, led by H. Johannes PRINCEN of the unrecognized *Setiakawan* (Solidarity) trade union; and a Forum for the Purification of People's Sovereignty, led by Gen. Hartono Resko DHARSONO, Indonesia's most prominent dissident. None had a significant impact on national elections or on the Suharto regime's political agenda. The Indonesian Democratic Union Party (*Partai Uni Demokrasi Indonesia*—PUDI) and the People's Democratic Party (*Partai Rakyat Demokras*—PRD) were launched in May and July 1996, respectively, but the Suharto government granted neither official status.

Given the scarcity of political alternatives under Suharto, various Muslim associations increasingly assumed a quasi-political character. These included the country's two largest Muslim organizations, the long-established NU and *Muhammadiyah,* the latter chaired by Amien Rais. In addition, an Association of Indonesian Muslim Intellectuals (*Ikatan Cendikiawan Muslim Indonesia*—ICMI) was formed in December 1990. The ICMI was widely regarded as the outgrowth of the president's desire to create a broad-based Muslim constituency that would be at least partially independent of the military. Its first chair was B. J. Habibie, a German-trained aeronautical engineer and staunch Suharto ally.

In 1998 this political landscape underwent a volcanic transformation. Suharto's departure from office in May and the Habibie government's decision to ease restrictions on political parties resulted in formal registration of nearly 140 new parties by late February 1999. A total of 48 subsequently met the requirements for offering candidates at the June 1999 DPR election, with the Indonesian Democratic Party of Struggle (PDI-P) of Megawati Sukarnoputri, the National Awakening Party (PKB) of Abdurrahman Wahid, and the National Mandate Party (PAN) of Amien Rais emerging as the principal anti-Golkar contenders. An anticipated alliance of the three was never formalized. Although 21 parties won at least 1 seat in the DPR, only 6 met the threshold of 10 seats (2 percent of the 500-seat body) required for contesting the next legislative election.

After the June 1999 election a loose coalition of ten or so predominantly Islamic parties emerged. Controlling over 160 DPR seats, the "Central Axis" (*Poros Tengah*) coalesced around Wahid as a presidential alternative to the incumbent B. J. Habibie and Megawati. In addition to the PKB and the PAN, parties associated with the axis included the PPP, the Crescent Star Party (PBB), the Justice Party (PK; now the Prosperous Justice Party—PKS), and the United Believers Awakening Party (PKU; see under PPP).

Twenty-four of the country's roughly 300 parties qualified for the April 2004 DPR elections: the 6 that had won at least 2 percent of the 1999 vote, plus 18 that had met membership and other requirements in at least two-thirds of the provinces. Only parties achieving 5 percent of the popular vote or 3 percent of the DPR seats at the April balloting were then eligible to nominate presidential candidates. In August 2004, in an unsuccessful effort to defeat front-runner Susilo Bambang Yudhoyono of the Democratic Party (PD) at the September presidential runoff, Golkar, the PDI-P, the PPP, and the new Prosperous Peace Party (PDS) established a loose Coalition of the Nation in support of President Megawati. Collectively, the 4 parties controlled over 300 seats in the 550-seat DPR, but Golkar, now led by Yudhoyono's vice presidential running mate, Jusuf Kalla, soon withdrew.

In early 2007, confronted by the prospect of being declared ineligible to contest the 2009 legislative election because they had not achieved the 3 percent vote threshold in 2004, some of the smaller parliamentary parties called for changes in the electoral law. In 2008 the DPR passed a new election law that, under its "transitional provisions," permitted the 9 previously ineligible parties to qualify. At the end of February 2008, over 100 parties were registered. At the end of May, however, following an initial vetting by the Ministry and Justice and Human Rights, the General Elections Commission announced that 51 of 64 potentially eligible parties (including the 16 parliamentary parties) had met all administrative requirements for the April 2009 legislative election, which included having at least 1,000 members, branches in 60 percent of the provinces, and chapters in 60 percent of all regencies and municipalities. In addition, at least 30 percent of all party nominees for the DPR must be women. In the end, 38 parties were officially registered to contest the election. Nine won seats.

An electoral law passed in October 2008 pronounced that only parties or coalitions that met one of two conditions—winning, in the April 2009 DPR election, 20 percent of the seats or 25 percent of the overall vote—could nominate presidential candidates for the July 2009 race. Independent candidates were not permitted.

Presidential Party:

Democratic Party (*Partai Demokrat*—PD). The centrist PD (also translated as the Democrats Party or Democracy Party) was formally established in 2002, largely to advance the cause of its principal founder, Lt. Gen. (Ret.) Susilo Bambang Yudhoyono, a former Golkar member who was serving at the time as coordinating minister for political and security affairs in the Megawati cabinet. Using Yudhoyono's popularity to build its base, the PD won an unexpected 7.5 percent of the vote and 56 seats in the DPR election in April 2004. A month earlier its founder, having declared in December 2003 that he would seek the presidency, had resigned from the cabinet. After finishing first in the initial round of the July presidential election, with just under 34 percent of the vote, Yudhoyono handily won the July runoff against Megawati, taking 60.9 percent. His closest advisers included Rachmat WITOELAR, a former Golkar secretary general, and two former PDI-P leaders, Heru LELONO and Suko SUDARSO.

The PD won a leading 148 seats in the April 2009 DPR election, based on a vote share of 26.8 percent. President Yudhoyono, backed by a coalition of over 20 parties, went on to win reelection in July.

Leaders: Susilo Bambang YUDHOYONO (President of the Republic and Chair of the Executive Board), Hadi UTOMO (Chair), Achmad MUBAROK (Deputy Chair), Anas URBANINGRUM (DPR Faction Leader), H. Marzuki ALIE (Secretary General).

Other Parties in the Governing Coalition:

Functional Group Party (*Partai Golongan Karya*—Golkar). A government-sponsored formation organized in 1964, the Joint Secretariat of Functional Groups (*Sekretariat Bersama Golongan Karya*—Sekber Golkar) began as a loose alliance of some 200 groups representing such functional interests as those of farmers, laborers, veterans, women, and youth. The largely military-led organization was technically not a party.

Although Golkar was labeled "toothless" by some observers, in October 1989 the Suharto regime called on the organization to play a more active role as a representative body. In the June 1992 legislative election Golkar won 68 percent of the vote and 282 of 400 elective seats in the DPR, while in May 1997 it captured 73 percent of the vote and 325 out of 425 legislative seats.

At a July 9–11, 1998, congress in Jakarta, in the first such open contest in the organization's history, State Minister Akbar TANJUNG won election as the group's new chair. The congress also abolished its board of patrons, which effectively removed Suharto from the party, and stripped two members of his immediate family of their official posts. Later in July, Golkar's Central Executive Council removed seven Suharto family members from their MPR seats.

Formally converted into a political party prior to the 1999 election campaign, Golkar finished second, with 21 percent of the vote and 120 seats in the DPR. Having been nominated in May as Golkar's presidential candidate, President Bacharuddin Jusuf Habibie withdrew shortly before the MPR balloting on October 20, the assembly having delivered what amounted to a no-confidence vote following his "accountability" speech of October 14. His candidacy had already been damaged by a major scandal that erupted in July 1999 over $70 million in public funds that had been diverted through the Bank Bali for Golkar's use, allegedly to buy votes. Following Habibie's withdrawal, most Golkar representatives supported the PKB's Abdurrahman Wahid, ensuring his election.

Subsequently, a number of Habibie supporters and others formed an "eastern caucus" dubbed Iramasuka or Iramasuka Nusantara—an acronym constructed from *Ir*ian *Ja*ya, *Ma*luku, *Su*lawesi, and *Ka*limantan, plus *Nusa Tenggara*.

In September 2002 Akbar Tanjung was convicted of corruption for diverting over $4 million in state funds to Golkar. He declined to resign as speaker of the DPR or as Golkar chair, however, pending appeal of his conviction, which was overturned by the Supreme Court in February 2004. The taint of corruption nevertheless may have contributed to his failure to win the party's 2004 presidential nomination. In a second-round intraparty vote in April, he was defeated by Gen. Wiranto, 315–227, despite the latter's indictment in Timor-Leste for "command responsibility" during the 1999 turmoil in East Timor. Wiranto named Salahuddin WAHID, brother of former president Abdurrahman Wahid, as his running mate and obtained the support of Wahid's PKB, but he finished third in the July presidential election, with 22 percent of the vote. At the April DPR election the party had had more success, winning a plurality of 127 seats on a 21.6 percent vote share.

Equally important for the party, the winning vice presidential candidate in 2004 was Golkar's Jusuf Kalla, who was then elected party chair in late December. His ascent had the additional consequence of separating Golkar from the other participants in the opposition Coalition of the Nation. As of mid-2008, Kalla was regarded as the party's likely presidential nominee in 2009, although Akbar Tanjung was also considered a possible contender. Golkar's second-place finish in the April 2009 DPR election, when it dropped to 106 seats, clearly undercut Kalla's prospects for the presidency. Nevertheless, negotiations with the PD over a renewed joint ticket failed to produce an agreement, leading Golkar and Wiranto's Hanura to combine forces. Kalla won only 12.4 percent of the presidential vote in July.

With a new leadership expected to be ushered in at the next national congress in October 2009, the leading candidates for chair were expected to be billionaire Aburizal BAKRIE, coordinating minister for people's welfare in the first Yudhoyono administration; Yuddy CHRISNANDI, a legislator; and media magnate Surya PALOH, chair of the Advisory Board. Suharto's youngest son, Hutomo "Tommy" Mandala PUTRA, despite having served a prison sentence for murder, also indicated that he intended to run. A sister, Siti Hadiyanti "Tutut" RUKMANA, a former party treasurer and social affairs minister in her father's last cabinet., was also regarded as a potential candidate, but she did not contest the election. In heated balloting, Bakrie won, defeating Paloh 296–240.

Leaders: Aburizal BAKRIE (Chair), Jusuf KALLA (Former Vice President of the Republic and 2009 presidential candidate), Agung LAKSONO (Coordinating Minister for People's Welfare and Deputy Chair of the Party),Theo SAMBUAGA (Deputy Chair), Priyo Budi SANTOSO (DPR Faction Leader), Sultan HAMENGKU BUWONO X (Governor of Yogyakarta), Idris MARHAM (Secretary General).

Prosperous Justice Party (*Partai Keadilan Sejahtera*—PKS). Also identified in English as the Justice and Prosperity Party, the PKS began as the Justice Party (*Partai Keadilan*—PK), which was formed in July 1998 and campaigned for the June 1999 election on a platform that included a call for racial and ethnic harmony and nondiscrimination. A moderate Islamic party, the PK won under 2 percent of the vote and seven seats in the DPR, after which it joined the PAN in organizing a parliamentary Reform Faction. The party's founding chair, Nur Mahmudi ISMAIL, resigned the leadership in May 2000 to concentrate on ministerial duties in the Wahid government.

Because the PK had not won sufficient DPR seats in 1999 to qualify for the 2004 DPR election, in 2002 the PK leadership organized an alternative party, the PKS, which succeeded in meeting the registration requirements. At the April 2004 election the PKS won an unexpected 7.3 percent of the vote and 45 seats, after which the party chair, Hidayat Nur Wahid, was elected chair of the MPR and resigned his party office. In the September 2004 presidential runoff the PKS threw its support to Susilo Bambang Yudhoyono, and in October it joined the new cabinet.

The PKS's Adang DARADJATUN, with 42 percent of the vote, failed to win the two-way contest for governor of Jakarta in August 2007. The PKS had greater success in the April 2009 DPR election, winning 57 seats; of the parties in the preceding DPR, only the PD and the PKS gained seats. The PKS then backed President Yudhoyono's reelection.

Leaders: Tifatul SEMBIRING (Minister of Information and Communication and Chair of the Party), Hilmi AMINIDIN (Chair of Advisory Board), Mustafa KAMAL (DPR Faction Leader), Hidayat NUR WAHID (2004–2009 MPR Chair), Anis MATTA (Secretary General).

National Mandate Party (*Partai Amanat Nasional*—PAN). Founded on August 23, 1998, by reformist Amien Rais of the *Muhammadiyah,* the PAN has advanced a program based on democracy; pluralism; nonsectarianism; nondiscrimination; women's equality; market economics; disengagement of the military from politics; and separation of executive, legislative, and judicial powers.

The PAN won only 7 percent of the June 1999 vote, for 34 seats in the DPR. Thereafter, Rais was a driving force behind formation of the "Central Axis" coalition. When the MPR convened in October, Rais was elected its chair, the third highest office (after president and vice president) in the state hierarchy.

At the April 2004 DPR election the PAN won only 6.4 percent of the vote but captured 53 seats. In July presidential balloting Rais finished fourth, managing only 15 percent of the vote, despite the backing of many moderate Muslim parties and having selected as his running mate Siswono Yudohusodo, a former Golkar member and Suharto minister who had himself been the initial presidential choice of the Indonesia Unity Party (PSI, below) and a number of smaller parties.

In April 2005 Amien Rais's candidate to succeed him as party chair, Sutrisno Bachir, defeated party cofounder and former finance minister Fuad BAWAZIER. In August, Bawazier resigned from the PAN, which, he asserted, had "abandoned its characteristic democracy." He later joined Gen. Wiranto's new Hanura party (below).

In the April 2009 DPR election the PAN won 46 seats. It then supported President Yudhoyono's reelection.

Leaders: Sutrisno BACHIR (Chair), Amien RAIS (Former Chair of the MPR), Hatta RADJASA (Coordinating Minister for the Economy), Asman ABNUR (DPR Faction Leader), Zulkifli HASAN (Minister of Forestry and Secretary General of the Party).

United Development Party (*Partai Persatuan Pembangunan*—PPP). In the face of sustained pressure from the government to simplify Indonesia's party system through fusion, four Islamic groups—the Muslim Scholar's Party of the NU, the Indonesian Islamic Party (*Partai Muslimin Indonesia*—PMI), the United Islamic Party of Indonesia (*Partai Syarikat Islam Indonesia*—PSII), and the Muslim Teachers' Party (*Persatuan Tarbijah Islamijah*—Perti)—merged into the PPP in 1973. Although the party remained faction ridden, its leadership generally supported government policies while seeking to suppress both radical elements and the more conservative NU faction.

During its first national congress, held in Jakarta in August 1984, the PPP formally adopted *Pancasila* as its sole ideology. However, elements within the NU, led by Abdurrahman Wahid, demanded that the group withdraw from "practical politics" and expressed dissatisfaction with the leadership of the PPP chair, Jailani NARO, who had formerly led the PMI. As a result, not only the NU but also the less influential *Syarikat Islam* severed their links with the PPP the following December, insisting that henceforth they would concentrate exclusively on social and religious activities.

The party's influence declined dramatically after the departure of the NU, and it did not recover for over a decade. It won 89 legislative seats in the 1997 elections, however, having benefited greatly from a split in the PDI (see PDI-P, above). At the June 1999 election it won 11 percent of the vote but a comparatively disproportionate share of 58 seats because of a vote-sharing agreement (*stembus akoord*) it had concluded with a number of smaller Islamic parties.

PPP leader Hamzah Haz was defeated in the October 1999 vice-presidential contest in the MPR, losing to Megawati. Subsequently named coordinating minister for people's welfare and eradication of poverty, he announced after only a month in office that he would leave the cabinet and concentrate on party affairs. Following Megawati's election to the presidency, on July 26, 2001, Haz was elected vice president by the MPR.

In the run-up to the 2004 elections the PPP's ranks were increased by merger or cooperation agreements with several smaller parties, including the United Believers Awakening Party (*Partai Kebangkitan Umat*—PKU), which is often rendered in English as the Islamic Awakening Party. The PKU had been launched in October 1998 by NU members and clerics committed to the adoption of Islamic law and opposed to the selection of a secularist as the next president. In announcing the "merger," PKU leader Asnawi LATIEF indicated that his party, which did not meet the requirements for competing in the 2004 DPR elections, did not plan to dissolve but to work in tandem with the PPP. Other parties adopting similar strategies were Ridwan SAIDI's New Masyumi Party (*Partai Masyumi Baru*—PMB), which derived its name from a Sukarno-era Consultative Council of Muslim Indonesians (*Majelis Syuro Muslimin Indonesia*), and the New Indonesia Party (*Partai Indonesia Baru*—PIB).

At the April 2004 legislative election the PPP finished third, with 58 DPR seats based on 8.2 percent of the vote. In the July presidential contest Hamzah Haz finished fifth, with 3 percent of the vote. A year later, dissatisfaction with Haz's continuing leadership led demonstrators to occupy party headquarters in a failed effort to convince the party's executive board to move up the date of the next party congress. When the congress was held, as scheduled, in February 2007, Suryadharma Ali was elected chair over Arief Mudatsir MANDAN, Achmad DIMYATI, and five other candidates.

With the April 2009 DPR election approaching, the PPP, the PDI-P, and Golkar held discussions on forming a "golden triangle" governing coalition, but the prospect dissolved in the wake of unsuccessful results at the polls and the competing presidential ambitions of the Golkar and PDI-P leaders. In the April 2009 election support for the PPP dropped, and the party lost more than one-third of its DPR seats, winning only 38. In July it backed President Yudhoyono for a second term.

Leaders: Suryadharma ALI (Minister of Religious Affairs and Chair of the Party), Hasrul ASWAR (DPR Faction Leader), Irgan Chairul MAHFIZ (Secretary General).

National Awakening Party (*Partai Kebangkitan Bangsa*—PKB). Launched in July 1998 by the NU, the PKB nevertheless supports secular government, a stance that led more conservative Muslims within the NU to organize other parties, including the PKU (see PPP, above). By mid-1999, however, growing opposition to a presidential bid by Megawati Sukarnoputri within various other Islamic and reform parties found them proposing the NU chair, Abdurrahman Wahid—familiarly, Gus Dur ("Older Brother Dur")—as their favored candidate even though the PKB had won only 51 DPR seats (on a 17 percent vote share) at the June election. With firm backing from Golkar and the "Central Axis" parties, he was elected by the MPR, 373–313 over Megawati, on October 20. Thereafter, Wahid's relations with the other leading parties and the Indonesian legislature grew increasingly fractious, culminating in his July 2001 removal from office. Wahid then dismissed the party chair, Mathori Abdul JALIL, for disloyalty.

The nearly blind Wahid had suffered two major strokes even before being elected president, and in 2004 his frail health disqualified him as a repeat candidate. As a consequence, the PKB ended up backing Golkar's Wiranto, who had selected the former president's brother and NU leader, Salahuddin Wahid, as his running mate.

At the April 2004 legislative election the PKB won about 10.6 percent of the vote (third place) but only 52 seats (sixth place). Within a year, a leadership dispute had split the party into two principal factions. Following decisions by party Chair Alwi SHIHAB and Secretary General Syaifullah YUSUF to join the Yudhoyono cabinet, both were forced to vacate their party offices. A congress in April 2005 elected Muhaimin Iskandar, a nephew of Wahid, to chair the party, but in October 2005 Shihab supporters held a competing convention that named Choirul ANAM as chair and Shihab as chair of the party's Executive Council. The December 2005 cabinet reshuffle saw the departure of Shihab, the retention of Yusuf, and the addition of Iskandar loyalist Erman SUPARNO as minister of manpower and transmigration. Some analysts viewed the changes as a step toward reconciliation, but in 2006 both factions continued to claim title to the party name.

Another rift occurred in 2008, when Wahid attempted to dismiss Iskandar. The Iskandar faction, however, was legally registered and in April 2009 won 28 seats (a loss of 25) in the DPR. It then supported President Yudhoyono's reelection in July. Former President Wahid died on December 30, 2009.

Muhaimin Faction Leaders: Muhaimin ISKANDAR (Minister of Manpower and Transmigration and Chair of the Party), Azis MANSYUR (Chief Patron), Marwan JAFAR (DPR Faction Leader), Mohammad Lukman EDY (Secretary General).

Gus Dur Faction Leaders: Ali Masykur MUSA (Chair), Yenni WAHID (Secretary General).

Other Parliamentary Parties:

Indonesian Democratic Party of Struggle (*Partai Demokrasi Indonesia–Perjuangan*—PDI-Struggle, or PDI-P). The Indonesian Democratic Party (PDI) was formed in January 1973 as a result of the government's exhortation to "simplify" Indonesia's party system. The party was organized through merger of the following five minority parties: the Indonesian Nationalist Party (*Partai Nasional Indonesia*—PNI), the Upholders of Indonesian Independence (*Ikatan Pendukung Kemerdekaan Indonesia*—IPKI), the Catholic Christian Party of Indonesia (*Partai Kristen Katolik Indonesia*), the (Protestant) Christian Party (*Partai Kristen Indonesia*—Parkindo), and the People's Party (*Partai Murba*—PM).

Having won 11 percent of the popular vote in 1987, the PDI was the most conspicuous gainer in the 1992 balloting, increasing its legislative representation from 40 to 56. Despite government objections, former president Sukarno's eldest daughter, Megawati Sukarnoputri, was elected party chair in December 1993.

In early 1995 a dissident group—charged by the party mainstream as being a product of infiltration by government agents—insisted that many members were linked to the banned Communist Party (PKI, below). These tensions came to a head in June 1996 when the progovernment PDI wing convened a party congress and elected Megawati's predecessor, Dr. SURYADI, as chair. When Megawati loyalists later attempted to retain the main PDI building in Jakarta, party activists clashed with security forces sent to evict them, resulting in a disputed number of fatalities, other casualties, and arrests. In September the Megawati faction was refused permission to register a list of candidates for the 1997 legislative election. With Megawati having advised supporters to vote for PPP candidates, the PDI won only 11 seats with 3 percent of the vote in the May 1997 elections.

In August 1998 the Supreme Court dismissed Megawati's lawsuit challenging her removal as PDI leader, and six days later clashes with the police occurred when her supporters tried to disrupt a congress of the progovernment faction in Palu. On October 8–10 in Denpasar, Bali, the pro-Megawati PDI faction held its own congress, at which she asserted that Indonesia had been "destroyed by parasites." Megawati subsequently registered her majority faction as a separate party, the PDI-Struggle.

At the June 1999 election the PDI-P captured a plurality of 153 seats in the DPR on a 37 percent vote share, while the rump PDI won only 2 seats. Although Megawati was considered the leading contender for the presidency, her decision to remain aloof from political alliances prior to the October meeting of the MPR, combined with the reluctance of many Islamic parties to support a woman candidate, ultimately cost her the victory. Rioting by some of her supporters immediately broke out but was calmed by her election as vice president. On July 23, 2001, upon President Wahid's removal from office, the MPR elevated Megawati to the presidency.

In the April 2004 DPR election the PDI-P fared poorly, winning 109 seats based on 18.5 percent of the vote. Seeking a full term as president three months later, Megawati finished second in the first round, winning 26 percent support, but at the September runoff she managed only 39 percent. In early 2005 a number of party reformers were reportedly seeking a candidate to replace her as party chair, but she won reelection "unanimously" in March. The dissidents were expelled in May and went on to form the Democratic Renewal Party (PDP, below) late in the year.

In the April 2009 parliamentary election the PDI-P finished third, winning 94 seats. In September 2007 the party had nominated Megawati as its July 2009 presidential candidate, but she finished a distant second, with 26.8 percent of the vote. Her husband, Taufik Kiemas, was expected to seek the post of MPR chair when the new parliament convened in October.

Leaders: Megawati SUKARNOPUTRI (Former President of the Republic and Chair of the Party), Taufik KIEMAS (Chair of the MPR), Fauzi BOWO (Governor of Jakarta), Tjahjo KUMOLO (DPR Faction Leader), Pramono ANUNG (Secretary General).

Great Indonesia Movement Party (*Partai Gerakan Indonesia Raya*—Gerinda). Gerinda was established in February 2008 as a vehicle for the presidential aspirations of Prabowo Subianto, former commander of the army's special forces unit (Kopassus) and a son-in-law of former president Suharto. Socialist in orientation, the party called for establishing a "people-based" economy. In July, shortly after Subianto's formal resignation from Golkar, the party named him as its nominee. When Gerinda managed to secure only 26 seats on a 4.6 percent vote share in the April 2009 DPR election and thereby failed to meet the threshold for nominating a candidate on its own, it entered into a coalition with the PDI-P. Together, the PDI-P and Gerinda nominated Megawati for president and Subianto for vice president. The ticket finished second in the July 2009 vote, winning 26.8 percent of the vote.

Leaders: Ir. SUHARDI (Chair), Prabowo SUBIANTO (2009 vice-presidential candidate), MOERDIONO (Chair of Advisory Board), Mijiyono HAYANTO (DPR Faction Leader), Ahmad MUZANI (Secretary General).

People's Conscience Party (*Partai Hati Nurani Rakyat*—Hanura). In December 2006 Gen. Wiranto, former minister of defense and 2004 Golkar candidate for president, announced the formation of Hanura, which was expected to become the vehicle for a 2009 presidential bid. In the April 2009 DPR election Hanura won 17 seats. It then joined Golkar in a coalition for the July presidential election, with Wiranto being named the ticket's candidate for vice president. Golkar's Jusuf Kalla and Wiranto finished third in the three-way race, winning only 12.4 percent of the vote.

Leaders: Gen. WIRANTO (Chair of the Party and 2009 vice-presidential candidate), Fauzi ACHMAD (DPR Faction Leader), Yus Usman SUMANEGARA (Secretary General).

Other Parties Represented in the 2004–2009 DPR:

Reform Star Party (*Partai Bintang Reformasi*—PBR). The moderate Islamic PBR began as the PPP-*Reformasi,* a youthful reform faction within the United Development Party that viewed the PPP leadership as too conservative. Formally established in September 2002 as a separate party led by popular Islamic preacher ZAINUDDIN M. Z., who was a former PPP vice chair, the PPP-Reform changed its name to the PBR in April 2003 to avoid a legal altercation over use of the PPP label.

Although Zainuddin was initially named the party's presidential candidate for 2004, the party won only 2.4 percent of the vote and 14 seats at the April 2004 DPR election and therefore did not meet the threshold for contesting the race. The PBR ultimately chose to support the PAN's Amien Rais in first-round balloting and then backed President Megawati in the second round.

In 2005 Zainuddin was unanimously reelected party chair despite differences with Zainal MAARIF, at that time a deputy speaker of the DPR. The rift continued to widen, however, with Maarif organizing a rival party congress and claiming the leadership. In April 2006 Zainuddin surrendered the chair in the interest of party unity and was succeeded by Bursah Zarnubi. In early 2007 Maarif attempted to relaunch the party after having been dismissed in 2006 for marrying a second wife. In March 2007 Zainuddin announced his intention to resign as chair of the party's Advisory Board because of differences with Zarnubi.

In December 2007 the party announced a name change, to the United Reform Star Party, in an effort to circumvent the 3 percent threshold for contesting the 2009 DPR election, but the change was made moot by passage of a new election law in 2008. The party won only 1.2 percent of the vote in April 2009 and therefore failed to obtain any seats in the DPR.

Leaders: Bursah ZARNUBI (Chair), Rusman H.M. ALI (Secretary General)

Prosperous Peace Party (*Partai Damai Sejahtera*—PDS). The PDS, which is sometimes rendered in English as the Peace and Prosperity Party, was established in October 2001. Although committed to *Pancasila,* the party membership is largely from the Christian minority and is led by a Christian preacher, Ruyandi Hutasoit. Although Hutasoit intended to seek the presidency in 2004, the PDS failed to meet the threshold for nominating him when it won only 2 percent of the vote and 13 seats at the April DPR election. Instead, the party chose to support President Megawati's reelection. In April 2009, with 1.5 percent of the vote, the party won no DPR seats

Leaders: Ruyandi Mustika HUTASOIT (Chair), Ferry REGAR (Secretary General).

Crescent Star Party (*Partai Bulan Bintang*—PBB). Defining itself as a democratic and modernist Islamic party with roots in the *Masyumi* party that was dissolved during the Sukarno era, the PBB won 13 seats and a 2 percent vote share at the June 1999 legislative election.

In April 2004 the PBB won about 2.6 percent of the vote and 11 seats in the DPR election. It supported Susilo Bambang Yudhoyono for president even though the party chair, Yusril Mahendra, was justice and human rights minister in the Megawati cabinet. Mahendra was named to the powerful post of state secretary in the Yudhoyono cabinet and served in that capacity until being replaced in the May 2007 reshuffle. In the DPR the PBB joined four smaller parties—the PPDK, the PP, the PPDI, and the PNIM (all below)—in forming the Democratic Star Pioneer faction.

In May 2005, with Mahendra having stepped down as chair, Malam S. Kaban was elected to replace him, defeating Hamdan Zoelva. Concerned that the PBB could not meet the requirements for competing in the 2009 election cycle, Zoelva later led an effort to organize a new formation, the Star Crescent Party (*Partai Bintang Bulan*—PBB), one possibility being that the two parties could then merge. The 2008 election law eliminated the need for the maneuver. The party won only 1.8 percent of the vote, however, and thus no DPR seats.

For the 2009 presidential election, Mahendra was the party's prospective nominee, but its lackluster performance in the DPR election excluded it from putting forth a candidate. An effort to have the relevant electoral law declared unconstitutional failed

Leaders: Malam S. KABAN (Chair), Hamdan ZOELVA (Deputy Chair), Yusril Ihza MAHENDRA (Chair of Advisory Board), Abdul Sahar HASSAN (Secretary General).

Democratic Nationhood Party (*Partai Demokrasi Kebangsaan*—PDK). The PDK was established in July 2002 as the National Democratic Unity Party (*Partai Persatuan Demokrasi Kebangsaan*—PPDK, also known in English as the United Democratic Nationhood Party). The PPDK drew support from reform-minded, nationalist members of the middle class. Its chair, Ryaas Rasyid, was minister of state for administrative reforms in the Wahid cabinet but resigned in January 2001 because he considered the government's regional devolution efforts to be insufficient. In the 2004 DPR election, the PPDK won 1.2 percent of the vote and four seats. It supported Golkar's Wiranto for president that July, which resulted in the departure of cofounder Andi Alfian MALLARANGENG. In an effort to avoid the threshold requirement for elections that was in effect at the time, the PPDK was relaunched as the PDK in October 2007.

In the April 2009 DPR election the PDK won only 0.6 percent of the vote and thus no seats.

Leaders: Muhammad Ryaas RASYID (Chair), ALIUDDIN HAMMERING (Secretary General).

Pioneer Party (*Partai Pelopor*—PP). The PP was established in August 2002 by Rachmawati Sukarnoputri, a younger sister of President Megawati, to advance her father's Marhaenist philosophy of "self-reliance and support for ordinary people." Having attacked Megawati's leadership, Rachmawati intended to seek the presidency herself but ended up supporting Amien Rais of the PAN when the PP managed to win only three DPR seats and less than 1 percent of the vote at the April 2004 DPR election. In January 2006 Rachmawati was named an adviser to President Yudhoyono.

In 2009 the PP won only 0.3 percent of the DPR vote and thus no seats. It supported President Yudhoyono's reelection in July 2009.

Leaders: Rachmawati SUKARNOPUTRI, Eke Surya SANTOSO (Chair), KRISTIYANO (Secretary General).

Concern for the Nation Functional Party (*Partai Karya Peduli Bangsa*—PKPB). The PKPB, which is also rendered in English as the National Concern Workers' Party, was founded in September 2002 with the support of former President Suharto and his eldest daughter, Siti Hardiyanti Rukmana. When the PKPB won only 2 percent of the vote and two DPR seats at the April 2004 legislative election, thereby precluding Rukmana's nomination for the presidency, the party decided to support Golkar's Wiranto. The PKPB's representatives chose to sit with the Golkar faction in the DPR.

The PKPB won only 1.4 percent of the vote in the April 2009 DPR election.

Leaders: R. HARTONO (Chair), Ari MARDJONO, Siti Hardiyanti RUKMANA, Hartarto SASTROSOENARTO (Secretary General).

Indonesian Justice and Unity Party (*Partai Keadilan dan Persatuan Indonesia*—PKPI). The PKPI began as the PKP, which was formed in mid-December 1998 by former Golkar members. One of its leaders, former general and defense minister Edi SUDRAJAT, had resigned from Golkar in November after having lost an election for Golkar chair the previous July. Another founder, Gen. Try Sutrisno, had served as Suharto's vice president from 1993 to 1998. The PKP won 1 percent of the vote and four seats in the DPR at the June 1999 election. Having reconstituted itself as the PKPI, in April 2004 it won only one seat. In the 2004 presidential contest the PKPI backed Susilo Bambang Yudhoyono.

Sudrajat died in December 2006 and was succeeded as chair by Meutia Swasono, minister of women's empowerment in the Yudhoyono cabinet. In 2009 the PKPI failed to retain its four DPR seats, having won only 0.9 percent of the vote. It backed President Yudhoyono's reelection in July.

Leaders: Meutia Farida SWASONO (Chair), Samuel SAMSON (Secretary General).

Indonesian Democratic Vanguard Party (*Partai Penegak Demokrasi Indonesia*—PPDI). Also identified in English as the Upholders of Indonesian Democracy Party, the PPDI was established in 2003. It won under 0.8 percent of the vote and one DPR seat at the April 2004 election and subsequently supported the PAN's Amien Rais for president.

Although the party was officially registered for the 2009 DPR election, an internal split threatened its prospects. It ended up winning only 0.1 percent of the vote.

Leaders: Mentik BUDIWIYONO (Chair), Joseph Lea WEA (Secretary General).

Indonesian National Party (Marhaenism) (*Partai Nasional Indonesia [Marhaenisme]*—PNIM). Formed in May 2002 by another of Sukarno's daughters, Sukmawati, the PNIM is a leading Marhaenist party, claiming descent from Sukarno's PNI, which he had established in 1927 and which was consolidated into the PDI in 1973. Sukmawati planned to compete for the presidency in 2004 against her sisters, the incumbent Megawati and the PP's Rachmawati, but her PNIM won only one DPR seat and 0.8 percent of the vote at the April DPR election. In the end, the PNIM backed the PAN's Amien Rais.

In December 2008 a former general and governor of Jakarta, SUTIYOSO, stated that the PNIM was prepared to support his run for the presidency in 2009, but the party's poor showing in the April 2009 DPR election, when it won only 0.3 percent of the vote, rendered its support moot.

Leaders: Sukmawati SUKARNOPUTRI (Chair), Ardi MUHAMMAD (Secretary General).

Other National Parties That Failed to Win DPR Seats in 2009:

Democratic Renewal Party (*Partai Demokrasi Pembaruan*—PDP). Also translated as the Renewal of Democracy Party, the PDP began as a reform group within the PDI-P, but its leaders were expelled in May 2005 after challenging Megawati's reelection as party chair. Charging that Megawati had turned away from Sukarno's teachings, the dissidents announced formation of the PDP the following December under the leadership of Roy B. B. Janis, who had previously served as an associate chair of the PDI-P. The PDP was officially registered in 2006. It won 0.9 percent of the vote in the 2009 DPR election.

Leaders: Roy B. B. JANIS (Executive Chair), Abdul MADJID (Chair of Advisory Council), Laksamana SUKARDI (Coordinator), Didi SUPRIYANTO (Secretary).

Indonesian Populist Fortress Party (*Partai Nasional Banteng Kemerdekaan Indonesia*—PNBKI). The PNBKI was established in 2002 as the *Partai Nasional Bung Karno* (incorporating in its title a nickname for former President Sukarno) by former PDI-P members who no longer supported President Megawati. Later renamed because of a new law prohibiting the naming of parties after individuals, it won 1.1 percent of the vote but no DPR seats in 2004. In 2009 it won 0.5 percent.

Leaders: Erros DJAROT (Chair), Zulfan LINDAN (Secretary General).

Indonesia Unity Party (*Partai Sarikat Indonesia*—PSI). The PSI was formed in December 2002 by eight ideologically diverse parties, each of which had won only one seat at the 1999 DPR election and which therefore did not meet the threshold for contesting the 2004 election. From the time of its formation the PSI was viewed as a coalition of convenience, and it attracted only 0.6 percent of the vote in 2004. Its 2004 presidential candidate, Siswono YUDOHUSODO, eventually became the running mate of the PAN's Amien Rais. In 2009 it won only 0.1 percent of the vote.

Leaders: H. MARDINSYAH (Chair), Nazir MUCHAMAD (Secretary General).

Seventeen other national parties, many of them newly registered since 2004, unsuccessfully contested the 2009 DPR election. Of them, only 2 won more than 1.0 percent of the vote: the **Ulema National Awakening Party** (*Partai Kebangkitan Nasional Ulama*—PKNU), established by former members of the PKB and chaired by Choirul ALAM, which won 1.5 percent, and the **National People's Concern Party** (*Partai Peduli Rakyat Nasional*—PPRN), led by Amelia Achmad YANI, which won 1.2 percent.

The other 15 unsuccessful parties were the following: the **Archipelagic Republic Party** (*Partai Republik Nusantara*—PRN), led by Letjen SYAHRIR; the **Freedom Party** (*Partai Merdeka*—PM), formed in 2002 by former government minister Adi SASONO; the **Indonesian Democratic Devotion Party** (*Partai Kasih Demokrasi Indonesia*—PKDI), led by Stefanus Roy RENING; the **Indonesian Nahdlatul Community Party** (*Partai Persatuan Nahdlatul Ummah Indonesia*—PPNUI), which emerged from the NU as the *Nahdlatul Ummat* Party and won five seats in 1999 under the leadership of Syukron MAKMUN; the **Indonesian Workers and Businessmen's Party** (*Partai Pengusaa dan Pekerja Indonesia*—PPPI), led by Daniel HUTAPEA; the **Indonesian Youth Party** (*Partai Pemuda Indonesia*—PPI), chaired by Hasanuddin YUSUF; the **Labor Party** (*Partai Buruh*—PB), led by labor union leader Mochtar PAKPAHAN, who had organized the National Labor Party (*Partai Buruh Nasional*—PBN) after being released from prison in 1998; the **National Front Party** (*Partai Barisan Nasional*—Barnas), chaired by Vence RUMANGKANG; the **National Sun Party** (*Partai Matahari Bangsa*—PMB), led by Imam ADDARUQUTNI, a former PAN member; the **New Indonesia Struggle Party** (*Partai Perjuangan Indonesia Baru*—PPIB), led by Nurmala Kartini SJAHRIR; the **Patriot Party** (*Partai Patriot*—PP), formed in 2001 and led by Yapto Sulistio SOERJOSOEMARNO; the **Prosperous Indonesia Party** (*Partai Indonesia Sejahtera*—PIS), led by Budiyanto DARMASTONO; the **Regional Unity Party** (*Partai Persatuan Daerah*—PPD), founded in 2002 and chaired by Oesman SAPTA; the **Sovereignty Party** (*Partai Kedaulatan*) led by H. Ibrahim BASRAH; and the **Workers' Struggle Party** (*Partai Karya Perjuangan*—PKP), led by Jackson KUMAAT.

Aceh Parties:

Aceh Party (*Partai Aceh*—PA). The PA was established in May 2008 through the conversion of the Free Aceh Movement (*Gerakan Aceh Merdeka*—GAM) into a legalized party.

The GAM, which had fought for Aceh's independence from 1976 until 2005, was virtually indistinguishable from the Aceh Sumatra National Liberation Front (ASNLF), which dated from 1989. The GAM leader, Hasan di Tiro, has lived in Sweden since 1979.

In February 2002 the GAM joined in peace talks in Geneva, Switzerland, that led to a December 9 cease-fire and peace agreement, under which the GAM was to begin disarming. Ultimately, however, the GAM continued to reject greater autonomy in place of independence, and in May 2003, following the breakdown of peace talks in Tokyo, Japan, President Megawati declared martial law in Aceh. In May 2004 martial law was downgraded to a state of civil emergency but not before a number of GAM activists had been convicted of treason and terrorism and sentenced to lengthy prison terms.

In the aftermath of the December 26, 2004, tsunami disaster, the GAM declared a cease-fire and dropped its demand for independence, which opened the way for a resumption of peace negotiations with the government. The peace agreement signed on August 15, 2005, effectively ended the secessionist conflict (despite the continuing presence of small proindependence militant groups), and by the end of the year the GAM had decommissioned its weapons and disbanded its armed wing, the *Tentara Nasional Aceh* (TNA). To aid in its political transformation the GAM established an Aceh Transition Committee (*Komite Peralihan Aceh*—KPA). On April 19–23, 2006, a number of GAM leaders, including the prime minister of the government-in-exile, Malik Mahmud (but not the 83-year-old Hasan di Toro), visited Aceh.

Following approval by the DPR of Aceh autonomy legislation, two GAM members, running as independents, were among the eight candidates contesting the provincial governor's race in December 2006: H. A. HUMAM, who was supported by the PPP as well as by the exiled GAM leadership, and Irwandi YUSUF, who was more closely associated with the KPA. The victorious Yusuf, who won 38 percent of the vote, was sworn in on February 8, 2007.

GAM's transformation into a legal political party made it eligible for legislative elections held in April 2009, when the PA was the clear leader among regional parties in contests for the provincial and district assemblies. Earlier, in October 2008, Hasan di Toro visited Aceh after three decades in exile.

Leaders: Muzzakir MANAF (Chair, Former GAM Commander), Hasan di TIRO and Malik MAHMUD (Patrons), Adnan BEURANSAH (Spokesperson), Muhammad YAHYA (Secretary General).

In addition to the PA, the following 5 Aceh-based parties were registered for the 2009 elections: **Acehnese People Party** (*Partai Rakyat Aceh*—PRA); **Peaceful, Prosperous Aceh Party** (*Partai Aceh Aman Sejahtera*—PAAS), **Independent Voice of the Acehnese Party** (*Partai Suara Independen Rakyat Aceh*—SIRA); **Sovereign Aceh Party** (*Partai Daulat Aceh*—PDA); **United Aceh Party** (*Partai Bersatu Aceh*—PBA).

Illegal and Insurgent Groups:

Communist Party of Indonesia (*Partai Komunis Indonesia*—PKI). Founded in the 1920s, the PKI was banned in 1966 in the wake of the failed 1965 coup attempt. It subsequently split into pro-Peking and pro-Moscow factions. A number of imprisoned party leaders were executed in 1985 and 1986 (some 15 years after being sentenced for their involvement in the 1965 revolt), and at present only a handful of underground PKI activists appear to be operating within the country. In April 1996 the government restored the suffrage rights of over 1 million people listed as having been involved in the 1965 PKI insurgency, although over 20,000 others continued to be barred from voting. Voicing support for the *reformasi* movement, in 1998 the party called for formation of a Patriotic and Democratic Alliance.

Three PKI members, all of whom had been in prison for over 30 years, were among 28 political prisoners freed by the Habibie government in August 1998. In May 2000 President Wahid called for revoking the country's ban on communist ideology, but the proposal was attacked by most political leaders. In February 2004 the Constitutional Court restored the political rights of former PKI members, but discrimination against members and their families remains common. In 2009 former party members were permitted to run for DPR seats.

Jemaah Islamiah (JI). In the days after the September 11, 2001, al-Qaida attacks on the United States, the shadowy *Jemaah Islamiah* (Islamic Congregation) emerged as the principal Southeast Asian terrorist organization. Operating from various cells located throughout the region, the JI was believed to have direct ties to al-Qaida. JI-attributed bombings and other plots have taken place or been uncovered in a number of countries, including the Philippines, Singapore, and Malaysia as well as Indonesia, which is generally regarded as the organization's home base. The JI has as an overarching goal the creation of a single, regional Islamic state.

The militant cleric Abu Bakar BASHIR (BAASYIR) has been labeled as the organization's spiritual leader—an accusation that he has denied. After serving four years in jail for subversion during the Suharto era, Bashir moved to Malaysia but subsequently returned to Indonesia, purportedly to promote the establishment of a regional Islamic state through his participation in an umbrella organization known as the **Indonesian Mujahidin Council** (*Majelis Mujaheddin Indonesia*—MMI).

Until the October 2002 bombing of a Bali tourist resort, which killed 202 people, the Megawati government refused to acknowledge an Islamic terrorist presence in Indonesia. Although Bashir was detained after the bombing, which had led the United States and the UN to declare the JI a terrorist organization, the government was unable to directly connect him to the attack. In September 2003 Bashir was convicted of crimes that included subversion for authorizing a series of bombings in December 2000 and for plotting to assassinate Megawati, who was vice president at the time, but in December the subversion conviction was overturned. He remained incarcerated for forgery and immigration violations, and upon being released on April 30, 2004, he was immediately rearrested for his alleged leadership of the JI and for his alleged involvement not only in the Bali case but also in the August 2003 bombing of a Marriott Hotel in Jakarta, which killed 12.

In August 2003 another allegedly key figure in JI operations, Riduan ISAMUDDIN (also known as HAMBALI), was apprehended by Thai officials, with assistance from the U.S. Central Intelligence Agency. Hambali, flown to the United States for interrogation, has since been held incommunicado, originally at an undisclosed location but more recently at the U.S. Guantánamo Bay detention center.

Among the three dozen suspects arrested for the Bali bombing, the JI-linked AMROZI bin Nurhasyim, his brother Ali GUFRON (MUKHLAS), and Imam SAMUDRA were convicted and sentenced to death in 2003. In July 2008 the Supreme Court rejected their appeals, and they were executed by firing squad on November 9. Bashir's trial, which began in late October 2004, concluded on March 3, 2005, when he was found guilty of conspiracy in the Bali bombing and sentenced to a prison term of 30 months (later reduced to 25). Bashir was released in June 2006; five months later the Supreme Court quashed his conviction.

In September 2004 a suicide bombing outside the Australian embassy in Jakarta killed 11. Azahari HUSIN and Noordin Mohammed TOP, both suspected JI members, were believed to have planned the attack and quickly climbed to the top of the regional "most wanted" list. In October 2005 suicide bombers again struck Bali, killing 44. A month later, Husin was killed by security personnel in East Java.

By then, some analysts were reporting a split in the JI between hardline militants and those who rejected the tactic of inflicting civilian casualties. In mid-2006 Top and other extremists formed an al-Qaida organization identified as **Tanzim Qaedat al-Jihad** (Organization for the Basis of Jihad).

In March 2006 Indonesian officials indicated that they had arrested some 270 alleged JI members since 2000, including Bashir's apparent successor, Abu RUSDAN. In June 2007 military leader Abu Dujana and political leader ZARKASIH (alias Zainuddin FAHMI) were captured. In April 2008 both were convicted of terrorism and give 15-year prison sentences.

The first major domestic terror attack in several years took place on July 17, 2009, when coordinated explosions inside Jakarta's Marriott and Ritz-Carlton hotels killed six foreigners and one Indonesian in addition to the two bombers. Noordin Top, generally considered the most wanted individual in Southeast Asia by police forces, was believed to be the mastermind of the bombings. He was killed by security personnel two months later.

Leaders: Ainal BAHRI (Abu DUJANA), ZULKARNAEN (Arif SUNARSO).

Malukan Sovereignty Front (*Front Kedaulatan Maluku*—FKM). Established in mid-2000, the largely Christian FKM has advocated independence for the so-called South Maluku Republic (*Republik Maluku Sarani*—RMS), which had been proclaimed on April 25, 1950. The FKM's most visible activity, raising the RMS flag each year on the anniversary of the independence declaration, has led authorities to arrest dozens of Malukans for subversion. This, in turn, has repeatedly contributed to violent clashes with security forces.

Those convicted of subversion have included FKM leaders Alex Manuputty, Moses Tuanakotta, and Samuel Waileruny. Manuputty fled to the United States in December 2003, following rejection of his appeal. In November 2004 Tuanakotta was sentenced to nine years in prison, after which Simon Saiya was named by exiled leaders in the Netherlands to head an RMS transitional government.

In April 2008 a district court convicted Johan TETERISA of treason and handed down a life sentence for leading a traditional war dance and waving an RMS flag during a visit to Ambon by President Yudhoyono in June 2007. Another 19 dancers had already received prison sentences of 10–20 years.

Leaders: Simon SAIYA (Chair), Alex MANUPUTTY (in exile), Samuel WAILERUNY, Moses TUANAKOTTA.

For a discussion of the **Free Papua Organization,** see the Annexed Territory section, below.

LEGISLATURE

Under constitutional changes passed in August 2002, Indonesia's **People's Consultative Assembly** (*Majelis Permusyawaratan Rakyat*—MPR) now comprises two bodies: the Regional Representatives Council (DPD), which functions as an upper house with limited powers related primarily to regional concerns, and the People's Representation Council (DPR), which performs ordinary legislative functions.

Initially, the MPR was an outgrowth of the Provisional People's Consultative Assembly (*Majelis Permusyawaratan Rakyat Sementara*—MPRS) appointed by President Sukarno in 1960. As of January 1999 its membership included the 500 members of the DPR, plus another 500 comprising additional Golkar and military representatives, unaffiliated regional delegates, and, in proportion to their respective shares of DPR seats, appointed members of the United Development Party and the Indonesian Democratic Party. Government-supportive members, including those elected by regional parliaments, held about 80 percent of the seats. Reforms passed by the DPR on January 28, 1999, reduced the membership to 700, including 135 regional representatives and 65 civic and social delegates in addition to the 500 DPR members.

The changes enacted in 2002 and implemented in 2004 restructured the MPR as, in effect, a joint session of the DPR and the DPD. Before the 2002 reforms, which instituted direct presidential elections, the MPR elected the president and vice president. As in the past, it must meet at least once every five years.

MPR Chair: Taufiq KIEMAS.

Regional Representatives Council (*Dewan Perwakilan Daerah*—DPD). The DPD was created by constitutional amendment in August 2002. Members (familiarly styled "senators") are indirectly elected for five-year terms on a nonpartisan basis by provincial assemblies and must convene at least once a year. The most recent election for 132 members (4 from each of Indonesia's 33 provinces) was held April 9, 2009.

Chair: Irman GUSMAN.

People's Representation Council (*Dewan Perwakilan Rakyat*—DPR). An outgrowth of the Mutual Cooperation House of Representatives (*Dewan Perwakilan Rakyat–Gotong Rojong*—DPRGR) named by President Sukarno in 1960, the DPR encompassed 425 elected members and 75 military appointees until the June 1999 election, at which time military representation was cut to 38 seats. Additional reforms passed in August 2002 eliminated all reserved seats while increasing the number of members to 550, effective from the 2004 election. Representatives are directly elected through a province-based proportional system that permits voters to cast ballots for individual candidates or parties, which must achieve a minimum threshold of 2.5 percent of the popular vote to claim seats.

For the April 9, 2009, election the size of the house was increased to 560 seats. Following the voting, the General Elections Commission (*Komisi Pemilihan Umum*—KPU), the Supreme Court, and the Constitutional Court all became involved in hearing disputes related to the awarding of seats. Although the initial election results were released in May, the KPU did not announce 546 "final" seat assignments until September 3. At that time a still-unresolved vote-counting issue led the KPU to delay announcing the winners of Papua Province's 10 seats; 4 other seats, although awarded to specific parties, remained temporarily unfilled because replacements for the parties' disqualified designees had been yet been named. The following party totals reflect the new house as sworn in on October 1, 2009: Democratic Party, 148; Golkar Party, 106; Indonesian Democratic Party of Struggle, 94; Prosperous Justice Party, 57; National Mandate Party, 46; United Development Party, 38; National Awakening Party, 28; Great Indonesia Movement Party, 26; People's Conscience Party, 17.

Speaker: Marzuka ALIE.

CABINET

[as of December 1, 2009]

President	Susilo Bambang Yudhoyono (DP)
Vice President	Boediono (nonparty)
Coordinating Ministers	
Economy	Hatta Radjasa (PAN)
People's Welfare	Agung Laksono (Golkar)
Political, Legal, and Security Affairs	Air Chief Mar. (Ret.) Djoko Suyanto (ind.)
Ministers	
Agriculture	Suswono (PKS)
Communication and Information	Tifatul Sembiring (PKS)
Culture and Tourism	Jero Wacik (DP)
Defense	Purnomo Yusgiantoro (ind.)
Energy and Natural Resources	Darwin Saleh (PD)
Finance	Mulyani Indrawati (ind,) [f]
Foreign Affairs	Marty Muliana Natalegawa (ind.)
Forestry	Zulkifli Hasan (PAN)
Health	Endang Rahayu Sedyaningsih (ind.) [f]
Home Affairs	Gamawan Fauzi (ind.)
Industry	M.S. Hidayat (Golkar)
Justice and Human Rights	Patrialis Akbar (PAN)
Manpower and Transmigration	Muhaimin Iskandar (PKB)
Maritime Affairs and Fisheries	Fadel Muhammad (Golkar)
National Education	Muhammad Nuh (ind.)
Public Works	Djoko Kirmanto (ind.)
Religious Affairs	Suyadharma Ali (PPP)
Social Affairs	Salim Segaf Al Jufri (PKS)
Trade	Mari E. Pangestu (ind.) [f]
Transportation	Freddy Numberi (PD)
Ministers of State	
Acceleration of Development in Disadvantaged Regions	Ahmad Helmi Faisal Zaini (PKB)
Administrative Reform	E.E. Mangindaan (DP)
Cooperatives and Small and Medium-Sized Enterprises	Syarifuddin Hasan (PD)
Environment	Gusti M. Hatta (ind.)
Public Housing	Suharso Manoarfa (PPP)
Research and Technology	Suharna Surapranata (PKS)
State Enterprises	Mustafa Abubakar (ind.)
Women's Empowerment	Linda A. Gumelar (ind.) [f]
Youth and Sports Affairs	Andi Mallarangeng (PD)
Attorney General	Hendarman Supandji (ind.)
Chair, National Development Planning Agency	Armida Alisjahbana (ind.) [f]
State Secretary	Sudi Silalahi (ind.)

[f] = female

COMMUNICATIONS

The Indonesian press, rigidly controlled under the Sukarno regime, was accorded relative freedom under President Suharto until early 1974, when riots in Jakarta triggered a government crackdown. Over the next quarter century more than 200 newspapers and periodicals were shut down, and others were ordered not to report on various matters, including regional independence movements.

The political reforms that followed President Suharto's resignation in 1998 led to increased press freedom. Numerous party newspapers began publishing, and soon after taking office in October 1999 President Wahid abolished the notorious Ministry of Information, which was soon replaced by a more tolerant State Information Dissemination Bureau.

In 2002 the legislature passed a restrictive media law that established a new regulatory body, the Indonesian Broadcasting Committee, with authority over ownership, licensing, advertising, and the content of news as well as entertainment programming. Severe restrictions have also been placed on cross-ownership of print and broadcast media. In July 2007, however, the Constitutional Court declared unconstitutional sections of the criminal code that had proscribed "public expression of feelings of hostility, hatred, or contempt toward the government." In addition, the court threw out a constitutional provision that criminalized defaming the president. In April 2009 Indonesia's Supreme Court overturned a verdict against *Time Magazine* that it had defamed President Suharto in a 1999 article by claiming that he and his family had accumulated $15 billion during his time in office.

In March 2008 the DPR passed a law criminalizing online pornography (defined as "contents that violate decency"), defamation, and subject matter that might "create hatred and enmity among different groups."

Press. The following are dailies published in Jakarta in Indonesian, unless otherwise noted: *Kompas* (520,000), liberal Catholic; *Pos Kota* (500,000), sensationalist; *Jawa Pos* (Surabaya, 120,000); *Suara Merdeka* (Semarang, 200,000); *Berita Buana* (150,000), sensationalist;

Pikiran Rakyat (Bandung, 150,000); *Surabaya Post* (Surabaya, 110,000); *Harian Umum AB* (80,000), official army paper; *Pelita* (80,000), Muslim; *Harian Analisa* (Medan, 80,000); *Waspada* (Medan, 60,000); *Jakarta Post* (50,000), in English; *Harian Indonesia/Indonesia Rze Pao* (40,000), in Chinese.

News agencies. The principal domestic service, with branches throughout the country, is the Indonesian National News Agency (Antara); the KNI News Service operates from Jakarta, as do the major foreign bureaus.

Broadcasting and computing. The number of broadcast outlets expanded rapidly after the change of government in 1998. The former government network, *Radio Republik Indonesia* (RRI), was converted to a public broadcasting service in 2000 and remains the largest radio source. *Televisi Republik Indonesia* (TVRI), which also became a public broadcasting service in 2000, employs an extensive relay system to reach the entire country. Since 1998 the number of commercial radio and television stations has increased manyfold.

As of 2008 there were 79.2 Internet users per 1,000 inhabitants.

INTERGOVERNMENTAL REPRESENTATION

Ambassador to the U.S.: Sudjadnan PARNOHADININGRAT.

U.S. Ambassador to Indonesia: Cameron R. HUME.

Permanent Representative to the UN: (Vacant).

IGO Memberships (Non-UN): ADB, APEC, ASEAN, BIS, G-20, IDB, Interpol, IOR-ARC, NAM, OIC, WCO, WTO.

ANNEXED TERRITORY

Papua (West Papua and Papua provinces). The western half of the island of New Guinea, Papua has an area of 159,375 square miles (412,781 sq. km.) and a population of 2.7 million (2006E). As a consequence of recent transmigration, mainly from Java, native Papuans now number only slightly more than half of the total. Jayapura is the principal city and the capital of Papua Province. Manokwari is the capital of West Papua Province (previously called West Irian Jaya). Both have elected governors as chief administrators and elected legislatures, the Papua People's Representative Council (*Dewan Perwakilan Rakyat Papua*) for Papua and the Regional People's Representative Council (*Dewan Perwakilan Rakyat Daerah*—DPRD) for West Papua. The territory's extensive resources include natural gas, gold, copper, nickel, and tropical woods.

Long known as Netherlands New Guinea and more recently as Irian Jaya, Papua is a former Dutch colony that was administered by Indonesia after May 1, 1963, under a UN-sponsored agreement. The territory had been retained by the Netherlands upon recognition of Indonesian independence in 1949 but was subsequently turned over to the United Nations on the understanding that administrative authority would be transferred to Indonesia pending self-determination before the end of 1969. Although Papuan representatives complained of oppression by Indonesia and expressed a desire to form an independent state, Indonesia staged an "act of free choice" during July and August 1969 by convening eight regional consultative assemblies, all of which voted for annexation to Indonesia.

In 1971 a "Provisional Revolutionary Government of West Papua New Guinea" was established by insurgents who in 1976 claimed to control about 15 percent of the territory in the eastern sector, adjacent to Papua New Guinea. Although the latter banned all anti-Jakarta movements, it sought the help of the UN High Commissioner for Refugees (UNHCR) in an effort to find third countries willing to grant Irian insurgents asylum. An offensive by the Indonesian Army against the **Free Papua Organization** (*Organisasai Papua Merdeka*—OPM) in 1984 provoked the flight of hundreds of Irian villagers into Papua New Guinea. A border cooperation agreement was signed in October 1985, but it did not end cross-border raids by Indonesian forces. In 1992 a new Status of Forces Agreement was concluded with Papua New Guinea that dealt with a number of security issues but stopped short of sanctioning joint military operations against guerrilla units.

In September 1998 the newly installed Habibie government and the OPM, led by Moses WERROR, announced a cease-fire, and in October the Indonesian military declared that Irian Jaya was no longer considered to be a "military operation zone." No authoritative casualty figures for the prolonged conflict exist, although civilian deaths may exceed 40,000; some less-than-objective sources have placed the number as high as 150,000–300,000.

In October 1999 the Habibie administration announced that the province of Irian Jaya was being divided into three—West, Central, and East Irian Jaya—to improve administration, delivery of services, and distribution of economic development assistance. Most independence advocates protested the change, condemning it as an effort to divide the population.

On June 4, 2000, some 3,000 representatives to a Papua People's Congress, chaired by Theys ELUAY, declared their desire to separate the territory from Indonesia. The Wahid administration, which had provided financial support for the Congress with the understanding that the body would not declare independence, immediately rejected Papuan sovereignty claims. Jakarta nevertheless ordered security forces to avoid violence in dealing with proindependence demonstrators, organized a fact-finding team to investigate alleged human rights abuses, and granted permission, at least temporarily, for Papuans to fly their own flag beneath that of Indonesia. In early July members of the Congress's Presidium met with Wahid, who continued to rule out secession. Eluay and other leaders of a Papuan Presidium Council (*Presidium Dewam Papua*—PDP) were subsequently charged with subversion for advocating independence, and their trial was ongoing at the time of President Wahid's removal from office. Although his successor, President Megawati, apologized for decades of repression in Papua and elsewhere, she, too, ruled out independence.

On October 23, 2001, the Indonesian legislature approved an autonomy structure for Papua (as the region was to be officially named as of January 1, 2002) under which some 70–80 percent of revenues from the exploitation of natural resources would be retained for local use. Although the OPM, under the leadership of Mathias WENDA, denounced the autonomy status and continued to press for an independence referendum, the cease-fire held despite sporadic clashes.

On April 21, 2003, a military court convicted seven officers and soldiers of kidnapping and murdering Theys Eluay in November 2001, but the brevity of the sentences—between two and three and a half years—drew considerable criticism. The proposed trifurcation of Papua, ostensibly to improve administration, was also rejected as an effort to split the independence movement, which refused to recognize the creation of West Irian Jaya Province. (Indonesia's Constitutional Court has ruled against any further division of Papua—see the Constitution and government section, above.)

In October 2005 the central government created a Papua People's Council (*Majelis Rakyat Papua*—MRP), comprising Papuan religious, traditional, and women's leaders, to which local officials appointed 42 members. PDP leader Willy MANDOWEN denounced the council as undemocratic and asserted that the people of West Papua would create their own assembly, one that "truly represents the cultural, tribal groups in West Papua." President Yudhoyono, for his part, expressed his hope that the 2005 Aceh peace process and resultant autonomy agreement would serve as a model for resolving the Papua dispute. Meanwhile, in May 2005 a court sentenced two individuals to 10 and 15 years in prison for having raised a West Papuan independence flag in December 2004.

In March 2006 Jakarta criticized Australia's decision to grant temporary visas to 43 Papuan refugees, mostly men associated with the independence movement who had fled Indonesia by boat. At midyear reports surfaced that a number of guerrilla leaders from the so-called West Papua National Army had decided to form a central command and continue their pursuit of independence, but by nonviolent means.

A July 2007 report by U.S.-based Human Rights Watch accused Indonesia security personnel of operating as a "law unto themselves" and committing human rights abuses, including murder, rape, and torture, during efforts to track down OPM guerrillas in Papua and West Papua (since April 2007, the official name of West Irian Jaya). In the same month, the Papuan Tribal Council called on the provincial government to accept the OPM's "Morning Star" flag as an official provincial symbol. The MPR also backed the proposal, despite Jakarta's continuing objection to independence symbols.

Meeting in Port Vila, Vanuatu, in March–April 2008, the leaders of 28 West Papuan groups established a **West Papua National Coalition for Liberation** (WPNCL), chaired by Gen. Richard YOWENI of the OPM's National Liberation Army (*Tentara Pembebasan Nasional*—TPN). Working from a secretariat based in Port Vila, the WPNCL hoped to generate increased international support for Papuan self-determination, but in August 2009 it was rebuffed by the Pacific Islands Forum (PIF) when it sought observer status in the organization. Vice Chair Otto ONDAWAME accused the PIF of hypocrisy because of its failure to address Papua's human rights and self-determination issues, while Secretary General Rex RUMAKIEK indicated that the effort to be included as part of the Pacific community would continue.

Meanwhile, low-level violent altercations between independence advocates and the authorities persist, including additional arrests and prosecutions for flying the banned "Morning Star" flag. In March 2009 Nicholas JOUWE, 85, an OPM founder, visited Indonesia after 40 years in exile in the Netherlands. He later met with government officials, including President Yudhoyono, who had requested Jouwe's return. The visit was interpreted as an effort to promote reconciliation, although four Dutch journalists accompanying Jouwe were detained for violating their tourist visas by covering a protest rally in Jayapura. Some 1,000 demonstrators demanded an independence referendum and called for a boycott of upcoming elections.

IRAN

Islamic Republic of Iran
Jomhori-e Islami-e Irân

Political Status: Former monarchy; Islamic Republic proclaimed April 1–2, 1979, on basis of referendum of March 30–31; present constitution adopted in a referendum of December 2–3, 1979.

Area: 636,293 sq. mi. (1,648,000 sq. km.).

Population: 70,495,782 (2006C); 73,653,000 (2008E)

Major Urban Center (2005E): TEHRAN (8,600,000).

Official Language: Persian (Farsi).

Monetary Unit: Rial (official rate December 1, 2009: 9,920.00 rials = $1US).

Supreme Religious Leader: Ayatollah Seyed Ali KHAMENEI; elected President October 2, 1981, and sworn in October 13, following the assassination of Mohammad Ali RAJAI on August 30; reelected August 16, 1985, and sworn in for a second four-year term on October 10; named Supreme Religious Leader by the Assembly of Experts on June 4, 1989, following the death of Ayatollah Ruhollah Musavi KHOMEINI on June 3.

President: Mahmoud AHMADINEJAD; popularly elected in a runoff on June 24, 2005, confirmed on August 3 by the Supreme Religious Leader, and sworn in before the legislature for a four-year term on August 6, succeeding Mohammad KHATAMI; reelected for another four-year term on June 12, 2009, confirmed by the Supreme Religious Leader on June 13, and inaugurated on August 5.

First Vice President: Vacant, following the resignation on July 24 of Esfandyar Rahim MASHAEE, who had been appointed by the president on July 16, 2009, to succeed Parviz DAVODI.

THE COUNTRY

A land of elevated plains, mountains, and deserts that is semiarid except for a fertile area on the Caspian coast, Iran is celebrated both for the richness of its cultural heritage and for the oil resources that have made it a center of world attention. Persians make up about one-half of the population, while the principal minority groups are Turks and Kurds, who speak their own languages and dialects. English and French are widely spoken in the cities. More than 90 percent of the people belong to the Shiite sect of Islam, the official religion. Prior to the 1979 Islamic revolution, women constituted approximately 10 percent of the paid labor force, with substantial representation in government and the professions. Since 1979 female participation in most areas of government has been limited, and many working women still serve as unpaid agricultural laborers on family landholdings. On the other hand, the government of President Ali Akbar Hashemi RAFSANJANI was less willing than its predecessor to enforce Islamic social codes, and women successfully ran for parliamentary seats. Educational and professional restrictions on women are less stringent than in a number of nearby Arab states.

Despite a steady increase in petroleum production, both the economy and the society remained basically agricultural until the early 1960s, when a massive development program was launched. During the next decade and a half, the proportion of GDP (exclusive of oil revenue) contributed by agriculture dropped by nearly 30 percent, Iran becoming a net importer of food in the course of a major population shift to urban areas. Under a 1973–1978 plan, agriculture was slated to expand along with industry and oil and gas production. Severe inflation and a substantial outflow of capital, among other issues, prevented these goals from being realized.

Conditions deteriorated during the 1980–1988 war with Iraq, as heavy infrastructure damage contributed to a sharp reduction in petroleum exports. The government subsequently relaxed the tight economic controls imposed during the war, its new free-market posture emphasizing (at least rhetorically) the privatization of state-run enterprises, curtailment of agricultural subsidies, and efforts to attract foreign investment. However, although the long-term potential remained strong (Iran's oil reserves were estimated at upward of 100 billion barrels), the economy was stressed through the mid-1990s by high inflation (exacerbated by cuts in state subsidies), rising unemployment, a fast-growing population, widespread corruption, a growing external debt burden, and food and housing shortages that sparked sporadic antigovernment demonstrations.

While GDP grew by 4 percent in 1997, growth slipped to 1 percent in 1998, primarily as the result of a dramatic drop in oil prices. By the end of 1998 annual inflation was estimated at 35 percent. Annual GDP growth averaged 4.6 percent in 2000–2001, mostly as the result of higher oil prices. Despite a downward revision of oil production quotas by the Organization of the Petroleum Exporting Countries (OPEC) in 2002, GDP growth of 4.8 percent was recorded. Also contributing to economic advances were increased privatization, tax incentives for corporations, and loosening of trade regulations. A dual exchange rate—one for state imports of many basic goods and another, much higher, for all other transactions—was eliminated with the adoption of a unified exchange rate in 2002.

High oil prices continued to buoy the economy, with annual average GDP growth of 6.2 percent in 2005–2008. While the International Monetary Fund (IMF) noted Iran's robust growth due to soaring oil prices, it urged authorities to use the additional revenue to sustain growth and create jobs in light of the rising unemployment rate, reported to be 18 percent. Meanwhile, the annual inflation rate was 20 percent. On a positive note, the IMF commended Iran for accelerating privatization efforts, particularly with its largest banks, and noted progress in structural and tax reforms and the reduction of energy subsidies. Annual GDP growth was expected to contract to 3.2 percent in 2009, according to the IMF, owing in large part to the global economic recession's negative effect on oil prices, as well as the government's significant increase in public expenditures, which contributed to double-digit inflation.

GOVERNMENT AND POLITICS

Political background. Modern Iranian history began with nationalist uprisings against foreign economic intrusions in the late 19th century. In 1906 a coalition of clergy, merchants, and intellectuals forced the shah to grant a limited constitution. A second revolutionary movement, also directed largely against foreign influence, was initiated in 1921 by REZA Khan, an army officer who, four years after seizing power, ousted the Qajar family and established the Pahlavi dynasty. Although Reza Shah initiated forced modernization of the country with Kemalist Turkey as his model, his flirtation with the Nazis led to the occupation of Iran by Soviet and British forces in 1941 and his subsequent abdication in favor of his son, Mohammad Reza PAHLAVI. The

end of World War II witnessed the formation of separatist Azerbaijani and Kurdish regimes under Soviet patronage; however, these crumbled in 1946 because of pressure exerted by the United States and the United Nations (UN). A subsequent upsurge of Iranian nationalism resulted in expropriation of the British-owned oil industry in 1951, during the two-year premiership of Mohammad MOSSADEQ.

In the wake of an abortive coup in August 1953, Mossadeq was arrested by loyalist army forces with assistance from the U.S. Central Intelligence Agency (CIA) and British intelligence operatives. The period following his downfall was marked by the shah's assumption of a more active role, culminating in systematic efforts at political, economic, and social development that were hailed by the monarchy as a "White Revolution." However, the priorities established by the monarch, which included major outlays for sophisticated military weapon systems and a number of "showcase" projects (such as a subway system for the city of Tehran), coupled with a vast influx of foreign workers and evidence of official corruption, led to criticism by traditional religious leaders, university students, labor unions, and elements within the business community.

In March 1975 the shah announced dissolution of the existing two-party system (both government and opposition parties having been controlled by the throne) and decreed the formation of a new National Resurgence Party to serve as the country's sole political group. In the face of mounting unrest and a number of public-services breakdowns in overcrowded Tehran, Emir Abbas HOVEYDA, who had served as prime minister since 1965, was dismissed in August 1977 and replaced by the National Resurgence secretary general, Jamshid AMOUZEGAR.

By late 1977 both political and religious opposition to the shah had further intensified. On December 11 a Union of National Front Forces was formed under Karim SANJABI, a former Mossadeq minister, to promote a return to the constitution, the nationalization of major industries, and the adoption of policies that would be "neither communist nor capitalist, but strictly nationalist." Conservative Muslim sentiment, on the other hand, centered on the senior mullah, Ayatollah Ruhollah KHOMEINI, who had lived in exile since mounting a series of street demonstrations against the "White Revolution" in 1963, and the more moderate Ayatollah Seyed Kazem SHARIATMADARI, based in the religious center of Qom. Both leaders were supported politically by the long-established Liberation Movement of Iran, led by Mehdi BAZARGAN.

By mid-1978 demonstrations against the regime had become increasingly violent, and Prime Minister Amouzegar was replaced on August 27 by the Senate president, Jaafar SHARIF-EMAMI, whose parliamentary background and known regard for the country's religious leadership made him somewhat unique within the monarch's inner circle of advisers. Unable to arrest appeals for the shah's abdication, Sharif-Emami was forced to yield office on November 6 to a military government headed by the chief of staff of the armed forces, Gen. Gholam Reza AZHARI. The level of violence nonetheless continued to mount; numerous Kurds in northwest Iran joined the chorus of opposition, as did the well-financed Tudeh Party, a communist group. The oil fields and major banks were shut down by strikes, bringing the economy to the verge of collapse. Thus, after an effort by Golam-Hossein SADIQI to form a new civilian government had failed, the shah on December 29 named a prominent National Front leader, Shahpur BAKHTIAR, as prime minister designate.

Ten days after Bakhtiar's formal investiture on January 6, 1979, the shah left the country on what was called an extended "vacation." On February 1, amid widespread popular acclaim, Ayatollah Khomeini returned from exile, and a week later he announced the formation of a provisional government under a Revolutionary Council, which was subsequently reported to be chaired by Ayatollah Morteza MOTAHARI. On February 11 Prime Minister Bakhtiar resigned, and Bazargan was invested as his successor by the National Consultative Assembly immediately prior to the issuance of requests for dissolution by both the assembly and the Senate.

Despite a series of clashes with ethnic minority groups, a referendum on March 30–31, 1979, approved the proclamation of an Islamic Republic by a reported 97 percent majority. A rising tide of political assassinations and other disruptions failed to delay the election on August 3 of a constituent assembly (formally called the Assembly of Experts) delegated to review a draft constitution that had been published in mid-June. The result of the council's work was subsequently approved in a national referendum on December 2–3 (see Constitution and government, below).

The most dramatic event of 1979 was the November 4 occupation of the U.S. embassy in Tehran and the seizure of 66 hostages (13 of whom were released on November 17, while another was freed for health reasons in early July 1980), apparently in an effort to secure the return of the shah for trial; he had been admitted to a New York hospital for medical treatment. The action, undertaken by militant students, was not disavowed by the Revolutionary Council, although the government appeared not to have been consulted. Prime Minister Bazargan felt obliged to tender his resignation the following day, without a successor being named. On December 4 the UN Security Council unanimously condemned the action and called for release of the hostages, while the International Court of Justice (ICJ) handed down a unanimous decision to the same effect on December 15. Both judgments were repudiated by Iranian leaders.

Notwithstanding the death of the shah in Egypt on July 27, 1980, and the outbreak of war with Iraq in late September (see Foreign relations, below), no resolution of the hostage issue occurred in 1980. American frustration at the lengthy impasse was partially evidenced by an abortive helicopter rescue effort undertaken by the U.S. Air Force on April 24, and it was not until November 2 that Tehran agreed to formal negotiations with Washington, proposing the Algerian government as mediator. The remaining 52 hostages were ultimately freed after 444 days of captivity on January 20, 1981, coincident with the inauguration of Ronald Reagan as U.S. president. In return for their freedom, Washington agreed (1) to abstain from interference in internal Iranian affairs; (2) to freeze the property and assets of the late shah's family pending resolution of lawsuits brought by the Islamic Republic; (3) to "bar and preclude" pending and future suits against Iran as a result of the 1979 revolution or the hostage seizure, with an Iran-U.S. Claims Tribunal to be established at The Hague, Netherlands; (4) to end trade sanctions against Tehran; and (5) to unfreeze $7.97 billion in Iranian assets.

Internal developments in 1980 were highlighted by the election of the relatively moderate Abol Hasan BANI-SADR, a former adviser to Ayatollah Khomeini, as president on January 25, and the convening of a unicameral assembly, the *Majlis-e Shoura-e Islami*, on May 28, following two-stage balloting on March 14 and May 9. On August 9 Bani-Sadr reluctantly agreed to nominate Mohammad Ali RAJAI, an Islamic fundamentalist, as prime minister after three months of negotiations had failed to yield parliamentary support for a more centrist candidate.

Despite the support of secular nationalists, political moderates, much of the armed forces, and many Islamic leftists, Bani-Sadr was increasingly beleaguered by the powerful fundamentalist clergy centered on the Islamic Republican Party (IRP) and its (then) secretary general, Chief Justice of the Supreme Court Ayatollah Mohammad Hossein BEHESHTI. The IRP had emerged from the 1980 legislative balloting in firm control of the *Majlis,* enabling the clergy, ultimately with the support of Ayatollah Khomeini, to undermine presidential prerogatives during the first half of 1981. Moreover, on June 1 an arbitration committee, which had been established in the wake of violent clashes on March 5 between fundamentalists and Bani-Sadr supporters, declared that the president had not only incited unrest but had also violated the constitution by failing to sign into law bills passed by the *Majlis.* Nine days later, Khomeini removed Bani-Sadr as commander in chief, and on June 22, following a two-day impeachment debate in the assembly that culminated in a 177–1 vote declaring him incompetent, the chief executive was dismissed.

On June 28, 1981, a bomb ripped apart IRP headquarters in Tehran, killing Ayatollah Beheshti, 4 government ministers, 6 deputy ministers, 27 *Majlis* deputies, and 34 others. Prosecutor General Ayatollah Abdolkarim Musavi ARDEBILI was immediately appointed chief justice, while on July 24 Prime Minister Rajai, with more than 90 percent of the vote, was elected president. Having been confirmed by Ayatollah Khomeini on August 2, Rajai named Hojatolislam Mohammad Javad BAHONAR (Beheshti's successor as leader of the IRP) as prime minister, the *Majlis* endorsing the appointment three days later. Meanwhile, in late July deposed president Bani-Sadr, accompanied by Massoud RAJAVI of the *Mujaheddin-e Khalq* (see Political Parties and Groups, below), had fled to Paris, where he announced the formation of an exile National Resistance Council.

On August 30, 1981, President Rajai and Prime Minister Bahonar were assassinated by an explosion at the latter's offices, and on September 1 the minister of the interior, Hojatolislam Muhammad Reza MAHDAVI-KANI, was named interim prime minister. On October 2 Hojatolislam Seyed Ali KHAMENEI, Bahonar's replacement as secretary general of the IRP and a close associate of Khomeini, was elected president with 95 percent of the vote. Sworn in on October 13, he accepted the resignation of Mahdavi-Kani on October 15, with Mir Hosein MUSAVI, the foreign minister, being named the Islamic Republic's fifth prime minister on October 31, following confirmation by the *Majlis.* President Khamenei was elected to a second four-year term on August 16, 1985, defeating two IRP challengers. On October 13, following nomination by the president, Musavi was reconfirmed as prime minister.

At *Majlis* elections on April 8 and May 13, 1988, reformists won a clear majority. The elections, which were boycotted by the sole recognized opposition party, the Liberation Movement of Iran, also highlighted the increasing power of *Majlis* speaker Hojatolislam Ali Akbar Hashemi Rafsanjani, who on June 2 was named acting commander in chief of the armed forces. On June 6 Rafsanjani was renamed to his parliamentary post, despite the reported efforts of Ayatollah Hussein Ali MONTAZERI, Khomeini's officially designated successor, to force him to concentrate exclusively on his military responsibilities.

On March 27, 1989, following a meeting of the Presidium of the Assembly of Experts at which the "future leadership of the Islamic Republic" was discussed, Montazeri, declaring his "lack of readiness" for the position, submitted his resignation as deputy religious leader. On June 3 the 89-year-old Khomeini died, the Assembly of Experts designating President Khamenei as his successor the following day. On July 28 Iranians overwhelmingly voted their approval of constitutional changes that abolished the office of prime minister and significantly strengthened the powers of the theretofore largely ceremonial presidency. On August 17 Speaker Rafsanjani, who had been elected to succeed Khamenei as chief executive, was sworn in before the *Majlis,* and two days later he submitted a 22-member cabinet list that secured final approval on August 29.

In nationwide elections on October 8, 1990, to the Assembly of Experts, supporters of President Rafsanjani won a majority of seats, thus dealing a major setback to hard-line leaders. Rafsanjani further depleted the hard-liners' influence by, ironically, making assembly membership contingent on successful completion of an Islamic law examination. Furthermore, in parliamentary balloting in April and May 1992 Rafsanjani supporters captured an unexpectedly large majority of the seats, aided in part by the pro-Rafsanjani Council of Guardians' elimination of a number of hard-line *Majlis* candidates in March.

On June 11, 1993, President Rafsanjani was reelected to a second four-year term. However, despite lackluster opposition from three challengers selected by the Council of Guardians from a list of 128 presidential candidates, he won only 63.3 percent of the vote, a severe decline from the 94.5 percent registered in 1989. The president's slippage was also evident when the *Majlis,* while approving the remainder of the reshuffled cabinet on August 16, voted against the reappointment of Mohsen NURBAKHSH as minister of economic affairs and finance. Notwithstanding the obvious legislative dissatisfaction with current policies, Rafsanjani subsequently named Nurbakhsh to the newly created post of vice president for economic affairs, which did not require approval by the *Majlis.*

Cuts in state subsidies and consequent price increases triggered a series of riots in several cities in 1994, the assembly authorizing police to "shoot to kill" in any subsequent outbreaks. An estimated 30 people died when police opened fire during a disturbance near Tehran in April 1995. Nevertheless, President Rafsanjani vowed to persevere with his free-market reform policies, although it was widely conceded that little progress had been achieved in making the economy more efficient or the government bureaucracy less corrupt.

Elections to a new *Majlis* were held on March 8 and April 19, 1996, the balloting failing to produce a clear-cut victor in the battle between conservatives and moderates for political dominance. The results reflected the continued "quiet power struggle" between President Rafsanjani and Ayatollah Khamenei, whose supporters had accused the administration of having "wandered" from the path set by the 1979 revolution. With political primacy still apparently hanging in the balance, attention subsequently focused on the presidential election scheduled for May 1997, ruling clerics having emphasized that no constitutional amendments would be considered to permit a third term for Rafsanjani.

In what was considered an extraordinarily high voter turnout of 88 percent, Hojatolislam Seyed Mohammad KHATAMI, a moderate cleric, won the May 23, 1997, presidential poll with 20 million votes (69.5 percent) to 9 million combined votes for the three other candidates, including second-place (25 percent) Ali Akbar NATEQ-NURI, the conservative speaker of the *Majlis*, who was supported by Ayatollah Khamenei and the Society of Combatant Clergy, the majority conservative faction of the *Majlis.* Khatami, backed by various leftist groups as well as the moderate Servants of Construction, reportedly did well among women, students, the urban middle class, and other voters who apparently desired an end to Iran's international isolation, an easing of Islamic "vigilantism," and economic reform. The *Majlis* approved Khatami's cabinet recommendations on August 20; meanwhile, outgoing President Rafsanjani was named as president of the newly expanded Council for the Expediency of State Decrees (see Constitution and government, below), which included former cabinet members rejected by Khatami.

The election of President Khatami in May 1997 precipitated an extended tug-of-war for political and economic control between his reformist camp, which enjoyed widespread popular support, and the conservative clerics, who retained broad institutional power, often in alliance with intelligence services and businessmen. For his part, Khatami steadfastly pursued the "rule of law" and a civil society marked by greater nonclerical participation in governing bodies, expanded freedoms for individuals and the media, and tolerance for divergent religious and political views (including the legalization of parties). He also steadfastly called for warmer ties with the West based on a "dialogue of civilizations" and attempted to convince neighboring states that Iran had no interest in establishing regional dominance. Conservatives tried to block democratization at many levels, including the *Majlis* (which forced the dismissal of several cabinet members) and the judiciary (which banned newspapers and took legal action against a number of reformists). The conservative cause appeared to receive a boost in the October 23, 1998, balloting for the Assembly of Experts, although their success was tainted by a relatively low turnout and the fact that many reform candidates had been barred from running by the conservative Council of Guardians. However, pro-Khatami candidates did very well in the municipal balloting of late February 1999, winning all of the seats on the Tehran Council and some 70 percent of the seats they contested overall. Significantly, Ayatollah Khamenei, often associated with the conservative cause, did not support hard-liners in their efforts to ban reform candidates in the local elections.

Reformist candidates reportedly won about 70 percent of the seats in *Majlis* elections of February–May 2000, but the new membership's legislative efforts faced constant resistance from the Council of Guardians and the judiciary. The reformists maintained their electoral momentum in June 2001, when President Khatami was reelected with a reported 78 percent of the vote against nine challengers. The reformists suffered a major defeat in local elections held on February 28, 2003, with conservative candidates winning majorities in most major cities, as former supporters of the reformists chose to stay away from the polls. The conservative Builders of an Islamic Iran Council won 14 of 15 city council seats in Tehran. Turnout in the capital was reported at about 10 percent, with turnout nationwide reported at 39 percent.

In parliamentary elections on February 20, 2004, conservatives won a sweeping victory after the Council of Guardians disqualified more than a third of the candidates. Some 80 incumbent reformist MPs were among those barred from standing for election. The Interior Ministry reported turnout at 28 percent in Tehran and 50.57 percent nationwide, the lowest since the 1979 revolution. After a second round, held on May 7 to determine remaining seats, the conservatives had secured at least 200 of 290 seats. Within the conservative majority, the Builders of an Islamic Iran Council controlled about 195 of those. Lesser-known reformists without formal ties to established political parties and associations were left with a small bloc of about 40 seats.

In the 2005 presidential elections, conservative candidate Mahmoud AHMADINEJAD, the mayor of Tehran, won a runoff vote against former president Rafsanjani on June 24, with 61.64 percent of the vote vs 35.93 percent, respectively, a difference of more than 7 million votes. Turnout for the runoff was reported at 59.72 percent compared to 62.66 percent in the first round (in which seven candidates competed). Reformist and former *Majlis* speaker Mehdi KARRUBI, who stood as a candidate in the first round on June 17, alleged rampant voter fraud and irregularities in an open letter to the supreme leader.

In the elections for the Assembly of Experts on December 15, 2006, conservatives retained control, the Council of Guardians having again disqualified a third of the candidates. Rafsanjani retained his seat, receiving the most votes of any Tehran candidate. In concurrent elections for local councils, moderate conservatives won the majority of seats, followed by reformists. Following the death in July 2007 of the speaker of the Assembly of Experts, Ali MESHKINI, Rafsanjani was elected on September 4 to fill the post.

Following the resignation of five ministers within four days, including the oil minister, the cabinet was reshuffled on August 12, 2007.

In parliamentary elections on March 14, 2008, conservatives repeated their strong performance of four years earlier, securing about 60 percent of the seats in the first round of balloting after the Council of Guardians disqualified nearly 40 percent of the reformist candidates, including many former *Majlis* members. Supporters of President Ahmadinejad won fewer seats than anticipated, owing in large part to gains by independent candidates, who won more than 30 percent of the seats. So-called pragmatic conservatives, who were said to be dissatisfied with Ahmadinejad's economic policies, also made a strong showing. Turnout nationwide was reported to be 60 percent, nearly 10 percent higher than in 2004. Following second-round balloting on April 25 to decide 82 seats, the pragmatic conservatives, or principlists, added nearly a dozen seats to the 42 they had secured in the first round. Ahmadinejad's supporters secured a total of 170 of the 290 seats, including at least 38 seats in the runoff. Overall, reformists gained 6 seats over the 40 they held following the 2004 elections, and independents secured 71 seats. Results for 3 seats were annulled by the Interior Ministry, though no reason was given. Reformists called for a recount after the first round; a subsequent investigation by the Council of Guardians validated the initial results.

President Ahmadinejad dismissed the ministers of economic affairs and the interior, replacing both on April 22, 2008. The new minister of interior, Ali KORDAN, was impeached by parliament for false claims he made about his education. Meanwhile, an aide to Ahmadinejad was fired for allegedly trying to bribe legislators to keep them from voting for impeachment. The subsequent vote was seen as underscoring parliament's increasing rift with Ahmadinejad (see Current issues, below).

On June 12, 2009, Ahmadinejad was reelected for a four-year term in controversial balloting in which he secured 62.63 percent of the vote, compared to 33.75 percent for his main rival, former prime minister Mir Hosein Musavi, a political moderate. Two other candidates received only a small percentage of the vote. Immediately after the results were announced and Ahmadinejad's victory subsequently confirmed by the supreme leader, violent protests broke out across the country in the wake of allegations of irregularities (see Current issues, below). After a partial recount of the votes, the Guardian Council confirmed the election results on June 29.

On July 16, 2009, the head of the Atomic Energy Organization, Gholamreza AGHAZADEH, resigned, and President Ahmadinejad replaced him in a reshuffled cabinet, naming one of his vice presidents, Esfandyar Rahim MASHAEE, as first vice president. The move prompted outrage from hard-line conservatives, who denounced the choice because of remarks Mashaee made in 2008 to the effect that Iranians were friends with Israelis. More significantly, Ahmadinejad insisted on retaining Mashaee over the objections of Supreme Leader Ayatollah Khamenei, who had been the president's foremost defender following the controversial election. (The first vice president is first in line to succeed the president if he dies or becomes incapacitated and also leads cabinet meetings in the president's absence.) However, on July 24 Ahmadinejad submitted to the pressure—ultimately, after the public broadcast of Khamenei's order on state television—and accepted Mashaee's resignation. Ahmadinejad was scheduled to be sworn in before the legislature by mid-August.

Constitution and government. The constitution of December 1979 established Shiite Islam as the official state religion, placed supreme power in the hands of the Muslim clergy, and named Ayatollah Ruhollah Khomeini as the nation's religious leader (*velayat-e faqih*) for life. The *velayat-e faqih* is also supreme commander of the armed forces and the Revolutionary Guard, can declare war, and can dismiss the president following a legislative request or a ruling of the Supreme Court. He is formally responsible for the "delineation" of national policies in all areas, although some de facto authority was assumed by other officials following Ayatollah Khomeini's death in 1989.

An elected 86-member Assembly of Experts appoints the country's spiritual leader and has broad powers of constitutional interpretation. (Members of the assembly are popularly elected for eight-year terms. Previously, only mullahs were permitted to run; however, revisions approved prior to the 1998 balloting permitted nonclerics to stand for the assembly, although their candidacies were still subject to approval by the Council of Guardians.) The president, the country's chief executive officer, is popularly elected for a maximum of two four-year terms. Members of the unicameral *Majlis,* to which legislative authority is assigned, also serve four-year terms. The post of prime minister was eliminated as part of basic law revisions approved by referendum in July 1989, the president being authorized to appoint members of the Council of Ministers, subject to legislative approval. The *Majlis* was also empowered to impeach the president by a one-third vote of its members and to request his dismissal by a two-thirds vote. In the event of a presidential vacancy, an election to refill the office must be held within 50 days.

A Council of Guardians, encompassing six clerics specializing in Islamic law appointed by the *velayat-e faqih* and six nonclerical jurists elected by the legislature from nominees selected by the High Council of the Judiciary, is empowered to veto candidates for the presidency, *Majlis,* and Assembly of Experts and to nullify laws considered contrary to the constitution or the Islamic faith. (No constitutional provision having been made for the vetting by the Council of Guardians of candidates in municipal elections, the *Majlis* established a special committee for that purpose prior to the February 1999 local balloting.) In addition, a Council for the Expediency of State Decrees, composed of six clerics and seven senior governmental officials, was created in February 1988 to mediate differences between the *Majlis* and the more conservative Council of Guardians. (The authority and size of the Expediency Council were expanded in March 1997 by Ayatollah Khamenei, transforming the Council from an arbitrative panel to an "august consultative body," comprising a wider range of members, such as technocrats and faction leaders.) There is also a Supreme Council for National Security, established under the 1989 constitutional amendments to replace the National Defense Council. The new council, which coordinates defense and security policies and oversees all intelligence services, comprises the president, who serves as chair, two members appointed by the *faqih,* the chief justice of the Supreme Court, the speaker of the *Majlis,* and several military and ministerial representatives. Political parties are technically authorized to the extent that they "do not violate the independence, sovereignty, national unity, and principles of the Islamic Republic."

The civil courts instituted under the monarchy were replaced by Islamic Revolutionary Courts, judges being mandated to reach verdicts on the basis of precedent or Islamic law. The legal code subsequently underwent numerous changes, and on several occasions Ayatollah Khomeini called for the purging of judges who were deemed unsuitable or exceeded their authority. In August 1982 it was announced that all laws passed under the former regime would be annulled if contrary to Islam, while on September 23 homosexuality and consumption of alcohol were added to an extensive list of capital offenses. Although individuals are guaranteed a constitutional right to counsel, summary trials and executions were common following the 1979 revolution, many victims being suspected leftists or guerrillas.

Iran is administratively divided into 30 provinces (*ostans*); in addition, there are about 400 counties (*shahrestan*) and nearly 900 municipalities (*bakhsh*). The first municipal elections ever were conducted in February 1999. Reformers hoped that substantial authority would eventually be shifted from the national government to the local councils.

Foreign relations. Although a charter member of the United Nations, Iran momentarily curtailed its participation in the world body upon the advent of the Islamic Revolution. It boycotted the 1979 Security Council debate on seizure of the U.S. embassy in Tehran but joined in UN condemnation of the Soviet presence in Afghanistan late in the year.

An active member of OPEC, Iran was long in the forefront of those urging aggressive pricing policies, as opposed to the more moderate posture of Saudi Arabia and other conservative members. After 1980, however, a combination of the world oil glut and the need to finance its war effort forced Iran to sell petroleum on the spot at market at prices well below those set by OPEC; concurrently, it joined Algeria and Libya in urging a "fair share" strategy aimed at stabilizing prices through drastic production cutbacks.

A major international drama erupted in late 1986 with the revelation that members of the U.S. Reagan administration had participated in a scheme involving the clandestine sale of military equipment to Iran, the proceeds of which were to be used to support anti-Sandinista *contra* forces in Nicaragua. In early 1989 relations with the West, which had recently improved, again plummeted when British authorities refused to enjoin publication of Salman Rushdie's *Satanic Verses,* a work considered deeply offensive to Muslims worldwide, with Khomeini issuing a death decree against the author in February.

Iran and its western neighbor, Iraq, have long been at odds over their borders, principally over control of the Shatt al-Arab waterway linking the Persian Gulf to the major oil ports of both countries (see Iraq map, p. 683). Although the dispute was ostensibly resolved by a 1975 accord dividing the waterway along the *thalweg* (median) line, Iraq abrogated the treaty on September 17, 1980, and invaded Iran's Khuzistan Province on September 22. Despite early reversals, Iran succeeded in retaining control of most of the larger towns, including the besieged oil center of Abadan, and by the end of the year the conflict had resulted in a military stalemate. The war had the immediate effect of accentuating disunity within the Islamic world, the more radical regimes of Libya, Syria, and South Yemen supporting Tehran, and the more conservative governments of Jordan, Egypt, and the Gulf states favoring Baghdad. (In March 2009 Iran and Iraq agreed on joint technical teams to demarcate the border.)

Despite mediation efforts by the United Nations, the Organization of the Islamic Conference, the Nonaligned Movement, and various individual countries, fighting continued, with Iran advancing into Iraqi territory for the first time in July 1982. Rejecting a cease-fire overture, Tehran demanded $150 billion in reparations, the ouster of the Saddam Hussein government, and Iraqi repatriation of expelled Shiites. By early 1984 Iranian forces had made marginal gains on the southern front, including capture of the bulk of the Majnoon oil fields north of Basra, with what was essentially a stalemate prevailing for the ensuing three years.

A renewal of Iranian military offensives in late 1987 proved futile, as Iraqi troops drove Iranian troops from Basra and half of the Iranian Navy was reported lost during fighting with U.S. battleships protecting oil tankers in the Gulf. In February 1988 the "war of the cities" recommenced, with Iran and Iraq bombarding each other's capitals and other densely populated centers. Thereafter, the combination of Iraq's increasing use of chemical weapons and major military supply shortages led Iran to agree to a cease-fire on July 18. Ensuing peace talks, mediated by the United Nations, were slowed by friction over the return of prisoners, the Iraqi demand for free passage through the Shatt al-Arab waterway, and Iranian insistence that Iraq be condemned for initiating the fighting. However, despite allegations by both sides that the other was rearming, the cease-fire continued into 1990, being succeeded by a peace agreement on what were essentially Iranian terms (i.e., a return to the 1975 accord) in the wake of the crisis generated by Iraq's seizure of Kuwait in August 1990. (Still, Iran contends that its "cessation of hostilities" agreement with Iraq has never been replaced by a formal peace accord.)

Iran played a somewhat ambivalent role during the Gulf drama of 1990–1991, declaring its "full agreement" with those condemning the Kuwaiti invasion but opposing the deployment of U.S. troops to the region. In September 1990 it denied that it had secretly agreed to help break the UN embargo by importing some 200,000 barrels a day of Iraqi crude oil. Subsequently, it provided "haven" for upward of 100 Iraqi warplanes upon commencement of Operation Desert Storm in January 1991. Iran retained the planes upon the conclusion of hostilities and a year later confiscated them in what it termed partial satisfaction of reparations stemming from the Iran-Iraq conflict.

As the Gulf crisis subsided, Iran's top two leaders, Ayatollah Khamenei and President Rafsanjani, appeared to have reached an unspoken understanding to cooperate in countering the influence of their more radical colleagues by seeking a reduction in friction with the United States and other Western powers, as well as with regional Arab governments, including Iraq. In the wake of Saddam Hussein's humiliating military defeat, Tehran voiced sympathy for Iraq's Shiites while insisting that it was providing no military support for the southern rebels. Iran appeared to try to position itself midway between two former antagonists: Iraq, which it wished to see weakened but not destroyed, and the United States, whose power it acknowledged but which it did not welcome as a permanent arbiter of Middle Eastern affairs.

In May 1991 the administration of George H. W. Bush announced that it would not welcome improved relations until Tehran used its influence to secure the release of hostages held by pro-Iranian groups in Lebanon. The Iranian foreign ministry indicated in return that the hostage issue might soon become a "non-problem," particularly if some $10 billion of impounded Iranian assets were released by Washington. Shortly thereafter, the United States agreed to resume purchasing Iranian oil, with the stipulation that all payments would go into an escrow account established by the ICJ.

In April 1991 Iran generated concern among its Persian Gulf neighbors by expelling Arab residents from Abu Musa, a small island in the middle of the waterway that, along with two adjacent islands, Large Tunb and Small Tunb, had long been viewed as belonging to the United Arab Emirates but had been jointly administered since Iranian occupation of Abu Musa in 1971. Iran subsequently rejected the Arab League's call for ICJ arbitration. (Iran has continued to maintain that it owns the islands. The Gulf Cooperation Council [GCC] has backed the Emirates' claim to the islands and has "demanded" that Iran enter into negotiations and end its "occupation" of Abu Musa.)

For the remainder of 1991 Tehran continued its efforts to emerge from political and economic isolation, hosting an international human rights conference in September and taking an active role in the release of the remaining American and British hostages in Lebanon. However, despite a U.S. agreement in December to compensate Iran $278 million for undelivered military equipment, further rapprochement was stymied by Tehran's opposition to U.S.-brokered Middle East talks and President Rafsanjani's condemnation of American efforts to persuade China and India to stop transferring nuclear equipment to Iran.

Further complicating relations with the United States was a decision in March 1995 by Conoco Inc., under heavy pressure from Washington, to abandon a proposed $1 billion contract with Iran for the development of offshore oil and natural gas fields, and the subsequent imposition by U.S. President Bill Clinton of a full embargo on U.S. trade and investment with Iran. Describing Iran as an "outlaw state" because of its alleged complicity in international terrorism and its pursuit, according to U.S. officials, of nuclear weapons capability, Washington also called upon Moscow and Beijing to forgo their respective plans to sell nuclear reactors to Iran for the production of electricity.

In January 1996 it was revealed that some $18 million had been approved for the American CIA to support efforts to "change the nature" of the Iranian government. Washington subsequently attempted to intensify pressure on Tehran by authorizing sanctions against foreign companies that invest significantly in Iran's oil and gas industries.

A German court appeared to support American charges that Iran had engaged in "state-sponsored terrorism" when it ruled in April 1997 that senior Iranian officials were involved in the 1992 assassinations of Iranian Kurdish separatists in a German restaurant. Bonn withdrew its ambassador to Tehran following the ruling, with other European Union (EU) members (except Greece) following suit. The EU's action, however, was temporary (the ambassadors returned in November) and did little to dissuade critics of the United States' unilateral policy of sanctions against Iran. Former U.S. national security advisers Zbigniew Brzezinski and Brent Scowcroft, for example, said the costly sanctions were not isolating Iran but were instead alienating American allies while driving Tehran and Moscow closer. Iran had reportedly been receiving Russian help with a ballistic missile program. According to the *New York Times*, Moscow agreed to withdraw support of the program under American and Israeli pressure in 1997. Meanwhile, in November the United States bought 21 Soviet-era MIG-29s from Moldova to keep them from being sold to Iran.

Washington seemed more receptive to rapprochement with Tehran following the election of moderate President Khatami in May 1997. At the end of July, Secretary of State Madeleine Albright confirmed that the United States would not oppose the construction of a transnational Central Asian gas pipeline that would cross northern Iran, the first major economic concession to Iran since the 1979 revolution. Tehran's relations with Iraq, Syria, and the Gulf states, especially Saudi Arabia, also improved following Khatami's victory.

In a televised interview in January 1998 President Khatami proposed cultural exchanges with the United States. He also expressed a willingness to reconsider Iran's severed relationship with the United States and, in reply, the U.S. State Department suggested direct negotiations. However, Iran's powerful conservative spiritual leader, Ayatollah Ali Khamenei, subsequently lashed out at the United States, reconfirming deep internal divisions in the Iranian leadership.

The most significant regional tension in 1998 involved neighboring Afghanistan, where Taliban forces launched a midyear campaign to gain control of those parts of the country previously held by opposition forces. Tehran, angered at the unexplained killing of a number of its diplomats in Afghanistan and concerned over the fate of the anti-Taliban Shiite community in the central area of that country, massed more than 200,000 troops along the border in September, and war seemed imminent. Both sides subsequently showed a degree of restraint; however, moderates in Tehran reportedly expressed the fear that a military venture would compromise Iran's hope to become the "gateway" for the economic markets opening up in Central Asia. Similar motivation also partially explained Tehran's announcement in September that it had disassociated itself from the *fatwa* against Salman Rushdie, a decision that prompted the reestablishment of full relations with the United Kingdom. President Khatami's "charm offensive" toward Europe subsequently included a visit to the Vatican in March 1999.

Toward the end of the Clinton administration in 1999–2000, trade restrictions against Iran were reduced, and Secretary of State Albright announced official "regret" over the U.S. role in the 1953 coup and for supporting Iraq in the 1980–1988 Iran-Iraq war. However, the new George W. Bush administration adopted a much less conciliatory stance in the first half of 2001, based on what it claimed was Iranian support for militant Palestinian groups, such as Islamic Holy War and Hamas, as well as Hezbollah guerrillas in Lebanon. (The Iranian government contended that it provides only "moral support" and humanitarian aid for such groups and does not belong on the U.S. list of state sponsors of terrorism.) Moderate Iranians had hoped that a new era in relations with Washington would develop following the U.S.-led campaign against al-Qaida and Taliban forces in Afghanistan in late 2001, Iran having reportedly supplied useful intelligence and other assistance to support that effort in light of its different view of Islam than that expressed by al-Qaida and the Taliban. However, expectations of rapprochement with Washington were dashed in January 2002, when President Bush accused Iran of forming, along with Iraq and North Korea, an "axis of evil" threatening global security. That characterization prompted widespread anti-American demonstrations in February, and President Khatami accused Washington of "bullying" many other countries in the world through its "war on terrorism." Nevertheless, the United States continued its pressure, with Bush in August accusing Iran of seeking to develop weapons of mass destruction and demanding that Russia cease assistance to Iranian nuclear activities. The EU, on the other hand, considered Iran's posture in a much less provocative light and launched new talks with Tehran on possible trade-liberalization measures.

Iran officially opposed the U.S.-led invasion of Iraq in 2003 but nevertheless welcomed the ouster of President Saddam Hussein and allowed Iraqi opposition figures to travel freely from Iran to northern Iraq on the eve of the war. Meanwhile, the U.S.-led campaign in Afghanistan against the Taliban removed another hostile regime on Iran's western border.

Iran has had close ties in Iraq to prominent Shiite political figures, especially those from the Supreme Council of Islamic Revolution in Iraq (SCIRI). Iran had provided refuge and assistance to SCIRI during the 1980–1988 Iran-Iraq war, arming the group's military wing, the Badr Brigade. Iran reportedly has operated an extensive intelligence network in Iraq and has provided support to Shiite mosques and influential religious charities. U.S. officials have accused Iran of "meddling" in Iraq and failing to police its border with Iraq.

Iran's nuclear program became the focus of international scrutiny following revelations—revealed in satellite photographs provided by the exiled *Mujaheddin-e Khalq* in August 2002 (see reference to MKO, under Political Parties, below)—that it had failed to disclose an elaborate underground uranium-enrichment facility in Natanz and a heavy-water plant in Arak. Iranian officials obstructed inspectors from the International Atomic Energy Agency (IAEA) and provided contradictory explanations to them when they inquired about the nature of Iran's nuclear program. Facing possible referral to the UN Security Council, Iran negotiated a tentative agreement in October 2003 with Britain, France, and Germany—acting as representatives of the EU—to allow more intrusive inspections and to divulge the full history of its program in return for access to civilian nuclear technology. Iran also volunteered to temporarily suspend uranium-enrichment activities while negotiations continued with the Europeans. In the meantime, additional questions were raised about the nature of Iran's nuclear program and the government's intentions when the IAEA found traces of highly enriched uranium. Iran insisted that its activities were solely for the purpose of producing electricity, but the United States accused Tehran of secretly working to build nuclear weapons.

Tensions over the nuclear issue heightened following the election of President Ahmadinejad in June 2005. Talks between Iran and European governments had made little progress, and Iran, dismissing European proposals as "insulting," announced that it would end its voluntary suspension of uranium-enrichment activities and would refuse further IAEA inspections. The Iranians reopened a uranium conversion plant in Isfahan in August 2005, declaring that it was fully within its rights under the Nuclear Non-Proliferation Treaty to pursue uranium enrichment and activities associated with it. On February 4, 2006, member states on the IAEA's board of governors voted to refer Iran to the UN Security Council for its failure to dispel concerns over its nuclear program. The Security Council urged Iran on March 29 to suspend uranium enrichment but did not threaten punitive sanctions amid reluctance voiced by Russia and China. Striking a defiant tone, President Ahmadinejad announced on April 11 that Iran had successfully enriched uranium at low levels, saying the country had taken a major step toward mastering nuclear technology. He reiterated the regime's view that Iran regarded uranium enrichment as an inalienable right under the Nuclear Non-Proliferation Treaty. In the first direct approach by an Iranian leader to a U.S. president since the hostage crisis of 1979, Ahmadinejad sent a letter to President Bush on May 8 criticizing U.S. foreign policy while expressing his country's readiness to defuse disagreement on the nuclear program. The letter was dismissed by the Bush administration as containing no concrete proposals to resolve the nuclear dispute.

In 2006 the United States reversed its long-standing policy and said on May 31that it was ready to hold direct talks with Iran on the nuclear issue and that it would join European governments in negotiations aimed at resolving the crisis. In a fresh diplomatic initiative, the United States, other permanent members of the UN Security Council, and Germany agreed to offer Iran a package of incentives if it suspended uranium enrichment and cooperated with IAEA inspectors. The proposal, which included offers of access to civilian nuclear technology, trade concessions, and some security assurances, was presented to Iran by an EU envoy in June. However, Iran insisted it would not respond to the offer until late August, despite Western demands for an answer within weeks. In August, Ahmadinejad said that Iran would not yield to international pressure to dismantle its nuclear program. Consequently, the Security Council unanimously voted on December 23 to impose sanctions on Iran. For its part, Iran condemned the resolution as illegal.

While the United States has said it would continue to seek a diplomatic solution to the nuclear dispute, it has refused to rule out possible military action. Iranian officials have warned that any U.S. or Israeli military action against its nuclear sites would result in retaliation against U.S. and Israeli targets. In March 2007 the UN Security Council unanimously agreed to tighten its sanctions as Iran continued to insist that it was developing its nuclear program solely for peaceful purposes. The UN resolution included a ban on arms sales to Iran and an expanded freeze on its assets. Iran again countered that the sanctions were illegal. Iranian and U.S. officials met in Baghdad in May 2007, in the most high-profile contact between them, but the talks focused on Iraq. Iran continued to maintain that it would not halt its nuclear research program, even as the Bush administration asserted that there would be "serious consequences" if Tehran did not end its enrichment process. In September the IAEA reported that it had reached agreement with Tehran on a "work plan" to resolve outstanding questions about nuclear activity, but Western diplomats continued to step up pressure on Iran. The EU decided to impose its own sanctions outside of those adopted by the UN because some countries wanted to distance themselves from the broader U.S. actions. Subsequently, in October the Bush administration announced sweeping new sanctions against Iran's Revolutionary Guard, accusing the guard of proliferating weapons of mass destruction and supporting terrorism through the guard's elite Quds division. The United States also called for other countries to stop doing business with four of Iran's largest banks. Iran's chief nuclear negotiator, Ali LARIJANI, resigned in October, reportedly over differences with Ahmadinejad on how to conduct the talks. Larijani had supported continuing talks with the West, whereas Ahmadinejad, now supported in his claim of a peaceful nuclear program by Russian President Vladimir Putin, was said to favor a more hard-line approach. Some analysts said the resignation was a sign of the supreme leader's support for Ahmadinejad's tough stance. By early November, the UN had agreed to consider yet another set of sanctions if Iran did not answer key questions by December about its nuclear program, though a month earlier the IAEA had said that it had no evidence Tehran was seeking nuclear arms. The nuclear issue received international attention in December after a U.S. National Intelligence Estimate (NIE) concluded that Iran had halted its nuclear weapons program in 2003, and that the program remained inactive, a major contradiction to the NIE's findings in 2005. Nevertheless, President Bush continued to defend his policy and reiterated that "all options are on the table." Iran, for its part, contended that the recent NIE report rendered all prior sanctions illegal. Meanwhile, it was reported that Iran and Russia had resolved all disagreements over payments for the Bushehr nuclear power plant and that Russia subsequently delivered fuel for the plant. The Bush administration backed Russia's supplying fuel rods to Iran because it meant Iran no longer needed enriched uranium.

In 2007 Iran and Nicaragua restored diplomatic relations and signed extensive trade agreements. Iran also entered into several economic agreements with Venezuela in 2007. A diplomatic dispute with Canada ended in December, when Iran expelled the Canadian ambassador for allegedly "breaching diplomatic protocols." Denmark closed its embassy in Tehran in 2008 following a student protest related to the reprinting in Danish newspapers of a controversial cartoon originally published in 2006 that depicted the prophet Mohammad. Iran had demanded an apology.

Tensions between Iran and the United States heightened in January 2008 amid claims that Iranian speedboats had threatened U.S. Navy ships in international waters in the Strait of Hormuz. The speedboats pulled away just as the navy vessels were about to fire on them, an incident that coincided with President Bush's trip to the Middle East. Meanwhile, in what was described as an "unexpectedly critical" report, the IAEA said that Iran had failed to give clear answers to Western intelligence agencies regarding a military link to its nuclear program. Iran called the allegations "baseless." In May the London-based Institute for Strategic Studies said that Iran's controversial nuclear program had spurred "a wave of interest" in atomic energy across the Middle East, with at least 13 countries already having announced plans to explore nuclear energy or revive existing programs.

Morocco suspended its diplomatic ties with Iran in March 2008 over public comments by an Iranian official that allegedly questioned the sovereignty of Sunni-majority Bahrain. Outrage by Sunni Muslims prompted Moroccan leaders to recall their envoy to Iran.

Meanwhile, Iran's relations with Iraq warmed in March 2008 during President Ahmadinejad's landmark visit to Baghdad, the first time an Iranian leader had traveled there since 1979. (It was also recorded as the first "full-fledged" state visit to Iraq by any foreign head of state since the U.S. invasion in 2003.) Ahmadinejad, in a direct denial of U.S. allegations, said that Iran was not arming Shiite militias in Iraq. Subsequently, the two countries signed several agreements, including some encompassing the development of mining and other industries. However, Iraq refused a $1 billion Iranian loan for projects to be headed by Iranian firms. In June Iraq's prime minister, Nouri al-Maliki, made a reciprocal visit to Iran.

In May 2008 the United States and Britain were considering what was described as "an overture for wide-ranging political talks" from Iran. The Western allies had renewed their offer of "incentives" if Tehran would suspend uranium enrichment and engage in negotiations on its nuclear program. However, Iran's continued development of its nuclear program, discerned by Israeli intelligence overflights, prompted one Israeli minister to warn that an attack on Iran's nuclear sites was becoming "unavoidable."

The nuclear issue continued to be the focal point of contention between Iran and the West. Though U.S. Secretary of State Condoleezza Rice in June 2008 said she would meet "any time, anywhere, on any issue" with her Iranian counterpart, it was conditioned on Iran's suspending its nuclear activity. However, Ahmadinejad stood firm, rejecting such pressure, and was quoted as saying there was nothing the West could do about it. Further pressure, including a warning from French president Nicolas Sarkozy, came in September. Following the election of U.S. president Barack Obama, who had sent a conciliatory message to Iran during his campaign, the new administration offered to hold direct talks with Iran, without preconditions. However, following the tumultuous 2009 presidential election in Iran, President Obama "kept his remarks about the Iranian election so cool and detached that Republicans quickly attacked him as showing weakness in the defense of democracy," the *International Herald Tribune* reported. Meanwhile, U.S. defense secretary Robert Gates remained skeptical about the possibility of relations between the two countries, particularly in the aftermath of Iran's successful test launch of a missile capable of striking U.S. and Israeli bases in the Persian Gulf. The test launch resulted in the Italian foreign minister canceling his trip (that same day) to Iran, after Ahmadinejad insisted the two meet at the launch site.

In May 2009 it was reported that Iran had built up a military force in Eritrea as a security measure against piracy in the Gulf of Aden, a major passageway for oil tankers.

Current issues. Prior to the 2004 parliamentary elections, the Council of Guardians undermined Iran's reformists, whose candidates won overwhelmingly in 2000, by banning more than 2,300 of the 8,200 aspiring candidates, including some 80 sitting members of parliament. (For further details on President Khatami and political events of 2000–2004, see earlier editions of the *Handbook*.) The reformist *Majlis* members held a sit-in in the lobby of parliament to protest the ban but failed to rally public support. Subsequently, one-third of the *Majlis* members offered their resignations. Following vague calls for compromise by the supreme religious leader, the Council of Guardians reinstated a small number of candidates, excluding those who were prominent reformist members of parliament. The ruling left reformists without candidates in more than 70 constituencies. The council gave no specific reasons for the disqualifications but accused the barred candidates of failing to uphold and respect the principles of the Islamic Republic and the authority of the supreme leader. Calling the ban a "bloodless coup," the largest reformist party, the Islamic Iran Participation Front (IIPF), boycotted the election. Cabinet ministers hinted that they might refuse to organize the election, but they eventually backed down from their threat. Subsequently, the relatively new conservative group, Builders of an Islamic Iran Council, secured a large majority in the February elections, clinching their status after second-round balloting in May. The Interior Ministry reported nationwide voter turnout at the lowest level since the 1979 revolution, though the Council of Guardians contended that the turnout was higher. In the wake of the overriding defeat for reformists, some argued for constitutional amendments to enhance the authority of elected representatives.

In the run-up to the 2005 presidential elections, the Council of Guardians again barred hundreds of candidates, including all women. Among the seven candidates, former president Rafsanjani led the first round of polling, with 21.01 percent. His failure to secure a majority forced an unprecedented runoff with Mahmoud Ahmadinejad, an obscure conservative and former officer in the Revolutionary Guard who became mayor of Tehran in May 2003. One of the reformist candidates, former *Majlis* speaker Mehdi Karrubi, who had finished behind Ahmadinejad by less than 1 percent after leading in earlier tallies, alleged vote-rigging, claiming involvement by the supreme leader's son. Rafsanjani's aides also alleged widespread irregularities and manipulations carried out by paramilitaries and militia. Ahmadinejad, who had promised to address social inequalities, won an overwhelming victory in the June runoff, securing nearly 62 percent of the vote despite reformists' efforts to set aside their uneasy relations with Rafsanjani and urging support for him to prevent "fascism."

With Ahmadinejad's election, the conservatives regained control of all the elected institutions, allowing the supreme leader to consolidate his power. The regime announced various efforts to tighten the enforcement of laws requiring women to follow Islamic dress code, but it has proved unable or unwilling to fully dismantle the limited social freedom developed under Khatami's tenure. Meanwhile, the U.S. military presence in neighboring Iraq and Afghanistan prompted the conservatives to invoke national security concerns, portraying the reformists as traitorous for questioning the premises of the theocracy and for reaching out to Western governments. With the reformists in disarray, high oil prices bolstering state revenues, and Shiite allies leading the government in Iraq, the supreme leader and the conservative clerical establishment appeared to face no immediate threat to their hold on power.

Ahmadinejad subsequently provoked international condemnation with his comments on Israel and the Holocaust. Quoting Ayatollah Knhomeini, the president said in a speech in October 2005 that Israel should be "wiped off the map." In December he said that the West "invented a myth that Jews were massacred" and suggested that Israel be moved to Europe or elsewhere. On the nuclear issue, Ahmadinejad sought to rally public opinion in Iran and throughout the Islamic world with populist rhetoric, accusing the West of pushing a double standard by tolerating other nuclear powers, including Israel, while singling out Iran for punishment.

Rifts began to develop domestically, as some pragmatic conservative members of parliament clashed with Ahmadinejad over a number of cabinet nominees and the president's proposed budget. Also, the supreme leader, in what was interpreted as a rebuke to Ahmadinejad's handling of international issues, set up an advisory council on foreign relations in 2006 with former foreign minister Kamal Kharrazi as its chair. The council was seen by some observers as an attempt to offset the brash approach of Ahmadinejad and pave the way for possible diplomatic solutions. Nevertheless, Iran did not back down from its intentions to proceed with development of its nuclear program (see Foreign relations, above). Others speculated that the supreme leader's naming of Kharrazi to the council was perhaps an indication of his dissatisfaction with Ahmadinejad.

Amid growing frustration with the president and his policies, students held a major demonstration in December 2006, denouncing Ahmadinejad as a "dictator." After the more conservative followers of Ahmadinejad did not fare as well as expected in the December 15 elections for the Assembly of Experts and the concurrent local elections, reformists appeared to take a more active role, buoyed by Rafsanjani having received the most votes in Tehran in the assembly elections. (Tehran was formerly seen as a stronghold for Ahmadinejad.) Rafsanjani further demonstrated his increasing influence by meeting with the British ambassador in Tehran in January 2007 over the nuclear issue, committing Iran to "any verifying measures by the responsible authorities," according to news reports. While some analysts said Rafsanjani was trying to avoid a major confrontation with the United States, others thought his actions resulted from the mounting influence of the reformists. Collaterally, in what was described as an unprecedented rebuke, 150 members of the *Majlis* signed a letter condemning the president's economic policies.

A measure adopted in 2007 by the *Majlis* to hold concurrent parliamentary and presidential elections was rejected by the Council of Guardians in April on the grounds that it would shorten the respective terms of office. In the run-up to parliamentary elections in 2008, various reformist groups began forming coalitions in the wake of divisions among many of the groups. The economy continued to dominate societal concerns amid widespread unemployment and a rising inflation rate. In May demonstrators protested against low wages and the lack of jobs, with thousands calling for the labor minister's resignation. Though Ahmadinejad had promised economic reforms, many factories had closed, and there were increasing reports of alleged government harassment of workers' advocates. The economic downturn was further exacerbated by Ahmadinejad's announcement, only several hours ahead of time, of gas rationing and a fuel-price increase, prompting violent riots. Meanwhile, the parliament rejected an emergency measure that would have postponed the rationing. Fearing that the rioting might spread, the government temporarily shut down the country's mobile phone network to prevent protesters from easily contacting each other to set up more demonstrations. The rationing was imposed in anticipation of possible U.S. sanctions over Iran's nuclear program, banning companies from selling oil to Iran. Subsequently, Venezuela agreed to sell oil to Iran.

In July 2007 the United States accused the Revolutionary Guard of assisting Iraqi militants in abducting and killing five U.S. soldiers in January. It also contended that militants were using explosive devices from Iran against coalition forces in the U.S.-backed war in Iraq. Ultimately, sanctions were announced against the Revolutionary Guard, the first time the United States had taken punitive steps against the armed forces of a sovereign country. News reports quoted Iran's interior minister as warning of a "crushing" response to any military attack against Iran. Meanwhile, domestic turmoil persisted throughout the year. Students staged a large demonstration in October, clashing with police during a speech by Ahmadinejad. The government cracked down on the media and other critics and dissenters. Additionally, there was a sharp escalation in cross-border fighting with Kurdish rebels, who claimed to have several thousand members seeking autonomy for Kurds in Iran near the border with Iraq (see Political Parties and Groups, below).

Despite increasing oil revenues, Iran's spiraling inflation and widespread unemployment made the economy the most important issue in the 2008 parliamentary elections. President Ahmadinejad's economic policies alienated many conservatives, who split into two main factions: the hard-line supporters of Ahmadinejad (and the Revolutionary Guard), who sought to maintain their hold on parliament; and a broad coalition of principlists, who were aligned with the clerics, Ali Larijani, the former chief nuclear negotiator, and Tehran's mayor, Mohammad Baqer QALIBAF. Reformists, too, were divided, the main coalition including 18 groups allied with former president Khatami and the National Trust Party of former *Majlis* speaker Mehdi Karrubi. More than 2,000 candidates from the Reformist Coalition were disqualified by the Council of Guardians, provoking widespread criticism. Similarly, the candidate list of the pro-reform National Trust Party was reduced by half. Thus conservatives, as expected, won an overwhelming majority of seats following two rounds of voting, though reformists were able to increase their representation somewhat over the number they had held in the outgoing parliament. Independents won a significant number of seats, but since none was reported to have appeared on the lists of any political groups, it was unclear as to which factions they ultimately aligned themselves with in the *Majlis*. According to observers, the parliament, though overwhelmingly conservative, would not be fully supportive of President Ahmadinejad, as the broad principlists were expected to form alliances with pro-reform factions to challenge the administration on economic policies that fueled public discontent. Just prior to the second round of elections, Ahmadinejad had dismissed the economic affairs and interior ministers in the wake of severe criticism of their alleged mismanagement and lack of accountability. The reshuffle reportedly marked a further consolidation of the power of the Revolutionary Guard, 12 former members of which were said to hold cabinet posts, while only one cleric retained a ministry title. The *International Herald Tribune* reported the elections as another "triumph for the supreme leader's consolidation of conservative authority," reinforcing Ayatollah Khamenei's claims of "political hegemony."

Tensions between parliament and Ahmadinejad heightened in late 2008, as the replacement interior minister was impeached in an episode reported by the *Washington Post* as a "tumultuous parliamentary session broadcast live on Iranian state radio. He caused a storm by linking the lawmakers opposing him to foreign groups and anti-Iranian governments, often referred to here as 'the enemy.'" Ahmadinejad, for his part, said the impeachment (over false education credentials) was illegal and "unfair." The ousted interior minister was the tenth to resign or be impeached since Ahmadinejad was elected in 2005.

Attention soon turned to the 2009 presidential election, amid growing public dissatisfaction with the economic policies of the Ahmadinejad adminstration, as unemployment and inflation continued to soar, along with prices, especially gas and housing. Meanwhile, major increases in state spending—particularly on the nation's nuclear program, with little domestic benefit, and increasing civil service wages and pensions ahead of the election—and Ahmadinejad's unpopular remarks about Israel and his denial of the Holocaust turned a significant portion of the population against him, according to observers. In March a political moderate who had not been active in politics for 20 years, former prime minister Mir Hosein Musavi, announced his candidacy for the June election. He gained the support of many reformists after their candidate, Mohammad Reza Khatami, former deputy speaker of parliament and a leader of the Islamic Iran Participation Front (*Jebhe-ye Mosharekat-e Iran-e Eslami*—IIPF), withdrew. (Khatami, who had only reluctantly become a candidate when pressured by reformists, stepped down to support Musavi.) While a few conservatives announced their endorsement of Musavi, most of his backers were avid reformists, though Musavi reportedly did not characterize himself as such. However, he campaigned on a platform of greater personal freedom and women's rights, and was said to be trying to gain ground with conservatives who had become disillusioned with Ahmadinejad. Two other challengers also entered the race: Mohsen REZAI, former commander of the Revolutionary Guard, described as an independent conservative, and former *Majlis* speaker Mehdi Karrubi of the National Trust Party. As the challengers began increasingly to use the online social networking site Facebook, the government on May 23 blocked the site, though it subsequently lifted the ban in response to public outcry. That same month Ayatollah Khamenei urged the populace not to vote for pro-Western candidates (i.e., the reformists). Meanwhile, in the midst of the presidential campaign, Iran successfully test-fired a medium-range missile capable of striking as far as Israel and U.S. bases in the Persian Gulf, according to news reports.

Immediately following the 2009 election, which Ahmadinejad won handily with nearly 63 percent of the vote, with an inordinately high turnout of 85 percent, according to official government results, Musavi denounced the outcome, claiming widespread fraud. The other two challengers also questioned the official outcome, alleging widespread abuses and vote rigging. As soon as the official results were announced (and subsequently confirmed by Ayatollah Khamenei), mass demonstrations erupted in Tehran and across the country, overwhelmingly by supporters of Musavi, resulting in violent clashes with police and plainclothes paramilitary *Basijis* and the arrests of more than 100 members of reformist groups who were charged with having organized the protests. Meanwhile, shortly before a victory rally for the president, Ahmadinejad praised the outcome of the election as "very accurate." Despite the president's remarks, reports surfaced of a crackdown on independent media in the country, as well as restrictions on mobile phone use for calls and text messaging, measures designed to prevent the organization of further demonstrations. As the protests were unfolding, Musavi and Mohammad Reza Khatami, brother of the former president, were said to have been taken into custody at their homes by security forces. Subsequently, challenger Mohsen Rezai, who won just 1.73 percent of the vote, and former speaker of parliament Ali Larijani, expressed their support for Ahmadinejad.

Within days of the initial protests in June 2009, the administration banned international media from covering demonstrations in Tehran after video was aired that showed police battling with supporters of Musavi, according to news reports. Meanwhile, similar reports said Iranian television aired rallies in favor of Ahmadinejad. As protests continued for several weeks, there were reports of journalists being beaten, and amateur video captured the shooting death of one female protester, prompting further international condemnation. In Tehran, stores closed, universities suspended classes, and security forces hurled tear gas inside Musavi's campaign headquarters. Unconfirmed estimates put the number of demonstrators killed at about 250 as of late June. On June 29, the Guardian Council of 12 clerics appointed to oversee elections dismissed all complaints and confirmed the official results.

While international officials and human rights organizations denounced the violence, the initial response to the 2009 election results was generally muted. U.S. secretary of state Hillary Clinton initially said that the United States hoped the election reflected "the genuine will and desire" of the Iranian people (though weeks later, U.S. president Obama said he was appalled and outraged by the violence in Iran). The Iranian government, for its part, accused Great Britain, the United States, and other Western nations of fueling the protests and otherwise interfering in Iran's affairs. The European Union (EU) "categorically rejected" all such allegations. Subsequently, Iran arrested several British embassy employees but later began releasing some of them.

In the weeks after the election, demonstrations continued to be met with resistance by security police, and the elite Revolutionary Guard was said by the *New York Times* to have emerged "as a driving force behind efforts to crush a still-defiant opposition movement." On July 16, 2009, President Ahmadinejad named minister Esfandyar Rahim Mashaee, his son-in-law, as first vice president, angering conservatives because of remarks Mashaee made in 2008 indicating that Iran was friends with Israel. Further, Ahmadinejad showed "rare defiance" to Supreme Leader Ayatollah Khamenei, the president's foremost defender following the controversial election, by refusing to dismiss Mashaee as Khamenei ordered. The president's refusal to obey marked a major rift among the hard-line conservatives, according to analysts, who said Ahmadinejad feared the hard-liners would try to exert power over the government. Meanwhile, leaders in parliament said the legislature planned to force Ahmadinejad to replace Mashaee. Ultimately, however, Ahmadinejad relented under the pressure and accepted Mashaee's resignation on July 24. A further rift developed between Khamenei, backed by the Revolutionary Guard and the hard-line clerics, and cleric and former president Ali Akbar Hashemi Rafsanjani, who delivered a sermon criticizing officials' handling of the post-election crisis. Rafsanjani thus "re-ignited the opposition, emerging as its leading patron," according to the Associated Press.

POLITICAL PARTIES AND GROUPS

Although political parties are permitted under the constitution, none was recognized following the formal dissolution of the government-sponsored Islamic Republican Party in June 1987, despite Tehran's announcement in October 1988 that such groupings would thenceforth be welcomed if they "demonstrated commitment to the Islamic system." A number of new political formations were identifiable during the *Majlis* elections of 1996, although it was carefully noted by the government that they were not official parties. Meanwhile, some former parties appeared to remain informally tolerated. Supporters of President Mohammad Khatami were reported in 1998 to have achieved recognition as the first full-fledged political party since the 1979 revolution (see Islamic Iran Solidarity Party, below), and several others also subsequently achieved legal status. However, the main political formations have continued to be organizations acting in a "pseudo-party" capacity by, among other things, presenting candidate lists for legislative elections without having sought formal party registration. Political parties in Iran tend to operate as small clubs, personal platforms, or loosely defined ideological associations rather than as large organizations with grassroots networks or formal, disciplined structures. Membership in one does not preclude membership in another, and the associations tend to lack detailed policy manifestos. Some appear before an election and quickly fade afterward.

Though many of the candidates contesting the 2008 *Majlis* elections ran as independents, four main lists of candidates were presented by two conservative and two reformist groupings. The conservative United Fundamentalist Front (or United Principlist Front) was led by deputy *Majlis* speaker Reza BAHONAR and speaker Gholam-Ali Haddad-Adel, both leaders of the Builders of an Islamic Iran Council. The group was comprised largely of staunch supporters of President Ahmadinejad. The other conservative grouping, the Inclusive Fundamentalist Coalition (or Broad Principlist Coalition), included principlists opposed to the president's economic and foreign policies, aligned with Ali Larijani, the former chief nuclear negotiator and former speaker of parliament; clerics; and the mayor of Tehran, Mohammad Baqer Qalibaf. The Reformists Coalition, led by Mohammad SALAMATI of the Islamic Revolution Mujaheddin Organization, included 18 groups allied with former president Khatami. The reformist National Trust Party, led by former *Majlis* speaker Mehdi Karrubi, included a number of candidates who were also allied with the Reformists Coalition. A Nationwide Coalition of Independent Candidates was also established in February 2008.

In 2009 the Guardian Council approved only four of the 476 potential candidates, men and women, for the Juen presidential election. Reformists were inclined to back former prime minister Mir Hosein Musavi, along with some conservatives who became increasingly angry with incumbent president Ahmadinejad over his domestic policies and inflammatory rhetoric.

Builders of an Islamic Iran Council (*Etelaf-e Abadgaran-e Iran-e Eslami*). This group, whose name is also translated as Developers of an Islamic Iran Council, first emerged in the local elections of February 2003, presenting largely unknown, younger candidates on the Tehran ballot with strong backing from senior conservatives in the political establishment. The party won control of the Tehran city council, which had been paralyzed by feuds among reformist council members. The council elected Mahmoud Ahmadinejad as mayor. The group in some cases operated under alternative names outside of Tehran. Employing vague slogans calling for economic progress and adherence to "Islamic values," the party launched a well-financed campaign for the 2004 parliamentary elections. With more than 2,300 reformist candidates barred from appearing on the ballot, the group secured a large majority of at least 195 seats in the *Majlis*. Divisions and defections have emerged within the party's bloc in parliament, sharply reducing the number of seats held by the party, although not affecting the overall conservative majority. A significant number of the newly elected MPs included former officers in the Revolutionary Guards. The most powerful figure in the party has been Gholam-Ali Haddad-Adel, son-in-law of the supreme leader, who was selected speaker of the *Majlis*. The group originally endorsed Mohammad Baqer Qalibaf, the former chief of police forces, before the first round of the 2005 presidential elections, but later backed Ahmadinejad in his successful bid. Although encompassing a range of views on economic policy but without a clear ideological vision, the group has become the most prominent conservative party, at least in the public arena.

The party has drawn membership from the Society of Islamic Engineers, which has roots in traditional conservative circles and helped publicize the Builders of an Islamic Iran Council. The deputy speaker of the *Majlis*, Reza Bahonar, comes from the society, as does Ahmadinejad. Following their election, the party's MPs adopted strident, populist language; impeached Khatami's transport minister; urged an uncompromising stance on the nuclear issue; and adopted measures hostile to foreign investment. The party has been widely perceived as a vehicle for the supreme leader, with the supreme leader's son, Mojtaba Khamenei, allegedly playing an influential role in the party.

In the run-up to the 2008 parliamentary elections, the conservatives were divided between the party's hard-line supporters of President Ahmadinejad and others who opposed his economic policies and brash approach to international issues. The party subsequently participated in the United Fundamentalist Front, which won 69 percent of the *Majlis* seats. Though Ahmadinejad has been recognized as a member of this group, he ran for president in 2009 as an independent.

Leaders: Gholam-Ali HADDAD-ADEL (Former Speaker of the *Majlis*), Mehdi KOUCHAKZADEH, Hossein FADAEI.

Society of Combatant Clergy (*Jame'e Rohaniat Mobarez*—JRM). This hard-line, conservative group has continued to exert influence within the political establishment, although, like other older conservative groups, it has been overshadowed on the public stage by the Builders of an Islamic Iran Council. Along with the Islamic Coalition Society (see below), the group vehemently opposed the reformist agenda and has remained committed to perpetuating the country's rigid political and cultural restrictions. With strong ties to the clergy, the party sees Iran as representing the interests of the Islamic world.

The JRM was formed in late the 1970s in support of the then-exiled Ayatollah Khomeini. (The JRM has often been referenced, as it was in recent *Handbooks,* as the Association of Combatant Clergy. The JRM abbreviation and translation of "Jame'e" as "society" has been adopted for this edition of the *Handbook* in order to assist the reader in differentiating between the conservative JRM and its influential moderate offshoot, the Assembly of Combatant Clergy [MRM; see below]. Readers are cautioned to assess news reports carefully, as the two groupings are routinely confused because of the similarity of their names.) The JRM served as the primary vehicle for clerical political representation following the installation of Khomeini as the nation's leader in 1979, with the JRM and Servants of Construction (SC) considered breakaway groups. Although the JRM essentially concurred with the SC in the mid-1990s regarding proposed economic reform, it argued that ultimate political authority should remain with the nation's religious leaders, adopting a conservative stance on such issues as proposed expanded press freedoms and reinstitution of a formal party system.

As of late 1995 the society was believed to control about 150 seats in the *Majlis*, giving it significant policy influence under the leadership of Speaker Ali Akbar Nateq-Nuri. Having apparently done poorly in the first round of voting for the new *Majlis* in March 1996, the JRM adopted a hard-line approach for the second round, denouncing "liberals" as a threat to the ideals of the 1979 revolution. According to a number of observers, that campaign was assisted by *Hezbollah* militants, who, among other things, reportedly disrupted meetings of "un-Islamic" groupings.

It was subsequently estimated that society supporters had secured about 110 seats in the new *Majlis* in 1996. Although this represented the loss of its former "overall majority," the JRM was nevertheless able to secure the reelection of Nateq-Nuri as speaker by a reported vote of 146–105. JRM adherents later served as the core of the new *Hezbollah* faction in the *Majlis,* with Nateq-Nuri unsuccessfully carrying the standard of the conservative clerics in the May 1997 presidential election. He received 7.2 million votes to 20 million for the victorious Mohammad Khatami. However, Nateq-Nuri was reelected as *Majlis* speaker in both 1997 and 1998. The JRM was not widely referenced in regard to the 1999 municipal balloting. Many of its 2000 *Majlis* candidates were presented in conjunction with the Islamic Coalition Society. The JRM did not endorse a candidate in the 2001 presidential balloting, thereby diluting the conservatives' chances of mounting an effective challenge to President Khatami. In the 2005 presidential elections, the group initially backed Ali Larijani, former director of the state television and radio monopoly and former chief nuclear negotiator, prompting criticism from Ahmadinejad's supporters that the group was causing divisions within the conservative camp.

By 2007 rifts reportedly had developed among some progovernment factions, with Nateq-Nuri criticized for not being conservative enough. In March, Nateq-Nuri said that he would not be a candidate in any election. In June 2008 Nateq-Nuri was detained by Iranian authorities for allegedly accusing some clerics of corruption.

In the run-up to the 2009 presidential election, a rift reportedly developed between Nateq-Nuri and group leader Mohammad Reza Mahdavi-Kani, with the former remaining silent on the candidacy of Ahmadinejad, while the latter spoke out in support of the president. Mahdavi-Kani's declaration angered members in the wake of an official vote that failed to reach the threshold for its public pronouncement of support for Ahmadinejad. Other members turned against the Ahmadinejad administration in the wake of soaring housing and gas prices and double-digit inflation.

Leaders: Ali Akbar NATEQ-NURI (Former Speaker of the *Majlis*), Assadollah BADAMCHIAN, Mohammad Reza MAHDAVI-KANI (Founder and General Secretary).

Islamic Coalition Society (*Jameyat-e Motalefe-ye Eslami*). An umbrella organization of hard-line conservative clerics and merchants with links to the late Ayatollah Khomeini, the Islamic Coalition Society is influential in the judiciary as well as the quasi-charitable foundations that, having originally been formed to aid war victims and the poor, now control much of the non-oil economic sector. Although consensus within the society opposes political liberalization, there reportedly has been factionalization concerning economic reform, which is endorsed by some of the business community. In the 2005 presidential elections, the party initially backed Ali Larijani but later withdrew its support in favor of Ahmadinejad, reportedly on the orders of the office of the supreme leader.

In the 2006 Assembly of Experts elections, the party supported candidates of the Society of Combatant Clergy. In advance of the 2008 parliamentary elections, the party backed the candidate list of the United Fundamentalist Front.

In the 2009 presidential election, the party supported Ahmadinejad.

Leaders: Hamid Reza TARAQQI, Habibollah ASGAROWLADI (Former Commerce Minister), Assadollah BADAMCHIAN (Deputy Secretary General), Mohammad Nabi HABIBI (Secretary General).

Islamic Iran Development and Justice Party (IIDJP). The principlist grouping held its first congress on December 13, 2007, with a stated goal of increasing public participation in politics. Concerns about unemployment, inflation, and social ills led to the formation of the party in the run-up to the 2008 parliamentary election, with party leaders expressing their support for Ali Larijani, who subsequently won a seat. In the 2009 presidential election, the party supported independent conservative Mohsen Rezai.

Leaders: Kamal DANESHYAR, Amir Ali AMIRI, Reza TALAINIK (Secretary General).

May 23 Movement. Prior to the reformist victory in the parliamentary elections of 2000, some 20 parties and organizations (including important student organizations) committed to political reform and broadly supportive of President Khatami formed the May 23 Movement. (The coalition was named in honor of Khatami's election victory, which occurred on May 23, 1997; it is also known as the Second Khordad Movement [or Front], the second day of the month of Khordad in the Iranian calendar corresponding to May 23.) Once in power, serious divisions within the coalition emerged, as reformists argued over how to respond to the successive vetoes of parliamentary bills and measures stifling dissent and press freedom. The coalition failed to agree on a unified candidate list in Tehran for the 2003 local elections. During the disputed 2004 parliamentary elections, members of the coalition were deeply divided over whether to boycott the vote or to participate in hopes of limiting the size of a conservative victory. Although the coalition leaders continued to hold meetings, they could not reach agreement on a single, reformist candidate for the 2005 presidential elections, splitting reformist votes during the first round. One of the group's early leaders, Abbas Abdi, is said to be among the most influential reformists in Iran. Abdi was also reported to be the first person to storm the U.S. embassy in Tehran, leading other students in the 1979 takeover and hostage crisis. Abdi subsequently joined the IIPF (below).

Islamic Iran Participation Front (*Jebhe-ye Mosharekat-e Iran-e Eslami*—IIPF). Established in December 1998 by pro-Khatami forces, the IIPF presented candidates in the 1999 municipal elections, some in coalition with the SC (below). For the 2000 *Majlis* balloting, it served as a core component of the May 23 Movement, subsequently reporting that approximately 80 of its members had been elected. The IIPF is led by Mohammad Reza Khatami, the brother of President Khatami. Several senior members of the party had been involved as student activists in the seizure of the U.S. embassy in 1979 but have since evolved into proponents of liberal democratic change. After the 2000 elections, members of the IIPF were the most outspoken advocates for sweeping reforms, arguing as cabinet ministers and MPs for greater media freedom, cultural openness, women's rights, environmental safeguards, and engagement with Western governments. Regarding economic policy, some elements of the IIPF and other reformists remain reluctant to embrace market reform measures.

Some prominent members of the party were targeted and harassed by the conservative judiciary, paramilitaries, and parallel security services. Abbas Abdi, who formerly was reported to have been a leader in the May 23 Movement (above) and among those who stormed the U.S. embassy in Tehran in 1979, was sentenced to four years in prison after publishing a poll in October 2002 showing a majority of Iranians supporting dialogue with the United States. Judges closed newspapers sponsored by the party, including *Sobh-e Emrooz*. Its editor, Saeed Hajarian, was a senior adviser to President Khatami when Khatami was shot and nearly killed in an assassination attempt in 2000. Hard-line paramilitaries sometimes broke up IIPF rallies and events. Frustrated with the obstruction of the Council of Guardians and judicial repression, IIPF members lobbied to confront the conservatives, advocating that Khatami resign or hold a referendum, but the president refused. By the end of Khatami's second term, the IIPF had concluded that reform within the parameters of the current system was unattainable and that the constitutional framework had to be amended to deliver genuine parliamentary democracy. During the crisis preceding the 2004 elections, in which most IIPF candidates were banned from appearing on the ballot, IIPF leaders wrote an unprecedented open letter to the supreme leader questioning the legitimacy of his rule and warning of a betrayal of the revolution. Out of power, some members have turned to promoting new civil society groups and civic education efforts. The party has sought to reach out to liberal activists in the banned but tolerated Liberation Movement of Iran led by Ibrahim YAZDI (see below). The party supported Mostafa Moin, former minister of scientific research in Khatami's cabinet, in the first round of the 2005 presidential elections. In the second round, the party endorsed Rafsanjani, largely as a vote against the conservative Ahmadinejad.

In 2007 divisions were reported over attempts to form a reformist coalition in advance of the 2008 *Majlis* election. However, following the government's barring most of the party's members from contesting the election, the IIPF participated in the Reformists Coalition, backing its list of candidates.

In 2009 the IIPF backed Mir Hosein Musavi for president. Following the disputed election, during a period of mass protests, reports surfaced that police had stormed IIPF party headquarters and arrested several people, including Mohsen Mirdamadi and Mohammad Reza Khatami, who was later released. (International journalists were banned from covering events in the city, and thus many reports remained unconfirmed.) Meanwhile, the group condemned the recent arrests and called on the government to release all political prisoners.

Leaders: Mohammad Reza KHATAMI (Former Deputy Speaker of the *Majlis*), Saeed HAJARIAN, Seyyed Safdar HOSEYNI, Azar MANSURI, ABBAS ABDI, Abdollah RAMEZANZADEH (Deputy Secretary General), Mohsen MIRDAMADI (Secretary General).

Islamic Revolution Mujaheddin Organization (IRMO). Described by some observers as the "third major grouping" (after the JRM and the SC) during the 1996 *Majlis* campaign, IRMO was supported by a number of leftist organizations and former parties. It was reportedly aligned to a certain degree with the SC in 1996, although its support was considered "feeble" in contrast to *Hezbollah*'s efforts on behalf of the SC's main rival, the JRM. IRMO supported Mohammad Khatami in the 1997 presidential election and served as one of the most liberal components of the May 23 Movement in the 2000 *Majlis* balloting. Although it supported Khatami in his reelection effort in 2001, IRMO subsequently distanced itself from the government by insisting upon more active resistance to the antireform influence of conservative clerics.

A prominent member of the party, university academic Hashem Aghajari, was convicted of apostasy and sentenced to death in November 2002 for a speech in which he questioned absolute clerical authority and called on Iranians to interpret the Koran for themselves. Following student demonstrations, the supreme leader intervened, ordering the courts to lift the death penalty. Aghajari was later sentenced to a five-year prison term. In the 2005 presidential elections, IRMO supported Mostafa Moin.

Most, if not all, of the party's candidates were reportedly among the thousands of reformists disqualified by the government prior to the 2008 parliamentary elections. Following the 2009 presidential election, IRMO leaders urged unsuccessful independent challenger Mir Hosein Musavi, whom the party supported, to form a new political party.

Leaders: Behzad NABAVI (Former Deputy Speaker of the *Majlis*), Mohsen ARMIN (Spokesperson), Mohammad SALAMATI (Secretary General).

Islamic Iran Solidarity Party. Reportedly recognized in 1998 as Iran's first legal post-1987 party, the Islamic Iran Solidarity Party was launched by a group of Khatami government ministers and other officials. Perhaps more than any other reformist organization, the party has fallen into disarray and possible irrelevance following recent victories by the conservatives in parliament and the presidency.

In 2006 Ebrahim ASGHARZADEH, former secretary general of the party (and reported to be among those who took Americans hostage in 1979), resigned, saying he would start a new group because the reformists had failed to understand the "real needs of the people." He subsequently formed the Front for Freedom and Equality (below). In the run-up to the 2008 parliamentary elections, the Islamic Iran Solidarity Party was reported to have participated in the Reformists Coalition. In September 2008, parliament considered, but subsequently rejected, an impeachment motion against Education Minister Ali Ahmadi over teacher pay issues.

Leaders: Reza RAHCHAMANI, Reza NORUZ-ZADEH, Ali Reza Ali AHMADI (Secretary General).

Front for Freedom and Equality. Ebrahim Asgharzadeh, formerly of the Islamic Iran Solidarity Party, established the new group in early 2008, denouncing weaknesses and shortcomings in the reformists' camp, with the goal of unseating "authoritarians" in the *Majlis*. Asgharzadeh, one of the few reformist candidates qualified by the government, ran on the Reformist Coalition list in the 2008 parliamentary election.

Leader: Ebrahim ASGHARZADEH.

Islamic Labor Party (ILP). An outgrowth of a workers' movement launched in the 1980s in opposition to Marxist groups, the ILP reported that 15 of its members had been elected to the *Majlis* in 2000 as part of the May 23 Movement. ILP leader Ali Reza Mahjoub is also head of the House of Workers, the nation's primary federation of unions. One of the few well-known reformists to return to the *Majlis* in 2005 balloting, Mahjoub managed to win a seat in the new parliament, representing a Tehran district (determined in a third round of voting that coincided with the first round of presidential polling on June 17).

In 2007 the party participated in protests demanding job security and rights for workers, including the right to form unions; it subsequently joined the Reformists Coalition in advance of the 2008 parliamentary elections. In the run-up to the 2009 presidential election, the ILP was among several reformist parties that pressed for a single candidate to represent their interests.

Leaders: Ali Reza MAHJOUB, Abolqasem SARHADIZADEH, Hosein KAMALI (Secretary General).

Assembly of Combatant Clergy (*Majma' Ruhaniun Mobarez*—MRM). The MRM was launched in 1988 by members of the Society of Combatant Clergy (JRM) who split from the parent group because of their objections over the JRM's unwillingness to support political liberalization. (The MRM was referenced as the Assembly of Militant Clerics in the 1999 *Handbook,* and its name has been routinely translated in news reports as the Association of Militant Clerics [or Clergy], the League of Militant Clerics, and other variations. See the section on the JRM, above, for an explanation of the naming conventions adopted for this edition of the *Handbook* to assist in identifying the two groups.)

Members of the MRM were prominent in the reformists' victory in 1988 *Majlis* balloting, although their influence declined following the 1992 balloting. The MRM returned to center stage on the political front with the surprise presidential victory in 1997 by MRM member Mohammad Khatami, who had been eased out of his position as minister of Islamic culture in 1992 after critics accused him of maintaining too liberal a stance regarding Western influences. A member of the May 23 Movement in the 2000 *Majlis* balloting, the MRM currently serves as one of the primary moderate groupings within the reform movement.

Within the May 23 Movement, the MRM favored a more gradualist approach to reform, seeking to work solely within the confines of the theocratic system and avoid antagonizing conservative institutions. The MRM opposed boycotting the 2004 elections and supported a rival presidential candidate in the 2005 presidential elections, backing party leader Mehdi Karrubi instead of the IIPF's Mostafa Moin. After losing in the first round of the election and alleging fraud, Karrubi resigned as the organization's secretary general to form his own party (see the National Trust, below). The MRM elected Mohammad Khatami to head its Central Council on August 8, 2005, days after he completed his second and final four-year term as president. Khatami has been associated with the party since the 1980s.

In 2008 MRM leader Seyyed Abdolvahed Musavi-Lari had a key role in the Reformists Coalition prior to the parliamentary elections. Khatami, for his part, announced that he would not be a candidate. In April Khatami announced that he was retiring from political activity, but he later decided to contest the 2009 presidential election. However, he withdrew in March 2009 to support Mir Hosein Musavi. In April the MRM voted against backing Ahmadinejad, due to a "variety of criticisms" against the president, according to the group's spokesperson.

Leaders: Seyyed Abdolvahed MUSAVI-LARI, Gholamreza MESBAHI (Spokesperson), Mohammad KHATAMI (Secretary General).

National Trust Party (*Etemaad-e Melli*). Shortly after the 2005 presidential election, Mehdi Karrubi, former parliamentary speaker and former leader of the MRM, registered the National Trust as a new party. Party founders included Rassoul MONTAJABNIYA, a former prominent member of the Assembly of Combatant Clergy, and Reza HAJATI, a former student activist. Karrubi also owns a newspaper that carries the party's name.

The reformist National Trust Party, which reportedly was allowed to field candidates for 55 percent of the seats in the 2008 parliamentary election, initially rejected overtures to join the Reformists Coalition formed in advance of the balloting. However, following its unsuccessful bid in the first round in March, the National Trust Party joined the Reformists Coalition for the second round in April. The loose coalition also included the **Democracy Party** (*Mardom Salari*), led by Mostafa KAVAKEBIAN.

In the run-up to the 2009 presidential election, a rift developed between the National Trust Party and backers of former president Khatami. Party leader Mehdi Karrubi subsequently announced his candidacy in May; he received 0.85 percent of the vote.

Leader: Mehdi KARRUBI (2005 and 2009 presidential candidate and Former Speaker of the *Majlis*).

Servants of Construction—SC (*Kargozaran-e Sazandegi*). The SC (also sometimes referenced as the Executives of Construction) was launched in January 1996 by 16 top members of the Iranian executive branch, leading to its being informally referenced as the "G-16." Widely viewed as allied with (then) President Rafsanjani, the SC founders called for continued economic reform and moderate political liberalization.

About 90–100 SC supporters were believed to have been elected to the *Majlis* in 1996, a strong "antiliberal" campaign on behalf of the JRM/*Hezbollah* having apparently prevented what some observers had expected to be a clear-cut SC victory. The SC supported Interior Minister Abdullah NOURI in his unsuccessful bid to be elected speaker of the new *Majlis*.

The SC supported Mohammad Khatami in the May 1997 presidential election. Although the *Majlis* subsequently approved all of Khatami's cabinet recommendations, some of the harshest debate was over two SC candidates, Nouri and Seyed Ataollah Mohajerani. Early in 1998 the conservative judiciary arrested some Khatami supporters, including the SC's Gholan Hussein Karbaschi, mayor of Tehran, for alleged corruption in an election backlash that was seen by pro-Khatami elements as an escalation of political warfare. The popular mayor, who had been a leading figure in Khatami's surprise presidential victory, was subsequently sentenced to 18 months in prison. By that time, however, the SC had reportedly elected him as its secretary general after the grouping had apparently been officially recognized as a party. After 7 months in jail, Karbaschi was pardoned in December 1999 by Ayatollah Ali Khamenei. The SC was subsequently reported to have been fractionalized on the issue of how close to remain aligned with the Khatami administration, some members criticizing the president for failing to take stronger action to challenge the prosecution of SC members by the conservative judiciary.

The SC presented candidates in the 1999 municipal elections, some in alliance with the IIPF. Nouri was the top vote-getter in the local balloting in Tehran, but later in the year he was sentenced to five years in prison for having questioned the powerful role of the religious hierarchy, his case becoming one of the most prominent of the reformist versus conservative battles.

The "centrist, economics-oriented" SC presented joint candidates with other members of the May 23 Movement for many of the seats in the 2000 *Majlis,* although SC candidates competed on an independent SC list for some seats in Tehran. Included in that group was Rafsanjani, who had stated his goal of returning to the speakership of the *Majlis.* Indicative of the ongoing lack of harmony between Rafsanjani and Khatami (as well as their respective supporters), Rafsanjani was also included on the candidate list of the conservative JRM. Although he was elected to the *Majlis,* Rafsanjani ultimately declined his seat in the wake of controversy surrounding electoral decisions in his favor on the part of the Council of Guardians. He, however, remained head of the influential Expediency Council. Meanwhile, the SC claimed representation in the *Majlis* of some 55 members. Following the SC's defeats in the municipal elections of 2003, the parliamentary elections of 2004, and Rafsanjani's crushing loss in the 2005 presidential vote, the group announced plans for a major reorganization and "restructuring" that would result in new leadership. Regardless, it will be difficult to alter the perception of the party as a failed platform for Rafsanjani.

The SC backed reformist coalition candidates in the 2008 *Majlis* elections and Mir Hosein Musavi in the 2009 presidential balloting.

Leaders: Mohammad HASHEMI, Hossein MARASHI (Spokesperson), Gholan Hussein KARBASCHI (Secretary General).

Liberation Movement of Iran (*Nehzat-e Azadi-e Irân*). A liberal Islamic grouping established in 1961 by Mehdi Bazargan, the Liberation Movement, also referenced as the Freedom Movement of Iran, supported the opposition religious leaders during the anti-shah demonstrations of 1978. Named prime minister in February 1979, Bazargan resigned in the wake of the U.S. embassy seizure the following November. Subsequently, he remained one of the most outspoken critics tolerated by the government. In a letter authored in November 1982, he accused the regime of responsibility for an "atmosphere of terror, fear, revenge, and national disintegration." *Nehzat-e Azadi,* which was linked to the Paris-based National Resistance Council, boycotted the legislative balloting in 1984 and in 1988 because of government-imposed electoral restrictions. In May 1988 the publication of a second letter from Bazargan to Ayatollah Khomeini highly critical of the government's war efforts and other "erroneous plans" led to the arrest of leading members of his party and of the Association for the Defense and Sovereignty of the Iranian Nation, which had been formed in opposition to continuation of the war with Iraq in March 1986 by Bazargan and others who had participated in the 1979 provisional government. Bazargan charged that the movement was not permitted to participate freely in the 1992 legislative campaign, and supporters were urged to boycott the 1993 presidential balloting.

Bazargan died of heart failure in January 1995, and his longtime assistant, Ibrahim Yazdi, was subsequently named as the movement's new secretary general. Yazdi later called on the government to permit the movement to present candidates in the March 1996 legislative elections. However, the Council of Guardians ruled that movement candidates per se would not be permitted to do so, although four members could run as independents. Those potential candidates subsequently declined to participate in the campaign to protest the council's decision. For his part, Yazdi argued that, while Iranians remained "loyal" to the "ideals" of the revolution, there was growing discontent over the government's "violation" of "rights and liberties." Yazdi was arrested in December 1997 (and later released) after signing a letter with 50 other government critics appealing for protection for Ayatollah Hussein Ali Montazeri, a cleric whose home was attacked by demonstrators after he questioned the authority of Ayatollah Khamenei. Montazeri had once been in line to succeed Ayatollah Khomeini (see Political background, above, for details). He has been under house arrest for several years for his remarks, prompting mass protests by his supporters in the city of Isfahan.

The Liberation Movement, a strong supporter of the reform tendency since 1997, was not permitted to present candidates in 2000 *Majlis* balloting, and the crackdown on the party by the conservative judiciary resulted in the arrest of some 60 party members in late 2000 and early 2001 on charges of seeking to overthrow the government in relation to, among other things, student unrest. The party was formally outlawed in July 2002. It condemned the Council of Guardians' ban on hundreds of reformist candidates in the 2004 parliamentary elections and speaks out frequently on human rights abuses. The most significant case has been that of Akbar Ganji, a journalist jailed in 2001 for reporting on an alleged conspiracy of assassinations orchestrated against dissidents. He was released after having served his full sentence in 2006, despite pressure for years by world leaders for his early release.

Since 2005, when Yazdi tried to run for president but was disqualified, the party has been tolerated, but by most accounts it has no influence in the affairs of the country.

In 2009 an activist member of the group was arrested for allegedly disseminating propaganda against the government.

Leader: Ibrahim YAZDI (Secretary General and Former Prime Minister).

Office for Consolidation of Unity (*Daftar-e Takhim-e Vahdat*). This student organization has served as a platform for outspoken critics of the regime and in 1999 led street demonstrations protesting a crackdown on press freedom. The organization played an important role in the 1979 revolution, supporting the seizure of the U.S. embassy, and many of its leaders participated in the taking of American hostages. The group allied itself with the May 23 Movement (Second of Khordad) but later broke ranks with President Khatami and the reformists, criticizing their refusal to confront the conservatives and arguing that the Islamic Republic is inherently undemocratic. Several leaders have been imprisoned since 1997. Ahmad BATEBI, a student demonstrator with no links to the organization's leadership, was imprisoned in 1999 after his photograph appeared in newspapers and on the cover of the *Economist* holding the bloodied T-shirt of a fellow student. He remains in prison, after having been allowed several furloughs for medical care; he was rearrested in 2006. In February 2007 Batebi's wife, a dentist, reportedly was "snatched from the street," arrested by men thought to be security and intelligence agents, according to Human Rights Watch. A government crackdown on student activists in midyear included the arrest of six members of the organization during a sit-in at a university in July and the subsequent use of tear gas against students protesting an appearance by President Ahmadinejad at the University of Tehran in October. Following the disputed 2009 presidential election, student members of the group in Great Britain protested, demanding the expulsion of the British ambassador from Tehran after Iranian leaders accused Western nations of being behind the post-election violence.

Devotees of the Party of God (*Ansar-e Hezbollah*). This is a hardline paramilitary organization known for breaking up antiregime street demonstrations and attacking those considered to be flaunting social restrictions imposed by the authorities. Its roots date back to the 1979 revolution, when gangs of urban poor organized as *Hezbollah* to support Ayatollah Khomeini. Most members are veterans of the Iran-Iraq war or former members of the Basij militia, which was formed by the revolutionary leadership. The group has been accused of carrying out political assassinations.

National Front (*Jebhe-e Melli*). The National Front was established in December 1977 as an essentially secular antiregime coalition of nationalist factions, including followers of former prime minister Mohammad Mossadeq. One of its founders, Shahpur Bakhtiar, was formally expelled upon designation as prime minister by the shah in late 1978; another founder, Karim SANJABI, resigned as foreign minister of the Islamic Republic in April 1979 to protest a lack of authority accorded to Prime Minister Bazargan. Prominent in the front is the long-standing **Iranian Nation Party** (INP), formed by Dariush FORUHAR, a former minister in the post-revolution Bazargan government. The INP (also sometimes referenced as the Iran People's Party) was tolerated by the government, despite remaining technically illegal. The party's newsletter regularly published harsh criticism of the regime, particularly in regard to human rights violations. Foruhar and his wife, Parvaneh ESKANDARI-FORUHAR, were murdered in November 1998, the killings ultimately being attributed to "rogue elements" within government security forces. Several INP members were arrested in July 1999 in connection with student unrest. For the 2000 *Majlis* balloting the INP, now led by Bahran NAMAZI, attempted to present joint candidates with the Liberation Movement of Iran and other groups in a Coalition of National Religious Forces in support of the reformist movement.

Party of the Masses (*Hezb-e-Tudeh*). Traditionally pro-Soviet, the communist Tudeh was formed in 1941, declared illegal in 1949, and went underground in 1953. A number of its leaders returned from exile in East Germany in early 1979. At a March 1981 Central Committee plenum, the party aligned itself with Ayatollah Khomeini's "anti-imperialist and popular line," while ending its support for separatist movements. Because of Tudeh's conservatism, a number of more radical communist groups also emerged. Tudeh was formally banned in April 1983 after several party officials confessed (some said they were coerced) to providing the Soviet Union with military and political information. On the other hand, a faction of the militia Fedayeen-e-Khalq joined Tudeh in support of the revolution. Its founder, Iraj ESKENDARI, died in East Germany in April 1985. Party cofounder Ehsan TABARI, who had been imprisoned and later fled the country, died in 1989, the same year 38 members of the party were executed along with thousands of other political prisoners. A dissident faction, calling itself the Iranian People's Democratic Party, was reportedly formed in Paris in February 1988. In 2007 the party's Web site listed addresses in Berlin and London, and the party leader was identified as Ali Khavari.

Party leader Dr. Nureddin KIANOURI died in 1990, following his imprisonment, along with that of his wife, Maryam Farman FARMAYAN, in 1983. The elderly couple was tortured, according to the record of what transpired. Farmayan, a major figure in the feminist movement in Iran and a founding member of the party's women's organization, died in 2008 at age 94.

Leader: Ali KHAVARI (Chair, in exile).

Among some of the other parties and groups are the Islamic Labor Welfare Party, the Youth Party, the Modernist Muslim Women's Association, and the Association of the Women of the Islamic Revolution.

The largest guerrilla group—which at one time claimed some 100,000 members but is now considered to have much less support—is the **Mujaheddin-e Khalq** ("People's Warriors," also referenced as the *Mujaheddin Khalq* Organization—MKO or MEK), founded in 1965 in opposition to the shah. Leftist but also Islamic, the *Mujaheddin* confined most of their activities after the revolution to urban areas, frequently engaging in street battles with the Revolutionary Guards and the regular army; many of the political assassinations of 1979–1982 were apparently carried out by its members. The political leader of the *Mujaheddin,* Massoud RAJAVI, accompanied former president Abol Hasan Bani-Sadr into exile in Paris in July 1981 but subsequently came under pressure from French authorities and left, with 1,000 of his followers, for Iraq in June 1986; within Iran, guerrilla leader Mussa KHIABANI was killed in February 1982, his successor being Ali ZARKESH. In mid-1988 the *Mujaheddin* captured three Iranian towns before the Iranian army drove them back into Iraq in early August. The 15,000-member guerrilla force reportedly met with stiff resistance from "locals" who considered its attacks on the weakened army treasonous. Subsequently, the *Mujaheddin* claimed that thousands of its adherents had been executed by government forces. In December 1991 many *Mujaheddin* members were arrested during a government crackdown on opposition street protests, while President Rafsanjani ordered air strikes against its bases in Iraq during the run-up to the 1992 balloting.

In late 1993 Tehran strongly criticized Paris's decision to permit Maryam RAJAVI (wife of Massoud Rajavi and recently elected, according to *Middle East International,* as "president of Iran" by the *Mujaheddin* executive committee) to remain, with 200 supporters, in France. In January 1994 some 17 *Mujaheddin* members were arrested for participating in a bombing in the Iranian capital, with leaders of the group denying complicity and accusing the government of routinely linking them to all such disturbances for political purposes. Later in the year the U.S. State Department accused the *Mujaheddin* of engaging in terrorism, Washington's animosity apparently stemming in part from *Mujaheddin* links to the Iraqi regime of Saddam Hussein. The group was reportedly used to assist Hussein's forces in crushing Kurdish and Shiite rebellions. In the summer of 1997, apparently as a gesture of goodwill toward the new moderate Khatami government, Israel ordered an end to *Mujaheddin* broadcasts via an Israeli-owned satellite. The *Mujaheddin,* now operating out of Iraq, claimed responsibility for sporadic attacks in Tehran in 2000 and 2001. Subsequently, the group was designated a foreign terrorist organization by the United States, Canada, Iraq, Iran, and the European Union. (In 2009 the Council of the European Union removed the group from the EU's terror list.)

In August 2002, the group's political wing, the National Council of Resistance of Iran (NCRI), presented satellite photographs and details of an underground uranium-enrichment center in Natanz and a heavy-water nuclear production facility in Arak. The satellite imagery prompted speculation that the group was supplied with intelligence from the United States or Israel, as it would lack sufficient resources to monitor Iran's nuclear activities. The revelations, subsequently confirmed by UN inspectors, indicated that Iran had made substantial progress in its nuclear research and renewed suspicions that the regime was pursuing a clandestine weapons project (possibly involving the purchase of materials and know-how from Pakistani scientists). The group lost its primary sponsor after the fall of Saddam Hussein and was briefly bombarded by U.S. forces. The MKO agreed to a cease-fire and was later disarmed and confined to designated camps under U.S. guard. Some 4,000 MKO members have remained under U.S. military supervision or "detention" at Camp Ashraf in Iraq, and, after a lengthy review by the U.S. State Department and the Federal Bureau of Investigation (FBI), none has been charged as suspected terrorists. The political wing, the NCRI, continues to enjoy support from a small number of parliamentary representatives in Europe and in the U.S. Congress.

Meanwhile, the U.S. State Department listed the NCRI as an "alias" for the exiles fighting in Iraq. Rajavi, described as the leader of the NCRI, met on separate occasions with leaders of Belgium and Norway, drawing criticism from Iran after Rajavi was quoted as saying the Iranian mullahs were a threat to the people of Iran and "to all humanity."

In 2007 as many as 3,800 members were said to be living in Iraq under some degree of supervision by the United States. Though Iraq was trying to evict the group for security reasons, the United States reportedly was reluctant to change course because the *Mujaheddin* were said to be providing important information about Iran's nuclear program.

Of the separatist groups, the largest is the primarily Sunni Muslim **Kurdish Democratic Party of Iran** (KDPI), also referenced as the Democratic Party of Iranian Kurdistan (DPIK), which was outlawed in August 1979. Campaigning under the slogan "Democracy for Iran, Autonomy for the Kurds," the KDPI, like the *Mujaheddin,* has been a principal target of government forces; its guerrilla wing is often referred to as the *Pesh Mergas* (as is a similar Kurdish group in Iraq). Its former secretary general, Abdur Rahman QASSEMLOU, was assassinated in Vienna in July 1989, while his successor, Sadeq SHARAFKANDI, and four KDPI colleagues were murdered in Berlin in September 1992. In 1993 German prosecutors charged that the Iranian government had been involved in the latter attack. (Former Iranian prime minister Bani-Sadr testified at a trial in Germany in 1996 that Ayatollah Khamenei had personally signed a death warrant for Sharafkandi.) Late in 1993 it was also reported that KDPI guerrillas had engaged government troops near the Iraqi border. Another KDPI leader, Ghafur HAMZEKI, was reported to have been assassinated in Baghdad in August 1994, while, in what was described as an effort to "crush" the guerrillas, Iranian bombers and missiles attacked KDPI bases in Iraq the following November. In May 1995 it was reported that Abdallah HASSANZADEH had replaced Mustafa HEJRI as KDPI leader and secretary general. The KDPI claimed that its fighters had been attacked by Iranian troops in late 1996 in the wake of the incursion by the Iraqi military into the Kurdish "safe haven" in northern Iraq. In April 1997 a German court ruled that unnamed senior Iranian officials were responsible for the 1992 assassinations in Berlin, a finding that strained Iran's relations with the EU as well as with Germany. Perhaps indicating a reduction in tensions between the KDPI and the government, the KDPI was described as openly supporting candidates in Kurdish-populated areas in the 1999 municipal elections. As of 2005 the secretary general of the Iraq-based KDPI was Mustafa HEJRI. In December 2006 the KDPI reportedly split into two factions: one led by Hejri, and a breakaway group led by Abdullah Hassan ZADEH, also in Iraq.

Another separatist group, identified as the **Party for a Free Life in Kurdistan**, also known as Pejak, was operating in 2007 just miles from Iran in the northern region of Iraq. It claimed responsibility for numerous cross-border attacks in Iran, including the killing of 24 Iranian soldiers in 2006 in retaliation for the deaths of 10 Iranian Kurds. The group, which some reports said was an offshoot of the Kurdistan Workers' Party in Iraq, claimed to have several thousand members living in its base camp in northern Iraq and identified two of its leaders as Akif ZAGROS and Gulistan DUGAN. In February 2007 three members of Pejak were killed by Iranian forces near the border with Turkey; earlier Pejak claimed it had shot down an Iranian helicopter. Despite ongoing clashes within Iran and Iraq, the U.S. State Department said in August that Pejak was not included on its list of foreign terrorist organizations but noted that its activities were being monitored. Subsequently, in April 2008 Pejak leaders, reported to be hiding in the mountains in Iraq, threatened bomb attacks inside Iran unless Tehran changed its anti-Kurdish policies. Recently, the *New York Times* reported that Pejak and the Kurdistan Workers' Party (PKK), recognized as a terrorist organization that has engaged in violent conflict with Turkey, "appear to a large extent to be one and the same, and share the same goal: fighting campaigns to win new autonomy and rights for Kurds in Iran and Turkey." The PKK's leader is Abdullah OCALAN (imprisoned in Turkey). In April 2009 the group was blamed for an attack on a police station in a western province bordering Iraq. A week later, Iranian forces attacked Kurdish villages near the border and inside Iraq that were thought to be Pejak strongholds, according to *Agence France-Presse*.

LEGISLATURE

The unicameral **Islamic Consultative Assembly** (*Majlis-e Shoura-e Islami*) has 290 members serving four-year terms. Members are popularly elected in multiple-member constituencies in which each voter votes for as many candidates as there are seats. (Successful candidates must receive a minimum percentage of the total votes. If some seats remain unfilled after the first round of balloting, a runoff round is held.) Political groups are permitted to present candidate lists, many of the leading groups serving in a quasi-party capacity. All candidates must be approved by the Council of Guardians, which regularly rejects many prospects. Five of the 290 seats are reserved for religious minorities, including 2 for Armenian Christians, 1 for Assyrian Christians, and 1 each for Jewish Iranians and Iranian Zoroastrians.

In the most recent election of March 14 and April 25, 2008, conservatives secured 170 seats; reformists, 46; and independents, 71. The results for 3 seats were annulled.

Speaker: Ali Ardeshir LARIJANI.

CABINET

[as of July 16, 2009]

President	Mahmoud Ahmadinejad
First Vice President	Vacant
Vice President, Chief of Cultural Heritage and Tourism	Hamid Baqaei
Vice President, Chief of the Iran Atomic Energy Organization (IAEO)	Ali Akbar Salehi
Vice President, Chief of Iran's Environmental Protection Organization	Fatemeh Vaezjavadi [f]
Vice President, Chief of the Islamic Revolution Martyrs Foundation	Massoud Zaribafan
Vice President, Chief of Management Development and Human Resources	Ebrahim Azizi
Vice President, Chief of the National Youth Organization	Mehrdad Bazrpash
Vice President, Chief of the Physical Training Organization	Mohammad Ali-Abadi
Vice President, Chief of the President's Office	Ali Saidlu
Vice President, Strategic Planning and Supervision Affairs	Amir Mansur Borqei
Ministers	
Agricultural Jihad	Mohammad Reza Eskandari
Commerce	Masoud Mir Kazemi
Communications and Information Technology	Mohammad Soleimani
Cooperatives	Mohammad Abbasi
Culture and Islamic Guidance	Mohammad Hossein Saffar Harandi

Defense	Brig.-Gen. Mohammad Mostafa Najjar
Economic Affairs and Finance	Seyed Shamseddin Hosseini
Education	Ali Reza Ali Ahmadi
Energy	Parviz Fattah
Foreign Affairs	Manouchehr Mottaki
Health	Kamran Baqeri Lankarani
Housing and Urban Development	Mohammad Saeedi Kia
Industry and Mines	Ali Akbar Mehrabian
Intelligence	Gholam Hosein Mohseni
Interior	Sadeq Mahsouli
Justice and Government Spokesperson	Gholam Hosein Elham
Labor	Mohammad Jahromi
Petroleum	Gholam Hosein Nozari
Roads and Transport	Hamid Behbahani
Scientific Research and Technology	Mohammad Mehdi Zahedi
Welfare and Social Affairs	Abdolreza Mesri

[f] = female

COMMUNICATIONS

Freedom of the press is provided for in the 1979 constitution, except in regard to violations of public morality and religious belief or impugning the reputation of individuals. Nevertheless, more than 20 newspapers were closed in August 1979, and drastic curbs were imposed on foreign journalists, including a ban on unsupervised interviews with government officials and a requirement that reporters apply for press cards every three months. In August 1980 Ayatollah Khomeini called for increased censorship, and on June 7, 1981, an additional seven publications were banned. Subsequently, on August 25, 1981, the *Majlis* passed a law making it a criminal offense to use "pen and speech" against the government. However, the Rafsanjani government permitted a degree of debate in the press on controversial issues, leading one correspondent to describe the situation as "lively but controlled." Critics of the regime called for an extension of press freedom, noting that newspapers were routinely shut down by the authorities for publishing "antigovernment" articles. The Khatami administration installed in 1997 issued permits to dozens of new publications, apparently hoping through public debate to strengthen independent institutions. The establishment of a more vibrant press was credited with the success of reformists in the February 1999 municipal elections. However, conservatives opposed to the new policy of openness continued to control the "Press Court," which ultimately determines the fate of newspapers. Journalism subsequently became one of the main battlefields in the conflict between reformists and conservatives. New restrictions on the press contributed to large-scale student demonstrations in July 1999.

Shortly after the 2000 legislative elections, the outgoing *Majlis* hurriedly approved a crude press-control law, which the conservative Council of Guardians ruled could not be overturned by the new reform-minded *Majlis*. Consequently, some 110 proreform publications were closed over a four-year period, and many journalists were arrested. Journalists and dissident voices sought refuge on the Internet, but the judiciary began cracking down on Web-based writers in 2003 and imposing stricter controls on Internet service providers. Nevertheless, some Farsilanguage Web sites based outside the country have managed to circumvent the restrictions. Blogging has also grown rapidly as a form of political and social protest, reducing the regime's ability to control the flow of information.

Numerous journalists and editors have been jailed in recent years. The plight of journalist Akbar GANJI, in particular, has gained international attention. Ganji's articles linking conservative authorities to the killing of dissidents led to his arrest and imprisonment in 2001. He was freed for a while but was rearrested in 2006.

In 2007 nine journalists remained behind bars. The watchdog Reporters Without Borders said in its 2007 report that Iran "continues to be the Middle East's biggest prison for the media." Gholan Hussein Karbaschi, leader of the Servants of Construction party and managing editor of the banned daily newspaper *Ham-Mihan*, faced libel and other charges in 2007; the reformist paper had been banned from 1997 to 2005 and had been briefly reinstated in 2007. In 2008 a journalist accused of being a member of a terrorist group called *Mardom Salari*, was sentenced to death. The government also closed down five news Web sites for allegedly "poisoning" public opinion in the run-up to parliamentary elections. In 2009 the case of Roxana SABERI, an Iranian-American journalist, captured international attention after she was arrested in January, found guilty of spying, and sentenced to eight years in prison. An appeals court subsequently found her guilty of lesser charges (all of which she denied) and gave her a two-year suspended sentence. She was freed in May.

Reporters Without Borders declared in 2009 that Iran "now ranks alongside China as the world's biggest prison for journalists," in the wake of the final election results in June and the subsequent demonstrations by the opposition. The watchdog group reported that 33 journalists and "cyber-dissidents" had been jailed as of June 21. The group also urged nations not to recognize the election results, "citing censorship and a crackdown on journalists," according to CNN. Other international media also reported on Iran's media censorship and blocking of Internet sites.

Press. Prominent newspapers aligned with the conservatives include *Jomhuri Islami*, hard-line conservative; *Kayhan* (Universe), hard-line conservative; *Resalat* (Message), considered more "pragmatic"; *Siasat-e Ruz*, hard-line; and *Ettela'at* and *Hamshari*, owned by the Tehran city council. Newspapers backed by reformists include *Sharqh* (East), which enjoys the most influence and reach; *Hambastegi, E'temad, Aftab-e Yazd,* the economic-focused *Donyaye Eqtesad,* and *Eqhbal*, associated with the IIPF; and *Entekhab* and *Farhang-e Ashti*. English-language dailies include the moderate *Iran News, Iran Daily*, and the conservative *Tehran Times*. The daily *Mardom Salari* was reported to be the newspaper of a Sunni group of the same name.

News agencies. In December 1981 the domestic Pars News Agency was renamed the Islamic Republic News Agency (IRNA). Following the July 1981 closing of Reuters' Tehran office, *Agence France-Presse* and Italy's ANSA were the only Western bureaus with operations in Iran. Reuters has subsequently reopened its facility in Tehran, and several other foreign bureaus are now represented, including the BBC and the New China News Agency (*Xinhua*). A small number of foreign journalists are allowed to reside in Iran; they must renew their visas every three months. Permission to travel to certain regions, including predominantly Kurdish areas and towns along the border with Iraq and Afghanistan, must be approved by the Ministry of Culture and Islamic Guidance and is often denied. In 2008 two other news agencies, *Matma* and *Salamat,* were licensed, bringing the total number of news agencies operating in the country to 16.

Broadcasting and computing. The Islamic Republic of Iran Broadcasting (IRIB), which answers directly to the office of the supreme leader (who appoints the director), operates a comprehensive monopoly on television and radio over two networks and home-service radio broadcasting in a variety of indigenous and foreign languages. IRIB has been frequently criticized by reformists for ignoring reformist voices or manipulating issues to favor conservative viewpoints. The reformist majority in the previous *Majlis* also alleged that the broadcaster had failed to fully account for its expenditures. From the outset of the U.S.-led war in Iraq in 2003, IRIB broadcast an Arabic-language program beamed into Iraq on terrestrial transmitters and throughout the Arab world by satellite. Iranian law prohibits commercial stations. A ban on the use of satellite television is sporadically enforced but widely flouted. Authorities have also attempted to jam satellite reception with mixed success. As of 2008 there were 313.7 Internet users per 1,000 inhabitants. Some estimates put the number of Farsi Web logs as high as 700,000, one of the highest blog sectors in the world. Aware of the popularity of the Internet, state authorities have carried out extensive censorship using filter software that blocks sites related to politics, women's rights, homosexuality, and pornography.

INTERGOVERNMENTAL REPRESENTATION

The United States severed diplomatic relations with Iran on April 4, 1980. Iranian diplomatic interests in Washington were handled by an interests section at the Algerian embassy until March 1992, when a successor section was established at the Pakistani embassy. The embassy of Switzerland handles U.S. interests in Iran.

Permanent Representative to the UN: Mohammad KHAZAEE.

IGO Memberships (Non-UN): CP, ECO, IDB, Interpol, IOM, IOR-ARC, NAM, OIC, OPEC, PCA, WCO.

IRAQ

Republic of Iraq
al-Jumhuriyah al-Iraqiyah

Note: Elections to the National Assembly were originally scheduled for January 19, 2010, but were subsequently postponed until March 7.

Political Status: Independent state since 1932; declared a republic following military coup that overthrew the monarchy in 1958; provisional constitution issued September 22, 1968, and substantially amended thereafter; de facto one-party regime ousted following invasion by U.S./UK-led forces in March 2003; interim constitution (Transitional Administrative Law) adopted by the U.S.-appointed Iraqi Governing Council on May 8, 2004, providing for popular election of a Transitional National Assembly; new constitution adopted by referendum on October 15, 2005, providing for popular election of a permanent National Assembly and a mixed presidential/parliamentary system.

Area: 167,924 sq. mi. (434,923 sq. km.).

Population: 22,017,983 (1997C); 29,488,000 (2008E).

Major Urban Centers (2005E): BAGHDAD (5,925,000), Irbil (Arbil, 3,216,000), al-Mawsil (Mosul, 1,325,000), Basra (1,250,000).

Official Languages: Arabic, Kurdish.

Monetary Unit: New dinar (market rate December 1, 2009: 1,150.05 new dinars = $1US).

President of the Presidency Council: Jalal TALABANI (Patriotic Union of Kurdistan); elected by the Transitional National Assembly on April 5, 2005, and inaugurated on April 7; reelected by the National Assembly on April 22, 2006, and sworn in on May 3 for a four-year term.

Vice Presidents of the Presidency Council: Adil Abd al-MAHDI (Supreme Council for the Islamic Revolution in Iraq) and Tariq al-HASHIMI (Iraqi Islamic Party); elected by the National Assembly on April 22, 2006, and sworn in on May 3 for a four-year term.

Prime Minister of the National Government: Nuri Jawad al-MALIKI (Islamic Call/United Iraqi Alliance); nominated by the president (upon the recommendation of the United Iraqi Alliance) on April 21, 2006, and approved by the National Assembly and sworn in (along with his new national unity government) on May 20 in succession to Ibrahim al-JAAFARI (Islamic Call/United Iraqi Alliance).

President of the Kurdish Region: Massud BARZANI (Democratic Party of Kurdistan); approved by the Iraqi Kurdistan National Assembly on June 12, 2005, and inaugurated for a four-year term on June 14; popularly elected on July 25, 2009, and inaugurated for another four-year term on August 20.

Prime Minister of the Kurdish Regional Government: Barham SALIH (Patriotic Union of Kurdistan); appointed by the president to form a new government (upon the nomination of the Kurdistan List) on September 30, 2009, and inaugurated on October 28 (following ratification by the Kurdistan Iraqi Parliament) in succession to Nechirvan BARZANI.

THE COUNTRY

Historically known as Mesopotamia ("land between the rivers") from its geographic position centered in the Tigris-Euphrates Valley, Iraq is an almost landlocked, partly desert country whose population is overwhelmingly Muslim and largely Arabic-speaking but also includes a Kurdish minority of over 4 million in the northeastern region bordering on Syria, Turkey, and Iran. A slim majority of Muslims are Shiite, although the government had long been Sunni-dominated prior to the 2003 U.S./UK-led invasion. Under Saddam Hussein's regime, women comprised about one-fifth of the paid labor force, nearly one-half of the agricultural workforce, and one-third of the professionals in education and health care. A moderate interpretation of Islamic law gave women equal rights in divorce, land ownership, and suffrage. Women were given the right to vote and run for office in the interim constitution adopted in 2004, although their ultimate rights regarding civil matters were the focus of intense debate during the 2005 negotiations for a permanent constitution.

Agriculture, which was characterized by highly concentrated land ownership prior to the introduction of land reform legislation in 1958, occupies about two-fifths of the population but produces less than one-tenth of the GNP. The most important crops are dates, barley, wheat, rice, and tobacco. Oil is the leading natural resource and, under normal conditions, accounts for over half of GNP. Iraq has known reserves of 115 billion barrels of oil, although many fields have yet to be explored. Iraq's reserves (estimated as high as 350 billion barrels) are believed to be among the four largest in the world. The predominantly Kurdish north is rich in oil, as is the mainly Shiite south. However, the central region (where most Sunnis live) has fewer proven reserves, an issue that has contributed significantly to recent difficulties in negotiating final political stability at the national level. Other important natural resources include phosphates, sulfur, iron, copper, chromite, lead, limestone, and gypsum. Manufacturing is not highly developed, although petrochemical, steel, aluminum, and phosphate plants were among heavy-industrial construction projects undertaken in the 1970s. During most of the 1980s the country experienced severe economic difficulty as a result of depressed oil prices and the heavy costs (including shortfalls in oil output) attributable to war with Iran. However, economic reforms launched in 1987, coupled with postwar optimism, helped propel GDP growth by 10 percent in 1988, the first positive rate since early in the decade.

Serious difficulties were encountered in 1990 in the form of economic sanctions imposed by the United Nations (UN) following Iraq's August 2 seizure of Kuwait. Subsequently, the unremitting air campaign launched by U.S.-led coalition forces in early 1991 was described as causing "near apocalyptic results" that relegated Iraq's infrastructure to a "preindustrial" condition. UN sanctions, most importantly an embargo on the export of Iraqi oil, continued into late 1996 because of what Western leaders considered Baghdad's failure to implement cease-fire resolutions fully. As of that time Iraq's economy and social services network remained in near-total collapse. Limited oil shipments resumed in December 1996 under the UN's "oil-for-food" plan, which helped control malnutrition and permit provisions of basic health services.

As of mid-2002 Iraq had earned an estimated $54 billion under the UN plan, producing nearly 2 million barrels per day, or 4 percent of global production, with the United States one of Iraq's leading customers. Nevertheless, conditions for the general population remained dismal. Child mortality had reportedly doubled since the Gulf war, and an estimated 30 percent of school-age children were no longer enrolled in school in a country that once boasted one of the highest literacy rates in the Arab world. Many members of the professional class had "fallen into poverty," and the Iraqi dinar had collapsed into "near worthlessness," which contributed to rampant unemployment. Meanwhile, serious conflict between Iraq and the UN over weapons inspections effectively barred progress toward ending sanctions.

The March 2003 invasion of Iraq by U.S./UK-led forces further damaged Iraq's infrastructure, although following the ouster of Saddam Hussein, the United States immediately pledged $20 billion for reconstruction. The World Bank, International Monetary Fund (IMF), and other international organizations promised an additional $18 billion. Oil production and exports resumed in the second half of 2003 but remained below prewar levels. Particularly damaging to production were numerous attacks on Iraq's oil pipelines, installations, and oil security personnel on the part (apparently) of disaffected supporters of the former Hussein regime and other Sunni insurgents as well as militant Islamists from other countries. The ongoing conflict also compromised rebuilding efforts, which were described as anemic by international critics of the United States. In 2003 Iraq's GDP declined by 41.4 percent, but it recovered in 2004 to grow by 46.5 percent before slowing dramatically to 3.7 percent growth in 2005 and 6.2 percent in 2006.

In 2006 the Office of the UN High Commissioner for Refugees (UNHCR) decried what it perceived to be an insufficient international response to the plight of Iraqi refugees. The UNHCR estimated that 1.9 million Iraqis had been displaced internally and 2 million externally (primarily to Syria and Jordan). Meanwhile, health experts estimated

that approximately three-quarters of the population lacked clean water or sanitation services.

The IMF extended its assistance to the Iraqi government in March 2007 in view of "some progress" in economic reform, particularly in the financial and banking sectors. However, the Fund called for improvements in the tax system, intensified efforts to fight widespread corruption, passage of a proposed hydrocarbons law that would regulate oil production and distribution of revenue, and, most importantly, negotiation of a political settlement that would curb sectarian violence.

Regarding the oil sector, officials of the Kurdish Regional Government in September 2007 signed exploration contracts with several U.S. and Canadian companies as the national hydrocarbons law remained stalled in the legislature. In 2008 the national government, which called the Kurdish initiative "illegal," announced that foreign companies would be invited to submit bids for oil and gas contracts for the first time in more than 30 years, although revenue-sharing within Iraq remained unresolved. Meanwhile, the IMF credited the government's "fiscal discipline" with having helped reduce annual inflation to 14 percent (down from 70 percent in 2006). Economic prospects also appeared to advance as security conditions improved in 2008, although public services remained "dilapidated" and the private sector "anemic."

Real GDP growth registered 10 percent for 2008, although declining oil prices in the second half of the year prompted cuts in government spending and pushed the budget into deficit after several years of surpluses. Meanwhile, corruption in government and the business sector continued to dampen the enthusiasm of foreign investors, who also urged passage of stalled legislation designed to promote privatization and reduce the inefficiency of state-run enterprises.

GOVERNMENT AND POLITICS

Political background. Having previously been conquered successively by Arabs, Mongols, and Turks, the region now known as Iraq became a British mandate under the League of Nations following World War I. British influence, exerted through the ruling Hashemite dynasty, persisted even after Iraq gained formal independence in 1932. The country continued to follow a generally pro-British and pro-Western policy until the overthrow of the monarchy in July 1958 by a military coup that cost the lives of King FAISAL II and his leading statesman, Nuri al-SAID. Brig. Gen. Abd al-Karim QASIM, leader of the revolt, ruled as head of a left-wing nationalist regime until he was killed in a coup on February 8, 1963, that brought to power a new military regime led by Lt. Gen. Abd al-Salam ARIF and, after Arif's accidental death in 1966, by his brother, Gen. Abd al-Rahman ARIF. The Arif regime terminated in a bloodless coup on July 17, 1968, which established Maj. Gen. Ahmad Hasan al-BAKR, a former premier and leader of the right wing of the Arab Socialist Renaissance Party (*Hizb al-Baath al-Arabi al-Ishtiraki*), as president, prime minister, and chair of the Revolutionary Command Council (RCC), which was designated the country's highest authority by the provisional constitution issued on September 22.

Under President Bakr a number of alleged plots were used as excuses to move against internal opposition. The most prominent took place in June 1973 when a coup attempt by Col. Nazim KAZZAR, head of national security, led to numerous arrests and executions. Domestic instability was further augmented by struggles within the Baath and by relations with the Kurdish minority.

The Kurds, under the leadership of Mullah Mustafa al-BARZANI, resisted most Baghdad governments in the two decades after World War II and, with Iranian military support, were intermittently in open rebellion from 1961 to 1975. A 1970 settlement with the Kurds ultimately broke down over distribution of petroleum revenues and exclusion of the oil-producing Kirkuk area from the proposed "Kurdistan."

In May 1974 Iraq and Iran agreed to a mutual withdrawal of troops along their common frontier, pending a settlement of outstanding issues. However, the Iraqi army subsequently launched a major offensive against the Kurdish rebels, and over 130,000 Kurds fled to Iran to escape the hostilities. Concessions were ultimately made on both sides in an agreement concluded in March 1975 during a meeting of the Organization of Petroleum Exporting Countries (OPEC) in Algiers; a "reconciliation" treaty was signed in Baghdad the following June. Iraq agreed to abandon a long-standing claim to the Shatt al-Arab waterway at its southern boundary with Iran and accepted a delimitation of the remaining frontier on the basis of agreements concluded prior to the British presence in Iraq. Iran, in return, agreed to cease all aid to the Kurds, whose resistance momentarily subsided. In mid-1976, however, fighting again erupted between Iraqi forces and the Kurdish *Pesh Merga* guerrillas, ostensibly because of the government's new policy of massive deportation of Kurds to southern Iraq and their replacement in the north by Arabs.

On July 16, 1979, President Bakr announced his resignation from both party and government offices. His successor, Saddam HUSSEIN, had widely been considered the strongman of the regime, and his accession to leadership of the Baath and the RCC came as no surprise. Earlier in the year, the Iraqi Communist Party (ICP) had withdrawn from the six-year-old governing National Progressive Front, following what Hussein himself had termed a purging of Communists from the government. Reports in late July of a "failed conspiracy" against the new president provided further evidence that he had effectively eliminated opponents from the RCC.

Although former president Bakr was known to be experiencing health problems, his resignation was apparently linked to differences within the RCC in regard to three policies: (1) containment not only of the Kurds but, in the aftermath of the Iranian Revolution, the increasingly restive Shiite community, led by Ayatollah Muhammad Bakr al-SADR until his execution in April 1980; (2) an Iraqi-Syrian unification plan (see Foreign relations, below), aspects of which Hussein found objectionable; and (3) suppression of the ICP, including the removal from the cabinet of its two ministers. Although a broad amnesty was proclaimed on August 16, 1979, Kurdish, Shiite, and Communist opposition to the Hussein government persisted and appeared to expand following Baghdad's September 17, 1980, abrogation of the 1975 Algiers agreement and the invasion five days later of Iran's Khuzistan Province, which yielded a debilitating conflict that was to preoccupy the regime for the next eight years (see Foreign relations, below).

Iraq also suffered extensive physical destruction from the Western-led Operation Desert Storm in early 1991, which had been precipitated by the Iraqi invasion of Kuwait the previous August. (For a chronology of relevant events, see the 1991 *Handbook,* Appendix A-II.) Upon formal termination of the conflict on March 3, Baghdad faced major rebellions by Kurds in the north and Shiites in the south, both of which were largely contained by early April. Many Shiite refugees fled into southeastern Iran, and the Kurds retreated into the mountainous northern region bordering Iran and Turkey. Late in the month autonomy talks were launched in Baghdad between Kurdish leaders and the Iraqi

government. Meanwhile, on March 23 President Hussein announced the formation of a new government, including the appointment of Saadoun HAMMADI to assume the prime ministerial duties theretofore performed by Hussein himself. On May 18 the Kurdish leadership reported that the regime had accepted its demands for a democratic government, separation of the Baath from the government, a free press, and elections. Moreover, on July 4 the National Assembly endorsed a bill providing for a limited democracy, wherein political party formations would be legalized but membership in the armed forces and security apparatus would continue to be limited to Baath members.

Although President Hussein formally approved the National Assembly bill on September 3, 1991, he subsequently retreated from liberalization measures and moved to consolidate power within a cabinet increasingly dominated by family members. On September 13 the president named Muhammad Hamzah al-ZUBAYDI to replace Hammadi as prime minister after Hammadi, whom analysts had described as the only independent in the regime, had called for a more conciliatory posture in negotiations with UN coalition members and the Kurds.

In January 1992, 80 military officers charged with participating in a coup attempt were executed along with 76 antiregime demonstrators. Four months later elections were held in the north to an Iraqi Kurdistan National Assembly. However, Baghdad immediately branded the poll as violating a constitutional prohibition of elections by armed groups; the Kurdish leaders defended the action as being in conformity with the 1970 autonomy agreement. On June 4 the new Kurdish Assembly named Fuad MASUM, a member of the political bureau of the Patriotic Union of Kurdistan (PUK), as the first Kurdish prime minister, and a Kurdish cabinet was appointed shortly thereafter. Masum resigned on March 18, 1993, amid reported discontent over fuel and food shortages in the north; he was succeeded on April 11 by Kosrat Abdulla RASUL, a popular veteran guerrilla fighter, who announced a new Kurdish cabinet on April 26. (The Kurdish coalition government collapsed in 1994 as renewed fighting broke out between the PUK and its long-standing rival, the Democratic Party of Kurdistan [DPK]. Kurdish territory was subsequently partitioned informally into PUK and DPK spheres of influence until the DPK invited Iraqi troops into the area to participate in an anti-PUK campaign in August 1996. See DPK under Political Parties and Groups, below, for details.) Meanwhile, President Hussein remained firmly in control of the Iraqi government, although growing popular discontent was reported, particularly in regard to the economic and social effects of UN sanctions in place since the Gulf crisis. A number of civilians and army officers (apparently including former supporters of the regime) were executed following the discovery of an alleged coup plot in August 1993, which may also have contributed to a surprise cabinet reshuffle on September 5 in which Prime Minister Zubaydi was replaced by Ahmad Hussein KHUDAYYIR, a longtime Baath member and close associate of the president who had served as finance minister since 1991.

Citing the damage inflicted on Iraq by the UN sanctions, President Hussein took formal control of the Iraqi administration on May 29, 1994, by assuming the additional post of prime minister in succession to Khudayyir, who retained the finance portfolio. Numerous ministerial changes were reported over the next 15 months as the regime faced continuing economic and political pressures.

In mid-August 1995 two of President Hussein's sons-in-law and their wives fled the country and accepted political asylum in Jordan. The most important of the defectors appeared to be Lt. Gen. Hussein Kamil al-MAJID, who, as head of the Iraqi weapons program, had been one of the most powerful figures in President Hussein's inner circle. Majid, reported to have been locked in an intense power struggle with Saddam Hussein's eldest son, Udai HUSSEIN, immediately called for the overthrow of the Hussein regime in order to have the UN sanctions lifted.

Apparently in part to counter perceptions that the defections represented a serious threat to the government's future, the RCC on September 7 amended the constitution to provide for popular confirmation of its chair as president of the republic. Three days later the National Assembly endorsed the RCC's "nomination" of Saddam Hussein for a seven-year presidential term, and a national referendum on October 13 produced a reported 99.96 percent "yes" vote on the question. Voter turnout was also announced at over 99 percent, a tribute, in the eyes of some observers, to the organizational capabilities of a "revitalized" Baath, which also supplied nearly all the candidates for new assembly elections in March 1996. Meanwhile, any genuine concern the regime may have felt as the result of the much-publicized defections of 1995 evaporated in February 1996 when Lt. Gen. Majid accepted a "forgiveness" offer from President Hussein, only to be killed in a gunfight shortly after his return to Iraq.

Following the recommendation of the RCC, the National Assembly on August 19, 2002, unanimously nominated President Hussein for another seven-year term. The government reported that 100 percent of those voting in a national referendum on October 15 approved the measure.

After declaring the Iraqi regime to be in violation of UN resolutions relating to inspections designed to determine Iraq's status in regard to weapons of mass destruction, the United States and the United Kingdom launched an invasion in March 2003 that resulted in the ouster of Hussein. (See Current issues, below, for additional information.) On April 21 U.S. Gen. (Ret.) Jay GARNER arrived to head a U.S. Office for Reconstruction and Humanitarian Assistance (ORHA), which, among other things, was to set up an Iraqi Interim Authority (IIA) as an advisory body to the ORHA. However, the Iraqis slated to participate in the authority (many of whom had just returned from exile) balked at the lack of day-to-day government responsibilities assigned to the proposed IIA. On May 6 U.S. President George W. Bush named L. Paul BREMER, a former U.S. ambassador, as head of the civil administration and the Coalition Provisional Authority (CPA). The UN Security Council endorsed the CPA's legal status as an occupying power in a resolution on May 22 and called upon the CPA (formally launched June 1) to facilitate a quick transition to Iraqi rule.

With membership determined by the CPA, a new Iraqi Governing Council (IGC) was established on July 13, 2003. The 25 members were carefully divided across religious and ethnic lines (13 Shiites, 5 Sunnis, 5 Kurds, 1 Assyrian Christian, and 1 Turkman). A rotating presidency was instituted for the IGC, which on September 1 announced the formation of a 25-member interim cabinet authorized to assist in drafting an interim constitution and preparing for elections for a transitional government. (The Arab League did not recognize the IGC as Iraq's legitimate government, although OPEC allowed the IGC oil minister to attend OPEC meetings.)

The draft interim constitution was presented on March 1, 2004, and was approved by the United States and the IGC on March 8. On June 28 the IGC was dissolved in favor of the new Iraqi Interim Government (IIG), which accepted the transfer of sovereignty from the CPA (as endorsed by the UN Security Council on June 8). Ayad ALLAWI, a Shiite from the Iraqi National Accord, was named prime minister of the interim administration, and Ghazi Ajil al-YAWAR, a Sunni, was named to the largely ceremonial post of interim president.

Elections to a 275-member Transitional National Assembly (TNA) were held on January 30, 2005, with the main Shiite coalition (the

United Iraqi Alliance [UIA]) securing 140 seats, followed by the Democratic Patriotic Alliance of Kurdistan (DPAK) with 75 and the multiethnic, multireligious Iraqi List (led by Allawi) with 40. (The main Sunni parties called for a boycott.) Concurrent balloting was held for a new Iraqi Kurdistan National Assembly, as well as for various regional councils.

After intense and often contentious negotiations, the TNA, on April 5, 2005, elected Jalal TALABANI, a Kurd from the PUK, as president of a new Presidency Council that also included Shiite and Sunni vice presidents. On April 7 the Presidency Council appointed Ibrahim al-JAAFARI, a Shiite from Islamic Call (*al-Dawah*, a party that was part of the winning UIA list), to head a new cabinet, which was inaugurated on May 3. On October 15 a proposed permanent constitution, drafted by a committee appointed by the TNA, was adopted by referendum with a "yes" vote of 79 percent. On December 15 elections for a permanent National Assembly (with 275 seats) were held, the UIA repeating its January victory by winning a plurality of 128 seats. The DPAK finished second with 53 seats, followed by the Iraqi Accord Front (IAF) with 44 and the Iraqi National List (INL, as the Iraqi List had been renamed) with 25. (Iraq's Sunni community participated more heavily in the December poll than it had in January; many of its votes were directed to the IAF or the Iraqi National Dialogue Front.)

Because the formation of a government depended on a two-thirds majority ratification in the National Assembly, several months passed before a cabinet could be submitted to the body for approval. The major problem involved divisions within the UIA over its choice for prime minister. Al-Jaafari won an internal poll within the alliance against Adil Abd al-MAHDI in February 2006 by just one vote. However, groups representing Kurds and Sunnis refused to participate in any national unity government with al-Jaafari as prime minister. Consequently, al-Jaafari was eventually forced to relinquish the premiership to a fellow *al-Dawah* candidate, Nuri Jawad al-MALIKI, who on May 20 formed a cabinet that included representatives from most of the major parties in the assembly. (The ministries of defense, interior, and national security were not filled until June 8.)

Six Shiite ministers representing the supporters of hard-liner Muqtada al-SADR (see Al-Sadr Movement under Political Parties and Groups) resigned from the cabinet on April 16, 2007. Further damaging governmental stability, the ministers from the IAF suspended their participation in the cabinet in August, while several INL ministers resigned their posts as directed by former prime minister Allawi. The IAF returned to the cabinet in July 2008, the al-Maliki administration having been strengthened by improving security conditions.

Constitution and government. Constitutional processes were largely nonexistent during the two decades after the 1958 coup, despite the issuance of a provisional basic law in 1968 and a 1971 National Action Charter that envisaged the establishment of local governing councils and the reconvening of a legislature. It was not until 1980 that elections were held for a unicameral National Assembly and a Kurdish Legislative Council, respectively. However, the Revolutionary Command Council (RCC), the nation's supreme authority since 1968, was not dissolved, effective power remaining concentrated in its chair, who continued to serve concurrently as president of the republic and commander in chief of the Armed Forces. (Amendments approved by the RCC in September 1995 directed that its chair's assumption of the presidency would henceforth be subject to the approval of the National Assembly and a national referendum.) RCC decrees had the force of law and were not automatically subject to any legislative or judicial review, although some bills were passed on to the assembly for approval. The RCC was also solely responsible for electing and dismissing its own members, who had to come from the leadership of the Baath. The judicial system was headed by a Court of Cassation and included five courts of appeal, courts of the first instance, religious courts, and revolutionary courts that dealt with crimes involving state security.

As a concession to northern minority sentiment, the Kurds in 1970 were granted autonomy as "defined by law," and in 1976 Iraq's 16 provincial governorates were expanded to 18, 3 of which were designated as Kurdish Autonomous Regions. However, it was not until after the 1991 Gulf war that Baghdad agreed to enter into a dialogue with Kurdish leaders to achieve meaningful implementation of what had been promised more than two decades earlier. After the new talks broke down, Kurdish groups in 1992 established an elected Iraqi Kurdistan National Assembly, which in turn selected a prime minister to oversee a Kurdish government broadly responsible for most services in the region until the collapse of Kurdish cooperation in 1994.

In January 1989 it was announced that the Iraqi constitution would be replaced prior to the National Assembly balloting of April 1; however, a draft of the new basic law did not appear until July 30, 1990, after having secured legislative approval 12 days before. The published version of the document provided for direct election of the president for an eight-year renewable term; replacement of the RCC by a 50-member Consultative Council, composed of an equal number of appointed and directly elected members; and the registration of new political parties, with a proviso that only the Baath would be permitted to have branches in the army and security forces. In a speech on March 16, 1991, Saddam Hussein declared that the time had come to begin building the "pillars" of the "new constitutional order" despite the many problems facing the country. On September 3, 1991, Hussein approved a law technically ending 23 years of one-party rule; however, the other changes were never submitted to a referendum.

The interim constitution adopted in March 2004 following the overthrow of Saddam Hussein in 2003 provided for an appointed Interim Iraqi Government (IIG) to assume sovereignty from the U.S.-led Coalition Provisional Authority (CPA) for a short time pending the election of transitional government bodies. The 275-member Transitional National Assembly (TNA—elected by popular vote on January 20, 2005) was authorized to elect the Presidency Council, dissolve the cabinet, and oversee the drafting of a new permanent constitution. The Presidency Council (elected in April 2005) was empowered to appoint the prime minister, cabinet, and members of the judicial council and to veto legislation passed by the assembly. Day-to-day governmental responsibility was given to the prime minister and the cabinet (installed in May 2005).

The TNA was supposed to produce a draft permanent constitution by August 15, 2005, but deep divisions regarding issues such as the role of Islam, the powers of regions under a federalist system, and the distribution of oil wealth pushed negotiations well past that deadline. Most Sunni representatives boycotted the discussion, in part due to their concern over proposed "regionalization" articles that Sunnis feared might lead to the eventual breakup of the country. However, some Sunni leaders accepted a last-minute agreement regarding future constitutional revision and encouraged Sunnis to participate in the referendum on October 15. The proposed constitution was approved by 79 percent of the voters, receiving overwhelming support in Shiite- and Kurdish-dominated areas. However, the new basic law almost failed as the result of a provision that it could not be passed if two-thirds of the voters in three provinces rejected it. The "no" vote easily exceeded the two-thirds threshold in two Sunni-dominated provinces but reached only about 55 percent in the third province where passage had seemed questionable.

The new 2005 permanent constitution codified Iraq as a federal republic with a mixed presidential/parliamentary system. Although regions (of which Kurdistan was recognized as one) were granted broad autonomy, the "unity of Iraq" was "guaranteed." A region was defined as comprising one or more provinces, leaving open the possibility of provinces joining together to form more powerful regions. (A Kurdish Regional Government [KRG] was subsequently formed in the provinces of Arbil, Suleimaniah, and Dohuk.) However, many of the provisions in that regard and other controversial areas were considered temporary at best because the constitution authorized the National Assembly to appoint a new panel following the upcoming legislative elections to propose additional changes and refinements to the constitution. Meanwhile, Islam was enshrined as the state religion (and a basic source of legislation), although freedom of religion was guaranteed. The directly elected National Assembly (one seat for every 100,000 inhabitants) was authorized to elect the president by a two-third's majority for a four-year term. Significant responsibilities (including the role of commander in chief of the armed forces) were reserved for the prime minister, nominated by the president upon the recommendation of the bloc with a majority of seats in the assembly.

In October 2006 the assembly passed legislation permitting provinces throughout the country to form regional administrations similar to the KRG. However, resistance reportedly remained strong among Sunnis, who feared that the nine predominantly Shiite provinces in the south might merge into a "super-region."

Foreign relations. After adhering to a broadly pro-Western posture that included participation in the Baghdad Pact and its successor, the Central Treaty Organization (CENTO), Iraq switched abruptly in 1958 to an Arab nationalist line that was subsequently largely maintained. Relations with the Soviet Union and other Communist-bloc countries became increasingly cordial after 1958, whereas diplomatic links with the United States (and temporarily with Britain) were severed in 1967. In 1979, however, Baghdad moved against Iraqi Communists, veering somewhat toward the West, particularly France, for military and development aid. The change in direction was reinforced following a June 7, 1981, Israeli air raid against the Osirak nuclear reactor being built outside Baghdad, France indicating that it would consider assisting in reconstructing the facility.

Relations with Arab states have fluctuated, although Iraq has remained committed to an anti-Israel policy. A leading backer of the "rejection front," it bitterly denounced the 1977 peace initiative of Egyptian President Sadat and the Camp David accords of September 1978, after which, on October 26, Syria and Iraq joined in a "National Charter for Joint Action" against Israel. This marked an abrupt reversal in relations between the two neighbors, long led by competing Baath factions. The "National Charter" called for "full military union," and talks directed toward its implementation were conducted in January and June 1979. At the latter session, held in Baghdad, presidents Assad of Syria and Bakr of Iraq declared that their two nations constituted "a unified state with one President, one Government and one Party, the Baath." However, the subsequent replacement of Bakr by Saddam Hussein, whom the Syrians had long considered an instigator of subversion in their country, coupled with Hussein's accusations of Syrian involvement in an attempted coup, abruptly terminated the rapprochement.

Relations with Tehran have long been embittered by conflicting interests in the Gulf region, including claims to the Shatt al-Arab and to three islands (Greater and Lesser Tunb and Abu Musa) occupied by Iran in 1971, as well as by Iranian support for Iraq's Kurdish and Shiite communities. Following the advent of the Khomeini regime in Iran in 1979, Iraq bombed a number of Kurdish villages inside Iran, and on September 22, 1980, having repudiated a 1975 reconciliation treaty, Iraq invaded its eastern neighbor. Despite overwhelming Iraqi air superiority and early ground successes, the Iranian military, reinforced by a substantially larger population with religious commitment to martyrdom, waged a bitter campaign against the Western-supplied Iraqi forces, the brief campaign projected by Hussein soon being reduced to a stalemate. In the course of the protracted conflict, numerous Iraqi cease-fire proposals were rebuffed by Tehran, which called for the payment of $150 billion in reparations and Hussein's ouster. It was not until a failed siege of the Iraqi city of Basra, coupled with an increasingly intense political struggle within Tehran, that Ayatollah Khomeini on July 20, 1988, called for a suspension of hostilities. A cease-fire was subsequently concluded with effect from August 20, although it was not until August 15, 1990, in the midst of the crisis generated by its seizure of Kuwait, that Iraq agreed to a comprehensive settlement based on the 1975 Algiers accord, a rejection of which by Baghdad had precipitated the lengthy conflict. A number of issues, including Iranian demands for reparations, subsequently remained unresolved, however, and a final peace accord was not signed, the status between the two countries being described as "no war, no peace."

The "annexation" of Kuwait in August 1990 was preceded by Saddam Hussein's delivery of a July 17 Revolution Day speech, during which the Iraqi president insisted that Kuwait had not only exceeded OPEC production quotas but had also stolen oil from Iraqi wells by "slant drilling." Other areas of contention were historic uncertainties regarding the precise demarcation of the Iraq-Kuwait border, plus the status of certain offshore territories (including Bubiyan Island) that had been operationally "loaned" to Iraq as a gesture of Arab solidarity during the Iran-Iraq war (see article on Kuwait). However, there was little international support for Baghdad's position, and the UN Security Council reacted strongly, demanding an unconditional withdrawal within hours of the Iraqi action on August 2, imposing a trade embargo on August 6, and approving on November 29 the use of any methods needed to force Iraqi compliance as of January 15, 1991. On January 16, following a five-month buildup of U.S. and allied military units, the UN coalition commenced offensive action, which yielded the liberation of Kuwait City on February 26–27 and a suspension of military operations on February 28, followed by Iraqi acceptance of terms for ending the conflict on March 3.

Although most coalition military units withdrew from the Gulf by mid-1991, the UN economic embargo remained in effect, in part because of U.S. displeasure at Saddam Hussein's continuance in office. Nevertheless, although Washington had long demanded that the Iraqi president step down, the George H. W. Bush administration did not wish to trigger dismemberment of the country. Thus, it stood aside as Iraqi forces crushed a Shiite insurrection in the south, and U.S. aid to the northern Kurds was confined largely to humanitarian supplies.

Seemingly encouraged by the coalition's unwillingness to intervene on behalf of either the Kurds or Shiites, the Hussein regime subsequently refused to comply with cease-fire provisions requiring its assistance in the location and destruction of Iraq's nonconventional weapons. Nevertheless, by October 1991 the International Atomic Energy Agency (IAEA) had accumulated enough information to charge that an Iraqi atomic weapon had been within 18 months of completion at the outset of the Gulf war and that enough material had survived allied bombing to allow the completion of other such weapons within five years. Consequently, on October 11 the Security Council approved additional restrictions, branded by Baghdad as "colonial," to prevent Iraq from ever again acquiring the means to build weapons of mass destruction.

During 1992 and early 1993 tension continued unabated between Baghdad and UN authorities. On August 27, 1992, U.S. and British warplanes began patrolling a southern "no-fly" zone below the 32nd parallel to protect Shiite Muslims from Iraqi air attacks. In January 1993 Iraq was obliged to remove surface-to-air missiles that had been moved into the zone, and a series of cross-border raids to retrieve abandoned military equipment from Kuwait were countered by retaliatory allied air strikes. Meanwhile, a northern "no fly" zone, similar to the one in the south, remained in effect to protect the Kurds, although Kurdish secession was effectively blocked by opposition from virtually all interested parties save for the Kurds themselves.

U.S. Tomahawk missiles struck the Iraqi intelligence headquarters in Baghdad on June 26, 1993; Washington claimed it had "compelling evidence" that Iraq had been involved in a plot to kill former president Bush in Kuwait several months earlier. Moreover, Western powers threatened further military action if the Hussein regime continued to resist measures designed to prevent the development of chemical and nuclear weapons and long-range missiles by the Iraqi military.

An estimated 70,000 Iraqi soldiers massed near the Kuwaiti border in early October 1994, prompting the United States to order "overwhelming" air power and send 40,000 of its troops back to the region in fear of a repetition of the 1990 invasion. In addition, the UN Security Council warned Baghdad against any further "provocative" behavior, and other Arab states (including some, such as Jordan, that had been relatively pro-Iraqi in the previous conflict) strongly condemned the Iraqi buildup. Consequently, the Iraqi forces quickly withdrew, and on November 10, in a major policy shift, the RCC issued a decree, signed by President Hussein and approved by the National Assembly, that accepted Kuwait's sovereignty, political independence, and territorial integrity, based on a recent UN border demarcation.

Despite Iraq's conciliatory measures, the Security Council kept its economic sanctions in place, the United States insisting it would not support their lifting until Baghdad had returned Kuwaiti property seized in 1990–1991, had accounted for numerous missing Kuwaitis (some presumed to still be held in Iraqi prisons), and had established permanent safeguards to protect the rights of the Kurds in the north and the Shiites in the south. Western powers also insisted on full compliance with the demands of the UN weapons monitors; concern focused on a perceived lack of candor from Baghdad regarding its biological weapons program.

In view of the enormous hardships being endured by the populace as the result of continued UN sanctions, the regime finally agreed in December 1995 to a UN Security Council plan permitting the sale of a limited amount of Iraqi oil to pay for food and medicine. (Baghdad had previously resisted the proposal, saying it represented a compromise of its sovereignty.) The Security Council gave its final approval to the project in May 1996, but implementation was delayed over U.S. concerns that appropriate monitoring mechanisms had not been established. Washington reluctantly accepted the arrangements for the oil sale in early August, but action was again suspended later that month when Iraqi troops entered Kurdish territory in the north at the invitation of the DPK. (See the DPK under Political Parties and Group for details.)

In early September 1996 the United States launched more than 20 cruise missiles at Iraqi air defense installations in the south as an "indirect punishment" for Iraq's recent military actions in the north. Tension escalated over the next several weeks as Washington dispatched aircraft carriers and additional troops to the Gulf and President Hussein threatened to fire upon Western planes patrolling the "no-fly" zones. Both sides subsequently retreated from the brink of open warfare, however, as Iraqi forces withdrew from the north and the United States discovered a paucity of support from its former coalition allies for renewed hostilities. Consequently, with Iraq facing a potentially catastrophic winter, attention again focused on the oil-for-food plan, which was finally implemented in mid-December. The plan authorized Iraq to sell $2 billion in oil over the next six months. Some of the revenue was earmarked for victims (primarily Kuwaitis) of Iraq's 1990 aggression; the Kurds were also scheduled to receive assistance. However, the bulk of the new income was slated for distribution (under UN supervision) throughout Iraq, where it was estimated that nearly 5,000 children had been dying each month from malnutrition or normally treatable diseases.

The UN Special Commission on Iraq (UNSCOM) reported in April 1997 that although progress was being made in the dismantling of weapons, Iraq was still not cooperating as fully as desired. The issue erupted into a major crisis in October when Baghdad threatened to block all further UN inspections unless the economic sanctions were lifted and U.S. personnel (described as a threat to Iraqi "national sovereignty") were removed from the UN teams. At the same time, new UNSCOM head Richard Butler (former Australian ambassador to the UN) reported that "no remotely credible account" had emanated from the Iraqi government regarding its former biological weapons program. In November the RCC ordered the expulsion of all U.S. inspectors, prompting Washington to send additional forces to the region and to solicit support for a possible military response. However, the United States found little enthusiasm for its plan among Arab states, many of whom accused the Clinton administration of applying a double standard by taking such a hard line toward Iraq but failing to pressure Israel to proceed with implementation of the peace accord with the Palestinians. Nevertheless, U.S. planes, ships, and soldiers continued to pour into the region in early 1998 in preparation for an attack, despite opposition from fellow Security Council members China, France, and Russia. With time apparently running out, UN Secretary General Kofi Annan met with Hussein in Baghdad in late February, finally securing the Iraqi president's signature on a memorandum of understanding permitting the resumption of inspections at all proposed sites, including the "presidential palaces" previously declared off-limits. Tensions having been reduced, at least temporarily, regional leaders subsequently launched a quiet campaign to pursue the reintegration of Iraq into the international community, while a number of countries, including France and Russia, continued to promote the lifting of the UN sanctions. Among other things, many countries were eager to join Iraq in oil and natural gas projects as soon as the sanctions were removed. Meanwhile, the new phase of the oil-for-food program permitted $5.2 billion in oil sales over the next six months.

Encouraged by the apparent moderation in the Iraqi stance on inspections, the United States in the spring of 1998 reduced its forces in the Gulf, and UNSCOM head Butler spoke of a possible breakthrough in negotiations with the Iraqi regime. However, a fresh crisis erupted in August when Baghdad, declaring its disarmament "complete," demanded a reduction in U.S. representation in UNSCOM and suspended cooperation with UNSCOM in some areas. The Security Council adopted a hard line toward the demands, and the Iraqi government subsequently announced it was ending all cooperation with UNSCOM until the UN sanctions were lifted and Butler was replaced as chief of the inspectors. A new U.S./UK assault on Iraqi sites appeared imminent in mid-November before Hussein, reportedly under heavy pressure from other Arab leaders, agreed to permit UNSCOM to return to work. Significantly, in addition to ordering a continued buildup of U.S. military capabilities in the region, President Clinton and other U.S. officials indicated that U.S. policy now sought a regime change in Iraq, not just "containment." To that end, the U.S. Congress authorized Clinton to allocate $97 million in military and financial assistance to Iraqi opposition groups.

In early December 1998 UNSCOM's Butler reported that the Iraqi government was not living up to its mid-November pledge of cooperation but was in fact refusing inspectors access to some sites and withholding requested documents. Consequently, on December 16, U.S. and UK forces launched Operation Desert Fox, an intensive bombing and missile campaign on military sites throughout Iraq. U.S. and UK officials said the attacks were designed to degrade the weapons capabilities of the Hussein regime and reduce its collateral threat to nearby countries, although China, France, and Russia (the other permanent members of the Security Council) criticized the action. Extensive damage was inflicted by the campaign (which ended on December 20), but Baghdad remained defiant, declaring a permanent cessation in its interactions with UNSCOM and announcing it would no longer respect the no-fly zones. Subsequently, Iraqi pilots routinely challenged the zones, prompting retaliatory strikes by U.S. forces, now operating under expanded rules of engagement and having been authorized to attack a wider array of targets, such as government buildings and communication facilities. U.S. and UK planes continued to pound Iraqi sites into May. However, the Security Council remained divided on how to proceed, support for military action having been further eroded by revelations that some UNSCOM inspectors had conducted intelligence-gathering activities for Washington while engaged in their inspection duties. (For subsequent developments in the dispute with the UN and the United States, see Current issues, below.)

As part of Baghdad's efforts to rejoin mainstream Arab activity, a free-trade pact was negotiated with Egypt in January 2001, while economic ties were promoted with Syria, one destination for inexpensive Iraqi oil. In addition, Iraq was formally reintegrated into the Arab League at the March 2002 summit, during which Baghdad pledged its support for Kuwaiti "sovereignty." Moreover, President Hussein continued to emphasize his regime's support for the Palestinian cause by, among other things, halting oil exports for one month in the spring of 2002 to protest Israeli actions.

The overthrow of Saddam Hussein's regime in April 2003 significantly altered the dynamics of Iraq's role in the region. The fall of Baghdad in just three weeks raised U.S. hopes that a post-Hussein Iraq would serve as an impetus for regional transformation in the Middle East, but the more immediate goal became stability in Iraq. The first step in building a new Iraqi government was the appointment of the IGC by the U.S.-led CPA. The creation of this body was met with skepticism by Iraq's Arab neighbors but was endorsed by Iran, which was willing to cooperate with the council because it included Iraqi Shiite parties that had been in exile in Iran. Following the dissolution of the CPA in 2004, Iraq's interim government, led by Ayad Allawi, cooperated with U.S.-led forces in an effort to defeat insurgents. Iraq's transitional and permanent governments, led, respectively by Ibrahim al-Jaafari and Nuri al-Maliki, continued Allawi's policy of cooperation with the United States.

In 2006 Prime Minister al-Maliki backed the full withdrawal of foreign troops by 2008. The United States, however, tied its withdrawal to security conditions in Iraq, not to a specific timetable. Meanwhile, tensions continued between Iraq and its neighbors over the flow of foreign insurgents into the country, while Sunni capitals in the region expressed concern over the implications of a Shiite-dominated government in Iraq.

In November 2006 President Talabani met with Iranian President Ahmadinejad in an attempt to solicit Iran's assistance in quelling the sectarian violence that had wracked Iraq since early in the year. Ahmadinejad pledged to assist "brother Iraq" but insisted that stability was dependent on the withdrawal of U.S.-led "occupation forces" from Iraq. Talabani also visited Syria in January 2007, diplomatic relations between Iraq and Syria having been resumed the previous November. Syria's President Assad declared that a "safe and secure Iraq" would be a "benefit" for Syria. Iran and Syria also were among some 16 countries from the region and the West that held a regional security conference in Baghdad in March, Iraqi Prime Minister al-Maliki imploring Iraq's neighbors to discontinue financial and military aid to militant groups in Iraq. Subsequently, some 60 countries meeting in Egypt in May adopted a five-year plan for Iraqi reconstruction and security. Concurrently, several creditor nations announced that they were forgiving additional Iraqi debt.

Tensions with Turkey intensified significantly in October 2007 when Turkish forces began cross-border shelling of suspected bases of the Kurdistan Workers' Party (PKK), which had been conducting a campaign against the government in Ankara since the late 1970s. Turkey in 2008 launched several more offensives against the PKK in Iraq, prompting criticism from the Iraqi government and messages of concern from Washington. However, state visits between Turkish and Iraqi officials continued, while a number of Sunni Arab countries (including Syria) also extended their diplomatic relations with the Shiite/Kurd–dominated Iraqi government. Among other things, the United Arab Emirates forgave some $7 billion of Iraqi debt. Meanwhile, Iran's president Mahmoud Ahmadinejad visited Iraq in March 2008, pledging additional economic assistance; in June, al-Maliki traveled to Iran, reportedly to discuss the regional implications of a possible permanent U.S. military presence in Iraq.

Friction developed with Syria in the second half of 2009 as the Iraqi government strongly objected to the border with Syria being used as a transit route for insurgents heading into Iraq. In September Iraq deployed troops along the border after several major bomb attacks in Baghdad and other locations.

Current issues. In December 1999 the UN Security Council authorized the establishment of the UN Monitoring, Verification, and Inspection Committee (UNMOVIC) to succeed UNSCOM and offered to suspend the UN sanctions against Iraq if Baghdad were to cooperate with the new disarmament body and the IAEA for 120 days. Although Iraq quickly rejected the proposal, Hans Blix of Sweden, a former IAEA director, was chosen in January 2000 as a compromise candidate to head UNMOVIC, and technical appointments to UNMOVIC in March were designed to produce a broad base of inspectors who would be perceived as less subservient to U.S. and UK influence than the UNSCOM inspectors had been. Nevertheless, Iraq displayed no inclination to let the new inspectors into the country, in part, according to some analyses, because international commitment to the sanctions appeared to be waning. President Hussein subsequently launched a "charm offensive" to reestablish regional ties, particularly through trade accommodations. In addition, he was seen as attempting to deflect attention from the Iraqi disarmament issue by adopting a vocal pro-Palestinian stance.

The tone of the Iraqi/UN impasse changed significantly with the installation of the George W. Bush administration in Washington in early 2001, the new U.S. president announcing he would give heightened attention to enforcement of the no-fly zones and otherwise intensify the pressure on Baghdad. Lending support to the call for renewed vigilance, UNMOVIC in March 2001 indicated that the Iraqi regime probably still retained the ability to deploy biological or chemical weapons.

Following the terrorist attacks on the United States in September 2001, President Bush quickly expanded the global U.S.-led "war on terrorism" to include the Iraqi situation, arguing that Iraqi weapons of mass destruction could someday end up in the hands of terrorists. Branding Iraq as a member (along with Iran and North Korea) of an "axis of evil," Bush directed the Central Intelligence Agency to use "all available tools" to overthrow Hussein. In mid-2002 the Bush administration started planning a U.S.-led invasion of Iraq if complete disarmament were not quickly forthcoming. Although Washington initially indicated it believed previous Security Council resolutions were sufficient to support military action against Iraq, the U.S. administration ultimately responded to domestic and international pressure and decided to seek another "last chance" resolution. Iraq having agreed in September to "unconditional" inspections (while continuing to maintain that it possessed no prohibited weapons or weapon-delivery systems), the Security Council on November 8, 2002, adopted Resolution 1441, which threatened Iraq with "serious consequences" if it failed to comply with the new inspection regime. UNMOVIC inspectors arrived in Iraq later in the month.

The growing possibility of the overthrow of the regime of Saddam Hussein presented a paradox for leaders in the Kurdish north, which in recent years had enjoyed de facto self-rule, the region having been divided into separate areas administered by the PUK and the DPK. For some Kurds, a war to remove Hussein actually appeared to represent a risk of relinquishing some of the authority currently exercised, although most of the Kurdish political organizations remained committed to the establishment of a federal Iraq. In addition, the Kurds were leery of Turkey's intentions should hostilities erupt. (Turkey, home to some 20 million Kurds, had battled its own Kurdish separatist movement since the early 1980s [see article on Turkey for details] and was naturally perceived as concerned that a breakup of Iraq could lead to renewed demands for creation of an independent Kurdistan.) Further complicating political and military assessment was the presence of major oil fields near the northern city of Kirkuk, controlled by the Hussein regime but claimed by the Kurds.

UN weapons inspectors arrived in Iraq in late November 2002 to resume the search for banned weapons. Meanwhile, Iraq gave the UN a list of its current weapons as well as information on its past weapons programs. However, the 12,000-page report was heavily criticized by the United States as being misleading and incomplete. The UN demanded greater cooperation from Iraq, citing numerous incidents of interference. Consequently, on December 19 the United States declared that Iraq was in breach of UN resolutions.

In January 2003 the inspectors discovered 12 unreported chemical warheads as well as Iraqi missiles that appeared to violate range limitations. However, Iraq subsequently pledged to be more forthcoming and cooperative, and opposition to the U.S. military buildup grew in France, Germany, and a host of other nations. In February UN inspectors reported that Iraq had agreed to the UN's use of aerial reconnaissance, and the inspectors asked for more time to complete their mission. However, the United States and the UK presented a draft UN Security Council resolution on February 24 that would have authorized military action against Iraq if the regime did not meet a deadline of March 17. By this point, the Security Council and NATO seemed locked into pro- and anti-invasion blocs. In response, the Bush administration announced that it would develop a "coalition of the willing" to pursue military action. The pro-war camp withdrew its draft UN resolution on March 17 in light of a threatened French veto. Meanwhile, as the United States and the UK deployed more troops to the region and conducted a diplomatic campaign to convince more countries that Iraq was in violation of its UN commitments, Arab leaders tried unsuccessfully to convince Hussein to resign and go into exile.

As the threat of invasion grew, the Iraqi regime undertook a number of steps designed to forestall military engagement. On February 4, 2003, Iraqi officials made an offer to renegotiate terms with the UN to address any remaining major concerns of the weapons inspectors. The regime also began destroying its stocks of the prohibited missiles in March. At the same time the country was divided into four military districts, each led by a relative or close ally of Hussein, and Iraq began defensive deployments of troops around Baghdad.

On March 20, 2003, the United States launched a series of missile attacks (the "shock and awe" initiative); American, British, Australian, and Polish troops began a ground offensive shortly thereafter. The coalition forces drove quickly into Iraq and engaged in both conventional and psychological warfare to convince the Iraqi military to surrender. Both efforts were successful, with the rapid advance to Baghdad being eased by the surrender of major Iraqi commands. Meanwhile, some of the most intense fighting of the war took place between coalition forces and Iraqi special militias known as the *Fedayeen* (martyrs) *Saddam*. (Some of the *Fedayeen* were reportedly non-Iraqis recruited on the eve of the campaign.) The U.S./UK coalition attempted, with limited success, to prompt a Shiite uprising in the South. However, Kurdish forces in the north operated effectively with U.S. special operations forces and airborne troops and were able to capture the key towns of Mosul and Kirkuk. By April 7 U.S. forces were in Baghdad; the last battle of the campaign took place in Hussein's hometown of Tikrit on April 14.

On May 1, 2003, President Bush declared an end to major combat operations, prematurely as it turned out. Subsequently, the U.S.-led coalition undertook efforts to create a stable interim government and restore security and infrastructure. However, the first attempts to develop a broad-based government failed because Iraqis could not agree on specific terms and opposed U.S. plans to keep the proposed IIA as a mainly advisory body. After the ORHA was deemed to have failed (particularly in view of a deteriorating security situation), new chief civilian leader Paul Bremer attempted to "de-Baathify" the government and military by dissolving the security forces, a decision that was later perceived to have had negative consequences.

Security continued to deteriorate as foreign fighters, former regime elements, and Iraqi Sunnis engaged in a bloody insurgency. A truck bomb destroyed the UN compound in Baghdad, leading to a UN withdrawal from Iraq, and car bombs and improvised explosives subsequently took a toll on coalition forces and Iraqi leaders. In a major development, Hussein's two sons were killed in a battle in Mosul in late July 2003. Meanwhile, efforts to identify or discover banned weapons produced no results, even after the deployment of the 1,000-member Iraq Survey Group, which was composed of U.S. and international weapons experts. (In January 2005 the Bush administration confirmed that no banned weapons or chemical agents had been found.)

Insurgents also began to kidnap foreign workers and Iraqi government and political figures. Over time, the insurgency appeared to become more organized, and many analysts concluded that one of the ringleaders was Jordanian-born Abu Musab al-ZARQAWI, who was known to have links to al-Qaida.

On December 13, 2003, Saddam Hussein was captured near Tikrit, and by January 2004 the coalition had captured or killed 42 of its 55 "most-wanted" former Iraqi leaders. Meanwhile, security improved in the Kurdish north and the Shiite south; the ongoing insurgency was concentrated in the central region in an area that became known as the Sunni Triangle.

During negotiations on the interim constitution in early 2004, the Shiites on the IGC demanded that the document be based on sharia (Islamic law); they also opposed a clause that permitted any three provinces to block a permanent constitution with a two-thirds vote in each of the three provinces. Because there were three Kurdish provinces, that provision gave the Kurds a de facto veto over the future constitution. However, the country's highest Shiite leaders eventually agreed to the "Kurdish veto." In return, a plan to use regional bodies to elect representatives to the TNA was revised in favor of direct elections.

In March 2004 Bremer announced the reconstruction of the Iraqi security forces in response to growing unrest in Fallujah among followers of Shiite cleric Muqtada al-SADR, the son of a popular cleric killed by the Hussein regime. After two sieges in April and May and a second assault, which included members of the new Iraqi security forces, Fallujah was returned to relative calm. Al-Sadr subsequently announced his intention to participate politically and to form a party.

Internal problems continued to plague the IGC and the CPA through 2004. (On May 17, 2004, the chair of the IGC, Izzedin SALIM, was assassinated.) Meanwhile, the credibility of the United States was undermined by revelations of a prisoner-abuse scandal at the U.S. military prison at Abu Ghraib in which U.S. troops mistreated and degraded Iraqi prisoners.

After contentious negotiations within the Sunni community, Muhsin Adb al-HAMID, leader of the Iraqi Islamic Party (the largest mainstream Sunni party), urged Sunnis to boycott the balloting for the TNA on January 30, 2005. The turnout was thereby only approximately 60 percent, although international observers described the balloting, dominated by the Shiite United Iraqi Alliance, as generally free and fair. The poll also marked the first time women voted in an Iraqi election.

On May 10, 2005, the TNA appointed a 55-member council to draft a new constitution. A deadline of August 15 was set for completion of the draft, which was scheduled for a national referendum on October 15 in preparation for new elections at the end of the year. However, the August 15 deadline was subsequently extended amid disagreement over, among other things, the extent of autonomy to be given to the three main regions. Sunnis in particular were concerned about extensive Shiite control of oil-rich areas in the south as well as possible Iranian influence over the southern provinces. Eventually, a draft constitution, which provided for the establishment of regional authorities, was submitted in time for a referendum on October 15 (see Constitution and government, above). The constitution was approved by 79 percent of the voters, although it was rejected in three provinces. The growing sectarian/ethnic political divide in Iraq was apparent; Sunni-dominated provinces overwhelmingly rejected the constitution, and Shiite- and Kurdish-dominated provinces voted in favor of it. In order for the constitution to be presented to the Iraqi people on time, a pledge was made to revisit the controversial aspects of the document once a permanent government was formed. The voting also reflected the differing views of Iraq's ethnic and sectarian communities on the nature of what post–Saddam Hussein Iraq should look like. The Kurds wanted confirmation of their regional autonomy, and, like the Kurds, most Shiites favored a federal Iraq. Sunnis, however, feared that extensive regional autonomy would produce a weak, decentralized Iraqi nation-state in which their interests would not be sufficiently protected. Meanwhile, the fact that most of Iraq's oil reserves were in the Shiite-dominated southern provinces and in the northern Kirkuk area (claimed historically by Iraqi Kurds) exacerbated internal tensions.

With the constitutional referendum completed, Iraq elected a permanent National Assembly on December 15, 2005. Iraq's Sunni Arab leaders concluded that their boycott of the January poll had been a mistake, and two Sunni-based political groupings were formed to contest the election—the Iraqi Accord Front (IAF) and the Iraqi National Dialogue Front. The IAF was dominated by the Iraqi Islamic Party, and the Dialogue Front was formed by secular, nationalist Sunnis (some with Baath backgrounds), who steadfastly opposed a federal Iraq.

Throughout 2005 violence in Iraq developed an increasingly sectarian tone, prompting speculation that Iraq was about to plunge into all-out civil war. Foreign troops and Shiites were targeted by insurgents, especially by followers—Iraqi and non-Iraqi—of Abu Musab al-Zarqawi (the Jordanian leader of "al-Qaida in Iraq" [see section on al-Qaida in article on Afghanistan for additional information]). Hopes that Iraq would stabilize in the near-term were dealt a severe blow on February 22, 2006, by the bombing in Samarra of the al-Askariya shrine, a Shiite holy site. The bombing confirmed for some observers that Iraq was in a civil war, and the civilian death toll rose dramatically in February and March.

As violence increased in the early months of 2006, contentious negotiations over the formation of the government continued. Despite the recent victory of the UIA, the premiership of Ibrahim al-Jaafari was unpopular with the DPAK and with Sunnis. Furthermore, al-Jaafari was not universally popular with all the factions within the alliance, and a standoff ensued between his *al-Dawah* group, the supporters of Muqtada al-Sadr, and other parties and independents who wanted to back another candidate. SCIRI proposed that its vice president, Adil Abd al-MAHDI, be nominated for prime minister by the UIA, but in an internal party ballot in February al-Jaafari defeated al-Mahdi by one vote (64–63). Thus, the UIA was left with a candidate for prime minister whom half the alliance opposed and who was unacceptable to other parties whose support was required to get the two-thirds majority needed to form a government. In April a representative of Grand Ayatollah Ali al-SISTANI brokered an agreement in which neither al-Jaafari nor Abd al-Mahdi would be the alliance candidate for prime minister, clearing the way for Nuri al-Maliki to serve as a compromise candidate. Al-Maliki was able to gain consensus within the factions of the alliance as well as approval from Sunni and Kurdish groups and Allawi's Iraqi National List.

On June 7, 2006, al-Zarqawi was killed in a U.S. air strike near Baquba. Observers, including President Bush, cautioned that violence in Iraq would likely continue, despite al-Zarqawi's death.

In the wake of sectarian violence that was claiming an average of 1,500 Iraqis per month, Prime Minister al-Maliki in June 2006 initiated a broad security operation designed, as a first step, to restore control in Baghdad. He also presented a national reconciliation plan directed in large part at Sunni insurgents. However, more than 3,000 Iraqis died in July, primarily at the hands of sectarian death squads. (Sunnis charged that Shiite militias were killing Sunnis under the cover of Iraqi security forces.) In September the U.S. defense department reported that the Shiite-Sunni fighting had spread from Baghdad and now represented a major element of the "core conflict" in Iraq. Many analysts questioned the ability of the al-Maliki administration to resolve the violence, although U.S. President Bush in November once again announced his support for the beleaguered prime minister.

Saddam Hussein was hanged in December 2006 following his conviction of crimes against humanity, including his ordering the execution of Shiites in the village of Dujail following an attempt on his life in 1982. (Hussein also faced numerous charges in other cases, although formal proceedings against him in those matters ceased after his death.) The events surrounding Hussein's execution appeared to further inflame Sunni passions, and sectarian violence continued unabated into 2007. Consequently, President Bush in late January announced that some 30,000 additional troops would be sent to Iraq as part of a military "surge" intended to restore security. At the same time, the United States reportedly began to enlist previously anti-U.S. Sunni tribal leaders in a campaign against al-Qaida forces, Bush once again linking the conflict in Iraq to the global "war on terrorism."

Prime Minister al-Maliki faced a serious political threat in August 2007 when the IAF and the INL suspended participation in his cabinet. As a result, al-Maliki in September reportedly intensified his efforts to placate Sunnis by releasing Sunnis who had been arrested in the recent crackdown and by endorsing proposed legislation that would permit former Baath members to return to government service. However, the hydrocarbons law (considered a crucial element in a lasting political settlement) remained unresolved in the assembly, and some political groups (including some Shiite followers of Muqtada al-Sadr and the predominantly Sunni supporters of former prime minister Allawi in the INL) called for dissolution of the assembly and new elections. Meanwhile, President Bush cited what he described as the success of the nine-month surge and urged continued support for the al-Maliki administration despite its failure to achieve many of the benchmarks established earlier to measure progress.

In mid-2007 the UN terminated UNMOVIC's mandate and also announced that the scope of the UN Assistance Mission for Iraq would be expanded to assist the Iraqi government in fostering political reconciliation as security conditions continued to improve. One so-called benchmark was reached in early 2008 with passage of legislation permitting many former Baath members to return to their jobs and resume political activity. A general amnesty was also issued for many of those detained in security sweeps of recent years. On the other hand, major fighting erupted in the spring between Iraqi security forces and Shiite militias (some possibly linked to al-Sadr) that had previously controlled many neighborhoods in Baghdad and other cities. The government's apparent success in those encounters strengthened al-Maliki's position and facilitated the IAF's return to the cabinet in July. Al-Maliki subsequently suggested that conditions had improved sufficiently to consider the potential withdrawal of most foreign troops from Iraq by 2011, but negotiations were reported regarding the possible permanent stationing of U.S. troops in the country (a controversial proposal within the Iraqi population). Although still loathe to produce a formal timetable for withdrawal, U.S. officials also expressed the hope that the "endgame" had been reached, although they were careful to acknowledge that recent gains remained "fragile" and "reversible," as evidenced by continued deadly bomb attacks throughout the country. Among the remaining outstanding political issues was the status of oil-rich Kirkuk, which the Kurds claimed should become part of the Kurdish autonomous region, even though some 40 percent of its population was Arab or Turkmen.

In September 2008 Iraqi forces assumed responsibility for security in Anbar Province, the "heartland" of the former Sunni insurgency, and in November the Status of Forces Agreement (SOFA) was concluded with the United States, providing for final U.S. withdrawal from Iraq within three years. Provincial elections on January 31, 2009, also provided evidence of potential stability after the national legislature finally agreed upon the extent of provincial authority. (The ongoing dispute over Kirkuk precluded balloting in its province, while the three Kurdish provinces voted in July for their autonomous regional legislature.) Parties and groups that had coalesced behind Prime Minister al-Maliki dominated the provincial elections as his Shiite supporters were joined by Sunnis expressing their appreciation for al-Maliki having reached across sectarian lines with recent policies.

In February 2009 new U.S. president Barack Obama announced an exit plan under which U.S. forces would be reduced in Iraq from 142,000 to 50,000 by August 2010. In early June Obama reassured Iraqis that the United States was not pursuing permanent military bases in Iraq and held "no claim" on Iraqi territory or resources. Later that month most U.S. combat troops withdrew from Baghdad and other major population centers. Although deadly insurgent attacks subsequently increased in number significantly as the U.S. presence declined, the Iraqi government in the fall described the security situation to be sufficiently controlled to permit national legislative elections in early 2010. Most noteworthy among the preelection political developments was al-Maliki's formal separation from the UIA (see below).

POLITICAL PARTIES AND GROUPS

Following the 1968 coup the dominant force within Iraq was the Arab Socialist Renaissance Party (*Hizb al-Baath al-Arabi al-Ishtiraki*), which under the National Action Charter of 1973 became the core of the regime-supportive National Progressive Front (NPF), subsequently the National Progressive and Patriotic Front (NPPF). (For details on the Baath, which was disbanded by the CPA following the ouster of Saddam Hussein in 2003, and other components of the NPPF, see the 2007 *Handbook*.) In the wake of the onset of the war with Iran in September 1980, various elements announced the formation of antigovernment groupings, all receiving support from abroad. A more inclusive opposition grouping, the 17-member Iraqi National Joint Action Committee (INJAC) was launched in Damascus in December 1990. During a summit in Damascus in August 1991 the INJAC called for efforts to "promote its actions inside Iraq." However, in December INJAC members rejected a plan that called for regional assistance in overthrowing the regime. Coordination of opposition activity passed in June 1992 to the Iraqi National Congress (INC, below).

On September 3, 1991, President Hussein nominally ended 23 years of de facto one-party rule by approving a measure that legalized opposition formations. However, there were no reports of such groups emerging subsequently in areas under government control.

Dissident groups met with top U.S. officials in August 2002 to try to present a coherent, cohesive front in anticipation of possible U.S.-led military action against the regime of Saddam Hussein, but, according to most accounts, the opposition remained fractious. Problems included objections by some groups over perceived INC domination, criticism by smaller Shiite organizations over apparent efforts by the Supreme Council of the Islamic Revolution of Iraq (SCIRI) to speak for the entire Shiite population, and concerns over the role of former Iraqi military officers, who may have been involved in human rights abuses while serving in Iraq but were now seeking a role in the potential new government.

The collapse of the Baath regime following the overthrow of the Hussein regime in 2003 and the banning of the party left a political vacuum in the country, which was filled by many formerly exiled parties, Muqtada al-Sadr's movement, Kurdish political organizations, and Sunni coalitions. Iraqi politics thereby became, for the most part, defined by ethnicity and sect. However, in preparation for the elections planned for early 2010 a number of groupings began to emphasize their cross-sectarian, multiethnic nature and commitment to national unity over "identity politics." The formation of the Iraqi National Alliance (INA) was announced in late August 2009 as a partial successor to the United Iraqi List (UIA), which had won a legislative majority in December 2005 and had subsequently dominated the government. The two leading components of the INA were the Supreme Islamic Iraqi Council (SIIC, as SCIRI had been renamed) and the Al-Sadr Movement. Although the INA clearly remained primarily a Shiite grouping, it also included several Turkman parties, the INC, and several small Sunni groups. Human Hamoudi of the SIIC was named INA leader, although he was not considered an automatic selection to be the alliance's candidate for prime minister. Other possible candidates included former prime minister Ibrahim al-Jaafari (who had led a National Reform Trend in the January 2009 provincial elections) and Iraqi vice president Adil Abd al-Mahdi. Significantly, Prime Minster al-Maliki's *al-Dawah* ultimately declined to join the INA, reportedly because the INA would not agree in advance that al-Maliki would be the INA's candidate for prime minister. Instead, al-Maliki announced that the State of Law coalition, which had been formed for the provincial elections, would be expanded for the national legislative poll. The coalition initially comprised some 40 parties and groups representing Shiites, Sunnis, Kurds, and Christians, with tribal leaders reportedly outnumbering clerics in its leadership. Among other things, al-Maliki pledged to support the "social diversity" of the country.

Parliamentary Parties and Groups:

United Iraqi Alliance (UIA). Formed in December 2004, the UIA was the brainchild of Grand Ayatollah Ali al-Sistani, the Shiite leader who wanted an umbrella organization for the major Shiite parties. Minor parties in the UIA include Hezbollah, a "Marsh Arab" Shiite grouping; the **Islamic Action Organization**, formed in the early 1960s and often referred to as the Islamic Task Organization (ITO); and the **Islamic Union of Iraqi Turkmen,** a grouping of Shiite Turkmen formed in 1991 and led by Abbas al-BAYATI. By the time of the January 30, 2005, balloting for the TNA, some 22 parties had reportedly joined the alliance. In the December 2005 assembly elections, the UIA was reported to have won a plurality of 128 seats. The alliance subsequently served as a core component of the national unity government, although it was reconstituted (at least partially) as the INA in 2009 (see above).

Supreme Islamic Iraqi Council (SIIC). The SIIC is the new name adopted in May 2007 by the Supreme Council for the Islamic Revolution in Iraq (SCIRI), which had also been referenced as the Supreme Assembly of the Islamic Revolution in Iraq (SAIRI). SCIRI was formed in 1982 as an umbrella for a number of Shiite groups, including the **Holy Warriors** (*al-Mujahidin*), which was founded in 1979 in Iran. (The Holy Warriors had claimed responsibility for a variety of attacks on Baghdad, and in March 1980 the RCC had decreed the death penalty for members of the organization.) Other founding members of SCIRI were Islamic Call (*al-Dawah*, see below); the **Islamic Action Organization,** an *al-Dawah* splinter group formed in 1980 under the leadership of Sheikh Taqi MODARESSI; the **Islamic Movement in Iraq,** led by Sheikh Muhammad Mahdi al-KALISI; and the **Islamic Scholars Organization,** led by Sheikh al-NASERI.

Each of the SCIRI components was awarded representation in the INJAC in 1990. In late December 1991 the INJAC debated and ultimately rejected a plan formulated by SCIRI leader Hojatolislam Said Muhammad Bakr al-HAKIM (a founder of the Holy Warriors), which called for Syrian, Iranian, and Turkish assistance in overthrowing the Hussein regime.

In early 1994 spokespersons for SCIRI called for UN intervention to protect the Shiite population in southern Iraq from a government military offensive. In early 1999 the United States indicated an interest in providing assistance to SCIRI as part of the new U.S. initiative to topple Saddam Hussein. However, SCIRI leaders based in Iran declined the offer because they did not want to collaborate with the INC.

SCIRI declined to attend the INC rejuvenation meetings in 1999. It subsequently claimed responsibility for attacks on Iraqi government targets in May 2000 and June 2001. Although SCIRI participated in the 2002 sessions designed to promote a unified anti-Hussein front in advance of a potential U.S.-led military campaign, it was not operating in tandem with the INC and argued that Iraqis themselves should overthrow the Hussein regime. SCIRI reportedly had up to 12,000 fighters at its command, most in Iran but some already in Iraq. When Saddam Hussein fell, SCIRI leaders began returning to Iraq and pledged cooperation with the U.S.-sponsored political process. SCIRI was one of the early participants in the IGC established by the CPA.

Following the overthrow of the regime of Saddam Hussein in 2003, the SCIRI militia (the Badr Brigade) regrouped as a political entity, the **Badr Organization,** which maintained close ties to SCIRI. SCIRI leader al-Hakim was assassinated in August 2003; he was succeeded by his nephew, Abd al-Aziz al-HAKIM.

Abd al-Aziz al-Hakim met in December 2006 in Washington with U.S. President Bush, whose administration appeared to be emphasizing ties with SCIRI (despite SCIRI's Iranian association) in an attempt to "marginalize" the supporters of Muqtada al-Sadr. The adoption of the SIIC rubric in May 2007 was also seen, in part at least, as another effort to underscore the moderate stance of the group in relation to the Sadrists, with whom the SIIC and the Badr Organization (a dominant element in Iraqi security forces) subsequently battled for control of southern Iraq.

The SIIC's fortunes declined in the January 2009 provincial elections as it lost dominance in several Shiite provinces. Abd al-Aziz al-Hakim, who had functioned as one of Iraq's most influential leaders by maintaining good relations with both the United States and Iran, died of illness in early 2009 just as the SIIC was forming the INA. He was succeeded as the SIIC leader shortly thereafter by his son, Amman al-Hakim.

Leaders: Amman al-HAKIM (Leader), Adil Abd al-MAHDI (Vice President of the Republic), Haithem al-HUSSAIN, Human HAMOUDI.

Islamic Call (*al-Dawah al-Islamiyah*). *Al-Dawah* was established in the 1950s with the support of Shiite leader Muhammad Bakr al-Sadr, who was executed by the Hussein regime in April 1980. Closely affiliated with the Iranian *Mujaheddin,* the Damascus-based *al-Dawah* claimed responsibility for seven assassination attempts on Saddam Hussein and for numerous bombings during the 1980s. Although it was a founding member of the INC, *al-Dawah* subsequently distanced itself from the congress because it was dissatisfied with its representation on the group's executive council. The United States refused to aid *al-Dawah*'s antiregime activities and some reports in April 1999 indicated that a deep political rivalry had developed between *al-Dawah* and the SCIRI leadership. By 2002 it was generally accepted that *al-Dawah* had broken away from SCIRI, and *al-Dawah* was not officially represented at the various Iraqi opposition meetings during 2002.

As a party in exile, *al-Dawah* had split into various branches in Tehran, Damascus, and London, but after the fall of Saddam Hussein its prominent leaders returned to Iraq and resumed political activity. Like SCIRI, whose leaders also returned from exile, *al-Dawah* cooperated with the U.S.-led occupation authority and gained representation on the IGC. Following the UIA's success in the January 2005 TNA balloting, Ibrahim al-Jaafari of *al-Dawah* was appointed prime minister. However, dissatisfaction with al-Jaafari's performance within the UIA eventually forced him to relinquish the post after elections for the permanent assembly in December 2005. In April 2006 al-Jaafari was replaced as the UIA candidate for prime minister by another *al-Dawah* member, Nuri al-Maliki. *Al-Dawah* formally withdrew from the UIA in August 2009, and al-Maliki subsequently focused on the State of Law coalition as the vehicle for his reelection effort.

Leaders: Nuri Jawad al-MALIKI (Prime Minister), Ali al-ADEEB.

Al-Sadr Movement. This group, an amorphous political, social, and military movement, coalesced around the personality of Shiite leader Muqtada al-Sadr, the son of Grand Ayatollah Mohammed Sadeq al-Sadr and a relative of Grand Ayatollah Mohammed Bakr al-Sadr, two prominent Iraqi Shiite clerics killed by Saddam Hussein's regime. After being underground since 1999, Muqtada al-Sadr rose to prominence almost immediately after the fall of Saddam Hussein in 2003. Al-Sadr did not have the religious credentials of his father, but he was able to claim his family's legacy. Although the majority of Iraqi Shiites backed the approach of the Shiite establishment toward the U.S. occupation of Iraq, Muqtada al-Sadr galvanized a minority of urban Shiite poor from East Baghdad's "Sadr City" (formerly known as Saddam City). After forming his own militia (the Mahdi Army), he also began to organize social services for Shiite communities.

Al-Sadr spurned the IGC, whose membership consisted of other Shiite parties such as SCIRI and *al-Dawah*. Throughout 2003 his followers opposed the presence of U.S.-led forces in Iraq, and tensions rose between occupying authorities and his movement. In early April 2004 full-blown hostilities erupted between al-Sadr's militia and U.S. forces in Sadr City, Najaf, and other Shiite population centers. U.S. forces prevailed then and also when another uprising broke out in August, the Mahdi Army suffering heavy losses. However, Al-Sadr survived the fighting, which enhanced his reputation among Shiites who opposed the continued U.S. presence. His political and military actions also challenged other Shiite groups and the establishment in Najaf. However, al-Sadr was never able to command the allegiance of the majority of Iraq's Shiites, who still followed Grand Ayatollah Ali al-Sistani.

The Al-Sadr Movement did not confront coalition forces in Iraq militarily after the August 2004 failed uprising. However, al-Sadr refused to participate in the January 2005 elections for the TNA, although the closely allied "National Independent Cadres and Elites" list won three seats. Throughout 2005 al-Sadr sought a political role and was persuaded to join the UIA list before the December 2005 poll.

With the formation of a national unity government in May 2006, al-Sadr's followers were awarded five ministries (agriculture, education, health, trade, and transportation). However, the Mahdi Army was subsequently implicated in widespread attacks on Sunnis during sectarian violence that dominated the rest of the year. Under reported heavy U.S. pressure, the al-Maliki administration directed security forces to target Madhi Army elements as part of the security operation launched in early 2007, and in April the Sadrist ministers resigned from the cabinet, denouncing Maliki's support for the U.S. "occupation forces." In May al-Sadr called upon his supporters to operate "peacefully" in pursuit of the withdrawal of U.S. forces, and in August he declared a "suspension" of Mahdi Army activities for six months, although some breakaway factions reportedly continued to operate militarily.

In September 2007 the Sadrist bloc announced its formal withdrawal from the UIA's legislative faction due to what it perceived as the government's failure to provide adequate services or security. The rupture was partly attributable, in the opinion of many analysts, to the ongoing friction between the Sadrists and the SIIC for influence in southern Iraq.

Al-Sadr extended the "cease-fire" in regard to the Mahdi Army in February 2008 for six months. However, fighting subsequently broke out between al-Sadr's supporters and government forces attempting to quash Shiite militias in Baghdad and elsewhere. (Some analysts suggested that breakaway factions of the Mahdi Army were operating outside al-Sadr's control at that point.) Al-Sadr again urged his forces not to target government institutions or forces, while decrying the government's "haphazard raids." As many as 1,000 may have died in the seven-week conflict before al-Sadr authorized Iraqi forces (but no U.S. troops) to deploy in Sadr City. Al-Sadr subsequently announced the formation of a new "social wing" for his movement and extended the cease-fire against U.S. troops indefinitely, while continuing to call for an immediate withdrawal of the U.S. presence from Iraq.

Emphasizing the movement's shift toward political and social activity, al-Sadr's supporters helped to launch the INA with the SIIC in preparation for the 2010 national legislative elections. However, al-Sadr remained in self-imposed exile in Iran.

Leaders: Muqtada al-SADR, Sheikh Salah al-UBAYDI, Nassar al-RUBAYI (Parliamentary Leader).

Islamic Virtue Party (*Hizb al-Fadilah*). *Al-Fadilah* is led by Muhammad al-Yacoubi, a former student of Mohammad Sadeq al-Sadr. The party is particularly strong in the Basra region of Iraq and advocates the establishment of a regional government in the Shiite south, as well as installation of Islamic religious law throughout Iraq. *Al-Fadilah* was part of the UIA during the January and December 2005 legislative elections and joined the national unity government in 2006. However, *al-Fadilah* withdrew from the UIA and the cabinet in March 2007 in a dispute over cabinet posts. The party contested several provincial elections in 2009 on its own.

Leaders: Sheikh Muhammad al-YACOUBI, Sheikh Arsad al-NASIRI, Bassam SHARIF.

Democratic Patriotic Alliance of Kurdistan (DPAK). The DPAK (or Kurdistan Alliance) was formed by the DPK, PUK, and other smaller groups in December 2004 to contest the January 2005 elections for the TNA. Other minor parties in the DPAK included the **Kurdistan Communist Party** (KCP), formed in 1993 and led by Kamal SHAKIR; the **Kurdistan Socialist Democratic Party** (KSDP), led by Muhammad Jahi MAHMUD; the **Kurdistan Toilers' Party,** formed in 1985 by dissidents from the Kurdistan Socialist Party under the leadership of Qadir AZIZ; the **Chaldean Democratic Union; the Iraqi Turkmen Brotherhood Party;** and the **Islamic Group of Kurdistan.**

The DPAK finished second in the January 2005 balloting with 75 seats and just over 25 percent of the vote, partly because of the widespread boycott of the election by Iraq's Sunni community. The PUK, DPK, and most of the other smaller DPAK parties presented a joint Kurdish National Democratic List for the January 2005 elections for the Iraqi Kurdistan National Assembly; the list won 104 of 111 seats.

PUK secretary general Jalal Talabani became president of Iraq after the January 2005 poll. In the December 2005 election for a permanent assembly, the DPAK again presented a joint ticket dominated by the DPK and PUK. Six other smaller parties joined the list, although the Kurdistan Islamic Union left to campaign on its own. Since more Sunni Arabs participated in the December elections than in January, the DPAK's seat total fell to 53 on a vote share of 21.7 percent. In addition to being an important component of the national government, the DPAK continued to dominate the Kurdish Regional Government.

The DPK and PUK presented a Kurdistani List for the July 2009 elections to the Kurdistan Iraqi Parliament, securing 59 seats on a 58 percent vote share. Meanwhile, the KCP and Toilers' Party participated in a Freedom and Social Justice List that also included the **Kurdistan Independent Work Party,** the **Kurdistan Pro-Democratic Party,** and the **Democratic Movement of Kurdistan Party.**

Democratic Party of Kurdistan (DPK). The DPK evolved from a KDP offshoot, the Kurdish Democratic Party (Provisional Leadership), which was formed in late 1975 following the Algiers agreement between Iraq and Iran and the collateral termination of aid to the Kurds by Iran and the United States. When Mullah Mustafa al-Barzani withdrew from the Kurdish insurgency (see Political background, above), the KDP splintered, and the Provisional Leadership declared itself the legitimate successor. It refused to cooperate with the National Front and undertook guerrilla activity through the military wing of the old party, the *Pesh Mergas* ("Those Who Face Death"). The Provisional Leadership consistently opposed government efforts to resettle Kurds in southern Iraq and engaged in clashes with its rival (the PUK, see below), and the Iraqi army. The group began to call itself the DPK following the death of Mullah Barzani in March 1979, although differences between "traditionalist" and "intellectual" factions continued.

In mid-July 1979 several hundred party members returned to Iraq from Iran, where they had resided since 1975. In the spring of 1980, however, there were reports that Iraqi Kurds (*Faili*), who had emigrated from Iran in the first half of the century, were being expelled at the rate of 2,000 a day. Collaterally, Massud Barzani, the son of Mullah Barzani and a leader of the DPK Iranian wing, voiced support for the Tehran regime because of collusion between "U.S. imperialism and its [Baath] lackeys . . . [in] relentlessly fighting against . . . our Shi'a brethren." A subsequent party congress in August 1981 concluded with a denunciation of the "fascist regime" in Baghdad and its "imperialist war."

In 1988 the DPK and the PUK served as the leading components of a new rebel coalition called the Kurdistan Front (KF) that also included the Kurdistan Socialist Party (KSP), the Kurdistan People's Party (a small Marxist grouping), and the IMIK (below). The DPK controlled the largest rebel force during the 1991 Kurdish uprising following the Gulf war and was represented at the Baghdad peace talks by Nechirvan BARZANI, a nephew of Massud Barzani and grandson of the KDP's founder. During the second half of 1991, the distance between Massud Barzani, who urged immediate negotiations with the Hussein regime, and the PUK's Jalal Talabani, who argued for continued military actions prior to talks, widened, thus hampering action by a coalition that had granted veto power to each of its members. (The revived KF by then included the Assyrian Democratic Party [a Kurdish-speaking Assyrian grouping], the Christian Union [another Assyrian formation], and the Kurdish Communist Party [KCP, an offshoot of the ICP, below].)

On May 19, 1992, the KF conducted an inconclusive election for executive leader, neither of the leading contenders (Massud Barzani and Jalal Talabani), with vote shares of 44.6 and 44.3 percent, respectively, being able to secure a majority; concurrently, a 105-seat Iraqi Kurdistan National Assembly was selected (see Legislatures, below). The DPK and the PUK decided to share power equally in the assembly as well as in a Kurdish "national government" located in Arbil. Moreover, immediately prior to an INC meeting in September 1992, the two groups agreed to place their guerrilla units under a single command. However, the accord was never implemented, and the DPK and PUK retained control of western and eastern "enclaves," respectively. Ongoing tension, fueled by the reported deep animosity between Barzani and Talabani, eventually erupted into open fighting in early 1994, and as many as 2,000 guerrillas were reported killed over the ensuing months. Although an agreement was announced in late November for a cease-fire leading up to new elections in May 1995, PUK forces shortly thereafter seized control of Arbil and expelled DPK representatives from the assembly and cabinet. Yet another cease-fire in the spring of 1995 also proved ineffective, and heavy fighting was reported to have broken out again in July, one correspondent describing the factions as "risking national suicide" at the time when unity was most crucial to Kurdish ambitions. Despite intense U.S. mediation efforts, the DPK/PUK infighting continued throughout the rest of the year and the first half of 1996 as each side retained control of its own territory and no region-wide governance was attempted.

Prompting intense international criticism, the DPK invited the Iraqi military to join it in a "final" offensive against the PUK in late August 1996. (DPK leaders subsequently argued that they had taken that action out of fear that the PUK was planning its own offensive in concert with Iranian forces, which had recently crossed the border to challenge guerrillas from the Kurdish Democratic Party of Iran.) Some 30,000 Iraqi soldiers moved into the north and quickly forced the PUK out of its stronghold in Salahuddin and toward the Iranian border.

On September 26, 1996, DPK leader Barzani announced the formation of a new coalition Kurdish government, led by Roz Nuri SHAWEZ of the DPK and including representatives from the IMIK and the KCP. Barzani also declared that the "temporary" military alliance with Baghdad had ended (Iraqi troops having already been withdrawn in the face of U.S. retaliatory measures in southern Iraq) and reiterated that he was not pursuing a separate political accord with the Iraqi regime. Subsequently, the PUK launched a counter-offensive and recaptured most of the territory it had recently lost. By late October the DPK and PUK were again reported to be discussing a cease-fire and the possible reactivation of regional authority.

The DPK withdrew from negotiations in March 1997, and KF cohesion was further corroded when new hostilities broke out the following month between the PUK and the IMIK. Kurdish affairs were additionally complicated in May when some 10,000 Turkish troops crossed into northern Iraq to attack camps of the Kurdish Workers' Party (PKK, see article on Turkey). Although Baghdad formally objected to the encroachment on its sovereignty, its protest was apparently not heartfelt enough to stimulate any other action. Despite UN and other international condemnation of its cross-border offensive, Turkey sent even more forces into Iraq in September, claiming, among other things, that it had been invited to do so by the DPK. Subsequently, the PUK launched what it called a "pre-emptive strike" against DPK strongholds in October; however, the cease-fire was subsequently reinstated (reportedly under heavy U.S. pressure), and the uneasy DPK/PUK territorial and military stand-off continued into 1998. At that time, it was estimated that there were approximately 10,000 DPK guerrillas loyal to Barzani, described as a publicity-shy "tribal leader" wary of Western influence in the region. Despite having been branded a "traitor" by other opposition groups for his brief collaboration with the Iraqi regime in 1996, Barzani was invited to Washington to meet with Talabani in the fall of 1998, their subsequent peace agreement reflecting U.S. recognition that the former remained a significant influence in the Kurdish region and thereby a necessary component of any effective anti-Hussein opposition. Among other things, the two Kurdish leaders agreed to share power in the region and to conduct new assembly elections in the second half of 1999. However, although "relative peace" transpired in the Kurdish-controlled regions, continued friction prevented new assembly balloting. Finally, in October 2002, the assembly reconvened amid a "display of friendship" between Barzani and Talabani, seemingly prompted by the prospect of the overthrow of Saddam Hussein and the concurrent need for Kurdish unity in discussions regarding a "post-Saddam" Iraq. (It has long been widely accepted that Kurdish sentiment overwhelmingly favors the creation of an independent Kurdish state. However, bowing to opposition to that concept from regional and Western capitals, the Kurdish groups in Iraq remain formally supportive of a federated Iraq with substantial regional autonomy.) As of late 2002, it was estimated that as many as 25,000 guerrillas were under the command of the DPK, which had governed northwestern Iraq on a de facto basis with an administration based in Arbil. (Most news reports currently reference this group as the Kurdish Democratic Party [KDP] in apparent recognition of its status as the genuine successor to the original KDP.)

Leaders: Massud BARZANI (President of the Kurdish Region), Jawhar Namiq SALIM, Masru BARZANI, Sami ABDURAHMAN, Hashyar ZUBARI.

Patriotic Union of Kurdistan (PUK). The PUK, which has received support from the Syrian Baath, resulted from the 1977 merger of Jalal Talabani's Kurdish National Union (KNU) with the Socialist Movement of Kurdistan and the Association of Marxist-Leninists of Kurdistan. The KNU had been formed in mid-1975 when Talabani, a left-wing member of the original KDP, refused to accept Mullah Barzani's claim that the Kurdish rebellion had come to an end. Supported by *Pesh Merga* units, Talabani subsequently attempted to unify guerrilla activity under his leadership, but the PUK suffered significant losses in June 1978 during skirmishes in northern Iraq with the DPK, which Talabani accused of having links to both the shah of Iran and the U.S. Central Intelligence Agency.

In January 1984 it was reported that an agreement had been concluded between the PUK and government forces that called for a cease-fire, assurances of greater Kurdish autonomy, and the formation of a 40,000-member Kurdish army to counter Iranian incursions into Iraqi Kurdistan. The agreement was never implemented, however, and Iran's Islamic Republic News Agency asserted in November 1986 that the PUK had entered into an alliance with the DPK to pursue a joint struggle against Baghdad.

PUK forces battled with supporters of the IMIK (below) in late 1993, PUK leaders calling the pro-Iranian fundamentalists "dangerous" and uncommitted to basic Kurdish aspirations. Two years later the PUK was locked in open conflict with the DPK, Talabani accusing arch rival Massud Barzani, among other things, of "hoarding" revenue generated by trade across the Turkish border. Like the DPK, the PUK was estimated to control about 15,000–25,000 fighters, leading observers to the conclusion that a military resolution of their dispute seemed unlikely. Meanwhile, Talabani, described, in contrast to Barzani, as a "garrulous jet-setter," was considered to have the stronger support among Western powers. The PUK, in which a core of urban intellectuals and leftists could still be identified, also exhibited policy differences with the DPK. The PUK's antitribal stance, for example, attracted support from peasant farmers embroiled in land disputes with long-standing tribal leaders. Following attacks by DPK/Iraqi forces in August and September 1996, the PUK was reported to have received military support from Iran, facilitating its subsequent counteroffensive. In September 1998 Talabani reconciled with Barzani during a meeting in Washington in the interest of presenting a united front against the Iraqi regime (see DPK, above, for additional information). Subsequently, the PUK exercised de facto authority in the eastern half of northern Iraq, designating the city of Sulaimani as its regional "capital," until the formation of the Kurdish Regional Government following the overthrow of the Hussein national government.

Leaders: Jalal TALABANI (President of the Republic and Leader of the Party), Barham SALIH (Prime Minister of the Kurdish Regional Government), Ahmad BAMARMI.

Iraqi National List (INL). Formerly known as the Iraqi List, the INL was formed by Interim Prime Minister Ayad Allawi in December 2004 in advance of the 2005 legislative balloting. The INL includes members of several parties and groups, including Allawi's INA, as well as some tribal leaders. Although mostly Shiite, the group formally presents itself as secular and nonsectarian. It campaigned on a platform of promoting national unity by bridging ethnic and religious differences, but it polled only 13.8 percent of the vote in the January 2005 poll, winning 40 seats in the 275-seat TNA. The INL was therefore unable to form a government, and Allawi was succeeded as prime minister by Ibrahim al-Jaafari of the United Iraqi Alliance.

In preparation for the December 2005 poll for a permanent National Assembly, the INL expanded to include the Iraqi Communist Party and former president Ghazi al-Yawar's *Iraqiyun* List. Nevertheless, it once again polled poorly; its representation fell to 25 seats with just 8 percent of the vote. The group may have suffered from the formation of Sunni-based lists that were running for the first time. Despite the poor showing, the INL retained representation in the subsequent national unity government.

In August 2007 the INL leaders directed INL ministers to resign from the cabinet to protest the perceived lack of reform efforts on the part of Prime Minister al-Maliki, with Allawi presenting himself as a candidate to return to the premiership. However, not all of the INL cabinet members followed the withdrawal directive.

The INL performed well in the January 2009 provincial elections, finishing second overall (behind the State of Law coalition and, significantly, ahead of the SIIC). Some INL members reportedly joined State of Law in advance of the 2010 national legislative poll.

Leader: Ayad ALLAWI (Former Interim Prime Minister).

Iraqi National Accord (INA). A predominantly Sunni grouping formed with support from Saudi Arabia following the Iraqi invasion of Kuwait, the INA was the focus of increasing attention in the mid-1990s in light of the disarray within the INC. The U.S. intelligence community in particular reportedly concluded that the INA represented one of the "most promising" of the Iraqi opposition formations, in part because its members included a number of defectors from the Iraqi military. The INA opened an office in Amman, Jordan, in February 1996 after King Hussein offered to support anti–Saddam Hussein efforts. An INA office also operated in Kurdish-controlled territory in northern Iraq until operations there were quashed by Iraqi troops in August–September 1996.

The INA was also one of the seven organizations deemed eligible by Washington in early 1999 to share in $97 million of U.S. aid designed to support antiregime activity. Subsequent reports regularly referenced the INA, which claimed clandestine support within the Iraqi military, as a member of the revamped INC. Although continuing to cooperate (from offices in London and Jordan) with the INC in attempting to establish a unified opposition front in 2002, the INA appeared to be making certain that it was identified as a separate grouping. Meanwhile, former INA members under the leadership of Tawfiq al-YASIRI and other former Iraqi military officers formed an Iraqi National Coalition to participate in opposition coordination efforts.

Leaders: Dirgham KADHIM, Ayad ALLAWI (Secretary General).

Iraqiyun List. Established in December 2004 by Interim President Ghazi Ajil al-Yawar, the *Iraqiyun* List comprised independents and members of small parties from across the political, ethnic, and religious spectrum. It supported a federal system for Iraq.

After the *Iraqiyun* List secured five seats in the TNA in January 2005, al-Yawar was named one of Iraq's two vice presidents. The *Iraqiyun* List joined the Iraqi National List for the December 2005 election for the permanent National Assembly.

Leader: Ghazi Ajil al-YAWAR (Former Vice President of the Republic).

Iraqi Communist Party—ICP (*al-Hizb al-Shuyui al-Iraqi*). Founded in 1934, the ICP was legalized upon its entrance into the National Front in 1973. However, in May 1978 the government executed 21 Communists for engaging in political activities within the armed forces (a right reserved exclusively to Baath members), and by March 1979 several hundred ICP members had either fled the country or relocated in Kurdish areas. With the party having withdrawn from the National Front, (then) RCC Vice Chair Saddam Hussein confirmed in April that Communists were in fact being purged.

In 1993 an ICP congress rejected a proposal that it transform itself into a more centrist grouping and instead reaffirmed its Marxist identity. The congress also elected Hamid Majid Musa as the new ICP secretary general.

The ICP was not included on the list of opposition groups approved by Washington to receive U.S. assistance in early 1999, and it did not participate in the 2002 meetings led by the INC, SCIRI, and other groups in the hope of creating a unified opposition front. However, Musa was appointed a member of the Governing Council following the fall of Saddam Hussein, and the ICP campaigned for the January 2005 legislative election under a **People's Union** list that also included non-ICP candidates. In the December 2005 poll, the ICP joined the Iraqi National List.

Leader: Hamid Majid MUSA.

Iraqi Accord Front (IAF). The IAF (also referenced as the Iraqi Consensus Front or *Tawafiq*) is a Sunni coalition that won 44 seats in the December 2005 assembly poll. The biggest party in the IAF is the IIP, but the front also includes the hard-line **General Council for the People of Iraq**, led by Adnan al-Dulaimi; and the **National Dialogue Council**, led by Sheikh Khalaf al-ILYAN. The IAF helped formulate the early 2006 national reconciliation and joined the subsequent unity government. However, in early August 2007 the IAF announced that its ministers were suspending their cabinet participation to protest the al-Maliki administration's failure to disband Shiite militias or to release Sunnis who had been "arbitrarily arrested" in the 2006–2007 crackdown on sectarian violence. The IAF also demanded a greater role for Sunnis in security policies overall.

Apparently responding to the recent government crackdown on Shiite militias, which, among other things, had targeted Sunnis, the IAF in April 2008 announced its plan to rejoin the government. Six IAF members (four from the IIP and two from the National Dialogue Council) were installed in the cabinet in July.

Leaders: Muhsin Abd al-HAMID, Salim al-JUBOURI, Adnan al-DULAIMI.

Iraqi Islamic Party (IIP). The IIP, formed in the 1950s, was suppressed during the reign of Saddam Hussein, and members of the party conducted an armed struggle against the regime. The IIP resurfaced after the fall of Saddam Hussein in 2003, and the party's secretary general, Muhsin Abd al-Hamid, was given a seat on the IGC. Leaders of the IIP called on followers to boycott the January 2005 legislative elections, but the party participated in the December 2005 poll as the main component of the IAF. (The IIP had caused some controversy among Sunni Arabs because of its support for the new constitution.)

Tariq al-HASHIMI, vice president of the republic, left the IIP to join Prime Minister al-Maliki's State of Law coalition in the second half of 2009.

Iraqi National Dialogue Front. This front, which contested the December 2005 legislative elections, is predominantly a Sunni political grouping, although its candidates included representatives from other ethnic and sectarian groups. It was formed to protest the IIP's acceptance of the draft constitution, which included provisions for regional authorities. The front's founder, Saleh al-Mutlaq, was the primary Sunni Arab negotiator on the constitutional drafting committee. The front secured just over 4 percent of the vote in the December 2005 poll, winning 11 seats.

Leader: Saleh al-MUTLAQ.

Kurdistan Islamic Union (KIU). Led by Salah al-Din Baha al-DIN, the KIU was part of the Kurdish Alliance in the January 2005 elections. The KIU dropped out of the Kurdish Alliance and ran on its own in the December 2005 poll, winning five seats and 1.3 percent of the vote. In the 2009 balloting for the Kurdistan Iraqi Parliament, the KIU led a Reform and Services List that won 13 seats. Other members of the coalition included the Islamic Group in Kurdistan, the KSDP (see DPAK, above), and the **Future Party.**

Iraqi Turkmen Front (ITF). A coalition of 26 small Turkmen parties and groups formed in 1995, the ITF advocated greater autonomy for the Turkmen ethnic group and official recognition as a minority. The ITF secured three seats in the January 2005 TNA elections, but its representation dropped to one seat after the December 2005 poll.

Leader: Faruk Abdullah Abd al-RAHMAN.

Other parties that secured representation in the National Assembly in the December 2005 poll included the *Mithal al-Alusi* **List for the Iraqi Nation;** the **Assyrian Democratic Movement** (*al-Rafidain*); the **Reconciliation and Liberation Bloc;** *al-Risaliyun,* described as closely allied with Muqtada al-Sadr; and the **Yazidi Movement for Reform and Progress.**

Other Parties and Groups:

Change (*Gorran*). This grouping was formed in opposition to the DPK-PUK alliance in the Kurdish region in early 2009. It surprised analysts by securing 25 seats in the July balloting for the Kurdistan Iraqi Parliament.

Iraqi National Congress (INC). The INC was launched by a number of largely Kurdish exile groups in Vienna, Austria, in June 1992. More than 70 delegates from 33 opposition groups attended the congress's first conference within Iraq in the northern city of Shaqlawah in September. During a second such conference in Salahuddin in October, 170 representatives from virtually all the antiregime formations elected a 3-member presidential council and a 26-member executive council. The participants also committed themselves to the nonviolent overthrow of Saddam Hussein and the establishment of a federal system that would permit a substantial degree of ethnic autonomy without partition of the country. Delegates to a third conference in 1993 established a constitutional council and approved diplomatic initiatives intended to secure broader international support for their efforts. At that time, many groups (including the DPK, PUK, SCIRI, IMIK, and INA) were presenting themselves as components of the INC. However, infighting subsequently disrupted INC cohesion, and by 1996 the group was described as in complete disarray (see the 2005–2006 *Handbook* for details).

In early 1999 Washington designated the INC as one of the groups eligible to receive U.S. aid in the effort to topple the Iraqi regime. Consequently, in an apparent effort to regroup, the INC held its first general meeting in nearly three years in London in April 1999. The session appointed an "interim collective leadership" to oversee the revitalization effort, although the seat reserved for SCIRI was not filled.

The United States briefly halted aid to the INC in early 2002 to protest perceived insufficient accounting of the estimated $18 million previously allocated to the INC. However, later in the year the INC's international profile again increased as speculation grew over the role of long-standing Iraqi opposition groups following the potential overthrow of Saddam Hussein. A few observers suggested that INC leader Ahmad Chalabi might serve an important role in a new government. At the same time, however, it appeared that many of the INC's major founding components no longer considered themselves members of the INC. SCIRI, for example, clearly was maintaining its distance from the INC, and the PUK, DPK, and INA were also regularly being referenced as operating outside of the INC umbrella.

Chalabi and other INC members entered Iraq during the U.S./UK-led invasion in early 2003. Despite losing the support of the United States for alleged improper financial dealings, Chalabi became deputy prime minister in the Transitional National Government. Chalabi's INC was briefly part of the UIA but campaigned outside the UIA in the December 2005 elections, failing to win any assembly seats.

Leaders: Ahmad CHALABI (Former Deputy Prime Minister), Gen. Najib al-SALHI.

Movement for Constitutional Monarchy. Led by a claimant to the Hashemite throne, which was abolished in 1958, this London-based movement was one of the groups declared eligible for special U.S. aid in early 1999. In 2002 it was described as a component of the INC. In the December 2005 poll the movement ran with Ahmad Chalabi's INC, but the list failed to win any seats.

Leaders: Sharif Ali ibn HUSSEIN, Salah al-SHAYKHLY.

Islamic Movement of Iraqi Kurdistan (IMIK). The Sunni Muslim IMIK, also referenced as the Kurdistan Islamic Movement (KIM), long served as the voice of the Islamic fundamentalist movement in northern Iraq. As a member of the Kurdistan Front, the IMIK reportedly won 4 percent of the vote in the May 1992 balloting for the Iraqi Kurdistan National Assembly. However, it subsequently rejected an offer from the DPK and the PUK to fill five seats in the new legislative body. In December 1993 intense fighting broke out between supporters of the IMIK and the PUK, followed by a reported "peace agreement" brokered by representatives of SCIRI in February 1994. Viewed as having Iranian support, the IMIK was subsequently reported to have agreed to participate in the new Kurdish government envisioned by the November 1994 DPK/PUK accord. However, when that plan collapsed, the movement, by then apparently controlling some territory near the Iranian border in its own right, was described as aligned with the DPK in ongoing confrontation with the PUK.

A serious split within the IMIK led to the creation of the more radical *Ansar al-Islam* (see below). Although the IMIK had originally been on the list of groups eligible for U.S. aid under the Iraq Liberation Act, assistance was reportedly denied following the terrorist attacks on the U.S. in September 2001, apparently out of concern in Washington over funding certain Islamist groupings.

Leaders: Sheikh Othman Abd al-AZIZ, Ahmad Kakar MAHMOUD, Sheikh Sadiq Abd al-AZIZ.

Ansar al-Islam (Supporters of Islam). A Kurdish extremist grouping launched initially as the *Jund al-Islam* (Army of Islam) by IMIK defectors and other fundamentalist militants in mid-2001, *Ansar al-Islam* was subsequently blamed for a number of violent episodes in northern Iraq. One of the group's adversaries—the PUK—alleged that *Ansar al-Islam,* which controlled several villages with a guerrilla force estimated at 400–1,000 fighters, was connected with the al-Qaida terrorist network of Osama bin Laden.

Leaders: Mullah Najm al-Din FARAJ (a.k.a. Mullah KREKAR), Ahson Ali Abd al-AZIZ, Abdullah al-SHAFII.

Kurdistan Islamic Group (KIG). Formed in 2001 by Muhammad Ali Bapir, the KIG, a conservative Sunni grouping, is comprised mainly of former members of the IMIK. The group was reportedly linked to *Ansar al-Islam* (an allegation denied by Bapir), and leaders were arrested by U.S. forces in 2003. In the January 2005 elections, the KIG secured two seats in the TNA.

Leader: Muhammad Ali BAPIR.

Al-Qaida in Iraq. This group is an outgrowth of the *Tawhid* insurgent/terrorist organization formed, under the leadership of Jordanian militant Abu Musab al-Zarqawi, to combat U.S.-led forces following the overthrow of the Hussein regime in 2003. *Tawhid*'s initial relationship to Osama bin Laden's al-Qaida was unclear, but in late October 2004 al-Zarqawi pledged his allegiance to bin Laden, who in turn endorsed al-Zarqawi as leader of al-Qaida in Iraq. Al-Zarqawi claimed responsibility for the antigovernment attacks in Jordan in late 2005 in what was perceived as an attempt to expand his group's influence beyond Iraq. Concurrently, references to the group as "al-Qaida in Mesopotamia" increased.

The U.S. government consistently referred to al-Qaida in Iraq as comprising "non-Iraqi terrorists," although most independent analysts concluded that Sunni Iraqi insurgents also participated in the activities of the group, which was reportedly involved in many attacks on U.S. and Iraqi forces. In addition, al-Zarqawi's followers targeted Shiite Iraqi civilians perceived to be cooperating with the United States or the Iraqi government, which apparently cost al-Qaida in Iraq much support among those sectors in the population that might otherwise have sympathized with its goals.

Al-Zarqawi was killed during a U.S. airstrike in June 2006, and he was reportedly later succeeded as leader of al-Qaida by Sheikh Abu Hamza al-MUHAJIR, an Egyptian referred to by U.S. officials under a different pseudonym—Abu Ayyub al-Masri. Al-Muhajir subsequently reportedly claimed the allegiance of 12,000 fighters, although many observers considered that figure to be inflated.

In 2007 the United States reportedly convinced a number of Sunni tribal leaders (who may have previously supported the Sunni insurgency) to join with U.S. and Iraqi forces in a sustained campaign against al-Qaida in Iraq. In the fall, bin Laden reportedly urged al-Qaida supporters in Iraq to avoid fueling sectarian violence, although the extent of his authority in that matter appeared questionable. Meanwhile, al-Qaida in Iraq continued to operate as part of an umbrella organization of Sunni insurgent groups known as the Islamic State of Iraq.

Major offensives were launched against al-Qaida in Iraq by U.S. forces in January 2008 and by Iraqi forces in May. Al-Qaida in Iraq was subsequently described as severely weakened.

Anbar Salvation Council. Also known as "Anbar Awakening," this group was formed in 2006 (apparently with the support of the al-Maliki administration) to represent progovernment Sunnis in Anbar Province. Components of the council in 2007 reportedly cooperated with U.S. and Iraqi forces in the campaign against al-Qaida fighters. One leader of the council, Sheikh Abd al-SATTAR Abu Reesha, was killed by a roadside bomb in September 2007.

The Awakening movement subsequently spread to other areas of Iraq as former Sunni insurgents joined the U.S.-led campaign against al-Qaida in Iraq. Members of numerous Awakening Councils (reportedly earning $300 per month from the United States) subsequently served as guards at checkpoints and buildings, their presence being credited as a major reason for the decline of violence in the country in 2008. In October 2008 the Shiite-dominated military assumed responsibility for the heavily armed councils in Baghdad. The following year a number of Sunni tribal leaders joined Prime Minister al-Maliki's State of Law coalition in anticipation of the 2010 legislative elections.

LEGISLATURES

The former bicameral parliament ceased to exist with the overthrow of the monarchy in 1958; legislative functions were subsequently assumed by the Revolutionary Command Council (RCC). On the basis of a bill approved by the RCC in March 1980, a unicameral National Assembly was established for which elections were first held in June, with subsequent balloting in October 1984, April 1989, March 1996, and March 2000.

Elections were also held in the "autonomous" northern region in September 1980, August 1986, and September 1989 to a 50-member Kurdish Legislative Council, which Baghdad continued to recognize despite balloting for a more inclusive Iraqi Kurdistan National Assembly in May 1992.

Following the ouster of Saddam Hussein in 2003, the interim constitution adopted in 2004 provided for a popularly elected 275-member Transitional National Assembly to serve until a permanent constitution was adopted permitting eventual election of a new assembly. The new constitution, approved by national referendum on October 15, 2005, provided for a unicameral **National Assembly** (also referenced as the Council of Representatives [*Majlis al-Nuwwab*]). The assembly comprises 275 members elected by proportional representation within the 18 provinces, whose seat distribution (based on population) ranges from 5 to 59. Twenty-five percent of the seats are reserved for women. The seat distribution following the first election on December 15, 2005, was as follows: the United Iraqi Alliance, 128 seats (the Supreme Council for the Islamic Revolution in Iraq, 29; supporters of Muqtada al-Sadr, 29; Islamic Call, 26; the Islamic Virtue Party, 16; and independents included on the alliance's list, 28); the Democratic Patriotic Alliance of Kurdistan, 53; the Iraqi Accord Front, 44; the Iraqi National List, 25; the Iraqi National Dialogue Front, 11; the Kurdistan Islamic Union, 5; the Reconciliation and Liberation Bloc, 3; *al-Risaliyun*, 2; *Mithal al-Alusi* List for the Iraqi Nation, 1; Iraqi Turkmen Front, 1; the Yazidi Movement for Reform and Progress, 1; and the Assyrian Democratic Movement, 1.

Speaker: Iyad al-SAMMARRAI.

Kurdistan Iraqi Parliament. Created after the collapse of a new autonomy agreement with the Iraqi government in late 1991, a unicameral Iraqi Kurdistan National Assembly, as then constituted, contained 105 seats, 5 of which were reserved for Christian Assyrians. A minimum vote share of 7 percent was necessary for non-Assyrian representation. Following the balloting of May 19, 1992, the Democratic Party of Kurdistan (DPK) and the Patriotic Union of Kurdistan (PUK) agreed to fill 50 seats each; 4 were awarded to the Assyrian Democratic Party and 1 to the (Assyrian) Christian Union. However, renewed Kurdish infighting subsequently precluded legislative activity. On October 4, 2002, the assembly reconvened for the first time in eight years as part of a reconciliation initiative launched in anticipation of possible U.S. military action against the Iraqi regime of Saddam Hussein.

Following the ouster of Hussein in 2003, the interim national constitution adopted in 2004 provided for new elections for a 111-member Iraqi Kurdistan National Assembly. The first balloting was held on January 30, 2005.

The regional legislature (which covers the Iraqi provinces of Dohuk, Irbil, and Suleimaniya) was renamed the Kurdistan Iraqi Parliament in 2009. One hundred of the 11 members (elected for a four-year term) are elected by party-list proportional balloting in a single nationwide constituency. The remaining 11 seats are reserved for minorities (5 for Turkmen, 5 for Christians, and 1 for Armenians), also elected by proportional balloting, except for the Armenian seat, which is majoritarian. At least 30 percent of the seats must be allocated to women.

In the balloting for the 100 general seats on July 25, 2009, the Kurdistani List (the DPK and PUK) won 59 seats; Change, 25; the Reform and Services List, 13; the Islamic Movement, 2; and the Freedom and Social Justice List, 1. The next election was scheduled for March 2010.

Speaker: Kamal KIRKUTI.

CABINET

[as of September 1, 2009]

Prime Minister	Nuri al-Maliki (Shiite, UIA)
Deputy Prime Minister (Economic Affairs)	(Vacant)
Deputy Prime Minister (Security Affairs)	Rafaa al-Issawi (Sunni, IAF)
Ministers	
Agriculture (Acting)	Akram al-Hakim
Communications	Faruq Abd al-Qadir Abd al-Rahman (Sunni, IAF)
Culture	Mahir Dali Ibrahim al-Hadithi (Sunni, IAF)
Defense	Gen. Abd al-Qader Jassim al-Obeidi (Sunni, ind.)
Education	Khudayer al-Khuzaie (Shiite, UIA)
Electricity	Karim Waheed (Shiite, ind.)
Environment	Narmin Uthman (Kurd, DPAK) [f]
Finance	Bayan Jabr (Turkmen Shiite, UIA [SIIC])
Foreign Affairs	Hushyar Zubari (Kurd, DPAK)
Health	Salih Mahdi al-Hasnawi (ind.)
Higher Education	Abd Diyab al-Ajili (Sunni, IAF)
Housing and Construction	Bayan Daza Ei (Kurd, DPAK) [f]
Human Rights	Wijdan Mikaeil (Christian, INL) [f]

Industry and Minerals	Fawzi al-Hariri (Kurd, DPAK) [f]
Interior	Jawad Kadem al-Bolani (Shiite, UIA)
Justice (Acting)	Safa al-Safi
Labor and Social Affairs	Mahmoud Mohammed Jawad al-Radhi (Shiite, UIA)
Migration and Displacement	Abdul-Samad Rahman Sultan (Shiite, UIA)
Municipalities and Public Works	Riyad Gharib (Shiite, UIA)
Oil	Hussein al-Shahristani (Shiite)
Planning	Ali Baban (Sunni, formerly IAF)
Science and Technology	Raed Fahmi Jahid (Sunni, INL)
Trade	Nuri al-Maliki (Shiite, UIA)
Transportation	Amir Abdel Jabbar Ismail (Shiite, UIA)
Water Resources and Irrigation	Abd al-Latif Rashid (Kurd, DPAK)
Youth and Sport	Jassim Mohammed Jafar (Shiite, UIA)
Ministers of State	
Civil Society Affairs	Thamir Jaffar Muhammad al-Zubaydi (Shiite, UIA)
Foreign Affairs	Muhammad Munajid al-Ifan al-Dulaymi (Sunni, IAF)
National Assembly Affairs	Safa al-Safi (Shiite, UIA)
National Dialogue	Akram al-Hakim (Shiite, UIA)
National Security	Sherwin al-Waili (Shiite, UIA)
Provincial Affairs	Khulud Sami Azarah al-Majun (Shiite, UIA) [f]
Tourism and Antiquities	Qahtan Abbas Numan (Shiite, UIA)
Women's Affairs	(Vacant)

[f] = female

Kurdistan Regional Government:

[as of October 28, 2009]

Prime Minister	Barham Salih (PUK)
Deputy Prime Minister	Azad Barwari (DPK)
Ministers	
Culture and Youth	Kawa Mahmoud Shakir
Education	Safeen Mohsin Dizayee
Electricity	(Vacant)
Endowment and Religious Affairs	Kamil Ali Aziz
Finance and Economy	Bayiz Saeed Mohammad Talabany
Health	Taher Abdullan Hussein Hawrami
Higher Education and Scientific Research	Dlawer al-Aldeen
Housing and Reconstruction	Kamaran Ahmed Abdullah
Interior	Abdul Karim Sultan Sinjari
Labor and Social Affairs	Asos Najib Abdullah [f]
Martyrs	Majid Hamad Amin Jamil
Municipalities and Tourism	Samir Abdullah Mustafa
Natural Resources	Abdullah Abdulrahman Abdullah
Pesh Merga Affairs	Jafa Mustafa Ali
Planning	Ali Osman Haji Badri Sindi
Trade and Industry	Sinan Abdulkhalq Ahmed Chalabi
Transportation and Communications	Anwar Jalabi Sabo
Secretary of the Cabinet	Mohammad Qaradaghi

[f] = female

COMMUNICATIONS

Press. Following the overthrow of the Hussein regime in 2003, the CPA and the interim and transitional Iraqi governments promoted the establishment of a free press. Several hundred small, often fleeting, newspapers were subsequently launched, many of them serving as outlets for Iraqi political parties. More than 150 journalists were killed in 2003–2007, and others were kidnapped, primarily by insurgents who particularly targeted local journalists working for foreign news sources. Intensified sectarian conflict in 2006–2007 also contributed to the imposition of press restrictions by the Maliki administration, especially in regard to what the government perceived as "inflammatory" reporting. Some foreign correspondents and Iraqi journalists who had fled the violence returned to the country in 2008 as security conditions improved. Under heavy domestic and international pressure, the government recently established a special police force to investigate violence against journalists.

The official government daily is *al-Sabah*. Another prominent daily in Arabic is *al-Hayat*.

News agencies. The domestic facility is the Iraqi News Agency (*Wikalat al-Anba al-Iraqiyah*); several major foreign bureaus maintain offices in Baghdad.

Broadcasting. The public broadcaster is the Iraqi Media Network, which operates the Radio of the Republic of Iraq and the *al-Iraqiyah* television station. As of 2008 there were 10 Internet users per 1,000 inhabitants.

INTERGOVERNMENTAL REPRESENTATION

Ambassador to the U.S.: Samir Shakir Mahmood SUMAIDA'IE.

U.S. Ambassador to Iraq: Christopher R. HILL.

Permanent Representative to the UN: Hamid al BAYATI.

IGO Memberships (Non-UN): AFESD, AMF, BADEA, CAEU, IDB, Interpol, LAS, NAM, OAPEC, OIC, OPEC, PCA, WCO.

IRELAND

Republic of Ireland
Éire

Political Status: Independent state since 1921; under republican constitution effective December 29, 1937.

Area: 27,136 sq. mi. (70,283 sq. km.).

Population: 4,239,848 (2006C); 4,412,000 (2008E).

Major Urban Centers (2006C): DUBLIN (506,211), Cork (119,418), Galway (72,414), Limerick (52,539).

Official Languages: Irish (Gaelic), English.

Monetary Unit: Euro (market rate December 1, 2009: 1 euro = $1.51US).

President (*Uachtarán na hÉireann*): Mary Patricia McALEESE (*Fianna Fáil*); elected on October 30, 1997, and inaugurated for a seven-year term on November 11, succeeding Mary ROBINSON (nonparty); reelected without opposition on October 1, 2004, and sworn in for a second seven-year term on November 11.

Prime Minister (*Taoiseach*): Brian COWEN (*Fianna Fáil*); nominated by the *Dáil* on May 7, 2008, and appointed by the president and sworn in the same day in succession to Patrick Bartholomew (Bertie) AHERN (*Fianna Fáil*), who had resigned on May 6.

THE COUNTRY

The present-day Irish Republic, encompassing 26 of Ireland's 32 historic counties, occupies all but the northeastern quarter of the Atlantic island lying 50 to 100 miles west of Great Britain. Animated by a

powerful sense of national identity, the population is approximately 88 percent Roman Catholic and retains a strong sense of identification with the Catholic minority in Northern Ireland. However, a constitutional provision according a privileged position to the Church was repealed by public referendum in 1972. In 2007 women constituted 42 percent of the paid labor force, concentrated in the clerical and service sectors; female participation in government, traditionally small, currently includes the largely ceremonial president, three other cabinet ministers, 12 of 60 senators, and about 13 percent of *Dáil* representatives.

Historically dependent on farming and animal husbandry, Ireland's economy continues to include a viable agricultural sector, which accounts for 4 to 5 percent of GNP, 7 percent of exports, and 15 percent of employment. Most farm activity centers on cattle raising and dairying; wheat, barley, sugar beets, and potatoes rank among the leading crops. The industrial sector now contributes about 36 percent of GNP, employs 27 percent of the workforce, and provides roughly 90 percent of export earnings. Exported manufactures include chemicals, computers and electrical machinery, clothing, and textiles as well as beverages and processed foods. Tourism is another significant source of foreign exchange. Leading trading partners include the United Kingdom, the United States, Belgium, and Germany.

Ireland has been a substantial net financial beneficiary of the European Community (EC, subsequently the European Union—EU) since it became a member in 1973. At the same time, an Industrial Development Authority has had considerable success in attracting foreign investment that helped to generate economic growth averaging 3 percent a year through the 1980s and also in improving the trade balance. During the 1990s Ireland experienced an economic surge, with GDP growth per annum through 1997 averaging 6.5 percent, by far the highest in the EU. In the second half of the decade foreign investment poured into the country, and the high-tech sector, most notably the computer industry, flourished, earning Ireland's economy the label "Celtic Tiger." Reversing a decades-old pattern, immigration began outpacing emigration, with much of the influx being returnees.

GDP growth for 1998 exceeded 8 percent, and Ireland was well positioned to meet the criteria for its entry into the European Economic and Monetary Union (EMU) in 1999, when economic expansion reached 8 percent. By July 2000, however, some analysts were expressing concern about an annualized inflation rate of 6.2 percent—more than double the average for the 11-country euro-zone—which was being fueled by rising wages and consumer demand, labor shortages, low interest rates, a housing boom, and expanding private-sector credit. GDP growth in 2000 remained the EU's highest, at about 9 percent, enabling the government to propose both substantial spending increases and tax cuts in its 2001 budget. The budget quickly drew a reprimand from the EU, however, because of what were characterized as its inflationary tendencies. GDP growth remained strong (6.9 percent) in 2002, although increased government spending produced a deficit after several years of surpluses. One contributor to the additional spending was a major decentralization initiative designed to ease congestion in Dublin by relocating government offices.

The Irish economy continued to demonstrate remarkable strength in 2005; real GDP increased by 5.9 percent according to the International Monetary Fund (IMF), while employment grew by more than 4 percent, with inward migration playing a significant role. In its 2006 budget, the government revealed plans for reduced taxes on low- and middle-income earners, accompanied by new restrictions on tax loopholes benefiting the wealthy. The IMF subsequently praised the country's low unemployment (4.4 percent in 2006), consistently high growth rate (5.7 percent in 2006), and fiscal balance. However, inflation (approximately 4 percent in 2006) remained above the euro-area average.

GDP expanded by 6 percent in 2007, but the global financial crisis punished the Irish economy severely in 2008, when plummeting property values and related credit issues contributed to contraction of 2.3 percent. As part of what the IMF described as a "painful adjustment," the government was forced to extended heavy support to the banking sector out of fear of a total collapse and to slash public sector wages in an effort to constrain a budget deficit that had reached 7 percent. It was subsequently predicted that GDP would contract by a staggering 7.5 percent in 2009, with unemployment soaring to double digits.

GOVERNMENT AND POLITICS

Political background. Ireland's struggle to maintain national identity and independence dates from the beginning of its conquest by England in the early Middle Ages. Ruled as a separate kingdom under the British Crown and, after 1800, as an integral part of the United Kingdom, Ireland gave birth to a powerful revolutionary movement whose adherents first proclaimed the Republic of Ireland during the Easter Week insurrection of 1916 and, despite initial failure, reaffirmed it in 1919. A measure of national independence was accorded by Great Britain through a treaty in December 1921. Under its terms, the 26 counties of Southern Ireland were granted dominion status, the 6 Protestant-majority counties of Northern Ireland electing to remain within the United Kingdom. The partition was regarded as provisional by the Irish Republic, which until 1998 remained formally committed to incorporation of the northern counties into a unified Irish nation. Under the historic multiparty Good Friday Agreement of April 10, 1998, however, the Irish government acknowledged, as stated in the accompanying British-Irish Agreement, "the legitimacy of whatever choice is freely exercised by a majority of the people of Northern Ireland with regard to its status, whether they prefer to continue to support the Union with Great Britain or a sovereign united Ireland."

Officially known as the Irish Free State from 1922 to 1937, Southern Ireland became the Irish Republic, or simply Ireland (*Éire*), with the entry into force of its present constitution on December 29, 1937. The era's dominant leader was Éamon DE VALÉRA of the Republican (*Fianna Fáil*) party, who served as prime minister for most of the period between 1932 and 1959 and was then president until 1973. Ireland's association with the British Commonwealth was gradually attenuated and finally terminated on April 18, 1949. For most of the next decade governmental responsibility tended to alternate between the *Fianna Fáil* and United Ireland (*Fine Gael*) parties, while from 1957 to 1973 the former ruled under the successive prime ministries of De Valéra (1957–1959), Sean F. LEMASS (1959–1966), and John M. LYNCH (1966–1973).

After calling a surprise election in February 1973, *Fianna Fáil* failed to retain its majority, and a coalition government of the *Fine Gael* and Labour parties was installed under the leadership of Liam COSGRAVE. Lynch returned as prime minister following a *Fianna Fáil* victory in an election held June 16, 1977, but on December 5, 1979, announced his intention to resign and six days later was succeeded by Charles J. HAUGHEY. Haughey's investiture was widely regarded as the most remarkable comeback in Irish political history: Although ultimately acquitted, he had been dismissed as Lynch's finance minister in 1970 and tried on charges of conspiring to use government funds to smuggle arms to the outlawed Irish Republican Army (IRA).

At the election of June 11, 1981, *Fine Gael* gained 21 lower house seats over its 1977 total, and on June 30 Dr. Garret FITZGERALD, by a three-vote margin, succeeded in forming a government in coalition with Labour. The new administration quickly increased taxes, announced spending cuts, and permitted higher interest rates, but on

January 27, 1982, its first full budget was defeated by a single vote. Following a new election on February 8, the Haughey-led *Fianna Fáil,* backed by three Workers' Party deputies and two independents, returned to office on March 9. Eight months later, unable to reverse economic decline and buffeted by a series of minor scandals within his official family, Haughey lost a no-confidence motion by two votes. The balance of power again shifted at an election on November 24, yielding the installation of another *Fine Gael*–Labour government under FitzGerald on December 14, 1982.

On October 22, 1986, FitzGerald survived a no-confidence motion by one vote, but he lost his parliamentary majority on December 10 with the resignation of a *Fine Gael* conservative. On January 21, 1987, the four-year-old coalition government fell over the issue of budget cuts, which Labour felt would impinge inequitably on welfare programs. At the ensuing general election of February 17 *Fianna Fáil* fell only three seats short of a majority, with a third Haughey administration being approved on March 10 by the barest possible margin on a vote of 83–82, with one abstention. On the basis of public opinion polls that suggested increased support for his administration, Haughey called an early election on June 15, 1989, but *Fianna Fáil*'s net loss of four parliamentary seats obliged him to join with the Progressive Democrats (PD), which had been formed by *Fianna Fáil* dissidents in 1985. On July 12 the *Fianna Fáil*–PD coalition won *Dáil* approval in an 84–79 vote, with Haughey returning as prime minister.

On December 3, 1990, Mary ROBINSON, a left-leaning lawyer who had long campaigned for birth control and legalized divorce, was inaugurated as president, after having defeated *Fianna Fáil* candidate Brian LENIHAN in runoff balloting on November 9. Lenihan, previously an odds-on favorite, had been dismissed from the Haughey administration in late October after confessing that he had lied in denying reports that in 1982 he had urged President Patrick J. HILLERY to act unconstitutionally in appointing a *Fianna Fáil* government without calling for a validating election.

In November 1991 Prime Minister Haughey, besieged by the alleged improprieties of associates, overcame an intraparty vote of no confidence led by his finance minister, Albert REYNOLDS, who was promptly sacked. However, on January 30, 1992, after being further buffeted by the revival of a 1982 wiretapping scandal, Haughey submitted his resignation, with Reynolds, on February 11, assuming the office that had eluded him three months before. Although *Fianna Fáil* was obliged to retain the PD as its coalition partner, eight former ministers were swept away in an abrupt conclusion to the Haughey era.

On June 18, 1992, a referendum was held on the Maastricht Treaty on more inclusive European union, which voters approved by a 69 percent majority. In a referendum on November 25, Irish voters registered nearly 60 percent majorities in favor of guaranteeing the right to travel to other EC states for abortion and the right to obtain information on abortion availability (enacted into law in March 1995). On a third question decided in November, however, voters opted by a similar majority against a proposed relaxation of Ireland's strict abortion proscription.

The *Fianna Fáil*–PD coalition collapsed in early November 1992 after Reynolds had accused PD leader Desmond O'MALLEY of giving "dishonest" evidence in an inquiry into fraud in the beef-exporting industry. Defeated by a Labour-proposed no-confidence motion on November 5, Reynolds was forced to call an early election on November 25 and saw his party slump to its worst postwar electoral showing. *Fine Gael* also lost ground sharply, while the Labour Party, under the charismatic leadership of Richard (Dick) SPRING, registered its best-ever result, albeit remaining third-ranked. Having spent the election campaign attacking Reynolds, Labour subsequently found that the new parliamentary arithmetic and the attractions of office dictated the party's first-ever coalition with *Fianna Fáil.* The new government, enjoying an unprecedented 36-seat overall majority, took office on January 12, 1993, with Reynolds continuing as prime minister, Spring becoming deputy prime minister and foreign minister, and Labour nominees being awarded five other posts.

Apparently secure in office, Reynolds was unexpectedly brought down in November 1994 after his nomination of the incumbent attorney general as High Court president drew Labour opposition because the nominee had been reluctant to authorize the extradition to the North of a Catholic priest accused of pedophile offenses. Amid great political drama, featuring accusations that Parliament had been misled, Reynolds resigned on November 17 and was replaced as *Fianna Fáil* leader by his finance minister, Bertie AHERN. However, attempts to reconstitute the previous coalition proved abortive, and on December 15 a three-party minority government was formed under the leadership of John BRUTON (*Fine Gael*) that included Labour and the small Democratic Left. The coalition commanded 82 of the *Dáil*'s 166 seats but could rely on the support of the Green Party deputy, whereas *Fianna Fáil* and the PD had a combined strength of only 78 seats and so would require the support of all five independents to challenge the government.

In light of the IRA's cease-fire announcement at the end of August 1994 (see Foreign relations, below), the *Dáil* voted on February 1, 1995, to revoke the 1976 Emergency Powers Act, which had enhanced special police powers in force since 1939. The retention of the original 1939 powers, on the grounds that they were needed to combat organized crime, drew strong criticism from civil liberties groups. (The 1976 powers were not reinstated when the IRA called off its cease-fire in February 1996.)

The Bruton government narrowly prevailed when it called on voters to sanction the legalization of divorce in a constitutional referendum on November 24, 1995. With *Fianna Fáil* giving only half-hearted backing to the proposed change, and with the Catholic Church exerting all its influence against, the outcome was a 50.3 percent victory for the affirmative. New statutes facilitating the division of properties in divorce took effect in February 1997.

With a scandal involving alleged payments to political figures reaching longtime *Fianna Fáil* leader Haughey, the government coalition headed by *Fine Gael* decided to call for early *Dáil* elections in 1997. However, the coalition of *Fine Gael,* Labour, and the Democratic Left failed to close a slight gap in opinion polls and lost to *Fianna Fáil* and the allied Progressive Democrats in balloting on June 6. While no party commanded an outright majority, *Fianna Fáil* won 77 seats and the Progressive Democrats 4 seats, enough to secure, with the support of a few independents, a confidence motion and to form a minority coalition government on June 26. Bertie Ahern thus became, at 45, Ireland's youngest prime minister.

On October 30, 1997, the *Fianna Fáil* candidate, Mary McALEESE, won the presidential election to succeed Robinson, who had declined to run for a second term and had stepped down in September to become the United Nations (UN) High Commissioner for Human Rights. Inaugurated on November 11, McAleese, a Catholic from Northern Ireland and professor of law at Queens University in Belfast, had trounced her four opponents with 45 percent of the vote on the first count and then received 59 percent in the runoff against the *Fine Gael* candidate, Mary BANOTTI.

On April 10, 1998, after 22 months of negotiations, the British and Irish governments won agreement on a historic multiparty peace accord for Northern Ireland (see Foreign relations, below, and the United Kingdom: Northern Ireland article). Prime Minister Ahern actively campaigned on behalf of the Belfast (Good Friday) Agreement, which received Parliament's overwhelming assent on April 22 and won the backing of 94.4 percent of republic voters (on a turnout of 56 percent) at a referendum on May 22. The approval constituted acceptance of constitutional changes voiding Ireland's claim to sovereignty in the North, although formal enactment of the amendments was delayed until the United Kingdom handed over devolved powers to the Northern Ireland Assembly and executive body on December 2, 1999.

In *Dáil* balloting on May 17, 2002, *Fianna Fáil* won 41.5 percent of the vote and 81 seats, while *Fine Gael* declined to 22.5 percent and 31 seats. Prime Minister Ahern was reappointed on June 6 to head another *Fianna Fáil*–PD government, which included many incumbent ministers.

Prior to the 2004 presidential election, a range of parties, including *Fianna Fáil, Fine Gael,* and *Sinn Féin,* supported the incumbent President McAleese. The Green Party tried to present Éamon RYAN for the presidency, but it was unable to garner support for his candidacy. As a result, no other candidate filed to run for the presidency by the October 1 deadline, and McAleese was thus officially declared reelected on October 1.

In the May 24, 2007, general election *Fine Gael* increased its vote share from 22.5 percent to 27.2 percent and picked up 20 more seats than in 2002. However, its seat gains came mostly at the expense of the Progressive Democrats and independents, and the Ahern-led *Fianna Fáil* won nearly the same vote share (41.6 percent) as in 2002 (41.5 percent) and retained 77 of its previous 81 seats (not counting the *Dáil* speaker elected as a *Fianna Fáil* member but serving without party affiliation). *Fianna Fáil* was therefore able to form a majority coalition government, appointed on June 14, 2007, under the continued leadership of Ahern, by joining forces with the Green Party (6 seats), Progressive Democrats (2 seats), and 4 independents.

In the wake of continued revelations at a tribunal investigating corruption allegations (see Current issues, below), Ahern resigned the premiership on May 6, 2008. On the following day Brian COWEN, who had been elected leader of *Fianna Fáil* in April, was nominated to the post by the *Dáil* and appointed by the president. Cowen quickly announced a reshuffled cabinet comprising the same parties as those in the Ahern administration.

Constitution and government. Under Articles 2 and 3 of the Irish constitution as adopted by plebiscite on July 1, 1937, the document applied to "the whole island of Ireland," with Parliament and the government accorded jurisdiction, at least in theory, over the entire "national territory." (As a consequence, residents of Northern Ireland have long been considered citizens of the republic and, accordingly, eligible to hold office in the South.) In the referendum of May 22, 1998, however, Irish voters approved substitute texts for Articles 2 and 3, as specified by the Good Friday Agreement concluded the previous month. The new Article 2 acknowledges "the entitlement and birthright of every person born in the island of Ireland . . . to be part of the Irish nation," but the new Article 3 also recognizes "that a united Ireland shall be brought about only by peaceful means with the consent of a majority of the people, democratically expressed, in both jurisdictions in the island." In addition, Article 3 authorizes creation of shared North-South executive institutions that "may exercise powers and functions in respect of all or any part of the island."

The constitution provides for a president (*Uachtarán na hÉireann*) directly elected for a seven-year term and for a bicameral legislature (*Oireachtas*) consisting of a directly elected lower house (*Dáil*) and an indirectly chosen upper house (*Seanad*) with power to delay, but not to veto, legislation. The *Seanad* may also initiate or amend legislation, but the lower house must approve all such proposals. Presidential and *Dáil* elections are conducted under the single transferable vote system, in which voters indicate their first choices on their ballots and are invited to indicate a preference order for the other candidates. Multiple "counts," in which candidates getting lower "first-choice" vote totals are eliminated and some votes are transferred to second choices, are often required to determine final electoral outcomes. The cabinet, which is responsible to the *Dáil,* is headed by a prime minister (*Taoiseach*), who is the leader of the majority party or coalition and is appointed by the president for a five-year term on recommendation of the *Dáil.* The president has the power to dissolve the *Dáil* on the prime minister's advice. The judicial system is headed by the Supreme Court and includes a Court of Criminal Appeal, a High Court (called the Central Criminal Court for criminal cases), and circuit and district courts. Judges are appointed by the president with the advice of the government and may be removed only by approval of both houses of the legislature.

Local government is based on 4 provinces (Connacht, Leinster, Munster, and part of Ulster), 27 counties (Tipperary counting as two for administrative purposes), and 5 county boroughs (Dublin, Cork, Galway, Limerick, and Waterford), each with elected governing bodies. Eight regional authorities have as part of their mandate coordinating EU matters.

On August 19, 1998, responding to a car bombing in Omagh, in the North, that claimed 29 lives and injured more than 200 people, Prime Minister Ahern proposed a controversial series of "extremely draconian" antiterrorism measures that included negating the right to silence and adding penalties for withholding information about terrorist crimes. Although opponents argued that the measures would violate human rights conventions, the Parliament passed the legislation in early September. Earlier, in November 1996, reacting to public fears of organized crime, voters had approved a referendum restricting the right to bail and giving police expanded authority to detain suspects.

Foreign relations. Independent Ireland has traditionally adhered to an international policy of nonalignment, remaining neutral throughout World War II and subsequently avoiding membership in any regional security structure, in part because of a reluctance to be a military partner of Britain. It has, however, been an active participant in the UN (since 1955), the EC/EU (since 1973), and other multinational organizations. In November 1992 it became an observer member of the Western European Union (WEU), following its endorsement of a defense/security dimension to European integration under the EU's Maastricht Treaty.

Beginning in 1969 Dublin's relations with the United Kingdom were complicated by persistent violence in Ulster and terrorism committed by both the IRA and ultra-unionists. Since the late 1970s the two governments have cooperated in security matters, but aspects of the Northern Ireland problem caused frequent strains. In an effort to improve relations, in 1981 Prime Ministers FitzGerald and Thatcher agreed to establish an Anglo-Irish Inter-Governmental Conference (AIIC) to discuss a range of mutual concerns. The conference convened in January 1982 but subsequently encountered a number of obstacles, including the Haughey government's opposition to UK proposals for devolution of power to the North, its unwillingness to endorse the British position during the UK-Argentinean Falklands conflict, and renewed IRA bombings in London. Further progress was, however, registered in discussions between the two prime ministers in November 1983, leading two years later to an Anglo-Irish Agreement that was subsequently ratified by the Irish and UK Parliaments. The pact established a "framework" within which Dublin would have an advisory role in the devolution of power to Northern Ireland but also acknowledged British sovereignty for as long as such status should be desired by a majority of the territory's inhabitants.

Relations between the two governments again worsened in the wake of the *Dáil*'s December 1987 ratification of the 1977 European Convention on the Suppression of Terrorism, which sanctioned the extradition of individuals charged with terrorist activity. Irish public opinion had opposed the convention because of British reluctance to modify its Diplock court system, whereby suspected terrorists could be summarily tried without juries in Belfast courts. As a result, "safeguards" were attached by the *Dáil,* including a stipulation that the Irish attorney general approve all extradition proceedings.

In April 1991 what had become a lengthy, but inconclusive, series of AIIC talks on the future of Northern Ireland were suspended in favor of a new initiative that called for negotiations between political leaders in the North and the Dublin government, followed by a renewal of talks between the British and Irish representatives. After a series of procedural delays, punctuated by a revival of sectarian violence, Irish ministers in June 1992 met with both Catholic and Protestant leaders from Northern Ireland for the first time since 1973. However, the republic's constitutional claim to the North again proved to be a crucial obstacle to progress, the talks being formally terminated in November in favor of a continuation of the AIIC process.

The advent of the *Fianna Fáil*–Labour coalition in January 1993 brought a change of tone in Dublin, which held out the prospect of Irish constitutional changes to accommodate the Northern majority. In May, President Robinson became the first Irish head of state to confer with a British monarch by meeting privately with Queen Elizabeth at Buckingham Palace. Familiar strains resurfaced during President Robinson's unofficial visit to Belfast the following month, when she met and shook hands with the *Sinn Féin* leader, Gerry ADAMS. Nevertheless, renewed impetus in UK-Irish consultations culminated in the Downing Street Declaration on Northern Ireland jointly issued by Prime Ministers Major and Reynolds on December 15, 1993.

Representing a new departure in Anglo-Irish relations, the declaration aimed at a cessation of hostilities in Northern Ireland. While assuming that "the people of the island of Ireland" might wish to opt for unification, it reiterated that "it would be wrong to attempt to impose a united Ireland in the absence of the freely given consent of a majority of the people of Northern Ireland." The Irish government then exerted its influence to bring *Sinn Féin* into the negotiating framework, as envisaged in the declaration, provided that *Sinn Féin* renounce violence. The government's efforts were rewarded by an IRA cease-fire announcement on August 31, 1994, after which *Sinn Féin* leader Adams was invited to Dublin, where in October the government launched an all-Ireland Forum for Peace and Reconciliation (FPR). The publication in February 1995 of a UK-Irish "framework document" setting out the parameters for all-party talks on Northern Ireland provided further impetus to the peace process.

A semi-official visit by Britain's Prince Charles on May 31–June 1, 1995, which included meetings with both President Robinson and Prime Minister Bruton, was the first by a member of the royal family since Irish independence in 1922. Nevertheless, Dublin's efforts to expedite formal all-party talks on Northern Ireland became stalled by the UK government's insistence on prior "decommissioning" of terrorist groups' arms. U.S. President Clinton, during a visit in November to London, Northern Ireland, and Dublin, helped the parties work around this impasse with the two governments agreeing to a "twin-track" approach under which decommissioning would be dealt with separately by an international commission chaired by former U.S. senator George J. Mitchell.

Mitchell's report in January 1996 concluded that decommissioning of arms prior to talks was unachievable but called on all groups to renounce violence in favor of democratic means. While both Dublin and London accepted the Mitchell "principles," London's collateral decision to hold elections in the North for a consultative Northern Ireland Forum on Political Dialogue prior to renewed talks was seen in Dublin as responsible for the IRA's decision in February to call off the cease-fire. Nevertheless, the Bruton government supported the British position that *Sinn Féin* could not participate in formal talks without a reinstatement of the cease-fire. The resumption of IRA violence in mainland Britain enabled Dublin to extract from London a firm date of June 10 for the start of talks, in return for accepting that a preceding forum election would be held in Northern Ireland. Following the polling on May 30, Bruton and Prime Minister Major of Britain jointly opened the talks at Belfast's Stormont Castle and by June 12 had persuaded the Unionist representatives to accept former senator Mitchell as plenary chair. Thereafter, the process became bogged down in familiar procedural wrangling.

On June 25, 1997, Prime Minister Bruton and British Prime Minister Tony Blair agreed on a detailed mechanism for arms decommissioning and the need for an IRA cease-fire, which was restored on July 20, 1997, clearing the way for *Sinn Féin* to enter the broad-based peace talks held in Belfast the following September. With progress made on several issues and the cease-fire continuing to hold, newly installed Prime Minister Ahern reaffirmed that the Irish Republic would consider dropping its claim to sovereignty over Northern Ireland, if approved by Irish voters in a constitutional referendum.

In January 1998 Ireland and Britain jointly issued a document entitled "Propositions on Heads of Agreement" that provided the framework for the Good Friday Agreement of April 10. The propositions put forward "balanced constitutional change" by both governments; establishment of a directly elected Northern Ireland Assembly and a North-South ministerial council; formation of British-Irish "intergovernmental machinery"; and "adoption of practical and effective measures" concerning such issues as prisoners, security, and decommissioning of arms. Conclusion of the Good Friday Agreement (for details, see the Northern Ireland article) was accompanied by a new British-Irish Agreement, which replaced the 1985 Anglo-Irish Agreement and committed both governments to carry through on the multiparty peace accord. On November 26 Tony Blair became the first UK prime minister to address the Irish Parliament, using the occasion to lobby for continuation of the peace process and for disarmament to begin.

The arms-decommissioning issue remained a sticking point, however, and the Good Friday Agreement was not fully implemented until December 2, 1999. The North-South Ministerial Council held its inaugural meeting on December 13, and four days later representatives of Ireland, the United Kingdom, the Channel Islands, the Isle of Man, and the devolved governments of Northern Ireland, Scotland, and Wales convened in London for the first session of the Council of the Isles. On the same day Prime Minister Blair hosted the first intergovernmental meeting under the British-Irish Agreement. Throughout 2000 and into 2001 Prime Minister Ahern remained actively involved in holding together the peace process in the face of IRA reluctance to begin active decommissioning. In March 2003 Ahern supported Blair's decision to postpone elections for the Northern Ireland Assembly in response to increasing violence in the North (the elections were held in November 2003). Ahern also participated in talks between the main Northern Irish political parties and the British and Irish governments in December 2003 and January 2004.

Relations between the Irish government and *Sinn Féin* and the IRA deteriorated sharply in late 2004 and early 2005 in the wake of allegations that the IRA was involved in massive money-laundering operations. The government launched raids on a number of alleged IRA locations and confiscated large sums of money, while criticizing *Sinn Féin* leaders for their perceived role (denied by *Sinn Féin*) in directing IRA activity. For his part, Prime Minister Ahern, long a champion of efforts to bring die-hard nationalists "in from the cold," was also reportedly upset by the *Sinn Féin* approach in the talks in December 2004 that failed to resolve the power-sharing dispute in Northern Ireland. However, in July 2005 the IRA announced that it would agree to permanently dismantle all of its weapons and allow two observers—a Catholic priest and a former president of the Methodist Church in Ireland—to witness the process. In September the disarmament was reported to have been carried out. However, the IRA's refusal to release details concerning the operation or to allow any visual documentation of the event fed the ongoing skepticism among members of Ian Paisley's Democratic Unionist Party (PUD). With the Democratic Unionists refusing to communicate with *Sinn Féin,* no resumption of negotiations regarding the sharing of power occurred. In April, UK Prime Minister Blair and Ahern gave the two sides until November 24, 2006, to form a government, declaring that if this deadline was not met they would dissolve the Northern Ireland legislature, terminate the salaries of those involved, and select other means for governance of the province.

On October 13, 2006, Ahern and Blair announced that their three-day meeting, held in St. Andrews, Scotland, with leaders of the major Northern Ireland political parties had led to the St. Andrews Agreement (see article on UK: Northern Ireland). It proposed a way forward for restoring devolved power through eventual restoration of the Northern Ireland Assembly. It also called for an executive power-sharing relationship between Unionist and Republican parties to be forged by November 24 and, if successful, for elections the following March. The parties reached sufficient understanding in November about power sharing as well as about the steps required by the agreement regarding policing and justice policy that elections were held on March 7, 2007. On March 26 the leading parties agreed to a shared executive arrangement, and on May 8 the first minister and deputy first minister were elected by the assembly, with other ministers being approved on May 12.

Debate on wider aspects of Irish external policy was stimulated by the publication in March 1996 of the first-ever government white paper on the subject, focusing on whether Ireland should abandon its long-standing military neutrality. Speaking in the *Dáil,* Foreign Minister Dick Spring hinted at Irish moves toward North Atlantic Treaty Organization (NATO) and WEU involvement. However, *Fianna Fáil* spokesmen reiterated the party's traditional opposition to participation in any military organization of which Britain was a member, referring with dread to the attendant possibility that British troops would return to Irish Republic soil. Despite a concern by opponents that ratification of the June 1997 Amsterdam Treaty on greater EU integration would ultimately commit Ireland to participation in a unified military force, Irish voters approved the treaty by referendum on May 22, 1998, with 62 percent voting in favor. In 1999 the Ahern government confirmed its interest in joining NATO's Partnership for Peace, which the *Dáil* authorized by a 112–24 vote on November 9, thereby permitting Irish forces to participate in training for multilateral "peace support, search-and-rescue and humanitarian missions." In 2000 Ireland agreed to commit 1,000 troops to a new EU Rapid Reaction Force, although the government secured an agreement that its troops would be deployed only in UN-sanctioned operations.

During the prelude to the 2003 U.S.-led invasion of Iraq, the Irish government permitted U.S. planes to use Shannon airport for stopovers and refueling. Although that decision prompted several large protests, the *Dáil* in March voted 77–60 to permit continued U.S. access to the airport.

Current issues. Following years of revelations about political favors and donations, tax evasion schemes, and various gifts to politicians, the climate of "sleaze" was cited by the Labour Party at the end of June 2000 when it introduced a no-confidence motion against the government. However, the government won a confidence motion by a vote of 84–80 on the strength of independent support.

In June 2001 the Ahern administration suffered a serious setback when Irish voters rejected the EU's Treaty of Nice, with 53.9 percent (of a low turnout of 35 percent) opposing further integration as well as institutional revisions needed to accommodate anticipated new members. A major voter concern appeared to be Ireland's potential loss of influence in a significantly expanded union (see the EU article). However, on October 19, 2002, voters approved the Nice treaty in a second referendum, 62.9 percent in favor and 37.1 percent opposed.

In January 2003 the Supreme Court ruled that non-Irish parents and relatives of children born in the country did not have an automatic legal right to remain in Ireland. This ruling was followed by a referendum in June in which voters overwhelmingly endorsed a constitutional amendment that prohibited the automatic extension of citizenship to non-EU babies born in Ireland. The court ruling and subsequent constitutional amendment were supported by the government as a means to end the practice of non-EU persons using residence in Ireland as a means to gain legal status within the union.

In June 2003 a commission found that Ahern and many other members of Parliament had violated limits on campaign spending in the 2002 elections. However, the commission ruled that the violations were not intentional and not criminal.

The June 11, 2004, elections for the European Parliament handed *Fianna Fáil* its worst electoral defeat in history as *Fine Gael* defeated the ruling party for the first time. The election also marked the first time that *Sinn Féin* won a seat in the EU body. Apparently in response to its poor showing, the administration in December announced a significant increase in public spending for retired workers, people with disabilities, and other sectors of the population.

Accusations of corruption plagued Ahern from the summer of 2006 through the May 2007 general election and into October 2007. In an August 2006 television interview, Ahern admitted to writing blank checks for *Fianna Fáil* party leaders while minister of finance (1991–1994) in the Haughey and Reynolds governments. In September a newspaper reported that while minister of finance in 1993 Ahern had allegedly also received payments from a wealthy businessman. A few days later Ahern admitted receiving these and other payments, describing them as loans. He also said that, while some persons making the payments had received government appointments, those decisions were made because the contributors were friends, not because money had changed hands. Ahern subsequently began to repay the contributors with 5 percent interest. Additional questions later arose over the source of a large deposit he had made into his bank account in 1994 and over whether he had paid market value for his Dublin house.

In December 2006 the Moriarty Tribunal, investigating the alleged financial improprieties of former *Fianna Fáil* prime minister Haughey, issued a scathing 600-page report on the corrupt practices of Haughey, the person who first named Ahern as minister of finance. Despite the timing of these and the preceding revelations, Ahern was required by the constitution to hold an election at least once every five years and thus had to call a general election before June 2007. Polls in April made continuation in government of *Fianna Fáil* and the Progressive Democrats look doubtful. However, the Mahon Tribunal (investigating allegations of Ahern's financial misdeeds) announced it was postponing its hearings until after the election, while on May 14 Ahern enhanced his image by being the first Irish leader to address a joint session of the British Parliament. Capitalizing on those developments (as well as on the nation's continued excellent economic conditions and the recent significant progress regarding Northern Ireland [see Foreign relations, above, for details]), *Fianna Fáil* secured only three fewer seats in the May 24 *Dáil* elections than it had in 2002.

On September 13, 2007, corruption issues returned to the forefront of attention as Ahern began several days of sworn testimony before the Mahon Tribunal. His testimony raised substantial doubt about the accuracy of his varied accounts in the early and mid-1990s. On September 26 Enda KENNY, *Fine Gael* leader, entered a motion of no confidence in the government on the basis of Ahern's dubious testimony. However, the motion was defeated 81–76, with the Green Party, Progressive Democrats, and 4 independents remaining in support of the government.

In March 2008 testimony before the tribunal, Ahern's former constituency secretary contradicted significant aspects of Ahern's earlier testimony, prompting Ahern's coalition partners to call for a clear explanation. On April 2 Ahern announced his intention to resign on May 6, a date that permitted him to address a joint session of the U.S. Congress on April 30 as previously scheduled. On his final day in office Ahern met with Northern Ireland's soon-to-retire First Minister Ian Paisley for a commemorative ceremony in which Ahern praised Paisley and, implicitly, himself for their roles in the return of self-rule to Northern Ireland.

Fianna Fáil's Brian Cowen, who had held numerous cabinet posts (most recently as deputy prime minister and finance minister), was nominated by the *Dáil* by a vote of 88–76 to succeed Ahern as prime minister in May 2008. Despite looming economic challenges (rising unemployment, declining revenues, and turbulent international markets), Cowen stated that his new government's first order of business was the national referendum due on June 12, 2008, regarding the EU's proposed Lisbon Treaty. Among the parties in Parliament, only *Sinn Féin* opposed ratification of the treaty, which was also endorsed by many business and labor leaders. However, 53.4 percent of the voters said "no" to the treaty, polling indicating that confusion over the meaning and implications of the treaty's provisions was a major factor in the result. In the immediate aftermath of the defeat, it was unclear how the Irish government would respond. Cowen appeared at first to rule out a second vote, and at a December meeting of the European Council—heads of the 27-member EU states—he presented the misgivings and doubts of the Irish people about the implications regarding taxes, military neutrality, and social policies of Ireland signing on to the Lisbon Treaty. In response, the council agreed that legal guarantees would be given to protect Irish sovereignty, and the Irish government set October 2, 2009, as the date for a second referendum, all the parliamentary parties except *Sinn Fein* again calling for a "yes" vote.

In the midst of the global financial crisis, which had hit Ireland particularly hard, public opinion polls from January 2009 onward showed a likely sizable margin of victory for ratification of the EU treaty as voters pondered the potentially negative economic consequences of a "no" vote. On a turnout of 59 percent, voters supported ratification 67 to 33 percent, thereby salvaging the EU's prospects. However, the vote appeared to do little to buoy sagging public support for the prime minister or even to give assurances of the survival of his government until the next scheduled election, in 2012. Within a week of the referendum, corruption charges associated with *Fianna Fáil* reemerged as John O'DONOGHUE resigned as speaker of the *Dáil* over a report of less than forthright disclosure of extravagant charges to his expense account. By mid-October the Green Party was threatening to leave the government to avoid being tainted by the corruption charges; it also voiced objections to the government's recent bank rescue plan.

POLITICAL PARTIES

Government Parties:

Fianna Fáil. Founded in 1926 by Éamon de Valéra, *Fianna Fáil* ("Soldiers of Destiny") advocates the peaceful ending of partition, the promotion of social justice, and the pursuit of national self-sufficiency. It held governmental responsibility in 1932–1948, 1951–1954, 1957–1973, 1977–1981, and March–November 1982, and was then in opposition for over four years. During this period Charles Haughey survived a number of challenges to his leadership, most notably from Desmond O'Malley (see PD, below), who withdrew from the party in 1985. O'Malley, sitting as an independent, was joined by one *Fianna Fáil* representative in voting to approve the Anglo-Irish Agreement in November 1985, the remainder of the party voting in opposition. Haughey returned as prime minister after the 1987 election, but the *Fianna Fáil* legislative plurality was reduced from 81 to 77 seats in the June 1989 balloting, creating, for the first time in Irish history, a governmental impasse. Consequently, Haughey turned to the PD and on July 12 formed *Fianna Fáil*'s first coalition government.

Haughey resigned in January 1992 and was succeeded by longtime party rival Albert Reynolds. In November the party suffered its worst electoral showing since World War II, winning only 68 seats, forcing Reynolds to seek support from the Labour Party (below). The coalition collapsed with Reynolds's resignation in November 1994, with *Fianna Fáil* going into opposition while remaining the largest parliamentary party. In the subsequent election of June 1997, however, *Fianna Fáil* increased its strength to 77 seats, enough for party chief Bertie Ahern to form a minority government in coalition with the PD and a few independents. Reynolds campaigned for but lost the party's nomination for the presidency in September 1997 to Mary McAleese, who won the nationwide election the following October.

In the 2002 legislative elections *Fianna Fáil* won 81 seats in the *Dáil* and 30 seats in the Senate. Ahern formed a new coalition government with the PD on June 6, 2002. McAleese was reelected president, without opposition, in October 2004. Following the 2007 elections *Fianna Fáil* held 77 seats in the *Dáil* (plus the officially nonpartisan chair), having overcome predictions of a poor showing that had been based on the ongoing financial scandals involving Ahern and former party leader Haughey.

In September 2007 Ahern announced that the party planned to reorganize on an all-Ireland basis that would include the six counties in Northern Ireland.

After Ahern announced his impending resignation in early April 2008, Deputy Prime Minister Brian Cowen was elected unopposed as the new party leader.

Leaders: Brian COWEN (Prime Minister and Party Leader), Mary COUGHLAN (Deputy Prime Minister), Mary McALEESE (President of the Republic), Séan DORGAN (General Secretary).

Green Party (*Comhaontás Glas*). Founded in December 1981 as the Ecology Party of Ireland by Christopher FETTES, *Comhaontás Glas* is an Irish expression of the European Green movement. The group adopted the name Green Alliance in 1983 but took its present name in 1987 to clarify its political status. It captured its first legislative seat at the June 1989 balloting, won a different seat in 1992, and has held 2 of Ireland's 15 European Parliament seats since 1994. The party backed the proposal legalizing divorce that was narrowly approved by referendum in November 1995.

In the June 1997 election the Green Party increased its strength to two seats. With its poll standing on the rise, the party's May 2000 convention featured a contentious debate over possible participation in a coalition government after the next election. The Green Party won six seats in the 2002 elections but did not join the government. It again won six seats in 2007 and, in view of the depletion of the Progressive Democrats, joined the new cabinet. That decision prompted the resignation as party leader of Trevor SARGENT, who had pledged not to enter government with *Fianna Fáil*.

Leaders: John GORMLEY (Party Leader), Dan BOYLE (Chair), Mary WHITE (Deputy Leader).

Progressive Democrats (*Dan Páirtí Daonlathach*—PD). The PD was organized in December 1985 by former *Fianna Fáil* legislator Desmond O'MALLEY as an alternative to a "party system . . . based on the civil war divisions of 65 years ago." Accused by critics of being a "Thatcherite," O'Malley called for fundamental tax reform, government tax cuts, and support for private enterprise. The party won 14 *Dáil* seats in 1987, 8 of which were lost in the 1989 election, after which it joined with *Fianna Fáil* in a coalition government. It withdrew in 1992, and at the resultant November legislative poll its representation rose from 6 seats to 10. O'Malley resigned as leader in October 1993 and was succeeded by Mary HANEY, the first female head of a significant Irish party. In the June 1997 elections the PD won 4 seats and joined *Fianna Fáil* in the new government. In the 2002 elections for the *Dáil,* the PD won 8 seats, and it subsequently formed another coalition government with *Fianna Fáil*.

Haney resigned as party leader in September 2006 in favor of Michael McDOWELL. Following the party's poor showing in the 2007 elections (only two seats won), a series of leadership shifts culminated in the election of Ciarán CANNON as new party leader in April 2008. By summer party leaders were talking publicly of disbanding the party. With O'Malley, Haney, and Cannon announcing their support for disbanding, delegates to a special party conference in November voted 201–161 to end the party's existence. Haney continued as minister of health, sitting as an independent, and the party continued to receive state subsidies through early 2009. In the June 2009 local elections, before which the party stopped receiving state funds, no candidate appeared on a ballot under the PD label, though more than 20 former members were elected as councilors on other party tickets. Shortly thereafter, the party presented its archive to a Dublin university.

Leader: Noel GREALISH (Caretaker).

Opposition Parties:

Fine Gael. *Fine Gael* ("Family of the Irish") was formed in September 1933 through the amalgamation of parties that had accepted the 1921 partition, led by *Cumann na nGaedheal* (the ruling party in 1923–1932). It advocates ultimate union with Northern Ireland, financial encouragement of industry, promotion of foreign investment, and full development of agriculture. Its inability to win a majority in the *Dáil* led to the formation of coalition governments with the Labour Party in 1948–1951, 1954–1957, 1973–1977, 1981–1982, and, under the premiership of Garret FitzGerald, 1982–1987. *Fine Gael*'s slump from 70 to 51 seats in the February 1987 election yielded the surprise resignation of FitzGerald, with former justice minister Alan DUKES being named opposition leader.

At the June 1989 election the party increased its parliamentary representation to 55, remaining in opposition. In November 1990 Dukes resigned and was replaced by his more rightist deputy, John Bruton. At the November 1992 balloting *Fine Gael*'s legislative representation fell to 45 seats, its poorest showing since 1948. Nevertheless, the political crisis of late 1994 enabled Bruton to form a three-party coalition government with Labour and the Democratic Left (see under Labour Party, below). In the June 1997 elections *Fine Gael* increased its strength to 54 seats, but the poor showing of Labour forced *Fine Gael* to return to opposition.

In mid-July 2000 Bruton proposed that *Fine Gael* and Labour consider a preelection pact before the next general election, but a Labour spokesman responded that his party preferred to campaign on its own platform. On January 31, 2001, Bruton lost a confidence vote among the party's MPs, and on February 9 Michael NOONAN, a former minister of justice, succeeded him as leader of the opposition. Noonan in turn resigned after *Fine Gael*'s poor performance in the 2002 balloting for the House of Representatives (31 seats on a 22.5 percent vote share); he was succeeded by Enda Kenny, a former minister of tourism and trade. Kenny led *Fine Gael* to an increase of 20 seats in the 2007 elections.

Leaders: Enda KENNY (Leader of the Opposition), Richard BRUTON (Deputy Leader), Tom HAYES (Parliamentary Chair).

Labour Party (*Páirtí Lucht Oibre*). Originating in 1912 as an adjunct of the Trades Union Congress (TUC), the Labour Party became a separate entity in 1930. It has traditionally advocated far-reaching social security and medical services, public ownership of many industries and services, better working conditions and increased participation of workers in management, expanded agricultural production, protection of the home market, and cooperation and ultimate union with Northern Ireland.

In October 1982 its leader in Parliament, Michael O'LEARY, resigned from the party following its rejection of his proposal that Labour commit itself to formation of a coalition government with *Fine Gael* should the Haughey government fall. His successor, Richard (Dick) Spring, promptly negotiated an interparty agreement that permitted a *Fine Gael*–Labour coalition to assume office on December 14. The coalition collapsed because of Labour's objection to budget cuts advanced by Prime Minister FitzGerald in January 1987. In opposition, Labour increased its parliamentary representation from 12 seats to 15 in the June 1989 balloting.

In 1990 Labour joined with the Workers' Party (below) in backing the successful presidential candidacy of Mary Robinson, who had twice been a Labour parliamentary candidate but had left the party in 1985. In November 1992 Labour achieved its best-ever election result, winning 33 seats. In January 1993 the party entered into a majority coalition with *Fianna Fáil* that collapsed in November 1994, largely at Labour's instigation. The party then renewed its alliance with *Fine Gael,* joining a three-party coalition that also included the Democratic Left (DL). However, in the June 1997 elections Labour's strength was cut to 17 seats, forcing its return to the opposition. The electoral decline precipitated the resignation of Dick Spring as party leader and the announcement by the Labour leadership that henceforth the party was prepared to discuss joining a governing coalition with any party.

For the 1997 election the Labour Party joined forces with the DL, but the coalition's total of 21 seats was significantly below the 37 seats won in the 1992 poll by the two parties combined. Following months of discussions, Labour and the DL formally merged in January 1999, with Labour leader Ruairí QUINN becoming leader of the unified party and the former DL president, Proinsias DE ROSSA, becoming party president. (For additional information on the DL, see the 2007 *Handbook*.)

Despite heightened expectations, Labour won only 20 seats in the May 2002 elections, and Quinn did not contest the party leadership post again when his term expired in October. He was succeeded by Pat RABBITTE, who resigned in August 2007 after the party had failed to improve in the balloting held the previous May.

Leaders: Eamon GILMORE (Party Leader), Joan BURTON (Deputy Leader).

Sinn Féin. The islandwide *Sinn Féin* ("Ourselves Alone") was formed in 1905 to promote Irish independence and won a majority of the Irish seats in the 1918 UK elections. In conjunction with the IRA, which had been created in 1919 to conduct a guerrilla campaign against British forces, *Sinn Féin* helped lead the revolutionary movement that produced the Irish Free State. Many members left both *Sinn Féin* and the IRA at the formation in 1922 of the *Cumann na nGaedheal* (see *Fine Gael,* above) and in 1926 of *Fianna Fáil*. Its influence substantially reduced, *Sinn Féin* continued its strident opposition to partition while serving as the political wing of the outlawed IRA. A long-standing policy dispute within the IRA eventually led traditional nationalists, committed to continued violence, to form the Provisional IRA in 1969, while the Marxist-oriented rump, primarily devoted to nonviolent political action, continued to represent the "Official" IRA. The rump changed its party name to *Sinn Féin*–The Workers' Party in 1977 to differentiate itself from the Provisional *Sinn Féin* created by the Provisional IRA. In 1982 the Marxists relinquished the *Sinn Féin* identification entirely to the "Provos" and became the Workers' Party (below). (The "Provisional" label is sometimes still used, particularly in reference to the IRA.)

In supporting the IRA's goal of establishing a unified "democratic socialist republic," *Sinn Féin* contested several elections with the proviso that no successful candidate would sit in the *Dáil,* which it did not consider legitimate. In the February 1982 balloting, none of *Sinn Féin*'s seven candidates was successful, and it did not contest the national election in November. In November 1986, however, a party conference in Dublin voted 429 to 161 in favor of ending the policy against taking up *Dáil* seats. Party President Gerry Adams received support in the action by other leaders, including the Army Council of the IRA, while a splinter group left the conference in protest (see Republican *Sinn Féin,* below). The change in policy won no *Dáil* seats until June 1997, when *Sinn Féin* won one. *Sinn Féin* also scored significant electoral success in Northern Ireland in 1997 (see United Kingdom: Northern Ireland article).

At a special party conference held in Dublin on May 10, 1998, *Sinn Féin* overwhelmingly endorsed the April 10 Good Friday Agreement and agreed to take up seats in the proposed Northern Ireland Assembly. Amid speculation that *Sinn Féin* might win sufficient seats at the next general election to warrant its inclusion in a coalition government, in July 2000 the party won the Sligo mayoralty, its first such victory in over three decades. In the 2002 elections *Sinn Féin* won five seats in the *Dáil*. The party also won its first seats in the EU Parliament in the 2004 elections, one from the republic and one from Northern Ireland. It secured four seats in the *Dáil* in 2007.

Leaders: Gerard (Gerry) ADAMS (President), Mary Lou McDONALD (Vice President), Declan KEARNEY (Chair), Dawn DOYLE (General Secretary).

Other Parties:

Socialist Party (SP). The SP was founded in September 1996 by trade unionists, Dublin community activists, and members of Militant Labour. Advocating public ownership and democratic socialist planning in key sectors of the economy, the islandwide, nonsectarian party won one *Dáil* seat in June 1997. In the parliamentary debate on the Good Friday Agreement of April 10, 1998, SP leader Joe Higgins called for "a democratic and socialist alternative" to the proposed constitutional changes and objected to seeking voter approval of the pact on May 22, arguing against holding simultaneous referenda on the Northern Ireland accord and the EU's Amsterdam Treaty. The SP won one seat in the 1997 and 2002 elections.

The SP supports the abolition of the office of president, and President McAleese's unopposed election in 2004 provided additional emphasis for the party's efforts. The SP lost its sole seat in the *Dáil* in 2007 when Higgins finished fourth (with 15 percent of the vote) in a three-seat constituency.

Leader: Joe HIGGINS.

Workers' Party (*Páirtí na nOibri*). Tracing its origin to the original *Sinn Féin* and known from 1977 until 1982 as *Sinn Féin*–The Workers' Party, the Workers' Party is a product of the independence and unification movements that have spanned most of the 20th century. Marxist in outlook and dedicated to the establishment of a united, socialist Ireland, the party captured its first *Dáil* seat in 20 years at the June 1981 election and expanded its representation to three at the February 1982 balloting. After slipping to two seats in November 1982, the party won four seats in 1987 and seven in 1989. In February 1992, however, six of the party's seven MPs, including its leader, Proinsias De Rossa, broke away to form the Democratic Left after their proposal to replace "Leninist revolutionary tactics" with "democratic socialism" was narrowly voted down at a party conference. The rump group failed to secure parliamentary representation in the elections from 1992 through 2007. Its Northern Ireland wing, formerly known as the Workers' Party Ireland Clubs, holds no seats in either the UK House of Commons or the Northern Ireland Assembly.

Leaders: Mick FINNEGAN (President), John LOWRY (General Secretary).

Republican Sinn Féin. The Republican *Sinn Féin* was formed at the parent party's 1986 conference by some 30 dissidents who were vehemently opposed to participation in a *Dáil* that did not include representatives from Northern Ireland. It is allegedly linked to Northern Ireland's violent Continuity IRA, although party leaders have denied any connection. The party president branded the IRA's May 2000 decision to put its arms dumps under international supervision as "an overt act of treachery."

Leaders: Ruairí Ó BRÁDAIGH (President); Des DALTON and Catherine Knowles McGUIRK (Vice Presidents).

Irish Republican Socialist Party (IRSP). Founded in 1974, the IRSP serves as the political wing of a fringe republican paramilitary group, the Irish National Liberation Army (INLA). The IRSP advocates a democratic socialist republic throughout all of Ireland's 32 counties. It opposed the April 1998 Good Friday Agreement as "a betrayal" that "institutionalizes sectarianism, fails to properly address the imperialist role that Britain has played . . . and locks the Irish people into a capitalist alliance." In August 1998, as urged by the party leadership, the INLA announced a cease-fire. In September 1999 the IRSP confirmed that it had drafted a nonaggression pact for presentation to the INLA and loyalist paramilitary groups in Northern Ireland.

Leaders: Willie GALLAGHER, Fra HALLIGAN.

Communist Party of Ireland—CPI (*Páirtí Cummanach na hÉireann*). An islandwide grouping first formed in 1921 and reestablished in 1933, the CPI split into northern and southern factions during World War II and remained separate until 1970. The party continues to advocate a united, socialist Ireland.

Leaders: Lynda WALKER (Chair), Eugene McCARTAN (General Secretary).

Other parties include several small religious and profamily parties, many of which were formed in opposition to the legalization of divorce in the constitutional referendum held in November 1995. Perhaps the most widely known is the **National Party,** founded in 1995 under the leadership of Nora BENNIS. Others include the **Christian Solidarity Party,** founded by Gerard CASEY in July 1994 as the Christian Centrist Party and now led by party president Cathal LOFTUS, and the **People of Ireland Party** (*Muintir na nÉireann Páirtí Teoranta*), founded in 1995 and led by Richard GREENE.

An **Independent *Fianna Fáil*** was established in 1970 by the late Neil BLANEY, a former *Fianna Fáil* minister, and, following his death, was led by his son Harry BLANEY from 1997 to 2002, when he retired and was replaced by his son Niall BLANEY. In 2006 Blaney announced he was joining *Fianna Fáil*; he was reelected to the *Dáil* on the *Fianna Fáil* ballot in the 2007 elections. Other parties with small followings include the **South Kerry Independent Alliance,** the **Natural Law Party,** the far-left **Socialist Workers' Party,** the anarchist **Workers' Solidarity Movement,** and **People Before Profit,** a left-wing alliance launched in October 2005 that received approximately 9,000 first-preference votes in the 2007 elections.

LEGISLATURE

The Irish **Parliament** (*Oireachtas*) is a bicameral body composed of an upper chamber (Senate) and a lower chamber (House of Representatives).

Senate (*Seanad Éireann*). The upper chamber consists of 60 members serving five-year terms. Eleven are nominated by the prime minister and 49 are elected—6 by graduates of the universities and 43 from candidates put forward by five vocational panels: cultural and educational interests, 5 seats; labor, 11; industry and commerce, 9; agriculture, 11; and public administration, 7. The electing body, a college of some 900 members, includes members of the *Oireachtas* as well as county and county borough councillors. The power of the Senate extends primarily to delaying for a period of 90 days a bill passed by the *Dáil*. Technically, the house does not function on the basis of party divisions; however, following the most recent balloting beginning July 24, 2007, its composition was as follows: *Fianna Fáil,* 28 seats; *Fine Gael,* 14; the Labour Party, 6; the Progressive Democrats (PD), 2; the Green Party, 2; *Sinn Féin,* 1; and independents, 7. (The PD disbanded in 2009, 1 member subsequently sitting with *Fine Gael* and the other as an independent.)

Chair (*Cathaoirleach*): Patrick MOYLAN.

House of Representatives (*Dáil Éireann*). The *Dáil* currently has 166 members (*teachtaí dála,* familiarly called TDs or deputies) elected by direct suffrage through a single-transferable-vote form of proportional representation for five-year terms, assuming no dissolution. At the most recent balloting, held on May 24, 2007, *Fianna Fáil* won 78 seats (reduced to 77 after the election of a deputy from the party as *Ceann Comhairle* [Chair or Speaker]); *Fine Gael,* 51; the Labour Party, 20; the Green Party, 6; *Sinn Féin,* 4; the Progressive Democrats (PD), 2; and independents, 5. (The 2 members elected on the PD ticket in 2007 sat as independents after the PD disbanded in 2009.)

Chair (*Ceann Comhairle*): Séamus KIRK.

CABINET

[as of September 1, 2009]

Prime Minister (*Taoiseach*)	Brian Cowen (FF)
Deputy Prime Minister (*Tánaiste*)	Mary Coughlan (FF) [f]
Ministers	
Agriculture, Fisheries, and Food	Brendan Smith (FF)
Arts, Sports, and Tourism	Martin Cullen (FF)
Communications, Energy, and Natural Resources	Eamon Ryan (GP)
Community, Rural, and *Gaeltacht* Affairs	Éamon Ó Cuív (FF)
Defense	Willie O'Dea (FF)
Education and Science	Batt O'Keefe (FF)
Enterprise, Trade, and Employment	Mary Coughlan (FF) [f]
Environment, Heritage, and Local Government	John Gormley (GP)
Finance	Brian Lenihan (FF)
Foreign Affairs	Micheál Martin (FF)
Health and Children	Mary Harney (ind.) [f]
Justice, Equality, and Law Reform	Dermot Ahern (FF)
Social and Family Affairs	Mary Hanafin (FF) [f]
Transport	Noel Dempsey (FF)

[f] = female

Note: FF = *Fianna Fáil;* GP = Green Party.

COMMUNICATIONS

Although free expression is constitutionally guaranteed, a Censorship of Publications Board under the jurisdiction of the Ministry of Justice is empowered to halt publication of books. Moreover, under the Broadcasting Act 1960, as amended in 1976 and interpreted by the Supreme Court in a July 1982 decision involving a ban against the Provisional *Sinn Féin,* individuals and political parties committed to undermining the state may be denied access to the public broadcasting media.

Press. All newspapers are privately owned and edited, but the Roman Catholic Church exerts considerable restraining influence. The following are English-language dailies published in Dublin, unless otherwise noted: *Sunday Independent* (282,000), pro–*Fine Gael*; *Sunday World* (284,000, including Northern Ireland); *Irish Independent* (161,000), pro–*Fine Gael*; *Evening Herald* (82,000), pro–*Fine Gael*; *The Irish Times* (119,000), independent; *The Star* (107,000), independent; *Sunday Tribune* (70,000), independent; *Irish Examiner* (Cork, 56,000), independent; *Sunday Business Post* (54,000), independent.

News agencies. There is no domestic facility, although a number of foreign bureaus maintain offices in Dublin.

Broadcasting and computing. Until mid-1990 *Radio Telefís Éireann* (RTE), an autonomous statutory corporation, operated all radio and television stations, including two television channels (both carrying advertising) and *Radió na Gaeltachta,* which broadcasts to Irish-speaking areas. In 1988 an Independent Radio and Television Commission (IRTC) was established, which in 1989 awarded a franchise for an independent television channel, TV3; at present there are also more than 20 commercial radio stations. In an attempt to preserve and nurture the growth of Ireland's native language, in 1997 the government began subsidizing the nation's first Gaelic-language television channel, *Teilifís na Gaelige*. As of 2008 there were 625.4 Internet users per 1,000 inhabitants.

INTERGOVERNMENTAL REPRESENTATION

Ambassador to the U.S.: Michael COLLINS.

U.S. Ambassador to Ireland: Daniel M. ROONEY.

Permanent Representative to the UN: Anne ANDERSON.

IGO Memberships (Non-UN): BIS, CEUR, EBRD, EIB, ESA, EU, Eurocontrol, IEA, Interpol, IOM, OECD, OSCE, PCA, WCO, WTO.

ISRAEL

State of Israel
Medinat Yisrael (Hebrew)
Dawlat Israil (Arabic)

Note: Information on Palestinian affairs, formerly included (until the 2008 edition) in this article under Occupied and Previously Occupied Territories, is now covered in the article at the end of the Governments section called the Palestinian Authority/Palestine Liberation Organization.

Political Status: Independent republic established May 14, 1948; under multiparty parliamentary regime.

Area: 8,463 sq. mi. (21,920 sq. km.), including inland water (172 sq. mi., 445 sq. km.).

Population: 5,548,523 (1995C); 7,341,000 (2008E). Area and population figures include East Jerusalem (27 sq. mi. [70 sq. km.] prior to subsequent unilateral expansion), which Israel occupied in 1967 and formally annexed in 1980 in an action not recognized by the United Nations or the United States (which maintains its embassy in Tel Aviv). Also included is a 444-square-mile (1,150 sq. km.) sector of the Golan Heights to which Israeli forces withdrew under a 1974 disengagement agreement with Syria and which was placed under Israeli law in December 1981. The figures do not include the Gaza Strip (most of which was turned over to Palestinian control in May 1994 prior to a total turnover in 2005) and the West Bank (from portions of which Israel began withdrawing in May 1994), which encompassed an area of about 2,320 square miles (6,020 sq. km.) and a combined population of approximately 3,449,000 in 2002.

Major Urban Centers (2005E): JERUSALEM (709,000, including East Jerusalem), Tel Aviv/Jaffa (375,000), Haifa (269,000), Rishon LeZiyyon (220,000), Ashdod (200,000).

Official Languages: Hebrew, Arabic. English, which was an official language under the British Mandate from the League of Nations, is taught in the secondary schools and is widely spoken.

Monetary Unit: New Shekel (market rate December 1, 2009: 3.77 shekels = $1US).

President: Shimon PERES (*Kadima*); elected by the *Knesset* in second-round balloting on June 13, 2007, and inaugurated for a seven-year term on July 15, succeeding Moshe KATSAV (*Likud*). (*Knesset* Speaker Dalia ITZIK [*Kadima*] had been serving in an acting presidential capacity since January 25, 2007. See Political background, below, for details.)

Prime Minister: Benjamin NETANYAHU (*Likud*); nominated by the president on February 20, 2009, to form a new government following the legislative elections of February 20 and sworn in as head of a new coalition government on March 31 in succession to Ehud OLMERT (*Kadima*), who had remained in a caretaker capacity after announcing his resignation on September 21, 2008.

THE COUNTRY

The irregularly shaped area constituting the State of Israel is not completely defined by agreed boundaries, its territorial jurisdiction being determined in part by military armistice agreements entered into at the conclusion of Israel's war of independence in 1948–1949. The territory under de facto Israeli control increased substantially as a result of Israel's military occupation of Arab territories in the Sinai Peninsula (since returned to Egypt), the Gaza Strip, the West Bank of the Jordan River (including the Old City of Jerusalem), and the Golan Heights following the Arab-Israeli War of 1967. (The Gaza Strip is now under Palestinian control, as are sections of the West Bank.) Those currently holding Israeli citizenship encompass a heterogeneous population that is approximately 80 percent Jewish but also includes important Arab Christian, Muslim, and Druze minorities. As of 2007 women

constituted 47 percent of the paid workforce, concentrated in agriculture, teaching, administration, and health care.

Following independence, Israel emerged as a technologically progressive, highly literate, and largely urbanized nation in the process of rapid development based on scientific exploitation of its agricultural and industrial potentialities. Agriculture has since diminished in importance but remains a significant economic sector, its most important products being citrus fruits, field crops, vegetables, and export-oriented nursery items. The industrial sector includes among its major components high-tech manufactures, cut diamonds, textiles, processed foods, chemicals, and military equipment. U.S. financial assistance, tourism, and direct aid from Jews in the United States and elsewhere are also of major economic importance.

Defense requirements generated a highly adverse balance of trade and contributed to a rate of inflation that escalated to more than 400 percent prior to the imposition of austerity measures in mid-1985. However, inflation declined dramatically to less than 16 percent in 1988, and Israel experienced one of the highest GDP growth rates in the world in the first half of the 1990s, while unemployment, which had peaked at more than 11 percent in 1992, dropped to 6 percent by the end of 1996. The conservative government installed in 1996 pursued pro-business policies (most notably extensive privatization of state-run enterprises) and a commitment to budget austerity. Nevertheless, growth slowed significantly in subsequent years, the downturn being attributed in part to a lack of progress in the Middle East peace process.

The economy rebounded dramatically in 2000, with GDP growth of 7.4 percent being achieved and inflation dropping to nearly zero. However, conditions subsequently reversed just as sharply in the wake of renewed government/Palestinian violence, the "burst of the technology bubble," and the collateral decline in the global economy. Deep recession was marked by GDP declines of 0.9 percent in 2001 and 1 percent in 2002. In the face of growing budget deficits, the administration proposed emergency spending cuts in 2002, prompting conflict within the government coalition.

Modest growth (1.3 percent) resumed in 2003, and GDP rose by 4 percent in 2004 and 5.2 percent in 2005. The International Monetary Fund (IMF) praised the government for reforming the pension system and accelerating privatization, although such measures prompted several large-scale strikes on the part of labor groups. In addition, unemployment remained unacceptably high, even though it dropped slightly from 10.4 percent in 2004 to 9.1 percent in 2005. In 2006 the IMF noted that recent macroeconomic policies and structural reforms had opened up Israel's economy, increased its competitiveness, and attracted foreign investment.

Despite the war with Hezbollah in Lebanon in mid-2006, GDP grew by an average of 5.3 percent annually in 2006–2007, while unemployment declined to 7.5 percent in the latter year. Inflation was nonexistent in 2006 but rose to 3.4 percent in 2007. Increased exports, the "innovative" technology sector, and heavy foreign investment were credited with underpinning the recent strong economic performance, which included a surplus in the government's budget in 2007.

Although GDP grew by 4.3 percent in 2008, the effects of the global economic crisis were apparent by the last quarter of the year as exports plummeted and the credit crunch depressed investment and strained the financial sector. The government consequently implemented a stimulus plan, established a new regulatory structure for capital markets, provided guarantees for exporters, and negotiated new wage and benefit packages with business and workers. Officials declared the economy to be in recovery by the fall of 2009, although growth of only 0.5 percent was predicted for the year, with unemployment of approximately 7 percent.

GOVERNMENT AND POLITICS

Political background. Israel's modern history dates from the end of the 19th century with the rise of the world Zionist movement and establishment of Jewish agricultural settlements in territory that was then part of the Ottoman Empire. In the Balfour Declaration of 1917 the British government expressed support for the establishment in Palestine of a national home for the Jewish people, provided that the rights of "existing non-Jewish communities" were not prejudiced. With the abrogation of Turkish rule at the end of World War I, the area was assigned to Great Britain under a League of Nations Mandate that incorporated provisions of the Balfour Declaration. British rule continued until May 1948, despite increasing unrest on the part of local Arabs during the 1920s and 1930s and Jewish elements during and after World War II. In 1947 the UN General Assembly adopted a resolution calling for the division of Palestine into Arab and Jewish states and the internationalization of Jerusalem and its environs, but the controversial measure could not be implemented because of Arab opposition. Nonetheless, Israel declared its independence coincident with British withdrawal on May 14, 1948. Although the new state was immediately attacked by Egypt, Syria, Lebanon, Jordan, and Iraq, it was able to maintain itself in the field, and the armistice agreements concluded under UN auspices in 1949 gave Israel control over nearly one-third more territory than had been assigned to it under the original UN resolution. A second major military encounter between Israel and Egypt in 1956 resulted in Israeli conquest of the Gaza Strip and the Sinai Peninsula. In two further Arab-Israeli conflicts, Israel seized territories from Jordan (1967) and from Egypt and Syria (1967 and 1973). Cease-fire disengagements resulted, however, in partial Israeli withdrawal from territory in the Syrian Golan Heights and the Egyptian Sinai. Withdrawal from the remaining Sinai territory, except for Taba (see Occupied and Previously Occupied Territories, below), was completed in April 1982 under a peace treaty with Egypt concluded on March 26, 1979. The Israeli sector of the Golan Heights, on the other hand, was placed under Israeli law on December 14, 1981.

The internal governmental structure of modern Israel emerged from institutions established by the British administration and the Jewish community during the Mandate. For three decades after independence, a series of multiparty coalitions built around the moderate socialist Israel Workers' Party (Mapai)—enlarged in 1968 to become the Israel Labor Party—governed with relatively little change in policy and turnover in personnel. Save for a brief period in 1953–1955, David BEN-GURION was the dominant political figure until his retirement in 1963. He was succeeded by Levi ESHKOL (until his death in 1969), Golda MEIR (until her retirement in 1974), and Yitzhak RABIN, the first native-born Israeli to become prime minister.

Prime Minister Rabin tendered his resignation in December 1976, following his government's defeat on a parliamentary nonconfidence motion, but he remained in office in a caretaker capacity pending a general election. On April 8, 1977, prior to balloting scheduled for May 17, Rabin was forced to resign his party post in the wake of revelations that he and his wife had violated Israeli law concerning overseas bank deposits. His successor as party leader and acting prime minister, Shimon PERES, proved unable to reverse mounting popular dissatisfaction with a deteriorating economy and evidence of official malfeasance. In a stunning electoral upset, a new reform party, the Democratic Movement for Change, captured a significant proportion of Labor's support, and the opposition *Likud* party, having obtained a sizable legislative plurality, formed the nucleus of a coalition government under Menachem BEGIN on June 19. Begin succeeded in forming a new governing coalition on August 4 after the *Likud* front had emerged with a one-seat advantage in the June 30 *Knesset* balloting.

Prime Minister Begin's startling announcement on August 28, 1983, of his intention to resign both his governmental and party positions for "personal reasons" (largely the death of his wife) was believed by many observers also to have been influenced by severe Israeli losses from the 1982 war in Lebanon (see Foreign relations, below). The Central Committee of *Likud*'s core party, *Herut,* thereupon elected Yitzhak SHAMIR as its new leader on September 1, and the constituent parties of the ruling coalition agreed to support Shamir, who, after failing in an effort to form a national unity government, was sworn in as prime minister on October 10.

Amid increasing criticism of the Shamir administration, particularly in its handling of economic affairs, five *Likud* coalition deputies voted with the opposition on March 22, 1984, in calling for legislative dissolution and the holding of a general election. In balloting on July 23, Labor (44 seats) marginally outpolled *Likud,* (41 seats). Extensive interparty discussion followed, yielding agreement on August 31 on the formation of a national unity coalition on the basis of a rotating premiership. Thus, Labor's Peres was approved as the new prime minister on September 13 with the understanding that he would exchange positions with Vice Prime Minister and Foreign Affairs Minister Shamir midway through a full parliamentary term of four years. On October 20, 1986, Shamir, in turn, became prime minister, with Peres assuming Shamir's former posts.

The election of November 1, 1988, conducted in the midst of a major Palestinian uprising (intifada) that had erupted in the occupied territories 11 months earlier, yielded an even closer balance between the leading parties, with *Likud* winning 40 *Knesset* seats and Labor 39. Conceivably, *Likud* could have assembled a working majority in alliance with a number of right-wing religious parties. However, most of the latter refused to participate in an administration that did not commit itself to legislation excluding from provisions of the law of return (hence from automatic citizenship) those converted to Judaism under Reform or Conservative (as opposed to Orthodox) auspices. As a result, Shamir concluded a new agreement with the Labor leadership, whereby he continued as prime minister and Peres assumed the finance portfolio in a government installed on December 22.

By early 1990 the coalition was under extreme stress because of divergent views on the terms of peace talks with the Palestinians. The principal differences turned on *Likud*'s insistence that no Arabs from East Jerusalem participate in the talks or in future elections and that Israel should be accorded a right of withdrawal from the negotiations should the Palestine Liberation Organization (PLO) become even remotely involved. There were also deep fissures within *Likud* itself, caused primarily by a group of hard-liners, including Industry and Commerce Minister Ariel SHARON, who were opposed to a Palestinian franchise. Following an angry exchange with Shamir in the *Knesset* on February 12, Sharon resigned from the cabinet. Ten days later the Labor Party issued an ultimatum to the prime minister to accept its peace formula (which called for at least one delegate each from Palestinian deportees and those maintaining partial residence in East Jerusalem) or face dissolution of the government. On March 12 Shamir dismissed Peres from the cabinet, prompting Labor's other ministers to resign. Three days later, in the wake of a successful nonconfidence motion (the first in Israeli parliamentary history), Shamir assumed the leadership of a caretaker administration. A lengthy period of intense negotiation followed, with Shamir on June 11 forming a *Likud*-dominated right-wing government whose two-seat majority turned on the support of dissidents from Labor and *Agudat Yisrael,* a periodic Labor ally. In November 1990 *Agudat Yisrael* formally joined the ruling coalition, increasing the government's *Knesset* majority to six.

In February 1992 former prime minister Rabin gained control of the Labor Party from longtime rival Peres, who had been unable since 1977 to lead Labor to the formation of a government in its own right. Four months later, in what was termed more of a *Likud* debacle than a Labor triumph, Labor won a plurality of 44 *Knesset* seats. It subsequently formed a new administration on July 12 in coalition with the recently organized *Meretz* (itself a coalition of three left-of-center parties) and the ultraorthodox Sephardi Torah Guardians (Shas).

On March 24, 1993, Ezer WEIZMAN, a former fighter pilot and former *Likud* hard-liner who had subsequently become a Labor Party leader and an outspoken advocate of peace with the Arabs, was elected by the *Knesset* as Israel's seventh president. The following day former deputy foreign minister Benjamin NETANYAHU, who called for "a much tougher line" in addressing the Palestinian issue, was elected in a party contest to succeed Shamir as *Likud* leader. The Labor/*Likud* split on the Palestinian question came into even sharper focus in September when Rabin signed the historic agreement with the PLO that launched the Palestinian self-rule process. (See the article on the Palestinian Authority/Palestine Liberation Organization for details.)

In mid-July 1994 two MPs from *Yiud,* a breakaway faction of the ultranationalist *Tzomet,* agreed to enter the Labor government; however, they were prevented from doing so until late December because of a High Court ruling that their action would contravene antidefection legislation. Their support gave the Labor coalition 58 of 120 *Knesset* seats. However, on February 3, 1995, the six *Knesset* representatives of Shas, which had withdrawn from the ruling coalition in March 1994, announced that they were formally returning to opposition because of worsening security and the status of Jewish settlers in the West Bank.

Attention subsequently focused on negotiations over the second agreement in the Palestinian autonomy process, which was signed on September 28, 1995, and endorsed (in a non-mandatory vote) by the *Knesset* by 61–59 on October 6. However, domestic and regional political affairs were soon thrown into turmoil when Rabin was assassinated on November 4 by a right-wing Israeli opposed to the peace process. (Rabin's assailant, Yigul AMIR, was sentenced to life imprisonment in March 1996.) Foreign Minister Peres assumed the position of acting prime minister upon Rabin's death and was formally nominated by the Labor Party on November 13 to proceed with forming his own cabinet. The leaders of Labor, *Meretz,* and *Yiud* signed another government agreement on November 21, and the new cabinet was approved by the *Knesset* the following day, at which time Peres became prime minister.

Likud's Netanyahu defeated Peres by a vote of 50.5 percent to 49.5 percent in the first-ever direct balloting for prime minister on May 29, 1996. The election turned primarily on security issues, as Netanyahu adopted a hard-line stance toward any further "concessions" to the Palestinians, categorically ruled out the eventual creation of an independent Palestinian state, and pledged additional support for the Jewish settlers in the West Bank. Although Labor led all parties by winning 34 seats in the concurrent *Knesset* elections, Netanyahu was subsequently able to form a coalition government comprising representatives from *Tzomet* and the newly formed *Gesher* (the two parties with whom *Likud* had presented joint *Knesset* candidates), Shas, The Third Way (a new centrist grouping), *Yisrael B'Aliya,* and two ultraorthodox groups (the National Religious Party [NRP] and United Torah Judaism [UTJ]). Netanyahu formally succeeded Peres as prime minister on June 18 after the *Knesset* approved the new government by a vote of 62–50.

In addition to growing pressure regarding the Palestinian question, Prime Minister Netanyahu confronted several other significant domestic problems in 1997 and early 1998. Most notable was the controversial demand by the Orthodox Jewish movement that it be formally confirmed as the ultimate authority concerning conversions to Judaism. (The Reform and Conservative movements, strongly represented in the United States, were seeking to have conversions completed under their auspices legally recognized in Israel.) With his coalition government so dependent on backing from Orthodox parties, Netanyahu initially announced support for legislation confirming the Orthodox monopoly; however, a special committee was subsequently established to attempt to produce a compromise position. The prime minister also faced dissension within *Likud* and growing restiveness over budget austerity, the latter contributing to the decision by *Gesher* to leave the coalition in January 1998. (The government's legislative majority was reduced to a razor-thin 61–59 by *Gesher*'s withdrawal.) In addition, the administration was buffeted in early 1998 by changes in the leadership of Mossad (Israel's external security apparatus, which had recently bungled an assassination attempt in Jordan) and the somewhat chaotic and incomplete distribution of gas masks during the most recent U.S./Iraqi crisis. Regarding that confrontation, the Israeli government had emphasized that, unlike in 1991, it had been prepared to respond militarily if it had been targeted by Iraqi missiles. On March 4, 1998, the *Knesset* by a vote of 63–49 reelected President Weizman, who had added a degree of political impact to the previously essentially ceremonial post by criticizing the Netanyahu government's handling of the peace process.

Under heavy international pressure, Prime Minister Netanyahu signed an accord with PLO Chair Yasir Arafat in late October 1998 calling for further Israeli withdrawals from West Bank territory (the so-called Wye agreement). However, implementation of the plan stalled in December as Netanyahu futilely attempted to address the growing popular demand for progress toward a resolution on the Palestinian front while maintaining the allegiance of the religious parties in his coalition, who steadfastly opposed any land-for-peace compromise and, in fact, urged additional construction of Jewish settlements in the occupied territories. The government also exhibited a lack of unity regarding policies to address the deteriorating economic climate. Consequently, in mid-December, Netanyahu, facing the threat of a no-confidence motion in the *Knesset,* agreed to early elections.

On May 17, 1999, Ehud BARAK of the Labor-led One Israel coalition was elected prime minister, defeating Netanyahu by 56–44 percent. (Three minor candidates had withdrawn shortly before the election.) Barak had staked out a more liberal peace posture than Netanyahu, announcing he would, if elected, revitalize the Wye agreement, initiate final status discussions with the Palestinians, withdraw Israeli forces from Lebanon within one year, and relaunch discussions with Syria regarding the Golan Heights. Barak had also emphasized his economic platform because domestic problems such as burgeoning unemployment, rising inflation, and declining growth appeared to be playing a greater role in voting considerations that year than in previous elections. In concurrent balloting for the *Knesset,* One Israel secured a plurality of 26 seats, followed by *Likud* (19 seats), Shas (17), *Meretz* (10), and 11 parties with 6 or fewer seats. Subsequently, in view of his poor showing (as well as *Likud*'s collective electoral decline), Netanyahu resigned as chair of *Likud* and was succeeded by his longtime rival, Ariel Sharon.

After difficult and extended negotiations (during which he ultimately abandoned efforts to form a "national unity" government with *Likud*), Barak on July 6, 1999, received *Knesset* confirmation of a new cabinet, including One Israel (Labor, *Gesher,* and *Meimad*), Shas, *Yisrael B'Aliya, Meretz,* the NRP, and the new Center Party. Barak immediately launched into intense diplomatic efforts to resolve the Palestinian conflict. However, his coalition proved fractious in regard to the peace initiatives, and Shas, *Yisrael B'Aliya,* and the NRP left the cabinet on July 9, 2000, to protest potential "concessions" to the Palestinians. On July 31 the government suffered another setback when Moshe KATSAV of *Likud* defeated Shimon Peres for the Israeli presidency by a vote of 63–37 percent. (President Weizman had resigned his post, ostensibly because of poor health, although he had recently been subjected to an investigation concerning gifts he had received as a cabinet member a decade earlier.) In addition, *Gesher*'s minister resigned from the cabinet on August 2.

Although he had survived several nonconfidence votes, Prime Minister Barak, faced with an apparent lack of support in the *Knesset* for his peace efforts, announced his resignation on December 9, 2000, and called for a special prime ministerial election as a national referendum of sorts on the matter. (Barak remained in his post in an acting capacity pending the new balloting.) In view of the outbreak of the "second intifada," the Israeli electorate illustrated its rightward shift on February 6, 2001, by electing the "hawkish" Sharon as prime minister by a 62.4–37.6 percent margin over Barak, who quickly resigned as Labor's leader.

Somewhat surprisingly, Labor agreed to join the national unity government formed by Sharon on March 7, 2001. *Likud*'s other coalition partners included Shas, *Yisrael B'Aliya,* the new One Nation, the UTJ (represented at the deputy ministerial level), and the new National Union-*Yisrael Beiteinu* (NU-YB) *Knesset* faction (see National Union under Political Parties, below, for details). On October 15 the NU-YB ministers announced their intention to leave the cabinet, having adopted an even harsher stance toward the Palestinian question than Sharon. However, their resignation was temporarily rescinded following the assassination by Palestinian militants of Tourism Minister Rechavam ZE'EVI, leader of the NU-YB, on October 17. After the NU-YB faction finally departed the cabinet on March 15, 2002, Sharon bolstered his government by appointing new ministers from the NRP and *Gesher.* However, Sharon dismissed the Shas and UTJ ministers on May 20 when they failed to support his austerity budget proposals, although the Shas ministers were reinstated on June 3 after the package passed on a second vote in the *Knesset. Gesher* leader David Levy resigned his post as minister without portfolio on July 29.

The Labor ministers resigned from the cabinet on October 30, 2002, because of their opposition to the allocation of funding for Jewish settlements in the West Bank and Gaza Strip. Faced with the potential collapse of his national unity government and the loss of a government majority in the *Knesset,* Prime Minister Sharon called for new *Knesset* elections to be held in early 2003.

On November 19, 2002, Maj. Gen. (Ret.) Avraham MITZNA, the mayor of Haifa, was elected as the new Labor leader. He subsequently proposed a "markedly dovish" approach to the Palestinian question, calling for the closure of Jewish settlements in the Gaza Strip, the immediate evacuation of Israeli forces from the region, and the eventual unilateral Israeli withdrawal from portions of the West Bank should a comprehensive peace agreement fail to materialize. Subsequently, Sharon was easily reelected as *Likud* leader over arch-rival Benjamin Netanyahu. Sharon pledged to maintain his hard line regarding negotiations with the Palestinians, announcing that negotiations would not proceed until all violence ceased.

Likud scored a major victory in the January 28, 2003, *Knesset* election, securing 38 seats compared to 19 seats for the Labor/*Meimad* coalition. Labor subsequently pulled out of negotiations regarding a new coalition government, and on February 28 Sharon formed a new cabinet comprising *Likud, Shinui,* the NRP, and the NU-YB. In June 2004 Sharon dismissed two NRP ministers who opposed his plan for unilateral Israeli disengagement from the Gaza Strip (see Current issues, below), placing the government in minority status in the *Knesset.* The coalition finally collapsed on December 1 when the *Knesset* rejected Sharon's proposed 2005 budget. (Sharon dismissed the *Shinui* ministers who voted against the budget.) On January 10, 2005, Sharon secured *Knesset* approval (by a vote of 58–56) for a new cabinet comprising *Likud,* Labor, and the UTJ, with Labor leader Peres being named vice prime minister in the new government.

In August 2005 the Sharon government began its unilateral disengagement from the Gaza Strip, which prompted the resignation of Finance Minister Netanyahu and opened up deep fissures within *Likud.* Subsequently, in November, the *Knesset* rejected Sharon's appointment of two *Likud* loyalists to his cabinet. Meanwhile, Amir PERETZ defeated Shimon Peres as leader of Labor in an internal party ballot, and Peretz subsequently promised to end the party's participation in Sharon's government. Sharon consequently called an election for early 2006 and then announced his resignation from *Likud* and the formation of a new party, *Kadima,* or "Forward."

In January 2006 Prime Minister Sharon suffered a debilitating stroke. His deputy, former Jerusalem mayor Ehud OLMERT, became acting prime minister (as prescribed by law). Olmert steered *Kadima* to a plurality of 29 seats in the March 28 *Knesset* balloting, while the coalition of Labor and *Meimad* won 19 seats and *Likud* fell to 12 seats. Subsequently, Olmert was named interim prime minister by the cabinet (effective April 14) when the cabinet on April 11 declared Sharon permanently incapacitated. Olmert was inaugurated as prime minister on May 4 as head of a coalition government (*Kadima,* Labor/*Meimad,* Shas, and the small Pensioners Party) that controlled 67 *Knesset* seats. Olmert expanded the coalition with the addition of *Yisrael Beiteinu* (which had separated from the National Union to campaign on its own in the recent legislative poll) to the cabinet in late October.

Former prime minister Shimon Peres (who had helped launch *Kadima*) was elected president of Israel with 86 votes in second-round balloting in the *Knesset* on June 13, 2007, after his two challengers from the first round dropped out of the race. Peres was inaugurated on July 15 after President Katsav had formally resigned effective July 2 as part of an apparent plea-bargaining arrangement involving charges of sexual harassment. (Katsav, at his own request, had been declared "temporarily incapacitated" by a *Knesset* committee in January in order to combat the charges, his presidential duties having been assumed at that time by *Knesset* Speaker Dalia ITZIK. In 2009 Katsav was indicted on rape and sexual harassment charges, his trial continuing as of November.)

The government's legislative majority in the *Knesset* diminished in January 2008 when *Yisrael Beiteinu* left the cabinet and declined further in July when three legislators defected from the Pensioner's Party. Prime Minister Olmert formally resigned on September 21 because of the impact of an ongoing corruption investigation on his ability to govern. However, he remained in his post in a caretaker capacity as Tzipi LIVNI, recently elected as a new *Kadima* leader, attempted to form a new coalition government. When Livni on October 26 declared that those negotiations had collapsed, President Peres announced that new *Knesset* elections would be held. Although *Kadima* secured a one-seat plurality in the balloting on February 10, 2009, Livni again proved unable to forge a center-left coalition, and *Likud*'s Benjamin Netanyahu was inaugurated on March 31 as head of a center-right government that comprised *Likud*, Labor, Shas, *Yisrael Beiteinu*, and Jewish Home (*Habayit Hayehudi*, a successor to the NRP). The new government was endorsed by 69 legislators on March 31, but its majority grew to 74 the following day when agreement was reached with the UTJ, which was assigned two deputy ministerial positions.

Constitution and government. In the absence of a written constitution, the structure of Israeli government is defined by fundamental laws that provide for a president with largely ceremonial functions, a prime minister serving as effective chief executive, and a unicameral parliament (*Knesset*) to which the government is responsible and whose powers include the election of the president. Under legislation passed in March 1992, in what some observers initially construed as an historic change in the country's electoral system, the *Knesset* approved a law providing for the direct election of the prime minister. However, that legislation was reversed in March 2001, and the prime minister is now once again appointed by the president upon the recommendation of the *Knesset*. The prime minister's term of office corresponds to that of the *Knesset*.

The role of Judaism in the state has not been formally defined, but the Law of Return of 1950 established a right of immigration for all Jews (with a few exceptions, such as criminals). The judicial system is headed by a Supreme Court, and there are five district courts in addition to magistrates' and municipal courts. Specialized courts include labor courts and religious courts with separate benches for the Jewish, Muslim, Druze, and Christian communities, while military courts are important in the occupied areas.

Israel is divided into six administrative districts (*mehozot*), each of which is headed by a district commissioner appointed by the central government. Regions, municipalities, and rural municipalities are the principal administrative entities within the districts.

Foreign relations. Israeli foreign relations have been dominated by the requirements of survival in an environment marked by persistent hostility on the part of neighboring Arab states, whose overt measures have ranged from denying Israel use of the Suez Canal (wholly mitigated upon ratification of the 1979 peace treaty) to encouraging terrorist and guerrilla operations on Israeli soil. Although initially committed to "nonidentification" between East and West, Israel encountered hostility from the Soviet Union and most other communist governments (Romania and Yugoslavia being the most conspicuous exceptions) and began to rely primarily on Western countries, principally the United States, for political, economic, and military support. A member of the United Nations since 1949, Israel has frequently incurred condemnation by UN bodies because of its reprisals against Arab guerrilla attacks and its refusal both to reabsorb or pay compensation to Arab refugees from the 1948–1949 war and to accept the internationalization of Jerusalem as envisaged in the 1947 UN resolution. (Enactment on July 30, 1980, of a law reaffirming a unified Jerusalem as the nation's capital evoked additional condemnation.)

In May 1974 a Golan disengagement agreement was concluded with Syria, while Sinai disengagement accords were concluded with Egypt in January 1974 and September 1975. Under the latter, Israel withdrew its forces from the Suez Canal and evacuated the Abu Rudeis and Ras Sudar oil fields. Both Egypt and the United States agreed to make a "serious effort" to bring about collateral negotiations with Syria for further disengagement on the Golan Heights (no such negotiations were initiated prior to the launching of U.S.-inspired Middle East peace talks in early 1991).

In what was hailed as a major step toward peace in the region, Egyptian President Anwar Sadat startled the world in November 1977 by accepting an Israeli invitation to visit Jerusalem. While Sadat yielded little during an unprecedented address to the *Knesset* on November 20, his very presence on Israeli soil kindled widespread hope that the lengthy impasse in Arab-Israeli relations might somehow be broken. Subsequent discussions produced potential bases of settlement in regard to the Sinai but no public indication of substantial rethinking of established positions, on either side, in regard to the West Bank and Gaza. Israel, in responding to Egyptian demands for a meaningful "concession," announced a willingness to grant Palestinians in Gaza and the West Bank "self-rule," coupled with an Israeli right to maintain military installations in the occupied territories. Egypt, on the other hand, rejected the idea of an Israeli military presence and continued to press for Palestinian self-determination.

The prospects for a meaningful accord fluctuated widely during the first eight months of 1978, culminating in a historic summit convened by U.S. President Jimmy Carter at Camp David, Maryland, on September 5. The unusually lengthy discussions yielded two major agreements—a "Framework for a Peace Treaty between Egypt and Israel" and a "Framework for Peace in the Middle East"—which were signed by President Sadat and Prime Minister Begin at the White House on September 17. In the course of subsequent negotiations in Washington, representatives of the two governments agreed on the details of a treaty and related documents, but the signing was deferred beyond the target date of December 17 because of disagreement about linkage to the second of the Camp David accords, which dealt with autonomy for the inhabitants of the West Bank and Gaza and provided for Israeli withdrawal into specified security locations. In addition, Egypt wished to modify an important treaty provision by an "interpretive annex," stating that prior commitments to other Arab states should have precedence over any obligations assumed in regard to Israel. Progress toward resolving the impasse was registered in early March 1979, and the treaty was formally signed in Washington on March 26, followed by an exchange of ratifications on April 25. In a set of minutes accompanying the treaty, the parties agreed that "there is no assertion that this treaty prevails over other treaties or agreements" and that, within a month after the exchange of instruments of ratification, negotiations would be instituted to define "the modalities for establishing the elected self-governing authority" for the Gaza Strip and West Bank. While no significant progress on autonomy for the two regions was immediately forthcoming, the sixth and final phase of withdrawal from the Sinai, save for Taba, was completed on schedule in April 1982.

On June 6, 1982, Israeli forces invaded Lebanon. While the immediate precipitant of the incursion appeared to have been the shooting on June 3 of Israel's ambassador to the United Kingdom, the attack was far from unanticipated in view of a substantial buildup of Israeli military strength along the border in May. Code-named "Peace for Galilee," the attack was initially justified by Israel as necessary to establish a PLO-free zone extending 40–50 kilometers inside Lebanon. By June 14, however, Israeli forces had completely surrounded Beirut, shortly after U.S. President Ronald Reagan had announced that he would approve the dispatch of 800–1,000 U.S. marines to participate in an international force that would oversee the evacuation of Palestinian and Syrian forces from the Lebanese capital. On August 6 U.S. envoy Philip Habib reached agreement, through Lebanese intermediaries, on the PLO withdrawal, which commenced on August 21.

In what was officially described as a "police action" necessitated by the assassination of Lebanese President-elect Bashir Gemayel on September 14, 1982, Israeli contingents entered West Beirut and took up positions around the Shatila and Sabra Palestinian refugee camps, where a substantial number of "terrorists" were alleged to have been left behind by the PLO. On September 18 it was revealed that a large-scale massacre of civilians had occurred at the hands of right-wing Phalangist militiamen, who had been given access to the camps by Israeli authorities. While the Israeli cabinet expressed its "deep grief and regret" over the atrocities, the affair generated widespread controversy within Israel, with Prime Minister Begin resisting demands for the ouster of Defense Minister Sharon as well as for the establishment of a commission of inquiry into the circumstances of the massacre. Following the largest protest rally in Israeli history in Tel Aviv on September 25, the prime minister reversed himself and asked the chief justice of the Supreme Court to undertake a full investigation. The results of the inquiry (published in February 1983) placed direct responsibility for the slaughter on the Phalangists but also faulted Sharon and several senior officers for permitting the militiamen to enter the camps in disregard for the safety of the inhabitants. In addition, while absolving the prime minister of foreknowledge of the entry, the commission expressed surprise, in view of "the Lebanese situation as it was known to those concerned," that a decision on entry should have been taken without his participation.

Talks between Israeli and Lebanese representatives on military withdrawal commenced in late December 1982 but became deadlocked on a number of issues, including Israeli insistence that it should continue to staff early-warning stations in southern Lebanon. On May 17, 1983, an agreement was concluded among Israeli, Lebanese, and U.S. negotiators that provided for Israeli withdrawal, an end to the state of war between Israel and Lebanon, and the establishment of a jointly supervised "security region" in southern Lebanon. Although unable to secure a commitment from Syria to withdraw its forces from northern and eastern Lebanon, Israel redeployed its forces in early September to a highly fortified line south of the Awali River. However, a number of attacks by guerrilla groups had concurrently been mounted against Israeli troops and contingents of the international peacekeeping force, and they culminated in simultaneous bomb attacks on U.S. and French detachments in Beirut on October 23 that left over 300 dead.

In March 1984, following departure of the multinational force from Beirut, the Lebanese government, under pressure from Syria, abrogated the troop-withdrawal accord, although the Israeli cabinet in January 1985 approved a unilateral three-stage withdrawal that was implemented in several stages over the ensuing six months. Despite the withdrawal announcement, Shiite Muslim militants in Lebanon mounted a terror campaign against the departing Israelis, who retaliated with an "iron-fist" policy that included the arrest and transfer to a prison camp in Israel of hundreds of Shiites. On June 14, 1985, militants hijacked an American TWA jetliner, demanding release of the prisoners in exchange for their hostages. After two weeks of negotiations, the Americans were freed, and Israel began gradual release of the Lebanese, both Israel and the United States insisting that the two events were unrelated. Meanwhile, negotiations had been renewed with Egypt to resolve the Taba dispute—a move that was condemned by *Likud* and was further jeopardized by the assassination of an Israeli diplomat in Cairo in August, by an Israeli air attack on the PLO's Tunis headquarters (in retaliation for the murder of three Israelis in Cyprus) in September, and by the killing of seven Israeli tourists in Sinai during October.

Throughout 1986 Peres (as prime minister until October 30 and as foreign minister thereafter) continued his efforts on behalf of a comprehensive peace settlement. An unprecedented public meeting in July with King Hassan of Morocco was described as "purely exploratory" but was viewed as enhancing the position of moderate Arab leaders, including Jordan's King Hussein, whose peace discussion with the PLO's Yasir Arafat had broken down in January. Late in the year, the Israeli government was hard-pressed to defend its role in the U.S.-Iranian arms affair, Peres insisting that Israel had transferred arms to Iran at Washington's request and was unaware that some of the money paid by Tehran had been diverted to Nicaraguan *contras*. The government was also embarrassed by the March 1987 conviction in a Washington court of Jonathan Jay POLLARD on charges of having spied for Israel. Defense Minister Rabin insisted that Pollard was part of a "rogue" spy operation set up without official sanction and that no one else had engaged in such activity since Pollard's arrest in 1985. However, the case aroused deep pro-Pollard feeling within Israel, and it was later reported that "state elements" had paid approximately two-thirds of Pollard's legal expenses. (Pollard, serving a life sentence in the United States, was granted Israeli citizenship in January 1996.)

During 1989 the government drew increasing criticism from international civil rights groups for actions triggered by the continuing intifada in the occupied territories. It also experienced a cooling of relations with Washington because of Prime Minister Shamir's failure to respond positively to the so-called "Baker plan" for Palestinian peace talks, the essentials of which corresponded to proposals advanced by former prime minister Rabin. By the end of the year the future of the occupied Arab lands had become increasingly critical because of an escalation of immigrants from the Soviet Union, some of whom were settling in the disputed areas.

With the launching of military action against Iraq by UN-backed forces in mid-January 1991, Israel came under attack by Soviet-made Scud missiles. U.S. President George H. W. Bush's administration thereupon dispatched two batteries of Patriot surface-to-air missiles to Israel, while urging Israeli authorities not to retaliate against Baghdad, lest it weaken the Arab-supported coalition. Having obliged with a posture of restraint, the Shamir government on January 22 requested that it be provided with $3 billion in compensation for damages, plus $10 billion in loan guarantees to resettle immigrants from the Soviet Union. Washington responded in late February by approving a $400 million housing loan guarantee, followed, in early March, by a $650 million aid package to help cover increased military and civil defense expenditures. On October 5, 1992, the U.S. Congress approved the $10 billion guarantee program after the new Labor government in Israel had announced that it would halt large-scale investment in the Jewish settlements in the occupied territories. On the same date a U.S. foreign aid appropriation bill was approved that included renewal of the annual $3 billion in economic and military aid earmarked for Israel in the wake of the 1978 Camp David accords.

Subsequently, in what was quickly branded a "public relations disaster," Israeli authorities on December 18, 1992, ordered the deportation of more than 400 Palestinians charged with being leaders of the fundamentalist Islamic Resistance Movement (see Hamas in the article on the Palestinian Authority/Palestine Liberation Organization) that had recently been responsible for a series of attacks on Israeli military personnel and civilians. Because Lebanon refused to accept the deportees, they were confined to a portion of the buffer strip inside the Lebanese border. The action drew almost universal condemnation from abroad, including demands by both the U.S. government and the UN Security Council that the group be returned to the occupied territories. Subsequently, Israel agreed to permit 10 (later 16) of those "wrongly deported" to return. In early February 1993 Israel also authorized the return of 100 of the others, with the remainder to be repatriated by the end of the year. The latter offer was resisted by the deportees, who demanded that all those remaining be released immediately, but was nonetheless implemented by the Israelis.

The Palestinian deportation issue proved particularly disruptive of lengthy Middle East peace talks that had begun in Madrid, Spain, on October 30, 1991, among Israeli, Lebanese, Syrian, and joint Jordanian-Palestinian delegations, with a number of other governmental and intergovernmental representatives present as observers. It was agreed at the meeting that further "two-track" negotiations would be held on Israeli-Palestinian and Israeli-Jordanian matters directed at an interim period of Palestinian self-rule and, eventually, a final settlement with Israel. However, no substantial progress was reported in three rounds of bilateral talks that concluded in mid-January 1992. Subsequently, the 19 participants in a revival of multilateral talks in Moscow on January 28–29 established working groups dealing with environment, water, disarmament and security, economic development, and refugee issues, although the Palestinians boycotted the meeting because of a dispute over the composition of its delegation. In addition, Syria and Lebanon refused to participate on the grounds that Israel had shown no territorial flexibility in the bilateral discussions.

In late June 1993, Hezbollah began launching rockets against Israeli Defense Force (IDF) and South Lebanese Army (SLA) targets in the South Lebanese "security zone." Within days the IDF began moving more troops into the area, and in mid-July the Israeli cabinet declared that the IDF would respond to any further attacks in the security zone or on its northern settlements. Hezbollah nonetheless launched a rocket attack on the Galilee panhandle late in the month. The IDF thereupon commenced bombing raids against reputed terrorist installations north of the security zone, causing widespread civilian casualties prior to a cease-fire on July 21. Further heavy fighting occurred in 1996, and public support in Israel for additional involvement in Lebanon subsequently reportedly declined, particularly after 73 Israeli soldiers were killed in a helicopter crash in February 1997. Consequently, although previous negotiations had always been based on the premise of a comprehensive regional settlement, the Netanyahu government in early 1998 proposed a "Lebanon first" strategy through which Israel would withdraw from Lebanon in return for stringent security guarantees. During the prime ministerial campaign in Israel in early 1999, Labor's Ehud Barak pledged to withdraw Israeli forces from Lebanon if elected, although he hoped it would be as part of a peace agreement with Syria and the Palestinians. The broader initiatives having stalled in early 2000, the Israeli *Knesset* in March voted to initiate a unilateral withdrawal, which was completed on May 24 (see article on Lebanon for additional information).

On August 19, 1993, some 14 months of secret talks in Norway between Israeli and PLO representatives yielded a Declaration of Principles on interim self-rule for Palestinians in the Israeli-occupied territories. The declaration provided for a five-year transitional period beginning with Israeli withdrawal from the Gaza Strip and Jericho and culminating in a transfer of authority in most of the rest of the West Bank in all matters, save foreign relations, defense, and "other mutually agreed matters" to "authorized Palestinians." Formalized in a historic signing by Israeli Prime Minister Rabin and PLO Chair Arafat in Washington on September 13, the process was targeted for completion by April 13, 1999.

A number of meetings to implement the Israeli/PLO accord were subsequently held in Egypt, but they failed to clear the way for commencement of the Israeli withdrawal from Gaza and Jericho on the agreed date of December 13. An initial dispute turned on Jericho's size, the Israelis proposing 21 square miles, with the PLO insisting on 39 square miles extending south to the Dead Sea. Subsequent disagreement centered on security provisions for Israeli settlers in Gaza, in addition to control over the passage of Palestinians from Egypt into Gaza and from Jordan into Jericho. These problems appeared to have been overcome in an agreement initialed by Israeli Prime Minister

Peres and PLO Chair Arafat in Cairo on February 9, 1994; however, the massacre of 29 worshippers at a Muslim mosque in Hebron by a follower of the late extremist Rabbi Meir KAHANE (see Kahane Lives, under Political Parties, below) brought the peace process to a sudden halt.

It was not until May 4, 1994, that a definitive accord implementing the 1993 declaration was signed in Cairo by Prime Minister Rabin and PLO Chair Arafat. Under the settlement, Israel was to withdraw from the Gaza Strip and Jericho within three weeks, legislative and executive powers for the two areas were to be assigned to a "Palestinian authority," and a 9,000-person Palestinian police force was to be established. On the other hand, Israel was to retain authority over Jewish settlements in Gaza, a military base on the Egyptian border, and external security. The actual degree of Palestinian autonomy was further constrained by annexes to the agreement that provided for an Israeli role at all levels of decision making for the territories. Nonetheless, Palestinian policemen entered the Gaza Strip on May 10, and on May 13 Israeli troops withdrew from Jericho, ending a 27-year occupation.

In a January 1994 meeting with President Clinton in Geneva, Syrian President Assad declared that he was ready for "normal, peaceful relations" with Israel. However, it was noted that peace would require significant concessions by Israel, including withdrawal from the Golan Heights. Israel appeared to respond on May 17 by offering to withdraw from the Golan in three phases over a five- to eight-year period in return for peace and normalized relations with its longtime adversary. However, observers were quick to note the sticking point: disagreement as to whether normalization or withdrawal should come first.

Israel was more successful in its quest for normalization with Jordan, U.S.-brokered contacts yielding another important White House ceremony on July 25, 1994, when King Hussein and Prime Minister Rabin signed a declaration ending the 46-year-old state of war between their two countries. On October 26 a peace treaty was signed, and it was ratified shortly thereafter by their respective legislatures. As called for by the treaty, diplomatic relations at the ambassadorial level were established on November 27. (The relationship was severely tested in September 1997 when Israeli intelligence officers attempted to assassinate Khaled MESHAL, a Hamas official in Amman. The attack on a Jordanian citizen enraged King Hussein, who threatened to break diplomatic relations and put two captured Mossad agents on trial. Prime Minister Netanyahu and other Israeli leaders reportedly made a secret visit to Amman in an effort to reduce tension, and the agents were returned to Israel in early October following the release of Hamas leader Sheikh Ahmed YASSIN and a large group of Jordanian and Palestinian prisoners from Israeli jails.)

Relations with most other Arab states (Iraq, Libya, and Sudan being conspicuous exceptions) improved measurably as the peace process gained momentum. In mid-1994 first-ever joint naval exercises, involving Israel, Egypt, Tunisia, Qatar, Canada, Italy, and the United States, were held off the Italian coast. In August a senior Israeli foreign ministry official visited Bahrain and Kuwait; in early September agreement was reached with Morocco and Tunisia on the establishment of liaison offices; and on September 30 the Gulf Cooperation Council (GCC) lifted the "secondary" and tertiary" aspects of its economic boycott of Israel, although retaining the ban on direct trade. In early November, Tansu Çiller became the first Turkish prime minister to visit Israel, and on December 26 Rabin became the first Israeli prime minister to visit Oman. Turkey and Israel also signed an agreement in August 1996 for the exchange of "technical expertise" on defense matters, a development that was criticized in many Arab capitals, and the two countries conducted a small, yet highly symbolic, joint military exercise in the Mediterranean in January 1998. In addition, Ehud Barak in October 1999 became the first Israeli prime minister to visit Turkey. Earlier, in an historic ceremony in Jerusalem on December 30, 1993, Israel and the Vatican had agreed to establish diplomatic relations. Representatives from both sides expressed the hope that a 2,000-year rupture between Christians and Jews could thus be overcome.

The funeral of Yitzhak Rabin in November 1995 attracted Israel's largest-ever gathering of foreign leaders, including several from prominent Arab states, underscoring, among other things, international concern that the assassinated prime minister would be difficult to replace in the ongoing Middle East peace process. However, despite the shock of his death, the withdrawal of Israeli troops from six more West Bank towns (as authorized in the second Israeli/PLO accord) proceeded smoothly throughout the rest of the year.

As was widely expected, Benjamin Netanyahu's election as Israeli prime minister in 1996 slowed progress on the Palestinian front. (See the article on the Palestinian Authority/Palestine Liberation Organization for details from 1996 through 1999.) A number of Arab states closed their offices in Israel following the outbreak of the "second intifada" in late 2000, and a March 2001 Arab League summit endorsed the Palestinian "right to resist" Israeli "aggression."

In early 2002 Saudi Arabia proposed the full normalization of relations between Israel and Arab states in return for complete Israeli withdrawal from the occupied territories. Arab leaders subsequently urged Washington to propose a specific timetable for creation of a Palestinian state, arguing that the lack of progress in resolving the Palestinian/Israeli conflict was generating widespread anti-U.S. sentiment in the Arab world. In April 2003, the Middle East Quartet (the European Union [EU], Russia, the UN, and the United States) formally unveiled the much-discussed "road map" toward a final comprehensive settlement of the Israeli-Palestinian dispute, calling for establishment of an "independent, democratic, and viable" Palestinian state. Final negotiations were slated for completion by the end of 2005, assuming Palestinian institutions had been "stabilized" and Palestinian security forces had proven adequate in combating attacks against Israel. Israeli Prime Minister Sharon offered "qualified" support for the road map, as did the *Knesset,* although the latter insisted that it be made clear that Palestinian refugees would not be guaranteed the right to return to their former homes in Israel. Meanwhile, in February 2004 the Sharon government had announced its intention to disengage unilaterally from the Gaza Strip, sending the message that it would not deal with Yasir Arafat's Palestinian Authority (PA) but instead would withdraw from Palestinian territories on its own terms. The decision was met with tacit approval from the George W. Bush administration, which, while preferring that major decisions be made within the context of a negotiated solution, viewed Yasir Arafat's leadership of the PA as the major obstacle to such a solution. Israel's disengagement from Gaza occurred over August and September 2005 and resulted in Sharon's voluntary exit from *Likud* to form *Kadima*.

Sharon's massive stroke in January 2006 left a degree of uncertainty in Israeli politics as his newly formed *Kadima*-led government seemed to rely heavily on his stature. Sharon's deputy, Ehud Olmert, assumed the prime ministership and was immediately faced with the implications of Hamas's sweeping win in the January 2006 Palestinian legislative elections. Among other things, the United States and Israel declared they would refuse to deal with an authority governed by Hamas. Meanwhile, Olmert's government faced the challenge of implementing its policy of "convergence"—including further unilateral disengagement from parts of the West Bank—which it presented successfully to Israeli electors in March.

In mid-July 2006 attention shifted to the Israeli-Lebanese border when Hezbollah conducted a cross-border raid and abducted two Israeli soldiers. Israel subsequently launched a series of air raids on Lebanon, targeting not just Hezbollah-controlled areas in the south of Lebanon but also Beirut and other cities. Civilian deaths in Lebanon rapidly mounted and reached 340 in the first week of bombings. The Israeli air force also bombed civilian infrastructure, including the Beirut airport, bridges, power plants, and fuel depots. Hezbollah, meanwhile, continued to fire rockets into northern Israel, killing 15 Israeli civilians. On August 14 Israeli troops began to withdraw from southern Lebanon in support of a resolution adopted on August 11 by the UN Security Council calling for an end to the hostilities. The resolution proposed that the UN Interim Force in Lebanon be expanded from 2,000 to 15,000 troops to assist in preserving order along the Israeli-Lebanese border while negotiations continued toward the disarmament of Hezbollah. It was reported that 117 Israeli soldiers had been killed in the conflict, while 41 Israeli civilians had died, primarily from the 4,000 rocket attacks launched by Hezbollah. Following the Israeli withdrawal, the Olmert government faced increasing domestic criticism in Israel for its perceived failure to have accomplished its main goal in the war—the removal of Hezbollah as a security threat. The anti-Hezbollah campaign also drew heavy criticism from most Arab states, particularly in regard to the killing of civilians and widespread damage to infrastructure throughout Lebanon. However, the United States firmly supported the initiative as a component of the "war on terrorism," and in mid-2007 Washington announced a new $30 billion, ten-year military-aid package for Israel.

In October 2007 Israeli jets reportedly bombed a desert site in Syria that some analysts concluded may have been a nascent nuclear reactor. (The charge was denied by Syria.) Nuclear issues also exacerbated tensions between Israel and Iran. Prime Minister Olmert traveled to Russia in October to urge Russian leader Vladimir Putin to agree to additional sanctions against Tehran in an effort to thwart Iran's perceived nuclear ambitions.

In early 2008 Olmert insisted that Iran was still pursuing nuclear weapons, and by midyear speculation was rampant concerning the possibility of an Israeli attack on Iranian nuclear facilities. On a more positive note, a series of indirect talks (through Turkish officials) was held in the summer with Syria regarding a potential peace settlement. Israel also reportedly offered to hold talks with the Hezbollah-dominated government in Lebanon, and a prisoner exchange was conducted in July.

The Israeli offensive in Gaza in December 2008–January 2009 (see Current issues, below, and the article on the Palestinian Authority/Palestine Liberation Organization for additional information) was strongly criticized by most Arab governments, and relations with Turkey were also strained by the matter. Following his installation as prime minister in March, Benjamin Netanyahu tried to shift the focus of international attention away from Palestinian affairs and toward Iran, whose perceived nuclear ambitions he characterized as Israel's top security concern. Netanyahu reportedly traveled to Moscow in September to ask the Russian government not to deliver surface-to-air missiles to Iran.

Current issues. Following his inauguration in July 1999, new Israeli Prime Minister Ehud Barak called for a comprehensive peace settlement with the Palestinians, Syria, and Lebanon within 15 months. Little progress was achieved by the spring of 2000, however, except for some redeployment of Israeli forces in the West Bank. In April, Barak appeared to accept the eventual creation of an independent Palestinian "entity" (he avoided using the word "state") comprising Gaza and 60–70 percent of the West Bank. However, he indicated a "majority" of the Jewish settlers in the disputed areas would remain under Israeli sovereignty. At the same time, popular sentiment in Israel appeared to be turning away from the proposed return of the Golan Heights to Syria, and the construction of additional Golan settlements (suspended since the previous December) resumed in April.

Faced with a collapsing coalition (see Political background, above), Barak attended a "make-or-break" summit with the PLO's Yasir Arafat and U.S. President Bill Clinton at Camp David in July 2000. Although agreement appeared close on several issues, the summit ended unsuccessfully when common ground could not be found regarding the status of Jerusalem and sovereignty over holy sites there. Although Barak subsequently indicated a willingness to endorse the establishment of two "separate entities" in Jerusalem, negotiations collapsed in October in the face of the second intifada and heavy reprisals by the Israeli military that included the use of assault helicopter and rocket attacks.

Barak's defeat by Ariel Sharon in the February 2001 special prime ministerial balloting appeared to doom prospects for any settlement soon, particularly in view of the fact that the new Bush administration in Washington had announced it did not consider itself in any way bound by the "parameters" endorsed previously by the Clinton administration. Sharon pledged that Jerusalem would remain "whole and unified" under Israeli sovereignty and that no Jewish settlements would be dismantled. Suicide bombings continued unabated in early 2002, and Israel in April launched an offensive of unprecedented scale that left it in control of most West Bank towns. When that initiative failed to restrain the suicide bombers, the Sharon government announced at midyear that it would begin to construct a "security fence" around the West Bank.

Not surprisingly, security issues dominated the January 2003 *Knesset* balloting. *Likud*'s solid victory appeared to indicate a repudiation of the "peace agenda" of Labor's new leader, Avraham Mitzna. At the same time, Sharon warned that "painful concessions" regarding Palestinian statehood would eventually be required.

In June 2004 the cabinet endorsed Sharon's plan for unilateral disengagement from Gaza, while Labor agreed to provide a safety net in the *Knesset* for Sharon in order to allow him to proceed toward disengagement. In October the *Knesset* endorsed the proposal by a vote of 67–47, and in February it approved $900 million in compensation for the Israeli settlers who faced displacement.

Following the death of Yasir Arafat in November 2004, the Israeli government called upon the new Palestinian leadership—headed by the new president, Mahmoud Abbas—to finally come to terms with "terrorism" on the part of Palestinian militants. However, momentum regarding Sharon's unilateral disengagement plan continued to grow, and forced evacuation of Israeli settlements from Gaza (and a few in the northern West Bank) were conducted in August–September 2005, marking the end of 38 years of Israeli occupation of the Gaza Strip. Staunch opposition to the Gaza disengagement from within Sharon's own *Likud*-led government compelled him to leave *Likud and* form *Kadima* in November 2006.

Prime Minister Sharon's stroke in January 2006 plunged Israel into a period of political uncertainty, especially given that he was leader of a new governing party that was barely three months old. Further difficulties rocked the Israeli government—with acting Prime Minister Ehud Olmert at the helm—when Hamas trounced Fatah in the Palestinian legislative elections in late January 2006.

Following his election success in the spring of 2006, Prime Minister Olmert promised that Israel's final borders would be drawn by 2010—unilaterally by Israel if he was unable to find a "Palestinian partner" other than Hamas with whom to negotiate a final treaty. He also praised the Israeli settlers in the West Bank and insisted that the larger settlements would be expanded. However, despite apparent majority popular support for Olmert's Palestinian stance, the administration faced growing criticism for its handling of the July–August conflict with Hezbollah in Lebanon; a leaked interim report from a special commission reportedly challenged Olmert's "judgment" and "prudence" in the matter. In addition, a number of scandals subsequently buffeted the cabinet, and corruption allegations apparently contributed to a demonstration in Tel Aviv in May 2007 by some 100,000 protesters demanding Olmert's resignation. Subsequently, operating with what was described as a "survival cabinet," Olmert appeared to base his future prospects on plans for renewed talks toward a comprehensive Middle East peace settlement, which were formally launched in the United States in November. By that time Olmert had signaled his readiness to discuss the eventual division of Jerusalem and the Israeli withdrawal from much of the West Bank as part of a final two-state settlement. However, *Likud*'s Benjamin Netanyahu, enjoying a recent surge in popularity polls, criticized the talks as a "continuation of one-sided concessions," while the rightist parties in the cabinet (Shas and *Yisrael Beiteinu*) also expressed concern about where the negotiations might lead.

Little progress was achieved in the first half of 2008 on the Palestinian front as conditions deteriorated sharply in Gaza. Meanwhile, domestic attention in Israel focused on new allegations of impropriety against Prime Minister Olmert in regard to cash payments he had allegedly received from a U.S. citizen during his tenure as minister of industry and trade. (Five corruption probes were underway at that point.) Labor leader Barak in June demanded that Olmert resign or face a nonconfidence motion in the *Knesset*. Barak withdrew his threat when Olmert announced he would call for new leadership elections within *Kadima*. Faced with devastatingly low popularity ratings, Olmert, who denied any wrongdoing, acceded to political reality by announcing at the end of July that he intended to resign and would not run in the upcoming *Kadima* elections. After winning a bruising party election in September, new *Kadima* leader Tzipi Livni faced a daunting challenge in attempting to forge a new coalition government and avoid early elections in order to pursue Olmert's recent diplomatic efforts with Hamas (which had recently endorsed a cease-fire) and Syria. Although Labor eventually appeared to accept Livni's overtures, Shas refused to join the proposed new coalition, thereby triggering the call for new elections.

Following the announcement of his resignation in September 2008, Prime Minister Olmert, serving in a caretaker capacity, dedicated the rest of his tenure to intensifying negotiations regarding Palestinian affairs, as well as broader regional tensions. However, talks with the Palestinians collapsed in December when the resumption of Hamas rocket attacks prompted a massive (and controversial) Israeli offensive against Gaza (see article on the Palestinian Authority/Palestine Liberation Organization for details). "Operation Cast Lead" (as the offensive was called) also muted the campaign for the February 2009 *Knesset* balloting and once again propelled security issues to the forefront of Israeli concerns. Although Livni and *Kadima* (along with Labor) strongly supported the Gaza initiative, Livni continued to call for a two-state solution to the Palestinian impasse. Meanwhile, *Likud*'s Benjamin Netanyahu, rising in popularity polls, pledged to end Hamas rule in Gaza and to concentrate more on improving the economic conditions of Palestinians than on political negotiations.

Both *Kadima* (28 seats) and a resurgent *Likud* (27 seats) claimed victory in the February 2009 poll, but it quickly became clear that Netanyahu enjoyed better prospects of forging a new government than Livni, particularly in light of reportedly severe friction between Livni and Labor's Barak. Netanyahu's first agreement was reached with the right-wing *Yisrael Beiteinu,* which had jumped to third place (ahead of

Labor) in the *Knesset* with 15 seats. Accord was subsequently achieved relatively easily by *Likud* with Shas, but significant opposition was reported within Labor over Barak's ultimate decision to join the *Likud*-led coalition.

Upon his inauguration in March 2009 as head of the new center-right government, Netanyahu pledged to pursue a "full peace" with the Palestinians, but skeptics expressed concern over the appointment of the very hawkish Avigdor LIEBERMAN, the leader of *Yisrael Beiteinu*, as minister of foreign affairs. The strength of the right-wing parties in his government also appeared to influence Netanyahu's subsequent resistance to heavy pressure from new U.S. president Barack Obama for a cessation of Jewish settlement construction in the West Bank and East Jerusalem. Meanwhile, formal talks with the Palestinians remained frozen as of November, a recent UN report having accused the Israeli military of war crimes and human rights abuses during the Gaza campaign. Domestically, attention at that time focused on the trials of former president Katsav (see Political background, above) and former prime minister Olmert, who had been indicted on corruption charges.

POLITICAL PARTIES

Government Parties:

Unity–National Liberal Party (*Likud–Liberalim Leumi*). The "Unity" rubric reflecting the contention that Israel was entitled to all land between the Jordan River and the Mediterranean, *Likud* was formed under the leadership of Menachem Begin in September 1973 in an effort to break the legislative monopoly of the Labor Alignment (see ILP, above). Joining in the grouping were the Herut-Liberal Bloc (*Gush Herut-Liberalim*—Gahal), composed of the *Herut* (Freedom) and Liberal parties, and the Integral Land of Israel movement. Peace to Zion (*Schlomzion*), Ariel Sharon's small right-wing party, entered *Likud* after the 1977 election. Although often maintaining a common outlook in regard to captured territory, the constituent parties subsequently differed somewhat on domestic policy, though theoretically tending to favor the denationalization of certain industries in the context of a free-enterprise philosophy.

In September 1985 *La'am* (For the Nation), a *Likud* faction that had been launched in 1969 from Rafi (a 1965 offshoot of Mapai, see ILP, above) by former prime minister David Ben-Gurion as the State List, merged with *Herut.* Prior to the 1988 election, two additional groups merged with *Likud:* the Movement for Economic Recovery/Courage (*Ometz*), founded in early 1984 by former Mapai member Yigael HURWITZ, and the Movement for Israel's Tradition (*Tenuat Masoret Yisrael*—Tami), an Oriental Orthodox party founded in 1981 as an offshoot of the NRP by Aharon ABU-HAZEIRA.

Relations between *Likud* leader Benjamin Netanyahu and former foreign minister David Levy became tense following the latter's loss to Netanyahu in the March 1993 party election. In early 1995 the situation worsened further, with Levy insisting that the adoption of a primary system to choose party candidates for the next election would marginalize the numerically dominant Sephardi community, of which he was a member. As a result, Levy formed a new party—*Gesher*—although he subsequently supported Netanyahu in the May 1996 prime ministerial balloting. *Likud* also agreed to present joint candidates with *Gesher* and *Tzomet* for the concurrent *Knesset* balloting on a platform that emphasized security as the "first condition" in any peace agreement and opposed the establishment of an independent Palestinian state as well as "land-for-peace" negotiations with Syria regarding the Golan Heights.

Surprising many observers, Netanyahu won the 1996 prime ministerial election with 50.5 percent of the vote. At the same time, the *Likud/Gesher/Tzomet* alliance garnered 25.1 percent of the *Knesset* votes, thereby securing 32 seats, 22 of which went to *Likud* under the formula previously established with its electoral partners. Meanwhile, within *Likud* the most contentious issue involved a cabinet post for Sharon, who had reportedly agreed not to challenge Netanyahu for party supremacy in return for a major ministry in the event of a *Likud* victory. Last-minute negotiations finally produced agreement on the creation of a new ministry of national infrastructure for Sharon, who became one of eight *Likud* members to join Netanyahu in the new cabinet. However, friction between Netanyahu and Sharon continued, as evidenced by Sharon's vote against the new Israeli/Palestinian accord when it was presented to the cabinet for approval by Netanyahu in January 1997. Benjamin Begin, Menachem Begin's son and a longtime opponent of territorial negotiations with the Palestinians, also voted against the agreement and resigned as minister of science to protest Netanyahu's decisions in the matter.

In June 1997 Finance Minister Dan MERIDOR, seen as a rival to Netanyahu within *Likud,* resigned his cabinet post, the fissure representing, in the opinion of many observers, growing disenchantment among some party faithful over a perceived lack of influence upon national policy. Potential factionalization was also apparent at the November party convention when Netanyahu's supporters pushed through a change whereby the former primary system for choosing legislative candidates was replaced by selection by the Central Committee, which was dominated by Netanyahu loyalists.

In January 1999 Netanyahu was named as *Likud*'s candidate for prime minister, securing 82 percent of the primary vote against Moshe ARENS. (Arens, one of Netanyahu's mentors and a former defense minister, had challenged Netanyahu in order to "stop the hemorrhaging" within the party.) By that time, several prominent *Likud* dissenters had defected to the new Center Party (below), while Benjamin Begin had founded his own party (see New *Herut,* below, under New Freedom) and decided to run for prime minister against Netanyahu.

Following his loss to Labor's Ehud Barak in the May 1999 balloting for prime minister, Netanyahu resigned as *Likud*'s leader. He was succeeded on an interim basis by Sharon, who was elected in a permanent capacity on September 3 with 53 percent support of the party membership over two other candidates. Netanyahu declined to challenge Sharon for the party's nomination for prime minister in the February 2001 election. However, in mid-2002 Netanyahu positioned himself for another run at *Likud* leadership, his supporters sponsoring a resolution that was approved by the Central Committee stating that the party would never support the creation of an independent Palestinian state. However, Sharon easily defeated Netanyahu in the November 28 leadership balloting. Despite their often bitter previous history, Netanyahu was named finance minister in the cabinet appointed in February 2003.

Although Sharon had survived several confrontations with dissident *Likud* members opposed to his plan for unilateral Israeli withdrawal from the Gaza Strip (which took place in August 2005), he left *Likud* in November and launched *Kadima.* Benjamin Netanyahu assumed leadership of *Likud* after Sharon's departure, winning an internal party ballot held in December 2005. *Likud*'s electoral fortunes were severely compromised by the launching of *Kadima*, and *Likud* won only 12 seats in the March 2006 *Knesset* balloting (down from 39 seats in 2003) on a vote share of 9 percent. However, Netanyahu easily won reelection as party leader in an August 2007 vote against far-right candidate Moshe FEIGLIN, a West Bank settler.

In December 2008 *Likud* associated itself with the right-wing, religious Zionist *Ahi Party*, which, as the Renewed Religious National Zionist Party, had participated, under the leadership of Ephraim EITAM, in the National Union in 2006, winning two of the nine seats secured by the NRP–National Union electoral coalition. (Eitam and Yitzhak LEVY had formed the Religious National Zionist Party prior to the 2006 balloting after they had split from the NRP in a dispute over policy regarding Gaza.) Netanyahu reportedly at first rebuffed Eitam's overtures on the ground that Eitam, a vehement supporter of the controversial Jewish settlements in the West Bank and East Jerusalem, was too hawkish. However, the affiliation (variously described as a merger or an electoral coalition agreement) with Ahi was ultimately accepted due to campaign budgetary advantages.

Likud rebounded dramatically in the 2009 *Knesset* balloting, securing 27 seats on a vote share of 21.6 percent and propelling Netanyahu to the prime ministership as head of a center-right coalition.

Leaders: Benjamin NETANYAHU (Prime Minister and Chair), Reuven RIVLIN (Speaker of the *Knesset* and 2007 presidential candidate), Zeev ELKIN (Parliamentary Leader).

Israel Labor Party—ILP (*Mifleget Ha'avoda Ha'yisra'elit*). The ILP was formed in January 1968 through merger of the Israel Workers' Party (*Mifleget Poalei Eretz Yisrael*–Mapai), a Western-oriented socialist party established in 1929 and represented in the government by prime ministers David Ben-Gurion, Moshe Sharett, Levi Eshkol, Golda Meir, Shimon Peres, and Yitzhak Rabin; the Israel Workers' List (*Reshimat Poalei Yisrael*–Rafi), founded by Ben-Gurion as a vehicle of opposition to Prime Minister Eshkol; and the Unity of Labor–Workers of Zion (*Achdut Ha'avoda–Poalei Zion*), which advocated a planned economy, agricultural settlement, and an active defense policy.

In January 1969 the ILP joined with Mapam (see *Meretz,* below) in a coalition known initially as the Alignment (*Ma'arakh*) and subsequently as the Labor Alignment (*Ma'arakh Ha'avoda*). The latter was technically dissolved upon Mapam's withdrawal to protest the formation of the national unity government, although the term was subsequently used to reference a linkage between Labor and *Yahad* (Together), a party led by former air force commander and former *Likud* leader Ezer Weizman, who had urged direct talks with Arab leaders until his retirement from partisan politics before the 1992 election.

Following the assassination of Prime Minister Rabin in November 1995, the party's Central Committee endorsed Shimon Peres, who had been serving as foreign minister and the lead Israeli negotiator regarding emerging Palestinian autonomy, to succeed Rabin as party leader and prime minister. Subsequently, in a significant policy change, the committee in April 1996 eliminated the long-standing section in the party platform that formally opposed the eventual creation of an independent Palestinian state.

Labor retained a slight majority in the May 1996 *Knesset* balloting, (securing 34 seats on the strength of 26.8 percent of the vote); however, Peres was narrowly defeated in the concurrent election for prime minister. Later in the year, amid reports of intraparty friction, Peres announced he would not run for prime minister in 2000 or for reelection as party chair.

In May 1997 the party rejected the proposed creation of a new post of party president for Peres, setting the stage for a subsequent "generational" change of leadership. In early June, Ehud Barak, a hawkish former army chief of staff and foreign minister under Peres, was elected as Labor's new leader with 57 percent of the votes, easily defeating runner-up Yossi BEILIN, a Peres supporter who garnered 29 percent of the vote. Barak subsequently attempted to move the ILP closer to the center of the political spectrum, and, after securing unanimous nomination in January 1999 as the party's candidate for prime minister, he announced in March that Labor would contest the upcoming legislative balloting in a One Israel coalition with *Gesher* and *Meimad.*

The ILP secured 23 of the 26 seats won by One Israel (20.2 percent of the vote) in the May 17, 1999, legislative elections, while Barak was elected prime minister with 56 percent of the vote. However, the ILP suffered a major blow when Peres was defeated by *Likud*'s Moshe Katzav for state president in July 2000, and Barak was soundly beaten in the special prime ministerial balloting in February 2001. Barak subsequently resigned as ILP leader, and new elections for that post were held in September 2001. Initial results showed Avraham BURG, the speaker of the *Knesset,* with a small majority over Benjamin BEN-ELIEZER, the current defense minister. However, Ben-Eliezer's supporters challenged the results, and after a partial rerun in December, Ben-Eliezer, a hard-liner regarding the Palestinian question, was declared the winner.

Gen. (Ret.) Avraham Mitzna, the mayor of Haifa, was elected leader of the ILP in November 2002 and subsequently proposed a "radical peace agenda" for the January 2003 *Knesset* balloting (which the ILP contested in a coalition with *Meimad*). Following a poor performance in the elections, Mitzna resigned the ILP leadership in May, and he was succeeded in an acting capacity by Peres. In December 2004 Labor joined Ariel Sharon's *Likud* to form a unity government in order to implement Israel's disengagement plan from the Gaza Strip.

In November 2005 Shimon Peres was replaced as the leader of Labor in an internal party ballot by left-wing union leader Amir PERETZ. Peretz had previously served as the leader of One Nation (*Am Ehad*), which had been formed in early 1999 by several dissident members of *Likud* with strong ties to organized labor. One Nation campaigned for the 1999 *Knesset* balloting in support of greater benefits for pensioners and workers. It secured two seats in the May 1999 legislative balloting on a vote share of 1.9 percent and three seats in the January 2003 balloting on a vote share of 2.8 percent. In 2004 Peretz, the longtime head of Israel's leading labor federation, announced the planned merger of *Am Ehad* with the ILP

Following his assumption of the Labor leadership post in 2005, Peretz stated his intention to reassert the party's traditional domestic socialist orientation. Labor concurrently left Prime Minister Sharon's government, prompting a call for an early election for March 2006, in which Labor/*Meimad* won the second-highest number of seats with 19. Peretz was subsequently appointed deputy prime minister and defense minister in the new government.

Peretz finished third in the first round of balloting for party leader in May 2007 after having faced severe criticism for his role in Israel's 2006 war with Hezbollah in Lebanon. In the subsequent runoff, Barak (returning to politics after a six-year absence) secured the leadership post with 51.2 percent of the vote against Ami AYALON, a former head of Israel's internal security who had promised to withdraw Labor from the government unless Prime Minister Olmert resigned. Upon being named deputy prime minister and defense minister, Barak pledged "level-headed" leadership, which included continued participation in the Olmert government, pending developments in proposed rejuvenation of negotiations with Palestinian leaders.

Following Prime Minister Olmert's resignation in September 2008, Barak indicated that Labor would participate in a coalition government led by new *Kadima* leader Tzipi Livni. However, friction was reported between the two leaders following the February 2009 *Knesset* balloting (in which Labor, running without *Meimad*, fell to 13 seats on a vote share of 9.9 percent), and Labor joined the *Likud*-led coalition government formed in March. (Labor's central committee approved the measure by a vote of 680–507.)

Leaders: Ehud BARAK (Chair and Defense Minister), Collette AVITAL (2007 presidential candidate), Daniel Ben SIMON (Parliamentary Leader), Eitan CABEL (General Secretary).

Israel Is Our Home (*Yisrael Beiteinu*). Founded in 1999 as a party representing the interests of immigrants to Israel from the former Soviet Union, *Yisrael Beiteinu* is led by Avigdor Lieberman, a former minister of the Sharon government. Adopting a hard-line stance on the Israeli-Palestinian conflict, the party won 4 seats in the May 1999 *Knesset* balloting with 2.6 percent of the vote, subsequently forming a single *Knesset* faction with the National Union (see below). However, in the 2006 *Knesset* polling *Yisrael Beiteinu* left the National Union coalition and campaigned on its own. It performed strongly and won 11 seats with 9 percent of the vote. The party joined the *Kadima*-led coalition government in October 2006, with Lieberman serving as deputy prime minister and heading the new strategic affairs ministry. However, *Yisrael Beiteinu* left the cabinet in January 2008 to protest the government's recent decision to resume negotiations with the Palestinians. In June, Lieberman criticized the Olmert government for conducting "shady political deals" to perpetuate itself.

Yisrael Beiteinu rose to third place in the February 2009 *Knesset* balloting by securing 15 seats on a vote share of 11.7 percent. Lieberman was subsequently named a deputy prime minister and minister of foreign affairs in the new *Likud*-led government.

Leaders: Avigdor LIEBERMAN (Chair), Yuri STERN, Robert ILATOV (Parliamentary Leader).

Sephardi Torah Guardians (*Shomrei Torah Sephardim*—Shas). An offshoot of *Agudat Yisrael* (below), Shas was formed prior to the 1984 *Knesset* balloting, in which it won four seats. It is an orthodox religious party that draws support from Jews of Oriental (Sephardi) descent from North Africa and the Middle East. In December 1984 the group withdrew from the national unity coalition in a dispute with the NRP over the allocation of portfolios, with the then Shas leader Yitzhak PERETZ subsequently returning to the interior ministry with a budget enhanced by a transfer of funds from religious affairs. Shas withdrew again in February 1987 over the issue of registering a U.S. convert as Jewish but rejoined the coalition after the 1988 election, in which it won six *Knesset* seats. Its representation was unchanged in the 1992 poll, after which it joined the Labor coalition. In September 1993 Shas leader Aryeh DERI was obliged to resign as interior minister after a lengthy inquiry into alleged corruption had yielded formal charges against him. The result was a six-month withdrawal of Shas from the government coalition, followed by the group's return to opposition status in February 1995.

Shas won 8.5 percent of the vote and 10 seats in the May 1996 *Knesset* balloting, thereby becoming the third-largest legislative party. Its success was in part attributed to the large Shas network of schools and social services, which had won growing grassroots support, even among relatively nonobservant Sephardic Jews. In June, Shas accepted an invitation to join the new Netanyahu government, in which its two portfolios included, not surprisingly, the ministries of labor and social affairs. In the national campaign of early 1999, Shas was described as "thoroughly domestic" in its political concerns and appeared to be surging in popularity, despite Deri's conviction in February on bribery and other charges. Shas won 17 seats on a 13 percent vote share in the May legislative balloting and joined Ehud Barak's subsequent Labor-led government.

Deri resigned as chair of Shas in June 1999. He was imprisoned in September 2000 after his four-year sentence was upheld by the appellate courts.

In the 2003 *Knesset* elections Shas won 11 seats. The party performed slightly better in 2006, gaining 12 seats, and Shas joined the *Kadima*-led coalition government formed by Prime Minister Olmert in May. In mid-2008 Shas threatened to support a nonconfidence motion against the Olmert government unless additional funds were allocated for religious schools and welfare payments. The party also strongly opposed any negotiations with Palestinian officials regarding the status of East Jerusalem.

Following Olmert's resignation in September 2008, Shas declined to join a proposed coalition government under the leadership of *Kadima*'s Tzipi Livni, who charged Shas with making "economically and diplomatically illegitimate demands" in return for participation. Shas won 11 seats in the February 2009 *Knesset* elections on a vote share of 8.5 percent and readily joined the subsequent *Likud*-led coalition government.

Leaders: Rabbi Ovadia YOSEF (Spiritual Leader), Eliyahu YISHAI (Chair and Deputy Prime Minister), Avraham MICHAELI (Parliamentary Leader).

Jewish Home (*Habayit Hayehudi*). *Habayit Hayehudi* is the rubric adopted by a group of parties in November 2008 who were attempting to unite various religious camps under the leadership, in part, of the **National Religious Party**—NRP (*Mifleget Datit Leumit*—Mafdal). Dedicated to the principles of religious Zionism, the NRP was formed in 1956 through the union of two older organizations, *Mizrahi* and the *Mizrahi* Workers (*Hapoel Hamizrahi*). The NRP subsequently evolved into a militantly nationalist group calling for outright annexation of the West Bank.

Formerly allied with Labor, the NRP went into opposition following the 1973 election because of a dispute over religious policy, but it subsequently reentered the government. In December 1976 Prime Minister Rabin ousted the 3 NRP cabinet members after 9 of the party's 10 legislative deputies had abstained on a no-confidence vote, thus precipitating a government crisis that led to a call for the May 1977 election. On the eve of the 1977 balloting, the NRP concluded a coalition with *Likud,* subsequently participating in the Begin government formed on June 20. The arrangement continued after the 1981 election, in which the NRP's representation fell from 12 to 6 seats. The electoral decline continued through 1984, when the NRP won only 4 seats.

Prior to the 1988 balloting (at which it won five seats) the NRP absorbed Heritage (*Morasha*), a religious grouping formed prior to the 1984 election by merger of the Rally of Religious Zionism (*Mifleget Tzionut Dati*—Matzad) with the Agudat Israel Workers (*Poalei Agudat Yisrael*). The party's legislative strength grew to six in 1992 and nine in 1996, and it secured two seats in the June 1996 government.

Underscoring the tenuous nature of the alliance between *Likud* and the ultra-religious parties, the NRP ministers voted against Prime Minister Netanyahu in January 1997 when the recent Israeli/Palestinian agreement was presented to the cabinet.

Zevulun HAMMER, longtime chair of the NRP and deputy prime minister in the Netanyahu cabinet, died in January 1998. He was succeeded as minister of education and culture and party chair by Yitzhak LEVY, the NRP secretary general. The NRP, by then considered the primary political voice of the Jewish settlers in the occupied territories, strongly opposed the Wye agreement of October 1998, contributing significantly to the subsequent collapse of the Netanyahu government.

The NRP secured five seats in the May 1999 *Knesset* balloting on a vote share of 4.2 percent. It left the new Barak government in mid-2000 in protest over discussion of the possible return of the Golan Heights to Syria. Effi Eitam, a brigadier general in the national reserves, succeeded Levy as NRP chair in April 2002 as the NRP prepared to join the Sharon government. In the 2003 *Knesset* poll the NRP won six seats, and the party again joined Prime Minister Sharon's government. However, Sharon's plan to disengage unilaterally from Gaza subsequently split the NRP, some of whose *Knesset* members joined the National Union (below) in February 2005. In the 2006 poll the NRP campaigned on a joint list with the National Union, with the combined slate winning nine seats on 7 percent of the vote. (Three of the seats went to members of the NRP).

The formation of *Habayit Hayehudi* in November 2008 was intended to involve the formal merger of the NRP and the National Union. However, the leaders of *Moledet* and *Tequma* (two major components of the National Union) objected to the slots proposed for their members on the *Habayit Hayehudi* candidate list and subsequently broke away to reform the National Union. Consequently, the *Habayit Hayehudi* ticket, which won three seats on a vote share of 2.9 percent in the 2009 poll, was essentially an NRP grouping, with the addition of *Tequma* members who opted to remain in the new party.

Leaders: Daniel HERSHKOWITZ (Chair), Zevulun ORIEV (Parliamentary Leader), Shalom JERBI (Secretary General).

United Torah Judaism (UTJ). Also known as the Orthodox Torah bloc, the UTJ was formed prior to the 1992 balloting as a coalition of the two parties below. It won four *Knesset* seats in 1992 and 1996, and one of its members was appointed deputy minister for housing and construction in the June 1996 Netanyahu government. The UTJ won five seats in the May 1999 legislative balloting on a vote share of 3.7 percent and subsequently agreed to support the Barak government in the *Knesset,* albeit without cabinet representation. The UTJ was given several deputy ministerial posts in the Sharon government in March 2001 but lost those positions in May 2002 when the UTJ opposed Sharon's emergency budget cuts. (Rabbi Eliezer SHACH, the longtime spiritual leader of the UTJ and its two component groupings, died in November 2001.)

The UTJ won five seats (on a vote share of 4.3 percent) in the 2003 *Knesset* balloting but resisted repeated invitations to join Sharon's subsequent coalition governments because of the presence of *Shinui* in the cabinet. However, after *Shinui* fell out with *Likud* in late 2004, the UTJ agreed to join the cabinet formed in January 2005. The two factions of UTJ briefly split in 2005 but reunited in time for the 2006 poll, in which the party won six seats on 4.7 percent of the vote.

The UTJ won five seats in the February 2009 *Knesset* balloting on a vote share of 4.4 percent. Although the party initially rebuffed an invitation to join the *Likud*-led coalition government installed on March 31 because of friction between the UTJ and *Yisrael Beiteinu*, the UTJ on April 1 signed an agreement with *Likud* under which the UTJ was given deputy ministerial posts in the ministries of health and education and leadership of the *Knesset*'s finance committee.

Leaders: Yaakov LITZMAN (Chair), Menachem Eliezer MOSES (Parliamentary Leader).

Union of Israel (*Agudat Yisrael*). A formerly anti-Zionist Orthodox religious party, *Agudat Yisrael* was allied prior to the May 1977 election with the *Poalei Agudat Yisrael* in the United Torah Front, which called for strict observance of religious law and introduced the no-confidence motion that led to Prime Minister Rabin's resignation in December 1976. The party's *Knesset* representation fell from four in 1981 to two in 1984 as a result of the loss of Oriental Jewish votes to the recently organized Shas. After winning five seats in 1988, *Agudat Yisrael* declined government representation at full ministerial level but agreed to the appointment of one of its representatives as deputy minister of labor and social affairs. It accepted a Jerusalem Affairs portfolio in November 1990 after Prime Minister Shamir agreed to endorse a number of its legislative objectives. *Agudat Yisrael* members secured four of the six seats that UTJ won in the 2006 *Knesset* polling.

Leader: Meir PORUSH.

Torah Flag (*Degel Hatorah*). Formed in 1988 by a group of *Agudat Yisrael* dissidents, the *Degel Hatorah* is a non-Zionist, ultra-orthodox religious party that captured two *Knesset* seats in the 1988 poll. Its members secured two of the six *Knesset* seats won by the UTJ in the 2006 *Knesset* polling.

Rabbi Auraham RAVITZ, leader of *Degal Hatorah* and a longtime member of the *Knesset*, died in early 2009.

Leader: Moshi GAFNI.

Opposition Parties:

Kadima (Forward). *Kadima* was formed by Prime Minister Sharon after he left *Likud,* then the leading party in the coalition government, in November 2005. Sharon's goal was a new centrist party that would grant him the freedom to carry out his policy of unilateral disengagement from Palestinian territories, a move that was staunchly opposed by some other members of *Likud.* Senior figures from Labor and *Likud* joined the new party, including Finance Minister Ehud Olmert (the former mayor of Jerusalem), justice minister Tzipi Livni (both from *Likud*), and former prime minister Shimon Peres (Labor). Following Sharon's debilitating stroke in January 2006, Olmert became acting prime minister.

Kadima won the largest number of seats (29 out of 120) in the March 2006 *Knesset* balloting. Its platform included a pledge to make further disengagements from Palestinian territory, although Jerusalem and the larger settlement blocs in the West Bank would remain under Israeli control.

Facing a growing corruption investigation (see Current issues, above), Olmert in July 2008 announced his intention to resign as prime minister. He also subsequently decided not to run as a candidate in the new election for *Kadima*'s leader, the post being narrowly won in balloting on September 17 by Tzipi Livni, theretofore deputy prime minister and a longtime rival of Olmert within the party. Livni, a centrist considered untainted by the corruption scandal, defeated runner-up Lt. Gen. (Ret.) Shaul Mofaz, a hawkish former army chief and current minister of transportation and road safety, by 43.1 percent of the vote to 42 percent. Mofaz had recently generated headlines by suggesting that an Israeli attack on Iran's nuclear facilities was "unavoidable."

Following Prime Minister Olmert's resignation in September 2008, Livni was unable to forge a new coalition government, necessitating early elections in February 2009. Although *Kadima* secured a plurality (28 seats) on a vote share of 22.5 percent, Livni proved unable to form a center-left government, and *Kadima* moved into opposition.

Olmert was indicated on three charges of corruption in late August 2009.

Leaders: Tzipi LIVNI (Party Leader and Leader of the Opposition), Shimon PERES (President of Israel), Lt. Gen. (Ret.) Shaul MOFAZ, Yohanan PLESNER, Eli AFLALO.

United Arab List (UAL). The UAL was formed prior to the 1996 *Knesset* elections by Arab groups hoping to increase the electoral clout of the estimated 1 million Israeli Arabs by presenting a joint list of candidates. Although reports agreed that one core component of the new grouping was the **Arab Democratic Party,** there was confusion regarding other participants. Israeli government publications said that the other two components of the UAL were the **Islamic Movement in Israel** and an **Arab Islamic List.**

The UAL won four seats in the 1996 balloting, as several other Arab groupings decided to present their own candidates. The UAL increased its representation in the May 1999 *Knesset* election to five seats on the strength of 3.4 percent of the vote but fell to two seats in 2003. In the 2006 *Knesset* election, the UAL ran on a single list with the **Arab Movement for Change,** led by Ahmad Tibi (see National Democratic Alliance [*Balad*], below, for earlier information). The combined grouping won four seats with just over 3 percent of the vote.

In early 2009 the Central Elections Committee banned the UAL and *Balad* from participating in the upcoming *Knesset* balloting on the grounds that the parties supported terrorism and refused to recognize Israel as a democratic Jewish state. Tibi called the proponents of the ban (primarily the far-right National Union and *Yisrael Beiteinu*) "fascists and racists" determined to have "a country without Arabs." The Supreme Court subsequently revoked the electoral ban, and the UAL–Arab Movement for Change List (named *Ra'am Ta'al*) retained its four seats in the February *Knesset* balloting on a vote share of 3.9 percent, having campaigned on a platform calling for Israeli withdrawal (including settlers) from the West Bank and establishment of a Palestinian state.

Leaders: Ibrahim SARSUR, Ahmad TIBI (Parliamentary Leader).

National Union (*Halchud HaLeumi*). Formed as an electoral alliance in early 1999 by *Moledet*, *Tequma* (see below), and New *Herut*, the right-wing National Union won four seats (two for *Moledet* and one each for *Tequma* and New *Herut*) in the May *Knesset* elections on the strength of 3 percent of the vote. Shortly thereafter, the National Union formed a joint *Knesset* faction with *Yisrael Beiteinu,* although the New *Herut* legislator objected to that initiative, and New *Herut* left the National Union. The National Union–*Yisrael Beiteinu* (NU–YB) faction joined the Sharon government in March 2001 but subsequently found itself to the right even of Sharon regarding the Palestinian question. On October 15 the NU–YB ministers, including Tourism Minister Rechavam Ze'evi of *Moledet,* announced their intention to resign from the cabinet. However, that decision was temporarily rescinded after Ze'evi was assassinated on October 17 by Palestinian militants. In March 2002 the NU–YB finally left the coalition, subsequent efforts by Sharon failing to persuade the ultrarightists to return.

In 2003 the NU–YB won seven seats in the Knesset election. The NU-YB *Knesset* faction expanded in 2005 when legislators Ephraim Eitam and Yitzhak Levy defected from the NRP and formed the Renewed Religious National Zionist Party, which joined the National Union.

Yisrael Beiteinu left the coalition prior to the 2006 *Knesset* balloting, in which the National Union ran with the NRP on one slate, which won nine seats (six for the National Union parties). An attempt was made to merge the NU and NRP into a single party in late 2008, but the initiative collapsed in a dispute over the proposed candidate list (see Jewish Home, above, for additional information). Meanwhile, Eitam's group aligned with *Likud* (see section on *Likud*). Consequently, the National Union ticket that won four seats in the February 2009 poll comprised *Moledet*, most of *Tequma*, and several smaller parties, including **Hatikva**, led by Aryeh ELDAD, and **Our Land of Israel** (*Eretz Yisrael Shelanu*), led by Rabbi Sholom Dov WOLPO and Baruch MARZEL.

Leader: Yaacov KATZ (Chair and Parliamentary Leader).

Homeland (*Moledet*). *Moledet* is an ultra-Zionist secular party founded in 1988 by a reserve major general, Rechavam Ze'evi, who called for annexation of the occupied territories and the ouster of their Arab inhabitants. In a controversial move that was opposed by several senior ministers, Ze'evi was appointed to the Shamir cabinet in February 1991, but the party went into opposition after the 1992 election, in which it increased its representation from two to three seats. In early July 1994 plans were announced for a merger of *Moledet* with the equally right-wing Renaissance (*Tehiya*) party. (For additional information on *Tehiya,* see the 2007 *Handbook.*)

Moledet won two seats in the 1996 *Knesset* balloting. Initially it was reported that the party was considering adopting a position of support for the government from outside the cabinet. However, that premise had collapsed by the end of the year, with the *Moledet* legislators presenting a token no-confidence motion in December to protest the government's negotiations regarding further troop withdrawals in the occupied territories.

Leader: Yaakov KATZ.

Revival (*Tequma*). Launched in late 1998 by spiritual leaders and activists among Jewish settlers in the occupied territories, *Tequma* subsequently joined the National Union electoral coalition with *Moledet* and New *Herut,* the right-wing parties having concluded they all would face difficulty passing the 1.5 percent vote threshold for *Knesset* representation running individually.

Leaders: Rabbi Menahem FELIBUS, Uri ARIEL, Benny KATZOVER, Zvi HENDEL.

Democratic Front for Peace and Equality—DFPE (*Hazit Democratit le-Shalom ve-Shivayon—Hadash*). The Democratic Front was organized prior to the 1977 election to present candidates drawn from the former New Communist List (*Rashima Kommunistit Hadasha*—Rakah), a section of the "Black Panther" movement of Oriental Jews, and a number of unaffiliated local Arab leaders. The DFPE retained its existing four *Knesset* seats in 1988, lost one in 1992, rebounded to five in 1996 (campaigning on behalf of an independent Palestinian state and "equality" for Israeli Arabs), and fell back to three in 1999 on a 2.6 percent vote share. The party, described as supported primarily by secular Israeli Arabs, retained its three seats in the 2003 and 2006 *Knesset* elections, and improved to four seats in the 2009 balloting on a vote share of 3.3 percent.

Leaders: Muhammad BAREKA (Chair), Hanna SWAID (Parliamentary Leader), Awdah BISHARAT (Secretary General).

Power–Democratic Israel (*Meretz–Yisrael Democrati*). *Meretz* was formed prior to the 1992 election as a coalition of the Civil Rights and Peace Movement—CRM (*ha-Tenua le-Zechouot ha-Ezrakh*—Ratz), the United Workers' Party (*Mifleget Hapoalim Hamenchedet*—Mapam), and *Shinu* (see below). The *Meretz* platform called for a phased peace settlement with the Palestinians, Jordan, Lebanon, and Syria, based on withdrawal from the occupied territories and guarantees for the security of Israel through interim agreements, security arrangements, and demilitarization. It also advocated religious pluralism, liberalization of the "law of return," the adoption of a bill of rights, equal status for women, and strict enforcement of antipollution legislation. *Meretz* won 12 *Knesset* seats in 1992 and 9 (Ratz, 4; Mapam, 3; and *Shinui*, 2) in 1996, having prior to the latter endorsed the creation of an independent Palestinian state and "land-for-peace" negotiations with Syria.

In February 1996 it was reported that Yossi SARID, a Ratz member and environmental minister in the Peres cabinet, had been elected to succeed Shulamit ALONI as *Meretz* chair. In early 1999 Ratz and Mapam agreed to a formal merger of their groupings, with *Meretz* becoming a political party rather than a coalition. Some *Shinui* members also participated in that initiative, although *Shinui* ultimately retained its own identity and campaigned on its own for the May 1999 *Knesset* elections, in which *Meretz* won ten seats on a vote share of 7.6 percent.

Meretz won six seats in the 2003 *Knesset* balloting on a vote share of 5.2 percent. Subsequently, it was announced that *Meretz* would merge with several other left-wing groups to form a new party, known as *Meretz-Yahad* ("Together"), which opposed Prime Minister Sharon's disengagement plan, calling instead for negotiations with the Palestinians toward a comprehensive settlement. Party leaders hoped to draw support from disaffected ILP members. However, in the 2006 *Knesset* election *Meretz-Yahad* won only five seats (on a 3.8 percent vote share), one less than *Meretz* had won in 2003 and just half of the representation it had after the 1999 election. In the 2009 *Knesset* elections *Meretz* ran on a joint list with the **New Movement** (*Tnu'a HaHadasha*), a new grouping of left-wing activists led by Tzali REGHEF. The New Movement–*Meretz* list won three seats (two for *Meretz*) on a vote share of 2.95 percent.

Leaders: Chaim ORON (Chair), Ilan GHILON (Parliamentary Leader).

National Democratic Alliance (*Balad*). This pro-Arab grouping is led by Azmi Bishara, a former member of Rakah who had been elected to the *Knesset* in 1996 on the Hadash list. In March 1999 Bishara, a Christian, announced his candidacy for prime minister, thereby potentially becoming the first non-Jew to run for that post. *Balad* campaigned primarily in opposition to perceived government discrimination against Israeli Arabs. It was subsequently reported that Ahmed Tibi, a Palestinian leader, had associated his Arab Movement for Change with *Balad.* Formed in early 1996 by Tibi (described as an adviser to Palestinian leader Yasir Arafat), the movement was one of the groupings expected to participate in the UAL. However, according to government publications, it presented its own candidates (unsuccessfully) in the 1996 *Knesset* elections before aligning with *Balad* for the 1999 balloting. (See UAL, above, for subsequent information on Tibi's party.)

Bishara withdrew from the prime minister's race shortly before the May 17, 1999, balloting; he did not specifically endorse Labor's Ehud Barak, but most Bishara supporters were expected to vote for Barak. *Balad* won two seats (filled by Bishara and Tibi) in the concurrent *Knesset* election. The *Knesset* stripped Bishara of his parliamentary immunity in November 2001, and the *Balad* leader went on trial in February 2002 on charges of "incitement to violence" by, among other things, a speech he had given in Syria supporting "popular resistance" on the part of Palestinians. (The charges were subsequently dropped after the courts ruled that Bishara's immunity had been in place when the statements were made.)

The Israeli government was unsuccessful in its efforts to have *Balad* disqualified from the 2003 *Knesset* balloting, in which *Balad* secured three seats on a 2.3 percent vote share. In 2006 *Balad* again won three seats. However, in April 2007 Bishara (by then resident abroad) reportedly resigned his *Knesset* seat after Israeli police confirmed that they were investigating him on suspicion of having "aided an enemy" during the 2006 war between Israel and Hezbollah in Lebanon. (Bishara had denounced Israel's actions in that conflict.)

Balad, described as supported mainly by secular Arab Israelis, faced another attempt to ban it from elections in 2009 (see UAL, above, for details). Following a Supreme Court ruling in its favor, *Balad* retained its three seats in the *Knesset* on a vote share of 2.5 percent.

Leaders: Azmi BISHARA (in exile), Jamal ZAHALKA (Chair and Parliamentary Leader).

Other Parties that Participated in the 2009 *Knesset* Elections:

Pensioners Party (*Gimla'ey Yisrael LaKneset*—Gil). Gil's primary concerns are domestic, and it pledges to protect pensioner rights, including the right to housing. It also advocates the enlargement of national health insurance and other services for pensioners. Gil stunned electoral observers in the 2006 *Knesset* poll by winning seven seats with nearly 6 percent of the vote. The party's ascent was underscored by its invitation to join the coalition government formed in May.

Three Gil legislators, led by Moshe SHARONI, quit the party in mid-2008 and formed a "Justice for Pensioners" faction in the *Knesset.* The defectors criticized Gil leader Rafi Eitan for failing to push the Olmert administration sufficiently in regard to proposed pension increases. Although two of the earlier defectors reportedly later rejoined Gil, the party fell dramatically to 0.5 percent of the vote in the February 2009 *Knesset* balloting.

Leader: Rafi EITAN.

Dimension (*Meimad*). Founded in the late 1980s by former NRP members who believed the parent grouping had become too right-wing, *Meimad* competed unsuccessfully in the 1992 *Knesset* elections. In February 1998 *Meimad* announced its intention to participate in the next legislative balloting as an "Orthodox but open-minded and open-hearted" grouping that could provide a voice for Zionists who supported the peace process. In early 1999 *Meimad* agreed to join the One Israel electoral coalition with the Labor Party and *Gesher. Meimad* secured 1 of the 26 seats won by One Israel in the May *Knesset* balloting, and leader Rabbi Michael Melchior was named to the subsequent Barak cabinet. *Meimad* ran in coalition with Labor in the 2003 and 2006 *Knesset* elections but opted out of that electoral alliance for 2009 in a dispute over where *Meimad* members would be placed on the candidate list. (*Meimad* had previously been assured of gaining seats via its placement in the lists.) *Meimad* contested the 2009 poll in alliance with the new **Green Movement,** a social-environmental party recently established under the leadership of Eran BEN-YEMINI and Al TAL. The new alliance won only 0.8 percent of the vote.

Leaders: Rabbi Michael MELCHIOR, Rabbi Yehuda AMITAL.

The Greens. One of several environmentally oriented parties established recently, The Greens won 1.52 percent of the vote in the 2006 *Knesset* poll, which would have been sufficient to secure representation in previous elections for which the threshold was 1.5 percent (raised to 2 percent for 2006). The party won some 50 seats in 22 municipalities in the November 2008 local elections but declined to 0.37 percent of the vote in the 2009 *Knesset* balloting.

Leader: Pe'er VISNER (Deputy Mayor of Tel Aviv).

Crossroads (*Tzomet*). Also known as the Zionist Revival Movement, *Tzomet* was formed by the defection of former army chief of staff Rafael EITAN from *Tehiya* prior to the 1988 balloting, in which it won two *Knesset* seats; *Tzomet* won eight seats in 1992 but split in 1994, when two of its legislators defected to form a separate faction, which in June took the name *Yiud* and subsequently joined the Labor coalition. *Tzomet* joined *Likud* and *Gesher* in an electoral coalition in early 1996, supporting Benjamin Netanyahu for prime minister and presenting joint *Knesset* candidates. *Tzomet* was allocated five of the *Knesset* seats won by the alliance in May, and Eitan was named deputy prime minister and minister of agriculture and rural development in the new cabinet formed in June. As was the case with several other ministers from hard-line groupings, Eitan voted against the accord providing for additional Israeli troop withdrawals from the West Bank when it was presented to the cabinet in January 1997. *Tzomet* contested the 1999 *Knesset* balloting on its own, securing only 0.1 percent of the vote. Former *Tzomet* leader Rafael Eitan drowned in November 2004. *Tzomet* won only 1,509 votes in the 2006 *Knesset* poll and 0.05 percent of the vote in 2009.

Leader: Moshe GREEN.

Other parties that presented candidates in 2009 included ***Ahrayut*** (Responsibility, 0.02 percent of the vote), which, under the leadership of Yaakov HESDAI, called for government restructuring through promulgation of a written constitution; ***Brit Olam*** (0.1 percent in 2006, 0.02 percent in 2009), a grouping led by Ofer LIFSCHITZ and Kinneret Golan HOZ that promotes improved relations between the Jewish and Arab communities; the ***Da'am* Workers Party** (0.1 percent of the vote in 2006, 0.08 percent in 2009), a largely Israeli Arab organization founded in 1995 by Jewish and Arab activists as an offshoot of the Communist Party of Israel and currently led by Asma AGBARIEH-ZAHALKA; the left-wing **Green-Leaf** (*Ale-Yarok*) party (1.2 percent of the vote in 2006, 0.39 percent in 2009), a grouping currently led by comedian Gil KOPATCH that promotes, among other things, the liberalization of marijuana laws; the ***Holocaust Survivors and Ale-Yarok Alumni*** (0.07 percent), led by Ohad SHEM-TOV and Moshe SASON; ***Koah Hakesef*** (Power of Money, 0.03 percent), a grouping led by Elizer LEVINGER that participated in the 2006 poll as the Party for the Struggle with the Banks; ***Koah LaHashpi'a*** (Strength to Influence, 0.11 percent), a new grouping dedicated to the rights of the disabled and led by Yochai DOK; ***Lazuz*** (Move, 0.02 percent), an anticorruption grouping led by Amnon ZE'EVI; ***Lechem*** (Bread, 0.02 percent in 2009), led by Yisrael TVITO; ***LEEDER*** (0.06 percent), led by Alexander RADKO; ***Lev*** (less than

0.01 percent), an immigrant grouping led by Ovadia FATCHOV; **Man's Rights in the Family Party** (0.03 percent), a grouping led by Yaakov SHLUSSER that participated in earlier elections as Justice for All (*Tsedek Lako)*; ***Or*** (Light, 0.02 percent), a secular grouping formed in 2008 under the leadership of author Yaron YADAN to pursue uniform education; **The Israelis** (*HaYisraelim,* 0.03 percent in 2009), a new party led by Gideon DORON in pursuit of a revamping of the *Knesset* structure to include constituency seats in addition to national proportional seats; ***Tzabar*** (0.14 percent), a youth-oriented party led by Boaz TOPOROVSKY; and ***Yisrael HaMithadeshet*** (Renewed Israel, 0.08 percent), currently led by Michael NUDELMAN;.

Other Parties:

Change (*Shinui*). The original *Shinui* movement under Amnon RUBINSTEIN joined in November 1976 with the Democratic Movement of former army chief of staff Yigael Yadin to form the Democratic Movement for Change (DMC), which, with 15 seats, emerged as the third-largest party in the 1977 election, after which it supported the Begin government. Following a split in the DMC in September 1978, the *Shinui* group and supporters of Transport and Communications Minister Meir AMIT withdrew to form the opposition Change and Initiative (*Shinui ve Yozma*—Shai). The DMC was formally dissolved in February 1981, its remnants regrouping with supporters of Shai to contest the June election under the *Shinui* label. A member of the national unity government after the 1984 balloting, *Shinui* withdrew from the coalition in May 1987. It presented a joint list with the New Liberal Party in 1988.

Two *Shinui* members were elected to the *Knesset* in 1996 as part of *Meretz.* However, *Shinui* in early 1999 opted to contest the upcoming *Knesset* balloting on its own under the leadership of Tommy LAPID, a political commentator and television personality who accepted the *Shinui* chairmanship in March. *Shinui*'s subsequent campaign was primarily devoted to opposing the increasing influence of ultra-orthodox parties. It secured six seats in the May 1999 *Knesset* balloting on a vote share of 5 percent. *Shinui* subsequently maintained a position of refusing to join any government that included any ultra-orthodox parties. Lapid resigned from the party in early 2006, and a number of *Shinui* members reportedly joined *Kadima.* The rump *Shinui* received only 4,675 votes in the March *Knesset* balloting. Lapid died in mid-2008.

New Freedom (*Herut Hahadasha*). New *Herut* was launched in 1998 by former *Likud* member Benjamin (Benny) BEGIN as a revival of the original *Herut,* which had been formed in the 1970s by his father, Menachem Begin. Benjamin Begin, a steadfast opponent of any "land-for-peace" agreement with the Palestinians, subsequently announced his candidacy for the prime ministerial election of May 1999. He also was a leading figure in the formation of the right-wing National Union electoral coalition with *Moledet* and *Tequma* for the concurrent *Knesset* balloting. However, Begin, who had withdrawn his prime ministerial candidacy shortly before the balloting, resigned his National Union leadership post following the. New *Herut* left the National Union when the Union agreed to form a single *Knesset* faction with *Yisrael Beiteinu,* the New *Herut* legislator thereby becoming a single-member faction. The party won less than 0.1 percent of the vote in the 2006 *Knesset* balloting.

Leader: Michael KLEINER.

Center Party. Formed in mid-1998 by Ronni MILO, a former mayor of Tel Aviv who had recently left *Likud* in opposition to the policies of Prime Minister Netanyahu, the Center Party subsequently attracted the support of other *Likud* dissenters, such as former finance minister Dan Meridor, as well as independents, such as Amnon LIPKIN-SHARAK, a former chief of the general staff of the Israeli Defense Force. Prior to joining the Center Party, Lipkin-Sharak had announced his intention to run for prime minister against Netanyahu. It initially appeared that Lipkin-Sharak would become the Center Party's nominee, but that designation ultimately went to Itzhak MORDECHAI, who joined the party shortly after being dismissed as defense minister by Netanyahu in January 1999. (The four prominent politicians in the Center Party had reportedly agreed to determine the strongest potential nominee among themselves and coalesce behind his candidacy.) Mordechai, arguing that Netanyahu was "incapable" of producing a permanent peace settlement, was attracting the support of about 25 percent of the voters, according to preelection public opinion polls. However, he withdrew from the race shortly before the election, throwing his support to Labor's Ehud Barak.

The Center Party won six seats in the May 1999 *Knesset* balloting on a vote share of 5 percent. It joined the original Barak cabinet but withdrew in August 2000. It joined the Sharon government in August 2001. In mid-2002 it was reported that several Center Party legislators were considering a return to *Likud.* Party leader Meridor also subsequently rejoined *Likud*, and the Center Party was subsequently described as defunct.

Movement for Israel and Immigration (*Yisrael B'Aliya*). *Yisrael B'Aliya* was originally launched in 1992 as the National Movement for Democracy and Aliya ("ingathering") as a means of promoting the economic well-being of the ex-Soviet immigrant community. *Yisrael B'Aliya* won six seats in the May 1999 legislative balloting on a vote share of 5.1 percent. After joining the subsequent Barak government, it left the cabinet in early August 2000 in opposition to consideration being given to a possible return of the Golan Heights to Syria. The party was awarded cabinet seats in the new Sharon government in early 2001, with Natan SHARANSKY serving as deputy prime minister. Following the poor showing of *Yisrael B'Aliya* in the January 2003 *Knesset* balloting (two seats on a 2.2 percent vote share), Sharansky resigned his cabinet post, with the stated goal of "rebuilding" the party. However, it was quickly announced that the deputies from *Yisrael B'Aliya* would "merge" with the *Likud* faction in the *Knesset.* Sharansky was subsequently named minister for diaspora affairs, but he resigned that post in May 2005 to protest Sharon's disengagement plan. *Yisrael B'Aliya* finally merged with *Likud* before the 2006 Knesset poll, and its former leader Sharansky subsequently served as a *Likud* representative in the *Knesset* before announcing his retirement from politics in October 2006.

Banned Party:

Kahane Lives (*Kahane Chai*). *Kahane Chai* is a derivative of Thus (*Kach*), which served as the political vehicle of Rabbi Meir KAHANE, founder of the U.S.-based Jewish Defense League. *Kach* elected its leader to the *Knesset* in 1984, after having competed unsuccessfully in 1977 and 1981. Linked to the activities of the anti-Arab "Jewish underground," the group advocated the forcible expulsion of Palestinians from both Israel and the occupied territories. It was precluded from submitting a *Knesset* list in October 1988, when the High Court of Justice ruled in favor of an Election Commission finding that it was "racist" and "undemocratic." Kahane was assassinated in New York in November 1990, with a number of his followers, including his son, Rabbi Binyamin Zeev KAHANE, subsequently forming *Kahane Chai.*

Baruch GOLDSTEIN, the Jewish settler who killed 29 Muslim worshippers at a Hebron mosque on February 25, 1994, was a Kahane disciple. On March 13 the Israeli cabinet voted to ban both *Kach* and *Kahane Chai,* although a subsequent official report on the incident found that Goldstein had acted alone.

Binyamin Kahane and his wife were killed in late December 2000 in a drive-by shooting allegedly conducted by Palestinian militants. In late 2001 the United States added *Kahane Chai* to its list of terrorist organizations, despite objections from the Israeli government. *Kahane Chai* was subsequently described as "highly visible" among Jewish settlers in the West Bank.

LEGISLATURE

The ***Knesset*** (Assembly or Congregation) is a unicameral legislature of 120 members elected by universal suffrage for four-year terms (subject to dissolution either by the *Knesset* itself or the prime minister [with the consent of the president]). The members are elected on a nationwide proportional basis, each voter casting one vote for the party or coalition of his or her choice. (The minimum vote percentage for a party to gain representation was raised from 1 percent to 1.5 percent in 1992 and to 2 percent in 2006.)

In the most recent balloting of February 10, 2009, *Kadima* won a plurality of 28 seats, followed by *Likud*, 27 seats; *Yisrael Beiteinu*, 15; the Israel Labor Party, 13; the Sephardic Torah Guardians (Shas), 11; United Torah Judaism, 5; the coalition (*Ra'am Ta'al*) of the United Arab List and the Arab Movement for Renewal, 4; the National Union, 4; the Democratic Front for Peace and Equality (*Hadash*), 4;

the New-Movement–*Meretz*, 3; Jewish Home (*Habayit Hayehudi*), 3; and the National Democratic Alliance (*Balad*), 3.

Speaker: Reuven RIVLIN.

CABINET

[as of November 1, 2009]

Prime Minister	Benjamin Netanyahu (*Likud*)
Vice Prime Ministers	Silvan Shalom (*Likud*) Moshe Ya'alon (*Likud*)
Deputy Prime Ministers	Ehud Barak (Labor) Avigdor Lieberman (*Yisrael Beiteinu*) Dan Meridor (*Likud*) Eliyahu Yishai (Shas)
Ministers	
Agriculture and Rural Development	Shalom Simhon (Labor)
Communications	Moshe Kahlon (*Likud*)
Culture and Sport	Limor Livnat (*Likud*) [f]
Defense	Ehud Barak (Labor)
Development of the Negev and Galilee	Silvan Shalom (*Likud*)
Economic Strategies	Benjamin Netanyahu (*Likud*)
Education	Gideon Sa'ar (*Likud*)
Environmental Protection	Gilad Erdan (*Likud*)
Finance	Yuval Shteinitz (*Likud*)
Foreign Affairs	Avigdor Lieberman (*Yisrael Beiteinu*)
Health	Benjamin Netanyahu (*Likud*)
Housing and Construction	Ariel Atias (Shas)
Immigrant Absorption	Sofa Landver (*Yisrael Beiteinu*) [f]
Improvement of Government Service to the Public	Michael Eitan (*Likud*)
Industry, Trade, and Labor	Binyamin Ben-Eliezer (Labor)
Intelligence	Dan Meridor (*Likud*)
Interior	Eliyahu Yishai (Shas)
Internal Security	Yitzhak Aharonovitz (*Yisrael Beiteinu*)
Justice	Yaakov Ne'eman (*Likud*)
Minority Affairs	Avishai Braverman (Labor)
National Infrastructures	Uzi Landau (*Yisrael Beiteinu*)
Public Diplomacy and the Diaspora	Yuli Edelstein (*Likud*)
Regional Cooperation	Silvan Shalom (*Likud*)
Religious Services	Yaakov Margi (Shas)
Science and Technology	Daniel Hershkovitz (*Habayit Hayehudi*)
Senior Citizens	Benjamin Netanyahu (*Likud*)
Social Affairs and Heritage	Meshulam Nahari (Shas)
Strategic Affairs	Moshe Ya'alon (*Likud*)
Tourism	Stas Misejnikov (*Yisrael Beiteinu*)
Transportation and Road Safety	Israel Katz (*Likud*)
Welfare and Social Services	Yitzhak Herzog (Labor)
Without Portfolio	Ze'ev B. Begin (*Likud*) Yossi Peled (*Likud*)

[f] = female

COMMUNICATIONS

Israeli newspapers are numerous and diversified, although many of the leading dailies reflect partisan or religious interests. Reporters Without Borders in early 2008 described the media as enjoying "genuine freedom," although there was a degree of military censorship on national security grounds. However, the journalism watchdog organization said that Israel's press freedom record was subsequently "badly tarnished" by military abuses against journalists in the Palestinian territories, particularly during the Gaza offensive of late 2008 and early 2009. The government was also criticized for banning access to Gaza by the media during that time.

Press. The following are dailies published in Hebrew in Tel Aviv, unless otherwise noted: *Yedioth Aharonoth* (300,000 daily, 600,000 Friday), independent; *Ma'ariv* (160,000 daily, 270,000 Friday), independent; *Ha'aretz* (65,000 daily, 75,000 Friday), independent liberal; *al-Quds* (Jerusalem, 50,000), in Arabic; *Davar* (39,000 daily, 43,000 Friday), General Federation of Labor organ; *Jerusalem Post* (Jerusalem, 30,000 daily, 50,000 Friday, not including North American edition published weekly in New York), in English; *Globes* (29,000), business organ; *Hatzofeh* (16,000), National Religious Front organ; *Hamodia* (Jerusalem, 15,000), *Agudat Yisrael* organ. There are also smaller dailies published in Arabic, Bulgarian, French, German, Hungarian, Polish, Romanian, Russian, voweled Hebrew, and Yiddish.

News agencies. The domestic agency is the News Agency of the Associated Israel Press (*'Itonut Yisrael Me'uchedet*—ITIM); numerous foreign bureaus also maintain offices in Israel, including the Jewish Telegraphic Agency of New York.

Broadcasting and computing. The commercial, government-controlled Israel Broadcasting Authority (*Reshut Hashidur Hayisra'elit*) provides local and national radio service over six programs, international radio service in 16 languages, and television service in Hebrew and Arabic. *Galei Zahal,* the radio station of the Israeli defense forces, broadcasts from Tel Aviv, as does the Israel Educational Television. As of 2008 there were 496.4 Internet users per 1,000 inhabitants.

INTERGOVERNMENTAL REPRESENTATION

Ambassador to the U.S.: Michael OREN.

U.S. Ambassador to Israel: James B. CUNNINGHAM.

Permanent Representative to the UN: Gabriela SHALEV.

IGO Memberships (Non-UN): BIS, EBRD, IADB, Interpol, IOM, PCA, WCO, WTO.

OCCUPIED AND PREVIOUSLY OCCUPIED TERRITORIES

The largely desert Sinai Peninsula, encompassing some 23,000 square miles (59,600 sq. km.), was occupied by Israel during the 1956 war with Egypt but was subsequently evacuated under U.S. and UN pressure. It was reoccupied during the Six-Day War of 1967 and, except for a narrow western band bordering on Suez, was retained after the Yom Kippur War of 1973. The Egyptian-Israeli peace treaty, signed in Washington, D.C., on March 26, 1979, provided for a phased withdrawal, two-thirds of which—to beyond a buffer zone running roughly from El Arish in the north to Ras Muhammad in the south—was completed by January 1980. Withdrawal from the remainder of the Sinai, to "the recognized international boundary between Egypt and the former mandated territory of Palestine," was completed on April 25, 1982 (three years from the exchange of treaty-ratification instruments), "without prejudice to the issue of the status of the Gaza Strip."

Title to Taba, a small Israeli-occupied area adjoining the southern port of Eilat, was long disputed. A 1906 Anglo-Egyptian/Turkish agreement fixed the border as running through Taba itself. However, a 1915 British military survey (admitted to be imperfect) placed the border some three-quarters of a mile to the northeast. A decision to submit the matter to arbitration was made during talks between Egyptian President Hosni Mubarak and Israeli Prime Minister Shimon Peres in Alexandria in September 1986. Two years later a five-member tribunal supported the Egyptian claim in regard to a boundary marker 150 yards inland from the shore, and in early 1989 Egypt acquired ownership of a luxury hotel on the beach itself, after agreeing to pay compensation to its owner.

Golan Heights. The mountainous Golan Heights, embracing a natural barrier of some 600 square miles (1,550 sq. km.) at the juncture of Israel and Syria southeast of Lebanon, was occupied by Israel during the 1967 war. Its interim status (including demarcation of an eastern strip under UN administration) was set forth in a disengagement agreement concluded with Syria in May 1974. In an action condemned by many foreign governments, including that of the United States, the area under Israeli military control was formally made subject to Israeli "law, jurisdiction, and administration" on December 14, 1981. The Israeli-controlled area is largely Druze-populated, with a minority of Jewish settlers; the number of inhabitants in mid-2006 was approximately 40,000.

Note: For information on the Gaza Strip (formerly occupied by Israel) and the West Bank (which currently contains Israeli settlements as well as Palestinian-controlled areas) see the article on the Palestinian Authority/Palestine Liberation Organization.

ITALY

Italian Republic
Repubblica Italiana

Political Status: Unified state proclaimed in 1861; republic established by national referendum in 1946; under parliamentary constitution effective January 1, 1948.

Area: 116,303 sq. mi. (301,225 sq. km.).

Population: 56,995,744 (2001C); 58,959,000 (2007E). The 2001 figure is de jure. The de facto figure is 57,110,144.

Major Urban Centers (2005E): ROME (2,539,000), Milan (1,284,000), Naples (996,000), Turin (870,000), Palermo (675,000), Genoa (591,000).

Official Language: Italian (German is also official in Trentino-Alto Adige).

Monetary Unit: Euro (market rate November 1, 2008: 1 euro = $1.51US).

President of the Republic: Giorgio NAPOLITANO (Democrats of the Left) elected by the electoral college on May 10, 2006, and inaugurated on May 15 for a seven-year term, succeeding Carlo Azeglio CIAMPI (nonparty).

President of the Council of Ministers: (Prime Minister): Silvio BERLUSCONI (People of Freedom); elected on April 13–14, 2008, and sworn in along with a new government on May 8 to succeed Romano PRODI (The Union).

THE COUNTRY

A peninsula rooted in the Alps and jutting into the Mediterranean for a distance of some 725 miles, the Italian Republic includes the large islands of Sicily and Sardinia and other smaller islands in the Tyrrhenian, Adriatic, Ionian, Ligurian, and Sardinian seas. Rugged terrain limits large-scale agriculture to the Po Valley, the Campagna region around Naples, and the plain of Foggia in the southeast. Among numerous socioeconomic cleavages, there is a vast difference between the industrialized north and the substantially underdeveloped south. Ethnically, however, the Italians form a relatively homogeneous society, the only substantial minority being the approximately 250,000 German-speaking persons in the province of Bolzano (Alto Adige, or South Tyrol), which is part of the region known as Venezia Tridentina from 1919 to 1947 and thereafter as Trentino-Alto Adige, whose more activist leaders have long sought a referendum on return of the province to Austrian sovereignty. Although Italian is the official language, regional variations of the standard Tuscan dialect exist, and in various parts of the country small minorities speak French, German, Ladin (similar to Romansch), Slovene, and Sard (Sardinian). Roman Catholicism is nominally professed by over 90 percent of the population; however, religious freedom is constitutionally guaranteed, and in March 1985 the Chamber of Deputies ratified a revised concordat with the Holy See that terminated Roman Catholicism's status as the state religion. In 2006 women constituted 40 percent of the paid labor force, concentrated mainly in education and the service sector; female participation in political leadership bodies has been estimated at 10 percent.

Italy, a founding member of the Economic and Monetary Union (EMU) of the European Union (EU), is the world's seventh largest economy. Though the "economic miracle" that characterized the lengthy boom period after World War II eventually faded, during the 1960s and 1970s, Italy's real GDP increased at a yearly average of 4.3 percent and its population at only 0.7 percent, allowing per capita income to double. GDP growth averaged 2.4 percent annually in 1976–1986 but only 1.4 percent over the following decade. Sluggish growth averaging 1.7 percent annually in 1998–1999 was followed by an upsurge to 3 percent in 2000, but annual growth declined to 2.2 percent in 2005, 1.5 percent in 2007, and –1 percent in 2008, amid rising inflation, appreciation of the euro, and the global economic recession. At present, the agricultural sector accounts for 2 percent of GDP, while industry contributes about 27 percent, and services, the balance.

Unemployment, a persistent problem, declined from 11.4 percent in1998 to 6.8 percent in 2008. Inflation reached 3.3 percent in 2008, the highest in 12 years, before falling to a 30-year low of just under 1 percent for 2009 in the wake of falling prices of goods and services as a result of the global recession. In recent years the government has targeted tax evasion in an effort to bring the economy in line with EU standards for member states and to help reduce the spiraling deficit. A slowing economy and increasing welfare costs contributed to the deficit as well, likely pushing the deficit beyond the EU limit of 3 percent of annual GDP in 2009.

GOVERNMENT AND POLITICS

Political background. Unified in the 19th century as a parliamentary monarchy under the House of Savoy, Italy fought with the Allies in World War I. Having succumbed in 1922 to the Fascist dictatorship of Benito MUSSOLINI, it entered World War II on the side of Nazi Germany in June 1940 and switched to the Allied side only after Mussolini's removal from office in 1943. Following a period of provisional government, the monarchy was abolished by popular referendum in 1946, and a new, republican constitution went into effect on January 1, 1948. A Communist Party (*Partito Comunista Italiano*—PCI) bid for national power under the leadership of Palmiro TOGLIATTI was defeated in the parliamentary election of April 1948, which established the Christian Democrats (*Partito della Democrazia Cristiana*—DC), then headed by Alcide DE GASPERI, as Italy's strongest political force. Luigi EINAUDI (DC) was elected as the country's first president in May 1948, being succeeded by Giovanni GRONCHI (DC) in 1955 and Antonio SEGNI (DC) in 1962, with the DC leading a succession of concurrent center-right coalition governments. The first important modification in this pattern occurred in 1962 with the formation by the DC's Amintore FANFANI of a center-left coalition that, under a policy of an "opening to the left" (*apertura a sinistra*), sought parliamentary support from the Socialist Party (*Partito Socialista Italiano*—PSI) and from 1964 usually included PSI ministers in the government. As part of the realignment, Giuseppe SARAGAT of the Democratic Socialist Party (*Partito Socialista Democratico Italiano*—PSDI) was elected to replace the ailing Segni as president in December 1964. Saragat was succeeded by Giovanni LEONE (DC) in 1971.

In a bitterly contested election in June 1976, the PCI registered unprecedented gains at the expense of the smaller parties, running a close second to the DC. While another DC-PSI government could technically have been formed, the Socialists had indicated during the campaign that they would no longer participate in a coalition that excluded the PCI. For their part, the Communists agreed to abstain on confirmation of a new cabinet in return for a "government role" at less than the cabinet level. As a result, former prime minister Giulio ANDREOTTI succeeded in organizing an all-DC minority government that survived chamber and senate confidence votes in August. Earlier, in July, Pietro INGRAO had become the first Communist in 28 years to be elected president of the lower house.

In January 1978 the Communists, Socialists, and members of the Italian Republican Party (*Partito Repubblicano Italiano*—PRI) withdrew their support of the Andreotti government following rejection by the DC of a renewed PCI demand for cabinet-level participation. Negotiations conducted by DC president Aldo MORO resulted, however, in

a compromise whereby the Communists settled for official inclusion in the ruling parliamentary majority and a guarantee that they would be consulted in advance on government policy. Andreotti, directed by President Leone to form a new government, organized a cabinet that, with only two changes from the preceding one, took office on March 13. Three days later, five-time prime minister Moro was abducted by the extremist Red Brigades; on May 9 his body was found in Rome after the government, with substantial opposition support, refused to negotiate with the terrorists. Moro had been considered a likely successor to President Leone, who on June 15, six months before the end of his term, resigned in the wake of persistent accusations of tax evasion and other irregularities. Following the interim presidency of Amintore Fanfani, Alessandro PERTINI of the PSI was sworn in as head of state on July 8.

The withdrawal of Communist support led to the collapse of the Andreotti government in January 1979 and, ultimately, to early but inconclusive elections in June, after which Francesco COSSIGA (DC) formed a three-party centrist government that survived a confidence vote in the chamber only because of abstentions by the Republicans and the PSI. In February 1980 the socialists withdrew their tacit parliamentary support, forcing the government to resign in March. Within days, however, the PSI agreed to participate in a new DC-led administration, and another three-party cabinet that included the Republicans took office in April. The second Cossiga government survived until September, when it was forced to resign after defeat of an economic reform package.

In October 1980 the PSI and PSDI concluded a "third force" agreement that did not, however, preclude a dialogue to "reconcile Christian and socialist values." Accordingly, the two parties and the Republicans joined a DC-led government under Arnaldo FORLANI that took office in October. Subsequently, it was revealed that a large number of leading officials, including several cabinet members, belonged to a secret Masonic lodge known as "P-2," which had been implicated in a variety of criminal activities. As a result of the scandal, Forlani was forced to submit his government's resignation in May 1981, and in June, Giovanni SPADOLINI of the PRI became the first non-Christian Democrat since 1945 to be invested as prime minister. The first Spadolini coalition, encompassing the four participants in the previous government plus the Liberals (*Partito Liberale Italiano*—PLI), lasted until August 1982, when the Socialists withdrew. Spadolini was able to form a new government that included the PSI, but differences over economic policy persisted, forcing a second collapse in November.

In December 1982 former prime minister Fanfani returned as head of a four-party coalition that included the DC, PSI, PSDI, and PLI. Although Fanfani succeeded in enacting a number of tax reforms, friction arose during the 1983 regional election campaign, and in April PSI leader Bettino CRAXI withdrew his party from the coalition, forcing a new parliamentary dissolution. In the election of June 1983, the Christian Democrats suffered their most severe setback since the party's formation, while the PCI also lost seats. The beneficiaries were the smaller parties, most notably the PRI . The PSI also gained, and on July 21 Craxi was asked to form Italy's first socialist-led administration. Rejecting repeated appeals from PCI leader Enrico BERLINGUER to join the Communists in a "democratic alternative" of the left, Craxi assembled a five-party government encompassing the Fanfani coalition plus the Republicans.

In October 1985, amid intense controversy surrounding the hijacking of the Genoa-based cruise ship *Achille Lauro* by Palestinian terrorists, Defense Minister Spadolini led a Republican withdrawal from the cabinet, precipitating Craxi's resignation. However, an accommodation was reached with Spadolini that permitted retroactive rejection of the government's resignation. Craxi again felt obliged to resign in June 1986, after an unexpected defeat on a local finance bill in which numerous coalition deputies played the role of secret-ballot defectors (*franchi tiratori,* or "snipers"), but he was eventually able to form a new government on the basis of the previous five-party alignment.

In February 1987 Craxi announced the "liquidation" of a 1986 pact with the DC that would have permitted them to lead the government for the last year of the parliamentary term; in March, with obvious reluctance, he submitted his resignation. After a series of abortive cabinet-building efforts, former prime minister Fanfani succeeded in organizing a minority administration that lasted only until late April; in a highly unusual move, the Christian Democrats voted to bring down their own government, leading President Cossiga (who had succeeded President Pertini) to call an early general election.

The June 1987 balloting yielded a significant shift of support from the PCI to the PSI, with a marginal gain for the DC and the parliamentary debut of Italy's Greens (*Federazione dei Verdi*—FdV). The Socialists strongly objected to the proposed choice of DC Secretary General Ciriaco DE MITA as prime minister, and President Cossiga somewhat unexpectedly called on the outgoing DC treasury minister, Giovanni GORIA, to head a revived five-party government that took office in July. Goria managed to retain coalition support only until March 1988, when the PSI and PSDI abstained on a controversial nuclear-power vote. Subsequently, after negotiating a record 200-page government program, De Mita, with PSI and PLI support, returned as head of a new administration. In October, De Mita succeeded in ending a 140-year tradition that permitted legislators to vote in secrecy on virtually all important measures. Thenceforth, budgetary matters, particularly, would no longer be subject to "sniper" attack, although secrecy was retained for selected issues, such as civil rights, abortion, and divorce, and for the electoral college selection of a president.

In May 1989 De Mita resigned as prime minister after being attacked by the PSI on a variety of economic and social issues. In July former prime minister Andreotti returned as head of an administration supported by the same five-party coalition as that of his predecessor. The government remained in power until March 1991, when Craxi's PSI withdrew its support, after which Andreotti fashioned a four-party coalition of the DC, PSI, PSDI, and PLI. It was Andreotti's seventh government.

The run-up to the general election of April 1992 was preceded by a number of significant changes in the Italian party system. Formation of the Democratic Party of the Left (*Partito Democratico della Sinistra*—PDS) as revisionist heir to the PCI prompted the collateral organization of a hard-line Communist Refoundation Party (*Partito della Rifondazione Comunista*—PRC). In addition, the long-dominant DC was severely challenged in the country's two major regions by the launching of the Northern League (*Lega Nord*—LN), with the Lombard League (*Lega Lombarda*—LL) at its core, and, in the south, by the emergence of an anti-Mafia grouping, The Network (*La Rete*). The new formations were the principal beneficiaries of the April balloting, in which the DC registered its poorest showing since World War II. On April 24 Prime Minister Andreotti announced his resignation, as did President Cossiga the following day, leaving the country without the constitutional capacity to form a new government. A prolonged deadlock over the selection of a new head of state ensued before being effectively broken by the assassination of the country's leading anti-Mafia judge, Giovanni FALCONE, on May 23. On May 25 a shocked electoral college, in its 16th round of voting, named the recently designated chamber speaker, Oscar Luigi SCALFARO (DC), as Cossiga's successor. Four weeks later, after nearly three months of political paralysis, the PSI's Giuliano AMATO succeeded, on the basis of the same four parties as his predecessor, in forming Italy's 51st postwar administration.

The traditional parties were severely damaged from early 1992 onward by the country's biggest postwar corruption scandal, which started in Milan and centered at first on disclosures that PSI officials had enriched party coffers by systematic abuse of public service contracts. Arrests began in February and continued throughout the year, amid evidence of wrongdoing at all levels of the center-left political establishment. Some 200 Italian parliamentarians were under criminal investigation by early 1993. Although gravely weakened by the widening scandal, the Amato government clung to office through public approval of eight referendums on April 18–19 that called for major political and economic reforms.

On April 22, 1993, Amato announced his resignation, and he was replaced on April 29 by the politically unaffiliated governor of the Bank of Italy, Carlo Azeglio CIAMPI, whose seven-party coalition government included 3 former Communists (now members of the PDS) and 1 Green. However, less than 24 hours later the last 4 resigned because of the chamber's unexpected refusal to lift Craxi's parliamentary immunity to corruption charges. On May 5 a new government was formed, 10 of whose 25 members were unaffiliated.

The "meltdown" of the postwar party structure accelerated in the run-up to a general election on March 26–27, 1994, and included the transformation of the once-dominant DC into the now-defunct Italian Popular Party (*Partito Popolare Italiano*—PPI). The result was a radically transformed parliament dominated by the right-wing Freedom Alliance (*Polo della Libertà*—PL), headed by the new *Forza Italia* formation of media tycoon Silvio BERLUSCONI. On May 11 Berlusconi was sworn in as prime minister of a five-party, right-wing government that included representatives of the LN and the "post-fascist" National Alliance (*Alleanza Nazionale*—AN).

Policy and personal strains quickly paralyzed the new government, however, culminating in the withdrawal of the LN and the resignation of Berlusconi on December 22, 1994. Shortly before his exit the prime minister had been called before Milan magistrates to answer charges of corrupt payments by parts of his business empire. Rebuffing Berlusconi's demand that he should be reappointed or new elections called, President Scalfaro appointed a nonparty banker, Lamberto DINI, as prime minister to head a cabinet of technocrats that took office on January 17, 1995, in the midst of an economic crisis. The discrediting of the old political elite reached new heights in September with the launching of judicial proceedings against Andreotti on charges of association with the Mafia. (He was ultimately acquitted of the final charge in October 1999 and is now a senator for life.)

Having survived a right-wing nonconfidence motion in October 1995 by striking a deal with the PRC, Dini submitted his resignation on December 30 after parliamentary passage of the 1996 budget. An attempt to form a reformist government by former merchant banker Antonio MACCANICO (then nonparty) foundered, whereupon new elections were called three years ahead of schedule. The contest saw the emergence of a broad "Olive Tree" (*Ulivo*) alliance of center-left parties that was headed by Romano PRODI (a former left-wing DC minister) and included the PPI, the ex-Communist PDS, and new parties founded by Dini and Maccanico.

The results of the balloting on April 20–21, 1996, gave the Olive Tree parties decisive pluralities in both houses; as a result Prodi on May 17 became prime minister of Italy's 55th postwar government—technically a minority administration, but with promised external support by the PRC. Although the cabinet was predominantly leftist, the government was firmly pro-EU and soon adopted austerity measures to meet the criteria for entry into the proposed EU EMU in 1999. Among other things, the government began to reduce a budget deficit of 6.8 percent of GDP to less than the 3 percent required for participation. In late November the Prodi government claimed an important initial success when the Italian lira was readmitted to the EU exchange rate mechanism after four years of nonparticipation.

The Prodi government survived its first crisis in April 1997 when the PRC refused to endorse military action to restore order in Albania, forcing Prodi to solicit the support of the center-right parties. A more serious challenge arose when Prodi in late September announced his proposed 1998 budget, which called for extensive additional retrenchment, including pension reductions and further welfare cuts. The PRC denounced the budget slashing, forcing Prodi to submit his resignation on October 9. However, public opinion turned on the PRC, which modified its stance sufficiently to permit reinstatement of the government. Subsequently, the Olive Tree alliance scored heavy victories in local elections in November.

Rejecting the proposed 1999 budget, the PRC again withdrew its support, and the government fell on October 9, 1998. Massimo D'ALEMA, leader of the Democrats of the Left (*Democratici di Sinistra*—DS, as the PDS had been renamed), the largest party in the parliament, was called upon to form a government after Prodi's attempts to regroup proved futile. D'Alema put together a multiparty government that included not only the first formerly Communist cabinet ministers since a unity government in 1947 but also former president Cossiga's recently organized Democratic Union for the Republic (*Unione Democratica per la Repubblica*—UDR), a center-right grouping of moderate democrats and Christian reformers. Sworn in on October 21, D'Alema retained several key ministers, including those who had been the architects of austerity, and pledged to pass the budget that had been Prodi's downfall.

D'Alema submitted his resignation on December 12, 1999, after losing the support of the small, three-party *Trifoglio* ("Clover") parliamentary alliance, which included Cossiga's new Union for the Republic (*Unione per la Repubblica*—UR). Asked to form a new administration by President Carlo Ciampi, who had handily won election as chief of state in May, D'Alema proposed a seven-party government that was largely unchanged except for the addition of the Prodi-sponsored Democrats (*Democratici*). However, D'Alema's second administration proved short-lived: Responding to major gains won by the resurgent center-right in regional elections, the prime minister resigned on April 17, 2000. President Ciampi then turned to former prime minister Amato, D'Alema's minister of treasury and budget, who succeeded in forming an eight-party Olive Tree government that was sworn in on April 26 and confirmed by the Chamber of Deputies two days later.

With Amato having removed himself from consideration, the Olive Tree endorsed Rome's mayor, Francesco RUTELLI, a Democrat, to lead the alliance into the 2001 general election. On the center-right, Silvio Berlusconi had apparently convinced most of the populace that the string of corruption charges against him were attributable more to overzealous prosecutors than to actual illegalities. Having reconfigured his Freedom Alliance as the House of Freedoms (*Casa delle Libertà*), on May 13 the former prime minister swept back into office with comfortable majorities in both houses of parliament. The victory had been widely predicted as Italy's complex political dynamics increasingly came to resemble, in effect, a two-party system: the center-right House of Freedoms alliance won 368 seats in the Chamber of Deputies (58.4 percent) and 177 in the Senate (56.2 percent of the elective seats), while the center-left Olive Tree took 247 (39.2 percent) in the lower house and 128 in the upper (40.1 percent). Berlusconi's cabinet, which was sworn in on June 11, included members of his *Forza Italia,* the AN, the LN, and two Christian Democratic parties, plus a handful of independents. Subsequently, the Christian Democrats merged as the Union of Christian and Center Democrats (*Unione dei Democratici Cristiani e dei Democratici di Centro*—UDC), and the small Italian Republican Party (PRI) decided to join the governing coalition.

Despite his electoral successes, Berlusconi faced charges that he had bribed judges in the mid-1980s to gain control of a food company, an attack that he said was politically motivated. (Prior convictions for bribing tax officials and for making illegal payments to Bettino Craxi's party in 1991 had already been overturned, and other charges had been dismissed.) In an undisguised attempt to undercut the prosecution, Berlusconi's parliamentary majority passed legislation allowing a defendant to request a change of venue if there were "legitimate suspicions" of judicial bias. However, the Supreme Court rejected Berlusconi's bid to move his corruption trial from Milan. Parliament then passed a bill giving immunity from prosecution to the top five officeholders—the president, the prime minister, the presidents of the senate and chamber, and the head of the Constitutional Court—during their tenure, which meant that the charges against Berlusconi would fall under the statute of limitations by the end of his current term. In January 2004 the Constitutional Court ruled the immunity law unconstitutional, and in April the trial resumed. In the end, Berlusconi was acquitted, although several of his closest colleagues were convicted of corruption and linked to organized crime.

On April 15, 2005, the UDC leader and deputy prime minister, Marco FOLLINI, withdrew his party from the cabinet, demanding policy and ministerial changes in the wake of major setbacks for the House of Freedoms parties in the local elections of April 3–4. As a consequence, Prime Minister Berlusconi tendered his resignation on April 20 but quickly fashioned a new government. He was sworn in once again on April 23 at the head of a reshuffled Council of Ministers (dubbed "Berlusconi II") that comprised all the House of Freedoms parties, including the UDC.

By the time the 2006 election campaign got under way, support for Berlusconi had been undermined by growing public discontent over Italy's anemic economy, Berlusconi's grip on the media, persistent charges of corruption against him and other government figures, and the continued presence of some 3,000 Italian troops in Iraq in support of the 2003 U.S. invasion. Nevertheless, the victory of a new coalition, the Union (*l'Unione*), headed by Prodi's center-left Olive Tree, in the April election was by a razor-thin margin in the chamber (49.8 percent over Berlusconi's 49.6 percent). Ironically, a new electoral law that Berlusconi had shepherded through parliament in December 2005 ended up giving Prodi's coalition a larger majority of chamber seats, 348–281, than would otherwise have been the case. The House of Freedoms actually won more votes in the senate (49.9 percent versus 49.8 percent), but the same electoral change handed the Union a 2-seat advantage.

Berlusconi initially refused to accede to Prodi, attributing the result to fraud, and opposed Prodi's choice of Giorgio NAPOLITANO, an 80-year-old former Communist and speaker of parliament, to succeed outgoing President Carlo Azeglio Ciampi. On May 10, 2006, Napolitano won approval by parliament and regional representatives for a seven-year term and appointed Prodi as prime minister. Prodi was sworn in with a new government on May 17.

By early 2007 public discontent with crime and a sluggish economy strained support for the Prodi government, especially in the senate, and prompted Union leaders to formulate a 12-point agenda that excluded more radical coalition priorities, including a proposal to grant legal rights to unwed and same-sex couples. This compromise initiative failed to prevent a major crisis in early March concerning Prodi's support for continuing the deployment of Italian peacekeepers in Afghanistan and for the expansion of a U.S. military base near Vicenza. After the senate rejected both proposals, Prodi tendered his resignation but accepted Napolitano's request to submit to a parliamentary vote of confidence. The crisis subsided on March 27 when the senate, having confirmed Prodi's tenure, narrowly approved both military measures.

Prodi's razor-thin majority dissolved on January 16, 2008, when Clemente Mastella of coalition partner UDEUR resigned following an investigation into allegations of corruption against him and his wife. Unable to muster a vote of confidence in the senate, Prodi tendered his resignation on January 24. On February 6 President Napolitano dissolved both houses of parliament and set early elections for April 13 and 14, in which the center-right grouping led by Berlusconi won 43.7 percent of the vote, compared with 38 percent for the center-left coalition led by Walter VELTRONI. Berlusconi was sworn in as prime minister, along with a new government, on May 8.

Constitution and government. The 1948 constitution, which describes Italy as "a democratic republic founded on work," established a parliamentary system with a president, a bicameral legislature, and an independent judiciary. The president, selected for a seven-year term by an electoral college consisting of both houses of parliament plus delegates named by regional assemblies, appoints the prime minister and, on the latter's recommendation, other members of the Council of Ministers; he may dissolve parliament at any time prior to the last six months of a full term. The Parliament consists of a Senate and a Chamber of Deputies; the two houses have equal legislative power, and both are subject to dissolution and the holding of new elections. The Council of Ministers is responsible to parliament and must resign upon passage of a vote of nonconfidence.

Under a modification to electoral arrangements approved by referendum in April 1993, proportional representation was replaced by predominantly "first-past-the-post," constituency-based elections. Subsequent parliamentary implementation of the mandate provided for single-member districts for both the senate and chamber, with 75 percent of the contests to be decided by plurality voting (hence no runoffs) and 25 percent by a system of proportional representation that would favor minor parties (subject, in the case of the Chamber of Deputies, to a vote threshold of 4 percent). A referendum held on April 18, 1999, called for abolishing the proportional component of chamber elections. Although 91 percent of those voting backed the measure, the turnout was 0.4 percent below the 50 percent threshold needed to make the result binding. A repeat referendum on May 21, 2000, attracted only 32 percent of registered voters.

The judiciary is headed by the Constitutional Court (*Corte Costituzionale*) and includes (in descending order of superiority) the Supreme Court of Cassation (*Corte Suprema di Cassazione*), assize courts of appeal (*corti d'assise d'appello*), courts of appeal (*corti d'appello*), tribunals (*tribunali*), district courts (*preture*), and justices of the peace (*giudici conciliatori*).

Italy's historically centralized system was substantially modified under the 1948 basic law, which called for the designation of 19 (later 20) administrative regions (*regioni*), 5 of which (Friuli-Venezia Giulia, Sicily, Sardinia, Trentino-Alto Adige, and Val d'Aosta) enjoy special status. Each region has its own administration, including an elected Regional Council (*Consiglio Regionale*). Since April 2000, voters have directly elected presidents in the 15 ordinary regions. (Each special region has its own constitutional provisions.) Subdivisions include 103 provinces and some 8,100 municipalities, all administered by locally elected bodies. In October 2001 a national referendum endorsed a devolution proposal under which the regions would assume greater authority in agriculture, education, health, and other areas. A November 2005 law amending the constitution was rejected by voters in a referendum held on June 25, 2006. The amendments, backed by Berlusconi's coalition and opposed by Prodi's governing coalition, would have transferred more authority to the regions in the areas of health, education, and law enforcement; increased the powers of the prime minister to include authority to dissolve parliament and appoint and dismiss ministers; and centralized the tax system. The amendments would have further diminished the powers of the president, already greatly limited under the constitution.

Foreign relations. Italian rule outside the country's geographical frontiers was terminated by World War II and the Paris Peace Treaty of 1947, by which Italy renounced all claims to its former African possessions and ceded the Dodecanese Islands to Greece, a substantial northeastern region to Yugoslavia, and minor frontier districts to France. A dispute with Yugoslavia over the Free Territory of Trieste was largely resolved in 1954 by a partition agreement whereby Italy took possession of Trieste city and Yugoslavia acquired the surrounding rural area. The essentials of the 1954 agreement were retained in a formal settlement concluded in 1975.

The province of Alto Adige (South Tyrol), acquired from Austria after World War I, was a periodic source of tension between the two countries. In June 1992 they were at last able to notify the United Nations (UN) that outstanding issues related to the South Tyrol question had been resolved. Under the settlement, South Tyrol (Bolzano) was to be given substantial provincial autonomy, including guarantees for use of the German language, within the broader autonomous region of Trentino-Alto Adige.

Internationally, Italy has been a firm supporter of the Atlantic alliance, the UN and its related agencies, and European integration, including the EC/EU. Rome has also attempted to forge a "special" relationship with the Arab world. Although affirming a need for action against terrorism, Italian authorities, in the wake of widespread anti-American street demonstrations, reacted coolly to the April 1986 U.S. bombing raid on Libya. By contrast, Italy endorsed a hard-line response to Iraq's seizure of Kuwait in 1990, and Italian forces joined the U.S.-led expedition that liberated Kuwait in early 1991. In early 2003, despite wide public protests, the Berlusconi government backed the U.S.-led ouster of Iraq's Saddam Hussein and later committed some 3,000 troops to the "coalition of the willing."

The post-1989 collapse of communism in Eastern Europe created some regional difficulties for Italy, notably an influx of refugees from Albania and later from former Yugoslavia. Responding to the new political realities, and in part to counter the economic power of reunited Germany, Italy sponsored the *Pentagonale* regional accord with Austria, Hungary, Czechoslovakia, and Yugoslavia; this became the *Esagonale* in 1991 with the accession of Poland, and in 1992, following the breakup of Yugoslavia, was relaunched as the Central European Initiative (CEI). In October 1994 Italy concluded a friendship and cooperation treaty with Russia.

As the former colonial ruler of Somalia, Italy displayed its concern at the descent of the country into anarchy in 1991 and provided 2,600 troops for the U.S.-led peacekeeping force in late 1992. In May 1993 it was one of the first to accord formal recognition to another former territory, the Ethiopian breakaway state of Eritrea. On a state visit to Addis Ababa in November 1997, then-President Scalfaro formally apologized for Italy's occupation of Ethiopia in 1936–1941.

The advent of the Berlusconi government in May 1994 challenged relations with Slovenia and Croatia deriving from the Italian right's desire to recover prewar Italian Istria; under Berlusconi, however, Italy confined itself to demanding compensation for Italians dispossessed after World War II, while the successor Dini government dropped Italy's veto on the conclusion of an EU-Slovenia association agreement. The compensation issue was resolved in 1998.

On the Bosnian conflict, Rome's policy of neutrality and negotiation was seen in some quarters as effectively pro-Serb, a charge rejected by the Italian Foreign Ministry. In September 1995 Italy denied permission for U.S. Stealth bombers to use Italian bases for strikes on Bosnian Serb targets, officially in protest against Italy's exclusion from the international Contact Group on Bosnia. In November, however, Italy agreed to assign 2,300 troops to the International Force (IFOR) to be deployed in Bosnia under the Dayton peace agreement. In the wake of an influx of Albanian refugees in early 1997, Italy led a 6,000-strong multinational force which, with UN backing, was credited with helping restore order in Albania. In 1998, having joined the Contact Group for the former Yugoslavia as its sixth member, Italy backed the sanctions imposed on Belgrade over the Kosovo crisis and in March 1999 joined the air campaign launched by the North Atlantic Treaty Organization (NATO) (see article on Serbia).

A G-8 summit of leading industrial nations that opened in Genoa on July 20, 2001, was met by an estimated 100,000 antiglobalization demonstrators, including a small minority of violent protesters. Rioting and the resultant police response led to some 300 injuries, the shooting death of a protester by police, nearly 300 arrests, considerable property damage, and an official investigation into possible police misconduct.

In his first foreign-policy address after becoming prime minister, Romano Prodi on May 18, 2006, denounced the war in Iraq as a "grave" mistake and withdrew remaining Italian forces from the country in December. Prodi renewed Italy's commitment to antiterror actions sanctioned by the UN and won approval to finance the Italian contingent of NATO peacekeeping forces in Afghanistan in 2007. In 2009 Italy became the first NATO member to respond to U.S. president Barack Obama's request for additional troops to fight the Taliban in Afghanistan.

Italian policy toward the EU and immigration constituted the principle foreign policy challenges after the 2008 elections. Long criticized for putting relations with the United States above those with the EU, Berlusconi also had to address the strong euro-skepticism espoused by the Northern League, a key member of his governing coalition. Anti-immigration sentiment in the Italian public was also at odds with the EU mandate for free movement of all citizens of member states within the EU. After Italy forced hundreds of people, apprehended as they approached Sicily aboard unseaworthy boats, to return to Libya in May 2009, the UN High Commissioner for Refugees (UNHCR) chided the Berlusconi government for violating the 1951 Geneva Convention by failing to establish whether some of the boat people were refugees. Even the Vatican, usually supportive of Berlusconi's policies, condemned the migrants' forced repatriation to Libya, a common conduit for Africans trying to reach Europe. An agreement between Italy and Libya to conduct joint naval patrols to stem the exodus of migrants went into effect in late May.

Current issues. Following his inauguration in May 2006, Prodi repeatedly faced serious challenges to his government's viability, initially related to Italy's economic problems. Faced with mounting scrutiny by EU finance ministers, Prodi quickly drew up a controversial plan to resolve the deficit and the public debt through a crackdown on tax evasion, which parliament narrowly approved in December. However, local elections in May 2007 confirmed the erosion of Prodi's political support, especially in the north, while his support held in the center of the country.

Economic hardship due to reduced purchasing power, caused by higher energy prices and rising taxes, granted Silvio Berlusconi's center-right a resounding victory in the 2008 election. The three-time prime minister and media tycoon had promised to cut taxes, privatize state-owned industries, and crack down on illegal immigration. A number of parties joined the center-right People of Freedom (*Il Popolo della Libertà*—PdL) coalition led by Berlusconi or the center-left coalition led by Walter Veltroni, suggesting a trend toward a two-party system. Political commentators attributed Berlusconi's victory as much to the center-left's ineptitude as to firm support for the center-right. By excluding several parties of the far left from the new Democratic Party (*Partito Democratico*—PD), center-left leaders lost an opportunity to present a broad front to counter the center-right's ability to exploit voters' frustrations with the sagging economy and the perceived threat posed by illegal immigrants. Further, the excluded leftist parties (see Political Parties, below) lost their seats in parliament, depriving the PD of a vital source of support.

Despite its clear majority in both houses of parliament, the center-right's stability was jeopardized by its dependence on support from the anti-immigrant and protectionist Northern League, even after Berlusconi's PdL was established as a political party in March 2009, absorbing some 13 parties, including the National Alliance. The merger created a large center-right party, mirroring the center-left's earlier creation of the PD and moving Italy further in the direction of a two-party system.

The ultra-right's influence on the new PdL and on Berlusconi's governing coalition was seen in police actions aimed mainly against illegal immigrants. Further, Berlusconi's refusal to condemn an initiative to reserve seats on Milan's public transportation for native Italians and his statement that his party did not envision "a multi-ethnic Italy" prompted outrage in Italy and abroad. The government's hard-line approach to immigration gained ground in May when the chamber passed a law imposing a $13,500 fine and deportation on illegal immigrants. Berlusconi's problems mounted in May when his wife filed for divorce, citing his philandering and plans to include several TV starlets in the PdL lists for European Parliament elections in June. Just days before the elections, opposition leaders called on the prime minister to resign after a court accused him of having paid his British lawyer to lie about Berlusconi's business investments in the 1990s.

Despite the controversies surrounding Berlusconi, two events in 2009 bolstered his grip on power: the center-left's disarray after its 2008 defeat and the prime minister's prompt outreach to the victims of the April 6 earthquake that killed almost 300, injured 1,500, and destroyed much of the city of l'Aquila and surrounding villages in the central region of Abruzzo.

The June elections for the European Parliament were widely seen as a referendum on Berlusconi's political fortunes. However, the recent scandals surrounding the prime minister had little impact on support for the PdL, which won 35 percent of the vote, for 29 of 72 seats for Italy, well ahead of the PD's 26 percent result, for 21 seats. The biggest winner in the polling was the right-wing National League, which doubled its percentage of the vote, to 10 percent, for 9 seats in the EU parliament.

Italy's election law, which enables small parties to gain political power by entering into coalitions, was the subject of a referendum held on June 21–22, 2009. Supported by advocates of a two-party system and opposed by Berlusconi and his governing allies in the Lega Nord, the referendum was largely ignored by voters. Although about three-quarters of respondents supported the referendum, a mere 20 percent of eligible voters turned out, far short of the 50-plus-1 percent quorum required for referendums to become law.

POLITICAL PARTIES

For more than four decades after World War II, the Italian political scene was dominated by the Christian Democrats (DC) on the center-right and the Italian Communist Party (PCI) on the left. The DC formed the major component of all postwar governments until 1994, while the PCI, although without government representation after 1947, remained the largest communist formation in Western Europe and by far the largest Italian opposition party. For most of the period, a number of smaller democratic socialist and reformist parties provided the Christian Democrats with sufficient (although varying) political allies to ensure continual center-left government and keep the Communists out of office. On the far right, reorganization of the prewar Fascist Party is constitutionally forbidden, although various postwar parties serving as vehicles for radical right-wing views have come together in what is now the National Alliance (AN).

The established postwar party structure came under increasing challenge in the 1980s, before effectively disintegrating in the early 1990s. On the left, the PCI reacted to the collapse of communism in Eastern Europe by becoming a democratic socialist party. On the right, increasing popular disgust with political corruption in Rome gave rise to various regional movements, especially in the north, seeking the breakup of Italy as a unitary state. On the center-left, the miring of many political leaders in financial and other scandals led to the conversion of the DC into the Italian Popular Party (PPI). This did not prevent a hemorrhage of Christian Democratic support in the 1994 election, which featured a three-way alliance structure of the right, center, and left, covering most significant parties. Since the 1996 elections this has become a two-way center-left versus center-right contest. In the 2008 election, all the significant parties joined Silvio Berlusconi's center-right coalition or Walter Veltroni's center-left coalition to create alignments that many Italians hoped would help stabilize the country's notoriously volatile political calculus. That hope flagged in February 2009,when Veltroni announced he had failed to unite the center-left and resigned as leader of the Democratic Party, weakening opposition to Berlusconi's center-right coalition.

Governing Coalition:

Fourteen years after winning his first general-election victory, media tycoon Silvio Berlusconi began his fourth term as prime minister following the election of April 13–14, 2008. He did so as leader of an unnamed, center-right coalition consisting of his newly created "union," the People of Freedom (*Il Popolo della Libertà*—PdL), and two regional parties, the Northern League (*Lega Nord*—LN), and the Movement for Autonomy Allied for the South (*Movimento per l'Autonomia Alleati per il Sud*—MPA).

Berlusconi's new coalition succeeded his **House of Freedoms** (*Casa delle Libertà*), created in September–October 2000, and Freedom Alliance (*Polo delle Libertà*—PL), formed prior to the 1994 balloting. Having taken power after the March 1994 election, the PL promptly suffered divisions, resulting in the exit of the LN in December and the collapse of the first Berlusconi government. Following the break with the LN, the remaining PL structure was retained for the April 1996 elections, although competition between Berlusconi and Gianfranco Fini, leader of the National Alliance (*Alleanza Nazionale*—AN), damaged its prospects of regaining power. While the PL's aggregate share of the proportional vote, at 44 percent, was above its comparable 1994 tally and 10 points higher than that obtained by the center-left Olive Tree alliance, the latter's gains in the constituency balloting and resultant plurality enabled it to form a minority government, to which the PL parties formed the main opposition. In the May 2001 election the House of Freedoms alliance, which had been joined by the New Italian Socialist Party (NPSI), won majorities in both houses of parliament, permitting Berlusconi to form a new center-right government, the only government to date that has lasted its entire five-year term (2001–2006). As the 2006 general election approached, the small Italian Republican Party (PRI) joined the House of Freedoms, but the alliance was narrowly defeated by the center-left Union coalition led by Romano Prodi.

After the People of Freedom was officially launched as a political party in March 2009, the governing coalition consisted of the PdL, the Northern League (LN), and the Movement for Autonomy Allied for the South (MPA).

People of Freedom (*Il Popolo della Libertà*—PdL). In an effort to coalesce Italy's myriad parties and movements of the right and center and as a response to the center-left's creation of the similarly inclusive, center-left Democratic Party (*Partito Democratico*—DP), Berlusconi launched the PdL coalition on November 18, 2007. At the time, the status of Berlusconi's *Forza Italia*—FI remained unclear. Following the January 2008 collapse of the center-left coalition government of Romano Prodi, Berlusconi agreed to form a joint list with Fini of the AN ahead of the April election.

On February 8, 2008, Berlusconi formed the new alliance, which also included FI, the AN, and several smaller parties that continued to exist as separate entities. The PdL subsequently garnered 37.4 percent of the vote, winning 276 seats in the chamber and 146 in the senate, making it Italy's largest political organization and the first to win more than 35 percent of the vote since Christian Democracy in 1979. (The AN was the second-largest ally in the PdL's legislative victory, winning 90 seats in the Chamber of Deputies and 48 in the Senate.)

Further bolstering the PdL's authority was the decision by the AN to merge with the PdL (alongside FI) in early March 2009, AN leaders citing the new "political force" that was under way. Ignazio La Russa, who had taken the AN helm after Gianfranco Fini became president of the Chamber of Deputies in 2008, said following the merger that the AN had no intention of being a faction within the PdL, insisting "if that were the case we would have remained a separate party." To further secure the PdL's stronghold, Berlusconi presided with much fanfare over the PdL's inaugural congress at the end of March, announcing the consolidation of the various parties, including some 13 minor groups and parties, into the PdL fold and what was described as "his increasing dominant leadership." News accounts described a rock-concert atmosphere at the venue in Rome, where Berlusconi announced the merger of his 15-year-old FI, along with the AN and others, into the PdL, under whose flag he was victorious as prime minister.

Among the parties and groups the PdL absorbed, following its formal establishment as a party in 2009, were: **Christian Democracy for the Autonomies**; the **Popular Liberals**, a breakaway faction of the UDC (below), led by Carlo GIOVANARDI; the **New Italian Socialist Party**, led by Gianni DE MICHELIS; the **Liberal Reformers**, a portion of the Liberal Democrats; **Decide!**, an association formed by Daniele CAPEZZONE; the **Circles of Freedom**, led by Michela Vittoria BRAMBILLA; the **Circles of Good Government;** the **Federation of Christian Populars**, founded by Mario BACCINI; **Italians in the World**, founded by Sen. Sergio DE GREGORIO; **Social Action**, originally called Freedom of Action, founded by Alessandra MUSSOLINI, granddaughter of Benito Mussolini; and **Libertarian Right**, formed by Luciano BUONOCORE. For further details about parties that merged into the PdL, see the 2008 *Handbook*.

Leaders: Silvio BERLUSCONI (Party President and Prime Minister of the Republic), Maurizio GASPARRI (Senate Leader), Fabrizio CICCHITTO (Chamber Leader), Sandro BONDI (Coordinator), Ignazio LA RUSSA (Coordinator), Denis VERDINI (Coordinator).

Northern League (*Lega Nord*—LN). The LN formed in February 1991 as a federation of the Lombard League (*Lega Lombarda*—LL) and sister parties in Emilio Romagna, Liguria, Piedmont, Tuscany, and Veneto. The party's name for the northern regions is "Padania" (the lands of the Po River), a term that the LN's parliamentary groups have included in their names.

Launched in 1979 and named after a 12th-century federation of northern Italian cities, the LL achieved prominence in the 1980s as the most conspicuous of several regional groups to challenge the authority of Rome, particularly its use of public revenues to aid the largely impoverished south. It advocated the adoption of a federal system with substantial regional autonomy in most areas, save defense and foreign policy. Its xenophobic and barely disguised racist outlook included a pronounced anti-immigrant posture.

The LN won 8.7 percent of the national vote in the 1992 general election and 8.4 percent as part of the PL in March 1994. Having joined the Berlusconi government in May, the LN pulled out in December amid much acrimony. In February 1995 it reestablished itself outside the PL and appended "Federal Italy" (*Italia Federale*) to its name, although a pro-Berlusconi faction that included party leader Umberto Bossi's longtime deputy and Berlusconi's interior minister, Roberto Maroni, left the party and reorganized as the Italian Federal League (*Lega Italia Federale*—LIF). Maroni and Bossi soon reconciled, and the LIF failed to establish itself as an alternative to the LN.

The LN contested the April 1996 legislative elections independently, increasing its support to 10.1 percent of the national proportional vote and winning 59 seats in the lower house and 27 in the senate, while becoming the strongest party in northern Italy. In opposition to the resultant center-left government, the LN convened a "parliament" in Mantua in late May, at which Bossi, flanked by green-shirted activists, reasserted the league's secessionist aims. When moderates within the party voiced doubts about the secessionist line, Bossi attracted much publicity in August by expelling their leader, former Chamber of Deputies president Irene Pivetti (subsequently of the UDEUR, below). In September Bossi led a three-day LN march and rally, the climax of which was a declaration of independence for the "Republic of Padania" and the formation of a provisional government. However, strong local opposition to the LN's aims, combined with warnings and appeals from senior politicians in Rome, apparently contributed to Bossi's subsequent announcement that he was prepared to negotiate new constitutional arrangements for northern Italy.

In January 1998 Bossi received a one-year suspended sentence for criminal incitement, and in July both he and Maroni received seven-month suspended sentences for resisting authorities and offensive behavior. Having reconciled with FI, the LN won a surprisingly small 3.9 percent of the proportional vote in 2001 as FI made significant inroads in the north.

Responding in part to anti-immigrant statements by the party leadership, in 2002 the Council of Europe issued a report describing the LN as "racist and xenophobic." In January 2004 Umberto Bossi resigned from the Council of Ministers because of inadequate progress on regional devolution. The LN nevertheless remained in the coalition, and in April 2005 the party's 28 deputies and 17 senators helped approve the "Berlusconi II" government. The LN saw minor losses in the April 2006 poll, winning 23 chamber and 13 senate seats.

The party subsequently softened its secessionist rhetoric and began to advocate federalism as the preferred means to securing greater regional autonomy. Riding a wave of anti-immigrant sentiment and disaffection with the center-left government, the LN emerged stronger than ever in the 2008 election, winning 8.3 percent of the vote—double its performance in 2006—and capturing 26 senate and 60 chamber seats. Reflecting its rising political status, the LN was awarded four cabinet posts.

Leaders: Umberto BOSSI (Federal Secretary), Angelo ALESSANDRI (Federal President), Federico BRICOLO (Senate Leader), Roberto COTA (Chamber Leader), Maurizio BALOCCHI (Administrative Secretary), Roberto CALDEROLI (Coordinator).

Movement for Autonomies (*Movimento per le Autonomie*—MPA). The MPA, which ran under the rubric Movement for Autonomy Allied with the South (*Movimento per l'Autonomia Alleati con il Sud*—MPA) in 2008 as a counterbalance to the Northern League within the center-right coalition, was founded on April 30, 2005, by Raffaele Lombardo, formerly president of the UDC in Catania and in the European Parliament. He left the party, citing its alleged failure to adequately represent the south's interests at the federal level. His decision to join forces with the Northern League came after Prodi's Union dropped from its list of legislative priorities the proposal to build a bridge over the Straits of Messina to join the mainland with Sicily. Lombardo and his supporters had long sought the bridge as a way to end Sicily's economic isolation.

In 2008 the MPA formed what was described as a political pact with the **Italy of the Center** (IdC), its leader, Vincenzo Scotti, becoming the president of the MPA.

With Berlusconi's promised support for the bridge project, the MPA joined his coalition in 2008, winning 2 senate seats and 8 chamber seats. In 2009 the party changed its name to Movement for Autonomies.

Leaders: Vincenzo SCOTTI (President), Raffaele LOMBARDO (Federal Secretary).

Parliamentary Opposition:

After less than two years in office, the government of Romano Prodi and his nine-party center-left *Unione* coalition failed to win a vote of confidence on January 24, 2008, after one of its constituent parties, UDEUR, defected in that month, eliminating the coalition's majority in the senate. Following the coalition's collapse, the center-left was handily defeated in the April 2008 poll (see Current issues, above) and returned to the opposition.

A new, unnamed center-left coalition replaced the Union, which was the latest iteration of the Olive Tree, the center-left coalition that was launched in mid-1995 mainly on the initiative of Prodi, a distinguished economics professor who had held ministerial office as a left-wing Christian Democrat and had joined the successor Italian Popular Party (PPI). By the time of the 1996 elections, the alliance included the centrist parties that had contested the 1994 elections as the Pact for Italy (*Patto per l'Italia*—PI) as well as the left-wing groupings of the 1994 Progressive Alliance (*Alleanza Progressista*—AP), notably the dominant ex-communist Democratic Party of the Left (DS). It also embraced two parties founded in early 1996, namely Italian Renewal (RI) and the now-defunct Democratic Union (*Unione Democratica*—UD), as well as the regional South Tyrol People's Party (SVP). In the April 1996 balloting the Olive Tree won a decisive plurality in both houses, with the result that the following month Prodi, who had campaigned under the banner of the *Lista Romano Prodi,* became prime minister of a minority center-left government that had assurances of external support from the Communist Refoundation Party (PRC, below).

After the fall of the Prodi government in October 1998 it was unclear if the Olive Tree would remain as a viable coalition inasmuch as the successor regime of Massimo D'Alema collaborated with Francesco Cossiga's more conservative Democratic Union for the Republic (UDR; see UDEUR under P-UDEUR, below) to form his government. In preparation for the upcoming European Parliament election, Cossiga left the UDR in January 1999 and subsequently established yet another party, the Union for the Republic (*Unione per la Repubblica*—UR), which, as part of the Clover (*Trifoglio*) parliamentary alliance with the Italian Democratic Socialists (SDI) and the Italian Republican Party (PRI, below), withdrew its support from the government in December 1999 and forced D'Alema's resignation. With an eye on the 2001 legislative elections, the Clover parties had questioned D'Alema's leadership and a number of proposed administrative changes he had announced, including bringing Romano Prodi's new Democrats into the government. D'Alema quickly formed a second, eight-party government with the addition of the Democrats and the continued participation of the reconfigured rump of the UDR, the UDEUR. Less than four months later, however, D'Alema again resigned, following the Olive Tree's losses to Silvio Berlusconi's forces in regional elections. The subsequent Amato government, with the SDI again participating, remained in office until the Olive Tree alliance, under Francesco Rutelli, suffered a major defeat in the May 2001 election.

After completing a five-year term as head of the European Commission, Prodi returned to active domestic politics. While maintaining the Olive Tree, he set about organizing a broader center-left coalition, initially called the Grand Democratic Alliance (*Grande Alleanza Democratica*—GAD) and then the Union, which was formed in 2005 in preparation for the 2006 election. During Italy's first "primary" election, held in October 2005, Prodi overwhelmingly defeated six challengers to become Union leader, capturing 74 percent of the votes. During the 2006 election Italian voters residing overseas elected six delegates and four senators running on a single Union ticket.

Now in the opposition, the unnamed center-left coalition, led by the Democratic Party (*Partito Democratico*—PD), continued to consolidate, decreasing its number of parties from the Union's nine to just two: the recently founded Democratic Party and the centrist-populist Italy of Values (*Italia dei Valori*—IdV).

Democratic Party (*Partito Democratico*—PD). Founded on October 14, 2007, during the presidency of Romano Prodi, the center-left PD resulted from the merger of the **Democrats of the Left** (*Democratici di Sinistra*—DS) and **Daisy–Democracy Is Freedom** (*Margherita–Democrazia è Libertà*—M-DL) in an effort to unify the center-left into a single entity. Six smaller parties also joined the PD and were subsequently fully absorbed (see below).

The 2008 election handed the PD 33.2 percent of the vote for the chamber and 33.7 percent for the senate. Following the collapse of his Union government and electoral defeat, on April 16, 2008, Romano Prodi resigned his leadership position in favor of Walter Veltroni, mayor of Rome and former DS leader. Although the PD remains the strongest center-left party, several factions have emerged that reflect the priorities of its two principal constituents. Former DS members and their supporters emphasize the party's social democratic roots and support affiliation with the European Socialist Party, while former Daisy advocates oppose that affiliation and continue to carry their Catholic and reformist standard.

Before the merger, the DS was the leading party of the Italian left. The party traced its roots to March 1990, when delegates to an extraordinary congress of the Italian Communist Party (*Partito Comunista Italiano*—PCI) voted to abandon the traditional name of the organization. At the final congress of the PCI, on February 3, 1991, it adopted a new name, the Democratic Party of the Left (*Partito Democratico della Sinistra*—PDS). In February 1998 the party shortened the name to its current title and abandoned the hammer and sickle as its symbol, replacing it with a rose and EU stars.

The other major party to merge into the PD, the M-DL, was formally constituted as a unified party in March 2002. It began in 2001 as the centrist *Margherita* alliance of four parties—The Democrats, the Italian Popular Party (PPI), Italian Renewal (RI), and the Democratic Union for Europe (see UDEUR under P-UDEUR, below)—intended to counterbalance the leftist DS within the Olive Tree. Under the leadership of Francesco Rutelli, the alliance won 14.5 percent of the proportional vote at the May 2001 election. The subsequent formation of the unified party was marred only by the decision of the UDEUR not to join it, in part because of objections to Rutelli's continued leadership.

Veltroni's quest to build a strong, unified party of the center-left collapsed in February 2009, when the party suffered heavy losses in regional elections in Sardinia. Veltroni resigned on February 21, leaving the center-left opposition in shambles and further strengthening Berlusconi's center-right coalition. Dario Franceschini, Veltroni's deputy, succeeded him as party leader.

(For more information on now-defunct subsets of the Democratic Party, including **Democrats of the Left** [*Democratici di Sinistra*—DS],

Daisy–Democracy Is Freedom [*Margherita–Democrazia è Libertà*—M-DL], and the **Italian Popular Party** [*Partito Popolare Italiano*—PPI], see the 2008 *Handbook.*)

Leaders: Dario FRANCESCHINI (Secretary), Anna FINOCCHIARO (Senate Leader), Antonello SORO (Chamber Leader).

Italy of Values (*Italia dei Valori*—IdV). Italy of Values was established in 1998 as a liberal democratic, law-and-order, reformist organization by Antonio Di Pietro, a former magistrate who had attracted national attention early in the decade for winning convictions against a number of national politicians in the "clean hands" (*Mani Pulite*) anticorruption campaign. Refusing to reestablish ties to the center-left Olive Tree (despite having initially lent support to Romano Prodi's Democrats) and rejecting participation in the center-right Berlusconi alliance, Di Pietro put forward his organization's own list, the *Lista Di Pietro–Italia dei Valori,* for the May 2001 elections. It failed to win any chamber seats, narrowly missing the 4 percent threshold for proportional seats, but retained 1 senate seat. For the 2004 European Parliament elections the IdV's two successful candidates were Di Pietro and former Communist leader Achille Occhetto. The party won 17 chamber and 4 senate seats in the 2006 election. The September 2006 defection from the party of Sen. Sergio DE GREGORIO reduced the Union's majority in the senate to a single seat.

IdV's electoral fortunes improved greatly in the 2008 election when it won 28 seats in the chamber and 14 in the senate. In the wake of the Democratic Party's poor showing in regional elections and its leadership shift, the IdV emerged as the opposition's most vocal critic of government policies.

Leaders: Antonio DI PIETRO (President), Felice BELISARIO (Senate Leader), Massimo DONADI (Chamber Leader).

Italian Radicals (*Radicali Italiani*—PR). The electoral affiliate of the **Radical Party** (*Partito Radicale*—PR) since 2002, the Italian Radicals party is a predominantly libertarian middle-class grouping advocating civil and human rights. The PR more formally identifies itself as a movement associated with the **Transnational Radical Party** (*Partito Radicale Trasnazionale*), which distances itself from national politics.

The PR's membership in the Chamber of Deputies increased from 4 seats in 1976 to 18 following the June 1979 election—by far the largest gain of any party. In November its secretary general, Jean FABRE, a French citizen, was sentenced by a Parisian court to a month in jail for evading conscription. In 1984, after having fled to France, PR deputy Antonio NEGRI was sentenced to 30 years' imprisonment for complicity in a variety of terrorist acts, although he and seven others were acquitted in January 1986 of being "moral leaders" of the Red Brigades and other extremist groups.

Gravitating to the right in the 1990s, the PR presented an unsuccessful Pannella List (*Lista Pannella*—LP) in the March 1994 poll as an ally of Berlusconi's Freedom Alliance. For the 1996 election, Pannella joined with television personality and critic Vittorio Sgarbi to present a *Lista Pannella-Sgarbi.* In the May 2001 balloting, the PR offered a *Lista Pannella-Bonino,* which attracted considerable attention in late April and early May when party leader Emma Bonino staged a hunger strike to protest the media's failure to cover her party's platform. The list failed to win seats in either house, although the *Lista Bonino* won two seats in the European Parliament in 2004.

Ahead of the 2008 election, the PR formed an electoral alliance with the PD, winning 3 seats on the Democratic Party list in the senate and 6 in the chamber. New leadership was elected at the PR party congress late in the year.

Leaders: Bruno MELLANO (President), Emma BONINO, Marco PANNELLA, Antonella CASU (Secretary).

Other Legislative Parties:

Union of the Center (*Unione di Centro*—UdC). The UdC was founded on December 8, 2007, by Pier Ferdinando Casini through the merger of his Union of Christian and Center Democrats (*Unione dei Democratici Cristiani e di Democratici Centro*—UDC) and the Rose for Italy (*Rosa per l'Italia*). The party was formed to unite like-minded centrist parties and attracted many minor parties and movements.

Frequently referenced simply as the Union of Christian Democrats, the UDC was initially established in December 2002 by a merger of the Christian Democratic Center (*Centro Cristiano Democratico*—CCD), the United Christian Democrats (*Cristiani Democratici Uniti*—CDU), and European Democracy (*Democrazia Europea*—DE). (For more information about the CCD, the CDU, and the DE, see the 2008 *Handbook.*) Prior to the 2001 general election the CCD and CDU had organized the *Biancofiore* ("White Flower") alliance, which won 3.2 percent of the proportional vote as a component of Berlusconi's House of Freedoms.

On occasion the UDC did not side with Prime Minister Berlusconi. In July 2003 it threatened to leave the governing coalition if the government blocked an investigation into possible corruption in his media empire. In September 2004 the nomination of the party president, Rocco Buttiglione, a fervent Catholic, to serve as European Commission vice president and commissioner for justice, freedom, and security was withdrawn because of controversial comments he had made about homosexuality and the role of women in the family.

In April 2005 the UdC's withdrawal from the government forced the prime minister's resignation. Subsequently, however, the party agreed to participate in a reshuffled cabinet. In 2006 the UDC won 39 chamber and 21 senate seats.

The UDC voted with Prodi's Union to keep Italian peacekeepers in Afghanistan and to allow expansion of a U.S. military base outside Vicenza. In December 2006 the UDC withdrew from the coalition, charging that the government was subject to undue influence by the Northern League and other far-right parties. However, in the 2007 local elections, the party presented a united front with the House of Freedoms, including far-right members of the coalition.

After the Prodi government's collapse in January 2008, the UDC moved closer to Berlusconi's coalition, prompting dissidents, under the leadership of Mario Baccini and Bruno Tabacci, to defect and create the Rose for Italy, also known as the White Rose (*Rosa Bianca*). This group drew support from Catholics who were disenchanted with both the center-right and center-left. Upon Berlusconi's refusal to allow the UDC to support but not join his nascent PdL party, the UDC left the center-right altogether.

On February 28, 2008, the Rose for Italy announced it would present a joint list with the UDC in the upcoming election under the Union of the Center designation, nominating Casini as its candidate for prime minister. The Christian Democratic Party and several other minor parties joined the UdC, which campaigned as an alternative to the expanding center-left and center-right coalitions. It was the only party not aligned with either coalition to win seats in both chambers: 35 deputies and 3 senators.

Leaders: Pier Ferdinando CASINI (Chamber Leader), Rocco BUTTIGLIONE (President), Giuseppe NARO (Secretary), Gianpiero D'ALIA (Senate Leader).

South Tyrolean People's Party (*Südtiroler Volkspartei*—SVP). The SVP is a moderate, autonomist grouping representing the German- and Ladin-speaking inhabitants of South Tyrol (Bolzano/Bozen or Alto Adige), where it is the largest party. In 1996 the SVP joined the Olive Tree alliance, with which it remained affiliated in May 2001, although it offered two candidate lists, the SVP list and the SVP–Olive Tree list. Together, they won 8 chamber and 5 senate seats. In 2004 the SVP ran with the Olive Tree alliance in the balloting for the European Parliament, winning one seat. The SVP won 5 seats in the senate and 4 in the chamber in 2006.

In 2008 the SVP lost ground, winning 4 seats in the Senate and 2 in the chamber.

Leaders: Luis DURNWALDER (President), Elmar Pichler ROLLE (Secretary).

Liberal Democrats (*Liberaldemocratici*—LD). A right-wing faction of M-DL established this party on September 18, 2007, upon the M-DL's decision to merge with the Democratic Party. Although the LD initially voiced support for Prodi's center-left government, it voted against it in the January 2008 confidence vote that led to the government's fall. After allying with Berlusconi's PdL on February 8, 2008, the LD won one seat in the senate and three in the chamber. Two elected LD members, including Lamberto Dini, later left the party to join the PdL. The two remaining LD deputies joined the "mixed" parliamentary group.

In November 2008 the party's deputies voted against Berlusconi's economic plan and withdrew its support for the government, returning to the center-left opposition. A faction of the LD joined the PdL in 2009.

Leader: Daniela MELCHIORRE (President), Italo TANONI (Coordinator).

Associative Movement Italians Abroad (*Movimento Associativo Italiani all'Estero*—MAIE). This party, which represents Italians residing in South America, succeeds Italian Associations in South America

(*Associazioni Italiane in Sud America*). In 2008 the party won 1 seat in the Senate and 1 in the chamber.

Leader: Riccardo MERLO.

Valdotanian Union (*Union Valdôtaine*—UV). This centrist party represents the Valle d'Aosta, where it is the largest party. It has been represented in parliament almost constantly since 1976 and has dominated the regional government for most of that time as well. The UV was founded in September 1946 as a close ally of the Christian Democratic Party until the mid-1950s, when it began strengthening its ties to the center-left. In 2006, after leaving the center-left coalition, the party lost its presence in parliament.

In 2008 the UV won one senate seat.

Leader: Ego PERRON (President).

Italian Republican Party (*Partito Repubblicano Italiano*—PRI). The oldest Italian political party still in existence under its original name, the PRI was founded in 1897, espousing Giuseppe MAZZINI's moderate leftist principles of social justice in a modern free society. In foreign policy it favors a pro-Western stance and continued membership in the Atlantic alliance. From June 1981 to November 1982 the PRI's political secretary, Giovanni Spadolini, served as the first non-Christian Democratic prime minister in 37 years; thereafter, the party continued its participation in center-left coalitions until going into opposition in April 1991. Having won 4.4 percent of the national vote in 1992, the PRI contested the March 1994 poll as principal member of the Democratic Alliance (*Alleanza Democratica*—AD), which won 1.2 percent of the national vote as part of the more inclusive AP. Having resigned the party leadership in 1988 and been reinstated in January 1994, Giorgio La Malfa again resigned in October 1994 before again being reinstated in March 1995.

In 1996 the Republicans joined with the Democratic Union (*Unione Democratica*—UD) of former PRI leader Antonio Maccanico as a minor element of the successful Olive Tree alliance. In December 1999, however, as part of the three-party "Clover" group, the PRI withdrew its support from Prime Minister D'Alema, which led to his resignation. At the June 1999 election for the European Parliament, it had offered a joint list with the Federation of Liberals (*Federazione dei Liberali*—FdL), which traced its roots to the conservative Italian Liberal Party (*Partito Liberale Italiano*—PLI), a minor participant in many of Italy's post–World War II governments, into the early 1990s. Subsequently, the PRI, under longtime leader Giorgio La Malfa, continued to call for formation of a liberal democratic alliance.

Following the May 2001 election La Malfa led the party into Berlusconi's House of Freedoms alliance, which precipitated a split in the party and formation by dissidents of the Movement of European Republicans (MRE). In April 2005 La Malfa joined the "Berlusconi II" cabinet as minister of EU policy. La Malfa and Party Political Secretary Francesco Nucara won seats in the chamber in 2006, running on the *Forza Italia* list.

The PRI formed an electoral alliance with the PdL ahead of the 2008 election, winning 2 chamber seats, again held by La Malfa and Nucara. However, the PRI declined to join the PdL when it became a party in 2009. Although it is no longer a member of the governing coalition, the PRI "loyally supports the majority in the current legislature, in full autonomy," Nucara explained to PHW.

Leaders: Francesco NUCARA (Political Secretary), Giorgio LA MALFA, Giancarlo CAMERUCCI.

Autonomy Liberty Democracy (*Autonomie Liberté Démocratie*). This center-left coalition was created for the 2006 election in the Valle d'Aosta, which is guaranteed one deputy and one senator under the constitution. The coalition included ten parties: **Alé Vallée**, **Alternative Greens** (*Verdi Alternativi*), **Alternative Left** (*Sinistra Alternativa*), **Committee of Valdaostans** (*Comité de Valdôtains*), the **DS** (*Gauche Valdôtaine*), the **IdV**, the **Daisy** (*La Margherita*), the **Communist Refoundation Party** (*Partito della Rifondazione Comunista*), **Rose in the Fist** (*Rosa nel Pugno*), and **Valle d'Aosta Alive** (*Vallée d'Aoste Vive*). The coalition won a single chamber seat in the 2008 poll.

Leaders: Carlo PERRIN, Roberto NICCO

Other Parties that Participated in the 2008 Elections:

Despite the ongoing trend toward consolidation of political parties of the center-left and center-right, more than 180 minor parties and groups participated in the 2008 election. Many of these were regional and local entities such as **The Other Sicily** (*L'Altra Sicilia*), the **Venetian Republic League** (*Liga Veneta Repubblica*), and the radical **Sardinian Action Party** (*Partito Sardo d'Azione*). Others represented special interests, such as **Defense of the Family** (*Difesa della Famiglia*) and the **Consumers' List** (*Lista Consumatori*), while a few, such as the **Movement of Young Activist Poets** (*Movimento Giovani Poeti d'Azione*) and **Dr. Cirillo's Party of the Existentially Impotent** (*Partito Impotenti Esistenziali Dr. Cirillo*), represented decidedly narrower interests.

The elections marked a turning point for some historically major parties. In December 2007, after Veltroni refused to bring the far left into his center-left coalition, the Communist Refoundation Party, Party of Italian Communists, Federation of the Greens, and Democratic Left—once powerful voices for labor and environmental interests in Prodi's Union—formed a coalition called The Left—The Rainbow (*La Sinistra—L'Arcobaleno*—SA) in an effort to maintain their presence in parliament. Their exclusion from the center-left proved disastrous because all four lost their seats in parliament, marking the first time communists were excluded from the legislature. After the election debacle, SA leader Fausto BERTINOTTI, a former leader of the Communist Refoundation Party and president of the Chamber of Deputies in 2006–2008, stepped down, and the SA dissolved.

The Democratic Left and factions of Communist Refoundation and the Party of Italian Communists subsequently formed a new alliance, **For the Left** (*Per la Sinistra*), in an unsuccessful effort to win seats in the European Parliament elections in June 2009

Communist Refoundation Party (*Partito della Rifondazione Comunista*—PRC). In February 1991 a dissident Communist Refoundation Movement (*Movimento di Rifondazione Comunista*) assembled in Rome to revive the old Communist Party, following the latter's conversion a week earlier to the PDS (see the DS, above). The new group was formally launched during a conference in Rome in May 1991; a month later Proletarian Democracy (*Democrazia Proletaria*—DP), a small party with roots in a 1976 leftist electoral alliance, voted to dissolve and join the new group.

Having won 5.6 percent of the vote in the 1992 Chamber of Deputies election, the PRC advanced to 6 percent in 1994 as a member of the Progressive Alliance (AP), from which it later distanced itself. In June 1995 the PRC was weakened by the defection of 14 of its 35 lower house deputies in protest at the alleged "isolationism" of the leadership. By mutual agreement, the rump PRC remained outside the center-left Olive Tree alliance in the April 1996 legislative elections, at which it increased its proportional vote to 8.6 percent. It then gave external backing to the minority Olive Tree government formed in May.

For more than two years the PRC was the key player in keeping the Prodi government in power, taking disagreements to the brink on several occasions over economic priorities (a 35-hour work week and a plan to stem unemployment in the south) and foreign policy issues (intervention in Albania and expansion of NATO). But the PRC was itself divided in these confrontations, notably when it nearly forced Prodi to resign in October 1997 but backed down when rank-and-file members protested the party's action. A year later, as the PRC withdrew its support of the 1999 budget and Prodi's coalition collapsed, the strains within the PRC split the party. A progovernment faction defected and formed the Party of Italian Communists (PdCI, below). In the May 2001 election the PRC won 3 senate and 11 chamber seats, all of the latter because of its 5 percent vote share in the proportional balloting. In the 2006 election the party rebounded, winning 41 chamber and 27 senate seats.

Following the party's failure to win any seats in parliament in 2008, party president Fausto Bertinotti resigned. At a congress held in July, the party elected a new secretary, Paolo Ferrero, who represented the party's left wing. The party remained divided along regional and factional lines. On January 24, 2009, a faction led by former PRC official Nichi VENDOLA left the party and formed the **Movement for the Left** (*Movimento per la Sinistra*—MpS) in an unsuccessful effort to draw other parties of the left to win seats in the June elections for the European Parliament.

Leader: Paolo FERRERO (Secretary).

Party of Italian Communists (*Partito dei Comunisti Italiani*—PdCI). Formed shortly after the PRC withdrew support of the Prodi government in October 1998, the PdCI was largely composed of PRC defectors led by Armando COSSUTTA, formerly the PRC president. However, the 21 deputies who followed Cossutta out of the PRC were insufficient to salvage the Prodi government. Subsequently, the

Communists reconciled themselves to being part of a coalition that included former Christian Democrats and received two cabinet posts in the D'Alema government, the first regime in half a century to include communists. The PdCI continued in the subsequent Amato administration and campaigned as part of the Olive Tree in 2001. After the 2006 election, during which the party won 16 chamber seats, Cossutta resigned as president and later left the party.

The PdCI left the SA coalition after the coalition's 2008 electoral debacle, wherein the PcCI and other coalition members lost all their seats in parliament and called for a new alliance of Italian communist parties.

Leaders: Oliviero DILIBERTO (Secretary), Antonino CUFFARO (President).

Federation of the Greens (*Federazione dei Verdi*—FdV). The FdV was officially launched in November 1986 as a union of regional green lists. In its first national election (June 1987) it took 1 senate and 13 chamber seats. After merging with the competing Rainbow Greens (*Verdi Arcobaleno*) in December 1990, the FdV in April 1992 improved its standing to 4 senate and 16 chamber seats on a national vote share of 2.8 percent. As a member of the Progressive Alliance in March 1994 its share slipped to 2.7 percent. The Greens won a 2.5 percent proportional vote share in the April 1996 legislative elections, following which Edo RONCHI of the FdV was appointed environment minister, a position he retained in the two D'Alema governments. Alfonso Pecoraro Scanio then served as minister of agriculture under Prime Minister Amato. The party won 9 senate and 8 chamber seats in May 2001 as part of the "Sunflower" alliance (with the Italian Democratic Socialists) within the Olive Tree. Although the FdV did not join in formation of the Olive Tree Federation in early 2005, it remained closely allied with the Olive Tree parties. The Greens won 15 chamber seats at the April 2006 election. For the senate contest, it joined with the PdCI (above) and the small **United Consumers** (*Consumatori Uniti*—CU), led by Bruno DE VITA, in a **Together with the Union** (*Insieme con L'Unione*) list that won 11 seats. In November 2006 a small number of Greens left the party and formed **Environmentalists for the Olive Tree** (*Ecologisti per l'Ulivo*), with the aim of merging into the Democratic Party the following year. The exodus left the party dominated by left-leaning members, led by president Alfonso Pecoraro Scanio, who was appointed minister of the environment in Prodi's cabinet.

In July 2008, after the FdV failed to win any seats as part of the SA coalition, Grazia Francescato replaced Pecoraro Scanio as party leader. In January 2009 the FdV formed a joint list for the European Parliament elections with the MpS, Democratic Left, and the Socialist Party but failed to win any seats.

Leader: Grazia FRANCESCATO (President).

Democratic Union for Consumers (*Unione Democratica per i Consumatori*—UD). Founded on September 11, 2007, by consumer advocates and former members of M-DL when it decided to merge with the Democratic Party, the UD supports labor unions and consumers' rights. Running on its own, the party failed to win seats in the 2008 election.

Leader: Bruno DE VITA (Secretary).

The Right (*La Destra*). This small, extreme-right party was founded in July 2007 by Francesco Storace, who left the National Alliance saying it had veered too far toward the center. It participated in a coalition with the Social Movement—Tricolor Flame in 2008 but failed to win any seats in the parliamentary election.

Leaders: Francesco STORACE (Secretary), Teodoro BUONTEMPO (President).

Pensioners' Party (*Partito Pensionati*—PP). Dating from 1987, the PP represents Italy's retirees. In 2004 it became the first such formation to win a seat in the European Parliament. A member of the Union coalition until it joined the PdL, the PP failed to win seats in the 2006 or 2008 national election.

Leader: Carlo FATUZZO (National Secretary).

Social Movement–Tricolor Flame (*Movimento Sociale–Fiamma Tricolore*—MS-FT). Led by Pino RAUTI, the MS-FT emerged from the minority profascism faction of the former MSI-DN, a majority of whose members opted in January 1995 to remain with the AN. Despite having fashioned a limited electoral agreement with the Berlusconi alliance, the party failed to win any chamber seats in the 2001 election, when it claimed only 0.4 percent of the lower house proportional vote. It failed to hold its one senate seat in 2006 and did not win any seats in 2008. Rauti subsequently withdrew from active politics.

Leader: Luca ROMAGNOLI (National Secretary).

Italy has numerous regional groupings, many of which allied with the **Northern League** and the **Autonomy Movement** for the 2006 and 2008 elections. Exceptions include the **Venetian Republic League** (*Liga Veneta Repubblica*), the **Lombard Alliance League** (*Lega Alleanza Lombarda*), and the Veneto-based **Northeast Project** (*Progetto Nordest*), which ran independently for both houses in 2006 and ran on the **People of Liberty** ticket in 2008

Other Parties:

Democratic Left (*Sinistra Democratica*—SD). This party, originally called Democratic Left for European Socialism, was founded on May 5, 2007, by Fabio Mussi and other members of Democrats of the Left who opposed that party's plan to merge with Daisy–Democracy Is Freedom to form the Democratic Party in October. The SD aims to solidify forces of the Italian left and work toward a unified European socialist movement.

Leaders: Fabio MUSSI, Claudio FAVA (National Coordinator).

Socialist Party (*Partito Socialista*—PS). Founded in 1892 as the Italian Socialist Party (*Partito Socialista Italiano* —PSI), the party saw the Communists (PCI) break away in 1921 and survived the suppression of the left during the fascist era. In 1947 a major split developed over the question of collaboration with the communists, a majority faction led by Pietro NENNI aligning itself with the PCI and a minority right-wing group led by Giuseppe Saragat forming what became the Italian Social Democratic Party (*Partito Socialista Democratico Italiano*—PSDI) in 1952. In opposition through the 1950s, the PSI participated in the so-called "opening to the left" from 1962, which eventually led to a coalition with the Christian Democrats. The PSI and PSDI merged in 1966 but split again in 1969, with the more conservative elements re-forming the PSDI.

Consistently the third-largest party in both houses of parliament, the PSI was a member of most governments in the 1970s and 1980s, with its leader, Bettino Craxi, becoming the first-ever PSI prime minister in 1983 and achieving a postwar record of incumbency before resigning in 1987. Craxi resigned as PSI general secretary in 1993, after 17 years in office, in the face of cautionary warrants indicating that he was under investigation on 50 charges of corruption and illicit party funding. In August, Craxi's parliamentary immunity was lifted.

In the wake of charges against numerous other PSI figures, the party slumped to 2.2 percent in the March 1994 parliamentary poll, which some PSI elements contested under the banner of the Democratic Alliance (see under PRI, above), following suit in the European Parliament balloting in June. In July, Craxi received a lengthy prison sentence while still facing other charges, along with about 30 other former PSI officials. (By mid-1999 Craxi, a fugitive in Tunisia, faced some 26 years in prison after multiple convictions. He died in January 2000.)

Seeking to recover its former constituency, the PSI transformed itself into the Italian Socialists (*Socialisti Italiani*—SI) in November 1994. For the April 1996 legislative elections the SI cooperated closely with the Italian Renewal (RI) within the broader Olive Tree alliance. In 1998 the PSDI, which had participated in many center-left coalition governments before losing all its lower house seats in 1994, remerged with the SI, with the conjoint grouping calling itself Italian Democratic Socialists (*Socialisti Democratici Italiani*—SDI). The SDI held one cabinet post in the first D'Alema government but as part of the "Clover" alliance (with the PRI and Francesco Cossiga's Union for the Republic) withdrew its support and forced the prime minister's resignation in December 1999. In February 2000, however, the SDI broke from the "Clover" group when Cossiga's party moved closer to Silvio Berlusconi's Freedom Alliance. Two months later it joined the Amato administration.

Prior to the 2001 national election the SDI joined with the Federation of the Greens (FdV, above) in *Il Girasole* ("Sunflower"), a sub-alliance within the Olive Tree that went on to win 16 senate and 18 chamber seats. In 2005 the party joined an alliance with the Italian Radicals called the Rose in the Fist (*Rosa nel Pugno*—RnP), which joined the center-left Union in November 2005. The alliance was undertaken to strengthen the hand of Italy's historical liberal, socialist, and lay movements in the 2006 general election. The party's platform stressed a range of goals focused primarily on social policy, including simplified divorce, access to the "morning after" contraceptive pill, legalization of civil unions for gay and heterosexual couples, and legalization of doctor-assisted suicide. The RnP won 18 chamber seats but no senate positions in the 2006 election.

In February 2006, **The Italian Socialists** (*I Socialisti Italiani*) came into being as a result of a schism within the New Italian Socialist Party (NPSI) between followers of NPSI leader Gianni De Michelis, who supported the party's membership in Berlusconi's governing coalition, and followers of Bobo Craxi, son of former socialist prime minister Bettino Craxi, who challenged the party's drift to the right. Following a court ruling in January 2006 in favor of De Michelis's leadership of the NPSI, Craxi founded The Socialists, which joined Prodi's Union coalition. The Socialists failed to win any seats in the 2006 election.

In March 2007 the party was renamed the Italian Socialists and joined the SDI in calling for a new "Socialist Constituency." Despite these earlier disputes, the NPSI also joined the PS.

In April 2007 Enrico Boselli, secretary of the SDI, who opposed the creation of the Democratic Party, launched a "Socialist Constituency" aimed at uniting Italy's disparate social-democratic parties. Subsequently, the constituency founded a new party, the Socialist Party. The party's goal was to reassemble Italian socialists after the collapse of the historic Italian Socialist Party into a single social-democratic party with strong ties to the European socialist movement.

Leaders: Enrico BOSELLI, Riccardo NENCINI (Secretary), Marco DI LELLO (National Coordinator).

Populars–UDEUR (*Popolari*—P-UDEUR). The UDEUR (Democratic Union for Europe/*Unione Democratica per l'Europa*) is the partial successor to the Democratic Union for the Republic (*Unione Democratica per la Repubblica*—UDR), which was formed in late 1997 by former president Francesco Cossiga. The UDR quickly attracted deputies and senators from centrist and conservative elements in other parties, including, in February 1998, the CDU and CCD (see above under UdC). Intended as Cossiga's vehicle for assembling moderate democrats and Christian reformers into the equivalent of the old Christian Democratic Party (the PPI's predecessor), the UDR played a pivotal role in the October 1998 formation of the D'Alema government, in which it was awarded three portfolios, including defense.

In January 1999 Cossiga announced his resignation as UDR chair, stating that he would be turning his attention to establishing an umbrella group for like-minded parties in preparation for the June 1999 European Parliament elections. Cossiga's resultant Union for the Republic (UR) joined with the SDI and PRI in the "Clover" parliamentary alliance and withdrew its support from the D'Alema government in December 1999. Meanwhile, the rump of the UDR reorganized in May as the UDEUR, remained in the government.

In the 2001 elections the UDEUR participated in the Olive Tree as part of the *Margherita* alliance, but in 2002 it remained aloof when the other *Margherita* parties decided to unify. Upon joining the Union coalition in 2004, the UDEUR revised its statute and added *Popolari* to its name. The party won 10 chamber and 3 senate seats in the 2006 election, holding two ministerial portfolios in the Prodi government.

Despite its small size, the UDEUR was the undoing of Prodi's government: its leader and Prodi's justice minister, Clemente Mastella, resigned on January 16, 2008, because of corruption charges and withdrew his party's support for the government on January 21. That led to the January 24 vote of no confidence in the senate that prompted Prodi's downfall.

In the run-up to the 2008 election both Berlusconi's People of Freedom and Casini's Union of the Center rejected Mastella's requests to merge UDEUR into their ranks. The party did not participate in the election.

Leader: Clemente MASTELLA (Secretary).

Christian Democratic Refoundation (*Rifondazione Democristiana*—RDC). Founded on October 1, 2006, by Publio Fiori, formerly of Christian Democracy for the Autonomies (above), the party aims to assume the mantle of the historic Christian Democratic Party (DC), which ruled Italy for most of the postwar period. While the party opposed the center-left coalition led by Prodi, it is not part of Berlusconi's center-right coalition. In early 2007 the party joined P-UDEUR and Christian Democracy (*Democrazia Cristiana*), a small group led by Giuseppe PIZZA in founding the "Christian Democratic Federation," with the aim of uniting the various parties and movements claiming to succeed the DC.

Leaders: Giovanni MEALLI (President), Publio FIORI (Secretary).

For more information on other parties active through 2006, see the 2008 *Handbook*.

Terrorist Groups:

In the second half of the 20th century Italy was often buffeted by political terrorism, with over 200 names having been used by groups committed to such activity. The most notorious of the left-wing formations, the **Red Brigades** (*Brigate Rosse*), was founded in 1969, reportedly in linkage with the West German Red Army Faction terrorists. The *Brigate Rosse* engaged in numerous killings during the late 1970s, including that of former prime minister Aldo Moro; subsequently, one of its offshoots, the **Union of Fighting Communists** (*Unione dei Comunisti Combattenti*—UCC), claimed responsibility for the 1987 murder of an air force general and the 1988 assassination of Sen. Roberto RUFFILLI, a leading ally of Prime Minister De Mita. In 1998 Renato CURCIO, a cofounder of the Red Brigades and its last leading figure behind bars, was freed from prison after serving 24 years of a 30-year sentence. In May 1999 the Red Brigades apparently resurfaced, claiming responsibility for assassinating Massimo D'ANTONA, an adviser to the minister of labor.

More recently, the Red Brigades have claimed responsibility for several murders, including the assassination in March 2002 of government economic adviser Marco BIAGI. Members continue to be apprehended, including Leonardo BERTULAZZI, who was arrested in Argentina in November 2002. The reputed head of logistics for the organization, he had been convicted in absentia in 1977 for kidnapping. In May 2004 the EU added the Red Brigades to its list of terrorist organizations.

Members of the **Politico-Military Communist Party** (*Partito Comunista Politico-Militare*), an offshoot of the Red Brigades, were arrested in February 2007 on charges of plotting to attack several domestic targets and assassinate current prime minister Berlusconi.

LEGISLATURE

The bicameral **Parliament** (*Parlamento*) consists of an upper house, the Senate, and a lower house, the Chamber of Deputies, of roughly equal power. A new electoral law passed in December 2005 restored the pre-1993 full proportional representation system for 617 out of 630 seats in 26 constituencies (autonomous Valle d'Aosta retains the first-past-the-post system for its single seat, while overseas Italian citizens elect the remaining 12 deputies). This legislation set minimum thresholds for parliamentary representation for a coalition (10 and 20 percent for the chamber and senate, respectively) and for a political party (4 percent for the chamber and 3 percent for the senate). When a coalition or a party with the largest number of votes fails to win 340 chamber seats, the law stipulates that it will receive enough "bonus" seats to reach the 340-seat level.

Senate (*Senato della Repubblica*). The upper house consists of 322 members elected to a five-year term (except for senators for life, currently numbering 7, including Giorgio Napolitano, who is inactive during his tenure as president) by universal suffrage under a proportional representation system that was proposed by the Berlusconi government and adopted on December 21, 2005 (recognizing coalitions winning at least 20 percent of the vote and including at least one party winning at least 3 percent of the vote, and parties winning at least 8 percent running independently or in a coalition winning less than 20 percent of the vote). Under a new "majority prize" provision, a coalition winning a majority of votes in a region will automatically be allocated no less than 55 percent of the region's seats, with the rest distributed among other qualifying coalitions and parties. The majority prize applies to all regions but Molise (which elects only 2 senators), Valle d'Aosta (1 senator), and Trentino-Alto Adige (which falls under a separate election law dividing its 6 seats evenly between Italian- and German-speaking senators). Under a law passed in December 2001, Italian citizens residing abroad elect 6 senators representing four districts: Europe; North and Central America; South America; and Africa, Asia, Oceania, and Antarctica.

The April 13–14, 2008, election produced the following results: Center-right coalition, 174 seats (People of Freedom, 147; Northern League, 25; Movement for Autonomy Allied for the South, 2); Center-left coalition, 132 (Democratic Party, 118; Di Pietro—Italy of Values, 14); Union of the Center, 3; South Tyrolean People's Party (present only in Trentino-Alto Adige), 2; South Tyrolean People's Party—Together for Autonomy (present only in Trentino-Alto Adige), 2; Associative Movement Italians Abroad (present only overseas), 1; and Valdotanian Union (present only in Valle d'Aosta), 1.

As of June 2009, senators were organized into the following parliamentary groups (senators may change their affiliation at any time): People of Freedom, 145 members; Democratic Party, 118; Northern League—Padania, 26; Italy of Values, 14; Union of the Center, South Tyrolean People's Party, and Autonomies, 11; and mixed, 8.

President: Renato SCHIFANI.

Chamber of Deputies (*Camera dei Deputati*). The lower house consists of 630 members directly elected to a five-year term by universal suffrage, with 617 seats distributed under the new proportional representation system (recognizing coalition lists with a 10 percent threshold that include at least one party receiving at least 2 percent of the vote, separate party lists with a 4 percent threshold, and parties representing linguistic minorities that win at least 20 percent of the vote in their corresponding regions). Valle d'Aosta elects 1 member, and overseas Italian citizens elect the remaining 12 deputies representing the same four districts as in the senate. Under the new majority prize provision, a coalition that receives a majority of the vote but less than 55 percent of the seats in Italy proper (340 out of 618) automatically is awarded the full 340 seats.

The April 13–14, 2008, election produced the following results: Center-right coalition, 344 (People of Liberty, 276; Northern League, 60; Movement for Autonomy Allied for the South, 8); Center-left coalition, 246 (Democratic Party, 217; Di Pietro—Italy of Values, 29); Union of the Center, 36; South Tyrolean People's Party (present only in Trentino-Alto Adige), 2; Autonomy Liberty Democracy (present only in Valle d'Aosta), 1; and Associative Movement of Italians Abroad (present only abroad), 1.

As of June 2009 deputies (who may change their affiliation at any time) were organized into the following parliamentary groups, which do not necessarily correspond to party names: People of Freedom, 271 members; Democratic Party, 216; Northern League–Padania, 60; Union of the Center, 35; Italy of Values, 27; mixed, 21; Movement for Autonomy, 8; linguistic minorities, 3; Liberal Democrats–MAIE, 3; Republicans, Regionalists, Populars, 3; and unaffiliated, 4.

President: Gianfranco FINI.

CABINET

[as of June 1, 2009]

Prime Minister	Silvio Berlusconi (PdL)
Ministers	
Agriculture and Forestry	Luca Zaia (LN)
Cultural Affairs	Sandro Bondi (PdL)
Defense	Ignazio La Russa (PdL)
Economic Development	Claudio Scajola (PdL)
Economy and Finance	Giulio Tremonti (PdL)
Education, Higher Education, and Research	Mariastella Gelmini (PdL) [f]
Environment and Marine Conservation	Stefania Prestigiacomo (PdL) [f]
Foreign Affairs	Franco Frattini (PdL)
Infrastructure and Transport	Altero Matteoli (PdL)
Interior	Roberto Maroni (LN)
Justice	Angelino Alfano (PdL)
Labor, Health, and Social Affairs	Maurizio Sacconi (PdL)
Ministers without Portfolio	
Equal Opportunity	Mara Carfagna (PdL) [f]
European Affairs	Andrea Ronchi (PdL)
Federal Reform	Umberto Bossi (LN)
Legislative Simplification	Roberto Calderoli (LN)
Parliamentary Relations	Elio Vito (PdL)
Program Implementation	Gianfranco Rotondi (PdL)
Public Administration and Innovation	Renato Brunetta (PdL)
Regional Affairs	Raffaele Fitto (PdL)
Tourism	Michela Vittoria Brambilla (PdL) [f]
Youth	Giorgia Meloni (PdL) [f]

[f] = female

COMMUNICATIONS

Although freedom of speech and press is constitutionally guaranteed, the collection and release of official news is centered in the Information Service of the Presidency of the Council of Ministers. Berlusconi's control of the three public television channels and outright ownership of the leading television and radio conglomerate, Mediaset, raised concerns about the availability of unbiased news coverage in Italy.

Press. Italy's 75 or so daily papers have a relatively low combined circulation. Several of the papers are owned or supported by political parties. Editorial opinion, influenced by the Catholic Church and various economic groups, leans heavily to the right of center. Most of the newspapers are regional, notable exceptions being the nationally circulated *Corriere della Sera, La Stampa, La Repubblica,* and *Il Giorno*. The following papers are published daily in Rome, unless otherwise noted: *Corriere della Sera* (Milan, 890,000), centrist; *La Repubblica* (750,000), center-left; *La Stampa* (Turin, 540,000), centrist; *La Gazzetta dello Sport* (Milan, 530,000), *Il Sole-24 Ore* (Milan, 420,000), business paper; *Il Giornale* (Milan, 350,000), center-right; *Il Messaggero* (340,000), center-right; *Il Resto del Carlino* (Bologna, 250,000), independent conservative; *La Nazione* (Florence, 200,000), right-wing; *Il Gazzettino* (Venice, 180,000), independent; *Il Giorno* (Milan, 170,000), independent; *Il Secolo XIX* (Genoa, 160,000), independent; *Il Mattino* (Naples, 140,000), independent; *Avvenire* (Milan, 130,000), Catholic; *Il Tirreno* (Livorno, 110,000), independent; *Giornale di Sicilia* (Palermo, 90,000), independent; *Il Manifesto* (80,000), leftist; *La Gazzetta del Mezzogiorno* (Bari, 80,000); *L'Unione Sarda* (Cagliari, 80,000).

News agencies. The leading domestic service is the Associated Press National Agency (*Agenzia Nazionale Stampa Associata*—ANSA); there is also a smaller Italian News Agency (*Agenzia Giornalistica Italia*—AGI), plus a number of specialized services. Numerous foreign bureaus maintain offices in the leading Italian cities.

Broadcasting and computing. Three nationwide radio broadcasting networks and three television channels are operated by *Radiotelevisione Italiana* (RAI), which is responsible to the Ministry of Communications. In 1995 voters approved partial privatization of RAI, although it took nearly a decade to pass implementing legislation. Over 2,000 private radio stations now broadcast locally, as do some 900 private television stations. The three principal private television channels are part of Mediaset, Silvio Berlusconi's media empire. As of 2008 there were 419.3 Internet users per 1,000 inhabitants.

INTERGOVERNMENTAL REPRESENTATION

Ambassador to the U.S.: Guilio TERZI.

U.S. Ambassador to Italy: David H. THORNE.

Permanent Representative to the UN: Cesare Maria RAGAGLINI.

IGO Memberships (Non-UN): ADB, AfDB, BIS, CDB, CEI, CERN, CEUR, EBRD, EIB, ESA, EU, Eurocontrol, G-8, G-10, G-20, IADB, IEA, Interpol, IOM, NATO, OECD, OSCE, PCA, WEU, WCO, WTO.

JAMAICA

Political Status: Independent member of the Commonwealth since August 6, 1962; under democratic parliamentary regime.

Area: 4,411 sq. mi. (11,424 sq. km.).

Population: 2,607,632 (2001C); 2,691,000 (2008E).

Major Urban Center (2005E): KINGSTON (575,000).

Official Language: English.

Monetary Unit: Jamaican Dollar (market rate December 1, 2009: 88.08 dollars = $1US).

Sovereign: Queen ELIZABETH II.

Governor General: Patrick ALLEN; sworn in on February 26, 2009, succeeding Kenneth Octavius HALL.

Prime Minister: Orette Bruce GOLDING (Jamaica Labour Party); sworn in on September 11, 2007, to succeed Portia SIMPSON MILLER (People's National Party) following legislative elections on September 3; formed new cabinet on September 14, 2007.

THE COUNTRY

Jamaica, whose name is derived from the Arawak Indian word *Xaymaca*, is a mountainous island located 90 miles south of Cuba. The third-largest island in the Caribbean, it is the largest and most populous of the independent Commonwealth nations in the area. About 77 percent of the population is of African descent; another 15 percent is of mixed Afro-European heritage. Population density is high, particularly in metropolitan Kingston, which contains more than 30 percent of the national total. The Anglican and Baptist creeds claim the most adherents, but numerous other denominations and sects are active. Women constitute approximately 46 percent of the official labor force, concentrated in agriculture and civil service, with a large proportion of the remainder serving as unpaid agricultural workers. As a consequence of male urban migration, more than one-third of all households are headed by women, with 70 percent of all children being born to single mothers.

The Jamaican economy is based on sugar, bauxite mining, and tourism, the last being the second leading earner of foreign exchange after remittances from Jamaican expatriates (who constitute an estimated one-quarter to one-third of the total Jamaican population). Agricultural products including rum, molasses, bananas, and citrus fruits also underpin the economy, as does a thriving informal sector based primarily on the illegal production and export of marijuana and, in recent years (according to some analysts), the transshipment of cocaine from South America to North America and Europe.

Since the mid-1970s the country has experienced severe economic difficulty, marked by high inflation, pervasive unemployment, a stifling foreign debt, and depression of the bauxite and sugar industries. Even before widespread devastation caused by Hurricane Gilbert in September 1988, the Seaga administration's acceptance of austerity measures mandated by the International Monetary Fund (IMF) had fueled growing public dissatisfaction with loss of services and decreased buying power. By late 1990 the one promising sector was the bauxite industry, which had launched a major expansion in both mining and refining because of increasing demand for aluminum. Subsequently, currency depreciation caused by deregulation of the foreign exchange market in September 1991 provoked a wave of protest by public-sector unions.

Inflation surged to 80.2 percent in 1991 but fell to single digits in the late 1990s. However, the economy otherwise remained severely distressed, as GDP declined annually in 1997–1999 while unemployment reached 16 percent in 1999. Increased tourism and rising demand for bauxite contributed in 2000 to the first expansion (0.5 percent) in five years. However, development prospects remained dim in view of extraordinarily high public debt, which appeared to preclude significant government investment in resolving widespread social problems such as income inequities, high illiteracy (30 percent), and rising crime and violence (linked to the drug trade as well as political turbulence).

Tourism revenues fell in the wake of the terrorist attacks in the United States in September 2001, and the economy was further buffeted by hurricanes and continued crime and violence. Growth subsequently remained slow by regional standards, registering 0.4 percent in fiscal year 2004–2006, 2.4 percent in 2006–2007, and 1.0 percent in 2007–2008. Meanwhile, official unemployment hovered at approximately 11 percent in 2007, while annual inflation reached nearly 20 percent in March 2008, mostly due to rising food and fuel prices.

Tourism, the bauxite/aluminum sector, and remittances were all severely distressed by the global economic crisis of 2008–2009, and GDP contraction of as much as 4–5 percent was predicted for 2009. The World Bank, Inter-American Development Bank, and other donors (including China) provided additional aid, but the government in mid-2009 was forced to pursue IMF lending for the first time since 1996 in order to offset declining public revenues and ongoing heavy debt repayment obligations.

GOVERNMENT AND POLITICS

Political background. A British colony from 1655 to 1962, Jamaica developed a two-party system before World War II under the leadership of Sir Alexander BUSTAMANTE and Norman W. MANLEY, founders, respectively, of the Jamaica Labour Party (JLP) and the People's National Party (PNP). A considerable measure of self-government was introduced in 1944, but full independence was delayed by attempts to set up a wider federation embracing all or most of the Caribbean Commonwealth territories. Jamaica joined the now defunct West Indies Federation in 1958 but withdrew in 1961 because of disagreements over taxation, voting rights, and location of the federal capital.

Bustamante became the nation's first prime minister at independence in 1962 and on his retirement in 1967 was succeeded by Donald SANGSTER, who died within a few weeks. His replacement, Hugh L. SHEARER, led the country until the 1972 election gave a majority to the PNP for the first time since independence and permitted Michael Norman MANLEY, son of the PNP's founder, to become prime minister. Manley remained in office following an impressive PNP victory in the election of December 1976, but when confronted by an economic crisis and mounting domestic insecurity, he was forced to call an early election in October 1980 that returned the JLP to power under the conservative leadership of Edward SEAGA. Benefiting from a surge of popularity occasioned by Jamaican participation in the invasion of Grenada, Seaga called an early parliamentary election for December 15, 1983, in which the JLP swept all seats in the wake of a PNP boycott occasioned by outdated voter rolls that allegedly favored the government party. In the face of highly adverse opinion poll results, the prime minister cited emergency conditions caused by Hurricane Gilbert to extend the parliamentary term beyond its normal five-year mandate but was unable to avert Manley's return to office in February 1989. A little more than a year later, opposition hopes that local balloting could be converted into a referendum against the administration were dashed as the PNP captured 11 of 12 disputed parish councils.

On March 15, 1992, Prime Minister Manley, who had been in poor health for several years, announced his retirement, effective March 23, at which time he was succeeded by his longtime deputy Percival (P. J.) PATTERSON. The PNP under Patterson won again in March 1993 and in December 1997 became the first Jamaican party to win a third consecutive term. In September 1998 local elections, the PNP won control in all 13 parish councils by taking 170 of 227 seats overall. Despite a significant reduction in its vote share and seats, the party maintained a majority in the legislative election on October 16, 2002, and Patterson formed a new cabinet on October 25. Patterson retired on March 30, 2006, and was succeeded by Portia SIMPSON MILLER, who had been elected PNP leader on February 25. The JLP returned to power after 18 years in opposition by winning 32 of 60 seats in the September 3, 2007, legislative elections, and new prime minister Bruce GOLDING, installed as the JLP leader in 2005, named an expanded 18-member cabinet on September 14.

Constitution and government. Under the 1962 constitution, the queen is the titular head of state. Her representative, a governor general

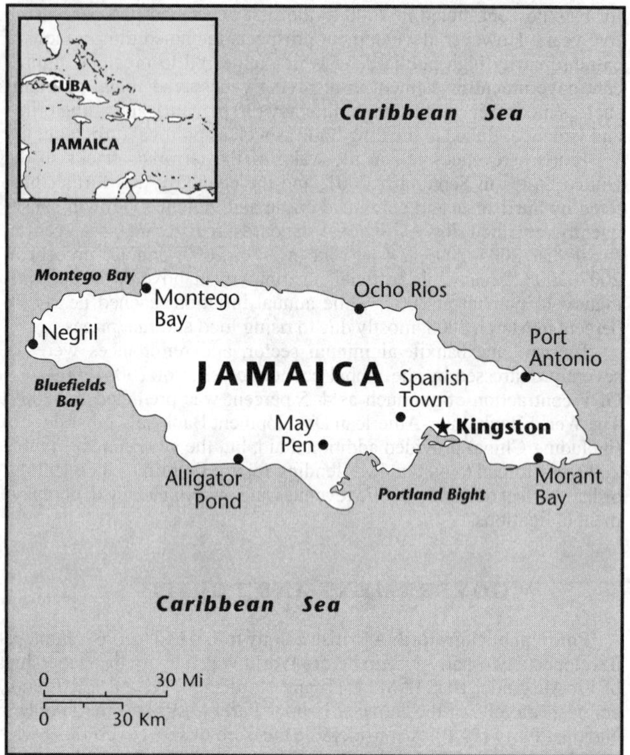

with limited powers, is advised, in areas bearing on the royal prerogative, by a six-member Privy Council. Executive authority is centered in a cabinet of no fewer than 12 members (including the prime minister), who are collectively responsible to the House of Representatives, the elected lower house of the bicameral Parliament; the upper house (Senate) is entirely appointive. The judicial system is headed by a Supreme Court with both primary and appellate jurisdiction. Judges of both the Supreme Court and a Court of Appeal are appointed by the governor general on the advice of the prime minister. There are also several magistrates' courts. For administrative purposes Jamaica is divided into 13 parishes and the Kingston and St. Andrew Corporation, a special administrative entity encompassing the principal urban areas.

In May 1991 Prime Minister Manley revealed that the government had mounted a constitutional review, including implementation of a change to republican status. The two leading parties had long agreed in the matter, the principal issue being whether the governor general should be replaced by a president with executive or ceremonial powers.

In September 1994 the search for an all-party consensus on constitutional reform foundered over a new issue: the PNP's move to dispense with the Privy Council as Jamaica's final court of appeal in favor of participation in a projected Caribbean Court of Appeal, the government arguing that the existing method of appeal was "culturally inappropriate and inconsistent" with Jamaica's sovereign status. Pressure for the change, which had been under discussion for some years, had intensified after the Privy Council had recommended that two individuals who had been under sentence of death for 14 years should, because of the lengthy delay, have their sentences commuted to life imprisonment. Prime Minister Patterson had responded that his administration was "unwavering" in its determination to execute convicted murderers. For its part, the opposition appeared to differ largely on procedural grounds, arguing that the government wished to alter the appellate process by simple legislative action without reference to the larger "package" of amendments that included a JLP-backed proposal for an independent police services commissioner. In March 1997 opposition leader Seaga declared that a future JLP government might withdraw from the Caribbean appellate body on the ground that its members' appointments had been politically biased.

In September 2004 Prime Minister Patterson announced that a referendum on republican status would be held by March 2005. The (then) opposition JLP responded that it would not support the move unless the abandonment of judicial appeals to the Privy Council was also submitted to the voters, and the referendum remained in abeyance.

In 2008 the new JLP administration proposed a constitutional revision that would set fixed dates for elections, replacing the current system, which allows the governor general to dissolve Parliament at any time and call for new elections within three months of the dissolution. However, no action had been taken by the fall of 2009 in regard to the proposed amendment, which would require approval by two-thirds of each legislative chamber and endorsement in a national referendum.

Foreign relations. Jamaica is a member of the United Nations and the Commonwealth as well as a number of regional organizations. Previously cordial relations with the United States were marred in July 1973 by Prime Minister Manley's declaration of U.S. Ambassador Vincent W. de Roulet as persona non grata. They were further exacerbated by Jamaican support for Cuban intervention in Angola in 1975 and by subsequent allegations of U.S. involvement in "destabilization" activities similar to those that had led to the ouster of the Salvador Allende regime in Chile.

The designation of Edward Seaga as prime minister in November 1980 signified a return to a pro-U.S. posture, the Cuban ambassador, in turn, being declared persona non grata and departing the country four days before the formal installation of the new government. Seaga was widely regarded as a prime mover behind the Reagan administration's 1981 Caribbean Basin Initiative, and ties to Washington were further strengthened by Jamaica's participation in the U.S.-led action in Grenada in October 1983. In contrast, Prime Minister Manley moved in late 1989 to reestablish relations with Havana.

In June 1994 Jamaica agreed to the anchoring of U.S. ships in its waters to determine if Haitian expatriates could qualify as refugees. In May 1997 an agreement was announced that would permit U.S. drug enforcement agents to pursue suspected traffickers into Jamaican airspace and territorial waters.

Relations with Haiti were suspended in March 2004 because of the presence of former president Jean-Bertrand Aristide, who had initially sought refuge in the Central African Republic and subsequently departed for exile in South Africa.

The Patterson and Simpson Miller administrations signed a number of agreements with Venezuela, including an August 2005 contract in which Venezuela offered Jamaica preferential prices for oil imports. Simpson Miller and Venezuelan president Hugo Chávez signed a memorandum of understanding in March 2007 to supply Jamaica with liquefied natural gas for electricity generation and bauxite/alumina production.

Current issues. Known affectionately as "Mama Portia" or "Sister P," Prime Minister Simpson Miller, Jamaica's first female premier, commanded widespread popular support at her inauguration in March 2006. However, a major financial scandal in the cabinet late in the year cost the PNP support (see the 2008 *Handbook* for details), although the government survived a no-confidence vote in the legislature.

The legislative elections scheduled for August 27, 2007, were postponed for a week due to Hurricane Dean, which heavily damaged the agricultural and mining sectors. Some analysts concluded that perceived foot-dragging on the part of the government in responding to the storm contributed to the JLP's narrow victory (only 3,000 votes separated it from the PNP in the nationwide total). Other issues of popular concern included ongoing economic stagnation and chronic crime and violence, much of it crime- and/or drug-related. (Jamaica has one of the highest murder rates in the world.) New prime minister Golding, considered a technocrat, quickly launched a series of anticrime measures and pledged to address corruption within the police force and the judiciary. Subsequently, both houses of the legislature endorsed retention of the death penalty as a means of combating the crime wave. However, by mid-2009 it had become clear that the failing economy had become the new administration's top priority. Among other things, Golding announced large-scale spending cuts and collateral tax increases, which were broadly criticized by the PNP.

POLITICAL PARTIES

Jamaica's two leading parties, the Jamaica Labour Party and the People's National Party, have similar trade union origins. Both are well organized and institutionalized, but personal leadership within them remains very important.

Government Party:

Jamaica Labour Party (JLP). Founded in 1943 by Alexander Bustamante, the JLP originated as the political arm of his Bustamante Industrial Trade Union. The more conservative of Jamaica's two leading parties, the JLP supports private enterprise, economic expansion, and a generally pro-Western international stance, but the party also identifies with black African states and other developing countries. Opposition to Prime Minister Seaga's leadership, particularly in regard to economic policy, contributed to the party's defeat in local elections in 1986, in the parliamentary poll of February 1989, and in municipal balloting in March 1990, with dissidents advancing the slogan "Three in a row, time to go." Seaga's principal opponents, a so-called "gang of five" led by Pearnel CHARLES, were unable to dislodge the JLP leader at the party's annual conference in June 1990 and were removed from the shadow cabinet during September and October. By late November all five had secured court injunctions banning the JLP executive from expelling them from membership in the party and deletion from its future candidate lists. Somewhat unexpectedly, Charles reasserted his loyalty to Seaga in July 1991, eliciting a bitter response from the party leader that he would be put "on probation." In March 1992 one of the dissidents, Karl Samuda, joined the PNP, while Charles was denied election to a deputy leadership post at the party's annual conference in July. Significantly, Charles and two of the other three remaining dissidents lost their seats in the March 1993 election. In September 1995 Samuda resigned from the PNP and was readmitted to the JLP a month later.

Although under attack by party opponents, Edward Seaga was reelected JLP leader on March 26, 1995. A month earlier Bruce Golding, the shadow finance minister and long considered Seaga's successor, had resigned as chair, reportedly after his supporters had asked Seaga to step down; subsequently Golding formed the rival NDM (below). Seaga was again confirmed as JLP leader at the party's annual conventions in 1999 and 2000.

The party was runner-up to the PNP in the election of December 18, 1997, winning only 10 House seats. Although the JLP increased its vote share and gained a total of 26 seats in legislative balloting in October 2002, the party's failure to displace the PNP as the ruling party reportedly prompted increasing internal criticism of Seaga. In mid-2004, Seaga announced that he would step down as JLP leader in November, and Golding (who had returned to the party) was elected his successor at a convention on February 20, 2005, and sworn in as Leader of the Opposition on April 21.

After nearly 20 years in the opposition, the JLP returned to power following the 2007 elections. The JLP also won local elections in December, gaining majorities in 9 of the 13 parish councils.

Leaders: Bruce GOLDING (Prime Minister and Party President), Karl SAMUDA (General Secretary).

Opposition Party:

People's National Party (PNP). Organized in 1938 by Norman W. Manley, the PNP became affiliated in 1943 with the Trade Union Council. After losing elections in 1945 and 1949 but winning those of 1955 and 1959, it came to power for the first time since independence in March 1972, following ten years in opposition. Headed until 1992 by Michael Manley (son of its late founder), the PNP is based on the National Workers' Union and draws its principal support from middle-class, intellectual, and urban elements. Committed to a program of "democratic socialism," the party was decisively defeated in the October 1980 election. It subsequently moved to the center, and in the 1986 municipal elections removed the word "socialism" from its manifesto, rejecting a proposed electoral alliance with the Workers' Party of Jamaica (WPJ), a communist grouping formed in 1978 (see the 2008 *Handbook* for information on the now defunct WPJ). Following its boycott of the 1983 balloting, the party functioned as an extraparliamentary opposition. Initially eschewing mass demonstrations in favor of "public forums," the PNP claimed a major role (along with the WPJ) in the unrest over fuel prices in January 1985, which was followed by mass PNP rallies in tourist areas and a successful campaign for the preparation of revised voter lists. The party won control of 11 of 13 parish councils in July 1986 (securing 126 of 187 seats overall) and decisively defeated the JLP in the parliamentary balloting of February 9, 1989, with a 56.7 percent vote share. It performed even better in the early election of March 30, 1993, winning 52 of 60 seats on a 60 percent vote share.

Former prime minister and PNP leader Michael Manley died on March 6, 1997. On December 18 his successor, P. J. Patterson, led the party to its third consecutive legislative victory with a marginal loss of two seats. Patterson managed to win a fourth victory for his party in legislative balloting in October 2002, although the PNP lost even more seats to the JLP. Reportedly because of the decreasing vote share of his party, Patterson subsequently declared that his current term would be his last, and he stepped down in favor of Portia Simpson Miller in March 2006; concurrently, Patterson announced his retirement from politics.

Following the PNP's loss in the September 2007 legislative election and its lackluster performance in the December local balloting, Simpson Miller faced a strong challenge for the party's leadership at the September 2008 party conference from Peter PHILLIPS, a former minister of national security, who pledged to return the PNP to its "socialist roots." However, Simpson Miller (the first woman to head one of the country's two main parties) was reelected by a small margin, and her supporters captured three of the PNP's vice-presidential positions as well.

Leaders: Portia SIMPSON MILLER (President of the Party, Leader of the Opposition, and Former Prime Minister); Angella BROWN-BURKE, Derrick KELLIER, Noel ARSCOTT, Fenton FERGUSON (Vice Presidents); Peter BUNTING (General Secretary).

Other Parties Competing in the 2007 Elections:

National Democratic Movement (NDM). The NDM was launched on October 29, 1995, by former JLP chair Bruce Golding, who had resigned in early September as opposition finance spokesperson. Golding, who had indicated earlier that he might challenge Edward Seaga for leadership of the JLP at its annual conference in November, declared that the new formation was needed to generate the "long-range stability without which there [could] be no significant investment and growth." Public opinion polls indicated that the NDM could attract 20 percent of the vote, as contrasted with 21 percent for the PNP and 18 percent for the JLP. However, the NDM lost all of its existing five seats in the legislative balloting of December 18, 1997. Golding stepped down from his leadership post in March 2000, and a May NDM conference selected as his successor Hyacinth BENNETT, who thereby became the first woman to head a Jamaican party. Before the legislative balloting in October 2002, the NDM initiated the formation of an electoral coalition called the New Jamaica Alliance (NJA) that also included the **Republican Party of Jamaica** (RPS), led by Denzil TAYLOR; and the **Jamaica Alliance for National Unity** (JANU), which had been launched the previous March by a church and civic group led by Rev. Al MILLER. The NJA failed to win any seats in legislative balloting.

In February 2005, Golding, who had returned to the JLP, was designated Seaga's successor and became leader of the opposition after winning a by-election on April 13.

The NDM contested only 10 seats in the September 3, 2007, elections, receiving fewer than 600 votes at the national level. (The NDM had threatened to boycott the poll after its principal candidate, Earle De Lisser, was not allowed to participate in televised debates between the JLP and PNP candidates.)

Leaders: Earle DE LISSER (Chair), Apollone REID (Vice President).

Imperial Ethiopian World Federation Incorporated Political Party (IEWFIPP). The IEWFIPP was launched in October 2001 as the nation's first Rastafarian party. It first presented candidates in the 2002 legislative election, pledging to abolish the constitution and the monarchy. The party also presented a small number of candidates in subsequent national and local elections but received only a handful of votes each time. Party founder Ras ASTOR BLACK ran as an independent (aligned with a Jamaica Alliance Movement) in the 2007 legislative elections. The IEWFIPP had only nine candidates in the 2007 race, most of them in Kingston, and received only 192 votes nationwide.

The only other party to receive votes (according to the electoral commission) in 2007 was the new **Jerusalem Bread Foundation,** whose single candidate received only nine votes.

Other Parties:

The following small parties contested elections in recent decades but did not contest the 2007 balloting: the **Jamaica-American Party**, founded in 1986; the **African Comprehensive Party**, founded in 1988; the **United Progressive Movement,** founded in 1993; **the Natural Law Party** (NLP), launched in 1996; and the **United People's Party** (UPP), created in 2000 by Antoinette HAUGHTON-CARDENAS, an attorney and former talk show host, in support of "family values" and "spiritual rebirth towards collective nation-building. (For more information on these parties, see the 2008 *Handbook.*)

LEGISLATURE

The bicameral **Parliament** consists of an appointed Senate and an elected House of Representatives. All spending bills must originate in the lower chamber.

Senate. The upper house presently consists of 21 members appointed by the governor general; 13 are normally appointed on advice of the prime minister and 8 on the advice of the leader of the opposition. After the 1983 election, however, the PNP refused to nominate opposition senators and expelled 2 party members who had accepted such appointments from Prime Minister Seaga as a means of protesting alleged electoral irregularities. The JLP adopted the same posture in the immediate wake of the 1993 poll.

Following the installation of the new 21-seat Senate on September 11, 2007, the Jamaica Labour Party held 13 seats, and the opposition People's National Party, 8.

President: Dr. Oswald HARDING.

House of Representatives. The lower house includes 60 members elected from single-member districts by universal adult suffrage for five-year terms, subject to dissolution. In the most recent election of September 3, 2007, the Jamaica Labour Party (JLP) won 32 seats and the People's National Party, 28. (Three by-elections were held in 2008 to fill JLP seats vacated because the legislators held dual citizenships, which is forbidden by the constitution. However, all three JLP legislators were reelected after having renounced their second citizenships [two U.S. and one Venezuelan]).

Speaker: Delroy CHUCK.

CABINET

[as of September 1, 2009]

Prime Minister	Bruce Golding
Ministers	
Agriculture and Fisheries	Christopher Tufton
Defense	Bruce Golding
Education	Andrew Holness
Finance and Public Service	Audley Shaw
Foreign Affairs and Foreign Trade	Kenneth Baugh
Health	Rudyard Spencer
Industry, Commerce, and Investment	Karl Samuda
Information and Telecommunications	Bruce Golding
Justice and Attorney General	Sen. Dorothy Lightbourne [f]
Labor and Social Security	Pearnel Charles
Mining and Energy	James Robertson
National Security	Dwight Nelson
Planning and Development	Bruce Golding
Transport and Works	Lester Michael Henry
Tourism	Edmund Bartlett
Water and Housing	Dr. Horace Anthony
Without Portfolio (Office of the Prime Minister)	Daryl Vaz
Youth, Sports, and Culture	Olivia Grange [f]

[f] = female

Note: All cabinet members belong to the Jamaica Labour Party.

COMMUNICATIONS

The press has traditionally been free of censorship and government control and is considered highly influential in the region.

Press. The following are published in Kingston: *Jamaica Gleaner* (250,000 daily, 900,000 Sunday); *Daily Star* (50,000 daily, 60,000 weekend); *Jamaican Observer* (50,000); *Jamaica Herald.*

News agencies. There is no domestic facility; AP, the Caribbean News Agency, and Reuters are among those with bureaus in Kingston.

Broadcasting and computing. The government-owned Television Jamaica Limited (formerly the Jamaica Broadcasting Company, JBC) controls the island's television facilities, while the Educational Broadcasting Service of the Ministry of Education provides radio and television service for the public schools. In mid-1989 the Manley administration scrapped its predecessor's plan to divest most JBC functions, while announcing that private interests would be permitted to operate a national television channel and a national radio station. The Golding administration announced plans in June 2008 to phase out the government's participation in commercial broadcasting and have the state's role limited to public broadcasting. There are currently three independent television stations and six independent radio stations.

As of 2008 there were 568.8 Internet users per 1,000 inhabitants.

INTERGOVERNMENTAL REPRESENTATION

Ambassador to the U.S.: Anthony Smith JOHNSON.

U.S. Ambassador to Jamaica: (Vacant).

Permanent Representative to the UN: Raymond O. WOLFE.

IGO Memberships (Non-UN): ACS, Caricom, CDB, CWTH, IADB, Interpol, IOM, NAM, OAS, OPANAL, SELA, WCO, WTO.

JAPAN

Nippon

Political Status: Constitutional monarchy established May 3, 1947; under multiparty parliamentary system.

Area: 145,850 sq. mi. (377,750 sq. km.).

Population: 127,768,843 (2005C); 127,801,000 (2008E).

Major Urban Centers (2005E): TOKYO (8,483,000), Yokohama (3,579,000), Osaka (2,629,000), Nagoya (2,215,000), Sapporo (1,881,000), Kobe (1,525,000), Kyoto (1,475,000), Fukuoka (1,401,000), Kawasaki (1,327,000), Saitama (1,176,000), Hiroshima (1,155,000), Sendai (1,025,000), Kitakyushu (993,000).

Official Language: Japanese.

Monetary Unit: Yen (market rate December 1, 2009: 86.68 yen = $1US).

Sovereign: Emperor TSUGUNOMIYA AKIHITO; ascended the throne on January 7, 1989, on the death of his father, Showa Emperor MICHINOMIYA HIROHITO.

Heir Apparent: Crown Prince NARUHITO.

Prime Minister: Yukio HATOYAMA (Democratic Party of Japan); elected by the Diet on September 16, 2009, following the general election of August 30, in succession to Taro ASO (Liberal Democratic Party), who had formally resigned with his cabinet earlier on September 16.

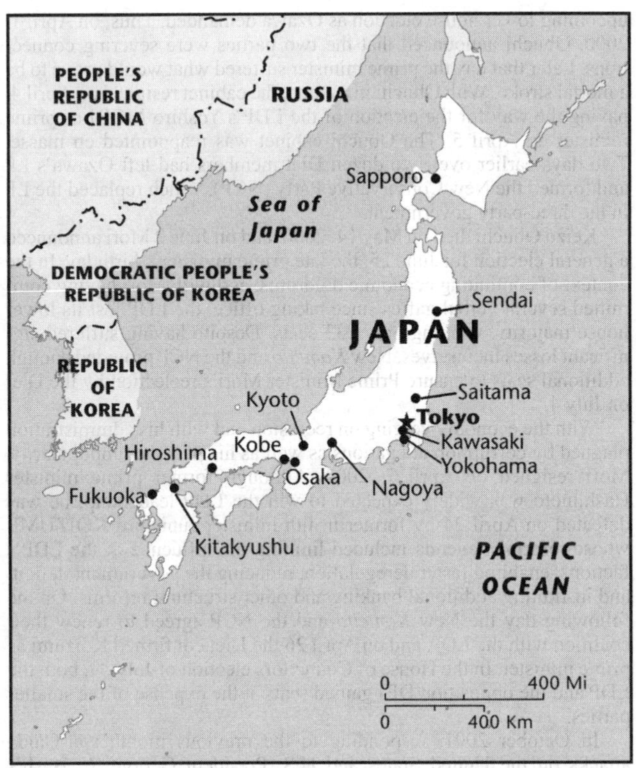

THE COUNTRY

Situated off the coast of Northeast Asia and stretching some 2,000 miles, the Japanese archipelago consists of over 3,000 islands, although the 4 main islands of Honshu, Hokkaido, Kyushu, and Shikoku account for 98 percent of the land area. While mountainous terrain has limited the farming acreage, the country's location has provided a stimulus to fishing, other maritime pursuits, and trading. The thickly settled, basically Mongoloid population is remarkably homogeneous; the only significant ethnic minority consists of 700,000 Koreans, most of whom are descended from some 2.5 million laborers brought to Japan in the period 1910–1945. The Ainu, an indigenous people concentrated on the northern island of Hokkaido, today number only about 50,000. Buddhism and Shintoism are the two major religions. Women constitute about 42 percent of the labor force but remain underrepresented in elective office. For example, women won only 11 percent of the seats in the August 2009 lower house election, the lowest proportion for major industrialized countries.

Japan's most remarkable achievement over the past 125 years has been its unique industrial development, which gave it undisputed economic primacy in Asia even before World War II. Growth between 1954, when prewar economic levels were first regained, and 1970 proceeded at an average rate, in real terms, of at least 10 percent annually, vaulting Japan past West Germany and into second place, behind the United States, among the world's largest economies. The role of agriculture in the Japanese economy has shrunk as those of industry and services have grown; full-time agricultural labor has declined since 1960 from 33 percent to 4 percent of the national workforce and now produces only 2 percent of GDP. Industry accounts for about 30 percent of GDP and 27 percent of employment, while services contribute 69 percent of GDP and 68 percent of employment.

During the 1990s average yearly expansion slumped to 1 percent as business investment declined and productivity increases proved inadequate. Beginning in 1997 Japan experienced its worst recession in over half a century. Growth of 2.8 percent was restored in 2000, but it dropped to 0.4 percent in 2001 and registered a decline of 0.3 percent in 2002. In 2003 growth returned to about 1.4 percent and the unemployment rate, after peaking at a record 5.5 percent early in the year, showed a modest drop. Alone among the major industrialized nations, Japan was also experiencing an extended period of deflation (averaging 1.3 percent a year in 2001–2004), leading the Bank of Japan to drop short-term interest rates to zero percent to stimulate investment. Although a mild recession in April–September 2004 temporarily set back expectations that the economy was emerging from the doldrums, real GDP rose by 1.9 percent in 2005, 2.0 percent in 2006, and then 2.3 percent in 2007. Meanwhile, deflation had ended, leading the Bank of Japan, in July 2006, to raise the interest rate (initially to 0.25 percent) for the first time in over five years. In 2008, however, the onset of the most extensive international financial crisis in the post–World War II era reversed the positive trend, leading Japan to record its first recession in seven years (see Current issues, below). For the year as a whole the economy contracted by 0.7 percent, with forecasts for 2009 varying from –3 percent to –7 percent

GOVERNMENT AND POLITICS

Political background. The armistice signed by Japan on September 2, 1945, concluded World War II and ended the era of modernization and imperial expansion that had begun with the Meiji Restoration in 1867. Stripped of its overseas territorial acquisitions, including Manchuria, Korea, Formosa (Taiwan), southern Sakhalin, and the Kuril Islands (in addition to the de facto loss of its "Northern Territories" to the Soviet Union—see Foreign relations, below), Japan was occupied by Allied military forces under Gen. Douglas MacArthur and entered a period of far-reaching social, political, and economic reforms overseen by U.S. occupation authorities. A constitution promulgated November 3, 1946, effective May 3, 1947, deprived Emperor HIROHITO of his claim to divine right and transformed Japan into a constitutional monarchy that expressly renounced war and the maintenance of military forces.

The Allied occupation was formally ended by a peace treaty signed in San Francisco on September 8, 1951, effective April 28, 1952; by its terms (still unrecognized by Moscow when the Soviet Union dissolved), the United States retained control of the Bonin and Ryukyu islands while informally recognizing Japan's "residual sovereignty" in those territories. Concurrently, a security treaty between Japan and the United States (modified in 1960 by a Treaty of Mutual Cooperation and Security) gave the latter the right to continue maintaining armed forces in and around Japan. The Bonin Islands were returned to Japanese administration in 1968, while reversion of the Ryukyus (including Okinawa) occurred in 1972.

For six decades Japan's political fortunes rested mainly with a small group of conservative politicians, civil servants, and businesspeople identified with the Liberal Democratic Party (LDP), established in 1955 by merger of the preexisting Liberal and Democratic parties. Dedicated both to free enterprise and to continued close association with the United States, the LDP was periodically challenged until the 1980s by leftist forces associated primarily with the Social Democratic Party of Japan—SDPJ (formerly the Japanese Socialist Party—JSP), the small Japanese Communist Party (JCP), and a wide but volatile extraparliamentary opposition, including trade union, student, and intellectual groups. LDP prime ministers during this period included Eisaku SATO (1964–1972); Kakuei TANAKA (1972–1974), whose tenure was cut short by charges of personal and financial irregularities; Takeo MIKI (1974–1976); Takeo FUKUDA (1976–1978); and Masayoshi OHIRA (1978–1980). Until 1993 LDP rule continued without interruption under prime ministers Zenko SUZUKI (1980–1982); Yasuhiro NAKASONE (1982–1987); Noburu TAKESHITA (1987–1989); Sosuke UNO (1989); Toshiko KAIFU (1989–1991); and Kiichi MIYAZAWA (1991–1993).

In the wake of a series of scandals and a mass exodus of party leaders, Prime Minister Miyazawa lost a no-confidence motion on June 18, 1993. In the ensuing lower house election of July 18 the LDP lost its parliamentary majority, although retaining a sizable plurality. Following the poll, an improbable seven-party coalition emerged that included the SDPJ and three new groups recently organized by LDP dissidents: the Japan Renewal Party (JRP), led by former LDP secretary general Ichiro OZAWA and former finance minister Tsutomu HATA; the Japan New Party (JNP); and the New Party Harbinger (*Shinto Sakigake*). On July 29 the coalition named as its choice for prime minister a conservative populist from the JNP, Morihiro HOSOKAWA, who secured parliamentary confirmation on August 6 over the LDP nominee, Yohei KONO, and thereby became Japan's first non-LDP prime minister since that party's formation. The new prime minister indicated that electoral reform would be his top priority.

In February 1994 SDPJ objections to higher indirect taxes were largely responsible for forcing Hosokawa into a humiliating modification of an economic stimulus package, thus provoking major coalition dissent over the 1994–1995 budget. In early April disclosures of alleged financial misconduct forced the prime minister to submit his resignation, thereby sparking a contentious succession battle. Tsutomu Hata of the JRP, the coalition parties' joint candidate, was elected on April 25, but his administration's viability was thrown into doubt when the SDPJ withdrew on April 26, thereby compelling Hata to form a minority cabinet dominated by his own party.

The SDPJ's action followed the formation, principally at the instigation of Ichiro Ozawa, of a new center-left parliamentary alliance called *Kaishin* (Innovation), which linked the JRP, the JNP, and the Democratic Socialist Party (DSP) with two new ex-LDP splinter groups. In late June, faced with almost certain defeat on an LDP-sponsored nonconfidence motion, Hata resigned, giving rise to interparty negotiations that yielded a coalition agreement between the LDP, the SDPJ, and *Shinto Sakigake.* On June 29 the Diet elected the SDPJ chair, Tomiichi MURAYAMA, prime minister over the candidate of the outgoing coalition, former LDP prime minister Kaifu. Five months later, the principal elements of the *Kaishin* alliance agreed to merge as *Shinshinto* (New Frontier Party).

Japanese political realignment was temporarily halted by a massive earthquake that caused some 5,000 deaths in Kobe and surrounding areas on January 17, 1995, followed by the release of deadly nerve gas in a Tokyo subway system on March 20. The latter incident, which resulted in ten deaths and injury to thousands of commuters, was the work of a millennial religious cult, *Aum Shinrikyo,* whose leader, Shoko ASAHARA, was arrested in May after an intensive manhunt.

In a House of Councilors election on July 23, 1995, the LDP and *Shinshinto* registered impressive gains while the SDPJ fell from second to third place, regaining only 16 of the party's 41 vacated seats. The LDP-SDPJ-*Sakigake* coalition nonetheless continued in office until January 5, 1996, when Prime Minister Murayama resigned, having been battered by a variety of economic and political problems. Murayama was succeeded on January 11 by the country's outspoken LDP trade minister, Ryutaro HASHIMOTO, at the head of a new administration of the same three parties.

Encouraged by the failure of *Shinshinto* to sustain its early promise as a "government in waiting," the prime minister called an early lower house election for October 20, 1995, and was rewarded by a significant increase in LDP representation to 239 seats in the 500-seat House of Representatives. The two smaller government parties both suffered heavy losses, in part because the new Democratic Party of Japan (DPJ) took 52 seats in its first election. Both the Social Democratic Party (SDP, formerly the SDPJ) and *Shinto Sakigake* declined to join a new LDP-dominated government, as did the DPJ, with the result that Hashimoto had to settle for a pledge of qualified external support from the SDP and *Shinto Sakigake* in return for formal policy consultation. On that basis, Hashimoto was reelected prime minister on November 7 and thereupon announced an exclusively LDP cabinet.

At the end of 1997 *Shinshinto* collapsed, with the DPJ quickly emerging as the largest opposition party. In May 1998 both the SDP and *Shinto Sakigake* decided to withdraw their support from the LDP at the end of the legislative session in June, but the announcement posed no threat to the LDP, which, owing to defections from other parties since the last election, once again controlled a majority of lower house seats.

The Hashimoto administration approached the July 12, 1998, election for half the House of Councilors with dim prospects amid economic turmoil triggered by what was then Japan's worst postwar recession (and the first since the oil shock of 1974). Furthermore, charges of bribery and other corruption had generated a series of resignations and dismissals within the Ministry of Finance and the central bank. On July 13, with the LDP having captured only 44 of the 60 contested seats it had previously claimed in the upper house, Prime Minister Hashimoto resigned. Foreign Minister Keizo OBUCHI succeeded him as party leader on July 24 and as prime minister, at the head of an "economic reconstruction Cabinet," on July 30.

Following protracted negotiations, in mid-January 1999 Prime Minister Obuchi announced formation of a coalition with Ichiro Ozawa's new Liberal Party (LP), a successor to *Shinshinto.* The following October, the recently organized New *Komeito* formally joined the government, guaranteeing a majority in both houses to Obuchi. In December, however, with a general election due in less than a year, the LP's Ozawa threatened to pull his party from the tripartite coalition unless Obuchi put forward legislation reducing the size of the House of Representatives. Obuchi relented and in January–February 2000 forced through the Diet a bill that cut 20 proportional seats from the 500-member lower house.

The LDP-LP relationship nevertheless remained tenuous, in part because the LDP would not support as many LP candidates for the upcoming lower house election as Ozawa demanded. Thus, on April 1, 2000, Obuchi announced that the two parties were severing connections. Later that day the prime minister suffered what would prove to be a mortal stroke. With Obuchi in a coma, the cabinet resigned on April 4, paving the way for the election of the LDP's Yoshiro MORI as prime minister on April 5. The Obuchi cabinet was reappointed en masse. Two days earlier over two dozen Diet members had left Ozawa's LP and formed the New Conservative Party (NCP), which replaced the LP in the three-party government.

Keizo Obuchi died on May 14, 2000, and on June 2 Mori announced a general election for June 25, the late prime minister's birthday. In the context of continuing economic doldrums, and with Mori having committed several verbal gaffes since taking office, the LDP lost its lower house majority, winning only 233 seats. Despite having suffered significant losses themselves, New *Komeito* and the NCP provided enough additional seats to ensure Prime Minister Mori's reelection by the Diet on July 4.

With the economy verging on recession and with his administration plagued by corruption allegations as well as his personal unpopularity, Mori resigned on April 7, 2001. Although former prime minister Hashimoto was widely expected to win the LDP leadership, he was defeated on April 24 by former health minister Junichiro KOIZUMI, whose reformist agenda included limiting the influence of the LDP's factions, enabling faster deregulation, reducing the government deficit, and instituting additional banking and other structural reforms. On the following day the New *Komeito* and the NCP agreed to renew their coalition with the LDP, and on April 26 the Diet confirmed Koizumi as prime minister. In the House of Councilors election of July 29, both the LDP and the opposition DPJ gained seats at the expense of the smaller parties.

In October 2001, responding to the previous month's al-Qaida attacks on the United States and U.S. President George W. Bush's announcement of a "war on terrorism," the Diet passed legislation that permitted the government to deploy warships to the Indian Ocean in support of U.S.-led operations in Afghanistan. Such noncombat deployment of Japan's Self-Defense Forces (SDF) remained controversial, however, and the issue became even more inflammatory in 2003 when Koizumi won approval to commit additional SDF personnel in support of the U.S.-led invasion of Iraq.

By late 2002 Koizumi's administration had failed to resolve the country's economic plight, in part because he proved unable to tame various LDP factions that differed with him over how to proceed with reform while simultaneously reinvigorating the economy. As a consequence, Koizumi's popularity dropped. Nevertheless, he handily defeated three challengers for the presidency of the LDP in September 2003 and then announced a general election for November 9. Aided by the LDP's absorption of the NCP shortly before the balloting, the LDP and New *Komeito* maintained a slightly reduced majority, but the DPJ, bolstered by a September merger with the LP, gained 40 seats, apparently confirming speculation that Japan was moving toward a two-party system. That possibility was further supported by the results of the July 11, 2004, election for half the House of Councilors: the DPJ won 50 seats and the LDP won 49, although together the latter and New *Komeito* retained an overall majority. On September 27 Prime Minister Koizumi announced a completely revamped cabinet.

On August 8, 2005, the prime minister called an early election following the defeat in the House of Councilors of reform legislation intended to privatize Japan Post—in effect, the largest savings bank in the world, with total assets of $2.9 trillion. Koizumi had staked his continuing leadership on privatizing the government agency because the overhaul stood at the center of his efforts to reform Japan's banking and financial sector while reducing the government's role and opening the industry to greater commercial— including foreign—participation. In the September 11 election the LDP registered the largest victory to date in Japan's post–World War II history, winning 296 seats and permitting Koizumi to pass his postal reform plan, which included dividing the agency into separate units responsible for mail delivery, banking, insurance, and management services.

On September 20, 2006, Cabinet Secretary Shinzo ABE was elected president of the LDP, winning 464 votes to 136 for Foreign Minister Taro ASO and 102 for Finance Minister Sadakazu TANIGAKI. Outgoing Prime Minister Koizumi had voluntarily stepped down after serving five years in office. The victory ensured Abe's election as prime minister by the Diet on September 26, when he introduced a new cabinet in which Foreign Minister Aso was the only holdover.

At the July 29, 2007, election for half the House of Councilors, the LDP lost its plurality in the upper house for the first time in the party's history. The opposition DPJ claimed 60 seats, for a total of 109, while the LDP won only 37, which dropped its representation to 83. The defeat for the Abe government came in the midst of corruption scandals, a series of ministerial gaffes, and the disclosure of massive errors in the public pension system (see Current issues, below). Despite a major cabinet reshuffle on August 27, pressure mounted for his resignation, and on September 12 Abe announced that he would step down. His successor as LDP president, Yasuo FUKUDA, a former cabinet secretary, easily won confirmation as prime minister on September 25.

Less than a year later, however, on September 1, 2008, Fukuda also resigned, beset by falling poll numbers, economic difficulties, and an inability to advance his legislative agenda because of opposition from the DPJ-controlled Senate. On September 22 the LDP elevated Taro Aso from LDP secretary general to party president by a two-to-one margin over four rivals, and he was confirmed as prime minister two days later.

Aso faired no better than Fukuda, however, and in early 2009, with Japan's economy succumbing to recession, his standing in public opinion polls dipped below 20 percent approval. In July, with the end of the lower house term approaching, Aso dissolved the House of Representatives and called an election for August 30. Dissatisfaction with LDP rule culminated in an unprecedented victory for the DPJ, which won 308 seats, compared to 119 for the LDP. On September 16 the DPJ's Yukio HATAYAMA won confirmation as prime minister at the head of a government that included the SDP and the People's New Party (PNP) as junior partners.

Constitution and government. The constitution of May 3, 1947, converted Japan from an absolute to a constitutional monarchy by transferring sovereign power from the emperor to the people and limiting the former to a "symbolic" and ceremonial role. In addition, the peerage was abolished and a range of civil rights enumerated, including freedom of thought and conscience, free and equal education, an absence of censorship, and impartial and public judicial procedures.

Legislative and fiscal authority are vested in a bicameral parliament (Diet) consisting of a dominant House of Representatives and an upper chamber, the House of Councilors, which has limited power to delay legislation. The cabinet, headed by a prime minister, is collectively responsible to the Diet and must resign on passage of a no-confidence vote in the House of Representatives unless the house is dissolved and a new election held. Judicial power is vested in an appointive Supreme Court and in lower courts as established by law.

Administratively, Japan is divided into 47 prefectures, each with an elected mayor or governor and a local assembly. Smaller municipal units have their own elected assemblies.

Constitutional amendments require a two-thirds majority of both houses and subsequent ratification by a majority vote in a popular referendum. In 1999 the Diet passed a bill authorizing the formation in each house of a Research Commission on the Constitution to consider "widely and comprehensively" the provisions of the basic law. The two committees convened for the first time in January 2000 and submitted their final reports in April 2005. The process culminated in the passage in 2007 of a national referendum bill, which set forth basic procedures for conducting a constitutional referendum. The bill will not enter into effect, however, until 2010.

Article Nine of the constitution, which prohibits "the threat or use of force" internationally and renounces the maintenance of armed forces and "other war potential" for such purposes, has been central to the ongoing consideration of whether the 1947 constitution should be amended or even replaced. Article Nine has been interpreted by the government as permitting the maintenance of Self-Defense Forces (SDF), currently totaling about 240,000 personnel. Presently, dispatch of SDF contingents abroad is limited to peacekeeping operations under the United Nations or, as in the case of the recent deployments to the Indian Ocean and Iraq, to the terms of specific legislation. In December 2006 the Diet voted to raise the status of the Defense Agency to that of a full ministry, but debate remains open as to whether the government should be granted a freer hand in deploying SDF forces overseas, including participation in mutual defense efforts.

Foreign relations. Japan was admitted to the UN in 1956 and belongs to all of its specialized and related agencies. As a leading industrialized country, Japan is also a member of such bodies as the Organization for Economic Cooperation and Development (OECD) and the Group of Seven/Group of Eight.

Japan's failure to offer a clear apology for its 1941 attack on Pearl Harbor has caused some lingering ill-feeling in the United States, as has, in Japan, Washington's refusal to apologize for the decision to drop atomic bombs on Hiroshima and Nagasaki in August 1945. Neither resentment has significantly affected Japan's continuing postwar reliance on the United States for its defense, and the 1960 mutual security treaty remains in effect.

In 1997 the two countries negotiated revised guidelines for military cooperation. For the first time Japan agreed to commit military personnel to overseas support during Far East crises. Without specifying a precise geographical purview, enabling legislation passed in 1999 permits Japan, in an emergency, to provide U.S. forces with fuel, food, and other logistic support plus access to Japanese civilian airports and ports. In addition, Japanese ships may assist in such activities as minesweeping in international waters, while members of the Japan SDF deployed abroad may carry weapons to defend themselves and Japanese civilians.

Perhaps the most troublesome aspect of the U.S.-Japan defensive alignment has been the American military presence in Okinawa. In December 1996 agreement was reached on a 20 percent reduction in the land utilized by the U.S. military, without, however, a reduction in the U.S. forces stationed on the island. In May 2006, following years of discussions, the two countries completed a plan for relocation of a U.S. Marine heliport to Nago, in the north, and the transfer by 2015 of 8,000 Marines to Guam, at a cost of $10.3 billion (60 percent to be paid by Japan). Also as part of force reorganization, all or part of five military facilities were to revert to Japanese control. Nevertheless, many Okinawans object to the continued U.S. presence—currently numbering over half of the 40,000–50,000 U.S. troops deployed in Japan—while recognizing its positive economic impact. Local resentment has been particularly fierce in response to criminal acts committed by U.S. servicemen against civilians. In 1995 Washington agreed to turn troops involved in such cases over to Japanese authorities.

In early 2004, in support of U.S. policy toward Iraq, SDF personnel were sent to provide humanitarian assistance and logistical support in Iraqi "safe areas." The deployment was vociferously condemned by the opposition and much of the public. In July 2006 Japan's 600 troops were withdrawn.

Controversial legislation passed in 1992 permitted, for the first time since World War II, the use of Japanese military personnel for international peacekeeping missions. Accordingly, a Japanese contingent was deployed with the UN mission in Cambodia and another was sent to Mozambique, but only to provide logistical support. Since 1996 Japanese troops have been assigned to the UN Disengagement Observer Force in the Golan Heights, but Tokyo declined to participate in other UN Security Council peacekeeping missions until Prime Minister Fukuda announced in June 2008 that Japan would contribute several "experts" to assist at the headquarters of the UN Mission in Sudan.

Issues related to Japan's imperialist past continue to affect relations with its neighbors, including Russia. The postwar normalization of relations with the Soviet Union proceeded slowly. Bilateral talks on a Japanese-Soviet peace treaty were instituted in 1972, but Soviet refusal to return the northern islands of Etorofu, Kunashiri, Shikotan, and Habomai, which were annexed after World War II, prevented any significant progress toward a treaty until the post-Soviet era. In 1996 Moscow and Tokyo agreed to resume negotiations on a peace treaty that would include resolution of the "northern territories" issue. In January 1998 a joint commission was formed to draft the text of a definitive accord, and in November, during the first state visit to Moscow by a Japanese head of government in 25 years, Prime Minister Obuchi and Russian President Boris Yeltsin reaffirmed a 2000 target date for completing the peace accord and ending the insular impasse.

Nevertheless, the issues remained unresolved a decade later. In December 2007 Russia seized four Japanese boats off Kunashiri for fishing without a permit. The captains and crew were all released by February 2008. In February 2009 Prime Minister Aso became the first Japanese prime minister since the end of World War II to visit Sakhalin Island, where he conferred with Russian president Dmitri Medvedev. The two pledged to accelerate efforts to find "an original and unconventional approach towards solving the sovereignty dispute by our generation," but the renewed sense of cooperation was undercut in June when Japan's House of Representatives unanimously approved a bill reasserting Japanese sovereignty over the islands. The Russian foreign ministry described the bill as "inappropriate and unacceptable," while the Russian State Duma rejected the idea of further talks on the issue unless the Diet reversed itself.

Normal relations with South Korea, but not with North Korea, were established in 1965–1966 after many years of hostility, which, in muted form, lingered because of Korean resentment over the Japanese occupation of 1910–1945 and over alleged discrimination against Koreans born and living in Japan. It was not until a visit by South Korean President Roh Tae Woo in May 1990 that the residual bitterness was substantially eased by Emperor Hirohito's tender of "deepest regret" for "the suffering . . . which was brought about by my country." During a state visit by South Korean President Kim Dae Jung to Japan in 1998, Emperor Akihito publicly communicated his "deep sorrow" for Japan's 35 years of colonial rule, while a concluding statement from the two governments included the first written "heartfelt apology" from Tokyo to Seoul.

In 1992 Tokyo admitted that the Japanese army had forced tens of thousands of Korean women to serve as "comfort women" (unpaid prostitutes) during World War II. In all, up to 200,000 women had been so enslaved in the territories occupied by Japan. To atone, in 1994 the Murayama government announced a ten-year commitment of $1 billion that, in part, would fund vocational training centers for women in neighboring countries. The first disbursements from a resultant Asian Women's Fund (of $18,500 each to 4 Filipino women) were made in 1996, but other comfort women and their organizations refused to accept payments that did not come directly from the Japanese government. When the program concluded in 2002, only 285 South Korean, Taiwanese, and Filipino women had received compensation. Additional outlays were provided from an unofficial government-backed fund for medical and welfare support. The issue resurfaced again in March 2007 following remarks by Prime Minister Abe in which he denied that the comfort women had been coerced, although he later expressed sympathy for the extreme difficulties they had faced.

In November 1996 the Japanese foreign ministry lodged a formal protest with South Korea because of a port facility being constructed in a group of small islands (called Takeshima by Japan and Tokto by South Korea) located midway between the two countries. Partly because of the territorial dispute, in January 1998 Tokyo scrapped a 1965 fishing treaty with its neighbor, but in September the two compromised on a treaty revision governing fishing zones and quotas. The Takeshima/Tokto issue has repeatedly flared up since then, including in April 2006 following Japan's announcement that it intended to conduct a hydrographic survey of the area, an announcement that was denounced by both South Korea and North Korea.

Relations with North Korea have been dominated by security concerns, especially after Pyongyang fired a three-stage missile over the Pacific in August 1998. The launch produced a strong rebuke from Tokyo, which temporarily froze food aid and development assistance to Pyongyang. North Korea's growing launch capability also contributed to Japan's September announcement that it would participate with the United States in research on a theater missile defense system (MDS).

Relations with Pyongyang were strained again in March 1999, when, in the first action of its kind since 1953, Japanese destroyers and other naval vessels chased and fired on two suspected North Korean spy ships in territorial waters. In December 2001 the Japanese coast guard intercepted a suspected North Korean spy ship within Japan's exclusive economic zone. An exchange of fire ended with the sinking of the North Korean vessel, which led Pyongyang to accuse Tokyo of "brutal piracy."

In October 2002, following a visit by Prime Minister Koizumi to North Korea and the latter's belated admission that it had kidnapped 13 Japanese citizens in the late 1970s and early 1980s to provide language instruction for government agents, Japan and North Korea restarted normalization talks in Kuala Lumpur, Malaysia. The two days of discussions made no progress, however, and further efforts were hindered by other developments, including Pyongyang's renewal of its nuclear weapons development program. In March 2003 North Korea objected to Japan's launch of two reconnaissance satellites and then, in December, to Tokyo's confirmation that it would move ahead with deployment of the MDS. A one-day visit to Pyongyang by Koizumi in May 2004 concluded without noticeable progress on any bilateral issues. In December 2005 Tokyo approved the joint development of sea-based missiles as part of the MDS.

In October 2006, responding to North Korea's October 9 underground nuclear weapons test, Japan imposed new unilateral sanctions. Steps included banning all imports from North Korea and preventing its ships from entering Japanese ports. Japan nevertheless remained a key participant in the six-party talks (with China, Russia, South Korea, and the United States) on dismantling North Korea's nuclear weapons program. With the talks having resumed in December 2006, and with Pyongyang having agreed to terminate development of its nuclear capabilities, discussions between Japan and North Korea resumed in June 2008 in Beijing. At that time North Korea agreed, among other tings, to reexamine the case of the abducted Japanese. Tokyo, in turn, agreed to ease sanctions.

Such steps toward comity came to another halt in 2009. On April 5 North Korea launched another rocket that it insisted was intended to carry a communications satellite into orbit, but Western observers declared that the launch was a failed military test. In response to broad international criticism of the launch, the North announced that it was once again quitting the six-party talks and would nullify all related agreements. On May 23 North Korea conducted its second nuclear weapons test, which was quickly followed by a series of short-range missile launches. Another series, labeled as a further provocation by Tokyo, followed in early July.

For many years Tokyo pursued a policy of "separating politics from economics" by trading extensively with both Taiwan and mainland China while according diplomatic recognition only to the former. Thus the Japanese were ill prepared for U.S. President Richard Nixon's opening to the People's Republic of China (PRC) in February 1972. Later that year Prime Minister Tanaka mounted a pathbreaking visit of his own to Beijing, during which he agreed to recognize the PRC as the sole legal government of China and to sever diplomatic (but not economic) relations with Taiwan. The rapprochement was formalized by the signing of a treaty of peace and friendship in Beijing in 1978.

In October 1992, during the first visit to the PRC by a Japanese monarch, Emperor Akihito acknowledged that Japan's wartime occupation had "inflicted great suffering on the people of China," but he yielded to domestic right-wing groups by stopping short of a formal apology. A November 1998 visit to Japan by Chinese President Jiang Zemin, the first by a Chinese head of state since World War II, failed to produce the expected formal, written Japanese apology for its 1937–1945 occupation. Instead, Prime Minister Obuchi repeated an expression of "deep remorse" that Prime Minister Murayama had voiced in 1995.

A persistent insular dispute has centered on the uninhabited Senkaku Islands (called the Diaoyutai Islands by China) located between Taiwan and Okinawa. Under Japanese control after the Sino-Japanese War of 1895, they were held by the United States from 1945 to 1972, when they were returned to Japan. In March 2004 Japan detained seven Chinese activists who had evaded Japanese patrols and landed on one of the disputed islands. In April 2006 the PRC strongly objected to a high-school textbook revision that identified the islands as definitively Japanese territory.

Beijing continues to express concern over U.S.-Japanese security guidelines and their potential implications regarding the defense of Taiwan, while Japan has criticized recent increases in PRC military spending. The PRC, like North and South Korea, also criticized Prime Minister Koizumi's repeated visits to the Yasukuni shrine honoring Japanese war dead, including a small number of convicted war criminals, and the adoption by Japanese schools of history textbooks that have minimized or ignored Japanese crimes during its occupation of the Korean peninsula, parts of China, and Southeast Asia before and during World War II.

In October 2006 newly elected Prime Minister Abe selected China for his first overseas visit. The following April, Chinese Premier Wen Jiabao traveled to Japan, and on May 6–10, 2008, Hu Jintao became the first Chinese president to visit Japan in a decade. Following the devastating May 12 earthquake in western China, Japan immediately offered aid, although China rejected Tokyo's initial plan to transport supplies to the stricken area using Air Self-Defense aircraft.

In recent decades Japan's ranking as one of the world's principal exporters has been a major factor in its international relations, particularly with the United States and Western Europe, both of which have taken steps against Japanese export penetration, particularly of automobiles and electronics. During U.S. President Bill Clinton's administration (1993–2001) trade wars were narrowly averted several times by the signing of last-minute accords. Beginning in 1999, accusations regarding Japanese steel exports and retaliatory American actions led both to seek redress before the World Trade Organization (WTO). In 2003 the WTO ruled against a U.S. law that permitted distribution of antidumping tariffs to U.S. steel firms. The WTO further ruled in 2004 that Japan and other affected countries could impose retaliatory tariffs. In another ruling favorable to Japan, in January 2007 the WTO ruled that U.S. antidumping duties on various goods, including some carbon steel products and ball bearings, were applied unfairly.

Current issues. By the time campaigning began for the July 2007 House of Councilors election, the Abe government's approval rating had dropped to 30 percent. On May 28 the minister of agriculture, forestry, and fisheries, Toshikatsu MATSUOKU, committed suicide rather than face questioning over alleged misuse of a political fund and involvement in bid-rigging related to public works projects. His replacement, Norihiko AKAGI, after only weeks on the job, was also embroiled in a funding scandal (he was ultimately forced to resign on August 1), and on July 3 Fumio KYUMA, after only six months in office as Japan's first postwar minister of defense, resigned after making remarks that were perceived as justifying the U.S. use of atomic bombs at the close of World War II. Other ministers had committed verbal gaffes that insulted women and those afflicted with Alzheimer's disease. Even more disturbing to the general public, earlier in the year the Social Insurance Agency, which is responsible for the public pension system, acknowledged that it had underpaid more than 200,000 retirees, that many more people had been improperly exempted from making contributions to the system, and that some 50 million premium payments had not been properly credited because of misplaced identification records. It therefore came as no surprise when voters turned control of the House of Councilors over to the DPJ-led opposition, which was thereby positioned to delay passage of Abe's legislative agenda.

Abe's decision to resign came in the midst of a parliamentary fight over extending Japan's commitment to naval refueling operations in support of the NATO-led mission in Afghanistan, but the pressure for him to resign had been mounting since the July election defeat. His successor, Prime Minister Fukuda, nearly 20 years older than Abe, was generally regarded as more supportive of the LDP's traditional factional structure, leading proreform advocates to lament that the government would conduct "business as usual." The opposition Democrats had other ideas, however, and their objections to the extension of the two-ship Indian Ocean support operation (a destroyer and a supply ship) led the government to announce the mission's suspension from November 1.

Although the Diet session had been scheduled to conclude on November 10, 2007, it was ultimately extended into 2008 as the government attempted to find a compromise that would permit renewal of the mission. In mid-November 2007 the House of Representatives, by a wide margin, passed a one-year extension that proposed limiting the mission to supplying oil and water, but the DPJ-led upper house refused to approve the measure. Finally, on January 11, 2008, the lower house overrode the upper house defeat by passing the bill with a two-thirds majority—the first time since 1951 that a bill had been passed over the objections of the House of Councilors. (The same maneuver was performed in December 2008 to enact another one-year extension.)

In subsequent months the DPJ continued to stymie government legislation, including an extension of a temporary "emergency" gas tax (which had been in effect for 30 years). On April 30, 2008, Prime Minister Fukuda again used his two-thirds majority in the lower house to reinstitute the tax. Adoption of another tax-related measure on May 13 required the same procedure. During the same period, the DPJ and its opposition allies repeatedly rejected or delayed the appointment of new Central Bank officials, and on June 1, the House of Councilors, for the first time under the 1947 constitution, passed a nonbinding censure motion against the prime minister, citing a recently introduced elderly health care and pension reform that, it claimed, overly burdened low-income individuals. The House of Representatives responded the following day by passing a confidence motion.

Only three months later, Fukuda resigned to avoid a "political vacuum" caused by the government's falling approval ratings and the DPJ's uncompromising opposition to key government legislation. Neither a major cabinet reshuffle undertaken by Fukuda in early August nor the subsequent announcement of a boost in government spending and tax cuts failed to alter the political landscape. Because it was widely expected that former foreign minister Taro Aso would succeed Fukuda, speculation immediately turned to whether the new prime minister would call a snap election, as demanded by the DPJ.

With the House of Representatives nearing the end of its four-year term, in July 2009 Prime Minister Aso called an election even though a DPJ victory was virtually assured by the public's dissatisfaction with the course of government. The state of the economy undoubtedly contributed to the LDP's unprecedented loss on August 30. Rapidly falling exports, rising food and commodity prices, and a loss of consumer confidence were already entrenched when Aso took office, and the economic picture quickly grew grimmer. In November 2008 the government announced that the economy was in recession. In December Aso proposed a $250 billion stimulus package of emergency measures that included supports for the financial system and was intended to supplement an earlier $300 billion package of proposed tax cuts, loan guarantees for businesses, and hiring incentives for employers. In early 2009 the strong value of the yen against the U.S. dollar and the euro continued to cut demand for Japanese exports, which were down by more than 45 percent in January, as further drops in production, corporate profits, business confidence, and wholesale prices generated fears that deflation would return. Data for the first quarter of the year ultimately showed a 4 percent drop in GDP, which amounted to an annualized decline of 15.2 percent—the steepest decline in Japan's post–World War II history.

The new DPJ-SDP-PNP government took office in September 2009 with the primary challenge of reinvigorating the economy. During the election campaign the DPJ had proposed to do so through such measures as increasing disposable household income, in part by instituting monthly child allowances, thereby boosting domestic demand and decreasing the economy's reliance on exports. The DPJ platform also called for creating jobs in agriculture, health care, and elder services and moving forward on negotiating a free-trade agreement with the United States. Other domestic tasks facing Prime Minister Hatoyama include reforming the government bureaucracy and revisiting the still-controversial changes made to the postal banking system by the Koizumi government.

Regarding Japan's relationship with the United States, the DPJ had campaigned against further extension of the refueling mission in the Indian Ocean and in favor of renegotiating the terms of the American military presence, including on Okinawa. Shortly before the election candidate Hatoyama caused a stir in Washington by writing in the *New York Times* that America's international dominance and style of capitalism might be approaching their end, but his first meeting with U.S. president Barack Obama, on the sidelines of the opening of the UN General Assembly in New York in September 2009, elicited mutual reassurances regarding the strength of the defense partnership, their commitment to confronting global warming, and the common goal of a nuclear-weapons-free world.

POLITICAL PARTIES

Throughout most of the postwar era, Japan's multiparty political structure featured the predominance of a single government party, the conservative Liberal Democratic Party (LDP), over a diversified opposition on the center and left of the political spectrum.

In November 1994 nine opposition groups united as *Shinshinto* (New Frontier Party). In addition to five LDP dissident formations, *Shinshinto* brought together the Japan New Party—JNP (*Nihon Shinto*), which had been formed by former prime minister Morihiro Hosokawa following his departure from the LDP in 1992; the Japan Renewal Party—JRP (*Shinseito*), formed in 1993 by former LDP secretary general Ichiro Ozawa; much of the Clean Government Party (*Komeito*), under Koshiro ISHIDA (discussed below under New *Komeito*); and the Democratic Socialist Party—DSP (*Minshu Shakaito-Minshato*) of Takashi YONEZAWA, the last being a 1961 right-wing offshoot of the Japan Socialist Party (JSP, subsequently the Social Democratic Party—SDP). But *Shinshinto,* initially headed by former LDP prime minister Toshiki Kaifu and then by Ozawa, never coalesced into a viable alternative to the LDP and by 1996 had lost impetus, being upstaged in the fall election campaign by the newly organized Democratic Party of Japan (DPJ) despite remaining the largest opposition group in the House of Representatives. In late 1997 *Shinshinto* dissolved, with many of its elements reforming as new parties in early 1998. A number of these soon afterward joined the DPJ, which now led the opposition.

Another *Shinshinto* successor, Ichiro Ozawa's Liberal Party (LP; see the DPJ, below), left the opposition and formed a governing coalition with the LDP in January 1999. At the start of April 2000 the LP resigned from the government, but the majority of the party's Diet members quickly established the New Conservative Party (NCP) and remained in alliance with the LDP. Six months earlier, the New *Komeito* had also joined the government.

Since then, evidence has mounted that Japan may be moving toward a two-party system. In 2004 the LDP gained strength through consolidation with the NCP, while the opposition DPJ increased its base by merging with the LP. Although New *Komeito* held its own as the third-ranked party, the once-powerful Japanese Communist Party (JCP) and SDP steadily lost ground: Since the July 2004 election for half the House of Councilors, neither the JCP nor the SDP could claim more than 9 seats in either house of the Diet, and in the August 2009 election for the lower house New *Komeito* fell to 21 seats.

Government Coalition:

Democratic Party of Japan—DPJ (*Nihon Minshuto*). The liberal DPJ was launched in September 1996 by a faction of the New Party Harbinger (*Shinto Sakigake*) led by Yukio Hatoyama and including the popular health and welfare minister, Naoto Kan. Grandson of a leader of the pre-1955 Democratic Party component of the LDP, Hatoyama had fallen out with the *Shinto Sakigake* leadership over electoral strategy. The new party quickly attracted parliamentary and popular support, winning 52 lower house seats in the October balloting, mostly at the expense of the SDPJ and what remained of *Shinto Sakigake*.

In March 1998 the New Party Fraternity—NPF (*Shinto Yuai*, or Amity Party), the Democratic Reform League—DRL (*Minshu Kaikaku Regno*), and the Good Governance Party—GGP (*Minseito*) voted to dissolve and join the DPJ. All had previously agreed to work with the DPJ in a parliamentary bloc called *Minyuren*.

The GGP had been established in January by the merger of three other parties: the Sun Party—SP (*Taiyo*), which had been formed in December 1996 by former prime minister Hata and a dozen lower house members who had left *Shinshinto*; the Voice of the People—VP (*Kokumin no Koe*); and the From Five Party (FFP) of former prime minister Morihiro Hosokawa. Like the NPF, the VP and FFP had emerged on January 4, 1998, from the ruins of *Shinshinto*.

Following the July 1998 election, the DPJ, supported in the House of Councilors by the affiliated **Shin-Ryokufukai** group, remained the largest opposition force in the Diet. In balloting for prime minister on July 30, Democratic leader Kan outpolled the LDP's Obuchi 104–103 in the upper house, but the LDP's majority in the lower house guaranteed Obuchi's election. At a DPJ convention in January 1999, Kan easily won reelection as party chief, despite earlier allegations of sexual misconduct. In September 1999, however, Kan lost his leadership to Secretary General Yukio Hatoyama by a runoff vote of 182–130.

In the June 2000 election the DPJ made major gains, advancing to 127 seats, 32 more than it had held before the balloting. In March 2001 the DPJ absorbed much of *Sakigake*, as the reconfigured rump of *Shinto Sakigake* had been named in 1998. (In 2002 the remaining elements of *Sakigake* formed the Environmental Political Party Green Assembly [*Kankyosenta Midori no Kaigi*], which dissolved in 2004.)

In September 2002 President Hatoyama won a narrow reelection victory over Naoto Kan, but a significant faction remained dissatisfied with his leadership. In December he resigned as president after other party leaders reacted strongly against his having unilaterally approached Ichiro Ozawa, then of the Liberal Party—LP (*Jiyuto*), about a merger aimed at uniting the opposition prior to the next general election. The DPJ's Diet delegation quickly replaced Hatoyama with Kan.

Ozawa had formed the LP in January 1998 following the breakup of *Shinshinto*. While the LP was reported at its founding to have attracted the greatest number of *Shinshinto* members (including 54 lower house representatives), it was viewed by many analysts as being unable to mount an effective campaign against the LDP because of its leader's autocratic style. Its membership in the lower house later fell to under 40, leaving it third among the opposition parties.

In January 1999 the LP joined the LDP in a coalition government, reuniting conservative forces that had separated upon Ozawa's departure from the LDP in 1993. Ozawa's insistence on LDP support for additional LP candidates in the upcoming general election contributed to a parting of ways on April 1, 2000, only hours before Obuchi's ultimately fatal stroke. Rejecting Ozawa's leadership, more than half the LP Diet members abandoned the party and quickly formed the New Conservative Party (NCP), which reestablished the LDP linkage. In the June 2000 election the LP fared considerably better than the NCP, winning 22 seats, 4 more than it had held in the House of Representatives prior to dissolution.

The forced resignation of DPJ President Hatoyama in December 2002 over his unauthorized contact with the LP's Ozawa probably delayed, but did not prevent, the parties' unification. The merger ultimately occurred on September 26, 2003, six weeks before a lower house election, in which the DPJ made significant gains, to 177 seats.

On May 10, 2004, Kan resigned as DPJ president, beset not only by an admission that he, like many other politicians, had not made all his required payments into the state pension plan but also by opposition from within the DPJ to his support for the LDP's pension reform bill. He was replaced on May 18 by the party's former secretary general, Katsuya OKADA, after the likely successor, Ichiro Ozawa, admitted six years of nonpayments into the pension plan.

In the House of Councilors election of July 2004 the DPJ won 50 seats, 1 more than the LDP, for a total of 83 seats, a gain of 24 over its total after the 2001 election. In late August Okada was elected to a two-year term as DPJ president, but the party's loss of more than one-third of its seats in the September 2005 general election led Okada to resign. His successor, the youthful Seiji MAEHARA, defeated Naoto Kan for the post, but on March 31, 2006, Maehara also resigned, accepting responsibility for the party's involvement in false accusations of financial impropriety directed against an LDP official. On April 7 the party's Diet members chose Ichiro Ozawa over Kan to fill the five-month balance of Maehara's term. In September, without challenge, Ozawa won a full term.

Capitalizing on public anger at the Abe government over financial and pension scandals, in July 2007 the DPJ won 60 of the 121 upper house seats up for election and thereby became the plurality party in the House of Councilors, with 109 of 242 seats, for the first time. (In September the upper house gave more votes to Ozawa than Fukuda for prime minister.) A crisis erupted in early November, however, when Ozawa resigned his leadership post after the DPJ refused to consider a grand coalition with the LDP. Two days later, at the urging of some party members, he withdrew his resignation.

By mid-2008, with the People's New Party (PNP), the New Party Nippon, and some independents having agreed to sit as a bloc with the DPJ in the House of Councilors, the DPJ effectively controlled 120 upper house seats, enough to delay, if not thwart, government legislation.

In September 2008 Ichiro Ozawa was elected unopposed to a two-year term as party president. On May 11, 2009, however, he resigned in response to a scandal involving illegal political donations. Although Ozawa himself was not implicated, a senior aide had been indicted in the case, which, Ozawa feared, would undercut the party's chances to defeat the LDP in the upcoming legislative election. Five days later the party's secretary general, Yukio Hatoyama, was elected party president, easily defeating party vice president Katsuya OKADA.

The August 2009 election saw the DPJ and its allies, the Social Democratic Party (SDP) and the PNP, convincingly defeat the LDP. The DPJ won 308 seats—a gain of 169 constituency seats and 26 block (proportional) seats—which permitted Hatoyama's election as prime minister.

Leaders: Yukio HATOYAMA (Prime Minister and President of the Party), Naoto KAN (Deputy Prime Minister), Tsutomu HATA and Kozo WATANABE (Supreme Advisers), Azuma KOSHIISHI (Caucus Leader in the House of Councilors), Ichiro OZAWA (Secretary General).

Social Democratic Party—SDP (*Shakai Minshuto*). Dating from 1945, the SDP was known until 1991 as the Japan Socialist Party (JSP) and then, until 1996, as the Social Democratic Party of Japan (SDPJ). The party long appeared to be more radical than its principal rival, the Japanese Communist Party, but a platform adopted in 1966 favored nonalignment, a nonaggression pact among the great powers, and a democratic transition from capitalism to socialism. In 1986 the party formally abandoned Marxist-Leninist doctrine.

Subsequently, the party's membership base was eroded by the decision of the pro-JSP *Sohyo* trade union federation to merge with the recently organized Private Sector Trade Union Confederation (*Rengo*). A platform revision in 1993 called for abandoning historic socialism in favor of what its then secretary general termed "a Japanese version of Western democratic socialism"; ending the party's opposition to Japan's Self-Defense Forces; dropping objections to the U.S.-Japan security and South Korean normalization treaties; and accepting nuclear power generation until safer sources of energy are found.

The SDPJ's lower house representation plummeted to 70 members in the June 1993 election (down from 136 in 1990), but the party remained second ranked and the LDP's overall defeat enabled the SDPJ to participate in the first non-LDP government in four decades. After leaving the new ruling coalition in April 1994, the SDPJ entered a coalition government with the LDP and *Shinto Sakigake* in June, providing Japan's first socialist prime minister, Tomiichi Murayama, since 1948.

In late 1994, 60 dissident members of the party's right wing, led by former chair Sadao YAMAHANA, formed a policy group within the SDPJ called the New Democratic Union—NDU (*Shin Minshu Rengo*). Early in 1995 Yamahana met with key members of three non-Socialist groups—Banri KAIEDA of the Democratic New Party Club (*Minshu Shinto Kurabu*), Takashi KURIHASHI of the Democratic Reform League, and Tatsuo KAWABATA of *Shinshinto*—to create a new third party, and 24 SDPJ and other MPs subsequently agreed to form the Democratic League–Democratic New Party Club (*Minshu Rengo–Minshu Shinto Kurabu*). However, in the wake of the January 17, 1995, Kobe earthquake and, two months later, the Tokyo subway attack, the participants suspended their efforts, with most of them ultimately finding their way to the new DPJ.

Of 41 SDPJ seats up for election in the upper house poll of July 23, 1995, only 16 were retained. Weakened in 1996 by the formation of the New Socialist Party (NSP, below) as well as the DPJ, the SDP suffered further electoral disaster in October, slumping to only 15 lower house seats. Fearing total domination by the LDP in a further coalition, the SDP opted instead to give qualified external support to a minority LDP government.

On May 30, 1998, the SDP announced it would end its loose alliance with the LDP at the end of the June legislative session. In the July upper house election, it recaptured only 5 of 12 contested seats it had previously held, but in June 2000 it increased its lower house membership to 19. Two months earlier, former prime minister Murayama had announced his retirement.

In the November 2003 lower house election the SDP won only six seats, which led longtime leader Takako Doi to resign as chair. Her deputy, Mizuho Fukushima, was named to succeed her. In February 2004 former party officials Kiyomi TSUJIMOTO and Masako GOTO received suspended sentences following their conviction on charges relating to diversion of state funds earmarked for staff secretaries.

The SDP gained one seat in the September 2005 general election. At a party convention held in February 2006, it vowed to continue its opposition to Prime Minister Koizumi's policies and any constitutional change that would weaken the renunciation of war. In the July 2007 upper house election the SDP won two proportional seats, giving it a total of five seats. In August 2009, allied with the DPJ, it retained seven lower house seats, but its share of the proportional vote fell to only 4.3 percent. The SDP then joined the DPJ-led government as a junior partner.

Leaders: Mizuho FUKUSHIMA (State Minister of Consumer Affairs and Food Safety, and Party Chair), Tomiichi MURAYAMA and Takako DOI (Honorary Leaders), Seiji MATAICHI (Vice Chair), Yasumasa SHIGENO (Secretary General).

People's New Party—PNP (*Kokumin Shinto*). The PNP was formed on August 17, 2005, under the leadership of former LDP legislator and Hashimoto faction leader Tamisuke Watanuki and others who objected to Prime Minister Koizumi's plan for postal privatization. Many of the members of the new party had previously belonged to the LDP's Kamei faction, whose leader, Shizuka Kamei, had argued that postal reform would come at the expense of rural and needy constituents. In the September lower house election the PNP retained four seats (two of them proportional), including Kamei's. In July 2007 it won two seats in the House of Councilors, thereby maintaining its upper house representation at four. The four chose to sit in the DPJ opposition bloc.

In the August 2009 House of Representatives election the PNP won three seats, despite losses by Watanuki and the party's secretary general, Hisaoki Kamei, and despite claiming only 1.7 percent of the proportional vote and no block seats. Following the election, Shizuki Kamei was named party leader, after which the PNP joined the new DPJ-led government.

Leaders: Shizuka KAMEI (State Minister of Financial Services and Postal Reform, and Party Leader), Tamisuke WATANUKI (Supreme Adviser), Hisaoki KAMEI (Adviser).

Principal Opposition Parties:

Liberal Democratic Party—LDP (*Jiyu-Minshuto*). Born of a 1955 merger between the former Liberal and Democratic parties, the conservative LDP attaches more importance to organization and financial power than to ideology. It has favored private enterprise, alliance with the United States, and expansion of Japanese interests in Asia.

The party leadership, generally drawn from the bureaucratic and business elites, was traditionally distributed among some dozen faction leaders, each of whom controlled from 10 to 50 votes in the Diet. In 1978, however, the party implemented a primary system for selecting candidates for its presidency, and that November, in the first runoff between two members of the same party in the Diet's history, Masayoshi Ohira defeated Prime Minister Takeo Fukuda for the leadership.

Ohira's successor, Zenko Suzuki, announced in October 1982 that he would not seek reelection because of rising dissent within the party. In a November primary Yasuhiro Nakasone secured 58 percent of the vote, thus ensuring his designation as prime minister. In October 1984 Nakasone became the first LDP president in 20 years to secure reelection. Ineligible for a further term, he was granted a one-year extension in September 1986, following the LDP's overwhelming parliamentary victory in July. He stood down from the party position in October 1987 and retired as prime minister in November, being succeeded in both positions by the party's secretary general, Noboru Takeshita.

Subsequently, numerous party officials were implicated in an insider trading scandal, Takeshita himself being forced to resign in favor of Sosuke Uno, who assumed office in June 1989. Buffeted by involvement in a sex scandal, coupled with unprecedented LDP defeats in Tokyo municipal elections and in a House of Councilors election, Uno announced his resignation after only 53 days in office and was succeeded in August by Toshiki Kaifu. Kaifu's own position was substantially weakened by an embarrassing LDP loss in the April 1991 Tokyo gubernatorial election, which led the party's powerful secretary general, Ichiro Ozawa, to resign. Six months later, Kiichi Miyazawa was chosen to succeed Kaifu as party leader.

In December 1992 the influence of the party's long-dominant Takeshita faction was reduced as the result of a major cabinet reshuffle and by the creation from its ranks of a new faction effectively headed by former secretary general Ozawa. Ozawa was one of a number of leaders to withdraw from the party prior to the July 1993 balloting, in which the LDP for the first time lost control of the lower house. On July 30 the battered party elected Yohei Kono as its new president. Although further weakened by postelection defections, the LDP rump seized the opportunity of a split in the new ruling coalition in April 1994 to establish an alliance with the Social Democrats and *Shinto Sakigake.* This resulted in the party's return to government in June as the dominant member of a three-party coalition.

In January 1996, in the wake of SDP leader Tomiichi Murayama's withdrawal as prime minister, the LDP's Ryutaro Hashimoto was elected to the post. The party's lower house representation advanced to 239 out of 500 in an October general election, permitting formation of a minority government with the external support of the SDP and New Party Harbinger (*Shinto Sakigake*). By fall 1997 the LDP had reestablished its majority through defections from other parties.

Hashimoto, although unopposed in reelection as party president in September 1997, resigned as prime minister and party leader on July 13, 1998, accepting full blame for the poor showing by the LDP in the previous day's upper house election. Following an intraparty campaign unprecedented in its openness, on July 24 Foreign Minister Keizo Obuchi defeated two other candidates to claim the LDP leadership, preparing the way for his election as prime minister on July 30.

Obuchi was reelected party leader in September 1999, freeing him to pursue an alliance with New *Komeito* (below). Obuchi's disabling stroke on April 1, 2000, immediately generated heated behind-the-scenes activity that culminated on April 5 in the elevation of the party's secretary general, Yoshiro Mori, to the LDP presidency and thus to the prime ministership.

In the June 25, 2000, lower house election the party lost its majority, winning only 233 seats in the 480-member chamber (it had held 271 of 500 seats before the balloting), but Mori continued in office with the support of coalition partners New *Komeito* and the New Conservative Party—NCP (*Hoshuto*). The latter had been formed in April 2000 by Transport Minister Toshihiro Nikai and 25 other members of Parliament who had abandoned the Liberal Party (LP; see DPJ, above) upon the LP's departure from the governing coalition.

Despite having survived parliamentary no-confidence votes in November 2000 and March 2001, Mori resigned on April 7, 2001. In the four-person contest to succeed him as LDP leader, Hashimoto, who was now head of the largest party faction, unexpectedly lost to Junichiro Koizumi, a reformer and former health minister who vowed to end the faction system. In voting on April 21–22 Koizumi won 123 of 141 party chapters, and his victory was confirmed on April 24 when he captured 51 percent of the 346 votes of Diet members. He was reelected, unopposed, to a two-year term on August 10, 2001, but over the next year his policies met frequent resistance from the heads of other powerful LDP factions. In March 2002 he lost a key ally, Koichi KATO, who fell victim to a tax-evasion scandal involving an aide.

In the September 20, 2003, election for the LDP presidency, Prime Minister Koizumi received over 60 percent support, defeating three other candidates: faction leader Shizuka Kamei, former transport minister Takao FUJII, and former foreign minister Masahiko Komura. In the subsequent November election for the House of Representatives the LDP won 237 seats. It then renewed its coalition with New *Komeito* and absorbed the NCP, which, having never won widespread support, had captured only 4 seats (down from 7 in 2000).

At the July 2004 House of Councilors election the LDP won 49 of 121 seats, slightly less than its target and 1 less than the DPJ. Its 114 total upper house seats (8 short of a majority) were supplemented by New *Komeito*'s 24. Following the replenishment, Chikage OGI, former NCP leader and transport minister, was elected the upper house's first female president.

In July 30, 2004, former prime minister Hashimoto announced that he would surrender the leadership of his faction, still the LDP's largest, as a consequence of a political contributions scandal. The move was seen as strengthening Prime Minister Koizumi's position within the party. In late September, shortly before announcing a cabinet reshuffle, Koizumi reorganized the party leadership.

The defeat of postal reform legislation in August 2005 had been proceeded by a major split within LDP ranks, with the result that 37 LDP legislators voted against the package in the lower house. Reform opponents Mitsuo HORIUCHI and Shizuka Kamei resigned as faction leaders, and Kamei then helped form the People's New Party (PNP, above). In the run-up to the September 2005 snap election, Prime Minister Koizumi refused to extend party backing to any of the rebels and instead ran other candidates, dubbed "assassins," against them. Most of the rebels were defeated. A number of those who had not formally resigned from the party prior to the election were expelled in October.

In September 2005 Sadakazu Tanigaki was elected leader of the former Ozata faction, Sadatashi OZATA having retired. Two months later, Yuji Tsushima was elected to head the former Hashimoto faction. Former health and welfare minister Yuya NIWA and Makoto Koga took control of the former Horiuchi faction. Former labor minister Bunmei Ibuki assumed leadership of the much-diminished Kamei faction. In October 2006 former foreign minister Nobutaka Machimura replaced former prime minister Mori as head of the Mori faction, the party's largest.

In June 2005 Koizumi had announced that he would step down as president of the party when his term ended in September 2006. By early 2006 three leading presidential candidates had emerged: Chief Cabinet Secretary Shinzo Abe, Foreign Minister Taro Aso, and Finance Minister Tanigaki. In the September 20 election, Abe, who was generally considered Koizumi's choice, won with 464 votes to 136 for Aso and 102 for Tanigaki. Six days later both houses of the Diet made Abe, 52, Japan's youngest postwar prime minister. His prospects for completing the term in office were dimmed in July 2007, however, when the LDP, for the first time in its history, lost its plurality in the House of Councilors. In the election for half the upper house the LDP won only 37 seats, for a total of 83. Under pressure, Abe resigned on September 12, and on September 23 the LDP elected Yasuo Fukuda, a former cabinet secretary, over Aso by a vote of 330–197. Fukuda quickly named three faction leaders, Bunmei Obuki, Sadakazu Tanigaki, and Toshiro Nikai, to key party posts. (In May 2008 the Tanigaki faction merged into the Koga faction.) He was then confirmed as prime minister on September 25.

Less than a year later, Fukuda resigned. On September 22, 2008, on his fourth attempt at the party presidency, Taro Aso was elected to the post with 351 of 527 votes. His opponents were Kaoru YOSANO, finance minister (66 votes); Yuriko KOIKE, a former environment minister (46); Nobuteru ISHIHARA, former LDP policy chief (37); and Shigeru ISHIBA, former defense minister (25 votes). Aso took office as prime minister on September 24, heading a substantially reconfigured cabinet. In January 2009 senior party member and former minister Yoshima Watanabe, citing the LDP's lack of commitment to political reform, resigned from the party. He subsequently formed the Your Party (below).

The LDP entered the 2009 election campaign with all opinion polls showing it far behind the DPJ. It ended up winning only 119 seats (a loss of 177) and taking only 26.7 percent of the proportional votes. On September 16 Taro Aso resigned both as prime minister and as party president. A party election on September 28 concluded with Sadakazu Tanigaki, 64, easily winning the party presidency over two 46-year-old candidates, former deputy minister of justice Taro KONO and legislator Yasutoshi NISHIMURA. Both of the younger candidates argued for a generational change in leadership and attacked the party's faction-based politics.

Leaders: Sadakazu TANIGAKI (President; Koga Faction), Taro ASO (Former Prime Minister; Aso Faction), Yasuo FUKUDA (Former Prime Minister; Machimura Faction), Yoshinobu SHIMAMURA (Leader in the House of Representatives), Shigeru ISHIBA (Chair, Policy Research Council; Tsushima Faction), Ryotaro TANOSE (Chair, General Council; Yamasaki Faction), Bunmei IBUKI (Former Secretary General; Ibuki Faction), Makoto KOGA (Koga Faction), Masahiko KOMURA (Former Foreign Minister; Komura Faction), Nobutaka MACHIMURA (Former Chief Cabinet Secretary; Machimura Faction), Toshihiro NIKAI (Former Minister of Economy, Trade, and Industry; Nikai Faction), Yuji TSUSHIMA (Tsushima Faction), Taku YAMASAKI (Yamasaki Faction), Tadamori OSHIMA (Secretary General).

New Komeito (New Clean Government Party). The New *Komeito* was formed by merger on November 7, 1998, of *Komei* with members of *Shinto Heiwa* (New Peace Party), which had disbanded earlier in the day.

The New *Komeito* is the latest incarnation of *Komeito* (Clean Government Party), which started as the *Komei* Political League, a political society, in 1961 and became a party in 1964. *Komeito* was a formal affiliate of the *Soka Gakkai* Buddhist organization until 1970, when the linkage became an informal one to broaden the party's appeal. *Komeito* long opposed the LDP on foreign policy, particularly with regard to retention of the Japan-U.S. Mutual Security Treaty, although it shifted its position in 1978 with respect to the country's Self-Defense Forces, which it had come to view as necessary for "protection of the territory." Having slipped to 45 seats in 1990, *Komeito*'s tally in the lower house rose to 51 in the July 1993 balloting, whereupon the party participated in both the Hosokawa and Hata non-LDP coalition governments before going into opposition in June 1994.

Sometimes also referred to as the New Clean Government Party, *Komei* was the smaller of two groups to emerge from *Komeito,* which disbanded in December 1994. The larger group, the *Komei* New Party, followed the *Komeito* chair, Koshiro Ishida, into *Shinshinto* five days later, while the smaller *Komei* held the loyalty of some 3,200 local assembly members and much of the *Komeito* delegation in the House of Councilors. Organized under the slogan "Reform Initiated Locally," it saw itself as the inheritor of *Komeito*'s "clean government" program, emphasizing grassroots democracy, humanism, protection of the global environment, and disarmament.

Following the breakup of *Shinshinto* in December 1997, some 18 members of the House of Councilors initially organized as the Dawn Club (*Reimei Kurabu*), which in January 1998 merged with *Komei,* while many *Shinshinto* lower house members formed *Shinto Heiwa* on January 4, 1998. *Shinto Heiwa* and another post-*Shinshinto* formation, the Reformers' Network Party—RNP (*Kaikaku Kurabu,* also known as the Reform Club), joined in a lower house alliance called the Peace and Reform Network, which soon constituted the second-largest opposition group in the House of Representatives.

Formation of the New *Komeito* by *Komei* and members of the defunct *Shinto Heiwa* in November 1998 served to broaden the alliance with the RNP in the lower house, where the two parties' 52 members formed a parliamentary group under the name *Komeito Kaikaku* (roughly, "Clean Government Reform"). At a convention on July 24, 1999, the party voted to join the LDP-LP alliance, but expansion of the governing coalition was delayed until October 5. (The RNP accompanied the New *Komeito* into the Obuchi government as a junior partner, but by then it had already been weakened by defections to other parties, and it lost all of its remaining 5 lower house seats in the next election.)

In the June 2000 lower house election New *Komeito* fared poorly, winning 31 seats, 11 fewer than it had held upon dissolution but enough to help ensure continuation of the governing alliance. By early 2001, however, the party was publicly dissatisfied with Prime Minister Mori's leadership, and on February 18 the New *Komeito* secretary general, Tetsuzo FUYUSHIBA, stated that it would leave the coalition if Mori did not resign soon, which he did less than two months later.

In the November 2003 election the party won 34 lower house seats. Following the July 2004 House of Councilors election, New *Komeito* held 24 seats in the upper house, where it ranked third. In September 2005 it lost 3 of its lower house seats, and following the July 2007 election its upper house delegation stood at 20.

Takenori Kanzaki, having served four terms as party leader, chose not to seek a fifth in 2006, and he was succeeded by Akihiro OTA in September. Wholesale leadership changes followed the defeat of the LDP–New *Komeito* government in the August 2009 election, in which Ota and the party's secretary general, Kazuo KITIGAWA, both lost their lower house seats. Having lost all 8 of its constituency seats, the party was left with only 21 block seats on the basis of 11.5 percent of the proportional vote.

Leaders: Natsuo YAMAGUCHI (Chief Representative), Tetsuo SAITO (Chair, Policy Research Council), Yoshihisa INOUE (Secretary General).

Japanese Communist Party—JCP (*Nihon Kyosanto*). Founded in the 1920s, the JCP traditionally relied on tight discipline to maximize its role in united front operations. Although "Eurocommunist" in outlook prior to the demise of the Soviet Union, the party focused primarily on domestic affairs, with an emphasis on the antinuclear issue. JCP strength in the House of Representatives crested at 39 in 1979 and fell to 15 after the 1993 poll.

No longer calling for abolition of the monarchy and immediate nationalization of core industries, the JCP attempted to recast itself as a democratic socialist party without abandoning its name. It had some success in the October 1996 lower house election, rising to 26 seats by attracting disaffected left-oriented former supporters of the SDP. It won 15 seats, for a total of 23 (a gain of 9), in the July 1998 upper house election, but won only 20 lower house seats in June 2000 and then fell to 9 in 2003. Its representation in the upper house also dropped to 9 after the July 2004 partial election. The party made no gains in the September 2005 lower house election, in which it claimed 9 block seats.

At the party's 24th Congress, held in January 2006, longtime leader Tetsuzo FUWA, citing age and health concerns as well as the need to "strengthen young energy" within party ranks, stepped down as chair of the Central Committee, a post that was temporarily left vacant. In July 2007 the JCP won only two seats in the House of Councilors, reducing its upper house representation to seven. Its platform for the August 2009 general election called for a "democratic revolution," foreign policy independence from the United States, and adoption of a rule-governed economy without "excessive probusiness policies." The JCP retained its nine block seats, based on 7.0 percent of the proportional vote.

Leaders: Kazuo SHII (Chair, Executive Committee), Tadayoshi ICHIDA (Head, Secretariat).

Other Parliamentary Parties:

Your Party (*Minna no To*). Formation of Your Party was announced on August 8, 2009, by Yoshimi Watanabe, a former state minister of administrative reform who had abandoned the LDP the preceding January because of opposition to the Aso government's policies, especially the slow pace of government reform. Watanabe called for reducing the control of the central government's bureaucracy, giving local governments more control, and reducing the size of both houses of the Diet. He also indicated that Your Party might cooperate with the DPJ if the DPJ won the September lower house election. At the polls Your Party won five seats, including three block seats based on a 4.3 percent share of the proportional vote.

Leaders: Yoshimi WATANABE (Chair), Keiichiro ASAO, Kenji EDA (Secretary General).

New Party Daichi—NPD (*Shinto Daichi*). Technically not a political party, New Party *Daichi* (Mother Earth) was established in August 2005 by former LDP member Muneo Suzuki, who had been convicted of bribery in 2003 but was free on bail. In the September 2005 lower house election Suzuki won a proportional seat and chose to sit as an independent.

In February 2008 a high court rejected Suzuki's appeal in the bribery case. He then appealed to the Supreme Court. Should the Supreme Court uphold his conviction and two-year prison sentence, he would be forced to vacate his Diet seat, which he retained in 2009 as an ally of the DPJ.

Leader: Muneo SUZUKI.

New Party Nippon—NPN (*Shinto Nippon*). Formed on August 21, 2005, by Nagano's governor, Yasuo Tanaka, the NPN attracted four LDP lower house members who opposed postal privatization. The party won 1 proportional seat in the lower house election of September 2005 and also held 1 seat in the House of Councilors, but in early July 2007 both representatives resigned from the party over policy differences with Tanaka. On July 29 Tanaka won his own seat in the House of Councilors. He subsequently chose to join the DPJ-led opposition bloc.

In August 2009 Tanaka won a seat in the lower house, where he chose to sit with the DPJ group.

Leader: Yasuo TANAKA.

Other Parties:

New Socialist Party—NSP (*Shin Shakaito*). The NSP was founded in March 1996 by left-wing elements of the SDP opposed to the latter's recent espousal of more moderate policies. It called in particular for the withdrawal of all U.S. forces from Okinawa and for a return to the old electoral system of multimember constituencies. Under the new system, the NSP failed to win a seat in the October lower house election, and it lost its 3 seats in the upper house in July 1998.

In July 1999 the party chair, Tatsukuni KOMORI, led an unofficial delegation of socialists to North Korea in an effort to promote diplomatic ties. Since then, the party has continued to promote dialogue with Pyongyang and to oppose U.S. foreign policy. It strongly objected to the use of Japan's Self-Defense Forces in Afghanistan and, later, in Iraq. In the 2005 lower house elections it cooperated with the SDP.

Leaders: Kimiko KURIHARA (President), Eiko TOMIYANA.

Other recently active minor parties include the leftist **Okinawa Masses Socialist Party** (*Okinawa Shakai Taishuto—Shadaito*), which was founded in 1950. The party's deputy leader, Keiko ITOKAZU, ran unsuccessfully as the opposition candidate in the November 2006 Okinawa gubernatorial election, but in 2007 she retained her seat in the national House of Councilors, where she sits as an independent. The **Greens Japan** (*Midori no Mirai;* literally, "Green Future") was formed in 2008 by merger of two parties: the Japan Greens, and the Rainbow and Greens. The **Happiness Realization Party** (*Kofuku Jitsugento*), led by Ryuho OKAWA, is associated with the Happy Science movement. It ran over 300 candidates in the August 2009 election, none successfully. The **Japan Renaissance Party** (JRP) was formed in 2008 by DPJ defector Hideo Watanabe, a member of the House of Councilors who subsequently chose to sit with the LDP. The JRP failed to retain its sole lower house seat in August 2009.

A variety of small right-extremist (*uyoku*) groups continue to function. Most are intensely nationalist "new wave" formations that espouse a revisionist view of Japan's imperialist history. There are also many small groups on the extreme left.

LEGISLATURE

The bicameral **Diet** (*Kokkai*) is composed of an upper chamber (House of Councilors) and a lower chamber (House of Representatives). Real power resides in the lower chamber, although amendments to the constitution require two-thirds majorities in both houses. Both houses vote for prime minister, but the lower house results prevail in the absence of a consensus.

House of Councilors (*Sangiin*). The upper chamber, which replaced the prewar House of Peers, is renewed by halves every three years, each member serving a six-year term. The chamber cannot be dissolved. An October 2000 electoral law reduced the membership from 252 to 247 effective from the July 2001 election, and another 5 seats were eliminated in 2004. At each election, 73 members are chosen from 47 prefectural districts, returning from 1 to 4 members, and 48 members are elected on a proportional basis from national party lists. As a result of the July 29, 2007, election, the Democratic Party of Japan (DPJ) and *Shin-Ryokufukai* held 109 seats (60 newly won); Liberal Democratic Party (LDP), 83 (37); New *Komeito,* 20 (9); Japanese Communist Party, 7 (3); Social Democratic Party, 5 (2); People's New Party (PNP), 4 (2); New Party Nippon, 1 (1); other, 1 (0); independents, 12 (7). Both the DPJ and the LDP subsequently recruited additional members for their party groups, which numbered 112 and 85, respectively, when the upper house convened in early August..

In the aftermath of the August 2009 lower house victory by the DPJ, its party group in the upper house numbered 118 (including the PNP representatives but excluding those from its other governing partner, the SDP, which chose to maintain its own caucus). The other significant change since 2007 was a drop in the number of independents to 4. The LDP-led group remained at 85 seats as of October 2009.

President: Satsuki EDA.

House of Representatives (*Shugiin*). An electoral reform bill adopted in 2000 specified that at the next election the existing 500-seat lower chamber would be reduced to 480 seats, of which 300 would be filled from single-member electoral districts by simple majority voting and 180 by proportional representation applied in 11 electoral blocks returning from 6 to 30 members. The term of office is four years. The election of August 30, 2009, produced the following results (block seats in parentheses): Democratic Party of Japan, 308 (87); Liberal Democratic Party, 119 (55); New *Komeito,* 21 (21); Japanese Communist Party, 9 (9); Social Democratic Party, 7 (4); Your Party, 5 (3); People's New Party, 3 (0); New Party *Daichi,* 1 (1); New Party Nippon, 1 (0); independents, 6.

Speaker: Takahiro YOKOMICHI.

CABINET

[as of October 15, 2009]

Prime Minister	Yukio Hatoyama
Deputy Prime Minister	Naoto Kan
Ministers	
Agriculture, Forestry, and Fisheries	Hirotaka Akamatsu
Defense	Toshimi Kitizawa
Economy, Trade, and Industry	Masayuki Naoshima
Education, Culture, Sports, Science, and Technology	Tatsuo Kawabata
Environment	Sakihito Ozawa
Finance	Hirohisa Fujii
Foreign Affairs	Katsuya Okada
Health, Labor, and Welfare	Akira Nagatsuma
Internal Affairs and Communications	Kazuhiro Haraguti
Justice	Keiko Chiba [f]
Land, Infrastructure, Transport, and Tourism	Seiji Maehara
State Ministers	
Abduction Issue	Hiroshi Nakai
Administrative Innovation	Yoshito Sengoku
Civil Service Reform	Yoshito Sengoku
Consumer Affairs and Food Safety, Social Affairs, and Gender Equality	Mizuho Fukushima (SDP) [f]
Economic and Fiscal Policy, and Science and Technology Policy	Naoto Kan
Financial Services	Shizuka Kamei (PNP)
National Strategy	Naoto Kan
Okinawa and Northern Territories Affairs, and Disaster Management	Seiji Maehara
Pension Reform	Akira Nagatsuma
Postal Reform	Shizuka Kamei (PNP)
Promotion of Local Sovereignty	Kazuhiro Haraguti
Chief Cabinet Secretary	Hirofumi Hirano
Chair, National Public Safety Commission	Hiroshi Nakai

[f] = female

Note: Except as noted, all cabinet members belong to the Democratic Party of Japan.

COMMUNICATIONS

News media are privately owned and free from government control.

Press. The Japanese press exerts a strong influence on public policy. The large newspapers publish numerous main editions a day as well as subeditions, and per capita circulation figures are among the highest in the world. The following three dailies, all of which publish in Tokyo, Osaka, and several other locations, constitute the "big three" national newspapers: *Yomiuri Shimbun* (10,100,000 morning, 3,970,000 evening), world's highest circulation; *Asahi Shimbun* (8,230,000 morning, 4,070,000 evening); *Mainichi Shimbun* (3,980,000 morning, 2,000,000 evening). Other prominent dailies include *Nihon Keizai Shimbun* (Tokyo and elsewhere, 3,000,000 morning, 1,700,000 evening), leading economic journal; *Chunichi Shimbun* (Nagoya, 2,700,000 morning, 750,000 evening); *Sankei Shimbun* (Tokyo and Osaka, 2,000,000 morning, 900,000 evening); *Nishi Nippon Shimbun* (Fukuoka, 830,000 morning, 190,000 evening); *Shizuoka Shimbun* (Shizuoka, 730,000 morning, 730,000 evening); *Tokyo Shimbun* (Tokyo, 660,000 morning, 350,000 evening).

News agencies. The leading domestic agencies are the Jiji Press, the Kyodo News Service, and Radiopress. In addition, many foreign agencies maintain offices in Tokyo and other leading cities.

Broadcasting and computing. There are two separate radio and television broadcasting systems. The Japan Broadcasting Corporation (*Nippon Hoso Kyokai*—NHK), a public entity operating nationwide radio and television networks as well as digital services, is financed mainly by subscription fees provided for under the Japanese Broadcasting Law. This system supplies over 6,000 stations, which reach approximately 99 percent of the population. In addition, there are nearly 200 independent members of the National Association of Commercial Broadcasters in Japan, who operate over 650 radio and 8,300 television stations financed through advertising revenues. Multiple ownership of the 100 radio and 125 television broadcasting companies by a single concern is prohibited.

As of 2008 there were 754 Internet users per 1,000 inhabitants.

INTERGOVERNMENTAL REPRESENTATION

Ambassador to the U.S.: Ichiro FUJISAKI.

U.S. Ambassador to Japan: John Victor ROOS.

Permanent Representative to the UN: Yukio TAKASU.

IGO Memberships (Non-UN): ADB, AfDB, APEC, BIS, EBRD, G-7/G-8, G-10, G-20, IADB, IEA, Interpol, IOM, OECD, PCA, WCO, WTO.

JORDAN

Hashemite Kingdom of Jordan
al-Mamlakah al-Urduniyah al-Hashimiyah

Note: In the wake of protracted legislative paralysis, King Abdullah II on November 23, 2009, ordered the dissolution of the House of Representatives and called for early elections. Prime Minister Nader Dahabi, whose government had been criticized for its handling of the recent economic downturn, resigned on December 9 and was succeeded by Samir Rifai, a businessman and former minister to the royal court. Rifai announced a new cabinet on December 14. Meanwhile, new elections were postponed until at least the last quarter of 2010 to permit the new government to enact electoral reforms.

Political Status: Independent constitutional monarchy established May 25, 1946; present constitution adopted January 8, 1952.

Area: 34,495 sq. mi. (89,206 sq. km.), excluding West Bank territory of 2,270 sq. mi. (5,879 sq. km.).

Population: 4,139,458 (1994C); 5,786,000 (2008E). Both figures exclude Palestinians in the West Bank, over which Jordan abandoned de jure jurisdiction in 1988.

Major Urban Center (2005E): AMMAN (2,378,000).

Official Language: Arabic.

Monetary Unit: Dinar (official rate December 1, 2009: 1 dinar = $1.41US).

Sovereign: King ABDULLAH ibn Hussein (King Abdullah II); assumed the throne on February 7, 1999, following the death of King HUSSEIN ibn Talal; coronation ceremony held on June 9, 1999.

Heir to the Throne: Undesignated. Prince HAMZEH ibn Hussein, half-brother of the king, had been designated crown prince on February 7, 1999, but on November 28, 2004, Abdullah stripped him of the crown, making the king's eldest son, 11-year-old Hussein, heir apparent.

Prime Minister: *(See headnote.)* Nader DAHABI, appointed by the king on November 22, 2007, to succeed Marouf BAKHET and sworn in with the new government on November 25, 2007.

THE COUNTRY

Jordan, a nearly landlocked kingdom in the heart of the Middle East, is located on a largely elevated, rocky plateau that slopes downward to the Jordan Valley, the Dead Sea, and the Gulf of Aqaba. Most of the land is desert, providing the barest grazing for the sheep and goats of Bedouin tribesmen, whose traditional nomadic lifestyle has largely been replaced by village settlement. With Israeli occupation in June 1967 of the territory on the West Bank of the Jordan River, the greater part of the country's arable area was lost. The population is mainly Arab, but numerous ethnic groups have intermixed with the indigenous inhabitants. Islam is the state religion, the majority being members of the Sunni sect. Less than 10 percent of Jordanian women are in the workforce, mainly in subsistence activities and trading; more than half are illiterate (as compared with 16 percent of men), with the percentage of women enrolled in school dropping dramatically at marriage age. Although enfranchised in 1974, female participation in government has been minimal. Some cabinets have included several female appointees; in addition, a woman was elected to the House of Representatives for the first time in 1993. Although no women won a seat in elections held June 17, 2003, six women were appointed to the house under a February 2003 amended law reserving six seats for them.

Jordan's economy and its political life have been dominated in recent times by dislocations and uncertainties stemming from the Arab conflict with Israel. The original East Bank population of some 400,000 was swollen in 1948–1950 by the addition of large numbers of West Bank Palestinian Arabs and refugees from Israel, most of them either settled agriculturalists or townspeople of radically different background and outlook from those of the seminomadic East Bankers. Additional displacements followed the Arab-Israeli war of June 1967. The society has also been strained by a 3.5 percent annual natural increase in population, rapid urbanization, scarce water resources, and the frustrations of the unemployed refugees, many of whom have declined assimilation in the hope of returning to "Palestine." (It has recently been estimated that over 50 percent of the people currently residing in Jordan are of Palestinian origin, about two-thirds of them still formally considered refugees.)

Agricultural production is insufficient to feed the population and large quantities of foodstuffs (especially grain) have to be imported, while many of the refugees are dependent on rations distributed by the UN Relief and Works Agency for Palestine Refugees in the Near East (UNRWA). Major exports include phosphates, potash, and fertilizers. Manufacturing is dominated by production of import substitutes, mainly cement, some consumer goods, and processed foods.

Although it is not an oil-producing country, Jordan was greatly affected by the oil boom of the 1970s and early 1980s. An estimated 350,000 Jordanians, including many professionals, took lucrative jobs in wealthy Gulf states, their remittances contributing significantly to the home economy. Lower-paying jobs in Jordan were filled by foreign laborers, primarily Egyptians. However, the subsequent oil recession led to the repatriation of many Jordanians and reduced assistance from other Arab countries. Consequently, the government agreed in April 1989 to an austerity program prescribed by the International Monetary Fund (IMF) in return for $100 million in standby funds and partial rescheduling of payments on its $8 billion external debt. Conditions were strained further as the result of the influx of more than 300,000 Palestinians expelled from Kuwait and Saudi Arabia following the 1991 Gulf war.

The government promoted its 1994 peace treaty with Israel as a crucial step toward economic development, and, indeed, the accord prompted an immediate influx of aid from the West, which had curtailed assistance because of Amman's stance during the Gulf crisis and war. Although Jordan lost key export markets in Iraq, under UN sanctions, and on the West Bank during the 1990s, its economy benefited from trade with other Arab states. Exports to the United States have grown since a bilateral free trade agreement took effect in 2001. GDP growth of 5 percent was recorded in 2002, dipping to 3.2 percent in 2003 but outpacing population growth for the first time in years. Jordan's external debt, however, neared $8 billion, further discouraging foreign investors who were already concerned about corruption in the public and private sectors. Annual GDP growth averaged 7 percent from 2003 to 2008, though unemployment and inflation remained high. The robust growth was attributed, in large part, to Jordan's far-reaching structural reforms, which included controlling public debt and increasing privatization. Also, strong performance in the construction and tourism sectors offset weaker demand for exports. In the wake of the global economic downturn, annual GDP growth was expected to contract to 3.5 percent in 2009. Meanwhile, the government guaranteed all bank deposits through the end of 2009 in an effort to maintain confidence in the economy, according to the prime minister.

GOVERNMENT AND POLITICS

Political background. The territory then known as Transjordan, which only included land east of the Jordan River, was carved out of the Ottoman Empire in the aftermath of World War I, during which Arabs, with the assistance of British forces, had rebelled against Turkish rule. British administration of the region was formalized under a League of Nations Mandate, which also covered the territory between the Jordan River and the Mediterranean (Palestine). Over the next two decades, gradual autonomy was granted to Transjordan under the leadership of ABDULLAH ibn Hussein, a member of the region's Hashemite dynasty who had been named emir by the British in 1921. Full independence came when Abdullah was proclaimed king and a new constitution was promulgated on May 25, 1946, although special treaty relationships with Britain were continued until 1957. The country adopted its current name in 1949, its boundary having expanded into the West Bank under an armistice concluded with Israel, with which Arab states had been in conflict since Britain relinquished its Palestinian mandate in 1948.

Following the assassination of Abdullah in 1951 and the deposition of his son TALAL in 1952, Talal's son HUSSEIN ascended the throne at the age of 16 and was crowned king on May 2, 1953. Hussein's turbulent reign was subsequently marked by the loss of all territory west of the Jordan River in the 1967 Arab-Israeli War (see Israel map, p. 642), assassination and coup attempts by intransigent Arab nationalist elements in Jordan and abroad, and intermittent efforts to achieve a limited modus vivendi with Israel. The most serious period of internal tension after the 1967 war involved relations with the Palestinian commando (fedayeen) organizations, which began to use Jordanian territory as a base for operations against Israel. In 1970 in what became known as Black September, a virtual civil war ensued between commando and royalist armed forces, with the fedayeen ultimately being expelled, primarily to Lebanon, in mid-1971. The expulsion led to the suspension of aid to Jordan by Kuwait and other Arab governments; it was restored following Jordan's nominal participation in the 1973 war against Israel.

In accordance with a decision reached during the October 1974 Arab summit conference in Rabat, Morocco, to recognize the Palestine Liberation Organization (PLO) as the sole legitimate representative of the Palestinians, King Hussein announced that the PLO would thenceforth have responsibility for the West Bank but stopped short of formally relinquishing his kingdom's claim to the territory. The Jordanian government was subsequently reorganized to exclude most Palestinian representatives, and the National Assembly, whose lower house contained 30 West Bank members, entered what was to become a ten-year period of inactivity (see Legislature, below).

In a move toward reconciliation with Palestinian elements, King Hussein met in Cairo in March 1977 with PLO leader Yasir ARAFAT, a subsequent meeting occurring in Jordan immediately after the September 1978 Camp David accords. In March 1979 the two met again near Amman and agreed to form a joint committee to coordinate opposition to the Egyptian-Israeli peace treaty, while in December the king named Sharif Abd al-Hamid SHARAF to replace Mudar BADRAN as head of a new government that also included six West Bank Palestinians. Sharaf's death on July 3, 1980, resulted in the elevation of Deputy Prime Minister Dr. Qasim al-RIMAWI, whose incumbency ended on August 28 by the reappointment of Badran. Following a breakdown of negotiations with Arafat in April 1983 over possible peace talks with Israel and a continued deceleration in economic growth, the king reconvened the National Assembly on January 9, 1984, and secured its assent to the replacement of deceased West Bank deputies in the lower house. The next day the king appointed Interior Minister and former intelligence chief Ahmed OBEIDAT to succeed Badran as prime minister in a cabinet reshuffle that increased Palestinian representation to 9 members out of 20. Obeidat resigned on April 4, 1985, the king naming Zaid al-RIFAI as his successor.

In mid-1988, after the outbreak of the intifada and following an Arab League call for PLO governance of the West Bank, Hussein abruptly severed all "legal and administrative" links to it, discontinued the five-year (1986–1990) aid package for its Palestinian population, and dissolved the House of Representatives. Subsequently, a declared intention to elect a house composed exclusively of East Bank members was suspended pending amendments to the electoral law.

On April 24, 1989, Prime Minister Rifai resigned because of widespread rioting in response to price increases imposed as part of the IMF-mandated austerity program. Three days later a new government, headed by Field Marshal Sharif Zaid ibn SHAKER (theretofore Chief of the Royal Court), was announced, with a mandate to prepare for a parliamentary balloting.

On November 8, 1989, following a campaign revealing continued support for the monarchy but intolerance of martial law and government corruption, Jordan held its first national election in 22 years. Urban fundamentalist and leftist candidates won impressive victories, generating concern on the part of a regime whose principal supporters had long been the country's rural conservatives. Nevertheless, following the election, the king lifted a number of martial law restrictions, appointed a new Senate, and reappointed Badran as prime minister. The cabinet that was announced on December 6 included six Palestinians but no members of the Muslim Brotherhood, despite the latter's strong electoral showing.

During the first half of 1990 the regime signaled continued interest in a more inclusive political process, meeting with Palestinian and Communist Party leaders and in April appointing a broadly representative group of individuals to a newly formed National Charter Commission. Subsequently, in a move indicative of popular support for Iraq's position in the Gulf crisis and the enhanced status of the Muslim fundamentalists, the king on January 1, 1991, named a prominent Palestinian, Tahir al-MASRI, and five Muslim Brotherhood members to the cabinet.

At a national conference on June 9, 1991, the king and the leaders of all the country's major political groups signed an annex to the constitution that granted parties the right to organize in return for their acceptance of the legitimacy of the Hashemite monarchy. Additional political reform was also expected with the appointment on June 18 of the liberal and (despite his Gulf war stance) generally pro-Western Masri to replace the conservative Badran as prime minister. However, Masri's attempt to form a broad-based coalition government foundered as the Muslim Brotherhood, excluded from his cabinet because of its strident opposition to Middle East peace negotiations, and conservatives, apparently concerned over accelerated democratization as well as their dwindling cabinet influence, joined in October to demand the government's resignation. Their petition, signed by a majority of the members of the (then recessed) House of Representatives being tantamount to a nonconfidence vote, Masri felt obliged to step down on November 16. Signaling a reassertion of monarchical control and an apparent slowdown in the pace of democratization, the king reappointed Shaker to head a new government, which, accommodating the conservatives but not the Brotherhood, survived a nonconfidence motion on December 16 by a vote of 46–27.

On April 1, 1992, King Hussein abolished all that remained of martial law regulations introduced in the wake of the 1967 Arab-Israeli war. Several months later the political party ban was formally lifted, and party registration began in December.

On May 29, 1993, Prime Minister Shaker was replaced by Abd al-Salam al-MAJALI, whose initial mission was to oversee the election of a new house. Although the balloting on November 8 was the first to be conducted on a multiparty basis, the effect was minimal, some of the new groups charging that electoral law changes and campaign restrictions had hindered their effectiveness. Only the Muslim Brotherhood's Islamic Action Front—IAF (*Jabhat al-Amal al-Islami*), with 16 seats, secured significant representation, while 47 independents, many of them expected to be broadly supportive of the king, were elected.

Majali was reappointed to lead the new government announced on December 1, 1993, his caretaker status being extended pending the outcome of the talks launched between Amman and Tel Aviv in the wake of the recent Israeli-PLO accord. On January 5, 1995, following the signing of the Jordanian-Israeli peace treaty (see Foreign relations, below), Majali stepped down as prime minister in favor of Shaker, whose new government was appointed three days later. Included in the 31-member cabinet were 17 house members, although the IAF, leader of the anti-treaty opposition, was again unrepresented.

As on three earlier occasions, Shaker, the king's cousin and longtime confidant, assumed the prime ministership in 1995 at a time of some difficulty for the regime. Although the government preferred to emphasize its economic plans, public attention focused primarily on the peace treaty, opposition to normalizing relations with Tel Aviv having been wider, or at least more vocal, than expected. However, the king adopted a relatively hard line toward the accord's opponents, stifling dissent somewhat, even at the expense, in the opinion of some observers, of a slowdown in the democratization process. Consequently, a conference planned by antitreaty Islamic, leftist, and nationalist parties for late May was banned by the government. Perhaps partly as a consequence, the impact of many of the parties was minimal when the first multiparty municipal elections were conducted on July 11–12, entrenched tribal influence dominating the balloting.

On February 4, 1996, King Hussein appointed Abd al-Karim KABARITI, another close friend of his and the former foreign affairs minister, to succeed Shaker. Once again the IAF was excluded from the new cabinet, although members of several other fledgling parties were given portfolios. Charged with revitalizing the economy, Kabariti imposed IMF-mandated reforms that led to increases in the price of bread, precipitating Jordan's worst unrest of the decade when riots broke out in August in the northern city of Karak and the poorer sections of Amman. While many of the demonstrators were arrested, the king later in the year quietly ordered a rollback in the price of bread and granted amnesty to those involved in the riots.

On March 19, 1997, Hussein dismissed Prime Minister Kabariti and reappointed Majali, whose primary task once again was to oversee the election of a new lower house. Most opposition parties and groups (including the Muslim Brotherhood) boycotted the November 4 balloting, citing new press restrictions and perceived progovernment bias in the electoral law. A number of prominent personalities, including former prime ministers Obeidat and Masri, also urged voters to stay away from the polls. Consequently, the balloting was dominated by progovernment, independent tribal candidates. On November 22 Hussein appointed a new 40-member House of Notables, none of whom was a member of the Islamist opposition. Meanwhile Majali remained as prime minister, although the cabinet was extensively reshuffled on February 17, 1998, in the wake of an outbreak of pro-Iraqi demonstrations, which had been quashed by security forces.

In mid-1998 it was confirmed that King Hussein was being treated for cancer, and on August 12 he delegated some authority to his brother, HASSAN ibn Talal, who had been crown prince and heir to the throne since 1965. On August 19 Prime Minister Majali submitted his government's resignation, and the following day Crown Prince Hassan appointed a new cabinet headed by Fayez TARAWNEH, a U.S.-educated economist and former chief of the royal court.

King Hussein, with his health declining rapidly, dismissed Hassan as his appointed successor on January 24, 1999, and replaced him with his eldest son, ABDULLAH. King Hussein died on February 7, and Abdullah assumed the throne the same day, becoming Abdullah II and taking an oath to protect "the constitution and the nation" before the National Assembly. (Formal coronation ceremonies were held on June 9.) On March 4 King Abdullah appointed a new 23-member cabinet headed by Abd al-Rauf al-RAWABDEH, a prominent proponent of economic reform. However, Rawabdeh, reportedly under pressure from the king and his government, resigned on June 18, 2000. Ali ABU al-RAGHEB, a businessman and former trade minister, was appointed to form a new government, which was sworn in on June 19.

On April 23, 2001, Abdullah announced the postponement of legislative elections scheduled for November. On July 22, he approved a new electoral law calling for the redrawing of voting districts, increasing the number of seats in the House of Representatives from 80 to 104 (later raised to 110 to accommodate a six-seat quota for women), and lowering the voting age from 19 to 18.

After elections on June 17, 2003, in which the IAF made a significant showing with 17 seats, a new 28-member cabinet, headed by al-Ragheb, was announced. Criticized for failing to bring about promised reform, al-Ragheb resigned in October and was replaced on October 25 by Faisal al-FAYIZ, formerly chief of the royal court.

On April 4, 2005, Fayiz resigned amid criticism of his slow pace of reform. The king appointed Adnan BADRAN, a 70-year-old academic, to replace him and reduced the number of cabinet positions as part of his effort to streamline government. Widely reported to be unpopular, the finance minister, Bassam AWADALLAH, resigned on June 15, forcing Badran to announce a shuffled cabinet on July 3 that included eight new ministers. Fifty-three legislators had threatened a no-confidence vote unless Badran overhauled his economic team and included more ministers from the south. The reshuffled cabinet included four women, and Adel QUDAH replaced Awadallah. Following bombings of three Amman hotels on November 9 (see Current issues, below), the king appointed Marouf BAKHET, Amman's ambassador to Israel, as national security chief. On November 24, Badran resigned amid reports that opinion polls rated the government the lowest of any administration after 200 days in office. The king named Bakhet, described as a reformer, to replace him. The cabinet was reshuffled on November 22, 2006. Bakhet and his new government were sworn in on November 27. In March 2007 the parliament approved a new law that requires political parties to have a founding membership of 500 rather than 50 in order to be legally recognized (see Current issues, below). A minor cabinet reshuffle occurred on September 2, 2007, following the July resignations of the health and water and irrigation ministers in the wake of a crisis involving contaminated drinking water.

Municipal elections on July 31, 2007, marking the first time Jordanians could elect city mayors, were boycotted by the IAF, which accused the government of vote rigging. Following elections to the lower house of parliament on November 20, 2007, supporters of the king, described as mainly Bedouins and centrists—all independents—secured an overwhelming majority of the 110 seats, with representation of the IAF reduced to six seats. On November 22 the king appointed Nader DAHABI to succeed Bakhet as prime minister. Dahabi, 61, a former transport minister and the head of an economic development zone, was sworn in with a new government (including eight members of the previous cabinet and four women) on November 25.

The cabinet was extensively reshuffled on February 23, 2009.

Constitution and government. Jordan's present constitution, promulgated in 1952, provides for authority jointly exercised by the king and a bicameral National Assembly. Executive power is vested in the monarch, who is also supreme commander of the armed forces. He appoints the prime minister and cabinet; orders general elections; convenes, adjourns, and dissolves the assembly; and approves and promulgates laws. The assembly, in joint session, can override his veto of legislation and must also approve all treaties. The House of Representatives is comprised of 110 members (increased from 80 in 2003) elected via universal suffrage, while members of the senate-like House of Notables are appointed by the king. The present multiparty system was authorized in a National Charter signed by the king and leaders of the country's major political movements in 1991. The judicial system is headed by the High Court of Justice. Lower courts include courts of appeal, courts of first instance, and magistrates' courts. There are also special courts for religious (both Christian and Muslim) and tribal affairs. Martial law, imposed at the time of the 1967 Arab-Israeli war, provided for military tribunals to adjudicate crimes against "state security." Although many other martial law elements—such as the ban on large public meetings and restrictions on the press and freedom of speech—were suspended by King Hussein in 1989 and 1991 decrees, the special courts were not abolished until martial law was totally repealed on April 1, 1992.

Local government administration is based on the five East Bank provinces (*alwiyah*) of Amman, Irbid, Balqa, Karak, and Man, each headed by a commissioner. The *alwiyah* are further subdivided into districts (*aqdiyah*) and subdistricts (*nawahin*). The towns and larger villages are governed by partially elected municipal councils, while the smaller villages are often governed by traditional village headmen (*mukhtars*). Under an election reform law adopted in 2007, all mayors and local councils are directly elected, except in Amman, where half the council members continue to be appointed by the king. The law also includes a 20 percent quota for women in local councils.

Foreign relations. Historically reliant on aid from Britain and the United States, Jordan has maintained a generally pro-Western orientation in foreign policy. Its pro-Iraqi tilt during the Gulf crisis and war of 1990–1991 (see below) was a notable exception, prompting the suspension of Western aid and imposition of a partial blockade of the Jordanian port of Aqaba to interdict shipments headed for Iraq in violation of UN sanctions. However, relations with the West improved rather quickly thereafter, several meetings between King Hussein and U.S. President Bill Clinton yielding preliminary agreement on external debt rescheduling and the resumption of aid.

Regional affairs have long been dominated by the Arab-Israeli conflict, Jordan's particular concerns being the occupation of the West Bank by Israel since 1967 and the related Palestinian refugee problem, both of which gave rise to policy disputes between King Hussein and PLO Chair Yasir Arafat. Jordan tended to be somewhat less intransigent toward Israel than many of its Arab neighbors. After initially criticizing the PLO for conducting secret talks with Israel, Hussein (who over the years had also had secret contacts with Israel) eventually endorsed the Israeli-PLO accord signed in September 1993. Subsequently, Jordanian and Israeli officials began meeting openly for the first time in decades to discuss such matters as water resources, the refugee problem, border delineation, and economic cooperation. Then, on July 25, 1994, King Hussein and Israeli Prime Minister Yitzhak Rabin signed a declaration ending the 46-year-old state of war between their two countries. The agreement was followed by the signing at the Jordanian-Israeli border on October 26 of a formal peace accord in which each nation pledged to respect the other's sovereignty and territorial integrity, based on a recently negotiated demarcation of their mutual border. Cooperation was also pledged on trade, tourism, banking, finance, and in numerous other areas. Significantly, President Clinton attended the treaty ceremony, promising substantial debt relief and increased aid to Jordan in return for its participation in the peace process. Arafat was conspicuously absent among the 5,000 invited guests, many Palestinians having been angered by the agreement's reference to Jordan's "special role" as "guardian" of Islamic holy sites in Jerusalem. However, the concern appeared to lessen somewhat in January 1995 when Jordan and the PLO signed an accord endorsing the Palestinian claim to sovereignty over East Jerusalem while also committing the signatories to wide-ranging cooperation in the financial, trade, and service sectors. In October 1996 King Hussein visited the West Bank for the first time since 1967, the trip apparently having been designed to underscore the king's support for the development of Palestinian autonomy under Arafat's direction. The king also played a significant intermediary role in the January 1997 agreement reached by Arafat and Israeli Prime Minister Benjamin Netanyahu regarding additional Israeli troop withdrawals from the West Bank.

Diplomatic relations with Egypt, suspended in 1979 upon conclusion of the latter's accord with Israel, were reestablished in September 1984. Prior to the Gulf crisis of the 1990s, relations with Saudi Arabia and other Middle Eastern monarchies were for the most part more cordial than those with such left-wing republics as Libya.

Relations with Syria have been particularly volatile, a period of reconciliation immediately after the 1967 war deteriorating because of differences over guerrilla activity. In September 1970 a Syrian force that came to the aid of the fedayeen against the Jordanian army was repulsed, with diplomatic relations being severed the following July but restored in the wake of the 1973 war. Despite numerous efforts to improve ties, relations again deteriorated in the late 1970s and early 1980s, exacerbated by Jordanian support for Iraq in the Gulf war with Iran. A cooperation agreement signed in September 1984 was immediately threatened by Syria's denunciation of the resumption of relations with Egypt; earlier, on February 22, relations with Libya had been broken because of the destruction of the Jordanian embassy in Tripoli, an action termed by Amman as a "premeditated act" by the Qadhafi regime. Thereafter, renewed rapprochement with Syria, followed by a resumption of diplomatic relations with Libya in September 1987, paved the way for a minimum of controversy during a November Arab League summit in Amman. A Syrian-Jordanian economic summit in February 1989 was preceded in January by a meeting between Hussein and Saudi Arabia's King Fahd to renegotiate an expiring agreement that in 1988 was reported to have provided approximately 90 percent of Jordan's foreign aid receipts.

Jordan's professed goal of maintaining neutrality in the wake of Iraq's occupation of Kuwait in 1990 was challenged by the anti-Iraqi allies who accused the regime of being sympathetic to Baghdad, citing the king's description of Saddam Hussein as an "Arab patriot" and Amman's resistance to implementing UN sanctions against Iraq. On September 19 Saudi Arabia, angered by King Hussein's criticism of the buildup of Western forces in the region, suspended oil deliveries to Jordan and three days later expelled approximately 20 Jordanian diplomats. Meanwhile, fearful that Jordan's location between Israel and Iraq made it a likely combat theater, King Hussein intensified his calls for a diplomatic solution, declared an intention to defend his country's airspace, and reinforced Jordanian troops along the Israeli frontier. In January 1991 Jordan temporarily closed its borders, complaining that it had received insufficient international aid for processing over 700,000 refugees from Iraq and Kuwait. Thereafter, in a speech on February 6, 1991, King Hussein made his most explicit expression of support for Iraq to date, assailing the allies' "hegemonic" aims and accusing the United States of attempting to destroy its neighbor. Following the war, the king quickly returned to a more moderate position, calling for "regional reconciliation" based on "forgiveness" among Arabs and a permanent resolution of the Palestinian problem.

In what was perceived as a further effort to rebuild relations with Arab neighbors, who before the war had provided annual aid estimated at $500 million, King Hussein called in late 1992 for the installation of a democratic government in Iraq. In May 1993 the king openly broke with Iraq, charging it with activities inimical to Jordanian interests and declaring his opposition to Saddam Hussein's continued rule. King Hussein also condemned the Iraqi buildup along the Kuwaiti border in October 1994 and, in August 1995, granted asylum to the members of President Hussein's family and governmental inner circle who had recently fled Iraq. In addition, he invited Iraqi opposition groups to open offices in Jordan. The king's unequivocal anti-Iraq stance assisted in the reestablishment of normal relations with all the Gulf states except Kuwait by August 1996, when he was greeted in Saudi Arabia by King Fahd for the first time since the 1990 invasion.

In December 1996 the United Nations implemented its "oil-for-food" deal with Iraq (see article on Iraq), which broke Jordan's informal "monopoly" on trade with its neighbor, and precipitated a decline in annual bilateral trade from $400 million in 1996 to just $250 million in 1997. As conflict loomed between the United States and Iraq in the early part of 1998, Amman managed to stay in the good graces of both countries by opposing any U.S. military attack while banning demonstrations in support of Iraq and calling on that country to abide by UN resolutions.

Efforts to normalize relations with Israel faced setbacks in early 1997 when Israel announced plans to build another settlement in East Jerusalem. Relations were in part assuaged when, following the shooting death of seven Israeli schoolgirls in Jordan on March 13 by a corporal in the Jordanian army, Hussein immediately responded by visiting the families of the Israeli schoolchildren and expressing sympathy for their losses. Nevertheless, relations again took a turn for the worse on September 25 when agents from the Israeli intelligence agency Mossad were caught in Amman attempting to poison Hamas leader Khaled Meshal. Furious at this attack on Jordanian soil, King Hussein demanded the antidote to the poison and threatened to break off relations with Israel. The Israeli government furnished the antidote and subsequently exchanged a large group of Jordanian and Palestinian prisoners held in Israel for the captured Mossad agents. (See Current issues, below, for subsequent developments.)

In February 2008 King Abdullah II met in Moscow with Russian president Vladimir Putin to enhance bilateral ties and begin talks on cooperation on a civilian nuclear energy program. The king also sought to incorporate Russia into the Middle East peace process initiated by the United States at its November 2007 summit in Annapolis, Maryland (see Current issues, below.) In March the king visited the United States, urging a long-term U.S. commitment to development in the region, and in August he became the first Arab leader to visit Iraq since the fall of Saddam Hussein. He announced plans to reopen Jordan's embassy in Iraq.

Current issues. The world was first alerted to the seriousness of King Hussein's health problems in August 1998, when he delegated broad powers to Crown Prince Hassan while undergoing extended treatment in the United States. Hassan quickly orchestrated the removal of the Majali government, which had become the focus of popular discontent over a number of issues, including the mishandling of a water crisis in Amman and the embarrassing overstatement of economic growth figures. The crown prince also launched a dialogue with the nation's political parties and groups (including the Muslim Brotherhood), which had remained marginalized as Jordan's proposed democratization program stalled under the influence of ongoing regional tensions, and pledged that the administration of Prime Minister Tarawneh would provide a "safety net" to protect the poor from the effects of IMF-mandated fiscal reforms. Moreover, Hassan subsequently attempted to effect changes at the top levels of the military, an initiative that angered Hussein, who returned in the fall to resume full monarchical authority. The perceived "meddling" in army matters was one of the reasons King Hussein cited for the dismissal of his brother as heir apparent in January 1999. Other factors reportedly included the king's long-standing interest in reestablishing a direct father-to-son line of succession and his belief that his eldest son Abdullah (married to a Palestinian woman) would ultimately prove a more popular leader than Hassan.

Representatives from some 75 countries (including nearly 50 heads of state) attended the funeral of King Hussein on February 8, 1999, underscoring the widespread respect he had earned for his peacemaking efforts and his skillful management of Jordanian affairs during his 46-year reign. World leaders also wanted to signal their support for King Abdullah II, a newcomer to the international stage suddenly forced into the role of a prominent participant in the Middle East peace process. The new king, who had been educated in the West and whose mother was from the United Kingdom, promised a more open government with fewer press restrictions and possible revision of the electoral code to facilitate greater party influence. However, he declared the economy to be his top priority, announcing his support for budget reduction and other reforms recommended by the IMF.

Immediately upon assuming the throne, King Abdullah announced that he was "absolutely committed" to peace with Israel, despite the fact that many Jordanians appeared to have become disenchanted with that particular aspect of his father's legacy. Underscoring its antimilitancy posture, the regime in the fall of 1999 ordered the closing of the Jordanian offices of Hamas and expelled several leaders of that Islamic fundamentalist movement, which spearheads hard-line anti-Israeli sentiment in the West Bank (and Gaza). In addition, security forces arrested a group of militants with reported ties to the alleged international terrorism organization of Osama bin Laden, charging the detainees with plotting to attack U.S. and Israeli targets. At the same time, Abdullah concentrated on improving ties with Syria, Lebanon, Kuwait, and other neighbors, and, in an apparent further attempt to promote Arab solidarity, called for the end of UN sanctions against Iraq.

The change in prime ministers in June 2000 was attributed to the perceived failure of the Rawabdeh government to achieve effective economic change as well as to Rawabdeh's reported "autocratic" style, which had apparently contributed to friction between his administration and the National Assembly. The appointment of Abu al-Ragheb as prime minister was generally well received, the business community in particular endorsing his stated goals of attracting foreign investment and promoting tourism. Investors also welcomed the country's accession to the World Trade Organization in April 2000 and the signing of a rare free trade agreement with the United States later in the year.

Meanwhile, political reform remained subordinate to the economic focus, King Abdullah reportedly relying even more heavily on secret security and intelligence services than his father had in the later years of his reign.

On June 16, 2001, the king dissolved the National Assembly in anticipation of new balloting for the House of Representatives, expected in November. However, in view of the roiling Israeli-Palestinian conflict, polling was postponed until September 2002. The king in August 2002 further delayed new elections until March 2003, citing "difficult regional circumstances" that included a potential U.S. attack on neighboring Iraq. Analysts suggested that the government feared "radical elements" might take advantage of surging anti-Israel and anti-U.S. sentiment within the Jordanian population to present a significant electoral challenge to the establishment unless regional tensions were reduced. Elections were finally held on June 17, 2003, two months after the fall of Baghdad to U.S.-led invading forces and the removal of Saddam Hussein from power. Progovernment legislators held a clear majority in the new legislature, but Islamist and tribal members opposed the king's promotion of women's rights. Reforms allowing women to initiate divorce, raising the legal age for marriage to 18, and stiffening penalties for "honor killings" of women were weakened or blocked by legislators arguing that such measures threatened family stability.

Popular opinion presented the government with a difficult act in maintaining strong ties with the United States, with King Abdullah II calling on Washington to establish a timetable for creation of a Palestinian state as a means of tempering Arab frustration over the lack of progress in the Middle East peace process. At the same time, Jordan was a solid supporter of the U.S.-led "war on terrorism" following the al-Qaida attacks on the United States in September 2001. In addition to contributing troops to peacekeeping forces in Afghanistan following the attempted ouster of the Taliban and al-Qaida, the government also announced in 2002 that it had thwarted planned attacks against U.S. and Israeli targets through several roundups of Islamic militants. However, critics of the government charged that the crackdown had undercut political liberalization by barring most public demonstrations, dampening legitimate dissent, and tightening restrictions on the media.

On October 28, 2002, Laurence Foley, senior U.S. diplomat, became the first Western official to be assassinated in Jordan. Of the 11 suspects tried for the crime, 8 were sentenced to death. Among them was Abu Musab al-ZARQAWI, who was tried in absentia and subsequently linked to the armed resistance to U.S. forces in Iraq. He was sentenced to death (in absentia) two more times for plotting failed attacks inside Jordan and at the border with Iraq. (Al-Zarqawi was killed in a U.S. airstrike near Baquba, Iraq, in June 2006.)

King Abdullah's effort to maintain Jordan's role as mediator in the Middle East resulted in the June 2003 summit he hosted in the Red Sea port of Aqaba with U.S. President George W. Bush, Israeli Prime Minister Ariel Sharon, and Palestinian National Authority (PNA) Prime Minister Mahmud Abbas in attendance to launch the U.S.-backed "road map" for peace.

U.S.-Jordanian relations were strained by the 2003 Iraq invasion, which Jordanians strongly opposed. In the run-up to war, Abdullah warned the United States and the United Kingdom that an attack on Iraq could lead to "regional destabilization." He ultimately adopted an ambivalent stance, accepting the stationing of U.S. forces near the Iraqi border while opposing the invasion. When Iraq's Sunnis boycotted legislative elections held January 30, 2005, the king warned of an impending "Shiite crescent" stretching from Iran to Lebanon that might destabilize the Sunni-led status quo in the Arab world. Relations with Iraq warmed in 2005 after King Abdullah agreed to pardon Iraqi Deputy Prime Minister Ahmed Chalabi, who had been sentenced in absentia by a Jordanian court in 1992 for bank fraud. In October 2005 the interim Iraqi prime minister visited Amman, and the two countries signed a security cooperation agreement. On November 9, 2005, near-simultaneous bombings in Amman at three hotels frequented by Westerners killed 60 people and injured more than 100, prompting King Abdullah to call for a "global strategy" against terrorism. Demonstrators filled the streets, denouncing the attacks and those who claimed responsibility: al-Zarqawi and al-Qaida (see al-Qaida under the article on Afghanistan). Eleven top officials, including the national security adviser, resigned on November 15, and days later Abdullah appointed Marouf Bakhet to the national security post. Vowing that he would not allow the attacks to derail the government's National Agenda for reform, the king subsequently named Bakhet—widely regarded as a proponent of change—as prime minister.

Amid increased tensions in the region, Jordan, at the request of the Iraqi government, closed its border with Iraq to all Arab citizens (including Jordanians) traveling to Iraq in early 2006, and it subsequently temporarily closed its border to Palestinian refugees. Meanwhile, tensions heightened inside Jordan as the government increased fuel prices in anticipation of the expiration of oil grants from Saudi Arabia, Kuwait, and the United Arab Emirates. Islamist groups' requests to hold demonstrations against the increases, set to end by 2007, were repeatedly denied by the government.

In the wake of the Palestinian election victory by Hamas in 2006, King Abdullah adopted a moderate approach, stating that Jordan would not "disregard the new Palestinian government before reviewing its agenda," and he continued to endorse Israeli-Palestinian negotiations. However, Jordan subsequently took a harder line, accusing Hamas of smuggling arms and plotting attacks inside the country. According to reports, Jordan was fearful that the "rising tide of radical Islam it sees originating from Iran" threatened its stability.

A woman convicted in the 2005 hotel bombings was sentenced to death in September 2006, shortly after a gunman was arrested in an unrelated incident in which he was charged with killing one tourist and wounding six other people, including a Jordanian police officer. In several other cases throughout the year, numerous people identified as belonging to various terrorist organizations, including al-Qaida, were sentenced to death or lengthy prison terms. Among those convicted were nine men involved in a 2005 rocket attack on a U.S. warship in the port of Aqaba and two al-Qaida members who were planning to carry out attacks on Jewish and U.S. targets during the millennium celebration.

Attention continued to focus on security concerns in 2007, with the sentencing of several more people convicted of plotting terrorist attacks and the trial of three Jordanian men accused of plotting to assassinate U.S. President George W. Bush during his 2006 visit to Amman. Addressing another significant issue—fuel prices—the government increased the minimum wage to help offset the rising prices. Among the more controversial topics was a new political parties law, which Islamic and other political groups protested vehemently, claiming it would severely reduce the number of parties in the country. Some observers said the new law, which requires parties to have at least 500 members from the kingdom's five governorates, actually united diverse parties for the first time. The IAF and other parties criticized King Abdullah for what they claimed was his failure to follow through on a recent pledge to institute more liberal political reforms, and more than two dozen groups staged a protest in April. Meanwhile, municipal elections, originally scheduled for July 17, were postponed to July 31. Nine IAF members were arrested for allegedly plotting against the government in the month leading up to the elections. The IAF boycotted the polling, alleging that the government allowed multiple voting by some members of the military.

In the November 20, 2007, parliamentary elections, the IAF fielded 22 candidates but secured only two-thirds of the seats it had won in 2003. Observers attributed the decline to rifts in the party and the IAF's inability to follow through on its long-held pledges to reduce poverty and unemployment. Independents loyal to the king won handily, though turnout was reported to be low (with reports of only 32 percent turnout in Amman). A large percentage of the population was said to oppose the current electoral laws, which they claimed allow for greater representation in progovernment districts. Opposition groups, including the IAF, had been pressuring the government for reforms to move toward proportional representation to ensure greater pluralism, including greater representation in districts heavily populated by Palestinians, but no government proposals were forthcoming. Hamas's rise to power in the Palestinian government was cited as key to the Jordanian government's lack of movement on electoral reforms in its effort to contain the republic's "restive Palestinian majority and an activist Islamic opposition," according to the *New York Times*. Following the parliamentary balloting, in which the government had rejected the IAF's request for international observers, the IAF again registered allegations of fraud; subsequently, 17 people were arrested on charges of vote tampering.

With his renewed support in the legislature, King Abdullah urged lawmakers to focus on education, health, housing, and public sector salaries. Additionally, the king continued to press for a two-state solution to resolve Palestinian-Israeli violence and the resumption of peace talks, as well as dialogue between Fatah and Hamas. Meanwhile, the king reiterated his "full support" for the Palestinian National Authority (also referenced as the Palestinian Authority) and sought international aid for the Palestinians in Gaza. Israeli Prime Minister Ehud Olmert was reported to have made a secret visit to Jordan earlier in 2007 to discuss bilateral relations. In November Jordan was represented at the U.S.-sponsored Middle East peace talks in Annapolis, Maryland.

Tensions in the region increased in January 2008 in the wake of Israel's blockade of Gaza, forcing many Palestinians to flee the dire situation there, lacking food, water, and electricity. Olmert's visit to Jordan in early January was harshly criticized by the IAF, despite the king's condemnation of Israeli "aggression" in Gaza. The government, for its part, accused the IAF of having a "special relationship" with Hamas. In March dozens of pro-Hamas marches, reportedly organized by the IAF, attracted thousands of Jordanians calling for Hamas to stage suicide attacks against Israel. In April five Islamists, four of whom were said to be members of the Hamas Islamic Resistance Movement (see Political Parties and Groups, below), were on trial for allegedly supplying secret military information to Hamas. In a major turnaround in August, Jordan made overtures to Hamas in an effort to rebuild a relationship, reportedly amid fears of a major influx of refugees, potentially leading to civil unrest, should U.S.-backed Middle East peace efforts collapse. The move by Jordan was said by analysts to have been an effort at maintaining a delicate balance between reaching out to Hamas and avoiding angering the United States and Israel. Further protests against Israel's blockade were organized by the IAF in Amman in November. Following Israel's attacks inside Gaza in late December, in response to Hamas's firing of rockets into southern Israel, tensions ignited within Jordan over the Gaza issue. When the speaker of parliament postponed a proposal by the IAF to dispatch an aid ship to Gaza, 21 members, including two from the IAF, walked out in protest. The IAF claimed the postponement was meant to block the aid effort, which would circumvent Israel's blockade of Gaza. The ship was ultimately dispatched in mid-January 2009.

Pressure for greater democratic reforms was brought to the forefront in January 2009 when 100 people, described as national and political leaders, said they had formed a "national front" to promote that agenda. Subsequently, the minister for political development, Musa al-MAAYTAH, promised further reforms and said the administration would embark on an "era of openness" with the Islamic opposition. Maaytah, who was part of an extensively reshuffled cabinet installed on February 23, was reported to have been appointed to underscore the government's commitment to political reforms. Another key appointment, which analysts saw as a signal of Jordan's "reluctance" to engage with Hamas, was Nayif al-QADI as interior minister, a post he had held in the late 1990s when he deported several Hamas members. The cabinet overhaul came at a time when inflation was approaching 13 percent and food and fuel prices were soaring. The prime minister retained his post in the reshuffle, which was aimed at stabilizing the economy in the wake of the global financial crisis.

In April 2009 three members of Hamas were convicted in a military court for participating in military training in Jordan, thus jeopardizing the kingdom's safety, according to authorities. Some news reports said that Jordan had accused the men of being spies. The men were sentenced to five years in prison, and two other defendants were acquitted. Hamas responded by requesting amnesty for the prisoners.

POLITICAL PARTIES AND GROUPS

Parties were outlawed prior to the 1963 election. Subsequently, an "official" political organization, the Arab National Union (initially known as the Jordanian National Union), held sway from 1971 to February 1976, when it was disbanded. On October 17, 1989, King Hussein announced that some party activity could resume but left standing a prohibition against party-affiliated candidacies for the November legislative election. The National Charter signed in June 1991 recognized the right of parties to organize, on condition that they acknowledge the legitimacy of the monarchy. Legislation formally lifting the ban on parties was approved by the National Assembly in July 1992 and by King Hussein on August 31. The first groups were recognized the following December.

Legal Parties:

National Constitutional Party (NCP). The NCP was officially formed on May 1, 1997, reportedly by nine pro-government parties and the **Jordanian Arab Masses Party** (*Hizb al-Jamahir al-Arabi al-Urduni*), the **Popular Unity Party** (*Hizb al-Wahdah al-Shabiyah*), and the **Jordanian Popular Movement.** (Some reports indicated that the component groupings had dissolved themselves in favor of the NCP, although their institutional status, as well as that of the NCP, subsequently remained unclear.) Under the slogan "rejuvenation, democracy, and unity," the NCP ran in the November elections on an agenda of peace with Israel, support for the IMF economic program, and the "Jordanization" of political life. It won only two seats. Many observers believe that the NCP was meant by its leaders to serve as a counterweight to the historical dominance of the Islamic, leftist and pan-Arabist movements. The formation of the NCP was one of the reasons that the Islamic and most of the leftist and pan-Arabist parties decided to boycott the elections.

In 2002 the NCP was one of five centrist parties that urged the government to carry out political reforms that would allow for less restrictive policies. The NCP joined a host of other parties in 2007 in a campaign opposing the government's political parties law.

Leaders: Abdul Hadi MAJALI (President of the Party and Speaker of the House of Representatives), Ahmad SHUNNAQ (General Secretary).

Islamic Action Front—IAF (*Jabhat al-Amal al-Islami*). The IAF was formed in late 1992 by the influential Muslim Brotherhood (below) as well as other Islamists, some of the latter subsequently withdrawing because of Brotherhood domination. Like the Muslim Brotherhood, the IAF promotes the establishment of a sharia–based Islamic state with retention of the monarchy. Although the IAF is generally perceived as opposing Israeli-PLO and Jordanian-Israeli peace talks, a significant "dovish" minority exists within the Front.

IAF leaders objected to electoral law changes introduced in mid-1993 and accused the government of interfering in the Front's campaign activities prior to the November house elections. However, after initially threatening to boycott the balloting, the Front presented 36 candidates, 16 of whom were elected. IAF candidates did not perform as well as anticipated in the July 1995 municipal elections, potential support having apparently gone instead to tribally-based parties. Subsequently, Front/Brotherhood leaders suggested that King Hussein was "trying to restore authoritarian rule." No IAF members were included in the new government announced in February 1996.

In view of the recently enacted press restrictions and continued complaints over electoral laws, the IAF boycotted the 1997 legislative balloting. A member of the IAF, Abd al-Rahim AKOUR, accepted a post in the new cabinet of June 2000 but was suspended from the party for that decision.

After winning 17 seats in the 2003 parliamentary elections, the IAF became the principal opposition party in the legislature. Following the suicide bombing attacks on hotels in Amman in 2005, which the IAF denounced, the Front urged the government to consider individual freedoms as it began drafting antiterror laws.

The victory of Hamas in the Palestinian elections in 2006 was seen by observers as likely to further widen the gap between hawks and doves in the IAF. The hawks, who contended that the government continued to marginalize Islamists, appeared to be strengthened by the Hamas victory, observers said. Subsequently, the IAF elected Zaki Said Bani-Irshayd, who was supportive of Hamas, as its new secretary general. (The dovish leader of the associated Muslim Brotherhood decided not to run for reelection in 2006.) A government crackdown on Islamists, including the dismissal of two deputies from the lower house of parliament, furthered the tensions between the government and the IAF, and resulted in a walkout by IAF deputies for several weeks in early 2007. The IAF continued lobbying for the elimination of the one-person, one-vote system (cited as an unfair system in multiple-candidate districts) and protested vehemently against a new law approved by the parliament in 2007, which required political parties to have a minimum of 500 members (instead of 50) in order to be officially recognized. Numerous other groups joined the IAF in a demonstration, in defiance of a government ban, against the political parties law, which they regarded as a "major setback to the country's democratic process." The IAF was highly critical of what it said was the king's lack of movement on promised political reforms, including a change to the press law involving imprisonment for journalists (later removed by legislators).

Also in 2007 the IAF elected the first Christian to its administrative board, but he resigned within a month. The IAF said the Christian member, who had been active in the group for years, probably resigned due to political and other pressures. Following its boycott of municipal elections in July (see Current issues, above), the IAF decided to participate in parliamentary elections in November. It secured only six seats, a significant erosion of power for what had been the leading opposition group in the lower chamber. The lack of support for the IAF was attributed to its inability to effect socio-economic changes and to rifts in the party between hawks and doves, the hawks opposing the doves decision to participate in polling, which the hawks believed would not be fair and transparent. Also, the hawks were said to be angered by the way the IAF candidates were chosen (without consultation with the full membership). Some observers said the party was facing "the biggest internal crisis in its history," furthered by Hamas's decision to form a Palestinian Muslim Brotherhood, prompting divisions in the IAF (see Muslim Brotherhood, below) between pro-Jordanian and pro-Hamas factions. In June the two factions resolved the contentious issue of whether Zaki Said Bani-Irshayd should retain his post as secretary general. He had been blamed by some for allegedly undermining the position of the group's parliamentary candidates in the 2007 elections, leading to a loss of IAF seats. Ultimately, Bani-Irshayd was allowed to retain his post, and four members who had resigned in protest returned, reportedly putting an end to the long-running conflict.

In March 2009 the IAF criticized Egypt for denying entry at the Rafa border crossing to 17 parliamentarians, including IAF members, who were on a mission to express solidarity with the people of Gaza. The IAF was also highly critical of Arab leaders who failed to accept an invitation to an emergency summit in Qatar to consider measures against Israel following the Gaza attacks.

Leaders: Hamza MANSUR, Abd al-Latif ARABIYAT, Ziad Abu GHANIMA, Jamil ABU-BAKR (Spokesperson), Rahil al-GHARAYIBAH (Deputy Secretary General), Zaki Said BANI-IRSHAYD (Secretary General).

Jordanian National Alliance Party—JNAP (*Hizb al-Tajammu al-Watani al-Urduni*). At the time of its recognition in December 1992, the JNAP was described as a "coalition of central and southern Bedouin tribes" with, as yet, no stated political or economic platform. It was subsequently viewed as essentially "pro-establishment" and supportive of King Hussein's position on Middle East peace negotiations, Secretary General Mijhim al-Khuraysha having previously served as an adviser to the king. In November 1993 the JNAP announced the formation of a Jordanian National Front (JNF) with *al-Yaqazah, al-Watan,* and the PJP (below).

The alliance was seen as primarily a parliamentary bloc (all members but the PJP being represented in the 1993 House of Representatives). The JNAP was represented in the February 1996 cabinet, but the party did not appear to play a role in the 1997 elections.

Leader: Mijhim al-KHURAYSHA (Secretary General).

Homeland Party (*Hizb al-Watan*). Two members of *al-Watan,* recognized in May 1993, were successful in the 1993 house balloting. Distancing itself from the other JNF components on the issue, *al-Watan* in late 1994 announced its opposition to the recent Jordanian-Israeli peace accord. Nevertheless, it was granted portfolios in the new cabinet announced in February 1996.

Leader: Hakam KHAIR (Secretary General).

Pledge Party (*Hizb al-Ahd*). One of the first parties to be recognized, the centrist *al-Ahd* supports a free market economy and development of a strong "national Jordanian identity" in which there would be "a clear distinction" between the Jordanian and Palestinian political entities. The *al-Ahd* secretary general, a former army chief of staff, was one of the party's two members elected to the house in 1993. He initially called for creation of a common front among centrist parliamentary parties as a counterbalance to the IAF. However, when parliamentary blocs were subsequently announced, *al-Ahd* was aligned not with the other centrist parties in the JNF but rather with a group of 15 independent deputies in a National Action Front (NAF), which was accorded five ministries in the government formed in January 1995. *Al-Ahd* was represented in the February 1996 cabinet.

Former secretary general of the party Abdul Hadi Majali, an early member of the Pledge Party, subsequently became the leader of the NCP (above).

In 2006 the Pledge Party was one of several groups that asked the government for permission to hold a protest march against U.S. President George W. Bush's upcoming visit.

Leader: Khaldun al-NASIR (Secretary General).

Awakening Party (*Hizb al-Yaqazah*). Two members of *al-Yaqazah,* including Secretary General Abd al-Rauf al-Rawabdeh, were elected to the House of Representatives in 1993. Rawabdeh was also appointed deputy prime minister in the subsequent Majali and Shaker cabinets; he was named prime minister by King Abdullah in March 1999.

Leader: Abd al-Rauf al-RAWABDEH (Secretary General).

Progress and Justice Party—PJP (*Hizb al-Taqaddumi wa-al-Adl*). The PJP was listed as one of the founding members of the JNF, which was primarily a parliamentary bloc, even though no PJP members were elected to the house in 1993.

Leader: Muhammad Ali Farid al-SAAD (Secretary General).

Democratic Unionist Arab Party—The Promise (*al-Hizb al-Wahdawi al-Arabi al-Dimuqrati—al-Wad*). The centrist *al-Wad* was formed in early 1993 as a merger of three unrecognized groups (the Democratic Unionist Alliance, the Liberal Unionist Party, and the Arab Unionist Party) with similar platforms regarding greater free market activity and the pursuit of foreign investment. Although *al-Wad* was recognized in February, it was subsequently reported to be in disarray as leaders of the founding groups squabbled over the new party's leadership posts.

Leaders: Talal al-UMARI (Assistant Secretary General), Anis al-MUASHIR (Secretary General).

Future Party (*Hizb al-Mustaqbal*). A conservative pan-Arabist grouping described as strongly supportive of the Palestinian intifada, *al-Mustaqbal* was recognized in December 1992. Many of its leaders are businesspeople and/or former government officials, including former secretary general Suliman Arrar, who had previously served as a cabinet minister and speaker of the House of Representatives, and former prime ministers Obeidat and Masri. The party boycotted the November 1997 elections.

In 2006 the Future Party joined several other parties in staging a protest against the November visit by U.S. President George W. Bush and against U.S. policies in the region.

Leaders: Yusuf GHAZAL (Deputy Secretary General), Abd al-Salam FREIHAT (Secretary General).

Communist Party of Jordan—CPJ (*al-Hizb al-Shuyui al-Urduni*). Although outlawed in 1957, the small pro-Moscow CPJ subsequently maintained an active organization in support of the establishment of a Palestinian state on the West Bank, where other communist groups also continued to operate. About 20 of its leaders, including (then) Secretary General Faik (Faiq) Warrad, were arrested in May 1986 for "security violations" but were released the following September. More than 100 members were detained for five months in 1989 for allegedly leading antigovernment rioting. One CPJ member, Isa Madanat, was elected to the House of Representatives in 1989 and the following spring he and several party associates participated in negotiations on the proposed National Charter, the January repeal of the nation's anti-Communist act having ostensibly put the CPJ on the same footing as other parties preparing for official recognition. After initially being rejected for legal party status in late 1992 on the ground that communism was "incompatible" with the Jordanian constitution, the CPJ was recognized in January 1993. By that time Madanat and his supporters had left the CPJ to form the JSDP (below, under JUDP).

Despite the opposition of its youth wing, the CPJ participated in November 1997 national elections.

Leader: Munir HAMARENEH (General Secretary).

Jordanian Arab Democratic Party—JADP (*al-Hizb al-Arabi al-Dimuqrati al-Urduni*). The JADP is a leftist group recognized in mid-1993, its supporters including former Baathists and pan-Arabists. The two JADP members who were elected in the 1993 house balloting subsequently joined a parliamentary bloc called the Progressive Democratic Coalition, which also included representatives from the JSDP and *al-Mustaqbal* as well as 18 (mainly liberal) independents. The JADP subsequently announced its opposition to any "normalization" with Israel without full "restoration of Palestinian rights," a stance that aligned the JADP with Palestinian groups opposed to the Israeli-PLO peace accord. The issue appeared to divide the party, some 17 members reportedly resigning in early 1995 in support of the PLO and in protest over a perceived "absence of democracy" within the JADP. One of the party's leaders, Muhammad Daudia, is a former cabinet minister.

Leaders: Muhammad DAUDIA, Muniz RAZZAZ.

Jordanian Baath Arab Socialist Party—JASBP (*Hizb al-Baath al-Arabi al-Ishtiraki al-Urduni*). The Baathists, who had supported a number of independent candidates in the 1989 house election, were initially denied legal status in December 1992 as the Baath

Arab Socialist Party in Jordan because of apparent ties to its Iraqi counterpart. However, the Interior Ministry reversed its decision in early 1993 after the grouping revised its name and offered "assurances of independence" from Baghdad. An Arab nationalist party that opposes peace talks with Israel as "futile," the JASBP presented three candidates in the 1993 house balloting, one of whom was elected. In late 1996 the government accused the JASBP of having helped to incite "bread riots," and a group of Baathists were arrested in connection with those events. However, some observers questioned the government's assertions, a correspondent for *Middle East International* describing the party as too "splintered and shrunken" to be capable of generating effective action. The newspaper *al-Dustur* reported on May 15, 1997, that the JASBP had formed an alliance with two other pan-Arabist parties—the **National Action Front** (*Haqq*), led by Muhammad al-ZUBI, and the **Arab Land Party,** led by Mohammad Al OURAN. The new grouping was reportedly called the **Nationalist Democratic Front** (NDF), led by Hamad al-FARHAN. The NDF parties did not boycott the November 1997 elections, and the JASBP won one seat in the lower house.

Leaders: Ahmad NAJDAWI, Abdullah al-AHMAR (Deputy Secretary General), Taysir al-HIMSI (Secretary General).

Jordan People's Democratic Party (*Hizb al-Shaab al-Dimuqrati al-Urduni*—Hashd). The leftist Hashd was formed in July 1989 by the Jordanian wing of the Democratic Front for the Liberation of Palestine (DFLP), a component of the PLO (see separate article). Its initial application for recognition was rejected because of its DFLP ties, but, as an independent "on a friendly basis" with the DFLP, the party was legalized in early 1993. Like the DFLP, the Hashd opposed the Israeli/PLO accord of September 1993 although it supports the peace process in general as a means of resolving the Palestinian problem. In 2002 the party rallied in support of Iraq prior to the U.S. invasion. In 2004 the party joined other groups in calling on Muslims worldwide to support Iran in the wake of U.S. involvement in the region.

Leader: Ahmad YUSUF (Secretary General).

Jordanian Unionist Democratic Party (JUDP). Formed in 1995 as a merger of the Jordanian Socialist Democratic Party—JSDP (*al-Hizb al-Dimuqrati al-Ishtiraki al-Urduni*) and the Jordanian Progressive Democratic Party—JPDP (*al-Hizb al-Taqaddumi al-Dimuqrati al-Urduni*), the JUDP supports "Arab unity, democracy, and social progress" and opposes the normalization of relations with Israel. The JSDP, whose secretary general (Isa Madanat) had been a former leader of the CPJ, had been recognized in early 1993 even though it had refused a government request to delete "socialist" from its name and references to "socialism" from its party platform. Meanwhile, the JPDP had been formed in late 1992 by the merger of three leftist groups—the Jordanian Democratic Party, the Palestinian Communist Labor Party Organization, and the Jordanian Party for Progress. (The latter subsequently withdrew from the JPDP, its leader later founding the Freedom Party, subsequently the Progressive Party, below.) The JPDP was recognized in January 1993 after its leaders bowed to government pressure and deleted references to socialist objectives from the party platform. Several leaders of the JPDP were former members of the Palestinian National Council.

The creation of the JUDP was widely attributed to the desire of its leftist components to develop a stronger electoral presence, their impact having been negligible in the 1995 municipal elections. However, in 1997 political differences precipitated the resignation of over 150 members, including former secretary general Mazen al-SAKET. The JUDP fielded four candidates in the November 1997 elections and won one seat.

In 2009 Musa al-Maaytah was named as minister of political development. It was unclear whether he was still affiliated with the JUDP.

Leaders: Isa MADANAT, Ali Abd al-Aziz AMER, Musa al-MAAYTAH (Secretary General).

Progressive Party. Formed in 1993 as the Freedom Party (*Hizb al-Hurriyah*) by a former official of the CPJ, this grouping is described as "trying to combine Marxist ideology with Islamic tradition and nationalist thinking." The Progressive Party participated in the 1997 lower house election boycott but was represented in parliament in 2003.

Leaders: Nael BARAKAT (Deputy Secretary General), Fawaz Mahmoud Muflih ZOUBIL (Secretary General).

Jordanian Democratic Popular Unity Party—JDPUP (*Hizb al-Wahdah al-Shabiyah al-Dimuqrati al-Urduni*). The leftist JDPUP was formed in 1990 by Jordanian supporters of the Popular Front for the Liberation of Palestine (PFLP, see article on the PLO). True to its PFLP heritage, the JDPUP opposes peace negotiations with Israel. The JDPUP joined the boycott of the 1997 lower house elections. In 2002 the JDPUP and five other opposition parties failed in their attempt to form a coalition, citing ideological differences. In 2007 the party was among several that protested the country's new political parties law. The party participated in the 2007 parliamentary elections.

Leader: Saeed THIYAB (Secretary General).

Democratic Arab Islamic Movement Party–Propagate (*Hizb al-Harakah al-Arabiyah al-Islamiyah al-Dimuqrati—Dua*). A liberal Islamist grouping founded in 1993, *Dua* was critical of the IAF and the Muslim Brotherhood for their "regressive" interpretation of the Koran. Both women and Christians were included in the party's initial temporary executive committee. *Dua* boycotted the 1997 lower house elections.

Leaders: Mahmoud Abu KHOUSAH, Munir JARRAR, Yusuf Abu BAKR (Secretary General).

Pan-Arab Action Front Party—PAAFP (*Hizb al-Jabhat al-Amal al-Qawmi*). Described as having close ties with Syria, the PAAFP was legalized in January 1994, its members reportedly including several prominent Palestinian hard-liners. Ideological differences subsequently led a faction of the PAAFP to form a new grouping, the **Nationalist Action Party**.

Leader: Muhammad al-ZUBI.

Liberal Party (*Hizb al-Ahrar*). Described as a "pro-peace" grouping, the Liberal Party is led by Ahmad al-Zubi, a prominent attorney. In mid-1995 al-Zubi was reportedly disbarred after having met with Israeli leaders, that penalty reflecting a strong bias against the recent peace accord in Jordanian professional groups such as the Bar Association.

Leader: Ahmad al-ZUBI.

Christian Democratic Party. The Christian Democratic Party was reportedly formed in part by a number of dissidents from the Jordan People's Democratic Party (*Hashd*) and the National Action Front (*Haqq*), as well as independents. At its founding in May 1997 the party announced that it would boycott the November elections to the lower house.

The first political party to be led by a woman was licensed by the government in March 2007. The centrist **Jordanian National Party** was formed by Muna HUSSEIN ABU-BAKR, a U.S.-educated biologist, to promote equal rights, among other things. She was arrested in 2008 on charges of selling counterfeit medicine. Also licensed in 2007 was the **United Jordanian Front Party**, founded in September by the interior minister, Eid al-FAYEZ, and Amjad MAJALI as a party for reform and modernization.

Other legal parties include the **al-Ansar Party,** a moderate grouping recognized in December 1995 and headed by Muhammad MAJALI; the **Arab Land Party,** which was organized in 1996 and contested the 1997 balloting under the leadership of Mohammad al-BATAYNEH, but later led by Muhammad al-ORAN; the **Jordanian Arab Constitutional Front Party,** led by Milhem al-TALL, who in 1989 election campaign called for Jordanian-Syrian union and participated in the 1997 boycott; the **Jordanian Peace Party,** a strong supporter of the peace process with Israel and headed by Shaher KHREIS; the **Green Party**, founded in 2000 by Mohammad BATAYNEH, who later served as energy minister; the **Jordanian People's Committees Movement,** launched in 2001 under the leadership of Khalid SHUBAKI; the **Jordanian Welfare Party,** launched in 2001 and led by Mohammad Rijjal SHUMALI; the **Progressive Arab Baath Party** (*Hizb al-Baath al-Arabi al-Taqaddumi*), led by Fouad DABOUR and said to have a political philosophy similar to that of the Syrian Baath Party; the **Ummah Party** (Community), led by Ahmed HANANDEH and recognized in June 1996 after reportedly having failed to convince other moderate parties to merge with it; the **Jordanian National Movement**, led by Samir AWAMLEH, was formed in 2004 and included 11 small parties in what was described as a pro-government centrist front; the **Prosperity** (*al-Rafah*) party, led by Mohammed AJRAMI after party infighting in 2002; the **Renaissance** (*al-Nahdah*) party, led by Mijhim al-KHURAYSHAH; the **New Dawn** (*al-Fajr al-Jadid*), a centrist party legalized in 1999; and the **Islamic al-Wasat** party, led by Marwan al-FAURI.

Other Groups:

Muslim Brotherhood (*al-Ikhwan al-Muslimun*). An outgrowth of the pan-Arab Islamic fundamentalist group of the same name established in Egypt in 1928, the Brotherhood has played a prominent role in Jordanian political affairs. It promotes the creation of an Islamic state based on strict adherence to Islamic law (sharia) but does not advocate abolition of the monarchy, having generally maintained a cooperative relationship with King Hussein.

Following an impressive showing in the 1989 elections, the Brotherhood was given ten seats on the National Charter Commission formed in April 1990. In November one of its leaders, Abd al-Latif Arabiyat, was elected speaker of the House of Representatives while five of its members entered the government on January 1, 1991. However, it was unrepresented in the subsequent Masri or Shaker cabinets, underscoring the rift between the Brotherhood and the government regarding Jordan's participation in the U.S.-led Middle East peace negotiations. In December 1992 members of the Brotherhood and other fundamentalists established the IAF (above) as their official political party. Primarily because of the Brotherhood's strong opposition to the 1994 peace treaty with Israel, it was not represented in the January 1995 cabinet, reports surfacing that King Hussein and Prime Minister Shaker pointedly had failed even to consult new Brotherhood leader Abd al-Majid THUNIBAT concerning the formation of the government. Indicative of the credibility of the Muslim Brotherhood as an opposition force, it was its decision to boycott the November 1997 elections that led other Islamic as well as non-Islamic opposition parties to also suspend their participation. The dovish Thunibat decided not to run for a fourth term as leader in 2006.

In 2007 the Muslim Brotherhood was caught up in the divisive issue of support for Hamas. The Brotherhood, as part of a 14-party Coordination Committee, wanted the group of diverse parties to meet and discuss the Palestinian crisis, but political differences among the parties eventually scuttled the Brotherhood's efforts. The Brotherhood was also described by observers as facing a crossroads in its relationship with Iran as a result of increasing sectarian tensions between Sunni and Shiite Muslims in the region.

Hamas's decision to establish a Palestinian Muslim Brotherhood in 2008 was seen as a turning point in its alignment with the Jordanian Brotherhood and as contributing to pro-Hamas and pro-Jordanian factions within the group. Meanwhile, rifts between hawks and doves (see IAF, above) led to the dissolution in February of the Brotherhood's Shura (consultative) Council (its highest decision-making committee); subsequently the hawks were elected to a narrow majority of a new council in March, though in a compromise move, Abd al-Latif Arabiyat, a dove, was chosen head of the council. At the same time, Haman Said, described as a hawk of Palestinian origin, was elected as the Brotherhood's new overall leader with the support of those in the group who backed Hamas. (His opponent, Salim Falahat, held the post of the director general.) Meanwhile, the government stated its increasing concerns about links between the Brotherhood and Hamas, fearing a security threat highlighted by the trial of five Islamists (see Current issues, above).

In advance of Pope Benedict XVI's visit to Jordan in May 2009, the Muslim Brotherhood demanded that the pope apologize for remarks he had made in 2006 about the Prophet Muhammad, which many Muslims found "insulting." Though the pope said he was "deeply sorry" about the reaction to his speech, he said the passage he quoted did not reflect his opinion. Pope Benedict was scheduled to meet with Muslim religious leaders at Amman's largest mosque. It was unclear whether Brotherhood members would be invited.

Leaders: Haman SAID, Abd al-Latif ARABIYAT (Head of the Shura Council), Muhammad Abd al-Rahman al-KHALIFA, Abd al-Munim ABU ZANT, Salim FALAHAT.

In January 1991 Islamic Jihad leader Sheikh Asad Bayyud al-TAMINI and **Islamic Liberal Party** leader Atta Abu RUSHTAH called for suicide attacks on Western targets, Rushtah subsequently being arrested by the Jordanian police. In addition, five party members were sentenced to death (two in absentia) in 1994 for allegedly plotting to assassinate King Hussein. In 1996 Rushtah was sentenced to three years in prison for allegedly slandering King Hussein.

Nearly 100 people identified as belonging to the **Prophet Mohammad Army** were arrested in mid-1991 in connection with a series of bomb attacks dating back more than a year. Although many of the detainees were subsequently released, 20 were convicted in November of crimes "against state security."

In 1992 four people (including two members of the House of Representatives) were convicted by a state security court of belonging to a new illegal organization called the **Vanguard of Islamic Youth** (*Shabab al-Nafir al-Islami*). They were subsequently pardoned by a royal amnesty that also applied to a group of detainees belonging to the **Islamic Resistance Movement** (Hamas), the fundamentalist organization based in the occupied territories (see under Israel: Political Groups in Occupied and Previously Occupied Territories). A wave of arrests was also reported in mid-1995 of members of an Islamist grouping called the **Renewal Party** (*Hizb al-Tajdid*.)

LEGISLATURE

The bicameral **National Assembly** (*Majlis al-Ummah*) consists of an appointed House of Notables and an elected House of Representatives. The assembly did not convene between February 1976 and January 1984, a quasi-legislative National Consultative Council, appointed by King Hussein, serving from April 1978 to January 1984.

House of Notables (*Majlis al-Ayan*). The upper chamber consists of 55 members appointed by the king from designated categories of public figures, including present and past prime ministers, twice-elected former representatives, former senior judges and diplomats, and retired officers of the rank of general and above. The stated term is four years although actual terms, until recently, have been irregular because of various royal decrees directed primarily at the elected House of Representatives, whose suspension requires a cessation of upper house activity.

The House of Notables appointed in January 1984 consisted of 30 members, while the body designated in November 1989 was expanded to 40 in keeping with a requirement that the upper house be half the size of its elected counterpart. The king formed a new 55-member upper chamber, including 7 women, on November 17, 2003, although activity remained suspended pending new elections to the House of Representatives. In the wake of bombings at three hotels in Amman on November 9, 2005, and the subsequent resignations of several government officials, the king dissolved the upper chamber on November 16 and appointed a new House of Notables on November 17.

The upper chamber was renewed on November 29, 2007.

President: Zaid al-RIFAI.

House of Representatives (*Majlis al-Nuwwab*). The lower chamber consists of 110 members elected from 45 districts containing 1 to 7 seats each. A small number of seats are reserved for members of the Christian and Circassian minorities and 6 for women. The constitutionally prescribed term of office is four years, although no full elections were held from 1967 to 1989 as the result of turmoil arising from Israel's occupation of the West Bank.

The house seated in 1967 contained 60 members (30 from West Jordan and 30 from East Jordan) elected in nonparty balloting. After being dissolved by the king in November 1974, its members were called back into session by royal decree in February 1976, at which time the king was authorized to postpone new elections indefinitely and call future special sessions as needed. However, the house did not meet again until January 1984. By-elections were held two months later to fill 8 vacant East Bank seats; it being deemed impossible to conduct elections in the West Bank, the 6 vacant seats from the occupied territory were filled by voting within the house itself. The house continued to meet in special session until its dissolution on July 30, 1988, following which King Hussein announced the severance of all legal and administrative ties with the West Bank. Consequently, the November 8, 1989, election of a new house (expanded to 80 members) excluded the West Bank. Political party activity remained proscribed, although the Muslim Brotherhood (defined as a charitable organization rather than a party) was permitted to present candidates, 20 of whom were elected.

The balloting conducted on November 8, 1993, was the first to be held on a multiparty basis since 1956, though most seats (47) were won by independents, with the largest opposition bloc being the Islamic Action Front (16 seats) and no other party holding more than 4 seats. With the Muslim Brotherhood/IAF and eight other parties boycotting the November 4, 1997, elections, only six political parties fielded a total of 22 candidates, with the vast majority of the 524 candidates running as independents and most of these representing pro-government and tribal interests.

King Abdullah dissolved the house on June 16, 2001, in anticipation of new elections in the fall. They were postponed repeatedly, until June 17, 2003. The number of seats was increased from 80 to 110 by a 2003 decree that also set aside 6 seats for women.

In the most recent elections of November 20, 2007, the Islamic Action Front won 6 seats, and independent candidates supportive of King Abdullah II won an overwhelming majority. *(See headnote.)*

Speaker: Abdul Hadi MAJALI.

CABINET

[as of October 1, 2009] *(see headnote)*

Prime Minister	Nader Dahabi
Ministers	
Agriculture	Said al-Masri
Culture	Sabri Rebihat
Defense	Nader Dahabi
Education, Higher Education, and Scientific Research	Walid al-Maani
Energy and Mineral Resources	Khaldoun Qteishat
Environment	Khalid al-Irani
Finance	Bassam al-Salim
Foreign Affairs	Nasir Judah
Health	Nayif al-Fayiz
Industry and Trade	Amer Hadidi
Interior	Nayif al-Qadi
Justice	Ayman Odeh
Labor	Ghazi Shubaykat
Municipal and Rural Affairs	Shihadeh Abu Hdeib
Planning and International Cooperation	Suhair al-Ali [f]
Political Development	Musa al-Maaytah
Public Sector Reform	Nancy Bakir [f]
Public Works and Housing	Alaa Batayneh
Religious Endowments and Islamic Affairs	Abdul Fattah Salah
Social Development	Hala Latouf [f]
Information and Communications Technology	Basim al-Rusan
Tourism and Antiquities	Maha Khatib [f]
Transportation	Sahel Majali
Water and Irrigation	Raed Abu Saud
Ministers of State	
Legal Affairs	Salim Khazaaleh
Media Affairs and Communications	Nabil Sharif
Parliamentary Affairs	Ghalib al-Zubi
Prime Ministry Affairs	Thouqan Qudah

[f] = female

COMMUNICATIONS

The press has long been subject to censorship, with publication of most papers having been suspended at various times for publishing stories considered objectionable by the government. In early 1989 the government purchased the two largest dailies, *al-Rai* and *al-Dustur,* but concerns that the takeover would result in further press censorship were eased in May when Prime Minister Shaker lifted press restrictions imposed in August 1988. Press freedom expanded somewhat under the National Charter approved in June 1991, and further liberalization was anticipated in conjunction with the legalization of political parties and other democratization measures. However, contrary to that expectation, the House of Representatives in late 1992 approved government-sponsored legislation requiring the licensing of journalists, forbidding criticism of the royal family or the military, and otherwise restricting press activities. The government has reportedly initiated some 40 court cases against journalists or publishers since a new press law was enacted in May 1993. In May 1997 the government announced amendments to the 1993 law that provided for heavy fines for various journalistic transgressions and increased the capital requirements for newspapers 25-fold. However, in January 1998 the Jordanian Supreme Court struck down the May 1997 amendments. The National Assembly in 1998 was considering the reimposition of some of the 1997 provisions, reportedly upon the recommendation of King Hussein; however, following his assumption of the throne in February 1999, King Abdullah indicated his intention to ease, rather than tighten, government influence over the press. Nevertheless, additional restrictions were imposed in late 2001 by royal decree, with journalists now facing prison terms for "sowing the seeds of hatred." The government defended the new penalties as necessary to maintain stability in light of regional and domestic tensions. The extent of press restrictions became apparent in February 2003, when three journalists for *al-Hilal* (Crescent), a weekly newspaper, received sentences ranging from two to six months for libeling and defaming the Prophet Muhammad.

In 2004 the first independent and private daily, *al-Ghad* (Tomorrow), began publishing. In 2006 the cabinet approved a new private weekly, *Dar al-Hayat*, published in English and Arabic.

In March 2007 the parliament adopted amendments to the press and publications law that allowed for heavy fines for journalists who committed perceived violations. However, following widespread criticism from media groups and human rights organizations, legislators struck down imprisonment for journalists for various offenses. According to the watchdog group Reporters Without Borders in 2008, state security police keep journalists "under pressure" despite King Abdullah's promise of democratic reforms.

Press. The following are Arabic dailies published in Arabic in Amman, unless otherwise noted: *al-Rai* (Opinion, 100,000), partially government-owned; *al-Aswaq* (Markets, 40,000); *al-Ghad* (Tomorrow, 55,000), privately owned; *Sawt al-Shaab* (Voice of the People, 30,000); *al-Dustur* (The Constitution, 70,000), partially government-owned; *al-Akhbar* (The News, 15,000); *The Jordan Times* (10,000), in English; *al-Arab al-Yawm* (Today's Arab), independent; *al-Masaiyah,* independent.

News agencies. The domestic facility is the government-owned Jordan News Agency (PETRA). Agence France-Presse, AP, Deutsche Presse Agentur (DPA), and Reuters are among the foreign bureaus that maintain offices in Amman.

Broadcasting and computing. Radio and television are controlled by the governmental Jordan Radio and Television Corporation (JRTV), although three private radio stations are permitted to broadcast. In 2007 an independent television station, ATV, under the same ownership as *al-Ghad*, was preparing to go on air. As of 2008 there were 260 Internet users per 1,000 inhabitants.

INTERGOVERNMENTAL REPRESENTATION

Ambassador to the U.S.: Zeid Bin Ra'ad al-HUSSEIN.

U.S. Ambassador to Jordan: Robert Stephen BEECROFT.

Permanent Representative to the UN: Mohammed F. al-ALLAF.

IGO Memberships (Non-UN): AFESD, AMF, BADEA, CAEU, IDB, Interpol, IOM, LAS, NAM, OIC, PCA, WCO, WTO.

KAZAKHSTAN

Republic of Kazakhstan
Qazaqstan Respublikasy

Political Status: Entered the Russian Soviet Federative Socialist Republic as autonomous republic on August 26, 1920; became constituent republic of the Union of Soviet Socialist Republics on December 5, 1936; declared independence on December 16, 1991; current constitution approved by referendum of August 30, 1995, effective from September 6.

Area: 1,049,155 sq. mi. (2,717,300 sq. km.).

Population: 14,953,100 (1999C); 15,658,000 (2008E). Emigration of ethnic Russians, Germans, and Ukrainians after independence, coupled with a declining birth rate (the lowest in Central Asia), has resulted in a net decrease from the 1989 total of 16,536,511.

Major Urban Centers (2005E): ASTANA (formerly Tselinograd and then Akmola, 333,000), Almaty (formerly Alma-Ata, 1,159,000). Formal transfer of the government from the former capital, Almaty, to Astana occurred in June 1998.

Official Language: Kazakh (replaced Russian in 1989); confirmed as official language in 1995 constitution, which also accords Russian special status as "the social language between peoples" while specifying that government officials are required to be proficient in Kazakh by the year 2010.

Monetary Unit: Tenge (official rate December 1, 2009: 148.64 tenge = $1US).

President: Nursultan Abishevich NAZARBAYEV; elected by the Supreme Soviet as its chair on February 22, 1990, succeeding K.U. MEDEUBEKOV (Communist Party of Kazakhstan); reelected on April 24; sworn in to newly created post of president on December 10, 1991, following popular election on December 1; confirmed in office until 2000 by referendum on April 29, 1995; elected for a seven-year term on January 10, 1999; reelected on December 4, 2005, and sworn in on January 11, 2006.

Prime Minister: Karim MASIMOV; promoted from deputy prime minister by the president and confirmed by Parliament on January 10, 2007, succeeding Daniyal AKHMETOV, who had resigned on January 8.

THE COUNTRY

The second largest of the former Soviet republics in area and the fourth largest (after Russia, Ukraine, and Uzbekistan) in population, Kazakhstan consists largely of a vast flatland, much of it desert, extending nearly 2,000 miles from the Altai Mountains in the east to the Caspian Sea in the west. It is bordered by Russian Siberia on the north, China on the east, and the republics of Kyrgyzstan, Uzbekistan, and Turkmenistan on the south. Its people are about 52 percent Turkic-speaking Kazakhs and 31 percent Russians, down from over 42 percent in 1960. Relations between the dominant Kazakhs and the country's ethnic Russian population deteriorated after independence, and as a result over 1.5 million ethnic Russians emigrated. Three-fifths of Kazakhstan's pre-independence German population of 946,000 likewise left the country, as did a large number of ethnic Ukrainians. Slightly less than half the current population is Sunni Muslim, with most of the rest being Russian Orthodox. Women constitute about 49 percent of the active labor force.

Prior to the breakup of the Soviet Union, Kazakhstan's northern tier of "virgin lands" produced most of the Union of Soviet Socialist Republics' (USSR) cattle and wool and a substantial amount of its wheat. Wheat, wool, and meat continue to be exported, with the agricultural sector currently contributing about 6 percent of GDP and employing 31 percent of the labor force. Kazakhstan ranked as one of the world's top wheat producers in 2008. Industry, which accounts for about 40 percent of GDP, is concentrated in hydrocarbon and mineral extraction, the most important sectoral exports being oil and gas, copper and other metals, and chemicals as well as machinery. The country's deposits of barite, chromite, lead, manganese, silver, tungsten, uranium, and zinc rank among the world's largest; other extractable resources include coal, copper, iron ore, gold, and titanium. Development of the vast Kazakh petroleum deposits, including those under the Caspian Sea, has attracted significant foreign investment.

As with the other former Soviet republics in Central Asia, Kazakhstan experienced a sharp economic reversal following independence: for 1990 to 1995 the World Bank calculated an average annual GDP contraction of more than 10 percent. In 1993 inflation peaked at over 2,100 percent. With assistance from the International Monetary Fund (IMF) and other multilateral agencies, Kazakhstan undertook a major restructuring program that saw majority shares in most state enterprises sold and virtually all state and collective farms placed in the hands of cooperatives, associations, or individual farmers. In 1996 the economy registered its first marginal expansion since independence.

Since a recession in 1998–1999, growth has been explosive, owing primarily to the petroleum sector. Additional oil and gas discoveries in 2001 and 2002 and significant foreign investment in Kazakhstan's energy sector have made the nation one of the world's leading energy suppliers. In late 2001 a new oil pipeline opened, linking Kazakhstan's largest onshore field, Tengiz, to the Russian Black Sea port of Novorossiysk, while construction began in 2004 on a $700 million pipeline to China. GDP expansion exceeded 9 percent annually in 2002–2005 and more than 10 percent in 2006, while an annual inflation rate of nearly 7 percent was recorded. In late 2008, Kazakh oil began flowing for the first time through the Baku-Tbilisi-Ceyhan pipeline route to the Turkish port of Ceyhan. Meanwhile, development began in the massive Kashagan field in the Caspian—reportedly the world's largest petroleum discovery in the last 30 years.

Annual GDP growth slowed to 3 percent in 2008 owing in large part to decreasing oil prices and the global economic crisis. As the recession deepened, growth was expected to contract in 2009 as well. In May 2009 the IMF urged the Kazakh government to strengthen the banking sector to restore public confidence in the financial system. On a positive note, the IMF commended the government for its progress in implementing the regulation of pension funds and for pledging to introduce measures to help reduce unemployment.

GOVERNMENT AND POLITICS

Political background. The Kazakh lands were controlled by Russia from 1730 to 1840 and, after a brief attempt at independence in 1917, became an autonomous Soviet republic in 1920 and a full union republic within the USSR in 1936. Kazakh leaders long acted in close concert with Moscow, and its current president had been viewed as a possible contender for the presidency of the Soviet Union. Thus, the Kazakh Republic approached secession from the USSR cautiously, issuing a declaration of state sovereignty only in October 1991 and withholding a declaration of independence until December 16.

In June 1989 Nursultan Abishevich NAZARBAYEV, chair of the Kazakhstan Council of Ministers, had been named first secretary of the Kazakh Communist Party. On February 22, 1990, Nazarbayev was elected to succeed K.U. MEDEUBEKOV as chair of the Supreme Soviet (head of state), a post to which he was reelected on April 24 following a legislative replenishment.

In late 1991 the Communist Party was renamed the Socialist Party of Kazakhstan, with Nazarbayev stepping down as its leader prior to being popularly elected president of the republic on December 1 and appointing a government headed by Sergei TERESHCHENKO. In early 1993 Nazarbayev became the acknowledged but unofficial leader of the new People's Union of Kazakhstan Unity (*Soyuz Narodnoye Edinstvo Kazakhstana*—SNEK), which on March 7, 1994, won a plurality of 33 directly elective seats in the 177-seat Supreme Council (*Kenges*). Some 220 prospective candidates, many assumed to be opponents of the president, had been denied participation in the election. The alignment of the *Kenges* thereafter depended on the "state list" and independent deputies (together, about 100), who were broadly pro-Nazarbayev. Tereshchenko was replaced as prime minister by Akezhan KAZHEGELDIN in October, amid presidential reproaches about the slow pace of economic reform.

A major political crisis erupted on March 6, 1995, when the Constitutional Court invalidated the 1994 poll because of numerous irregularities. The *Kenges* responded on March 11 by adopting a constitutional amendment enabling the legislature to overrule the court, but the latter refused to accept the action as lawful. The president appeared to back down by accepting the resignation of the Kazhegeldin government, dissolving the *Kenges,* and announcing a new election, which a substantial majority of deputies opposed. He then recaptured the initiative by calling an April 29 referendum at which he obtained a 95 percent mandate for the extension of his presidential term to December 2000. In a further referendum on August 30, Nazarbayev secured 89 percent support for a new constitution strengthening presidential powers.

Ruling by decree, President Nazarbayev dismissed the Constitutional Court in October 1995 and introduced a new government structure that enlarged his personal staff and pared down the number of ministries and state committees. Elections to the two legislative chambers created under the new constitution were held in early December, followed by runoff balloting. The January 1996 opening of the legislature, in which SNEK and its allies remained dominant, marked the end of rule by presidential decree.

On October 10, 1997, President Nazarbayev announced the resignation of Prime Minister Kazhegeldin and appointed Nurlan BALGIMBAYEV, head of the state oil company, as the new prime minister. The cabinet announced several days later retained a number of incumbents in key posts, although several senior members were replaced in a reshuffle announced on February 20, 1998.

Adoption of constitutional amendments by a joint session of Parliament on October 7, 1998 (see Constitution and government, below) was followed on January 10, 1999, by a premature presidential election in which the incumbent received 79.8 percent of the votes cast. His closest competitor, Serikbolsyn ABDILDIN of the Communist Party, won 11.7 percent. Several potential candidates, including former prime minister Kazhegeldin, had been ruled ineligible for violating a law against participation in meetings of unregistered organizations. (In September 2001 Kazhegeldin was sentenced, in absentia, to ten years in prison for abuse of power and bribery.) As required by the constitution, the Balgimbayev cabinet resigned following the election, with Balgimbayev then being reconfirmed as prime minister on January 21.

On July 7, 1999, President Nazarbayev announced that elections for the Senate and the Assembly would be conducted in September and October, respectively. The recently formed presidential party, Fatherland (*Otan*), which in March had absorbed the Party of People's Unity (successor to the SNEK), emerged from the Assembly elections of October 10 and 24 holding a plurality of 23 seats, with the pro-government Civic Party of Kazakhstan claiming 13 and independents (many of them progovernment), 22. The opposition was led by the current Communist Party (*Kommunisticheskaya Partiya Kazakhstana*—KPK), which won only 3 seats in the expanded 77-seat body. As with the January presidential election, the Organization for Security and Cooperation in Europe (OSCE) refused to validate the results, citing campaign irregularities.

On October 12, 1999, Kasymzhomart TOKAYEV, theretofore the foreign minister, was formally nominated as prime minister by the president and confirmed by Parliament, replacing Balgimbayev, who had resigned on October 1 to return to his previous post as head of the state oil monopoly. Prime Minister Tokayev resigned on January 28, 2002, citing the need for "new ideas" in government. He was succeeded by Imangali TASMAGAMBETOV, previously a deputy prime minister.

Expressing concerns about a lack of democratic progress, a number of government officials participated in the launching of the moderate Democratic Choice of Kazakhstan (*Demokraticheskii Vybor Kazakhstana*—DVK) movement in November 2001, provoking their dismissal. In the following year two prominent DVK founders—Galymzhan ZHAKIYANOV, who had been fired as governor of the northern Pavlodar region, and Mukhtar ABLYAZOV, a former minister of economy and trade—were sentenced to jail terms for having abused their former offices. (Ablyazov received a presidential pardon in April 2003 and retired from politics; Zhakiyanov was not paroled until January 2006.)

Prime Minister Tasmagambetov resigned on June 11, 2003, accusing the lower house of "crude violations of voting procedure" during a May 19 confidence vote that his government had won. Tasmagambetov was succeeded on June 13by Daniyal AKHMETOV, former governor of the Pavlodar region.

Meanwhile, under the terms of a restrictive political party law that had come into force in July 2002, several opposition parties had been officially "liquidated." Others had decided not to seek reregistration, while the Ministry of Justice had used the law's technical provisions to block the registration of new opposition groups. Only 12 parties were eligible to contest the September 19–October 3, 2004, Assembly election, in which the pro-presidential *Otan* won a commanding 42 of 77 seats. The only opposition seat was won by the Democratic Party of Kazakhstan "White Road" (*Ak Zhol*), a DVK splinter. *Otan* also dominated the Senate replenishment of August 19, 2005.

Of some two dozen prospective presidential candidates, five made it onto the ballot of December 4, 2005. President Nazarbayev won 91.1 percent of the vote, while the principal opposition candidate, former Assembly speaker Zharmakhan TUYAKBAI, collected only 6.6 percent. Having been sworn in for another term on January 11, 2006, Nazarbayev reappointed Prime Minister Akhmetov.

In 2006 the pro-presidential party *Otan*—later renamed *Nur Otan* (roughly, Light of the Fatherland)—increased its total of Assembly seats to 57 out of 77 by absorbing three allied parties.

On January 10, 2007, Deputy Prime Minister Karim MASIMOV was named prime minister and Akhmetov was appointed minister of defense. On June 20 President Nazarbayev dissolved the Assembly and called a snap election. At the August 18 voting the renamed *Nur Otan* won all 98 directly elected seats (with 88.4 percent of the vote) under a proportional representation system that had been instituted by constitutional amendment in May. No other party achieved the 7 percent threshold for representation. In Senate balloting on October 4, 2008, *Nur Otan* won all 16 indirectly elected seats.

Constitution and government. The constitution approved by referendum on August 30, 1995, was independent Kazakhstan's third in less than four years. It provided for a strong, popularly elected president with powers to appoint the prime minister (subject to parliamentary confirmation) and to dissolve the bicameral legislature. Parliament may remove the president, for treason or medical incapacity, by a three-fourths vote of a joint session.

The constitution guarantees private property and permits private ownership of land while retaining state control of water and other natural resources. It also provides for a Constitutional Council as the highest legal body, its members being appointed jointly by the chairs of the legislative houses and the president. The president may veto council decisions. A Supreme Court is the highest judicial body for criminal, civil, and other cases originating in the courts of general jurisdiction.

Kazakhstan encompasses a total of 16 "administrative-territorial units": 14 regions (*oblystar*), the capital, and Almaty, each governed by an elected council (*maslikhat*) and an executive body, the latter headed by a governor (*akim*) appointed by the president on the recommendation of the prime minister. Councils and executive bodies also function at lower administrative levels. The city of Baykonur (formerly Leninsk), which borders the Russian-run Baykonur space center, is under Russian administration.

Amendments adopted by parliament on May 18, 2007 and promulgated on May 21 limited future presidents—but not the current incumbent—to two terms in office. Beginning in 2012 the presidential term will be five years instead of seven. Other amendments, effective in 2007, increased the size of both houses of parliament—to 47 seats in the Senate, and to 107 in the Assembly, with 98 of those elected by proportional representation and the remainder appointed by the Assembly of the Peoples of Kazakhstan, an advisory body on ethnic matters that had been established by presidential decree in 1995.

Foreign relations. Kazakhstan became a sovereign member of the Commonwealth of Independent States (CIS) on December 21, 1991. By early 1992 it had established diplomatic relations with a number of foreign countries, including the United States. In March it was admitted to the United Nations, and it joined the IMF and World Bank in July. It also joined the Conference on (later Organization for) Security and Cooperation in Europe (CSCE/OSCE) and in May 1994 became a signatory of the NATO Partnership for Peace program. In January 1995 Kazakhstan signed a partnership and cooperation accord with the European Union, and the following December it joined the Organization of the Islamic Conference. It has also participated in the Economic Cooperation Organization. In 1996, Kazakhstan applied for membership in the World Trade Organization (WTO) and began to negotiate bilateral market access agreements with WTO members. Though Kazakhstan aimed to fulfill basic requirements for membership by the end of 2007, Kazakhstan's WTO membership had not been approved as of July 2008.

With Soviet nuclear weapons stationed inside Kazakhstan, disarmament became a leading foreign policy issue for the new republic. During a 1992 Washington visit, President Nazarbayev indicated that Kazakhstan was prepared to accede to the 1968 Nuclear Non-Proliferation Treaty (NPT) and agreed to sign a revised version of the Strategic Arms Reduction Treaty (START) initially concluded by U.S. president George H.W. Bush and Soviet president Mikhail Gorbachev in July 1991. Both actions were formalized during a visit by U.S. vice president Al Gore in December 1993. Thereafter, the United States provided technical and financial aid, including funds for dismantling nuclear weapons. On May 24, 1995, the Kazakh foreign ministry announced that all the country's nuclear weapons had been transferred to Russia or destroyed.

Regionally, the Caspian Sea has been a major focus of attention for Kazakhstan and the other littoral states, Russia, Azerbaijan, Turkmenistan, and Iran. Meeting in Moscow in July 1998, Nazarbayev and Russian president Boris Yeltsin signed the first of several bilateral agreements concerning Caspian Sea boundaries and development, thereby clearing the way for exploitation of underlying oil reserves. In 2001 Kazakhstan and Azerbaijan concluded a related agreement, which, like the Kazakh-Russian accords, was harshly attacked by another littoral state, Iran. In April 2002 and October 2007, the leaders of the littoral countries held inconclusive meetings in an effort to resolve their differences over Caspian rights. In June 2008, Turkmenistan and Azerbaijan settled a long-term land dispute, improving relations among the littoral states and increasing pressure, particularly on Iran and Russia, to resolve remaining issues that continue to impede the exploitation of the valuable energy reserves.

Economic integration has also been a major regional consideration. In January 1994 an economic union with Uzbekistan and, six days later, Kyrgyzstan was announced. In July the scope of the new Central Asian Economic Union was extended to include cooperation in defense, foreign policy, and social affairs. In March 1998 Tajikistan agreed to join the union, which four months later adopted the name Central Asian Economic Community. Subsequently renamed the Central Asian Cooperation Organization (CACO), it welcomed Russia as the fifth member in October 2004. A year later, the CACO agreed to merge into the Eurasian Economic Community (EAEC), which began in 1996 as a CIS Customs Union of Belarus, Kazakhstan, Kyrgyzstan, and Russia.

In April 1996 Kazakhstan, Kyrgyzstan, Russia, and Tajikistan undertook jointly with China to oppose separatist, terrorist, and Islamic fundamentalist activities in Central Asia. Beijing's main interest was to ensure the isolation of the Muslim Uygur (Uighur) minority in Xinjiang Uygur Autonomous Region, bordering Kazakhstan, but the rise of militant Islamic groups throughout Central Asia had become a major concern among the "Shanghai Five" states (so called from the site of their 1994 initial gathering).

With the continuing conflict in Afghanistan as a backdrop, the Shanghai Five defense ministers, meeting in Astana in March 2000, pledged their cooperation against terrorism. A month later, Nazarbayev joined the presidents of Kyrgyzstan, Tajikistan, and Uzbekistan in signing a mutual security agreement to combat terrorism, extremism, and other threats. In May 2001 Kazakhstan and the other members of the CIS Collective Security Treaty (Armenia, Belarus, Kyrgyzstan, Russia, and Tajikistan) authorized formation of a joint rapid reaction force, and in June 2001 the Shanghai Five plus Uzbekistan established the Shanghai Cooperation Organization. In April 2003 the six signatories of the CIS security treaty formed the Collective Security Treaty Organization.

The country's global profile was heightened by its support for the U.S.-led "war on terrorism" and the October 2001 invasion of Afghanistan, which elevated several Central Asian republics to the status of Washington's "newest strategic partners." Among other things, Kazakhstan granted overflight permission to U.S. planes, which were also permitted to use Kazakh airfields for refueling and emergency landings. In January 2009 Kazakhstan agreed to allow U.S. non-military cargo to traverse the country en route to Afghanistan to supply American troops there.

The depletion of the Aral Sea, as a result of river diversions executed by the Soviet Union in the 1960s, and concern over reclamation efforts led to regional cooperation between among the five Central Asian countries in May 2008.

In March 2009, another diplomatic effort among the Central Asian nations resulted in the implementation of a regional Nuclear Weapons Free Zone. In April, during a state visit by Iran's president, Mahmoud Ahmadinejad, whose nuclear program has prompted concern in the West and in much of the Middle East, President Nazarbayev offered a site in Kazakhstan for a global nuclear fuel repository.

Current issues. Beginning in 2005 President Nazarbayev made an annual bid for Kazakhstan to become the first Central Asian state to chair the OSCE. However, many member states opposed the bid due to Kazakhstan's poor record on human rights and its perceived lack of democratic reforms. Nevertheless, at the 2007 OSCE meeting in Spain, 56 member states voted unanimously to grant Kazakhstan the OSCE chair for 2010, the decision coming just three months after Kazakhstan's governing party won all 98 available seats in the Assembly. OSCE monitors subsequently concluded that despite alleged irregularities in 40 percent of the polling stations visited, the elections moved Kazakhstan forward "in its evolution toward a democratic country" and did not affect Kazakhstan's future chairmanship. Meanwhile, critics continued to assert that Nazarbayev had succeeded in making Kazakhstan a one-party state within a "cosmetically democratic" framework.

Attention in 2008 turned to the deepening global economic recession, the president announcing in October a $10 billion plan to stabilize the nation's financial sector. Further action in 2009 resulted in the nationalization of two failing banks and devaluation of the currency by 18 percent. In an address to the nation in March, Nazarbayev pledged to continue creating jobs and investing in the nation's infrastructure despite the severe economic downturn. On April 2, however, Prime Minister Masimov announced a 30-percent pay cut and 50-percent workforce reduction in the state's public holding company. Other public sector institutions, such as the state-owned airline and the oil and gas company KazMunaiGas, reduced their workforce by 15 percent. Meanwhile, the governing *Nur Otan* asked all parties to sign a memorandum of cooperation, waiving the right to protest during the crisis. The party unveiled its doctrine for the 2012 presidential election at a party congress held in Astana in May 2009. Four opposition parties and groups—the Communist Party of Kazakhsan (KPK), the National Social Democratic Party (NSDP), Free (*Azat*), and Forward! (*Alga!*)—refused to sign the memorandum and began holding talks on forming a democratic coalition.

POLITICAL PARTIES

In September 1991 the ruling Communist Party of Kazakhstan (KPK) renamed itself the Socialist Party of Kazakhstan (SPK) and adopted a platform of political pluralism and cautious economic reform. President Nazarbayev, the former KPK leader, withdrew from the SPK before his reelection in December 1991, and the party subsequently declined in importance. Nazarbayev was later associated with the Party of People's Unity of Kazakhstan (PPU), which was generally regarded as a "presidential" party prior to its 1999 merger with the newly established *Otan.*

The Kazakhstan Democratic Party "Citizen" (*Azamat*) was launched in April 1996 as an opposition movement aspiring to a government "of honest and competent people." *Azamat,* which did not register as a party until June 1999, was the first opposition grouping to feature eminent public figures in its leadership, including former government official and SPK chair Petr SVOIK. In February 1998 the current KPK, the SPK, *Azamat,* the nationalist *Azat* movement, and a number of other opposition groups formed a People's Front of Kazakhstan that suspended its activities ten months later, in the midst of the presidential campaign. By then, another movement, For Fair Elections, had been formed by *Azamat,* the KPK, and the Green Party (see *Tabiyghat,* below), among others. In mid-October a number of For Fair Elections leaders were arrested for participating in meetings of the unregistered movement, which ultimately led to their disqualification from presidential candidacy.

In July 1999 the KPK, the recently formed Republican People's Party of Kazakhstan (*Respublikanskaya Narodnaya Partiya Khazakhstana*—RNPK) of former prime minister Akezhan Kazhegeldin, and three public movements formed an opposition bloc, *Respublika,* to contest the October 1999 Assembly election on a platform that included abolition of the strong presidency and its replacement with a parliamentary system. Following the election, the KPK, RNPK, *Azamat,* Green Party, and various public associations formed an oppositionist Forum of Democratic Forces of Kazakhstan (*Forum Demokraticheskikh Sil Kazakhstana*—FDSK), which demanded that authorities invalidate the results for both parliamentary houses.

Launched in November 2001 as a movement, the Democratic Choice of Kazakhstan (DVK; see *Alga!,* below) brought together members of the opposition from a number of parties and movements—among them, the KPK, RNPK, and FDSK—and a number of government officials concerned over the slow pace of democratization. As a consequence of their involvement, the government officials were quickly dismissed. In another attempt to consolidate opposition forces, in December 2001 leaders of the RNPK, *Azamat,* and the newly established Kazakhstan People's Congress (*Narodnyi Kongress Kazakhstana*—NKK) announced that they were forming a United Democratic Party (UDP), but the UDP failed to cohere and was never registered.

Generating further criticism for its autocratic approach in dealing with political opponents, the government adopted a new Law of Political Parties in June 2002 that required a party to have 50,000 members, representing all regions, to obtain legal standing (the previous threshold had been 3,000 members). The new legislation also prohibited parties based on religion, ethnicity, or gender, and authorized the government to abolish any that did not register within two months of formation, failed to contest two consecutive elections, or failed to obtain 3 percent of the vote in an election. In response to the legislation, a number of opposition formations, including *Azamat,* the NKK, and the RNPK, refused to reregister and were therefore "compulsorily liquidated." Several others were denied registration, ostensibly for failing to meet technical provisions of the new law. They included the National Democratic Party "People's Wisdom" (*Yel Dana*), despite changing its name from the Democratic Party of Women of Kyrgyzstan and opening its membership to men.

A total of 12 parties were registered in time to contest the September–October 2004 legislative election, but only 4 parties met the 7 percent threshold needed to qualify for any of ten proportional seats. Following the election, the KPK, DVK, and the Democratic Party of Kazakhstan "White Road" (*Ak Zhol*) announced formation of an opposition Coordinating Council of Democratic Forces. Subsequently, in March 2005, most of the opposition parties established a Bloc of Democratic Forces "For Fair Kazakhstan" under former Assembly speaker and *Otan* member Zharmakhan Tuyakbai, who was designated as the bloc's 2006 presidential contender.

In September 2005 *Otan, Asar,* the Agrarian Party (APK), the Civic Party (GPK), the Democratic Party of Kazakhstan (see NSDP, below), and *Rukhaniyat* formed the pro-presidential People's Coalition of Kazakhstan in support of President Nazarbayev's reelection. Headed by Dariga Nazarbayeva of *Asar,* the coalition announced formation of a Democratic Union on December 6, 2005, two days after Nazarbayev's reelection. In the following year *Asar,* the APK, and the GPK merged into *Otan,* which in December 2006 adopted the new name *Nur Otan.* Further consolidations took place before the August 2007 Assembly election, in which *Nur Otan* took every seat in the lower house election. Seven of the eight registered parties contested the election but did not pursue it in court. Since the 2007 election, *Nur Otan* has dominated Kazakhstan's government at all levels.

Presidential Party:

People's Democratic Party "Light of the Fatherland" (*Narodno Demokraticheskaya Partiya "Nur Otan"*). On January 10, 1999, former prime minister Sergei Tereshchenko, head of the reelection campaign for President Nazarbayev, announced that he planned to form the Republican Political Party "Fatherland" (*Otan*), which would adhere to "democratic and parliamentarian principles." *Otan* was officially launched at a founding congress on March 1, with Tereshchenko being named acting chair when Nazarbayev declined the leadership on constitutional grounds. Merging into *Otan* were the Party of People's Unity of Kazakhstan (PPU), the Kazakhstan Liberal Movement, the Democratic Party of Kazakhstan, and the For Kazakhstan–2030 Movement.

Beginning in February 1993 as a sociopolitical movement called the Union of People's Unity or the People's Union of Kazakhstan Unity (*Soyuz Narodnoye Edinstvo Kazakhstana*—SNEK), the PPU later emerged as a pro-government political party. With its leadership composed primarily of officials who had been associated with the Communist Party of Kazakhstan, it inherited much of the organization of the former ruling party. It advocated gradual economic reform and political pluralism. It also sought to serve as a bridge between the country's ethnic groups while opposing dual citizenship and language rights for ethnic Russians. Registered for the March 1994 legislative balloting, the PPU won a small plurality, amid claims of fraud. It remained the dominant party as the result of legislative balloting in 1995 and 1996 and supported Nazarbayev's reelection in 1999.

Otan emerged from the 1999 lower house election as the plurality party, with 23 seats. In September 2002 the People's Cooperative Party of Kazakhstan, which had been formed in 1994 as a pro-Nazarbayev formation with a predominantly rural base, merged with *Otan;* it had won 1 Assembly seat in 1999. The Republican Political Labor Party, which had been established in 1995, also merged with *Otan* in 2002.

At the 2004 Assembly election *Otan* won a majority, achieving 61 percent of the party list vote and taking 42 of the 77 seats. Shortly thereafter, however, the speaker of the Assembly, Zharmakhan Tuyakbai, described the election as a "disgraceful farce" in which voters' rights were violated. He then resigned from *Otan* and joined the opposition.

In July 2006 *Otan* and the Republican Party "All Together" (*Asar*) agreed to merge. The *Asar* party had been established in September 2003 by the president's eldest daughter, Dariga NAZARBAYEVA, a prominent figure in the country's mass media industry. *Asar* had reportedly grown to be Kazakhstan's second-largest party (after *Otan*) by the time of the September–October 2004 Assembly election, in which it won four seats.

Meeting in November 2006, congresses of both the Agrarian Party of Kazakhstan—APK (*Qazaqstan Agrarlyk Partiyasi*) and the Civic Party of Kazakhstan (*Grazhdanskaya Partiya Kazakhstana*—GPK/ *Qazaqstan Azamattlyk Partiyasi*) also agreed to merge into *Otan.* The APK, founded in 1999 and pledging support for farmers and private land ownership, had won 3 seats in the 1999 Assembly election. In 2004 it and the GPK formed the Bloc of the Agrarian and Civic Parties "Agrarian Industrial Workers Union" (AIWU) to contest the Assembly election, in which the AIWU won 11 seats, second to *Otan.* The progovernment GPK had been formed in 1998 at the initiative of entrepreneurs in mining and heavy industry. In 1999 it had won 13 Assembly seats.

At an extraordinary congress held in late December 2006, *Otan,* which had raised its Assembly representation to 57 seats by absorbing *Asar,* the APK, and the GPK, changed its name to *Nur Otan.* On July 4, 2007, at a party congress in Astana, President Nazarbayev assumed the chairmanship, citing the constitutional amendments passed two months earlier. In the August 2007 snap Assembly election, the party claimed all 98 seats.

Dariga Nazarbayeva who had been appointed deputy chair of *Nur Otan* after its merger with *Asar*, was removed from her position in 2007. Meanwhile, her husband, Rakhat ALIYEV, was charged with corruption and dismissed as deputy prime minister. Observers then speculated that Nazarbayev's second daughter, Dinara, and her husband, Timur KULIBAEV would rise to power. In late 2007, however, the president dismissed Kulibaev without explanation as deputy head of a state company, signaling what appeared to be a fall from favor. In early 2008, Aliyev, in exile in Austria, was tried in absentia for kidnapping, conspiring to overthrow the government, and a host of other charges. He was sentenced to two 20-year terms in prison, but Austria refused to extradite him.

Despite its internal problems, *Nur Otan* continued to promote itself as the party that fostered stability and economic growth.

Leaders: Nursultan Abishevich NAZARBAYEV (Chair and President of the Republic), Darkhan KALETAYEV (First Deputy Chair).

Other Registered Parties:

Democratic Party of Kazakhstan "White Road" (*Qazaqstan Demokratiyalyk Partiyasi "Ak Zhol"*). *Ak Zhol,* whose English-language variants include "Bright Path" and "Light Way," was formed in March 2002 by several defectors from the recently organized opposition movement Democratic Choice (see *Alga!*, below). Although *Ak Zhol* also took a position in moderate opposition to the government, its critics asserted that it was the product of a government effort to establish an officially approved opposition party. One of the founders, Oraz ZHANDOSOV, had previously served as deputy prime minister, and in January 2003 he was appointed as a presidential aide. Another founder, former Security Council secretary and ambassador to Russia Altynbek SARSENBAYEV, was named minister of communications in July 2004; he stepped aside as the September election approached and then resigned on September 20, in the course of a ministerial reorganization that, in effect, eliminated his position. A third founder, Assembly member Bulat ABILOV, was convicted of slandering a fellow MP in July 2004 and given a suspended sentence, which precluded his running for reelection.

At the September–October 2004 balloting *Ak Zhol* finished second to *Otan* in terms of the party list vote, but its 12 percent share was only good enough for a single Assembly seat—the only seat won by the opposition. Alikhan Baimenov, who had headed the *Ak Zhol* party list, immediately stated that he would not take up the seat as a protest against the conduct of the "illegitimate" election.

In early 2005 *Ak Zhol* split over policy differences and direction. As a consequence, a faction called the "True *Ak Zhol"* (see Free, below) formed in late April. In the December 2005 presidential election Baimenov finished third, with only 1.6 percent of the vote. In October 2006, however, following a meeting with President Nazarbayev, Baimenov announced that he would assume his Assembly seat in the interest of building a political consensus.

In December 2006 *Ak Zhol* and the Justice Party (*Adilet*) announced a cooperation agreement, and in July 2007 the two merged under the *Ak Zhol* banner. *Adilet* had begun as the Democratic Party of Kazakhstan (DPK), which was registered in June 2004. Led by Maksut NARIKBAYEV, long a champion of legal reform and head of the "For Legal Kazakhstan" movement, the centrist party won one constituency seat in the 2004 Assembly election but less than 1 percent of the party list vote. *Ak Zhol* won 3 percent of the vote in the 2007 elections. The party claimed about 150,000 members prior to the election, but in 2008 acknowledged a decrease in its membership. The party advocates maintaining good relations with *Nur Otan* in order to achieve change; toward that end, it signaled its intention to sign *Nur Otan*'s March 2009 memorandum of cooperation between the parties.

Leader: Alikhan BAIMENOV (Chair).

Free (*Azat*). The founding congress of the Democratic Party of Kazakhstan "True White Road" (*Qazaqstan Demokratiyalyk Partiyasi "Naghyz Ak Zhol,"* later renamed *Azat*) was held in April 2005, following its split with the leadership of the *Ak Zhol*. It was headed by three *Ak Zhol* cochairs—Abilov, Sarsenbayev, and Zhandosov. Unlike the *Ak Zhol,* the *Naghyz Ak Zhol* gave its support to For Fair Kazakhstan's Zharmakhan Tuyakbai in the 2005 presidential race (see NSDP, below).

On February 13, 2006, Sarsenbayev, his driver, and a bodyguard were found murdered. At the end of August a former national security agent received a death sentence (commuted to life in prison) for planning the attack, while nine other defendants, all but one a security agent, were sentenced to between three years and life in prison.

In December 2006 founder Bulat Abilov went on trial for fraud involving an investment fund. In July he had been convicted of assaulting a police officer and given a three-year suspended sentence. The political opposition claimed that the charges were politically motivated.

In June 2007, *Naghyz Ak Zhol* announced it would merge with the NSDP. Within a week, however, parliament barred political parties from forming electoral blocs. Both parties failed to obtain seats in the August Assembly election. On February 29, 2008, *Naghyz Ak Zhol* voted to rename itself *Azat,* which means "free," in order to better distinguish itself from *Ak Zhol* (though its name duplicates that of an earlier nationalist group). *Azat* claimed to be the true opposition party and sought to exert political pressures on the government from its position outside Parliament.

The party called for nationwide demonstrations in February 2009, demanding the government's resignation over its handling of the financial crisis. However, officials refused to permit any public rally, except for one gathering in a small square in Almaty.

Another criminal case against Abilov, along with leaders of *Alga!* and the Communist Party, resumed in a district court in Almaty in March 2009. The three opposition figures were accused of aiding two murder suspects to gain asylum abroad. In April, leaders of Azat, NSDP, *Alga!* and the KPK met to explore the formation of what Abilov termed "an efficient political alliance." Abilov declared his willingness to lead such a coalition as a presidential candidate in 2012.

Leader: Bulat ABILOV (Chair).

Communist Party of Kazakhstan (*Kommunisticheskaya Partiya Kazakhstana*—KPK/*Qazaqstan Kommunistik Partiyasi*). A faction of the old ruling KPK opposed its conversion into the Socialist Party of Kazakhstan (*Sotsialisticheskaya Partiya Kazakhstana*—SPK) in September 1991 and eventually achieved legal registration as the new KPK in February 1994. The party favored close economic ties with other ex-Soviet republics, restoration of state ownership, welfare, and equality of ethnic groups. In 1996, the KPK eliminated references in its manifesto to "the struggle for proletarian dictatorship and the reinstatement of the USSR."

Party leader Serikbolsyn Abdildin finished second, with 11.7 percent of the vote, in the 1999 presidential election. The KPK won only three Assembly seats the following October, when it accused the pro-government Civic Party and the Agrarian Party, in particular, of vote manipulation.

In early 2004 differences over funding sources led supporters of Vladislav Kosarev to leave the KPK and establish the Communist People's Party (KNPK, below). In July the KPK and the newly registered DVK party (see *Alga!*, below) agreed to form an electoral bloc, "Democratic Choice of Kazakhstan," which won only 3.4 percent of the party list vote and no seats in the September Assembly election. The KPK boycotted the August 2007 Assembly election, protesting the institution of party-list balloting, Abdildin calling the election "a farce."

The KPK and *Alga!* partnered again in 2009 to form a radical bloc called Democracy. The two parties also held talks on creating a broader opposition coalition with the NSDP and Azat. The KPK, NSDP, and Azat refused to sign the memorandum on interparty consolidation initiated by *Nur Otan* in March.

Leader: Serikbolsyn ABDILDIN (First Secretary).

Communist People's Party of Kazakhstan (*Kommunisticheskaya Narodnaya Partiya Kazakhstana*—KNPK/*Qazaqstan Kommunistyk Khalyk Partiyasy*). The KNPK was registered in June 2004 by dissident KPK members who accused Serikbolsyn Abdildin of accepting suspect funds. The KNPK won 2 percent of the party list and no seats in the 2004 Assembly election. Its 2005 presidential candidate, maverick parliamentary deputy Yerasyl ABYLKASYMOV, won only 0.3 percent of the vote. In August 2007 the KNPK won only 1.3 percent of the Assembly vote. The KNPK holds a Marxist-Leninist platform that has been modified for Kazakhstan's current economic realities.

Leader: Vladislav KOSAREV (First Secretary).

National Social Democratic Party (NSDP). Founded in September 2006 by former speaker of the Assembly and 2005 presidential candidate Zharmakhan Tuyakbai and registered in January 2007, the NSDP has been described by its leader as "a party of principled opposition to the current political course of the country's leadership." As an extension of the For Fair Kazakhstan movement, the party has as its primary goal the "country's fundamental political modernization and democratic state building."

In June 2007 the NSDP announced its plan to merge with *Naghyz Ak Zhol*, though the merger was barred by parliament. In the August 2007 Assembly election, the NSDP finished second, but its 4.5 percent vote share was below the 7 percent threshold for seats.

At a forum of the democratic opposition in April 2009, attended by the NSDP, Azat, the KPK, and *Alga!*, Tuyakbai called on the parties to organize a coalition to lead the nation out of its economic and political crisis.

Leader: Zharmakhan TUYAKBAI (Chair).

Party of Kazakhstan's Patriots (PKP). Established in August 2000 by Gani Kasymov, an Assembly deputy and 1999 independent candidate for president, the PKP reregistered in 2003. In April 2004 the Officers' Union of Kazakhstan, an association of war veterans, joined the party, which was unsuccessful in the 2004 Assembly election, winning under 1 percent of the party list vote. In August 2007 the PKP won 0.8 percent of the vote.

Although the PKP supported President Nazarbayev's reelection in December 2005, it has differed with the government on some issues. Kasymov, now a senator, has been outspoken on environmental and human rights issues. In January 2009, in comments critical of the proposed amendments on mass media regulation, he was quoted as saying, "We have reached a point where we have no opposition parties in the country, do we want to destroy newspapers too?"

Leader: Gani KASYMOV (Chair).

Social Democratic Party "Village" (*Aul*). *Aul* was first registered in March 2000 by parliamentary deputy Gani Kaliyev in support of rural dwellers and agro-industry. The party was reregistered in April 2003 but won under 2 percent of the party list vote and no Assembly seats in the 2004 election. It did, however, win a Senate seat in 2005. In August 2007 it captured 1.5 percent of the national vote. In 2009, the party remained active in promoting legislation on rural and agricultural issues.

Leader: Gani KALIYEV (Chair).

Spirituality (*Rukhaniyat*). *Rukhaniyat* was registered in October 2003 under the leadership of writer Altynshash Dzhaganova, head of Kazakhstan's Migration and Demographics Agency. In 1995 she had founded the Revival of Kazakhstan Party, which the Ministry of Justice refused to register in April 2003. As a result, Dzhaganova organized *Rukhaniyat* to advance a socially oriented program based on spiritual revival. The party, largely supportive of President Nazarbayev, won less than 1 percent of the party list vote in 2004 and finished last in August 2007, with under 0.4 percent.

Leader: Altynshash DZHAGANOVA (JAGANOVA).

Unregistered Parties:

Homeland (*Atameken*). With support from the National Union of Entrepreneurs and Employers, *Atameken* held its founding congress in October 2006 and applied for registration in December. Generally supportive of President Nazarbayev, its leaders described the organization as a center-right, market-oriented party of the middle class. The party has been crippled by infighting. Its chair, Yerjan Dosmuhamedov, has been denounced by the party and lives abroad.

Leader: Yerjan DOSMUHAMEDOV (Chair).

Forward! (*Alga!*). *Alga!* is the successor to the People's Party "Democratic Choice of Kazakhstan" (*Demokraticheskii Vybor Kazakhstana*—DVK/*Qazaqstannyn Demokratiyalyk Tandau*), which was deregistered in January 2005.

The DVK was considered more moderate than the Forum of Democratic Forces (FDSK) when it was launched as a movement in November 2001 by a number of government officials, including Minister of Labor Alikhan Baimenov, who were promptly dismissed. In March 2002 Baimenov and other DVK founders, including former deputy prime minister Oraz Zhandosov, departed to form *Ak Zhol.*

Two prominent DVK founders—Galymzhan Zhakiyanov, who had been dismissed as governor of the northern Pavlodar region, and Mukhtar Ablyazov, another former minister—were convicted in 2002 on charges of abuse of power. Critics of the government charged that the trials were politically motivated. Ablyazov was granted a presidential pardon in April 2003 and retired from politics, but Zhakiyanov, who had been sentenced to serve a seven-year prison term, remained incarcerated until January 2006.

After repeated attempts to register as a nonprofit organization, the DVK was ultimately registered as a political party in May 2004. In July it joined the KPK in forming the KPK-DVK electoral bloc, the Opposition People's Union, which was unsuccessful in the subsequent Assembly election.

In January 2005 an Almaty court ordered the DVK dissolved for promoting civil disobedience. Party leaders planned to appeal to a higher court but ultimately sought to form a successor party, Forward, DVK! (*Alga, DVK!*), although "DVK" was dropped from the name by the July 2005 founding congress. Since then, *Alga!* has repeatedly had its registration application denied by the Ministry of Justice, but its chapters and coordinating committee remain active. In 2009 the group was again in coalition with the KPK and participating in discussions to join an opposition bloc with *Azat* and the NSDP.

Leaders: Asylbek KOZHAKHMETOV (Founder), Vladimir KOZLOV (Chair, Coordinating Committee).

Tabiyghat Party. The "green" *Tabiyghat* Party held its constituent congress in March 2006 under the leadership of environmental advocate Mels Yeleusizov. *Tabiyghat* (Nature) had been established as a nongovernmental organization in the early 1990s but has frequently been associated with opposition causes, particularly through the Party of Social Justice and Ecological Revival *"Tabiyghat"* and then the Green Party. Yeleusizov, who was disqualified as a 1999 presidential candidate because he had been convicted of participating in an unauthorized For Fair Elections meeting, ran in 2005 as an independent but won only 0.3 percent of the vote.

Leader: Mels YELEUSIZOV.

Banned Organizations:

In October 2004 the Supreme Court labeled the following as terrorist organizations and banned them: **al-Qaida; the Kurdistan Worker's Party;** the **Islamic Movement of Uzbekistan;** and the **Islamic Party of East Turkestan,** based in China's Xinjiang Uygur Autonomous Region. The latter two organizations are no longer in operation as of 2008. Another group, the **Hizb ut-Tahrir,** which has sought to establish an Islamic state in the region but has not been directly linked to terrorist activities, was banned in March 2005; a number of its alleged members have been prosecuted by Kazakhstan in recent years. The **Jamaat (Community) of Mujahedins** was added to the list of organizations banned for terrorist activities by the Kazakh Prosecutor-General's Office in October 2006, after extremist religious literature and ammunition connected to the group were reportedly found in the nation's capital.

LEGISLATURE

The 1995 constitution provides for a bicameral **Parliament,** which replaced the unicameral Supreme Council (*Kenges*).

Senate (*Senat*). The Senate has 47 members, increased from 39 following constitutional amendments of 2007. Of these, 15 are appointed by the president and 32 indirectly elected by officials representing the country's regions, Astana, and Almaty. Constitutional amendments passed in 1998 increased senatorial terms from four years to six, with half the elected seats renewable every three years. Members of the progovernment *Nur Otan* constitute the largest party bloc. In the replenishment on August 19, 2005, *Nur Otan* won 10 of the 16 seats. The other 6 were allocated as follows: Independents, 3; Civic Party of Kazakhstan (GPK),1; Social Democratic Party "Village," 1; and Republican Party "All Together" (*Asar*), 1;. The GPK and *Asar* subsequently merged with *Nur Otan.*

In balloting on October 4, 2008, for half of the indirectly elected seats, *Nur Otan* won all 16 seats.

Chair: Kasymzhomart TOKAYEV.

Assembly (*Majilis*). The Assembly has 107 members, increased from 77 according to constitutional amendments promulgated in May 2007. Constitutional changes approved in 1998, effective from the 1999 election, increased Assembly membership from 67 to 77 by adding 10 proportional seats filled from among those parties receiving at least 7 percent of the party list vote. At the same time, the term of office was raised from four to five years. Successful candidates had to win a majority of the votes cast in their districts, which often necessitated runoffs. The constitutional amendments of 2007 eliminated district seats. In the snap election of August 18, 2007, *Nur Otan* won all 98 directly elective seats. The other 9 members were indirectly elected on August 15-18 by the 350-member advisory Assembly of the Peoples of Kazakhstan.

Chair: Ural MUKHAMEDZHANOV.

CABINET

[as of June 1, 2009]

Prime Minister	Karim Masimov
First Deputy Prime Minister	Umirzak Shukeyev
Deputy Prime Minister	Yerbol Orynbayev
Deputy Prime Minister	Serik Akhmetov
Ministers	
Agriculture	Akylbek Kurishbayev
Culture and Information	Kul-Muhammed
Defense	Daniyal Akhmetov
Economy and Budget Planning	Bakhyt Sultanov
Education and Science	Zhanseit Tuymebayev
Emergency Situations	Vladimir Bozhko
Energy and Mineral Resources	Sauat Mynbayev
Environmental Protection	Nurgali Ashimov
Finance and State Revenues	Bolat Zhamishev
Foreign Affairs	Marat Tazhin
Industry and Trade	Aset Isekeshev
Internal Affairs	Serik Baymaganbetov
Justice	Rashid Tusupbekov
Labor and Social Welfare	Gulshara Abdykalikova [f]
Public Health	Zhaksylyk Doskaliyev
Tourism and Sports	Temirkhan Dosmukhanbetov
Transport and Communications	Abelgazy Kysainov

[f] = female

COMMUNICATIONS

Although the constitution prohibits censorship, most media outlets are directly or indirectly controlled by presidential family members or loyalists; President Nazarbayev's family controls the powerful Khabar Agency, the country's leading media company., Opposition journalists can be targeted under libel and other criminal statutes for such offenses as insulting the honor of the president, undermining national security, encouraging violence, or inciting ethnic or religious hatred. July 2006 amendments to the existing media law prohibit journalists from working in their profession for three years if the authorities shut down their publication or broadcast facility, restrict the reuse of a closed facility's name, and require media outlets to reregister if they change their circulation, address, or editor.

In its campaign for the OSCE chairmanship, Kazakhstan pledged to reform its laws governing media. The legislature approved some amendments to the nation's media law in January 2009, but an OSCE official noted that Kazakhstan's media regulation "still fails to meet several international standards." The nation's media market remained monopolistic, and confiscation and closure remained threats to opposition press. Journalists commonly faced legal retribution for publishing classified information or criticizing officials. One legislator won a judgment of $200,000 in a libel suit against the editor of *Taszhargan*, an opposition paper. When the editor refused to pay, he was jailed for five days. In April 2009 the Assembly took up legislation on Internet regulation.

Press. In 1999 the government announced that it would stop funding of most official newspapers, exceptions being *Kazakhstanskaya Pravda* and *Yegemen Kazakhstan.* Nevertheless, many newspapers continue to receive government stipends. The following are dailies published in Almaty in Russian, unless otherwise noted: *Karavan* (250,000), Khabar weekly; *Vremya* (Time, 125,000), weekly; *Novoye Pokoleniye* (New Generation, 50,000), Khabar weekly; *Kazakhstanskaya Pravda* (Kazakhstan Truth, 35,000), government organ; *Yegemen Kazakhstan* (Sovereign Kazakhstan, 30,000), government organ, in Kazakh; *Express K* (20,000); *Delovaya Nedelya* (Business Week, 16,000), weekly; *Uygur Avazi* (Voice of Uygur, 10,000), twice-weekly, government organ, in Uygur. *Karavan* may be the most widely circulated newspaper in Central Asia.

An opposition weekly, *Respublika,* was founded in 2000 and by 2002 reportedly had a circulation of 18,000, despite having been subjected to a number of formal actions and unofficial intimidation. In an effort to circumvent closure, the paper has appeared under various other names. Other opposition papers include *Azat* and *Versiya. Aina Plyus* was shut down in 2006.

News agencies. The former domestic facility, the Kazakh Telegraph Agency, was abolished in September 1997. The Kazakh Information Agency (Kazinform) currently offers government information. The Russian agency Interfax is among the foreign services offering news from Kazakhstan.

Broadcasting and computing. The official Kazakh Radio and Kazakh Television broadcast primarily in Kazakh and Russian. Over 100 additional television and several dozen radio stations also broadcast.

As of 2008 there were 110 Internet users per 1,000 inhabitants.

INTERGOVERNMENTAL REPRESENTATION

Ambassador to the U.S.: Erlan IDRISSOV.

U.S. Ambassador to Kazakhstan: Richard E. HOAGLAND.

Permanent Representative to the UN: Byrganym AITIMOVA.

IGO Memberships (Non-UN): ADB, CIS, EBRD, ECO, IDB, Interpol, IOM, OIC, OSCE, WCO.

KENYA

Republic of Kenya
Jamhuri ya Kenya

Political Status: Independent member of the Commonwealth since December 12, 1963; republic established in 1964; de facto one-party system, established in 1969, recognized as de jure by constitutional amendment on June 9, 1982; multiparty system approved by constitutional amendment on December 20, 1991.

Area: 224,960 sq. mi. (582,646 sq. km.).

Population: 28,686,607 (1999C); 35,052,000 (2008E).

Major Urban Centers (2005E): NAIROBI (urban area, 2,725,000); Mombasa (798,000).

Official Language: English (Kiswahili is the national language).

Monetary Unit: Kenya Shilling (principal rate December 1, 2009: 74.85 shillings = $1US).

President: Emilio Mwai KIBAKI (Party of National Unity) elected by popular vote on December 27, 2002, and inaugurated on December 30, 2002, for a five-year term, succeeding Daniel Teroitich arap MOI (Kenya African National Union), who had served as president since 1978; reelected on December 27, 2007, and sworn in for a second five-year term on December 30, 2007.

Vice President: Stephen Kalonzo MUSYOKA (Orange Democratic Movement–Kenya); appointed by the president on January 8, 2008, to succeed Arthur Moody AWORI (National Rainbow Coalition of Kenya), who had served as vice president since 2003.

Prime Minister: Raila Amolo ODINGA (Orange Democratic Movement) appointed by the president on April 13, 2008, and sworn in on April 17.

THE COUNTRY

An equatorial country on the African east coast, Kenya has long been celebrated for its wildlife and such scenic attractions as the Rift Valley.

The northern part of the country is virtually waterless, and 85 percent of the population and most economic enterprises are concentrated in the southern highlands bordering on Tanzania and Lake Victoria. The African population, mainly engaged in agriculture and stock-raising, embraces four main ethnic groups: Bantu (Kikuyu, Kamba, Luhya), Nilotic (Luo), Nilo-Hamitic (Masai), and Hamitic (Somali). Non-African minorities include Europeans, Asians (mainly Indians and Pakistanis), and Arabs. In addition to Kiswahili and English, the most important languages are Kikuyu, Luo, and Luhya. A majority of the population is nominally Christian (approximately 40 percent is Protestant, and 30 percent is Catholic), but approximately 35 percent adheres to traditional religious beliefs; there is also a growing Muslim minority currently comprising 6 to 10 percent of the population.

Although the services sector now accounts for approximately 65 percent of Kenya's GDP, Kenya's economy continues to depend heavily on agriculture. Agricultural production declined prior to 2003 and now accounts for less than 26 percent of the GDP (compared to 33.9 percent in 1984). This trend is particularly troubling because the vast majority of Kenyans rely on subsistence farming. (Women produce more than men in the sector.) The main cash crops are tea, coffee, sisal, pyrethrum, and sugar. The coffee and tea sectors, once export leaders, are in steady decline; coffee has gone from being the first to the fourth major source of foreign exchange earnings since the late 1980s. Coffee production has fallen steadily due to high production costs, inefficient methods of cultivation, and corruption in the government-controlled cooperatives. In 2005 an acute drought struck much of the northern and eastern parts of Kenya and agricultural production declined in these areas. Approximately 2.5 million people (10 percent of the population) faced the risk of starvation, and the crisis required an international relief effort to contain.

The manufacturing sector has been growing and now represents about 20 percent of GDP; important industries include food processing, the production of textiles and clothing, and oil refining (almost entirely of imported crude). Tourism represents about 13 percent of GDP and is the second largest source of foreign exchange. In 2005 the Kenyan government reported that tourism rose nearly 16 percent above 2004 levels, an indication that the industry had recovered from the adverse effects of the 2002 terrorist attacks in Mombasa, which led to a 1.5 percent decline in the country's GDP. These gains, coupled with general improvements in the tertiary sector, fueled relatively steady growth until the outbreak of violence following the disputed 2007 presidential election when tourism declined over 60 percent. Kenya's GDP expanded steadily from 4.9 percent in 2004 to 5.8 percent in 2005 and 6.1 percent in 2006; it peaked at 7 percent in 2007. In the aftermath of the post-election unrest and the turmoil in the world economy in the last quarter of 2008, growth fell to 2.0 percent. Inflation remained high over this period, with rates averaging over 10.5 percent annually since 2003; the rate surged to 14.5 percent in 2006. Inflation fell to 9.8 percent in 2007 despite expansion of public sector spending during the election year. In 2008 prices skyrocketed again in the face of worldwide increases in energy and food prices, with inflation averaging over 13 percent.

Although Kenya's economy was long considered one of the continent's healthiest, it has been subject since the mid-1980s to numerous pressures, including fluctuating fuel and commodity prices, an external debt of about $5 billion, high rates of natural population increase (currently estimated at 2.56 percent annually), escalating inflation, and large foreign exchange losses attributed to irregular banking activity. Kenya is still considered the banking, communications, and business center of East Africa, but the banking sector and the country's transportation infrastructure suffered greatly from the corruption and neglect under the Moi regime. Health and educational services also deteriorated significantly, while unemployment rose steadily. (The government's official estimate placed unemployment at 15 percent, while others estimate the rate at close to 40 percent.) Kenya has one of the highest infant mortality rates in the world, and more than half the population lives on less than $1 a day. Per capita annual income was $1,835 in 2006.

Kenya's relations with foreign financial donors were strained in the 1990s. Unsatisfied with the Moi regime's response to their economic conditions for aid (austerity) and political prescriptions (instituting party pluralism and eradicating corruption), donors suspended aid payments in November 1991. The World Bank released some $350 million in frozen aid funds in April 1993, but only after a tumultuous period when President Moi initially agreed to a strict economic liberalization program then reneged before finally acquiescing. Relations with both the International Monetary Fund (IMF) and the World Bank remained uncertain during the remainder of the decade.

The IMF greeted the December 2002 election of a new government with the hope that it might lift a 2001 loan freeze if the new government made progress in addressing the deficit, public sector corruption, and privatization of state enterprises. But the new government's elimination of fees for public schools, its increase in salaries and perks for senior civil servants, and pay raises for members of the National Assembly increased the public deficit. (The overall balance of tax revenue and public spending fell from 0.1 percent in 1995 to –2.9 percent in 2006.) By November 2003 the IMF approved a $277 million loan despite the government's difficulty in controlling deficits and its delays in privatizing state-run enterprises. In November 2004 the World Bank agreed to assist the government in an audit of bank projects in which corruption was suspected. The Goldenberg and Anglo-Leasing scandals and the government's heavy-handed treatment of the press (see Political background and Communications, below) in 2006 caused the IMF and the World Bank to delay indefinitely the disbursement of a three-year, $327 million loan. In March 2007 the World Bank's progress report for Kenya was favorable, which restarted the flow of loans and grants under the Bank's 2004–2007 Country Assistance Strategy, but the report still emphasized the need for strong anticorruption measures to be integrated into the program. The IMF adjusted the total amount of the 2003 loans to $237 million in 2007 and released the final installment of $59 million in November 2007. By 2009 the World Bank had over $1 billion invested in national and regional development projects in Kenya. The IMF extended $209 million in May 2009 to ease the shock to the Kenyan economy brought on by high fuel, food, and fertilizer prices and the decline in demand for Kenyan exports during the global economic contraction.

Kenya suffered one of the worst droughts in decades when the seasonal rains failed to appear in late 2005 or in early 2006. In the eastern and northern regions of the country up to 80 percent of the livestock died, and approximately 3 million people faced starvation. In October 2006 the return of seasonal rains brought severe flooding and displaced tens of thousands of Kenyans and Somali refugees in the northern and eastern area of the country. Drought conditions prevailed again in 2009 increasing the chances that famine may grip parts of East Africa in 2010.

GOVERNMENT AND POLITICS

Political background. Kenya came under British control in the late 19th century and was organized in 1920 as a colony (inland) and a protectorate (along the coast). Political development after World War II was impeded by the Mau Mau uprising of 1952–1956, which was inspired primarily by Kikuyu resentment that Europeans controlled much of the country's best land. Further difficulties arose in the early 1960s because of tribal and political rivalries, which delayed agreement on a constitution and postponed the date of formal independence within the Commonwealth until December 12, 1963. An election held in May 1963 had already established the predominant position of the Kenya African National Union (KANU), led by Jomo KENYATTA of the Kikuyu tribe, who had previously been imprisoned and exiled on suspicion of leading the Mau Mau insurgency. Kenyatta accordingly became the country's first prime minister and subsequently, upon the adoption of a republican form of government on December 12, 1964, its first president. The principal opposition party, the Kenya African Democratic Union (KADU), dissolved itself and merged with KANU in 1964. However, a new opposition party, the Kenya People's Union (KPU), emerged in 1966 under the leadership of the leftist Jaramogi Oginga Ajuma ODINGA, whose forced resignation as vice president in April 1966 caused a minor split in the ruling party and led to a special election in which the new group won limited parliamentary representation.

Both President Kenyatta and Vice President Daniel Teroitich arap MOI, a member of the small Kalenjin ethnic group, were unopposed for reelection in September 1974. Kenyatta died on August 22, 1978, and was immediately succeeded, on an interim basis, by Moi, who, as the sole KANU candidate, was declared president on October 10 to fill the remainder of Kenyatta's five-year term.

A veneer of apparent stability was shattered by an attempted coup by members of the Kenyan Air Force on August 1, 1982. Loyal military and paramilitary units quickly crushed the rebellion, and the government announced the disbanding of the existing air force. President Moi dissolved the National Assembly on July 22, 1983, and called for a premature general election. The balloting was conducted on September 26, although Moi on August 29 was guaranteed a return to the National Assembly as an unopposed candidate and reelected to another presidential term as KANU's sole candidate for the office. Thereafter, he dealt harshly with rebel leaders, 12 of whom were executed in 1985.

In early 1986 the government launched a crackdown on dissidents and dealt forcefully with unrest within the university community in late 1987. Internal and external critics continued to charge the government with human rights abuses. Notwithstanding such controversies, the government experienced little real electoral challenge in early 1988. As the only candidate presented by KANU on February 27, Moi was declared reelected, again without the formality of a public vote, while party preselection eliminated most dissenters from assembly balloting on March 21. Several days later, Moi replaced his longtime vice president, Mwai KIBAKI, with the relatively unknown Dr. Josephat KARANJA. However, in April 1989 the assembly, apparently with the tacit support of the president, declared its nonconfidence in Karanja, who resigned on May 1. Moi immediately appointed George SAITOTI to the position, noting that his new deputy, who had earned praise for his handling of economic affairs, would retain the finance portfolio.

In February 1990 Foreign Minister Robert OUKO, whose popularity was viewed by many as having eclipsed that of the president, was assassinated before he could complete a highly publicized investigation of government and KANU corruption. Although domestic unrest intensified following the incident, in May Moi once again rejected calls for introduction of a multiparty system, insisting that such a change would exacerbate tribal cleavage. A KANU conference in December 1990 reendorsed the one-party system, while in February 1991 the government refused to recognize a National Democratic Party (NDP) organized by former vice president Odinga. However, multiparty advocates regrouped in midyear as the Forum for the Restoration of Democracy (FORD), which, with widening popular support, continued the struggle for liberalization despite harassment by the authorities.

The administration's image was further tarnished on November 19, 1991, when Nicholas Kiprono BIWOTT, one of the president's closest political allies, was dismissed from the cabinet after an outside investigator had described him as a prime suspect in the Ouko murder. Shortly thereafter, international lenders and Western capitals informed Nairobi that economic assistance would be frozen until political and economic reforms were implemented. In response, Moi reluctantly reversed his position on multiparty pluralism, and following constitutional revision effective December 20, several new parties were legalized, prompting a number of cabinet and KANU officials to resign and join the opposition.

On October 28, 1992, Moi dissolved the National Assembly in preparation for the as yet unscheduled elections. Describing the action as his "secret weapon," Moi apparently sought to capitalize on the recent splintering of FORD into two factions, FORD–Kenya (FORD–K) and FORD–Asili (FORD–A), over the choice of a presidential candidate. In presidential balloting on December 29 Moi was challenged by two former vice presidents, Kibaki, founder of the Democratic Party (DP), and Odinga, leader of FORD–K, as well as FORD–A leader Kenneth MATIBA and four other candidates. Although winning only 36 percent of the vote, Moi easily outpolled his three top challengers. Meanwhile, in simultaneous legislative balloting KANU secured 100 assembly seats, well ahead of FORD–K and FORD–A, which won 31 seats each. Domestic and international observers criticized the polling as tainted by KANU intimidation tactics, electoral fraud, and vote rigging. Subsequently, on January 4, 1993, the two FORD groups and the DP, the latter controlling 23 assembly seats, announced the formation of an opposition coalition to "nonviolently" force the holding of new elections. However, only the DP honored a pledge not to sponsor candidates against other opposition parties. As a result, the coalition was in disarray in a by-election on June 27, 1994, that gave KANU 3 of 7 seats. More importantly, an increasing number of disillusioned opposition MPs were crossing over to KANU, with the latter edging toward the two-thirds majority needed for constitutional revision.

The government's violent crackdown on dissidents in late 1996 signaled both an intensification of Moi's desire to suppress the proreform movement and the apparent ascendancy of hard-liners within KANU. In early February 1997 the administration, citing "emergency" drought conditions, imposed the Preservation of National Security Act, which granted the government broad emergency powers, including the right to curtail political party activity. Thereafter, widespread antigovernment demonstrations were reported in late February 1997, and in April the ambassadors of 14 countries issued a joint statement condemning the government for using excessive force to suppress the continuing unrest and calling on the administration to remove restrictions on the opposition's freedoms of speech and assembly.

In mid-April 1997 the constitutional reform movement appeared to gain new focus when a number of prominent opposition leaders took part in a meeting of the National Convention Assembly (NCA), a proreform movement theretofore led by activist religious groups. For their part, KANU leaders dismissed the NCA as a "grouping of tribalists," and the NCA's attempt to convene a meeting of its executive wing was banned.

Under pressure from both domestic and international observers, President Moi on June 1, 1997, pledged to review the colonial-era laws that allowed security personnel to use force against illegal demonstrations; nevertheless, reports of government-initiated violence continued. Consequently, on July 17 the opposition announced its intention to launch a campaign of protest demonstrations culminating in a general strike in August. In response, the administration announced that it would establish a bipartisan parliamentary commission to review the constitution and expunge those laws designed to suppress the opposition. Real progress remained elusive, however, as the government rejected demands that NCA representatives be included on the commission.

On August 28, 1997, President Moi organized a meeting of over 120 KANU and opposition parliamentarians at which the two sides launched the Inter-Party Parliamentary Group (IPPG) to serve as a vehicle for drafting electoral reform measures. Subsequently, IPPG negotiators forged a series of draft constitutional amendments, which were approved by the legislature in late October and early November and signed into law by Moi on November 7. Meanwhile, the government approved the registration of 12 new parties, including, after some delay, Safina, a grouping launched in early 1995 by Paul MUITE (an opposition MP) and the noted paleontologist Dr. Richard LEAKEY (see Political Parties, below). On November 10 Moi dissolved the assembly, and the following day the government announced that presidential and legislative elections would be held in late December.

At the presidential balloting held December 29–30, 1997, President Moi won another five-year term by outdistancing a field of 14 candidates. The incumbent secured approximately 40 percent of the vote, while his nearest competitor, the DP's Kibaki, captured 31.1 percent. Meanwhile, in simultaneous legislative elections, KANU narrowly retained its majority, securing 113 seats. The DP finished second, with 41 seats overall, while a total of ten parties gained representation. Deriding the polling as fraudulent, a number of opposition officials immediately called for new elections, and Kibaki filed suit to have the results overturned. Dismissing criticism of the electoral process, on

January 8, 1998, Moi named a new government, which did not, however, include a vice president.

The terrorist bombing of the U.S. embassy in Nairobi on August 7, 1998, and the resulting death of 247 Kenyans and 11 U.S. citizens caught the Moi government off guard. Security concerns surfaced again in early 1999 when it was revealed that a Kurdish militant, Abdullah Öcalan, had entered Kenya without going through proper immigration procedures, only to be captured and transported out of the country by Turkish security agents acting without Nairobi's consent. On February 18 Moi dismissed three top security officials and reshuffled his government in an apparent response to the incident.

Among those affected by the cabinet changes was finance minister Simeon NYACHAE, the government's most prominent anticorruption campaigner, who resigned from the government rather than accept a lesser post. Nyachae's demotion reportedly surprised observers, as it appeared to undermine the government's claims of greater economic accountability on the eve of fresh negotiations with the IMF. On April 3 Moi reappointed George Saitoti as vice president. (Saitoti had held the post until December 1997, after which Moi had left the post vacant, prompting speculation that his next deputy would be his hand-chosen successor.)

President Moi pulled a political rabbit out of his hat in June 1999 when he enticed Dr. Richard Leakey (a prominent member of the Safina opposition party) to join the administration as cabinet secretary and head of the civil service. Leakey and his economic reform team were subsequently given high marks for probity and enthusiasm, although it remained unclear whether progress would be sufficient for the IMF and World Bank (who were demanding improved fiscal discipline, privatization, and anticorruption measures) to resume aid. That question became moot in April 2001 when Leakey resigned after powerful groups within the government had blocked his anticorruption efforts.

On June 12, 2001, Moi appointed Raila ODINGA (the former vice president's son) and other members of the NDP to his cabinet, thereby forming a "coalition" government. (In March 2002 KANU and the NDP formally merged.)

Moi in July 2002 selected Uhuru KENYATTA, the son of independence leader Jomo Kenyatta, as his preferred successor. However, public sentiment subsequently appeared to be turning solidly against KANU, which was expected to face a serious electoral challenge in December from a united opposition. On August 30, 2002, Moi dismissed Saitoti, who had earlier opposed Moi's selection of Kenyatta as his presidential successor. (The post remained vacant until November 4, when Moi appointed Wycliffe Musalia MUDAVADI from KANU as the new vice president.) In the meantime four cabinet ministers, including Odinga, resigned from the cabinet over Moi's selection of Kenyatta, and, with Saitoti, joined the opposition (see Political Parties, below). Moi dissolved the assembly on October 26, 2002, prior to the elections and before it had an opportunity to review proposed changes to the constitution drafted by the constitutional review commission. Moi dissolved the constitutional commission the following day, and on October 28 he barred delegates from convening.

The results of the presidential and legislative balloting on December 27, 2002, swept KANU out of power in a decisive victory for the "Super Alliance" of the National Rainbow Coalition (NARC), an umbrella group of opposition parties. The NARC presidential candidate, Mwai Kibaki, secured 62.3 percent of the vote, while Moi's handpicked successor, Uhuru Kenyatta, captured only 31.2 percent. The remaining three presidential candidates won less than 6.4 percent of the vote. In the legislative elections, the constituent parties of NARC captured a majority of 125 of the 210 elected seats. KANU finished second with 64 seats and became the official opposition party for the first time. Five other parties secured seats in the National Assembly.

President Kibaki was inaugurated on December 30, 2002, and had a cabinet in place by January 6, 2003. Vice President Michael Kijana WAMALWA died of a serious illness on August 23, 2003. Kibaki named Arthur Moody AWORI the new vice president on September 25, 2003.

The NARC government, in its first major policy initiative in 2003, eliminated the fees for public primary schools and made school compulsory. NARC's campaign pledges for economic revival proved more difficult to realize because the graft and oppression of the Moi regime had left the Kenyan economy in bad shape. The economy, transportation infrastructure, and the once-strong banking and financial services sector were in serious disrepair. International pressure to eliminate corruption in the public and private sectors and to privatize state enterprises, resisted by Moi for years, forced action when the new government needed foreign aid and loans to deliver on its promises to revive the economy. President Kibaki promised to create 500,000 new jobs every year, a pledge that proved impossible because acts of terrorism and severe drought weakened the tourism and agriculture sectors early in his term. Moreover, the government made slow progress in the privatization of government-controlled enterprises, which had long been sources of political patronage and graft.

The NARC coalition pledged to crack down on public sector corruption with a zero-tolerance campaign platform. In 2003 President Kibaki was under popular and international pressure to end corruption and prosecute some of the worst abusers under the Moi regime. In early February 2003 Kibaki dismantled entrenched political patronage networks by purging senior civil service and security forces members and reassigning others. Soon thereafter, he dismissed the chief executives of three state enterprises. Kibaki opened the new session of the National Assembly on February 18, 2003, with the remarkably frank admission that "[c]orruption has undermined our economy, our politics, and our national psyche" and pledged to address the issue by introducing legislation. (A new law and code of ethics were later adopted requiring senior government officials to declare their assets upon entering and exiting office.) Within days of the speech Kibaki suspended the chief justice of the High Court pending an investigation into allegations of corruption and torture of prisoners. Kibaki also named a high-profile anti-graft crusader, John GITHONGO (former head of Transparency International in Kenya), as his anticorruption chief.

In March 2003 the government opened a public inquiry, closely followed by the news media and the Kenyan people, into the infamous Goldenberg International corruption scandal that first surfaced in the 1990s. The inquiry addressed a scheme whereby nearly $600 million was siphoned from the public coffers of the central bank to the Goldenberg firm (and, by implication, to a string of government officials) in the form of export credits and state subsidies for gold and jewelry exports that never existed. (As of 2008, however, few public officials under investigation had been formally indicted or put on trial.)

In October 2003 Kibaki, in the wake of a report issued by a special commission investigating the conduct of the Kenyan judiciary, suspended 6 of the 9 judges in the court of appeals, 17 out of the 36 high court judges, and 82 of the 254 magistrates on grounds of "corruption, unethical conduct, and other forms of misbehavior."

By December 2003, however, problems with the government's own anticorruption record emerged in press accounts of new irregularities in government procurement. By May 2004 additional allegations surfaced over irregularities in procurement contracts for police telecommunications equipment, forensic laboratories, and a new passport system (dubbed the Anglo-Leasing scandal). In July British High Commissioner Sir Edward Clay publicly criticized the Kibaki government for its renewed tolerance for the corrupt practices of the past and an appetite among senior government officials within the NARC coalition for the trappings of office. The British, United States, and European Union (EU) governments immediately stepped up diplomatic pressure on Nairobi to investigate and prosecute any wrongdoing. The IMF and World Bank joined the chorus of donors calling for zero tolerance for corruption and an end to lavish perks for senior government officials.

In a bid to shore up support for his government in the face of bitter factional infighting among the major parties within NARC, President Kibaki reshuffled the cabinet on June 30, 2004, and formed a "government of national unity" by including key opposition party leaders, including members of KANU and FORD–People.

On February 7, 2005, John Githongo resigned from his post as anticorruption chief, citing pressure from within the cabinet to close his investigations of the procurement irregularities. The United States immediately suspended $2.5 million in anticorruption aid to Kenya. President Kibaki reshuffled the cabinet again on February 14, 2005, transferring some cabinet ministers and announcing a number of changes in the civil service in response to the mounting pressure from foreign governments, and on February 16, 2005, government prosecutors filed charges against six former government officials implicated in the procurement scandals.

In the wake of the no-vote for the referendum on constitutional reform in November, Kibaki dismissed his entire cabinet on November 23; 7 of the 28 cabinet ministers campaigned against the proposed constitution (see Constitution and government, below). Political turmoil ensued as Kibaki announced the names of his new cabinet on national television on December 8 only to have many of the newly appointed officials refuse to serve. Final cabinet appointments were made on December 13.

In 2006 more details of the Goldenberg and Anglo-Leasing corruption scandals surfaced and threatened to bring down Kibaki's government. John Githongo, living in exile in the United Kingdom, alleged in a public letter to President Kibaki that the Kenyan government had issued phony contracts to a nonexistent British firm to upgrade its passport system and forensic science laboratories (the Anglo-Leasing scandal). The "Githongo Report" alleged that up to 30 members of the government had participated in the scheme, including Vice President Moody Awori, who denied any wrongdoing. In the fallout George Saitoti (education minister), Kiraitu MURUNGI (energy minister), and David MWIRARIA (finance minister) resigned their cabinet positions in February 2006. Githongo also claimed that the money raised by graft was intended to fund the forthcoming election campaign.

By November the charges against Saitoti and Murungi were dropped or dismissed, and Kibaki reappointed them to their previous cabinet posts. David Mwiraria also returned to the cabinet in July 2007 but with a new portfolio (environment and natural resources). (Critics alleged that Kibaki was reluctant to jettison political allies who could deliver critical support in the 2007 elections.) Additionally, Kibaki refused to recall the National Assembly until March 22, 2006, out of fear that the parliament would pass a vote of no confidence.

Despite his pledge in 2002 to serve only for one term, Kibaki indicated in 2006 that he would seek reelection in 2007 under the banner of a new, but unnamed party. The formation by Kibaki's remaining supporters in government of a new splinter party, National Rainbow Coalition of Kenya (NARC–K), which drew Kibaki loyalists in the cabinet and National Assembly into its fold from the fractured NARC coalition's constituent parties, called into question the viability of the NARC government's election mandate. After five members of parliament died in an airplane crash in April 2006 (including two assistant cabinet ministers), the by-election held to replace them in July 2006 was the first electoral contest featuring NARC–K candidates. With Kibaki's endorsement and campaign support, the NARC–K candidates took three of the five seats. Kibaki did not formally join NARC–K, however, despite the party's public endorsement of him for another term in January 2007, choosing instead to keep his choice of reelection vehicle open until the formation of the Party of National Unity (PNU) in September 2007.

Kibaki dismissed two cabinet ministers in early October 2007 after NARC party leaders shifted their support to other presidential candidates before the presidential and legislative campaigns. Kibaki dissolved parliament on October 22 in preparation for the December general elections.

In legislative balloting on December 27, 2007, 23 parties won seats in the National Assembly. The Orange Democratic Movement (ODM), an opposition party with origins in the 2005 constitutional referendum fight, secured a plurality of 99 seats; the PNU, 43 seats; Orange Democratic Movement–Kenya (ODM–K), 16; KANU, 14; Safina, 5; NARC–K, 4; FORD–People, 3; and NARC, 3. Fifteen other parties won 2 seats or fewer. The parliamentary elections were overshadowed, however, by the post-election chaos surrounding the presidential balloting held on the same day. The Electoral Commission of Kenya (ECK) hastily declared incumbent president Mwai Kibaki the winner over challenger Raila Odinga, despite allegations by opposition leaders and international observers of widespread irregularities and a flawed result. Kibaki was declared the winner by the ECK with 46 percent of the vote; Raila Odinga, the ODM candidate, placed second with 44 percent. Kalonzo MUSYOKA of ODM–K polled 9 percent. Six other candidates failed to poll more than 1 percent combined. Ethnic violence over the disputed results led to thousands of causalities and widespread unrest and provoked a police crackdown on demonstrations (see Current issues, below).

President Kibaki was hurriedly sworn in for a second term on December 30. He installed a partial cabinet on January 8 and named Kalonzo Musyoka as vice president. Following protracted negotiations between Kibaki and the ODM's Raila Odinga over a power-sharing arrangement (see Current issues, below), Kibaki acquiesced in broad changes in the structure of executive power and agreed that Odinga would serve as the Kenya's first prime minister in an agreement signed on February 28. On April 13 they jointly appointed a new, expanded cabinet, with 42 seats divided according to the strength of the two camps. The cabinet, the largest in Kenya's history, was sworn in on April 17.

Lands minister Kipkalya KONES died in an airplane crash on June 10. Finance Minister Amos KIMUNYA resigned on July 8 after a vote of nonconfidence passed several days before in the National Assembly. Kimunya had presided over the ministry during the sale to the Libyan government of a hotel property owned by the Kenyan government. The appearance of irregularities surrounding the sale and Kimunya's initial denials of rumors that the property had been sold prompted the action by parliament.

Kibaki reshuffled the cabinet on January 23, 2009, giving Deputy Prime Minister Uhuru Kenyatta the finance portfolio, bringing Amos Kimunya back into the cabinet as trade minister, and appointing a new minister for roads. Justice minister Martha KARUA resigned from the cabinet on April 6. The minister for Nairobi's development was elevated to the justice portfolio and a replacement minister was appointed.

Constitution and government. The 1963 constitution has been amended several times, mainly in the direction of increased centralization and the abrogation of checks and balances that were originally introduced at the insistence of the tribal and party opposition. Originally designated by the assembly, the chief executive is now popularly elected for a five-year term. In case of a presidential vacancy, the vice president (a presidential appointee) serves pending a new election, which must be held within 90 days. The National Assembly, initially bicameral in form, was reduced to a single chamber in 1967 by merger of the earlier Senate and House of Representatives. The president can dissolve the body and call a new election; a nonconfidence vote also results in dissolution, with both presidential and legislative balloting mandated within 90 days. All candidates for election to the assembly were required to be members of KANU prior to the December 1991 amendment, which authorized multiparty balloting. The judicial system is headed by the Kenya Court of Appeal and includes the High Court of Kenya, provincial and district magistrates' courts, and Muslim courts at the district level. Under controversial amendments approved in 1988 the president, who had been accorded the right in 1986 to replace the auditor and attorney generals, was further empowered to dismiss court of appeal and high court judges; concurrently, police were authorized to hold uncharged detainees for up to 14 days. An amendment passed in August 1992 required that successful presidential candidates secure 25 percent of the vote in at least five of the eight provinces. Defended by the government as a means to avoid election of a solely regional candidate, the law was criticized by the opposition for unduly favoring the incumbent, whose support was drawn from a number of small, geographically widespread tribes. Amendments in 1997 permitted the formation of a coalition government, mandated a broad review of the constitution, and expanded the number of directly elected seats in the assembly from 188 to 210.

A constitutional review commission continued work in 2002 on a new draft constitution, projected to propose the establishment of a bicameral legislature and creation of the post of prime minister. President Moi dissolved parliament for the 2002 elections before any action was taken.

A popular plank of the NARC government electoral platform promised to deliver a new constitution that would reduce the powers of the president within six months, with a deadline of June 2003. The mistrust between the National Alliance of Kenya (NAK) and Liberal Democratic Party (LDP) party factions of NARC (see Political Parties, below), however, led to a stalemate over the formula for the diminution of executive power. Raila Odinga of the LDP rallied support for the creation of a robust prime minister in a constitutional arrangement similar to that of France. President Kibaki and his closest advisors in the NAK wing of NARC lost their enthusiasm for specific arrangements that would force the executive to substantively share power with another single figure, and for other reforms that might weaken NARC's ability to maintain its electoral advantage. A constitutional review conference opened on April 30, 2003, in the Bomas of Kenya, comprised of all the members of the National Assembly plus 406 delegates, but the divisions over a new power-sharing formula only sharpened during the proceedings. The promised deadline passed without approval of a new constitution, and popular agitation over the stalemate presented the NARC with a serious crisis, as a majority of Kenyans expected concrete reforms to prevent future abuses of executive power associated with the graft, corruption, and oppression of the previous regime. The situation became more polarized with the suspicious murder in September 2003 of Crispin MBAI, a key figure in the negotiations over executive power sharing at the Bomas conference and a close associate of Odinga.

The stalemate continued into 2004 as the "Mt. Kenya" faction of the NAK wing of NARC sought assembly review and amendment of the Bomas draft, which supported the Odinga/LDP view of executive power sharing and was approved in March by most of the 629 delegates to the review conference. The LDP wing countered that the draft could only be passed or defeated in toto, a position also favored by a majority of the delegates who attended the review conference. The government withdrew from the conference and sought passage of legislation that would permit the assembly to amend the Bomas draft. On June 28, 2004, President Kibaki announced that the 2004 revised date for a new constitution would also be missed. Riots broke out at pro-Bomas constitutional rallies in Nairobi and Kisumu as riot police moved to enforce a ban on antigovernment protests.

In 2005 the debate continued to rage in the assembly, where a Parliamentary Select Committee on Constitutional Review (PSC) was formed to consider the status of changes to the Bomas draft. The LDP pulled out of the PSC after six of its party members were removed from the committee. Eventually, the NAK wing of NARC prevailed as the assembly amended the Bomas draft to weaken the prime minister, retain a powerful presidency, and maintain a unicameral legislature. The changes also altered the basis for the administration of Kenya's provinces; previous arrangements would be changed to create elective district administration with accountability to the central government. On July 22, 2005, the National Assembly approved the key terms of the revised constitution bill. A national referendum on the new constitution, required by a ruling of the High Court before a new constitution could have effect, was held on November 21, 2005.

The proposed constitution's key elements included provisions for land reform, women's rights, and the further establishment of regional religious courts. (Christian and other religious courts would be created to work in tandem with the Kadhi, or Muslim, courts, which apply religious law to issues such as personal status, marriage, and divorce.) Absent from the proposed constitution, generally referred to as the Wako draft, were provisions to establish a prime minister and to return to a bicameral legislature.

The referendum, which became known as the Banana and Orange Referendum (because the many illiterate voters were asked to choose from a symbol of a banana if they approved of the new constitution and an orange if they opposed it), was hotly contested. Both sides held a series of political rallies that were marred by violence; at least eight people were killed. The referendum ballot on November 21, 2005, drew a 53 percent voter turnout. The Wako draft constitution was soundly defeated, with approximately 58 percent voting against and only 42 percent favoring its passage. The failure dealt a blow to Kibaki's leadership and threatened the viability of his government.

The political settlement that emerged on February 28, 2008, following the political turmoil and ethnic violence over the disputed December 2007 presidential elections led to a constitutional reform bill—the National Accord and Reconciliation Act—which passed on March 18, 2008. The act codified the new post of executive prime minister and created two deputy prime ministers. On December 16, 2008 parliament passed a bill eliminating the Electoral Commission (ECK) and providing for the establishment of an interim commission as recommended by the Kriegler Report. A bill to create a special tribunal to try perpetrators of election violence, as recommended by the Waki Report, however, failed to pass in February 2009 (see Current issues).

Administratively, Kenya is divided into 40 rural districts grouped into seven provinces: Central, Coast, Eastern, North, Rift Valley, Western, and North Eastern, exclusive of the Nairobi Extra Provincial District, which comprises the Nairobi urban area.

Foreign relations. Generally avoiding involvement in "big power" politics, Kenya devoted its primary attention following independence to regional and continental affairs, supporting African unity and liberation movements in southern Africa. Regionally, it signed the Treaty for East African Cooperation in Kampala, Uganda, on June 6, 1967, providing for the formal launching of the East African Community (EAC) on December 1. The grouping (initially perceived as a model for multinational economic integration) was designed to preserve and expand arrangements established under British colonial rule in areas such as transportation and communications. Supporters also envisioned eventual creation of a common market, and the East African Development Bank (EADB) was established as a related institution (see article on EADB under Regional and Subregional Development Banks). However, the EAC achieved little success, in part due to ideological differences between Kenya and socialist Tanzania and a variety of disputes between Kenya and Uganda. The EAC was terminated in mid-1977 amid significant acrimony over distribution of its assets and collateral developments, including Tanzania's decision to close its border with Kenya. In November 1983 final agreement was reached regarding the EAC assets, and the Kenyan-Tanzanian border was reopened; relations with Dar es Salaam were further stabilized by the reestablishment of diplomatic relations in December. Relations with Uganda also improved in the immediate wake of the November agreement, although new tensions subsequently arose, with each country accusing the other of harboring insurgents and Nairobi exhibiting what some observers described as an "obsession" with perceived Ugandan hostility.

In 1994 the three former EAC members established a Tripartite Commission for East African Cooperation with the hope of reviving integrationist sentiment, and in 1996 Francis MUTHAURA, Kenya's former ambassador to the United Nations, was named executive secretary of the commission's new secretariat, headquartered in Arusha, Tanzania. Kenya was subsequently viewed as the leading proponent of cooperation, and a treaty for the formal reactivation of the EAC had been drafted by the spring of 1999. The proposed accord called for the gradual reduction of tariffs between members and establishment of a common external tariff as initial steps toward a possible monetary union and even, in the minds of the most ardent integrationists, eventual political federation. The presidents of the three countries involved were scheduled to meet to approve the new treaty by the end of 1999. However, considerable negotiation reportedly was necessary on details of the plan; Tanzania expressed concern that it would be overwhelmed by Kenya's much larger economy, and continental leaders wondered how a revived EAC would interact with other groupings, such as the Common Market for Eastern and Southern Africa (Comesa) and the Southern African Development Community (SADC), which were promoting larger free-trade blocs. Meanwhile, Rwanda and Burundi were eager for membership once the EAC was relaunched successfully. (For details on the subsequent formal reestablishment of the EAC and the expansion to include Rwanda and Burundi, see separate article on the EAC in the Intergovernmental Organization section.) In 2004 the three EAC principals signed a customs union agreement that established a common external tariff, but left room for exceptions, which in 2007 materialized as Tanzanian requests to exempt pharmaceuticals, transport buses, millstones, and wheat. Comesa also moved to adopt a customs union in May 2007 with the common tariffs set to be in place by December 2008.

Kenyan-Somali relations frequently have been strained by the activities of nomadic Somali tribesmen (*shiftas*) in Kenya's northeastern provinces and by long-standing Somalian irredentist claims. They reached a nadir in mid-1977 with the outbreak of hostilities between Somalia and Ethiopia in the latter's Ogaden region, when a Kenyan spokesperson declared that an Ethiopian victory would be "a victory for Kenya." It was not until July 1984 that President Moi paid his first state visit to Mogadishu, in the course of which an agreement was concluded on border claims and trade cooperation, with Moi offering to help Somalian President Siad Barre "find a peaceful solution" to the dispute with Addis Ababa. The following September, several hundred ethnic Somali members of an exile group, the Northern Frontier District Liberation Front (NFDLF), responded to a government amnesty and returned to Kenya, declaring that the organization's headquarters in Mogadishu, Somalia, had been closed. Subsequently, in early December, Kenyan and Somalian representatives concluded a border security agreement, while other top *shifta* leaders responded to a second general amnesty in July 1985, declaring an end to the years of "banditry." With the subsequent collapse of the central state in Somalia, border incidents nonetheless continued throughout the 1990s and into the next century.

In early 1992 Nairobi, seeking to repair strained regional relations, signed cooperation agreements with Ethiopia and Sudan. Furthermore, on May 8 Nairobi established formal relations with Pretoria, and in June Moi became the first African head of state to visit South Africa in 21 years. Meanwhile, the encampment of approximately 300,000 Somalian, 70,000 Ethiopian, and 30,000 Sudanese refugees along Kenya's borders was described by the regime as an economic burden and source of insecurity. In August the United Nations High Commission for Refugees (UNHCR) criticized Kenya for detaining thousands of refugees in squalid conditions in Nairobi and Mombasa. Thereafter, in January 1993, amid rumors that it was considering an involuntary repatriation and describing the refugee situation as increasingly untenable, Kenya urged the UNHCR to hasten their departure.

On November 28, 2002, terrorists bombed an Israeli-owned hotel in Mombasa, killing 11 Kenyans and three Israeli tourists. On the same day a shoulder-launched missile was fired at an Israeli airliner but missed its target. In December al-Qaida claimed responsibility for the attacks as it had for the 1998 bombing of the U.S. Embassy in Nairobi.

President Kibaki's new government faced renewed pressure from the United States and the United Kingdom in 2003 to crack down on terrorist activity in Kenya with new internal security measures and reforms in the Kenyan security services. The United States threatened cuts in foreign aid to Kenya to encourage the new government, which reorganized the key security units responsible for antiterrorist intelligence. Both the United States and the United Kingdom announced in late May 2003 heightened security alerts for travel to Kenya, and British Airways and the Israeli airline El Al temporarily suspended flights. The travel alerts, warning of increased risk of a terrorist attack, were a blow to the Kenyan tourist industry already reeling from the November 2002 bombing and missile attacks. The alerts and threats of aid reduction prompted the government to submit a controversial Suppression of Terrorism Act in July 2003, which when introduced in the assembly was greeted with alarm by many government and opposition members, Muslim community leaders from the Coast and Mombasa, and leaders in human rights organizations; it prompted hundreds of protesters in Nairobi. The bill, which proposed to strengthen the government's powers of detention of persons and permit searches without court authorization, was blocked by an assembly committee. Since 2003, Kenya's cooperation with the United States antiterrorism policies for East Africa, while not complete (Kenya has refused to support immunity for U.S. personnel from war crimes prosecution), has nonetheless been substantial. Accordingly, direct aid to Kenya from the United States has increased since 2005, despite U.S. concerns over the persistence of public sector corruption.

Nairobi advanced its regional security objectives in East Africa in 2003 by signing in March a Strategy and Plan of Action for implementing a security agreement reached with Tanzania and Uganda in 2001. In May 2003 two Kenyan army battalions were deployed on the border with Somalia to guard against infiltration by potential terrorists, and in June the government responded to the heightened terror alerts by suspending flights to Somalia. As the violence escalated in Mogadishu and southern Somalia in early 2006 and as the drought conditions in the region worsened, these forces increasingly faced large numbers of refugees attempting to enter Kenya. By September 2006, with over 34,000 new refugees encamped in Kenya along the Somali border, the military was put on high alert and intensified patrols of territorial waters to fend off illegal shipments of arms and disrupt the transit of other illicit materials tied to terrorist cells among the Somali Islamic militias. The Kenyan military quietly cooperated with both Ethiopian and U.S. military forces in December strikes against the Somali militias by Ethiopian forces, offering intelligence assistance and air reconnaissance (this support of U.S. and Ethiopian forces was controversial and angered elements of Kenya's Muslim community). In January the Kenya-Somali border was closed. In the aftermath Human Rights Watch issued a report that accused Kenya of assisting the United States in rounding up Somali refugees suspected of ties to the Islamic militias and turning them over to Ethiopian authorities for detention.

In October 2006 President Kibaki appointed former president Daniel arap Moi as a special peace envoy for East Africa to assist in mediating the conflicts in Somalia and Sudan.

As part of its broad diplomatic and economic initiative toward Africa, the People's Republic of China (PRC) pursued increased bilateral ties with Kenya in 2006. PRC President Hu Jintao visited Kenya during his tour of Africa in 2006, and PRC diplomats offered expanded foreign aid and improved trade relations and sought in return Kenya's recognition of the PRC's One-China policy in regard to Taiwan. Expanded relations with China held the promise for Kenyan leaders of a new influx of foreign investment without the human rights and anticorruption conditions attached to U.S., U.K., IMF, or World Bank assistance. In April 2007 a delegation of nearly 100 Chinese business executives accompanied by PRC trade diplomats visited Nairobi; in August the Kenyan foreign ministry announced the opening of a new trade section in the Kenyan embassy in Beijing and assigned a trade attaché to the post.

Kenya experienced tremendous international pressure following the disputed 2007 presidential election. An EU election observation team immediately alerted the international community that there were irregularities and serious flaws in the tabulation of results at some polling locations and in the final counts certified by the ECK. As the unrest over the disputed presidential results spread across the country, fears of escalating ethnic violence between Luo and Kikuyu tribe members in major urban centers and between Kalenjin and Kikuyu in the Rift Valley, and the potential for continuing political and economic chaos, spurred a rapid, but uncoordinated diplomatic intervention. The strongest concerns were voiced by East African leaders and Western democracies, such as the United States, the EU (especially the United Kingdom), Canada, Australia, and international financial and security organizations, including the World Bank and the United Nations. Pressure form neighboring heads of state in East Africa and threats by Western governments to suspend aid, deny visas, freeze assets, and prosecute human rights cases finally convinced Kenyan elites that a domestic settlement was necessary to avert collapse of the constitutional order and to restore the regime's international legitimacy.

President Kibaki attended the first Africa-India summit in New Delhi in early April 2008. The summit was organized by the Indian government to counter the growing influence of China in Africa. The Indian government promised to lower import tariffs on African goods, increase direct foreign aid, and double the amount for loans to African governments.

Ironically, once he became prime minister, Raila Odinga engineered pressure from Nairobi on Zimbabwe's president Robert Mugabe to reach a power-sharing agreement with his rival in that country's disputed presidential election.

Current issues. Much of the Kibaki government's activity in 2007 was undertaken with an eye toward the dissolution of the parliament with the general elections scheduled for the end of the year. Public spending was increased (including investment in long overdue infrastructure projects and a substantial pay raise for civil servants), which fueled inflationary pressures in an economy where energy prices hit record highs and drought pushed up the price of food. Kibaki announced in September the formation of a new party coalition backing his reelection campaign, the Party of National Unity (PNU). The PNU was formed to replace the defunct NARC coalition that won the 2002 general election but included many of the same constituent parties that were still allied with Kibaki (who is Kikuyu). It also included the support of KANU after behind-the-scenes deal making by former president Moi.

The ODM, an opposition coalition that formed to defeat the Wako constitution referendum in late 2005, took steps in September 2006 to transform itself into a political party. The ODM's leaders spent many months wrangling over which of its many powerful and ambitious political figures should be the nominee in the presidential election. By August 2007 the factional disputes cost ODM the support of its KANU wing and split the remaining wings of the party in two, with the strongest faction rallying behind the presidential candidacy of Raila Odinga (who is Luo) and another faction backing the candidacy of Kalonzo Musyoka (who is Kamba). With three major candidates in the race, each from a different ethnic group, the scramble by party operatives to knit together the necessary cross-ethnic political alliances began in "the season of defections," when the party affiliations of political figures changed at a dizzying pace as they sought to pick a party that would get them a nomination and a seat in parliament.

Odinga gained momentum in the presidential race during September and early October and surged ahead of Kibaki in public opinion polls, with Musyoka running a distant third; but the polls showed the two major candidates pulling closer as the campaigns went into full swing after the dissolution of the parliament in late October. Kibaki's campaign platform emphasized his record on economic growth and development, his coalition's commitment to national unity instead of "tribalism," a commitment to leave no region or province lagging behind others, and an extension of free public school to secondary education. He also promised that the government would double investment in the nation's transportation, communication, and utility infrastructure. Odinga made constitutional reform and "majimbo" (increased autonomy for provincial governments) the center of his platform. He promised, if victorious, to resurrect the Bomas draft constitution and institute a federal system within six months, and to improve infrastructure and health care. Musyoka promised to fight poverty and public corruption, improve health care, expand free education, and adopt an "economic federalism."

Prior to the election, Kibaki appointed all new members to the ECK (including his family lawyer), except for the chair whom he reappointed. Odinga's ODM camp warned that Kibaki, who had close ties to former president Moi and other politicians threatened by regime change and ongoing anticorruption investigations, was preparing to rig the presidential election. Kibaki's preelection maneuvers and allegations of conspiracy by the opposition led to a highly charged atmosphere when the polls opened on December 27, 2007.

The ODM won a plurality in the parliamentary elections, but the presidential balloting was marred by sporadic violence. Chaos ensued when irregularities occurred at several polling sites in Central Province (Kibaki and Kikuyu strongholds), which did not report results at the same time as other areas of the country. In other cases, results announced at the constituency level did not match the results later reported by the ECK. The ECK declared Kibaki the winner in the presidential election without an official explanation of the balloting irregularities. Odinga declared that he had won and that the election had been rigged. On December 30 Kibaki was hurriedly sworn in for a second term, despite warnings from the EU election monitoring team that the results were highly irregular and deeply flawed. Soon thereafter, Odinga and other ODM leaders threatened to take their protest over the disputed elections into the streets of Kenya's major cities. More disturbing were violent attacks by Luo and Kalenjin on Kikuyus who had settled in the western parts of the country. The worst violence occurred in and around Eldoret in the Rift Valley, where ethnic Kalenjin militias targeted and killed Kikuyus, including people who had sought shelter in a church, which the attackers burned down, killing many inside. The ethnic violence sparked reprisals by Kikuyu on Luo communities in several large cities including the capital Nairobi. Luos counterattacked, and the entire country was threatened by escalating ethnic violence and the internal displacement of Kenyans evicted by the hostilities or displaced by fears of more violence. Before the unrest subsided, estimates put the number of dead at more than 1,200 and the displaced at more than 300,000.

Efforts to mediate between the Kibaki and Odinga camps began almost immediately with the World Bank's country director Colin Bruce attempting to broker a memorandum of understanding on an election inquiry and a power-sharing arrangement; these negotiations were soon taken over by the African Union chair and president of Ghana John Kufuor. The negotiations broke down, however, when Kibaki announced cabinet appointments on January 8 and refused to sign any brokered agreements for power sharing.

In the midst of calls for massive protests organized by the ODM in Nairobi, Mombasa, Kisumu, and other large cities around the country, the assembly convened on January 15. The longtime speaker of parliament was displaced by an ODM candidate in the first session. Meanwhile, the government warned that the opposition's planned "mass action" rallies were a violation of the preelection ban on public rallies and would be suppressed by force. Security forces fired tear gas and live rounds to break up several rallies. ODM leaders condemned these actions, but they switched tactics and announced a boycott on business interests allied with Kibaki and the PNU.

Former UN secretary general Kofi Annan stepped in to take over the mediation efforts later in January and scored a breakthrough when he convinced Kibaki and Odinga to meet together January 24 for the first time since before the election. The two leaders and their negotiating teams met throughout February but made little progress. As international pressure to come to an agreement mounted, the goals and demands of the two sides remained far apart. With intervention from U.S. secretary of state Condoleezza Rice and the Ugandan and Tanzanian presidents, Annan was finally able on February 28 to get the two sides to sign a two-page memorandum of understanding that put in place a power-sharing arrangement between Kibaki and Odinga. The arrangement created an executive prime ministership (and two deputy prime ministerships) to be occupied by Odinga and included a pledge to share cabinet positions. Final agreement on the size of the cabinet (eventually 42 ministers, the largest cabinet in Kenya's history) and the actual appointments was delayed until April 13 because the two sides squabbled over details for six weeks and almost dissolved the agreement. The threat of renewed violence eventually convinced both leaders to overcome the final obstacles and implement a grand coalition government.

As part of the power sharing agreement a series of independent commissions was established to study and report on the irregularities in the election and to investigate the post-election violence. The reports and recommendations of these commissions dominated political calculations for the coalition partners well into 2009.

The first of these reports was produced by an Independent Electoral Review Commission (IREC), which was chaired by South African jurist Johann Kriegler. Released in September 2008, the Kriegler Report found a dizzying array of ballot irregularities attributable to both ODM and PNU operatives as well as ECK regional poll staff rendering any chance of recovering a definitive winner of the presidential election impossible. Moreover the polls excluded a third of eligible voters while counting votes from more than one million deceased persons. The IREC's final recommendation was a complete overhaul of the ECK or its abolishment and replacement by an interim election board independent from government interference. A bill amending the constitution to abolish the ECK and replace it with an Interim Independent Election Commission (IIEC) passed in December.

The second and even more contentious group released its report on October 15. The Commission of Inquiry into Post–Election Violence (CIPEV), chaired by Justice Philip Waki, investigated the horrifying attacks, reprisals, and general mayhem wrought by ethnic militias following the presidential polls, in some cases perpetrated at the behest of political and business leaders. The Waki Report concluded that some attacks were spontaneous in origin but soon morphed into organized violence, while others were planned in advance and executed by ethnic militias organized and funded by political and business elites at the highest national and regional levels. Moreover, state security forces ignored internal staff reports that warned of possible violence and deliberately took advantage of the chaos to perpetrate additional human rights violations. As part of the documentation of the crimes, Waki produced a large body of evidence and handed over a sealed envelope to Kofi Annan that reportedly contained the names of prominent politicians and business leaders, most notably some members of the cabinet, who should face further investigation by a special tribunal. Waki's recommendation gave the government 90 days to act on its own to create a special tribunal independent of the judiciary and attorney general and with international representation. If the government failed to act on this timeline he requested than Annan turn the envelope over to the International Criminal Court in The Hague for further investigation.

While both men initially pledged to implement the Waki report, the political ramifications of the sealed envelope soon put strains on both President Kibaki and Prime Minister Odinga's political alliances and therefore on their ability to work together to get past the crisis. Part of Odinga's ODM leadership and electoral support came from areas where some of the most shocking violence occurred in the Rift Valley—and these political allies, threatened by the potential for being named in the sealed envelope, began to maneuver for leverage in order to avoid the possibility of prosecution. For Kibaki's part, his closest political and business elite allies were also threatened, as rumors after the election placed members of the Mungiki criminal syndicate in the presidential State House to plan reprisals for the attacks on Kikuyu communities. Kibaki signaled that the tribunal might be empowered to grant amnesty for all crimes, which galvanized opposition against a special tribunal constitutional bill in parliament by reform MPs who feared yet another government investigation that served to quash prosecutions and give impunity to corrupt politicians. Together with those MPs who feared prosecution or political cronies whose careers were tied to such persons, these reform MPs defeated the special tribunal bill put forward by the government in February 2009 (following the first of several extensions on the deadline granted by Annan).

As the government stalled or sought further schemes for undermining the independence of a tribunal, several other international reports were released that further deepened the sense that corrupt Kenyan public officials were systematically escaping justice. The most important of these was a statement from the UN official rapporteur on extrajudicial executions in Kenya, which alleged that Kenyan police and military personnel had engaged in systematic torture and execution over a number of years, and had escaped punishment by complicity from officials charged with oversight and investigation. In the same month, two human rights activists were murdered in broad daylight by gunmen in Nairobi not long after calling attention to the same pattern of abuse and impunity for police "death squads."

In July Annan, out of patience that the government would create a tribunal with appropriate power and independence, turned the sealed envelope over to an ICC prosecutor, despite the announcement by Kibaki and Odinga that they would form a Truth and Reconciliation Commission to explore the pattern of ethnic violence surrounding Kenyan elections since the advent of party pluralism.

POLITICAL PARTIES

Before its unprecedented defeat in the face of a united opposition in the 2002 national elections, the ruling **Kenya African National Union** (KANU) had dominated the government structure and political life of Kenya since independence. KANU's one-time principal rival, the **Kenya People's Union** (KPU), was proscribed in 1969, although a one-party system was not formally mandated until 1982. Under mounting domestic and external pressure, President Moi and KANU endorsed pluralism in December 1991, and a number of other parties were legalized in the ensuing months.

On August 5, 1992, prospects for an opposition upset of the incumbents in presidential and legislative elections later that year were severely undermined when Masinde MULIRO, a prominent **Forum for the Restoration of Democracy** (FORD) leader who advocated opposition unity, died. One month later, torn by debate over the nomination of a presidential candidate, FORD broke into two competing factions.

On November 30, 1995, members of FORD–K, FORD–A, the DP, and Safina launched an Opposition Alliance to defeat KANU, but intraparty disputes plagued the opposition in 1996 and 1997. In March 1997 an Opposition Solidarity was formed by former FORD–K leader Raila Odinga in concert with the FORD–A's Kenneth MATIBA and Ngengi MUIGAI, a DP faction leader. Meanwhile, the Opposition Alliance claimed to have drafted FORD–K and DP faction leaders Michael Kijana Wamalwa and Mwai Kibaki, respectively, as well as FORD–A's Joseph Martin SHIKUKU. However, the fledgling Alliance–Solidarity rivalry was almost immediately overshadowed by the emergence of the National Convention Assembly (NCA), a proreform grouping. At the NCA's inaugural national convention in April Kivutha KIBWANA was appointed chair, and the group's executive committee drafted a number of well-known opposition figures, including Kibaki, Richard Leakey, Koigi Wa WAMWERE, and Islamic Party of Kenya (IPK) leader Sheikh Khalid Salim Ahmed BALALA.

In late August 1997 President Moi denounced the NCA as the instigator of the violent unrest gripping the country. Moreover, despite the NCA's subsequent decision to suspend protest activities to allow the government to fulfill its pledge to introduce reforms, the group was banned from holding meetings. In the face of violent dispersal of its meetings by government security forces, the NCA announced its intention to boycott presidential and legislative balloting. On the other hand, the Opposition Alliance had reportedly "folded up its umbrella," to distance itself from the ongoing violence and in response to the government's reform promises. The NCA subsequently continued to be an important stakeholder and government critic in the reform process by articulating alternate plans to those proposed by KANU.

A number of opposition alliances were formed in 2002 in preparation for the December presidential and legislative balloting. In February several groups (including the DP, FORD–K, NCA, the **United Democratic Movement** (UDM), and a faction of FORD–A) launched a **National Alliance for Change** (NAC), which was later restyled as the **National Alliance of Kenya** (NAK) under the party registration for the **National Party of Kenya** (NPK). Concurrently, FORD–People, Safina, the Kenya National Democratic Alliance (KENDA), the NLP, and others established the People's Coalition of Kenya (PCK), also sometimes referenced as the "Third Force for Change." In mid-October the NAK and PCK joined the newly formed **Liberal Democratic Party** (LDP) and its so-called "Rainbow Alliance" of former KANU and NDP faction leaders in an even larger opposition alliance called the **National Rainbow Coalition** (NARC), also referred to as the "Super Alliance." However, the selection of Kibaki as the NARC's presidential candidate caused problems with FORD–People leader Simeon Nyachae, who withdrew his party from the alliance and launched his own presidential campaign. These 15 opposition parties in the "Super Alliance" were held together by a Memorandum of Understanding (MoU) signed before the December 2002 elections by the leadership of the constituent parties of the NAK and the LDP, who agreed, if victorious, to divide cabinet positions equally in consultation among the party leaders and to name the LDP's Raila Odinga as prime minister once a new constitution was adopted.

After the election, President Kibaki unilaterally named NAK and LDP ministers to his NARC cabinet in early 2003 without regard to the preelection agreement. Moreover, the NARC eight-member Summit of NAK and LDP politicians did not convene, and within the first three months some members of the new government were questioning the Summit's utility. By late spring of 2003 heated disputes erupted between Kikuyu Mt. Kenya elements of NAK and Luo LDP leader Odinga, in league with the Luhya NARC politicians (who together constituted a "Western Alliance"), over the diminution of executive power in the new draft constitution, which the Mt. Kenya faction sought to derail. By August Kibaki publicly opposed the creation of a premiership, stating before a NARC parliamentary meeting, "there can never be two governments." The bitter ethnic and factional infighting jeopardized the long-anticipated constitutional reform process and threatened to bring down the government because of the size of the LDP voting bloc in the assembly (59 elected seats).

President Kibaki attempted to quell the NARC infighting by decreeing in December 2003 that all the parties in the coalition were dissolved and called for new party elections to transform NARC into a single party. The LDP and FORD–K ignored the demand and boycotted a February 2004 meeting convened to reach a new consensus on power sharing and to plan the dissolution of the constituent parties (see below). By March, FORD–K leader Musikari KOMBO asked Kibaki to halt the recruitment drive begun by Charity K. NGILU to avoid irreparable harm and avoid violent clashes between party activists. Subsequently, none of the NARC member parties unilaterally disbanded their organizations, although Kibaki distanced himself from official status as leader of the DP.

The opposition KANU and FORD–People in the meantime allied in a **Coalition for National Unity** (CNU), which presented the factions within the NARC with opportunities to selectively seek the opposition's support on issues that divided the government. Odinga and the LDP exploited this opportunity by garnering KANU's support for the Bomas conference constitutional draft that endorsed curbing the power of the presidency, devolving power to district authorities, and creating a prime minister post. President Kibaki also exploited this opportunity on June 30, 2004, when he announced a cabinet reshuffle that produced a "government of national unity" by bringing in ministers from the opposition parties and demoting or removing key LDP cabinet members. By the end of 2004 many LDP MPs had crossed over to sit with the opposition parties in the assembly.

By mid-2005 the parliamentary groups of NARC were in disarray as members of the government and opposition camps crossed party lines to forge temporary and unstable alliances, and groups of MPs openly contemplated the formation of new political parties and party alliances in anticipation of the 2007 elections. The run-up to the constitutional referendum in November 2005 intensified this instability and maneuvering for political advantage.

Opposition to the November 2005 constitutional referendum united under the banner of the "Orange Team"; the "no" vote was symbolized by an orange. Building on the defeat of the proposed constitution, the LDP and KANU leadership, the power brokers behind the Orange Team, took steps to form a coalition, the **Orange Democratic Movement** (ODM). As a coalition of political notables and their parties and ethnic networks, ODM was subject to factional infighting even as its supporters were positioning the ODM to win control of the government in the 2007 elections. Neither the institutional structure nor the party leadership was finalized before August 2007, and only after major elements of the grouping left the coalition (KANU) or split from the main leadership to form a factional group (ODM–K, see below) behind the presidential candidate Stephen Kalonzo Musyoka.

In response to members of his own cabinet defecting to ODM, President Kibaki announced in March 2006 that he no longer considered NARC a viable party and that he identified with (but never formally joined) the newly formed **National Rainbow Coalition of Kenya** (NARC–K) party. ODM, KANU, and other opposition parties responded to the president's statement and his subsequent support for NARC–K candidates in the July 2006 by-elections by challenging the legitimacy of his government and calling for a vote of no confidence in parliament.

Given the close margins on votes of no confidence in parliament, the July 24, 2006, by-elections for five assembly seats (to replace the five MPs who died in an April 2006 airplane crash) were hotly contested by the new NARC–K party and the opposition KANU and LDP elements of ODM. NARC–K candidates prevailed in three of the five constituencies; KANU candidates won the other two. The balloting was marred by charges of vote buying, violence, and allegations that government aircraft were used to transport campaigning NARC–K politicians and that government vehicles were used to ferry voters to the polls. LDP and KANU party leaders called on the Electoral Commission of Kenya (ECK) to nullify the results, and ECK officials complained of "the wanton violation of electoral rules by the Government."

The first eight months of 2007 were driven by the shifting alliances of political candidates and ethnic power brokers as the strategic logic of the presidential election system (whereby successful candidates must secure 25 percent of the vote in at least five of the eight provinces) and Kenya's political and ethnic geography (whereby the major ethnic groups are largely concentrated in the various regions) made necessary.

President Kibaki worked to shore up his weakest alliances and reached out to former adversaries (like former president Daniel arap Moi) and pursued tactics designed to split the opposition. The latter proved fruitful as the major candidates vying for the ODM presidential nomination wrangled with one another over candidate selection mechanisms and control of party positions and organs; the infighting ultimately split the broad coalition into rival factions (ODM and ODM–K, see below) and drove KANU out of the ODM camp altogether. The eventual ODM flag bearer was Raila Odinga, a veteran of many campaigns, parties, and coalitions in Kenyan politics. Not to be outdone, Odinga openly and successfully courted government ministers and MPs to rally to the ODM banner and adopted campaign positions and forged political alliances that knitted together support from ethnic power brokers across the regions.

On September 16, 2007, Kibaki finally unveiled his reelection coalition under the banner of the **Party of National Unity** (PNU), an umbrella coalition of parties and the successor to the NARC coalition formed in 2002. As the PNU nominations process for parliamentary constituencies was subsequently bogged down by so many parties vying for a share of the nominations slate in November, affiliate parties and candidates began to make contingency plans so they could be on the ballot even if they failed to secure the PNU label. Other PNU-affiliated politicians succumbed to the appeals and promises of opposition leaders and bolted from the PNU and its affiliate parties. The ODM also lost to rival camps some politicians who had failed to win nomination by the party.

By December 27 there were nearly 2,550 registered candidates from 108 political parties (with a record 269 female candidates) eligible to run for the 210 elected seats in parliament. One parliamentary constituency had 33 separate candidates vying for a single seat. Unlike the presidential balloting held simultaneously, the parliamentary polling was conducted in relative calm and with few allegations of irregularities.

Once the PNU and ODM camps reconciled their bitter dispute over the presidential elections and the ethnic violence subsided, a grand coalition government emerged, with power sharing between rival presidential candidates and division of seats in an expanded cabinet. The practical result left only one opposition party among 23 in the legislature. All other parties were either part of the government or allied with government parties. An opposition caucus began to emerge in May 2008, however, which drew together nearly 65 politicians from some of the smaller parties and disgruntled MPs from the coalition parties.

The passage of a political parties bill in July 2008 requiring a stronger organizational basis for parties and more mass membership from each constituency across the nation created a scramble by parties to comply or face deregistration. If strictly enforced the law could reduce the number of parties certified to contest the next national election.

Government Parties:

The Orange Democratic Movement (ODM). Originally known as the Orange Team, ODM began as a coalition of disparate political actors who came together in their opposition to the November 2005 constitutional referendum. ODM took shape after the referendum as an unsteady partnership between the LDP and KANU and the smaller LPK, allied by their common desire to defeat President Kibaki in the 2007 election. As a consequence, ODM lacked a common ideology or political philosophy and was best understood throughout 2006 as a pure opposition coalition. In the beginning ODM had no institutional structure and suffered from infighting among the leaders, many of whom were actively plotting paths for securing the ODM endorsement for the presidential nomination. Among the notable political figures who sought the ODM nomination for president were Raila Odinga (LDP), William Ruto (KANU), Najib Balala (LDP), Uhuru Kenyatta (KANU), Stephen Kalonzo Musyoka (LDP), Musalia Mudavadi (LDP), Julia Ojiambo (LPK), and Joseph Nyaga.

In September 2006 ODM registered as a political party under the initials ODM–K and began to create party organs to contest the 2007 elections, but as it did so the tensions between the party notables seeking the ODM presidential nomination and between the constituent parties increased. The formal structures included a plenary, a National Executive Council, a National Election Board, and a Council of Elders (later renamed the Consensus Committee). Disagreements about how the presidential nominee should be selected, whether by a direct vote of party delegates or by consensus, lingered well into July 2007, with the various candidates shifting their position on the method they preferred as their fortunes rose and fell. They also fought bitterly within the party over attempts to fill party offices with their loyalists. In June KANU leader Uhuru Kenyatta began pressing for clarification on the nature of the party itself, whether it was a coalition of parties or whether ODM would replace its constituent parties. Unhappy with the answers about KANU's membership, outmaneuvered for the ODM presidential nomination, and in a fight over control of KANU's legal status, Kenyatta pulled KANU out in late July. In September KANU joined the PNU and endorsed Kibaki.

Eventually the party settled on a direct vote by delegates to select the presidential candidate. Soon thereafter the rivalry for the ODM nomination between Musyoka and Odinga boiled over, with Musyoka bolting from LDP to the LPK in early August 2007 and refusing to permit the Registrar of Societies to install a new slate of leaders for ODM. The schism resulted in Musyoka forming a separate party and running as a presidential candidate under the original, registered party designation, ODM–K (see below). Odinga, Ruto, Mudavadi, and other leaders immediately acquired the rights to the ODM designation, registered their slate of leaders, and condemned Musyoka and Ojiambo for dividing the movement and thereby strengthening Kibaki's hand. In the meantime they actively courted stronger ties with NARC and NAK leader Charity Ngilu, in part as a hedge against losing support from Kamba voters following the departure of Musyoka. (Musyoka and Ngilu are both Kamba.) Odinga secured the party nomination on September 1 at a party nominating convention. He established the ODM Pentagon as the party's top strategic organ. Other members of the Pentagon included Ruto, Mudavadi, Najib Balala, and Joseph Nyaga.

Charity Ngilu joined the ODM Pentagon in late October after publicly endorsing Odinga in early October and subsequently being dismissed from the cabinet by Kibaki. Ngilu secured Odinga's agreement that she would contest her parliamentary constituency under the NARC banner, however. Another cabinet member, John KOECH, left KANU to join ODM in October and was also subsequently dismissed from the cabinet by Kibaki. (Koech later defected to ODM–K in November after failing to win an ODM nomination in his constituency.) After backing Odinga's candidacy in September, KADDU party chair Cyrus Jirongo withdrew his support in early November citing ODM's hostility to KADDU's attempt to run candidates in constituencies contested by ODM candidates.

ODM selected its candidates for parliament in primaries held in mid-November. The party then offered candidates in 190 constituencies in the December parliamentary elections and secured 99 seats in the National Assembly. Raila Odinga was credited with 44 percent of the national vote for president in the ECK official tally of results, which Odinga publicly disputed. Odinga and the ODM alleged that the election was rigged and immediately took steps to instigate massive public protests in Nairobi and other major urban centers in Western Province (the Luo tribe and ODM party stronghold), as ethnic violence erupted against Kikuyu peoples in Luo and Kalenjin majority regions in the west and the Rift Valley.

With a plurality in the National Assembly, the ODM elected one of their own MPs, Kenneth Marende, as the speaker after the National Assembly convened in January in the midst of unrest over the disputed presidential election. Two ODM MPs were murdered in late January, reducing the party's overall seat count to 96. (The speaker is ex officio and, thus, vacated his constituency seat.) In June by-elections, the ODM retained its three seats. ODM cabinet minister Kipkalya Kones and an ODM assistant minister died in a plane crash in June. These seats were retained by the ODM in a September by-election.

After the tenth parliament convened in January, ODM and MPs from PICK, PDP, and UDM forged alliances, which, with Charity Ngilu's NARC, gave the parties a solid plurality of the National Assembly votes. None of the ODM's selections for cabinet posts, however, except for the UDM representative, came from the Rift Valley or the Kalenjin tribe, which created a split during the election between Odinga and the Kalenjin politicians who backed ODM candidates, including William Ruto.

Leaders: Raila ODINGA (Party leader, Prime Minister of the Republic, and 2007 presidential candidate), Henry KOSGEY (Chair), Peter Anyang' NYONG'O (Secretary General), Omingo MAGARA (Treasurer), William RUTO, Wycliffe Musalia MUDAVADI (Former Vice President of the Republic), Najib BALALA, Joseph NYAGA, Fred GUMO (Consensus Committee Chair), Richard OTIENO (Elections Board Chair).

Liberal Democratic Party (LDP). The LDP was launched in October 2002 by politicians who had formed the "Rainbow Alliance" faction within KANU and had left the party mainly in protest over President Moi's selection of Uhuru Kenyatta as his preferred successor for the presidency. The disaffected included former vice president George Saitoti and former cabinet ministers Raila Odinga, Kalonzo Musyoka, William ole NTIMAMA, and Awiti ADHU. Nearly simultaneously the LDP leaders opened negotiations with the leadership of the NAK to form the "Super Alliance" National Rainbow Coalition (NARC) to defeat the ruling KANU party in the presidential and legislative elections. The LDP's base of support came from the western provinces, which when combined with the NAK's base in central Kenya and the Rift Valley gave the NARC a chance to win pluralities in enough provinces to secure the success of a NARC presidential candidate. The LDP and NAK signed the MoU in late October 2002 to cement the alliance before the December balloting. In the MoU they reached agreement on a broad platform of issues, including having a new constitution in place by June 2003 and a post-election formula for the division of jobs and power sharing.

President Kibaki, however, ignored the MoU's equality formula when he appointed the new cabinet, and with all the jockeying for power by the notables in the LDP, the LDP did not select one among equals to spearhead the NARC Summit, the supreme NARC party organ. Disputes within the NARC over the division of executive power between the president and a premier in the draft constitution further convinced Odinga and other LDP leaders that the LDP was being systematically undercut by a Mt. Kenya faction of Kikuyu and NAK power brokers close to Kibaki.

The LDP openly defied President Kibaki's attempts in 2004 and 2005 to dissolve the constituent parties of NARC in favor of creating a single party with individual membership. When Kibaki brought members of the opposition KANU and FORD–People into the cabinet (at the expense of LDP leaders, some of whom were demoted), in June 2003, LDP MPs crossed over to sit with the opposition in the National Assembly, declaring that the LDP was leaving the government. None of the LDP cabinet ministers, however, resigned from the government at that time.

In early 2005 the LDP actively sought alliances with other parties and groups in anticipation of the 2007 elections. The rivalries and presidential aspirations among LDP notables, however, made it difficult to schedule party elections. By June the party's National Executive Council postponed scheduled party elections indefinitely pending a revision of nomination and elections rules.

Also in June 2005, LDP MPs announced that they would once again sit with the other NARC MPs in the National Assembly. In March 2006, LDP officially broke from NARC when LDP MPs crossed over to the opposition's benches and signaled their support for ODM. (Only Mutinda Mutiso and former education minister George Saitoti remained on the government side.)

LDP named Paddy Ahenda as party nominee for the 2007 presidential elections. The nomination elections were marked by corruption and apathy and were ultimately nullified by the formation of ODM. By mid-2006, other LDP notables (e.g., Odinga, Balala, Musyoka, and Mudavadi) were actively preparing bids for the ODM nomination for president.

Stephen Kalonzo Musyoka, frustrated by the ODM infighting, which left him unlikely to secure the presidential nomination, left the LDP to join the LPK and then formed ODM–K in August 2007. LDP party chair David Musila and Secretary General Joseph Kamotho also quit the LPD during the ODM factional fighting over the presidential nomination and reverted to membership in NARC.

By September 2007, as the presidential nominations were decided and the ODM parliamentary constituency primary elections were organized, the LDP had largely been subsumed by the ODM.

Leaders: Joseph KHAMISI (Vice Chair), Andrew LIGALE (Deputy Secretary General), Paddy AHENDA, Raila ODINGA, Wycliffe Musalia MUDAVADI (Former Vice President of the Republic), Najib BALALA, William ole NTIMAMA, Ochilo Mbogo AYACKO, Otieno KAJWANG'.

Party of National Unity (PNU). Fashioned as a umbrella coalition of parties that supported the reelection of President Kibaki, PNU was organized in September 2007 on the model of the National Rainbow Coalition formed to contest the 2002 election. As a result, some PNU politicians had a direct affiliation with the party, while others maintained their individual affiliations with parties that were corporate members or affiliates of PNU.

The PNU was composed of more than 18 parties, groups, and notables, including the partner party, KANU. Uhuru Kenyatta, KANU's leader, endorsed Kibaki for president, and, unlike other member parties in the PNU coalition, he secured an early agreement to run candidates independently of PNU for parliamentary and civic elections under KANU's banner. The major parties, besides KANU, enlisted under PNU were NARC–K, FORD–K (including the splinter group NEW FORD–K), FORD–People, the DP, Safina, Shirikisho Party Kenya (SPK), and Sisi Kwa Sisi (SKS). PNU also included minor parties such as the Social Party for the Advancement of Reforms Kenya (SPARK), Mazingira Green Party of Kenya (MPK), Saba Saba Asili, the Independent Party, and the Agano Party, among others.

PNU ultimately nominated 135 candidates to contest constituencies and made agreements with partner parties running candidates in the same or other constituencies. In the December 2007 election, PNU won 43 seats outright and, via its alliances, had the support of more than 93 seats. With 46 percent of the vote, the ECK declared President Kibaki the winner of the presidential election. In subsequent by-elections in June and September 2008, PNU picked up 3 additional seats.

Leaders: Mwai KIBAKI (Party leader and President of the Republic), George SAITOTI (Chair and Former Vice President of the Republic), Noah WEKESA (First Vice Chair), Jimmy ANGWENYI, Jamleck KAMAU, Chirau Ali MWAKWERE, and George NYAMWEYA (Vice Chairs), Karate MOORING (Secretary General), Mohamoud MOHAMMED (Treasurer).

Kenya African National Union (KANU). Originally drawing most of its support from Kenya's large Kikuyu and Luo tribes, KANU was formed in 1960, established its leading position in the election of May 1963, and subsequently broadened its constituency through absorption of the Kenya African Democratic Union (KADU) and the African People's Party (APP), both supported by smaller tribes. KANU principles include "African Socialism," centralized government, racial harmony, and "positive nonalignment."

Following President Moi's lead, KANU in December 1990 voted to retain the one-party system; however, on December 3, 1991, a special congress endorsed the president's about-face on the issue. A number of KANU adherents, including 11 National Assembly members, subsequently switched allegiance to new opposition parties, primarily FORD (below).

During the run-up to presidential and legislative balloting in late 1992 the party attempted to portray itself as a "stable alternative" to what it described as an internally divided, tribal opposition. On the other hand, it continued to suffer from a steady flow of defections as well as accusations that it was supporting Kalenjin tribesmen who were considered responsible for initiating ethnic clashes in the Rift Valley. Faring poorly in Nairobi, Nyanza, and Central Province, the party lost over half of its seats in assembly elections on December 29. Nevertheless, KANU retained an assembly majority, securing 100 seats, not including the 12 seats designated for presidential appointment.

In 1996 KANU was bolstered by the addition of a number of former opposition members as well as three legislative by-election victories. However, several factions subsequently emerged, notably KANU–A, ostensibly more open to political reform and internal party democracy; and KANU–B, which tended to reflect more centralized and traditionalist perspectives. With Moi's renomination for another (and possibly final) presidential term a foregone conclusion, the main issue within KANU in late 1996 was the selection of his vice presidential running mate for the 1997 campaign. Although George Saitoti retained a degree of support for continuing in office, it was reported that he and his supporters in the KANU–B faction (including Nicholas Biwott and party secretary general Joseph KAMOTHO) were being challenged by Simeon Nyachae, a cabinet minister, and his KANU–A colleagues.

At an October 1996 meeting the internecine competition reached a head as the two camps clashed over internal election policies, with the KANU–A wing seeking the introduction of a nationwide internal balloting system (apparently with the anticipation of snaring the secretary generalship) while KANU–B demanded continuation of the local branch elections (from which victors are chosen for top posts). For his part, President Moi came down firmly behind the

KANU–B faction, either demoting or ousting KANU–A ministers in a sweeping government reshuffling in January 1997.

In early 1998 Moi called on the party to rally behind constitutional reform efforts and pledged to expand KANU's dialogue with FORD–K and the National Development Party (NDP), a previously minor grouping that had been pushed into the limelight when former FORD–K leader Raila Odinga had joined it in December 1996. Meanwhile, a third faction (KANU–C) emerged within the party under the leadership of Kipruto arap Kirwa and other "youth-oriented" activists. Angered at the organizational efforts of the Kirwa faction, Moi called on KANU dissidents to quit the party in June; subsequently, Kirwa and his associates withdrew from the constitutional review process. (In January 1999 they formally broke with the party and formed the UDM [see below].)

The supremacy of the KANU–B faction within the party and government was reinforced by the February 1999 cabinet reshuffling, which included the demotion of Nyachae (who then left the government and, ultimately, the party [see FORD–People, below]). However, a number of prominent KANU–B leaders were subsequently accused of corruption in a report published by the assembly in May 2000.

Growing cooperation between KANU and the NDP led to the inclusion of several NDP members (including Odinga) in the cabinet in June 2001. Subsequently, in March 2002, the NDP decided to merge into KANU, with Odinga becoming KANU's secretary general. However, severe internal problems arose in July when President Moi selected Uhuru Kenyatta as his preferred successor. Odinga subsequently helped form the so-called Rainbow Alliance within KANU in conjunction with several other disaffected former leaders, including Saitoti, who had been ousted as vice president of the republic in August.

President Moi's selection of Kenyatta (who was formally nominated at a party congress in October) was designed to put a Kikuyu candidate on the party ballot and maintain Moi's control over the party after he exited the presidency. The ploy split KANU and drove out the Rainbow dissidents. The Alliance formally left KANU in October to form the LDP (see above). NARC's nomination of Mwai Kibaki in October pitted two Kikuyu candidates as the presidential frontrunners, a fact that magnified the importance of the votes brokered by the other ethnic leaders in the LDP.

More KANU old guard resigned after the party's defeat in the December 2002 elections, throwing the party into turmoil. By April 2003, Moi announced that he would step down as party chair later in the year. Stepping into the role of official opposition party leader in the assembly, Kenyatta named a shadow KANU cabinet in June. At the September KANU executive meeting, Moi kept his pledge and resigned as chair without naming a successor. Kenyatta was subsequently named acting chair in April 2004.

KANU's party elections were held at a party congress in early 2005. Kenyatta took the chair in a landslide victory over rival faction leader Nicholas Biwott; Biwott disputed the outcome and moved to set up a rival KANU faction dubbed the New KANU Alliance Party. (This faction was given control over KANU's government registration by the Registrar of Societies and the ECK during a battle over the party's relationship to ODM in late 2006 through June 2007.)

As the principal opposition party uniting the Orange Team against the November 2005 constitutional referendum, KANU played a dominant role in shaping the ODM (see above). KANU signaled its willingness to work with their ODM partners to nominate a single opposition candidate for president and worked with ODM partners in the July 2006 by-elections, with KANU representatives picking up two of the five contested seats in parliament.

In parliament KANU MPs aggressively challenged President Kibaki's paper-thin and disorganized majority. For instance, in March 2006 six KANU members resigned their seats in the powerful House Business Committee after complaining that the government was underrepresenting KANU in committee assignments.

Kenyatta grew increasingly disenchanted with KANU's place within ODM in 2007, however, as it became clear that he was not likely to secure the ODM nomination for president and that other ODM leaders were inclined to move ODM away from a coalition of parties model toward a unified party structure. In June 2007 he delayed filing presidential candidacy papers with the ODM party organs pending a clarification on whether ODM was a coalition or a party and whether the parties had status as corporate members. (After a meeting of his KANU faction in Kasaranu, Kenyatta secured an understanding within ODM's leadership that seats in a new government would be divided according to a set formula with 40 percent given to KANU.)

In the meantime, Biwott's faction actively maneuvered to support Kibaki in the elections (with the aid of Daniel arap Moi's rehabilitation by Kibaki and Moi's active deal brokering) and met at a Mombasa delegates meeting in June to continue the quest to take KANU outside ODM. Ultimately, the fight with Biwott for control over the KANU's registration forced Kenyatta's hand by July; moreover, Moi worked tirelessly behind the scenes to reconcile the factions, restore the party registration to Kenyatta's faction, and split KANU permanently from ODM (as Raila Odinga was getting the upper hand in the ODM nomination fight). By August Kenyatta announced that KANU was out of ODM and would run its own candidates in the legislative elections. Kenyatta also announced that he would not run for president but would instead support the reelection of Kibaki (the last a vindication for the king-making activities of Moi and a huge boost to Kibaki's reelection bid).

In September Kenyatta took part in the discussions forming the PNU coalition to reelect Kibaki, but KANU was given a special dispensation as a partner party and allowed to run candidates against PNU candidates in parliamentary races under the KANU banner.

Running candidates in 91 constituencies under its own banner, KANU won 14 seats in the parliamentary election in December 2007. Four KANU MPs were named to the cabinet in April 2008, including Kenyatta as deputy prime minister.

After yet another failed attempt to wrest back control of KANU the leadership, Nicholas Biwott was elected party leader of a new party, the National Vision Party, on December 22, 2008.

Leaders: Uhuru KENYATTA (Chair and 2002 presidential candidate), Marsden MADOKA (Vice Chair), Chris Okemo (Vice Chair), Julius ole SUNKULI (Secretary General), Joseph NKAISERRY (Deputy Secretary General), Gideon NDAMBUKI (National Organizing Secretary), Billow KERROW (Treasurer), Justin MUTURI (Chief Whip), Kipyator Nicholas BIWOTT, Daniel T. arap MOI (Former President of the Republic and of the Party).

Safina. Safina was launched in May 1995 by an opposition group that included Dr. Richard Leakey, a former director of the Kenya Wildlife Service. The group, which applied for registration on June 20, said that it would work with others to establish a viable alternative to KANU. However, a ruling party MP filed a suit in late July to block legalization of the formation on the grounds that its name (translated as "Noah's Arc") was "repugnant to good religious values." The emergence of Leakey (a second-generation white Kenyan) as head of an opposition group reportedly appeared to "unnerve both President Moi and KANU leaders." Among other things, Leakey had been successful in attracting foreign backing for his scientific activities and had served to heighten international awareness of Kenya's domestic turmoil. For its part, the government declared it had no intention of conferring legitimacy on a party "backed by foreigners."

Following his release from prison in December 1996, opposition activist Koigi Wa Wamwere joined Safina and called on the government to recognize the grouping. Official opposition to Safina remained strong, however, and in February 1997 security forces violently thwarted an attempt by party members to convene a meeting. Thereafter, Safina militants were reportedly deeply involved in the organization of antigovernment demonstrations, and at midyear Leakey, Paul Muite, and other party officials joined the NCA's executive wing.

In October 1997 Safina's bid for legalization was again rejected by the government; however, under pressure from moderate opposition leaders, the Moi administration reversed itself, and in November Safina was registered. Although legalized too late to forward a presidential candidate, Safina participated in the December 1997 legislative balloting, capturing three seats.

At Safina's first national convention on September 5, 1998, party delegates elected Farah Maalim interim chair and Mwandawiro MGHANGA secretary general. In addition, the party subsequently chose Josephine Odira SINYO to assume the parliamentary post vacated by Leakey, who had been restored to directorship of the wildlife service. Safina's cohesion subsequently suffered from Leakey's decision to join the KANU administration (see Current issues, above) and from a scandal involving alleged corruption on the part of key leaders.

Safina took part in the PCK negotiations to join forces with the NAK and LDP to form the NARC Super Alliance, but Paul Muite, like Simeon Nyachae of FORD–People, pulled out of NARC almost immediately after NARC refused to institute an electoral college to nominate a single candidate for the presidency. However, Muite has positioned Safina in support of President Kibaki's government by denouncing cabinet members who campaigned against the November 2005 constitutional referendum and by taking the unusually aggressive stance of publicly defending the Kibaki government's raid on *The Standard* newspaper (see Communications, below). Muite described the IMF and World Bank threats to withhold funds as "senseless and uncalled-for fodder for the donors to fight the government."

In September 2007 Safina affiliated with the PNU coalition to contest the parliamentary and presidential elections but never came to a formal agreement for corporate membership. As a result, Safina ran candidates under its own banner in the December parliamentary elections when it put forward candidates in 88 constituencies but secured only 5 seats in the National Assembly.

Safina announced in August 2008 that it was joining forces with SKS and Saba Saba Asili to form the **Progressive Parties Alliance** (PROPA). The alliance, which also included several youth movements, sought to fill a gap in central Kenya for a party based more on reform and social democratic ideology than on ethnic alliances.

Leaders: Paul MUITE (Chair), Peter MUNYA (Secretary General), Dome WAMAGATA (National Coordinator).

National Rainbow Coalition of Kenya (NARC–Kenya or NARC–K). NARC–K claimed to be a "political vehicle" that would enable the current Kenyan leadership a "fresh start" to achieve "true Kenyan independence." Launched in June 2006 and composed primarily of former members of NARC and the DP who remain loyal to President Kibaki, NARC–K seeks to free itself from the political corruption that plagued the country under President Moi and the scandals and factional infighting that have marred the Kibaki presidency. Although billed as a multiethnic party, the leadership derives most of its support from the Kikuyu ethnic group, and skeptics have charged that the formation of NARC–K is little more than a political maneuver designed to bring the DP into power under a different name. (Kibaki is the founder of DP, see below.) At the very least, the formation of NARC–K appeared to be an attempt to reconstitute the DP with the objective of attracting wider support within the Mt. Kenya region. Complicating matters further was Kibaki's ambiguous relationship with NARC–K. Kibaki stated that he identified with NARC–K, and Vice President Moody Awori (a Kibaki ally) declared that President Kibaki was "behind the inspiration of leaders knitting together the values, policies and vision of the party." However, Kibaki was noticeably absent from NARC–K's first public meeting, and he never registered as a member of the party. Kibaki's reluctance may be explained by the risk to his government of his joining NARC–K, and thereby endangering the constitutional status of his fragile government elected under the NARC banner. Moreover, Kibaki may have lost the support of FORD–People and other ministers if he announced for NARC–K.

Despite this ambiguity, the NARC–K leadership endorsed Kibaki as its presidential choice on January 7, 2007. When Kibaki subsequently spurned the invitation to run under the NARC–K banner and organized the PNU party coalition in September 2007, NARC–K joined as a corporate member of the new party. Soon thereafter many NARC–K notables, including Moody Awori, left the party to affiliate directly with PNU.

In the turmoil over the PNU nominations process, however, Martha Karua and Matua Katuku maneuvered to assume control over the NARC–K party registration. This effort created a safe haven for politicians allied with Kibaki: if they failed to secure the direct PNU nomination, aspirants could fall back to a NARC–K nomination and stand for election against the PNU choice.

NARC–K ran candidates in 59 constituencies and secured four seats under its own banner in the 2007 parliamentary election. Karua won a seat under the PNU label, was named to the cabinet by Kibaki after the election, and was part of Kibaki's negotiation team for brokering the power-sharing agreement between Kibaki and Odinga. She is jockeying with KANU's party leader, Uhuru Kenyatta, for the upper hand within the PNU alliance in the bid to be Kibaki's successor and the PNU's presidential candidate in 2012.

Leaders: Martha KARUA (Chair), Matua KATUKU (Secretary General), Danson MUNGATANA (Treasurer), Mohammed KUTI, Judah METITO, Yasin TWAHA.

Forum for the Restoration of Democracy for the People (FORD–People). FORD–People was launched by Kenneth Matiba in October 1997, thus ending his battle with Martin Shikuku for control of FORD–A. Reportedly the most distinguishing salient feature of the FORD–People's charter (in comparison to the FORD–A's) is an intraparty electoral system wherein its candidates' nominations "will be under direct primary elections."

Upon Matiba's retirement in December 1998, his son Raymond MATIBA allegedly assumed control over the party; however, it was not immediately clear in what capacity the younger Matiba would function.

In December 2001 FORD–People invited former KANU minister Simeon Nyachae to join the party and serve as its presidential candidate. FORD–People subsequently participated in the formation of the PICK and NARC groupings. Nyachae pulled out of NARC almost immediately, however, after NARC refused to institute a primary to nominate a single candidate for the presidency. Nyachae ultimately ended up pursuing his own candidacy in the December 2002 election, a decision that reportedly caused serious rifts within FORD–People.

Nyachae and the other elected FORD–People ministers sat in opposition within the National Assembly, pledging to vote with NARC when it made good decisions. Nyachae was eventually brought into the cabinet by President Kibaki when he formed the government of national unification in June 2004. At a December 2004 party conference Kipkalya Kones, Reuben Oyondi, and Farah Maalim were elected chair, vice chair, and secretary general, respectively.

In preparation for the 2007 presidential elections, FORD–People met with FORD–Kenya with the aim of reviving the original FORD party. The talks were aimed at reaching an agreement on the process of determining a joint presidential nominee. Farah Maalim proclaimed that the "differences between party members have been ironed out and all were now united." The parties intended to play down the importance of reaching an agreement on a new constitution and instead made economic development, energy resources, and drought recovery the primary issues for FORD–People. Ultimately, the parties remained separate. Simeon Nyachae, roads and public works minister, announced in June 2006 that he planned to leave politics and not stand for election in 2007.

The FORD–People leadership found the NARC–K leadership team unacceptable as electoral partners, a factor which may have been decisive in Kibaki choosing not to embrace NARC–K as the banner behind his reelection campaign. FORD–People joined under the PNU banner for the 2007 elections.

Like other PNU allied parties however, FORD–People chose to run under its own banner in some 41 constituencies and ultimately won three seats in the National Assembly in the December 2007 election. One FORD–People MP, Henry Obwocha, was appointed to the coalition cabinet.

Leaders: Simeon NYACHAE (2002 presidential candidate and Leader), Reuben OYONDI (Vice Chair), Farah MAALIM (Secretary General), Henry OBWOCHA (Deputy Secretary General, Party Whip), Francis Munyialo OPAR (Party Organizing Secretary), Dominic MUTHUURI (Treasurer), Kimani WANYOIKE (Former Secretary General and 1997 presidential candidate).

Democratic Party (DP). The DP, which draws support largely from the sizable Kikuyu ethnic group, was formed in January 1992 by a number of former government officials, including Mwai Kibaki, a long-standing ally of President Moi who had recently resigned from the government and KANU to protest the administration's failure to address widespread official corruption. Kibaki challenged the Moi government on a number of economic issues, especially its continued allocation of funds to inefficient government-owned operations.

At the DP's annual meeting in November 1992 Kibaki's presidential candidacy was unanimously supported; in balloting in late December the DP standard-bearer finished third while party legislative candidates won 23 seats. In early January 1993 the DP agreed to form an electoral coalition with FORD–A and FORD–K, which displayed little effective cohesion in a by-election five months later.

Confronted with the DP's dire financial condition, its main factions agreed to shelve their differences and reelected Kibaki chair at a congress in March 1997. However, a number of party members subsequently signaled their interest in campaigning as the group's standard-bearer in the forthcoming presidential elections. The most noteworthy bid came from Charity Ngilu, a prominent assemblywoman, who joined the SDP (and later formed the NPK) after Kibaki received the group's nomination.

In early 1998 the DP accused propresidential militants of orchestrating the outbreak of ethnic violence in the Rift Valley, alleging that supporters of Kibaki's presidential bid were being targeted. (On January 23 the party had filed suit to have the balloting nullified.) Thereafter, the DP sought to form a multiparty, opposition government-in-waiting; however, subsequent negotiations among opposition leaders quickly fell apart, and in April the DP named a shadow cabinet composed of its own members. In October the DP overwhelmingly supported a non-confidence motion against the government; however, as many as three of its legislators were alleged to have broken with the party on the issue. Kibaki subsequently continued to reject the assembly's constitutional review process, believing that it unfairly represented the interests of KANU and President Moi.

By 2002, the DP, under Kibaki's direction, played a key role in stitching together the NAC, NAK, and subsequently victorious NARC opposition party alliances to defeat KANU. Kibaki's election as president left him in the dual position of DP chair and NARC party boss. By December 2003 President Kibaki chose to distance himself publicly from any official role in the DP as he battled to dissolve the various parties within NARC in favor of direct NARC membership (see above). The DP, however, did not disband and continues to maintain a formal organization chaired by Kibaki, despite his public statements that the party ceased to exist after the formation of the NAK and despite his calls for DP members to support NARC.

At a June 2005 DP meeting in Nairobi, which was called to revitalize the party, 40 party leaders, who were members of the assembly, failed to attend, including President Kibaki, David Mwiraria, Chris MURUNGARU, Martha KARUA, Peter NDWIGA, and Kiraitu MURUNGI. The delegates who attended pledged to strengthen the party and avoid its personalization; however, by March 2006 it appeared that their efforts had failed. After announcing the formation of NARC–K, President Kibaki declared that DP "had ceased to exist." The DP's national governing council unanimously voted to remove President Kibaki as its leader and endorsed Rose Waruhiu to act as chair until the National Delegates Council in July 2006 (former ministers and party notables David Mwiraria, Chris Murungaru, and Kiraitu Murungi were suspended from the party in April). Waruhiu maintained that the party would not be dissolved and would field candidates in the 2007 general election either independently or with other political parties. Meanwhile, the party supported Kibaki, NARC, and the Government of National Unity formed when Rail Odinga and the LDP split with the NARC government in 2004.

DP leaders were solidly behind Kibaki's bid for reelection. They also actively engaged in the NARC revival efforts in July 2007 and benefited from the defection of several politicians from the NARC–K and KANU rosters as alliances shifted in the run-up to the elections. The DP later joined Kibaki's PNU as a corporate member in September 2007. DP leaders, however, like leaders of some other PNU corporate affiliate parties, chose to run parliamentary candidates under the party's own banner, despite pressure from PNU notables to stay within the PNU's nominations framework. Several prominent politicians, including Muriuki Karue and Ngenye Kariuki from NARC–K, defected from other PNU parties to join DP during the run-up to the nominations.

In the December 2007 election, the DP ran candidates in 86 constituencies but won only 2 seats in the National Assembly. None of the PNU cabinet seats were allotted to the DP MPs.

Leaders: Joseph MUNYAO (Acting Chair), (Vice Chair), George NYAMWEYA (Secretary General), Rachael KAMWERU (Deputy Secretary General), Karisa MAITHA (Treasurer), David MWENJE (Deputy Treasurer), Yacob HAJJI (Organizing Secretary).

New Ford Kenya (New FORD–K). Formed as a splinter group from FORD–K in 2007, New FORD–K forged an alliance with the PNU in September 2007 to contest the December 2007 elections but later choose to run candidates under the party's own banner. Two New FORD–K candidates won seats in the December 2007 parliamentary election, and Peter Shitanda was appointed to the cabinet.

Leaders: Peter Soita Shitanda (Chair), Boni KHALWALE.

Sisi Kwa Sisi (SKS). SKS purports to transcend religious barriers by uniting supporters of Islamic Party–Kenya and the Mungiki sect (the party's name is translated as "us among us"). The party won two seats in the 2002 legislative balloting and pledged to work with the NARC coalition to secure political and economic reforms.

In September 2007 the SKS joined the PNU coalition to contest the parliamentary and presidential elections but eventually choose to list its candidates separately in constituencies where it nominated candidates. SKS candidates won 2 seats in the December 2007 parliamentary election, but none of the PNU cabinet seats were allotted to SKS MPs.

SKS announced in August 2008 that it was joining forces with Safina and Saba Saba Asili to form the **Progressive Parties Alliance**—PROPA.

Leaders: John Rukenya KABUGUA (Chair), Moffat Muia MAITHA, William Gitau KAABOGO.

Forum for Restoration of Democracy–Asili (FORD–A). The Kikuyu-dominated FORD–Asili (Kiswahili for "Original") was formally launched on October 13, 1992, by Kenneth Matiba and Martin Shikuku, a popular Luhya politician and former FORD interim secretary general. Matiba, who had suffered a stroke while under detention in 1990, returned from recuperation in London in May 1992 to a "hero's welcome." Immediately thereafter he announced his interest in becoming FORD's presidential candidate, thus aggravating an already contentious leadership struggle. In early September Matiba and Shikuku boycotted FORD's inaugural congress, at which Jaramogi Odinga, as expected, was selected the party's presidential candidate, and one month later FORD–A was founded.

On November 17, 1992, Matiba outpolled Shikuku for the group's nomination, and in nationwide presidential balloting in December he finished second with 26 percent of the vote. In simultaneous legislative balloting the party won 31 seats, tying FORD–K. On January 4, 1993, the party joined in a coalition with FORD–K and the DP to contest KANU's electoral victories and "coordinate activities." On April 8 the party was declared the official opposition party by the assembly speaker, and in early May Matiba, as minority leader, named a shadow government with Shikuku in the vice presidential slot. However, in June FORD–A lost the assembly leadership when a party legislator defected to KANU. During 1994 the party leadership fell into disarray, with the still ailing Matiba openly sparring with Shikuku (whom some accused of being a KANU "mole") and with several MPs deserting to the government formation.

In March 1996 it was reported that Shikuku had lost his position as FORD–A secretary general to Kimani WANYOIKE while George NTHENGE had also been defeated (by Stephen Musila) in his bid to retain the party chair.

Amid reports that Matiba and Shikuku had established separate headquarters, Matiba's faction held its own intraparty elections in May 1997. Subsequently, however, the polling was challenged in court by Shikuku and nullified. In June Matiba announced that he no longer recognized the legitimacy of the Moi government and resigned from the parliament. Thereafter, Matiba's alliance with the Opposition Solidarity and Shikuku's ties with the Opposition Alliance appeared to have superceded their allegiance to what *Africa Confidential* described as the "catastrophically split" FORD–A. In October Matiba formed the FORD–People (see above). Shikuku announced his desire to run for the presidency in 2002 but was not one of the candidates on the December ballot.

In the 2002 elections some FORD–A leaders joined the NARC coalition under the NAK wing (John Michuki was subsequently appointed to the cabinet). The party also ran candidates for the National Assembly under the FORD–A party banner, independent of NARC, and secured 2 seats.

In 2005 party officials publicly asked Martin Shikuku to revamp the party as divisions both within the party and with FORD–People threatened to make FORD–A irrelevant in the upcoming 2007 elections. Julius Masiva (a Uasin Gishu branch official) charged that "Shikuku risks losing political credibility if he is going to leave the party to die. He should implement the views of the members." There was concern that the party would lose its official status as a registered party for failing to give returns as required by the Ministry of Justice and Constitutional Affairs.

Heading into the 2007 elections the status of FORD–Asili's political alignments was unclear. Martin Shikuku threw his support behind the ODM ticket. Kenneth Matiba, on the other hand, declared in December as a presidential candidate under the Saba Saba Asili banner (see below).

Running its candidates independent of either the ODM or PNU nomination slates, FORD–A secured 1 seat in the National Assembly in the 2007 parliamentary election, but none of the PNU cabinet seats were allotted to the FORD–A MP.

Leaders: Martin SHIKUKU (Chair and 1997 presidential candidate), John MICHUKI, Ivuti MWANGU, Francis KAGWIMA, Wanguhu NGANGA.

Forum for Restoration of Democracy–Kenya (FORD–K). The Luo-dominated FORD–K is the most direct outgrowth of the Forum for Restoration of Democracy (FORD), which was characterized by its multiparty founders in August 1991 as a "discussion group" in deference to the ban on political parties other than KANU. Despite seeming widespread support, FORD experienced problems in formulating a comprehensive platform and establishing a permanent party structure following its legalization in December 1992. Leadership disputes contributed to the difficulties; one faction supported the presidential ambitions of Martin Shikuku while another aligned itself with Jaramogi Oginga Ajuma Odinga, the aging former vice president of the republic, who succeeded in being named interim chair, with Shikuku as interim secretary general. However, the picture clouded further in May 1992 when Kenneth Matiba, a Kenyan businessman recently returned from London, announced his presidential candidacy.

At FORD's inaugural congress on September 4, 1992, Odinga was selected as the party's presidential candidate. However, Shikuku and Matiba supporters boycotted the congress and subsequently broke off to form FORD–Asili (FORD–A, see above). In early April 1993, despite a declaration of support by 51 opposition legislators for Odinga's assumption of the opposition leadership, the assembly speaker recognized FORD–A's Matiba. At the same time, intraparty opposition to Odinga's continued stewardship surfaced, with Kikuyu followers of (then) Deputy Chair Paul MUITE, an Odinga critic and de facto leader of the FORD–K's "young turks," reportedly defecting to the FORD–A and DP, (see above). (Muite subsequently became a founder of Safina, see above.)

In late June 1993 Odinga became leader of the opposition after a FORD–A legislator defected to KANU, and on July 15 he named a shadow cabinet. However, his subsequent efforts to improve relations with the Moi administration split the party, as supporters, led by his son, Raila Odinga, accused the anti-Moi faction aligned with Muite and (then) Secretary General Gitobu IMANYARA of seeking to gain control of the party. On September 18 the FORD–K national executive council stripped Imanyara of his post and named Munyua WAIYAKI as his replacement. The following day Muite resigned as deputy chair, and on September 21 Imanyara quit the party, announcing plans to launch a "new democratic opposition movement."

Following Odinga's death on January 20, 1994, (then) Deputy Chair Michael Kijana Wamalwa, a favorite of the late leader's sons, Raila and Oburu ODINGA, was named party chair. In June 1995 Secretary General Waiyaki resigned to help form the United Patriotic Party (UPP, below). Subsequently, a schism developed because of a leadership contest between Wamalwa and Raila Odinga. In December Odinga disregarded a court ruling banning internal party elections by having himself proclaimed chair at meetings in Kisumu and Nairobi (but not in Mombasa, where the police intervened). Wamalwa reacted by announcing that his faction would sponsor grassroots balloting in May and June. Relations between Wamalwa and Odinga sunk to a new low in early April 1996 when an extraordinary party congress, convened specifically to settle their leadership dispute, disintegrated into a riot after a party mediator, citing Wamalwa and Odinga's intransigence on procedural disagreements, declared their intraparty electoral contest "null and void" and resigned. Subsequently, on April 15 Wamalwa's supporters dismissed Odinga's claim that he had captured the party leadership. Friction continued throughout the year, culminating in Odinga's announcement in December that he was resigning from the party and joining the NDP. (On March 12 FORD–K officials openly supported a KANU candidate in a by-election contest with Odinga for the seat the latter had vacated when he left the party.)

At a FORD–K national delegates' conference on January 26, 1997, Wamalwa, James ORENGO, and Rachid MZEE were reelected chair, first vice chair, and second vice chair, respectively. Wamalwa was one of four prominent opposition leaders put under house arrest in May for their alleged roles in organizing antigovernment demonstrations. Subsequently, however, Wamalwa's opposition colleagues sharply criticized him after he met with President Moi to declare his intention to establish a dialogue with KANU.

Wamalwa's relations with KANU improved dramatically in 1998, and in October FORD–K legislators helped vote down a nonconfidence motion against the government. On the other hand, the October vote highlighted a split in the party between Wamalwa and a faction led by Orengo, who had tabled the motion. Wamalwa's ambivalent attitude toward KANU and what was considered by many his lackluster leadership style continued to cause dissension within the party, and Orengo attracted considerable publicity. Meanwhile, another anti-Wamalwa figure in the party, George KAPTEN, died under mysterious circumstances in 1999.

FORD–K was heavily involved in 2002 in the formation of a large anti–KANU opposition front, first NAK then the NARC Super Alliance, but Orengo launched his own presidential bid through the SDP (below). Wamalwa was named vice president by President Kibaki in January 2003 but died in August. Musikari Kombo, a Luhya like Wamalwa, became acting chair of the party until he was elected at a subsequent party conference.

After forestalling a challenge to his leadership of the party from Mukhisa Kituyi (who later left FORD–K for NARC–K) in December 2005, Kombo took steps in 2006 to broaden the national appeal of the FORD–K party. In March he opened a party office in the Thika district to build support in the central province. More significantly, Kombo initiated talks with party members to "synergize the FORD family" for the purpose of campaigns and electoral support. Talks with Simeon Nyachae and the FORD–People yielded encouraging results while negotiations with FORD–A were stymied by FORD–A's own internal divisions (see above). Kombo has also entered a dialogue with DP and NPK leaders to reinvigorate the NARC party organs in the wake of the formal launch of NARC–K and the exodus of cabinet ministers and MPs from NARC.

FORD–K leader Kombo played an important role in the negotiations that established the PNU, and the party joined the PNU coalition as a corporate member. In November 2007 Kipruto arap Kirwa defected from NARC–K, of which he was a vice chair, to join FORD–K. FORD–K won a single seat under its own banner in the December parliamentary election, but a PNU cabinet seat was not allotted to the FORD–K MP.

In 2007 a splinter party, **New FORD–Kenya,** emerged with the support of Soita Shitanda, the housing minister.

Leaders: Musikari N. KOMBO (Chair), John MUNYES (Secretary General), Otieno K'OPIYO (Deputy Secretary General), Jael MBOGO (Organizing Secretary), David SIMIYU.

Mazingira Green Party of Kenya (MPK). In April 2003 the noted environmental and human rights activist and assistant cabinet minister for environment Wangari Maathai formed the Green Party in the mold of Green parties in Europe. In 2004 Dr. Maathai was awarded the 2004 Nobel Peace Prize. She initially resisted invitations to join the NARC or NARC–K groupings because of a desire to see a new generation of leaders and to promote environmental issues.

In 2007 the party joined forces with other parties in President Kibaki's PNU coalition, in part to give Maathai a chance to win a seat in parliament. Running candidates under its own banner, the party secured only one seat in the December 2007 parliamentary election and received no cabinet appointments.

Leaders: Mwangi MAKANGA (Chair), Wangari MAATHAI, Sirus RUTEERE.

Orange Democratic Movement–Kenya (ODM–K). The ODM–K emerged in August 2007 from factional battles within the Orange Democratic Movement over the nomination of one of the party's many notables to be the candidate for president in the 2007 elections (see above). Outmaneuvered by Raila Odinga and his factional supporters for the ODM nomination, Stephen Kalonzo Musyoka, who controlled the party's official registration papers, established ODM–K, forcing Odinga and the remaining ODM leadership to register ODM separately.

Musyoka was nominated as the ODM–K presidential candidate on August 31, with LPK party chair Julia Ojiambo as his designated vice presidential candidate. ODM–K's new leadership summit consisted of Musyoka, Ojiambo, and Kennedy Kiliku, head of the NLP (see below).

The ODM–K contested seats in 133 constituencies, winning 14 in the December 2007 parliamentary election. Musyoka ran in the presidential election and was credited with 9 percent of the national vote in the disputed results released by the ECK. Soon after the election, Musyoka allied the party with Kibaki and the PNU. Kibaki then chose Musyoka as his vice president and minister for home affairs. After Kibaki and Odinga announced the power-sharing agreement, ODM–K retained three seats in the cabinet.

Leaders: Kalonzo MUSYOKA (Party Leader, Vice President of the Republic, and 2007 presidential candidate), Samuel POGHISIO (Chair), Mutula KILONZO (Secretary General), David RIMITA (Election Board Chair), Joseph KHAMISI.

Labour Party of Kenya (LPK). The LPK joined the Orange Team in opposing the constitutional referendum and allied itself with the LDP/KANU elements in the ODM in anticipation of the 2007 national elections. The LPK stood to gain 20 percent of the positions in government under the power-sharing scheme devised between the LDP, KANU, and LPK for power sharing if the ODM won the 2007 elections.

As the ODM factional infighting heated up in 2007 over the presidential nomination selection process, party leader Julia Ojiambo allied the LPK with Stephen Kalonzo Musyoka, who subsequently joined the LPK when he broke company with ODM leaders to form the ODM–K in August 2007. Like KANU, the LPK was opposed to ODM moving toward individual rather than corporate membership.

Although a founding member of NARC, the LPK controlled no seats in the assembly after the 2002 legislative balloting.

Leaders: Julia OJIAMBO (Chair), Stephen Kalonzo MUSYOKA (2007 ODM–K presidential candidate).

National Rainbow Coalition (NARC). The NARC was fashioned out of the October 2002 Super Alliance between the 14-party National Alliance for Kenya (NAK)—a restyled version of the National Alliance for Change—and the newly formed **Liberal Democratic Party** (LDP) and its Rainbow Alliance of KANU/NDP dissidents. From the beginning this grouping of politicians, ethnic interests, and wide-ranging political ideologies was one of political expedience more than enduring ties or shared policy goals. *Africa Confidential* framed NARC's inherent challenge: "[I]t isn't a party, it's a loose alliance of individuals and 15 parties. Its members range from leftists and trade unionists to 'tribal rights' ethnic chauvinists who have found common political cause."

Uniting the opposition to defeat the ruling KANU necessitated constructing a "big tent." NAK and LDP achieved this with the 2002 preelection MoU that equally divided job responsibilities and cabinet positions should NARC prevail. The NARC platform promised to revive the economy and create hundreds of thousands of jobs, crack down on official corruption (and get foreign aid flowing again), ratify a new constitution that limited presidential power within six months, and institute free universal primary education.

After the NARC electoral victory the underlying tensions within the coalition began to appear almost immediately. President Kibaki never convened the NARC Summit, the top party organ made up of the constituent major party leaders, after the election, and the LDP neglected to designate one of its leaders as its Summit representative, perhaps due to the difficulty of choosing faction leaders. From the very beginning the ethnic rivalries, dissension over broken MoU promises, and the division of power undermined the cohesion of NARC in government.

President Kibaki's efforts throughout 2004 and 2005 to fashion a more cohesive NARC by dissolving the constituent parties and opening NARC to an individual rather than a corporate basis for membership had the opposite effect. His move to invite opposition members into the government and demote several LDP cabinet members exacerbated the tensions and drove some LDP assembly members to sit with the opposition parties. The February 5, 2004, NARC party meeting in Nanyuki, convened to plan the dissolution of the constituent parties and broker a new consensus on power sharing, failed when only a fraction of the invited delegates attended. At a second Nanyuki meeting in April, members of the NARC committee for corporate membership voted down the plan to dissolve the member parties in favor of individual membership. The LDP, FORD–K, UDM, and IPK representatives voted in favor of retaining corporate membership, the FORD–A and SPARK delegates took a middle position, the DP representative remained neutral, and only the SDP and PPF leaders supported dissolution of parties and individual membership.

Calls for NARC party elections slated to begin February 26–27, 2005, at local levels, March 1 at the constituency level, and ending on March 11 were eventually scuttled. Opposition from three NARC factional leaders—Charity Ngilu (NPK), Raila Odinga (LDP), and Musikari Kombo (FORD–K)—led to a court battle over the NARC constitution.

In January 2005, 73 members of the assembly from the NAK wing of NARC formed a new lobby called National Reform Initiative (NARI) in response to their dissatisfaction with the pace and tenor of the government's economic, land, constitutional, and social service reforms. With the LDP wing of the coalition already in open rebellion, this left the future parliamentary cohesion of NARC in jeopardy. By mid-2005 National Assembly members from the Coast Province were openly meeting to discuss the formation of a regional party, further undermining NARC's cohesion.

The major party organs of NARC were the Summit, created by the MoU, the Party Council, and the Parliamentary Group. In theory the NARC Summit achieved some measure of party and ethnic balance among the coalition partners. The Summit consisted of the DP's Kibaki (Kikuyu), LDP's Odinga (Luo), Moody Awori (Luhya), and Najib Balala (Coast and Muslims), UDM's Kipruto KIRWA (Kalenjin), and the NPK's Charity Ngilu (Kamba). All of these organs fell away because of factional tensions. In practice NARC had two de facto secretariats, one unofficial group loyal to Kibaki and another official group under the leadership of Ngilu.

The movement of the LDP into opposition and the formation of NARC–K in 2006 further divided NARC and undermined its viability. President Kibaki declared NARC "dead," and Ngilu retorted that the newly formed NARC–K was little more than the DP with a different name and should not be confused with the NARC, which was still the ruling government party. At least 80 MPs left the coalition, including Mutua Katuku and Alex KIBAKI (President Kibaki's son), as well as many cabinet ministers.

Leaders of the NPK, DP, and FORD–K met in June 2006, after the formal launch of NARC–K, to discuss reinvigorating the NARC party organs after Kibaki distanced himself politically from the coalition.

The NARC revival effort was renewed a year later in the maneuvering to strengthen the party in preparation for the 2007 presidential and legislative elections. Party representatives met three times in meetings chaired by Noah Wekesa to rewrite the coalition's constitution; the last meeting included representatives of constituent members DP, FORD–K, FORD–A, UDM, SPARK, the PPF, plus representatives of the independent parties Mazingira Green Party of Kenya and Saba Saba Asili, and a representative from the LPK (part of ODM–K, see above). Most of these parties supported Kibaki's reelection.

Notably, the NARC party chair, Charity Ngilu, and other official party leaders declined to attend or review the new constitution and would not surrender NARC's registration certificate to others, thus keeping Kibaki from using NARC as his umbrella for contesting the 2007 elections. Ngilu, the heath minister until her dismissal from the cabinet in October 2007, broke with Kibaki and moved closer to the ODM leadership in August 2007, finally joining the ODM senior leadership group, Pentagon, in October, but with agreement that she had the option to stand for election to the new parliament under the NARC banner.

NARC put forward 73 candidates, including Ngilu, for constituencies, but won 3 seats in the National Assembly in the December 2007 election. After the election NARC was formally allied with the ODM and President Kibaki and Prime Minister Odinga appointed Ngilu to the cabinet with the water and irrigation portfolio.

Leaders: Charity NGILU (Chair), Fidelis NGULI (Secretary-General), Bartha Mbata MBUVI (Vice Chair), Noah WEKESA

(Council and Coordinating Committee Chair), Alex MUREITHI, Wanjala WELIME (Elections Board Chairs).

National Alliance Party of Kenya (NAK)/**National Party of Kenya** (NPK). The NPK was launched in June 2001 under the leadership of Charity Ngilu, who had been the SDP presidential candidate in 1997. The NPK announced that it would work toward "gender equality" and "good governance" while "fighting poverty, ignorance and disease."

By 2002 Ngilu had moved the NPK into the NAC grouping to help launch the restyled NAK, turning over to the opposition alliance the party registration for the NPK to avoid delays or obstruction in party certification from the Moi government.

The NAK brought together 14 parties under one tent (with the NAK as one of the two pillars of NARC, the other being the LDP). Before the LDP joined forces with the NAK to form NARC, Ngilu was in line to receive the prime minister's post under the anticipated new constitution. Once LDP's Rainbow Alliance entered the scene, the premiership was promised to Raila Odinga of the LDP. Ngilu was named a cabinet minister by President Kibaki, was made chair of NARC, and was selected to sit on the NARC Summit.

In the party dissolution crisis that followed in 2004, Ngilu initially supported Kibaki on the question of individual or corporate membership in NARC, but by early 2005 she and other NPK party leaders had reversed course and registered the NPK independently again. The NPK joined the LDP and FORD–K in asking the courts to block the March 2005 NARC effort to dissolve the constituent parties and hold direct NARC party elections. The High Court, however, ruled against the injunction and cleared the way for NARC to hold grassroots elections. NPK was not consulted during the creation of the NARC–Kenya party, and Ngilu challenged the legitimacy of the new party by suggesting that NARC–K was little more than the DP in a different form. After running for parliament under the NARC banner in the 2007 election, the NPK party largely lies dormant.

Leaders: Titus MBATHI (Chair), Fidelis NGULI (Secretary General), Charity K. NGILU (1997 presidential candidate), Cecily MBARIRE.

United Democratic Movement (UDM). The UDM was formed in 1998 under the leadership of Kipruto arap Kirwa, whose organization of an anti-Moi faction within KANU had cost him his post of assistant minister of agriculture in May. In early 1999 the group released a leadership roster, which reportedly included legislators thought to be KANU supporters. (Consequently, President Moi presented a motion that would forbid sitting assembly members to launch new groups.) The Moi administration suppressed UDM's formal registration.

UDM leaders took part in the 2002 negotiations to create the NAK and NARC (see above), and in return Kirwa was named agriculture minister in the NARC administration following the 2002 election. Kirwa formally registered UDM in March 2003. One impetus for the UDM is to provide a party to champion the interests of the Kalenjin ethnic group, according to party Secretary General Stephen Tanis.

In the 2004–2005 NARC party dissolution battles, UDM leaders supported maintaining corporate membership for the parties within NARC. By 2006 the future of UDM was uncertain. Kipruto Rono arap Kirwa (party leader and minister of agriculture) was embroiled in an alleged corruption scandal, and the party's influence at the national level appeared diminished. Moreover, Kirwa and Stephen Tanis allied themselves first with NARC–K and then the PNU after its formation in September 2007 before the elections. Kirwa eventually joined FORD–K, by then affiliated with the PNU, but he failed to win a seat in the National Assembly under that banner.

By the end of the parliamentary balloting, the UDM had secured one seat in the National Assembly and had forged an alliance with the ODM. The lone party MP, Helen Sambili, was named to a cabinet post in the grand coalition that emerged in April 2008.

Leaders: Nathaniel CHEBELION (Party leader), Helen Jepkemoi SAMBILI.

Government-Supportive Parties:

Chama Cha Uzalendo (CCU). A socialist party, the CCU secured two seats in the 2007 parliamentary election.

Leaders: Maur BWANAMAKA (Chair), P.L.O. LUMUMBA (Secretary General), Gitobu IMANYARA, Wavinya NDETI.

Party of Independent Candidates of Kenya (PICK). One of the earliest fringe parties after the advent of party pluralism, PICK was founded by a Nairobi businessman, John Harun Mwau, who styled himself as the PICK party boss.

PICK candidates won 2 seats in the December 2007 parliamentary election. The party is allied with the ODM but has no representation in the coalition cabinet.

Leaders: G.N. MUSIMI (Chair), F. OLIEWO (Vice Chair), F. NGUGI (Secretary), John Harun MWAU, Clement WAIBARA.

Kenya African Democratic Union–Asili (KADU–A). KADU–A won 1 seat in the National Assembly in the December 2007 election.

Leader: Francis BAYA.

Kenya National Democratic Alliance (KENDA). Like the SDP, KENDA's initial policy statements concerned human rights issues, the party calling for, among other things, an end to detention without trial and political imprisonment. Legalized in early 1992, KENDA secured no assembly representation in December 1992, and its presidential candidate, Mukara NG'AND'A, captured only 0.11 percent of the vote.

In 1997 Koigi wa Wamwere campaigned for the presidency under the KENDA banner when his party, Safina, was unable to forward a candidate.

In 2006 KENDA was revived by one of the businessmen implicated in the Goldenberg scandal, Kamlesh Pattni, in a move some critics speculated was a bid to win his election to parliament, boosting his chances for securing immunity from prosecution. Pattni also founded an organization named Hand of Hope to aid unemployed youth in a bid to overcome resistance from some of the party's left-leaning original membership.

KENDA campaigned for the 2007 parliamentary elections as if it were a formal affiliate of PNU, a relationship PNU denied because of Pattni's implication in the Goldenberg scandal. The party won 1 National Assembly seat.

Leaders: Kamlesh PATTNI (Chair), Joram KARIUKI (Vice Chair), Bernard KALOVE (Secretary General), Linah KILIMO, Koigi wa WAMWERE (1997 presidential candidate).

National Labor Party (NLP). The NLP has served as a safety valve or "briefcase party" for Kenyan politicians who need a platform for office-seeking when other avenues are blocked. In 2005 Joseph Kiliku had open discussion with the LDP's Stephen Kalonzo Musyoka about the latter using the party as a vehicle for his run for the presidency in 2007. (Musyoka eventually won nomination under the ODM–K banner.) Kiliku also sought to use his party, without success, as a platform for a revitalized Third Progressive Force (TPF). Kiliku later joined ODM–K's party summit.

NLP won 1 seat in the National Assembly in the December 2007 parliamentary election, and the party's MP affiliated with the ODM rather than the ODM–K/PNU alliance.

Leaders: Joseph Kennedy KILIKU (Chair), Walter OSEBE, Daniel Mogaka RAGU.

People's Democratic Party (PDP). The PDP won 1 seat in the National Assembly in the December 2007 election. The party's MP affiliated with the ODM rather than the ODM–K/PNU alliance.

Leader: Richard ONYONKA.

People's Party of Kenya (PPK). Launched to pursue "radical social democracy" and led by Harun Waweru, the PPK won 1 seat in the National Assembly in the December 2007 election. The party's MP affiliated with the ODM rather than the ODM–K/PNU alliance.

Leaders: Harun WAWERU (Chair), David MWAURA.

Opposition Parties:

Kenyan African Democratic Development Union (KADDU). KADDU is a small party with support in the Luhya districts of Kenya. Party leader Cyrus Jirongo declared in early August 2007 that he was a candidate for president but later pledged his support to the ODM's Raila Odinga, who had named Musalia Mudavadi, a Luhya, his vice president-designate. By early November Jirongo withdrew his support, however, charging the ODM was taking his party's support for granted.

Despite fielding candidates in 97 parliamentary constituencies the party won one seat in the National Assembly election in December 2007. Because KADDU was not affiliated with any of the parties in the coalition government, however, it is the only party that can be designated the "official opposition."

Leader: Cyrus JIRONGO (Chair).

Other Parties and Groups:

Saba Saba Asili. A splinter party formed in anticipation of the 2007 elections from elements of FORD–Asili, Saba Saba Asili (the name literally means "Seven Seven Original" in Kiswahili) negotiated to join the PNU coalition. Kenneth Matiba sought the party's nomination to run for president in 2007; by early December, however, party leaders urged Matiba to exit the race, citing inadequate financial resources and time to run an effective campaign. None of the party's candidates won a parliamentary constituency, and Matiba drew negligible support in the presidential polling.

Saba Saba Asili announced in August 2008 that it was joining forces with Safina and SKS to form the **Progressive Parties Alliance** (PROPA).

Leaders: Kenneth MATIBA (2007 presidential candidate), Ngengi MUIGAI (Chair), Mohammed KUSOMA (National Director), Joseph KANGUCHU (Organizing Secretary).

Shirikisho Party of Kenya (SPK). Shirikisho was a little-known regional group that claimed 1 seat in the 1997 legislative balloting and retained the 1 seat in the 2002 election. The party draws it support from the Coast Province.

In 2005 allegations of misappropriation of funds granted from the Center for Multiparty Democracy surfaced from former party treasurer Mwakio NDAU. SPK party leader Harry Kombe met in Nairobi with a small number of LDP and KANU assembly members who expressed interest in joining SPK. At the same time, party leaders spurned a plan by the Third Progressive Force to form a new Coast Province party and entertained talks of forming a coalition before the 2007 elections with the LDP and FORD–K representatives.

In July 2007, David MWIRARIA, returning to Kibaki's cabinet after resigning in February 2006 under suspicion of corruption, announced that he was leaving NARC–K to join the SPK. Transport minister Chirau Ali Mwakwere had previously left NARC–K in June to join the SPK (he had been one of the NARC–K vice chairs). Both continued to actively support Kibaki's reelection bid and worked to steer SPK into the Party of National Unity (PNU) coalition backing Kibaki. Chirau Ali Mwakwere won an assembly seat in the 2007 elections under the PNU party label.

The SPK favored greater autonomy for the provinces; SPK leaders pushed the PNU to make concessions in Kibaki's platform on this issue of concern, and some junior party leaders threatened to form a splinter group to advocate for federalism.

Leaders: Lina Mkasi BUNI (Chair), Abubakar YUSUF (Secretary General), Kassim JUMA (Organizing Secretary), Chirau Ali MWAKWERE, Harry KOMBE.

Minor groups who put forward candidates or who were referenced in the 2002 or 2007 election campaigns included the **AGANO Party,** led by David Mwaura WAIHIGA; the **Chama Cha Uma Party** (CCU), led by David Ng'ethe WAWERU (2002 and 2007 presidential candidate); the **Chama Cha Majimbo Na Mwangaza** (CCM), led by Leslie MWACHIRO; the **Islamic Party of Kenya** (IPK), led by Mohammed KHALIFA; the **Kenya Citizens Congress** (KCC); the **Kenya National Congress** (KNC), led by S. Kathini Maloba CAINES; the **Kenya Patriotic Trust Party** (KPTP), led by Joseph KARANI Ngacha (2007 presidential candidate); the **Kenya People's Party** (KPP), led by Pius MUIRU (2007 presidential candidate); the **Kenya Social Congress** (KSC), led by Mathius Ondeyo NYARIBARI; the **Kenya Union of National Alliance for Peace,** led by Wilson Nyakundi Abuga; the **New Aspirations Party of Kenya,** led by Mathew Okwanda; the **Republican Liberty Party** (RLP), led by Zachariah Momanyi Matayo; the **Republican Party of Kenya** (RPK), led by Jeremiah Nixon Kukubo (2007 presidential candidate); the **Social Democratic Party** (SDP), led by James Aggrey ORENGO (2002 presidential candidate); the **Social Party for the Advancement of Reforms Kenya** (SPARK), led by Joseph Owuor NYONG'O; the **United People's Congress,** led by Charles Barongo Nyakeri; the **Workers Congress Party of Kenya,** led by Nazlin Omar RAJPUT (2007 presidential candidate); and the **National Progressive Party** (NPP).

Other recently emerging groups include the **Alliance for Democracy** (*Muungano wa Ukombozi*); **Chama Cha Mwananchi** (CCM), a party of former political prisoners and government critics, led by Dick KAMAU; the **Generations Alliance Party of Kenya** (GAP–K), formed in January 2006 and led by Gerald Thuita; the **Grand National Union**, led by Mwangi KIUNJURI; the **Independent Party**, led by Kalembe NDILE; the **Kenya National Patriotic Party** (KNPP), led by Salim MWIROTHO; **Labour Party Democracy,** led by Mohamed Ibrahim NOOR; and the **Wakulima Party,** registered in October 2004.

LEGISLATURE

The unicameral **National Assembly** currently consists of 210 members elected by universal suffrage in single-seat constituencies for five-year terms, plus 12 members appointed by the president and two ex officio members (the speaker of the National Assembly and the attorney-general), for a total of 224 members of parliament. Prior to the expansion of the Assembly in 1997, there were 188 elected and 12 appointed members. From 1966 to the relegalization of political pluralism in December 1991, only KANU had been permitted to offer legislative candidates.

Following the December 27, 2007, balloting the 210 elected seats were distributed as follows (appointed seats appear in parentheses): Orange Democratic Movement, 99 (6); Party of National Unity, 45 (3); Orange Democratic Movement–Kenya, 16 (2); Kenya African National Union, 14(1), Safina, 5; National Rainbow Coalition of Kenya, 4; the Forum for the Restoration of Democracy–People, 3; National Rainbow Coalition, 3; Chama Cha Uzalendo, 2; Democratic Party, 2; New Ford Kenya, 2; Party of Independent Candidates of Kenya, 2; Sisi Kwa Sisi, 2; the Forum for the Restoration of Democracy–Asili, 1; the Forum for the Restoration of Democracy–Kenya, 1; Kenya African Democratic Development Union, 1; Kenya African Democratic Union–Asili, 1; Kenya National Democratic Alliance, 1; Mazingira Green Party of Kenya, 1; National Labor Party, 1; People's Democratic Party, 1; People's Party of Kenya, 1; United Democratic Movement, 1. In by-elections held on June 11, the Party of National Unity secured two additional seats to raise its total to 47, and the Orange Democratic Movement retained three seats to preserve its plurality of 99 elected seat. In by-elections held on September 25, 2008 the Orange Democratic Movement retained 2 seats. In by-elections held on August 27, 2009 the Orange Democratic Movement retained 2 seats. The next election is scheduled for 2012.

Speaker: Kenneth Otiato MARENDE (ex officio).

CABINET

[as of October 1, 2009]

President	Mwai Kibaki (PNU)
Vice President	Kalonzo Musyoka (ODM-K)
Prime Minister	Raila Odinga (ODM)
Deputy Prime Minister	Uhuru Kenyatta (PNU; KANU)
Deputy Prime Minister	Musalia Mudavadi (ODM)
Ministers of State in the President's Office	
Defense	Yusuf Mohamed Haji (PNU; KANU)
Provincial Administration and Internal Security	George Saitoti (PNU)
Ministers of State in the Vice President's Office	
Immigration and Registration of Persons	Gerald Otieno Kajwang (ODM)
National Heritage and Culture	William Ole Ntimama (ODM)
Ministers of State in the Prime Minister's Office	
Planning, National Development, and Vision 2030	Wycliffe Ambetsa Oparanya (ODM)
Public Service	Dalmas Anyango Otieno (ODM)
Ministers	
Agriculture	William Ruto (ODM)

Cooperative Development and Marketing	Joseph Nyagah (ODM)
Development of Northern Kenya and other Arid Lands	Ibrahim Elmi Mohamed (ODM)
East African Community	Amason Kingi Jeffah (ODM)
Education	Samson Ongeri (PNU; KANU)
Energy	Kiraitu Murungi (PNU)
Environment and Mineral Resources	John Njoroge Michuki (PNU)
Finance	Uhuru Kenyatta (PNU; KANU)
Fisheries Development	Paul Nyongesa Otuoma (ODM)
Foreign Affairs	Moses Wetangula (PNU)
Forestry and Wildlife	Noah Wekesa (PNU)
Gender and Children Affairs	Esther Murugi Mathenge (PNU) [f]
Higher Education, Science, and Technology	Sally Jepngetich Kosgey (ODM) [f]
Home Affairs	Kalonzo Musyoka (ODM-K)
Housing	Peter Soita Shitanda (PNU; New FORD–K)
Industrialization	Henry Kiprono Kosgey (ODM)
Information and Communications	Samuel Poghisio (ODM-K)
Justice, National Cohesion, and Constitutional Affairs	Mutula Kilonzo (PNU; ODM–K)
Labor	John Munyes (PNU)
Lands	Aggrey James Orengo (ODM)
Livestock Development	Mohamed Abdi Kuti (PNU; NARC–K)
Local Government	Musalia Mudavadi (ODM)
Medical Services	Peter Anyang Nyong'o (ODM)
Nairobi Metropolitan Development	Robinson Njeru Githae ()
Planning and National Development	Henry Onyancha Obwocha (FORD–People)
Public Health and Sanitation	Beth Wambui Mugo (PNU) [f]
Public Works	Chris Obure (ODM)
Regional Development Authorities	Fredrick Omulo Gumo (ODM)
Roads	Franklin Bett (ODM)
Special Programs	Naomi Shaban (PNU; KANU) [f]
Tourism	Najib Balala (ODM)
Trade	Amos Kimunya (NARC)
Transport	Chirau Ali Mwakwere (PNU; SPK)
Water and Irrigation	Charity Ngilu (ODM; NARC) [f]
Youth and Sports	Hellen Jepkemoi Sambili (UDM) [f]
Attorney General	Amos Wako

[f] = female

Note: Two parties are listed for ministers whose parties are constituent parts of PNU.

COMMUNICATIONS

Following the 2002 election, Kenya made significant strides in advancing free speech and developing a free press. The press grew noticeably bolder, publishing news articles and analysis critical of the government as a matter of routine and without the fear of intimidation or reprisals that were ever present under the Moi regime. Broadcasting was also a government monopoly until recently (see below).

The government introduced a bill in July 2004 that would have prevented ownership by the same media company of electronic and print versions of the same publications under the banner of avoiding media monopolies. Kenya's two largest news dailies also have electronic versions and are parts of larger media companies with television and/or radio divisions. In the face of opposition from the trade association for the media companies, the bill was dropped. In January 2004 the government arrested 15 news vendors on charges of selling publications that did not print the name and address of the publisher on the first or last pages, a violation of laws governing the publication of newspapers.

A government raid of *The Standard* newspaper and its sister television station KTN in March 2006, however, led many observers to question President Kibaki's commitment to free speech. The raids appeared to have been prompted by an article in *The Standard* claiming that a senior opposition figure had secret talks with President Kibaki. John Michuki, the minister for internal security, defended the attack by warning journalists working in Kenya that "if you rattle a snake, you must be prepared to be bit by it!" Rumors persist that the raid was led by government-hired mercenaries.

Press. Newspapers are privately owned. Although newspapers evince a range of opinions, many are financially controlled by Europeans or by individuals who are close to political elites. The National Rainbow Coalition (NARC) attempted to launch a daily newspaper in 2004, but the venture, which would have been entitled *The Dawn*, failed to raise the necessary funds to finance the start-up costs. In September 2007, a company with ties to Kibaki, Transcentury Ltd., bid on a 40 percent equity stake in the *Kenya Times*.

The following are English-language dailies published in Nairobi, unless otherwise noted: *Nation* (170,000 daily, 170,000 Sunday), independent; *Taifa Weekly* (70,000), weekly, in Kiswahili; *The Standard* (70,000 daily, 90,000 Sunday), moderate; *The People* (40,000); *Taifa Leo* (57,000), in Kiswahili; *Taifa Jumapili* (56,000), weekly, in Kiswahili; *Kenya Times* (52,000), KANU organ; *Kenya Leo* (6,000), KANU organ, in Kiswahili.

News agencies. The domestic facility is the Kenya News Agency (KNA); a number of foreign agencies also maintain bureaus in Nairobi.

Broadcasting and computing. The Kenya Broadcasting Corporation (KBC) was formed in 1989 as a state agency to succeed the Voice of Kenya and the Voice of Kenya Television; it operates over an area extending from Nairobi to Kisumu, as well as from the coastal city of Mombasa. Kenya Times Media Trust (KTMT), a joint venture of KANU, U.S.-based CNN, and Australian Rupert Murdoch, set up channel 62, a 24-hour commercial subscription service in 1989. Citizen TV, a commercial station, operates in Nairobi and surrounding areas. Nation Radio/TV, the commercial TV and radio stations owned by Nation Media Group, was founded in 1999. Stellagraphics TV (STV) was formed in 1998 as a commercial station operating in Nairobi; in 2007 the Kenyatta family acquired a 45 percent share in the station. Kenya Television Network (KTN-TV), formed in 1990, is a commercial station operating in Nairobi and Mombasa and is owned by the Standard Group, publisher of *The Standard* newspaper. Citizen Radio/Television is another independent commercial broadcaster owned by Royal Media Services. A number of FM commercial radio stations broadcast from Nairobi; nationwide there are over a hundred FM radio stations.

As of 2008 there were 86.7 Internet users per 1,000 inhabitants.

INTERGOVERNMENTAL REPRESENTATION

Ambassador to the U.S.: Peter N.R.O. OGEGO.

U.S. Ambassador to Kenya: Michael E. RANNEBERGER.

Permanent Representative to the UN: Zachary D. Muburi MUITA.

IGO Memberships (Non-UN): AfDB, AU, BADEA, Comesa, CWTH, EAC, EADB, IGAD, Interpol, IOM, IOR-ARC, NAM, PCA, WCO, WTO.

KIRIBATI

Republic of Kiribati
I Kiribati

Political Status: Formerly the Gilbert Islands; became a British protectorate in 1892; annexed as the Gilbert and Ellice Islands Colony in 1915, the Ellice Islands becoming independent as the state of Tuvalu in 1978; present name adopted upon becoming an independent member of the Commonwealth on July 12, 1979.

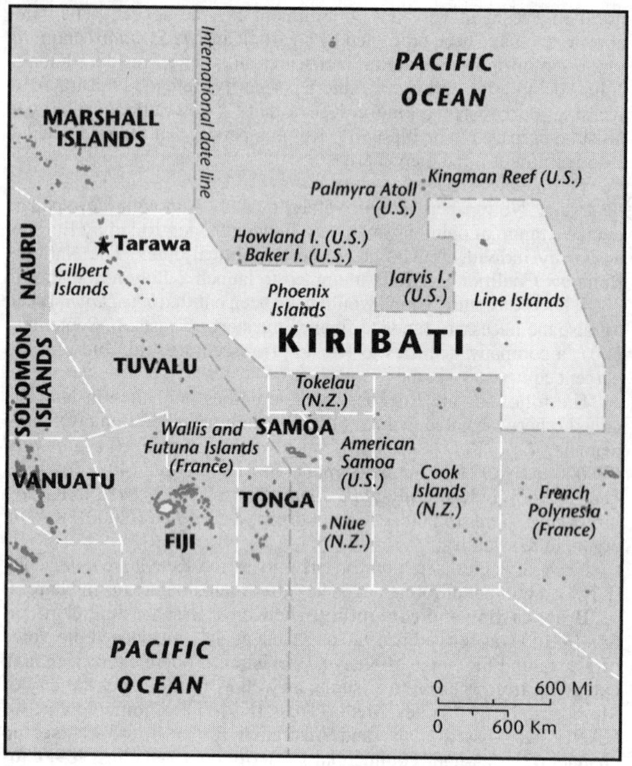

Area: 313 sq. mi. (811 sq. km.).

Population: 92,533 (2005C); 99,000 (2008E); neither figure includes upward of 2,500 Kiribati nationals living abroad.

Major Urban Center (2005E): BAIRIKI (South Tarawa, 48,000).

Official Language: I-Kiribati (Gilbertese); English is also widely spoken.

Monetary Unit: Australian Dollar (market rate December 1, 2009: 1.08 dollars = $1US). The British Pound is also in circulation.

President (*Beretitenti*): Anote TONG (*Boutokaan te Koaua*); popularly elected on July 5, 2003, succeeding Teburoro TITO (*Maneaban te Mauri*), whose government had been defeated in a confidence vote on March 28; reelected on October 17, 2007.

Vice President (*Kauoman-ni-Beretitenti*): Teima ONORIO (*Boutokaan te Koaua*); appointed by the president on July 10, 2003, succeeding Beniamina TINGA (*Maneaban te Mauri*); reappointed on October 23, 2007.

THE COUNTRY

Apart from Ocean Island (Banaba) in the west, Kiribati consists of three widely dispersed island groups scattered over 2 million square miles of the central Pacific Ocean: the Gilbert Islands and Ocean (Banaba) Island on the equator; the Phoenix Islands to the southeast; and the Line Islands still farther east and both north and south of the equator. The Gilbert group comprises Abaiang, Abemama, Aranuka, Arorae, Beru, Butaritari, Kuria, Maiana, Makin, Marakei, Nicunau, Nonouti, Onotoa, Tabiteuca, Tamana, and Tarawa. The Phoenix group encompasses Birnie, Enderbury, Gardner, Hull, Kanton (formerly Canton), McKean, Phoenix, and Sydney. The Line group embraces Kiritimati (Christmas), Fanning, Malden, Starbuck, Vostock, and Washington, as well as Millennium (formerly Caroline) and Flint, which in 1951 were leased to commercial interests on Tahiti. (The renaming of Caroline in August 1997 was intended to draw attention to the contention that Kiribati, having arbitrarily moved the international date line several hundred miles to the east, was to be the first nation over which the sun would rise on January 1, 2000.) Not all of the islands are inhabited and several attempts at settlement have been abandoned because of drought conditions, with potable water throughout the area often described as being as "precious as gasoline."

Most of the country's national income was traditionally derived from phosphate mining on the most western island, Banaba. By the time of independence, however, the phosphate supply was largely exhausted, although some $70 million in mining royalties had been invested in Europe. Mining ceased at the end of 1979, causing the loss of some 500 jobs. Fishing grounds in the area are said to be among the richest in the world, although the first commercial fishing vessel, built in Japan, was not put into service until 1979. Thereafter, significant income was realized from the sale of fishing licenses, although earnings of $40 million in 1998 were reported in early 2008 to have fallen to around $20 million.

In early 2008 Kiribati announced that some 72,000 sq. mi. in the Phoenix group had been declared a marine protected area (the world's largest) to ensure its biological diversity and sustainability.

Real GDP has fluctuated markedly in recent years, rising by 12.6 percent in 1998 but dropping to zero growth in 2005 and showing only marginal gains thereafter. Part of the difficulty has stemmed from an adverse trade balance that increased steadily from $26.8 million in 1998 to $80.5 million in 2004 (more recent data is not available, as of mid-2009).

GOVERNMENT AND POLITICS

Political background. The Gilbert and Ellice Islands Colony was under the jurisdiction of the British High Commissioner for the Western Pacific until 1972, when a governor was appointed from London. In 1975 the Ellice Islands became the separate territory of Tuvalu, prior to the achievement of independence in 1978. At a constitutional conference in London in early 1979, the British government refused a request by the Banabans, most of whom had been resettled on Rabi (Rambi) Island in the Fiji group during World War II and had since become Fijian citizens, that Ocean Island be separated from the Gilberts, and the latter, with Ocean Island included, became independent as a republican member of the Commonwealth on July 12.

Upon independence the former chief minister, Ieremia T. TABAI, assumed office as president of the republic and on July 20 appointed Teatao TEANNAKI as vice president. Following the first post–independence legislative election of March 26, 1982, Tabai was returned to office in presidential balloting conducted May 4. The government fell, however, on December 10 when the House of Assembly rejected, for the second time in two days, a bill that would have retroactively legitimized 5 percent salary raises for six public officials who, through an oversight, had erroneously benefited from a pay hike granted civil servants earlier in the year. In accordance with Kiribati's somewhat unusual constitutional practice, interim administration was assumed by a three-member Council of State chaired by the chair of the Public Service Commission, Rota ONARIO. Tabai was reelected on February 17, 1983, following legislative balloting on January 12 and 19, and on February 18 reappointed most members of his previous administration.

On May 12, 1987, following the election of a new House of Assembly on March 12 and 19, Tabai was again reelected, defeating his vice president, Teatao Teannaki, and the opposition candidate Teburoro TITO with a 59 percent share of the vote.

With the support of Tabai (who was ineligible for a further term), Teannaki secured the presidency on July 3, 1991, defeating his principal competitor, Roniti TEIWAKI, by a vote margin of less than 5 percent. Teannaki was, however, obliged to resign on May 24, 1994, when the parliamentary opposition, which had accused his administration of financial irregularities, successfully introduced a no-confidence motion. Government authority thereupon passed again to a Council of State, pending a new legislative election and the designation of a successor president. However, a constitutional crisis erupted when one of the Council's members refused to step down at the expiration of his term on May 28 and was forcibly removed from office by his colleagues (see Current issues, below).

In balloting held July 21–29, 1994, the incumbent Gilbertese National Progressive Party won only 7 assembly seats as contrasted with 13 for the opposition Christian Democratic (subsequently Christian Democratic Unity) Party, which in the wake of the election attracted enough support from independents to capture all four presidential nominations. Thereafter, Teburoro Tito won a decisive 51 percent vote share (half again as much as the runner-up) at a popular election on September 30 and was sworn in as chief executive on October 1. He was elected to a second term on November 27, 1998, easily defeating Dr. Harry TONG and Amberoti NIKORA.

In November 2002 Tito's legislative grouping, the *Maneaban te Mauri* (MTM) party, lost control to the opposition *Boutokaan te Koaua*—BTK (Supporters of the Truth). However, by early 2003 the BTK was reported to have "fractured," and on February 24 Tito won reelection by narrowly defeating the BTK's Taberannang TIMEON. Little more than a month later, on March 28, Tito was obliged to resign after failing, in a close vote, to secure approval of a $700,000 supplemental budget.

In the legislative balloting of May 9 and 12, 2003, the MTM secured an initial plurality and appeared to have a solid majority after a number of independents subsequently affiliated themselves with the MTM. Nonetheless, at the ensuing presidential election of July 5, with Timeon ineligible after losing his house seat, the BTK's Anote TONG defeated his brother and new MTM standard-bearer, Dr. Harry Tong, by some 1,000 votes. Anote Tong was reelected in controversial balloting on October 17, 2007, following legislative elections on August 22 and 30 in which the BTK secured strong majority support.

Constitution and government. For a small country, Kiribati has a relatively complex constitution (part of the UK Kiribati Independence Order 1979) that includes a number of entrenched provisions designed to safeguard individual and land rights for the Banabans. It provides for an executive president (*beretitenti*) who must command the support of a legislative majority. Upon passage of a no-confidence motion, the president must immediately resign, transitional executive authority being exercised by a Council of State composed of the chair of the autonomous Public Service Commission, the chief justice, and the speaker of the House of Assembly, pending a legislative dissolution and the holding of a general election. Subsequent to each such election, the House must propose no fewer than three and no more than four candidates for the presidency from its own membership, the final selection being made by nationwide balloting. If the presidency is vacated for reasons other than a loss of confidence, the vice president (*kauoman-ni-beretitenti*), originally appointed by the president from among his cabinet associates, becomes chief executive, subject to legislative confirmation. The cabinet includes the president, the vice president, and no more than ten other ministers (all drawn from the assembly), plus the attorney general, and is collectively responsible to the legislature.

The unicameral House currently consists of 44 elected members, an additional member named by the Banaban Rabi Council of Leaders, and the attorney general, ex officio if he is not an elected member. The speaker has no voting rights and must be elected by the House from outside its membership. The normal legislative term is four years. The judicial system encompasses a Court of Appeal, a High Court, and local magistrates' courts, the last representing the consolidation of former island, lands, and magistrates' courts. There is a right of appeal to the Judicial Committee of the UK Privy Council in regard to the High Court's interpretation of the rights of any Banaban or member of the Rabi Council. The nominated Banaban member of the House need not be a Kiribati citizen, while all expatriates with ancestors born in Banaba before 1900 may register as electors or stand for election as if resident on the island.

Foreign relations. Kiribati became a member of the Commonwealth upon independence, but its international contacts are otherwise quite limited. In March 1984 diplomatic relations (backdated to 1979) were established with Tuvalu, augmenting links established earlier with Australia and the United Kingdom, while New Zealand appointed a high commissioner in early 1989. The country joined the International Monetary Fund in June 1986 but did not request UN membership until April 1999, being admitted to the world body in September. Kiribati opened its first overseas diplomatic mission by posting a high commissioner in Suva, Fiji, in September 2001.

Under a 1979 treaty, the United States agreed to relinquish all claims to territory in the Phoenix and Line island groups, except for Palmyra. Included were Canton and Enderbury, previously under joint US-UK administration, but from which the British had already withdrawn. The parties also agreed that no military use of the islands by third parties would be permitted without joint consultation and that facilities constructed by the United States on Canton, Enderbury, and Hull islands would not be so used without U.S. approval. In mid-1996 President Tito urged neighboring states to reject a developer's offer to provide a $100 million development trust fund in return for their acquiescence in a plan to buy privately owned Palmyra for the storage of high-level nuclear waste.

Modest developmental assistance has been provided by Australia, Japan, New Zealand, the United Kingdom, the United States, and the Asian Development Bank. A 1985 agreement allowing Russian fishing boats within the archipelago's continental shelf lapsed in October 1986, and Kiribati subsequently enacted legislation to detain crews as well as vessels in cases of poaching within its exclusive economic zone, which Royal New Zealand Air Force planes aid in policing.

In May 1995 relations between Kiribati and the United States were strained because of Kiribati's failure to participate in Nuclear Non-Proliferation Treaty (NPT) negotiations in New York. (Washington refused to accept Kiribati's assertion that it lacked resources to send a delegate to the meeting on the ground that external resources were available to assist small nations in such activities.)

In early 1998 it appeared that the future of a Chinese satellite tracking facility in Bonriki in eastern Tarawa might be jeopardized by the transfer of the controlling authority from the People's Republic of China (PRC) Science Commission to the People's Liberation Army. By mid-1999 the issue had become sensitive because of indications that the principal purpose of the facility might be to monitor a theater missile defense system under construction by the United States on Kwajalein in the Marshall Islands.

On November 7, 2003, the Tong administration established diplomatic relations with the Republic of China (Taiwan), saying that it wished to retain existing relations with the PRC; however, the PRC promptly severed relations. The action was preceded by dismantlement of the satellite tracking station, the withdrawal of Chinese medical personnel, and the termination of PRC funding for the construction of a sports stadium. Subsequently, in August 2004, President Tong accused Beijing of attempting to destabilize his government, although his brother, as opposition leader, stated that he viewed Taiwan as a greater threat to Kiribati than the PRC.

In March 2006 Kiribati received an unrestricted grant of $1 million from Japan. The action came several months after Kiribati had refused an Australian government request to join a campaign to banish "scientific" whaling.

Current issues. The constitutional crisis of mid-1994 pointed up a deficiency in Kiribati's basic law, since it was by no means clear that the Council of State possessed the power of self-replenishment. The issue was further complicated by the fact that the country's chief justice was himself a Council member, which meant that a legal challenge in the matter would have to be submitted to a temporary judge brought in from Australia or New Zealand.

In recent years Kiribati has become increasingly concerned about the impact of long-term elevation of the sea level because of global greenhouse emissions. In September 1997 the president of a Smaller Island States (SIS) summit in Rarotonga, Cook Islands, declared that both Tuvalu and Kiribati would "sink beneath the waves" if estimates of sea-level rise were to be realized, and in June 2008, with Kiribati's highest point less than six feet above sea level, President Tong called for international assistance in a phased evacuation of his country's residents.

POLITICAL PARTIES

Traditionally, there were no formally organized parties in Kiribati; instead, ad hoc groups tended to form in response to specific issues or in support of particular individuals. Thus, a grouping known as the Mouth of the Kiribati People (*Wiia I-Kiribati*) was significantly involved in the 1982 defeat of the Tabai government but subsequently became moribund. Prior to the 1991 assembly balloting, the only recognizable party was a Christian People's Party (*Mwaneaba*), organized in August 1985 by a number of Catholic opposition legislators following the failure of a no-confidence motion against President Tabai on the Soviet fishing treaty. Prior to the 1991 presidential poll two additional groups emerged: a Gilbertese National Progressive Party (GNPP), launched to support the (ultimately successful) candidacy of Vice President Teatao Teannaki, and a Kiribati United Party (KUP), to further the candidacy of Tewareka TENTOA, whose name was not on the four-man list approved by the assembly. For the 1994 campaign a Protestant-oriented Christian Democratic Party (CDP) was launched in support of Teburoro Tito's successful candidacy, thereafter becoming the nucleus of a Christian Democratic Unity Party (CDUP), which also included the GNPP. The first three groups below were the principal contenders at the 2007 elections.

Boutokaan te Koaua—BTK (Supporters of the Truth). Theretofore in opposition, the BTK won the presidency in July 2003, despite failing to obtain a majority in its own right at a legislative poll two months earlier; it secured a majority in 2007.

Leaders: Anote TONG (President of the Republic), Ieremia TABAI (Chair).

Maurin Kiribati Party (MKP). The centrist MKP has been a coalition partner of the BTK since 2003, with the MKP's Nabuti Mwemwenikarawa serving as minister for finance and economic development. Mwemwenikarawa finished second in the 2007 presidential elections with approximately one-third of the votes.

Leaders: Banuera BERINA, Nabuti MWEMWENIKARAWA (2007 presidential candidate).

Maneaban te Mauri—MTM (Protect the Maneaba). Composed of supporters of former president Teburoro Tito, the MTM was the governing party during his administration but is currently in opposition. Following the party's poor showing in the August 2007 legislative poll, neither of the MTM's main presidential contenders—Dr. Harry Tong (defeated in the 2003 presidential race by his brother, Anote Tong) and Tetana TAITAI—received the necessary endorsement from the House of Assembly to be an official candidate in the October balloting.

Leaders: Teburoro TITO (Former President of the Republic), Dr. Harry TONG (2003 presidential candidate).

In late 2007, former minister of finance and economic development Taanete MAMAU announced that he and five other members of the House of Assembly had formed a new **Kiribati Independent Party** (KIP).

LEGISLATURE

The unicameral **House of Assembly** (*Maneaba ni Maungatabu*) currently consists of 44 (increased from 40 for the 2007 elections) elected members plus a nominated representative of Banabans resident on Rabi and the attorney general, ex officio. The normal legislative term is four years.

Since party affiliations in Kiribati are extremely loose and fluid ("independent" legislators may declare affiliation with a party after elections and affiliations can be easily changed at other times), legislative election results are difficult to quantify, and reports on party affiliations often vary widely (even in government sources). Following the balloting of August 22 and 30, 2007, the following distribution of elected seats was reported: *Boutokaan te Koaua* (BTK), 18; *Maneaban te Mauri* (MTM), 7; and independents, 19. However, other news reports indicated that at least several of the successful candidates belonged to the BTK-supportive Maurin Kiribati Party (MKP), one of whose legislators later became a presidential candidate. Based on several seemingly reliable news reports following the inauguration of the new assembly (at which point independents were eligible to declare party affiliation), the approximate distribution of seats was BTK, 28; MTM, 7; MKP 5; independents, 6.

Speaker: Taomati IUTA.

CABINET

[as of July 1, 2009]

President	Anote Tong
Vice President	Teima Onorio [f]
Ministers	
Commerce, Industry, and Cooperatives	Ioteba Redfern
Communications, Transport, and Tourism Development	Naatan Teewe
Education, Youth, and Sport Development	Teima Onorio [f]
Environment, Lands, and Agricultural Development	Martin Tofinga
Finance and Economic Development	Nabuti Mwemwenikarawa
Foreign Affairs and Immigration	Anote Tong
Health and Medical Services	Natanera Kirata [f]
Human Resources Development	Bauro Tongaai
Internal Affairs and Social Development	Amberoti Nikora
Line and Phoenix Islands Development	Tawita Temoku
Natural Resources Development	Tetabo Nakara
Public Works and Utilities	James Taom

[f] = female

COMMUNICATIONS

Press. The following are published on Tarawa: *Te Uekera* (5,000), published weekly in English and I-Kiribati by the government's Broadcasting and Publications Authority; *Te Itoi ni Kiribati* (2,300), Catholic monthly newsletter in I-Kiribati; *Te Kaotan te Ota* (1,700), Protestant quarterly newsletter in I-Kiribati; *Kiribati Newstar,* weekly, in English and I-Kiribati, established in 2000.

Broadcasting and computing. The government-operated Radio Kiribati transmits in Gilbertese, Tuvaluan, and English. In late 1993 the House of Assembly legalized the private ownership of radio stations, although the country's first FM station, launched in 1998 by former president Ieremia Tabai, was closed down on the ground that it was being operated without a license.

As of 2008 there were 20.7 Internet users per 1,000 inhabitants.

INTERGOVERNMENTAL REPRESENTATION

Kiribati was admitted to the United Nations in September 1999, although it has not opened a permanent mission at UN headquarters in New York. To date Kiribati has also not opened an embassy in Washington, D.C.

U.S. Ambassador to Kiribati: C. Steven McGANN (resident in Fiji).

Permanent Representative to the UN: (Vacant).

IGO Memberships (Non-UN): ADB, CWTH, PC, PIF.

KOREA

Chosŏn

Political Status: Politically divided; Democratic People's Republic of Korea under Communist regime established September 9, 1948; Republic of Korea under anti-Communist republican regime established August 15, 1948.

THE COUNTRY

Korea is a mountainous peninsula projecting southeastward from Manchuria between China and Japan. Whether viewed in terms of race, culture, or language, the population is extremely homogeneous. The literacy rate is more than 90 percent. For further details see the separate discussions of the Democratic People's Republic of Korea and the Republic of Korea, which follow.

POLITICAL HISTORY

A semi-independent state associated with China from the seventh century A.D., Korea was annexed by Japan in 1910 and tightly controlled by Tokyo until Japan's defeat in World War II. The northern half of Korea was integrated with the Japanese industrial complex in Manchuria, while the southern half remained largely agricultural. Although the restoration of an independent Korea "in due course" was pledged by U.S. President Franklin Roosevelt, Britain's Prime Minister Winston Churchill, and Nationalist Chinese President Chiang Kai-shek at the Cairo Conference in 1943, the need for prompt arrangements to receive the surrender of Japanese military forces in 1945 led to a temporary division of the country into Soviet (northern) and U.S. (southern) occupation zones along the line of the 38th parallel. Efforts by the two occupying powers to establish a unified Korean provisional government shortly became deadlocked, and the issue of Korea's future was referred to the UN General Assembly on U.S. initiative in 1947.

A UN Temporary Commission was set up to facilitate elections and the establishment of a national government but was denied access to the Soviet-controlled zone. UN-observed elections were accordingly held in the southern half of Korea alone in May 1948, and the Republic of Korea (ROK) was formally established on August 15; a separate, Communist-controlled government, the Democratic People's Republic of Korea (DPRK), was established in the North on September 9. The UN General Assembly refused to recognize the latter action and declared the ROK as the lawful government of the nation. Soviet troops withdrew from the DPRK in December 1948, and U.S. forces left the ROK in June 1949.

On June 25, 1950, five months after U.S. Secretary of State Dean Acheson had delineated a Pacific "defense perimeter" that did not include Korea, DPRK troops invaded the ROK in an attempt to unify the peninsula by force. U.S. forces promptly came to the assistance of the southern regime, and the UN Security Council, meeting without the USSR, called on all member states to aid the ROK. A total of 16 UN members subsequently furnished troops to a UN Unified Command established by the Security Council in July 1950 and headed initially by U.S. Gen. Douglas MacArthur (later by Gens. Matthew B. Ridgway and Mark Clark). The intervention of some 300,000 Chinese Communist "volunteers" on the side of the DPRK in late 1950 produced a military stalemate, and an armistice agreement was eventually signed in Panmunjom on July 27, 1953, establishing a cease-fire line and a four-kilometer-wide demilitarized zone (DMZ) bisecting Korea near the 38th parallel.

Negotiations in Geneva in 1954 failed to produce a settlement, and relations between the two countries were governed thereafter by the 1953 agreement, under which a Military Armistice Commission representing the former belligerents (including China) continued to meet in Panmunjom. Chinese military forces withdrew from the DPRK in 1958, but UN forces (now exclusively American) remain in the South. The United States initiated troop cutbacks from 1970 through 1972 and proposed to the UN Security Council in June 1975 that the UN Command in Korea be dissolved, but no action was taken on the proposal. In February 1977 the U.S. Jimmy Carter administration announced a "phased withdrawal" of U.S. combat personnel, but the plan was reversed in mid-1979 because of reports that the DPRK army held a numerical superiority in men and tanks far in excess of earlier estimates.

Political relations between North and South have alternated between overt hostility and mutual tolerance. Contacts regarding the problem of families separated by the political division of the country began in September 1971 under the auspices of the Red Cross societies of the respective countries. Talks directed toward peaceful reunification were initiated in July 1972 and resulted in the establishment of a North-South Coordinating Committee, which convened in October and continued to meet on a regular basis until August 1973, when negotiations were unilaterally broken off by the DPRK.

Following the North's acceptance of an appeal by ROK President Park Chung Hee to reopen discussions, representatives of the two Koreas met in Panmunjom in February 1979 in preparation for broader negotiations. After three brief sessions, however, the talks ended over differences regarding representation and the level at which future negotiations should be conducted. Meanwhile, by 1979 the ROK had charged the DPRK with 43,000 violations of the 1953 armistice, while the DPRK had charged the ROK with over 217,000 violations.

In January 1980 Pyongyang and Seoul agreed to a series of working-level talks designed to prepare for a first-ever meeting of their prime ministers. Ten working-level sessions were held during the ensuing eight months without agreement on an agenda for a high-level meeting, and North Korea terminated the discussions in September. A number of social and economic issues were addressed following a resumption of working-level discussions in 1983, with little substantive result, save for a limited number of family reunions conducted in Seoul and Pyongyang under Red Cross auspices in September 1985. Sporadic political-military talks were ritualistically suspended by the North during annual U.S.–South Korean "Team Spirit" military exercises.

Inconclusive economic cooperation talks were also held in 1984–1985, in addition to a series of preliminary interparliamentary discussions in July–September 1985. The interparliamentary meetings were resumed in August 1988 but quickly became bogged down.

On January 1, 1989, North Korea's Kim Il Sung called, for the first time (albeit indirectly), for a summit meeting with his South Korean counterpart. The overture was accepted three weeks later by ROK President Roh Tae Woo, but in early February Pyongyang suspended further discussions because of Seoul's refusal to cancel the round of "Team Spirit" exercises scheduled for March. A year later, Kim extended the initiative, calling for "total openness of both North and South," including the sanctioning of "free and mutual visits." Roh again responded affirmatively and offered to invite North Korean, Chinese, and Soviet observers to scaled-down "Team Spirit" maneuvers. Pyongyang, however, continued to insist on cancellation of the exercises.

The prospect of a prime ministerial meeting surfaced in mid-1990, following a stunned North Korean reaction to a summit between Soviet President Mikhail Gorbachev and ROK President Roh in San Francisco, but the first-ever chiefs of government meeting in Seoul on September 4–7 ended inconclusively. North Korean Premier Yon Hyong Muk called for an arms control/nonaggression pact that would limit each side to a standing army of 10,000 men and require the withdrawal of U.S. forces; in addition, he demanded the release of South Korean students who had been jailed for traveling illegally to the North, an end to "Team Spirit" exercises, and a common application for admission to the UN. South Korean Prime Minister Kang Young Hoon aimed at a more gradual cultivation of bilateral relations through a mutual exchange of military information, establishment of a hotline between defense ministers, the conclusion of an economic cooperation agreement, freer travel across the common border, and simultaneous entry into the UN of the two Korean states. Additional sessions were held in October and December 1990, without significant movement.

In May 1991 North Korea abandoned its insistence on common representation at the UN, and on September 17 both Koreas were admitted to the world body. In late October the fourth round of prime ministerial talks were held in Pyongyang, again without notable progress. In contrast, the fifth round in Seoul concluded on December 13–14 with a historic nonaggression pact and an agreement to meet again in mid-February to work toward a nuclear-free Korea. In signing the December accord, which called for formal termination of the 1950–1953 war, the North Korean government for the first time officially recognized its southern counterpart.

Ratifications of the December accords were exchanged during the sixth round of premierial talks in Pyongyang in February 1992, clearly indicating that Pyongyang had abandoned its long-standing demand for "one Korea" achieved through "liberation of the South." A month later, at the seventh premierial session, the participants agreed to establish a Joint Nuclear Control Committee, while during the eighth round in mid-September the participants announced agreements on nonaggression, cross-border exchanges, and establishment of a North-South Joint Reconciliation Commission.

Despite these positive developments, relations soon foundered once again, in part over North Korea's refusal to permit inspections by the International Atomic Energy Agency (IAEA) at a number of nuclear sites—a dispute that, during succeeding years, became enmeshed in matters of foreign aid and U.S.-DPRK diplomatic relations (for details, see the Foreign relations section of the DPRK article). The death of Kim Il Sung in July 1994, shortly before a planned first DPRK-ROK presidential meeting, brought progress to a halt.

In April 1996, after North Korea had threatened to withdraw from the 1953 armistice, U.S. President Bill Clinton and ROK President Kim Young Sam proposed that quadripartite talks, with China as the fourth participant, be initiated in an effort to conclude a definitive peace treaty. The following September Seoul broke off all North-South contacts following the discovery in South Korean waters of an abandoned North Korean submarine, and in July 1997 a military clash in the DMZ further threatened the renewed peace effort. Nevertheless, following a preliminary four-power meeting in August, on December 9–10 representatives of the four met in Geneva, Switzerland, to begin peace negotiations, while in February 1998 North Korea indicated its willingness to begin a dialogue with political parties and civic organizations in the South. In March a second four-party session in Geneva descended into procedural wrangling and disagreements over the withdrawal of U.S. troops, but on April 11, at the DPRK's suggestion, Pyongyang and Seoul held their first ministerial meeting in four years, in Beijing, the purpose being to discuss agricultural aid to the North. The talks ultimately broke down over South Korea's insistence that aid was contingent on North Korea's willingness to discuss family reunification.

On June 23, 1998, for the first time in seven years, officers of the UN Command and the DPRK army held talks in Panmunjom, despite South Korea's capture, the previous day, of a North Korean midget submarine that had become entangled in fishing nets. (Nine bodies were discovered on board when the submarine was opened.) A second, empty five-man sub was found in July.

Four-power talks resumed on October 21–24, 1998, with subcommittees being created to consider ways to establish a "peace regime" and to reduce peninsular tension. Despite the sinking of yet another suspected DPRK spy vessel in December, the fourth formal four-power session was held January 19–22, 1999. The focus of a fifth session, held April 24–28, was humanitarian aid to the North, which had been suffering a devastating famine since 1995. A sixth round held on August 5–9 made little headway, the diplomatic emphasis having shifted toward bilateral negotiations between, on the one hand, the two Koreas and, on the other, North Korea and Washington.

Progress toward improved North-South relations was threatened by a June 15, 1999, naval battle in the Yellow Sea—the first such encounter since the 1953 armistice—that resulted in the sinking of a North Korea gunboat, the death of an estimated 30 North Korean sailors, and additional damage to ships on both sides. Tensions had risen earlier in the month when North Korean vessels began accompanying crab-fishing boats into a buffer zone around the Northern Limit Line (NLL), established at the time of the 1953 armistice.

Prompted by a South Korean offer of additional fertilizer deliveries to aid famine recovery, North Korea agreed to attend family reunification talks in Beijing on June 22, 1999, but after two brief sessions the talks broke down on July 3, as Pyongyang demanded an apology for the Yellow Sea incident. On September 2 North Korea unilaterally declared an extension of its territorial waters to 40 miles (65 km) south of the NLL, prompting Seoul to announce the following day that it fully intended to defend the disputed area.

Although the North rejected a January 3, 2000, proposal from South Korea's President Kim Dae Jung to foster economic cooperation, a speech delivered by Kim on March 9 in Berlin, Germany, offered massive aid for building the North Korean economy if intergovernmental dialogue resumed. Only a week later secret talks between Seoul and Pyongyang reportedly opened in Beijing, leading to a surprise announcement on April 10 that South Korea's President Kim would meet North Korea's Kim at a first-ever summit in June.

Following five rounds of preparatory negotiations, the historic meeting took place June 13–15, 2000, in Pyongyang. On June 14, noting "the lofty wishes of the Korean people," the two leaders signed an accord that declared their intention to work toward peaceful national unification, authorized family reunions and eventual repatriation of long-term political prisoners, and promoted a "balanced development" of their economies as well as accelerated social, cultural, health, environmental, and sports exchanges. The accord also called for a continuing dialogue, including a reciprocal visit to Seoul by Kim Jong Il "at an appropriate time."

The foreign ministers of the two Koreas conferred for the first time during the July 2000 forum of the Association of Southeast Asians Nations, held in Bangkok, Thailand. Ministerial-level discussions continued July 29–31 in Seoul and August 29–September 1 in Pyongyang. The latter session concluded with an agreement permitting the ROK and DPRK military establishments to open a dialogue. Both delegations also approved additional family reunion meetings in Mt. Keumgang, a resort just north of the DMZ. Renewals of rail and highway links were also approved. The North-South defense ministers met in late September, with the first working-level military sessions following in November and December. The inaugural meeting of an Inter-Korean Economic Cooperation Promotion Committee convened on December 28.

Apparently because of the less-than-conciliatory stance of the new U.S. George W. Bush administration, North Korea postponed a fifth round of North-South talks that had been scheduled for March 2001. The session was ultimately held in Seoul on September 15–18 and was followed by a mostly unproductive November 9–14 round in Mt. Keumgang. Objecting to the heightened security instituted in Seoul following the September 11, 2001, attacks on the United States, Pyongyang delayed the seventh session until August 12–14, 2002. In the interim, another altercation near the NLL had resulted in the sinking of a South Korean patrol boat and casualties on both sides.

Several additional rounds of ministerial-level talks were convened between October 2002 and October 2003, a period that also saw the continuation of family reunions in Mt. Keumgang, the opening of the first road link between North and South in February 2003, and completion of the first rail connection across the DMZ in June 2003. In the same month, groundbreaking occurred for an industrial complex in Kaesong, in the North, to house South Korean manufacturing firms. The first tenant in the industrial park began operations in December 2004, and by 2009 100 firms were reportedly employing over 38,000 North Koreans.

The 14th round of cabinet-level talks, held May 5–7, 2004, was followed by a meeting of senior military leaders on May 26 and by a June 4 agreement to reduce tensions at the DMZ and near the NLL. Such positive developments were more than offset, however, by continuing hostility between Washington and Pyongyang. Following the latter's assertion in October 2002 that it had not abandoned its nuclear weapons program, as it had agreed to do in 1994, fuel oil shipments to the North were halted. Pyongyang then reopened its Yongbyon nuclear facility, ordered the last IAEA inspectors to leave the country, and announced its withdrawal from the Nuclear Non-Proliferation Treaty (NPT). The consequent diplomatic crisis was marked by heightened rhetoric from Pyongyang, which further stated that it would abrogate the 1992 Joint Declaration on the Denuclearization of the Korean Peninsula.

The North nevertheless gave way on its demand for bilateral discussions with the Bush administration and agreed to participate in the opening of six-party nuclear talks in Beijing on August 27–29, 2003, involving both Koreas, China, Japan, Russia, and the United States. (For details of subsequent six-party developments, see the DPRK article.)

In August 2004 the North canceled an additional round of North-South cabinet-level talks because 469 North Korean refugees had been flown to South Korea from Vietnam. (The number of defectors rose to 1,900 in 2004, dropped back to 1,400 in 2005, but rose again thereafter, setting a record of 2,800 in 2008; an estimated 100,000 to 300,000 illegal migrants may be living in China and elsewhere.) After a ten-month lapse, working-level discussions, held in Kaesong, resumed on May 16–19, 2005, and on June 22–23 a 15th round of cabinet-level meetings was conducted in Seoul. In addition to further bilateral military talks and a tenth meeting of the Inter-Korean Economic Cooperation Promotion Committee, July saw the restoration of private North-South telephone links, 60 years after they had been severed. The 18th cabinet-level session, held April 21–24, 2006, in Pyongyang, concluded with issuance of an eight-point statement that, among other things, supported joint development of the Han River estuary and of zinc and magnesite mines in the North. The two Koreas also appeared to be moving closer toward resolving a complaint from Seoul that the North continues to hold up to 600 prisoners of war, dating back to the 1950–1953 conflict, as well as nearly 500 abductees. Progress on that and all other fronts came to a halt, however, at the July 11–13 19th session in Pusan, when the North cut the talks short. The walkout occurred because South Korea, disgruntled by recent DPRK missile tests and Pyongyang's withdrawal from the six-party talks, would not discuss additional food and fertilizer aid.

A 20th ministerial session was ultimately held February 27–March 2, 2007, after the North had once again rejoined the six-party talks and agreed to dismantle its nuclear weapons program. The talks concluded with announcements that family reunions, suspended since the previous July, would resume, that the Red Cross would be consulted about the missing prisoners of war and abductees, and that long-delayed test runs of two cross-border trains—the first since 1950—would proceed. With considerable fanfare in the South, the rail journeys across the DMZ took place on May 17, following adoption of security arrangements at a meeting of high-level military personnel. Two days later, for the first time since the Korean War, a commercial cargo ship from the North entered a South Korean port.

The next ministerial-level session took place in Seoul from May 29 to June 1, 2007, but ended unfavorably when the ROK refused to release a shipment of food aid until the DPRK acted on its six-party pledge to begin shutting down its nuclear program. Late in the month, the DPRK renewed its commitment to shutting down its Yongbyon facility, and on June 26 the South announced that it would resume rice deliveries. On July 14, 2007, IAEA inspectors visited Yongbyon, and four days later the IAEA confirmed that all nuclear operations at the facility had been discontinued.

The renewed spirit of cooperation led Seoul to repeat a call for a second leadership summit, which the North accepted on August 5, 2007, although the meeting of Kim Jong Il and Roh Moo Hyun was postponed from August 28–30 because of severe flood damage in the North. The second summit ultimately took place at Pyongyang on October 2–4, at the conclusion of which the leaders released a Declaration on the Advancement of South-North Korean Relations, Peace, and Prosperity. Highlights of the declaration included a call to accelerate creation of a peninsular economic bloc, a decision to schedule a defense ministers meeting as part of a continuing effort to reduce military tensions, a commitment to work toward conclusion of a Korean War peace treaty and denuclearization, and an agreement to establish a maritime Special Peace and Cooperation Zone. In addition, the Inter-Korean Economic Cooperation Promotion Committee was to be upgraded to a Joint Committee for Inter-Korean Economic Cooperation. Improvements in transportation, communications, infrastructure, agricultural cooperation, and health and medical services were also targeted, and a joint ship-building venture was announced. On November 14–16, in the first such meeting since 1992, DPRK Prime Minister Kim Yong Il and ROK Prime Minister Han Duk Soo met in Seoul to advance toward the goals set forth at the October summit. Later in the month, the two countries' defense ministers also met.

In the following six months, further progress in North-South relations awaited fulfillment of Pyongyang's commitment to begin dismantling its nuclear facilities and provide an accounting of its weapons programs. Deadlines of December 31, 2007, and then February 28, 2008, were not met. Meanwhile, South Korea had elected a new president, Lee Myung Bak, who appeared more willing than his immediate predecessors to take the North to task not only for its failure to meet its six-party obligations but also for its human rights record. On June 26 the DPRK presented a partial nuclear accounting to China, and a day later it destroyed the cooling tower at its Yongbyon facility, which made renewed North-South negotiations likely. Although the six-party talks reconvened in Beijing on July 10, bilateral relations were set back once again on July 11 when a South Korean tourist, a member of a group staying at Mt. Keumgang, was shot dead on a beach by North Korean troops. On August 3 the DPRK announced that the number of South Korean personnel permitted at the resort would be slashed.

On October 2 and 27, 2008, in the first official meeting since the inauguration of President Lee, military delegations from the North and South conferred, but in November the North announced that it was suspending rail freight shipment from Kaesong, was cutting nonmilitary phone lines, and would reintroduce stringent border-crossing restrictions. The ostensible precipitant was the continuing distribution by South Korea civic groups of propaganda leaflets sent across the border via helium balloons.

On January 30, 2009, the North stated that it would no longer honor agreements previously concluded with Seoul and that it considered their maritime border accord void. Relations continued to spiral downward following an April 5 rocket launch by the North—Pyongyang identified it as a launch vehicle for a satellite, while most international observers described it as a military test—that provoked criticism from the UN Security Council. Reacting to widespread international condemnation, on April 14 the DPRK announced that it was once again quitting the six-party talks and nullifying all related agreements. As a result, all IAEA inspectors were expelled from Yongbyon. On May 15 the North also voided wage and rent agreements governing the Kaesong industrial zone. It then insisted that wages be quadrupled (to about $300 a month per worker) and that the rent for the complex's land be raised from $16 million a year to $500 million.

On May 25, 2009, two days after conducting a second nuclear weapons test and initiating a series of short-range missile launches, Pyongyang withdrew from the 1953 armistice, prompting the South to announce that it would participate in a U.S.-led Proliferation Security Initiative that authorized the interception and inspection of ships suspected of carrying military and other materials forbidden under sanctions regimes. The North indicated that it would regard any such intervention as an act of war.

Less than three months later, however, Pyongyang once again appeared to be retreating from its hard-line position. Tense relations with the United States were somewhat eased in early August 2009 by Pyongyang's decision, through the intercession of former U.S. president Clinton, to release two American journalists who had been convicted of what North Korea called an illegal border crossing. The death of former South Korean president Kim Dae Jung, on August 18, then provided an opportunity for the North to send a high-level delegation to the South to pay its respects. The delegation met briefly with President Lee, and within days the two Koreas agreed to resume family reunions in September–October after a two-year lapse. During the same period the North released a handful of detained South Koreans—a Hyundai employee in Kaesong who had criticized that DPRK government and four fishermen who had allegedly strayed into North Korean waters—and indicated a willingness to resume tours to Mt. Keumgang.

DEMOCRATIC PEOPLE'S REPUBLIC OF KOREA

Chosŏn Minchu-chui Inmin Konghwa-guk

Political Status: Communist people's republic established September 9, 1948.

Area: 46,540 sq. mi. (120,538 sq. km.).

Population: 21,213,378 (1993C,); 23,872,000 (2008E).

Major Urban Centers (1993C): PYONGYANG (3,255,388 [2008C]), Nampo (731,000), Namhung (710,000), Chongjin (582,000), Kaesong (334,000).

Official Language: Korean.

Monetary Unit: Won. The won is not readily convertible. As of December 1, 2009, the official exchange rate was 143.05 won = $1US. However, news reports continued to reference black market rates of more than 3,000 won = $1US.

Chair of the National Defense Commission: KIM Jong Il (KIM Chŏng-il); served as de facto head of state from the death of President KIM Il Sung (KIM Il-sŏng) on July 8, 1994, until election to a five-year term by the Supreme People's Assembly on September 5, 1998; reelected on September 3, 2003, and on April 9, 2009.

President of the Presidium of the Supreme People's Assembly: KIM Yong Nam; elected to the newly created office by the Supreme People's Assembly on September 5, 1998; reelected on September 3, 2004, and on April 9, 2009.

Premier: KIM Yong Il; elected by the Supreme People's Assembly on April 11, 2007, succeeding PAK Pong Ju; reelected on April 9, 2009.

THE COUNTRY

A land of mountains and valleys, the Democratic People's Republic of Korea (DPRK) is located in East Asia, bordering in the north on the People's Republic of China and the Russian Federation and in the south on the Republic of Korea (ROK). Its people, like those in the ROK, are characterized by ethnic and linguistic homogeneity, tracing their origins to the Mongols and the Chinese. Traditionally, Koreans followed Buddhism and Shamanism, but after the establishment of the Communist regime, religion declined as a factor in North Korean life. Preaching Christianity and other religions can be a capital offense. Women constitute an estimated 44 percent of the active labor force and hold 16 percent of the seats in the current Supreme People's Assembly.

The DPRK has more plentiful natural resources than the ROK and inherited a substantial industrial base from the Japanese occupation, but the Korean conflict of 1950–1953 destroyed much of the economic infrastructure. The Soviet-type economy was reconstructed at a high rate of growth with substantial Soviet and Chinese aid. At present, more than 90 percent of the economy is socialized, agricultural land and production remain collectivized, and state-owned enterprises continue to produce the vast majority of manufactured goods. Recently, however, the government has permitted farmers and others to retain income from legal "sideline activities," such as kitchen gardens, while a "special economic zone" was established in Rajin-Sonbong in 1991 to facilitate joint ventures with foreigners. In 1998 the government agreed to form a partnership with South Korea's Hyundai to develop scenic Mt. Keumgang, on the southeast coast, as a tourist resort; to proceed with a number of other joint ventures; and to build during the next ten years an industrial park for branches of various South Korean firms. As of 2009, the industrial complex in Kaesong housed about 100 South Korean companies and employed some 38,000 North Koreans; completion was expected in 2012.

The agricultural sector is dominated by production of rice, maize, and other grains for domestic consumption. Heavy industry includes the manufacture of steel, other metallurgical products, and cement. Ore deposits include coal, iron, gold, silver, magnesite, copper, and lead. Light manufacturing has been of increasing importance since the breakup of the Soviet Union forced economic reorganization, and textiles now constitute a principal source of export earnings. China ranks as North Korea's main trading partner.

Economic data on the DPRK remain difficult to obtain, and those released by the government often are not comparable with those for other countries. According to Pyongyang, the economy suffered drastic declines in the 1990s, with the GDP dropping by over 27 percent in 1994 and by more than 18 percent in 1995 and again in 1996. Despite some $1 billion in international food and other aid from South Korea and elsewhere, as many as 1.5 million people may have died from starvation or related disease from 1995 to 1998.

Agriculture employed just under 30 percent of the labor force and accounted for 30 percent of GDP in 2002, with industry contributing 38 percent. In 1999 the economy reportedly grew for the first time in a decade, expanding by 6.2 percent. According to South Korea's central bank, growth continued, albeit at a slower pace, through 2005, which registered a 3.8 percent gain. GDP contracted by 1.1 percent in 2006 and another 2.3 percent in 2007 before registering 3.7 percent growth in 2008, partly because of increased agricultural yields.

GOVERNMENT AND POLITICS

Political background. A provisional "people's republic" was established in the northern half of Korea under Soviet auspices in February 1946, and the Democratic People's Republic of Korea was formally organized on September 9, 1948, following proclamation of the Republic of Korea in the South. Both the government and the ruling Korean Workers' Party (KWP), which superseded the Communist Party in 1949, were headed by KIM Il Sung, a Soviet-trained Communist.

Suggesting that North Korean political authority might be passing from Kim Il Sung to his son, KIM Jong Il, the younger Kim was appointed to what was one of the country's most powerful posts, chair of the National Defense Commission (NDC), on April 9, 1993. Kim Il Sung died on July 8, 1994, but no action on succession was forthcoming until October 8, 1997, when Kim Jong Il was named KWP general secretary. The state presidency remained vacant.

Uncontested elections to the 687-member Tenth Supreme People's Assembly (SPA) were held on July 26, 1998, with the Central Election Committee reporting a voter turnout of 99.85 percent. At its first session on September 5 the new legislature, which included 60 generals among its membership, approved a number of constitutional changes (see Constitution and government, below) and reelected Kim Jong Il as NDC chair. Kim was thereby confirmed as de facto head of state, the state presidency having been abolished in deference to the memory of Kim Il Sung, whom the new preamble to the constitution described as the country's "eternal President." On the same day KIM Yong Nam, theretofore foreign minister, was named to the newly created post of president of the Assembly's Presidium, and Vice Premier HONG Song Nam was elevated to the premiership, succeeding KANG Song San, who had served as premier since 1984.

In a surprise statement on April 10, 2000, the two Koreas announced that Kim Jong Il and President Kim Dae Jung of South Korea would hold a summit in Pyongyang in mid-June. The announcement came in the midst of an unprecedented DPRK foreign relations initiative that included conclusion of a new friendship treaty with Russia in February, reestablishment of relations with Australia in May, and an unexpected visit by Kim Jong Il to China in late May—his first trip abroad in 17 years. During the historic June 13–15 summit in Pyongyang, the two Korean leaders called for, among other things, eventual national reunification and economic cooperation (see the preceding Korea article for details).

Pro forma balloting for the SPA on August 3, 2003, saw all 687 members elected unopposed. In its first session on September 3 the new legislature reelected Kim Jong Il as NDC chair and approved the selection of PAK Pong Ju, formerly the chemical industry minister, as premier. Pak was succeeded by KIM Yong Il, theretofore the minister of land and marine transport, on April 11, 2007. No official explanation was offered for Pak's dismissal, although some observers cited his apparent advocacy of a limited incentive-based wage system as part of an effort to raise the standard of living.

Kim Jong Il and South Korean President Roh Moo Hyun met in a second summit in Pyongyang October 2–4, 2007 (see the Korea article). On November 14–16 Prime Minister Kim met in Seoul with his South Korean counterpart in the first meeting of DPRK-ROK prime ministers in 15 years.

The election of the 12th SPA, initially scheduled for September 2008, was held on March 9, 2009; as in the past, only one KWP-endorsed candidate appeared on each district's ballot. No official reason was advanced for the six-month postponement, although observers attributed the delay to the rumored adverse health of Kim Jong Il, who reportedly suffered a stroke in August 2008. There were additional unconfirmed reports of a second stroke in October. Kim, described as looking frail, appeared at the opening of the new SPA on April 9, at which time he was reelected NDC chair. SPA Presidium Chair Kim Yong Nam and Premier Kim Yong Il were also reelected.

Constitution and government. From 1948 to 1972 the DPRK's nominal head of state was the chair of the Presidium of the Supreme People's Assembly; the office was, however, of substantially less consequence than that of premier. Under the constitution of December 1972 executive authority was vested in the president of the republic. In addition, a "super cabinet," the Central People's Committee, oversaw operation of the Administration Council, a cabinetlike body headed by the premier.

Constitutional changes adopted on September 5, 1998, by the SPA included abolition of the state presidency. Although the SPA remains the highest state organ, its authority to determine questions of war and peace passed to the ten-member NDC, whose chair now serves as head of state. The Central People's Committee and the Standing Committee were abolished, with most of their duties and powers being assigned to a newly created SPA Presidium that ranks as the "highest organ of state power" between full SPA sessions. The Presidium also assumed responsibility for diplomatic functions, including ratifying and abrogating treaties, that had previously been under the purview of the state presidency; the Presidium's president, the second highest DPRK official, "represents the state" and receives credentials of foreign representatives. The Administration Council was replaced by a smaller Cabinet that not only functions as the SPA's "administrative and executive" body but also has additional authority for governmental management. The premier, who "represents the government of the DPRK," is assisted by vice premiers. The judicial system is headed by the Central Court and includes a People's Court and local courts. Judges are elected by the SPA.

Administratively, the DPRK is divided into nine provinces and four special municipalities (Pyongyang, Nampo, Najin Sonbong, and Kaesong). Smaller units of local government include cities, urban districts, and counties. Each unit has its own people's assembly with a people's committee that, in addition to serving as the "local sovereign power organ" between assembly sessions, functions as the local administrative and executive body.

Foreign relations. The most important foreign policy issue for the DPRK has long been reunification of the peninsula, but the promising initiatives of the early 1970s failed to bear fruit.

The most striking rupture in North-South relations came in October 1983 after a bomb attack in Yangon, Myanmar, that killed four South Korean cabinet ministers. After two captured DPRK army members confessed to having been ordered to attack the South Korean delegation, including President Chun Doo Hwan, Yangon withdrew recognition of the DPRK and both Seoul and Washington demanded a public apology. Pyongyang, however, persisted in denying any responsibility for the incident. (For subsequent North-South developments, see the preceding article.)

The country has gone through a number of phases in relations with the Soviet Union/Russian Federation and the People's Republic of China (PRC). Close links with the Soviet Union were cultivated until 1964, while a generally pro-Chinese period came to an end during the PRC's "Cultural Revolution" in the second half of the 1960s. Subsequently, the Kim Il Sung regime maintained a somewhat ambivalent position, steadfastly proclaiming a policy of *Juche,* or self-reliance, while depending on both the Soviet Union and the PRC for aid.

In September 1995 Moscow formally terminated a defense treaty dating from 1961. Pyongyang responded that the treaty had been "as good as nullified" by the collapse of the Soviet Union and welcomed a proposal for a new nonmilitary cooperation agreement with the Russian Federation. In February 2000, during a visit to the North Korean capital by Russian Foreign Minister Igor Ivanov—the first such visit by a leading Russian official since Moscow had granted diplomatic recognition to South Korea a decade earlier—the two states concluded a friendship treaty that the SPA ratified in April. Meanwhile, on June 3–7, 1999, Kim Yong Nam had led the first high-level visit to the PRC since Beijing had extended diplomatic recognition to South Korea in 1991. During Kim Jong Il's May 2000 trip to Beijing, he conferred with both President Jiang Zemin and Premier Zhu Rongji, who reportedly offered some $1 billion in additional aid but also encouraged cooperation with South Korea, restraint in weapons and missile development, and economic reform.

In April 1992 North Korea reversed a six-year refusal to permit inspection of its nuclear facilities by the International Atomic Energy Agency (IAEA). Although inspectors were permitted to visit some nuclear sites, the government refused to open others and in March 1993 threatened to withdraw from the Nuclear Non-Proliferation Treaty (NPT), to which it had acceded in 1985. On April 1 the IAEA notified the UN Security Council of North Korea's "noncompliance" with the NPT and requested a food and fuel embargo. While remaining defiant, Pyongyang soon called for discussions with Washington to secure an end to the impasse.

In July 1993 U.S.-DPRK negotiators in Geneva concluded an agreement whereby Pyongyang would resume talks with the IAEA, and Washington would consider aid for the construction of nonmilitary light-water reactors. In August North Korea granted access to five "declared" sites, but not to two others in its Yongbyon nuclear complex. No further progress was registered until February 1994, when the DPRK agreed to unimpeded inspection of all seven sites, although not of two suspected nuclear waste dumps that could potentially yield a supply of bomb-grade material. In a formal pact concluded on October 21, 1994, Washington agreed to extend diplomatic recognition, arrange for financial assistance (estimated at some $4.6 billion) for the construction of two modern nuclear reactors, and supply 500,000 tons of fuel oil a year during the switchover. (Subsequently, it was agreed that South Korea would meet 70 percent of the cost and Japan another 20 percent, with the balance to be provided by the United States and others.) For its part, Pyongyang agreed to freeze all of its nuclear activities, provide safe storage for some 8,000 spent nuclear fuel rods, and accept full IAEA inspection after significant progress had been made toward construction of the new facilities. In December, at the conclusion of a two-day meeting in San Francisco, representatives of the United States, South Korea, and Japan agreed to set up a multilateral consortium, named the Korean Peninsula Energy Development Organization (KEDO), to oversee financing of the U.S.-DPRK nuclear accord.

A deadline of April 21, 1995, for finalizing the October 1994 nuclear accord was not met, primarily because of Pyongyang's insistence that the replacement light-water reactors be of U.S. rather than of South Korean manufacture. In June, however, the DPRK accepted a face-saving proviso that the reactors be of "the advanced version of U.S.-origin design and technology." A groundbreaking ceremony was held in the east coast town of Sinpo on August 9, 1997. By then, the European Union had joined KEDO.

Meanwhile, the DPRK continued to deny IAEA inspectors access to some laboratory sites. In August 1998 reports surfaced that U.S. intelligence had discovered yet another underground weapons site. Despite Pyongyang's initial demands for monetary compensation in return for opening the Kumchangri complex, a series of bilateral talks produced in March 1999 a joint statement in which the North Korean regime agreed to provide access to the site beginning in May. For its part, U.S. President Bill Clinton's administration pledged additional food and agricultural aid. An initial inspection of the Kumchangri facilities on May 20–24, 1999, and a repeat inspection a year later revealed that they were incomplete and posed no security threat.

In mid-1999 rumors began emerging that North Korea was preparing to test a longer-range version of a missile it had fired on August 31, 1998, over Japan and into the Pacific. U.S.-DPRK talks on North Korea's missile program had begun in 1996, with the most recent round having ended inconclusively in March 1999. Two months later, former U.S. secretary of defense William Perry visited Pyongyang, reportedly offering additional economic assistance and diplomatic ties if the DPRK showed sufficient restraint in its nuclear weapons and missile programs. Despite initial recalcitrance, in August Pyongyang agreed to postpone indefinitely further missile flight tests and to participate in additional bilateral sessions on the matter.

On September 17, 1999, Washington announced that it would soon ease the embargo that had been in place since 1953, the principal exception being for military-related goods and technology. A week later Pyongyang formally announced a suspension of ballistic missile testing. Several subsequent negotiating sessions focused on ways of improving relations and on prospects for higher-level discussions.

On June 19, 2000, President Clinton finally lifted economic sanctions against the DPRK. Talks on the missile program resumed in Kuala Lumpur, Malaysia, in July and November but ended with the United States refusing to meet the DPRK's request for $1 billion a year in compensation for ending missile sales. For years the cash-strapped North had been considered the world's leading exporter of rockets and related technology, and in August Kim Jong Il himself had confirmed sales to Iran and Syria. U.S. Secretary of State Madeleine Albright and DPRK Foreign Minister PAEK Nam Sun met for the first time on July 28 during a session of the Association of Southeast Asian Nations in Bangkok, Thailand. On October 23 Albright became the most senior U.S. official ever to visit the North.

The change of U.S. administration in January 2001 clearly chilled relations between Washington and Pyongyang, and they worsened throughout 2002, which began with U.S. President George W. Bush identifying the DPRK, along with Iraq and Iran, as part of an "axis of evil." The North also continued to be angered over U.S. insistence on IAEA inspection of all nuclear facilities. On August 7 U.S. officials attended the first pouring of concrete for a nuclear power plant under the 1994 KEDO agreement, but relations took on a darker cast during an October 3–5 visit by U.S. Assistant Secretary of State James Kelly to Pyongyang: The DPRK proclaimed that it had continued its nuclear weapons program in violation of the agreement. On November 15 KEDO announced that it would suspend future deliveries of heavy fuel oil to the North, pending progress on the nuclear weapons issue. With the rhetoric on both sides escalating, Pyongyang ordered all IAEA inspectors to leave the country, restarted the Yongbyon nuclear reactor, and in April 2003 formally withdrew from the NPT. As a direct consequence of Pyongyang's decisions, work on the two KEDO reactors was ultimately suspended, and the project was officially terminated in June 2006.

On August 27–29, 2003, in an effort to diffuse the crisis, six-party talks involving the two Koreas, the United States, the PRC, Japan, and Russia opened in Beijing, with additional rounds taking place on February 25–27 and June 23–26, 2004. By then, the general consensus was that Pyongyang had sufficient plutonium for up to eight nuclear warheads.

Following a year of political gamesmanship, a fourth six-party round opened in Beijing on July 26, 2005, and continued until a recess on August 7. When the talks resumed on September 13–19, the DPRK indicated its intention to renew participation in both the NPT and the IAEA's safeguards regime, but no additional progress was reported at the opening of the fifth round, held November 9–11. Less than a month later, the DPRK announced a boycott of further six-party sessions until the United States ended financial sanctions that it had imposed in response to the DPRK's alleged money laundering, smuggling, and counterfeiting of U.S. currency.

Until the nuclear weapons impasse brought the program to a halt, Pyongyang and Washington had regularly discussed the fate of the 8,000 U.S. servicemen still listed as missing in action from the Korean conflict. Some 40 joint exhumations took place during 1996–1999, but further efforts stopped in late 1999 because Washington refused to accept any linkage, as demanded by the North, to additional economic assistance. In June 2000 the two sides reached agreement on a plan for further excavations, the first of which took place on June 25, the 50th anniversary of the start of the Korean War. Between 1996 and North Korea's termination of the program in June 2005, the remains of over 200 individuals were recovered. More recently, remains of 6 U.S. servicemen were turned over to a visiting U.S. delegation in April 2007.

In an abrupt reversal of policy, the DPRK had sought during 1990 to establish relations with Japan, although it demanded that Tokyo apologize for its 35 years of colonial rule and match the $500 million in economic compensation given to South Korea when Tokyo and Seoul normalized relations in 1965. The apology was forthcoming at the January 30, 1991, launching of normalization talks, although Japan rejected the demand for compensation. Little was accomplished before the DPRK terminated discussions in November 1992. The following May, to Tokyo's consternation, North Korea test-fired a medium-range missile over the Sea of Japan.

In June 1998 the DPRK suspended a 1997 program under which Japanese-born spouses of Korean men had been allowed to visit their homeland. Earlier, Japan had dismissed the results of an unsuccessful North Korean investigation into the whereabouts of ten or more Japanese who had allegedly been kidnapped in the 1970s and 1980s to teach North Korean agents. Relations with Japan took yet another downturn with the DPRK's August 1998 missile launching, which prompted Tokyo to temporarily freeze food aid and development assistance, including its share of KEDO funding. North Korea insisted that the vehicle was a satellite launcher, which U.S. intelligence later admitted may have been the case. Tokyo announced in May 1999 that it would release its KEDO funding.

In December 1999, meeting in Beijing, representatives of the DPRK and Japan agreed, after a seven-year hiatus, to resume the suspended normalization talks. The normalization process, which nevertheless failed to advance over the next two years, was set back again in December 2001 when the Japanese coast guard sank a suspected North Korean spy ship in Japan's exclusive economic zone, an act that the North characterized as "brutal piracy." On September 17, 2002, in an effort to reenergize the diplomatic process, Japanese Prime Minister Junichiro Koizumi traveled to Pyongyang, where, for the first time, the DPRK admitted having abducted Japanese citizens between 1977 and 1983. Kim Jong Il also expressed a willingness to permit full IAEA inspections and to maintain a moratorium on the DPRK's missile testing beyond 2003. In return, Koizumi apologized for Japan's colonial occupation and offered to provide economic assistance following normalization of relations.

Although ministerial-level talks resumed in October 2002, the event was overshadowed by the revelation, earlier in the month, of North Korea's continuing nuclear weapons program and by a visit to Japan of five of the nationals who had been abducted more than two decades earlier. The decision of the five to remain in Japan led to a further rupture. A visit by Japan's Prime Minister Koizumi in May 2004 accomplished little. Bilateral talks resumed February 4–8, 2006, but no progress occurred with regard to normalization, the abduction issue, or the DPRK's nuclear and missile programs.

On July 5, 2006, North Korea launched seven rockets over the Sea of Japan, one of them a 6,000-kilometer-range *Taepo Dong-2* ballistic missile that failed less than a minute into its flight. On July 15 the UN Security Council passed a resolution condemning the tests, demanding renewal of the ballistic missile test moratorium and North Korea's return to the six-party talks, and advising all UN members to prevent the transfer to the DPRK of missile-related technology, materials, and financing. On October 9, in an action that even its closest ally, China, branded "flagrant and brazen," North Korea conducted its first underground nuclear test near Punggye, in the mountainous northeast. The Security Council responded with another condemnatory resolution.

Having captured the world's attention once again, on October 31, 2006, Pyongyang did an about-face, announcing that it was prepared to return to the six-party negotiations, and the fifth round resumed in Beijing on December 18–22. Although the initial session accomplished little, at the next, held February 8–13, 2007, the North stated that it was prepared to shut down the Yongbyon reactor once again, inventory all nuclear programs, and permit IAEA inspections. In return, the DPRK would receive 50,000 tons of heavy fuel (with another 950,000 tons to come, following the North's closure of all its nuclear facilities), both the United States and Japan would reopen normalization talks, and Washington would facilitate the release of $25 million in North Korean assets that had been frozen in a Macao bank as a consequence of U.S. financial sanctions.

The February 2007 breakthrough in the six-party talks on North Korea's nuclear program did not immediately produce results. In fact, North Korea abruptly ended the opening session of the sixth round of talks, held March 19–22, because its $25 million remained frozen in Macao's Banco Delta Asia (BDA). North Korea, seeking reentry into the global financial system, insisted that the funds be transferred from the BDA to another international bank. Until late June, however, arrangements for transferring the funds remained incomplete, largely because the U.S. Treasury Department had blacklisted the BDA for money laundering. Reputable banks, wary of sanctions mandated by U.S. law, were unwilling to accept a transfer without explicit approvals from the U.S. Treasury and State departments.

On June 26–29, following the transfer of the funds via a Russian bank, the DPRK permitted IAEA inspectors to visit Yongbyon as the first step toward shutting down the nuclear facility. On July 14 the IAEA confirmed that the Yongbyon reactor and other related facilities at the site had been shut down. South Korea had already agreed to resume shipments of food aid and heavy fuel oil to the North. The first six-party session since March was held in Beijing on July 18–20, with a follow-up session taking place on September 27–30. Pyongyang agreed that by the end of the year it would disable all facilities at Yongbyon and disclose all its nuclear programs. Although the North began disabling Yongbyon in November, the deadline was not met.

On June 27, 2008, North Korea destroyed the cooling tower at its Yongbyon nuclear facility, a day after delivering to China the much-anticipated accounting of its nuclear weapons program. Two key elements were missing from the declaration, however: details about its existing nuclear bombs and a response to U.S. assertions that Pyongyang has a uranium enrichment program. Nevertheless, the accounting was sufficient to evoke a positive reaction from the other countries in the six-party talks, and U.S. President Bush quickly announced that the United States would lift some sanctions and begin the process of removing North Korea from its list of state sponsors of terrorism. Working-level talks between Japan and North Korea also resumed in June, at which time Tokyo agreed to ease sanctions and Pyongyang agreed, among other things, to reexamine the case of the abducted Japanese.

On July 10–12, 2008, after a nine-month pause, the six-party talks reconvened. Although North Korea complained that fuel oil shipments were lagging behind schedule, it agreed to complete nuclear disablement by October. The session concluded with a working group having been assigned to draw up detailed verification procedures for the North's nuclear accounting. Meanwhile, on July 11 bilateral relations with South Korea had suffered yet another setback when North Korean guards shot and killed a South Korean tourist who was part of a group visiting Mt. Keumgang.

Progress toward dismantling Yongbyon was subsequently halted once again until the United States, on October 11, 2008, finally removed the DPRK from its list of state sponsors of terrorism. North Korea thereupon agreed to resume tearing down the Yongbyon facility and permit inspections. In November, however, it restricted inspectors from taking soil and other test samples. It also announced its intention to close the border with the South, apparently over continuing dissatisfaction with the conservative South Korean president, Lee Myung Bak. Six-party talks on December 8–11 failed to make progress on verification protocols.

Current issues. The DPRK's relations with South Korea and the international community in general rapidly deteriorated in late 2008 and early 2009. Having announced on January 30, 2009, that it was abrogating agreements previously concluded with Seoul and would not honor the Northern Limit Line that defined their maritime border in the

Yellow Sea, on April 5 the North launched another *Taepo Dong*-2 rocket. Pyongyang insisted that the launch carried a communications satellite into orbit, but Western observers saw no evidence of a new satellite and declared the launch an unsuccessful military test, the second and third stages of the rocket having failed to separate. The North responded to broad international condemnation of the launch by announcing on April 14 that it would not tolerate such "unbearable insults" and that it was once again quitting the six-party talks and nullifying all related agreements. As a result, all IAEA inspectors were expelled from Yongbyon, and the North claimed that it was going to resume reprocessing fuel rods. On April 24 the UN Security Council's sanctions committee proposed additional financial and trade penalties. The DPRK conducted a second, larger nuclear weapons test on May 23, 2009, which was quickly followed by a series of short-range missile launches and an announcement on May 25 that it was withdrawing from the 1953 armistice. On June 12, responding to the nuclear test, the UN Security Council unanimously voted to tighten sanctions against the North and authorized all UN member states to inspect ships suspected of carrying weapons or nuclear technology to or from the North.

All of these developments were accompanied by what has become a familiar barrage of overblown rhetoric directed by Pyongyang against South Korea and the United States. Analysts speculated that several factors may have contributed to the North's behavior. First, the regime may have wanted to present a symbolic show of force to greet the incoming Barack Obama administration in the United States. Second, North Korea's belligerence may have reflected Kim Jong Il's desire to demonstrate to hard-line elements of the North Korean military that he still adhered to a "military first" strategy. Support from the military is almost certainly linked to the question of succession. In early June South Korean media reported that Kim, 67, had named the youngest of his three sons, the Swiss-educated KIM Jong Un, 26, as his successor. Kim Jong Un holds a relatively low-level position with the NDC, and his father reportedly requested that North Korean higher-ups pledge their loyalty to the designee. Shortly after, a report surfaced that the elder Kim was suffering from pancreatic cancer, which would add greater urgency to securing his mini-dynasty. Other figures who have apparently advanced to the higher ranks of power include Kim Jong Il's brother-in-law, JANG Song Taek, who was appointed to the NDC in April. Generally regarded as a key adviser to Kim Jong Il, Jang is seen by some as a possible mentor, or even a power broker, should Kim Jong Un assume leadership in the near future.

In late July 2009 Pyongyang paused its heated rhetoric to suggest that although it regarded the six-party process as dead, it was willing to engage in bilateral negotiations, presumably with Washington. This announcement came less than a week after the North, reacting to U.S. Secretary of State Hillary Clinton's characterization of the regime as "unruly children," described her as unintelligent and a "funny lady" who sometimes resembles a "primary schoolgirl and sometimes a pensioner going shopping."

Pyongyang soon had more positive comments, however, regarding Secretary Clinton's spouse, former president Bill Clinton, who arrived in Pyongyang on August 4, 2009, in an unannounced private mission to seek the release of two U.S. television journalists, Chinese-American Laura Ling and Korean-American Euna Lee. The journalists, both employed by former U.S. vice president Al Gore's Current TV news channel, had been reporting on North Korean refugees when they were apprehended in March along the Tumen River border with China. North Korean authorities claimed that the two women had illegally crossed into the DPRK. Both were convicted in a closed trial on June 8 and sentenced to 12 years of hard labor, although subsequent reports indicated that they were actually being held at a "guesthouse" in Pyongyang and that a "remorseful acknowledgement" of their alleged misdeed by Washington might facilitate their release. Although President Clinton had no official standing and carried no official message from the White House, he was regarded as the most senior U.S. official to enter the North since Secretary of State Albright's visit in 2000. Clinton's trip was widely seen as a coup for the North, which had reportedly rejected Vice President Gore as an emissary. In the end, following a lengthy meeting with Clinton, Kim Jong Il issued a pardon for the journalists, who flew back to the United States on a private jet with Clinton.

Thereafter, Pyongyang appeared ready to ease relations with the South, in part by resuming family reunion visits, tours of Mt. Keumgang, and crossborder transportation to the Kaesong industrial park. During a visit by Chinese premier Wen Jiabao in early October 2009 to mark 60 years of diplomatic relations between Beijing and Pyongyang, the North also restated its willingness to pursue denuclearization of the Korean peninsula through bilateral and multilateral negotiations. For its part, Washington appeared willing to engage in bilateral talks, but only about North Korea's return to the six-party forum.

POLITICAL PARTIES

Democratic Front for the Reunification of the Fatherland (DFRF). The DFRF is an umbrella grouping of the dominant KWP, two smaller parties (below), and a number of mass organizations, including the General Federation of Trade Unions of Korea, the Korean Democratic Women's Union, the Kim Il Sung Socialist Youth League, and the Union of Agricultural Working People of Korea.

Chief of the Secretariat: KIM Wan Su.

Korean Workers' Party—KWP (*Chosŏn No-dong Dang*). Founded in 1949 through merger of the existing Communist Party and the recently established National Party, the KWP controls all political activity in the DPRK through an overlapping of party, executive, and legislative posts. Although party congresses are to meet every five years, the last one to convene, the sixth, met October 10–14, 1980, nearly a decade after the fifth. Between congresses, a Central Committee (encompassing 171 members and 141 alternates as of April 1998) acts on its behalf. In turn, the Central Committee names a Politburo. Kim Jong Il is the only remaining member of the five-man Politburo Presidium designated at the 1980 congress, one member having been dismissed and three having died.

On October 8, 1997, Kim was named to the additional post of general secretary, an office that had been vacant since Kim Il Sung's death. Other party organs include a Central Military Commission and a Secretariat.

General Secretary: Mar. KIM Jong Il.

Korean Social Democratic Party—KSDP (*Chosŏn Sahoeminju-dang*). The KSDP was launched in November 1945 as the Democratic Party, acquiring substantial support in both urban and rural areas prior to the flight of most of its leaders to the south in 1946. The party assumed its current name in 1981.

Leader: KIM Yong Dae (Chair of Central Committee).

Chongdoist Chungu Party—CCP (*Chondogyo Ch'ong-udang*). Sometimes translated as the Young Friends Party, the CCP descended from a prewar anti-Japanese group of religious (*Chondo,* or "Heaven's Way") nationalists. The Young Friends enjoyed a degree of autonomy until the Korean conflict, when it was brought under effective KWP control.

Leader: RYU Mi Yong (Chair of Central Committee).

LEGISLATURE

The unicameral **Supreme People's Assembly** (*Choe Ko In Min Hoe Ui*) is elected from a single slate of KWP members and party-approved nominees. Although the five-year term of the Ninth Assembly technically expired in 1995, an extended period of mourning for Kim Il Sung was given as the reason for having postponed the election of the 687-member Tenth Assembly until July 26, 1998. The new assembly convened on September 5 to approve constitutional amendments and to elect the state and legislative leaderships. One of the changes to the basic law abolished the assembly's Standing Committee, which had previously conducted the body's business between sessions, and replaced it with a 17-member Presidium. The 12th SPA was elected March 8, 2009.

President of the Presidium: KIM Yong Nam.
Chair: CHOE Thae Bok.

CABINET

[as of October 15, 2009]

Premier	Kim Yong Il
Vice Premiers	Kwak Pom Gi
	O Su Yong
	Pak Myong Son
	Pak Su Gil
	Ro Tu Chol

Ministers

Agriculture	Kim Chang Sik
Capital City Construction	Kim Ung Gwan
Chemical Industry	Ri Mu Yong
Coal Industry	Kim Hyong Sik
Commerce	Kim Pong Chol
Construction and Building-Materials Industries	Tong Chong Ho
Culture	Kang Nung Su
Education	Kim Yong Jin
Electric Power Industry	Ho Taek
Electronics Industry	Han Kwang Bok
Extractive Industries	Kang Min Chol
Finance	Pak Su Gil
Fisheries	Pak Thae Won
Food Procurement and Administration	Mun Ung Jo
Foreign Affairs	Pak Ui Chun
Foreign Trade	Ri Ryong Nam
Forestry	Kim Kwang Yong
Labor	Jong Yong Su
Land and Environmental Protection	Pak Song Nam
Land and Marine Transport	Ra Tong Hui
Light Industry	Ri Ju O
Machine-Building Industry	Jo Pyong Ju
Metal Industry	Thae Bong
Mining Industry	Kang Min Chol
Oil Industry	Kim Hui Yong
People's Armed Forces	Kim Yong Jun
People's Security	Ju Sang Song
Posts and Telecommunications	Ryu Yong Sop
Public Health	Choe Chang Sik
Railways	Jon Kil Su
State Construction Control	Pae Tal Jun
State Inspection	Kim Ui Sun
Urban Management	Hwang Hak Won
Chair, Physical Culture and Sports Guidance Committee	Pak Hak Son
Chair, State Planning Commission	Ro Tu Chol
Director, Central Statistics Bureau	Kim Chang Su
President, Central Bank	Ri Kwang Gon
President, National Academy of Sciences	Pyon Yong Rip
Director, Cabinet Secretariat	Kim Yong Ho

COMMUNICATIONS

All news media are censored by the KWP and staffed by KWP-approved personnel. Reporters Without Borders has ranked the DPRK as the world's leading violator of press rights.

Press. Reliable circulation figures remain unavailable. The following are dailies published in Pyongyang, unless otherwise noted: *Rodong Shinmun* (Labor Daily), organ of the KWP Central Committee; *Rodongja Shinmun* (Workers' Daily), organ of the General Federation of Trade Unions; *Minju Chosun* (Democratic Korea), organ of the SPA; *Chosun Inmingun* (Korean People's Army); *Korea Today,* monthly in Chinese, English, French, Russian, and Spanish.

News agencies. The Korean Central News Agency (KCNA) is the official government news service. Russia's ITAR-TASS has a bureau in Pyongyang.

Broadcasting. The DPRK Radio and Television Broadcasting Committee controls all stations. Internet access is very limited and highly censored.

INTERGOVERNMENTAL REPRESENTATION

At present, there are no diplomatic relations between the United States and the Democratic People's Republic of Korea.

Permanent Representative to the UN: SIN Son Ho.

IGO Memberships (Non-UN): NAM.

REPUBLIC OF KOREA

Taehan-min'guk

Political Status: Independent republic established August 15, 1948; present constitution approved in national referendum of October 27, 1987, effective February 25, 1988.

Area: 38,309 sq. mi. (99,221 sq. km.).

Population: 47,254,000 (2005C); 48,616,000 (2008E). The 2005 figure does not include an adjustment for underenumeration.

Major Urban Centers (2005E): SEOUL (9,572,000), Pusan (3,566,000), Taegu (2,625,000), Inchon (2,567,000), Taejon (1,467,000), Kwangju (1,451,000), Ulsan (928,000).

Official Language: Korean.

Monetary Unit: Won (market rate December 1, 2009: 1,161.10 won = $1US).

President: LEE Myung Bak (Grand National Party); elected December 19, 2007, and sworn in for a five-year term on February 25, 2008, succeeding ROH Moo Hyun (previously *Uri* Party; initially Millennium Democratic Party).

Prime Minister: CHUNG Un Chan (Grand National Party); nominated by the president on September 3, 2009, and confirmed by the National Assembly on September 28, succeeding HAN Seung Soo (Grand National Party).

THE COUNTRY

Characterized by mountainous terrain in the north and east and broad plains in the south, the Republic of Korea (ROK) is densely settled. A majority of its population is concentrated in the southern section, although approximately one-quarter are residents of the capital, Seoul, which is located within 30 miles of the demilitarized zone (DMZ) that separates it from the Democratic People's Republic of Korea (DPRK). The people are ethnically homogeneous, tracing their heritage to Mongol and Chinese origins. Buddhism, Shamanism, and Christianity are the important religions; the ROK has one of the largest Christian populations in Asia, numbering in excess of 17 million. Women constitute 42 percent of the active labor force, concentrated in wholesale and retail trade, food and lodging, manufacturing, and education. Fourteen percent of the seats in the current National Assembly are held by women.

Unlike the DPRK, the ROK did not begin the post–World War II period with a substantial industrial base, and postwar growth was cut short by the Korean conflict of 1950–1953. Subsequently, however, industrial expansion was rapid, and by the mid-1970s the agricultural sector (agriculture, fishing, and forestry) had been surpassed by manufacturing as a contributor to GDP. Agriculture now employs 7 percent of the labor force and accounts for only 3 percent of GDP. Farming is devoted primarily to grain production, chiefly rice; ocean fishing, both for domestic markets and export, is also important. Industry (manufacturing, mining, construction, and utilities), which employs about 26 percent of workers and contributes 39 percent of GDP, is concentrated in electronics, transport equipment (including ships), machinery, ferrous metals, chemicals, processed foods, and textiles. South Korea's relatively scarce mineral resources include deposits of coal and iron.

During the 1980s South Korea experienced an average annual economic growth rate of 9.5 percent, making it one of the world's fastest-growing economies. The 1990–1997 rate of 7.2 percent was only slightly less impressive, enabling it, in 1996, to join the Organization for Economic Cooperation and Development as a "developed" state. In the second half of 1997, however, the bankruptcies of a number of important conglomerates (*chaebols*) devastated the financial sector,

and the value of the won, which had already been damaged by the spreading financial crises elsewhere in East Asia, plummeted against the U.S. dollar, dropping by half for the year. Collaterally, South Korea's foreign-exchange reserves fell drastically, prompting the International Monetary Fund (IMF) to offer in December a record $58 billion stabilization package in return for a commitment to economic reform, including corporate restructuring. During 1998 the economy contracted by 6.7 percent and unemployment more than doubled, but by the end of the year a trade surplus had helped Seoul rebuild its foreign reserves from $9 billion to $50 billion, the won had rebounded, interest rates had dropped, and the government had repaid the first $3 billion installment on the IMF loan.

Far exceeding expectations, South Korea's economy recorded growth of 10.9 percent in 1999 and 9.3 percent in 2000, while unemployment rapidly declined. The GDP expanded by a more modest 3.8 percent in 2001, largely because of economic slowdowns in major export markets, but rebounded to a 7.0 growth rate in 2002. After registering a 3.1 percent gain in 2003, GDP growth averaged 4.5 percent in 2004–2005 and 5.1 percent in 2006–2007. South Korea directly felt the international financial crisis and resultant recession in the last quarter of 2008, when GDP fell by 5.1 percent. For the first quarter of 2009 Seoul reported a gain of 0.1 percent but predicted that for the year as a whole the GDP would drop by about 2 percent.

GOVERNMENT AND POLITICS

Political background. Syngman RHEE, a conservative president, dominated ROK politics from the establishment of the republic on August 15, 1948, until student-led demonstrations against ballot tampering forced his resignation in 1960. Plagued by administrative chaos, the liberal successor government of President YUN Po Sun and Prime Minister CHANG Myon was overthrown in a bloodless military coup led by Maj. Gen. PARK Chung Hee and four other officers on May 16, 1961. The National Assembly was dissolved, the constitution suspended, and all political parties disbanded, with General Park assuming executive powers under a military junta called the Supreme Council for National Reconstruction. As a step toward the reestablishment of civilian rule under a revised constitution, General Park and other leading officers retired from the army preparatory to seeking elective office. Park and his newly formed Democratic Republican Party (DRP) won the presidential and legislative elections held in 1963, and constitutional rule was formally restored with Park's inauguration as president in December.

President Park was reelected in 1967 and again in 1971, when he won a narrow victory over opposition candidate KIM Dae Jung. Shortly thereafter, Park declared a state of national emergency and extracted from the National Assembly, over strong opposition, emergency powers that gave him virtually unlimited authority to regulate the economy and limit constitutional freedoms in the interest of national security.

Responding to increased political tension, Park abruptly proclaimed martial law in October 1972. A new constitution, approved in a referendum held under martial-law restrictions, provided for a powerful president, to be designated by a directly elected National Conference for Unification (NCU), and a weak legislature with one-third of its membership appointed by the NCU. Park was reconfirmed by the NCU in December, and a legislative election held in February 1973 completed the nominal return to constitutional government.

Opposition to the so-called *Yushin* (Revitalizing) Constitution of 1972 grew slowly, with the government responding to recurring protests by increasingly repressive measures. Park was returned for a further six-year term in 1978, and the DRP, although failing to capture a plurality of votes in a December election, retained control of the National Assembly.

Following the October 1979 expulsion from the National Assembly of opposition leader KIM Young Sam for having criticized the Park regime in a *New York Times* interview, the entire legislative opposition resigned in protest. At that point student demonstrations, begun in the aftermath of an August labor protest, expanded into riots. Later that month Park and five companions were assassinated at the direction of KIM Jae Kyu, chief of the Korean Central Intelligence Agency (KCIA). Although anticipating military backing for a government takeover, the KCIA's Kim was instead arrested by army authorities within hours of the assassination.

Park was immediately succeeded by the prime minister, CHOI Kyu Hah. He was elected by the NCU in December 1979 to complete Park's term, quickly revoked his predecessor's emergency decrees, and declared an amnesty that freed 1,646 prisoners. Control of the country was, however, largely in the hands of Lt. Gen. CHUN Doo Hwan, head of the Defense Security Command, who had taken control of the armed forces in what amounted to a coup.

A widespread series of labor strikes in April 1980 escalated in May into mass student demonstrations. The government responded by arresting Kim Dae Jung and a number of other opposition leaders, provoking a popular uprising in the southern city of Kwangju. In late May, after heavy fighting and at least 200 deaths, the Kwangju insurrection was suppressed by government forces.

President Choi resigned in August 1980 and was soon succeeded by Chun Doo Hwan, who had resigned his commission before being elected president by the NCU. A new constitution, approved by a reported majority of 91.6 percent in a referendum, came into effect in October, at which time the existing National Assembly was dissolved and its functions assumed, on an interim basis, by an appointive Legislative Council for National Security. Kim Dae Jung, meanwhile, had been condemned to death for sedition. In January 1981, after worldwide appeals for clemency, his sentence was commuted to life imprisonment. The sentence was further reduced to 20 years in 1982 and eventually suspended, and Kim was permitted to seek medical treatment in the United States the following December.

In January 1981 President Chun rescinded martial law, which had been in effect since the Park assassination, and announced that a presidential election would be held in February, following balloting for an electoral college. Chun's newly formed Democratic Justice Party (DJP) secured 70 percent of the electoral college seats, and he was reinstalled as president in March. In the subsequent National Assembly election, the DJP obtained 151 of 276 seats.

In December 1984 a number of opposition politicians formed the New Korea Democratic Party (NKDP), which won nearly 25 percent of the seats in National Assembly election in February 1985. Shortly before, Kim Dae Jung and Kim Young Sam had been placed under house arrest.

Amid intensifying public disorder associated with demands for constitutional reform, in June 1987 ROH Tae Woo, who had been formally endorsed by the DJP as its choice to succeed President Chun, reversed policy and unexpectedly announced that virtually all of the opposition's reform demands would be met, including the call for direct presidential election. In July Chun resigned as DJP leader so that he could carry out his remaining official duties from a "supra-partisan position." In a cabinet reshuffle three days later he removed all of the party incumbents. At the end of August a committee of government and opposition representatives reached agreement on the essentials of a new constitution, which was overwhelmingly approved by both the National Assembly and the South Korean voters in October.

Although a unified opposition might have won the December 1987 presidential poll, neither Kim Young Sam nor Kim Dae Jung was willing to defer to the other. As a result, Roh obtained 35.9 percent of the vote, with Kim Young Sam and Kim Dae Jung winning 27.5 percent and 26.5 percent, respectively; KIM Jong Pil, a former prime minister under President Park, ran fourth with 7.9 percent.

The assembly poll of April 1988 gave only a plurality (125 of 299 seats) to the DJP. A preelection agreement by Kim Dae Jung and Kim Young Sam to merge their forces had again failed, with Kim Jong Pil's recently organized New Democratic Republican Party (NDRP) securing the balance of power with 35 seats. In December President Roh dismissed most of the ministers prominently associated with the previous regime.

In a startling political realignment, in February 1990 the DJP merged with Kim Jong Pil's NDRP and Kim Young Sam's Reunification Democratic Party (RDP) to form the Democratic Liberal Party (DLP), which immediately controlled nearly three-fourths of the assembly. In March 1991, despite a major drop in support for the Roh administration's domestic policies, the DLP secured a major political victory by winning more than half the contests in South Korea's first local legislative elections in three decades. It performed even better in voting for provincial and metropolitan assemblies in June, winning nearly two-thirds of the races.

Buffeted by charges of corruption and economic mismanagement, the DLP saw its representation plunge to 49 percent in the National Assembly election of March 1992, although it subsequently attracted enough defectors from other parties to claim a majority. Kim Dae Jung's opposition Democratic Party (DP) increased its strength by nearly one-third, to 97 seats, but the most dramatic showing was the 31 seats won by the Unification National Party (UNP), which had been formed only weeks before by Hyundai tycoon CHUNG Ju Yung.

In the watershed election of December 1992, Kim Young Sam, with a vote share of 42 percent, became the first nonmilitary candidate in three decades to win election as South Korean president. His former opposition colleague, Kim Dae Jung, received 34 percent, while Chung Ju Yung of the United People's Party (the reorganized UNP), drew 16 percent. The day after his inauguration in February 1993, Kim named a regionally dispersed cabinet that excluded former government officials. Earlier in the month Hyundai tycoon Chung had been indicted for using some $63 million in corporate funds for campaign purposes. (Subsequently convicted, he would be granted amnesty in August 1995.)

In March 1995 Kim Jong Pil, having left the DLP, formed the conservative United Liberal Democrats (ULD). In September Kim Dae Jung launched the National Congress for New Politics (NCNP), which immediately became the strongest opposition party by virtue of DP defections. In December, in apparent pursuit of a new image, the DLP changed its name to the New Korea Party (NKP).

The National Assembly election of April 1996 saw the NKP's plurality slip to 139 seats, with the NCNP winning 79 and the ULD, 50. The disintegrating DP was reduced to 15 seats. In August, at the conclusion of South Korea's "trial of the century," former presidents Chun Doo Hwan and Roh Tae Woo were found guilty of mutiny, treason, and corruption during the excesses and illegalities that began with the 1979 coup and extended beyond the 1980 Kwangju suppression. For the more profound crimes Chun was sentenced to death and Roh to 22 and a half years in prison. In December an appellate court commuted Chun's sentence to life imprisonment and reduced Roh's prison term to 17 years.

The South Korean party system displayed continued volatility in the run-up to the presidential election of December 1997, in which former dissident Kim Dae Jung, heading an NCNP-ULD coalition, secured a 40.3 percent plurality; his closest competitor, with 38.8 percent, was former prime minister LEE Hoi Chang of the recently formed Grand National Party (GNP), an amalgamation of the NKP and the DP. Four days later President Kim Young Sam pardoned Chun Doo Hwan and Roh Tae Woo, an action endorsed by his successor but criticized by others as an affront to the prodemocracy movement.

In February 1998 President Kim Dae Jung, as he had agreed to do before the election, nominated the ULD's Kim Jong Pil to be the next prime minister, but the GNP-led assembly rejected the nominee because of his participation in past authoritarian regimes. Undaunted, Kim Dae Jung named Kim Jong Pil as acting prime minister to head a new government that included a number of representatives of the "old guard." Nevertheless, the dispute persisted, tying up legislative proceedings and effectively blocking most of the administration's program. With the country in the midst of a major economic crisis and with the public growing increasingly hostile to the opposition's recalcitrance, the GNP finally relented and in August approved Kim Jong Pil's appointment. By early September defections from the GNP had given the governing coalition a working majority in the National Assembly.

President Kim undertook his first major cabinet reshuffle in May 1999, replacing the majority of his ministers in an effort to reinvigorate his economic reform program despite delaying tactics by the GNP. At the same time Kim continued to espouse his "sunshine" policy of peaceful political engagement and economic and cultural cooperation with North Korea, although improving relations were threatened by a June 15 naval battle in the Yellow Sea and North Korea's subsequent unilateral extension of its territorial waters. Kim again reshuffled his cabinet in January 2000, naming 11 new ministers concurrent with National Assembly approval of the ULD's PARK Tae Joon as successor to Prime Minister Kim Jong Pil, who had announced his resignation to prepare his party for the upcoming legislative election.

In February 2000 LEE Han Dong, a former GNP faction leader and the newly elected ULD leader, announced that his party would move into opposition because Kim Dae Jung's new Millennium Democratic Party (MDP, successor to the NCNP) had failed to honor its commitments, particularly consideration of constitutional changes that would replace the existing strong presidency with a parliamentary system. The break was less than complete, however, with Prime Minister Park remaining at the head of the cabinet.

On April 10, 2000, three days before the national election, President Kim stunned the opposition by announcing a June summit with North Korean leader Kim Jong Il in Pyongyang. Although the MDP recorded significant gains on April 13, the GNP retained its plurality, a mere 4 seats short of a legislative majority. The ULD suffered major losses, winning only 17 seats, 33 fewer than it had won in 1996.

Prime Minister Park resigned on May 19, 2000, in response to a court ruling that he had accepted bribes while chair of the giant Pohang Iron and Steel and had then evaded taxes. Three days later, President Kim nominated the ULD's Lee Han Dong as Park's successor, unofficially sealing a renewal of the MDP-ULD partnership.

During the historic June 13–15, 2000, summit in Pyongyang, the leaders of the two Koreas called for, among other things, greater economic cooperation and eventual national reunification. On October 13, in recognition of his efforts to promote democracy and human rights and to achieve "peace and reconciliation" with the DPRK, Kim Dae Jung was awarded the 2000 Nobel Peace Prize.

In March 2001 President Kim undertook a major cabinet reshuffle in which the ULD received three portfolios in an effort to cement the MDP-ULD relationship. Shortly thereafter, the small Democratic People's Party (DPP) announced that it would join the coalition, thereby giving the government a slim majority in the National Assembly.

On September 4, 2001, the entire cabinet resigned following passage in the National Assembly of a nonconfidence motion against Minister of Unification LIM Dong Won. Joining the GNP in voting for the motion was the ULD, effectively announcing its departure from the government. The revamped cabinet presented on September 7 retained Lee Han Dong as prime minister, precipitating his expulsion from the ULD. In National Assembly by-elections a month later, the MDP lost its slim legislative majority.

With two of his sons under investigation for bribery and tax evasion (they were ultimately convicted, fined, and sentenced to prison), Kim Dae Jung resigned from the MDP on May 6, 2002, as did half a dozen cabinet ministers on the following day. In August the GNP cemented a legislative majority with by-election victories in 11 of 13 contests. On October 5, having rejected two previous nominees, the National Assembly approved former Supreme Court justice KIM Suk Soo as prime minister.

Polls initially gave Lee Hoi Chang a clear advantage going into the December 2002 presidential election, but the race was made considerably closer in late November when the leading third-party candidate, CHUNG Mong Joon, the head of South Korea's Football Association and a son of the Hyundai founder, left the race in favor of the MDP's

ROH Moo Hyun. Although Chung withdrew his support the day before the election, apparently because of policy differences with regard to North Korea, Roh won with 48.9 percent of the vote in a come-from-behind victory over Lee, who took 46.6 percent and, shortly thereafter, retired from politics. On January 22, 2003, President-elect Roh nominated as prime minister a former officeholder (1997–1998), GOH Kun, who was approved by the National Assembly on February 26, a day after Roh's inauguration. The president then named a substantially reconfigured cabinet dominated by academics and managers.

The initial months of Roh's presidency were marred by two ongoing scandals, one involving the illegal channeling through a Hyundai subsidiary and the Korean Development Bank of some $100–$200 million to the North Korean government to entice its participation in the June 2000 summit, and the other involving alleged insider trading and accounting fraud by the country's leading *chaebols,* including Hyundai, Samsung, and the SK Group. An investigation into the summit scandal led to the June indictment of two former government ministers, LIM Dong Won and PARK Jie Won, both of whom were ultimately found guilty, and the chair of Hyundai, CHUNG Mong Hun, who committed suicide in August. By then, public support for Roh was dropping sharply, not only because of the scandals but also because of an economic downturn, an April decision to commit South Korean troops to a noncombat role in support of the U.S. invasion of Iraq, and a lack of progress in negotiations with the DPRK. Roh proposed holding a public referendum on his presidency, but the National Assembly, dominated by his opponents, dismissed the gesture as unconstitutional.

In September 2003 several dozen reform-minded legislators abandoned the MDP (as did Roh himself), and in late October they named their new formation the *Uri Dang* (Our Party). In the same month an investigation was launched into charges that prominent members of the MDP and GNP had accepted illegal donations prior to and soon after the 2002 presidential election. On December 4 the National Assembly, in the first such action since 1954, overrode Roh's veto of a bill establishing an independent investigation into the donations. Among those ultimately charged with receiving illegal contributions were leaders in both the GNP and MDP, including a chief aide to President Roh.

On March 12, 2004, following several days of acrimonious debate, the National Assembly, led by the GNP and Roh's former party, the MDP, voted 173–2 to impeach the president for corruption, economic mismanagement, and violation of political neutrality. The last charge involved his having urged voters to support the *Uri* Party in the upcoming general election. Prime Minister Goh assumed the president's duties, pending a decision by the Constitutional Court on Roh's removal from office.

Amid rising public support for Roh, in the April 15, 2004, National Assembly election the *Uri* Party claimed a majority of 152 seats in the 299-seat legislature, with the GNP finishing second and the MDP seeing its representation shrink from more than 60 seats to 9. A month later, on May 14, the Constitutional Court dismissed the corruption and economic mismanagement cases against President Roh. Further, the court ruled that Roh's minor electioneering violation was insufficient to warrant impeachment. Roh thereupon resumed his office, and six days later he joined the *Uri* Party.

On May 24, 2004, Prime Minister Goh tendered his resignation, which was accepted on the following day. On June 8 the president nominated as Goh's successor the *Uri* Party's LEE Hae Chan, who was confirmed on June 29.

A January 2, 2006, cabinet reshuffle was followed on March 14 by the resignation of Prime Minister Lee, whose propriety had been called into question by his playing a round of golf on the very day, March 1, when a nationwide railway workers' strike began. Deputy Prime Minister HAN Duck Soo headed the government until the confirmation of HAN Myeong Sook (*Uri* Party) on April 19. A former minister of the environment, Han thereby became the ROK's first woman prime minister.

In furtherance of her presidential aspirations, Han resigned as prime minister on March 7, 2007, and two days later President Roh nominated as her successor Han Duck Soo (*Uri* Party), who was confirmed by the National Assembly on April 2. By then, however, the *Uri* Party had lost dozens of defectors as the center-left struggled to find a candidate capable of besting the GNP in the presidential election scheduled for December 2007.

On October 2–4, 2007, President Roh and North Korean leader Kim Il Jong met in the second North-South summit (see the Korea article for details), although the occasion was marked by considerably less fanfare than the 2000 summit. In a follow-up meeting, Prime Minister Han welcomed North Korea's prime minister, Kim Yong Il, to Seoul on November 14–16. It was the first meeting of North-South prime ministers in 15 years.

With the *Uri* Party having dissolved in August 2007, and with most of its members having moved to the new center-liberal United New Democratic Party (UNDP), the December 19 presidential election essentially became a three-way contest among the GNP's LEE Myung Bak, the UNDP's CHUNG Dong Young, and former GNP chair Lee Hoi Chang, running as an independent. The conservative Lee Myung Bak won convincingly, securing 48.7 percent of the vote, followed by Chung with 26.1 percent and Lee Hoi Chang with 15.1 percent. Turnout was 63.2 percent, a historic low, but the front-runner secured a record margin of victory for a direct presidential election. In January he nominated as prime minister HAN Seung Soo, a former foreign minister, who was confirmed by the National Assembly on February 29, four days after Lee's inauguration.

The National Assembly election of April 9, 2008, secured a majority for the GNP, which won 153 of the 299 seats. The United Democratic Party (UDP), formed by merger of the UNDP and the DP in February, finished second, with 81 seats, while Lee Hoi Chang's new Liberty Forward Party (LFP) won 18.

By mid-2009, however, public opinion polls reflected a growing dissatisfaction with President Lee and the GNP (see Current issues, below). In an effort to revive support, on September 3 Lee named a new prime minister, CHUNG Un Chan, and six other new ministers. Chung, the president of Seoul National University and a Princeton-trained economist, was confirmed by the National Assembly on September 28.

Constitution and government. The 1987 constitution (technically the ninth amendment of the country's 1948 basic law) sets forth a variety of guarantees, including freedom of press and assembly, the right of habeas corpus, labor's right to organize and strike, and the prohibition of detention without a court order. In addition, the armed forces are enjoined to observe "political neutrality."

The president, who is directly elected for a single five-year term, appoints a prime minister (subject to legislative confirmation) and, on the prime minister's recommendation, a State Council of 15–30 members from which heads of executive ministries are drawn. Members of the unicameral National Assembly serve four-year terms, are specifically authorized to investigate government affairs, and enjoy complete immunity for activity inside the house. By a two-thirds vote of the membership the assembly may impeach the chief executive, although removal from office requires the concurrence of the Constitutional Court.

The three-tiered judiciary includes at its apex a Supreme Court, with regional appellate high courts and district courts operating at the lower levels. Within the district level are city and county courts and a family court. Justices of the Supreme Court, named by the president and confirmed by the assembly, serve six-year terms. A separate Patent Court was added to the system in 1998, along with the first district-based Administrative Court to handle tax, labor, and similar cases. In addition, a Constitutional Court rules on the constitutionality of legislation, hears petitions on constitutional questions, and also has in its purview impeachments, disputes involving state agencies and local governments, and cases related to the dissolution of political parties.

Administratively, the country is divided into 16 "local authorities": the capital of Seoul and 6 additional metropolitan areas (Inchon, Kwangju, Pusan, Taegu, Taejon, and Ulsan), 8 mainland provinces, and the island province of Cheju. The provinces are divided into counties, cities, towns, and townships. Provincial governors and local executives are directly elected.

Foreign relations. Before its admission to the United Nations in September 1991 the ROK maintained a permanent observer at the world organization's New York headquarters and participated in the activities of many of its specialized agencies. The designation of Seoul as the site for the 1988 Olympics reflected South Korea's growing acceptance as a member of the international community, while a thriving export program strengthened economic ties with a variety of trading partners.

Relations with the DPRK and the United States have long been the most sensitive areas of external concern for the ROK. Communication between Seoul and Pyongyang has fluctuated widely in recent years, sporadic talks alternating with hostile exchanges on a variety of issues. Both sides are formally committed to reunification but have adopted differing (and occasionally shifting) positions on the means of achieving it. Low points in relations occurred in October 1983, when North Korean agents killed four South Korean cabinet ministers in a bomb attack in Myanmar, and in November 1987 with the destruction by North Korean agents of a South Korean airliner en route from Bahrain to Seoul. Subsequently, in the wake of global reverses suffered by Communist regimes, tensions eased, and in September 1990 a series of talks were launched at the prime ministerial level that culminated in the nonaggression pact of December 1991 (see Korea article).

In the most serious incursion in nearly three decades, a party of North Korean military personnel and espionage agents came ashore in September 1996 from a submarine that had run aground. Eleven were found dead, 1 was captured alive, and 11 were hunted down and killed by early November, with the loss of 8 South Korean soldiers (several shot by friendly fire) and 4 civilians. Pyongyang initially rejected South Korean protests at the incursion, which cost the South Korean defense minister his job, but after lengthy discussions with U.S. officials the North Korean government issued a surprisingly contrite apology at the end of December.

The subsequent reduction in tension helped open the door for substantive talks among DPRK, ROK, Chinese, and U.S. representatives on a proposed permanent peace settlement for the peninsula. The successful June 2000 DPRK-ROK summit in Pyongyang—the first meeting of the top leaders of the two Koreas—portended a new era of direct North-South bilateral contacts. Since 2003 the ROK has also joined the DPRK, the People's Republic of China (PRC), Japan, Russia, and the United States in intermittent six-party talks aimed at resolving the crisis over the DPRK's nuclear weapons program. In 2008–2009, however, the DPRK, reacting in part to the inauguration of the more conservative Lee Myung Bak administration, announced that it was abrogating the 1953 armistice, declared the six-party process dead, disavowed all military and other agreements with Seoul, conducted a second underground nuclear weapons test as well as numerous missile tests, and moved to restart its nuclear plant at the Yongbyon nuclear complex (for details, see the preceding DPRK article).

Relations with Japan, formally restored in 1965 after 14 years of negotiation, have been constrained by Korean bitterness over the pre-1945 occupation and Tokyo's treatment of resident Koreans. For its part, Japan was long critical of Seoul's record on human rights and then curtailed economic assistance after the abduction of Korean opposition leader Kim Dae Jung from Japan in 1973. A state visit to Japan by Chun Doo Hwan in September 1984, the first by a South Korean president, elicited a ritual apology from Emperor Hirohito for "the unfortunate past between us." President Roh visited Tokyo in May 1990 and again in November 1992, but President Kim canceled a meeting at UN headquarters with Japanese Prime Minister Tomiichi Murayama in October 1995 after the latter referred to his country's occupation of the Korean peninsula as "legally valid."

Further complicating relations with Tokyo has been the issue of Korean and other "comfort women" forced into unpaid prostitution during World War II by the Japanese military (see Japan article). Then in February 1996 a long-standing dispute over sovereignty of an uninhabited small island group in the Sea of Japan (called Tokto by the Koreans, Takeshima by the Japanese, and the Liancourt Rocks by Western navigators) reignited, leading both countries to declare 200-mile exclusive economic zones encompassing the disputed islands. In January 1998 Japan unilaterally terminated a bilateral fishing treaty because of the insular dispute, but eight months later the two governments reached agreement on a new treaty that included a compromise on the issue of fishing zones in the contested area. An October state visit by President Kim Dae Jung to Tokyo reinforced the fisheries pact and also produced a joint statement that included a Japanese expression of "deep remorse and a heartfelt apology" for its 1910–1945 occupation. Historical differences continue to flare up, however, over such matters as the treatment of Korea in Japanese history textbooks, while in April 2006 South Korea denounced Japan's announcement that it intended to conduct a hydrographic survey of the Tokto area. In April 2008 President Lee Myung Bak traveled to Japan, where he and Japanese Prime Minister Yasuo Fukuda attempted to ease bilateral relations. They agreed to resume talks, after a four-year hiatus, on an economic partnership agreement. A summit with Japanese Prime Minister Taro Aso (the fifth such event) on January 11–12, 2009, focused on economic coordination.

Normalization of relations with the Soviet Union, long of lesser priority, was severely impaired by the destruction of a civilian Korean airliner in September 1983, after the plane had strayed off course and passed over Soviet missile installations on the Kamchatka peninsula. A meeting between Presidents Roh Tae Woo and Mikhail Gorbachev in San Francisco on June 4, 1990, preceded mutual diplomatic recognition on September 30 and a historic first visit to Moscow by President Roh in December. In August 1992 relations were also normalized with the PRC, and in late September President Roh traveled to Beijing for the first official visit by a South Korean head of state.

Relations with the United States were temporarily strained in the late 1970s not only by the repressive policies of the Park regime but by revelations of widespread Korean influence peddling in U.S. congressional circles. Anti-American sentiment in the ROK, most dramatically symbolized by arson attacks on U.S. cultural centers in Kwangju and Pusan in the early 1980s, came mainly from opposition politicians, students, and religious leaders, who argued that support for President Chun inhibited the emergence of a truly democratic system. In mid-1987, however, Chun's acceptance of constitutional reform was reported to have stemmed in part from strong U.S. diplomatic pressure.

During a brief visit to Washington in July 1999 Kim Dae Jung requested revision of a 1979 agreement with Washington that prevented Seoul from developing surface-to-surface missiles with a maximum range greater than 180 kilometers. Reacting to North Korea's missile program, Kim requested that the limit be extended to 300 kilometers. In January 2001 Seoul announced that it was moving forward on its missile development program, and in January 2002 the Ministry of Defense signed a contract with U.S. manufacturer Lockheed Martin to purchase its Army Tactical Missile System. At the same time, however, Seoul opposed deployment in South Korea of a theater missile defense system, as proposed by the United States.

The withdrawal of U.S. troops from South Korea, initiated in 1990 because of a lessened threat from the Soviet Union, was suspended in October 1992 upon emergence of the North Korean nuclear inspection issue. Although small reductions later resumed, some 37,500 U.S. troops remained until 2005, when the force was cut to 30,000. Troop levels were scheduled to decline to 25,000. At the beginning of November 2004 South Korean troops assumed full responsibility for policing the DMZ, and in 2007 the allies agreed that wartime control of ROK forces would pass to South Korean commanders in 2012.

In April 2003 the National Assembly voted to send South Korean troops to provide noncombat assistance in Iraq, a move that the president supported despite differences with Washington over its hard-line policy toward North Korea. In May some 650 military engineers and medics were dispatched to Iraq. In February 2004 authorization was given to deploy an additional 3,000 troops, thereby making South Korea's the third-largest military contingent, after those of the United States and the United Kingdom. Because of a worsening security environment, the additional deployment did not begin until August 2004. In December 2005 the National Assembly voted to extend the mission through 2006 but to reduce South Korea's commitment to about 2,200 personnel. A further reduction, to 650 troops, was announced in 2007, with the National Assembly then approving a final extension of the reduced mission. The last South Korean troops returned home in December 2008. Meanwhile, Seoul had announced that it would remove its military personnel (60 medics and 150 engineers) from Afghanistan before the end of 2007. In July the Taliban had abducted 23 South Korean hostages, 2 of whom it executed. The remaining 21 were all released by the end of August following negotiations that concluded with a South Korean pledge to remove its troops (a decision that had already been made, Seoul insisted) and to keep Korean missionaries from entering Afghanistan.

In October 2006 the South Korean foreign minister, BAN Ki Moon, was named UN secretary general.

Current issues. President Lee's first year in office was marked by a precipitous decline in public support. He had come into office promising to streamline government, aid over 7 million debt-ridden consumers, stimulate the economy through such measures as business tax cuts and privatization, and marshal private funding for construction of a controversial $16 billion, 2,000-kilometer Grand Korean Waterway intended to connect the country's major rivers. He also vowed to improve relations with the United States and to adopt a tougher, more pragmatic approach toward North Korea, which undoubtedly contributed to the DPRK's increasing belligerence. He faced, however, strong opposition in the National Assembly to many of his economic goals and to passage of a U.S.-ROK free trade agreement that had been negotiated by the preceding administration

To make matters worse, barely a month into office President Lee made a serious miscalculation. In April 2008 he visited U.S. President George W. Bush, at which time South Korea agreed to lift a ban on the import of U.S. beef. The ban had first been imposed in December 2003, in response to the discovery in one U.S. cow of bovine spongiform encephalopathy (BSE), or mad cow disease. At the time, South Korea was the third-largest buyer of U.S. beef. On several occasions in 2006 and 2007 Seoul had again allowed American beef to be imported, but on each occasion Korean inspectors had soon discovered bones or bone fragments in the shipments, which violated the import terms and resulted in renewal of the ban. With the lifting of the ban in April 2008, the two governments hoped to remove a principal obstacle (the other involving automobiles) to consideration of the free trade agreement by the U.S. Congress.

What President Lee did not count on, however, was the furor that resulted at home from the beef agreement. Thousands of protesters took to the streets in what became a series of daily demonstrations that threatened the longevity of the government. In early June the entire cabinet offered to resign, while the opposition launched a boycott of National Assembly sessions. President Lee ended up apologizing for mishandling the agreement and on July 7, 2008, replaced the ministers in charge of health and welfare, food and agriculture, and education and science. Beef imports finally resumed late in the year, after the United States had accepted tighter restrictions on beef from older cattle.

Meanwhile, the free trade pact, which had been signed in June 2007, was still pending in both the Korean and U.S. legislatures. In November 2008, however, the election of Barack Obama to the U.S. presidency brought the ratification process to a halt. Obama had described the free trade agreement as "badly flawed" during his campaign, and in January 2009 the incoming secretary of state, Hillary Clinton, confirmed that it would have to be renegotiated.

Although the U.S. decision constituted a major setback for the Lee administration, a more immediate concern was the ongoing world financial crisis and recession. In September 2008 the government had introduced a tax-cut plan in an effort to boost the economy, and a month later it announced that it would spend $3.8 billion to support the construction and housing industry. At the end of the month the National Assembly approved $130 billion in loan guarantees and other supports for a host of South Korean banks, in part to improve liquidity and aid small businesses. Meanwhile, the central bank had introduced the first of several interest rate cuts. A cabinet reshuffle in January 2009 included the replacement of the minister of finance. In March the government announced a supplementary budget intended to create jobs, support low-income wage earners, and provide economic stimulus through investments in information technology, infrastructure, the environment, and "eco-friendly" projects. Although the ROK ended up showing 0.1 percent growth in GDP in the January–March quarter, the government anticipated a loss of about 2 percent for the full year.

On May 27, 2009, former president Roh Moo Hyun committed suicide. In the final years of his term Roh's popularity had plummeted as a result of a laggard economy, the failure of the "sunshine" policy toward North Korea to bear fruit despite billions of won in aid, and continuing governmental and private-sector corruption that extended to the highest ranks of Hyundai, the SK Group, Samsung, and other corporations. (In August 2008, as has become a tradition before Liberation Day festivities, President Lee, a former executive in the Hyundai conglomerate, issued over 340,000 pardons or other dispensations, including pardons for Hyundai chief CHUNG Mong Koo and SK Group executive CHEY Tae Won.) The taint of corruption had also extended to Roh's family. On May 14 his elder brother had been sentenced to four years in prison for bribery, and his only son was under investigation. His wife had admitted accepting $1 million from a businessman to pay what was described as a personal debt, while the same supporter had reportedly given another $5 million—without his knowledge, Roh claimed—to his son and his brother's son-in-law while Roh was in office. Roh, who had entered office in 2003 with a reputation as a corruption fighter and insisted on his innocence, had himself been questioned at length by authorities less than a month before his death.

Another former president, Kim Dae Jung, 85, died on August 18, 2009, prompting North Korea to send representatives to Seoul to pay their respects to the architect of the "sunshine" policy. During the visit to the South, DPRK representatives met with President Lee. Shortly after, Pyongyang agreed to permit a resumption of family reunion visits, tours of Mt. Keumgang, and crossborder transportation to the Kaesong industrial park. During the same period the North released a handful of recently detained South Koreans, including four fishermen who had allegedly strayed into North Korean waters.

The cabinet changes in September 2009 partly reflected the GNP's concern that without a governmental shakeup it would have no more success at upcoming by-elections for the National Assembly than in April, when it had failed to win any of the five open seats. Although the new prime minister, Chung Un Chan, who is considered a potential presidential candidate in 2012, drew the most attention, another key change was the selection of the chair of the Joint Chiefs of Staff, Gen. KIM Tae Young, to be minister of national defense. Kim's predecessor, Gen. LEE Sang Hee, had criticized President Lee for cutting in half a requested increase in the defense budget.

POLITICAL PARTIES

In the five years before 1972 South Korea had what was essentially a two-party system of the Democratic Republican Party (DRP), formed in 1963 as an electoral mechanism for the ruling military junta, and the New Democratic Party (NDP), organized in 1967 as a coalition of opposition elements. The imposition of emergency decrees and alteration of the electoral system under the 1972 constitution strongly favored progovernment groups, with the DRP becoming a personal vehicle for President Park Chung Hee. The existing parties were dissolved following the constitutional referendum of October 1980.

In the March 1981 National Assembly election, eight parties obtained legislative representation, the Democratic Korea Party (DKP) emerging as the largest opposition group, second to President Chun Doo Hwan's Democratic Justice Party (DJP). In February 1985 the New Korea Democratic Party (NKDP) displaced the DKP as the principal opposition formation, and soon afterward the two merged under the NKDP label.

In April 1987 the two leading dissidents, Kim Dae Jung (then under house arrest) and Kim Young Sam, joined a majority of the NKDP legislators in announcing the formation of a new opposition group, the Reunification Democratic Party (RDP); however, Kim Dae Jung withdrew from the RDP in October to launch the Peace and Democracy Party (PDP) in support of his bid for the presidency. In early 1990 President Roh Tae Woo's DJP, Kim Young Sam's RDP, and Kim Jong Pil's New Democratic Republican Party (NDRP) joined to form the regime-supportive Democratic Liberal Party (DLP).

In September 1991 the opposition Democratic Party (DP), founded by RDP members who had refused to join the DLP, expanded to accommodate Kim Dae Jung's New Democratic Party (NDP). The latter had been formed in April 1991 by merger of Kim's PDP and the Party for a New Democratic Alliance (PNDA), an RDP rump led by LEE Ki Taek. In 1992 Hyundai mogul Chung Ju Yung formed the Unification National Party (UNP), which had some success in the March National Assembly election and then reorganized as the United People's Party—UPP (*Tongil Minju Dang*) in support of Chung's unsuccessful presidential candidacy.

In March 1995 Kim Jong Pil, having left the DLP, formed the United Liberal Democrats (ULD), and six months later Kim Dae Jung returned to active politics after a three-year absence and launched the National Congress for New Politics (NCNP), which attracted a substantial number of DP defectors and thereby became the largest opposition formation. Prior to the April 1996 National Assembly election the DLP restyled itself as the New Korea Party (NKP), and in November 1997, with another presidential election approaching, the NKP and the DP joined forces as the Grand National Party (GNP) in support of candidate Lee Hoi Chang.

In January 2000 the NCNP merged into the newly organized Millennium Democratic Party (MDP). In 2003 deep divisions within the MDP led a reform-minded group to depart and form the *Uri* Party, which went on to claim a slim majority in the National Assembly election of April 2004. The National Election Commission reported that 25 parties were registered before the contest, but only 6—the *Uri* Party, the GNP, the Democratic Labor Party (DLP), the MDP, the ULD, and the National Alliance 21 (NA21)—won representation, and all of the rest, mainly regional formations, failed to meet the alternative requirement, 2 percent of the vote, needed to guarantee their continued registration. In May 2004 the NA21 was disbanded by its leader and sole National Assembly member, Hyundai heir Chung Mong Joon, who had organized the party in November 2002 as his personal presidential vehicle. In February 2006 the ULD, which had seen many of its members defect to the new People First Party (PFP), announced its intention to merge into the GNP. As of mid-2006, only the *Uri* Party and the GNP could claim a significant national following.

By July 2007 the *Uri* Party had lost more than half its National Assembly delegation to defections. The Democratic Party (DP, the renamed MDP) had already joined forces with a group of former *Uri*

Party members to form Centrist United Democratic Party (CUDP), but the CUDP changed its name back to the DP following the August formation of the United New Democratic Party (UNDP) and the latter's absorption of the balance of the *Uri* legislators when that party dissolved later in the month. With the GNP having won the presidency in December 2007, the UNDP and the DP merged in February 2008 as the United Democratic Party (UDP) to contest the April National Assembly election, in which 16 parties were eligible to compete. The UDP finished second to the GNP, while a new party, Lee Hoi Chang's Liberty Forward Party (LFP), finished third and the Park Geun Hye Coalition (PGHC), a group of former GNP members loyal to former GNP chair PARK Geun Hye (the daughter of Park Chung Hee), came in fourth. In July 2008 the UDP dropped "United" from its name and thereby became the newest Democratic Party (DP).

Governing Party:

Grand National Party—GNP (*Hannara Dang*). The "progressive conservative" GNP was formed in November 1997 by merger of the New Korea Party—NKP (*Shin Hankuk Dang*) and the Democratic Party—DP (*Minju Dang*).

The NKP had been called the Democratic Liberal Party—DLP (*Minju Dayu Dang*) from its founding in 1990 until December 1995, when the conservative DLP leadership endorsed a decision by President Kim Young Sam to redesignate the party in an effort to shake off the taint of past corruption, including a slush fund scandal involving Roh Tae Woo. In the April 1996 National Assembly election the NKP lost its overall majority, taking a plurality of 139 seats on a 34.5 percent vote share, but the subsequent adhesion of defectors, mainly from the DP, and independents restored its majority.

In February 1995 the DP had absorbed an earlier NKP, a minor party that was formed by DLP dissidents in October 1992 and had itself absorbed the New Political Reform Party—NPRP (*Shin Jungchi Gaihyok Dang*) before joining the DP. In the April 1996 balloting the DP suffered near annihilation: it won only 15 seats, down from 97 in 1992 and 5 less than the minimum required for official group status. Several of its assembly members promptly defected to President Kim's NKP.

The newly formed GNP was runner-up to the NCNP/ULD at the December 1997 presidential poll, with candidate Lee Hoi Chang winning 38.7 percent of the vote. In August 1998 most of the party leadership, including President CHO Sun, resigned following the GNP's failure to elect its candidate for speaker of the National Assembly, and by early September 1998 defections had cost the party its legislative majority.

In preparation for the April 2000 assembly election, party leader Lee withheld nominations from a number of GNP legislators who had been associated with former president Kim Young Sam or with the earlier military dictatorship. In February 2000 many of this "old guard" were central to formation of the Democratic People's Party—DPP (*Minkook Dang*), which won 2 seats in April. The GNP won 133 seats, 4 short of a majority, on a 39.0 percent vote share, but subsequent defections from other parties, coupled with by-election victories in October 2001 and August 2002, gave it more than half the seats.

Before the December 2002 presidential election the GNP attempted to win back the support of its most prominent defectors, including members of the DPP, which had participated in the ruling MDP-ULD coalition from April 2001 until the dismissal of DPP legislator Han Seung Soo as foreign minister in January 2002. Han rejoined the GNP in October 2002. A month later Park Geun Hye, daughter of the late Park Chung Hee and a former GNP vice president, also rejoined the party. She had left in early 2002 and in May had formed the short-lived Korean Coalition for the Future (KCF). In the 2002 presidential election Lee Hoi Chang again finished second, with 47 percent of the vote, and he announced his retirement shortly thereafter.

In March 2004 Park Geun Hye replaced the party chair, CHOE Byung Yol, whose leadership had been undermined by the 2002 illegal fund-raising scandal. In the April 2004 National Assembly election the GNP lost its majority, winning 121 seats and under 36 percent of the party list vote. It had considerable success in subsequent by-elections, however, and by the end of 2005 it had picked up an additional 6 seats. Meanwhile, Park had won election to a full two-year term at the party convention in July 2004.

In February 2006 KIM Hak Wan, the only remaining National Assembly member from the United Liberal Democrats (*Jayu Minju Yonmaeng*), announced that his party would merge into the GNP before the local elections at the end of May. The conservative ULD had been formed by Kim Jong Pil in March 1995, following his withdrawal from the DLP. After having won 50 seats in the National Assembly in 1996 and having participated in several subsequent governments, its fortunes declined. In April 2004 it won only 4 seats, and in 2005 many members joined the new People First Party (see Liberty Forward Party, below).

On May 20, 2006, while campaigning for local candidates, party leader Park was slashed by a knife-wielding assailant, and the GNP may have benefited from a sympathy vote at the polls: on May 31 it captured six of seven major mayoral contests and six of nine governorships. In mid-June Park stepped down as chair to pursue the party's endorsement for the national presidency. As of mid-2007, polls indicated that either she or the GNP's other leading candidate, former Seoul mayor Lee Myung Bak, were likely to carry the GNP to victory in December, although the departure in March 2007 of a third prospective candidate, former Gyeonggi Province governor Sohn Hak Kyu, had cost the GNP some support. By then, by-election victories had raised the party's National Assembly delegation to 128 seats—a plurality, in view of recent defections from the *Uri* Party. On August 20 Lee Myung Bak narrowly won the party's presidential endorsement over Park.

In early November 2007 GNP founder and former candidate Lee Hoi Chang entered the race as a conservative independent, but despite his winning 15.1 percent of the December vote, Lee Myung Bak easily won the presidency, with 48.7 percent. The GNP also won the April 2008 National Assembly election, claiming 153 of 200 seats.

In July 2008 Park Hee Tae defeated Chung Mong Joon for the party chair. Efforts were already under way to woo back some 30 members of the National Assembly who, as supporters of former chair Park Geun Hye, had left the GNP in a dispute over party endorsements for the April election. The 30 had won election either as members of the Park Geun Hye Coalition (below) or as independents, and about half of them ultimately rejoined the GNP. Park Geun Hye herself remained a major figure in the party, even though a confidant, HWANG Woo Yea, lost a contest for legislative floor leader in May 2009 to Lee supporter Ahn Sang Soo.

By mid-2009, despite holding 168 National Assembly seats, the GNP had lost its advantage over the Democrats in public opinion polls. In April by-elections it had failed to win any of 5 open assembly seats, which contributed to President Lee's decision to appoint a new prime minister and revamp the cabinet in September. Collaterally, with party chair Park Hee Tae having stepped down to contest a National Assembly by-election in October, Chung Mong Joon assumed the vacated post.

Leaders: LEE Myung Bak (President of the Republic), CHUNG Un Chan (Prime Minister), CHUNG Mong Joon (Chair), PARK Geun Hye (Former Chair), PARK Hee Tae (Former Chair), KANG Jae Sup (Former Chair), AHN Sang Soo (National Assembly Floor Leader), OH Se Hoon (Mayor of Seoul), KIM Hyung O (National Assembly Speaker).

Other Parliamentary Parties:

Democratic Party—DP (*Minju Dang*). The current Democratic Party was formed as the United Democratic Party (UDP) by merger on February 12, 2008, of the United New Democratic Party (UNDP) and the existing Democratic Party (DP). At the time, the UNDP held 135 seats in the National Assembly, while the DP held only 6. In the April 2008 election the UDP won 81 seats. It then reverted to the "Democratic Party" at a convention in July.

The preexisting DP (not to be confused with the earlier DP that was involved in forming the GNP in 1997) had been launched by Kim Dae Jung in January 2000 as the "reformist populist" Millennium Democratic Party—MDP (*Saecheonnyeonminju Dang*), which then dropped "Millennium" from its name in August 2005. The MDP was successor to the centrist National Congress for New Politics—NCNP (*Sae Jungchi Kukmin Hoiee*), which dated from September 1995 and had quickly displaced a previous Democratic Party as the leading opposition grouping by drawing to its ranks 54 assembly members who had sided with Kim in a power struggle with former DP president Lee Ki Taek. Standing on an anticorruption platform, in the April 1996 assembly election the NCNP won 79 seats on a 25.3 percent vote share concentrated in Kwangju and the surrounding province of Chonnam (South Cholla). Kim Dae Jung was elected president in December 1997 with a plurality of 40.3 percent.

In August 1998 the New Party by the People (NPP) merged with the NCNP. The NPP had been launched in November 1997 by the former governor of Gyeonggi Province, RHEE In Je, following his loss of the NKP presidential nomination to Lee Hoi Chang. Rhee ran third in the 1997 presidential balloting, with 19.2 percent of the vote.

In January 2000 the NCNP simultaneously dissolved and merged into the MDP. In the April National Assembly election the new party captured 115 seats and 35.9 percent of the vote, second to the GNP. President Kim subsequently convinced four independent assembly members to join the party's ranks. Beset by factional infighting, scandals involving members of his government and his family, and by-election losses in October 2001 that cost the MDP its slim legislative majority, President Kim resigned the party presidency in November 2001. Six months later he left the party, as did six cabinet ministers.

In April 2002 Roh Moo Hyun, victor in a series of regional party primaries, emerged as the MDP's 2002 presidential candidate, but his prospects were dimmed by further by-election losses in August. On November 25, however, one of the three leading presidential nominees, Chung Mong Joon of the newly formed NA21, withdrew in favor of Roh, who won the December election with 49 percent of the vote.

Soon afterward, sharp divisions emerged between reform-minded Roh supporters and the party's "old guard." As a consequence, Roh and three dozen members of the National Assembly resigned from the MDP in September 2003. Those departing included the MDP chair, CHYUNG Dai Chul, and another prominent leader, Chung Dong Young, who became chair of the new *Uri* Party. Chyung was among the most prominent politicians subsequently convicted of receiving illegal contributions during 2002–2003.

Following Roh's departure, the MDP joined the opposition and supported Roh's impeachment in March 2004. At the same time, some members of the party strongly objected to readmitting a number of former members who had defected to other parties prior to the 2002 presidential election. Those seeking readmission included SHIN Nak Kyun, who had recently headed the NA21.

The MDP entered the April 2004 National Assembly election holding some 60 seats, but it emerged from the balloting having won only 7 percent of the proportional vote and 9 seats. As a consequence, the party's chair, Chough Soon Hyung, resigned. In April 2006 the secretary general of what was now named the DP, JO Jae Hwan, was charged with accepting a $400,000 bribe from a would-be mayoral candidate who wanted the party's endorsement.

The pending merger of the DP and the New Party for Centrist Reform and Alliance (NPCRA) was announced in early June 2007 and confirmed on June 27, with the resultant party, tentatively named the Centrist United Democratic Party (CUDP), to be launched in July. The NPCRA had been established in early May 2007 by 20 members of the National Assembly who, in opposition to President Roh, had abandoned the *Uri* Party en masse in early February. Leaders included KIM Han Gill, the former *Uri* floor leader in the National Assembly. In announcing formation of the CUDP, Kim and DP leader PARK Sang Cheon attacked efforts by other liberals to form a broader alliance. Remaining members of the *Uri* Party, in turn, attacked the CUDP as a "small-scale alliance" incapable of challenging the GNP.

In early August 2007 a handful of former DP legislators left the CUDP and joined 80 *Uri* defectors in forming the UNDP. Leading figures included former GNP leader SOHN Hak Kyu and former *Uri* Party leader Chung Dong Young, both presidential aspirants. The *Uri* Party (Our Party, *Uri Dang*), initially called the New Party for Participatory Citizens, had been established in September 2003 by dissident members of the MDP who supported President Roh Moo Hyun and objected to the "old guard" policies represented by regionalism and close connections to the country's major corporations. In the April 2004 National Assembly election the party won a slim majority, 152 seats. A month later, following the Constitutional Court decision that reinstated him to the presidency, Roh Moo Hyun joined the party. In March 2005, however, the *Uri* Party lost its majority in the National Assembly when 2 legislators surrendered their seats because of electoral violations. In by-elections in April the party failed to win any of the 6 contested seats, 5 of which it had previously held. It was equally unsuccessful in October, when it failed to win any of 4 open seats. The party then suffered unprecedented losses in the May 2006 local elections, when it won only one provincial governorship and no major mayoral races. By early 2007 the party was sharply divided between Roh loyalists and various anti-Roh factions. In January–February some 30 National Assembly members resigned from the party. In late February, recognizing that his continued membership was adversely affecting the party's standing, President Roh resigned his affiliation, as several previous presidents had done in the final year of their terms. By the end of June 2007 the *Uri* Party had seen its National Assembly delegation drop to 73. (For a more complete history of the *Uri* Party, see the discussion of the UNDP in the 2008 edition of the *Handbook*.)

On August 18, 2007, the UNDP absorbed the last members of the *Uri* Party, which had overwhelmingly voted to disband, and thereby became the plurality party in the National Assembly, with 143 seats. (Critics attacked the UNDP as little more than a renamed *Uri* Party.) An effort by the UNDP to unite the center-left prior to the December presidential election failed, however, when the balance of the CUDP refused to accept the UNDP's decision to welcome pro-Roh members from the *Uri* Party. Instead, the remaining CUDP leaders changed the party's designation back to the DP and announced that they would field their own presidential candidate. In mid-October Rhee In Je won the nomination over several other candidates, chiefly KIM Min Seok. Chough Soon Hyung had dropped out of the race in September, charging Rhee with violating campaign rules, and ultimately backed the UNDP's Chung Dong Young after failing to convince Rhee to leave the race. (Rhee finished sixth, with 0.7 percent of the vote. In April 2008, having been denied endorsement by the UDP because of his history of defections, he was elected to the National Assembly as an independent. Chough joined the new Liberty Forward Party, below.)

The UNDP primary concluded on October 15, 2007, with the announcement that Chung, having received 44 percent of the vote, would be the party's presidential nominee. Sohn Hak Kyu finished second, with 34 percent, while President Roh's preferred candidate, former prime minister Lee Hae Chan, garnered only 22 percent of the vote. In the December election Chung finished second, with 26.1 percent of the vote. The election of Sohn as party chair in January 2008 prompted the resignation of Lee Hae Chan from the party.

The decision of the UNDP and the DP to unite as the UDP in February 2008 did not prevent a GNP victory in the April legislative election, at which the merged party won only 25.1 percent of the vote. The party's 2007 presidential candidate, Chung Dong Young, won election as an independent, while former UNDP chair Sohn Hak Kyu retired from politics after losing his race. At the party's July 2008 national convention former *Uri* leader Chung Sye Kyun, with 58 percent of the vote, was elected DP chair over CHOO Mi Ae (27 percent) and Chyung Dai Chul (16 percent).

Leaders: CHUNG Sye Kyun (Chair), PARK Sang Cheon (Former Chair of the Premerger DP), CHUNG Dong Young (2007 UNDP presidential nominee), LEE Kang Rae (Leader in the National Assembly).

Liberty Forward Party—LFP (*Jayou Seonjin Dang*). The LFP was established on February 1, 2008, by former GNP leader and presidential candidate Lee Hoi Chang, who had run in December 2007 as an independent and had finished third, with 15 percent of the vote. Formation of the conservative LFP was announced in preparation for the upcoming National Assembly election. A week later, the People First Party—PFP (*Gukmin Jungsim Dang*) merged into the LFP, which consequently held a total of 8 legislative seats at that time.

The PFP had been formed in October 2005 by the governor of South Chungchong Province, Sim Dae Pyung, and several National Assembly members. At its formal inauguration in January 2006, Sim and assembly independent SHIN Kook Hwan were elected cochairs, while Rhee In Je, who had run for president in 1997 as the candidate of the New Party by the People and had later joined the ULD, was given the responsibility of leading the PFP into the May 2006 local elections. Two other former ULD legislators had also joined the new party, but a merger with the ULD fell through.

In the April 2008 election the new LFP won 18 seats, for third place. It later joined with the liberal Renewal of Korea Party (RKP, below) to form a working group, the Forward and Creative Alliance, in the National Assembly. In June 2008 it was rumored that in an effort to shore up support for his faltering government, President Lee Myung Bak was considering offering the prime ministership to the LFP's Sim Dae Pyung, a former governor of South Chungchong Province. Lee Hoi Chang, however, dismissed talk of a conservative alliance.

Leaders: LEE Hoi Chang, SIM Dae Pyung (Chair), RYU Keun Chan (National Assembly Floor Leader), CHOUGH Soon Hyung, YOO Jay Kun.

Park Geun Hye Coalition—PGHC (Chinbak Yeondae). Also referenced as the Pro-Park Alliance, the PGHC was organized by supporters of the GNP's Park Geun Hye, who had narrowly lost the contest for the GNP's nomination for the December presidential election. Loyal to Park, who herself remained in the GNP, many had been denied the

GNP's endorsement for the April 2008 National Assembly election. In the balloting the party finished fourth, with 14 seats. Subsequently, the rift in the GNP was partially mended, and several former GNP members were welcomed back.

The PGHC lost an additional three National Assembly seats, leaving it with five, in May 2009 when the Supreme Court upheld the conviction of Suh Chung Won, a party coleader, for accepting money from KIM No Sik and YANG Jung Rye for placing them on the candidate list. Suh, sentenced to 18 months in prison, went on a hunger strike to protest the decision.

Leaders: SUH Chong Won, KIM Eul Dong.

Democratic Labor Party—DLP (*Minjunodong Dang*). Organized by labor activists in January 2000, the DLP campaigned on a platform that included political reform and advocacy of workers' interests. One of the founders, Kwon Young Gil, had captured 1.2 percent of the vote in the 1997 presidential race as the candidate of the People's Victory.

In the April 2000 election the party drew only 1.2 percent of the vote and won no seats. As a result, on April 17 the National Election Commission canceled its registration. At a special convention on May 20, however, the party announced that it was being "reborn" as a progressive party and would lead a civic effort to eliminate government corruption. Many of its leaders have also served in the leadership of the Korean Confederation of Trade Unions.

In a second run for the presidency, Kwon finished third in 2002, with 3.9 percent of the vote. In the April 2004 election the DLP attracted considerable support from voters who were disaffected with "old guard" politics, winning 13 percent of the party list vote for a total of eight proportional seats. It also won 2 district seats. Because the party's constitution prohibits individuals from leading both the party and its parliamentary delegation, Kwon stepped down as DLP president at a party convention in June. His successor, KIM Hye Kyung, resigned after the October 2005 by-elections, at which the DLP failed to retain a seat won in April 2004. In February 2006 MOON Sung Hyun, the interim president, retained the post by defeating CHO Seung Soo in a party runoff. In December 2006 two members of the DLP were among five individuals charged with spying for North Korea.

In September 2007 Kwon Young Gil again won the party's presidential endorsement, defeating SIM Sang Jeong with 53 percent of the primary vote. In the December election he finished fifth, attracting only 3.0 percent of the vote. As a consequence of the party's poor results, the leadership offered to resign en masse, and party founders Sim and Roh Hoe Chan were named to head an emergency committee, with Sim then becoming interim leader. In February 2008, however, both Sim and Roh, leaders of the party's minority People's Democracy faction, left to form the New Progressive Party (below) when the majority National Liberation faction refused to adopt a proposed reform program that would have altered a pro-Pyongyang stance and expelled party members who had been implicated in spying for the North. In the April National Assembly election the DLP won only five seats.

Legislator Kang Ki Kab was elected DLP chair over LEE Soo Ho at a party runoff in July 2008.

Leaders: KANG Ki Kab (Chair), KWON Young Gil (2007 presidential candidate).

Renewal of Korea Party—RKP (*Changjo Hangkuk Dang*). The liberal RKP, which is also commonly called the **Creative Korea Party** (CKP), was established at the end of October 2007 and registered in November. Its principal founder, Moon Kook Hyun, a former chief executive of the Yuhan-Kimberley pharmaceutical company, finished fourth in the December presidential contest, with 5.8 percent of the vote. Moon's refusal to align with the UNDP for the election eventually led to a split in the party. In the April 2008 National Assembly election the RKP won only three seats.

Afterward the party became embroiled in a controversy over one of its proportional representatives. LEE Han Jung, unbeknownst to the party leaders, had been under criminal investigation. A further controversy involved accusations that Lee was among the politicians who had allegedly "bought" seats by making generous donations to parties. In September 2008 Lee was sentenced to two years in prison.

Leaders: MOON Kook Hyun (Chair), KIM Yong Chun.

New Progressive Party (NPP). The NPP was established in February 2008 by the moderate faction of the DLP (above) headed by Sim Sang Jeung and Roh Hoe Chan following the DLP's rejection of a reform proposal that would have ended the DLP's strong pro-Pyongyang policy. In the April National Assembly election the NPP failed to win any seats, having narrowly missed the 3 percent threshold for proportional representation. It did, however, win an April 2009 by-election after the DLP agreed to back its nominee, CHO Seung Soo, in order to defeat the GNP candidate.

Leaders: ROH Hoe Chan (Chair), LEE Deok Woo, SIM Sang Jeung.

Other Parties:

The following small parties were also registered at the time of the April 2008 National Assembly election: **Arts and Culture Party,** led by KIM Won Young; **Chamjuin Yunhap,** led by KIM Sun Mi; **Christian Love Party** (CLP), led by CHOI Su Hwan; **Citizen's Party,** led by CHOI Yong Ki; **Economic Republican Party,** led by HUH Kyung Young, who had won 0.4 percent of the 2007 presidential vote; **Economy & Unification Party,** led by AHN Dong Uk; **Family Party for Peace and Unity,** led by KWAK Jeong Hwan; **International Green Party,** led by LEE Wae Won and CHEONG Jae Bok; **Korean Society Party,** led by KUM Min, who had won 0.1 percent of the 2007 presidential vote; **Liberty Peace Party,** led by LEE Tae Hui; **National Security Party,** led by LEE Geon Gai; **National Unity for Harmony and Advancement,** led by HEO Sul; **Party for Advanced Korea,** led by JANG Suk Chang; **Professional Coalition Party,** led by OH Ho Seok; **Righteous Korea Party,** led by KANG Seung Kyu; **Sinmirae Political Party,** led by KIM Ho Il; **System and Future Party,** led by JI Man Won; and **Unification Korea Party,** led by AHN Kwang Yang. With the exception of the CLP, which was registered in 2004, all had been registered since 2006.

LEGISLATURE

The present **National Assembly** (*Kuk Hoe*) is a unicameral body of 299 members elected for four-year terms. In the most recent election of April 9, 2008, 245 seats were filled by direct election from single-member constituencies, while 54 were distributed proportionally among those parties winning at least 5 district seats or 3 percent of the party vote. The results (direct/proportional breakdowns in parentheses) were as follows: Grand National Party (GNP), 153 (131, 22); United Democratic Party (UDP), 81 (66, 15); Liberty Forward Party (LFP), 18 (14, 4); Park Geun Hye Coalition (PGHC), 14 (6, 8); Democratic Labor Party, 5 (2, 3); Renewal of Korea Party (RKP), 3 (1, 2); independents, 25. In July 2008 the UDP was renamed the Democratic Party (DP). After the election, nearly three dozen members of the assembly were charged with electoral law violations. As of mid-2009, a number had lost their seats as a consequence; some cases remained before the courts.

As of July 2009 the GNP held 168 seats, having wooed back a number of members who, as a consequence of an intraparty dispute, had run as independents or as members of the PGHC. The DP held 84 seats; the Forward and Creative Alliance (a floor group comprising the LFP and the RKP), 20; the DLP, 5; the PGHC, 5; the RKP, 1, who had refused the join the LFP/RKP floor group; and the New Progressive Party, which had won an April 2009 by-election, 1. Eight members claimed no affiliation, and there were 7 vacancies. There were no provisions for refilling proportional seats that had been vacated because of electoral law violations, although a challenge to the relevant section of the law by affected parties was expected to make its way to the Supreme Court.

Speaker: KIM Hyong O.

CABINET

[as of October 15, 2009]

Prime Minister	Chung Un Chan
Minister for Special Affairs	Jo Ho Young
Ministers	
Culture, Sports and Tourism	Yu In Chon
Education, Science, and Technology	Ahn Byong Man
Environment	Lee Maan Ee
Food, Agriculture, Forestry, and Fisheries	Jang Tae Pyoung
Foreign Affairs	Yu Myung Hwan
Gender Equality	Paik Hee Young [f]

Health, Welfare, and Family Affairs	Jeon Jae Hee [f]
Justice	Lee Kwi Nam
Knowledge Economy	Choi Kyung Hwan
Labor	Yim Tae Hee
Land, Transport, and Maritime Affairs	Chung Jong Hwan
National Defense	Gen. Kim Tae Young
Public Administration and Security	Lee Dal Gon
Strategy and Finance	Yoon Jeung Hyun
Trade	Kim Jong Hoon
Unification	Hyun In Taek

[f] = female

COMMUNICATIONS

Freedom of the press prevails, although corporate conglomerates control many media outlets. In June 2006 the Constitutional Court ruled unconstitutional parts of recently enacted laws that sought to limit domination by corporate giants.

The British Broadcasting Corporation has described the Republic of Korea as being at "the leading edge of the digital revolution" in communications.

Press. South Korea has upward of 100 general dailies, about 20 of which are national in scope. Unless otherwise noted, the following are Seoul dailies published in Korean, although many also offer English-language pages and Internet editions: *Chosun Ilbo* (Korea Daily, 2,380,000); *Joong-ang Ilbo* (Central Daily, 2,300,000); *Dong-A Ilbo* (East Asia Daily, 2,150,000); *Hankuk Ilbo* (Korea Daily, 2,000,000); *Kyung-hyang Shinmun* (Kyung-hyang News, 730,000); *Hankyoreh Shinmun* (Korean People's News, 500,000); *Seoul Shinmun* (Seoul News, 500,000); *Korea Herald* (150,000), in English; *Korea Times* (100,000), in English.

News agencies. The principal domestic facility is the United News Agency (*Yonhap Tong Shin*). A number of foreign agencies maintain offices in Seoul.

Broadcasting and computing. The publicly owned Korean Broadcasting System (*Hankuk Pangsong Kongsa*) is a nationwide, noncommercial radio and television network. The public Munwha Broadcasting Corporation (MBC) and the American Forces Korea Network also offer radio and television programming. In addition, several private television corporations operate. Cable and satellite services are widely available.

As of 2008 there were 765 Internet users per 1,000 inhabitants.

INTERGOVERNMENTAL REPRESENTATION

Ambassador to the U.S.: HAN Duck-soo.

U.S. Ambassador to Republic of Korea: D. Kathleen STEPHENS.

Permanent Representative to the UN: PARK In-kook.

IGO Memberships (Non-UN): ADB, AfDB, APEC, BIS, EBRD, G-20, IADB, IEA, Interpol, IOM, OECD, PCA, WCO, WTO.

KOSOVO

Republic of Kosovo
Republika e Kosovës (Albanian)
Republike Kosovo (Serbian)

Note: The decision of the *PHW* editors to devote a separate article to the Republic of Kosovo, despite its ambiguous international status, acknowledges its recognition by over 60 countries but does so without prejudice regarding the Republic of Serbia's insistence that Kosovo remains a de jure province of that country. The International Court of Justice is currently considering the legitimacy of Kosovo's unilateral declaration of independence.

Political Status: Autonomous district of Kosovo (and Metohija) within the Serbian constituent republic of the communist Federal People's Republic of Yugoslavia (instituted November 29, 1945); autonomous province within the Serbian constituent republic of the Socialist Federal Republic of Yugoslavia (proclaimed April 7, 1963) and then of the Federal Republic of Yugoslavia (proclaimed April 27, 1992); placed under administration of the United Nations Interim Administrative Mission in Kosovo (UNMIK) from June 14, 1999, by authorization of UN Security Council Resolution 1244; autonomous province of the "state union" of Serbia and Montenegro (while remaining under UNMIK administration), which was established February 4, 2003, and then of the independent Republic of Serbia, established June 5, 2006; independence from Serbia unilaterally declared on February 17, 2008, in an action denounced by Serbia, which continues to regard Kosovo and Metohija as an inalienable autonomous province; constitution of the Republic of Kosovo adopted by the Assembly of Kosovo on April 9, 2008, with effect from June 15.

Area: 4,211 sq. mi. (10,908 sq. km.).

Population: 1,956,196 (1991C); 2,000,000 (2008E).

Major Urban Centers (2007E): PRIŠTINA (PRISHTINË, 168,000), Prizren (110,000), Mitrovica (Mitrovicë, 70,000), Peć (Pejë, 70,000).

Official Languages: Albanian and Serbian. Bosnian, Roma, and Turkish are official at the municipal level and as otherwise provided by law.

Monetary Unit: Euro (market rate December 1, 2009: 1 euro = \$1.51US). The Serbian dinar continues to circulate in areas where the population is mostly ethnically Serb.

President: Fatmir SEJDIU (Democratic League of Kosovo); elected president of UNMIK-administered Kosovo by the Assembly of Kosovo on February 10, 2006, following the death of President Ibrahim RUGOVA (Democratic League of Kosovo) on January 21 and the interim incumbency of Assembly Speaker Nexhat DACI (then Democratic League of Kosovo); resigned January 9, 2008, but reelected on the same day to a full five-year term by the legislature; became president of the Republic of Kosovo upon declaration of independence, February 17, 2008.

Prime Minister: Hashim THAÇI (Democratic Party of Kosovo); endorsed as prime minister of UNMIK-administered Kosovo by the Assembly of Kosovo and assumed office on January 9, 2008, following the legislative election of November 17, 2007, in succession to Agim ÇEKU (then nonparty); became prime minister of the Republic of Kosovo upon declaration of independence, February 17, 2008.

THE COUNTRY

The landlocked Republic of Kosovo, bordered by Serbia on the north and northeast, Macedonia on the southeast, Albania on the southwest, and Montenegro on the west, encompasses about 12 percent of Serbia's area before the separation. The terrain is predominantly mountainous and hilly, the principal exception being the Metohija (Dukagjin) basin in the west. The population is 92 percent ethnic Albanian, with the Serb minority constituting about 5.3 percent; other minorities include Bosniacs, Turks, Romanies, Montenegrins, and Croats. Approximately 90 percent of the citizenry profess Islam; the principal minority religions are Serbian Orthodox (7 percent) and Roman Catholic (3 percent).

Long subsidized by the other regions of Yugoslavia, the underdeveloped Kosovar economy suffered in the late 1990s from a campaign of ethnic cleansing by the Yugoslavian military, at the direction of the government of President Slobodan Milošević, a Serb. Beginning in early 1998 escalating violence in Kosovo led to a renewal of international sanctions against Yugoslavia and then to a bombing campaign authorized by the United Nations Security Council and conducted, primarily against the constituent Republic of Serbia, by the North Atlantic Treaty Organization (NATO) in March–June 1999. Following the cessation of hostilities, a donor conference of over 100 countries and agencies pledged some \$2 billion in reconstructive, humanitarian, and administrative assistance for Kosovo.

Under the supervision of the postconflict UN Mission in Kosovo (UNMIK), the Kosovo Trust Agency privatized many state-owned

enterprises, a legacy of the Yugoslav socialist era. At present, agriculture contributes about one-fifth of GDP, as does industry, with services accounting for the balance. Leading agricultural products include wheat and other grains, vegetables, and fruits. A significant portion of the countryside remains forested. Industry has traditionally centered on extraction and processing of ores, chiefly lead, silver, and zinc, but in recent decades a lack of investment in equipment and infrastructure has hurt output. Kosovo is believed to have the world's fifth-largest reserves of lignite, and there are also deposits of bauxite, chromium, and other metals. Other important industries are food processing and construction. Leading exports include minerals, processed metals, and scrap metal. In the years immediately before independence was declared, foreign assistance and remittances from Kosovars working abroad amounted to nearly half the GDP. Together, the two continue to account for over one-quarter of GDP. About 45 percent of the population lives in poverty, on under $2 a day.

Following a recessionary period in 2002–2003, Kosovo's GDP grew by 3.3 percent in 2004, 0.6 percent in 2005, 3.8 percent in 2006, and 5.0 percent in 2007. The declaration of independence in February 2008 had little immediate impact on the overall economy, which grew by 5.4 percent for the year as a whole. Historically high unemployment continued unabated, at about 44 percent. Projected growth for 2009, 3.5 percent, was not significantly affected by the ongoing international recession, primarily because the country's exports amount to only 6 percent of GDP and because the government increased public expenditures by an estimated 40 percent.

GOVERNMENT AND POLITICS

Political background. Considered their historic homeland by Serbians, what became Kosovo-Metohija was absorbed by the Ottoman Empire in the late 14th century, following the Ottoman victory at the battle of Kosovo Polje. Kosovo was briefly part of an independent Albania in 1913–1914, after which it was included in Serbia and then, from December 1918, the Kingdom of the Serbs, Croats, and Slovenes. Formally renamed Yugoslavia on October 3, 1929, the highly centralized, Serb-dominated monarchy was attacked and occupied by Nazi Germany and Fascist Italy in April 1941. Communist-inspired Partisans, led by Marshal Josip Broz Tito, a Croat, opposed the occupation with Allied support and assumed power at the end of World War II, establishing a "federal people's republic" that included within the constituent Serbian republic an autonomous district of Kosovo and Metohija, with newly defined borders, in which ethnic Albanians constituted a majority. Although the Autonomous Province of Kosovo and Metohija was granted increased responsibilities under 1963 and 1974 federal constitutions, it remained subservient to the government of the Serbian constituent republic.

Long-standing ethnic strife between Serbians and Albanians led members of both ethnic communities to relocate and generated sometimes-violent protests. In July 1989, contrary to the federal constitution, Serbia effectively stripped Kosovo (and Vojvodina) of autonomous status. When the Kosovo Assembly demanded that the province be elevated to republican status within Yugoslavia, Serbia dissolved the legislature. The ethnic Albanian delegates to the assembly nevertheless attempted to declare Kosovo a constituent republic within the Yugoslav federation. Kosovo's autonomous status within Serbia was restored, but the move was insufficient to satisfy Kosovo's ethnic Albanian majority. On October 19, 1991, the Kosovar legislature, citing an independence referendum held the previous month, declared an independent "Republic of Kosovo" that was recognized only by neighboring Albania. Meanwhile, the Yugoslav federation, beset by independence pressures in other constituent republics, was disintegrating: between June 1991 and March 1992 Croatia, Slovenia, Macedonia, and Bosnia and Herzegovina all declared independence, leaving Montenegro and Serbia as the rump Yugoslavia.

Ethnic Albanians, resisting Serbian attempts to impose political, social, and educational control, established their own underground administration. Elections to the Kosovo Assembly in May 1992, won by the pro-independence Democratic League of Kosovo (*Lidhja Demokratike e Kosovës*—LDK), were condemned as illegal by Belgrade. Nevertheless, on May 25 the LDK leader, Ibrahim RUGOVA, was proclaimed president of the "Republic of Kosovo." The local situation deteriorated in December 1994 when Serbian security forces carried out the most sweeping wave of arrests since 1990 in an effort to eliminate the unauthorized police force created by the ethnic Albanians. Tension intensified further in mid-1995 when the Belgrade government announced that Serb refugees from Croatia's Krajina would be resettled in Kosovo.

As early as 1992 the most militant Kosovar separatists had formed loosely linked guerrilla bands that eventually became the Kosovo Liberation Army—KLA (*Ushtria Çlirimtare e Kosovës*—UÇK). Many of its commanders favored not just separation from Yugoslavia but union in a Greater Albania. Following the murder of four Serbian policemen in February 1998 by KLA members, a retaliatory Serb security operation killed 24 ethnic Albanian villagers, many apparently by summary execution. In March some 50,000 protesters demonstrated in Priština, while the United States and the European Union (EU), among others, condemned the excessive use of force and the UN Security Council imposed an arms embargo on Yugoslavia. Despite a series of diplomatic missions to Belgrade and Priština, the Serbian crackdown continued, provoking additional demonstrations and calls by regional neighbors and the international Contact Group on former Yugoslavia (Britain, France, Germany, Russia, and the United States as well as the UN and the EU and, later, Italy) for restraint and the opening of talks on Kosovar autonomy. Later in March, ethnic Albanians, in addition to casting ballots for the shadow "Republic of Kosovo" legislature, reelected the LDK's Ibrahim Rugova as shadow president, although some ethnic Albanian parties boycotted the vote, partly in opposition to Rugova's advocacy of passive resistance in the effort to achieve Kosovar independence.

With daily demonstrations continuing in the province, U.S. diplomats convinced Yugoslav President Milošević and Rugova to meet for the first time in May 1998. Although both sides agreed to initiate weekly talks in Priština, the violence in Kosovo continued to escalate as Serbian army and paramilitary security forces, sweeping through Kosovar villages, met strong resistance from the rapidly expanding KLA. In June Milošević rejected diplomatic efforts by U.S. negotiator Richard Holbrooke and Russian President Boris Yeltsin, who sought the inclusion of the KLA in negotiations, a cease-fire, and withdrawal of Serbian forces from Kosovo. By then, reports of civilian massacres, torture, and other human rights violations committed by Serbian contingents were regularly surfacing, contributing to the prospect of NATO intervention. In October, facing the threat of imminent NATO air strikes, Milošević agreed to begin withdrawing military and security forces from Kosovo and to allow entry of 2,000 international observers supervised by the Organization for Security and Cooperation in Europe (OSCE). In November, however, Belgrade barred members of the UN's International Criminal Tribunal for the former Yugoslavia (ICTY) from entering Kosovo to investigate allegations of extrajudicial killings.

Although fighting intensified again in mid-December 1998, late in the month both sides accepted a local cease-fire brokered by the head of the OSCE mission. In January 1999, despite renewed threats from NATO, widespread hostilities resumed. The worst atrocity of the conflict to date occurred when Serbian forces executed 45 civilians from the village of Račak.

In February 1999 peace talks between Serbian officials and ethnic Albanians—including KLA representatives—opened in Rambouillet, France. Cosponsored by France and the United States, the negotiations were aimed at winning approval of a proposal by the Contact Group that, while acknowledging Serbian sovereignty in Kosovo, envisaged almost complete administrative autonomy for the province, the withdrawal of all but 1,500 Serbian border troops, the rapid disbanding of the KLA, and formation of a new, ethnically balanced police force. In March the Kosovar delegation signed the pact, but the Serbian delegation continued to reject the presence of NATO peacekeepers. Holbrooke met with Milošević in Belgrade March 22–23 in a final, futile diplomatic effort to avoid war.

On March 24, 1999, NATO forces from eight countries initiated Operation Allied Force, the most extensive air campaign in Europe since the close of World War II. In the following weeks allied bombing extended throughout Yugoslavia in an effort to force the Milošević regime to accept the Rambouillet agreement. Amid increasing allegations of massacres and other war crimes in Kosovo, Serbian forces stepped up a widespread campaign of "ethnic cleansing" that saw the entire Albanian population forced from some cities and villages, creating an immediate refugee crisis at the borders of Albania and Macedonia. By the end of April the refugee exodus was swelling toward 750,000, with additional hundreds of thousands displaced within the province itself.

On May 6, 1999, the Group of Seven (G-7) countries plus Russia (G-8) proposed a peace plan providing for "deployment in Kosovo of effective international civil and security presences" and formation of an interim provincial administration under the UN Security Council. On June 3 President Milošević accepted the terms of an amended peace agreement offered by President Martii Ahtisaari of Finland and Russia's Viktor Chernomyrdin, including the deployment in Kosovo (but not the rest of Serbia) of a UN-sponsored, NATO-dominated peacekeeping contingent (Kosovo Force, or KFOR) expected to number some 50,000 troops. The agreement also called for the complete withdrawal of the Serbian army, police, and paramilitary forces from Kosovo.

On June 10, 1999, NATO suspended its bombing campaign and the UN Security Council adopted Resolution 1244, authorizing international troop deployment and the establishment of an interim civilian administration in Kosovo. The resolution also reaffirmed Yugoslavia's "sovereignty and territorial integrity" but echoed previous calls for "substantial autonomy and meaningful self-administration in Kosovo." Meanwhile, on May 27 the ICTY had indicted President Milošević and four others, including Yugoslavia's interior minister and army chief of staff, for crimes against humanity related to events in Kosovo.

On June 14, 1999, the UN Security Council received a plan for the civil Kosovo administration. The EU would supervise reconstruction, and the OSCE would oversee institution building. Humanitarian and administrative matters would primarily fall in the purview of the Office of the UN High Commissioner for Refugees (UNHCR) and a newly established UN Interim Administration in Kosovo (UNMIK), respectively. On June 20, with the Yugoslav army having completely withdrawn from Kosovo, NATO formally concluded its bombing campaign. On the same day NATO and the KLA signed an agreement providing for KLA demilitarization, although Hashim THAÇI, the KLA leader, refused to renounce the eventual goal of Kosovar independence. Most of the 1 million or more Kosovo Albanian refugees and displaced persons were already returning to their homes, contributing to the collateral flight from the province of ethnic Serbs, many of whom feared reprisals.

In July 1999 UNMIK established a consultative, multiethnic Kosovo Transitional Council (KTC), although the LDK's Rugova initially refused to participate because not all the parties in his shadow government were included. In December UNMIK announced formation of an Interim Administrative Council (IAC) of Rugova, Thaçi, and Rexhep QOSJA of the United Democratic Movement (*Lëvizja Bashimit Demokratike*—LBD); a fourth seat on the IAC was reserved for a representative of the Serb community, which refused to participate. By then, forensic specialists from the ICTY were already exhuming bodies from mass graves in Kosovo. (Late in the year, the Albanian death toll was estimated at 4,000–5,000, considerably less than originally projected.) On April 18, 2000, the Eurocorps, with troop contingents from Germany, Spain, France, Belgium, and Luxembourg, took over control of the Kosovo peacekeeping effort from NATO, but KFOR was encountering increasing difficulty in preventing violent clashes between Albanian and Serb communities.

Municipal elections in Kosovo were held on October 28, 2000, under UNMIK supervision. Participation by ethnic Serbs was minimal. Rugova's LDK finished first, well ahead of Thaçi's recently formed Democratic Party of Kosovo (*Partia Demokratike e Kosovës*—PDK). A new 120-member Assembly of Kosovo was elected on November 17, 2001, with the LDK winning a plurality of 47 seats. Thaçi's PDK finished with 26 seats, and the multiparty Serb Return Coalition (*Koalicija Povratak*—KP) took 22. After opening its first session on December 10 the assembly, with its limited provisional powers, elected a seven-member administrative presidency, but it failed to elect a provincial president. It wasn't until March 4 that Rugova received the two-thirds vote required for election. Under a power-sharing arrangement, Bajram REXHEPI of the PDK was named prime minister.

On February 4, 2003, Serbia and Montenegro dissolved Yugoslavia and established a "state union" with a new Constitutional Charter, under which Kosovo's status remained substantially unchanged.

In the second election for the Kosovar assembly, held October 23, 2004, President Rugova's LDK again finished first, winning 47 seats, followed by Thaçi's PDK with 30. For the most part Kosovo's Serb community boycotted the balloting, with most of the 10 reserved Serb seats being awarded to a Serb List for Kosovo and Metohija (*Srpska Lista za Kosovo i Metohiju*—SLKM) that included members of the KP. On December 3 the newly convened legislature reelected Rugova as president and confirmed a minority government headed by Ramush HARADINAJ of the Alliance for the Future of Kosovo (*Aleanca për Ardhmërinë e Kosovës*—AAK), which had finished third, with 9 seats, in the October legislative election. The selection of Haradinaj, a former KLA commander, caused the Serbian government to withdraw from the first-ever direct talks with Kosovar officials, which had opened in Vienna, Austria, on October 14, 2003.

Haradinaj's tenure as Kosovo's prime minister proved short: on March 8, 2005, he resigned and shortly afterward surrendered to the ICTY to face charges that included crimes against humanity. (His trial, which began in March 2007, concluded in April 2008 with an acquittal.) His successor, the less controversial Bajram KOSUMI, also of the AAK, was confirmed by the legislature on March 23.

Less than a year later, on January 21, 2006, President Rugova died of cancer, which began a series of leadership changes. Nexhat DACI, speaker of the Kosovo Assembly, served as acting president until February 10, when the legislature elected Fatmir SEJDIU of the LDK as president. Prime Minister Kosumi then resigned on March 1, under pressure for stronger leadership during UN-mediated negotiations over Kosovo's future political status. On March 10 President Sejdiu named as prime minister Agim ÇEKU, a former officer in the Croatian Army and more recently a general in the Kosovo Protection Corps.

In February 2006 the UN convened talks in Vienna on Kosovo's future status. Representatives of France, Germany, Italy, Russia, the United Kingdom, and the United States also attended. Serbia's position remained that Kosovo was part of its territory, while Kosovar leaders insisted that the only viable political solution was independence. Progress toward resolution of the political status question was sidetracked immediately by disagreement over more minor issues regarding division of power regionally, and economic, cultural, and religious matters.

On June 3, 2006, Montenegro declared its independence, and the separate Republic of Serbia was proclaimed two days later; UNMIK-administered Kosovo as well as Vojvodina remained autonomous provinces of Serbia. Also in June, Serbia's government unveiled a proposal dubbed "the platform" that offered Kosovo greater autonomy within Serbia for 20 years while preserving Belgrade's control over foreign affairs, borders and customs, monetary policy, protection of Serb religious and cultural matters, and human rights. Kosovo's ethnic Albanian leaders rejected Serbia's proposal outright. The platform also received little support from the parties convened in Vienna.

On March 26, 2007, having stated earlier in the month that he saw no chance of achieving a compromise by the Serbian and Kosovar governments, UN Special Envoy Martii Ahtisaari submitted to the UN

Security Council his plan for Kosovo's "supervised independence." It called for creation of a constitutional commission to draft a basic law that would require approval by two-thirds of the Kosovo assembly. UNMIK's mandate would expire, but in an arrangement similar to Bosnia and Herzegovina's, an international representative would have veto power over decisions of the Kosovar government.

The Ahtisaari plan paid particular attention to the status of the minority Serb population. (With only a fraction of the estimated 200,000 Serbs who had fled Kosovo since 1999 having returned, ethnic Albanians outnumbered ethnic Serbs by an estimated 1.8 million to 120,000.) Serbs would be granted broad governmental powers in six municipalities, each of which could receive direct aid from Serbia. In addition, Serbs and other minorities would be guaranteed seats in the legislature.

Although the Kosovo Assembly voted its approval of the Ahtisaari plan in early April 2007, Serbia rejected it. Moreover, Russia pledged to use its veto power on the Security Council to derail any plan the Serbian government found unacceptable. Several other regional countries, including Greece and Romania, also expressed reservations. With a December 2007 deadline looming for reaching a final decision, representatives of the Serbian and Kosovar governments, including the presidents and prime ministers of both jurisdictions, met in New York on September 28 for face-to-face discussions, although Serbia warned of "unforeseeable consequences" if the process concluded with Kosovo's unilateral declaration of independence. Between then and November 26 five additional negotiating rounds were held either in Belgium or Austria. Serbia's final offer of self-government except in foreign relations, defense, and border control was rejected by Kosovo, the only significant point of agreement being that both would avoid threats and violence.

On November 17, 2007, the PDK won a plurality of 37 seats in an election for the Assembly of Kosovo. The LDK finished second, with 25 seats, a net loss of 22 from its previous total. Six ethnic Serb parties split the 10 seats set aside for Serbs; seven other minority parties won a total of 14 seats. Voter turnout was only 43 percent. On January 9, 2008, the new legislature reelected Fatmir Sejdiu as president and then endorsed Thaçi as prime minister of a coalition cabinet comprising the PDK, the LDK, the ethnic Serb Independent Liberal Party (*Samostalna Liberalna Stranka*—SLS), and the Kosovo Democratic Turkish Party (*Kosova Demokratik Türk Partisi*—KDTP).

On February 17, 2008, addressing the assembly, Prime Minister Thaçi declared Kosovo to be "proud, independent, and free" as a "democratic, multiethnic state moving rapidly toward EU and Euro-Atlantic integration." The declaration of independence was condemned by Serbia. The following day, Albania, France, the United Kingdom, and the United States were among the first countries to recognize Kosovo. On April 9 the assembly adopted a constitution by a vote of 103–0, and it entered into effect on June 15.

Constitution and government. Kosovo's constitution identifies the country as a secular state adhering to the principles of religious freedom and freedom of expression except as limited by law "to prevent encouragement or provocation of violence and hostility on grounds of race, nationality, ethnicity, or religion." Except for a similar limitation, freedom of the media is guaranteed and censorship prohibited. Freedom of association is also protected unless a court determines that an organization or activity threatens constitutional order; violates human rights; or encourages ethnic, national, racial, or religious hatred.

Until the constitution entered into effect on June 15, 2008, Kosovo was administered by UNMIK and "provisional institutions of self-government," which had been established by UNMIK in accordance with a May 15, 2001, Constitutional Framework for Provisional Self-Government. Under the framework, the authority of the presidency to manage foreign relations was limited by a need to set policy "in coordination with" the special representative of the UN secretary general (SRSG). Under the constitution, the president, who is indirectly elected by the national legislature for a five-year term, "represents the unity of the people," represents the country internally and externally, and guarantees the "constitutional functioning" of the republic's institutions. He serves as command-in-chief of the Kosovo Security Force and, in consultation with the prime minister, may declare a state of emergency. Election of the president requires a two-thirds majority in the assembly, but if no candidate achieves that goal on the first two ballots, the two front-runners proceed to a third ballot in which a simple majority prevails. The 120-member, unicameral Assembly of Kosovo has retained its preexisting structure, which includes 20 seats reserved for ethnic minorities, including 10 Serbs. The assembly sits for a four-year term, subject to early dissolution. The government is headed by a prime minister who commands a majority in the assembly. The cabinet must include minority representation.

The judiciary includes a Supreme Court, district courts, and municipal courts. An independent Constitutional Court serves as "final interpreter" of the constitution. Administratively, Kosovo encompasses 7 districts (*distrikt, rreth*), subdivided into 35 municipalities (*komuna, opština*).

With regard to Kosovo the 2006 Serbian constitution affirms the "equality of all citizens and ethnic communities in Serbia" and adds that Kosovo and Metohija is "an integral part of the territory of Serbia," albeit with "substantial autonomy." On May 11, 2008, Serbia conducted national and municipal elections, including in the mainly northern, Serb-dominated areas of Kosovo. Although UNMIK branded the municipal elections as illegal, on June 28, the anniversary of the 1389 battle of Kosovo Polje, the Serb representatives from 26 municipalities convened in Mitrovica as a 45-member Assembly of the Community of the Municipalities of the Autonomous Province of Kosovo and Metohija. Self-declared competencies of the body include directing and coordinating activities of participating municipalities; proposing relevant legislation to Serbia's National Assembly; adopting "declarations, resolutions, and proposals"; and taking positions with regard to national authorities operating in the province.

Foreign relations. As of October 2009, Kosovo had been recognized by 62 countries plus Taiwan. Twenty-two of the EU's 27 members had granted Kosovo recognition, a notable exception being Spain, which, in view of the decades-old separatist movement in the Basque region, expressed concern that Kosovo's unilateral separation from Serbia would be viewed as a precedent. Serbia was particularly incensed at the mid-October 2008 decision of neighboring states Montenegro and Macedonia to recognize Kosovo. Of the 15 former Soviet republics, only the Baltic states (Estonia, Latvia, and Lithuania) have granted recognition. Non-European states doing so included Australia, Canada, Japan, Saudi Arabia, and the United States.

The Kosovar government had indicated at independence that it would quickly seek membership in the UN, but no application had been submitted by August 2008. Admission requires approval by at least two-thirds (128) of the members—a level unlikely to be achieved in the immediate future. Moreover, Russia, which is not only Serbia's principal European ally but also a target of violent separatist movements in Chechnya and elsewhere in the Caucasus region, refused recognition and stated that, as a permanent member of the Security Council, it would veto Kosovo's membership in the UN unless and until the dispute with Serbia is resolved. China, another country with veto power, also declined to recognize Kosovo. On June 29, 2009, Kosovo was formally admitted to the International Monetary Fund and the World Bank Group.

Since December 2006 Kosovo has been a member of the Central European Free Trade Association (CEFTA), along with Albania, Bosnia and Herzegovina, Croatia, Macedonia, Moldova, Montenegro, and Serbia. The CEFTA agreement had been signed by UNMIK on behalf of Kosovo. Given that Kosovar independence has been recognized by more than the necessary two-thirds of the states in the Council of Europe, membership in that organization is expected in the near future.

Current issues. Despite recognition from the Western powers, Kosovo's international legal status remains uncertain. In contrast, when Timor-Leste achieved independence from Indonesia in 2002 after a period of UN administration, most of the world's countries, including Indonesia, quickly granted recognition, and Timor-Leste achieved UN membership when the General Assembly convened six months later. Kosovo's case, Serbia has argued, is very different and raises issues of sovereignty and territorial integrity. On August 15, 2008, Serbia's foreign minister announced that Belgrade would ask the International Court of Justice (ICJ) for an advisory ruling on the legality of Kosovo's unilateral declaration of independence. He added that the current Serbian government would "accept any opinion that comes from the ICJ." In early October the UN General Assembly approved the referral to the court, which then offered all UN members six months to submit written statements on the question, followed by a three-month period for submission of rebuttals. On July 29, 2009, the ICJ further announced that public hearings on the matter would begin on December 1, 2009.

Should the ICJ ultimately rule in favor of Serbia's claim, Kosovo would certainly not revoke its independence declaration, and should the court rule for Kosovo, hard-line Serbs (both in Kosovo and Serbia proper) would certainly protest and probably demand the resignation of Belgrade's comparatively moderate government. As for membership in the UN and the OSCE, Kosovo's Deputy Prime Minister Hajredin

KUÇI has indicated that his government would apply when political circumstances were more favorable.

UNMIK, now headed by SRSG Lamberto Zannier, an Italian, continues to maintain a presence in Kosovo, although the nature of the mission has shifted to some degree. The EU's economic development "pillar" concluded on June 30, 2008, and was replaced by a civilian crisis management mission, the Rule of Law Mission in Kosovo (EULEX), led by a retired French general, Yves de Kermabon. The focus of the new mission is providing assistance in establishing police, justice, and customs services. The original OSCE assignment, the Democratization and Institution Building Pillar, remains in place under the direction of Austrian diplomat Werner Almhofer. In addition, the February declaration of independence stated that Kosovo would "invite and welcome" a continuing NATO leadership role in an interim military presence. In response to Serb protests in the wake of the declaration, NATO troops moved to secure the northern border, and they continued to provide security thereafter. In mid-March 2008 clashes in the ethnically divided city of Mitrovica resulted in some 80 casualties, including the death of one KFOR soldier. As of October 2009, over 12,600 troops from 32 countries remained in Kosovo as part of the KFOR/NATO contingent.

On February 26, 2009, the ICTY, in its first judgment related to the 1999 Kosovo conflict, convicted five former Yugoslav and Serbian officials of crimes against humanity but acquitted Milan Milutinović, a former Serbian president. Sentences ranged from 15 to 22 years in prison. Other Serbs have been convicted by Serbia's war crimes court, which is also hearing cases in which former KLA members have been accused of victimizing ethnic Serbs. In June Bulgaria briefly detained former prime minister Agim Çeku on the basis of a Serbian warrant that accused him of having committed war crimes. A Bulgarian court ordered his release.

The UNHCR has reported that between 2000 and 2007 over 17,800 ethnic Serbs and other minorities returned from internal displacement in Kosovo or from exile, but that number pales beside the estimated 200,000 Serbs who had fled the 1999 conflict and its aftermath. Furthermore, in 2008 only about 500 additional refugees returned to Kosovo. Speaking before the UN Security Council in June 2009, the foreign minister of Serbia, Vuk Jeremić, asserted that a principal reason that many ethnic Serbs were not exercising their right to return was the failure of the Kosovo Property Agency to resolve more than 40,000 claims submitted by ethnic Serbs for illegally seized property. Kosovo's foreign minister, Skender HYSENI, in addition to disputing the UNHCR figures, categorized Jeremić's assertion as "science fiction."

POLITICAL PARTIES

Prior to the declaration of independence from Serbia, ethnic Albanian parties in Kosovo uniformly refused to participate in national elections, and most ethnic Serb parties in Kosovo boycotted Kosovar elections. Over two dozen organizations contested the Kosovo elections of October 2004. The parliamentary and local elections held in November 2007 were contested by 25 parties, 2 coalitions, and 36 "citizens' initiatives," including an assortment of Serb parties and initiatives vying for reserved minority seats. With a 5 percent threshold established for proportional representation in the assembly, many of the smaller national parties sought alliances with the principal formations, all of which are on the center-right or right of the political spectrum.

Government Parties:

Democratic Party of Kosovo (*Partia Demokratike e Kosovës*—PDK). More radical than the moderate Democratic League of Kosovo (LDK, below), the PDK was established as the Party of Democratic Progress in Kosovo (*Partia e Progresit Demokratik të Kosovës*—PPDK) in September–October 1999 by Hashim Thaçi, leader of the Kosovo Liberation Army—KLA (*Ushtria Çlirimtare e Kosovës*—UÇK). The KLA's increasing importance to a Kosovo settlement had been recognized by its participation in the February–March 1999 Rambouillet, Paris, peace talks, although Adem DEMAÇI, its political spokesperson, refusing to accept any resolution short of independence, argued against attendance and resigned from the KLA leadership. In March a Serbian judge issued an arrest warrant for KLA chief Thaçi, who had been tried in absentia and sentenced to ten years in prison for his activities. Shortly thereafter, the KLA named Thaçi as prime minister of a proposed provisional Kosovar government.

At a PPDK congress in May 2000 the party changed its name to the PDK. In November 2001 it won 26 assembly seats, with Bajram Rexhepi becoming prime minister of Kosovo in March 2002. Following the October 2004 assembly election, in which it again finished second, with 30 seats, the PDK chose to remain outside the governing coalition.

In the November 2007 assembly election the PDK list won 34.3 percent of the vote and thus a plurality of 37 seats. Having recognized that they could not meet the 5 percent threshold for assembly seats, several small parties had signed coalition agreements with the PDK. As a result, Edita TAHIRI, leader of the **Democratic Alternative of Kosovo** (*Aleancë Demokratike të Kosovës*—ADK), and Emrush XHEMAJLI of the **People's Movement of Kosovo** (*Lëvizja Popullore e Kosovës*—LPK) were awarded assembly seats from the PDK list. Other agreements had been signed with the **Liberal Party of Kosovo** (*Partia Liberale e Kosovës*—PLK), led by Gjergj DEDAJ, who was named a deputy minister in the Thaçi government, and the **Social Democratic Party of Kosovo** (*Partisë Social-Demokratike të Kosovës*—PSDK), then led by Kaqusha JASHARI. In April 2008 the PSDK named former prime minister Agim Çeku as party chair, a post that he was formally elected to in June.

Leaders: Hashim THAÇI (Prime Minister and Chair of the Party), Hajredin KUÇI (Vice Chair), Fatmir LIMAJ (Vice Chair), Rrustem MUSTAFA (Vice Chair), Bajram REXHEPI (Former Prime Minister and Vice Chair of the Party), Ramë BUJA (Assembly Leader), Jakup KRASNIQI (Speaker of the Assembly and Secretary General of the Party).

Democratic League of Kosovo (*Lidhja Demokratike e Kosovës*—LDK). The LDK, founded in 1989, remains the largest Albanian party. Advocating the creation of an independent, demilitarized republic, it won an overwhelming preponderance of seats in a "constituent republican assembly" for the province in 1992, after which the LDK leader, Ibrahim Rugova, was proclaimed president of a self-declared "Republic of Kosovo." The group boycotted all Yugoslavian and Serbian elections before independence.

Rugova, who consistently advocated nonviolence and a negotiated settlement of the Kosovo issue with Belgrade, was reelected president, with over 90 percent of the vote, in the "Republic" elections of March 1998. Collaterally, the LDK again won most of the seats in the shadow legislature. In the November 2001 election and again in October 2004 the LDK won a leading 47 seats in the Kosovo Assembly, which retained Rugova as president until his death on January 21, 2006. Assembly Speaker Nexhat Daci served as acting president until Fatmir Sejdiu was elected president by the assembly on February 10.

The fallout from Rugova's death led to divisions within the party and the removal of Speaker Nexhat Daci and Deputy Prime Minister Adem Salihaj from leadership posts in early 2006. Daci and Salihaj went on to form the Democratic League of Dardania (LDD, below).

In the November 2007 assembly election the LDK finished second, with 22.6 percent of the vote and 25 seats, a net loss of 22 from its previous total. Two parties in coalition with the LDK were the **Christian Democratic Party for Integration** (*Partia Demokristiane për Integrim*—PDKI), a 2007 splinter from the PShDK (below) led by Zef MORINA, and the **New Party of Kosovo** (*Partisë së Re të Kosovës*—PReK), led by Bujar BUKOSHI. Morina and Bukoshi both received assembly seats. In June 2009 the PDKI and the PShDK agreed to reunite.

It took three ballots for the assembly to reelect President Sejdiu in January 2008. On the first two ballots, when he received 62 and 61 votes, respectively, he fell well short of the required two-thirds majority, but on the third, with only a simple majority required, he won with 68.

Leaders: Fatmir SEJDIU (President of Kosovo and Chair of the Party), Eqrem KRYEZIU and Kolë BERISHA (Vice Chairs), Lutfi HAZIRI (Vice Chair and Assembly Leader), Ramë MANAJ (Secretary General).

Independent Liberal Party (*Samostalna Liberalna Stranka*—SLS). The ethnic Serb SLS was organized in August–September 2006 in Mitrovica under the leadership of Slobodan Petrović. The SLS cast itself as multiethnic in orientation and announced its preference for Kosovo's remaining part of Serbia, but it did not take a hard line on the issue.

In the November 2007 assembly election the SLS won three of the ten seats reserved for Serbs. The party went on to form a floor group in cooperation with three other minority parties. It became the sole Serb party to join the government.

Leaders: Slobodan PETROVIĆ (Chair), Ajdar ILJAZI (Vice Chair), Saša RAŠIĆ (Minister of Community and Return), Bojan STOJANOVIĆ (Assembly Leader).

Kosovo Democratic Turkish Party (*Kosova Demokratik Türk Partisi*—KDTP). The KDTP was established in 1990 to represent the ethnic Turkish population. In November 2007 it won three Kosovo Assembly seats, as it had in the previous two elections, and joined the Thaçi government.

Leaders: Mahir YAĞCILAR (Minister of Environment and Spatial Planning), Enis KERVAN, Müfera SINIK.

Other Assembly Parties:

New Kosovo Alliance (*Aleanca Kosova e Re*—AKR). The AKR was formed in March 2006 by wealthy and controversial businessman Behxhet Pacolli, reputedly Kosovo's richest politician. The conservative party favors laissez-faire capitalism, a secular state, lower taxes, individual freedom and responsibility, and adoption of a presidential system. It won 12.3 percent of the assembly vote and was awarded 13 seats in 2007, for third place.

Leaders: Behxhet PACOLLI (Chair), Ibrahim GASHI (Vice Chair), Ibrahim MAKOLLI (Vice Chair and Assembly Leader), Rrahim PACOLLI (Secretary).

Democratic League of Dardania (*Lidhja Demokratike e Dardanisë*—LDD). The center-right LDD, whose name incorporates a historical name for Kosovo, was formed in January 2007 by former assembly speaker Nexhat Daci and other dissidents from the LDK. Daci had lost an LDK leadership election to Fatmir Sejdiu. At its formation the LDD held 7 seats in the assembly. In the November 2007 election the coalition of the LDD and the Albanian Christian Democratic Party of Kosovo (below) won 11 seats.

Leaders: Nexhat DACI (Chair); Besa GAXHERRI, Xhemajl HYSENI, and Adem SALIHAJ (Vice Chairs); Lulzim ZENELI (Secretary and Assembly Leader).

Albanian Christian Democratic Party of Kosovo (*Partia Shqiptare Demokristiane e Kosovës*—PShDK). Dating from 1990, the PShDK mainly represents Catholic ethnic Albanians in Kosovo but includes some Muslims in its ranks. The party attracted little support in the October 2000 municipal elections in Kosovo, finishing with only a 1.2 percent vote share.

After the 2004 Kosovo Assembly election the PShDK was awarded 2 seats. Shortly thereafter, a major rift resulted in a disputed February 2005 party convention at which a majority faction replaced leader Mark Krasniqi with Tadej RODIQI. The Krasniqi wing subsequently held its own convention. The party remained split thereafter, with the anti-Krasniqi wing ultimately forming the PDKI (above, under LDK).

With the November 2007 election approaching, the PShDK announced that it would compete nationally in coalition with the LDD despite a previous association with the LDK. The alliance won 11 seats. After the election, longtime leader Krasniqi, 87, was succeeded by Ton Marku.

On June 11, 2009, the PShDK and the PDKI signed an agreement on reuniting, with a new leadership and party name to be determined at a future unification congress.

Leaders: Ton MARKU (Chair), Nikë GJELOSHI and Mark KOMANI (Vice Chairs), Mark KRASNIQI.

Alliance for the Future of Kosovo (*Aleanca për Ardhmërinë e Kosovës*—AAK). The AAK was launched in May 2000 by Ramush Haradinaj, a former KLA commander, as a political alliance that incorporated a number of smaller Kosovar parties, including the Parliamentary Party of Kosovo (*Partija Parlamentare e Kosovës*—PPK). A conservative party that placed itself ideologically in "the modern European center," the PPK was a principal rival of Ibrahim Rugova's LDK in the early 1990s.

In November 2001 the AAK won eight assembly seats; in 2004 it won nine. Party Chair Haradinaj headed the coalition government formed in December 2004 but resigned in March 2005 to face war crimes charges before the ICTY. He was succeeded by the AAK's Bajram Kosumi, who previously had been a leader of the PPK and the United Democratic Movement (*Lëvizja Bashimit Demokratike*—LBD). Kosumi resigned as prime minister on March 1, 2006.

In the November 2007 assembly election the AAK won ten seats. Its candidate for president, Naim Maloku, finished second in the January 9, 2008, election.

On April 3, 2008, the ICTY acquitted Haradinaj of war crimes.

Leaders: Ramush HARADINAJ (Chair); Ahmet ISUFI, Bajram KOSUMI, and Naim MALOKU (Vice Chairs); Ardian GJINI (Assembly Leader).

Serb Democratic Party of Kosovo and Metohija (*Srpska Demokratska Stranka Kosova i Metohije*—SDSKiM). The SDSKiM was organized in June 2005 on the basis of the Citizens' Initiative of Serbia (*Gradjanska Inicijativa Srbija*—GIS). Despite the objections of the Serbian government, the GIS had contested the Serbian set-aside seats in the 2004 Kosovo Assembly election, winning two of them.

In January 2005 party founder Slaviša Petković accepted the post of minister for returns and communities in the Kosovo Council of Ministers. He resigned in November 2006 and was replaced by the SDSKiM's Branislav Grbić, who in July 2007 announced formation of a new ethnic Serbian party, the New Democracy (below). In the November election the SDSKiM won 3 seats.

Leaders: Slaviša PETKOVIĆ, Vladimir TODOROVIĆ.

Vakat Coalition (*Koalicija "Vakat"*). Vakat was established in June 2004 by three parties: the **Democratic Party of Bosniacs** (*Demokratska Stranka Bošnjaka*—DSB/*Partia Demokratike e Boshnjakëve*), the **Democratic Party Vatan** (*Demokratska Stranka Vatan*—DSV/*Partia Demokratike Vatan*), and the **Bosniac Party of Kosovo** (*Bošnjačka Stranka Kosova*—BSK/*Partia Boshnjake e Kosovës*). The DSB was registered in 2001. Both the DSV and the BSK began as local branches of the Party of Democratic Action (below) and became parties earlier in 2004. In the October Kosovo Assembly election Vakat won three seats. It then joined the "6+" parliamentary group of non-Serb minority representatives.

In the 2007 election Vakat again won 3 seats and continued as part of what was now the "7+" assembly group.

Leaders: Xhezair MURATI (DSB, Chair of 7+), Sadik IDRIZI (DSV), Husnija BESKOVIĆ (BSK).

Party of Democratic Action (*Stranka Demokratske Akcije*—SDA/ *Partia e Aksionit Demokratik*). Established in 1990 as a branch of the Yugoslavian SDA, the Kosovo SDA primarily represents the Bosniac community, as do its current counterparts in Bosnia and Herzegovina, Montenegro, and the Sandžak and Preševo regions of Serbia. In the October 2004 Kosovo Assembly election the SDA Kosovo won 1 seat.

In April 2007 SDA chair Numan Balić, despite his support for independence, opposed the plan put forward by Martii Ahtisaari because, he asserted, it did not adequately address the needs of non-Serb minorities in Kosovo. In the November assembly election he claimed one of the party's 2 seats. Both representatives chose to sit with the AAK floor group.

Leaders: Numan BALIĆ (Chair), Vezira EMRUŠ.

New Democratic Initiative of Kosovo (*Iniciativa e Re Demokratike e Kosovës*—IRDK). In the 2004 Kosovo Assembly election the IRDK contested the seats set aside for the Roma, Ashkali, and Egyptian communities. It won 2 seats. In 2007 it won one and chose to sit with the AAK assembly group.

Leader: Xhevdet NEZIRAJ (Member of the Assembly).

Seven additional ethnic minority parties won seats in the 2007 assembly election. The **Citizens' Initiative of Gora** (*Gradjanska Inicijativa Gore*—GIG), representing the Gorani community and led by Murselj HALILI, claimed one. The **Democratic Ashkali Party of Kosovo** (*Partia Demokratike Ashkali e Kosovës*—PDAK), led by Sabit RRAHMANI, won 3 seats, a gain of two from 2004. The ethnic Serb **New Democracy** (*Nova Demokratija*—ND) was formed in July 2007 by former SDSKiM leader Branislav GRBIĆ, who claimed the party's sole assembly seat. The following also won 1 seat each: the **Serb Kosovo-Metohija Party** (*Srpska Kosovsko Metohijka Stranka*—SKMS), led by Dragiša MIRIĆ; the **Serb People's Party** (*Srpska Narodna Stranka*—SNS), led by Mihailo ŠĆEPANOVIĆ; the Serb **Union of Independent Social Democrats of Kosovo and Metohija** (*Savez Nezavisnih Socijaldemokrata Kosova i Metohije*—SNSKiM), led by Lubiša Živić; and the **United Roma Party of Kosovo** (*Partia Rome e Bashkuar e Kosovës*—PReBK), led by Zylfi MERXHA.

Other Parties:

Reformist Party ORA (*Partia Reformiste ORA* ["Hour" or "Time"]). ORA was established in 2004 by media entrepreneur Veton SURROI as a reformist initiative with an economic focus. It contested the October 2004 Kosovo Assembly election as the Citizens' List "ORA" (*Lista Qytetarë "ORA"*), winning 6 percent of the vote and seven seats, and was organized as a party in December. In 2007 it won only 4.1 percent of the vote, insufficient for seats, which prompted

Surroi to resign the party leadership. In March 2008 Vice Chair Teuta Sahatqija was elected as his successor, following unsuccessful discussions with former prime minister Agim Çeku about joining ORA and assuming the leadership.

Leaders: Teuta SAHATQIJA (Chair); Gazmend MUHAXHERI, Naim HOXHA, and Besnik KRAJKU (Vice Chairs); Nazim JASHARI (Secretary).

Serb List for Kosovo and Metohija (*Srpska Lista za Kosovo i Metohiju*—SLKM). With the October 2004 Kosovo Assembly election approaching, Oliver Ivanović led formation of the SLKM, which included his own Return Coalition (*Koalicija Povratak*—KP) as well as the national Democratic Party and Serbian Renewal Movement. The Return Coalition had been organized by a group of national Serbian parties prior to the 2001 Kosovo Assembly election on a platform that called for an end to Serbian emigration from Kosovo, the return of those Serbs displaced during the Kosovo conflict, an accounting of those missing, a return of Serbian property, and measures to ensure Serb safety and freedom of movement. The only Serb political group to participate in the November election, it finished third, winning 22 seats.

Because of the low turnout of Serb voters (most Serb parties boycotted the election), the SLKM won only 0.2 percent of the October 2004 vote, but that was sufficient to claim eight of the ten seats reserved for Serbians. At the urging of Serbia's government, the SLKM did not contest the November 2007 elections. Ivanović currently serves as a state secretary in Serbia's government.

Leader: Oliver IVANOVIĆ (Chair).

Other eligible parties that failed to win seats in the 2007 assembly election were the **Albanian Republican Party** (*Partia Republikane Shqiptare*—PRS); the **Kosovo Ecological Party** (*Partia Ekologjike e Kosovës*—PEK); the **Justice Party** (*Partia e Drejtësisë*—PD), led by Sylejman ÇERKEZI; the **National Front** (*Balli Kombëtare*—BK); and the **National Movement for the Liberation of Kosovo** (*Lëvizja Kombëtare për Çlirimin e Kosovës*—LKÇK).

LEGISLATURE

The **Assembly of Kosovo** (*Kuvendit të Kosovës/Skupštine Kosova*) comprises 120 representatives, 100 of whom are directly elected on a proportional basis from among those parties winning at least 5 percent of the vote. Ten minority seats are reserved for Serbs; 4 for Ashkali, Romani, and Egyptians; 3 for Bosniacs; 2 for Turks; and 1 for Gorani. All members serve four-year terms.

In the most recent election of November 17, 2007, the Democratic Party of Kosovo won 37 seats; the Democratic League of Kosovo, 25; the New Kosovo Alliance, 13; the alliance of the Democratic League of Dardania and the Albanian Christian Democratic Party of Kosovo, 11; and the Alliance for the Future of Kosovo, 10. Six ethnic Serb parties split the 10 seats set aside for Serbians: the Independent Liberal Party, 3; the Serb Democratic Party of Kosovo and Metohija, 3; New Democracy, the Serb Kosovo-Metohija Party, the Serb People's Party, and the Union of Independent Social Democrats of Kosovo and Metohija, 1 each. Seven other minority parties won a total of 14 seats: the Democratic Ashkali Party of Kosovo, 3, including 2 reserved minority seats; the Kosovo Democratic Turkish Party, 3 (2 minority seats); the Vakat Coalition, 3 (2 minority seats); the Party of Democratic Action, 2 (1 minority seat); and the Civic Initiative of Gora, the New Democratic Initiative of Kosovo, and the United Roma Party of Kosovo, 1 minority seat each.

President: Jakup KRASNIQI.

CABINET

[as of October 15, 2009]

Prime Minister	Hashim Thaçi (PDK)
Deputy Prime Ministers	Hajredin Kuçi (PDK)
	Ramë Manaj (LDK)
Ministers	
Agriculture	Idriz Vehapi (PDK)
Culture, Youth, and Sport	Valton Beqiri (LDK)
Community and Return	Saša Rašić (SLS)
Defense	Fehmi Mujota (PDK)
Economy and Finance	Ahmet Shala (PDK)
Education, Science, and Technology	Enver Hoxhaj (PDK)
Energy and Mining	Justina Pula-Shiroka (PDK) [f]
Environment and Spatial Planning	Mahir Yağcilar (KDTP)
Foreign Affairs	Skender Hyseni (LDK)
Health	Alush Gashi (LDK)
Interior Affairs	Zenun Pajaziti (PDK)
Justice	Nekibe Kelmendi (LDK) [f]
Labor and Social Welfare	Nenad Rašić (SLS)
Local Governance	Sadri Ferati (LDK)
Public Services	Arsim Bajrami (PDK)
Trade and Industry	Lutfi Zharku (LDK)
Transport and Communication	Fatmir Limaj (PDK)

[f] = female

COMMUNICATIONS

The 2008 constitution guarantees media freedom and prohibits censorship except in situations involving incitement of ethnic, national, racial, or religious hostility or violence.

Press. The following are among the dailies published in Priština in Albanian: *Bota Sot* (World Today); *Gazeta Express* (Express Gazette), tabloid format; *Koha Ditore* (Daily Time), leading newspaper, founded in 1997; *Kosova Sot* (Kosovo Today); *Lajm* (News), tabloid format; *Zëri* (Voice).

Broadcasting. Kosovo's public broadcaster, *Radio Televizioni e Kosovës* (RTK), was established in 1999 by the OSCE and the European Broadcast Union and more recently authorized by act of the Assembly of Kosovo in 2006. Editorially independent, it transmits a mix of news, educational programming, and entertainment terrestrially and by satellite in Albanian, Serbian, and three other languages. RTK encompasses one television channel and two radio stations, Radio Kosovo and the youth-oriented Blue Sky Radio. In all, there are some two dozen television stations, although only a few transmit nationally, and nearly 100 radio stations.

INTERGOVERNMENTAL REPRESENTATION

As of October 15, 2009, the Republic of Kosovo had been recognized by 62 countries plus the Republic of China, or Taiwan. It had not yet applied for UN membership.

Ambassador to the U.S.: Avni SPAHIU.

U.S. Ambassador to Kosovo: Christopher William DELL.

KUWAIT

State of Kuwait
Dawlat al-Kuwayt

Political Status: Constitutional hereditary emirate; independent since June 19, 1961, save for occupation by Iraq from August 2, 1990, to February 26, 1991.

Area: 6,880 sq. mi. (17,818 sq. km.).

Population: 2,213,403 (2005C), including 880,774 Kuwaitis and 1,332,629 non-Kuwaitis; 3,604,000 (2008E). The 2005 figure is not adjusted for underenumeration.

Major Urban Centers (2005E): KUWAIT CITY (32,000), Salmiya (145,000), Hawalli (107,000).

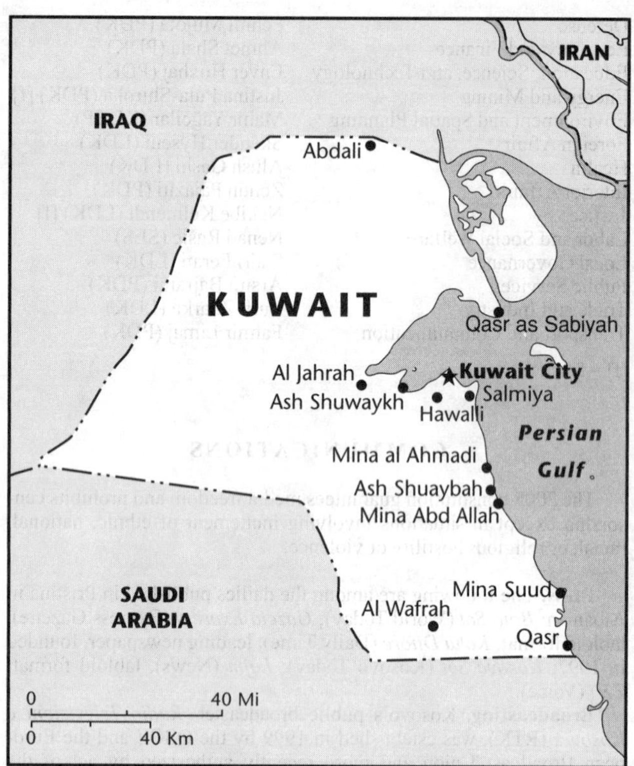

Official Language: Arabic.

Monetary Unit: Dinar (official rate December 1, 2009: 1 dinar = $3.47US). In May 2007 Kuwait abandoned the dinar's peg to the dollar, instead pegging it to a basket of international currencies.

Sovereign (Emir): Sheikh Sabah al-Ahmad al-Jabir al-SABAH; inaugurated on January 29, 2006, after unanimous confirmation the same day by the National Assembly, following the abdication on January 24 of Sheikh Saad al-Abdallah al-Salim al-SABAH, who became emir on January 15 upon the death of his cousin, Sheikh Jabir al-Ahmad al-Jabir al-SABAH.

Heir Apparent: Sheikh Nawaf Ahmad al-Jabir al-SABAH; appointed crown prince by his brother, emir Sheikh Sabah al-Ahmad al-Jabir al-Sabah on February 7, 2006, replacing Sheikh Sabah al-Ahmad al-Jabir al-SABAH.

Prime Minister: Sheikh Nasser Muhammad al-Ahmad al-SABAH; appointed February 7, 2006, by his uncle and predecessor, emir Sheikh Sabah al-Ahmad al-Jabir al-SABAH and sworn in with a new government on February 20; reappointed by the emir on May 20, 2008, and sworn in with a new government on May 28; reappointed as head of a new government on December 17 following the resignation of the government on December 1; reappointed by the emir on May 20, 2009, following early legislative elections on May 16 and appointed a new government on May 29.

THE COUNTRY

Located near the head of the Persian Gulf, Kuwait is bordered on the north and west by Iraq and on the south by Saudi Arabia. It shared control of a 2,500-square-mile Neutral Zone with the latter until the area was formally partitioned in 1969, with revenues from valuable petroleum deposits in the zone being divided equally by the two states. An extremely arid country, Kuwait suffered from an acute shortage of potable water until the 1950s, when the installation of a number of desalination plants alleviated the problem.

About 95 percent of native Kuwaitis, who constitute less than 35 percent of the country's population, are Muslims; an estimated 70 percent belong to the Sunni sect and the remainder are Shiites. The noncitizen population, upon which the sheikhdom has long depended for a labor pool, is composed chiefly of other Arabs, Indians, Pakistanis, and Iranians who settled in Kuwait after World War II. Some 97 percent of native Kuwaitis are employed in the public sector, which accounts for 75 percent of GDP. Women comprise approximately 31 percent of the paid labor force; those who are native Kuwaitis are concentrated in health care and education, with the remainder primarily employed as teachers and domestic servants. In 2005 women were granted the right to vote and to hold elected office, but the debate on the matter revealed a deep split, even among women, in the Kuwaiti populace, many of whom still hold to traditional customs. There is also a distinct rift between rural tribal society and what has been described as the "urban oligarchy" dominated by the ruling family.

Kuwait's petroleum reserves, reported as 101.5 billion barrels in 2004, comprise 10 percent of proven global reserves. (However, in 2006 oil-industry reports claimed authorities had been exaggerating, and that reserves were actually about 48 billion barrels.) The oil sector was nationalized in 1975, and Kuwait had become, prior to the Iraqi invasion and occupation of 1990–91, a highly developed welfare state, providing its citizens with medical, educational, and other services without personal income taxes or related excises. In May 2005 the Kuwaiti government granted a $171 monthly pay raise to tens of thousands of workers and pensioners to help them meet the rising cost of living.

Surging oil prices and the relative political stability in the region since the fall of Iraqi ruler Saddam Hussein in April 2003 have bolstered Kuwait's booming economy: a $23 billion budget surplus was reported in 2005. Yet non-oil revenues continued to lag, prompting the International Monetary Fund (IMF) in May 2005 to urge a value-added tax. Annual GDP growth, about 10 percent in 2004, averaged 7.8 percent in 2005–2006.

The IMF in 2006 noted progress in structural reforms, "albeit at a slow pace," as well as increased privatization, particularly in telecommunications, airlines, and infrastructure. In light of Kuwait's plans to expand oil production (see Current issues, below) and soaring oil revenue, the IMF urged the government toward greater fiscal transparency and economic diversity through private sector development to help absorb the fast-growing labor force. Also in 2006, the parliament approved a one-time payment of $692 to each citizen to help meet the cost of living.

Against the recommendation of the IMF, Kuwait dropped its currency peg to the weakened U.S. dollar in May 2007 and instead pegged the dinar to a basket of international currencies. Annual GDP growth was about 7 percent as a result of increased oil production in response to global demand. Robust growth continued in 2008, with annual GDP of 6.4 percent, again due to greater oil production and strong growth in the non-oil sector. In an effort to reduce the inflation rate (averaging about 7 percent annually in 2007–2008), the central bank in March capped consumer loans in an effort to curb citizens' large personal debt. Also in 2008 the government initiated plans for $50 billion worth of improvements in its oil and gas industries.

While the economy remained fairly strong despite the global financial crisis, Kuwait's financial system was set back as the stock exchange index fell by 50 percent, the country's third-largest bank lost $1.4 billion, and the largest investment firm defaulted on most of its $3 billion debt, according to the IMF. Fund managers forecast a decline in 2009 annual GDP by 1.2 percent, owing to a decrease in oil production and an accompanying downturn in the non-oil sector. On a more positive note the IMF commended Kuwaiti authorities for their generous assistance to low-income countries both within and outside the region. Meanwhile, fund managers reiterated their recommendations for Kuwaiti authorities to accelerate introduction of a value-added tax, expedite structural reforms, and reduce dependency on oil revenue.

GOVERNMENT AND POLITICS

Political background. Kuwait's accession to complete independence in 1961 was preceded by a period of close association with Great Britain that began in the late 19th century when the then-semiautonomous Ottoman province sought British protection against foreign invasion and an extension of Turkish control. By treaty in 1899, Kuwait ceded its external sovereignty to Britain in exchange for financial subsidies and defense support, and in 1914 Britain recognized Kuwait as a self-governing state under its protection. Special treaty relations continued until the sheikhdom was made fully independent by agreement with reigning Emir Abdallah al-Salim al-SABAH on June 19, 1961. Iraqi claims to Kuwaiti territory were rebuffed shortly afterward by the dispatch of British troops at Kuwait's request and were subsequently reduced to a border dispute that appeared to have been substantially resolved in 1975.

On August 29, 1976, the government of Sheikh Jabir al-Ahmad al-SABAH resigned in the wake of alleged "unjust attacks and denunciations against ministers" by members of the National Assembly. Sheikh Sabah al-Salim al-SABAH, who succeeded Emir Abdallah in 1965, responded on the same day by dissolving the assembly, suspending a constitutional provision that would have required a new election within two months, and instituting severe limitations on freedom of the press. On September 6 Sheikh Jabir, who succeeded Emir Sabah in 1977, formed a new government that was virtually identical in membership to the old.

Observers attributed the drastic measures of 1976 to the impact of the Lebanese civil war upon Kuwait, which then counted some 270,000 Palestinians among its nonnative population. The continuing exclusion of immigrant elements from political life accounted in large part for the lack of significant political change during the remainder of the decade, despite growing dissatisfaction among some groups, most noticeably Shiite Muslims, upon commencement of the Iranian revolution in early 1979.

Following a return to the earlier constitutional practice, a nonparty poll for a new National Assembly was held on February 23, 1981. Five days later, the heir apparent, Sheikh Saad al-Abdallah al-Salim al-SABAH, who had first been appointed in 1978, was redesignated as prime minister. He was reappointed on March 3, 1985, after balloting on February 20 for a new assembly that was itself dissolved on July 3, 1986, in the wake of a series of confrontations between elected and ex officio government members over fiscal and internal security issues. Echoing the events of 1976, the emir postponed new elections and implemented strict press controls.

In early 1989 a group of ex-parliamentarians, led by former speaker Ahmad Abd al-Aziz al-SADUN, launched a petition drive to revive the 1962 constitution and restore the National Assembly, reportedly gathering over 30,000 signatures by December. The government's response was that it was pursuing a "new form of popular participation" centered on a National Council of 50 elected and 25 appointed members to serve as a surrogate for the former legislature for the ensuing four years. The opposition nonetheless continued to insist on revival of the earlier body and mounted a largely successful boycott of National Council balloting on June 10, in which all of the contested seats were won by government supporters.

The Iraqi invasion of August 2, 1990, resulted in the flight of virtually all members of the country's ruling elite. In March 1991 they returned, amid massive physical destruction, to face widespread demands for meaningful representative government. Opposition leaders vehemently denounced the composition of a new government formed on April 20 as little more than an extension of its predecessor, in which all major posts were held by members of the royal family. The emir responded with a promise that elections to a new National Assembly would be held in 1992, and on July 9 the interim National Council was reconvened with orders to discuss and organize the elections. Meanwhile, the regime was buffeted by foreign and domestic criticism of its postwar policies, including the perfunctory trials of alleged Iraqi collaborators and the expulsion of tens of thousands of non-Kuwaiti citizens. Subsequently, the government commuted the death sentences of convicted collaborators, promised defendants the right to a fair trial, and on August 14 created criminal appeals courts.

National Assembly balloting was held on October 5, 1992, with candidates considered opponents of the government capturing a majority of the seats. Sheikh Saad resigned as prime minister two days later but was reappointed by the emir on October 12, despite growing demands from the opposition that someone else be named to the post. On the other hand, in a significant concession to the opposition, six members of the assembly were named to the new cabinet announced on October 17. The cabinet was also extensively reshuffled on April 13, 1994, the new government subsequently announcing it would move ahead with economic reforms, including privatization.

In addition to intensifying Kuwait's "siege mentality" the October 1994 border confrontation with Iraq (see Foreign relations, below) also exacerbated the sheikhdom's budget difficulties, the government in 1995 announcing plans to impose new fees on many public services in an effort to control the deficit. On the political front, attention focused on the conflict between the National Assembly and the government over whether the assembly had the right to review decrees issued during its 1986–1992 hiatus. Legislators were also pressing for the prosecution of former officials, most of whom are members of the royal family, on corruption charges. In part, the schism reflected the influence of Islamic fundamentalists within the assembly, 39 of whose 50 elected deputies in 1994 endorsed an appeal, subsequently rejected by the government, to make Islamic religious law (sharia) the sole source of Kuwaiti law. Growing fundamentalist support was also noted within the population as a whole, although many young Kuwaitis were described as having "embraced" Western culture as the outgrowth of a belief that the country's survival hinged on continued strong ties with the United States and Europe.

Following the balloting for a new assembly on October 7, 1996, it was reported that 17–22 "solidly progovernment" candidates had been elected with the remainder including an estimated 14–18 representatives from the generally antigovernment Islamist camp. The prime minister again entered a pro forma resignation on October 8, but he was reappointed on October 12 and his new, moderately reshuffled government was sworn in on October 15.

Sheikh Saad and his cabinet resigned on March 15, 1998, as legislators continued to press various ministers on several fronts (see Current issues, below). However, the emir immediately reappointed Sheikh Saad as prime minister, and a new, substantially reshuffled government was announced on March 23.

The cabinet again resigned on January 29, 2001, and substantial debate was reported within the ruling family over the makeup of the next government. On February 17, 2001, the cabinet included eight new members and, significantly, oil and finance ministers who were not members of the ruling family. Although aging Prime Minister Saad remained the titular head of government, many of his responsibilities were turned over to the deputy prime minister, Sheikh Sabah al-Ahmad al-Jabir al-SABAH, the brother of the emir. With age and illness taking a toll on the ruling family, the question of succession weighed heavily on the state.

On June 1, 2003, four ministers resigned to stand for election. After the assembly elections on July 5, 2003, Sheikh Sabah was appointed prime minister, replacing the heir apparent, Sheikh Saad al-Abdallah al-Salim al-Sabah, and separating the post from the crown prince for the first time in a move that made the prime minister more accountable to the people. Meanwhile, Islamists and pro-government candidates swept to victory, crushing the pro-Western liberals and the full cabinet resigned, in a routine move, the day after the elections. The responsibility for forming a new government fell to the deputy prime minister and foreign minister, reportedly because Sheikh Saad had been ill for some time, and a new cabinet was installed on July 17, 2003. Despite the more conservative trend, the assembly did grant women the right to vote for the first time in the country's history in May 2005, and in June the first woman was appointed to the cabinet.

A group of former Salafists formed what they described as Kuwait's first political party in 2005, a move that was unsettled since political parties are officially illegal (see Political Parties, below).

Upon the death of Sheikh Jabir on January 15, 2006, cabinet ministers immediately proclaimed the crown prince, Sheikh Saad, as the new emir. Several days later, however, it was reported that the ruling family proposed that the prime minister and de facto ruler, Sheikh Sabah, be appointed emir in place of the ailing Sheikh Saad. On January 23 the cabinet asked the National Assembly to hold a special session to discuss whether Sheikh Saad was fit to rule, and the following day a letter of abdication from the emir was delivered to the legislators. On January 29 the assembly voted unanimously in favor of Sheikh Sabah, who took the oath of office the same day. The cabinet resigned the following day. On February 7 the emir appointed 65-year-old Sheik Nasser Muhammad al-Ahmad al-SABAH (the emir's nephew) as prime minister and 68-year-old Sheik Nawaf Ahmad al-Jabir al-SABAH (the emir's brother) as crown prince and heir apparent. The prime minister and the new government were sworn in on February 20. Following a dispute with opposition legislators over proposed changes to electoral districts (see Current issues, below), the emir dissolved the National Assembly on May 21, after an unprecedented walkout a week earlier by 29 members and their equally surprising demand that they be allowed to question the prime minister about the controversial electoral proposal. The information minister resigned in protest in the midst of the dispute and was replaced on May 14. Following dissolution of the assembly, the emir called for new elections, which were held on June 29, a year ahead of schedule. A new cabinet was sworn in on July 11 and shortly thereafter approved the controversial electoral reform measure, which parliament approved on July 17.

The cabinet resigned on March 4, 2007. On March 25 the emir appointed a new cabinet, again headed by Sheik Nasser al-Sabah. The new government, which reportedly included ten members of the previous government and four Islamists, was sworn in on April 2. The cabinet was reshuffled on October 28. The entire cabinet resigned on March 17, 2008, and the emir called for new, early elections on May 17. Islamists won a plurality, with 21 of 50 seats, a gain of 2 seats from the previous election. Liberal candidates won 7 seats. Though 27 women contested the elections, none won a seat. On May 20 the emir reappointed Prime Minister Sheik Nasser al-Sabah, who included two women in his reshuffled cabinet of May 28. It was the first election under a new law that reduced the number of voting districts from 25 to 5. The cabinet resigned on November 25, 2008, in order to prevent yet another attempt by the legislature to question the prime minister (see Current issues, below). Prime Minister Nasser al-Sabah was reappointed on December 17 to head a new government following the resignation of the government on December 1.

The cabinet was reshuffled on January 12, 2009. In yet another move to circumvent lawmakers' attempt to question the prime minister, the government resigned on March 16, and the emir dissolved parliament on March 18 and called for early elections. The second parliamentary elections within a year were held on May 16, with Sunnis losing ground to liberals, as Islamists secured 11 seats, down from 21 in the previous election. In a historic first, four women—all described as academics—won seats in the assembly. Prime Minister Nasser al-Sabah was reappointed on May 20 and named a reshuffled cabinet, with the key posts of defense, finance, and foreign affairs unchanged, on May 29.

Constitution and government. The constitution promulgated in 1962 vests executive power in an emir selected from the Mubarak line of the ruling Sabah family, whose dynasty dates from 1756. The emir rules through an appointed prime minister and Council of Ministers, while legislative authority is shared by the emir and a National Assembly that is subject to dissolution by decree. The judicial system, since its revision in 1959, is based on the Egyptian model and includes a Constitutional Court, courts of the first degree (criminal assize, magistrates', civil, domestic, and commercial courts), and a Misdemeanors Court of Appeal. The domestic court, which deals with cases involving such personal matters as divorce and inheritance, is divided into separate chambers for members of the Sunni and Shiite sects, with a third chamber for non-Muslims. Civil appeal is to a High Court of Appeal and, in limited cases, to a Court of Cassation. Although the 1962 basic law theoretically accorded equal rights to men and women, an election law adopted at the same time precluded women from voting or holding elected office. After decades of controversy over the elimination of these proscriptions, the assembly amended the country's election law on May 16, 2005, granting women the right to vote in and contest parliamentary and local elections for the first time in the country's history.

Foreign relations. As a member of the Arab League, Kuwait has closely identified itself with Arab causes and through such agencies as the Kuwait Fund for Arab Economic Development and the Organization of Arab Petroleum Exporting Countries has contributed to the economic development of other Arab countries. In 1967 it launched a program of direct aid to countries experiencing hardship as a result of conflict with Israel. In 1981 Kuwait joined five other regional states in forming the Gulf Cooperation Council (GCC).

Dominating external concerns in the 1980s was the Iran-Iraq war, which curtailed oil exports and generated fear of Iranian expansionism in the event of a victory for the Khomeini regime. After a number of attacks on shipping by both participants and a decision by Washington to increase its naval presence in the Gulf, Kuwait, which had previously declined an offer of American tanker escort, proposed in April 1987 that a number of its vessels be transferred to U.S. registry. The reflagging provided enhanced security for oil shipments but was interpreted as solidifying the sheikdom's pro-Iraqi posture. Diplomatic relations between Kuwait and Iran were eventually restored in November 1988, three months after the Iran-Iraq cease-fire.

Despite its support of Iraq during the latter's conflict with Iran, the emirate had experienced periodic strain with Baghdad long before the Gulf crisis of August 1990. For many decades Iraq had laid intermittent claim to all of Kuwait on the basis of its status within the Ottoman province of Basra at the turn of the century. However, the merits of such a case were substantially weakened by an Iraqi agreement in 1963 to respect the independence and sovereignty of its southern neighbor. Unresolved by the 1963 accord was the question of boundary demarcation, in regard to which earlier diplomatic references had been quite vague. Nor was the land boundary the only problem: Iraq had also claimed offshore territory, including, most importantly, Bubiyan Island, which dominated access to the Iraqi port and naval base of Umm Qasr via the Khor Abdallah waterway. The boundary uncertainties also lent a degree of credibility to claims that Kuwait was encroaching on Iraqi oil fields, allegedly by "slant drilling," while Baghdad had long complained of the failure of the Gulf emirates, including Kuwait, to hold to OPEC-mandated oil production quotas. Such problems were unaddressed by Security Council Resolution 687, which provided the basis of a formal cease-fire between Iraqi and UN forces. (For a chronology of events associated with the Gulf war, see p. 969 in the 1991 *Handbook*.)

In June 1991 the Kuwaiti government withdrew its diplomats from Algeria, Jordan, Mauritania, Sudan, Tunisia, and Yemen, saying that it was "reducing" relations with the six countries because of their lack of support during the Gulf crisis. Meanwhile, a ten-year military cooperation agreement signed with the United States on September 19 authorized the United States to stockpile military equipment and provided its navy with port access; however, the accord did not sanction the permanent stationing of troops. The agreement came in the immediate aftermath of an Iraqi "invasion" of Bubiyan Island that, although easily repelled by Kuwaiti forces, had heightened Kuwait's anxiety about the Hussein regime.

In February 1992 a UN border commission issued a draft document on delineation of the Kuwait-Iraq border, which included the division of Umm Qasr. Observers described the commission's recommendations as an attempt to punish Iraq for its invasion. On November 23 the UN commission revised the border even further north, giving Kuwait complete control of the naval base as well as additional oil fields in the area, effective January 15, 1993. However, Iraq strongly objected to the decision and sent troops into the disputed territory in early January (ostensibly to retrieve weapons), with friction over the issue contributing to a brief resumption of allied air attacks on Iraqi military targets. Subsequently, Kuwait sought and received Western assurance that the 2,000 American troops still in the emirate would be quickly reinforced if Baghdad maintained a confrontational posture.

On April 14, 1993, George H. W. Bush received an enthusiastic reception on his arrival for a three-day visit to the emirate. Subsequently, there were reports of an Iraqi plot to assassinate the former U.S. president, with 14 people charged in the matter being placed on trial in early June. As the result of what U.S. President Bill Clinton termed "compelling evidence" of Iraqi involvement in such a plot, the United States launched a missile attack against Baghdad on June 26. (Subsequent reports suggested that the evidence in question was seriously flawed, although a number of Iraqis were among those ultimately convicted in the case.)

In November 1993 Kuwait signed a ten-year defense cooperation agreement with Russia, similar to post–Gulf war pacts with Britain, France, and the United States. A trade and investment agreement with Russia in November 1994 was considered, in part, an outgrowth of Kuwait's announcement several months earlier that it intended to buy some $800 million in Russian armaments.

The specter of another Iraqi incursion was raised in early October 1994 when Iraqi troops were once again deployed near the Kuwaiti border. However, Baghdad retreated quickly from its threatening stance in the face of Western military preparations and dropped a long-standing claim to its "19th province" by formally recognizing Kuwait's sovereignty in early November, including acceptance of the UN's recent demarcation of the border between the two countries. The Kuwaiti government called the recognition "a step in the right direction," although tension remained high, with Kuwait charging that more than 600 of its nationals were still being held as "hostages" in Iraqi jails. Meanwhile, Kuwait agreed to the permanent stationing on its territory of a squadron of U.S. warplanes.

Not surprisingly, Kuwait remained uncompromising in its anti-Iraq stance in 1997, even though Gulf neighbors Qatar and the United Arab Emirates were promoting the "rehabilitation" within the Arab world of the regime in Baghdad. Consequently, in early 1998 Kuwait was the only Arab state to unequivocally endorse U.S. plans to take military action against Baghdad in the wake of the recent breakdown of UN inspections there. Additional U.S. troops and warplanes were granted staging rights in Kuwait, with an attack unleashed on Baghdad in December.

In early September 2000, in conjunction with renewed Iraqi complaints of Kuwaiti oil "theft," tensions rose significantly. The UN

Security Council agreed that Kuwait ultimately should be awarded $15.9 billion in reparations for the 1990–1991 occupation. However, relations improved significantly following the Arab League Summit in March 2002 at which Iraq reportedly agreed to honor Kuwait's independence and territorial integrity. Tensions continued to escalate between Kuwait and Baghdad until after the United States defeated Saddam Hussein, and Kuwait was on board to support creation of a new government in Iraq in 2005. As recently as February 2005 there were reports of a series of gunfights between Islamist groups described as armed extremists and Kuwaiti security forces. These militant groups were reportedly tied to al-Qaida, suggesting that Kuwait has some security concerns in the war against terrorism. Relations appeared to have improved with Jordan and Palestinian officials since the end of the Gulf war, and in May 2005 Kuwait agreed to send 150 soldiers to Sudan as part of the UN peacekeeping mission to help end civil war.

Following further conflict between Palestinians in Gaza and Israel, and U.S. efforts to mediate a peace accord, the president of the Palestinian Authority, Mahmoud Abbas, engaged in talks with Kuwait in October 2007 ahead of a summit hosted by the United States in November. Kuwait was reported to be "conspicuous by its absence" at that summit, with no official reason given. U.S. president George W. Bush visited Kuwait in January 2008 to hold "broad" talks with the emir in an effort to gain Arab support for the Middle East peace initiative. Meanwhile, Kuwait remained strong in its pro-Palestinian Authority (PA) stance and in March urged Hamas to give up its control in Gaza.

In July 2008 Kuwait named its first ambassador to Iraq since the 1991 Gulf war. In December, China and Kuwait agreed to expand cooperation on economic and energy issues.

In early 2009 several members of Kuwait's parliament protested Israel's attacks on Palestinians in the Gaza Strip, in response to Hamas's rocket attacks in southern Israel. In March the head of Kuwait's national intelligence service was allowed to enter the town of Ramallah, near Jerusalem, as a guest of the PA, but the Israelis refused to allow him entry to the Temple Mount after he insisted on being escorted only by PA members.

Current issues. A significant change for the country occurred in 2003 when Sheikh Sabah was appointed as prime minister, marking the first time in Kuwait's history that the crown prince did not hold the post. The aging emir and Sheikh Saad, the former prime minister and official heir apparent, were widely reported to be in ill health, resulting in questions about the next generation of Kuwaiti leaders.

Tensions eased to a great extent in Kuwait after U.S. and coalition forces toppled the regime of Iraqi ruler Saddam Hussein in April 2003, greatly relieving security issues for Kuwait. However the government has downplayed the arrests of suspected al-Qaida terrorists in the intervening years and repeated clashes between government security forces and Islamic militants as the acts of a select few. Kuwait has pledged to help support the new Iraqi government in its efforts to achieve stability.

In an unexpected move on May 16, 2005, the National Assembly granted women the right to vote for the first time in the country's history. The prime minister, who had been pushing for the amendment to Kuwait's election law, said women could become cabinet ministers, the first being sworn in on June 20. (Islamist lawmakers protested loudly as she took her oath, while liberals applauded the move.) The assembly's 35–23 vote, with 1 abstention, came after decades of heated debates, demonstrations, and riots, and a 2002 decree by the emir insisting that women be given full political rights by 2003. Ultimately, the government invoked a rarely used urgency order to push the measure through in one session, despite heated arguments by Islamists. The Islamists did include a requirement that "females abide by Islamic law," which has been widely interpreted to mean there would be separate polling places for men and women. The granting of full suffrage to women was hailed throughout the West as a "victory for democracy." Shortly after the vote, the speaker of the assembly called for further, though unspecified, steps toward democracy in Kuwait.

The governmental changes of January 2006 (see Political background, above) reportedly caused a rift between the two branches of the royal family, a majority of whom believed the crown prince, Sheik Saad, was too ill to rule. They instead endorsed the prime minister, Sheikh Nasser al-Sabah, and the cabinet took the issue to the assembly for resolution, citing a constitutional procedure that would allow the transfer of power for health reasons if two-thirds of lawmakers approved. Adding to the weeklong leadership crisis, the two branches of the ruling family—the Jabirs and the Salims—were pitted against each other in what observers reported was "an extraordinary public battle for control." The tensions underscored the longtime rivalry between Sheik Sabah and Sheik Saad, and upset the tradition of alternating leadership between the two royal branches. (Sheikh Saad died in 2008.)

Meanwhile, the upheaval postponed for an indefinite time a significant assembly vote on the $8.5 billion Project Kuwait, in which international companies would help boost oil production in the northern region of the country. (The project was ultimately scrapped in 2008.)

More political turmoil ensued in May 2006 when the assembly prepared to vote on a bill to reduce the number of electoral districts, with reformist members backing a plan to cut the number of districts from 25 to 5. However, the majority supported a government-endorsed plan that would reduce the number of districts to 10 but would first refer the measure to the constitutional court for a ruling on its legality. The move to refer the measure to court was seen as a delaying tactic, since court action could take months or years, giving the government what critics said was an advantage through alleged vote-buying in the next election. The delay would also allow the government to maintain the 25 districts while demonstrating it had attempted to change the system, observers said. Prior to the vote, 29 opposition members shocked those in chambers by walking out, leaving the "stunned" cabinet members behind until an opposition crowd outside the chambers jeered them into leaving as well. In an unprecedented move, the 29 opposition members demanded that they be allowed to question the prime minister about the proposed electoral law changes. The next day, with the reformists boycotting, the assembly voted 33–1 to send the controversial measure to the court. A week later, on May 21, 2006, the emir dissolved the assembly and called for parliamentary elections on June 29, a year ahead of schedule. Liberal reformists, campaigning on an anti-corruption platform, and Islamists reportedly won a total of 33 seats, with the support of many women's groups participating for the first time in elections. On July 17 parliament approved the redrawing of 25 electoral districts to create 5 larger ones, making it difficult for vote buying to influence elections, according to observers. The electoral revisions were hailed as a victory by advocates of democratic reforms.

Accusations of improprieties continued to fuel political tensions in July 2006, resulting in the dismissal of the energy minister, who was accused of tampering with the parliamentary elections. In December the minister of information resigned in the wake of charges that he tried to restrict media freedom and failed to cooperate with parliament. The full cabinet resigned on March 4, 2007, reportedly to avoid a planned no-confidence vote in the assembly against the health minister, who is a member of the royal family. The emir named a new government on March 25, retaining his nephew, Sheik Nasser Muhammad al-Ahmad al-Sabah, as prime minister, and putting ruling family members in the key ministries of defense, foreign affairs, interior, and oil. The oil minister, who was accused of financial irregularities, resigned in June, and the health minister resigned in August. Tensions continued to escalate between the cabinet and the National Assembly, the ministers blaming the powerful legislature for its "disabling" interference in government. Following a cabinet reshuffle in October, the newly appointed oil minister resigned within weeks, and further political turmoil ensued as ministers continued to battle the assembly over social welfare policies.

The political situation was exacerbated when, in events unusual in Kuwait, a rift developed between the Shiite minority and the ruling Sunni majority. Tensions increased significantly after two Shiite lawmakers delivered a eulogy in February 2008 for a slain Lebanese Hezbollah leader who had been killed by a car bomb in Syria. Kuwait claimed that the slain man was a terrorist who had killed Kuwaitis during a 1988 hijacking. Reports surfaced in early March of the arrests of other Shiite members of parliament and at least one political activist. Meanwhile, the cabinet, which sought to contain benefits to Kuwaiti citizens in its efforts to diversify the oil-rich economy, continued to clash with opposition lawmakers. Subsequently, the entire cabinet resigned in March after a dispute with parliament over additional pay increases for civil servants, the cabinet having already approved a significant monthly raise. Two days later the emir dissolved parliament and called for new elections on May 17, 2008.

Economic and social issues dominated the 2008 elections, in which Islamists maintained their hold on the National Assembly, winning slightly less than half of the total seats, with the Islamic Salafi Alliance gaining the most with ten seats. Shiite candidates won 5 seats, 1 more than in the previous election. Despite the frustration of women candidates' failing to win a seat, two women were named to the new cabinet, again headed by Sheik Nasser al-Sabah. On June 1 two Islamist members of parliament walked out in protest of the two women cabinet ministers who sit in parliament, because the women were not wearing headscarves. The new cabinet included representatives from the four major tribes, two Shiite ministers, and one liberal minister. Four ministers from the ruling family retained their posts. The entire cabinet resigned on November 25, under pressure from the assembly, in order to prevent lawmakers from questioning the prime minister about his alleged mismanagement of the government and his decision to allow a controversial Iranian Shiite Muslim cleric to enter Kuwait despite a legal ban. The assembly wanted to vote on the matter but was preempted by the government's resignation, which the emir accepted. News reports said the resignation also "cast doubt" on a government plan to shore up the stock market in the wake of demonstrations by local investors who had lost money, their protests prompting the government to temporarily close the exchange.

Further accusations against the prime minister led the government to resign on March 16, 2009, again derailing legislators' efforts to question the prime minister, primarily about what the Islamists alleged was misuse of public funds. Parliamentary debate had stalled a proposed stimulus package, which had the backing of the cabinet and the ruling family. The emir subsequently dissolved the assembly on March 18 and scheduled early elections for May 16. Ten days following the dissolution of parliament, and thus absent official opposition, the government approved by "a decree of urgency" a $5.2 billion stimulus package.

In the run-up to the 2009 election, two members of parliament were arrested after they publicly criticized the ruling family. Meanwhile, fundamentalists called for women to boycott the election. Of the 210 candidates vying for 50 seats, 16 were women, and for the first time in the country's history, women were elected, securing 4 seats. Meanwhile, Sunnis lost more than half of their representation, winning only 11 seats, while liberals and independents made noteworthy gains. Observers noted, however, that Islamists were still able to form a significant parliamentary bloc in alliance with tribal members. On May 20 the emir asked Prime Minister Nasser al-Sabah to form a new government, surprising some observers who had suggested he would be replaced as a result of the dispute with parliament that had prompted the snap election.

POLITICAL PARTIES

Although political parties are not legal in Kuwait, a number of political "groupings," many of them loosely organized, have been permitted to function in public without restriction. More candidates in the 2003 National Assembly balloting were identifiable as supported by several of the groupings below. The government in mid-2004 acknowledged that political parties are likely to fully develop at some point, but no specific encouragement appears forthcoming.

Prior to the 2006 elections several opposition groups and independents reportedly participated in a loose alliance named Kuwait Rally. Among those in the alliance were the ICM, the KDF, and others described as fundamentalists.

In advance of the 2009 parliamentary elections, a group of former legislators led by a veteran opposition member of parliament, Ahmad al-SAADUN, participated as the Popular Bloc, also referenced as the Popular Action Bloc. Other groups that participated included the two Shiite alliances, the National Islamic Alliance and the Justice and Peace Alliance, led by Hassan NASEER.

Islamic Constitutional Movement (ICM). A moderate Sunni Muslim organization with reported ties to the Muslim Brotherhood in other Arab states such as Egypt and Jordan, the ICM has called for the "adjustment" of all Kuwaiti legislation so as not to "conflict" with sharia (Islamic religious law). In conjunction with the Kuwaiti Democratic Forum (KDF, below), the ICM led the prodemocracy movement that developed in Kuwait following the expulsion of Iraqi troops in early 1991, with a call for new assembly elections and formation of a more representative cabinet. However, ICM leaders subsequently stressed that they sought "small steps, not jumps" in liberalization and did not question the authority of the royal family. Several ICM members were victorious in the 1992 and 1996 assembly balloting, but lost seats in the 2003 election.

In May 2006 the ICM reportedly dismissed leader Ismail al-SHATTI after he reportedly refused to resign as transport minister following his pro-government vote to sending a draft electoral law to the constitutional court (see Current issues, above). The ICM opposed the move, along with thousands of Kuwaitis who protested in front of the National Assembly in late May.

The ICM increased its representation from two seats in 2003 to six seats in 2006, a change attributed to the group's broad support among women. In July 2006 al-Shatti was named minister of state for cabinet affairs, and in October he was also referenced as a deputy prime minister, in addition to his other portfolio. ICM spokesperson Muhammad Abdullah Hadi al-Olaim was named to the cabinet in the March 2007 reshuffle. The group lost three seats in the 2008 legislative elections, but al-Olaim retained his key cabinet posts in oil, electricity, and water. Al-Olaim was replaced in February 2009, and the ICM won only one seat in the May legislative election.

Leaders: Sheikh Jasim Muhalhal al-YASIM, Muhammad Abdullah Hadi al-OLAIM (Spokesperson), Nasir al-SANI, Badr al-NASHI (Secretary General).

Kuwaiti Democratic Forum (KDF). The secularist, center-left KDF was initially described as the best organized of Kuwait's political groupings, with a membership based primarily in urban areas. Several KDF leaders (including "veteran leftist" Ahmad al-Khatib), who had been instrumental in the growth of the prodemocracy movement following the Gulf crisis, were elected to the assembly in October 1992, where they aligned with Islamic representatives in a campaign to make the royal family "more accountable." However, Khatib did not run for reelection in 1996.

KDF leader Abdallah Nibari, described as a "leading liberal member of the opposition" in the assembly, was wounded in an apparent assassination attempt in June 1997. Nibari had been critical of the government's handling of recent large military contracts, contending "middlemen" were being exorbitantly enriched by the process. KDF lost its parliamentary representation in the 2003 assembly balloting when Abdallah Nibari lost his seat. The group participated in the 2009 parliamentary election but did not win any seats.

Leaders: Ahmad al-KHATIB, Abdallah NIBARI.

Islamic Salafi Alliance (ISA). This hard-line Sunni group appears to have replaced the Islamic Popular Group (IPG) among the major Sunni Muslim organizations. The so-called scientific Salafis also fall under this umbrella and are known as the Salafi Movement. It advocates social reform and a return to "true Islam." The Salafi gained some seats in the 2003 assembly balloting. The group conducted a public campaign in 2005 in an effort to thwart the government's restoration of voting rights to women. In 2006 the group supported the proposed reduction in the number of electoral districts and reportedly won two seats in the assembly. In the 2008 assembly elections the ISA was reported to have won ten seats. In the 2009 election the group won two seats.

Leader: Khalid al-ISSA.

Islamic National Alliance (INA). The INA, whose leader was elected to the assembly in October 1992, represents Kuwaiti Shiites. The INA reportedly derived from the Cultural Social Society (*Jamiyat al-Thaqafah al-Ijtimayah*), established by forces loyal to the Iranian revolution of 1979. However, Shiite pressure has been described as less severe on the Kuwaiti government than on other neighboring regimes (such as the one in Bahrain) in part because some Shiite leaders in Kuwait are participating in the political process while others remain wealthy supporters of the ruling family.

Following episodes of vandalism against Sunni bookstores in January 2008, the ISA publicly condemned the attacks and urged Shiites and Sunnis to present a united front against attempts to stir up sectarian violence. The group won one seat in the 2009 election.

Leader: Adnan Sayid Abd al-Samad Sayid ZAHIR.

Nation Party (*Hizb Al-Ummah*). This group was formed on January 29, 2005, by former Salafists "to promote pluralism and a multiparty system of government" and is described as the first true political party ever formed in Kuwait. The group has called for the removal of foreign troops from Kuwait. Since the constitution and Kuwaiti laws do not provide for the establishment of political parties, the government has not been quite sure how to deal with the group. The founders of the group were called in for questioning by police at the end of January "for violating the public gatherings law," according to a party official. In February the government imposed a travel ban on all 15 party members. All 15 members were acquitted of the public gatherings violations in May, although party official Hakim al-Mutairi was fined for circulating publications without proper authorization. Three party members said they would run in the 2006 assembly elections, though leaders said the party would boycott the elections, alleging the elections would be fraudulent. In May 2006 the party announced its backing of full political rights for women, becoming the first Sunni Muslim group to do so.

A proposal for a draft law permitting the establishment of political parties in Kuwait received the backing of party leaders in July 2007. The party participated in the 2008 parliamentary elections but did not win any seats.

The party boycotted the 2009 parliamentary elections, citing lack of progress in political reforms.

Leaders: Dr. Mohammed al-HADRAN, Hakim al-MUTAIRI, Self al-HAJIRI, Fayssal al-HAMAD (Secretary General).

National Democratic Movement (NDM). Launched in May 1997 by some 75 founding members (reportedly including national legislators and cabinet ministers), the NDM announced it would pursue broader "personal freedoms" for Kuwaitis as well as new legislation designed to give the assembly a greater role in overseeing government contracts. A number of NDM members were elected in the 2003 assembly balloting.

Leaders: Ahmad BISHARA, Khaled al-MUTAIRI.

Other groups include the **Justice and Development Movement**, founded by young political activists in 2005 under the leadership of Nasser Yousouf al-ABDALI to promote democracy and tribal confederations. Following the 2009 legislative elections, al-Abdali protested alleged voting irregularities, along with members of the KDF and the Nation Party.

LEGISLATURE

A **National Assembly** (*Majlis al-Ummah*) was organized in 1963 to share legislative authority with the emir, although it was dissolved by decree of the ruler from August 1976 to February 1981 and from July 1986 to October 1992. Under the 1962 basic law, the assembly encompasses 50 representatives (originally, 2 each from 25 constituencies) elected for four-year terms, in addition to ministers who, if not elected members, serve ex officio. Only literate, adult, native-born males over 21 years old whose families have resided in Kuwait since 1920 have been allowed to vote, although as of 2005 women have been allowed to participate as candidates and voters in assembly elections. Under a new election law adopted in 2006, 10 representatives are chosen from each of 5 constituencies.

Balloting for the most recent assembly was conducted on May 16, 2009. In a field of 210 candidates, 16 of them women, independents won 21 seats; Sunni Islamists, 13; liberals, 7; Shiite Islamists, 6; and the Popular Bloc, 3. Four women were elected.

Speaker: Jassim al-KHURAFI.

CABINET

[as of June 1, 2009]

Prime Minister	Sheikh Nasser al-Muhammad al-Ahmad al-Sabah
First Deputy Prime Minister	Sheikh Jabir Mubarak al-Hamad al-Sabah
Deputy Prime Minister	Sheikh Muhammad Sabah al Salim al-Sabah
Deputy Prime Minister for Legal Affairs	Rashed Abdul Mohsen al-Hammad
Deputy Prime Minister for Economic Affairs	Sheikh Ahmad Fahad al-Amad al-Jair al-Sabah
Ministers	
Awqaf and Islamic Affairs	Rashed Abdul Mohsen al-Hammad
Commerce and Industry	Ahmad Rashed al-Haroun
Communications	Muhammad Mohsen al-Busairi
Defense	Sheikh Jabir Mubarak al-Hamad al-Sabah
Education and Higher Education	Mudhi Abdulaziz al-Homoud [f]
Electricity and Water	Bader Shebib al-Shuraiaan
Finance	Mustafa Jasim al-Shimali
Foreign Affairs	Sheikh Muhammad Sabah al-Salim al-Sabah
Health	Hilal Musaed al-Sayer
Information	Sheikh Ahmad Abdullah al-Ahmad al-Sabah
Interior	Lt. Gen. Sheikh Jabir Khalid al-Jabir al-Sabah
Justice	Rashed Abdul Mohsen al-Hammad
Oil	Sheikh Ahmad Abdullah al-Ahmad al-Sabah
Public Works and Municipalities	Fadhel Safar Ali Safar
Social Affairs and Labor	Muhammad Mohsen al-Ifasi
Ministers of State	
Cabinet Affairs	Roudhan Abdul Aziz al-Roudhan
Housing and Administrative Development	Sheikh Ahmad Fahad al-Amad al-Jair al-Sabah
Municipal Affairs	Fadhel Safar Ali Safar
National Assembly Affairs	Muhammad Mohsen al-Busairi

[f] = female

COMMUNICATIONS

The emir suspended constitutional guarantees of freedom of the press on August 29, 1976. Following the National Assembly election of 1981, censorship was relaxed, permitting the reemergence of what the *New York Times* called "some of the most free, and freewheeling, newspapers in the region." However, in conjunction with the dissolution of the assembly in July 1986 the government imposed new press restrictions, subjecting periodicals to prior censorship and announcing it would suspend any newspapers or magazines printing material "against the national interest." The government also continued its drive to bring more Kuwaitis into the news media and deported an estimated 40 journalists from other Arab countries to open jobs for nationals.

In January 1992 the government lifted the 1986 censorship codes in conjunction with an agreement by the major press groups to self-monitor the content of their publications, and the press was subsequently described as having returned to the vitality and relative openness of the early 1980s, with direct criticism of the emir remaining as the only proscription.

In May 2006 the parliament approved a new press law that prohibits the arrest or detainment of journalists unless there is a Supreme Court verdict making such action necessary. The law also allows citizens whose application for a publishing license is rejected to sue the government. In addition, the law forbids jailing journalists unless they criticize the emir, threaten to overthrow the government, or commit religious offenses. The changes, approved unanimously after strenuous debate, reverse provisions of a 1961 press law. Despite the new law, most publications reportedly continued to refrain from publishing articles critical of the government out of fear of reprisals.

In 2007 the editor of *al-Watan* and one of the paper's reporters were fined for allegedly publishing an article about a corrupt judge. Also, three cases were brought against the weekly *al-Shaab* for allegedly printing political articles (its license restricts it to stories on arts and culture), according to the watchdog Reporters Without Borders. In 2008 the government rescinded the licenses of *al-Shaab* and *al-Abraj* and fined the editors. The former was again accused of printing political material, and the latter was accused of defaming the prime minister.

Press. The following dailies (in Arabic, unless otherwise noted) are published in Kuwait City: *al-Anba* (The News, 107,000); *Rai al-Amm* (Voice of the People, 87,000, published in Shuwaikh); *al-Qabas* (Firebrand, 80,000); *al-Siyasah* (Policy, 80,000); *al-Watan* (Homeland, 60,000); *Kuwait Times* (28,000), in English; *Arab Times* (42,000), in English; and *al-Jamahir* (83,000). A weekly, *al-Risalah* (The Message), is published in Shuwaikh. During the 1990–1991 Iraqi occupation a number of clandestine newsletters were issued on an irregular basis, including one that was converted at liberation into a full-fledged tabloid, *26th of February,* with a circulation of 30,000; however, the paper suspended publication in March 1991 because it lacked a government license.

News agencies. The domestic facility is the Kuwait News Agency—KUNA (*Wakalat al-Anba al-Kuwayt*); in addition, numerous foreign agencies maintain bureaus in Kuwait City.

Broadcasting and computing. The Radio of the State of Kuwait and Kuwait Television (*Tilifiziyun al-Kuwayt*) are both controlled by the government. In November 2002 Kuwait closed the office of *al-Jazira* satellite television station, which broadcasts from Qatar, officially for "security reasons," though it also reportedly accused the station of lacking objectivity. In May 2005 the station was allowed to resume broadcasts. As of 2008 there were 342.6 Internet users per 1,000 inhabitants.

INTERGOVERNMENTAL REPRESENTATION

Ambassador to the U.S.: Shaikh Salem Abdullah al-Jaber al-SABAH.

U.S. Ambassador to Kuwait: Deborah K. JONES.

Permanent Representative to the UN: Abdullah Ahmed Mohamed al-MURAD.

IGO Memberships (Non-UN): AfDB, AFESD, AMF, BADEA, BDEAC, CAEU, GCC, IDB, Interpol, LAS, NAM, OAPEC, OIC, OPEC, PCA, WCO, WTO.

KYRGYZSTAN

Kyrgyz Republic
Respublika Kirgizstan (Russian)
Kyrgyz Respublikasy (Kyrgyz)

Political Status: Designated autonomous republic of the Russian Soviet Federative Socialist Republic on February 1, 1926; became constituent republic of the Union of Soviet Socialist Republics (USSR) on December 5, 1936; Republic of Kyrgyzstan proclaimed December 13, 1990; independence from the USSR declared by the Kyrgyz Supreme Soviet August 31, 1991; new constitution introduced on May 5, 1993; current edition of constitution approved by referendum on October 21, 2007.

Area: 76,640 sq. mi. (198,500 sq. km.).

Population: 4,822,938 (1999C); 5,294,000 (2008E).

Major Urban Center (2005E): BISHKEK (formerly Frunze, 851,000).

Official Languages: Kyrgyz, Russian. Kyrgyz is the "state language."

Monetary Unit: Som (official rate December 1, 2009: 43.94 soms = $1US).

President: Kurmanbek BAKIYEV; named acting president and acting prime minister by the bicameral Supreme Council on March 24, 2005, succeeding, Askar A. AKAYEV, who had fled the country earlier the same day and whose formal resignation was accepted by the Supreme Council on April 11; elected president on July 10 and sworn in on August 14 for a five-year term; reelected to a second term in early voting on July 23, 2009, and sworn in on August 2.

Prime Minister: Igor CHUDINOV (*Ak Zhol*); appointed prime minister by Supreme Council on December 24, 2007, succeeding Acting Prime Minister Iskenderbek AIDARALIYEV (nonparty), who had replaced Almazbek ATAMBAYEV (Social Democratic Party of Kyrgyzstan) after his resignation on November 28.

THE COUNTRY

A mountainous country in eastern Central Asia, Kyrgyzstan is bounded on the northwest by Kazakhstan, on the east by China, on the south by Tajikistan, and on the southwest by Uzbekistan. Approximately 65 percent of the population is Turkic-speaking Kyrgyz, 14 percent Uzbek, and 13 percent Russian, with substantially smaller minorities of other ethnic groups; the dominant religion is Sunni Islam. Women make up about 42 percent of the labor force and 26 percent of the current national legislature.

The agricultural sector, which accounts for about 32 percent of GDP and employs 36 percent of the workforce, is now dominated by wheat production. Production of sugar beets, potatoes, and vegetables has also expanded since independence, while livestock and wool output have dropped significantly. Industry contributes about 20 percent of GDP and employs 19 percent of workers. In 1997 production began at the Kumtor gold mine, which ranks among the ten largest in the world. Other extractable resources include natural gas, petroleum, coal, lead, tungsten, mercury, and uranium. Manufacturing focuses on food processing, metallurgy, clothing and other textiles, and machine building. In addition to gold, leading exports include textiles, metals, mineral products, food products, and machinery. Hydroelectricity is sold primarily to neighboring Kazakhstan and Uzbekistan.

Kyrgyzstan experienced a major economic disruption upon the breakup of the Soviet Union in 1991, as Kyrgystan introduced one of the more aggressive restructuring and liberalization programs among the former Soviet republics. The country suffered a 51 percent contraction in GDP from 1991 to 1995, with inflation soaring to more than 1,300 percent in 1993. Agro-industry was particularly hard hit, experiencing a 90 percent decline in the production of most commodities. Beginning in 1995, however, overall economic growth resumed, and by 1998 the government had privatized the majority of state enterprises, restructured the financial industry, and introduced a liberal trade and capital exchange regime.

Following a slowdown triggered largely by the Russian financial crisis of 1998, growth averaged over 5 percent annually in 2000–2001. In part because of a temporary reduction in gold extraction, 2002 saw no growth, but in 2003 and again in 2004 GDP expanded by 7 percent. The economy contracted by 0.2 percent in 2005 but grew by about 3 percent in 2006, 8.5 percent in 2007, and 7.6 percent in 2008, as gold production recovered. At the same time, however, soaring prices for imported commodities fueled inflation that reached 25 percent for that year. The international financial crisis and recession that extended into 2009 compounded Kyrgystan's economic difficulty by reducing both trade and remittances from workers abroad, leading the International Monetary Fund (IMF) to project that growth for the year would not exceed 1 percent. Simultaneously, difficulties in the energy and power sector, including a water shortage, have hindered hydroelectric production. Policy for further economic growth is partly based on the development of Kyrgyzstan's hydrocarbon reserves, in conjunction with Russia's natural gas monopoly, Gazprom.

GOVERNMENT AND POLITICS

Political background. Conquered by Russia between 1855 and 1876, the territory then called Kyrgyzia mounted an unsuccessful revolt against Bolshevik rule before being incorporated into the Russian Soviet Federative Socialist Republic as an autonomous *oblast* (region) in 1924. It was designated an autonomous republic in 1926 and a constituent republic of the Soviet Union in 1936.

As Soviet discipline began to weaken in the late 1980s, Kyrgyzstan became the scene of Central Asia's worst pre-independence ethnic violence, with at least 300 people killed in Kyrgyz-Uzbek clashes in mid-1990. The "Soviet Socialist" component of the republic's name was formally abandoned in December 1990. Independence from the Soviet Union was declared on August 31, 1991, by the Kyrgyz Supreme Soviet, following the failed coup against Soviet president Mikhail Gorbachev in Moscow and a collateral attempt by Soviet authorities to remove the Kyrgyz executive president, Askar AKAYEV.

On October 28, 1990, the Supreme Soviet had elected Akayev from a field of six candidates to the newly created post of president, and on October 12, 1991, he was popularly elected to a five-year presidential term with Feliks KULOV as his running mate. On January 22, 1991, Nasirdin ISANOV, theretofore vice president, had been named head of the cabinet (de facto prime minister). Following Isanov's death in an automobile accident on November 29, Tursunbek CHYNGYSHEV was designated his successor.

On December 10, 1993, Vice President Kulov resigned after being accused of complicity in a scheme to embezzle the country's gold reserves. The Chyngyshev government lost a legislative confidence vote over the same issue three days later, with Apas JUMAGULOV being confirmed as head of a new administration on December 17.

On January 30, 1994, voters overwhelmingly backed an economic reform program advanced by President Akayev, but undiminished opposition by former Communists led the president's supporters to threaten a legislative boycott. In September the Jumagulov government resigned but continued in a caretaker capacity.

In another referendum on October 22, 1994, a large majority of voters approved the abolition of the existing legislature and the creation

of a much smaller bicameral body. Elections on February 5 and 19, 1995, were contested by over 1,000 candidates, many of them independents but some representing 12 political parties. The voting was largely along clan/ethnic lines, with most of the new deputies being conservative-minded survivors of the Communist-era bureaucracy.

The reappointment of Jumagulov as prime minister on April 5, 1995, signaled President Akayev's intention to pursue his reform program. When conservative elements in the legislature succeeded in September in blocking the president's request for an extension of his mandate to 2001, he called an early presidential election for December 24 and registered a commanding 71.6 percent victory over two other candidates. Moreover, in a referendum on February 10, 1996, Akayev secured 94 percent endorsement for constitutional amendments that substantially increased presidential powers and abolished the post of vice president (which had remained vacant since December 1993). Having submitted his resignation following the referendum, Jumagulov was again reappointed prime minister on March 4.

On March 24, 1998, Prime Minister Jumagulov resigned, ostensibly for health reasons, and he was succeeded the following day by Kubanychbek JUMALIEV, previously head of presidential administration. On September 3, faced with what he labeled foot-dragging by the conservative Supreme Council on key legislation, such as legalization of private land ownership, President Akayev announced a referendum to restructure the bicameral legislature and reduce its authority in several areas, including budget deliberations. On October 17 some 90 percent of those voting assented.

On December 23, 1998, with the som having depreciated significantly because of the recent Russian economic crisis and Moscow's devaluation of the ruble, the Jumaliev government resigned at the president's request. Two days later Jumabek IBRAIMOV, chair of the State Property Fund, succeeded Jumaliev. Ibraimov died on April 4, 1999, however, and was succeeded on an acting basis on April 12 by former deputy prime minister Amangeldy MURALIYEV, who had been serving as governor of the Osh *oblast*. Muraliyev was confirmed as prime minister on April 21.

On November 12, 1999, President Akayev announced first-round parliamentary elections for February 20, 2000. The conduct of the balloting drew wide criticism from international observers and the opposition, however, not least because the Central Electoral Commission (CEC) had disqualified several opposition party lists on technicalities. One of the principal antigovernment leaders, former vice president Feliks Kulov of the recently organized Dignity (*Ar-Namys*) party, lost under highly questionable circumstances at runoff balloting on March 12, and ten days later authorities arrested him for offenses allegedly committed during his 1997–1998 tenure as minister of national security.

A military court acquitted Kulov on August 7, 2000, but the verdict was annulled by a higher court on September 11. Although widely considered a leading opposition candidate in the presidential election scheduled for October 29, Kulov later refused to take a mandatory Kyrgyz language proficiency test and was therefore disqualified, leaving Socialist Party "Fatherland" (*Ata-Meken*) candidate Omurbek TEKEBAYEV as President Akayev's principal opponent. At the election Akayev won 75 percent of the vote against five challengers; Tekebayev finished second, with 14 percent.

Following President Akayev's inauguration on December 9, 2000, the Muraliyev cabinet resigned, as required by the constitution, and on December 21 Kurmanbek BAKIYEV, theretofore a southern regional governor, was named as prime minister.

On January 22, 2001, the retrial of Feliks Kulov concluded with another guilty verdict, followed by imposition of a seven-year prison sentence. On March 26 Kulov appealed the decision to the Supreme Court, which upheld his conviction and sentence on July 19.

In January 2002 the government arrested Azimbek BEKNAZAROV, an outspoken legislator from the south and a critic of a 1999 Sino-Kyrgyz treaty that had ceded territory to China (see Foreign relations, below). During his trial on charges of having abused his authority while chairing an investigative committee, many of Beknazarov's southern supporters took to the streets, and at a demonstration held March 17–18 in Jalal-Abad's district of Aksy, security forces killed five demonstrators. Although convicted in May and given a short sentence, Beknazarov received amnesty under a bill passed in June. (In December a military court convicted two prosecutors and two interior department officials of offenses related to the Aksy incident, but the convictions were subsequently overturned.)

On May 22, 2002, in the midst of antigovernment protests that condemned not only the prosecution of Beknazarov but also ratification of the border treaty and the government's mishandling of the March demonstrations, Prime Minister Bakiyev and his cabinet resigned. President Akayev immediately appointed Nikolay TANAYEV, first deputy prime minister under Bakiyev, as acting prime minister. Tanayev was confirmed in the post in a permanent capacity on May 30.

On February 2, 2003, three-fourths of those voting approved a constitutional referendum that had been called by the president less than a month before. The changes returned the national legislature to a unicameral Supreme Council, effective as of the election scheduled for 2005, and also called for eliminating all party list (proportional) seats. In a separate question that asked whether Akayev should remain in office until the expiration of his term in late 2005, 79 percent gave him a vote of confidence, despite the previous year's turmoil.

At the election for the new 75-member Supreme Council on February 27 and March 13, 2005, only 6 seats went to members of the opposition, many of whom had been excluded from competing on technical grounds. The release of preliminary results quickly led to peaceful protests, beginning in Osh and Jalal-Abad and spreading elsewhere in the south. On March 21, however, the southern demonstrations turned violent, and protesters began assembling in Bishkek. On March 24 a crowd estimated at 5,000 marched on government offices, looters took to the streets, and President Akayev and his immediate family fled to Russia. On the same day, protesters freed Feliks Kulov from prison and the outgoing bicameral legislature named former prime minister Bakiyev, leader of the multiparty opposition People's Movement of Kyrgyzstan (PMK), as acting president and acting prime minister. On March 25 Bakiyev appointed a new cabinet that included Kulov as minister of security, although Kulov resigned only five days later. Meanwhile, the issue of legislative legitimacy had been resolved in favor of the newly elected Supreme Council. Both houses of the bicameral legislature therefore dissolved themselves on March 28–29.

On April 4, 2005, Askar Akayev, from Moscow, tendered his resignation, which the Supreme Council accepted on April 11. In a presidential election on July 10 Bakiyev won 89.5 percent of the vote against the national ombudsman, Tursunbay BAKIR-UULU, and four other candidates. Kulov, having been appointed first deputy prime minister on May 16, had withdrawn as a presidential candidate after receiving assurances that he would be named to head the next cabinet. Appointed acting prime minister on August 15, Kulov won parliamentary confirmation as prime minister on September 1, although in late September the legislature rejected several ministerial nominees put forward by the

Bakiyev-Kulov "tandem." The completed cabinet was finally sworn in on December 20.

Relations between the Bakiyev-Kulov government and the Supreme Council were often antagonistic in the following months, and in early May 2006 the cabinet members submitted their resignations en masse (except for Kulov, who had been urged not to by his colleagues) in response to legislative criticism of most ministers' individual performances. President Bakiyev rejected the resignations but on May 10, bowing to the demands of a growing opposition, announced a number of key changes, including new deputy prime ministers (one of whom was ultimately rejected by the legislature), a new head of presidential administration, and a new chief of the National Security Service.

In April 2006 many key opposition leaders formed the For Reforms (*Za Reformy*) movement in an effort to pressure the government to adopt constitutional reforms that had been promoted during the "Tulip Revolution" of March 2005. In the first week of November street demonstrations in Bishkek succeeded in pressuring Bakiyev and the legislators to approve constitutional changes that reduced the president's powers and called for election of a new 90-seat legislature in which half the seats would be proportionally elected and in which the party with the greatest representation would name the next prime minister.

On December 19, 2006, the Kulov government resigned, reportedly to speed up the holding of a new legislative election. Instead, the resignation threatened to generate a constitutional crisis because no party held sufficient seats in the Supreme Council to name a new prime minister. President Bakiyev responded by threatening to dissolve the legislature unless it restored a number of presidential powers, including designation of a prime minister. On December 30, on a temporary basis, the Supreme Council did as requested. Bakiyev signed the changes into law on January 15, 2007, and quickly named Kulov to form a new administration, but the Supreme Council rejected his selection on January 18 and again on January 25.

On January 29, 2007, Bakiyev named the acting minister of agriculture, Azim ISABEKOV, prime minister, and the legislature concurred. Isabekov's tenure was short, however, and he resigned on March 29 after Bakiyev rejected his decision to fire a number of ministers as a gesture to the opposition. The following day, Bakiyev named opposition moderate Almazbek ATAMBAYEV of the Social Democratic Party of Kyrgyzstan (*Partiya Sotsialdemokraticheskaya Kyrgyzstana*—PSDK) to head a reshuffled cabinet that won approval on April 10.

With the Constitutional Court having ruled on September 17, 2007, that the constitutional changes of November and December 2006 were unconstitutional as they had not been approved by referendum, President Bakiyev called a referendum on further changes (see Constitution and government, below). On October 21, the new edition of the constitution and accompanying changes to the electoral law both officially won 77 percent approval, although there were numerous allegations of polling irregularities. The next day, before promulgating the package of amendments, President Bakiyev dissolved the Supreme Council—a power revoked in the new edition of the constitution. On October 24 the cabinet resigned, as required by the constitution, and parliamentary elections were scheduled for December 16.

Initially, the Atambayev government remained in place pending the election; however, Atambayev resigned on November 18, 2007, after criticizing President Bakiyev and was replaced as acting prime minister by Iskenderbek AIDARALIYEV, then the first deputy prime minister. The resignation was prompted by the perception that Bakiyev was attempting to control both the executive and legislative branches through his part in establishing a new presidential "True Path" Popular Party (*Ak Zhol*) before calling the constitutional referendum.

Both the referendum on the changes to the constitution and the December 2007 elections proved controversial, with the Organization for Security and Cooperation in Europe (OSCE), which monitored the polls, declaring that the elections "failed to meet a number of OSCE standards." Only three parties were elected to the enlarged Supreme Council, with *Ak Zhol* winning 71 of the 90 seats. The only opposition party to win seats was the PSDK, with 11. Vote rigging was claimed by other leading opposition parties, including *Ata-Meken,* which finished second in the vote count (8.7 percent) but failed to meet a regional threshold requirement and was therefore denied seats. In its first session, the new legislature elected Igor CHUDINOV (*Ak Zhol*) as prime minister on December 24.

Following a March 2009 ruling by the Constitutional Court that, in accordance with the October 2007 changes to the constitution, a presidential election had to be held before the end of October 2009, the Supreme Council scheduled national voting for July. Six candidates, including the incumbent, appeared on the ballot. Although most of the leading opposition parties, loosely unified in a United People's Movement (UPM) that had been formed the preceding December, collectively agreed to endorse former prime minister Atambayev as their sole candidate, Temir SARIEV, leader of the *Ak Shumkar* (White Falcon) party broke from the group and declared his candidacy. On July 23 President Bakiyev won an easy victory, taking 76.4 percent of the vote. Atambayev withdrew on election day, claiming massive voter fraud, and finished in second place.

Constitution and government. The post of executive president was created by the Supreme Soviet in 1991, although the constitution of the former Communist system was not superseded until May 5, 1993. In approving the 1993 document, the legislature agreed to President Akayev's demand that a provision calling for adherence to the moral values of Islam be dropped; equality of rights and treatment is guaranteed for all ethnic groups.

As amended in 1994, the constitution provided for a bicameral legislature and a popularly elected president, both serving for five-year terms. Amendments approved by referendum in February 1996 and October 1998 tended to strengthen the presidency. Yet another referendum, held February 2, 2003, approved restoration of a unicameral Supreme Council as of 2005 and eliminated party list seats.

The package of constitutional amendments adopted on November 8, 2006, and signed the following day by the president expanded the powers of the legislature at the expense of the president, who, for example, would no longer be able to select the prime minister. Instead, the party commanding the most votes in the council would name the prime minister, subject to presidential approval. The document also called for expanding the council to 90 seats, half to be filled on a proportional basis. In contrast, the amendments approved on December 30, 2006, and signed by the president on January 15, 2007, restored a number of presidential powers, including authority to name the prime minister and other cabinet members. April 2007 saw violent demonstrations opposing the new constitutional reforms and calling for the introduction of a proportional representation system for parliamentary elections. Then, on September 17, 2007, the Constitutional Court threw out the 2006 amendments on the grounds that they should have been submitted to a referendum, which led President Bakiyev to call a referendum on additional changes to the constitution as well as a revised electoral law. Held only a month later, on October 21, the referendum reintroduced party list voting, on the basis of a single national constituency. Electoral reforms also required parties entering the Supreme Council to reach a threshold of 5 percent of national votes and to obtain at least 0.5 percent of the vote in each of the country's seven regions and the cities of Bishkek and Osh. The latter provision effectively eliminates regional parties from representation

The president, who is popularly elected, is limited to two terms in office. He serves as commander-in-chief as well as head of state and has broad powers of appointment. He can also initiate referendums and may call an early legislative election following two no-confidence votes in the government. The prime minister, as head of government, must command a majority in the 90-seat Supreme Council and be approved by the president. The legislature may remove the president from office by a three-fourths vote, may dissolve itself by a two-thirds vote, and may override presidential objections to legislation, by a two-thirds vote in most cases or by a three-fourths vote in certain defined areas.

The judicial structure is headed by a Constitutional Court charged with ensuring the constitutionality of executive and legislative acts, and by a Supreme Court as the highest organ of civil, criminal, and administrative justice. Judges of the local courts are appointed by the president on the proposal of the Judicial Council, and justices of the Supreme and Constitutional courts are elected by parliament after being endorsed by the president and hold their positions until they reach retirement age.

Administratively, Kyrgyzstan comprises seven regions (*dubans* or *oblasts*)—Batken, Chuy, Issyk-Kul, Jalal-Abad, Naryn, Osh, and Talas—plus the city of Bishkek. Local and regional assemblies are directly elected. They in turn elect local executives.

Foreign relations. Kyrgyzstan became a sovereign member of the Commonwealth of Independent States (CIS) on December 21, 1991. It joined the United Nations on March 2, 1992, with admission to the IMF and World Bank following in May and September, respectively. Kyrgyzstan subsequently became a member of the Conference on (later Organization for) Security and Cooperation in Europe (CSCE/OSCE) and, as a predominantly Muslim country, of the Organization of the

Islamic Conference. In June 1994 Kyrgyzstan acceded to NATO's Partnership for Peace program, under which Kyrgyz troops have regularly participated in joint military exercises.

In January 1994 Kyrgyzstan became the third member of the Central Asian Economic Union (CAEU), which had been launched by Kazakhstan and Uzbekistan. In February 1995 the CAEU was given a formal ministerial framework, and its role was extended to cover defense, foreign affairs, and social policy. It also began addressing such regional issues as drug-smuggling, the allocation of scarce water resources, and infrastructural development. In July 1998, with Tajikistan having agreed to join, the CAEU adopted the name Central Asian Economic Community, which then became the Central Asian Cooperation Organization (CACO) in March 2002. In January 2006 the CACO merged into another regional grouping, the six-member Eurasian Economic Community (EAEC) of Belarus, Kazakhstan, Kyrgyzstan, Russia, Tajikistan, and Uzbekistan.

Kyrgyzstan also participated in the six-member CIS Collective Security Treaty (with Armenia, Belarus, Kazakhstan, Russia, and Tajikistan), which in 2001 agreed to base a Collective Rapid Reaction Force in Bishkek; in April 2003 the six treaty members reconfigured their association as the Collective Security Treaty Organization (CSTO).

The formation of the CSTO was largely a response to concerns about Islamic fundamentalism, terrorism, and drug-trafficking in the region. Earlier, in the mid-1990s, China, Kazakhstan, Kyrgyzstan, Russia, and Tajikistan had begun meeting as the so-called "Shanghai Five," which had as its focus border issues, regional stability, and security concerns involving Islamic militancy. In 2001 Uzbekistan joined the grouping, which redesignated itself as the Shanghai Cooperation Organization (SCO), with a formal SCO charter then being signed in 2002. Central Asian summits have repeatedly seen the participants pledge cooperation against terrorism and Islamic extremism.

In Kyrgyzstan, the most serious related incidents occurred in 1999 and 2000. In August 1999 a force numbering in the hundreds took 20 or so hostages in Batken. With assistance from Russia and Kazakhstan, the government launched a counteroffensive that ultimately included bombing runs in Tajikistan, to where the insurgents, who were linked to the Islamic Movement of Uzbekistan (see the Uzbekistan article), had retreated. A negotiated release of the final hostages occurred in October. In August and September 2000 bands of militants, variously numbered from a handful to over 200 according to Kyrgyz officials, reportedly crossed the border from Tajikistan and were met by defense units. Tajik officials denied that the militants had been based in Tajikistan.

In 1999–2000 Uzbekistan began laying land mines along its border with Kyrgyzstan to stop incursions and drug-trafficking. The issue appeared resolved in mid-2004, when Uzbekistan began clearing the mines, which had caused civilian injuries on both sides. Meanwhile, protracted negotiations on delimiting the Uzbek-Kyrgyz border were continuing. Relations were further damaged in 2005 when Kyrgyzstan refused to extradite 29 refugees (out of more than 400) who had fled across the border in May to escape what was widely labeled a massacre of protesters in Uzbekistan's Andizhan region. The definition of this 130 km border is still incomplete, while disputes in Isfara Valley have delayed completion of delineation with Tajikistan. However, Kyrgyzstan did ratify the Kyrgyz-Kazakh border demarcation treaty on April 11, 2008, following promises of increased imports of subsidized oil and wheat, as well as further foreign investment from Kazakhstan.

Economic difficulties and the allocation of natural resources have also repeatedly contributed to tensions among regional states. During 1999, for example, shipment of natural gas from Uzbekistan to Kyrgyzstan was temporarily discontinued for nonpayment; when deliveries resumed, Tashkent unilaterally raised the price. In June 1999 Kyrgyzstan cut off water supplies to Kazakhstan because the latter had failed to deliver coal shipments as payment. In April 2006 representatives of the regional governments met in Berlin, Germany, in a cooperative effort to conclude an agreement on sharing water and hydroelectricity, two of Kyrgyzstan's principal resources. In exchange, Kyrgyzstan reportedly sought more secure supplies of coal, oil, and natural gas from Kazakhstan and Uzbekistan.

In August 1999 President Akayev signed a Sino-Kyrgyz treaty that ceded to China some 360 square miles of territory. Ratification of the treaty by both houses of the Kyrgyz legislature in May 2002 was met with widespread protests. Final demarcation of the border with China was accomplished in 2004.

President Akayev responded to the September 2001 al-Qaida attacks against the United States and the resultant U.S.-led campaign in Afghanistan by declaring Kyrgyzstan to be a "frontline state" in the war against terrorism, drug-trafficking, and Islamic extremism. Having approved U.S. and NATO use of the Manas airport, in September 2003 Kyrgyzstan reached agreement with Moscow on establishing a Russian air base in nearby Kant. Speaking at the latter facility in August 2004, Foreign Minister Askar AITMATOV characterized Russia as Kyrgyzstan's "main strategic partner."

In July 2006 negotiations concluded on continued U.S. use of the Manas facility, establishing an annual rate of $17.5 million, a considerably higher rent than the previous $2.6 million per year. The presence of U.S. and NATO forces remained controversial, however, and on February 19, 2009, the Supreme Council voted 78–2 to deny U.S. access to the facility, which had been handling up 15,000 troops transfers a month in and out of Afghanistan. Less than a month later, the parliament also voted to close Manas to other countries fighting in the U.S.-led coalition. The status of the base nevertheless remained under discussion, and on June 22 Washington and Bishkek concluded a revised agreement under which Manas would function as a "transit center," with the U.S. paying $60 million annually and also committing $36 million to upgrading the air traffic control system and other infrastructure. The Supreme Council ratified the pact on June 30.

Current issues. With the *Ak Zhol* party in full control of the legislature and advancing such policy objectives as the privatization of the energy sector, President Bakiyev appeared to have consolidated control over both the legislative and executive branches following the elections of December 2007 and July 2009. In May 2008 Bakiyev reshuffled several members of his government in appointments that were generally seen as augmenting his power, specifically in the selection of the new defense minister, Bakyt KALIEV. During the same month, in a reportedly premeditated move, the parliamentary speaker Adakhan MADUMAROV resigned and was replaced by Aitibai TAGAEV. Tagaev is reported to be loyal to Bakiyev and lack major political ambitions.

Following the 2007 election, the opposition refused to recognize the legitimacy of the new Supreme Council, with *Ata-Meken* immediately promising "large-scale" protests, accusing the CEC of "falsifying the results" in Osh, and stating that the elections "were conducted dishonestly, with flagrant violations of legislation." Supporters of *Ata-Meken* began a hunger strike protesting the election results, and 20 people were arrested. This initial protest advanced, with the formation on January 21, 2008, of the opposition For Justice Movement (FJM). The FJM proceeded to set up a "Public Parliament" in Bishkek. Then in February, Azimbek BEKNAZAROV, a leader of the opposition Party of National Restoration "Banner" (*"Asaba"*) opposition, announced formation of a Revolutionary Committee. On April 12, both the Revolutionary Committee and the FJM organized a popular gathering in Bishkek, where they presented a resolution demanding new elections, declaring the current parliament illegitimate. The broader UPM was formed in December but failed to dent the Bakiyev government's authority despite repeated accusations of corruption, nepotism, lack of reform, and economic failure. In the six-candidate presidential race, no challenger reached double digits, according to the official results. In addition to the incumbent, Almazbek Atambayev (8.4 percent), and Temir Sariev (6.4 percent), the election was contested by Toktaim UMETALIEVA, chair of the Association of Nongovernmental and Nonprofit Organizations of Kyrgyzstan (1.1 percent); Nurlan MOTUEV, leader of the *Joomart* (The Generous) Movement (0.9 percent); and Jenishbek NAZARALIEV, a physician and member of *Asaba* (0.8 percent).

In January 2009 the chief-of-staff of the presidential administration, Medet SADYRKULOV, resigned and was rumored to be joining the opposition. On March 12 Sadyrkulov died in what was officially labeled a car crash, leading some opposition elements to assert that he had been assassinated for political reasons. Also in March, FJM coordinator Alikbek JEKSHENKULOV was arrested on charges related to financial abuse during his 2005–2007 tenure as foreign minister and to the December 2007 murder of a Turkish national. Insisting on his innocence, Jekshenkulov described the charges as politically motivated. His trial began in June 2009.

During negotiations with the United States over the Manas air base, Kyrgyzstan was also negotiating additional aid from Russia, which in early 2009 offered investment capital of $1.7 for infrastructure projects as well as over $650 million in the form of direct aid, debt cancellation, and low-interest loans. Despite some media speculation abroad that Russia was interested in gaining access to the Manas air base or in using its influence with the Kyrgyz government as a bargaining chip in its own negotiations with the new Barack Obama administration in the

United States, Moscow endorsed the "transit center" agreement concluded in June as necessary to the continuing war against the Taliban in Afghanistan. In August, during a CSTO meeting, Moscow and Bishkek agreed that Russia could base its own small "military contingent" in southern Kyrgyzstan, presumably in Osh or Batken. The facility, which is to include a training center for Kyrgyz as well as Russian personnel and will be associated with the CSTO's Collective Operational Reaction Forces (CORF), is seen as securing access to Russian forces stationed in Tajikistan and as helping to counter the Islamist threat to the region. In addition to its air base in Kant, Russia maintains the Marevo Communications Center of the Russian Navy in the Chu Oblast and a center for testing naval equipment at Lake Issyk-Kul.

POLITICAL PARTIES

The previously dominant Kyrgyz Communist Party withdrew from the Communist Party of the Soviet Union on August 28, 1991, at which time its property within Kyrgyzstan was nationalized and its funds frozen; three days later it was disbanded. From then until the departure of President Akayev in March 2005, party affiliation did not have a significant impact on government leadership, despite the presence of a vocal opposition.

According to the Ministry of Justice, 19 parties were registered in March 1999. An electoral code adopted at that time restricted eligibility for the 2000 legislative elections to parties active for at least 12 months before the balloting. A number of newer parties circumvented the restriction by forming electoral blocs with older parties. A total of 9 parties and 2 blocs offered approved party lists for the February–March 2000 balloting. The principal bloc was the pro-government Union of Democratic Forces (*Soyuz Demokraticheskikh Sil*—SDS), which included among its participants the Social Democratic Party of Kyrgyzstan (PSDK), and former prime minister Amangeldy Muraliyev's Unity Party of Kyrgyzstan (*Birimdik*). The SDS list finished second to the Party of Communists of Kyrgyzstan (PKK) in the proportional vote, attracting a 19 percent share.

In April 2001, 9 opposition parties formed the People's Patriotic Movement. Many of its participants remain active, including Feliks Kulov's *Ar-Namys*, the Communist Party of Kyrgyzstan (CPK), the Freedom Party (*Erkindik*), the New Kyrgyzstan party (then called the Agrarian Labor Party of Kyrgyzstan), the PKK, the Poor Nation Party (*Kairan-El*), and the Socialist Party "Fatherland" (*Ata-Meken*). In August 2002 over 20 opposition parties and nongovernmental organizations announced the formation of a Movement for the Resignation of President Askar Akayev and Reforms for the People.

In January 2004 a number of leading opposition parties—among them *Erkindik, Kairan-El,* the Party of National Restoration "Banner" (*Asaba*), and the Progressive Democratic Party "Free Kyrgyzstan" (ErK)—established an ideologically diverse electoral bloc, For the People's Power (*Za Vlast Narodna*). The alliance subsequently announced that it would support former prime minister Kurmanbek Bakiyev for president in 2005. In September 2004, looking toward the legislative election expected in February 2005, the People's Power parties were joined by both Communist parties (the CPK and PKK) and New Kyrgyzstan in forming a People's Movement of Kyrgyzstan—PMK (*Narodnoe Dvizhenie Kyrgyzstana*), an electoral alliance that pledged to work for free and fair elections. The PMK held a constituent conference in early November, at which time Bakiyev was elected chair of the movement.

Earlier, in May 2004, a Civic Union "For Fair Elections" was announced by *Ar-Namys, Ata-Meken,* the "Poor and Unprotected" People's Party (*Bei Becharalar;* see PSDK, below), and the PSDK. Described as a centrist "third force" positioned between strongly progovernment parties and the regime's most vocal opponents, the grouping designated as its leader Misir ASHURKULOV, an associate of President Akayev who was dismissed as Security Council secretary shortly thereafter. In October 2004, by which time there were at least 40 registered parties, Bakiyev's PMK and For Fair Elections declared that they would join forces. Although the opposition leadership had no expectations that it would win a victory at the February–March 2005 legislative election, the systematic disqualification of opposition candidates, who ended up winning only half a dozen of the 75 seats, directly contributed to the Tulip Revolution of March 24.

By early 2006 the number of registered parties had surpassed 70. The PMK had registered in May 2005 as a bloc that later redefined itself as the Sociopolitical Movement of Kyrgyzstan. Most members, in April 2006, participated in forming the pro-presidential National Forum for Support of Democratic Reforms and Legality, chaired by Tabyldy OROZALIYEV of the recently formed Republican Party of Labor and Unity (see under *Ak Zhol*). The National Forum was initially described as including 13 parties and 20 public movements.

In January 2006 a new People's Coalition of Democratic Forces encompassing 7 parties, 2 blocs, and 9 nongovernmental organizations was established to promote constitutional and social reforms, including the adoption of a parliamentary system of government; among the participants were *Ar-Namys, Ata-Meken, Kairan-El,* My Country (*Moya Strana;* see under *Ak Zhol*), the PKK, and the PSDK. In succeeding months the People's Coalition was increasingly viewed as disenchanted with the Bakiyev-Kulov government, and in April it gave birth to the opposition For Reforms (*Za Reformy*) movement. Following the legislature's rejection in January 2007 of his reappointment as prime minister, Feliks Kulov joined and was subsequently appointed leader of the For Reforms opposition. While For Reforms organized the majority of protests during 2006, it dissolved in March 2007 as leading opposition figures became unwilling to support Kulov, opposing his views on forcing Bakiyev to resign before his term expired. This left a still-divided opposition that included *Ata-Meken*, the newly formed *Ak Shumkar* party, the CPK, Kulov's *Ar-Namys* party, and the short-lived successor to For Reforms, the For One Kyrgyzstan Movement (formed predominantly of *Asaba*, PSDK, and *Kairen El* parties), which ceased activities in September 2007.

Meanwhile, a number of Bakiyev supporters, led by Topchubek TURGUNALIYEV of *Erkindik,* announced a "revival" of the now-defunct PMK through the formation of the For Political Stability and Unity movement. This was then superseded by the formation of the presidential *Ak Zhol* party in October 2007, which absorbed many affiliates of For Political Stability and Unity.

While the number of registered parties increased again in 2007 to 101, only 50 officially indicated their intention to contest the December 16 elections. Of these, 22 applied for registration with the CEC, but 10 failed to meet the requirements, most often because of problems with candidate lists. Three parties—Ak Zhol, the PSDK, and the PKK—met the thresholds for winning parliamentary seats. Although Ata-Meken easily exceeded the 5 percent national threshold, winning 9.3 percent of the vote and finishing second, it failed to win the minimum of 0.5 percent in each region.

In January 2008 some of the leading opposition parties, including *Ak Shumkar, Ata-Meken, and Ar-Namys,* joined other organizations in establishing the **For Justice Movement**—FJM (*Akyikat Ichun*), which named former foreign minister Alikbek Jekshenkulov as its coordinator. A broader **United People's Movement**—UPM (also frequently referred to as the United National Movement or the United Opposition Movement) was formed in December 2008 by a diverse group that included the FJM. It announced on April 20, 2009, that it intended to field a single candidate in the July presidential election. The UPM numbered among its participants *Ak Shumkar, Asaba, Ata-Meken,* the Green Party, the National Democratic Party "Great Unity" (*Uluu Birimdik*), the PSDK, and the United Kyrgyzstan movement, although *Ak Shumkar* was expelled in May following its decision to nominate its chair as a candidate for the presidency. After the election the UPM began discussions on establishing a more unified structure, including its possible but—given the ideological diversity of its participating organizations-unlikely merger into a single party.

In 2008 the legislature set about tightening registration requirements in a deliberate effort to reduce the number of parties. Registration now requires that a party have branches in all regions, Bishkek, and Osh, each with at least 200 members.

Presidential Party:

True Path Popular Party (*Ak Zhol Eldik Partiyasi*). The founding congress of *Ak Zhol* (*Ak Jol;* also translatable as "White Road" and "Bright Path") was held October 15, 2007. The party was in part an outgrowth of a civic movement, For the Constitution, Reform, and Development, that had been organized a month earlier to promote adoption of constitutional revisions. At its founding congress *Ak Zhol* initially named Kurmanbek Bakiyev as its chair, a position he could not hold while serving as president of the republic.

Prior to the December 2007 elections, which it dominated with 47 percent of the vote and 71 parliamentary seats, it absorbed the Republican Party of Labor and Unity (*Emgek Zhana Birimdik*) and My

Country (*Menim Ata-Jurtum/Moya Strana*), along with other parties from the PMK and the For Political Stability and Unity movement, which it superseded. Labor and Unity had been established in August 2005 by key Bakiyev supporters, including the well-known writer Yuruslan TOYCHUBEKOV, who had served as the president's campaign manager, and Kurmanbek TEMIRBAYEV. Often referenced in English as the Party of Action, the center-right My Country party dated from October 1998.

In April 2009 the party expelled one of its deputy chairs, Elmira IBRAIMOVA, for criticizing President Bakiyev, who was unanimously endorsed for reelection on May 1.

Leaders: Avtandil ARABAYEV and Vladimir NIFADYEV (Deputy Chairs), Igor CHUDINOV (Prime Minister).

Major Opposition Parties:

Social Democratic Party of Kyrgyzstan (*Partiya Sotsial-demokraticheskaya Kyrgyzstana*—PSDK). The PSDK was launched in 1993 with the political endorsement of President Akayev. Supporting the government's reformist, promarket line, it won representation in the 1995 legislative elections and was a leading component of the SDS in 2000. Its chair, Almazbek Atambayev, was a 2000 presidential nominee, winning about 6 percent of the vote, for third place.

In October 2004 the PSDK absorbed the "Poor and Unprotected" People's Party (*El Partiyasi "Bei Becharalar"*). Appealing to intellectuals, the disadvantaged, and students, the leftist, reform-minded *Bei Becharalar* had been registered in December 1995. Its leaders had included Daniyar USENOV, who served as first deputy prime minister from mid-2006 until the end of March 2007, and Melis ESHIMKANOV, who had won about 1 percent of the vote in the 2000 presidential election and was later named head of the state-run radio and television.

In the run-up to the 2007 parliamentary election the PSDK faced controversy when the Central Election Commission (CEC) canceled Edil BAYSALOV's registration as a parliamentary candidate. Baysalov had photographed a printed ballot paper and posted it on the Internet during a visit to a polling station in his capacity as a member of the CEC. The CEC then decided to scrap [the 2.7 million ballot papers and ordered the PSDK to pay for new ones. In the election the party finished second, winning 5.8 percent of the vote and 11 seats.

In April 2009 the United People's Movement UPM) selected Atambayev as its presidential candidate. Although he withdrew from the contest on election day, alleging voter fraud, he finished second, winning 8.4 percent of the vote. Following the election, the PSDK and fellow UPM member *Ata-Meken* (below) pursued discussions on a possible merger.

Leaders: Almazbek ATAMBAYEV (Chair and 2009 UPM presidential candidate), Bakyt BESHIMOV (Parliamentary Leader).

Socialist Party "Fatherland" (*Socialisticheskaya Partiya "Ata-Meken"*). The center-left Socialist Party was founded in 1992 by a nationalist faction of the Progressive Democratic Party "Free Kyrgyzstan" (ErK, below). It failed to meet the 5 percent threshold for claiming party list seats in the 2000 Legislative Assembly balloting, although its chair, Omurbek Tekebayev, won election in a single-mandate district and was subsequently elected deputy speaker of the body. Following the disqualification of Feliks Kulov, he was widely considered to be the leading opposition presidential contender for the October 2000 election, at which he finished second, with 14 percent of the vote.

Briefly speaker of the Supreme Council, Tekebayev resigned in February 2006 after criticizing the government's commitment to rapid reform. He was a principal architect of the For Reforms opposition movement that took shape two months later. In the run-up to the December 2007 legislative election, the socialists forged an electoral alliance with *Ak Shumkar.* The alliance was viewed as the opposition's best opportunity to challenge *Ak Zhol*. Despite winning the second largest proportion of the vote, it failed to gain a seat in the new legislature because it did not meet the 0.5 percent threshold in each of the country's regions.

Leaders: Omurbek TEKEBAYEV (Chair), Asiya SASYKBAYEVA.

Ak Shumkar ("White Falcon"). *Ak Shumkar* was organized as an opposition parliamentary faction in April 2007. In late October its leaders forged an electoral alliance with *Ata-Meken* to contest the December parliamentary election, but in the run-up to the 2009 presidential election personal differences between the party's chair, Temir Sariev, and the UPM candidate, Almazbek Atambayev, resulted in *Ak Shumkar*'s decision to nominate Sariev, dividing the opposition. As a consequence, the party was expelled from the UPM. Sariev, a founder and initial cochair of the For Justice Movement (FJM), finished third in the July election, with 6.4 percent of the vote.

Leader: Temir SARIEV (Chair and 2009 presidential candidate).

Ar-Namys ("Dignity" or "Honor"). *Ar-Namys* was organized in July 1999 by one of Kyrgyzstan's leading oppositionists, former vice president Feliks Kulov, who had resigned as Bishkek mayor in April to protest corruption and antidemocratic tendencies in the Akayev administration. The party quickly emerged as one of Kyrgyzstan's largest.

Because *Ar-Namys* had not existed long enough to offer its own party list for the February 2000 election, it attempted to qualify by joining with the Democratic Movement of Kyrgyzstan (*Demokraticheskoye Dvizhenie Kyrgystana*—DDK), which put Kulov at the head of its list. (Founded in 1990, the DDK initially served as an umbrella for various pro-democracy and pro-independence groups, but was registered as a political party in 1993.) When the DDK list was disqualified, Kulov ran in a single-mandate district, reportedly winning some 40 percent of the vote on February 20 but then, in balloting fraught with accusations of official misconduct, losing in the runoff on March 12. Ten days later, in the context of continuing demonstrations demanding that the election be nullified, he was arrested and charged with abuse of power and other offenses during his tenure as minister of national security in 1997–1998.

Considered a leading opposition candidate for president, Kulov was disqualified in September 2000 when he refused to take the mandatory Kyrgyz language test. Having already announced a pre-election alliance with *Ata-Meken,* Kulov later agreed to head Omurbek Tekebayev's campaign. In January 2001 and May 2002 he was convicted of various crimes and sentenced to prison. He was nevertheless regarded as a potential contender for the presidency in 2005. Having been freed during the regime-changing demonstrations of March 24, 2005, Kulov later saw his convictions thrown out by the courts. He served as President Bakiyev's first prime minister from 2005 until rejected for reappointment by the Supreme Council in January 2007.

Having failed to win a seat in the December 2007 parliamentary election, *Ar-Namys* joined with the *Ata-Meken* and *Asaba* parties in claiming that the election was marred by vote rigging. While Kulov remained party chair, he accepted a government appointment as coordinator of small- and medium-scale electricity generation programs on May 5, 2008.

Leaders: Feliks KULOV (Chair), Emil ALIYEV (Deputy Chair).

Party of National Restoration "Banner" (*Partiya Natsionalnovo Vozrozhdeniya "Asaba"*). Named with reference to a Kyrgyz military banner, *Asaba* was launched in November 1991 by a nationalist faction of the DDK (see *Ar-Namys*) that supported creation of a sovereign, democratic state and protection of the Kyrgyz economy and political interests. One of its leaders, Azimbek Beknazarov, whose 2002 trial was a precipitating factor in the March riots in the south, was regarded as a possible 2005 presidential contender before *Asaba* and other opposition parties endorsed former prime minister Bakiyev in 2004.

A former prosecutor general, Beknazarov stated in May 2006 that his principal goal was constitutional reform. In January 2008, with *Asaba* having failed to win any seats in the December 2007 election, Beknazarov joined in forming a **Revolutionary Committee** of opposition leaders whose aim was to act in a "very radical manner" to force President Bakiyev to resign for failing to meet people's expectations after the March 2005 revolution.. Beknazarov unexpectedly resigned as the party chair in April 2008 and was succeeded by his deputy, Sovetbek JAMALDINOV. Beknazarov his since served as coordinator of the UPM. In June 2009 the party elected a new chair, Salmor Dyikanov.

Although *Asaba* supported UPM presidential candidate Atambayev in 2009, the party's Jenishbek NAZARALIEV, a physician, also ran as an independent, but he withdrew on election day and finished last with 0.8 percent of the vote.

Leaders: Salmor DYIKANOV (Chair), Azimbek BEKNAZAROV (UPM Coordinator), Turat DYUSHEYEV.

Freedom Party (*Erkindik*). Announced in February 2000 by former members of the Progressive Democratic Party "Free Kyrgyzstan" (ErK, below) who rejected the leadership of Tursunbay Bakir-uulu, *Erkindik* (Freedom) was officially registered in late April and held a founding congress a month later, at which time Topchubek Turgunaliyev (previously a founder of ErK) succeeded Adylbek KASYMOV as leader.

On September 1, 2000, Turgunaliyev and seven others were convicted of a 1999 plot to assassinate President Akayev, with Turgunaliyev, labeled the "mastermind" by the government, receiving a 16-year prison sentence. Leading opposition politicians quickly protested the conviction and sentence as politically motivated. President Akayev later granted a pardon to Turgunaliyev, due to Turgunaliyev's deteriorating health. In late 2003 Turgunaliyev praised Georgia's "Rose Revolution" and suggested that it might serve as a model for Kyrgyzstan.

A key member of the PMK from 2004 and subsequently a strong supporter of President Bakiyev, Turgunaliyev spearheaded a campaign to dissolve the Supreme Council and hold new legislative elections. In May 2006 he announced formation of a new pro-reform **Blessed Kyrgyzstan** (*Kuttuu Kyrgyzstan*—KK) movement, which was described as including over ten parties. In 2007 he helped organize the pro-Bakiyev For Political Stability and Unity movement, but later joined the opposition. *Erkindik* registered for the December parliamentary election but failed to pass the required thresholds for representation.

In late 2008–2009 Turgunaliyev became a UPM leader, serving as chair of its Committee against Political Persecution. As a consequence of his participation in a protest march following Bakiyev's reelection in July 2009, he was held in jail for 15 days.

Leader: Topchubek TURGUNALIYEV (Chair).

Green Party of Kyrgyzstan. Founded in 2006 by Erkin Bulekbayev, the Green Party has been a consistent opposition voice. The party was denied a place on the 2007 parliamentary ballot. Bulekbayev has been jailed for charges ranging from insulting the honor and dignity of the president to fomenting disorder and ethnic hatred during an April 2009 march demanding the expulsion of Kurds.

Leader: Erkin BULEKBAYEV (Chair).

National Democratic Party "Great Unity" (*"Uluu Birimdik"*). Registered in August 2005, *Uluu Birimdik* (Solidarity) was described as appealing to owners of small and medium-size businesses as well as the "rural intelligentsia." It participated in formation of the UPM and opposed President Bakiyev's reelection in 2009.

Leader: Emilbek KAPTAGAYEV (Chair).

Other Parties:

Party of Communists of Kyrgyzstan (*Partiya Kommunistov Kyrgyzstana*—PKK). The PKK was launched in June 1992 as the successor to the former ruling Kyrgyz Communist Party, which had been disbanded in August 1991. Registered in September 1992, the party enjoyed significant support in the state bureaucracy. A majority of successful candidates in the February 1995 legislative elections reportedly belonged to or had close ties to the party. PKK leader Absamat MASALIYEV was runner-up in the December 1995 presidential poll, winning 24.4 percent of the vote.

Despite having suffered defections in 1999 (see CPK, below), the PKK won a plurality of party list seats (5 of 15) in the 2000 Legislative Assembly election, taking 28 percent of the vote on a platform that included the reconstitution of the Soviet Union. Its contender for president in 2000, Ishak Masaliyev (Absamat's son), failed the mandatory Kyrgyz language test.

In July 2004 longtime party leader Absamat Masaliyev died, and two months later his deputy, Bakytbek BEKBOYEV, was elected his successor, defeating fellow MP Nikolay Baylo. Bekboyev lost the post the following December, partly due to an internal dispute over energy policy, and was replaced by Baylo. Leadership subsequently passed to Ishak Masaliyev, who in 2007 appeared to favor the moderate reform posture of the For One Kyrgyzstan movement. Masaliyev was reelected to a five-year term as leader in November 2008.

In the December 2007 parliamentary election the PKK barely passed the 5 percent threshold and won 8 seats. In the 2009 presidential contest it endorsed President Bakiyev's reelection.

Leaders: Ishak MASALIYEV (Chair and Parliamentary Leader), Nikolai BAYLO.

Communist Party of Kyrgyzstan—CPK (*Kommunistov Partiya Kyrgyzstana*). Formation of the CPK was announced in August 1999 by dissidents within the Party of Communists (PKK, above) who had accused PKK leader Absamat Masaliyev of cooperating with ideological enemies and defending corrupt officials. In 2004 party founder Klara Adzhibekova proposed reunification, an offer rejected by the PKK in the absence of an apology. The CPK registered to contest the December 2007 parliamentary election but failed to meet technical requirements and was disqualified by the Central Election Commission.

Leader: Klara ADZHIBEKOVA.

Democratic Party "Turan." *Turan,* an old Iranian name for Central Asia, registered as a political party in 2007 and contested the December 2007 election. The party was perceived both as a personal vehicle for former deputy speaker of the Supreme Council Tayirbek Sarpashev and a "fake" opposition party aiming to split the anti-Bakiyev vote.

Leader: Tayirbek SARPASHEV (Chair).

New Force (*Novaya Sila*—NS). Registered in October 1994 as the Women's Democratic Party of Kyrgyzstan (*Demokraticheskaya Partiya Zhenshchin Kyrgyzstana*—DPZK), the NS—more formally known as the Democratic Party of Women and Youth "New Force"—adopted its present name in November 2003, at which time it opened its membership to men as well as women.

Broadly supportive of the Akayev government, the DPZK received two party list seats based on a 13 percent vote share (including President Akayev's vote) at the February 2000 election. In 2003 the NS chair, Tokon Shailiyeva, was named governor of Issyk-Kul, but she was replaced by the new government in March 2005.

In the 2007 election NS campaigned to increase the profile of women and disadvantaged groups, but it won less than 1 percent of the national vote and thus no parliamentary seats.

Leaders: Tokon SHAYLIEVA (Chair), Lyubov SAFONOVA.

New Kyrgyzstan (*Jany Kyrgyzstan*—JK). Based in southern Osh, the leftist, rural-oriented JK was registered in 1994 as the Agrarian Labor Party of Kyrgyzstan (*Agrarno-Trudovnaya Partiya Kyrgyzstana*—ATPK). Its initial goal was preventing a breakdown in agricultural infrastructure and overcoming what its founders perceived as a crisis in agro-industry. The party's Usen Sydykov, a populist, was disqualified as a parliamentary candidate before the 2000 elections and again in 2002 after having received a near-majority in the first round of a by-election. Sydykov subsequently served as President Bakiyev's head of presidential administration until being transferred in May 2006, although he remained a key presidential adviser.

Ismail ISAKOV, a former secretary of the Security Council who had resigned in October 2008 because he differed with President Bakiyev on foreign policy matters, lost his position as JK secretary general in December 2008 because he had made overtures to the opposition and supported formation of the UPM. In 2009, although the JK supported Bakiyev's reelection, Isakov announced his intention to run for president (he later withdrew), which led to his expulsion from the party in May.

Leader: Usen SYDYKOV (Founder).

Progressive Democratic Party "Free Kyrgyzstan" (*Progressivno-Demokraticheskaya Partiya "Erkin Kyrgyzstan"*—ErK). The ErK (an acronym meaning "will") was founded in 1991 as a splinter group of the Democratic Movement of Kyrgyzstan (DDK) on a platform of moderate nationalism and support for a liberal market economy. It was weakened in 1992 by secession of the more nationalist *Ata-Meken* (above), its subsequent attempts to build a pro-democracy bloc making little progress.

ErK's founder, Topchubek Turgunaliyev, was campaign manager for Medetkan SHERIMKULOV in the December 1995 presidential election but was arrested (for insulting the incumbent) shortly before the polling, in which Sherimkulov placed last of three candidates. In January 1997, in what his supporters charged was a politically motivated case, Turgunaliyev was convicted of embezzlement during his tenure as rector of Bishkek Humanitarian University. He was released from prison in November 1998 and later joined *Erkindik* (above)., which broke from ErK in February 2000.

In April 2000 ErK Chair Tursunbay Bakir-uulu accepted responsibility for the party's failure to win any party list seats at the 2000 national election. He subsequently announced his intention to run for president in October, but he received under 1 percent of the vote. After being elected by the Legislative Assembly in November 2002 to serve as Kyrgyzstan's first ombudsman, Bakir-uulu resigned as ErK's formal leader, although he remained its dominant figure. In July 2005 he finished second in the presidential election, winning 4.0 percent of the vote.

In December 2007 ErK failed to meet the threshold for parliamentary seats, and in 2008 Bakir-uulu lost his bid for a second term as ombudsman. Initially endorsed by the party as its 2009 presidential candidate, he stepped aside upon being named Kyrgyzstan's ambassador to Malaysia. He had also been serving as cochair of Kyrgyzstan's Union of Muslims.

Leaders: Tursunbay BAKIR-UULU, Muradil JANJALBEKOV and Yuruslan ISTANOV (Deputy Leaders).

Other parties that made it onto the ballot for the December 2007 Supreme Council election were the **Party of the Unaffiliated "Aalam"** (Universe) and **Glas Naroda** (*"El Dobushu,"* People's Voice). Among the disqualified parties were the following: **Jany Mezgil** (New Time), led by Askar BAZARKULOV; the **National Patriotic Party "Peace"** (*"Tynchtyk"*), which was registered in 2006 under the leadership of Ismail KOCHKOROV; the **Party of Farmers of Kyrgyzstan,** led by Kuttubek ASYLBEKOV; the **Party of Veterans and Youth of Kyrgyzstan,** led by Abdygul CHOTBAYEV; the **Party of War Veterans in Afghanistan and Participants in Other Local Military Conflicts** (*Politicheskaya Partiya Veteranov Vojny b Afghanistane i Uchastnikov Drugikh Lokalnykh Boyelykh Konflicktov*—PPVVAA), led by Akbokon TASHTANBEKOV; **Rodina** (Homeland), led by Kadyrjan BATYROV; **Taza Koom** (Clean Society), which had been led by Abdygany ERKEBAYEV, speaker of the opposition's "public parliament," until it endorsed President Bakiyev's reelection in 2009; and **Zamandash** (Compatriot), whose leader, Muktarbek OMURAKUNOV, was detained by authorities in July 2008 because of his alleged involvement in an improper procurement contract while press secretary of the State Committee for Migration and Employment.

The **Poor Nation Party** (*Kairan-El Partiyasi*), founded in 1999, continues to be led by Doornbek SADYRBAEV, who ran for the Supreme Council in 2007 on the *Asaba* list. Former prime minister Amangeldy Muraliyev is currently a leader of the opposition movement **United Kyrgyzstan,** which was established in June 2008 by a number of individuals who had previously been associated with former president Akayev.

Banned Organizations:

In November 2003 the Supreme Court banned four Islamic fundamentalist organizations: the **Hizb-ut-Tahrir;** the **East Turkestan Islamic Party** (*Sharq Turkestan Islam Partiyasy*); the **East Turkestan Liberation Organization** (*Sharq Azzat Turkestan*); and the **Islamic Party of Turkestan**, also known as the **Islamic Movement of Uzbekistan** (IMU). In May 2006 a skirmish along the Kyrgyz-Tajik border left at least four dead, allegedly members of the *Hizb-ut-Tahrir* and IMU. Smuggling of weapons may have been involved.

LEGISLATURE

The Soviet-era unicameral legislature of 350 members was replaced in 1995 by a bicameral Supreme Council comprising a 70-member (later reduced to 45 members) Assembly of People's Representatives (*El Okuldor Palatasy*) and a 35-member (later increased to 60 members) Legislative Assembly (*Myizan Chygaru Palatasy*). Members of both houses were directly elected for five-year terms. Whereas the Assembly of People's Representatives consisted of nonprofessional deputies who represented the nation's regional/ethnic communities, the Legislative Assembly met in standing session to handle the day-to-day workload of the parliament. The constitutional referendum of February 2003 endorsed restoration of a unicameral legislature, the **Supreme Council** (*Jogorku Kenesh*), effective from the next election.

A first round of balloting on February 27, 2005, concluded with 31 of the legislature's 75 seats being filled; runoff balloting was then held on March 13. Most candidates ran as independents. Following the ouster of President Akayev, many members of the former opposition called for throwing out the election results and reseating the bicameral legislature. On March 28–29, 2005, however, the Assembly of People's Representatives and the Legislative Assembly both dissolved in favor of the new Supreme Council, which was organized into deputy groups that typically reflected regional and ethnic biases as well as ideological orientation and party affiliation.

Elections for an expanded 90-seat legislature were held on December 16, 2007, with all seats filled on the basis of national party lists. Party list requirements included 30 percent representation for women, 15 percent for those under 35, and 15 percent for various ethnic minorities. The election produced the following distribution of seats: *Ak Zhol,* 71 seats; the Social Democratic Party of Kyrgyzstan, 11; and the Party of Communists of Kyrgyzstan, 8.

Speaker: Aitibai TAGAEV.

CABINET

[as of October 15, 2009]

Prime Minister	Igor Chudinov
First Deputy Prime Minister	Omerbek Babanov
Deputy Prime Minister	Uktomhan Abdullaeva [f]
Ministers	
Agriculture, Water Economy, and Processing Industry	Iskenderbek Aidaraliev
Culture and Information	Sultan Raev
Defense	Bakytbek Kaliev
Economic Development and Trade	Akylbek Japarov
Education and Science	Abdulda Musaev
Emergencies	Kamchibek Tashiev
Finance	Marat Sultanov
Foreign Affairs	Kadyrbek Sarbaev
Health	Marat Mambetov
Industry, Energy, and Fuel Resources	Ilyas Davidov
Interior	Moldomusa Kongantiev
Justice	Nurlan Tursunkulov
Labor and Social Welfare	Nazgyl Tashpaeva [f]
Transportation and Communication	Nurlan Sulaimanov
Head, Prime Minister's Administration	Nurlan Aytmurzaev
Chair, State Committee for Customs	Nurlan Akmatov
Chair, State Committee for Migration and Employment	Aigul Ryskulova [f]
Chair, State Committee for National Security	Murat Sutalinov
Chair, State Committee for State Property	Tursun Turdumambetov
Chair, State Committee on Taxes and Collections	Ahmatbek Keldibekov

[f] = female

COMMUNICATIONS

Government censorship was explicitly rejected in a 1994 presidential decree, and in 1998 constitutional amendments approved by referendum included a provision forbidding the legislature from imposing restrictions on press freedoms. Nevertheless, opposition newspapers, particularly *Res Publica,* encountered frequent problems with the authorities under President Akayev, including fines and suspension of publication for such alleged offenses as libel and insulting officials. This led to frequent self-censorship, which, according to a recent report by Reporters Without Borders, persists.

A new Law on TV and Radio Broadcasting signed by President Bakiyev on June 3, 2008, strengthened the government's control over the media. The law provided the president with the authority to appoint all board members of the National Television and Radio Company (NTRC), which dominates the airwaves, and also allows state bodies to revoke broadcasting licenses without the participation of the courts. Reporters Without Borders said the law effectively "wrecks efforts undertaken to make [NTRC] a public and not a state company." It was equally critical of the 2009 presidential campaign, in which the OSCE also cited the incumbent's "unfair advantage" in coverage and media bias.

Press. The following are published at least five times a week in Bishkek: *Slovo Kyrgyzstana* (Kyrgyz Word, 110,000), government organ, in Russian; *Delo No* (Case Number, 50,000), weekly, in Russian; *Vechernyi Bishkek* (Bishkek Evening News, 20,000 daily, 50,000 weekend), in Russian; *Zaman Kyrgyzstan* (Kyrgyz Herald, 15,000), weekly, in Kyrgyz; *Res Publica* (Republic, 10,000), independent, in Russian and English; *Times of Central Asia,* weekly, in English. Opposition newspapers include *Alibi, De Facto,* and *Open Politics.*

News agencies. The government facility is the Kyrgyz National News Agency (Kabar), headquartered in Bishkek. AkiPress and 24.kg are independent agencies, as is *Zamandash* Press, which was established in 2008 with a focus on economic, labor, financial, and related news. Russia's Interfax and ITAR-TASS also maintain bureaus in the capital.

Broadcasting and computing. The government's Kyrgyz National Television and Radio Broadcasting Corporation is the leading broadcaster, although its transmissions do not yet cover the entire country. A number of independent stations have recently started transmitting, mainly from the capital. Some areas also receive broadcasts from Russian Public Television.

As of 2008 there were 157 Internet users per 1,000 inhabitants.

INTERGOVERNMENTAL REPRESENTATION

Ambassador to the U.S.: Zamira Beksultanovna SYDYKOVA.

U.S. Ambassador to Kyrgyzstan: Tatiana C. GFOELLER-VOLKOFF.

Permanent Representative to the UN: Nurbek JEENBAEV.

IGO Memberships (Non-UN): ADB, CIS, EBRD, ECO, IDB, Interpol, IOM, OIC, OSCE, PCA, WCO, WTO.

LAOS

Lao People's Democratic Republic
Sathalanalat Paxathipatai Paxaxôn Lao

Political Status: Fully independent constitutional monarchy proclaimed October 23, 1953; Communist-led people's democratic republic established December 2, 1975; present constitution adopted August 14, 1991.

Area: 91,428 sq. mi. (236,800 sq. km.).

Population: 5,621,982 (2005C); 6,008,000 (2008E).

Major Urban Center (2005E): VIENTIANE (Viangchan, 730,000).

Official Language: Lao (English is considered the business language in government circles).

Monetary Unit: New Kip (market rate December 1, 2009: 8,465.00 new kips = $1US). The Thai baht also circulates.

President: CHOUMMALY SAYASONE; elected by the National Assembly for a five-year term on June 8, 2006, to succeed KHAMTAY SIPHANDONE.

Vice President: BOUNNHANG VORACHIT; elected by the National Assembly for a five-year term on June 8, 2006, to succeed CHOUMMALY SAYASONE.

Prime Minister: BOUASONE BOUPHAVANH; approved by the National Assembly on June 8, 2006, to succeed BOUNNHANG VORACHIT.

THE COUNTRY

The wholly landlocked nation of Laos sits between Vietnam and Thailand but also shares borders with Cambodia, China, and Myanmar (Burma). Apart from the Mekong River plains adjacent to Thailand, the country is largely mountainous, with scattered dense forests. Tropical monsoons provide a May–October wet season that alternates with a November–April dry season. The population is divided among three major groups: about 56 percent Lao-Loum (valley Lao), 34 percent Lao-Theung (mountainside Lao), and 9 percent Lao-Soung (mountaintop Lao); the Lao-Theung and Lao-Soung have long protested the disproportionate economic and political influence of the lowland population. Tribal minorities include non-Khmer-speaking groups in the southern uplands and Hmong and Yao in the northern mountains. Although most ethnic Lao, especially the valley Lao, follow Hinayana (Theravada) Buddhism, most of the tribal minorities practice animism. Lao is the official language, while English has supplanted French within government circles. Pali, locally known as *Nang Xu Tham,* a Sanskrit language of Hindu origin, is generally used by priests. About one-third of the population is illiterate, according to the government. Women constitute 50 percent of the active labor force and hold 25 percent of the seats in the National Assembly.

Laos remains one of Asia's poorest countries, with an estimated per capita income of $580 in 2007, according to World Bank calculations. Some 77 percent of the labor force is engaged in agriculture (predominately at the subsistence level), which continues to account for 42 percent of GDP. Rice, the principal food staple, grows on the large majority of the farmed land, while coffee has become an increasingly important export crop; other crops include maize, tobacco, cotton, and citrus fruits. Opium, nominally subject to state control, is an important source of income in Hmong hill areas. Industry as a whole (including mining, construction, and utilities) accounts for 32 percent of GDP, with services contributing the balance, 26 percent. Since 2005 copper has emerged as the leading mining export, followed by gold. There are also deposits of silver, tin zinc, and gemstones as well as large quantities of high-quality iron ore in Xieng Khouang Province.

Wood products, principally timber and logs, traditionally accounted for the largest share of exports, but in recent years manufactured garments have become more important. Electricity also contributes significantly to foreign earnings, with Laos pinning much of its hopes for economic development on additional efforts to tap the hydroelectric potential of the Mekong basin. Remittances from expatriate Laotians remain a significant income source, and tourism has also become increasingly important.

Although the Communist regime that gained power in 1975 instituted strict socialist policies, including the creation of large agricultural cooperatives, in the 1990s it promoted a return to family farming, encouraged private enterprise and foreign investment, privatized nonstrategic state-owned enterprises, and began reorganizing "strategic" companies, including banks and utilities, to compete commercially. Economic growth averaged more than 6 percent from 1987 to 1997 but declined in 1998 and 1999, when weak fiscal and monetary policies, coupled with the regional economic downturn, led to triple-digit inflation and a drastic drop in the value of the kip. By mid-2000, however, the kip had stabilized and inflation had been checked to around 10 percent, according to the government. For 2000–2003 GDP growth averaged 5.9 percent annually. The rate of growth, which rose to 6.4 percent in 2004 and 7.1 percent in 2005, peaked at 8.1 percent in 2006 before dropping slightly, to 7.9 percent, in 2007.

GOVERNMENT AND POLITICS

Political background. Laos became a French protectorate in 1893 and gained limited self-government as an Associated State within the French Union on June 19, 1949. Although the French recognized full Lao sovereignty on October 23, 1953, the Communist-led Vietminh—supported within Laos by the so-called *Pathet Lao* (Land of Lao), the military arm of the Lao Communist movement—mounted a war of "national liberation" in 1954 in conjunction with its operations in Vietnam. Hostilities were ended by the Geneva Accords of 1954, and the last French ties to Laos lapsed in December of that year.

Pro-Western or conservative governments held power from 1954 to 1960, except for a brief interval in 1957–1958 when neutralist Prime Minister SOUVANNA PHOUMA formed a coalition with Prince SOUPHANOUVONG, his half-brother and leader of the pro-Communist Lao Patriotic Front (*Neo Lao Hak Xat*—NLHX).

In April 1960 the Lao army, headed by Gen. PHOUMI NOSAVAN, gained control of the government through a fraudulent National Assembly election. A coup in August by a group of neutralist officers under Capt. KONG LE led to the reinstatement of Souvanna Phouma as prime minister, but a countercoup led by General Phoumi brought about the installation four months later of a rightist administration headed by Prince BOUN OUM NA Champassak. In an effort to defuse the fighting and avoid deeper involvement by the great powers, a 14-nation conference was convened in Geneva in May 1961, and the rightists, neutralists, and NLHX eventually agreed to join a coalition government that took office under Souvanna Phouma in June 1962.

Renewed factional feuding nevertheless led to the withdrawal of the NLHX ministers over the next two years and the continuation, with North Vietnamese support, of the Communist insurgency based in the north. The NLHX refused to participate in an election held in July 1965, the results of which left Souvanna Phouma in control of the National Assembly. Military encounters between the government and the *Pathet Lao* (formally renamed the Lao People's Liberation Army in 1965) continued thereafter, with the *Pathet Lao* retaining control of the northeast and working closely with North Vietnamese forces concentrated in the area.

Peace talks between the *Pathet Lao* and the Souvanna Phouma government resumed in 1972, and in February 1973 cease-fire proposals put forward by the latter were accepted. A political protocol signed the following September provided for a provisional coalition government and a joint National Political Consultative Council (NPCC) empowered to advise the cabinet. On April 5, 1974, King SAVANG VATTHANA signed a decree appointing the coalition government, thus formalizing the end of a decade of bitter warfare. Prince Souvanna Phouma was redesignated prime minister, while *Pathet Lao* leader Prince Souphanouvong (the "Red Prince") was named president of the NPCC.

In May 1975, following the fall of Cambodia and South Vietnam to Communist insurgents, *Pathet Lao* forces moved into the Laotian capital of Vientiane and began installing their own personnel in government posts while subjecting both military and civilian supporters of the neutralist regime to political "reeducation" sessions. Three months later,

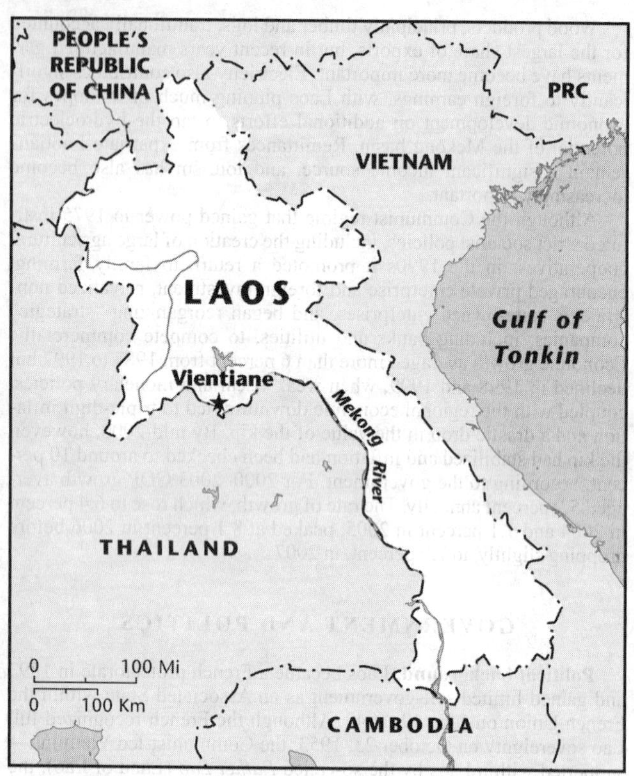

on August 23, the formal "liberation" of Vientiane was announced. On December 2, at a People's Congress called by the Lao Patriotic Front, the monarchy was abolished, the 19-month-old coalition government of Prince Souvanna Phouma was terminated, and the Lao People's Democratic Republic (LPDR) was established. Concurrently, Souphanouvong was designated head of state and chair of a newly established Supreme People's Assembly, while KAYSONE PHOMVIHAN, secretary general of the Lao People's Revolutionary Party (LPRP), was named prime minister.

Souphanouvong resigned his state posts after reportedly having suffered a stroke in September 1986; he was succeeded as head of state (on an acting basis) by PHOUMI VONGVICHIT, theretofore a deputy chair of the Council of Ministers. The presidency of the republic was thus separated from the chairmanship of the assembly.

The government, in emulation of both Moscow and Hanoi, subsequently retreated from its hard-line socialist posture, decentralizing economic planning in favor of greater free-market activity. Some degree of political liberalization also ensued, culminating in a Supreme People's Assembly election in March 1989. Although non-LPRP candidates were permitted, all candidates required the advance approval of the Lao Front for National Construction (LFNC).

On August 14, 1991, the assembly unanimously approved the LPDR's first constitution. The basic law provided for a strong presidency, to which ministerial chair Kaysone Phomvihan was elected on August 15, with Gen. KHAMTAY SIPHANDONE being named prime minister. Promulgation of the constitution was preceded by a number of legislative measures that provided for a New Economic Mechanism, which sought to reconcile a continued belief in central economic planning with the requirements of a market economy, taking China's recent change of economic course as its model.

President Kaysone died on November 21, 1992. Four days later the renamed National Assembly elected the number three man in the party hierarchy, NOUHAK PHOUMSAVAN, to the presidency, while Prime Minister Khamtay, the second-ranked leader, was named on November 24 to succeed Kaysone as party president.

The sixth LPRP congress in March 1996 took a more cautious approach to economic reform while tightening the grip of the military on the country's political structures. Notably, the party removed Deputy Prime Minister KHAMPHOUI KEOBOUALAPHA, a leading proponent of privatization and other market reforms, from both the Politburo and Central Committee. A government reorganization in April included the elevation of Gen. SISAVATH KEOBOUNPHANH, previously minister of agriculture and forestry, to the new post of state vice president.

On February 24, 1998, the newly elected National Assembly designated Prime Minister Khamtay as President Nouhak's successor, moved Vice President Sisavath to the prime ministership, and brought in the LFNC chair, OUDOM KHATTIGNA, as vice president. Oudom died on December 9, 1999, with no successor being named in subsequent months.

The seventh LPRP congress, held March 12–14, 2001, introduced few changes in the aging hierarchy and was followed on March 27 by the National Assembly's election of the outgoing minister of defense and a deputy prime minister, CHOUMMALY SAYASONE, to the vacant vice presidency. The legislature also confirmed the nomination of BOUNNHANG VORACHIT, theretofore the finance minister and a deputy prime minister, to head a new cabinet.

The National Assembly election of February 24, 2002, concluded once again with LPRP candidates winning all but one seat, which went to an independent, the minister of justice. The president, vice president, and prime minister were all retained in office by vote of the new parliament on April 9. On January 15, 2003, however, the government's economic team was shuffled. In an apparent response to internal security concerns, on the following October 1 the National Assembly approved Politburo member BOUASONE BOUPHAVANH to be Laos's fourth deputy prime minister.

The eighth LPRP congress, held March 18–21, 2006, marked the departure of Khamtay Siphandone, 82, from the party leadership and presaged his retirement as president two months later, following the National Assembly election of April 30. His successor in both roles was Choummaly Sayasone, 70, who was elected president at the first session of the new National Assembly on June 8. On the same day, Bounnhang Vorachit was elevated to the vice presidency and Bouasone Bouphavanh was confirmed as prime minister.

Constitution and government. The 1991 constitution redefined the country's political and economic systems as well as the rights and duties of citizens, but it preserved a one-party state under the umbrella of the LFNC. The National Assembly, which is elected for a five-year term, names the president for a term of equal duration and approves a cabinet headed by a prime minister whose authority is substantially less than that of the former Council of Ministers chair.

In the wake of the 1975 takeover, judicial functions were assumed by numerous local "people's courts," with a People's Supreme Court subsequently being added. The president of the Supreme Court is chosen by the National Assembly; all other judges are named by the legislature's Standing Committee. The country is divided into 17 provinces (*khoueng*) and the municipality of Vientiane. The state president names provincial governors, the municipal mayor, and the governor of Saysomboun. Provinces are subdivided into districts, each of which has an appointed chief administrator.

Foreign relations. Laos's neutrality in major power issues ended with the 1975 declaration of the LPDR. In late 1978 Laos strongly supported Soviet-backed Vietnam's ouster of the Pol Pot government in Cambodia, subsequent reports indicating that Laotian troops had joined Vietnamese forces in fighting the regrouped *Khmers Rouges*. Although Laos condemned China's incursion into Vietnam in February 1979 and broke off relations with Beijing over the issue, it backed the Soviet intervention in Afghanistan ten months later. Relations with China were restored in 1989.

After a lengthy series of skirmishes, Lao-Thai relations hit a nadir in late 1987 when fighting broke out over disputed border territory. A series of high-level talks in late 1990 led to a mutual troop withdrawal from border areas in March 1991. Five months later the two governments concluded a border security and cooperation settlement and agreed to complete the repatriation of some 60,000 Lao refugees from Thailand.

April 1994 saw the inauguration of the first bridge across the lower Mekong River, providing a major road link between Vientiane and northern Thailand and thus giving landlocked Laos easier access to southern Thai ports. A year later Cambodia and Vietnam joined Laos and Thailand in establishing the Mekong River Commission to develop the river basin, and in September 1996 Vientiane and Bangkok set up a joint boundary commission to delineate a definitive border. In April 2000 Laos joined China, Myanmar, and Thailand in completing a treaty governing navigation on the upper Mekong.

During the Vietnam War, American forces tried to cut off the flow of North Vietnamese troops and supplies passing through Laos and Cambodia into South Vietnam. As part of that effort the U.S. military flew some 580,000 bombing missions over Laos, dropping more tonnage than fell on Europe during World War II. The United States broke off diplomatic relations with Laos in 1975, and contacts at the ambassadorial level did not resume until 1992.

Recent U.S.-Lao diplomatic activity has addressed two ongoing U.S. concerns: efforts to curtail the narcotics trade and the ongoing search for several hundred U.S. servicemen listed as missing in action in Laos during the Vietnam War. Vientiane's cooperation on these issues contributed to Washington's 1995 announcement that it was lifting its 20-year aid embargo, thus making Laos eligible for assistance from the U.S. Agency for International Development (USAID) and paving the way for further normalization of bilateral relations.

Although the George W. Bush administration concluded a minor trade agreement with Laos in September 2003 and pledged to pursue reestablishing "Normal Trading Relations" (NTR), in 2004 congressmen in the U.S. president's own party voiced strong opposition because of Laos's human rights record, including alleged abuse of prisoners and the Hmong minority (see Current issues, below). NTR status was ultimately approved by both houses of the U.S. Congress in 2004, but only because it was incorporated into an essential piece of trade legislation.

In July 1992 Laos signaled its desire for greater regional economic and political integration by signing the 1976 Treaty of Amity and Cooperation in Southeast Asia of the Association of Southeast Asian Nations (ASEAN). That move paved the way for ASEAN membership, which was approved in June 1997. Vientiane hosted its first ASEAN summit on November 27–30, 2004.

Current issues. The June 2006 change in the top leadership was so well programmed that it was hardly a change at all, with Choummaly Sayasone, Bounnhang Vorachit, and Bouasone Bouphavanh each merely climbing one rung higher in the government hierarchy. As an unnamed "foreign observer" remarked to an *Agence France-Presse* reporter during the March LPRP congress, "more of the same" could be expected, given that "there is no pressure from outside, there is no organized dissident movement, and there is no movement inside."

If there is any remaining internal opposition to the government, it lies in the north among remote Hmong bands, some of whom still receive financial support from a U.S.-based expatriate community. (After the conclusion of the Vietnam War the United States resettled more than 100,000 Hmong, including Gen. VANG PAO, who had led a U.S.-funded anticommunist guerrilla insurgency.) The government continues to be accused of human rights abuses, and even genocide, in its efforts to suppress the remaining Hmong. The charges have been leveled not only by Americans and other anticommunists but also by various human rights groups, including Amnesty International, which issued a March 2007 report titled *Laos: Hiding in the Jungle—Hmong under Threat*.

In December 2006 Thailand's Prime Minister Surayud Chulanot and Laos's Bouasone Bouphavanh agreed to the repatriation of some 6,650 Hmong from refugee camps in Thailand, despite objections from the Office of the United Nations High Commissioner for Refugees, among others. The Hmong issue took another turn in early June 2007, when Vang Pao, then 76, and nine other individuals were charged in the United States with violating the U.S. Neutrality Act by plotting to overthrow the Laotian government. The group allegedly conspired to buy arms, including automatic weapons and surface-to-air missiles, prior to launching an assault. (In May 2009 a federal judge rejected a dismissal motion by the defense.) Within days, the Thai government deported another 160 Hmong refugees to Laos. In May Thailand had announced that it would henceforth consider fleeing Hmong as "illegal migrants" and repatriate them quickly.

On June 20, 2008, World Refugee Day, some 5,000 Hmong, after spending a year in detention, walked away from Huai Nam Khao camp in Thailand's Petchabun Province to protest the repatriation agreement. The international aid organization Doctors Without Borders (*Médecins Sans Frontières*—MSF) subsequently reported that on June 22 some 800 of the Hmong were forcibly returned to Laos. Thai officials, however, stated that the repatriation was "voluntary." Most of the other protesters had returned to the refugee camp.

As of August 2009, the army-run camp reportedly still held 4,700 Hmong, while another 150 were being held at an immigration detention center in Nong Khai, Thailand. Although the United States has provided funding for both facilities, primarily through humanitarian organizations, current U.S. policy permits further Hmong immigration only on a case-by-case basis. Human rights organizations continue to express concern that an estimated 2,000 of the Hmong had historical connections to the U.S. Central Intelligence Agency and are therefore at risk if returned. Although the Laotian government assured Thai authorities in May 2009 that voluntary returnees would not be persecuted, it continued to reject international monitoring of the process. Also in May, the MSF withdrew its personnel to protest what it described as overt efforts by the Thai army to pressure the Hmong to withdraw asylum requests and accept repatriation. Thailand reportedly repatriated some 2,900 Hmong in the first seven months of 2009 and planned to return another 4,600 shortly.

POLITICAL PARTIES

In 1979 the **Lao Front for National Construction** (LFNC) succeeded the Lao Patriotic Front (*Neo Lao Hak Xat*—NLHX) as the umbrella organization for various social as well as political groups committed to national solidarity. The most recent LFNC congress was held May 15–16, 2006.

President: SISAVATH KEOBOUNPHANH.

Leading Party:

Lao People's Revolutionary Party—LPRP (*Phak Pasason Pativat Lao*). Known prior to the Communist seizure of power as the People's Party of Laos (*Phak Pasason Lao*), the LPRP is the Communist core of the LFNC.

The seventh party congress, held March 12–14, 2001, was attended by 452 delegates, who unanimously reelected General Khamtay to another term as LPRP president, expanded the Central Committee from 49 to 53, and added 3 new Politburo members, for a total of 11.

With Khamtay having announced his retirement, the eighth congress, held March 18–21, 2006, renamed the office of president as secretary general—its original title until a 1991 change—and elected Choummaly Sayasone to the post. The 498 delegates replaced one-third of the Central Committee, now comprising 55 members, but made only 2 changes in the Politburo, including the addition of its first female, Pany Yathothu, a Hmong.

Secretary General: CHOUMMALY SAYASONE.

Other Members of Politburo: Gen. ASANG LAOLY (Deputy Prime Minister), BOUASONE BOUPHAVANH (Prime Minister), BOUNNHANG VORACHIT (Vice President of the LPDR), Maj. Gen. DOUANGCHAY PHICHIT (Minister of National Defense), PANY YATHOTHU, Gen. SAMANE VIYAKHET (Former Chair, National Assembly), Gen. SISAVATH KEOBOUNPHANH (Former Prime Minister), SOMSAVAT LENGSAVAD (Deputy Prime Minister), THONGLOUN SISOULITH (Minister of Foreign Affairs), THONGSING THAMMAVONG (Chair, National Assembly).

LEGISLATURE

Under the 1991 constitution the Special People's Assembly was renamed the **National Assembly** (*Sapha Heng Xat*). The most recent election for 115 members (from candidates approved by the Lao Front for National Construction) was held on April 30, 2006. Two independent candidates won seats, while the Lao People's Revolutionary Party won the other 113. Under the constitution, representatives are to serve five-year terms, but recent elections have been held at roughly four-year intervals.

Chair: THONGSING THAMMAVONG.

CABINET

[as of October 15, 2009]

Prime Minister	Bouasone Bouphavanh
Deputy Prime Ministers	Asang Laoly
	Maj. Gen. Douangchai Phichit
	Somsavat Lengsavad
	Thongloun Sisoulith
Ministers	
Agriculture and Forestry	Sitaheng Lathsaphone
Communication, Transport, Post, and Construction	Sommath Pholsena
Education	Somkoth Mangnormek
Energy and Mining	Soulivong Daravong
Finance	Somdy Douangdy

Foreign Affairs	Thongloun Sisoulith
Industry and Commerce	Nam Viyaket
Information and Culture	Mounkeo Oraboun
Justice	Chaleum Yapaoheu
Labor and Social Welfare	Onchanh Thammavong [f]
National Defense	Maj. Gen. Douangchai Phichit
National Security	Thongbane Sengaphone
Public Health	Ponemek Daraloy
President's Office	Souban Srithirat
Prime Minister's Office	Douangsavat Souphanouvong
	Khamouan Boupha
	Onneua Phommachanh
	Phouthong Saengakhom
	Xaysengly Tengbriachue
Prime Minister's Office, Head of Government Secretariat Committee	Cheuang Sombounkhanh
Prime Minister's Office, Head of National Tourism Authority	Somphong Mongkhonvilay
Prime Minister's Office, Head of Public Administration and Civil Service Authority	Bounpheng Mounphosay [f]
Prime Minister's Office, Head of Science, Technology, and Environment Organization	Bountiem Phissamay
Prime Minister's Office, Head of Water Resources and Environment Agency	Khempheng Pholsena [f]
Prime Minister's Office, President of National Mekong River Committee	Khamluad Sitlakon
Head of Cabinet Office	Soubanh Sritthirath
President, Committee for Planning and Investment	Soulivong Daravong
President, State Control and Inspection Commission	Asang Laoly
Governor, Central Bank	Phouphet Khamphounvong

[f] = female

COMMUNICATIONS

All media are tightly controlled by the government or the LPRP, although in July 2008 a draft of a new media law under consideration by the National Assembly called for permitting private ownership of newspapers. The change has yet to be implemented.

Press. Laotian newspapers have limited circulation and scope. Current publications include *Lao Dong* (Labor, 50,000); *Paxaôn* (The People, 30,000), LPRP organ; *Vientiane Mai* (New Vientiane, 3,000), organ of the local LPRP; and *Vientiane Times* (3,000), in English.

News agencies. *Khaosan Pathet Lao* (KPL), the domestic agency, is a government organ issuing daily bulletins in Lao, English, and French. Russian and Vietnamese agencies as well as Reuters have representatives in the capital. The proposed new media law would allow foreign bureaus to open their own offices.

Broadcasting and computing. The government offers national and international radio service through National Radio of Laos. Lao National Television broadcasts through two stations. Some viewers also receive Lao Television 3, a joint venture of the government and a Thai company.

As of 2007 there were approximately 17 Internet users per 1,000 people. As of that same year there were about 252 cellular mobile subscribers per 1,000 people.

INTERGOVERNMENTAL REPRESENTATION

Ambassador to the U.S.: Phiane PHILAKONE.

U.S. Ambassador to Laos: Ravic Rolf HUSO.

Permanent Representative to the UN: Kanika PHOMMACHANH.

IGO Memberships (Non-UN): ADB, ASEAN, Interpol, NAM, OIF, PCA.

LATVIA

Republic of Latvia
Latvijas Republika

Political Status: Absorption of independent state by the Soviet Union on August 5, 1940, repudiated by the Latvian Supreme Council on May 4, 1990; resumption of full sovereignty declared August 21, 1991, and accepted by USSR State Council on September 6.

Area: 24,938 sq. mi. (64,589 sq. km.).

Population: 2,377,383 (2000C); 2,262,000 (2008E).

Major Urban Centers (2005E): RIGA (715,000), Daugavpils (110,000), Liepaja (85,000).

Official Language: Latvian.

Monetary Unit: Lats (official rate December 1, 2009: 1 lats = $2.02US). Following its accession to the European Union in 2004, Latvia announced that it hoped to adopt the euro as its national currency by 2008, later adjusting the forecasted adoption to no earlier than 2012. The lats was pegged to the euro in January 2005.

President: Valdis ZATLERS (nonparty); elected by the *Saeima* on May 31, 2007, and sworn in for a four-year term on July 7, 2007, succeeding Vaira VIKE-FREIBERGA (nonparty).

Prime Minister: Valdis DOMBROVSKIS (New Era); nominated by the president on February 26, 2009, and confirmed by the *Saeima* on March 12 to succeed Ivars GODMANIS (Latvia's First Party and Latvia's Way Union), who had resigned on February 20.

THE COUNTRY

The second-largest of the former Soviet Baltic republics, Latvia is bordered on the north by Estonia, on the east by Russia, on the southeast by Belarus, and on the south by Lithuania. In 2005 an estimated 58.8 percent of the population was Latvian, 28.6 percent Russian, 3.8 percent Belarusian, 2.6 percent Ukrainian, 2.5 percent Polish, and 1.4 percent Lithuanian.

Since World War II the country has become largely urbanized, with an industrial capacity that includes steel and rolled ferrous metal products. Cattle and dairy farming are the principal agricultural activities. Natural resources include extensive deposits of peat and gypsum, in addition to forests that have long yielded substantial sawn timber output.

Ramshackle after five decades of Soviet rule, the Latvian economy was severely dislocated by the postindependence transition from command to free-market policies, experiencing sharp declines in industrial and agricultural output, as well as food and energy shortages. Between 1990 and 1993 GDP contracted by an estimated 50 percent, inflation averaged nearly 200 percent a year (peaking at 958 percent in 1992), and unemployment rose to 20 percent. There were signs of recovery in 1994 (with real GDP growth of 2 percent and inflation down to 35 percent), although Latvia lagged behind its two Baltic neighbors in implementing privatization measures. Growth was impeded in 1995 by a series of bank failures and collateral difficulties in the broader financial sector, despite real GDP growth of 8.6 percent in 1997 following implementation of a tight monetary policy and other reforms supported by the International Monetary Fund (IMF) and the World Bank. Meanwhile, inflation had declined to 8.4 percent for 1997.

The Russian financial crisis in the second half of 1998 adversely affected the Latvian economy, with GDP growth slipping to 3.6 percent for the year and heading into negative figures in early 1999. However, international confidence in the economy remained strong, as underscored by Latvia's accession to the World Trade Organization (WTO) in February 1999 and positive comments from the European Union

(EU) concerning Latvia's requested membership. Although GDP growth for 1999 was negligible at 0.1 percent, it averaged 6 percent annually from 2000 to 2003. However, Latvia was the "poorest" of the ten countries that joined the EU in May 2004. By that time, more than 60 percent of Latvia's trade was conducted with EU members.

Growth of 8.5 percent was registered in 2004 and 10.2 percent in 2005, with per capita GNP having risen more than 50 percent since 1995. However, persistent inflation at roughly 7 percent in 2005–2006 and 15.4 percent in 2008 precluded Latvia's plans to join the euro zone, with adoption unlikely before 2013. Meanwhile, inflation, easy credit, and buoyant house prices created unsustainable consumption levels, prompting a severe recession. GDP grew by 11.5 percent in 2006 and by 9.6 percent in 2007 but was expected to decrease by 15 percent in 2009, following a contraction of 4.6 percent in 2008.

GOVERNMENT AND POLITICS

Political background. Conquered by the Livonian branch of the Teutonic Knights in the 13th century, subjected to Polish domination in the 16th, partly ruled by Sweden in the 17th, and absorbed by Russia in the 18th, Latvia came under Bolshevik control in 1917, prior to German occupation in February 1918. Restored to power after German withdrawal in December, the Bolsheviks were defeated by British naval and German army units in March 1919, and a democratic successor regime was recognized by the Soviets in August 1920 under the Treaty of Riga. Admitted to the League of Nations in September 1921, Latvia adopted a new constitution in May 1922, but the country succumbed to a military-backed coup by the prime minister, Karlis ULMANIS, in May 1934. Latvia was obliged to conclude a treaty of mutual assistance with the Soviets in October 1939 and was formally incorporated into the USSR on August 5, 1940.

On January 11, 1990, the Latvian Supreme Soviet voted to abolish constitutional clauses according a "leading role" to the Communist Party, and on February 15 it condemned the 1940 annexation in favor of a "free and independent State of Latvia" as part of a restructured Soviet Union. The recently formed Latvian Popular Front secured a clear majority in legislative balloting in March and April, and on May 3 the chair of the Supreme Soviet Presidium, Anatolijs V. GORBUNOVS, became head of state by being elected chair of what was redesignated as the Supreme Council; concurrently, the deputy chair of the Popular Front, Ivars GODMANIS, was named prime minister, in succession to Edvzīns BRESIS.

In a March 3, 1991, referendum, 73.68 percent of the participants voted for independence, which was formally declared on August 21 when hard-liners attempted a coup in Moscow. After securing the crucial endorsement of Russian President Boris Yeltsin, the independence of all three Baltic republics was, in the wake of the failed coup, accepted by the new USSR State Council on September 6.

In elections to a restored Latvian Parliament (*Saeima*) on June 5–6, 1993, the recently organized Latvian Way (*Latvijas Cekļš*—LC) won nearly a third of the votes and a plurality of 36 of 100 seats. On July 7, in the third round of balloting, the *Saeima* elected Guntis ULMANIS of the Latvian Farmers' Union (*Latvijas Zemnieku Savienība*—LZS) as president of the republic, and on July 20 the *Saeima* confirmed the LC's Valdis BĪRKAVS as head of a governmental coalition that included the LZS.

The Bīrkavs government resigned on July 14, 1994, following the withdrawal of the LZS because a promise to impose protectionist duties on food imports had not been kept. After a government proposed by the right-wing Latvian National Conservative Party (*Latvijas Nacionā Konservatā Partija*—LNNK) had been rejected by the *Saeima* on August 18, a new coalition was approved on September 15 under the premiership of Māris GAILIS of the LC.

Elections to the *Saeima* on September 30 and October 1, 1995, produced a fragmented legislature amid greatly reduced LC support, with nine parties winning representation and the 18-seat tally of the centrist Master Democratic Party (*Demokrātiskā Partija Saimnieks*—DPS, or *Saimnieks*) giving it narrow plurality status. A subsequent attempt to form a conservative coalition was voted down by the *Saeima,* which also rebuffed a government proposed by the *Saimnieks* leader, Ziedonis ČEVERS. President Ulmanis then called on a nonparty businessman and former agriculture minister, Andris ŠĶĒLE, who on December 21 obtained parliamentary endorsement (70–24) for a predominantly center-right, eight-party coalition that included the DPS, the LC, and the moderate conservative parties. Least comfortable in the new administration was the Latvian Unity Party (*Latvijas Vienības Partija*—LVP), consisting largely of former Communists, whose conservative orientation quickly brought it into conflict with the more reform-minded parties in the ruling coalition. On the other hand, the prime minister himself enjoyed considerable public support for his aim of achieving financial stability and accelerating the privatization program. Backed by most of the coalition parties, President Ulmanis secured parliamentary election for a second three-year term on June 18, 1996, winning on the first ballot with 53 votes against 25 for Ilga KREITUSE (the *Saeima* speaker and candidate of *Saimnieks*) and a total of 19 for two other candidates.

The increasing assertiveness of the *Saimnieks* as the largest coalition partner subsequently served as a source of instability, as evidenced in late September and early October 1996 by the ouster of Kreituse as *Saeima* speaker (on September 26) and the resignation a week later of her husband, Aivars KREITUSS, as finance minister, amid much internal party acrimony (see Political Parties, below). On October 21, moreover, *Saimnieks* leader Čevers resigned as deputy prime minister, claiming that the prime minister had authoritarian tendencies and that the 1997 draft budget was unfair to "ordinary people," his exit leaving the party with only one cabinet representative.

Turmoil continued into 1997 when Šķēle resigned on January 20 over criticism of his choice of a finance minister by President Ulmanis. The latter, however, renominated Šķēle, and the reinstated prime minister formed another diverse coalition of the LC, LNNK, LZS, DPS, and the Fatherland and Freedom Alliance (*Tēvzemei un Brīvībai*—TB) committed to quickening the pace of economic reform, pursuing foreign investment, and approving the nation's first balanced budget. The new cabinet was installed on February 13. However, Šķēle, increasingly at odds with the parties forming his coalition government (which had lost five ministers by mid-1997 to resignations), resigned again on July 28. The coalition subsequently nominated Economics Minister Guntars KRASTS of the recently merged TB/LNNK to succeed him, the *Saeima* confirming the appointment on July 28.

In April 1998 Krasts dismissed his economics minister, a member of the DPS; the four other DPS ministers immediately quit the coalition, charging the government with responsibility for deteriorating relations with Moscow. At legislative elections on October 3, the newly formed People's Party (*Tautas Partija*—TP), led by popular former prime minister Šķēle, secured a plurality of 24 seats, followed by the LC, 21 seats; the TB/LNNK, 17; and the Popular Harmony Party (*Tautas Saskaņas Partija*—TSP), 16. Meanwhile, in the wake of continued DPS infighting, the former leading legislative party managed only 2 percent of the vote and, consequently, did not win a single seat. Subsequently, nearly two months of negotiations failed to produce an agreement for participation in a new government by the TP, which insisted that Šķēle be named prime minister. Consequently, on November 26 the *Saeima* approved a minority government comprising the LC, TB/LNNK, and the New Party (*Jauna Partija*—JP, which held eight legislative posts) under the leadership of the LC's Vilis KRIŠTOPANS. The coalition as initially constituted appeared extremely fragile, however, and in February 1999 the Latvian Social Democratic Alliance (*Latvijas Socāldemokratu Apvienāba*—LSDA) was added to the cabinet, its 14 seats giving the government a majority in the *Saeima*.

Seven rounds of voting were required before the *Saeima* was able on June 17, 1999, to agree on Vaira VIKE-FREIBERGA, a well-respected scholar and independent, as the next president. Meanwhile, difficulties continued within the government, and on July 4 Prime Minister Krištopans resigned in response to what he called "an atmosphere of distrust" within the coalition. On July 16 the *Saeima* approved a new TP, TB/LNNK, and LC government led by the TP's Šķēle. That coalition also proved restless, however, and Šķēle resigned on April 12, 2000. The president on April 25 named the LC's Andris BERZĪNS to head a cabinet that, as constituted on May 5, also included the TB/LNNK, TP, and JP. Although the JP formally withdrew from the government in early 2001, two JP ministers retained their post; they subsequently became members of the new Latvia's First Party (*Latvijas Pirmā Partija*—LPP).

Surprisingly, the LC failed to secure representation in the October 5, 2002, *Saeima* balloting, which was dominated by the recently formed, center-right New Era (*Jaunais Laiks*—JL), the pro-Russian for Human Rights in United Latvia (*Par Cilvē ka Tiesībām Vietnotā Latvijā*—PCTVL), and the TP. The JL leader Einars REPŠE, a former central bank head, was approved on November 7 to head a coalition government comprising the JL, LPP, TB/LNNK, and the new Greens' and Farmers' Union (*Zaļo un Zemnieku Savienība*—ZZS). On June 20, 2003, President Vike-Freiberga was reelected by a vote of 88–6, having won the endorsement of nearly all the major parties.

The LPP withdrew from the government in late January 2004 following a dispute between Prime Minister Repše and Deputy Prime Minister Ainārs ŠLESERS of the LPP. Having lost its legislative majority, the government resigned on February 5. Indulis EMSIS of the ZZS was confirmed by the *Saeima* on March 9 to lead a minority government comprising the ZZS, LPP, and TP. It was widely believed that a minority government was approved in order to preclude lengthy negotiations during a time of historic developments for Latvia (which was seeking North Atlantic Treaty Organization [NATO] and EU membership; see Foreign relations, below). The Emsis government resigned on October 25, 2004, after, among other things, the TP voted against the proposed 2005 budget. Aigars KALVĪTIS of the TP (a former economy minister) was approved by the *Saeima* on December 2 to head a majority government comprising the TP, LPP, JL, and ZZS. In April 2006 all JL members of the cabinet resigned after recordings of phone conversations of Transport Minister Ainārs Šlesers were revealed that suggested his possible involvement in a vote-buying scandal in the Jurmala City Council elections. Šlesers was forced to resign, but all other members of the LPP retained their cabinet posts. The JL's abandonment of the government coalition was an early move leading up to the October 2006 *Saeima* elections.

Despite the scandals and ruptures in the government, the TP and its coalition partners secured a slim majority of 51 seats in the *Saeima* balloting on October 7, 2006. In order to improve the government's legislative position, Prime Minister Kalvītis invited the TB/LNNK, which had often previously voted with the government, to join the TP, ZZS, and the LPP and LC, who had run in a LPP-LC coalition in the elections, in the new cabinet that was approved by the *Saeima* on November 7.

On May 31, 2007, the *Saeima* elected Dr. Valdis ZATLERS, an independent supported by the four government parties, to succeed President Vike-Freiberga, who had served the maximum of two consecutive terms. Zatlers defeated Aivar ENDZIŅŠ of the Harmony Center, who also had the support of the JL and PCTVL, by a vote of 58 to 39.

Following widespread protests in November 2008, Prime Minister Kalvītis announced the resignation of the government, effective December 5, although the cabinet remained in place in a caretaker capacity. Former prime minister Ivars Godmanis of the LPP-LC (now a formally merged party) succeeded Kalvītis on December 20 as head of a reshuffled cabinet comprising the same parties as in the previous government.

The Godmanis government resigned on February 20, 2009, however, following riots in the capital, which were provoked by a drastic contraction in economic growth, income, and employment. President Zatlers nominated Valdis DOMBROVSKIS of the JL to succeed the prime minister on February 26. A new JL-led government, including the ZZS, the TB-LNNK, the TP, and the PS, was installed on March 12.

Constitution and government. Partially reactivated in 1990 prior to formal independence from the Soviet Union, Latvia's 1922 constitution was fully restored in July 1993, confirming the state as a democratic, parliamentary republic with popular sovereignty exercised through a directly elected parliament (*Saeima*). The 100-member body elects the state president by an absolute majority for a four-year term (amended from three years by the *Saeima* on December 4, 1997), which may be followed by one consecutive renewal. The government, headed by a prime minister, serves at the pleasure of Parliament, which also confirms the appointment of judges; however, the latter may be dismissed only by decision of the Supreme Court, as the highest judicial body.

Foreign relations. Soviet recognition of the independence of the three Baltic states on September 6, 1991, paved the way for their admission to the Conference on (later Organization for) Security and Cooperation in Europe (CSCE/OSCE) on September 10 and admission to the United Nations on September 17. Prior to the Soviet action, diplomatic recognition had been extended by a number of governments, including, on September 2, that of the United States, which had never recognized the 1940 annexations. The path toward foreign recognition was eased on September 4 with the passage of legislation providing for the return of foreign property seized after the Soviet takeover. Latvia was admitted to the IMF on May 19, 1992, and to the World Bank on August 9.

Regionally, Latvia concluded a Baltic Economic Cooperation Agreement with Estonia and Lithuania in April 1990. Under the accord, joint ventures were authorized, assuming foreign equity of no more than 50 percent. On September 24, 1991, the three states also reached agreement on a customs union that authorized free trade and visa-free travel among their respective jurisdictions, although implementation of its provisions proceeded very slowly. At the political level, Latvia participated with Estonia and Lithuania to revive cooperation that had existed under the prewar Baltic Council. It was also a founding member of the broader Council of the Baltic Sea States in 1992. In 1997 Latvia moved closer to its stated goal of becoming a member of the Central European Free Trade Agreement (CEFTA) when Warsaw approved a free trade agreement with Riga.

A postindependence objective of securing the withdrawal of Russian troops was complicated by Moscow's intense criticism of alleged discrimination against ethnic Russians in Latvia (see Current issues, below). Western pressure persuaded Moscow to adhere to an August 1994 deadline for withdrawal, subject to Russian retention of the Skrunda communications base for at least four years and with Latvia guaranteeing the social benefits of retired Russian military personnel. Dismantling of the Skrunda base began in late 1998.

Latvia became a signatory of NATO's Partnership for Peace in February 1994, subsequently reiterating its desire for full membership and also for accession to the EU. In the latter context, Latvia and the other two Baltic states in July 1995 became the first ex-Soviet republics to sign association agreements with the EU, offering the prospect of eventual full accession. On October 13 Latvia became the first of the three to submit a formal application for EU membership. However, an EU report issued in December 1996 was critical of Latvia in several respects, most notably for what the EU described as extensive corruption at all levels of government.

Latvia joined the two other Baltic nations in rejecting Russia's offer of a unilateral security guarantee in 1997. Latvian-Russian relations subsequently remained strained partly because of territorial disputes, which had appeared headed for resolution in October 1997. Eighteen months of discussion yielded a draft border demarcation agreement, which was approved by the Latvian cabinet in December 1997, but Moscow failed to endorse the accord in an attempt to delay Latvia's accession to the EU and NATO. (A final demarcation treaty was signed in Moscow in March 2007.)

Collaterally, Prime Minister Krasts pressed for quicker economic reform, which was considered a prerequisite to meeting Latvia's top foreign policy objectives of becoming a member of NATO and the EU. The European Commission asserted that Latvia had met the political criteria for admission but still did not have a sufficiently competitive economy. Consequently, in December 1997 Latvia was not among the six nations formally invited by the EU to begin entry negotiations in the spring of 1998, although it was included among five nations designated as the potential "second wave" of new EU members. Earlier, NATO did not invite Latvia to become a member when it named three candidate nations in July 1997 for the first-round expansion in 1999, but it specifically identified the Baltic states (and two other nations) as strong prospects for membership in the future. On January 16, 1998, the Baltic states and the United States signed a Charter of Partnership, a nonbinding agreement that was seen as supporting the three states' NATO candidacy but hardly guaranteeing it.

Riga's global integrationist desires advanced in October 1998, when the WTO unanimously invited Latvia to become the first Baltic nation to join. The EU later indicated it might be willing to begin preaccession talks with Latvia by the end of 1999, provided Riga continued to make progress on economic reforms. In December 2002, Latvia and nine other countries were formally invited to join the EU. The administration of Prime Minister Repše, installed in late 2002, successfully guided Latvia through the final stages of its accession to NATO and the EU, despite internal divisions regarding Repše's leadership style. A national referendum in Latvia on September 21, 2003, endorsed accession with a 67 percent "yes" vote, and Latvia joined the EU on May 1, 2004. The *Saeima* subsequently approved the proposed new EU constitution on June 6. Earlier, on March 29, Latvia had also become a member of NATO after having adopted a number of reforms, including increased spending on the military.

Latvia supported President George W. Bush in his Iraq policy in 2003, deploying some 130 troops to support the U.S./UK-led coalition in Iraq following the fall of Saddam Hussein. Latvia's defense minister indicated in June 2007 that most Latvian troops would leave Iraq by July. Latvia doubled its troop deployments to Afghanistan after it withdrew from Iraq, in accordance with NATO obligations. Commitment to NATO partnerships was further underscored by the government's announcement in June that Latvia was willing to serve as a base for components of the American missile shield system proposed to protect Europe and the United States in the event of a nuclear attack.

President Zatlers visited Ukraine with a large business delegation on June 25, 2008, to formalize a cooperation agreement between the two allies, emphasizing their shared history and potential for further commercial exchange. Meanwhile, relations with Russia remained strained as Russia granted ethnic Russian minorities in Latvia and Estonia the right to enter Russia without visas. Latvia and neighboring Estonia predicted that integration would falter in their countries if ethnic Russians could travel to Russia as de facto citizens. They also charged Russia with hypocrisy for pushing the Baltic governments to involve Russians in the political process while subtly undermining the naturalization process. Latvia also strongly protested against Russia's war with Georgia in August 2008. The episode caused particular concern given the presence of a sizable and potentially disgruntled ethnic Russian minority in Latvia, as Russian president Medvedev had pledged to advance the interests of Russian citizens "wherever they are." (Many Baltic Russians, who would otherwise be stateless, hold Russian passports.)

Current issues. One of the most difficult internal issues for Latvia has been that of entitlement to citizenship. In contrast to Estonia and Lithuania, where they are far less numerous, ethnic Russians account for more than a quarter of Latvia's overall population, a considerably reduced figure since independence from Russia in 1991, when more than a third of the population was Russian. Tension between the two groups has long been exacerbated by the inability of most Russians to speak Latvian and the fact that Soviet émigrés constituted a privileged economic class under communism. Thus, a major question has been the citizenship status of first-generation residents, many of whom arrived in accordance with a Kremlin-directed effort to weaken Latvian national identity.

Strategies for Latvia's continued economic development and increased European integration dominated party platforms leading up to the 2006 *Saeima* elections. The controversial campaign season witnessed a vote-buying scandal that prompted the resignation of several government officials and an investigation into charges of fraud and money laundering against the mayor of Ventspils. New Era in particular adopted a strong anticorruption stance but was unable to overcome the governing coalition's record on stability, EU and NATO accession, and economic growth. Upon installation of his new government in November, Prime Minister Kalvītis of the TP became the first incumbent prime minister to be returned to power since independence.

Relations with Russia remained fragile, in part due to the Kalvītis and Godmanis governments' inclusion of the nationalist TB/LNNK, which supported stricter language laws and demonstrated with other nationalist parties against Russian meddling in internal affairs following riots in Estonia after the removal of the World War II Soviet Bronze Soldier memorial in May 2007 (see article on Estonia).

Valdis Zatlers, the new president inaugurated in July 2007, was initially not expected to be as influential as former president Vike-Freiberga, a widely popular American-raised former professor and savvy diplomat. However, he surprised observers with his strong support for anticorruption activists in 2007. In early November an estimated 7,000–9,000 Latvians demonstrated against the government's dismissal of the chief of the Corruption Prevention and Combating Bureau (KNAB), which had questioned campaign spending by the TP. The protest, which called for dissolution of the government, was among the largest since independence. Despite dwindling popularity and parliamentary parties' increased adoption of independent positions, the TP had passed the annual budget on October 24, a day after the prime minister survived a vote of no confidence.

However, mass protests in response to inflation and the apparently political prosecution of the KNAB chief, Aleksejs LOSKUTOVS, led to further political instability in November 2007 and forced a reorganization of government, with Prime Minister Kalvītis announcing later that month that the government would resign, effective December 5. Ivars Godmanis of the LPP-LC, Latvia's first postindependence prime minister and interior minister of the outgoing government, was appointed by the president on December 17 and confirmed by the *Saeima* on December 20, addressing issues of law and order and oversight as central to his agenda.

The KNAB attracted controversy again in 2008, as Loskutovs was unable to account for a large amount of money seized in recent corruption cases, prompting some legislators to call for his resignation. By October, Loskutovs' role in the missing monies remained unclear. A new director was appointed in early 2009.

Public anger soon turned its focus from corruption to perceived government incompetence as the Latvian economy was expected to contract by 15 percent in 2009, precipitating the downfall of the LPP-LC–led government. Following protests that evolved into major riots in the capital, Riga, the president declared that the government had lost the confidence of the public and that he would allow voters to opt for an early election by referendum unless the government was restructured from within the *Saeima*. The LPP-LC government resigned on February 20 and was replaced on March 12 by a new JL-led coalition, which included the Civic Union (*Pilsoniskā Savienība*—PS) as well as the TB/LNNK, the ZZS, and the TP, which had been coalition partners in the previous government. The new government, headed by Prime Minister Valdis Dombrovskis, held 64 seats. The new government aimed to restore public finances through significant budget cuts, which were mandated by the IMF. The IMF had granted the government a credit line worth $10.5 billion in December 2008 in order to prevent the breakdown of the economy and the currency's link to the euro. The currency remains at risk of devaluation.

POLITICAL PARTIES

In January 1990 the then Latvian Supreme Soviet revoked the political monopoly of the Latvian Communist Party (*Latvijas Komunistu Partija*—LKP), which was banned on the declaration of independence in August 1991. Having spearheaded the reassertion of national identity, the broadly based Latvian Popular Front spawned a wide array of new and revived parties, with the *Saeima* election of June 1993 being contested by 23 parties or alliances and that of September–October 1995 by 19. The trend continued in the two subsequent elections to the *Saeima*, in 1998 and 2002, in which 21 and 20 parties or alliances, respectively, campaigned. In 2002 only 6 parties met the 5 percent voter support threshold to win seats in the *Saeima*. Similarly, 19 parties campaigned on the October 2006 electoral ballot, with just 7 mustering the electoral clout to send MPs to the *Saeima*.

Government Parties:

New Era (*Jaunais Laiks*—JL). Also referenced as New Time, the JL was launched in February 2002 under the leadership of Einars Repše, who had resigned in November 2001 from his longtime post as president of the central bank, where he had gained popularity for having helped maintain the stability of Latvia's currency. Describing itself as "liberal-right," New Era pledged to combat corruption and drug smuggling, support "honest businessmen," and pursue EU and NATO membership.

The JL secured a plurality of 26 seats in the October 2002 legislative balloting, with Repše serving as prime minister until early 2004, when the coalition dissolved. New Era joined the ruling coalition led by the People's Party in October 2004, but resigned in protest in April 2006 over allegations that members of the LPP (see LC-LPP, below), a coalition partner, were involved in a municipal vote-buying scandal. Following its exit from government, the JL took 16.38 percent of the vote in the 2006 *Saeima* elections, narrowing its share of seats to 18.

Incoming prime minister Godmanis in December 2007 broached the possibility of including the JL in his new government, but JL leaders expressed doubt that the ruling coalition could sustain public confidence. The government eventually resigned in response to discontent with its economic management on February 20, 2008. A JL-led coalition took office on March 12 following discussions between Valdis Dombrovskis and the president, who nominated Dombrovskis to the position on February 26. The government remained fragile, with economic policy set to dominate the agenda until the next election.

At the most recent party congress, held February 28, 2008, the party pledged to support the EU economic recovery plan and allocation of EU funds for economic development in Latvia. The JL gained just 6.6 percent and one seat in the 2009 European Parliament elections.

Leaders: Valdis DOMBROVSKIS (Prime Minister), Solvita ABOLTINA (Chair), Einars REPŠE (Council Chair), Guntis ULMANIS (Former President of the Republic), Edgars JAUNUPS (General Secretary).

People's Party (*Tautas Partija*—TP). Founded in May 1998 by former prime minister Andris Šķēle, the People's Party won a plurality in the October general election, securing 24 seats on a vote share of 21.2 percent. Self-described as center-right, the party's motto and symbol emphasize "a family of three," parents plus three children, which is the size of the family unit the party says the Latvian economy should be able to sustain. The party, considered probusiness, favors close cooperation with the Baltic states and membership in NATO, the EU, and the WTO. The party's initial success was attributed to the popularity of Šķēle, who was largely credited with Latvia's recent economic recovery. Despite the resignation of the New Era party from the ruling coalition in April 2006, the TP won a plurality of 23 seats in the legislative balloting on a vote share of 19.6 percent.

Following the resignation of Prime Minister Kalvītis in late 2007, the TP retained many cabinet positions as a partner in the Godmanis government. After that government's resignation in 2008, the TP joined the new coalition led by the JL under Prime Minister Dombrovskis. The TP lost its sole seat in the European Parliament in the 2009 balloting.

Leaders: Māris KUČINSKIS (Chair), Maris ARBERGS (Deputy Chair), Aigars KALVĪTIS (Former Prime Minister), Andris ŠĶĒLE (Former Prime Minister).

Greens' and Farmers' Union (*Zalo un Zemnieku Savienī*—ZZS). The center-right ZZS, a pro-EU, pro-NATO grouping, was formed by a merger of the two parties below ahead of the 2002 legislative poll, in which the ZZS won 12 seats. Former prime minister Vilis Krištopans was subsequently described as a leader of the ZZS, as was Ingrīda Ūdre (formerly of the New Party), who was elected speaker of the *Saeima* in November 2002. A strong coalition partner of the ruling People's Party, the ZZS secured the second-largest vote share in the 2006 *Saeima* elections with 16.7 percent, granting it 18 seats. It remained a partner in the subsequent LC-LPP and JL governments. The ZZS objected to spending cuts that would harm its agricultural constituency in late 2008 and 2009 and was expected to resist the new government's austerity measures in 2009 and 2010. The ZZS won just 3.71 percent of the vote in the 2009 EU polling.

Leaders: Augusts BRIGMANIS (Chair), Ingmārs LĪDAKA (Deputy Chair), Gundars DAUDZE (Speaker of the *Saeima*).

Latvian Farmers' Union (*Latvijas Zemnieku Savienība*—LZS). The LZS continues the tradition of a similarly named organization founded in 1917 and prominent in the interwar period until banned in 1934. It resumed activity in July 1990. As suggested by its name, it is primarily devoted to defending rural interests, taking a somewhat conservative position on the nationality issue. Having won 12 seats in the 1993 balloting (with 10.6 percent of the vote), the LZS slipped to 8 seats and 6.3 percent in the 1995 election, which it contested in alliance with the LKDS (below, under LZP) and the **Democratic Party of Latgale** (*Latgales Demokrātiskā Partija*—LDP), the latter based in the underdeveloped eastern region of Latvia. In 1996 former members of the LVP joined the LZS, giving it 13 seats in the Parliament. However, the party failed to win any seats in the election of October 1998. New party leaders were elected in March 2001, with Guntis Ulmanis, former president of the republic and theretofore honorary chair of the LZS, retiring from the party in the fall. Augusts Brigmanis was reelected party chair at the March 2006 party congress. His only potential competitor, Mārtiņš Roze, informed the party that his duties as minister of agriculture prevented him from considering additional leadership responsibilities.

Leaders: Augusts BRIGMANIS (Chair), Mārtiņš ROZE (Vice Chair), Ingrīda ŪDRE (Vice Chair and Former Speaker of the *Saeima*), Jānis LAPÓE (General Secretary).

Latvian Green Party (*Latvijas Zalā Partija*—LZP). Founded in 1990, the LZP endorsed a Green List at the 1993 election, which captured only 1.2 percent of the vote. Despite the party's lack of parliamentary representation, the LZP named a member as the minister of state for environmental protection. The party also obtained representation at the junior level in the center-right government formed in December 1995, having contested the recent election in alliance with the LNNK. The LZP was part of the coalition government formed by Prime Minister Šķēle. but was not included initially in the succeeding Krasts coalition of August For the June 1998 elections the LZP joined an electoral alliance with the **Latvian Christian Democratic Union** (*Latvijas Kristīgi Demokratu Savienība*—LKDS), but the grouping failed to win any seats. The party's fortunes rose in July 2002 when the LZP party congress voted to merge with the LZS, forming the Greens' and Farmers' Union (ZZS).

Following the collapse of the Repše government in early 2004, the LZP's Indulis Emsis was named prime minister until December.

Leaders: Gundars DAUDZE (Speaker of the Ninth *Saeima*) Indulis EMSIS (Former Speaker of the Ninth *Saeima* and Former Prime Minister), Viesturs SILENIEKS (Cochair), Raimonds VĒJONIS (Cochair).

For Fatherland and Freedom/LNNK (*Tēvzemei un Brīvībai/LNNK*—TB/LNNK). Founded at a joint congress of the Fatherland and Freedom Alliance (*Apvienāba Tēvzemei un Brīvībai*—TB) and the Latvian National Conservative Party (*Latvijas Nacionālā Konservatīvā Partija*—LNNK) on June 21, 1997, the TB/LNNK is a right-wing nationalistic formation favoring repatriation of aliens, stringent laws on citizenship, and protection of the "purity of the Latvian language," although it maintains a pro-EU and pro-NATO posture.

The TB and the LNNK had been members of the National Bloc (*Nacionālā Bloc*), a parliamentary alliance of conservative parties (including the LZP, LZS, LKDS, and LVP) launched in September 1994. Although the National Bloc components for the most part contested the 1995 election independently, all joined the ensuing center-right coalition government and backed the successful reelection bid of President Ulmanis of the LZS in June 1996.

The LNNK had evolved from the Latvian National Independence Movement (*Latvijas Nacionālā Neatkarības Kustība*—LNNK), which was founded in 1988 and adopted the LNNK abbreviation in 1994. Ultranationalist and anti-Russian, the LNNK insisted that state benefits should be limited to ethnic Latvians and that no more than 25 percent of non-Latvians should be recognized as citizens. It won 15 seats on a 13.6 percent vote share in 1993 but was somewhat discredited by the far-right agitation of successful LNNK candidate Joahims ZIGERISTS. On the president's invitation, LNNK attempted to form a right-wing government in August 1994 but was rebuffed by the *Saeima*. For the fall 1995 election the LNNK formed an unlikely alliance with the Latvian Green Party, their joint list winning only 8 seats on a 6.3 percent vote share.

The TB was an alliance of several far-right groups that allegedly received support from right-wing extremists in Germany. The TB won 5.4 percent of the vote and 6 seats in 1993, rising to 11.9 percent and 14 seats in 1995, thus becoming the strongest National Bloc member. After party leader Māris Grīnblats had tried and failed to form a government, the TB agreed to join a center-right coalition headed by a nonparty prime minister.

The TB/LNNK nominated Guntars Krasts, a pragmatic businessman, for prime minister in July 1997 when the Šķēle coalition government unraveled. In August 1998 the party blocked enactment of amendments that would have liberalized the citizenship law and organized a referendum on a more restrictive policy at the general election of October 1998, which was rejected by voters. Also, with 17 seats on a 14.6 percent vote share, the party fared worse in the election than its components did as separate parties in 1995. The TB/LNNK fell to 5.4 percent of the vote and only 7 seats in the 2002 legislative poll, taking a minority partner position in the new government. Despite refusing to participate in the coalition formed in 2004, the TB/LNNK worked with the ruling alliance on several issues following New Era's exit from the coalition in April 2006. The 2006 party platform called for reduced income taxes, a higher minimum salary for income tax collection, and restriction of Latvian citizenship. The TB/LNNK joined the government formed in November 2006, following elections the previous month in which it secured 8 seats on a vote share of 6.94 percent.

TB/LNNK candidates were cool toward negotiating the border question with Russia and resisted the settlement terms in 2007 (see Current issues, above). The party endorsed the commissioning of a monument to victims of Soviet rule in 2008. A high-profile party dissenter, Ģirts Valdis Kristovskis, exited the party to form the new PS (below) in February 2008, apparently prompting a group of subsequent defections from the TB/LNNK. The party secured 7.45 percent of the vote in the European parliamentary voting in 2009, losing three of its four seats. It placed fifth in the polling.

Leaders: Māris GRĪNBLATS (Parliamentary Chair, Former TB Chair, and Former Deputy Prime Minister), Guntars KRASTS (Former Prime Minister), Roberts ZĪLE (Council Chair).

Civic Union (*Pilsoniskā Savienība*—PS). A prominent TB/LNNK dissenter, Ģirts Valdis Kristovskis, reportedly led an exodus from that party in February 2008, founding the PS with JL member Sandra Kalniete in April. The new party emphasized support for the KNAB and countering corruption. The PS joined the JL government in March 2009. The PS drew the largest number of votes in the 2009 EU elections, with 24.3 percent of the vote and two seats.

Leaders: Sandra KALNIETE (Chair, Cofounder, Former European Commissioner, Former Foreign Minister), Ģirts Valdis KRISTOVSKIS (Cofounder), Anna SEILE (Parliamentary Chair), Ilma CEPANE (Deputy Parliamentary Chair).

Opposition Parties:

Latvia's First Party and Latvia's Way Union (*Latvijas Pirmās Partijas un Partijas "Latvijas Ceļš" Vēlēšanu Apvienība*—LPP-LC). After failing to win any seats in the *Saeima* in 2002, Latvia's Way (LC) joined forces with the LPP to run on a common ballot for the 2006 elections. While the LPP and the LC held similar positions on economics, the LPP has influenced the bloc's identity as a center-right Christian party.

During the 2006 parliamentary poll the LPP-LC alliance secured ten seats on an 8.58 percent vote share. A joint congress conducted after elections in November 2006 chose former prime minister Andris Bērziņš of the LC as chair of the party coalition. In a joint conference on August 25, 2007, the LPP-LC officially became a single party, also incorporating two small, previously unknown regional parties, Vidzeme Union and We of Our Region. The LPP-LC was installed as head of a governing coalition under Ivars Godmanis on December 17, 2007, following the resignation of the TP-led government. Prime Minister Godmanis resigned on February 20, 2009, in response to voter frustration with the government's economic management. The LPP-LC placed fourth and maintained its one seat in the European Parliament in the 2009 elections.

Leaders: Andris BERZĪNŠ (Parliamentary Chair and Former Prime Minister), Jānis DUKŠINSKIS (Deputy Parliamentary Chair), Dzintars JAUNDŽEIKARS (Deputy Parliamentary Chair), Ivars GODMANIS (Former Prime Minister).

Latvia's First Party (*Latvijas Pirmā Partija*—LPP). A center-right, Christian grouping, known as the "clergyman" party because of the number of pastors among its members, the LPP was founded in May 2002. One of its leaders was Ēriks JĒKABSONS, a Lutheran minister who had returned to Latvia after having fled the USSR for the United States in 1987. Many former members of the New Party (*Jauna Partija*—JP) joined the LPP. The JP had been founded in March 1998. One of its founders was the popular composer Raimond PAULS, who was elected chair at the party's first congress. With a membership dominated by center-left young professionals, the party won eight seats in the general election of October 1998 on a vote share of 7.3 percent. After Krištopans resigned in July 1999, the JP moved into opposition, but it rejoined the government in May 2000.

In January 2001 it was announced that the JP had changed its name to the New Christian Party (*Jauna Kristigo Partija*—JKP), representing the grouping's greater religious orientation. Friction with the other coalition members culminated in late January with a group of JP/JKP legislators voting against the administration's proposed laws on pensions and real estate taxes. JKP leader Ingrīda ŪDRE announced the party was withdrawing from the government, but Justice Minister Ingrinda LABUCKA and Reform Minister Jānis KRUMINS chose to retain their posts. This split appeared to precipitate JKP's collapse and the subsequent formation of the pro-EU, pro-NATO LPP, which took ten seats and a 9.5 percent vote share on the 2002 parliamentary ballot. The LPP suffered a setback when Transport Minister Ainārs Šlesers was forced to step down in March 2006 after recorded phone calls suggested possible involvement in a vote-buying scheme in Jurmala City Council elections. The LPP remained in government despite New Era demands for its removal.

Latvian Way (*Latvijas Ceļš*—LC). Displaying a center-right political posture and a liberal-conservative socioeconomic orientation, the group was formed prior to the 1993 balloting and viewed by many Latvians as a "*nomenklatura*" party because of the former careers of many of its members. Nevertheless, its dominant parliamentary position enabled it to lead successive coalition governments, its 32.4 percent vote share in 1993 yielding a plurality of 36 seats. Having slumped to 17 seats in the 1995 election, the LC became a junior partner in the subsequent government before assuming a dominant role in the minority government formed in November 1998 following the October balloting, in which the LC had picked up 4 additional seats. The LC, a pro-EU and pro-NATO grouping, did poorly in the 2001 municipal elections, its loss of support being attributed to growing public disenchantment with the national government. Further distress followed the 2002 *Saeima* balloting as the LC fell to 4.9 percent of the vote, taking no seats. The party's most recent congress was on August 18, 2007, prior to its merger with the LLP.

Harmony Center (*Saskaņas Centrs*—SC). Formed in July 2005, the SC is an alliance of the Popular Harmony Party, the Latvian Socialist Party, and the newly formed New Center. Its first chair was Riga city councilor and New Center chair, Sergejs DOLGOPOLOVS. Dolgopolovs, who was expelled from the National Harmony Party in 2004 after a fractious struggle with longtime leader Jānis JURKANS, abdicated the SC chairship in favor of journalist Nils Ušakovs a few months after the alliance's founding. The SC performed well in its electoral debut, taking 14.42 percent of the vote in the 2006 elections and winning 17 seats in the *Saeima*.

The party was later challenged in the weeks leading up to the May 2007 presidential elections as outgoing president Vike-Freiberga questioned the leftist SC's loyalty to Latvia in a radio interview. In her criticism of the party, the president noted the SC's softer line toward Russia and evidence of financing irregularities. In response, the SC threatened to sue, arguing that the popular president's distrust of the party undermined its presidential candidate, Aivars Endziņš. More moderate than the PCTVL, the SC favors national unity and free language choice in children's education. The SC emerged as the most popular party based on polls of voter support in mid-2009, suggesting that it would be to the party's advantage to remain in opposition until the next election, in order to challenge the government without bearing any responsibility for the economic crisis. The party opposed proposed cuts to the pensions system and sought to preserve social services. The SC purportedly sought to woo PCTVL voters in 2009 by publishing Russian-language materials with favorable analyses of Latvia's Soviet past, while taking a harder line in Latvian papers. The SC placed second in the 2009 EU parliamentary elections with 19.57 percent of the vote and two seats.

Leaders: Jānis URBANOVIČS (Chair), Valērijs AGESINS (Deputy Chair), Aleksandrs GOLUBOVS (Deputy Chair), Nils UŠAKOVS.

New Center (*Jaunais Centrs*—JC). The JC was founded by Sergejs Dolgopolovs after he was expelled from the National Harmony Party by former head Jānis Jurkans in 2004. Its program suggests a progressive income tax, reduced defense spending, expanded social entitlements, and relaxed requirements for naturalization. The JC also promotes economic growth through improved state support of business and decentralized government administration.

The January 2007 party congress focused on drawing up plans for merging with the SC.

Leaders: Sergejs DOLGOPOLOVS (Chair), Leonid KURDJUMOVS (Vice Chair).

Popular Harmony Party (*Tautas Saskaņas Partija*—TSP). Also rendered as the National Harmony Party, the TSP is the remnant of the Harmony for Latvia-Rebirth (*Saskaņa Latvijai-Atdzimšana*) grouping that remained after the formation of the breakaway Political Union of Economists (*Tautsaimnieku Polilitiskā Apvienāba*—TPA). (The TPA was launched in March 1994 by 4 of the 13 *Saeima* delegates elected by Harmony for Latvia-Rebirth. For the fall 1995 balloting, the TPA considered an alliance with the DPS but eventually opted to stand independently, failing to win representation.)

Eschewing ethnic Latvian nationalism, the TSP advocates the coexistence of Latvians and non-Latvians, with entrenched rights for minority groups. In the 1995 election the TSP won 6 seats on a 5.6 percent vote share; in July 1996, however, two TSP deputies followed a breakaway group that opted for merger with *Saimnieks*. As a result the four-strong TSP contingent no longer met the minimum requirement of 5 seats for recognition as a parliamentary group and so technically became independents. The party regained its standing as a legislative faction when a member of the LSP joined its ranks in September 1997.

After the TSP split from the PCTVL, it tried to become the dominant voice of Latvia's minorities. But in the European Parliament elections in June 2004, the party failed to reach the 5 percent threshold, while former alliance partner PCTVL earned 1 seat. The TSP also failed to reach the 5 percent threshold for seats in the Riga City Council during the March 2005 election.

Leaders: Jānis URBANOVIČS (Chair), Valērijs AGEŠINS (Deputy Chair), Aleksandrs BARTAŠEVIČS (Deputy Chair).

Latvian Socialist Party (*Latvijas Socālistiska Partija*—LSP). The LSP was launched in 1995 to represent the interests of the non-Latvian population and to urge the adoption of Russian as Latvia's second official language. The LSP's most prominent figure was Alfrēds Rubiks, the former leader of the Latvian Communist Party who had run on the Equality ticket in June 1993 despite the fact that he was in prison awaiting trial for supporting the failed August 1991 coup on the part of hard-liners in Moscow. Rubiks was elected to the *Saeima*, but the new body rejected his credentials. In July Rubiks was sentenced to eight years of imprisonment for conspiracy to overthrow the government in 1991. Nevertheless, he headed the LSP list in the 1995 balloting, in which the party won 5 seats on a 5.6 percent vote share. Still in prison, Rubiks was also a candidate in the June 1996 presidential contest, receiving five votes in the *Saeima* balloting. He was released from prison in 1997. In 1998 the LSP joined other leftist parties in the For Human Rights in United Latvia (PCTVL) alliance, which enjoyed solid electoral success through 2002. Along with the TSP, the LSP split from the PCTVL in 2003. Despite reports that three other left-wing parties planned to join in the SC, the LSP indicated its intention to maintain its separate identity. (The LSP ran under the SC banner in the 2006 elections, taking 4 of the 17 SC seats.)

Leader: Alfrēds RUBIKS.

For Human Rights in United Latvia (*Par Cilvēka Tiesībām Vienotā Latvijā*—PCTVL). The PCTVL was first referenced in 1998 when the Popular Harmony Party, Latvian Socialist Party, and Equality, which had no hope as individual parties of meeting the 5 percent threshold for legislative representation, attempted to form an electoral coalition to contest the October balloting under the PCTVL rubric. However, the government declined to register the PCTVL, citing what it perceived to be a lack of appropriate endorsement by all the governing bodies of the component parties. Consequently, all the candidates envisioned for the PCTVL ticket were instead presented solely under the TSP banner. One of the main campaign issues for the candidates was pursuit of liberalization of the citizenship and language laws so as to better serve the interests of the Russian-speaking population.

The pro-Moscow PCTVL was permitted to run as a coalition in the 2002 legislative balloting. The alliance's platform endorsed membership in the EU, despite Equality opposition, but was perceived as ambivalent regarding NATO. Although the PCTVL came in second in the legislative poll with 25 seats on a 19 percent vote share, its pro-Moscow stance on many issues precluded it from participation in subsequent coalitions. The PCTVL split in 2003 when first the TSP, and then the LSP, exited over programmatic and apparent personal differences. Members of these breakaway parties who still supported the PCTVL registered a new party, BITE (*Brīvā Izvēle Tautu Eiropā*, or Free Choice in People's Europe), which subsequently joined the PCTVL coalition. During the European Parliament elections of 2004, the PCTVL won a seat that was filled by Tatjana Ždanoka. In 2006 the PCTVL took 6.03 percent of votes, securing 6 seats in the ninth *Saeima*.

Despite a long history of fractures, the affiliated parties of the PCVTL voted in May 2007 to officially merge into a single party, and were joined by the Latvian Social Democratic Workers' Party (see LSDSP, below) in January 2009. During the current legislative term the PCTVL has sought to extend Latvian citizenship to those born in Latvia and foreign residents over 60 years old, and grant suffrage to noncitizens. The party was one of the few in government not to sign the economic stabilization program in December 2008. The PCTVL was third and retained its sole seat in the European Parliament in the 2009 polling.

Leaders: Jakovs PLINERS (Chair), Juris SOKOLOVSKIS (Deputy Chair).

Free Choice in People's Europe (*Brīvā Izvēle Tautu Eiropā*—BITE). The BITE was formed under the leadership of Jakovs Pliners by members of the Popular Harmony Party and Latvian Socialist Party after those parties exited from the PCTVL alliance in 2003. The new party promptly joined the PCTVL in 2003. Given that its founding and leadership has been guided by the PCTVL, BITE's platform should be understood as the same as the parent organization, which is to provide equal rights to all residents, ease naturalization requirements, and allow the Russian language to be used in official spheres.

The BITE merged with Equality in May 2007.

Leader: Jakovs PLINERS.

Equality (*Līdztiesība*). Representing the interests of Russian speakers in newly independent Latvia, Equality secured seven seats in the 1993 legislative balloting on a 5.8 percent vote share. The grouping appeared to have been succeeded in 1995 by the LSP, particularly when a joint candidate list was presented under the LSP rubric for the 1995 legislative balloting. However, Equality, also often referenced as the Equal Rights Movement, in fact maintained its separate identity, becoming a core component of the PCTVL in 1998. Some members, including party leader Sergejs DIMANIS, subsequently pushed for a formal merger with the TSP but were rebuffed, prompting Dimanis's resignation as party leader. He was succeeded by Tatjana Ždanoka, noted for her prominent anti-independence stance in the late 1980s and later for her intensely anti-EU sentiments. A number of prospective Equality candidates for the 2002 PCTVL electoral list were not permitted to run because of their previous association with the Communist Party.

European MP Ždanoka remains a vocal, pro-Russian opponent of Latvian independence. Equality merged with the BITE party in May 2007.

Leaders: Vladimir BUZAYEV (Chair), Tatjana ŽDANOKA.

Society for Other Politics (*Sabiedrība Citai Politikai*—SCP) The SCP is a center-left group that was formed in 2008 by defections from the People's Party. It currently has two representatives in the parliament, Aigars STOKENBERGS and Artis PABRIKS. The SCP secured 3.85 percent of the vote in the 2009 EU balloting.

Leader: Gatis KOKINS (President).

Other Parties Contesting the 2006 Legislative Elections:

Latvian Social Democratic Workers' Party (*Latvijas Socāldemokrātiskā Strādnieku Partija*—LSDSP). Initially formed in 1904 and Latvia's leading party in the 1920s, the LSDSP was relaunched in 1989. However, it secured less than 1 percent of the vote in the 1993 legislative poll. The LSDSP participated in the 1994 municipal elections in various alliances with numerous other small groupings.

In the 1995 national legislative balloting the LSDSP was part of a "Labor and Justice" coalition that also included the Latvian Democratic Labor Party (*Latvijas Demokrātiskā Darba Partija*—LDDP) and others. The LDDP, formed in April 1990, is a minority breakaway faction of the Latvian Communist Party. In 1995 the LDDP announced (prior to the election) that its name had been changed to the Latvian Social Democratic Party (*Latvijas Socāldemokrātiskā Partija*—LSDP), although the LDDP rubric was still referenced for the legislative balloting, at which the Labor and Justice coalition failed to gain representation on a 4.6 percent vote share. (The LSDP rubric was used consistently following the election.)

The LSDSP, LSDP, and others formed a **Latvian Social Democratic Alliance** (*Latvijas Socāldemokrātu Apvienī*—LSDA) for the 1998 legislative elections, surprising observers by securing 12.8 percent of the vote and 14 seats. In May 1999 the LSDSP and LSDP formally merged, with the LSDSP rubric being retained. In public opinion polls in late 2000, the LSDSP was ranked as the most popular party, and it performed well in the March 2001 municipal elections, eventually forming a coalition with the TB/LNNK to govern the Riga City Council. However, the party's fortunes were reversed in late 2001 when a group of its legislators bolted to form the Social Democratic Union (see below) in protest over, among other things, the reported autocratic style of LSDSP Chair Juris BOJĀRS. Although considered "pro-Moscow," the left-wing LSDSP formally endorsed Latvia's membership in the EU and NATO. The LSDSP lost its legislative representation at the 2002 *Saeima* balloting after securing only 4 percent of the vote, and dropped to a 3.5 percent vote share in the 2006 parliamentary elections. In mid-2008 the party reportedly began negotiating conditions for a merger with the PCTVL. However, the party planned to field independent candidates in 2009 following its most recent congress in June 2008. The LSDSP received only 3.8 percent of the vote and no seats in the 2009 European Parliament elections.

Leaders: Jānis DINEVIČS (President), Ansis DOBELIS (General Secretary), Guntars JIRGENSONS (Chair).

The Patriotic Fatherland Party (*Politiskā Patriotiskā Stradnieku Apvienība "Dzimtene"*—PPSP). Founded in March 2004 as an alliance of Latvian Youth Party, United Social Democratic Party, United Social Democratic Party Welfare, and the Conservative Party, the PPSP supported Latvian withdrawal from Iraq and an anticorruption platform, and it won 2.08 percent of the vote during the 2006 *Saeima* balloting.

Leader: Jānis KUZINS (Chair, Latvian Youth Party).

All for Latvia (*Visu Latvijai*—VL) The VL, a radical nationalist youth organization, was transformed into a political party in January 2006 under the leadership of Raivis Dzintars. Its platform includes expelling people who are disloyal to the country and strengthening the role of the Latvian language in society. The VL supported the Estonian government's decision to remove the Bronze Solider (see article on Estonia) and attempted to initiate debate regarding the removal of its counterpart, the Victory Monument, which commemorates Soviet World War II soldiers in Latvia. During the 2006 parliamentary elections, the VL took 1.48 percent of the vote. The last party congress was held on December 7, 2008, in Riga. The party manifesto argued for the expansion of compulsory instruction in the Latvian language, as well as other nation-centered learning objectives. The party secured 2.81 percent of the vote in the 2009 EU elections.

Leaders: Raivis DZINTARS and Imants PARADNIEKS (Co-Chairs).

Latvian Democrats (*Demokrāti.lv*—LD). Known as the New Democrats (*Jaunie Demokrāti*—JD) until the *Demokrāti.lv* designation was adopted at a congress on March 28, 2009, the LD belongs to an umbrella of European parties—the EU Democrats—that seek to address transparency and accountability of issues within the EU by giving European voters a greater role in decision making. The JD received 1.27 percent of votes in the parliamentary poll of 2006.

Leader: Edgars JANSONS.

Pensioners and Seniors Party (*Pensionāru un Senioru Partija*—PSP). Formed to defend pensioner interests, the PSP took 0.79 percent of votes in the 2006 *Saeima* balloting.

Popular Union "Centrs" (*Politiskā Apvienība "Centrs"*). This electoral alliance was formed for the 2002 legislative balloting by the LDP, Labor Party, the **Latvian Farmers Party,** and the **Party of Latvia's Freedom** (led by Odisejs KOSTANDA). The alliance won only 0.6 percent of the vote, below the 5 percent requirement for seats in the *Saeima,* and apparently failed to register any returns following the 2006 legislative poll.

Latvian Democratic Party (*Latvijas Demokrātiskā Partija*—LDP). The LDP is a successor to the Master Democratic Party (*Demokrātiskā Partija Saimnieks*—DPS), itself a descendant of the prewar Democratic Center Party (*Demokrātiskā Centra Partija*—DCP), which was relaunched in 1992 and won 5 seats in the 1993 legislative balloting on a 4.8 percent vote share. The DCP subsequently became simply the Democratic Party before merging with another group in 1994 under the *Saimnieks* rubric (signifying a traditional source of authority, also sometimes rendered in English as "In Charge"). Taking a liberal position on economic issues and exhibiting a moderate national policy orientation, *Saimnieks* won a narrow plurality of 18 seats with 15.1 percent of the vote in the fall 1995 parliamentary election. After its chair, Ziedonis Čevers, had failed to form a government, *Saimnieks* opted to join a broadly conservative coalition headed by a nonparty prime minister, although strains with other participants were apparent in 1996. In June 1996 the *Saimnieks* speaker of the *Saeima,* Ilga Kreituse, was runner-up (with 25 votes) in the parliamentary balloting for the post of state president.

The DPS was strengthened in July 1996 by its absorption of the small Republican Party (unrepresented in the *Saeima*) and by the defection to it of two deputies of the TSP. Internal strains surfaced on September 13, however, when the party council voted to expel the *Saimnieks* finance minister, Aivars Kreituss, for disregarding party policy and for having used his ministerial position to set up a campaign fund for his wife, Ilga, in her candidacy for the presidency. Kreituse showed solidarity with her husband by resigning from the party four days later, with the result that on September 26 she was ousted from the *Saeima* speakership, to which another *Saimnieks* nominee was elected. Collaterally, *Saimnieks* became increasingly opposed to the policies of the government to which it belonged, with Čevers resigning as deputy premier in October. Aivars and Ilga Kreituse went on to form the **Labor Party** (*Darba Partija*—DP) (see 2008 *Handbook*).

Although the DPS had been the leading party following the 1995 elections, factionalism had weakened it by the time of the general election of October 1998, when it won less than 2 percent of the votes and lost representation in the *Saeima,* prompting party chair Čevers to resign. The grouping adopted the LDP rubric in November 1999.

Leaders: Andris AMERIKS (Chair), Juris CELMIŅŠ (Deputy Chair).

Other small parties registered for the 2006 *Saeima* elections included **Māra's Land** (*Maras Zeme*), a right-wing party that won a 0.48 vote share; the **Euroskeptics** (*Eiroskeptiķi*), an anti-EU group that garnered 0.37 percent of the votes; **Our Land** (*Mūsu Zeme*), an anti-EU right-wing party that received 0.23 percent of the votes; the **Social Justice Party** (*Sociālā Taisnīguma partija*), a leftist grouping that won 0.17 percent of the votes; the **Union of National Strength** (*Nacionālā Spēka Savienība*), a hard-line nationalist group that had a 0.13 percent vote share; **Latvian Latvia** (*Latviešu Latvija*), a nationalist group that took 0.12 percent of the votes; and the **Fatherland Union** (*Tēvzemes Savienība*), which also received 0.12 percent of the votes. An additional group, **Victory** (*Uzvara*), led by Vladimirs LINDERMANS, was banned as a branch of Russia's National Bolshevik Party.

Parties Founded since the 2006 Elections:

Libertas.lv. The Latvian branch of the wider Libertas.eu movement was founded on March 28, 2009, ahead of elections to the EU Parliament. The group opposed the EU Lisbon treaty and advocated a more transparent, democratic EU in which a greater proportion of laws and taxes were passed by a majority of elected representatives. The party finished eighth in the 2009 European Parliament election with 4.31 percent of the vote.

Leader: Guntars KRASTS (Chair, Member of European Parliament, and Former Prime Minister of Latvia).

New Latvia (*Jaunie Latvija*—JP). Taking a name associated with 18th-century Latvian nationalism, the center-right JP was founded on March 28, 2009. The platform issued at the founding congress emphasized government efficiency, tax reform, individual work ethic, social inclusion, and a practical approach to foreign policy that coordinated economic policy throughout the region. Education was a key issue, with the party advocating five years of mandatory secondary education.

Leader: Didzis ŠMITS.

Action Party (*Rīcības Partija*—RP). The RP formed in order to protest perceived government failings in economic management in

2009, participating in the Riga protests that precipitated the fall of the Godmanis-led coalition in February 2009. The RP was supported by 0.2 percent of voters in mid-2009.

Leader: Normunds GROSTIŅŠ.

LEGISLATURE

The Latvian **Parliament** (*Saeima*) is a unicameral body of 100 members with a four-year mandate (extended from three years by a constitutional amendment approved on December 4, 1997) elected by universal suffrage for citizens according to proportional representation. (The threshold was increased to 5 percent for individual parties and 7 percent for coalitions in February 1998.) The election of October 7, 2006, resulted in the seats being distributed as follows: People's Party, 23; Greens' and Farmers' Union, 18; New Era, 18; Harmony Center, 17; Latvia's First Party/Latvia's Way Union, 10; For Fatherland and Freedom/LNNK, 8; For Human Rights in United Latvia, 6.

Speaker: Gundars DAUDZE.

CABINET

[as of September 1, 2009]

Prime Minister	Valdis Dombrovskis (JL)
Ministers	
Agriculture	Janis Duklavs (ZZS)
Culture	Ints Dālderis (TP)
Defense	Imants Legis (PS)
Economy	Artis Kampars (JL)
Education and Science	Tatjana Koke (ZZS) [f]
Environment	Raimonds Vējonis (ZZS)
Finance	Einars Repše (JL)
Foreign Affairs	Māris Riekstiņš (TP)
Health	Baiba Rozentāle (TP)
Interior	Linda Mūrniece (JL) [f]
Justice	Mariks Seglins (TP)
Regional Development and Local Government	Edgars Zalāns (TP)
Transport	Kaspars Gerhards (TB-LNNK)
Welfare	Uldis Augulis (ZZS)

[f] = female

COMMUNICATIONS

Press. The first "informal" (i.e., independent) publications began to appear in 1988, of which the most popular (in Latvian, Russian, and English editions) became the Popular Front's *Atmoda* (Awakening). Reporters Without Borders ranked Latvia 7th, along with five other countries, out of 173 nations in its 2008 index of press freedoms. The Communist Party press monopoly was outlawed in 1990, at which time *Diena* (Day) was launched in Latvian and Russian, with a circulation that quickly rose to more than 100,000, but more recently has been about 75,000. Other papers currently published in Riga (Latvian dailies, unless otherwise noted) include *Lauku Avīze* (Country Newspaper, 90,000), weekly; *SM-Segodnya* (SM-Today, 65,000), in Russian; *Neatkarīgā Cīna* (Independent Struggle, 63,000); *Rigas Balss* (Riga Voice, 57,000), in Latvian and Russian; *Vakara Zinas* (Evening News, 53,000); *Labrit* (Good Morning, 36,000), in Latvian and Russian; *The Baltic Times* (12,000); *Biznes i Baltja* (Business and the Baltics, 19,000); *Chas Lilit,* weekly, in Russian; *Sovietskaya Latviya* (Soviet Latvia, 71,300); *Neatkarīga Rita Avīze*; *Dienas Bizness* (Daily Business, 15,000), weekly.

News agencies. The Latvian Telegraph Agency (*Latvijas Telegrafa Agentura*—LETA) is a Reuters affiliate; it participated in the formation of a regional service, *Baltija,* in 1990.

Broadcasting and computing. Radio Latvia broadcasts two programs in Latvian and Russian, as well as in Swedish and English; as of 1999, programming was also available from 16 independent stations. Latvian TV cooperates with British (BBC, MTV), German (ZDF), and U.S. (CNN) networks, as well as with individual stations in Poland, France, and Finland. An independent TV station was licensed in 1996. A media law in 1998 required that 51 percent of all radio and television broadcasts be of European origin and that 40 percent be broadcast in Latvian. As of 2008 there were 606.3 Internet users per 1,000 inhabitants.

INTERGOVERNMENTAL REPRESENTATION

Ambassador to the U.S.: Andrejs PILDEGOVICS.

U.S. Ambassador to Latvia: Judith Gail GARBER.

Permanent Representative to the UN: Normans PENKE.

IGO Memberships (Non-UN): BIS, CBSS, CEUR, EBRD, EIB, EU, Interpol, IOM, NATO, NIB, OSCE, PCA, WCO, WTO.

LEBANON

Republic of Lebanon
al-Jumhuriyah al-Lubnaniyah

Note: Former prime minister Saad Hariri, designated by the president to form a government following the June 2009 legislative elections, was sworn in on November 9 as head of a new coalition government that included 15 ministers from Hariri's March 14 Alliance, 10 ministers from the parliamentary opposition (including representatives from Hezbollah and al-Amal), and 5 independents.

Political Status: Independent parliamentary republic proclaimed November 26, 1941, with acquisition of de facto autonomy completed upon withdrawal of French troops in December 1946.

Area: 4,036 sq. mi. (10,452 sq. km.).

Population: 4,143,000 (2008E). Estimates vary widely; the most recent official figure (2,126,325 in 1970), which excluded Palestinian refugees, was based on a population sample and was much lower than UN estimates of the period. In recent years the UN appears to have accepted the 1970 figure, discarding most of its previous estimates for the late 1970s and early 1980s.

Major Urban Centers (2005E): BEIRUT (1,300,000), Tarabulus (Tripoli, 215,000), Saida (Sidon, 151,000), Tyre (120,000).

Official Language: Arabic (French is widely used).

Monetary Unit: Lebanese Pound (market rate December 1, 2009: 1,501.50 pounds = $1US).

President: Gen. Michel SULIEMAN (Maronite Christian); elected and inaugurated for a six-year term by the National Assembly on May 25, 2008, to succeed Gen. Emile LAHOUD.

Prime Minister: Fouad SINIORA (Sunni Muslim); appointed by the president on June 30, 2005, to succeed Najib MIKATI; nominated to continue as prime minister by the March 14 Alliance in May 2008; formed a new government on July 11, 2008; remained as prime minister of a caretaker government following elections of June 7, 2009 (see Headnote, above).

THE COUNTRY

Lebanon is bounded on the west by the Mediterranean Sea, on the north and east by Syria, and on the south by Israel. A long-standing presumption of roughly equal religious division between Christians and Muslims is no longer valid because of a high birthrate among the latter. (No formal census has been conducted since 1932 for fear that the results might provoke political unrest.) The largest Muslim sects are the Shiites and the Sunni, each traditionally encompassing about one-fifth of the permanent population, although recent estimates place the number

of Shiites at approximately 40 percent of the entire population and 70 percent of the Muslim population. The Druze number nearly 200,000, and Christian sects include Maronites, Orthodox Greeks, Greek Catholics, Orthodox Armenians, and Armenian Catholics. An estimated 350,000 Palestinian refugees live in long-standing camps in Lebanon. Women comprise about 30 percent of the paid labor force and are concentrated in lower administrative, commercial, and educational sectors.

Because of a commercial tradition, Lebanon's living standard until the mid-1970s was high in comparison to most other Middle Eastern countries and developing nations in general. The leading contributor to national income was the service sector, encompassing banking, insurance, tourism, transit trade, income from petroleum pipelines, and shipping. Industrial development, though largely limited to small firms, was also important, the principal components being food processing, textiles, building materials, footwear, glass, and chemical products. However, the civil war that erupted in 1975 and 1976 severely damaged the economy, with 1976 GNP dropping 60 percent compared to 1974. In addition, casualties and dislocations among the civilian population yielded an estimated loss of two-thirds of skilled industrial workers. Although nearly half the plunge in GNP had been recovered by 1978, renewed turmoil contributed to further decline prior to the full-scale Israeli invasion in mid-1982. By 1985 some 70 percent of the country's production had come to a halt, 35 percent of all factories had been destroyed, 80 percent of industrial workers had been laid off, and the national debt had grown by 700 percent in four years to $30.4 billion. The budget deficit grew from $1 billion in 1981 to $10 billion in 1984, absorbing one-third of the gross national product. The agricultural sector declined by 36 percent in 1984 alone, while most government income from customs duties disappeared and the once-stable Lebanese pound lost more than 99 percent of its 1982 value by late 1989.

Although inflation and unemployment continued to run at 100 and 30 percent, respectively, the country's economic future was viewed with cautious optimism following the appointment of multibillionaire Rafiq Hariri as prime minister in October 1992 after the end of the civil war. The United Nations estimated the war's damage at about $25 billion. Lebanon experienced a heavy inflow of foreign investment as it attempted to rebound from the devastation caused by the war. GDP, up about 75 percent since 1990, grew by 4 percent in 1997, with annual inflation running at 8.5 percent. Although described by the World Bank as having made a "remarkable" recovery in the 1990s, the economy remained negatively influenced by high external debt, a growing budget deficit, and severe unemployment.

Consequently, GDP growth began to plummet to only 1 percent in 1999 and fell to –0.5 percent in 2000, influenced by a plodding bureaucracy, corruption, and resistance by vested interests to reform. Economic growth rebounded from 2 percent in 2001 to 7.5 percent in 2004. Lebanon's recovering GDP growth was due to stronger regional goods exports. The depreciation of the U.S. dollar, to which the Lebanese pound is pegged, also strengthened economic competitiveness. The economy also suffered severely from Israeli air attacks in July and August 2006, during the Israel-Hezbollah conflict. About 8 percent of the Lebanese population lived in extreme poverty before the 2006 hostilities; the percentage rose considerably after the bombing campaigns. The Economist Intelligence Unit estimated that the country's economy contracted 6.4 percent in 2006, mainly because of damages from the conflict, which were estimated by the World Bank to be $730 million. The International Monetary Fund (IMF) pledged around $7.8 billion in aid to assist Lebanon in rebuilding infrastructure damaged during the war. The GDP was stronger than expected in 2007, rising 3.8 percent. Nevertheless, Lebanon's growth remained below potential, and unemployment remained high at 9.2 percent in 2007. The country's crippling external debt dropped from 173 to 165 percent of GDP in 2007. In 2008 the GDP grew by only 2 percent, while inflation reached 8.1 percent. Despite the global economic recession of 2008–2009, the IMF reported that Lebanon's economy was growing significantly more in 2009 than the projected 4 percent.

GOVERNMENT AND POLITICS

Political background. Home to the Phoenicians in the third millennium B.C., Lebanon was later subjected to invasions by the Romans and the Arabs, with Turkish control being established in the 16th century. During the 19th century Mount Lebanon, the core area of what was to become the Lebanese Republic, acquired a special status as a result of European intervention on behalf of various Christian factions. Following the disintegration of the Ottoman Empire after World War I, the country became a French mandate under the League of Nations, France adding to Mount Lebanon areas detached from Syria to enlarge the country's area and its Muslim population. Independence, proclaimed in 1941 and confirmed in an agreement with Free French representatives in 1943, was not fully effective until the withdrawal of French troops in 1946, following a series of national uprisings during the tenure of the republic's first president, Bishara al-KHURI. The National Pact of 1943, an unwritten understanding reflecting the balance of religious groups within the population at that time, provided for a sharing of executive and legislative functions in the ratio of six Christians to five Muslims. Although this arrangement helped moderate the impact of postwar Arab nationalism, the country was racked by a serious internal crisis in the summer of 1958 that led to the temporary landing of U.S. Marines at the request of President Camille CHAMOUN. The crisis was alleviated in July 1958 by the election of a compromise president, Gen. Fuad CHEHAB, who was acceptable to the dissident leadership. Internal stability was further consolidated by the peaceful election of Charles HELOU as president in 1964.

Although Lebanon was an active participant in only the first Arab-Israeli war, Palestinian guerrilla groups based in southern Lebanon began launching attacks on Israel in the mid-1960s. In November 1969 Yasir ARAFAT, who had emerged as chair of the Palestine Liberation Organization (PLO) the previous February, met with representatives of the Lebanese Army in Cairo, Egypt, to conclude a secret pact under which Lebanon recognized the right of Palestinians to engage in action against the Jewish state, with the military agreeing to facilitate movement of commandos through border zones. Although the so-called Cairo Agreement was subsequently amended to restrict Palestinian activity, a sharp increase in the number of cross-border raids, particularly after the expulsion of the Palestinian guerrilla groups from Jordan in 1970 and 1971, generated Israeli reprisals and, in turn, demands from the Christian right that the Lebanese government restrain the commandos.

Serious fighting between the Maronite right-wing Phalangist Party and Palestinian guerrilla groups erupted in Beirut in April 1975, exacerbated by growing tensions between status quo and antistatus quo factions. The status quo forces, mainly Maronite, opposed demands by nationalists, most of whom were Muslim, who wanted the government to identify more closely with the Palestinians and other pan-Arab causes, and also demanded revisions in Lebanon's political system to reflect Muslim population gains. The conflict escalated further in 1976, causing widespread destruction and the virtual collapse of the economy. In March a group of Muslim army officers, calling for the resignation of President Sulayman FRANJIYAH, mounted an abortive coup, and on April 9 regular Syrian army units intervened in support of the Lebanese leadership following its break with the leftists headed by Kamal Jumblatt. The Syrian intervention permitted the election by the Lebanese parliament on May 8 of Ilyas SARKIS to succeed President Franjiyah.

During a meeting in Riyadh, Saudi Arabia, on October 17 and 18, 1976, Syrian president Assad and Egyptian president Anwar Sadat agreed on the establishment of a definitive cease-fire, commencing October 21, to be maintained by a 30,000-man Arab Deterrent Force (ADF) theoretically directed by President Sarkis but actually under Syrian control. Despite appeals from Iraq and Libya for a limit on Syrian participation, the plan was approved during an Arab League summit meeting in Cairo on October 25 and 26. By late November, hostilities had largely ceased, and on December 9 President Sarkis designated Salim Ahmad al-HUSS to form a new government (Prime Minister Karami tendered his resignation on September 25).

Notwithstanding the assassination of Druze leader Jumblatt on March 16, which negated efforts by President Sarkis and Prime Minister Huss to secure agreement on constitutional reform, an uneasy truce prevailed throughout much of the country during 1977. The principal exception was the southern region, where fear of Israeli intervention prevented deployment of Syrian-led peacekeeping units. Thus insulated, rightist forces made a strenuous effort to bring the entire border area under their control, but they were rebuffed in the coastal sector, which remained in Palestinian hands.

The formation of a new Israeli government under Likud's Menachem Begin in June 1977 resulted in an escalation of support for the Phalange-led Maronite militia, which now called for withdrawal of the Syrian-led ADF from Lebanese territory. As a result, the political situation during 1978 became more complex, and the level of conflict intensified. On March 15 Israeli forces invaded southern Lebanon in an attempt to "root out terrorist bases" that had supported a guerrilla raid four days earlier on the highway between Haifa and Tel Aviv. Less than a month later, the UN Security Council authorized the dispatch of an Interim Force in Lebanon (UNIFIL) to assist in restoring peace to the area.

On April 18, 1979, Maj. Saad HADDAD, commander of some 2,000 Christian militiamen loyal to the rightist Lebanese Front, proclaimed an "independent free Lebanese state" consisting of an eight-mile-wide strip of southern Lebanon along the Israeli border. The move was prompted by the deployment of units of the Lebanese army, which Haddad had accused of complicity with both Syria and Palestinian guerrillas, alongside UNIFIL forces in the south. A week later, the Israeli government, which was providing matériel to Haddad's troops, announced that it would initiate preemptive strikes in response to continuing infiltration from Lebanon. On June 6, in the context of increased Israeli shelling, "search-and-destroy" missions, and air strikes, the PLO and the National Movement stated that they would remove their forces from the port city of Tyre as well as villages throughout the south in order to protect the civilian population. In both June and September, Israeli and Syrian jet fighters dueled south of the Litani River (below the so-called red line, beyond which Israel refused to accept a Syrian presence), while UNIFIL forces were, at various times throughout the year, attacked by all sides, despite a series of UN-sponsored cease-fires. The situation was no better in Beirut and farther north. On the right, Phalangist, National Liberal Party (NLP), Armenian, and Franjiyah loyalists clashed; on the left, intrafactional fighting involved Nasserites, members of the Arab Socialist Union, Arafat's Fatah and other Palestinian groups, and forces of the Syrian Socialist Nationalist Party. Meanwhile, Syrian troops found themselves fighting elements of the right, the left, and increasingly militant pro-Iranian Shiites.

By mid-1981, in addition to the largely emasculated Lebanese military, the Syrian presence, and the sporadic incursion of Israeli units, it was estimated that more than 40 private armies were operating throughout the country, including Amal, a military wing of the Shiite community, which had grown to a force of some 30,000 men engaged largely in operations against the Palestinians and Lebanese leftist groups sympathetic to Iraq. The most important engagements during the first half of the year, however, occurred between Syrian forces and Phalangist militiamen in Beirut and in the strategically important town of Zahlé in the central part of the country. In the course of the fighting in Zahlé, the Israeli air force intervened to assist Phalangist forces against Syrian air attacks. As Israeli attacks in Lebanon intensified and PLO guerrilla actions increased in Israel, U.S. presidential envoy Philip Habib arranged a cease-fire between Israeli and PLO forces. The uneasy peace ended on June 6, 1982, when Israel again attacked PLO forces in Lebanon, supposedly in retaliation for an unsuccessful assassination attempt by a Palestinian gunman on the Israeli ambassador to Britain. In little more than a week, the Israeli army succeeded in encircling PLO forces in West Beirut while driving the Syrians back into the eastern Bekaa Valley. Subsequently, on August 6, U.S. envoy Habib announced that agreement had been reached on withdrawal of the PLO from Lebanon, the actual evacuation commencing on August 21 and concluding on September 1.

On August 23, 1982, Maronite leader Bashir GEMAYEL was designated by the Lebanese Assembly to succeed President Sarkis; however, the president-elect was assassinated in a bombing of the Phalangist Party headquarters on September 14. The assassination of Gemayel was followed, on September 16–18, 1982, by the massacre of numerous inhabitants of the Sabra and Shatila Palestinian refugee camps in Beirut, where a group of fighters had allegedly been left behind by the PLO. While the perpetrators of the massacre were right-wing Phalangist militiamen, they had been given access to the camps by Israeli authorities, whose de facto complicity generated intense controversy within Israel and widespread condemnation from abroad. Bashir's brother, Amin Pierre GEMAYEL, was named on September 21 as his replacement and was sworn in two days later. The new president promptly reappointed Prime Minister Wazzan, whose new government was announced on October 7.

During late 1982 and early 1983 the presence of a multinational peacekeeping force of U.S., French, Italian, and British units helped stabilize the situation in the vicinity of Beirut, while direct negotiations between Israeli and Lebanese representatives yielded, with U.S. participation, a troop withdrawal agreement on May 17, 1983, that included provision for the establishment of a "security region" in southern Lebanon. The agreement was strongly opposed by Lebanese Arab nationalists and by Syria, which refused to discuss the withdrawal of its own forces from northern and eastern Lebanon, and Israel began construction in August of a defense line along the Awali River, to which it redeployed its troops in early September. The action was followed by a resurgence of militia activity in West Beirut, clashes between pro- and anti-Syrian groups in the northern city of Tripoli, and fighting between Druze and Phalangist forces in the Chouf Mountains and elsewhere.

A series of "national reconciliation" talks, involving all the leading factions, commenced in Geneva, Switzerland, in late September 1983, but they were adjourned six weeks later, following simultaneous bomb attacks on the headquarters of the U.S. and French peacekeeping contingents in Beirut. Subsequently, the Western peacekeeping forces were withdrawn, and on March 5 Lebanon, under strong pressure from Syria, abrogated the unratified withdrawal accord concluded ten months earlier.

In March 1985 a rebellion broke out within the Lebanese Forces against the political leadership of the Phalange and its ostensible leader, Amin Gemayel. Deeply opposed to the president's close ties to Syria, the anti-Gemayel forces seized much of the Maronite-held sector of Beirut, the area around the port of Junieh, and the mountains north of the capital. The rebellion was led by Samir GEAGEA, a young Phalangist commander who had led the raid in which Tony Franjiyah had been slain in 1978. Geagea's forces, styled the "Independent Christian Decision Movement," called for a confederation of sectarian-based mini-states and rejected an appeal in April by 50 of Lebanon's senior Christian leaders for intercommunal talks to achieve national reconciliation. In May, reportedly under pressure from Syria, Phalangist officials removed Geagea as head of their executive committee; his successor, Elie HOBEIKA, who reportedly had commanded the forces that perpetrated the Sabra and Shatila massacres in 1982, immediately affirmed the "essential" Syrian role in Lebanon and Lebanon's place in the Arab world.

Within Muslim-controlled West Beirut, the Shiite Amal militia fought several battles against the Nasserite *al-Murabitun,* the Palestinians, and its former ally, the Druze-led Progressive Socialist Party (PSP); it also continued the struggle against government forces across the Green Line in East Beirut. In April a coalition of Amal and PSP forces defeated *al-Murabitun* and seized control of West Beirut. Subsequently, Amal opened a campaign against Palestinian forces in Beirut and laid siege to two Palestinian refugee camps. The renewed "war of the camps" precipitated an emergency session of the Arab League Council in June, which called for a cease-fire, and, under pressure from Syria, Amal agreed to withdraw its forces.

While the siege of the camps was momentarily lifted, Amal and the PSP repeatedly clashed during the ensuing three months for control of Beirut. Damascus attempted to end the fighting between its Lebanese allies with a security plan drawn up under the auspices of Syrian vice president Khaddam in September. According to the plan, the Lebanese army and police would end the rule of sectarian militias in Beirut under supervision of Syrian observers. Earlier, although the various militias continued their struggle for control of the city, PSP leader Walid JUMBLATT and Amal chief Nabih BERRI had launched a National Unity Front that included the Lebanese Communist Party, the Baath, the PSNS, and 50 independent political leaders, several of them Christian. Formed under Syrian auspices, the Front called for a political program rejecting partition, confessionalism, or other division of the country.

In mid-September 1985 the northern city of Tripoli became the scene of some of the most violent clashes in the civil war. The chief protagonists were the Islamic Unification Movement, allied with pro-Arafat Palestinians against the pro-Syrian Arab Democratic Party. Although surrounded by Syrian forces, Tripoli had become the base of an anti-Syrian coalition that Damascus wished to destroy. As a result of the fighting, 80 percent of the city's 400,000 inhabitants fled.

Events in southern Lebanon were dominated by the redeployment of Israeli troops and its consequences. During the phased departure, militant Shiites stepped up guerrilla activity against the Israelis. In retaliation, as part of its "iron fist" policy, Israel seized several hundred men from Shiite villages and imprisoned them in Israel. To obtain their release, a fundamentalist Shiite faction hijacked an American TWA airliner en route from Athens to Rome, forced the plane to land in Beirut, and removed the passengers to various locations throughout the city. After 17 days the hostages were released through the intercession of Amal leader Berri. Concurrently, Israel began a gradual release of the Shiites, both the United States and Israel denying that there was any link between the two actions.

The departure of the Israelis precipitated bloody clashes among Shiite, PSP, Palestinian, and Maronite forces seeking to gain control of the evacuated areas. However, most Maronite and Palestinian forces were defeated, the southern part of the country falling largely under Shiite control, with PSP forces confined to traditionally Druze enclaves.

Although the Israeli occupation of Lebanon officially ended on June 6, 1985, numerous Israeli security advisors remained with the South Lebanese Army (SLA), which retained control of a narrow border strip, with Israel continuing its policy of hot pursuit of forces that continued their attacks on the SLA.

During 1986 the military alignments within Lebanon underwent substantial (in some cases remarkable) change. In January, following the conclusion of a December 28 "peace agreement" in Damascus between Druze leader Jumblatt, Shiite leader Berri, and Phalangist leader Hobeika, Lebanese Forces units commanded by Hobeika were decisively defeated in heavy fighting north and east of Beirut by hardline Phalangists loyal to his predecessor, Samir Geagea. After Hobeika had fled to Paris (although returning within days to Damascus), both Jumblatt and Berri called for the removal of President Gemayel, who declared that he was "not the problem" and would refer the accord to the National Assembly, which contained a Christian majority. In the south, numerous clashes occurred in ensuing months between Palestinian and Lebanese groups, on the one hand, and opponents of the Israeli-backed SLA on the other, with increased anti-Israeli guerrilla activity by an Islamic Resistance Front that included the pro-Iranian Hezbollah, a radical Shiite group that had refused to endorse the December agreement. By the end of the year, it was apparent that the more moderate Amal had lost many of its militiamen to Hezbollah. Of greater consequence, however, was the reappearance of numerous PLO guerrillas, many of whom had returned via the Phalangist-controlled port of Junieh, north of Beirut. In November the Palestinians surged from refugee camps near Sidon and, in heavy fighting, forced Amal units to withdraw from hillside positions around the adjacent town of Maghdousheh. Druze leader Jumblatt, who had previously supported the Palestinians, immediately announced that his forces would join with other pro-Syrian leftist groups to "confront jointly any attempt by the Palestinians to expand outside their camps." By early 1987 the "war of the camps" had returned in the north, while fighting broke out in Beirut between Shiites and their intermittent Druze allies, prompting a renewed intervention by Syrian army forces to restore a semblance of order to the battle-scarred capital.

The assassination, in a helicopter bombing on June 1, 1987, of Prime Minister Karami reportedly shocked a country already traumatized by seemingly endless bloodshed. Although Karami had earlier declared his wish to resign because of an inability to resolve the nation's political and economic crises, he had been one of Lebanon's most durable and widely respected Muslim leaders.

The most important development during the latter half of 1987 was the increased influence of Hezbollah, which had supplanted Amal in many of the poorer Shiite areas, particularly in the south. During early 1988 the group also moved to augment its strength in the suburbs of West Beirut, provoking violent clashes with Amal that were contained in May by the second deployment of Syrian army units to the area in 15 months. Further conflict between the two Shiite groups broke out in southern Lebanon in October and in Beirut in early January 1989, after Amal had entered into a peace agreement with the PLO. However, on January 30, during a meeting convened in Damascus by high-level Syrian and Iranian representatives, a cease-fire was concluded, under which Hezbollah agreed to accept Amal's primacy in the south.

Meanwhile, the political process in Lebanon had come to a virtual standstill. The National Assembly failed to secure a quorum to elect a successor to President Gemayel, despite a compromise agreement in Damascus on September 21, 1988, in support of a Christian deputy, Michel DAHER. Maronite leaders immediately denounced Syrian "imposition" of the candidate, and, bowing to pressure before leaving office on September 22, Gemayel appointed an interim military government headed by Gen. Michel AOUN, the commander in chief of the Lebanese Army. Pro-Syrian Muslim groups responded by branding the action a military coup and pledged their continued support of the Huss administration, which, following the resignation of its Christian members, continued to function on a caretaker basis in Muslim West Beirut.

Bitter fighting resumed between Lebanese Army and Muslim forces in Beirut in March 1989 in the wake of an attempted Christian naval blockade of ports controlled by Druze and Muslim militias, with General Aoun declaring a "war of liberation" against Syria. Fighting subsequently broke out between units of the Lebanese Army reporting to Aoun and Geagea's Lebanese Forces, placing Lebanese civil war for the first time squarely within the Christian community.

In late September 1989, 62 of the 70 survivors of the 99-member assembly elected in 1972 met in Taif, Saudi Arabia, to discuss a peace plan put forward by the Arab League that called for transfer of most executive powers of the traditionally Maronite Christian president to the Sunni Muslim prime minister, an end of sectarianism in the civil and military services, and an increase in legislative seats to permit more accurate representation of the country's varied socioreligious groupings. Aoun rejected the plan in late October because it did not call for an immediate Syrian troop withdrawal. Nevertheless, the assembly members convened at the northern town of Qlaiaat on November 5 to ratify the Taif accord and elect René MOUAWAD as the new president. Less than three weeks later, on November 17, President Mouawad was assassinated, with the legislators assembling again on November 24 to elect Ilyas HRAWI as his successor. On the following day Prime Minister Huss formed a new government that was carefully balanced between Muslim and Christian officeholders.

Despite Aoun's objection, President Hrawi on September 21, 1990, approved a series of constitutional amendments implementing the Taif accord, and in mid-October Lebanese and Syrian forces ousted the renegade general from his stronghold in East Beirut. Subsequently, most other militia units withdrew from the vicinity of the capital, and on December 20 Hrawi asked Umar KARAMI, the brother of the former prime minister, to form a "government of the second republic," the composition of which was announced on December 24 and accorded a parliamentary vote of confidence on January 9, 1991.

In early 1992 a severe decline in the value of the Lebanese pound yielded an escalation in prices that triggered mass protests by consumers. With no relief forthcoming, the Confederation of Trade Unions (CTU) launched a general strike on May 6 (the fourth in two months), in response to which Prime Minister Karami submitted his government's resignation. On May 7 the CTU suspended the strike, and on May 16 Rashid al-Sulh, who had served as prime minister 17 years earlier, formed a new government that won a vote of confidence from the National Assembly on May 29. On October 31, following the country's first general election in 21 years, Rafiq HARIRI, a wealthy businessman who held dual Lebanese-Saudi citizenship, formed a government that contained representatives of most of the former militias with the conspicuous exception of Hezbollah and the (Maronite) Lebanese Forces.

In mid-July 1993 Israel launched an extensive bombing campaign of both military and civilian targets in and north of its self-proclaimed security zone in response to a series of attacks by Palestinian and Hezbollah forces opposed to the Middle East peace talks. In early August regular Lebanese army units, with apparent backing by both the U.S. and Syrian governments, were deployed to the south in an effort to maintain a cease-fire that had taken somewhat tenuous effect on July 31. However, additional clashes in late August included two Hezbollah ambushes that yielded a number of Israeli deaths and renewed Israeli air strikes against Hezbollah installations. In mid-November the guerrillas launched a major offensive against SLA positions.

On October 17, 1995, the assembly approved a "one-time" amendment to the constitutional provision limiting presidents to a single six-year term, President Hrawi's stay in office thereby being extended for three years (until November 24, 1998). Legislative elections were held in August and September 1996, with progovernment (and by implication, Syrian-backed) candidates dominating. However, the balloting generated much more controversy than expected. Among other things, the government was accused of intimidating and/or bribing voters, unconstitutionally restructuring the sensitive Mount Lebanon voting district, and harassing opponents, who pointed to the presence of some 35,000 Syrian soldiers as evidence of how limited Lebanese autonomy really was. Following the election, Hrawi invited Hariri on October 24 to form a new government. However, the cabinet was not announced until November 7, Syrian intervention having reportedly been required to settle differences among Hrawi, Hariri, and Berri regarding ministerial seats. Although some new cabinet members were appointed, the changes did not appear to reflect any significant revision of government philosophy.

Labor unrest in March 1996 prompted the government to impose a state of emergency banning public demonstrations. Also during the first part of the year the cycle of attacks and retaliatory strikes between Hezbollah guerrillas and Israeli forces intensified, and on April 11 the Israeli government launched the Grapes of Wrath campaign against suspected Hezbollah locations throughout southern Lebanon and on the outskirts of Beirut. More than two weeks of Israeli air raids and shelling displaced some 400,000 people, caused widespread damage, and left more than 200 Lebanese civilians dead. Many of the casualties occurred when Israeli rockets hit a UN Palestinian refugee camp in Qana; although Israel (facing severe international criticism) claimed the incident had been a mistake arising from "technical errors," UN personnel assigned to review the matter concluded that the Israeli interpretation was difficult to accept. In any event, a five-nation monitoring group (France, Israel, Lebanon, Syria, and the United States) was established to oversee a cease-fire against civilian targets brokered as of April 26.

Heavy fighting resumed in 1997 in southern Lebanon, as it became apparent that Hezbollah's military capacity had increased to the point of making an indefinite standoff possible. At the same time, Israeli public opinion turned against their military's involvement in Lebanon, the death of 73 soldiers in a February helicopter crash helping convince many Israelis that they had become mired in their own "Vietnam."

In May and June 1998 the first municipal balloting in 35 years took place and included the Christian parties, many of which had boycotted the 1992 and 1996 elections. Observers described the voting as "fairly clean," an important assessment for the nation's fledgling democratic system in view of the controversy surrounding the 1996 national poll. On October 15 the National Assembly unanimously elected Gen. Emile LAHOUD, the army chief of staff, as the next head of state, after eliminating only the day before the constitutional provision that required state officials to resign their positions six months prior to running for office. Following his inauguration on November 24, Lahoud asked Hariri to stay on as head of a new cabinet, but the prime minister ultimately declined over what he described as Lahoud's "inappropriate" involvement in the selection of ministers. Lahoud on December 2 appointed former prime minister Huss to the post for the fourth time; the new "technocratic" cabinet (containing only two incumbents) was announced on December 4 and received the required legislative vote of confidence on December 17.

In May 2000, Israeli forces unilaterally withdrew from southern Lebanon. Within weeks, the United Nations demarcated a "line of withdrawal" between Lebanese territory on the one side and Israel and the Golan Heights on the other and declared Israel's withdrawal complete. Hezbollah claimed, however, that the "Sheba farms," a 25-square-kilometer patch of land on the Israeli-occupied Golan Heights, was actually part of Lebanon and that continued "resistance" to "Israeli occupation" was therefore justified. Under pressure from Hezbollah and Syria, the Lebanese government officially claimed Sheba farms, thus endorsing the "resistance," and declined to post Lebanese army troops to the border with Israel and the Golan Heights.

Later in 2000 national elections brought Hezbollah into parliament and Rafiq Hariri back to the premiership. Over the next three years, Syria would gradually reduce the public profile of its military presence in Lebanon by moving forces from Beirut to the Biqa Valley and by reducing the overall size of its Lebanese contingent, all the while strengthening its political and economic domination of the country. Meanwhile, Hezbollah fighters harassed Israeli forces in the Sheba farms area and responded to Israeli military overflights by sending unpiloted drones into Israeli airspace and firing antiaircraft guns at angles that permitted debris to rain down on Israeli border towns.

In March 2002 Syrian president Bashar al-Assad made an official visit to Lebanon, calling on his close ally President Lahoud. Relations between Lahoud and Prime Minister Hariri, never good, deteriorated steadily during their joint incumbencies. Hariri had employed part of his vast personal fortune in spearheading the reconstruction of downtown Beirut, controversially increasing the country's national debt. Lahoud (and Syria) tolerated Hariri's premiership out of grudging respect for his ties to France, Saudi Arabia, and the United States and his ability to prime the pump of economic reconstruction.

By mid-2004 speculation ran rife concerning who would succeed Lahoud. By August Syria had made the decision: Emile Lahoud would remain in office three years beyond his legal mandate (thus requiring amendment of the constitution). Hariri bitterly opposed the extension, but was ordered by Assad to comply. He did so but subsequently resigned, setting in motion a dramatic series of events leading ultimately to his assassination in February 2005.

The February 14, 2005, assassination of Hariri united citizens across the political spectrum, and hundreds of thousands of protesters took to the streets of Beirut to demand an end to Syrian military occupation of Lebanon and an international inquiry into the assassination. The largest protest occurred on March 14, four weeks after the assassination, when as many as 1.5 million demonstrators crowded the streets of Beirut. Prime Minister Karami, who resigned his post two weeks after the assassination, was replaced on April 19 by Najib Mikati, who formed a caretaker government to oversee national elections. International pressure and Lebanese protesters obliged Syria to withdraw the last of its forces on April 26. Meanwhile, retired general Michel Aoun, an arch foe of Syria, returned to a hero's welcome after 14 years in exile and announced his intention to compete in the forthcoming elections. Saad Hariri, the son of the assassinated former prime minister, in alliance with Druze leader Walid Jumblatt, unveiled his own list of candidates. Unable to agree with Hariri and Jumblatt on terms for a unified list of anti-Syrian candidates, Aoun formed his own list in alliance with pro-Syrian Christian politicians from northern Lebanon.

National elections in June 2005 produced mixed results. An alliance of anti-Syrian groups, called the March 14 Alliance, won 72 of parliament's 128 seats. Although Aoun emerged as Lebanon's leading Maronite political figure, Hezbollah increased its parliamentary strength in alliance with Amal, and Lebanon's Maronite community insisted that Lahoud be kept in office as a symbol of Christian political status, notwithstanding his close relationship with Syria. Confusion over Lebanon's political direction was punctuated by car bombings that killed several critics of Syria, including journalist Samir QASEER, former Communist Party leader George HRAWI, and journalist-parliamentarian Jibran TUENI and injured anti-Syrian journalist May CHIDIAC and caretaker defense minister Elias MURR, a former ally of Syria who backed Aoun in the election.

President Lahoud's weakened status seemed at first to advantage former general Michel Aoun, but Aoun and the March 14 Alliance did not trust each other, making the ex-general a questionable near-term replacement or eventual successor to Lahoud. The parliament called in February 2006 for Lahoud to vacate the presidency by March 14, 2006. Aoun rejected the call of the March 14th Alliance for Lahoud's ouster and reached out to Shiites by means of a February 2006 accord between Aoun's "Free Patriotic Movement" and Hezbollah. After 15 years of exile in France, Aoun's backing of Lahoud and outreach to Hezbollah signified his recognition of the central role Damascus continued to play in Lebanon and his need for Syrian acquiescence were he ever to succeed Lahoud.

Hezbollah's insistence on retaining its arms and status as the Lebanese resistance contributed to the political stalemate. As part of an ongoing "National Dialogue" begun in early 2006, Lebanon's top 14 political leaders agreed in March 2006 that the Sheba farms were Lebanese lands, irrespective of the June 2000 edict of the United Nations.

Some Lebanese leaders reportedly believed that Israeli withdrawal from this sliver of land on the Golan Heights might be the key to Hezbollah's disarmament and the full deployment of the Lebanese Armed Forces to the country's southern border.

At the end of Lahoud's presidency on November 23, 2007, the National Assembly was deadlocked and unable to elect a new president for six months. On May 9, 2008, Hezbollah launched attacks in Beirut and took control of the Western sector within a few hours. The fighting between Hezbollah and March 14 Alliance supporters spread throughout the country and continued for two weeks. A compromise between Hezbollah and the March 14 coalition resulted in the election of General Michel SULEIMAN to the presidency on May 25, 2008. He took office immediately.

Legislative elections were held on June 7, 2009, and resulted in a decisive victory for the March 14 Alliance, which won 71 of 128 seats. Saad HARIRI, son of assassinated former prime minister Rafiq Hariri, was appointed prime minister on June 27, a move widely seen as a sign of agreement among the various adversarial political blocs in Lebanon. Hariri insisted that no losing candidates for legislative seats in the June elections be appointed to the cabinet. He also insisted ministerial portfolios be rotated among political parties, bringing him in direct conflict with FPM leader Michel Aoun, who insisted FPM caretaker communications minister Jebran Bassil be reappointed to the position. The opposition in the National Assembly rejected Hariri's proposed government, which included 15 ministers from the March 13 coalition, 10 ministers from the Hezbollah-led opposition bloc, and 5 ministers appointed by the president. Hariri handed the president his resignation on September 10 (see Current issues, below).

Constitution and government. Lebanon's constitution, promulgated on May 23, 1926, and often amended, established a unitary republic with a president indirectly elected by the legislature, a unicameral legislature elected by universal suffrage, and an independent judiciary. Under the National Pact of 1943, the principal offices of state were divided among members of the different religious communities. The president, traditionally a Maronite Christian, is elected to a six-year term by a two-thirds majority of the legislature, while the prime minister is a Sunni Muslim formally nominated by the president following endorsement by a legislative majority. The speaker is by convention a Shiite Muslim. The Taif accord, incorporated in 1989, provides for an equal number of Christian and Muslim parliamentary deputies. The National Assembly is comprised of 128 seats; legislators are elected directly to maximum four-year terms.

Lebanon is administratively divided into six provinces (*muhafazat*), each with a presidentially appointed governor who rules through a Provincial Council. The judicial system is headed by 4 courts of cassation and includes 11 courts of appeal and numerous courts of the first instance. Specialized bodies deal with administrative matters (Council of State) and with the security of the state (Court of Justice) and also include religious courts and a press tribunal.

Foreign relations. A member of the United Nations and the Arab League, Lebanon has traditionally pursued a foreign policy reflecting its self-image as a democratic Arab state with a significant Christian population, a country serving as a "bridge" between the West and the balance of the Arab world. From 1948 until 1975 the salient characteristics of this approach were good relations with the West (particularly the United States and France), an arm's-length relationship with Arab nationalists and the Palestinian resistance, a cordial (if wary) relationship with Syria, and conflict avoidance with Israel. In 1948 the country participated in the first Arab-Israeli war but did the absolute minimum in terms of combat. Its 1949 armistice with Israel restored the 1922 Palestine-Lebanon border as an armistice demarcation line. Although Lebanon and Israel remained technically at war, the Israel-Lebanon Mixed Armistice Commission under UN auspices was a model of Arab-Israeli cooperation. For nearly 20 years the Lebanese–Israeli frontier was unfenced and quite peaceful. Lebanon avoided involvement in the Arab-Israeli wars of 1956, 1967, and 1973.

The catastrophic defeat of Arab armies in the June 1967 war and the rise of an independent Palestinian resistance movement posed a new challenge to Lebanon's foreign policy. In 1948 some 100,000 Palestinian refugees had made their way into Lebanon to be housed in UN-run camps. In the late 1960s and early 1970s Palestinian fighters from these camps and from Jordan and Syria began to establish a "state within a state" in southern Lebanon, a largely Shiite area of subsistence farms and poor villages all but neglected by Lebanon's Christian, Sunni, and Druze political elite. The Lebanese government tried simultaneously to appease Palestinian fighters intent upon raiding and firing into Israel while persuading Israel (through the West) that it harbored no aggressive intent and was itself a victim. Growing Palestinian-Israeli violence exposed deep fissures in Lebanon's body politic, as Muslims and Druze generally sympathized with Palestinian fighters while Christians (especially Maronites) generally resented the Palestinian presence. Lebanon's descent into civil war in 1975 reflected the failure of foreign policy to preserve domestic tranquility in a country lacking consensus on the vital issue of national identity.

Lebanon's reputation for moderation and its tradition of effective participation in the United Nations made it the object of international interest, sympathy, and occasional intervention during its 15-year civil war. UN observers were deployed to the southern part of the country before, during, and after Israel's 1982 invasion. Multinational forces consisting mainly of American and French troops tried to stabilize the country in 1982 and 1983. The UN Secretariat exerted considerable effort in 2000 to confirm the full withdrawal of Israeli forces from Lebanon by actually drawing a line of withdrawal.

In the end, however, Syrian intervention and influence proved decisive. From 1990 to 2005 Syria was Lebanon's suzerain, and Lebanese foreign policy reflected Syria's vital interests. When Syrian interests dictated that the Lebanese government endorse Hezbollah's "resistance" to Israeli occupation—even after the occupation ended in May 2000—the government complied. Israel's unilateral withdrawal from Lebanon had seemingly robbed Syria of a convenient way to remind Israel—through violence along the Lebanon-Israel frontier—that there could be no peace without the return of the Golan Heights. When Hezbollah and Syria claimed that the Sheba farms, a small piece of the Golan Heights, was actually part of Lebanon and therefore an appropriate object of continued "resistance," the Lebanese government complied, although a map of Lebanon on the country's currency clearly showed the Sheba farms to be part of the Israeli-occupied Golan Heights—that is, part of Syria.

In August 2004 Syria dictated the extension of President Emile Lahoud's term of office. This action produced UN Security Council Resolution 1559 in September, calling for the withdrawal of foreign forces, free elections, and the disarmament of the militias. Lebanon's parliament nonetheless approved Lahoud's extension, and Prime Minister Hariri resigned and began organizing opposition to Syria. Lahoud immediately appointed veteran politician Omar Karami as prime minister. The adoption of UN Security Council Resolution 1559 in September 2004 also placed the Lebanese government in an awkward position with the international community. The government objected to the UN demand for the removal of Syrian forces until the independence movement forced Syria to end its military presence there. Even after elections in June 2005 produced a majority opposed to Syrian suzerainty, the resolution's call for the disarmament of militias presented a potentially explosive dilemma. Hezbollah's electoral success among Lebanon's Shiite community and its decision to join a cabinet headed by Fouad SINIORA seemed to dictate that the incoming government would continue to define the party's armed wing as the "Lebanese resistance" rather than a "militia," thereby raising the possibility of increasing tensions between Lebanon's freely elected, post–"Syrian occupation" government and the West—particularly the United States, which considers Hezbollah a terrorist organization. Indeed, on the eve of his visit to the United States in April 2006, Lebanese Prime Minister Fouad Siniora indicated that he would inform President George W. Bush of Lebanon's position that Israel should withdraw from the Sheba farms, a position that Hezbollah took in response to demands that it disarm and terminate its military role. Lebanon's government remained deadlocked over demands by the anti-Syrian coalition in parliament for the removal of Lahoud from office, reflecting the protracted nature of Lebanon's relationship with Syria.

Lebanon's internal peace was visibly shaken by the July–August 2006 war between Israel and Hezbollah. On July 12, 2006, Hezbollah fighters crossed into Israel, took two Israeli soldiers prisoner and ambushed an Israeli tank that had entered Lebanon in pursuit. Hezbollah also began launching rocket volleys in the direction of Nahariya, Haifa, and other Israeli locations in response to concentrated Israeli air attacks on Lebanese infrastructure and populated areas believed to shelter Hezbollah's leaders, weapons, and fighters. The Siniora government, a U.S. ally, was powerless to stop Israeli air strikes and deployment of forces into southern Lebanon to combat Hezbollah. Israel was determined to see Hezbollah's military capabilities destroyed despite mounting civilian casualties, which resulted in international outcry and demands for a UN-sponsored ceasefire. On August 11, 2006, the UN Security Council adopted Resolution 1701 to end the fighting between Israel and Hezbollah. Three days later, the fighting ended with a truce. By August 17, Lebanese troops began moving toward the Israeli border. UNIFIL was expanded, Hezbollah fighters were removed from the border, and reconstruction began. Saudi Arabia, the United States, and other Western countries pledged substantial reconstruction funds to strengthen the Siniora government and counterbalance Iran's funding of Hezbollah's reconstruction efforts in heavily damaged Shiite population centers in southern Lebanon and southern Beirut. An international peacekeeping mission arrived to help maintain a fragile peace.

Syria made clear its opposition to Lebanese cooperation with a UN investigation (and potential tribunal) of the murder of Rafiq Hariri and was reportedly behind the November 21, 2006, murder of Pierre Amin Gemayel, the anti-Syrian minister of industry. Ten days earlier five Shiite ministers representing Hezbollah and Amal had resigned from the government. Siniora refused to step down as president and continued to govern with a cabinet that included no Shiite representatives. Nevertheless, Syria formally recognized Lebanon on October 15, 2008. Also, in 2008 international pressure was brought to bear on Israel to withdraw from the Sheba farms as a way to weaken Hezbollah's defense. U.S. secretary of state Condoleeza Rice met with UN Secretary-General Ban Ki-Moon in May to discuss the proposal. The United States and France advocated mediation to resolve the issue.

In April 2009 Lebanon and France approved a new security agreement that increased cooperation to curb terrorism, drug trafficking, and illegal immigration. A second agreement, whereby France agreed to provide training and technical advice on prison operations, was also concluded in April. In May U.S. vice president Joe Biden visited Lebanon, the most senior U.S. official to visit the nation in 25 years. He indicated that U.S. aid would depend on legislative election results and the composition of the next government.

Current issues. In May 2007 the Lebanese army launched an attack on the headquarters of the militant Fatah al-Islam group near the Nahr al-Barid Palestinian refugee camp after militants had opened fire on soldiers in nearby Tripoli. In June Defense Minister Elias Murr declared that the militants had been defeated; however, fresh fighting broke out in July. The overall death toll was at least 246. Violence against the Lebanese Armed Forces in northern Lebanon increased in the summer and fall 2008. In late September and October 2008 Syria began amassing military forces on its northern border with Lebanon, raising fears that Syria intended to use the increasing violence as an excuse to invade Lebanon. Car bombs exploded in northern cities in late September, and many believed the attacks were linked to Syrian intelligence agencies because President Assad had warned that northern Lebanon was "a base for extremism and . . . a danger for Syria."

The Special Tribunal for Lebanon charged with investigating the assassination of Hariri convened in the Netherlands in March 2009. In April the body ordered four pro-Syrian Lebanese generals, who had been held since September 2005 in connection with the assassination, freed, stating there was insufficient evidence linking them to the crime.

After resigning when his proposed government was rejected by the assembly, Hariri was renonminated on September 16, 2009, and talks began immediately to form a government (see Headnote, above). Negotiations centered on whether or not to preserve the traditional 15-10-5 structure of the cabinet. Meanwhile, outgoing prime minister Siniora's caretaker government remained in office.

POLITICAL PARTIES AND GROUPS

Lebanese parties have traditionally been ethnic and denominational groupings, rather than parties in the Western sense, with seats in the National Assembly distributed primarily on a religious, rather than on a party, basis. The compromise government formed in July 2008 included members of the March 14 Alliance and Hezbollah and its allies. That government continued in office after the June 2009 elections.

The March 14 Alliance: An alliance of anti-Syrian groups, this bloc was formed after the assassination of Rafiq Hariri and united citizens across the political spectrum, which led to massive protests in Beirut. The protests ultimately led to Syria's withdrawal from Lebanon. The legislative elections held in June 2009 resulted in the Alliance winning 71 of 128 seats. Saad Hariri was appointed prime minister, but as of October 2009, he had been unable to form a new government (see Current issues, above). Hariri's longtime ally, Walid JUMBLATT, announced in August 2009 that he was leaving the March 14 Alliance to join the president's bloc in any future cabinet.

Leaders: Saad HARIRI (Prime Minister; Future Movement); Fares SOUAID (Secretary General; Lebanese Forces).

Future Movement (*Tayyar al-Mustaqbal*). This party was formed by the late Rafiq Hariri after he resigned as prime minister. Hariri was assassinated in February 2005, sparking the demonstrations that led to the withdrawal of Syrian troops from Lebanon. To protest the extension of President Lahoud's tenure, this movement became the largest bloc in the March 14 Alliance and is now led by Saad Hariri, the son of the slain prime minister. The FM won 26 seats in the June 2009 legislative elections. Saad Hariri was subsequently nominated the new prime minister, although as of October 2009, a new government had not been installed (see Current issues, above).

Leader: Saad HARIRI.

Phalange Party (*al-Kataib al-Lubnaniyah/Phalanges Libanaises*). Also known as the Lebanese Social Democratic Party, this organization was founded in 1936 by Pierre Gemayel as a militant Maronite organization. The party was deeply involved in provoking the 1975 civil war. Phalangist leader Amin Gemayel became president of Lebanon in 1982, following the assassination of his brother, Bashir Gemayel. Amin Gemayel went into exile in 1988 at the end of his term, after which the Phalangist movement lost direction and broke into different factions, thus losing its predominant role in the Lebanese political landscape. Amin Gemayel returned to Lebanon in mid-2000 and subsequently accused other leaders of the Phalange Party of being "too cooperative" with Syria. On November 21, 2006, Pierre Amin Gemayel, the staunchly anti-Syrian minister for industry and son of former president Amin Gemayel, was assassinated. The Phalange Party won five seats in the June 2009 legislative elections.

Leader: Amin GEMAYEL (Former President).

Lebanese Forces Party. Organized as a Maronite militia by Bashir Gemayel in 1976 and subsequently commanded by Samir Geagea, the Lebanese Forces was licensed as a political party in 1991. In March 1994 the party was banned, and a number of members (including Geagea's deputy, Fouad MALIK) were arrested because of alleged involvement in the February bombing of a Maronite church north of Beirut. On April 21 Geagea was arrested and charged with complicity in the November 1990 assassination of Maronite rival Dany Chamoun. In June 1995 Geagea and a codefendant, Karim KARAM, were found guilty and sentenced to death for the 1990 killing, but the sentences were immediately commuted to life imprisonment at hard labor. Subsequently, in 1996, Geagea was also charged with the assassination of Prime Minister Karami in 1987. Following the 2005 election, the Lebanese parliament passed legislation to release Geagea from prison. In the June 2009 legislative elections, the Lebanese Forces won five seats.

Leader: Samir GEAGEA.

National Liberal Party—NLP (*Hizb al-Ahrar al-Watani/Parti National Libéral*). The NLP, a largely Maronite right-wing grouping founded in 1958, rejected any coalition with Muslim groups with Palestinian involvement. It repeatedly called for the withdrawal of Syrian troops from Lebanon and argued that only a federal system could preserve the country's unity. Periodic clashes between NLP and Phalangist militias culminated in early July 1980 in a major defeat for National Liberal forces. The NLP lost considerable influence in the first decade of the twenty-first century, despite the return from exile of its leader Dory Chamoun in 1998, the older brother of former leader Dany Chamoun, who was assassinated in October 1990. Chamoun was the only NLP representative elected in the June 2009 legislative elections.

Leader: Dory CHAMOUN.

Henshag Party. This Armenian party allied with the Future Movement in 1996. It won two seats in the 2009 legislative elections.

Leader: Serge TORSAKISSIAN..

Jamaa al-Islamiya Party. This fundamentalist Sunni group was founded in 1964. It won one seat in the 2009 legislative elections.

Leader: Imad al-HOUT.

Ramgavar Party. This Armenian Party allied with the Future Movement in 1996. It won one seat in the 2009 legislative elections.
Leader: Jean OGASSAPIAN.

National Bloc (*al-Kutlah al-Wataniyah/Bloc National*). The National Bloc, a Maronite party formed in 1943, has been opposed to military involvement in politics. In 2008 Carlos Edde called for the disarmament of Hezbollah and reconciliation between all Lebanese factions. The National Bloc won no seats in the 2009 legislative elections.
Leader: Carlos EDDE.

Opposition Parties:

Party of God (*Hizb Allah*, commonly rendered *Hezbollah*). Hezbollah, a Shiite group, announced its formation in 1985, stating its goal was to establish an Islamic state in Lebanon. Hezbollah subsequently assumed the major role in the "war of liberation" against Israeli forces in southern Lebanon, widely believed to be financed by Syria and Iran. By 1996, however, Hezbollah had earned significant grassroots support within the Shiite populace because of its network of health and other social services. Therefore, it was considered less "subservient" to Syria, although the party bowed to pressure from Damascus by agreeing to present joint candidates with Amal for the 1996 legislative balloting.

Although Hezbollah formally endorsed the "liberation" of Jerusalem through jihad (holy war) and condemned Western culture and political influence, its primary goal was the withdrawal of Israeli troops from southern Lebanon. Following the unilateral withdrawal of Israeli forces from southern Lebanon in 2000, Hezbollah was widely viewed in the Middle East as having engineered the first Arab "victory" in the long-standing conflict with Israel.

In late 2001 the United States, having included Hezbollah on its list of terrorist organizations, called on countries to freeze Hezbollah's financial assets. However, as expected, the Lebanese government rejected the U.S. demand, calling Hezbollah's anti-Israeli stance legitimate "resistance" and praising the organization for its social programs. The European Union also declined to include Hezbollah on the list of organizations that it considers supportive of terrorism.

The adoption of UNSC Resolution 1559 which called for "the disbanding and disarmament of all Lebanese and non-Lebanese militias," put pressure on Hezbollah, particularly after the assassination of Rafiq Hariri. However, Hezbollah performed well in the 2005 parliamentary elections, winning 35 seats as part of a coalition with Amal. In July 2005 Hezbollah agreed to join a government, heading a ministry for the first time. On November 11, 2006, Hezbollah and its allies in the cabinet resigned from the Siniora government.

On May 6, 2008, the pro-U.S. March 14 government issued two directives designed to undermine Hezbollah's military autonomy. In response, Hezbollah took control of West Beirut on May 9. The fighting in Beirut marked the first time Hezbollah had used its military weapons against the Lebanese people. As a result, the popularity of the group fell. A compromise between Hezbollah and the March 14 Alliance led to the election of Gen. Michel Sulieman as president in late May and the creation of a new cabinet in July.

In June 2009 Hezbollah and its allies in the Loyalty to the Resistance Bloc won 13 seats in the National Assembly. Hezbollah subsequently led the effort to reject incoming Prime Minister Saad Hariri's proposed government in September 2009.
Leader: Sayyed Hassan NASRALLAH (Secretary General).

Amal (*Amal*). Amal, an acronym for *Afwaj al-Muqawa al-Lubnaniyah* (Groups of the Lebanese Resistance), which also means "hope," was founded by Imam Musa SADR as the militia of the Movement of the Disinherited. Although allied with the Palestinian left during the civil war, Amal subsequently became increasingly militant on behalf of Lebanon's Shiites, many of whom had been forced from their homes in the south, and in support of the Iranian revolution of 1979.

After the 1982 Israeli invasion, several pro-Iranian offshoots of Amal emerged as well-organized guerrilla movements, among them Hezbollah, which operated against U.S., French, and Israeli forces with great effectiveness. A "war of words" developed between Amal and Hezbollah prior to the 1996 legislative balloting, and it initially appeared that they would present competing candidates (unlike in 1992). However, reportedly under pressure from Syrian leaders, the two groups finally agreed (a week before the balloting) on a joint accord and national list, which secured nearly all the seats in southern Lebanon. Amal leader Nabih Berri was subsequently reelected speaker of the National Assembly. Amal has been largely disarmed in recent years, as Hezbollah presented the primary military opposition to Israeli forces in southern Lebanon. Amal opposed the Syrian withdrawal of 2005. Following the parliamentary elections of 2005, Berri was reelected speaker of the National Assembly. Most of Amal's support today comes from coastal cities in Lebanon's south. Following the 2005 election, Amal joined Hezbollah in the Lebanese cabinet, but on November 11, 2006, it supported Hezbollah's decision to leave the Siniora government. Amal allied itself with Hezbollah and other opposition parties in the legislative elections of June 2009. The party won 13 seats.
Leader: Nabih BERRI (President of the Party and Speaker of the National Assembly).

Syrian Socialist Nationalist Party (*Parti Socialiste Nationaliste Syrien*—PSNS). Organized as the Syrian Nationalist Party in 1932 in support of a "Greater Syria" embracing Iraq, Jordan, Lebanon, Syria, and Palestine, the PSNS was considered a rightist group until 1970. Also known as the Syrian People's Party, it was banned from 1962 to 1969 after participating in an attempted coup in December 1961. The party split into factions in the 1970s but reunited by the end of the decade. In 2005 the PSNS allied with Hezbollah in a pro-Syrian bloc, blaming Israel for the assassination of Rafiq Hariri. In June 2009 the PSNS won two seats in the legislative elections.
Leader: Ali QANSO.

Free Patriotic Movement—FPM (*Tayyar al-Watani al-Hurr*). This party is led by Michel Aoun, former general in the Lebanese Army, who served as the provisional prime minister of one of two governments that contended for power in the final years of the civil war. Most of its leadership and support comes from Lebanon's Christian community. Aoun led the FPM from abroad while he was exiled in Paris. He returned to Lebanon in May 2005 to run in the legislative elections held in May and June. The Free Patriotic Movement and its allies won 21 seats in the 128-member National Assembly. The party left the March 14 Alliance in 2006 and joined the opposition. The FPM won 19 seats in the June 2009 legislative elections. In September 2009 the FPM helped prevent approval of incoming Prime Minister Saad Hariri's proposed cabinet because it denied Aoun the right to nominate the party's ministers.
Leader: Michel AOUN.

Marada Movement. The Marada Movement originated as a militia during the civil war, when it was known as the Marada Brigade. The militia became firmly pro-Syrian in the late 1970s. It was launched as a political party in 2006, when it allied with the pro-Syrian opposition. Its supporters are primarily Christian. The party won four seats in the June 2009 legislative elections.
Leader: Suleiman FRANJIEH.

Tashnaq Party. The Tashnaq Party, or the Armenian Revolutionary Federation, is the most influential of the three Armenian political parties in Lebanon. The party was founded in 1890 and operates in countries with significant Armenian populations. Before the Lebanese Civil War, the party was aligned with the Phalangist Party; in 2000 the Tashnaq split with Rafiq Hariri and in parliamentary elections that year won only 1 seat. The Tashnaq boycotted the 2005 elections and lost all seats. Although courted by Saad Hariri in 2009, the Tashnaq joined the pro-Syrian bloc and won two seats in the legislature.
Leader: Hoviq MEKHITARIAN (Chair).

Lebanese Democratic Party (*Hizb al-dimuqrati al-lubnani*). The Lebanese Democratic Party was founded by Talal Arslaw, a Druze, in 2001. It won two seats in the June 2009 legislative elections.
Leader: Talal ARSLAW.

Baath Party: The Baath Party was founded in Syria in the 1940s to unify all Arabs in one country. The Lebanese branch remains closely affiliated with the Syrian branch. The Baath Party won two seats in the June 2009 legislative elections.
Leader: Assem QANSO.

Other Parties

Progressive Socialist Party—PSP (*al-Hizb al-Taqaddumi al-Ishtiraki/ Parti Socialiste Progressif*). Founded in 1948, the PSP is a largely Druze group that advocates a socialist program with nationalist and anti-Western overtones. Relations between former party president

Kamal Jumblatt and President Assad of Syria soured in the 1970s, before the Syrian intervention of April 1976. Jumblatt was assassinated in March 1977, and the party leadership shifted to his son, Walid, who subsequently became a Syrian ally and during the Israeli occupation established close ties with the Shiite Amal organization (see above). The alliance ended in early 1987, when the PSP intervened on the side of the PLO in the war of the camps in Beirut. The PSP became steadily more vocal in its opposition to the Syrian presence in Lebanon and opposed the three-year extension given by the National Assembly for President Lahoud's term.

The PSP allied itself with the March 14 movement after the assassination of Rafiq Hariri and won 11 seats in the June 2009 elections as part of the March 14 bloc. However, Walid Jumblatt, leader of the party, announced on August 3, 2009, that the PSP would align itself with the president, rather than the March 14 bloc, in the incoming government. This substantially reduced the majority won by the March 14 bloc in the June legislative elections and weakened the movement's influence in the incoming cabinet.

Leader: Walid Kamal JUMBLATT.

Lebanese Communist Party—LCP (*al-Hizb al-Shuyui al-Lubnani/Parti Communiste Libanais*). The LCP was founded in 1924 as the Lebanese People's Party, banned in 1939 by the French Mandate Authority, and legalized in 1970. Although primarily Christian in the first half-century of its existence, the party became predominantly Muslim in the wake of the civil war. Its longtime secretary general, George Hrawi, also served as a vice president of the National Movement. In June 2005 Hrawi, who had left the Communist Party, was assassinated. This made him the third prominent anti-Syrian politician killed that year.

Leader: Khaled HADADEH (Secretary General).

For information on the **al-Waad Party**, see the 2008 *Handbook*.

Note: For a discussion of Palestinian groups formerly headquartered in Lebanon, see article on the PLO.

LEGISLATURE

The former Chamber of Deputies, which in March 1979 changed its name to the **National Assembly** (*Majlis al-Nuwwab*), is a unicameral body elected by universal suffrage for a four-year term (subject to dissolution) through a proportional system based on religious groupings. The National Pact of 1943 specified that the speaker be a Shiite Muslim. The distribution of seats was on the basis of a 6:5 Christian to Muslim ratio until 1990 when, in implementation of a provision of the Taif accord, the total number of seats was raised from 99 to 108, with half assigned to each group. That ratio was maintained in 1996, when the number of seats was increased to 128.

Candidates are not presented as nominees of political parties but on lists supportive of prominent politicians or alliances of political organizations. The March 14 Alliance, an anti-Syrian coalition, polled successfully in the 2009 elections, winning 71 of 128 seats. Hezbollah, Amal, the Free Patriotic Movement, and their allies won 57 seats. Amal's Nabih Berri was subsequently reelected speaker by the new assembly.

Speaker: Nabih BERRI.

CABINET

The cabinet is traditionally divided into a 15-10-5 structure, granting the majority party 15 ministers, the opposition 10, and the president, 5.

[as of October 1, 2009]

Prime Minister	Fouad Siniora (Sunni, Future Movement)
Deputy Prime Minister	Elias Murr (Greek Orthodox, Suliemanally)
Deputy Prime Minister	Issam Abu Jamra (Greek Orthodox, Hezbollah ally)
Ministers	
Administrative Reform	Ibrahim Shamseddine (Shiite, March 14)
Agriculture	Elie Skaf (Greek Orthodox, Hezbollah ally)
Culture	Tamam Slam (Sunni, March 14)
Defense	Elias Murr (Greek Orthodox, Sulieman ally)
Displaced Persons	Raymond Audi (Greek Orthodox, March 14)
Economy and Trade	Mohammad Safadi (Sunni, March 14)
Education and Higher Education	Bahia Hariri (Sunni, March 14) [f]
Energy and Water	Alan Taborian (Armenian, Hezbollah ally)
Environment	Antoine Karam (Maronite, March 14)
Finance	Mohamad Chatah (Sunni, March 14)
Foreign Affairs and Emigrants	Fawzi Salloukh (Shiite, Hezbollah)
Industry and Oil	Ghazi Zaayter (Shiite, Hezbollah ally)
Information	Tareq Mitri (Greek Orthodox, March 14)
Interior and Municipalities	Ziad Baroud (Maronite, Sulieman ally)
Justice	Ibrahim Najjar (Greek Orthodox, March 14)
Labor	Mohammed Feneish (Shiite, Hezbollah ally)
Public Health	Mohamed Jawad Khalifé (Shiite, Hezbollah ally)
Public Works and Transport	Ghazi Hani Aridi (Druze, March 14)
Social Affairs	Mario Aoun (Maronite, Hezbollah ally)
Telecommunications	Gibran Bassil (Maronite, Hezbollah ally)
Tourism	Elie Marouni (Maronite, March 14)
Youth and Sports	Talal Arslan (Druze, Hezbollah ally)
Ministers of State	
	Yussef Tagla (Catholic, Sulieman ally)
	Khaled Qabbani (Sunni, March 14)
	Nassib Lahoud (Maronite, March 14)
	Jean Ogasapian (Armenian, March 14)
	Wael Abu Faour (Druze, March 14)
	Ali Qanso (Shiite, Hezbollah ally)

[f] = female

Note: The current cabinet is a caretaker government that remained in place following the June 2009 legislative elections (see Headnote, above).

COMMUNICATIONS

For a time, relative to other Middle Eastern countries, in Lebanon the press was traditionally free from external controls, but Syrian troops forced suspension of a number of newspapers in December 1976. Following the imposition of formal censorship on January 1, 1977, most suspended newspapers were permitted to resume publication; a number of newspapers and periodicals decided to publish from abroad. Between March and July 1994 the government also banned political broadcasting by private stations. In its 2008 annual index on freedom of the press, Reporters Without Borders ranked Lebanon 66th, along with Botswana, out of 173 countries.

Press. The following are published daily in Beirut in Arabic, unless otherwise noted: *al-Nahar* (78,000), independent; *al-Anwar* (The Light, 59,000), independent; *al-Safir* (The Envoy, 50,000), independent; *al-Amal* (Hope, 35,000), Phalangist; *al-Hayat* (Life, 32,000), independent; *al-Dunya* (The World, 25,000); *al-Liwa* (The Standard, 15,000); *al-Mustaqbal* (The Future), founded by Rafiq Hariri; *al-Sharq* (The East, 36,000); *al-Nida* (The Appeal, 10,000), Communist; *al-Jaridah* (The News, 22,000), independent; *Daily Star,* independent (English); *L'Orient–Le Jour* (French, 23,000), independent; *Le Soir* (French, 17,000).

News agencies. The principal domestic facility is the National News Agency (*Wakalat al-Anba al-Wataniyah*). In addition, most foreign bureaus maintain offices in Beirut.

Broadcasting and computing. The government-controlled Radio Lebanon (*Idhaat Lubnan/Radio Liban*) broadcasts nationally in Arabic, Armenian, English, and French and internationally to three continents. Television Lebanon (*Tilifiziyun Lubnan/Télé Liban*) broadcasts over three channels. In addition, the chaotic conditions of the lengthy civil war prompted the unlicensed launching of some 100 radio and 20 television stations that the government, since early 1992, has been attempting to shut down. In 1994 a law was enacted that revoked the monopoly held by Television Lebanon and Radio Lebanon over licensed broadcasting and laid the legal groundwork for the operation of privately owned television and radio stations. In 1996 the government approved new licensing regulations that were expected to result in the closing of about two-thirds of television and radio stations. However, the enterprises in jeopardy continued to operate, pending a government review of the new code, which had prompted domestic and international complaints regarding attempted "press muzzling."

Today there are several legal private television and satellite channels. Some, such as Manar TV (operated by Hezbollah) and Future TV (operated by the Future Movement), were founded by political organizations. Others include the Lebanese Broadcasting Corporation, New TV, and the National Broadcasting Network. As of 2008 there were 225.3 Internet users per 1,000 inhabitants.

INTERGOVERNMENTAL REPRESENTATION

Ambassador to the U.S.: Antoine CHEDID.

U.S. Ambassador to Lebanon: Michele J. SISON.

Permanent Representative to the UN: Nawaf SALAM.

IGO Memberships (Non-UN): AFESD, AMF, BADEA, IDB, Interpol, LAS, NAM, OIC, OIF, PCA, WCO.

LESOTHO

Kingdom of Lesotho

Political Status: Traditional monarchy, independent within the Commonwealth since October 4, 1966.

Area: 11,720 sq. mi. (30,355 sq. km.).

Population: 1,872,721 (2006C); 2,741,000 (2008E), even without the exclusion of expatriate workers in South Africa (approximately 150,000 in 1999), the 2006 figure would appear to reflect substantial underenumeration

Major Urban Center (2005E): MASERU (185,000).

Official Languages: English, Sesotho.

Monetary Unit: Loti (official rate December 1, 2009: 7.33 maloti = $1US). The loti is at par with the South African rand, although under a Tripartite Monetary Area agreement concluded between Lesotho, Swaziland, and South Africa on July 1, 1986, the rand has ceased to be legal tender in Lesotho.

Sovereign: King LETSIE III; became king upon the dethronement of his father, King MOSHOESHOE II. on November 6, 1990; voluntarily abdicated upon his father's return to the throne on January 25, 1995; became king again on February 7, 1996, following the death of his father on January 15; took coronation oath on October 31, 1997.

Prime Minister: Bethuel Pakalitha MOSISILI (Lesotho Congress for Democracy); sworn in on May 29, 1998, following intraparty caucus election, replacing Ntsu MOKHEHLE (Lesotho Congress for Democracy); formed new government on June 3, 1998; formed new government on June 11, 2002, following legislative balloting of May 25; formed new government on March 2, 2007, following legislative balloting on February 17.

THE COUNTRY

Lesotho, the former British High Commission territory of Basutoland, is a hilly, landlocked enclave within the territory of South Africa. The Basotho people, whose vernacular language is Sesotho, constitute more than 99 percent of the population, which includes small European and Asian minorities. About 80 percent of the population is nominally Christian. The economy is largely based on agriculture and stock raising; diamond mining, which in the late 1970s accounted for more than half of export earnings, was discontinued in 1982 but was resumed in the early 2000s after the discovery of several high-value gems. Lesotho is highly dependent on South Africa, its main trading partner, which employs 80 percent of the country's wage earners and is the principal supplier of energy. Because of the unusual employment pattern, women are primarily responsible for subsistence activities, although they are unable by custom to control household wealth.

Economic growth was stagnant in the early and mid-1980s, partly because of prolonged droughts that depressed agricultural output and compounded problems of unemployment, landlessness, and inflation. However, real GDP growth averaged 6 percent annually from 1987 to 1997, under the influence of an expanding manufacturing sector, a collateral growth in exports, and the economic effect of investment in the massive Lesotho Highlands Water Project (LHWP, see Foreign relations, below). Severe political disruption in 1997 and 1998 (see Political background, below) contributed to a 3.6 percent decline in real GDP in fiscal year April 1998–March 1999. In December 1999 the government, in conjunction with the International Monetary Fund (IMF), announced a new economic recovery program designed to attract foreign investment, diversify the manufacturing base, enhance tourism, privatize state-run enterprises and otherwise promote the private sector, reform tax policy, and overhaul the financial sector. In early 2001 the IMF approved a new three-year assistance package but warned that the country continued to face a serious HIV/AIDS problem, as well as widespread unemployment and poverty. Other observers cited rampant corruption in the government and civil service as a barrier to effective economic and political reform.

The economy was severely compromised in 2001 and 2002 as the result of massive food shortages resulting from drought and soil degradation. Agricultural production subsequently increased, although food shortfalls continued into 2007, and rising food prices contributed to high inflation and burgeoning governmental budget deficits.

Annual GDP growth averaged 3 percent from 2005–2007, due in large part to significant growth in the textile industry and diamond production. Drought hit again in 2007, prompting the UN to appeal for massive international assistance for what it described as the most severe conditions in 30 years. Widespread poverty and the high incidence of HIV/AIDS continued to be major concerns, despite a concerted government effort to address the latter. By April 2008 the United States and other international donors had pledged some $19 million in food aid to address the crisis. Strong GDP growth of about 5 percent was recorded in 2008, owing largely to the textile and clothing industry, but economic growth was expected to contract to around 2 percent in 2009 in the wake of the global economic crisis and a significant decrease in demand for garments. Food prices increased, as did inflation and unemployment. On a positive note, in 2009 the government began a pilot program that provided grants to assist some 5,000 orphans and vulnerable children. An expanded version of the program was planned for 2010.

GOVERNMENT AND POLITICS

Political background. United under MOSHOESHOE I in the mid-19th century, Basutoland came under British protection in 1868 and was governed from 1884 by a British high commissioner. A local consultative body, the Basutoland Council, was established as early as 1903, but the decisive move toward nationhood began in the mid-1950s and culminated in the attainment of full independence within the Commonwealth as the Kingdom of Lesotho in 1966. MOSHOESHOE II, the country's paramount chief, became king of the new state, and Chief Leabua JONATHAN, whose Basutoland National Party (BNP) had won a legislative majority in the preindependence election, became prime minister.

A trial of strength between the king and prime minister erupted in 1966 when the former's attempt to gain personal control over both foreign and domestic policy led to rioting by opposition parties; after being briefly confined to his palace, the king agreed to abide by the

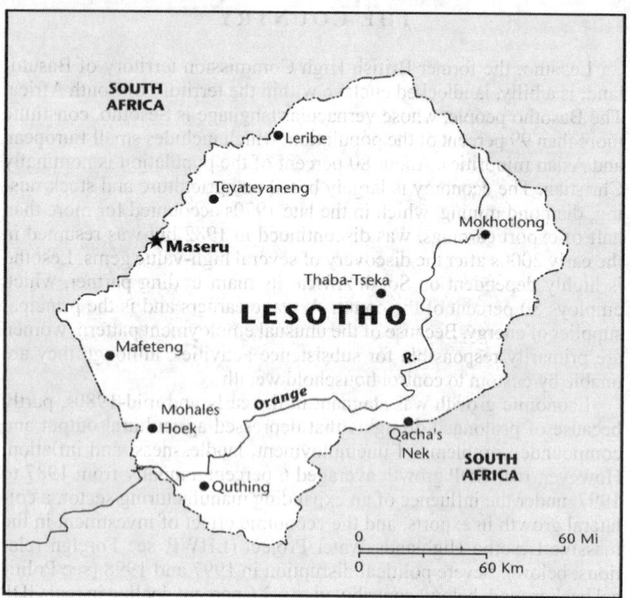

constitution. Further internal conflict followed the 1970 election, in which the opposition Basotho Congress Party (BCP) appeared to have outpolled the BNP. Voting irregularities were cited to justify the declaration of a state of emergency, a consequent suspension of the constitution, and the jailing of opposition leaders. Subsequently, the detainees were released, and the king, who had gone into exile, returned. The state of emergency was ultimately lifted in July 1973, but, in the wake of a coup attempt in January 1974 against his increasingly unpopular regime, the prime minister introduced new internal security measures (patterned after similar measures in South Africa) that proscribed the transmittal of outside funds to political groups within the country and authorized the jailing of individuals for 60 days without legal assistance. Between 1979 and 1982 numerous armed clashes were reported with the Lesotho Liberation Army (LLA), a guerrilla group affiliated with the outlawed "external" wing of the BCP under Ntsu MOKHEHLE, who claimed from exile that he was Lesotho's true leader on the basis of the election results invalidated in 1970.

In late 1984 the prime minister was mandated by an extraordinary general meeting of the BNP to call for a legislative election, and, with effect from December 31, the king dissolved an interim assembly that had been appointed after the abortive 1970 balloting. Following refusal by the five leading opposition parties to participate in the voting scheduled for September 17 and 18, 1985, Chief Jonathan announced that a formal poll would be unnecessary and declared all the BNP nominees elected unopposed.

On January 20, 1986, the Jonathan regime was toppled in a relatively bloodless coup led by Maj. Gen. Justin M. LEKHANYA, commander in chief of the Lesotho Paramilitary Force (LPF). Among the factors reportedly contributing to the coup were an economic blockade by South Africa (see Foreign relations, below) and power struggles within the BNP and the LPF. A decree issued on the day of the coup conferred executive and legislative powers on the king, who was to act in conjunction with a six-member Military Council and the Council of Ministers. On January 24 the king swore in Lekhanya as chair of the Military Council, with a largely civilian Council of Ministers being installed three days later. In February the king declared an amnesty for political offenders, and in March he banned all political activity pending the establishment of a new constitution. The new government quickly concluded a security pact with Pretoria and began to retreat from the Communist-bloc relations established by Chief Jonathan in the last years of his rule. (Chief Jonathan died in 1987.)

A new crisis erupted in early 1990 following the dismissal and arrest on February 19 of three Military Council members, two of whom were cousins of the king. Moshoeshoe refused to approve the appointment of replacement members and in a publicized letter to Lekhanya demanded an explanation for the arrests. The general responded two days later by declaring that supreme authority would "for the time being" be vested in himself and other members of the council, though the king would remain head of state. On February 22 he announced a major cabinet reshuffle that involved the dismissal of 9 of 18 ministers, including the king's brother, Chief Mathealira SEEISO, from his post as interior minister. On March 5 the council formally validated the action against the monarch, who left the country on March 10 for a "brief sabbatical" in the United Kingdom. The king was dethroned on November 6, and his son, Letsie David SEEISO, was sworn in as King LETSIE III on November 12 after his accession had been approved by an assembly of 22 traditional chiefs.

On April 30, 1991, General Lekhanya was overthrown in a bloodless coup and replaced as chair of the Military Council by Col. Elias Phisoana RAMAEMA. Thereafter, an unsuccessful attempt to depose Ramaema on June 17 led to the arrest of 18 senior military officers, and, in an unrelated action, Lekhanya was placed under house arrest from August 2 to September 17 for allegedly plotting a return to power.

In April 1992 the former king announced that he would be returning to Lesotho in late May, apparently against the wishes of the Military Council. Complicating the situation was a report that King Letsie III was prepared to abdicate in favor of his father. During talks brokered by the Commonwealth secretariat in London in June, it was agreed that Moshoeshoe could return as head of the royal family, but not as monarch, and on July 20 he was accorded a warm reception in Maseru after a two-year absence.

After several postponements, a general election was held on March 27, 1993, in which the previously outlawed BCP swept all 65 National Assembly contests, both General Lekhanya and BNP leader Evaristus SEKHONYANA being among the defeated. Although the results were disputed by the BNP, which subsequently rejected an offer of two nominated Senate seats, Ntsu Mokhehle was installed as head of a BCP government on April 2.

In mid-November 1993 coup rumors were sparked when the government's attempts to fulfill its promise to integrate former LLA soldiers into the Royal Lesotho Defense Force (RLDF) resulted in a confrontation between the latter's senior and junior officers. Furthermore, the RLDF's unwillingness to acquiesce to the new administration was, at least nominally, the catalyst for clashes between rival factions of the RLDF in January 1994. On April 14 dissident soldiers assassinated Deputy Prime Minister Selometsi BAHOLO and seized four other cabinet ministers for four hours in apparent response to government plans to investigate the January violence.

On August 17, 1994, King Letsie announced that he had removed the government of Prime Minister Mokhehle and that the country would be run by an appointed provisional council prior to the scheduling of new elections. The action was immediately challenged by thousands of rock-throwing protesters in a march on the royal palace, while a four-nation summit involving the leaders of Botswana, Zimbabwe, and South Africa was convened in Pretoria late in the month in an effort to resolve the crisis. On September 14 a meeting between the king and Mokhehle yielded an agreement that reinstated the latter and called for the abdication of the former in favor of his deposed father. A bill that provided for the monarchial transfer was approved on November 17, with Moshoeshoe II returning to the throne on January 25, 1995. Paralleling the reaccession of King Moshoeshoe, the more important outcome was his son's agreement to restore democracy, lacking which South Africa had threatened an economic blockade of the landlocked enclave. Subsequently, South Africa's deputy foreign secretary termed the Lesotho settlement "the first success of the Organization of African Unity's regional approach to conflict resolution."

On January 15, 1996, King Moshoeshoe was killed in an automobile accident while returning from a late-night visit to his cattle herds in the royal village of Matsieng, and on February 7 Crown Prince Letsie David ascended the throne for the second time as King Letsie III. The 32-year-old Letsie promised to "abstain from involving the monarchy in any way in politics or with any political parties or groups."

In late 1996 and early 1997 Lesotho's political landscape was dominated by a highly publicized struggle between Prime Minister Mokhehle and Molapo QHOBELA, the leader of the BCP's "modernizing" wing and deputy chief of the party's National Executive Commission (NEC). The NEC denounced Mokhehle's governance and voted to strip Mokhehle of his party leadership posts as the first step in an apparent effort to gain control of the government; however, in mid-April 1997 the High Court reinstated Mokhehle on an interim basis and ordered him to hold intraparty elections by the end of July. On June 7 Mokhehle and 37 BCP legislators defected from the BCP and announced the formation of the Lesotho Congress for Democracy (LCD). Furthermore, Mokhehle asserted that he would continue as prime minister, citing the

LCD's control of a majority of the assembly seats. Consequently, on June 11 the BCP suspended its participation in the assembly, asserting that Mokhehle's "coup" was a blatant attempt to avoid the proposed intraparty balloting. In October Mokhehle's deputy, Bethuel Pakalitha MOSISILI, met with Botswanan, South African, and Zimbabwean leaders who had been charged by the Southern African Development Community (SADC) with mediating the political stalemate. Thereafter, dismissing the BCP's continued attacks on its legitimacy, the LCD hosted the official coronation of King Letsie III on October 31.

In early 1998 Prime Minister Mokhehle announced that he would not run for reelection in balloting scheduled for May, citing declining health, and on February 27 the legislature was dissolved in anticipation of the polling. In elections on May 23 approximately 400 candidates from 12 parties vied for posts in the enlarged 80-seat assembly. Although the polling was initially described as "free and fair" by the SADC and Lesotho's Independent Electoral Commission (IEC), the LCD's capture of 78 seats (the BNP being credited with 1, and 1 remaining vacant) was immediately denounced as fraudulent by the opposition, whose subsequent demand for a recount was rejected by the IEC. On May 28 Mosisili was elected prime minister by an LCD intraparty caucus, and on June 4 a new government was sworn in. Nevertheless, opposition calls for an annulment of the elections continued. In late July the Court of Appeals ruled that only the king could annul elections.

On August 4, 1998, opposition demonstrators occupied the grounds outside the royal palace. On August 11 the SADC named a South African judge, Pius LANGA, to head an international team (referred to thereafter as the Langa Commission) charged with investigating the charges of electoral fraud. Meanwhile, tensions continued to mount at the royal palace, where several people were killed during clashes between the opposition and security forces and progovernment activists. On August 26 the Langa Commission released an interim report in which it accused the IEC of mishandling the vote tallying, and, under pressure from South Africa, the government agreed to a vote recount. However, on September 11, mutinous soldiers arrested more than 20 senior military officials after the dismissal of a military leader with alleged sympathies for the antigovernment demonstrators. Furthermore, the commander of the military, Lt. Gen. Makhula MOSAKENG, was forced to resign at gunpoint. On September 22, South Africa and Botswana, acting under the auspices of the SADC, deployed approximately 800 troops to Maseru at the request of Prime Minister Mosisili, who reportedly feared a coup attempt by the rampaging soldiers. The SADC forces were greeted by stiff resistance from the mutinous soldiers as well as opposition militants and were unable to gain control of Maseru until September 29, by which time dozens of people had been killed and the city severely damaged by looting and burning.

By early October 1998 a majority of the RDLF had returned to the barracks, and between October 2 and 14 the SADC organized government and opposition negotiations that yielded an agreement to create a transitional executive committee that would operate parallel to the government and assist in organizing new elections in 15 to 18 months. The negotiators also agreed to restructure the IEC, draft a new code of conduct for political parties, and create guidelines for equitable access to media outlets for all political groups. Furthermore, it was concluded that Prime Minister Mosisili would remain in office during the transitional phase and that SADC forces would remain for an indefinite period. On December 9 a 24-member Interim Political Authority (IPA) was sworn in, and the following day two opposition party members were elected cochairs of the new body.

SADC peacekeeping forces completed their withdrawal in mid-May 1999, supporters describing the military intervention of the previous year as an "outstanding success." At the same time, the IPA expressed confidence that it would meet its deadline of organizing national elections by mid-2000, when the original IPA mandate was due to expire. Under pressure from international mediators concerned over potential delays, the IPA and the government in December 1999 reached an agreement to hold elections sometime in 2000, with the IPA mandate to be extended indefinitely until balloting was conducted. However, a planned election date in May 2000 was quickly scrapped as the IPA and the government argued over proposed restructuring of the parliament. The IPA and the government subsequently charged each other with attempting to delay the elections, although neutral observers suggested that it was the government that appeared to have the most to gain from such tactics. Plans to conduct the balloting in early 2001 also proved unrealistic in view of disagreement over voter registration and the addition of legislators selected via proportional representation to the assembly.

In legislative balloting on May 25, 2002, the LCD won a new term in office, and on June 11 Mosisili formed an all-LCD cabinet. Four more ministers were announced on July 11.

On April 30, 2005, the nation's first local elections were held, with a government stipulation that one-third of the elected seats be filled by women. Seven opposition parties tried to have the elections postponed, claiming irregularities, which some observers said may have affected voter turnout (reported to be about 30 percent). Though an official breakdown of results was not released, electoral officials announced May 9 that the LCD won "by a large margin," followed by independents, the opposition Basotho National Party (BNP) and the Lesotho People's Congress (LPC), and unspecified smaller parties. Failed elections were reported in 15 districts, attributed to the death of candidates, and new elections were to be scheduled to replace them.

Following the resignation from the LCD of Communications Minister Thomas THABANE and 17 others on October 9, 2006, King Letsie dissolved parliament on November 24 and called for early assembly elections on February 17, 2007. The LCD won a majority in balloting deemed free and fair by some international observers but vehemently contested by opposition parties (see Current issues, below). Prime Minister Mosisili retained his post and was sworn in on February 23. He named a new government on March 2, retaining most of the ministers from the previous government.

Constitution and government. Under the 1966 constitution, which was suspended in January 1970, Lesotho was declared to be an independent monarchy with the king functioning as head of state and executive authority being vested in a prime minister and cabinet responsible to the lower house of a bicameral parliament. In April 1973 an interim unicameral body was established, encompassing 22 chiefs and 71 nominated members. A return to bicameralism was voted in 1983, but the bill was never implemented and was voided after the 1986 coup by the Military Council, which announced the vesting of "all executive and legislative powers in HM the King"; the latter action was reversed by the council prior to the exile of Moshoeshoe in March 1990, the new monarch appearing to possess only ceremonial authority.

On July 4, 1991, a National Constituent Assembly approved the draft of a new constitution, which was promulgated following the legislative election of March 1993. The revised basic law restored the bicameral system and returned executive authority to a cabinet headed by a prime minister, without conclusively resolving the issue of the monarch's role. The judicial system consists of a High Court, a Court of Appeal, and subordinate courts (district, judicial commissioners, central, and local). Judges of the High Court and the Court of Appeal are appointed on the advice of the government and its Judicial Service Commission. Local government is based on nine districts, each of which is administered by a commissioner appointed by the central government. In April 1997 the assembly approved a constitutional amendment that established an Independent Electoral Commission (IEC).

Foreign relations. Lesotho's foreign policy was long determined less by its membership in the United Nations, the Commonwealth, and the Organization of African Unity (OAU, subsequently the African Union—AU) than by its position as a black enclave within the white-ruled Republic of South Africa. While rejecting the South African doctrine of apartheid and insisting on the maintenance of national sovereignty, the Jonathan government for some years cultivated good relations with Pretoria. Subsequent events, however, led to a noticeable stiffening in Maseru's posture. Following South Africa's establishment of the adjacent Republic of Transkei in October 1976, Lesotho requested a special UN Security Council meeting on the matter, complaining that its border had been effectively closed in an "act of aggression" designed to force recognition of Transkei. Subsequently, South African prime minister Pieter Botha accused Maseru of harboring militants from the African National Congress (ANC) among the approximately 11,000 South African refugees living in Lesotho. Friction over Chief Jonathan's refusal to expel the ANC supporters culminated in South Africa's institution of a crippling economic blockade, ostensibly to block cross-border rebel activity, on January 1, 1986. Pretoria denied charges of complicity in the subsequent overthrow of Chief Jonathan but lifted the border controls one week later when the new military regime flew 60 ANC members to Zimbabwe. The new relationship with South Africa was further demonstrated by the signature in October of a treaty authorizing commencement of the $2 billion Lesotho Highlands Water Project (LHWP), which had been under consideration for more than two decades. The three-phase project, expected to take 25 to 30 years to complete, will divert vast quantities of water to South Africa's arid Transvaal region in return for the payment of substantial royalties. (The project has been the attention of intense scrutiny recently in light of bribery charges against foreign contractors. In May 2002 a former chief executive of the LHWP was sentenced to a lengthy prison term for fraud and accepting bribes, while Canadian, French, and German companies were fined for paying bribes. The first phase of the project was completed in the early 2000s.)

In an attempt to broaden its international support both regionally and abroad, Lesotho has been an active member of the Southern African Development Coordination Conference (SADCC, subsequently the SADC), a body created in 1980 to lessen members' economic dependence on the then white-ruled regime. However, in view of its vulnerability to South African influence, Maseru, unlike other SADCC governments, did not seek sanctions against Pretoria for its apartheid policies. Rather, on May 21, 1992, the two governments formally established diplomatic relations.

In January 1994 the interwoven nature of relations between Lesotho and South Africa was evidenced by Pretoria's immediate and forceful response to the unrest in Maseru. Although the Commonwealth was subsequently credited with brokering an accord between the combatants, observers cited pressure from a task force created by South African president F. W. de Klerk and other southern African leaders as the reason for the speedy resolution of the dispute. Thereafter, speculation about the possible merger of the two countries continued, with the *Christian Science Monitor* quoting local observers as saying that, if not for the monarchy, Lesotho would be "swallowed up" by South Africa. In 2001 it was reported that relations between the South African government and Lesotho's royal family were strained because of the former's failure to "come clean" on a "massacre" allegedly committed by its paratroopers during the SADC's intervention in 1998. However, relations subsequently improved (apparently influenced by the successful 2002 legislative elections in Lesotho), culminating in a new cooperation protocol through which South Africa agreed to provide economic aid and technical assistance. In 2005 troops from Lesotho were being trained for use in future UN and SADC missions. Late that year, Prime Minister Mosisili visited China amid pledges by both countries for political and economic cooperation.

In 2009 Lesotho asked South Africa to reconsider its overhaul of a program to benefit textile manufacturers, in effect ending an export incentive. Analysts said the decision "puts South Africa on a "collision course" with export-dependent Lesotho.

Current issues. Although tension between the government and the opposition was reported in advance of the May 2002 legislative poll, the balloting was deemed generally free and fair by international observers, the new mixed system (which included 40 members elected on a proportional basis) having succeeded in providing minority parties with a significant legislative voice. Nevertheless, the government continued to face severe pressures from food shortages (accompanied by high prices that triggered street protests in November 2003) and the HIV/AIDS crisis (an estimated 31 percent of the population was infected). In November 2005 the government announced a plan to offer free HIV/AIDS testing to the entire population.

In January 2006 Foreign Affairs Minister Monyane Moleleki was wounded by gunfire near his home shortly after he had attended a national conference of the LCD, during which tensions reportedly heated up over the accession issue, with Moleleki seen as one of the main contenders for leadership of the party. Another attack in August resulted in the death of a member of parliament. In October cabinet minister Thomas Thabane and 17 other LCD members, expressing their lack of confidence in the government, resigned from the LCD to form a new party, the All Basotho Convention (ABC), pledging to reduce poverty and improve the economy, among other things. The defections left the LCD without a majority, prompting King Letsie to dissolve parliament and call for early elections. Hours after parliament was dissolved, another attack was reported in the capital at the home of another cabinet minister who was also considered to be vying for LCD leadership. The attack resulted in the death of an aid worker, whose vehicle was reportedly mistaken for that of the minister.

Following the king's scheduling of legislative elections in February 2007, the opposition complained they did not have enough time to prepare. Subsequently, the LCD and the ABC formed arrangements with the NIP and the LWP, respectively, in which the predominant party would contest only the single-member constituencies, while the smaller parties would submit party lists only for compensatory seats. The proportional lists, however, reportedly included members of the larger party. The alliances were established so that the smaller party's supporters would vote for the larger party's candidates in constituency voting, and in exchange, the larger party's supporters would vote for the smaller party in compensatory balloting. These agreements prompted criticism from UN observers who said such alignments resulted in the "deliberate manipulation" of the electoral system, which was meant to maximize party participation in parliament. Further, opposition groups challenged the LCD's arrangement in which it had selected candidates against the wishes of NIP leader Anthony MANYELI. Following the LCD's securing a majority in single-round balloting, a number of parties—including the ACP, BNP, NIP, MFP, and ABC—staged a sit-in outside the parliament, backed by tens of thousands of demonstrators protesting alleged fraud in some constituencies and the electoral commission's allocation of proportional seats in the assembly. The groups argued that Manyeli should submit his own list of parliamentary candidates in new elections. The government, for its part, stood firm, observers noting that it could not afford to give up seats gained in the alliance, which would result in the significant erosion of its overwhelming majority.

In June 2007 a curfew was imposed in the capital in the wake of what the government described as "politically motivated" attacks on the homes of three ministers and against ABC leader Thomas Thabane. No one was injured. Thabane attributed the turmoil to widespread discontent with the election results. Shortly thereafter, the government announced that it had thwarted a coup attempt by some members of the military, and a radio journalist was also implicated for allegedly reading on air a letter from a group of soldiers threatening the government. Observers believed the curfew was meant to undermine the "potential political threat" from opposition groups. As tensions increased and several parties staged further mass protests, including a boycott by some businesses, the SADC was called upon to resolve the dispute through mediation. Meanwhile, five people, including three members of the military and the radio journalist, were charged with treason in connection with the alleged coup plot.

In October 2007 the LCD had an initial meeting with the SADC but then refused further meetings. Subsequently, however, both the government and Thabane backed the mediation efforts and agreed to meet with SADC in February 2008. Thabane reiterated that he did not dispute that the LCD had won the most seats, but he claimed that the allocation of seats through proportional representation had been misused since not enough seats were awarded to smaller parties. Meanwhile, the SADC mediator, former Botswana president Ketumile Masire, was reportedly not optimistic about resolving the dispute through mediation. The matter was subsequently taken to Lesotho's Supreme Court. In October the government warned opposition parties against "stirring unrest" by organizing a rally to protest the disputed assembly seats. Further fueling the debate, Justin Metsing Lekhanya, the former military leader and head of the Basotho National Party, called the parliament "illegitimate," based on the government's alleged abuse of the electoral system to obtain additional seats. Meanwhile, opposition leader Thomas Thabane urged the prime minister to hold new elections to resolve the issue.

On a positive note, international organizations and the United States announced greater financial assistance for Lesotho's efforts to combat HIV/AIDS, and China in 2008 pledged to provide additional medical teams. The number of those infected reportedly had fallen from 31 percent in 2003 to 26 percent in 2008, due in large part to the government's testing program and offers of free counseling and medicine in the past two years.

After the SADC failed to resolve the electoral dispute, the government was reportedly was no longer interested in 2009 in mediation efforts. With tensions still heightened over the impasse, an attack on the prime minister's home in April was described by the government as an assassination attempt. The prime minister was not hurt, but three gunmen were killed by police after a group of armed men stormed the residence on April 22. Two suspects were arrested, though their identities and motives were not immediately known. The opposition parties quickly condemned the attacks.

POLITICAL PARTIES

Political party activity was banned in March 1986 following the January coup that ended nearly 20 years of dominance by the Basotho National Party (BNP). Subsequently, the BNP joined four former opponents (the BCP, UDP, BDA, and CPL) in an informal "Big Five" alliance to demand that the ban be lifted in preparation for a return to civilian government. Ten days after the coup of April 30, 1991, the Military Council announced that party activity could resume as long as it did not degenerate into "divisive politics." However, it was not until nearly two years thereafter that a general election was authorized.

The 11 parties that had competed individually in the 1998 legislative balloting (the LCD, BCP, BNP, MFP, SDU, NPP, NIP, KBP, LEP, PFD, and CDP) were accorded 2 seats each on the Interim Political Authority (IPA) that was established in late 1998. The UDP and the LLP, which had contested the 1998 election as an alliance, each received 1 seat on the 24-member IPA.

In May 1999 a number of small parties (the PFD, NPP, NIP, KBP, CDP, CPL, and SDP) announced formation of an anti-LCD grouping called the Khokanyana-Phiri Democratic Alliance. In August another antigovernment grouping, the Setlamo Democratic Alliance, was formalized by the BNP, BCP, MFP, UDP, LLP, and LEP, which had been operating together informally since the beginning of the year.

Parliamentary Parties:

Lesotho Congress for Democracy (LCD). The LCD was launched by Prime Minister Ntsu Mokhehle, the (then) BCP interim president, on June 7, 1997, one month before the BCP was scheduled to hold intraparty elections for his post and just two days after a BCP spokesperson had labeled him "permanently incapacitated." Subsequently, Mokhehle cited the LCD's control of a majority of the legislative posts (38 seats) as the basis for his continued control of the government. In early 1998 Bethuel Pakalitha Mosisili, theretofore deputy party leader, was elected to succeed Mokhehle as party leader, the latter declining to run for reelection due to poor health. (Mokhehle died in January 1999.)

Party infighting was reported in 2000, culminating in violence between rival factions in October that precipitated police intervention. Some observers suggested the friction underscored a split between the youthful, possibly more progressive, supporters of Mosisili and a conservative faction led by Shakhana MOKHEHLE, brother of the LCD founder. Subsequently, Mosisili was elected for another five-year term as party leader. Mokhehle was defeated 717–710 in his reelection bid by Sephiri Motanyane, described as a close associate of Mosisili's. Prominent LCD leaders, including Deputy Prime Minister Kelebone Maope and several other cabinet members, charged that the elections had been "rigged" and vowed to take the matter to court. Maope's faction left the party in September 2001 to form the Lesotho People's Congress (below). In April 2005 it was reported that the LCD had won the country's first locally held elections.

In 2007 the LCD formed an alliance with the NIP for the legislative elections. Under the arrangement, the LCD contested only the constituencies, and the NIP submitted party lists for compensatory seats but included LCD members on the NIP lists. However, it was subsequently reported that eight members of the NIP contravened the arrangement by contesting constituency seats against LCD candidates. (In one constituency this reportedly cost the LCD a seat.) Following the election, the NIP joined other parties in protesting the allocation of seats, claiming that the NIP alliance with the LCD was invalid because NIP leader Anthony Manyeli had rejected it (see NIP, below for details). A court of appeals subsequently upheld the LCD's arrangement with the NIP. However, a definitive ruling from the Supreme Court was expected in mid-2008.

Leaders: Bethuel Pakalitha MOSISILI (Prime Minister and Party Leader), Motiohi MOENO (Deputy Secretary General), Enoch Sephiri MOTANYANE (Secretary General).

National Independence Party (NIP). The NIP was formed in late 1984 by a former cabinet member who resigned from the Jonathan government in 1972. In an election manifesto issued in March 1985, the NIP called for establishing diplomatic relations with South Africa and severing links with Communist countries. In mid-1992 it criticized the government for scheduling elections "prematurely" and announced that it would boycott the balloting then scheduled for November. The party failed to win seats in the 2002 assembly elections.

In 2007 the LCD reportedly "went behind the back" of NIP leader Anthony Manyeli to form an alliance with deputy leader Dominic Motikoe over constituency and compensatory polling (see LCD, above). Manyeli, who had rejected the arrangement, joined other parties' leaders in protest after the election, claiming that the parliamentary seats were unfairly allocated. The protesting parties contended that the LCD received more seats than it had legitimately won (through its allegedly invalid arrangement with the NIP) and that some parties did not get the compensatory seats they deserved. The NIP's claim against its alliance with the LCP was ultimately decided in favor of the LCP by a court of appeals, overturning a High Court ruling in favor of Manyeli. However, the Lesotho constitution states that High Court decisions regarding political elections cannot be appealed. Subsequently, the NIP and other parties asked the SADC to review the situation (see Current issues, above).

Leaders: Anthony MANYELI (Chair), Dominic MOTIKOE (Deputy Chair).

All Basotho Convention (ABC). Vowing to fight poverty and bring about economic change, former minister Thomas Thabane, once considered a likely successor to Prime Minister Mosisili, formed the ABC in 2006 with 17 other LCD dissidents after he resigned from the LCD on October 9. The decline in the LCD majority was seen by observers as the impetus behind King Letsie's decision to dissolve parliament in November in the wake of a possible no-confidence vote and to call early legislative elections in February 2007. The ABC formed an alliance with the LWP in which the ABC supported the LWP in the proportional balloting in the 2007 election, much as the LCD had done with the NIP. Both alliances were criticized for violating the spirit of proportional balloting, prompting numerous protests.

Leaders: Thomas THABANE (President), Sello Clement MACHAKELA (Deputy President), Nyane MPHAFI (Secretary General).

Lesotho Workers' Party (LWP). The LWP was formed in August 2001 by left-wing trade unionists and other labor leaders. The party formed a controversial electoral alliance with the ABC in the 2007 legislative elections (see ABC, above).

Leader: Billy MACAEFA.

Alliance of Congress Parties (ACP). The ACP was formed in 2006 by the two parties below and a faction of the BCP, led by Ntsukunyane MPHANYA, in advance of the February 2007 legislative election.

Basutoland African Congress (BAC). The BAC was launched in early 2002 by a breakaway faction of the BCP in a dispute over leadership. BAC founder Molapo Qhobela was suspended from his leadership post in 2003 after he allegedly made unilateral changes to the party's constitution.

Rifts in the party were reported between the Qhobela faction and those favoring BAC leader Khauhelo RALITAPOLE, and in January 2007 a pro-Qhobela faction split off, forming the **Basutoland African National Congress.**

Lesotho People's Congress (LPC). The LPC was established in October 2001 by an LCD breakaway group led by former deputy prime minister Kelebone Maope.

Leaders: Kelebone MAOPE (Party Leader), Shakhane MOKHEHLE (Secretary General).

Basotho Congress Party (BCP). Strongly antiapartheid and pan-Africanist in outlook, the BCP (formerly the Basutoland Congress Party) was split, following the abortive 1970 election, by the defection of (then) deputy leader Gerard P. RAMOREBOLI and several other members, who defied party policy and accepted nominated opposition seats in the interim National Assembly.

Banned in 1970, the main branch of the BCP continued to oppose the Jonathan government, claiming responsibility in the late 1970s for numerous armed attacks on police and BNP-supportive politicians. Concurrently, a Lesotho Liberation Army (LLA) of 500–1,000 operated, under external BCP direction and allegedly with South African support, in the country's northern mountains and from across the border. Despite overtures from the new regime in early 1986, the LLA called for revival of the 1966 constitution as a condition for abandoning antigovernment activity. However, in early 1989 external leader Ntsu Mokhehle returned to Lesotho, along with about 200 BCP supporters, presumably because of Pretoria's satisfaction with the current military government. Meanwhile, although the BCP remained committed to the establishment of a constitutional democracy, the LLA, apparently of no further use to South Africa, was reportedly reduced to a few "rag-tag" dissidents.

Mokhehle and other party members attended the opening of the constituent assembly in June 1990, despite their earlier support of a boycott. Subsequently, the party was rumored to be interested in Lesotho's incorporation into South Africa. Formerly a socialist party, the BCP in its 1993 election manifesto declared its commitment to a mixed economy.

Controversy rocked the BCP in 1996 as the rift between the party's conservative elders and the younger, so-called modernizers widened. At a party congress in March delegates elected a new 12-member National Executive Commission (NEC). In addition, "conservative" Deputy Prime Minister Bethuel Pakalitha Mosisili, a potential Mokhehle successor, secured the party vice presidency, outpolling the incumbent, modernizer Molapo Qhobela. However, Qhobela and his supporters promptly filed suit to have the balloting overturned, alleging that the conservative elders had rigged the elections. Subsequently, in May four prominent modernizer cabinet ministers, including Qhobela and Tseliso MAKHAKHE, were ousted from the government. One week later two other ministers aligned with them quit the cabinet.

In November 1996 the High Court ruled in favor of the Qhobela faction, annulling the March NEC polling and charging the members of the previous NEC with preparing new elections. In fresh balloting for the NEC on January 24, 1997, the modernizers retained their seats, reflecting their reportedly overwhelming numerical dominance within the party. On February 16 the remaining links between the two factions were fractured when the Mokhehle government ignored Qhobela's attempts to mediate an end to a police mutiny and violently squashed the rebellion. The progressives' dismay with Mokhehle was further compounded by testimony at South Africa's Truth and Reconciliation Commission (see separate article on South Africa) that, according to *Africa Confidential,* appeared to substantiate long-held rumors that Mokhehle and his LLA forces had cooperated with the apartheid-era regime's "death squads." At a BPC meeting on February 28 party delegates voted to remove Mokhehle from the party presidency; however, on April 18 the High Court reversed Mokhehle's ouster, declaring that it violated the BCP's charter and directing Mokhehle to serve as interim president (his term having expired in January) until new party-wide elections could be held.

On June 7, 1997, Mokhehle announced that he and 37 other BCP legislators were leaving the party to form the LCD. On July 27 party delegates elected Qhobela as the BCP's new leader. Subsequently, on December 1 the Khauta KHASU-led Democratic Movement for Reconstruction (DMR) announced that it was disbanding so that its members could rejoin the BCP. (Khasu, former BCP deputy leader G. P. Ramoreboli, and Phoka CHAOLANE had been expelled from the BCP in 1992.)

In December 1998 Khauhelo Ralitapole, leader of the BCP's Women's League, was named cochair of the IPA.

Another rift over party leadership developed in 1999 among party officials Tseliso Makhakhe, Sekoala Toloane, and Ntsukunyane Mphanya, who all sought to unseat Qhobela. In early 2001 two different executive committees—one led by Molapo Qhobela, former minister of foreign affairs and heretofore president of the BCP, and the other by Makhakhe, former minister of education—claimed legitimate control of the party. Following a court's decision to accord the pro-Makhakhe faction the legitimate use of the BCP rubric, the pro-Qhobela faction broke away in early 2002 to form the Basutoland African Congress. Makhakhe stepped down from his leadership post in 2002 to give others the opportunity to head the party. For the 2007 legislative elections, Mphanya and his supporters participated in the launching of the ACP. Meanwhile, the BCP proper presented its own candidates and secured one proportional seat.

Leader: Sekoala TOLOANE.

Basotho National Party (BNP). Organized in 1959 as the Basutoland National Party, the BNP has counted many Christians and chiefs among its members. It traditionally favored free enterprise and cooperation with South Africa while opposing apartheid. In the mid-1970s, however, it began co-opting policies originally advanced by the BCP, including the establishment of relations with Communist states and support for the ANC campaign against Pretoria. Growing internal division was reported in 1985 over who would succeed the aging chief Jonathan as prime minister. One faction was dominated by the paramilitary Youth League, armed and trained by North Korea, which reportedly planned a government takeover. The Youth League was disarmed and officially disbanded in a confrontation with the Lesotho Paramilitary Force on January 15, 1986, prior to the LPF-led coup of January 20. Although the BNP's national chair was named finance minister in the post-Jonathan administration, supporters of Chief Jonathan were barred from political activity. Chief Jonathan was detained briefly after the coup, released, and then placed under house arrest in August along with six BNP supporters for activities allegedly threatening national stability. They were released in September by order of the High Court with an admonition to refrain from political activity. The former prime minister died in April 1987.

On October 18, 1995, BNP leader Evaristus Retselisitsoe Sekhonyana was sentenced to two years' imprisonment or a heavy fine after being convicted of sedition for having urged armed resistance to military units during the August unrest. Sekhonyana assumed a leading role in the interparty negotiations that were held in the aftermath of the September 1998 uprising; however, he died on November 18. At a BNP congress in March 1999, former military leader Justin Metsing Lekhanya was elected as the new party leader. In the 2002 legislative elections the BNP became the second-largest party in the assembly (21 seats) and the main opposition grouping. In 2005 the government rejected a proposal from the BNP to form a government of national unity.

In 2007 the BNP won 3 seats through proportional representation.

Leaders: Justin Metsing LEKHANYA (Party Leader and former military ruler of the country), Leseteli MALEFANE (Secretary General).

Basotho Democratic National Party (BDNP). Founded in November 2006 by former BNP member Thabang Nyeoe, the BDNP stated its commitment to "the creation of a living democracy" in Lesotho.

Leaders: Thabang NYEOE, Joang MOLAPO, Pelele LETSOALA (Secretary General).

Marematlou Freedom Party (MFP). A royalist party, the MFP has long been committed to enlarging the king's authority. In other respects, its position has been somewhere between the BCP and the BNP. An offshoot Marematlou Party (MP), formed in 1965 and led by S. S. Matete, reemerged with the MFP in 1969. One of its members, Patrick Lehloenya, accepted a cabinet post as minister to the prime minister in late 1975, subsequently becoming minister of health and social welfare. The party's (then) president, Bennett Makalo KHAKETLA, was appointed minister of justice and prisons in the cabinet formed after the 1986 coup.

Party leader Vincent Moeketse Malebo and LWP leader Billy Macaefa were scheduled to face trial in mid-2008 on contempt of court charges. The reason for the charges was unclear.

Leaders: Vincent Moeketse MALEBO, Tsitso LEANYA, Seth MAKOTOKO.

The **Basotho Batho Democratic Party,** formed in 2006, and the **Popular Front for Democracy,** led by Lekhetho RAKUNE, each secured 1 seat in the 2007 legislative election.

Other Parties that Participated in the 2007 Parliamentary Elections:

Kopanang Basotho Party (KBP). Lesotho's first feminist party, *Kopanang Basotho* (Basotho Unite) was launched in mid-1992 to protest what it called "repressive and discriminatory" laws against women. By the end of the year it reportedly had a membership of some 30,000. Party leader Limakatso NTAKATSANE died in 2002.

United Party (UP). In late February 1996 United Party leader Makara Azael Sekautu and two soldiers were arrested for their roles in a botched coup attempt that government officials alleged had been planned since September 1995. Sekautu was released in 1998 and reportedly ran for a legislative seat as part of a UDP/LLP/UP electoral alliance. However, official government election results referenced the coalition as including only the UDP and LLP, and the UP did not secure representation on the IPA. The UP contested the 2002 assembly balloting without success.

Leader: Makara Azael SEKAUTU.

The **Lesotho Educational Party,** led by Thabo S. PITSO; the **New Lesotho Freedom Party,** led by Manapo Majara P. KHOABANE; the **Christian Democratic Party**, led by Ernest RAMOKOENA; and the **Social Democratic Party**, described upon its formation in 1998 as a "youth" party under the leadership of Masitise SELESO, also nominated candidates for the 2007 legislative elections.

Other Parties:

National Progressive Party (NPP). The NPP was launched on October 22, 1995, by Chief Peete Nkoebe Peete, who had previously been a deputy leader of the BNP but had had a falling-out with Chief Sekhonyana. Peete declared that the new group would function in the tradition of the BNP's founder, Chief Leabua Jonathan.

Leader: Chief Peete Nkoebe PEETE.

United Democratic Party (UDP). The UDP was formed in 1967 by two progovernment members of the BCP. However, in a 1982 manifesto the party called for the establishment of full diplomatic relations with Pretoria, the expulsion from Lesotho of all South African political refugees, and opposition to trade sanctions against the Botha regime. In early 1985 UDP leader Charles Mofeli branded the projected legislative balloting as a "farce" and accused Prime Minister Jonathan of attempting to create a one-party state. Mofeli was also one of the most vocal critics of the successor military regime, being detained briefly in 1987 for condemning its "abuse of power." (Mofeli died in January 2008.) The UDP contested the 1998 legislative balloting in an alliance with the **Lesotho Labour Party**. (There have been no recent references to the latter.)

Leaders: Mthuthuzeli PATRICK, Molomo NKUEBE (Secretary General).

LEGISLATURE

The bicameral parliament established under the 1966 constitution was dissolved in the wake of alleged irregularities in the election of January 27, 1970. An interim assembly of 22 chiefs and 71 nominated members, named on April 27, 1973, was dissolved as of December 31, 1984. Subsequent arrangements called for a Senate of 22 chiefs and an assembly of 60 elected and up to 20 nominated members. Since none of the opposition parties nominated candidates for balloting to have been conducted on September 17–18, 1985, Chief Jonathan canceled the poll and declared the BNP candidates elected unopposed. The 1983 Parliament Act, on which the action was based, was voided following the 1986 coup.

At present the **Parliament** is a bicameral body consisting of a nonelective Senate and an elective National Assembly.

Senate. The Senate contains 22 chiefs and 11 nominated members. A restructuring of the Senate (to make the body more "democratic" and "representative") was proposed for consideration by the Interim Political Authority (IPA), established in late 1998. However, little further information on proposed changes had surfaced as of 2005.

The Senate was renewed on March 9, 2007.

President: Morena Letapata MAKHAOLA.

National Assembly. In the election of May 23, 1998, approximately 400 candidates competed for 80 lower-house seats (an increase of 15 since the 1993 polling). The Lesotho Congress for Democracy (LCD) won 78 seats, the Basotho National Party (BNP) secured a sole position, and 1 seat was left vacant. The next election initially was not scheduled until 2003; however, early elections were envisioned as part of the late-1998 agreement negotiated between the government and the opposition following the military intervention of the SADC. After several postponements, balloting was conducted in 2002 for a new assembly, with 80 members elected on a "first-past-the-post" system complemented by 40 members selected by proportional vote.

In the most recent balloting of February 17, 2007, the seat distribution was as follows: the LCD, 61 (all in single-member constituencies); the National Independence Party, 21 (all proportional seats in alliance with the LCD); the All Basotho Convention (ABC), 17 (all in single-member constituencies); the Lesotho Workers Party, 10 (all proportional seats in alliance with the ABC); the BNP, 3 (all proportional seats); the Alliance of Congress Parties, 2 (all proportional); the Basotho Batho Democratic Party, 1 (proportional); the Basotho Congress Party, 1 (proportional); the Basotho Democratic National Party, 1 (proportional); the Marematlou Freedom Party, 1 (proportional); the Popular Front for Democracy, 1 (proportional); and vacant, 1.

An election was repeated in one constituency on June 30, 2007, as a result of the death of the candidate in that district before the February balloting. A member of the LCD was elected, bringing the total number of LCD seats to 62.

Speaker: Nthohi MOTSAMAI.

CABINET

[as of October 1, 2009]

Prime Minister	Bethuel Pakalitha Mosisili
Deputy Prime Minister	Archibald Lesao Lehohla
Ministers	
Agriculture and Food Security	Lesole Mokoma
Communications, Science, and Technology	Mothejoa Metsing
Defense and National Security	Bethuel Pakalitha Mosisili
Education and Training	Mamphono Khaketla [f]
Employment and Labor	Refiloe Masemene
Finance and Development Planning	Timothy Thahane
Foreign Affairs	Mohlabi Tsekoa
Forestry and Land Reclamation	Ralechate Mokose
Gender, Youth, and Sports	Mathabiso Lepono [f]
Health and Social Welfare	Mphu Keneiloe Ramatlapeng [f]
Home Affairs and Public Safety; Parliamentary Affairs	Archibald Lesao Lehohla
Industry, Trade, and Marketing	Popane Lebesa
Justice, Human Rights, and Correctional Services	Mpeo Mahase-Moiloa [f]
Law and Constitutional Affairs	Mpeo Mahase-Moiloa [f]
Local Government	Pontso Suzan Matumelo Sekatle [f]
Natural Resources	Monyane Moleleki
Prime Minister's Office	Motloheloa Phooko
Public Service	Semano Henry Sekatle
Public Works and Transport	Tsele Chakela
Tourism, Culture, and Environment	Lebohang Ntsinyi [f]

[f] = female

COMMUNICATIONS

While freedom of expression is guaranteed in the Constitution of Lesotho, Reporters Without Borders has reported that the government often targets the independent media. Censorship was imposed when a member of the British royal family visited in 2003 because of the Lesotho government's concern about its image abroad, according to Reporters Without Borders. The watchdog group also cited alleged intimidation of and attacks on journalists who reported on a rift in the ruling party in 2006 and 2007. The Media Institute of Southern Africa arranged for armed security guards to protect the homes of some journalists following the 2007 assembly elections because of alleged intimidation. A radio journalist charged with treason (later reduced to sedition) in June 2007 (see Current issues, above), was released in 2008 after his sentence was suspended and he paid a token fine. Also in June the government issued an order to all state agencies not to buy advertising in the independent weekly *Public Eye* in what Reporters Without Borders referred to as a disguised form of censorship and an abuse of authority. In 2008 radio Harvest FM, an organ of the All Basotho Convention, was suspended for three months following complaints of defamation by the communications minister.

Press. The following are published in Sesotho in Maseru, unless otherwise noted: *Moeletsi oa Basotho* (Mazenod, 20,000), Catholic weekly; *Leselinyana la Lesotho* (Light of Lesotho, 15,000), published fortnightly in Morija by the Lesotho Evangelical Church; *Lentsoe la Basotho* (14,000), weekly government organ; *Lesotho Today* (7,000), government organ in English; *The Mirror* (4,000), independent weekly in English; *Lesotho Weekly; Makatolle,* weekly; *Our Times*, weekly in English; *Mphatlatsane* (4,000), daily; *Mopheme* (The Survivor); *Public Eye*, a weekly. The MoAfrika press group also publishes a weekly independent newspaper, *MoAfrika*, in Sesotho.

News agency. The state-run Lesotho News Agency (LENA), originally established in 1983, was relaunched in August 1990.

Broadcasting and computing. The Lesotho National Broadcasting Service (LNBS) operates the government-owned, commercial Radio Lesotho, which transmits in Sesotho and English; MoAfrika press group operates an independent radio station in Maseru; and private FM stations include the People's Choice, Joy Radio, Harvest FM, and Catholic Radio, as well as Khotoso Radio, operated by the National University of Lesotho. As of 2008 there were 35.8 Internet users per 1,000 inhabitants.

INTERGOVERNMENTAL REPRESENTATION

Ambassador to the U.S.: David Mohlomi RANTEKOA.

U.S. Ambassador to Lesotho: Robert B. NOLAN.

Permanent Representative to the UN: Motlatsi RAMAFOLE.

IGO Memberships (Non-UN): AfDB, AU, BADEA, CWTH, Interpol, NAM, SADC, WCO, WTO.

LIBERIA

Republic of Liberia

Political Status: Independent republic established in 1847; under de facto one-party system starting in 1878; martial law imposed on April 25, 1980, following coup of April 12; new constitution approved by national referendum on July 3, 1984 (with full effect from January 6, 1986 [the date of the inauguration of the new president]); constitution effectively voided by rebel action in mid-1990; Interim Government of National Unity (supported militarily by the Economic Community of West African States Monitoring Group [Ecomog]) sworn in November 22, 1990; State Council of Liberian Transitional National Government sworn in March 7, 1994; new six-member State Council sworn in September 1, 1995, following cease-fire agreement of August 19; amended version of 1995 cease-fire agreement signed by faction leaders on August 16, 1996, after 1995 accord was rendered moot by an outbreak of violence in April; constitution of 1986 reaffirmed by the National Assembly on August 6, 1997, following presidential and legislative balloting on July 19; transitional government established October 14, 2003, following settlement of a civil war; new elected government installed January 16, 2006.

Area: 43,000 sq. mi. (111,369 sq. km.).

Population: 2,101,628 (1984C); 3,929,000 (2008E).

Major Urban Center (2005E): MONROVIA (571,000).

Official Language: English.

Monetary Unit: Liberian Dollar (market rate December 1, 2009: 66.55 dollars = $1US). The U.S. dollar also circulates.

President: Ellen JOHNSON-SIRLEAF (Unity Party); elected in second-round balloting on November 8, 2005, and inaugurated on January 16, 2006, for a six-year term to succeed the Chair of the National Transitional Government, Charles Gyude BRYANT (Liberia Action Party).

Vice President: Joseph N. BOAKAI (Unity Party); elected in second-round balloting on November 8, 2005, and inaugurated on January 16, 2006, for a term concurrent with that of the president, succeeding the Vice Chair of the National Transitional Government, Wesley Momo JOHNSON (United People's Party).

THE COUNTRY

Facing the Atlantic along the western bulge of Africa, Liberia is a country of tropical rain forests and broken plateaus. Established as a haven for freed American slaves, it became an independent republic in 1847, more than a century before its neighbors. A small (3–5 percent of the population) "Americo-Liberian" elite, which traced its descent to the settlers of 1820–1840, subsequently played a significant role in Liberian affairs while being gradually assimilated into the rest of the population, which is currently divided into some 16 principal tribes speaking nearly 30 native languages. About 10 percent of the population is Christian and 10–20 percent Muslim; the remainder practices indigenous religions and traditional customs. Women comprise approximately 40 percent of the labor force, mainly in agriculture; female participation in government, traditionally minimal, has increased since the 1980s.

The Liberian economy is dependent on exports of iron ore, rubber, and timber, plus smaller quantities of diamonds and coffee. In 1989 iron ore accounted for more than half of export revenue, although the industry employed only 2 percent of the labor force. Industrial development also included diverse smaller enterprises centering on commodities such as processed agricultural goods, cement, plastic explosives, beverages, and refined petroleum. In addition, Liberia provided a "flag of convenience" for about 2,450 ships, or approximately one-fifth of the world's maritime tonnage.

During the decade preceding the collapse of the Doe regime in 1990, a decline in world commodity prices combined with mismanagement of state enterprises to produce a severe fiscal crisis. In response, the government attempted to privatize national industries, mounted an anticorruption campaign, and promoted an agriculture-based "green revolution." Complicating the situation was the suspension of aid in 1986 by the International Monetary Fund (IMF) because of Monrovia's failure to make scheduled payments on its external debt, which exceeded $1.7 billion by mid-1990. Of far greater consequence was the subsequent carnage caused by civil war and the interim government's lack of fiscal resources because of rebel activity.

The administration installed in mid-1997 pledged to focus its economic rehabilitation efforts on advancement of the private sector and reduction of the high unemployment rate. Real GDP grew by 20 percent in 1999, although per capita income reportedly remained at only one-third of prewar levels and unemployment was widespread. Subsequently, the Liberian economy suffered from the country's increasing international isolation resulting from the government's perceived role in the burgeoning subregional conflict (see Foreign relations, below). Among other things, the unrest led to a UN embargo on diamond sales (integrally related to arms traffic), a halt to many donor-financed development projects, and delays in the government's proposed fiscal reforms.

Intensified fighting in 2002 led to a dramatic decline in GDP in 2003 and created severe food and energy shortages and substantial internal and external displacement of large segments of the population. In March 2003 the IMF suspended Liberia because of the Taylor administration's failure to pay its dues and repay loans. However, the negotiation of a cease-fire and installation of a national transitional government in the second half of 2003 prompted international donors in February 2004 to pledge $520 million in humanitarian and economic assistance. Growth of 2.4 percent and 5.3 percent was achieved in 2004 and 2005, respectively.

Following the 2005 elections, the country's fragile economic recovery continued. In order to repair the country's reputation for financial mismanagement, the new administration launched a series of reforms in early 2006 designed, among other things, to increase the collection of unpaid taxes, improve auditing processes, and computerize the banking system. In exchange for the renewal of foreign aid, donor organizations and states created the Governance and Economic Management Assistance Program (GEMAP), under which international experts were designated to assist members of the new Liberian government. (GEMAP officials were required to countersign all major government expenditures, a condition that generated significant resentment among Liberians.)

In April 2006 the IMF announced that Liberia was one of 11 countries that had qualified for debt relief under the Heavily Indebted Poor Countries (HIPC) initiative. (Liberia's foreign debt stood at about $3.2 billion.) As evidence of the daunting task facing the new government, it was estimated that 50 percent of the population survived on less than $1 per day. In addition, some estimates placed unemployment as high as 80 percent.

GDP grew by 8 percent in 2006 and 9.5 percent in 2007, much of the expansion being tied to additional foreign aid. Inflation remained at approximately 10 percent in the latter year. Meanwhile, increased tax revenues, reductions in the bloated civil service bureaucracy, and additional debt relief from Germany, the United Kingdom, the United States, South Africa, and China were expected to permit the government to

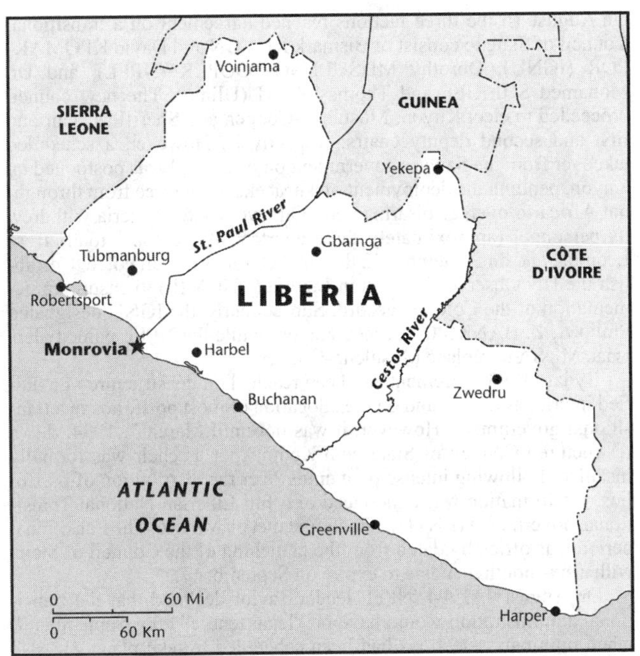

expand spending on infrastructure improvements. Acknowledging that significant progress had been achieved by the Johnson-Sirleaf administration but cautioning that annual per capita GDP ($195) remained below prewar levels, the IMF normalized relations with Liberia in 2008 and approved new support. Growth of 7.1 percent was registered in 2008 despite the effects of rapidly rising food and fuel prices, which pushed inflation to 20 percent in the fall.

GOVERNMENT AND POLITICS

Political background. Liberia's political origins stem from a charter granted by the U.S. Congress to the American Colonization Society in 1816 to establish a settlement for freed slaves on the west coast of Africa. The first settlers arrived in 1822 with the financial assistance of U.S. President James Monroe, and in 1847 Liberia declared itself an independent republic under an American-style constitution. During the late 19th and early 20th centuries, such European powers as Britain, France, and Germany became involved in the country's domestic affairs and laid claim to portions of Liberian territory. After World War I, however, American political and economic influence was reestablished, with Firestone assuming operation in 1926 of the world's largest rubber plantation in Harbel.

Relative stability characterized internal politics under the guidance of the True Whig Party (TWP), which ruled continuously for more than a century after coming to power in 1878. Political authority was strongly centralized under the administration of President William V. S. TUBMAN, who was elected in 1944 on a platform calling for the promotion of foreign economic investment and the unification of the country via integration of the Americo-Liberian population and tribal groups. Following Tubman's death in 1971, his successor, William Richard TOLBERT Jr., attempted to maintain Tubman's policies. However, limited economic imagination, insensitivity to popular feeling among indigenous Liberians, and allegations of maladministration and corruption contributed in the late 1970s to growing domestic opposition, including a wave of illegal strikes. Widespread rioting in Monrovia in April 1979 over a proposed increase in the price of rice prompted Congress to grant emergency powers to Tolbert, while later in the year municipal elections were postponed and tough labor laws were enacted to end the work stoppages.

Despite legalization in January 1980 of the People's Progressive Party (PPP), the country's first formal opposition in more than two decades, President Tolbert responded to a call for a general strike by PPP leader Gabriel Baccus MATTHEWS in March by asserting that the party had planned an "armed insurrection." Matthews and other PPP leaders were arrested, but on April 12, two days before their trial was to begin, a coup led by junior officers overthrew the government, President Tolbert and more than two dozen others being killed. A People's Redemption Council (PRC), chaired by Master Sgt. Samuel Kanyon DOE, was established, and on April 13 the PRC announced a civilian-military cabinet that included Matthews as foreign minister. On April 22, following a series of military trials, a number of former government and TWP officials were publicly executed by firing squad. Three days later, the PRC suspended the constitution and instituted martial law.

In April 1981 the PRC appointed a 25-member commission to draft a new constitution, in keeping with Doe's promise of a return to civilian rule by April 1985. After a number of postponements for the avowed purpose of registering and educating voters, a constitutional referendum was held on July 3, 1984. On July 20 Doe announced that the document had been accepted, and the following day he abolished the PRC and merged its membership with 57 hand-picked civilians to form an Interim National Assembly. Although the new assembly immediately elected him as its president, Doe characterized the status as temporary and announced that he would present himself as a candidate in a national election to be held in October 1985.

Because of restrictions imposed by the government-appointed electoral commission, neither Matthews nor the chair of the constitutional commission, Dr. Amos SAWYER, was allowed to campaign for the presidency in 1985, with their parties also being disqualified from presenting legislative candidates. As a result, three substantially weaker groups challenged Doe's recently launched National Democratic Party of Liberia (NDPL). Amid widespread allegations of electoral fraud and military intimidation, Doe claimed victory in the October 15, 1985, balloting on the basis of a reported 50.9 percent presidential vote share, while the NDPL was awarded 73 of the 90 assembly seats.

In June 1987, as part of an apparent effort to consolidate his power, President Doe dismissed four Supreme Court justices, thereby drawing criticism that he had exceeded his constitutional authority. Three months later the government reported that it had thwarted a coup attempt masterminded by former foreign minister Matthews.

During 1988 the regime continued to crack down on real or imagined opponents. In March, William Gabriel KPOLLEH, president of the Liberian Unification Party (LUP), was charged with leading a coup attempt, and in July Doe's former PRC deputy, J. Nicholas PODIER, was slain in the wake of another alleged overthrow effort (reportedly the ninth since 1980).

In late 1989 a number of villages in the northeastern border region of Nimba County were overrun by a group of about 150 rebels led by Charles Chankay TAYLOR, who five years earlier had escaped from custody in the United States after being charged with the theft of Liberian government funds. In January 1990 the fighting assumed a tribal character, with the rebels (styling themselves the National Patriotic Front of Liberia [NPFL]) attacking members of the president's Krahn ethnic group and government forces retaliating against Nimba's principal tribe, the Gio. By early June what had begun as a seemingly minor insurrection had expanded into a major threat to the Doe regime. After steady progress in a series of engagements with Liberian army units, rebel troops advanced on Monrovia, and by mid-July a "reign of terror" was reported in the capital, with both sides allegedly engaging in atrocities against ethnic opponents and unarmed civilians. Meanwhile, an Independent NPFL (INPFL), which had broken with the Taylor group in February under the leadership of Prince Yormic JOHNSON, emerged as a major "third force" that succeeded in gaining control of central Monrovia on July 23.

With neither the United Nations nor the Organization of African Unity (OAU, subsequently the African Union—AU) taking action to ameliorate the conflict, the Economic Community of West African States (ECOWAS) organized a 4,000-man peacekeeping force styled the ECOWAS Monitoring Group (Ecomog), which arrived in Monrovia on August 25, 1990. The intervention was welcomed by Johnson but was bitterly denounced by Taylor, who insisted that the force had been assembled to avert defeat of the Doe regime by the NPFL.

On September 11, 1990, President Doe was killed by members of the Johnson group as the apparent result of an argument that had broken out during a meeting arranged by Ecomog. Government forces nonetheless continued their defense of the heavily fortified executive mansion under the presidential guard commander, Brig. Gen. David NIMLEY. During the next several days four individuals (Johnson, Taylor, Nimley, and the former constitutional commission chair, Amos Sawyer, who headed an Interim Government of National Unity [IGNU] from exile in Banjul, Gambia) proclaimed themselves president, with the last being recognized, on an interim basis, by ECOWAS on November 22. Six days later the three warring factions within Liberia concluded a cease-fire agreement in Bamako, Mali, and declared their intention to participate in a national conference to establish an interim government. Although Taylor was reported to have signed the accord only because of pressure from his two principal backers, Libya and Burkina Faso, the suspension of hostilities generally held into 1991, with the three faction leaders (including Gen. Hezekiah BOWEN, who had succeeded Nimley as head of the Armed Forces of Liberia [AFL]), agreeing to meet in Lomé, Togo, on March 15 to pave the way for a transitional regime. At the last moment, however, Taylor refused to attend without the participation of elected representatives from Liberia's 13 counties, all but one of which his forces claimed to control. A compromise structure was eventually agreed upon, providing for a president and two vice presidents (representing the IGNU, NPFL, and INPFL, respectively). However, there was little immediate progress toward implementation of the plan, and Ecomog experienced mounting pressure to move militarily against the obdurate Taylor. On June 30 the stalemate appeared to have been broken in the course of a meeting attended by Taylor, Sawyer, and five West African heads of government in Yamoussoukro, Côte d'Ivoire, that yielded agreement on the establishment of a commission to organize a national election.

Although fighting subsided in July–August 1991, Taylor took no action to disarm his forces as mandated by the Yamoussoukro accord, while Johnson on August 6 announced that the INPFL was withdrawing from the tripartite regime. Faced with Taylor's hostility toward the composition of the Ecomog force, Côte d'Ivoire offered to seek Ecomog's replacement by a UN contingent, but the idea was rejected by Sawyer on August 19. Renewed hostilities thereupon broke out in the form of clashes between NPFL units, which had entered Sierra Leone in support of local dissidents, and Sierra Leonean troops, who were accompanied by a group from former president Doe's Krahn tribe that had styled itself the United Liberation Movement of Liberia for Democracy (Ulimo). Nonetheless, peace talks resumed in Yamoussoukro on September 16 and 17, yielding a new stand-down commitment by the Liberian factions in return for an Ecomog restructuring (primarily in response to NPFL charges that it was Nigerian-dominated).

A fourth summit in Yamoussoukro on October 29–31, 1991, drew a pledge by the NPFL to withdraw from Sierra Leone, disarm its forces, and relinquish Liberian territory under its control to Ecomog. It was also agreed that a buffer zone would be established between Liberia and Sierra Leone and that the Liberian election would be held within six months. On November 8 Johnson's INPFL announced that it would rejoin the interim government, although Ulimo leader Raleigh SEEKIE repudiated the peace agreement. While additional disagreements, including a refusal by both the NPFL and INPFL to honor new banknotes issued by the Sawyer administration, surfaced by early 1992, a 13-member interim election commission was sworn in on January 13 with instructions to prepare for legislative and presidential balloting in August. A week later, in his annual message to Monrovia's Interim Assembly, President Sawyer offered NPFL leader Taylor the vacant post of vice president in the interim government on the condition that Taylor join in effective implementation of the most recent Yamoussoukro accord. However, no response was reported.

On April 7 and 8, 1992, ECOWAS representatives met in Geneva, Switzerland, with Sawyer, Taylor, the vice president of Nigeria, and the presidents of Burkina Faso, Côte d'Ivoire, and Senegal. The group reaffirmed its support of Yamoussoukro IV, including establishment of the Ecomog buffer zone. On April 14 Taylor renounced the agreement, calling it "unbalanced and unsatisfactory," but on April 29 he reversed himself. On April 30 Ecomog began deployment in border areas theretofore controlled by the NPFL.

In August 1992 heavy fighting broke out between NPFL and Ulimo forces, and in September the NPFL accused Ecomog of supporting the NPFL's ostensibly Sierra Leone-based opponents. Fighting also erupted in October in Monrovia between NPFL and Ecomog units. By early 1993 the ECOWAS contingent appeared to have gained the upper hand, and in March the NPFL was driven (briefly as it turned out) from its stronghold of Gbarnga, with its control of the hinterland having been reduced from more than 90 percent to less than 40 percent. In early April Ecomog troops drove Taylor's forces from the strategic port city of Buchanan, and in May the southeastern port of Greenville also fell, confining the NPFL's maritime access to the small town of Harper near the border with Côte d'Ivoire.

On July 25, 1993, in Cotonou, Benin, Liberia's leading combatants (the NPFL, Ulimo, and Ecomog) signed an OAU/UN-brokered peace accord, and on August 1 the lengthy conflict appeared to end, Taylor advising his followers (somewhat prematurely) "to return to your towns and villages and begin to rebuild your lives. The war is over." On August 16 the three factions reached agreement on a transitional Council of State to consist of Bismark KUYON and David KPOMAKPOR (IGNU), Dorothy MUSULENG-COOPER (NPFL), and Dr. Mohamed SHERIFF and Thomas ZIAH (Ulimo). The new council proceeded to elect Kuyon, Musuleng-Cooper, and Sheriff as chair and first and second deputy chairs, respectively. However, a scheduled takeover from the Sawyer government on August 24 was postponed by Kuyon, pending the deployment of a peacekeeping force from throughout Africa to oversee disarmament. One week later Nigeria withdrew its personnel (approximately three-quarters of the force total) from Ecomog, and on September 22 the UN Security Council voted to establish the UN Observer Mission in Liberia (UNOMIL) to ensure implementation of the Cotonou accord. Subsequently, the IGNU designated Philip A. Z. BANKS to succeed Kuyon, while the NPFL named Gen. Isaac MUSA to replace Musuleng-Cooper.

By late 1993 agreement had been reached on the structure of a unified interim assembly and on the allocation of most portfolios in a transitional government. However, it was not until March 7, 1994, that a restructured Council of State with Kpomakpor as chair was formally installed. Following intense bargaining over the distribution of portfolios, the formation was announced of a full Liberian National Transitional Government (LNTG), which first met on May 16. The transitional period was officially dated from the launching of the Council of State, with a six-month mandate to expire on September 7.

On August 4, 1994, NPFL leader Taylor declared that the transitional administration would have no "legal tenure" after September 7, when multiparty elections had been scheduled to take place. He also demanded a cabinet reshuffle, claiming that several key ministers who had been expelled from the NPFL for criticizing his leadership no longer could be counted as representing the NPFL.

On September 7, 1994, Taylor joined AFL leader Bowen and Lt. Gen. Alhaji G. V. KROMAH, the leader of Ulimo's Mandingo-based Muslim faction (Ulimo-M), in a meeting on Lake Volta near Akosombo with Ghana's President Jerry Rawlings and representatives of Ecomog, the OAU, and the UN secretary general. Five days later, an agreement was signed calling for an immediate end to hostilities; continuance until October 10, 1995, of the transitional government, headed by a new five-member Council of State; and the holding of presidential and legislative elections within a year. During the Akosombo meeting, however, the NPFL dissenters, led by Labor Minister Thomas WOEWEIYU, overran the NPFL headquarters in Gbarnga, forcing Taylor to seek temporary refuge in Côte d'Ivoire.

In October 1994 both UNOMIL and Ecomog forces were substantially reduced, prospects for an end to the lengthy Liberian conflict having receded. On November 6 the Ghanaian and Nigerian governments (the largest contributors to Ecomog) convened a "last ditch" meeting in Accra that included, in addition to the signatories of the Akosombo accord, Gen. Roosevelt JOHNSON, leader of Ulimo's Christian-oriented Krahn faction (Ulimo-K); Dr. George E. S. BOLEY, head of the Krahn-based Liberian Peace Council (LPC); François MASSAQUOI, commander of the Lofa Defense Force (LDF); and Woeweiyu, representing the NPFL dissidents. However, the meeting adjourned on November 29 with no agreement on the membership of a reconstituted Council of State.

Despite the failure of the November 1994 talks, follow-up discussions were launched in Accra in December, with the major warring groups (the NPFL, Ulimo-K, Ulimo-M, AFL, LNC, LDF, and the Woeweiyu dissidents [now styled the Central Revolutionary Council–NPFL]) participating. On December 22 agreement was reached on a cessation of hostilities as of December 28 and on a Council of State to include one representative each from the NPFL, Ulimo, the AFL, and the LNC, with a fifth member to be selected by the NPFL and Ulimo from traditional chiefs. It was further agreed that the Council of State would give way to an elected government on January 1, 1996, after multiparty elections on November 1, 1995.

On January 25, 1995, the warring groups agreed to expand the Council of State from five to six members, but they continued to disagree as to its composition and adjourned the talks indefinitely on January 31. Subsequently, on February 6, Ghanaian mediators rejected a Taylor proposal for another five-man council to be chaired by an elderly traditional chief, Tamba TAYLOR (no relation to the NPFL leader), with Charles Taylor as first vice chair, Ulimo-M's Kromah as second vice chair, and the AFL's Bowen as third vice chair. It was not until August 19 that agreement on the makeup of the new council was reached and a seemingly conclusive cease-fire was declared. The six members inaugurated in Monrovia on September 1 included Charles

Taylor, G. V. Kromah, Dr. George E. S. Boley, and three civilians—Chief Tamba Taylor, Oscar QUIAH, and Wilton S. SANKAWULO, a former university professor and newspaper columnist, who was named council chair.

On September 3, 1995, the Council of State announced the formation of a new Transitional Government. Twelve days later the UN Security Council voted unanimously to extend UNOMIL's mandate to January 31, 1996, and in October Ecomog responded positively to an appeal from its chair, President Rawlings of Ghana, for a fourfold increase in its troop level to oversee disarmament and demobilization of the various warring factions.

On April 6, 1996, renewed fighting broke out throughout Monrovia, sparked by the attempted arrest of Ulimo-K leader Johnson by NPFL and Ulimo-M fighters. Although Johnson's headquarters were easily taken, he escaped capture, and his forces and Krahn defectors from other factions took up arms throughout the city. By April 9 Johnson and his fighters, with several hundred hostages in tow, had been forced to retreat to their Monrovia barracks; however, systematic looting continued amid anarchic conditions in the capital.

On April 10, 1996, with extremely intense fighting reported around the U.S. embassy (where thousands of Liberian civilians and foreigners were reported to have sought refuge), the United States ordered the deployment of a warship to the Liberian coast to support an evacuation effort begun the previous day. On the same day the warring faction leaders agreed to a cease-fire; however, it was immediately abandoned after Johnson refused to surrender to Ecomog forces. On April 16 anti-Johnson militiamen laid siege to his base. Three days later a second cease-fire was announced, and on April 21 the Ulimo-K released the majority of its hostages. Furthermore, Ecomog commanders reported that they had secured the perimeter of Monrovia in an effort to stanch the flow of arms and fighters. Nevertheless, intense fighting reportedly continued.

An ECOWAS summit scheduled for May 8, 1996, in Ghana was canceled after a number of member states and faction leaders refused to attend; for his part, Charles Taylor claimed he and his "government" troops were needed in Monrovia to maintain order. Citing frustration with the "intransigence" of the warring faction leaders, Ghanaian President Rawlings threatened to withdraw Ecomog troops if peace negotiations were not promptly launched.

At ECOWAS's annual summit in July 1996, its members pledged to organize Liberian elections within nine months. With fighting reported to have subsided, ECOWAS representatives and all of the faction leaders met in mid-August in Abuja, Nigeria, where they agreed to a revised version of the 1995 accord. The faction leaders also unanimously elected Ruth PERRY, a senator during the Doe era, to replace Sankawulo as chair of the Council of State. The cease-fire agreement was highlighted by a proposed schedule for disarmament and demobilization (from November 22, 1996, to January 31, 1997), dissolution of the factions (January 31, 1997), presidential and legislative elections (May 31, 1997), and the inauguration of a new government (June 15, 1997). On August 31 the UNOMIL mandate was extended, and on September 3 Perry was inaugurated, thus becoming the first-ever female African head of state.

Adding muscle to the August 1996 accord, ECOWAS threatened to impose sanctions on "any person or group obstructing the implementation" of the cease-fire agreement. Meanwhile, the United States pledged to finance the anticipated expansion of Ecomog troop strength. Subsequently, amid reports of mass starvation in those areas already cleared of fighters, Ecomog troops began deploying weeks ahead of the scheduled November start of the disarmament process. However, an assassination attempt against Charles Taylor at the presidential palace on October 31 resulted in suspension of Council of State activities and underscored the fragility of the cease-fire. Nevertheless, registration of political parties continued through the end of the year in preparation for the general elections scheduled for May 1997.

In mid-January 1997 the Council of State reconvened for the first time since the attempt on Taylor's life. Meanwhile, Ecomog's Nigerian leadership increased pressure on the former combatants to turn in their arms. Consequently, the disarmament campaign, which had theretofore elicited only a trickle of returns, accelerated to near conclusion by the end of the month, and on February 1 all the armed factions were declared officially dissolved. In mid-February presidential and legislative balloting was scheduled for May 30, and a seven-member electoral commission was established. Two weeks later, Taylor, Kromah, and Boley resigned from the Council of State to begin preparations for the presidential election. In early March, President Perry appointed former information minister Henry ANDREWS as president of the electoral commission, and on April 2 the commission was officially sworn in. Meanwhile, former UN official and international banker Ellen Johnson-Sirleaf emerged as Taylor's primary competition for the presidency in the wake of the splintering of an anti-Taylor coalition, the Alliance of Seven Parties (see Political Parties and Groups, below). In addition, 11 others registered as presidential candidates, and at least 13 parties announced their intention to compete for legislative posts. In mid-May the balloting was postponed to July.

In presidential and legislative balloting on July 19, 1997, Taylor and the restyled National Patriotic Party (NPP) overwhelmed their opponents, with Taylor and his vice presidential running mate, Enoch DOGOLEA, capturing approximately 70 percent of the votes and the NPP securing majorities in both the House of Representatives and the Senate. Although some analysts had forecast a tight race between Taylor and Johnson-Sirleaf, Taylor's well-financed campaign, his veiled threats to recommence fighting if he were to lose the elections, and his election-eve apology for his role in the civil war proved too much for Johnson-Sirleaf. She received just 9 percent of the vote, and the UP was also a distant second in legislative polling. International observers described the balloting as generally fair. However, a number of domestic critics characterized the balloting as irreparably tainted by irregularities. On August 2 Taylor and Dogolea were inaugurated, and by mid-month Taylor had finished appointing a predominantly NPP cabinet.

In 1998 President Taylor wielded an increasingly heavy hand in response to domestic criticism, shutting down opposition media outlets, purging dissenters from the government, and, according to critics, covertly supporting violent attacks on opposition foes. In mid-September dozens of people were reportedly killed in Monrovia when presidential forces attempted to arrest General Johnson, who had refused to release his grip on a section of the capital and was suspected of plotting to overthrow the government. During the fighting, Johnson and his entourage fled to the U.S. embassy, where they were allowed to enter only after Taylor's forces attacked and killed 2 of Johnson's associates and wounded 2 U.S. personnel. The following day, Johnson, Lt. Gen. Alhaji Kromah of the All-Liberia Coalition Party (ALCOP), and approximately 20 others were charged with treason. Subsequently, Johnson and Kromah escaped from the country (the former by U.S. helicopter), and neither of the 2 men, nor half of their codefendants, appeared at the opening of their trial in November. (In April 1999, 13 of the "coup plotters" were sentenced to 10 years in prison.)

At a July 1999 weapons-destruction ceremony, President Taylor declared the end of a "dark chapter" in Liberian history. (More than 200,000 people had died in the civil war.) It soon became clear, however, that many of Taylor's opponents had not given up their fight, as evidenced by guerrilla activity on the part of the Liberians United for Reconciliation and Democracy (LURD) in the northwest. In August 2000 the administration charged a number of opposition figures (many in exile) with treason in connection with ongoing "dissident" activities. However, facing heavy international pressure for both his domestic policies and his involvement in regional conflicts (particularly involving Sierra Leone), Taylor amnestied many of his opponents and urged them to return to Liberia to assume a role in the political process. Although a fragile peace in Sierra Leone offered some respite for Taylor and other participants in the interlocking regional disputes, the LURD offensive continued into early 2002. Opposition leaders also accused the administration in the first half of 2002 of increasingly repressive (and sometimes violent) measures against dissident voices in the media and elsewhere. In addition, international human rights activists charged Liberian security forces with numerous violations that were seen as contributing to a deteriorating political climate. Meanwhile, additional pressure was applied to the government by another recently launched rebel group, the Movement for Democracy in Liberia (MODEL).

In January 2003 the government announced that new presidential and legislative elections would be held in October. However, LURD/MODEL fighters launched an offensive in February that neared Monrovia in April, causing a mass exodus from the capital and making it clear that normal political activity was an impossibility without a cease-fire.

As the rebels reached Monrovia in June 2003, peace negotiations were launched in Accra, Ghana. On June 17 the Accra accord was signed, calling for withdrawal of the rebels to the north of Monrovia, deployment of an international peacekeeping force, and the resignation of President Taylor in favor of a transitional government. Within days, however, Taylor reneged on his pledge to resign, and the rebels again advanced on Monrovia. Complicating matters for President Taylor was an indictment from the UN-sponsored court in Sierra Leone charging him with 17 counts of crimes against humanity in connection with his alleged role in that nation's recently resolved conflict.

Near the end of July 2003, ECOWAS authorized the deployment of peacekeeping forces under the banner of the ECOWAS Mission in Liberia (ECOMIL), and some 3,250 ECOMIL troops (mainly from Nigeria) were dispatched to Monrovia in early August. Under intense international pressure, Taylor finally resigned on August 11 and left Liberia for Nigeria. Vice President Moses Zeh BLAH assumed presidential authority on an acting basis, and he quickly negotiated (on August 18) a new cease-fire and a so-called Comprehensive Peace Agreement with the rebels. In accordance with the peace plan, a national transitional government was installed on October 14, with Charles Gyude BRYANT of the Liberia Action Party (LAP) as chair. His cabinet comprised members of the pro-Taylor Government of Liberia (GOL), the LURD, the MODEL, and representatives of civic organizations. At the same time, a 76-member National Transitional Legislative Assembly (NTLA) was installed for a two-year period pending new legislative and presidential elections. Bryant dedicated his administration to the task of bringing Liberia "back from the brink of self-destruction." Priorities included the disarmament (with help from the UNMIL) of the former warring factions and assistance for some 300,000 internal or external refugees (as of November 2004). Sporadic clashes between Muslims and Christians in several areas of the country also contributed to the government's difficulties. In addition, the administration's image was subsequently tarnished by revelations of alleged financial irregularities.

In the first round of presidential balloting on October 11, 2005, George WEAH of the Congress for Democratic Change (CDC) led 22 candidates with 28.3 percent of the vote. Ellen Johnson-Sirleaf of the UP finished second with 19.8 percent. However, Johnson-Sirleaf handily won the runoff balloting on November 8 with 59.4 percent of the vote. Meanwhile, in the October 11 balloting for the House of Representatives, the CDC led all parties with 15 seats. Since her party did not command a legislative majority, Johnson-Sirleaf (the first democratically elected female leader of a national government in Africa) formed a cabinet that included independents and members of several small parties.

Constitution and government. The former Liberian constitution, adopted July 26, 1847, was modeled, save in the matter of federalism, after that of the United States. Executive authority was vested in the president, who was limited by a 1975 amendment to a single eight-year term, excluding time spent completing the unexpired term of a predecessor. The bicameral Congress consisted of an 18-member Senate and a 65-member House of Representatives.

The constitution approved in July 1984, with effect from President Doe's inaugural in January 1986, did not differ significantly from its predecessor. Rather than being elected for eight years, the president was restricted to a maximum of two six-year terms, while the legislature was restyled the National Assembly. The Senate was increased to 26 members and the House was reduced to 64. Suffrage was extended to all adults. The 1984 law also provided for relatively simple registration of political parties, with prohibitions against those considered dangerous to "the free and democratic society of Liberia." Administratively, the country was divided into 9 counties and 5 territories, with lesser units encompassing 30 cities and 145 townships. The number of counties has subsequently increased to 15.

Some of the provisions of the 1984 constitution were superseded by the Comprehensive Peace Agreement of 2003 and the Electoral Reform Act of 2004, which, among other things, established guidelines for elections to a new Senate and House of Representatives (see Legislature, below) and for new presidential/vice presidential balloting.

Foreign relations. Many of the guiding principles of the OAU originated with President Tubman, who held a prominent position among moderate African leaders dedicated to peaceful change and noninterference in the internal affairs of other countries. President Tolbert was similarly respected in international forums, with the result that the April 1980 coup and his assassination were widely condemned throughout the world.

Liberia's traditional friendship with the United States was reflected both in the extent of U.S. private investment and in the existence of a bilateral defense agreement. Neither proved to be seriously threatened after 1980, despite initial U.S. criticism of the PRC takeover. The Doe government's essentially pro-Western posture was reflected in its cool treatment of the Libyan and Soviet ambassadors (the latter being expelled in October 1983 for alleged involvement in an antigovernment conspiracy), while in July 1985 relations with Moscow were severed for "gross interference" stemming from links between student activists and the Soviet embassy in Monrovia. In May 1987, on the other hand, the Soviet embassy was permitted to reopen in the context of a Liberian overture to the Eastern bloc, while in mid-1989 Doe renewed ties with former close confidant Muammar Qadhafi of Libya.

The core group of rebels led by Charles Taylor in early 1990 was reported to have been given commando training in Burkina Faso and Libya, while the initial point of entry into Nimba appeared to have been from neighboring Côte d'Ivoire. Although the United States maintained formal neutrality in the conflict, it appeared somewhat embarrassed by its support of the Doe regime and suspended trade concessions to Liberia in early May. Concurrently, the United States dispatched a naval flotilla to the region to evacuate American citizens wishing to leave. In March 1991, despite a continued display of reluctance to become involved in Liberian internal affairs, the United States was reported to have worked behind the scenes to persuade the NPFL's Taylor to participate in the roundtable discussions that yielded the abortive cease-fire of May 1991 and the equally abortive peace agreement of the following October.

In mid-1998 Liberia accused Guinea of attempting to destabilize Liberia through its role in Ecomog. Monrovia's diplomatic offensive against Guinean officials (who denied the charges) coincided with a heightening of tension between the Taylor administration and the Ghanaian and Nigerian governments over Monrovia's alleged support of rebels who were fighting the ECOWAS-backed government of Sierra Leone. In early 1999 the United States declared that it had uncovered evidence of Liberia's support for those rebels, and shortly thereafter Nigeria withdrew its remaining troops from Liberia, asserting that it could no longer maintain a mission there while Monrovia supported attacks against Nigerian troops in Sierra Leone.

An armed incursion from Guinea into northwestern Liberia was reported in April 1999, prompting a state of emergency in Lofa County. Under ECOWAS mediation, a tripartite commission was subsequently formed to attempt to reduce friction in the diamond-rich areas at the conjunction of the borders of Liberia, Guinea, and Sierra Leone. Consequently, a degree of stability ensued, permitting the final Ecomog contingents to leave Liberia in October and the borders to be reopened with Sierra Leone (in October) and Guinea (in February 2000). However, major fighting erupted again in mid-2000 along the border with Guinea, the Liberian government accusing the Guinean government of supporting anti-Taylor elements that had loosely coalesced as the LURD. Skirmishes continued into 2001, exacerbating already extensive refugee problems. Among other things, Liberian refugees in Guinea claimed they were being mistreated by the Guinean military, which in turn argued that the refugees were helping Guinean rebels (see article on Guinea for additional information). Meanwhile, President Taylor faced growing international pressure for his apparent continued support of the rebel Revolutionary United Front (RUF) in Sierra Leone. The complicated subregional conflict pitted the militaries of Guinea and Sierra Leone, Liberian rebels, and certain tribal groups (notably the Kamajors) from Sierra Leone on one side against the Liberian army and rebel groups from Guinea and Sierra Leone on the other. Much of the fighting involved control of rich mining areas, diamond production permitting various factions to buy armaments for their military campaigns.

In May 2001 the United Nations imposed an embargo on Liberian trade in diamonds and arms and barred senior Liberian officials from international travel as a means of encouraging Taylor's disengagement from the civil war in Sierra Leone. Combined with other pressure (including the suspension of development aid from the European Union [EU]), the UN initiative appeared to have the desired effect in contributing to a tentative resolution of the situation in Sierra Leone (see article on Sierra Leone for details). However, fighting between the LURD and the Liberian government continued into 2002, relations between Guinea and Liberia remaining tense until a somewhat surprising meeting in late February of the presidents of Liberia, Guinea, and Sierra Leone at which agreement was reached on enhanced border security, repatriation of refugees, and reactivation of the Mano River Union.

The intensification of the civil war in Liberia in late 2002 and early 2003 exacerbated tensions with regional powers as well as with the broader international community. Ghana, Nigeria, and Sierra Leone attempted to mediate a cease-fire as rebel forces moved on Monrovia, while many Western capitals urged President Taylor to resign. (Relations with the United States had deteriorated in late 2002 when evidence emerged that al-Qaida financiers may have been profiting from the Liberian diamond-smuggling trade.)

The UN endorsed the ECOWAS peacekeeping force in early August 2003, but by September ECOMIL had been superseded by a new UN force of 11,500 called the UN Mission in Liberia (UNMIL). Meanwhile, the United States pressed Nigeria to turn Taylor over to the UN for possible prosecution on charges related to his alleged activities in Sierra Leone.

In November 2005 the UN expanded the mandate of UNMIL to include the capture of Charles Taylor and his transfer to the UN Special Court for Sierra Leone. In December the UN renewed sanctions that prohibited travel for some 60 Liberians who were suspected of involvement in the conflict in Sierra Leone. Meanwhile, the United States supported the continuing efforts to demobilize the militia groups in Liberia in 2005–2006, pledging some $200 million for the effort and providing American military advisors to help train a new security force.

After a lengthy campaign by a range of international bodies, on March 25, 2006, the Nigerian government announced that it would honor a request to extradite Taylor to stand trial before the UN Special Court for Sierra Leone. Taylor briefly escaped on March 28, but he was recaptured the following day. He was transferred to Monrovia, and then to the Special Court in Freetown, Sierra Leone. Upon Johnson-Sirleaf's request, Taylor was subsequently transferred to The Hague to stand trial so that his presence in Sierra Leone did not destabilize the region. (The Special Court was also moved to The Hague for the trial.) Taylor's trial opened in early 2008 and, following several delays, was not expected to conclude until 2010, Taylor's lawyers having started their defense in mid-2009. Meanwhile, Taylor's son, Charles TAYLOR Jr., was sentenced to 97 years in prison following his conviction in a U.S. court on torture charges similar to his father's. The younger Taylor, who was born in the United States, was the first person to be tried under a 14-year-old law permitting prosecution of U.S. citizens for torture committed abroad.

Liberia's primary regional concern in 2009 was the situation in Guinea, where unrest emanating from the recent military coup threatened, in the opinion of some analysts, stability throughout the region. Liberian president Johnson-Sirleaf played a prominent leadership role in efforts to implement an agreement in Guinea that would lead to a return to civilian government.

Current issues. The 2005 presidential runoff pitted George Weah, a former soccer star who ran a populist campaign and enjoyed the support of some elements of the former Taylor regime, against Ellen Johnson-Sirleaf, a long-standing member of the anti-Taylor opposition and a former World Bank official who was championed as the candidate who could best restore Liberia's international ties and garner much-needed foreign reconstruction aid. Weah initially alleged fraud surrounding his loss in the second round, although EU and ECOWAS observers described the balloting as generally free and fair and the national election commission dismissed Weah's complaints. Liberian security forces and UN peacekeepers used tear gas and riot batons to disperse protest demonstrations by Weah's supporters shortly after the balloting. Even more violent demonstrations broke out in December after Weah delivered a speech that was highly critical of the elections and Johnson-Sirleaf. However, in order to defuse the situation, Weah later in the month announced he had accepted his defeat and urged his supporters to do likewise.

Despite ongoing political tension throughout the country and the diversity of the new legislature, lawmakers in early 2006 indicated a willingness to work with the Johnson-Sirleaf administration. All of the new president's cabinet appointments were approved by March, as were most of her initial legislative proposals. The international community also responded positively to the completion of the elections (see The Country, above).

Lengthy delays and apparent corruption in the judicial system led to an escalation of mob justice and vigilantism in 2006. Meanwhile, a South African–style Truth and Reconciliation Commission (TRC) began in October to gather testimony from victims and alleged war criminals from the earlier conflict. Although the commission suspended its activities in January 2007 due to a lack of funds, the government subsequently announced a broad investigation of former government officials on fraud and corruption charges.

In April 2007 the UN Security Council lifted the remaining sanctions on the diamond trade in Liberia in exchange for the country becoming a partner in the Kimberley Process, which had been designed to prevent export of "blood diamonds" from conflict areas. The Liberian government announced in July that it would begin to issue new licenses for the diamond sector. Meanwhile, at midyear, the UNMIL reported that more than 60,000 former fighters had been integrated into job-training programs. However, later in the year the UNMIL reported a "broad range of human rights concerns," particularly in regard to the "decrepit" judicial system.

Much attention in early 2008 focused on the first public hearings on the recently reactivated TRC, although critics described the commission as "toothless" because of its lack of prosecutorial powers. Additionally, tensions were reported regarding the "opening of old wounds," especially in light of the fact that many of the alleged perpetrators continued to hold public office. The government also faced significant challenges later in the year regarding rising fuel and food prices as well as revelations of ongoing corruption. Nevertheless, the administration drew praise for its economic reforms and was described in one international report issued in October as the "fastest-improving state" in Africa.

The TRC presented its final report to the legislature in mid-2009, although many analysts described the findings as flawed and representative of the "differing agendas" of the members of the commission. Among the controversial elements was a call for President Johnson-Sirleaf to be barred from office because she had for a brief time in 1989 supported Charles Taylor's insurgency. (Johnson-Sirleaf earlier in 2009 had apologized to the TRC for her actions, saying she had been fooled about Taylor's "true intentions.") The legislature subsequently postponed action on the report until 2010. Meanwhile, concern grew over the increasing role being played by Liberia as a transit point for regional drug trafficking, while the opposition criticized the administration for ineffectiveness in combating corruption in business and government.

POLITICAL PARTIES AND GROUPS

For more than a century prior to the 1980 coup, an Americo-Liberian elite had dominated Liberia's politics through the True Whig Party (TWP), most of whose leaders were subsequently assassinated or executed.

Upon the PRC's assumption of power in 1980, political party activity was suspended, a ban that was extended in December 1982 to any individual or group "caught making unfavorable speeches and pronouncements against the government." The ban was repealed in July 1984, although only the NDPL, LAP, LUP, and Liberia Liberal Party (LLP) were permitted to contest the election of October 15, 1985.

In anticipation of presidential and legislative elections, the Alliance of Seven Parties was formed in February 1997 by the LAP, LUP, NDPL, TWP, LPP, UP, and UPP. On March 24 the alliance held intraparty primary elections to choose a presidential candidate for the upcoming elections; however, the victory of the LAP's Cletus Wotorson was immediately challenged, and both the UPP and LPP withdrew from the coalition, claiming that the LAP had engaged in fraud and vote buying. With the alliance in disarray, the LPP, LUP, and TWP announced in June that they had switched their allegiance to UP presidential candidate Ellen Johnson-Sirleaf (although the LPP ultimately fielded its own candidate). Likewise, a coalition of the three most prominent Krahn parties—the LPC, NDPL, and the Krahn faction of Ulimo (Ulimo–K)—proved unable to reach agreement on campaign tactics and splintered. Later, one manifestation of efforts to forge an anti-Taylor alliance was the Collaborating Political Parties (CPP), whose members included the ALCOP, FDP, LAP, LINU, LPP, NDPL, PDPL, PPP, RAP, TWP, UP, and UPP.

Some 22 parties and groupings registered to contest the 2005 legislative and presidential elections. However, in May 2007 the national elections commission suspended 9 parties for failing to maintain headquarters in Monrovia as required by the constitution. The affected parties included the PPP, LPL, LERP, RULP, IDP, NPL, UDA, PDPL, and the dormant **United Democratic Party**. The parties, who strongly challenged suspensions, were given two months to establish a presence in the capital. Subsequently, in June, 8 parties (the FDP, NDPL, PDPL, RAT, TWP, ULD, LERP, and LPL) announced the formation of a loose collaborative body called the Forum for Political Party Leaders (FOPPAL) as a proposed means for small parties to build consensus on national issues.

Legislative Parties:

Congress for Democratic Change (CDC). Formed in 2005 and led by former soccer star George Weah, the CDC is a populist party with broad appeal among Liberia's poor. In the 2005 legislative balloting, it became the largest party in the House with 15 seats.

The CDC splintered in March 2006 when Samuel TWEAH Jr., the chair of the American branch of the party, resigned, along with other leading CDC figures, citing financial irregularities and a dispute over whom the party should have supported for speaker of the House. Further tensions within the party were reported in 2007 when party leaders decided to endorse several LAP candidates in legislative by-elections as part of a collaborative initiative between the parties.

Several smaller parties (including the LP and NDPL) in 2009 were reportedly considering alignment with the CDC for the 2011 elections.

Leaders: George WEAH (Party President and 2005 presidential candidate), Lenn Eugene NAGBE (Secretary General), Acarous GRAY (Assistant Secretary General).

Liberty Party (LP). Formed in 2005, the LP is led by Charles Brumskine, who placed third in the 2005 presidential polling with 13.9 percent of the vote. The LP secured nine seats in the 2005 House elections, making it the second largest party in the chamber.

At a party congress in February 2006, Brumskine announced that he would not stand as the party's presidential candidate in the 2011 elections. A new slate of party leaders was elected, including a new national chair, Israel Akinsanya. Subsequently, Brumskine indicated that the LP might cooperate with the CDC in the 2011 elections.

Leaders: Charles BRUMSKINE (Party President and 2005 presidential candidate), Israel AKINSANYA (Chair).

Coalition for the Transformation of Liberia (COTOL). Formed in July 2005 as an electoral coalition by the three parties below and the LAP in preparation for the October presidential and legislative balloting, the COTOL chose the LAP's Varney G. Sherman as its presidential candidate. Sherman placed fifth in the first round of balloting with 7.8 percent of the vote. Most of the COTOL components supported George Weah in the presidential runoff. Meanwhile, the COTOL became the largest Senate grouping with seven seats; it also won eight seats in the House.

Tensions were reported within the COTOL in 2006 as the LAP sought electoral alliances outside of the coalition for upcoming legislative by-elections. The LAP finally withdrew from the COTOL in December, although renewed LAP/LUP cooperation was reported in mid-2009 (see UP, below, for details).

Leaders: Isaac F. MANNEH (Chair), Napoleon TOQUE (Vice Chair), Varney G. SHERMAN (2005 presidential candidate).

Liberia Unification Party (LUP). Organized in 1984 by Gabriel KPOLLEH, former president of the Monrovia Public School Teachers' Association, the LUP was initially viewed as a potential "Trojan horse" by the NDPL. Kpolleh surprised many observers by backing the LAP-led legislative boycott in 1985, with all four of the party's assembly members refusing to take their seats. In March 1988 the party's leader and deputy leader were arrested on charges of plotting to overthrow the government and were given ten-year prison sentences the following October. Kpolleh was released in 1991 and was later assassinated, although the LUP remained active.

Leader: Isaac F. MANNEH (Chair).

True Whig Party (TWP). Founded in 1868 and Liberia's ruling party until banned in the wake of the 1980 coup, the TWP was revived in 1991. Many members of the TWP defected to either the CDC or the UP prior to the 2005 elections.

Leaders: Peter VUKU (Chair), Othello R. MASON (Secretary General).

People's Democratic Party of Liberia (PDPL). The PDPL was represented by George Toe WASHINGTON in the 1997 presidential balloting. The PDPL broke with the other parties in COTOL and supported Ellen Johnson-Sirleaf in the 2005 presidential runoff.

Leaders: Napoleon TOQUE (Chair), G. Narrison TOULEE (Secretary General).

Liberia Action Party (LAP). The LAP was organized by Tuan WREH, a former supporter and political confidant of General Doe, who was subsequently joined by a number of Tolbert-era officials, including ex–finance minister Ellen Johnson-Sirleaf. In 1985 the LAP emerged as the NDPL's primary challenger following disqualification of the UPP, winning two Senate and eight House seats. However, it decided to boycott legislative proceedings because of the detention of Johnson-Sirleaf and other party leaders for their alleged role in the 1985 coup attempt. In early 1986 Wreh and another LAP member were expelled from the party for agreeing to take their seats in defiance of the boycott. Johnson-Sirleaf, though pardoned in May 1986, fled to the United States claiming her life was in danger after her rearrest in July.

The subsequent naming of an LAP member, David FARHAT, to Doe's cabinet failed to abate the party's antigovernment criticism. The group derided the arrival of U.S. financial experts in early 1988 as a "disgrace to Africa, and Liberia in particular" and in September joined with the UP in condemning the government's banning of student politics. In mid-1989 the leaders of the LAP, UP, and UPP issued a joint communiqué calling on Doe to enact economic and political reforms and return to the tenets of the 1984 constitution. The government responded by dismissing Farhat from his position as finance minister, despite his being credited with increasing budgetary restraint and the repayment of U.S. loans. The LAP's Jackson F. DOE (no relation to the former chief executive) was widely believed to have been the actual winner of the 1985 presidential contest; he was reported in 1990 to have been executed by order of rebel leader Charles Taylor.

At a meeting of the Alliance of Seven Parties in March 1997, the LAP's presidential candidate, Cletus Wotorson, was chosen as the coalition's standard-bearer. However, charges that the primary had been rigged in his favor led to the splintering of the Alliance and prompted the LAP's most prominent member, Ellen Johnson-Sirleaf, to defect to the UP.

In 2003 LAP Chair Charles Gyude BRYANT was chosen as chair of the new transitional government, although he subsequently suspended his party activity to avoid the appearance of favoritism. In December 2006 the LAP announced its departure from the COTOL, but in mid-2009 the party appeared headed for cooperation with the LAP and UP for the 2011 elections.

Leaders: Varney SHERMAN, Cletus WOTORSON (President of the Senate and 1997 presidential candidate), Alex TYLER (Speaker of the House of Representatives).

Unity Party (UP). The UP was formed by Dr. Edward B. KESSELLY, who had served as local government minister in the Tolbert administration and subsequently chaired the PRC's Constituent Advisory Assembly. The party elected one senator and two representatives in the 1985 balloting. In November 1988 Kesselly claimed that the government was attempting to "frame" him in an effort to squelch his anticorruption protests. (Kesselly died in 1993.)

In April 1997 former finance minister and UN official Ellen Johnson-Sirleaf defected from the LAP and joined the UP to campaign for the presidency. The addition of Johnson-Sirleaf gave the UP newfound prominence and, subsequently, the backing of the TWP, LUP, and a number of LPP members. Despite early polling showing her with a higher popularity rating than Taylor, Johnson-Sirleaf and the UP's poorly financed efforts were ultimately no match for the NPP.

In late 1998 the UP pledged to continue participating in the electoral process if the government would guarantee the security of its candidates. In August 2000 the government issued an arrest warrant for Johnson-Sirleaf for her alleged role in dissident activities in Lofa County. However, she was granted amnesty in July 2001, and she returned to Monrovia in September.

Johnson-Sirleaf was one of the candidates to lead the NTLA in 2003 but failed to gain sufficient support. After she was chosen as the UP's 2005 presidential candidate, a number of prominent members of other parties reportedly defected to the UP in solidarity with her.

In mid-2009 reports surfaced of a planned "merger" of the UP with the LAP and LUP in order to present joint candidates in the 2011 presidential and legislative balloting. It was expected that Johnson-Sirleaf would head the presidential ticket, with the LAP's Varney Sherman as her running mate.

Leaders: Charles CLARKE (Chair), Ellen JOHNSON-SIRLEAF (President of the Republic), Joseph BOAKAI (Vice President of the Republic), Walter WISNER (Secretary General).

Alliance for Peace and Democracy (APD). Formed as a coalition in advance of the October 2005 elections by the two parties below, the APD chose the LPP's Togba-Nah Tipoteh as its presidential candidate. He placed ninth in the first round of balloting with 2.3 percent of the vote.

Leader: Marcus DAHN (Chair).

Liberian People's Party (LPP). The LPP was organized by former members of the Movement for Justice in Africa (Moja), whose leader, Togba-Nah Tipoteh, had been dismissed from the cabinet for alleged complicity in a countercoup attempt in August 1981. Moja was a left-nationalist, Pan-Africanist formation organized in 1973 and banned in 1981, at which time Tipoteh went into exile. LPP leader Amos Sawyer, former chair of the PRC's national constitutional commission, was also charged with plotting against the regime in August 1984, although the allegation was widely interpreted as an attempt by General Doe to discredit a leading rival for the presidency in 1985. Reportedly in retaliation for Sawyer's subsequent unwillingness to accept an offer to campaign as General Doe's running mate, an audit was initiated in early 1985 of his financial dealings as constitutional commission chair, thus permitting the electoral commission to deny registration to the LPP. In 1988 Sawyer testified against the Doe regime before a U.S. congressional committee considering revocation of Liberia's preferential trade status. In November 1990 he was named to head the ECOWAS-supported caretaker government, thereby reportedly earning the disapproval of some LPP stalwarts. Meanwhile, Tipoteh, an avowed supporter of Prince Johnson, returned to Monrovia in mid-1991 to preside over Moja's relaunching as a paramilitary formation styled the Black Berets/Moja, which was later disbanded.

The LPP was significantly fractionalized in regard to the 1997 presidential elections, partly due to the competing presidential ambitions of Sawyer, Tipoteh, and George Klay KIEH Jr., another LPP founder. The party initially intended to back a joint opposition candidate forwarded by the Alliance of Seven Parties. However, following the alliance's nomination of Cletus Wotorson, Tipoteh declared that the alliance's primary had been fraudulent and announced the withdrawal of the LPP from the grouping. Tipoteh then served as the LPP standard-bearer in the presidential balloting, although Sawyer, former LPP chair Dusty Wolokolie, and other prominent LPP members supported various other candidates. Sawyer, Wolokolie, and others were subsequently expelled from the LPP. Meanwhile, Edwin DENNIS-WEAH, a prominent attorney, was selected by the LPP's national committee to succeed James LOGAN as secretary general, Logan reportedly having become disillusioned with the political infighting. For his part, Kieh resigned from the LPP and subsequently formed a New Deal Movement (below) that included a number of other disgruntled former LPP members.

Tipoteh subsequently served as the primary spokesperson within Liberia for the LPP (which also has an active branch in the United States), earning a reputation as one of the nation's leading anti-Taylor voices. Meanwhile, some LPP leaders (including Dennis-Weah and Chair John KARWEAYE) remained outside Liberia as of mid-2002, as did numerous leaders from other opposition parties concerned over what they perceived as a deteriorating security situation in Liberia and increasingly heavy-handed behavior by the administration and security forces.

Leaders: Togba-Nah TIPOTEH (1997 and 2005 presidential candidate), Richard S. PANTON.

United People's Party (UPP). A centrist outgrowth of the precoup People's Progressive Party (PPP) and viewed as the most serious threat to the NDPL, the UPP was organized by former PPP leader Gabriel Baccus Matthews, who had been dismissed as foreign minister in November 1981 because of opposition to a pro-U.S. posture by the Doe regime and had left the government again in April 1983 after serving for a year as secretary general of the cabinet. Although meeting legal requirements for registration, the UPP was not permitted to participate in the 1985 balloting because of its leader's "socialist leanings," and the party unofficially supported Jackson Doe of the LAP in the presidential race. A number of leading officials subsequently quit the party because of the exiled Matthews's unwillingness to join an opposition coalition in March 1986, which induced the government to permit his return from the United States and rescind its proscription of the LAP in late September.

The UPP's Wesley Johnson was chosen as vice chair of the transitional government in 2003.

Leaders: Marcus DAHN (Chair), Wesley JOHNSON.

National Patriotic Party (NPP). Restyled the National Patriotic Party in 1997, the small rebel group launched by Charles Taylor in Liberia's northeastern region in 1989 was originally called the National Patriotic Front of Liberia (NPFL). The NPFL dissidents reportedly included a number of former Liberian soldiers who had fled abroad after the 1985 coup attempt. The NPFL succeeded in gaining control of most of Liberia, except for the capital, by mid-1992, although it experienced reverses thereafter (see Political background, above). Charles Taylor received an enthusiastic reception upon his arrival in Monrovia to take a seat on the Council of State in September 1995.

In accordance with the 1996 peace pact, on January 31, 1997, the NPFL's military wing was officially dissolved. On February 1 the interim National Patriotic Association of Liberia (NAPAL) was formed and charged with overseeing the transformation of the NPFL's political wing, the National Patriotic Party, into a legal political party, and in April the NPP was officially registered. Charles Taylor and the NPP scored easy electoral victories in July 1997, and, following his inauguration in August, the new president named a government dominated by NPP stalwarts.

The NPP provided the main base of support for Taylor in the subsequent civil war, although Taylor's actions appeared to undercut popular support for the NPP. Following Taylor's departure from Liberia in August 2003, many NPP members reportedly continued to support him, and he reportedly remained in contact with them. However, other NPP stalwarts disassociated themselves from Taylor and joined other parties.

In the first round of the 2005 presidential balloting, the NPP's Roland Massaquoi placed sixth with 4.1 percent of the vote. Meanwhile, Taylor's wife, Jewel HOWARD-TAYLOR, was elected to the Senate.

Taylor was extradited from Nigeria in March 2006 and placed in the custody of the UN's Special Court for Sierra Leone (see Foreign relations, above, for further details).

It was reported in mid-2009 that other parties (including the UP and CDC) wee wooing NPP members in advance of the 2011 elections, thereby creating factionalization within the NPP.

Leaders: Charles Chankay (Ghankay/Gankay) TAYLOR (Former President of the Republic, under UN arrest), Lawrence GEORGE (Acting Chair), Roland MASSAQUOI (2005 presidential candidate), Francis GARLAWOLO, John WHITFIELD (Secretary General).

New Deal Movement (NDM). The NDM was launched in 1999 by a number of former LPP members, including George Klay Kieh Jr., a professor who had found his goal of running for president of the republic blocked by senior LPP leaders. The NDM achieved formal party status in mid-2002. Kieh received 0.5 percent of the vote in the first round of presidential balloting in 2005.

Leaders: George Klay KIEH Jr. (2005 presidential candidate), T. Wilson GAYE (Chair).

All-Liberia Coalition Party (ALCOP). The ALCOP was formed in November 1996 by Ulimo-M leader Lt. Gen. Alhaji Abraham G. V. Kromah, who said that the new party would serve as a vehicle for ethnic Krahns and Mandingos. Although Kromah claimed to have completely disarmed his militants by the end of January 1997, a raid on his headquarters in February unearthed an arms cache, and he was briefly detained.

In September 1998 Kromah was indicted for allegedly plotting a coup against Charles Taylor. Subsequently, Kromah fled the country, and he ignored a summons to appear in court in November. In April 1999 former Ulimo-M members clashed with government forces in northern Liberia; however, the government's allegations that Kromah was behind the incursion from Guinea remained unconfirmed. In August members of the hitherto unknown Joint Forces for the Liberation of Liberia (JFLL), a group reportedly formed by former Ulimo-M members, clashed with security forces and briefly kidnapped foreign aid workers.

Kromah received 7.8 percent of the vote in the first round of the 2005 presidential polling.

Leaders: David KORTIE (Chair), Lt. Gen. Alhaji Abraham G.V. KROMAH (1997 and 2005 presidential candidate).

National Democratic Party of Liberia (NDPL). Essentially a Krahn-based party, the NDPL was formed in August 1984 to support the policies and projected presidential candidacy of General Doe. Amid widespread opposition charges of fraud in the 1985 election, the NDPL, in addition to electing Doe, was awarded an overwhelming majority of seats in both houses of the National Assembly.

NDPL candidate Winston Tubman came in fourth in the first round of the 2005 presidential balloting with 9.2 percent of the vote. Two posts in the subsequent Johnson-Sirleaf administration were given to members of the NDPL.

Several senior NDPL members reportedly recently defected to the UP.

Leaders: Nyandeh SIGH (Chair), Harry MONIBA (1997 presidential candidate), Winston TUBMAN (2005 presidential candidate).

National Reformation Party (NRP). The NRP was formed by Martin Sheriff in 1996. However, in 2005 Bishop Alfred Reeves was the party's presidential candidate with Sheriff serving as the vice presidential candidate. Reeves, a Christian prelate, and Sheriff, a leading Muslim, campaigned on a platform of religious harmony and a return to morality. Reeves received 0.3 percent of the vote in the first round of balloting, last among the 22 candidates. The NRP supported George Weah in the presidential runoff.

Leaders: Bishop Alfred REEVES (2005 presidential candidate), Martin SHERIFF (2005 vice presidential candidate and 1997 presidential candidate).

United Democratic Alliance (UDA). Formed prior to the 2005 elections as a coalition of the three small parties below, the UDA presented the LINU's John Morlu as its presidential candidate. He ran a populist campaign that emphasized nonviolence and pledged to end corruption and improve social services. Morlu received 1.2 percent of the vote in the first round of balloting. The LINU and LEDP supported George Weah in the second round.

Leaders: Aaron WESSEH (Chair), John MORLU (2005 presidential candidate).

Liberia National Union (LINU). The LINU was formed by former vice president of the republic and NDPL executive Harry MONIBA in 1996 as a party for the Lofan and Gbandi peoples. Moniba unsuccessfully contested the 1997 presidential elections as the LINU candidate. Moniba died in 2004, and John Morlu was elected as the party's new leader at a congress in May 2005. Morlu subsequently attempted to broaden the appeal of the party outside of its traditional base.

Leaders: John MORLU (Party Leader and 2005 presidential candidate), Aaron WESSEH (Chair), Jerome GEORGE (Secretary General).

Liberia Education and Development Party (LEDP). A Christian party, the LEDP was formed in 2004 as a vehicle for the planned presidential bid of Rev. Hananiah Zoe. However, Zoe subsequently agreed to join the UDA and supported John Morlu for the 2005 presidential balloting.

Leaders: Rev. Hananiah ZOE, Benedict MATADI (Chair).

Reformation Alliance Party (RAP). Formed in 1996, the RAP unsuccessfully contested the 1997 presidential elections. In July 2005 Dr. H. Boima FAHNBULLEH Jr., the RAP 1997 presidential candidate (and a former foreign minister), resigned from the party. The RAP split with the other UDA parties and endorsed Ellen Johnson-Sirleaf in the 2005 presidential runoff.

Leader: Losine N. SARYON.

Other Parties that Participated in the 2005 Elections:

Liberia Equal Rights Party (LERP). At a party convention in August 2005, delegates elected Joseph Korto as the LERP candidate for the 2005 presidential election. He won 3.3 percent of the vote (seventh place) in the first round of balloting. The LERP supported Ellen Johnson-Sirleaf in the November runoff.

Leader: Joseph KORTO (2005 presidential candidate).

Reformed United Liberia Party (RULP). The RULP was formed in 2005 by William "Shad" Tubman, the son of former president William Tubman. The younger Tubman received 1.6 percent of the vote in the first round of the subsequent presidential poll, while the RULP failed to secure any seats in the legislative elections. The RULP supported Ellen Johnson-Sirleaf in the 2005 presidential runoff but subsequently charged that the UP had failed to honor a prerunoff agreement that would have provided a cabinet position for the RULP.

Leaders: William "Shad" TUBMAN (2005 presidential candidate), Peter S. MENYOU.

Progressive Democratic Party (Prodem). Formed in 2004, Prodem was initially composed mainly of former LURD members, including former LURD leader Sekou Conneh, who was chosen as the party's 2005 presidential candidate. Conneh received only 0.6 percent of the vote in the first round of the presidential election, and the party did not gain any seats in the legislative elections. Following the November presidential runoff, Conneh was prominent in successful efforts to convince George Weah's supporters to accept the decision of the election commission to declare Ellen Johnson-Sirleaf as the victor.

Testifying before the TRC in mid-2008, Conneh denied any wrongdoing during the civil war, despite allegations of atrocities on the part of LURD fighters. Conneh argued he should be considered a hero for having helped to initiate the downfall of Charles Taylor.

Leaders: Sekou CONNEH (2005 presidential candidate), Amara KROMAK (Chair), Jackie C. DEVINE (Secretary General).

National Party of Liberia (NPL). The NPL, whose support was reportedly centered in the Lofa region, was formed in 2005 by former senator Armah Jallah, who received 0.4 percent of the vote in the first round of the 2005 presidential poll. The NPL endorsed George Weah in the runoff.

Leader: Armah JALLAH (Party Founder and 2005 presidential candidate).

Union of Liberian Democrats (ULD). Formed in 2005 by Dr. Robert Kpoto, the ULD is a mainly Lofan grouping. In September 2005 senior members of the ULD reportedly broke away to form a new party—the **Progressive Independent Movement of the ULD** (PIMULD). The PIMULD supported the COTOL and Varney Sherman in the October 2005 elections, and both the ULD and the PIMULD endorsed George Weah in the November runoff. (Kpoto had received just 0.4 percent of the vote in the first round of the presidential poll.)

Leaders: Dr. Robert KPOTO (Party Founder and 2005 presidential candidate), George J. TARN (Chair).

Other parties and groups that participated in the 2005 elections include the **Free Democratic Party** (FDP), formed in 1996 and led by Ciapha GBOLLIE, George BORWAH, and David FARHAT (2005 presidential candidate); the **Freedom Alliance Party of Liberia** (FAPL), led by Margaret THOMPSON (2005 presidential candidate); the **Labor Party of Liberia** (LPL), led by Joseph WOAH-TEE (2005 presidential candidate); the **Liberia Destiny Party** (LDP), led by Nathaniel BARNES (2005 presidential candidate); the **Liberia First Group** (LFG), formed in 2005 and led by former LPP chair Dusty WOLOKOLIE and LPP figure Commany WESSEH (the LFG supported the UP and Ellen Johnson-Sirleaf in the 2005 elections); and the **National Vision Party** (NATVIPOL), led by George M. KAIDII, who was also the party's 2005 presidential candidate.

The **Liberia National Alliance** (LNA) consists of the **Progressive People's Party** (PPP) and the **Independent Democratic Party** (IDP). The LNA presented PPP leader Chea CHEAPOO as its 2005 presidential candidate.

Other Parties and Groupings:

Liberians United for Reconciliation and Democracy (LURD). The LURD claimed responsibility for antigovernment guerrilla activity launched in northwestern Liberia in mid-1999. A number of former Ulimo fighters reportedly participated in the organization of the LURD, and, as had been the case with Ulimo, Krahn-Mandingo infighting was subsequently reported within the new grouping. The Liberian government accused the Guinean government of supplying arms to the LURD, which appeared to include several anti-Taylor factions left over from the Liberian civil war as well as anti-Taylor elements from the complicated conflict in Sierra Leone. The LURD subsequently became the largest anti-Taylor group in Liberia, its fighters ultimately pressuring Taylor to leave the country in August 2003 (see Political background, above, for details).

In January 2004, Aisha CONNEH (the daughter of the president of Guinea and the wife of Sekou Damate Conneh, who had been named chair of the LURD in 1999) reportedly attempted unsuccessfully to gain control of the LURD in cooperation with Chayee DOE (the younger brother of former Liberian president Samuel Doe). Chayee Doe was subsequently killed, while Sekou Conneh was reportedly suspended from the party. The LURD disbanded in late 2004, and many of its members reportedly joined Prodem (above), which chose Sekou Conneh as its 2005 presidential candidate.

Liberia Peace Council (LPC). Organized in 1993, the LPC was a largely Krahn group that engaged in numerous clashes with the NPFL in southeastern Liberia. In January 1996 the LPC was cited by observers as the only faction to have complied with the disarmament provisions of the August 1995 peace accord. However, such claims were subsequently undermined by reports of LPC-NPFL clashes, and in October LPC militants were accused of attempting to assassinate Charles Taylor.

In early 1997 the LPC participated in the Alliance of Seven Parties. However, following the factionalization of the Alliance and breakup of the informal Krahn coalition, the LPC forwarded its chair, Dr. George BOLEY, as its presidential candidate. In early 1999 it was reported that Boley had fled the country in fear of attack by Taylor's security forces. The LPC subsequently disbanded, and many of its members, including Boley, reportedly joined the NDPL.

Movement for Democracy in Liberia (MODEL). Supported primarily by members of the Krahn ethnic group who had previously been core constituents of former president Samuel Doe, MODEL was launched in 2001 and quickly emerged as a major anti-Taylor rebel force during the 2002–2003 civil war. MODEL leader Thomas Yaya NIMELY was named foreign minister under the peace agreement of August 2003. MODEL disbanded in late 2004 under an agreement that also involved the LURD and pro-Taylor groups. Nimely chose not to form a political party, urging his supporters to join existing parties.

United Liberation Movement of Liberia for Democracy (Ulimo). Ulimo was initially a formation drawn primarily from the Krahn tribe of former president Doe. As such, it opposed the granting of concessions to the rebels by ECOWAS and Amos Sawyer's interim government. By 1994 Ulimo had split into two factions: a Krahn-based Christian group (Ulimo-K), led by Gen. Roosevelt Johnson; and a Mandingo-based Muslim group (Ulimo-M), led by Lt. Gen. Alhaji G. V. Kromah. (The former was sometimes referenced as Ulimo-J and the latter confusingly [and incorrectly] as Ulimo-K.)

In early 1996 forces aligned with Johnson fought with Ecomog troops in Tubmanburg after the former refused to comply with the disarmament provisions of the 1995 peace accord. Subsequently, on March 11, 1996, Ulimo-K's Executive Council and military commanders issued a joint statement announcing the dismissal of Johnson as party chair in favor of Brigadier Gen. William KARYEE, citing Johnson's inability to forward the peace process as the reason for his ouster.

Krahn fighters from the AFL and LPC reportedly defected to Ulimo-K during the fighting that ensued after militiamen loyal to the NPFL and Ulimo-M attempted to arrest Johnson on April 6, 1996. Thereafter, amid intense fighting in the capital, Johnson, who continued to be recognized as the faction's de facto leader, was flown to Ghana on May 3 by U.S. helicopters to attend an ECOWAS peace summit then scheduled for May 8.

Under pressure from international observers, on June 11, 1996, Ulimo-K agreed to disarm, and in August a faction spokesperson claimed that the group's militiamen had turned over their weapons to Ecomog troops. Moreover, in late September the two Ulimo factions reportedly agreed to a cessation of their mutual hostilities. However, in early October Ulimo-K fighters agreed to end their armed blockade of the highways leading to Tubmanburg and Cape Mount (where thousands of starving citizens were subsequently discovered) only under pressure from the Council of State and ECOWAS. Meanwhile, Ulimo-M leader Kromah announced his intention to compete in the May 1997 presidential elections as the candidate of the new ALCOP.

Johnson's efforts to form an electoral coalition with the LPC and NDPL failed in early 1997; subsequently, Ulimo-K candidates performed poorly in balloting in July. In August, Johnson was appointed minister of rural development; however, Johnson continued to criticize the Taylor administration, accusing the president in early 1998 of filling the military with former NPFL militiamen. In March, Johnson was the target of what he described as the third recent attempt on his life; concurrently, it was reported that Taylor had removed Johnson from the cabinet with the goal of naming him to an overseas post (ambassador to India). Thereafter, clashes between Ulimo-K militants and presidential forces were reported in neighborhoods controlled by Johnson, and in September an all-out attack by Taylor's troops forced Johnson and his family and close associates to seek refuge in the U.S. embassy, from where they were subsequently airlifted out of the country.

Many members of Ulimo were reportedly involved in the formation of the LURD in 1999. Subsequently, in 2004, Johnson died in exile in Nigeria. Most reports suggested that both Ulimo factions were defunct as of 2005.

LEGISLATURE

The **National Assembly** established by the 1984 constitution was a bicameral body consisting of a Senate and a House of Representatives, both elected by universal adult suffrage. Following the collapse of the Doe administration, the assembly was nominally superseded by interim bodies established by the Sawyer and Taylor regimes. Subsequently, in accordance with the 1993 Cotonou agreement, a 35-member Transitional Legislative Assembly (TLA) composed of representatives of the principal warring factions was inaugurated on March 7, 1994. On July 17, 1997, the TLA approved legislation that limited legislative terms to four years.

Balloting for the Senate and the House of Representatives was held on July 19, 1997, although those bodies ceased to function as a result of the civil war in the early 2000s. Under the terms of a recently completed peace agreement, an appointed 76-member National Transitional Legislative Assembly was established on October 14, 2003. Twelve seats were accorded to the pro-Taylor Government of Liberia (GOL), 12 to the Liberians United for Reconciliation and Democracy, 12 to the Movement for Democracy in Liberia, 18 to established political parties, 7 to representatives of civic organizations, and 15 to the nation's counties (1 for each of the 15 counties).

Under the terms of the 2003 peace agreement and the Electoral Reform Law of 2004, new elections were held for both houses of the assembly on October 11, 2005.

Senate. The Senate comprises 30 members (2 from each of the 15 countries) directly elected in a single round of voting. (The top two vote-getters in each county are declared the victors.) According to the guidelines adopted for the 2005 balloting, the first-place finishers in each county were elected for nine-year terms, the second-place finishers for six-year terms. All subsequent elections will be for nine-year terms. In the balloting on October 11, 2005, the Coalition for the Transformation of Liberia won 7 seats; the Unity Party, 4; the National Patriotic Party, 3; the Congress for Democratic Change, 3; the Alliance for Peace and Democracy, 3; the Liberty Party, 3; the National Democratic Party of Liberia, 2; the All Liberia Coalition Party, 1; the National Reformation Party, 1; and independents, 3.

President: Cletus WOTORSON.

House of Representatives. The lower house comprises 64 members directly elected from single-member constituencies in single-round plurality voting for six-year terms. In the balloting on October 11, 2005, the Congress for Democratic Change secured 15 seats; the Liberty Party, 9; the Unity Party, 8; the Coalition for the Transformation of Liberia, 8; the Alliance for Peace and Democracy, 5; the National Patriotic Party, 4; the New Deal Movement, 3; the All Liberia Coalition Party, 2; the National Democratic Party of Liberia, 1; the National Reformation Party, 1; the United Democratic Alliance, 1; and independents, 7.

Speaker: Alex TYLER.

CABINET

[as of October 1, 2009]

President	Ellen Johnson-Sirleaf (UP) [f]
Vice President	Joseph N. Boakai (UP)
Ministers	
Agriculture	Florence Chenoweth
Commerce and Industry	Miata Beysolow [f]
Defense	Brownie Samukai
Education	Joseph Korto
Finance	Augustine K. Ngafuan
Foreign Affairs	Olubanke King-Akerele [f]
Gender Development	Vabah Gayflor [f]
Health and Social Welfare	Walter Gwenigale
Information, Culture, and Tourism	Laurance K. Bropleh
Internal Affairs	Ambulai B. Johnson

Justice and Attorney General	Christiana Tah [f]
Labor	Tiawon Gongloe
Lands, Mines, and Energy	Eugene Shannon
National Security	Victor Helb
Planning and Economic Affairs	Amara Konneh
Posts and Telecommunications	Jeremiah Sulunteh
Public Works	Samuel Kofi Woods
Transportation	Alphonso Gaye
Youth and Sports	Etmonia Tarpeh [f]
Ministers of State	
Economic and Legal Affairs	Morris Saytumah
Presidential Affairs (Acting)	Edward McClain
Without Portfolio	Natty B. Davis II

[f] = female

COMMUNICATIONS

The Doe regime did not impose formal press censorship upon the installation of the PRC in 1980, although the *Daily Observer* (the country's main paper) was repeatedly closed subsequent to its founding in 1981. Several other papers were also shut down in 1988–1990. In August 2000 the government ordered formal censorship of news reporting on the fighting in Lofa County, and reporters from the *Daily News* were arrested and charged with "espionage" in February 2001 in regard to an article that challenged government expenditures. Meanwhile, human rights and media organizations reported heavy pressure on journalists and publications that were critical of the government from 1999 to mid-2002. Freedom of the press has generally been perceived as a genuine component of the nation's democratic transition since 2003, although occasional attacks on journalists by "uncontrolled" members of various groups have been reported.

Press. The following are issued in Monrovia: *Daily Observer* (30,000), independent; *The Herald* (3,000), Catholic weekly; *The New Liberian* (2,000), published daily by the Ministry of Information; *Footprints Today,* founded 1984; *Sun Times,* founded 1985. By early 1991 a number of new papers had been launched, including *The Inquirer* (independent), the *New Times, The Torchlight,* and *The Patriot,* a pro-Taylor organ. In addition the INPFL had commenced publication of *Scorpion.* Among other newspapers are the *Monrovia News,* the *New Democrat* (independent), the *Analyst* (independent), and the *Daily News.*

News agency. The official facility is the Liberian News Agency (Lina); *Agence France-Presse, Deutsche Presse Agentur,* Reuters, and UPI are represented in Monrovia.

Broadcasting. The government-controlled Liberian Broadcasting Corporation (LBS) operates one commercial radio station (ELBC) and one commercial television station (ELTV), while the government-operated Liberia Rural Communications Network (LRCN) transmits from three radio outlets (ELRG, ELRV, and ELRZ). Additional radio programming is offered by the Liberian-American-Swedish Minerals Company (Lamco) station ELNR, the Sudan Interior Mission's religious station ELWA, and a Voice of America transmitter in Monrovia. The government's heavy hand on the print media was extended to radio and television in 2000 when the private *Star* radio station and the Catholic-oriented *Radio Veritas* were shut down in March for broadcasts critical of the regime. Also, in August a British *Channel Four* TV crew was charged with "spying" while preparing a documentary linking President Taylor to diamond smuggling and gunrunning in Sierra Leone. Following an international outcry, the crew was freed. As of 2008 there were 5.3 Internet users per 1,000 inhabitants.

INTERGOVERNMENTAL REPRESENTATION

Ambassador to the U.S.: M. Nathaniel BARNES.

U.S. Ambassador to Liberia: Linda THOMAS-GREENFIELD.

Permanent Representative to the UN: Marion V. KAMARA.

IGO Memberships (Non-UN): AfDB, AU, BADEA, ECOWAS, Interpol, IOM, MRU, NAM, WCO.

LIBYA

Great Socialist People's Libyan Arab Jamahiriya
al-Jamahiriyah al-Arabiyah al-Libiyah al-Shabiyah al-Ishtirakiyah al-Uzma

Political Status: Independent state since December 24, 1951; revolutionary republic declared September 1, 1969; name changed from Libyan Arab Republic to Libyan Arab People's Republic in 1976; present name adopted March 2, 1977.

Area: 679,358 sq. mi. (1,759,540 sq. km.).

Population: 5,678,484 (2003C, provisional); 6,283,000 (2008E). Both figures include nonnationals.

Major Urban Centers (2003C): TARABULUS (TRIPOLI, 1,197,000), Banghazi (Benghazi, 680,000), Misratah (Misurata, 351,000), Surt (Sirte, 162,000). (Many secretariats have reportedly been relocated recently to Sirte—about 400 miles east of Tarabulus—and other cities.)

Official Language: Arabic.

Monetary Unit: Dinar (official rate December 1, 2009: 1.19 dinar = $1US).

Revolutionary Leader (De Facto Head of State): Col. Muammar Abu Minyar al-QADHAFI (Col. Moammar GADDAFY); assumed power as Chair of Revolutionary Command Council (RCC) following coup d'état of September 1, 1969; became prime minister in January 1970, relinquishing the office in July 1972; designated General Secretary of General People's Congress concurrent with abolition of the RCC on March 2, 1977, relinquishing the position March 1–2, 1979.

Secretary General of General People's Congress: Mubarak Abdullah al-SHAMIKH; appointed by the General People's Congress on March 4, 2009, to succeed Miftah Muhammad KUAYBAI.

Secretary General of General People's Committee (Prime Minister): Al-Baghdadi Ali al-MAHMUDI; appointed by the General People's Congress on March 5, 2006, to succeed Shukri Muhammad GHANIM; reappointed on March 4, 2009.

THE COUNTRY

Extending for 910 miles along Africa's northern coast, Libya embraces the former Turkish and Italian provinces of Tripolitania, Cyrenaica, and Fezzan. Some 95 percent of its territory is desert and barren rockland, and cultivation and settlement are largely confined to a narrow coastal strip. Tribal influences remain strong within a population that is predominantly Arab (with a Berber minority) and almost wholly Sunni Muslim in religion. Arabic is the official language, but Italian, English, and French are also spoken. The government has made efforts in recent years to increase the education of females (about 50 percent of whom are reportedly illiterate), and women comprised 21 percent of the official labor force in 1996, up from less than 9 percent in the 1980s. Female representation in government continues to be minimal.

Libya's reputation as a country largely devoid of natural resources was rendered obsolete by the discovery of oil in the late 1950s; the ensuing development of export capacity resulted in its achieving the highest per capita GNP in Africa (more than $8,600 in 1980). However, world market conditions subsequently reduced the country's oil revenue from a high of $22 billion in 1980 to $5 billion in 1988, with per capita GNP declining to less than $5,500 through the same period. Oil production (about 1.6 million barrels per day) accounts for more than 95 percent of export income, the primary market being Western Europe. Other industry has been limited by the weakness of the domestic market, uneven distribution of the population, and a shortage of skilled manpower. Recent large-scale development has focused on building chemical and steel complexes, in addition to the

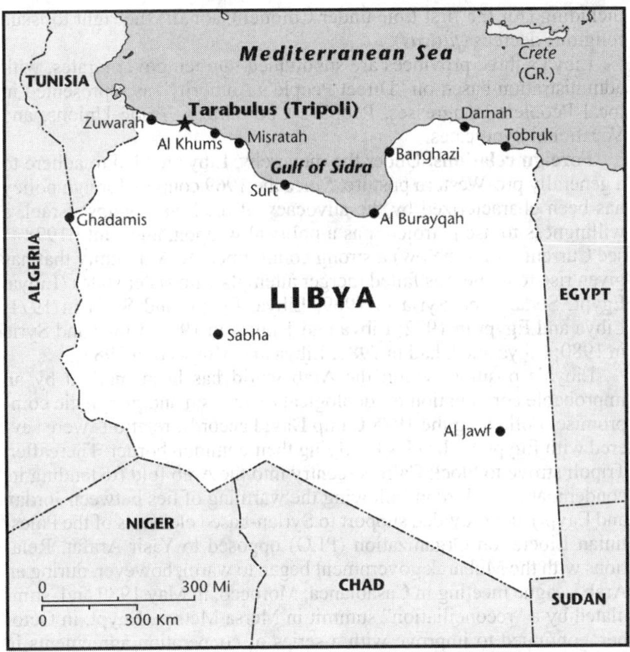

controversial Great Man-Made River Project, a $30 billion plan to pipe water from aquifers deep below the Sahara Desert to coastal areas. Described as the world's largest irrigation project, the long-term scheme inaugurated in mid-1991 has provided for significant agricultural expansion as well as bountiful drinking water to major cities. Due to limited rainfall and an insufficient labor pool resulting from migration to the cities, agriculture currently contributes only minimally to domestic output. Barley, wheat, tomatoes, olives, citrus, and dates are the primary crops.

After decades of rigid state control of the economy, liberalization measures, including the promotion of limited private enterprise, were introduced in 1988. Results were initially viewed as encouraging, but domestic opposition was kindled by concurrent government efforts to eliminate food subsidies, reduce state employment, and trim financing for medical, educational, and other social programs. Consequently, about 70 percent of the economy remains under government control, and much of the populace still relies heavily on various subsidies. Falling oil prices in 1998 contributed to a devaluation of the dinar in November and cutbacks in the proposed 1999 budget before economic pressures were eased by the return of high oil prices in the second half of 1999 and 2000. Early in the 21st century, leader Muammar al-Qadhafi's perceived resistance to even modest free-market reforms constrained foreign investment.

Economic affairs, particularly in regard to the West, changed dramatically in September 2004 when the United States lifted most of its long-standing unilateral sanctions against Libya. Western companies immediately began to negotiate substantial oil contracts with Tripoli in conjunction with pledges from the Qadhafi regime to enact broad economic policy changes (see Foreign relations and Current issues, below). Real GDP growth of 5 percent in 2004 and 6.3 percent in 2005 reflected improved performance mainly in the non-oil sector, particularly construction, transportation, hotels, and trade. In 2006 the International Monetary Fund (IMF) cited the government's efforts to ease trade restrictions, the recent move toward a market economy, and continuing overall economic progress, including GDP growth of 5.6 percent. Following Libya's withdrawal from the Heavily Indebted Poor Countries (HIPC) initiative, the IMF encouraged the government to structure its creditor agreements with other poor countries on terms similar to those of the HIPC. The IMF also encouraged Libya to better manage its oil revenue, restructure its public banks, and move forward with structural reforms.

In 2007 a U.S.-based consultant hired by Qadhafi to assess Libya's economy reported that the country's schools, hospitals, and infrastructure were "in serious disrepair" despite the nation's oil wealth. Additionally, unemployment was in double digits. With the help of the aforementioned consultant and several others, Qadhafi embarked on a long-term plan to modernize the economy. GDP growth of 6.8 percent in 2007 was attributed in large part to high oil prices and growth in the oil sector. Robust growth continued in 2008, with annual GDP of 6 percent, but the economy was expected to contract by about 1 percent in 2009, owing to a sharp decline in oil prices, reduced limits set by the Organization of Petroleum Exporting Countries (OPEC), and the global economic crisis. However, analysts expected the economy to rebound in 2010, with annual growth of 6.1 percent forecast. Meanwhile, the European Union (EU) agreed to extend its financial cooperation program with Libya until 2013.

GOVERNMENT AND POLITICS

Political background. Successively ruled by the Phoenicians, Greeks, Romans, Arabs, Spaniards, and others, Libya was under Ottoman Turkish control from the middle of the 16th century to the beginning of the 20th century. It was conquered by Italy in 1911 and 1912 and was ruled as an Italian colony until its occupation by British and French military forces during World War II. In conformity with British wartime pledges and a 1949 decision of the UN General Assembly, Libya became an independent monarchy under Emir Muhammad IDRIS al-Sanussi (King IDRIS I) on December 24, 1951. A constitution promulgated two months earlier prescribed a federal form of government with autonomous rule in the three historic provinces, but provincial autonomy was wiped out and a centralized regime instituted under a constitutional amendment adopted in 1963.

The 1960s witnessed a growing independence in foreign affairs resulting from the financial autonomy generated by rapidly increasing petroleum revenues. This period marked the beginnings of Libyan radicalism in Third World politics and in its posture regarding Arab–Israeli relations. Increasingly, anti-Western sentiments were voiced, especially in regard to externally controlled petroleum companies and the presence of foreign military bases on Libyan soil. The period following the June 1967 Arab–Israeli conflict saw a succession of prime ministers, including the progressive Abd al-Hamid al-BAKKUSH, who took office in October 1967. His reforms alienated conservative leaders, however, and he was replaced in September 1968 by Wanis al-QADHAFI. The following September, while the king was in Turkey for medical treatment, a group of military officers led by Col. Muammar al-QADHAFI seized control of the government and established a revolutionary regime under a military-controlled Revolutionary Command Council (RCC).

After consolidating his control of the RCC, Colonel Qadhafi moved to implement the goals of his regime, which reflected a blend of Islamic behavioral codes, socialism, and radical Arab nationalism. By June 1970 both the British and U.S. military installations had been evacuated, and in July the Italian and Jewish communities were dispossessed and their members forced from the country. In June 1971 an official party, the Arab Socialist Union (ASU), was organized, and in September the Federation of Arab Republics (a union of Egypt, Libya, and Syria) was approved by separate referenda in each country. The federation, while formally constituted at the legislative level in March 1972, became moribund shortly thereafter. Meanwhile, the regime had begun acquiring shares in the country's petroleum industry, resorting to outright nationalization of foreign interests in numerous cases; by March 1976 the government controlled about two-thirds of oil production.

Periodically threatening to resign because of conflicts within the RCC, Colonel Qadhafi turned over his prime-ministerial duties to Maj. Abd al-Salam JALLUD in July 1972 and was in seclusion during the greater part of 1974. In August 1975 Qadhafi's rule was seriously threatened by a coup attempt involving army officers—some two dozen of whom were ultimately executed; a number of drastic antisubversion laws were promptly enacted. In November a quasi-legislative General National Congress (renamed the General People's Congress [GPC] a year later) was created, while in March 1977 the RCC and the cabinet were abolished in accordance with "the installation of the people's power" under a new structure of government headed by Colonel Qadhafi and the four remaining members of the RCC. The political changes were accompanied by a series of sweeping economic measures, including limitations on savings and consolidation of private shops ("nests of exploitation") into large state supermarkets, which generated middle-class discontent and fueled exile-based opposition activity. The government was further reorganized at a meeting of the General People's Congress in March 1979, Colonel Qadhafi resigning as secretary general (but retaining his designation as revolutionary leader and supreme commander of the armed forces) in favor of Abd al-Ati UBAYDI, who was in turn replaced as secretary general of the General People's Committee (prime minister) by Jadallah Azzuz al-TALHI.

At a congress session in January 1981, Secretary General Ubaydi was succeeded by Muhammad al-Zarruq RAJAB, who, in February 1984, was replaced by Miftah al-Usta UMAR and named to succeed Talhi as secretary general of the General People's Committee. Talhi was returned to the position of nominal head of government in a major ministerial reshuffle announced on March 3, 1986; in a further reshuffle on March 1, 1987, Talhi was replaced by Umar Mustafa al-MUNTASIR.

In October 1990 a government shakeup was undertaken that included the appointment of Abd al-Raziq al-SAWSA to succeed Umar as secretary general of the General People's Congress and Abu Zaid Umar DURDA to succeed Muntasir as head of the General People's Committee. Durda was reappointed in November 1992 while Sawsa was replaced by Zanati Muhammad al-ZANATI. The 1992 reorganization was otherwise most noteworthy for the designation of Muntasir, a moderate who had earlier cultivated a good working relationship with the West, as the equivalent of foreign secretary.

The sanctions imposed by the United Nations in 1992 (see Foreign relations, below) subsequently contributed to what was widely believed to be growing domestic discontent with the regime. Internal difficulties were most sharply illustrated by an apparent coup attempt in early October 1993, reportedly involving thousands of troops at several military locations. Although loyalist forces quashed the revolt in about three days, the government was described as "severely shaken" by the events.

In a cabinet reshuffle on January 29, 1994, Abd al-Majid al-QAUD was named to succeed Durda as secretary general of the General People's Committee. Qaud was succeeded on December 29, 1997, by Muhammad Ahmad al-MANQUSH, who was reappointed along with most other senior ministers in a cabinet reshuffle on December 15, 1998. On March 1, 2000, Manqush was succeeded by Mubarak Abdullah al-SHAMIKH, Colonel Qadhafi concurrently ordering a sharp reduction in the number of ministries in the name of further devolution of power to local "people's" bodies. Shamikh remained in his post during a reshuffle on October 1, 2000, but was replaced in a subsequent reorganization on June 13, 2003, by Shukri Muhammad GHANIM, theretofore the secretary for economy and trade. The secretary for public security, Nasr al-Mabruk ABDALLAH, was suspended on February 18, 2006, after a violent protest a day earlier at the Italian embassy in Benghazi. Six new secretaries were added to the cabinet, and Ghanim was dismissed, in a reorganization on March 5, 2006, when the former assistant secretary general of the General People's Committee, Al-Baghdadi Ali al-MAHMUDI, was appointed to succeed Ghanim. The cabinet was reshuffled on January 22, 2007, and again on March 3, 2008. Following the renewal of the General People's Congress March 1–4, 2009, an extensive reshuffle of the General People's Committee took place on March 4, 2009, with al-Mahmudi retained as secretary general and former intelligence chief Mussa KUSSA named to the foreign liaison post. Abdurrahman Muhammad SHALGAM, who had been foreign minister for eight years, was named Libya's representative to the UN Security Council, and the previous assistant secretary general Mubarak Abdullah al-Shamikh, was appointed speaker of the General People's Congress.

Constitution and government. Guided by the ideology of Colonel Qadhafi's *Green Book,* which combines elements of nationalism, Islamic theology, socialism, and populism, Libya was restyled the Great Socialist People's Libyan Arab Jamahiriya in March 1977. The *Jamahiriyah* is conceived as a system of direct government through popular organs interspersed throughout Libyan society. A General People's Congress is assisted by a General Secretariat, whose secretary general serves as titular head of state, although effective power has remained in Colonel Qadhafi's hands since the 1969 coup. Executive functions are assigned to a cabinet-like General People's Committee, whose secretary general serves as the equivalent of prime minister. The judicial system includes a Supreme Court, courts of appeal, courts of the first instance, and summary courts. In 1988 the government also established a People's Court and a People's Prosecution Bureau to replace the unofficial but powerful "revolutionary courts" that had reportedly assumed responsibility for nearly 90 percent of prosecutions. In what was seen as an effort to placate the expanding Islamic fundamentalist movement, Colonel Qadhafi in April 1993 called for more widespread implementation of sharia (Islamic religious law), and in February 1994 the General People's Congress granted new powers to the country's religious leaders, including (for the first time under Colonel Qadhafi) the right to issue religious decrees (*fatwas*).

Libya's three provinces are subdivided into ten governorates, with administration based on "Direct People's Authority" as represented in local People's Congresses, People's Committees, Trade Unions, and Vocational Syndicates.

Foreign relations. Under the monarchy, Libya tended to adhere to a generally pro-Western posture. Since the 1969 coup its foreign policy has been characterized by the advocacy of total war against Israel, a willingness to use petroleum as a political weapon, and (until 1998—see Current issues, below) a strong commitment to Arab unity that has given rise to numerous failed merger attempts with sister states (Libya, Egypt, Sudan, and Syria in 1969; Libya, Egypt, and Syria in 1971; Libya and Egypt in 1972; Libya and Tunisia in 1974; Libya and Syria in 1980; Libya and Chad in 1981; Libya and Morocco in 1984).

Libya's position within the Arab world has been marked by an improbable combination of ideological extremism and pragmatic compromise. Following the 1978 Camp David accords, relations were severed with Egypt, both sides fortifying their common border. Thereafter, Tripoli strove to block Cairo's reentry into the Arab fold (extending its condemnation to Jordan following the warming of ties between Jordan and Egypt) and provided support to Syrian-based elements of the Palestinian Liberation Organization (PLO) opposed to Yasir Arafat. Relations with the Mubarak government began to warm, however, during an Arab League meeting in Casablanca, Morocco, in May 1989 and, stimulated by a "reconciliation" summit in Mersa Metruh, Egypt, in October, continued to improve with a series of cooperation agreements in 1990 and the opening of the border between the two countries in 1991. By mid-decade, Egypt had become what one correspondent described as Libya's most important potential "bridge to the West," Cairo's supportive stance reflecting the importance of Libya as a provider of jobs for Egyptian workers and the value attached by the Mubarak regime to Colonel Qadhafi's pronounced antifundamentalist posture.

Relations with conservative Morocco, broken following Tripoli's 1980 recognition of the Polisario-backed government-in-exile of the Western Sahara, resumed in 1981. Ties with neighboring Tunisia, severely strained during much of the 1980s, advanced dramatically in 1988, the opening of the border between the two countries precipitating a flood of option-starved Libyan consumers to Tunis. Regional relations stabilized even further with the February 1989 formation of the Arab Maghreb Union (AMU), although Colonel Qadhafi remained a source of controversy within the ineffective and largely inactive grouping.

A widespread expression of international concern in the 1980s and 1990s centered on Libyan involvement in Chad. Libya's annexation of the Aozou Strip in the mid-1970s was followed by active participation in the Chadian civil war, largely in opposition to the forces of Hissein Habré, who in 1982 emerged as president of the strife-torn country. By 1983 Libya's active support of the "National Peace Government" loyal to former Chadian president Goukhouni Oueddei (based in the northern Tibesti region) included the deployment of between 3,000 and 5,000 Libyan troops and the provision of air support for Oueddei's attacks on the northern capital of Faya-Largeau. Although consistently denying direct involvement and condemning the use of French troops in 1983 and 1984 as "unjustified intervention," Qadhafi agreed in September 1984 to recall "Libyan support elements" in exchange for a French troop withdrawal. The agreement was hailed as a diplomatic breakthrough for Paris but was greeted with dismay by Habré and ultimately proved to be an embarrassment to the Mitterrand government because of the limited number of Libyan troops actually withdrawn. Subsequently, in March 1987, the militarily superior Qadhafi regime suffered the unexpected humiliation of being decisively defeated by Chadian government forces, which captured the air facility at Quadi Doum, 100 miles northeast of Faya-Largeau, and forced the Libyans to withdraw from all but the Aozou Strip, leaving behind an estimated $1 billion worth of sophisticated weaponry.

In early August 1987, Chadian forces, in a surprise move, captured Aozou, administrative capital of the contested border area, although the town was subsequently retaken by Libya. Skirmishes continued as the Islamic Legion, comprised largely of Lebanese mercenaries, attacked Chadian posts from bases inside Sudan, with Libyan jets supporting counteroffensives in the Aozou Strip. A year later, Libya reportedly had lost 10 percent of its military capability, although it retained most of the disputed territory.

In July 1989 the Organization of African Unity (OAU, subsequently the African Union—AU) sponsored negotiations between President

Habré and Colonel Qadhafi, which set the stage for the signing of a peace treaty by the countries' foreign ministers on August 31. The treaty called for immediate troop withdrawal from the disputed territory, exchange of prisoners of war, mutual "noninterference," and continued efforts to reach a permanent settlement. Relations subsequently deteriorated, however, with Habré accusing Libya of supporting Chadian rebels operating from Sudan.

Following the ouster of the Habré regime in December 1990, new Chadian president Idriss Déby announced in early 1991 that a "new era" had begun in relations between Chad and Libya, the belief being widespread that Libya had supplied arms and logistical support (but not personnel) to the victorious Chadian rebels. However, Déby subsequently described the Aozou issue as still a "bone of contention" requiring resolution by the International Court of Justice (ICJ). Consequently, in February 1994 the ICJ ruled by a vote of 16–1 that Libya had no rightful claim to the Aozou Strip or any other territory beyond the boundary established in a 1955 treaty between Libya and France. On May 30 the lengthy dispute ended with Libya's withdrawal and a symbolic raising of the Chadian flag. Shortly thereafter, Colonel Qadhafi received President Déby in Tripoli for the signing of a friendship and cooperation treaty, which, among other things, provided for a Libyan–Chadian Higher Joint Committee to discuss mutual concerns. Following the inaugural meeting of the Committee in July, (then) Chadian prime minister Kassiré Koumakoyé announced his country's support for Libyan efforts to have UN economic sanctions lifted.

Relations with the West have been problematic since the 1969 coup and the expulsion, a year later, of British and U.S. military forces. Libya's subsequent involvement in negotiations between Malta and the United Kingdom over British naval facilities on the Mediterranean island contributed to a further strain in relations with London. In December 1979 the United States closed its embassy in Tripoli after portions of the building were stormed and set afire by pro-Iranian demonstrators, while in May 1981 the Reagan administration ordered Tripoli to shut down its Washington "people's bureau" in response to what it considered escalating international terrorism sponsored by Colonel Qadhafi. Subsequent U.S.–Libyan relations were characterized as "mutual paranoia," with each side accusing the other of assassination plots amid hostility generated by U.S. naval maneuvers in the Gulf of Sirte, which Libya has claimed as an internal sea since 1973.

Simultaneous attacks by Palestinian gunmen on the Rome and Vienna airports on December 27, 1985, brought U.S. accusations of Libyan involvement, which Colonel Qadhafi vehemently denied. In January 1986 President Ronald Reagan announced the freezing of all Libyan government assets in U.S. banks, urged Americans working in Libya to depart, banned all U.S. trade with Libya, and ordered a new series of air and sea maneuvers in the Gulf of Sirte. (U.S. officials charged that Libya was harboring members of the Revolutionary Council of Fatah, the radical Palestinian grouping led by Abu Nidal and allegedly behind the 1985 attacks. See PLO article for further details.) Three months later, during the night of April 14, eighteen F-111 bombers based in Britain, assisted by carrier-based attack fighters, struck Libyan military targets in Tripoli and Benghazi. The action was prompted by what Washington termed "conclusive evidence," in the form of intercepted cables, that Libya had ordered the bombing of a Berlin discotheque nine days before, in the course of which an off-duty U.S. soldier had been killed. The U.S. administration also claimed to have aborted a planned grenade and machine-gun attack on the American visa office in Paris, for which French authorities ordered the expulsion of two Libyan diplomats.

Tripoli's adoption of a more conciliatory posture during 1988 did not yield relaxation of tension with Washington, which mounted a diplomatic campaign against European chemical companies that were reported to be supplying materials for a chemical weapons plant in Libya. Despite Libyan denial of the charges, reports of U.S. readiness to attack the site were believed to be the catalyst for a military encounter between two U.S. F-14s and two Libyan MiG-23 jets over the Mediterranean Sea on January 4, 1989, which resulted in downing of the Libyan planes. Concern subsequently continued in some Western capitals over the alleged chemical plant (the site of a much-publicized fire in March 1990), as well as Libya's ongoing efforts to develop nuclear weapons. Suspicion also arose over possible Libyan involvement in the bombing of Pan Am Flight 103, which blew up over Lockerbie, Scotland, in December 1988, and the crash of a French DC-10 in Niger near the Chad border in September 1989.

Colonel Qadhafi was described as maintaining an "uncharacteristically low profile" following the August 1990 Iraqi invasion of Kuwait (which he publicly criticized) and the U.S.-led Desert Storm campaign against Iraqi forces in early 1991. However, the respite from the international spotlight proved short-lived as the investigations into the Lockerbie and Niger plane explosions once again focused Western condemnation on Libya.

In October 1991 the French government issued warrants for six Libyans (one of them a brother-in-law of Colonel Qadhafi) in connection with the Niger crash, while American and British authorities announced in mid-November that they had filed charges against two Libyan nationals in connection with the Pan Am bombing. In early December the Arab League Council expressed its "solidarity" with Libya in the Lockerbie matter and called for an inquiry by a joint Arab League–UN committee. Two days later a Libyan judge declared that the two suspects were under house arrest and that Tripoli would be willing to send judicial representatives to Washington, London, and Paris to discuss the alleged acts of terrorism.

On January 21, 1992, the UN Security Council unanimously demanded extradition of the Lockerbie detainees to either Britain or the United States and insisted that Libya aid the French investigation into the Niger crash. Although Libya announced its willingness to cooperate with the latter demand, which involved no extradition request, it refused to turn over the Lockerbie suspects, declaring it would try the men itself. Consequently, the Security Council ordered the imposition of selective sanctions, including restrictions on air traffic and an embargo of shipments of military equipment as of April 15.

On May 14, 1992, in partial compliance with the Security Council, Libya announced that it would sever all links with organizations involved in "international terrorism," admit UN representatives to verify that there were no terrorist training facilities on its soil, and take action to preclude the use of its territory or citizens for terrorist acts. In addition, a special session of the General People's Congress in June agreed that the Lockerbie suspects could be tried in a "fair and just" court in a neutral country as suggested by the Arab League. However, the Security Council reiterated its demand for extradition to the United States or United Kingdom, ordered that the sanctions be continued, and warned that stiffer measures were being considered. After mediation efforts by UN Secretary General Boutros Boutros-Ghali failed to resolve the impasse, the Security Council voted on November 11, 1993, to expand the sanctions by freezing Libya's overseas assets and banning the sales to Libya of certain oil-refining and pipeline equipment. The sanctions were subsequently regularly extended, although the Security Council rejected a U.S. proposal for a total oil embargo.

Libya continued to face heavy pressure from the United States in 1996. In April, U.S. defense secretary William Perry warned that force would be used if necessary to prevent Libya from completing an alleged underground chemical weapons plant.

After more than a year of failed efforts to negotiate a resolution of the Lockerbie impasse, Libya finally agreed in March 1999 to send the two suspects (Abd al-Basset al-MEGRAHI and Lamin Khalifah FHIMAH) to the Netherlands to face a trial under Scottish law before three Scottish judges, though Qadhafi had argued that they be tried in a neutral country. Colonel Qadhafi's acceptance of the plan apparently was predicated on assurances that the trial would not be used to attempt to "undermine" his regime. For their part, Washington and London appeared to compromise on the issue of the trial's location, in part at least, out of recognition that international support for continued sanctions was diminishing. The Security Council announced that the UN sanctions had been suspended as soon as the suspects arrived in the Netherlands on April 5. However, unilateral U.S. sanctions remained in place as long as Libya stayed on Washington's official list of countries perceived to be "state sponsors of terrorism."

An antiterrorism court in Paris convicted in absentia six suspects in the Niger plane crash case, including Abdallah SENOUSSI, Qadhafi's brother-in-law, in March 1999 and issued warrants for their arrest, which could be enforced only if they left Libya. Meanwhile, Colonel Qadhafi had also permitted German investigators to question Libyan intelligence officers concerning the 1986 Berlin disco bombing, although prosecution of the case had been thrown into disarray in 1997 when the main witness apparently recanted his previously incriminating testimony against alleged Libyan operatives. (Four defendants were convicted of the Berlin bombing in October 2001, the court also accepting the prosecution's argument that the Libyan secret service had been involved in planning the attack.)

In July 1999 full diplomatic relations were reestablished with the United Kingdom, which had severed ties after a British policewoman was killed during an anti-Qadhafi demonstration outside the Libyan mission in London. (It had been argued that the policewoman was killed by gunfire directed from the mission at the demonstrators.) Resolution of the dispute included Libya's agreement to cooperate in the investigation and to pay compensation to the victim's family.

The Lockerbie trial opened in May 2000, and on January 31, 2001, Megrahi was convicted of murder in connection with the bombing, the judges having accepted the admittedly circumstantial evidence that he had been at the airport when the bomb was planted and that he was working for Libyan intelligence at the time. Megrahi was sentenced to life in prison, but Fhimah returned to Libya after being acquitted. (For subsequent developments see Current issues, below.)

In July 2007 U.S. President George W. Bush, in a move marking further normalization of relations between the two countries, nominated the first U.S. ambassador to Libya in nearly 35 years. However, several Democrats in the U.S. Congress held up confirmation of the nominee for more than a year pending Libya's full reparations to families of Lockerbie victims.

Relations with France were normalized in July 2007 following Libya's release of five Europeans and one Palestinian, the medics having been imprisoned (and tortured) for eight years after they were found guilty of infecting children with the AIDS virus. The deal to release the medics had been brokered by French President Nicholas Sarkozy and his wife, though Sarkozy initially denied the promise of an arms deal was involved. (In December, however, Sarkozy welcomed Colonel Qadhafi in a full state visit and the two countries signed an arms deal worth nearly $10 billion.) Tripoli's role as a potential peacemaker was further enhanced in 2007 as a result of its having hosted two meetings with rebel groups from the Darfur region of Sudan and an AU-UN summit in September aimed at ending the Darfur conflict.

In January 2008 Libya joined the UN Security Council after the U.S. dropped its objections. Libya thus became the sole representative of the Middle East and Africa on the Security Council, a move not entirely welcomed by Saudi Arabia (where the king had alleged an assassination attempt by Qadhafi) and South Africa (whose leader and Qadhafi had a "personal confrontation" at the 2007 AU summit in Ghana). The EU in March made overtures to increase its relations with Tripoli, and later that month President Bush sought congressional approval to exempt Libya from a law that allowed victims of terrorism to seize the U.S. assets of state sponsors of the attacks. With increasing investment by U.S. oil companies in Libya, the Bush administration was concerned that without such a provision, Libya, among other states, would be discouraged from fighting terrorism. Despite its improved relations with the United States, Libya rejected, along with most other African countries, the U.S. proposal to move its Africa Command military headquarters anywhere in Africa.

Also in 2008, a federal judge in Washington ruled that the Libyan government and six officials must pay $6 billion in damages to the families of seven U.S. citizens killed in the 1989 Niger crash. (Though Libya had never claimed responsibility, in 2004 it agreed to make reparations of $170 million to the families of 170 victims.) In February 2009 Colonel Qadhafi was installed as chair of the AU, the appointment coinciding with his increasing role of peace broker, as he continued mediation efforts, most recently in connection with conflicts in Sudan, Niger, and Mauritania.

Relations with Switzerland deteriorated in March 2009, when, in an odd diplomatic feud, Libya disrupted oil deliveries to Switzerland, withdrew $7 billion from Swiss banks, recalled some of its diplomats, and ultimately sued over Swiss allegations that one of Qadhafi's sons, Hannibal, and his wife beat two of their servants at a luxury hotel in Geneva. The younger Qadhafi was arrested and briefly detained before being allowed to return to Libya. Tripoli, however, charged that the action violated international rules of diplomatic relations. Meanwhile, Italy offered to try to mediate on Libya's behalf.

In a meeting with Qadhafi's son, al-Saif al-Islam Qadhafi, in April 2009 in Washington, U.S. Secretary of State Hillary Clinton said she would pursue stronger ties with Libya. Meanwhile, *The New York Times* reported that Libya, after having abandoned its WMD, was unhappy with the "payoff" from its deal with the United States, Libyan officials "insisting that the United States had done too little too reward Libya's concessions."

Current issues. Colonel Qadhafi announced in the late 1990s that he was turning his focus away from pan-Arabism and toward pan-Africanism, having described most other Arab states as "defeatist" in dealing with the West and Israel. The quixotic Libyan leader attended his first OAU summit in 20 years in July 1999 to promote his new vision and hosted a special summit in September to address proposed changes in the charter that would permit creation of OAU peacekeeping forces. Subsequently, Qadhafi participated prominently in efforts to resolve the conflicts in Sudan and Democratic Republic of the Congo and served as a mediator in the war between Eritrea and Ethiopia. However, Libya's image as a potential continental unifier suffered a severe blow in late September 2000 when scores of black African workers died in a series of attacks by Libyans on nonnational workers in a suburb of Tripoli. (Underscoring the continued deterioration of the African initiative, in 2003 Libya recalled its troops from the Central African Republic, a trade agreement with Zimbabwe collapsed, and Qadhafi abolished the ministry for African unity.)

In early 2001 Colonel Qadhafi criticized the conviction of one of the defendants in the Lockerbie trial (see Foreign relations, above) as politically motivated. However, by that time it was widely accepted that the Libyan government had not supported any terrorist activities or groups in several years and was genuinely interested in reintegration into the global community. Qadhafi had also improved his international image by cooperating extensively with the U.S.-led "war on terrorism," by freeing a number of political prisoners and by indicating a willingness to discuss the proposed payment of compensation to the families of the victims of the Lockerbie bombing.

Qadhafi subsequently continued his drive to improve Libya's international standing, and the initiative appeared to reach critical mass with an August 2003 announcement of final resolution of the Lockerbie affair. Under the carefully crafted language of the settlement, Libya accepted "responsibility for the actions of its officials" and agreed to pay an estimated $10 million (in three installments) to each of the families of the 270 killed in the attack. The UN Security Council formally lifted UN sanctions against Libya in September, permitting payment of the Lockerbie settlements to begin. In January 2004 Libya also agreed to pay a total of $170 million to the families of those killed in the 1989 Niger plane crash. The final piece of the puzzle appeared to be put in place in September 2004 when Libya agreed to pay $35 million to the non-U.S. victims of the 1986 bombing in Berlin.

Meanwhile, dramatic progress was also achieved regarding the other long-standing area of intense Western concern, that is, Libya's perceived pursuit of weapons of mass destruction (WMD). In December 2003 the United States and UK announced that after nine months of secret negotiations Qadhafi had agreed to abandon all WMD programs and to permit international inspectors to verify compliance. (Some analysts suggested that the process had been accelerated by the aggressive stance taken by the U.S. Bush administration against Iraq.) Washington announced in February 2004 that it would permit flights to Libya and allow U.S. oil companies to launch talks with Tripoli aimed at further exploitation of oil fields. Many U.S. commercial sanctions were lifted the following April, and in October the European Union (EU) removed its embargo on arms sales to Libya, and other economic sanctions. Underscoring the dramatic transformation of the West's perception of Qadhafi, he was visited in 2004 by the British, French, and German heads of state, and a number of U.S. companies were awarded permits in 2005 for oil exploration. Collaterally, the Libyan regime, which celebrated its 35th year in power in 2004, pledged sweeping economic reforms to broaden trade and expand investment opportunities. Libya officially remained on the U.S. list of terrorist-sponsoring states, possibly in part to permit investigation of charges by Saudi Arabia that then-Crown Prince Abdallah (now king) had been the target of an assassination plot, but Libya and Saudi Arabia reestablished diplomatic relations in late 2005.

In a diplomatic move that observers said was also meant to send a message to Iran and North Korea (both developing nuclear capabilities), the United States restored full relations with Libya on May 15, 2006. The United States also removed Libya from its list of state sponsors of terrorism (the latter requiring congressional approval within 45 days). Some of the families of Lockerbie bombing victims were angered, however, that they had not been notified first and demanded that the U.S. Congress ensure Libya fulfilled its financial commitment to them. (Libya halted its final payment to the families until it was removed from the list of states sponsoring terrorism.) With diplomatic ties restored, further restrictions on American oil companies were lifted, allowing for increased exploration. For its part, Libya opened bidding on its oil reserves to international companies in an effort to boost production over the next ten years and bring in a projected $7 billion.

In January 2007 it was reported that the government planned to lay off 400,000 civil servants (though that figure was later revised to 120,000) in an effort to reduce government spending and encourage private sector development. Those who lost their jobs were to be paid their full salary for three years or up to $40,800 in loans to start a new business. Meanwhile, Qadhafi was said to be embarking on an extensive economic modernization plan (see The Country, above, for details).

The Lockerbie bombing was back in the headlines in June 2007 when a Scottish judicial panel issued a ruling upon completion of its three-year investigation that Megrahi, the only person convicted in the case, should be granted a new appeal. The panel stated that "a miscarriage of justice may have occurred," citing questions about the testimony of one witness, among other details of the case. (A legal effort to release a secret intelligence report, which observers said would result in the freeing of Megrahi, was rejected by a British court in March 2008. In April 2009, he remained in prison in Scotland, serving a life sentence pending appeal. Libya sought his extradition, as he reportedly was suffering from cancer and had only a short time to live.) Megrahi was released from prison by the Scottish government on August 20, 2009, on compassionate grounds due to his dire prognosis. His return to Libya, where he was greeted by a celebratory crowd, prompted international outrage. As of November, Megrahi was still alive.

Qadhafi's son, al-Saif al-Islam Qadhafi, who many believe may succeed his father as head of state, publicly proposed a new constitution or "social contract" that would institute an independent judiciary, a free press, and a central bank. No further progress was reported on his proposal, which would also incorporate sharia law; nevertheless it was seen as a noteworthy sign that Libya might pursue gradual reforms.

A troubling domestic issue brought international attention in January 2008 when Tripoli announced it would go through with plans for a mass expulsion of some 1 million illegal immigrants—most of whom were workers from poor African countries—despite harsh criticism by Amnesty International. The human rights organization said some of those expelled would face torture in their home countries. Meanwhile, the Italian government entered into an agreement with Tripoli for joint patrols of Libya's coast to deter those who engage in human trafficking. (Nearly 17,000 migrants were believed to have traveled by sea from Libya to Italy in 2007.)

A major reshuffling of the General People's Committee in March 2009 was originally planned in accordance with measures proposed by Colonel Qadhafi to reduce the size of government and distribute the country's oil wealth directly to the people. However, the General People's Congress, concerned that the plan wouldn't work, failed to support it. The subsequent restructuring of the "cabinet" drew criticism for having retained many of the same members. Most notable among the changes, observers said, was the appointment of former intelligence chief Mussa Kussa, a longtime Qadhafi loyalist, as foreign minister, effectively allowing him to speak for the leader. Kussa was seen as a strongman in the regime and among those who played a key role in Qadhafi's decision to abandon WMD. Meanwhile, though there were media reports that a draft constitution would be released at the end of February, that did not materialize.

In March 2009, in a move that again demonstrated Libya's willingness to change its policies, according to Human Rights Watch, the government released two political prisoners who had been sentenced to 12 and 15 years, respectively, in 2007 after they tried to organize a commemorative gathering for protesters who had been killed in clashes with police. Libya also released dozens of other political prisoners (see Libyan Islamic Fighting Group under Political Parties, below). In April, at the urging of the EU, Libya further addressed a major issue of concern dating to 2008 when it ordered stricter supervision of its coastline to prevent further illegal migration, following the drowning of some 200 migrants during a storm off the coast in March.

POLITICAL PARTIES

Under the monarchy, all political parties were banned. In 1971 an official government party, the Arab Socialist Union (ASU), was founded with the Egyptian ASU as its model. The formation was designed primarily to serve as a "transmission belt," helping implement government decisions at local levels and serving to channel local concerns upward to the central government; however, there was no public reference to it after 1975. At present all parties are proscribed, Colonel Qadhafi arguing that their legalization would only lead to disorder.

Opposition Groups:

National Front for the Salvation of Libya (NFSL). Formation of the NFSL was announced in Khartoum, Sudan, on October 7, 1981, under the banner "Finding the democratic alternative." In September 1986 the Front published a list of 76 regime opponents that it claimed had been assassinated in exile, and in January 1987 it joined with a number of other exile formations in establishing a joint working group during a meeting in Cairo, Egypt. The NFSL also participated in the formation of the LNLA (below), which, however, announced its independent status in early 1994.

Operating out of Egypt and the United States, the NFSL was in the forefront of efforts to coordinate anti-Qadhafi activity in the first half of the 1990s, including a conference in Washington in late 1993 attended by most of the regime's leading opponents. However, a "statement of principles" of a proposed front was not negotiated.

In early 1994 it was reported that the NFSL had begun to transmit its antiregime radio program, the *Voice of the Libyan People,* via European Satellite. The program had previously been intermittently broadcast by shortwave radio from neighboring countries. In 1997 the NFSL issued a report alleging that more than 300 Qadhafi opponents had been killed by government operatives abroad or by domestic security forces between 1977 and 1994. In mid-2004 NFSL leaders warned Western leaders that the Qadhafi regime continued to hold political prisoners despite the country's improved international reputation.

Jabal MATAR, described as leader of the NFSL's "military wing," and Muhammad MAGARIAF, the group's secretary general, have been missing since 1990, according to Amnesty International, which reported that the two "disappeared" in Cairo.

The group held a national conference in 2005 but declined to participate in a second national conference in March 2008 in London, saying on its Web site that the Front was "keen to distance itself" from going into the details of information that "need not be disseminated, in the interest of national action."

Leaders: Ibrahim SAHAD, Mahmud DAKHIL, Muhammad Fayiz JIBRIL.

Libyan National Liberation Army (LNLA). The LNLA was formed in Chad in 1988 as a paramilitary unit organized with covert U.S. backing to destabilize the Libyan government. The existence of the army, comprising an estimated 600–700 Libyan soldiers taken prisoner by Chadian forces and subsequently molded into an anti-Qadhafi force, became known following the overthrow of the Habré regime in late 1990. Washington quickly airlifted the Libyan *"contras"* out of Chad after the fall of Ndjamena, U.S. embarrassment over the affair increasing as the LNLA participants entered a "floating exile." About 250 eventually returned to Libya, the rest reportedly finding temporary asylum in Zaire and, subsequently, Kenya. In late 1991 some of the guerrillas were reported to have been moved to a Central Intelligence Agency (CIA) training base in the United States, and in April 1992 LNLA members participated in an NFSL congress in Dallas, Texas. Two years later, as the apparent result of a policy dispute, the LNLA severed its links to the NFSL. There has been little subsequent information regarding any LNLA activity.

Leaders: Col. Khalifa HIFTER, Braek SWESSI.

In May 1996 a number of opposition groups reportedly issued a statement condemning the "despotic practices" of the Qadhafi regime, according to the *Africa Research Bulletin,* which said signatories included the **Libyan Constitutional Union,** the **Libyan Nationalist Organization,** and the **Libyan Democratic Nationalist Grouping.** Also listed were a **Movement for Change and Reform** (a nationalist grouping) and the **Libyan Islamic Group,** an underground but nonviolent organization that has been compared to groups such as the Muslim Brotherhood in Egypt. A number of supporters of the Libyan Islamic Group (including professors and other professionals) were reportedly arrested in Benghazi and other northeastern cities in mid-1998. Another group reportedly involved in clashes with security forces is the **Islamic Martyrs Movement,** whose reputed leader Muhammad al-HAMI, was believed to have been killed by government security forces in July 1996. (Abdullah AHMAD subsequently was identified as a spokesperson for the movement.) The grouping, described as comprising Libyan veterans of the Afghan war operating out of the mountains near Benghazi, claimed that it had wounded Qadhafi in an attack on his motorcade on the night of May 31–June 1, 1998. (The government denied that such an attack had taken place.) Meanwhile, the formation of the **Libyan Patriots Movement** had been announced in London in January 1997, founders calling for the ouster of Colonel Qadhafi and creation of a "free Libya" based on free-market economic principles. In April 1998 the movement reportedly staged an attack on security forces in Benghazi.

In August 2000 the formation of a new external opposition grouping—the **National Reform Congress**—was reported as a vehicle for promoting a multiparty system in Libya.

A group identified as the **Libyan Islamic Fighting Group** (LIFG) reportedly clashed with Libyan security forces more than a decade ago, when the group was also referenced as the Libyan Militant Islamic Group—LMIG. It is an Islamic fundamentalist grouping that had been linked to the antigovernment disturbances in northeastern Libya in March 1996 and had claimed that it had planned an assassination of Colonel Qadhafi. The Libyan leader subsequently criticized the United Kingdom for permitting the group to maintain operations in London in view of the group's avowed goal of overthrowing the Libyan government. In 2001 the LIFG was included on the U.S. list of terrorist organizations whose assets were to be frozen. A number of LIFG members remained in prison in Libya in 2002.

The United States and the UK reportedly helped Libya in 2006 in a crackdown on group members to prevent militants from plotting attacks against Qadhafi and against U.S. forces in Iraq. In late 2006 the LIFG, then led by Abdallah al-SADIQ, said the government had released 60 of the group's members who had been held on allegations of promoting violence. The action reportedly followed months of negotiations between Libyan authorities and the group's leader, Numan bin-UTHMAN, in which the government tried to persuade the group to disband. The LIFG members were freed after they reportedly agreed to renounce violence. In November 2007 the LIFG was reported to have pledged allegiance to the terrorist group al-Qaida. In a tape recording purportedly made by Ayman al-ZAWAHIRI, al-Qaida's second-in-command, the presumed leader of the LIFG, Abu Laith al-LIBI, confirmed the group's new allegiance. However, bin-Uthman, who was reported to be living in London, claimed that al-Libi represented only one faction of the LIFG, a branch that had been based for years in Afghanistan. Al Libi, who was linked to a failed coup attempt against Qadhafi in 1994, was killed in Pakistan in February 2008, the *Washington Post* reporting at the time that the LIFG was defunct. In 2009 Libyan officials said dozens of the group's prisoners had been released.

LEGISLATURE

The Senate and House of Representatives were dissolved as a result of the 1969 coup, Colonel Qadhafi asserting that all such institutions are basically undemocratic, "as democracy means the authority of the people and not the authority of a body acting on the people's behalf."

A government decree of November 13, 1975, provided for the establishment of a 618-member General National Congress of the ASU to consist of the members of the Revolutionary Command Council and leaders of existing "people's congresses," trade unions, and professional groups. Subsequent to its first session held January 5–18, 1976, the body was identified as the **General People's Congress** (GPC). The GPC was last renewed March 1–4, 2009, comprising 468 members.

Secretary General: Mubarak Abdullah al-SHAMIKH.

CABINET

[as of November 1, 2009]

Secretary General, General People's Committee (Prime Minister)	Al-Baghdadi Ali al-Mahmudi
Secretaries	
Agriculture, Livestock, and Marine Resources	Abu-Bakr Mabruk al-Mansuri
Education, Higher Education, and Research	Abdul Kabir al-Fakhri
Finance and Planning	Abd-al-Hafid Mahmud al-Zulaytini
Foreign Liaison and International Cooperation	Mussa Kussa
Health and Environment	Mahmoud Muhammad Hijazi
Industry, Economy, and Trade	Muhammad al-Huwayj
Justice	Mustafa Muhammad Abd-al-Jalil
Public Security and Interior	Lt. Gen. Abd-al-Fattah Yunis al-Ubaydi
Public Utilities	Matuq Muhammad Matuq
Social Affairs	Ibrahim al-Zarruq Sharif
Transport	Muhammad Ali Zidan

COMMUNICATIONS

In October 1973 all private newspapers were nationalized, and censorship remains heavy. Despite claims in 2006 by a Libyan media company, encouraged by Col. Qadhafi's son, Sayif al-Islam al-Qadhafi, that the government was prepared to allow private media within the year, Reporters Without Borders found no such changes taking place. To the contrary, the watchdog organization stated in its 2008 report that "the regime is deaf to all criticism and remains repressive."

Press. The country's major daily, *al-Fajr al-Jadid* (The New Dawn, 40,000), is published in Tripoli in Arabic, by JANA. Also published daily in Arabic in Tripoli are the "ideological journal" *Al-Zahf al-Akhdar* (The Green March), *Al Jamahiriya,* and *Al Shams*. The daily *Tripoli Post* is published in English.

News agencies. The official facility is the Jamahiriya News Agency (JANA). Italy's ANSA and Russia's ITAR-TASS maintain offices in Tripoli.

Broadcasting and computing. Radio and television transmission in both Arabic and English is under the administration of the Great Socialist People's Libyan Arab Jamahiriya Broadcasting Corporation. There is a private television station, *Al Libiya,* via satellite. The Voice of America also broadcasts in the country. As of 2008 there were 51.3 Internet users per 1,000 inhabitants.

INTERGOVERNMENTAL REPRESENTATION

There were no diplomatic relations between Libya and the United States until June 2004, when, in the wake of perceived progress toward the resolution of several long-standing areas of severe contention (see Foreign relations and Current issues, above), Washington announced it would open a liaison office in Tripoli.

Ambassador to the U.S.: Ali Suleiman AUJALI.

U.S. Ambassador to Libya: Gene Allan CRETZ.

Permanent Representative to the UN: Abdurrahman Mohamed SHALGHAM.

IGO Memberships (Non-UN): AfDB, AU, AFESD, AMF, AMU, BADEA, CAEU, Comesa, IDB, Interpol, IOM, LAS, NAM, OAPEC, OIC, OPEC, PCA, WCO.

LIECHTENSTEIN

Principality of Liechtenstein
Fürstentum Liechtenstein

Political Status: Independent principality constituted in 1719; current constitution promulgated October 5, 1921; established diplomatic association with Switzerland in 1919 and customs and currency association in 1923.

Area: 61.8 sq. mi. (160.475 sq. km.).

Population: 34,600 (2004 National Registration); 36,000 (2008E). Both figures include more than 10,000 resident aliens.

Major Urban Centers (2005E): VADUZ (5,010), Schaan (5,700).

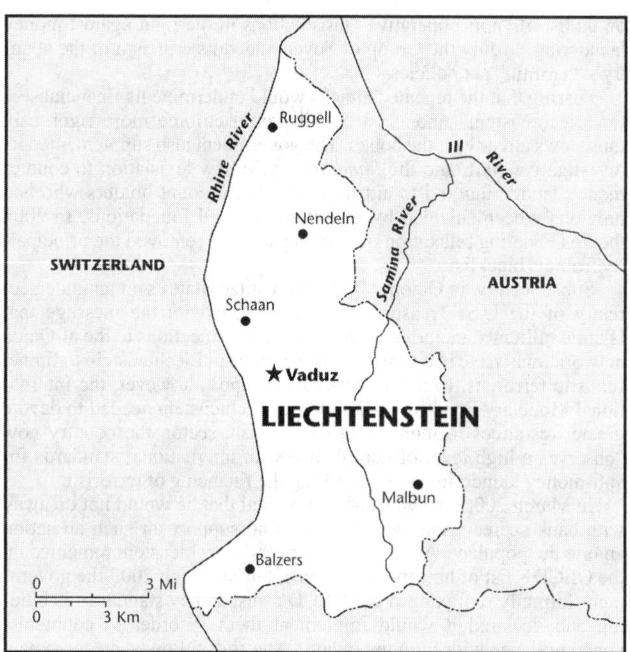

Official Language: German (Alemannic).

Monetary Unit: Swiss Franc (market rate December 1, 2009: 0.95 francs = $1US).

Sovereign: Prince HANS-ADAM von und zu Liechtenstein II; assumed the executive authority of the sovereign on August 26, 1984; acceded to the throne at the death of his father, Prince FRANZ JOSEF II, on November 13, 1989. (On August 15, 2004, Prince Hans-Adam turned over most day-to-day governmental responsibility to Crown Prince Alois.)

Heir Apparent: Crown Prince ALOIS von und zu Liechtenstein.

Prime Minister (Chief of Government): Klaus TSCHÜTSCHER (Fatherland Union); nominated by the *Langtag* and appointed by Prince Hans-Adam on March 25, 2009, following the general election of February 8, succeeding Otmar HASLER (Progressive Citizens' Party).

THE COUNTRY

A miniature principality on the upper Rhine between Austria and Switzerland, Liechtenstein has a predominantly Roman Catholic population whose major language, Alemannic, is a German dialect. Approximately one-third of the current population are resident aliens, most of whom have sought employment in the service sector.

Once dependent on agriculture, which currently employs less than 2 percent of the population despite the continuing importance of dairying and cattle breeding, Liechtenstein underwent considerable industrialization in the post–World War II era, with an emphasis on metallurgy and light industry. Notable products include dental appliances and precision machinery, most of which are exported, principally to Switzerland and the member countries of the European Union (EU). The principality is chiefly known, however, as one of the world's leading "offshore" banking and finance centers, with a history of confidentiality and of low tax rates that have attracted some 80,000 trust and holding companies, virtually all of which maintain no physical presence in the country. At present, the financial industry provides some 40 percent of revenue and has helped Liechtenstein's per capita GNP rank among the world's highest. In recent years external pressure has forced the government to support efforts to end money laundering and the abuse of banking secrecy (see Current issues, below). Collaterally, the government has attempted to boost tourism and foreign investment in order to improve Liechtenstein's status as a "business center."

GOVERNMENT AND POLITICS

Political background. The Principality of Liechtenstein, whose origins date back to the 14th century, was established in its present form in 1719. Part of the Holy Roman Empire and after 1815 a member of the German Confederation, it entered into a customs union with Austria in 1852; following the collapse of the confederation in 1866, the principality in 1868 declared permanent neutrality. Formally terminating the association with Austria in 1919, Liechtenstein proceeded to adopt Swiss currency in 1921, and in 1923 entered into a customs union with Switzerland, which continues to administer the principality's customs and provides for its defense and diplomatic representation. Liechtenstein's neutrality was respected in both world wars of the 20th century.

In August 1984, in an unusual action, the aging Prince FRANZ JOSEF had assigned his official responsibilities, without abdication of title, to Prince HANS-ADAM, a business school graduate. When Franz Josef died on November 13, 1989, after a 51-year reign that had made him the world's most durable monarch, he was immediately succeeded by his 44-year-old son.

From 1938 until April 1997 the government was a coalition of the Progressive Citizens' Party (*Fortschrittliche Bürgerpartei*—FBP) and the Fatherland Union (*Vaterländische Union*—VU). At the election of February 1993 the FBP, after 15 years, had regained its status as the largest parliamentary party from the VU but it was limited to a 12-seat plurality in an expanded body of 25 members when the environmentalist Free List (*Freie Liste*—FL) unexpectedly met the 8 percent threshold for representation, winning 2 seats with 10.4 percent of the vote. However, the *Landtag* was dissolved by Prince Hans-Adam in September after Prime Minister Markus BÜCHEL fell victim to a nonconfidence motion brought by his own FBP in protest against his leadership methods. At the ensuing October election the VU secured a majority of 13 seats (with a vote share of 50.1 percent), while the FBP fell back to 11 seats (44.2 percent) and the Free List slipped to 1 seat (8.5 percent). In December the VU's Mario FRICK formed a new coalition administration, with the FBP's Thomas BÜCHEL succeeding him as deputy chief of government. The VU also increased its vote in communal elections in January 1995, winning the mayoralty of Vaduz after nearly 70 years of FBP control.

Snap *Landtag* elections (nine months early) were held in January–February 1997, with the only change in distribution being the loss of one FBP seat to the FL. Although negotiations were expected to produce another coalition cabinet as a matter of course, the FBP announced in March that it was leaving the government, ostensibly to create an "effective opposition." Consequently, a new all-VU government under Frick's leadership—the first one-party administration since 1938—was nominated by Prince Hans-Adam and installed on April 9 upon approval by the *Landtag*.

At the election of February 9 and 11, 2001, the opposition FBP won 49.9 percent of the vote and gained 3 *Landtag* seats over its previous total, for a majority of 13, guaranteeing the designation of party leader Otmar HASLER as the next chief of government. The VU took 41.1 percent, for 11 seats, and the Free List captured 8.8 percent and 1 seat. The new legislature confirmed Hasler and an all-FBP cabinet on April 5.

The prince subsequently continued promoting a constitutional reform plan designed to strengthen the monarchy's powers, including giving him the authority to appoint judges with legislative concurrence (rather than the other way around), to dismiss the government or dissolve the *Landtag* without explanation, and to impose emergency rule. Many legislators, in contrast, wanted to limit the monarchy's existing powers, and a minority was known to favor creation of a republic. Hans-Adam repeatedly called for his proposed reforms to be put before the voters, while warning that he would go into exile if a referendum concluded with a negative vote. He even asserted that without the present royal house and its wealth—his personal fortune was estimated at $4–6 billion—the principality might have little recourse but to seek a union with either Switzerland or Austria to find a successor who would be willing to meet the costs of maintaining the monarchy. In a national referendum on March 14 and 16, 2003, voters approved the prince's demands with a 64 percent "yes" vote. On August 15, 2004, Hans-Adam (following his father's example) transferred most executive power to his son, Crown Prince ALOIS, although Hans-Adam remained monarch and head of state.

The FBP fell to a plurality of 12 seats in the general election of March 11 and 13, 2005, prompting the return of an FBP-VU coalition, again headed by Hasler, on April 21. The coalition stayed together following the February 8, 2009, general election, but the VU's Klaus

TSCHÜTSCHER was appointed prime minister because the VU had secured 2 more seats than the FBP.

Constitution and government. Under the constitution adopted October 5, 1921, and amended following a referendum in 2003 (see above), the monarchy is hereditary in the male line and the sovereign exercises legislative power jointly with a unicameral Diet (*Landtag*), which is elected every four years by direct suffrage under proportional representation, assuming no dissolution. The chief of government (*regierungschef*) is appointed by the sovereign from the majority party or group in the Diet. The government, which is responsible to both the sovereign and the Diet, also includes a deputy chief (*regierungschef-stellvertreter*) and three additional government councilors (*regierungsräte*) elected by the Diet itself. Elections are held in two constituencies (Oberland and Unterland), while administration is based on 11 communes (*gemeinden*). The judicial system consists of civil, criminal, and administrative divisions: the first two include local, Superior, and Supreme Courts, while the third encompasses an Administrative Court of Appeal (for hearing complaints about government officials and actions) and a State Court, both of which consider questions of constitutionality.

The enfranchisement of women at the national level, supported by both major parties and approved unanimously by the legislature, was narrowly endorsed by male voters in 1984, after having been defeated in referenda held in 1971 and 1973. Approval at the local level was also voted in eight communes, with approval in the remaining three following in 1986. Following the 2009 balloting women held 6 of 25 seats in parliament, and 2 of the 5 government ministers were women.

Foreign relations. Liechtenstein maintains an embassy in Bern but is represented elsewhere by Swiss embassies and consulates through an agreement dating from October 27, 1919. Long a participant in a number of United Nations (UN) specialized agencies, Liechtenstein decided only in December 1989 to seek admission to the UN. The application was approved in 1990. Previously an associate member of the European Free Trade Association (EFTA) because of its customs union with Switzerland, the principality became EFTA's seventh full member on May 22, 1991. The country does not have a standing army but has long been preoccupied with European defense strategy and is an active participant in the Organization for (formerly Conference on) Security and Cooperation in Europe (OSCE/CSCE).

While not making a formal territorial claim, Liechtenstein in 1992 reopened the question of the extensive lands once owned by the grand duke in what was then Czechoslovakia. Ten times the size of Liechtenstein itself, these ducal estates had been confiscated in 1919 by the fledgling Czechoslovak Republic, which in 1938, under Axis pressure, had agreed to return half and to pay compensation for the remainder. The agreement was repudiated by the post–World War II Communist regime and found no more favor with the post–communist government in Prague. In mid-2001 Liechtenstein submitted its complaint to the International Court of Justice (ICJ). In February 2005 the ICJ refused to rule on the question.

Switzerland's surprise application in 1992 for membership in the European Community/European Union (EC/EU) caused difficulties for Liechtenstein, which faced the possibility of having to follow suit if it wished to preserve the 1923 customs union between the two states. Of particular concern were proposed labor-mobility rules. Liechtenstein instead favored membership in the proposed European Economic Area (EEA) between the EU and most EFTA countries.

The situation subsequently became even more complicated when Swiss voters rejected ratification of the EEA treaty, a development that effectively blocked progress on that nation's EU membership proposal as well (see article on Switzerland). In December 1992 55.8 percent of the Liechtenstein voters endorsed EEA membership, but EEA participation had to be deferred pending renegotiation of the customs union. Another national referendum, this time to approve the revised arrangement with Switzerland, was approved by 55.9 percent of those voting in April 1995, with Liechtenstein then acceding to the EEA on May 1.

In 2003 Liechtenstein initially refused to approve expansion of the EEA to include the Czech Republic and Slovakia because of the lingering dispute over the post–World War II agreements. Prince Hans-Adam subsequently lifted his veto against the proposed EEA expansion on the condition that negotiations to resolve the dispute would be renewed.

In May 2000 the Bank for International Settlements (BIS) included the principality on its list of offshore facilities having lax supervision, and a month later the independent Financial Action Task Force (FATF), which had been established with the support of the Organization for Economic Cooperation and Development (OECD), placed Liechtenstein on its list of "noncooperative" jurisdictions in the fight against money laundering. In July the Group of Seven added its criticism of the country's "harmful" tax policies.

Fearing that the repeated attacks would undermine its financial sector, Liechtenstein announced that it would enforce more rigorously those laws already on the books. The government also supplemented its investigative staff, and the *Landtag* passed new legislation to counter money laundering and to aid in identifying account holders who had previously been shielded by intermediaries and foundations. In 2001 the FATF, noting relaxation of banking secrecy, removed the principality from its blacklist.

Subsequently, in October 2002, the United States sent an undersecretary of the U.S. Treasury to Liechtenstein with the message that Islamic militants, including financiers with connections to the al-Qaida network, may have been using bank accounts in Liechtenstein to funnel funds to terrorists. In a September 2003 report, however, the International Monetary Fund found that while Liechtenstein needed to devote greater resources to monitoring its financial sector, the country now "observes a high level of compliance with international standards for anti-money laundering and combating the financing of terrorism."

In March 2006 Crown Prince Alois said that he would not do away with bank secrecy, stating that there is no support for such an action among the populace. As of September 2007 Liechtenstein remained on the OECD's list of harmful tax havens, but in March 2009 the government formally reorganized the OECD transparency standards as binding and declared it would implement them in order to counteract noncompliance with foreign tax laws. The shift followed an agreement with the United States to exchange information on individuals' banking practices upon request from the United States, provided Liechtenstein courts deem the request legitimate. The government subsequently initialed a similar agreement with Germany and signed one with the United Kingdom.

Current issues. With their endorsement in the national referendum of March 2003, the voters effectively turned Prince Hans-Adam into what was described as Europe's sole absolute monarch. The prince's detractors described his vastly enhanced powers as equivalent to "dictatorial" authority, and the Council of Europe threatened to impose sanctions because of the perceived threat to the democratic process. Tension over the matter was only partly defused by the assumption of substantial executive authority by Crown Prince Alois in 2004. Hans-Adam later reportedly indicated that he did not expect to abdicate completely for perhaps 20 more years.

Internationally, Liechtenstein has stepped up its efforts to establish free trade agreements with a number of countries, usually in cooperation with the other EFTA members, namely Iceland, Norway, and Switzerland. The four countries—none of which is a member of the EU—signed a trade agreement with the Southern African Customs Union in July 2006 and entered into a trade agreement with South Korea in September 2006. The group also began negotiations for a similar trade agreement with India in March 2007 and has undertaken talks with Thailand and Malaysia.

In September 2007 the OECD again branded Liechtenstein an uncooperative tax haven. Its controversial bank secrecy practices faced additional international challenges in February 2008 when German officials relied on records stolen from the Liechtenstein Group Trust (LGT), a bank owned by the royal family, to pursue hundreds of German citizens suspected of using secretive LGT trusts and foundations to evade taxes. Within weeks, the records were also being used in similar investigations in the United States and United Kingdom. Initial reactions in Liechtenstein were defensive and hostile. However, by summer's end, with elections scheduled for February 2009 and the secrecy issue threatening the regional economic integration of the principality's high-tech and manufacturing industries, Prince Alois and Prime Minister Hasler announced their readiness to respect international standards regarding financial transparency. (They did so formally in March 2009—see above).

With public disquiet growing over the banking scandal, including the revelation that some 1,000 Germans had used their Liechtenstein accounts to evade taxes totaling the equivalent of more than a billion dollars, Prime Minister Hasler's FBP slipped to 43.5 percent of the vote in the February 2009 legislative elections, finishing second to the VU. However, the VU, which won a majority (13 of 25 seats) and could have formed a cabinet on its own, opted to form another coalition government with the FBP. The new government continued on the path of implementing OECD standards for banking transparency and endorsed bilateral agreements with Germany and the United Kingdom to that effect. On another diplomatic front, in July 2009 the government established formal relations with the Czech Republic, renewing hope that the long-standing territorial dispute between the two countries might someday be resolved.

POLITICAL PARTIES

Government Parties:

Fatherland Union (*Vaterländische Union*—VU). Considered the more liberal of the two major parties, the VU (sometimes referred to as the Patriotic Union) was formed with substantial working-class support in 1917 as the People's Party (*Volkspartei*), which controlled the government for the decade 1918–1928. Having adopted its present name in 1936, it served as the junior coalition partner of the FBP (above) from 1938 to 1970, when it won a majority of legislative seats. It lost its coalition seniority in 1974, regained it in 1978, lost it in February 1993, and regained it again the following October. It formed its own government in April 1997 after the FBP voluntarily moved into opposition. Following the February 2001 election, it declined to reestablish a coalition with the victorious FBP. However, it rejoined the government in April 2005 after securing 10 seats (on a 38 percent vote share) in the March general election. After winning an outright majority of 13 seats on 47.6 percent of the vote in the February 2009 balloting, the VU took the prime leadership position in the new coalition with FBP.

Leaders: Klaus TSCHÜTSCHER (Prime Minister), Adolf HEEB (President), Hans-jörg GOOP (Party Secretary).

Progressive Citizens' Party (*Fortschrittliche Bürgerpartei*—FBP). Founded in 1918 as the basically conservative Citizens' Party (*Bürgerpartei*) and sometimes identified as the Bourgeois Party, what subsequently became the FBP held a majority of legislative seats from 1928 to 1970 and from 1974 to 1978. Starting in 1938 it participated with the VU (below) in Europe's longest-serving government coalition. After 15 years as the junior coalition partner, it regained seniority in February 1993 under the premiership of Markus Büchel but lost it in the year's second election in October, when the FBP list was headed by Josef BIEDERMANN. Following the 1997 election, at which it won a disappointing 10 seats, the FBP withdrew from the coalition government to sit in opposition. Having won 13 seats at the February 2001 election, the FBP formed a one-party administration in early April. However, after slipping to 12 seats (on a 49 percent vote share) in 2005, it reestablished the coalition with the VU. The coalition continued after the February 2009 election but with the VU in the leadership role, the FBP's vote share having declined to 43.5 percent, good for 11 seats.

Leaders: Martin MEYER (Deputy Prime Minister), Otmar HASLER (Former Prime Minister), Marcus VOGT (President), Elmar KINDLE (Vice President).

Opposition Party:

Free List (*Freie Liste*—FL). Less conservative than the traditional parties, the social democratic, environmentalist FL was formed prior to the 1986 election, at which it narrowly failed to secure the 8 percent vote share necessary for parliamentary representation; it again fell short in 1989, in part because 3 percent went to a new Liechtenstein Nonparty List (*Überparteiliche Liste Liechtensteins*—ÜLL). The party finally passed the threshold in the February 1993 balloting, securing 10.4 percent of the vote and two *Landtag* seats. It lost one of those seats the following October, regained it in 1997, and then fell back to a single seat in the February 2001 election before rebounding to three seats (on a 13 percent vote share) in March 2003. After again winning three seats on 13 percent of the vote in the March 2005 balloting, the FL fell back to just one seat with 8.9 percent of the vote in the February 2009 general election. Unlike all its previous elections, the FL declared in its 2009 campaign that it would be willing to join a government coalition. However, both the VU and FBP said they would not join forces in government with the FL.

Leaders: Claudia HEEB-FLECK, Egon MATT.

LEGISLATURE

The **Diet** (*Landtag*) is a unicameral body currently consisting of 25 members directly elected for four-year terms (barring dissolution) on the basis of universal suffrage and proportional representation. In the balloting of February 8, 2009, the Fatherland Union won 13 seats; the Progressive Citizens' Party, 11; and the Free List, 1.

President: Arthur BRUNHART.

CABINET

[as of September 1, 2009]

Prime Minister	Klaus Tschütscher (VU)
Deputy Prime Minister	Martin Meyer (FBP)
Ministers	
Construction and Public Works	Martin Meyer (FBP)
Cultural Affairs	Aurelia Frick (FBP) [f]
Economic Affairs	Martin Meyer (FBP)
Education	Hugo Quaderer (VU)
Environmental Affairs, Land Use, Planning, Agriculture, and Forestry	Renate Muessner (VU) [f]
Family and Equal Opportunity	Klaus Tschütscher (VU)
Finance	Klaus Tschütscher (VU)
Foreign Affairs	Aurelia Frick (FBP) [f]
General Government Affairs	Klaus Tschütscher (VU)
Home Affairs	Hugo Quaderer (VU)
Justice	Aurelia Frick (FBP) [f]
Public Health	Renate Muessner (VU) [f]
Social Affairs	Renate Muessner (VU) [f]
Sports	Hugo Quaderer (VU)
Transport and Telecommunications	Martin Meyer (FBP)

[f] = female

COMMUNICATIONS

Press. The following are published in Vaduz: *Liechtensteiner Woche* (14,000), Sunday; *Liechtensteiner Vaterland* (9,000), daily VU organ; *Liechtensteiner Volksblatt* (9,000), daily FBP organ.

News agency. The Press and Information Office of the Liechtenstein Government (*Presse und Informationsamt der Fürstlichen Regierung*) issues periodic press bulletins.

Broadcasting and computing. The only transmitter is that of Radio Liechtenstein, which was launched in 1995; reception is otherwise from Swiss facilities. As of 2008 there were 659.6 Internet users per 1,000 inhabitants.

INTERGOVERNMENTAL REPRESENTATION

Ambassador to the U.S.: Claudia FRITSCHE.

U.S. Ambassador to Liechtenstein: Donald Sternoff BEYER, Jr.

Permanent Representative to the UN: Christian WENAWESER.

IGO Memberships (Non-UN): CEUR, EBRD, EFTA, Interpol, OSCE, PCA, WTO.

LITHUANIA

Republic of Lithuania
Lietuvos Respublika

Political Status: Independence from Russia declared February 16, 1918; absorption of independent state by the Soviet Union on August 3, 1940, repudiated on March 11, 1990, by the Lithuanian Supreme

Council; independence recognized by the USSR State Council on September 6, 1991; current constitution approved by referendum of October 25, 1992.

Area: 25,174 sq. mi. (65,200 sq. km.).

Population: 3,483,972 (2001C); 3,343,000 (2008E). Substantial emigration occurred in the 1990s, as evidenced by a 1989 census count of 3,674,802, which continued after the 2001 tally.

Major Urban Centers (2005E): VILNIUS (541,000), Kaunas (364,000), Klaipėda (188,000), Šiauliai (130,000), Panevėžys (116,000).

Official Language: Lithuanian.

Monetary Unit: Litas (official rate December 1, 2009: 2.28 litai = $1US). The litas was pegged to the euro as of February 2, 2002. Lithuania joined the European Union in 2004, although the target date for adopting the euro has recently been pushed back to 2013.

President: Dalia GRYBAUSKAITĖ (nonparty); elected in first-round balloting on May 17, 2009, and inaugurated for a five-year term on July 12 to succeed Valdas ADAMKUS (nonparty).

Prime Minister: Andrius KUBILIUS (Homeland Union-Lithuanian Christian Democrats); nominated by the president on November 28, 2008, confirmed by the parliament on November 30, and sworn in on December 9 to succeed Gediminas KIRKILAS (Lithuanian Social Democratic Party); renominated on July 15, 2009, and approved by parliament on July 16 following presidential elections.

THE COUNTRY

The largest of the former Soviet Baltic republics, Lithuania is bordered on the north by Latvia, on the east by Belarus, on the south by Poland, and on the southwest by the detached Russian region of Kaliningrad. At the 2001 census 83.5 percent of the population was Lithuanian, 6.7 percent Polish, 6.3 percent Russian, and 1.2 percent Belarusan. About 79 percent are Roman Catholic, and 4 percent Russian Orthodox, while 16 percent professed no religion.

Following World War II the country passed from a largely agricultural to a substantially industrialized country, with a population that was two-thirds urban in 1986. As of 2008 the industrial sector accounted for 32.2 percent of GDP, with paper, plastics, synthetic fibers, and sulfuric acid being leading products. Services accounted for about 63.3 percent, while agriculture contributed only 4.5 percent of GDP. Cattle raising and dairy farming, in addition to grain and sugar beet cultivation, are the principal agricultural activities. Natural resources include forest tracts and relatively extensive peat reserves. In 2008 the majority of exports went to the European Union (EU), although Russia was the single largest importer of Lithuanian goods at 16.1 percent, followed by Latvia, Germany, and Poland. Russia remains the leading source of Lithuania's imports, accounting for 30.1 percent.

Economic disruption prompted by political change resulted in a 50 percent fall in GDP between 1990 and 1993, average annual inflation of 200 percent, and an estimated unemployment rate of 15 percent by early 1994. Recovery in 1995 yielded economic growth of 3 percent, an inflation rate reduced to 15 percent, and the first trade surplus since independence. GDP growth had risen to 7.3 percent in 1997 before declining to 5.1 percent in 1998 as the Russian financial crisis started to take a toll on Lithuanian exports. At the same time, inflation declined dramatically 8.8 percent in 1997 and to 5.1 percent the following year. The continuing regional impact of the Russian crisis contributed to an economic contraction of 3.9 percent in 1999, but 2000 saw 3.9 percent growth. With eventual EU accession as a goal, successive governments accelerated structural reforms, including bank privatization, tax rationalization, and restructuring of the energy sector. In 2002 the administration also announced broad changes in the nation's pension system. GDP grew by 8.9 percent in 2003, while unemployment fell to 12.4 percent. Overall, economic conditions were satisfactory enough to permit Lithuania's EU accession in 2004. GDP grew by approximately 7.5 percent in 2006, while unemployment fell to 5.4 percent in 2006, down from 8.3 percent the previous year. However, inflation subsequently forced the target date for adoption of the euro to be postponed to at least 2012. GDP growth in 2007 was 8.8 percent, slowing to 3.3 percent in 2008. A severe contraction of 15 percent was expected in 2009 following the deepening of the global economic crisis, and a recovery was not expected before 2011.

GOVERNMENT AND POLITICS

Political background. One of the leading states of medieval Europe, with domains extending as far south as the Black Sea, Lithuania was merged with Poland during the 16th century and subsequently absorbed by Russia during the Polish partitions of the 18th century. World War I brought with it four years of German occupation. Following the November 1918 armistice, many countries recognized the restoration of Lithuanian independence, which had been declared on February 16 despite the continuing presence of German forces. A democratic government was established in May 1920, but for several more years Lithuania remained beset by Bolshevik, czarist, and Polish interventions, with Vilnius, the capital, being occupied by Poland in 1920 and Kaunas thereupon being declared the provisional capital. A 1926 coup produced the dictatorship of Antanas SMETONA, who remained in power until World War II.

A secret protocol of the German-Soviet "friendship" treaty of September 1939 assigned the greater part of Lithuania to the Soviet sphere of influence; after being compelled to assume the status of a Soviet Socialist Republic in July 1940, the country was formally incorporated into the Soviet Union on August 3, along with Estonia and Latvia. The initial period of Soviet control was marked by executions and the deportation to Siberia of tens of thousands of Lithuanians. German reoccupation quickly followed the onset of German-Soviet hostilities in June 1941, one consequence being the subsequent decimation of Lithuania's Jewish population. Reimposed at the end of World War II, the Soviet annexation was never recognized by Britain and the United States.

In elections to the Lithuanian Supreme Soviet in late February and early March 1990, a majority of seats were won by candidates backed by the Lithuanian Reform Movement (*Sajūdis*), a secessionist formation that cut across ideological lines. On March 11 *Sajūdis* chair Vytautas LANDSBERGIS defeated Algirdas BRAZAUSKAS, the Communist incumbent chair of the Supreme Soviet Presidium, in balloting for the chair of what was now styled the Supreme Council. Following the election of Landsbergis, the council designated Kazimiera Danutė PRUNSKIENĖ, a *Sajūdis*-endorsed Communist, to succeed Vytautas SAKALAUSKAS as chair of the Council of Ministers (prime minister). Later the same day, Lithuania became the first

Soviet republic to declare its independence by repudiating the 1940 annexation and announcing a Provisional Fundamental Law of the Republic of Lithuania, an action that was immediately rejected by Moscow. In April the Soviet Union imposed an economic blockade on the country, and on June 29, following a meeting of Landsbergis and Prunskienė with President Mikhail Gorbachev in Moscow, the council approved a temporary suspension of its independence declaration. However, subsequent negotiations proved fruitless, and on January 2, 1991, Chair Landsbergis announced an end to the moratorium.

Prime Minister Prunskienė resigned on January 8, 1991, following widespread opposition to price increases that she had authorized. Three days later Soviet army troops moved to occupy key government buildings in Vilnius, precipitating clashes that resulted in the deaths of 14 civilians and injuries to 700. The Lithuanians responded by refusing to participate in the referendum on the Union Treaty on March 17, mounting instead a February 9 poll on independence that elicited a "yes" vote of 90.47 percent. A number of other incidents involving Soviet troops followed, prior to Moscow's acceptance of independence for all three Baltic republics on September 6 in the wake of the failed August coup by hard-liners in Moscow.

Chair Landsbergis attempted to secure sweeping new executive powers in a referendum on May 23, 1992, but a participation rate of less than half of the electorate doomed the proposal. Prime Minister Gediminas VAGNORIUS, who had succeeded Prunskienė following the five-day interim incumbency of Albertas ŠIMINAS, resigned, effective May 28, 1992, because of "destructive left-wing forces" that were allegedly inhibiting government efforts "to stabilize the economy, reform the legal system, and manage the country's finances." However, he continued in office on a caretaker basis until the approval of a new government under Aleksandras ABIŠALA on July 23. In the country's first election since independence, held in two stages on October 25 and November 15, 1992, Lithuanian voters turned away from *Sajūdis* and awarded a parliamentary majority to the Brazauskas-led Lithuanian Democratic Labor Party (*Lietuvos Demokratinė Darbo Partija*—LDDP), which had been formed in 1990 by the secessionist wing of the Lithuanian Communist Party. In a simultaneous referendum, the electorate gave 78 percent approval to a new constitution. On November 25 Brazauskas was elected chair of Parliament (*Seimas*) and, as such, acting president of the republic. Confirmed in office by direct balloting on February 15, 1993, he named Adolfas ŠLEŽEVIČIUS on March 10 to succeed Abišala as prime minister.

A major political crisis developed in January 1996 over disclosures that the prime minister had withdrawn his personal savings of roughly $34,000 from a Lithuanian bank two days before its operations had been suspended by the central bank because of financial irregularities. Denying any wrongdoing, Šleževičius rejected opposition calls for his resignation and was backed by the LDDP council. However, eroding support among LDDP deputies culminated on February 8 with the *Seimas* approving, by 94 votes to 24, a presidential decree calling for his resignation, whereupon Laurynas Mindaugas STANKEVIČIUS, the minister of administrative reforms and municipal affairs, was named to succeed him. Following the parliamentary endorsement of Stankevičius a week later, a new LDDP government was announced by the president on February 23.

Despite a limited economic upturn in 1996, the LDDP government went down to a comprehensive defeat in legislative elections on October 20 and November 10, retaining only 12 seats out of the 137 filled. The turnout was only 53 percent in the first round and little more than 40 percent in the second. In a decisive swing to the right, the Homeland Union (Lithuanian Conservatives) (*Tėvynės Sąjunga [Lietuvos Konservatoriai]*—TS[LK]), which had been launched in 1993 as a partial successor to *Sajūdis,* won an overall majority of 70 seats, while other center-right parties also polled strongly. Meanwhile, in four referenda held on October 20, assorted LDDP proposals for constitutional and electoral reform all failed to obtain majority support.

The TS(LK) leader, former chair Landsbergis, was accordingly elected unopposed to the powerful post of chair of the *Seimas* when it reconvened on November 25, 1996, following confirmation that the TS(LK) had opted to govern in alliance with the Lithuanian Christian Democratic Party (*Lietuvos Krikščionių Demokratų Partija*—LKDP) rather than alone. Negotiations between the two parties yielded a formal coalition agreement by early December, and on December 10 a new government received legislative endorsement by 87 votes to 21 and was sworn in. Headed by former prime minister Vagnorius, it included 11 additional TS(LK) ministers and 3 from the LKDP, with two portfolios being allocated to the Lithuanian Center Union (*Lietuvos Centro Sąjunga*—LCS).

The TS(LK) continued its steady political progress in the March 1997 local elections, securing 33 percent of the seats, compared to 14 percent for the LDDP. Seven candidates contested the subsequent presidential election, with incumbent Brazauskas having declined to run for reelection. In first-round balloting on December 21, Artūras PAULAUSKAS, a former prosecutor, secured 44.7 percent of the vote, followed by Valdas ADAMKUS with 28 percent and TS(LK) leader Landsbergis with 16 percent. With Landsbergis's support, Adamkus squeaked out a victory in the second round of balloting on January 4, 1998, winning 50.3 percent of the vote. Adamkus, who had worked for Lithuanian independence during four decades in exile in the United States, was inaugurated on February 26. Prime Minister Vagnorius submitted his resignation, but Adamkus subsequently reappointed him to head a reshuffled cabinet that was confirmed by the *Seimas* on March 10.

Vagnorius's reappointment initially appeared to signal continuity in the government's emphasis on economic reform and anticorruption measures. However, over the next year severe discord developed between Adamkus and Vagnorius on several fronts, most notably the president's contention that his office should be accorded greater responsibility in the interest of the "modernization of the state." Adamkus also urged that greater authority be given to elected local officials, arguing that the TS(LK) administration had adopted a "Soviet-style" approach to government that imposed policies from the top. Consequently, in mid-April Adamkus announced that he had lost confidence in Vagnorius and urged him and his cabinet to resign. Although the prime minister argued that he was being unfairly vilified for having resisted Adamkus's attempts to "usurp" power, he announced his resignation on April 30 and was replaced on an interim basis by Social Welfare and Labor Minister Irena DEGUTIENĖ. Adamkus then tapped the TS(LK) mayor of Vilnius, Rolandas PAKSAS, who was confirmed as prime minister on May 18, and a new cabinet of TS(LK), LKDP, LCS, and independent ministers was sworn in on June 12. The new administration proved short-lived, however, with Paksas resigning on October 27 because of his opposition to sale of a one-third stake in the country's largest enterprise, the Mažeikiai oil refinery, to U.S.-based Williams International. The ministers of economy and finance also resigned, although the majority of the cabinet as well as President Adamkus supported the arrangement. When Paksas's interim replacement, Degutienė, declined the prime ministership, Adamkus instead nominated Andrius KUBILIUS of the TS(LK), who was confirmed by the *Seimas* on November 3. Five days later the LCS announced that it was leaving the government, although its one minister instead quit the party and remained in the cabinet.

Following a poor showing by the TS(LK) in the March 2000 local election, a group of about a dozen deputies led by former prime minister Vagnorius established a Moderate Conservative faction within the *Seimas,* thereby costing the TS(LK) its majority status. Formation of the Moderate Conservative Union (*Nuosaikiųjų Konservatorių Sąjunga*—NKS) followed in May. In the same month, President Adamkus announced a legislative election for October 8, and the LDDP, the Lithuanian Social Democratic Party (*Lietuvos Socialdemokratų Partija*—LSDP), and two smaller parties agreed to forge an electoral alliance headed by former president Brazauskas. In the October balloting Prime Minister Kubilius's TS(LK) won only 9 seats (down from 70 in 1996), while the A. Brazauskas Social Democratic Coalition (*A. Brazausko Socialdemokratinė Koalicija*—ABSK) won a plurality of proportional seats. Nevertheless, the ABSK parties' overall total of 51 deputies proved insufficient to form a government. President Adamkus then turned to former prime minister Paksas and his four-party "New Policy" (*Naujosios Politikos*) bloc of the Lithuanian Liberal Union (*Lietuvos Liberalų Sąjunga*—LLS), the New Union (Social Liberals) (*Naujoji Sąjunga* [Socialliberalai]—NS[SL]), the LCS, and the Modern Christian Democratic Union (*Moderniųjų Krikščionių Demokratų Sąjunga*—MKDS). Confirmed for the second time as prime minister on October 26, Paksas announced that his new administration's priorities would be education, economic liberalization and tax reform, government restructuring, and European integration.

However, discord over economic policy and privatization brought a quick end to Paksas's tenure. On June 18, 2001, the NS(SL) leader and *Seimas* chair, Artūras Paulauskas, called for Paksas to step down; collaterally, the six NS(SL)-selected cabinet ministers resigned. Paksas tendered his own resignation two days later, with the LLS minister of the economy, Eugenijus GENTVILAS, then assuming Paksas's duties on an acting basis. The end to Prime Minister Paksas's second brief term in office came about not only because of policy differences between his LLS and Artūras Paulauskas's NS(SL) but also because of the two leaders' political rivalry. On July 3 the *Seimas* confirmed former president Brazauskas as prime minister at the head of a coalition of the LSDP (with which the LDDP had merged in January) and the NS(SL), the new cabinet being announced on July 5.

In first-round presidential balloting on December 22, 2002, President Adamkus led 17 candidates with 35.5 percent of the vote, followed by Paksas (19.7 percent) and Paulauskas (8.3 percent). However, Paksas defeated Adamkus in the runoff election on January 5, 2003, with 54.7 percent of the vote. Prime Minister Brazauskas was reconfirmed on March 6 to head another (only slightly reshuffled) LSDP-NS(SL) coalition government.

In late 2003 President Paksas became embroiled in a controversy concerning his alleged links with a shadowy figure, Yurii BORISOV, who was reputed to have ties to organized crime (see Current issues, below). After a special legislative committee alleged that Paksas had, in addition to other charges, jeopardized national security, impeachment proceedings were launched in December, resulting in six formal charges against Paksas in February 2004. After Paksas rejected calls for his resignation, the *Seimas* on April 6 found him guilty by large margins of three charges and removed him from office. As mandated by the constitution, Paulauskas (the chair of the *Seimas*) assumed presidential authority on an acting basis.

The first round of a new presidential election was held on June 13, 2004, with Adamkus winning 30.7 percent of the vote, followed by Kazimiera PRUNSKIENĖ of the Union of the Peasants and New Democracy Party (*Valstiečių ir Naujosios Demokratijos Partiju Sąjunga*—VNDPS) with 21.4 percent. (Prunskienė was supported by Paksas after the *Seimas* had ruled that Paksas could not be a candidate.) Adamkus secured the presidency in a second round on June 27 with 52.6 percent of the vote.

Following Lithuania's accession to the EU on May 1, 2004, the recently formed Labor Party (*Darbo Partija*—DP) burst onto the electoral scene with a strong performance in the June 2004 elections for the European Parliament. It continued its ascendancy in the *Seimas* balloting on October 10 and 24, leading all parties with 39 seats. After lengthy negotiations, Prime Minister Brazauskas was reappointed to head a new coalition government (inaugurated on December 14) comprising the DP, LSDP, NS(SL), and VNDPS.

In April 2006 the ruling coalition barely survived a crisis when the NS(SL) pulled out and removed its members from the cabinet. This action was precipitated when coalition partners voted to oust parliamentary chair and NS(SL) member Artūras Paulauskas in a no-confidence vote on April 11. In the ensuing negotiations among the remaining coalition partners, the DP won the vacated cabinet post for social security and labor, while the Lithuanian National Farmers' Union (*Lietuvos Valstiečių Liaudininkų Sajunga*—LVLS, as the VNDPS had been renamed) won the prestigious foreign affairs ministry. However, the government collapsed in late May when the DP withdrew from the coalition amid severe internal party turmoil (see Current issues and Political Parties, below). Prime Minister Brazauskas tendered his resignation on June 1, and President Adamkus nominated Finance Minister Zigmantas BALCYTIS as acting prime minister. After Balcytis failed to secure a majority of legislative votes to make the appointment permanent, President Adamkus subsequently tapped Defense Minister Gediminas KIRKILAS, who was confirmed by the *Seimas* on July 4, 2006. A new minority cabinet (comprising the LSDP, LVLS, LCS, and the recently formed Civil Democracy Party [*Pilietinės Demokratijos Partija*—PDP]) was approved on July 18 with the government subsequently depending upon TS members to honor their agreement not to obstruct the minority government from ruling. The NS(SL) rejoined the governing coalition in February 2008, ahead of elections slated for October 12.

Widespread discontent with the rapidly souring economy led to the defeat of the ruling LSDP-led coalition in balloting on October 12 and 16, 2008. The TS-LKD emerged the winner with 45 seats, and composed a government led by Andrius KUBILIUS, including the LRLS, the LCS, and the recently formed National Revival Party (*Tautos Prisikėlimo Partijos*—TPP) (see Political Parties, below). The inclusion of the TPP reflected the strength of populist sentiment against the establishment parties, and support for the TS-LKD and the TPP was echoed in the June 2009 elections to the European Parliament.

On May 17, 2009, Dalia GRYBAUSKAITĖ won the first round of presidential elections with 51.7 percent of votes, convincingly besting her nearest opponent, Algirdas BUTKEVICIUS of the LSDP, who won 11.9 percent. Grybauskaitė took office on July 12. Kubilius was reappointed as prime minister on July 15.

Constitution and government. The 1992 constitution accords primacy, as representing the sovereignty of the people, to a Parliament (*Seimas*) elected for a four-year term, although significant powers, particularly in the sphere of foreign policy, are allocated to the president, who is directly elected for a five-year term. The president appoints the prime minister and, on the latter's nomination, other ministers, all subject to the approval of the *Seimas*. The judicial structure is headed by a Constitutional Court and a Supreme Court, whose judges are selected by the *Seimas* from presidential nominations. Members of district and local courts are appointed by the president.

Government at the local level currently encompasses 10 counties (*apskritys*), which are centrally directed and supervised; 44 rural and 12 urban municipalities, which are self-governing; and 500 neighborhoods. The 56 self-governing units elect local councils, with each council then selecting an executive.

Foreign relations. Soviet recognition of the independence of the Baltic states on September 6, 1991, paved the way for admission of the three to the Conference on (later Organization for) Security and Cooperation in Europe (CSCE/OSCE) on September 10 and admission to the United Nations on September 17. More than 30 governments had recognized Lithuania during late August, though Washington's failure to do so until September 2 visibly annoyed Chair Landsbergis.

Regionally, Lithuania concluded a Baltic Economic Cooperation Agreement with Estonia and Latvia in April 1990. On September 24, 1991, the three states also reached agreement on a customs union that authorized free trade and visa-free travel among their respective jurisdictions, although implementation of its provisions proceeded very slowly. Lithuania was also a founding member of the broader Council of the Baltic Sea States in 1992.

On July 31, 1991, President Landsbergis and Russian President Boris Yeltsin signed an agreement giving Russia rights of transit across Lithuania to its Baltic enclave of Kaliningrad. Subsequently, on February 16, 1992, Landsbergis demanded that former Soviet troops be withdrawn from Kaliningrad on the grounds that their presence had become a "historic anachronism." While firmly rejecting this demand, Russia entered into negotiations on the withdrawal of its troops from Lithuania, where a referendum on June 14 gave 90 percent endorsement to the government's position. Yeltsin responded on September 8 by agreeing to a full withdrawal by August 31, 1993. Despite some last-minute uncertainty, the deadline was met by the Russians, with President Brazauskas having waived a $140 billion compensation claim lodged by his predecessor. Under an economic cooperation agreement concluded on March 6, Russia undertook to supply oil, natural gas, and nuclear energy to Lithuania in exchange for agricultural and manufactured goods. In October 1999 the *Seimas* ratified a border treaty that had been negotiated in 1997, but in June 2000 the legislature also passed a resolution seeking compensation for 50 years of Soviet occupation, the cost of which was later estimated at $20 billion. Relations nevertheless remained cordial, with Presidents Adamkus and Vladimir Putin taking a common tack in March 2001 on the status of Kaliningrad and the free movement of the region's residents through Lithuania.

Independent Lithuania moved quickly to reestablish historically close relations with Poland, concluding on January 13, 1992, a joint Declaration on Friendly Relations and Cooperation that included a number of economic and ecological provisions and confirmed the existing border between the two countries. In April 1994 President Lech Wałęsa became the first Polish head of state to visit Lithuania in over a century, signing a treaty of friendship and cooperation in Vilnius. In February 1995 President Brazauskas paid a reciprocal visit to Warsaw, which was followed in September by a bilateral accord envisaging that Lithuania would accede to the Central European Free Trade Agreement (CEFTA/Visegrad Group). Lithuania's relations with Moscow-aligned Belarus were more problematic: an economic cooperation agreement concluded on April 2, 1992, included a confirmation of the existing border, but a widely quoted statement by the Belarus defense minister in March had included territorial claims on Lithuania. Relations with Belarus were further complicated when all three Baltic nations condemned the widespread fraud and repression leading up to the March 2006 elections, which resulted in the reelection of President Alyaksandr Lukashenka.

A prime ministerial visit to Israel in October 1994 was intended to consolidate a government apology made the previous month for Lithuania's wartime role in the Nazi genocide of European Jewry. The visit followed heated controversy over the decision of the immediate post-Soviet government to exonerate convicted war criminals on the grounds that Soviet-era trials had been coercive and lacking due process. Under international pressure, incoming President Brazauskas had in March 1993 announced a review of pardons issued by the previous government. Tension between Lithuania and Israel again flared when in March 2006 the Vilnius District Court found Nazi collaborator Algimantas Dailidė guilty of genocide, but failed to impose any punishment due to the defendant's poor health and old age.

Having joined the Council of Europe in May 1993, Lithuania became a signatory of the North Atlantic Treaty Organization's (NATO) Partnership for Peace in January 1994, subsequently reiterating its desire for full membership and also for eventual accession to the EU. In the latter context, Lithuania and the other two Baltic states in July 1995 became the first ex-Soviet republics to sign "Europe" (i.e., association) agreements with the EU, offering the prospect of eventual full membership, for which Lithuania submitted a formal application on December 8.

Lithuania was not among the three countries invited in July 1997 by NATO to join the alliance in 1999, strong Russian objections to such expansion contributing significantly to NATO's decision to proceed slowly. However, NATO officials announced that they considered Lithuania and the other two Baltic states to be strong candidates for eventual membership. Lithuanian leaders were also disappointed (albeit not surprised) that Lithuania was not included on the list of countries invited in December by the EU to begin membership negotiations in 1998. However, the EU agreed that talks would continue toward Lithuania's inclusion in the "second wave" of expansion. In October 1999 the EU abandoned the second wave concept and then announced in December that Lithuania could proceed with accession negotiations.

The three Baltic states signed the U.S.-Baltic Charter of Partnership on January 16, 1998, in which Washington affirmed the three nations' sovereignty (without making any military commitments), supported the integration of the trio into Western institutions, and approved three bilateral working groups to advance cooperation. In December the Lithuanian Parliament abolished the death penalty and also began to consider the possible closure of the Ignalina nuclear power plant, which EU members considered obsolete and dangerous; both actions were considered necessary to improve EU membership prospects for Lithuania. In September 1999 Lithuania agreed to decommission one of Ignalina's two reactors by 2005, contingent on receiving sufficient aid toward the $2.5 billion cost.

Lithuania was formally invited in November 2002 to join NATO, and the EU issued a similar invitation in December. On May 10 and 11, 2003, 91 percent of Lithuanian voters approved of joining the EU in a national referendum. On March 10, 2004, the *Seimas* approved NATO accession by a vote of 100–3, and Lithuania joined NATO on March 29. EU accession followed on May 1, and in November Lithuania became the first EU member to approve (by an 84–4 vote in the *Seimas*) the proposed (and ultimately unsuccessful) new EU constitution. The *Seimas* also ratified the EU's new proposed Lisbon Treaty in May 2008. As of 2008, euro adoption was expected no earlier than 2013. Lithuania's European involvement continued in other ways as it participated in a number of NATO operations, including missions in the Balkans and Afghanistan. Lithuania also contributed 330 troops to support the U.S./UK-led coalition in Iraq following the ouster of Saddam Hussein. The last Lithuanian troops left Iraq at the end of 2008, while 16 additional Lithuanian troops joined the 100-strong force in Afghanistan that fall.

Lithuania's relationship with the United States is expected to remain cooperative, with President Obama emphasizing his continued support for Lithuanian security in a conference call in June 2009. U.S. attempts to seek rapprochement with Russia, however, could encourage anxiety on the part of the conservative government. While President Grybauskaitė has indicated her intention to engage Russia in a measured way, relations, which have been strained since Lithuania's independence, are unlikely to improve substantially, particularly as Russia seeks to maintain Lithuania's dependence on its energy sector.

Current issues. Two paramount domestic challenges facing Lithuania recently have been corruption and government instability. In October 2003 documents were discovered that allegedly linked President Paksas to Yurii BORISOV, an ethnic Russian alleged to have ties with organized crime. Among other things, it was alleged that Paksas had granted Borisov dual citizenship, despite reported concerns from Lithuanian security services that Borisov might have been involved in smuggling arms. President Paksas's critics charged that Borisov had contributed heavily to Paksas's political finances. In November an emergency session of the *Seimas* established a special committee to investigate the matter, and in December the *Seimas* accepted the committee's report alleging that Paksas had jeopardized national security. After Paksas was removed from office by the *Seimas* in April, the *Seimas* ruled that Paksas could not participate in the upcoming balloting to fill the presidency. In October 2004 Paksas was acquitted of criminal charges of revealing state secrets, and he vowed to return to politics. However, that goal appeared to be compromised in November when a court in Vilnius found Borisov guilty of blackmailing Paksas while Paksas was president.

In June 2005 the leader of the Labor Party, Viktor USPASKICH, was dismissed from the post of economy minister after being charged with fraudulent campaign finance practices. In April 2006 the *Seimas* ousted NS(SL) leader Artūras Paulauskas from the office of speaker, accusing him of insufficient efforts to curb abuse of power within the *Seimas*. The speaker's party responded by leaving the government. After President Adamkus expressed no confidence in two DP ministers, Prime Minister Brazauskas resigned as well, saying the coalition could no longer function. Finance Minister Balcytis failed to secure *Seimas* support to extend his acting prime ministership, and President Adamkus nominated Defense Minister Kirkilas to replace him and form a new cabinet. Nevertheless, the government remained fragile, with parties opposed to early elections but frequently in conflict over policy direction. Kirkilas barred the DP from rejoining the ruling parties until all corruption investigations were resolved.

In addition to the campaign finance scandal, the DP was often viewed as being a friend of the Russian state. The ouster of Viktor Uspaskich had added significance because as economy minister he would have been responsible for overseeing negotiations with Russia for the sale of stock in Lithuania's sole oil refinery, which the Russians reportedly wanted to buy below market value. In May 2006 it was announced that a Polish company would be the buyer, after which the Russian pipeline supplying the refinery suffered a rupture. Critics accused Russia of deliberately inflicting the damage, which was not expected to be repaired until 2009, if at all, since the refinery had been quickly refitted to use tankers for oil shipments in what was seen as a strategic move by Lithuania for greater energy independence.

Energy remained a key concern in 2009, as the EU mandated closing of an outdated nuclear power plant by the end of the year, raising domestic concerns that electricity supply and prices would subsequently challenge ordinary Lithuanians, as well as render Lithuania dependent on a single source for energy. In July Baltic and Polish energy companies agreed to develop a nuclear plant on the same site by 2015. In the meantime, groups including UTT argued that the deadline for closure should be extended.

Lithuania continued to experience government instability throughout 2007. The coalition expanded to include the NS(SL) in February 2008, giving it a slight majority. However, policy disagreements within the LSDP and ideological diversity within the coalition slowed government progress, particularly in responding to the economic crisis. The speaker of the *Seimas,* Viktoras MUNTIANAS, was forced to resign in March in the wake of bribery charges.

Despite public aversion to corruption, parties accused of impropriety, such as the DP, remained popular, and a number of populist parties gained strength ahead of the 2008 balloting, in tandem with strikes by public sector workers and teachers demanding wage hikes in a difficult economic climate. This prompted the organization by celebrities of the new, centrist TPP in an effort to ensure moderate government (see Political Parties, below). Nonetheless, the TS-LKD won the 2008 balloting. The resultant center-right coalition government that came into power in October 2008 enacted a crisis package during its first session in December 2008.

The victory of former EU commissioner Grybauskaitė in the 2009 presidential elections was largely attributed to her reputation as a competent manager who operated above ideological considerations. She is reported to have a plan for reorganizing the cabinet. The president also endorsed cuts in pensions and family benefits in an effort to shore up the country's finances, guaranteeing lively political debate in the *Seimas* during 2009–2010. The conservative government was reappointed by Grybauskaitė and confirmed by the parliament on July 16.

POLITICAL PARTIES

The constitutional revision of March 11, 1990, effectively revoked the monopoly of the Lithuanian Communist Party (*Lietuvos Komunistų Partija*—LKP). In August 1991 the party itself was banned and its property confiscated, although its secessionist wing had long since withdrawn to form the Lithuanian Democratic Labor Party (LDDP; see LSDP). Legislation was approved in early 1999 for government funds to be allocated to parties demonstrating backing from at least 3 percent of the voters.

Government Parties:

Homeland Union-Lithuanian Christian Democrats (*Tėvynės Sąjunga-Lietuvos Krikščionys Demokratai*—TS-LKD) The TS-LKD was formed as **In the Name of Lithuania** (*Vardan Lietuvos*—VL) in February 2008 by the TS and LKD as an electoral coalition designed to improve rightist prospects ahead of the October legislative balloting. The parties officially merged in May 2008 and decisively won elections in October that year, taking 19.7 percent of votes and 45 seats, with the social democratic rival, the LSDP, following with 25 seats. The TS-TKD leads the governing coalition with the TPP, LRLS, and LCS and adopted its current name in May 2008. It won a 26.1 percent plurality of votes in the June 2009 European Parliament elections.

Leaders: Andrius KUBILIUS (Prime Minister and TS Chair), Valentinas STUNDYS (LKD Chair) Jurgis RAZMA (Parliamentary Elder), Valentinas STUNDYS (Deputy Elder), Arvydas VIDŽIŪNAS (Deputy Elder).

Homeland Union (*Tėvynės Sąjunga*—TS). The TS is the current name of the party formerly known as the Homeland Union (Lithuanian Conservatives) (TS [*Lietuvos Konservatoriai*]—TS[LK]), which was launched on May 1, 1993, as a partial successor to the Lithuanian Reform Movement (*Sajūdis*), the party that had spearheaded the independence campaign. Under the leadership of Vytautas Landsbergis, the broadly based *Sajūdis* was the leading formation in the elections of February and March 1990 but in the face of economic adversity suffered a stinging defeat in 1992, winning only 20.5 percent of the vote. Although the TS(LK) presented itself as a right-of-center party, it indicated that its ranks would be open to former Communists.

Benefiting from the deep unpopularity of the then ruling LDDP, the TS(LK) rose to power in the fall 1996 election with a 30 percent vote share, but Landsbergis finished a disappointing third with 15.7 percent of the vote in the first round of the presidential balloting in December. The TS(LK) renewed its 1996 coalition agreement with the Lithuanian Christian Democratic Party (LKDP; see LKD, below) in January 1999; the Lithuanian Center Union (LCS, above) also remained in the government until departing in November 1999, shortly after the TS(LK)'s Andrius Kubilius had been confirmed as prime minister, in succession to Rolandas Paksas.

Following a poor showing in the March 2000 local election, a group of about a dozen deputies loyal to former TS(LK) prime minister Gediminas Vagnorius established a Moderate Conservative faction within the *Seimas,* thereby costing the TS(LK) its majority status. Formation of the NKS splinter (below) followed. In the October 2000 parliamentary election the TS(LK) won only one constituency seat but won eight more on an 8.6 percent proportional vote share.

In November 2003 the TS(LK) absorbed the LDS (below). In February the party dropped the "Lithuanian Conservatives" from its name and became known simply as the TS. In the October 2004 legislative balloting, the TS won 25 seats, thereby becoming the second-largest grouping in the *Seimas.* After DP deputies resigned from the government in May 2006, the LSPD-led government no longer controlled a legislative majority government without the cooperation of the TS, which remained outside the cabinet. However, in response to concerns that the party's support for the government was harming its standing with the TS base voters, the TS ended its official support for the government in September 2007. Members of the party went further in their opposition in April 2008, pushing for a vote of no confidence in the prime minister (see Current issues, above).

Leaders: Andrius KUBILIUS (Prime Minister, Chair, and 2002 presidential candidate), Vytautas LANDSBERGIS (Former President of the Republic), Rasa JUKNEVIČIENĖ (Deputy Chair), Arvydas VIDŽIŪNAS (General Secretary), Irena DEGUTIENĖ and Jurgis RAZMA (Parliamentary Leaders).

Lithuanian Rightist Union (*Lietuvos Dešiniųjų Sąjunga*—LDS). The LDS was formed in October 2001 by merger of four small parties, none represented in the current *Seimas*: the Homeland People's Party (*Tėvynės Liaudies Partija*—TLP), the Independence Party (*Nepriklausombyės Partija*—NP), the Lithuanian Democratic Party (*Lietuvos Demokratų Partija*—LDP), and the Lithuanian Freedom League (*Lietuvos Laisvės Lyga*—LLL).

The TLP held its founding congress in December 1999 under the leadership of Laima ANDRIKIENĖ. Described by one of its founders as a "classical right-wing party," the LDS supports European integration, market economics, and close cooperation with the TS(LK), Christian Democrats, and other like-minded formations. The LDS was absorbed by the TS(LK) in 2003 (see TS, above).

Leaders: Arūnas ŽEBRIŪNAS (Chair), Laima ANDRIKIENĖ, Saulius PEČELIŪNAS (LDP), Valentinas ŠAPALAS (NP), Antanas TERLECKAS (LLL).

Lithuanian Christian Democrats (*Lietuvos Krikščionys Demokratai*—LKD). The LKD was formed in May 2001 by merger of the Lithuanian Christian Democratic Party (*Lietuvos Krikščionių Demokratų Partija*—LKDP) and the Christian Democratic Union (*Krikščionių Demokratų Sąjunga*—KDS).

The LKDP had been organized in 1989 as the revival of a pre-Soviet party originally formed in 1905. It ran third in the 1992 balloting on a joint list with the Lithuanian Democratic Party (LDP; see LDS, above) and the Lithuanian Union of Political Prisoners and Deportees (LPKTS, below). It won a total of 16 seats, for second place, in 1996 and joined the TS(LK)-led coalition government. In the October 2000 election, however, it secured only 2 seats. A month later the party chair, Zigmas ZINKEVIČIUS, resigned over what he labeled as secret merger negotiations being conducted by the party's board chair, Algirdas SAUDARGAS, with the KDS. A smaller formation, the KDS had won a single parliamentary seat in 1992, 1996, and 2000; its deputy, Kazys Bobelis, had also won 4 percent of the vote in the 1997 presidential balloting. The LKD improved its performance in the 2007 local elections and sought even better electoral prospects with its May 2008 merger with the TS.

Leaders: Kazys BOBELIS (2002 and 2004 presidential candidate), Valentinas STUNDYS (Chair), Kazimieras KUZMINSKAS (Deputy Chair).

National Revival Party (*Tautos Prisikėlimo Partijos*—TPP). Founded in May 2008 by entertainment producer and personality Arūnas Valinskas, the TPP sought to capitalize on voter apathy toward parliamentary parties and advance a centrist program in support of strategic relationships with Europe and the United States. The TPP announced that it would "seek to have Lithuania become a leader among the Baltic States." The party's first congress lacked the required 1,000 founding members, despite generally positive attitudes toward the party among the public and the support of many Lithuanian celebrities. However, the party filed the required papers with the justice ministry in June 2008, targeting disaffected voters in order to prevent UTT Chair Rolandas Paksas from returning to power in a populist revolt. The new party proved remarkably successful in its first balloting in October of that year, securing 15.1 percent of votes, 16 seats, and three cabinet portfolios as a member of the ruling coalition. The TPP chair, Arūnas Valinskas, was named speaker of the *Seimas* and is a noted celebrity, having starred in TV shows for 22 years and organized the first beauty contest for a women's prison in Lithuania, Miss Captivity.

Despite initial momentum, the TPP won only 1.01 percent of votes in the June 2009 European Parliament elections, in which 20.9 percent of the Lithuanian electorate voted.

Leaders: Arūnas VALINSKAS (Founder, Chair, and Speaker of the *Seimas*), Laimontas DINIUS (Parliamentary Elder), Jonas STANEVIČIUS (First Deputy Elder), Donalda MEIŽELYTĖ SVILIENĖ (Deputy Elder), Aleksandr SACHARUK (Deputy Elder).

Liberal and Center Union (*Liberalųir Centro Sąjunga*—LCS). Formed in March 2003 via the merger of the three parties below, the LCS is also referred to as the Liberal Centrists. LCS leader Artūra Zoukas was reelected as mayor of Vilnius in June 2003, though he later faced allegations that he accepted bribes in exchange for municipal influence. In response, nine LCS legislators rejected Zoukas's leadership and formed the new LRLS (below).

The LCS gained 18 seats in the October 2004 legislative elections, but the merger lapsed in 2005. The electoral coalition subsequently saw its representation fall to 8 seats and 5.3 percent of votes in the 2008 elections. Following the expulsion of LLS members by the LCS members, the union was in ruins in 2009, despite the exit of the combative former LCS chair, Artūra Zoukas, who did not stand for reelection during the LCS congress on June 27, 2009 (see LCS, below). Both major parties retained an electoral interest in preserving the coalition, although party members charged that the leadership prolonged divisions in order to preserve their positions in the existing hierarchies. Leverage for any future negotiations belonged to the LLS in 2009, which enjoyed higher public support. The LCS lost both of its seats in the June European Parliamentary elections.

Leaders: Gintautas BABRAVIČIUS (LCS Chair and Deputy Mayor of Vilnius), Artūra ZOUKAS (Former LCS Chair, Parliamentary Elder, and Mayor of Vilnius), Vytautas BOGUŠIS (Deputy Elder), Žilvinas ŠILGALIS (Deputy Elder).

Lithuanian Liberal Union (*Lietuvos Liberalų Sajunga*—LLS). The founding congress of the moderately right-wing LLS took place in November 1990, but the party failed to win any parliamentary seats in 1992. In 1996 it garnered one. Following a solid performance in the March 1997 local elections, the LLS attempted to position itself as a leader of Lithuanian centrists, broadening its appeal beyond its base in the business community. In December 1999 former prime minister Rolandas Paksas, having resigned from the TS(LK), joined the LLS and quickly ascended to chair.

In the October 2000 election the party made major gains, winning 17.3 percent of the proportional vote, second only to the ABSK. The LLS then led the New Policy bloc in forming a government under Paksas (see Political background, above), but the coalition dissolved in June 2001 when the NS(SL) parted ways with the LLS. In early September, pressured by the party's governing body, Paksas resigned as party chair. At an extraordinary congress held on October 27 Paksas was defeated in his campaign for chair but accepted the post of first deputy chair. In late December 2001 Paksas and ten other deputies announced that they intended to leave the LLS, in part because of a dispute about selecting the party's standard-bearer for the 2002 presidential race. In March the LLS defectors formed the LDP (see UTT, below). The then chair, Eligijus MASIULIS, saw the former chair of the LCS, Artūra Zoukas, as an obstacle to complete the union with the LCS, and subsequently joined the Lithuanian Republic Liberal Movement (*Lietuvos Respublikos Liberalų Sajūdis*—LRLS), which was formed in 2006.

Progress in reuniting with the LCS seemed more likely with the ascendance of Gintautas Babravičius, Zoukas's successor, who was viewed as less divisive. The leadership for the LLS appeared to be vacant following Masiulis's switch to the LRLS.

Lithuanian Center Union (*Lietuvos Centro Sąjunga*—LCS). The LCS originated in 1992 as the Lithuanian Center Movement (*Lietuvos Centro Judėjimas*—LCJ), which contested the 1992 election on a promarket platform and won 2 *Seimas* seats. Registered as the LCS in 1993, the party went on to win 13 seats in 1996 and then joined the center-right TS(LK) coalition government in December. In the subsequent presidential election it backed Valdas Adamkus.

In November 1999 LCS Chair Romualdas OZOLAS announced that the LCS was breaking with the government; in response, the LCS minister of justice, Gintautas Babravičius, left the party and remained in the cabinet. In the October 2000 election the LCS won only two seats, which led to Ozolas's resignation. As part of the New Policy bloc, it joined the second Paksas government. The party's most recent congress was held on June 27, 2009, in which Gintautas Babravičius, then the deputy mayor of Vilinus, replaced Artūra Zoukas, mayor of Vilinus, as chair. Babravičius emphasized the strategic advantages of a full merger of the LCS constituent parties.

Leaders: Gintautas BABRAVIČIUS (Chair and Deputy Mayor of Vilinus), Artūra ZOUKAS (Mayor of Vilinus and former chair).

Modern Christian Democratic Union (*Moderniųjų Krikščionių Demokratų Sąjunga*—MKDS). The constituent congress of the MKDS was held in April 2000 following the decision of the "modern" faction of the Lithuanian Christian Democratic Party (LKDP) to part ways with the "conservative" faction. Differences had emerged in fall 1999, but the LKDP held together until after the March 2000 local elections. The MKDS won one parliamentary seat in October 2000 and has now been absorbed.

Lithuanian Republic Liberal Movement (*Lietuvos Respublikos Liberalų Sajūdis*—LRLS). Also widely referenced as simply the Liberal Movement, the LRLS was formed in early 2006 after nine LCS legislators rejected the leadership of LCS Chair and Vilnius Mayor Artūras Zoukas. However, at the LRLS congress in June 2007, the party endorsed a united liberal ballot for the 2008 *Seimas* elections. In response to the motion, the LCS replied that LRLS members were welcome to return to the party at will.

Despite the apparent failure of the motion, the LRLS won 5.7 percent of votes and 11 seats in the October 2008 general election and was included in the cabinet after joining the ruling coalition. The party continues to operate independently of the LCS. In 2009 it appeared that the LRLS was not a successor party to the LLS, despite the fact that some of the LLS leadership, notably Eligijus Masiulis, had migrated to the LRLS, and media references to the LLS continued in 2009. The LRLS won 7.16 percent of votes and one seat in the 2009 European Parliament balloting,

Leaders: Petras AUSTREVICIUS (Chair), Eligijus MASIULIS (Deputy Chair and Minister for Transportation and Communication), Mindaugus SADAUSKUS (Secretary General), Audrius ENDZINAS (Parliamentary Elder), Erikas TAMAŠAUSKAS (Deputy Elder), Dalia TEIŠERSKYTĖ (Deputy Elder).

Opposition Parties:

Lithuanian Social Democratic Party (*Lietuvos Socialdemokratų Partija*—LSDP). The present LSDP was established by merger in January 2001 of the existing LSDP and the Lithuanian Democratic Labor Party (*Lietuvos Demokratinė Darbo Partija*—LDDP). Together, they had formed the backbone of the A. Brazauskas Social Democratic Coalition (*A. Brazausko Socialdemokratinė Koalicija*—ABSK), which had been established to present a consolidated list for the proportional component of the October 2000 legislative election. The other ABSK participants were the NDP, VNDPS, and LRS.

The premerger LSDP was formed in 1896 and reestablished in 1989, winning a 5.9 percent vote share in the 1992 balloting. The LDDP was formed in 1990 by a faction of the former Lithuanian Communist Party (LKP) that initially supported Soviet President Gorbachev's reformist program and subsequently endorsed independence for Lithuania. The LDDP scored a surprising victory in the 1992 parliamentary balloting, winning 42.6 percent of the vote on a platform of gradual transition to a market economy; the party's leader, Algirdas Brazauskas, was subsequently confirmed as president. Considerable party turmoil accompanied the government crisis and ouster of Prime Minister Adolfas ŠLEŽEVIČIUS in early 1996, which led to disastrous returns in the subsequent *Seimas* election: LDDP representation fell to 9.5%.

In the October 2000 election the ABSK won a 31 percent vote share. Following the January 2001 LSDP-LDDP merger, Brazauskas had sufficient leverage to form a new administration with the NS(SL) when the latter party's coalition with the LLS dissolved in June. The LSDP presented joint candidates with the NS(SL) in the 2004 legislative balloting, after which Brazauskas continued as prime minister. The NS(SL) left the government in April 2006, and the ruling LSDP/LVLS/DP coalition collapsed due to DP resignations on June 1. Gediminas Kirkilas, then the national defense minister, was nominated by President Adamkus to form a new LSPD-led minority government. Brazauskas, now retired, subsequently endorsed Kirkilas for the party chair. He was elected to the position during the 2007 party congress, though he was expected to be less influential than his predecessor. Nevertheless, following the party's third place finish in the October 2008 elections with 25 seats and 11.7 percent of votes, the LSPD profile improved. As the chief opposition party, it benefitted because the government faced the brunt of popular anger regarding the economic crisis. The LSDP increased its representation from 2 to 3 seats and its vote share to 18.14 percent in the June 2009 European Parliament elections.

Leaders: Algirdas BUTKEVIČIUS (President and Parliamentary Elder), Vytenis Povilas ANDRIUKAITIS (Vice President), Irena ŠIAULIENĖ (First Deputy Elder), Juozas OLEKAS (Deputy Elder), Gediminas KIRKILAS (Former Prime Minister and Former Chair), Algirdas Mykolas BRAZAUSKAS (Former Prime Minister and Former Chair).

Lithuanian National Farmers' Union (*Lietuvos Valstiečių Liaudininkų Sąjunga*—LVLS). The LVLS is the name adopted in February 2006 by the Union of the Peasants and New Democracy Parties (*Valstiečiųir Naujosios Demokratijos Partiju Sąjunga*—VNDPS). The VNDPS had formed on December 15, 2001, by merger of the Lithuanian Peasants' Party (*Lietuvos Valstiečių Partija*—LVP) and the New Democracy Party (*Naujosios Demokratijos Partija*—NDP), which had formed a joint faction in the *Seimas* following the October 2000 election.

The LVP, which traced its origins to 1905, had been revived as the Lithuanian Peasants' Union (*Lietuvos Valstiečių Sąjunga*—LVS) in 1990 and adopted the LVP designation in 1994. It won one constituency seat in the 1996 parliamentary election and then four in 2000. In March 2001 the party suffered a split when a delegation from Kaunas was not seated at a party congress because two of its leaders had been expelled the previous month for criticizing the leadership of the party chair, Ramūnas Karbauskis. Most of the Kaunas delegation reportedly joined the LSDP in protest. The LVP subsequently helped confirm Prime Minister Brazauskas.

The NDP had been launched as the Lithuanian Women's Party (*Lietuvos Moterų Partija*—LMP) in February 1995 under the leadership of Kazimiera Prunskienė, former head of the Soviet-era Association of Women of Lithuania as well as prime minister in 1990 and 1991. In 1992 the Lithuanian Supreme Court ruled that she had been a conscious collaborator with the KGB, which she denied. The LMP won one seat in the 1996 election, after which it adopted the NDP designation. In 2000 the NDP campaigned as part of the ABSK coalition. It won two single-member constituency seats and one proportional seat but left the coalition shortly thereafter.

In the legislative elections in October 2004, the VNDPS alliance won 6.6 percent of the popular vote and ten seats. Kazimiera Prunskienė, the party's candidate, won 47.4 percent of votes in the second round of presidential elections in June 2004, dipping to 3.9 percent in the first round of presidential elections in May 2009. The party held three parliamentary seats following the 2008 balloting and won 1.83 percent of votes in the 2009 European Parliament elections.

Leaders: Ramūnas KARBAUSKIS (President), Kazimiera Danutė PRUNSKIENĖ (Honorary Chair and presidential candidate in 2004 and 2009).

New Union (Social Liberals) (*Naujoji Sąjunga* [*Socialliberala*]—NS[SL]). The left-of-center NS(SL) was established in late April 1998 by Artūras Paulauskas, a prosecutor who had easily surpassed rivals in the first round of the January 1998 presidential contest but had then finished second in runoff balloting. Prior to the 2000 parliamentary election the NS(SL) joined the LLS, LCS, and MKDS in announcing that after the balloting they would attempt to form a "New Policy" (*Naujosios Politikos*). Backed by President Adamkus, the New Policy program advocated liberal democracy, a market economy, and social activism. After the October balloting, in which the NS(SL) finished third, the partners entered government under the LLS's Rolandas Paksas. The coalition foundered in June 2001, however, with Paulauskas calling for Paksas to step down and with all six NS(SL) cabinet ministers resigning. Later in the month Paulauskas negotiated a coalition agreement with the LSDP and joined the new government.

Paulauskas played a leading role in the 2003–2004 impeachment crisis, serving as interim president following the ouster of President Paksas. The NS(SL) later presented joint candidates with the LSDP in the 2004 legislative elections. Following the impeachment, Paulauskas chose to return to his duties as chair of the *Seimas,* a post he would lose in a no-confidence vote on April 11, 2006. Bereft of leadership, the NS(SL) withdrew from the ruling coalition. The party reentered government in February 2008, with one of its members, Algirdas MONKEVIČIUS, being named the new education and science minister in June 2008. However, after winning just one seat and 3.6 percent of votes in the October 2008 balloting, the party returned to the opposition. The NS(SL) won 3.37 percent of votes for the European Parliament in 2009.

Leaders: Artūras PAULAUSKAS (Chair and Environment Minister), Vaclovas KARBAUSKIS, Vaclav STANKEVIČ, Vaidas PLIUSNIS (General Secretary).

Labor Party (*Darbo Partija*—DP). Formed by ethnic Russian businessman Viktor Uspaskich in 2003, the DP is a populist party that supports increased pensions and higher wages for workers and once touted itself as an alternative to some established parties perceived to be tainted by corruption. After the DP secured 28.44 percent of the vote in *Seimas* elections on October 10, 2004, Uspaskich was named minister of the economy in the government installed in December 2004. However, he was compelled to resign in June 2005 in response to allegations that he faced a conflict of interest between his governmental position and his business affairs. Nevertheless, the DP remained in government, winning additional cabinet portfolios in April 2006 when the NS(SL) withdrew from the ruling coalition. In response to aggressive maneuverings by Uspaskich, seven DP party members in the *Seimas* left the party in May 2006 and helped to form the PDP (below).

Allegations of unorthodox accounting and kickbacks to DP legislators as well as lawmakers from other parties led Uspaskich to self-imposed exile in Moscow in May 2006. Uspaskich returned to Lithuania in September 2007; he was promptly arrested and two days later placed under house arrest for six months. Uspaskich returned in order to run for a vacant legislative position and possibly stage a political comeback while campaigning from his home, but he failed to secure the seat. In July 2008 a Vilnius court withheld an electoral commission subsidy worth 2.5 million litas due to the allegations regarding the party's financial practices.

The DP continued to be dogged by corruption allegations in 2008 and 2009, and saw its legislative seat share fall to ten after competing in an electoral coalition with the heretofore unknown **Youth Party**. The coalition garnered 9.0 percent of votes. The DP won 8.58 percent of votes in the June 2009 EU balloting, losing four of its five seats.

Leaders: Jonas PINSKUS (Chair), Loreta GRAUŽINIENĖ (Former Acting Chair), Viktor USPASKICH (Former Chair).

For Order and Justice (*Už Tvarka ir Teisinguma*—UTT). The UTT was formed as an electoral coalition of the two groups below in 2004 following President Paksas's removal from office. The coalition was reportedly designed to minimize voter backlash against Paksas's LDP; there was also concern that the LDP might be prevented from presenting its own candidates without a partner. The UTT won 10 seats in the *Seimas* in the October poll on a vote share of 11.4 percent. The UTT alliance performed well in the 2007 local elections and won 12.7 percent votes and 15 seats in the October 2008 election. The party continues to endorse a platform of nationalism, social solidarity, and Christian values, and took 11.92 percent of votes and 2 seats in the European Parliament elections in June 2009.

Leaders: Rolandas PAKSAS (Chair and Former President of the Republic), Valentinas MAZURONIS and Remigijus AČAS (Parliamentary Leaders).

Liberal Democratic Party (*Liberalų Demokratų Partija*—LDP). Formed in March 2002 by former prime minister Rolandas Paksas and other LLS defectors, the center-right Liberal Democratic Party pledged to support the business sector and to guarantee "order in the state."

Paksas was elected president of the republic in 2003 but was removed from office in 2004 (see Political background and Current issues for details). The LDP supported the VNDPS candidate in the 2004 presidential poll after Paksas was ruled ineligible to run.

Leaders: Rolandas PAKSAS (Chair, Former Prime Minister, and Former President of the Republic), Valentinas MAZURONIS (First Deputy Chair).

Lithuanian People's Union "For Fair Lithuania" (*Lietuvos Liaudies Sąjunga "Už Teisingą Lietuvą"*—LLS). The LLS was formed in 2000 by Julius Veselka, who ran successfully as a "self-nominated" candidate in the 2000 legislative elections. The LLS won 11 percent of the vote in the 2002 local elections.

Leader: Julius VESELKA.

Lithuanian Poles' Electoral Action (*Lietuvos Lenkų Rinkimų Akcija*—LLRA). The LLRA began as the Lithuanian Polish Union (*Lietuvos Lenkų Sąjunga*—LLS), an ethnic grouping that won four *Seimas* seats in 1992. As the LLRA, it retained only one seat in 1996 but secured two in 2000 and 2004. In the 2008 elections it garnered 4.8 percent of votes and three seats. Following the European parliamentary elections in June 2009, the LLRA joined the European Conservatives and Reformists (ECR) grouping founded with leadership from the British Tories in the European Parliament on June 22.

Leaders: Valdemar TOMAŠEVSKI and Leokadija POČIKOVSKA (Members of Parliament), Waldemar TOMASZEWSKI (Member of European Parliament).

Other Parties:

Civil Democracy Party (*Pilietinės Demokratijos Partija*—PDP) The PDP was formed in mid-2006 by legislators from the DP (who were dissatisfied with the leadership of the DP's former chair, Viktor Uspaskich, and related DP scandals) and the LDP. The party continued to command limited support ahead of the 2008 elections and was viewed as ripe for a possible merger with the LVLS or the LSDP. The PDP failed to secure any seats in the October 2008 elections or the June 2009 European Parliament election, in which it won 1.31 percent of votes. No merger plans had been revealed as of mid-2009.

Leader: Algimantas MATULEVIČIUS (President).

Front Party (*Frontas Partija*). Also referenced as A Pro-Lithuania Front, the leftist Front Party was founded in May 2008 by Algirdas Paleckis, an LSDP dissident who had recently been ejected from that party. The new party promoted "milder" redistributive policies and indexed wages and pensions based on inflation. Although Paleckis said he was not specifically recruiting from the LSDP, a number of that party's members subsequently joined the new grouping. The party adheres to a broadly anti-establishment, leftist program and won 2.37 percent of votes in the June 2009 European Parliament elections, garnering a seat for its chair.

Leader: Algirdas PALECKIS (Founder).

Samogitians Party (*Zematis Partija*). Founded to advance the Samogitian dialect for professional, official, and private use, as well as to secure recognition of the Samogitians as a distinct nationality, the party was denied registration due to low support in 2008. The justice ministry also argued that the party's platform, if realized, could lead to federalism by granting official recognition to a regional minority language. The party won 1.23 percent of votes in the 2009 European Parliament balloting.

Party of Trade Unions (*Sąjunga Partija*). Founded in 2008 by former social democrat Kęstutis Juknis, the party registered with the ministry of justice in June of that year, aiming to become the primary political party for Lithuania's trade unions. No additional activity had been reported as of mid-2009.

Leader: Kęstutis JUKNIS (Founder and Chair).

Lithuanian Russian Union (*Lietuvos Rusų Sąjunga*—LRS). An ethnic party representing the Russian minority, the LRS was registered in 1995 but failed to win representation in the 1996 parliamentary election. It won 3 proportional seats in 2000 as part of the ABSK. It subsequently backed formation of the LSDP-NS(SL) government. The LRS received 2 seats in the elections for the Vilnius City Council in April 2007. The LRS received less than 1 percent of the vote in the 2008 parliamentary balloting.

Leaders: Sergejus DMITRIJEVAS, Vladimiras ORECHOVAS, Jurgis UTOVKA.

"Young Lithuanians," New Nationalists and Political Prisoners Union (*"Jaunosios Lietuvos," Naujųjų Tautininkų ir Politinių Kalinių Sąjunga*—JLNTPKS). Previously known as the Lithuanian National Party "Young Lithuania" (*Lietuvių Nacionalinė Partija "Jaunoji Lietuva"*), the rightist JLNTPKS retained its one parliamentary seat in the October 2000 election, but won no seats in 2004 despite fielding five candidates for single-member districts. However, a 2007 survey gave the JLNTPKS 4 percent of electorate support. The grouping gained 1.75 percent of the vote in the 2008 legislative elections.

Leader: Stanislovas BUŠKEVIČIUS (Chair).

Other parties contesting recent elections included the **Christian Conservative Social Union** (*Krikščionių Konservatorių Socialinė Sąjunga*—KKSS), which won 2 percent of the vote; the **Lithuanian Freedom Union** (*Lietuvos Laisvės Sąjunga*—LLaS), a hard-right party led by Vytautas ŠUSTAUSKAS that received 0.28 percent of the vote in 2004; the **Lithuanian Union of Political Prisoners and Deportees** (*Lietuvos Politinių Kaliniųir Tremtinių Sąjunga*—LPKTS), which won one parliamentary seat in 1992 and 1996 but was unsuccessful in 2000 and 2004 despite a loose alliance with the TS(LK); and the **Lithuanian Center Party** (*Lietuvos Centro Partija*—LCP), which won less than 1 percent in the 2008 parliamentary elections..

Additional minor parties include the **Lithuanian Socialist Party** (*Lietuvos Socialistų Partija*—LSP). In late 2000 an additional small party, the **Lithuanian Life's Logic Party** (*Lietuvos Gyvenimo Logikos Partija*—LGLP), reportedly saw its ranks swelled by supporters of neofascist leader Mindaugas MURZA, whose repeated efforts to register his **Lithuanian National Socialist Party** (*Lietuvių Nacionalsocialinės Partija*—LNP) had been denied on the grounds that it contributed to ethnic hostility. Murza left the LGLP in August 2001 and became chair of the LNDP in May 2002. For information on the **Lithuanian National Union** (*Lietuvių Tautininkų Sąjunga*—LTS), **Lithuanian National Democratic Party** (*Lietuvos Nacional-demokratų Partija*—LNDP), and the **Moderate Conservative Union** (*Nuosaikiųjų Konservatorių Sąjunga*—NKS), see the 2008 *Handbook*. For more details on the **Lithuanian Rightist Union** (*Lietuvos Dešiniųjų Sąjunga*—LDS) and the **Lithuanian Freedom Union** (*Lietuvos Laisvės Sąjunga*—LLaS), see the 2009 *Handbook*.

LEGISLATURE

The former Supreme Council (*Aukščiausioji Taryba*) was redesignated as the **Parliament** (*Seimas*) on July 7, 1992, with a complement of 141 members, of whom 71 are currently elected from single-member constituencies and 70 are elected from party lists by proportional representation subject to a 5 percent threshold. Under changes enacted in June 1996, voters became entitled, with effect from the fall 1996 election, to record a preference for individual candidates on the party lists.

The election on October 12 and 26, 2008, produced the following totals: Homeland Union-Lithuanian Christian Democrats secured 45 seats; the Lithuanian Social Democratic Party, 25; the National Revival Party, 16; the For Order and Justice coalition, 15; the Lithuanian Republic Liberal Movement, 11; the Labor Party and Youth Coalition, 10; the Liberal and Center Union, 8; Lithuanian Poles' Electoral Action, 3; Lithuanian National Farmers' Union, 3; New Union (Social Liberals), 1; independents, 4.

The next election was scheduled for October 12, 2012.

Speaker: Arūnas VALINSKAS.

CABINET

[as of September 1, 2009]

Prime Minister	Andrius Kubilius (LSDP)
Ministers	
Agriculture	Kazimieras Starkevičius (TS-LKD)
Culture	Remigijus Vilkaitis (TPP)
Economy	Dainius Kreivys (TS-LKD)
Education and Science	Gintaras Steponavičius (LRLS)
Energy	Arvydas Sekmokas (ind.)
Environment	Gediminas Kazlauskas (TPP)
Finance	Ingrida Šimonytė (ind.) [f]
Foreign Affairs	Vygaudas Ušackas (ind.)
Health	Algis Čaplikas (LCS)
Interior	Raimundas Palaitis (LCS)
Justice	Remigijus Šimašius (ind.)
National Defense	Rasa Juknevičienė (TS-LKD) [f]
Social Security and Labor	Rimantas Jonas Dagys (TS-LKD)
Transportation and Communication	Eligijus Masiulis (LRLS)

[f] = female

COMMUNICATIONS

During the Soviet period all media outlets were required to endorse Communist ideology. Censorship was abolished in 1989. In 2008 Reporters Without Borders rated Lithuania 16, along with the Czech Republic, the Netherlands, and Portugal, out of 173 countries in press freedom.

Press. The following are dailies published in Vilnius in Lithuanian unless otherwise noted: *Lietuvos Rytas* (Lithuania's Morning, 50,000), weekly edition in Russian; *Respublika* (Republic, 50,000); *Kauno Diena* (Kaunas's Day, 50,000); *Kurier Wilenski* (Vilnius Courier, 32,000), in Polish; *Lietuvos Aidas* (Echo of Lithuania); *Echo Litvy* (Echo of Lithuania), in Russian.

News agency. The Lithuanian Telegraph Agency (ELTA) is state-owned, servicing the local press in Lithuanian and Russian. The only English-language facility is the Baltic News Service (BNS), which operates in all three Baltic countries.

Broadcasting and computing. Lithuanian Television and Radio Broadcasting (*Lietuvos Radijas ir Televizija*) is the supervising agency. Lithuanian Radio broadcasts in Lithuanian, Russian, Polish, Yiddish, Belarusan, and Ukrainian, while Lithuanian Television offers programs in Lithuanian, Russian, Polish, Belarusan, and Ukrainian. There are also three dozen independent radio and TV outlets. As of 2008 there were 550 Internet users per 1,000 inhabitants.

INTERGOVERNMENTAL REPRESENTATION

Ambassador to the U.S.: Audrius BRUZGA.

U.S. Ambassador to Lithuania: Anne Elizabeth DERSE.

Permanent Representative to the UN: Dalius ČEKUOLIS.

IGO Memberships (Non-UN): BIS, CBSS, CEUR, EBRD, EIB, EU, Interpol, IOM, NATO, NIB, OSCE, PCA, WCO, WTO.

LUXEMBOURG

Grand Duchy of Luxembourg
Grousherzogdem Lëzebuerg (Letzeburgish)
Grand-Duché de Luxembourg (French)
Grossherzogtum Luxemburg (German)

Political Status: Constitutional monarchy, fully independent since 1867; in economic union with Belgium since 1922.

Area: 998 sq. mi. (2,586 sq. km.).

Population: 439,539 (2001C); 475,000 (2008E).

Major Urban Centers (2005E): LUXEMBOURG-VILLE (Lützelburg, 77,000), Esch-sur-Alzette (28,000).

Official Language: Letzeburgish. As a general rule, French is used for administrative purposes, and German for commerce.

Monetary Unit: Euro (market rate December 1, 2009: 1 euro = $1.51US).

Sovereign: Grand Duke HENRI; ascended to the throne October 7, 2000, on the abdication of his father, Grand Duke JEAN.

Heir Apparent: Prince GUILLAUME, son of the grand duke; proclaimed by the grand duke on December 18, 2000.

President of the Government (Prime Minister): Jean-Claude JUNCKER (Christian Social People's Party); sworn in as the head of a Christian Social–Socialist Workers' coalition by the grand duke on January 20, 1995, succeeding Jacques SANTER (Christian Social People's Party) on the latter's appointment as president of the European Commission; sworn in again on August 7, 1999, following election of June 13 and negotiation of a coalition with the Democratic Party; sworn in for a third term on August 2, 2004, after legislative elections on June 13 and the approval of a revived Christian Social–Socialist Workers' coalition; sworn in for a fourth term on July 23, 2009, after legislative elections on June 7 and approval of another Christian Social–Socialist Workers' coalition.

THE COUNTRY

Located southeast of Belgium between France and Germany, the small, landlocked Grand Duchy of Luxembourg is a predominantly Roman Catholic country whose native inhabitants exhibit an ethnic and cultural blend of French and German elements. Linguistically, both French and German are widely spoken; the local language, Letzeburgish, is a West Frankish dialect. About one-third of the population now consists of immigrants, while a tight labor market has benefited *fortaliers,* cross-border workers from neighboring countries.

Luxembourg is highly industrialized. Iron and steel products have long been mainstays of the economy and still account for nearly one-third of total exports. A drastic downturn in the industry in the mid-1970s led not only to a major, successful restructuring and modernization plan, but also to economic diversification, focusing on the production of such goods as rubber, synthetic fibers, plastics, chemicals, and small metal products. Luxembourg also became an international financial center, the number of banks rising from 13 in 1955 to more than 150 as of 2007. Stock transactions, insurance, and reinsurance have also become of major importance, and Luxembourg currently accommodates more than 9,000 holding companies. Female labor force participation was 59.5 percent in 2008, with women holding 12 of 60 seats in the Chamber of Deputies following the 2009 election. Four of the current 15 government ministers are women, occupying 8 of 28 ministries. Agriculture, which occupies only 2 percent of the labor force, consists primarily of small farms devoted to livestock raising, although viticulture is also of some prominence. Trade is largely oriented toward Luxembourg's neighbors and fellow participants in the Benelux Economic Union and the European Union (EU, formerly the European Community—EC).

After three decades of burgeoning prosperity, Luxembourg entered an economic deceleration in the early 1990s as recession struck Belgium, France, and Germany, its three most important trading partners. Nevertheless, the principality maintained a positive GDP growth rate and in 1994 resumed solid expansion that soared to 7.5 percent in 2000. Having entered the EU's Economic and Monetary Union (EMU) in 1999, which was expected to reduce some of the grand duchy's competitive advantages, Luxembourg undertook financial-sector diversification, particularly in Internet-related services. GDP growth averaged only 2.9 percent in 2003 but rebounded in 2004 to 4.5 percent, apparently under the influence of recent reforms initiated by the government (see Current issues, below). Luxembourg also continued to enjoy one of the lowest budget deficits in the EU (1 percent of GDP) as well as one of the lowest unemployment rates (3.9 percent in 2004). The country's budget deficit nearly doubled in 2005, however, to 1.9 percent and unemployment rose to 4.2 percent. The International Monetary Fund (IMF) blamed growth in social expenditures for the rising budget deficit.

In October 2006 the government's draft budget projected a GDP growth rate of 5.5 percent of GDP, a rate double the European average. The government also projected a budget deficit for 2007 of 0.9 percent and an even smaller deficit of 0.8 percent by 2009.

The global financial turmoil of 2008 pulled Luxembourg's open economy into a recession. Real GDP fell by 0.9 percent in 2008 and was projected to decline by as much as 5.0 percent in 2009, despite a government stimulus initiative. In addition, unemployment was expected to climb to 6.9 percent in 2009 (from 4.0 percent in 2008), while inflation was expected to decline in response to sagging consumer demand and import prices. At present, Luxembourg enjoys the world's highest per capita income.

GOVERNMENT AND POLITICS

Political background. For centuries Luxembourg was dominated and occupied by foreign powers, until the Congress of Vienna in 1815 declared it a grand duchy subject to the king of the Netherlands. On Belgium's secession from the Netherlands in 1830, the greater part of Luxembourg went with it (today constituting the Belgian province of the same name); the remainder was recognized as an autonomous neutral state in 1867 and came under the present ruling house of Nassau-Weilbourg in 1890, when the link with the Netherlands was formally severed. An economic union with Belgium was established in 1922, but Luxembourg retains its independent political institutions under a constitution dating from 1868.

Since World War II political power has been exercised by a series of coalition governments in which the Christian Social People's Party (*Chrëschtlech Sozial Vollekspartei*—CSV) has traditionally been the dominant element. For 15 years beginning in 1959, the government was led by Pierre WERNER, who formed coalitions with both the Socialist Workers' Party of Luxembourg (*Lëtzebuergesch Sozialistesch Arbechterpartei*—LSAP) and the Democratic Party (*Demokratesch Partei*—DP). A month after the 1974 election, however, the latter two formed a new government under DP leader Gaston THORN. After the 1979 election a fairly lengthy period of intraparty negotiation resulted in the formation of a CSV-DP government and the return of Werner as prime minister.

Following the 1984 election, at which the CSV remained the largest party but the LSAP registered the greatest gain, a new round of negotiations led to a revived center-left CSV-LSAP coalition under former finance minister Jacques SANTER. In the 1989 poll, the three leading parties lost three seats each, with Santer forming a new bipartisan government after the CSV had retained its plurality in the Chamber of Deputies.

As in 1989, Luxembourg's 1994 national and European Parliament elections were held together to signify the principality's deep commitment to the cause of European unity. Economic policy questions dominated the campaigning for both elections, which produced only marginal shifts in the party balance. A month later, in July, Prime Minister Santer was unexpectedly named the compromise choice to take over the European Commission presidency in January 1995. His successor as prime minister was another CSV finance minister, Jean-Claude JUNCKER.

In the June 1999 election both governing parties suffered losses—four seats in the case of the LSAP, enabling the DP to negotiate an agreement with the CSV that brought it into the government for the first time in 15 years. The new Juncker cabinet, sworn in in August, included the DP's president, Lydie POLFER, as vice prime minister as well as minister of foreign affairs and external commerce.

On October 7, 2000, Grand Duke JEAN, 79, who had reigned since his mother's abdication in 1964, stepped aside in favor of his son, Grand Duke HENRI. In preparation for his accession, Henri had been designated as his father's "lieutenant-representative" in 1998. In December 2000 he followed tradition and named his eldest son, Prince GUILLAUME, as heir apparent.

In the June 13, 2004, legislative elections, the CSV remained the dominant party and Juncker announced a new coalition government with the LSAP on July 31. In the June 7, 2009, balloting the CSV won a 26-seat plurality and, after a month of negotiations, formed another coalition government with the LSAP, sworn in on July 23 with Juncker again as prime minister.

Constitution and government. Luxembourg's 1868 constitution has been repeatedly revised to incorporate democratic reforms, to eliminate the former status of "perpetual neutrality," and to permit devolution of sovereignty to international institutions. Executive authority is exercised on behalf of the grand duke by the prime minister and the cabinet, who are appointed by the sovereign but are responsible to the legislature. Legislative authority rests primarily with the elected Chamber of Deputies, although until 2008 the grand duke could veto laws. A nonelective Council of State serves as an advisory body to the Chamber. Deputies are elected on a proportional basis from four electoral constituencies (north, center, south, and east).

The judicial system is headed by the Superior Court of Justice and includes a Court of Assizes for serious criminal offenses, district courts, and justices of the peace. There are also administrative and special social courts and, since 1996, a Constitutional Court. Judges are appointed for life by the grand duke. The country is divided into 3 districts, 12 cantons, and 116 communes. The districts function as links between the central and local governments and are headed by commissioners appointed by the central government.

Foreign relations. Luxembourg's former neutral status was abandoned after the German occupation of World War II. The country was a founding member of the United Nations (UN) and a leader in the postwar consolidation of the West through its membership in Benelux, the North Atlantic Treaty Organization (NATO), the EC/EU, and other multilateral organizations. Relations with Belgium have long been close.

In 1992 the Chamber of Deputies overwhelmingly approved the EU's Maastricht Treaty. During negotiations of the EU's Treaty of Nice in 2000, Luxembourg joined other small EU states in trying to retain their long-standing level of influence and power in view of planned EU expansion. Prime Minister Juncker, who assumed the six-month presidency of the EU's European Council in January 2005, put his political career on the line by campaigning strongly for Luxembourg to approve the proposed EU constitution. Juncker, reportedly widely respected in EU circles, announced he would resign as prime minister if voters rejected the EU initiative. Consequently, a national referendum on the question on July 10 received a 56.5 percent "yes" vote, making Luxembourg one of the few countries in which a direct popular vote approved the controversial EU initiative.

Luxembourg has continued to support both NATO and the development of an autonomous European security and defense identity. The Juncker government approved NATO expansion at the 2002 Prague summit. Meanwhile, Luxembourg supported the creation of a European Rapid Reaction Force (ERRF) designed to give the EU the ability to quickly respond to humanitarian and other security crises. Luxembourg initially pledged 100 troops for the new force. It has also supported increased European cooperation on defense-industrial issues, including the design and production of military aircraft and major arms systems. Such cooperation was seen as a means to protect domestic steel and other manufacturing industries. Luxembourg strongly opposed the U.S./UK-led invasion of Iraq in 2003 and subsequently reaffirmed its support for development of an "autonomous" EU defense capability that would not be inordinately subjected to U.S. pressure.

Luxembourg faced challenges in the early 2000s regarding how its financial sector operated. Within the EU, the United Kingdom and France were particularly vocal in fighting for full information exchange between national tax authorities as the best means of stopping tax evasion on savings income, whereas Luxembourg argued that maintaining its banking secrecy was a necessity to avoid flight of investment accounts to offshore facilities. At the same time, Luxembourg, as well as a number of other countries and offshore dependencies, were pressured by the United States into relaxing bank secrecy rules and cooperating in tax fraud investigations. In January 2001 Luxembourgian banks began withholding taxes on investments from U.S. sources. In 2003 Luxembourg reached a compromise agreement with the EU under which a 15 percent withholding tax was to be enforced beginning in 2004. (The rate was scheduled to increase gradually to 35 percent by 2010.) Yielding to international pressure, Luxembourg, together with Austria and Switzerland, agreed in March 2009 to loosen secrecy laws and cooperate with foreign tax authorities.

Current issues. In early 2006 the Juncker government was preoccupied with the attempted hostile takeover of Luxembourg-based steel manufacturer Arcelor by the Indian-owned Mittal Steel. Arcelor, the world's largest steel producer, had been formed in 2001 by merger of Luxembourg's Arbed with French and Spanish corporations. The proposed takeover raised concerns over foreign ownership of businesses that are seen as critical to the region. The Indian government accused European governments opposed to the sale—including Spain and France as well as Luxembourg—of discrimination and warned that blocking the sale could harm global trade talks. Arcelor, with 6,000 workers, is the largest employer in Luxembourg, and the Luxembourg government, with a 6.7 percent interest, is the company's largest shareholder. Despite Juncker's opposition to the takeover, parliament on March 17 rejected a change in the country's corporate takeover laws that would have made it more difficult for the acquisition to succeed. In June the Juncker government abruptly changed its position, announcing that it supported the Arcelor-Mittal merger. While it would sell some of its shares in Arcelor, it planned to retain a 2.7 percent stake in the postmerger company. As of September 2007, merger arrangements remained incomplete.

The Juncker government has also continued to vigorously negotiate with the European community over complaints about the country's tax laws. In July 2006 the government promised to remove tax exemptions given to certain holding companies after EU regulators held the exemptions to be illegal. A month earlier, however, Prime Minister Juncker had blocked value-added tax (VAT) reforms that were backed by all other EU members. The reforms called for taxing services at the rate in place in the country where the service is consumed rather than, as at present, in the country of origin. Since Luxembourg's 15 percent VAT is the lowest in the EU, many large service companies in the telecom and electronic commerce industries, such as AOL and Amazon.com, have established their European headquarters in Luxembourg, contributing some €300 million ($225 million) annually to government coffers. The proposed reforms, which Junker again vetoed in June 2007, would likely have a severe impact on revenues.

In February 2008 parliament passed a bill legalizing euthanasia and assisted suicide for the terminally ill, putting Luxembourg's stance in line with Belgium and Netherlands. The bill's approval was viewed as a defeat for Prime Minister Juncker, whose party had opposed the legislation. The bill was subsequently vetoed by the grand duke, but the Chamber nullified the veto and, in December 2008, approved a constitutional amendment removing the grand duke's veto power.

The Juncker-led CSV maintained its predominant position in the June 2009 legislative balloting in part because Juncker was credited with adept handling of financial affairs and resisting as far as practical international pressure over the Grand Duchy's bank secrecy laws.

POLITICAL PARTIES

With an electoral system based on proportional representation, for decades Luxembourg has been ruled by coalition governments headed by the Christian Social Party or the Democratic Party allied with each other or with the Socialist Workers' Party.

Government Parties:

Christian Social People's Party (*Chrëschtlech Sozial Vollekspartei—CSV/Parti Chrétien Social*—PCS). Formed in 1914, Luxembourg's strongest single party traditionally drew its main support from farmers, Catholic laborers, and moderate conservatives. Often identified as a Christian Democratic grouping, the CSV endorses a centrist position that includes support for the monarchy, progressive labor legislation, assistance to farmers and small business owners, church-state cooperation, and an internationalist foreign policy. The dominant partner in most postwar coalitions, the CSV most recently won 38.0 percent of the vote and 26 seats in the June 7, 2009, election. Jean-Claude Juncker, who has served as prime minister since 1995 (making him Europe's longest-serving leader), subsequently formed another coalition government with the LSAP.

Leaders: Jean-Claude JUNCKER (Prime Minister), François BILTGEN (President), Diane ADEHM (Vice President), Marie-Josée FRANK (Vice President), Marco SCHANK (Secretary General).

Socialist Workers' Party of Luxembourg (*Lëtzebuergesch Sozialistesch Arbechterpartei*—LSAP/*Parti Ouvrier Socialiste Luxembourgeois*—POSL). Founded in 1902, the LSAP draws its major support from urban lower- and lower-middle-class voters, particularly those affiliated with trade unions. It advocates extension of the present system of social legislation and social insurance, and supports European integration, NATO, and the UN. In 1971 a conservative wing split off to form the Social Democratic Party, which was dissolved in 1983.

After 15 years of government partnership with the CSV, in 1999 the LSAP finished third in the balloting and returned to opposition as Prime Minister Juncker established a center-right government with the second place DP. Following the election of June 13, 2004, the LSAP was again invited to form a coalition government with the CSV. The coalition was renewed following the 2009 balloting, in which the LSAP won 21.6 percent of the vote and 13 seats.

Leaders: Alex BODRY (President), Yves CRUCHTEN and Jacqueline REITER (Vice Presidents), Romain SCHNEIDER (Secretary General).

Opposition Parties:

Democratic Party (*Demokratesch Partei*—DP/*Parti Démocratique*—PD). The DP includes both conservatives and moderates and draws support from professional, business, white-collar, and artisan groups. Also referred to as the Liberals, the party is committed to free enterprise, although it favors certain forms of progressive social legislation. It is mildly anticlerical and strongly pro-NATO. It participated in the Werner government prior to the 1984 election, after which it went into opposition. It won 11 Chamber seats in 1989 and 12 in 1994. Having moved ahead of the Socialist Workers' Party in the June 1999 election, winning 15 seats, the DP negotiated a coalition agreement with the CSV. In the June 13, 2004, elections the DP fell to 16.1 percent of the vote and 10 seats, and it declined further in the 2009 balloting to 15.0 percent of the vote and 9 seats.

Leaders: Claude MEISCH (President), Anne BRASSEUR (First Vice President), Simone BEISSEL (Vice President), Guy DALEIDEN (Vice President), George GUDENBURG (Secretary General).

Alternative Democratic Reform Party (*Alternativ Demokratesch Reformpartei/Parti Réformiste d'Alternative Démocratique*—ADR). This party was initially organized in 1957 as the Five-Sixths Action Committee (*Aktiounskomitee "5/6-Pensioun fir Jidfereen"*), the name referencing its support for an across-the-board introduction in the private sector of pensions worth five-sixths of final salary (the level then operative for public employees). In November 1992 it adopted the name Action Committee for Democracy and Pension Justice (*Aktiounskomitee fir Demokratie a Rentengerechtegkeet—ADR/Comité d'Action pour la Démocratie et la Justice Sociale*—CADJS). After winning five Chamber seats in 1994, seven in 1999, and five in 2004, the party in 2006 changed its name again (to the current form) in an apparent attempt to foster a broader position in mainstream politics. The ADR won four seats on 8.1 percent of the vote in the 2009 balloting.

Leader: Roby MEHLEN (President).

The Greens (*Déi Gréng/Les Verts*). Organized at a June 1983 congress as the Green Alternative (*Gréng Alternativ Partei/Parti Vert-Alternatif*), The Greens won two legislative seats in 1984 but in 1986 suffered a major split. The party again won two seats in 1989 and then added three more in 1994 before reuniting with the Green Ecological Initiative List (*Gréng Lëscht Ekologesch Initiativ*—GLEI) in 1995. Its current program advocates environmental protection, democracy, social justice, human rights, and similar causes. In the June 1999 election it won five seats in the Chamber of Deputies, and it won seven seats in 2004 and 2009.

Leader: François BAUSCH (Parliamentary Group President).

The Left (*Déi Lénk/La Gauche*). The constituent congress of The Left took place on January 30, 1999, culminating efforts to overcome previous cleavages and organize political forces to the left of the social democratic DP and The Greens. Participants included the KPL (below), DP dissidents, trade unionists, and members of other small left-wing parties, including the Revolutionary Socialist Party (*Parti Socialiste Révolutionnaire*—PSR) and the New Left (*Neue Linke/Nouvelle Gauche*—MNG). In the legislative election of June 1999 the new grouping won one seat in the Chamber of Deputies. In local balloting in Esch-sur-Alzette in April 2000 The Left finished third, with 12.8 percent of the vote, enabling it to join a majority coalition with the DP and The Greens. The Left's André HOFFMAN resigned his seat in the Chamber of Deputies to join Esch-sur-Alzette's council of aldermen, with the KPL's Aloyse BISDORFF thereupon succeeding him in the national legislature. Bisdorff was subsequently succeeded by Serge URBANY. The Left received 1.9 percent of the vote in the June 2004 elections but won no seats. Its vote percentage rose to 3.3 in the 2009 balloting, resulting in The Left winning one seat.

The Left has no formal leadership positions; the organization's first ordinary congress in May 2000 elected a 45-member *Nationale Koordination/Coordination Nationale,* which subsequently selected an 11-member *Koordinationsbüro/Bureau de Coordination*.

Other Parties Contesting the 2009 Legislative Elections:

Communist Party of Luxembourg (*Kommunistesch Partei vu Lëtzebuerg*—KPL/*Parti Communiste Luxembourgeois*—PCL). Established in 1921, the historically pro-Soviet KPL draws its main support from urban and industrial workers and some intellectuals. It advocates full nationalization of the economy and was the only Western European Communist party to approve the Soviet invasion of Czechoslovakia in 1968. The KPL suffered a loss of three of its five parliamentary seats in the 1979 election, retaining the two that remained in 1984. Its longtime leader, René URBANY, died in 1990, and the party lost its sole remaining Chamber seat in 1994. Many Communist Party officials joined The Left party after the 1994 elections, and the KPL decided not to contest the elections. The KPL received only 0.9 percent of the vote in the 2004 legislative poll and 1.5 percent in 2009.

Leaders: Ali RUCKERT (President).

Citizens' List (*Biergerlëscht/Liste des Citoyens*). Formed in early 2009 in anticipation of the June elections, Citizens' List displayed a decidedly single-issue focus on increased pension rights. The party placed two candidates on the 2009 ballot. One was Aly Jaerling, a former ADR member of parliament who left the ADR in 2006 to sit as an independent in protest over the ADR's decision to broaden its issue focus beyond pensions and in objection to the ADR's nationalist appeals. The other was Jean ERSFELD, former leader of the now defunct FPL (see below). Neither candidate was elected, as the Citizens' List won only 0.8 percent of the vote.

Leader: Aly JAERLING.

Other Parties:

Free Party of Luxembourg (*Frai Partei Lëtzebuerg*—FPL). Led by Jean ERSFELD, the FPL received 0.12 percent of the vote in the June 2004 elections. However, it did not field candidates in 2009 and is now defunct.

LEGISLATURE

Legislative responsibility is centered in the elected Chamber of Deputies, but the appointive Council of State retains some vestigial legislative functions.

Council of State (*Der Staatsrat/Conseil d'État*). The council consists of 21 members appointed for life; 7 are appointed directly by the grand duke, while the others are appointed by him on proposal of the council itself or of the Chamber of Deputies.

President: Alain MEYER.

Chamber of Deputies (*Chamber vum Deputéirten/Châmbre des Députés*). The Chamber currently consists of 60 deputies elected for five-year terms (subject to dissolution) by direct universal suffrage on the basis of proportional representation.

In the June 7, 2009, elections the Christian Social People's Party won 26 seats; the Socialist Workers' Party of Luxembourg, 13; the Democratic Party, 9; the Greens, 7; the Alternative Democratic Reform Party, 4; and The Left, 1.

President: Laurent MOSAR.

CABINET

[as of September 1, 2009]

Prime Minister and Minister of State	Jean-Claude Juncker (CSV)
Vice Prime Minister	Jean Asselborn (LSAP)
Ministers	
Administrative Simplification	Octavie Modert (CSV) [f]
Agriculture, Viticulture, and Rural Development	Romain Schneider (LSAP)
Civil Service and Administrative Reform	François Biltgen (CSV)
Communications	François Biltgen (CSV)
Cooperation and Humanitarian Affairs	Marie-Josée Jacobs (CSV) [f]
Culture	Octavie Modert (CSV) [f]
Defense	Jean-Marie Halsdorf (CSV)
Economy and Foreign Trade	Jeannot Krecké (LSAP)
Equality of Opportunity	Françoise Hetto-Gaasch (CSV) [f]
Family and Integration	Marie-Josée Jacobs (CSV) [f]
Finance	Luc Frieden (CSV)
Foreign Affairs	Jean Asselborn (LSAP)
Health	Mars Di Bartolomeo (LSAP)
Higher Education and Research	François Biltgen (CSV)
Housing	Marco Schank (CSV)
Interior and Territorial Planning	Jean-Marie Halsdorf (CSV)
Justice	François Biltgen (CSV)
Middle Classes and Tourism	Françoise Hetto-Gaasch (CSV) [f]
National Education and Professional Training	Mady Delvaux-Stehres (LSAP) [f]
Parliamentary Relations	Octavie Modert (CSV) [f]
Religious Affairs	François Biltgen (CSV)
Social Security	Mars Di Bartolomeo (LSAP)
Sports	Romain Schneider (LSAP)
Sustainable Development and Infrastructure	Claude Wiseler (CSV)
Treasury	Jean-Claude Juncker (CSV)
Work, Employment, and Immigration	Nicholas Schmit (LSAP)
Ministers Delegate	
Civil Service and Administrative Reform	Octavie Modert (CSV) [f]
Economic Solidarity	Romain Schneider (LSAP)
Sustainable Development and Infrastructure	Marco Schank (CSV)

[f] = female

COMMUNICATIONS

All news media are privately owned and are free of censorship.

Press. The following newspapers are published daily in the capital, unless otherwise noted: *Luxemburger Wort/La Voix du Luxembourg* (85,000), in German and French, Catholic, CSV organ; *Tageblatt/ Zeitung fir Lëtzebuerg* (Esch-sur-Alzette, 30,000), in German and French, LSAP affiliated; *Le Républicain Lorrain* (15,000), in French; *Lëtzebuerger Journal* (10,000), in German, Democratic organ; *Zeitung vum Lëtzebuerger Vollek*, KPL organ, in German.

News agencies. There is no domestic facility; a number of foreign bureaus, including AP, UPI, and *Agence France-Presse,* maintain offices in Luxembourg-Ville.

Broadcasting and computing. Broadcasting is dominated by RTL Group, a privately owned international media company that was formed in 2000 by merger of the Luxembourg-based CLT-UFA—the continent's largest commercial broadcaster—and the television branch of London-based Pearson. In addition, Luxembourg is home to the *Société Européenne des Satellites* (SES), one of the world's leading satellite service providers.

As of 2008 there were 805.3 Internet users per 1,000 inhabitants.

INTERGOVERNMENTAL REPRESENTATION

Ambassador to the U.S.: Jean-Paul SENNINGER.

U.S. Ambassador to Luxembourg: (Vacant).

Permanent Representative to the UN: Sylvie LUCAS.

IGO Memberships (Non-UN): ADB, BLX, CEUR, EBRD, EIB, EU, Eurocontrol, IEA, Interpol, IOM, NATO, OECD, OIF, OSCE, PCA, WCO, WEU, WTO.

MACEDONIA

Republic of Macedonia
Republika Makedonija

Note: The country was admitted to the United Nations in April 1993 as "The former Yugoslav Republic of Macedonia," although international usage of this title (particularly in regard to capitalization) has varied, with the abbreviation FYROM sometimes being invoked. As of mid-2009 no resolution had been achieved in the dispute with Greece over use of "Macedonia" in the country's official name.

Political Status: Former constituent republic of the Socialist Federal Republic of Yugoslavia; independence proclaimed under constitution of November 17, 1991, on the basis of a referendum conducted September 8.

Area: 9,928 sq. mi. (25,713 sq. km.).

Population: 2,022,547 (2002C); 2,049,000 (2008E).

Major Urban Center (2005E): SKOPJE (476,000).

Official Languages: Macedonian, Albanian. Macedonian, with a Cyrillic alphabet, is further designated as the official language for international relations. Albanian, with a Latin alphabet, became an official language under a 2001 constitutional revision that authorized that status for any language spoken by at least 20 percent of the population. Moreover, in local jurisdictions other languages used by at least 20 percent of the citizens are considered official. (Local authorities may also permit additional languages to be used in public interactions with the government.)

Monetary Unit: New Macedonian Denar (market rate December 1, 2009: 40.80 denars = $1US).

President: Gjorge IVANOV (Internal Macedonian Revolutionary Organization–Democratic Party for Macedonian National Unity); directly elected in second-round balloting on April 5, 2009, and sworn in for a five-year term on May 12, succeeding Branko CRVENKOVSKI (Social Democratic Union of Macedonia).

Chair of the Council of Ministers (Prime Minister): Nikola GRUEVSKI (Internal Macedonian Revolutionary Organization–Democratic Party for Macedonian National Unity); approved by the Assembly and sworn into office on August 26, 2006, following the election of July 5 and 19, succeeding Vlado BUČKOVSKI (Social Democratic Union of Macedonia); formed new government on July 7, 2008, following the legislative elections in June.

THE COUNTRY

The former Yugoslavian component of historical Macedonia is a landlocked country bordered on the east by Bulgaria, on the north by Serbia and Montenegro, on the west by Albania, and on the south by Greece. According to the 2002 census, 64.2 percent of the population is ethnic Macedonian and 25.2 percent ethnic Albanian, with Turks, Roma, Serbs, Bosniaks, Vlachs, and others forming smaller groups. Most of the Macedonian majority supports the Macedonian Orthodox (Christian) Church; the Albanians are predominantly Muslim. Demography contributes to the ethnic tensions within the country. The higher birthrate among the ethnic Albanian, Turkish, and Roma communities is frequently cited by ethnic Macedonian nationalist politicians as eroding the nature of the state as the homeland of the "Macedonian people." Equally important is the depopulation of the countryside; two-thirds of Macedonian towns and villages continue to see long-term population decline because of internal migration, primarily to Skopje. The perception that rural areas are underfunded has contributed, in part, to past ethnic conflict.

Agriculture accounted for about 11 percent of GDP and roughly 20 percent of employment in 2008, the principal crops being fruits, vegetables, grains, and tobacco. The industrial sector, contributing about 27 percent of GDP and 30 percent of employment, principally exports iron and steel, footwear and clothing, nonferrous metals, tobacco products, and beverages (especially wine). Women constitute 40 percent of the labor force. Extractable resources include lignite, copper, lead, and zinc. Serbia, Germany, Greece, Italy, and Russia are Macedonia's leading trading partners.

The poorest of the former Yugoslav republics, Macedonia was economically distressed in the postindependence period by regional conflict and the disruption of established trading links with neighboring countries. Industrial and agricultural production declined sharply, yielding GDP contraction of about one-third in 1990–1993, during which inflation averaged 600 percent per year and unemployment rose to 40 percent. Beginning in 1994 the government initiated a structural reform program suggested by the International Monetary Fund (IMF) and World Bank; initiatives included liberalization of trade regulations, modernization of customs procedures, privatization of state-run enterprises, and reform of the financial sector. In 1998 Macedonia applied for membership in the World Trade Organization (WTO) and the Central European Free Trade Association (CEFTA), joining the former in April 2003 and the latter in February 2006.

Severe difficulties have continued since independence, however, including a dearth of foreign investment, continued and steady high unemployment (roughly 35 percent), and increasing poverty (nearly one quarter of the population lives below the poverty line). The ethnic Albanian Muslim minority has been disproportionally affected by economic problems, generating additional resentment in a segment of the population already embittered over perceived "second class" treatment.

GDP plummeted by 4 percent in 2001 and by 2 percent in 2002, but steady growth of over 3 percent annually was achieved in 2003–2005. The IMF approved a new three-year aid package in September 2005, while the European Union (EU) formally declared Macedonia as a candidate for EU membership in December. Among other things, EU accession appeared dependent on a resolution of the name dispute with Greece (see Current issues, below). Growth of 5.0 percent and 4.8 percent was registered in 2007 and 2008, respectively, but the effects of the global economic crisis were expected to produce GDP contraction in 2009. In addition, corruption remained a problem (Transparency International in 2006 had rated Macedonia among the most corrupt countries in Europe), while unemployment in mid-2009 surpassed 32 percent, one of the highest rates in Europe. (The rate was more than 50 percent for those under 30 years of age.)

GOVERNMENT AND POLITICS

Political background. Greater geographic Macedonia was contested between rival Balkan empires until its incorporation into the Ottoman Empire. Ottoman rule lasted five centuries prior to the Second Balkan War and the Treaty of Bucharest of 1913, which divided most of the territory between Greece and Serbia, the respective portions being known as Aegean (or Greek) Macedonia and Vardar Macedonia (the latter after the region's principal river). A much smaller portion (Pirin Macedonia) was awarded to Bulgaria. After World War I Vardar Macedonia (South Serbia) became part of the Kingdom of the Serbs, Croats, and Slovenes, later renamed Yugoslavia in October 1929. In 1944 it was accorded the status of a constituent republic of the communist-ruled federal Yugoslavia.

Following Belgrade's endorsement of a multiparty system in early 1990, Vladimir MITKOV of the newly styled League of Communists of Macedonia–Party of Democratic Change (*Sojuz na Komunistite na Makedonija–Partija za Demokratska Preobrazba*—SKM-PDP) was named president of the republic's State Presidency, pending a general election. The balloting for a 120-member Assembly, conducted in three stages on November 11 and 25 and December 9, was marked by ethnic tension between the Macedonian and Albanian communities and yielded an inconclusive outcome: the opposition Internal Macedonian Revolutionary Organization–Democratic Party for Macedonian National Unity (*Vnatrešno Makedonska Revolucionerna Organizacija–Demokratska Partija za Makedonsko Nacionalno Edinstvo*—VMRO-DPMNE) won a plurality of 37 seats, compared with 31 for the second-place SKM-PDP, and a total of 25 for two Albanian groups. As a result of the stand-off, Kiro GLIGOROV of the SKM-PDP (subsequently the Social Democratic Union of Macedonia [*Socijaldemokratski Sojuz na Makedonija*—SDSM]) was named to succeed Mitkov as president.

On January 25, 1991, the Assembly unanimously adopted a declaration of sovereignty that asserted a right of self-determination, including

secession from Yugoslavia. On September 8, 75 percent of the republic's registered voters (with most Albanians abstaining) participated in a referendum that endorsed independence by an overwhelming margin. On November 17 the Assembly approved a new constitution, and on December 24 Macedonia joined Bosnia and Herzegovina, Croatia, and Slovenia in seeking recognition from the European Community (EC, subsequently the EU). The ethnic Albanians reacted in January 1992 with a 99.9 percent vote in favor of territorial and political autonomy for the Albanian-majority regions in western Macedonia. While Belgrade tacitly recognized Macedonian autonomy by handing over border posts to Macedonian army units on March 15 and withdrawing its own military forces from the republic 11 days later, most foreign governments withheld recognition because of Greek protests over the country's name (see Foreign relations, below).

A mid-1992 cabinet crisis resulted in the formation of a new coalition headed by Branko CRVENKOVSKI of the SDSM and including the Party for Democratic Prosperity (*Partija za Demokratski Prosperitet/Partia për Prosperitet Demokratik*—PDP/PPD), a primarily ethnic Albanian party. The new government introduced short-term emergency economic measures, including devaluations of the denar in October and December. Meanwhile, in light of an influx of some 60,000 refugees from the war in Bosnia and Herzegovina, the Assembly in October approved a 15-year residency requirement for Macedonian citizenship, which was modified to eight years in 2003.

The prime importance attached by the government to securing full international recognition helped to ensure the survival of the disparate ruling coalition, which had been mandated to cement national unity. Nevertheless, underlying tensions between the ethnic Macedonian and ethnic Albanian communities surfaced in 1993 amid accusations of Albanian separatism, and in early 1994 the PDP/PPD split into moderate and nationalist factions, the former remaining in the government and the latter joining the opposition.

In the October 1994 presidential election Gligorov secured easy reelection as the candidate of an SDSM-led alliance, winning 78.4 percent of the valid votes cast (52.4 percent of the total electorate), against 21.6 percent for the nominee of the VMRO-DPMNE, Ljubčo GEORGIEVSKI. In the two-stage legislative election the SDSM-led alliance won 95 of the 120 seats and then opted to maintain the coalition with the PDP/PPD under the continued premiership of Crvenkovski. The opposition parties claimed that both the presidential and legislative elections had been riddled with fraud, a view that received some support from international observers.

On October 3, 1995, President Gligorov suffered serious injuries in a bomb attack on his car in Skopje that resulted in two fatalities. Accepting responsibility for failure to protect the president, Dr. Ljubomir FRČKOVSKI resigned as interior minister, attributing the assassination attempt to an unnamed "multinational financial and economic corporation in a neighboring state," assisted by Macedonian nationals. In accordance with the constitution, the speaker of the Assembly, Stojan ANDOV, leader of the Liberal Party of Macedonia (*Liberalna Partija na Makedonija*—LPM), became acting president, serving until Gligorov resumed his duties in January 1996.

In a major cabinet reshuffle in February 1996, Prime Minister Crvenkovski dropped the LPM from the ruling coalition, ignoring specific advice from the president that its previous party composition should be retained. The new lineup, which included Frčkovski as foreign minister, thus featured the dominant SDSM together with lesser participation by the PDP and the Socialist Party of Macedonia (*Socijalistička Partija na Makedonija*—SPM). Andov responded to the ouster of his party by resigning as speaker, being succeeded in March by Tito PETKOVSKI of the SDSM. An LPM attempt in April to force an early election was easily rebuffed, given the government's comfortable parliamentary majority. The SDSM won a plurality of council seats as well as mayoralties in municipal elections in late 1996, the biggest challenge coming from a coalition of right-wing groupings.

In February 1997 an estimated 3,000 ethnic Macedonian students protested against a law permitting the Albanian language to be used in teaching at Skopje University's teacher college, reflecting nationalistic sentiment that the government should not yield to perceived separatism on the part of ethnic Albanians. In March the EU formally expressed concern over rising ethnic tensions. Rioting, resulting in 3 deaths, 100 wounded, and 500 arrests, erupted in July in Gostivar over the right to fly the Albanian flag at municipal buildings in ethnic Albanian areas.

Despite ethnic unrest and a financial scandal allegedly implicating government officials, the government survived a confidence vote in March 1997. The financial scandal was caused by the collapse of a pyramid scheme in which 30,000 people may have lost as much as $60 million. The assembly approved a major cabinet reshuffle on May 29, with Prime Minister Crvenkovski pledging to concentrate on economic reforms and anticorruption measures.

The problems of ethnic Albanians in Kosovo subsequently spilled over into Macedonia, including a series of car bomb explosions in January and February 1998 that were disputably claimed by the Kosovo Liberation Army—KLA (*Ushtria Çlirimtare e Kosovës*—UÇK). President Gligorov said in early March that the army had prepared a plan for a large-scale movement of Kosovars through Macedonia to Albania in case open war broke out. Meanwhile, the leaders of several ethnic Albanian parties were charged in mid-March with violating (during a pro-Kosovo rally) Macedonian laws limiting the display of Albanian nationalist symbols. In addition, the mayors of Tetovo and Gostivar were imprisoned for flying the Albanian flag over municipal buildings. In response, the PDP and the Democratic Party of Albanians (*Demokratska Partija na Albancite*—DPA/*Partia Demokratike Shqiptare*—PDSh—DPA/PDSh), under the leadership of longtime Albanian nationalist Arben XHAFERI, threatened to withdraw from governmental institutions.

The legislative election in October–November 1998 gave a majority of 62 seats to the VMRO-DPMNE and its electoral partner, the newly formed, probusiness Democratic Alternative (*Demokratska Alternativa*—DA). A governmental crisis was averted after the election, when Prime Minister–designate Georgievski negotiated a coalition agreement that included the DPA/PDSh, theretofore perceived as a more militant segment of the Albanian population than the more mainstream PDP/PPD. Georgievski's new VMRO-DPMNE-DA-DPA/PDSh government pledged to further integrate Albanians into Macedonian institutions and society as a whole. Pardons were granted for several Albanian figures charged with political crimes, including the mayors of Tetovo and Gostivar.

In presidential balloting to replace the retiring Gligorov, the VMRO-DPMNE candidate, Boris TRAJKOVSKI, captured 52.9 percent of the second-round vote in November 1999, outdistancing the SDSM's Tito Petkovski, who had finished first in the initial round. Trajkovski's victory came with the support of the DA and the DPA/PDSh, both of which had fielded their own candidates in the first round. Official confirmation of Trajkovski's victory was delayed, however, when the Supreme Court ordered that a revote be held in selected precincts because of ballot stuffing and other irregularities. The results of the reballoting proved nearly identical to the previous totals, and Trajkovski was inaugurated on December 15.

In November 2000, the DA, citing the slow pace of economic reform, announced its withdrawal from the governing coalition, putting the administration in jeopardy. In August the administration had weathered the defection of six VMRO-DPMNE legislators to the Internal Macedonian Revolutionary Organization–True Macedonian Reform Option (*Vnatrešno Makedonska Revolucionerna Organizacija–Vistinska Makedonska Reformska Opcija*—VMRO-VMRO), but it now needed to negotiate a new coalition agreement in order to survive. With additional support from independent deputies (including four defectors from the DA), a new alliance of the VMRO-DPMNE, the DPA/PDSh, and the LPM received parliamentary assent.

In February 2001 fighting erupted in Tanusevçi, on the border with Kosovo, precipitated by members of the Albanian National Liberation Army—NLA (*Ushtrisë Çlirimtare Kombëtare*—UÇK) led by Ali AHMETI. By mid-March fighting had spread to the Tetovo area, leading the UN Security Council to pass a unanimous resolution condemning "extremist violence" as "a threat to the security and stability of the wider region." In April the DPA and PDP, both having condemned the NLA, began discussions with the government on possible constitutional changes that would address the status of ethnic Albanians. In May the Assembly, by a vote of 104–1, approved formation of a national unity government that, in addition to the three parties in the previous Georgievski administration, included the SDSM, the PDP, the VMRO-VMRO, and the Liberal-Democratic Party (*Liberalno-Demokratska Partija*—LDP), which incorporated elements of the LPM. Fighting nevertheless escalated in succeeding weeks, and as of June some 65,000 ethnic Albanians had fled to Kosovo to escape the conflict.

A Western-brokered peace agreement (the Ohrid Framework Agreement) was achieved on August 13, 2001. Two weeks later NLA members began surrendering their arms to a 3,500-member NATO force, which had entered the country at the request of President Trajkovski. With NATO's "Operation Essential Harvest" achieving a partial disarmament on schedule, on September 6 the Assembly formally approved the peace accords. The pact called in part for constitutional revisions that would excise the privileged status accorded the Macedonian majority and grant official status to other languages with a native-speaking population of at least 20 percent, effectively making Albanian a second official language. The Assembly finally enacted a package of related constitutional amendments on November 16. Five days later, declaring that the national unity government had achieved its aim of restoring domestic stability, the SDSM and LDP resigned from the administration, which was quickly joined by the New Democracy Party (*Nova Demokratija*—ND).

In the parliamentary election of September 15, 2002, former prime minister Branko Crvenkovski's SDSM led a ten-party alliance, the Coalition for Macedonia Together (*Koalicija za Makedonija Zaedno—Koalicija* ZMZ), to a near-majority of 60 seats in the 120-seat *Sobranje*. Prime Minister Georgievski's VMRO-DPMNE and its principal ally, the LPM, managed to win only 33 seats. The Democratic Union for Integration (*Demokratska Unija za Integracija/Bashkimit Demokratik për Integrim*—DUI/BDI), chaired by former Albanian National Liberation Army leader Ali Ahmeti, won 16 seats and joined a new Crvenkovski coalition government, which was confirmed by the national Assembly (*Sobranje*) and took office on November 1.

On February 26, 2004, President Trajkovski and six of his staff members were killed in a plane crash near Mostar in Bosnia and Herzegovina. In the first round of elections to choose Trajkovski's successor on April 14, Prime Minister Crvenkovski of the SDSM and Sasko KEDEV of the VMRO-DPMNE advanced, leaving behind two ethnic Albanian candidates. (Former interior minister Ljube BOSKOVSKI was barred from running as an independent because he had not fulfilled a constitutional residency requirement, while Arben Xhaferi, the DPA/PDSh chair, withdrew.) Crvenkovski won the April 28 runoff with 62.7 percent of the vote and was sworn in as president on May 12, Assembly Speaker Ljubčo JORDANOVSKI having served in the interim as acting president. Interior Minister Hari KOSTOV succeeded Crvenkovski as prime minister and was sworn in on June 2, after a parliamentary vote of confidence. On November 15, however, Kostov resigned in protest against corruption and nepotism within the coalition. He was replaced by Vlado BUČKOVSKI, who also took over as SDSM chair. On December 17 the Assembly approved Bučkovski's coalition government, which included the DUI/BDI.

Parliamentary elections were held on July 5 and July 19, 2006. VMRO- DPMNE, leading a broad coalition, won 45 seats, defeating rival coalitions led by the SDSM and DUI/BDI. Negotiations between the VMRO-DPMNE's Nikola GRUEVSKI, the prospective prime minister, quickly brought the New Social Democratic Party (*Nova Socijal Demokratska Partija*—NSDP), the SPM, and the LPM into government. However, the search to find a partner from the country's three ethnic Albanian parties proved more protracted. Following unsuccessful negotiations with the DUI/BDI and PDP/PPD, an agreement was made with the DPA/PDSh. The cabinet was inaugurated on August 26 following approval by the *Sobranje* on the same day.

In 2007 both the SDSM and DUI/BDI coalitions broke apart, leading to broader support for the government with the PDP/PDD and several smaller parties joining the ruling coalition. Nevertheless, the government was unable to secure sufficient legislative support to enact economic reforms and proposals regarding the ethnic Albanian minority. The government faced an additional setback in April 2008 when Greece vetoed the expected offer of NATO membership for Macedonia, citing the continued name dispute. The VMRO-DPMNE and allied parties consequently voted for an early election in 2008, hoping for a "mandate" to enact change.

Despite problems during the polling (see Current Issues, below), the VMRO-DPMNE secured a decisive victory in the June 2008 elections, with its coalition winning an outright majority with 63 seats. Prime Minister Gruevski subsequently formed a new government with the DUI/BDI that was also supported by the Party for a European Future (*Partija za Evropska Idnina*—PEI). As a result, the government was backed by 82 legislators, more than the two-thirds necessary to enact constitutional reforms.

Gjorge IVANOV of the VMRO-DPMNE finished first among seven candidates in the first round of presidential balloting on March 22, 2009, with 35.0 percent of the vote, followed by the SDSM's Ljubomir FRČKOSKI with 20.5 percent. Ivanov won the runoff with Frčkoski on April 5 with 63.1 percent of the vote.

Constitution and government. The constitution proclaimed in November 1991 defines Macedonia as a state based on citizenship, not ethnicity, and specifically rules out any territorial claims on neighboring countries. The Albanian minority, however, asserted that the preamble and dozens of provisions of the basic law accorded privileged status to the ethnic and religious Macedonian majority. This perception contributed to the violent events of 2001 and led to enactment of a series of corrective amendments later that year. The principal changes were a revised preamble referring to nonethnic Macedonian communities as citizens; a requirement that certain legislation obtain minority group approval as well as passage by the full legislature (a "double majority"); provision for additional official languages in areas where native speakers constitute 20 percent of the population; and proportional representation of ethnic Albanians in the Constitutional Court, public administration, and security forces.

The constitution provides for a directly elected president serving a five-year term as head of state and a cabinet, headed by a prime minister, owing responsibility to a unicameral national Assembly (*Sobranje*). The Assembly is elected for a four-year term by a combination of majority and proportional voting. Ultimate judicial authority is vested in a Supreme Court, with a Constitutional Court adjudicating constitutional issues.

In 2002 the Assembly approved legislation providing for the devolution of greater authority to local government, effectively granting a measure of self-rule to ethnic Albanian regions. In other measures to integrate ethnic Albanians into national life, legislators passed a controversial law granting status as a state university to the underground Albanian-language university in Tetovo. A new citizenship law passed in 2003 enabled foreign nationals to qualify for citizenship after 8 rather than 15 years of legal residence.

In 2004 the Assembly passed a redistricting law cutting the number of administrative districts from 123 to 84, in 16 of which Albanians claimed a majority. The law, which was in accordance with the 2001 Ohrid peace accords, gave local authorities greater powers in regional planning, finance, and health care. The measure was opposed by many ethnic Macedonians, who feared that redistricting could lead to partition of the country along ethnic lines, but a November referendum to annul the legislation was boycotted by many parties and groups and therefore failed by nearly half to obtain the necessary 50 percent participation rate. Further proposals advanced by Gruevski in 2007 to reform the electoral system by adding 13 guaranteed seats for non-Albanian ethnic minorities and émigré Macedonians living abroad have been stalled by opposition in parliament.

Foreign relations. Recognition of Macedonia by the EC/EU was stalled by the insistence of Greece that recognition be conditioned on Macedonia's changing its name. Greece based its position on historical considerations, including the fact that its own northernmost province is also named Macedonia. Thus, the EC/EU foreign ministers declared at a meeting in May 1992 that the community was "willing to recognize

Macedonia as a sovereign and independent state within its existing borders and under a name that can be accepted by all parties concerned." Outside of the EC/EU, Turkey was unmoved by Greece's concerns, having extended recognition to Macedonia on February 6. On August 6 Russia also recognized the new republic.

On December 11, 1992, the UN Security Council authorized the dispatch of some 700 UN peacekeeping troops and military observers to the Macedonia-Serbia/Kosovo border in an effort to prevent the fighting in Bosnia and Herzegovina from spreading to the south. Subsequently, the Clinton administration in the United States, which had consistently refused to commit ground forces to the Bosnian theater, indicated that it was willing to participate in the Macedonian peacekeeping effort, and on June 18, 1993, the first troops of an eventual 500-strong U.S. contingent arrived to join the UN Preventive Deployment Force (UNPREDEP). The force's mandate was renewed at six-month intervals thereafter, with its size increasing to 1,150 by November 1996.

Disagreements with Greece, including the nomenclature dispute, continued throughout the 1990s. After the Skopje government formally applied for UN membership on January 7, 1993, a partial Greek concession permitted the new state to join the UN in April as "The former Yugoslav Republic of Macedonia." Under the compromise, a definitive name as well as a related dispute over the use of Alexander the Great's Star of Vergina symbol on the Macedonian flag would have to be negotiated. The new republic was not permitted to fly its flag outside UN buildings until a 1995 U.S.-UN-brokered agreement settled on an acceptable flag design.

Strains with Greece were aggravated by the return to power of a socialist government in Athens in October 1993. Greek Prime Minister Andreas Papandreou was incensed by the decision of the leading EU states in December to recognize Macedonia, and on February 16, 1994, after Washington had extended recognition, Athens imposed a controversial partial trade embargo on Macedonia, cutting the landlocked republic off from the northern Greek port of Salonika (Thessaloniki), its main import-export channel, for all goods except food and medicine.

UN and U.S. mediation brought Macedonia's dispute with Greece to partial resolution on September 13, 1995, when the respective foreign ministers initialed an agreement in New York covering border definition, revision of the Macedonian constitution to exclude any hint of territorial claims, and the design of the Macedonian flag, which incorporated a sun with rays to replace the disputed star. Following ratification by the Macedonian Assembly, the accord was formally signed in Skopje on October 15, whereupon Greece lifted its trade embargo. In light of the accommodation with Greece, Macedonia was admitted to full membership in the Organization for Security and Cooperation in Europe (OSCE) on October 12, 1995, and to the Council of Europe a week later. Despite the Skopje-Athens 1995 agreement, the Greek government, throughout the rest of the decade and into the next, strongly opposed the "Republic of Macedonia" name preferred, with equal resolution, by its northern neighbor.

Moves by the Skopje government to counter a developing Belgrade-Athens axis on Balkan matters included the cultivation of relations with Bulgaria, which had recognized Macedonia in January 1992, and with Turkey. However, the Bulgarian policy encountered difficulty in April 1994 when a Bulgarian minister broke off a visit to Macedonia because of Skopje's insistence on the existence of a distinct Macedonian language. Reflecting the traditional Bulgarian view that Macedonians are really Bulgarians (and their language a variant of Bulgarian), the Bulgarian minister's action reminded the international community that Bulgaria had recognized Macedonia, but not the Macedonian nationality. The two governments appeared to bridge their differences in early 1999, negotiating a compromise on the language question, which had been blocking Bulgaria's ratification of some 20 bilateral agreements. Bulgaria also provided military aid to the Macedonian army, which lacked armor or heavy weapons, in the form of tanks, howitzers, spare parts, and ammunition from surplus stocks. Relations remained cordial in 2000 despite Sofia's banning of an ethnic Macedonian party, the United Macedonian Organization (*"Ilinden"*), which generated outraged protests by nationalistic groups in Macedonia. During a May visit to Skopje, Bulgarian President Petar Stoyanov signed nine bilateral accords and urged continuing friendship and mutual respect. Despite support for the Macedonian state, the Bulgarian government continues to deny aspects of ethnic Macedonian identity, language, and history. This was underscored on July 24, 2006, when Bulgarian Minister of Foreign Affairs Ivailo Kalfin noted that "aggression towards the Bulgarian nation or history on behalf of the Macedonian authorities" might limit Bulgaria's support for Macedonian membership in the EU following its own accession on January 1, 2007.

The Belgrade-Athens axis and Serb claims on Macedonian territory militated against a natural alignment between the Macedonians and Serbs, even though Skopje and Belgrade reached a mutual recognition accord in April 1996 and despite widespread sympathy within Macedonia for Serbia in the Yugoslav conflicts. The NATO bombing campaign launched against Yugoslavia in March–June 1999 precipitated the temporary flight of more than 250,000 ethnic Albanians into Macedonia from Kosovo. Most ethnic Macedonians, concerned over the broader regional implications of greater autonomy for the Albanian Kosovars, reportedly opposed the NATO action, while ethnic Albanians in Macedonia called upon the government to provide their confreres with massive assistance. In addition, some ethnic Albanians in Macedonia indicated they might join the KLA in combating Serbian forces, raising the specter of a spillover of the conflict into Macedonia, long considered a "firewall" against further spread of the Balkan fighting. However, the DPA/PDSh's Xhaferi successfully appealed for calm among ethnic Albanians in Macedonia, while the government dutifully accepted the temporary deployment of some 12,000 NATO forces in Macedonia as part of the peacekeeping force proposed for Kosovo.

In view of the Kosovo conflict, most UN members had wanted UNPREDEP to continue to function, but China vetoed a further extension of the mission beyond February 28, 1999. The decision appeared directly related, despite Beijing's denials, to Skopje's establishment of relations with Taiwan in January, an action that caused China to sever ties to Macedonia. Some members of the Georgievski government had argued that recognition of Taiwan would produce a much-needed inflow of foreign investment, on top of foreign aid, from the island, but the results did not meet expectations. Skopje renewed diplomatic ties with Beijing on June 18, 2001, as a consequence of which Taiwan immediately broke relations with Macedonia.

In early 2001 Macedonia indicated that it would no longer pursue new diplomatic ties to countries that refused to recognize the country's designation as the "Republic of Macedonia." (The United States officially recognized Macedonia by its constitutional name, the Republic of Macedonia, in 2004.) Meanwhile, negotiations with Athens over the name issue continued, even while economic ties between the neighbors moved forward. In November 1999, for example, Greece and Macedonia concluded an agreement on construction of a $90 million oil pipeline between Thessaloniki and Skopje, while in April 2000 the National Bank of Greece was one of three foreign investors to purchase Macedonia's largest bank from the government. In May 2002 the Greek and Macedonian defense ministers concluded a military cooperation agreement. (Military ties with the West were subsequently further strengthened by Macedonia's contribution of 40 soldiers to the U.S.-led force in Iraq and 140 troops to the NATO mission in Afghanistan.)

In December 2006 the name dispute was exacerbated when Skopje airport was named "Aleksandar Makedonski Airport," resulting in protests from the Greek government and a rebuke from the EU. The most recent attempted compromise to solve the name dispute, proposed by the European Parliament on June 5, 2007, would have the country referred to as *"Republika Macedonija–Skopje,"* but the term was rejected by the Macedonian government.

The unilateral declaration of independence by Kosovo in February 2008 and subsequent recognition by the United States and majority of EU members were met with caution in Macedonia. Despite pressure by the DPA/PDSh and DUI/BDI for formal recognition, the government limited itself to proceeding with a commission to demarcate the common border. On October 9, 2008, Macedonia formally recognized Kosovo's independence.

The name dispute with Greece took center stage once more in April 2008, when Macedonia's bid to join NATO was formally vetoed by Greece pending the resolution of the issue. The Greek government warned that it would similarly oppose any EU application by Macedonia while the question remained open. The resulting public anger among ethnic Macedonians was widely credited by domestic media as one factor in the VMRO-DPMNE's electoral victory in 2008. (Prime Minister Gruevski had promised not to "trade off" changing the state's name for NATO and EU admission.)

In November 2008 Macedonia filed a complaint with the International Court of Justice arguing that Greek actions to block Macedonian membership in the EU and NATO were contrary to the 1995 interim agreement between the two countries. Tensions were increased further by the Gruevski government's decision to name the country's north-south highway after Alexander the Great, to name the main soccer stadium in Skopje after Phillip II of Macedonia, and to commission a 22-meter statue of Alexander to be placed in the main square of Skopje. Negotiations between Macedonia and Greece continued in 2009 over the potential compromise name of "Republic of Northern Macedonia."

Current issues. Ethnic tensions have diminished since the conflict in 2001 but have not been completely resolved. Although the NLA officially disbanded in September 2001, NATO's Operation Essential Harvest was able to collect some, but not all, of the group's arsenal. Operation Amber Fox, beginning in September, was intended to protect the international monitors who were assigned to oversee implementation of the provisions of the Ohrid accords. Initially authorized for three months, the operation was extended several times before being succeeded on December 14, 2004, by Operation Allied Harmony. Meanwhile, the government pushed forward with related legislation, including an amnesty bill that passed in March 2002 and a series of language laws that won approval in June.

Macedonia formally submitted its application for EU membership in 2004. Continued adherence by all parties to the Ohrid accords was considered vital to future progress on that front. EU concern was raised when the OSCE criticized the conduct of the March 2005 local elections, but the European Commission deemed Macedonia a "worthy candidate" in November and the EU summit granted official candidate status in December. Nevertheless, substantive negotiations for admission have not yet begun, in part because of the dispute between Greece and Macedonia over the latter's name.

The 2006 election was judged to be generally free and fair, although the process was marred by outbreaks of violence as well as allegations of electoral irregularities. Prime Minister Gruevski's inclusion of the DPA/PDSh in the ensuing government deepened rifts among the political parties representing ethnic Albanians. Outbreaks of ethnic and political violence were subsequently reported, including a rocket-powered grenade attack on the central building of the government in August 2007. The key provisions of the Ohrid accords continued to be implemented, but only slowly and with some opposition among ethnic Macedonians. Among other things, certain elements within the Albanian community expressed a preference for union with Kosovo, and former members of the NLA called for a referendum to allow the village of Tanusevci (one of the flash points of the 2001 war) to accede to Kosovo. Police raids in November 2007 and April 2008 seized small but significant caches of weapons reportedly held by NLA splinter groups.

On another front, unemployment continued to spur emigration, notably to Bulgaria: during 2000–2007 more than 75,000 Macedonian citizens applied for Bulgarian passports (including former prime minister Ljubčo Georgievski, who was granted Bulgarian citizenship). As a result, accusations arose in Macedonia that the Bulgarian government was attempting an assimilation policy that would lead to Macedonia's "suicide."

The June 2008 Assembly elections were again tarnished by outbreaks of violence as well as by allegations of voter intimidation, ballot stuffing, and other irregularities. Much of the conflict was between supporters of the DPA/PDSh and DUI/BDI and included street fighting, shootings, and bombings, resulting in at least one death. OSCE monitors noted "serious irregularities" in the election and rated the conduct of 9 percent of polling stations in predominantly ethnic Macedonian areas as "bad" or "very bad." The figure rose to 32 percent in ethnic Albanian majority regions. Irregularities in the June 2 polling at some stations led to the State Electoral Commission invalidating the results in some districts, and a revote was held on June 15. Following new irregularities in this second round, a third round of voting was held in some districts on June 29.

In view of the difficulties that marred the 2008 legislative elections, the EU indicated that open, free, and peaceful presidential elections in 2009 would be a precondition for progress to continue regarding EU membership for Macedonia. These conditions were largely met, although turnout declined from over 1 million voters in the first round to 750,000 in the second round, largely reflecting a boycott by ethnic Albanian voters. Collaterally, the domestic media and Albanian political leaders reported rising ethnic tensions, in part stemming from divisions along ethnic lines regarding the continuing dispute with Greece, which is seen as hindering Macedonia's chances to join the EU and NATO. (A Gallup poll released in February 2009 showed that a majority of both ethnic Macedonian and ethnic Albanian citizens see membership in the EU as desirable. However, if such membership required changing the name of the state, only 3 percent of ethnic Macedonians said they would agree, compared to 69 percent of ethnic Albanians.)

Prime Minister Gruevski replaced several cabinet ministers in July 2009, the reshuffle reportedly reflecting concern over the recent economic downturn and internal party differences (particularly over how to proceed in regard to the EU). Another cabinet shake-up was rumored to be in the offing for the fall following the release of a report from the European Commission regarding Macedonia's status. Meanwhile, Gruevski expressed hope that the election of a new socialist government in Greece in early October might lead to greater flexibility in negotiations over the name dispute. On October 14, 2009, the European Commission recommended that membership negotiations be opened with Macedonia, while urging Gruevski's government to resolve the name issue with Greece. Greek foreign minister Dimitris DROUTSAS has stated that the Greek government will approve the negotiations only after the name dispute is resolved.

POLITICAL PARTIES

For four and a half decades after World War II, the only authorized political party in Yugoslavia was the Communist Party, which was redesignated in 1952 as the League of Communists of Yugoslavia (in Serbo-Croatian, *Savez Kumunista Jugoslavija*—SKJ). In 1989 non-Communist groups began to emerge in the republics, and in early 1990 the SKJ approved the introduction of a multiparty system, thereby triggering its own demise. In Macedonia the party's local branch, the League of Communists of Macedonia (*Sojuz na Komunistite na Makedonija*—SKM), had been succeeded by the SKM-PDP in 1989 (see SDSM, below).

Nearly three dozen parties offered candidates for the 1998, 2002, 2006, and 2008 elections, on their own, in coalitions, or both.

Government and Government-Supportive Parties:

Coalition for a Better Macedonia (*Koalicija za Podobra Makedonija*—KzPM). Established in preparation for the 2008 legislative election, the KzPM is an electoral list of 19 parties in continuation of the 2006 "National Unity" coalition that was also led by the VMRO-DPMNE. Both the 2006 and 2008 lists were frequently referred to as the "VMRO-DPMNE coalition" in local media.

The KzPM included a number of small ethnic parties, many of which had previously supported the opposition in 2006. Their joining the KzPM reflected Prime Minister Gruevski's interest in reforming the parliament by adding dedicated seats for ethnic minorities. Smaller coalition members included the **Democratic Party of the Bosniaks** (*Bošnjačka Demokratska Partija*—BDP), the **Democratic Party of Serbs in Macedonia** (*Demokratska Partija na Srbite vo Makedonija*—DPSM), the **Democratic Party of Turks** (*Partija za Dviženje na Turcite vo Makedonija*—PDTM), the **Democratic Union of the Roma** (*Demokratska Unija na Romite*—DUR), the **Internal Macedonian Revolutionary Organization–Macedonia** (*Vnatrešno Macedonska Revolucionerna Organizacija-Makedonija*—VMRO-Makedonija), the **Party of Democratic Action of Macedonia** (*Stranka na Demokracka Akcija na Makedonija*—SDA), the **Party of the Greens** (*Partija na Zelenite*—PZ), the **Party of Justice** (*Partija na Pravata*), the **Party for Full Emancipation of the Roma** (*Partija za Celosna Emancipacija na Romite*—PCER), the **Party for Integration of the Roma** (*Partija za Integracija na Romite*—PIR), the **Party of Vlachs of Macedonia** (*Stranka na Vlasite od Makedonija*—SVD), the **People's Movement of Macedonia** (*Narodno Dviženje za Makedonija*—NDM), the **Union of Roma in Macedonia** (*Sojuz na Romite na Makedonija*—SRM), the **Worker's Agricultural Party of the Republic of Macedonia** (*Rabotničko Zemjodelska Partija na Republika Makedonija*—RZPRM), and the **United Party for Emancipation** (*Obedineta Partija za Emancipacija*—OPE), a union of two former Roma parties: the Party for Complete Emancipation of Roma and the United Party of Roma from Macedonia.

Internal Macedonian Revolutionary Organization–Democratic Party for Macedonian National Unity (*Vnatrešno Makedonska Revolucionerna Organizacija–Demokratska Partija za Makedonsko Nacionalno Edinstvo*—VMRO-DPMNE). The VMRO is named after a historic group (founded in 1893) that fought for independence from the Ottoman Empire. The DPMNE, launched by Macedonian migrant workers in Sweden, merged with the VMRO in June 1990.

The VMRO-DPMNE, with significant support within the ethnic Macedonian population, strongly endorsed a revival of Macedonian cultural identity, its nationalistic stance being broadly perceived as anti-Albanian and right-wing, despite the group's description of itself as representing the "democratic center." The party won a plurality of 39 seats in the 1990 Assembly, subsequently serving as the main opposition to the Communist-led government. The VMRO-DPMNE's presidential candidate in 1994, Ljubčo Georgievski, gained 21.6 percent of the vote against the SDSM's Kiro Gligorov. However, the VMRO-DPMNE boycotted the second round of the 1994 legislative balloting, alleging fraud in the first round, in which it had been credited with no seats.

The VMRO-DPMNE competed for many of the single-member district seats in the 1998 legislative balloting in an alliance with the Democratic Alternative (below) called "For Changes." It emerged from that balloting with 49 seats, having led all parties in the proportional contest with 28.1 percent of the vote. By that time, the VMRO-DPMNE appeared to have substantially moderated its platform, presenting itself as dedicated to "reconciliation and progress" and earning description as a "neo-liberal" party. Nevertheless, it was still a surprise when Georgievski invited the DPA, a hard-line ethnic Albanian grouping, to join his new government. Georgievski was reelected president of the party at a May 1999 congress.

The VMRO-DPMNE presidential candidate, Boris Trajkovski, won the 1999 election over the SDSM candidate, taking 52.9 percent of the vote in second-round balloting on November 14. He had finished second, with 20.6 percent, in the first round two weeks earlier, when the DA and DPA had offered their own candidates. In the September–October 2000 local elections, a VMRO-DPMNE/DA alliance won the majority of mayoralties.

In August 2000 six VMRO-DPMNE deputies defected to the new Internal Macedonian Revolutionary Organization–True Macedonian Reform Option. The government's legislative majority was briefly threatened three months later when the DA left the governing coalition, but within days Georgievski announced the inclusion of the LPM, which, with added independent support, permitted the administration to remain in power.

The party did poorly in the 2002 legislative elections, winning less than 25 percent of the vote (although Boris Trajkovski remained in the mostly ceremonial position of president). The poor showing, and the rise of Nikola Gruevski to leadership of the party, resulted in July 2004 in supporters of Georgievski leaving the VMRO-DPMNE to form the VMRO-NP (below). Dosta DIMOVSKA, a former party vice president and former minister of the interior, similarly led her supporters to found the Democratic Republican Union for Macedonia (*Demokratski Republički Sojuz za Makedonija*—DRUM). In a fraud-related scandal in 2004, Vojo MIHAJLOVSKI was removed from his position as party secretary.

The split by much of the party's conservative wing effectively moved the VMRO-DPMNE closer to the political center. The VMRO- DPMNE led a coalition with some 13 other (mostly smaller) parties for the 2006 Assembly balloting, winning 38 seats (out of a total of 45 for the coalition). Success has allowed the VMRO-DPMNE to subsequently absorb eight smaller political parties, including the League for Democracy (*Liga za Demokratija*), the Internal Macedonian Revolutionary Organization–True Macedonian Reform Option (*Vnatrešno-Makedonska Revolucionerna Organizacija–Vistinska Makedonska Reformska Opcija*—VMRO-VMRO), the DRUM, and the Agricultural People's Party of Macedonia (*Zemjodelska Narodna Partija na Makedonia*—ZNPM).

Following the 2006 elections, the VMRO-DPMNE's reform agenda was stymied by opposition in parliament. As a result, in April 2008 it led government parties in calling for early elections.

Leaders: Nikola GRUEVSKI (President of the Party and Chair of the Council of Ministers); Gjorge IVANOV (President of the Republic); Trajko SLAVEVSKI, Gordana JANKULOVSKA (Vice Presidents of the Party); Martin PROTOGER (General Secretary).

Socialist Party of Macedonia (*Socijalistička Partija na Makedonija*—SPM). Formerly called the Socialist League–Socialist Party of Macedonia (*Socijalistički Sojuz–Socijalistička Partija na Makedonija*—SS-SPM), the SPM is the successor to the local branch of the former "popular front" grouping, the Socialist League of the Working People of Yugoslavia (in Serbo-Croatian, *Socijalistički Savez Radnog Narodna Jugoslavija*—SSRNJ). For the 1990 elections the SPM formed a partial alliance with the Party for the Total Emancipation of Roma in Macedonia (*Partija za Celosna Emancipacija na Romite vo Makedonija*—PCERM), led by Faik ABDI, which obtained one seat under the SPM umbrella and retained it in 1994. Meanwhile, the SPM won eight seats as part of the SM alliance with the SDSM. Following the death of Kiro POPOVSKI, Ljubisav Ivanov-Dzingo was elected SPM leader in May 1996.

In the wake of the collapse of the SM in 1996, the SPM contested the proportional seats and some of the single-member district seats in the 1998 Assembly balloting in coalition with the PCERM and the Democratic Progressive Party of the Roma in Macedonia (*Demokratska Progresivna Partija na Romite od Makedonija*—DPPRM) as well as some smaller ethnic parties. The SPM won one constituency seat, but the coalition, the Movement for Cultural Tolerance and Civic Cooperation, won only 4.7 percent of the proportional vote and therefore no proportional seats. For the 2000 local elections the SPM entered an SDSM-led alliance.

The SPM retained its single seat in the 2002 Assembly poll. Subsequently, in December 2003, it announced the formation of a coalition called the Third Way that also included the Democratic Alternative (below) and the Democratic Union (below). The SPM joined the VMRO-DPMNE's electoral bloc in 2006, winning three seats in parliament and entering the coalition government. It retained these seats in 2008.

Leaders: Ljubisav IVANOV-DZINGO (President), Blagoje FILIPOVSKI.

Democratic Union (*Demokratski Sojuz*—DS). The DS was founded on March 25, 2000, by former minister of the interior Pavle Trajanov. Identifying itself as a "law and order" party, its program emphasizes the rule of law, the territorial integrity of Macedonia, and an "effective campaign against organized crime, corruption, and drugs." It entered into a coalition with the Socialist Party of Macedonia in 2005 and then joined the SPM in coalition with the VMRO-DPMNE. In the 2008 elections it took one seat in parliament.

Leader: Pavle TRAJANOV (President).

Democratic Renewal of Macedonia (*Demokraticka Obnova na Makedonija*—DOM). The DOM was founded in November 2005 by former LDP member Liljana Popovska. In 2008 elections it retained its single seat in parliament.

Leader: Liljana POPOVSKA.

Democratic Union for Integration (*Demokratska Unija za Integracija/Bashkimit Demokratik për Integrim*—DUI/BDI). The DUI/BDI was formed in June 2002 by Ali Ahmeti, the former head of the Albanian National Liberation Army—NLA (*Ushtrisë Çlirimtare Kombëtare*—UÇK), which had been dissolved in late September 2001 as a consequence of the August peace accord with the government. The principal focus of the DUI/BDI, according to its chair, was the full implementation of the provisions of the Ohrid accords.

In June 2002 the DUI/BDI reportedly entered into merger talks with the **National Democratic Party** (*Nacionala Demokratska Partija/Partisë Demokratike Kombëtar*—NDP/PDK), another Albanian party led by Kastriot HAXHIREXHA and comprising former members of the NLA. However, the parties ultimately contested the 2002 Assembly balloting independently. In 2003 Haxhirexha and Ahmeti announced the merger of the two groups, but other NDP/PDK members disavowed that action, denouncing Haxhirexha, a former critic of the Ohrid accords, for having abandoned the NDP/PDK's "pursuit of federalism." Claiming "no common interest" with the DUI/BDI, the rump NDP/PDK elected new leaders, including Basri HALITI as chair; Xhegair SHAQIRI, the legislator elected under the NDP/PDK banner in 2002, briefly joined the DUI/BDI but then returned to the NDP/PDK. Some reports in the run-up to the 2006 elections referenced the DUI/BDI-NDP/PDK as presenting candidates, although the NDP/PDK also presented its own candidates, indicating that the split between NDP/PDK factions continued.

In the 2006 parliamentary elections the DUI/BDI led an electoral bloc that included the PDP/PPD and the Democratic League of Bosniaks. The DUI/BDI won 14 seats, establishing it as the strongest ethnic Albanian party in parliament. Although the VMRO-DPMNE initially approached it with regards to joining the government, it ultimately chose DPA/PDSh as a partner. The DUI/BDI responded with protests, roadblocks, and mass rallies. The conflict between VMRO-DPMNE and DUI/BDI, which claimed that the government was failing to uphold the Ohrid accords, led to a lengthy boycott of parliament by the latter from January 26 through August 2007, precipitating a political crisis. In May 2007 Menduh Thaçi threatened to remove the DPA/PDSh from the government coalition if the VMRO-DPMNE reached a political agreement with the DUI/BDI, reflecting continued rivalry and conflict between ethnic Albanian political parties. In July 2007 Fazli VELIU, a member of the DUI parliamentary group and one of the founders of the National Liberation Army, suggested that renewed military struggle was a possibility if Kosovo failed to receive independence and ethnic Albanians failed to receive equality within Macedonia. The DUI/BDI leadership subsequently criticized Veliu's statement that "thousands" of ethnic Albanians in Macedonia were ready to take up arms to defend Kosovo.

In the 2008 Assembly election the party took 18 parliamentary seats, strengthening its position as the leading ethnic Albanian party. After negotiations with both the DPA/PDSh and DUI/BDI, the VMRO-DPMNE (which possessed sufficient legislative strength to rule alone) brought the latter into the ruling coalition government, even though previous disagreements between the two parties (particularly over the recognition of Kosovo) remained unresolved. In response to reports of rising ethnic Albanian frustration in 2009, the DUI/BDI urged its coalition partners in the ruling government to find a compromise with Greece over the name dispute by the end of the year. The DUI/BDI still defended the Ohrid Agreement as resolving key minority demands, though the party suggested that implementation might be hastened.

The DUI/BDI's Agron Buxhaku won 7.5 percent of the vote in the first round of the 2009 presidential poll.

Leaders: Ali AHMETI (Chair), Agron BUXHAKU (2009 presidential candidate), Gezim OSTREMI.

Party for a European Future (*Partija za Evropska Idnina*—PEI). The PEI is a centrist party that advocates deeper integration with NATO and the EU. The party was formed in March 2006 by Fijat Canoski. In 2006 and 2008 it won a single seat in parliament. Although it did not receive a cabinet position following the 2008 balloting, the PEI pledged legislative support for the government.

Leader: Fijat CANOSKI.

Other Parliamentary Parties:

Sun–Coalition for Europe (*Sonce–Koalicija za Evropa*). The *Sonce Koalicija* is a continuation of the **Coalition for Macedonia Together** (*Koalicija Za Makedonija Zaedno—Koalicija* ZMZ), which was created in 2002 by the SDSM, LDP, and smaller parties and was renewed for the 2006 elections. Several of the smaller ethnic parties that had been members of the *Koalicija* ZMZ, however, joined the VMRO-DPMNE electoral list in 2008 to support proposed changes that would see greater minority representation in parliament. In addition to the parties below, the *Sonce* coalition included the **Democratic Union of Vlachs from Macedonia** (*Demokratski Sojuz na Vlasite ot Makedonija*—DSVM); the **Green Party of Macedonia** (*Zelena Partija na Makedonia*—ZPM); **New Alternative** (*Nova Alternativa*—NA), a splinter from the VMRO–People's Party; and the **Party of Pensioners of the Republic of Macedonia** (*Partija na Penzionerite na Republika Makedonija*—PPRM).

The Sonce coalition won 27 seats in the 2008 Assembly balloting, which the domestic media generally regarded as a subpar performance.

Social Democratic Union of Macedonia (*Socijaldemokratski Sojuz na Makedonija*—SDSM). The SDSM was the name adopted in 1991 by the League of Communists of Macedonia–Party of Democratic Change (*Sojuz na Komunistite na Makedonija–Partija za Demokratska Preobrazba*—SKM-PDP), which had been launched in 1989 as successor to the SKM. Although the SKM-PDP had run second to the VMRO-DPMNE in the 1990 legislative poll, its nominee, Kiro Gligorov, was subsequently designated president of the republican presidency.

The SDSM was the largest component of the Union of Macedonia (*Sojuz na Makedonija*—SM), an electoral alliance formed for the 1994 presidential and legislative balloting by the SDSM, SPM, and LPM, the three non-Albanian parties of the post-1992 government. The SM supported the SDSM's Gligorov in his successful bid for a second presidential term in 1994, and the SM secured 95 seats (58 for the SDSM) in the controversial concurrent legislative poll, with the SDSM's Branko Crvenkovski remaining as prime minister of the subsequent SM-led government. However, friction developed within the SM, leading to the departure of the LPM from the government in a February 1996 reshuffle. The SM was subsequently described as having collapsed, and minimal cooperation between the SDSM and the SPM was reported in the 1998 legislative elections, from which the SDSM emerged with only 27 seats. (One of the seats credited to the SDSM was won in coalition with the Social Democratic Party of Macedonia [SDPM], which had won a seat in 1994.)

In the 1999 presidential contest the SDSM candidate, former Assembly speaker Tito Petkovski, finished first in the first round, with 32.7 percent of the vote, but lost in the November runoff to the governing coalition's candidate. In May 2000 the SDSM and the LDP concluded a cooperation agreement for the upcoming local elections and the next general election. The League for Democracy soon joined the alliance, and all three immediately called for new elections. An SDSM-led rally in Skopje in mid-May attracted 40,000 people, who heard Crvenkovski charge the government with corruption, failure to raise the standard of living, and an inability to fulfill its election promises. However, a year later the SDSM agreed to join a national unity government, although it withdrew in November 2001, noting that the unity government had accomplished its immediate goal of achieving domestic stability.

In 2004 Crvenkovski was elected president of the republic as the candidate of the *Koalicija* ZMZ. The coalition was renewed for the 2006 Assembly election, at which the SDSM won 23 of the coalition's 32 seats. The defeat resulted in an internal shake-up within the party, with party leader Vlado Bučkovski being removed after losing a no-confidence vote and with Crvenkovski sidelined within the party. In the November 2006 party elections Radmila Sekerinska became the first female leader of a major Macedonian political party since independence.

Following the announcement in April 2008 of early elections, the SDSM organized the *Sonce* coalition, pledging to achieve NATO membership and begin the first steps in EU accession talks by the end of the year. *Sonce*'s poor performance in the June 2008 elections led Sekerinska (and other senior party members) to announce their resignations from their posts in July. Although a temporary party leadership was appointed, Crvenkovski's role was strengthened and he resumed leadership of the party after finishing his presidential term in May 2009.

Leaders: Branko CRVENKOVSKI (President of the Party and Former President of the Republic), Ljubomir FRČKOSKI (2009 presidential candidate), Andrej PETROV (Secretary), Zoran ZAEV (Vice President).

New Social Democratic Party (*Nova Socijal Demokratsčka Partija*—NSDP). The NSDP was formed in November 2005 by former members of the SDSM who sought a more centrist social democratic party. Its party platform is broadly pro-Western and technocratic, stressing Macedonian membership in the EU, improved relations with the United States, investment in "information and communication technology," and the need for economic development. In the 2006 legislative elections the party won seven seats and was subsequently invited to join the government, assuming the ministries of both defense and the economy. In 2008 the party joined the opposition prior to the elections, taking three seats in parliament.

Leaders: Tito PETKOVSKI (President), Predrag TRPESKI (Vice President).

Liberal-Democratic Party (*Liberalno-Demokratska Partija*—LDP). The centrist LDP was formed in January 1997 by what proved to be a temporary merger of the LPM (below) and the Democratic Party of Macedonia (*Demokratska Partija Makedonija*—DPM). The DPM had been registered in July 1993 under the leadership of a Communist-era prime minister but unexpectedly failed to have much impact in the 1994 balloting. When the DPM and LPM merged as the LDP, the DPM's Petar Goševl became leader of the new formation.

The LDP won only four seats in the 1998 legislative poll, securing 7.0 percent in the proportional balloting; Goševl resigned as chair in January 1999 in view of that poor electoral performance. In 2000 the LPM was reestablished as a separate party, taking with it three of the four LDP parliamentary deputies. In May 2000 the LDP joined the SDSM in an electoral alliance for the September local elections and the 2002 Assembly election.

The LDP's participation in the *Koalicija* ZKM contributed to the coalition's success in the 2004 presidential election. In 2006 the party won five seats in parliament. The coalition's poor showing led, in 2007, to party leader Risto PENOV's resignation and a decision for the party to leave the *Koalicija* ZKM, positioning the party for an independent bid in the expected 2010 elections. The 2008 early elections, however, saw the party remain in coalition with its previous partners. It received four seats in parliament.

The LDP's Nano Ruzin won 4.1 percent of the vote in the first round of the 2009 presidential balloting.

Leaders: Jovan MANASIEVSKI (President), Nano RUZIN (2009 presidential candidate), Petar GOŠEV.

Liberal Party of Macedonia (*Liberalna Partija na Makedonija*—LPM). The LPM was organized initially as the Alliance of Reform Forces of Macedonia (*Sojuz na Reformskite Sili na Makedonija*—SRSM), an affiliate of the federal Alliance of Yugoslav Reform Forces (in Serbo-Croatian, *Savez Reformskih Snaga Jugoslavije*—SRSJ). In the 1990 balloting it was allied in some areas with the Young Democratic and Progressive Party (in Serbo-Croatian, *Mlas Demokratska Progresivna Partija*—MDPS), which it later absorbed, adopting the name Reform Forces of Macedonia–Liberal Party (*Reformskite Sili na Makedonija–Liberalna Partija*—RSM-LP) in 1992. Using the shorter LPM rubric, the party won 29 seats in the 1994 election as part of the Union of Macedonia (SM; see under SDSM, below) and continued to be a component of the ruling coalition. However, growing friction with the dominant SDSM culminated in ejection of the LPM from the coalition in February 1996, whereupon party leader Stojan Andov resigned as speaker of the legislature and committed the LPM to vigorous opposition.

A 1997 merger with the Democratic Party of Macedonia (DPM) to form the Liberal-Democratic Party (LDP) ended in 2000, when the LPM reemerged as a separate organization. In November 2000 the revived party joined the governing coalition led by the VMRO-DPMNE.

The LPM participated in the electoral bloc led by the VMRO-DPMNE for the 2006 assembly poll, winning two seats in parliament and subsequently participating in government. In 2008 it moved to join the opposition, stating dissatisfaction with the government's progress in obtaining NATO and EU membership.

Leaders: Borche STOJANOVSKI (President), Ristana LALCESKA (Vice President).

Democratic Party of Albanians (*Demokratska Partija na Albancite/Partisë Demokratike Shqiptare*—DPA/PDSh). The DPA/PDSh was formed in mid-1997 by the merger of the Party for Democratic Prosperity of Albanians in Macedonia (*Partija za Demokratski Prosperitet na Albancite vo Makedonija*—PDPA) and the People's Democratic Party (*Narodna Demokratska Partija*—NDP). The NDP was an ethnic Albanian grouping that resulted from a split between the moderate majority of the ethnic Albanian Party for Democratic Prosperity and an antigovernment minority, led by Ilijaz Halimi, at a congress of the parent party in February 1994. The NDP became the largest nongovernment party after the October–November elections, at which it won four seats, but lost that status when the LPM joined the opposition in February 1996.

The PDPA had been launched in April 1995 as another breakaway from the PDP by a group opposed to the parent party's participation in the government coalition. Its leader was Arben Xhaferi, a spokesperson for the militant Albanian population who had spent many years in the separatist movement in Kosovo before establishing a base in Tetovo in western Macedonia and being elected as an independent to the Macedonian legislature.

The government allegedly refused to recognize the DPA/PDSh after its formation in 1997 on the grounds that the grouping supported unconstitutional demands on behalf of the Albanians. In fact, official government reports on the 1998 legislative election referenced the grouping as the PDPA/NDP, which contested the balloting in partial alliance with the PDP. Following the election, the use of the DPA/PDSh title appeared to gain the government's sanction, particularly after the DPA/PDSh, which had won 11 legislative seats, agreed to join the subsequent VMRO-DPMNE-led coalition government. Xhaferi, described by the *Christian Science Monitor* as the "flint" that could "set Macedonia afire," called his accord with the VMRO-DPMNE's Ljubčo Georgievski "a small miracle." The DPA/PDSh was not officially registered under that name until July 2002.

Following its entrance into the government, the DPA/PDSh appeared to moderate its course, although Deputy Chair Menduh Thaçi remained one of the more hard-line advocates for Albanian rights. In the 1999 presidential election the party's candidate, Muharem NEXIPI, finished fourth, with 14.8 percent of the vote; in the second round, the DPA/PDSh threw its support to the successful VMRO-DPMNE candidate. The DPA/PDSh won 7 seats in the 2002 Assembly poll, but from April 2005 through January 2006 the delegates boycotted parliamentary sessions in protest of "manipulated results" in the 2005 local elections. In the 2006 parliamentary elections the DPA/PDSh ran independently, winning 11 seats. After failing to reach an agreement with the DUI/BDI, the VMRO-DPMNE negotiated for the DPA/PDSh's entrance into the government.

There were reports during the 2008 Assembly election of violence between members of the DPA/PDSh and the DUI/BDI and of serious electoral irregularities in several districts with a majority of ethnic Albanians. The DPA/PDSh rejected the results of the second round of voting on June 15 but accepted the third round, while accusing the DUI/BDI of fostering division and violence within the Albanian community. Meanwhile, merger discussions with the PDP/PPD proved unsuccessful, although PDP/PPD leader Abduljhadi Vejseli and a significant faction of the PDP/PPD joined the DPA/PDSh (see PDP/PPD below for details).

The DPA/PDSh's Mirushe Hoxha won 3.1 percent of the vote in the first round of presidential balloting in 2009.

Leaders: Menduh THAÇI (Chair), Abduljhadi VEJSELI (Vice President), Imer ALIU, Mirushe HOXHA (2009 presidential candidate), Ernad FEJZULLAHU (Secretary General).

Other Parties Participating in the 2008 Legislative Elections:

Party for Democratic Prosperity (*Partija za Demokratski Prosperite/Partia për Prosperitet Demokratik*—PDP/PPD). The PDP/PPD was one of the principal vehicles for supporting ethnic Albanian interests in Macedonia after its May 1990 launch. Subsequent to the 1990 election (in which it won 25 seats), it absorbed a smaller party with the same abbreviation, the Popular Democratic Party of Ilijaz Halimi.

After joining the government in 1992, the PDP/PPD underwent a split at a February 1994 congress between progovernment moderates, led by Dželadin MURATI, and antigovernment nationalists, led by Halimi, who subsequently reorganized as the NDP (see DPA, above). Dubbing itself the "Party of Continuity," the rump PDP/PPD came into sharp conflict with its coalition partners in mid-1994 over the conviction of a group of alleged Albanian separatists, including the honorary president of the PDP/PPD, Mithat EMINI.

Having lost ground in the October–November 1994 Assembly balloting, the PDP/PPD continued as a government party, although it participated in a boycott of the Assembly by ethnic Albanian deputies from February to July 1995 in protest against a law banning use of Albanian in passports and identity cards. During this period another antigovernment faction broke away as the PDPA (also under the DPA, above), with the rump PDP/PPD remaining in the government coalition.

The PDP/PPD contested the 1998 legislative balloting in partial coalition with the DPA/PDSh (PDPA/NDP), securing 14 seats. However, the PDP/PPD subsequently switched governmental roles with the DPA/PDSh, moving into opposition while the DPA/PDSh joined the new VMRO-DPMNE–led cabinet. Following the poor showing of the party's 1999 presidential candidate, Muhamed HALILI, who finished sixth with 4.2 percent of the vote, the party leadership was replaced virtually en masse in April 2000, President Abdurahman HALITI giving way to Imer IMERI (Ymer YMERI). Although the party competed in the first round of the local elections in 2000, it pulled out of the second round, alleging major irregularities.

With the departure of the DA from the government in November 2000, Imeri apparently agreed to support the opposition in its bid to replace the Georgievski coalition, but he changed his mind when several of the party's Assembly members objected. Subsequent talks with the DPA/PDSh's Xhaferi and the VMRO-DPMNE about joining the government broke down in late December, in part because a hard-line faction demanded that the proposed private Albanian-language university in Tetovo be a state institution and that use of the Albanian language be permitted in the National Assembly—demands that the government was not prepared to accept at that time. Early in 2001 speculation rose that the PDP/PPD and the DPA/PDSh might merge, but that was before the outbreak of hostilities between militant

Albanians and the government. International pressure reportedly led the PDP/PPD to join the May 2001 national unity administration.

In May 2002 Haliti returned to the party presidency following Imeri's resignation for health reasons. Secretary General Muhamed Halili was expelled a month later for criticizing Haliti. The PDP/PPD won two seats in the 2002 Assembly poll.

In the 2006 legislative elections the party ran in an electoral bloc with the DUI/BDI, winning three seats. The DUI/BDI's conflict with the VMRO-DPMNE resulted in a boycott of parliament in 2007 by both the DUI/BDI and PDP/PPD. Fears that the PDP/PPD was becoming marginalized prompted it to break its coalition in May 2007. On June 12 the PDP/PPD formally entered the government, where it attempted to moderate relations between the VMRO-DPMNE and the DUI/BDI.

The PDP/PPD performed poorly in the June 2, 2008, legislative elections, taking less than 1 percent of the vote and no seats. Party leader Abduljhadi Vejseli consequently proposed a full merger with the DPA/PDSh, and PDP/PPD members were encouraged to vote for the DPA/PDSh in the revotes held on June 15 and June 29. However, the merger proposal provoked a backlash within the PDP/PPD that prompted Vejseli to leave the party and join the DPA/PDSh.

Sefedin Haruni was appointed president of the PDP/PPD in August 2008 and confirmed at a party congress in December. In June 2009 Haruni joined other Albanian political figures (including Hisni SHAQIRI, a former prominent parliamentarian and current leader of the NDU/BDK, below) in calling for extensive constitutional changes to Macedonia beyond those laid out in the Ohrid Framework. Among other things, they proposed the creation of a "bi-national" state under a federal structure.

Leaders: Sefedin HARUNI (Leader), Arianit HOXHA (Secretary General).

Minor parties participating in the 2008 elections include the **Fathers' Macedonian Organization for Radical Renewal–Vardar-Aegean-Pirin** (*Tatkovinska Makedonska Organizatsija za Radikalna Obnova–Vardar-Egej-Pirin*—TMORO-BEP, a reference to one of the early names of the 19th-century VMRO), the **VMRO–Democratic Party** (*VMRO–Demokacija Partija*), the **Movement for National Unity of Turks** (*Dvizhenje za Nacionalno Edinstvo na Turcite*), the **Party of Free Democrats** (*Partija na Slobodni Demokrati*—PSD), the **Radical Party of the Serbs in Macedonia** (*Radikalna stranka na Srbite vo Makedonija*—RSSM), the **Union of Tito's Left Forces** (*Sojuz na Titovi Levi Sili*—STLS), and the **National Democratic Union** (*Nacionalna Demokratska Unija/Bashkimi Demokratik Kombëtar*—NDU/BDK). None of these parties was able to obtain 1 percent of the total vote.

Other Parties:

New Democracy (*Nova Demokratija/Demokracia e Re*—ND/DR). The ND/DR was formed in September 2008 as a new party representing Albanian interests by Imer Selmani, former vice president of the DPA/PDSh, and other DPA/PDSh members (including a number of legislators) who cited policy differences with the DPA/PDSh leadership for their defection. Selmani won 15 percent of the vote in the first round of the 2009 presidential election, finishing ahead of the candidates from rival ethnic Albanian parties. The ND/DR was subsequently reported to have five legislators within its membership.

Leaders: Imer SELMANI (Chair and 2009 presidential candidate), Sulejman RUSHITI.

Democratic Alternative (*Demokratska Alternativa*—DA). Formed in March 1998 by Vasil Tupurkovski, the Macedonian member of the final Yugoslavian State Presidency, the DA presented a strongly "probusiness" platform. It contested many of the single-member district seats in the October legislative election in the "For Changes" alliance with the VMRO-DPMNE and won 10.1 percent of the vote in the proportional balloting. Having secured 13 legislative seats, the DA was accorded six posts in the subsequent coalition government led by the VMRO-DPMNE.

Tupurkovski finished third in the 1999 presidential race, with 16 percent of the vote. In the 2000 local elections the party again ran in alliance with the VMRO-DPMNE, but on November 24 it left the governing coalition, ostensibly because of the slow pace of economic reform. Personality differences between Tupurkovski and Prime Minister Georgievski may also have contributed to the rupture. As a consequence, four of the party's legislators immediately departed to sit as independents while continuing their support for the government, and three others defected to the VMRO-DPMNE after the new year. In the 2006 parliamentary elections it won no seats and took less than 2 percent of the national vote; it did not compete in the 2008 elections.

Leaders: Vasil TUPURKOVSKI (Chair), Savo KLIMOVSKI (Former Speaker of the Assembly).

Internal Macedonian Revolutionary Organization–People's Party (*Vnatrešno Makedonska Revolucionerna Organizacija–Narodna Partija*—VMRO-NP). The VMRO-NP was formed in Skopje in July 2004 by supporters of former VMRO-DPMNE chair and prime minister Ljubčo Georgievski. The VMRO-NP is a conservative party whose platform closely resembles the VMRO-DPMNE. In the 2006 parliamentary elections it won six seats, but three members of parliament subsequently left the party. Its former leader, Ljubčo Georgievski, took Bulgarian citizenship in 2006, resigned as party president in 2007 (though retaining an honorary position as "party leader"), and subsequently entered Bulgarian politics as a mayoral candidate for Blagoevgrad. In May 2008 the state election commission revoked the party's candidate list, citing that the group missed submission deadlines.

Leaders: Marjan DODEVSKI (Acting President), Ljubcho GEORGIEVSKI (Party Leader).

LEGISLATURE

The present Macedonian **Assembly** (*Sobranje*) is a directly elected unicameral body of 120 members, elected for a four-year term through proportional representation from six electoral districts, each with 20 seats. Prior to 2002, 85 of the legislators were directly elected in two-round (if necessary) majoritarian balloting in single-member districts; the other 35 were elected on a nationwide proportional basis, with seats distributed to parties winning at least 5 percent of the national vote.

Following the election of June 2, 15, and 29, 2008, the seat distribution was as follows: the Coalition for a Better Macedonia, 63 (the Internal Macedonian Revolutionary Organization–Democratic Party for Macedonian National Unity, 53; the Socialist Party of Macedonia, 3; the Democratic Union, 1; Democratic Renewal of Macedonia, 1; the Democratic Party of Serbs in Macedonia, 1; the Democratic Party of Turks, 1; the United Party for Emancipation, 1; the Party of Democratic Action of Macedonia, 1, and the Internal Macedonian Revolutionary Organization-Macedonia, 1); the Sun–Coalition for Europe, 27 (the Social Democratic Union of Macedonia, 18; the Liberal-Democratic Party, 4; the New Social Democratic Party, 3; New Alternative, 1; the Liberal Party of Macedonia, 1); the Democratic Union for Integration, 18; the Democratic Party of Albanians, 11; and the Party for a European Future, 1.

Speaker: Trajko VELJANOSKI.

CABINET

[as of September 1, 2009]

Prime Minister	Nikola Gruevski (VMRO-DPMNE)
Deputy Prime Minister	Zoran Stavreski (VMRO-DPMNE)
Deputy Prime Minister (Economy)	Vladimir Peshevski (VMRO-DPMNE)
Deputy Prime Minister (EU Integration)	Vasko Naumovski (VMRO-DPMNE)
Deputy Prime Minister (Ohrid Agreement Implementation)	Abdulhakim Ademi (DUI/BDI)
Ministers	
Agriculture, Forestry, and Water Supply	Ljupcho Dimovski (SPM)
Culture	Elizabeta Kancevska Milevska (VMRO-DPMNE) [f]
Defense	Zoran Konjanovski (VMRO-DPMNE)
Economy	Fatmir Besimi (DUI/BDI)
Education and Science	Nikola Todorov (VMRO-DPMNE)
Environment and Physical Planning	Nexhati Jakupi (DUI/BDI)
Finance	Trajko Slavevski (VMRO-DPMNE)
Foreign Affairs	Zoran Stavreski (VMRO-DPMNE)
Health	Bujar Osmani (DUI/BDI)
Informatics and Technology	Ivo Ivanovksi (VMRO-DPMNE)

Internal Affairs	Gordana Jankulovska (VMRO-DPMNE) [f]
Justice	Mihajlo Manevski (VMRO-DPMNE)
Labor and Social Policy	Xhelal Bajrami (DUI/BDI)
Local Self-Government	Musa Xhaferi (DUI/BDI)
Transport and Communications	Mile Janakieski (VMRO-DPMNE)
Without Portfolio	Nezhdet Mustafa (SPM)
Without Portfolio	Hadi Neziri (PDTM)
Without Portfolio	Vele Samak (ind.)

[f] = female

COMMUNICATIONS

Freedom of the press is protected by the constitution.

Press. Macedonia has experienced turbulence, contraction, and conglomeration in print media since 2002. The three largest Macedonian-language dailies—*Dnevnik, Utrinski Vesnik,* and *Vest*—were acquired by a German media conglomerate, *Westdeutsche Allgemeine Zeitung* (WAZ) at the end of 2002. The decline of rival dailies led to concerns over the possibility of a print media "monopoly," eased in 2006 by the emergence of new independent papers.

The following are dailies published in Skopje in Macedonian unless noted otherwise: *24 Chasa* (100,000, included as an insert in several publications), *Dnevnik* (50,000), *Shpik* (50,000), *Utrinski Vesnik* (30,000), *Koha* (27,000), in Albanian; *Vest* (15,000). (Reported circulation figures are contested between the various publications and media organizations.) There are also a number of smaller national and local papers published daily, weekly, or fortnightly in Macedonian, Albanian, Turkish, and Romani, as well as national weekly magazines (*Forum, Kapital, Makedonsko Sonce,* and *Puls*). The government provides subsidies to all print media, but many publications reportedly suffer from financial difficulties. These difficulties may explain the growing Internet presence of newspapers and the emergence of news Web sites, the latter including einnews.com and maknews.com.

News agencies. There are two news agencies: the state-owned Macedonian Information Agency and the privately owned Makfak.

Broadcasting and computing. Broadcasting is still dominated by the state-run *Makedonska Radio-Televizija* (MRT), formerly Radio-Television Skopje (*Radiotelevizija Skopje*), which provides both terrestrial and satellite service. Independent stations, largely unlicensed, also broadcast.

INTERGOVERNMENTAL REPRESENTATION

Ambassador to the U.S.: Zoran JOLEVSKI.

U.S. Ambassador to Macedonia: Philip Thomas REEKER.

Permanent Representative to the UN: Slobodan TAŠOVSKI.

IGO Memberships (Non-UN): BIS, CEI, CEUR, EBRD, Eurocontrol, Interpol, OIF, OSCE, PCA, WCO, WTO.

MADAGASCAR

Republic of Madagascar
Repoblikan'i Madagasikara (Malagasy)
République de Madagascar (French)

Note: President Andry Rajoelina announced a new cabinet, again led by Prime Minister Monja Roindefo, on September 8, 2009, but its composition was rejected by the three main opposition forces (led by former presidents Marc Ravalomanana, Didier Ratsiraka, and Albert Zafy). After further negotiations, on November 13 Eugene Mangalaza was inaugurated as the new "consensus" prime minister, and two "copresidents" (representing the Ravalomanana and Zafy camps) were appointed later in the month. However, the allocation of portfolios in the planned national unity cabinet subsequently proved contentious, with Rajoelina refusing to participate in the negotiations. On December 18 Rajoelina declared the power-sharing agreement void and unilaterally appointed Col. Vital Albert Camille as prime minister, prompting widespread international criticism.

Political Status: Established as the Malagasy Republic within the French Community in 1958; became independent June 26, 1960; military regime established May 18, 1972; name of Democratic Republic of Madagascar and single-party system adopted in new constitution and Socialist Revolutionary Charter approved by national referendum on December 21, 1975; present name adopted in the new constitution of the Third Republic (codifying multiparty activity first authorized by presidential decree of March 1990) that was approved by national referendum on August 19, 1992, but was subsequently the subject of extensive political conflict; federal system established by constitutional amendments approved by national referendum on March 15, 1998, and promulgated on April 8; federal system restructured by constitutional amendments passed by referendum on April 4, 2007, and promulgated April 28; transitional government following a coup on March 17, 2009.

Area: 226,657 sq. mi. (587,041 sq. km.).

Population: 12,092,157 (1993C); 20,221,000 (2008E).

Major Urban Center (2005E): ANTANANARIVO (1,581,000).

Official Languages: Malagasy, French, English.

Monetary Unit: Ariary (official rate December 1, 2009: 1,934.50 ariarys = $1US). The ariary replaced the Madagasy Franc in mid-2003.

President: Andry RAJOELINA (Young Malagasies Determined); installed as president of the High Authority of the Transition on March 21, 2009, after his predecessor, Marc RAVALOMANANA (I Love Madagascar) surrendered power to a military directorate on March 17.

Prime Minister: *(See headnote.)* Monja ROINDEFO Zafitsimivalo (National Movement for the Independence of Madagascar); assumed office March 17, 2009, after being appointed as head of a transitional government by the president of the High Authority of the Transition on February 7; succeeding Gen. Charles RABEMANANJARA (I Love Madagascar).

THE COUNTRY

The Republic of Madagascar, consisting of the large island of Madagascar and five small island dependencies, is situated in the Indian Ocean off the southeast coast of Africa. The island is renowned for its biodiversity and its treasure trove of unique plant and animal species. Although the population includes some 18 distinct ethnic groups, the main division is between the Asian Mérina people (the largest ethnic group [26 percent of the population]) of the central plateau and the sub-Saharan peoples of the coastal regions (*côtiers*). The Malagasy language is of Malayo-Polynesian origin, yet reflects African, Arabic, and European influences. The population is about 36 percent Christian (predominantly Roman Catholic in the coastal regions, Protestant on the plateau) and about 9 percent Muslim, while the remaining 55 percent adhere to traditional beliefs. The nonindigenous population includes some 30,000 Comorans and smaller groups of French, Indians, Pakistanis, and Chinese. Women constitute more than 45 percent of the labor force, performing the bulk of subsistence activity. However, due largely to matriarchal elements in precolonial Malagasy culture, females are significantly better represented in government and urban managerial occupations than their mainland counterparts.

Agriculture, forestry, and fishing account for about two-fifths of Madagascar's gross domestic product (GDP) but employ more than four-fifths of the labor force, the majority at a subsistence level. Leading export crops are coffee, cloves, and vanilla, while industry is concentrated in food processing (notably seafood) and textiles. Mineral resources include deposits of graphite, nickel, chromium, and gemstones (particularly sapphires), in addition to undeveloped reserves of bauxite, iron, titanium, and petroleum.

In the 1970s much of the country's economic base, formerly dominated by foreign businesses, was nationalized by a strongly socialist regime. However, in the face of mounting external debt, worsening trade deficits, and capital flight, the administration in 1980 abandoned its formal commitment to socialism and called for assistance from the

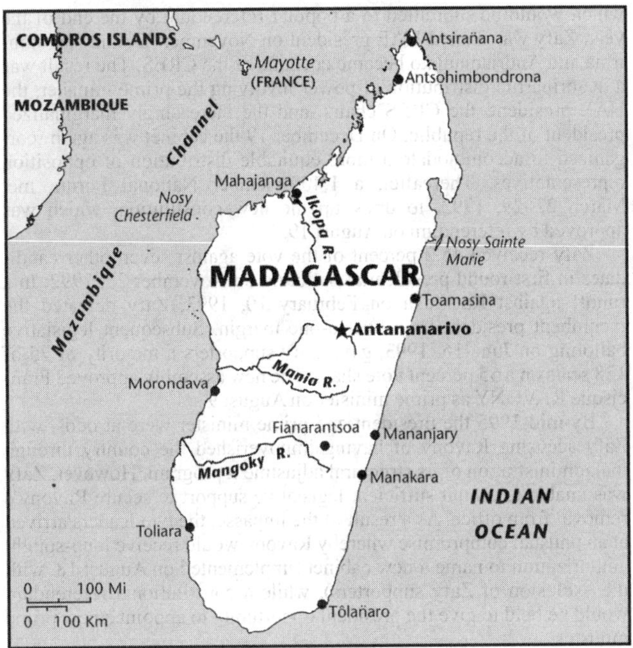

International Monetary Fund (IMF), the World Bank, and U.S. and European donors. In addition, budget austerity, currency devaluations, and measures to reduce food imports by boosting agricultural production were introduced. Although foreign creditors applauded such actions, no measurable economic progress was subsequently achieved, with economic reforms aggravating the decline of living standards in urban areas.

In 1992 the IMF and the World Bank temporarily suspended aid to Madagascar, calling for additional austerity measures and widespread economic reform. The government adopted (nominally at least) an adjustment strategy in 1994 focusing on privatizing state-run enterprises, deregulating various sectors, and liberalizing restrictions on foreign investment. Following a period of sustained growth in the late 1990s, the country suffered a series of economic shocks. By 2000 it was reported that an estimated 75 percent of the population lived in poverty and that the health and education infrastructures were dilapidated. The lingering effects of three cyclones in early 2000 and weak export prices made the economy a key issue in the controversial 2001 presidential campaign (see Political background, below).

In 2002 the GDP declined by 12.7 percent, and inflation spiked to 15.4 percent, as a result of violence and uncertainty associated with the contested presidential election. The new administration subsequently enjoyed consistent international support, in part because of its measures to support economic liberalization, encourage foreign investment, and eliminate corruption. In 2003 the economy began to recover, with GDP growing by 9.6 percent and inflation declining to 2.7 percent with the introduction of a new currency, the ariary. The IMF dispersed a $100 million credit for economic restructuring and arranged several multimillion dollar grants for economic reforms in 2002. Arrangements for substantial multilateral debt relief were concluded with the IMF and World Bank in 2004.

GDP growth fell to 5.3 percent in 2004, in part because of the effects of a devastating cyclone. Inflation remained around 11 percent in 2005 and 2006 because of high world commodity prices. However, analysts subsequently predicted significantly positive economic developments for Madagascar, based on expanded foreign investment and the country's accession in May 2006 to the Southern African Development Community (SADC), which was expected to expand regional trade opportunities. Meanwhile, aid from the World Bank and the European Union (EU) was earmarked for infrastructure projects (mostly the construction of roads) and programs designed to reduce poverty.

GDP growth rebounded to 6.3 percent in 2007 and 7 percent in 2008. The nation's mining sector expanded due to the discovery of nickel, copper, and platinum deposits and the development of chromite and ilmenite mines. With a $3.3 billion investment by the Japanese firm, Sumitomo, and other foreign backers, a nickel mine, said to be the world's largest, opened in Tamatave in November 2007. In March 2008 oil production began in Madagascar for the first time in 60 years. Despite economic growth, Madagascar remained one of the world's poorest countries, with a malnutrition rate of 38 percent, according to the United Nations.

As in 2002, Madagascar's political crisis of 2009 resulted in a significant drop in foreign investment, development aid, and revenue from tourism. Government services such as sanitation were halted for long periods amid the uncertainty of the transition. At the same time, a third straight year of severe drought in the south, several major cyclones, and the steep increase in food prices contributed to a humanitarian emergency, with nearly two-thirds of the population facing food insecurity. A sharp decline in global demand for vanilla further weakened the country's agrarian sector. The IMF projected a slight decline in GDP of 0.2 percent for 2009.

GOVERNMENT AND POLITICS

Political background. During the 18th century and most of the 19th century, Madagascar was dominated by the Mérina people of the plateau. However, after a brief period of British influence, the French gained control and by 1896 had destroyed the Mérina monarchy. Renamed the Malagasy Republic, it became an autonomous state within the French Community in 1958 and gained full independence on June 26, 1960, under the presidency of Philibert TSIRANANA, a *côtier* who governed with the support of the Social Democratic Party (*Parti Social Démocrate*—PSD).

Tsiranana's coastal-dominated government ultimately proved unable to deal with a variety of problems, including ethnic conflict stemming from Mérina opposition to the government's pro-French policies. In addition, economic reverses led to a revolt in 1971 by peasants in Tulear Province, while students, dissatisfied with their job prospects in a stagnating economy, mounted a rebellion in early 1972. Having acknowledged his growing inability to rule in May, Tsiranana abdicated his duties as head of state and chief of government in favor of Maj. Gen. Gabriel RAMANANTSOA, a Mérina, who was confirmed for a five-year term by a referendum held October 8.

An attempted coup by dissident *côtier* officers led to Ramanantsoa's resignation on February 5, 1975; his successor, Col. Richard RATSIMANDRAVA, a Mérina, was assassinated six days later, with Brig. Gen. Gilles ANDRIAMAHAZO assuming the leadership of a Military Directorate. Andriamahazo was in turn succeeded on June 15 by Cdr. Didier RATSIRAKA, who as foreign minister had been instrumental in reversing Tsiranana's pro-Western policies in favor of a more Soviet-oriented and vigorously pro-Arab agenda from May 1972. Subsequently, on December 21, 1975, voters approved a Socialist Revolutionary Charter and a new constitution that called for the establishment of a National Front for the Defense of the Malagasy Socialist Revolution (*Front National pour la Défense de la Révolution Socialiste Malgache*—FNDR) as an overarching political formation. The voters also designated Ratsiraka, a *côtier*, for a seven-year term as president of the newly styled Democratic Republic of Madagascar; thereby he continued his role as chair of a Supreme Revolutionary Council (*Conseil Suprême de la Revolution*—CSR) that had been established in 1972.

The new Ratsiraka government formed on January 11, 1976, was designed to reflect a regional balance of both military and civilian elements. The government was reconstituted on August 20 following the accidental death of Prime Minister Joël RAKOTOMALALA on July 30 and his replacement by Justin RAKOTONIAINA on August 12. Local elections, the first since the constitutional revision, began in March 1977 and were dominated by the Vanguard of the Malagasy Revolution (*Antoky'ny Revolosiona Malagasy*—Arema), established by Ratsiraka a year earlier as the main FNDR component. Arema members also filled 112 of the 137 positions on the FNDR's single list of National Assembly candidates, which was approved by a reported 90 percent of voters on June 30. Ratsiraka subsequently appointed a new cabinet, headed by Prime Minister Lt. Col. Désiré RAKOTOARIJAONA.

President Ratsiraka was popularly reelected to a seven-year term on November 7, 1982, by a four-to-one margin over Monja JAONA of the National Movement for the Independence of Madagascar (*Mouvement National pour l'Indépendqnce de Madagascar*—Monima), who had campaigned on a platform attempting to capitalize on growing domestic insecurity. Assembly elections scheduled for 1982 were postponed until August 23, 1983, at which time more than 500 candidates from FNDR-affiliated groups were allowed on the ballot. Arema secured 117 seats on the basis of a 65 percent vote share.

In August 1985 an army raid in Antananarivo killed 19 leaders of the country's 10,000-member *kung fu* sect, which was reported to be plotting a revolution. However, this hard-line approach failed to deter burgeoning opposition to administration policies among students, civil servants, and some FNDR members.

On February 12, 1988, Lt. Col. Victor RAMAHATRA (theretofore minister of public works) was named to succeed Colonel Rakotoarijaona as prime minister. While the latter's resignation was officially attributed to "health reasons," observers noted he had recently given the impression of distancing himself from the president.

With the FNDR increasingly unable to maintain control of its constituent groups, the scheduled 1988 assembly elections were postponed, ostensibly to permit their being held simultaneously with presidential balloting in November 1989. However, under powers granted by a constitutional amendment approved by the assembly in December 1988, Ratsiraka moved the presidential election up to March 12, 1989. Aided by disunity within the opposition, which fielded three candidates, Ratsiraka was reelected to another term, albeit with a reduced majority (63 percent) and with waning support in Antananarivo and other urban areas. The opposition remained in disarray after it announced a boycott of the election but then decided at the last minute to participate without having reached agreement on common candidates. Arema had little trouble maintaining its large majority in assembly balloting on May 28.

After the government thwarted a coup attempt in Antananarivo in July 1989, party leaders became increasingly critical of the administration's policies. In early 1990 President Ratsiraka issued a decree that abolished mandatory participation in the FNDR as of March 1. A number of new parties immediately emerged, six of which joined with the Christian Council of Churches of Madagascar (*Fikambanan'ny Fiangonana Kristiana Malagasy*—FFKM) in sponsoring a National Meeting for a New Constitution on May 23. Ten days earlier, three people had been killed and some two dozen injured in a coup attempt by the Republican Committee for Public Safety (*Comité Républican pour le Salut Publique*), whose 15 members reportedly included individuals involved in the 1989 coup attempt. Thereafter, highly publicized FFKM-opposition party conferences held August 16–19 and December 5–9 demanded abolition of the CSR, the formation of an all-party transitional government, and the convening of a constituent assembly to define the institutions of a Third Republic. Ratsiraka responded in January 1991 by announcing that he had asked the government to present a series of proposals to the assembly to bring the constitution into closer conformity with the "national and international context."

On July 28, 1991, following seven weeks of strikes and demonstrations in Antananarivo by the opposition Living Forces (*Forces Vives/Hery Velona*) group, Ratsiraka dissolved the government and announced that he would call for constitutional reform by the end of the year. On August 8 he appointed as prime minister the mayor of Antananarivo, Guy Willy RAZANAMASY, who, after being granted extensive executive powers, proclaimed a desire to lead his country "down the tortuous and difficult road to democracy." However, an interim government announced by Razanamasy on August 26 included no representatives from the FFKM or *Hery Velona,* which was composed of 16 political parties, including the National Union for Development and Democracy (*Union Nationale pour le Développement et la Démocratie*—UNDD) led by Dr. Albert ZAFY, Manandafy RAKOTONIRINA'S Movement for Proletarian Power (*Mpitolona ho'amin'ny Fanjakan'ny Madinika*—MFM), and Rev. Richard ANDRIAMANJATO's now-defunct Congress Party for Madagascar Independence-Renewal (*Parti du Congrès del'Indépendance de Madagascar-Renouveau*—AKFM-*Fanavaozana).* As a result, the opposition launched a general strike and organized a protest rally in the capital of some 300,000 persons, bringing economic life to a sudden halt. In the wake of Ratsiraka's loss of control, Zafy, the leader of *Hery Velona*, set up a shadow government, proclaiming himself as the prime minister and the *Haute Autorité*, a political body composed of the parties in the *Hery Velona*, as the national assembly.

In the wake of continued unrest, Ratsiraka and Razanamasy agreed on October 29, 1991, to the formation of a new unity government that would include representatives of opposition formations, religious groups, and the armed forces. In addition, both the CSR and the assembly transferred their functions to the transitional High State Authority (*Haute Autorité d'État*—HAE) and a Committee for Economic and Social Recovery (*Comité pour le Redressement Économique et Social*—CRES). On October 31 Ratsiraka and the *Hery Velona* signed the Panorama Convention, which established a transitional government. The terms of the convention left Ratsiraka as president but transferred most of his powers to the HAE and CRES, promising a new constitution, which would be submitted to a popular referendum by the end of the year. Zafy was named HAE president on November 23, and Rakotonirina and Andriamanjato became cochairs of the CRES. The result was a quadripartite distribution of power involving the prime minister, the HAE president, the CRES chairs, and the increasingly marginalized president of the republic. On December 19 the cabinet was again reorganized to accommodate a more equitable distribution of opposition representatives. Thereafter, a 1,400-member National Forum met March 22–29, 1992, to draw up the new constitution, which was approved by referendum on August 19.

Zafy received 45.2 percent of the vote against seven other candidates in first-round presidential balloting on November 25, 1992. In a runoff against Ratsiraka on February 10, 1993, Zafy defeated the incumbent president by a two-to-one margin. Subsequent legislative balloting on June 16, 1993, gave Zafy supporters a majority of 75 of 138 seats on a 55 percent vote share. The new assembly approved Francisque RAVONY as prime minister on August 9.

By mid-1995 the president and prime minister were at odds, with Zafy accusing Ravony of having impoverished the country through maladministration of its structural adjustment program. However, Zafy was unable to mount sufficient legislative support to secure Ravony's removal from office. As a result of the impasse, the two leaders arrived at an unusual compromise whereby Ravony would receive long-sought authorization to name a new cabinet (implemented on August 18, with the exclusion of Zafy supporters), while a constitutional referendum would be held to give the president opportunity to appoint a new prime minister.

Despite complaints of a return to authoritarianism, Zafy won a 63 percent "yes" vote in the referendum of September 17, 1995, and on October 30 he appointed Emmanuel RAKOTOVAHINY to succeed Ravony, who had resigned on October 13. Rakotovahiny's cabinet, appointed on November 10, was dominated by members of Zafy's UNDD, although the ongoing dispute regarding economic policy was underscored by the fact that the sentiments of the new finance minister, Jean-Claude RAHERIMANJATO, echoed those of former prime minister Ravony, not Zafy. That controversy came to a head in early May 1996 when IMF director Michel Camdessus, during a visit to Antananarivo, announced that the government as constituted was not suitable to negotiate new agreements with the IMF and World Bank. Consequently, on May 17, the assembly passed a motion of no-confidence in the government by a vote of 109–15. Although Rakotovahiny challenged the constitutionality of the vote, he submitted his resignation on May 20, and on May 28 Zafy appointed Norbert RATSIRAHONANA, chief judge of the High Constitutional Court, as the new prime minister. The cabinet announced by Ratsirahonana on June 5 was again comprised primarily of UNDD members, and many legislators boycotted Ratsirahonana's subsequent policy address to the assembly to protest the government's failure to alter its economic approach.

The executive/legislative conflict culminated on July 26, 1996, in a 99–39 assembly vote to remove Zafy from office on grounds that he had violated his oath of office by taking numerous actions contrary to the constitution and the "interests of the entire Malagasy people." Zafy challenged the legality of the decision, charging that the assembly was attempting a "constitutional coup." However, on September 5 the High Constitutional Court upheld the assembly's action and appointed Prime Minister Ratsirahonana, serving as interim president until new elections could be held, appointed an interim government (including representatives from a number of factions and parties) on September 13. Later in the month he presented the government's revised economic policy to IMF officials.

Fifteen candidates contested the presidential balloting on November 3, 1996. The front-runner was former president Ratsiraka (who had returned in late September from 18 months of self-imposed exile in Paris), with 36.6 percent of the vote. He was followed by Zafy, 23.4 percent; Herizo RAZAFIMAHALEO (head of the Leader–*Fanilo* party), 15 percent; Ratsirahonana, 10 percent; and National Assembly Speaker Rev. Richard ANDRIAMANJATO, 5 percent. Runoff balloting between Ratsiraka and Zafy took place on December 29, Razafimahaleo having thrown his support to the former. Preliminary results showed Ratsiraka ahead by about 30,000 votes, but Zafy alleged fraud during vote tabulation. However, on January 30, 1997, Ratsiraka was proclaimed president by virtue of a 51 percent share of the second-round polling. On February 21 Ratsiraka named Pascal RAKOTOMAVO, a business executive and Arema official, as prime minister. One week later Rakotomavo formed a new multiparty government.

On July 15, 1997, the High Constitutional Court approved the government's proposal to push back the next legislative elections (originally scheduled for mid-1997) to May 1998. Consequently, the term of the National Assembly (then set to expire in August) was extended to mid-1998. For its part, the opposition rejected the government's claim that the additional time was necessary to properly prepare for the balloting, calling the delays "illegal." Relations between the president and his opponents plummeted when he announced plans to organize a constitutional referendum on his proposal to return Madagascar to its pre-1995 provincial system. On February 4, 1998, opposition legislators failed in their effort to impeach Ratsiraka over the matter, and on March 15 the referendum was approved by a narrow margin (50.96 percent). The constitution of the Third Republic entered into force on April 8, providing for a federal system comprising six provincial governments. At the same time, opponents of Ratsiraka accused him of attempting to consolidate power in a "presidential regime." (Under the new constitution the president could name the prime minister and other members of government without reference to the assembly and could dissolve the assembly without any provision for an automatic subsequent election. Whereas previously representative groups nominated 30 senators for appointment by the president, the president could appoint the senators without them having to be nominated by groups. The amendments also left largely to presidential interpretation the relationship between the central and provincial governments.)

In legislative balloting on May 17, 1998, Arema captured 63 seats. The next largest bloc of seats, 32, went to a group of independent, but predominantly propresidential, candidates. After further defections to Arema by a number of former moderate opposition groups, propresidential legislators reportedly controlled at least 90 percent of the assembly posts (albeit in a body whose powers had been diminished by the March constitutional amendments). On July 6 a power struggle between Prime Minister Rakotomavo and Deputy Prime Minister Rajaonarivelo culminated in the resignation from the government of the latter along with 17 other ministers. Unable to govern and constitutionally obligated to resign following assembly elections, Rakotomavo left office on July 22. The following day the president appointed Tantely René Gabrio ANDRIANARIVO, an Arema stalwart and former deputy prime minister, to replace Rakotomavo. On July 31 a new government was named in which Arema controlled all the key portfolios, underscoring the extent to which President Ratsiraka and Arema had secured political control. On the other hand, the administration's economic recovery program continued to falter, with its halting privatization efforts and apparent unwillingness to adhere to international reform prescriptions undermining its chances of securing much needed financial aid. In late 1998 new economic initiatives were announced, with a focus on customs and revenue collection reforms accompanying further privatization pledges.

In March 1999 opposition activists ignored the government's refusal to grant them permission to organize a protest march and demonstrated in Antananarivo. It was widely believed that the unrest in the capital was the start of an intensive campaign to unseat the president. However, the opposition remained disorganized, as evidenced by Arema's successes in the first provincial government elections on December 3, 2000, in which Arema won a majority in all provinces except Antananarivo, and in the first Senate election on March 18, 2001, in which Arema secured 49 of the 60 elected seats. However, a number of smaller parties subsequently endorsed the presidential candidacy of Marc RAVALOMANANA, the supermarket magnate and mayor of Antananarivo who had gained strong support among the middle class with his promises to spur economic growth.

There were six candidates in the presidential election on December 16, 2001, and balloting produced highly controversial and destabilizing results. The government reported that no candidate had secured 50 percent of the votes and that a runoff was required between President Ratsiraka (officially credited with 41 percent of the first-round votes) and Ravalomanana, who had been credited with a front-running 46 percent. However, Ravalomanana, supported by the I Love Madagascar (*Tiako I Madagasikara*—TIM) party, claimed he had in fact won nearly 52 percent of first-round votes, setting the stage for massive political turmoil in early 2002. Ravalomanana's supporters poured into the streets of the capital in late January to protest the government's ruling that a second round of balloting was required. International observers concluded that massive tampering had occurred in the initial official tabulations.

As demonstrations continued, Ravalomanana declared himself president on February 22, 2002, and began installation of his own cabinet under the leadership of Jacques SYLLA. Ratsiraka responded by declaring a national state of emergency on the same day and martial law on February 28. Ravalomanana ignored the declaration of martial law, forming a government without resistance from the army or the security forces. On March 4 the pro-Ratsiraka governors of the five provinces declared that they were autonomous from Antananarivo and established their "capital" in Ratsiraka's home town of Toamasina with the support of five of the six provinces' governors. The army then split its support between the rival candidates. Conditions deteriorated in March as groups loyal to the two parallel governments clashed violently in Antananarivo, control of which was ultimately gained by Ravalomanana's forces, while many of his supporters were arrested, tortured, or killed in the provinces. Negotiations in Senegal in April pointed toward a compromise settlement. However, on April 16 the administrative chamber of the Supreme Court declared the initial published results of the December 16 voting void and ordered a recount, which, as reported by the High Constitutional Court, showed that Ravalomanana had won a first-round majority of 51.5 percent. Ravalomanana was formally inaugurated on May 6, becoming the first elected Mérina president. He subsequently sent the army to regain control of the provinces, replacing provincial governors with special presidential delegates. Ratsiraka refused to accept the legitimacy of that situation and continued to fight it. However, the United States officially recognized Ravalomanana as president of Madagascar on June 26, and similar action by France on July 3 sealed the fate of Ratsiraka, who left the country on July 5 for eventual exile in France.

On June 18, 2002, President Ravalomanana reappointed Sylla as prime minister. Hopes for reconciliation were dashed when the new cabinet excluded Ratsiraka's supporters, with the exception of one Arema minister. In the next month, President Ravalomanana used his power to appoint 30 senators, but Arema retained a majority in the Senate. Early legislative elections were held on December 15, 2002, with Ravalomanana's TIM party winning a majority of 103 seats in the 160-seat assembly. The Patriot Front, an electoral alliance supporting Ravalomanana, gained an additional 22 seats, while Arema's representation declined to 3 seats. Significantly, 23 deputies were elected as independents. The elections were the first in which foreign monitors were allowed to observe the polling. Following the balloting, Sylla was reappointed prime minister on January 12, 2003.

Judicial proceedings against members of the former government exacerbated political divisions in late 2002 and 2003. Arema politicians were arrested and interrogated on the pretext of corruption investigations. In August 2003 Ratsiraka and two former Central Bank officials were tried and sentenced in absentia to ten years hard labor for allegedly embezzling $8.25 million from the bank during the crisis. The former Arema prime minister and the secretary-general of the party also received sentences in 2003.

In early 2004 there was a major cabinet reshuffle to incorporate leaders of other parties, and Ravalomanana released some prisoners convicted of crimes committed during the political crisis of 2002. The attempted reconciliation brought little political benefit to the government, however, largely due to a downturn in the economy. Nevertheless, Ravalomanana managed to neutralize the challenges to his reelection. Pierrot RAJAONARIVELO, the exiled Arema leader, was twice barred from entering the country to register his candidacy before the official deadline. Another opposition figure, retired Gen. ANDRIANAFIDISOA (known as General FIDY), had his candidacy nullified by the High Constitutional Court after he failed to pay the registration fee. The president was easily reelected on December 3, 2006 and subsequently appointed Gen. Charles Rabemananjara as prime minister, marking the first time in Madagascar's post-independence history that Mérina highlanders filled both the presidential and prime ministerial offices.

The TIM then expanded its majority in the assembly to 106 out of 127 seats in balloting on September 23, 2007. The national opposition parties managed to capture only 1 seat in the lower house, with the remainder going to independents. Since the former ruling party Arema remained in disarray, Madagascar's opposition parties had become small, fragmented, and driven by personalities. The only significant electoral setback for the TIM during this period came when Andry Rajoelina defeated the TIM candidate to become mayor of Antananarivo on December 12, 2007. The opposition fared badly in the Senate balloting of April 20, 2008, when TIM swept every seat.

By late 2008, Rajoelina began to galvanize popular discontent, just as Ravalomanana himself had as mayor of the capital. With his opposition movement, Young Malagasies Determined (*Tanora malaGasy Vonona*—TGV), demonstrating relentlessly against the Ravalomanana regime, Rajoelina declared himself Madagascar's leader on January 31, 2009. In the ensuing power struggle, the elected president gradually lost support within the urban population. His support within the military also dwindled after several incidents in which security forces fired into crowds of protestors. Ravalomanana succumbed on March 17, handing power to a military tribunal, which in turn handed it to Rajoelina. Although constitutionally too young to qualify for the presidency, Rajoelina suspended parliament on March 18, and installed himself as head of the High Authority of the Transition (HAT) on March 21 (see Current issues, below). Monja ROINDEFO Zafitsimivalo was appointed prime minister on March 17 and a transitional government was formed on April 18.

Constitution and government. Under the 1992 constitution, which was substantially amended by referenda in 1995 and 1998 (see Political background), the president is directly elected for a five-year term, renewable twice, by runoff between the two leading contenders if such is needed to secure a majority. Cabinet leadership is assigned to a prime minister, previously responsible to the legislature but now appointed by the president (from a legislative list) and subject to dismissal by the president. The bicameral Parliament consists of a Senate of both indirectly elected and presidential appointees and a National Assembly of deputies directly elected by proportional representation. While the president can dissolve the assembly, it retains the power to pass a motion of censure and require the prime minister and the cabinet to step down.

In 1995 Madagascar's former six provinces were replaced by 28 regions. The former 111 prefectures (*fivondronana*) were replaced by 148 departments and the former 1,252 subprefectures (*firaisana*) by 1,400 communes, of which 45 were urban.

The constitutional amendments of 1998 effectively reversed the changes incorporated in 1995, restoring a federal system with six semi-autonomous provinces. The amended document also included provisions for the establishment of regional and communal districts; however, as of mid-2006 no further progress toward their creation had been reported. Authority over regional representatives and budget allocations was centralized in the national government under President Ravalomanana.

A package of constitutional amendments was approved by referendum on April 4, 2007. These revisions once again abolished the six provinces, replacing them with 22 regions. In addition, the constitution recognized English as an official language, alongside Malagasy and French; allowed the president to legislate by decree in national emergencies; and upheld President Ravalomanana's economic policy, the Madagascar Action Plan (MAP).

Under Madagascar's existing constitution, the president must be no less than 40 years of age, and thus Rajoelina was not legally entitled to hold the office until 2014. The High Authority of the Transition announced the goal of enacting a new constitution and electoral code in advance of presidential elections, which, according to the current constitution, were to be held in October 2010.

Foreign relations. During the Tsiranana administration, Madagascar retained close economic, defense, and cultural ties with France. In 1973, however, the Ramanantsoa government renegotiated all cooperation agreements with the former colonial power, withdrew from the Franc Zone, and terminated its membership in the francophone Common African and Malagasy Organization. Over the next several years the government repudiated a number of agreements with the Republic of South Africa, established diplomatic relations with communist nations, and announced pro-Arab policies. In 1979 the government offered the former Israeli embassy in Antananarivo to the Palestine Liberation Organization as a base for local activity, while support was consistently offered to African liberation movements.

Subsequently, there was a drift toward the West. Ambassadorial links with Washington were restored in November 1980 after a lapse of more than four years, and aid agreements were negotiated with the United States, France, Japan, and a number of Scandinavian countries. On the other hand, talks were initiated in Moscow in 1984 on improving trade with the Soviet Union, and agreements to strengthen bilateral relations with China were announced in 1986.

In a dramatic policy reversal in mid-1990, economic and air links were established with South Africa as President Ratsiraka, heralding President F.W. de Klerk's "courageous" efforts to reverse apartheid laws, sought Pretoria's aid in developing Madagascar's mineral and tourism industries. In September 1998 Ratsiraka attended an international conference in Durban, thus becoming the first Malagasy head of state to visit South Africa. Subsequent regional negotiations focused on Madagascar candidacy for SADC membership (achieved in 2005).

Following the disputed presidential election of 2001, several countries terminated diplomatic relations with Madagascar and the country was suspended from meetings of the African Union (AU) for over a year. In June 2002 the Ravalomanana government was recognized by the United States; France and Senegal followed suit one month later, and the administration gradually established substantial international support. The presidents of Germany and France visited Madagascar in 2006; in July, French president Jacques Chirac apologized for the actions of French troops during a 1947 revolt against French rule. In January 2007 a high EU official confirmed the union's support for Madagascar during a visit. The introduction of English as an official language underscored the nation's closer relations with English-speaking countries, especially the United States. At the same time, Madagascar's foreign policy increasingly reflected strong Asian influence in the region. In June 2008 the president met with foreign donors, including China and India, to showcase the nation's economic growth and secure aid for poverty reduction efforts. Madagascar also received foreign assistance to deal with environmental challenges, including a $20 million debt-for-nature deal with France. The island nation also committed to selling 9 million tons of carbon offsets to fund forest protection.

The international community condemned the unseating of President Ravalomanana in March 2009. The AU suspended Madagascar on March 20, and foreign diplomats boycotted Andry Rajeolina's inauguration as head of the transition authority the following day. No state extended recognition to the new regime. Several nations suspended non-humanitarian foreign aid, and the United States halted development funding through the Millennium Challenge Corporation. The UN, AU, and SADC mediated negotiations between four political groupings in Madagascar, which broke down in May. In June, the SADC appointed Joaquim Chissano, former president of Mozambique, to mediate a new round of talks. In July, Rajoelina attended an EU summit in Brussels, but failed to persuade the EU to restore aid before the restoration of constitutional order.

Current issues. By 2008, President Ravalomanana came under increasing criticism for corruption and dictatorial tendencies. The president, a wealthy businessman, appeared to use the authority of the office to enhance the interests of his Tiko company. Perhaps his most unpopular initiative was to lease three million acres of arable land to the South Korean company Daewoo, which planned to practice export-oriented agriculture. When the negotiations became public in November 2008, critics questioned the appropriateness of such a sizable giveaway to a foreign company at a time of economic crisis and widespread food insecurity.

The mayor of Antananarivo, Andry Rajoelina, capitalized on the president's floundering popularity. The former disc jockey and owner of the Vivo radio and television stations became Ravalomanana's most visible critic. In December, Vivo TV aired an interview with Didier Ratsiraka, in which the exiled former leader called for open revolt against the government. Ravalomanana reacted by shutting down the TV station on December 13. For the next three months, protests took place in the capital almost daily. More than 40 people were killed on January 26, 2009, as security forces opened fire on rioting crowds. On January 31, Rajoelina demanded the president's resignation and proclaimed that he would henceforth lead the nation. Ravalomanana in turn used his prerogative to sack the mayor on February 3. Undaunted, Rajoelina announced on February 7 that he had asked Monja ROINDEFO of the Monima party to become prime minister of a transitional government. That day, the presidential guard shot more than 20 protesters to death.

As the showdown continued, the army grew unwilling to put down the ongoing demonstrations. In March, mutinying soldiers ousted the defense minister and army chief of staff, and a coup appeared imminent. Rajoelina demanded the president's arrest on March 14. In a televised address on March 15, Ravalomanana declared that a national referendum would be held. His proposal arrived too late to allay an armed challenge to his continued rule. Soldiers loyal to the opposition occupied a presidential palace and the central bank building on March 16. On March 17, Ravalomanana announced that he was stepping down, dissolving the government, and transferring power to a self-chosen group of four senior military officials. The officers, however, declined to become a ruling directorate and instead invited Rajoelina to form a transitional government. The High Constitutional Court approved the transfer of power on March 18. Rajoelina was installed as head of state at a swearing-in ceremony on March 21, notable for the absence of invited foreign dignitaries. The new leader committed to new elections within two years. On March 31, he named 44 members to the High Authority of the Transition, with himself as its president. The transitional body was made up of representatives of numerous political parties and most of the country's geographical regions; its precise function and powers remained somewhat ambiguous.

Government functions were drastically curtailed amid the political crisis. Uncollected trash piled up in the streets of the capital, and development and aid projects came to a halt as foreign donations were frozen. A cyclone that moved down the coast of the island in April and a punishing drought in the south contributed to a dire humanitarian emergency. Meanwhile Ravalomanana, now exiled in South Africa, vowed to return and insisted he was still legally in charge. His supporters, terming themselves "legalists," demonstrated in the capital, even after a ban on protests imposed by Rajoelina in April.

The UN, AU, and SADC convened crisis talks between four main parties in Malagasy politics: the Rajoelina and Ravalomanana camps as well as representatives of former leaders Didier Ratsiraka and Albert Zafy. The negotiations appeared close to an agreement on a consensual transition leading to all-party elections, but Ratsiraka, demanding amnesty for his supporters accused of crimes during the 2002 crisis, walked out on May 23 and the talks broke down. On June 3, a court sentenced Ravalomanana in absentia to four years in jail on corruption charges stemming from the president's 2008 purchase of a $60 million presidential jet. Finally on August 9, negotiations hosted by Mozambican president Joaquim Chissano between Rajoelina, Ravalomanana, Ratsiraka, and Zafy resulted in an agreement that called for elections within 15 months, a general amnesty, and the creation of government of national unity led by an agreed-upon prime minister and three deputy prime ministers. However, the three former presidents subsequently rejected Rajoelina's effort to develop a new unity government in September. *(See headnote.)*

POLITICAL PARTIES AND GROUPS

While Madagascar has long featured multiple parties, they were required under the 1975 constitution to function as components of a national front (see Arema, below). The requirement was rescinded under a decree that became effective on March 1, 1990. A number of new groups promptly emerged, several of which participated in the launching of a loosely structured anti-Ratsiraka coalition that resulted from church-sponsored conferences later in the year. By early 1992 two opposition tendencies were evident: a relatively moderate grouping centered on the MFM (see PMDM/MFM, below), which evidenced a gradualist approach to constitutional change, and a more intransigent Living Forces group, led by the UNDD's Albert Zafy, which only grudgingly agreed to participate in the transitional regime but went on to capture the presidency in late February 1993 and a majority of legislative seats in mid-June.

By March 1998 two large opposition coalitions claimed the services of the leading anti-Ratsiraka politicians. The Panorama Group was organized in September 1997 under the leadership of former prime minister Ravony and was described as a counterbalance to the more radical Union of Democratic Active Forces (*Union des Forces Vives Démocratique*—UFVD), which was formed in early 1998 by Zafy. However, these coalitions were superseded in 2001 when most anti-Ratsiraka elements informally coalesced behind the presidential candidacy of Marc Ravalomanana.

Following the formation of Zafy's National Reconciliation Committee in 2002, several opposition parties agreed to form a parliamentary coalition to promote a "third way" between the progovernment TIM and the antigovernment Arema. The resultant grouping was named the **Parliamentary Solidarity for Democracy and National Union** (*Solidarité des Parlementaires pour la Défense de la Démocratie et de l'Unité National*—SPDUN). The SPDUN, which included most of the parties that had supported Ravalomanana in the 2002 presidential election, announced its intention to serve as the "loyal opposition" to the Sylla government. Included in the SPDUN were the AKFM-*Fanavaozana*, the RPSD-Nouveau, the PMDM/MFM, and the AVI. Rev. Richard Andriamanjato of the AKFM-*Fanavaozana* and Jean Eugené VONINAHITSY of the RPSD-Nouveau were chosen as co-leaders of the SPDUN. The MFM also subsequently became a member before exiting the grouping (along with the AVI) in 2006.

In September 2005 three opposition groupings formed another loose coalition called the **3 National Forces** (*3 Forces Nationale*—3FN), led by former president Zafy. The 3FN consisted of Zafy's CRN (below), the SPDUN, and the **Rally of National Forces** (*Rassemblement des Forces Nationales*—RFN), led by Rev. Rafimanaheja EDMOND. (The RFN's constituent elements included the AKFM, Leader-*Fanilo*, and the *Fihavanantsika*, led by Rev. Daniel RAJAKOBA.) The 3FN led a series of protests against the government in October and December 2005 and sought a transitional coalition government prior to the 2006 presidential polling. The government responded by holding a national conference on May 29, 2006, but the opposition parties declined to participate because of the president's refusal to consider their demands.

In 2006 the 3FN focused on electoral reforms ahead of the December presidential election, a demand echoed by other parties, most presidential candidates, and the two most powerful civil society organizations, the FFKM (Malagasy Council of Churches) and the CNOE (National Committee of Election Observers). However, in the second half of 2006, the 3FN lost influence. The RFN's Razafimahefa Edmond resigned his 3FN leadership position in July 2006, accepting a post in the Reformed Protestant Church of Jesus Christ, an organization in the FFKM and an important source of support for the president. The 3FN was also internally divided between moderates and radicals, who differed on whether to boycott the presidential election.

The emergence of Rajeolina as a national figure led to a new realignment of the nation's party system in 2009 as both Rajeolina and Ravalomanana deputized politicians from smaller parties. Monja ROINDEFO, Chair of Monima, became prime minister under the High Authority of the Transition; meanwhile, the MFM's Manandafy RAKOTONIRINA attempted to form a government loyal to the exiled Ravalomanana. Rakotonirina was arrested April 29.

Government Party:

Young Malagasies Determined (*Tanora malaGasy Vonona*—TGV). This group began in 2007 as a vehicle for Andry Rajoelina' campaign for mayor of Antananarivo. Rajoelina is a former disc jockey and successful entertainment and advertising entrepreneur. His party's acronym, TGV—which also refers to the French high-speed train—was soon applied as a monicker for Rajoelina himself, capturing his relentless determination and the rapidity of his ascent. Rajoelina defeated an experienced TIM politician for the mayoralty of the capital, and shortly mounted a challenge to Ravalomanana himself. The president temporarily shut down Rajoelina's Vivo TV station in December 2008, after it aired an incendiary interview with the exiled former president Didier Ratsiraka. The incident raised Rajoelina's profile and catalyzed the street protest movement that ultimately brought Ravalomanana down. The TGV demonstrations, complete with pop music and a festival atmosphere, attracted a large number of youthful supporters. Considering that roughly half of Madagascar's population is under the age of 21, Rajoelina's successful courtship of urban youth gave him a substantial amount of leverage.

As of 2009, the TGV party had developed little formal infrastructure. The ministers Rajoelina selected for his provisional government mostly belonged to other parties or were independents. It remains to be seen whether Rajoelina's movement evolves into a lasting political party with a more traditional structure.

Leader: Andry RAJOELINA (President of the High Authority of the Transition).

Other Parties and Groups:

I Love Madagascar (*Tiaho I Madagasikara*—TIM). A "political association," TIM was formed to support the presidential campaign of Marc Ravalomanana, the businessman who had been elected mayor of Antananarivo in 1999 as an independent. Ravalomanana's candidacy was also endorsed by numerous other parties, including the AVI, RPSD, PMDM/MFM, and *Grad-Iloafo*. TIM became a formal party in mid-2002 and became the majority party in the assembly following the 2002 legislative elections, when it received 34.3 percent of the vote and 103 seats.

In 2005 an internal power struggle emerged within the TIM, and Prime Minister Jacques Sylla failed to be reelected as the party's secretary general at a congress in January 2005. Reports suggested that Ravalomanana feared Sylla would challenge him in the next presidential election and therefore wanted to dismiss the prime minister. Nevertheless, the two continued to work together, as a rift between Ravalomanana and then assembly speaker Jean Lahiniriko in 2006 moved to the forefront of party friction. Lahiniriko, who had become increasingly critical of the government, was sacked as speaker of the National Assembly in May 2006, having faced criticism for praising Iran's nuclear program. Lahiniriko was also ejected from the TIM. He subsequently ran as an independent in the 2006 presidential poll, finishing second to Ravalomanana with 11.68 percent of the vote. He formed a new party in February 2007 (see below).

By 2008 the party had achieved complete political dominance, controlling the national legislature and local politics. However, the rising protests against President Ravalomanana unraveled the party's control over Malagasy politics, and after the incidents of January 26 and February 7, 2009, in which security forces killed scores of demonstrators, the momentum decisively shifted to Andry Rajoelina and his TGV movement. Shortly after attaining power in March, Rajoelina dissolved the legislature and took over the office of the prime minister, effectively wiping out what remained of the TIM's power base in the national government. Representatives of the TIM, now referred to in the press as "the Ravalomanana faction," participated in the internationally mediated four-party negotiations throughout 2009. Arguably, Ravalomanana and his party stood to gain the most from efforts to construct a consensus solution to the nation's political impasse. That solution grew more complicated after Ravalomanana was sentenced in absentia on corruption charges in June, and three former officials in the TIM government were accused of responsibility for a bomb attack in the capital in July.

Leaders: Marc RAVALOMANANA (Former President of the Republic), Charles RABEMANANJARA (Former Prime Minister), Yvan RANDRIASANDRATRINIONY (President of the Party and Former President of the Senate), Fetison ANDRIANIRINA (Lead negotiator).

Leader–*Fanilo*. Launched in 1993 by a group of self-styled "non-politicians," Leader–*Fanilo* opposed President Zafy in the September 1995 referendum and expelled Trade and Tourism Minister Henri RAKOTONIRAINY for accepting cabinet reappointment two months later.

Party leader Herizo Razafimahaleo finished third in the first round of the 1996 presidential balloting with 15 percent of the vote and fourth in 2001 with 4.2 percent. (Three Leader–*Fanilo* cabinet members resigned from the government in early October 2001 after Razafimahaleo announced his intention to campaign for the presidency.) Razafimahaleo's 2006 presidential campaign emphasized the lack of separation between President Ravalomanana's company, Tiko, and TIM. Razafimahaleo finished fourth in the balloting with 9.05 percent of the vote.

Leader-*Fanilo* was the only nationally organized party, apart from the TIM, to win an assembly seat in the 2007 balloting, when Jonah Parfait Prezaly was elected. On July 25, 2008, the opposition party suffered a significant loss with the death of Herizo Razafimahaleo. He was succeeded as president by historian Manassé Esoavelomandroso, theretofore the party's secretary general. Andry Rajoelina named Prezaly to the High Authority of the Transition in March 2009.

Leaders: Manassé ESOAVELOMANDROSO (President), Alain RAKOTOMAVO (Secretary General), Jonah Parfait PREZALY.

Rally for Socialism and Democracy (*Rassemblement pour le Socialisme et la Démocratie*—RPSD). The RPSD is the current incarnation of the Social Democratic Party (*Parti Social Démocrate*—PSD) that was legalized in March 1990 as a revival of the party originally formed in 1957 by Philibert Tsiranana. (The group is still frequently referenced under the PSD rubric.) Although initially sympathetic to the Ratsiraka government, in the second half of 1990 the party moved into opposition. The party's prestige was bolstered by the addition of former MFM leaders Franck Ramarosaona and Evariste Marson in 1990 and 1992, respectively. The RPSD supported Albert Zafy in the second presidential round (after a bid by Marson had failed in the first) and went into opposition after the June 1993 assembly poll. Jean Eugène VONINAHITSY, RPSD secretary general and vice president of the National Assembly, received 2.79 percent of the vote in the first round of the 1996 presidential election.

The RPSD won 11 assembly seats in May 1998, and thereafter reportedly joined Arema's legislative alliance. In late 2000, however, relations between Arema and the RPSD were strained when Voninahitsy was arrested on charges of insulting the head of state and "putting out false information." Earlier, he had criticized Ratsiraka for purchases made by the state. The RPSD left Arema's legislative faction by late 2000 and supported opposition candidate Marc Ravalomanana in the 2001 presidential campaign. Disaffected members left the RPSD to join the Patriotic Front (FP) prior to the 2002 assembly elections. The RPSD allied itself with the TIM in the election and secured 5 seats in the polling.

In 2003 RPSD dissidents led by former secretary general Voninahitsy left the party to form a new group, the New RPSD or **RPSD-Nouveau** (RPSD-*Vaovao*), which was active in the anti-Ravalomanana protests of October 2005. Voninahitsy was subsequently convicted of corruption and sentenced to two years in jail in December 2005. He was expected to run in the 2006 presidential race but was arrested on additional charges in February 2006 and received a four-year jail sentence, which was upheld by an appeals court in June 2008. The RPSD did not field a candidate in the 2006 presidential election, but a former RPSD leader, Philippe TSIRANANA, son of former president Philibert Tsiranana, stood as an independent. The RPSD-Nouveau expressed disapproval of the constitutional reforms approved by referendum in 2007. Marson was appointed to the High Authority of the Transition on March 31, 2009. He opposed any power-sharing arrangement involving Ravalomanana in the transition.

Leader: Evariste MARSON (President).

One Should Be Judged By One's Works (*Asa Vita Ifampitsanara*—AVI). In May 1998 the AVI won 14 assembly seats as a moderate opposition party under the leadership of former prime minister and interim president Norbert Ratsirahonana. Subsequently, however, the AVI joined the Arema-led propresidential legislative alliance. In the 2001 presidential campaign, Ratsirahonana withdrew his candidacy in late October and endorsed Marc Ravalomanana. In 2002 the AVI joined Ravalomanana's first government as part of the now-defunct pro-Ravalomanana Patriot Front (*Firaisankinam-Pirenenai*—FP) formed in conjunction with former RPSD members. The FP secured 20 of the coalition's 22 seats in that year's legislative elections. In late 2003 the AVI began to distance itself from the president and joined the opposition group the SPDUN (which it left in March 2006). Ratsirahonana publicly denounced the national conference in June 2005. The AVI leader formally split from the president in October 2006, claiming Ravalomanana had become a dictator, and entered that year's presidential election as the AVI candidate, winning 4.2 percent of the vote. The poor showing weakened the party's position among the opposition. Ratsirahonana was a major supporter of Andry Rajoelina's struggle to unseat Ravalomanana, standing by the new leader's side as he assumed power on March 17, 2009, and arguing his claim before the High Constitutional Court. He was subsequently named to the High Authority of the Transition.

Leader: Norbert RATSIRAHONANA (Secretary General).

Militant Party for the Development of Madagascar (*Parti Militant pour le Développement de Madagascar*—PMDM/MFM). The PMDM/MFM is a successor name for the Movement for Proletarian Power (*Mouvement pour le Pouvoir Prolétarien/Mpitolona ho'amin'ny Fanjakan'ny Madinika*—MFM) formed in 1972 by student radicals who helped to overthrow President Tsiranana. Although it continues to be referenced by its earlier Malagasy initials, the party adopted its current name at a 1990 party congress.

The MFM initially opposed the Ratsiraka government and remained outside the FNDR framework until 1977. The group won three assembly seats in 1983 and seven in 1989. Party leader Manandafy Rakotonirina placed second in the 1989 presidential balloting with 19 percent of the vote. As an opposition party, the MFM was part of the movement that forced Ratsiraka from power in 1991. The party completed a conversion from Marxism to liberalism in the 1990s, supporting the establishment of a market economy and a Western-style multiparty system.

MFM leader Rakotonirina, who stood as a first-round presidential contender in 1992, supported Albert Zafy in the second round. Following the legislative poll of June 1993, the MFM went into opposition. It supported prime minister and interim president Norbert Ratsirahonana in the 1996 presidential balloting but reportedly swung back over to the government camp following the May 1998 legislative elections. The MFM supported opposition candidate Marc Ravalomanana in the 2001 presidential campaign, and Rakotonirina was influential in Ravalomanana's controversial decision to declare victory and take to the streets after the first round of voting. Rakotonirina later became a special adviser to President Ravalomanana. In the 2002 elections the MFM won two seats in the National Assembly.

Despite its initial closeness to Ravalomanana, the MFM subsequently shifted to the opposition, joining the SPDUN (from which it withdrew in March 2006) and. The party denounced the national conference in 2005 (see CRN, below) and declared unconstitutional Ravalomanana's decision to move the presidential election date to December 2006. As an independent candidate in that election, Rakotonirina won 0.33 percent of the vote. The MFM won no seats in the 2007 legislative voting.

On April 20, 2009, while in exile in Johannesburg, Ravalomanana declared MFM's Rakotonirina his nominee to be Madagascar's next prime minister. Rakotonirina released a partial list of ministers for a prospective legalist government on April 28. but was arrested at an Antananarivo hotel by a militia loyal to Rajoelina. The 70-year-old Rakotonirina was incarcerated at Mantasoa.

Leader: Manandafy RAKOTONIRINA.

Vanguard of the Malagasy Revolution (*Avant-Garde de la Révolution Malgache/Antoky'ny Revolosiona Malagasy*—Arema). Arema was organized by Didier Ratsiraka in 1976 and subsequently served as the nucleus of the National Front for the Defense of the Malagasy Socialist Revolution (*Front National pour la Défense de la Révolution Socialiste Malgache*—FNDR), which was renamed the Militant Movement for Malagasy Socialism (*Mouvement Militant pour le Socialisme Malgache*—MMSM) in mid-1990. The 1975 constitution provided for organization of the FNDR as the country's overarching political entity, with a variety of "revolutionary associations" permitted to participate in elections as FNDR components. However, three FNDR members (the MFM, Vonjy, and Monima) initiated joint antigovernment activity, beginning in early 1987, and contested the 1989 presidential and legislative elections as the equivalent of opposition formations, thus dissolving the FNDR's political monopoly.

After losing the 1992 presidential election, Ratsiraka eventually moved to Paris, France. He remained a force in Malagasy politics, regularly criticizing the Zafy administration and what he described as the nation's political "chaos." In 1993 he formed the Vanguard for Economic and Social Recovery (*Avant-Garde pour le Redressement Économique et Social*—ARES) as a successor to Arema; however, his supporters and media groups continue to use the Arema acronym and earlier title.

Ratsiraka regained the presidency in February 1997. On November 29 of that year, at Arema's first party congress since taking power, Deputy Prime Minister Pierrot Rajaonarivelo was elected to the secretary general's post vacated by Ratsiraka. The party also reportedly adopted the Malagasy title, *Andry sy Riana Enti-Manavotra an'i Madagasikara,* or Supporting Pillar and Structure for the Salvation of Madagascar; however, the Arema acronym remained in common use.

In legislative balloting in May 1998 Arema and its allies secured an overwhelming mandate (its forces reportedly controlled approximately 90 percent of the assembly seats). Meanwhile, intraparty relations between Rajaonarivelo and Prime Minister Rakotomavo reached a nadir on July 6 when Rajaonarivelo and 17 of his ministerial allies withdrew from the cabinet, thereby paralyzing the government and effectively destroying Rakotomavo's chances for reappointment.

In 2000–2001 disagreements were reported between Arema's liberal wing, headed by Rajaonarivelo, and the "orthodox" wing, represented by ministers Nivoson Jacquit Rosat SIMON and Boniface LEVELO.

Following the violence surrounding the 2001 presidential election, Arema lost substantial public support. Ratsiraka and other senior Arema figures, including Secretary General Pierrot Rajaonarivelo, went into exile in France. In the legislative balloting in 2002, Arema secured only three seats, and it boycotted local elections in 2003. In 2003 Rajaonarivelo was sentenced in absentia to five years in prison on several charges involving his alleged abuse of office while deputy prime minister. His sentence was reduced to three years in 2005.

Arema was significantly weakened in 2006 by internal divisions over whether to support Pierrot Rajaonarivelo's presidential candidacy and whether to advocate the revision of the electoral code, with those supporting the status quo arguing that the code had been instituted by Didier Ratsiraka and therefore should be accepted. Reports subsequently indicated a growing split in the party, with one faction loyal to the exiled leadership and a second group (led by Assistant Secretary General Pierre RAHARIJOANA) eager to distance itself from the exiles.

In 2006 Rajaonarivelo called upon the government to issue an amnesty to potential candidates, such as himself, whose sentences would otherwise preclude them from participating in the upcoming presidential poll. Rajaonarivelo, considered Ravalomanana's main opponent, officially announced his candidacy for the presidential election in May. However, he was convicted in absentia of embezzlement of public funds in August and sentenced to 15 years of hard labor and barred from holding office. Rajaonarivelo twice attempted to return to Madagascar to register his candidacy, but the Malagasy authorities blocked his return and the High Constitutional Court denied his candidacy. Arema then announced that it would boycott the election. In 2007 Arema was divided, with factions supporting each of the two exiled leaders, Ratsiraka and Rajaonarivelo. The pro-Ratsiraka contingent challenged the standing of the interim national secretary, Pierre Houlder RAMAHOLIMASY. Arema won no seats in the 2007 legislative election.

Ratsiraka was instrumental in sparking the crisis that resulted in the overthrow of Ravalomanana. His televised interview calling for insurrection against the government led to the shutdown of Rajoelina's Viva television network in December 2008. Rajoelina, who had received early financial backing from Rajaonarivelo for his business enterprises, was perceived by numerous analysts as a front for the exiled Arema leaders. Arema initially supported the coup, but Ratsiraka later condemned it. Rajaonarivelo returned from exile in April 2009, stating that he hoped to foster national reconciliation. Arema was one of the four parties represented in UN-mediated talks on the crisis, but Ratsiraka pulled out of the negotiations in May, demanding amnesty for his supporters as a condition of his participation.

Leades: Adm. Didier RATSIRAKA (Former President of the Republic, in exile), Pierrot Jocelyn RAJAONARIVELO (Secretary General), Pierre Houlder RAMAHOLIMASY (Interim National Secretary).

National Reconciliation Committee (*Comité pour la Réconciliation Nationale*—CRN). The CRN was launched in 2002 by former president Albert Zafy and other prominent former officials in an attempt to foster a solution to the "post-election crisis," pitting the supporters of former president Ratsiraka against the supporters of President Ravalomanana.

Zafy had led the National Union for Development and Democracy (*Union Nationale pour le Développement et la Démocratie*—UNDD), a party originally organized in 1955 and revived by Zafy in 1998. The UNDD stridently denounced "corruption" under the Ratsiraka regime. In 1990 Zafy organized the Living Forces coalition (*Forces Vives/Hery Velona*), an alliance of 16 opposition parties, trade unions, and religious groups, whose agitation prompted the dissolution of the Ratsiraka government in 1991. This grouping was sometimes referred to as the Living Forces Rasalama Coalition (*Cartel Hery Velona Rasalama*—Cartel HVR). Zafy was then named to head the High State Authority under the Provisional Government and elected president in 1993. UNDD members came to dominate the cabinet in 1995 and 1996, until Zafy was impeached in September 1996. Prior to presidential balloting in 1996, a number of parties disavowed their *Forces Vives* membership, and Zafy lost narrowly to Ratsiraka in the second-round balloting.

In legislative balloting in May 1998, what remained of the pro-Zafy grouping competed under the banner of the recently established **Action, Truth, Development, and Harmony** (*Asa Fahamarianana Fampandrosoana Arinda*—AFFA). Six AFFA candidates, including Zafy, were elected. The AFFA supported Zafy in the 2001 presidential election but failed to gain any seats for itself in the 2002 legislative balloting.

Zafy and the CRN never formally recognized the legitimacy of Marc Ravalomanana's presidency and advocated for a transitional regime to govern before new elections were held lest the problems of 2001–2002 be repeated. At the national conference in June 2005, the CRN advocated creating a "parallel government." In December 2006 Zafy's property was raided by the police as part of the government's investigation of General Fidy's alleged November coup attempt; the police sought to locate and arrest Zafy.

Despite Ravalomanana's reelection, the CRN continued to press for a national reconciliation. Zafy traveled to Paris in July 2007 for a series of closed meetings with ex-president Ratsiraka and other former officials.

Zafy took part in the negotiations mediated by the UN and the AU after the March 2009 coup. The former president advocated for an inclusive, consensual basis for a democratic transition, calling for a truth and reconciliation commission based on the South African model.

Leaders: Dr. Albert ZAFY (Former President of the Republic), Emmanuel RAKOTOVAHINY (Chairman and Former Prime Minister).

National Movement for the Independence of Madagascar/Madagascar for the Malagasy Party (*Mouvement National pour l'Indépendance de Madagascar/Madagasikara Otronin'ny Malagasy*—Monima). A left-wing nationalist party based in the south, Monima (also called *Monima Ka Miviombio*—Monima K) withdrew from the National Front FNDR in 1977, charging it had been the victim of electoral fraud. Its longtime leader, Monja JAONA, was under house arrest from November 1980 to March 1982, at which time he brought the group back into the FNDR and was appointed to the Supreme Revolutionary Council (CSR). He joined the 1982 presidential election as Commander Ratsiraka's only competitor, winning almost 20 percent of the vote. That December he was again placed under house arrest for activities "likely to bring about the fall of the country." He was released in mid-August 1983, after undertaking a hunger strike, and returned to the legislature as one of Monima's two representatives. The party's poor showing (less than 4 percent of valid votes cast) in 1983 was partly attributed to uncertainty, prior to Jaona's release, as to whether it would participate. Jaona won 3 percent in the 1989 presidential balloting and became Monima's sole assembly representative. Monima's deputy general secretary, René RANAIVOSOA, resigned from the party in June 1990, following a dispute with Jaona, and established the **Democratic Party for Madagascar Development** (*Parti Démocratique pour le Développement de Madagascar*—PDDM/ADFM).

In March 1992 Jaona was seriously wounded during a pro-Ratsiraka demonstration. Monima's influence decreased after Jaona's death. The party reportedly endorsed President Ratsiraka's reelection bid and did not support Ravalomanana in the 2002 crisis.. In the 2002 and 2007 assembly balloting, Monima won no seats. Jaona's son, Monja ROINDEFO Zafitsimilavo, stood as an independent in the 2006 presidential election and came in last.

Andry Rajeolina announced that Roindefo would serve as prime minister of his transitional administration on February 7, 2009. Roindefo's position became official in March, after Rajeolina was installed as leader. Monima defended the legality of the transfer of power, asserting that it was supported by popular demand. In June, the party spoke out against the involvement of the SADC in mediation efforts, and opposed extending amnesty to either Ravalomanana or Ratsiraka.

Leaders: Monja ROINDEFO (Chair), Gabriel RABEARIMANANA (Secretary General).

Socialist and Democratic Party for the Union of Madagascar (*Parti Socialiste et Démocratique pour l'Union à Madagascar*—PSDUM). This party was launched on February 3, 2007, by Jean Lahiniriko, speaker of the National Assembly from 2003 to 2006. During a visit to Iran in April 2006, Lahiniriko congratulated the Tehran government on the success of its nuclear program. His comment was not meant to represent official state policy; nevertheless, some of his fellow legislators accused him of treason. Lahiniriko was removed from office and expelled from the ruling TIM party. He then vowed to challenge incumbent Marc Ravalomanana for the presidency. Running as an independent, he finished second with 11.65 percent in the December 2006 vote, carrying his home province of Toliara. As he launched his new party, he warned that "a programmed return of dictatorship" was threatening Madagascar. He ran as a PSDUM candidate for assembly in September 2007 and was soundly defeated by the TIM candidate, although he disputed the returns.

Lahiniriko declared his support for Rajoelina just before the demonstrations of January 26, 2009. Lahiniriko and another party leader, former government minister Julien Reboza, were named to the High Authority of the Transition on March 31.

Leaders: Jean LAHINIRIKO (Former Speaker of the Assembly), Julien REBOZA (National Secretary).

Three recently formed parties fielded candidates in the 2006 presidential election: **Union** (*Tambatra*), whose candidate, Pety RAKOTONIAINA, was sentenced in October 2007 to five years in prison for stealing state-owned cars; **Our Madagascar** (*Madagasikarantsika*), boasting the first female presidential candidate, Elia RAVELOMANANTSOA; and **Good Governance Madagascar** (*Fihavanantsika*), supporting Daniel RAJAKOBA. Other minor parties include the **Fihaonana Confédération des Societés pour le Développement**, led by Guy Willy Razanamasy; the Republican Party of Madagascar (PRM), led by Roger Ralison; and the pro-Arema party, the **Toamasina Tonga Saina** (TTS). Roland RATSIRAKA (the nephew of the former president, the mayor of Toamasina, and a member of the TTS) ran as an independent candidate in the 2006 presidential election and came in third with 10.09 percent of the votes, only to be jailed on charges of embezzlement in April 2007. He was released with a deferred sentence after six months.

For more information on the Congress Party for Madagascar **Independence–Renewal** (*Parti du Congès* de *l'Indépendance de Madagascar–Renouveau*—AKFM-*Fanavaozana*), see the 2008 *Handbook*.

LEGISLATURE

The 1992 constitution provides for a bicameral **Parliament** (*Parlement*) consisting of a Senate and a National Assembly. Both houses were suspended immediately following the coup of March 17, 2009.

Senate (*Sénat*). Prior to the constitutional amendments of April 2008, the Senate had 60 elected members (10 representing each of the six provinces) and 30 appointed members. Arema won 49 of the 60 elected seats in the balloting of March 18, 2001, and President Ratsiraka made appointments the following month. After taking power in 2002, President Ravalomanana used his constitutional power to replace the appointed senators, mostly with members of his new I Love Madagascar party.

As of 2008, Madagascar's upper house has 33 members: 22 (1 from each region) are elected by electoral colleges comprised of regional and municipal officials, and 11 are appointed by the president. The term of office is six years. In legislative elections held on April 20, 2008, I Love Madagascar received all the elective seats.

National Assembly (*Assemblée Nationale*). The lower house encompasses 127 members, who are directly elected by proportional representation for five-year terms. President Ravalomanana dissolved the assembly in July 2007, claiming that its composition did not represent the national makeup following the constitutional reforms approved by referendum on April 4, 2007. The results of the balloting on September 23, 2007, were as follows: I Love Madagascar, 106 seats; Leader–*Fanilo*, 1 seat; independents, 20.

CABINET

[as of September 1, 2009] *(see headnote)*

Prime Minister	Monja Roindefo Zafitsimivalo
Ministers	
Civil Service, Labor, and Social Laws	William Noelson
Commerce	Jean-Claude Rakotonirina
Communication and Culture	Gilbert Raharizatovo
Economy and Industry	Richard Fienena
Energy	Jean Rodolph Ramanantsoa
Environment and Forests	Mariot Jean Florent Rakotovao
Finance and Budget	Benja Johasy Razafimahaleo
Foreign Affairs	Ny Hasina Andriamanjato
Health and Family Planning	Henri Ranaivoarisoa
Higher Education and Scientific Research	Athanase Tongavelo
Interior	Manantsoa Masimana
Justice and Keeper of the Seals	Christine Razanamahasoa [f]
National Defense	Col. Noel Rakotonandrasana
National Education	Julien Razafimanazato
Population and Social Affairs	Nadine Ramaroson [f]
Posts, Telecommunications, and New Technology	Augustin Razafinarivo Andriamananoro
Public Security	Remy Sylvain Organes Rakotomihantarizaka
Territorial Management and Decentralization	Hajo Herivelo Andrianiainarivelo
Tourism and Crafts	Irene Victoire Andreas [f]
Transport	Roland Ranjatoelina
Water	Nirhy-Lanto Andriamahazo
Secretary of State	
Gendarmerie	Col. Claude Ravelomanana

[f] = female

COMMUNICATIONS

Media censorship in Madagascar was formally lifted in March 1989. Madagascar's Communication Code of 1990 provided further liberalization but made defamation and insult punishable by up to six months in prison. In its 2008 annual index of press freedom, Reporters Without Borders ranked Madagascar 94, along with Burundi, out of 173 countries. According to an April 2009 report by the organization, Madagascar's new government has censored coverage of opposition protests in the state-run press. The fact that both Marc Ravalomanana and Andry Rajoelina own radio and television stations was a significant factor in the recent power struggle.

Press. In 2006 there were 14 privately owned major daily newspapers, including *Midi-Madagasikara* (21,000), in French; *Madagascar Tribune* (12,000), in French and Malagasy; *Maresaka* (5,000), independent, in Malagasy; *L'Express de Madagascar* (10,000), a bilingual independent; and *La Gazette de la Grande Ile* (15,000), independent. President Ravalomanana owns the daily, *Le Quotidien. Dans Les Media Demain* (4,000) is a French weekly. The publication director of *La Gazette de la Grande Ile* was given three prison sentences in 2005 in separate libel cases.

News agencies. In June 1977 the government replaced the existing *Agence Madagascar-Presse* with the *Agence Nationale d'Information "Taratra"* (Anta). A number of foreign bureaus maintain offices in the capital.

Broadcasting and computing. In 1999 *Radio Nationale Malagasy,* a government-owned, commercial network, in addition to a number of private facilities, serviced some 3.3 million receivers, while *Télévision Nationaly Malagasy* offered programming for approximately 424,000 receivers in 2003. President Ravalomanana owns a TV and radio station (managed by his daughter), Madagascar Broadcasting System (MBS), which was set up ahead of the presidential election in 2001. National state radio and TV also came under his control in March 2002, while many private radio stations in the capital are owned by pro-Ravalomanana politicians. There are over 240 licensed radio stations, and 37 television stations actively broadcasting.

As of 2008 there were 16.5 Internet users per 1,000 inhabitants.

INTERGOVERNMENTAL REPRESENTATION

Ambassador to the U.S.: Jocelyn RADIFERA.

U.S. Ambassador to Madagascar: R. Niels MARQUARDT.

Permanent Representative to the UN: Zina ANDRIANARIVELO-RAZAFY.

IGO Memberships (Non-UN): AfDB, AU, BADEA, Comesa, Interpol, IOC, IOM, IOR-ARC, NAM, OIF, SADC, WCO, WTO.

MALAWI

Republic of Malawi

Political Status: Independent member of the Commonwealth since 1964; republic under one-party presidential rule established July 6, 1966; constitution amended on June 22, 1993, to provide for multiparty activity following national referendum of June 15; new constitution enacted provisionally as of May 16, 1994, and adopted permanently (as amended) on May 18, 1995.

Area: 45,747 sq. mi. (118,484 sq. km.).

Population: 9,933,868 (1998C); 13,897,000 (2008E).

Major Urban Centers (2005E): LILONGWE (676,000), Blantyre (715,000), Mzuzu (107,000).

Official Language: English. (Chichewa is classified as a national language.)

Monetary Unit: Kwacha (official rate December 1, 2009: 142.12 kwacha = $1US).

President: Bingu wa MUTHARIKA (Democratic Progressive Party); popularly elected (as a member of the United Democratic Front) on May 20, 2004, and inaugurated for a five-year term on May 24, succeeding Bakili MULUZI (United Democratic Front); reelected on May 19, 2009, and inaugurated for a second five-year term on May 22.

First Vice President: Joyce Banda (United Democratic Front); popularly elected on May 19, 2009, and inaugurated for a five-year term on May 22, succeeding Cassim CHILUMPHA (United Democratic Front).

Second Vice President: Vacant following the resignation of Chakufwa CHIHANA (Alliance for Democracy) on February 24, 2004.

THE COUNTRY

Malawi, the former British protectorate of Nyasaland, is a landlocked southeastern African nation bordering the western side of 360-mile-long Lake Malawi (formerly Lake Nyasa). The country's name is a contemporary spelling of "Maravi," which historically referenced the interrelated Bantu peoples who inhabit the area. The main tribal groups are the Chewas, the Nyanja, and the Tumbuka. It is estimated that 80 percent of the population is Christian and 13 percent Muslim, with the remainder, except for a very small Hindu population, adhering to traditional African beliefs. A small non-African component includes Europeans and Asians. Three-quarters of adult females are subsistence agricultural workers, while the number of households headed by women has increased in recent years as men have relocated to pursue cash-crop labor.

About 85 percent of the population is engaged in agriculture, the most important cash crops being tobacco, tea, peanuts, sugar, and cotton. Agriculture accounts for 40 percent of the nation's GDP and 80 percent of export revenues. Development efforts have focused on integrated rural production, diversification in light industry (particularly agriprocessing and import substitution), and improved transportation facilities.

Although credited by the mid-1980s with being one of the few African states with a grain surplus, Malawi continued to suffer high rates of malnutrition, infant mortality, and poverty—a paradox widely attributed to an agricultural system favoring large estate owners. The economy was further stressed by chronic unemployment, trade imbalances, persistent inflation, and external debt pressures, prompting the government in the early 1990s to adopt adjustment measures sponsored by the International Monetary Fund (IMF), including the privatization of state enterprises. The reforms contributed to an economic resurgence in the mid-1990s. However, a downturn subsequently ensued, due in part, according to the IMF, to a slackening in the pace of reform as well as a slowdown in agricultural demand. Real GDP growth fell to 1.7 percent in 2000, with inflation steadying at 45 percent. In 2001 GDP declined by 4.1 percent, before posting a small recovery in 2002 and growing by 4.4 percent in 2003. In addition, inflation was brought down to 10 percent in 2003.

In 2000 Malawi was approved for $1 billion in debt reduction under the World Bank's Heavily Indebted Poor Countries (HIPC) initiative, and the IMF provided a $65 million loan for poverty reduction. However, excessive government spending, corruption, and the slow pace of economic reforms led international donors, including the World Bank, IMF, United States, and European Union (EU), to suspend some economic aid during 2001–2002, although humanitarian assistance continued in light of Malawi's worsening food crisis (caused by drought in some areas and severe flooding in others). Poor harvests in 2004 left some 5 million Malawians dependent on food aid, although agricultural production improved significantly in 2005. Meanwhile, the EU resumed full economic and development aid, including support for ports, hydroelectric facilities, and direct financial contributions to limit the government's deficit. In April 2006 the IMF reported that the new government had made progress in regard to economic reforms and approved a three-year, $59 million aid program (contingent on continued reform and the meeting of certain economic benchmarks). The World Bank also approved aid to develop rural infrastructure.

Although global tobacco prices fell, record corn prices and harvests spurred GDP growth of 8.5 percent in 2006. Meanwhile, Malawi was certified to have met the goals to qualify for additional debt relief under the HIPC. (More than 90 percent of the country's external debt, or $3.1 billion, has been forgiven.) In 2007 GDP growth was 7.4 percent, while inflation continued to fall to 8.1 percent. The economy was helped by sales of a surplus corn crop and new foreign investment, including a $185 million uranium mining project undertaken by an Australian firm. In addition, the IMF provided $18 million as part of the country's Poverty Reduction and Growth Facility agreement. Despite the improving economic conditions, the government notified the UN that Malawi

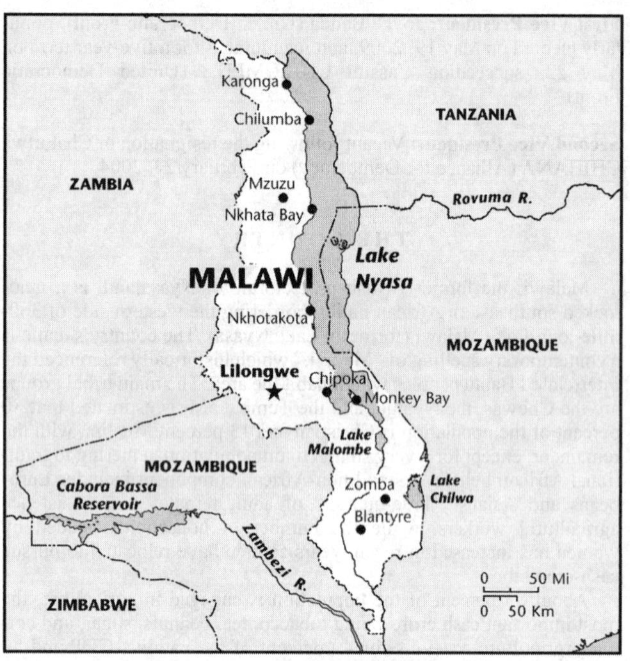

would not be able to meet its target of reducing poverty by 50 percent by 2015.

The EU pledged to provide Malawi $677 million in economic assistance over a six-year period beginning in 2008. The Millennium Challenge Cooperation announced that Malawi was eligible to receive economic aid for poverty reduction programs from the organization. In 2008 Malawi's GDP growth was 7.1 percent, while inflation was 8.7 percent. That year, Malawi ranked 168 in the world in terms of per capita income (GNI) at $289. At least 65 percent of the population was reported to live below the poverty level and unofficial estimates put the unemployment rate at 45.5 percent. In response to rising fuel process, the IMF agreed to a $77.1 million loan in December 2008, $51.4 million of which was available for immediate disbursal.

GOVERNMENT AND POLITICS

Political background. Under British rule since 1891, the Nyasaland protectorate was joined with Northern and Southern Rhodesia in 1953 to form the Federation of Rhodesia and Nyasaland. Internal opposition to the federation proved so vigorous that a state of emergency was declared, with nationalist leaders H. B. M. CHIPEMBERE, Kanyama CHIUME, and Hastings Kamuzu BANDA being imprisoned. They were released upon the attainment of internal self-government on February 1, 1963, and dissolution of the federation at the end of that year. Nyasaland became a fully independent member of the Commonwealth under the name of Malawi on July 6, 1964, and a republic two years later, with Prime Minister Banda being installed as the country's president.

The early years of the Banda presidency were marked by conservative policies, including the retention of white civil service personnel and the maintenance of good relations with South Africa. Younger, more radical leaders soon became disenchanted, and in 1965 a minor insurrection was led by Chipembere, while a second, led by Yatuta CHISIZA, took place in 1967. Both were easily contained, however, and Banda became entrenched as the nation's political leader.

In March 1983 Dr. Attati MPAKATI of the Socialist League of Malawi (one of the two principal exile groups) was assassinated in Zimbabwe. In May, Orton CHIRWA, the former leader of the other main exile organization (the Malawi Freedom Movement—Mafremo) was found guilty of treason and was sentenced to death. (Chirwa had been jailed, along with his wife and son, since December 1981.) Subsequent appeals in December 1983 and February 1984 were denied, and Chirwa, who claimed that he and his family had been abducted from Zambia to permit their arrest, became an object of international human rights attention. Bowing to the pressure, Banda commuted the sentence to life imprisonment in June 1984. (Chirwa died in 1992 under unclear circumstances.)

In an apparent response to pressure from international aid donors, President Banda instructed the National Assembly in December 1991 to "make a final decision" on unipartyism, albeit prefacing his call for debate by commending the "successes" of his Malawi Congress Party (MCP), which had voted for a continuation of the existing system only three months before. Thus, despite the country's first mass protests against MCP rule in May 1992, no opposition groups were permitted to present candidates in legislative balloting on June 26–27. Somewhat unexpectedly, given another MCP vote against pluralism on October 2, President Banda on October 18 announced plans for a national referendum to decide Malawi's future political structure. On June 15, 1993, 63.5 percent of those participating voted in favor of a multiparty system.

On October 13, 1993, 11 days after Banda underwent emergency brain surgery, the office of the president announced the formation of a three-member Presidential Council, thus rejecting the opposition's call for a "neutral" president to rule in Banda's absence. The council was comprised of the MCP's recently appointed secretary general, Stephen Gwandanguluwe CHAKUAMBA Phiri, as well as MCP stalwarts John TEMBO and Robson CHIRWA. Nevertheless, preparations for the May 1994 multiparty balloting continued, with the assembly approving constitutional amendments reforming the electoral process and presidency (see Constitution and government, below) and authorizing the formation of two transitional bodies: the National Consultative Council (NCC) and the National Executive Council (NEC), charged with electoral preparation and oversight.

In early December 1993 the Presidential Council ordered the disarmament of the Malawi Young Pioneers (MYP), an MCP-affiliated paramilitary group whose recent killing of two regular army soldiers had exacerbated tensions between the two armed forces. The ensuing crackdown, resulting in 32 deaths and the reported flight of 1,000 pioneers to Mozambique, was denounced by the NCC, which accused the Presidential Council of having "lost control." Consequently, on December 7 a still visibly ailing Banda dissolved the Presidential Council and reassumed presidential powers. Shortly thereafter, Banda appointed a new defense minister, Maj. Gen. Wilfred John MPONERA, who, on January 7, 1994, announced the completion of MYP disarmament.

In the country's first multiparty election on May 17, 1994, voters decisively rejected bids by Banda and two other presidential candidates in favor of Bakili MULUZI of the United Democratic Front (UDF). In simultaneous legislative balloting, the UDF also led the field, although it fell short of a majority by five seats. Four days after his inauguration on May 21, President Muluzi announced a coalition government in which two minor parties—the Malawi National Democratic Party (MNDP) and the United Front for Multiparty Democracy (UFMD)—were allocated one portfolio each.

On July 21, 1994, the MCP and the Alliance for Democracy (Aford) announced the formation of a shadow government that included Banda's former second in command, John Tembo, as finance minister. However, the MCP-Aford pact was effectively terminated when Aford president Chakufwa CHIHANA accepted an appointment by Muluzi as second vice president designate and three other Aford members joined an expanded cabinet on September 24. Constitutional revision was required to accommodate Chihana's appointment (see Constitution and government, below).

In response to domestic and international criticism of the size of his cabinet, Muluzi reshuffled it and reduced its size from 35 to 32 members on July 16, 1995. A more significant change occurred on July 27, when the UDF and Aford announced that they had signed an agreement to form a coalition government. However, in December relations between the two groups cooled when Aford leader Chihana accused the government of "lacking transparency" and failing to combat corruption.

On December 23, 1995, former president Banda and his five codefendants were acquitted of all charges relating to the murder of "reformist" politicians in 1983 (see MCP in Political Parties and Groups, below). Shortly thereafter, Banda apologized for the "pain and suffering" that had occurred while he was in office. However, he continued to deny personal responsibility, instead blaming "selfish individuals" in his government. Meanwhile, the new UDF-led government continued to press inquiries into a wide range of abuses that were alleged to have taken place under Banda's rule. Ultimately, although official scrutiny remained leveled at some of Banda's former confidants, investigative fervor in general dissipated substantially upon Banda's death on November 25.

On May 2, 1996, Chihana resigned from the government, saying that he wanted to concentrate on his party responsibilities. Six Aford cabinet ministers refused to comply with Chihana's demand that they resign from the government as well, and they declared themselves "independents." In response, Aford and the MCP suspended their participation in the assembly, accusing the UDF of attempting to secure a legislative majority by "poaching" their representatives as cabinet ministers. Assembly activity subsequently remained blocked (the UDF proving unable to muster a quorum) until April 1997, when Aford and the MCP ended their boycott after President Muluzi agreed to pursue constitutional amendments that would "prevent political horse trading and chicanery." However, the matter was not resolved on July 24, when Muluzi appointed a new cabinet that still included Aford representatives against the wishes of Aford leaders.

On June 15, 1999, President Muluzi was reelected to a second five-year term with 51.37 percent of the vote, compared to 44.3 percent for runner-up Chakuamba, the joint MCP/Aford candidate. (Aford's Chihana had served as Chakuamba's vice presidential running mate.) In concurrent legislative polling the UDF secured a plurality of 93 of 193 seats. The opposition accused the government of numerous irregularities, including manipulation of the media and the voter registration process as well as vote rigging. The losing candidates also argued that a runoff should have been held because Muluzi's vote total had not surpassed the level of 50 percent of the registered voters. Although the international community generally accepted the balloting as free and fair and the courts in Malawi upheld the results, Chakufwa Chihana of Aford, the MCP/Aford vice presidential candidate, called for a campaign of civil disobedience to protest the government's actions. Muluzi's critics also challenged the cabinet he appointed on July 1 for containing too many ministers (21 of 36) from the southern part of the country, the UDF stronghold.

Corruption charges prompted the appointment of new cabinets in March and November 2000, although many incumbents were simply given new portfolios. Meanwhile, severe intraparty infighting continued to hamper both the MCP and Aford, as evidenced by their poor showing in the November 2000 local elections, which were dominated by the UDF, albeit in the context of a low voter turnout. Muluzi's second term was marked by a bitter dispute over proposed constitutional changes to allow a president to seek a third term. The initial proposal failed to gain the needed two-thirds majority in the assembly in 2002, and a second effort in the legislature was rebuffed in 2003. The UDF attempted to have the measure brought to the public in a national referendum. However, it became clear that the constitutional amendment would fail because of widespread opposition, and the referendum request was withdrawn. Muluzi subsequently announced that he would not seek a third term. Instead he handpicked his successor, economist Bingu wa MUTHARIKA, who had run as a presidential candidate in 1999 for the defunct United Party (UP).

Presidential polling in 2004 was delayed by two days as a result of complaints by opposition parties that some 1 million voters, including many of their supporters, had been purged from the list of eligible voters. However, the High Court accepted the government's explanation that only double registrations and ineligible voters had been eliminated from the rolls.

In January 2004 a coalition of seven small parties, calling itself *Mgwirizano* (Unity), was launched to present Chakuamba as a joint presidential candidate. However, President Mutharika was reelected in balloting on May 20 with 35.9 percent of the vote, compared to 27.1 percent for Tembo (the MCP candidate) and 25.7 percent for Chakuamba. In concurrent legislative balloting, the MCP secured 60 seats, followed by the UDF with 49. Opposition parties and candidates challenged the legitimacy of the polling. However, Chakuamba withdrew his objections and accepted the post of minister of agriculture in the new Mutharika government, which also included the UDF, the National Democratic Alliance, the *Mgwirizano* coalition, and independents. Many independent legislators agreed to support the UDF in the assembly, some 23 of them subsequently joining the UDF. Additional realignments occurred after a dispute within the UDF prompted Mutharika to form a new party (see Current issues, below). As part of his anti-corruption campaign, the president dismissed 35 senior government officials between 2004 and 2006.

Mutharika announced a new economic plan in 2007 designed to enhance the country's agricultural sector through new investments in technology and infrastructure. Tensions between the president and individual government ministers led to four cabinet reshuffles in the period 2004–2008, with Mutharika assuming the portfolios of minister of agriculture and food security, and of education, science, and technology.

On May 16, 2009, the president dissolved the cabinet ahead of national elections. In the presidential elections on May 19, Mutharika was reelected with 66.4 percent of the vote. Tembo placed second with 30.3 percent. Five other minor party candidates received less than 1 percent each in polling that was criticized by some domestic and foreign monitors (see Current issues, below). In legislative balloting held on the same day, the DPP won an outright majority in the assembly with 113 seats. A new cabinet was appointed on June 15. Only eight ministers were retained from the previous cabinet. Mutharika's brother Peter was appointed minister of justice and constitutional affairs and the president retained the portfolio of agriculture and food security. Islamic groups protested the new cabinet because it included only two Muslims, as opposed to the seven in the previous government.

Constitution and government. The constitution of July 6, 1966, established a one-party system under which the MCP was accorded a political monopoly and its leader extensive powers as head of state, head of government, and commander in chief. Originally elected to a five-year presidential term by the National Assembly in 1966, Hastings Banda was designated president for life in 1971.

Following approval of a multiparty system in a national referendum on June 15, 1993, the assembly on June 22 amended the basic law to permit the registration of parties beyond the MCP. In November further revision abolished the life presidency and repealed the requirement that presidential candidates be MCP members. Following the return of ailing President Banda to active status in early December, an additional amendment was enacted to provide for an acting president in case of the president's incapacitation.

A new constitution (proposed by a National Constitutional Conference) was approved by the assembly on May 16, 1994, and entered into effect provisionally for one year on May 18. The new basic law incorporated the 1993 amendments, while also providing for a new Constitutional Committee and a Human Rights Commission. It also authorized the eventual creation of a second legislative body (the Senate) no sooner than 1999. However, in January 2001, much to the consternation of opposition parties and some civic organizations, the assembly revised the basic law to eliminate reference to the proposed Senate. The government argued that the creation of the Senate would have burdened the country's fragile economy, but opponents claimed that the administration was in reality primarily concerned that the new body would have had the power to impeach the president. Following review and refinement by the Constitutional Conference, the new constitution was once again approved by the assembly and promulgated as a permanent document on May 18, 1995. One of the amendments approved by the assembly in November 1994 provided for a presidentially appointed second vice president. The first vice president is elected as a running mate to the president and assumes the presidency if that office becomes vacant. The president is not required to designate a second vice president, but any such appointment must be made outside the president's political party.

The 1995 constitution provided for a Western-style judicial system, including a Supreme Court of Appeal, a High Court, and magistrates' courts. No mention is made of the so-called traditional courts (headed by local chiefs), which had been restored in 1970. For administrative purposes Malawi is divided into 3 regions, and 28 districts, which are headed by regional ministers and district commissioners, respectively.

Foreign relations. Malawi under President Banda's leadership sought to combine African nationalism with multiracialism at home and a strongly pro-Western and anticommunist position in world affairs. Citing economic necessity, Malawi was one of the few black African states to maintain uninterrupted relations with white-ruled South Africa. A consequence of the linkage was a September 1986 meeting in Blantyre, during which the leaders of Mozambique, Zambia, and Zimbabwe reportedly warned Banda to change his policies, particularly concerning alleged Malawian support for Renamo rebels in Mozambique. Banda, while denying the allegations, nevertheless quickly concluded a joint defense and security pact with Mozambique. The government also reaffirmed its commitment to an effort by the Southern African Development Coordination Conference (SADCC, subsequently the Southern African Development Community—SADC) to reduce dependence on South African trade routes. To that end, Malawi in 1987 agreed to increase shipments through Tanzania, with which it had established diplomatic ties in 1985 despite long-standing complaints of Tanzanian aid to Banda's opponents. Relations with Zambia had also been strained by Malawi's claim to Zambian territory in the vicinity of their common border.

In 1994 the new Muluzi administration moved quickly to strengthen regional ties, the president traveling to Zimbabwe, Zambia, and Botswana. In addition, Malawi and Mozambique created a joint commission to locate and repatriate former rebels located in the opposite state. Malawi also endeavored to improve relations and security ties with the United States. In June 2003 five suspected al-Qaida terrorists were turned over to U.S. custody.

President Mutharika's anticorruption campaign won international praise from European states, the United States, and international organizations such as the IMF and the World Bank. As a result, donors increased aid and assistance to the government, Malawi receiving about $60 million annually in U.S. economic aid in 2005 and 2006. Concurrently, Malawi's exports to the United States increased dramatically through the African Growth and Opportunity Act (AGOA), which eliminated U.S. tariffs on more then two-thirds of Malawian exports.

Following record maize harvests in 2006 and 2007, the government purchased excess crops from farmers to donate to Swaziland and Lesotho following a widespread drought. Malawi also increased sales of maize to Zimbabwe to record levels—400,000 tons per year. The two countries signed an economic cooperation agreement in May 2006, despite international criticism that closer ties undermined efforts to democratize Zimbabwe.

Relations between Malawi and China were strained in 2006 after Malawi refused an invitation to participate in a 2006 conference called by China in an effort to convince a group of African countries to break off diplomatic and economic relations with Taiwan. Instead of accepting the Chinese overtures, Malawi, Burkina Faso, Gambia, Sao Tome and Principe, and Swaziland signed a joint declaration of support in 2007 for Taiwan. Among other things, Taiwan since 2002 has provided financial and technical support to Malawi for a number of programs designed to improve education and health care, including an initiative to combat the spread of HIV/AIDS.

In January 2008 Malawi announced the suspension of diplomatic relations with Taiwan and the initiation of new ties with China. China subsequently pledged $287 million in new economic aid for Malawi. Chinese officials also promised new infrastructure assistance. The new relationship was expected to be especially beneficial to Malawi's tobacco sector, the largest in Africa, because China accounted for one-third of worldwide tobacco. In May Malawi and Zambia agreed on a joint electrification program whereby Malawi would provide power to remote areas along the border of the two countries. Malawi agreed to deploy 50 police officers to the Darfur region of Sudan as part of the UN–African Union peacekeeping force and pledged an additional 800 troops. In September Malawi withdrew recognition of the Polisario Front government in the Western Sahara and instead called for a negotiated settlement over the disputed region.

In 2009 foreign minister Yang Jiechi became the first senior Chinese official to visit Malawi and he announced a $90 million loan for economic development during the trip.

Current issues. Following the 2004 elections, new president Mutharika launched a broad anticorruption campaign that earned praise (and additional aid) from donors such as the EU and the United States. However, the initiative generated a rift between Mutharika and former president Muluzi, some of whose close allies (including several UDF leaders) were arrested on corruption charges. (Critics of Mutharika accused him of using the new anticorruption bureau as a personal political tool.) Consequently, supporters in the assembly of Muluzi (who remained leader of the UDF after leaving the presidency) began to block legislation presented by the Mutharika administration. The conflict culminated in the president's decision in February 2005 to quit the UDF and form a new Democratic Progressive Party (DPP), which attracted a number of Mutharika's supporters within the UDF and other parties and prompted significant legislative realignment.

In March 2005 the UDF and MCP attempted without success to impeach Mutharika for inappropriate use of government funds. At the same time, it was reported that the government was contemplating an investigation of former president Muluzi's alleged acquisition of millions of dollars during his presidential tenure. Relations between the executive and legislative branches deteriorated further when Mutharika moved his offices into the new assembly building, forcing the assembly to return to its old headquarters. Opposition parties (led by the UDF) again attempted to start impeachment proceedings against the president in June, and, in apparent retaliation, Mutharika removed the UDF's Cassim Chilumpha from his cabinet post, although Chilumpha remained vice president. Collaterally, Mutharika announced a cabinet reshuffle that raised the number of ministers from 27 to 33 so that he could include some of his independent supporters.

The assembly formally approved the start of impeachment proceedings in mid-October 2005, but the High Court ordered them stopped after pro-Mutharika demonstrations deteriorated into "riots" in which opposition legislators were reportedly attacked. In any event, it had been widely expected that the impeachment motion would not have garnered the two-thirds assembly vote required for success. In addition, analysts suggested that much of the population considered the impeachment initiative a waste of time and resources, particularly in view of the nation's severe food crisis. Among other things, the assembly's blockage of the administration's proposed budget compromised the distribution of emergency food supplies. (The budget had also called for a pay raise of more than 350 percent for the president.)

The government conducted another string of arrests in November 2005 as part of its anticorruption campaign. Among those charged were two legislators who had led the recent impeachment drive and Vice President Chilumpha. However, the High Court ruled that Chilumpha could not be brought up on criminal charges while serving as vice president. In February 2006 Mutharika attempted to dismiss Chilumpha for "undermining the government," but the High Court declared the president lacked the constitutional authority for such a move. At the end of April, Chilumpha and some 12 others (including senior members of the UDF) were arrested on treason charges, the administration accusing them of having plotted the assassination of Mutharika. The charges against most of those arrested were quickly dropped, but Chilumpha remained under house arrest along with two codefendants. Meanwhile, former president Muluzi was arrested on corruption charges in July, but he was released the following day after all charges were dismissed.

The restrictions on Vice President Chilumpha's house arrest were gradually relaxed as his trial began in January 2007. (The case proceeded slowly and continued into the fall because of repeated motions and challenges by the defense.) Meanwhile, the crackdown on the UDF continued, as three party officials were arrested on charges of treason in January, and Michael Sata, the leader of Zambia's main opposition group, was refused entry into Malawi in March. The police asserted that the Zambian leader intended to aid the UDF in antigovernment activities. The incident prompted criticism that security forces had become too politicized.

In June 2007 the Supreme Court upheld the article in the constitution that declared that any member of parliament who switched parties could be expelled and forced to stand for office in a by-election. The ruling was expected to affect at least 70 members of the legislature, although the government indicated that it would take more than six months to organize that many by-elections. Opposition members of parliament initially blocked debate on the government's proposed budget in an effort to force the by-elections. A compromise was finally reached in September that allowed passage of the budget in return for subsequent legislative debate on the management of new polling.

In February 2008 opposition parties boycotted the opening of the assembly and insisted that debate over by-elections be the first priority of the parliament. Only 6 of the 105 opposition deputies attended the opening of the legislature. In May the government arrested a number of opposition figures, including former president Muluzi, on charges that they were plotting a coup. Also charged were former senior military leaders and the secretary general of the UDF, Kennedy MAKWANGWALA. Opposition leaders decried the arrests as part of an intimidation campaign ahead of presidential and legislative elections scheduled for 2009. All were subsequently released on bail. Also in May, Mutharika initiated the parliamentary budgetary session despite the ongoing opposition boycott. Meanwhile, the government announced a 17 percent increase in pay for civil servants in an effort to prevent a general strike. The UDF nominated Muluzi as its presidential candidate at a party congress in May, although concerns were raised over his eligibility because presidents were limited to two consecutive terms. Muluzi and his supporters contended that the wording of the constitution allowed more than two terms as long as they were not consecutive. The nation's constitutional court ruled that Muluzi was ineligible, leaving the UDF without a candidate in the presidential balloting (see Political Parties, below).

In the presidential and legislative balloting, concerns were raised over the number of voters who were turned away from the polls in some precincts. Protests were also lodged to the electoral commission over the use of state media to support the ruling Mutharika and the ruling DPP (see Communications, below). However, most domestic and foreign observers asserted that the balloting was generally free and fair. The polling marked the first time in Malawi that a woman, Loveness Gondwe of the New Rainbow Coalition (see Political parties, below), ran for the presidency. Although Gondwe did not win, Joyce Banda of the DPP became the country's first female vice president. Also in May 2009, it was announced that long-delayed local elections would be held in 2010.

POLITICAL PARTIES AND GROUPS

For nearly three decades prior to the 1993 national referendum, the Malawi Congress Party (MCP) was the only authorized political group, and it exercised complete control of the government. On June 29, 1993, the constitution was amended to allow for multiparty activity, and on August 17 the government announced that the first groups had been authorized to function as legal parties.

The **Mgwirizano** (Unity) coalition was formed in January 2004 by seven small parties opposed to the UDF and the rule of President Muluzi. The coalition included the Republican Party, the People's Progressive Movement, the Movement for Democratic Change, the People's Transformation Party, the Malawi Democratic Party, the National Unity Party, and the Malawi Forum for Unity and Development. It fielded a slate of candidates for the legislative election and chose Gwanda Chakuamba as the coalition leader and main presidential candidate. (John Malewezi also ran as a candidate for the People's Progressive Movement.) Following the legislative elections, some member parties decided to support newly elected President Mutharika after he reached out and incorporated party members in a coalition government. However, the coalition dissolved in February 2005 with the resignation of Chakuamba and the formation of the Democratic Progressive Party (see below).

Legislative Parties:

Democratic Progressive Party (DPP). The DPP was launched in February 2005 by President Bingu wa Mutharika and other UDF dissidents who opposed UDF president Muluzi. Disaffected members of other parties and a number of independents also joined the DDP, which as of mid-2006 was credited with controlling some 74 assembly seats. DPP Vice President Gwanda Chakuamba was dismissed from the cabinet and expelled from the party in September 2005 after he strongly criticized President Mutharika. Ralph KASAMBARA was dismissed as attorney general in 2006 and left the party to form the **Congress for Democrats** (CODE). Chakuamba's successor as party vice president, Uladi MUSSA, was also dismissed in January 2007 on charges that he was attempting to launch a new political party. Mussa was replaced by the party's Secretary General Heatherwick Ntaba, who was also the chief political adviser to Mutharika.

Mutharika was reelected president of the republic in May 2009 during elections in which the DPP secured 113 seats and an outright majority in the assembly.

Leaders: Bingu wa MUTHARIKA (President of the Republic and Party President), Joyce Banda (Vice President of the Republic), Hetherwick NTABA (Party Vice President).

United Democratic Front (UDF). The UDF was founded in April 1992 by former MCP officials who operated clandestinely until October, when they announced their intention to campaign for a multiparty democracy. A party congress on December 30, 1993, chose UDF chair Bakili Muluzi to be the UDF's presidential candidate. Meanwhile, the UDF leaders were embarrassed by allegations, attributed to the MCP, that they had engaged in anti-opposition activities while MCP members.

Muluzi defeated incumbent president Banda and two other candidates in March 1994 with a 47.3 percent plurality of the vote. In the legislative balloting the UDF won a plurality of 84 of 177 seats. Muluzi was reelected with 51.37 percent of the vote in 1999, while the UDF increased its legislative plurality to 93 out of 193 seats in 1999.

Beginning in 2000, the party suffered serious internal divisions, leading to the formation of the anti-Muluzi NDA (below). In 2003, dissident members of the UDF left the party to form a new entity, the People's Progressive Movement (PPM), led by former UDF party vice president Aleke Banda. In the 2004 legislative elections the UDF lost its plurality and became the second-largest party (49 seats) in the assembly behind the MCP.

Following the 2004 presidential election, a leadership struggle emerged between Muluzi, who remained party president, and his handpicked successor as Malawi's president, Bingu wa Mutharika. Among other things, Muluzi's supporters objected to elements of the broad anticorruption efforts by Mutharika, who in February 2005 left the UDF to form the DPP (above).

The UDF led the subsequent effort to impeach President Mutharika, although its legislative representation had reportedly fallen to 30 by mid-2006 due to defections to the DPP. In addition, many UDF leaders faced corruption charges pressed by the Mutharika administration (see Current issues, above). Muluzi announced in March 2007 that he intended to be the UDF candidate for the presidency in 2009, and he won the party's nomination at a convention in April 2008. The subsequent ruling by the constitutional court that Muluzi was ineligible to run led many UDF supporters to back MCP candidate John Tembo (see below). In the legislative balloting the UDF secured 17 seats. Many party members blamed the UDF's poor performance on Muluzi's failed presidential effort.

Leaders: Bakili MULUZI (President of the Party and Former President of the Republic), Kennedy MAKWANGWALA (Secretary General), Friday Jumbe.

Malawi Congress Party (MCP). The MCP is a continuation of the Nyasaland African Congress (NAC), which was formed in 1959 under the leadership of President H. Kamuzu Banda. Overtly pro-Western and dedicated to multiracialism and internal development, the party was frequently criticized for being excessively conservative. It held all legislative seats prior to the multiparty poll of May 1994, when it ran second in both the presidential and legislative races.

On August 25, 1994, Banda retired from politics although he retained the title of MCP president for life. The 1994 vice presidential candidate, Stephen Chakuamba, assumed leadership of the party. Thereafter, in early 1995, the party was shaken by the arrests of Banda, John Tembo (longtime Banda associate and MCP leader), and others for alleged involvement in the killing 12 years earlier of Dick MATENJE and several other MCP cabinet ministers. At the time of his death, Matenje had headed an increasingly popular reform wing within the party that had clashed with Tembo and his supporters. Banda, Tembo, and their codefendants in the murder trial were acquitted on all charges in December. Related charges against Cecilia KADZAMIRA, Banda's longtime companion who had been the country's "official hostess" during the latter part of the Banda regime, had been dismissed prior to trial on technical grounds. However, the government continued to press the case by appealing the verdict to the High Court, which ultimately upheld the acquittal. Meanwhile, Tembo and Kadzamira were arrested in September 1996 on charges of conspiracy to commit murder in connection with an alleged plot to assassinate cabinet members in 1995. They were quickly released on bail, and it was subsequently unclear if the case would be pursued. Similar ambiguity existed regarding fraud charges against Tembo and Kadzamira stemming from alleged malfeasance during the accumulation of the vast Banda "economic empire." Banda himself had been the focus of a corruption investigation in early 1997, but the case was dropped later in the year when it became apparent that the former president had little time to live.

Conflict between Banda's supporters and MCP "reformists" continued through 1997, with the latter clearly gaining the ascendancy at the party convention in July. In a surprisingly decisive vote of 406–109, Tembo was defeated in the race for MCP president by Chakuamba, who immediately declared his intention to run for president of the republic in 1999, insisting that the MCP should merge with Aford (below) to present the strongest possible challenge to the UDF. However, the proposed merger was shelved in the wake of objections from MCP veterans, including Tembo, who had been elected unopposed as MCP vice president.

In intraparty polling in January 1999, Chakuamba defeated Tembo in a contest to decide who would be the MCP's standard-bearer in midyear presidential balloting. Subsequently, Chakuamba rejected suggestions that he choose Tembo as his running mate and named Aford's Chakufwa Chihana to his campaign ticket. On February 8 an electoral alliance for the presidential race between the two parties was officially inaugurated. Meanwhile, pro-Tembo activists staged demonstrations to protest what they (and reportedly Tembo) considered an affront. The MCP/Aford ticket finished second (with 44.3 percent of the vote) in the June presidential ballot, while the MCP secured 66 seats (on 33.82 percent of the vote) in the legislative poll. Meanwhile, tension between Chakuamba and Tembo continued, and in late May Tembo called upon

Chakuamba to step down as party leader. In early June, Chakuamba called for an MCP boycott of the opening session of parliament, but his request was ignored and he was given a one-year suspension from the house (later voided by the High Court). On June 24 Speaker Sam Mpasu endorsed Tembo as new leader of the opposition in parliament, a decision that was subsequently challenged by Chakuamba.

The MCP infighting continued unabated into 2000, and the rival factions held separate conventions in August at which Chakuamba and Tembo were each declared party chair. However, the following summer the High Court nullified the parallel conventions. Meanwhile, the Chakuamba faction, which announced it had expelled Tembo and his supporters from the party, pursued ties with the NDA, the newly formed antigovernment grouping, while the Tembo faction was perceived as cooperating more and more with the administration. Chakuamba subsequently joined the Republican Party (below) in December 2003. the MCP became the largest party in the assembly after the 2004 elections, but Tembo lost his presidential bid. MCP Secretary General Kate KAINGA-KALULUMA joined the new Mutharika government and subsequently left the MCP to join the DPP. Subsequently, the MCP cooperated with the UDF's attempt to impeach President Mutharika, although internal MCP dissension was reported regarding that and other issues. (A dissident faction led by Respicius DZANJALIMODZI reportedly challenged Tembo's supporters for party supremacy.)

In 2007 Tembo rejected a proposal from the UDF to rally behind a single candidate in the 2009 presidential elections. Under the proposal, Tembo would have run as the vice presidential candidate with Muluzi as the presidential contender. Dissatisfied with Tembo's leadership, former party vice president Nicholas DAUSI and at least 60 MCP members and elected officials left the party in 2008 to join the DPP.

During the 2009 elections the MCP campaigned on a pledge to implement a universal subsidy for all farmers. Tembo placed second in the presidential balloting and the MCP became the second largest party in the legislature with 27 seats, although it lost more than half its former seats. After the balloting many MCP officials who criticized Tembo, including party spokesperson Ishmael Chafukira, who had called for the presidential candidate's resignation, were removed from their positions.

Leaders: John TEMBO (Party Leader and 2004 presidential candidate), Louis CHIMANGO (Speaker of the National Assembly).

Alliance for Democracy (Aford). Aford was launched in Lilongwe on September 21, 1992, by trade union leader and prodemocracy advocate Chakufwa Chihana, who at the time of the group's founding was awaiting trial on sedition charges. The grouping was led by a 13-member interim committee that included civil servants, academics, and businesspeople. Although Aford described itself as "not a party but a pressure group," the government on November 7 declared membership in the group illegal. In late December many of its members were arrested during demonstrations ignited by the sentencing of Chihana to three years imprisonment.

In March 1993 a spokesperson for the Zimbabwean-based Malawi Freedom Movement (Mafremo) announced that the group had dissolved and had merged with Aford. (Mafremo, in the wake of the 1981 arrest and imprisonment of its leader, Orton CHIRWA, had been relatively inactive until an early 1987 attack on a police station near the Tanzanian border that was attributed to the group's military wing, the Malawi National Liberation Army. Although initially based in Dar es Salaam, Mafremo had subsequently been reported to have secured Zimbabwean support through the efforts of a new leader, Dr. Edward YAPWANTHA, who was expelled from Zimbabwe in mid-1990, apparently as a result of improved Malawian-Zimbabwean relations.)

In mid-1994, Chihana, who had been granted a sentence reduction and released two days before the multiparty referendum, pressed President Banda to resign in favor of an MCP-UDF-Aford transitional government. In August Aford turned back a merger bid from another opposition party—the Congress for the Second Republic (CSR)—asserting an interest in the CSR's then exiled leader, Kanyama CHUIME, but not the party.

Following its third-place showing in the 1994 assembly balloting, Aford declined an invitation to participate in a government coalition with the UDF, which was five seats short of a legislative majority. On June 20 Aford signed a memorandum of understanding with the MCP, in which the two groups committed themselves to preservation of "the endangered national unity and security of the country." However, in September Chihana joined the Muluzi government as second vice president designate, while three other Aford members accepted cabinet posts. Although Chihana rejected reports that the party was defecting to the UDF, in January 1995 Aford announced the dissolution of its alliance with the MCP.

Relations between the UDF and Aford deteriorated over the next year, and on May 2, 1996, Chihana, who had criticized the UDF on several points in December 1995, resigned from the second vice presidency, ostensibly to devote more time to party affairs. In June it was reported that an Aford national congress had voted to withdraw from the government coalition and had ordered its members in the cabinet to resign their posts. However, most of the ministers refused to leave the government, and it was reported that at least six members of the Aford executive council rejected the decision to separate from the coalition with the UDF. In response, Chihana called for the ouster of the "renegade" members, who, according to some reports, were by then referring to themselves as "independents." The issue remained clouded throughout 1997 as the new cabinet announced in July included not only the previous Aford ministers but also several other Aford members. Meanwhile, at the party's annual congress in December, Aford delegates voted against a merger with the MCP that had been advocated by many within the Chihana camp.

In June 1998 two Aford legislators, Joseph MSEKAWANTHU and Edward MUSYANI, declared their independence from the party, charging that the party's dictatorial" leadership policies had marginalized them. In October Aford officially acknowledged having decided to compete for the presidency on a joint ticket with the MCP, and in February 1999 Chihana agreed to campaign for the vice presidency on a ticket led by MCP leader Chakuamba. Aford was credited with 10.52 percent of the vote and 29 seats in the June 1999 assembly balloting.

Intraparty fighting continued in 2000–2001 in regard to issues such as the future of the alliance with the MCP and whether the party should cooperate with the government. While the faction around Chihana was reportedly in favor of continuing an antigovernment stance, another wing pressed to discontinue the alliance with the MCP and form a national unity government with the UDF. Aford won only 6 seats in the 2004 elections and supported the subsequent Mutharika government after Chihana was appointed minister of agriculture and food security, a post he left in February 2005. Four of Aford's legislators reportedly defected to the DPP in 2005. In June 2006 Chihana died in South Africa; he was succeeded as party leader by Chipimpha Mughogho. At a party conference in December, Aford officials voted to expel members who did not support Mughogho as Aford leader. In October 2007 Dindi Gowa NYASULU was elected president of Aford at a congress that was marred by the death of 26 Aford delegates who perished in a bus accident on the way to the convention.

Nyasulu was the Aford presidential candidate in the 2009 balloting. He placed last among the six contenders with less than 1 percent of the vote. In the concurrent assembly polling, Aford secured only one seat.

Leaders: Dindi Gowa NYASULU (President), Khwauli MSISKA (Secretary General).

Malawi Forum for Unity and Development (MAFUNDE). MAFUNDE was formed in 2002 under the leadership of George MNESA to fight corruption and end food shortages. The party failed to gain seats in the 2004 balloting, but it secured one seat in the 2009 assembly election.

Leader: George Mnesa.

Maravi People's Party (MPP). Formed in 2007, the MPP initially opposed Mutharika and the DPP. When MPP secretary general and party cofounder Paul Maulidi attempted to form an electoral alliance with the ruling DPP, he was ousted from the party and replaced by Yusuf Haudi (Maulidi subsequently joined the DPP). The MPP gained one seat in the 2009 assembly elections. After the elections, the MPP announced it would support Mutharika and the DPP.

Leader: Yusuf Haudi (Acting Secretary General).

Other Parties that Contested the 2009 Legislative Election:

Congress for National Unity (CONU). The CONU is led by a cleric who received .51 percent of the vote in the 1999 presidential poll. The CONU also participated unsuccessfully in the 1999 legislative balloting. In the 2004 elections CONU gained one seat in the assembly. CONU failed to secure any seats in the 2009 balloting.

Leaders: Bishop Daniel NKHUMBWE (1999 presidential candidate), Silvester White CHABUKA (1999 vice presidential candidate).

Republican Party (RP). The RP was formed in 2004 by Gwanda Chakuamba, Stanley Masauli, and other opponents of John Tembo from the MCP. Using the RP as the nucleus of the anti-Muluzi coalition *Mgwirizano*, Chakuamba placed third in the 2004 presidential balloting with 25.7 percent of the vote. He subsequently joined the government as minister of agriculture and food security. In the legislative elections, the RP became the third largest party with 15 seats.

In March 2005 Chakuamba resigned from the RP, along with a number of RP members, to join the new DPP. Chakuamba initially announced the dissolution of the RP, but the RP's executive council rejected the proposed "merger" with the DPP. The executive committee agreed that the RP would remain in the government.

Following his dismissal from the government and the DPP in September 2005, Chakuamba attempted to reassert control over the RP. However, he was formally expelled from the RP in October, and he subsequently announced the formation of the **New Republican Party** (NRP) and pledged to support Muluzi of the UDF in the 2009 presidential elections (see below).

In the 2009 elections Stanley Masauli was the RP presidential candidate. He placed fourth among the six candidates, but received less than 1 percent of the vote. The RP failed to secure any seats in the concurrent assembly elections.

Leaders: Anastansia MSOSA (Party Chair), Stanley MASAULI (2009 Presidential Candidate).

New Republican Party (NRP). The NRP was formed in October 2005 by former Republican Party leader Gwanda Chakuamba (see above). The NRP initially backed Muluzi, but when the UDF candidate was declared ineligible in April 2009, Chakuamba endorsed Mutharika, reportedly in hopes of broadening the appeal of the party. The NRP did not gain any seats in the 2009 legislative balloting.

Leader: Gwanda CHAKUAMBA.

People's Progressive Movement (PPM). Formed in 2003 by former UDF vice president Aleke Banda and other UDF members opposed to their party's Muluzi faction, the PPM joined the *Mgwirizano* coalition for the 2004 elections, gaining six seats in the assembly. Party member and former vice president of the republic John MALEWEZI ran as a presidential candidate for the PPM in 2004, placing fifth with just 2.5 percent of the vote. In 2005 a number of PPM members joined the DPP, although the PPM retained its status as an independent party. The party endorsed Mutharika in the 2009 presidential balloting.

Leader: Mark KATSONGA (Party Leader).

Movement for Genuine Democratic Change (MGODE). The MGODE, created in October 2003 by former members of Aford, joined the *Mgwirizano* coalition prior to the 2004 presidential and legislative elections, gaining three seats in the assembly balloting. In 2005 it was reported that the MGODE had been absorbed into the DPP, however the party registered as an independent grouping for the 2009 assembly elections. It did not secure any seats in the polling.

Leaders: Sam Kandodo BANDA (Party President), Greene MWAMONDWE (Chair), Rodger NKWAZI (Secretary General).

Malawi Democratic Party (MDP). The MDP was legalized shortly after its formation in mid-1993, its leader running a distant fourth in the presidential balloting of May 17, 1994. Although having won no legislative seats, the MDP held the economic planning portfolio during the first four months of the Muluzi government and was given the housing portfolio in August 1995.

The MDP leadership reportedly called for the government's resignation in July 1995 after the party lost its sole post in a cabinet reshuffling. Two months later, the MDP's president and vice president, Kampelo Kalua and Unandi Banda, were arrested on intimidation charges; however, the two were subsequently acquitted.

Kalua received only 1.43 percent of the vote in the 1999 presidential vote, while no MDP legislative candidates were successful in the 1999, 2004, or 2009 election. The party supported Tembo of the MCP in the presidential balloting.

Leaders: Kampelo KALUA (President and 1994 and 1999 presidential candidate), Unandi BANDA (Vice President), Lyson MILANZI (1999 vice presidential candidate).

New Rainbow Coalition (NARC). Formed in March 2008 on the eve of presidential and legislative balloting, NARC supported the creation of a federal system in Malawi. A long-time member of Aford and legislator in the assembly, Loveness Gondwe formed NARC after Aford refused to support her presidential bid. Gondwe was NARC's presidential choice (and Malawi's first female presidential candidate). She placed fifth in the polling and NARC failed to gain any seats in the assembly.

Leaders: Loveness GONDWE (2009 presidential candidate), Beatrice MWALE (2009 vice-presidential candidate).

Other parties that contested the May 2009 legislative elections included the **People's Transformation Party** (Petra), which gained one seat in the 2004 balloting, but failed to gain any representation in 2009 and whose presidential candidate Kamuzu CHIBAMBO placed third; the **National Unity Party** (NUP), formed in 2005 and led by Harry CHIUME; the **New Congress for Democracy** (NCD), launched in 2004 by former MCP members and led by Hetherwick NTABA, who joined the Mutharika government as minister of health after the election (it was subsequently reported that Ntaba had joined the DPP and that the NCD had been dissolved); the **Pamodzi Freedom Party** (PFP), established in 2002 and led by Rainsford NDIWO; **Congress of Democrats** (CODE), led by Ralph KASAMBARA; the **Malawi Forum for Unity and Development** (MAFUNDE), formed in June 2002 and led by George MNESA; and the **United Democratic Party** (UDP), formed in 2005 by Kenedy Solomon KALAMBO.

Other Parties:

National Democratic Alliance (NDA). The NDA was originally launched in early 2001 as a "pressure group" designed to promote "good governance" and to combat potential revision of the constitution that would permit President Muluzi to run for a third term. The new grouping also criticized the government's economic policies and urged installation of a "unity government" that would include the MCP. The NDA was founded by several dissident UDF members, the most prominent being Brown Mpinganjira, a longtime Muluzi loyalist who had been dismissed from the cabinet in November and arrested on corruption charges in late December. Mpinganjira, who had once been considered a possible successor to Muluzi, accused the government of trumping up the charges against him because of his outspoken opposition to a third term for Muluzi. The charges were subsequently dropped for lack of evidence.

At the inception of the NDA, Mpinganjira and the other UDF "rebels" insisted that they were still UDF members and that they were not trying to establish a new party. However, the UDF quickly expelled Mpinganjira and three other UDF legislators from the party for their NDA association. In late February 2001 another prominent UDF member, James Makhumula, also left the party in favor of association with the NDA, of which he eventually was named national chair. (Makhumula, a prominent and wealthy businessman, had been regarded as the "chief financier" of the UDF.)

Apparently in response to growing support for the NDA, the assembly in June 2001 passed an "antidefection law," which stated that legislators leaving the party under whose banner they were elected thereby forfeited their seats. In November the assembly voted to expel Mpinganjira and six others for violation of the new law. However, the High Court ordered the legislators reinstalled. Subsequently, the NDA was granted legal party status in preparation for the 2004 elections. Mpinganjira placed fourth in the 2004 presidential election with 8.7 percent of the vote, while the NDA gained eight seats in the assembly balloting. Reports in 2006 indicated that Mpinganjira had rejected an invitation to merge his party with the DPP. Instead the NDA leader was linked to the UDF, while other NDA deputies in fact joined the DPP. The NDA was reported to be defunct prior to the 2009 balloting.

Leaders: Brown MPINGANJIRA (President and 2004 presidential candidate), James MAKHUMULA (Chair).

LEGISLATURE

Members of the unicameral **National Assembly** normally sit for five-year terms. From 1978 through 1992 candidates had to be approved by the MCP. The first multiparty balloting was held on May 17, 1994, for an enlarged body of 177 members. The number of legislators was increased to 193 for the balloting of July 15, 1999. In legislative balloting on May 19, 2009, the Democratic Progressive Party secured 113 seats; the Malawi Congress Party, 27; the United Democratic Front, 17; Alliance for Democracy, 1; Malawi Forum for Unity and Development, 1; the Malawi People's Party, 1; and independents, 38. One seat was not filled during the balloting and a by-election was scheduled for later in

2009. There were 40 women elected to the assembly in 2009, up from 27 in the previous election.

Speaker: Louis CHIMANGO.

CABINET

[as of July 1, 2009]

President	Bingu wa Mutharika (DPP)
Vice President	Joyce Banda (DPP)
Second Vice President	(Vacant)
Ministers	
Agriculture and Food Security	Bingu wa Mutharika (DPP)
Defense	Sidik Mia
Development Planning and Cooperation	Abi Shawa
Education, Science, and Technology	George Chaponda (DPP)
Finance	Ken Edward Kandodo (DPP)
Foreign Affairs and International Cooperation	Eta Elizabeth Banda (DPP) [f]
Health	Moses Chirambo (DPP)
Home Affairs and Internal Security	Aaron Sangala
Industry, Trade, and Private Sector Development	Eunice Kazembe [f]
Information and Civic Education	Leckford Mwanza (DPP)
Irrigation and Water Development	Ritchie Bizwick Muyewa (DPP)
Justice and Constitutional Affairs	Peter Mutharika (DPP)
Labor and Vocational Training	Yunus Mussa (UDF)
Lands, Housing, and Surveys	Peter Nelson Mwanza (DPP)
Local Government and Rural Development	Goodall Gondwe (DPP)
Natural Resources and Energy	Grey Malunga
Persons with Disabilities and the Elderly	Bessie Reen Kachere [f]
Tourism and Wildlife	Anna Kachikho [f]
Transport and Public Works	Khumbo Kachali (DPP)
Women and Child Development	Patricia Kaliati (DPP) [f]
Youth, Sports, and Culture	Lucius Kanyumba

[f] = female

COMMUNICATIONS

Press. Most newspapers are privately owned and operated. There is no formal censorship, but the government's refusal to tolerate any form of criticism was reflected in a 1973 decree that journalists who printed material "damaging to the nation's reputation" were liable to life imprisonment. In 1992 the press law was amended, reducing sentences for such crimes to five years; in addition, previously stringent restrictions on foreign journalists appeared to have been relaxed. In March 1993, on the other hand, opposition newspapers launched by Aford and the UDF were reported to have been banned. However, subsequent constitutional amendments eased press restrictions, and by November 1993 there were reportedly 12 newly licensed opposition newspapers. Censorship remains a problem; two journalists were arrested after publishing a story in which they suggested that the president was afraid of ghosts and had moved out of the presidential mansion because he believed it to be haunted. On March 15, 2005, the journalists were charged with publishing false stories and causing ridicule to the president. In the 2007 budget, opposition members of parliament managed to reduce funding of the state broadcasting companies to a symbolic one kwacha because of claims that the media had become organs of the government. Media groups protested the arrest of three employees of Joy Radio on May 19, 2009, election day, for unlawful campaigning, and the Malawi Electoral Commission criticized the state radio and television station for failing to provide equal access to all parties during the 2009 balloting. In its 2008 ratings of global press freedom, Reporters Without Borders ranked Malawi 70, along with Benin and Tanzania, out of 173 countries, but noted that the country had improved from its ranking of 92 in 2007.

The following are published in Blantyre, unless otherwise noted: *Boma Lathu* (100,000), Department of Information monthly in Chichewa; *Moni* (39,000), monthly in English and Chichewa; *Malawi News* (30,000), opposition weekly in English and Chichewa; *The Daily Times* (22,000), opposition daily in English; *Odini* (Lilongwe, 12,000), Catholic fortnightly in English and Chichewa; *The Independent* (10,000), independent weekly; *Malawi Democrat,* Aford publication; *Michiru Sun,* independent daily; *The New Express,* independent weekly; *Nation,* progovernment daily; *Mirror,* weekly; *Chronicle,* independent weekly; and *The Dispatch,* independent daily.

News agency. The domestic facility is the Malawi News Agency (Mana).

Broadcasting and computing. Radio service in English and Chichewa is provided by the statutory and semicommercial Malawi Broadcasting Corporation (MBC) and the privately owned Capital Radio Company. In July 1995 the government signed an agreement with TV3 of Malaysia to establish a television service by March 1996; however, Lilongwe canceled the deal in May 1996, citing the slow pace of implementation and poor equipment quality. Subsequent efforts to begin broadcasting were slowed by financial problems, although Television Malawi formally came into existence in 1999. As of 2008 there were 21.3 Internet users per 1,000 inhabitants.

INTERGOVERNMENTAL REPRESENTATION

Ambassador to the U.S.: Hawa Olga NDILOWE.

U.S. Ambassador to Malawi: Peter William BODDE.

Permanent Representative to the UN: Steve Dick Tennyson MATENJE.

IGO Memberships (Non-UN): AfDB, AU, BADEA, Comesa, CWTH, Interpol, NAM, SADC, WCO, WTO.

MALAYSIA

Note: The capitalized portions of non-Chinese names in this article are frequently the more familiar components, rather than "family" names in the Western sense.

Political Status: Independent Federation of Malaya within the Commonwealth established August 31, 1957; Malaysia established September 16, 1963, with the addition of Sarawak, Sabah, and Singapore (which withdrew in August 1965).

Area: 127,316 sq. mi. (329,749 sq. km.), encompassing Peninsular Malaysia, 50,806 sq. mi. (131,588 sq. km.); Sarawak, 48,050 sq. mi. (124,450 sq. km.); Sabah, 28,460 sq. mi. (73,711 sq. km.).

Population: 23,274,690 (2000C, incorporating adjustment for underenumeration, including Peninsular Malaysia, 18,599,699; Sabah, 2,603,485; Sarawak, 2,071,506); 27,711,000 (2008E).

Major Urban Centers (2007E): KUALA LUMPUR (1,390,000), Kelang (Klang, 735,000), Ipoh (630,000). The new administrative capital, Putrajaya, is 25 miles south of Kuala Lumpur.

Official Language: Bahasa Malaysia.

Monetary Unit: Ringgit (official rate December 1, 2009: 3.38 ringgit = $1US).

Paramount Ruler: Sultan MIZAN Zainal Abidin ibni al-Mahum Sultan Mahmud al-Muftaki Billah Shah (Sovereign of Terengganu); elected for a five-year term on November 3, 2006, by the Conference of Rulers; sworn in on December 13 and formally installed on April 26, 2007, succeeding Tuanku SYED Sirajuddin ibni al-Marhum Syed Putra Jamalullail (Sovereign of Perlis).

Deputy Paramount Ruler: Sultan ABDUL HALIM al-Muadzam Shah (Sovereign of Kedah); elected November 3, 2006, and sworn in on December 13 for a term concurrent with that of the paramount ruler, succeeding Sultan MIZAN Zainal Abidin ibni al-Mahum Sultan Mahmud al-Muftaki Billah Shah (Sovereign of Terengganu).

Prime Minister: Mohamad NAJIB Abdul Razak (United Malays National Organization); appointed on April 3, 2009, and sworn in the same day to succeed ABDULLAH bin Ahmad Badawi (United Malays National Organization), who had resigned on April 2; formed new government on April 9.

THE COUNTRY

Situated partly on the Malay Peninsula and partly on the island of Borneo, Malaysia consists of 11 states of the former Federation of Malaya (Peninsular, or West Malaysia) plus the states of Sarawak and Sabah (East Malaysia). Thailand and Singapore are the mainland's northern and southern neighbors, respectively, while Sarawak and Sabah share a common border with the Indonesian province of Kalimantan. The multiracial population is comprised predominantly of Malays (50 percent), followed by Chinese (24 percent), non-Malay tribals (11 percent), and Indians and Pakistanis (7 percent). Although the Malay-based Bahasa Malaysia is the official language, English, Tamil, and several Chinese dialects are widely spoken. Islam is the state religion, but the freedom to profess other faiths is constitutionally guaranteed. Minority religious groups include Buddhists (19 percent), Christians (9 percent), and Hindus (6 percent). The status of women is largely determined by ethnic group and location, urban Malay women being better educated than their rural counterparts. Overall, women comprise 36 percent of the active workforce, concentrated in services and manufacturing.

Traditionally a leader in the production of rubber, palm oil, and tin, Malaysia continues to be the world's principal supplier of palm oil and a significant source of rubber and tin. In the past decade, however, these and other commodity exports, including petroleum, liquefied natural gas, and saw logs and sawn timber, have been superseded in importance by manufactures—chiefly semiconductors and electrical equipment and appliances, which together account for about 50 percent of export earnings. Other exports include chemicals and chemical products, metal manufactures, petroleum products, optical and scientific equipment, and textiles, clothing, and footwear. Agriculture now contributes only about 10 percent of GDP and employs 13 percent of the labor force, while industry accounts for 45 percent of GDP and 36 percent of jobs.

In mid-1991 the government introduced a New Development Policy (NDP) as successor to the New Economic Policy (NEP) of the 1970s and 1980s. The NDP, which set as a national goal the achievement of fully developed status by the year 2020, placed substantially less emphasis than its predecessor on transferring corporate assets to the *bumiputras* ("sons of the soil"), comprising Malays and other indigenous peoples, while providing added incentives for both foreign and domestic investors.

In 1990–1997 Malaysia ranked as one of the world's most rapidly expanding economies, with an average annual GDP growth rate of 8.7 percent. By late 1997, however, Malaysia had succumbed to the East Asian economic crisis, and in 1998 the economy contracted by 7.4 percent—its worst downturn since independence. It rebounded rapidly, however, registering a 6.1 percent gain in GDP for 1999. Growth in 2002–2008 remained robust, averaging 5.7 percent annually.

Though the government approved an economic stimulus package of nearly $2 billion in late 2008 in response to the global economic crisis, the International Monetary Fund (IMF) forecast a contraction of Malaysia's economy in 2009, perhaps by as much as 3.5 percent. The downturn was due largely to a sharp decline in exports, plant closings, and the subsequent loss of manufacturing jobs. On a more positive note, the IMF expected economic growth to recover somewhat in 2010, increasing by 1.3 percent.

GOVERNMENT AND POLITICS

Political background. Malaysia came into existence as a member of the Commonwealth on September 16, 1963, through merger of the already independent Federation of Malaya with the self-governing state of Singapore and the British Crown Colonies of Sarawak and Sabah. The Malay states, organized by the British in the 19th century, had achieved sovereign status in 1957, following the suppression of a long-standing communist insurgency. Tunku ABDUL RAHMAN, head of the United Malays National Organization (UMNO) and subsequently of the Alliance Party, became Malaya's first prime minister and continued in that capacity after the formation of Malaysia. Singapore, with its predominantly Chinese population, had been ruled as a separate British colony and became internally self-governing in 1959 under the leadership of LEE Kuan Yew of the People's Action Party (PAP). Its inclusion in Malaysia was terminated in August 1965, primarily because the PAP's attempt to extend its influence beyond the confines of Singapore was viewed as a threat to Malay dominance of the federation.

In May 1969 racial riots in Kuala Lumpur led to a declaration of national emergency. A nine-member National Operations Council was given full powers to quell the disturbances, but parliamentary government was not fully restored until February 1971. Meanwhile, communist guerrillas, relatively quiescent since 1960, had begun returning from sanctuaries across the Malaysian-Thai border, and by early 1974 they were once again posing a serious threat to domestic security. In the context of a vigorous campaign against the insurgents, an August election resulted in an impressive victory for Prime Minister ABDUL RAZAK bin Hussein's newly styled National Front (*Barisan Nasional*) coalition of ethnic and regional parties, which left only two of the eight opposition parties with seats in the lower house of Parliament.

In January 1976 Abdul Razak died and was succeeded by the deputy prime minister, HUSSEIN bin Onn, who was also designated chair of the National Front. Under Hussein's leadership the front retained overwhelming control of the federal House of Representatives in an early election in July 1978. In May 1981, however, Hussein announced that for health reasons he would not stand for reelection as UMNO president, and he was succeeded in June by the party's deputy president, MAHATHIR bin Mohamad, who formed a new government following his designation as prime minister in July.

In early elections in 1982 and 1986 the National Front continued to win easy victories. In early 1987, however, a major crisis surfaced within UMNO as it prepared for a triennial leadership poll in April. Accusing Mahathir of tolerating corruption, mismanagement, and extravagant spending, Deputy Prime Minister MUSA bin Hital joined with a number of other prominent UMNO figures in supporting the candidacy of Trade and Industry Minister Tengku RAZALEIGH Hamzah for the party presidency. After an intensely fought campaign,

Mahathir defeated Razaleigh by a mere 43 of 1,479 votes, with Abdul GHAFFAR bin Baba outpacing Musa by an even closer margin for the deputy presidency. The party thereupon divided into two factions, a "Team A" headed by the prime minister and a dissident "Team B."

In February 1988 Peninsular Malaysia's High Court ruled that UMNO was an illegal entity under the country's Societies Act because members of 30 unregistered branches had participated in the April 1987 balloting. Former prime ministers Abdul Rahman and Hussein bin Onn, on behalf of the Team B dissidents, thereupon filed for recognition of a new party (UMNO-Malaysia) but were rebuffed by the Registrar of Societies on the grounds that the High Court order had not yet become effective. Mahathir, applying on February 13 (the date of deregistration), was granted permission to begin the process of legalizing a government-supportive "new" UMNO (UMNO-*Baru*). Subsequently, the government secured legislation authorizing the transfer of UMNO assets to UMNO-*Baru* and also saw enacted a series of constitutional amendments rescinding the right of the High Court to interpret acts of parliament.

The prime minister subsequently invited Razaleigh and Musa to join UMNO-*Baru*. While both dissidents initially rejected the offer, their somewhat uneasy alliance collapsed in January 1989, when Musa accepted reentry into the government formation. Razaleigh subsequently announced that the successor to Team B, *Semangat '46* (Spirit of '46, after the year of UMNO's founding), had formed a coalition with the opposition *Parti Islam* (Pas) that, with the addition of two smaller formations, was registered in May as the Muslim Unity Movement (*Angkatan Perpaduan Ummah*—APU).

Although the National Front was for the first time faced with a seemingly viable opposition, the latter secured only 53 of 180 seats in the federal parliamentary balloting of October 1990. At the state level, however, the opposition won control in Kelantan and ousted UMNO's chief minister in Penang.

In November 1993 Finance Minister ANWAR Ibrahim emerged as Prime Minister Mahathir's most likely successor by replacing Ghaffar bin Baba as UMNO deputy president. In December Mahathir followed tradition by naming Anwar deputy prime minister.

In parliamentary elections in April 1995 the National Front scored a landslide victory, capturing 162 of 192 seats in an unprecedented vote share of 64 percent (compared with 53 percent in 1990). In addition, front parties won overwhelming majorities in 10 of the 11 contested state assemblies. A year later the governing alliance in Kelantan between Pas and *Semangat* '46 collapsed, Razaleigh Hamzah having announced in May his intention to return to UMNO. Shortly thereafter the fundamentalist Pas, which still held a legislative majority in Kelantan, was forced by the federal government to suspend a plan to introduce a harsh Islamic criminal code similar to the one imposed by the Taliban in Afghanistan.

In the second half of 1997, differences between Mahathir and his deputy began to surface in their approaches to the regional financial crisis that was drawing Malaysia into its grasp. Mahathir, an economic nationalist, attributed the crisis to foreign-currency traders and speculators, who were abetting international institutions and foreign powers that wanted to "recolonize" the country. In contrast, Anwar, a proponent of the global marketplace, responded to the crisis by introducing, beginning in December and continuing into 1998, a series of austerity and financial reform measures, including a relaxation of racial quota laws to allow the country's Chinese and Indian minorities greater participation in Malay-dominated companies.

In September 1998 Mahathir dismissed his former protégé from the cabinet, and later he removed him as deputy president of UMNO. Anwar quickly opened a campaign against Mahathir under the banner of *reformasi,* the call for political reform that had accompanied President Suharto's resignation in Indonesia earlier in the year. Mahathir then stated that he had removed Anwar because of "moral misconduct," alluding to widely circulated rumors that Anwar had engaged in both homosexual and heterosexual liaisons.

On September 20, 1998, addressing a crowd variously estimated at between 30,000 and 50,000—the country's largest opposition rally in three decades—Anwar called for Mahathir to resign. Later that day he was arrested under the Internal Security Act (ISA), which was also invoked in the following days to detain a number of Anwar supporters. On September 29 Anwar appeared in court with a black eye and other bruises, alleging that police had beaten him unconscious and inflicted serious injuries. On October 24 rock-throwing protesters and police engaged in the most violent street confrontation of the crisis.

By late October 1998 Anwar faced five counts of sodomy as well as five of corruption for using his office to interfere with official investigations into his activities. In April 1999 Anwar was convicted of corruption and sentenced to six years (later reduced to four years) in prison. The verdict sparked renewed rioting by Anwar's supporters.

Meanwhile, in January 1999 Mahathir had reshuffled his cabinet, naming former foreign minister ABDULLAH bin Ahmad Badawi to the post of deputy prime minister.

Anticipating that Mahathir might call a snap election before the expiration of the legislature's term in 2000, the principal opposition parties announced in June 1999 that they would join forces. The resultant Alternative Front (*Barisan Alternatif*—BA)—subsequently the **People's Alliance** (*Pakatan Rakyat*—PR)—included Pas, the Democratic Action Party (DAP), the small Malaysian People's Party (*Parti Rakyat Malaysia*—PRM), and the new National Justice Party (*Keadilan*), which had been formed in early April by Anwar's wife, Wan AZIZAH Wan Ismail, an eye surgeon and political novice.

In late November 1999 the opposition, led by Pas, registered significant gains at the polls, but the National Front nevertheless won more than enough seats to maintain its two-thirds majority in the House of Representatives. Accordingly, Mahathir took the oath of office for his fifth term in December, after which he named Deputy Prime Minister Abdullah as his preferred successor to head UMNO upon his eventual retirement.

In August 2000 the High Court in Kuala Lumpur convicted Anwar of sodomy and pronounced an additional nine-year prison sentence.

On October 31, 2003, Prime Minister Mahathir handed the prime ministership over to Abdullah Badawi, who took a cautious approach to ministerial changes until confirming his support at the polls in an early election held March 21, 2004. The National Front captured 198 of 219 seats in an expanded House of Representatives, while Pas saw its numbers diminish to 7. A new cabinet was sworn in on March 30.

In September 2004, with his sodomy conviction having been overturned on final appeal, Anwar Ibrahim was released from prison. Under the terms of his 1999 corruption sentence, he remained barred from holding public office until 2008. As an adviser to the People's Justice Party (*Parti Keadilan Rakyat*—PKR), of which his wife Wan Azizah was president, Anwar helped unify the opposition ahead of the 2008 general election. In voting on March 8, the opposition People's Front (later changed to People's Alliance (*Pakatan Rakyat*) won 82 seats in parliament, depriving the governing National Front of a two-thirds majority for the first time since 1969 and winning control of state governments in Perak and four other states.

Under increasing pressure by the governing party to leave office early, Abdullah resigned as prime minister on April 2, 2009. The BN's Mohamad NAJIB Abdul Razak. Najib was named prime minister on April 3, 2009, and named a reshuffled cabinet on April 9, including mostly UMNO members, but also representatives of six other parties.

Constitution and government. The constitution of Malaysia is based on that of the former Federation of Malaya, as amended to accommodate the special interests of Sarawak and Sabah, which joined in 1963. It established a federal system of government under an elective constitutional monarchy. The administration of the 13 states (11 in the west, 2 in the east) is carried out by rulers or governors acting on the advice of State Executive Councils. Each state has its own constitution and a unicameral State Assembly that shares legislative powers with the federal Parliament. The supreme head of the federation is the paramount ruler (*Yang di-Pertuan Agong*), who exercises the powers of a constitutional monarch in a parliamentary democracy. He and the deputy paramount ruler (*Timbalan Yang di-Pertuan Agong*) are chosen for five-year terms by and from among the nine hereditary rulers of the Malay states, who, along with the heads of state of Malacca, Penang, Sabah, and Sarawak, constitute the Conference of Rulers (*Majlis Raja Raja*). In 1993, with the reluctant agreement of the rulers, constitutional amendments were enacted that curbed royal legal immunities; a further restriction in 1994 ended the paramount ruler's authority to block legislation.

Executive power is vested in a prime minister and cabinet responsible to a bicameral legislature consisting of a partially appointed Senate with few real powers and an elected House of Representatives. Ultimate judicial authority is vested in a Federal Court (formerly called the Supreme Court); Peninsular and East Malaysia have separate high courts. An intermediary Court of Appeal was established by constitutional amendment in 1994. The pattern of local government varies to some extent from state to state.

The federal government has authority over such matters as external affairs, defense, internal security, justice (except Islamic and native law), federal citizenship, finance, commerce, industry, communications, and transportation. Sarawak and Sabah, however, enjoy guarantees of autonomy with regard to immigration, civil service, and customs matters.

State and Capital	*Area (Sq. Mi.)*	*Population (2007e)*
Johor (Johor Bahru)	7,330	3,299,000
Kedah (Alor Star)	3,639	1,907,000
Kelantan (Kota Bahru)	5,765	1,399,000
Melaka (Malacca)	637	732,000
Negeri Sembilan (Seremban)	2,565	987,000
Pahang (Kuantan)	13,886	1,475,000
Perak (Ipoh)	8,110	2,113,000
Perlis (Kangar)	307	221,000
Pulau Pinang (George Town)	399	1,490,000
Sabah (Kota Kinabalu)	28,460	2,689,000
Sarawak (Kuching)	48,050	1,957,000
Selangor (Shah Alam)	3,148	2,781,000
Terengganu (Kuala Terengganu)	5,002	1,060,000
Federal Territories		
Kuala Lumpur	94	1,429,000
Labuan (Victoria)	35	98,000
Putrajaya	18	7,250*

*Population as of February 2001

Foreign relations. From the early 1960s, Malaysia was a staunch advocate of regional cooperation among the non-Communist states of Southeast Asia, and it has been an active member of the Association of Southeast Asian Nations (ASEAN) since the organization's inception in 1967. Although threatened by leftist insurgency in the first two decades of independence, Malaysia committed itself to a nonaligned posture. At the same time, it maintained links with Western powers, Britain, Australia, and New Zealand all pledging to defend the nation's sovereignty and assisting Malaysia against Indonesia's armed "confrontation" policy of 1963–1966. Britain, Australia, New Zealand, Malaysia, and Singapore are further linked through the Five Power Defense Arrangement.

Tensions with Indonesia again arose in 1979 over Malaysia's decision to force Indochinese refugees back to sea, a development that Jakarta condemned as causing the inundation of its own shores by "boat people." A year later Malaysia proclaimed an exclusive economic zone extending up to 200 miles from its territorial sea boundaries as defined in newly drawn maps. Protests were immediately registered by China, Indonesia, the Philippines, Singapore, Thailand, and Vietnam, the last having recently dispatched troops to occupy jointly claimed Amboyna Island, northeast of Sabah.

In February 1982 Malaysia became the first neighboring state to recognize Indonesia's "archipelagic" method of defining territorial seas by means of lines drawn between the outermost extensions of outlying islands. In return, Indonesia agreed to respect Malaysian maritime rights between its peninsular and Borneo territories, and in 1984 the two countries concluded a joint security agreement that strengthened a 1972 accord. In January 1994 talks between Malaysia and Indonesia ended without resolution of conflicting claims to two islands, Sipadan and Ligitan, off the east coast of Borneo, although the two sides agreed to settle the dispute in accordance with principles of international law. In December 2002 the International Court of Justice (ICJ) awarded both islands to Malaysia, but since then access to surrounding waters in the Sulawesi Sea has become a persistent irritant.

Prime Minister Mahathir was a frequent critic of the United States and the only major head of government to decline U.S. president Bill Clinton's invitation to attend a summit of the Asia-Pacific Economic Cooperation (APEC) in Seattle in 1993 on the grounds that Washington sought to dominate the Asian countries. However, Mahathir held talks on "bilateral and regional issues" with President Clinton in 1994.

In January 1998 Jakarta received assurances that Indonesians holding valid temporary work permits in Malaysia would be exempt from a recently announced "Operation Go Away," the expulsion of tens of thousands of mainly illegal foreign workers who had been welcomed during Malaysia's economic boom. A large percentage of illegal workers were Indonesian, however, and the Mahathir government moved quickly to begin deporting them. The most violent incident occurred on March 26 at the Seminyeh repatriation camp, where rioting claimed nine lives. Subsequently, several dozen members of Indonesia's Acehnese minority, fearing reprisals related to a decades-old separatist conflict in Aceh district, sought asylum by breaking into a handful of foreign missions in Kuala Lumpur. Although Brunei, French, and Swiss officials quickly permitted Malaysian authorities to remove the Acehnese, in August some 20 who had sought refuge at the U.S. embassy and the offices of the UN High Commissioner for Refugees were granted asylum by Denmark and Norway.

In 2004–2005 Malaysia's threatened expulsion of up to 1.5 million illegal immigrant workers, most of them Indonesian, again drew protests from Jakarta. In late May 2005 Malaysia, faced with an unexpected labor shortage, reversed the policy.

Relations with Singapore, which were cool following Singapore's withdrawal from the Federation of Malaya in August 1965, improved in subsequent years. In 1995, for example, the two agreed on the joint manufacture and marketing of military equipment, in addition to the formation of a common force for UN peacekeeping purposes.

Recent relations have not been without controversy, however. In April 1998 the two states agreed to submit to the ICJ competing claims to the islet of Pulau Batu Putih (*Pedra Branca*) off the coast of Johor. On May 23, 2008, the ICJ found that sovereignty over the island had passed to Singapore.

Relations with the United States were strained somewhat in 2001, despite Prime Minister Mahathir's condemnation of the September 2001 al-Qaida attacks on New York and Washington, D.C.. In October the prime minister criticized the U.S. military campaign against al-Qaida in Afghanistan (and before leaving office in 2003 he was a vocal opponent of the U.S. invasion of Iraq.)

In September 2001 Malaysia and Singapore agreed to settle differences over such matters as water supplies to Singapore and the use of Malaysian airspace by Singapore's aircraft. Little additional progress was achieved through 2003, however, because Singapore sought to resolve open issues as a package. In December 2004 the two countries launched new talks, which also focused on releasing Malaysian workers' pension funds held by Singapore and on building a bridge to replace the outdated causeway that connects Singapore to the mainland. In April 2006, however, Malaysia scrapped plans for the bridge, construction of which Singapore continued to link to restoration of full airspace rights as well as to a 20-year commitment from Malaysia for 1 billion cubic meters of sand for reclamation.

Relations with China have been particularly strong in recent years, despite competing claims to the Spratly Islands. Both sides have endorsed a code of conduct for all claimants. In May 2004 Prime Minister Abdullah, fresh from his March election victory, traveled to China to promote closer business and trade ties.

Regionally, Malaysia has advanced the idea of a broad East Asian Economic Community (EAEC) and hosted the first East Asian summit in 2005.

Following Prime Minister Najib's appointment in 2009, relations with the United States warmed, and in May U.S. secretary of State Hillary Clinton declared that relations between the two countries were excellent, with cooperation in security matters as well as trade and investment.

Current issues. In 2006, former prime minister Mahathir continued to make headlines, attacking his chosen successor, Prime Minister Abdullah, for not securing the large infrastructure projects that Mahathir favored, notably, construction of a new bridge to Singapore. Mahathir was apparently preparing to challenge Abdullah at the next UMNO congress, but his effort failed in September 2008.

Malaysia's opposition parties made gains in the elections of March 8, 2008, stripping the ruling National Front of its two-thirds majority in parliament and winning control of five state governments. Slow economic growth, rising crime, and uneasiness over racial restrictions on minorities were said to be factors, along with allegations of government corruption and nepotism.

Meanwhile, Anwar Ibrahim, the former deputy prime minister and key opposition figure, returned to the political stage in 2008 for the first time since his arrest a decade earlier. Anwar and his People's Alliance (*Pakatan Rakyató—PR*), aimed to overturn Malaysia's long-standing system of ethnic-based privileges and end what Anwar termed the "dangerous politics of racism." The PR also sought to abolish the Internal Security Act, which permits indefinite detention without trial.

Anwar's decade-long ban from holding office expired on April 14, 2008. Shortly afterward, he announced his intention to forge a parliamentary majority by persuading enough legislators to cross over to the PR. Meanwhile, in July, Anwar was again charged with sodomy, although the public seemed to believe the charge was politically motivated. On August 28, Anwar, won a by-election for the parliamentary seat relinquished by his wife, Wan Azizah Wan Ismail, president of the People's Justice Party (*Parti Keadilan Rakyat*—PKR), a PR coalition member. In the days before September 16, his previously announced deadline for an opposition takeover of the government, Anwar announced that he had firm commitments from more members of parliament than necessary, but he refused to name them out of fear that they would face harassment. When the takeover failed to happen, Anwar lost credibility within his party, and the media claimed that the opposition was losing momentum.

Prime Minister Abdullah was also facing pressure within his party. After he announced his plan to hand over his office to Deputy Prime Minister Najib Abdul Razak in 2010, UMNO leaders complained that the party could lose its stronghold unless the transition occurred sooner.

In February 2009, Najib, for his part, was behind a takeover by the ruling National Front (BN) of the Perak state legislature, the fourth largest in the country, with three PR lawmakers backing the BN. A constitutional crisis unfolded as both the BN and PR coalitions claimed a majority. First Minister Mohammad NIZAR Jamaluddin of the Pan-Malaysian Islamic Party (PAS, a member of the PR coalition) called for the assembly to be dissolved, and later demanded a no-confidence vote be held in order to force the BN to prove its majority. Neither request was granted, and the Sultan of Perak called for Nizar's resignation. When Nizar refused, the Sultan swore in a new First Minister from UMNO. Subsequently, the assembly was effectively sidelined for months as lawsuits proceeded.

Following Najib's appointment as prime minister on April 3, he held little influence over the opposition, as the PR won two of three by-elections on April 7. Najib's new cabinet, named on April 9, included six parties, but none from the opposition.

In his first month in office, Najib took steps to modify Malaysia's racially based New Economic Policy by eliminating the requirement for some foreign investors to form partnerships with ethnic Malays. The policy shift reflected the need to attract greater investment at a time of financial crisis, but also highlighted the governing party's hopes to shore up the support of ethnic minorities, especially the Chinese and Indian communities, which had begun to favor the PR and which viewed the original requirement for investors as economic discrimination.

The electoral crisis in Perak culminated on May 7, when men widely assumed to be plainclothes police physically removed the State Assembly Speaker V. SIVAKUMAR of DAP and arrested several other opposition legislators. Photos and video clips of the incident circulated on the Internet, compounding the government's embarrassment. On May 11, the high court sided with the PR, ruling as unconstitutional the opposition's having been denied the chance to call a no-confidence vote, but the court of appeal overturned this ruling on May 22. The PR appealed this ruling to the nation's highest court, while the BN refused to dissolve the assembly and call new elections. The issue dominated the Najib administration's first months, raising what some observers said were questions about the government's commitment to democratic reforms. Meanwhile, Anwar Ibrahim was scheduled to go on trial for sodomy for the second time beginning in July.

POLITICAL PARTIES

Malaysia's political system has long been dominated by the National Front coalition. Numerous opposition coalitions have formed, but until 2008, none had ever posed a meaningful threat to the UMNO-led alliance.

A right-of-center Muslim Unity Movement (*Angkatan Perpaduan Ummah*—APU), centered on a loose alliance of the Pan-Malaysian Islamic Party (Pas) with Razaleigh Hamzah's *Semangat '46,* was formed in May 1989 but made few inroads against the National Front in the October 1990 election. Another alliance, the People's Might (*Gagasan Rakyat*), which included the Democratic Action Party (DAP), the Malaysian People's Party (PRM), the Indian Progressive Front (IPF), and the Sabah United Party (PBS), was officially registered in 1992, by which time two additional parties had joined. The departure of several parties before the 1995 general election weakened the *Gagasan Rakyat*, and Razaleigh's return to UMNO in May 1996 led to the demise of *Semangat '46* and, ultimately, of the APU.

In September 1998, following the ouster and arrest of Anwar Ibrahim, two loose opposition coalitions emerged: the Coalition for a People's Democracy (*Gagasan Demokrasi Rakyat*), chaired by Tian Chua, and the People's Justice Movement (*Gerakan Keadilan Rakyat—Gerak*), chaired by Fadzil Nor of Pas. The two shared overlapping memberships that encompassed various social and reform organizations as well as several political parties. Out of this organizing came the Alternative Front (*Barisan Alternatif*—BA), an ideologically incongruous grouping that won 42 seats in the November 1999 election. With the DAP having withdrawn from the BA in 2001, the coalition won only 7 seats in the March 2004 general election.

The opposition began to gain momentum in the March 2008 election, stripping the National Front of its two-thirds parliamentary majority and taking 5 out of 13 state governments. Energized by the return of Anwar Ibrahim to political life, the successor coalition to the BA, now called the **People's Alliance** (*Pakatan Rakyat*—PR), seemed to have reached the brink of power in Malaysia (see Current issues, above).

Government Coalition:

National Front (*Barisan Nasional*—BN). Malaysia's leading formation since its launching in 1973, the BN is a coalition of parties representing the country's leading ethnic groups. The nucleus of an earlier coalition, organized in 1952 as the Alliance Party, was Tunku Abdul Rahman's United Malays National Organization (UMNO). With the establishment of Malaysia, the alliance was augmented by similar coalitions in Sarawak and Sabah, the number of participating organizations totaling 11 in 1990, prior to the withdrawal of the Sabah United Party (PBS). By mid-1994, with the addition of 3 PBS splinters—the PDS (renamed the UPKO in 1999), the PBRS, and the SAPP (see discussions of all three, below)—the BN encompassed 14 parties. In 2001 the People's Justice Movement (Akar) voted to merge with UMNO, and in 2002 the PBS rejoined the BN.

In April 1995, in addition to the National Front's overwhelming victory at the federal level, member parties captured 10 of the 11 state legislatures up for election. By September 1996, *Barisan Nasional* controlled 12 of the country's 13 state assemblies, the sole exception being Kelantan's.

The BN retained its two-thirds legislative majority in the 1999 and 2004 elections. However, in the March 2008 vote, a strong showing by the People's Front (*Pakatan Rakyat*) brought the opposition to within 30 seats of controlling the House of Representatives, and the BN lost control of four state assemblies.

Leaders: Mohamad NAJIB Abdul Razak (Prime Minister), TENGKU Adnan Mansor (Secretary General).

United Malays National Organization—UMNO (*Pertubuhan Kebangsaan Melayu Bersatu*). The leading component of the ruling National Front, UMNO has long supported the interests of the numerically predominant Malays while acknowledging the right of all Malaysians, irrespective of racial origins, to participate in the political, social, and economic life of the nation. Party officials are selected by indirect election every three years.

In April 1987 Prime Minister Mahathir bin Mohamad retained the presidency by a paper-thin margin after an unprecedented internal contest. The intraparty struggle culminated in deregistration of the original party in February 1988, in the wake of which the pro-Mahathir faction organized the "new" UMNO (UMNO-*Baru*). The dissidents, led by Razaleigh Hamzah, were denied an opportunity to regroup as UMNO-Malaysia. In 1989 Mahathir launched a partially successful campaign to woo back the dissidents. The party dropped "*Baru*" and restored its original name in 1997.

In the November 1999 federal election UMNO won 71 seats, 17 fewer than in 1995, which analysts attributed to a loss of support among Malay backers of Anwar Ibrahim, who had been ousted as deputy president in September 1998. In December, having already announced that he was serving his final term as prime minister, Mahathir named Deputy Prime Minister Abdullah Badawi as his preferred successor.

In May 2001 the People's Justice Movement (*Angkatan Keadilan Rakyat*—Akar) overwhelmingly voted to disband and join UMNO. Akar, formed in 1989 by former members of the Sabah United Party (PBS), had participated in the National Front since July 1991.

With Mahathir having stepped down from party and government posts in October 2003, Abdullah Badawi led UMNO to victory at the polls in March 2004, when the party won 110 lower house seats. Mahathir subsequently denounced the policies of his successor and briefly quit the party in the wake of the BN's setbacks in the 2008 balloting, hoping to create pressure on Abdullah to step down. Abdullah responded in July by announcing that Deputy Prime Minister Najib Razak would succeed him in June 2010. However, following increasing pressure from party members for Abdullah to step down, he resigned in 2009. At the party's congress in March 2009, Najib was unanimously elected party president, and a week later, he was sworn in as Malaysia's sixth prime minister. Najib pledged to reform the party, which was widely acknowledged to be in danger of losing its dominance.

Leaders: Mohamad NAJIB Abdul Razak (Prime Minister and President of the Party); MUHYIDDIN Mohamed Yasin (Deputy Prime Minister and Deputy President of the Party); Ahmad Zahid Hamidi, Hishammuddin Hussein, Shafie Apdal (Vice Presidents).

Malaysian Chinese Association—MCA (*Persatuan China Malaysia*). The MCA supports the interests of the Chinese community but is committed to "moderation" and the maintenance of interracial goodwill and harmony. More conservative than the Chinese opposition DAP, it has participated in the governing alliance continuously since 1982.

For 13 years, the MCA's representation in parliament has been stable at around 30 seats. However, that number dropped to 15 after the March 2008 election. Taking responsibility for the poor showing, party president ONG Ka Ting declined to seek reelection. At the party congress in October, transport minister Ong Tee Keat (no relation) won the party presidency, and Ng Yen Yen, the minister of tourism, became the first female vice president of a major National Front party.

Ong announced a plan to revive grassroots participation in the party and assess the performance of party leaders. Meanwhile, Ong came under criticism as transport minister in connection with the ministry's handling of the Port Klang Free Zone development, an industrial park that has faced major cost overruns.

Leaders: ONG Tee Keat (President), NG Yen Yen (Vice President), NG CHUA Soi Lek (Deputy President).

United Traditional Bumiputra Party (*Parti Pesaka Bumiputra Bersatu*—PBB). Founded in 1983, the PBB traces its origins to the Sarawak Alliance of *Bumiputra*, a mixed ethnic party; *Pesaka*, a Dayak and Malay party; and the Sarawak Chinese Association. The PBB won a plurality of 19 seats in the 1983 Sarawak state assembly election and subsequently formed a coalition government with the Sarawak Native People's Party (PBDS; see the PRS, below) and the SUPP (below). This coalition, dominated by the PBB, has controlled Sarawak's government ever since, with PBB president Abdul Taib Mahmud serving as the state's chief minister for 27 years.

In 2004 the party won 11 seats in the House of Representatives, and in 2008 it added 3 more. In May 2006 the party won all 35 seats it contested in the state assembly elections.

Leaders: Abdul TAIB Mahmud (Chief Minister of Sarawak and President of the Party); ABANG Johari Tun Abang Openg and Alfred JABU Anak Numpang (Deputy Presidents), AWANG Tengah Ali Hassan and Douglas UGGAH Embas (Senior Vice Presidents).

Malaysian People's Movement Party (*Parti Gerakan Rakyat Malaysia*). Based in Pulau Pinang (Penang), *Gerakan* is a social democratic party that has attracted many intellectual supporters, especially in the Chinese community. It was organized in 1968 by TAN Chee Khoon, who left the party after the 1969 election to form the now-defunct Social Justice Party (*Parti Keadilan Masyaraka*—Pekemas). The party was weakened by a leadership dispute in 1988 that saw numerous members defect to the MCA and two of its vice presidents resign. It retained five seats in the House of Representatives in 1990, increased its membership to ten in March 2004, but dropped to two in 2008. That year, the party also lost control of the state government in Penang, which it had led for many decades.

In April 2007, Lim Keng Yaik retired after 26 years of party leadership. Former Penang Chief Minister Koh Tsu Koon was named acting president and officially elected at the party's 2008 congress. Koh called for the party to reinvent itself after its poor showing in the 2008 election. With the party's power diminishing, several prominent members quit, and some members advocated pulling out of the BN coalition.

Leaders: KOH Tsu Koon (President), LIM Keng Yaik (Adviser), CHANG Ko Youn (Deputy President).

Malaysian Indian Congress—MIC (*Kongresi India Malaysia*). The leading representative of the Indian community in Malaysia, the MIC was founded in 1946 and joined the alliance in 1955. S. Samy Vellu first won the party presidency in 1979. In March 2009, he was reelected to an 11th term, but later declared he would step down early after naming a successor late in the year.

The MIC won seven House seats in the 1995, 1999, and March 2004 elections, but its parliamentary representation dropped to three in the 2008 vote. The Hindu Rights Action Force (HINDRAF, see below), a non-government group banned by the home ministry in 2008, has posed a challenge to the MIC's leadership among Malaysia's Indian population.

Leaders: S. Samy VELLU (President); G. PALANIVEL (Deputy President); S. SUBRAMANIAM (Secretary-General).

Sarawak People's Party (*Party Rakyat Sarawak*—PRS). Registered in October 2005, the PRS traces its origin to a leadership dispute that split the now-defunct Sarawak Native People's Party (*Parti Bansa Dayak Sarawak*—PBDS).

The PBDS had been organized in 1983 by a number of legislators from the Sarawak National Party (SNAP, below) who wished to affiliate with a purely ethnic Dayak party. The new formation was accepted as a National Front partner in January 1984 and formed a coalition state government with the PBB, SNAP, and the SUPP (below) the following March. In the 1999 and 2004 national elections it won 6 seats.

The 2003 decision of longtime party leader and cabinet member Leo MOGGIE anak Irok to retire led to a protracted leadership dispute ultimately won by James Masing. As a consequence, the PBDS was deregistered on October 22, 2004, by which time the new PRS was already being organized under SIDI Munan. As expected, Masing's PBDS faction joined the new party, with Masing being named president shortly thereafter. In June 2005 the PRS was accepted into the federal National Front.

In January 2006 the PRS and another National Front party, the SPDP (below), announced their intention to merge, but discussions were ultimately postponed, first because of the May 2006 state election, in which the PRS won eight of the nine seats it contested, and then because of a leadership dispute within the PRS. Masing was reelected president at a conference in December 2006, while Larry SNG Wei Shien claimed leadership of a faction loyal to former deputy president SNG Chee Hua, his father. Masing expelled Sng from the party in April 2008. The split appeared to have driven many former PRS members into the ranks of the opposition PKR.

Leader: James Jemut MASING (President).

Sarawak United People's Party—SUPP (*Parti Bersatu Rakyat Sarawak*). The SUPP was organized in 1959 as a left-wing Sarawak party. Although the SUPP began as a Chinese ethnic party, it recently opened its membership and has become one of Malaysia's most diverse parties. It won 16 seats in the Sarawak assembly election of 1991 and in 1996, as part of a coalition with the other Sarawak-based National Front parties, won 57. In November 1999 it won eight seats in the House of Representatives. That number dropped to six in the 2004 and 2008 national elections. In May 2006 it won 11 state legislative seats, unexpectedly losing 8 of those it contested as part of the National Front. The party, beset by infighting, was expected to make major changes in its leadership team before the next state election.

Leaders: George CHAN Hong Nam (President of the Party and Deputy Chief Minister of Sarawak), LAW Hieng Ding (Deputy President), SIM Kheng Hui (Secretary General).

Sarawak Progressive Democratic Party—SPDP (*Parti Demokratik Maju Sarawak*). The SPDP was established in November 2002 following a leadership crisis in the Sarawak

National Party (SNAP, below) that led to SNAP's deregistration. Several months before, William Mawan had been elected president of SNAP, but a competing SNAP faction had refused to accept the decision. Within days of SNAP's deregistration, Mawan announced formation of the multiracial SPDP, which was soon accepted into the National Front as SNAP's replacement. In the 2004 and 2008 general elections the SPDP won four seats, and in May 2006 it won eight at the state level. In 2009 the party was trying to form new branches outside Sarawak. In June 2008, the SPDP and PRS agreed to merge. However, grassroots opposition to the plan, and Anwar Ibrahim's challenge to the sitting government, slowed the process.

Leader: William MAWAN Ikom (President).

Sabah United Party (*Parti Bersatu Sabah*—PBS). A predominantly Kadazan party with a Roman Catholic leader, the PBS was founded by defectors from the now-moribund Sabah People's Union (*Bersatu Rakyat Jelata Sabah*—Berjaya) in 1985. Appealing to urban, middle-class voters disaffected with the Berjaya-led government, it won a majority of state assembly seats in April. Having been admitted to the National Front in 1986, in 1988 the PBS announced a "loose alliance" with fellow National Front member *Gerakan.*

The PBS retained control of the Sabah assembly in a state general election in July 1990, but less than a week before the federal legislative poll of October 1990 it withdrew from the National Front and went into opposition. In what some viewed as an act of political retaliation, the party president, Joseph Pairin Kitingan, was arrested by federal authorities in early 1991. His conviction on corruption charges led to a fine of approximately $4,600.

In 1993 the PBS attracted almost half of the state assembly contingent of the United Sabah National Organization (USNO), immediately prior to that party's long-envisaged merger with UMNO. In an early state election in 1994 the PBS obtained a plurality of seats but because of subsequent defections was obliged to yield to a National Front administration. It won only 17 of 48 seats in the 1999 state election and then lost 2 to defections.

The PBS was readmitted to the National Front in January 2002, and in the March 2004 election won 4 seats in the federal House of Representatives and 13 in the Sabah legislature. It currently has 3 federal MPs.

Leaders: Joseph PAIRIN Kitingan (Former Chief Minister of Sabah and President of the Party); Maximus ONGKILI, YEE Moh Chai, and ALIUDDIN Mohamad Tahir (Deputy Presidents); Radin MALLEH (Secretary General).

United Pasok Momogun Kadazandusun Murut Organisation (UPKO). Reviving the name of a Sabah party from the 1960s, a congress of the Sabah Democratic Party (*Parti Demokratik Sabah*—PDS) voted in 1999 to adopt the UPKO designation. The PDS had been organized in 1994 by withdrawal from the PBS of a group of dissidents led by Deputy President Bernard Dompok. The original UPKO had been established by the 1964 merger of the *Pasok Momogun* party and the United National Kadazan Organization (UNKO), but the party dissolved in 1967.

Intended to unite the majority Kadazandusun community and the Murut population of Sabah, the current UPKO subsequently indicated its willingness to discuss mergers not only with other Sabah-based National Front parties but also with the PBS. UPKO won four lower house seats at the 2004 and 2008 general elections. The party has been active on issues of immigration and citizenship; in April 2009 it set up an office to help local Sabahans obtain the national identity card.

Leaders: Bernard DOMPOK (President), Wilfred BUMBURING (Deputy President).

United Sabah People's Party (*Parti Bersatu Rakyat Sabah*—PBRS). The PBRS was launched in 1994 by Joseph Kurup, theretofore secretary general of the PBS. In the 1999 national election Kurup came within a few hundred votes of unseating PBS President Joseph Pairin Kitingan. In 2002 a leadership dispute ended with a decision by the Registrar of Societies that Kurup was the legitimate president. His challenger, Jeffrey Kitingan, was then expelled by the party. (He joined the PKR in October 2006.)

In the 2008 election, Kurup won the party's only seat in parliament, running unopposed after an officer rejected the nomination papers of PKR candidate Danny Anthony ANDIPAI. Subsequently, Malaysia's Election Court declared the vote null and void, but a federal court upheld his election on March 13, 2009.

Leaders: Joseph KURUP (President), ELLRON Angin (Deputy President).

People's Progressive Party of Malaysia—PPP (*Parti Kemajuan Rakyat Malaysia*). Centered in Ipoh, where there is a heavy concentration of Chinese, the multiracial, left-wing PPP was organized in 1955. In 1996 the Registrar of Societies approved a new constitution for the party, which thereupon adopted the name *Parti Progressif Penduduk Malaysia (Baru),* or PPP (New). However, a four-year-old dispute over the party leadership continued. In September 1999 the High Court annulled the presidency of M. Kayveas, who had been elected in 1993, and threw out the 1996 constitutional changes, at which time the party reverted to its original name. Kayveas quickly obtained a stay from the Court of Appeal, which confirmed him as president in November. Kayveas was reelected president in September 2005. The PPP won one seat in parliament in the 2004 general election, but none in 2008. In May 2009 the party expelled a member of its supreme council, alleging that he used bribes to gain political support from party division leaders.

Leaders: M. KAYVEAS (President), PADUKA Anaitullah (Deputy President).

Liberal Democratic Party—LDP (*Parti Liberal Demokratik*). A Chinese-dominated party based in Sabah, the LDP formed in 1989 and joined the National Front in 1991. In 1999 it captured one seat in the House of Representatives; it lost the seat in 2004, but V. K.Liew won it back in 2008. Liew was appointed deputy minister in the prime minister's department in April 2009.

Leaders: V.K. LIEW (President), CHIN Su Phin (Deputy President).

Parliamentary Opposition:

People's Alliance (*Pakatan Rakyat*—PR). The Democratic Action Party (DAP), Pan-Malaysian Islamic Party (Pas), and People's Justice Party (PKR), along with the Malaysian People's Party (PRM; see below under PKR), organized the Alternative Front (*Barisan Alternatif*—BA) in 1999. The BA put forth Anwar Ibrahim as a candidate for prime minister in that year's election, although the former Mahathir deputy was incarcerated after his corruption conviction. The DAP withdrew from the BA in September 2001 because of opposition to Pas's Islamic agenda, and in the 2004 national election the BA won only 7 seats.

The three parties adopted the People's Alliance designation following their successful cooperation in the March 8, 2008, general elections. By agreeing not to compete with each other, the PR won control of 5 out of Malaysia's 13 state assemblies and overturned the BN's two-thirds majority in the House of Representatives. On April 1, the party leaders announced that they would solidify their relationship under the PR banner. Despite vast differences in their ideologies, the three parties agree on the nation's need for transparent and egalitarian governance.

Anwar Ibrahim reentered parliament on August 28, 2008, and took over leadership of the PR and the PKR (below) from his wife, Dr. Wan Azizah Wan Ismail. At first, Anwar set out to engineer enough defections from BN MPs to allow the PR to capture the government. That plan failed, but the opposition coalition demonstrated increasing strength in 2009. The PR won two of three by-elections on April 7. Moreover, the electoral crisis in Perak proved a major embarrassment for Najib and the BN, increasing the opposition's hope that it could consolidate a majority of popular support before the next general election (see Current Issues, above).

Leader: ANWAR Ibrahim.

Democratic Action Party—DAP (Parti Tindakan Demokratik). A predominantly Chinese, democratic socialist party, the DAP is a 1965 offshoot of the ruling People's Action Party (PAP) of Singapore.

In 1987 a number of DAP politicians, including parliamentary opposition leader Lim Kit Siang, were arrested and held without trial for "provoking racial tensions." In 1989 Lim was released from jail and the party agreed to cooperate with the APU in upcoming elections, although refusing to join the coalition because of its

Muslim orientation. The DAP went on to win 20 seats in the House of Representatives in 1990 but saw its representation plummet to 9 in 1995.

In August 1998 Lim Guan Eng, deputy secretary general of the party and son of Lim Kit Siang, was sentenced to prison on charges of sedition relating to a political pamphlet he had written. An effort by the elder Kim to mount support for his son led critics to charge the secretary general with nepotism and dictatorial actions. Kim responded by suspending the party's vice chair, treasurer, and publicity secretary, all of whom subsequently helped found the MDP (below).

Lim Guan Eng was released from prison in August 1999. Three months later, as part of the Alternative Front, the DAP won only 10 seats in the national election, although it remained the leading legislative opponent of various National Front parties in a majority of states. Taking responsibility for the poor national showing, the elder Lim resigned as party secretary general—a post he had held for three decades—but he was immediately named party chair.

In September 2001, objecting to Pas's call for establishing an Islamic state, the DAP withdrew from the BA. In the March 2004 election, the DAP kept its distance from Pas and went on to win 12 seats, thereby becoming the leading opposition party once again. At a party congress in September Lim Kit Siang stepped down as chair. His son Lim Guan Eng was elected secretary general.

The DAP returned to cooperating with Pas and the PKR in the 2008 voting, winning 28 lower house seats, and subsequently in the People's Alliance (PR). In September, Lim Kit Siang called on Prime Minister Abdullah to call a special session of parliament to vote on a no-confidence measure. A DAP parliamentarian, Teresa KOK, along with a journalist and a popular blogger, were arrested on September 12 under the Internal Security Act (ISA). The party called the arrests politically motivated and demanded the abolition of the ISA. In March 2009 DAP national chair Karpal Singh was charged with sedition; he in turn accused the government of using the sedition laws selectively against political opponents.

The political conflict in Perak came to a head on May 7, 2009, when the state assembly speaker, V. SIVAKUMAR of DAP, was abducted from the podium. Lim Kit Siang compared the dramatic scene to the race riots of May 1969 and called on Malaysians to "remember May 7 until we have removed the hegemony" of BN.

Leaders: LIM Kit Siang (former chair), KARPAL Singh (Chair), LIM Guan Eng (Secretary General).

Pan-Malaysian Islamic Party (*Parti Islam SeMalaysia*—Pas). An Islamic party with a strong rural base, Pas participated in the governing coalition in 1973–1977 but since then has been in opposition. Pas has governed Kelantan State continuously since 1990. It increased its federal legislative representation from 7 to 27 seats in 1999, rising to lead the opposition and also capturing Terengganu State.

Pas membership is open only to Muslims, and the party prohibits women candidates at the state and federal levels. Officially, the party seeks the establishment of an Islamic state, but its leaders have stated that should it win control of the federal government and introduce Islamic law, non-Muslims could be tried in accordance with the country's current secular legal system. In Kelantan, non-Muslims are exempt from some of the strictest aspects of sharia (Islamic) law.

In June 2002 the party's president, the moderate Fadzil Mohamad NOR, died. His immediate successor as party leader, Abdul Hadi Awang, a more radical Islamist and longtime supporter of Afghanistan's ousted Taliban regime, announced in July that Islamic law would be strictly enforced in Terengganu State, where he served as chief minister until Pas was ousted in the March 2004 state election. Nationally, it saw its lower house representation plummet to 6 seats. A loss in a state by-election in December 2005 reduced the party's majority in the Kelantan assembly to a single seat.

Party elections held in June 2005 were notable for the success of more moderate politicians. Although Abdul Hadi Awang had no challengers, the new deputy president and all three vice presidents were regarded as reformers. The party election of June 2007 reconfirmed the ascendancy of the "young Turks," led by Deputy President Nasaruddin Mat Isa, although the presidency was again uncontested.

In 2008, Pas won control of the state of Kedah, expanded its majority in Kelantan, and joined coalition governments in two other states with its People's Alliance partners. In an effort to broaden the party's base, Pas toned down its rhetoric about imposing Islamic law and pledged to uphold social equality and freedom of religion. Its relative success at attracting Chinese and Indian support with a more moderate image reflected the shifts in the country's racial and political dynamics.

Abdul Hadi was reelected to his post, again uncontested, in May 2009. Internal debates reflected a division between party moderates committed to the People's Alliance and conservatives open to cooperation with UMNO.

Leaders: ABDUL HADI Awang (President of the Party and Former Chief Minister of Terengganu), NIK ABDUL AZIZ Nik Mat (Spiritual Leader of Pas and Chief Minister of Kelantan), NASARUDDIN Mat Isa (Deputy President), KAMARUDDIN Jaafar (Secretary General).

People's Justice Party (*Parti Keadilan Rakyat*—PKR). The PKR resulted from the August 2003 merger of the National Justice Party (*Parti Keadilan Nasional*—PKN) and the Malaysian People's Party (*Parti Rakyat Malaysia*—PRM).

Announced in April 1999 by Wan Azizah Wan Ismail as a centrist, multiracial formation, the PKN was organized by supporters of Anwar Ibrahim in an effort to unite anti-Mahathir forces. The party was largely an outgrowth of the nonparty Movement for Social Justice (*Pergerakan Keadilan Sosial*—Adil), which had been announced by Wan Azizah the previous December as a vehicle for reform. Anwar indicated from prison that he would not officially join the party. As part of the BA, *Keadilan* won five lower house seats in November 1999. It unexpectedly picked up a sixth, at the National Front's expense, in a November 2000 by-election.

Formerly the Malaysian People's Socialist Party (*Parti Socialis Rakyat Malaysia*—PSRM), the PRM was a left-leaning party that never held legislative seats. Its former leader, KASSIM Ahmad, was arrested in 1976 on suspicion of having engaged in communist activities and was not released until 1981. Another leader, Syed Husin Ali, was similarly detained without trial under the country's Internal Security Act from 1974 until 1980. In 1989 the party changed its name back to its pre-1970 title as part of an effort to assume a more moderate position.

In July 2002 the PRM and *Keadilan* signed a memorandum of understanding on their eventual merger as the PKR, which was accomplished in August 2003. However, the Registrar of Societies did not formally approve the move until after the March 2004 election, at which the PKN retained only 1 seat. Its representation ballooned to 31 in 2008, making it the second strongest party in the parliament.

At the party's fourth congress, held in May 2007, Wan Azizah was reelected president. Anwar, concerned that his election might result in the party's deregistration, decided not to run, although all understood that he would step into a leadership role when the ban on his holding office expired in April 2008. Wan Azizah resigned her parliament seat on July 31 to allow her husband to run in a by-election, which he won handily. Anwar rejoined parliament on August 28 and assumed leadership of the People's Alliance (*Pakatan Rakyat*).

In May 2009, in what the party termed "an unprecedented move for a political party in Malaysia," the PKR announced the adoption of direct "one-member one-vote" election of all party officials. Party president Wan Azizah returned to a prominent role as party spokesperson in 2009. With her husband scheduled to go on trial on a sodomy charge in July, Azizah was prepared to assume surrogate leadership once more.

Leaders: Wan AZIZAH Wan Ismail (President), ANWAR Ibrahim, SYED HUSIN Ali (Deputy President), TIAN Chua.

Other Parties:

Sabah Progressive Party—SAPP (*Parti Maju Sabah*). Formally registered in 1994, the SAPP is a Chinese formation that was admitted to the National Front after splitting from the PBS. It won two seats in the 1999 balloting. In September 2002 one of the seats was vacated when the Election Commission found the party's president guilty of corrupt electoral practices. In March 2008 the SAPP won two seats in the House of Representatives.

Party president Yong Teck Lee threatened in June 2008 to file a no-confidence motion against Prime Minister Abdullah Ahmad Badawi. The motion did not go forward, but on September 17, SAPP withdrew from the BN to become an independent party. Deputy president Raymond TAN, who was also deputy chief minister of Sabah, subsequently quit the party and, later joined *Gerakan*.

Leaders: YONG Teck Lee (President), LIEW Teck Chan, Eric Enchin MAJIMBUN (Deputy Presidents), Richard YONG We Kong (Secretary General).

Indian Progressive Front—IPF (*Barisan Kemajuan India SeMalaysia*). The IPF was launched in 1990 by M.G. PANDITHAN, who had been an MIC vice president until ousted by Samy Vellu. The IPF supported the National Front for the 1999 and 2004 elections. Although the MIC opposed the party's inclusion in the front, Vellu and Pandithan reconciled in April 2007. Pandithan died on May 29, 2008, and his wife, Jayashree Pandithan, took over his position as party leader. However, after the Registrar of Societies nullified her election in February 2009, the group devolved into factions. Prime Minister Abdullah Badawi attempted to heal the divide, dangling a potential offer to join the National Front if the party reconciled.

Leader: Jayashree PANDITHAN.

Malaysian Dayak Congress—MDC (*Kongres Dayak Malaysia*). Established in May 2005, primarily by former members of the deregistered PBDS, the MDC was formed to advance the Dayak community. It sought to contest the May 2006 Sarawak state elections but had not yet been officially registered. Its candidates therefore ran under the SNAP banner. In April 2008 the Home Ministry refused to register the party.

Leaders: Nicholas BAWIN (President Pro Tempore), Johnical RAYONG NGIPA (Deputy President Pro Tempore), Louis JARAU PATRICK (Secretary General Pro Tempore).

Malaysian Democratic Party—MDP (*Parti Demokratik Malaysia*). The MDP was formed in 1999 by a number of DAP members who objected to what they considered Lim Kit Siang's autocratic policies. Officially registered in October, it contested, without success, 11 lower house seats in the November election on a multiracial, multicultural, and prodemocracy platform. In 2004 it ran in only one constituency. Party leader Wee Choo Keong was elected a member of Parliament for the Wangsa Maju township in Kuala Lumpur, running under the PKR banner, in the 2008 election.

Leader: WEE Choo Keong (Secretary General).

Malaysian Indian Muslim Congress (*Parti Kongres Indian Muslim Malaysia*—Kimma). Kimma was founded in 1977 as a means of uniting Malaysia's Indian Muslims. Kimma has long sought the equivalent of *bumiputra* status for Indian Muslims.

In the 2004 election the party supported the National Front candidates, but it has been rejected for front membership half a dozen times. In August 2008, after then-party president MUHAMMED ALI Naina Mohd, suggested that the party should switch its allegiance to the *Pakatan Rakyat,* Kimma's youth chief and 850 young members reportedly quit the party.

Leader: SYED IBRAHIM Kader (President).

Malaysia Makkal Sakthi Party (MMSP). Established in 2009 under the leadership of R.S. Thanenthiran, formerly the national coordinator of the Hindu Rights Action Force (HINDRAF, see below), the MMSP represents a division within the HINDRAF movement, although another HINDRAF leader, P. Waythamoorthy, agreed to be listed as deputy president. The Registrar of Societies approved the new party on May 11, less than two months after it had applied. Thanenthiran said the new party would remain independent of the National Front and Pakatan Rakyat for the time being, but would be willing to join whichever coalition could satisfy the aspirations of Malaysia's Indian community.

Leaders: R.S. THANENTHIRAN (President), P. WAYTHAMOORTHY (Deputy President), Kannan RAMASAMY (Secretary General).

Sarawak National Party—SNAP (*Parti Kebangsaan Sarawak*). Long a leading Sarawak party, SNAP ran in the 1974 federal election as an opposition party, capturing nine seats in the lower house. Supported largely by the Iban population of Sarawak, it joined the National Front at both the state and federal levels in 1976. In 1996 and 2001 it joined the PBB, SUPP, and PBDS in dominating the Sarawak state balloting. In November 1999 it won four seats in the national election.

On November 5, 2002, SNAP was formally deregistered as a consequence of a leadership dispute, dating from the preceding April, in which the party's deputy president, Peter TINGGOM Karmarau, had challenged its longtime president, James WONG Kim Ming. In August an extraordinary party meeting had elected William Mawan Ikom as successor to Wong, who refused to accept what he termed a "coup d'état." Within days of the deregistration, which Wong planned to challenge, Mawan announced formation of the Sarawak Progressive Democratic Party (SPDP).

The deregistration was suspended by the Court of Appeal in April 2003, permitting SNAP to compete in the March 2004 national election, in which it failed to win any of the seven seats it contested. With the deregistration appeal not yet resolved, SNAP won one state seat in May 2006. It contested six lower house seats in 2008.

Leaders: Edwin DUNDANG Bugak (President), TING Ling Kiew (Deputy President).

State Reform Party—Star (*Parti Reformasi Negeri*). Led by a former Sarawak state cabinet member and senior vice president of SNAP, Star was registered as a party in 1996. It ran a small number of unsuccessful candidates in the lower house balloting of 1999 and 2004. Star chose not to contest the May 2006 state election after failing to arrange an acceptable seat allocation with other opposition parties. Its leader, Patau Rubis, was formerly a vice president of SNAP.

Leader: PATAU Rubis (President).

There are numerous other small parties. The **Malaysian Islamic Council Front** (*Barisan Jemaah Islamiah SeMalaysia*—Berjasa) is a Kelantan-based party organized in opposition to Pas following the latter's withdrawal from the government in 1977. The **Malaysian Justice Movement** (*Parti Angkatan Keadilan Insan Malaysia*—AKIM) was launched in 1995 by a number of *Semangat '46* and Pas dissidents. Sabah opposition parties include the **Sabah People's Unity Front** (*Parti Barisan Rakyat Sabah Bersekutu*), the **Sabah People's United Democratic Party** (*Parti Demokratik Setiasehati Kuasa Rakyat Bersatu Sabah*—Setia), and the **United Pasok Nunkragang National Organization** (*Pertubuhan Kebangsaan Pasok Nunkragang Bersatu*—Pasok).

Other small parties registered for the March 2004 election were the **Community Coalition Congress Party** (*Parti Kongres Penyatuan Masyarakat*), the **Malaysian Punjabi Party** (*Parti Punjabi Malaysia*), and the **Malaysian Workers' Party** (*Parti Pekerja-Pekerja Malaysia*).

The Malaysian Indian United Party (MIUP) was founded in 2007, but did not field candidates in the 2008 election. Journalist Manuel Lopez formed the **Malaysian Indian Democratic Action Front** (MINDRAF) in 2009 with the intention of serving Malaysia's Indian community and addressing issues such as the plight of people without identification papers. It is not related to the HINDRAF movement (see below).

Illegal Organization:

Hindu Rights Action Force—HINDRAF (*Barisan Bertindak Hak-Hak Hindu*). This union of non-governmental organizations, formed to advocate for the rights of Malaysia's Indian community, captured the nation's attention in November 2007. The group held a massive rally near the Petronas Twin Towers in Kuala Lumpur, without obtaining a government permit, to protest the legacy of social and economic discrimination against Indians and the destruction of Hindu temples. Police arrested more than 200 people, and 5 leaders were later detained without charges for more than a year under the Internal Security Act. The unusual street demonstration galvanized Malaysia's ethnic minorities and played a significant role in the loss of support for the National Front in the 2008 polling. Citing a threat to public order, Home Minister Syed Hamid Albar declared HINDRAF an illegal organization in October 2008. Prime Minister Najib freed the five detained leaders during his first month in office.

Radical Islamic Group:

Malaysian Mujahideen Group (*Kumpulan Mujahideen Malaysia*—KMM). The shadowy KMM, which advocates Malaysia's conversion to an Islamic state, was apparently organized in 1998 as the Malaysian Militant Group (*Kumpulan Militan Malaysia*). It is regarded as an affiliate of the Indonesian-based terrorist group **Jemaah Islamiah.**

A number of alleged KMM members have been jailed under Malaysia's Internal Security Act, which permits detention without trial. In many cases the KMM detainees have been Pas members, including Nik Adli Nik Abdul Aziz Nik Mat, son of the chief minister of Kelantan, who was held from August 2001 until October 2006.

Leaders: ZULKIFLI bin Hir (resident in Philippines), NIK ADLI Nik Abdul Aziz Nik Mat.

LEGISLATURE

The federal **Parliament** (*Parliamen Malaysia*) is a bicameral body consisting of a Senate and a House of Representatives.

Senate (*Dewan Negara*). The upper chamber consists of 70 members: 44 appointed by the paramount ruler (including 2 senators from the Federal Territory of Kuala Lumpur and 1 each from Labuan and Putrajaya) and 2 selected by each of the 13 state legislatures. Members serve once-renewable three-year terms. The Senate is never dissolved, new elections being held by the appropriate state legislative assembly as often as there are vacancies among the elected members. As of May 2009, 60 seats were occupied as follows: National Front, 55 (United Malays National Organization, 34; Malaysian Chinese Association, 8; Malaysian Indian Congress, 5; Malaysian People's Movement Party, 2; United Traditional Bumiputra Party, 2; People's Progressive Party, 1; Sarawak United People's Party, 1; United *Pasok Momogun Kadazandusun Murut* Organization, 1; Sarawak Progressive Democratic Party, 1); People's Alliance, 4 (Pan-Malaysian Islamic Party, 3; People's Justice Movement, 1); minority representatives, 1. The remaining 10 seats were not filled.

President: Abdul Hamid PAWANTEH.

House of Representatives (*Dewan Rakyat*). The lower house currently has 222 elected members. The term of the House is five years, subject to dissolution. Elections are by universal adult suffrage, but the voting is weighted in favor of the predominantly Malay rural areas, with some urban (mainly Chinese) constituencies having three to four times as many voters as their rural counterparts.

In the most recent election of March 8, 2008, the National Front (BN) won 140 seats (United Malays National Organization, 79; Malaysian Chinese Association, 15; United Traditional Bumiputra Party, 14; Sarawak People's Party, 6; Sarawak United People's Party, 6; Sarawak Progressive Democratic Party, 4; United *Pasok Momogun Kadazandusun Murut* Organization, 4; Malaysian Indian Congress, 3; Sabah United Party, 3; Malaysian People's Movement Party, 2; Sabah Progressive Party, 2; United Sabah People's Party, 1; and Liberal Democratic Party, 1.) The opposition People's Front won 82 seats, distributed as follows: People's Justice Party, 31; Democratic Action Party, 28; and Pan-Malaysian Islamic Party (Pas), 23.

The Sabah Progressive Party subsequently departed from the BN, and one Pas lawmaker elected switched to independent affiliation.

Following several by-elections in 2009, the BN held 138 seats; the opposition People's Alliance (*Pakatan Rakyat*—PR), 81; and independents, 3.

Speaker: PANDIKAR Amin Mulia.

CABINET

[as of June 1, 2009]

Prime Minister	Mohamed Najib Abdul Razak (UMNO)
Deputy Prime Minister	Muhyiddin Mohamed Yasin (UMNO)
Ministers	
Agriculture and Agro-Based Industry	Noh Omar (UMNO)
Defense	Ahmad Zahid Hamidi (UMNO)
Domestic Trade and Consumer Affairs	Ismail Sabri Yaakob (UMNO)
Education	Muhyiddin Mohamed Yasin (UMNO)
Energy, Green Technology, and Water	Peter Chin Fah Kui (SUPP)
Federal Territories	Raja Nong Chik Zainal Abidin (independent)
Finance	Mohamed Najib Tun Abdul Razak (UMNO)
Foreign Affairs	Anifah Aman (UMNO)
Health	Liow Tiong Lai (MCA)
Higher Education	Mohamed Khaled Nordin (UMNO)
Home Affairs and Internal Security	Hishammuddin Hussein (UMNO)
Housing and Local Government	Kong Cho Ha (MCA)
Human Resources	S. Subramaniam (MIC)
Information, Communications, and Culture	Rais Yatim (UMNO)
International Trade and Industry	Mustapha Mohamed (UMNO)
Natural Resources and Environment	Douglas Uggah Embas (PBB)
Plantation Industries and Commodities	Bernard Giluk Dompok (UPKO)
Prime Minister's Office, in charge of Economic Planning	Nor Mohamed Yakcop (UMNO)
Prime Minister's Office, in charge of Islamic Affairs	Jamil Khir Baharom (UMNO)
Prime Minister's Office, in charge of Legal Affairs and Parliament	Mohamad Nazri Abdul Aziz (UMNO)
Prime Minister's Office, in charge of Unity Affairs and Performance Management	Koh Tsu Koon (Gerakan)
Rural and Regional Development	Mohamed Shafie Haji Apdal (UMNO)
Science, Technology, and Innovations	Maximus Ongkili (PBS)
Second Minister of Finance	Ahmad Husni Hanadzlan (UMNO)
Tourism	Ng Yen Yen (MCA) [f]
Transport	Ong Tee Keat (MCA)
Women, Family, and Community Development	Shahrizat Abdul Jalil (UMNO) [f]
Works	Shaziman Abu Mansor (UMNO)
Youth and Sports	Ahmad Shabery Cheek (UMNO)

[f] = female

COMMUNICATIONS

Journalists are subject to arrest under the Internal Security Act (ISA), Official Secrets Act, and Sedition Act, and the home minister is empowered "at any time by notification in writing" to alter a newspaper license. Self-censorship as well as official censorship is common. In February 2006 the government suspended publication of the *Sarawak Tribune* after it reprinted satirical Danish editorial cartoons that caricatured the Prophet Muhammad. A popular blogger and editor of the Malaysia Today Web site was detained under the ISA on September 12, 2008. He was released three weeks later, but subsequently was charged with sedition for allegedly making defamatory remarks about a government official.

Party newspapers of the People's Justice Party (*Parti Keadilan Rakyat*—PKR) and Pan-Malaysian Islamic Party (*Parti Islam SeMalaysia*—Pas), both members of the People's Alliance, were banned on March 23, 2009, two weeks before legislative by-elections. Prime Minister Najib lifted the bans on April 3, his first day in office.

Press. The following, unless otherwise noted, are dailies published in Kuala Lumpur: *Berita Harian* (350,000 daily; 420,000 Sunday, published as *Berita Minggu*), in Malay; *Utusan Malaysia* (240,000), UMNO-controlled organ, in Malay; *Sin Chew Jit Poh* (Selangor, 230,000 daily; 230,000 Sunday), in Chinese; *The Star* (Selangor, 220,000 daily; 250,000 Sunday, published as *Sunday Star*), MCA organ, in English; *Chung Kuo Pao* (210,000), in Chinese; *New Straits Times* (190,000 daily; 190,000 Sunday, published as *New Sunday Times*), founded 1845, in English; *Nanyang Siang Pao* (180,000 daily, 220,000 Sunday), in Chinese; *Tamil Nesan* (35,000 daily, 60,000 Sunday), in Tamil.

News agencies. The domestic facility is the state-run Malaysian National News Agency (Bernama); a number of foreign agencies maintain offices in Kuala Lumpur.

Broadcasting and computing. The Ministry of Information is empowered to revoke the license of any broadcaster who transmits materials "conflicting with Malaysian values." Government services are provided by Radio Television Malaysia (RTM), which operates about 30 radio stations and 2 television networks. A limited number of private companies also provide broadcast services.

As of 2008 there were 558 Internet users per 1,000 inhabitants.

INTERGOVERNMENTAL REPRESENTATION

Ambassador to the U.S.: Jamaludin bin JARJIS.

U.S. Ambassador to Malaysia: James R. KEITH.

Permanent Representative to the UN: HAMIDON Ali.

IGO Memberships (Non-UN): ADB, APEC, ASEAN, BIS, CWTH, IDB, Interpol, IOR-ARC, NAM, OIC, PCA, WCO, WTO.

MALDIVES

Republic of Maldives
Dhivehi Jumhuriyah

Political Status: Former British protectorate; independent since July 26, 1965; sultanate replaced by republican regime November 11, 1968; present constitution promulgated August 7, 2008.

Area: 115 sq. mi. (298 sq. km.).

Population: 299,968 (2006C); 311,000 (2008E).

Major Urban Center (2005E): MALÉ (88,000).

Official Language: Dhivehi.

Monetary Unit: Maldivian Rufiyaa (market rate December 1, 2009: 12.80 rufiyaa = $1US).

President: Mohamed NASHEED (Maldivian Democratic Party); elected for a five-year term in a runoff election on October 29, 2008, and inaugurated on November 11, succeeding Maumoon Abdul GAYOOM (Maldive People's Party).

Vice President: Mohammed Wahid HASSAN Manik (National Unity Party); elected on October 29, 2008, and inaugurated on November 11 for a term concurrent with that of the president.

THE COUNTRY

The Republic of Maldives is a 500-mile-long chain of small, low-lying coral islands in the Indian Ocean, southwest of India's tip. Grouped into 20 atoll clusters, the more than 1,200 islands (only about 200 are inhabited) have vegetation ranging from scrub to dense tropical forest. The population displays mixed Sinhalese, Dravidian, and Arab traits. The official language, Dhivehi, is related to Sinhalese. Islam is the state religion, most of the population belonging to the Sunni sect. Women make up 41 percent of the active labor force, but only 5 were elected to the 77-seat national legislature in 2009.

The economy was traditionally dependent on fishing, which continues to lead the islands' exports but accounts for only 8 percent of GDP and 8 percent of employment. Agriculture, hunting, and forestry add another 4 percent to GDP. In recent years fishing has been surpassed in importance by a booming tourism sector. Tourist arrivals surpassed 615,000 in 2004; dropped to 395,000 in 2005 as a consequence of the December 2004 Indian Ocean tsunami; recovered to 600,000 in 2006, and set a record of 675,000 in 2007, led by visitors from the United Kingdom, Italy, Germany, France, Japan, and China. The international financial crisis in the last quarter of 2008 meant that the number of arrivals grew by only 1.1 percent for 2008, to 683,000, and were down by about 10 percent in the first half of 2009. Manufacturing, which contributes about 7 percent of GDP and employs 18 percent of the active labor force, is limited, the most important products being canned fish and garments. Cottage industries and handicraft production are also significant sources of employment and income. The government dominates most economic activity, but private sector participation has been increasingly encouraged.

Gross national income grew steadily in 1995–2004, a decade during which annual GDP expansion averaged about 6.7 percent. The economy was hit severely, however, by the December 2004, tsunami. About 100 people died, and damage to infrastructure and housing was estimated at $375 million—about half the country's GDP for 2004. Fourteen islands suffered what the International Monetary Fund (IMF) labeled "virtually complete destruction"; 3 of the 14 were abandoned. Despite an inflow of international aid from the World Bank and other institutions as well as individual countries, Maldives saw its economy contract by 4.6 percent in 2005, although it recovered in 2006, when growth accelerated to 19 percent. The rate of expansion was a more stable 6.6 percent for 2007. For 2008 the IMF projected GDP growth at 6.5 percent and the rate of inflation more than doubling to 15 percent, largely because of increased prices for food and petroleum.

GOVERNMENT AND POLITICS

Political background. Subjected to a brief period of Portuguese domination in the 16th century, the Maldives came under British influence in 1796 and was declared a British protectorate in 1887. Internal self-government was instituted in 1960, and full independence was achieved on July 26, 1965, following negotiations with the United Kingdom covering economic assistance and the retention of a British air facility on southern Gan Island. The centuries-old Maldivian sultanate, which had been temporarily replaced by a republican form of government in 1953–1954, was then reinstated until 1968, when the Maldives again became a republic in accordance with the outcome of a national referendum.

Having been initially appointed prime minister in 1972, Ahmed ZAKI was redesignated in February 1975 but was removed from office and placed under arrest in March. President Ibrahim NASIR assumed executive responsibilities, and Zaki was banished. The change in governmental structure was then codified by a constitutional revision.

After 21 years of rule, President Nasir announced in mid-1978 that he would not seek reelection, despite a parliamentary request that he continue in office. The Majlis (Citizens' Assembly) thereupon nominated as his successor Transport Minister Maumoon Abdul GAYOOM, who had once been banished and once imprisoned for criticizing Nasir's administration but had since become the country's first permanent representative to the United Nations. Prior to Gayoom's installation in November, outgoing President Nasir pardoned a number of those under house arrest or banished, including former prime minister Zaki, who subsequently served as UN representative. The Majlis renominated President Gayoom for additional terms in 1983 and 1988, with confirmation by referendum.

In November 1988 the islands withstood an attempted coup by more than 400 mercenaries (reportedly members of the Sri Lankan People's Liberation Organization of Tamil Eelam), who landed in Malé, attacked government troops, and caused at least 12 deaths. In response, India dispatched some 1,600 paratroopers, who quickly restored order. A trial of 73 individuals involved in the affair concluded in August 1989 with 17 sentenced to death and the rest to lengthy prison terms. In mid-September, however, President Gayoom commuted the death sentences, including that imposed on the coup leader, Maldivian businessman Abdulla LUTHUFEE, to life imprisonment.

In 1993 President Gayoom's renomination was unexpectedly challenged by his brother-in-law, Ilyas IBRAHIM. Gayoom reportedly defeated Ibrahim by an informal vote of 28–18 in the Majlis, which then proceeded to nominate Gayoom as its official unanimous candidate. Ibrahim was charged with illegally attempting to influence members of the Majlis and fled the country prior to being sentenced in

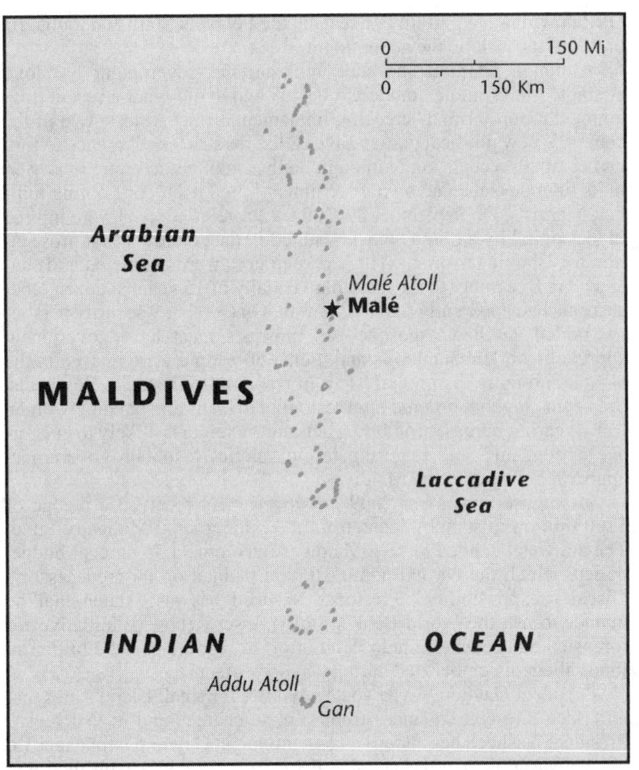

absentia to 15 years' imprisonment. Gayoom was inaugurated for a fourth term in November, following endorsement by referendum.

Amid growing calls for political reform, especially for the legalization of party activity, in December 1994 contests for the 40 elective seats in the Majlis drew 229 candidates, all standing as independents. Those elected included several leaders of the "proreform" movement, notably former ministers Abdulla KAMALUDHEEN and Ahmed MUJUTABA.

Ilyas Ibrahim returned to house arrest in Maldives in 1996 but was released in 1997, his case apparently having influenced the way presidential balloting in the legislature (now termed the People's Majlis) was to be conducted under a new constitution that was promulgated on January 1, 1998. Although four others sought the presidential nomination during secret balloting in the legislature in September 1998, President Gayoom received a unanimous endorsement. Following confirmation by referendum, he took the oath of office for a fifth term in November. In a surprising but, for Maldives, not unprecedented development, the new cabinet introduced by President Gayoom included his erstwhile adversary Ilyas Ibrahim as well as Abdulla Kamaludheen.

The People's Majlis election of November 1999 saw a nearly 50 percent turnover in the elected membership, with two government ministers, including Kamaludheen, being among the defeated. A total of 129 independent candidates contested the election.

In 2003 President Gayoom won unanimous endorsement for a sixth term. He was confirmed by 90.3 percent of the voters on October 17 and sworn in on November 11.

On August 13, 2004, the president declared a state of emergency following demonstrations demanding the release of political prisoners, some of whom had been detained since protesting the deaths of several prisoners at the hands of security personnel in September 2003. When the state of emergency was lifted on October 10, 2004, nearly 80 of the 185 who had been arrested in August were still being held.

Legislative elections to the 50-seat People's Majlis, originally scheduled for December 31, 2004, but postponed because of the Indian Ocean tsunami, were held on January 22, 2005. Although all candidates were required to run as independents, reform advocates performed strongly. Those endorsed by the Maldivian Democratic Party (MDP), an opposition party then based in Sri Lanka, captured 18 of the 42 elective seats.

In the context of a presidentially sanctioned political reform process, on May 28, 2004, voters cast ballots for a partially elected People's Special Majlis that was assigned the task of drafting another new constitution. Further, on June 2, 2005, the People's Majlis unanimously passed legislation legalizing the formation of political parties. The MDP quickly registered and immediately became the principal opposition to President Gayoom's newly organized Maldive People's Party (*Dhivehi Rayyithunge* Party—DRP).

In August 2005 demonstrators again demanded the release of political prisoners. The authorities responded by arresting more than 130, including the MDP chair, Mohamed NASHEED (familiarly called Anni), who had returned from exile in April. Nasheed faced charges of terrorism and sedition. In October Jennifer LATHEEF, daughter of exiled MDP founder Mohamed LATHEEF, was convicted of inciting a riot in September 2003 and sentenced to ten years in prison. Four codefendants had already received comparable prison terms. In August 2006, however, Jennifer Latheef was released from house arrest, as was Mohamed Nasheed in September. The releases came in the context of "Westminster House" talks, chaired by the United Kingdom's high commissioner to the Maldives, between the government and the opposition.

On August 18, 2007, some 62 percent of those voting in a national referendum on the structure of government indicated support for maintaining a strong presidency, while the balance favored a parliamentary system. After four years of work, the People's Special Majlis approved a new constitution on June 26, 2008, and on August 7 it was signed by the president. The day before, Gayoom had pardoned a number of prisoners, including others who had been convicted of terrorism in connection with the September 2003 unrest.

Voting in the country's first multiparty presidential election, held October 8, 2008, Maldivians gave a plurality of 40.3 percent to the incumbent, President Gayoom, and 24.9 percent to the second-place finisher, the MDP's Mohamed Nasheed. Finishing third, with 16.7 percent of the vote, was former attorney general and independent candidate Hassan SAEED of the New Maldives movement. In the resultant two-way runoff on October 29, Nasheed won 53.7 percent of the vote to Gayoom's 45.3 percent. Inaugurated on November 11, President Nasheed named a multiparty cabinet to serve with him and his vice president, Mohammed Wahid HASSAN Manik of the National Unity Party (NUP).

The country's first multiparty legislative election, for an expanded 77-seat People's Majlis, was held May 9, 2009, with revoting in one district on July 11. The DRP won a leading 28 seats, while its ally, the People's Alliance (PA), won 7. The president's MDP, which outpolled the DRP by 30.8 percent of the vote to 24.6 percent, took 26 seats, with independents claiming most of the balance.

Constitution and government. Following adoption of a republican constitution in 1968, the Maldivian government combined constitutional rule with de facto control by members of a small hereditary elite. The 1998 basic law, having been drafted over a 17-year period by a Citizens' Special Majlis, was approved by the president on November 20, 1997, effective January 1, 1998. Like its predecessor, this constitution provided for a unicameral legislature, now called the People's Majlis (People's Assembly), controlled by an elected majority. The legislature nominated the president for a five-year term, with confirmation required by popular referendum. The president appointed other leading officials, including those entrusted with overseeing the legal system, which is based on Islamic law (sharia).

Changes introduced by the 1998 basic law included multicandidate competition in the People's Majlis for its presidential nomination, parliamentary immunity from prosecution, expansion of ministerial powers, and greater citizens' rights. In addition to the ordinary legislature, the 1998 constitution provided for a People's Special Majlis (previously the Citizens' Special Majlis) to draft or amend a constitution. Either the president or the People's Majlis could convene a People's Special Majlis, whose membership included the 50 members of the People's Majlis, an additional 42 elected members (2 per administrative district and 2 from Malé), 8 presidential appointees, and the members of the cabinet.

The new constitution approved by the People's Special Majlis in June 2008 and signed by President Gayoom in August retains a strong presidential system but reduces some powers and limits the president to two terms in office. It provides for a two-way runoff should no presidential candidate achieve 50 percent of the vote in a first round. A president must be the child of Maldivian citizens and must practice the Sunni branch of Islam. Cabinet ministers are named by the president but must receive legislative endorsement. The People's Majlis, now wholly elected using a first-past-the-post system, was expanded from 50 to 77 seats.

The 2008 constitution also enumerates a broad range of human rights, including freedom of speech, assembly, and association, and provides for the separation of executive, legislative, and judicial powers. The judicial system encompasses a Supreme Court, a High Court, and trial courts. Independent bodies are to be established for human rights, defense, police, elections, and corruption investigations. The constitution prohibits ministers from having private businesses, one immediate consequence being that four cabinet members tendered their resignations on August 6, 2008.

The current constitution includes no provision for a People's Special Majlis. In general, constitutional amendments require the assent of three-fourth of the full People's Majlis and the signature of the president, although the legislature may call for a referendum if the president does not assent to a change.

There are 20 atoll-based administrative divisions. The capital constitutes a separate, centrally administered district. In the past, each atoll was governed by a presidentially appointed atoll chief (*verin*), who was advised by an elected committee. Under the 2008 constitution, all divisions are to be "administered decentrally." As authorized by law, the president may create constituencies, posts, and councils, with the members of all councils to be elected democratically. Each council may then elect a president and vice president to serve as administrative officers for the jurisdiction.

Foreign relations. An active participant in the Nonaligned Movement, the Republic of Maldives has long sought to have the Indian Ocean declared a "Zone of Peace," with foreign (particularly nuclear) military forces permanently banned from the area. Thus, despite the adverse impact on what was an already depressed economy, the government welcomed the withdrawal of the British Royal Air Force from Gan Island in 1976 and rejected a subsequent Soviet bid to establish a base there. The republic became a "special member" of the Commonwealth in July 1982 and a full member in June 1985. In addition to an emphasis on regional affairs—Maldives is a founding member of the South Asian Association for Regional Cooperation (SAARC)—the Gayoom government took an active role addressing such environmental issues as global warming, particularly with regard to its impact on small island states.

India remains the Maldives's closest international partner and the only country with which Malé has a defense cooperation agreement. Most ambassadors to Maldives reside in Sri Lanka, although Bangladesh, India, Pakistan, and Sri Lanka have high commissioners in Malé. For financial reasons Maldives maintains a limited number of diplomatic missions, including those at UN headquarters in New York, in Sri Lanka, and in the United Kingdom. In May 2008 it opened a new embassy in Saudi Arabia.

Current issues. The peaceful transfer of power from President Gayoom to President Nasheed in November 2008 won wide international praise. Given a divided opposition, many observers had considered it unlikely that Gayoom would be at the polls, but he was undercut by the disintegration of his cabinet, primarily over budgetary and development issues. July and August 2008 saw the resignations of a dozen ministers, including finance head Gasim IBRAHIM, reputedly the country's wealthiest businessman. Although Gayoom managed a plurality in the first round of presidential balloting on October 8, Mohamed Nasheed drew the support of the other four presidential candidates (including Ibrahim) for the second round three weeks later, which contributed to Gayoom's defeat.

Newly inaugurated President Nasheed came into office pledging to fight corruption, improve healthcare, build infrastructure on outlying atolls, and privatize state trading companies. He faced a host of other problems, including a growing illegal narcotics trade, economic inequalities, housing shortages, and inadequate construction capacity to meet the demands of the tourism industry. But between his inauguration and the May 2009 People's Majlis election, Nasheed's governing style became as much an issue as his agenda. After serving as a special adviser for only 100 days, Hassan Saeed resigned, charging that the president was not taking his advice. Opponents were quick to charge Nasheed with nepotism and heavy-handedness. In May 2009 he dismissed two cabinet members. Attorney General Fathimath Diyana SAEED had accused him of abuse of power and improperly trying to influence the May voting. Minister of Civil Aviation and Communication Mohamed Jameel AHMED had "fail[ed] to make progress," but he had also accused appointees of abusing their authority. Given that Nasheed's predecessor had tightly controlled the government for three decades, it was unsurprising that the new administration was inexperienced and prone to missteps. Nevertheless, the success of Gayoom's DRP in winning a plurality of seats in the People's Majlis undoubtedly provided a check on the government.

Although Islam is the state religion, the government has long attempted to promote "moderate Islam" and avoid what a recent government report termed "creeping fundamentalism." At least two of the country's new political parties have called for stricter adherence to fundamentalist precepts, and although neither is likely to come to power, in its final days the Gayoom government found itself confronting militant Islamists. On September 29, 2007, 12 foreign tourists were injured in the capital by a bomb, which resulted in the country's first prosecution for Islamic terrorism. Three perpetrators were convicted and sentenced in December to the maximum penalty of 15 years; a dozen other suspects had apparently fled to Pakistan. On October 9 security personnel raided an illegal mosque—all mosques must have government approval—on Himandhoo Island. Some 50 people were injured in the assault and more than 60 arrested. In response to these developments, President Gayoom ordered new restrictions, including banning women from wearing burqas, prohibiting acts and statements "likely to encourage extremism," and requiring foreign clerics to obtain government approval before entering Maldives.

In August–September 2009 the government received a pledge of $100 million in standby loans from the International Monetary Fund. The aid was intended to help Maldives overcome a 34 percent budget deficit, which the current administration blamed on its predecessor's "fiscal irresponsibility." President Nasheed has also stated that he intends to ask the World Bank's Stolen Asset Recovery initiative for forensic and accounting help in an effort to recover over $2 billion in funds allegedly embezzled during Gayoom's tenure.

President Gayoom was a vocal advocate for small island states that may face dire consequences from climate change, and in that regard President Nasheed has attempted to continue in Gayoom's footsteps. In November 2008 he advanced the idea of a sovereign wealth fund that would be used for land purchases abroad: Maldives's inhabited islands average only 1.5 meters above sea level, and rising oceans could wipe the country from the map. Furthermore, in March 2009 Nasheed announced plans for using wind, solar, and biomass power generation that, in combination with carbon offsets, would make Maldives the world's first carbon-neutral country by 2020.

POLITICAL PARTIES

On June 2, 2005, at President Gayoom's request, the People's Majlis unanimously passed a reform allowing the registration of political parties, which had long been banned in Maldives. Parties seeking registration must submit the signatures of at least 3,000 members.

In May 2008 a National Unity Alliance (NUA) of five opposition groups—the Maldivian Democratic Party (MDP), the Islamic Democratic Party (IDP), the Social Liberal Party (SLP), the *Adhaalath* Party, and the New Maldives (NM)—failed to agree on selection of a single opposition candidate to compete against President Gayoom in the upcoming presidential election. The NUA had been organized in 2007, in part to press for an interim government before new elections. In mid-2008 the Maldivian National Congress (MNC) became the NUA's sixth member. The cabinet sworn in on November 12 included five parties plus the NM movement.

As of the May 2009 legislative election, 13 parties had been registered. Eleven offered candidates, and 5 won seats.

Governing Coalition:

Maldivian Democratic Party (MDP). Efforts to establish a legal MDP date back to at least 2001, when the government refused to register it. As a result, the MDP was based in Colombo, Sri Lanka, from 2003 until officially registered in the Maldives in June 2005. The Majlis elected in 1999 reportedly included 7 MDP supporters; 18 representatives elected in January 2005 had run with MDP endorsements. Following legalization of political parties, the center-right MDP assumed leadership of the parliamentary opposition. In May 2006 the party president, Ibrahim ISMAIL, resigned over tactical issues.

In November 2006 officials arrested 100 MDP members and supporters, ostensibly to avert a violent demonstration, and later charged the acting MDP president, Ibrahim Hussein Zaki, with treason for delivering a speech in which he voiced support for protesting fishermen. The charge was later downgraded to committing "enmity, contempt, and disharmony." In April 2007 the MDP was fined, not for the first time, for holding illegal gatherings, this time to welcome home Majlis member Mariya Ahmed Didi, who in March had received from the U.S. State Department an International Woman of Courage Award for her advocacy of women's rights.

In June 2007 Hussain Zaki unexpectedly lost a multicandidate party election to a former attorney general, Mohamed MUNAVVAR. In a subsequent primary to determine the MDP's 2008 presidential nominee, Mohamed Nasheed (Anni) won 68 percent of the vote, defeating Munavvar (21 percent) and Reeko MOOSA (9 percent). Nasheed, having taken 24.9 percent of the first-round presidential vote for second place, went on to defeat the incumbent and claim the presidency with 53.7 percent.

In the May 2009 legislative election the MDP finished second, with 26 seats, despite claiming a plurality of votes, 30.8 percent.

Leaders: Mohamed NASHEED (President of the Republic), Mariya Ahmed DIDI (Chair), Ibrahim Hussein ZAKI (Acting President), Hamid Abdul GHAFOOR (Secretary General).

National Unity Party—NUP (*Gaumee Itthihaad*). The NUP, which is also sometimes referenced in English as the National Alliance Party (NAP), was established in mid-2008 by former education minister Mohamed Wahid Hassan. Initially the party's presidential candidate, Hassan formed an alliance with the MDP and was named by the MDP's Mohamed Nasheed as his running mate for the October election. In the May 2009 legislative election the NUP won only 0.3 percent of the vote and no seats.

Leaders: Mohamed Wahid HASSAN Manik (Vice President of the Republic), Mohamed RASHEED (Minister of Economic Development), Musthafa LUTHFEE (Minister of Education).

Dhivehi Qaumee Party (DQP). The DQP (Maldives National Party) originated in the New Maldives (NM) movement, which was formed by former attorney general Hassan Saeed and former foreign minister Ahmed Shaheed, both of whom had resigned from the government in August 2007 and had criticized President Gayoom for delaying democratic reforms. Another prominent member was Mohamed Latheef, a founder of the MDP who had returned from exile in January 2007. The NM called for a left-leaning agenda, including adoption of a 35-hour work week, a minimum wage, and universal health insurance.

In 2008 Saeed sought the presidency as an independent and finished third, with 16.7 percent of the vote, in the first round. Shaheed, his running mate, was subsequently reappointed as foreign minister by President Nasheed, and Saeed became an adviser to Nasheed. After only 100 days in office, however, Saeed resigned because the new president was not heeding his advice.

In May 2009 the newly registered DQP won 3.5 percent of the national vote and two seats in the People's Majlis.

Leaders: Hassan SAEED (2008 presidential candidate), Ahmed SHAHEED (Minister of Foreign Affairs).

Republican Party (*Jumhooree* Party—JP). The JP was founded in May 2008 by Ahmed Nashid, an associate of former finance minister Gasim Ibrahim. Presidential aspirant Ibrahim, who resigned from the cabinet and the DRP (below) in mid-July, joined the JP in August and was quickly named its presidential candidate. By then, the JP had reportedly become the largest opposition party in the People's Majlis, with nine seats.

Ibrahim finished fourth in the 2008 presidential election, winning 15.2 percent of the vote as the candidate of the Republican Coalition, which also included *Adhaalath* and the Maldives National Congress (MNC, below). Ibrahim and his running mate, Ahmed Ali SAWAAD, were invited to join the Nasheed cabinet, and a third JP member, Fathimath Diyana Saeed, was named attorney general. Ibrahim resigned in December 2008, however, and in May 2009 Saeed was dismissed by President Nasheed for writing letters that criticized the government. Subsequently, the JP threatened to take the MDP for court for not fulfilling their coalition agreement regarding the number of JP members in the cabinet.

In the May 2009 People's Majlis election the JP won one seat.

Leaders: Ahmed NASHID, Gasim IBRAHIM, Mohamed SHIHAB (Minister of Home Affairs).

Justice Party (*Adhaalath* Party). The Justice Party was registered in August 2005. Islamic in orientation and including among its membership a number of Muslim clerics and scholars, the party backed demands for the release of political prisoners and governmental reform. Some members have called for adoption of strict sharia law and the death penalty for Muslims who convert to other religions. The party endorsed Gasim Ibrahim of the JP for president in 2008 but in July 2009 signed a coalition agreement with the MDP for the next local council elections. In May the party had won under 1 percent of the vote and no People's Majlis seats.

Leaders: Sheikh Hussain RASHID AHMED (President), Abdul Majeed BARI (Minister of Islamic Affairs), Sheikh Mohamed SHAHEEM Ali Saeed.

Social Liberal Party (SLP). Former MDP president Ibrahim Ismail announced his intention to organize the SLP in late 2006, but it was not registered until September 2007. The party called for constitutionally guaranteed freedoms and equal distribution of wealth. Ismail finished last in the first round of the October 2008 presidential election with 0.8 percent of the vote. The party won only 0.4 percent of the vote in the May 2009 national election.

Leaders: Mazlan RASHEED, Ibrahim ISMAIL (2008 presidential candidate), Hassan LATHEEF (Minister of Human Resources, Youth, and Sports).

Parliamentary Opposition:

Dhivehi Rayyithunge Party (DRP). Registered shortly after the legalization of parties, the DRP (Maldive People's Party) was established by President Gayoom. Its members included the cabinet and the government-supportive members of the People's Majlis and the People's Special Majlis. The party held its first congress April 19–21, 2006, at which time Gayoom was formally elected party chair by a vote of 887–33 over reform activist Ali SHAFEEQ.

A number of more youthful party leaders, including Ahmed Shaheed, Mohamed Jameel, and Hassan Saeed, headed a proreform "New Maldives" caucus that, at least initially, claimed the support of President Gayoom. Leaders of a more conservative faction included Ilyas Ibrahim, Ismail Shafeeu, and Thasmeen Ali. The resignations from the cabinet in August 2007 of Shaheed, Jameel, and Saeed came amid accusations that the president was hindering democratic reform. In late October Saeed left the DRP and declared his intention to seek the presidency in 2008 (see NM, above). President Gayoom won the party's endorsement for reelection but lost an October runoff in which he took 45.3 percent of the vote.

In the May 2009 People's Majlis election the DRP won a slim plurality of seats (28) despite receiving fewer votes—24.6 percent of the total—than the MDP.

Leaders: Maumoon Abdul GAYOOM (Chair of the Party and Former President of the Maldives), Ahmed Thasmeen ALI Deputy Leader and (2008 vice-presidential candidate), Ilyas IBRAHIM (Former Minister of Health), Ismail SHAFEEU (Former Minister of Defense).

People's Alliance (PA) Organized by Abdulla Yamin, a half-brother of President Gayoom, the PA endorsed Gayoom for reelection in 2008 and then ran in the May 2009 People's Majlis election as a partner of the DRP, winning 5.0 percent of the vote and 7 seats.

Leader: Abdulla YAMIN.

Other Parties:

Islamic Democratic Party (IDP). The IDP was officially registered in December 2005. Party President Umar Naseer, decrying what he considers the excesses of "liberal" democracies, has advocated instituting an "Islamic democracy" based on sharia. He finished fifth in the first round of the October 2008 presidential election, winning only 1.4 percent of the vote. The party finished even less well in 2009, with 0.1 percent of the People's Majlis vote.

Leaders: Umar NASEER (President of the Party and 2008 presidential candidate), Ahmed RIZWEE (2008 vice-presidential candidate).

The **Maldives Social Democratic Party** (MSDP), led by Reeko Ibrahim MANIK, endorsed President Gayoom for reelection in 2008. Both the MSDP and the **People's Party** (PP), led by Ahmed RIYAZ, chose not to contest the 2009 legislative election. The **Poverty Alleviating Party** (PEP), led by Ahmed SALEEM, was registered in September 2008, as was the **National Alliance** (NA), led by Mohamed WAHEED. The **Maldives National Congress** (MNC), chaired by Mohamed NAEEM, ran with the Republican Coalition in 2008. In 2009 it won less than 0.1 percent of the national vote.

LEGISLATURE

Prior to adoption of the 2008 constitution, the Maldivian **People's Majlis** was a unicameral body of 50 members: 8 appointed by the president and 42 popularly elected as independents (2 from Malé and 2 from each of the 20 administrative districts). The country's first multiparty election, for a 77-seat People's Majlis, was held May 9, 2009, with revoting in one district on July 11. The results were as follows: *Dhivehi Rayyithunge* Party, 28 seats; Maldivian Democratic Party, 26; People's Alliance, 7; *Dhivehi Qaumee* Party, 2; Republican Party, 1. Representatives, all of whom are now elected from districts drawn on the basis of population, serve five-year terms.

Speaker: Abdullah SHAHID.

CABINET

[as of December 15, 2009]

President	Mohamed Nasheed (MDP)
Vice President	Mohamed Wahid Hassan (NUP)
Ministers	
Agriculture and Fisheries	Ibrahim Didi (MDP)
Civil Aviation and Communication	Mahmood Razee (MDP)
Defense and National Security	Ameen Faisal (MDP)
Economic Development	Mohamed Rasheed (NUP)
Education	Mustafa Luthfee (NUP)
Finance and Treasury	Ali Hashim (MDP)
Foreign Affairs	Ahmed Shaheed (DQP)
Health and Family	Aminath Jameel (MDP) [f]
Home Affairs	Mohamed Shihab (JP)
Housing, Transport, and Environment	Mohamed Aslam (MDP)
Human Resources, Youth, and Sports	Hassan Latheef (SLP)
Islamic Affairs	Abdul Majeed Bari (*Adhaalath*)
Tourism, Arts, and Culture	Ahmed Ali Sawaad (JP)
Attorney General	Husnu Suood (MDP)

[f] = female

COMMUNICATIONS

After a brief flirtation with freedom of the press in 1990, the Gayoom government reversed itself, outlawing all but officially sanctioned publications and jailing a number of journalists. The country's only opposition daily, *Minivan Daily,* founded by opposition leader Mohamed Nasheed, was repeatedly targeted. In 2006, however, Gayoom began proposing reforms, including increased press freedoms. and in May 2006 the minister of information stated that radio and television broadcasting would be opened to the private sector. Nevertheless, self-censorship was common and the government retained the authority to prosecute journalists and shut down publications and media outlets "if any undesirable outcome arises due to the publication of an article or statement." By mid-2008, in anticipation of the upcoming presidential election, the government broadcasting facilities had already agreed to provide equal access for all candidates. In June 2009 President Nasheed proposed broadcasting legislation that would establish a supervisory Broadcasting Commission.

Press. Most news publications are in Dhivehi, but many include English pages. The following are published in Malé: *Haveeru Daily* (4,500); *Aafathis* (3,000), daily; *Jamaathuge Habaru* (Community News, 1,500), monthly; *Adduvas,* independent weekly; *Miadhu News,* daily; *Minivan Daily* (Independence Daily). In February 2008 printing of the official English-language weekly, *Maldives News Bulletin,* was discontinued in favor of online publication.

News agencies. The Haveeru News Service (HNS) and the Hiyama News Agency operate in Malé. The government also maintains a Maldives News Bureau.

Radio, television, and computing. The government dominates broadcasting through the Voice of Maldives radio facility and Television Maldives. Private ownership of stations has been permitted since 2007.

As of 2008 there were 235.2 Internet users per 1,000 inhabitants.

INTERGOVERNMENTAL REPRESENTATION

Ambassador to the U.S.: (Vacant).

U.S. Ambassador to the Maldives: Patricia A. BUTENIS.

Permanent Representative to the UN: Abdul Ghafoor MOHAMED.

IGO Memberships (Non-UN): ADB, CWTH, CP, IDB, Interpol, NAM, OIC, SAARC, WCO, WTO.

MALI

Republic of Mali
République du Mali

Political Status: Independent republic proclaimed September 22, 1960; military regime established November 19, 1968; civilian rule reestablished under constitution approved in 1974 and promulgated June 19, 1979; 1974 constitution suspended on March 26, 1991, and replaced by interim Fundamental Act on March 31; multiparty constitution drafted by National Conference in July–August 1991, approved by popular referendum on January 12, and formally proclaimed on February 14, 1992.

Area: 478,764 sq. mi. (1,240,000 sq. km.).

Population: 9,790,492 (1998C); 12,717,000 (2008E).

Major Urban Center (2005E): BAMAKO (1,995,000).

Official Language: French. Bambara, Fulfuldé, Songhai, and Tamasaq are also commonly spoken.

Monetary Unit: CFA franc (official rate December 1, 2009: 434.59 CFA francs = $1US). The CFA franc, previously pegged to the French franc, is now permanently pegged to the euro at 655.957 CFA francs = 1 euro.

President: Amadou Toumani TOURÉ (nonparty); popularly elected in second-round balloting on May 12, 2002, and inaugurated for a five-year term on June 8 to succeed Alpha Oumar KONARÉ (Alliance for Democracy in Mali); reelected in first-round balloting on April 29, 2007, and inaugurated for a second five-year term on June 8.

Prime Minister: Modibo SIDIBÉ (nonparty); appointed by the president on September 28, 2007, to succeed Ousmane Issoufi MAIGA (nonparty), who resigned on September 27, 2007.

THE COUNTRY

Of predominantly desert and semidesert terrain, landlocked Mali stretches northward into the Sahara from the upper basin of the Niger and Senegal rivers. The country's lifeline is the Niger River, which flows northeastward past Bamako, Ségou, and Timbuktu in Mali and then southeastward through Niger and Nigeria to the Gulf of Guinea. Mali's overwhelmingly Muslim population falls into several distinct ethnic groups, including the Bambara and other southern peoples, who are mostly farmers, while the Peul, or Fulani, as well as the Tuareg pursue a primarily nomadic and pastoral existence on the fringes of the Sahara. Women constitute only about 15 percent of the formal workforce; female involvement in politics has traditionally been minimal.

Approximately 80 percent of the economically population is dependent on agriculture and fishing, with cotton, peanuts, and livestock being the leading sources of foreign exchange. Although the country was once dubbed the potential "breadbasket of Africa," Mali's food output in recent decades has been severely depressed by periodic droughts, locust infestations, and land mismanagement. However, a

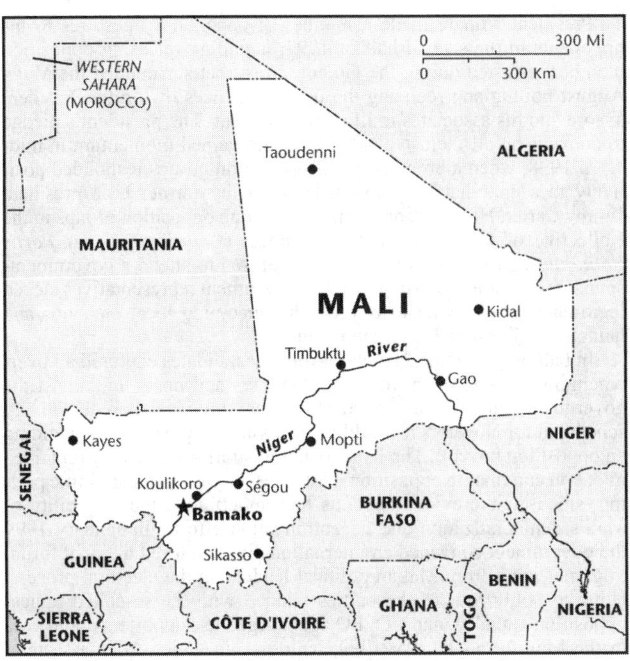

return to agricultural self-sufficiency became a top priority for the Traoré government, which in its later years tried to boost production by loosening price and marketing controls. Industrial activity is concentrated in agro-processing, some enterprises having recently been privatized as part of an overall retreat from state dominance of the economy. Extraction of minerals such as uranium, bauxite, ferronickel, phosphates, and gold, while drawing the interest of international investors, has been hindered by inadequate transport and power facilities. Some progress toward economic reconstruction has been registered with assistance from a variety of foreign sources, although Mali remains one of the world's dozen poorest countries.

In September 1993 the International Monetary Fund (IMF) and World Bank agreed to provide Mali with a four-year aid plan. Within two months the IMF suspended the program but reversed itself in March 1994 and approved an immediate disbursement of funds to help dampen economic and social turmoil generated by devaluation of the CFA franc two months earlier. Annual GDP growth averaged about 5.7 percent from 1995 to 2000, with inflation falling into negative figures in 1999–2000. Among other things, the IMF urged an increased pace of privatization, harmonization of investment regulations and business laws, and greater efficiency in collection of tax revenues, which could permit increased social spending. In August 1999 the IMF approved a three-year loan to assist the government in its economic reform program, and additional aid was approved in 2000 and 2001. In 2003 Mali completed a series of economic reforms and restructuring under the IMF's Heavily Indebted Poor Countries (HIPC) initiative, and, as a result, the country was granted $417 million in debt relief. In 2004 Mali received a three-year IMF grant of $6.3 million to support continuing economic reforms. Record gold and agricultural production in the early 2000s helped maintain strong economic growth, which averaged 5 percent annually in 2000–2004. Inflation remained low, at less than 1 percent in 2003, but the government's deficit rose as spending on infrastructure, including roads, increased significantly. Rising fuel prices and falling cotton prices constrained growth in 2005. However, gold production continued to increase.

In 2006 the World Bank approved additional debt relief for Mali and provided other credits to support agriculture as well as poverty-reduction efforts, and the United States provided $461 million for infrastructure improvement programs. Growth of 5.3 percent was achieved in 2006 but dropped to 2.8 percent in 2007 and 4.2 percent in 2008. It is expected to drop further to around 3 percent in 2009 due to decreased gold production. Inflation was 1.4 percent in 2007 but jumped to 9.2 percent in 2008 due to high oil and food prices. It is expected to drop to 3 percent in 2009. Meanwhile, the government granted oil exploration licenses to two foreign companies in exchange for a commitment from the companies to invest more than $11 million in the Malian economy over a four-year period and continues to pursue external investment to develop its petroleum industry. One such company, Eni SPA, an Italian oil and gas company, announced in January 2009 that it will start drilling five wells in mid-year.

GOVERNMENT AND POLITICS

Political background. Mali, the former French colony of Soudan, takes its name from a medieval African kingdom whose capital was located near the present capital city of Bamako. As a part of French West Africa, Soudan took part in the general process of post–World War II decolonization and became a self-governing member state of the French Community in 1958. Full independence within the community was achieved on June 20, 1960, in association with Senegal, with which Soudan had joined in January 1959 to form a union known as the Federation of Mali. However, Senegal seceded from the federation on August 20, 1960, and on September 22 Mali proclaimed itself an independent republic and withdrew from the French Community.

Mali's government, led by President Modibo KEITA of the Soudanese Union/African Democratic Rally (*Union Soudanaise/Rassemblement Démocratique Africain*—US/RDA), gradually developed into a leftist, one-party dictatorship with a strongly collectivist policy at home and close ties to the Soviet bloc and the People's Republic of China. In late 1968 the Keita regime was ousted in a bloodless coup d'état led by Lt. Moussa TRAORÉ and Capt. Yoro DIAKITÉ under the auspices of a Military Committee of National Liberation (*Comité Militaire de Libération Nationale*—CMLN).

Reversing the economic policies of the Keita government, the military regime pledged that civil and political rights would soon be restored. However, further centralization of the military command took place in 1972 following the trial and imprisonment of Captain Diakité and two associates for allegedly plotting another coup. Subsequent coup attempts were reported in 1976 and 1978, the latter involving a reputed pro-Soviet faction of the CMLN that opposed a projected return to civilian rule under a constitution approved in 1974.

After a five-year period of transitional rule by the CMLN, civilian government was formally restored on June 19, 1979, when General Traoré was elected, unopposed, to a five-year term as president and prime minister. Earlier, in March, the Malian People's Democratic Union (*Union Démocratique du Peuple Malien*—UDPM) had been formally constituted as the country's sole political party. In 1982 the presidential term was increased to six years, resulting in the reelection of Traoré coincident with pro forma legislative balloting on June 9, 1985. Three days earlier the president had carried out a cabinet reshuffle that included the designation of Dr. Mamadou DEMBELE as prime minister. The latter office was abolished in the course of a further cabinet shakeup, on June 6, 1988, that preceded assembly renewal on June 26.

Widespread opposition to harsh conditions under the Traoré regime erupted into rioting in Bamako and other towns during January 1991 and continued into February and March amid mounting demands for the introduction of a multiparty system. On March 26 Traoré was ousted by an army group under the leadership of Lt. Col. Amadou Toumani TOURÉ, who formed a 17-member Council of National Reconciliation (*Conseil de la Réconciliation Nationale*—CRN). On March 30 the CRN joined with anti-Traoré political leaders in establishing a Transitional Committee for the Salvation of the People (*Comité de Transition pour le Salut du Peuple*—CTSP), comprised of 10 military and 15 civilian members. On April 2 the CTSP announced the appointment of Soumana SACKO, a highly respected senior official of the UN Development Program, as prime minister. The cabinet that was announced two days later consisted largely of "unknown" technocrats, with military officers being awarded a number of key portfolios.

On April 5, 1991, the CTSP authorized the formation of political parties and declared its intention to rule for a nine-month period ending with a constitutional referendum and multiparty elections. Traoré supporters were subsequently purged from the government and military, and, following a failed attempt to liberate the imprisoned former president in June, a coup attempt by the then territorial administration minister, Maj. Lamine DIABIRA, failed in mid-July.

At a National Conference on July 29–August 14, 1991, charged by the CTSP with the founding of a "third republic" based on "legality and freedom," 1,000 delegates from 42 parties and 100 associations drafted a new constitution, which the government pledged to put to a referendum on December 1 in anticipation of multiparty elections in early 1992. However, in November the government extended the transition period to March 26, 1992, citing difficulties in establishing an electoral system and its inability to guarantee safe polling sites for voters in the north, where Tuareg insurgents had long been active.

On January 12, 1992, the new basic law was approved by 98.35 percent of referendum participants. One week later the Alliance for Democracy in Mali (*Alliance pour la Démocratie au Mali*—Adema) won a majority of seats in municipal balloting. Both polls, as well as legislative balloting in February–March, were marred by low voter turnout, coupled with allegations of electoral fraud and inappropriate CTSP support for Adema. In addition, a number of parties protested a reported CTSP decision to assign Tuareg groups uncontested legislative seats as an outgrowth of a National Peace Pact concluded with the rebels on March 25. Nonetheless, after a one-month postponement, Adema leader Alpha Oumar KONARÉ led eight competitors in first-round presidential balloting on April 12 and went on to defeat Tréoulé Mamadou KONATÉ by a 40 percent margin two weeks later. On June 8 Younoussi TOURÉ, a former Central Bank president, was named to succeed Sacko as prime minister.

On May 18, 1993, the Supreme Court upheld death sentences that had been passed on former President Traoré and three associates for causing the "premeditated murder" of 106 persons during prodemocracy riots in the capital in March 1991. Meanwhile, an escalation of student riots, which had commenced seven months earlier, yielded arson attacks on a number of public installations, including the National Assembly building. On April 9, in response to the unrest, President Konaré announced the resignation of the Touré government and appointed defense minister Abdoulaye Sekou SOW to head a new administration.

On November 7, 1993, citing austerity concerns, Prime Minister Sow downsized his fledgling cabinet; however, Adema membership in the reshuffled, technocratic government grew as its members replaced three nonparty ministers. On December 9 the government confirmed reports that an imprisoned former Traoré aide, Lt. Col. Oumar DIALLO, and five others had been charged with plotting to "topple democratic institutions" and "dispose" of anyone opposed to Diallo's release.

On February 2, 1994, Sow became the second consecutive prime minister to resign amid student protests over government spending decisions. Collaterally, Sow echoed his predecessor that Adema members had undermined his premiership. Two days later President Konaré named an Adema member, Ibrahim Boubacar KEITA, as the new prime minister. On February 6 the cabinet was thrown into disarray when ministers from the National Congress for Democratic Initiative (*Congrès National d'Initiative Démocratique*—CNID) and the Rally for Democracy and Progress (*Rassemblement pour la Démocratie et le Progrès*—RDP) resigned, with CNID leader Mountaga TALL accusing the administration of having "marginalized" non-Adema ministers. Subsequently, the government named by Keita on February 7 included only 16 members, 11 from Adema, and 5 from minor parties.

The military conflict between the government and Tuaregs unofficially ended in June 1995 when the last active rebel group, the Arab Islamic Front of the Azawad, halted its guerrilla campaign and announced its interest in peace negotiations. In November the government announced that approximately 20,000 Tuareg refugees had returned from exile in Mauritania. By February 1996 more than 3,000 former rebels had reportedly been integrated into the armed forces.

On March 4, 1997, President Konaré dissolved the assembly in anticipation of assembly elections in April. The first of two rounds of balloting was held on April 13; however, the polling was marred by reported gross irregularities, including a shortage of balloting papers. Consequently, on April 25 the Constitutional Court annulled the first-round results and indefinitely postponed the second round. At the same time, the court ordered that preparations for presidential polling continue, thus ignoring opposition threats to boycott such balloting if it preceded the assembly balloting.

In presidential elections on May 11, 1997, Konaré garnered 95.9 percent of the vote, overwhelming his sole opponent, Mamadou Maribatourou DIABY of the small Unity, Development, and Progress Party (*Parti pour l'Unité, le Développement, et le Progrès*—PUDP). Eight other opposition candidates boycotted the polling, which was marked by a low voter turnout and antigovernment demonstrations. Subsequently, in two rounds of legislative balloting on July 20 and August 3, Adema candidates also easily dominated an electoral field depleted by an opposition boycott. On September 13 Konaré reappointed Prime Minister Keita, who rejected opposition calls for a "unity" government and named a cabinet on September 16 that was dominated by propresidential parties and moderate opposition groups.

President Konaré made a number of conciliatory gestures to his opponents in the second half of 1997, including releasing opposition members arrested during the violent unrest that surrounded the May–August polling and reducing the death sentences of former President Traoré and his associates to life imprisonment. The president's pledge to convene an all-inclusive national forum gained momentum in mid-April 1998, when a broad range of opposition groups responded positively to a conciliatory proposal brokered by former U.S. president Jimmy Carter. However, on April 20 hard-line opposition groups in the Collective of Opposition Political Parties (*Coordination des Partis Politiques de l'Opposition*—COPPO) refused to attend a government-sponsored summit, asserting that the government representatives lacked legitimacy and vowing to boycott the upcoming local elections and launch a civil disobedience campaign.

In balloting on June 21, 1998, Adema candidates captured an overwhelming number of mayoral and local council posts. In August the government announced that further local polling, then tentatively scheduled for November, would be postponed in the hopes of avoiding an opposition boycott. The Konaré administration reportedly remained intent on convincing opposition hard-liners to participate in future polling, since their previous boycotts had undermined the credibility of Mali's democratization and decentralization efforts. In January 1999 the government convened an internationally monitored national forum to garner input from Malian political leaders on the electoral process. However, only four of the parties aligned with the so-called radical opposition attended, and COPPO again urged its supporters not to vote in the May 2 and June 5, 1999, balloting, in which Adema secured about 60 percent of the seats on local councils.

Prime Minister Keita resigned on February 14, 2000, to campaign for the 2002 presidential election and was succeeded the following day by Mande SIDIBÉ, one of President Konaré's economic advisors. The cabinet announced on February 21 included 15 new ministers. The president had announced he would not attempt to circumvent the two-term limit despite encouragement from his supporters, and reportedly Touré who was gearing up for a presidential run. At midyear COPPO leaders announced plans to present a coalition opposition candidate in the campaign. Indeed, Touré resigned from his army post in September 2001 as required by law to be able to run for the presidency in 2002.

Forty parties signed a "pact of good conduct" in January 2001 in preparation for the 2002 balloting. However, late in the year President Konaré suspended plans for a referendum on new electoral laws approved by the assembly in mid-2000 based on recommendations from the 1999 national forum. In February 2002 the assembly adopted new electoral legislation that did not require a referendum, paving the way for first-round presidential balloting in late April and legislative elections in July. Most parties agreed to participate in the polls despite daunting challenges, including economic malaise resulting from depressed export prices and ongoing inadequacies in the health and education sectors.

Prime Minister Sidibé resigned on March 18, 2002, to contest the upcoming presidential election. He was succeeded by former president Modibo Keita. In the first round of balloting on April 28, Touré, backed by a number of parties, finished first among more than 20 candidates. He was elected president on May 12 by securing about 64 percent of the vote in a runoff against Soumaïla CISSÉ of Adema. Touré appointed Mohamed Ag AMANI (nonparty) as the new prime minister on June 9; on June 15 a new "national unity" cabinet was named that included members of a number of parties as well as independents. One of President Touré's first acts was to pardon former President Traoré in an attempt to promote national unity and reconciliation..

In controversial assembly balloting on July 14 and 28, 2002, Hope 2002 (*Espoir 2002*) (an alliance of parties upset over the conduct of the first round of the presidential poll) won 66 seats, followed by the Alliance for the Republic and Democracy (a coalition that included Adema and others) with 51 seats, and Alternation and Change (a coalition of parties that had supported Touré in the presidential balloting) with 10.

In by-elections on October 20, 2002, Adema won all 8 seats being contested and became the largest single party in the assembly with 53 seats. Hope 2002, with 66 seats, combined with 19 presidential-supportive deputies to create a stable presidential majority within the legislature.

Local elections on May 30, 2003, were relatively free of the problems that had surrounded the 2002 presidential and assembly elections. In part due to a government campaign to encourage voting, turnout was high, and more than 20 parties won seats, and Hope 2002 secured a majority of the mayoral posts.

Prime Minister Ag Amani resigned on April 28, 2004, and was replaced by former transport minister Ousmane Issoufi MAIGA (non-party). Maiga formed a new cabinet on May 2.

As the candidate of the new Alliance for Democracy and Progress (*Alliance pour la Démocratie et le Progrès*—ADP), President Touré was reelected to a second term in the first round of balloting on April 29, 2007, with 68 percent of the vote, followed by former Prime Minister Ibrahim Boubacar Keita of the FDR with only 19 percent. A voter registration drive produced more than 500,000 new voters for the balloting, although turnout for the poll was only 36 percent. President Touré had little problem securing reelection, especially since the new propresidential ADP now included Adema and the UDD. Opposition parties condemned the balloting as fraudulent, but international observers generally described the poll as free and fair.

Touré subsequently reappointed Prime Minister Maiga and most of the incumbent cabinet ministers. The ADP also dominated the two-round assembly balloting in July, capturing 113 seats while the coalition led by the FDR won 30, the African Solidarity for Democracy and Independence (*Solidarité Africaine pour la Démocratie et l'Indépendence*—SADI) won 4, and independent candidates took another 15. Maiga resigned from the prime minister post on September 27, and was replaced the next day by Modibo SIDIBÉ, a technocrat without a leadership role in any political party.

President Touré reshuffled the cabinet on April 9, 2009, reappointing Sidibé and moving several of the prime minister's political allies into key cabinet position. This move was believed to send a message to party leaders in Adema and the ADP coalition that the president is not yet interested in advancing a prospective successor for the 2012 presidential election but rather in maintaining technocrats capable of carrying out the president's policy priorities. The reshuffle also came shortly before municipal elections on April 26, 2009. Voter turnout was low at about 45 percent, and Adema/PASJ and URD candidates were the top winners, securing 3,186 seats (29.65 percent) and 1,935 seats (17.94 percent) respectively.

Constitution and government. The constitution adopted at independence was abrogated by the military in November 1968. A new constitution was approved by referendum on June 2, 1974, but did not enter into force until June 19, 1979. The constitution drafted by the National Conference of July 29–August 14, 1991, and approved by referendum on January 12, 1992, replaced the interim *Acte Fondamental* that the CTSP had promulgated in April 1991 following abrogation of the 1974 document. The current basic law includes an extensive bill of individual rights, a charter for political parties, guarantees of trade union and press freedoms, and separation of executive, legislative, and judicial powers. A directly elected president, who may serve no more than two five-year terms, appoints a prime minister and other cabinet members, who are, however, responsible to a popularly elected unicameral National Assembly. The judicial system is headed by a Supreme Court, which is divided into judicial, administrative, and fiscal sections. There is also a nine-member Constitutional Court, while a High Court of Justice is empowered to hear cases of treason.

Mali is administratively divided into eight regions, the eighth being created in May 1991 by the halving of a northern region as a concession to Tuareg separatists. The regions, headed by appointed governors, are subdivided into 46 districts (*cercles*) and 282 counties (*arrondissements*), also administered by appointed officials. Most municipalities have elected councils, which have been given increased authority in connection with the government's recent decentralization program.

Foreign relations. Reflecting a commitment to "dynamic nonalignment," Mali improved its relations with France, Britain, the United States, and other Western nations under General Traoré. It also cultivated links to China and Russia and emerged as a dynamic regional player through the leadership of former president Konaré as chair of the Economic Community of West African States (Ecowas) in 1999, as head of the African Union (AU) from September 2003 to February 2008, and for his efforts to resolve civil conflicts in Sierra Leone and Côte d'Ivoire.

For two decades Mali was locked in a dispute with Burkina Faso (formerly Upper Volta) over ownership of the 100-mile long, 12-mile wide Agacher strip between the two countries. The controversy, which triggered a number of military encounters (including a four-day battle in December 1985), was finally settled by a ruling in late 1986 from the International Court of Justice that divided the disputed territory into roughly equal parts, with the border being defined in accordance with traditional patterns of nomadic passage. Both governments responded quickly to a subsequent land clash between local groups in 2006. Similar clashes involving Mauritania were followed by a border demarcation agreement in May 1988.

Relations with Libya cooled due to the latter's involvement in the Chadian civil war. In early 1981 a number of Libyan embassy personnel in Bamako were expelled; relations were further exacerbated by the expulsion of some 2,500 Malian workers from Libya in 1985 as part of Qadhafi's drive to reduce its dependence on foreign labor. Subsequently, Mali charged Libya with supporting Tuareg insurgents in northern Mali. In August 2006 Libya announced that it would close its consulate in the northeast region of Kidal in Mali. The consulate was opposed by many in Mali who perceived it as an effort by Libya to expand its influence in the region. However, relations have since improved with Mali's membership in the Community of Sahelo-Saharan States (*Communauté des États Sahélo–Sahariens*), which is backed by Libya, and by Qadhafi's rise to the presidency of the African Union in Feburary 2009.

In January 1991 the Algerian government mediated a truce between the Malian government and moderate Tuareg party leaders. International diplomatic efforts were credited with generating tripartite agreements among Algeria, Mali, and Niger in 1992, which resulted in the repatriation of thousands of Tuaregs from Algeria in August 1993 and the creation of accommodation centers in Algeria for exiles fleeing the countries' drought and civil unrest. Negotiations between Mali and Algeria in February 1995 yielded an accord on border security issues. In July 2003 Islamic militants in Algeria held a group of European tourists hostage in a remote region of Mali, which they released on August 8 following negotiations led by former Tuareg rebels. Mali subsequently agreed to increase border security with Algeria and to increase antiterrorism cooperation with Algeria, Chad, and Niger. Algeria also assisted the Malian government and Tuareg rebels to reach another peace deal after the mutiny in the Kidal region in July 2006. The countries remain close partners in combating Islamist extremist activity in the region; Algeria recently increased its military aid to Mali following a visit of Mali's defense minister to Algiers in April 2009.

Relations with France warmed under President Sarkozy but remained challenged by France's increasingly strong anti-immigration policies. In 1998, the two countries created a joint commission to repatriate Malians living illegally in France, and the French government agreed to fund programs to help the returning Malians reintegrate into society.

Relations with Côte d'Ivoire were strained following a coup attempt in that country in January 2001. Ivorian authorities reportedly unofficially implied that Mali and Burkina Faso had backed the overthrow effort, and many Malians living in Côte d'Ivoire at the time were attacked when the armed rebellion began in 2002.

The United States considers Mali an important ally in the region because of its democratic government and its commitment to fight terrorism. The growing presence of foreign Islamic extremists, mainly from Pakistan and Afghanistan, prompted the Malian government in 2004 to seek international counterterrorism aid, prompting U.S. military advisers to initiate an antiterrorism training program for the Malian armed forces. This followed several U.S.-sponsored military training exercises in Mali and several years of U.S. security assistance in the form of equipment and financial aid. The government also gave permission for U.S. special operations units to undertake antiterrorism missions in the north of the country, where Algerian militants had reportedly established a presence. The United States subsequently announced it would use its Malian base as a headquarters for regional antiterrorism efforts.

Mali signed a broad economic agreement with China in early 2006, and China was Mali's top export destination. In return for increased exports of cotton from Mali to China, China agreed to expand investment in Mali's agriculture, tourism, and telecommunications sectors. China's President Hu Jintao visited Mali in February 2009, further expanding bilateral relations.

Current issues. Tuareg rebels renewed their fight against the government by launching attacks on several cities and military bases in the north in May 2006. In July an accord was announced, but sporadic fighting continued; reports indicated that groups backed by al-Qaida, known as Al-Qaida in the Islamic Maghreb (AQIM), had established camps in northern Mali..Another pact was signed in February 2007 under the auspices of Algeria in which the Tuaregs agreed to disarm in exchange for their integration into the military and government economic investment in the region. By March more than 600 rebels had turned over their arms and become part of the national security forces. However, some disaffected Tuaregs kidnapped 40 military personnel in late 2007 in the northeast of the country. All have since been released, and the government has taken steps to address the political demands of the remaining rebels, now called the Tuareg Alliance for Change of Northern Mali (*Alliance Touareg Nord–Mali pour le Changement*—ATNMC) and led by Ibrahim Ag BAHANGA, in part due to fear that they will build alliances with armed Islamist groups in the region. With Libya's assistance, a truce was signed between the government and ATNMC in April 2008.

Since then, Ag Bahanga and his loyalists continued sporadic attacks, though Ag Bahanga fled to Libya in February 2009 as a result of a government military offensive to defeat those Tuaregs refusing to abide by the 2006 accord and subsequent truce. President Touré has continued to reach out to other Tuareg leaders, further isolating Ag Bahanga, and recently formed a new Saharan security force made of primarily of former Tuareg rebels. Government forces continued to struggle to rout the disaffected Tuaregs and AQIM loyalists and to curb drug and illegal-immigrant smuggling through its vast territory. In February 2009 four European tourists were kidnapped in eastern Mali. Meanwhile, the AQIM was reportedly responsible for the murder of a British tourist in northern Mali in late May 2009 and for killing several dozen Malian soldiers on July 4, 2009.

In 2009 the government of Mali continued to struggle with the privatization of several major parastatals; the effort was slowed by the worldwide recession that began in 2008, though the government announced in July 2009 that it sold a majority stake in its public telecommunications company (Sotelma) to Maroc Telecom. Since Mali is the leading cotton producer in sub-Saharan Africa, the proposed sale of the national cotton company, the *Compagnie Malienne pour le Développement des Textiles* (CMDT)—which the government wanted to divide into four regional units before privatization—was particularly controversial, which has caused a decrease in cotton production over the last few years. The government completed negotiations with the IMF over the country's 2008–2011 poverty reduction and growth facility (PRGF) in May 2008 Mali is expected to meet its development targets over the next few years, significantly increasing investment in education, agricultural production, and oversight over the mining sector.

Due to rising international food prices, the government of Mali introduced a six-month suspension of customs on rice imports in April 2008 to avoid civil unrest. Meanwhile, the major political actors began to look towards the 2012 presidential elections. The constitution limits presidents to two consecutive terms of office, preventing President Touré from standing for reelection in 2012. However, some speculated that President Touré would attempt, with ADP support, to amend the constitution to allow for a third consecutive term. Similarly, as former president Konaré finished his tenure as head of the African Union in early 2008 and returned to Mali, some surmised that he could attempt to run for president again in 2012, as the constitution does not expressly prohibit former presidents who have left office from running again.

Islamic religious leadership and some other civil society groups strong protested a new family law passed by the Malian National Assembly on August 3, 2009. The law stipulated new social and legal rules that some Malian Muslims considered contrary to Koranic teaching, such as making women and men equal before the law, expanding inheritance rights for widows and female children, outlawing marriage of girls younger than 18 years old, and no longer recognizing traditional Muslim marriages as legal. After weeks of protests, President Touré announced that he would not sign the law but would send it back to the National Assembly for further study.

POLITICAL PARTIES

Sixteen political parties grouped into five alliances are currently represented in Mali's national assembly, though others are active at the local government level. The only authorized party prior to the March 1991 coup was the **Malian People's Democratic Union** (*Union Démocratique du Peuple Malien*—UDPM), but was dissolved in the wake of Traoré's ouster. Public demonstrations that preceded the 1991 coup were orchestrated by a number of groups (including Adema), which were linked by a Coordination Committee of Democratic Associations and Organizations, which joined the CRN in forming the CTSP on March 30, after which both it and the CRN were dissolved, and on April 5 the CTSP authorized the formation of political parties. By late 1991 approximately 50 formations, many with links to pre-1968 political personalities or groups, had applied for legal status, though only 27 parties presented legislative candidates in 1992.

In May 1992, representatives of 13 parties announced the formation of a **Front to Safeguard Democracy** (*Front Sauvegarde de la Démocratie*—FSD) under the reported leadership of the US/RDA's Tréoulé Konaté and the RDP's Almamy SYLLA to oppose Adema. In August 1995 a number of senior leaders left the group following a dispute with Konaté. In October 1996 Adema formed a progovernment alliance, the **National Convention for Democracy and Progress** (*Convention Nationale pour la Démocratie et le Progrès*—CNDP), which included the CDS, Parena, and others, and the formation of another opposition alliance, the **Rally for Patriotic Forces** (*Rassemblement pour les Forces Patriotiques*—RFP), was reported. A number of opposition parties boycotted the 1997 legislative balloting after the president refused to reschedule presidential elections (held on May 11) until after assembly polling.

In 1998 the differences between the hard-line and moderate opposition widened. Loosely coalesced under the banner of the **Collective of Opposition Political Parties** (*Coordination des Partis Politiques de l'Opposition*—COPPO), the former rejected the administration's plans for an all-inclusive national forum and demanded both a reform of the electoral system and direct talks with the president. However, despite a proposal brokered by former U.S. president Jimmy Carter requiring the Konaré government to reformulate the electoral commission, reschedule municipal elections, and revise the electoral list in exchange for the opposition's agreement to recognize the results of the 1997 elections, the COPPO alliance subsequently fell apart. Meanwhile, in late January 1999 three centrist groups—the COPP, PDP, and UDD—formed a **Convention for the Republic and Democracy** (*Convention pour la République et la Démocratie*—CRD) under the leadership of Mamadou GAKOU.

In 2000 and 2001 tension between the government and most opposition parties significantly thawed, and by June 2000 almost all of the parties that boycotted the 1997 polling decided to contest the 2002 presidential and legislative elections. In connection with the balloting, three main electoral coalitions emerged. The first was the **Alliance for Alternation and Change** (*Alliance pour L'Alternance et le Changement*—ACC), which consisted of some 28 parties (including Parena, the US/RDA, UFDP, BDIA, MIRIA, RAMAT, and PDR) and provided President Touré a political base in the assembly. The second coalition was the **Alliance for the Republic and Democracy** (*Alliance pour la République et la Démocratie*—ARD), which included Adema, the UDD, and others. Adema and the UDD each presented their own candidates in the first round of the presidential poll but then cooperated in the presidential runoff and legislative balloting. The third grouping was **Hope 2002** (*Espoir 2002*), which was formed by some 15 parties (including the CNID, RPM, MPR, and RDP) following the first round of the presidential balloting, which Hope 2002 described as "rigged" in favor of Adema. Hope 2002 supported Amadou Touré in the second round of the presidential poll. In the legislative elections, Hope 2002 became the largest single group within the assembly, though none of the three coalitions won a clear majority, and President Touré formed a consensus government that faced no serious opposition for the following two years.

In 2005 Mali's National Assembly passed a new statute on political parties that tightened regulation on the creation, organization, and financing of parties and requires all parties to be registered in more than one person's name.

For the 2007 presidential and legislative elections, more than 40 parties came together to form the **Alliance for Democracy and Progress** (*Alliance pour le Démocratie and le Progrès*—ADP) to support Touré's reelection. Both Touré and the ADP easily won the presidential and legislative elections. However, political disunity within ADEMA-PASJ and other Malian parties since the 2007 balloting presented a formidable challenge to Touré's government, a trend which will likely accelerate as President Touré's term comes to an end in 2012 and party leaders within Adema jockey for the party's nomination. The conflict will be complicated by an informal political association of Touré supporters known as the **Citizens' Movement** (*Mouvement Citoyen*—MC). The group came into existence around the time of Touré's 2002 election and boasts membership from a variety of political parties and civil society organization. The MC is currently led by Hamed Diané SÉMÉGA. In January 2008, several prominent members of the RPM broke off to form a new political party, called the **Front for Mali's Development** (*Front pour le Développement du Mali–Mali Niéta Jekulu*—FDM/MNJ).

Government Parties:

Alliance for Democracy and Progress (*Alliance pour le Démocratie et le Progrès*—ADP). Formed to support the incumbent

Amadou Toumani Touré in the presidential election, the ADP included more than 40 parties. Touré won the April 2007 balloting and the ADP won a strong majority (113 seats) in the subsequent July legislative elections.

Leaders: Dioncounda TRAORÉ (Speaker of the National Assembly), Mountaga TALL.

Alliance for Democracy in Mali/Pan African Party for Liberty, Solidarity, and Justice (*Alliance pour la Démocratie au Mali/ Parti Pan-Africain pour la Solidarité et la Justice*—Adema/PASJ). A principal organizer of anti-Traoré demonstrations and subsequently among those groups represented in the CTSP, Adema registered for legal status in April 1991. Adema candidates won substantial majorities in all three 1992 elections, securing 214 municipal council seats and 76 National Assembly seats. Adema also captured the presidency on April 26 with a 70 percent second-round vote share.

At the party's first congress on July 8–14, 1993, dissident members released a manifesto calling for the "appointment to positions of responsibility [within the party] . . . of competent men and women of integrity" and the "destruction of the old state apparatus." Moreover, former prime ministers Touré and Sow both cited subversive activities by "radical" elements within Adema as among their reasons for resigning from the party. Observers attributed the intraparty friction to a conflict between members identifying with the former prime ministers and favoring integration of non-Adema political groups into the government and a smaller faction advocating Adema's unilateral rule.

At a party congress on September 25–27, 1994, founding member and Chair Mohamed Lamine Traoré lost his post in an action spearheaded by Prime Minister Ibrahim Boubacar Keita, who had hinted at dramatic party changes at his investiture. Subsequently, Traoré, Secretary General Mohamedoun DICKO, and a number of other senior members resigned from the party; two months later the dissidents launched MIRIA (below).

In February 1996 Adema signed a cooperation agreement with Parena, a newly founded group led by former Konaré ministers and dissidents from the CNID, which called for the establishment of a committee to implement a joint government program and electoral alliance pact.

At an Adema congress on December 5–6, 1997, debate on how to reintegrate disenfranchised opposition groups into the political process dominated the agenda. In 1998 relations between Adema and the majority of its hard-line opponents grew more distant. On the other hand, at a much heralded summit in May, Adema and representatives of the MPR (below) discussed adopting cooperative tactics to avert further violence.

In February 1999 Adema held its fifth national congress amid reports that it was divided by intraparty squabbling. Although Konaré reportedly emerged from the congress heralding the health of his party, continued factionalization was subsequently reported between Keita's supporters and his critics, led by Secretary General Ali Nouhoun DIALLO. Despite such opposition, Keita was reelected as party chair in October. He resigned from all his party duties, however, in October 2000 in reaction to the advances registered by the "reformist" wing. Keita then launched his own formation, the RPM (below). In March 2002, in a bitterly contested party election, Adema chose Soumaïla Cissé over former Prime Minister Mandé Sidibé to be the party's presidential candidate. However, Cissé was defeated in the second round of the presidential poll. Subsequently, Adema's parliamentary majority was reduced from 128 seats to 53 in legislative balloting, although the party remained the largest single group in the assembly. The electoral decline led to infighting within the party, and Cissé led a group of dissident members in the formation of a new rival party, the URD (below).

In 2006 former defense minister Soumaylou Boubèye MAIGA announced he intended to seek Adema's nomination for the 2007 presidential election. However, Adema subsequently was instrumental in the formation of the ADP, which endorsed President Touré. Maiga consequently ran in the election as the leader of a small grouping, Convergence 2007, and was endorsed by the "rival" FDR (see below). In the 2007 legislative balloting, Adema won 51 of the ADP's 113 seats and became the largest party in the assembly. Party leader Dioncounda Traoré was subsequently elected president of the assembly.

Adema's ninth annual convention in March 2008 demonstrated growing divisions within the party due to political fallout from the 2007 elections following Maiga's defection to the Convergences 2007 coalition. Adema/PASJ candidates in the April 2009 municipal elections were the top winners, securing 3,186 seats (29.7 percent) and won the majority in all regions and four out of six communes in Bamako city.

Leaders: Alpha Oumar KONARÉ (Former President of the Republic), Dioncounda TRAORÉ (President of the National Assembly and President of the Party), Marimata DIARRA, Mandé SIDIBÉ (Former Prime Minister).

Union for the Republic and Democracy (*Union pour la République et la Démocratie*—URD). Launched in 2003 by former members of Adema who supported former presidential candidate Soumaïla Cissé, the URD is a centrist party that supports secularism and economic reforms. The URD won 34 seats in the 2007 legislative election and held its second party congress in April 2008. Cissé publicly expressed confidence in party president Younoussi Touré, dashing the presidential aspirations of the party's second vice president, Oumar Ibrahim Touré. URD candidates won the second largest number of seats in the April 2009 municipal elections, securing 1,935 seats (17.9 percent).

Leaders: Soumaïla CISSÉ (Founder and former presidential candidate), Younoussi TOURÉ (Party President), Lassana KONÉ (Secretary General).

Union for Democracy and Development (*Union pour la Démocratie et le Développement*—UDD). Running on a platform calling for "security, good citizenship, and clean streets," the UDD, whose founder, Moussa Balla Coulibaly, was an official in the Traoré government, won 62 seats in the 1992 municipal elections.

In 1999 it was reported that the Socialist Party for Progress and Development had merged into the UDD. In late 2001 Coulibaly was nominated as the UDD's presidential candidate in the 2002 polling. Coulibaly was eliminated in the first round, and the UDD supported Soumaïla Cissé of Adema in the second round.

Leader: Moussa Balla COULIBALY (Chair and 2002 presidential candidate).

National Congress for Democratic Initiative (*Congrès National d'Initiative Démocratique*—CNID). Launched in 1990 as the National Committee for Democratic Initiative (*Comité National d'Initiative Démocratique*), the CNID was included in the April 1991 formation of the CTSP in recognition of its role in the overthrow of the Traoré regime. In 1992 the party, supported by a predominantly youthful constituency, secured 96 municipal and 9 National Assembly seats. On April 12 Mountaga Tall, the party's 35-year-old presidential candidate, finished third in the first presidential round, with 11.41 percent of the vote.

On March 26, 1995, on the eve of the party's first conference, a group of dissidents reacted to the expulsion of ten governing committee members by holding a rival conference of the "true" CNID (see Parena, below).

In 1998 the CNID emerged as one of the most prominent of the radical opposition groups, organizing boycotts of the June polling and allegedly attempting to interfere with polling. The group's stance toward the government reportedly softened in 2000 and 2001, and the CNID participated in presidential and legislative polling in 2002. Tall finished fifth as the CNID's candidate in the first round of presidential balloting in 2002 with 3.75 percent of the vote. The CNID subsequently joined Espoir 2002 for the legislative poll, reportedly securing 13 of Espoir 2002's seats.

The CNID's representation was reduced to seven seats following the 2007 assembly elections, in which it participated in the ADP. The party has since suffered from a rift among its senior leadership over party activities in part of Bamako city.

Leaders: Mountaga TALL (Chair), Fanta Mantchini DIARRA (Senior Deputy), N'Diaye BAH (Secretary General).

Sudanese Union/African Democratic Rally (*Union Soudanaise/Rassemblement Démocratique Africain*—US/RDA). The Malian wing of the RDA was formed in the aftermath of an RDA convention in Bamako in 1946. Supported by a rural constituency, the group came to power with the formation of Modibo Keita's post-independence government in 1960 but went underground following his ouster in 1968.

At a special congress in January 1992, the US/RDA split over the selection of a presidential candidate. Members initially selected Tréoulé Mamadou KONATÉ, the son of an RDA founder and an advocate of purging "Stalinism" from the party, but the party leadership ultimately repudiated the action, nominating instead former UN official Baba Hakib HAIDARA. Subsequently, both stood as candidates, with Konaté outpolling his rival in the first round but securing only 30 percent of the second-round vote in a contest with Alpha Oumar Konaré. In October 1995 Konaté was killed in a car crash, and in January 1996 the party ousted Secretary General Mamadou Bachir Gologo in favor of Mamadou Bamou TOURÉ.

In mid-May 1998, 29 senior US/RDA members led by political secretary Daba DIAWARA issued a statement allying themselves with party leader Seydou Badian KOUATÉ, who, in defiance of the US/RDA's official stance, had declared that the group should recognize the government and participate in the local elections scheduled for June. Touré then attempted to suspend the 29 members, who, in turn, rejected the legitimacy of his leadership, asserting that his earlier unwillingness to implement reconciliation initiatives approved by the party's governing organs had undermined his authority. The moderate tendency of the US/RDA participated in the 1999 local elections.

The US/RDA supported former president Amadou Touré's presidential campaign in 2002. It reportedly won three seats as part of the ACC in the 2002 legislative balloting. In August 2003, Mamadou Bamou Touré resigned as secretary general of the party.

Leader: Mamadou Bachir GOLOGO (President).

Patriotic Movement for Renewal (*Mouvement Patriotique pour le Renouveau*—MPR). The MPR, which describes itself as a descendant of the UDPM, was legalized in January 1995. Because of its ties to former President Traoré, the party was reportedly widely denigrated until 1997, when it assumed a prominent role in the opposition camp. In May 1998 at a highly publicized meeting with Adema, MPR representatives reportedly agreed to cooperate in efforts to control political violence. Collaterally, the MPR pressed the government to expedite the trials of the former president and his associates. Subsequently, following the splintering of the US/RDA in mid-1998, one observer described the MPR as the most "stable" of the moderate opposition groups. Nevertheless, in January 1999 MPR activists clashed with security forces when the former attempted to march from their own meeting to the site of the national forum.

The MPR was described by *Africa Confidential* in 1999 as being "openly aligned" with the imprisoned Traoré but committed to the pursuit of "national reconciliation." Indeed, in 2000 the group decided to participate in presidential and legislative elections in 2002, nominating Choguel MAIGA for president. Maiga received 2.71 percent of the vote, and the MPR joined Espoir 2002 for the subsequent legislative balloting.

Leader: Choguel MAIGA (President and 2002 presidential candidate).

Other minor parties in the ADP include the **Democratic Bloc for African Integration** (*Bloc Démocratique pour l'Intégration Africaine*—BDIA), a liberal party formed in 1993 under the leadership of Youssouf TRAORÉ that won three seats in the 2002 assembly elections and one in 2007; the **Alternation Bloc for Renewal, Integration, and African Cooperation** (*Bloc des Alternances pour la Renaissance, l'Intégration, et la Coopération Afrique*—BARICA), formed in 2004; the **Movement for African Independence, Renewal, and Integration** (*Mouvement pour l'Indépendence, la Renaissance, et l'Intégration Africaine*—MIRIA), established by dissident members of Adema, including Mohamed Lamine TRAORÉ; the **National Rally for Democracy** (*Rassemblement National pour la Démocratie*—RND), established in 1997 and led by Abdoulaye Garba TAPO; the **Solidarity and Progress Party** (*Parti de la Solidarité et du Progrès*—PSP); and the **Citizens' Party for Renewal** (*Parti Citoyen pour le Renouveau*—PCR), formed in July 2005.

Opposition Parties:

Front for Democracy and the Republic (*Front pour la Démocratie et la République*—FDR). The FDR was formed by some 16 parties in advance of the 2007 elections to oppose the reelection of President Touré. Former defense minister and Adema member Soumaylou Boubèye MAIGA and RPM leader Ibrahim Boubacar Keita were the main forces behind the creation of the new coalition. The FDR ran presidential candidates from four of its member parties, including the small, newly formed Convergence 2007, led by Adema dissident Soumaylou Maiga, in an unsuccessful effort to force a runoff election. It has so far proved unable to contest the dominance of the ADP and President Touré, as it lost many seats in the 2007 elections. The party did, however, pick up a seat in a March 2008 by-election in Sikasso.

Leaders: Ibrahim Boubacar KEITA, Tiéblé DRAMÉ, Soumaylou Boubèye MAIGA, Mamadou SANGARÉ (2007 presidential candidates).

Rally for Mali (*Rassemblement pour le Mali*—RPM). Launched initially in February 2001 as "Alternative 2000," the RPM was a breakaway faction from Adema supportive of former Prime Minister Ibrahim Kéita, who left Adema in October 2000 and placed third in the first round of the 2002 vote with 21.03 percent. The RPM gained 46 seats in the 2002 legislative balloting as part of Espoir 2002. In September Keita was elected president of the assembly, but he resigned from that post in 2007 to run for president again, placing second in the first round with 19.15 percent of the vote. Several key members of the RPM broke away from the party in January 2008 to form the base of a new Malian political formation, the FDM/MNJ (see entry, below). The RPM won 773 seats (7.17 percent) in the April 2009 municipal elections, the third largest number in the country.

Leaders: Ibrahim Boubacar KÉITA (2002 and 2007 presidential candidate and former President of the National Assembly), Bocary TRETA (Secretary General).

Front for Mali's Development (*Front pour le Développement du Mali–Mali Niéta Jekulu*—FDM/MNJ). Created in January 2008 with 23 members, most of whom were from the RPM but represented a variety of political movements within the country. The group claimed to form as a response to the poor governance under Touré in the spirit of the March 26, 1991, coup d'état that ousted Gen. Traoré from power. The group has come out strongly against Touré and the ADP's efforts to change the constitutional term limit for sitting presidents from two to three terms.

Leader: Harouna SISSOKO (President).

Party for National Renaissance (*Parti pour la Renaissance Nationale*—Parena). Active since March 1995, Parena was officially launched on September 18 after its founders, CNID dissidents Capt. Yoro Diakité and Tiéblé Dramé, lost their five-month legal battle for control of that party. A number of Parena leaders were former or current Konaré government ministers, a status reflected in the signing of the Parena-Adema cooperation pact in February 1996. Parena participated in the cabinet announced in 1997 but declined to accept any posts in the February 2000 government. Meanwhile, Diakité was reported to have formed a new party (see BARA, below).

In 2001 Parena distanced itself from Adema, and Dramé became the party's presidential candidate in 2002, finishing fourth in the first round of balloting with 3.99 percent of the vote. Parena reportedly won one of the ACC seats in the 2002 legislative poll. Dramé was the party's candidate in the 2007 presidential poll, in which he placed third with 3.04 percent of the vote.

Leaders: Tiéblé DRAMÉ (2007 presidential candidate and Party President), Amidou DIABATE (Secretary General).

Democratic and Social Convention (*Convention Démocratique Sociale*—CDS). The self-styled "centrist" CDS was launched by Mamadou Bakary Sangaré Kabakoro in 1996. Unlike its moderate opposition party peers, the CDS chose not to participate in the government named in September 1997, although it participated in the 1999 local elections. Sangaré received 2.21 percent of the vote in the first round of presidential balloting in 2002. The CDS joined the FDR in 2007 and Sangaré ran as one of the four presidential candidates from the coalition. He placed fifth in the balloting.

Leader: Mamadou Bakary SANGARÉ (2007 presidential candidate).

African Solidarity for Democracy and Independence (*Solidarité Africaine pour la Démocratie et l'Indépendence*—SADI). Established in 2002 prior to the presidential elections, the SADI presented Oumar MARIKO as its presidential candidate. He received less than 1 percent of the vote in the first-round balloting. In the subsequent legislative elections, the SADI won six seats. Mariko was also the party's candidate in 2007 and placed fourth in the first round of balloting with 2.7 percent of the vote. SADI legislative candidates won four seats in the July 2007 elections.

Leaders: Cheick Oumar SISSOKO, Oumar MARIKO (2002 and 2007 presidential candidate).

Other Groups:

Party for Democracy and Progress (*Parti pour la Démocratie et le Progrès*—PDP). On February 8, 1994, the PDP leadership agreed to abandon its cabinet posting, reversing an earlier decision to ignore CNID and RDP calls for an opposition boycott. However, Boubacar Karamoko COULIBALY, the youth and sports minister, refused to resign, saying he would remain as an independent. In April 1994 dissidents led by Karim TRAORE broke from the PDP to form the **Malian Alliance for Democracy and Progress–Dambe** (*Alliance Malienne pour la Démocratie et le Progrès-Dambe*—AMDP-Dambe).

Leader: Mady KONATÉ.

Block of Alternatives for African Renewal (*Bloc des Alternatives pour le Renouveau Africain*—BARA). Formed in 1999 under the direction of Capt. Yoro Diakité, a former leader of Parena, the BARA pledged to pursue "unity" and "African integration." In 2001 BARA was reportedly working with the UDD and the CND to support the presidential bid of UDD chair Moussa Balla Coulibaly. In December 2003 BARA announced its opposition to President Touré's government, though it held no seats in the National Assembly.

Leaders: Capt. Yoro DIAKITÉ (Chair), Inza COULIBALY (Secretary General).

Union of Democratic Forces for Progress (*Union des Forces Démocratiques pour le Progrès*—UFDP). The UFDP was launched in 1991 under the leadership of Demqo DIALLO, a prominent human rights advocate and champion of efforts to oust Moussa Traoré. A pro-Konaré grouping, the UFDP joined the CNDP in 1997 and criticized antigovernment protesters. Diallo died in June 2001, and a July national congress of the party (now also sometimes referred to as the Union of Forces of Progress) elected Shaka Diarra as the new chair. The UFDF failed to gain any seats in the 2007 legislative elections.

Leaders: Shaka DIARRA (Chair), Youssouf TRAORE (Secretary General).

In the 2007 presidential election, Sidibé Aminata DIALLO was the candidate of the **Movement for Environmental Education and Sustainable Development** (*Rassemblement pour l'Éducation á l'Énvironnement et Développement Durableé*—REDD), while Madiassa MAGUIRAGA was the candidate of the **Popular Party for Progress** (*Parti Populaire pour le Progrès*—PPP). Both candidates received less than 1 percent of the vote. (Diallo was Mali's first female presidential candidate.) Mamadou Maribatourou Diaby, the incumbent's sole challenger in the 1997 presidential balloting, was a member of the **Unity, Development, and Progress Party** (*Parti pour l'Unité, le Développement, et le Progrès*—PUDP). Diaby also ran unsuccessfully for the presidency in 2002. Other minor parties include the **Civic Society** (*Société Civique*—SC); the **Movement for Democracy and Development** (*Mouvement pour la Démocratie et le Développement*—MPDD); the **Party for Unity and Progress** (*Parti pour l'Unité et le Progrès*—PUP), led by former UDPM official Nock Ag ATTIA; the **Popular Movement for Development** (*Mouvement Populaire pour le Développement*—MPD); the **Soudanese Progress Party** (*Parti Soudanais du Progrès*—PSP), which is led by African Development Bank consultant Oumar Hammadoun DICKO and which was awarded two assembly seats in 1992 by the Supreme Court after successfully suing Adema for electoral fraud.

In August 1998 members of the **Barefooted Ones** (*Pied Nus*), a Muslim sect led by Cheikh Ibrahim Khalil KANOUTE, killed a judge in Dioila for imprisoning one of their colleagues and then clashed with local security officials. Seeming to go into hibernation for many subsequent years, members of the groups reportedly killed a woman in January 2008 in a village about 25 miles (40 km) northeast of Bamako. The group reportedly rejects all forms of Western and modern influences and has protested against the government's adherence to internationally prescribed economic structural adjustment programs.

In November 2001 the former leader of the PDP, Idrissa TRAORE, formed the **Party for Democracy and Self-Sufficiency** (*Parti pour la Démocratie et l'Autosuffisance*—PDA). Other active parties include the **National Democratic Convention** (*Convention Nationale Démocrate*—CND); the **Convention for Progress and the People** (*Convention pour le Progrès et le Peuple*—COPP), led by Mamadou Gakou; the **Malian Rally for Labor** (*Rassemblement Malien pour le Travail*—RAMAT), which won two seats in the 2002 legislative elections under the leadership of Abdoulaye MAKO; and the **Party for Democracy and Renewal** (*Parti pour la Démocratie et le Renouveau*—PDR), which won one seat in the 2002 assembly balloting under the leadership of Adama KONE. Other minor parties in Hope 2002 included **the Party for Independence, Democracy, and Solidarity** (*Parti pour l'Indépendence, la Démocratie, et la Solidarité*—PIDS), formed by dissenters from the US/RDA in September 2001 and led by Daba DIAWARA; and the **Rally for Democracy and Labor** (*Rassemblement pour la Démocratie et le Travail*—RDT), formed in 1991 and led by Amadou Ali NIANGADOU.

For information on the Azwad Liberation Front (*Front pour la Libération de l'Azaouad*—FLA), and the Movements and Fronts of Azawad (*Mouvements et Fronts Unifiés de l'Azaouad*—MFUA), see the 1996 *Handbook*. For more information on the Rally for Democracy and Progress (*Rassemblement pour la Démocratie et le Progrès*—RDP), see the 2008 *Handbook*.

LEGISLATURE

Following the March 1991 coup, the UDPM-dominated legislature was dissolved, with its powers assigned to the CTSP. The current **National Assembly** (*Assemblée Nationale*) contains 147 members serving (subject to dissolution) five-year terms. Legislators are directly elected in two-round balloting (as necessary) from 125 constituencies. Following balloting on July 1 and 22, 2007, the Alliance for Democracy and Progress held 113 seats, (the Alliance for Democracy in Mali/Pan African Party for Liberty, Solidarity, and Justice, 51; the Union for the Republic and Democracy, 34; the Patriotic Movement for Renewal, 8; the National Congress for Democratic Initiative, 7; the Union for Democracy and Development, 3; the Alternation Bloc for Renewal, Integration, and African Cooperation, 2; the Solidarity and Progress Party, 2; the Movement for African Independence, Renewal, and Integration, 2; the Democratic Bloc for African Integration, 1; the National Rally for Democracy, 1; the Citizens' Party for Renewal, 1; and the Soudanese Union/African Democratic Rally, 1); the Front for Democracy and the Republic 15 (the Rally for Mali, 11; the Party for National Renaissance, 4); the African Solidarity for Democracy and Independence, 4; and independents, 15.

President: Dioncounda TRAORÉ.

CABINET

[as of October 1, 2009]

Prime Minister	Modibo Sidibé
Ministers	
Agriculture	Agathane Ag Alassane
Communications and Technology	Diarra Mariam Flantié Diallo [f]
Culture	Mohamed el Moctar
Defense and Veterans	Natié Pleah
Economy and Finance	Sanoussi Touré
Employment and Vocational Training	Ibrahima N'Diaye
Energy and Water	Mamadou Igor Diarra
Environment and Sanitation	Tiémoko Sangaré
Equipment and Transportation	Hamed Diane Semega
Foreign Affairs and International Cooperation	Moctar Ouane
Health	Oumar Ibrahim Touré
Housing and Urbanism	Gakou Salimata Fofona [f]
Industry, Investment, and Commerce	Ahmadou Abdoulaye Diallo
Internal Security and Civil Protection	Gen. Sadio Gassama
Justice and Keeper of the Seals	Maharafa Traoré
Labor, State Reforms, and Relations with Institutions	Abdoul Wahab Berthe
Livestock and Fisheries	Diallo Madeleine Ba [f]
Malians Abroad and African Integration	Badra Alou Macalou

Mines	Abou-Bakar Traoré
Primary Education, Literacy, and National Languages	Salikou Sanago
Promotion of Women, Children, and the Family	Maiga Sina Damba [f]
Secondary and Higher Education and Scientific Research	Siby Ginette Bellegarde [f]
Social Development, Solidarity, and the Elderly	Sékou Diakité
Territorial Administration and Local Communities	Gen. Kafougouna Koné
Tourism and Arts and Crafts	N'diaye Bah
Youth and Sports	Hamane Niang

COMMUNICATIONS

Press. Though Mali is considered to have one of the freest presses in Africa, its impact has long been limited because of widespread illiteracy (80–90 percent). Until the 1990s, little opportunity to publish dissenting or adversarial material. A teacher was convicted in June 2007 of slander against the president and five journalists were subsequently convicted of lesser charges for writing about the story. In its 2008 annual index of press freedom, Reporters Without Borders ranked Mali 31st along with Ghana, Greece and Cypress, out of 173 countries.

The following are published in Bamako: *L'Essor-La Voix du Peuple* (3,500), government daily; *Le Républicain,* independent daily; *Le Soudanais*; *Nouvel Horizon* and *Le Soir de Bamako,* independent dailies; *Liberté,* weekly; *L'Observateur; L'Aurore,* biweekly; *Info-Matin,* proopposition daily; and *Le Continent,* weekly. *Les Echos* (25,000), initially a progovernment bimonthly, subsequently a daily, was launched in March 1989. There are approximately 40 privately-owned newspapers in the country.

News agencies. The National Information Agency of Mali (ANIM) and the Malian Publicity Agency (AMP) were merged in 1977 to form the official *Agence Malienne de Presse* (Amap); *Agence France-Presse* and a number of other foreign agencies maintain bureaus in Bamako.

Broadcasting and computing. Mali has approximately 27 government and regional radio stations and 203 private stations and two television broadcast stations. *Radiodiffusion-Télévision Malienne* (RTM) broadcasts news bulletins and programs in French, English, and the principal local languages. The staff of a private radio station were arrested in October 2003 and charged with "slander and incitement to violence" by the government. The arrests were criticized by press groups and opposition parties. As of 2008 there were 15.7 Internet users per 1,000 inhabitants.

INTERGOVERNMENTAL REPRESENTATION

Ambassador to the U.S.: (Vacant).

U.S. Ambassador to Mali: Gillian A. MILOVANOVIC.

Permanent Representative to the UN: Oumar DAOU.

IGO Memberships (Non-UN): AfDB, AU, BADEA, BOAD, CILSS, ECOWAS, IDB, Interpol, IOM, NAM, OIC, OIF, UEMOA, WCO, WTO.

MALTA

Republic of Malta
Repubblika ta'Malta

Political Status: Became independent within the Commonwealth on September 21, 1964; republic declared by constitutional amendment on December 13, 1974.

Area: 122 sq. mi. (316 sq. km.).

Population: 404,039 (2005C); 410,000 (2008E).

Major Urban Centers (2005E): VALLETTA (7,100), Birkirkara (22,600), Sliema (12,700).

Official Languages: Maltese, English; Italian is also widely spoken.

Monetary Unit: Euro (market rate December 1, 2009: 1 euro = $1.51US). The euro became Malta's official currency on January 1, 2008, at a fixed rate of 1 euro = 0.4293 Maltese lira.

President: George ABELA (Malta Labour Party); elected on April 1, 2009, to a five-year term by the House of Representatives and sworn in on April 4, succeeding Edward (Eddie) FRENCH ADAMI (Nationalist Party). (Presidents resign from their parties upon election.)

Prime Minister: Lawrence GONZI (Nationalist Party); sworn in on March 23, 2004, to replace Edward FENECH ADAMI (Nationalist Party), who had resigned the same day to run for the presidency; sworn in for a second term on March 11, 2008, following the legislative election of March 8.

THE COUNTRY

Strategically located in the central Mediterranean some 60 miles south of Sicily, Malta comprises the two main islands of Malta and Gozo in addition to the small island of Comino. The population is predominantly of Carthaginian and Phoenician descent and of mixed Arab-Italian cultural traditions. The indigenous language, Maltese, is of Semitic origin. Roman Catholicism is the state religion, but other faiths are permitted.

Malta has few natural resources, and its terrain is not well adapted to agriculture. Historically, the country was dependent upon British military installations and expenditures, which were curtailed upon expiry of a 1972 Anglo-Maltese defense agreement in 1979. The most important industry was ship repair, but the government sought to encourage diversification while at the same time soliciting external budgetary support in lieu of the former British subsidy. These efforts were initially successful, the economy yielding in 1974–1979 double-digit rates of real per capita growth, comfortable current account surpluses, and declining unemployment. Growth slowed thereafter but remained at a healthy annual average of 5.3 percent in the decade 1985–1994 as Malta established itself as a major freight entrepôt, financial center, and tourist destination. However, budget deficits prompted the government installed in 1996 to restrain spending, accelerate the privatization of several state-run enterprises, and expand economic incentives designed to attract foreign investment and promote industrial development. The new government elected in September 1998 pledged to pursue membership in the European Union (EU), its predecessor having preferred negotiations toward a free trade agreement with the EU rather than full-fledged accession. In 1999 the government introduced austerity measures to reduce the 8.6 percent budget deficit as part of efforts to join the EU, which was achieved in 2004.

Malta's entry into the EU was expected to improve the nation's economy on a variety of fronts. Already some two-thirds of Malta's trade was with EU states, and membership was expected to improve tourism and increase manufacturing exports (the two main components of the Maltese economy). In addition, the government pledged to undertake a program of privatization and enhanced tax administration as a precondition for membership. In return, Malta was granted exemptions designed to protect several economic sectors, primarily agriculture and industry.

After several years of economic decline or stagnation, Malta's economy grew by 3.3 percent in both 2005 and 2006. The budget presented in October 2006 for fiscal 2007 projected a reduced budget deficit of 2.8 percent, safely under the eurozone limit of 3 percent and an essential step in Malta's successful effort to adopt the euro at the start of 2008. The switch to the euro was believed to have contributed to an estimated increase in inflation to 4 percent in 2008. GDP grew by 1.6 percent in 2008 but was projected to decline by 1.5 percent in 2009 as the tourism and manufacturing sectors suffered the effects of the global recession. In addition, unemployment was expected to climb from 5.8 percent in 2008 to 6.9 percent in 2009.

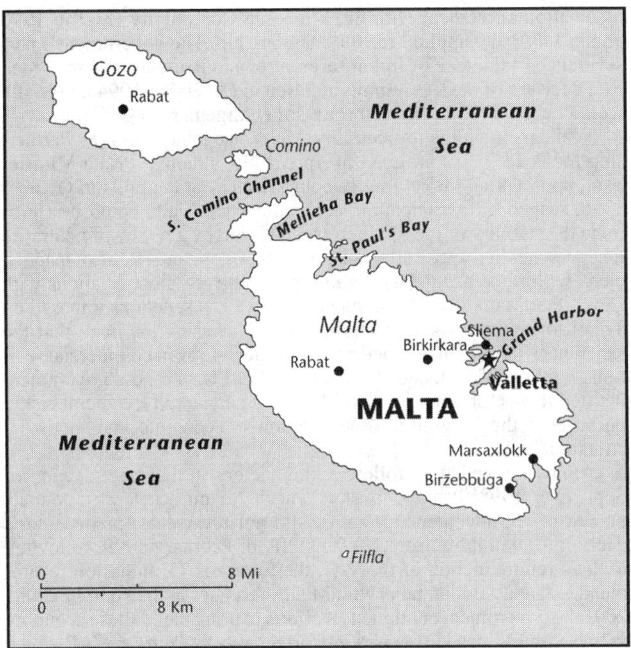

GOVERNMENT AND POLITICS

Political background. Malta has a long history of conquest and rule by foreign powers. It first came under British control in 1800, possession being formalized by the Treaty of Paris in 1814, and its strategic importance being enhanced by the opening of the Suez Canal in 1869. Ruled by a military governor throughout the 19th century, it experienced an unsuccessful period of internal autonomy immediately following World War I. Autonomy was abolished in 1933, and Malta reverted to its former status as a Crown Colony. A more successful attempt at internal self-government was initiated in 1947, after Malta had been awarded the George Cross by Britain for its resistance to Axis air assaults during World War II. In 1956 the islanders voted three to one in favor of full integration with Britain, as proposed by the ruling Malta Labour Party (MLP), led by Dominic (Dom) MINTOFF. However, British reservations, combined with a change of government in Malta, resulted in the submission in 1962 of a formal request for independence within the Commonwealth by Prime Minister Giorgio BORG OLIVIER of the Nationalist Party (*Partit Nazzjonalista*—PN), who led the islands to full sovereignty on September 21, 1964. The first post-independence change of government came in the 1971 election, which returned the MLP and Mintoff to power. Disenchanted with the British connection, Mintoff led Malta to republican status within the Commonwealth in December 1974.

The MLP retained its legislative majority in the elections of 1976 and 1981. The results of the 1981 poll were challenged by the opposition PN, which had won a slim majority of the popular vote and which, after being rebuffed in an appeal for electoral reform, instituted a boycott of parliamentary proceedings. In a countermove to the boycott, Prime Minister Mintoff declared the 31 Nationalist-held seats vacant in April 1982, with the PN subsequently refusing to make by-election nominations. In March 1983, however, PN leader Edward FENECH ADAMI agreed to resume parliamentary activity on the basis of a commitment from Mintoff to discuss changes in the electoral law.

The interparty talks were suspended in July 1983 in the wake of increasingly violent antigovernment activity and the adoption of a legislative measure that prohibited the charging of fees by private schools and indirectly authorized the confiscation of upwards of 75 percent of the assets of the Maltese Catholic Church. During 1984 the conflict erupted into a major confrontation between church and state, with the Catholic hierarchy ordering the closure of all schools under its jurisdiction—half the island's total—in September. The schools reopened two months later, with Vatican officials agreeing in April 1985 to the introduction of free education over a three-year period in return for government assurances of noninterference in teaching and participation in a joint commission to discuss remaining church-state issues, including those regarding church property.

Meanwhile, in December 1984 Mintoff had stepped down as prime minister in favor of Karmenu MIFSUD BONNICI. The church-state dispute was officially resolved in July 1986, while in January 1987 both the MLP and the PN supported constitutional changes that included modification of the electoral law to ensure that a party winning a majority of the popular vote would have a parliamentary majority.

In the bitterly contested 1987 election, Labour, as in 1981, won 34 of 65 legislative seats, but, after 16 years in office, lost control of the government because the PN had obtained a popular majority and was therefore awarded additional seats. Thus, PN leader Fenech Adami became prime minister. Earlier in the year, at the conclusion of her five-year term, President Agatha BARBARA had yielded her office, on an acting basis, to the Speaker of the House of Representatives, Paul XUEREB. Xuereb retained the position from February 1987 until the House elected the PN's Dr. Vincent TABONE as his successor in April 1989.

In the election of February 1992 the PN won 34 legislative seats with a vote share of 51.8 percent, while the MLP obtained 31 seats with 46.5 percent. Five days later, Fenech Adami formed a new government in which all senior ministers were retained, although in a number of cases with altered portfolios. In 1994 former PN leader Ugo MIFSUD BONNICI was sworn in as Malta's fifth president.

In March 1995 Fenech Adami carried out a major cabinet reshuffle, bringing in a younger generation of ministers as part of a strategy to retain power in the next general election. However, the prime minister's decision to call an early election for October 1996 proved a miscalculation. Labour unexpectedly outpolled the PN 50.7 to 47.8 percent in fiercely contested balloting that drew a record turnout of 97 percent. Although the PN won 34 elective seats to Labour's 31, the 1987 constitutional amendment entitled Labour to 4 additional seats, handing it a parliamentary majority. The new Labour government was sworn in under the premiership of Alfred SANT, a Harvard-educated former physicist.

Fulfilling one of its major domestic campaign promises, the Sant government in July 1997 abolished the country's 15 percent value-added tax (VAT), which had been introduced in 1995. Subsequently, the opposition argued that this reversal had contributed to the growing economic problems of budget deficits, rising inflation, and increased unemployment.

The government's single-seat majority evaporated when former prime minister Mintoff, Sant's aging MLP predecessor, deserted the party on two votes relating to a development project in Mintoff's district. Plagued by resignations, bitter attacks from Mintoff, and dissatisfaction within the MLP over Sant's failure to follow traditional patronage policies and his perceived drift to the right, the prime minister called an election for September 1998, three years early. The PN emerged with 35 seats to the MLP's 30, permitting the PN's Fenech Adami to return as prime minister. In March 1999, voting along straight party lines, the House of Representatives elected as president the PN's Guido DE MARCO, until then the deputy prime minister and foreign minister.

Membership in the EU became one of the main priorities of Fenech Adami's government. In response to criticism from the anti-EU MLP, Fenech Adami called a nonbinding referendum on EU membership that was held on March 8, 2003. Although those voting endorsed membership by 53.65 to 46.35 percent, Sant and other MLP leaders argued that the closeness of the vote, when combined with the 9 percent of the eligible voters who did not cast a ballot, meant that the majority of Maltese opposed accession. In response, Fenech Adami called for elections on April 12, 2003, just four days before Malta was to sign the accession treaty, to affirm support for membership. Turnout was 96.2 percent. The PN received 51.8 percent of the vote and 35 seats, while the MLP won 47.5 percent and 30 seats. Malta signed the EU accession treaty on April 16 and formally entered the EU a year later, on May 1, 2004.

Having decided to seek the presidency, Fenech Adami resigned as prime minister on March 23, 2004. He was replaced by Lawrence GONZI (PN), who reshuffled and expanded the cabinet to form a new government that was sworn in on the same day as Fenech Adami's resignation. Fenech Adami, elected president by the House of Representatives on March 29, was sworn into office on April 4.

In the national legislative election on March 8, 2008, the PN outpolled the MLP by a slim margin in the national vote, even though the PN won only 31 seats, compared to 34 for the MLP, based on the results within the voting districts. Consequently, under a special constitutional provision designed to deal with such a situation (see Legislature, below), the PN was awarded 4 more seats, giving it a 35–34 majority. President Adami subsequently reappointed Gonzi as prime minister, and Gonzi was sworn in on March 11. His cabinet was approved and sworn in the following day. Meanwhile, the 23 local council elections also held on March 8 resulted in the PN securing majorities in 12 councils and the MLP in 11.

In January 2009 Prime Minister Gonzi announced that his government would take the unprecedented step of endorsing an opposition party member for president. On April 1 Gonzi made official the government's nomination of George ABELA of the MLP for president. The House of Representatives unanimously approved Abela on the same day, and he was sworn in on April 4.

Constitution and government. The 1964 constitution established Malta as an independent parliamentary monarchy within the Commonwealth, with executive power exercised by a prime minister and cabinet, both appointed by the governor general but chosen from and responsible to parliament. By constitutional amendment, the country became a republic on December 13, 1974, with an indirectly elected president of Maltese nationality replacing the British monarch as de jure head of state. The president serves a five-year term, as does the prime minister, subject to the retention of a legislative majority. The parliament consists of a unicameral House of Representatives elected on the basis of proportional representation every five years, assuming no prior dissolution. Under an amendment adopted in February 1987, the party winning a majority of the popular vote is awarded additional House seats, if needed to secure a legislative majority.

The judicial system encompasses a Constitutional Court, a Court of Appeal, a Criminal Court of Appeal, and lower courts. The president appoints the judges for the Constitutional Court and the Court of Appeal. There was little established local government in Malta until 1993, when a Local Councils Act (subsequently amended) was passed. In 2001 provisions for local councils were incorporated into the constitution. At present, there are 68 directly elected local councils, 54 on the island of Malta and 14 on Gozo.

Foreign relations. After independence, Maltese foreign policy centered primarily on the country's relationship with Great Britain and thus with the North Atlantic Treaty Organization (NATO). A ten-year Mutual Defense and Assistance Agreement, signed in 1964, was abrogated in 1971 by the Mintoff government. Under a new seven-year agreement, concluded in 1972 after months of negotiation, the rental payments for use of military facilities by Britain were tripled. Early in 1973 Mintoff reopened the issue, asking additional payment to compensate for devaluation of the British pound, but he settled for a token adjustment pending British withdrawal from the facilities in March 1979. Rebuffed in an effort to obtain a quadripartite guarantee of Maltese neutrality and a five-year budgetary subsidy from France, Italy, Algeria, and Libya, the Mintoff government turned to Libya. During ceremonies marking the British departure, the Libyan leader, Col. Muammar al-Qadhafi, promised "unlimited" support. In the course of the following year, however, the relationship cooled because of overlapping claims to offshore oil rights, and in September 1980 an agreement was concluded with Italy whereby Rome guaranteed Malta's future neutrality and promised a combination of loans and subsidies totaling $95 million over a five-year period. In 1981 Malta also signed neutrality agreements with Algeria, France, and the Soviet Union.

In December 1984 Prime Minister Mintoff announced that the defense and aid agreement with Italy would be permitted to lapse in favor of a new alignment with Libya, which would undertake to train Maltese forces to withstand "threats or acts of aggression." Six months later the maritime issue was resolved, the International Court of Justice establishing a boundary 18 nautical miles north of a line equidistant between the two countries.

In March 1986 Prime Minister Mifsud Bonnici met with Colonel Qadhafi in Tripoli in what was described as an effort to ease the confrontation between Libya and the United States in the Gulf of Sidra. In August the Maltese leader stated that his government had warned Libya of the approach of "unidentified planes" prior to the April attack by U.S. aircraft on Tripoli and Benghazi, although there was no indication that Libyan authorities had acted on the information.

Upon assuming office in May 1987, Prime Minister Fenech Adami indicated that the military clauses of the 1984 agreement with Libya would not be renewed, although all other commitments would be continued. Cooperation between the two countries at the political and economic levels was reaffirmed in 1988, with Libya renewing its $38 million oil supply pact with Malta late in the year.

A member of the United Nations, the Conference on (later Organization for) Security and Cooperation in Europe (CSCE/OSCE), and a number of other international organizations, Malta concluded an association agreement with the European Community (EC) in 1970 and in July 1990 applied for full membership. The government's perseverance in the face of initial reservations in Brussels was rewarded by a decision of the EU summit in Essen in December 1994 that Malta would be included in the next round of enlargement negotiations.

While maintaining its neutrality, Malta also joined NATO's Partnership for Peace (PfP) program in April 1995, although Prime Minister Sant, upon taking office after Labour's victory at the polls in October 1996, suspended participation, contending that Malta could best promote the stability of the Mediterranean region by a policy of neutrality that was neither anti-European nor anti-American. He also made it clear, with reference to past Labour governments' close relations with Libya, that Malta would continue to observe UN sanctions imposed on Tripoli over the Lockerbie affair, while expressing the hope that the sanctions would soon be lifted so that Maltese-Libyan commercial relations could be developed. In regard to the EU, the new government insisted it was "still not time" for Malta to pursue full EU membership because of the "fragility" of the nation's "economic and industrial structure."

Almost immediately following his victory in the snap election of September 1998, Prime Minister Fenech Adami accelerated Malta's pursuit of EU membership, but he did not reverse his predecessor's decision to withdraw from NATO's PfP. In February 1999, following Malta's reintroduction of the VAT, the European Commission recommended that accession talks with Malta start later in the year. In 2000–2002 the government continued its efforts to bring the Maltese economy in line with EU standards, sparking further attacks from the MLP, which argued that EU accession would freeze crucial foreign investment, decimate Malta's manufacturing and agricultural sectors, and raise administrative costs. In 2003 Malta signed the EU accession treaty, along with nine other aspirant countries, and Malta joined the EU on May 1, 2004. Although the MLP had opposed Maltese inclusion in the EU, it joined the NP in supporting accession to the eurozone in 2008 with the expectation that adopting the euro would increase tourism and foreign investment.

Current issues. European parliamentary elections on June 12, 2004, showed that EU membership remained a contentious issue. Each of the major parties ran a full slate of candidates, and there were a number of fringe and independent candidates as well. The MLP, which ran a Euro-skeptic campaign, outpolled the ruling PN, while the small pro-EU green-oriented Democratic Alternative (*Alternattiva Demokratika*—AD) performed much better than expected. The MLP received 48.4 percent of the vote and three seats, and the PN, 39.8 percent and two seats. The AD gained no seats but had its highest electoral vote in history at 9.3 percent.

As a step toward adoption of the euro, it was announced in April 2005 that the Maltese lira would participate in the European Central Bank's (ECB) Exchange Rate Mechanism II. This move mandated strong fiscal discipline, together with a degree of influence by the ECB in Malta's financial affairs. In May 2007 the European Commission, citing Malta's "high degree of convergence with the euro area," endorsed Malta's adoption of the euro from January 1, 2008, and in July the EU Council confirmed the decision.

In March 2006 it was announced that Malta would hold talks with Italy and Libya to discuss joint oil exploration in the Mediterranean. Malta's strategic location has also played an important role in another recently developing issue—the arrival of a wave of illegal immigrants from Africa, many attempting to make their way through Malta to the European mainland. More than 1,800 arrived in 2005 alone. Housing (or sometimes confining) the immigrants has stretched the nation's resources and generated resentment among many Maltese. The issue led to a dispute between Malta and Spain in June 2006 when Malta, claiming that it already had more than its share of illegal immigrants, declined to allow ashore 51 African immigrants who had been rescued by a Spanish fishing boat.

During the campaign for the March 2008 legislative elections, Prime Minister Gonzi's PN ruled out the possibility of forming a coalition with the pro-environmentalist AD. The election contest thereby became a debate principally between the PN and MLP, despite increased public attention on immigration issues and the emergence of two new political parties (the National Action and Empire Europe) with strong anti-immigrant positions. The incumbent PN campaigned on its economic achievements (including the budget deficit reduction) and pledged to reduce income taxes. The MLP focused on proposed anti-corruption measures. Following the PN's complicated (and razor-thin) victory (see Legislature, below, for details), Gonzi pledged that his new center-right government would, among other things, pursue privatization of the Maltese shipyards and other state-owned enterprises. After lengthy negotiations, an agreement was announced in July by the PN and MLP to cooperate through a new special committee in the House of Representatives designed to facilitate compromise on outstanding issues. The accord was considered a victory for the MLP, which had long complained of being left out of the decision-making process during the last 20 years of PN rule.

The MLP scored a resounding victory in the June 2009 balloting in Malta for the European Parliament by securing 55 percent of the vote, compared to 40 percent for the PN and only 2.3 percent for the AD. Most analysts attributed the MLP's surge to dissatisfaction among the populace over rising unemployment and steady increases in the cost of living. The MLP also led in concurrent balloting for one-third of the nation's local councils, although the PN performed better than it did in the EU poll.

POLITICAL PARTIES

Government Party:

Nationalist Party (*Partit Nazzjonalista*—PN). Advocating the retention of Roman Catholic and European principles, the PN brought Malta to independence. It formerly supported alignment with NATO and membership in the EC, but because of a constitutional pact with Labour in February 1987 it adopted a neutral foreign policy. The party obtained 50.9 percent of the vote in the 1981 election without, however, winning control of the legislature. In the 1987 balloting it again obtained only a minority of elective seats, but under the February constitutional amendment was permitted to form a government because of its popular majority.

The Nationalists retained power in the 1992 election but were unexpectedly defeated in 1996, when their share of the popular vote slipped from 51.8 to 47.8 percent. The PN returned to power in the election of September 1998 with a vote share of 51.8 percent. In the April 2003 elections, the PN won 51.8 percent and 35 seats. In March 2004 Edward Fenech Adami, theretofore the prime minister, was elected president, and PN Vice Chair Lawrence Gonzi became prime minister.

Although the PN finished second in seat totals to the MLP in the 2008 legislative poll, it secured a plurality of the nationwide votes (49.34 percent) and was therefore awarded additional seats to give it a slim parliamentary majority and continued governmental control.

Leaders: Lawrence GONZI (Prime Minister of Malta and Chair of the Party), Tonio BORG (Deputy Prime Minister), Paul Borg OLIVIER (Secretary General).

Opposition Party:

Malta Labour Party—MLP (*Partit Laburista*). In power from 1971 to 1987, the MLP advocated a socialist and "progressive" policy, including anticolonialism in international affairs, a neutralist foreign policy, and emphasis on Malta's role as "a bridge of peace between Europe and the Arab world." The party has periodically complained of intrusion by the Catholic Church into political and economic affairs.

In the election of December 1981 the MLP's vote share fell to 49.1 percent from 51.2 percent in 1976, but without loss of its three-seat majority in the House of Representatives; its vote share fell further, to 48.8 percent, in 1987, when it moved into opposition, and continued its decline, to 46.5 percent, in 1992, prompting former prime minister Karmenu Mifsud Bonnici to announce his retirement as party leader. His successor, Alfred Sant, initiated a modernization of the party's organization and policies while maintaining the MLP's commitment to neutrality and opposition to EU accession. Labour returned to power in 1996, winning 50.7 percent of the popular vote, but was ousted when it secured only 47 percent in September 1998. In the 2003 elections the MLP received 47.5 percent of the vote and 30 seats. As a result of the election, Sant resigned as party leader, but he was subsequently reelected to the post. Sant resigned again following the March 2008 legislative poll, in which the MLP had won a majority of seats (34) but finished second (with 48.79 percent of the votes) to the PN as far as the total vote was concerned. Sant was succeeded as MLP leader by Joseph Muscat, a 34-year-old member of the European Parliament, who won the June 6 party leadership election on the second ballot. In January 2009 Prime Minister Gonzi announced his government would nominate MLP member George Abela for the Maltese presidency. Abela officially resigned from the party to pave the way for his accession to the post on April 1.

Leaders: Joseph MUSCAT (Leader); Anglu FARRUGIA and Toni ABELA (Deputy Leaders); Stefan ZRINZO AZZOPARDI (President); Jason MICALLEF (General Secretary).

Other Parties that Contested the 2008 Legislative Election:

Democratic Alternative (*Alternattiva Demokratika*—AD). An ecologically oriented grouping launched in 1989, the AD, also referenced as the Maltese Green Party, ran a distant third in the 1992 balloting, securing no legislative seats on a vote share of 1.7 percent. It was again unsuccessful in 1996, when its vote share slipped to 1.5 percent, and in September 1998, when it won 1.2 percent of the vote. In the 2003 elections the AD received only 0.7 percent of the vote, and, after the AD won only 1.3 percent in 2008, Harry VASSALO resigned as party leader.

Leaders: Arnold CASSOLA (Chair), Mario MALLIA and Stephen CACHIA (Deputy Chairs), Victor GALLEA (General Secretary).

National Action (*Azzjoni Nazzjonali*—AN). The AN was launched on June 9, 2007, under the leadership of former Nationalist Party MP Josie Muscat. Although the party claimed neither leftist nor rightist ideology, it put forth a platform aimed at restricting immigration, preserving traditional Maltese values, implementing flat-rate taxes, and reforming existing political institutions. The party also sought direct election of the president, a reformed electoral system, and increased political autonomy for Gozo. After the AN received a meager 0.5 percent of the vote in the March 2008 legislative elections, Muscat announced his resignation as party leader; however, as he was the only one nominated for the leadership position at the party assembly in May, he continued in the position.

Leaders: Josie MUSCAT (Leader), Anglu XUEREB (Deputy Leader), Wayne HEWITT (General Secretary), Antonio BARTOLO (President of the Executive).

Four other parties fielded candidates in 2008. All received fewer than 100 votes. The largest was **Empire Europe** (*Imperium Europa*—IE), a new radical right party with pan-Europeanism as its core principle, led by Normal LOWELL.

LEGISLATURE

The **House of Representatives** (*Il-Kamra Tad-Deputati*) consists of 65 elective members returned for a five-year term (subject to dissolution) on the basis of proportional representation applied in 13 electoral districts. The constitution requires that the party obtaining the highest number of votes nationwide must also end up with a legislative majority, assuming only two parties win seats. Consequently, if a party wins the nationwide vote but trails in seats awarded in the district results, it is given enough additional seats to reach a majority.

In the most recent election, held March 8, 2008, the Nationalist Party (PN) secured only 31 seats compared to the Malta Labour Party's 34 in the district balloting. However, since the PN had won a greater percentage of the nationwide vote, it was subsequently awarded 4 additional seats to give it a majority in the House, whose membership was thereby temporarily increased to 69.

Speaker: Louis GALEA.

CABINET

[as of September 1, 2009]

Prime Minister	Lawrence Gonzi
Deputy Prime Minister	Tonio Borg
Ministers	
Education, Culture, Youth, and Sport	Dolores Cristina [f]
Finance, Economy, and Investment	Tonio Fenech
Foreign Affairs	Tonio Borg
Gozo	Giovanna Debono [f]
Infrastructure, Transport, and Communications	Austin Gatt

Justice and Home Affairs	Carmelo Mifsud Bonnici
Resources and Rural Affairs	George Pullicino
Social Policy	John Dalli

[f] = female

COMMUNICATIONS

Freedom of the press prevails. Many print and broadcast outlets are owned by political parties, unions, or the Catholic Church.

Press. The following are Maltese-language dailies published in Valletta, unless otherwise noted: *It-Torca* (*The Torch*, 30,000), General Workers' Union weekly; *L-Orizzont* (25,000), General Workers' Union daily; *Il-Mument* (25,000), Nationalist Party weekly; *The Times* (23,000 daily, 35,000 Sunday), in English; *In-Nazzjon* (20,000), Nationalist Party daily; *The Malta Independent* (18,000), in English; *Lehen Is-Sewwa* (10,000), Catholic weekly; *Alternattiva Zghazagu*, pro-DA weekly. Business newspapers include *The Malta Business Weekly* and *The Malta Financial and Business Times*.

News agencies. There is no domestic facility; a number of foreign services, including ANSA, *Agencia EFE*, AP, and Reuters, maintain bureaus in Valletta.

Broadcasting and computing. In 1991 a broadcasting bill restructured Xandir Malta, which theretofore provided radio and television services under supervision of the Malta Broadcasting Authority, into an independent corporation; the bill also authorized the launching of ten private commercial radio stations, a number of community radio stations, and a cable television network. Since then, the number of stations has grown considerably, with both cable and satellite television widely available.

As of 2008 there were 487.9 Internet users per 1,000 inhabitants.

INTERGOVERNMENTAL REPRESENTATION

Ambassador to the U.S.: Mark MICELI-FARRUGIA.

U.S. Ambassador to Malta: Douglas W. KMIEC.

Permanent Representative to the UN: Saviour F. BORG.

IGO Memberships (Non-UN): CEUR, CWTH, EBRD, EIB, Eurocontrol, EU, Interpol, IOM, NAM, OSCE, PCA, WCO, WTO.

MARSHALL ISLANDS

Republic of the Marshall Islands

Note: President Litokwa Tomeing was ousted by losing a confidence motion by a vote of 17–15 in the House of Representatives on October 21, 2009, following a prolonged power struggle with former president Kessai Note. House Speaker Jurelang Zedkaia was inaugurated as the new president on November 2 after defeating Note in a House vote for the position by a vote of 17–15. Meanwhile, Alvin Jacklick succeeded Zedkaia as speaker.

Political Status: Sovereign state in free association with the United States (which retains authority with regard to defense) since October 21, 1986.

Area: 70 sq. mi. (181 sq. km.).

Population: 50,848 (1999C); 59,000 (2008E).

Major Urban Center (2005E): DALAP-ULIGA-DARRIT (Majuro Atoll; 26,000).

Official Languages: English, Marshallese.

Monetary Unit: U.S. Dollar (see U.S. article for principal exchange rates).

President: *(See headnote.)* Litokwa TOMEING (Our Islands); elected by the House of Representatives on January 7, 2008, to succeed Kessai H. NOTE (United Democratic Party), following legislative election of November 20, 2007.

THE COUNTRY

The Marshalls consist of a double chain of coral atolls, encompassing 33 islands and more than 850 reefs, within the Pacific region known as Micronesia, some 2,000 miles southwest of Hawaii. The two chains are about 80 miles apart, the eastern (which includes the capital, Majuro) being known as the Rataks ("Sunrise") Chain and the western (which includes Bikini, Eniwetak, and Kwajalein) being known as the Ralik ("Sunset") Chain. More than 90 percent of the inhabitants are indigenous Marshallese. Christianity is the principal religion, with adherents of Roman Catholicism the most numerous. Copra products long dominated exports, although a decline in copra oil prices in the early 1980s led to a severe trade imbalance. The sale of fishing licenses and income from fishing-related services now make up a significant portion of external earnings. Financial assistance from the United States (currently at about $50 million a year) is a crucial component of government revenue for a country whose GDP declined by nearly 25 percent in 1995–2001, with debt servicing equaling about 40 percent of budget outlays and far exceeding export earnings. For several years the unemployment rate has been relatively unchanged at around 30 percent. Nonetheless, the economy grew by about 4.0 percent in 2002 before receding by 1.8 percent in 2003, then rising again by 5.9 percent in 2004 before declining by an average of 1.5 percent in 2005–2008. With consumer price increases in the latter span averaging 4.3 percent, the government in July 2008 felt obliged to declare a state of economic emergency (see Current issues, below).

GOVERNMENT AND POLITICS

Political background. Purchased by Germany from Spain in 1899, the Marshalls were seized in 1914 by Japan and retained as part of the mandate awarded by the League of Nations in 1920. The islands were occupied by U.S. forces near the end of World War II and (along with the Caroline and Northern Mariana islands) became part of the U.S. Trust Territory of the Pacific in 1947. In 1965 a Congress of Micronesia was established, with the Marshalls electing 4 of the 21 members of its House of Representatives. Subsequently the Marshall Islands district drafted its own constitution, which came into effect on May 1, 1979. Three years later the Republic of the Marshall Islands (RMI) concluded a Compact of Free Association with the United States, which was declared to be in effect on October 21, 1986, following ratification by the U.S. Congress and final approval by the islands' government. Under the Compact, the RMI is a fully sovereign state, save with regard to defense, which was to remain a U.S. responsibility for at least a 15-year period; it is also obligated to "consult" with Washington regarding major foreign policy matters.

The islands' first president was Amata KABUA, who first assumed office on May 1, 1979, and was subsequently reelected to four successive four-year terms. He died on December 20, 1996, while undergoing medical treatment in Honolulu, Minister of Transportation Kunio D. LEMARI being named acting president pending legislative designation of a successor. In balloting within the House of Representatives (*Nitijela*) on January 14, 1997, Imata KABUA (a cousin of Amata and a minister without portfolio in the previous government) was elected to fulfill the remainder of Amata Kabua's term. In the legislative poll of November 15, 1999, the United Democratic Party (UDP) won a first-ever majority for an opposition group and on January 3, 2000, named Kessai H. NOTE, theretofore *Nitijela* speaker, to succeed Kabua as president.

On January 15, 2001, President Note survived a no-confidence motion, 19–14, brought by Imata Kabua and six other senators dissatisfied, in part, by the government's preparations for negotiating a successor agreement to the 1986 Compact. President Note, addressing the legislature after the vote, described it as a "wake-up call" to the cabinet.

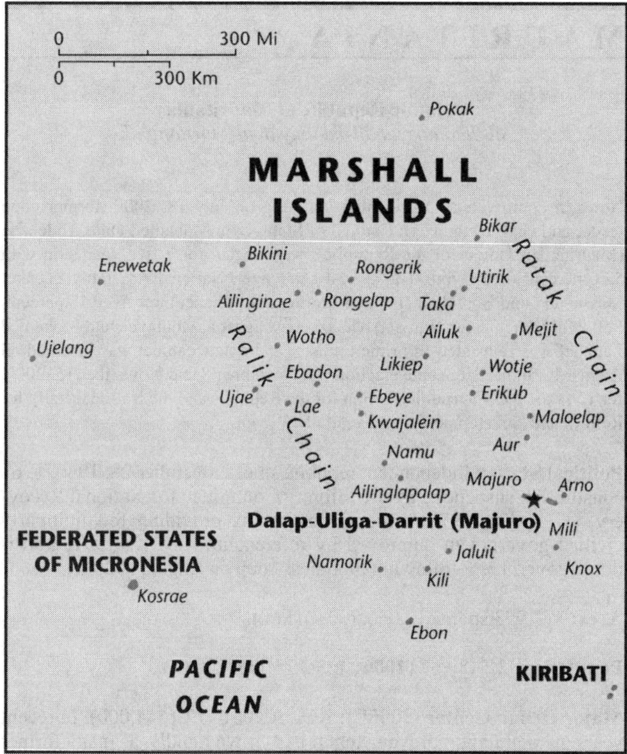

On November 1, 2002, after several rounds of negotiations, the U.S.'s George W. Bush administration and the Note government initialed on Majuro a new 20-year Compact, although the Marshalls entered reservations with regard to specific monetary figures, pending completion of ongoing negotiations on the Military Use and Operating Rights Agreement governing future use by the United States of defense facilities on Kwajalein Island.

In early 2003 RMI and U.S. negotiators reached agreement on lease renewal for the Kwajalein Missile Range (renamed the Ronald Reagan Missile Defense Test Site in 2001), and on May 1 they signed a new Compact that would provide the Marshalls with economic aid for the ensuing two decades and preserved the right of RMI citizens to enter, reside, and work in the United States without visas.

On November 17, 2003, the UDP secured a 20-seat majority in the *Nitijela,* and on January 4, 2004, President Note won reelection by a 20–9 House vote over Justin DeBRUM. However, his bid for a third term was rejected on January 7, 2008, by the *Nitijela*, which elected its speaker, Litokwa TOMEING, as his successor.

Constitution and government. The 1979 constitution provides for a bicameral parliament whose popularly elected lower house, the *Nitijela,* performs most legislative functions. The 33-member body selects from its own ranks an executive president, who serves for the duration of the four-year parliamentary term. There is no specific provision for succession should the presidential office become vacant, as happened following the death of Amata Kabua in December 1996. The upper house is a council of 12 traditional chiefs who make recommendations with regard to customary law and practice. Municipalities are governed by elected magistrates and councils, while villages follow traditional forms of rule.

Foreign relations. The effective degree of Marshalls' autonomy in foreign affairs is not entirely clear. In early 1987 the *Nitijela* debated whether to endorse the Treaty of Rarotonga that called for the establishment of a South Pacific Nuclear Free Zone, but, unlike the Federated States of Micronesia (see FSM article), it failed to take action in the matter after a Washington official had termed adherence "inappropriate" given the U.S. obligation under the Compact to defend the Marshalls, coupled with its own decision not to sign the document.

In December 1990 the UN Security Council formally abrogated the U.S. Trusteeship in respect to the Marshall Islands, the Federated States of Micronesia, and the Commonwealth of the Northern Marianas, and in September 1991 both the FSM and the Marshalls were admitted to the United Nations. In May 1992 the Marshalls became the 161st member of the International Monetary Fund and the 157th member of the World Bank. Regionally, the RMI belongs to the Asian Development Bank, the Pacific Community, and the Pacific Islands Forum.

Following independence, the Marshalls joined a number of Pacific neighbors in attempting to attract investors by the sale of passports to Asians. By mid-1996 the practice was officially suspended in the wake of complaints by allegedly disadvantaged Marshallese businesses and objections by the U.S. State Department on the impact of such sales on the Compact provision granting islanders the right of entry into the United States. Because of the problem, Washington initiated a policy late in the year of denying entry to passport holders whose places of birth were other than the Marshalls.

In November 1998 the Marshalls established diplomatic relations with Taiwan, hoping thereby to attract both trade and investment. Already linked to the People's Republic of China (PRC), the RMI government hoped that a "two-Chinas" policy might be possible; however, the PRC, saying that the Marshalls "must correct their mistake," severed relations three weeks later.

In recent years, the Marshalls has joined a number of its low-lying neighbors in warning of the consequences of an anticipated rise in sea levels because of global warming. It demonstrated its concern by hosting a 16-nation conference on the issue sponsored by the UN Food and Agriculture Organization in early 2007.

Current issues. The revised Compact of Free Association with the United States covering 2003–2023 provides for some $960 million in grants, an annual contribution of $7 million toward a trust fund, and services to be provided by various U.S. agencies, including the Federal Aviation Administration, the Federal Emergency Management Agency, and the U.S. Agency for International Development's Office of Disaster Assistance. In 2005 concern was expressed over the adequacy of the trust fund upon the expiration of grant assistance in 2023. The response from Washington was that income from the trust fund was never intended to match the level of grant support. An indication of the Marshall's economic difficulty surfaced in February 2006, when the minister of finance announced a suspension of disbursement from the government's general fund because of a shortfall between spending and revenue from tax collection.

In April 2006 the government supported a lawsuit by residents of Bikini against the United States for nonpayment of approximately $560 million of a 2001 award by the Marshall Islands Nuclear Claims Tribunal. The award totaled $563,315,500, of which the tribunal was able to pay Bikinians only $2,279,000 because of inadequate U.S. funding. Far more serious was the prospect of an estimated shortfall of $17–21 million in public utility costs that in mid-2009 helped trigger the declaration of economic emergency. Also contributing was a collapse in copra prices (after a banner year in 2008) and a plummeting tourist sector after Japan Airline had curtailed flights in response to the halt of a popular scuba-diving program on Bikini Atoll.

In early 2008 residents of Kwajalein Atoll rejected extension of a land-use agreement with the U.S. Defense Department for the Reagan Test Site, insisting that they be given $19 million in annual rent rather than the $15 million offered by the Pentagon. While the $4 million difference seemed relatively minor, the islanders appeared steadfast, even if the stalemate resulted in closure of the facility. The dispute prompted a split between President Tomeing, who favored conciliatory talks with Washington over the issue, and his influential foreign minister, Tony DeBRUM, who, as a legislator from Kwajalein, called for a confrontational posture. Faced with the potential loss of a confidence vote, Tomeing took the unusual approach of bringing five opposition members into a drastically reshuffled cabinet in April 2009. *(See headnote.)*

POLITICAL PARTIES

Traditionally there were no formal parties in the Marshalls. In the 1991 balloting, however, an Our Islands "presidential caucus" chaired by Amata Kabua defeated a Ralik-Ratak Democratic Party organized by Tony DeBrum, a former Kabua protégé.

Our Islands (*Ailon Kein Ad*—AKA). An outgrowth of the earlier Our Islands caucus, the AKA was formally launched in 2002. In 2008, as part of a coalition styled the **United People's Party** (UPP), it supported the successful presidential candidacy of Litokwa Tomeing, who had defected from the UDP prior to the November 2007 legislative poll.

Leaders: Litokwa TOMEING (President of the Republic), Christopher LOEAK, Tony DeBRUM.

United Democratic Party (UDP). The main opposition grouping prior to the legislative poll of November 1999, the UDP supported the successful presidential candidacy of Kessai Note in 2000 and his reelection in 2004.

Leader: Kessai H. NOTE (Former President of the Republic).

LEGISLATURE

Technically, a bicameral system prevails, although only the lower house, the *Nitijela,* engages in normal legislative activity.

Council of Chiefs (Council of *Iroij*). The council is composed of 12 traditional leaders who tender advice on matters affecting customary law and practice.

Chair: Iroij Kotak LOEAK.

House of Representatives (*Nitijela*). The *Nitijela* comprises 33 members (called senators) directly elected for four-year terms from 24 electoral districts. In the most recent election of November 19, 2007, *Ailon Kein Ad* won 17 seats; the United Democratic Party, 13; and independents, 3.

Speaker: Jurelang Z. ZEDKAIA.

CABINET

[as of July 1, 2009] *(see headnote)*

President	Litokwa Tomeing (AKA)
Ministers	
Assistance to the President	Maynard Alfred (UDP)
Education	Nidel Lorak (AKA)
Finance	Jack Ading (AKA)
Foreign Affairs and Trade	John Silk (UDP)
Health and Environment	Amenta Matthew (AKA) [f]
Internal Affairs and Welfare	Norman Matthew (AKA)
Justice	David Kramer (AKA)
Public Works	Mattian Zackhras (UDP)
Resources and Development	Ruben Zackhras (UDP)
Transportation and Communications	Kenneth Kedi (UDP)

[f] = female

COMMUNICATIONS

Press. There is a weekly *Marshall Islands Journal* (3,700), which has been self-deprecatingly dubbed "the world's worst newspaper," as well as an official *Marshall Islands Gazette,* both issued on Majuro; the *Kwajalein Hourglass* (2,000) is published twice weekly on Kwajalein.

Broadcasting and computing. Radio Marshalls (WSZO) broadcasts from Majuro. Subscription-only television service is provided by the Marshall Islands Broadcasting Corporation. In addition, the U.S. Department of Defense offers radio and television programming for its personnel on Kwajalein Island.

As of 2008 there were 36.3 Internet users per 1,000 inhabitants.

INTERGOVERNMENTAL REPRESENTATION

Ambassador to the U.S.: Banny DeBRUM.

U.S. Ambassador to the Marshall Islands: Martha Larzelere CAMPBELL.

Permanent Representative to the UN: Phillip MULLER.

IGO Memberships (Non-UN): ADB, Interpol, PC, PIF.

MAURITANIA

Islamic Republic of Mauritania
al-Jumhuriyah al-Islamiyah al-Muritaniyah

Note: In controversial presidential balloting on July 18, 2009, former coup leader and chair of the High Council of State, Gen. Mohamed Ould Abdelaziz (Mauritanian Union for the Republic), was elected for a five-year term with 52.6 percent of the vote. His closest challenger, National Assembly Speaker Massaoud Ould Boulkheir (Popular Progressive Alliance), received 16 percent. Following the inauguration of Abdelaziz on August 5, Moulaye Ould Mohamed Laghdaf was reinstated as prime minister and a new cabinet was installed on August 11. In partial Senate elections on November 8 and November 15, 2009, for 17 seats, the Mauritanian Union for the Republic and the National Rally for Reform and Development won a total of 13 seats.

Political Status: Independent republic since November 28, 1960; 1961 constitution suspended by the Military Committee for National Recovery on July 20, 1978; present constitution, providing for multiparty civilian government, approved by referendum July 12, 1991; transitional government following bloodless coup on August 6, 2008.

Area: 397,953 sq. mi. (1,030,700 sq. km.).

Population: 2,548,157 (2000C); 3,357,000 (2008E).

Major Urban Center (2005E): NOUAKCHOTT (644,000). In recent years the population of Nouakchott has grown rapidly, as many former nomads have taken up permanent residence in the capital since the 1970s.

Official Language: Arabic. (Three languages of the Black African community—Poular, Soninke, and Wolof—are constitutionally designated as national languages. French, an official language until 1991, is still widely spoken, particularly in the commercial sector. In addition, in 1999 the government designated French as the "language for science and technical subjects" in Mauritanian schools.)

Monetary Unit: Ouguiya (official rate December 1, 2009: 262.00 ouguiyas = $1US).

Interim President: *(See headnote.)* Ba Mamadou MBARE, acceded from Senate President in accordance with constitutional order on April 15, 2009, following the resignation the same day of chair of the High Council of State, Gen. Mohamed Ould ABDELAZIZ.

Prime Minister: *(See headnote.)* Moulaye Ould Mohamed LAGHDAF, appointed by the chair of the High Council of State on August 14, 2008, to succeed Yahya Ould Ahmed el-WAGHF (National Pact for Development and Democracy), who was ousted in the bloodless coup on August 6; named new government on August 31; reinstated with new transitional government on June 26, 2009.

THE COUNTRY

Situated on the western bulge of Africa, Mauritania is a sparsely populated, predominantly desert country, overwhelmingly Muslim and, except in the south, Arabic in language. The dominant Beydane (Arabic for "white") Moors, descendants of northern Arabs and Berbers, have been estimated as constituting one-third of the population, with an equal number of Haratines (mixed-race descendants of black slaves) having adopted Berber customs. Black Africans, the most important tribal groups of which are the Toucouleur, the Fulani, the Sarakole, and the Wolof, are concentrated in the rich alluvial farming lands of the Senegal River valley. They have recently claimed to account for a much larger population share than is officially acknowledged, their case being supported by the government's refusal to release pertinent portions of the last two censuses. Racial tension, exacerbated by government "arabization" efforts, has contributed to internal unrest and conflict with several neighboring nations. Further complicating matters has been the de facto continuation of slavery, officially banned in 1980 but still

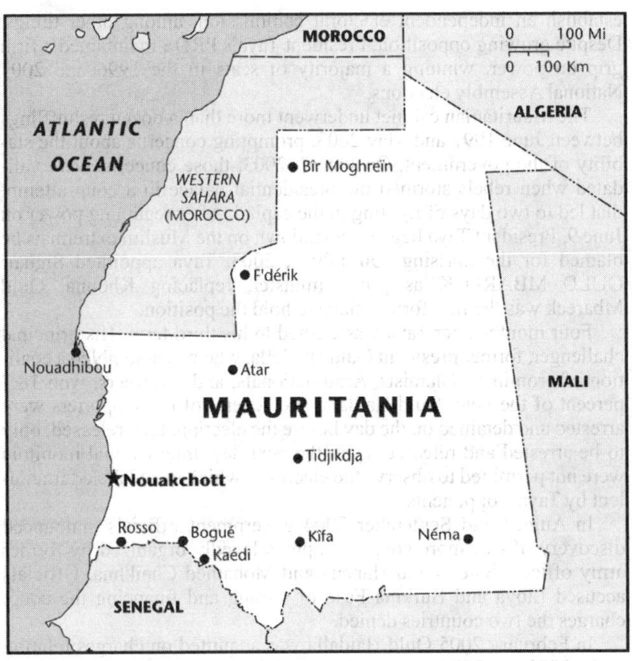

reportedly encompassing an estimated 100,000–400,000 Haratines and blacks in servitude to Arab masters.

Before 1970 nearly all of the northern population was engaged in nomadic cattle raising, but the proportion had shrunk to less than one-quarter by 1986. Prolonged droughts, desertification, the loss of herds, and more recently, a devastating locust attack in 2004 that wiped out about half of the country's crops, have driven more Mauritanians to urban areas, where many depend on foreign relief aid. Many Mauritanians seek their livelihood in other countries.

The country's first deep water port, financed by China, opened near Nouakchott in 1986. Mauritania's coastal waters are among the richest fishing grounds in the world and generate more than half of its foreign exchange, although the region is also routinely fished by foreign trawlers.

To secure aid from international donors, the government initiated numerous economic reforms, including privatization of state-owned enterprises, promotion of free market activity, and currency devaluation. The government also endorsed political liberalization, although genuine progress in that regard has been minimal, while international lenders called for measures to address the unequal distribution of wealth. More than 50 percent of the population lives in poverty, and the social services sector is considered grossly inadequate.

In 2002 the International Monetary Fund (IMF) and the World Bank announced debt relief of $1.1 billion for Mauritania. In 2003 exploratory tests indicated the presence of offshore oil fields, prompting investments from international oil companies. Annual GDP growth of 5.6 percent and 5.2 percent, respectively, was reported in 2003 and 2004. Following the military coup in August 2005, the transitional government "swiftly embarked on a course of macroeconomic stabilization and reforms," according to the IMF, resulting in a decline in inflation from 17 percent at the beginning of the year to single digits in the last quarter and an overall strengthening of the economy. In 2006 Mauritania began exporting crude oil, with daily production reportedly averaging 54,000 barrels per day, contributing to a significant increase in annual growth (about 10 percent) in 2007. The IMF commended the transitional government for its efforts toward transparency and for its plans to curtail government spending and to budget oil revenue for anti-poverty programs. Mauritania received debt relief totaling more than $400 million in 2007 from the IMF, the World Bank, and other international organizations. Annual GDP growth of about 5 percent in 2008 was expected to slow to about 3 percent in 2009, owing in large part to a decrease in donor revenue following what observers said was a lack of progress in restoring democracy after the August 2008 bloodless coup. The global financial crisis also negatively affected Mauritania, as iron and oil prices declined sharply, and key investors pulled out of the planned privatization of country's largest mining company. Meanwhile, the government instituted price controls on food and fuel. Resolution of the political crisis (see Current issues, below) was said by analysts to be the key to restoring the depressed economy in 2010, analysts said.

GOVERNMENT AND POLITICS

Political background. Under nominal French administration from the turn of the century, Mauritania became a French colony in 1920, but de facto control was not established until 1934. It became an autonomous republic within the French Community in 1958 and an independent "Islamic Republic" on November 28, 1960. President Moktar OULD DADDAH (died October 14, 2003), who led the country to independence, established a one-party regime with predominantly Moorish backing and endorsed a policy of moderate socialism at home combined with nonalignment abroad. Opposition to his 18-year presidency was periodically voiced by northern groups seeking union with Morocco, inhabitants of the predominantly black south who feared Arab domination, and leftist elements in both student and trade union organizations.

Under an agreement concluded in November 1975 by Mauritania, Morocco, and Spain, the Ould Daddah regime assumed control of the southern third of Western (Spanish) Sahara on February 28, 1976, coincident with the withdrawal of Spanish forces and Morocco's occupation of the northern two-thirds (see map and discussion under entry for Morocco). However, an inability to contain Algerian-supported insurgents in the annexed territory contributed to the president's ouster in a bloodless coup on July 10, 1978, and the installation of Lt. Col. Mustapha OULD SALEK as head of state by a newly formed Military Committee for National Recovery (*Comité Militaire de Recouvrement National*—CMRN). Ould Salek, arguing that the struggle against the insurgents had "nearly destroyed" the Mauritanian economy, indicated that his government would be willing to withdraw from Tiris El-Gharbia (the Mauritanian sector of Western Sahara) if a settlement acceptable to Morocco, Algeria, and the insurgents could be found. However, the overture was rejected by Morocco, and in October the Algerian-backed Popular Front for the Liberation of Saguia el Hamra and Rio de Oro (Polisario) announced that the insurgency would cease only if Mauritania were to withdraw from the sector and recognize Polisario's government in exile, the Saharan Arab Democratic Republic (SADR).

In March 1979 Ould Salek reiterated his government's desire to extricate itself from the conflict but dismissed several CMRN members known to favor direct talks with Polisario. Subsequently, on April 6 he dissolved the CMRN itself in favor of a new Military Committee for National Salvation (*Comité Militaire de Salut National*—CMSN) and relinquished the office of prime minister to Lt. Col. Ahmed OULD BOUCEIF, who was immediately hailed as effective leader of the Nouakchott regime. On May 27, however, Ould Bouceif was killed in an airplane crash and was succeeded (following the interim incumbency of Lt. Col. Ahmed Salem OULD SIDI) by Lt. Col. Mohamed Khouna OULD HAIDALLA on May 31.

President Ould Salek was forced to resign on June 3, and the CMSN named Lt. Col. Mohamed Mahmoud Ould Ahmed LOULY as his replacement. Colonel Louly immediately declared his commitment to a cessation of hostilities and on August 5, after three days of talks in Algiers, concluded a peace agreement with Polisario representatives. While the pact did not entail recognition of the SADR, Mauritania formally renounced all claims to Tiris El-Gharbia and subsequently withdrew its troops from the territory, which was thereupon occupied by Moroccan forces and renamed Oued Eddahab.

On January 4, 1980, President Louly was replaced by Col. Ould Haidalla, who also continued to serve as chief of government. The following December Ould Haidalla announced that, as a first step toward restoration of democratic institutions, his largely military administration would be replaced by a civilian government headed by Sid Ahmad OULD BNEIJARA. Only one army officer was named to the cabinet announced on December 15, while the CMSN published a draft constitution four days later that proposed establishment of a multiparty system.

The move toward civilianization was abruptly halted on March 16, 1981, as the result of an attempted coup by a group of officers (who were allegedly backed by Morocco), and Prime Minister Ould Bneijara was replaced on April 26 by the army chief of staff, Col. Maaouya Ould Sidahmed TAYA. A further coup attempt, involving an effort to abduct President Ould Haidalla at Nouakchott airport on February 6, 1982, resulted in the arrest of Ould Bneijara and former president Ould Salek, both of whom were sentenced to ten-year prison terms by a special tribunal on March 5.

On March 8, 1984, in a major leadership reshuffle, Taya returned to his former military post, and the president reclaimed the prime ministry, to which was added the defense portfolio. The following December Ould Haidalla was ousted in a bloodless coup led by Colonel Taya, who assumed the titles of president, prime minister, and chair of the CMSN.

Amid increasingly vocal black opposition to Moorish domination, Colonel Taya announced plans in mid-1986 for a gradual return to democratic rule (see Constitution and government, below), and local councils were elected in the country's regional capitals in December. However, north-south friction persisted, with 3 Toucouleur officers being executed and some 40 others imprisoned for involvement in an alleged coup attempt in October 1987.

Although the Taya regime was subsequently charged with systematic repression of opponents, particularly southerners, elections were held for councils in the principal townships and rural districts in January 1988 and 1989, respectively. New elections to all the municipal councils, originally planned for late 1989 but postponed because of a violent dispute with Senegal (see Foreign relations, below), were held in December 1990. Meanwhile, racial tension remained high because of reports that security forces had imprisoned thousands of black army officers and government officials, several hundred of whom had allegedly been executed or tortured to death. Although the government claimed that the arrests had been made in connection with a coup plot, opponents charged that the regime was merely intensifying an already virulent antiblack campaign.

On April 15, 1991, Colonel Taya surprised observers by announcing that a referendum would be held soon on a new constitution, followed by multiparty presidential and legislative elections. The draft constitution was released on June 10 by the CMSN, approved with a reported "yes" vote of nearly 98 percent in a national referendum on July 12, and formally entered into effect on July 21. Four days later the CMSN adopted legislation on the legalization of political parties, six of which were quickly recognized, including the regime-supportive Democratic and Social Republican Party (*Parti Républicain Démocratique et Social*—PRDS). On June 29 Colonel Taya declared a general amnesty for detainees held on state security charges, thereby somewhat mollifying black hostility.

In presidential balloting on January 24, 1992, Colonel Taya, as the PRDS nominee, was credited with winning 63 percent of the vote; his principal challenger, Ahmed OULD DADDAH, received 33 percent. Ould Daddah, the previously exiled brother of former president Moktar Ould Daddah, was supported by a number of the new political parties, including the influential Union of Democratic Forces (*Union des Forces Démocratiques*—UFD), which challenged the accuracy of the official election results.

On February 10, 1992, five opposition parties requested postponement of National Assembly elections scheduled for March 6 and 13 to avoid a repetition of what they claimed had been massive fraud in the presidential poll. Their appeal rejected, 6 of the 14 opposition groups, including the UFD, boycotted the balloting, in which the PRDS won an overwhelming majority of seats on a turnout of little more than a third of the electorate.

In indirect senatorial balloting on April 3 and 10, 1992, the participants were further reduced to the PRDS and the small Avante-Guard Party (*Parti Avant-Garde*—PAG). The PAG received none of the available seats, as contrasted with 36 for the PRDS and 17 for independents. On April 18, following Colonel Taya's inauguration as president, Taya yielded the office of prime minister to a young technocrat, Sidi Mohamed OULD BOUBACAR, who announced the formation of a new government on April 20.

In 1994 the government party won control of 172 of the 208 municipal councils (as compared to 19 for independents and 17 for the UFD), prompting opposition charges of extensive electoral fraud. The opposition also questioned the results of the April Senate replenishment, in which the PRDS won 16 of 17 seats. In September it was reported that President Taya had dropped his military title in pursuit of a more civilian image. At the same time, the government launched a crackdown on Islamic "agitators," fundamentalists having reportedly gained converts by providing much-needed social services in urban areas.

Taya dismissed Ould Boubacar on January 2, 1996, replacing him with Cheikh el Avia Ould Mohamed KHOUNA. The December 12, 1997, elections won President Taya another six-year term, with an official 90 percent of the vote. The UFD and several other opposition parties boycotted the balloting in objection to the regime's failure to establish an independent electoral commission, among other things. Despite growing opposition, President Taya's PRDS maintained a firm grip on power, winning a majority of seats in the 1996 and 2001 National Assembly elections.

The Mauritanian cabinet underwent more than a dozen reshufflings between June 1997 and May 2003, prompting concerns about the stability of the government. On June 7, 2003, those concerns were validated when rebels stormed the presidential palace in a coup attempt that led to two days of fighting in the capital. After regaining power on June 9, President Taya began a crackdown on the Muslim extremists he blamed for the uprising. On July 7, 2003, Taya appointed Sighair OULD MBARECK as prime minister, replacing Khouna. Ould Mbareck was the first former slave to hold the position.

Four months later Taya was elected to his third term. His principal challenger, former president Ould Haidalla, who had assembled a coalition of prominent Islamists, Arab nationals, and reformers, won 18.7 percent of the vote. Ould Haidalla and several of his supporters were arrested and detained on the day before the election, then released, only to be arrested and released again the next day. International monitors were not permitted to observe the elections, which were labeled fraudulent by Taya's opponents.

In August and September 2004 government officials announced discovery of two more coup attempts, allegedly organized by former army officers Saleh Ould Hanena and Mohamed Cheikhna. Officials accused Libya and Burkina Faso of arming and financing the coup, charges the two countries denied.

In February 2005 Ould Haidalla was acquitted on charges relating to the 2003 and 2004 attempted coups. Four soldiers were found guilty and sentenced to life in prison. A bloodless coup was staged on August 3, 2005, when Taya was in Saudi Arabia attending the funeral of King Fahd. A group of security and army officers led by Col. Ely Ould Mohamed VALL established themselves as the ruling Military Council for Justice and Democracy (MCJD) with Vall as head of state. On August 5 the parliament was dissolved. Mbareck resigned as prime minister on August 7 and was immediately replaced by Ould Boubacar, ambassador to France, who resigned from the former ruling PRDS party on August 9. A new cabinet, described as consisting primarily of technocrats, was announced on August 10.

In keeping with their promise of a quick return to a civilian government, the leaders of the junta presented constitutional amendments in a national referendum in June 2006 that provided for new legislative and presidential elections. Balloting for the National Assembly was held on November 19 and December 3, while senate elections were held on January 21 and February 4, 2007. Many of the successful candidates in both houses were technically independents (see Current issues, below, for details), although a coalition of opponents of the Taya regime called the Coalition of Forces of Democratic Change (*Coalition des Forces des Changement Démocratique*—CFCD) secured 38 seats in assembly elections. Women held 18 percent of seats in the assembly and 16 percent of seats in the senate, close to the junta's goal of 20 percent participation by women.

Among 20 candidates in first-round presidential balloting on March 11, 2007, only 8 ran under the banner of political parties. Sidi Mohamed Ould Cheikh ABDALLAHI, an independent, won with 53 percent of the vote in the runoff election on March 25 (with the support of half of the first-round candidates), defeating Ahmed Ould Daddah of the Rally of Democratic Forces (*Rassemblement des Forces Démocratiques*—RFD), who garnered 47 percent. Abdallahi appointed Zeine Ould ZEIDANE, who had finished third in the balloting, as prime minister on April 20. The new government, which was formed on April 28, reportedly was made up largely of technocrats and at least four members of the Popular Progressive Alliance (*Alliance Populaire et Progressive*—APP).

Abdallahi was reported to have been among the founding members of the National Pact for Development and Democracy (*Pacte National pour le Développment et le Démocratie*—PNDD) in early 2007, sometime after the presidential election. The party, formed by independents and supporters of Abdallahi from small political parties, subsequently became the governing party. On May 6, 2008, Abdallahi appointed Yahya Ould Ahmed el-WAGHF as prime minister, and on May 11 el-Waghf reshuffled the cabinet. Though dominated by the PNDD, the cabinet included for the first time a small number of opposition party representatives. El-Waghf resigned along with the entire cabinet on July 3 in advance of a scheduled no-confidence vote by parliament, but he was immediately reappointed by the president. A new, expanded cabinet, consisting entirely of PNDD members, was named on July 15.

On August 6, 2008, Abdallahi was deposed in a bloodless coup led by the head of the Presidential Guard, Gen. Mohamed Ould ABDELAZIZ, who formed an 11-member High Council of State. Abdallahi, el-Waghf, and the minister of the interior, Mohamed Ould RZEIZIM, were arrested, with all but Abdallahi subsequently released. On August 14 Abdelaziz appointed Moulaye Ould Mohamed LAGHDAF, a diplomat, as prime minister. Laghdaf formed a new government on August 31, retaining four ministers from the previous government. On April 15, 2009, Ba Mamadou MBARE, the president of the Senate, became interim head of government, following the resignation of Abdelaziz, who stepped down to contest the presidential elections that had been set for June 6. Opposition parties threatened to boycott the balloting amid claims that junta leaders had ensured Abdelaziz's election, since all candidates approved by the Constitutional Court were reportedly pro-junta. Subsequently, both sides reached agreement on a new election date of July 18 (and August 1, if a runoff was necessary), and former president Abdallahi was asked to name a unity government, with Laghdaf as prime minister, on June 26. The new government retained 13 ministers and added 13 ministers from the opposition. Meanwhile, the High Council of State adopted the rubric Superior Council of National Defense, and on June 27 Abdallahi officially resigned as president. (*See headnote*.)

Constitution and government. The constitution of May 23, 1961, which had replaced Mauritania's former parliamentary-type government with a one-party presidential system, was formally suspended by the CMRN on July 20, 1978. A Constitutional Charter issued by the Military Committee confirmed the dissolution of the National Assembly and the Mauritanian People's Party (*Parti du Peuple Mauritanien*—PPM) and authorized the installation of the committee's chair as head of state until such time as "new democratic institutions are established."

In December 1980 the CMSN published a constitutional proposal that was to have been submitted to a referendum in 1981. However, no balloting was held prior to the coup of December 1984. Subsequently, Colonel Taya indicated that the military would prepare for a return to democracy through a program called the Structure for the Education of the Masses that would involve the election of councilors at the local level to advise the government on measures to improve literacy, social integration, and labor productivity. In the series of municipal elections conducted in 1986–1990, voters chose from multiple lists of candidates approved by the government, although no formal political party activity was permitted.

The 1991 constitution declared Mauritania to be an "Islamic Arab and African republic," guaranteed "freedom of association, thought, and expression," and conferred strong executive powers on the president, including the authority to appoint the prime minister. Directly elected by universal suffrage in two-round voting, the president was allowed to serve an unlimited number of six-year terms. The new basic law also established a bicameral legislature (comprising a directly elected National Assembly and an indirectly elected Senate), as well as constitutional, economic and social, and Islamic councils.

The legal system traditionally reflected a combination of French and Islamic codes, with the judiciary encompassing a Supreme Court; a High Court of Justice; courts of first instance; and civil, labor, and military courts. In June 1978 a commission was appointed to revise the system according to Islamic precepts, and in March 1980, a month after the replacement of "modern" codes by Islamic law (sharia), the CMSN established an Islamic Court consisting of a Muslim magistrate, two councilors, and two *ulemas* (interpreters of the Koran). Earlier, in October 1978, a special Court of State Security had been created. The 1991 constitution provided for an independent judiciary, with sharia serving as the "single source of law."

The Military Council for Justice and Democracy (MCJD), formed by the leaders of the August 2005 coup, maintained the 1991 constitution, supplementing it with a military council "charter" that stipulated the MCJD held power over the executive and legislative branches, dissolved the parliament, and gave the MCJD advisory power over the Constitutional Council. Constitutional amendments proposed by the transitional government were overwhelmingly approved by voters (97 percent) in a June 25, 2006, referendum to limit a president to two terms of five years each and set a maximum age limit of 75 for a president, among other things.

For administrative purposes the country is divided into 12 regions, plus the capital district of Nouakchott, and 32 departments; in addition, 208 urban and rural districts (areas populated by at least 500 inhabitants) were created in October 1988.

Foreign relations. Mauritania has combined nonalignment in world affairs with membership in such groupings as the Arab League (since 1973) and, as of 1989, the Arab Maghreb Union (AMU). Following independence, economic and cultural cooperation with France continued on the basis of agreements first negotiated in 1961 and renegotiated in 1973 to exclude special arrangements in monetary and military affairs. As a consequence, French military advisers were recalled and Mauritania withdrew from the Franc Zone, establishing its own currency. In late 1979 a limited number of French troops and military instructors returned to ensure Mauritania's territorial integrity following Nouakchott's withdrawal from Western Sahara and the annexation of its sector by Morocco.

Mauritania's settlement with the Polisario Front was followed by restoration of diplomatic relations with Algeria, which had been severed upon Algiers' recognition of the Saharan Arab Democratic Republic (SADR) in 1976. During 1980–1982 Nouakchott maintained formal neutrality in Polisario's continuing confrontation with Morocco, withholding formal recognition of the SADR but criticizing Rabat's military efforts to retain control of the entire Western Sahara. In 1983 Colonel Ould Haidalla concluded a Maghreb Fraternity and Cooperation Treaty with Algeria and Tunisia that was implicitly directed against Rabat and Tripoli. On the other hand, declaring that the conflict in the Western Sahara had "poisoned the atmosphere," Colonel Taya subsequently attempted to return Mauritania to its traditional posture of regional neutralism. While still maintaining its "moral support" for the SADR, which it officially recognized in 1984, the Taya regime normalized relations with Morocco and Libya, thereby balancing growing ties with Algeria that included the signing of a border demarcation agreement in April 1986.

Relations with Senegal were tense after an April 1989 incident when violence erupted between villagers along the border, provoking race riots in both nations' capitals that reportedly caused the death of nearly 500 people and injury to more than 1,000. During the ensuing months an estimated 170,000–240,000 Mauritanian expatriates fled Senegal, while Mauritania reportedly expelled 70,000 Senegalese and 40,000 of its own black residents. Mauritania and Senegal severed diplomatic relations in August, with each country accusing the other of instigating further violence. Although the countries restored ties in April 1992 and the border was partially reopened the following November, tension continued as black Mauritanians charged they were being prevented from returning to Mauritania, and Senegal attributed widespread "banditry" along the border to the refugee situation. Despite several flare-ups, relations between the two countries improved after Senegal's president Abdoulaye Wade expressed his support for the Taya regime, following the 2003 coup attempt in Mauritania, and extradited a suspected coup plotter to Mauritania. (In November 2007 Mauritania, Senegal, and the United Nations High Commissioner for Refugees [UNHCR] signed a tripartite agreement to initiate the return of thousands of black Mauritanian refugees.)

Mauritania has also had strained relations with Mali, whose black-dominated Traoré regime accused Nouakchott in the late 1980s of supporting antigovernment activity among its ethnically Berber Tuareg population. Following the resolution of the Tuareg situation in the mid-1990s, relations with Mali have warmed.

Mauritania attracted an unusual amount of international attention because of its support for Iraq in the 1990–1991 Gulf crisis, causing Western donors to sharply curtail aid to Nouakchott. However, assistance was subsequently restored, apparently reflecting Western support for the Taya regime's strong antifundamentalist posture. The government distanced itself from Iraq, expelling Baghdad's ambassador in October 1995 amid reports of a coup plot among "pro-Baathist" elements. Among other things, the policy shift contributed to improved relations with Gulf Arab states.

In November 1995 Nouakchott announced plans to open an "interest" office in Tel Aviv as part of what was expected to be eventual restoration of full relations with Israel. The action was condemned by some hard-line Arab states, including Libya, which recalled its ambassador and discontinued all aid to Mauritania. However, Tunisian mediation in early 1997 helped restore relations between Mauritania and Tripoli.

In late 1999 the Taya government completed the foreign policy reversal started in mid-decade by severing relations with Iraq and becoming only the third Arab state (after Egypt and Jordan) to establish full diplomatic relations with Israel.

French officials have been critical of Mauritania's human rights record, but relations between the two countries improved after France offered support to the Taya regime following the 2003 coup attempt.

The government has cooperated with the United States in several counterterrorism training programs beginning in 2003. Such programs target al-Qaida–affiliated groups operating in Mauritania and several neighboring countries. In a major decision, Mauritania announced in December that it was withdrawing from the Economic Community of West African States (ECOWAS); analysts suggested that Nouakchott had grown increasingly concerned over the possibility that the non-Francophone countries in ECOWAS would adopt a common currency to the detriment of the ouguiya. Subsequently, the Taya administration declared that it would focus on affairs in northern Africa, particularly through the proposed rejuvenation of the Arab Maghreb Union, rather than on its relations with its southern neighbors. (As a result, Nouakchott was described in 2000 as having informally accepted the premise that the Western Sahara would remain a province of Morocco.)

Regional tensions increased in August and September 2004 after President Taya accused Libya and Burkina Faso of arming renegade soldiers allegedly preparing to topple the Taya regime in two separate coup attempts. Both countries denied the accusations.

Following the August 2005 coup, Colonel Vall pledged to maintain Mauritania's relations with Israel. The African Union (AU) suspended Mauritania's membership the day after the coup but readmitted the country on April 10, 2007, following democratic elections.

After the bloodless coup in 2008, Algeria and Nigeria condemned the coup, while Libya expressed its support for the junta. Morocco and Senegal were reported to have "shown understanding," while a French minister canceled a planned visit in October after the junta refused to release the deposed president from house arrest.

Israel closed its embassy in Nouakchott on March 6, 2009, after the junta asked the ambassador to leave in the wake of Israel's recent retaliatory attacks against Palestinians in the Gaza Strip. Mauritania, one of only three Arab countries to have diplomatic ties with Israel (Egypt and Jordan being the others), withdrew its ambassador from Israel in February.

Current issues. President Taya's 2003 victory came amid widespread allegations of fraud, but his critics declined to pursue the matter through legal channels. French observers were not invited to monitor the elections, as they had done in 2001, and several opposition members, including Taya's main opponent, were arrested in the days leading up to the vote, prompting a warning from Human Rights Watch of a climate of "harassment of opposition members."

The crackdown on Islamists and other Taya opponents intensified, and subsequently in the spring of 2005 the government arrested 30 alleged terrorists accused of attempting to destabilize the country. The government claimed to have linked many of the prisoners to a group affiliated with al-Qaida. However, opponents and some human rights groups charged that Taya was using Western fears of terrorism as an opportunity to silence his opponents. Training and financing for the crackdown came partly from the United States as part of its own counterterrorism efforts. Human rights groups cautioned that increasing tensions between Taya and Islamic groups, fueled by the impending infusion of oil money, could further destabilize the country.

On June 16, 2005, gunmen ambushed a remote military outpost in northern Mauritania, killing 15 soldiers. An al-Qaida affiliate in Algeria called the Salafi Group for Call and Combat (see article on Algeria) claimed responsibility for the attack. The group said the ambush was meant to avenge the imprisonment of Islamists in Mauritania.

Taya had become "despotic" since taking power and was "deeply unpopular," not only for his imprisonment of dissidents (Islamists, in particular), but also because of his perceived discrimination against Mauritania's poorer Arab population, according to *Middle East International.* The coup staged by a group of military officials on August 3, 2005, when Taya was out of the country, had significant domestic support—marked by exuberant street celebrations—and, ultimately, international acceptance, including financial support for promised elections. Col. Ely Ould Mohamed Vall, who, as president of the Military Council for Justice and Democracy became head of state after the MCJD's takeover, immediately announced broad-ranging plans for democratic reform. He offered assurances that the transitional government would be in place for no longer than two years, and that neither he nor anyone in the MCJD would participate in elections scheduled in 2006 (local and parliamentary) and 2007 (presidential). In addition, he announced a general amnesty for political prisoners; implemented a constitutional referendum (see Constitution and government, above); and allowed Taya—in exile in Qatar—to return to Mauritania if he chose, though barring him from the 2007 presidential elections. While the coup initially met with international condemnation, attitudes soon softened, and in early 2006 the European Union (EU) offered some $7 million to support the transition, with other contributions reportedly coming from France, Spain, and Egypt. The United States was also reported to be working with the junta to organize multiparty elections as soon as possible. As of April, according to a Mauritanian census, nearly 1 million voters had been registered. Perhaps the most significant change under Colonel Vall's initial tenure was the amending of the constitution to set term limits for a president, eliminating the power of a "president-for-life," and bringing the country closer to civilian rule with the introduction of multiparty elections.

The transitional government banned leaders of the junta from standing as candidates in the 2006 assembly balloting. A number of Islamic parties were also proscribed, though their members were permitted to run as independents. At the same time, party leaders claimed that the Taya regime could also find a way back to power by fielding so-called independent candidates. Parties opposed to the former Taya regime and independents won the most seats. The CFCD, led by Ahmed Ould Daddah's RFD party, secured the largest single bloc of seats and was subsequently perceived as the primary opposition grouping. Also notable was the success of Islamists in gaining seats. The elections were described as the first free and transparent elections since independence.

Following the election of President Abdallahi in March 2007, attention turned to key domestic issues. Abdallahi, who once held a ministerial post in the Taya regime but later fell out of favor and spent a year under house arrest, vowed to fight poverty and injustice—key planks of Ould Daddah's campaign as well. Abdallahi was backed by numerous parties once loyal to Taya and was also widely regarded as the candidate favored by the junta. Abdallahi's choice for prime minister was Zeine Ould ZEIDANE, an economist who had headed the central bank under the Taya regime and had been retained by the junta in that post to carry out reforms recommended by the IMF and the World Bank.

It was reported sometime after the election that Abdallahi had formed a new political party, the PNDD, which he would not chair since the constitution, as amended in 2006, prohibits a president from doing so. However, he chose Yahya Ould Ahmed el-WAGHF as the party's leader, outlined its platform, and welcomed independents and former members of the ruling party. Opposition and smaller parties vehemently opposed the formation of this "presidential majority" party, claiming that it would involve the "squandering" of public money and lead to corruption, despite government assurances of neutrality. In August, as part of its further efforts toward democratic reform, the government announced that it had licensed 18 new political parties (see Other Parties and Groups under Political Parties, below, for details). The president also undertook a major reshuffle of the military, removing members of the former ruling junta. Addressing another area of domestic concern, the National Assembly passed legislation imposing fines and prison terms for practitioners of slavery. (Though slavery was banned in 1980, a large number of Mauritanians are still believed to be enslaved; see The Country, above).

Trials began in 2007 for more than 20 Islamists allegedly linked to al-Qaida, some of whom were accused in the 2005 attack on military garrisons and others who were alleged to have received training in Algeria from groups connected to al-Qaida. In December two French tourists were killed by gunmen believed to be affiliated with al-Qaida; a few days later three Mauritanian soldiers were killed in a similar attack at the border with Algeria. Concerns about these events and other terrorist activity in North Africa resulted in the cancellation by France of a major tourist event, the Dakar Rally, which included a route through Mauritania. President Abdallahi, for his part, promised to continue Mauritania's policy of supporting U.S. antiterrorism efforts in North Africa, and the assembly created an antiterrorism body. Further terrorist activity was reported in February 2008 when the Israeli embassy in Nouakchott was attacked, resulting in injury to three people at a nearby café. Among the eight people arrested was one who allegedly belonged to a group linked to al-Qaida. Meanwhile, Israel said it had no plans to close its embassy in Mauritania.

Domestic discontent, spurred by rising food prices and attacks by extremist groups in 2008, were cited as among factors that led President Abdallahi to replace Zeidane as prime minister in May. In addition, the administration had been criticized for not representing the majority parties in parliament (Zeidane's cabinet was mainly technocrats and members of the APP). Though the new prime minister, the PNDD's Yahya Ould Ahmed el-Waghf, included several opposition parties in his reshuffled cabinet, the RFD refused to participate in a unity government. RFD leader Ahmed Ould Daddah, in rejecting the offer, said the opposition parties had essentially been invited to sign on to the president's political program. Within months, el-Waghf was facing a no-confidence vote in parliament, initiated by disaffected PNDD members who said the prime minister had chosen government members affiliated with the former Taya regime, in addition to naming opposition members to the cabinet. President Abdallahi said it was "astonishing" that members of the majority party would vote against the government, but ultimately the censure vote was not held. Following the turmoil, el-Waghf resigned in July, along with the entire cabinet, but he was reappointed by the president. The new cabinet, named within two weeks, comprised only members of Abdallahi's PNDD. Disaffection with Abdallahi and his perceived ineptitude in curbing high food prices, coupled with allegations of corruption against him, ultimately led 48 members of the PNDD to resign on August 4. Two days later, Abdallahi fired several members of his elite Presidential Guard, including its head, Gen. Abdelaziz, who had backed Abdallahi in his bid for the presidency. Hours after the security staff were dismissed, Abdelaziz staged a bloodless coup, with soldiers surrounding the palace. Abdallahi, el-Waghf, and the interior minister were immediately placed under arrest. State-run radio and television were shut down, and the country was returned to military rule. Police dispersed, without violence, throngs of citizens outside the palace, and Abdelaziz took over as chair of an 11-member High Council of State. Despite Abdelaziz's pledge that he would hold elections at some unspecified future date, the African Union, the EU, the UN, and the United Sates immediately condemned the coup and called for a return to constitutional rule. Further, the United States announced it was suspending aid, and Mauritania's biggest bilateral donor, the French Agency for Development, suspended all non-emergency funding.

The interior minister and the former prime minister were released on August 11, 2008, but Abdallahi remained in custody. The following day, the junta authorized laws granting its members the right to rule and giving them "the necessary powers to reorganize and manage state affairs during the period needed for the organization of presidential elections," according to published reports. A separate decree named Mohamed Lemine Ould GUIG, a former prime minister in the Taya regime, as secretary general of the High Council of State. Two days later Abdelaziz named Laghdaf as prime minister. Observers noted his choice of a former ambassador for prime minister and his anti-Islamist stance as elements that would appeal to the West, and the United States in particular. However, Washington refused to recognize the military government.

Laghdaf's new cabinet retained four key ministers from the previous government—defense, justice, economy, and finance—and all members reportedly were from parties that supported the coup. Those parties were said to include the RFD and a reformist Islamist party led by Mohamed Jemil Ould. Meanwhile, members of the PNDD, APP, and UFP, as well as some civil societies, formed a group called the National Front for the Defense of Democracy (*Avant National pour la Défense de la Démocratie*—FNDD) to voice opposition to the coup. Despite conflicting sentiments among parties, the coup appeared to have the support of the majority of members of parliament, as more than two-thirds from both chambers signed a declaration praising the junta.

On September 2, 2008, the assembly named a council to try Abdallahi on charges of corruption and obstructing parliament. (An attempt by parliament before the coup to hold a special session to conduct the corruption probe had been blocked by Abdallahi.) The former president's supporters claimed that the allegations were a front that gave the military leaders an excuse to stage the coup. Meanwhile, the assembly also launched an investigation of Abdallahi's wife, who had been accused of stealing public funds. Meanwhile, it was reported that another former coup leader and associate of Abdelaziz, Col. Vall, had returned to Mauritania on September 1.

Turmoil continued on another front in 2008 as al-Qaida in the Maghreb denounced the coup and called for a "holy war" in Mauritania, saying that the junta leaders had been acting in concert with the "infidels" of Israel, the United States, and France. Al-Qaida also called for the restoration of a caliphate in the country and denounced Mauritania further for its diplomatic ties to Israel. On September 15 al-Qaida militants killed 12 Mauritanian soldiers in what news reports said was an attempt by the terrorist group to avenge the coup. That same day the National Assembly voted to hold elections within 12 to 14 months. Meanwhile, General Abdelaziz vowed to crack down on al-Qaida.

In mid-September 2008, General Abdelaziz rejected an ultimatum by the AU that Mauritania restore constitutional order by October 6 and reinstate President Abdallahi, or else face sanctions. A "democratic convention" scheduled for December was boycotted by the opposition, the FNDD saying that participation would be the equivalent of recognizing the junta. In January 2009 the junta announced that a presidential election would be held on June 6, Abdelaziz having announced earlier that he would not be a candidate. Meanwhile, Abdallahi, who had been released from custody—reportedly to avert EU sanctions—said he would accept the outcome of a new election only if the army abdicated authority and constitutional order were restored. Mass demonstrations protesting his release were reported, with Abdallahi claiming that the rallies were arranged by the junta, while some observers said public opinion was mixed.

Moving forward with plans for a new government, the junta formed an independent electoral commission in March 2009 to supervise the upcoming presidential election. Further, Abdelaziz resigned on April 15, and the following day Senate president Ba Mamadou Mbare moved into the position of interim head of government. Contrary to his earlier statements, Abdelaziz decided to run for president (as an independent), along with challengers Kane Hamidou Baba, vice president of the RFD; Ibrahima Moctar Sarr, leader of the AJD-MR (see Political Parties, below); and former prime minister Sighair Ould Mbareck. Opposition parties threatened to boycott the balloting, claiming that all the candidates were pro-junta, and during demonstrations supporting former president Abdallahi, hundreds of protesters were reportedly beaten by police. The elections were postponed while efforts were under way to persuade opposition parties to participate. Subsequently, as tensions increased, Senegalese president Abdoulaye Wade helped avert a political crisis by mediating talks in Dakar between junta leaders and the chairs of the FNDD and the RFD. In early June an agreement was reached not only on a new election date of July 18 (and August 1, if a runoff was necessary), but also on the formation of a transitional unity government, with Laghdaf retained as prime minister and a cabinet that included equal numbers of opposition and government ministers. Meanwhile, the High Council of State adopted the rubric Superior Council of National Defense, and on June 27 Abdallahi, in accordance with the agreement reached in Senegal, officially resigned as president. At the end of the month, the AU dropped its sanctions against Mauritania, citing its efforts to restore democracy. Meanwhile, another former coup leader, Col. Vall, announced his candidacy in the upcoming election. Vall, a cousin and former ally of Abdelaziz, condemned the most recent coup, saying it was "wrong and there was no reason for it." A month before the election, assembly speaker Massaoud Ould Boulkheir announced his candidacy under the banner of the opposition FNDD; a few days later, Mohamed Jemil Ould Mansour of the National Rally for Reform and Development (RNRD) announced his candidacy. Other parties, including new ones formed ahead of the election, subsequently named candidates, bringing the field to ten. (*See headnote.*)

Three weeks before the election, al-Qaida of the Islamic Maghreb claimed responsibility for the killing of an American aid worker in Nouakchott.

POLITICAL PARTIES

Mauritania became a one-party state in 1964, when the Mauritanian People's Party (*Parti du Peuple Mauritanien*—PPM/*Hizb al-Shah al-Muritani*) was assigned legal supremacy over all governmental organs. The PPM was dissolved following the coup of July 1978. Although partisan activity was not permitted, some candidates in municipal elections in 1986–1990 were linked to various informal groups.

The constitution approved in July 1991 guaranteed "freedom of association," and subsequent legislation established regulations for the legalization of political parties. Groups based on race or region were proscribed, while Islamic organizations were declared ineligible for registration on the ground that Islam belonged to "all the people" and could not be "claimed" by electoral bodies.

In view of the near-total dominance of the Democratic and Social Republican Party (PRDS) in recent national and municipal elections, legislation was adopted in late 2000 providing for a degree of proportional representation in the 2001 assembly balloting and concurrent local polls. It was also announced that all parties securing at least 1 percent of the votes in the municipal elections would receive government financing (based on their total vote) and that "equal access" to the state-controlled media would be provided to opposition parties.

Following the coup of August 3, 2005, most political parties and groups backed the transitional junta. Though the Republican Democratic

Party for Renovation (*Parti Républicain Démocratique Rénové*—PRDR), as the PRDS had been renamed, initially denounced the coup, within little more than a month it appeared willing to support the junta, and in September it abolished the post of party chair that had been held for 15 years by former president Taya. The junta continued to restrict Islamist groups, but their members were allowed to run as independents in legislative and municipal elections. Five groups, including the Party for Democratic Convergence (PDC) and Action for Change (AC), were banned in 2005 because the junta regarded them as being Islamist organizations.

In advance of parliamentary and presidential elections in 2006 and 2007, respectively, various parties and groups formed alliances, though whatever electoral agreements they had were unclear.

A minor alliance formed in March 2006 to represent the "progressive left" was referenced as the Rally of the Forces of Progress. It included the Democratic and Social Union and members of the banned Party for Democratic Convergence. Another minor alliance formed in late 2006, the National Union for Democratic Change, reportedly included four parties, two of which had been banned. The group's stated goal was to support all ethnic groups.

The Coalition of Forces of Democratic Change (*Coalition des Forces des Changement Démocratique*—CFCD), formed in mid-2006 and led by Ahmed Ould Daddah, included parties and independents opposed to the former Taya regime. The 11 affiliated parties and groups were the RFD, the FP, the APP, the UFP, the HATEM, the RD, the UPSD, the Centrist Reformers, El Sawab, the Movement for Direct Democracy, and the Rally for Mauritania. Members in the coalition presented their own candidates in the first round of assembly balloting but agreed to support only the top vote-getter from the first round in the second round. Parties associated with the CFCD were credited with winning 38 seats in the assembly. Formal CFCD candidates were presented for the Senate, winning 3 seats, although individual members of the RFD, the HATEM, the UFP, and the APP, some in alliance with independents, were credited with winning a total of 12 seats. While the coalition members had initially agreed to present a single candidate in the 2007 presidential election, that pact fell apart when four component parties presented presidential candidates. Additional friction occurred when the APP leader, Massaoud Ould Boulkheir, decided to support Abdallahi in the second round, while the UFP leader, Mohammed Ould Maaloud, chose to back Ould Daddah.

The National Rally of Independents, formed prior to the 2006 assembly elections, was comprised largely of members of the former ruling PRDR. Of the 41 independents who won seats in the assembly, 39 were reportedly associated with the National Rally of Independents. (The remaining two independents were reported to be supportive of the CFCD.)

In February 2007 the RD withdrew from the CFCD to join a new coalition called *El-Watan* to support Ould Haidalla's presidential bid. The other parties allied with *El-Watan* were the FP and the Rally for Mauritania.

In early January 2007, 17 parties and groups formerly associated with the Taya regime, including the PRDR, formed a loose coalition called *Al-Mithaq*. Among the other parties participating in the coalition were the UDP, the RDU, and the Alternative (*l'Alternative*). *Al-Mithaq* formally backed Abdallahi in the presidential election, although some members of the former ruling party in the coalition ran as independents.

Following the bloodless coup of 2008, the PNDD, APP, and UFP, as well as some civil societies, formed the National Front for the Defense of Democracy (*Avant National pour la Défense de la Démocratie*—FNDD) in opposition to the coup. It later included the RNRD.

The **Alternative Party**, a pro-junta party formed in January 2009, backed Mohamed Yehdi Ould for president. The party's chair, Moctar HACEN, was a former minister and former member of the PRSD. In May 2009, in the run-up to the presidential election scheduled for June but postponed to July, the **Mauritanian Union for the Republic** was formed. The new party, which was founded by legislators who supported the coup, named junta leader Gen. Mohamed Ould Abdelaziz as chair. (*See headnote.*)

National Pact for Development and Democracy (*Pacte National pour le Développment et le Démocratie*—PNDD). Formed by President Sidi Mohamed Ould Cheikh Abdallahi following his election (as an independent) in March 2007, the party is also referenced as the PNDD-ADIL. Aside from Abdallahi's naming Yahya Ould Ahmed el-Waghf to head the party, little has been reported about the platform or which groups signed on to Abdallahi's move to consolidate government authority in the executive and legislative branches (the PNDD was reported to hold a majority of seats in parliament and all of the cabinet posts under Abdallahi's tenure as president). Some 40 party dissidents were reported to be responsible for calling for the no-confidence vote against Prime Minister el-Waghf in 2008, criticizing him for not representing the will of the electorate by including opposition members and others said to be aligned with the Taya regime in the government.

Just prior to the coup on August 6, 2008, some 48 members of the party resigned in the wake of mounting criticism of Adballahi's ability to effect change and allegations of corruption against him.

PNDD member Boidiel Ould Houmeid was among those who organized the FNDD to speak out against the August 2008 coup (see Current issues, above). Following the 2008 coup el-Waghf was imprisoned for six months; his release in June 2009 was among the conditions set forth by the opposition during negotiations in Senegal in May (see Current issues, above).

Leaders: Yahya Ould Ahmed el-WAGHF (Chair and Former Prime Minister), Sidi Mohamed Ould Cheikh ABDALLAHI (Former President of the Republic), Sidi Mohamed Ould MAHAM, Boidiel Ould HOUMEID.

Rally of Democratic Forces (*Rassemblement des Forces Démocratiques*—RFD). The RFD was formed in 2001 by former members of the Union of Democratic Forces (*Union des Forces Démocratiques*—UFD), which had been legalized in October 1991 under the leadership of Hadrami Ould KHATTRY and had originally encompassed a number of diverse opposition groups whose desire to oust the Taya regime appeared to be their only common bond. Widely viewed as the strongest opposition formation, the UFD supported Ahmed Ould Daddah, half-brother of former Mauritanian president Moktar Ould Daddah, in the January 1992 presidential election while spearheading the subsequent legislative boycotts. In May 1992 it was announced that the supporters of Ahmed Ould Daddah had been incorporated into the union, which was reported thereupon to have adopted the name of Union of Democratic Forces–New Era (*Union des Forces Démocratiques–Ere Nouvelle*—UFD-EN). However, news reports often continued to use the original name when referencing the group.

The party remained highly critical of the government; Ahmed Ould Daddah, who was elected UFD president in June 1992, charged that official harassment was impeding "normal" party activity. After Ould Daddah was reconfirmed as leader in early 1993, several prominent members left the party and formed the UDP. More serious were the announced defections in June 1994 of two of the union's most important components, *El-Hor,* which formed the Action for Change and the Movement of Independent Democrats (*Mouvement des Démocrates Indépendants*—MDI), which joined the PRDS.

The UFD was one of only two opposition parties (the UDP being the other) to contest the municipal elections in early 1994, gaining a majority in 17 of the country's 208 local councils. It boycotted the 1992 legislative poll but obtained one senate seat in 1994. The UFD competed unsuccessfully in the first round of 1996 legislative balloting but boycotted the second round, charging that the government had "tampered" with voting lists to excise supporters of the opposition.

In October 2000 the government banned the UFD-EN, accusing the party of inciting violence in connection with pro-Palestinian street demonstrations. Supporters subsequently launched the RFD, which won three assembly seats in the 2001 legislative balloting and control of four districts in municipal polls. Ahmed Ould Daddah was unanimously elected as president of the RFD in January 2002.

In April 2002 RFD won one seat in partial Senate elections, the first of Taya's radical opposition ever to do so. A year later, in May 2003, a senior RFD member was arrested in the wake of the U.S.-led attack on Iraq and subsequent crackdown on Mauritanian Islamic groups. That same month the government appointed a close associate of Ahmed Ould Daddah, Abdellahi Ould Souleimana Ould CHEIKH SIDYA, to a cabinet position in an apparent attempt to gain some RFD support.

In 2004 Ahmed Ould Daddah was charged with helping to finance the opposition Knights of Change (see below), a movement in exile that reportedly advocated the armed overthrow of the Taya government. Daddah was later acquitted.

The RFD refused to join the new government of Prime Minister el-Waghf in May 2008, and in July the party further indicated its unhappiness with the current administration by aligning itself with those in parliament who proposed a no-confidence vote against the prime minister, prompting his resignation. (The president reappointed el-Waghf, and the no-confidence vote was never held.)

Though the RFD initially supported the 2008 junta, it later announced that it would boycott the upcoming presidential election, calling it a "masquerade." However, the RFD subsequently agreed to participate, following a compromise agreement between junta leaders and political parties. Dissident vice president Kane Hamidou Baba announced his bid for presidency without the backing of the RFD, which endorsed Ould Daddah instead.

Leaders: Ahmed OULD DADDAH (President of the Party and 1992, 2003, 2007 and 2009 presidential candidate), Kane Hamidou BABA (Vice President of the Party and 2009 presidential candidate).

Republican Democratic Party for Renovation (*Parti Républicain Démocratique Rénové*—PRDR). This party is a successor to the Democratic and Social Republican Party (*Parti Républicain Démocratique et Social*—PRDS). The PRDS was launched in support of President Taya by a longtime associate, Cheikh Sid Ahmed Ould BABA, who resigned from the cabinet and military in mid-1991 to concentrate on party politics. As the PRDS nominee, Taya won the January 1992 presidential poll by a substantial margin, and the PRDS assumed essentially unchallenged political control by winning large majorities in the subsequent elections for the National Assembly and the Senate, which were boycotted by most opposition groups. The party also dominated the municipal and senate balloting of early 1994.

In March 1995 the PRDS absorbed the MDI, led by Bechir el-HASSEN, which had left the UFD (below) in June 1994.

The party won 70 of 79 seats in the 1996 legislative balloting on its own right and was also considered to enjoy the support of the seven independent legislators (some of whom were former PRDS members) and the RDU representative in the assembly. Taya was reelected as party leader at the second national congress held in November 1999. The PRDS won 64 of 81 seats in the assembly in the 2001 balloting and 15 out of 18 open seats in the April 2004 partial senate elections. In 2003 President Taya won his third term in office.

Following the August 3, 2005, coup, Colonel Vall named PRDS member Sidi Mohamed Ould Boubacar as prime minister, and Boubacar quit the party on August 9. The PRDS initially objected to the junta, calling on its members to support the former regime. A few days later, however, it reportedly reversed itself and gave approval to the ruling MCJD. Support for Taya, widely reported to be a repressive leader who imprisoned dissidents, particularly Islamists, had waned over the years, and his policy of engagement with Israel angered Arab nationalists, observers said. On September 19 the party took the further step of abolishing the chair that Taya had held for 15 years. In October the party held an extraordinary congress and reportedly changed its name to the Republican Democratic Party for Renovation. However, the actions of the congress were canceled in November by a Mauritanian court, which also ordered the party's assets seized pending the outcome of a dispute within the party over whether an audit should have been conducted during the congress. Further turmoil was evidenced when the party's Islamist wing, led by Abdou MAHAM, severed its ties the same month, reportedly to join the Rally for Democracy and Unity (*Rassemblement pour la Démocratie et l'Unité*—RDU). On November 25 the PRDS elected Ethmane Ould Cheikh Abou Ali Maali, Mauritania's ambassador to Kuwait, as president. The party further distanced itself from Taya by announcing its opposition to the diplomatic ties with Israel that the former president had established.

Leaders: Ethmane Ould Cheikh Abou Ali MAALI (President), Cheikh El Avia Ould Mohamed KHOUNA (Former Prime Minister), Rachid Ould SALEH (Former Speaker of the National Assembly), Bela Ould MAKIYA (Secretary General).

Rally for Democracy and Unity (*Rassemblement pour la Démocratie et l'Unité*—RDU). Led by the mayor of Atar who had served as a cabinet minister under Mauritania's first president, the RDU supported President Taya in the January 1992 presidential campaign, but, after winning one seat in the first round of the March assembly election, broke with the government and boycotted the second round, as well as the subsequent senate race. However, as of the 1996 legislative elections, in which it retained its seat, the RDU was once again described as allied with the PRDS, and the RDU leader was named an adviser to the president in the government announced in December 1998. In the 2004 Senate elections, the RDU won one seat.

The RDU, which had been critical of the 2005 coup, soon reversed its position and supported the military junta, saying it hoped the junta could return stability to the country and lead Mauritania to democracy.

Leader: Ahmed Moktar Sidi BABA.

Union for Democracy and Progress (*Union pour la Démocratie et le Progrès*—UDP). The UDP was legalized in June 1993, its ranks including prominent ex-UFD members, some of whom had also served in the administration of Mauritania's first president, Moktar Ould Daddah. UDP leaders pledged to work toward "restoration of national unity," which, in contrast to government policy, appeared to be aimed at conciliation with black Mauritanians. However, despite its professed multiracial stance, the UDP has recently been described as continuing, for the most part, to represent conservative Moorish interests.

The UDP participated in the 1994 municipal balloting, although it did not gain control of any of the 19 local boards for which it offered candidates, party leaders reportedly having encouraged supporters to vote for whichever opposition candidate had the best chance of defeating the PRDS candidate. Said to be suffering from internal dissension, the UDP won no seats in the 1996 legislative poll. When UDP leader Hamdi OULD MOUKNASS was appointed as a presidential adviser in December 1997, the UDP moved into a position as a government-supportive party. At the same time, some party members had reportedly aligned with the FPO, the recently organized leading opposition coalition.

Hamdi Ould Mouknass died in September 1999 and was succeeded as UDP president in May 2000 by his daughter, Naha Mint Mouknass, who thereby became one of the few female party leaders in the Arab world. She was also named a presidential adviser, reaffirming the rump UDP's ties to the government.

Leaders: Naha Mint MOUKNASS (President), Sheikh Saad Bouh CAMARA, Ahmed OULD MENAYA (Secretary General).

Union of Progressive Forces (*Union des Forces Progressives*—UFP). Formed by former members of the UFD, the UFP, whose leadership includes former Marxists, called for dialogue with the PRDS in order to "improve the political atmosphere." The new party won three seats in the 2001 assembly balloting. In 2003 the UFP supported Ould Haidalla for president and joined other opposition groups in complaining of fraud following the Taya victory. The party considered boycotting the 2004 Senate elections but ultimately participated with two nominees. Both lost, one by a narrow margin, to PRDS candidates. In 2005 the party demanded the return of Mauritanian exiles and an end to slavery in the country, precepts it pushed for in the transitional program following the August coup.

Party chair Mohammed Ould Maaloud received 4.08 percent of the vote in the first round in the 2007 presidential election; he supported Ould Daddah in the second round.

The UFP opposed the August 2008 coup, and Maaloud became a leader of the opposition grouping FNDD.

Leaders: Mohammed Ould MAALOUD (Party Chair and 2007 presidential candidate), Kadiata Malick DIALLO (Vice Chair), Mohamed Moustafa Ould BADREDDINE.

Popular Front (*Front Populaire*—FP). The FP, formerly referenced as the Popular and Democratic Front (*Front Populaire et Démocratique*—FPD), is led by former minister Mohamed Lemine Chbih Ould Cheikh Malainine, who finished second (with 7 percent of the vote) as an independent candidate in the December 1997 presidential polling. Malainine, a Muslim spiritual leader, was elected chair of the FP at its first congress in April 1998.

In early 2001 Malainine announced that the FPD would participate in the October legislative balloting, eliciting criticism from the UFD-EN. Despite Malainine's apparently conciliatory gesture toward the government, he was arrested in April on charges of conspiring with Libya to commit acts of terrorism and sentenced to five years in prison. Amnesty International described Malainine as a "prisoner of conscience" and charged that his arrest was merely an attempt to "stifle" the opposition. The sentence was also strongly condemned by other opposition parties. In October 2002 the FP formed, with the Cavaliers for Change and RFD, the United Opposition Framework (UOF), which sought dialogue on democratic reform between the government and opposition groups.

In July 2006, in the run-up to legislative elections, FP leader Malainine helped form the CFCD. In the first round of the 2007 presidential election, he ran as an independent, finishing with less than 1 percent of the vote.

Leaders: Mohamed Lemine Chbih Ould Cheikh MALAININE (President and 2007 presidential candidate), Mohamed Fadel SIDIYA, Badi Ould IBNOU.

Popular Progressive Alliance (*Alliance Populaire et Progressive*—APP). A number of APP members were arrested in early 1997 on "conspiracy" charges emanating from the group's allegedly "pro-Libyan" tendencies. The APP boycotted the 2001 elections. On August 1, 2004, Massaoud Ould Boulkheir, the former leader of the dissolved Action for Change, was elected president of the APP, replacing Mohamed El-Hafedh Ould Ismail. That same month the party won two seats in Nouakchott in the partial senate elections. In the first round of the 2007 presidential election, Boulkheir placed fourth with 9.8 percent of the vote and pledged to support the new president (despite his ties with the CFCD, led by Ahmed Ould Daddah).

The party was among several that called on the government in 2007 to sever ties with Israel.

The APP opposed the 2008 bloodless coup, and in 2009 Boulkheir ran for president as the candidate of the FNDD.

Leaders: Massaoud Ould BOULKHEIR (Chair, Speaker of the Assembly, and 2007 and 2009 presidential candidate), El Khalil Ould TEYIB (Vice Chair).

Mauritanian Party of Union and Change (*Parti Mauritanien pour l'Union et le Changement*—HATEM). This party originated in 2003 as a military organization referenced as the **Knights of Change** (*Umat*), led by former army colonel Saleh Ould Hanena. The Knights had staged several failed coup attempts against President Taya, and Hanena was accused of being the mastermind behind the 2003 plot. In February 2005 Hanena was sentenced to life imprisonment, but he was released by the new junta later that year.

The group became a political party in 2006 and changed its name to HATEM. In the first round of the 2007 presidential election, Hanena won 7.65 percent of the vote. He and his Islamist supporters backed Ould Daddah for president in the second round.

The party, along with the APP and El Sawab, among others, urged the new government in 2007 to break diplomatic ties with Israel.

In 2009 as many as 57 senior members of the pro-junta party resigned and formed a new group, **Patriotic Sphere of Influence**.

Leader: Saleh Ould HANENA (2007 and 2009 presidential candidate).

Socialist and Democratic Popular Union (*Union Populaire Socialiste et Démocratique*—UPSD). A conservative Moorish group recognized in late September 1991, the UPSD is also identified as the Social and Popular Democratic Union (*Union Démocratique Sociale et Populaire*—UDSP). It is led by Mohamed Mahmoud Ould Mah, a former mayor of Nouakchott, who, at the time of his election to that post in 1986 was a member of the UND. Ould Mah was accorded a presidential vote share of 1.36 percent in January 1992 and 0.7 percent in December 1997. The UPSD supported Ahmed Ould Daddah in the 2003 presidential election, when Daddah ran under the banner of the RFD.

Leader: Mohamed Mahmoud OULD MAH (1992 and 1997 presidential candidate).

Other parliamentary parties are the Alternative (*l'Alternative*); the National Rally for Democracy, Liberty, and Equality; the Democratic Renovation Party (RD); and the Union of the Democratic Center.

Other Parties that Participated in Recent Elections:

El Sawab ("The Correct," "The Right Track"). El Sawab, formed in May 2004 by politicians close to former head of state Mohamed Khouna Ould Haidalla, said it had an "original" society program. The party, which was officially recognized in July 2004, opposed Taya's regime. It was described in 2008 as a Baathist party that opposed Mauritania's support for Israel and called on the media to "expose the Zionists" in Mauritania.

Leaders: Abdelsalam Ould HOURMA (Chair), Cheikh Sidi Ould HANENNA, Mohamed Ould GUELMA.

Party for Democratic Convergence (PCD). Many Mauritanians refer to the PCD as "Haidalla's friends," referring to former president Mohamed Khouna Ould Haidalla, but the Arabic initials, formed in May 2004, reveal another allegiance: they spell El Hamd, literally, "praise to God." The PCD is composed of a wide range of groups that were persecuted under the Taya regime, including many black Mauritanians, Islamic radicals, and those who supported the 2003 coup attempt. The vice president of the group, former Nouakchott mayor Mohamed Jemil Ould MANSOUR, an accused Islamic radical, was arrested in 2003 but escaped from prison during the coup attempt and fled to Belgium. There Mansour helped found the **Mauritanian Forum for Reform and Democracy**, along with other political exiles from the 2003 coup. Upon returning to Mauritania, Mansour was arrested again and then released.

Ould Haidalla, who had challenged Taya in the November 2003 presidential election, was arrested two days after the election, and in December he was convicted of plotting a coup against Taya. Ould Haidalla, who denied the charges, received a suspended sentence. In 2005 he was acquitted on charges relating to attempted coups in 2003 and 2004. Also in 2005 the ruling junta refused to recognize the PCD because it contended the party advocated the monopoly of Islam in politics. Party leaders denied it had Islamist links, despite having religious leaders among its members. In the first round of the 2007 presidential election, party leader Isselmou Ould Moustapha was officially credited with 0.24 percent of the vote. It was unclear why he appeared on the ballot under the PCD banner since the PCD had been banned. In the same election, Ould Haidalla ran as an independent, receiving 1.73 percent of the vote in the first round.

Leader: Isselmou Ould MOUSTAPHA (2007 presidential candidate).

National Union for Democracy and Development (*Union Nationale pour la Démocratie et le Développement*—UNDD). Formed by Sen. Tidjane Koita after he left the AC in 1997, the UNDD has been described as the "moderate opposition" and a proponent of dialogue between the PRDS and the more strident anti-regime groups. None of the UNDD's candidates was successful in the 2001 assembly balloting.

Leader: Tidjane KOITA.

Mauritanian Renewal Party (*Parti Mauritanien pour le Renouvellement*—PMR). Shortly after legalization of the PMR, also referenced as the **Mauritanian Party for Renewal and Concord** (PMRC), in mid-September 1991, its leaders charged that inappropriate links had been formed between the PRDS and long-standing national and municipal leaders, placing other groups at a disadvantage in forthcoming elections. The PMR, however, won 1 seat in the 1992 legislative balloting. In the 1997 presidential balloting, PMR leader Moulaye al-Hassan OULD JEYDID finished third with less than 1 percent of the vote.

In April 2001 the government announced the recognition of a new party also named the Mauritanian Renewal Party, led by Atiq OULD ATTIA.

In 2007 leaders Ould Jeydid and Rajel dit Rachit MOUSTAPHA each received less than 1 percent of the vote as presidential candidates representing the PMRC and the PMR, respectively. The relationship between the two parties was unclear.

Alliance for Justice and Democracy (*Alliance pour la Justice et la Démocratie*—AJD)—**Movement for Renovation** (*Mouvement pour la Rénové*—MR). The AJD was formed in 2000 by Massoud Ould Boulkheir, former leader of the outlawed Action for Change, and other AC dissidents. The AJD was officially recognized in 2001. It opposed the Taya regime on the issue of recognition of Israel, the AJD urging the government to cut all ties with Israel, and it appealed for a fair resolution to the problems of Mauritanian refugees in Senegal. Boulkheir was the AJD's presidential candidate in 2003.

The AJD boycotted the 2006 constitutional referendum, saying the proposed amendments did not adequately address the issue of slavery, among other things.

According to the *Africa Research Bulletin*, a leading figure in FLAM (see below), Ba Mamadou BOCAR, was elected AJD vice president in August 2007. The party was subsequently referenced as having merged with the MR and as having "integrated" FLAM—Renovation (see below). It was unclear what the latter association meant.

Ibrahima Moctar Sarr ran as an independent in the 2007 presidential balloting, receiving just under 8 percent of the vote; he supported Ould Daddah in the second round.

Leaders: Ibrahima Moctar SARR (President and 2007 and 2008 presidential candidate), Kebe ABDOULAYE, Alpha DIALLO, Cisse Amadou CHEIKH (Secretary General).

Party for Liberty, Equality, and Justice (*Parti pour la Liberté, l'Egalité, et la Justice*—PLEJ). The PLEJ was founded in 1991 by Ba Mamadou Alassane, a former ambassador and cabinet minister who was among the first black Africans to head a political party in Mauritania. The PLEJ's main concerns are the return of Mauritanian refugees from Senegal and the elimination of racism in Mauritania. In 1997 party member Kane Amadou Moctar was one of four candidates who challenged Taya in the presidential election.

In the first round of the 2007 presidential election, Alassane received less than 1 percent of the vote; he supported Ould Daddah in the second round.

Leaders: Ba Mamadou ALASSANE (Chair and 2007 presidential candidate), Daouda MBAGNIGA.

Other parties and groups that participated in recent elections include the **Third Generation** (*Parti de la Troisienne Generation*—PTG), led by Lebat OULD JEH; the **Social Democratic Party**, formed in 2005 by Mohamed Salek Ould DIDAH; the **Rally for Mauritania**, formed in 2005 by Cheikh Ould HORMA; the **Mauritanian Party for the Defense of the Environment** (*Parti Mauritanien pour la Défense de l'Environment*—PMDE), established in 2003 by Mohamed Ould DEL-LAHI; the **Mauritanian Party of Liberal Democrats** (*Parti Mauritanien des Libéraux Democrates*—PMLD), led by Moustapha Ould LEMRABOTT; and the **Party of Labor and National Unity** (*Parti du Travail et de l'Unité Nationale*—PTUN), led by Ali Bouna Ould OUENINA and Mohamed Ould EL BAH.

Other Parties and Groups:

National Party for Democracy and Development. The government-supportive party, also referenced as the **National Convention for Justice and Development**, was established in January 2008 over the strident objections of the opposition and smaller parties, party leaders assuring that since President Abdallahi was not the chair, the party was not violating the constitution. The new party, reportedly founded by political activists and some members of the RDU, was based on support for President Abdallahi and his programs. The party chair, Yahya Oud Ouakef, serves as the secretary general of the presidency in Abdallahi's administration.

In March 2008, following talks with Prime Minister Zeidane, a senior official of the Communist Party of China met with the party chair to reiterate China's support for interparty relations.

Leaders: Yahya Ould OUAKEF (Chair), Sahla bint Ahmad ZAYID.

Among the 18 new parties licensed by the government in August 2007 were the **Work and Equality Party**; the **Mauritanian Hope Party**, founded by women and led by Tahi bint LAHBIB, it aims to have women make up half of its membership; the **Conservative Party**; the **Mauritania National Congress**; the **National Rally for Reform and Development** (RNRD), an Islamist party whose leaders include Mohamed Jemil Ould Mansour and Zainab bint DADEH, a former Baath party member; the **Alternation and Consultation Party**; and the **Coalition for Democracy in Mauritania**. Also licensed was the **Direct Democracy Movement**, which had been banned in 2005 but whose members reportedly aligned themselves with the CFCD prior to the 2006 assembly elections. The newly licensed party, also reportedly led by Ould Mansour, was described as reformist rather than Islamist, in accordance with the political parties law, although it was reported to be an offshoot of the Muslim Brotherhood (see Mauritanian Islamic Movement, below).

Democratic Center Party (*Parti du Centre Démocratique*—PCD). The Democratic Center Party, also referenced as the Mauritanian Party of the Democratic Center (PCDM), supported Ahmed Ould Daddah in the January 1992 presidential balloting after its own leader withdrew from the race. The party was referenced in 2005 as being among several parties meeting with CMJD officials to discuss the transitional democratic process and reforms.

Leaders: Benba Ould Sidi BADI, Mamouni Ould Moktar EMBARAK.

African Liberation Forces of Mauritania (*Forces de Libération Africaine de Mauritanie*—FLAM). Organized in 1983 in opposition to what were perceived as repressive policies toward blacks, FLAM was believed responsible for an "Oppressed Black" manifesto that in 1986 was widely distributed within Mauritania and at the nonaligned summit in Zimbabwe. Based partly in Dakar, Senegal, the group also condemned reprisals against blacks by the Taya regime following an alleged coup attempt in 1987. Many FLAM supporters were reported to be among those who fled or were expelled to Senegal in 1989. Subsequently engaged in guerrilla activity, FLAM leaders announced in July 1991 that they were suspending "armed struggle" in response to the government's general amnesty and promulgation of a new Mauritanian constitution. FLAM endorsed Ahmed Ould Daddah in the January 1992 presidential election, after which it renewed its antigovernment military campaign near the Senegalese border. Leaders of the group stated in early 1995 that they were neither secessionists nor terrorists, reiterating their support for the establishment of a federal system that would ensure an appropriate level of black representation in government while protecting the rights of blacks throughout Mauritanian society. In early 2001 the FLAM called upon the international community to exert pressure on the Mauritanian government to address the issue of black refugees remaining in Senegal and Mali as the result of the 1989 exodus.

The group, along with the Patriotic Alliance and other anti-Taya organizations, again pledged to give up its armed struggle following the 2005 coup.

In February 2006 a breakaway group formed under the rubric **FLAM—Renovation,** reportedly planning to join in the political process in Mauritania, though it was unclear how it intended to do so (see AJD-MR, above). The breakaway group, issuing a report from Senegal, called on the government to address the refugee issue.

FLAM had called for a boycott of the constitutional referendum in 2006 and criticized the approved amendments on the grounds that they did not adequately address the issue of slavery, among other things. According to FLAM's Web site, the group has never participated in an election in Mauritania because FLAM's "standard conditions," including issues like human rights, slavery, and refugees, have not been met. In June 2007 a group of Mauritanian expatriates living in New York filed a suit against Taya, alleging torture and other human rights violations. The suit included claims by two black Mauritanians that they were among the victims of "ethnic cleansing" under the Taya regime.

In November 2007, following the signing of a tripartite agreement by Mauritania, Senegal, and the UNHCR to allow for the return of thousands of black Mauritanian refugees, FLAM raised concerns about the country's ability to handle the influx.

Leader: Samba THIAM (President).

Patriotic Alliance (a.k.a. Democratic Alliance). Several Mauritanian political groups created the Patriotic Alliance on July 10, 2004. It is allegedly affiliated with Ould Haidalla and those responsible for the failed 2003 coup. In February 2005 Senegal deported a leader of the Patriotic Alliance, Ely Ould SNEIBA, to Mali. Sneiba later was convicted in absentia by a Mauritanian court and sentenced to five years for his role in the coup attempt. In July 2005 Sneiba was granted political asylum in Belgium.

In 1994 security forces accused a number of previously unknown extremist organizations, including **Call to Islam** and the **Mauritanian Islamic Movement** (*Hasim*) of conspiring to overthrow the government. As part of its antiterrorism efforts, backed by the United States, the Mauritanian government in October 2004 arrested three leaders of the Mauritanian Islamic Movement—Mohamed El-Hacen Ould DEDOW, Moctar Ould Mohamed MOUSSA, and Mohamed Jemil Ould Mansour—on charges of subversion. Mansour, who was later listed as the leader of the **Centrist Reformers**, described as moderate Islamists, has been named as among the leaders of several parties or groups.

Additional parties include the **Democratic and Social Union** (*Union Démocratique et Sociale*—UDS), which was led by Isselmou Ould HANEFI and boycotted the 2006 parliamentary elections; the **National Party for Unity and Democracy** (*Parti National pour l'Unité et la Démocratie*—PNUD); the **Mauritanian Liberal Democrats,** led by Mustapha OULD LEMBRABET; the **Mauritanian Labor Party,** led by Mohamed Hafid OULD DENNA; the **Democratic Alliance,** led by Mohamed Ould Taleb OTHMAN; the **National Renaissance Party** (*Parti de la Renaissance Nationale*—PRN), led by Mohamed Ould Abdellaki Ould EYYE; the **National Pact** (*Pacte National*—PN), led by former PRDS member Mohamed Abdallah OULD KHARCY; and the **Popular Initiatives Rally**, which supported the 2008 junta, led by Mohamed SALEM.

In 2009 Ould Mansour, formerly of the PCD, ran for president under the banner of the National Rally for Reform and Development, allied with the FNDD. In November 2008 the **Union of Democratic Youth** was formed under the leadership of Jeddou Ould AHMAD, with a platform of anti-terrorism. The party supported the August 2008 coup.

LEGISLATURE

The 1991 constitution provides for a bicameral legislature consisting of an indirectly chosen Senate and a popularly elected National Assembly. The parliament was dissolved by the Military Council for

Justice and Democracy following the August 3, 2005, coup. Constitutional amendments approved in a public referendum on June 25, 2006, included provisions for restoring the **Parliament**.

Senate (*Majlis al-Shuyukh*). The Senate is renewed by thirds every two years for six-year terms, with 53 of its 56 members selected by the country's mayors and municipal councilors and 3 seats representing Mauritanians abroad chosen by the elected senators.

In the most recent election on January 21 and February 4, 2007, the seat distribution was as follows: the Rally of Democratic Forces (RFD), 5; the Republican Democratic Party for Renovation, 3; the Coalition of Forces of Democratic Change, 3; the Mauritanian Party of Union and Change (HATEM), 2; the Union of Progressive Forces (UFP), 1; the RFD/UFP, 1; the RFD/Independents, 1; the HATEM/Independents, 1; the Union for Democracy and Progress/Independents, 1; the People's Progressive Alliance /Independents, 1; independents, 34. (*See headnote.*)

President: Vacant.

National Assembly (*Majlis al-Watani*). In 2006 the size of the assembly was increased from 81 to 95 seats, 14 of which are elected nationally in proportional balloting on a party basis and 81 of which are elected in 45 regional constituencies. The mixed voting system is majoritarian in single-member and two-seat constituencies, with proportional representation in constituencies of 3 or more seats. All members are elected for five-year terms.

In the most recent balloting on November 19 and December 3, 2006, the seat distribution was as follows: the Coalition of Forces of Democratic Change, 38 (the Rally of Democratic Forces [RFD], 15; the Union of Forces of Progress [UFP], 8; the Popular Progressive Alliance, 5; the Mauritanian Party of Union and Change, 2; the HATEM/APP, 2; the RFD/UFP, 2; the Democratic Renovation Party, 2; the Popular Front, 1; the Socialist and Democratic Popular Union, 1); the Republican Democratic Party for Renovation, 7; the Rally for Democracy and Unity, 3; the Union for Democracy and Progress, 3; the Union of Democratic Center, 1; the Alternative, 1; the National Rally for Democracy, Liberty, and Equality, 1; independents, 41.

Many members of the legislature reportedly joined the new National Pact for Development (PNDD), formed in March 2007. Before the bloodless coup on August 6, 2008, the PNDD was said to have held 50 of the assembly's 95 seats, but it was unclear which groups had aligned themselves with the governing party.

Speaker: Massaoud Ould BOULKHEIR.

CABINET

[as of July 1, 2009] (*see headnote*)

Prime Minister	Moulaye Ould Mohamed Laghdaf
Ministers	
Civil Service, Labor, and Professional Training	Hacen Ould Liman Amar Jowar
Communications and Relations with Parliament	Ahmed Ould Ahmed Abd (opposition)
Culture, Youth, and Sport	Sidi Ould Samba
Defense	Yedali Ould Cheikh (opposition)
Economic Affairs	Sidi Ould Tah
Equipment and Transport	Diop Cheikh Baidy (opposition)
Finance	Sidi Ould Salem (opposition)
Fisheries	Hacenna Ould Ely
Foreign Affairs and Cooperation	Mohamed Mahmoud Ould Mohamedou
Handicrafts and Tourism	Bamba Ould Dermane
Health	Zeinabou Mint Mohamed (opposition) [f]
Housing and Town and Country Planning	Mohamed Lemine Ould El Mamy (opposition)
Industry and Mines	Diabira Fousseynou (opposition)
Interior and Decentralization	Mohamed Ould Rzeyzim (opposition)
Islamic Affairs and Education	Maktar Ould Mohamed Moussa (opposition)
Justice	Ahmadou Tidjane Bal
Minister Delegate to the Prime Minister in Charge of Environment	Othmane Ould Cheikh Ahmed Aboul Maali
National Education	Ahmed Ould Bah
Oil and Energy	Camara Bakary Haroun (opposition)
Rural Development	Sy Adama
Secretary General of the Government	Ba Ousmane
Secretary of State in Charge of Arab Maghreb Union Affairs	Amar Ould Mohamed Lemine (opposition)
Secretary of State in Charge of Modernization of the Administration and Information Technology and Communication	Sidi Ould Mayouf
Secretary of State in Charge of Professional Training	El Moktar Ould Ahmed Ould Bousseif (opposition)
Water Resources and Sanitation	Mohamed Lemine Ould Aboye
Women's Affairs, Children, and Families	Mariem Baba Sy (opposition) [f]

[f] = female

COMMUNICATIONS

All news media were owned and operated by the government until mid-1991, when legislation recognizing the principle of freedom of the press was passed in conjunction with the country's new constitution. However, the new law precluded the news media from "encouraging intolerance between tribes or races," and the government reportedly banned the September 1991 issue of the *Mauritanie Demain* because the monthly magazine had reported on the alleged torture of black political detainees. In the weeks leading up to the 2003 presidential elections, authorities shut down four weekly newspapers. In March 2005 a freelance journalist was charged with "damaging the public image" of Mauritania and imprisoned after he interviewed a woman said to be a runaway slave, prompting protests from international organizations devoted to protecting the rights of journalists. In 2006 the transitional government adopted a new media law that abolished the requirement that newspapers obtain a government permit before they were allowed to publish. Also, the government pledged to allow private radio and TV stations to operate by the end of 2007.

The watchdog group Reporters Without Borders declared in its 2008 annual report that "freedom of press is alive and well" in Mauritania, citing the return to civil liberties following the election of President Sidi Mohamed Ould Cheikh Abdallahi in 2007.

State-run radio and television were shut down in the wake of the bloodless coup on August 6, 2008. It was unclear how long they would be blocked.

Press. The following are published in Nouakchott: *Ach Chaab,* government daily in Arabic and French; *Mauritanie Nouvelle,* independent in French; *La Calame,* independent weekly in French; *La Tribune,* independent weekly in French; *Eveil-Hebdo,* independent weekly in French; *Journal Officiel,* government semimonthly in French; and *Akhbar Nouakchott*, independent daily in French and Arabic.

News agencies. The government facility is *Agence Mauritanienne de l'Information* (AMI); *Agence France-Presse* also maintains an office in Nouakchott.

Broadcasting and computing. The state-owned *Office de Radiodiffusion et Télévision de Mauritanie* (ORTM) broadcasts to radio receivers in Arabic, French, and indigenous tribal languages, as well as to about 323,000 television sets in Arabic and French. As of 2008 there were 18.7 Internet users per 1,000 inhabitants.

INTERGOVERNMENTAL REPRESENTATION

Ambassador to the U.S.: (Vacant).

U.S. Ambassador to Mauritania: Mark M. BOULWARE.

Permanent Representative to the UN: Abderrahim OULD HADRAMI.

IGO Memberships (Non–United Nations): AfDB, AFESD, AMF, AMU, AU, BADEA, CAEU, CILSS, IDB, Interpol, IOM, LAS, NAM, OIC, OIF, WCO, WTO.

MAURITIUS

Republic of Mauritius

Political Status: Constitutional monarchy under multiparty parliamentary system established upon independence within the Commonwealth on March 12, 1968; became a republic on March 12, 1992.

Area: 790 sq. mi. (2,045 sq. km.).

Population: 1,179,137 (2000C); 1,273,000 (2008E).

Major Urban Centers (2005E): PORT LOUIS (151,000), Beau Bassin/Rose Hill (109,000), Vacoas-Phoenix (107,000), Curepipe (84,000), Quatre Bornes (81,000).

Official Language: English (French is also used, while Creole is the lingua franca and Hindi the most widely spoken).

Monetary Unit: Mauritian Rupee (official rate December 1, 2009: 29.30 rupees = $1US).

President: Sir Anerood JUGNAUTH (Mauritian Socialist Movement—MSM); elected by the National Assembly on October 7, 2003, to complete the five-year term (which began on February 25, 2002) of Karl Auguste OFFMANN (Mauritian Socialist Movement), who had resigned on September 30, 2003, as part of the power-sharing agreement negotiated in 2002 by the MSM and the Mauritian Militant Movement; unanimously reelected by the National Assembly on September 19, 2008, for a five-year term.

Vice President: Angidi Verriah CHETTIAR (Mauritius Labour Party); elected by the National Assembly on August 24, 2007, for a five-year term to succeed Raouf BUNDHUN (nonparty).

Prime Minister: Navin RAMGOOLAM (Mauritius Labour Party); named prime minister on July 5, 2005, in succession to Paul Raymond BÉRENGER (Mauritian Militant Movement) following legislative election of July 3.

THE COUNTRY

The island of Mauritius, once known as Ile de France, is situated 500 miles east of Madagascar, in the southwestern Indian Ocean (see map, above); Rodrigues Island, the Agalega Islands, and the Cardagos Carajos Shoals (St. Brandon Islands) also are national territory. (Mauritius also claims Diego Garcia and other islands in the Chagos Archipelago, currently controlled by the United Kingdom as part of the British Indian Ocean Territory [see Foreign relations, below, for details].) The diversity of contemporary Mauritian society is a reflection of its history as a colonial sugar plantation. African slave laborers were imported initially, and they were followed by the migration of Indians (who now constitute two-thirds of the population), Chinese, French, and English. Religious affiliations include Hinduism, to which 48 percent of the population adheres; Christianity (predominantly Roman Catholicism), 24 percent; and Islam, 17 percent. Women are significantly engaged in subsistence agriculture, although they comprise only 32 percent of the paid labor force. Twelve women served in the National Assembly and two of those in the cabinet as of 2009.

Sugar production, to which over 90 percent of the arable land was devoted in the 1960s, traditionally accounted for an overwhelming proportion of the country's export earnings. However, rapidly falling prices after 1975 created severe economic difficulties that were partly overcome by expanded activity in the country's export processing zone (EPZ), by means of which investors were given tax and other incentives to set up ventures aimed at production for export. Excellent sugar harvests in the 1980s, expanded tourist activity, and increased exports of manufactured goods, coupled in 1989 with the opening of a local stock exchange and the authorization of offshore banking activity, subsequently yielded substantial economic growth. Most sales in sugar and other commodities are to the European Union (EU) under trade provisions of the Lomé Convention. However, South Africa has recently begun to vie with France as the leading supplier of goods to Mauritius, and economic ties have been expanded with a number of other southern African nations.

The overall strong economic performance in the 1990s led some experts to reference a "Mauritian miracle" and to describe the country as a "case study" in the successful management of a developing country that pursued "investor-friendly" policies. GDP growth averaged 5.7 annually from 1996–1999, although it measured only about 3 percent in 1999 because of the effects of a severe drought on agricultural production. Government initiatives focused on promoting offshore banking, information technology, garment manufacturing, and tourism (about 500,000 visitors annually). Job creation programs received top priority because unemployment grew from a negligible 1.5 percent in 1995 to a disturbing 8 percent in early 2001. The job situation may have contributed to the unrest in Port Louis in February 1999 (see Current issues, below); skeptics claimed that the wealthiest segment of the population had benefited disproportionately from recent growth and that significant tension continued to exist between the underprivileged Creole population and the Hindu majority.

Success in the sugar and tourism industries led to economic growth of 4.5 percent in 2003–2004. However, unemployment reached 10.2 percent, and ongoing budget deficits contributed to debt. Moreover, threats to the sugar and textile industries (see Current issues, below) reportedly troubled voters in the July 2005 legislative balloting.

Apparently responding to reforms, which lowered rates for both individuals and corporations, the economy rebounded in 2006 and 2007. The country continued to attract significant foreign investment. Reforms lowered average tariffs from 19.9 percent in 2001 to just 6.6 percent in 2007, while the financial services sector, valued at $35.86 billion, continued to draw foreign investment. The country's main trading partners were the United Kingdom, India, France, and China. In 2008 real per capita income increased to $6,400—one of the highest levels in Africa. That year GDP growth was 5.2 percent, inflation 8.8 percent, and unemployment 7.8 percent. Meanwhile, in 2008 China announced the construction of a $730 million industrial park on the island, the largest direct foreign investment (see Current issues, below). A 2009 World Bank report ranked Mauritius 24 out of 181 countries and best in Africa for business and investment. The global economic crisis slowed the economy in late 2008 and early 2009, and GDP growth was expected to slow to less than 1 percent (see Current issues, below).

GOVERNMENT AND POLITICS

Political background. Because of its location, Mauritius had strategic importance during the age of European exploration and expansion, and the Dutch, French, and English successively occupied the island. France ruled Mauritius from 1710 to 1810, when Britain assumed control to protect its shipping during the Napoleonic wars. Political evolution began as early as 1831 under a constitution that provided for a Council of Government, but the franchise was largely restricted until after World War II. The postwar era also witnessed the introduction of political parties and increased participation in local government.

An election under a system of internal parliamentary democracy initiated in 1967 revealed a majority preference for full independence, which was granted by Britain on March 12, 1968, with Sir Seewoosagur RAMGOOLAM of the Independence Party (IP) as prime minister. A state of emergency, occasioned by an outbreak of severe communal strife between Muslims and Creoles, was lifted in 1970, although new disorder brought its reimposition from December 1971 to March 1978.

Under constitutional arrangements agreed upon in 1969, the mandate of the existing Legislative Assembly was extended by four years. In the election of December 20, 1976, the radical Mauritian Militant Movement (*Mouvement Militant Mauricien*—MMM), led by Anerood JUGNAUTH and Paul BÉRENGER, won a plurality of legislative seats, but the IP and the Mauritian Social Democratic Party (*Parti Mauricien Social-Démocrate*—PMSD) formed a coalition that retained Prime Minister Ramgoolam in office with a slim majority. In the country's second postindependence balloting on June 11, 1982, the incumbent parties lost all of their directly elective seats, Jugnauth proceeding to form an MMM-dominated government on June 15.

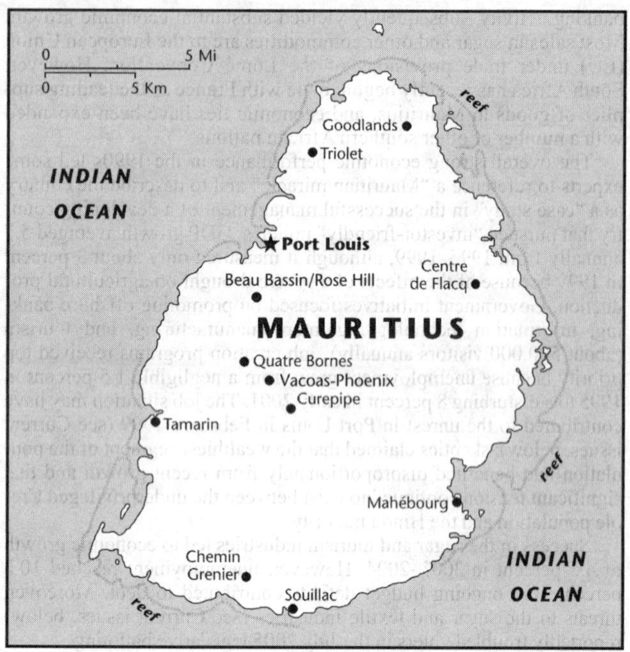

In the wake of a government crisis in March 1983, which yielded the resignation of 12 ministers, including Bérenger, and the repudiation of the prime minister by his own party, Jugnauth and his supporters regrouped as the Mauritian Socialist Movement (*Mouvement Socialiste Mauricien*—MSM) and, in alliance with Ramgoolam's Mauritius Labour Party (MLP) wing of the IP and the PMSD, won a decisive legislative majority in a new election held August 21.

In February 1984 Ramgoolam's successor as MLP leader, Sir Satcam BOOLELL, was relieved of his post as minister of economic planning, whereupon the MLP voted to terminate its support of the MSM. However, 11 Labour deputies, under the leadership of Beergoonath GHURBURRUN, refused to follow Boolell into opposition and remained in the government alliance (initially as the Mauritian Workers' Movement—MWM and later as the Mauritian Labour Rally—RTM).

In municipal council balloting on December 8, 1985, the opposition MMM won 57.2 percent of the vote, decisively defeating the coalition parties, who captured only 36.8 percent, while the MLP was a distant third with 5.4 percent. Although insisting that the MMM victory represented a rejection of Jugnauth's policies, Bérenger did not immediately call for the government to resign. However, such an appeal was made in the wake of a major scandal at the end of the month, which stemmed from the arrest on drug charges of four coalition members at Amsterdam's Schipol Airport. Subsequently, the MLP agreed to reconcile with the MSM, and Boolell was awarded three portfolios and the post of second deputy prime minister in a cabinet reorganization August 8, 1986.

At an early election on August 30, 1987, called largely because of favorable economic conditions, a reconstituted Jugnauth coalition consisting of the MSM, the MLP, the RTM (subsequently absorbed by the MSM), the PMSD, and the Rodriguan People's Organization (*Organisation du Peuple Rodriguais*—OPR) retained power by capturing 41 of 62 elective legislative seats. In August 1988, however, the PMSD, whose leader, Sir Gaëtan DUVAL, had frequently been at odds with the coalition mainstream in domestic and foreign policy, withdrew from the government, forcing Jugnauth to form a new cabinet whose assembly support had fallen to a majority of 10. Two months later the largely urban-based coalition suspended participation in municipal balloting to avoid the embarrassment of a major defeat, with the MMM (allied with several small parties) winning all of the seats in a two-way contest with the PMSD.

In an effort to strengthen his parliamentary position, Jugnauth in July 1990 concluded an electoral pact with the opposition MMM. However, the move angered a number of his fellow MSM ministers, as well as MLP leader Boolell. In August, after the government narrowly failed to secure the 75 percent approval necessary to make the country a republic within the Commonwealth, Jugnauth dismissed the dissident ministers and announced that he would continue as head of a minority administration with the parliamentary support of the MMM. A month later the MMM formally joined the government, with its president, Dr. Prem NABABSINGH, named deputy prime minister.

At an early election on September 15, 1991, the governing alliance won 59 of 62 legislative seats, far in excess of the 75 percent required to implement a change to republican status, which was approved by the Legislative Assembly on December 10, with effect from March 12, 1992. By agreement between the coalition's leading parties, Sir Veerasamy RINGADOO, who had been appointed governor general in January 1986, was designated nonexecutive president of the new republic for three months; he was succeeded on June 30 by the MMM's Cassam UTEEM.

In a cabinet reshuffle on August 18, 1993, Bérenger, who had been openly critical of government policies, was ousted as foreign minister. Two months later he was removed as MMM secretary general by the party's Political Bureau, which named Jean-Claude DE L'ESTRAC as his successor. However, the action was reversed on October 23 by the MMM Central Committee, which proceeded to name a new, pro-Bérenger party leadership. On November 16 Bérenger crossed the aisle to sit with the opposition, although he formally rejected the opposition leadership on the grounds that he had no electoral mandate for such a role. A year later Bérenger and De L'Estrac resigned as MPs; only the former regained his seat in by-elections in January 1995.

After the MLP had in January 1995 rebuffed Prime Minister Jugnauth's offer of power sharing, the PMSD agreed in early February to join the coalition, which then encompassed the MSM, MTD, OPR, and the Mauritian Militant Renaissance, despite opposition from a number of leading PMSD members, with a cabinet realignment following on February 13. An early election was then called after Jugnauth had failed to secure passage of a constitutional amendment to introduce a variety of languages (Hindi, Urdu, Tamil, Marathi, Telegu, Chinese, and Arabic) into the educational curriculum. The Creole opposition strongly opposed the amendment, which also provoked the withdrawal not only of the recently appointed PMSD members but also of the OPR representative, thus effectively shrinking the government coalition.

In an outcome not dissimilar to Prime Minister Jugnauth's 1982 electoral victory, an opposition MLP-MMM alliance swept the legislative balloting of December 20, 1995, with the MLP's Dr. Navin RAMGOOLAM, son of former prime minister Sir Seewoosagur Ramgoolam, forming a new government on December 31. It consisted of 13 MLP ministers, 9 MMM ministers (including Bérenger as deputy prime minister and foreign minister), and 1 OPR representative at the junior ministerial level. However, Bérenger was dismissed from the cabinet on June 20, 1997, and most of the other MMM ministers resigned their posts in protest. After reportedly failing to convince the PMSD to participate in the government, Ramgoolam on July 2 formed a new cabinet, which included only MLP ministers except for 1 OPR member and 1 independent (Dr. Ahmed Rashid BEEBEEJAUN, who had recently left the MMM rather than give up his portfolio for land transport, shipping, and public safety). Meanwhile, President Uteem was reappointed to another term, although his relationship with the MMM (which had promoted his initial appointment) remained unclear. Ramgoolam reshuffled his cabinet on October 25, 1998, reportedly to enhance the role of young MLP legislators in the government after an alliance formed between Bérenger's MMM and Jugnauth's MSM. The prime minister also attempted to shore up his control by including the recently formed Xavier Duval Mauritian Party (PMXD) in a cabinet reshuffle on September 26, 1999. However, in the legislative balloting on September 11, 2000, the MSM-MMM electoral coalition soundly trounced the MLP-PMXD alliance, securing 54 of the 62 elected seats. Consequently, Jugnauth returned as prime minister on September 17 to lead with Bérenger a MSM-MMM coalition government, which required Jugnauth to resign after three years and Bérenger to assume the premiership.

On February 15, 2002, President Uteem resigned after he refused to approve an antiterrorism law recently passed by the National Assembly. (Uteem argued that the new legislation could undermine national sovereignty in the name of U.S. security concerns.) He was replaced by Vice President Angidi Verriah Chettiar, who resigned on February 18 after he also refused to sign the bill into law. In accordance with the constitution, Chief Justice Arriranga PILLAY replaced Chettiar as the interim president on February 18 and subsequently signed the controversial legislation. On February 25 the National Assembly elected Karl Auguste OFFMANN and Raouf BUNDHUN as the president and vice president, respectively.

On September 29, 2002, the OPR won 10 of 18 seats in the new Rodrigues Regional Assembly, while the Rodrigues Movement won the remaining 8 seats.

Although many observers doubted the MSM-MMM "marriage" of 2000 would survive, Bérenger assumed the premiership on October 1, 2003, and Jugnauth took the largely ceremonial presidency on October 7. The most noteworthy of Bérenger's subsequent cabinet changes was the appointment of Pravind Kumar JUGNAUTH (the son of Anerood Jugnauth) as deputy prime minister and finance minister.

At balloting for 62 elected members of the National Assembly on July 3, 2005, the Social Alliance (led by the MLP) won 38 seats, while the alliance of the MSM and the MMM won 22 and the OPR won 2. Prime Minister Bérenger resigned on July 5 and was succeeded the same day by MLP leader Navin Ramgoolam, who formed a new cabinet comprising (for the most part) the parties that had formed the Social Alliance. The Social Alliance also swept municipal balloting in October, winning 122 of 124 seats in five towns, including all 30 seats in the capital, Port Louis. It also won the majority of mayoral contests.

In regional balloting in December 2006, the Rodriguan Movement (*Mouvement Rodriguais*—MR) gained a majority in the Regional Assembly after two decades of dominance of island politics by the Rodriguan People's Organization (*Organisation du Peuple Rodriguais*—OPR).

Although new presidential balloting was technically due in 2007, the government postponed the election until 2008, arguing that President Jugnauth was entitled to a full five-year term. The MSM appeared comfortable with that decision but strongly objected to the MLP's insistence that new vice-presidential elections should proceed as scheduled in 2007. Nevertheless, Prime Minister Ramgoolam nominated former vice president Chettiar to the post in August 2007, and the appointment was endorsed by the MLP-dominated assembly. In September former prime minister Paul Bérenger of the MMM was appointed opposition leader in the assembly, following the resignation of Nando Bodha of the MSM (see Political Parties, below).

Ramgoolam dismissed the foreign minister in March 2008 after the minister publicly criticized the coalition government. The prime minster then took over the foreign ministry portfolio, but carried out a major cabinet reshuffle on September 13 in which four new ministers were appointed and thirteen ministers had their portfolios altered. Ramgoolan gave up the foreign affairs ministry, but took over as minister of defense and home affairs. The cabinet continued to be dominated by the MLP and the reshuffle was reportedly an effort to improve the government's popularity ahead of the 2010 legislative balloting. On September 19 Jugnauth was unanimously reelected president by the assembly in balloting that had been postponed for a year.

Constitution and government. The Mauritius Independence Order of 1968, as amended the following year by the Constitution of Mauritius (Amendment) Act, provided for a unicameral system of parliamentary government with executive authority exercised by a prime minister appointed by the governor general (as the representative of the Crown) from among the majority members of the Legislative Assembly. In December 1991 the assembly approved a change to republican status as of March 12, 1992, with an essentially titular president, appointed by the assembly to a five-year term, replacing the queen as head of state. The change also included creation of an indirectly elective vice presidency. The legislature (known under the present basic law as the National Assembly) includes a Speaker, 60 representatives directly elected from three-member districts on the main island, plus 2 from Rodrigues, and the attorney general, if not an elected member. In addition, up to 8 "best loser" seats may be awarded on the basis of party or ethnic underrepresentation as indicated by shares of total vote and total population, respectively. Judicial authority, based on both French and British precedents, is exercised by a Supreme Court, four of whose five judges (excluding the chief justice) preside additionally over Appeal, Intermediate, District, and Industrial court proceedings. There are also inferior courts and a Court of Assizes. In conformity with the practice of a number of other small republican members of the Commonwealth, final appeal continues to be to the Judicial Committee of the Privy Council in London.

Nine districts constitute the principal administrative divisions, with separate administrative structures governing the Mauritian dependencies. The Agalega and Cargados Carajos islands are ruled directly from Port Louis, while Rodrigues Island has a central government under a resident commissioner. On the main island, municipal and town councils are elected in urban areas and district and village councils in rural areas.

In 1991 a Rodrigues Local Council, comprising 21 members appointed by the minister for Rodriguan affairs, was established to exer-cise a degree of autonomy on Rodrigues. However, its mandate expired in 1996 amid political infighting concerning the issue. Subsequently, in November 2001, the National Assembly authorized creation of an elected Rodrigues Regional Assembly (see Legislature, below). In addition to enjoying the same authority as that of local bodies on the main island, the new Regional Assembly was empowered to propose bills to the National Assembly and to oversee development projects and otherwise administer internal initiatives.

Foreign relations. Mauritius maintains diplomatic relations with most major foreign governments. One principal external issue has been the status of Diego Garcia Island, which was considered a Mauritian dependency until 1965, when London transferred administration of the Chagos Archipelago to the British Indian Ocean Territory (BIOT). The following year, Britain concluded an agreement with the United States whereby the latter obtained use of the island for 50 years. Following independence in 1968 Mauritius pressed its claim to Diego Garcia, while international attention was drawn to the issue in 1980 when Washington announced that it intended to make the island the chief U.S. naval and air base in the Indian Ocean. In July the Organization of African Unity unanimously backed Port Louis's claim, but efforts by Prime Minister Ramgoolam to garner support from the UK government were rebuffed.

In July 1982 Britain agreed to pay $4 million in compensation for its 1965–1973 relocation of families from the Chagos islands to Mauritius. In accepting the payment, Port Louis reversed its position in regard to Diego Garcia and insisted that existence of the U.S. base violated a 1967 commitment by the United Kingdom (denied by London) that the island would not be used for military purposes. The Diego Garcia issue resurfaced in 1989 when U.S.-Soviet détente seemed to reduce the strategic significance of the base and encourage those who supported regional demilitarization. In September a British Foreign and Commonwealth Office official stated that London did not "look unfavorably" on the Mauritian claim. In October Mauritius charged that the accidental bombing of the island by a U.S. fighter plane had endangered nearby civilian aircraft. The installation proved to be of major value to U.S. forces during the Gulf war of early 1991, and the British position thereafter appeared to harden, London's high commissioner to Port Louis declaring in mid-November that the question of British sovereignty over the Chagos Archipelago was "not negotiable." The issue surfaced again in 1996 when the Ramgoolam government demanded a share of the proceeds from fishing permits issued by the BIOT, while stressing that any such income should not be defined as rent for, and thus acceptance of, the U.S. naval base on Diego Garcia. In October 2000 the British High Court ruled that some 2,000 inhabitants of Diego Garcia and other islands of the Chagos Archipelago had been "unlawfully removed" to Mauritius prior to independence, possibly opening the way for the return of Chagossians to all of the islands in question except, notably, Diego Garcia. (The Creole-speaking Chagossians have not assimilated well into mainstream Mauritian society; many of them live in poverty.) Suits have been filed for substantial UK and U.S. financial support for the proposed return, while Mauritius has continued to press its claim to sovereignty over the islands. In 2004 lawyers representing the Chagossians petitioned Queen Elizabeth to permit the Chagossians to return to the Chagos Archipelago and to compensate them further for the UK's previous "unlawful actions." The petition also requested that the UK rebuild the infrastructure on the islands to permit the resumption of fishing and agriculture. In 2006 the UK High Court ruled in favor of the return of the Chagossians. The ruling was appealed by the UK Foreign Office, but the Court of Appeal affirmed the original decision. Chagossians were allowed to return to any of some 65 islands in the archipelago, but not Diego Garcia. Since many of the Chagossians had assimilated well in Mauritius, it was expected that only a small number would actually return to the islands, which had been uninhabited for more than 30 years.

Many years earlier, in June 1980, the Ramgoolam government had announced that it was amending the country's constitution to encompass the French-held island of Tromelin, located some 350 miles to the north of Mauritius, thus reaffirming a claim that Paris had formally rejected in 1976. In December 1989 the Jugnauth administration announced that it would seek a ruling on Tromelin from the General Assembly's Committee on Decolonization. Six months later French President François Mitterrand, during a tour of the Indian Ocean region, agreed to Franco-Mauritian discussions on the future of the island, although its status remained unchanged as of 2007.

Mauritius is a member of the Indian Ocean Commission (IOC). In February 1995 it hosted a ministerial meeting to form a regional economic bloc, the Indian Ocean Rim Association for Regional Cooperation (IOR-ARC), which first met in Mauritius in March 1997. In August 1995 Mauritius became a member of the Southern African Development Community (SADC). It is also a member of the Common Market for Eastern and Southern Africa (Comesa). Mauritius is pushing for trade expansion through the IOR-ARC because it finds the IOC and Comesa ineffective.

In an effort to overcome reductions in EU subsidies for Mauritian exports of sugar and textiles, the Ramgoolam government signed the U.S.-Mauritian Trade and Investment Framework in September 2006. The accord reduced tariffs on trade between the two countries and led to a rise in Mauritian exports to the United States, with total trade between the two countries at $237 million in 2007. Meanwhile, the government signed an interim trade agreement with the EU in December 2007. Also in December, Mauritius and India signed a 30-point antiterrorism agreement, which focused on efforts to curtail financial support for illegal organizations and activities.

In appreciation for continued Chinese investment, in March 2008 business leaders chartered the Mauritian Council for the Promotion of Peaceful Reunification of China to support unification of China and Taiwain. In May Mauritius donated $300,000 for the victims of the earthquake in southwest China. Nonetheless, there were tensions over China's growing influence (see Current issues). In July the two countries signed a series of bilateral economic agreements. Meanwhile, Mauritius and Singapore signed an accord whereby the latter agreed to provide government-to-government training and aid to improve the Mauritian public service sector. In August Mauritius opposed the SADC Gender Protocol which set, among other goals, a requirement that women comprise 50 percent of all government posts and elected offices by 2015. Mauritian delegates argued that the protocol would require the country's constitution to be changed and replace existing equal rights measures with quota systems.

During a February 2009 visit to Mauritius, Chinese president Jintao Hu announced that his country would invest $260 million to expand the country's main airport.

Current issues. The long-disenfranchised Creole population rioted in February 1999 after a popular singer died in police custody. Underlying the violence was friction between Creoles, the mixed-blood descendants of African slaves who constitute about 30 percent of the population, and Hindus, the dominant force in government and the extended public sector. The Ramgoolam administration was also buffeted by the resignation of several top officials tainted by scandal, as well as by drought-induced economic decline. Consequently, in August the prime minister felt compelled to dissolve the National Assembly and call for new elections in September, four months early. The MSM and MMM quickly concluded an unbeatable electoral alliance, based on an agreement that former prime minister Jugnauth would reassume the reins of government for three years, with Bérenger serving as prime minister the following two years. The new administration appeared to have the support of the private sector, notably the sugar companies and the Catholic Church. Jugnauth declared the economy and internal security to be his top priorities.

In October 2003 Bérenger, a Creole, became the nation's first non-Hindu prime minister. He pledged to make economic progress the top priority of his administration, but rising unemployment and inflation subsequently appeared to erode support for the MSM-MMM alliance. Further complicating matters for the government were setbacks in the sugar industry (the EU announced sharp cutbacks in the prices it would pay for foreign sugar) and the textile sector (Chinese factories had become intense competitors). As a result, the MLP-led Social Alliance of former prime minister Navin Ramgoolam regained the confidence of its old constituencies with its populist platform and won the July 2005 legislative poll. However, Ramgoolam's new government quickly faced daunting challenges, as a steep rise in oil prices combined with ongoing problems in the sugar and textile industries to buffet the country in 2006 with what commentators regularly referred to as an "economic triple shock." The government subsequently sought to expand the financial, tourism, and information technology sectors. Among other things, customs duties were reduced and financial firms were given additional incentives, prompting an increase in foreign investment. In addition, the government encouraged additional flights to and from India and China and supported an expansion of the cruise industry. (More than 600,000 tourists visited Mauritius in 2006.) Low wages and English-language capabilities also continued to contribute to growth in the call center and telecommunications sectors, with more than 150 foreign companies now operating in the island.

The MSM opposed the assembly's selection of a new vice president in 2007, arguing that vice-presidential balloting should have been delayed until 2008 in conjunction with the decision made in regard to the president. Among other things, the opposition suggested that MLP control of the vice presidency for a year might help to consolidate the power of the MLP-led electoral coalition in advance of the 2010 balloting. (Former vice president Bundhun had been unaffiliated.)

A multi-million-dollar manufacturing-park project undertaken by China created tension among residents and farmers in Terre Rouge, near Port Louis. More than 100 families were forced to relocate to accommodate a 521-acre industrial area. The issue reflected larger tensions on the island, where half of foreign workers were Chinese; citizens felt that foreign firms were taking local jobs.

In February 2008 Jacob Zuma, leader of the South African National Congress, attempted to intervene in a court case in Mauritius over evidence that could be used against him in a corruption case involving a French arms firm. In June the Mauritian constitutional court rejected Zuma's request to suppress the evidence.

In an effort to prevent a recession because of a decline in tourism and textile exports, in 2009 the government announced a $330 million stimulus package that provided funds for infrastructure programs, as well as business loans and grants. In March 2009 the government was forced to lend the national air carrier, Air Mauritius, more than $52 million to prevent bankruptcy. Foreign investment in construction projects also fell significantly between 2008 and 2009.

POLITICAL PARTIES

A large number of political parties have contested recent Mauritian elections (more than 70, presenting more than 640 officeseekers in 2005); few, however, have run candidates in most constituencies, and only a very limited number have secured parliamentary representation. By 2008 there were more than 60 recognized parties. Because most of the groups are leftist in orientation, ideological differences tend to be blurred, with recurrent cleavages based largely on pragmatic considerations. Although assembly elections were scheduled for 2010, the main parties began talks for electoral coalitions in 2008 in anticipation that early elections might be called in 2009.

Government and Government-Supportive Parties:

Mauritius Labour Party (MLP). A Hindu-based party, the MLP (also referenced as the Workers' Party [*Parti des Travailleurs*—PTr]), under the leadership of Seewoosagur Ramgoolam, joined the country's other leading Indian group, the Muslim Action Committee (CAM), in forming the Independence Party (IP) prior to the 1976 election. Collectively, the MLP and the CAM won an overwhelming majority of 47 legislative seats in the 1967 preindependence balloting, whereas the IP retained only 28 in 1976 and lost all but 2 in 1982 (both awarded to the MLP on a "best loser" basis). A condition of the MLP joining the 1983 government alliance was said to be the designation of Ramgoolam as president upon the country's becoming a republic; following failure of a republic bill in December 1983, the longtime MLP leader was named governor general.

In February 1984, after MLP leader Sir Satcam Boolell was relieved of his post as minister of planning and economic development, the party went into opposition. It reentered the government in August 1986, with Boolell as second deputy prime minister. In September 1990 the MLP again moved into opposition, Seewoosagur Ramgoolam's son, Navin, succeeding Boolell as party leader and assuming the post of leader of the opposition. On the basis of a preelectoral accord with the MMM's Paul Bérenger, the younger Ramgoolam became prime minister following the MLP-MMM victory in December 1995. The MLP-MMM coalition dissolved in mid-1997 with Ramgoolam subsequently remaining the head of an all-MLP (with the exception of one OPR minister) cabinet. At that point the MLP was described as holding a majority of 35–37 seats in the assembly. With the MMM aligning with the MSM for the September 2000 assembly balloting, the MLP was left with only the PMXD and several small parties as electoral partners, their coalition securing 36.6 percent of the vote but only 6 of the 62 elected seats.

The **Rally for Reform** (*Rassemblement pour la Réforme*—RPR) joined the MLP prior to the 2005 legislative elections. The RPR was launched in August 1996 by a dissident faction of the MSM led by Rama Sithanen (a former finance minister) and Sheila Bappoo (who had briefly been MSM secretary general). It formed an alliance with the PMSD for the October 1996 municipal elections, the combined list polling some 25 percent of the vote. In the September 2000 assembly balloting, the RPR was aligned with the MLP-PMXD coalition. Its leaders, Rama SITHANEN and Sheila BAPPOO, both subsequently gained cabinet posts in the MLP-led government after the 2005 elections.

For the 2005 assembly elections, the MLP led a Social Alliance (Alliance Social) that included the new MSD, the PMXD, the MR, and the MMSN. In 2006 former vice president Angidi Verriah Chettiar was chosen as the honorary president of the party. He was subsequently appointed vice president of the republic in 2007. In 2009 it was reported that the MLP was endeavoring to develop an electoral alliance with Creole groups such as the **Federation of Mauritian Creoles** (*Fédération des Créole Mauricians*—FCM) ahead of the 2010 assembly elections in an effort to undermine the electoral base of the MMM.

Leaders: Dr. Navin RAMGOOLAM (Prime Minister and Leader of the Party), Ahmed Rashid BEEBEEJAUN (Deputy Prime Minister and Deputy Party Leader), Etienne SINATAMBOU (President), Angidi Verriah CHETTIAR (Vice President of the Republic and Honorary President of the Party), Devanand VIRAHSAWMY (Secretary General).

Xavier Duval Mauritian Party (*Parti Mauricien Xavier Duval*—PMXD). A by-product of interfamily conflict within the PMSD (below), the PMXD is led by Xavier Luc Duval, the son of the late PMSD leader, Sir Gaëtan Duval. Following his split with his uncle, Hervé Duval (the current PMSD leader), and the formation of the PMXD, Xavier Luc Duval was elected to the National Assembly in a by-election on September 19, 1999, on a MLP-PMXD ticket. He was subsequently named minister of industry, commerce, corporate affairs, and financial services in the new MLP-led cabinet announced on September 26, and the party ran in alliance with the MLP in the September 2000 legislative poll, Duval securing 1 of the "best loser" seats in the assembly following that poll. When the MLP's Navin Ramgoolam became prime minister in 2005, he named Xavier Luc Duval one of his three deputy prime ministers (a position that was subsequently retitled vice-prime minister in 2008). In 2009 the PMXD launched a political weekly, *Le Populaire*.

Leaders: Xavier Luc DUVAL, Jacques PANGLOSE (Secretary General), Regina MAUDER (Mayor of Quatre-Bornes), Cader HOSENALLY.

Republican Movement (*Mouvement Républicain*—MR). The MR was founded on the eve of the October 1996 municipal balloting, in which its leader, Rama Valayden, won a local council seat. Valayden had presented himself as an heir to the policies pursued by the late Sir Gaëtan Duval of the PMSD. The MR aligned with the MSM-MMM coalition in the September 2000 balloting, one MR member reportedly securing a seat as an alliance candidate. In May 2001 the MR decided to end its support for the government, and subsequent press reports referred to the MR as an "opposition party." The MR participated in the MLP-led Social Alliance in 2005, and Rama Valayden was named attorney general and minister of justice and human rights in the new Ramgoolam government. In 2006 the MR's Mirella Chauvin was elected mayor of Beau Bassin/Rose Hill, the second largest city in Mauritius. The MR was expected to remain part of the electoral alliance with the MLP.

Leaders: Rama VALAYDEN, Sada ETWAROO, Mirella CHAUVIN (Mayor of Beau Bassin/Rose Hill).

Mauritian Militant Socialist Movement (MMSM). The MMSM is a radical Hindu group led by former agriculture minister Madun Dullo. It participated in the MLP-PMXD electoral alliance in the September 2000 assembly poll and the MLP-led Social Alliance in 2005. Dullo was dismissed as foreign minister in March 2008, and reports indicated that the MMSM would withdraw its support from the coalition government. In 2009 the MMSM was reportedly in discussions with the MMM to form an electoral coalition for the planned 2010 assembly balloting.

Leader: Madun DULLO.

Social Democratic Movement (*Movement Social-Démocrate*—MSD). The MSD was formed in March 2005 by four MSM legislators (including two who had recently resigned from the cabinet) to protest the proposed continuation of the MSM-MMM electoral alliance. The new party joined the Social Alliance for the July legislative balloting and was expected to ally with the MLP in the 2010 balloting.

Leaders: Anil BAICHOO, Mukeshawr CHOONEE.

Mauritian Social Democratic Party (*Parti Mauricien Social-Démocrate*—PMSD). Composed chiefly of Franco-Mauritian landowners and middle-class Creoles, the PMSD initially opposed independence but subsequently accepted it as a fait accompli. Antisocialist at home and anticommunist in foreign affairs, it has long been distinguished for its Francophile stance. The party was part of the Ramgoolam government coalition until 1973, when it went into opposition. It won 23 legislative seats in the 1967 election but retained only 8 in 1976, when it reentered the government. Reduced to 2 "best loser" seats in 1982, it won 4 on an elective basis in 1983 and 1987. The party withdrew from the alliance in August 1988 following a dispute over fiscal policy.

The party was awarded 1 "best loser" seat following the 1991 election. In January 1994 Sir Gaëtan Duval, the leader of the PMSD, failed in an attempt to persuade Prime Minister Jugnauth to form a common front to block the threatened electoral alliance between the MLP and the MMM. At a party congress on May 22 he turned the leadership over to his son, Xavier Luc Duval, under whom the PMSD retreated visibly from its theretofore rightist posture. The party joined the MSM-led coalition in February 1995, with the younger Duval being given the industry and tourism portfolios; however, the move was opposed by the PMSD Central Committee, which in April called on Duval to resign from the government (a move which he undertook only in October for a quite different reason—his opposition to the proposed language amendment). The episode reflected a growing rift between the two Duvals, with Sir Gaëtan subsequently withdrawing from the PMSD to form the Gaëtan Duval Party (*Parti Gaëtan Duval*—PGD). As the PGD candidate he reentered the assembly on a "best loser" basis after the December elections. Because the PMSD had failed to gain representation, the elder Duval effectively resumed its leadership until his death in May 1996, when his seat in the legislature passed to his brother, Hervé Duval. It was reported that Prime Minister Ramgoolam had approached Hervé Duval with a proposal to join the government in late June 1997 following the split in the MLP-MMM coalition. However, the PMSD leader decided to align instead with the MMM in the short-lived National Alliance opposition grouping, a decision that apparently exacerbated Duval's differences with Xavier Luc Duval, who subsequently formed his own grouping, the PMXD (above). In balloting in 2000 the PMSD was described as associated with the coalition led by the MSM and MMM. (Hervé Duval's supporters have also been referenced as the *Vrai Bleus* [True Blues].) The party joined the MSM-MMM electoral coalition for the 2005 assembly balloting. In September 2006 the PMSD switched its support to the governing MLP-led coalition, reportedly in hopes of gaining a cabinet post.

Leaders: Maurice ALLET (President), Hervé DUVAL, Clifford EMPEIGNE.

Opposition Parties:

Mauritian Socialist Movement (*Mouvement Socialiste Mauricien*—MSM). The MSM was organized initially on April 8, 1983, as the Militant Socialist Movement (*Mouvement Socialiste Militant*) by Prime Minister Jugnauth following his expulsion, in late March, from the MMM. Prior to the 1983 election, the MSM, with the MLP, the PMSD, and the OPR, formed a coalition that secured a clear majority of legislative seats. In February 1984 the MLP withdrew from the alliance, although a number of its deputies remained loyal to the government.

The MSM secured 26 of the 41 elective seats won in August 1987 by the reconstituted five-party alliance, from which the PMSD withdrew a year later. The MLP again moved into opposition following an electoral agreement between the MSM and MMM in July 1990, with the new MSM-led alliance winning 59 of 62 elective seats in September 1991. In a disastrous loss in December 1995, all of the MSM deputies, including Jugnauth, lost their seats. However, the MSM formed a coalition with the MMM for the snap legislative elections in September 2000 and secured 54 of the elected seats with 51.7 percent of the vote.

Pravind Kumar Jugnauth succeeded his father as leader of the MSM in April 2003. In 2004 he called for retention of the MSM-MMM electoral alliance in the 2005 assembly balloting, prompting several prominent MSM members to quit the party to form the new MSD (above). In 2006 the MSM's Nando Bodha was named the official leader of the parliamentary opposition in the National Assembly. However, he resigned from that post in 2007 after the PMSD withdrew its support. Tensions grew within the MSM-MMM coalition in March 2008 over the MSM's demand that should the coalition win the next election, the new prime minister would be the younger Jugnauth, the current MSM party chair. Reports in 2009 indicated that the two parties were unable to agree on terms for a coalition. Also in 2008 the MSM celebrated its twenty-fifth anniversary with a series of public events designed to highlight the party's positions prior to the 2010 assembly elections.

Leaders: Sir Anerood JUGNAUTH (President of the Republic), Pravind Kumar JUGNAUTH (Former Deputy Prime Minister and Chair of the Party), Nando BODHA (Former Leader of the Opposition), Dr. Beergoonath GHURBURRUN, Emmanuel Jean Leung SHING (Secretary General).

Mauritian Militant Movement (*Mouvement Militant Mauricien*—MMM). The leadership of the MMM was detained during the 1971 disturbances because of its "confrontational politics," which, unlike that of other Mauritian parties, was intended to cut across ethnic-communal lines. Following the 1976 election, the party's leadership strength was only 2 seats short of a majority; in 1982, campaigning in alliance with the Mauritian Socialist Party, it obtained an absolute majority of 42 seats.

In March 1983, 12 members of the MMM government of Anerood Jugnauth, led by Finance Minister Paul Bérenger, resigned in disagreement over economic policy and because they and their supporters believed that Creole should be designated the national language. Immediately thereafter, Jugnauth was expelled and proceeded to form the MSM (above), which, with its allies, achieved a decisive victory in the August 21 election.

Prior to the 1987 balloting, Bérenger, long viewed as a Marxist, characterized himself as a "democratic socialist." However, he was unsuccessful in securing an assembly seat on either a direct or "best loser" basis. The party itself campaigned as the leading component of a Union for the Future alliance, which included two minor groups, the **Democratic Workers' Movement** (*Mouvement des Travaillistes Démocrates*—MTD), then led by Anil Kumar BAICHOO and later by Sanjeet TEELOCK; and the **Socialist Workers' Front** (*Front des Travailleurs Socialistes*—FTS). On July 17, 1990, the MMM concluded an electoral accord with the MSM and MTD and formally entered the Jugnauth government on September 26.

In October 1993 Bérenger was briefly ousted as MMM secretary general, but he was returned to office by the party's Central Committee, which proceeded to expel the anti-Bérenger majority of Political Bureau members, including Prem Nababsingh and Dharmanand Goopt FOKEER, theretofore MMM president and chair, respectively, who remained members of the Jugnauth administration. In April 1994 Bérenger concluded an electoral pact with Navin Ramgoolam of the MLP under which, in the event of a coalition victory, Ramgoolam was to become prime minister and Bérenger his deputy. Two months later Nababsingh and his supporters formally left the MMM to organize the Mauritian Militant Renaissance.

Bérenger resigned his parliamentary seat on November 29, 1994, after having charged the MSM of manipulating the 1991 election, despite having been a government minister at the time. He regained his MP status in a by-election in January 1995 and became deputy prime minister and foreign minister as a result of the MLP-MMM victory in December 1995. However, Bérenger was relieved of his cabinet posts in June 1997, and the MMM moved into opposition when all but one of the party's nine other ministers resigned from the government.

In August 1997 Bérenger spearheaded the organization of a National Alliance (*Alliance Nationale*—AN) in an apparent attempt to improve his chances of securing the top governmental post in the next election. In addition to the MMM, the AN comprised the PMSD, the RPR, and the MMSM. However, the grouping did poorly in an April 1998 by-election (the AN candidate finished third with 16 percent of the vote), and a correspondent for the *Indian Ocean Newsletter* described the AN as "having been shot at dawn." Bérenger subsequently joined with Jugnauth in late 1998 to announce a MMM-MSM "federation" that would present joint candidates in the next general election and share governmental responsibility in the event of success. The federation was formally established in January 1999, and, as expected, Bérenger assumed a deputy post in the coalition with the understanding that he would be named to a similar rank in a Jugnauth-headed government. Following the landslide victory of the MSM-MMM coalition in the September 2000 balloting, Bérenger was named deputy prime minister, with the understanding that he would succeed Jugnauth as prime minister in three years. Bérenger also negotiated a similar proposed arrangement with Pravind Jugnauth of the MSM prior to the 2005 balloting.

On April 8, 2006, Bérenger resigned his position as leader of the opposition in the assembly because relations between the MMM and the MSM had deteriorated following the MMM-MSM coalition's defeat in the 2005 elections.

In May 2007 the MMM launched a campaign to attract younger, professional voters after a new Central Committee was elected. The effort was part of a larger initiative to remake the image of the party in advance of upcoming local and national elections. In September Bérenger was appointed leader of the opposition in the assembly. Reports indicated that the MMM and the MSM were unable to form a coalition because of the demand by the MSM's that party leader Pravind Jugnauth be prime minister, if a MMM-MSM coalition won the next election. In November 2008 Bérenger launched an initiative to reform the Mauritian electoral system by adopting a proportional system of representation.

Leaders: Paul BÉRENGER (Opposition Leader and Former Prime Minister), Premnath RAMNAH (Former Speaker of the National Assembly), Ahmed Sulliman JEEWAH (Party President), Rajesh BHAGWAN (General Secretary), Jaya Krishna CUTTAREE (Deputy Party Leader).

Rodriguan People's Organization (*Organisation du Peuple Rodriguais*—OPR). The OPR captured the two Rodrigues Island seats in the 1982 and 1983 balloting and, having earlier indicated that it would support the MSM-Labour alliance, was assigned one cabinet post in the Jugnauth government of August 1983; it retained the post after the ensuing two elections. The OPR again won Rodrigues's two elective parliamentary seats in 1995, despite its affiliation with the Jugnauth administration. It joined the resultant MLP-led government, although its customary full ministerial responsibility for Rodrigues affairs was downgraded to junior level under the prime minister. The OPR regained the full cabinet authority for Rodrigues affairs in the new government announced in July 1997. The party again secured the two elective seats from Rodrigues in the 2000 and 2005 legislative polls.

In 2006 two OPR deputies in the Regional Assembly defected to the opposition **Rodriguan Movement** (*Mouvement Rodriguais*—MR) (below), which gave the MR a majority in the assembly and forced Louis Serge Claire to resign as chief commissioner. Clair subsequently became the leader of the opposition in the assembly, and the OPR remained in opposition following regional elections in 2006.

Leaders: Louis Serge CLAIR (Former Rodrigues Island Minister, Leader of the Opposition in the Regional Assembly and Leader of the Party), Jean Alex Nancy (Secretary), J. Benoit JOLICOEUR.

Rodriguan Movement (*Mouvement Rodriguais*—MR). A regional rival of the OPR favoring U.S.-style federalism rather than separation, the MR was awarded two "best loser" seats following both the 1995 and 2000 legislative polls. Following the defection of two OPR deputies and the loss of that party's majority in the Regional Assembly in 2006, MR member Johnson Roussety was appointed chief commissioner of the island. The MR subsequently won a majority in the 2006 regional elections, and Roussety was reappointed.

Leaders: Johnson ROUSSETY (Chief Commissioner of Rodrigues), Nicolas VON MALLY (Party Leader).

Other Parties and Groupings:

Green Party (*Les Verts*). The Green Party was reportedly aligned with the MSM-MMM electoral coalition in the September 2000 legislative balloting, and party leader Sylvio Louis MICHEL was named minister of fisheries in the new cabinet. For the 2005 balloting, the party joined the MLP-led electoral alliance, but failed to gain any seats.

Leader: Sylvio Louis MICHEL.

Resistance and Alternative. A center-left grouping launched in March 2005, Resistance and Alternative argued that the "big parties" had failed to solve the nation's problems. In 2008 the party endeavored unsuccessfully to force the government to end ongoing negotiations with the EU over a new trade pact. Party leader Ashok SUBRON emerged as one of the main critics of the government's 2009 economic stimulus plan.

Leader: Ashok SUBRON (Secretary General).

Party of God (*Hizbullah*). The Islamic party *Hizbullah* obtained 1 assembly seat as a "best loser" in the December 1995 election. (Some subsequent reports referenced the seat as belonging to the **Mauritian Liberal Movement** [*Mouvement Libéral Mauricien*—MLM], described as *Hizbullah*'s "ally.") Reportedly draining Muslim support from the MMM, *Hizbullah* was credited with 5 percent of the vote in the September 2000 poll but did not receive a "best loser" seat. Party leader Ceeal MEEAH was held for three years on murder charges before being released in 2003. The party led an effort to replace the "best loser" system with one based on ethnic representation. Reports in 2005 indicated that some officials in the party began using a new name, the **Mauritian Solidarity Front** (*Front Solidarite Mauriciene*—FSM)

Leader: Ceeal MEEAH.

Mauritian Socialist Party (*Parti Socialiste Mauricien*—PSM). The original PSM was formed in 1979 by the withdrawal from the MLP of a group of dissidents led by Harish Boodhoo. It was dissolved in May 1983 by absorption into the MSM, and Boodhoo was named deputy prime minister. In January 1986 Boodhoo resigned his government post in the wake of a disagreement with Prime Minister Jugnauth over drug policy, and he withdrew from the assembly the following November. Subsequently, he mounted an opposition campaign in his newspaper, *Le Socialiste*, and in June 1988 announced the PSM's revival. Boodhoo was aligned with the MSM-MMM alliance for the September 2000 balloting. However, the PSM apparently withdrew its support for the government in early 2002, and Boodhoo subsequently attempted to forge an opposition coalition. In the 2005 elections, many PSM members supported the MSM.

Leader: Harish BOODHOO.

Muslim Action Committee (*Comité d'Action Musulman*—CAM). The CAM has long represented the interests of the Indian Muslim community. Reports on the September 2000 legislative poll referenced a **Mauritian Action Committee** (*Comité d'Action Mauricien*—also CAM). It was not clear if any relationship existed between the two groups. In 2003 members of the Muslim Action Committee reportedly launched a new party called the **Muslim League** under the leadership of Farook Mohammed BACCUS. The CAM failed to gain any representation in the 2005 elections.

Leader: Youssuf MOHAMMED (President).

National Mauritian Movement (*Mouvement National Mauricien*—MNM). Led by an ex-police chief who had criticized Prime Minister Ramgoolam's handling of the riots in Port Louis in early 1999, the right-wing MNM campaigned for the 2000 legislative balloting on a platform urging voters to renounce the country's "old parties." (Some confusion may exist over the name of this grouping, some electoral reports also referencing a **National Democratic Movement [Raj Dayal]**.) The MNM did not secure any seats in the 2005 assembly balloting.

Leader: Col. Raj DAYAL.

In addition, there are two far-left organizations that remain active: **The Struggle** (*Lalit*), led by Lindsey COLLEN, and the **Socialist Workers' Party** (*Parti Socialiste Ouvriére*—PSO), whose secretary general is Didier EDMOND. In 2005 *Lalit* called for the United States to close its military base on Diego Garcia and for all of the Chagos Archipelago to be returned to Mauritian sovereignty.

Other parties participating in the September 2000 or 2005 assembly elections were the **Agricultural Planting Movement** (*Mouvement Planteur Agricole*—MPA); **Authentic Mauritian Movement** (*Mouvement Authentique Mauricien*—MAM); **Liberal Action Party** (*Parti Action Libéral*—PAL); **Mauritian Democracy** (*Démocratie Mauricienne*—DM); **Mauritian Democratic Movement** (*Mouvement Démocratique Mauricien*—MDM); **Mauritius Party Rights** (MPR); **National Democratic Movement** (*Mouvement Démocratique National*—MDN); **NouvoLizur,** a grouping led by former cabinet minister Joceline MINERVE which, among other things, supports "Chagossian rights"; **Party of the Mauritian People** (*Parti du Peuple Mauricien*—PPM); **Socialist Workers Movement** (*Mouvement Travailliste Socialiste*—MTS); **Tamil Council** (TC); and the **Mauritian Union** (*Union Mauricienne*—UM).

LEGISLATURE

The Mauritian **National Assembly** is a unicameral body containing 62 elected deputies (3 from each of the 20 constituencies on the main island and 2 from Rodrigues Island), plus up to 8 appointed from the list of unsuccessful candidates under a "best loser" system designed to provide "balanced" ethnic and political representation. The legislative term is five years, subject to dissolution. In the National Assembly elections held on July 3, 2005, the Social Alliance (led by the Mauritius Labor Party) won 38 of the 60 elected seats from the main island, the other 22 going to a coalition led by the Mauritian Socialist Movement (MSM) and the Mauritian Militant Movement (MMM). The Rodriguan People's Organization (OPR) won the 2 elected seats on Rodrigues Island. In the subsequent "best loser" distribution of appointed seats for the assembly, the Social Alliance was accorded 4 additional seats; the MSM-MMM coalition, 2; and the Rodriguan Movement, 2.

Speaker: Rajikeswur PURRYAG.

Rodrigues Regional Assembly. As authorized by a constitutional amendment approved by the National Assembly in November 2001, the Rodrigues Regional Assembly comprises 18 members, 12 elected from six constituencies on a first-past-the-post system and 6 elected on a proportional basis. In balloting for the assembly on December 10, 2006, the Rodriguan Movement secured 10 seats and the Rodriguan People's Organization, 8 seats.

Chair: Joseph Chenlye LAMVOHEE.

CABINET

[as of June 1, 2009]

Prime Minister	Navinchandra Ramgoolam (MLP)
Deputy Prime Ministers	Ahmed Rashid Beebeejaun (MLP)
Vice-Prime Ministers	Charles Gaëtan Xavier Luc Duval (PMXD)
	Rama Krishna Sithanen (MLP)
Ministers	
Agro-Industries, Food Protection and Security	Satya Faugoo (MLP)
Business, Enterprise and Cooperatives	Mahess Gowreesoo (MLP)
Civil Service Affairs and Administrative Reforms	Balkissoon Hookoom (MLP)
Consumer Protection and Citizens Charter	Sylvio Hock Sheen Tang Wah Hing (MLP)
Defense and Home Affairs	Navinchandra Ramgoolam (MLP)
Education, Culture and Human Resources	Vasant Kumar Bunwaree (MLP)
Environment and National Development	Lormus Bundhoo (MLP)
Finance and Economic Development	Rama Krishna Sithanen (MLP)
Foreign Affairs, International Trade, and Regional Cooperation	Arvin Boolell (MLP)
Health and Quality of Life	Rajeshwar Jeetah (MLP)
Housing and Lands	Abu Twalib Kasenally
Industry, Science and Research	Dharambeer Gokhool (MLP)
Information Technology and Telecommunications	Mohammad Asraf Ally Dulull (MLP)
Justice and Human Rights; Attorney-General	Jaya Rama Valayden (MR)
Labor, Industrial Relations, and Employment	Jean François Chaumiere (MLP)
Land Transport and Shipping	Anil Kumar Bachoo (MLP)
Local Government, Rodrigues and Outer Islands	James Burty David (MLP)
Public Infrastructure	Anil Kumar Bachoo (MLP)
Renewable Energy and Public Utilities	Ahmed Rashid Beebeejaun (MLP)

Social Security, National Solidarity, Senior Citizen Welfare, and Reform Institutions	Sheilabai Bappoo (MLP) [f]
Tourism, Leisure, and External Communications	Charles Gaëtan Xavier Luc Duval (PMXD)
Women's Rights, Child Development, and Family Welfare	Indranee Seebun (MLP) [f]
Youth and Sports	Satyaprakash Ritoo (MLP)

[f] = female

COMMUNICATIONS

The traditionally free Mauritian press was subject to censorship under the state of emergency imposed in 1971, but restrictions were lifted on May 1, 1976. Radio and television are under the semipublic control of the government-appointed Independent Broadcasting Authority. In its 2008 report, Reporters Without Borders asserted that press freedoms in Mauritius were similar to those in Western, developed countries and ranked Mauritius 47, along with Poland, Romania and South Korea, out of 173 countries in freedom of the press.

Press. The following are published daily in Port Louis in English and French, unless otherwise noted: *Weekend* (85,000), weekly; *Le Mauricien* (35,000); *Cinq Plus* (30,000), weekly; *L'Express* (30,000); *Le Quotidien* (30,000); *Le Dimanche* (25,000), weekly; *Mauritius Times* (13,500), weekly; *Le Nouveau Militant* (6,000), MMM weekly; *Chinese Daily News* (5,000), in Chinese; *China Times* (3,000), in Chinese; *Maurice Soir* (2,000), in French; *The Sun,* MMM organ; *Vani,* PSM weekly.

Broadcasting and computing. The Mauritian Broadcasting Corporation operates two national radio networks and four television channels, along with two pay television stations. Private radio stations were authorized in 2000, and several stations operate from Port Louis. Approximately 93 percent of Mauritian homes had a television in 2005, and all television owners pay a monthly fee of $3. As of 2008 there were 220.3 Internet users per 1,000 inhabitants.

INTERGOVERNMENTAL REPRESENTATION

Ambassador to the U.S.: (Vacant).

U.S. Ambassador to Mauritius: (Vacant).

Permanent Representative to the UN: Somduth SOBORUN.

IGO Memberships (Non-UN): AfDB, AU, BADEA, Comesa, CWTH, Interpol, IOC, IOM, IOR-ARC, NAM, OIF, PCA, SADC, WCO, WTO.

MEXICO

United Mexican States
Estados Unidos Mexicanos

Political Status: Independence originally proclaimed 1810; present federal constitution adopted February 5, 1917.

Area: 761,600 sq. mi. (1,972,544 sq. km.).

Population: 103,263,388 (2005C), including an adjustment for underennumeration; 106,683,000 (2008E).

Major Urban Centers (2005E): MEXICO CITY (Federal District, 8,795,000), Guadalajara (1,645,000), Tijuana (1,474,000), Ciudad Juárez (1,454,000), Heroica Puebla de Zaragoza (1,428,000), León (1,183,000), Monterrey (1,132,000), Chihuahua (743,000), Acapulco (682,000), Mexicali (616,000), Veracruz (481,000).

Official Language: Spanish.

Monetary Unit: New Peso (market rate December 1, 2009: 12.86 pesos = $1US).

President: Felipe CALDERÓN Hinojosa (National Action Party); elected July 2, 2006, and inaugurated on December 1 for a six-year term, succeeding Vicente FOX Quesada (Nacional Action Party).

THE COUNTRY

Extending southeastward from the U.S. border to the jungles of Yucatán and Guatemala, Mexico ranks third in size and second in population among North American countries and holds comparable rank among the countries of Latin America. Its varied terrain encompasses low-lying coastal jungles, a broad central plateau framed by high mountain ranges, and large tracts of desert territory in the north. The people are mainly of mixed Indian and Spanish (*mestizo*) descent, with minority groups of pure Indians and Caucasians. Despite the predominance of Roman Catholicism, constitutional separation of church and state has prevailed since 1857, with links to the Vatican in abeyance until 1992 (see Foreign relations, below). About one-fourth of the population is still engaged in agriculture, which now contributes less than 6 percent of GDP. In 2000 women constituted 37 percent of the nonagricultural labor force, concentrated mainly in trade, manufacturing, and domestic service; in the export-oriented border factories (*maquiladoras*), more than 80 percent of the workforce is female. As of mid-2009, 2 of 19 cabinet secretaries were women, as were 28 percent of the Chamber of Deputies and 20 percent of the Senate.

Industrialization has been rapid since World War II, but its benefits have been unevenly distributed, and much of the rural population remains substantially unaffected. The GNP grew by a yearly average of 16 percent during 1972–1975, with the growth rate declining to a still-impressive 8 percent in 1978–1981. Subsequently, the economy fell into deep recession, with unserviceable foreign debt, massive capital flight, widespread unemployment, and rampant inflation. Successive International Monetary Fund (IMF) interventions slowed the decline in 1983–1984, but by mid-1986, in the wake of a disastrous earthquake in Mexico City the preceding September and a collapse in oil prices, crisis conditions had returned, with inflation surging to more than 140 percent in 1987. The government responded late in the year with a number of initiatives, including an innovative buy-back plan for foreign debt and an Economic Solidarity Pact (*Pacto de Solidaridad Económica*—PSE) among government, management, and labor to hold down prices and wages. Bolstered by a dramatic decline in inflation to less than 20 percent in 1989, coupled with modest GNP growth, the Carlos Salinas administration sought a reported $1 billion from its international lenders in 1990 for oil, electric power, and communications development. Further invigorating Salinas's economic agenda were windfall oil revenues from the Persian Gulf crisis ($3 billion) and anticipated income from the privatization of telecommunications, banking, and the iron and steel industries ($3–$5 billion in the short term, plus the potential repatriation of an estimated $50 billion that reportedly went overseas during earlier nationalization schemes).

An economic growth rate of 3.6 percent in 1991 was considered highly satisfactory, given a 2.2 percent growth in population and a recession in the United States; however, the rate receded to 2.6 percent in 1992 (albeit with a further decline in inflation to 15.5 percent) and to less than 1 percent in 1993. During 1994 inflation declined further to 7.1 percent, while economic growth was estimated at 3.3 percent. In December the country was engulfed by a fiscal crisis that prompted a $50 billion U.S.-led rescue package in January 1995. By late 1995 it was evident that the slump would be far worse than in 1982, with a decline of between 3.5 and 5 percent in GDP, inflation of more than 40 percent, and a doubling of official unemployment to 6.6 percent (as contrasted with a business association figure of 10.4 percent and union estimates as high as 35 percent). GDP showed a gain of 5.2 percent for 1996, with inflation dipping to under 30 percent for the year. GDP growth continued strong during the next two years, at 7 percent in 1997 and 4.8 percent in 1998, but inflation remained high at more than 18 percent. The economy grew by 3.7 percent in 1999 and then soared by

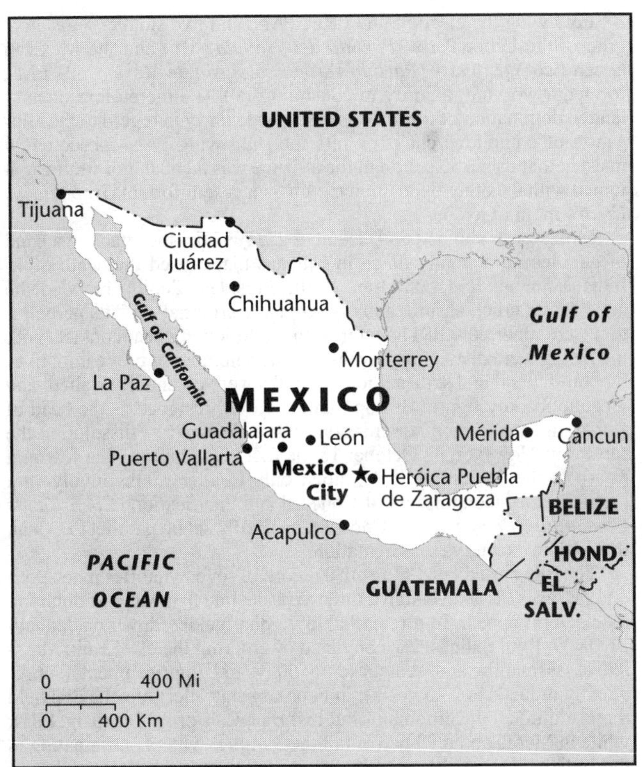

6.9 percent in 2000. In early 2001, however, growth stalled, in large part because of weakness in the U.S. economy but also because of a decline in *maquiladora* activity as the result of Chinese competition. By mid-2001 the inflation rate had dropped below 7 percent, but GDP contracted by 0.3 percent before improving by 0.7 percent in 2002, 1.3 percent in 2003, and 4.4 percent in 2004. In 2005 GDP declined by 3 percent, but more surprising was that year's inflation rate of 3.3 percent, which was the lowest since such records began 36 years earlier. Inflation rose to 4.1 percent in 2006, with GDP growth standing 4.8 percent for the same year. GDP growth was 3.3 percent in 2007 and 1.3 percent in 2008. Mexico's economy was expected to suffer in response to the recession in the US and the outbreak of swine flu in 2009, with the IMF predicting a sharp contraction of 7.3 percent amidst falling exports and tourism. Inflation reached 3.7 percent in 2007 and rose to 6.5 percent in 2008, although a decline to 3.5 percent was expected in 2009. The IMF reflected general confidence in Mexico's economic management by granting a flexible credit line valued at $47 billion in April 2009; those flexible conditions were granted to just one other country, Poland, that year.

GOVERNMENT AND POLITICS

Political background. The territory that is now Mexico was conquered by Spain in the 16th century. Mexico proclaimed its independence in 1810 and the establishment of a republic in 1822. The country was ruled by Gen. Antonio López de SANTA ANNA from 1833 to 1855, a period that encompassed the declaration of Texan independence in 1836 and war with the United States from 1846 to 1848. Archduke MAXIMILIAN of Austria, installed as emperor of Mexico by Napoleon III in 1865, was deposed and executed by Benito JUAREZ in 1867. The dominant figure during the latter years of the nineteenth century was Gen. Porfirio DÍAZ, who served as president from 1877 to 1910.

Modern Mexican history dates from the Revolution of 1910, which shattered an outmoded social and political system and cleared the way for a generally progressive republican regime whose foundations were laid in 1917. From 1928 political life was dominated by a nationwide grouping known since 1946 as the Institutional Revolutionary Party (*Partido Revolucionario Institucional*—PRI), which purported to carry forward the work of the 1917 constitution.

Luis ECHEVERRÍA Alvarez, who assumed the presidency in 1970, adopted the slogan "Upward and Forward" (*"Arriba y Adelante"*) as a rallying cry for his program of reform, which sought to overcome inequitable distribution of income, widespread alienation and unrest, scattered urban and rural violence, and a visible erosion in the prestige, if not the power, of the PRI. Echeverría's efforts were opposed both by the right, because of a feeling that the traditional favoritism shown to business interests was waning, and by the left, because of a conviction that the reform was a sham.

In the presidential election of July 4, 1976, Finance Minister José LÓPEZ Portillo, running as the PRI candidate, obtained 94.4 percent of the popular vote against a group of independents, no opposition party having presented an endorsed candidate. Soon after his inauguration on December 1, the new chief executive introduced a far-reaching program of political reform that resulted in three previously unrecognized parties, including the Mexican Communist Party, being conditionally legalized prior to the legislative election of July 1979, after which all three were granted seats in the Chamber of Deputies according to their vote totals.

A left-wing coalition, the Unified Socialist Party of Mexico (*Partido Socialista Unificado de México*—PSUM), formed in November 1981 by the Communists and four smaller parties, failed to gain ground against the entrenched PRI in the July 1982 balloting. The ruling party captured all but one elective congressional seat and saw its presidential candidate, former minister of programming and budget, Miguel de la MADRID Hurtado, win 74.4 percent of the vote in a field of seven nominees. During the ensuing four years the PRI was buffeted by an unprecedented, if minor, set of electoral losses to the rightist National Action Party (*Partido Acción Nacional*—PAN). In the lower house election of July 1985 PAN won 9 elective seats, while in a supplementary distribution under proportional representation the leftist parties gained substantially more seats than in 1982.

At a congress in October 1987 the PRI ratified the selection of former planning and budget minister Carlos SALINAS de Gortari as its 1988 presidential candidate. Although seemingly assured of victory, Salinas was credited with a bare 50.4 percent vote share in the balloting of July 6, 1988. His three competitors, Cuauhtémoc CÁRDENAS Solórzano of the leftist National Democratic Front (*Frente Democrático Nacional*—FDN), PAN's Manuel CLOUTHIER, and Rosario IBARRA de la Piedra of the far-left Revolutionary Workers' Party (*Partido Revolucionario de los Trabajadores*—PRT), immediately brought charges of widespread fraud, which in September were rejected by the Congress sitting as an electoral college to review the results.

In the legislative and gubernatorial elections of August 18, 1991, the PRI won 31 of 32 available Senate seats and 290 of 300 directly contested Chamber seats. It was also declared the winner in all six state governorship contests, although two of the victors were forced to withdraw because of manifest voting irregularities. Subsequent gubernatorial, state, and municipal elections in 1992–1993 showed a pattern of eroding PRI support, occasional opposition successes, frequent violence, and continual opposition charges of fraudulent electoral practice. Following disclosures that the PRI had received large financial donations from the beneficiaries of privatization, party chair Genaro BORREGO Estrada in March 1993 announced a limit on individual contributions; later that month he was removed from office by President Salinas. The president, seeking to respond to domestic and international criticism of Mexican political practice, then initiated other PRI leadership changes and introduced electoral reform measures that were approved by Congress in September (see Constitution and government, below). Meanwhile, the government had come under strong censure for its unconvincing response to the killing on May 25 of the archbishop of Guadalajara, Cardinal Juan Jesús POSADAS Ocambo, who was caught in an apparent shootout between rival drug gangs at the city's airport.

In November 1993 the PRI leadership endorsed Luis Donaldo COLOSIO Murrieta, the social development secretary and a Salinas loyalist, as the party's presidential candidate for the 1994 election. However, a state of crisis generated by the eruption of a major insurgency in the southern state of Chiapas in January 1994 was compounded by the assassination of Colosio in the northern border city of Tijuana on March 23. The replacement PRI candidate, Ernesto ZEDILLO Ponce de Léon (another Salinas loyalist but regarded as more conservative than Colosio), was duly elected president on August 21, but with the PRI's lowest-ever share of the popular vote, while simultaneous congressional elections yielded significant gains for opposition parties. Even more ominous for the PRI was a near sweep by PAN of executive and legislative races in the state of Jalisco on

February 12, 1995, and the party's capture of the Guanajuato governorship on May 28. Meanwhile, the assassination of PRI Secretary General José Francisco RUIZ Massieu on September 28, 1994 prompted an ever-widening inquiry into possible linkage with the Colosio killing and speculation as to ties between political figures and drug traffickers.

On February 28, 1995, Raúl SALINAS de Gortari, the former president's older brother, was arrested for allegedly masterminding the Ruiz Massieu killing, with Carlos Salinas announcing a brief hunger strike two days later in defense of his "personal honor" before departing for what appeared to be voluntary exile in the United States. Subsequently, additional questions arose as to the activities of the dead man's brother, Mario RUIZ Massieu, who submitted his resignation as deputy attorney general after accusing senior PRI officials of hindering an investigation into the affair. He was arrested in Newark, New Jersey, on March 3 as he attempted to board a plane for Spain. Mexican authorities stated that almost $7 million had been credited to his accounts in various U.S. banks and charged him with falsifying evidence regarding the murder to protect Raúl Salinas. During ensuing months Mexico sought unsuccessfully to secure extradition of the ex-prosecutor, a fourth and final appeal being rejected by a U.S. magistrate on December 22, even though Washington sought his deportation as an undesirable alien. (He committed suicide in September 1999 immediately prior to a scheduled federal court appearance on drug and wiretapping charges.)

Earlier, the PRI's electoral fortunes had shown scant signs of recovery. In August 1995 PAN retained control of Baja California (where the PRI in 1988 had experienced its first state-level defeat), its third victory of the year out of four such contests. By mid-November both PAN and the leftist Democratic Revolutionary Party (*Partido de la Revolución Democrática*—PRD) had substantially increased their local representation, although the PRI succeeded in retaining the governorship of Michoacán, a PRD stronghold. The ruling party was subsequently embarrassed in the state of Guerrero, whose governor, Rubén FIGUEROA Alcocer, was obliged to resign on March 12, 1996, after being accused of attempting to cover up a police massacre of 17 opposition peasants. Meanwhile, PAN had pulled out of electoral reform talks with the PRI, although the PRD, which had earlier withdrawn from the discussion, returned to the negotiating table, paving the way for a tentative agreement on April 15 by parties holding 70 percent of federal legislative seats.

Meanwhile, the outbreak of insurgent activity in the southernmost state of Chiapas continued under the direction of an indigenous formation styling itself the Zapatista National Liberation Army (*Ejército Zapatista de Liberación Nacional*—EZLN). Led by a charismatic *mestizo* using the alias "Subcomandante Marcos," the group issued a "Declaration of the Lacandona Jungle" that sought redress from "a dictatorship of more than 70 years."

On January 1, 1996, the Zapatistas announced the creation of a Zapatista National Liberation Front (*Frente Zapatista de Liberación Nacional*—FZLN), which was characterized as "a new political force with its base in the EZLN" that would work for the "transforming of Mexico." A month later the government and the EZLN reached agreement on a draft charter expanding the rights of Indians, thus clearing the way for a peace accord. However, the pact was threatened in late May, when the Zapatistas declared a "red alert" in areas under their control because of alleged military provocations by the government. The rebels again withdrew from the peace process but agreed on June 10 to return following the release of two high-ranking Zapatista leaders who had been captured in February. Meanwhile, an even more radical Popular Revolutionary Army (*Ejército Popular Revolucionario*—EPR) had emerged in the southern state of Guerrero. With no apparent links to the EZLN, EPR guerrillas mounted an attack on police and military installations in four Mexican states on August 28 that left 13 dead and 23 wounded. On September 1 President Zedillo pledged to combat the new rebel force with the "full force of the state."

By late 1996 the government also faced continued erosion in its political strength in the rest of the country. PAN and the PRD both made significant inroads against PRI dominance in elections held in the states of Coahuila and México, winning a number of mayoralties. In addition, public opinion polls indicated that the PRI faced a genuine challenge in retaining its legislative majority in the national elections scheduled for mid-1997 and could also lose the concurrent first-ever direct balloting for mayor of Mexico City (considered the second-most influential office in the country). On July 6, 1997, the PRI retained only 238 of 500 lower house seats and yielded the Mexico City mayoralty to the PRD's Cárdenas Solórzano.

Following the election, the PRD, PAN, and two smaller legislative groups, the Labor Party (*Partido del Trabajo*—PT) and the Mexican Green Ecologist Party (*Partido Verde Ecologista de México*—PVEM), formed a working majority to constrain the PRI's theretofore unchallenged domination of the lower house, particularly in regard to the allocation of committee chairs. While the right-wing PAN subsequently insisted that its participation in the alliance was tactical, not strategic, it joined with the other opposition members in a semiformal *Grupo de los Cuatro* in mid-October.

Mexico was stunned on December 22, 1997, by the attack of a band of gunmen on a small village in Chiapas that caused the death of 45 Indians, including 15 children. While President Zedillo branded the attack as "a cruel, absurd, and unacceptable criminal act," its perpetrators were reportedly PRI adherents. In the following year contacts with the EZLN were distinctly uneven. Despite a number of peace initiatives by both federal and state authorities, talks were essentially stalled, and on June 8 a key figure, Bishop Samuel RUIZ, resigned as the head of Conai, the negotiation commission, which declared its dissolution the same day. However, on October 18 the EZLN announced that it would return to the bargaining table, albeit only to attend talks involving a parliamentary Commission of Concord and Pacification (*Comisión de Concordia y Pacificación*—Cocopa), originally set up parallel to Conai, that had no executive representation.

The PRI closed out 1998 with a record of seven victories in ten governors' races, thus reversing a three-year decline that had cast doubt on its electoral appeal. In a remarkable verdict handed down on January 21, 1999, Raúl Salinas was convicted of ordering the 1994 Ruiz Massieu assassination and sentenced to 50 years' imprisonment (subsequently reduced to 27.5 years). In February state elections the PRI held three additional governorships but lost Baja California Sur to the PRD, while in March about 90 percent of the 3 million voters participating in the Indian rights plebiscite (the "Consultation for the Recognition of the Rights of Indian Peoples and the End of the War of Extermination") voiced support for the Zapatista program, including explicit constitutional recognition of Indian rights.

The election of July 2, 2000, was a watershed event in Mexican political history. Although consistently trailing in the public opinion polls, Vicente FOX Quesada of the right-wing PAN, in a coalition with a number of smaller parties called Alliance for Change, succeeded in defeating the PRI nominee, Francisco LABASTIDA Ochoa, 43 percent to 36 percent. In the 500-member Chamber of Deputies, the Alliance for Change won a substantial plurality of 223 seats, and in the 128-member Senate the PRI's former majority of 77 seats was reduced to a plurality of 60, with the Alliance for Change gaining a close second at 51. The PRD, heading a six-member Alliance for Mexico City, retained control of the capital, electing Andrés Manuel LÓPEZ Obrador to the office from which Cárdenas had resigned to run for the presidency.

President Fox's initial high approval rating of 79 percent had declined to 48 percent by January 2002 and to 30 percent by January 2004. The effect of a downturn in the U.S. economy, together with increased competition from Chinese manufacturing, posed great obstacles to the Fox administration. In addition, a highly touted tax reform package, which was expected to raise overall revenues, met immediate opposition. In his dealings with the legislature, observers argued that President Fox, while effective at promoting his goals, had displayed a lack of political skill in nurturing them to fruition.

The most notable achievement of President Fox's first year in office was the passage of an Indigenous Rights Bill. Fox had begun his tenure by offering concessions to the Zapatistas, including the closure of military bases in Chiapas. Subcomandante Marcos and 23 other members of the EZLN "General Staff" responded with a march on Mexico City, where they lobbied for the enactment of the proposed legislation and sent EZLN leaders to address the Congress on March 28, 2001 (despite the opposition of Fox's party). The bill, passed in late April, authorized constitutional changes prohibiting discrimination based on factors including race, religion, or gender; permitting election of indigenous officials by standard electoral practices; guaranteeing the right to preserve Indian languages and cultures; and offering indigenous peoples preferential use of such natural resources as wood and water within their territories. As a consequence of PAN-supported amendments, the legislature frustrated the expectations of the Zapatistas and other indigenous groups by limiting their legal control over land and giving states authority to specify conditions of such control. Subcomandante Marcos labeled it a "grave insult" that "sabotages the process of reconciliation" and the EZLN refused to resume peace talks with the government. In late 2003 they declared political autonomy in 30 of their indigenous municipalities.

In addition to developments in the municipalities, the 2003 general congressional balloting yielded significant changes in the political landscape. The PAN representation plummeted, while that of the PRI rose to just short of a majority. The biggest surprise, however, was the success of the PRD in nearly doubling its contingent from 52 to 95, thereby generating a de facto three-party system while enhancing López Obrador's presidential prospects.

Although the front-runner during much of the 2006 presidential campaign, PRD presidential candidate López Obrador faltered, narrowly losing the July 2 poll to the PAN's Felipe CALDERÓN Hinojosa by 0.5 percent of the vote. López Obrador immediately disputed the close election (Calderón's margin of victory was less than 250,000 votes), demanded a national recount of the ballots, and alleged widespread election irregularities. The allegations were brought to the Instituto Federal Electoral (IFE), Mexico's highest court for election disputes, for a ruling. On July 6, 2006, the institute declared Felipe CALDERÓN Hinojosa the winner. López Obrador oversaw massive street protests that lost popular support over time, but he continued to dispute the outcome of the election in 2008 (see Current issues, below). The PAN also emerged from the 2006 elections as the largest party in Mexico's Senate and Chamber of Deputies though its seat share remained well short of a majority.

The most significant change to President Calderón's cabinet during the first half of his term occurred on November 4, 2008, when Juan Camilo MOURIÑO Terrazas, a powerful interior minister regarded as Calderón's likely choice to succeed him, died in a plane crash in the center of Mexico City. Investigators ruled out foul play in the accident.

Since 2006 the PRI has been resurgent, gaining several state governorships and, in the July 5, 2009, midterm elections, gaining a majority (in coalition with the small PVEM) in the Chamber of Deputies. This development marked the first time a political grouping has had an absolute majority in the chamber since 2007. The PRI finished first in the July 5 legislative election with 36.7 percent of the vote, followed by the PAN, with 28.0; the PRD, with 12.2; the PVEM, with 6.5; the PT, with 3.6; the New Alliance Party (*Partido Nueva Alianza*—Panal), with 3.4; Democratic Convergence (*Convergencia por la Democracia*—CD), with 2.4; and Socialdemocracy (*Socialdemócrata*), with 1.0.

Constitution and government. Under its frequently amended constitution of February 5, 1917, Mexico is a federal republic consisting of 31 states (each with its own constitution, elected governor, and legislative chamber) plus a Federal District, whose chief executive (formerly appointed, but elected as of 1997) is advised by 365 elected councilors. The president is directly elected for a single six-year term. Since 2000 only one, rather than both, parents of presidential contenders must be native-born Mexicans. There is no vice president. Mexico has no constitutionally defined line of succession should the president resign or become incapacitated; in that event, the Congress chooses the next president by secret ballot.

The bicameral Congress, consisting of an elected Senate and Chamber of Deputies (both under a mixed direct and proportional system), was long confined by the party system to a secondary role in the determination of national policy; at present, however, with different parties controlling the legislative and executive branches, its influence has drastically increased. The judicial system is headed by a 21-member Supreme Court, which has four divisions: administrative, civil, labor, and penal. The justices of the Supreme Court are appointed for life by the president with the approval of the Senate. Lower courts include collegiate and single-judge circuit courts, district courts, and jury courts. The basis of local government is the municipality (*municipio*).

State and Capital	*Area (sq. mi.)*	*Population (2008E)*
Aguascalientes (Aguascalientes)	2,112	1,146,000
Baja California Norte (Mexicali)	26,997	3,108,000
Baja California Sur (La Paz)	28,369	573,000
Campeche (Campeche)	19,619	796,000
Chiapas (Tuxtla Gutiérrez)	28,653	4,533,000
Chihuahua (Chihuahua)	94,571	3,358,000
Coahuila (Saltillo)	57,908	2,621,000
Colima (Colima)	2,004	583,000
Durango (Durango)	47,560	1,547,000
Guanajuato (Guanajuato)	11,773	5,038,000
Guerrero (Chilpancingo)	24,819	3,136,000
Hidalgo (Pachuca)	8,036	2,415,000
Jalisco (Guadalajara)	30,535	7,024,000
México (Toluca)	8,245	14,583,000
Michoacán (Morelia)	23,138	3,954,000
Morelos (Cuernavaca)	1,911	1,649,000
Nayarit (Tepic)	10,417	968,000
Nuevo León (Monterrey)	24,792	4,013,000
Oaxaca (Oaxaca)	36,275	3,549,000
Puebla (Puebla)	13,090	5,577,000
Querétaro (Querétaro)	4,421	1,727,000
Quintana Roo (Chetumal)	19,387	1,325,000
San Luis Potosí (San Luis Potosí)	24,351	2,479,000
Sinaloa (Culiacán)	22,486	2,656,000
Sonora (Hermosillo)	70,291	2,509,000
Tabasco (Villa Hermosa)	9,756	2,052,000
Tamaulipas (Ciudad Victoria)	30,650	3,200,000
Tlaxcala (Tlaxcala)	1,511	1,134,000
Veracruz-Llave (Veracruz)	27,683	7,233,000
Yucatán (Mérida)	14,827	1,924,000
Zacatecas (Zacatecas)	28,283	1,377,000
Federal District		
Ciudad de México	579	8,792,000

Foreign relations. A founding member of the United Nations, the Organization of American States (OAS), and related organizations, Mexico has generally adhered to an independent foreign policy based on the principles of nonintervention and self-determination. One of the initiators of the 1967 Treaty for the Prohibition of Nuclear Weapons in Latin America (Treaty of Tlatelolco), it is the only non–South American member of the Latin American Integration Association (ALADI) and the only OAS state to have continually maintained formal relations with Cuba. In return, Mexico was the only major Latin American country for which Castro refused to train guerrillas. In late 1998 the Cuban leader did, however, condemn Mexican membership in the North American Free Trade Agreement (NAFTA) (see below), although he subsequently retreated from the position following the momentary withdrawal of Mexico's ambassador to Havana.

Under President de la Madrid the country continued to exercise a leadership role in the region, despite a diminution of influence because of its economic difficulties. As a participant in the Contadora Group, which also included Colombia, Panama, and Venezuela as original members, Mexico took the group's agenda for regional peace to both South America and the United States. U.S. military policy in Central America continued to be a major source of strain in the traditionally cordial relationship between Mexico and its northern neighbor, with the Mexican chief executive tending to emphasize socioeconomic bases of regional instability, and President Ronald Reagan citing "Soviet-Cuban terrorism" as the source of difficulty. Other disagreements between the two countries have centered on border issues, such as air pollution, drug trafficking, and U.S. efforts to control illegal immigration.

In 1988–1989 the United States pledged to support Mexico's efforts to enact economic reforms and negotiate a debt reduction agreement, with Washington describing the results of both as "models" for debtor nations. Meanwhile, U.S.-Mexico commercial relations continued to expand; in November 1989 the leaders of the two nations signed a trade accord, and in September 1990 Mexico, in a dramatic reversal of its traditional posture, formally requested the opening of free trade talks. Thereafter, Canada, which had concluded a free trade agreement with the United States in December 1989, was invited to participate in the discussions, which commenced in mid-1991 and concluded with agreement on the precedent-shattering NAFTA on August 11–12, 1992. In August 1993 certain contentious labor and environmental subclauses were clarified by further agreement, enabling NAFTA to secure ratification by the Mexican Congress in December and to come into effect on January 1, 1994. (Benefits from NAFTA have recently disappointed expectations due to U.S. strategic concerns regarding terrorism and illegal immigration.) In late 1993 Mexico also joined with Colombia and Venezuela (the so-called Group of Three) in a regional trade pact intended to create an economic market encompassing some 145 million people. In December 2000 the Mexican Senate ratified a free trade agreement with Guatemala, Honduras, and El Salvador that had been concluded six months earlier.

During a European tour in mid-1991, President Salinas had an unprecedented audience with Pope John Paul II that led to the reestablishment of diplomatic relations with the Vatican on September 21, 1992, after a 126-year hiatus. The action came after a series of amendments to Mexico's 1917 constitution that voided a long-standing ban on religious bodies and conferred new rights in such matters as dress and voting by church officials. In January 1999 the pope paid his fourth visit to Mexico, despite tension over the government's birth control policies and handling of the Chiapas insurgency.

Counternarcotics policy has been a continuing subject of cooperation and contention between the United States and Mexico. In 1997, during a period of increased U.S. assistance in combating the drugs trade, the head of Mexico's antidrug agency, Gen. Jesús GONZÁLEZ Rebollo, was arrested on charges of collusion with traffickers. In the wake of the U.S. action, opposition legislators charged the Zedillo administration with sacrificing Mexican interests to Washington's agenda. Further fueling the controversy was the charge by a high-ranking U.S. Drug Enforcement Agency official in mid-1997 that Colombian drug activities had been "eclipsed" by those of the Mexican cartels. U.S.-Mexico cooperation in counter-trafficking declined, and the government of Vicente Fox did not seek to increase it during the first half of the 2000s.

President Fox was the first foreign leader with whom incoming President George W. Bush met in 2001, and he was invited to Washington for a high-profile state visit in September of that year. Following the September 11, 2001 attacks, however, relations with Mexico became a much lower priority for the Bush administration, and the U.S. president's promises to pursue immigration and other reforms in the U.S. Congress languished. Relations with the United States grew more distant after President Fox refused to back U.S. policy in Iraq, while opposing as "inadequate" most overtures by President Bush on resolving the status of Mexican nationals in the United States (who were said to account for approximately 60 percent of all illegal immigrants).

President Calderón later indicated that he would implement the outgoing president's policy affecting all Mexican citizens facing criminal charges in the United States: they would be subject to extradition orders, regardless of whether they had faced a Mexican Court. In 2006 Mexico extradited 60 people to its northern neighbor. In the first two months of 2007, 17 more were sent.

Motions for increased cooperation between the neighbors continued as President Bush visited Mexico in March 2007 at the conclusion of his five-country tour of Latin America. At his press conference, the president pledged to push the Congress to approve a comprehensive immigration reform package (see article on America in the 2008 *Handbook*); to increase efforts to stem demand for illegal drugs in the United States as well as restricting supplies from Latin America; and to combat arms trafficking from the United States to gangsters in Mexico and Central America.

Following Bush's visit, the (outgoing) president of Argentina, Néstor Kirchner, and his wife Cristina Fernández (the president-elect following Argentina's October 2007 poll) visited Mexico in July 2007, extending an invitation to Mexico for full membership in Mercosur, the South American customs union of which Mexico is currently an associate partner. The president of Brazil, Lula da Silva, followed with the same offer. President Calderón and President da Silva signed several commercial agreements to advance bilateral trade. In August 2009 President Calderón visited Brazil, where the two governments pledged to increase trade ties.

The most important issue on the Mexican foreign policy agenda in 2008 was securing concessions from the U.S. Congress regarding some of their demands on the Mérida Initiative, a framework for U.S. counter-drug assistance worth $1.4 billion over three years, benefiting Mexico, the Dominican Republic, Haiti, and Central American countries. Initially, the U.S. Congress insisted that Mexican soldiers be tried before civil rather than military courts, but this condition, as well as many others, was softened. The State Department was required to certify that Mexico's human rights record was improving before being allowed to release 15 percent of military assistance.

The Calderón government actively promoted Mexican engagement in the region through 2008. Calderón joined Chilean Michele Bachelet in prioritizing Plan Puebla Panamá (PPP), a project in which wealthier Latin American states invest in their poorer neighbors, particularly on infrastructure projects to link nations' transportation, energy and communications networks. Although the press widely saw this as an effort to construct a promarket alternative to Chávez's ALBA project (see Venezuela), the PPP also reflected Mexico's desire to build refineries in Central America to handle Mexican crude oil. This was expected to benefit Mexican production and slow immigration from Central America into Mexico.

Venezuela and Mexico have been trying to repair the diplomatic breach that led to the withdrawal of their respective ambassadors in 2005. Relations improved with the reappointment of ambassadors to both countries in August 2007, but on April 3, 2008, President Chávez announced his intention to nationalize the cement industry, one of the prominent producers being owned by Cementos Mexicanos (CEMEX), a private Mexican company. On August 18, 2008, the deadline for negotiations lapsed and the cement industry was nationalized.

On March 1, 2008, a Revolutionary Armed Forces of Colombia (FARC) camp in Ecuador was bombed by Colombian forces (see Colombia and Ecuador entries). In addition to killing prominent FARC leaders, four Mexican students who were at the camp were also killed. The students were in Ecuador for a seminar on "Bolivarian Thinking," and parents of the deceased claim the students went to the camp to listen to peace proposals. Mexican intelligence suggested that a FARC cell within Mexico arranged for the trip to Ecuador and that the students may have been representing the FARC or drug traffickers.

An increase in drug-related crime near the two countries' border, including an October 11, 2008, grenade and gunfire attack on the U.S. consulate in Monterrey, revived Mexico as a top concern of U.S. policymakers in 2008 and 2009. Between October 2008 and August 2009, Mexico hosted visits from Bush administration secretary of state Condoleezza Rice, Joint Chiefs of Staff Chairman Adm. Michael Mullen, Obama administration secretary of state Hillary Clinton, Attorney General Eric Holder, Secretary of Homeland Security Janet Napolitano, "Drug Czar" Gil Kerlikowske, and, on two occasions, President Obama himself. The principal focus of all of these meetings was law enforcement and security cooperation.

The week before his January 20, 2009, inauguration, President-elect Obama met with President Calderón in Washington; Obama's remarks at this event raised concerns among the Mexican delegation that he might seek to revise the NAFTA free trade agreement, but the new president took no steps in that direction during his first months in office. In April Obama visited Mexico City, where he praised Calderón's security efforts and spoke of "a new era of cooperation and partnership" between the two countries. Obama and Canadian prime minister Stephen HARPER were in Guadalajara in August 2009 for a North American Summit; on this occasion Obama made clear that U.S. reforms to immigration law would not be coming in the short term, and expressed concern about respect for human rights in Mexico's fight against drug cartels.

U.S.-Mexican military and police cooperation continued to deepen within the framework of the Mérida Initiative in 2009. In March Secretary of State Clinton announced the opening of a Bilateral Implementation Office in Mexico City, charged with coordinating U.S.-Mexican cooperation against drug gangs. In April the Mexican Navy participated in its first joint exercise with the United States. The U.S. Congress later approved a supplemental appropriation giving Mexico an additional $420 million in June, well beyond the $66 million the Obama administration had requested. The additional money was allocated to hasten delivery of military equipment by moving up expenditures originally planned for 2010.

U.S. expressions of concern about security have occasionally offended Mexican sensibilities. A January 2009 report by the Defense Department's Joint Forces Command identified Mexico and Pakistan as the two failing states with the highest probability of needing a sudden U.S. intervention. That month, outgoing CIA Director Michael Hayden named Mexico and Iran as the United States' two most urgent foreign policy challenges. Adm. Mullen implied in March that U.S. tactics employed in Iraq and Afghanistan might have relevance to operations Mexico. Some Mexican politicians also voiced complaints that the Obama administration's chosen ambassador, Carlos PASCUAL, was a renowned expert in framing U.S. policy toward failed states.

Current issues. The disputed presidential election on July 2, 2006, led to massive protests throughout July, as presidential candidate and Mexico City mayor López Obrador and his partisans implored supporters to take to the streets of Mexico City. The crisis deepened at the beginning of August after López Obrador stepped up his charge that the election was "fraudulent" and urged his hundreds of thousands of supporters to begin "pacific civil resistance" by setting up camps throughout Mexico City's main square (*Zócalo*) to "occupy permanently" the central city.

Nevertheless, the importance of the protests diminished and attention turned to the government's "war on crime." President Calderón oversaw an unprecedented increase in the Mexican Army's counter-drug role, dispatching 45,000 troops along with 30,000 federal police to hard-hit cities, where in many cases they effectively replaced corrupt, ineffective, or overwhelmed police forces. These forces confronted five principal drug cartels, who resisted the offensive and competed with each other for increasingly limited territory, using extremely violent tactics that claimed progressively more civilian lives. The cartels are the Arellano Félix or Tijuana organization; the factions of Joaquín "El Chapo" GUZMÁN and the BELTRÁN LEYVA brothers within the Sinaloa cartel; the Gulf cartel, also known as "*Las Zetas*" or "*La Compañía;*" and the Michoacán-based "*La Familia.*" In March 2009, Sinaloa cartel leader Guzmán appeared in *Forbes* magazine's list of the richest people in the world.

Narcotrafficking-related deaths totaled 2,700 in 2007 and 5,600 in 2008. This figure surpassed 5,000 by early September 2009. Other types of violence increased as well, with official records of kidnapping showing a 35 percent jump between 2006 and 2007. In 2008, roughly three to four people were kidnapped in Mexico daily, six to seven times the number in Colombia and roughly three to four times the number in Venezuela. The hardest-hit states in 2008 were Chihuahua, whose capital, Ciudad Juárez, is now one of the most violent cities in the world; Sinaloa; and Baja California Norte.

While Calderón's security policy has not succeeded in reducing drug and organized crime violence, it has been popular. By September 2009, Calderón's approval rating stood at 68 percent, almost double his vote share in the 2006 presidential election, though support for the PAN was far lower, as indicated by its poor showing in the July 2009 legislative elections (see Political Background).

In July 2008 14-year-old Fernando MARTÍ, the son of a prominent Mexican businessman, was kidnapped and murdered. The death led to such significant pressure that Mexico City mayor Marcelo EBRARD, a supporter of López Obrador, agreed to meet with President Calderón for the first time. Investigations into the Martí kidnapping later uncovered the involvement of corrupt Mexico City police.

Concerns about crime led President Calderón, along with judicial, legislative, and state authorities, to sign a common "National Accord for Security, Justice and Legality" on August 21, 2008. Nine days later, hundreds of thousands of Mexicans took to the streets to protest crime and insecurity, calling on the state to do more. The budget that President Calderón sent to the Congress in September included a more than 30 percent increase in security and justice expenditure. This announcement was punctuated by a September 15 attack that shocked the nation: the *La Familia* cartel's indiscriminate launching of two grenades into a crowded Independence Day celebration in central Morelia, the capital of Michoacán, which killed 7 people and wounded over 100.

In October 2008 the PRI continued a series of electoral victories that began shortly after the disputed 2006 presidential election, winning gubernatorial contests in Guerrero (which it took from the PRD) on the 5th and Coahuila on the 19th. On October 28 the Chamber of Deputies approved legislation making reforms to PEMEX (Petróleos de México), Mexico's state-owned petroleum company. The bill granted PEMEX more autonomy and allowed private corporations to serve as subcontractors, but did not overcome opposition to allowing joint ventures with foreign corporations. In July the PRD had run a referendum in a number of states for supporters to vote on whether PEMEX should be privatized; the results were an overwhelming "no." Despite the unrepresentative sample of PRD partisans in the referendum, the move is not politically possible, and Calderón has indicated he does not desire a PEMEX privatization. However, PEMEX, which produces 35 percent of government revenue, has lost productive capacity as a result of underinvestment and government diversion of PEMEX income into areas such as food subsidies.

November 2008 was a particularly difficult period for Mexico's beleaguered public security apparatus. The SIEDO, the 400-person elite unit of the attorney general's office charged with combating organized crime, was found to have been compromised by six senior officials in the pay of the Beltrán Leyva faction of the Sinaloa cartel, and its director was arrested. Victor Gerardo GARAY, the chief of a national police force, the Federal Preventive Police (PFP), was later revealed to have brought women into a Jacuzzi, given them cocaine, and demanded a payoff from drug gang members after personally raiding their mansion in October. The two scandals increased pressure on Public Security Secretary Genaro GARCÍA LUNA. Despite Garcías notoriously poor relations with the army, he was compelled to accept the nomination of an active-duty general as a vice minister. Earlier that month, another key security policymaker, Interior Secretary Juan Camilo Mouriño, died in an airplane crash (See Political Background).

In January 2009, faced with a global economic slowdown, particularly reduced demand from the United States, President Calderón proposed a $4.4 billion stimulus package seeking to boost demand by about 1 percent of GDP. Security, meanwhile, was again the prominent concern in February, as drug gangs killed an army general assigned to head the police in Cancún, engaged in a prolonged firefight with the Army in Chihuahua, and forced the resignation of the police chief in Ciudad Juárez. Meanwhile demonstrators in several cities, widely alleged to be organized by drug gangs, demanded that the Army be withdrawn from the anti-drug mission. In April, however, the Mexican presidency indicated that the Army would be on Mexico's streets playing a counter-drug role at least until 2013.

Following the outbreak of the H1N1 "Swine Flu" virus, which originated in the country, the disease spread quickly through the population. All public facilities were shut down at the end of April and the first several days of May, compounding the country's economic woes and dimming prospects for tourism that year.

In April and May authorities arrested several party leaders, mayors, and other state officials on charges of ties to drug cartels. Opposition parties, particularly the PRD, argued that they were unfairly singled out for the arrests, claiming that the PAN was seeking to sully their reputations ahead of the July 2009 legislative elections. President Calderón insisted that the political affiliation of the raids' targets was a coincidence. The arrests proved not to provide the PAN with any political advantage, however, as the ruling party lost a significant share of votes to the PRI in the July 5 voting (See Political Background).

In August Mexico's Congress passed, and President Calderón signed, a law legalizing possession—but not the sale—of small quantities of drugs. The Bush administration had strongly opposed such a measure at the end of Vicente Fox's presidency in 2006; to the surprise of many observers, the Obama administration did not offer an opinion on the new law.

POLITICAL PARTIES

Mexican politics for more than seven decades after the late 1920s featured the dominance of a single party, the Institutional Revolutionary Party (PRI), which for much of the period enjoyed virtually unchallenged control of the presidency, the Congress, and state governments. The situation changed dramatically, however, as a result of the election of July 2, 2000.

Parties must now capture a mandated minimum of 2 percent of the total vote in a national election to maintain their registrations. In 2006 eight additional parties were recognized by the Federal Electoral Institute (*Instituto Federal Electoral*—IFE) after crossing the vote share threshold. One party, Socialdemocracy, lost its recognition following the 2009 elections.

Presidential Party:

National Action Party (*Partido Acción Nacional*—PAN). Founded in 1939 and dependent on urban middle-class support, the long-time leading opposition party has an essentially conservative, proclerical, and probusiness orientation, and favors limitations on the government's economic role. It has traditionally been strongest in the north and west of the country. Largely because of fragmentation within the leftist opposition, PAN was, until recently, the main beneficiary of erosion in PRI support. In 1982, despite losing all but 1 of its directly elective Chamber seats, the party's proportional representation rose from 39 to 54, with party spokespeople claiming that they had been denied a number of victories as the result of PRI electoral fraud. Similar claims were made after the 1985 election, in which PAN gained 9 directly elective Chamber seats and a number of mayoralties, and was widely acknowledged to have gained the majority of votes in two gubernatorial races awarded to the PRI. The party ran third in both the presidential and legislative balloting of July 1988.

On July 2, 1989, Ernesto RUFFO Appel, PAN's Baja California Norte gubernatorial candidate, captured the party's first governorship. In November 1990 PAN again accused the PRI of fraud after it had secured landslide victories in state and local balloting.

The party secured its first Senate seat in the August 1991 balloting, despite a drop in Chamber representation from 101 to 99. The most startling development, however, was in the Guanajuato gubernatorial race, in which the official victor, a PRI hard-liner, was induced to defer to the interim incumbency of PAN's Carlos MEDINA Plascencia. The party registered another notable gain by winning the state governorship of Chihuahua in July 1992. However, a number of influential party dissidents insisted that the victories were achieved through a policy of rapprochement with the PRI and vowed to respond to the *"salinista"* drift by formation of a breakaway party.

In the August 1994 presidential balloting the PAN candidate, Diego FERNÁNDEZ de Cevallos, came in second with 25.9 percent of the popular vote, while PAN representation in the Chamber rose to 119 seats and in the enlarged Senate to 25. Far more impressive was the stunning defeat inflicted on the PRI in Jalisco on February 13, 1995, with PAN capturing the governor's office, the Guadalajara mayoralty, and an overwhelming majority of state legislative seats. In mid-March Secretary General Felipe Calderón Hinojosa defeated Ruffo Appel in a contest to succeed Carlos CASTILLO Peraza as party president. Calderón Hinojosa was himself succeeded on March 6, 1999, by Luis BRAVO Mena.

PAN contested the 2000 election in a coalition with the Mexican Green Ecologist Party (PVEM, below) styled the Alliance for Change (*Alianza por el Cambio*), which succeeded in winning the presidency and a plurality of 223 seats in the Chamber of Deputies. In the following year the party won several additional governorships, a number of which were lost in 2004.

In July 2006 Calderón Hinojosa, a member of the party's conservative wing, defeated the PRD's López Obrador for the presidency by the narrowest of margins (35.9 to 35.4 percent). PAN emerged from the 2006 election as the largest party in both the Senate, with 52 seats, and in the Chamber of Deputies, with 206 seats.

Despite the party's good fortune in the previous election, the grouping's viability has been threatened by tension between Calderón and the party president, Manuel ESPINO Barrientos. Espino has pushed for Mexican membership in the Christian Democratic Organization of the Americas (*Organización Demócrata Cristiana de América*), of which he is also president, and recently attracted Cuban protests for his overtures to the Cuban community in Miami. The poor showing of PAN in the local elections following the 2006 presidential elections provided an opportunity for Espino to step down and be replaced on December 9, 2007, by Germán MARTÍNEZ Cázares, who is more loyal to the president. On June 9, 2008, Santiago CREEL Miranda stepped down as the leader of PAN in the Senate. Creel had been President Fox's preferred candidate in the 2006 party primary and is a potential candidate for the presidency in 2012.

The PAN performed poorly in the July 5, 2009, midterm elections. With 28.0 percent of the vote the party finished second, more than 8 points behind the PRI, and its representation in the Chamber of Deputies dropped from 206 to 143 members. The party won only 1 of 6 state governorship contests; of the 5 losses, 2 were in states that had previously had PAN governors.

Martínez quit the party presidency shortly after the election debacle. On August 11 the party chose President Calderón's former private secretary, César NAVA, as its new president. Nava ran unopposed and gained sufficient votes among party delegates despite opposition from Creel and Espino.

Leaders: Felipe CALDERÓN Hinojosa (President of Mexico), César NAVA (President of the Party), Vicente FOX Quesada (Former President of Mexico).

Other Congressional Parties:

Institutional Revolutionary Party (*Partido Revolucionario Institucional*—PRI). Founded in 1929 as the National Revolutionary Party (*Partido Nacional Revolucionario*—PNR) and redesignated in 1938 as the Mexican Revolutionary Party (*Partido de la Revolución Mexicana*—PRM), the PRI took its present name in 1946. As a union of local and state groups with roots in the revolutionary period, it was gradually established with a broad popular base and retains a tripartite organization based on three distinct sectors (labor, agrarian, and "popular"), although in 1978 it was officially designated as a "workers' party." While the PRI's general outlook may be characterized as moderately left-wing, its membership includes a variety of factions and outlooks. Since the early 1980s controversies surrounding electoral outcomes have led to internal turmoil, which in late 1986 resulted in the formation of the Democratic Current (*Corriente Democrática*—CD) faction under the leadership of Cuauhtémoc Cárdenas Solórzano and former party president Porfiro Muñoz Ledo, which called for more openness in PRI affairs, including the abolition of secrecy (*tapadismo*) in the selection of presidential candidates. In June 1987, five months after a shake-up in which half of the party's 30-member Executive Committee was replaced, the PRI withdrew recognition of the CD and in 1988 Cárdenas accepted the presidential nomination of the National Democratic Front (FDN; see under PRD, below), prior to organizing the PRD.

The precipitous decline of the PRI's presidential vote (94.4 percent in 1976, 71.0 in 1982, 50.4 in 1988), coupled with diminished congressional representation, prompted Carlos Salinas in the wake of the 1988 campaign to pledge thorough reform of the party apparatus, which Secretary General Manuel CAMACHO Solís characterized as being ridden by "bureaucratization, autocracy, [and] corruption." The issue intensified in the wake of charges that the central government had provided upward of $10 million to finance the PRI's unsuccessful Baja California Norte gubernatorial campaign in 1989. Thus, during the party's 14th National Assembly in Mexico City in September 1990, Salinas persuaded the delegates to adopt a series of measures that included direct and secret balloting for most leadership posts and the selection of a presidential candidate by a democratically elected convention rather than by the outgoing chief executive.

In March 1993 controversy over donations to the PRI from newly privatized enterprises led to the appointment as party chair of Fernando ORTIZ Arana, who the following month dismissed six of the seven PRI Executive Committee members. Notwithstanding the 1990 Assembly decisions, the PRI's first 1994 presidential candidate, Luis Donaldo COLOSIO Murrieta, was effectively chosen by Salinas, as was Ernesto ZEDILLO Ponce de León, following Colosio's assassination in March 1994. This continuance of the so-called *destape* ("unveiling") tradition of nomination by the presidential incumbent was condemned by the PRI's Democracy 2000 (*Democracia 2000*) faction but did not prevent Zedillo from being elected in August, albeit with a record low share (48.8 percent) of the popular vote. On September 28 the PRI's newly appointed secretary general, José Francisco RUIZ Massieu, was assassinated in Mexico City. A little over a year later, on October 13, 1995, a disaffected Camacho Solís, who had been passed over as the PRI's 1994 presidential nominee, quit the party to work for "real political change."

In the election of July 6, 1997, the PRI for the first time lost control of the Chamber of Deputies and also failed to capture the newly elective mayoralty of Mexico City. On March 17, 1999, the party's president, Mariano PALACIOS Alcocer, and its secretary general, Carlos ROJAS Gutiérrez, both resigned, ostensibly to reduce the role of the party hierarchy in selecting its 2000 presidential candidate. Earlier, President Zedillo had announced that he would break tradition by not designating his successor, proposing instead an open primary in fall 1999. On March 30 José Antonio GONZÁLEZ Fernández, who had resigned as labor and social welfare secretary on March 18, was elected party president following the withdrawal from the race of Rodolfo ECHEVERRÍA Ruiz, who complained of favoritism toward his opponent by senior party members.

Following Vicente Fox's stunning defeat of Francisco LABASTIDA Ochoa on July 2, 2000, Dulce María SAURI Riancho, who had been appointed in November 1999 to succeed González as party president, submitted her resignation, but she was persuaded to stay on pending the designation of a successor. In the next year the PRI lost several governorships, and by November 2001 it held only 17 of 31. Meanwhile, it was facing an internal leadership struggle pitting its traditionalists (dubbed the *dinosaurios* by opponents and the media) against a reform-oriented wing (the *técnicos*). In April 2001 several prominent PRI members, including former party president Genaro BORREGO Estrada, announced that they were considering forming a new party, the "Renaissance Movement" (*Movimiento Renacimiento*), later in the year. An open election for the PRI presidency was held in February 2002, with Roberto MADRAZO Pintado, a former Tabasco governor, narrowly defeating Beatriz PAREDES Rangel, then president of the Chamber of Deputies.

A serious intraparty row erupted in late 2003 between Madrazo and the party's secretary general, Elba Esther GORDILLO, who also served as bloc leader in the Chamber of Deputies, albeit as an advocate of cooperation with the PRN. As a result of the dispute, Gordillo lost her Chamber leadership, and she subsequently withdrew to launch her own formation, the New Alliance Party (below).

The PRI contested the 2006 election in a coalition with the PVEM (below) styled the **Alliance for Mexico** (*Alianza por México*). Since its third place finish in that election, the PRI has been a principal beneficiary of the decline in support for President Calderón's PAN, picking up a number of governorships. (As of September 2009, the PRI had 19 of the country's 32 governorships.) The PRI has generally cooperated with the president on major initiatives in 2008. Of particular note is the PRI's support of private company participation in off-shore drilling. The PRI plan seems to go further in opening up the petroleum sector in Mexico than does the government plan, which indicates the continued importance of technocrats within the party. However, the PRI has more recently campaigned with more populist themes, tapping into Mexicans' economic anxiety.

With voters turning away from the PAN, and the PRD riven by infighting, the PRI was the overwhelming winner of the midterm election on July 5, 2009. With 36.7 percent of the vote, the party saw its representation in the Chamber of Deputies jump from 106 to 237 seats. Thanks to its alliance with the PVEM, the PRI gained control of a majority of the lower house.

On August 25 the PRI chose Francisco ROJAS Gutiérrez, a party veteran and close associate of former President Salinas, to lead its majority bloc in the Chamber of Deputies. Rojas ran unopposed. The leader of the party's Senate bloc, Manlio Fabio BELTRONES, has been one of the most outspoken critics of President Calderón's security policies.

Leaders: Beatriz PAREDES Rangel (President of the Party), Roberto MADRAZO Pintado (Former President of the Party and 2006 presidential candidate), Francisco ROJAS Gutiérrez (Bloc Leader in the Chamber of Deputies) Manlio Fabio BELTRONES (Bloc Leader in the Senate).

Democratic Revolutionary Party (*Partido de la Revolución Democrática*—PRD). The PRD was launched in 1988 by Cuauhtémoc Cárdenas, who had previously led the dissident Democratic Current (CD) within the PRI and had placed second in the July presidential balloting as standard-bearer of the National Democratic Front (*Frente Democrático Nacional*—FDN) coalition. Other participants in the FDN included the PVE (see PVEM), PARM, and PPS (below), the Social Democratic Party (*Partido Social Demócrata*—PSD), the Movement Toward Socialism (*Movimiento al Socialismo*—MAS), and the Mexican Socialist Party (*Partido Mexicano Socialista*—PMS).

The PMS had been launched in March 1987 by merger of Mexico's two principal leftist groups, the Unified Socialist Party of Mexico (*Partido Socialista Unificado de México*—PSUM) and the Mexican Workers' Party (*Partido Mexicano de los Trabajadores*—PMT), and three smaller formations. Recognized by the Soviet Union as the country's official Communist Party, the PSUM dated from the November 1981 merger of the Mexican Communist Party (*Partido Comunista Mexicano*—PCM) with four smaller groups. (The PCM, formed in 1919, was accorded legal recognition from 1932 to 1942 and was thereafter semi-clandestine until returned, conditionally, to legal status in 1978.) Having survived intense leadership disputes that followed the 1981 merger, the mainstream faction of the PSUM led an electoral front for the July 1985 balloting that included among its participants the PMT and the Popular Socialist Party (PPS, below). None won directly elective Chamber seats, although the PSUM was awarded 12 proportional seats; the PPS, 11; and the PMT, 6.

Following the 1987 launch of the PMS, discussions with the FDN during the latter half of the year failed to yield agreement on a joint candidate for the 1988 presidential election. As a result, the PMS nominated Herberto CASTILLO of the PMT. It was not until early June 1988 that Castillo withdrew in favor of the FDN's Cuauhtémoc Cárdenas, who a month later narrowly lost to the PRI's Carlos Salinas in a widely disputed election. Formation of the PRD as a unified party followed, with a variety of additional political and social organizations joining the CD, PMS, and MAS.

The newly formed PRD's July 1989 loss to the PRI in the Michoacán gubernatorial balloting was widely viewed as the result of fraudulent vote tallying. Subsequently, PRD members occupied municipal buildings and commandeered public roads, leading to clashes with PRI adherents and government forces that continued into 1990. Meanwhile, the party, which had been denied legalization on a national basis in June, sought international assistance in investigating the alleged political assassination of some 60 of its members since 1988.

In early 1990 the PRD accused PRI "reactionaries" of kidnapping prominent party member Leonel GODOY and threatening Jorge CASTANEDA. In November, defying a new law criminalizing false fraud accusations, it claimed that the PRI had employed "all known forms of violating the vote" in capturing elections in México and Hidalgo states. The PRD's México state vote fell from 1.2 million for Cárdenas alone in 1988 to 200,000 for all PRD candidates in 1990. Meanwhile, observers described the January 1991 resignation of a PRD leader, Jorge ALCOCER, who accused Cárdenas of being "authoritarian and intolerant," as symptomatic of the dissension that had wracked the party since the 1988 balloting. In the August 1994 presidential balloting Cárdenas came in third with 16.6 percent of the popular vote, while PRD representation in the Chamber rose to 71 seats and in the enlarged Senate to 8 seats.

In June 1996 the PRD became the first Mexican party not only to place selection of its leadership in the direct vote of its members but also to confer the franchise on all registered voters who opted to join on polling day. Andrés Manuel López Obrador, PRD leader in Tabasco, defeated two other candidates for the party presidency in July.

At the election of July 6, 1997, the PRD placed second in the Chamber of Deputies, with 125 seats, while Cárdenas Solórzano became the first elected mayor of Mexico City. In February 1999 the PRD claimed its third governorship, winning Baja California Sur from the PRI.

For the 2000 election, Cárdenas Solórzano resigned his mayoralty for a renewed presidential bid, but he ran a distant third as head of a multiparty Alliance for Mexico (*Alianza por México*), which included the Labor Party, Democratic Convergence, Nationalist Society Party, and Social Alliance Party (all below). For the Mexico City race the five were joined by the PCD in an Alliance for Mexico City (*Alianza por la Ciudad de México*).

The PRD, which had been supportive of the Fox regime, severed its links with the federal government in early 2004 because of its conviction that the administration had been orchestrating charges of corruption in the capital to damage the presidential prospects of its popular incumbent mayor, López Obrador (who was elected mayor in December 2000). Following massive popular demonstrations in support of López Obrador, President Fox in April 2005 suspended charges against the mayor, who, at the conclusion of a bitterly contested campaign, was narrowly defeated by the PAN's Calderón Hinojosa in the July 2006 presidential poll.

For the 2006 campaign, the PRD formed a grouping with the PT and CD (see below), styled the Coalition for the Good of All (*Coalición por el Bien de Todos*). Despite losing the 2006 presidential elections, the PRD was the second largest party in the Chamber of Deputies with 25 percent of the seats.

The PRD split over how to respond to the narrow Calderón victory, as radicals supported López Obrador's street protests and his creation of a "legitimate" government, while moderates were willing to engage the government. The divisions were evident in the March 16, 2008, elections for PRD president, which pitted Jesús ORTEGA of the moderate New Left (*Nueva Izquierda*) against Alejandro ENCINAS, who supports López Obrador. With 70 percent of the ballots counted and accusations of fraud from both sides, the party annulled the election after setting and missing several deadlines for releasing the results. The resultant embarrassment was magnified given the party's argument that the PRI and the PAN used electoral fraud to deny the PRD electoral victories in the 1988 and 2006 presidential elections. It also strengthened critiques of the PRD, particularly loyalists of López Obrador, as being "anti-institutional" and "revolutionary." Finally, on November 12, 2008, the national elections tribunal ruled in favor of Ortega, in a victory for the moderates.

In December 2008, the PRD's national congress decided not to form alliances with other parties for the 2009 midterm elections. The party held a primary to choose candidates on March 15, and New Left candidates generally fared worse than supporters of López Obrador.

For his part, López Obrador campaigned against moderate PRD candidates in some districts, openly supporting candidates from the Labor Party and Democratic Convergence. On July 5, 2009, the divided party fared badly at the polls, finishing a distant third with 12.2 percent of the vote, as its representation in the lower house of Congress fell from 126 to 71 seats.

Following its July 5 debacle, on August 11 the PRD chose Encinas to head its shrunken bloc in the Chamber of Deputies. Though weakened as of mid-2009, the PRD remained strong in Mexico City, where Marcelo Ebrard was serving as mayor.

Leaders: Andrés Manuel LÓPEZ Obrador (Former Mayor of Mexico City and 2006 presidential candidate), Jesús ORTEGA (President of the Party), Alejandro ENCINAS (Bloc Leader in the Chamber of Deputies), Carlos NAVARRETE Ruiz (Bloc Leader in the Senate), Cuauhtémoc CÁRDENAS (former presidential candidate).

Mexican Green Ecologist Party (*Partido Verde Ecologista de México*—PVEM). An outgrowth of the National Ecologist Alliance (*Alianza Ecologista Nacional*), Mexico's Greens initially adopted the name Green Ecologist Party (PVE) upon formally entering the political arena in 1987. Having failed to obtain registration in time for the 1988 election, the PVE participated in the FDN. A dispute over the party name led to its registration as the Ecologist Party of Mexico (PEM) for the 1991 election, but the party narrowly failed to secure the minimum necessary to gain full legal status. It assumed its present name in 1993.

The PVEM president, Jorge GONZÁLEZ, received 0.9 percent of the vote in the August 1994 presidential poll and failed to win congressional representation. However, it won 6 Chamber seats in 1997, on a vote share of 4 percent. The party went on to secure 5 Senate and 15 Chamber seats as an ally of PAN in 2000, although its leadership had come under fire from like-minded groups for abandoning environmental issues in its pursuit of electoral success. It won 2 additional lower house seats in 2003, but in early 2004 became entangled in a bribery scandal stemming from a tape-recorded solicitation by González, the party president. In 2008, the party made advocacy of the death penalty, especially for kidnappers, a signature issue, which caused the European Green Party to withdraw its recognition of the PVEM as a "green" party.

The PVEM contested the 2006 election in a coalition with the PRI styled the **Alliance for Mexico** (*Alianza por México*). It maintained this alliance for the 2009 legislative elections, finishing fourth and winning 21 seats in the Chamber of Deputies.

Leaders: Jorge Emilio GONZÁLEZ Torres (President of the Party and 1994 presidential candidate), Francisco AGUNDIS Arias (Congressional Leader).

Labor Party (*Partido del Trabajo*—PT). A moderate leftist formation founded in 1990 by a number of organizations, the PT won 1.2 percent of the vote in the 1991 congressional poll. In the August 1994 presidential contest Cecilia SOTO González fought a vigorous campaign that drew support away from the more established PRD and gave her 2.7 percent of the national vote. Ten PT candidates were elected to the Chamber of Deputies in 1994, 7 in 1997, 8 in 2000, and 6 in 2003.

In 2006 the PT joined the CD (below) in a grouping with the PRD styled the **Coalition for the Good of All** (*Coalición por el Bien de Todos*). While the PRD pulled out of this coalition, effectively dissolving it, for the 2009 legislative elections Andrés Manuel López Obrador, the PRD's 2006 presidential candidate, campaigned on behalf of some PT candidates, some of whom had been close advisors during his candidacy and his tenure as Mexico City mayor. The PT finished fifth in July 5, 2009, voting for the Chamber of Deputies, and holds 13 seats.

Leaders: Alberto ANAYA Gutiérrez (Congressional Leader), Sen. Ricardo MONREAL Ávila.

New Alliance Party (*Partido Nueva Alianza*—Panal). Panal was launched in 2005 by former PRI secretary general Elba Esther Gordillo, following a falling out with the PRI leadership. Gordillo also controls the National Education Workers' Syndicate (*Sindicato Nacional de Trabajadores de la Educación*—SNTE), the largest labor union in Latin America. Panal finished sixth in the 2009 legislative elections, maintaining its 9 seats in the Chamber of Deputies.

Leaders: Fermín TRUJILLO Fuentes (Secretary General), Elba Esther GORDILLO (Former PRI Secretary General and Former Secretary of Education), Jorge KAHWAGI Macariblo (President of the Party), Roberto CAMPA Cifrián (2006 presidential candidate).

Democratic Convergence (*Convergencia por la Democracia*—CD). Now generally referenced simply as *Convergencia* following a party assembly held in 2002, the CD began in 1997 as a civil association with a social democratic orientation. It was registered as a *"Partido Político Nacional"* in June 1999 under former Veracruz governor Dante Delgado and other PRI dissidents. In the 2000 election it ran as part of the earlier Alliance for Mexico, winning one Senate and two Chamber seats. It won five lower house seats in 2003.

In 2006 the CD participated in the **Coalition for the Good of All** (*Coalición por el Bien de Todos*) with the PT and PRD (both above). In the 2009 legislative elections, which followed the coalition's dissolution, CD finished seventh, barely maintaining its legal status with 2.4 percent of the vote. It holds 6 seats in the Chamber of Deputies.

Leaders: Luis MALDONADO Venegas (President of the Party), Dante DELGADO Rannauro (Former President of the Party), Cuauhtémoc VELASCO Olivia (President of the National Council), Pedro JIMÉNEZ León (Secretary General).

Other Parties:

Socialdemocracy (*Socialdemócrata*). Founded in 2006, Socialdemocracy participated in the 2006 election under the name of Social Democratic and Farmer Alternative Party (*Partido Socialdemócrata y Campesina*—PASC); it later changed its name to the Social Democratic Alternative Party (*Partido Alternativa Socialdemócrata*—PAS). PAS obtained 2.7 percent of the votes, securing 4 congressional seats. In May 2007 PAS dropped Farmer (*Campesina*) from its title. A self-styled moderate-left (*nueva izquierda*) party, PAS platform issues included clean air, minority rights, and a free market that is sensitive to the social challenges of globalization. The party's founder, Patricia MERCADO, a well-known feminist activist, broke with the party in 2008 and formed a new political movement, the **Alternative Movement** (*Movimiento Alternativa*—MA), which did not participate in the 2009 midterm elections. In those elections, Socialdemocracy failed to meet the 2 percent vote threshold and lost both its congressional representation and its legal status.

Leader: Alfredo BEGNÉ Guerra (President of the Party).

Popular Socialist Party (*Partido Popular Socialista*—PPS). Led by Vicente LOMBARDO Toledano until his death in 1968, the PPS is Marxist in orientation and draws support from intellectuals, students, and some labor elements. In the election of July 1976, PPS leader Jorge CRUIKSHANK García became the first opposition candidate to win a Senate seat since 1929. In the wake of charges that a "deal" had been made concerning the seat, a majority of the party voted, at the annual PPS Congress in December, for more forceful opposition to the PRI. Nevertheless, the Socialists failed to present a presidential candidate in 1982, choosing instead to support PAN's nominee; in legislative balloting the PPS lost its Senate seat but retained its 11 proportionally awarded Chamber seats. In 1983 the party won a number of state legislative seats from the PRI and in 1985 was again awarded 11 Chamber seats, on a proportional basis, as part of the PSUM-led alliance (see under PRD, above). It supported Cárdenas as a member of the FDN alignment in 1988 and obtained 12 lower house seats in the 1991 proportional allocation.

In August 1994 the party's Marcela LOMBARDO Otero received only 0.5 percent of the presidential vote, and the party subsequently failed to win congressional representation.

In 1997 the PPS lost its registration as a national political party, but is currently registered as a national political association under the Popular Socialist (*Popular Socialista*) designation.

Leader: Cuauhtémoc Amezcua DROMUNDO (Secretary General).

For more information on the now-defunct **Mexican Social Democratic Party** (*Partido Social Demócrata Mexicano*—PSDM), see the 2008 *Handbook*. For more information on the **Revolutionary Workers' Party** (*Partido Revolucionario de los Trabajadores*—PRT), the **Nationalist Society Party** (*Partido de la Sociedad Nacionalista*—PSN), and the **Social Alliance Party** (*Partido Alianza Social*—PAS, see the 2009 *Handbook*.

Paramilitary Groups:

Zapatista National Liberation Army (*Ejército Zapatista de Liberación Nacional*—EZLN). Initial accounts of the January 1994 uprising in Chiapas (see Political background, above) suggested that the rebels numbered upward of 1,000 men seeking economic relief for Mexico's "dispensable" indigenous groups. Ideologically, the EZLN appeared somewhat unique in not invoking traditional leftist (Marxist-Leninist) jargon. In early 1996 the group announced the launching of a "sister organization," the **Zapatista National Liberation Front** (*Frente Zapatista de Liberación Nacional*—FZLN), which was not, however, to be construed as a "formal" political party and would not contest elections; the latter group staged a peaceful, unarmed march in Mexico City on September 12, 1997.

A march by EZLN leaders to Mexico City in February–March 2001 culminated in a controversial invitation to address the Congress of Deputies on March 28. The EZLN speakers urged passage of the Indigenous Rights Bill, although the Zapatistas ultimately rejected the version of the bill that passed in late April as offering insufficient autonomy and land rights. As a consequence, the EZLN refused to negotiate with the Fox government.

In late 2003 "Subcomandante Marcos" was reported to have resigned as rebel representative, although appointed co-leader of a Chiapas "good government" municipal board. The former spokesperson later led a tour of various Mexican cities in 2006 to generate popular support ahead of the elections. The group has been less active nationally in recent years, though it remains a political force in several municipalities of Chiapas.

Leaders: "Subcomandante MARCOS," Javier ELORRIAGA (FZLN).

Popular Revolutionary Army (*Ejército Popular Revolucionario*—EPR). The EPR was apparently launched in 1994 as a coalition of a dozen-odd minor leftist factions allied with the peasant-based Revolutionary Workers' Party and Clandestine Popular Union–Party of the Poor (*Partido Revolucionario Obrerista y Clandestino de Unión Popular–Partido de los Pobres*—PROCUP-PDLP). PROCUP was founded in the 1970s by radicals under the leadership of Oaxaca University rector Felipe MARTÍNEZ Soriano, who has been imprisoned since 1990 for involvement in the killing of two security guards at a Mexican newspaper office. The PDLP, dating from 1967, was a largely moribund clandestine formation before being revived by merger with PROCUP. In 1991 PROCUP claimed responsibility for a series of bombings of the Mexico City offices of a number of international corporations and was charged in 1994 with the kidnapping of Alfred Harp Helu, the chair of Mexico's largest bank, for whose release his family paid a $30 million ransom.

During 1996 the ERP was reported to have killed 26 soldiers or police officers while extending its activities into more than half of Mexico's 31 states. At a secret press conference in August 1996 it announced formation of a 14-organization **Popular Democratic Revolutionary Party** (*Partido Democrático Popular Revolucionario*—PDPR) that would serve as its political wing. Three months earlier the PROCUP-PDLP reportedly had dissolved.

Relatively quiescent after 1997, the ERP resurfaced in May 2002 when it appeared responsible for the killing of two police officers 95 miles east of Acapulco. More recently, President Fox indicated in mid-2004 that the group was still active, while media reports suggested that it had spawned a number of splinter formations, particularly in the south. Between July and September 2007, the ERP claimed responsibility for explosions in PEMEX fields as well as in a Sears company. The group has carried out few armed actions since 2007, but issues periodic political statements, including a 2009 endorsement of a small movement urging voters in the midterm elections to turn in blank ballots. A struggling, year-long effort to mediate between the EPR and the government ended in April 2009, when the mediating committee quit for lack of progress.

Leaders: "Comandante OSCAR," "Comandante VICENTE," "Comandante ANTONIO."

Popular Insurgent Revolutionary Army (*Ejército Revolucionario Insurgente Popular*—ERIP). The formation of the ERIP was announced in November 1996 by a group claiming to represent "peasants, Indians, workers, and businesspeople." The ERIP, which called for the resignation of the Zedillo administration and the convening of a national congress to draft a new constitution, said it would operate in northern and central Mexico as a "complement" to the southern-based EZLN and EPR.

For more information on guerilla groups active in the 1990s, see the 2008 *Handbook*. For information on the **Insurgent People's Revolutionary Army** (*Ejército Revolucionario del Pueblo Insurgente*—ERPI), please see the 2009 *Handbook*.

LEGISLATURE

The **Union Congress** (*Congreso de la Unión*) consists of a Senate and a Chamber of Deputies, both elected by popular vote. When Congress is not in session, limited legislative functions are performed by a Permanent Committee of 18 senators and 19 deputies elected by their respective houses. Legislators cannot serve consecutive terms.

Senate (*Cámara de Senadores*). The upper chamber contains 128 members, the number having been doubled with the election, for six-year terms, of 96 senators in 1994. In 1997, 32 senators were elected for three-year terms. In 2000 all 128 seats were renewed for the first time, half by majority vote in each state and the Federal District, one-quarter by assignment to the leading minority candidate in each of the 32 jurisdictions, and one-quarter by national proportional representation. Following the election of July 2, 2006, minor defections in the Senate resulted in the following breakdown as of mid-2009: the National Action Party held 51 seats; the Institutional Revolutionary Party, 32; the Democratic Revolutionary Party, 26; the Mexican Green Ecologist Party, 6; the Labor Party, 5; the Democratic Convergence Party, 5; independents, 3. The Senate presidency changes monthly.

Chamber of Deputies (*Cámara de Diputados*). The lower chamber presently contains 500 members elected for three-year terms, including 200 seats distributed on a proportional basis among parties winning more than 2 percent of the vote nationwide. Following the election of July 5, 2009, the Institutional Revolutionary Party held 237 seats; the National Action Party, 143; the Democratic Revolutionary Party, 71; the Mexican Green Ecologist Party, 21; the Labor Party, 13; New Alliance, 9; and the Democratic Convergence Party, 6.

President: Francisco Javier RAMÍREZ Acuña.

CABINET

[as of October 1, 2009]

President	Felipe Calderón Hinojosa
Secretaries	
Agrarian Reform	Abelardo Escobar Prieto (PAN)
Agriculture, Livestock, Rural Development, Fishing, and Food	Francisco Javier Mayorga Castañeda (PAN)
Communications and Transport	Juan Francisco Molinar Horcasitas (PAN)
Economy	Gerardo Ruiz Mateos (PAN)
Energy	Georgina Kessel Martínez [f]
Environment and Natural Resources	Juan Rafael Elvira Quezada (PAN)
Finance and Public Credit	Agustín Carstens Carstens (PAN)
Foreign Affairs	Patricia Espinosa Cantellano [f]
Health	José Ángel Córdova Villalobos (PAN)
Interior	Fernando Francisco Gómez Mont Urrueta (PAN)
Labor and Social Welfare	Javier Lozano Alarcón (PAN)
National Defense	Gen. Guillermo Galván Galván
Navy	Adm. Mariano Francisco Saynez Mendoza
Public Education	Alonso Lujambio Irazábal (PAN)
Public Safety	Genaro García Luna
Public Service	Salvador Vega Casillas (PAN)
Social Development	Ernesto Cordero Arroyo (PAN)
Tourism	Rodolfo Elizondo Torres (PAN)
Attorney General	Arturo Chávez Chávez (PAN)

[f] = female

Note: President Calderón appointed a number of independent specialists to his cabinet. All ministers known to be members of a party are identified above.

COMMUNICATIONS

Most press and broadcasting media are privately owned but operate under government regulation.

Press. The print media were traditionally subsidized, directly and indirectly, by the government. In addition to deriving 60–80 percent of their advertising revenue from official sources, newspapers and magazines commonly published, without attribution, materials prepared by public officials. Moreover, the low salaries paid reporters reflected an understanding by management that incomes were typically supplemented by officeholders. In 1982, however, the government introduced legislation making such payments to reporters a criminal offense while substantially reducing official advertising; the loss of advertising revenue, coupled with increases in the price of newsprint, resulted in the closure of nearly three dozen papers during the recession of the mid-1990s. Journalists have been heavily targeted in recent years by drug cartels who punish reporting on their activities and related official corruption. In the first nine months of 2009 5 Mexican journalists were killed, and at least 24 have been killed since 2000; self-censorship is consequently routine. The most important dailies, published in Mexico City unless otherwise noted, are the following: *El Heraldo de México* (374,000), conservative; *Esto* (350,000); *La Prensa* (208,000 daily, 172,000 Sunday), liberal; *Excélsior* (200,000), conservative; *Reforma* (145,000); El *Financiero* (135,000), financial; *El Norte* (Monterrey, 134,000 daily, 155,000 Sunday); *Ovaciones* (130,000 morning, 100,000 evening); *El Universal* (94,000 daily, 136,000 Sunday), center-left; *El Sol de Tampico* (Tampico, 77,000); *El Sol de México* (76,000); *Diario de México* (76,000); *Uno Más Uno* (60,000), left-wing; *El Occidental* (Guadalajara, 49,000); *Novedades* (43,000 daily, 44,000 Sunday), independent. *Proceso* is a widely circulated center-left weekly newsmagazine.

News agencies. AMI (*Agencia Mexicana de Información*), Notimex (*Noticias Mexicanas*), Notipress (*Noticias de Prensa Mexicana*), and *Noti-Acción* are the principal Mexican news agencies. A number of foreign agencies maintain bureaus in Mexico City.

Broadcasting and computing. Radio and television are privately owned but operate under the supervision of several governmental regulatory bodies. Of the more than 750 TV stations (including cable outlets), the progovernment *Televisa* reaches virtually the entire country and dominates the ratings, although an independent challenger, *Televisión Azteca,* was launched in 1993. As of 2008 there were 217.1 Internet users per 1,000 inhabitants.

INTERGOVERNMENTAL REPRESENTATION

Ambassador to the U.S.: Arturo SARUKHÁN Casamitjana.

U.S. Ambassador to Mexico: Carlos PASCUAL.

Permanent Representative to the UN: Claude HELLER.

IGO Memberships (Non-UN): ACS, ALADI, APEC, BCIE, BIS, CDB, EBRD, G-20, IADB, Interpol, IOM, OAS, OECD, OPANAL, PCA, SELA, WCO, WTO.

FEDERATED STATES OF MICRONESIA

Political Status: Sovereign state in free association with the United States (which retains authority with regard to defense) since October 21, 1986.

Land Area: 271 sq. mi. (701 sq. km.).

Population: 107,008 (2000C); 110,000 (2008E).

Major Urban Centers (2005E): PALIKIR (Pohnpei, 6,600), Weno (Chuuk, 12,300), Kitti (Pohnpei, 6,800), Nett (Pohnpei, 6,300), Kolonia (Pohnpei, 5,000).

Official Language: English. The principal native languages are Kosrean, Pohnpeian, Trukese, and Yapese.

Monetary Unit: U.S. Dollar (see U.S. article for principal exchange rates).

President: Emanuel (Manny) MORI; elected by the Congress on May 11, 2007, and sworn in on the same day for a four-year term, succeeding Joseph J. URUSEMAL.

Vice President: Alik L. ALIK; elected by the Congress on May 11, 2007, and sworn in on the same day for a term concurrent with that of the president, succeeding Redley KILLION.

THE COUNTRY

The Federated States of Micronesia (FSM), with the Republic of Palau at their western extremity, occupy the archipelago of the Caroline Islands, some 300 miles to the east of the Philippines. The constituent states are the island groups (from west to east) of Yap, Chuuk (formerly Truk), Pohnpei (formerly Ponape), and Kosrae, each of which has its own indigenous language, with English as the official language of the Federation. Most inhabitants of the more than 600 islands are of either Micronesian or Polynesian extraction. Roman Catholicism predominates among the largely Christian population. Subsistence farming and fishing are the principal economic activities, with tourism of increasing importance. GNP per capita was reported to have fallen by 1.4 percent in real terms during 1990–1999 before rising by 8.4 percent in 2000. Growth then declined to an average of 2.0 percent annually through 2008. This current period of declining growth included a disastrous typhoon in April 2004 with a number of tidal storms thereafter; wavering disbursement of Compact assistance from the United States (which, however, totaled nearly $90 million for fiscal 2009); and little hope for subsequent improvement because of the global economic slump. More than half of the tax-paying wage earners are government employees, with most of the remainder dependent on spending by either government or government workers. The paucity of job prospects has heightened emigration to the United States, where FSM citizens can work without visas.

GOVERNMENT AND POLITICS

Political background. Purchased by Germany from Spain in 1899, the Carolines were seized in 1914 by Japan and retained as part of the mandate awarded by the League of Nations in 1920. The islands were occupied by U.S. forces in World War II and (along with the Marshall and Northern Mariana islands) became part of the U.S. Trust Territory of the Pacific in 1947. In 1965 a Congress of Micronesia was established, with the Carolines electing 14 of the 21 members of its House of Representatives. Following acceptance of a 1975 covenant authorizing creation of the Commonwealth of the Northern Mariana Islands, the remaining components of the Trust Territory were regrouped into six districts, four of which in July 1978 approved a constitution of the FSM that became effective on May 10, 1979. In October 1982 the FSM concluded a Compact of Free Association with the United States, which was declared to be in effect on November 3, 1986, following ratification by the U.S. Congress and final approval by the FSM government. Under the compact, the FSM is a fully sovereign entity, save with regard to defense, which was to remain a U.S. responsibility for a minimum of 15 years; it was also obligated to "consult" with Washington on major foreign policy matters.

On May 15, 1987, John R. HAGLELGAM was sworn in as the FSM's second president, succeeding Tosiwo NAKAYAMA. Haglelgam was unable to stand for a second term because of his failure to secure reelection to the Congress on March 5, 1991, and on May 11 Bailey OLTER, formerly vice president under Nakayama, was elected his successor. Olter was elected to a second term on May 11, 1995. In November 1996 the Congress ruled that President Olter, who had recently suffered a stroke, was unable to fulfill his responsibilities and directed Vice President Jacob NENA to serve as acting president. Subsequently, it was determined that Olter would be unable to return to office, and on May 8, 1997, Nena was formally installed for the balance of his four-year mandate. Olter died in February 1999.

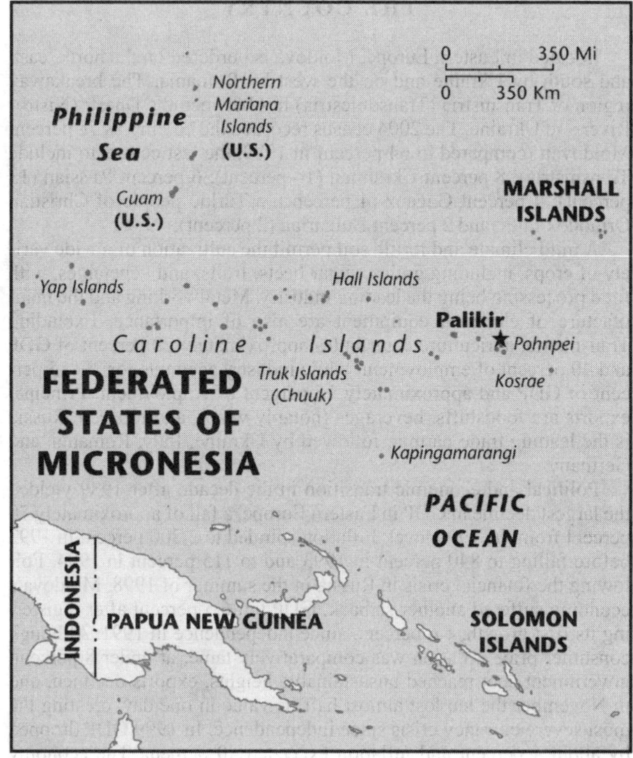

In the election of May 12, 1999, Vice President Leo A. FALCAM was elected to the presidency by the Congress, all 14 members of whom had been returned to office in nationwide balloting on March 2. However, both President Falcam and former president Nena lost their seats at the full legislative replenishment of March 4, 2003, and on May 10 the Congress elected Joseph J. URUSEMAL as chief executive.

Following an extension of the 1986 Compact, a successor was signed on May 1, 2003, and approved by the U.S. Congress in November. The present compact calls for annual grants of $76.2 million, in addition to $16 million annually for a Micronesian trust fund.

President Urusemal failed in a reelection bid after the congressional election of March 6, 2007, Emanuel (Manny) MORI, a longtime critic of the current compact, being named to replace him on May 11.

Constitution and government. The 1979 constitution provides for a unicameral Congress of 14 members, referred to as senators. One senator is elected from each state for a four-year term, while the others are elected for two-year terms from single-member districts delineated on a population basis. The president and vice president, who serve four-year terms, are selected by the Congress from among the four-year senators, the vacated seats being refilled by special election. The individual states have elected governors and legislatures, the latter encompassing a bicameral body of 38 members for Chuuk (a 10-member Senate and a 28-member House of Representatives) and unicameral bodies of 27, 14, and 10 members, respectively, for Pohnpei, Kosrae, and Yap. The state officials serve for four years, save that legislative terms on Chuuk and Pohnpei are staggered. Municipalities are governed by elected magistrates and councils, while villages follow traditional forms of rule.

State	*Area (sq. mi.)*	*Population (2007E)*
Chuuk	45.6	53,900
Kosrae	42.3	8,100
Pohnpei	132.4	35,500
Yap	46.7	11,400

In late 2000 local voters overwhelmingly endorsed creation of a fifth state, Faichuk, encompassing eight islands, with a population of about 20,000, that currently constitute part of Chuuk. In addition, sentiment has mounted for a constitutional amendment that would provide for direct election of the president and vice president. However, no action had been taken in either matter by late 2009.

Foreign relations. As in the case of the Marshall Islands, FSM's political autonomy is seemingly constricted by the U.S. retention of authority in defense matters and its right of "consultation" in foreign affairs. Nevertheless, the FSM parted company with both Majuro and Washington in endorsing the Treaty of Rarotonga that called for the establishment of a South Pacific Nuclear Free Zone. Like its neighbor, FSM is a member of the Asian Development Bank, the Pacific Community, and the Pacific Islands Forum.

In December 1990 the UN Security Council formally abrogated the U.S. Trusteeship with respect to the FSM, the Northern Marianas, and the Marshall Islands, and in September 1991 both the Marshalls and the FSM were admitted to the United Nations. In June 1993 the FSM was admitted to the International Monetary Fund and the World Bank.

Current issues. A leading issue in recent years has been the alleged political "dominance" of Chuuk (Truk), which holds nearly half of the FSM congressional seats. The controversy was reportedly a precipitant of impeachment proceedings against Chuuk Governor Gideon DOONE in 1989 that involved a variety of charges, including misuse of government funds. The governor was eventually acquitted of the charges in January 1990, but nearly two decades later, the state's status remained at issue, as evidenced by support from Chuuk's Faichuk region for separation as a fifth state.

Following the conclusion of Compact renewal in 2003, Washington has periodically called for guarantees that the support it provides is being properly dispensed. The problem came to a head in 2008, with 11 cases of missing or misallocated funds being referred to the FSM Department of Justice, and led to implementation of a Fundware Financial Management System (FFMS) in early 2009.

POLITICAL PARTIES

There are, at present, no formal parties in the FSM, political activity tending to center on regional (state) alignments.

LEGISLATURE

The FSM **Congress** is a 14-member body, 4 of whose members are elected on a statewide basis for four-year terms, while 10 are selected on a population/district basis for two-year terms. The most recent election for the four-year terms was on March 6, 2007. The most recent election for the two-year terms was on March 3, 2009.

Speaker: Isaac V. FIGIR.

CABINET

[as of July 1, 2009]

President	Emanuel (Manny) Mori
Vice President	Alik L. Alik
Secretaries	
Education	Casiano Shoniber
Finance and Administration	Finley S. Perman
Foreign Affairs	Lorin S. Robert
Health and Social Services	Vita Akapito Skilling [f]
Justice and Attorney General	Maketo Robert
Resources and Development	Peter M. Christian
Transportation, Communications, and Infrastructure	Francis I. Itimai

[f] = female

COMMUNICATIONS

Press. *The National Union* (5,000) is a government-sponsored information bulletin that appears twice monthly; there is also a *Chuuk News Chronicle* and a *Micronesia Focus,* both published in Pohnpei, and a bimonthly *Island Tribune* that began publication in late 1997. In March 1997, the FSM Congress called for deportation of Canadian-born Sherry

O'Sullivan, the editor since 1994 of the independent monthly, *FSM News,* on the ground that she had disregarded "local customs, traditions, and culture" by publishing accounts of "widespread bribery" and other malpractices at election time.

Broadcasting and computing. There is a radio station on each of the four principal islands that broadcasts in English and the local language; there are also television stations on Chuuk, Pohnpei, and Yap.

As of 2008 there were 144.9 Internet users per 1,000 inhabitants.

INTERGOVERNMENTAL REPRESENTATION

Ambassador to the U.S.: Yosiwo P. GEORGE.

U.S. Ambassador to the Federated States of Micronesia: Peter Alan PRAHAR.

Permanent Representative to the UN: Masao NAKAYAMA.

IGO Memberships (Non-UN): ADB, PC, PIF.

MOLDOVA

Republic of Moldova
Republica Moldova

Note: Marian Lupu, the presidential candidate of the governing Alliance for European Integration (APIE), failed to gain the 61 votes needed for election in balloting in the Parliament on November 10 and December 7, 2009. Consequently, Acting President Mihai Ghimpu remained in the post until new parliamentary elections are held (constitutionally precluded until mid-2010) or until the constitution is revised (as proposed by the APIE) to permit presidential election by majority vote in the Parliament.

Political Status: Formerly the Moldavian Soviet Socialist Republic, a constituent republic of the Union of Soviet Socialist Republics; declared independence as the Republic of Moldova on August 27, 1991; became sovereign member of the Commonwealth of Independent States on December 21, 1991; new constitution approved on July 28, 1994, and entered into force on August 27.

Area: 13,000 sq. mi. (33,670 sq. km.).

Population: 3,388,071 (2004C); 3,420,000 (2008E).

Major Urban Centers (2005E): CHIȘINĂU (formerly Kishinev, 596,000), Tiraspol (185,000), Tighina (125,00), Bălți (123,000).

Official Language: Moldovan.

Monetary Unit: Moldovan leu (official rate December 1, 2009: 11.11 leu = $1US).

President (Acting): *(See headnote.)* Mihai GHIMPU (Liberal Party); named acting president (due to his position as speaker of Parliament) by Parliament on September, 11, 2009, to succeed Vladimir VORONIN (Party of Communists of the Republic of Moldova), who had resigned the same day.

Prime Minister: Vladimir FILAT (Liberal Democratic Party of Moldova); nominated by the acting president (upon the recommendation of the four-party Alliance for European Integration) on September 17, 2009, following the legislative election of July 29 and inaugurated on September 25 (following approval of his government by Parliament the same day) to succeed Zinaida GRECIANÎI (Party of Communists of the Republic of Moldova), who had announced her resignation on September 10 (effective September 14). (Justice Minister Vitalie PÎLOG [Liberal Party] served as acting prime minister from September 14–25, 2009, having been appointed to the post on September 10 by outgoing president Vladimir Voronin.)

THE COUNTRY

Located in Eastern Europe, Moldova is bordered on the north, east, and south by Ukraine and on the west by Romania. The breakaway region of Transnistria (Transdniestria) lies between the Dnestr (Nistru) River and Ukraine. The 2004 census recorded the country as 78 percent Moldovan (compared to 64 percent in 1989, the last census to include Transnistria); 8 percent Ukrainian (14 percent); 6 percent Russian (13 percent); 4 percent Gagauz (4 percent), a Turkic people of Christian Orthodox faith; and 2 percent Bulgarian (2 percent).

A mild climate and fertile soil permit the cultivation of a wide variety of crops, including grains, sugar beets, fruits, and vegetables, with food processing being the leading industry. Metalworking and the manufacture of electrical equipment are also of importance. Excluding Transnistria, agriculture contributes approximately 20 percent of GDP and 40 percent of employment, while industry accounts for 20–25 percent of GDP and approximately 15 percent of employment. Principal exports are foodstuffs, beverages (notably wine), and tobacco. Russia is the leading trade partner, followed by Ukraine, Italy, Romania, and Germany.

Political and economic transition in the decade after 1989 yielded the largest decline in GDP in Eastern Europe, a fall of approximately 70 percent from the 1990 level. Inflation spiraled to 2,200 percent in 1992 before falling to 840 percent in 1993 and to 115 percent in 1994. Following the financial crisis in Russia in the summer of 1998, Moldova's economy suffered another setback. GDP fell 6.5 percent after registering its first growth, 1.6 percent, since independence in 1991. Although consumer price inflation was comparatively tame, at under 8 percent, government debt reached unsustainable heights, exports declined, and in November the leu lost almost half its value in one day, creating the most severe currency crisis since independence. In 1999 GDP dropped by about 4 percent and inflation exceeded 40 percent. The economy recovered in 2000, with growth of 1.9 percent and with inflation halved. Late in the year the International Monetary Fund (IMF) and World Bank agreed to resume lending, conditioned upon Parliament's passing a debt restructuring plan that the government had negotiated with the European Bank for Reconstruction and Development (EBRD and approving a new civil code (adopted in 2002) favoring free-market principles..

GDP rose by an average of 7.1 percent annually in 2002–2005, although growth slipped to approximately 4 percent in 2006. Inflation dipped from 15.7 percent in 2003 to 11.9 percent in 2005 before rising to 14.1 percent in 2006.

In January 2006 Russian energy giant Gazprom temporarily cut off natural gas deliveries to Moldova—which is almost completely dependent on its neighbors for energy—and doubled the price of gas. In March the Russian government banned imports of Moldovan wine, citing health and quality issues. The wine ban was particularly painful because, previously, Moldovan wine sales approached 15 percent of GNP, and it exported approximately 80 percent of its wine to Russia. The result was a trade deficit with Russia approaching $200 million in 2006, compared to a roughly $90 million surplus in 2005. (Russian President Vladimir Putin announced an end to the wine ban in November 2006, but Russia continued to delay imports of Moldovan wine into 2007.)

Although the IMF expressed concern with the lack of structural reform, in 2006 it released a statement in which it noted, "Moldova's European aspirations have provided much-needed momentum to the authorities' structural reform efforts and commitment to combat corruption." The World Bank reported in 2006 that "GDP growth is no longer reducing poverty," particularly rural poverty. Roughly half the population lives off subsistence farming. Those who do produce a surplus have difficulty getting it to market, as the country's road network is deficient and agricultural purchase prices are low. Moreover, with an average wage of only about $129 per month, Moldova reportedly has the lowest standard of living in Europe. One clear result of the economic difficulties is that 600,000 Moldovans (one in four adults) have left the country to look for work, principally in Russia and Italy. Remittances back home from workers abroad amounted to an estimated $950 million in 2007, accounting for over 35 percent of GDP. The steady rise in food prices, at 15 percent for 2007 and accelerating in 2008, threatened to reverse gains made in reducing urban and rural poverty given that the average household in Moldova spends over a third of its earnings on food. Meanwhile, GDP growth of 5 percent and 7.2 percent was reported in 2007 and 2008, respectively.

In the first half of 2009 remittances from abroad fell by approximately 30 percent under the effects of the global financial crisis. The

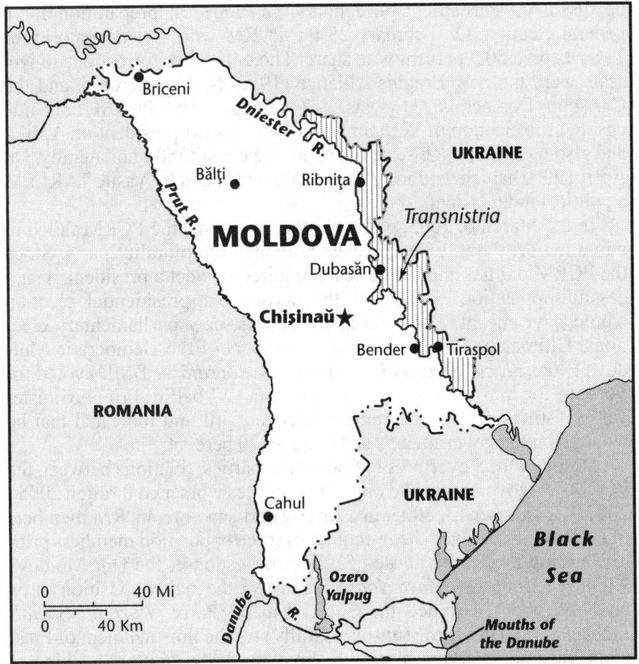

fall in remittances and corresponding drop in consumer demand contributed to a 25 percent contraction in the manufacturing and construction sectors, although agriculture remained steady. Consequently, the IMF and the Moldovan government predicted that GDP might plummet by more than 9 percent for the full year.

GOVERNMENT AND POLITICS

Political background. Historical Moldova lay between the frontiers of the Russian, Habsburg, and Ottoman empires and was the object of numerous invasions and territorial realignments, including incorporation in Greater Romania from 1918 to 1940. Present-day Moldova encompasses the territory of the pre-1940 Moldavian Autonomous Soviet Socialist Republic, which was located within Ukraine and which was joined to all but the northern and southern portions of Bessarabia upon detachment of the latter from Romania in 1940. With its redrawn borders, the redefined Moldavian SSR became a constituent republic of the Soviet Union.

On July 29, 1989, Mircea SNEGUR was elected chair of the Presidium of the republican Supreme Soviet. Although a member of the Politburo of the Communist Party of Moldova (*Partidul Comunist din Moldova*—PCM), he subsequently endorsed the nationalist demands of the Popular Front of Moldova (*Frontul Popular din Moldova*—FPM), which had been launched earlier in the year. The language law of 1989 asserted a "Moldo-Romanian" identity, and in 1990 the Moldovan flag was adapted from the Romanian tricolor.

On August 19, 1990, the Turkic-speaking Gagauz minority in the southern part of the country responded to the prospect of union with Romania by announcing the formation of a "Republic of Gagauzia." On September 2 the Slavic majority in the eastern Dnestr valley followed suit, proclaiming a "Pridnestrovskian Moldavian Soviet Socialist Republic" (changing to Pridnestrovskian Moldavian Republic [*Pridnestrovskaia Moldavskaia Respublica*] in 1991, commonly called either Transnistria or Transdniestria in English). The Supreme Soviet thereupon went into emergency session, naming Snegur to the new post of executive president on September 3 and empowering him to introduce direct rule "in regions not obeying the constitution." Despite continued unrest, including a pitched battle between police and secessionist militia at a bridge over the Dnestr River on November 2, the situation eased late in the year after political intervention by Soviet President Mikhail Gorbachev.

On August 22, 1991, in the wake of the failed Moscow coup against Gorbachev, PCM First Secretary Grigory YEREMEY resigned from the Politburo of the Communist Party of the Soviet Union (CPSU), and on August 23 President Snegur, who had opposed the Moscow hard-liners, effectively banned the PCM. On August 27 Moldova declared its independence and two days later established diplomatic relations with Romania. In October 1991 the leading pro-unification FPM faction came out in opposition to Snegur and called for a boycott of the presidential election set for December 8. Snegur was nevertheless reelected as the sole candidate in a turnout officially given as 82.9 percent, this time drawing his main political support from the pro-independence Agrarian Democratic Party of Moldova (*Partidul Democrat Agrar din Moldova*—PDAM).

In March 1992 ethnic conflict again erupted. Igor SMIRNOV, the president of Transnistria, called for mobilization of all men between ages 18 and 45. Concurrently, his deputy, Aleksandr KARAMAN, asserted the "very real danger . . . of a Moldovan variant of Yugoslavia" and insisted that the only viable solution would be a confederal republic in which Moldovans, Russians, and Gagauz would have separate autonomous territories. For his part, President Snegur offered special economic status to the Transnister region but rejected the concept of a separate republic. Local Red Army units stationed in the region intervened for Transnistria, escalating the conflict from September 1991 to July 1992. In July 1992 a cease-fire was signed and Russian Federation troops entered the region to act as monitors for the agreement.

Initial enthusiasm in Moldova and Romania for unification faded quickly, with public opinion polls in Moldova showing that no more than 10 percent of the population supported union. On January 7 President Snegur called for a referendum on unification to be held, appealing for strengthened Moldovan independence. The referendum split pro- and anti-unionist deputies, the referendum call ultimately being defeated by one vote. On August 3 Snegur was granted decree powers for the ensuing year to facilitate economic reforms, and in February 1994 his administration indicated that it sought accommodation with Transnistria on the basis of substantial autonomy for the region, including its own legislative body and the use of distinctive political symbols.

The parliamentary election of February 27, 1994, yielded an overall majority for the PDAM and was followed on March 6 by a referendum in which a reported 95.4 percent of participants voted for maintaining Moldova's separation from both Romania and Russia. A further national unity government under the continued premiership of the PDAM's Andrey SANGHELI obtained legislative approval on April 5, its first major act being the introduction of a new devolutionary constitution in August, effectively removing union with Romania as an option, except as a long-term aspiration.

Fortified by an IMF loan, the Moldovan government in March 1995 embarked on a major privatization program to dispose of some 1,500 state enterprises. However, resistance to privatization remained prevalent within the state bureaucracy, while opposition parties forecast an outbreak of widespread corruption. Principally because of such opposition within the PDAM, President Snegur in July launched the Party of Rebirth and Conciliation of Moldova (*Partidul Renaşterii şi Concilierii din Moldova*—PRCM).

Although Prime Minister Sangheli was able to announce on August 1, 1995, that the five-year Gagauz conflict was over (see Constitution and government, below), the Transnister problem remained more intractable. President Snegur entered into direct talks with Smirnov, but little progress was made in 1995. On December 24 a territorial referendum yielded an 82.7 percent majority in favor of a draft independence constitution and of separate membership in the Commonwealth of Independent States (CIS). Although the constitution was promulgated in January 1996, the Moldovan government's quest for a political accommodation with the Pridnestrovskian Moldavian Republic leadership was boosted on January 19 when President Snegur secured the signatures of his Russian and Ukrainian counterparts on a joint statement asserting that the Transnister region was part of Moldova but should have special status. Further talks between Snegur and Smirnov culminated in an agreement on June 17 defining the region as "a state-territorial formation in the form of a republic within Moldova's internationally recognized borders." This tortuous wording appeared to satisfy both sides' core demands, although detailed implementation and ratification were expected to be difficult processes. Meanwhile, withdrawal of the Russian 14th Army proceeded slowly, with the Russian military authorities citing various hindrances.

On the domestic political front, President Snegur launched his campaign for reelection in November 1996. A key feature of his platform was that Moldova should move to a more presidential form of government, particularly in respect to authority to appoint and dismiss ministers. The president faced obstruction from the opposition-dominated Parliament, which in February voted down a presidential proposal to change "Moldovan" to "Romanian" as the constitutional descriptor of the official language.

Backed by a PRCM-initiated "Civic Movement," Snegur headed the poll in the first round of presidential elections held on November 17, 1996, winning 38.7 percent of the vote against eight other candidates. In second place, with 27.7 percent, came Petru LUCINSCHI, the parliamentary speaker and unofficial PDAM candidate. Enlivened by a phone-tapping scandal and PDAM allegations that the president's supporters were attempting to rig the outcome, the second round of voting on December 1 featured a runoff between Snegur and Lucinschi, with the latter receiving the formal endorsement not only of the PDAM but also of the Party of Communists of the Republic of Moldova (*Partidul Comuniştilor din Republica Moldova*—PCRM). The outcome was a decisive victory for Lucinschi, who obtained 54 percent of the vote. After Lucinschi was inaugurated on January 15, 1997, he nominated Ion CIUBUC, an economist, to succeed Sangheli. On January 24 the Parliament approved the new government, whose members were selected, according to Ciubuc, not in regard to their political affiliation but rather for their "professional" abilities. The new prime minister pledged that his administration would focus on economic reforms.

Balloting for a new Parliament was held on March 22, 1998, with the PCRM winning a plurality of 40 seats, followed by the pro-Snegur Democratic Convention of Moldova (*Convenţia Democrată din Moldova*—CDM) with 26 seats, the pro-Lucinschi bloc For a Democratic and Prosperous Moldova (*Pentru o Moldovă Democratică şi Prosperă*—PMDP) with 24 seats, and the Party of Democratic Forces (*Partidul Forţelor Democratice*—PFD) with 11 seats. A center-right coalition consisting of the CDM, PMDP, and PFD, called the Alliance for Democracy and Reforms (*Alianţa pentru Democraţie şi Reforme*—ADR), formed a new government on April 21, with Ciubuc as premier. However, unable to stem a growing economic crisis, Ciubuc resigned on February 1, 1999, leaving the ADR deadlocked over his successor. President Lucinschi advanced Serafim URECHEAN for prime minister; however, the prospective premier's effort to form a government of technocrats failed, and he withdrew on February 17. Two days later the president nominated Deputy Prime Minister Ion STURZA for the premiership. Parliament approved Sturza's cabinet on March 12, needing an absentee ballot from Ilie ILASCU, a legislator imprisoned by Transnistria since 1992, to secure a confidence vote.

The Sturza government fell on November 9, 1999, when the Christian Democrats (*Frontul Popular Creştin Democrat*—FPCD) and a handful of independents (four of whom had left the PMDP a month earlier) joined the Communists in passing a vote of no confidence, citing the government's economic failures. The move followed the defeat several days earlier of a government-sponsored bill to privatize the wine and tobacco industries, rejection of which caused the IMF and the World Bank to suspend release of further loans and credits. A struggle between the president and the legislature ensued, with the latter rejecting two nominees for prime minister and Lucinschi not even submitting the name of his third choice when it became apparent that Parliament would again reject the cabinet. With the president having vowed to dissolve the legislature if it turned down another nominee, on December 21 Parliament approved a largely nonparty government led by Dumitru BRAGHIŞ, theretofore deputy minister for the economy and reform.

What remained of the former governing alliance, the ADR, broke apart in April 2000 when the principal component of the PMDP, Parliament Speaker Dumitru DIACOV's Movement for a Democratic and Prosperous Moldova (*Mişcarea o Moldovă Democratică şi Prosperă*—MMDP), announced its reconfiguration as the Democratic Party of Moldova (*Partidul Democrat din Moldova*—PDM) and its independence from President Lucinschi and his efforts to strengthen the presidency through constitutional amendment. The struggle over Moldova's system of government took a different direction in July, when Parliament, overriding Lucinschi's vehement veto, overwhelmingly passed constitutional changes that included indirect election of the president by the legislature. A corresponding election law promulgated in October mandated that a presidential candidate would need a three-fifths majority to secure a victory.

In December 2000 neither the PCRM's Vladimir VORONIN nor Pavel BARBALAT, chair of the Constitutional Court, succeeded in marshaling the 61 votes required to win the presidency. Barbalat, who was backed by Diacov's PDM, Snegur's CDM, and the Christian Democrats, repeatedly failed to break 40 votes, while Voronin came no closer than 59 (in a third ballot on December 6). A center-right parliamentary boycott prevented a quorum and thus a fourth ballot on December 21, and on December 26 the Constitutional Court ruled that President Lucinschi had the "right and duty" to order new elections. Accordingly, he dissolved Parliament on January 12, 2001, in preparation for a general election. On February 25 the PCRM won a clear majority of 71 seats on a 50.7 percent vote share. The only other formations to win seats were the new Braghiş Alliance (19 seats, 13.3 percent) and the Christian Democrats (11 seats, 8.3 percent). The PCRM landslide ensured the election of Voronin as Moldova's next president on April 4 and also gave it enough seats to amend the constitution unilaterally. On April 19 Parliament endorsed a new cabinet headed by Vasile TARLEV, a political independent.

In the March 6, 2005, parliamentary elections, the PCRM failed to win a majority but, with 56 seats, remained the plurality party. Since the PCRM did not win the 61 seats required to elect a president, a successful opposition boycott of the subsequent presidential election would have meant, after two failed ballots, new parliamentary elections. Ultimately, however, enough members of the Democratic Moldova Bloc (*Blocul Electoral "Moldova Democrată"*—BMD) voted for Voronin for him to be reelected on the second ballot. Prime Minister Tarlev formed a new government later in April and indicated that he would trim the government's staff size by 70 percent.

Despite initial overtures to opposition parties, relations between the PCRM-led government and opposition parties worsened through 2005–2007. On October 13, 2005, in a strictly partisan vote, PCRM members of Parliament removed the immunity of three opposition members prior to charging them with abuse of office. In response, the Our Moldova Alliance (*Alianţa Moldova Noastră*—AMN), the main opposition party, on November 24 joined the Social Liberal Party (*Partidul Social-Liberal*—PSL) in calling (unsuccessfully) for the impeachment of President Voronin. charging him with "breaking laws, flouting a ruling of the European Court of Human Rights, offending the Romany ethnic minority with epithets used in relation to the opposition, and promoting his own candidate to the post of Chişinău mayor."

Local elections in 2007 (held in 2006 in autonomous Gagauzia) resulted in political setbacks for the PCRM, amid what the U.S. embassy termed "intimidation of candidates, unequal access to and coverage in the media for all parties, misuse of administrative resources, reports of improper campaigning near voting stations, government bias in favor of ruling-party candidates, and irregularities in voter lists." Particularly symbolic was the loss of the mayoral race in Chişinău to the Liberal Party (*Partidul Liberal*—PL) candidate, Dorin CHIRTOACĂ. Although the PDM and AMN saw only modest gains in the district elections, many of the smaller opposition political parties saw significant gains or obtained district seats for the first time, with nearly 30 percent of district seats held by members of the smaller parties or by independents. The Tarlev government subsequently became increasingly unpopular due to its problems in implementing economic and political reforms. Consequently, Tarlev stepped down as prime minister on March 19, 2008, stating the need for "new individuals" to lead the country. Deputy Prime Minister Zinaida GRECIANÎI subsequently became Moldova's first female prime minister. Upon taking office, she changed over a third of the cabinet and pledged to focus on economic development and European integration.

The PCRM won 60 seats in the April 5, 2009, legislative balloting, leaving it 1 shy of the 61 seats (a three-fifths majority) needed to elect a president on its own. Consequently, balloting in Parliament on May 20 and June 3 failed to elect a president, necessitating a new legislative poll on July 29 at which the PCRM declined to 48 seats, compared to 53 seats for the opposition (the PDM, AMN, PL, and the recently formed Liberal Democratic Party of Moldova [*Partidului Liberal Democrat din Moldova*— PLDM]), which coalesced as the Alliance for European Integration (*Alianţa Pentru Integrare Europenă*—APIE) and pledged to form a new government.

President Voronin resigned effective September 11, 2009, and he was succeeded in an acting capacity by the PL's Mihai GHIMPU, who had recently been elected speaker of Parliament. At the request of the APIE, Ghimpu on September 17 nominated PLDM leader Vladimir FILAT to form a new government, which, as approved with 53 votes in Parliament on September 25, included members of the four APIE parties. *(See headnote.)*

Constitution and government. A new constitution, replacing the 1977 Soviet-era text, secured legislative approval on July 28, 1994, and entered into force on August 27 (the third anniversary of independence). It described Moldova as a "presidential, parliamentary republic" based on political pluralism and "the preservation, development, and expression of ethnic and linguistic identity." Executive power continues to be vested in a president, who was directly elected until constitutional changes passed in July 2000 (over President Lucinschi's veto) transformed the country into a parliamentary republic" and led to passage in

September–October of a law establishing procedures for indirect election by the unicameral Parliament. (A three-fifths majority is required for a president to be elected. After two failed ballots, new legislative elections must be held, although only two legislative elections can be held in a single calendar year.) The president nominates the prime minister, subject to approval by the Parliament, which is elected for a four-year term. Passage of a nonconfidence motion in the Parliament forces the resignation of the Council of Ministers. Other constitutional clauses proclaim Moldova's permanent neutrality and proscribe the stationing of foreign troops on the national territory.

The 1994 constitution authorized "special status" for both the Gagauz region in the south and the Transnister region, where separatist activity had broken out in 1990. Statutes providing broad autonomy to Gagauz-Yeri (Gagauzia, *Găgăuzia*) went into effect in February 1995, with referendums the following month to determine which villages wished to be part of the special region. Subsequently, direct elections for a 35-member regional People's Assembly were held in May–June, as was the direct election of a regional executive leader (*bashkan*), who was authorized to carry out quasi-presidential responsibilities.

Meanwhile, the status of Transnistria remained unresolved. In December 1995 Transnistrians overwhelmingly endorsed an independence constitution, and in December 2006, 97 percent voted in a referendum to seek independence. In May 1997, however, the Moldovan and Transnister leaders, meeting in Moscow, agreed to participate in a single state, although the dynamics of the region's "special status" remained to be defined. In Kyiv, Ukraine, in July 1999 Smirnov and Lucinschi signed a declaration on normalizing relations that committed both sides to a single "economic, judicial, and social sphere within Moldova's existing borders." Nevertheless, subsequent claims by Transnistria that Chişinău ignored its needs and opinions soon led to a renewal of demands for independence. At present, a strong president who also serves as prime minister leads Transnistria's government; under changes introduced in 2000, a 43-member, unicameral parliament replaced a bicameral legislature.

In December 2001 Parliament passed a law on local administration that would have replaced Moldova's counties with a district system, but the Constitutional Court declared the measure unconstitutional in March 2002. In January 2003 the government approved new legislation replacing 9 provinces and 2 autonomous regions introduced in 1999 with a structure that now encompasses 32 districts, 3 municipalities (Tighina and Bălţi as well as the capital), the Autonomous Territorial Unit of Gagauzia, and Transnistria. Local administrative units include communes and cities.

Foreign relations. Moldova's first international action following independence in 1991 was to establish diplomatic relations with Romania. On January 16, 1992, Hungary became the first foreign country to exchange ambassadors with the former Soviet republic, although some 70 others, including the United States, had by then recognized Moldovan independence. On March 2 Moldova was admitted to the UN and on April 27 was formally offered membership in the IMF and World Bank. It also joined the Conference on (later Organization for) Security and Cooperation in Europe (CSCE/OSCE).

Possible union with Romania was placed on the agenda by the creation of a parliamentary-level National Council of Reunification in late 1991, while in 1992 government-level meetings were instituted on the basis of a treaty of friendship and cooperation. A growing preference in Moldova for independence meant that by mid-1993 reunification had ceased to be a practical political option. However, spurred by Romania's eagerness to join the North Atlantic Treaty Organization (NATO) and settle border issues, Moldova and Romania agreed in April 1997 to resume talks on a basic treaty, which was finally initialed on April 28, 2000, by the countries' foreign ministers. Despite seven years of further negotiation, in 2008 the treaty remained unsigned, in part because Romania has refused to accept references to a separate Moldovan language.

On March 16, 1994, during a visit to Brussels for talks with officials from NATO and the EU, President Snegur signed NATO's Partnership for Peace, while the Moldovan Parliament on April 8 finally ratified membership in the CIS and its economic union. Although Moldovan participation in CIS military or monetary integration was ruled out, the CIS ratification indicated cautious alignment with Moscow, with the aim in particular of securing the long-sought departure of the Russian Fourteenth Army from Transnistria.

In July 1995 Moldova became the first CIS member to be admitted to the Council of Europe. In December it signed military cooperation agreements with the United States and Ukraine, having concluded a friendship and cooperation treaty with the latter in 1992. A border treaty was concluded with Ukraine in 1999, but objections from factions within the Moldovan Parliament left it unratified until 2001.

In November 1996 Moldova was admitted to membership of the Central European Initiative. In 1997 the government announced its support for negotiations with the EU toward associate membership, perhaps leading eventually to full membership. Regionally, in October 1997 Moldova joined Georgia, Ukraine, and Azerbaijan in forming the GUAM group.

Moldova subsequently made efforts to reach beyond purely regional issues. In September 2003, for example, it began participating in postwar security operations in Iraq at the invitation of the U.S. government. In addition, in January 2004 Moldova agreed to participate in UN peacekeeping operations, subsequently contributing soldiers to missions in Liberia, Côte D'Ivoire, and Sudan.

In recent years Moldova's foreign relations have directly reflected its internal conflicts to an unusual degree. With large ethnic populations who identify with Romania and Russia, relations with those two countries have been at the forefront of Moldovan foreign policy. Relations with Romania were strained over suggestions by Moldovan President Voronin that "greater" Moldova included the Romanian province of Moldova. Romanian President Ion Iliescu in January 2004, called the idea "a falsification of historical reality and an expression of revisionist inclinations." And while Moldovan Foreign Minister Andrei STRATAN said in February that Moldova wanted to renew negotiations on a bilateral treaty with Romania, Romania rejected any treaty talks that did not include discussion of the "special relationship" between Romanian and Moldovan identities.

Not coincidentally, Moldova's relations with Russia have often been the inverse of its relations with Romania. While President Voronin (a former KBG officer) was considered pro-Russian when he first took office, he gradually adopted more anti-Russian positions, largely as a result of the conflict in Transnistria. In April 2004 Voronin emphasized that Moldova's relations with Russia were still good, with only the Transnister issue being a problem. But Russia has repeatedly declined to sign a "Declaration on Stability and Security for the Republic of Moldova" sought by Voronin. Russia maintains that such a guarantee of Moldovan sovereignty would be possible only if Moldova guaranteed a peaceful settlement of the Transnister issue.

Moldova's desire for integration with the EU received a setback on March 10, 2004, when Ivan Borisavljevic, the European Commission's envoy to Moldova, said that there were serious obstacles on the road to accession, including the Transnistria conflict, corruption, poverty, and lack of genuine reforms. He estimated it might be 10–15 years before Moldova was ready for integration talks. A recent report by the EU was critical of the slow pace of reform, stressing "the need for Moldova to redouble efforts to implement democratic reforms in crucial areas such as respect for human rights, freedom of the media, and respect for the rule of law, including independence of the judiciary." In February 2005 Moldova signed an "action plan" with the European Union (EU) to bring the country closer to EU standards. The action plan involved a wide range of political, economic, and judicial reforms.

Relations with Russia worsened in January 2006, when Russia cut off supplies of natural gas to Moldova after the latter declined to accept a 100 percent increase in prices. In mid-January, the two countries agreed on a less dramatic increase in prices. In March, however, the Russian government banned the import of wine from Moldova and Georgia, purportedly for health reasons. In fact, most analysts characterize Russia's move as retaliation for Moldova's and Georgia's position opposing Russia's entry into the World Trade Organization (WTO) until Russia stops supporting separatists in those two countries and removes troops from their territory. Relations improved in 2007 as both the Moldovan and international media reported rumors of feelers by both Moldova and Russia to resolve the Transnister problem.

Romania's accession to the EU on January 1, 2007, raised new issues with Moldova. Romanian President Traian Băsescu has urged Moldovan admission to the EU and offered Romanian assistance toward this goal. He stated in June 2007 that this would effectively "bring the Romanian people together under the umbrella of the European Union." Voronin, however, had declared in December 2006 that Romanian offers of assistance were "interference in the domestic affairs of a sovereign state." An agreement to open new Romanian consulates in the Moldovan towns of Bălţi and Cahul was reversed in March 2007 by the Moldovan foreign ministry, which complained that Romania had released inflated figures regarding Moldovans seeking Romanian citizenship. Relations worsened in December 2007 with the expulsion of two Romanian diplomats and when Voronin and Romanian officials traded accusations over the continued delay in ratifying the basic treaty and border treaty between the two states. In July 2008 relations improved when it was announced that the Romanian consulate in Cahul would open in exchange for a Moldovan consulate in Iasi.

The pro-Western coalition government installed in September 2009 set further integration with the EU as one of its chief priorities in foreign affairs. Meanwhile, acting president Mihai Ghimpu, while acknowledging past personal convictions for a union with Romania, stressed that unification was not a goal for the new government. In response, Russian far-right political leader Vladimir Zhirinovsky called for immediate Russian recognition of the independence of Transnistria, a statement widely interpreted in Moldova as suggesting possible Russian opposition to continued EU expansion in the region. Romanian former foreign minister Adrian Cioroianu suggested that the Moldovan government effectively ignore the status of Transnistria while pursuing other aspects of European integration, this statement in turn seen as evidence of continued Romanian desire for unification.

Current issues. The status of the Transnister region has been a major focus of attention since independence. Chişinău has insisted that the region remain an integral part of Moldova, while Transnister leaders have fluctuated between demanding outright independence and proposing a confederal system that would grant the region autonomy. Transnister leader Igor Smirnov, who called for the two sides to approach each other as "independent nations," dismissed a draft federative plan proposed by former Russian prime minister Yevgeni Primakov in September 2000. Independence advocates also continued to insist that Russian forces remain in place, whereas in November the OSCE expressed concern that the process of withdrawing Russian troops (then numbering about 2,600), as agreed at the 1999 OSCE summit in Istanbul, had yet to begin in earnest. The Russian pullout finally began in late 2001, just a week before Smirnov's December 9 reelection as Transnister president. The Russian withdrawal, however, did not continue.

In 2002 the OSCE issued a draft report calling for a federalized Moldova, with parts of the country having a right to their own legislation and constitution, although the Moldovan constitution and laws would have priority, while the OSCE would provide peacekeeping troops. After the United States announced its support for the plan, OSCE-sponsored talks got under way in August, but little progress ensued.

Russia once again promised the OSCE that it would remove its troops from Transnistria by the end of 2003. Although the Moldovan government, concerned that unguarded weapon stocks would fall into the hands of separatists, initially asked Russia to remain, President Voronin in November 2003 reversed course and refused to sign a Russian-backed plan to extend the stay of the troops. Separatist leader Smirnov promptly threatened to block the withdrawal of Russian troops. In December Voronin said he supported U.S. secretary of state Colin Powell's call for an international peacekeeping force, but Russia continued to reject that proposal, arguing that Russian troops needed to remain in the region to protect Russia's "national security" interests.

In July 2004 the separatists in Transnistria raised tensions by shutting down schools in the region that taught Moldovan in Latin script. Transnister militia even surrounded a boarding school and refused to allow OSCE staff to deliver food and water, a tactic described by an OSCE official as "simply inhumane." Consequently, Voronin called Smirnov and his colleagues a "group of transnational criminals" and broke off negotiations. In early August the separatists blocked rail lines between Transnistria and Moldova, and they subsequently announced that they were mobilizing reserves for the "Transnister Army." Smirnov collaterally declared that Transnistria "is marching on the road to setting up an independent, sovereign state." In October Russia stated it would not leave Transnistria until the issue is resolved.

Legislation proposed by the Moldovan government in the spring of 2005 reportedly would have given the region autonomous status within the Moldovan Republic, although banking, armed forces, customs, and foreign policy would have remained under Moldovan authority. Meanwhile, the United States backed a Ukrainian proposal for Transnistria that proposed free elections under the aegis of the EU, the OSCE, the United States, and Russia, as well as replacement of Russian peacekeeping forces with international forces. Transnistria agreed to rejoin talks in mid-May 2005 but declined to allow OSCE inspectors access to the region.

While none of the 2005 progressed significantly, Moldova—with the support of the United States and the EU—increased pressure on separatists by gaining the agreement of Ukraine in March 2006 to refuse exports from Transnistria unless they were approved by Moldovan customs. The separatist government, whose finances derive primarily from those exports, responded by instituting a blockade of train traffic at the border, which continued to be subject to transit disputes involving Russia as well as Moldova and Ukraine. (In October 2005 the EU agreed to a two-year mission to help Moldova and Ukraine monitor their border and train border guards to prevent smuggling.)

Despite such pressures, the Transnister Republic government reported that a referendum on September 17, 2006, showed that 95 percent of those participating voted against reunification with Moldova, and 97 percent favored "independence, with the ultimate goal of union with Russia." The most recent parliamentary elections, held on December 11, 2005, resulted in an upset victory for the Renewal party over the Republic party (see Transnistrian Parties under Political Parties, below), while the presidential election in December 2006 concluded with another term for Smirnov, who secured 82 percent of the vote.

Russian political and economic support for Transnistria subsequently remained crucial. Russian interests in Transnistria were one factor in Russian president Vladimir Putin's decision to announce the suspension of the Adapted Conventional Armed Forces in Europe Treaty on July 14, 2007, following Western protests over the continued presence of Russian troops in the region. However, reports of Russian irritation over corruption in Transnistria, plus a pro-Russian shift by Moldovan president Voronin in his disputes with Romania, led to widespread discussion in the Moldovan and international media that both Chişinău and Moscow were pressuring Transnister leaders to negotiate a permanent resolution to the region's status.

In October 2007 Voronin proposed a plan for both Moldova and Transnistria to demilitarize (eliminating the small Moldovan army), to broaden economic and communication links, and to allow international observers to monitor the situation. In March 2008 Moldovan media reported that the crucial issue in obtaining Russian support to resolve the Transnistrian conflict was Moscow's requirement for a formal repudiation of any future Moldovan membership in NATO. Voronin met with Smirnov in April 2008 for the first time in seven years, agreeing on further talks to "gradually" resolve the conflict. In the wake of the Russian-Georgian War of mid-2008, however, Smirnov in September called instead for Transnistria's formal independence and expressed confidence that Russia would support the "120,000 Russian citizens" living in Transnistria.

Protesters (estimated at 15,000 in Chişinău alone) took to the streets throughout Moldova after the results of the April 2009 legislative elections were announced, claiming fraud on the part of the ruling PCRM. Demonstrators broke through police lines in the capital, and part of the parliament building and the office of the president were burned. Several hundred protesters were injured in the subsequent police crackdown, and at least three died in custody. Amnesty International accused the government of tolerating police brutality and torture in suppressing the demonstrators, which most analysts characterized as spontaneous and student-led, although President Voronin blamed the unrest on Romania. Meanwhile, the OSCE observers described the elections as generally free and fair, but concern was raised over the fraud allegations and the need was stressed for further "democratic reforms."

The problems following the April 2009 election appeared to undercut support for the PCRM in the July reballoting, especially after PCRM leader Marian LUPU defected, along with a number of other legislators, to the PDM. Eight years of communist rule came to an end with the installation of the APIE government in September under Vladimir Filat, a prominent businessman who pledged to pursue further integration with the EU and to introduce major reforms designed to combat the recent economic collapse. Filat also indicated that his administration would strengthen ties with Romania and seek the withdrawal of Russian troops from Transnistria and their replacement with international peacekeepers. In response, Transnistrian leader Smirnov announced plans to expand his region's armed forces.

POLITICAL PARTIES

Since independence, Moldovan parties have frequently formed electoral blocs to contest parliamentary elections, but none have lasted more than one national election cycle. In 1994 the Electoral Bloc "Socialist Party and Unity Movement" (*Blocul Electoral "Partidul Socialist şi Mişcarea 'Unitate-Edinstvo'"*—PSMUE) finished second to the then-dominant (but now defunct) Agrarian Democratic Party of

Moldova (*Partidul Democrat Agrar din Moldova*—PDAM), and the Peasants and Intellectuals Bloc (*Blocul Ţăranilor şi Intelectualilor*) finished third. In 1998 the pro-Snegur, rightist Democratic Convention of Moldova (*Convenţia Democrată din Moldova*—CDM) won 26 seats and the pro-Lucinschi bloc For a Democratic and Prosperous Moldova (*Pentru o Moldovă Democratică şi Prosperă*—PMDP) took 24, enabling them, in conjunction with the 11 seats held by the Party of Democratic Forces (PFD; see under PSL), to form a center-right coalition, the Alliance for Democracy and Reforms (*Alianţa pentru Democraţie şi Reforme*—ADR) that installed Ion Ciubuc as prime minister. A year later the ADR backed Ion Sturza's government, but by the end of the year fractures within the unwieldy alliance had reduced it to minority status. The protracted effort to elect a successor to President Lucinschi in 2000 and the ultimate decision to call an early legislative election for February 2001 brought an end to what remained of the ADR, the CDM, and the PMDP as parties repositioned themselves. For that election the principal opposition formation, which finished a distant second to the Party of Communists (PCRM), was the multiparty Braghiş Alliance.

Moldova's unusually high bar for representation in Parliament (see Legislature, below, for details) continued to encourage the formation of electoral blocs. In July 2003 Our Moldova Alliance (AMN) was formed by merger of the Social Democratic Alliance (ASD), successor to the Braghiş Alliance; the Liberal Party (PL); and the Alliance of Independents (AI). In May 2004 the three primary center-left opposition parties—the AMN, the Democratic Party of Moldova (PDM), and the Social Liberal Party (PSL)—announced the formation of the Democratic Moldova Bloc (BMD). By January 2005, however, two months before the next legislative election, cracks were already showing in the alliance. Three members of the former Braghiş Alliance announced they were running on the Party of Communists (PCRM) list. The following October, 30 senior members of the AMN, including former prime minister Braghiş, left the party to form a new Party of Social Democracy (PDS).

Nine parties, 2 electoral blocs, and 12 independent candidates contested the March 2005 parliamentary elections, with only the PCRM, BMD, and Christian Democratic People's Party (PPCD) meeting the threshold for representation. Twelve parties and 5 independent candidates contested the April 2009 parliamentary election (recent electoral law changes having barred bloc participation), with the PCRM, the PLDM, AMN, and PL meeting the threshold. Following the failure by parliament to elect a president, 8 parties contested the new elections in July, with the PCRM, PLDM, AMN, PL, and ADM meeting the threshold.

Government Parties:

Liberal Democratic Party of Moldova (*Partidului Liberal Democrat din Moldova*—PLDM). The PLDM was founded in December 2007 by Vladimir Filat, a legislator who had left the PDM in September 2007, citing differences with the party leadership. In April 2008 the PLDM began a petition drive to change presidential elections to uninominal, direct elections, thereby confronting the PCRM and emerging as the most vocal opposition party. In the April 2009 elections the PLDM took 12.4 percent of the vote and won 15 seats. In the July balloting the PDLM gained 18 seats on a vote share of 16.6 percent.

Leader: Vladimir FILAT (Prime Minister and President of the Party).

Liberal Party (*Partidul Liberal*—PL). The PL (which should not be confused with the party of the same name that joined in forming the AMN in 2003; see below) was established in 1993 as the center-right Party of Reform (*Partidul Reformei*—PR), which changed its name to the PL in April 2005. The PL supports national unity, withdrawal of Russian forces, and integration into Western institutions.

The PR won 2.4 percent of the vote in the 1994 parliamentary election and 0.5 percent in 1998. In 2001 it joined the National Romanian Party (*Partidul Naţional Român*—PNR) in the Electoral Bloc "Faith and Justice" (*Blocul Electoral "Credinţa şi Dreptate"*—BECD), which won 0.7 percent. It did not compete in 2005. In June 2007 the PL's Dorin Chirtoacă, 28, unexpectedly won election as mayor in Chişinău.

In the April 2009 elections the PL emerged as a significant political force, taking 13.1 percent of the vote and winning 15 seats. In the July balloting it again secured 15 seats (on a vote share of 14.7 percent).

Leaders: Mihai GHIMPU (Acting President of the Republic, Chair of the Party, Speaker of Parliament), Dorin CHIRTOACĂ.

Democratic Party of Moldova (*Partidul Democrat din Moldova*—PDM). The PDM was established in April 2000 as successor to the movement "For a Democratic and Prosperous Moldova" (*Mişcarea "Pentru o Moldovă Democratică şi Prosperă"*—MMDP). The centrist movement had been formed in February 1997 to promote the policies of President Lucinschi. Its leader, Dumitru Diacov, the former deputy speaker of the Parliament, had left the PDAM along with a group of other legislators in a policy dispute over support for the government. For the May 1999 local elections the MMDP joined the Party of Progressive Forces of Moldova (PFPM; see PSRM, below), the Social Political Movement "New Force" (*Mişcarea Social-Politică "Forţă Nouă"*), and an unregistered wing of the Social Democratic Party of Moldova (PSDM, below) under Gheorghe Sima to form the Centrist Alliance of Moldova (*Alianţa Centristă din Moldova*—ACM), which finished second to the Communist-led BCAS bloc.

In October 1999 the decision of four members of the MMDP's legislative delegation to sit as independents cost the government of Prime Minister Sturza its majority.

The formation of the PDM marked Speaker of Parliament Diacov's formal split with President Lucinschi, Diacov having strongly argued against the adoption of a presidential form of government. In 2001, running independently, the PDM failed to win any seats in Parliament. In the 2005 election the PDM won eight seats as a component of the BMD.

In February 2008 the PDM and the **Social Liberal Party** (*Partidul Social-Liberal*—PSL) announced a merger. The PSL was formed in May 2001 under the leadership of Oleg Serebrian. In December 2002 it absorbed the Party of Democratic Forces (*Partidul Forţelor Democratice*—PFD), whose chair, Valeriu MATEI, had finished fifth in the first round of the 1996 presidential election. The center-right PSL favored domestic political reform and integration with the EU. It won three parliamentary seats in 2005. The merger with the DPM was announced as prompted by the need to create a unified opposition party to the PCRM.

In the April 2009 elections the PDM won only approximately 3 percent of the vote. However, the party's fortunes were transformed in June, following the dissolution of parliament and announcement of new elections. Marian Lupu, a prominent member of the PCRM, left that party after stating that "reform from within was not possible." Lupu subsequently joined the PDM as de facto leader, bringing with him about a dozen sitting members of the PCRM parliamentary delegation and a substantial electoral base. Consequently, the PDM won 13 seats in the July balloting on a vote share of 12.5 percent. Subsequently, Lupu became the presidential candidate of the APIE for the balloting scheduled for late October. *(See headnote.)*

Leaders: Marian LUPU (Chair and Former Speaker of Parliament), Dumitru DIACOV (Former Chair), Oleg SEREBRIAN (Vice Chair and Former Chair of the PSL), Ion STURZA (Vice Chair).

Our Moldova Alliance (*Alianţa Moldova Noastră*—AMN). The AMN was formed in July 2003 by a joining of three parties: the Social Democratic Alliance (*Alianţa Social Democrată*—ASD), the Liberal Party (*Partidul Liberal*—PL), and the Alliance of Independents of the Republic of Moldova (*Alianţa Independenţilor din Republica Moldova*—AIRM). The ASD was a successor to the Braghiş Alliance, a group of factions in Parliament supporting former prime minister Dumitru Braghiş, who became a cochair of the AMN. The Liberal Party had itself been established only a year earlier by the merger of Mircea Snegur's Party of Rebirth and Reconciliation of Moldova (*Partidul Renaşterii şi Concilierii din Moldova*—PRCM), the National Peasant Christian-Democratic Party (*Partidul Naţional Ţărănesc Creştin Democrat din Moldova*—PNŢCDM) of former prime minister Valeriu MURAVSCHI (1991–1992), and the Social Liberal Union "Force of Moldova" (*Uniunea Social-Liberală Forţa Moldova*).

The AIRM, formed in October 2001, was led by Serafim Urechean, mayor of Chişinău. The AMN was quickly joined by the People's Democratic Party of Moldova (*Partidul Democrat-Popular din Moldova*—PDPM) and two other small parties. On October 24, 2005, the AMN faced a crisis when 30 members of the national political council, led by Braghiş, announced they were quitting the alliance over policy changes that moved the alliance further to the right. Braghiş soon announced that he was forming a new party (see Party of Social Democracy of Moldova, below).

The AMN formed the core of the center-left Electoral Bloc "Democratic Moldova" (*Blocul Electoral "Moldova Democrată"*—BMD) in the 2005 parliamentary elections. The bloc, which also included the

PDM and PSL, won 28.5 percent of the vote and 34 seats. The AMN was accorded 23 of the seats, although some parliamentarians subsequently left the party's formal voting group to sit as independents due to dissension within the party. The three BMD components ran separately in the June 2007 local elections.

The AMN won 9.8 percent of the vote and 11 seats in the April 2009 legislative elections but declined to a 7.4 percent vote share and 7 seats in the July balloting.

Leader: Serafim URECHEAN (President).

Opposition Party:

Party of Communists of the Republic of Moldova (*Partidul Comuniştilor din Republica Moldova*—PCRM). The PCRM is a successor to the Soviet-era Communist Party of Moldova (*Partidul Comunist din Moldova*—PCM). The latter was suspended in August 1991 but achieved legal status in September 1994 as the PCRM even though many former Communists had by then opted for the Socialist Party of Moldova (PSM, below) as the successor to the former ruling grouping. The party was not legalized until after the 1994 legislative balloting, but it subsequently attracted defectors from other parties.

In 1996 the PCRM sought to build an alliance of "patriotic popular forces" for the fall presidential election, in which party leader Vladimir Voronin finished third in the first round with 10.3 percent of the vote. The PCRM then backed the successful second-round candidacy of Petru Lucinschi and was awarded two ministries in the new government of Ion Ciubuc. Hard-liners within the PCRM announced in February 1997 they were leaving the party to form a new grouping under the old PCM banner, Voronin dismissing the dissenters as "chameleons."

During the legislative campaign of late 1997 and early 1998 the PCRM called for the "rebirth of a socialist society," in which a "pluralist economy" would be supported by a "strengthened" state sector. Party leaders also expressed support for renewed linkage of the sovereign republics that had emerged following the breakup of the Soviet Union as well as close political and military ties with Russia. The PCRM led all parties in the March 1998 balloting with 30 percent of the vote, which earned it a plurality of 40 seats, including 9 non-PCRM supporters.

For the 1999 local elections it spearheaded formation of a Communist, Agrarian, and Socialist Bloc (*Blocul Comuniştilor, Agrarienilor şi Socialiştilor*—BCAS) that also finished first in total district and local council seats. Participants included the PDAM and the Party of Socialists (PSRM, below). In the 2001 election the PCRM won 71 seats, enabling it to elect its chair as president.

The PCRM did not fare as well in the 2005 parliamentary elections, winning only 56 seats. Lacking enough votes to ensure the reelection of Voronin as president, and threatened with a boycott of the presidential election by opposition parties, the PCRM reached out to members of the Democratic Moldova Bloc to gain enough votes to ensure Voronin's reelection. The 2007 local elections saw the PCRM weaken further, slipping from holding 615 district council seats nationwide to 465. Most notably, in Chişinău the PCRM lost the mayoral election. In 2008, however, the party and local coalition allies secured over a third of the seats for the People's Assembly in the autonomous region of Gagauzia, interpreted in the domestic press as arresting the party's decline.

The PCRM won 49.5 percent of the vote and 60 seats in the April 2009 parliamentary elections, falling one seat short of the three-fifths majority necessary to elect a president on its own. In the July balloting the PCRM declined to 44.7 percent of the vote and 48 seats, prompting Voronin's resignation from the presidency and the party's move into opposition status.

Leaders: Vladimir VORONIN (Chair of the Party and Former President of the Republic), Maria POSTOICO (Parliamentary Leader), Eugenia OSTAPCIUC (Former Parliamentary Leader), Marc TKACIUK (Secretary, PCRM Central Committee).

Other Parties that Participated in Both 2009 Legislative Elections:

Christian Democratic People's Party (*Partidul Popular Creştin Democrat*—PPCD). A pro-Romanian party, the PPCD was known until December 1999 as the Christian Democratic People's Front (*Frontal Popular Creştin Democrat*—FPCD). The FPCD was a February 1992 continuation of the former Popular Front of Moldova (*Frontul Popular din Moldova*—FPM), which was formed in 1989 and became the dominant political group following the eclipse of the Communist Party of Moldova in mid-1991. In May 1993 the party's Executive Committee appointed Iurie Roşca as its chair in place of former prime minister Mircea DRUC, who lived in Romania and had become a Romanian citizen. The FPCD won 9 parliamentary seats on a vote share of 7.3 percent in the February 1994 election, subsequently reiterating its commitment to eventual union with Romania. The party backed the unsuccessful reelection bid of President Snegur in 1996.

The FPCD broke with the CDM alliance in March 1999 when it boycotted the confidence vote that installed the Sturza government. The FPCD insisted on four portfolios in the government instead of the two it was offered and, as a result, received none. In November it voted with the Communists against the Sturza government, and in December it supported the Braghiş cabinet.

At a December 1999 party congress the renamed PPCD deleted from its manifesto an insistence on Romanian national unity and instead called for Moldovan integration within Europe and "the fulfillment of national unity in full agreement with the will of the people." In June 2000 the party's vice chair, Valentin DOLGANIUC, and a group of supporters resigned, accusing the party chair of creating an "atmosphere of intolerance and dictatorship" and of abandoning the party's principals through an alliance with the PCRM. Roşca subsequently commented that he viewed eventual unification with Romania as inevitable. The PPCD won 11 parliamentary seats in February 2001.

With the PCRM growing increasingly critical of Russia, the PPCD continued to move closer to the ruling party. Roşca even indicated in April 2005 that he would consider joining the cabinet. This led some party members to join other opposition parties, including, in December 2006, former party vice president Sergiu BURCA, who left for the PSL. After the 2005 elections PPCD seats in Parliament remained at 11; however, several deputies subsequently re-registered as independents.

The PPCD took 3.0 percent of the vote in the April 2009 elections and declined to 1.9 percent in July.

Leaders: Iurie ROŞCA (Chair of Executive Committee), Vlad CUBREACOV (Vice Chair and Parliamentary Leader), Ştefan SECĂREANU (Vice Chair), Ignat VASILACHE (Secretary General).

Social Democratic Party (*Partidul Social Democrat*—PSD). This party was previously known as the Social Democratic Party of Moldova (*Partidul Social-Democrat din Moldova*—PSDM), one of many Moldovan parties to claim a social democratic orientation following independence. The PSDM contested the 1994 election as the core component of the Social Democratic Electoral Bloc (*Blocul Social-Democrat*—BSD), which secured 3.7 percent of the votes, barely missing the 4 percent threshold for parliamentary representation. In 1997 the party suffered a major split, when a wing supporting President Lucinschi separated and formed the United Social Democratic Party of Moldova (*Partidul Social-Democrat Unit din Moldova*—PSDUM) in conjunction with four other groups. In the 1998 election the PSDM, running on its own, won 1.9 percent of the vote, while the electoral alliance of the PSDUM and two other organizations received 1.3 percent. The PSDM subsequently reunited; a dissident group led by the PSDUM's former chair, Gheorghe Sima, ran as part of the Centrist Alliance of Moldova in the 1999 local elections. In 2001 the PSDM won 2.5 percent of the vote.

Prior to the March 2005 elections, the PSDM accused the ruling PCRM of illegally and unethically controlling the Central Election Commission and the country's media to block access by opposition parties. The commission rejected the PSDM charges. Running without an electoral bloc in 2005, the PSDM marginally improved its showing, earning 2.9 percent of the vote.

In June 2008 the PSDM merged with the Party of Social Democracy of Moldova (*Partidul Democraţiei Sociale din Moldova*—PDSM). Founded on April 15, 2006, and led by former prime minister Dumitru Braghiş, the PDSM was formed by disgruntled former members of Our Moldova Alliance. It adopted a social democratic agenda and advocated strong partnerships with the Russian Federation, the United States, and the EU. The party also called for closer relations with Romania and an ultimate withdrawal from the CIS. The PDSM's strong showing in the 2007 district elections left it the fourth-largest opposition party, albeit considerably behind the PDM, AMN, and PPCD.

Upon the 2008 merger of the PSDM and PDSM, the new grouping, which subsequently drew away a faction of the UCM (below) as well, was renamed the PSD, with Braghiş assuming leadership of the new party. In the April 2009 elections the PSD received 3.7 percent of the vote, failing to pass the threshold. In June the leadership of the PSD and UCM announced that the parties would merge by the end of 2009, calling for other centrist parties to join as well. The PSD won 1.9 percent of the vote in the July legislative poll.

Leaders: Dumitru BRAGHIŞ (Chair), Eduard MUŞUC (Secretary General).

Other Parties that Participated in the April 2009 Legislative Elections Only:

Centrist Union of Moldova (*Uniunea Centristă din Moldova*—UCM). Founded in 2000 on a platform that called for adherence to the rule of law and creation of a civil society, the UCM was initially led by Ion MOREI, until he joined the Tarlev cabinet as minister of justice. It won one parliamentary seat in 2001 as part of the Braghiş Alliance but took only 0.8 percent of the vote in 2005. For the April 2009 election, the UCM included members of the PLD and PUM on the UCM candidate list in an effort to combine the parties' support and pass the threshold into parliament without violating the recent ban on electoral blocs. However, the UCM list secured only 2.8 percent of the vote.

Leader: Vasile TARLEV (Chair).

Party of Law and Justice (*Partidul Legii şi Dreptăţii*—PLD). The PLD began as the Party of Social and Economic Justice (*Partidul Dreptăţii Social-Economice din Moldova*—PDSEM), which was formed in February 1998 in time for the March parliamentary elections. The party was badly embarrassed when 16 of its candidates withdrew from the party and the election in protest against the alleged authoritarian rule of the party leader, Marina LIVIŢCHI, who was accused of misappropriating charitable donations for her election campaign. The party received less than 2 percent of the vote in 1998 and was completely marginalized in the 1999 local elections.

With Gen. Nicolae Alexei as its new leader, the PDSEM ran in the 2005 elections on a platform advocating European integration, closer relations with Romania, and popular election of the president. The party failed to improve on its previous performance, winning only 1.7 percent of the vote. In the 2007 district, municipal, city, and village council elections, the renamed PLD won less than 1 percent of the total vote. The PLD did not register for the April 2009 elections, instead negotiating with the UCM for some PLD party members to be included on the UCM candidate list.

Leader: Gen. Nicolae ALEXEI.

Humanist Party of Moldova (*Partidul Umanist din Moldova*—PUM). A conservative party, the PUM was registered in February 2006. The party ran in the local elections of 2007 on a platform that stressed the restoration of "human dignity," with attention to social morals, faith, and economic conditions in the country. The PUM did not register for the April 2009 elections, instead negotiating with the UCM for PUM members to be included on the UCM candidate list.

Leader: Ion MEREUŢA (Chair).

"European Action" Social-Political Movement (*Mişcarea Social-Politică "Acţiunea Europeana"* —MAE). Founded in 2007, the MAE officially called for Molodvan integration into the EU. Many party supporters also reportedly supported the unification of Moldova with Romania. In the April 2009 election the MAE's candidate list included members of the small **National Liberal Party** (*Partidul Naţional Liberal*—PNL). The list won only 1.0 percent of the vote.

Leader: Anatol PETRENCU (Chair).

Republican Party of Moldova (*Partidul Republican din Moldova*—PRM). Established in 1999 under Ion CURTEAN, the PRM joined the PSRM in the *"Edinstvo"* electoral bloc for the 2001 parliamentary election. It won only 0.04 percent of the vote in 2005 and 0.09 percent of the vote in April 2009.

Leader: Ioan CURTEAN (Chair).

Conservative Party (*Partidul Conservator*—PC). Founded in 2006, the PC called for decentralization of governmental authority. It won 0.29 percent of the vote in the April 2009 elections.

Leader: Natalia NIRCA.

Party of Spiritual Development "United Moldova" (*Partidul Dezvoltării Spirituale "Moldova Unită*—PDSMU). Founded in 2005, the PDSMU called for, among other things, greater inclusiveness for women. In the April 2009 election it won 0.22 percent of the vote. It did not formally contest the July balloting but encouraged party members to support the PSD.

Leader: Ana TCACI (Chair).

Other Party that Participated in the July 2009 Legislative Elections Only:

Ecologist Party of Moldova "Green Alliance" (*Partidul Ecologist "Alianţa Verde" din Moldova*—PEAVM). The PEAVM, which had participated in the 2007 elections on its own, ultimately withdrew from the April 2009 balloting, calling upon its supporters to vote for the PLDM. The PEAVM officially returned to the electoral arena for the July balloting, in which it won 0.4 percent of the vote.

Leader: Vladimir BRAGA.

Other Parties:

Electoral Bloc "Motherland" (*Blocul Electoral "Patria-Rodina"*—BEPR). The BEPR was formed in January 2005 by two left-wing parties: the Party of Moldovan Socialists (PSRM) and the Socialist Party of Moldova (PSM). The bloc advocated closer relations with Russia, self-determination for Transnistria, and elimination of the office of president. It opposed accession to the EU and closer relations with the West. The bloc earned only 4.97 percent of the vote in parliamentary elections in 2005, well below the threshold for representation.

Leader: Boris MURAVSCHII.

Party of Socialists of the Republic of Moldova "Patria-Rodina" (*Partidul Socialiştilor din Republica Moldova*—PSRM). The PSRM was organized in 1997 by former PSM members Eduard Smirnov, Valentin KRILOV, and Veronica Abramciuc. In 1996 Abramciuc, running as an independent, had finished last in the presidential race. The party won only 0.6 percent of the national vote in the 1998 parliamentary election. For the February 2001 election it joined the Republican Party of Moldova (PRM, below) and the Party of Progressive Forces of Moldova (*Partidul Forţelor Progresiste din Moldova*—PFPM), which had been established in October 1999 under Valeriu EFREMOV, in forming the Unity Electoral Bloc (*Blocul Electoral "Edinstvo"*).

For the 2007 local elections PSRM joined forces with the Social Movement *"Ravnopravie"* (MSPRR, below) in the Electoral Bloc *"Patria-Rodina–Ravnopravie."*

Leaders: Veronica ABRAMCIUC and Eduard SMIRNOV (Cochairs).

Socialist Party of Moldova (*Partidul Socialist din Moldova*—PSM). Established in 1992 by former members of the proscribed Communist Party (PCM), the pro-Russian PSM ran for Parliament in 1994 as part of the PSMUE electoral bloc, winning 28 seats on a 21.8 percent vote share. The resultant Socialist Union (*Unitatea Socialistă*) parliamentary faction then aligned with the dominant PCRM. In 1996, however, the PSM fell into disarray over the presidential election, in which most of the leadership backed Prime Minister Sangheli but others preferred Petru Lucinschi. With a number of deputies having deserted the party and formed the PSRM, the four-party Socialist Union list won only 1.8 percent of the vote in 1998. In the 1999 local elections the PSM, running independently, fared no better. In 2001 the party joined the Braghiş Alliance.

In the 2007 local elections the PSM ran on its own in a limited number of city and village council races.

Leader: Victor MOREV (Chair).

Motherland-Moldova (*Patria-Moldova*—PM). The PM was formed in September 2007 by merger of the Labor Union "Motherland" (*Uniunea Mundi "Patria-Rodina"*—UMPR) and an organization of Moldovans abroad, the *Asociaţia "Patria-Moldova."* The UMPR dated from 1999, when it was formed by a former PSDM leader, Gheorghe Sima, who then participated in the Centrist Alliance of Moldova (ACM; see under PDM, above). In 2001 the UMPR was part of the Braghiş Alliance. In the 2005 parliamentary election the UMPR won 0.9 percent of the vote. By 2009 the PM had apparently dissolved, with the UMPR under Sima initially registering for the April elections but subsequently withdrawing.

Leaders: Andrei ŢĂRNĂ (Chair), Gheorghe SIMA (Deputy Chair).

Republican Popular Party (*Partidul Popular Republican*—PPR). Founded in 1999 as the Peasants' Christian Democratic Party (*Partidul Ţărănesc Creştin Democrat din Moldova*—PŢCDM), the party changed its name at a party conference in May 2005 to the PPR. The party runs on a platform of improving conditions for the peasants of Moldova, in part through subsidized government loans. More specifically, it has called for a new Parliament of 51 members, each elected individually; for popular election of the president; and for a dramatic reduction in the size of government by cutting the number of ministries down to 6 at most.

The PŢCDM collected 1.4 percent of the vote in 2005. The PPR did not compete in 2009 but stated its support for the UCM.

Leader: Nicolae ANDRONIC (Chair).

Socio-Political Republican Movement "Equality" (*Mişcarea Social-Politică Republicană "Ravnopravie"*—MSPRR). A far-left party, the MSPRR advocates closer relations with Russia and Ukraine, seeks introduction of Russian as an official language, and opposes reunification with Romania. The party won 2.83 percent of the vote in the 2005 parliamentary elections (up from 0.4 percent in 2001), failing to win any seats.

In late 2008 talks were launched with the leadership of the UCM over a potential merger, but no accord was reached. However, the MSPRR in early 2009 announced its support for the UCM in the upcoming legislative 2009 elections, creating friction within the party that led to the ouster of Chair Valerii Klimenko in March. (Some party members maintained that Klimenko remained the legal chair.)

Leaders: Boris SHAPOVALOV (Chair), Valerii KLIMENKO (Former Chair).

Additional parties registered at the time of the 2009 local elections were the **Party "For People and Country"** (*Partidul "Pentru Neam şi Ţară"*—PPNŢ), the **Agrarian Party of Moldova** (*Partidul Agrar din Moldova*—PAM); the **European Party** (*Partidul European*—PE); and the **Movement of Professionals "Hope"** (*Mişcarea Profesioniştilor "Speranţa-Nadejda" din Moldova*—MPSNM), which had been part of the Braghiş Alliance.

Transnistrian Parties:

Renewal (*Obnovleniye*). Established in 2000 as a nongovernmental organization, Renewal competed in the 2000 and 2005 Transnistrian parliamentary elections before becoming officially registered as a party in 2006. Having won 7 seats in 2000 (when most of the victors were officially nonpartisan, although supportive of President Smirnov), Renewal became the majority party in December 2005, winning 23 seats and gaining additional support from allied parties, which won 6 more. Probusiness in orientation, it has campaigned for full independence from Moldova; political reform, including adoption of a parliamentary rather than presidential system; and integration with Europe.

Leaders: Yevgeni SHEVCHUK (Speaker of Parliament), Mikhail BURLA.

Republic (*Respublika*). Long the center of power in Transnistria, Republic began as a social association and emerged as the government party under the leadership of Igor Smirnov and Grigori MARACUTSA, Transnistria's president and parliamentary speaker, respectively. In the December 2005 election, however, Republic won only 13 seats, losing its majority status, after which Maracutsa was replaced as speaker.

Leaders: Gen. Aleksandr KOROLYOV, Vladimir RILYAKOV.

Transnistria's political party system is becoming increasingly complex, with more than half a dozen new parties registering in 2006–2007 alone. Some are closely associated with particular business interests. Among the more prominent of the current parties are the **Patriotic Party of Pridnestrovie,** chaired by Oleg SMIRNOV, son of the president; the **Social Democratic Party of Pridnestrovie,** which, led by Aleksandr RADCHENKO, is the principal advocate of full union with Moldova; and the **Pridnestrovie Communist Party,** whose candidate for president in 2006, Nadezhda BONDARENKO, finished second, with 8 percent of the vote. Several other parties have close ties to established parties in Russia.

LEGISLATURE

In May 1991 the unicameral Supreme Soviet was redesignated as the **Parliament** (*Parlamentul*), which is elected for a four-year term by proportional representation from a single nationwide district. There are currently 101 members. Previously, the thresholds to gain representation were 6 percent for individual parties, 9 percent for two-party coalitions, and 12 percent for three-party blocs. Changes to the electoral code in 2008 banned coalitions, although some parties circumvented the ban in the April 2009 elections by having candidates from several parties run on the list of one of the parties. The thresholds were changed prior to the July 2009 balloting to 3 percent for independents and 5 percent for parties.

Following the April 5, 2009, elections, the seats were distributed as follows: the Party of Communists of the Republic of Moldova (PCRM), 60; the Liberal Party (PL), 15; the Liberal Democratic Party of Moldova (PLDM), 15; and Our Moldova Alliance (AMN), 11. However, the newly-elected parliament was unable to elect a president of the republic, and new legislative elections were held on July 29, after which the seats were distributed as follows: the PCRM, 48: PLDM, 18; PL, 15; the Democratic Party of Moldova, 13; and the AMN, 7.

Speaker: Mihai GIMPU.

CABINET

[as of September 25, 2009]

Prime Minister	Vladimir Filat (PLDM)
Deputy Prime Ministers	Valeriu Lazăr (PDM)
	Iurie Leancă (PLDM)
	Ion Negrei (PL)
	Victor Osipov (AMN)
Ministers	
Agriculture and Processing Industry	Valeriu Cosarciuc (AMN)
Construction and Regional Development	Marcel Răducan (PDM)
Culture	Boris Focşa (PDM)
Defense	Vitalie Marinuţa (PL)
Economy	Valeriu Lazăr (PDM)
Education	Leonid Bujor (AMN)
Environment	Gheorghe Şalaru (PL)
External Affairs and European Integration	Iurie Leancă (PLDM)
Finance	Veaceslav Negruţă (PLDM)
Health	Vladimir Hotineau (PLDM)
Information Technology and Communications	Alexandru Oleinic (AMN)
Internal Affairs	Victor Catan (PLDM)
Justice	Alexandru Tănase (PLDM)
Social Protection, Family, and Children	Valentina Buliga (PDM) [f]
State Minister	Victor Bodiu (PLDM)
Transport and Roads	Anatol Şalaru (PL)
Youth and Sports	Ion Ciobanu (PL)

[f] = female

COMMUNICATIONS

Although the constitution guarantees freedom of the press, reports by nongovernment media monitoring groups in Moldova have charged that the government tightly controls the country's electronic media, resulting in coverage biased toward the ruling PCRM. Indeed, according to the Canada-based International Freedom of Expression Exchange and the Committee to Protect Journalists, during 2003, opposition media reporting on government corruption or other topics considered troublesome "endured police raids, the confiscation of archival material, detentions, and interrogations" as well as efforts to discourage advertisers. The Parliament passed a new Audiovisual Code in 2006, promising more press freedom and privatization of national media stations. In 2007, however, the government closed two radio stations, Antena C and BlueStar, as well as one television channel, Euro TV. Analysts noted that the stations had broadcast reports critical of the government and that closure came in advance of local elections. A report in 2007 by Freedom House, a U.S.-based human rights organization, placed Moldova in the category of "unfree states" in its assessment of media independence. Reporters Without Borders in 2008 criticized a "worsening" media climate, including government use of criminal investigations against media outlets. In 2009 the OSCE noted complaints that the Moldovan government on multiple occasions restricted travel or access by journalists. This included both the deportation of Romanian journalists accused of involvement in organizing protests against the April election results, and the detention or house arrest of Moldovan journalists.

Press. The following are Moldovan dailies published in Chişinău, unless otherwise noted: *Moldova Suverenă* (Sovereign Moldova, 100,000), government organ; *Nezavisimaya Moldova* (Independent Moldova, 60,000), independent, in Russian; *Flux* (Flux, 60,000), weekly; *Viaţă Satuli* (Life of the Village, 50,000), triweekly government organ; *Timpul* (Times, 36,000); *Tinerimea Moldovei/Molodezh Moldovy* (Youth of Moldova; 16,000 Romanian, 2,000 Russian); *Ţara* (Homeland, 18,000), PPCD organ; *Trudovoi Tiraspol* (Working Tiraspol, 7,500), antigovernment Russian organ. An Internet media presence is growing. Online news sources include reporter.md and infoprim.md.

News agency. The domestic facility is the National News Agency "Moldpres" (*Agenţia Naţională de Presă*), headquartered in Chişinău.

Broadcasting and computing. In 1994 a presidential decree ordered a consolidation of broadcast activity into a new State Radio and Television Company of Moldova (*Compania de Stat Teleradio-Moldova*). Private commercial radio and television stations also broadcast or relay Romanian and Russian transmissions.

As of 2008 there were 233.9 Internet users per 1,000 inhabitants.

INTERGOVERNMENTAL REPRESENTATION

Ambassador to the U.S.: Nicolae CHIRTOACA.

U.S. Ambassador to Moldova: Asif CHAUDHRY.

Permanent Representative to the UN: Alexandru CUJBA.

IGO Memberships (Non-UN): BSEC, CEI, CEUR, CIS, EBRD, Eurocontrol, Interpol, IOM, OIF, OSCE, WCO, WTO.

MONACO

Principality of Monaco
Principauté de Monaco

Political Status: Independent principality founded in the 13th century; constitutional monarchy since 1911; present constitution promulgated December 17, 1962 (amended in April 2002).

Area: 0.70 sq. mi. (1.81 sq. km.).

Population: 32,020 (2000C); 34,000 (2008E).

Major Urban Center (2005E): MONACO-VILLE (1,100).

Official Language: French.

Monetary Unit: Euro (market rate December 1, 2009: 1 euro = $1.51US). Although not a member of the European Union (EU), Monaco was authorized by the EU to adopt the euro as its official currency and mint a limited supply of Monégasque euro coins.

Sovereign: Prince ALBERT II; acceded to the throne April 6, 2005, following the death of his father, Prince RAINIER III; formally installed in two-part process on July 12 and November 19, 2005.

Heiress Presumptive: Princess CAROLINE Louise Marguerite Grimaldi, elder sister of the sovereign.

Minister of State: Jean-Paul PROUST; assumed office June 1, 2005, following nomination by the sovereign to succeed Patrick LECLERCQ.

THE COUNTRY

A tiny but celebrated enclave on the Mediterranean coast nine miles from Nice, Monaco is surrounded on three sides by France. The principality is divided into four districts: Monaco-Ville (the capital, built on a rocky promontory about 200 feet above sea level), Monte Carlo (the tourist quarter), La Condamine (the business district around the port), and Fontvieille (the industrial district). A majority of the citizenry is of foreign origin, primarily French or Italian. Monégasques constitute approximately 19 percent of the population and speak their own language, a combination of French and Italian. Roman Catholicism is the state religion, and French is the official language, although other European languages, in addition to Monégasque, are also spoken.

The principality's main sources of income are tourism, import-export trade, its services as a financial center, corporate and indirect taxes, and an expanding industrial base. Shipping is also of growing importance, while gambling, despite the renown of the Monte Carlo Casino and the success of the American-style Loew's Monte Carlo, has recently accounted for no more than 4 percent of the country's income. Such light industrial products as plastics, processed foods, pharmaceuticals, glass, precision instruments, and cosmetics yield about one-third of the GDP. Customs, postal services, telecommunications, and banking are governed by an economic union with France established in 1956.

Concerted land reclamation efforts begun in the 1960s succeeded in expanding the principality's total area by some 23 percent in the following 40 years, with some of the new acreage sold for private development consistent with the government's urban master plan. A new convention center, the Grimaldi Forum, opened in 2000 as part of a more recent effort to attract such business-related activities as conferences and seminars. Development interests also include Internet-based services and expansion of the Port de la Condamine.

In general, the principality's economic status reflects that of France. Monaco is also directly dependent on the French labor force; each business day an estimated 40,000 French workers cross the border, more than doubling the population. Although the government does not routinely publish economic statistics, the per capita income is understood to be one of the highest in the world.

A period of stagnation in the mid-1990s was followed by significant recovery and sustained growth starting in 1997. Growth was estimated at 2.5–3.0 percent in 2008, and the effects on Monaco's economy of the global downturn were expected to be relatively minor in 2009.

GOVERNMENT AND POLITICS

Political background. Ruled by the Grimaldi family since 1297, the Principality of Monaco has maintained its separate identity in close association with France, under whose protection it was placed in 1861. A 1918 treaty stipulated that Monégasque policy had to conform with French political, military, naval, and economic interests. A further treaty of July 17, 1919, provided for Monaco's conversion to an autonomous state under French guidance should the reigning prince die without leaving a male heir. New conventions redefining the French-Monégasque relationship were signed in 1963 in response to the principality's status as a tax refuge, and the earlier treaties were superseded in 2005 (see Foreign relations, below, for details).

In the 1960s Prince RAINIER III, who had acceded to the throne in 1949, embarked on a three-year struggle with shipping magnate Aristotle S. Onassis for control of the *Société des Bains de Mer* (SBM), a corporation that owns the Monte Carlo Casino, main hotels, clubs, restaurants, and considerable Monégasque real estate. Monaco gained control of the company in 1967 by buying out Onassis's majority shareholdings.

World attention focused briefly on the principality again in 1982, following the death of Princess GRACE (the former American actress Grace Kelly) as the result of an automobile accident in the Côte d'Azur region. Subsequently, the passing of the princess was viewed as representing a fiscal as well as personal loss for Monégasques, whose economy, based in large part on tourism, had recently stagnated, with income from both real estate and gambling receding sharply over previous years.

Elections to the National Council in January 1993 appeared to mark a movement toward more competitive politics, although groupings remained electoral lists rather than parties as such. In December 1994 Paul DIJOUD (a former French ambassador to Mexico) was sworn in as Monaco's minister of state (chief minister) in succession to Jacques

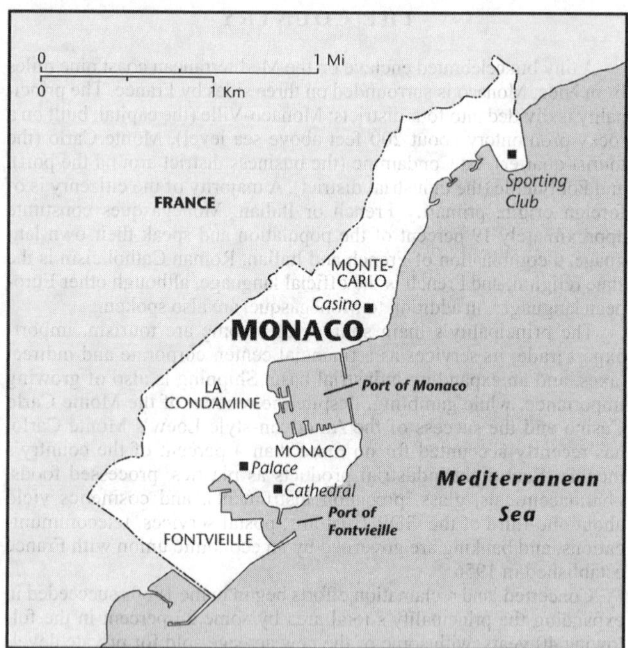

DUPONT. Dijoud was succeeded on February 3, 1997, by Michel LÉVÊQUE, another long-standing member of the French diplomatic corps who had most recently served as ambassador to Algeria. Elections on February 1 and 8, 1998, resulted in the capture of all council seats by the list of the National and Democratic Union (*Union Nationale et Démocratique*—UND), which had dominated every council election since its formation in 1962.

On January 1, 2000, Patrick LECLERCQ succeeded Michel Lévêque, who had retired as minister of state. Like his predecessors, Leclercq had a long history of diplomatic service to France, including, most recently, as ambassador to Spain.

The UND's long domination of the National Council came to a surprisingly dramatic end in the balloting of February 6, 2003, when it secured only 3 of the 24 seats in the National Council. The Union for Monaco (*Union pour Monaco*—UPM) list, presented by three allied parties, secured the other 21 seats.

Prince Rainer died on April 6, 2005, after an extended illness, and he was succeeded immediately by his son, ALBERT Alexandre Louis Pierre, who became Prince ALBERT II. Subsequently, the new sovereign named Jean-Paul PROUST, a former chief of police in Paris, to succeed Leclercq as minister of state. The current heiress presumptive is Albert's elder sister, Princess CAROLINE Louise Marguerite Grimaldi.

The election of February 3, 2008, closely mirrored the 2003 election, with the UPM, now a coalition of only two parties, again winning 21 seats.

Constitution and government. As amended in 2002, the 1962 constitution (replacing the one of 1911) vests executive power in the hereditary prince or princess, grants universal suffrage, outlaws capital punishment, and guarantees the rights of association and trade unionism. The sovereign rules in conjunction with a minister of state, who is assisted by a cabinet (Council of Government), whose members, like the minister of state and all other palace personnel, are appointed by the sovereign.

Traditionally, the legislature (the National Council) has had few powers, although the 2002 constitutional amendments authorized the council to review budgets, introduce members' private bills, and ratify certain treaties and other international agreements. Advice on constitutional, treaty, and other matters may be offered by a 7-member Crown Council, while a 12-member State Council advises the sovereign in such areas as legislation, regulations, and law and order.

Municipal affairs in the four *quartiers* are conducted by a 15-member elected Communal Council (*Conseil Communal*), with the mayor of Monaco-Ville presiding. The judiciary includes a Supreme Court of five full and two deputy members, all named by the sovereign on the basis of nominations by the National Council and other institutions. In addition, a Review Court considers appeals based on alleged violations of law. At lower levels there are a district court, a labor court, a court of the first instance, and a court of appeals. The majority of judges are French nationals.

The 2002 amendments in part focused on succession to the throne, an issue that had come to the forefront because Prince Albert (Prince Rainier's son) had never married and thereby had no legitimate male heirs. (Prince Albert has recently acknowledged having fathered two illegitimate children, but they are precluded from the line of succession.). Under the 2002 revisions, which technically entered into effect upon French ratification in 2005 of a 2002 treaty (see Foreign relations, below), the long-standing principle of male primogeniture was modified to permit succession by a female sibling and her descendants in the event a reigning sovereign leaves no direct, legitimate male heir.

Foreign relations. Monaco's foreign relations were traditionally controlled by France, based on treaties from the early 1900s (see Political background, above, for details). However, those treaties were superseded by a new "Treaty adapting and confirming relations of friendship and co-operation between the French Republic and the Principality of Monaco," which was signed in Paris on October 24, 2002, and ratified by France on October 13, 2005. Most significantly, the new treaty ended Monaco's subservience to French policy, replacing it with the principle of sovereign equality in the context of historically "close and privileged relations." Furthermore, a new "Convention to adapt and develop administrative co-operation between the French Republic and the Principality," signed in November 2005 as a replacement for a 1930 convention, gave preference in senior government and civil service appointments to Monégasques. Consultation with Paris on major appointments remains the rule, but such senior positions as minister of state are no longer filled on a pro forma basis by French nationals. The principality participates indirectly in the European Union (EU) by virtue of its customs union with France. Prior to joining the United Nations (UN) in 1993, it maintained a Permanent Observer's office at UN headquarters in New York and had long belonged to a number of UN specialized agencies.

In 1994 Monaco signed an agreement with France providing for coordinated action against money laundering and requiring Monégasque banks and other institutions to report dubious financial transactions to the authorities. However, dissatisfaction with Monaco's progress in this regard surfaced in 1998 when young reformist judges alleged that the old guard was being lax in its prosecution. Consequently, overruling Prince Rainier, Paris appointed new prosecutors and chief judges. Stung by criticism (*Le Monde* characterized Monaco as a "refuge for cheats"), the government released a report in January 1999 denying that inappropriate activity was prevalent in the principality and attacking the "myth" of Monaco as a "superficial playground." In part, the report was seen as a component of the government's campaign to gain membership in the Council of Europe, which at first reportedly considered Monaco as neither fully sovereign nor sufficiently democratic. In October 2004, in consideration of the 2002 treaty revisions, an ongoing legal reform process, and the successful conduct of the 2003 legislative election under a new election law, Monaco was admitted to the Council of Europe.

Pressure on the principality increased in February 2008 after German officials bribed a bank official in Liechtenstein to release private bank records, which exposed many German nationals who were evading taxes. Monaco's practices fell under more scrutiny because Liechtenstein, in addition to Monaco, was among those cited by the Organization for Economic Cooperation and Development (OECD) as retaining harmful tax policies. In March 2009, however, Monaco bowed to international pressure and agreed to follow OECD regulations on tax evasion. Subsequently, the principality was removed from the "black list" and placed on a "gray list," pending implementation of reforms. Minister of State Jean-Paul Proust subsequently announced that Monaco planned to take actions necessary to be removed from the gray list by the end of the year.

Current issues. The 2003 National Council election was widely viewed as a generational battle between the "young lion," Stéphane VALÉRI of the UPM coalition, and the UND's longtime leader, National Council President Jean-Louis CAMPORA, who had served in the council for 30 years. The overwhelming UPM victory was also attributed to the electorate's desire for "modernization."

Prince Rainier's death in 2005 marked the end of a remarkable 56-year reign in which he had shepherded Monaco from a gambling "toy town" into an economically lively and diverse state. As expected,

Prince Albert pledged to continue his father's policies, although the new government he subsequently appointed included a new department for external affairs, underscoring the need for the principality to keep pace with the fast-changing European landscape. In that context, Monaco began systematically (but slowly) reviewing and adopting some 200 Council of Europe conventions in an effort to cement its broader ties to Europe. The conventions, which cover legal, social, economic, institutional, and diplomatic concerns, also necessitated reform of many domestic laws and codes.

Under Prince Albert, Monaco continued to focus on expanding its economy, with shipping and cruise-ship tourism, in particular, showing strong growth prior to the global financial crisis that began in 2008. The nation's ongoing positive economic performance appeared to buttress support in the February 2008 elections for the governing UPM, which secured 53 percent of the vote, compared to 40 percent for the UND-led Rally and Issues for Monaco and 7 percent for Monaco Together (see Political Parties, below, for additional information).

Some analysts view a lack of office space and affordable housing as inhibiting more rapid expansion. In response, the government has begun efforts to create new office space on underutilized land. In addition, in 2006 the principality requested bids on a new, ten-year land reclamation project that would add 25 acres and possibly 4,000 residents to Monaco. However, in 2008 environmentalists alleged that the expansion could extensively damage the ecosystem. Prince Albert an ardent environmentalist, suspended the project in December 2008, pending a review of the environmental impact. Also reflecting the prince's environmental concerns, in March 2009 Monaco agreed to work toward zero emissions of carbon.

POLITICAL PARTIES

Although a party system is slowly developing, at present there is no political party law distinguishing parties from other associations. Nor is there public funding of parties except for small reimbursements to help cover election expenses. As explained by a 2007 report by the Monitoring Committee of the Council of Europe: "The primary function of a party in the Principality is not to attain power and thus enter government . . . but only to contribute to the management of the State's affairs whilst permanently seeking a compromise between the will of the Prince and the expectations of Monégasques as represented by the National Council."

In the absence of formal political parties, Monaco's politics were until recently dominated for nearly four decades by the **National and Democratic Union** (*Union Nationale et Démocratique*—UND). Formed in 1962 through the merger of the National Union of Independents (*Union Nationale des Indépendants*) and the National Democratic Entente (*Entente Nationale Démocratique*), the UND won all 18 National Council seats in the elections of 1968, 1978, 1983, and 1988. In 1993, when the UND captured 15 seats, it was sometimes informally referenced as the Campora List (*Liste Campora*), reflecting the leadership of Jean-Louis Campora, who was elected president of the new council to succeed long-term UND leader Jean-Charles REY. Two seats were also won in 1993 by the Médecin List (*Liste Médecin*), led by Jean-Louis MÉDECIN, the former mayor of Monaco-Ville. The UND list was credited with winning all the seats in the 1998 elections in competition with lists from the **National Union for the Future of Monaco** (*Union Nationale pour l'Avenir de Monaco*—UNAM) and the **Rally for the Monégasque Family** (*Rassemblement de la Famille Monégasque*—RFM).

In 2003 the UNAM, the **Promotion of the Monégasque Family** (*Promotion de la Famille Monégasque*—PFM, as the RFM had been renamed), and the **Union for the Principality** (*Union pour la Principauté*—UP) combined forces under an opposition Union for Monaco (*Union pour Monaco*—UPM) list. Led by former UND member Stéphane Valéri, now of the UP, the UPM won 21 of 24 seats, with the balance going to the UND list of the Rally for Monaco (*Rassemblement pour Monaco*—RPM).

In January 2006 the PFM, led by René GIORDANO, left the UPM. Also during 2006 UND councilor Christine PASQUIER-CIULLA formed her own **Monégasque Party** (*Parti Monégasque*—PM), while in September former UNAM vice chair Claude BOISSON and the UP's Vincent PALMARO established the **Principality, Ethics, and Progress** (*Principauté, Éthique, et Progrès*—PEP) party.

On February 3, 2008, the UPM, now comprising only the UP and the UNAM, repeated its 2003 win, securing 21 seats as Valéri urged voters to support the "evolution" of UPM programs. The conservative coalition called the Rally and Issues for Monaco (*Rassemblement et Enjeux pour Monaco*—REM), consisting of the RPM (led by Guy MAGNAN) and the **Values and Issues** (*Valeurs & Enjeux*) party (led by Laurent NOUVION) won 3 seats. A third coalition (Monaco Together [*Monaco Ensemble*—ME]), which included the PFM, **Monégasque Synergy** (*Synergie Monegasque*—SM), and the **Association of Non-Attached Monégasques** (*Association des Nom Inscrits Monégasques*—NIM), also took part in the election but won no seats with only about 7 percent of the vote. The PM did not participate in the election because it did not have a slate of at least 13 candidates as required by law. The PEP candidates ran under the banner of the RPM.

LEGISLATURE

The **National Council** (*Conseil National*) is a 24-seat unicameral body elected via direct universal suffrage for a five-year term. Councilors are elected from one multimember national constituency, and voters can vote for up to 24 candidates. Sixteen seats are filled by the top vote-getters, with the balance then being chosen by proportional representation from those lists receiving at least 5 percent of the vote. (The proportional element was introduced in 2002 at the request of the Council of Europe.) In the most recent election on February 3, 2008, the seat distribution was as follows: the Union for Monaco, 21 (Union for the Principality, 15; National Union for the Future of Monaco, 6); and the Rally and Issues for Monaco, 3.

President: Stéphane VALÉRI.

CABINET

[as of July 1, 2009]

Minister of State	Jean-Paul Proust
Councilors	
Finance and Economy	Sophie Thevenoux [f]
Foreign Affairs	Franck Biancheri
Health and Social Affairs	Jean-Jacques Campana
Interior	Paul Masseron
Public Works, Environment, and Urban Affairs	Gilles Tonell

COMMUNICATIONS

Given Monaco's small population and its location, most residents depend on French mass media for much of their information. A law on freedom of the media was passed in July 2005.

Press. The principality publishes an official *Journal de Monaco,* a weekly that includes new laws and decrees; other publications include the weekly *Monaco Hebdo* (3,000) and the monthly *Observateur de Monaco* and *Gazette de Monaco.* French newspapers are widely read, and special Monaco editions of *Nice-Matin* and *L'Espoir de Nice* are published in Nice.

News agency. *Agence France-Presse* is the principal international facility.

Broadcasting and computing. Of the three local radio stations, *Radio Monte Carlo* (RMC) has long been predominant. The only television station, *Télé Monte Carlo,* is owned by a French company. *Monaco Télécom,* partly owned by the state, holds the public service broadcasting license and offers the only cable television service. *Monaco Info,* a cable channel, is a government news service.

As of 2008 there were 672.5 Internet users per 1,000 inhabitants.

INTERGOVERNMENTAL REPRESENTATION

Monaco maintains consuls general in Washington and New York, while the U.S. consul general in Nice, France, also services U.S. interests in Monaco.

Ambassador to the U.S.: Gilles Alexandre NOGHÈS.

U.S. Ambassador to Monaco: Charles H. RIVKIN.

Permanent Representative to the UN: Isabelle F. PICCO.

IGO Memberships (Non-UN): CEUR, Eurocontrol, Interpol, OIF, OSCE.

MONGOLIA

Monggol Ulus

Note: Prime Minister Sanj Bayar, citing ill health, resigned from office on October 25, 2009. Four days later, the State Great Hural confirmed Minister of Foreign Affairs Sukhgaatar Batbold (Mongolian People's Revolutionary Party) as his successor.

Political Status: Independent since 1921; Communist People's Republic established November 26, 1924; multi-party system introduced by constitutional amendment of May 11, 1990; current constitution adopted January 13, 1992, in effect from February 12.

Area: 604,247 sq. mi. (1,565,000 sq. km.).

Population: 2,373,493 (2000C); 2,659,000 (2008E).

Major Urban Centers (2005E): ULAANBAATAR (Ulan Bator, 936,000), Erdenet (82,000), Darhan (64,000), Choybalsan (40,000).

Monetary Unit: Tugrik (market rate December 1, 2009: 1,453.00 tugriks = $1US).

Official Language: Khalkha Mongol.

President: Tsakhiagiyn ELBEGDORJ (Democratic Party), popularly elected for a four-year term on May 24, 2009, and sworn in on June 18, succeeding Nambaryn ENKHBAYAR (Mongolian People's Revolutionary Party).

Prime Minister: *(See headnote.)* Sanj BAYAR (Mongolian People's Revolutionary Party); appointed by the State Great Hural on November 22, 2007, succeeding Miyeegombo ENKHBOLD (Mongolian People's Revolutionary Party); reappointed by the State Great Hural on September 11, 2008, and formed new government on September 22.

THE COUNTRY

Traditionally known as Outer Mongolia (i.e., that portion of historic Mongolia lying north of the Gobi Desert), the present country of Mongolia occupies a vast area of steppe, mountain, and desert between the Russian Federation on the north and the People's Republic of China on the south. Khalkha Mongols make up 82 percent of the population. The remainder are other Mongol groups (often speaking their own dialects); Turkic-speaking peoples; and Chinese, Russian, and Tungusic minorities. Until 1989 the state restricted religious functions, although guaranteeing freedom of religion. Lamaist Buddhism is the prevalent faith, practiced by an estimated 40 percent of the population, even though its leadership was largely wiped out by antireligious activity in 1937–1939. Islam is practiced by the small Kazakh minority (4 percent), and there are also small numbers of Christians and shamanists. Some 51 percent of the active labor force is female, but women constitute only 4 percent of the legislators elected in 2008.

The Mongolian economy was traditionally pastoral, and agriculture, especially animal husbandry, continues to account for 19 percent of GDP while employing 34 percent of the domestic labor force. Moreover, manufacturing is largely devoted to processing agricultural products into such goods as cashmere and textiles. The nonservice economy is largely driven by ore extraction and processing, chiefly of copper and gold, which together accounted for 60 percent of the country's export earnings in 2005. One of the world's largest copper-molybdenum facilities is located in Erdenet, while full production at the massive Oyu Tolgoi copper-gold mine was expected to begin by 2011 (see Current issues, below). Other mineral resources include uranium, fluorspar, coal, tungsten, and recently discovered petroleum. The services sector accounts for roughly 42 percent of GDP and employs about 60 percent of the labor force. More than 33 percent of the population lives below the poverty line.

For decades Mongolia relied heavily on Soviet aid, and the breakup of the Soviet Union precipitated a severe economic crisis in the first half of the 1990s. As Mongolia began privatizing state-owned enterprises, financial assistance from the West and international institutions helped support an economic recovery, with annual GDP growth averaging over 3 percent in 1996–1999. The growth rate fell to 1.1 percent in 2000–2001, largely as a consequence of adverse weather, but soared to 10.8 percent in 2004 and 9.9 percent in 2007, as world prices for copper and gold rose and livestock production recovered.

In the wake of the global financial crisis, commodity prices declined dramatically in 2008, inflation soared to an estimated 28 percent, and tax revenue declined. Nearly $1 billion in foreign aid, including $300 million in agriculture credits from Russia, helped keep the government functioning during the crisis. Annual GDP growth in 2009 was expected to slow to around 2 percent, with prices for copper and other commodities remaining low. On a positive note, the IMF in April 2009 approved an arrangement for loaning $229 million to the government in stages. The program's goal was to keep government deficits below 6 percent of annual GDP, strengthen the banking sector through further regulation and supervision, and cut some social spending without reducing aid to the poorest people in the country.

GOVERNMENT AND POLITICS

Political background. The home of such legendary figures as Genghis Khan and Tamerlane, Mongolia fell under Chinese control in the 17th century and continued under Chinese suzerainty for over 200 years. The fall of the Manchu dynasty resulted in a brief period of independence from 1911 until 1919, when Chinese hegemony was reestablished. Two years later Mongolian revolutionary leaders Sukhe BATOR and Horloogiyn CHOYBALSAN (Khorloin CHOIBALSAN) defeated the Chinese with Soviet assistance and established permanent independence.

Initially, a constitutional monarchy was created under Jebtsun Damba KHUTUKHTU, but following his death in 1924 the Mongolian People's Party (founded in 1921) was renamed the Mongolian People's Revolutionary Party (MPRP), and the Mongolian People's Republic was proclaimed as the first Communist state outside the Soviet Union. Rightist influences, including a major revolt in 1932, were suppressed, and Choybalsan gained the ascendancy in 1934–1939, after which he continued to dominate both party and government until his death in 1952.

Yumjaagiyn TSEDENBAL was named chair of the Council of Ministers in 1952 and, after a two-year period of apparent political eclipse, succeeded Dashiyn DAMBA as MPRP first secretary in 1958. In addition, in 1974 he was named chair of the Presidium of the People's Great Hural. In 1984 Tsedenbal was relieved of his government and party posts, reportedly because of failing health, with Jambyn BATMÖNH being named MPRP secretary general. Upon designation as Presidium chair in December, Batmönh relinquished the chair of the Council of Ministers to Dumajiyn SODNOM. Both were reconfirmed following the 19th MPRP Congress in 1986.

In obvious response to the unprecedented pace of political change in Eastern Europe, the regime in December 1989 permitted the organization of an opposition Mongolian Democratic Union (MDU), which mounted a series of demonstrations calling for political and economic reforms. In February 1990 some 300 MDU adherents organized the Mongolian Democratic Party (MDP), which was tacitly recognized by Batmönh via a greeting to its initial congress. A number of other opposition groups also emerged.

At an MPRP Central Committee plenum in March 1990 the entire Politburo was replaced, with Gombojavyn OCHIRBAT succeeding Batmönh as party leader. Later in the month, the minister of foreign economic relations, Punsalmaagiyn OCHIRBAT (no relation to the party leader), succeeded Batmönh as head of state, and Sharavyn GUNGAADORJ replaced Sodnom as chair of the Council of Ministers. Significantly, neither was a member of the MPRP top leadership.

In May 1990 the Great Hural approved constitutional amendments that formally abandoned the one-party system and provided for a proportionally elected standing body (Little Hural) to complement the existing legislature. At the ensuing election in July–August the MPRP

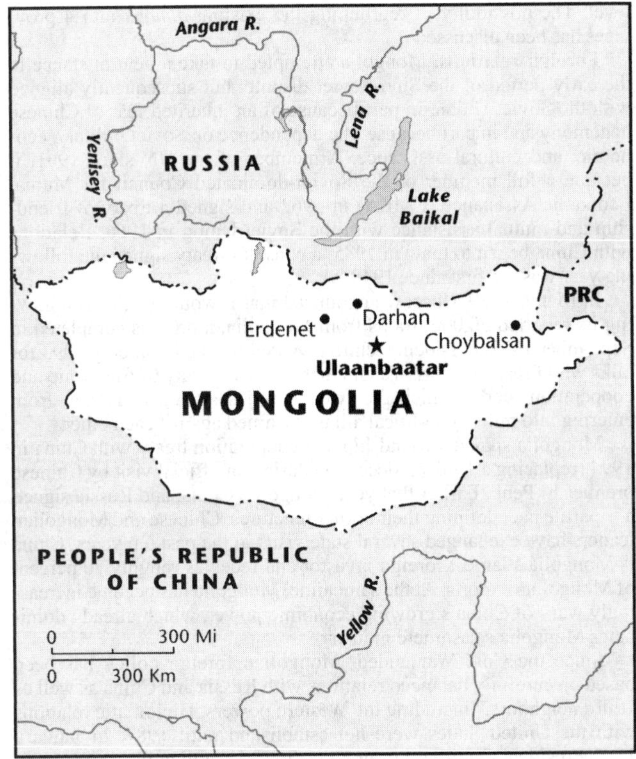

won approximately four-fifths of the seats in the Great Hural and nearly two-thirds of those in the Little Hural, but a three-party opposition Coalition of Democratic Forces also won representation. In September the Great Hural named Punsalmaagiyn Ochirbat to the new post of state president and elected Radnaasümbereliyn GONCHIGDORJ of the recently organized Mongolian Social Democratic Party (MSDP) as state vice president and chair of the Little Hural. A week later Dashiyn BYAMBASÜREN succeeded Gungaadorj as chief of government (now termed prime minister) and on the following day named a "coalition" government that did not, however, include representatives of the MDP.

In June 1992, under a new constitution, an election for a reinstituted unicameral legislature saw the MPRP capturing 71 of 76 seats even though opposition parties won 40 percent of the vote. In July the Great Hural elected a free-market economist, Puntsagiyn JASRAY, as prime minister, and in August an all-MPRP administration was announced.

In April 1993 a special MPRP congress refused to nominate President Ochirbat for popular reelection, selecting instead Lodongiyn TUDEV, editor of the party newspaper *Ünen*. As a result, Ochirbat agreed to stand as joint candidate of the MSDP and the Mongolian National Democratic Party (MNDP), and on June 6 he retained the presidency, winning 57.8 percent of the vote.

The legislative poll of June 30, 1996, marked the end of more than seven decades of communist rule. A recently organized Democratic Union (DU), led by the MNDP and the MSDP, defeated the MPRP by an unexpected two-to-one margin. Thirty days later the coalition's leader, Mendsaikhan ENKHSAIKHAN, formed a new government. However, the MPRP quickly regained a dominant position in the provincial and municipal elections of October 1996. Moreover, the MPRP's Natsagiyn BAGABANDI overwhelmed incumbent president Ochirbat, the DU nominee, by 60.8 percent to 29.8 percent in the May 1997 presidential election.

In January 1998 the Great Hural approved a measure that would permit its members to serve concurrently as government ministers. In April the governing organs of the MNDP and MSDP both recommended that the DU chair, Tsakhiagiyn ELBEGDORJ of the MNDP, assume the prime ministership, leading Prime Minister Enkhsaikhan to tender his resignation. A week later, the Great Hural endorsed Elbegdorj by a vote of 61–5. For more than a month, however, parliamentary infighting led to rejection of several ministerial nominees, with the cabinet that was ultimately assembled consisting entirely of legislators.

In late May 1998 the MPRP precipitated a parliamentary crisis when its delegation began a boycott of the Great Hural following approval (subsequently rescinded) of a merger involving the bankrupt public Renovation Bank with a private bank. With the legislative process paralyzed by the boycott, in July the Great Hural passed a no-confidence motion 42–33, and as a consequence the prime minister resigned a scant three months after taking office.

With the Elbegdorj cabinet staying on as caretakers, the DU leadership and the MPRP's Bagabandi were soon at loggerheads. The president repeatedly rejected the coalition's nominee for prime minister, Davaadorgjiyn GANBOLD of the MNDP. On August 31, 1998, the president accepted DU nominee Rinchinnyamiin AMARJARGAL, the outgoing minister of foreign affairs, but on September 2 the Great Hural defeated the nomination 36–35. Before the end of the month the president had rejected two additional nominees, while on October 2 the country was deeply shaken when an apparent MNDP compromise candidate, Sanjaasürengiyn ZORIG, who had been a principal leader of the prodemocracy movement in 1989–1990, was killed in his home. The political stalemate continued, with Ganbold again being rejected by the president for a sixth and a seventh time, and the DU refusing to nominate any of six potential candidates deemed acceptable by Bagabandi.

On November 24, 1998, the Constitutional Court ruled for the second time in less than a month that the constitution prohibited members of the Great Hural from serving as prime minister or in the cabinet. The decision apparently helped break the impasse, and on December 9, having received the imprimatur of both the DU and the president, Janlav NARANTSATSRALT, the mayor of Ulaanbaatar, was easily confirmed as prime minister. The Great Hural nevertheless rejected the majority of his initial cabinet nominees and withheld approval of the final four until January 1999.

Barely six months later, Narantsatsralt lost the support of the entire MNDP-dominated cabinet, which threatened to resign and accused him of jeopardizing national interests in a letter he had sent, without prior ministerial consultation, to a Russian official regarding terms for the sale of Russia's share in the Erdenet copper-molybdenum joint venture. Having lost a legislative no-confidence vote 41–22 on July 23, Narantsatsralt tendered his resignation the following day and was succeeded in an acting capacity by Foreign Minister Nyamosor TUYA. On July 30 the State Great Hural gave swift approval, this time, to President Bagabandi's prime ministerial nominee, Amarjargal, who resigned from the legislature and immediately won confirmation by a vote of 50–2. The cabinet approved on September 2 was substantially unchanged.

With the electorate searching for a measure of stability and firmer leadership, in the general election of July 2, 2000, the MPRP swept back into power, capturing 72 of the 76 seats in the State Great Hural. The sole MNDP seat was won by former prime minister Narantsatsralt, while the MSDP, running on its own, won none. Nambaryn ENKHBAYAR, chair of the MPRP and a member of the State Great Hural, was confirmed as prime minister on July 26, and an MPRP cabinet won legislative approval on August 9. The legitimacy of Enkhbayar's appointment was ultimately resolved in May 2001, when President Bagabandi accepted constitutional amendments permitting legislators to serve as cabinet members.

President Bagabandi won a second term in the election of May 20, 2001, taking 58 percent of the vote. His chief opponent, Radnaasümbereliyn Gonchigdorj (36.6 percent), stood as the candidate of the Democratic Party (DP), which had been formed the preceding December by merger of the MNDP, the MSDP, and three smaller parties.

In 2003 the DP and the Motherland–Mongolian Democratic New Socialist Party (M-MDNSP), led by gold magnate Badarch ERDENEBAT, formed the Motherland Democratic Coalition (MDC), which was joined by the Civil Will Republican Party (CWRP) in March 2004. In the June 27 parliamentary election the MDC won 34 seats, only 2 less than the governing MPRP. With neither group able to claim a majority in the legislature, protracted negotiations on forming a new government ensued. On August 13, 2004, the legislators unanimously elected the outgoing prime minister, Nambaryn Enkhbayar, as chair of the State Great Hural, and on August 20 former prime minister Tsakhiagiyn Elbegdorj of the DP/MDC was again appointed prime minister. It took another month for the MPRP and MDC to reach agreement on an equal division of cabinet posts, with a "Grand Coalition Government" subsequently sworn in on September 28. However, in December the M-MDNSP withdrew from the MDC, which soon led to the dissolution of the coalition and to the dismissal in February 2005 of the two M-MDNSP ministers.

With President Bagabandi prohibited from seeking a third term, the MPRP nominated Nambaryn Enkhbayar as its presidential candidate in the May 22, 2005, election. Enkhbayar won with 53.4 percent of the vote, defeating former prime minister Mendsaikhan Enkhsaikhan of the DP (19.7 percent) and three other candidates.

On January 11, 2006, all ten MPRP ministers resigned from the coalition cabinet, and two days later the State Great Hural voted to dissolve the government. Four key votes in favor of dissolution were cast by members of the DP, including Enkhsaikhan, former prime minister Janlav Narantsatsralt, and Mishig SONOMPIL. An effort by the MPRP to forge a "national unity" government was rejected by the DP, though Enkhsaikhan, Narantsatsralt, and Sonompil all accepted posts in the new cabinet of MPRP chair Miyeegombo ENKHBOLD, who was confirmed as prime minister by the legislature on January 25. The three maverick ministers were expelled from the DP and formed the National New Party (NNP). Also joining the coalition government were the Motherland Party (formerly the MDNSP), the Republican Party (RP), and the People's Party (PP).

On November 5, 2007, Prime Minister Enkhbold resigned after he was ousted as MPRP party chair in October in favor of the incumbent secretary general, Sanj BAYAR. On November 22 the State Great Hural confirmed Bayar as prime minister, and he appointed a coalition cabinet including members of the Civil Will Party (CWP), the National New Party (NNP), and the Republican Party (RP).

In legislative elections on June 29, 2008, the MPRP won a majority of seats. DP leaders questioned the integrity of the vote, prompting a violent demonstration on July 1 and a legislative boycott that prevented the incoming parliament from reaching a quorum for more than two months (see Current issues, below). When the Hural finally convened, it reappointed Bayar as prime minister on September 11. The DP accepted an offer from Bayar and the MPRP to join the new government, which was sworn in on September 22.

In the presidential election on May 24, 2009, DP leader and former prime minister Tsakhiagiyn Elbegdorj, who also had the backing of the CWP and the Mongolian Green Party (MGP), defeated the incumbent Enkhbayar on a narrow vote share of 51 percent. Elbegdorj, the first non-MPRP president in the country's history, was sworn in for a four-year term on June 18.

Constitution and government. The constitution adopted in 1960 left intact the guiding role of the MPRP, whose highly centralized leadership also dominated the state administration. The national legislature (People's Great Hural) was identified as the supreme organ of government but typically met only for a brief annual session to approve measures submitted by the Council of Ministers. The Presidium of the Hural represented the legislature between sessions, and its chair served as head of state.

In March–May 1990 a number of constitutional changes were debated and approved, including renunciation of the "guiding role" of the MPRP in favor of a multiparty system, conversion of the Presidium chair into a state presidency, and the creation of a vice presidency. Selected by the Great Hural, the vice president was to serve as ex officio chair of a new standing assembly (Little Hural).

The current constitution, adopted on January 13, 1992, returned legislative power to a single chamber, known as the State Great Hural, whose 76 members are elected by universal suffrage for four-year terms. In June 2008, for the first time, Mongolians elected legislators by proportional representation rather than a winner-take-all vote.

The powers of the State Great Hural include appointing and dismissing the prime minister and other administrative officials. A popularly elected president serves as head of state for a four-year term; should no presidential candidate receive a majority of the votes cast, a two-way runoff is held. The president can veto legislative decisions (subject to override by a two-thirds majority), nominates the prime minister in consultation with the largest legislative party, and serves as commander-in-chief of the armed forces. A Supreme Court sits at the apex of the judicial system, while a Constitutional Court is charged with ensuring the "strict observance" of the basic law and with resolving constitutional disputes.

Mongolia is divided into 21 provinces (*aymguud* or *aimags*), each subdivided into counties and *baghs,* plus the capital city of Ulaanbaatar, subdivided into districts and *horoos.* At the provincial and capital level the prime minister appoints governors (*dzasag darga*) nominated by elected hurals. Each county (*soum*) and district (*khoron*) also elects a hural, while "General Meetings of Citizens" function at the lowest administrative tier. A local governor is nominated by each subdivision's legislative body and appointed by the governor of the next highest level. The possibility of regrouping the existing *aimags* into 4 provinces has been discussed.

Foreign relations. Mongolia attempted to take a neutral stance in the early period of the Sino-Soviet dispute, but subsequently aligned with the Soviet Union, in part because of an inherited fear of Chinese hegemony and in part because of a dependence on Soviet military, economic, and cultural assistance. A member of the UN since 1961, it became a full member of the Soviet-dominated Council for Mutual Economic Assistance (CMEA) in 1962 and signed a treaty of friendship and mutual assistance with the Soviet Union in 1966. Relations with China began to thaw in 1985; a consular treaty signed the following year was the first since 1949.

In March 1989 Moscow announced that it would begin withdrawing its reported 50,000 troops from Mongolia, a process completed in September 1992. President Ochirbat visited Russia in January 1993 for talks with President Boris Yeltsin that yielded a treaty of friendship and cooperation, under which the two countries agreed to refrain from entering into military-political alliances aimed against each other.

Mongolia signed a friendship and cooperation treaty with China in 1994 (replacing a 1962 predecessor) during an official visit by Chinese premier Li Peng. Earlier that year Mongolia, China, and Russia signed a tripartite pact defining their border junctures. Chinese and Mongolian leaders have exchanged several state visits in the past ten years. China is Mongolia's largest foreign investor and receives roughly 70 percent of Mongolian exports. At the same time, Mongolia has become increasingly wary of China's growing economic power, which already dominates Mongolia's cashmere industry.

Since the Cold War ended, Mongolian foreign policy has been based on carefully balanced relations with Russia and China as well as "third neighbors," including the Western powers. Diplomatic relations with the United States were not established until 1987. In January 1991 President Ochirbat became the first Mongolian head of state to travel to the United States, where he met with President George H. W. Bush and signed a bilateral trade agreement. The nation was soon admitted into the Asian Development Bank along with the World Bank and the IMF. More recently, Mongolia has frequently been in accord with Washington on foreign policy matters, including the "war on terrorism."

In the mid-2000s Mongolian troops joined coalition forces in Iraq following the U.S. invasion, and Mongolia also deployed some military trainers to Afghanistan. Visits in 2005 by U.S. secretary of defense Donald Rumsfeld and President George W. Bush (the first sitting U.S. chief executive to do so) marked a significant shift in relations.

In 2008 enhanced economic cooperation between Mongolia and Russia was evidenced by Mongolia's importing almost all of its oil from Russia. In March 2009 Russian prime minister Vladimir Putin offered $300 million in credits to Mongolia's agriculture industry. While Putin was visiting Mongolia in May, the two nations agreed to develop a rail network extending to the Oyu Tolgoi and Tavan Tolgoi mines. Under the deal, Russian firms would receive licenses to mine both sites. In addition, Russia sought to develop and extract Mongolian uranium deposits.

Current issues. The 2008 elections for the State Great Hural were the nation's first to be conducted by proportional representation. Returns from the balloting came in slowly, and in the delay, the MPRP announced that it had won a majority of the 76 seats, albeit by only one seat. DP leader Elbegdorj alleged fraudulent activity, and other opposition parties joined the DP in demonstrations in Ulaanbaatar on July 1. That evening, a violent crowd overwhelmed police and set fire to the MPRP building and the adjacent Cultural Palace. Five people were killed and several hundred were arrested. President Enkhbayar declared a four-day state of emergency, shutting down all radio and television transmissions except for the government-run channel. Official election results announced on July 14 supported the MPRP's majority, with ten seats unassigned pending recounts. Nine days later 25 of 27 DP deputies walked out of the opening session of the State Great Hural, making a quorum impossible and preventing new members from being sworn in. In early August the DP demanded the resignation of the head of the elections commission before party members would return and parliament could reconvene. While the legislature was blocked, a group of MPRP and DP members acted as an interim government by consulting on urgent national affairs. After Prime Minister Bayar agreed to invite the DP into a coalition government, the DP legislators ended their walkout on August 28. Bayar was reappointed as prime minister on September 11 and named a new government that included only the DP and the MPRP on September 28.

In the run-up to the 2009 presidential campaign, Elbegdorj, who had stepped down as DP chair, was nominated to challenge Enkhbayar in the May election. Some observers likened Elbegdorj's campaign, with its message of political change and an end to corruption, to the successful 2008 campaign of U.S. president Barack Obama. Like Obama, Elbegdorj drew much of his electoral strength from young and urban voters. He was aided by the support of small parties, including the CWP and MGP, which chose not to divide the opposition vote by running their own candidates. In the polling on May 24, Elbegdorj won with 51 percent of the vote. Enkhbayar conceded defeat immediately, relieving concerns about a repeat of the 2008 post-election violence. When Elbegdorj was sworn in on June 18, he became the first head of state in Mongolia's history as an independent nation who did not belong to the MPRP. World leaders congratulated Mongolia on the peaceful transfer of power.

The main domestic issues facing the new administration in 2009 were the development of the nation's mineral resources and the equitable distribution of profits from mineral extraction. The Oyu Tolgoi (Turquoise Hill) copper-gold deposit, among the world's richest, was slated to be developed by a Canadian firm and to create tens of thousands of jobs. However, a final deal was held up in the State Great Hural for several years as lawmakers debated how to determine the government's share of the project. During the presidential campaign, both the DP and the MPRP pledged a proportion of mining profits to the Mongolian people. The DP proposed an allowance similar to the oil dividends paid annually to citizens of the U.S. state of Alaska by the state government. A bill creating a public corporation to distribute these shares was introduced in June 2009. President Elbegdorj opposed taking an equity stake in Oyu Tolgoi, preferring to leave the industry in private hands, but in July DP lawmakers proposed a 34 percent stake for the government, as the State Great Hural was under great pressure to conclude a deal swiftly. On August 25, a special session of parliament overwhelmingly approved terms for the Oyu Tolgoi investment agreement, granting the government a 34 percent stake in the project and repealing the 68 percent windfall profits tax. In September the finance minister announced that the government would create a sovereign wealth fund from its share of the revenues from Oyu Tolgoi, fulfilling the promise to distribute part of the profits to the population. Government and industry representatives signed the agreement on October 6 in Ulaanbaatar.

POLITICAL PARTIES

Until 1990 the Mongolian People's Revolutionary Party (MPRP) was the country's only authorized political formation. On March 23, 1990, the People's Great Hural ended the party's monopoly, and in June 1996 the MPRP lost to the Democratic Union—DU (*Ardchilsan Kholboo,* also translated as the Democratic Alliance), a loose four-party coalition of the Mongolian National Democratic Party (MNDP), the Mongolian Social Democratic Party (MSDP), the Mongolian Religious Democratic Party (MRDP), and the Mongolian Green Party (MGP), each of which backed its own candidates.

As of March 2000, Mongolia had 24 registered parties. Thirteen individual parties, 2 two-party coalitions, and 1 three-party coalition contested the July 2000 general election, which overwhelmingly returned the MPRP to power. Prior to provincial and local elections held three months later, a significant coalescence of forces occurred. The MPRP's principal opponents were a six-party Coalition of Democratic Forces (the "Big Six"), led by the MNDP and the MSDP, and another eight-party grouping led by the Civil Will Party (CWP) and the Mongolian Republican Party (MRP). In December 2000 the MNDP and MSDP led the formation of a new Democratic Party (DP), while the CWP and the MRP merged in February 2002 as the Civil Will Republican Party (CWRP). In December 2003, however, the merger fell apart and the MRP reemerged as the Republican Party (RP). In June 2003 the DP and the Motherland–Mongolian Democratic New Socialist Party (M-MDNSP) had announced formation of the Motherland Democratic Coalition—MDC (*Ekh Oron Ardchilsan Evsel*), which the rump CWRP ultimately decided to join.

Thus, in the June 2004 election the MPRP, unlike in 2000, faced a unified front of the major opposition parties, which won 44.7 percent of the national vote and emerged with sufficient seats to demand a role in the new government. In December 2004 the M-MDNSP (renamed Motherland in 2005) withdrew from the MDC, which was disbanded on December 26.

Only parliamentary parties may nominate candidates for the state presidency. Those offering candidates in 2005 were the DP, Motherland, the MPRP, and the RP. With the addition of the recently formed People's Party (PP) in December 2005, Mongolia had 22 registered parties. Dissidents from the DP later formed the National New Party (NNP).

Government Parties:

Democratic Party—DP (*Ardchilsan Nam*). The DP was formed on December 6, 2000, by the merger of six parties and groups: the Mongolian National Democratic Party (MNDP), which dated from the 1992 merger of four opposition parties, including the Mongolian Democratic Party (MDP) of Sanjaasürengiyn Zorig; the Mongolian Social Democratic Party (MSDP), which ultimately broke away and reregistered as a separate party in January 2005 (see below); the Mongolian Democratic Party (MDP), which traced its roots to Zorig's earlier MDP and which had been formed in January 2000 by disaffected members of the MNDP; the Mongolian Democratic Renewal Party (MDRP), which was founded in 1994 and had participated in the "Big Six" coalition for the October 2000 provincial and local elections; the Mongolian Religious Democratic Party (MRDP), a Buddhist party established in 1990 and later participated in the DU coalition; and a faction of the Mongolian Traditional United Party (MTUP).

The DP's founding chair was Dambyn Dorligjav of the MNDP and a former minister of defense. The party's 2001 presidential candidate, former MSDP chair Radnaasümbereliyn Gonchigdorj, finished second, with 36.6 percent of the vote.

In the June 2004 State Great Hural election the DP, in an electoral alliance with the MDC, won 26 of the MDC's 35 seats. The MDC and the MPRP then formed a coalition government led by the DP's Tsakhiagiyn Elbegdorj. However, in late December the MDC dissolved shortly after the DP's national committee voted to overhaul the party's leadership and replace former prime minister Mendsaikhan Enkhsaikhan with Gonchigdorj. Enkhsaikhan nevertheless remained the party's 2005 candidate for president, finishing second with19.7 percent of the vote.

In February 2006 Enkhsaikhan, former prime minister Janlav Narantsatsralt, and Mishig Sonompil were dismissed from the party after casting deciding votes against the Elbegdorj government and then accepting cabinet posts in the new MPRP government.

At the party congress on March 30–April 1, 2006, former prime minister Elbegdorj was elected chair over Erdeniin Bat-Uul and two other candidates. In November 2007 the DP was the sole parliamentary party to oppose the designation of the MPRP's Bayar as prime minister.

Following the 2008 balloting for the State Great Hural, Elbegdorj challenged the results and accused the MPRP of stealing the election. For weeks, a walkout by all but two of the party's legislators blocked the seating of a new parliament. The two members who did not join the boycott, Bat-Uul and B. BAYBAYAR, were threatened with expulsion. However, while the legislature remained in limbo, members of the MPRP and DP worked as a de facto interim government and the DP subsequently joined a new government with the MPRP in November.

N. Altankhuyag was elected party chair in 2008, Elbegdorj having stepped down in August. Elbegdorj subsequently was tapped as the party's flagbearer for the 2009 presidential election. He became the first Mongolian president from a party other than the MPRP.

Leaders: Tsakhiagiyn ELBEGDORJ (President of the Republic), N. ALTANKHUYAG (Chair), Erdeniin BAT-UUL, Dambyn DORLIGJAV, D. ERDENEBAT (General Secretary).

Mongolian People's Revolutionary Party—MPRP (*Mongol Ardyn Khuv'sgalt Nam*). For nearly seven decades the MPRP (known until 1924 as the Mongolian People's Party—MPP) was organized along typical communist lines, its tightly centralized structure nominally subject to party congresses meeting at five-year intervals. An elected Central Committee met twice yearly, and a Politburo and Secretariat served as principal policymaking bodies.

An extraordinary party congress in 1990 abolished the Politburo in favor of a Central Committee Presidium, with the incumbent general secretary redesignated as Presidium chair. In that year's general election the MPRP secured more than 80 percent of Great Hural seats. Further structural changes were introduced at a party plenum in 1992: a 169-member Little Hural replaced the Central Committee and the

Presidium's functions were transferred to an 11-member Leadership Council, headed by a general secretary.

In 1993 the party's presidential candidate, Lodongiyn Tudev, editor of the party newspaper, lost to the incumbent, Punsalmaagiyn Ochirbat, who had maintained nominal MPRP membership despite being denied renomination and running as a joint candidate of the MNDP and MSDP.

In a further loss, the MPRP's legislative representation plummeted to 25 seats in the 1996 election, a loss of 46 from its 1992 total. In 1997, however, the party's chair, Natsagiyn Bagabandi, won a landslide presidential victory, defeating President Ochirbat, who had formally resigned from the party to run as the Democratic Union candidate.

In 1999 a contemporary Mongolian People's Party (MPP) merged with the MPRP, although a number of party dissidents continued to claim the MPP name. (The MPP was founded in 1991.)

In the July 2000 general election the MPRP won 72 of 76 seats in the State Great Hural, after which the party chair, Nambaryn Enkhbayar, won easy confirmation as prime minister. In local elections in October, the MPRP controlled all 21 provincial legislatures.

In June 2004 the party won 46.5 percent of the national vote but lost half its seats in the State Great Hural. Shy of a legislative majority, the MPRP courted the three parliamentary independents but was unsuccessful and therefore entered into negotiations with the opposition MDC for a coalition government. Ultimately, Prime Minister Enkhbayar agreed to step down and was elected chair of the legislature.

In May 2005 Enkhbayar was elected president, succeeding Bagabandi. A month later, following Enkhbayar's mandatory resignation as party chair, the MPRP elected Miyeegombo Enkhbold, mayor of Ulaanbaatar, as his successor. Enkhbold became prime minister in January 2006 after ten MPRP ministers resigned from the Elbegdorj government, forcing its collapse. A wave of public protest followed, as the formerly communist MPRP stood accused of undermining democracy.

In June 2007 the MPRP's Tsend Nyamdorj resigned as chair of the State Great Hural shortly after the Constitutional Court ruled that he had acted unconstitutionally in amending laws. At the party's congress in October, the secretary general, Sanj Bayar, successfully challenged Enkhbold for the party chair, winning 57 percent of the votes. As a consequence, Enkhbold resigned as prime minister and was succeeded by Bayar.

On July 1, 2008, the MPRP won a majority in legislative elections, but following accusations of vote fraud, an angry throng set fire to the MPRP building. President Enkhbayar declared a state of emergency to deal with the violent protest. Subsequently, the MPRP maintained a majority of seats, though recounts in 10 constituencies were delayed for several months. In the 2009 presidential election, the MPRP was defeated for the first time since popular elections for that office began in 1990. The defeat of President Enkhbayar by the DP's Tsakhiagiyn Elbegdorj led to some internal criticism of the party's strategy and turnover of its local leadership. Some younger party members sought to open the party to new reformist leadership and wider debate of strategy and policy. The party also considered changing its name to the Mongolian Democratic Development Party but ultimately retained the original rubric.

Leaders: Sanj BAYAR (Prime Minister and President of the Party), Nambaryn ENKHBAYAR (Former President of Mongolia), Miyeegombo ENKHBOLD (Deputy Prime Minister), Tsend NYAMDORJ (Former Chair of the State Great Hural), Yondon OTGONBAYAR (General Secretary).

Other Legislative Parties:

Civil Will Party—CWP (*Irgenii Zorig Nam*). The centrist CWP was registered in March 2000 under the leadership of Sanjaasuren Oyun, sister of the slain MNDP activist, and cabinet member Sanjaasürengiyn Zorig. The CWP campaigned in coalition with the MGP (below) for the July 2000 election, with Oyun winning its only seat.

In September 2000 Oyun was elected chair of an eight-party opposition coalition to contest the October 2000 provincial and local elections. Participants included the Mongolian Republican Party (MRP), the Mongolian Liberal Democratic Party (MLDP), the Mongolian Civil Democratic New Liberal Party, and the Party for Mongolia (PM), which was established by Luvsandambyn DASHNYAM in 1998 and which agreed to join the CWP in December 2000. For the 2001 presidential election the CWP nominated Dashnyam, who captured only 3.5 percent of the vote.

In February 2002 the CWP and the MRP merged to form the Civil Will Republican Party—CWRP (*Irgenii Zorig Najramdakh Bügd Nam*), but they separated in December 2003 (see the RP, below), although the CWRP retained "Republican" in its name when it reregistered in April 2004. It then entered the national election campaign as part of the MDC, winning two State Great Hural seats. In January 2006 the party reestablished itself as the CWP.

Despite the objections of some members, in 2007 the party decided to join the MPRP-led coalition government. Oyun accepted the post of foreign minister under Prime Minister Bayar. She won the party's only seat in the 2008 parliamentary election. In the 2009 presidential election, the CWP supported Elbegdorj, Oyun expressing hope that he would help reconcile the nation's partisan divide.

Leader: Sanjaasuren OYUN.

Mongolian Green Party—MGP (*Mongolyn Nogoon Nam*). The MGP was organized in 1990 as the political arm of the Mongolian Alliance of Greens. It competed as part of the DU in 1996 but failed to win any seats. For the July 2000 election it was allied with the CWP, but for the October provincial and local elections the MGP participated in the six-party Coalition of Democratic Forces. Unlike its fellow coalition members, however, it later announced that its agenda prevented it from joining in the DP merger. In 2001 the MGP supported the presidential candidacy of the DP's Gonchigdorj. It ran six unsuccessful candidates for the State Great Hural in 2004.

Officially, the party did not take part in the 2008 elections for the State Great Hural, yet one of its leaders, D. Enkhbat (also endorsed by the CMP, below), was declared the winner of a seat in Bayangol after a lengthy investigation of the vote. He quickly formed a Green Group in the State Great Hural to advocate for ecological approaches to the mining industry.

In 2009 the Green Party supported the DP's Tsakhiagiyn Elbegdorj for president.

Leader: D. ENKHBAT.

Other Parties that Participated in Recent Elections:

Civil Movement Party (CMP). The CMP was established in 2006 by a coalition of nongovernmental organizations, including the Just Society Civil Movement, led by Jalbasüren BATZANDAN. The party registered in 2007 and participated in the 2008 legislative election but failed to win a seat. Batzandan and his deputy, Otgonjargal MAGNAI, were arrested on suspicion of instigating the post-election demonstrations on July 1, 2008, that led to the burning of MPRP headquarters. Both denied the charges. They were detained for nearly two months before being released. Subsequently, Batzandan and Magnai joined the DP. Nyamaa Davaa was named party chair in November. Davaa, a former director of Anod Bank, was arrested on December 11, 2008, along with two bank associates and held for more than six months without charges before being released in June 2009.

Leader: Nyamaa DAVAA.

Motherland Party (*Ekh Oron Nam*). Motherland began as the Mongolian Democratic New Socialist Party (*Mongoliin Ardchilsan Shine Sotsialist Nam*—MDNSP). The MDNSP was organized in 1998 under the auspices of Badarch Erdenebat, wealthy director general of the Erel Company, which had profited from the duty-free export of gold. The new formation quickly attracted defectors from other parties, including the MPRP.

In mid-1999 the MDNSP and the Mongolian Workers' Party (*Mongolyn Ajilchny Nam*—MWP) announced formation of a leftist Motherland coalition in support of a return to state regulation and coordination of industry, coupled with sustainable social development. Although the MWP offered its own candidates in the July 2000 election, Erdenebat ran under the banner of the Motherland-MDNSP (M-MDNSP), winning the organization's sole seat.

The M-MDNSP supported President Bagabandi's 2001 reelection but in June 2004 ran as part of the MDC, from which it withdrew at the end of December, in part because of Erdenebat's presidential aspirations. He served as minister of defense in the Elbegdorj cabinet until February 2005 and finished fourth, with 11.4 percent of the vote, in the May presidential election as candidate of Motherland, as the party had been renamed in January. Erdenebat served in the Enkhbold cabinet of 2006–2007 but lost his seat in parliament in the 2008 election.

Leaders: Badarch ERDENEBAT (Chair), N. CHULUUNBAATAR (Secretary General).

National New Party—NNP (*Ündesnii Shine Nam*). The NNP was formed by Janlav NARANTSATSRALT and Mendsaikhan Enkhsaikhan following theirexpulsion from the DP for joining the MPRP government in February 2006. Narantsatsralt died in November 2007.

The NNP retained two cabinet posts in the Bayar government formed in 2007. The party participated in the 2008 legislative elections but won no seats. Its ministers were dropped from the cabinet in September 2008.

Leaders: Ts. TSOLMON, Mendsaikhan ENKHSAIKHAN.

People's Party—PP (*Ard Tümnii Nam*). Organized in November 2005 by former DP deputy chair Lamjay GÜNDALAI, the PP was registered a month later, at which time Gündalai held its only seat in the State Great Hural. In January 2006 Gündalai joined the MPRP-led Enkhbold government, but he was dismissed a year later. Gündalai rejoined the DP in April 2008.

Republican Party—RP (*Bügd Najramdahk Nam*). The RP traces its origins to the 1992 launching of the Mongolian Capitalists' Party, which changed its name to the Mongolian Republican Party (MRP) in 1997. In January 2000 the MRP was one of nine non-parliamentary parties that discussed organizing a "third force" coalition to contest the national election, in which it failed to win any seats.

In early 2002 the MRP merged with the CWP (above) to form the Civil Will Republican Party (CWRP), but the MRP reemerged as the RP in December 2003 because of its leaders' opposition to contesting the 2004 national election in alliance with the DP. The RP ran 35 candidates in another loose "third force" effort, but longtime leader Bazarsadiin Jargalsaikhan won its only victory.

In May 2005 Jargalsaikhan won 13.9 percent of the vote in the presidential election. He joined the Enkhbold coalition cabinet in January 2006 as minister of industry and commerce but left in February 2007 because of discontent with mining law reforms that he had advocated. He lost his Hural seat in the 2008 election.

Leader: Bazarsadiin JARGALSAIKHAN

Other Parties:

Mongolian Social Democratic Party—MSDP (*Mongolyn Sotsial Ardchilsan Nam*). The MSDP called at its inaugural congress in March 1990 for a just and humane society patterned on the values espoused by social democratic parties in the West. The party's legislative representation fell from 7 (overall) in 1990 to 1 in 1992, but it won 12 State Great Hural seats in 1996 as part of the DU. One of its leaders, Radnaasümbereliyn Gonchigdorj, served as state vice president and Speaker of the State Great Hural before running as a DP candidate for president. The party lost all its State Great Hural seats in the July 2000 election and in September agreed to merge with the MNDP. The DP resulted in December.

In December 2004, however, objecting to DP policies, the MSDP separated from the DP. It was reregistered as a separate party on January 20, 2005, although the DP protested the restoration of the party's name. The MSDP held a party congress in March 2008 but did not field candidates in the elections for the State Great Hural.

Leaders: Adyagiin GANBAATAR (Chair), Ts. SAIKHANBILEG (Secretary General).

Other parties registered for the 2008 election included the Progressive Party, the Freedom Enforcement Party, the Mongolian Democratic Movement Party, the Mongolian Conservative United Party, and the Mongolian Liberal Party.

For more information on the **Mongolian National Unity Party** (*Mongolyn Undesnii ev Negdliin Nam*—MNUP), the **Mongolian Traditional United Party** (*Mongolyn Ulamjlaliin Negdsen Nam*—MTUP), as well as additional parties founded in 2000 or earlier, see the 2008 *Handbook*.

LEGISLATURE

State Great Hural (*Ulsyn Ikh Khural*). The 76 members of the Great Hural are popularly elected for four-year terms.

In the most recent election on June 29, 2008, Mongolia introduced a new voting system based on party lists. Parties winning at least 5 percent of the national vote are awarded seats on a proportional basis. Following the election, the seat distribution was as follows: the Mongolian People's Revolutionary Party (MPRP), 39; Democratic Party (DP), 25; Civil Will Party (CWP), 1; and independents, 1. Following recounts for 10 disputed seats, the seat distribution as of May 2009 was as follows: the MPRP, 45; DP, 27; CWP, 1, Mongolian Green Party, 1, independents, 1; vacant, 1.

Chair: Damdin DEMBEREL.

CABINET

[as of September 1, 2009] *(see headnote)*

Prime Minister	Sanj Bayar (MPRP)
First Deputy Prime Minister	Norovlin Altanhuyag (DP)
Deputy Prime Minister	Miyeegombo Enkhbold (MPRP)
Ministers	
Defense	Luvsanvandan Bold (DP)
Education, Culture, and Sciences	Yondon Otgonbayar (MPRP)
Environment	Luimed Gansukh (DP)
Finance	Sangajabyn Bayartsogt (DP)
Food, Agriculture, and Light Industry	Tunjin Badamjunai (MPRP)
Foreign Affairs	Sukhgaatar Batbold (MPRP)
Health	Sanbuu Lambaa (DP)
Justice and Home Affairs	Tsendlin Nyamdorj (MPRP)
Minerals and Energy	Dashdorj Zorigt (MPRP)
Roads, Transportation, Construction and Urban Development	Khaltmaa Battulga (DP)
Social Welfare and Labor	Tugsjargal Gandi (MPRP) [f]
Chief of Government Secretariat	Badraa Dolgor (MPRP) [f]

COMMUNICATIONS

The 1992 constitution guarantees freedom of the press and the right "to seek and receive information." However, journalists can be prosecuted for disclosing state secrets, and press freedom groups such as Globe International have charged that censorship and harassment of reporters hinder the development of independent journalism. The central government's leading newspapers, *Ardyn Erh* and *Zasgiyn Gazryn Medee,* were privatized in early 1999. A 2005 law ordered the conversion of state-run broadcast outlets into public service companies.

Press. The following are published at least five days a week in Ulaanbaatar, unless otherwise noted: *Serüüleg* (Alarm Clock, 29,000), weekly tabloid; *Udriyn Sonin* (Daily News, 14,000), formerly the government-run *Ardyn Erh* (People's Power); *Zuunii Medee* (Century's News, 8,000), formerly *Zasgiyn Gazryn Medee* (Government News); *Ünen* (Truth, 8,000), MPRP organ; *Unuudur* (Today, 5,000); *Mongolyn Medee* (Mongolian News, 3,000); *Mongol Messenger,* English-language weekly, owned by state-run Montsame agency; *UB Post,* English-language weekly.

News agencies. The state-run Mongolian News Agency (*Mongol Tsahilgaan Medeeniy Agentlag*—Montsame) is the principal domestic facility in Ulaanbaatar. The Russian agencies ITAR-TASS and RIA-Novosti and China's *Xinhua* also have offices in the capital.

Broadcasting and computing. Mongolian Radio (*Mongol Yaridz*) broadcasts domestically; its Voice of Mongolia offers an overseas service. Since the 1990s private radio stations have also been established. Although cable television is available in larger towns, and local stations have been established in the largest cities, the central Mongolian Television (*Mongol Televiz*) remains dominant. As of 2008 there were 124.9 Internet users per 1,000 inhabitants.

INTERGOVERNMENTAL REPRESENTATION

Ambassador to the U.S.: Bekhbat KHASBAZAR.

U.S. Ambassador to Mongolia: Jonathan S. ADDLETON.

Permanent Representative to the UN: Enkhtsetseg OCHIR.

IGO Memberships (Non-UN): ADB, EBRD, Interpol, IOM, NAM, *SCO*, WCO, WTO.

MONTENEGRO

Republic of Montenegro
Republike Crne Gore

Political Status: An autonomous principality formally independent of the Ottoman Empire in 1878; declared a kingdom in 1910; incorporated as part of the Kingdom of the Serbs, Croats, and Slovenes, which was constituted as an independent monarchy on December 1, 1918, and formally renamed Yugoslavia on October 3, 1929; constituent republic of the communist Federal People's Republic of Yugoslavia instituted November 29, 1945, and then of the Socialist Federal Republic of Yugoslavia proclaimed April 7, 1963; constituent republic, along with Serbia, of the Federal Republic of Yugoslavia proclaimed April 27, 1992, and of the "state union" of Serbia and Montenegro established February 4, 2003, under new Constitutional Charter; Republic of Montenegro established June 3, 2006, following an independence referendum on May 21; new constitution adopted by the legislature (sitting as a Constituent Assembly) on October 19, 2007, and promulgated October 22.

Area: 5,333 sq. mi. (13,812 sq. km.)

Population: 627,000 (2008E).

Major Urban Centers (2005E): PODGORICA (formerly Titograd, 140,000).

Official Languages: Montenegrin; however, in areas established by national minorities, their languages (Albanian, Bosnian, Croatian, Serbian) are also accorded official status.

Monetary Unit: Euro (market rate December 1, 2009: 1 euro = $1.51US). The euro has been legal tender in Montenegro since January 1, 2002.

President: Filip VUJANOVIĆ (Democratic Party of Socialists of Montenegro); served as Montenegrin prime minister 1998–2002; elected chair of the Montenegrin Assembly on November 5, 2002, following the legislative election of October 20, and thus became acting president upon the resignation of President Milo DJUKANOVIĆ on November 25; elected president for a five-year term on May 11, 2003, and inaugurated June 13. Reelected president in the first postindependence presidential election in Montenegro on April 6, 2008, on the first round, winning nearly 52 percent of the vote, and inaugurated May 20.

Prime Minister: Milo DJUKANOVIĆ (Democratic Party of Socialists of Montenegro); nominated by the president on February 20, 2008, and confirmed by the legislature on February 29; nominated for a second term on May 7, 2009, following the March 29 parliamentary elections, and reconfirmed by the legislature on June 10.

THE COUNTRY

Montenegro is a Balkan republic, mostly mountainous, with a 180-mile coastline along the Adriatic Sea. The terrain, part of the Karst Plateau, is renowned for its rugged scenery. The country is bordered by Albania to the south, Serbia to the east, and Bosnia and Herzegovina to the north. Montenegrins constitute approximately 43 percent of the population, Serbs approximately 32 percent, Bosniaks about 8 percent, Albanians 5 percent, and various other ethnic groups (e.g., Croats and Roma) the remainder. Eastern Orthodox Christianity predominates, although there is a large Muslim minority, given the long regional occupation by the Ottoman Empire.

Industrial production, which was badly damaged by the United Nations (UN) economic sanctions imposed against Yugoslavia in the 1990s, is concentrated in hydroelectricity generation; the extraction and processing of raw materials, especially bauxite (reserves of bauxite may be surpassed in size only by Russian deposits), and also coal, lumber, and salt; and production of aluminum and steel. Processing of tobacco and food is also a major manufacturing activity. The industrial sector as a whole employs approximately 30 percent of the total workforce, compared to 68 percent for services. Agriculture and livestock production remain important despite employing only 2 percent of the workforce. Cereals, tobacco, grapes, figs, and olives are the major cash crops; poultry, lamb, goat, and beef are the primary meat products. Only about 14 percent of the total area of the country is suitable for cultivation. Another 54 percent is covered with forest or woodlands. Tourism, concentrated along the Adriatic coastline, makes up a fifth of the country's GDP and has been targeted for expansion. At independence, Montenegrin leaders claimed that GDP had grown 5 percent in 2005, with inflation at 1.8 percent, and that the budget deficit was 1.9 percent of GDP. In 2007 real GDP growth reached 7 percent. Challenges include rebuilding neglected infrastructure, curbing public-sector corruption, boosting private-sector employment, and suppressing the enormous black-market sector that developed during the period of sanctions. Foreign investment, particularly in finance and tourism, has grown since independence, and in 2007 Montenegro had the third highest investment per capita ratio in Europe. Growth continued at 7.5 percent for 2008 as a whole, despite slowing toward the end due to the global finance crisis. The International Monetary Fund has estimated an annual growth of 2 percent in 2009. Economic development has addressed the widespread unemployment of the 1990s, although unemployment in early 2009 was still approximately 11 percent. An overarching goal is integration into the European Union (EU), which the government hopes to negotiate by 2012.

GOVERNMENT AND POLITICS

Political background. Following centuries of national struggle against the Ottoman Empire, an autonomous Montenegrin principality emerged over the 16th and 18th centuries. As with Serbia, in the 19th century Montenegro broke all but nominal ties to the Ottomans, finally achieving formal independence in 1878. The newly independent state was both an ally and rival to Serbia, with Prince (later, King) NIKOLA I himself hoping to unify Serbian-inhabited lands. Montenegro's incorporation on December 1, 1918, into the Kingdom of the Serbs, Croats, and Slovenes under the Serbian House of Karadjordjević led to a brief civil war. Uniting Serbia and Montenegro with the Croatian, Dalmatian, and Bosnian and Herzegovinian territories previously ruled by Austria-Hungary, the new entity (formally styled Yugoslavia on October 3, 1929) was ruled as a highly centralized, Serb-dominated state until occupied by Nazi Germany and Fascist Italy in April 1941. Resistance was led by two rival groups, the proroyalist Chetniks and the communist-inspired Partisans, the latter led by Josip Broz TITO, a Croat who sought to enlist all the country's national groups in the liberation struggle. Near the end of the war Tito became prime minister in a "government of national unity," and on November 29 the monarchy was abolished and a Federal People's Republic of Yugoslavia, based on the equality of the country's principal national groups, was proclaimed. In January 1953, under a new constitution, Tito was elected president of the republic.

Aided by Western arms and economic support, Yugoslavia maintained its autonomy throughout the Stalin era and beyond. Internally, seeking its own "road to socialism," Yugoslavia had become the first East European country to evolve institutions that moderated the harsher features of communist rule. A federal constitution promulgated in 1963 consolidated a system of "social self-management"; it also expanded the independence of the judiciary, increased the responsibilities of the federal legislature and those of the country's six constituent republics (Bosnia and Herzegovina, Croatia, Macedonia, Montenegro, Serbia, and Slovenia) and two autonomous provinces (Kosovo and Vojvodina), and widened freedom of choice in elections.

When Marshal Tito died in May 1990, the leadership of state and party passed to collegial executives—the state presidency and the Presidium of the Central Committee of the League of Communists of Yugoslavia (*Savez Komunista Jugoslavija*—SKJ), respectively. Through the 1980s the federal state presidency and the presidency of the party Presidium rotated on an annual basis among the constituent republics without appreciable dispute.

Economic ills in 1990 set off a series of events that led to the dissolution of greater Yugoslavia into the independent states of Croatia, Slovenia, Bosnia and Herzegovina, and Macedonia, with only Serbia and Montenegro remaining in a diminished federation. In February 1992 Serbia and Montenegro agreed to join in upholding "the principles of a common state which would be a continuation of Yugoslavia." In April a rump Federal Assembly adopted the constitution of a new Federal

Republic of Yugoslavia (FRY), under which elections for a successor assembly were held in Serbia and Montenegro.

In 1996 the Democratic Party of Socialists of Montenegro (*Demokratska Partija Socijalista Crne Gore*—DPS) achieved a majority in elections for the separate Montenegrin Assembly. On July 15, 1997, Slobodan MILOŠEVIĆ, constitutionally barred from running for a third term as president of Serbia, was elected unopposed as the Yugoslav federal president. However, he continued to face electoral threats to his power.

In Montenegro, a split in the Milošević-allied ruling DPS precipitated a 1997 presidential election. On February 21 Montenegrin Prime Minister Milo DJUKANOVIĆ attacked Milošević in a press interview, which, along with his calls for an independent foreign policy and currency for Montenegro, resulted in Djukanović's forced resignation as DPS vice president on March 26. The pro-Djukanović faction of the party responded on July 11 by sacking a key Milošević ally, state and DPS President Momir BULATOVIĆ, although a month later the pro-Bulatović faction engineered his return as party leader at a DPS congress. In the midst of this turmoil Montenegrin Assembly Speaker Svetozar MAROVIĆ announced Montenegrin presidential elections for the fall. Following a ruling by the Constitutional Court, both Djukanović and Bulatović were permitted to run. Although Bulatović, one of eight candidates, claimed a narrow plurality of votes over Djukanović in first-round voting on October 5, Djukanović defeated the two-term incumbent by a mere 5,000 votes in a runoff on October 19.

The new president took office on January 13, 1998, despite violent protests by Bulatović supporters. Through mediation by Yugoslav Prime Minister Radoje KONTIĆ (a Montenegrin), on January 21 the demonstrators agreed to settle for early legislative elections in May 1998. A transitional government under the leadership of the DPS's Filip VUJANOVIĆ was appointed on February 4. It included 17 ministers from Djukanović's DPS faction, 7 from the opposition, and 4 independents; the Bulatović faction of the DPS as well as the pro-independence Liberal Alliance of Montenegro (*Liberalni Savez Crne Gore*—LSCG) refused to participate.

On May 19, 1998, former Montenegrin president Bulatović was named prime minister of Yugoslavia. On May 31, however, Montenegrin voters awarded 49.5 percent of the vote and a majority of seats in the Montenegrin Assembly to President Djukanović's For a Better Life electoral coalition, while Bulatović's recently organized Socialist People's Party of Montenegro (*Socijalistička Narodna Partija Crne Gore*—SNP) claimed 36 percent of the vote and emerged as the leading opposition party. Montenegro's interim prime minister, Vujanović, was reappointed on July 16 to head a government encompassing the three coalition partners: the DPS, the People's Party (*Narodna Stranka*—NS), and the Social Democratic Party of Montenegro (*Socijaldemokratska Partija Crne Gore*—SDP).

In 1999 Montenegrin President Djukanović continued his efforts to distance his administration from federal policies in regard to Kosovo, particularly "ethnic cleansing" of ethnic Albanians, which had precipitated military action by the United States and other North Atlantic Treaty Organization (NATO) countries (see Serbia article for details). Even though Montenegro was not exempt from the NATO air campaign, and despite rumors that the Serbian military was preparing to depose him, on April 21 Djukanović rejected orders that the Montenegrin police be placed under the command of the FRY army. Djukanović accused Milošević of using "the pretext of the defense of the country" to displace the civil government. Later, the republican government proposed replacing the federal republic with a looser association in which Montenegro would set its own foreign and military policy and establish independent currency controls.

In July 2000 Milošević's allies pushed through the Federal Assembly constitutional changes designed to maintain his hold on power. The changes included directly electing the president, permitting the incumbent to serve two additional four-year terms, and putting organization of elections under the FRY instead of the individual republics. Although the Montenegrin Assembly described the changes as "illegal" and "a gross violation of the constitutional rights of the Republic of Montenegro," the legislators rejected a proposal for an immediate referendum on Montenegrin independence. In late July Milošević called elections for September, even though his presidential term would not expire until July 2001. The governing coalition in Montenegro quickly announced that it would boycott the balloting. The federal election of September 24 was followed by two weeks of turmoil that concluded with the demise of the Milošević regime and the inauguration on October 7 of Vojislav KOŠTUNICA.

On December 28, 2000, the NS withdrew from Montenegro's governing coalition in opposition to further movement toward independence. Four months later, President Djukanović entered the Montenegrin Assembly election of April 22, 2001, banking on a strong vote for separation from Serbia, but his DPS-SDP alliance failed to achieve more than a slight plurality against a coalition of the SNP, the NS, and the Serbian People's Party (*Srpska Narodna Stranka*—SNS). Three seats short of a majority, Djukanović turned to the Liberal Alliance, which agreed to extend external support to a new Vujanović cabinet, but the government's minority status soon forced the president to backtrack on plans for an immediate independence referendum.

On March 14, 2002, the governments of the Federal Republic of Yugoslavia and its two constituent republics announced an "agreement in principle" that would bring the history of Yugoslavia as such to an end, with its replacement by a "state union" to be called Serbia and Montenegro. Over the objections of parties that wanted a separate and independent Serbia, the Serbian legislature ratified the accord 149–79 on April 9. The same day, the Montenegrin legislature voted in favor of the agreement 58–11, despite strong opposition from the SDP and the previously government-supportive LSCG, both of which favored Montenegrin independence. Four SDP-affiliated ministers quickly resigned from the Montenegrin cabinet, and on April 19 Prime Minister Vujanović submitted his resignation, announcing that his government no longer commanded a legislative majority. At President Djukanović's request, Vujanović attempted to fashion another government, but he was unable to do so, and in July the president called for an early legislative election. Meanwhile, on May 31 both chambers of the Federal Assembly had approved the state union agreement by wide margins.

The Montenegrin Assembly election of October 20, 2002, saw a list headed by the DPS win 39 of 75 seats, compared to 30 for an opposition coalition. Following the election, caretaker Prime Minister Vujanović was elected speaker of the Montenegrin legislature. On November 25 Milo Djukanović resigned as president of Montenegro, and a day later Speaker Vujanović, in his new capacity as acting president, nominated Djukanović for the prime ministership (the office he had previously held from 1991 to 1998). Vujanović then ran in the Montenegrin presidential election of December 22. Although he won an overwhelming majority, an opposition boycott held the turnout under 50 percent, invalidating the results and forcing a similarly unsuccessful revote on February 9, 2003. In response, the Montenegrin Assembly eliminated the 50 percent requirement, and on May 11 Vujanović was elected president with 63 percent of the vote. Meanwhile, on January 8 Djukanović had been confirmed as prime minister.

On January 27 and 29, 2003, the Serbian and then the Montenegrin assemblies approved the Constitutional Charter for the state union of Serbia and Montenegro. The Federal Assembly concurred on February 4 (by votes of 26–7 in the upper chamber and 84–31 in the lower), thereby excising Yugoslavia from the political map. Under the charter a new state union Assembly was elected by and from among the members of the FRY, Serbian, and Montenegrin legislatures, and the new Assembly in turn elected the DPS's Marović, the only candidate, as state union president and chair of the Council of Ministers on March 7.

Under their 2003 EU-backed state union agreement, both Serbia and Montenegro had the right to vote on the question of independence in three years. On May 21, 2006, by a vote of 55.5 percent to 44.5 percent (half a percentage point above the EU threshold for approval), Montenegrins chose independence. Two weeks later, on June 3, the Montenegrin Assembly declared independence. On June 5, although many Serbians were unhappy with what they viewed as an abrupt divorce, the Serbian National Assembly declared Serbia to be the independent successor state to the state union, as had been agreed upon under the charter, and thereby extinguished the last remnants of the former Yugoslavia.

In the Montenegrin election of September 10, 2006, a coalition led by the DPS and SDP won a majority of 41 seats in the expanded 81-seat Montenegrin legislature. A multiparty opposition Serbian List, headed by the SNS, won 12 seats, while another ethnic Serbian coalition led by the SNP won 11. The new Movement for Change (*Pokret za Promjene*—PzP) also won 11 seats. On October 3 President Vujanović revealed that Prime Minister Djukanović had decided not to seek reappointment as prime minister, although he would remain at the helm of the DPS. A day later, Vujanović asked the minister of justice, Željko ŠTURANOVIĆ, to form a new government, and on November 10 the legislature confirmed the revamped Council of Ministers. However, on January 31, 2008, Šturanović resigned, citing health issues. Djukanović reassumed the office of the prime minister in February.

On April 6, 2008, sitting president and DPS candidate Filip Vujanović was reelected for another term in the first presidential elections since independence. In the first round of voting, Vujanović (51.9 percent of the vote) won an absolute majority over the Serb List candidate Andrija MANDIĆ (19.6 percent), PzP candidate Nebojša MEDOJEVIĆ (16.6 percent), and SNP candidate Srdjan MILIĆ (11.9 percent). Vujanović was inaugurated for his second term on May 21, 2008.

In January 2009 Djukanović proposed early elections although the sitting parliament had a year of its term remaining. Djukanović argued that new elections would provide a four-year mandate for a government to negotiate EU membership. The parliament voted for dissolution by a thin majority, the opposition arguing that the government hoped to use early elections to avoid voter retaliation for slowing economic growth.

In the parliamentary election of March 29, 2009, the Coalition for a European Montenegro (*Koalicija za Evropska Crna Gora*—KzECG) of the DPS, SDP, Bosniak Party (*Bošnjačka Stranka*—BS), and Croat Civic Initiative (*Hrvatska Gradjanska Inicijativa*—HGI) won 48 out of 81 seats; they were subsequently joined in forming a government by the Democratic Union of Albanians (*Demokratska Unija Albanaca*—DUA/*Unioni Demokratih i Shqiptarëve*—UDSh), a small Albanian political party with 1 seat. The SNP led the opposition with 16 seats, while the New Serb Democracy (*Nova Srpska Demokracija*—NSD) won 8 and the PzP won 5, with the remaining 3 seats being split between small Albanian political parties. Djukanović was reconfirmed for an additional term as prime minister on June 10.

Constitution and government. Yugoslavia under successive postwar constitutions remained a communist one-party state until the emergence of a variety of opposition groups at the republican level in early 1990. The constitution of the Federal Republic of Yugoslavia, adopted on April 27, 1992, provided for a bicameral Federal Assembly, encompassing a Chamber of Republics (with equal representation for Serbia and Montenegro) and a Chamber of Citizens apportioned on the basis of population. The federal president was elected to four-year terms by the assembly until July 2000, when the legislature passed constitutional changes that instituted direct elections for the presidency as well as for the Chamber of Republics. The president was expected to nominate a prime minister from the other constituent republic.

The Constitutional Charter of the state union of Serbia and Montenegro was formally adopted in February 2003 and lasted until both countries chose independence in 2006. It established a presidency with circumscribed powers, although the head of state also served as chair of the Council of Ministers, in which Serbians and Montenegrins shared executive responsibilities. The president was elected by and answerable to the unicameral legislature, the Assembly of Serbia and Montenegro, which comprised 91 Serbian and 35 Montenegrin deputies. The Court of Serbia and Montenegro comprised an equal number of judges from each republic. Each of the constituent republics had a popularly elected president and unicameral assembly, with a prime minister nominated by the former and confirmed by the latter. The judicial systems included Constitutional and Supreme Courts as well as lower-level courts.

Article 60 of the Constitutional Charter specified that after three years a member state could choose to initiate steps toward independence, which had to be approved by referendum in the initiating state. When Montenegro ultimately chose independence, as the charter specified, Serbia became the successor to the state union internationally, thereby inheriting the former federation's membership in the UN and all other international and financial organizations.

At independence, Montenegrins had yet to craft a process for drafting and approving a new constitution for the republic. The legislature postponed adoption of a new constitution until after the September 2006 general elections. The new basic law was approved by the assembly, sitting as a Constituent Assembly, on October 19, 2007, and promulgated on October 22. Under the constitution the president will continue to be elected for a five-year term and the current assembly is to remain as constituted. The legislative term, subject to early dissolution, is four years. The government is to be headed by a prime minister nominated by the president and confirmed by the legislature. The judiciary includes a Constitutional Court and a Supreme Court. The document failed, however, to satisfy the demands of most ethnic Serbs (see Current issues, below).

Foreign relations. As a constituent republic of the Federal Republic of Yugoslavia in the 1990s and then of the state union, Montenegro suffered from the international sanctions imposed because of the Serbian-led involvement in the Bosnian conflict, the Kosovo crisis, and Belgrade's failure to produce war crimes fugitives, especially Ratko Mladić (see the Serbia article). Following the defeat of Slobodan Milošević in 2000, the new Yugoslav government moved broadly to reestablish its international linkages. FRY was formally reintegrated into the UN on November 1 and into the Organization for Security and Cooperation in Europe (OSCE) on November 27. In April 2003 it joined the Council of Europe, and two months later it applied for membership in NATO's Partnership for Peace (PfP) program.

Just days after the declaration of independence, President Vujanović sent a letter to the UN seeking membership for Montenegro. The United States, the EU and its member nations, Russia, China, and many other governments quickly recognized Montenegrin independence shortly thereafter. The UN admitted Montenegro as its 192nd member on June 28, 2006, not long after Montenegro became the 56th member of the OSCE. It has subsequently been admitted to the International Monetary Fund, the World Bank, and other UN-related organizations, and in May 2007 it became the newest member of the Council of Europe. Two months earlier, Montenegro and the EU initialed a Stabilization and Association Agreement, regarded as the first step toward eventual EU membership. The Montenegrin government applied for NATO membership on November 5, 2008. It formally began the EU integration process by applying for membership on December 15, 2008.

Despite both historical ties to Serbia and divided domestic popular opinion, the Montenegrin government recognized the independence of Kosovo on October 9, 2008. Serbia subsequently expelled the Montenegrin ambassador to Belgrade, with relations sinking to their lowest level since Montenegrin independence.

Current issues. Despite the removal of the independence issue from the agenda, in mid-2006 the opposition parties seized on cultural anxieties raised by the slim margin of victory recorded by the proindependence forces in the May referendum. For example, petition drives demanding dual Montenegrin-Serbian citizenship sprang up soon after the votes were counted, although the Serbian government showed no inclination to automatically confer citizenship on all Montenegrins who declared themselves to be Serbs. Meanwhile, the pro-independence Bosniak and Albanian leadership were dismayed that the Constitutional Court had struck down the Minority Rights Act, which guaranteed seats in the assembly to minority groups based on their proportion in the population (one seat for groups less than 5 percent of the population; three seats for ethnic groups over 5 percent), even if they fell below the usual electoral threshold. The act had been passed just ten days before the referendum, after these leaders had made the bill a condition for their support of independence.

While the government began building the new country's international relations, it was already clear that progress toward achieving key goals—most particularly, entry into the EU and NATO—depended first and foremost on adoption of a new constitution. But the closeness of the September 2006 assembly election, which produced a slim majority for the DPS-SDP tandem and its allies, left the legislature sharply divided on a number of hot-button issues for the minority communities, especially the Serb population. Their concerns included whether minority representation should be guaranteed not only in the legislature but also in the government bureaucracy and agencies, how much autonomy minorities would be accorded with respect to education and cultural matters, and whether Serbian should remain the official language. Disputes also raged over state symbols, including the national coat-of-arms, the national anthem, and the design of the flag. Slavic Montenegrins remained divided between those who espouse a historical and unique Montenegrin identity and those who support a Montenegrin identity close to or part of a larger Serbian identity (e.g., proposing that the official language be called "Montenegrin-Serbian.") Many of the latter view themselves as ethnic Serbs within historical Montenegro and seek dual citizenship as Serbian citizens. The Serbian government in 2007 opened the possibility for recognizing such, but the DPS opposes any widespread implementation of dual citizenship.

The parliamentary drafting committee, assisted by the OSCE, succeeded in enumerating a variety of basic rights, such as freedom of speech, press, assembly, and association as well as presumption of innocence and the right to a fair and public trial. The committee also laid out a governmental structure based on the division of powers among executive, legislative, and judicial branches, complete with a system of checks and balances. In early April 2007 the assembly, after a week of heated debate, adopted a draft document that included alternatives proposed by minority representatives, and a period of "public debate" ensued. By August, however, neither the government majority nor the opposition appeared willing to compromise on the remaining issues. Apart from the concerns of the ethnic minority parties, the largest opposition party, the PzP, demanded that the government agree to a snap election upon adoption of the constitution. The DPS-SDP refused, and it began to appear unlikely that the constitution would receive the two-thirds vote needed for enactment by the legislature. If that route to adoption had remained blocked, a simple majority in a national referendum could have determined adoption or rejection. In the end, the PzP and the BS voiced support for the proposed constitution, which, with 55 votes in favor and 21 against, achieved the two-thirds tally needed for passage. Most ethnic Albanian representatives abstained, while the Serbs voted in opposition.

Milo Djukanović's decision to leave government in 2007 temporarily removed the main target of the opposition. His reinstatement as prime minister in February 2008 led, however, to renewed accusations that the government leadership has used its position for personal enrichment. Djukanović continues to be reviled by many opponents, who have labeled him as corrupt (Italian officials have accused him of tobacco smuggling) and tyrannical. Nevertheless, as the acknowledged architect of Montenegrin independence, he remains the country's most prominent politician internationally. Despite having been in high office since the early 1990s, Djukanović is only in his 40s, and he may well have a role in advancing Montenegro's integration into the European community.

Questions of symbolism continue to play a role in politics. The 2007 constitution made Montenegrin the official language of the country. Polls in that year showed that over 50 percent of the country preferred to refer to the language as Serbian, a position backed by the pro-union opposition. In June 2008 the SPD proposed that the capital be moved to the historic royal capital of Cetinje (recognized as such within the 2007 constitution), a move criticized by the SNS. In June 2009 a new Montenegrin Latin alphabet was announced as standard, replacing the existing Serbian Latin and Cyrillic alphabets; in July, a new official standard for the language was announced.

The ongoing financial crisis has reemphasized efforts to diversify the country's economy. Extremely high rates of foreign investment have helped to develop a growing tourism sector, but this has not fully replaced the industrial stock built during the Yugoslavia era. The foreign-owned Kombinat Aluminijuma Podgorica aluminum processing facility alone accounted for 15 percent of the country's GDP in 2008 and approximately 30 percent of its exports, but it relies on government subsidies. The threatened closure of the plant in 2009 without further government aid has reignited debates about the environmental impact of existing socialist industries, the role of foreign investment, and preferential industrial subsidies on electricity.

POLITICAL PARTIES

For four-and-a-half decades after World War II, Yugoslavia's only authorized political party was the Communist Party, which was redesignated as the League of Communists of Yugoslavia (*Savez Komunista Jugoslavija*—SKJ) in 1952. The collapse of Communist rule in 1989 and 1990 led to the formation of a large number of successor and other parties, including several "federal" groupings that sought, without success, to preserve the Yugoslav federation (see the 1994–1995 edition of the *Handbook*, p. 991).

In Montenegro, the Democratic Party of Socialists of Montenegro (DPS), successor to the League of Communists of Montenegro, has headed the government since the party's formation in the early 1990s, most recently in alliance with the smaller Social Democratic Party of Montenegro (SDP). Joined by the People's Party (NS), they contested the May 1998 Montenegrin election as the For a Better Life (*Da Živimo Bolje*—DŽB) alliance but chose to boycott the federal elections of September 2000, leaving the field to the republic's opposition parties, principally the Socialist People's Party of Montenegro (SNP) and the Serbian People's Party (SNS). With the NS having left the government in late December 2000, the DPS and the SDP formed the Victory Is Montenegro–Milo Djukanović Democratic Coalition (*Pobjeda Je Crne Gore–Demokratska Koalicija Milo Djukanović*) to contest the April 2001 Montenegrin election, in which it won 42 percent of the vote and a plurality of 36 seats. The SNP and the SNS were joined by the NS in the opposing, anti-independence Together for Yugoslavia (*Zajedno za Jugoslaviju*) coalition, which finished second, with 41 percent of the vote and 33 seats. In 2002 the DPS and the SDP formed the Democratic List for European Montenegro–Milo Djukanović (*Demokratska Lista za Evropsku Crnu Goru–Milo Djukanović*), which won 48 percent of the vote and 39 seats. The SNP, SNS, and NS ran as the Together for Changes *(Zajedno za Promjene*), which won 38 percent and 30 seats.

In 2006 the assembly opposition parties—the SNP, SNS, and NS-which had been joined in 2004 by the newly organized Democratic Serbian Party (DSS), were allied in support of maintaining the state union with Serbia and against the May 21, 2006, independence referendum. Their pro-union grouping was defeated by an electoral coalition of pro-independence DPS and SDP voters, with significant support from the Liberal Party of Montenegro (LPCG) and the ethnic Albanian and Bosniak party leaders and voters.

For the March 2009 parliamentary election 6 coalitions and 11 individual parties offered candidate lists.

Government Parties:

Coalition for a European Montenegro (*Koalicija za Evropski Crna Gora*—KzECG). The KzECG is the latest variation in a series of coalitions led by the DPS starting in 1998, initially as an anti- Milošević grouping. In 2009 the coalition included the DPS, HGI, BS, and SDP. In the March 2009 elections the KzECG won 51.9 percent of the vote and 48 seats (47 in the national proportional vote, and 1 of the seats elected by the ethnic Albanian minority). This secured a majority in parliament.

Democratic Party of Socialists of Montenegro (*Demokratska Partija Socijalista Crne Gore*—DPS). The DPS is the successor to the League of Communists of Montenegro. In December 1992 it retained a majority in the Montenegrin legislative poll with 44 percent of the vote and finished fourth in the federal lower house. In November 1996 it increased its federal representation and maintained its majority at the republican level, winning 45 seats. Historically very close to Slobodan Milošević, the party suffered from intense internal squabbling as increasingly anti-Milošević Prime Minister Milo Djukanović narrowly beat Momir Bulatović in the 1997 Montenegrin presidential election and ousted him from the party leadership. The party split in January 1998, with the Bulatović faction forming the SNP (below).

In May 1998 the DPS won 30 of the For a Better Life coalition's 42 legislative seats. Despite overtures from the anti-Milošević Democratic Opposition of Serbia alliance, the DPS chose to boycott the September 2000 federal elections, a major tactical error that left the anti-independence SNP in unchallenged control of the Montenegrin delegation to the federal Chamber of Citizens. In the April 2001 Montenegrin Assembly election the DPS-led Victory Is Montenegro coalition finished first but required the external support of the Liberal Alliance (see LPCG, below) to organize a government.

At the October 2002 republican election the DPS won 30 of the Democratic List's 39 seats. An effort in late 2002 by President Djukanović and Prime Minister Filip Vujanović to, in effect, exchange jobs was finally accomplished in 2003. The DPS also held the office of state union president and was the leading Montenegrin party in the state union assembly, although it fully intended to lead Montenegro to independence.

The DPS introduced the independence referendum legislation in the assembly. After the Constitutional Court ruled the Minority Rights Act unconstitutional, the DPS leadership offered guaranteed slots in the assembly to several of the minority parties provided they join the DPS in an election coalition. It also promised to pursue legislation or a constitutional provision to undo the court ruling and reinstate the guaranteed legislative seats for ethnic minority parties.

In the September 2006 parliamentary election the DPS led the Coalition for a European Montenegro–Milo Djukanović (*Koalicija za Evropsku Crnu Goru–Milo Djukanović*), which also included the SDP and the Croat Civic Initiative, to a slim majority of 41 seats. In April 2008 the DPS candidate for the presidency, Filip Vujanović, was reelected in the first round with almost 52 percent of the vote, surprising analysts who had predicted two rounds of elections. In March 2009 the DPS won 35 seats as part of the Coalition for a European Montenegro list.

Leaders: Milo DJUKANOVIĆ (Prime Minister and President of the Party), Filip VUJANOVIĆ (President of the Republic), Željko ŠTURANOVIĆ (Vice President of the Party), Filip VUJANOVIĆ (Vice President), Miodrag RADUNOVIĆ, Miodrag VUKOVIĆ (Parliamentary Whip).

Social Democratic Party of Montenegro (*Socijaldemokratska Partija Crne Gore*—SDP). Dating from the 1992 merger of three parties (two social democratic and one communist), the SDP was strongly pro-independence. It won one federal parliamentary seat in 1996. In the May 1998 Montenegrin legislative election, it won five seats as part of the For a Better Life coalition and joined the resultant government. It boycotted the 2000 federal election but again ran in coalition with the DPS in the April 2001 Montenegrin election. In October Ranko Krivokapić was elected party president, succeeding Žarko RAKČEVIĆ. In October 2002 the SDP won nine Montenegrin Assembly seats as part of the Democratic List.

The SDP was once again in coalition with the DPS in 2006, both for the independence referendum and the September parliamentary election, at which it won seven seats. In the March 2009 elections the SDP won nine seats as part of the Coalition for a European Montenegro list.

Leaders: Ranko KRIVOKAPIĆ (President of the Party and of the Montenegrin Assembly); Ivan BRAJOVIĆ, Vujica LAZOVIĆ, Rifat RASTODER (Vice Presidents).

Croat Civic Initiative (*Hrvatska Gradjanska Inicijativa*—HGI). The HGI was organized in 2002 prior to the October municipal elections in Tivat, in which it won four seats. The first Croat party to officially function in Montenegro since before World War II, it named Dalibor BURIĆ its first chair. It supported the independence referendum in 2006 and then in August agreed to join in the coalition formed by the DPS and SDP for the legislative election. It won one seat. Again competing with a DPS-led coalition in the March 2009 elections, the HGI won one seat as part of the coalition's list.

Leaders: Marija VUČINOVIĆ (President), Božo NIKOLIĆ (Member of the Assembly).

Bosniak Party (*Bošnjačka Stranka*—BS). The BS was established in February 2006 by merger of the Bosniak Muslim Alliance, the International Democratic Union, the Bosniak Democratic Alternative, and the Party of National Equality. With the independence referendum looming, the BS was seen as a vehicle for negotiating with both sides to achieve the most favorable terms for the Bosniak minority, which was split on the issue, in part because the Bosniak communities in the Sandžak region straddle the border between Serbia and Montenegro. In the end, the party chair, Rafet Husović, supported independence.

Afterwards, the BS rejected an overture by the DPS to join its coalition for the September 2006 parliamentary election and instead formed a coalition with the Liberal Party, the Liberals and Bosniak Party–"Correct in the Past, Right in the Future" (*Liberali i Bošnjačka Stranka–"Ispravni u Prošlosti, Pravi za Budnućnost"*), which won three seats. In December 2006 Husović called for the equality of Montenegrins, Serbians, and Bosniaks in their "mother country."

Although not officially a party leader, the Sandžak politician Harun HADŽIĆ has been closely linked to the BS.

In the March 2009 elections, the BS joined the DPS-led Coalition for a European Montenegro. It won three seats as part of the coalition's list.

Leaders: Rafet HUSOVIĆ (President and Minister without Portfolio), Ejup NURKOVIĆ (Vice President), Suljo MUSTAFIĆ (Leader of Assembly Delegation).

Democratic Union of Albanians (*Demokratska Unija Albanaca*—DUA/*Unioni Demokratih i Shqiptarëve*—UDSh). In the 2002 legislative election the DUA ran as the Democratic Coalition "Albanians Together" (*"Albanci Zajedno"*), which won two seats reserved for the Albanian community. The coalition included two other ethnic Albanian parties, the DSCG and the PPD (both discussed below). In April 2001 the three had run independently, with the DUA and the DSCG each winning one seat.

In 2006 the DUA supported independence but chose to run alone in the parliamentary election, in which it won one seat and then joined the governing coalition. In the March 29, 2009, elections the DUA again ran alone, winning 1.5 percent of the vote and one of the seats in parliament reserved for election by the ethnic Albanian minority.

Leader: Ferhat DINOŠA (Chair and Minister for Human and Minority Rights).

Opposition Parties:

Socialist People's Party of Montenegro (*Socijalistička Narodna Partija Crne Gore*—SNP). The SNP was formed in early 1998 by Momir Bulatović following his rupture with the DPS. It held its first congress in March 1998, at which 150 members of a governing committee were elected. In the republican election of May 1998 the party came in second, with 29 seats.

Under FRY Prime Minister Bulatović, the party maintained strict support for Slobodan Milošević through the September 2000 election. Because the governing Montenegrin coalition boycotted the balloting, the SNP virtually swept the Montenegrin polls, winning 19 of the republic's 20 upper house seats and 28 seats in the lower house. With Bulatović having resigned the federal prime ministership following Milošević's concession, the party's vice chair, Zoran ŽIŽIĆ, was selected as his successor by newly installed President Koštunica in late October.

The chair passed from Momir Bulatović to an opponent, Predrag BULATOVIĆ (no relation), at a party congress in February 2001, after which the SNP formed the Together for Yugoslavia alliance with the SNS and the NS (below) to contest the April Montenegrin legislative election. Following the June 2001 extradition to The Hague of Milošević to stand trial before the International Criminal Tribunal for the former Yugoslavia (ICTY), Prime Minister Žižić resigned in protest, but he was succeeded in mid-July by another SNP member, Dragiša Pešić, who remained in office until FRY was replaced by the state union. In the 2002 republican election the party won 19 of the 30 seats claimed by the Together for Changes coalition.

The SNP joined the other opposition parties in street protests against the DPS-SDP government throughout 2004 and the boycott of parliament in the same year. The SNP also spearheaded the pro-union coalition in opposition to the 2006 independence referendum. After the vote for independence, Predrag Bulatović steered the party toward a pragmatic "constructive dialogue" on postindependence platform issues, especially the need for a draft constitution, support for more democratic institutions, and engagement with the path toward European integration.

Negotiations toward a pre-election coalition with the other opposition parties were complicated by charges by SNP leaders of "poaching" tactics by the other opposition parties, especially the SNS, directed at SNP voters. In the end, the SNP and SNS formed separate coalitions, with the SNP leading the **SNP-NS-DSS Koalicija**, which won 11 parliamentary seats, 8 of them by the SNP. As a result of the poor showing, Bulatović resigned as chair in October. At the party's Fifth Congress, held in late November, Srdjan Milić defeated Dragiša Pešić and Borislav GLOBAREVIĆ for the leadership. Three deputy chairs were named in January 2007. Milić, nominated by the party for the 2008 presidential election, took almost 12 percent of the vote in the first round, placing fourth.

In the March 29, 2009, elections the SNP won 16.83 percent of the vote, for 16 seats in parliament.

Leaders: Srdjan MILIĆ (Chair); Milorad BAKIĆ, Vasilije LALOŠEVIĆ, and Dragiša PEŠIĆ (Deputy Chairs).

New Serb Democracy (*Nova Srpska Demokratija*—NSD). The NSD was formed in January 2009 as a merger between the Serbian People's Party (*Srpska Narodna Stranka*—SNS) and the People's Socialist Party of Montenegro (*Narodna Socijalistička Stranka Crne Gore*—NSS).

The Serbian People's Party was registered as a party in March 1998 by a dissident faction of the NS (below). Although the party continued to support the Milošević regime through the Kosovo crisis, some local party leaders refused to support the federal president's reelection in 2000. A party congress in February 2001 elected former NS leader Božidar Bojović as chair, succeeding Zelidrag NIKČEVIĆ. In October 2002 the SNS won six seats in the Montenegrin legislature. A year later Bojović was replaced by current leader Andrija Mandić and quickly formed the DSS.

The SNS joined the prounion coalition in opposition to the 2006 independence referendum. Postreferendum news accounts alleged that SNS party members attributed the success of the referendum vote to the support of ethnic minority voters and therefore demonstrated increased hostility toward ethnic minorities, especially Bosniaks, in Serb-dominated areas.

After independence, SNS leaders positioned the party to advocate for policies aimed at protecting the status of Serbs in Montenegro. The SNS launched a petition drive advocating dual Serbian citizenship for Montenegrin Serbs, and party leaders publicly called for measures to preserve cultural autonomy and proportional representation in political institutions for Serbs. It parted ways with a key ally, the SNP, prior to the September 2006 election and instead headed the Serbian List–Andrija Mandić (*Srpska Lista–Andrija Mandić*), which included another frequent ally, the Montenegrin branch of the xenophobic Serbian Radical Party (see SSR, below), as well as the Democratic Party of Unity (DSJ, below), the NSS, and a nongovernmental organization, the Serb National Council (*Srpsko Naradno Veće*—SNV). The SNS won 8 of the list's 12 seats, with each of the other four organizations in the coalition claiming 1. Mandić was reelected president in December 2006. As PzP president, he has endorsed strongly pro-Serbian policies, including opposition to the 2007 constitution (for formally changing the national language to Montenegrin from Serbian) and organizing rallies against any Montenegrin recognition of Kosovo's independence. Mandić himself has taken dual Montenegrin and Serbian citizenship. In the 2008 presidential elections the SNS-led Serbian List nominated Mandić as a common candidate, taking second place with almost a fifth of the vote. Following the government's decision to recognize an independent Kosovo in October 2008, the SNS led the Serbian List in a boycott of parliamentary functions.

The NSS was established in February 2001 by supporters of former FRY prime minister Momir Bulatović following his ouster from the SNP. The party failed to attract significant support in the April 2001 Montenegrin Assembly election, capturing less than 3 percent of the vote and therefore winning no seats. In 2002 it ran as a component of the Patriotic Coalition for Yugoslavia (*Patriotska Koalicija za Jugoslavia*—PK), which also included the Serbia-based Yugoslav United Left and Serbian Radical Party, but again failed to meet the 3 percent threshold. In 2006, as a component of the Serbian List, the NSS won one parliamentary seat.

The unified NSD won 9.2 percent of the vote in March 2009, securing 8 seats.

Leaders: Andrija MANDIĆ (President); Goran DANILOVIĆ (Deputy President); Emil LABUDOVIĆ, Slaven RADULOVIĆ, and Strahinja BULAJIĆ (Vice-Presidents).

Movement for Change (*Pokret za Promjene*—PzP). The PzP began as a nongovernmental organization, the Group for Change (*Grupa za Promjene*—GzP), which was a significant participant in public discourse from its founding in 2002. Modeled on Serbia's G17 Plus think tank of economists, the GzP focused in part on ending corruption in the public sector, which it attributed primarily to the dominance of the DPS under Milo Djukanović. Its principal leaders, Executive Director Nebojša Medojević and Chair Svetozar JOVIĆEVIĆ, ranked among Montenegro's most respected public figures in the period leading up to independence. Many of its members appeared to support independence, but the GzP itself did not take a stand on the referendum.

Registered as a party in July 2006, the PzP surprised most observers by winning 11 legislative seats in September. As part of the opposition, it has frequently been allied with the leading Serbian parties, although it supported adoption of the 2007 constitution. Medojević, the party's candidate in the 2008 presidential elections, took third place with almost 17 percent of the vote in the first round. In the March 29, 2009, elections the party took approximately 6 percent of the vote and 5 seats.

Leaders: Nebojša MEDOJEVIĆ (Chair); Branko RADULOVIĆ , Dušanka TUŠUP, and Zoran MARSENIĆ (Deputy Chairs).

New Democratic Force (*Nova Demokratska Snaga/Forca e Re Demokratike*—FORCA). *FORCA* was founded in October 2005 as a local ethnic Albanian political party in the coastal town of Ulcinj. *FORCA* subsequently expanded into other municipalities with a substantial ethnic Albanian minority. In the September 2006 parliamentary elections *FORCA* won 0.7 percent of the vote and no seats. In the March 29, 2009, elections, it won 1.9 percent of the vote and one of the seats elected by the ethnic Albanian minority.

Leader: Nazif CUNGU (Chair).

Albanian List (*Albanski List/Lista Shqiptare*—AL/LS). The AL/LS is an electoral alliance of two small ethnic Albanian parties: the **Democratic Alliance of Montenegro** (*Demokratski Savez u Crnoj Gori*—DSCG), led by Mehmet BARDHI, and the Podgorica-based **Albanian Alternative** (*Albanska Alternativa/Alternativa Shqiptare*—AL/AS). In the September 2006 parliamentary elections both the DSCG and AL/AS each won a single seat in parliament. In the March 29, 2009, elections the combined AL/LS won 0.9 percent of the national vote, and as a coalition won a single seat in parliament from those elected by the ethnic Albanian minority.

Albanian Coalition–Perspective (*Albanska Koalicija–Perspektiva/Koalicioni Shqiptar–Perspektiva*—AKP/KSP). Founded in February 2009 by dissident factions from several existing ethnic Albanian parties, the AKP/KSP won 0.8 percent of the vote and one seat in parliament from among those elected by the ethnic Albanian minority.

Leader: Amir HOLLAJ.

Other Parties that Participated in the 2009 Elections:

People's Coalition (*Narodjačka Koalicija*—NK). The NK electoral alliance was formed by the NS and DSS in February 2009; negotiations for a larger conservative coalition with the SNP or NSD were initiated but failed to reach an agreement. In the March 29, 2009, elections the NK took 2.9 percent of the vote, failing to pass the threshold.

People's Party (*Narodna Stranka*—NS). Historically an intensely pan-Serbian formation, the NS supported the maintenance of Montenegro's ties with Serbia. It won 14 seats and 13 percent of the vote in the December 1992 Montenegrin election. In November 1996 an NS coalition with the Liberal Alliance (see LPCG, below) called the People's Accord (*Narodna Sloga*) won 19 seats in the Montenegrin legislature as well as 8 federal seats. In March 1997 differences over continuing support for the coalition led supporters of the party's vice chair, Božidar Bojović, to attempt expulsion of the president, Novak KILIBARDA, who was moving closer toward accepting Montenegrin independence. Kilibarda's NS joined the DPS in forming the For a Better Life coalition shortly before the May 1998 Montenegrin election, in which it won 7 seats. In the same month the Bojović faction registered a new pro-Belgrade party, the SNS. Kilibarda joined the governing Montenegrin coalition as a deputy prime minister.

In March 2000, rejecting Kilibarda's pro-independence stance, the NS replaced him with Dragan Šoć, the Montenegrin minister of justice. On December 28, objecting to the latest independence moves by President Djukanović, the NS left the governing coalition and subsequently allied itself with the SNP for the April 2001 election. (Kilibarda, meanwhile, had established the **People's Accord of Montenegro** [*Narodna Sloga Crne Gore*—NSCG], which has not played a notable role in Montenegrin politics.) In October 2002 it won five assembly seats as part of the Together for Changes coalition.

After independence, the NS leaders rebuffed SNS proposals for a Serbian List in favor of working to preserve the broader prounion coalition with the SNP and DSS. In the September 2006 election the NS won 2 of the SNP-NS-DSS Coalition's 11 seats and then formed a 3-member parliamentary floor group with the DSS representative.

Leaders: Predrag POPOVIĆ (Chair), Dragan ŠOĆ, Budimir DUBAK.

Democratic Serbian Party (*Demokratska Srpska Stranka—*DSS). This Montenegrin-based version of Serbia's DSS was launched by former NS and SNS party leader Božidar Bojović in December 2003. The DSS joined the opposition parties' street protests against the DPS-SDP government throughout 2004. The DSS also joined the pro-union coalition in opposition to the 2006 independence referendum. After the referendum DSS leaders rebuffed calls from the SNS for a Serbian list to contest the 2006 parliamentary elections, advocating instead for preservation of the larger pro-union coalition of parties.

Leaders: Ranko KADIĆ (Chair), Božidar BOJOVIĆ.

Liberal Party of Montenegro (*Liberalna Partija Crne Gore—*LPCG). The LPCG was established on October 31, 2004, under the leadership of Miodrag Živković, the former chair of the Liberal Alliance of Montenegro (*Liberalni Savez Crne Gore—*LSCG), following his expulsion from the LSCG in September.

Established in 1990 as a strong supporter of independence for Montenegro, the LSCG won 13 seats in the 1992 republican elections but failed to approach that total in subsequent contests. It won 6 seats in the April 2001 assembly election, after which it supported formation of a minority DPS-SDP government. Only a year later, however, it withdrew its support over objections to formation of the state union. In the resultant October 2002 Montenegrin election its representation fell to 4 seats, even though it had made major gains in municipal elections. In the May 2003 three-way republican presidential contest, Živković finished second, with 30 percent of the vote.

In 2004 the party split, largely over the issue of independence, leading to the Liberal Alliance chair's expulsion in September. On March 24, 2005, delegates to an extraordinary conference of the LSCG voted to end the Liberal Alliance party's existence. Longtime party leader Slavko PEROVIĆ condemned Montenegro's intelligentsia and opposition for abandoning their mission, and attacked the Djukanović regime as "mafia-ridden."

With the LSCG now defunct, LPCG leader Živković set his new party in support of independence but continued opposition to the alleged criminality and abuse of power by the Djukanović regime. (In July 2004 he had been found guilty of libeling the prime minister with salacious accusations.) It ran in alliance with the BS in 2006, winning only one seat.

For the 2009 elections the LPCG formed an electoral alliance with the **Democratic Center** (*Demokratskog Centra—*DC), the **For a Different Montenegro Coalition** (*Za Drugačiju Crnu Goru—*ZDCG). The ZDCG took 2.71 percent of the vote in the March 29, 2009, elections, failing to pass the threshold.

Leaders: Andrija POPOVIĆ (Chair), Miodrag ŽIVKOVIĆ.

Party of Serb Radicals (*Stranka Srpskih Radikala—*SSR). The SSR began as the Montenegrin branch of Serbia's Serbian Radical Party (*Srpska Radikalna Stranka—*SRS), which was founded in February 1991 by Vojislav Šešelj, the radical pan-Serbian leader being tried by the ICTY for crimes against humanity. The SRS, a quasi-fascist advocate of "Greater Serbia" that emphasizes the importance of its "leader" (*vodj*), is a leading party in Serbia's legislature.

The Montenegrin SRS joined the Serbian List in the run-up to the 2006 election and came away with one seat. In December it adopted its current name because the inclusion of Šešelj's name in the party's formal title violated Montenegro's law on political parties. Although legally independent of Serbia's SRS, the SSR leadership has stated that in all other respects they are the same.

The Serbian List coalition fractured before the 2009 elections, with several new formations emerging. A new **Serb National List** (*Srpska Nacionalna Lista—*SNL) included the SSR; the **Serbian People's Party** (*Stranka Srpski Narodnjaka—*SSN), a faction of the SNS led by Dobriolo Dedeić; and the **Serbian National Council** (*Srpsko Narodno Veče—*SNV), led by Momcilo Vuksanović. In the March 29, 2009, elections the SNL received 1.3 percent of the vote, failing to pass the threshold.

Leaders: Duško SEKULIĆ (Chair), Bojan STRUNJAŠ.

Other parties participating in the March 29, 2009, elections included **the Party of Pensioners and Disabled People of Montenegro** (*Stranka Penzionera i Invalida Crne Gore*); the **Bosniaks and Muslims Together, as One** (*Bošnjaci i Muslimani zajedno, jedno*); the **Fatherland Serbian Party** (*Otadzhbinska Srpska Stranka*); the **Montenegrin Communists** (*Crnogorski komunisti*); and the ethnic Albanian **Party of Democratic Prosperity** (*Partija Demokratskog Prosperiteta/Partia e Prosperitetit Demokratik*).

Other Parties:

Civic Party of Montenegro (*Gradjanska Partija Crne Gore—*GPCG). The small GPCG joined the Democratic List for European Montenegro prior to the October 2002 election and was awarded one assembly seat. In 2003 it supported independent presidential candidate Dragan HAJDUKOVIĆ, who won 4 percent of the vote.

Party leader Krsto PAVIĆEVIĆ was outspoken in his criticism of the DPS leadership following a ruling of the Constitutional Court in July 2006 striking down the Minority Rights Act. He opined that because the court was under the political control of the DPS, the court's action should be reversed by Prime Minister Djukanović to maintain good faith with the ethnic Bosniak and Albanian parties.

For the September 2006 parliamentary election the GPCG ran as part of the **Civic List** (*Gradjanska Lista*) along with Hajduković's newly formed **Green Party** (*Zeleni Partija*). In October, with the Civic List having failed to obtain even 1 percent of the national vote, the GPCG's principal officers, including Krsto Pavićević, Petar BOKAN, and Slobodan MEDENICA, resigned. The party is not currently active at the national level and did not enter the March 2009 parliamentary elections, but it does hold elected municipal seats.

Leaders: Milorad DAPČEVIĆ, Nedjeljko DJUROVIĆ, Džoni HODŽIĆ, Davor KLASIĆ.

Democratic Party of Unity (*Demokratska Stranka Jedinstva—*DSJ). The DSJ is a new party registered in mid-2006 by Zoran Žižić, who was previously vice chair of the SNP. Žižić left the SNP when that party declined to join the Serbian List coalition in the run-up to the September 10 polls. Failing to reach a coalition accord with the SNP or the Serbian List, the DSJ did not enter the March 2009 elections.

Leader: Zoran ŽIŽIĆ (Chair and Member of the Assembly).

For a list of other small parties that participated in the 2006 elections, see the 2009 *Handbook*.

LEGISLATURE

Assembly of the Republic of Montenegro (*Skupština Republike Crne Gore*). The 81 members of the assembly (sometimes referred to as parliament) are elected to four-year terms by proportional representation. Parties must meet a 3 percent threshold to qualify for 76 national seats; the Albanian minority elects 5 other representatives. Results for the election of March 29, 2009, were as follows: Coalition for a European Montenegro, 48 seats (Democratic Party of Socialists of Montenegro, 35; Social Democratic Party, 9; Bosniak Party, 3; Croat Civic Initiative, 1); Socialist People's Party of Montenegro, 16; New Serb Democracy, 8; Movement for Change, 5; Albanian Coalition–Perspective, 1; Albanian List (Democratic Alliance of Montenegro and Albanian Alternative), 1; Democratic Union of Albanians, 1; New Democratic Force, 1.

President: Ranko KRIVOKAPIĆ.

CABINET

[as of October 1, 2009]

Prime Minister	Milo Djukanović (DPS)
Deputy Prime Minister	Svetozar Marković (DPS)
Deputy Prime Minister	Igor Lukšić (DPS)
Deputy Prime Minister for Economic Policy and Finance	Vujica Lazović (SDP)

Ministers

Agriculture, Forestry, and Water Management	Milutin Simović (DPS)
Culture, Sports, and Media	Branislav Mićunović (DPS)
Defense	Boro Vučinić (DPS)
Economic Development	Branko Vujović (DPS)
Education and Science	Sreten Škuletić (DPS)
Finance	Gordana Djurović (DPS) [f]
Foreign Affairs	Milan Roćen (DPS)
Health,	Miodrag Radunović (DPS)
Human and Minority Rights	Ferhat Dinoša (DUA)
Interior Affairs and Public Administration	Ivan Brajović (SDP)
Justice	Miraš Radović (ind.)
Labor and Social Welfare	Suad Numanović (DPS)
Maritime Affairs, Transportation, and Communications	Andrija Lompar (SDP)
Tourism and Environmental Protection	Predrag Nenezić (DPS)
Urbanism and Environmental Protection	Branimir Gvozdenović (DPS)
Without Portfolio	Slavoljub Stijepović (DPS)
	Rafet Husović (BS)

[f] = female

COMMUNICATIONS

Press. The following are dailies published in Podgorica in Serbo-Croatian or Montenegrin, unless otherwise noted: *Vijesti* (20,000); *Dan,* opposition (15,000); *Pobjeda,* state-run (8,000); *Republika* (3,000); and *Monitor*, weekly.

News agencies. An independent news agency, MNNews, operates from Montenegro.

Broadcasting and computing. Montenegro has a state-funded broadcasting service, *Radio-Televizija Crne Gore,* that offers two radio and two television networks as well as satellite service. There are also numerous privately owned stations.

As of 2008 there were 472.4 Internet users per 1,000 inhabitants.

INTERGOVERNMENTAL REPRESENTATION

Ambassador to the U.S.: Miodrag VLAHOVIĆ.

U.S. Ambassador to Montenegro: Roderick W. MOORE.

Permanent Representative to the UN: Nebojša KALUDJEROVIĆ.

IGO Memberships (Non-UN): CEI, CEUR, EBRD, Eurocontrol, Interpol, IOM, OSCE, PCA, WCO.

MOROCCO

Kingdom of Morocco
al-Mamlakat al-Maghribiyah

Political Status: Independent since March 2, 1956; constitutional monarchy established in 1962; present constitution approved March 1, 1972.

Area: 274,461 sq. mi. (710,850 sq. km.), including approximately 97,343 sq. mi. (252,120 sq. km.) of Western Sahara, two-thirds of which was annexed in February 1976 and the remaining one-third claimed upon Mauritanian withdrawal in August 1979.

Population: 29,891,708 (2004C); 31,599,000 (2008E).

Major Urban Centers (2005E): RABAT (1,654,000), Casablanca (2,957,000), Fez (967,000), Marrakesh (840,000), Oujda (406,000).

Official Language: Arabic.

Monetary Unit: Dirham (official rate December 1, 2009: 7.57 dirhams = $1US).

Sovereign: King MOHAMED VI, became king on July 23, 1999, following the death of his father, HASSAN II.

Heir to the Throne: Crown Prince MOULAY HASSAN.

Prime Minister: Abbas EL FASSI (*Istiqlal*), appointed by King Mohamed on September 19, 2007, replacing Driss JETTOU (nonparty).

THE COUNTRY

Located at the northwest corner of Africa, Morocco combines a long Atlantic coastline and Mediterranean frontage facing Gibraltar and southern Spain. Bounded by Algeria on the northeast and (following annexation of the former Spanish Sahara) by Mauritania on the south, the country is topographically divided into a rich agricultural plain in the northwest and an infertile mountain and plateau region in the east that gradually falls into the Sahara in the south and southwest. The population is approximately two-thirds Arab and one-third Berber, with small French and Spanish minorities. Islam is the state religion, most of the population adhering to the Sunni sect and following the Maliki school. Arabic is the language of the majority, most others speaking one or more dialects of Berber; Spanish is common in the northern regions and French among the educated elite. Women comprise 35 percent of the paid labor force, concentrated mainly in textile manufacture and domestic service; overall, one-third of the female population is engaged in unpaid family labor on agricultural estates. Increasing numbers of women from upper-income brackets have participated in local and national elections, but have obtained minimal representation. Women were allocated 30 seats in the House of Representatives in advance of the September 2007 elections in an attempt to address this issue. After that election, seven women were appointed to cabinet positions, up from five in the previous administration. In the 2009 local election women gained just over 3,400 seats as the result of legislation that guaranteed women a minimum of 12 percent of the total seats. This was an increase in representation of 250 percent over the 2003 balloting.

The agricultural sector employs approximately 40 percent of the population; important crops include cereals and grains, oilseeds, nuts, and citrus fruits. One of the world's leading exporters of phosphates, Morocco also has important deposits of lead, iron, cobalt, zinc, manganese, and silver; overall, mining accounts for about 45 percent of export receipts. The industrial sector emphasizes import substitution (textiles, chemicals, cement, plastics, machinery), while tourism and fishing are also major sources of income. Trade is strongly oriented toward France, whose economic influence has remained substantial. Since the early 1980s the economy has suffered from periodic droughts, declining world demand for phosphates, rapid urbanization, and high population growth. Unemployment remains a problem, with youth and talent seeking opportunity in Europe. Reports from the International Monetary Fund (IMF) and World Bank noted that Morocco's economic growth has been steady despite its failure to meet targets in growth, investment, and exports. Continued dependence on the agricultural sector of the economy remains a problem.

Living conditions remain low by regional standards, and wealth is poorly distributed. However, with its low inflation rate and cheap labor pool, Morocco is considered by some as a potential target for substantial investment by developed (particularly European) countries. To encourage such interest, the government continues to privatize many state-run enterprises, address the high (44.9 percent) illiteracy rate, and reform the stock market, tax system, and banking sector. However, the pace of reform remains somewhat sluggish.

A more costly wage structure and higher oil subsidies contributed to a rapidly rising budget deficit and a concomitant drop in the GDP growth rate to 1.2 percent in 2005. However, a 2004 free trade

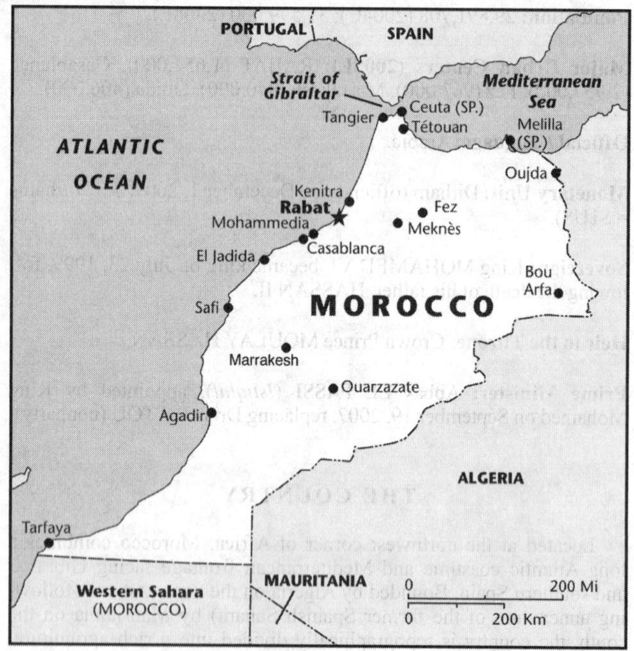

agreement with the United States (see Foreign relations, below) took effect in January 2006, improving prospects for increased direct foreign investment. Concurrently, Morocco's decision to allow private purchase of shares in the largest state-owned bank and the state telecommunications company further enhanced the climate for foreign capital. A widespread drought in 2007 hindered grain production that year and the following one (see Current issues, below). Remittances from workers abroad and steady tourist receipts helped the economic picture, although there were concerns that recent terrorist attacks and the discovery of a series of militant cells during 2007 and 2008 would have a negative impact on tourism.

Although in 2008 the agricultural sector recovered from the droughts of previous years, the worldwide economic crisis constrained growth as remittances from Moroccans living abroad declined by 9.7 percent, while exports were down 34 percent and imports fell by 23 percent. Nonetheless, GDP grew by 5.3 percent in 2008, while inflation remained low at 2 percent. Meanwhile, unemployment rose to 10.2 percent. GDP growth was expected to rise to more than 6 percent in 2009.

GOVERNMENT AND POLITICS

Political background. Originally inhabited by Berbers, Morocco was successively conquered by the Phoenicians, Carthaginians, Romans, Byzantines, and Arabs. From 1912 to 1956 the country was subjected to de facto French and Spanish control, but the internal authority of the sultan was nominally respected. Under pressure by Moroccan nationalists, the French and Spanish relinquished their protectorates, and the country was reunified under Sultan MOHAMED V in 1956. Tangier, which had been under international administration since 1923, was ceded by Spain in 1969.

King Mohamed V tried to convert the hereditary sultanate into a modern constitutional monarchy but died before the process was complete. It remained for his son, King HASSAN II, to implement his father's goal in a constitution adopted in December 1962. However, dissatisfaction with economic conditions and the social policy of the regime led to rioting at Casablanca in March 1965, and three months later the king assumed legislative and executive powers.

In June 1967 the king relinquished the post of prime minister, but the continued hostility of student and other elements led to frequent governmental changes. A new constitution, approved in July 1970, provided for a partial resumption of parliamentary government, a strengthening of royal powers, and a limited role for political parties. Despite the opposition of major political groups, trade unions, and student organizations, an election for a new unicameral House of Representatives was held in August 1970, yielding a progovernment majority. However, the king's failure to unify the country behind his programs was dramatically illustrated by abortive military revolts in 1971 and 1972.

A new constitution was overwhelmingly approved by popular referendum in March 1972, but the parties refused to enter the government because of the monarch's reluctance to schedule legislative elections. After numerous delays, elections to communal and municipal councils were finally held in November 1976, to provincial and prefectural assemblies in January 1977, and to a reconstituted national House of Representatives in June 1977. On October 10 the leading parties agreed to participate in a "National Unity" cabinet headed by Ahmed OSMAN as prime minister.

Osman resigned on March 21, 1979, ostensibly to oversee reorganization of the proroyalist National Assembly of Independents (RNI), although the move was reported to have been precipitated by his handling of the lengthy dispute over the Western Sahara (see Disputed Territory, below). He was succeeded on March 22 by Maati BOUABID, a respected Casablanca attorney.

On May 30, 1980, a constitutional amendment extending the term of the House of Representatives from four to six years was approved by referendum, thus postponing new elections until 1983. The king indicated in June 1983 that the legislative poll, scheduled for early September, would be further postponed pending the results of a referendum in the Western Sahara to be sponsored by the Organization of African Unity (OAU, subsequently the African Union—AU). On November 30 a new "unity" cabinet headed by Mohamed Karim LAMRANI was announced, with Bouabid, who had organized a new moderate party eight months earlier, joining other party leaders in accepting appointment as ministers of state without portfolio.

The long-awaited legislative poll was finally held on September 14 and October 2, 1984, with Bouabid's Constitutional Union (UC) winning a plurality of both direct and indirectly elected seats, while four centrist parties collectively obtained a better than two-to-one majority. Following lengthy negotiations, a new coalition government, headed by Lamrani, was formed on April 11, 1985.

Although King Hassan appeared to remain popular with most of his subjects, domestic opposition leaders and Amnesty International continued to charge the government with human rights abuses and repression of dissent, including the alleged illegal detention and mistreatment of numerous leftists and Islamic extremists arrested in 1985 and 1986. On September 30, 1986, the king appointed Dr. Azzedine LARAKI, former national education minister, as prime minister, following Lamrani's resignation for health reasons.

Attributed in large measure to improvements in the economy, calm ensued, with domestic and international attention focusing primarily on the Western Sahara. Thus, a national referendum on December 1, 1989, overwhelmingly approved the king's proposal to postpone legislative elections due in 1990, ostensibly to permit participation by Western Saharans following a self-determination vote in the disputed territory.

In mid-1992, amid indications that the referendum might be delayed indefinitely or even abandoned, the government announced that forthcoming local and national elections would include the residents of Western Sahara as participants. On August 11 King Hassan reappointed Lamrani as prime minister and announced a "transitional cabinet" to serve until a postelection cabinet could be established under new constitutional provisions (see Constitution and government, below).

The basic law revisions were approved on September 4, 1992, by a national referendum, which the government hailed as a significant step in its ongoing democratization program. Widespread disbelief greeted the government's claim that 97.5 percent of the electorate had participated and that a 99.9 percent "yes" vote had been registered.

In balloting for directly elective house seats, delayed until June 25, 1993, the newly established Democratic Bloc (*Koutla*), a coalition of center-left opposition groups led by the old-guard *Istiqlal* party and the Socialist Union of Popular Forces (USFP), secured 99 seats. They won only 15 more in the September 17 voting in electoral colleges made up of local officials, trade unionists, and representatives of professional associations. Meanwhile, the National Entente (*Wifaq*), a group of center-right royalist parties, increased its representation from 116 in the first round of balloting to 195 after the second. The Democratic Bloc subsequently charged that the indirect election encompassed widespread fraud, an allegation that received some support from international observers.

Although King Hassan rejected the Democratic Bloc's demand that the results of the indirect poll be overturned, he did propose that the bloc participate in the formation of a new cabinet, the first of what

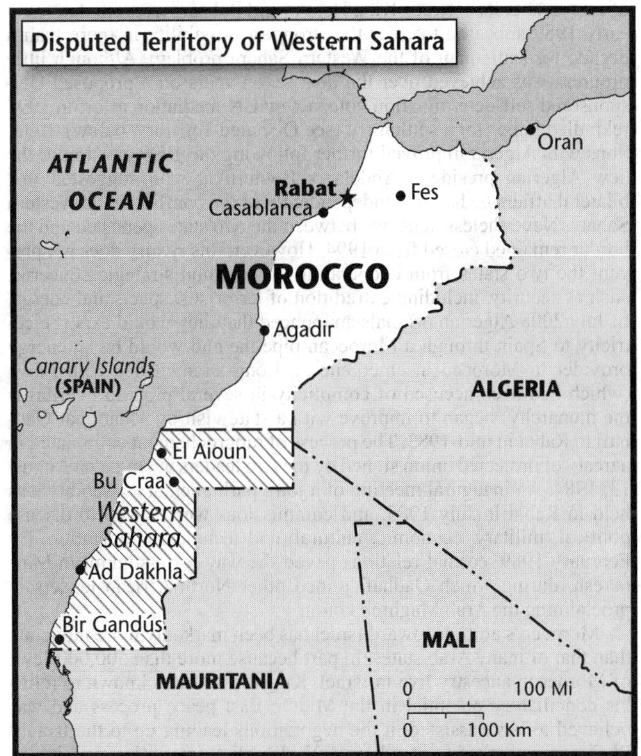

the king envisioned as a series of alternating left-right governments. The offer was declined because of the monarch's insistence that he retain the right to appoint the prime minister and maintain de facto control of the foreign, justice, and interior portfolios. Consequently, Lamrani formed a new nonparty government on November 11.

With his poor health again cited as the official reason for the change, Lamrani was succeeded on May 25, 1994, by former foreign minister Abdellatif FILALI, a longtime close adviser to the king. On June 7 Filali presented the monarch with a ministerial list unchanged from that of his predecessor, while King Hassan continued to seek Democratic Bloc leadership of a new coalition government. The negotiations eventually collapsed in early 1995, in part because of the king's wish that Driss BASRI, long-term minister of state for interior and information, remain in the cabinet. The opposition parties had objected to Basri's influence for many years, charging that he had sanctioned human rights abuses and tolerated electoral fraud. Nonetheless, Basri retained the interior post on February 28 when Filali's new government, including 20 members of the National Entente, was announced.

Despite his failure to draw the leftist parties into the government, the king continued to pursue additional democratization, particularly regarding the proposed creation of an upper house of the legislature that, theoretically, would redistribute authority away from the monarchy to a certain degree. The king's proposal was affirmed by a reported 99.56 percent "yes" vote in a national referendum on September 13, 1996, most opposition parties having endorsed the amendment (see Constitution and government, below, for details).

Local elections were held on June 13, 1997, with seats being distributed along a wide spectrum of parties and no particular political dominance being apparent. Such was also the case with the November 14 balloting for a new House of Representatives as the *Koutla*, *Wifaq*, and a bloc of centrist parties each won about one-third of the seats. On the other hand, the indirect elections to the new House of Councilors revealed a decided tilt toward the *Wifaq*, not a surprising result considering its long-standing progovernment stance.

Continuing to pursue an alternating left-right series of governments, King Hassan was subsequently able to finally persuade the Democratic Bloc to assume cabinet control, and on February 4, 1998, he appointed Abderrahmane YOUSSOUFI of the USFP (which had won the most seats in the House of Representatives) as the next prime minister. As formed on March 14, the new cabinet included representatives from seven parties, although the King's supporters (most notably Basri) remained in several key posts.

King Hassan, whose health had been a concern since 1995, died of a heart attack on July 23, 1999; Crown Prince SIDI MOHAMED succeeded his father immediately, the official ceremony marking his enthronement as King MOHAMED VI being held on July 30. Shortly thereafter, Driss Basri, who was nicknamed "The Butcher" by human rights activists and had presided over a period of government crackdowns on the opposition, was dismissed as minister of the interior and moved to Paris, where he died in August 2007. The new king confirmed his support for Prime Minister Youssoufi and his government. The cabinet was reshuffled on September 6, 2000, with Youssoufi retaining the top post, but the new king replaced him with an independent, Driss JETTOU, in 2002.

Parliamentary elections in September 2007 maintained a conservative government. After a record low turnout of 37 percent, the party *Istiqlal*, a member of the Democratic Bloc, took control. Abbass EL FASSI was appointed prime minister on September 19, 2007, and on October 15 formed a cabinet that reflected the king's desire for a moderately conservative, reformist government.

Prior to local balloting in June 2009 the newly formed Party of Authenticity and Modernity (PAM), which included a number of members of the House of Representatives who had defected from other parties, announced it would join the opposition (see Current issues, below). PAM placed first in the local elections, followed by *Istiqlali* in the contest to select more than 28,000 local councillors. During the balloting, Fatima Zahra Mansouri of the PAM became the first woman elected mayor of a major city, Marrakech, and only the second woman ever elected to lead a city in Morocco. In July there was a minor cabinet reshuffle which brought the Popular Movement (MP) into the government and expanded the number of ministers from the USFP and the RNI. The reshuffle was undertaken in order to maintain the government's majority in the legislature following the defection of deputies to PAM. As a result, the government had the support of 200 of the 325 deputies in the House. In regional balloting in September, the PAM won the chairmanship of four of the eight regions.

Constitution and government. Morocco is a constitutional monarchy, the crown being hereditary and normally transmitted to the king's eldest son, who acts on the advice of a Regency Council if he accedes before age 20. Political power is highly centralized in the hands of the king, who serves as commander in chief and appoints the prime minister; in addition, he can declare a state of emergency, dissolve the legislature, veto legislation, and initiate constitutional amendments. Constitutional revisions approved in 1992 empowered the prime minister, instead of the king, to appoint and preside over the cabinet (albeit still subject to the king's approval); broadened the authority of the House of Representatives to include, inter alia, the initiation of confidence motions and the launching of investigations; and established new Constitutional and Economic/Social Councils. The preamble of the basic law was also altered to declare "the kingdom's attachment to human rights as they are universally recognized."

Until recently, legislative power had been nominally vested in a unicameral House of Representatives, one-third of whose members were indirectly designated by an electoral college. The new upper house (House of Councilors), provided for in the 1996 referendum, is elected indirectly from various local government bodies, professional associations, and employer and worker organizations. All members of the House of Representatives are now elected directly. Included in the new legislature's expanded authority is the power to censure the government and to dismiss cabinet members, although such decisions can still be overridden by the king.

The judicial system is headed by a Supreme Court (*Al-Makama al-Ulia*) and includes courts of appeal, regional tribunals, magistrates' courts, labor tribunals, and a special court to deal with corruption. All judges are appointed by the king on the advice of the Supreme Council of the Judiciary.

The country is currently divided into 49 provinces and prefectures (including four provinces in Western Sahara), with further division into municipalities, autonomous centers, and rural communes. The king appoints all provincial governors, who are responsible to him. In addition, the basic law changes of September 1996 provided for 16 regional councils, with some members elected directly and others representing various professional organizations.

Foreign relations. A member of the UN and the Arab League, Morocco has been chosen on many occasions as a site for Arab and African Islamic conferences at all levels. It has generally adhered to a nonaligned policy, combining good relations with the West with support for African and especially Arab nationalism. Morocco has long courted economic ties with the European Union (EU, formerly the European Community—EC), although its request for EC membership was politely rebuffed in 1987 on geographic grounds. An association agreement was negotiated in 1995 and signed in 1996 with the EU, which reportedly had begun to perceive the kingdom as the linchpin of a European campaign to expand trade with North Africa. Morocco also joined the EU's European Neighborhood Policy and in this context developed an Action Plan, finalized in July 2005, which defined mutual priorities and objectives in the areas of political, economic, commercial, justice, security, and cultural cooperation. These objectives included negotiating an agreement on liberalized trade, pursuing legislative reform, applying human rights provisions, managing migration flows more effectively, and signing a readmission agreement with the EU and developing the energy sector. The action plan also called for an enhanced dialogue on combating terrorism.

In July 2008 France launched a new initiative, the Union for the Mediterranean, a regional group of European, Middle Eastern, and North African countries that gave Morocco a leading role. In addition, the Moroccan government has long been interested in formalizing its relationship to the EU as an advanced status partner, which would allow Moroccans greater access to EU labor markets. France strongly supported Morocco's bid and promoted its application.

Relations with the United States have been friendly, with U.S. administrations viewing Morocco as a conservative counter to northern Africa's more radical regimes. An agreement was signed in mid-1982 that sanctioned, subject to veto, the use of Moroccan air bases by U.S. forces in emergency situations. Periodic joint military exercises have since been conducted, with Washington serving as a prime supplier of equipment for Rabat's campaign in the Western Sahara. In 2004 the United States and Morocco signed a free trade agreement that went into effect in 2006. As a result, exports from Morocco to the United States increased from $445.8 million in 2005 to $878.5 million in 2008, while imports rose from $480.8 million to $1.44 billion. U.S. secretary of defense Donald Rumsfeld visited Morocco in February 2006 and praised the king for his cooperation with U.S. counterterrorism efforts. (Morocco is a signatory to the U.S.-led Trans-Sahara Counterterrorism Initiative, a seven-year program worth $500 million.) Anti-U.S. protesters, particularly the Moroccan Association for Human Rights, expressed displeasure that domestic political freedoms and human rights in Morocco were apparently left off the agenda for discussion. There were suggestions that Morocco had offered to host the new U.S.-Africa command, AFRICOM, although this was denied by the Moroccan Foreign Affairs Ministry. Accepting such a sensitive proposal posed difficulties for the Moroccan regime given the robust criticism of the U.S. government accepted by the general population. The United States, however, continues to view Morocco as a key ally in combating terrorism.

During early 1991 Rabat faced a delicate situation in regard to the Iraqi invasion of Kuwait the previous August. Many Arab capitals were critical of King Hassan for contributing 1,700 Moroccan troops to the U.S.-led Desert Shield deployment in Saudi Arabia and other Gulf states; domestic sentiment also appeared to be strongly tilted against Washington. However, the king defused the issue by permitting a huge pro-Iraq demonstration in the capital in early February and by expressing his personal sympathy for the Iraqi people during the Gulf war. His middle-of-the-road approach was widely applauded both at home and abroad.

Morocco's role in regional affairs has been complicated by a variety of issues. Relations with Algeria and Mauritania have been marred by territorial disputes (until 1970, Morocco claimed all of Mauritania's territory). The early 1970s brought cooperation with the two neighboring states in an effort to present a unified front against the retention by Spain of phosphate-rich Spanish Sahara, but by 1975 Morocco and Mauritania were ranged against Algeria on the issue. In an agreement reached in Madrid on November 14, 1975, Spain agreed to withdraw in favor of Morocco and Mauritania, who proceeded to occupy their assigned sectors (see map) on February 28, 1976, despite resistance from the Polisario Front, an Algerian-backed group that had proclaimed the establishment of an independent Saharan Arab Democratic Republic (SADR). Following Mauritanian renunciation of all claims to the territory in a peace accord with Polisario on August 5, 1979, Moroccan forces entered the southern sector, claiming it, too, as a Moroccan province.

Relations with Algeria were formally resumed in May 1988 prior to an Arab summit in Algiers on the uprising in the Israeli-occupied territories. The stage was thus set for diplomatic activity, which in the wake of first-ever talks between King Hassan and Polisario representatives in early 1989 appeared to offer the strongest possibility in more than a decade for settlement of the Western Sahara problem. Although little progress was achieved over the next seven years on a proposed UN-sponsored self-determination vote, a new UN mediation effort in 1997 rekindled hopes for a settlement (see Disputed Territory, below). Relations with Algeria improved further following the 1999 election of the new Algerian president, Abdelaziz Bouteflika, who suggested that bilateral affairs be handled independently of the conflict in the Western Sahara. Nevertheless, tensions between the two states persisted and the border remained closed from 1994. However, this rivalry does not prevent the two states from cooperating on common strategic concerns, such as security, including extradition of terrorist suspects and energy. In July 2008 Algerian officials announced that they would export electricity to Spain through a Moroccan pipeline and would be an energy provider to Morocco in emergencies. Long strained ties with Libya (which had been accused of complicity in several plots to overthrow the monarchy) began to improve with a state visit by Muammar Qadhafi to Rabat in mid-1983. The process of rapprochement culminated in a treaty of projected union signed by the two leaders at Oujda on August 13, 1984. An inaugural meeting of a joint parliamentary assembly was held in Rabat in July 1985, and commissions were set up to discuss political, military, economic, cultural, and technical cooperation. By February 1989, cordial relations paved the way for a summit in Marrakesh, during which Qadhafi joined other North African leaders in proclaiming the Arab Maghreb Union.

Morocco's attitude toward Israel has been markedly more moderate than that of many Arab states, in part because more than 500,000 Jews of Moroccan ancestry live in Israel. King Hassan was known to relish his conciliatory potential in the Middle East peace process and was believed to have assisted in the negotiations leading up to the Israeli/PLO agreement of September 1993. Israeli Prime Minister Yitzhak Rabin made a surprise visit to Rabat on his return from the historic signing in Washington, his talks with King Hassan being heralded as an important step toward the establishment of formal diplomatic relations between the two countries.

In late 2001 relations between Morocco and Spain were strained by disagreements over illegal immigration, fishing rights, and smuggling. In July 2002 the countries were involved in a brief military standoff over an uninhabited islet (called Perejil by Spain, Leila by Morocco, and claimed by both) off the coast of Ceuta. With U.S., EU, and Egyptian mediation, the two sides agreed to withdraw their troops from the islet and begin cooperating on various issues. The March 2004 bombings in Madrid, which were partly perpetrated by Moroccan immigrants, encouraged the states to coordinate security policy and exchange counterterrorism intelligence. Tensions eased dramatically when Spain's conservative government was replaced by the Spanish Socialist Workers Party in March 2004, but the relationship is still fragile. When Spain's King Juan Carlos visited Ceuta in November 2007, Morocco protested by recalling its ambassador from Spain.

In March 2009 Morocco broke off diplomatic relations with Iran, following statements by an Iranian official critical of Bahrain. The remarks prompted widespread outrage among Sunnis. The severance followed the recall of the Moroccan envoy to Iran in February because of that country's criticism of Morocco and reports in Rabat of Iranians endeavoring to undermine the monarchy. Also in March, Morocco expelled four foreign missionaries on the grounds they were illegally attempting to convert Muslims to Christianity.

Morocco withdrew from Libya's fortieth anniversary celebrations in September 2009 in protest over the appearance of Polisario leader Mohamed Abd al-Azziz (see Disputed territories, below). However, the following month the two countries signed a range of bilateral economic agreements to expand cooperation in tourism, air travel, and various industries.

Current issues. Leader of the *Istiqlal* Party Abbas EL FASSI overcame rumors that he was unlikely to be chosen as the new prime minister due to his alleged involvement in the 2002 Al-Najat scandal during his tenure as employment minister. (Several Moroccan officials were charged with supporting a scheme by the company, which allegedly sought to employ 30,000 Moroccans. Thousands of applicants paid for costly medical exams in order to be approved, only to later find the jobs did not exist.)

The El Fassi government, however, remains unstable since the governing coalition holds only 45 percent of the seats in parliament. However, a new political advocacy group, Movement for All Democrats (*Mouvement pour tous les Démocrates*—MTD), was launched in 2008 and expected to support progovernment agendas (see Political Parties, below).

Past abuses of human rights, including the disappearance of dissenters, seem to have diminished. The status of women in Moroccan society has been officially reformed, with the legal age for marriage raised from 15 to 18 and polygamy virtually outlawed. However, the government and king remain highly sensitive to critique, fining and imprisoning journalists in recent cases (see below).

As 2005 came to a close, a Moroccan truth commission—formally called the Equity and Reconciliation Commission (IER)—released its final report on alleged human rights abuses during the reign of King Hassan. The commission, described as the first of its kind in the Arab world, had been set up in January 2004. The commission reported that between independence in 1956 and the end of Hassan's rule in 1999, nearly 600 people were killed, and opposition activists were systematically suppressed, with numerous instances of torture and disappearances. Many prodemocracy activists, including the Moroccan Association for Human Rights, criticized the panel for its policy of withholding the names of those found responsible for the abuses and for not recommending prosecution of the perpetrators. The hearings were televised throughout the country, an event unprecedented in the region.

Palace officials have been concerned by the rise of radical Islamists who have been spurred on by the Iraq War. Several suicide attacks on one day in early 2003 in Casablanca killed more than 40 people. Some 2,000 Moroccans were convicted of the bombings, with several given death sentences and others long prison terms. A new antiterrorism law was swiftly passed amid concerns in the media that increased powers of detention and surveillance would erode the gains in human rights. Although a survey by the U.S.-based Pew Research Center indicated that 45 percent of Moroccans had a favorable view of Osama bin Laden (compared with 65 percent in Pakistan and 55 percent in Jordan), Moroccans seemed to support the government's efforts to crack down on perpetrators of political violence. Also encouraging was the government's initiation of a new housing program and renewed efforts to industrialize the northern coast, recognition that poverty and joblessness in the slums had created potential breeding grounds for radicalism.

Despite government efforts to address the problem, much of the population continued to live in dire poverty, while militancy appeared to be increasing in the poor shanty towns around the country's major cities. In March and April 2007, police raids on a series of militant cells in Casablanca resulted in some members exploding themselves to avoid capture. In August 2007 a young suicide bomber attacked a bus of tourists in Meknes. The palace was also alarmed by a change of designation by the militant Algerian organization *Groupe Salafiste pour la Predication et Combat* (GSPC) to al-Qaida in the Islamic Maghreb (AQIM) in January 2007, suggesting potential regionwide cooperation among militant groups. Since then, the government has made several high-profile preventive arrests, reporting in July 2008 that it had found 55 terrorist cells since 2003. One such alleged cell included the Islamist political party the Civilized Alternative (*Al-Badil al-Hadari*). In February 2008 officials arrested 32 members of the group including leader Mustapha Mouatassime and revoked its legal status for suspected ties to clandestine extremist groups, including al-Qaida.

The rate of unemployment continued to be a thorny issue, as unemployed graduates frequently protested outside parliament, demanding government jobs. In December 2005 several students set themselves on fire during such a protest, reportedly yelling "a civil service job or death." While none died, a number were badly burned. Official figures estimated that 9.9 percent of the population was unemployed in 2007, revealing an increase from the previous year, which was due largely to the impact of a drought on the agricultural sector. The drought, along with a stagnating economy and the rising cost of food and fuel, led to riots in 2007 and 2008. Hundreds of people protested unemployment in the port city of Sidi Ifni in May and June of 2008.

Journalism watchdog groups cite a series of government actions as examples of an increasingly regressive stance on media freedom. In July 2007 a Moroccan court jailed five activists for criticizing the monarchy, giving each one a four-year prison sentence and a 10,000-dirham fine. In February 2008 a computer engineer was sentenced to three years in jail for posting a satirical profile of Prince Moulay Rachid to the social networking site Facebook. In May 2008 Moroccan authorities banned a program by the television network Al Jazeera about the Maghreb region in Rabat, and in June a Moroccan court ordered the newspaper *al Jarida al Oula* to stop publishing victim testimony from the IER. In July the government jailed a human rights activist for false reporting after he said authorities killed and raped protestors during the riots in Sidi Ifni. The government disputed the claim and also fined Al Jazeera for disseminating the allegation. Morocco has also been criticized by international NGOs for its decision to imprison Sahrawi human rights campaigners who had been involved in demonstrations in the Western Sahara in 2005. Furthermore, Morocco's continued detention of terrorist suspects has drawn criticism from human rights groups.

In March 2009 the government initiatied a broad campaign against what it described as subversives, including homosexuals and Shiite Muslims. A number of Shite schools were closed, while dozens of known Shiites were arrested, as were at least 20 homosexuals. Reports indicated that the campaign was a response to calls in several newspapers for greater tolerance for Shiites and homosexuals.

The government launched a new round of talks with public sector unions in October 2009. The unions primarily sought higher wages, and the discussions foreshadowed negotiations scheduled to begin in December with private sector unions. The government also proposed new legislation to extend unemployment benefits to include medical and social security coverage. The new law was an attempt to end nine years of negotiations between unions and the government over unemployment benefits. In December the government announced plans for the creation of a fund to provide support to divorced women whose husbands refuse to make alimony payments.

POLITICAL PARTIES

Governing Coalition:

Democratic Bloc (*Bloc Démocratique*). Launched in May 1992 to promote the establishment of a "healthy democracy within the framework of a constitutional monarchy," the Democratic Bloc or *Koutla* ("coalition") currently includes the following three groups: the Socialist Union for Popular Forces (*Union Socialiste des Forces Populaire*—USFP), Independence Party (*Parti de l'Istiqlal, or Istiqlal*—PI), the Party of Progress and Socialism (*Parti du Progrès et du Socialisme*—PPS). Together with the National Assembly of Independents (*Rassemblement National des Indépendants*—RNI) they form the governing coalition.

All of the bloc's founding members, except the PPS, urged voters to abstain from the September 1992 constitutional referendum, and in February 1993 ceased participation in the national commission created to supervise upcoming legislative elections. The protesters charged that the commission was failing to pursue the electoral law revision necessary to ensure "free and fair elections." However, all of the bloc's components participated in the 1993 balloting, securing 114 seats overall, with affiliated labor organizations winning 6 more. Most of the bloc's success (99 seats) came in the direct election, leading to its contention that the results of the indirect election had been "falsified." After protracted debate, the bloc in November rejected King Hassan's invitation to name most of the ministers in a new government, insisting that it should be given a right of veto over all appointments. However, after its components secured 102 seats in the 1997 balloting for the House of Representatives, the *Koutla* agreed to lead a new coalition government, which was appointed in March 1998 under the leadership of the USFP's Abderrahmane Youssoufi. After the elections in September 2007, *Koutla* parties narrowly retained control of the government despite a poor overall showing (105 seats, down from 134 in the previous election). In September 2007 *Istiqlal*'s Abbas El Fassi became prime minister and coalition leader, succeeding independent Driss Jettou, who had governed since October 2002. The formation of the Party of Authenticity and Modernity (*Parti Authenticité et Modernité*—PAM) in 2008 (see below) led to a number of defections from all of the parties of the bloc.

Leader: Abbas EL FASSI (*Istiqlal*).

Independence Party (*Parti de l'Istiqlal, or Istiqlal*—PI). Founded in 1943, *Istiqlal* provided most of the nation's leadership before independence. It split in 1959, and its members were relieved of governmental responsibilities in 1963. Once a firm supporter of the throne, the party now displays a reformist attitude and only supports the king on selected issues. Stressing the need for better standards of living and equal rights for all Moroccans, it has challenged the government regarding alleged human rights abuses. In July 1970 *Istiqlal* formed a National

Front with the UNFP (below) but ran alone in the election of June 1977, when it emerged as the then leading party. It suffered heavy losses in both the 1983 municipal elections and the 1984 legislative balloting.

In May 1990 *Istiqlal* joined the USFP (below), the PPS (see below), and the OADP (below) in supporting an unsuccessful censure motion that charged the government with "economic incompetence" and the pursuit of "antipopular" and "antisocial" policies. In November 1991 *Istiqlal* announced the formation of a common front" with the USFP to work toward "establishment of true democracy," and the two parties presented a joint list in 1993, *Istiqlal*'s 118 candidates securing 43 seats in the direct *Majlis* poll. *Istiqlal* was the leading party in the June 1997 local elections but fell to fifth place in the November house balloting. In the 2007 elections, *Istiqlal* won 52 seats, more than any other party. Its secretary general Abbas El Fassi was named prime minister in September 2007.

The party placed second in local balloting in June 2009 and secured 5,292 seats, or 19 percent of total, on local and regional councils.

Leaders: Abbas EL FASSI (Secretary General). Hachmi EL FILALI, Abou Bakr KADIRI, Abdelkrim GHALLAB, Mohamed BOUCETTA, M'hamed DOUIRI (Presidential Council).

Socialist Union of Popular Forces (*Union Socialiste des Forces Populaire*—USFP). The USFP was organized in September 1974 by the UNFP-Rabat Section (see UNFP, below), which had disassociated itself from the Casablanca Section in July 1972 and was accused by the government of involvement in a Libyan-aided plot to overthrow King Hassan in March 1973. The USFP subsequently called for political democratization, nationalization of major industries, thorough reform of the nation's social and administrative structures, and the cessation of what it believed to be human rights abuses by the government. It secured the third-largest number of legislative seats in the election of June 1977 but withdrew from the House in October 1981 in protest at the extension of the parliamentary term. A year later it announced that it would return for the duration of the session ending in May 1983 so that it could participate in the forthcoming electoral campaigns. The majority of nearly 100 political prisoners released during July–August 1980 were USFP members, most of whom had been incarcerated for alleged antigovernment activities in 1973–1977.

After 52 of its 104 candidates (the USFP also supported 118 *Istiqlal* candidates) won seats in the June 1993 *Majlis* balloting, the union was reportedly divided on whether to accept King Hassan's offer to participate in a coalition government, the dispute ultimately being resolved in favor of the rejectionists. Subsequently, the USFP was awarded only 4 additional house seats in the September indirect elections. First Secretary Abderrahmane Youssoufi resigned his post and departed for France in protest over "irregularities" surrounding the process. The party also continued to denounce the "harassment" of prominent USFP member Noubir EL-AMAOUI, secretary general of the **Democratic Confederation of Labor** (*Confédération Démocratique du Travail*), who had recently served 14 months in prison for "insulting and slandering" the government in a magazine interview.

Youssoufi returned from his self-imposed exile in April 1995, apparently in response to overtures from King Hassan, who was again attempting to persuade leftist parties to join a coalition government. Although observers suggested that the USFP would soon "redefine" the party platform and possibly select new leaders, a July 1996 congress simply reconfirmed the current political bureau. Meanwhile, one USFP faction was reportedly attempting to "re-radicalize" the party under the direction of Mohamed BASRI, a longtime influential opposition leader. In June 1995 Basri returned from 28 years in exile, during which he had been sentenced (in absentia) to death three times.

The USFP was the leading party in the November 1997 house balloting, securing 57 seats and distancing itself somewhat from its *Koutla* partner *Istiqlal* (32), with which it had been considered of comparable strength. Subsequently, the 74-year-old Youssoufi (once again being referenced as the USFP first secretary) was named by King Hassan to lead a new coalition government, although many younger USFP members reportedly opposed the party's participation. Internal dissent continued, as some radical members charged Youssoufi and the party administration with acting timidly in government and failing to push for further reforms in state institutions. Demands for a leadership change were reportedly voiced in the party congress in March 2001, especially by younger members and those associated with labor unions. However, Youssoufi managed to retain his post, prompting some members to leave the party to form the **National Ittihadi Congress** (CNI, below). USFP was the leading party in the 2002 elections, winning 50 seats. In 2003 Youssoufi resigned and Mohamed El Yazghi took over as first secretary. USFP came in with the largest losses in the 2007 elections; it won only 38 seats, down from 50 seats in 2007. In December of 2007, El Yazghi resigned his party leadership post following disagreements over the 2008 budget. However, El Yazghi was appointed minister of state in October 2007 and retains that position. Abdelwahed RADI and Fathallah OUALALOU ran for first secretary, and Radi was elected at a party congress in November 2008.

In local balloting in June 2009 the USFP won 3,266 seats or 11.6 percent of the total.

Leader: Abdelwahed RADI (First Secretary).

Socialist Democratic Party (*Parti Socialiste et Démocratique*—PSD). The PSD was established in October 1996 by OADP members who disagreed with that group's rejection of King Hassan's proposed constitutional changes. The party won six seats in 2002 balloting. In December 2005 the party decided to dissolve itself and integrated into the USFP.

Leaders: Abdessamad BELKEBIR, Mohamed Habib TALEB, Aissa QUARDIGHI (Secretary General).

Party of Progress and Socialism (*Parti du Progrès et du Socialisme*—PPS). The PPS is the successor to the **Moroccan Communist Party** (*Parti Communiste Marocain*), which was banned in 1952; the **Party of Liberation and Socialism** (*Parti de la Libération et du Socialisme*), which was banned in 1969; and the **Party of Progress and Socialism** (*Parti du Progrès et du Socialisme*—PPS), which obtained legal status in 1974. The single PPS representative in the 1977 chamber, Ali YATA, was the first Communist to win election to a Moroccan legislature. The fourth national congress, held in July 1987 in Casablanca, although strongly supportive of the government's position on the Western Sahara, criticized the administration's recent decisions to privatize some state enterprises and implement other economic liberalization measures required by the International Monetary Fund (IMF). However, by mid-1991 the PPS was reported to be fully converted to *perestroika,* a stance that had apparently earned the party additional support within the Moroccan middle class. In late 1993 Yata unsuccessfully urged his Democratic Bloc partners to compromise with King Hassan in formation of a new government.

Ali Yata, who had been reelected to his post of PRP secretary general in mid-1995, died in August 1997 after being struck by a car. Ismail Alaoui was elected as the new secretary general. In March 2002 the PPS and the PSD (above) announced that they had launched the **Socialist Alliance** (*Alliance Socialiste*) and that they were planning to cooperate in the legislative poll in September. In that election the PPS collected only 11 seats. The PPS won 1,102 seats in local balloting in June 2009.

Leader: Ismail ALAOUI (Secretary General).

National Assembly of Independents (*Rassemblement National des Indépendants*—RNI). The RNI was launched at a Constitutive Congress held October 6–9, 1978. Although branded by left-wing spokesperson as a "king's party," it claimed to hold the allegiance of 141 of 264 deputies in the 1977 chamber. Subsequent defections and other disagreements, both internal and with the king, resulted in the party's designation as the "official" opposition in late 1981. It won 61 house seats in 1984, thereafter returning to a posture of solid support for the king and the government. RNI leader Ahmed Osman, a former prime minister and former president of the House of Representatives, is one of the country's best-known politicians and is also the son-in-law of the former king. Previously affiliated with the National Entente, the RNI participated (as did the MNP) in the November 1997 elections as an unaligned "centrist" party (winning 46 seats) and subsequently agreed to join the *Koutla*-led coalition government named in early 1998. In 2002 RNI won 41 seats. RNI sustained few losses in the 2007 elections and emerged with 39 seats.

In April 2007 Ahmed Osman was ousted by younger members who organized an extraordinary congress and demanded a successor be found. In May 2007 Mustafa Mansouri was elected as the new president after Ahmed Osman agreed not to nominate himself again. Mansouri became the speaker of the House of Representatives in October 2007.

The RNI placed third in local balloting in June 2009 with 4.112 seats or 14 percent of all positions.

Leader: Mustafa MANSOURI (Chair).

Popular Movement (*Mouvement Populaire*—MP). Organized in 1958 as a monarchist party of Berber mountaineers, the MP was legally recognized in 1959. The MP was a major participant in government coalitions of the early 1960s. It secured the second-largest number of legislative seats in the election of June 1977 and was third-ranked after the 1984 and 1993 elections. In October 1986 an extraordinary party congress voted to remove the MP's founder, Mahjoubi Aherdane, from the post of secretary general, replacing him with Mohand Laenser. Aherdane subsequently formed a new Berber party (see MNP, below). It is known to be loyal to the monarchy and still draws its support base from rural Berber areas. In the 2002 elections the MP won 27 seats and Laenser was named minister of agriculture. In 2006 the MP absorbed the **Popular National Movement** (*Mouvement National Populaire*—MNP) and the **Democratic Union** (*Union Démocratique*—UD) (see below) and saw large gains in the 2007 elections. MP won 41 seats and became the third largest party in the House of Representatives. The MP won 2,213 seats in local council elections in June 2009. It joined the government following a cabinet reshuffle in July in which Laesner was appointed a minister of state without portfolio.

Leader: Mohand LAENSER (Secretary General).

Popular National Movement (*Mouvement National Populaire*—MNP). The MNP was organized in October 1991 by longtime Berber leader Mahjoubi Aherdane, who was ousted as secretary general of the MP in 1986. The new party won 25 house seats in 1993. A number of MNP members left the party in mid-1996 to form the MDS (below). The MNP won 19 seats in the 1997 balloting for House of Representatives, having shed its National Entente orientation. Ahmed MOUSSAOUI, the minister of youth and sports, was expelled from the MNP in April 2001 and was subsequently reported to have joined the UD. The MNP won 18 seats in 2002. In 2006 it rejoined the MP party.

Leader: Mahjoubi AHERDANE (Secretary General).

Democratic Union (*Union Démocratique*—UD). UD is a center-leaning Berber party. In 2006 it joined the MP party.

Leader: Bouazza IKKEN.

Legislative Parties:

Party of Authenticity and Modernity (*Parti Authenticité et Modernité*—PAM). PAM was formed in August 2008 by Fouad El Himma, a childhood friend of Mohamed VI who had previously led another coalition, the **Movement for All Democrats** (*Mouvement pour tous les Démocrates*—MTD). PAM was created by a merger of five smaller parties: Alliance of Freedom (ADL), the Citizens' Initiatives for Development (ICD), the Covenant Party (Al Ahd), the Environment and Development Party (PED), and the National Democratic Party (PND). Its stated purpose is to limit the fragmentation of the Moroccan political environment and prevent the rise of Islamist parties.

In January 2009 the PND (see below) withdrew from the PAM after the party failed to win any seats in by-elections the previous September. PAM joined the opposition prior to the June local elections, reportedly as a means to demonstrate its independence from the monarchy. The grouping placed first in the balloting and secured 21.5 percent of the seats. It then won control of 4 of the 8 regions in regional balloting in September. By the end of 2009 some 89 deputies in the House of Representatives had switched their allegiance to PAM, making the party the largest in the chamber. PAM secretary general Mohammed Cheikh Biadillah was elected speaker of the House of Councilors in October.

Leaders: Fouad El HIMMA, Mohammed Cheikh BIADILLAH (Secretary General and Speaker of the House of Councilors).

Alliance of Freedom (*Alliance des Libertés*—ADL). The ADL was created in 2002 by Ali Bel Haj as a moderate, reformist party. It went on to win four seats in the legislative balloting that year. The ADL only secured one seat in the 2007 elections.

Leader: Ali BEL HAJ.

Citizens' Initiatives for Development (*Initiatives Citoyennes pour le Développement*—ICD). The ICD was formed in 2002 by defectors from the MNP (see below).

Leader: Mohammed BENHAMMOU.

Covenant Party (*Parti Al Ahd*), The Covenant Party was established in 2002 by former members of the MP and the MNP. The party listed its candidates with the PND (below) in the 2007 elections to win a collective 14 seats in the legislature.

Leader: Najib EL OUAZZANI.

Party of Environment and Development (*Parti de l'Environnement et du Développement*—PED). PED is a progressive party founded in 2002 to promote sustainable development and environmental preservation. The party won two legislative seats in 2002 and five in 2007.

Leader: Ahmed AL ALAMI.

National Democratic Party (*Parti National Démocrate*—PND). The PND was founded as the Democratic Independents (*Indépendants Démocrates*—ID) in April 1981 by 59 former RNI deputies in the House of Representatives. At the party's first congress on June 11–13, 1982, its secretary general, Mohamed Arsalane al-JADIDI, affirmed the PND's loyalty to the monarchy while castigating the RNI for not providing an effective counterweight to the "old" parties. In the 2007 elections, the party ran its candidates with the Covenant Party (see below). Together they won 14 legislative seats. The PND was one of the founding parties of the PAM in 2008, but then withdrew in January 2009.

Leaders: Abdallah KADIRI, Thami KHYARI (Secretary General).

Justice and Development Party (*Parti de la Justice et du Développement*—PJD). The PJD was formerly known as the **Popular Constitutional and Democratic Movement** (*Mouvement Populaire Constitutionnel et Démocratique*—MPCD). The MPCD was a splinter from the Popular Movement. It won 3 legislative seats in 1977 and none in 1984 or 1993. In June 1996 the moribund MPCD was rejuvenated by its merger with an unrecognized Islamist grouping known as **Reform and Renewal** (*Islah wa al-Tajdid*), led by Abdelillah BENKIRANE. The Islamists were allocated 3 of the MPCD's secretariat seats, and Benkirane was generally acknowledged as the party's primary leader. He announced that his supporters had relinquished their "revolutionary ideas" and were now committed to "Islam, the constitutional monarchy, and nonviolence." The party won 9 seats in the House of Representatives in 1997, while Benkirane was successful in a by-election on April 30, 1999. The PJD has gained popularity, taking 42 seats in the House of Representatives in 2002, having won in most districts where it was permitted to run a candidate. In local elections in 2003, it scaled back the candidates it presented, with new leader Saad Eddine OTHMANI explaining that the party did not want to scare off foreign investors with high-profile wins.

The PJD was expected to make major gains in the 2007 parliamentary elections and many viewed the party as a test case for an Islamist parliamentary victory. While the party fielded candidates in just 50 constituencies in 2002, the PJD campaigned in 94 constituencies in the September elections. Although the party won the largest share of the vote, it took only 46 legislative seats—6 fewer than *Istiqlal*. Despite its status as the second largest party, the PJD was not included in the governing coalition.

In July 2008 the party membership chose Abdelillah Benkirane, a well-known moderate and former leader of the Reform and Renewal party, as its new secretary general. Benkirane, who supports the monarchy, aimed to turn the party away from an overtly religious agenda.

The PJD came in sixth in local balloting in the June 2009 elections and secured only 5.5 percent of the seats, although the party did well in urban areas where it gained 16 percent of the posts.

Leader: Abdelillah Benkirane (Secretary General).

Constitutional Union (*Union Constitutionelle*—UC). Founded in 1983 by Maati Bouabid, UC is a moderate party that emphasizes economic self-sufficiency. Said to have royal support, the party won 83 house seats in 1984. UC's representation fell to 54 seats in 1993, although it retained a slim plurality and one of its members was elected president of the new house. Bouabid died in November 1996, exacerbating problems within a party described as already in disarray. UC was the second leading party in the November 1997 house balloting, winning 50 seats, but dropped to 16 in 2002. In the 2007 elections, UC won 27 seats. In the June 2009 local elections, the UC won 1,307 seats.

Leader: Mohamed ABIED (Secretary General).

Democratic Forces Front (*Front des Forces Démocratiques*—FFD). Launched in 1997 by PRP dissidents, the FFD won nine seats in the November house balloting, and its leader was named to the March

1998 cabinet. In 2007 the party again won nine seats. It has endeavored unsuccessfully to enact legislation to abolish the death penalty in Morocco.

Leader: Thami KHYARI (National Secretary).

Democratic and Social Movement (*Mouvement Démocratique et Social*—MDS). Launched in June 1996 (as the National Democratic and Social Movement) by MNP dissidents, the right-wing Berber MDS is led by a former policeman. The party held seven seats following the 2002 balloting for the House of Representatives. The party had nine seats after the 2007 elections.

Leader: Mahmoud ARCHANE (Secretary General).

Unified Socialist Party (*Parti Socialiste Unifié*—PSU). This party has had several incarnations, initially as the Organization of Democratic and Popular Action (*Organisation de l'Action Démocratique et Populaire*—OADP). Claiming a following of former members of the USFP and PPS, the OADP was organized in May 1983. It obtained 1 seat in 1984 balloting and 2 seats in 1993. A new 74-member Central Committee was elected at the third OADP congress, held November 5–6, 1994, in Casablanca.

The OADP was one of the few major parties to oppose the king's constitutional initiatives of 1996, some of its members subsequently splitting off to form the PSD (see above) because of the issue. The OADP won four seats in the November 1997 *Majlis* elections. Although the OADP was a member of the ruling Democratic Bloc, it was not listed as having any members in the March 1998 cabinet. OADP sources defined the group's stance as one of "critical" support of the coalition government. In 2002 it merged with other groups to form the United Socialist Left (*Gauche Socialiste Unifiée*—GSU).

In 2005 GSU reformed to create PSU. In the 2007 elections it ran in electoral coalition with the **Party of the Democratic Socialist Avant-Garde** (*Parti de l'Avant-Garde Démocratique Socialiste*—PADS) and the National Congress Party, collectively winning six seats.

Leader: Mohamed MOUJAHID (Secretary General)

National Congress Party (*Congrès National Ittihadi*—CNI). The CNI was founded in 2001 by USFP dissidents.

Leader: Abdesalam EL AZIZ (Secretary General).

Party of the Democratic Socialist Avant-Garde (*Parti de l'Avant-Garde Démocratique Socialiste*—PADS). Formed by USFD dissidents in 1991, PADS boycotted the 1997 elections on the ground that its members had been harassed by the government. In 2007 PADS formed a union with the National Congress Party (see above) and the Unified Socialist Party (see above) and took six seats in the legislature.

Leader: Ahmed BENJELLOUNE

Workers' Party *(Parti Travailliste)*. This left-wing party was established in May 2006. It was set up by trade unionists and old militants from the USFP. Among its founders was Abdelkrim Benatiq, who was close to the former prime minister, Abderrahman Youssoufi. The Workers' Party won five legislative seats in the 2007 election.

Leader: Abdelkrim BENATIQ.

Other Parties and Groups:

Other parties, a number of which won seats in 2002, 2006, and 2007 include the **Action Party** (*Parti de l'Action*—PA), led by Mohammed EL IDRISSI; the small but longstanding **Democratic Party for Independence** (*Parti Démocratique pour l'Indépendance* or *Parti de la Choura et de l'Istiqlal*, or *Choura*—PDI), led by Abdelwahed MAACH; the **Moroccan Liberal Party** (*Parti Marocain Libéral*—PML), led by Mohammed ZIANE; the **Moroccan Union for Democracy** (*Union Marocaine pour la Démocratie*—UMD), led by Abdellah AZMANI; the **National Ittihadi Congress** (*Congrès National Ittihadi*—CNI), a breakaway group from the USFP led by Abdelmajid BOUZOUBAA; the **National Party for Unity and Solidarity** (*Parti National pour l'Unité et la Solidarité*—PNUS), led by Muhammad ASMAR; the **Party of Citizens' Forces** (*Parti des Forces Citoyennes*—PFC), led by Abderrahim LAHJOUJI; the **Party of Reform and Development** (*Parti de la Réforme et du Développement*—PRD), led by former RNI member Abderrahmane EL KOHEN; the **Party of Renewal and Equity** (*Parti du Renouveau et de l'Equité*—PRE), led by Chakir ACHEHBAR; the **Renaissance and Virtue Party** *(Parti de la Renaissance et de la Vertu)*, an Islamist party set up in December 2005 by a former member of the PJD, led by Mohamed KHALIDI; and the **Social Center Party** (*Parti du Centre Social*—PCS), led by Lachen MADIH.

For more information on the **Popular National Movement** (*Mouvement National Populaire*—MNP) and groups active through the 1990s, see the 2008 *Handbook*.

Clandestine Groups:

Justice and Welfare (*Adl wa-al-Ihsan*). The country's leading radical Islamist organization, *Adl wa-al-Ihsan* was formed in 1980. Although denied legal party status in 1981, it was informally tolerated until a mid-1989 crackdown, during which its founder, Sheikh Abd Assalam Yassine, was placed under house arrest and other members were imprisoned. The government formally outlawed the group in January 1990; two months later, five of its most prominent members were given two-year prison terms, and Yassine's house detention was extended, touching off large-scale street disturbances in Rabat. Although the other detainees were released in early 1992, Yassine remained under house arrest, with King Hassan describing extremism as a threat to Moroccan stability. An estimated 100 members of *Adl wa-al-Ihsan* were reportedly among the prisoners pardoned in mid-1994, although Yassine was pointedly not among them. He was finally released from house arrest in December 1995 but was soon thereafter placed under "police protection" for apparently having criticized the government too strenuously. (Among Yassine's transgressions, in the eyes of the government, was his failure to acknowledge King Hassan as the nation's supreme religious leader.) His house arrest prompted protest demonstrations in 1998 by his supporters, whom the government also charged with responsibility for recent protests among university students and a mass demonstration in late December 1998 protesting U.S.–UK air strikes against Iraq. Although the group remained proscribed, Yassine was released from house arrest in May 2000. He reportedly continued to be critical of the royal family and the government, but based on Yassine's rejection of violence, the government tolerated the group's activities. However, in May 2006 the government arrested hundreds of *Adl wa-al-Ihsan* members across the country, apparently in reaction to rumors that the party had planned an uprising. Those rounded up were later freed, but party members claimed that materials such as computers and books had been seized from party offices.

In a separate matter, Yassine's daughter, Nadia YASSINE, head of the organization's feminist branch, was charged with insulting the monarchy after she gave an interview to a Moroccan newspaper in June 2005, in which she asserted that the monarchy "was not suitable for Morocco," that a republic would be preferable, and that the king's regime was likely to collapse soon. She faced up to five years in prison. After the United States expressed opposition to her prosecution, her trial was postponed indefinitely.

Despite the postponement, authorities have continued to put pressure on the party. In July 2006 *Adl wa-al-Ihsan* member Hayat Bouida was allegedly abducted and tortured for three hours by six intelligence agents in Safi, a city 300 kilometers south of Casablanca. In May 2007 she was stabbed by two intelligence agents in front of her house. In March 2008 more than 20 members of the group were arrested and several were prosecuted. In July 2009 Abdel Wahed Hilali, a half brother of Nadia Yassine, was arrested on charges of drug smuggling. Also in July eight members of the group were arrested for illegal activities. By 2009 authorities estimated that there were approximately 200,000 members of *Adl wa-al-Ihsani* throughout Morocco.

Leaders: Sheikh Abdessalam YASSINE, Fathallah ARSLANE (Spokesperson).

LEGISLATURE

The constitutional amendments of September 1996 provided for a bicameral **Parliament** (*Barlaman*) comprising an indirectly elected House of Councilors and a directly elected House of Representatives. Previously, the legislature had consisted of a unicameral House of Representatives, two-thirds of whose members were directly elected with the remainder being selected by an electoral college of government, professional, and labor representatives.

House of Councilors (*Majlis al-Mustasharin*). The upper house consists of 270 members indirectly elected for nine-year terms (one-third of the house is renewed every three years) by local councils, regional councils, and professional organizations. In the first election on December 5, 1997, the National Assembly of Independents won 42 seats; the Democratic and Social Movement, 33; the Constitutional Union, 28; the Popular Movement, 27; the National Democratic Party, 21; the Independence Party, 21; the Socialist Union of Popular Forces, 16; the Popular National Movement, 15; the Action Party, 13; the Democratic Forces Front, 12; the Party of Progress and Socialism, 7; the Socialist Democratic Party, 4; the Democratic Party for Independence, 4; and various labor organizations, 27. In the election to renew one-third of the house on September 15, 2000, the National Assembly of Independents won 14 seats; the Popular National Movement, 12; the National Democratic Party, 10; the Popular Movement, 9; the Constitutional Union, 8; the Independence Party, 7; the Democratic and Social Movement, 6; the Democratic Forces Front, 5; the Socialist Union of Popular Forces, 3; the Party of Renewal and Progress, 2; the Action Party, 2; the Socialist Democratic Party, 2; the Democratic Party for Independence, 1; and various labor organizations, 3.

Speaker: Mohammed Cheikh BIADILLAH.

House of Representatives (*Majlis al-Nawwab*). The lower house has 325 members directly elected on a proportional basis for five-year terms. (Under electoral law revision of May 2002, 30 seats were set aside for women; those seats were to be contested on a proportional basis from national lists for the September 2002 balloting, while the other 295 seats were to be elected on a proportional basis from 92 multimember constituencies.) Following legislative elections on September 7, 2007, the distribution of seats was: Independence Party (*Istiqlal*), 52; Party of Justice and Development, 46; Popular Movement, 41; National Assembly of Independents, 39; Socialist Union of Popular Forces, 38; Constitutional Union, 27; Party of Progress and Socialism, 17; Union of the National Democratic Party and al-Ahd (Covenant), 14 (National Democratic Party-Al-Ahd Union, 8; Al-Ahd, 3; National Democratic Party, 3); Democratic Forces Front, 9; Democratic and Social Movement, 9; Electoral Coalition of the Union of the Democratic Socialist Avant-Garde, the National Congress Party and the Unified Socialist Party, 6; Workers' Party, 5; Party of Environment and Development, 5; Renewal and Equity Party, 4; Socialist Party, 2; Moroccan Union for Democracy, 2; Party of Citizens' Forces, 1; Alliance of Freedom, 1; Development and Citizenship Initiative, 1; Party of Renaissance and Virtue, 1; Independents, 5.

Speaker: Mustapha MANSOURI.

CABINET

[as of December 1, 2009]

Prime Minister	Abbas El Fassi (*Istiqlal*)
Minister of State	Mohamed El Yazghi (USFP)
Minister of State	Mohand Laenser (MP)
Ministers	
Agriculture, Rural Development, and Marine Fisheries	Aziz Akhenouch (MP)
Communication, Spokesman of the Government	Khalid Naciri (PPS)
Culture	Bensalem Himmich (USFP)
Employment and Vocational Training	Jamal Aghmani (USFP)
Energy, Mining, Water, and Environment	Amina Benkhadra (ind.) [f]
Equipment and Transport	Karim Ghellab (*Istiqlal*)
Finance and Economy	Salaheddine Mezouar (RNI)
Foreign Affairs and Cooperation	Taieb Fassi Fihri (ind.)
Foreign Trade	Abdellatif Maâzouz (ind.)
General Secretary of the Government	Abdessadek Rabiі (ind.)
Habous (Religious Endowments) and Islamic Affairs	Ahmed Toufiq (ind.)
Health	Yasmina Baddou (*Istiqlal*) [f]
Housing and Urban Planning	Ahmed Taoufiq Hejira (*Istiqlal*)
Industry, Trade, and New Technologies	Ahmed Chami (USFP)
Interior	Chakib Benmoussa (ind.)
Justice	Abdelwahed Radi (USFP)
National Education, Higher Education, Staff, Training, and Scientific Research	Ahmed Akhchichine (PAM)
Relations with Parliament	Mohamed Saad Alami (*Istiqlal*)
Social Development, the Family, and Solidarity	Nouzha Skalli (PPS) [f]
Tourism, Handicrafts, and Social Economy	Mohamed Boussaid (RNI)
Youth and Sports	Moncef Belkhayat (RNI)
Ministers Delegate (Ministries)	
Moroccans Living Abroad	Mohammed Ameur (USFP)
General and Economic Affairs	Nizar Baraka (*Istiqlal*)
National Defense	Abderrahmane Sbaï (ind.)
Modernization of the Public Sector	Mohamed Abbou (RNI)
Secretaries of State	
Foreign Affairs and Cooperation	Mohammed Ouzzine (MP)
	Latifa Akherbach (ind.) [f]
Handicrafts	Anis Birou (RNI)
Interior	Saad Hassar (ind.)
Secondary Education	Latifa Labida (ind.) [f]
Territorial Development	Abdeslam Al Mesbahi (*Istiqlal*)
Water and Environment	Abdelkébir Zahoud (*Istiqlal*)

[f] = female

COMMUNICATIONS

Press. Moroccan newspapers have a reputation for being highly partisan and outspoken, although those incurring the displeasure of the state face reprisal, such as forced suspension, and government control has at times been highly restrictive. The following are published daily in Casablanca in French, unless otherwise noted: *Le Matin du Sahara* (100,000), replaced *Le Petit Marocain* following government shutdown in 1971; *al-Alam* (Rabat, 100,000), *Istiqlal* organ, in Arabic; *L'Opinion* (Rabat, 60,000), *Istiqlal* organ; *Maroc Soir* (50,000), replaced *La Vigie Marocaine* in 1971; *al-Maghrib* (Rabat, 15,000), RNI organ; *al-Mithaq al-Watani* (Rabat, 25,000), RNI organ, in Arabic; *al-Anbaa* (Rabat, 15,000), Ministry of Information, in Arabic; *al-Bayane* (5,000), PRP organ, in French and Arabic; *Libération*, USFP organ; *al-Ittihad al-Ishtiraki,* USFP organ, in Arabic; *Risalat al-Umma,* UC organ, in Arabic; *Anoual* (Rabat), OADP weekly, in Arabic; *al-Mounaddama*, in Arabic. *Al-Mouharir,* a USFP organ, and *al-Bayane* were suspended in the wake of the June 1981 riots in Casablanca. The latter was permitted to resume publication in mid-July but, having had a number of its issues confiscated in early 1984 because of its reporting of further Casablanca disturbances, it was suspended again from October 1986 until January 1987. Two months later, the government seized an issue of *Anoual,* apparently in response to its coverage of prison conditions, and took similar action against *al-Bayane* in January 1988 because of its stories on problems in the educational system and recent demonstrations at Fez University. The USFP's *al-Ittihad al-Ishtiraki* was also informed that it would be censored because of its coverage of the student disturbances. In mid-1991 the government banned distribution of the first issue of *Le Citoyen,* a weekly established by political dissidents to promote government reform. Following the enthronement of the reform-minded King Mohamed VI in 1999, the government somewhat relaxed its grip on the print media. However, from 2000 through mid-2002 various issues of *Le Journal,* the independent weekly *L'Economiste, Maroc-Hebdo,* the Islamist weekly *Risalat al-Foutawah, Le Reporter al-Moustaquil, Le Quoditien du Maroc, Chamal, Demain,* and *Al-Sahifa* were banned. Domestic and international journalists' organizations criticized a libel law adopted in April 2002, accusing the government of eroding civil and press liberties by making it easier to file libel suits. In May 2006 Human Rights Watch issued a report critical of tightening controls on the press, citing recent harassment of independent news weeklies that had questioned government policies. In August 2007 alone three journalists were called into court for countering the monarchy. This included Ahmed BENCHEMSI, editor of the Arabic language weekly *Nichane* (Forthright), and of its French-language sister publication *Tel Quel* (As It Is), who was charged with showing disrespect towards the monarchy. A restrictive press law grants the mandate for these prosecutions. While the El Fassi government has pledged to reform it, no action had been taken as of mid-2008. In its 2008 annual index of freedom of the press, Reporters Without Borders ranked Morocco 122 out of 173 countries.

News agencies. The Moroccan Arab News Agency (*Wikalat al-Maghrib al-Arabi*—WMA), successor to the former *Maghreb Arabe Presse,* is an official, government-owned agency. Most major foreign agencies maintain offices in Rabat.

Broadcasting and computing. Broadcasting is under the supervision of the Broadcasting Service of the Kingdom of Morocco (*Idhaat al-Mamlakat al-Maghribiyah*). The government-controlled *Radiodiffusion-Télévision Marocaine* provides radio service over three networks (national, international, and Berber) as well as commercial television service; transmission by a private television company was launched in 1989. In addition, the Voice of America operates a radio station in Tangier. As of 2008 there were 330.4 Internet users per 1,000 inhabitants.

INTERGOVERNMENTAL REPRESENTATION

Ambassador to the U.S.: Aziz MEKOUAR.

U.S. Ambassador to Morocco: Samuel Louis KAPLAN.

Permanent Representative to the UN: Mohammed LOULICHKI.

IGO Memberships (Non-UN): AfDB, AFESD, AMF, AMU, BADEA, EBRD, IDB, Interpol, IOM, LAS, NAM, OIC, OIF, PCA, WCO, WTO.

DISPUTED TERRITORY

Western Sahara. The region known since 1976 as Western Sahara was annexed by Spain in two stages: the coastal area in 1884 and the interior in 1934. In 1957, the year after Morocco attained full independence, Rabat renewed a claim to the territory, sending irregulars to attack inland positions. In 1958, however, French and Spanish troops succeeded in quelling the attacks, with Madrid formally uniting Saguia el Hamra and Rio de Oro, the two historical components of the territory, as the province of Spanish Sahara. Mauritanian independence in 1960 led to territorial claims by Nouakchott, with the situation being further complicated in 1963 by the discovery of one of the world's richest phosphate deposits at Bu Craa. During the next dozen years, Morocco attempted to pressure Spain into relinquishing its claim through a combination of diplomatic initiatives (the UN first called for a referendum on self-determination for the Sahrawi people in 1966), direct support for guerrilla groups, and a legal challenge in the International Court of Justice (ICJ).

Increasing insurgency led Spain in May 1975 to announce that it intended to withdraw from Spanish Sahara, while an ICJ ruling the following October stated that Moroccan and Mauritanian legal claims to the region were limited and had little bearing on the question of self-determination. Nevertheless, in November King Hassan ordered some 300,000 unarmed Moroccans, in what became known as the Green March, to enter the territory. Although Spain strongly objected to the action, a tripartite agreement with Morocco and Mauritania was concluded in Madrid on November 14. As a result, Spanish Sahara ceased to be a province of Spain at the end of the year; Spanish troops withdrew shortly thereafter, and Morocco and Mauritania assumed responsibility for Western Sahara on February 28, 1976. On April 14 Rabat and Nouakchott reached an agreement under which Morocco claimed the northern two-thirds of the region and Mauritania claimed the southern one-third.

The strongest opposition to the partition was voiced by the Popular Front for the Liberation of Saguia el Hamra and Rio de Oro (Polisario, see below), which in February 1976 formally proclaimed a government-in-exile of the Sahrawi Arab Democratic Republic (SADR), headed by Mohamed Lamine OULD AHMED as prime minister. Whereas Polisario had originally been based in Mauritania, its political leadership was subsequently relocated to Algeria, with its guerrilla units, recruited largely from nomadic tribes indigenous to the region, establishing secure bases there. Neither Rabat nor Nouakchott wished to precipitate a wider conflict by operating on Algerian soil, which permitted Polisario to concentrate militarily against the weaker of the two occupying regimes and thus to aid in the overthrow of Mauritania's Moktar Ould Daddah in July 1978. On August 5, 1979, Mauritania concluded a peace agreement with Polisario in Algiers, but Morocco responded by annexing the southern third of Western Sahara. Meanwhile, Polisario launched its first raids into Morocco, while continuing a diplomatic offensive that by the end of 1980 had resulted in some 45 countries according recognition to the SADR.

During a summit meeting of the Organization of African Unity (OAU) in Nairobi, Kenya, in June 1981, King Hassan called for a referendum on the future of the disputed territory, but an OAU special implementation committee was unable to move on the proposal because of Rabat's refusal to engage in direct negotiations or to meet a variety of other conditions advanced by Polisario as necessary to effect a cease-fire. As a result, conflict in the region intensified in the second half of the year.

At an OAU Council of Ministers meeting in Addis Ababa, Ethiopia, on February 22, 1982, a SADR delegation was, for the first time, seated, following a controversial ruling by the organization's secretary general that provoked a walkout by 18 member states, including Morocco. For the same reason, a quorum could not be declared for the next scheduled Council of Ministers meeting in Tripoli, Libya, on July 26, or for the 19th OAU summit, which was to have convened in Tripoli on August 5. An attempt to reconvene both meetings in November, following the "voluntary and temporary" withdrawal of the SADR, also failed because of the Western Sahara impasse, coupled with disagreement over the composition of a delegation from Chad. Another "temporary" withdrawal of the SADR allowed the OAU to convene the long-delayed summit in Addis Ababa in May 1983 at which it was decided to oversee a referendum in the region by the end of the year. Morocco's refusal to meet directly with Polisario representatives forced postponement of the poll, while the 1984 Treaty of Oujda with Libya effectively reduced support for the front's military forces. Subsequently, Moroccan soldiers crossed briefly into Algerian soil in "pursuit" of guerrillas, while extending the area under Moroccan control by 4,000 square miles. The seating of a SADR delegation at the twentieth OAU summit in November 1985 and the election of Polisario Secretary General Mohamed Abd al-AZZIZ as an OAU vice president prompted Morocco's withdrawal from the organization.

At the sixth triennial Polisario congress, held in "liberated territory" in December 1985, Abd al-Azziz was reelected secretary general; he subsequently appointed a new 13-member SADR government that included himself as president, with Ould Ahmed continuing as prime minister. The following May a series of "proximity talks" involving Moroccan and Polisario representatives concluded at UN headquarters in New York with no discernible change in the territorial impasse. Subsequently, Rabat began construction of more than 1,200 miles of fortified sand walls that forced the rebels back toward the Algerian and Mauritanian borders. Polisario, while conceding little likelihood of victory by its 30,000 fighters over an estimated 120,000 to 140,000 Moroccan soldiers, nonetheless continued its attacks, hoping that the economic strain of a "war of attrition" would induce King Hassan to enter into direct negotiations—a position endorsed by a 98–0 vote of the forty-first UN General Assembly. The UN also offered to administer the Western Sahara on an interim basis pending a popular referendum, but Rabat insisted that its forces remain in place. In 1987 the SADR reported an assassination attempt against Abd al-Azziz, alleging Moroccan complicity. Rabat denied the allegation and suggested that SADR dissidents may have been responsible.

Following the resumption of relations between Rabat and Algiers in May 1988, which some observers attributed in part to diminishing Algerian support for Polisario, progress appeared to be developing toward a negotiated settlement of the militarily stalemated conflict. On August 30, shortly after a new SADR government had been announced with Mahfoud Ali BEIBA taking over as prime minister, both sides announced their "conditional" endorsement of a UN-sponsored peace plan that called for a cease-fire and introduction of a UN peacekeeping force to oversee the long-discussed self-determination referendum. However, agreement was lacking on the qualifications of those who would be permitted to participate in the referendum and whether Moroccan troops would remain in the area prior to the vote. Underlining the fragility of the negotiations, Polisario launched one of its largest attacks in September before calling a cease-fire on December 30, pending face-to-face talks with King Hassan in January 1989. Although the talks eventually broke down, the cease-fire continued throughout most of the year as UN Secretary General Javier Pérez de Cuéllar attempted to mediate an agreement on referendum details. However, Polisario, accusing Rabat of delaying tactics, initiated a series of attacks in October, subsequent fighting being described as some of the most intense to date in the conflict. Another temporary truce was implemented in March 1990, and in June the UN Security Council formally authorized creation of a Western Saharan mission to supervise the proposed referendum. However, it was not until April 29, 1991, that the Security Council endorsed direct UN sponsorship of the poll, with the General Assembly approving a budget of $180 million, plus $34 million in voluntary contributions, for a UN Mission for the Referendum in Western Sahara (referenced by its French acronym, MINURSO). The mission's charge included the identification of bona fide inhabitants of the territory, the assembly of a voting list, the establishment of polling stations, and supervision of the balloting itself. The plan appeared to be in jeopardy when fierce fighting broke out in August between Moroccan and Polisario forces prior to the proposed deployment of MINURSO peacekeeping troops; however, both sides honored the UN's formal cease-fire date of September 6.

By early 1992 the broader dimensions of the Western Sahara conflict had significantly changed. The collapse of the Soviet Union and heightened internal problems for Polisario's principal backers, Algeria and Libya, created financial and supply problems for the rebels. At midyear it was estimated that more than 1,000 rank and file had joined a number of dissident leaders in defecting to Morocco. Meanwhile, Morocco had moved tens of thousands of settlers into the disputed territory, thereby diluting potential electoral support for Polisario. In addition, the proposed self-determination referendum, which the UN had planned to conduct in February, had been postponed indefinitely over the issue of voter eligibility, Polisario leaders charging that UN representatives had compromised their impartiality through secret dealings with Rabat. An unprecedented meeting, brokered by the UN at El Aaién between Moroccan and Polisario representatives, ended on July 19, 1993, without substantial progress. The main difficulty lay in a dispute about voting lists, Polisario insisting they should be based on a census taken in 1974 and Morocco arguing that they should be enlarged to include the names of some 100,000 individuals subsequently settling in the territory.

A second round of face-to-face talks, scheduled for October 1993, was cancelled at the last moment when Polisario objected to the presence of recent defectors from the front on the Moroccan negotiating team. Although the prospects for agreement on electoral eligibility were regarded as slight, MINURSO began identifying voters in June 1994 with the hope that balloting could be conducted in October 1995. Registration proceeded slowly, however, and UN officials in early 1995 protested that the Moroccan government was interfering in their operations. In April, UN Secretary General Boutros Boutros-Ghali reluctantly postponed the referendum again, sentiment reportedly growing within the UN Security Council to withdraw MINURSO if genuine progress was not achieved shortly.

In May 1996 the Security Council ordered a reduction in MINURSO personnel, UN officials declaring an impasse in the voter identification dispute and observers suggesting that hostilities could easily break out once again. However, face-to-face contacts between Polisario and Moroccan officials resumed in September, but no genuine progress ensued. It was reported that only 60,000 potential voters had been approved, with the cases of some 150,000 other "applicants" remaining unresolved at the end of the year.

New UN Secretary General Kofi Annan made the relaunching of the UN initiative in Morocco one of his priorities in early 1997 and in the spring appointed former U.S. Secretary of State James Baker as his personal envoy on the matter. Baker's mediation led to face-to-face talks between Polisario and representatives of the Moroccan government in the summer, culminating in the announcement of a "breakthrough" in September. Essentially, the two sides agreed to revive the 1991 plan with the goal of conducting the self-determination referendum in December 1998. They also accepted UN "supervision" in the region pending the referendum and agreed to the repatriation of refugees under the auspices of the UN High Commissioner for Refugees. MINURSO resumed the identification of voters in December 1997; however, the process subsequently again bogged down, with most observers concluding that the Moroccan government bore primary responsibility for the foot-dragging. Annan launched what he said would be his final push for a resolution in early 1999, calling for the resumption of voter registration at midyear leading up to a referendum by the end of July 2000.

In September 1999 several pro-independence riots in Western Sahara were suppressed by what some saw as an overreaction by the police, who beat and arrested scores of demonstrators. The heavy-handedness of the security forces reportedly strengthened the resolve of King Mohamed VI to oust the "old guard" of the Moroccan regime, especially Interior Minister Driss Basri. Although the new king later espoused a more flexible stance toward the Western Sahara issue, UN special envoy Baker noted in April 2000 that he remained pessimistic about the prospects of a resolution of the conflict, citing Morocco's insistence that Moroccan settlers in Western Sahara be eligible in the proposed referendum. In September 2001 Polisario rejected Baker's proposal to grant the Western Sahara political autonomy rather than hold an independence referendum. Recent interest in oil drilling in the region reportedly further complicated the matter. In November 2002 King Mohamed described the notion of a self-determination referendum as "obsolete." In mid-2004 the UN Security Council adopted a resolution urging Morocco and Polisario to accept the UN plan to grant Western Sahara self-government. Morocco rejected the proposal and continued to insist that the area be granted autonomy within the framework of Moroccan sovereignty. In August 2005 Polisario released 404 Moroccan prisoners, the last of the soldiers it had captured in fighting. The front said it hoped that the gesture would lead to Moroccan reciprocity and then a peace settlement. In November 2005 the king renewed his call for autonomy for the region within the "framework of Moroccan sovereignty," but the Polisario Front quickly rebuffed what it referred to as the king's "intransigence."

The stalemate lasted into 2006. Morocco continued to administer the annexed territory as four provinces: three established in 1976 (Boujdour, Es-Smara, El-Aaiún) and one in 1979 (Oued ed-Dahab). The SADR administers four Algerian camps, which house an estimated 165,000 Sahrawis, and claims to represent some 83,000 others who remain in the Western Sahara. Morocco has called for the relocation of the Sahrawis to a third country.

In April 2007 the Moroccan government submitted a proposal called the "Moroccan Initiative for Negotiating an Autonomy Status for the Sahara," to UN Secretary General, Ban Ki-Moon. Under this proposal the territory would become an autonomous region and would enjoy a measure of self-government but within the framework of the kingdom's sovereignty and national unity. The idea of autonomy was encouraged by both the United States and France, who viewed it as the most workable solution to the crisis. At the same time, however, Polisario submitted its own proposal to the UN, called "Proposal of the Frente Polisario for a Mutually Acceptable Political Solution Assuring the Self-Determination of the People of Western Sahara," which called for "full self-determination through a free referendum with independence as an option." Morocco and Polisario agreed to attend UN-sponsored talks in June 2007, a groundbreaking development given that this was the first time in ten years that the two sides had sat down at the same table. In 2008 the UN envoy was quoted saying that independence was not an option for the Western Sahara, a comment that had the Polisario Front and the Algerian government crying foul. In April 2008 the UN renewed its mission in the region for another year, and the stalemate that had persisted in the last three attempts at negotiation between the parties continued. In August 2009 Morocco resumed informal negotiations with the Polisario Front under UN sponsorship. However, Algeria subsequently accused Morocco of responsibility for delaying the resumption of official talks.

Sahrawi Front:

Popular Front for the Liberation of Saguia el Hamra and Rio de Oro (*Frente Popular para la Liberación de Saguia el Hamra y Rio de Oro*—Polisario). Established in 1973 to win independence for Spanish (subsequently Western) Sahara, the Polisario Front was initially based in Mauritania, but since the mid-1970s its political leadership has operated from Algeria. In consonance with recent developments throughout the world, the once strongly socialist Polisario currently promises to institute a market economy in "the future Sahrawi state," except in regard to mineral reserves (which would remain state property). The front also supports "eventual" multipartyism, its 1991 congress, held in Tindouf, Algeria, pledging to draft a "democratic and pluralistic" constitution to present for a national referendum should the proposed self-determination vote in the Western Sahara go in Polisario's favor. In other activity, the Congress reelected longtime leader Mohamed Abd al-Azziz as secretary general of the front and thereby president of the SADR. However, in August 1992 the defection to Morocco of the SADR foreign minister, Brahim HAKIM, served to point out the increasingly tenuous position of the rebel movement. Subsequently, a new SADR government in exile announced in September 1993 was most noteworthy for the appointment of hard-liner Brahim GHALI as defense minister.

In 1995 Polisario reportedly was still threatening to resume hostilities if the UN plan collapsed. However, it was widely believed that the front's military capacity had by then diminished to about 6,000 soldiers.

The Ninth Polisario Congress, held August 20–27, 1995, reelected Abd al-Azziz as secretary general and urged the international community to pressure the Moroccan government regarding its perceived stonewalling. In September a new SADR government was announced under the leadership of Mahfoud Ali Larous Beiba, a former SADR health minister. On October 12 the first session of a SADR National Assembly was convened in Tindouf, its 101 members having been elected via secret ballot at local and regional "conferences." A new SADR government was named on January 21, 1998, although Beiba remained as prime minister and a number of incumbents were reappointed. Beiba was succeeded in 1999 by Bouchraya Hamoudi Bayoun, who was in turn succeeded in 2003 by Abdelkader Taleb Oumar.

In the summer and fall of 2005, many Sahrawis had began referring to their campaign against Morocco as an *"intifada,"* and Abd al-Azziz called for assistance from South Africa's Nelson Mandela and U.S. President George W. Bush in resolving the Western Sahara standoff.

In 2008 SADR announced that it sought bids for offshore oil exploration, but it received little foreign interest because of concerns over the longterm legal status of any contracts.

Secretary General: Mohamed Abd al-AZZIZ (President of the SADR).

Prime Minister of the SADR: Abdelkader Taleb OUMAR.

MOZAMBIQUE

Republic of Mozambique
República de Moçambique

Political Status: Former Portuguese dependency; became independent as the People's Republic of Mozambique on June 25, 1975; present name adopted in constitution that came into effect on November 30, 1990.

Area: 309,494 sq. mi. (801,590 sq. km.).

Population: 20,530,714(2007C); 20,861,000 (2008E). The 2007 figure is preliminary.

Major Urban Center (2005E): MAPUTO (1,122,000).

Official Language: Portuguese (a number of African languages are also spoken).

Monetary Unit: Metical (market rate December 1, 2009: 30.80 meticals = $1US). The "new metical" was introduced in 2006 at the rate of 1 new metical = 1,000 old meticals.

President: Armando Emilio GUEBUZA (Mozambique Liberation Front); elected on December 1–2, 2004, and inaugurated on February 2, 2005, to succeed Joaquim Alberto CHISSANO (Mozambique Liberation Front).

Prime Minister: Luisa Dias DIOGO (Mozambique Liberation Front); appointed by the president on February 17, 2004, to succeed Dr. Pascoal Manuel MOCUMBI (Mozambique Liberation Front), who earlier had announced his intention to resign; reappointed by the president on February 3, 2005, following presidential and legislative elections on December 1–2, 2004.

THE COUNTRY

Mozambique lies on the southeast coast of Africa, its contiguous neighbors being Tanzania on the north; Malawi and Zambia on the northwest; and Zimbabwe, South Africa, and Swaziland on the west and south. Mozambique's varied terrain comprises coastal lowlands, central plateaus, and mountains along the western frontier. The country is bisected by the Zambezi River, which flows southeastward from the Zambia-Zimbabwe border. The population, while primarily of Bantu stock, is divided into several dozen tribal groups, most speaking distinct local languages or dialects. About 40 percent of the population is Christian, and approximately 20 percent is Muslim. About one-quarter of the population practices traditional religions. Catholic and Anglican churches, many of which were closed following independence, have regained influence as a result of the government's retreat from a rigidly Marxist-Leninist orientation. Women constitute 48 percent of the labor force, primarily in the agricultural sector; there are a number of female ministers, including the prime minister, in the current cabinet and 89 members of the assembly are women (35.6 percent). In 2008 the United Nations ranked Mozambique as 175 out of 179 countries in its human development index.

Agriculture remains the mainstay of the economy, employing two-thirds of the workforce and providing the principal cultivated exports: cashew nuts, cotton, sugar, and tea. Seafood is also an important export. Following independence, agricultural output declined—particularly in production of sugar and cotton as well as of such minerals as coal and copper—as the government introduced pervasive state control and the Portuguese community, which possessed most of the country's technical and managerial expertise, left the country. In the early 1980s, however, the government began to encourage limited private ownership, foreign investment, and the development of family-owned and operated farms. For the most part, industry has been limited to processing agricultural commodities, although significant deposits of natural gas, as well as bauxite, iron, manganese, tantalite, uranium, and other ores, await exploitation.

The economy contracted sharply from 1982 to 1986, as insurgency and drought inflicted widespread death and deprivation that necessitated massive emergency food imports and other aid. Subsequently, a recovery program sponsored by the International Monetary Fund (IMF) contributed to moderate economic growth, although social conditions, particularly in rural areas, remained dismal as the result of rebel activity.

In June 1993 international donors pledged some $70 million to aid the estimated 4 million internally displaced Mozambicans and to launch a massive repatriation program in light of progress toward resolution of the longstanding civil war. However, returning refugees faced grim economic conditions, as reflected by an average annual per capita income of less than $80 (the world's lowest, according to the World Bank). The imposition by the government of fiscal austerity and other reforms subsequently sparked an impressive recovery, GDP growing by more than 10 percent annually from 1996 to 1999 and Mozambique becoming the "darling" of the IMF and World Bank, which had helped to negotiate substantial debt relief packages. However, despite having returned to food self-sufficiency, Mozambique remained among the lowest-ranked nations regarding development, and poverty was widespread, much of the population living in small villages lacking electricity or running water. The widespread effects of severe flooding slowed GDP growth in 2000 to 2.1 percent, while inflation registered 12.7 percent for the year. The economy recovered in 2001, however, with real GDP rising by 13.9 percent. Through mid-2002, the World Bank, the IMF, and the World Trade Organization continued to praise the country's economic performance and the government's policies.

Growth continued through 2003, propelled by expansion in manufacturing, construction, and service industries. In 2004 the World Bank provided $790 million in grants for debt relief. In addition, the IMF pledged $7.7 million in assistance over a three-year period to support government efforts to reform and restructure the economy. (Banking reform and intensified privatization efforts were requested.) The IMF also approved $110 million to fund construction of a major railway in Zambezi Province as a conduit for manufactured goods and passengers to the interior of the country.

In 2005 it was reported that GDP had increased annually by an average of 8 percent over the past ten years, one of the highest long-term growth rates in Africa. Collaterally, the poverty rate had declined from 69 percent of the population in 1997 to 54 percent in 2005. A report that year by 18 donor nations indicated that the government's

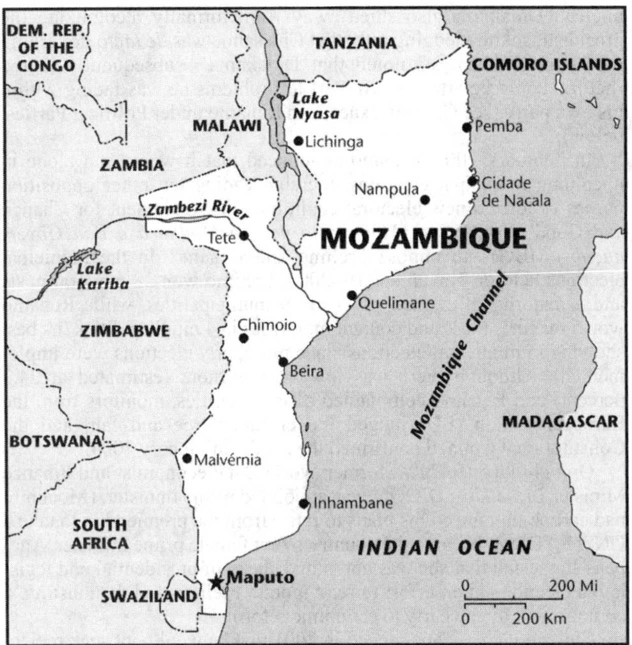

anticorruption campaign had made little progress. However, the government had privatized more than 1,200 state-owned corporations by 2007, and several large projects, including titanium and coal mines, natural gas fields, and an ammonia and phosphate plant, continued to attract significant foreign investment. The government received $506.9 million from the U.S. Millennium Challenge Corporation to improve infrastructure, including road construction and enhancements to the water and sewage systems.

In 2008 the government announced a $3 billion effort, funded mainly by foreign investments, to develop Mozambique as a tourist destination. The government was also praised by the World Bank for its economic programs, and through 2008, the Bank provided $60 million annually for 17 infrastructure projects. Meanwhile, Portugal cancelled Mozambique's $390 million debt, Ireland pledged $290 million over a four-year period for poverty reduction, and France promised $1 million to improve government services. GDP growth was 6.5 percent, and inflation 11.2 percent, up from 7.9 percent the year before. Unemployment remained above 20 percent, and as high as 60 percent in some areas. The 2008-2009 global economic slowdown was estimated to slow GDP growth in 2009 to 5 percent as foreign investment was reduced, but higher agricultural output was expected to somewhat offset the economic decline. In June 2009 the European Commission agreed to provide $598 million in aid to Mozambique, while the World Bank and other donors pledged $446 million to improve healthcare.

GOVERNMENT AND POLITICS

Political background. Portuguese hegemony was established early in the 16th century, when Mozambican coastal settlements became ports of call for traders from the Far East. However, it was not until the Berlin Congress of 1884–1885 that Portuguese supremacy was formally acknowledged by the European powers. In 1952 the colony of Mozambique became an Overseas Province and, as such, was constitutionally incorporated into Portugal. In 1964 armed resistance to Portuguese rule was initiated by the Mozambique Liberation Front (*Frente de Libertação de Moçambique*—Frelimo), led by Dr. Eduardo MONDLANE until his assassination by Portuguese agents in 1969. Following Mondlane's death, Samora MACHEL and Marcelino DOS SANTOS overcame a bid for control by Frelimo Vice President Uriah SIMANGO and were installed as the movement's president and vice president, respectively. After the 1974 coup in Lisbon, negotiations in Lusaka, Zambia, called for the formation of a new government composed of Frelimo and Portuguese elements and for the attainment of complete independence in mid-1975. The agreement was challenged by leaders of the white minority, who attempted to establish a white provisional government under right-wing leadership. After the collapse of this rebellion on September 10, 1974, most of the territory's 250,000 whites migrated to Portugal or South Africa.

On June 25, 1975, Mozambique became an independent "people's republic," with Machel assuming the presidency. Elections of Frelimo-sponsored candidates to local, district, provincial, and national assemblies were held during September–December 1977. In an apparent easing of its commitment to Marxist centralism, the government took steps in the early 1980s to separate government and party cadres. However, a government reorganization in March 1986 reestablished party domination, with the Council of Ministers being divided into three sections, each directed by a senior member of the Frelimo Political Bureau.

On July 26, 1986, Mário Fernandes da Graça MACHUNGO, an economist who had overseen recent liberalization of the economy, was sworn in as prime minister, a newly created post designed to permit President Machel to concentrate on defense of the regime against the Mozambique National Resistance (*Resistência Nacional Moçambicana*—Renamo), which had grown from a relatively isolated opponent to an insurgent force operating in all ten provinces. Machel, who had remained a widely respected leader despite the country's myriad problems, died in a plane crash on October 19 and was succeeded on November 6 by his longtime associate, Foreign Affairs Minister Joaquim Alberto CHISSANO. Chissano extended the economic liberalization policies initiated by his predecessor, overtures to the West for emergency and development aid generally being well received. However, domestic progress remained severely constrained by Renamo attacks on civilians and the concurrent destruction of farms, schools, and health facilities.

In part to seek accommodation with the rebels, Frelimo abandoned its commitment to Marxism-Leninism in July 1989. A year later, direct talks with Renamo representatives were launched in Rome, Italy, and in August 1990 Frelimo's Central Committee endorsed the holding of multiparty elections in 1991.

On November 2, 1990, following extensive National Assembly debate, a new, pluralistic constitution was adopted. Subsequently, a tenuous cease-fire negotiated with Renamo on December 1 broke down, the rebels withdrawing from the Rome talks. The talks resumed in May 1991, and five months later the rebels agreed to halt armed activity, to drop demands for a UN transitional government, and to recognize the government's authority. For its part, the government agreed to procedures by which Renamo could function as a political party following a formal cease-fire.

After several weeks of deadlock in the ninth round of the Rome talks, the parties finally agreed on a protocol, which was signed March 12, 1992. It provided for election to the Assembly of the Republic by proportional representation; the holding of simultaneous legislative and presidential balloting; the formation of a National Electoral Commission, one-third of whose members would be named by Renamo; and government assistance to Renamo in establishing itself as a political grouping in every provincial capital. After another delay, the round continued with a June 10 agreement on the formation of a unified, nonpartisan army; the specifics of a cease-fire; and transitory arrangements before the general election. On August 5 Chissano and Renamo leader Gen. Afonso DHLAKAMA held their first ever face-to-face meeting, and on August 7 they reached an accord on a cease-fire and electoral preparations. Subsequently, despite reports of Renamo intransigence and an increasingly restive national army, Chissano and the rebel leader signed a peace treaty in Rome on October 4, ending the 16-year conflict. Included in the treaty were provisions for a cease-fire, multiparty elections within a year, the establishment of a 30,000-member army drawn equally from the existing forces, a political amnesty, and Western-financed repatriation of refugees. Five days later the assembly approved the treaty and the launching of the UN's Operation in Mozambique (*Operação des Naões Unidas em Moçambique*—ONUMOZ), a peacekeeping force with responsibility for disarming both combatants, integrating troops into the new armed forces, organizing elections, and securing trade routes.

In April 1993 the UN Security Council voiced "serious concern" over implementation of the October 1992 accord because of a shortfall in funds for deployment of peacekeeping troops and the withdrawal of Renamo members from the cease-fire and control commissions established under the treaty. Renamo subsequently indicated that it would not return to the commissions until a number of logistical problems had been resolved and some $15 million to support its political activities had been received.

On June 3, 1993, the commissions resumed meeting, and on June 21 the disarmament program was launched. Two months later the Joint Commission for the Formation of the Mozambique Defense Armed Forces announced that it had reached agreement on creation of the inclusive Mozambique Defense Armed Forces. In addition, an August 27–September 3 meeting between Chissano and Dhlakama, their first since 1992, yielded an accord on territorial administration, following Renamo's retreat from insistence that it be given jurisdiction over the provinces it controlled. At a further meeting on October 16–20 the two agreed on the establishment of a 20-member electoral commission (to be composed of ten government appointees, seven Renamo officials, and three from other opposition parties). Thereafter, the peace process continued to advance as the government and Renamo settled electoral law differences and formally agreed to a demobilization plan that would commence on November 30 and continue for six months.

By mid-January 1994 over 50 percent of the rebels were reported to have arrived at demobilization sites. By contrast, the government was widely criticized for a compliance level of only 19 percent. Nonetheless, President Chissano, responding to a Security Council call for a transfer of power to democratically elected officials by the end of November, announced that the country's first multiparty balloting would take place on October 27–28.

At the long-deferred balloting (extended by one day to October 29), President Chissano was a clear victor, polling 53.7 percent of the vote, compared to 33.7 percent for his principal opponent, Renamo's Dhlakama. While the legislative outcome was much closer (129–112), no opposition members were named to the government subsequently formed under former foreign minister Pascoal Manuel MOCUMBI.

Under pressure from the opposition and international donors to broaden its definition of what constituted a viable polling district, the assembly, with Renamo support, approved a constitutional amendment in November 1996 that provided for the establishment of a local government electoral system wherein communities with a functioning administration and a "reasonable" local tax base would participate in polling. In early 1997 Renamo reversed itself, threatening to stalemate the assembly and boycott elections if the scope of the polling was not expanded. Nevertheless, in March 1997 the assembly approved the creation of a nine-member, bipartisan national elections commission, which it charged with preparing for balloting. In June it was announced that elections would be held in 23 cities and 10 towns (1 in each of the provinces) in December, one year after originally scheduled. Balloting was subsequently postponed until May 1998 and, once again, in March 1998 to June 30.

After months of threats, in April 1998 the partners in the Coordinating Council of the Opposition formally announced their intention to boycott the local polling, citing the government's unwillingness to allow their representatives to participate in the commission that was investigating alleged electoral roll fraud. The opposition's subsequent efforts to garner support for their boycott plans appeared to have succeeded dramatically, as on June 30 less than 20 percent of the electorate was reported to have participated in the balloting. In the immediate aftermath of the elections, during which Frelimo candidates easily overwhelmed a field of independent competitors, the opposition declared the polling "null and void" and threatened to launch a civil disobedience campaign if the results were upheld. Subsequently, however, the Renamo- led opposition announced that it would not hinder the efforts of the newly elected officials, asserting that it was turning its attention to preparing for general elections in 1999.

Chissano once again defeated Dhlakama (52.3–47.7 percent) in the presidential poll conducted on December 3–5, 1999, while Frelimo won 133 seats in the concurrent assembly balloting, compared to 117 seats for Renamo and its recently formed opposition alliance called the Renamo/Electoral Union (Renamo/*União Electoral*—Renamo/UE). After the Supreme Court rejected a Renamo/UE call for nullification of the results, Chissano was sworn in for another five-year term on January 15, 2000. Two days later he reappointed Mocumbi to head a new all-Frelimo cabinet, which was described as bringing "fresh blood" into the government while retaining the "tested core" of the previous administration.

Tension between the government and the opposition rose significantly in November 2000, when more than 40 people were killed during countrywide protest demonstrations called by Renamo. Although it was later announced that the Chissano and Dhlakama had agreed to form consultative "working committees," and the government pledged to consider Renamo's preferences in appointing governors in the disputed provinces, the exact form of this accommodation remained unclear. Dhlakama also shied away from formally recognizing the president, acknowledging only that Chissano "was *de facto* governing the country." Analysts noted that Dhlakama's subsequently muted rhetoric could be attributed in part to problems he was facing within his own party (see Current issues, and Renamo under Political Parties, below).

In February 2003 Renamo announced that it would run alone in upcoming municipal elections, thereby leading ten other opposition parties to form a new electoral coalition—the Movement for Change and Good Governance (*Movimento para a Mudança e Boa Governação*—MBG)—to oppose Frelimo and Renamo. In the municipal elections held on November 19, 2003, Frelimo won 28 mayoral posts and a majority of council posts in 29 municipalities, while Renamo won 5 mayor's races and council majorities in 4 municipalities (its best showing in municipal elections since multiparty elections were implemented). Although there was low voter turnout (estimated at 24.2 percent) and Renamo complained of irregularities, monitors from the European Union (EU) judged the elections free and fair, and the Constitutional Council confirmed the results in January 2004.

On February 19, 2004, former World Bank economist and Finance Minister Luisa Dias DIOGO was appointed prime minister. (Mocumbi had earlier announced his plans to retire from the premiership to take a UN job.) Diogo became the country's first female prime minister. Analysts suggested that she was appointed ahead of presidential and legislative elections in an effort to reinvigorate Frelimo and demonstrate a commitment by the party to economic reform.

Chissano having announced in 2001 that he would not seek reelection in 2004, Frelimo chose Armando GUEBUZA as its presidential candidate. In balloting on December 1–2, Guebuza won 63.74 percent of the vote. His closest rival was Dhlakama, who received 31.72 percent of the vote. In concurrent legislative balloting, Frelimo won 62.03 percent of the vote and 160 seats, while Renamo won 29.73 percent and 90 seats. None of the other 23 parties received more than 2 percent of the vote. Both the presidential and legislative elections were heavily criticized by the opposition and international observers. Renamo protested to the Constitutional Council, and its deputies initially refused to take their seats in the assembly. Nonetheless, on January 20, 2005, the council certified the results. Diogo was reappointed as prime minister on February 3, and she subsequently formed a new cabinet of Frelimo appointees.

In March 2007 Guebuza conducted two cabinet reshuffles in an effort to improve the government's popularity. In particular, Guebaza replaced his brother-in-law, Defense Minister Gen. (ret.) Tobias DAI, who had been heavily criticized following an explosion at a military facility (see Current issues, below). The president named as Transport and Communications minister Paulo ZUCULA, whose management of relief efforts following flooding in January and February was widely acclaimed (see Current issues, below).

In local and regional elections in November 2008 (see Current issues, below) Frelimo won 42 of the 43 mayoral contests and secured majorities on all 43 municipal councils. Renamo protested the results, which were judged as generally free and fair by both domestic and international observers. It called for a second round of voting in several contested regions; however, the constitutional court certified the original results. New presidential and legislative elections were scheduled for October 28, 2009 (see Current issues, below).

Constitution and government. The 1975 constitution characterized the People's Republic of Mozambique as a "popular democratic state" while reserving for Frelimo "the directing power of the state and society," with decisions taken by party organs to be regarded as binding on all government officials. A subsequent constitution, adopted in August 1978, set as a national objective "the construction of the material and ideological bases for a socialist society." The president of Frelimo served as president of the republic and chief of the armed forces, while an indirectly elected People's Assembly was designated as the "supreme organ of state power."

The basic law approved by the assembly in November 1990 contained no reference to Frelimo or leadership of the working class, while "People's" was dropped from the state name. It provided for a popularly elected president serving a maximum of two five-year terms. The Council of Ministers continued to be headed by a presidentially appointed prime minister, with national legislators selected on a proportional basis in multiparty balloting. In addition to freedom of association and of the press, the new document guaranteed various human and civil rights, including the right to private property and the right to strike. A Supreme Court heads an independent judiciary.

A number of constitutional amendments were approved by the Assembly of the Republic in November 2004, although most of the basic elements of the 1990 text remained intact. (The president continued to hold the power to appoint the prime minister, cabinet ministers, and provincial governors.) The amendments reaffirmed the authority of the Constitutional Council (established in 2003) to rule on the constitutionality of legislation and to validate election results. Other changes provided for an Ombudsman (appointed by a two-third's majority in the assembly) to investigate allegations of misconduct by state officials, for the election of provincial assemblies (beginning in 2008), and for the establishment of an advisory Council of State (comprised of automatic members [such as former presidents, former assembly presidents, and the runner-up in the most recent presidential election], as well as members appointed by the president and the assembly). Although the new council was given no formal decision-making authority, the president was required to consult with the council on a broad range of matters, including the conduct of elections. The basic law revisions also removed the president's immunity from prosecution by authorizing impeachment by a vote of two-thirds of the assembly.

The governors of the country's ten provinces are appointed by the president, who may annul the decisions of provincial, district, and local assemblies. The city of Maputo (which has provincial status) is under the administrative direction of a City Council chair. Legislation in 2006 provided for the creation of elected assemblies for the ten provinces, the size of the assemblies to be determined by population. In 2008 the number of municipalities with elected mayors and assemblies was increased from 33 to 43.

Foreign relations. Avowedly Marxist in orientation until mid-1989, the Frelimo government was for many years the beneficiary of substantial economic, technical, and security support from the Soviet Union, Cuba, East Germany, and other Moscow-line states. However, links with the West began to increase in 1979. The UK and Brazil extended credit, and in 1982 Portugal resumed relations that had ceased in 1977 as a result of the nationalization of Portuguese holdings. Relations with the United States, troubled since 1977 by charges of human rights abuses, reached a nadir in 1981 with the expulsion of all U.S. embassy personnel for alleged espionage. Relations were reestablished in July 1983, and President Machel made a state visit to Washington in September 1985, securing economic aid and exploring the possibility of military assistance. President Chissano was similarly received in March 1990 by President George H. W. Bush, who promised an unspecified amount of U.S. aid for reconstruction and development. Meanwhile, in 1984 Mozambique had been admitted to the IMF and World Bank, signifying a desire on Maputo's part to become a more active participant in the world economy.

Despite its prominence as one of the Front-Line States committed to majority rule in southern Africa, Mozambique maintained economic links to white-dominated South Africa as a matter of "realistic policy," with some 40,000 Mozambicans employed in South African mines and considerable revenue derived from cooperation in transport and hydroelectric power. However, relations were severely strained by South African support for the Renamo insurgents in the 1980s. In a 1984 nonaggression pact, the "Nkomati Accord," South Africa agreed to stop aiding Renamo in return for Mozambique's pledge not to support the African National Congress (ANC) in its guerrilla campaign against the South African minority government. The accord proved ineffective, however, as growing rebel activity fostered Mozambican suspicion of continued destabilization attempts by its white-ruled neighbor. In August 1987 the two countries agreed that the pact should be reactivated, prompting an unprecedented meeting between President Chissano and South African President Botha in September 1988, at which Botha again promised not to support the insurgents. In 1990 President Chissano announced that he was convinced that the new government in Pretoria had indeed halted its support of Renamo and that the two countries could now concentrate on economic cooperation.

The civil war also dominated Maputo's relations elsewhere in the region. The Zimbabwean government, declaring "If Mozambique falls, we fall," sent an estimated 10,000 troops to combat the Renamo rebels, particularly in the transport corridor to Beira, which played a central role in the Front-Line States' effort to reduce dependence on South African trade routes. In December 1986 Tanzanian President Mwinyi also agreed to make troops available to Mozambique, as did Malawi following a dispute over alleged Renamo bases within its borders (see Malawi article). In 1992 Zimbabwean president Robert Mugabe, along with Italian officials, played a major role in brokering the peace accord that was signed in Rome in October.

By early 1993 approximately 1.7 million Mozambicans had taken refuge in neighboring countries, Malawi housing 1.1 million. On June 12 Mozambique and the UN High Commission for Refugees (UNHCR) formally inaugurated a repatriation operation (beginning with exiles in Zimbabwe), which observers described as the largest ever in Africa, and by August 19 Mozambique had signed repatriation agreements with Malawi, Swaziland, and Zambia. The repatriation program was formally terminated on November 21, 1995, at which time the UNHCR announced that more than 1 million refugees had returned home.

The most surprising foreign policy development of 1995 was Mozambique's admission to the Commonwealth as the group's 53rd member. Its entry on a unique and special case basis had been urged by its anglophone neighbors as a means of enhancing regional trade, most importantly in cashew nuts, which critics insisted was effectively controlled by Indian and Pakistani interests.

In 1996 Mozambique negotiated security agreements with Malawi, Swaziland, and Zimbabwe in an effort to squelch the border violence attributed to *Chimwenje,* a shadowy grouping of Zimbabwean dissidents who were allegedly led and trained by former Renamo militiamen from bases along their shared borders (for more information on *Chimwenje,* see article on Zimbabwe). Meanwhile, following approximately a year of negotiations, Mozambique signed an agreement with South Africa in May that provided South African farmers with access to Mozambican agricultural land. The deal was opposed by both Renamo leaders and Frelimo activists, who charged that "exporting white farmers to Mozambique" was favored by South Africa's ANC as a means of freeing up land for black settlement. At the same time, South Africa and Mozambique inaugurated the Maputo Corridor Development Project with the aim of redeveloping the trade route between Johannesburg and Maputo and refurbishing the latter's harbor. In 2002 the government initiated a program to resettle white farmers from Zimbabwe whose land had been expropriated.

Relations between Mozambique and the United States have improved in recent years. In 2002, Chissano, along with the leaders of Botswana and Angola, met with U.S. President George W. Bush in Washington, D.C., in a summit on development of the region. Mozambique is part of the U.S. Africa Growth and Opportunity Act (AGOA) that offers preferential trade opportunities to African states. Relations with European states also remained strong, with both France and Russia agreeing in 2002 to cancel portions of Mozambique's debt. Meanwhile the EU increased direct annual aid to Mozambique to $131 million per year through 2007.

In 2002 and 2003 Mozambique conducted a series of cooperative military exercises with Portugal. (The two countries also have an agreement whereby soldiers from Mozambique are trained in Portugal.) Although the relationship between the two countries subsequently remained essentially strong, friction developed in 2005 over the proposed takeover by Mozambique of a hydroelectric plant on the Zambesi River for which the Portuguese government held 85 percent financial responsibility. New President Guebuza refused to accept the amount of back debt that Portugal demanded be paid by Mozambique prior to the transfer of ownership, and, although a tentative agreement was announced in late 2005, it was not implemented until Mozambique paid Portugal $700 million in November 2007. Meanwhile, the Guebuza administration reached out to a broad range of other potential donors for assistance, achieving success most notably with China, Germany, and India. China agreed in 2007 to give Mozambique $2.5 million in military equipment and to provide training for Mozambican military officers annually at Chinese military academies.

In 2007 South Africa decided to reopen an investigation into the 1986 death of President Machel because of suspicions that the apartheid regime had been involved in the plane crash that had killed the Mozambique leader. Meanwhile, a South African soldier was killed along with five Mozambicans in June while participating in a joint operation to destroy mines and leftover military ordnance from Mozambique's civil war.

Political violence against Zimbabweans in South Africa led more than 10,000 refugees to flee to Mozambique in May 2008. The Mozambican government declared a state of emergency and established refugee camps along the border to accommodate the exodus. In December Mozambique and China signed an agreement to increase military cooperation and collaboration. Meanwhile, China granted Mozambique $1.5 million to upgrade its military equipment.

Mozambique and Portugal signed an agreement in February 2009 to expand cooperation in the areas of law enforcement and criminal justice. Also in February Mozambique and India signed two new economic agreements and India granted Mozambique a $25 million line of credit to improve industry and infrastructure.

Current issues. During the 2004 presidential campaign, divisions within Frelimo emerged between the supporters of Armando Guebuza (the Frelimo candidate) and Chissano. The new cabinet appointed following Guebuza's victory contained many new members and appeared to represent an attempt by the new president to break with Frelimo's "old guard." In addition to purging many *"Chissanoistas"* from their former posts throughout government ranks, Guebuza also launched a broad anticorruption initiative that often focused on members of the former administration. (Guebuza described the "remoralization" of government as his top priority.) Tensions between Frelimo and Renamo also remained high, although Dhlakama (who continued to refuse to accept the validity of the 2004 election results) agreed to take his seat on the new Council of State in December 2005 on the grounds that too many critical governmental decisions were being made without appropriate opposition influence. Underscoring the ongoing friction, a bipartisan assembly commission, established in 2005 to propose electoral law reforms, disbanded in April 2006 without reaching agreement.

President Guebuza continued to consolidate power through 2006 by, among other things, creating the National Civil Service Authority to oversee public servants, including hiring and promotion. Whereas the civil service had previously operated under the ministry of state administration, the new agency reported directly to the president. Opposition leaders and independent media criticized the new body as a means for the president to reward supporters and ensure control over the civil service.

Widespread flooding caused by Cyclone Favio in February 2007 left 29 dead and forced more than 90,000 from their homes. In March an explosion at a military weapons depot left 104 dead and injured more than 500. The incident was the third explosion at the facility since 1985, and the government faced widespread criticism over its unwillingness to launch an investigation into the base or the explosions.

Arguing that the opposition had not been allowed to contribute to the legislation, Renamo denounced the 2006 electoral law that provided for the election of provincial assemblies. Nonetheless, Renamo and its allies pledged to participate in the polling, which was rescheduled for 2008. In March 2007 Renamo opposed minor electoral law reforms that dealt with municipal balloting, which was also scheduled for 2008. In October former president Chissano became the first person to be awarded the $5 million Mo Ibrahim Prize for Achievement in African Leadership for his reconciliation efforts.

In March Cyclone Jokwe struck the north and central coasts, leaving 17 dead and more than 60,000 homeless or in need of food aid. By the winter, the UN estimated that more than 350,000 Mozambicans required food aid as a result of the storm. In April 2008 Amnesty International issued a report that criticized the Mozambican police for excessive force and extrajudicial killings. The Mozambican media reported at least 26 vigilante slayings in 2007 and 2008. The killings were reportedly linked to the security forces. In response to rising fuel prices, the government approved a $280-million biofuels project in which 44,500 acres would be used to grow sugarcane to produce ethanol. Renamo campaigned in the 2008 local elections outside of the electoral coalition that it led in the 2004 balloting. The party experienced a significant number of defections prior to, and after, the local elections (see Political parties, below) in which it lost the five mayorships that it had controlled. Continuing internal strife among the opposition parties led analysts to predict Frelimo would sweep the 2009 presidential and legislative balloting.

POLITICAL PARTIES

For its first 15 years of independence Mozambique was a one-party state in which the Mozambique Liberation Front (Frelimo) was constitutionally empowered to guide the operations of government at all levels. However, after extensive national debate, the government concluded in 1990 that a "significant minority" of the population desired a multiparty system. Consequently, constitutional revision in October guaranteed freedom of association, with subsequent legislation establishing the criteria for party legalization. Following President Chissano's February 6, 1991, announcement that legislation sanctioning political party formations (approved in January) was now in effect, a number of groups announced their intention to hold inaugural congresses, and by January 1994, 13 political parties had been legally recognized. Some 25 parties contested the 2004 legislative elections, while 16 contested the 2008 local balloting.

Government Party:

Mozambique Liberation Front (*Frente de Libertação de Moçambique*—Frelimo). Founded in 1962 by the union of three nationalist parties and led by Dr. Eduardo Mondlane until his death in 1969, Frelimo engaged in armed resistance to Portuguese rule from 1964 to 1974, when agreement on independence was reached. At its third national congress in 1977, the front was designated a Marxist-Leninist party (directed by a Central Committee, a Political Bureau, and a Secretariat), but at the fourth party congress in 1983 economic philosophy began to shift toward the encouragement of free-market activity. Following the death of Samora Machel in October 1986, the Central Committee designated his longtime associate, Joaquim Alberto Chissano, as its political leader.

Frelimo retreated even further from Marxist doctrine at the group's fifth congress in 1989. Terming itself the vanguard of "the Mozambican people" rather than a "worker-peasant alliance," the party opened its membership to many formerly excluded groups, such as private property owners, the business community, Christians, Muslims, and traditionalists. The congress also called for a negotiated settlement with Renamo, bureaucratic reform, and emphasis on family farming rather than state agriculture.

Although President Chissano easily defeated Renamo's Afonso Dhlakama in the 1994 election, Frelimo as a party performed much more poorly, barely securing a majority of legislative seats. On a regional basis the results were quite mixed, the party substantially outpolling Renamo in the south, while being decisively defeated in the center and trailing marginally in the north.

In what was described as a break with "old guard" leadership, five of the Frelimo Central Committee's six members were replaced on July 24, 1995, and Manuel Tome was appointed as the party's new secretary general. In spite of these changes, corruption charges continued to dog the party. Observers attributed Frelimo's subsequent endorsement of a proposal to limit the geographic scope of municipal elections to weak support beyond its southern base. Challenged only by small opposition groups and independent candidates, Frelimo dominated balloting for local posts in June 1998. It secured 48.5 percent of the vote and 133 seats in the December 1999 legislative balloting.

During a party congress in June 2002, Chissano was reelected as Frelimo chair. However, former parliamentary leader Armando Guebuza was elected as the new secretary general and the party's 2004 presidential candidate despite the fact that Chissano had supported Herder MUTEIA for the post. Guebuza was elected president in the 2004 balloting, and Frelimo increased its seats in the assembly to 160. Significant friction was subsequently reported between President Guebuza and former members of the Chissano administration (see Current issues, above).

Guebuza further consolidated his control over Frelimo at a party congress in November 2006. His close supporters gained dominance of the 160-member party central commission and the 17-member political commission, the main decision-making body of Frelimo. Meanwhile, Guebuza loyalist Filipe Paunde was elected general secretary of the party. A party congress in July 2008 chose candidates to compete in municipal and regional elections. Reports indicated that the majority of candidates were Guebuza supporters. In September Guebuza was chosen as Frelimo's presidential candidate for the 2009 balloting at a party contest where the incumbent ran unopposed. In November Frelimo won a resounding victory in local elections throughout the country.

Leaders: Armando GUEBUZA (President of the Republic and Secretary General), Luisa Dias DIOGO (Prime Minister), Joaquim Alberto CHISSANO (Former President of the Republic and Honorary Party President), Filipe PAUNDE (General Secretary), Manuel TOME (Parliamentary Leader), Edson MACUACUA (Party Spokesperson).

Opposition Party:

Mozambique National Resistance/Electoral Union (*Resistência Nacional Moçambicana/União Electoral*—Renamo/UE). Formed in mid-1999, the Renamo/UE electoral alliance secured 38.8 percent of the vote and 117 seats in the December legislative balloting, a surprisingly good result in the opinion of most analysts after what was generally viewed as a minimalist campaign that lacked a coherent platform. (Distribution according to component parties, which included those indented below as well as Unamo, was unavailable, although the influence of the non-Renamo parties was considered minimal, and most seats certainly went to Renamo members.) Collaterally, Renamo/UE presidential candidate Afonso Dhlakama won 47.7 percent of the votes in the presidential balloting in 1999.

Renamo contested municipal elections independently in 2003, but Renamo/UE ran in the presidential and legislative elections in 2004. The alliance was hurt by the defection of Renamo members to form the Party for Peace, Development, and Democracy (see below) and the loss of Unamo (see below). In July 2007 Renamo announced that it would contest future elections without its coalition partners, thereby ending the electoral alliance. Nonetheless, the member parties pledged to continue political cooperation in opposition to Frelimo. Prior to the 2008 local elections party leaders decided against allowing Daviz SIMANGO, the popular **National Convention Party** (see below) mayor of Beira, from seeking reelection. Simango led a mass defection from Renamo. Reports indicated that at least ten Renamo deputies in the assembly resigned from the party. Simango campaigned as an independent and won another term and subsequently launched a new party, the **Mozambique Democratic Movement** (*Movimento Democrático de Moçambique*—MDM). Dhlakama was chosen as Renamo's candidate for the 2009 presidential balloting.

Leaders: Gen. Afonso Macacho Marceta DHLAKAMA (Chair), Manecas DANIEL (Vice Chair), Maximo DIAS (Chair of the Renamo/UE General Assembly), Ossufo MOMADE (Secretary General).

Mozambique National Resistance—MNR (*Resistência Nacional Moçambicana*—Renamo). Also known as the *Movimento Nacional da Resistência de Moçambique* (MNRM) and as the André Group, after its late founder, André Matade MATSANGAI, Renamo was formed in the early 1970s primarily as an intelligence network within Mozambique for the white Rhodesian government of Ian Smith. Following Rhodesia's transition to majority rule as "Zimbabwe" in 1980, Renamo developed into a widespread anti-Frelimo insurgency, relying on financial support from Portuguese expatriates and, until the early 1990s, substantial military aid from South Africa. The 20,000-member Renamo army, comprising Portuguese and other mercenaries, Frelimo defectors, and numerous recruits from the Shona-speaking Ndau ethnic group, operated mainly in rural areas, where it interdicted transport corridors and sabotaged food production. Widely condemned for terrorist tactics, including indiscriminate killing and mutilation of civilians, Renamo, although largely stalemating the government militarily, generally failed to gain external recognition. In an apparent attempt to foster its nationalist image, Renamo launched an "Africanization" program in 1987 that included replacements for white Portuguese at its Lisbon-based headquarters. Further image-building took place at the 1989 Renamo congress, which revamped the movement's internal bodies. The congress also declared that Renamo was no longer intent on overthrowing the government but was seeking instead a peace settlement under which it could participate as a recognized "political force" in free elections resulting from constitutional revision. However, the Renamo leadership appeared disconcerted when, in 1990, the government agreed to hold such elections. Thereafter, despite a December 1, 1990, cease-fire, Renamo's military activities continued, thus supporting a widely held view that apart from its advocacy of a multiparty system the group lacked a political agenda.

When rebel strikes coincided with the reopening of peace talks in March and May 1991, there was speculation that party president Gen. Afonso Dhlakama had lost control over some of his forces. Thereafter, in negotiations with the government in Rome, Renamo, weakened by dwindling finances and pressed by South Africa, the UK, and the United States to negotiate seriously, signed the first of a series of concessionary protocols. By mid-1992 it was apparent that the lengthy rebellion was drawing to a close.

While Dhlakama failed in his bid to win the presidency from Chissano in December 1994, the results of the legislative poll left Renamo only marginally second to Frelimo. In May 1995 President Chissano stated that, while Dhlakama could not be styled leader of the opposition (because he was not an elected member of the People's Assembly), he would be accorded "dignified status."

Although Renamo's legislative initiatives were blocked in the Frelimo-controlled assembly in 1995–1996, observers credited Dhlakama with continuing to enhance both the group's and his own political viability. In November 1996 Renamo legislators reportedly gave unanimous support to a constitutional amendment altering local election laws. In early 1997, however, the party reversed itself, threatening to boycott upcoming balloting unless the 1996 bill was repealed. Amid escalating tensions, the party organized nationwide antigovernment demonstrations in May 1997.

Although Renamo officials publicly insisted that they had no interest in returning to an armed struggle, arson attacks and disruption of the water supply were reported in July 1997. Subsequently, Dhlakama denounced the government's use of force to suppress the unrest, reportedly warning that Renamo would not rule out using force to defend itself against government "aggression."

Citing the need for the party to be "more flexible," Dhlakama forced the ouster of Secretary General Jose de CASTRO and Assistant Secretary General Albino FAIFE in January 1998. João Alexandre was subsequently named to Castro's former post. A split was reported in 2000 between those Renamo members, including a number of legislators, who appeared to be interested in negotiating a settlement with Frelimo, and those led by Dhlakama, who at midyear were still refusing to accept the results of the December 1999 legislative and presidential elections. In September 2000 the party's former legislative leader, Raul DOMINGOS, was expelled for "having collaborated with Frelimo" and for "corruption" during secret talks he allegedly held with the government. (Some analysts noted that Domingos had previously been seen as a possible successor to Dhlakama.)

Allegedly facing increasing dissent within the party, Dhlakama nevertheless was reelected as Renamo's president in November 2001.

At a subsequent party congress, a ten-member political committee was created as a means to decentralize party leadership and broaden the party's appeal. In the 2004 presidential elections, Dhlakama again ran as the party's candidate, receiving 31.74 percent of the vote. The Renamo-led electoral alliance won 29.73 percent of the vote in the concurrent legislative elections, its representation declining from 117 to 90 seats in the assembly. Renamo deputies initially boycotted the assembly to protest perceived irregularities in the polling, but, after the Constitutional Council upheld the results, the deputies were seated in January 2005.

A number of regional and local Renamo leaders reportedly defected to Frelimo in 2006, apparently in the hope of improving their chances in the upcoming provincial and municipal elections. Partially in response to losses within the party, the senior Renamo leadership decided to contest upcoming regional and local elections without its coalition partners in an effort to gain greater representation at the provincial and municipal levels.

Led by Sebastiao JANOTA and Saimon MUTERO, a group of Renamo dissidents formed a splinter group, the Renamo National Salvation Junta (*Junta Nacional de Salvação da Renamo*—JNSR) in 2008. The JNSR reportedly sought to replace Dhlakama and institute a number of party reforms, including greater financial transparency and openness in internal Renamo elections.

Leaders: Gen. Afonso Macacho Marceta DHLAKAMA (President), Ossufo QUITINE (Legislative Leader), Fernando MAZANGA (Spokesperson), João ALEXANDRE (former Secretary General), Ossufo MOMAD (Secretary General).

Mozambican Social Democratic Party (*Partido Moçambicano da Social Democracia*—PMSD). The PMSD was launched as political heir to the Mozambican Nationalist Movement (*Movimento Nacionalista Moçambicana*—Monamo) at the conclusion of Monamo's first congress in May 1992. Monamo had been founded in 1979 by exiled former Frelimo members led by Máximo Dias, who in 1973–1974 had attempted to persuade the Lisbon government to negotiate with the insurgents. In the late 1980s Monamo merged with the West German–based Mozambique National Independent Committee (*Comité Nacional Independente de Moçambique*—Conimo) to form the Mozambican Political Union (*União Política Moçambicana*—Upomo). In 1989 the group called for an immediate cease-fire under UN auspices, the departure of foreign troops, and the holding of national elections. Upomo operated until adoption of the 1990 constitution, after which Dias returned to Mozambique and Monamo reportedly decided to seek legal party status on its own. (Despite the formal change of name in 1992, the Monamo acronym continues in use.)

Monamo/PMSD participated in the 1994 balloting in a Patriotic Alliance (*Aliança Patriótica*—AP) with the FAP (immediately below) that won 1.95 percent of the vote.

In 2006 Dias reportedly threatened to leave the Renamo/UE coalition because of the dominance of Renamo. (He contended that Renamo consistently appointed its own members to any vacant party or government posts.) In July 2007 Dias announced that he intended to dissolve Monamo/PMSD and create a new humanitarian nongovernmental organization. However, Monamo/PMSD contested the 2009 local balloting, led by Dias.

Leader: Dr. Máximo Diogo José DIAS (Secretary General).

Patriotic Action Front (*Frente de Acção Patriótica*—FAP). Founded in 1991, FAP was a proponent in 1992 of delaying multiparty elections and naming a two-year transitional government. Ahead of the 2008 municipal elections, FAP announced it would not run any of its own members, and would support the Renamo candidates.

Leaders: José Carlos PALAÇO (President), Raulda CONCEIÇÃO (Secretary General).

National Convention Party (*Partido de Convenção Nacional*—PCN). In October 1992 the *Indian Ocean Newsletter* described the PCN as a possible "third force" between Frelimo and Renamo. Amid nationwide debate in late 1992–early 1993 on the implementation of the October peace treaty provisions, the party urged the government to adhere to the timetable that called for elections in late 1993. The PCN, led by Lutero Simango, son of former national vice president Uriah Simango, was also linked to controversial former chief of staff Col. Gen. Sebastião MABOTE, who became a vocal critic of the regime after his ouster from the government in 1991 for alleged participation in a coup plot. In 2008 the PCN and Renamo split over the candidacy of PCN member Daviz SIMANGO, the incumbent mayor of Beira, when Renamo stalwarts were able to run a member of their party, Manuel Perreira, for the post. Simango campaigned as an independent, won the election, and went on to form his own party, the **Mozambique Democratic Movement** (see below).

Leaders: Lutero SIMANGO (Chair), Inácio CHIRE, Luís GUIMARÃES, Abel Gabriel MABUNDA (Secretary General).

Mozambique People's Progress Party (*Partido de Progresso do Povo Moçambicano*—PPPM). The PPPM held its inaugural congress in July 1992 and was legalized in December. In 1993 supporters of its then vice president, Miguel Mabote, withdrew to form the PT (below). The PPPM won 1.06 percent of the vote in the 1994 legislative poll. Reportedly displeased with its influence within the Renamo-led coalition, in 2008 the PPPM was instrumental in the formation of a new electoral alliance, the Democratic Alliance of Veterans for Development (see below). It broke with Renamo and pledged to support the Frelimo candidate in the 2009 presidential balloting. It ran as an independent party in the 2009 local balloting.

Leaders: Dr. Padimbe KAMATI (President), Che ABDALA (Secretary General).

United Democratic Front (*Frente Democrática Unida*—FDU). The FDU was formed in late 1994 by Mariano Janeiro Turbina, former head of the defunct Mozambique Federal Party and theretofore commander of an anti-Frelimo guerrilla force in central Mozambique. The FDU did not participate in the 2009 municipal elections.

Leader: Mariano Janeiro TURBINA.

United Front of Mozambique–Democratic Convergence Party (*Frente Unida de Moçambique–Partido de Convergência Democrática*—Fumo-PCD). Linked to Germany's Christian Democrats, Fumo-PCD held its inaugural congress in Maputo in January 1993. The party secured 1.39 percent of the legislative votes in 1994. It joined the Renamo/UE in 1999 despite the objection of Fumo-PCD founder Domingos Arouca, who resigned from the party's presidency in protest. A June 2000 Fumo-PCD congress offered Arouca the position of "honorary president," but he angrily refused the post. The death of Arouca on January 3, 2009, at age 80, reportedly enhanced party president Jose Samo GUDO's control over Fumo-PCD. Fumo-PCD did not run any candidates in the 2008 local elections.

Leaders: Jose Samo GUDO (President), Pedro LOFORTE (Secretary General).

The other minor parties participating in the Renamo/UE were the **Mozambique Independents Alliance**, led by Ernesto SERGIO and Khalid Hussein MAHOMED; the **National Unity Party**, led by Hipóloto de JESUS; and the **Ecological Party of Mozambique** (*Partido Ecologista de Moçambique*—Pemo).

Other Groups that Contested the 2004 Legislative Elections:

Party for Peace, Democracy, and Development (*Partido para a Paz, Democracia, e Desenvolvimento*—PPDD). Formed in 2003 by disaffected members of Renamo, including Raul Domingos, the PPDD is a liberal party that promotes nonpartisanship in public administration. At the first party congress on October 4, 2003, Domingos was nominated to run for the presidency in 2004. He placed third in the balloting with 2.73 percent of the vote. The PPDD also came in third in the concurrent legislative elections with 2 percent of the vote. Most analysts believe that the PPDD pulled votes away from Renamo. The party hoped to continue to build its base through provincial and municipal elections in 2008 and then challenge Renamo as the main opposition party. In 2008 the ruling Senegalese Democratic Party (PDS) pledged to provide monetary and technical assistance to the PPDD in the 2008 local elections and the 2009 legislative balloting. The PPDD participated in the 2008 municipal balloting, placing third, behind Frelimo and Renamo, in overall votes. Following the local elections, Domingos reportedly offered to merge the PPDD with Renamo if Afonso Dhlakama resigned as leader of Renamo.

Leader: Raul DOMINGOS.

Movement for Change and Good Governance (*Movimento para a Mudança e Boa Governação*—MGB). The MGB was an electoral alliance formed prior to the 2004 elections to rally behind a single candidate for the presidency and to pool resources for the legislative elections. The MGB consisted of Unamo and the small **Party of All Mozambican Nationalists** (*Partido de Todos os Nativos Moçambicanos*—Partonamo). In the legislative elections, the MGB received 0.36 percent of the vote. The MGB did not campaign as a unified group in the 2008 municipal elections.

Leader: Carlos Alexandre REIS (Chair and 2004 presidential candidate).

Mozambican National Union (*União Nacional Moçambicana*—Unamo). Reportedly then in control of three battalions of rebel fighters in Zambezia province, Unamo was formed in 1987 by a Renamo breakaway faction. Subsequently, some of its leaders appeared to be operating from Malawi, while others established an office in Lisbon. However, by late 1990, Unamo forces stationed along the Malawian border were reported to be "on good terms" with the government. Meanwhile, political leaders had returned from exile in anticipation of Unamo being recognized as a legal party, spokespersons indicating it would participate in upcoming legislative contests but would endorse President Chissano in his reelection bid.

In March 1991 the party formally characterized itself as a social democratic "peaceful organization" with 20,000 members and offices in nine provinces. One year later it was the first opposition party granted legal status. However, in August 1992 party president Carlos Alexandre Reis was imprisoned for financial crimes for which he had been convicted and sentenced in absentia seven years earlier.

In April 1994 Unamo was alleged to be financing *Rombezia,* an armed group in northern Mozambique led by Manuel ROCHA and Octavio CUSTODIO, which was descended from the African National Union of Rombezia (*União Nacional Africana da Rombezia*—UNAR). UNAR was believed to have been formed by the Portuguese secret police in the 1960s to promote an independent state in the Rovuma and Zambezia provinces (which gave the grouping its name).

Unamo secured only 0.73 percent of the vote in the 1994 legislative balloting and subsequently announced it was forming the extraparliamentary United Salvation Front (*Frente Unida de Salvação*—FUS) with the PSLD, PPPM, PT, Pacode, Pimo, and the Democratic Renewal Party (PRD). However, in 1999 Unamo chose, as did the PPPM and the PRD, to participate in the Renamo/UE, while the other FUS members either ran alone or joined different coalitions. In 2004, however, Unamo joined the MGB, while Reis ran as the Unamo candidate for the presidency. He received

0.9 percent of the vote. In the 2008 local elections, Unamo secured one council seat. It appealed the election results, alleging fraud, but Unamo's bid for new balloting was rejected by the constitutional court.

Leaders: Carlos Alexandre REIS (President), Florencia João Da SILVA (Secretary General).

Democratic Union (*União Democrática*—UD). UD was formed in 1994 as a coalition of Panade, Palmo, and the **National Party of Mozambique** (*Partido Nacional de Moçambique*—Panamo), led by Marcos JUMA and Chabane ASSANE. It secured 5.15 percent of the vote in the December legislative poll, thereby gaining nine seats and becoming only the third party, behind Frelimo and Renamo, to gain representation. (Earlier editions of the *Handbook* incorrectly assigned those seats to the Democratic Union of Mozambique [*União Democrática de Moçambique*—Udemo], a former separatist group in northern Mozambique.) However, Palmo left UD in mid-1999, and the rump coalition of Panade and Panamo managed only 1.48 percent of the vote (and consequently no seats) in the December balloting. UD only received 0.34 percent of the vote in the 2004 legislative elections. Juma reportedly led Panamo to join the Constructive Opposition Bloc in 2006. The UD did not participate in the 2008 municipal elections.

Leaders: José Chicuarra MASSINGA, Marcos JUMA.

National Democratic Party (*Partido Nacional Democrático*—Panade). Panade was launched in late 1992 by José Massinga, a former foreign ministry official who was discharged in 1979 for alleged links to the U.S. intelligence network. The party's platform, based on "Christian values and human dignity," reportedly mirrored the teachings of activist Catholic bishops in central Mozambique. The group was legalized in 1993.

Leader: José Chicuarra MASSINGA.

Liberal Democratic Party of Mozambique (*Partido Liberal Democrático de Moçambique*—Palmo). Reportedly seeking legal recognition in late 1990, Palmo criticized the nonindigenous population for "controlling" the economy to the detriment of "original" (black) Mozambicans. At the party's first congress on May 6–11, 1991, Martins Bilal won a hotly contested presidential contest over Dr. António Palange. Consequently, another prominent leader, Casimiro Miguel Nhamithambo, resigned from the party, criticizing it for "lacking democracy" and launching a breakaway group (PSLD, below).

In July 1998 a dispute between Bilal and Palange split Palmo, with Bilal claiming that the party's national committee had suspended Palange, whose recent assumption of the UD leadership mantle had given him increased national prominence. For his part, Palange asserted that the committee had lacked a quorum and that it was Bilal who had in fact been dismissed from the party for financial malpractice. In November Palange was formally expelled from Palmo. He subsequently launched his own formation (CDU, below).

Palmo had filled five of the nine legislative seats won by UD in 1994. However, it split from UD in August 1999, securing 2.47 percent of the vote and no seats in the December poll. In balloting in 2004, Palmo received 0.30 percent of the vote. Palmo did not field candidates in the 2008 municipal balloting.

Leaders: Martins Luis BILAL (Chair), Antonio MUEDO (Secretary General).

Labor Party (*Partido Trabalhista*—PT). The PT was formed in 1993 by a breakaway faction of the PPPM. In early 1997 the party's vice president and secretary general were expelled for allegedly embezzling PT funds. The PT contested several municipal races but failed to win any seats in 2003. The PT won 0.56 percent of the legislative vote in 1994, 2.69 percent in 1999, and 0.47 percent in 2004. In 2006 the PT was reported to have joined the Constructive Opposition Bloc led by Pimo. Party President Miguel MABOTE emerged as a leading critic of the government after the army-arsenal explosion in 2007 (see Current issues, above). The PT failed to gain any offices in the 2008 municipal elections.

Leaders: Miguel MABOTE (President), Luis MUCHANGA (Secretary General).

Social, Liberal, and Democratic Party (*Partido Social, Liberal e Democrático*—PSLD). The PSLD was formed by former Palmo leader Casimiro Nhamithambo, who complained of the parent group "lacking democracy." The PSLD, also referenced by the initials SOL, was a founding member in early 1999 of the Mozambican Opposition Union (*União Moçambicana da Oposição*—UMO), which its supporters hoped would serve as an electoral front for as many as a dozen parties. Nhamithambo initially served as the UMO secretary general, but he resigned from that post later in the year as the result of friction with Wehia RIPUA, the leader of another UMO component, the **Mozambique Democratic Party** (*Partido Democrático de Mocambique*—Pademo). Although Nhamithambo announced at that time that the PSLD would remain in UMO despite the dispute, the PSLD ultimately contested the December 2000 legislative poll on its own, winning 2.02 percent of the vote. (Only three groups finally ran under the UMO banner: Pademo, the **Democratic Congress Party** [*Partido do Congresso Democrático*—Pacode], and the **Democratic Party for the Reconciliation of Mozambique**. Meanwhile, UMO supported Renamo's Afonso Dhlakama in the presidential race after Ripua's candidacy was disallowed due to faulty nomination papers.) In 2004 the PSLD won 0.46 percent of the legislative vote.

Leader: Casimiro Miguel NHAMITHAMBO.

Independent Party of Mozambique (*Partido Independente de Moçambique*—Pimo). Described as a "thinly disguised Islamic party," Pimo won 1.23 percent of the legislative vote in 1994 and 0.71 percent in 1999. Pimo leader Yaqub Sibinde attempted to run for president in 1999, but his nomination was declared invalid by the Supreme Court. In 2003 Pimo won three posts in municipal elections in predominately Islamic areas. In 2004 Sibinde ran for the presidency and received 0.91 percent of the vote. In the concurrent legislative elections, Pimo received 0.59 percent of the vote. In 2006 Sibinde was reported to have formed an opposition alliance of 18 minor parties called the **Constructive Opposition Bloc**. Besides Pimo, other members of the bloc included the PT and Panamo. Pimo gained one council seat in the 2008 municipal elections.

Leaders: Yaqub Neves Salomão SIBINDE, Magalhaes IBRAMURGY (General Secretary).

Democratic Liberal Party of Mozambique (*Partido Democrático Liberal de Moçambique*—Padelimo). Formed in 1998, Padelimo won 0.80 percent of the vote in the 1999 legislative balloting and 0.12 percent in 2004.

Leader: Joaquim José NYOTA.

Social Broadening Party of Mozambique (*Partido de Ampliação Social de Moçambique*—Pasomo). Pasomo won 0.05 percent of the legislative vote in 1999 and 0.52 percent in 2004.

Leader: Helder Francisco CAMPIRA.

Green Party of Mozambique (PVM). Formed in 1997, the PVM (also known as *Os Verdes* [The Greens]) split into two factions prior to the 1999 elections, one supportive of membership in Renamo/UE and the other committed to an independent campaign. In 2004 the independent faction gained 0.33 percent in legislative elections.

Leader: Armando Bruno João SAPEMBE.

Other parties or groups that contested the 2004 legislative elections included the **Broad Opposition Front** (*Frente Alargada da Oposição*—FAO), a coalition of conservative parties that included the small **Liberal Front** (*Frente Liberal*—FL) and received 0.25 percent of the vote; the **Party of Freedom and Solidarity,** which received 0.88 percent of the vote; the **National Reconciliation Party** (PARENA), which received 0.6 percent of the vote; the **Ecological Party–Land Movement,** which received 0.4 percent of the vote; and the **Congress of United Democrats** (*Congresso dos Democratas Unios*—CDU), formed in January 2002 by António PALANGE following his expulsion from Palmo. A number of other minor parties also received less than 1 percent of the vote. In 2008 the FL and PARENA formed the **National Democratic Alliance** (*Alianca Nacional Democrática*—AND) to compete in the municipal elections. AND also included two other small parties, the **Democratic Reconciliation Party** (*Partido de Reconcilliação Democrática*—PAREDE), led by Joaquina Joaaquim Notiço; and the **Independent Social-Democratic Party** (PASDI).

Other Parties and Groups:

Mozambique Democratic Movement (*Movimento Democrático de Moçambique*—MDM). The MDM was formed in 2009 by former Renamo members led by Daviz Simango. Simango was elected mayor of Beira as an independent in 2008. The MDM drew support from independents and former opposition members. Reports indicated that at least four Renamo deputies in the assembly had defected to the MDM. Simango was selected as the MDM presidential candidate for 2009.

Leader: Daviz SIMANGO.

In June 2008 four small parties announced the creation of an electoral alliance—the **Democratic Alliance of Veterans for Development** (*Aliança Democrática de Antigos Combatentes para o Desenvolvimento*—ADACD)—to compete in future municipal and legislative elections. The ADACD included the **Mozambique People's Progress Party** (*Partido de Progresso do Povo Moçambicano*—PPPM), the **Democratic Congress Party** (*Partido do Congresso Democrático*—Pacode), the **Mozambique Socialist Party** (*Partido Socialista de Moçambique*—PSM), and the **Union for Reconciliation** (*Partido da União para a Reconciliação*—PUR), (see below). ADACD was led by PSM general secretary Joao da Rosa LIKALAMBA, and it pledged to support the Frelimo candidate in the 2009 presidential election. The ADACD failed to qualify for the 2008 municipal elections.

Mozambique Communist Party (*Partido Comunista de Moçambique*—Pacomo). The formation of Pacomo was announced on April 12, 1995. Reports in 2008 indicated that the party was defunct.

Leader: Almeida TESOURA.

Minor parties that competed in the 2008 municipal balloting include the **Group for Democracy in Beira** (*Grupo para a Democracia de Beira*—GDB), an independent local grouping in Beria, which won seven council seats in the 2008 balloting; the **Natives and Residents of Manhica** (*Naturais e Residentes da Vila da Mahiça*—NATURMA); the **Party of Union for Mundança** (*Partido de União para Mundança*—UM); **Together for the City** (*Juntos pela Cidade*—JPC), a regional grouping that ran only in Maputo; the **Group for Change in Marromeu** (*Grupo para Mundança de Marromeu*—GMM), active only in Marromeu; and the **Organization of Independent Candidates of Nacala** (*Organização dos Candidatos Independentes de Nacala*—OCINA).

Other minor parties that did not participate in the 2008 municipal balloting include the **Democratic Alliance of Mozambique** (*Aliança Democrática de Moçambique*—ADM), led by José Pereira BRANQUINHO; the **Democratic Confederation of Mozambique** (*Confederação Democrática de Moçambique*—CDM), led by Domingos CARDOSO; the **Mozambique Agrarian Party** (*Partido Agrário de Moçambique*—PAM); the **Mozambican Socialist Party** (*Partido Socialista de Moçambique*—PSM), led by Joao da Rosa LIKALAMBA; the **Revolutionary Party of the United Socialist People of Mozambique** (*Partido Revolucionário do Povo Socialista Unido de Moçambique*—Prepsumo); the **Social Democratic Party** (*Partido Social Democrático*—PSD), led by Cárlos MACHEL; the **Union for Reconciliation** (*Partido da União para a Reconciliação*—PUR); and the **Waterworkers and Farmers of Mozambique** (*Regedores e Camponeses de Moçambique*—Recamo), led by Arone SIJAMO.

LEGISLATURE

A People's Assembly (*Assembleia Popular*), consisting of Frelimo's then 57-member Central Committee, was accorded legislative status in an uncontested election in December 1977. The body was increased to 210 members in April 1983 by the addition of government ministers and vice ministers, provincial governors, representatives of the military and of each province, and ten other citizens. While its term was not constitutionally specified, the original mandate was set by law at five years. The lengthy poll eventually conducted in August–December 1986 was for 250 deputies, indirectly elected by provincial assemblies from a list of 299 candidates presented by Frelimo. The name of the body was changed to the Assembly of the Republic in the 1990 constitution, which also provided for future elections to be conducted by direct universal suffrage on a multiparty basis.

Assembly of the Republic (*Assembleia da República*). The current legislature is a unicameral body of 250 members elected on a proportional basis for five-year terms. Parties must secure 5 percent of the vote on a nationwide basis to gain representation. In the balloting of December 1–2, 2004, the Mozambique Liberation Front won 160 seats and the Mozambique National Resistance/Electoral Union, 90.

President: Eduardo MULEMBWE.

CABINET

[as of June 1, 2009]

Prime Minister	Luisa Dias Diogo [f]
Ministers	
Agriculture and Rural Development	Soares Nhaca
Development and Planning	Aiuba Cuereneia
Education and Culture	Aires Bonifacio Aly
Energy	Salvador Namburete
Environmental Coordination	Alcinda Abreu
Finance	Manuel Chang
Fisheries	Cadmiel Muthemba
Foreign Affairs and Cooperation	Oldemiro Baloi
Health	Paulo Ivo Garrido
Industry and Commerce	Antonio Fernando
Interior	José Pacheco
Justice	Maria Benvida Levy [f]
Labor	Helena Taipo [f]
Mineral Resources	Esperanca Bias [f]
National Defense	Felipe Jacinto Nyusi
President's Office with Responsibility for Diplomatic Affairs	Francisco Caetano J. Madeira
President's Office with Responsibility for Parliamentary Affairs	Isabel Manuel Nkavandeka [f]
Public Works and Housing	Felicio Zacarias
Science and Technology	Venancio Simao Massingue
State Administration	Lucas Chomera
Tourism	Fernando Sumbana Júnior
Transport and Communications	Paulo Zucula
War Veterans' Affairs	Feliciano Salomao Gundana
Women and Social Action Coordination	Virgília B. N. Santos Matabele [f]
Youth and Sports	David Simango

[f] = female

Note: All of the above are members of the Mozambique Liberation Front.

COMMUNICATIONS

Press. After having maintained strict control of the media since independence, the government in 1990 permitted substantial press liberalization. In late 1991 a press law was ratified, giving existing publications six months to reregister in accordance with new provisions, including revised ownership rules. In July 2001 the New York–based Committee to Protect Journalists reported that Mozambican journalists were exhibiting a degree of self-censorship in regard to investigations into corruption because of intimidation emanating from the November 2000 murder of a reporter from the independent daily, *Metical,* which subsequently went out of business. Among other things, journalists complained that the government's investigation of the murder lacked intensity. In its annual report on press freedom in 2008, Reporters Without Borders ranked Mozambique 90, a decline from its ranking of 73 in the previous year. The following are published in Maputo and Beira, respectively: *Notícias* (33,000), government controlled, and *Diário de Moçambique* (16,000). In 1993 *Mediacoop,* a cooperative publishing venture founded by a group of independent journalists, launched *Mediafax,* a daily, and in early 1994, *Savana,* a weekly. Other publications include the progovernment weekly *Domingos* (25,000) and the pro-Renamo *Imparcial.*

News agencies. The official facility is the Mozambique Information Agency (*Agência de Informação de Moçambique*—AIM); a number of international agencies are represented in Maputo.

Broadcasting and computing. Government broadcast facilities include *Rádio Moçambique* and *Televisão de Moçambique.* As of 2008 there were 15.6 Internet users per 1,000 inhabitants.

INTERGOVERNMENTAL REPRESENTATION

Ambassador to the U.S.: Amelia Matos SUMBANA.

U.S. Ambassador to Mozambique: (Vacant).

Permanent Representative to the UN: Daniel ANTÓNIO.

IGO Memberships (Non-UN): AfDB, AU, BADEA, CPLP, CWTH, IDB, Interpol, IOR-ARC, NAM, OIC, SADC, WCO, WTO.

MYANMAR (BURMA)

Republic of the Union of Myanmar
Pyihtaungsu Thamada Myanmar Naingngandaw

Political Status: Independent republic established January 4, 1948; military-backed regime instituted March 2, 1962; one-party constitution of January 4, 1974, abrogated upon direct assumption of power by the military on September 18, 1988, at which time the words "Socialist Republic" (*Socialist Thamada*) were dropped from the country's official name; official title in English changed from Union of Burma to Union of Myanmar on May 27, 1989; new constitution, ratified through referendum of May 10 and 24, 2008, and promulgated May 29, 2008.

Area: 261,789 sq. mi. (678,033 sq. km.).

Population: 35,306,189 (1983C); 50,214,000 (2008E). The 1983 figure includes nonresident nationals but excludes adjustment for underenumeration.

Major Urban Centers (2007E): NAYPYIDAW (NAY PYI TAW, 420,000); Yangon (Rangoon, 4,090,000), Mandalay (960,000). In November 2005 the military regime began moving government offices to the vicinity of Pyinmana, 320 miles north of Yangon, the former capital. The newly built capital was officially designated Naypyidaw on March 27, 2006. City population estimates vary widely.

Official Language: Myanmar (Burmese).

Monetary Unit: Kyat (UN operational rate of exchange as of December 1, 2009: 6.41 kyats = $1US).

Chair, State Peace and Development Council: Sr. Gen. THAN SHWE; former vice chair of the State Law and Order Restoration Council (SLORC); assumed roles of SLORC chair and prime minister in succession to Gen. SAW MAUNG following the latter's resignation on April 23, 1992; became chair of the State Peace and Development Council (SPDC) on November 15, 1997, when it replaced the SLORC; stepped down as prime minister on August 25, 2003.

Vice Chair, SPDC: Sr. Gen. MAUNG AYE; appointed to revived position of vice chair of the SLORC on April 27, 1994; became vice chair of the SPDC on November 15, 1997.

First Secretary, SPDC: Lt. Gen. TIN AUNG MYINT OO; appointed on October 24, 2007, succeeding Lt. Gen. THEIN SEIN.

Prime Minister: Lt. Gen. Thein SEIN; appointment as acting prime minister announced on May 18, 2007, due to medical incapacity of Prime Minister Lt. Gen. SOE WIN; confirmed as prime minister on October 24, following the death of Soe Win on October 12.

THE COUNTRY

Myanmar, the largest country on the Southeast Asian mainland, has an extensive coastline running along the Bay of Bengal and the Andaman Sea. It shares a land border with Bangladesh and India in the west, China in the north, and Laos and Thailand in the east. Dominating the topography are tropical rain forests, plains, and mountains that rim the frontiers of the east, west, and north. Nearly three-quarters of the population is concentrated in the Irrawaddy (Ayeyawady) basin in the south.

More than 70 percent of the country's inhabitants are Burman. Karens (Kayins, about 7 percent) are dispersed over southern and eastern Myanmar, while Shans (9 percent), Thai in origin, are localized on the eastern plateau; Chins, Kachins, Mons, and Rakhines (Arakanese), totaling about 1 million, are found in the north and northeast. In addition, about 400,000 Chinese and 120,000 Indians and Bangladeshi are concentrated primarily in the urban areas. The various ethnic groups speak many languages and dialects, but the official Myanmar (Burmese), which is related to Tibeto-Chinese, is spoken by the vast majority. About 90 percent of the population professes classical Buddhism (Theravada Buddhism), the state religion; minority religions include Islam (4 percent), Christianity (4 percent), Hinduism (3 percent), and animism. Women make up an estimated 46 percent of the active labor force. Female representation in the present military-dominated government is rare.

Although the country is rich in largely unexploited mineral resources (including hydrocarbons, silver, zinc, copper, lead, nickel, antimony, tin, and tungsten), its economy is heavily dependent on agriculture, which accounts for 44 percent of GDP and employs nearly two-thirds of the labor force. Teak and other hardwoods, and pulses and beans are among the major exports, and agriprocessing remains the leading industry, although production of textiles and garments has become more important as a source of export earnings. Production of natural gas from offshore fields is expanding; base metals, ores, and gemstones also contribute to national income. On the whole, the industrial sector contributes about 20 perent of GDP. Officially, most economic activity other than food production is conducted by state-owned enterprises, but smuggling and the black market provide most consumer goods. There is also a thriving trade in opium, grown primarily in the "Golden Triangle" at the border juncture with Laos and Thailand, and in methamphetamines.

Calculations of GDP growth vary widely, with most international agencies regarding the government's figure of 8.4 percent annually during the 1996–2001 Five-Year Plan as inflated. For 2005–2006 average annual growth was reported to be about 13 percent.. The International Monetary Fund (IMF) projected growth of 5 percent for 2009 and 4 percent for 2010. Sanctions imposed by the international community have contributed to chronic economic distress marked by high inflation (over 35 percent in 2007), a nearly unmanageable external debt, the depletion of foreign exchange, and import constraints that have exacerbated the shortages of goods and spare parts for manufacturing.

GOVERNMENT AND POLITICS

Political background. Modern Burma was incorporated into British India as a result of the Anglo-Burmese wars of 1824–1886 but in 1937 was separated from India and granted limited self-government. During World War II Japan occupied the country and gave it nominal independence under a puppet regime led by anti-British nationalists, who subsequently transferred their loyalties to the Allied war effort.

The Anti-Fascist People's Freedom League (AFPFL), a coalition of nationalist forces, emerged as the principal political organization in 1945. Under the AFPFL, various groups and regions joined to form the Union of Burma, which gained full independence from the British in January 1948 and for a decade maintained a parliamentary democracy that was headed for most of that period by Prime Minister U NU. In May 1958 the AFPFL dissolved into factional groups, precipitating a political crisis that, four months later, forced Nu to resign in favor of a caretaker government headed by Gen. NE WIN, commander-in-chief of the armed forces.

Ne Win scheduled elections in 1960, and the Nu faction of the AFPFL returned to power under the name of the Union Party. However,

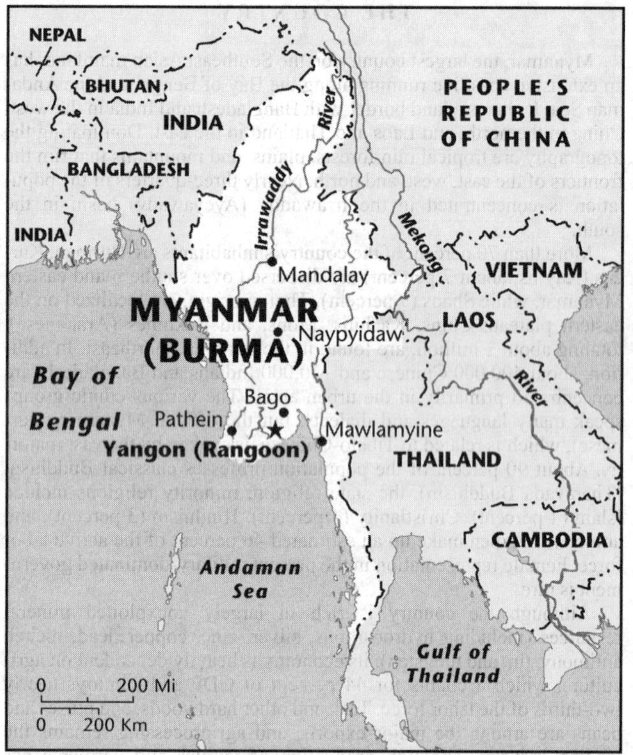

problems involving internal security, national unity, and economic development led Ne Win to mount a coup d'état in March 1962, after which a Revolutionary Council of senior army officers ran the government. A Burma Socialist Program Party (BSPP) was launched by the council the following July. In January 1974, after 12 years of army rule, the Ne Win government adopted a new constitution and revived the legislature as a single-chambered People's Assembly.

At a special BSPP congress in 1976 the party's general secretary, SAN YU, severely castigated his colleagues for the economic malaise that the country had long endured, and in February 1977 Prime Minister SEIN WIN was among those denied reelection to the party's Central Committee. In March a new cabinet was organized with MAUNG MAUNG KHA as prime minister, and a new People's Assembly was elected in January 1978. At its inaugural session in March the assembly designated an enlarged State Council chaired by Ne Win, who was thereby reconfirmed as president.

At the BSPP's fourth congress in August 1981, Ne Win announced his intention to resign as president while retaining his post as party chair. Following a legislative election in October, the assembly approved San Yu as his successor. In November 1985, after another pro forma legislative election, the regime's third most powerful figure, party General Secretary AYE KO, was formally designated vice president.

Serious student-led disturbances erupted in the capital in 1988, leading to an extraordinary BSPP congress that concluded with both Ne Win and San Yu resigning from the party leadership. In July the People's Assembly named the new BSPP chair, SEIN LWIN, to succeed San Yu as state president and chair of the State Council, while Maung Maung Kha stepped down as prime minister in favor of Thura TUN TIN. Student leaders thereupon mounted a campaign to press for President Sein Lwin's resignation, which culminated in a popular outpouring of more than 100,000 demonstrators in Yangon. Shortly thereafter, Sein Lwin was replaced as both president and party chair by the attorney general, Dr. MAUNG MAUNG. Like his predecessors, Maung Maung was a longtime associate of Ne Win.

On September 18, 1988, soon after the BSPP and the legislature had called for a multiparty general election, the military again seized power. The president was relieved of office, and the army commander, Gen. SAW MAUNG, assumed the chair of a new State Law and Order Restoration Council (SLORC). The Defense Service Intelligence director, Brig. Gen. KHIN NYUNT, assumed the post of SLORC first secretary. On September 21 Saw Maung became prime minister, presiding over a new cabinet composed, with one exception, of military figures. Although few restrictions were placed on the formation of opposition parties, many of their supporters were severely repressed, and all public gatherings of more than four individuals were banned.

By the end of February 1989 over 200 parties had been legalized, although the electoral campaign for a new People's Assembly was largely a contest between the government's National Unity Party (NUP, successor to the BSPP) and the National League for Democracy (NLD), led by AUNG SAN SUU KYI, the daughter of the "founder of modern Burma," AUNG SAN, who had been assassinated in 1947 on the eve of independence. On May 27, 1990, voters awarded a massive victory to the NLD, which secured more than 80 percent of the seats. Humiliated by the NUP's showing, 2.1 percent of the seats, the SLORC leadership refused to let the assembly convene.

The naming in October 1991 of Aung San Suu Kyi as recipient of the Nobel Peace Prize focused world attention on the repressive policies of the SLORC and triggered a wave of domestic demonstrations on behalf of the opposition leader, who had been held in detention since July 1989. The government responded by shutting down universities, arresting numerous protestors, and mounting a dry-season campaign against dissident minorities, especially Karen insurgents on the Thai border.

In April 1992, Saw Maung, who was reported to be in poor mental health, was succeeded as prime minister by Gen. THAN SHWE. Following his installation, the new SLORC leader stated that he intended to release all those who had been imprisoned "for political reasons," although only about half of an estimated 2,000 such persons had been freed by December. Aung San Suu Kyi remained under house arrest as the SLORC continued its systematic delegalization of opposition parties.

In May 1992 the SLORC announced that a "coordination meeting" would be convened to pave the way for a National Convention to draft a new constitution. Most opposition groups were excluded from the preparatory process for the convention, which opened in January 1993 but was subject to a series of adjournments.

In July 1995 Aung San Suu Kyi was freed. Following her release, she called for conciliation between the democracy movement and the SLORC leadership, but in November the NLD delegation (only 86 members out of 703) pulled out of the National Convention, insisting that the body had displayed scant interest in democratic reform. In March 1996 the convention began what would turn out to be an eight-year hiatus.

In advance of a planned NLD congress in May 1996, the government arrested some 260 party members, limiting the number of attendees to 18. Some 500–800 NLD supporters were arrested when they attempted to hold another congress at Aung San Suu Kyi's house in September. Intensifying conflict between students and the government culminated in weeklong demonstrations in Yangon and Mandalay in early December, which prompted the government to close the universities once again and reimpose Aung San Suu Kyi's house arrest. NLD activists continued to be targeted by the regime's security forces throughout the first half of 1997; however, in late September the NLD held its first authorized congress since 1995, with Aung San Suu Kyi in attendance. Shortly thereafter the cycle of arrests and imprisonments began anew and continued through early 1998.

During the mid-1990s, SLORC had mounted a series of successful attacks on longtime insurgents. In January 1995 the military captured Manerplaw, the headquarters of the rebel Karen National Union (KNU), which was followed by the fall of the KNU's last stronghold in Kawmoora, on the Thai border. In March Gen. BO MYA resigned as commander of the Karen National Army (KNA), although continuing as chair of the KNU. Also in March, the Karenni National Progressive Party (KNPP) abandoned its armed struggle, leading SLORC officials to claim that 14 of 16 rebel groups had now laid down their arms. Most of the remaining military opposition came from the Mong Tai Army (MTA) of Shan drug warlord KHUN SA. Eight months later Khun Sa announced his "retirement" as MTA chief, and in January 1996 his troops began their formal surrender. In April the government announced that Khun Sa would neither be tried for his crimes nor extradited to the United States to face charges of drug trafficking.

Negotiations between the regime and KNU collapsed in early 1997, and government forces immediately launched an offensive against the remaining rebel bases. Sporadic fighting was reported throughout the rest of the year and into early 1998, with thousands of refugees fleeing into Thailand.

On November 15, 1997, the SLORC was dissolved and immediately replaced by the "permanent" State Peace and Development Council (SPDC), which thereupon announced a cabinet reshuffling. Subsequently, Khin Nyunt ordered the detention of a number of former cabinet officials and their supporters on corruption charges. A further cabinet reshuffling occurred in December.

Although the SPDC approved an NLD party congress held in May 1998 at Aung San Suu Kyi's residence, the military blocked attempts by the NLD leader to visit supporters outside the capital. In September Suu Kyi and nine other activists carried out a threat to initiate a "People's Parliament." Calling themselves the Committee Representing Elected Lawmakers, they declared all junta laws and proclamations invalid, demanded the release of all political prisoners, and stated their intention to act as a parliament until the Constituent Assembly was allowed to meet. Meanwhile, the SPDC continued what had become its biggest crackdown against the opposition since early in the decade. By October nearly 900 NLD members had been detained. In August–September 2000 Aung San Suu Kyi twice tried to venture outside Yangon but was again prevented from doing so.

In November 2001 the government hierarchy underwent its most significant changes since the formation of the SPDC four years earlier. SPDC Secretary WIN MYINT was dismissed, as were the three deputy prime ministers. Several additional cabinet changes were announced, and 10 of 12 regional military commanders were reassigned. Although the SPDC did not explain its actions, observers concluded that the changes had served to strengthen the hands of Than Shwe and SPDC Vice Chair Sr. Gen. MAUNG AYE.

During the same period a UN special envoy to Myanmar, Malaysian diplomat Razali Ismail, was attempting to facilitate prisoner releases and discussions between the opposition and the SPDC. The military regime had begun releasing detained NLD members, including, in August, the party's chair and vice chair, AUNG SHWE and TIN OO, but in December Aung San Suu Kyi described the negotiators as still engaged in confidence-building. At the end of the year an estimated 1,500 political prisoners continued in custody. On May 6, 2002, Suu Kyi was unconditionally released from house arrest, although the SPDC gave no indications that it was any more willing to consider democratic reforms.

Two months earlier, in March 2002, the SPDC had reported the discovery of a planned coup led by Ne Win's son-in-law AYE ZAW WIN. Ne Win and his daughter SANDAR WIN, wife of the alleged ringleader, were placed under house arrest. On September 26 Aye Zaw Win and his three sons were sentenced to hang for treason. (Although the Supreme Court confirmed the sentences in August 2003, executions, in deference to the country's Buddhist heritage, are rarely carried out.) Ne Win, age 91, died in December 2002.

On May 30, 2003, a convoy carrying Aung San Suu Kyi and supporters was attacked near Mandalay. The attack, reportedly by a mob of up to 2,000, was orchestrated by the government-supportive Union Solidarity and Development Association (USDA). Shortly after, the NLD leader was placed in "protective custody" until transferred to her home on September 26. The regime's actions provoked widespread international outrage.

On August 25, 2003, the SPDC announced a major cabinet reshuffle that saw Than Shwe turn over the prime ministership to Khin Nyunt, who was replaced as SPDC first secretary by the former second secretary, Lt. Gen. SOE WIN. Five days later the new prime minister announced that the long-adjourned National Convention would reconvene as the first element of a "seven-step road map" to democracy that would also include a referendum on a new constitution, legislative elections, and the selection of state leaders by the resultant People's Assembly.

Meeting in Nyaunghnapin Camp in Hmawby Township, outside Yangon, the National Convention reconvened on May 17, 2004, with SPDC Second Secretary Lt. Gen. THEIN SEIN as chair. The 1,088 delegates included representatives of political parties, ethnic groups ("national races"), workers, farmers, the intelligentsia, and state service personnel, plus "invited delegates" from state "Special Regions" and former insurgent groups that had "exchanged arms for peace." Conspicuously absent were NLD representatives, who refused to participate until the regime released Aung San Suu Kyi and NLD Vice Chair Tin Oo from house arrest.

On October 19, 2004, Prime Minister Khin Nyunt was "permitted to retire" and reportedly placed under house arrest, with Soe Win assuming the cabinet leadership. At the same time, Thein Sein was elevated to SPDC first secretary. During the same period the SPDC began another major reorganization of the military command structure as well as a purge of the military intelligence apparatus, previously headed by Khin Nyunt, who was convicted of corruption and bribery in July 2005 and sentenced to 44 years in prison, although his sentence was apparently suspended and he was returned to house arrest. Ministerial-level changes also occurred on August 11, 2005, and May 15, 2006, and in mid-June 2006 eight deputy ministers retired or were relieved of their responsibilities.

In late 2006 the KNU demanded that the military halt an offensive in the east that had brought an end to a two-year-old de facto cease-fire and had reportedly displaced 10,000 Karens. (In March the Norwegian Refugee Council had estimated that Myanmar had 540,000 internally displaced people, the largest number of any country in Asia.) The government justified its offensive against the KNU and other ethnic groups as a response to a number of small bomb blasts, which were also blamed on exile groups. The most serious incident occurred on May 7, 2005, in the capital; according to official sources, three bombs killed 19 people and injured 150.

On May 18, 2007, with Soe Win undergoing medical treatment, Thein Sein was identified as acting prime minister. He officially succeeded the deceased Soe Win on October 24, when the SPDC also announced the appointment of Lt. Gen. TIN AUNG MYINT OO as SPDC first secretary.

On August 15, 2007, the SPDC announced major price hikes for fuels—66 percent for gasoline, 100 percent for diesel, and 500 percent for natural gas—triggering a series of protests led initially by the 88 Generation Students group. As September approached, Buddhist monks increasingly took control of what gradually became the first public uprising against the government since 1988. Antigovernment protests spread across the urban landscape, with some 100,000 people demonstrating. On September 25 the SPDC imposed a curfew, outlawed gatherings of more than five people, and sent troops and the police into the streets to quell demonstrations. USDA-organized militias—the *Swan-ar Shin* (Masters of Force)—also clashed with the protesters. Between September 26 and 28, the government reported the deaths of 10 demonstrators and the arrest of some 2,100. The country's principal Internet service provider was shut down, as were all cellular telephone networks. By September 30, with government forces having raided and cordoned off several monasteries in Yangon, the protest movement had succumbed.

Efforts by UN under-secretary general for political affairs Ibrahim Gambari to bring the government and the opposition to the negotiating table met with scant success until late October 2007. The curfew and ban on assembly were lifted on October 20, and within a week a government representative had met with Aung San Suu Kyi. On November 8 Gambari released a statement on behalf of Suu Kyi, who indicated she was "ready to cooperate with the government in order to make this process of dialogue a success." On November 13 Gambari told the UN Security Council that the SPDC had taken steps toward establishing a "substantive dialogue" on human rights concerns. Nevertheless, no progress was made during a series of meetings between the government and Suu Kyi.

Although Suu Kyi's annually renewed house arrest technically expired in May 2009, at that time she was being held at Insein Prison in Yangon since being formally charged earlier in the month with harboring for two days an uninvited American who had swum to her lakeside home. Suu Kyi was convicted on August 11 and sentenced to three years in prison, but Gen. Than Shwe commuted the sentence to another 18 months under house arrest.

Meanwhile, the government pushed forward with its "Road Map for Democracy." Between July 18 and September 3, 2007, a final National Convention session completed "basic principles" for a new constitution. A 54-member, government-appointed State Constitution Drafting Commission then produced a complete text that was published on April 9, 2008, approved by referendum on May 10 and 24, and promulgated by the SPDC on May 29. The next stage in the road map was slated to be fulfilled in 2010 by elections for a new bicameral Union Parliament as well as state and regional assemblies.

Constitution and government. The 1974 constitution was adopted with the stated objective of making Burma a "Socialist Republic" under one-party rule. It provided for a unicameral People's Assembly as the supreme organ of state authority and for a State Council comprising 14 representatives from the country's major political subdivisions plus 15 additional members (including the prime minister) elected from the assembly. The State Council and its chair, who was also state president, served four-year terms, concurrent with that of the assembly. The prime minister was designated by the Council of Ministers, which was elected by the assembly from its own membership, following nomination by the State Council. All of these institutions were abolished upon direct assumption of power by the military in September 1988.

A new constitution was promulgated on May 29, 2008, following passage with 92 percent voter support, according to the SPDC. In addition to creating a republic, the constitution provides for a multiparty political system, the election of a bicameral Union Parliament, the indirect election of a president, and establishment of an independent judiciary. It also ensures a "national political leadership role" for the military, which it recognizes as the ultimate protector of the constitution and accords "the right to independently administer and adjudicate all affairs of the armed forces." In both houses of the Union Parliament and in the country's 14 state and regional assemblies 25 percent of the seats are reserved for military designees.

The president is elected by members of the Union Parliament sitting as a tripartite Electoral College comprising (1) representatives of the states and divisions, with an equal number from each; (2) representatives elected from township constituencies on the basis of population; and (3) members of the defense services. The three groups each select a vice president, with the one who then receives the most votes from the full Electoral College assuming the executive presidency for a five-year term; the other two vice presidents serve a concurrent term. The president may be impeached for treason, breach of the constitution, misconduct, or "inefficient discharge of duties." Impeachment requires support by two-thirds of the full membership of both parliamentary houses.

With the concurrence of the Union Parliament, which can only reject the nominees for cause, the president is empowered to name government ministers and the justices of the supreme court. The president also names the commander-in-chief of the defense services, with the "proposal and approval" of the National Defense and Security Council (NDSC). The 11-member NDSC comprises the president and the 2 vice presidents; the speakers of the upper and lower houses; the commander-in-chief and his deputy; the minister of foreign affairs; and the ministers of defense, home affairs, and border affairs, all three of whom must be army officers. Thus, the military holds at least six seats on the NDSC. In the event of a national emergency, the president turns authority over to the commander-in-chief, who may rule with full presidential, legislative, and judicial powers and may suspend the rights of citizens. Following termination of the emergency, the NDSC is responsible for running the government until the conclusion of new elections, which must be held within six months.

The Supreme Court sits at the apex of the judiciary, followed by a system of high courts in the states and regions, courts of self-administered zones and divisions, and district and township courts. The constitution also provides for separate courts-martial to adjudicate defense service personnel. A Constitutional Tribunal is responsible for interpreting the constitution, reviewing the constitutionality of legislation, reviewing the actions of executive authorities, and resolving constitutional disputes between jurisdictions. Constitutional amendment requires 75 percent support from the Union Parliament, with the added proviso that amendments to specified sections of the basic law must then receive the assent of half of all eligible voters in a referendum.

Local government is based primarily on seven states (Chin, Kachin, Kayah, Kayin, Mon, Rakhine, Shan) and seven regions (Ayeyawady, Bago, Magway, Mandalay, Sagaing, Tanintharyi, Yangon), plus the Union Territory of Naypyidaw. The states and regions (previously called divisions) are divided into townships, which are subdivided into urban wards and village tracts. The 2008 constitution also recognizes five "self-administered zones" (Danu, Kokang, Naga, Pa Laung, and Pa-O) and one "self-administered division" (Wa), each comprising specified townships within a particular state or region. Each state and region elects an assembly. The executive is headed by a chief minister, who is nominated by the president and approved by the respective legislature. The union territory is directly administered by the president.

Foreign relations. Nonalignment was the cornerstone of Burmese foreign policy from 1948 through the end of the Cold War in the early 1990s, and until quite recently the country's participation in most intergovernmental organizations, including the UN and its specialized agencies, was marginal. In 1979 Burma announced its withdrawal from the Nonaligned Movement, indicating that it would consider participation in an alternative organization committed to "genuine nonalignment." In 1992, however, it rejoined the existing group. In 1997 Myanmar was admitted to the Association of Southeast Asian Nations (ASEAN), partly in an effort by neighboring states to foster "constructive engagement" with the SPDC.

In 1949 Burma became the first noncommunist country to recognize the People's Republic of China, with which it shares a 1,200-mile border. The two signed a Treaty of Friendship and Mutual Nonaggression in 1960, following settlement of a long-standing border dispute. By 1967, however, leftist terrorism, aimed at instituting a Chinese-style "Cultural Revolution," was increasingly resented by the Burmese and led to a severe deterioration in Sino-Burmese relations that lasted into the next decade.

Relations with Bangladesh worsened in mid-1978 because of an exodus from Burma of some 200,000 Rohingya Muslims who, according to Dhaka, had been subjected to an "extermination campaign." Later, it appeared that Muslim leaders had encouraged the flight in part to publicize their desire to establish the Rakhine (Arakan) region as an Islamic state; meanwhile, the number of refugees living in makeshift camps on the Bangladeshi side of the border had reportedly risen to more than 260,000 by March 1992. Repatriations began in September 1992; however, many Rohingyas were reluctant to return, while some of those who did were reported to be members of a terrorist Rohingya Solidarity Organization (*Kalarzo*) that was responsible for the killing of 16 Myanmar troops in May 1994. By September 1995 most refugees had been repatriated, although more than 20,000 remained in Bangladesh as of early 1998. Myanmar subsequently announced it would guarantee the safety of any additional voluntary returnees. In January 2000 Yangon rejected reentry for some 14,000 refugees, whom it claimed were not Myanmar, but in April 2004 the two governments agreed that the remaining Rohingyas would be repatriated. Nevertheless, most have refused to leave or have not received authorization from Myanmar. In February 2009 Myanmar's foreign minister told an ASEAN meeting that Myanmar would accept Rohingya migrants if they declared themselves to be ethnic Bengalis.

A dispute between Bangladesh and Myanmar over territorial boundaries in the Bay of Bengal has recently flared up. Dating back to 1974, the dispute has taken on added significance because of possible oil and natural gas deposits under the sea.

In October 1994 Myanmar concluded a friendship pact with Thailand, but relations have remained cool. Insurgent refugee camps are still located on Thai soil, and Myanmar military forces have repeatedly crossed the border in pursuit of guerrillas. In October 1999 Thai authorities freed the five Myanmar perpetrators of a hostage incident at the Myanmar embassy in Bangkok, leading an angered SPDC to close the Thai-Myanmar border until late November. In contrast, in January 2000 Thailand earned the SPDC's praise for a swift, deadly response when a small Kayinni group called God's Army took some 700 hostages at a hospital near the border. In June 2001, four months after another cross-border clash had led to a series of bilateral meetings, Myanmar and Thai leaders agreed to resolve border issues and to jointly fight drug production and smuggling. Difficulties continued into 2002, however, and the border was closed from May to October. In July 2003 the Thai government announced plans to relocate all Myanmar dissidents to refugee camps near the border.

In April 1997 the United States announced the imposition of economic sanctions against Myanmar, largely because of its repression of prodemocracy advocates. In 1998 the United States and Japan approved a grant of $3.8 million to the UN Drug Control Program to help eliminate opium poppy cultivation in Myanmar, but Washington continued its ten-year-old policy of refusing to make direct grants to the Yangon regime. Later that month, in response to the Bill Clinton administration's October 1996 ban on travel to the United States by junta leaders, Yangon denied permission for the U.S. ambassador to the UN, Bill Richardson, to enter Myanmar. In April 2000 the European Union (EU) announced that it was freezing assets of Myanmar officials in addition to increasing sanctions.

Following the protests of 2007, further sanctions were applied by both the United States and the EU. On May 1, 2008, the U.S. Treasury froze the assets of state-owned firms in Myanmar, adding to the sanctions of October 2007 in which the Treasury froze the financial assets of members of the military regime, while the EU widened its sanctions against Myanmar, adding a ban on imports of timber, gemstones, and precious metals in response to the military junta's crackdown on prodemocracy groups.

In mid-2000 the SPDC was condemned, not for the first time, by the International Labor Organization (ILO) for using forced labor and was also accused at an international conference in Nepal of having more child soldiers—at least 50,000, according to a Save the Children spokesperson—than any other country in the world. On November 16 the ILO, for the first time in its 81-year history, urged its members to impose sanctions against a country. In March 2002, in an effort to diffuse continuing criticism, the government signed an agreement permitting the ILO to monitor compliance through a new liaison office in Yangon. An action plan drawn up in May 2003 by ILO representatives and the government remained largely unimplemented, and in June 2005 the ILO once again called for sanctions. In February 2007 the government agreed not to act against individuals who bring complaints of forced labor before the ILO. Since then, including in September 2009, the ILO has convened a series of meetings with government personnel to raise awareness of the issue.

In May 2001 Pakistan's Chief Executive Pervez Musharraf visited Myanmar. The trip was noteworthy in that he was the first head of government, apart from ASEAN and Chinese leaders, to visit the country in 12 years. Visits by other foreign leaders remain infrequent, although in March 2006 A.P.J. Abdul Kalam became the first president of India to visit Myanmar. Six months later, India and Myanmar concluded a security agreement, after which New Delhi extended military aid to Yangon. In February 2007 the SPDC attacked a border camp controlled by a faction of the National Socialist Council of Nagaland, one of numerous Indian separatist groups that have established external bases from which they conduct raids into India.

On September 29, 2006, for the first time in its history, the UN Security Council discussed human rights and internal developments in Myanmar. On January 12, 2007, however, Russia and China vetoed a Security Council resolution that called on the SPDC to release political prisoners, permit free expression and political activity, and end human rights violations and military action against ethnic minorities. The resolution had been sponsored by the United States and the United Kingdom. In June 2007 the International Committee of the Red Cross added its voice to those condemning the SPDC for human rights abuses.

On June 26–27, 2009, Ibrahim Gambari visited Myanmar for the eighth time in his capacity as special representative of the UN secretary general. In general, his visits have focused on democratization. On July 3–4 Secretary General Ban Ki-moon paid a second visit to Myanmar—his first had come in the wake of the 2008 cyclone—at which time Sr. Gen. Than Shwe promised that the planned 2010 elections would be free and fair. The secretary general was not permitted to meet with Aung San Suu Kyi.

Current issues. On May 3, 2008, Cyclone Nargis hit Myanmar's Irrawaddy region. By May 15 the UN estimated the number of severely affected people to be between 1.6 and 2.5 million. In late June Myanmar raised the death toll to 84,500, with another 53,800 missing. A subsequent report from ASEAN put the cost of reconstruction and relief at $1 billion.

The government's initial response to the disaster provoked strong international criticism. Visas for aid workers were initially withheld, and it took 20 days for the government to agree to allow all aid workers, regardless of nationality, into the country. Amnesty International reported that on May 30 authorities began evicting families from government-run cyclone relief camps, fearing the "tented villages" could become permanent. U.S. Navy ships with relief supplies left Myanmar's coast on June 5 after failing to receive permission for their helicopters to enter Myanmar air space. Then in July, with the eviction campaign continuing, accusations emerged that the authorities were forcing cyclone survivors to do menial labor in exchange for food, while aid was still reportedly prevented from reaching areas in need. Despite the international criticism, the UN reported on July 10 that a total of 50 countries had pledged around $175 million to support relief, recovery, and rehabilitation efforts, with the United Kingdom and United States the largest donors.

In the midst of the cyclone crisis, the SPDC proceeded with its scheduled referendum on the new constitution, although voting in the most adversely affected regions was postponed from May 10 until May 24. No international election monitors were permitted into Myanmar, and the reported 98 percent turnout, with 92 percent approval, legitimized expectations that the poll would be seriously flawed. In February Sr. Gen. Than Shwe had signed a law that threatened penalties for opposing the measure. Under the Referendum Law for the Approval of the Draft Constitution, anybody who publicly critiqued the referendum faced a fine and a three-year prison sentence.

Periodically, the SPDC grants amnesty to thousands of prisoners—9,000 in September 2008, 7,100 in September 2009—but relatively few of them fall into the category of political prisoners. An estimated 2,200 political prisoners remain incarcerated. Moreover, courts throughout the country continue to convict dissidents and sentence them to decades-long prison sentences for crimes that most other countries would consider noninfractions or, at worst, minor offenses, such as drawing cartoons critical of SPDC members or breaching "public order." Among those currently serving sentences of more than 60 years are leaders of the September 2007 protests, including MIN KO NAING of the 88 Generation Students and ASHIN GAMBIRA of the Alliance of All Burmese Buddhist Monks.

The August 2009 conviction of Aung San Suu Kyi for harboring American John Yettaw was interpreted by international observers as a means of preventing her involvement in the 2010 elections. Yettaw, sentenced to a seven-year prison term for illegally visiting Suu Kyi, was released on August 15 through the intercession of U.S. Sen. James Webb, the first member of the U.S. Congress to visit Myanmar in a decade and the first to have a meeting with Than Shwe. Although Webb's visit, part of a tour through Southeast Asia, was unofficial, he stated that he saw it as potentially "laying the foundation of goodwill and confidence-building" between Yangon and Washington. The new U.S. president, Barack Obama, was believed to be considering a change in his predecessor's stringent policies toward Myanmar, although prospects for even a modest thaw were undoubtedly complicated by recent reports that the SPDC has discussed obtaining nuclear technology from North Korea and may be building a secret nuclear reactor and reprocessing plant. In September U.S. secretary of state Hillary Clinton nevertheless announced that the Obama administration was in fact ready to engage in direct talks with the SPDC, but without weakening sanctions. Suu Kyi reportedly supported the policy change.

During 2009 the SPDC continued a three-year military offensive against the KNU. Largely as a result of the decades-old conflict, some 400,000 Karens live in refugee camps across the border in Thailand. (According to the Office of the UN High Commissioner for Refugees, between 2005 and 2008 some 30,000 Myanmar refugees were resettled from Thai camps, 21,500 of them in the United States.) Although information about army activities is very hard to obtain and nearly impossible to confirm, there have been recent reports of offenses against ethnic Chinese in northeastern Kokang as well as reports that an offensive against Wa insurgents was about to be undertaken. In addition, a report by Human Rights Watch in January called attention to the plight of the Chin minority, adjacent to India, where army abuses were described as including forced labor, summary executions, torture, food shortages, and sexual exploitation.

POLITICAL PARTIES AND GROUPS

At the time of the 1962 coup, the most important Burmese parties were U Nu's Union Party (*Pyidaungsu* Party); the opposition Anti-Fascist People's Freedom League; and the procommunist National United Front, with its major affiliate, the Burmese Workers' Party. Although a number of their leaders were imprisoned, the parties continued to exist until March 1964, when the Revolutionary Council banned all but its own Burma Socialist Program Party (BSPP). Following the September 1988 coup, the party ban was rescinded, and the BSPP reorganized as the National Unity Party (NUP).

Over 200 political organizations were registered prior to the May 1990 Constituent Assembly election, although many were little more than discussion groups. Following the overwhelming victory of the opposition National League for Democracy (NLD), the military regime not only refused to convene the new assembly but also withdrew recognition from nearly all opposition formations. Fewer than a dozen parties, most of them government supportive, participated in the intermittent 1993–1996 sessions of the National Convention, which was to draw up a new constitution. The convention reconvened annually between May 2004 and the final session, which concluded on September 3, 2007, having produced 15 chapters of "basic principles." Convention sessions were attended by a number of additional political organizations that had negotiated cease-fire agreements with the SPDC, but the entire process was tightly controlled by the military, leaving some ethnic groups dissatisfied with their inability to introduce substantive amendments. The principal opposition parties, the NLD and the Shan Nationalities League for Democracy, refused to participate because NLD leaders Aung San Suu Kyi and Tin Oo remained under house arrest.

The 2008 constitution provides for the formation of political parties within a "genuine and discipline-flourishing multiparty democratic system" (Chapter X). Party registrations may be revoked for receiving foreign assistance, abusing religion, or "directly or indirectly contacting or abetting" terrorists or insurgent groups in armed rebellion against the state.

As of September 2009 the SPDC had yet to promulgate a party registration law. Some of the 17 ethnic groups that had concluded cease-fire agreements with the SPDC were expected to restructure into parties and contest the anticipated 2010 elections, and other new parties were expected to register as well. Considerable attention was given to an announcement in September 2009 by THAN THAN NU and NAY YEE BA, both of them daughters of former prime ministers, that they planned to organize a Democratic Party prior to the elections, and there were also reports that a military "proxy party," the National Politics Party, would also be formed.

National Convention Participants:

National Unity Party—NUP (*Taingyintha Silonenyinyutye* Party). An outgrowth of the former BSPP, the NUP was launched in September 1988. Unlike the practice under BSPP rule, members of the armed forces have been specifically excluded from membership. The party won only 10 of 485 available seats at the Constituent Assembly balloting of May 1990.

A closely associated **Union Solidarity and Development Association** (USDA), founded in 1993 and currently headed by Maj. Gen. HTAY OO (also the minister of agriculture and irrigation), was described by the *Far Eastern Economic Review* in 1998 as a more inclusive "quasi-political party established under the guise of a community-assistance organization." In May 2003 the USDA was accused of organizing the attack against Aung San Suu Kyi's motorcade, and it has since been used to suppress, sometimes violently, other antijunta activities. According to the government, the USDA has a membership of some 22 million, although it continues to be known in the vernacular by a derogatory abbreviation, *Kyant Phut* (translatable as "monitor lizard" or, roughly, "stupid reptile").

Leader: KHIN MAUNG KYI (Secretary General).

The following parties have also supported the military regime and uniformly condemned the NLD's announcement of the "People's Parliament" in 1998: the **Khami National Solidarity Organization** (also known as the Mro National Solidarity Organization); the **Lahu National Development Party,** based in the Lahu tribe of eastern Shan State; the **Kokang Democracy and Unity Party;** the **Union Kayin League** (Union Karen League); the **Union Pa-O National Organization,** based in west-central Shan State; and the **Wa National Development Party.**

Also participating in one or more of the reconvened National Conventions of 2004–2007, at the invitation of the SPDC, were a number of additional groups, known as the "cease-fire groups," some of which had split off from still-active insurgent formations and had "exchanged arms for peace." The invited groups included the **Arakanese Army;** the **Burmese Communist Party (Rakhine Group),** a remnant of the Communist Party that was outlawed in 1953 and later dissolved along ethnic lines; the **Democratic Karen Buddhist Association** (see KNU, below); the **Haungthayaw Special Region Group** from Kayin State; the **Homein Region Welfare and Development Group;** the **Kachin Defense Army** (formerly a battalion in the Kachin Independence Army) of Shan State Special Region 5; the **Kachin Independence Organization** (KIO) of Kachin State Special Region 2; the **Kayinni National Progressive Party Dragon Group** (see KNPP, below); the **Kayinni National Progressive Party (Hoya Splinter);** the **Kayinni National Unity and Solidarity Organization** (*Ka Ma Sa Nya*); the **Manpan Regional Militia Group;** the **Mon Armed Peace Group (Chaungchi Region);** the **Mon (Splinter) Nai Saik Chan Group;** the **New Mon State Party;** the **Phayagon Special Region Group,** also from Kayin; the **Shan State National Army** (SSNA), which broke from the Mong Tai Army (MTA) of Shan drug warlord Khun Sa in 1995; the **Shan State Nationalities People's Liberation Organization** (SNPLO); and the **Shwepyiaye (MTA) Group.** All of these organizations claimed predominantly ethnic or regional support. In many cases their ideological orientations remained problematic. Some expressed support for Aung San Suu Kyi and the NLD, and all opposed to at least some aspects of the government's constitutional proposals. Some have denied allegations of continuing involvement in drug trafficking.

During 2005, in the context of continuing hostilities in Shan State, the SSNA and the SNPLO announced that they had ended their cooperation with the government and were joining the insurgent Shan State Army–South (see below). By the end of 2005, however, the SSNA had surrendered. The SNPLO surrendered on August 3, 2008, and announced its intention to form a Shan State party to enter the 2010 elections. As of September 2009 the KIO was divided between factions that supported and opposed participation in the anticipated 2010 elections.

The government-supportive **United Wa State Party** (UWSP) and the associated United Wa State Army (UWSA), are both led by BAO YU XIANG (PAU YU CHANG). The UWSA is reputedly the country's leading producer of opium, heroin, and methamphetamines. Reportedly numbering as many as 25,000, with another 10,000 in associated village militias, the UWSA has operated with considerable autonomy within the Golden Triangle. Although Bao Yu Xiang has recently asserted that poppy cultivation has been eliminated in the area under UWSA control, in November 2008 the U.S. State Department described the UWSA as the "largest and most powerful drug trafficking organization in Southeast Asia."

Opposition Parties:

National League for Democracy (NLD). Registered as a political party in September 1988, the NLD was an outgrowth of the Democracy and Peace (Interim) League (DPIL), which had been formed by a number of leading dissidents a month earlier. Its founding president, AUNG GYI, withdrew to form the Union National Democratic Party (UNDP) after having called, unsuccessfully, for the expulsion from the DPIL of a number of alleged communists. (The UNDP was deregistered in 1992.)

Following her return to Burma in April 1988, the party's first general secretary, Aung San Suu Kyi, became the regime's most vocal and effective critic. Both she and fellow NLD leader Tin Oo were arrested in July 1989 and declared ineligible to compete in the May 1990 balloting, which produced an overwhelming victory for the NLD, tacitly allied with some 21 ethnic-based regional parties. The NLD's two other principal leaders, KYI MAUNG and CHIT KHAING, were arrested in September 1990.

In April 1991 the SLORC announced that the NLD's Central Committee had been "invalidated," thus technically removing the four leaders from their party positions. Kyi Maung and Tin Oo were released from prison in March 1995, while Suu Kyi was freed from house arrest in July. Kyi Maung left the NLD in 1997, reportedly because of a dispute with Suu Kyi.

In July 1997 SLORC leader Khin Nyunt met with NLD chair Aung Shwe, and on September 27–28 NLD delegates were permitted to hold the group's first congress with Suu Kyi in attendance in two years. An authorized NLD Congress on May 27–28, 1998, at her residence was attended by 400 party members. In the following months, however, in response to the NLD's threat to call a "People's Parliament," the regime began a series of crackdowns against the party that included hundreds of detentions, closure of many local offices, and forced resignations. In all, tens of thousands of party members may have been forced to resign in 1998–1999. Suu Kyi was again placed under de facto house arrest from September 2000 until May 2002.

On May 30, 2003, following a violent attack on an NLD motorcade by government supporters, Suu Kyi was taken into "protective custody." An unclear number of NLD members—initial reports indicated 4, but some subsequent accounts said 60 or more—were killed by the mob. Suu Kyi's house arrest resumed on September 26. On April 13, 2004, Aung Shwe and U Lwin were released, leaving Suu Kyi and Tin Oo as the only senior NLD members in detention. A month later the NLD refused to participate in the reconvened National Convention until both were freed.

As part of a wider amnesty for 9,000 prisoners, described by Amnesty International as mostly drug dealers and petty criminals, WIN TIN, one of the founders of the NLD, was released from prison in September 2008 along with several other NLD members. Described as Myanmar's longest-serving political prisoner, Win Tin had been incarcerated since 1989. Several dozen NLD members were among the 7,000 prisoners released in September 2009.

The 2008 constitution includes as a condition for presidential eligibility that a candidate as well as the individual's parents, spouse, and natural children and their spouses cannot owe allegiance to a foreign country. Because Suu Kyi's late husband, Michael Aris, was British, she would be excluded from seeking the office. Both she and Tin Oo remain under house arrest, with the latest year-long extension being given to Tin Oo in February 2009. Suu Kyi's house arrest was not renewed in May 2009. At the time, however, she was being held in a prison after being charged with harboring in her home an uninvited American. In August she was convicted, but a three-year prison sentence was commuted to another 18 months of house arrest.

In April 2009 the NLD indicated that it would participate in the 2010 elections but only if the SPDC released all political prisoners, amended the 2008 constitution to meet democratic standards, and agreed to let the international community supervise the elections.

Leaders: AUNG SAN SUU KYI (De Facto Leader), AUNG SHWE (Chair), TIN OO (Vice Chair), KHIN MAUNG SWE (Chair, Central Information Committee), U LWIN (General Secretary).

Shan Nationalities League for Democracy (SNLD). Established in 1988, the SNLD won 23 seats in the 1990 Constituent Assembly balloting, second only to the NLD. Its leader, Khun Tun Oo, has been a key opposition figure both in Shan State and on the national scene, where he participated in the "People's Parliament" and conferred repeatedly with UN and EU representatives. The SNLD refused to participate when the National Convention reconvened in May 2004.

In February 2005 the group's chair and secretary were among nearly a dozen individuals charged with treason, insurrection, and other offenses. In November Tun Oo was convicted and sentenced to spend the rest of his life in prison. Eight others also received lengthy sentences. The SNLD and NLD made a joint call for a "no" vote in the 2008 referendum on the new constitution and have denounced the result.

Leaders: KHUN TUN OO (Chair), SAI SAW AUNG (Secretary).

Like the SNLD, the other seven parties of the **United Nationalities Alliance** also boycotted the reconvened National Convention in 2004–2007: the **Arakan League for Democracy,** which won 11 seats in the 1990 Constituent Assembly election and whose chair, SAW MRA AUNG, was elected leader of the "People's Assembly" in 1998 by the Committee Representing Elected Lawmakers; the **Chin National League for Democracy,** which won 2 seats in 1990; the **Kachin State National Congress for Democracy,** which won 3 seats in 1990; the **Karen National Congress for Democracy;** the **Kayah State All Nationalities League for Democracy,** which won 2 seats in 1990; the **Mon National Democratic Front** (also identified in some sources as the Mon National League for Democracy), which won 5 seats in 1990; and the **Zomi National Congress,** which won 2 seats in 1990. In August 2008 these parties were joined by the SNLD and the NLD in addressing a letter to government authorities and the UN office in Yangon to request a meeting with the UN Special Envoy Ibrahim Gambari. This request was refused.

Dissident Groups:

88 Generation Students. Named after the 1988 uprising organized by the group's leaders, many 88 Generation members have been subjected to lengthy prison terms, and human rights groups have catalogued a number of claims of torture. The unofficial leader of the group is MIN KO NAING (Paw U TUN), who has won numerous human-rights awards for his nonviolent campaign for democracy. He was arrested in 1989 and was released in November 2004 after 15 years in prison. Along with four other key members, he was detained again in September 2006. In January 2007 all five were released, without explanation.

The 88 Generation Students was directly involved in organizing the 2007 protests. Dozens, including Min Ko Naing, were arrested as a consequence and in November 2008 were convicted in various courts and sentenced to as much as 65 years in prison for incitement and "disturbing public tranquility."

Leaders: MIN KO NAING, KYAW MIN YU, NILAR THEIN, THIN THIN AYE.

Alliance of All Burmese Buddhist Monks (AABBM). The AABBM, which has termed the military an "enemy of the people," was a prime mover behind the September 2007 prodemocracy demonstrations. Its leader, Ashin Gambira, was sentenced in November 2008 to 12 years in prison for offenses that included insulting religion and committing "crimes against the peace." He was later convicted of additional offenses, with 56 years being added to his prison term.

Leader: Ashin GAMBIRA.

In July 2008 a group calling itself the **Vigorous Burmese Student Warriors** (VBSW) claimed responsibility for a bomb that exploded outside a Yangon office of the USDA.

Insurgent Groups:

During the first half of the 1990s the military regime eliminated or arranged cease-fires with most of the country's longtime military insurgents, although negotiations with several groups subsequently broke down. After 2004, only a few remained militarily active. (For a more complete accounting of insurgent groups active prior to 1995, see the 1993 and 1994–1995 editions of the *Handbook.*)

Karen National Union (KNU). With origins dating back to 1947, the KNU and its military wing, the Karen National Liberation Army (KNLA), operated as one of the more effective minority-based insurgent groups into the 1990s. The KNU declared a unilateral cease-fire in March 1995, following the loss of its Manerplaw headquarters in January and its base in Kawmoora a month later. In early 1997, however, talks between the KNU and the government broke down, with the army quickly renewing its campaign against remaining KNU bases. In March 1999 KNU guerrillas reportedly executed ten or more immigration officials who had been captured the previous month near the Thai border.

Earlier, a splinter group calling itself the **Democratic Karen Buddhist Organization** (DKBO) had broken away from the largely Christian KNU. With the support of government forces, the DKBO's military wing, the Democratic Karen Buddhist Army (DKBA), spearheaded several assaults in 1997–1998 on KNU refugee camps in Thailand. The KNU responded in March 1998 by attacking DKBA bases in Myanmar. As the Democratic Karen (or Kayin) Buddhist Association, the group was invited by the government to participate in the reconvened National Convention in 2004. Since then, KNU and the DKBO have continued to clash.

At a ten-day party congress held in late January 2000, Bo Mya stepped down as KNU chair in favor of the party's former secretary general, SAW BA THEIN SIEN, who indicated that the party intended to adopt "political means" rather than use force of arms to achieve its goals.

A fringe KNU group, God's Army, took 700 hostages at a hospital in Ratchaburi, Thailand, in January 2000, demanding an end to an anti-Karen offensive in the Thai-Myanmar border region. All 10 hostage-takers died in an assault by Thai forces a day later. Dating from 1997 and probably numbering no more than 150 men, the cultlike God's Army was ostensibly led by 12-year-old twins, Johnny and Luther HTOO. It apparently disbanded in October 2000, with the Htoo brothers being granted asylum in Thailand in January 2001.

On January 16–22, 2004, Bo Mya led a delegation that held peace talks in Yangon with Prime Minister Khin Nyunt. Although a loose agreement on establishing a cease-fire was reportedly reached, no official pact had been signed by midyear, and skirmishes continued to occur. At a congress held November 18–December 8 Bo Mya, reportedly in poor health, was replaced as vice chair but remained in charge of defense. The cease-fire came to an end after Khin Nyunt's removal from office in October 2004.

In May 2006 a renewed government offensive against KNU supporters drew widespread international criticism as well as calls for a new cease-fire and renewed negotiations. Bo Mya died on December 24, 2006. In February 2007 a KNU splinter led by HTAIN MAUNG signed a peace agreement with the government, and two months later reports surfaced of a major defeat for the KNU at the hands of the army and DKBO forces.

On February 17, 2008, Secretary General PADOH MAHN SHA of the KNU was shot dead in his home. Thai police reported the assailants were Karen, although government culpability was suspected, albeit without evidence. In late 2008 the KNU elected its theretofore vice chair, Tamla Baw, as chair and his daughter, Zipporah Sein, as secretary general. Since then, the KNU has repeatedly sought to draw international attention to the military offensive being conducted against Karens by the SPDC.

Leaders: Gen. TAMLA BAW (Chair), David THARCKABAW (Vice Chair), Zipporah SEIN (Secretary General).

Karenni National Progressive Party (KNPP). With a predominantly Kayinni membership, the KNPP was established in 1957. It concluded an agreement with the SLORC in March 1995 but in mid-1996 took up arms again and remained in active opposition in 2004, although two splinter groups had concluded cease-fire agreements with the SPDC and, on that basis, were invited to send delegates to the reconvened National Convention.

The KNPP held cease-fire discussions with the government in 2007 but failed to reach an agreement. In June 2007 it sponsored a meeting of ethnic groups that were still engaged in armed resistance. Attendees represented the KNU, the Shan State Army–South (below), the **Chin National Front**, and the **Arakan Liberation Party.**

Leaders: KHU OO REH (Secretary), Maj. AUNG MYAT (Military Commander).

Shan State Army–South (SSA-S). Dating from 1964, the Shan State Army established the Shan State Progressive Party (subsequently the Shan State Peacekeeping Council) in 1972, although the two later separated. In April 1998 Amnesty International, in a report quickly ridiculed by the SPDC, accused the Myanmar army of torturing or killing hundreds of Shans and forcing at least 300,000 to flee their homes in 1996–1997 as part of its effort to cut off support for the SSA. Although the SSA-North concluded a peace agreement with the SPDC, the SSA-South remained in militant opposition to the government. It was joined by the Shan State National Army in 2005 and was declared to be a terrorist organization by the SPDC in August 2006. In mid-2009 there was considerably speculation that the SPDC, having achieved measurable gains in a recent offensive against ethnic Karens, was planning to launch a campaign against the SSA-S before the end of the year.

Leader: Col. YAWD SERK (Commander).

Among the groups reputedly engaged in drug manufacture and trafficking is the **Shan United Revolutionary Party,** an offshoot of the Mong Tai Army that rejected the latter's surrender to government forces.

Exile Groups:

A number of exile opposition groups currently function. Most support a **National Coalition Government of the Union of Burma** (NCGUB), a shadow government that was established in 1991 and is currently led from exile by Dr. SEIN WIN, a cousin of Aung San Suu Kyi. The government was most recently elected by exiled legislators at a congress held January 20–23 in Malahide, Ireland.

In April 2006 the government declared the NCGUB, the All Burma Student Democratic Front (ABSDF), the Federation of Trade Unions Burma (FTUB), and the National League for Democracy–Liberated Areas (NLD-LA) to be terrorist organizations.

All Burma Student Democratic Front (ABSDF). The ABSDF was founded in 1988 by disaffected students. In March 1998 the Yangon regime accused the ABSDF of organizing a plot to assassinate government leaders and bomb government buildings and foreign embassies. The ABSDF denied the charge, responding that it had decided in 1997 to abandon armed conflict in favor of "nonviolent, political defiance." Earlier, ABSDF leader KO AUNG TUN was imprisoned for 15 years for writing a history of the Burmese student movement.

The ABSDF held its Eighth Congress in December 2006. More recently, in September 2009 it joined the 88 Generation Students and the All-Burma Monks' Alliance in a statement urging the junta to end its assaults against ethnic minority groups.

Leaders: THAN KE (Chair), MYO WIN (Vice Chair), Sonny MAHINDER (General Secretary).

Other exile groups include the **Democratic Party for a New Society,** the **People's Defense Front,** the **Burma Women's Union,** and the **Network for Democracy and Development.** In February 2004 they joined with the ABSDF and a number of other groups to organize an umbrella **Democratic Alliance of Burma.** Additional formations include the **National Council of the Union of Burma** (NCUB) and the **Federation of Trade Unions Burma** (FTUB), which was established in 1991; both are led by PYITHIT NYUENT WAI (a.k.a. MAUNG MAUNG). Among the leaders of the **National League for Democracy–Liberated Areas** (NLD-LA) is NYO OHN MYINT. The nonprofit **U.S. Campaign for Burma** is headed by Executive Director KO AUNG DIN. Overlapping memberships are common. In April 2005, an exile group based in Australia and led by SAI SOE NYUNT declared the independence of the Federated Shan States.

LEGISLATURE

The former People's Assembly (*Pyithu Hluttaw*), elected in November 1985, was abolished by the military government on September 18, 1988. On March 1, 1989, the government issued an election law for a new Constituent Assembly, which excluded from either voting or presentation as candidates all members of the armed forces, members of religious orders, those who "abuse religion for political purposes," persons associated with insurgent groups, and citizens enjoying "the rights and privileges of a subject or citizen of a foreign power."

In the election of May 27, 1990, 93 parties competed for 485 of 492 assembly seats (polling being barred in 7 constituencies for security reasons). The National League for Democracy won an overwhelming majority of 392 seats, compared to 10 for the government-backed National Unity Party. (For a complete listing of the 25 other parties that won at least 1 seat, see the 1999 or earlier editions of the *Handbook.*) The assembly was not permitted to convene.

The 2008 constitution provides for a bicameral legislature, the **Union Parliament** (*Pyidaungsu Hluttaw*), comprising a 224-member **National Assembly** (*Amyotha Hluttaw*) and a 440-member **People's Assembly** (*Pyithu Hluttaw*). States and regions are equally represented by 12 members each in the upper house, in which an additional 56 seats are reserved for members of the military, chosen by the commander-in-chief. Members of the lower house are to be elected from township-based districts according to population; 110 seats (25 percent) are reserved for the military. The first elections for both houses are scheduled to take place in 2010.

CABINET

[as of December 15, 2009]

Prime Minister	Lt. Gen. Thein Sein
Ministers	
Agriculture and Irrigation	Maj. Gen. Htay Oo
Commerce	Brig. Gen. Tin Naing Thein
Communications, Posts, and Telegraphs	Brig. Gen. Thein Zaw
Construction	Maj. Gen. Khin Maung Myint (acting)
Cooperatives	Maj. Gen. Tin Htut
Culture	Maj. Gen. Khin Aung Myint
Defense	Sr. Gen. Than Shwe
Development Affairs	Col. Thein Nyunt
Education	Chan Nyein
Electric Power No. 1	Col. Zaw Min
Electric Power No. 2	Maj. Gen. Khin Maung Myint
Energy	Brig. Gen. Lun Thi
Finance and Revenue	Maj. Gen. Hla Tun
Foreign Affairs	Maj. Gen. U Nyan Win
Forestry	Brig. Gen. Thein Aung
Health	Kyaw Myint
Home Affairs	Maj. Gen. Maung Oo
Hotels and Tourism	Maj. Gen. Soe Naing
Immigration and Population	Maj. Gen Maung Oo (acting)
Industry No. 1	Aung Thaung
Industry No. 2	Maj. Gen. Nyan Win
Information	Brig. Gen. Kyaw Hsan
Labor	Aung Kyi
Livestock and Fisheries	Brig. Gen. Maung Maung Thein
Mines	Brig. Gen. Ohn Myint

National Planning and Economic Development	Soe Tha
Progress of Border Areas and National Races	Col. Thein Nyunt
Rail Transport	Maj. Gen. Aung Min
Religious Affairs	Brig. Gen. Thura Myint Maung
Science and Technology	Thaung
Social Welfare, Relief, and Resettlement	Maj. Gen. Maung Maung Swe
Sports	Brig. Gen. Thura Aye Myint
Transport	Maj. Gen. Thein Swe
Armed Forces Commander-in-Chief	Sr. Gen. Than Shwe
Joint Chief-of-Staff of the Armed Forces	Gen. Shwe Mahn
Air Force Commander-in-Chief	Lt. Gen. Myat Hein
Army Commander-in-Chief	Vice Sr. Gen. Maung Aye
Navy Commander-in-Chief	Maj. Gen. Nyan Tun
Commander, Coastal Military Command	Brig. Gen. Khin Zaw Oo
Commander, Eastern Military Command	Brig. Gen. Yar Pyae
Commander, Northern Military Command	Brig. Gen. Soe Win
Commander, Northeast Military Command	Brig. Gen. Maung Shein
Commander, Southern Military Command	Brig. Gen. Hla Min
Commander, Western Military Command	Brig. Gen. Thaung Aye

COMMUNICATIONS

The Revolutionary Council banned all publication of privately owned foreign newspapers in 1966. Under the 1974 constitution, all newspapers remained heavily censored. At present, all media are directly controlled by the government or strictly supervised. The international organization Reporters Without Borders has ranked Myanmar among the world's ten worst countries when it comes to press freedoms and as a "black hole" in terms of Internet access.

Press. Since 1988 the principal daily published in Yangon has been the official government organ, *Myanama Alin/New Light of Myanmar* (called *Loketha Pyithu Neizin/Working People's Daily* until April 1993), in Myanmar (400,000) and English (15,000). Other government-controlled dailies published in the capital are *Botahtaung* (The Vanguard), in Myanmar; *Guardian*, in English; and *Kyehmon* (The Mirror), in Myanmar. Irregular clandestine papers include the *Dawn News Bulletin,* published by the All Burma Student Democratic Front. There also is an opposition electronic newspaper, *BurmaNet News.*

News agencies. The domestic facility is the official Myanmar News Agency—MNA (Myanmar The Din Zin). Several foreign agencies maintain offices in Yangon. Mizzima News, based in New Delhi, India, was established by exiled journalists in 1998.

Broadcasting and computing. Programming is controlled by the state-owned Myanmar TV and Radio Department (MTRD), formerly the Burma Broadcasting Service, which transmits in Myanmar, English, and a variety of local languages. TV Myanmar broadcasts, with the aid of relays and satellite, can be received throughout the country; a second station has limited coverage. An opposition Democratic Voice of Burma, based in Oslo, Norway, was cited by Reporters Without Borders for its "outstanding coverage" of the 2007 protests in Myanmar.

As of 2008 there were 2.2 Internet users per 1,000 inhabitants.

INTERGOVERNMENTAL REPRESENTATION

Ambassador to the U.S.: (Vacant).

U.S. Ambassador to Myanmar: (Vacant).

Permanent Representative to the UN: Than SWE.

IGO Memberships (Non-UN): ADB, ASEAN, Interpol, NAM, WCO, WTO.

NAMIBIA

Republic of Namibia

Note: President Hifikepunye Pohamba (South West Africa People's Organization of Namibia—SWAPO) was reelected for a five-year term on November 27–28, 2009, with a vote share of 76.4 percent. In concurrent elections for the National Assembly, the SWAPO won 54 of 72 seats. The opposition Rally for Democracy and Progress, participating for the first time in national elections, secured 8 assembly seats, and the party's president, Hidipo Hamutenya, placed a distant second in presidential balloting, with a 10.9 percent of the votes.

Political Status: Former German territory assigned to South Africa under League of Nations mandate in 1920; declared to be a United Nations responsibility by General Assembly resolution adopted October 27, 1966 (resolution not recognized by South Africa); subject to tripartite (Angolan-Cuban-South African) agreement concluded on December 22, 1988, providing for implementation from April 1, 1989, of Security Council Resolution 435 of 1978 (leading to UN-supervised elections on November 1 and independence thereafter); independence declared on March 21, 1990.

Area: 318,259 sq. mi. (824,292 sq. km.).

Population: 1,826,854 (2001C); 2,101,000 (2008E). Both area and population figures include data for Walvis Bay (see Political background and Foreign relations, below).

Major Urban Center (2005E): WINDHOEK (282,000).

Official Language: English.

Monetary Unit: Namibian Dollar (official rate December 1, 2009: 7.33 dollars = $1US). Introduced on September 13, 1993, the Namibian dollar is at par with the South African rand, which is also legal tender in Namibia.

President: (*See headnote.*) Hifikepunye POHAMBA (South West Africa People's Organization of Namibia); popularly elected on November 15–16, 2004, and inaugurated for a five-year term on March 21, 2005, to succeed Samuel (Sam) Daniel Shafilshuna NUJOMA (South West Africa People's Organization of Namibia).

Prime Minister: Nahas ANGULA (South West Africa People's Organization of Namibia); appointed by the president following parliamentary elections on November 15–16, 2004, and sworn in on March 21, 2005, to succeed Theo-Ben GURIRAB (South West Africa People's Organization of Namibia).

THE COUNTRY

Bordered on the north by Angola and Zambia, on the east by Botswana, on the southeast and south by South Africa, and on the west by the Atlantic Ocean, Namibia consists of a high plateau bounded by the uninhabited Namib Desert along the Atlantic coast, with more desert land in the interior. The inhabitants are of diversified origins, although the Ovambo constitute by far the largest ethnic group (a majority of 51 percent in the 1981 census, slightly less than 50 percent on the basis of a 1986 estimate). A substantial exodus has reduced the white population, traditionally engaged in commercial farming and ranching, fish processing, and mineral exploitation, from approximately 12 percent to 6.6 percent. Other groups include the Kavango, the Herero, the Damara, the Nama, and those classified as "coloured." The country is one of the world's largest producers of diamonds, which yield about half of export earnings, and uranium; copper, lead, zinc, tin, and other minerals are also available in extractable quantities. These resources yielded substantial economic growth during the 1970s; subsequently, falling mineral prices, extended periods of drought, and internal insecurity caused a severe recession, marked by 40–50 percent unemployment, 13–16 percent inflation, and severe budgetary problems. In July 1990 international donors committed $200 million to help offset a $270 million fiscal shortfall caused by South Africa's withdrawal from the economy. GDP growth averaged 5 percent annually in 1990–1993 and 3 percent annually in 1994–1999. Economic policies have focused on further exploitation of the country's rich fisheries, export manufacturing, promotion of private investment, and programs designed to ameliorate the severe maldistribution of wealth and an unemployment rate estimated to be as high as 35 percent. A 2002 agreement to allow Namibian craft to fish in South African territorial waters further expanded the sector.

Steady economic growth continued in the early 2000s, with GDP increasing by an average of 3–4 percent annually. Significantly, inflation fell to 5 percent by 2004 (from 8.8 percent in 1997) after the Bank of Namibia cut interest rates from 12.75 percent to 5 percent over a four-year period.

In addition to continued mineral exploitation and fishing, international firms have invested $800 million in the development of natural gas fields. Long-term plans are to use the fields to produce electricity for export to surrounding states, including South Africa. In an effort to ameliorate unemployment and poverty, the government launched a controversial land redistribution program in 2004 (see Current issues, below) in order to increase farm ownership among black Namibians. The program continued to be of regional interest in 2006, with Namibia and four other nations meeting in Pretoria in March for a conference on the subject. Despite the economic challenges of an unemployment rate exceeding 20 percent and widespread poverty, real GDP growth averaged 4.2 percent in 2005–2007, owing mainly to buoyant diamond production, according to the International Monetary Fund (IMF). While overall economic performance remained strong and debt declined, growth was insufficient to create new jobs. The IMF in 2007, while commending Namibia's overall economic progress, emphasized the need for authorities to develop the non-mining sector to help reduce poverty. The prevalence of HIV/AIDS, affecting an estimated 20 percent of the population, continued to be a major concern, though the outlook improved somewhat with the government's development of a strategy to address the disease. The IMF also cited progress in the implementation of education reforms, financial assistance to farmers in the wake of a major drought, and the establishment of an anticorruption commission. Economic growth contracted to 3 percent in 2008, owing in large part to a downturn in the mining sector as a consequence of the global financial crisis. Sharp increases in food and fuel prices pushed inflation to nearly 11 percent.

The IMF commended Namibia for its prudent fiscal policies in recent years and urged the administration to "remain vigilant" in the wake of the continuing global downturn and to "press ahead" with structural reforms and diversification. GDP was expected to decline to about 0.4 percent in 2009, reflecting a significant decrease in the diamond and tourism sectors as a result of global financial turmoil.

GOVERNMENT AND POLITICS

Political background. South West Africa came under German control in the 1880s, except for a small enclave at Walvis Bay, which had been annexed by the United Kingdom in 1878 and subsequently became a part of South Africa. Having occupied the whole of South West Africa during World War I, South Africa was granted a mandate in 1920 to govern the area under authority of the League of Nations. Declining to place the territory under the UN trusteeship system after World War II, South Africa asked the UN General Assembly in 1946 for permission to annex it; following denial of the request, Pretoria continued its rule on the strength of the original mandate.

Although the international status of the territory and the supervisory authority of the United Nations were repeatedly affirmed in advisory opinions of the International Court of Justice (ICJ), the court in 1966 declined on technical grounds to rule upon a formal complaint by Ethiopia and Liberia against South Africa's conduct in the territory. The UN General Assembly then terminated the mandate in a resolution of October 27, 1966, declaring that South Africa had failed to fulfill its obligations. A further resolution on May 19, 1967, established an 11-member UN Council for South West Africa, assisted by a UN commissioner, to administer the territory until independence (originally set for June 1968) and to prepare for the drafting of a constitution, the holding of an election, and the establishment of responsible government. The council was, however, refused entry by the South African government, which contended that termination of the mandate was invalid. South Africa subsequently disregarded a number of Security Council resolutions to relinquish the territory, including a unanimous resolution of December

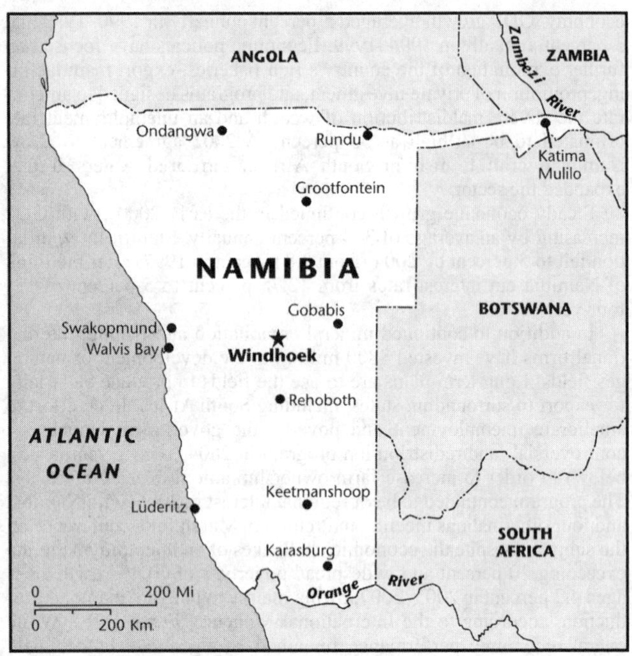

1974 that gave it five months to initiate withdrawal from Namibia (the official name adopted on December 16, 1968, by the General Assembly).

Beginning in the mid-1960s, South Africa attempted to group the black population into a number of self-administering tribal homelands ("Bantustans"), in accordance with the so-called Odendaal Report of 1964. Ovamboland, the first functioning Bantustan, was established in October 1968, but its legitimacy was rejected by the UN Security Council. Fully implemented, the partition plan would have left approximately 88,000 whites as the largest ethnic group in two-thirds of the territory, with some 675,000 black inhabitants confined to the remaining third.

Both the Organization of African Unity (OAU, subsequently the African Union—AU) and the South West Africa People's Organization (SWAPO) consistently pressed for full and unconditional self-determination for Namibia. In May 1975, however, Prime Minister John Vorster of South Africa stated that while his government was prepared to "exchange ideas" with UN and OAU representatives, it was not willing to accede to the demand that it "acknowledge SWAPO as the sole representative of the Namibian people and enter into independence negotiations with the organization."

On September 1, 1975, the South African government convened a constitutional conference in Turnhalle, Windhoek, on the future of the territory. SWAPO and other independence groups boycotted the conference and organized demonstrations against it. As a result, the Ovambos, with approximately half of the territory's population, were represented by only 15 of 135 delegates. At the second session of the conference, held in March 1976, Chief Clemens KAPUUO, then leader of the Herero-based National United Democratic Organization, presented a draft constitution that called for a bicameral legislature encompassing a northern chamber of representatives from Bantu areas and a southern chamber that would include representatives from the coloured and white groups. During the third session of the conference in August, a plan was advanced for the creation of a multiracial interim government to prepare Namibia for independence by December 31, 1978. Despite continued opposition from SWAPO, the conference's constitution committee unanimously approved a resolution on December 3 that called for establishment of the interim government within the next six months.

A draft constitution calling for representation of the territory's 11 major racial and ethnic groups was approved by the Turnhalle delegates on March 9, 1977, and was subsequently endorsed by 95 percent of the white voters in a referendum on May 17. However, it continued to be opposed by SWAPO as well as by a group of diplomats representing the five Western members of the UN Security Council (Canada, France, the Federal Republic of Germany, the United Kingdom, and the United States). The Western delegation visited Windhoek on May 7–10 and subsequently engaged in talks with South African Prime Minister Vorster in Cape Town, in the course of which it indicated that the Turnhalle formula was unacceptable because it was "predominantly ethnic, lacked neutrality, and appeared to prejudice the outcome of free elections." The group added, however, that the appointment of an administrator general by the South African government would not be opposed insofar as it gave promise of contributing to "an internationally acceptable solution to the Namibia question." For his part, Vorster, prior to the appointment of Marthinus T. STEYN as administrator general on July 6, agreed to abandon the Turnhalle proposal for an interim government, accept the appointment of a UN representative to ensure the impartiality of the constituent election in 1978, and initiate a withdrawal of South African troops to be completed by the time of independence. He insisted, however, that the South African government had no intention of abandoning its jurisdiction over Walvis Bay and certain islands off the South West African coast. (Governed as part of South Africa until 1922, when it was assigned to South West Africa for administrative purposes, Walvis Bay was reincorporated into South Africa's Cape Province in August 1977.)

During November and December 1977 representatives of the diplomatic group engaged in inconclusive discussions with leaders of SWAPO and of the black African "Front-Line States" (Angola, Botswana, Mozambique, Tanzania, and Zambia). The main problem concerned South African security forces within Namibia, SWAPO asserting that their continued presence would influence the outcome of the projected election despite a UN presence. Nonetheless, Administrator General Steyn moved energetically to dismantle the territory's apartheid system, including abolition of the pass laws and the Mixed Marriages Act, in preparation for the 1978 balloting.

On March 27, 1978, Chief Kapuuo, who had assumed the presidency of the Democratic Turnhalle Alliance (DTA, see Political Parties, below), was shot and killed by unknown assailants on the outskirts of Windhoek. The assassination removed from the scene the best-known tribal figure apart from SWAPO leader Sam NUJOMA, who denied that his group had been involved. Three days later the Western nations presented Prime Minister Vorster with revised proposals calling for a cease-fire between SWAPO guerrillas and the 18,000 South African troops in the territory. The latter force would be expected to gradually decrease to 1,500, with UN troops being positioned to maintain order in preparation for Constituent Assembly balloting. South Africa accepted the plan on April 25 after receiving assurances that the status of Walvis Bay would not be addressed until after the election, that the reduction of its military presence would be linked to "a complete cessation of hostilities," and that some of its troops might be permitted to remain after the election if the assembly so requested. On July 12 SWAPO agreed to the Western plan, which had also been endorsed by the Front-Line States. The UN Security Council approved the plan on July 27, but Pretoria reacted bitterly to an accompanying resolution calling for the early "reintegration" of Walvis Bay into South West Africa and subsequently announced that its own final approval would be deferred. In early September South African Foreign Minister P. W. Botha denounced the size of the proposed UN military force for the territory, and two weeks later he indicated that his government had reversed itself and would proceed with an election of its own before the end of the year. Undaunted, the Security Council on September 29 approved Resolution 435, which called for the formation of a 7,500-member UN Transitional Assistance Group (UNTAG) to oversee free and fair elections, while declaring "null and void" any unilateral action by "the illegal administration in Namibia in relation to the electoral process." Administrator General Steyn nonetheless proceeded to schedule balloting for a Constituent Assembly, which on December 4–8, without SWAPO participation, gave the DTA 41 of 50 seats.

In May 1979 the South African government agreed to the Constituent Assembly's request that the body be reconstituted as a National Assembly, although without authority to alter the status of the territory. Collaterally, conflict between SWAPO guerrilla forces and South African troops intensified, the latter carrying out a number of preemptive raids on SWAPO bases in Angola and Zambia. By midyear negotiations between UN and South African representatives had not resumed, Pretoria having rejected a contact group proposal to establish bases for SWAPO forces in Namibia as a counter to South African installations. In an effort to break the deadlock, Angolan President António Agostinho Neto, a few weeks before his death in September, proposed the creation of a 60-mile-wide demilitarized zone along the Angolan-Namibian border to prevent incursions from either side. He also pledged that Angola would welcome a UN civilian presence to ensure that any guerrillas not wishing to return to Namibia to participate in an all-party election would be confined to their bases.

Although Pretoria agreed to "the concept" of a demilitarized zone, discussions during 1980 failed to yield agreement, and on November 24 UN Secretary General Kurt Waldheim called for a meeting in Geneva in January 1981 to discuss all "practical proposals" that might break the lengthy impasse. Earlier, DTA spokesperson had urged repeal of the General Assembly's 1973 recognition of SWAPO, arguing that the root of the problem lay in the fact that "the UN is required to play a neutral role in respect of implementation but at the same time is the most ardent protagonist of SWAPO."

During 1981–1982 units of both the South West Africa Territorial Force (SWATF) and the South African Defence Force (SADF) conducted numerous "search and destroy" raids into Angola, Pretoria insisting that the withdrawal of Cuban troops from the latter country was a necessary precondition of its own withdrawal from Namibia and the implementation of a UN-supervised election. Thus, Prime Minister Botha declared at a Transvaal National Party congress in September 1982 that his government would never accede to Namibian independence unless "unequivocal agreement [could] first be reached" on the linkage issue. Subsequently, an Angolan spokesperson indicated that a partial withdrawal of Cuban forces was possible if Pretoria would agree to reduce the size of its military presence to 1,500 troops and discontinue incursions into his country. The overture prompted a secret but inconclusive series of talks between Angolan and South African ministerial delegations on the island of Sal in Cape Verde in early December, the South African foreign minister subsequently asserting that responsibility for a Cuban withdrawal was "the task of the Americans."

In November 1983 a Multi-Party Conference (MPC) of seven internal groups, including the DTA, was launched in Windhoek in an effort to overcome the standoff. Although the "Windhoek Declaration of Basic Principles" that was issued on February 24, 1984, did little more than reaffirm the essentials of the earlier UN plan, South African Prime Minister Botha announced in March that his government would be willing to enter into negotiations with all relevant parties to the dispute, including the Angolan government and UNITA, the Angolan rebel movement that enjoyed de facto SADF support. However, the overture was rejected by SWAPO on the ground that only Namibian factions should be involved in independence discussions. Collaterally, Angola offered to participate as an observer at direct negotiations between SWAPO and Pretoria. Two months later Zambian President Kenneth Kaunda and South West African Administrator General Willem VAN NIEKERK jointly chaired a meeting in Lusaka that was attended by representatives of South Africa, SWAPO, and the MPC, while a meeting between van Niekerk and SWAPO president Nujoma was held in Cape Verde on July 25. Although unprecedented, the bilateral discussions also proved abortive, as did subsequent talks involving Washington, Luanda, SWAPO and/or Pretoria; progress on the issue was further inhibited in mid-1985 by evidence of continued U.S. and South African support for UNITA.

After lengthy discussion with the MPC, on June 17, 1985, Pretoria installed a Transitional Government of National Unity (TGNU), with a cabinet, 62-member legislature, and Constitutional Council of representatives from the MPC parties. Having largely excluded Ovambos, the new administration was estimated to command the support of perhaps 16 percent of the population and was further limited by Pretoria's retention of veto power over its decisions; not surprisingly, international support for the action was virtually nonexistent. While the TGNU's "interim" nature was stressed by Pretoria, which mandated a formal constitution within 18 months, stalled negotiations with Angola and continued SWAPO activity provoked South African intimations that the arrangement could lead to a permanent "regional alternative to independence."

In early 1986 Pretoria proposed that independence commence August 1, again contingent upon withdrawal of the Cubans from Angola. The renewed linkage stipulation, termed by the United Nations as "extraneous," prompted both Angola and SWAPO to reject the plan as nothing more than a "public relations exercise." In September a UN General Assembly Special Session on Namibia strongly condemned South Africa for effectively blocking implementation of the UN plan for Namibian independence and called for the imposition of mandatory sanctions against Pretoria; however, U.S. and UK vetoes precluded the passage of such resolutions by the Security Council.

During 1987 South Africa continued to seek Western recognition of the TGNU as a means of resolving the Namibian question. However, even within the TGNU, differences emerged regarding a draft constitution and the related question of new elections to second-tier legislative bodies.

In 1988 the long drawn-out dispute moved toward resolution. A series of U.S.-mediated negotiations among Angolan, Cuban, and South African representatives that commenced in London in May and continued in Cairo, New York, Geneva, and Brazzaville (Republic of the Congo) concluded at UN headquarters on December 22 with the signing of an accord that linked South African acceptance of Resolution 435/78 to the phased withdrawal, over a 30-month period, of Cuban troops from Angola. The agreement provided that the resolution would go into effect on April 1, 1989, with deployment of UNTAG (approximately 7,100 individuals from 22 countries). As ratified by the Security Council on February 16, the timetable further provided that South African troop strength would be reduced to 1,500 by July 1, followed by the election of a constituent assembly on November 1 and formal independence for the territory by April 1990.

Ten groups were registered to contest the slightly deferred Constituent Assembly election of November 7–11, 1989, with SWAPO winning 41 of 72 seats and the DTA winning 21. On February 16, 1990, the assembly elected Nujoma to the presidency of the new republic. He was sworn in by UN Secretary General Pérez de Cuéllar during independence ceremonies on March 21, with Hage GEINGOB being installed as prime minister of a 20-member cabinet.

In July 1993 Namibia and South Africa agreed to joint administration of Rooikop Airport at Walvis Bay, and on August 18 South African President F. W. de Klerk announced that his government had agreed to relinquish its claim to the port. The actual withdrawal on March 1, 1994, was hailed as completing the process of Namibian independence.

On July 18, 1994, Windhoek's already battered economic record was dealt a further blow when the auditor general released a report criticizing the Nujoma government for widespread financial mismanagement and accusing three ministries of criminal fraud. However, on December 6, one day before Namibia's first presidential and legislative elections since independence, South African President Nelson Mandela announced his country's plans to forgive Namibia's $190 million debt. Thereafter, propelled by Mandela's timely largesse and SWAPO's enduring image as the party of independence, President Nujoma and SWAPO legislative candidates easily outpaced the opposition in balloting on December 7–8, capturing approximately 76 percent of the presidential vote and 53 assembly seats. Nujoma's sole competitor, Mishake MUYONGO of the renamed DTA of Namibia (who received 23 percent of the vote), cited SWAPO's dominance in the north and declared that the elections left Namibia divided along ethnic lines. Although SWAPO captured the two-thirds assembly majority necessary to amend the constitution, Nujoma had announced earlier that any proposed changes would be submitted to popular referendum. SWAPO reportedly gained control of 27 of 45 local councils in the February 1998 balloting, followed by the DTA of Namibia with 9.

On October 16, 1998, the SWAPO-dominated National Assembly approved a constitutional amendment that granted President Nujoma the opportunity to compete for a third presidential term and increased the powers of the office. On October 30 the assembly voted against a DTA of Namibia proposal to hold a popular referendum on the bill, despite its earlier pledges to the contrary, and on November 19 the National Council also passed the third-term amendment, leaving final approval to Nujoma, who signed the bill into law in 1999. Despite continued opposition objections to the constitutional revamping, Nujoma was easily reelected for a third term in balloting on November 30–December 1, 1999, securing 76.8 percent of the vote, while SWAPO maintained its assembly dominance in concurrent legislative balloting. In late March 1999 Nujoma slightly reshuffled his government, appointing several prolabor deputy ministers in what observers described as an apparent attempt to counter the formation of a new party, the Congress of Democrats (CoD), by Ben ULENGA, a former independence fighter and trade unionist who had recently left SWAPO as the result of his opposition to the third term for Nujoma. The CoD, which called for an anticorruption drive among public officials and for the withdrawal of Namibian troops from the Democratic Republic of the Congo (DRC), was expected by some observers to offer SWAPO its first genuine electoral challenge, perhaps enough to cost the ruling party its comfortable legislative majority. However, SWAPO easily maintained more than enough seats to permit constitutional revision at will.

Although President Nujoma volunteered in April 2001 to seek a fourth term if he believed that popular will favored such a decision, late in the year he announced that he had ruled out another term. Meanwhile, tension was reported between Nujoma and Prime Minister Geingob, resulting in the appointment of Theo-Ben GURIRAB to the premiership in August 2002. (Geingob declined Nujoma's offer of another cabinet post.)

In May 2004 a SWAPO party convention nominated Hifikepunye POHAMBA (the minister of lands, resettlement, and rehabilitation) as the party's presidential candidate in the November elections. Pohamba was challenged by six other candidates, including Ben Ulenga of the CoD. Pohamba received 76.3 percent of the vote in the November 15–16, 2004, elections, with his closest rival being Ulenga with 7.34 percent. None of the other candidates received more than 5.2 percent. In the concurrent legislative elections, SWAPO maintained its dominance, winning 55 of the 72 seats. Following the elections, a new cabinet composed of SWAPO members was chosen, with Nahas ANGULA, the former minister of higher education, training, and employment creation, as prime minister. In October 2006 a new ministry for veterans affairs was created. The cabinet was reshuffled on April 8, 2008, and was again dominated by SWAPO members. An interim attorney general was appointed on September 9, 2008, assuming that role from the portfolio of the minister of justice.

Constitution and government. On February 9, 1990, the Constituent Assembly approved a liberal democratic constitution that became effective at independence on March 21. The document provides for a multiparty republic with an executive president, selected initially by majority vote of the legislature (but by direct election thereafter) for a maximum of two five-year terms. (An amendment was approved in 1998 to permit incumbent President Nujoma to serve a third term, although the two-term limit will still exist for future presidents.) The bicameral legislature encompasses a National Assembly elected by proportional representation for a five-year term and a largely advisory National Council consisting of two members from each geographic region who are elected by regional councils for six-year terms. A Council of Traditional Leaders advises the president on the utilization and control of communal land. Provision is made for an independent judiciary, empowered to enforce a comprehensive and unamendable bill of rights, considered to be the centerpiece of the document. Capital punishment and detention without trial are outlawed. The basic law also calls for a strong affirmative action program.

Regional and local units of elective government, delineated on a purely geographical basis, are to function "without any reference to the race, colour, or ethnic origin" of their inhabitants.

Foreign relations. At independence Namibia became the 50th member of the Commonwealth and shortly thereafter the 160th member of the United Nations. For economic reasons, it was deemed necessary to continue trading with South Africa; at the same time it viewed continuance of Pretoria's apartheid policies as precluding the establishment of normal diplomatic relations. Thus South Africa was permitted to maintain a mission in Windhoek that did not have the status of a full-fledged embassy.

In September 1990 it was reported that discussions (South Africa rejected the term "negotiations") had begun on the future status of South African–controlled Walvis Bay, title to which was claimed in both countries' constitutions. The talks continued in March 1991 without yielding agreement, Pretoria indicating that the only concession it would consider would be some form of joint administration of the enclave, but in November the two governments agreed to establish an interim joint administration committee. On August 21, 1992, the Walvis Bay Joint Administrative Body was formally launched. Meanwhile, neither government retreated from its territorial claim, with South Africa insisting that it would withhold a final decision until after it had formed a postapartheid government. However, on August 16, 1993, in a major decision of the multiparty forum convened to decide on the future of South Africa, the South African government delegation agreed under pressure from the African National Congress and other participants to transfer the Walvis Bay enclave to Namibia. South Africa, however, refused in November 2000 to continue negotiations with Namibia on the precise position of the Orange River border between the two countries. In 2006 the two countries agreed to a draft plan for the use of water from the river, though agreement on the exact boundary had not been reached as of mid-2008.

A seemingly less consequential dispute with a neighboring country has turned on the status of Sedudu, a small island in the middle of the Chobe River along the southern border of Namibia's Caprivi Strip. The island had been assumed to be part of Botswana until 1992, when Namibia advanced a claim that yielded a number of armed skirmishes in the area. Following an unsuccessful mediation attempt by President Robert Mugabe of Zimbabwe, the two nations agreed in early 1995 to forward the dispute to the ICJ. On December 15, 1999, the ICJ ruled in favor of Botswana regarding Sedudu, and Namibia announced that it would accept the decision.

In an effort to end illegal trading across its border with Angola (which had been closed since September 1994), Windhoek ordered troops to fire at vehicles attempting to cross the frontier in 1995. Encountering continued insecurity along the border, Namibian authorities decided in September to create a "control unit" in support of defense and police efforts to monitor contraband traffic. On the other hand, a meeting between Namibian and Angolan officials in March 1996 was described as "positive," and in April Namibia welcomed the arrival of UN troops in southeastern Angola, suggesting that when the peacekeepers had established themselves, the border might be reopened. (The border was reopened in 1999.) In July 1997 an international human rights group accused the Nujoma administration of being responsible for the disappearance of over 1,700 Angolans since the 1994 crackdown.

In August 1998 President Nujoma confirmed speculation that Namibian forces had been sent to the Democratic Republic of the Congo at the request of the DRC's president, Laurent Kabila, to help Kabila's army fight Rwandan-backed rebels. While effectively acknowledging domestic critics' assertions that his office had acted unilaterally, Nujoma attributed his decision to join Angola and Zimbabwe in aiding the DRC to the "spirit of Pan-Africanism, brotherhood and international solidarity." Thereafter, in late October the DRC rebellion topped the agenda of Nujoma's summit with South African President Mandela. The latter had been a critic of involving the forces of the members of the Southern African Development Community (SADC) in the violence. The country's involvement with the conflict in DRC was widely criticized by the Namibian opposition during 1999 and 2000. Following the assassination of Kabila in 2001, Namibian troops were withdrawn under the auspices of a UN agreement.

In February 2001 Namibia joined Angola and Zambia in the establishment of a tripartite mechanism aimed at improving security along their mutual borders, Windhoek having continued to provide the Angolan government with military support in the campaign against UNITA. After the cease-fire agreement between the Angolan government and UNITA (see article on Angola), the Namibian government began repatriating Angolan refugees, with 20,000 having been returned by the end of 2003.

In 2001 descendants of Hereros killed by the Germans during their occupation of the country filed a suit in the United States against the German government, seeking $2 billion in reparations. Although the suit was dismissed in 2004, Germany formally apologized for the role played by its colonial officials in the 1904–1907 Herero uprising against German rule. Nonetheless, relations between Germany and Namibia remain close, and Germany continues to be a leading Namibian donor.

Relations between Namibia and Brazil increased significantly during Nujoma's tenure as president. Brazilian companies were contracted to explore the edges of Namibia's continental shelf in order to determine the country's formal oceanic boundaries. In addition, under the terms of the 2002 Naval Cooperation Agreement, Brazil provided assistance to construct a naval port at Walvis Bay and to train Namibian naval officers in return for the purchase of Brazilian-built vessels for the Namibian navy. Namibia has also developed closer military ties with Russia. A 2001 bilateral military accord called for Russian technical and military assistance and the eventual purchase of Russian-built MiG fighters.

In late 2005, following President Pohamba's visit to Beijing, relations with China were enhanced as the two countries signed extradition and trade agreements, and China pledged continued economic and social assistance to Namibia. In 2006 Namibia and Zimbabwe signed extradition treaties to assist each other in legal and criminal matters.

Russian officials visited Namibia in 2007, resulting in discussions on a joint venture to produce and sell uranium to meet future needs in the development of nuclear power plants. North Korea was also engaging in closer relations with Namibia, owing in part to the latter's uranium stores. (Namibia was said to be the fifth-largest producer in the world). In March 2008 Kim Yom Nam, North Korea's second-most senior leader, attended the inauguration in Windhoek of the new presidential residence, built by North Korea at a cost of $125 million.

Current issues. Following approval of the constitutional amendment granting President Sam Nujoma the opportunity to compete for a third presidential term, Windhoek's attention in late 1998 turned to the intertwined issues of regional council elections (November 30) and secessionist activity in the Caprivi Strip region. Observers ascribed low voter participation in regional polling to both apathy and the adherence of DTA of Namibia supporters to a boycott called by the party in protest of the government's refusal to postpone balloting in those regions affected by the alleged uprising. (See Caprivi Liberation Front under Illegal Groups in Political Parties and Groups, below, for additional information.)

After the 2004 elections, which were initially described as free and fair by foreign observers, opposition groups took the electoral commission of Namibia to court over alleged irregularities. The charges were prompted by the discovery of uncounted ballots that had been removed from polling places. A recount in March 2005 confirmed the SWAPO victory, although opposition parties gained a small number of additional votes. Otherwise, the electoral developments were most noteworthy for the smooth presidential transition to Pohamba after 15 years of rule by the "father of the nation," Sam Nujoma.

Also in 2004 the government intensified its program to redistribute land from white-owned farms to landless blacks. Previous efforts had been based on the voluntary sale of land and had resulted in the transfer of approximately 10 percent of the country's 7,000 white-owned farms to members of the majority population (and the resettlement of some 25,000 people). The government's new plan called for the expropriation of about one-third of the remaining white-owned farms, although the government pledged that owners would be compensated. In 2005 the budget for land purchases was doubled to $8 million, and Namibia received $10.4 million from Germany for training and technical assistance for the new farmers (although not for land costs). In 2006 the government was still grappling with ways to improve the program and speed its implementation. Another issue still unresolved in 2006 pertained to the discovery of eight mass graves in late 2005, reported to be the remains of SWAPO liberation fighters killed the day the UN resolution on Namibian independence was signed. Government officials called for a "truth commission" but no plans were forthcoming on whether to exhume the bodies or how to deal with the graves. More mass graves were discovered in October.

In August 2006 President Pohamba, in a surprise announcement, called for draft legislation that would allow the country to hold its first constitutional referendum. Such legislation would require approval by a two-thirds majority in both houses of parliament. While Pohamba did not specify what issue the referendum would address, observers said it would likely be a proposal to replace the post of prime minister with that of vice president to establish an automatic line of succession to the president and to prevent ruling party in-fighting over selection of a presidential candidate. Though Pohamba said such legislation would be in place by 2008, no action had been taken by mid-2009.

Corruption continued to be an issue of major concern in 2008, highlighted in a survey released by the Namibia Institute for Democracy, which reported an increase in alleged corruption in the government and public sectors and cited the judiciary for its lack of speed in resolving cases.

Accusations of fraud and illegal practices were frequently exchanged between members of SWAPO and dissidents who broke away from the governing party to form the Rally for Democracy and Progress (RDP). The former senior SWAPO members were reviled by the party, which purged its central committee of anyone whose name appeared on a list linked to the RDP (see Political Parties and Groups, below). Collaterally, in a move described as ushering in a new era in SWAPO's history, longtime SWAPO leader Sam Nujoma handed over party leadership to President Pohamba and lined up the president's likely successor by bringing former prime minister Hage Geingob back into the leadership fold as vice president of the party. Subsequently, attention in 2008 turned to the presidential and assembly elections in 2009; SWAPO initiated its campaign in April, stating its intention to increase its parliamentary seats from 55 to 71. A month earlier the elections commissioner and three of his top officials were suspended, critics claiming that now that the director was an impartial administrator, SWAPO had him removed. The elections director subsequently was reported to have joined the RDP. The dismissals led to the postponement of a local by-election that was deemed to be of special importance to SWAPO in one of its first contests against members of the breakaway RDP; however SWAPO members secured all but one of the seats in the thrice-postponed by-election.

In the run-up to the 2009 elections, President Pohamba approved in December 2008 a 24 percent salary increase for all political officeholders, and in early 2009 he granted pay increases for civil servants, a move that was seen by some analysts as a "stimulus" to the economy during the global financial downturn. In March President Pohamba received SWAPO's bid to stand for reelection as president of the republic, and the party was reported to have the support of half of the voting population, according to a recent survey. However, observers noted that a significant number of voters remained undecided, leaving open the possibility of a more widely contested election. (*See headnote.*)

Meanwhile, widespread flooding over four months in early 2009 affected more than 200,000 people, with 102 reported dead and 82,000 in need of food aid due to the huge loss of crop land and livestock, particularly in the north. The government estimated it would need $240 million to clean up after the disaster, and the UN sought urgent funds to help flood victims.

POLITICAL PARTIES AND GROUPS

Government Party:

South West Africa People's Organization of Namibia (SWAPO). Consisting mainly of Ovambos and formerly known as the Ovambo People's Organization, SWAPO was the largest and most active South West African nationalist group and was recognized prior to independence by the United Nations as the "authentic representative of the Namibian people." Founded in 1958, it issued a call for independence in 1966 and subsequently initiated guerrilla activity in the north with the support of the OAU Liberation Committee. Further operations were conducted by the party's military wing, the People's Liberation Army of Namibia (PLAN), from bases in southern Angola. A legal "internal wing" engaged in political activity within Namibia, although it was the target of arrests and other forms of intimidation by police and South African military forces. SWAPO's co-founder, Andimba TOIVO JA TOIVO, was released from 16 years' imprisonment on March 1, 1984, and was immediately elected to the organization's newly created post of secretary general. In February 1988, at what was described as the largest such meeting in the movement's history, 130 delegates representing about 30 branches of SWAPO's internal wing reaffirmed their "unwavering confidence" in the exiled leadership of Sam Nujoma and their willingness to conclude a cease-fire in accordance with implementation of the UN independence plan. Nujoma returned to Namibia for the first time since 1960 on September 14, 1989, and was elected president of the new republic by the Constituent Assembly on February 16, 1990.

At a party congress in December 1991, the first since the group's inception, delegates reelected Nujoma and Rev. Hendrik Witbooi party president and vice president, respectively, while Moses GAROËB captured the secretary generalship from Toivo ja Toivo. The congress also elected a new Central Committee (enlarged from 38 to 67 members) and adopted a revised constitution, expunging references to the PLAN and changing descriptions of the group from a "liberation movement" to a "mass political party."

In presidential and legislative balloting in December 1994 President Nujoma and SWAPO legislative candidates captured approximately 70 percent of the vote. However, some internal friction was subsequently reported between Nujoma loyalists and the party's "pragmatists" over Nujoma's allegedly heavy-handed direction of party affairs. Thereafter, in what observers described as a possible shift of power to the group's younger leaders, in April 1996 Deputy Minister of Foreign Affairs Netumbo NANDI-NDAITWAH was named party secretary general. She replaced Garoëb, who had resigned days earlier.

In May 1997, at SWAPO's second congress since independence, party delegates adopted a resolution supporting amendment of the constitution to allow Nujoma a third presidential term. In addition, SWAPO Vice President Witbooi retained his post, staving off a challenge by Prime Minister Hage Gottfried Geingob, while cabinet member and Nujoma confidante Hifikepunye Pohamba was elected secretary general.

On the eve of the extraordinary party congress of August 29–30, 1998, Ben Ulenga, Namibia's high commissioner to Britain and a SWAPO central committeeman, resigned from his overseas post to protest the plans to allow Nujoma a third term as well as the deployment of Namibian troops in the DRC. Ulenga's public denouncement of the Nujoma amendment, the first by a ranking SWAPO member, colored the late August proceedings, at which the congress rebuffed calls from party dissidents for a debate on the issue and formally approved the proposed bill. In November the party voted to suspend Ulenga, who had recently led "like-minded" colleagues in the formation of a self-described bipartisan grouping. (In early 1999 Ulenga launched the Congress of Democrats, below.)

Meanwhile, in regional council balloting in December 1998 SWAPO easily won the majority of the posts in polling marked by low voter turnout. In the legislative election in November–December 1999 the party got 76.1 percent of the vote and won 55 seats in the National Assembly, and Nujoma was reelected president with 76.8 percent of the vote.

At the August 2002 congress, the party's politburo underwent a significant change. Some analysts noted that new prime minister Theo-Ben Gurirab, new SWAPO vice president Hifikepunye Pohamba, and new secretary general Ngarikutuke Tjiriange were among the possible successors to Nujoma, who had announced in late 2001 that he would not seek a fourth presidential term.

In May 2004 Pohamba was chosen as Nujoma's successor at a party conference. Nujoma was reelected as party president for a three-year term. SWAPO was successful in the November legislative elections; Gurirab subsequently was elected speaker of the assembly, and Nahas Angula was appointed prime minister.

Party infighting erupted in 2005 after SWAPO secretary and deputy works minister Paulas KAPIA was accused in a scandal involving state funds (the opposition claimed Nujoma was involved as well; he denied the allegations). Kapia resigned his government post and his assembly seat, and was suspended from the party. Some observers suggested that it was President Pohamba who had forced the resignation of Kapia, a Nujoma protégé; subsequently, Nujoma returned Kapia to the party payroll. The rift between "Nujomaists" and backers of former foreign minister Hidipo HAMUTENYA, who took over Kapia's assembly seat, deepened after Jesaya NYAMU, a leading party member for some 40 years (and loyal to Hamutenya), was dismissed from the party in late 2005 for alleged "serious misconduct." The vote to oust him reportedly divided the party between backers of Nujoma and Hamutenya, with some observers speculating that Hamutenya might throw his support to Pohamba in an effort to remove Nujoma from the party presidency.

Nujoma retained party leadership in 2006, despite accusations by some party officials that the elections were fraudulent. Tensions increased in 2007, the rival factions now including those who backed Pohamba, in addition to supporters of Nujoma and Hamutenya. Because of the fractured party and lack of support from many cabinet ministers still loyal to Nujoma, observers said Pohamba was unable to lead the country effectively. Pohamba's uncertain status in the party contributed to the postponement of the next congress from midyear to November 2007. By the time the congress convened, however, Nujoma had decided to give up his party position after decades at the helm and to withdraw from active politics, thus handing off control to Pohamba (and to a slate of party officers tapped by Nujoma). The congress was also notable for the absence of party cofounder Toivo ja Toivo from the party's central committee, along with other high-ranking party members. (Though Toivo ja Toiva had been rumored at the time to have joined a new party started by Hamutenya and other dissidents—the Rally for Democracy and Progress—he denied it.) Reportedly, the list of breakaway RDP members had somehow been supplied to SWAPO, resulting in a great deal of acrimony toward the dissidents and the purge of the party's central committee in a scheme engineered by Nujoma to reward SWAPO loyalists. Collaterally, the startup of the RDP (see below) coincided with the election of the new SWAPO slate, including former prime minister Hage Geingob as the party's vice president. Pohamba was elected as party president, with Geingob, a political moderate, described as the likely successor to Pohamba as Namibia's president. (Geingob subsequently was given a ministerial post in 2008.) The party also elected its first female secretary general, justice minister Pendukeni Iivula-Ithana.

In the run-up to a by-election in the newly incorporated town of Omuthiya in early 2008, Pohamba called for a boycott of businesses owned by RDP members. SWAPO also postponed the by-election for several months, reportedly to fend off an initial electoral victory for the RDP, but also due to the dismissal of the elections commissioner over unspecified irregularities. SWAPO ultimately won the poll with a reported 90 percent of the vote.

In 2008 the elections director, Philemon KANIME, who had been a member of SWAPO for nearly 50 years, was suspended from his job (and subsequently not reappointed) after he had been accused of illegally registering the new RDP (below). Kanime then joined the RDP.

In 2009 SWAPO denied allegations of violence against the APP (below). In February the party suspended three members who were allegedly involved with the RDP. In March the party nominated President Pohamba as its standard-bearer in the presidential elections slated for November, despite what were described as "behind the scenes" attempts to oust him. (*See headnote.*)

Leaders: Hifikepunye POHAMBA (President of the Republic and Party President), Hage GEINGOB (Former Prime Minister and Party Vice President), Theo-Ben GURIRAB (Speaker of the National Assembly), Rev. Hendrik WITBOOI, Nangolo MBUMBA (Deputy Secretary General), Pendukeni IIVULA-ITHANA (Secretary General).

Other Legislative Parties:

DTA of Namibia. The grouping known as the Democratic Turnhalle Alliance (DTA) until adoption of the abbreviated form in November 1991 was launched in the wake of the Turnhalle Conference as a multiracial coalition of European, coloured, and African groups. Advocating a constitutional arrangement that would provide for equal ethnic representation, the DTA obtained an overwhelming majority (41 of 50 seats) in the Constituent Assembly balloting of December 4–8, 1978, and was instrumental in organizing the Multi-Party Conference in 1983. Its core formations were the white-based Republican Party (RP), organized in October 1977 by dissident members of the then-dominant South West Africa National Party (SWANP), and the Herero-based National United Democratic Organization (NUDO), which had long advocated a federal solution as a means of opposing SWAPO domination. (For a list of other groups participating in the formation of the DTA, see the 1999 *Handbook.*)

At a Central Committee meeting on November 30, 1991, DTA officials announced the transformation of the coalition into an integrated political party. The committee also reelected the party leaders to permanent positions, adopted a new constitution, and announced that the group would thenceforth be known as the DTA of Namibia.

An intraparty chasm between former RP leader Dirk MUDGE and a faction led by party president Mishake MUYONGO and information secretary Andrew MATJILA widened in the wake of the DTA of Namibia's poor showing in regional and local council elections in November–December 1992. At a central committee meeting in February 1993, the Muyongo faction pressed Mudge to resign, arguing that his former ties to South Africa had contributed to the party's loss of electoral support from all but small-town whites and the Herero and Caprivi communities. In April Mudge announced that he would be vacating his parliamentary seat, insisting that he had made the decision for purely personal reasons and would retain the DTA of Namibia chair. In mid-1994 Matjila broke with the party, and less than a year later Mudge resigned his party post and bowed out of politics. Thereafter, in balloting in December, Muyongo secured only 23 percent of the presidential vote, while the party's parliamentary representation fell to 15 seats, the DTA of Namibia claiming that there had been widespread voting irregularities.

On August 25, 1998, the DTA of Namibia's Executive Committee suspended Muyongo from the party presidency and named Vice President Katuutire Kaura interim party leader after Muyongo called for the secession of the Caprivi Strip region from Namibia. Muyongo subsequently assumed control of the militant Caprivi Liberation Movement (see CLF, under Illegal Groups, below).

The legislative elections on November 30–December 1, 1999, proved nearly disastrous for the DTA of Namibia as the party secured less than half the seats it had won in 1994, winning only 9.5 percent of the vote and 7 seats in the National Assembly. In the presidential election, Kaura received 9.6 percent of the vote. In early April 2000 the DTA of Namibia and the UDF formed an opposition coalition when the negotiations with the CoD broke down.

The DTA of Namibia won 4 seats in the 2004 legislative elections while its presidential candidate, again Kaura, placed third with 5.2 percent of the vote. The defections of DTA of Namibia members to the RP and NUDO hurt the party most in the December Regional Council elections, where voters split among the three parties, giving SWAPO its greatest success ever in such balloting. The DTA of Namibia secured 2 seats in the 2004 legislative balloting.

In 2005 Katuutire Kaura was elected party president, and Alois Gende won the post of secretary general over McHenry Venaani, 27, who had also challenged Kaura for the party presidency. Early in 2007 the DTA proposed a "grand coalition" of opposition parties, a notion that did not interest the RP, CoD or NUDO.

Venaani, a member of parliament, announced in March 2008 that he would not contest any party office at the central committee meeting to be held later in the year, citing his desire to keep the party unified. Rifts had begun to develop after constituents in the Kavango region called for Kaura to step down and expressed their support for Venaani. Two months earlier, party stalwart Rudolf KAMBURONA resigned from the DTA after 32 years, saying he wanted to concentrate on farming, rejecting speculation that he was going to join the RDP (below). Meanwhile, observers noted growing dissatisfaction within the party with Kaura's leadership. Nevertheless, Kaura was reelected along with other party leaders at the DTA congress in November 2008, the only surprise being the election of Venaani as secretary general, according to observers.

In January 2009 some tribal members claimed that the government had refused drought aid to tribe members who belonged to parties other than SWAPO. The government denied the allegations. Venaani also demanded that the agencies that distributed the food stop claiming that the relief came directly from SWAPO.

Leaders: Katuutire KAURA (President and 2004 presidential candidate), Johan DE WAAL, Philemon MOONGO (Vice President), Willem de KLERK, McHenry VENAANI (Secretary General).

United Democratic Front (UDF). The UDF is led by Justus Garoëb, longtime head of the **Damara Council,** which withdrew from the MPC in March 1984; chair of the group was Reggie DIERGAARDT, leader of the **Labour Party,** a largely coloured group that was expelled from the DTA in 1982 but participated in the MPC subsequent to its November 1983 meeting. Two small leftist groups were also Front members: the **Communist Party of Namibia** (CPN) and the Trotskyist **Workers' Revolutionary Party** (WRP). The UDF ran a distant third in the November 1989 election, winning four assembly seats. In balloting during November–December 1992 the party was unable to lessen the gap between itself and the two major parties, capturing only 1 of 13 regional council seats.

In a November 1993 action opposed by other clan chiefs, UDF president Garoëb was enthroned as the king of Damara. Thereafter, observers attributed Garoëb's failure to participate in the December 1994 presidential balloting, despite a pledge to the contrary, to the UDF's poor financial condition. Meanwhile, the party, securing only 2 percent of the vote, lost two of its 4 assembly seats.

In late 1998 a UDF spokesperson denounced SWAPO's legislative efforts to grant Nujoma a third term. The UDF won 2 seats in the 1999 National Assembly election, while Garoëb secured 3 percent of the vote in the presidential poll.

In the 2004 presidential balloting Garoëb gained 3.8 percent of the vote, and the UDF won 3 seats in the assembly.

The UDF, along with several other opposition parties, was unsuccessful in calling for postponement of by-elections in one constituency in 2008 because of alleged irregularities.

Leaders: Justus GAROËB (King of Damara, President of the Party, and 2004 presidential candidate), Eric BIWA (Chair).

Congress of Democrats (CoD). The CoD was launched in March 1999 by former SWAPO stalwart Ben Ulenga, who had been suspended by SWAPO in 1998 after he criticized efforts to permit President Nujoma to run for a third term and had formed a grouping styled Forum for the Future. Included in the CoD's platform were calls for a smaller cabinet and the withdrawal of Namibian troops from the DRC. The CoD won 9.9 percent of the votes in the legislative elections held on November 30–December 1, 1999. It won 7 seats in the National Assembly and became the official parliamentary opposition, supplanting the DTA of Namibia. Ulenga received 10.5 percent of the vote in the presidential election.

The CoD lost support in the 2004 elections; Ulenga only received 7.34 percent of the presidential vote while the party fell to 5 seats. Factionalism within the party was reported in 2007, with some members continuing to call for new leadership following failed party elections in May. The election was declared void due to fraud and other irregularities (Ulenga defeated his challenger by 14 votes). Though Ulenga said he would step down based on what had happened during the party election, he apparently retained the leadership post amid the discord. Ignatius Shixwameni, leader of the main faction within the CoD and the party's secretary general, formed a splinter group that broke away in late 2007 and became the basis for the new All People's Party (see below).

Kala GERTZE, one of the CoD's founding members and its secretary general from 2004–2007, died from asthma in March 2008. Infighting continued through July 2008, despite a High Court ruling that the party hold a congress in five months. The court subsequently ruled that if the two factions could not agree on a chairperson to oversee the party's elections, the Law Society of Namibia would appoint a candidate. Ultimately, Ulenga retained his post as party president, defeating Nora SCHIMMING-CHASE, a faction leader and the party's former vice president, in balloting at a party congress in November. Elma Dienda, an assembly member who reportedly was a Schimming-Chase supporter, was elected party treasurer.

Leaders: Ben ULENGA (President and 2004 presidential candidate), Elma DIENDA (Treasurer), Gretchen BOOIS (Deputy Secretary General), Tsudao GURIRAB (Secretary General).

Monitor Action Group (MAG). A conservative, predominantly white grouping, the MAG won 1 assembly seat in December 1994. The MAG received 0.7 percent of the vote in the legislative election on November 30–December 1, 1999, and won one seat in the National Assembly.

In the 2004 polls Jacobus Pretorius received 1.2 percent of the presidential vote, while the party retained its single seat in the assembly.

A proposal by the MAG in 2007 that all opposition parties consider uniting behind one candidate in the 2009 presidential election was met with "guarded, lukewarm and even slightly hostile" responses from other parties, according to *Africa Confidential.*

Leaders: Jacobus W. F. ("Kosie") PRETORIUS (Party Chair and 2004 presidential candidate), Jurgie VILJOEN.

National Unity Democratic Organization (NUDO). Led by the Herero High Chief, Kuaima Riruako, former members of NUDO left the DTA of Namibia (and his seat in parliament) in 2003 to reestablish their Herero-based party. In the 2004 elections, NUDO secured 4.79 percent of the vote and 3 seats in the assembly. Riruako came in third with 5.2 percent of the vote in the presidential poll. Party leader Chief Kuaima Riruako resigned his National Assembly seat on February 1, 2008, saying he wanted to "focus his energies on other matters," including recruiting more supporters for NUDO across the country. He retained his post as party chair.

In January 2009 a youth leader in the party called on the government to make an early announcement of the dates of the presidential and legislative elections, rather than waiting until the customary two months ahead of time, to give candidates and parties time to adequately prepare.

Leaders: Chief Kuaima RIRUAKO (Party Chair and 2004 presidential candidate), Tumbee TJOMBE (Vice President), Asser MBAI (Secretary General).

Republican Party (RP). Originally part of the DTA, the RP was reestablished as an independent party in 2003 under the leadership of Henk Mudge, the son of Dirk Mudge, the leader of the former Republican Party within the DTA. The conservative RP won 1.9 percent of the vote in the 2004 elections and gained a seat in the assembly for the first time. In addition, the younger Mudge ran as a presidential candidate; he came in fifth with 1.95 percent of the vote. Secretary General Carola ENGELBRECHT was dismissed in 2005 for allegedly discussing the party's internal affairs in public.

Joseph Kauandenge, formerly of the DMC and NMIC (below), was reported in 2005 to be an adviser to RP president Henk Mudge.

In October 2008 the party claimed that four of its members, including Vice Chair Clara Gowases, were illegally arrested for distributing flyers urging voters to boycott an upcoming regional by-election. The party members were released after a few hours. The party subsequently boycotted the by-election.

Leaders: Henk MUDGE (President and 2004 presidential candidate), Clara GOWASES (Vice Chair), Cap GAESEB (Acting Secretary General).

Other Parties Participating in the 2004 Legislative Elections:

Namibia Democratic Movement of Change (DMC). Established by former DTA of Namibia member Frans Goagoseb, the DMC received 0.53 percent of the vote in the 2004 legislative poll. The party-hopping Joseph Kauandenge, who at one time was a youth leader for the DTA and subsequently was a member of NUDO, was said in 2005 to be an adviser to the RP's president (above). However, in June 2007 he was reported to have joined the DMC and was elected secretary general.

Leaders: Frans GOAGOSEB (President), Joseph KAUANDENGE (Secretary General).

South West Africa National Union (SWANU). Formerly coordinating many of its activities with SWAPO's internal wing, the Herero-supported SWANU joined with the Damara Council and a number of smaller groups to form a multiracial coalition in support of the Western "contact group" solution to the Namibian problem. SWANU's president, Moses KATJIOUNGUA, participated in the 1983 MPC meeting and in September 1984 was reported to have been replaced as party leader by Kuzeeko Kangueehi, who indicated that the group would leave the MPC, with a view to possible merger with SWAPO. In October, on the other hand, Katjioungua was again identified as holding the presidency, with Kangueehi described as the leader of a dissident faction (subsequently styled SWANU-Left). The incumbent's anti-SWAPO orientation was reflected by his inclusion in the "national unity" cabinet of 1985. A founding member of the Democratic Coalition of Namibia (DCN), SWANU abruptly dropped out of the grouping in November 1994 while Katjioungua stayed within the DCN. SWANU formed an electoral alliance with the **Workers' Revolutionary Party** (below), which received less than 0.5 percent of the vote in the legislative election on November 30–December 1, 1999.

SWANU secured less than 1 percent of the vote in the 2004 legislative elections.

At the party's congress in November 2007, Usutuaije Maamberua, a former finance secretary, was elected party president. In recent years the party has been campaigning for reparations from Germany for alleged atrocities committed under German rule more than 100 years ago, similar to reparations paid to Jewish people who suffered at the hands of the Nazis.

In advance of the 2009 parliamentary elections, SWANU presented its ten-point platform in February, calling for a "socialist, transformationist, revolutionary approach" to government.

Leaders: Usutuaije MAAMBERUA (President), Dr. Rihupisa KANDANDO (National Chair), Kuzeeko KANGUEEHI, Hitjevi Gerson VEII, Tangeni IYAMBO (Secretary General).

Other Parties and Groups:

Rally for Democracy and Progress (RDP). One of three parties formed within months of each other in the run-up to the 2009 elections, the RDP was established on November 17, 2007, as a result of rifts within SWAPO. Former senior SWAPO members, including Hidipo HAMUTENYA and Jesaya Nyamu, both former ministers, and Kandi Hehova, a former chair of SWAPO's National Council, launched the party with pledges to eradicate poverty and unemployment and improve health and education services, areas in which they believed SWAPO had failed to make significant progress. They denied some analysts' description of RDP as a tribal party.

Another factor that observers said led to the formation of the new party was Hamutenya's dismissal from his ministerial post following his having contested the SWAPO presidency in 2004 against Pohamba. Hamutenya had been a SWAPO loyalist for 46 years, having served on SWAPO's central committee for 30 years.

In its first electoral test in a local by-election in April 2008, the party fared poorly; SWAPO won overwhelmingly. Another by-election in the new town of Omuthiya, which had been scheduled for February 2008, was postponed until late April, observers saying that SWAPO was trying to postpone a likely RDP victory. SWAPO did not want the RDP to win in its first contest (see SWAPO, above). Following a large RDP rally in July, the by-election was postponed again until September, the RDP winning only one seat while SWAPO won the remaining six. Observers described the defeat as a serious blow to the RDP, since most of its leaders are from Omuthiya and its surrounding regions. Subsequently, the RDP, alleging "political anarchy," called on the government to resign and hold early elections. Violence broke out in another constituency in November, when hundreds of SWAPO supporters allegedly prevented the RDP from holding a rally and several reportedly were beaten.

At the party's congress in December 2008, former foreign minister Hidipo Hamutenya, who had been dismissed by President Nujoma in 2004, was elected party president.

Leaders: Hidipo HAMUTENYA (President), Steve BEZULDENHOUT (Vice Chair), Kandi HEHOVA, Jesaya NYAMU (Secretary General).

All People's Party (APP). Licensed on January 22, 2008, the APP was established ahead of the 2009 elections by former minister and former CoD secretary general Ignatius Shixwameni and his brother, Herbert Shixwameni, following the former's leadership dispute with CoD president Ben Ulenga. Other members were said to be defectors from SWAPO, DTA, and NUDO, with the party's stronghold in the northern Kavango region. The stated goals were to unite a broad, national base in a "truly democratic party" and to fight to wipe out poverty, unemployment, and inequality. If successful in presidential elections, the leaders pledged to set up a welfare state, providing free education and access to decent housing.

The party's first rally, held in March 2008, was reported to be a "huge success," with thousands attending in the Kavango region.

Leaders: Ignatius SHIXWAMENI (Interim Chair), Herbert SHIXWAMENI, Stephanus SWARTBOOI (Interim Deputy Chair), Portia KONDOMBOLO, Linus MUCHILA, Hildegade HAMBIRA.

Democratic Party of Namibia (DPN). Formed in July 2008 by Solomon Dawid Isaacs, a former SWAMU member who lived in exile from the 1960s to 1978, the party's stated mission is to address the marginalization of minority groups, particularly in the south. Isaacs said the DPN supports equal distribution of wealth and redistribution of land or "regaining" ancestral lands.

Leader: Solomon Dawid ISAACS (Interim Chair).

Workers' Revolutionary Party (WRP). The Trotskyite WRP was formed in 1989 and was part of the UDF. The WRP contested the 1994 legislative election and received 0.19 percent of the vote. For the 1999 balloting, the WRP formed an electoral alliance with SWANU (above).

In November 2007 party leader Hewat Beukes harshly criticized insurance companies following alleged racist comments and other complaints about firms' profits allegedly made at the expense of the poor, during a public parliamentary hearing on insurance firms in Namibia.

Leaders: Werner MAMUGWE, Hewat BEUKES.

Federal Convention of Namibia (FCN). Strongly opposed to the UN independence plan, the FCN was organized by J. G. A. (Hans) DIERGAARDT, a former minister of local government and leader of the **Rehoboth Free Democratic Party** (*Rehoboth Bevryder Demokratiese Party*—RBDP). The RBDP was an outgrowth of the former Rehoboth Liberation Front (RLF), which endorsed the partition of Namibia along ethnic lines and obtained 1 assembly seat in 1978 as representative of part of the Baster community, composed of Afrikaans-speaking people with European customs. The RFDP was an original member of the MPC but in 1987 joined the SWANP in opposing the draft constitution endorsed by other transitional government members. However, following the Constituent Assembly election in 1989, in which the party secured one seat, FCN members subsequently participated on the team that drafted the new constitution.

In 1994 the FCN chose former Women's Party (WP) leader Hileni LATVIO as its presidential candidate; however, Latvio failed to register her candidacy by the appropriate date and was denied an extension. The FCN won less than 0.5 percent of the vote in the 1999 legislative elections and won no seats. Diergaardt, party chair, died in 1998 at age 70.

Namibia Movement for Independent Candidates (NMIC). The NMIC was launched in July 1997 on a platform stressing the need to incorporate Namibian youths into the political process. In September 1998 NMIC became affiliated with the DTA of Namibia (above). Party leader Joseph Kauandenge subsequently had a leading role in several parties, most recently in the DMC and RP (above).

Illegal Groups:

Caprivi Liberation Front (CLF). Formed in 1994, the CLF has sought autonomy or independence for the Caprivi Strip, a narrow portion of northern Namibia that juts about 250 miles into central Africa, touching the borders of Angola, Botswana, Zambia, and Zimbabwe. The strip, theretofore part of the British protectorate of Bechuanaland (subsequently Botswana), was ceded to Germany, colonial ruler of South West Africa, in 1890 as part of a land swap that included Britain's assumption of control in Zanzibar. The region is part of the former ancestral kingdom of Barotseland, which also included portions of Zambia, Botswana, and Zimbabwe. In the 1970s and 1980s the strip was used by South African forces as a base for military activities against independence fighters in Namibia as well as against the Angolan government.

In 1998 the Namibian government reported that a security sweep had uncovered training bases in Caprivi for the CLF-affiliated Caprivi Liberation Army (CLA). Several thousand Caprivians subsequently fled to Botswana, including Mishake Muyongo, the CLF/CLA leader who been dismissed from both SWAPO and the DTA of Namibia for his secessionist sentiments. In early August 1999 a small group of alleged CLA members attacked security locations in the town of Katima Mulilo, the fighting leaving at least 16 dead. The insurgents were quickly routed, but the Namibian government declared a state of emergency in the region for three weeks and implemented what critics described as a heavy-handed crackdown that allegedly included the abuse of detainees. Among the factors reportedly fueling antigovernment sentiment among Caprivians (primarily from the Lozi ethnic group) is the political and economic dominance of Ovambos in Namibia.

In August 2007 ten men, all Namibian citizens, including CLF leader Mishake Muyongo, were found guilty of high treason in the 1999 attempt to overthrow the government in the Caprivi region and establish a separate state. The men were among alleged CLA members who crossed the border into Angola in 1998 to obtain arms, returning to CLA training camps in northern Namibia, according to the government. All of the men, claiming they were not Namibian, refused to recognize the court's authority. They were sentenced to prison terms ranging from 30 to 32 years, and all ten appealed their convictions. (Two other men accused in the same case were acquitted in June 2007.) In February 2009, police arrested Albius Moto LISELI, who they claimed was an associate of Muyongo and a participant in the insurgency. He was also charged with high treason. Another leader in the secessionist movement, John MABUKU, who had fled with Muyongo, died in exile in Botswana in 2008.

Leader: Mishake MUYONGO (under asylum in Denmark).

United Democratic Party (UDP). The UDP (with the CLA as its military wing) was founded in 1985 by Mishake Muyongo. The UDP, subsequently led by Crispin Matongo following his resignation from the CoD, was affiliated with the DTA until 1999. Matongo, who had been banned from Namibia, returned in 1990 and served as the country's prison commissioner for six years. After his retirement in 1996 he became chair of the UDP, which shared the CLF's goal of self-rule for the Caprivi Strip. In 2006 Matongo, a cousin of Muyongo, tried to revive the UDP. However, in September the government declared the UDP illegal and banned it from holding any meetings in the country.

Leader: Crispin MATONGO.

LEGISLATURE

The Namibian **Parliament** consists of an indirectly elected National Council and a National Assembly whose voting members are directly elected.

National Council. The largely advisory upper house is a 26-member body containing 2 members from each of 13 regional councils; the term of office is six years. The national body launched its first session on May 11, 1993, following regional and local elections on November 29–December 4, 1992 After SWAPO gained control of 12 of the 13 regional councils in balloting on November 30–December 1, 2004, the distribution of seats in the National Council was as follows: South West Africa People's Organization of Namibia, 24; the Democratic Turnhalle Alliance of Namibia, 1; and the United Democratic Front, 1.

President: Asser Kuveri KAPERE.

National Assembly. The 72 members of the current lower house were initially elected on November 7–11, 1989, to the Namibian Constituent Assembly, which at independence assumed the functions of an ordinary legislature with a five-year mandate. Following the most recent balloting of November 15–16, 2004, the distribution of seats was as follows: the South West Africa People's Organization of Namibia, 55; the Congress of Democrats, 5; the Democratic Turnhalle Alliance of Namibia, 4; the National Unity Democratic Organization, 3; the United Democratic Front, 3; the Republican Party, 1; and the Monitor Action Group, 1. In addition to the elected members, up to 6 nonvoting members may be named by the president. (*See headnote.*)

Speaker: Dr. Theo-Ben GURIRAB.

CABINET

[as of May 1, 2009] (*see headnote*)

Prime Minister	Nahas Angula
Deputy Prime Minister	Dr. Libertina Amathila [f]
Ministers	
Agriculture, Water, and Rural Development	John Mutorwa
Attorney General (interim)	Albert Kawana
Defense	Maj. Gen. Charles Namoloh
Education	Nangolo Mbumba
Environment and Tourism	Netumbo-Nandi Ndaitwah [f]
Finance	Saara Kuugongelwa-Amathilia [f]
Fisheries and Marine Resources	Abraham Iyambo
Foreign Affairs	Marco Hausiku
Health and Social Services	Richard Kamwi
Home Affairs and Immigration	Rosalia Nghidinwa [f]
Information and Communication Technology	Joel Kaapanda
Justice	Pendukeni Iivula-Ithana [f]
Labor	Immanuel Ngatjizeko
Lands, Resettlement, and Rehabilitation	Alpheus Naruseb
Mines and Energy	Errki Nghimtina
Presidential Affairs	Albert Kawana
Regional and Local Government and Housing	Jerry Ekandjo
Safety and Security	Nickey Iyambo
Trade and Industry	Hage Geingob
Veterans Affairs	Ngarikutuke Tjiriange
Women's Affairs and Child Welfare	Marlene Mungunda [f]
Works and Transport	Helmut Angula
Youth, Sport, and Culture	Willem Konjore

[f] = female

COMMUNICATIONS

Although there are generally few restrictions on the press, in 2001 the government forbade state agencies and institutions from advertising or purchasing *The Namibian* in response to articles that were critical of the government. The watchdog group Reporters Without Borders has described Namibia as "one of the African countries that most respect freedom."

In March 2009 opposition parties claimed that the government's cancellation of a call-in talk show was the beginning of a crackdown on the media in advance of legislative elections later in the year. It was reported that the show's cancellation "appeared to be a reaction to" the opposition Rally for Democracy and Progress—RDP.

Press. The following newspapers are English dailies published in Windhoek, unless otherwise noted: *New Era* (25,000), weekly; *Die Republikein* (12,000), DTA organ in Afrikaans, English, and German; *The Namibian* (11,000); *Windhoek Observer* (10,000), weekly; *Allgemeine Zeitung* (5,000), in German; *Windhoek Advertiser,* daily (5,000); *Namibia Economist; Namibia News; Namibia Today,* pro-SWAPO; *Tempo,* weekly; *Namib Times,* biweekly, published in Walvis Bay; *The New Era,* government biweekly; and the regional *Caprivi Vision.* In 2005 former Namibian president Nujoma sued *The Namibian* for $658,000 over allegations the newspaper had implicated him in a financial scandal. Media observers said Nujoma's suit was a "blatant attempt to muzzle the media" and could result in the demise of the paper if Nujoma won. As of mid-2008 the status of the case remained unclear.

News agencies. A Namibian Press Agency (Nampa) was launched by SWAPO in November 1987; the Italian-based Inter Press Service (IPS) and the South African Press Association maintain offices in Windhoek.

Broadcasting and computing. The Namibian Broadcasting Company (NBC), formerly the South West Africa Broadcasting Company (SWABC), is accountable to the Ministry of Information and Broadcasting, although with a mandate to operate as an independent service. However, in October 2002 President Nujoma ordered the NBC to stop broadcasting foreign programs. In addition, during the 2004 elections opposition parties charged that the NBC provided the government party, SWAPO, with a disproportionate share of airtime and refused some requests to broadcast opposition advertisements. Radio broadcasts, which commenced in 1979, are transmitted over eight channels in 11 regional languages; television service, initiated in 1981, broadcasts in English, with a commitment to add ethnic languages when feasible. The country's first private commercial radio station commenced operation in April 1994. As of 2008 there were 53.3 Internet users per 1,000 inhabitants.

INTERGOVERNMENTAL REPRESENTATION

Ambassador to the U.S.: Patrick NANDAGO.

U.S. Ambassador to Namibia: Gail Dennise MATHIEU.

Permanent Representative to the UN: Kaire Munionganda MBUENDE.

IGO Memberships (Non-UN): AfDB, AU, Comesa, CWTH, Interpol, NAM, SADC, WCO, WTO.

NAURU

Republic of Nauru
Naoero

Political Status: Independent republic since January 31, 1968; special membership in the Commonwealth changed to full membership on May 1, 1999.

Area: 8.2 sq. mi. (21.3 sq. km.).

Population: 9,919 (1992C); 10,000 (2008E). At the time of the 1983 census, only 4,964 of 8,042 inhabitants were declared to be native Nauruans.

Major Urban Centers: None; the *Domaneab* ("meeting place of the people"), which is the site of the Nauru Local Government Council, is located in Uaboe District, while government offices are located in Yaren District.

Official Languages: English, Nauruan.

Monetary Unit: Australian Dollar (market rate December 1, 2009: 1.08 dollars = $1US).

President: Marcus STEPHEN; elected by Parliament on December 19, 2007, succeeding Ludwig SCOTTY; returned to office following legislative election of April 26, 2008.

THE COUNTRY

An isolated coral island in the west-central Pacific, Nauru is located just south of the equator between the Marshall and Solomon Islands. The present population consists of some 60 percent indigenous Nauruans (a mixture of Micronesian, Melanesian, and Polynesian stocks), 25 percent other Pacific islanders, 8 percent Chinese, and 7 percent Australians and other Caucasians. Habitation is mainly confined to a fertile strip of land ringing a central plateau composed of very high-grade phosphate deposits. For several decades this mineral wealth yielded one of the world's highest per capita incomes, which, however, declined from a peak of over $17,000 in 1975 to scarcely more than $8,000 a decade later. For 1998, the UN estimated annual GDP per capita at under $3,000, and the overall GDP continued its decline. According to the government, 1999 saw a recovery, with estimated growth of 3 percent, but the rate of expansion in 2000 dropped to under 1 percent, and in April 2004 Nauru sought Australian help to avoid bankruptcy.

Income from the government-owned Nauru Phosphate Company was intended to provide an investment fund against the time, originally thought to be around 2010, when the phosphate deposits would be exhausted. However, a variety of difficulties, including widespread fiscal mismanagement, led to drastic depletion of the fund. To compensate, Nauru turned to offshore banking accounts, which, however, led to accusations by the Organization for Economic Cooperation and Development (OECD) and others that it had become a center for tax evasion and money laundering, and on March 27, 2003, Parliament passed legislation abolishing the practice (see Current issues, below).

GOVERNMENT AND POLITICS

Political background. A former German colony, Nauru became a British League of Nations mandate in 1919, with Australia as the administering power. The Japanese occupied the island during World War II and transported most of the inhabitants to Truk, where fewer than two-thirds survived the hardships of forced labor. In 1947 Nauru was made a UN Trust Territory under joint administration of the United Kingdom, Australia, and New Zealand, with Australia again serving as de facto administering authority. Local self-government was gradually accelerated, and in 1966 elections were held for members of a Legislative Council with jurisdiction over all matters except defense, external affairs, and the phosphate industry. Pursuant to the council's request for full independence, Australia adopted the Nauru Independence Act in November 1967, and the trusteeship agreement was formally terminated by the United Nations, effective January 31, 1968. The arrangements for independence were negotiated by a delegation led by Hammer DeROBURT, who had been head chief of Nauru since 1956 and who became the new republic's first president by legislative designation on May 18, 1968. Relations with the Commonwealth were defined by an agreement announced on November 29, 1968, whereby Nauru became a "special member" entitled to full participation in the organization's activities, except meetings of the Commonwealth heads of government. President DeRoburt, reelected in 1971 and 1973, was replaced by Bernard DOWIYOGO following a legislative election in December 1976.

Although reconfirmed following a parliamentary election in November 1977, Dowiyogo resigned in January 1978 because of a deadlock over budgetary legislation. Immediately reelected, Dowiyogo resigned again in mid-April after the opposition had blocked passage of a bill dealing with phosphate royalties. He was succeeded by Lagumot HARRIS, who in turn resigned on May 11 because of an impasse on an appropriations bill. Harris was succeeded, on the same day, by former president DeRoburt, apparently as the result of a temporary defection by an opposition representative.

The remarkable spectacle of three presidents in one month was accompanied by intense debate on the economic future of Nauru upon exhaustion of its phosphate deposits. Exports of the commodity had been declining for several years, and both public and private groups had engaged in substantial overseas investment, including a retail and office complex on Saipan in the Marianas and a 53-story office building in Melbourne, Australia.

DeRoburt was reelected in 1980 and 1983 but was forced to yield office to Kennan Ranibok ADEANG during a ten-day loss of his parliamentary majority in October 1986 and for a four-day period in the wake of an election on December 6. He was sworn in for a ninth term on January 27, 1987, following redesignation by a new parliament elected three days earlier.

DeRoburt again fell victim to a no-confidence vote on August 17, 1989, Kenas AROI being designated his successor. However, Aroi was obliged to resign on December 12 to seek medical treatment in Australia, and Dowiyogo returned for a third time as chief executive.

Legislative balloting on November 15, 1992, yielded a standoff between supporters of President Dowiyogo and Beraro DETUDAMO, a protégé of former president DeRoburt, who had died on July 15. After intense negotiations, Dowiyogo succeeded in forging a ten-member coalition of the nominally independent members.

On November 22, 1995, following a legislative poll the day before, Parliament reelected former president Lagumont Harris over Dowiyogo by a 9–8 vote. However, Dowiyogo was reappointed by Parliament on November 7, 1996, only to be ousted himself on November 26 in favor of Adeang, who in turn lost a confidence motion soon thereafter, prompting the appointment of Reuben KUN as acting president. Following new legislative elections on February 8, 1997, Kinza CLODUMAR, a former finance minister, was appointed president on February 12. He was ousted by a no-confidence vote on June 17, 1998, and succeeded by Dowiyogo, who assumed office for a fifth term. Dowiyogo himself lost a no-confidence motion on April 27, 1999, and was succeeded by René HARRIS, a member of Parliament since 1977 and former head of Nauru's national phosphate corporation.

President Harris was reelected following legislative balloting on April 8, 2000, but was obliged to resign on April 19 because of factional differences, with Dowiyogo being returned to office on April 20. Dowiyogo's sixth term in office ended with passage of a no-confidence motion on March 30, 2001, at which time René Harris resumed the presidency.

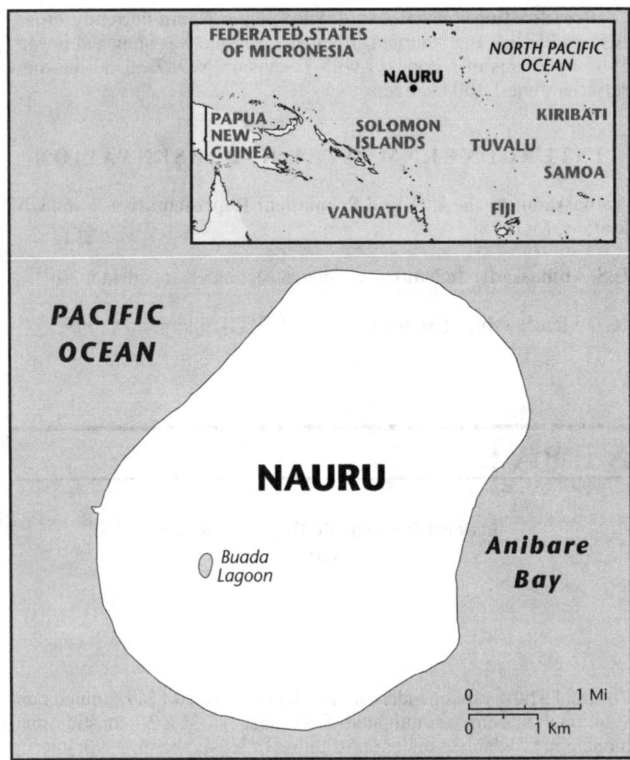

Harris was defeated in a no-confidence vote on January 8, 2003, with Dowiyogo sworn in as his successor the following day. However, the Nauru Supreme Court (sitting in Australia) ruled that the vote for Dowiyogo was invalid because it had been called without the presence of Harris and his ministers. With the Harris group in attendance, the vote was split 9–9. Following a period of confusion that included Harris's return to the presidency for one day, Dowiyogo defeated Clodumar on a 9–8 vote and was reinvested on January 20. However, he died after undergoing heart surgery in Washington, D.C., on March 20 and was succeeded on an acting basis by Derog GIOURA.

Another general election was held on May 3, 2003, and on May 29 Ludwig SCOTTY was installed as president. On August 8 Scotty was ousted and replaced by Harris; however, on June 22, 2004, Harris was in turn replaced by Scotty. On October 1, Scotty dissolved Parliament and in the ensuing general election on October 23 was accorded a new majority that permitted his reinvestiture. Scotty was again reconfirmed on August 28, 2007, following an early legislative poll on August 24, but he lost a no-confidence vote on December 18 and was succeeded the following day by Marcus STEPHEN. (René Harris died of a heart attack on July 4, 2008.)

President Stephen, after declaring a state of emergency because of a parliamentary impasse, survived a snap election on April 26, 2008, and was reinvested on April 28.

Constitution and government. Nauru's constitution, adopted by an elected Constitutional Convention on January 29, 1968, and amended on May 17 of the same year, provides for a republic whose president combines the functions of head of state and chief of government. The unicameral Parliament, consisting of 18 members popularly elected for three-year terms (assuming no dissolution), selects the president from among its membership; the president in turn appoints a number of legislators to serve as a cabinet that is responsible to Parliament and is obligated to resign as a body in the event of a no-confidence vote.

The island is administratively divided into 14 districts, which are regrouped into 8 districts for electoral purposes. An elected Local Government Council of nine members (one of whom is designated Head Chief) shares administrative responsibilities with Parliament.

In April 2007 voters went to the polls to elect members of a constitutional convention that would debate the findings of an Independent Commission on Constitutional Review appointed a year earlier to assess the country's 39-year-old basic law. In its report, the commission recommended that the president be popularly elected, that the legislative speaker not be a member of Parliament, that a Public Service Commission be established, that an independent director of audit be appointed, and that judicial appeals to the High Court of Australia be abolished. After acceptance by the convention, the recommendations were reviewed in early 2009 by a parliamentary Select Committee, which submitted its report for further debate the following June. Final action by the electorate was expected in late 2009.

Foreign relations. Nauru maintains formal diplomatic relations with about a dozen foreign governments, primarily through representatives accredited to Australia and Fiji. In January 1998, on the 30th anniversary of Nauru's independence, President Clodumar announced that the country would apply for membership in the United Nations. (A formal request was issued in April 1999 with admittance to the world body in September.) Long a member of the UN Economic and Social Commission for Asia and the Pacific and of the South Pacific Forum (SPF, now the Pacific Islands Forum), Nauru acceded in August 1982 to the South Pacific Regional Trade Agreement (Sparteca), under which Australia and New Zealand had agreed to permit the duty-free entry of a wide variety of goods from SPF member countries. Its principal international tie, however, has been with the Commonwealth. Under special membership status negotiated following independence, Nauru was permitted to participate in a wide range of Commonwealth activities and was eligible for technical assistance. Full membership was accorded on May 1, 1999.

In January 1992 Nauru joined with sister island nations Kiribati and Tuvalu, and the New Zealand dependencies of the Cook Islands and Niue, to form a Small Island States (SIS) grouping to address a number of common concerns, including global warming, the negotiation of fishing rights in their 200-mile Exclusive Economic Zones (EEZs), and the possibility of renting airspace to planes overflying their countries.

During 1995 Nauru adopted the hardest line of all regional countries in opposing France's decision to resume nuclear testing at Mururoa Atoll in September. It was one of four countries and territories to boycott the Tahiti Games in August because of the issue, with President Dowiyogo, who had previously supported New Zealand's World Court bid to stop the tests, traveling to Paris with other regional leaders in an unsuccessful effort to secure cancellation.

In July 2002 Nauru and the Republic of China (Taiwan) ended two decades of diplomatic relations as the Harris government and the People's Republic of China agreed to establish formal ties. The Harris administration, attempting to justify its about-face, cited the alleged interference of a Taiwanese envoy in a recent parliamentary by-election, although most observers attributed the shift to an expectation that Beijing would provide substantially more economic aid than Taipei. However, little aid was forthcoming, and in May 2005 the Scotty administration resumed relations with Taiwan.

Since 2001, two issues have dominated Nauru's foreign relations: its role as an offshore banking center, which drew charges of money laundering from the United States and the OECD, and its cooperation with Australia in the temporary housing of refugee "boat people" (see Current issues, below).

Current issues. Since 1998, with virtual exhaustion of Nauru's phosphate deposits and the squandering of its phosphate trust assets in a series of failed investments, the country's economy has been in crisis. The decline was briefly arrested with an influx of offshore banking transactions, Russian deposits alone amounting to $70 billion, according to the U.S. Treasury Department. Responding to what became an OECD-led chorus of complaints, Parliament passed an anti–money laundering bill in August 2001. Nonetheless, Nauru remained on the OECD's uncooperative list because of little concrete action against an estimated 400 shell banks, and in March 2003 offshore banking was outlawed. However, the action failed to dispel recurrent charges of corruption that yielded an average of two executive turnovers a year in the period 1999–2004. It was not until May 2008 that Washington indicated partial acceptance of the anticorruption effort by withdrawing two of its reporting and compliance conditions.

Meanwhile, Nauru had entered into a series of agreements with Australia for the detention of large numbers of "boat people" whom Canberra did not wish to admit as refugees. In 2001 Nauru agreed to accept 240 Iraqis who had been rescued at sea by a Norwegian freighter; subsequently, it accepted A$10 million to house 400 Afghans who had also sought to settle in Australia. Later, as the number of asylum seekers, including a group of Sri Lankans, rose to 1,200, the payment increased to a total of A$31 million, a sum approximately that of the island's GDP. The arrangements, part of Australia's "Pacific Solution" for migrants, were not intended to be permanent, and in late 2003 a group of detainees staged a hunger strike to press consideration of their claim by Canberra. The strike was called off in early 2004, after Australia agreed to review their cases and New Zealand said it would accept some of the refugees on humanitarian grounds.

In early 2008 Australia announced that it would close its detention center on the island and accept those remaining as immigrants. The move had a negative effect on Nauru's economy, which had benefited from payments of an estimated A$100 million over a five-year period. As a result, Canberra agreed to fund a limited resumption of phosphate mining and provide A$29 million in developmental assistance for fiscal 2009. However, long-term issues remain unresolved, including a lack of arable land that has necessitated reliance on imports for 90 percent of the island's food and the threat of inundation by global warming. As a result, in the course of Nauru's celebration of the 40th anniversary of independence, calls were issued for reannexation by Australia, an action (appearing unlikely of acceptance in either jurisdiction) that would permit islanders to improve their condition by residence and work in the larger country.

POLITICAL PARTIES

Until 1976 there were no political parties in Nauru. Following the election of December 1976 at least half of the new Parliament claimed membership in the Nauru Party, a loosely structured group led by Bernard Dowiyogo and consisting primarily of younger Nauruans opposed to some of President DeRoburt's policies. The party won 9 of 18 seats in the election of November 1977 but became moribund thereafter.

Following the election of January 1987, it was reported that eight members of Parliament had joined an opposition Nauru Democratic Party under the leadership of former president Kennan Adeang. A subsequent report indicated that Dowiyogo's supporters had formed a Democratic Party, with supporters of former president Lagumot Harris having launched another Nauru Party. None, however, developed into effective organizations.

In 2001 a **Nauru First** (*Naoero Amo*) party was organized by a group of activists, including David ADEANG, Dr. Kieren KEKE, and Marlene MOSES, in opposition to both the Dowiyogo and René Harris camps. A second new formation, the **Center Party,** also emerged under the leadership of former president Kinza Clodumar.

LEGISLATURE

The unicameral **Parliament** of 18 members is popularly elected for a three-year term, subject to dissolution. Voting is compulsory for those over 20 years of age. The most recent election was on April 26, 2008.

Speaker: Riddell AKUA.

CABINET

[as of July 1, 2009]

President	Marcus Stephen
Ministers	
Assisting the President	Dr. Kieren Keke
Civil Aviation	Ludwig Scotty
Commerce, Industry, and Environment	Frederick Pitcher
Education	Roland Kun
Finance and Sustainable Development	Dr. Kieren Keke
Fisheries and Marine Resources	Roland Kun
Foreign Affairs	Dr. Kieren Keke
Health and Sport	Mathew Batsiua
Home Affairs	Marcus Stephen
Justice	Mathew Batsiua
Nauru Phosphate Royalties Trust	Marcus Stephen
Public Service	Marcus Stephen
Transport and Communications	Sprent Dabwido

COMMUNICATIONS

Press. The *Bulletin* (750), weekly in English and Nauruan; *Central Star News,* fortnightly; *The Visionary,* periodical published by Nauru First.

Broadcasting. Government-owned Radio Nauru currently broadcasts in English and Nauruan. Television service was launched in May 1991 by means of a contract with Television New Zealand that now services some 1,100 receivers.

INTERGOVERNMENTAL REPRESENTATION

Ambassador to the U.S. and Permanent Representative to the UN: Marlene MOSES.

U.S. Ambassador to Nauru: C. Steven McGANN (resident in Fiji).

IGO Memberships (Non-UN): ADB, CWTH, Interpol, PC, PIF.

NEPAL

Federal Democratic Republic of Nepal
Nepál

Political Status: Independent monarchy established 1769; limited constitutional system promulgated December 16, 1962; constitutional monarchy proclaimed under constitution of November 9, 1990; interim constitution promulgated January 15, 2007, changing country's official name from Kingdom of Nepal to State of Nepal; monarchy formally ended and federal democratic republic proclaimed May 28, 2008, by a Constituent Assembly.

Area: 54,362 sq. mi. (140,797 sq. km.).

Population: 23,151,423 (2001C); 28,762,000 (2008E).

Major Urban Center (2005E): KATHMANDU (804,000).

Official Language: Nepali.

Monetary Unit: Nepalese Rupee (market rate December 1, 2009: 74.10 rupees = $1US).

President: Ram Baran YADAV (Nepali Congress); elected by the Constituent Assembly on July 21, 2008, and sworn in on July 23, following the abolition of the monarchy on May 28, and the abdication of King GYANENDRA on June 11.

Vice President: Paramananda JHA (Madhesi People's Rights Forum Nepal), elected by the Constituent Assembly on July 19, 2008, and sworn in on July 23.

Prime Minister: Madhav Kumar NEPAL (Communist Party of Nepal [United Marxist-Leninist]); elected by the Constituent Assembly on May 23, 2009, and sworn in on May 25, succeeding Pushpa Kamal DAHAL (Communist Party of Nepal [Maoist]).

THE COUNTRY

Landlocked between India and Tibet in the central Himalayas, Nepal is renowned for its mountainous landscape dominated by several of the world's highest peaks and for the prowess of its Gurkha regiments, who have served in the British and Indian armies. It encompasses three distinct geographic zones: a southern plain known as the Terai, a central hill region with many rivers and valleys, and a northern section dominated by high mountains. The country is inhabited by more than 50 tribes, who fall into two main ethnic groupings, Mongolian and Indo-Aryan. The majority of the population, particularly in the south, is Hindu in religion and linked in culture to India. The northern region, adjoining Tibet, is mainly Buddhist, but throughout the country Hindu

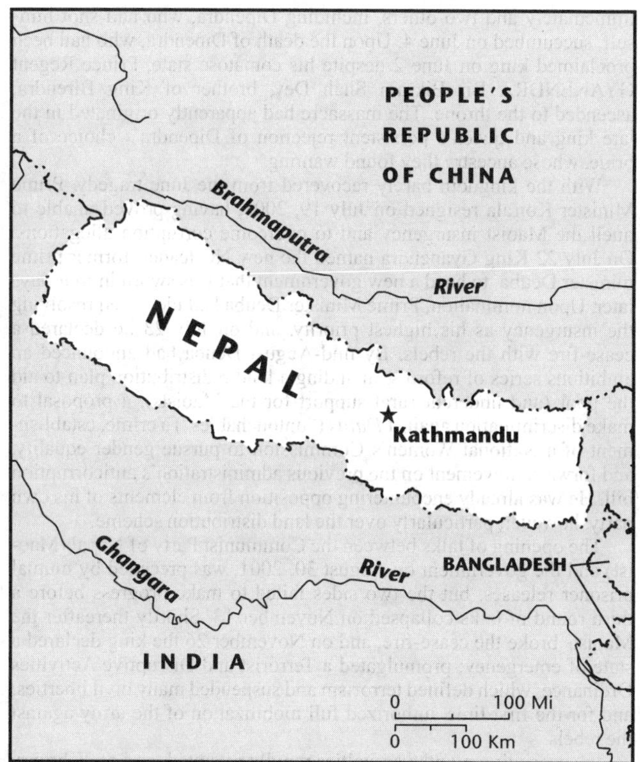

and Buddhist practices have intermingled with each other and with shamanism. In 1998 women constituted 40 percent of the labor force, almost entirely in agriculture; however, female participation in government has been minimal.

With gross national income per capita of approximately $1,060 in 2007 (computed to reflect purchasing power parity between countries) and with 50 percent illiteracy (higher for females), Nepal is considered one of the world's least-developed nations. Moreover, Nepal suffers from a severely unequal distribution of wealth: according to some estimates, average income in the "hill country" is less than 10 percent that of the capital region.

Agriculture continues to employ 75 percent of the labor force and to account for about a third of GDP. Industry, which contributes about one sixth of GDP, is oriented toward processed foods and other nondurable consumer goods, industrial development being hindered by rudimentary communication and transportation facilities. Natural resources include timber (despite extensive deforestation in some areas), mica, and coal, while there is increasing emphasis on the export potential of hydropower. At present, leading exports include woolen carpets, ready-made clothing, and such agricultural products as pulses, jute, and grain. Another significant source of foreign exchange is remittances from Nepalese employed abroad. India remains Nepal's principal trading partner, although an effort has been made to expand trade relations particularly in East Asia.

GDP growth averaged about 5 percent annually in the 1990s, during which extensive foreign aid from individual countries and such organizations as the World Bank supported a wide variety of projects, including construction of roads, railways, and hydroelectric facilities. In 2000–2001 growth continued at a 5.6 percent rate, but an escalating Maoist insurgency contributed to a 0.6 percent drop in output in the following fiscal period. Annual GDP growth averaged about 3 percent in 2003–2007, increasing to 5.6 percent in 2008 on the strength of a good growing season, more tourism, and the dissolution of the Maoist insurgency. Annual growth was expected to contract to about 4 percent in 2009, largely due to a decline in exports and the higher cost of oil imports, as well as a decline in remittances because of the global economic downturn. On a positive note, the World Bank helped to develop and finance numerous programs to support the peace process, commercialization of the agriculture sector, and expansion of the electricity sector.

GOVERNMENT AND POLITICS

Political background. Founded in 1769 by the Gurkha ruler Prithvi NARAYAN Shah as a kingdom comprising 46 previously sovereign principalities, Nepal was ruled by Narayan's descendants until the 1840s, when the Rana family established an autocratic system that, under hereditary prime ministers, lasted until 1951. A revolution in 1950, inspired in part by India's independence, restored the power of King TRIBHUVAN Bir Bikram Shah Dev and initiated a period of quasi-constitutional rule that continued after 1955 under the auspices of Tribhuvan's son, King MAHENDRA Bir Bikram Shah Dev.

A democratic constitution promulgated in 1959 paved the way for an election that brought to power the socialist-inclined Nepali Congress (NC) under Biseswar Prasad KOIRALA. In December 1960, however, the king charged the new government with misuse of power, dismissed and jailed its leaders, suspended the constitution, banned political parties, and assumed personal authority. A new constitution promulgated in 1962 and amended in 1967 established a tiered *panchayat* (assembly) system of representative bodies that was held to be more in keeping with Nepal's traditions. The "nonparty" system encountered persistent opposition, despite reconciliation efforts that included Koirala's release from detention.

King BIRENDRA Bir Bikram Shah Dev, who succeeded to the throne in 1972, accorded high priority to economic development but encountered difficulty in combining monarchial rule with pressures for political liberalization.

In 1979, after prolonged demonstrations, King Birendra announced that a referendum would be held to determine whether the nation favored revision of the *panchayat* structure or its replacement by a multiparty system. In May 1980 Nepalese voters rejected reintroduction of a party system, and in December the king proclaimed a number of constitutional changes, including direct, nonparty election to the National Assembly.

In the wake of economic distress caused by the March 1989 lapse of crucial trade and transit treaties with India (see Foreign relations, below), the banned NC called for dissolution of the government. Inspired by events in Eastern Europe, the NC and seven communist groups joined in February 1990 to form a Movement for the Restoration of Democracy that sought multiparty elections and an end to the *panchayat* system. In April, amid a mounting "People's Movement" (*Jana Andolan*), King Birendra reluctantly agreed to the appointment of the NC president, Krishna Prasad BHATTARAI, to head an interim cabinet that included three of Bhattarai's colleagues, three communists, two independent human rights activists, and two royal nominees. In May the king declared an amnesty for all political prisoners (most of whom had campaigned for party legalization) and delegated legislative power to the Bhattarai cabinet, the assembly having been dissolved in April. Shortly thereafter, he approved the government's nominees to a Constitutional Recommendation Commission and in September accepted the commission's draft of a new basic law, formally promulgated on November 9.

On May 12, 1991, in the country's first multiparty general election since 1959, the NC won control of the new House of Representatives, although Bhattarai lost his seat. As a result, the party's strongly anti-communist general secretary, Girija Prasad KOIRALA (brother of the former prime minister), was named to head a new administration. Subsequently, the NC was seriously weakened by differences between Prime Minister Koirala and his predecessor, and in July 1994, when he could not secure endorsement of an overview of government policies and programs, Koirala submitted his resignation.

In the election held in November 1994 the Communist Party of Nepal (Unified Marxist-Leninist)—CPN (UML) won a plurality of 88 seats in the 205-member lower house, and its leader, Man Mohan ADHIKARI, was sworn in as prime minister. In June 1995, however, the NC tabled a no-confidence motion that the National Democratic Party (*Rashtriya Prajatantra* Party—RPP), theretofore a crucial CPN (UML) ally, announced it would support. Two days later, at Adhikari's request, the king dissolved the National Assembly. The action was protested by the NC, the rightist RPP, and the royalist Nepali Goodwill Party (*Nepal Sadbhavana* Party—NSP), which collectively held 106 legislative seats. In August the Supreme Court ruled the action unconstitutional, and the prime minister resigned following rejection of a confidence motion in September. The NC's Sher Bahadur DEUBA then formed the country's first coalition administration, encompassing the NC, RPP, and NSP.

The Deuba coalition government remained vulnerable to potential shifting alliances, especially among the RPP ministers, and the prime minister was forced to resign in March 1997, after losing a confidence motion by two votes. The king invited former prime minister Lokendra Bahadur CHAND (1983–1986, 1990) of the RPP to form a new government, which included the CPN (UML), RPP, and NSP. Following local elections in May, elements within the RPP as well as opposition parties charged the victorious CPN (UML) with having committed election fraud and other irregularities. By late September the RPP had split into factions led by Chand and former prime minister Surya Bahadur THAPA (1963–1964, 1965–1969, 1979–1983). When Chand lost a confidence motion in October, he resigned, with Thapa then becoming prime minister for the fourth time and naming a new government that included the RPP and NSP. The NC subsequently joined the cabinet in another reshuffle, but the coalition remained unstable, and in January 1998 Thapa asked the king to dissolve the parliament and call new elections. The CPN (UML) and the Chand faction of the RPP objected and instead called for a special legislative session to consider a no-confidence motion. As a result, the RPP expelled the Chand group, which immediately formed a "New RPP." Meanwhile, the king had referred the issue to the Supreme Court, which in February recommended convening the House of Representatives. On February 20 the government survived a no-confidence motion by only three votes. In April, Prime Minister Thapa resigned in accordance with a power-sharing arrangement with the NC.

Former NC prime minister G.P. Koirala was sworn in on April 15, 1998, as the head of a three-person minority government, the NC being the plurality party in the House following a March split in the CPN (UML). The latter party had lost more than half its MPs to a new Communist Party of Nepal (Marxist-Leninist)—CPN (ML) in a dispute over the water-sharing treaty concluded with India in 1996. On April 18 Koirala secured a confidence vote and three days later introduced an expanded cabinet.

A cabinet reshuffle in August 1998 marked formation of an NC-led coalition with the new CPN (ML), which had demanded in return for its support review of the 1950 Indo-Nepal Peace and Friendship Treaty; withdrawal of Indian troops from the disputed Kalapani border area, where they had been posted since the 1962 Sino-Indian war; and repatriation to Bhutan of the nearly 100,000 Bhutanese refugees of Nepali descent who had been sheltered in camps in southeast Nepal since 1990 (see Foreign relations, below). In December, charging that the NC had failed to honor its commitment, the CPN (ML) withdrew from the government, prompting Prime Minister Koirala to recommend that the lower house be dissolved. The NC and the CPN (UML) then agreed to form an interim, pre-election government—Nepal's sixth in four years—that was sworn in with the additional participation of the NSP. The interim administration won a confidence vote in January 1999, and a day later the king dissolved the House of Representatives and announced that a general election would be held in May.

With the left split by the CPN (UML)–CPN (ML) rupture, and with Prime Minister Koirala having announced that he would step aside in favor of his longtime intraparty rival, former prime minister K.P. Bhattarai, the NC swept to victory in the May 3 and 17, 1999, election. Despite the objections of all the major parties except the NC, the election had been conducted in two phases to ensure adequate security in the western and central regions, site of a Maoist "People's War" insurgency, which largely relied on support from the illiterate, impoverished peasantry in the hinterlands. With the NC having won a majority of 111 seats in the lower house, Bhattarai was sworn in as prime minister on May 31. Nevertheless, internecine warfare continued between NC President Koirala and Prime Minister Bhattarai, even though the two septuagenarians had committed themselves to preparing a "younger generation" of leaders. On March 16, 2000, one day before a scheduled vote by the NC parliamentarians would have ousted him from office, Bhattarai announced to the lower house that he would submit his resignation to the king. On March 18 Koirala easily defeated former prime minister Deuba in the NC's first-ever open leadership election, and on March 20 the king appointed him prime minister for the fourth time.

In February 2001 Koirala included members of Deuba's NC faction in a reshuffled cabinet, but after two months of parliamentary boycotts and disruptions led by the opposition CPN (UML), King Birendra prorogued both houses of the legislature on April 5.

On June 1, 2001, Nepal experienced an unprecedented trauma when Crown Prince DIPENDRA Bikram Shah Dev killed most of the royal family, including King Birendra and Queen AISHWARYA, with an automatic weapon during a family get-together at the palace. Eight died immediately and two others, including Dipendra, who had shot himself, succumbed on June 4. Upon the death of Dipendra, who had been proclaimed king on June 2 despite his comatose state, Prince Regent GYANENDRA Bir Bikram Shah Dev, brother of King Birendra, ascended to the throne. The massacre had apparently originated in the late king and queen's persistent rejection of Dipendra's choice of a bride, whose ancestry they found wanting.

With the kingdom barely recovered from the June tragedy, Prime Minister Koirala resigned on July 19, 2001, having proved unable to quell the Maoist insurgency and to overcome corruption allegations. On July 22 King Gyanendra named the new NC leader, former prime minister Deuba, to head a new government that was sworn in four days later. Upon nomination, Prime Minister Deuba had identified resolving the insurgency as his highest priority, and on July 23 he declared a cease-fire with the rebels. By mid-August Deuba had announced an ambitious series of reforms, including a land redistribution plan to aid the poor (and undercut rural support for the Maoists), a proposal to make discrimination against *Dalits* ("untouchables") a crime, establishment of a National Women's Commission to pursue gender equality, and forward movement on the previous administration's anticorruption bill. He was already encountering opposition from elements of his own party, however, particularly over the land distribution scheme.

The opening of talks between the Communist Party of Nepal (Maoist) and the government on August 30, 2001, was preceded by mutual prisoner releases, but the two sides failed to make progress before a third round of talks collapsed on November 13. Shortly thereafter the Maoists broke the cease-fire, and on November 26 the king declared a state of emergency; promulgated a Terrorist and Disruptive Activities Ordinance, which defined terrorism and suspended many civil liberties; and for the first time authorized full mobilization of the army against the rebels.

In succeeding months casualties rapidly mounted, and on February 21, 2002, Deuba easily marshaled the two-thirds lower house majority needed to extend the state of emergency for another three months. Responding to criticism from the opposition as well as from international human rights advocates, on April 4 the government somewhat relaxed the state of emergency to permit greater press freedom and to allow public political meetings. Meanwhile, the Maoists widened their attacks on the country's infrastructure, including communications facilities, water supplies, dams, bridges, schools, and health clinics. By late May the death toll from the six-year insurgency had risen to 4,000–5,000, up from about 1,800 the preceding October.

In May 2002 Koirala supporters within the NC, charging that Deuba had failed to consult them before requesting a second extension of the state of emergency, prepared to join the parliamentary opposition in rejecting the proposal. Facing defeat, Prime Minister Deuba convinced King Gyanendra to dissolve the House of Representatives on May 22, a decision that was attacked by most parties and led several NC ministers to resign from Deuba's caretaker cabinet. In late May the NC disciplinary committee expelled Deuba from the party for three years. In turn, Deuba supporters called a convention for June 16–19 and proceeded to expel Koirala. On September 17 the Election Commission determined that the Koirala faction had the right to the NC title, and on September 23 Deuba registered a new Nepali Congress (Democratic)—NC (D).

With a backdrop of the increasingly intense Maoist insurgency, on October 4, 2002, King Gyanendra dismissed the Deuba government for "incompetence," postponed the early legislative election that had been scheduled for November 13, and temporarily assumed executive powers. On October 11 he named former prime minister L.B. Chand of the promonarchy RPP to head a nonparty government, which was then expanded in mid-November.

On January 29, 2003, following extensive negotiations conducted by Minister of Physical Planning and Construction Narayan Singh PUN, the Chand government and the CPN (Maoist)—CPM-M—agreed to a new cease-fire and peace talks, which opened in the capital on April 27. A second round was held on May 9, but by then the cease-fire was beginning to break down. Facing student-led antigovernment demonstrations and the continuing refusal of the major political parties to join in his peace efforts, on May 30 Prime Minister Chand resigned.

On June 4, 2003, the king named as prime minister the RPP's S.B. Thapa (his fifth term) after rejecting the candidate of a five-party opposition Joint People's Movement (JPM), Madhav Kumar NEPAL, the CPN (UML)'s general secretary. Like its predecessor, the all-RPP cabinet introduced on June 1 was denounced as illegitimate by the NC, the CPN (UML), and the other JPM parties, who accused the king of undermining multiparty democracy through "regression." Many in the opposition advocated recalling the dismissed House of Representatives—although there was no constitutional provision for doing so—as well as forming an all-party government.

A third round of peace talks on August 17–19, 2003, made no significant progress as the Maoists continued to insist that a constituent assembly be elected to draft a new constitution. On August 27 the CPN-M leader, Pushpa Kamal DAHAL (Comrade PRACHANDA), issued a statement announcing an end to both the talks and the cease-fire, and in succeeding months the violence escalated once again as the insurgents demonstrated their ability to attack throughout the country. The CPN-M also continued its efforts to organize administrative machinery in the districts it claimed to control.

On May 7, 2004, Prime Minister Thapa resigned "to pave the way for national consensus," and on June 2 the king reappointed former prime minister Deuba—the country's 14th prime minister in 14 years. Shortly thereafter, the CPN (UML), contending that opposition-supported antigovernment street demonstrations were no longer "meaningful," withdrew from the JPM. On July 5 the Deuba cabinet was expanded to include the CPN (UML), the RPP, and the NSP, in addition to Deuba's NC (D).

At the beginning of 2005 the government remained in disarray. The NC frustrated by the king's unwillingness to compromise with the opposition, had joined the CPN (UML) in calling for creation of a republic, while other parties had decided to support the Maoists' demand for election of a constituent assembly and their inclusion in an interim government. On February 1 King Gyanendra dismissed the Deuba government, reintroduced a state of emergency, placed many political leaders under house arrest, ordered the army into the streets of the capital, and suspended press and other freedoms. Having vowed to "restore peace and effective democracy in this country within the next three years," on February 2 he named a cabinet of loyalists under his leadership. Although the state of emergency was lifted on April 29, 2005, a number of civil restrictions remained in effect. The cabinet was expanded on July 15 by the addition of several other loyalists, all the major political parties having rejected the king's proposal that they put forward nominees.

On May 8, 2005, the country's leading opposition parties announced formation of a "Seven-Party Alliance" (SPA), adopting a roadmap to the restoration of democracy that included reinstating the dissolved House of Representatives and forming a unity government. Participating in the SPA were the NC; the NC (D); the CPN (UML); the NSP (Anandi Devi), an NSP splinter formed in 2003; People's Front Nepal (*Janamorcha Nepal*—JMN); the Nepal Workers' and Peasants' Party (NWPP); and the United Left Front (ULF), at that time a five-party grouping of small communist parties. Together, the SPA parties had held all but about a dozen of the 205 seats in the dissolved House of Representatives. Among other actions, the SPA's coordinating committee began organizing prodemocracy demonstrations in Kathmandu and elsewhere.

Responding to overtures from the SPA, including indications that the participating parties were ready to consider formation of a constituent assembly that would draft a new constitution, on September 3, 2005, the Maoists' Prachanda announced a three-month unilateral cease-fire. Subsequent talks between the SPA and the Maoists led to a November 22 announcement of a 12-point agreement designed to end the king's "autocracy" and move toward election of a constituent assembly. The cease-fire was extended on December 2 but ended on January 2, 2006, because of lack of response by the government.

Municipal elections on February 8, 2006, were boycotted by the SPA, while Maoist threats against candidates and voters contributed to a low turnout. With the Maoists in control of an estimated three-fourths of the countryside and with the roads into Kathmandu again blockaded, the SPA began a general strike on April 6. In the wake of public protests, King Gyanendra on April 24 announced that he would reinstate the House of Representatives and asked the SPA to assume responsibility "for taking the nation on the path to national unity and prosperity, while ensuring permanent peace and safeguarding multiparty democracy." On April 26 the SPA nominated veteran NC leader G.P. Koirala for prime minister. On the same day, the Maoists announced another cease-fire. The House of Representatives convened on April 28. Two days later, the House unanimously approved a resolution endorsing formation of a constituent assembly.

On May 18, 2006, the House of Representatives assumed all legislative powers; stripped most governmental rights and responsibilities from the king, including his role as commander in chief; and delegated executive authority to a Council of Ministers responsible to the House. In their first face-to-face meeting, held June 16, 2006, Prime Minister Koirala and Comrade Prachanda, joined by other Maoist negotiators and representatives of the SPA, concluded an agreement that called for implementing the November 2005 agreement and a cease-fire code of conduct that had been signed on May 26. The new agreement expressed a commitment to "democratic norms and values" and provided for the immediate drafting of an interim constitution, to be followed by formation of an interim government in which the CPN-M would participate. On November 28 the government and the CPN-M signed, along with a UN representative, a tripartite agreement calling for the Nepalese Army to return to barracks, for the 30,000–40,000 soldiers of the Maoist People's Liberation Army to be confined to several camps, and for a comparable number of arms from each side to be locked away under UN supervision.

Following protracted negotiations, a draft interim constitution was approved by the SPA and the CPN-M in December 2006 and promulgated on January 15, 2007, by the House of Representatives. The legislature was immediately superseded by a unicameral Interim Legislature-Parliament of 330 members, including 83 representatives of the CPN-M. An Interim Council of Ministers, including Maoists, assumed office on April 1.

An election for a Constituent Assembly to draft a new constitution was set for November 22, 2007, having been postponed from June. However, on September 18 the Maoists resigned from the government over the issue of abolishing the monarchy, and their continuing demands for the declaration of a republic in advance of the referendum contributed to a further postponement of the polling. They subsequently rejoined the government in December, and on December 23, the CPN-M and the government parties signed an agreement that included support for establishing a federal democratic republic at the first meeting of the Constituent Assembly, once its 601 members were chosen. Meanwhile, five small royalist parties formed the United Inclusive Front to oppose the republican trend, and former prime minister Thapa of the RPP campaigned in favor of retaining the monarchy.

The elections to the Constituent Assembly were finally held on April 10, 2008, the elections commission estimating voter turnout of 60 percent. Both first-past-the-post and proportional representation systems were employed, with the CPN-M winning the most seats (220), Twenty-six of the remaining 381 seats were to be appointed by the future Council of Ministers. During the first session of the new Constituent Assembly on May 28, Nepal was declared a federal democratic republic, with delegates voting 560–4 to abolish the monarchy. King Gyanendra confirmed on June 2 that he would abdicate the throne, and he left the palace on June 11. On June 26 Prime Minister Koirala resigned, effective upon the election of a new president. On July 19 the assembly elected Vice President: Paramananda JHA as vice president. On July 21 the assembly, in a second round of voting, elected Ram Baran YADAV as president. He asked the CPN-M to form a government, and Pushpa Kamal Dahal, known as Prachanda, was named prime minister on August 18.

Prachanda's brief tenure ended in May 2009 in the wake of turmoil over the reintegration of the Maoist People's Liberation Army (PLA), resulting in Prachanda's firing the army chief of staff (see Current issues, below). The CPN (UML) resigned from the coalition government on May 3, and Prachanda resigned on May 4. The Maoists subsequently obstructed parliament with walkouts and heckling, and slowed the economy with strikes and other demonstrations. The Constituent Assembly nevertheless formed a coalition government and, with the Maoists boycotting, elected Madhav Kumar NEPAL of the CPN (UML) as prime minister on May 23, after agreement was reached that included the NC and the MPRF in the new unity government. Nepal gradually filled out his new government with ministers from several parties.

Constitution and government. The *panchayat* system in operation prior to the May 1980 referendum provided for a hierarchically arranged parallel series of assemblies and councils encompassing four different levels: village (*gaun*) and town (*nagar*), district (*jilla*), zone (*anchal*), and national (*Rashtriya Panchayat*). The members of the village and town assemblies were directly elected, members of the other bodies being indirectly elected by bodies directly below them in the hierarchy. The constitutional changes introduced in December 1980 provided for direct, rather than indirect, election to a nonpartisan National Assembly; designation of the prime minister by the assembly, rather than by the king; and parliamentary responsibility of cabinet members.

Under the 1990 constitution the remaining vestiges of the *panchayat* system were abandoned in favor of multiparty parliamentary government, with the king's role substantially curtailed. Executive powers were exercised jointly by the king and a Council of Ministers, the latter headed by a prime minister who, although named by the king, had to command a majority in the popularly elected lower house of Parliament, the House of Representatives. An upper chamber, the National Assembly, contained both indirectly elected and nominated members. The constitution could be amended by a two-thirds majority of the lower house, save for entrenched provisions dealing with such matters as human rights, the basic structure of the governmental system, and the rights of parties. Treaties and other major state agreements required approval by a two-thirds majority of both houses in joint session. The judicial hierarchy encompassed district courts, appellate courts, and a Supreme Court with powers of constitutional review.

The May 18, 2006, proclamation by the House of Representatives, which stripped King Gyanendra of his rights and powers, specified that the House was "sovereign . . . until another constitutional arrangement is made." Executive authority was delegated to the Council of Ministers, which was responsible to the House. The House also assumed full authority over the Nepalese Army (renamed from Royal Nepal Army), made the king's property and income subject to taxation, and declared Nepal to be a secular state. Further, the proclamation declared that the 1990 constitution and prevailing laws "shall be nullified to the extent of inconsistency" with the proclamation. An additional measure passed on June 10 specifically stripped the king of the veto and of his power to sign legislation into law.

The 167-article interim constitution adopted in January 2007 enumerated a wide range of "fundamental rights," including those of free expression, assembly, and equal protection. It endowed the Council of Ministers with executive authority and stated that "no power regarding the governance of the country shall be vested in the king," but it stopped short of naming the prime minister as head of state. The interim constitution also established a unicameral Interim Legislature-Assembly pending election of a Constituent Assembly tasked with determining the fate of the monarchy and drafting a permanent constitution. The existing judicial system was left in place. Amending the interim constitution required a two-thirds vote of the legislature, which in late December 2007 passed an amendment endorsing establishment of a federal republic. The Constituent Assembly, at its inaugural session on May 28, 2008, formally created the republic, abolishing the monarchy entirely after 239 years.

The Fifth Amendment to the interim constitution was approved by the Council of Ministers on June 25, 2008, and adopted by the Constituent Assembly on July 13. This provision allows for the formation of a government through a simple majority vote of the Constituent Assembly. It creates a national president and vice president, although their powers are not specified, executive power being vested in the prime minister. According to the amendment, the president, vice president, prime minister, and Constituent Assembly chair and vice chair are to be selected on the basis of a political understanding; however, if such understanding cannot be reached, they can be elected by a simple majority vote in the assembly. A Constituent Assembly majority is required to remove a prime minister from office through a no-confidence vote. The amendment also stipulates that the leader of the opposition shall be a member of the Constitutional Council.

Administratively, Nepal is divided into 5 development regions, 14 zones, 75 districts, nearly 4,000 villages, and 36 municipalities. Among the issues the Constituent Assembly must negotiate is the structure of a federal system for the nation, including the number of states or provinces, the borders between them, their relationship to the nation's ethnic composition, and their degree of autonomy.

Foreign relations. Although historically influenced by Britain and subsequently by India, Nepal has endeavored to strengthen its independence, particularly after India's annexation of the adjacent state of Sikkim in 1975. Thus, Kathmandu adopted a policy of nonalignment and has sought a balance in regional relations. Nepalese leaders have moved to involve not only India and China, but also Bangladesh, Bhutan, and Pakistan in cooperative endeavors, with primary emphasis on water resource development.

In November 1979, a major issue in relations with China was apparently resolved by the signing in Beijing of an agreement defining Nepal's northern frontier. The agreement was hailed as a model for the potential settlement of outstanding border disputes between China and the neighboring states of India and Bhutan.

Relations with India plummeted in 1989 as a result of an impasse over trade and transit agreements upon which the Nepalese economy was highly dependent. Factors influencing India's reluctance to renew the treaties included recent Nepalese arms purchases from China, the levying of a 55 percent tariff on Indian goods, and the enactment of legislation requiring non-Nepalese to obtain work permits. The agreements were revived following an announcement by Prime Minister Bhattarai in 1990 that his government had postponed receipt of the latest Chinese arms shipment "to accommodate Indian sensitivities on [the] issue." An additional series of agreements covering trade, transit, border control, agriculture, and cultural exchanges were signed in December 1991.

In January 1996 the Nepalese and Indian foreign ministers signed an agreement in Kathmandu calling for a joint hydroelectric project in the Mahakali River basin. The $5 billion undertaking was bitterly opposed by a faction of the CPN (UML), which joined other left-wing groups in mounting widespread public protests that nevertheless failed to prevent ratification of the Indo-Nepal Mahakali Integrated Development Treaty in September. Passage was somewhat eased by the conclusion in mid-August of an agreement allowing Nepal transit rights across northeastern Indian territory to ports in Bangladesh.

Since the early 1990s successive governments have expressed concern about an influx of ethnic Nepalese from nearby Bhutan. Although some claimed to be descendants of 19th-century settlers, Bhutanese authorities insisted that most had relocated to Bhutan in the 1980s and were illegal immigrants. Preliminary talks on resolving the problem were held in Kathmandu in October 1993, and in April 1994 an agreement was reached on how to categorize the more than 90,000 Bhutanese of Nepalese origin stranded in eastern Nepal. However, subsequent bilateral talks failed to resolve the dispute, despite international pressure mounted to address the plight of the refugees living in UN-run camps, and it wasn't until October 2003 that an agreement was reached that was to permit repatriation of about three-fourths of the ethnic Nepalese in one of the seven refugee camps in Nepal. In the end, however, Bhutan demurred. (During 2008–2009 more than 15,000 were resettled from the camps, most in the United States For additional details, see the article on Bhutan in this edition of the *Handbook*.)

On January 23, 2007, the UN Security Council established a UN Mission in Nepal (UNMIN) to help maintain the cease-fire, monitor sequestration of arms by the Maoists and the Nepalese Army, and help oversee the Constituent Assembly election.

The United States continued to list the Maoists (now called the Unified Communist Party of Nepal (Maoist)) as a terrorist organization in 2009. A State Department official said in June that the party would be removed from the terrorist list if it renounced violence, curtailed the violent activities of the Young Communist League, and worked to conclude the peace process.

Also in June 2009, Nepali media reported an incursion by the Indian border security force, the Seema Surakshya Bal (SSB), in the Dang district. The SSB reportedly forced more than 2,000 people from their homes.

Current issues. Some 13,100 people died during the decade-long Maoist insurgency, nearly half of them civilians. During the last years of the conflict, casualties and reports of human-rights violations escalated. The Maoists were accused of committing abuses, such as hostage-taking, use of children as combatants, torture, and the killing of captives. At the same time, the Nepalese Army and the police allegedly engaged in arbitrary detentions, torture, summary executions, and "the disappearance" of Maoist sympathizers, threatening societal stability.

Difficulties persisted even after the peace accord of 2006 and the inclusion of the CPN-M in the government. Opponents accused the Maoists of failing to keep their commitments, including dismantling parallel local governments, stopping tax collections in areas under their control, and eliminating trials by the "people's courts" they had set up. By February 2007, though nearly 31,000 Maoist combatants had turned in only 3,400 weapons, few observers regarded that as a credible number. In addition, intimidation of political opponents reportedly continued, often by members of the Maoist youth wing, the Young Communist League.

Following the election of a Constituent Assembly in April 2008 and the official abolition of the monarchy in May, the stunning transition of the CPN-M from rebel army to governing party accomplished many of the goals of the armed struggle, the most significant of which was the overthrow of Nepal's monarchy. The Maoists' agenda was somewhat unclear as they began to exercise state power in cooperation with other parties, while at the same time, comments by former prime minister Prachanda and other Maoist leaders raised doubts about the party's commitment to parliamentary government and a democratic system. Mutual suspicion and political wrangling delayed the Constituent Assembly from beginning its work on the new constitution. Among the challenges to the peace process was the fate of the Maoist People's Liberation Army (PLA). Nearly 20,000 former PLA fighters remained in temporary quarters under United Nations supervision, while the government sought to determine how to integrate them into society. Maoist officials strongly advocated the PLA's joining the Nepali army. However, coalition partners of the Maoists (now renamed the Unified Communist Party of Nepal (Maoist)), such as the NC and the CPN (UML), opposed combining the two fighting forces, fearing that the PLA cadres might politicize the national defense forces, undermining the peace process and threatening to set off new conflict. Army officials, led by Gen. Rookmangud KATAWAL, resisted plans to assimilate PLA troops. Subsequently, Prime Minister Prachanda fired Katawal on May 3, 2009. However, President Yadav intervened that same day, overturning the general's dismissal. The CPN (UML) immediately pulled out of the coalition government, and Prachanda resigned the next day. The UCPN-M then organized a series of crippling strikes across the country, effectively shutting down the Constituent Assembly for more than a month, and the party demanded that the president's order be reversed. The Maoists claimed that the president had acted beyond his constitutional authority and that civilian control of the military was at stake.

In the wake of Prachanda's resignation, 22 of the 24 political parties represented in the Constituent Assembly, comprising 350 of its 601 members, agreed to a coalition government led by the CPN (UML), with its senior leader, Madhav Kumar Nepal, nominated as prime minister. Nepal, who lost his bid for an assembly seat in 2008, had become a member of parliament in early 2009 after the resignation of a party colleague. Considered an ideological moderate, Nepal was touted as a skilled negotiator who could bring rival parties together. He pledged to work toward the conclusion of the peace process with the Maoists and toward the completion of a new constitution. Meanwhile, the process of forming a coalition cabinet was lengthy and awkward as several parties refused to join because of dissatisfaction with the portfolios offered them. The Madhesi People's Rights Forum (MJF) subsequently split into progovernment and opposition factions. The government's growing pains, including the deteriorating security situation and the Maoists' obstruction of parliament, contributed to a perception among observers that the coalition was fragile and that considerable effort would be required to stabilize the government before progress could be made on a new constitution. The Constituent Assembly was scheduled to come up with a final draft of a new constitution by May 2010.

POLITICAL PARTIES

Political formations were banned by royal decree in 1960, although de facto party affiliations continued. The 1990 constitution prohibited restrictions on political parties. At the time of the 1999 election, there were 101 recognized parties, of which 30 offered candidates. Only 6 parties captured 3 percent or more of the vote, a requirement for designation as a "national party."

In May 2003, seven months after King Gyanendra had dissolved the House of Representatives, with no new election in sight, the Nepali Congress (NC), the Communist Party of Nepal (Unified Marxist-Leninist)—CPN (UML), the Nepali Goodwill Party (Anandi Devi), the Nepal Workers' and Peasants' Party (NWPP), and the People's Front Nepal (JMN) formed an opposition "Joint People's Movement" (JPM) that won the support of half a dozen other parties. In June 2004 the CPN (UML) left the JPM, and in July it joined a multiparty cabinet that excluded the remaining JPM members. The king's assumption of power in February 2005 led directly to the May 8 formation of the "Seven-Party Alliance" (SPA) of the original five JPM parties, the NC (Democratic), and the United Left Front of smaller communist parties. The subsequent decision of the king to recall the 1999 House of Representatives put the SPA in power and began the road toward bringing the Communist Party of Nepal (Maoist)—CPN (Maoist) into the interim government and electing a Constituent Assembly.

A total of 62 parties applied to the Election Commission for formal recognition prior to the assembly election. By late July 2007 about 40 had been registered and assigned election symbols. A total of 25 parties won seats in the Constituent Assembly, including several new parties, such as the 3 parties of the United Democratic Madhesi Front (UDMF).

Government Parties:

Communist Party of Nepal (Unified Marxist-Leninist)—CPN (UML) (*Nepala Kamyunishta Parti* [*Ekikrit Marksbadi ra Leninbadi*]). Sometimes referenced as the United (or Unified) Communist Party of Nepal (UCPN), the CPN (UML) was formed in 1991 by merger of two factions of the Communist Party of Nepal: CPN (Marxist) and the CPN (Marxist-Leninist). In April 1990 the CPN (Marxist) and the CPN (ML) joined with five other leftist formations, including three pro-Soviet CPN factions, a pro-Chinese group, and the NWPP (below), in a United Leftist Front in support of the restoration of democracy. This diverse grouping became moribund prior to the 1991 poll.

In May 1991 Man Mohan Adhikari was elected head of the CPN (UML) parliamentary group and therefore leader of the opposition. Following the November 1994 election, he was reelected parliamentary leader and was then sworn in as prime minister of Nepal's first communist government. He was obliged to resign after losing a no-confidence vote in September 1995. The CPN (UML) subsequently participated in the coalition government formed by Prime Minister Chand in March 1997 before joining that of Prime Minister Koirala in December 1998.

In March 1998 more than half the CPN (UML) legislators left the parent grouping and reorganized under the former CPN (ML) title to protest the 1996 water-sharing agreement with India. In February 2002 the bulk of the CPN (ML) rejoined the parent party, although a faction remained independent as the "reconstituted" CPN (ML) (see below). The CPN (ML)'s secretary general, Bamdev Gautam, immediately resumed a leadership role in the CPN (UML)

In April 1999 former prime minister Adhikari, the party's candidate for prime minister in the upcoming election, died. In the May election the CPN (UML) won 71 seats, down from the 88 it had claimed in 1994. In early 2001 the CPN (UML) was largely responsible for legislative boycotts and disruptions that led the king to prorogue both houses of parliament in April.

The party's former general secretary, Madhav Kumar Nepal, was a principal organizer of the Joint People's Movement in 2003. Having left the JPM following Prime Minister Deuba's reappointment, in July 2004 the CPN (UML) joined an expanded four-party cabinet, in which Bharat Mohan Adhikari served as deputy prime minister until the entire government was dismissed on February 1, 2005.

The party won the third highest number of seats in the Constituent Assembly election in April 2008, splitting the left-wing vote with other communist groupings, including the victorious Maoists. Jhalanath Khanal was elected party chair at a convention in February 2009, defeating K.P. Oli. The party left the Maoist-led government in May after Prime Minister Prachanda, the Maoist leader, dismissed the army chief of staff without consulting the other government parties. Prachanda then resigned, and the CPN(UML) was invited to form a new government. M.K. Nepal was elected as prime minister, and party members assumed several key ministries. The party subsequently was divided in its stance toward the Maoists, as some members criticized the new government's decision to overturn the former government's decision to fire the army chief, contrary to a key Maoist demand (see Current issues, above).

Leaders: Madhav Kumar NEPAL (Prime Minister), Jhalanath KHANAL (Chair), Bamdev GAUTAM (Vice Chair), Bidhya BHANDARI (Vice Chair), Ashok RAI (Vice Chair), K. P. Sharma OLI, Ishwor POKHAREL (General Secretary).

Nepali Congress (NC). Founded in 1947, the NC long sought abolition of the *panchayat* system and defied the regime by holding a national convention in Kathmandu in March 1985, after which it launched a civil disobedience movement (*satyagraha*) to press for the release of political prisoners and for party legalization. Following widespread popular agitation that began in February 1990, NC President K.P. Bhattarai was asked to head a coalition government pending nationwide balloting in May 1991. Although the NC won 110 of 205 House seats in 1991, Bhattarai failed to secure reelection and hence was obliged to yield the office of prime minister to G.P. Koirala, who served until 1994. Sher Bahadur Deuba served as prime minister in a coalition government from 1995–1997. Koirala returned as prime minister in April 1998, although his cabinet appointees provoked considerable intraparty controversy over the inclusion of what some members considered "corrupt" ministers who had served in previous administrations.

During the parliamentary campaign of 1999 Koirala announced that, to foster party unity, he would step aside in favor of Bhattarai, who returned as prime minister when the NC, on a 38 percent vote share, won a clear majority of 111 seats in the House of Representatives.

Conflict between Bhattarai and supporters of Koirala, who had retained the party presidency, nevertheless continued, forcing Bhattarai to resign on March 16, 2000, a day before a scheduled intraparty vote would have turned him out of office. Meeting two days later for the party's first open leadership election, the parliamentarians, as expected, selected Koirala as their leader by a 69–43 vote over Deuba. Accordingly, King Birendra redesignated Koirala as prime minister on March 20.

Leadership disputes within the NC continued to simmer. On August 8, 2000, Koirala dismissed the minister of water resources, Khum Bahadur KHADKA, for demanding that Koirala step aside as party president. Khadka drew support for the principle of "one man, one office" from former prime ministers Deuba and Bhattarai, but Koirala remained firm in his dual roles.

Although Koirala beat back another challenge by Deuba's supporters at a party convention in January 2001, he resigned as prime minister on July 19. Deuba then defeated Secretary General Sushil Koirala, 72–40, for the party leadership and was designated by the king to be prime minister.

The stark division between the Koirala and Deuba factions persisted, culminating in the May 2002 decision by the NC disciplinary committee to expel Deuba for failing to consult the party before seeking parliamentary extension of the country's state of emergency. Deuba supporters then expelled Koirala at a June 16–19 "general convention." The fissure ultimately led Deuba to register his faction as the Nepali Congress (Democratic)—NC (D) following a decision by the Election Commission that the Koirala faction held title to the Nepali Congress name. At the time, the NC (D)'s membership included 40 of the NC representatives who had been elected to the lower house in 1999.

In the months following the king's October 2002 decisions to dissolve the House of Representatives and replace Prime Minister Deuba with the National Democratic Party's L.B. Chand, the NC joined the CPN (UML) and other, smaller parties in challenging the constitutionality of the moves. The NC was a prime mover in formation of the JPM in April–May 2003 and of the SPA two years later. The NC (D) also joined the SPA. Deuba had been reappointed prime minister for a third time in June 2004, only to be dismissed once again on February 1, 2005, placed under house arrest, and convicted by a corruption commission. However, he was released in February 2006 and went on to regain leadership of the NC(D) parliamentary delegation.

With election of a Constituent Assembly in the offing, the NC and the NC (D) reunited on September 25, 2007. A collateral decision to support a republic form of government led former prime minister Bhattarai to resign from the party. The NC won 110 of 601 Constituent Assembly seats in April 2008, reflecting a decline from the party's historic levels of popular support, especially in the Terai region of southern Nepal. The party joined the coalition government headed by Madhav Kumar Nepal in May 2009. Koirala angered some in the party by nominating his daughter Sujata KOIRALA for the post of foreign minister. In June in a contested election for leader of the party's parliamentary group, Ram Chandra Poudel defeated former prime minister Deuba.

Leaders: Ram Baran YADAV (President of Nepal), Girija Prasad KOIRALA (President of the Party), Sher Bahadur DEUBA (Former Prime Minister), Ram Sushil KOIRALA, Ram Chandra POUDEL (Vice President of the Party).

Madhesi People's Rights Forum Nepal (*Madheshi Janadhikar Forum*—MJF). The MJF began in 1997 as a civic organization advocating for the rights of Madhesis—the indigenous people who make up the majority in Nepal's southern plain—to self-determination. The MJF organized an uprising and general strike in January 2007, in protest of the interim constitution, which they said ignored the interests of marginalized groups. The situation in the Terai escalated into violence that claimed roughly 50 lives.

In August, the MJF signed an agreement with the government on 22 points. However, a faction of the group opposed the agreement. Later, the MJF declared that the government had failed to fulfill the agreement and called for militant protests around November 22, the scheduled date for the Constituent Assembly election. A second wave of violence arose in the Terai in February 2008. That month the MJF joined the Terai Madhesh Democratic Party (*Tarai Madhesh Loktantrik* Party—TMLP, below) and Goodwill Party (Sadbhavana Party—SP, below) to form the United Democratic Madhesi Front (UDMF). Following this uprising, the government agreed to several of the UDMF demands, including the creation of an autonomous Madhesi state within Nepal. The UDMF parties were also allowed to register for the Constituent Assembly election, although the deadline had passed. In its first electoral contest, the MJF won 52 seats, making it the fourth largest party in the assembly, and joined the government led by Prachanda and the Maoists. Party leader Upendra Yadav won the post of foreign minister.

Following Prachanda's resignation in May 2009, incoming prime minister Nepal offered the deputy prime minister position to Bijay Kumar GACHCHHADAR, the leader of the MJF parliamentary group, without the approval of the MJF executive committee. This led to a bitter division, resulting in the expulsion of Gachchhadar and six others and their withdrawal from the government coalition. Gachchhadar, however, claimed the support of a majority of the party's lawmakers. His faction continued to participate in the government and later received two additional ministerial portfolios (see MJF-G, below). Yadav accused the leaders of the CPN (UML) and Nepali Congress of intentionally provoking a split in the MJF.

Leader: Upendra YADAV.

Madhesi Peopleís Rights Forum NepalóGachchhadar (*Madheshi Janadhikar Forum (Gachchhadar)*—MJF-G). A faction of the indigenous Madhesi People's Rights Forum (MJF, above), the MJF-G began in 2009, when Bijay Kumar Gachchhadar accepted the position of deputy prime minister under Madhav Kumar Nepal. The MJF leadership had asked Nepal not to appoint any party members without the party's formal approval. Gachchhadar refused to decline the high office and claimed leadership of the party, asserting that a majority of MJF constituent assembly members supported him. He and the other dissidents then split from the party.

Leader: Bijay Kumar GACHCHHADAR (Deputy Prime Minister).

Terai Madhesh Democratic Party (*Tarai Madhesh Loktantrik Party*—TMLP). An ethnic and regional party founded in 2008 by former NC leader Mahanta Thakur, the TMLP demands, with the MJF and the Sadbhavana Party, that Nepal be declared a federal republic, with the Madhesis granted an autonomous province, and that Madhesis and all ethnic groups be given proportional representation in all state organizations. The party came in fifth in the Constituent Assembly voting, winning 20 seats. It joined the government for the first time in June 2009.

Leaders: Mahanta THAKUR (Chair), Hridayesh TRIPATHI.

National Democratic Party (*Rashtriya Prajatantra* Party—RPP). A monarchist party comprising largely former *panchayat* members and supporters, the RPP was formed in 1992 by merger of two groups (both calling themselves the National Democratic Party), one led by S.B. Thapa and the other led by L.B. Chand. The unified RPP won 20 legislative seats in the 1994 election. It entered the government as a member of the NC-led coalition in September 1995, but factionalism within the RPP contributed to the government's instability. The demise of the coalition in March 1997 led to Chand's designation as prime minister in a CPN (UML)-RPP-NSP cabinet that survived less than seven months before being replaced by an RPP-NSP (and subsequently NC) government under Thapa. In January 1998 the RPP expelled former prime minister Chand and nine supporters for threatening to back a no-confidence vote against Prime Minister Thapa, who had asked the king to dissolve the House of Representatives. The rebel group quickly formed a "New RPP," commonly called the RPP (Chand).

The RPP won 11 percent of the vote and 11 seats in the May 1999 election, while the RPP (Chand) claimed a meager 3 percent and no seats. The Thapa and Chand groups merged in January 2000. After the dismissal of the Deuba government in October 2002, the king reappointed former prime minister Chand to that office, but Chand resigned in late May 2003 and was in turn replaced by former prime minister Thapa. The change further widened the rift between the Chand and Thapa factions in the party, and in December 2003 the RPP called for Thapa's resignation for undermining multiparty democracy. Thapa ultimately resigned in May.

By late 2004 the rupture within the RPP appeared complete. Although Chand and the party's president, P.S. Rana, were continuing their efforts to hold the party together, Thapa had stated his intention to form a new party, which was launched in March 2005 as the *Rashtriya Janshakti* Party (RJP, below). The departure of Thapa supporters did not, however, end factionalism within the RPP. In September the RPP announced that it would support the "prodemocracy agitation" led by the SPA, but in December half a dozen RPP members were in the reshuffled cabinet announced by the king.

In January 2006 President Rana ousted ten members of the party's central committee, including six cabinet ministers. The royalist dissidents ultimately formed the RPP (Nepal) [see below]. With nine seats, the RPP became the largest opposition party in the interim parliament. Party divisions, as well as the RPP's opposition to ending the monarchy, weakened its showing in the Constituent Assembly balloting; the party won eight seats. It subsequently joined the UML-led government in June 2009.

Leaders: Pashupati Shumsher RANA (President), Lokendra Bahadur CHAND (Former Prime Minister), Deepak BOHARA, Parshu Ram KHAPUNG.

Communist Party of Nepal (Marxist-Leninist)—CPN (ML). On March 5, 1998, 46 of the CPN (UML)'s 89 House members, led by former deputy prime minister Bamdev Gautam and others, left the parent grouping and formed the CPN(ML). The split occurred primarily because of the dissidents' opposition to the water-sharing arrangements in the 1996 Indo-Nepal Mahakali Integrated Development Treaty. Describing the new formation as a party of the progressive left, its leaders voiced support for nationalism and democracy while labeling the United States imperialist and India a "regional hegemonist."

The CPN (ML) joined the NC in the government of August–December 1998; its departure over policy differences guaranteed the administration's collapse. Despite winning 7 percent of the vote in May 1999, the party failed to capture any lower house seats.

In August 2001 the CPN (ML) and the CPN (UML) agreed to discuss reunification, although the February 2002 decision to proceed was rejected by some CPN (ML) leaders. They then restructured the party, which was sometimes referred to as the CPN (ML)-Reorganized or CPN (ML)-Reconstituted. At a party convention in January 2007 a rift developed in the CPN (ML) central committee, with a faction led by Rishi Kattel subsequently helping to start the a new party, the CPN (Unified). The CPN (ML) formed a United Left Front with two other CPN splinters and joined the Seven-Party Alliance in the Koirala government. Competing independently for the Constituent Assembly in 2008, it won eight seats.

Leader: Chandra Prakash MAINALI (General Secretary).

Communist Party of Nepal (United)—CPN (United—U). The CPN (United) traces its origin to the pro-Moscow branch of the original CPN, which was launched in 1949 but suffered repeated fractures beginning in 1982. In 1991 the CPN (Democratic), led by Bishnu Bahadur MANANDHAR; the CPN (Varma) of K.N. VARMA; and the CPN (Amatya), led by Tulsi Lal AMATYA, formed a unified party, the CPN (United). In December 1993 Amatya broke from the CPN (United) and led his faction into the CPN (UML).

In 1998 the party formed a United Marxist Front (UMF) with the small CPN (Marxist), led by Prabhu Narayan CHAUDHARI. In 2001 the Varma faction joined the CPN (UML).

Although the CPN (United) and the CPN (Marxist) merged in September 2005, the party split in late 2006. Chaudhari and Manandhar resigned, and the CPN (United) reestablished in 2007 under the leadership of Chandra Dev Joshi. With the CPN (Unity Center) and the CPN (Marxist-Leninist), it formed the United Left Front, which joined the governing Seven-Party Alliance. In 2008 the United Left Front dissolved as the CPN (Unity Center) and joined the CP (Maoist). The CPN (United) won seats for five members in the Constituent Assembly. Party leader Ganesh Shah was given a ministry portfolio in the Maoist-led government. The party boycotted the election of a new prime minister in May 2009.

Leaders: Chandra Dev JOSHI (President), Thakur Prasad SHARMA, Ganesh SHAH.

Other Legislative Parties:

Unified Communist Party of Nepal (Maoist)—UCPN-M. Established in 1994 by a breakaway faction of the CPN (Unity Center), in 1996 the CPN-M launched the "People's War" insurgency, which continued and intensified for ten years. In August 2000 the CPN-M announced that it had formed a People's Liberation Army. It also set up a "United People's Revolutionary Council" as a quasi-central government for the areas under its control.

Despite having rejected previous government overtures, in early 2000 the Maoists indicated they would be willing to open discussions related to a 32-point list of demands. At the first round of peace talks with the Deuba government on August 30, 2001, Maoist representative Krishna Bahadur Mahara pressed for an end to the monarchy, formation of an interim government, establishment of a constituent assembly to draft a new constitution, and the release of all Maoist prisoners. No significant progress was made before they abruptly ended a four-month-old cease-fire in November. The January–August 2003 cease-fire and resultant peace talks also came to nothing, as the Maoists continued their insistence on elections for a constituent assembly. In the following 18 months the insurgency expanded its reach and its tactics, initiating general strikes and, on more than one occasion, blockading Kathmandu.

In early 2005 a significant rift over strategy emerged between party General Secretary Prachanda and party ideologue Baburam Bhattarai, who advocated opening lines of communication with parties agitating against King Gyanendra's assumption of power. In July, however, Bhattarai and two close associates, his wife, Hisila YAMI (a.k.a. RAHUL), and Dinanath SHARMA (a.k.a. ASHOK), were reinstated to their posts. With opposition to King Gyanendra's "autocratic monarchy" mounting, secret talks between the CPN-M and the SPA began even before the September 2005 unilateral Maoist cease-fire. Further discussions then led to the November 2005 12-point plan for restoring democracy and bringing the CPN-M into the political mainstream. In early May 2006 one of the first measures of the new Koirala government was to end the party's proscription.

The June 16, 2006, eight-point agreement with the new government, accomplished following the first face-to-face meeting between Prime Minister Koirala and Prachanda, granted the Maoists much of what they had been seeking, including the election of a constituent assembly in the near future and a role in an interim government, while committing them to dissolving the rural governments they had formed and to permitting international supervision of their army and weapons prior to the election. A comprehensive peace agreement followed in November, ahead of the promulgation of the interim constitution on January 15, 2007. The CPN-M, effecting a transformation from a guerrilla army to a political party, joined the Interim Legislature-Parliament with 83 seats. In September 2007, having failed to obtain full cabinet support for declaring a republic and for electing all constituent assembly seats on a proportional basis, the CPN-M withdrew its four ministers from the government. It rejoined the government at the end of the year after winning a commitment from the Council of Ministers to support establishment of a republic.

Having accomplished their objectives of taking down the monarchy and bringing about the formation of the constituent assembly, the Maoists proceeded to take first place in the election on April 10, 2008, securing 220 of the assembly's 575 elected seats. On August 15, the assembly elected Prachanda to the office of prime minister.

In January 2009, the party merged with the Communist Party of Nepal (Unity Center-Masal). Renaming itself the Unified Communist Party of Nepal (Maoist), the party formally renounced the "Prachandapath"—the leader's adaptation of Maoist principles to Nepalese conditions—as its guiding doctrine.

The party advocated for the integration into Nepal's army of its nearly 20,000 PLA combatants, who were confined to temporary quarters under UN monitoring. When President Yadav overturned Prachanda's dismissal of the army chief of staff on May 3, 2009, Prachanda claimed the move exceeded the president's constitutional authority and threatened civilian control of the military. He resigned the following day, and the party shifted to the opposition, launching intense protests. Maoist partisans stormed parliament on May 18 and boycotted the election for a new prime minister. Subsequently, they prevented parliament from sitting for a month through daily obstruction, insisting that the president's order be nullified. Meanwhile, Prachanda and his supporters argued for concluding the peace process and the drafting of a new constitution.

Leaders: Pushpa Kamal DAHAL (a.k.a. Comrade PRACHANDA) (Chair and Former Prime Minister), Dev GURUNG, Krishna Bahadur MAHARA, Baburam BHATTARAI, Mohan Baidya KIRAN.

Sadbhavana Party (SP). This party splintered off from the Nepal Goodwill Party (Anandi Devi) (*Nepali Sadbhavana* Party [Anandi Devi]—NSP-A, below) in 2007. It joined the United Democratic Madhesi Front (UDMF) in 2008. Its leader, Rajendra Mahato, had been general secretary of NSP-A and a cabinet minister. Mahato announced his resignation from the interim parliament on January 19, 2008, accusing the government of ignoring the demands of the Madhesis. He was elected to the Constituent Assembly along with eight others from his party, and he was appointed minister of commerce in Prachanda's cabinet. On May 3, 2009, the party withdrew from the Maoist-led government in protest of Prachanda's firing the army chief of staff. The party chose not to enter the UML-led government due to disagreement over how many and which portfolios it would be assigned.

Leader: Rajendra MAHATO.

People's Front Nepal (*Janamorcha Nepal*—JMN). The JMN began as the electoral front for the Communist Party of Nepal (Unity Center Mashal)—CPN (UCM) (*Ekata Kendra Mashal*), formation of which was announced in April 2002 by the leaders of the CPN (Unity Center) and the CPN (*Mashal*). The CPN (Unity Center) was formed in 1990 from the merger of four left-wing factions and organizations. During the 1990s both the CPN (Unity Center) and the CPN (*Mashal*) established electoral fronts. In 1991 the Unity Center's United People's Front/Nepal (*Samyukta Janmorcha Nepal*—SJN) won 9 seats in the House election. In 1994 the party split, one faction forming the radical CPN (Maoist), above, which took with it an allied SJN faction. The CPN (*Mashal*) subsequently formed the National People's Front (*Rashtriya Jana Morcha*—RJM) for electoral purposes. In the May 1999 election the RJM won 5 seats despite capturing only 1 percent of the vote.

Prior to the 1999 lower house election the SJN's Amik Sherchan spearheaded formation of a "Coordination Committee" of eight leftist organizations including the CPN (*Mashal*) and its affiliated RJM; the NWPP; the National People's Movement Coordination Committee (NPMCC); and four parties that later formed the United Left Front—the CPN (ML), the CPN (United), the CPN (Marxist), and the CPN (MLM). In February 2000 all nine leftist parties jointly announced a protest program with the aim of pressuring the government to control essential commodity prices, fight corruption, and protect national interests.

The April 2002 decision to form the CPN (UCM) was followed in July by an announcement that the SJN and the RJM would also merge as the JMN. In 2006, this group became a member of the governing Seven-Party Alliance. However, rifts developed between the JMN and the CPN (UCM) . The JMN (KC), led by Chitra Bahadur K.C., left the SPA and registered in 2007 as the reconstituted Rashtriya Jana Morcha (RJM, below). Another JMN faction, the JMN (Ale), led by Chitra Bahadur Ale, later joined in forming the CPN (Unified). A third JMN group retained the JMN designation, remaining part of the SPA and, in April 2008, winning seven seats in the Constituent Assembly. The party was reconstituted in January 2009 and opposed the merger of Unity Center Mashal with CPN (Maoist). It retained the JMN name.

Leader: Dan Bahadur BISHWOKARMA.

Nepal Goodwill Party (Anandi Devi) (*Nepali Sadbhavana* Party [Anandi Devi]—NSP [Anandi Devi] or NSP-A). This party was originally formed as the NSP, to promote the interests of the Madhesi inhabitants of the Terai. It has sought redelineation of the southern constituencies on the basis of population and the granting of citizenship to all persons settled in Nepal before adoption of the 1990 constitution. The NSP won 3 House seats in 1994 after winning none in 1991 and was awarded one portfolio in the Deuba government of September 1995. In December 1998 the NSP entered the NC-CPN (UML) coalition administration as a junior partner. In the May 1999 election the NSP won 5 seats on a 3 percent vote share.

In January 2002 the party's longtime president, Gajendra Narayan SINGH, died. Differences subsequently emerged over who should fill party posts. At a divisive national convention in March 2003 one faction supported Singh's widow, Anandi Devi SINGH, for the presidency, while another backed the acting president, Deputy Prime Minister Badri Prasad MANDAL. As a consequence, the party split. In April 2004 the Supreme Court upheld an August 2003 Election Commission decision that awarded the NSP title to the Mandal faction, with the other faction becoming the NSP (Anandi Devi). The latter helped form the opposition JPM in 2003 and was among the first of Nepal's mainstream parties to call for election of a constituent assembly as a means of resolving the Maoist insurgency.

In June 2007 the NSP and the NSP (Anandi Devi) reunited, retaining the latter designation, but a faction led by cabinet minister Rajendra MAHATO sought recognition as a separate party. In September the Election Commission denied the request, prompting Mahato to resign from the party and the government. He and his supporters nevertheless remained active in the Terai agitation and continued to use the NSP designation until renaming their splinter the Sadbhavana Party (SA, above), allied with the Madhesi People's Rights Forum (MJF, above).

In August 2008 an ailing Anandi Devi was ousted from the party, reportedly as a result of the party's winning only two seats in the 2008 Constituent Assembly balloting. The party withdrew from the Maoist-led government in February 2009.

Leader: Sarita GIRI.

National Democratic Party (Nepal) (*Rashtriya Prajatantra* Party [Nepal]—RPP [Nepal]). The RPP (Nepal) is a faction of the RPP (above) that approved participating in King Gyanendra's government after the king deposed the democratic government in 2005. In January 2007 it absorbed two other small parties: the *Rashtriya Prajatantra* Party (*Rastrabadi*), or RPP (Nationalist), led by Rajeshwor DEVKOTA, itself an earlier splinter from the RPP; and the *Nepal Bidwat Parishad,* led by Jit Bahadur ARJEL.

At the inaugural session of the Constituent Assembly on May 28, 2008, the RPP (Nepal)'s four members cast the only votes against forming a republic. The right-wing party continued to favor popular referendums on restoring the monarchy and on whether Nepal should be a secular or a Hindu state.

Leader: Kamal THAPA.

National People's Front (*Rastriya Janamorcha*—RJM). This party began as electoral front of the CPN (Mashal) in the 1990s. It merged with the political front of another CPN splinter in 2002 to form the People's Front Nepal (*Janamorcha Nepal*—JMN, above). After the JMN joined the governing Seven-Party Alliance in 2006, Chita Bahadur K.C. led a faction out of the party and reclaimed the name of the RJM. The party held 3 seats in the Interim Legislature-Parliament and four seats in the 2008 Constituent Assembly. The RJM was the first party in the Constituent Assembly to oppose any type of federal structure for the Nepalese republic. **The party maintains that federalism, especially if enacted along ethnic or caste lines,** could lead to the disintegration of national unity. instead, the party advocates decentralization within the existing unitary system.

Leaders: Chitra BAHADUR K.C. (Chair), Dilaram ACHARYA.

Nepal Workers' and Peasants' Party—NWPP (Nepal *Majdoor Kisan* Party). An advocate for the poor and working people, the NWPP began as a Maoist formation but currently advocates nonalignment and a mixed economy. Most of the party's support lies in its stronghold in the Bhaktapur area. It doubled its lower house strength from 2 to 4 seats in 1994 but won only 1 in May 1999. The NWPP was a member of the Seven-Party Alliance but declined an invitation to join the government. It agreed to sign the December 2007 23-point agreement with the Maoists despite objections. It won 4 seats in the 2008 Constituent Assembly election.

In February 2009 the party proposed that Nepal's 14 existing zones become separate states in a federal structure with a president as head of state and government. It opposed federalism based on castes or ethnic communities.

Leader: Narayan Man BIJUKCHHE ("Rohit").

National People's Force Party (*Rastriya Janshakti* Party—RJP). The RJP was launched in March 2005 by former prime minister S.B. Thapa, whose long and complicated history of rivalry with former prime minister L.B. Chand over control of the RPP culminated in his decision to form a new party. Although a royalist, in May 2006 Thapa, arguing in favor of "political stability," backed the legislative proclamation that stripped King Gyanendra of his powers. Subsequently, the RJP and RPP began discussions on reunification, although the RJP registered separately for the Constituent Assembly election, in which it was awarded three seats. S.B. Thapa had been included in the RPP's delegation to the Interim Legislature-Parliament.

Leader: Surya Bahadur THAPA (President), Prakash Chandra LOHANI (Vice President).

National People's Liberation Party (*Rastriya Janamukti* Party). An ethnically based party founded in 1990 by the indigenous leaders M. S. Thapa and Gore Bahadur Khapangi, the party favors a federal system based on autonomous ethnic federal units. The party won 2 seats in the 2008 Constituent Assembly balloting.

Leaders: M.S. THAPA (Chair), Bayan Singh RAI (General Secretary).

Communist Party of Nepal (Unified)—CPN (Unified). Formed in 2007, the CPN (Unified) brought together three splinter groups from other communist organizations: the Chitra Bahadur ALE wing of the JMN; the Rishi KATTEL wing of the CPN (ML); and the faction of the

CPN (MLM Center) led by Sitaram TAMANG. The new party assumed the 2 seats in the Interim Legislature-Parliament that had been assigned to the JMN (Ale) and subsequently won 2 seats in the Constituent Assembly.

Leader: Ram Singh SHRIS.

Nepali People's Party (*Nepali Janata Dal*). This party was formed in 1995, intending to work for the emancipation of Dalits, Janjatis, and other disadvantaged groups in Nepalese society, including women. The party won two Constituent Assembly seats in 2008. Supporting the contention that President Yadav exceeded his authority by overturning the move to fire the army chief of staff, Nepali Janata Dal boycotted the election of a new prime minister in May 2009.

Leaders: Hari Charan SHAH (Chair), Kabi Raj TIMILSINA (Vice Chair).

Federal National Democratic Forum (*Sanghiya Loktantrik Rastriya Manch*). This party, first registered in early 2008, is an umbrella organization of state councils and other groups, some of them armed, representing Nepal's indigenous ethnic groups or *janajati*, such as the Limbus. Reflecting its ethnic base, the party advocates for self-determination, a federal system based on autonomous regions, and proportional representation of diverse populations in government. The party won two seats in the Constituent Assembly.

Leader: Kumar LINGDEN.

In addition, the following parties each won 1 Constituent Assembly seat: **Socialist Democratic People's Party Nepal** (*Samajwadi Prajatantrik Janata* Party *Nepal*), led by Prem Bahadur SINGH; **Nepal Democratic Socialist Party** (*Nepal Loktantrik Samajbadi Dal*), represented by Laxmilal CHAUDHARY; **Dalit Janjati Party**, representing low-caste *Dalits* and other marginalized peoples, led by Bishwendra PASAWAN; **Nepal Family Party** (*Nepal Parivar Dal*), a utopian socialist party that envisions Nepal as one family, represented by Eknath DHAKAL; **Nepa National Party** (*Nepa Rastriya* Party), represented by Buddha Ratna MANANDHAR, an ethno-nationalist party supporting the linguistic and cultural rights of the Newar community; and **Chure Bharwar National Unity Party Nepal** (*Chure Bhawar Rastriya Ekta* Party *Nepal*), the front of a regional defense organization, led by Keshab MAINALI.

For more information on the **Communist Party of Nepal (Marxist-Leninist-Maoist Center)**—CPN (MLM Center), see the 2008 *Handbook*.

Other Parties that Participated in Recent Elections:

Nepal Green Party (Nepal *Hariyali* Party—NHP). Formed in 1996, the NHP is committed to a "clean environment and clean government" and to a free-market economy. It also favors maintaining a multiparty democracy within the context of a constitutional monarchy. It ran 45 candidates for the lower house in 1999, but none were successful. It also failed to win a seat in the Constituent Assembly.

Leader: Kuber SHARMA.

Nepal Samata Party (NSP). The NSP was formed in 2002 by then government minister Narayan Singh Pun, who had been elected to the House of Representatives as an NC member. In 2003, while serving under Prime Minister Chand, Pun was widely credited with bringing the CPN (Maoist) to the negotiating table. In December 2005 he was named minister of land reform in King Gyanendra's cabinet. The party also participated in the February 2006 local elections. As a consequence, in April 2006 Pun was formally expelled from the NC delegation to the reinstituted House. Pro-monarchist, the NSP registered in 2007 for the upcoming Constituent Assembly election but won no seats. Pun died on February 21, 2008.

Leaders: Pasang Goparma SHERPA (Chair), Moti Prasad Rana MAGAR (General Secretary).

Ethnic Organizations:

In the past, indigenous and other ethnic organizations played little part in national politics per se, but the success of the Maoist insurgency in 2006 and the subsequent adoption of an interim constitution generated demands from many for federalism, self-determination, and ethnic autonomy.

A principal instigator of the insurgency in the Terai that began in January 2007 was an offshoot of the CPN (Maoist), the **Janatantrik Terai Mukti Morcha** (JTMM), which sought an independent Terai. The group has several armed and active wings. The more moderate **Madhesi People's Rights Forum** (*Madhesi Janadhikar* Forum—MJF, above) entered the electoral arena in 2008 and became a force in the Constituent Assembly and the government. Another group, the **Khumbuwan National Front** (*Khumbuwan Rashtriya Morcha*—KRM), representing the Limbu population in the east, also left the CPN (Maoist), with which it had been associated for a number of years. The **Tharu Kalyankari Sabha** (TKS) sought autonomy for the Tharu people.

In the wake of the unrest in the Terai, a nonpartisan umbrella organization representing 54 indigenous groups (*Janajatis)*, the **Nepal Federation of Indigenous Nationalities** (NFIN), chaired by Pasang SHERPA, opened discussions with the government. Its demands included use of a strictly proportional voting system for the Constituent Assembly. On August 30, 2007, the MJF and the government announced a 22-point agreement that included provision for a federal constitutional structure, but the nature of that federalism is highly contentious.

LEGISLATURE

The 1990 constitution provided for a bicameral Parliament (*Sansad*) consisting of a permanent upper house, the **National Assembly** (*Rashtriya Sabha*), of 60 indirectly elected and appointed members, and a 205-member directly elected **House of Representatives** (*Pratinidhi Sabha*) with a five-year mandate. The proclamation of sovereignty by the House of Representatives on May 18, 2006, effectively suspended the National Assembly's governmental role. The lower house was dissolved by the king on May 22, 2002, and reinstated on April 28, 2006.

When the House promulgated the interim constitution on January 15, 2007, both houses of Parliament "automatically cease[d] to subsist." At the same time, a 330-member **Interim Legislature-Parliament** came into existence, encompassing a combination of 209 legislators from the previous Parliament—excluded were the king's nominees and those who had supported his assumption of power—plus party nominees. The three largest parties—the Nepali Congress, the Communist Party of Nepal (Unified Marxist-Leninist), and the Communist Party of Nepal (Maoist)—held roughly the same number of seats. Nine other parties were represented, including the Nepali Congress (Democratic), which reunited with the Nepali Congress in September.

As called for in the interim constitution, the tenure of the Interim Legislature-Parliament came to an end upon formation of the **Constituent Assembly**. In addition to drafting a new constitution, the assembly was to act as a unicameral legislature for two years. The assembly has 601 members: 240 directly elected in districts, through the "first-past-the-post" method; 335 elected by proportional representation on the basis of party lists; and 26 named by the Council of Ministers to represent indigenous and marginalized groups.

In the election on April 10, 2008, for 575 seats, the seat distribution was as follows: the Communist Party of Nepal (Maoist), 220; Nepali Congress, 110; Communist Party of Nepal (Unified Marxist-Leninist), 103; Madhesi People's Rights Forum, 52; Terai Madhesh Democratic Party, 20; Sadbhavana Party (Mahato), 9; National Democratic Party, 8; Communist Party of Nepal (Marxist-Leninist), 8; People's Front Nepal, 7; Communist Party of Nepal (United), 5; National Democratic Party (Nepal), 4; National People's Front, 4; Nepal Workers' and Peasants' Party, 4; National People''s Force Party, 3; National People's Liberation Party, 2; Communist Party of Nepal (Unified), 2; Nepal Goodwill Party (Anandi Devi), 2; Nepali People's Party, 2; Federal National Democratic Forum, 2; independents, 2; Socialist Democratic Peoples' Party Nepal, 1; Dalit Janajati Party, 1; Nepal Family Party, 1; Nepal National Party, 1; Nepal Democratic Socialist Party, 1; and Chure Bhawar National Unity Party Nepal, 1.

The 26 seats appointed by the Council of Ministers were distributed as follows: the Communist Party of Nepal (Maoist), 9; Nepali Congress, 5; Communist Party of Nepal (Unified Marxist-Leninist), 5; Madhesi People's Rights Forum, 2; Sadbhavana Party, Nepal Workers' and Peasants' Party, 1; People's Front Nepal, 1; Terai Madhesh Democratic Party, 1; and Communist Party of Nepal (Marxist-Leninist), 1.

In by-elections in six constituencies on April 10, 2009, the additional seats were distributed as follows: Unified Communist Party of Nepal (Maoist), 3 seats; Nepali Congress, 1; Communist Party of Nepal (Unified Marxist-Leninist), 1; and Madheshi People's Rights Forum, 1.

Chair: Subash Chandra NEMWANG.

CABINET

[as of September 1, 2009]

President	Ram Baran Yadav (NC)
Vice President	Paramananda Jha (MJF)
Prime Minister	Madhav Kumar Nepal (CPN-UML)
Deputy Prime Minister	Bijay Kumar Gachchhadar (MJF-G)
Ministers	
Agriculture and Cooperatives	Mrigendra Kumar Singh (MJF-G)
Commerce and Supplies	
Defense	Bidhya Bhandari (CPN-UML) [f]
Education	Ram Chandra Kuswaha (TMLP)
Energy	Prakash Sharan Mahat (NC)
Environment, Science, and Technology	Thakur Prasad Sharma (CPN-U)_
Federal Structure, Constituent Assembly, Paliamentary Affairs and Culture	Minendra Rijal (NC)
Finance	Surendra Pandey (CPN-UML)
Foreign Affairs	Sujata Koirala (NC) [f]
Forests and Soil Conservation	Deepak Bohara (RPP)
General Administration	Rabindra Shrestha (CPN-UML)
Health and Population	Umakant Chaudhary (NC)
Home Affairs	Bhim Rawal (CPN-UML)
Industry	Mahendra Yadav (TMLP)
Information and Communication	Shankar Pokharel (CPN-UML)
Irrigation	Balkrishna Khand (NC)
Labor and Transport	Mohammad Aftab Alam (NC)
Land Reforms and Management	Dambar Bahadur Shrestha (CPN-ML)
Local Development	Purna Kumar Sherma (NC)
Peace and Reconstruction	Rakam Chemjong (CPN-UML)
Physical Planning and Works	Bijay Kumar Gachchhadar (MJF-G)
Tourism and Civil Aviation	Sharat Singh Bhandari (MJF-G)
Water Resources	Bishnu Poudel (CPN-UML)
Women, Children, and Social Welfare	Vacant
Youth and Sports	Ganesh Nepali (TMLP)

[f] = female

COMMUNICATIONS

The 1990 constitution endorsed freedom of the press, most importantly by outlawing prior censorship, although on occasion the government attempted to restrict independent media from disseminating news it considered sensationalist or unverified. More severe restrictions accompanied recent states of emergency, and journalists were detained under anti-terrorism ordinances and acts. During the Maoist insurgency a significant number were tortured or killed, either by the police and the military for supporting the Maoist cause or by Maoists for spying or other alleged offenses.

Along with other constitutionally guaranteed rights, freedom of the press was suspended, by order of the king, when a state of emergency was reinstituted on February 1, 2005. According to Reporters Without Borders, over 400 journalists were arrested during the following year. The harsh restrictions were abolished, however, following the restoration of multiparty government in April–May 2006. The 2007 interim constitution lists freedom to publish and broadcast as a fundamental right, subject to "reasonable restrictions on any act which may undermine the sovereignty and integrity of Nepal or which may endanger the harmonious relations subsisting among the peoples of various castes, tribes or communities, or on any act of sedition, defamation, contempt of court or incitement to an offence; or on any act which may be contrary to decent public behavior or morality."

In 2009 the watchdog International Freedom of Expression eXchange (IFEX) reported that "press freedoms in Nepal continue to face a serious threat despite the hope that restoration of democratic rule would improve the situation." It cited attacks on journalists, some deadly, and the disappearance in 2007 of a journalist who had been accused by the government and later released on bail.

Press. For its size, Nepal has an unusually large number of newspapers, including some 140 dailies and several hundred weeklies. The following are published daily in Kathmandu: *Gorkha Patra* (75,000), government organ, in Nepali; *Nepali Hindi Daily* (60,000), pro-Indian, in Hindi; *Kathmandu Post* (30,000), in English; *Rising Nepal* (20,000), government organ, in English.

News agencies. The domestic facility is the government's *Rastriya Samachar Samiti* (RSS); AP, UPI, *Agence France-Presse, Deutsche Presse-Agentur,* Reuters, *Xinhua,* and Kyodo News Service are among the organizations that maintain bureaus in Kathmandu.

Broadcasting and computing. A government broadcasting monopoly ended in the mid-1990s, and limited private FM radio and television service is increasingly common. Radio Nepal and the Nepalese Television Corporation are owned and operated by the government. As of 2008 there were 17.3 Internet users per 1,000 inhabitants.

INTERGOVERNMENTAL REPRESENTATION

Ambassador to the U.S.: Shankar Prasad SHARMA.

U.S. Ambassador to Nepal: (Vacant).

Permanent Representative to the UN: Gyan Chandra ACHARYA.

IGO Memberships (Non-UN): ADB, Interpol, IOM, NAM, SAARC, WCO, WTO.

NETHERLANDS

Kingdom of the Netherlands
Koninkrijk der Nederlanden

Political Status: Constitutional monarchy established 1814; under multiparty parliamentary system.

Area: 13,103 sq. mi. (33,936 sq. km.).

Population: 15,987,075 (2001C); 16,403,000 (2008E). Since 1971 population records have been maintained by means of a continuous accounting system rather than by total enumerations, the 2001 figure being derived from a January compilation of system components.

Major Urban Centers (2005E): AMSTERDAM (739,000), Rotterdam (596,000), The Hague (seat of government, 468,000), Utrecht (276,000), Eindhoven (209,000).

Official Language: Dutch.

Monetary Unit: Euro (market rate December 1, 2009: 1 euro = $1.51US).

Sovereign: Queen BEATRIX Wilhelmina Armgard; ascended the throne April 30, 1980, upon the abdication of her mother, Queen JULIANA Louise Emma Marie Wilhelmina.

Heir Apparent: WILLEM-ALEXANDER, Prince of Orange.

Prime Minister: Jan Peter BALKENENDE (Christian Democratic Appeal); sworn in as head of a three-party coalition on July 22, 2002, following general election of May 15, succeeding Willem (Wim) KOK (Labor Party); formed new three-party coalition government on May 27, 2003, following general election of January 22; formed a two-party minority government on July 7, 2006, after the Democrats 66 withdrew support from the previous government; formed a new three-party coalition government on February 22, 2007, following the general election of November 22, 2006.

THE COUNTRY

Facing the North Sea between Belgium and Germany, the Netherlands (often called "Holland," from the name of one of its principal provinces) is noted for the dikes, canals, and reclaimed polder lands providing constant reminder that two-fifths of the country's land area lies below sea level. The largely homogeneous, Germanic population is divided principally between Catholics (31 percent) and Protestants (21 percent), with 40 percent declaring no religious affiliation in 1999. In 2007 women constituted 47 percent of the labor force, concentrated in the services sector; women currently occupy more than one-third of the seats in each parliamentary chamber and head 4 of 16 ministries.

The Netherlands experienced rapid industrialization after World War II, although the industrial sector is now limited to approximately 22 percent of the labor force as compared with 74 percent in the services sector. The traditionally important agricultural sector employs fewer than 4 percent but is characterized by highly efficient methods of production, which are amply rewarded by the common agricultural policy of the European Union (EU, formerly the European Community—EC), of which the Netherlands was a founding member. Leading agricultural products include potatoes, vegetables, sugar beets, wheat, and pork. Since there are few natural resources except large natural gas deposits, most nonagricultural activity involves the processing of imported raw materials. Refined petroleum, chemicals, steel, textiles, and ships constitute the bulk of industrial output. Principal exports include machinery and transport equipment, chemicals and petroleum products, and food. Germany, Belgium, France, and the United Kingdom rank as leading trading partners.

In the early 1980s the economy was stagnating under the influence of persistently high budget deficits necessitated, in part, by the nation's extensive welfare system, which, among other things, provided disability payments to more than 1 million workers. However, a labor/business pact in 1982 established the basis for significant governmental cost-cutting, private-sector promotion, wage moderation, and more flexible employment regulations. As a result, the economy grew at a real average rate of 1.9 percent during 1985–1994. GDP grew by 3.8 percent in 1997 and 4.1 percent in 1998, while inflation remained at about 2 percent annually and unemployment fell to under 5 percent in 1998. The Netherlands thereby easily met the economic criteria required for its participation in the launching of the EU's Economic and Monetary Union (EMU) on January 1, 1999.

GDP growth in 1999 and 2000 held steady at more than 3 percent as inflation remained under control and unemployment continued to decline, reaching 3.6 percent in 2000. However, the economy subsequently deteriorated, with growth of only 1 percent in 2001, 0 percent in 2002, and –1 percent in 2003. Meanwhile, inflation and unemployment climbed to nearly 6 percent in 2002. In addition, the budget surplus of the late 1990s (which had permitted tax reduction) was replaced by a deficit that the Dutch government forecast would reach 3.25 percent of GDP in 2004, thereby creating difficulty for the administration regarding EMU fiscal guidelines. The economy appeared to begin a recovery in 2004 (growth of 1.1 percent), although unemployment continued to rise.

The International Monetary Fund (IMF) cited budgetary restraint and stronger exports as the main factors resulting in further improvement in the country's economy during 2005, when GDP grew another 1.1 percent. GDP subsequently grew even faster, by 3 percent in 2006 and 2.5 percent in 2007, which the IMF attributed to fiscal consolidation, stability-oriented macroeconomic policies, and structural reforms. Meanwhile, unemployment rates continued to improve, dropping from 5.0 percent in 2005 to 4.1 percent in 2006 and 3.4 percent in 2007. However, the economy fell into recession in the second quarter of 2008 as a result of the global financial crisis, to which Netherlands was particularly vulnerable because of its robust financial sector and international connections. Among other things, the government nationalized the holdings of the Fortis bank in Netherlands and injected massive amounts of capital into the banking and affiliated sectors overall. The government also introduced a substantial stimulus package in early 2009. GDP contraction of more than 4 percent was predicted for 2009, although unemployment appeared to be remaining relatively low. Although analysts expected at least minimal economic growth to be reestablished in 2010, the IMF warned that reductions in the country's generous health benefits and pensions would be required to secure long-term stability in light of the rapidly aging population.

GOVERNMENT AND POLITICS

Political background. Having declared independence from Spain in 1581 at the time of the Counter Reformation, the United Provinces of the Netherlands were ruled by hereditary *stadhouders* (governors) of the House of Orange until the present constitutional monarchy was established under the same house at the close of the Napoleonic period. Queen JULIANA, who had succeeded her mother, WILHELMINA, in 1948, abdicated in favor of her daughter BEATRIX in April 1980.

Following World War II the Netherlands was governed by a succession of coalition governments in which the large Catholic People's Party (*Katholieke Volkspartij*—KVP) typically played a pivotal role prior to its merger into the more inclusive Christian Democratic Appeal (*Christen-Democratisch Appèl*—CDA) in 1980. Coalitions between the KVP and the Labor Party (*Partij van de Arbeid*—PvdA) were the rule until 1958, when the latter went into opposition, the KVP continuing to govern in alliance with smaller parties of generally moderate outlook. A center-right coalition headed by Petrus J. S. DE JONG assumed office in April 1967 and was followed by an expanded center-right government formed under Barend W. BIESHEUVEL in 1971.

The inability of the Biesheuvel government to cope with pressing economic problems led to its early demise in July 1972 and to an election four months later. A 163-day interregnum then ensued before a PvdA-led government organized in May 1973 by Johannes (Joop) M. DEN UYL emerged as the first Dutch administration dominated by the political left. It survived until March 1977, when it collapsed in the wake of a bitter dispute between PvdA and CDA leaders over compensation for expropriated land. After another extended interregnum (the longest in the nation's history), Andreas A. M. VAN AGT succeeded in organizing a government of his CDA and the People's Party for Freedom and Democracy (*Volkspartij voor Vrijheid en Democratie*—VVD) in late December.

In the election of May 1981 the center-right coalition lost its legislative majority and was replaced by a grouping that included the CDA, PvdA, and center-left Democrats 66 (*Democraten 66*—D66), with van Agt continuing as prime minister. The comfortable legislative majority thus achieved was offset by sharp differences over both defense and economic policy, and the new government collapsed in May 1982. The principal result of balloting in September was a loss of 11 seats by the D66 and a gain of 10 by the VVD. Ruud F. M. LUBBERS was installed as head of another center-right government in November following his succession to the CDA leadership in October. Contrary to opinion poll predictions, the CDA won a plurality in the lower house election of May 1986, Lubbers being returned as head of a new center-right government in July.

Lubbers was forced to resign on May 2, 1989, following coalition disagreement over funding for an ambitious environmental plan, although he remained in office in a caretaker's capacity pending new elections. Because of its perceived antienvironmental posture, the VVD's parliamentary representation dropped from 27 to 22 seats in the balloting on September 6, with the PvdA becoming the CDA's partner in a new center-left administration sworn in on November 7 under Lubbers's leadership. His continuation in office was made possible by a commitment to the PvdA to increase antipollution and social welfare expenditures, financed largely by the imposition of a "carbon dioxide" tax on business firms and a freeze on defense spending in 1991. While the subsequent course of events in Eastern Europe permitted an actual cutback in projected military expenses, the overall economic situation deteriorated.

The May 1994 general election marked the withdrawal from Dutch politics of Prime Minister Lubbers, who failed to gain the presidency of the European Commission in June. (The U.S. government vetoed his candidacy for the post of secretary general of the North American Treaty Organization [NATO] in 1995, but Lubbers was named to head the UN Office of the High Commissioner for Refugees in 2000.) The CDA campaign in 1994 was headed by Elco BRINKMAN, party leader in the Second Chamber. With Lubbers's departure, the CDA suffered its worst-ever defeat, losing a third of its support. The PvdA also lost ground, but it replaced the CDA as the largest parliamentary party, while substantial gains were registered by the VVD and D66. Far-right and far-left parties also gained seats, and two new pensioners' movements made their chamber debuts. In light of the new parliamentary arithmetic, the outcome of lengthy postelection negotiations was, as expected, the formation in August 1994 of a three-party coalition of the PvdA, VVD, and D66, with Willem (Wim) KOK becoming the first Labor prime minister since 1977.

The new coalition committed itself to a four-year program of retrenchment in social, defense, and other government spending, although deeper welfare cuts were deferred for two years at the PvdA's behest. In addition, the governing parties were broadly united in desiring to meet the "Maastricht criteria" for participation in a single European currency toward the end of the century.

With the government having received wide international praise for the "Dutch model" of sustained economic growth, substantial job creation, and an effective social services sector, the PvdA and the VVD improved their positions in the May 6, 1998, Second Chamber elections, although the D66 slipped significantly. The new government announced by Kok on August 3 comprised six ministers each from the PvdA and the VVD and three from the D66, with the coalition controlling 97 of the 150 seats in the *Tweede Kamer*.

On May 19, 1999, the cabinet resigned following the defeat by one vote in the *Eerste Kamer* of a bill sponsored by the D66 that would have permitted national "corrective referendums" to veto certain economic and social legislative decisions. However, on June 2 the three parties agreed to resume the coalition and to back a revised "consultative referendum" bill under which referendum results would not be binding.

Although the three-party governing coalition flirted with collapse in May 1999, two years of relative stability followed.

At the same time, the Netherlands attracted international attention, as it had so frequently in the past, for legalizing controversial social practices. In 2001 it became the world's first country to permit same-sex marriages, and a year later another first-of-a-kind law legalizing euthanasia entered into effect.

On August 26, 2001, Prime Minister Kok confirmed that he would step down, with the party then turning to its parliamentary leader, Ad MELKERT, to lead it into the 2002 elections. Following local balloting in March 2002, however, it appeared that prospects for Labor's continuation in office were declining, given the increasing strength of the CDA and the emergence, farther to the right, of an anti-immigrant populist party, the List Pim Fortuyn (*Lijst Pim Fortuyn*—LPF).

Prime Minister Kok and his cabinet resigned on April 16, 2002, in response to a report that criticized the Dutch military for failing to prevent the July 1995 massacre at the Bosnian "safe haven" of Srebrenica. The government continued to serve in a caretaker capacity until the May 15 general election. Despite the shock of the assassination of LPF leader Pim FORTUYN on May 6, the leaders of the major parties agreed to hold the balloting as scheduled, with the CDA (led by Jan Peter BALKENENDE) securing a plurality of 43 seats in the *Tweede Kamer,* followed by the LPF (26 seats), VVD (24), and PvdA (23).

A CDA/LPF/VVD coalition government was formed on July 22, 2002, under Balkenende's leadership. However, it resigned on October 16 as a result of differences over the proposed expansion of the EU, a power struggle within the LPF, and increasing economic difficulties. In early balloting for the *Tweede Kamer* on January 22, 2003, the CDA again achieved a slim plurality (44 seats versus 42 for the PvdA). The CDA initially sought to form a coalition with the PvdA, but negotiations fell apart due primarily to personal animosity between the leaders of the parties. After protracted negotiations, a CDA/VVD/D66 coalition was announced on May 27, with Balkenende retaining the premiership.

On June 29, 2006, the Balkenende government collapsed after several weeks of infighting among the three parties in the coalition government. The smallest of the three parties, the D66, withdrew its support for the government after its calls for the resignation of Immigration and Integration Minister Rita VERDONK of the VVD were rebuffed. An interim minority government of the CDA and the VVD was installed on July 7.

Although many analysts had predicted a major defeat for the CDA at the hands of the PvdA, the CDA lost only 3 of its seats in the November 22, 2006, *Tweede Kamer* balloting, while the PvdA lost 9 of its seats. Most electoral gains were registered on the extremes, as the extreme-left Socialist Party (*Socialistische Party*—SP) won 25 seats (up from 9 in 2003) and new extreme right-wing Party for Freedom (*Party voor de Vrijheid*—PVV) won 9 seats. After more than two months of negotiations, Balkenende was able to construct a broad-spectrum coalition government comprising the CDA, PvdA, and the Christian Union (*ChristenUnie*—CU), which was installed on February 22, 2007.

Constitution and government. Originally adopted in 1814–1815, the Netherlands' constitution has been progressively amended to incorporate the features of a modern democratic welfare state in which the sovereign exercises strictly limited powers. Under a special Statute of December 29, 1954, the Kingdom of the Netherlands was described as including not only the Netherlands proper but also the fully autonomous overseas territories of the Netherlands Antilles and Suriname, the latter ultimately becoming independent in 1975. On January 1, 1986, the island of Aruba formally withdrew from the Antilles federation, becoming a separate, self-governing member of the kingdom.

Political power centers in the parliament, or States General (*Staten Generaal*), consisting of an indirectly elected First Chamber (*Eerste Kamer*) and a more powerful, directly elected Second Chamber (*Tweede Kamer*). Either or both chambers may be dissolved by the sovereign prior to the holding of a new election. Executive authority is vested in a Council of Ministers (*Ministerraad*) appointed by the sovereign but responsible to the States General. An advisory Council of State (*Raad van State*), comprised of the queen and crown prince plus a number of councillors appointed by the queen upon nomination by the Second Chamber, is consulted by the executive on legislative and administrative policy. The judicial system is headed by a Supreme Court and includes five courts of appeal, 19 district courts, and 62 cantonal courts.

For administrative purposes the Netherlands is divided into 12 provinces, the most recent, Flevoland, having been created on January 1, 1986, from land formed under the more than half-century-old Zuider Zee reclamation project. Each province has its own elected council, which elects an executive, and a sovereign commissioner appointed by the queen. At the local level there are approximately 640 municipalities, each with a council that designates aldermen to share executive responsibilities with a crown-appointed burgomaster.

Foreign relations. Officially neutral before World War II, the Netherlands reversed its foreign policy as a result of the German occupation of 1940–1945 and became an active participant in the subsequent evolution of the Western community through the Benelux Union, NATO, the Western European Union, the EC/EU, and other West European and Atlantic organizations. A founding member of the UN, the Netherlands also belongs to all of the UN's specialized agencies. The country's principal foreign policy problems in the postwar period stemmed from the 1945–1949 transition to independence of the Netherlands East Indies (Indonesia); Jakarta's formal annexation in 1969 of West New Guinea (Irian Jaya); and continued pressure, including numerous acts of terrorism, by South Moluccan expatriates seeking Dutch aid in the effort to separate their homeland from Indonesia.

A major foreign affairs issue with profound domestic repercussions turned on the NATO decision in late 1979 to modernize and expand its nuclear arsenal. After intense debate in the Second Chamber, the Dutch acceded to the wishes of their allies but indicated that they would postpone local deployment of 48 cruise missiles in the hope that a meaningful arms control agreement with the Soviet bloc could be negotiated. In the absence of such an agreement, a treaty with the United States authorizing deployment of the missiles by mid-1989 was finally ratified by the Netherlands in February 1986. However, preparations for installation of the missiles were suspended prior to the signing of the U.S.-Soviet intermediate-range nuclear force treaty in December 1987 and were formally terminated upon acceptance of the treaty by the States General in March 1988.

On December 15, 1992, the States General completed its ratification of the EC's Maastricht Treaty on economic and political union. However, the Netherlands' enthusiasm for European integration did not extend to participation in the "Eurocorps" military force inaugurated by France and Germany in 1992. Instead, the Netherlands on March 30, 1994, signed an agreement with Germany providing for the creation of a 30,000-strong Dutch-German joint force that would be fully integrated into NATO and open to other NATO members. The new joint force was formally inaugurated in August 1995, with staff headquarters in Münster, Germany.

Amsterdam took offense in November 1995 when the U.S. government vetoed the candidacy of former prime minister Ruud Lubbers for the post of NATO secretary general, reportedly because of Lubbers's record of concern about German dominance in Europe. Nevertheless, the Netherlands, which had previously committed troops to peacekeeping efforts in Bosnia, assigned 2,100 troops to the NATO-commanded International Force (IFOR) under the Dayton peace accords. The Kok administration was also a solid supporter of NATO action against Yugoslavia in early 1999.

The Hague is home to the International Court of Justice and the UN-sponsored International Criminal Tribunals for the former Yugoslavia and Rwanda (see the discussion under the UN Security Council). A Dutch air base also served as the trial site for two Libyans accused of the 1988 bombing of Pan Am flight 103 over Lockerbie, Scotland; the Dutch government had permitted the base to be regarded as Scottish territory for the duration of the trial, which concluded with one guilty verdict and one acquittal in early 2001.

Although the Netherlands had contributed naval resources to the U.S.-led UN coalition in the 1991 Gulf War, support for the U.S./UK-led invasion of Iraq in 2003 was tepid (at best) in many quarters. Although the government initially deployed 1,700 troops to the Iraqi campaign, those forces were withdrawn in 2005. However, in February 2006 the Dutch parliament bowed to entreaties of U.S. and NATO officials and agreed to send up to 1,700 troops to Afghanistan as part of a NATO reconstruction mission.

Dutch voters took a dramatic step back from European integration when a larger-than-expected 61.5 percent of voters rejected the EU constitution in a referendum in June 2006. Prime Minister Balkenende's government had conducted a campaign in favor of the treaty, and Balkenende subsequently announced that any future consideration was to take place in the legislature rather than by referendum. The government announced approval of the treaty in July 2008 after both houses of parliament provided large majorities voting in support.

Current issues. Events prior to the May 2002 balloting for the *Tweede Kamer* were dominated by the sudden emergence as a major political force of flamboyant Pim Fortuyn, whose promotion of a populist mix of liberal policies (such as the improvement of public services) and rightist positions (such as heavy curbs on immigration and restrictions on rights for ethnic minorities) had struck a chord within a Dutch population increasingly concerned over deteriorating economic conditions and rising crime. Following Fortuyn's assassination on May 6 by an animal rights and environmental activist, consideration was given to postponing the balloting. However, all the major party leaders consented to proceeding as scheduled, with the LPF (the party formed by Fortuyn) winning 26 seats and joining the CDA and VVD in a center-right coalition government. Internal leadership struggles within the LPF quickly compromised the stability of the party and the government, prompting early elections in January 2003. Although the LPF seat total fell to 8 in that balloting and the party lost its cabinet status, some of its proposals regarding immigration and crime had become official government policy.

Upon formation of the CDA/VVD/D66 coalition in May 2003, Prime Minister Balkenende promised a crackdown on drug trafficking and other crimes. His administration also tried to combat a burgeoning fiscal crisis through proposed liberalization of labor regulations and reductions in longstanding welfare and pension benefits. However, those measures were met with stiff resistance by trade unions and other elements of society accustomed to the consensus-building approach previously employed in advance of major shifts in economic policies. Despite the government's austerity measures, it was predicted that the budget deficit would exceed 3 percent of GDP and thereby place the Netherlands in violation of the EU's growth and stability pact. (The Dutch government had previously been among the sharpest critics of similar French and German transgressions.) The gathering difficulties culminated in the opposition parties securing a solid majority of the Dutch seats in the June 2004 European Parliament elections. Another factor in the government's poor showing was public opposition to the administration's solid support for U.S. policy in Iraq.

The intertwined issues of immigration and rising anti-Muslim sentiment moved dramatically to the forefront again in November 2004 when Theo van GOGH, a filmmaker who had recently released a movie that focused on Islam's treatment of women, was assassinated, allegedly by an Islamic radical. Numerous anti-Muslim disturbances broke out in the wake of the murder, further threatening the Netherlands' long-time reputation for tolerance. In early 2005 the government announced that stricter qualifications would be imposed on potential immigrants regarding their knowledge of the nation's history and culture. Concurrently, an extensive campaign to combat terrorism was launched, and a number of alleged Islamic militants were either arrested or deported. The immigration and terrorism issues were widely believed to have been major factors in the 61.5 percent "no" vote registered by the Dutch electorate in a national referendum in June on the question of whether the proposed new EU constitution should be approved. (The government and most major parties had called for a "yes" vote.)

In May 2006 Immigration and Integration Minister Rita Verdonk of the VVD announced that she was considering revoking the citizenship of Ayaan HIRSI ALI, a member of the legislature and an immigrant from Somalia, for having allegedly lied on her application for asylum. After public uproar, the government ultimately decided to allow Hirsi Ali to retain her Dutch citizenship, though she had already resigned her legislative seat and accepted a job at the American Enterprise Institute, a conservative think tank in the United States. The D66 party, the smallest member of the governing coalition, demanded the resignation of Verdonk in exchange for its continuing participation in the government. Verdonk was also under fire from D66 for her proposals to require Dutch to be the only language spoken in the streets of Holland. When Verdonk refused to resign, the D66 on June 29 left the coalition; Prime Minister Balkenende consequently announced the resignation of his government and set the stage for new elections to be held approximately a year before originally scheduled.

Former Prime Minister Ruud Lubbers was called on to negotiate a new government, and within a week an interim minority government comprising the CDA and VVD was installed. The so-called rump cabinet focused on preparation for the new elections and presentation of the 2007 budget.

The CDA's better-than-anticipated performance in the November 2006 legislative balloting was in part attributed to recent economic recovery, which had pushed real annual GDP growth to nearly 3 percent. Meanwhile, the seat gains by the extreme-left and extreme-right parties forced Prime Minister Balkenende to form a broad new government in February 2007 covering the center-left to the center-right. Compromises in both directions were apparent in the new government's pledges to scrap plans to privatize Schiphol Airport, to remain part of the U.S. Joint Strike Fighter project, to avoid parliamentary inquiry into Dutch support for the Iraq War, and to increase investment in education, health, childcare, and the environment. The government also promised to pardon asylum seekers resident in country since 2001, a reversal of a policy that had almost brought down the government in December 2006 when Rita Verdonk had refused a legislative demand that she freeze expulsions until a new government could consider the issue of a general pardon. The *Tweede Kamer* approved the pardon in June 2007.

Immigration issues, especially with respect to Muslims, subsequently remained in the spotlight. Geert WILDERS, leader of the new right-wing PVV, announced he was making a short film portraying the Koran as a source of violence and terrorism. The government denounced the film and met with Muslim leaders to calm the situation in anticipation of the film's release in the spring of 2008. After Dutch television refused to air the film, entitled *Fitra,* Wilders released it on the Internet, leading to the closing of the Dutch embassy in Afghanistan and calls for boycotts of Dutch products. To the relief of the government, however, the film drew little reaction from Dutch Muslims. Although a court ruling in early 2009 appeared to pave the way for Wilders to be prosecuted for hate speech (see section of the PVV under Political Parties, below, for details), the PVV continued to rise in popularity, stunning many analysts by finishing second in the European Parliament elections in June with 17 percent of the vote. Although the CDA led all parties in that balloting with 19 percent of the vote, the three-party governing coalition lost 6 of the 16 seats it had previously held.

Another major focus of attention in 2009 was the effort by the government to combat the strongly negative effects of the global financial crisis (see The Country, above, for details). In a related development, the Dutch government joined the UK in pressuring Iceland to agree to repay the nearly 1 billion euros in savings that were lost when Icelandic banks collapsed.

POLITICAL PARTIES

The growth of the Dutch multiparty system, which emerged from the tendency of political parties to reflect the interests of particular religious and economic groups, has been reinforced by the use of proportional representation.

Government Parties:

Christian Democratic Appeal (*Christen-Democratisch Appèl*—CDA). Party organization in the Netherlands has long embraced a distinction between confessional and secular parties, although the former experienced a gradual erosion in electoral support. Partly in an effort to counter the anticonfessional trend, the CDA was organized in December 1976 as an unprecedented alliance of the Catholic People's Party (*Katholieke Volkspartij*—KVP) and two Protestant groups, the Anti-Revolutionary Party (*Anti-Revolutionaire Partij*—ARP) and the Christian Historical Union (*Christelijk-Historische Unie*—CHU). The KVP was founded in 1945 as a centrist party supported primarily by Roman Catholic businesspeople, farmers, and some workers. It endorsed many social welfare programs while favoring close cooperation between spiritual and secular forces in the community. The ARP, founded in 1879, was the nation's oldest political organization, drawing its principal strength from Calvinist businesspeople, white-collar workers, and farmers. The CHU was formed in 1908 by a dissident faction of the ARP. Traditionally more centrist than the parent party, it shared the ARP's Calvinist outlook.

The three constituent parties, which had presented joint lists at the May 1977 parliamentary election, agreed in October 1980 to merge into a unified political grouping. Led by Ruud Lubbers, the CDA obtained a plurality of legislative seats in both 1986 and 1989, aligning itself with the Liberals on the earlier occasion and with Labor on the latter. Under the new leadership of Elco Brinkman for the May 1994 poll, the CDA lost a third of its support (falling from 35.3 to 22.2 percent of the vote) and was reduced to the status of second strongest Second Chamber party. Brinkman resigned as CDA leader in August.

A period of "uncertainty and wrangling" developed within the CDA in the wake of the 1994 electoral decline, the right wing appearing to gain ascendancy in 1997 with selection of Jaap de HOOP SCHEFFER as new party leader. In the May 1998 Second Chamber balloting, the CDA slipped to 29 seats (down from 34) on a vote share of 18.4 percent, although it rebounded strongly to finish first in the March 1999 provincial elections and, thus, in selection of the new First Chamber two months later. De Hoop Scheffer resigned as parliamentary leader in September 2001, citing inadequate support from the party. He was succeeded by Jan Peter Balkenende.

Positioning itself as a "reasoned choice" between the radically conservative LPF (below) and the social-democratic PvdA, the CDA led all parties by securing 43 seats in the May 2002 election to the *Tweede Kamer*. Balkenende subsequently formed a coalition government with the LPF and VVD, but the government collapsed three months later due to divisions within the LPF. Balkenende formed another coalition (this time with the VVD and the D66) following the January 2003 general election, in which the CDA again finished first with 44 seats.

In municipal elections in March 2006, the CDA showed a moderate loss of support, winning 16.9 percent of the vote, a drop of 3.4 percent over the 2002 elections, apparently as a result of an underperforming economy and unpopular pension and health care reforms.

After the June 29, 2006, cabinet crisis and the installation of a minority interim government of the CDA and VVD on July 7, new elections were held in November. The CDA won 26.5 percent of the vote and 41 seats. Balkenende formed a new government in coalition with PvdA and CU in February 2007.

Leaders: Jan Peter BALKENENDE (Prime Minister), Pieter van GEEL (Parliamentary Chair), Peter VAN HEESWIJK (Chair).

Labor Party (*Partij van de Arbeid*—PvdA). The Labor Party was formed in 1946 by a union of the former Socialist Democratic Workers' Party with left-wing Liberals and progressive Catholics and Protestants. It favored democratic socialism and was a strong supporter of the UN and European integration. The party program stressed the importance of equality of economic benefits, greater consultation in decision making, and reduced defense spending. In October 1977, against the advice of its leadership, the party's national congress voted in favor of the establishment of a republican form of government for the Netherlands. During the same period, the PvdA strongly opposed both nuclear power generation and the deployment of cruise missiles. Subsequent policy considerations focused on employment; strengthening social security, health care, and education; transport infrastructure; and debt reduction.

In the May 1994 general election the PvdA slipped from 31.9 to 24.0 percent of the vote but overtook the CDA as the largest Second Chamber party with 37 seats. It won 45 seats (on a 29 percent vote share) in May 1998. The PvdA's seat total slipped badly to 23 in the May 2002 balloting for the *Tweede Kamer,* but the party rebounded to 42 seats in January 2003, making it the second largest party in the country.

In municipal elections in March 2006, the PvdA showed a sharp increase in support, raising its share of the vote by 7.6 percent to 23.4 percent from the 2002 elections. Some analysts predicted that the PvdA would be the main beneficiary of the resignation in June 2006 of the Balkenende government, since recent opinion polls projected that the PvdA would win the largest share of parliamentary seats if a snap election were held. Those forecasts proved premature, however. With the economy rebounding and the CDA losing only 3 seats in the November election, the PvdA lost 9 seats. However, its 33-seat total kept it as the second largest party in the parliament, which was enough to make it the most viable partner for the CDA in the new government.

Leaders: Wouter BOS (Deputy Prime Minister and Leader), Mariëtte HAMER (Parliamentary Chair), Lilianne PLOUMEN (Chair).

Christian Union (*ChristenUnie*—CU). The Christian Union dates from January 2000, when the Reformational Political Federation (*Reformatorische Politieke Federatie*—RPF) and the Reformed Political Union (*Gereformeerd Politiek Verbond*—GPV) agreed to unify. Appealing to both Calvinists and interdenominational Christians, the RPF had been formed in 1975; it obtained 2 Second Chamber seats in 1981 and 1982, 1 in 1986 and 1989, and 3 in 1994 and 1998. Established in 1948, the more conservative, Calvinist GPV long supported a strong defense policy and the Atlantic alliance but opposed any subordination to a supranational governmental body. It won 2 Second Chamber seats in each of the last three general elections prior to the launching of the CU.

Following the merger, the Christian Union controlled 4 seats in the First Chamber and 5 seats in the Second Chamber. The GPV and RPF factions in the Second Chamber formally merged in March 2001. The Christian Union won 3 seats in the *Tweede Kamer* in 2002 as well as 2003. After winning nearly 4 percent of the vote and 6 seats in the *Tweede Kamer* in November 2006, the CU joined the Balkenende-led governing coalition.

Leaders: André ROUVOET (Deputy Prime Minister), Arie SLOB (Parliamentary Chair), Peter BLOKHUIS (Chair).

Opposition Parties:

Socialist Party (*Socialistische Partij*—SP). The left-wing SP increased its vote share from 0.4 percent in 1989 to 1.3 percent in the May 1994 Second Chamber poll, returning two deputies. In preparation for the May 1998 elections, party leaders argued that there was "too much poverty" in the country and criticized a perceived widening of the gap between the rich and poor. It won 3.5 percent of the votes, for five seats. The SP also offered a progressive agenda, in contrast to the LPF, for the 2002 and 2003 elections for the *Tweede Kamer,* securing 9 seats both times. In 2005 the SP opposed the proposed new EU constitution.

The SP won 5.7 percent of the votes in the March 2006 municipal elections (more than doubling its number of seats). In the 2006 *Tweede*

Kamer election the SP won 25 seats, a gain of 16, making it the third largest party in parliament.

Leaders: Agnes KANT (Parliamentary Chair), Jan MARIJNISSEN (Chair).

People's Party for Freedom and Democracy (*Volkspartij voor Vrij heid en Democratie*—VVD). The forerunners of the VVD included the prewar Liberal State and Liberal Democratic parties. Organized in 1948, the party drew its major support from upper-class businesspeople and middle-class, white-collar workers. Although it accepted social welfare measures, the VVD was conservative in outlook and strongly favored free enterprise and separation of church and state.

The party lost ground in both the 1986 and 1989 elections, on the latter occasion going into opposition for the first time since 1982. In the May 1994 balloting, however, the VVD advanced from 14.6 to 19.9 percent of the vote and then entered into a governing coalition with the PvdA and D66 in August. The VVD struck a popular chord with its tough line on immigration and asylum seekers, overtaking the CDA as the strongest party in provincial elections in March 1995. The VVD's Second Chamber seat total rose from 31 to 38 in the May 1998 poll (based on 25 percent of the vote), although it fell to second place behind the CDA in the provincial elections of March 1999. The rise of the LPF (below) cost the VVD in the May 2002 general election, at which VVD representation fell to 23 seats.

Jozias van AARTSEN became party leader when the VVD joined the coalition government in July 2002 and former party leader Garrit ZALM left the post to become minister of finance. Van Aartsen resigned his position after the party performed poorly in the municipal elections of March 2006, and Mark Rutte was elected new party leader on May 31, defeating Immigration and Integration Minister Rita Verdonk for the post.

Verdonk was at the center of the controversy that brought down the government in late June 2006, as the D66 left in protest over her actions in the Hirsi Ali affair (see Current issues, above). Although the VVD remained a partner in the interim minority government that followed, the November election saw the VVD vote share drop to 14.7 percent and its seat total to fall to 22, a loss of 6. Verdonk stirred another government crisis in December 2006, and when she continued to press her anti-immigrant criticisms of the VVD, the party expelled her in September 2007. Rather than resign her parliamentary seat, she decided to sit as an independent and subsequently formed a new political group called Proud of the Netherlands (*Trots op Nederland*—TON).

Leaders: Mark RUTTE (Parliamentary Chair), Ivo OPSTELTEN (Chair).

Party for Freedom (*Party voor de Vrij heid*—PVV). The PVV grew out of a one-man faction in the *Tweede Kamer* in 2004 by Geert Wilders, who had resigned from the VVD in a dispute with party leaders over Turkey's possible entry into the EU but had refused to resign his legislative seat. Wilders subsequently continued to promote anti-immigration policies and other right-wing causes. For the 2006 legislative poll, the Euro-skeptic PVV presented itself as a free-market, low-tax party and an advocate of conformity to Judeo-Christian cultural traditions. The PVV surprised observers by securing 9 seats in the *Tweede Kamer* on a vote share of 5.9 percent.

In January 2009 an appeals court ruled that Wilders should be prosecuted for inciting hatred against Muslims by comparing Islam to Nazism (see Current issues, above, for additional information). He was also temporarily barred from entering the UK on the grounds that he was a threat to "community harmony and therefore public safety." (A UK immigration tribunal overturned the ban in October.)

Even though the PVV had called for the European Parliament to be dissolved, the party presented candidates for the elections to that body for the first time in June 2009. In a surprising outcome, the PVV finished second in that balloting with 17 percent of the vote, securing 4 of 25 seats. Dutch prosecutors subsequently announced that Wilders' hate speech trial would begin in January 2010.

Leader: Geert WILDERS (Parliamentary Chair and Party Chair).

Green Left (*GroenLinks*—GL). The GL was organized as an electoral coalition prior to the 1989 balloting by the Evangelical People's Party (*Evangelische Volkspartij*—EVP), the Radical Political Party (*Politieke Partij Radikalen*—PPR), the Pacifist Socialist Party (*Pacifistisch Socialistische Partij*—PSP), and the Netherlands Communist Party (*Communistische Partij van Nederland*—CPN). It became a permanent party in 1991, when each of its constituent groups voted to disband.

The GL more than doubled its previous representation when it won 1 *Tweede Kamer* seat on a 7.3 percent vote share in 1998. After retaining the 11 seats in the 2002 elections, GL representation fell to 8 seats in 2003 and to 7 in 2006.

Leaders: Femke HALSEMA (Parliamentary Chair), Henk NIJHOF (Chair).

Democrats 66 (*Democraten 66*—D66). Formed in 1966 as a left-of-center party, the D66 favored the dropping of proportional representation and the direct election of the prime minister. Its stand on other domestic and foreign policy questions was similar to that of the PvdA. It changed its name from Democrats '66 to Democrats 66 in 1986. The party's lower house representation rose from 9 seats in 1986 to 12 in 1989, the latter figure being doubled in 1994 on a vote share of 15.5 percent.

In May 1999 the D66 caused the near collapse of the government when its proposal for "corrective referendums" (to override certain parliamentary decisions) was defeated by one vote in the upper house. The matter was resolved in early June when the D66 accepted a compromise that opened the way for nonbinding referendums.

The D66's representation fell to 7 seats in the May 2002 Second Chamber balloting, down from 14 in 1998. Although the party secured only 6 seats in the January 2003 election, the D66 became something of a "kingmaker" when it provided the necessary legislative majority for the new coalition government led by the CDA and the VVD.

The D66 withdrew its support for the Balkenende coalition government in June 2006, resulting in the collapse of the government. The immediate cause of the party's withdrawal was the failure of the VVD's Rita Verdonk to resign as immigration minister (see Current issues for details), but the party also objected to the Balkenende government's support for sending additional Dutch troops to Afghanistan.

The D66's electoral decline continued in the 2006 legislative poll, in which it won only 3 seats on a 2.0 percent vote share.

Leaders: Alexander PECHTOLD (Parliamentary Chair), Ingrid van ENGELSHOVEN (Chair).

Party for the Animals (*Party voor de Dieren*—PvdD). Founded in 2002 as an advocate for animal rights, the party won 0.5 percent of the *Tweede Kamer* vote in 2003. However, it secured 2 seats in the Second Chamber in 2006 (on a vote share of 1.8 percent), thus becoming the first party principally devoted to animal welfare to gain entry into parliament.

Leader: Marianne THIEME (Parliamentary Chair and Party Chair).

Political Reformed Party (*Staatkundig Gereformeerde Partij*—SGP). Dating from 1918, the SGP is an extreme right-wing Calvinist party that bases its political and social outlook on its own interpretation of the Bible. It advocates strong legal enforcement, including the use of the death penalty, and is against supranational government, which it feels opens society to corrupting influences. Since 1993 women have been banned from active membership.

The SGP retained its existing 3 Second Chamber seats in the 1989 election but slipped to 2 in May 1994 before rebounding to 3 in 1998. It frequently cooperated with the GPV and RPF (see Christian Union), including presentation of joint lists for European Parliament balloting. The SGP won 2 seats in the *Tweede Kamer* in 2002, 2003, and 2006 (on a vote share of 1.6 percent).

Leaders: Bas J. van der VLIES (Parliamentary Chair), Arie VAN HERTEREN (Chair).

Other Parties that Participated in the 2006 Elections:

List Pim Fortuyn (*Lijst Pim Fortuyn*—LPF). The LPF was established as Livable Rotterdam (*Leefbaar Rotterdam*—LR) by political maverick Pim Fortuyn prior to the March 2002 local elections, at which the party succeeded in winning control of the Rotterdam council. The LR platform emphasized an end to immigration and a reversal of anti-discrimination guarantees for ethnic minorities. (Among other things, Fortuyn described Islam as "backwards.") The party was renamed the LPF in preparation for the May 2002 general election.

Fortuyn was assassinated on May 6, 2002, nine days before the scheduled legislative balloting, in which the LPF performed remarkably well, winning 26 seats. The LPF subsequently joined the CDA and VVD in a coalition government, but the party soon spun into disarray amid a bitter internal leadership battle and several scandals. Voters in the January 2003 balloting for the *Tweede Kamer* punished the LPF, which won only 8 seats. Underscoring continued party infighting, the 8 LPF members of the *Tweede Kamer* announced their "resignation" from the party in August 2004 in a dispute with the party leadership. The LPF subsequently campaigned in 2005 against the proposed new EU constitution. In the 2006 election the LPF ran under the name "Fortuyn" and won less than 1 percent of the vote and no seats. The party subsequently announced its dissolution at the national level effective January 2008, although it continued to function at the local level.

Leader: Olaf STUGER (Chair).

In September 2006 Marcos PASTORS (a Rotterdam city council member) and Joost EERDMANS (a member of parliament elected on the List Pim Fortuyn in 2002) established **One Netherlands** (*Eén NL*) with a program similar to that of List Pim Fortuyn. The new party outpolled Fortuyn in the November balloting, receiving 0.64 percent of the vote, but fell short of the threshold required for a seat in the *Tweede Kamer*. Meanwhile, the **United Seniors Party** (*Verenigde Senioren-partij*—VSP) under leader Herman TROOST polled 0.13 percent in the balloting.

Eleven other parties and lists, none receiving more than 0.05 percent of the vote, were on the November 2006 ballot. They were the **Ad Bos Collective**, led by Ad BOS; the **Party for the Netherlands** (*Partij voor Nederland*—PVN), led by Hilbrand NAWIJN; **List 21**, led by Arif POTMIS; **Transparent Netherlands** (*Nederland Transparant*—NLTrans), led by Gerrit de WIT; the **Green Free Internet Party** (*Groen Vrij Internet Partij*—GVIP), led by Wernard BRUINING; the **Liberal Democratic Party** (*Liberaal Democratische Partij*—LibDem), led by Sammy of Tuyll van SEROOSKERKEN; the **Blanco List**, led by Robert VERLINDEN; the **Continuous Direct Democracy Party** (*Continue Directe Democratie Partij*—CDDP), led by Rob VERBOOM; the **Love Respect Freedom Party**, led by Dander van der SLUIS; the **Solid Multicultural Party** (*Solide Multiculturele Partij*—SMP), led by Max SORDAM; and **Tamara's Open Party** (*Tamara's Open Partij*—TOP), led by Tamara BERGFELD.

Other Parties:

Center Democrats (*Centrum Democraten*—CD). Despite its name, the CD was actually an extreme right-wing group that urged a total ban on third world immigration. Having in 1989 regained the 1 lower house seat it had lost in 1986, it advanced to three seats in May 1994, winning 2.5 percent support by capitalizing on popular concern about the changing ethnic composition of Dutch society, particularly the doubling of political asylum admissions from 20,000 in 1992 to 40,000 in 1993. In the May 1998 Second Chamber poll it won only 0.6 percent of the vote and no seats. Party Chair Johannes (Hans) JANMAAT died in 2002, leaving the party's future in doubt.

The Greens (*De Groenen*). Founded in 1983 as a federation of local parties, the conservative Greens won 1 upper House seat in 1995 on an independent list and retained it in May 1999. Although the party failed to capture any upper or lower House seats in 2003, it remained active at the local level.

Leader: Paul FRERIKS (Chair).

Friesian National Party (*Fryske Nasjonale Partij*—FNP). Established in 1962 as a regional party advocating the interest of the people in the province of Friesland, the FNP has a member—Hendrik ten HOEVE—who holds a seat in the *Eerste Kamer* under the party label of the Independent Senate Group.

In 2004 Paul van BUITENEN (a former member of the European Commission) launched **Transparent Europe,** which secured 2 seats in the June 2004 balloting for the European Parliament on an antifraud and antiwaste platform. (For a list of other small parties that were active in the 1990s and/or early 2000s, see the 2007 *Handbook*.)

LEGISLATURE

The **States General** (*Staten Generaal*) is a bicameral body consisting of an indirectly elected First Chamber and a directly elected Second Chamber.

First Chamber (*Eerste Kamer*). The 75 members of the upper house are indirectly elected by the country's 12 provincial councils for four-year terms. Following the provincial balloting of March 7, 2007, elections to the First Chamber on May 29 gave the Christian Democratic Appeal 21 seats; the Labor Party, 14; the People's Party for Freedom and Democracy, 14; the Socialist Party, 12; the Christian Union, 4; The Green Left, 4; the Political Reformed Party, 2; the Democrats 66, 2; the Party for the Animals, 1; and the Independent Senate Group, 1.

President: Yvonne TIMMERMAN-BUCK.

Second Chamber (*Tweede Kamer*). The lower house consists of 150 members directly elected (in a single nationwide district under a pure proportional representation system) for four years, subject to dissolution and, under certain circumstances, term extension. The threshold for a party or list to secure representation is 0.67 percent of the national vote. Following the most recent election of November 22, 2006, the Christian Democratic Appeal held 41 seats; the Labor Party, 33; the Socialist Party, 25; the People's Party for Freedom and Democracy (VVD), 22; the Party for Freedom, 9; the Green Left, 7; the Christian Union, 6; the Democrats 66, 3; the Party for the Animals, 2; and the Political Reformed Party, 2. (One of the PvdA legislators was expelled from the party in September 2007 and subsequently sat in the *Tweede Kamer* as an independent. [See section on the VVD in Political Parties, above, for details.])

Chair: Gerdi VERBEET.

CABINET

[as of November 1, 2009]

Prime Minister	Jan Peter Balkenende (CDA)
Deputy Prime Ministers	Wouter Bos (PvdA)
	André Rouvoet (CU)
Ministers	
Agriculture, Nature, and Food Quality	Gerda Verburg (CDA) [f]
Defense	Elmert van Middelkoop (CU)
Development Cooperation	Bert Koenders (PvdA)
Economic Affairs	Maria van der Hoeven (CDA) [f]
Education, Culture, and Science	Ronald Plasterk (PvdA)
Environmental and Spatial Planning	Jacqueline Cramer (PvdA) [f]
European Affairs	Frans Timmermans (PvdA)
Finance	Wouter Bos (PvdA)
Foreign Affairs	Maxime Verhagen (CDA)
Foreign Trade	Frank Heemskerk (PvdA)
General Affairs	Jan Peter Balkenende (CDA)
Health, Welfare, and Sport	Ab Klink (CDA)
Housing, Communities, and Integration	Eberhard van der Laan (PvdA)
Interior and Kingdom Relations	Guusje ter Horst (CU)
Justice	Ernst Hirsch Ballin (CDA)
Social Affairs and Employment	Piet Hein Donner (CDA)
Transport, Public Works, and Water Management	Camiel Eurlings (CDA)
Youth and Families	André Rouvoet (CU)

[f] = female

COMMUNICATIONS

Press. Newspapers are free from censorship and are published by independent commercial establishments. There is strict separation between managerial and editorial boards. The following are published daily in Amsterdam, unless otherwise noted: *De Telegraaf* (800,000), independent; *Het Algemeen Dagblad* (Rotterdam, 277,000), independent; *De Volkskrant* (288,000), independent Roman Catholic; *Eindhovens Dagblad/Brabants Dagblad* ('s-Hertogenbosch, 300,000); *NRC Handelsblad* (Rotterdam, 237,000), liberal; *Friesch Dagblad* (Leeuwarden, 190,000); *De Gelderlander* (Nijmegen, 190,000), independent Roman Catholic; *Haagsche Courant* (The Hague, 150,000), independent; *De Stem* (Breda, 150,000), Roman Catholic; *Dagblad Tubantia/De Twentsche Courant Tubantia* (Enschede, 150,000); *Noordhollands Dagblad* (Alkmaar, 150,000); *Utrechts Nieuwsblad*

(Utrecht, 140,000); *De Limburger* (Maastricht, 140,000), Roman Catholic; Nieuwsblad van het Noorden (Groningen, 130,000), independent; *Eindhovens Dagblad* (Eindhoven, 130,000), Roman Catholic; *Trouw* (120,000), Calvinist; *Rotterdams Dagblad* (Rotterdam, 120,000); *Leeuwarder Courant* (Leeuwarden, 110,000), independent progressive; *Het Parool* (89,000), independent.

News agencies. The Netherlands News Agency (*Algemeen Nederlands Persbureau*—ANP) is an independent agency operated in The Hague and Amsterdam on a cooperative basis by all Dutch newspapers; numerous foreign bureaus maintain offices in The Hague.

Broadcasting and computing. Public broadcasting by seven associations is coordinated by the Netherlands Broadcasting Corporation (*Nederlandse Omroep Stichting*—NOS) and the Netherlands Programming Corporation (*Nederlandse Programma Stichting*—NPS). The five national public service radio stations are privately owned, as are a dozen regional and several hundred local stations. Public television is available on three channels, and another two are commercial. In addition, cable networks provide foreign commercial and public broadcasts. As of 2008 there were 865.5 Internet users per 1,000 inhabitants.

INTERGOVERNMENTAL REPRESENTATION

Ambassador to the U.S.: Renée JONES-BOS.

U.S. Ambassador to the Netherlands: Fay HARTOG-LEVIN.

Permanent Representative to the UN: Hermanus SCHAPER.

IGO Memberships (Non-UN): ADB, AfDB, BIS, BLX, CERN, CEUR, EBRD, EIB, ESA, EU, Eurocontrol, G10, IADB, IEA, Interpol, IOM, NATO, OECD, OSCE, PCA, WCO, WEU, WTO.

RELATED TERRITORIES

The bulk of the Netherlands' overseas empire disappeared with the accession of Indonesia to independence after World War II and the latter's subsequent acquisition of West New Guinea (Irian Jaya). Remaining under the Dutch Crown were the two Western Hemisphere territories of Netherlands Antilles and Suriname, the latter of which became independent on November 25, 1975. As of January 1, 1986, the island of Aruba was politically detached from the Antilles federation, joining it as an internally self-governing territory (see following articles).

ARUBA

Note: In legislative balloting on September 24, 2009, the opposition Aruban People's Party (AVP/OLA) won 48 percent of the vote and 12 of 21 seats, while the governing People's Electoral Movement was reduced to 8 seats. Mike Eman of the AVP/OLA, which had campaigned on a platform calling for repeal of a recent business tax and other measures to combat rising unemployment, was inaugurated as prime minister along with his new cabinet on October 30.

Political Status: Formerly part of the Netherlands Antilles; became autonomous in internal affairs on January 1, 1986.

Area: 74.5 sq. mi. (193 sq. km.).

Population: 90,508 (2000C); 107,000 (2008E).

Major Urban Center (2005E): ORANJESTAD (30,000).

Official Language: Dutch. English, Spanish, and Papiamento (an Antillean hybrid of mainly Portuguese and Spanish that is common to the Leeward Islands) are also spoken.

Monetary Unit: Aruban Guilder (official rate December 1, 2009: 1.79 guilders = $1US). The guilder (also called the florin) is at par with the Netherlands Antilles guilder, which is pegged to the U.S. dollar.

Sovereign: Queen BEATRIX Wilhelmina Armgard.

Governor: Fredis P. (Freddy) REFUNJOL; invested on May 7, 2004, succeeding Olindo KOOLMAN.

Prime Minister: (*See headnote.*) Nelson Orlando ODUBER (People's Electoral Movement); sworn in on October 30, 2001, following the election of September 28, succeeding Jan Hendrik Albert (Henny) EMAN (Aruban People's Party); reappointed following election of September 23, 2005.

THE COUNTRY

Aruba is a Caribbean island situated approximately 16 miles off the northeast coast of Venezuela and 50 miles west of Curaçao. Like other former Dutch dependencies in the area, its population is largely of mixed African ancestry, with minorities of Carib Indian and European extraction. Roman Catholicism is the dominant religion. Tourism is presently of primary economic importance. The island's only oil refinery, owned by a subsidiary of the U.S. oil giant Exxon Mobil, was closed down in March 1985. However, it was rehabilitated by a subsidiary of the U.S. Coastal Corporation later in the decade and remains a significant source of income, as does transshipment of petroleum. Economic growth averaged greater than 4 percent annually in 1996–1999, with annual inflation averaging about 0.7 percent. A downturn began in 2000, with growth for the year declining to 0.6 percent in 2006 before rebounding to 2.1 percent in 2007. The tourism sector was adversely affected by the September 2001 terrorist assaults on the United States, which contributed to a 4 percent decline in GDP for the year. A further decline in tourism resulted from publicity surrounding the disappearance of American Natalee Holloway in May 2005 (see Current issues, below). However, from 2006 to 2008 a recovery in tourism along with what the International Monetary Fund (IMF) defined as "robust" activity in the construction and utility sectors contributed to an economic rebound.

GOVERNMENT AND POLITICS

Political background. Like Curaçao and Bonaire, Aruba became a Dutch possession in 1634 and remained so, save for a brief period of British control during the Napoleonic wars, until participating in constitutional equality with the Netherlands as part of the Netherlands Antilles in 1954.

However, a majority of the islanders disliked what was perceived as both political and economic domination by Curaçao and entered into lengthy discussions with Dutch authorities that resulted in the achievement of formal parity with the Netherlands and Netherlands Antilles, under the Dutch crown, on January 1, 1986. Upon the assumption of domestic autonomy, the assets and liabilities of Aruba and the five remaining members of the federation were divided in the ratio 30–70, Aruba agreeing to retain economic and political links to the Netherlands Antilles at the ministerial level for a ten-year period. (Full independence was initially projected for 1996 but tentative agreement was reached in July 1990 for the island to maintain its existing status indefinitely rather than move on to independence. References to the 1996 independence date were removed from the related constitutional documents completely in April 1995.)

Pre-autonomy balloting on November 22, 1985, yielded victory for a four-party coalition headed by J. H. A. (Henny) EMAN of the center-right Aruba People's Party (AVP) over the People's Electoral Movement (MEP), then led by "the architect of Aruba's transition to . . . eventual independence," Gilberto (Betico) CROES. Following the election of January 7, 1989, a three-party government was formed, led by the MEP's Nelson ODUBER. The coalition continued in office after the election of January 8, 1993, although the AVP outpolled the MEP. Oduber resigned on April 17, 1994, after disagreements with his coalition partners, and Eman returned as head of a new government coalition that included the small Aruban Liberal Organization (OLA) following a general election on July 29.

The legislature was dissolved on September 15, 1997, in the wake of a dispute between the AVP and its coalition partner, with the OLA offering to form a caretaker coalition with the MEP. However, the governor general refused the request. A general election on December 12 failed to resolve the impasse, the parliamentary distribution remaining unchanged. Subsequent negotiations continued until April 16, 1998,

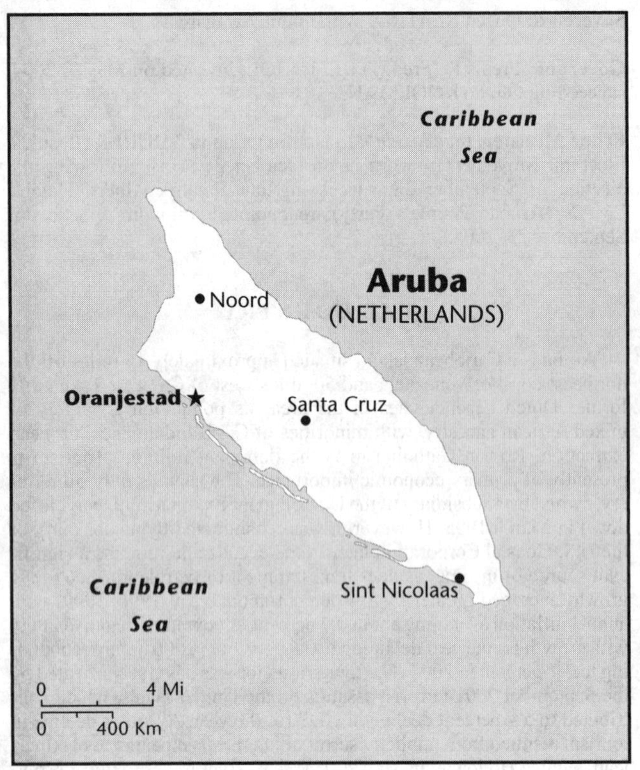

when the former coalition partners reached agreement on a new government.

The AVP/OLA government again collapsed in June 2001 when the two OLA members resigned after voicing objections to the AVP's plan to convert the tourism ministry into a semiprivate agency. Early elections were therefore held on September 28, with the MEP winning a majority of 12 seats, setting the stage for the return of MEP leader Oduber to the prime minister's post on October 30. Oduber remained in office following the election of September 23, 2005, at which the MEP retained control with 11 seats. *(See headnote.)*

Constitution and government. The Dutch sovereign is titular head of state and is represented in Aruba by an appointed governor. Domestic affairs are the responsibility of the prime minister and other members of the Council of Ministers, appointed with the advice and approval of a unicameral *Staten* (legislature) of 21 deputies. Control of foreign affairs and defense is vested in the Council of Ministers in The Hague, with an Aruban minister plenipotentiary sitting as a voting member in matters affecting the island. Judicial authority is exercised by a local court of first instance, with appeal to a joint Court of Appeal of the Netherlands Antilles and Aruba, and ultimate appeal to the Supreme Court of the Netherlands in The Hague.

Current issues. Aruba's tourist industry, already depressed by U.S. travelers' concern over terrorism, was further weakened by the disappearance in May 2005 of 18-year-old Holloway, who was with a group from Alabama celebrating their high school graduation. Three men seen leaving a bar with her were arrested on June 23 but were subsequently released. Publicity over the matter was unabated, in part because of a number of trips to the island by the missing girl's mother, who accused local authorities of inept handling of the case. Unable to bring the matter to a successful conclusion, the Oduber administration in early 2007 asked the Netherlands to assume responsibility for further inquiry, with Dutch officers given full investigative powers. However, no new developments were subsequently reported, despite the temporary redetention late in the year of the girls' male companions.

The IMF has stated that Aruba's financial system is "generally sound," while cautioning that reliance on tourism for 50 percent of its GDP makes it vulnerable to external shocks, such as the global recession of 2008–2009. The IMF has therefore recommended "immediate action" to shore up the health care system, "rationalize" the civil service, implement tax reform, and establish appropriate conditions for attracting private investment.

POLITICAL PARTIES

Leading Parties:

People's Electoral Movement (*Movimento Electoral di Pueblo*—MEP). Founded in 1971 and a member of the Socialist International, the MEP was in the forefront of the struggle for self-government. It won a plurality of 10 *Staten* seats in 1989. Two were lost in 1993, but the MEP was able to form a governing coalition with the NDA and APP prior to the withdrawal of both in April 1994. In the 2001 election the MEP won 12 seats, 1 of which was lost in 2005.

Leaders: Nelson Orlando ODUBER (Prime Minister *[see headnote]* and Leader of the Party), Hyacintho R. (Rudy) CROES.

Aruban People's Party (*Arubaanse Volkspartij*—AVP/*Partido di Pueplo Arubano*—PPA). Like the MEP, the AVP advocated separation of Aruba from the Netherlands Antilles. A member of the Christian Democrat International, it formed a coalition government that included the APP and NDA after the 1985 balloting but was forced into opposition in 1989. It increased its vote share by 23 percent in 1993, exceeding that of the MEP, but could do no better than to tie its opponent's nine seats. It formed a new government in coalition with the OLA after the 1994 election, which was revived in May 1998 but fell in June 2001. In the September election it won 6 *Staten* seats, adding 2 more in 2005.

Leaders: Jan Hendrik Albert (Henny) EMAN (Former Prime Minister), Michiel Godfried EMAN.

Aruban Patriotic Party (*Arubaanse Patriottische Partij*—APP/*Partido Patriótico Arubano*—PPA). Organized in 1949, the APP has opposed full independence for the island. It won 2 parliamentary seats in 2001 but lost both in 2005.

Leader: Benedict (Benny) Jocelyn Montgomery NISBETT.

Aruban Liberal Organization (Organisatie Liberaal Arubaanse/*Organisacion Liberal Arubano/Organisashion pa Liberashou di Aruba*—OLA). The OLA won 2 *Staten* seats in 1994, thereupon joining the government as the AVP's junior partner in a coalition that was formally terminated in September 1997 but revived in April 1998. In the 2001 election the OLA won 1 seat, which it lost in 2005.

Leader: Glenbert François CROES (Former Deputy Prime Minister).

Also winning seats in the 2005 election were the **Network of Eternal Democracy** (*Red Eternal Democratico*—RED), led by Fr. Rudy LAMPE, and the **Aruban Patriotic Movement** (*Movimento Patriotico Arubana*—MPA), led by Monica Kock ARENDS, who was described as Aruba's first female party leader. The **Real Democratic Party** (*Partido Democracia Real*—PDR), led by Andin BIKKER, failed to secure representation in 2005, although it came within 20 votes of success in one district. Other parties include the **National Democratic Action** (*Acción Democratico Nacional*—AND), led by Pedro Charro KELLY; the **Aruban Democratic Alliance** (*Aliansa Democratico Arubano*—ADA), led by Robert Frederick WEVER; and the **Concentration for the Liberation of Aruba** (*Conscientisacion y Liberacion Arubano*—CLA), led by Mariano Duvert BLUME.

LEGISLATURE

The unicameral **States** (*Staten*) consists of 21 members elected for four-year terms, subject to dissolution. In the most recent balloting, held on September 23, 2005, the People's Electoral Movement won 11 seats; the Aruban People's Party, 8; the Aruban Patriotic Movement and Network of Eternal Democracy, 1 each. The next election was scheduled for September 25, 2009. *(See headnote.)*

President: Mervin Glorinda RAS.

CABINET

[as of June 1, 2009]

Prime Minister	Nelson Orlando Oduber
Deputy Prime Minister	Marisol Tromp-Lopez [f]
Ministers	
Education	Marisol Tromp-Lopez [f]
Finance and Economic Affairs	Nilo J. J. Swaen
General Affairs and Foreign Relations	Nelson Orlando Oduber

Justice	Hyacintho Rudy Croes
Public Health and the Environment	Candelario A. S. D. (Booshi) Wever
Social Affairs and Infrastructure	Marisol Tromp-Lopez [f]
Sports, Culture Integration, Community Development, and Labor	Tai Foo Ramon Lee
Tourism and Transportation	Edison (Eddy) Briesen
Minister Plenipotentiary to the Hague	Francisco (Fredo) W. Croes
Minister Plenipotentiary to Washington, DC	Jocelyne Croes [f]

[f] = female

COMMUNICATIONS

Press. The following are dailies published in Oranjestad: *El Diario* (17,000), in Papiamento; *Amigoe di Aruba* (12,000, including Netherlands Antilles), in Dutch; *The News* (10,000), in English; *Aruba Today/ Bon Dia Aruba* (10,000), in English and Papiamento.

News agencies. The Netherlands News Agency (*Algemeen Nederlands Persbureau*—ANP) and the Associated Press (AP) maintain offices in Oranjestad.

Broadcasting and computing. There are nine privately owned radio stations (one devoted to evangelical and cultural broadcasting), with television provided by the commercial Tele-Aruba. As of 2008 there were 227.6 Internet users per 1,000 inhabitants.

INTERGOVERNMENTAL REPRESENTATION

Foreign relations are for the most part conducted through the Netherlands Ministry of Foreign Affairs in The Hague, although there is a Minister Plenipotentiary in the Netherlands Embassy in Washington, and the United States maintains a Consulate General's Office on Curaçao (Netherlands Antilles) that also serves Aruba.

IGO Membership (Non-UN): *ACS*, Interpol.

NETHERLANDS ANTILLES

De Nederlandse Antillen

Note: The dissolution of the Netherlands Antilles was most recently scheduled for October 10, 2010, at which time Curaçao and Sint Maarten were slated to achieve autonomous status within the kingdom (like Aruba), while Bonaire, Saba, and Sint Eustatius were slated to be integrated into Netherlands proper as municipalities.

Political Status: Former Dutch dependency; became autonomous in internal affairs under charter of the Kingdom of the Netherlands, effective December 29, 1954.

Area: 309 sq. mi. (800 sq. km.), encompassing Curaçao (171 sq. mi.), Bonaire (111 sq. mi.), Sint Maarten (Dutch portion, 13 sq. mi.), Sint Eustatius (8 sq. mi.), Saba (5 sq. mi.).

Population: 175,653 (2001C), excluding Aruba; 197,000 (2008E).

Major Urban Center (2005E): WILLEMSTAD (urban area, 76,000).

Official Language: Dutch and Papiamento (an Antillean hybrid, principally of Portuguese and Spanish, that is common in the Leeward Islands). English and Spanish are also widely spoken.

Monetary Unit: Netherlands Antilles Guilder (official rate December 1, 2009: 1.79 guilders = $1US). The guilder is pegged to the U.S. dollar.

Sovereign: Queen BEATRIX Wilhelmina Armgard.

Governor: Dr. Fritz M. de los SANTOS GOEDGEDRAG; invested on July 1, 2002, to succeed Dr. Jaime M. SALEH.

Prime Minister: Emily DE JONGH-ELHAGE (Antillean Restructuring Party); sworn in March 26, 2006, succeeding Etienne YS (Antillean Restructuring Party), following election of January 27.

THE COUNTRY

The Netherlands Antilles currently consists of one group of two islands and another of three islands, located 500 miles apart in the eastern Caribbean. The southern islands of Curaçao and Bonaire lie off the northwest coast of Venezuela, while the northern (Leeward) islands of Sint Maarten (the northern portion of which is part of the French department of Guadeloupe), Sint Eustatius (also known as Statia), and Saba are some 200 miles east of Puerto Rico. Approximately 85 percent of the population is of mixed African ancestry, the remainder being of Carib Indian and European derivation. Roman Catholicism is dominant in the southern islands and Saba, while Protestantism is most prevalent on Sint Eustatius and Sint Maarten. The economy has long been dependent on the refining of crude oil from Venezuela and Mexico, although most facilities (centered in Curaçao) have recently been operating at less than 50 percent capacity; as a result, tourism and offshore banking activities are of increasing importance. Agriculture is relatively insignificant because of poor soil and little rainfall.

Hurricane Luis in September 1995 devastated the Leeward Islands, particularly Sint Maarten, where an estimated three-quarters of the buildings were destroyed. The related loss of hotel accommodations contributed to a 14.5 percent decline in tourist arrivals in 1995, during which GDP grew by 1.3 percent, inflation rose further to 2.8 percent, and unemployment was virtually unchanged. GDP declined slightly in 1996 and 1997 and increased by only 0.4 percent in 1998; meanwhile, unemployment rose to 16.7 percent in 1998, the International Monetary Fund (IMF) blaming the poor economic performance on the government's failure to reduce its budget deficit or enact other reforms envisioned in an IMF-endorsed reform package discussed in 1997. By 2008 growth revived to 3.2 percent and was forecast to increase marginally thereafter, albeit with heightened inflation because of increased oil prices.

GOVERNMENT AND POLITICS

Political background. The Leeward Islands (including Aruba, see previous article) became Dutch possessions in 1634, while the Windward Islands passed to uninterrupted Dutch control in the early 19th century. Long administered as a colonial dependency, the (then) six-island grouping was in 1954 granted constitutional equality with the Netherlands and Suriname (which became independent in 1975) as an autonomous component of the Kingdom of the Netherlands.

Given the geographical range of the grouping, political differences have traditionally been island-based, necessitating highly unstable coalition governments. Thus, Prime Minister Silvio ROZENDAL, installed following an election in June 1977, was forced to resign in April 1979, in the wake of a legislative boycott by Aruban representatives. After balloting in July, a new three-party government was formed by Dominico MARTINA of the Curaçao-based New Antilles Movement (*Movimentu Antiá Nobo*—MAN), but in September 1981 the People's Electoral Movement (MEP) of Aruba again withdrew its support, as talks began in The Hague concerning the island's constitutional future. A governmental stalemate ensued that was not resolved by a general election in June 1982, although Martina remained in office until redesignation as head of a five-party coalition that excluded the MEP the following October. In March 1983 agreement was reached on the assumption of Aruban *status aparte* in January 1986, with full independence in 1996, but the Martina government was weakened by the withdrawal of the conservative National People's Party (*Partido Nashonal di Pueblo*—PNP) in August and eventually collapsed in June 1984. On September 20 the NVP's Maria LIBERIA-PETERS, heading another five-party coalition that included neither the MAN or MEP, became the islands' first female prime minister. However, she was defeated in an election held November 22, 1985, in preparation for Aruba's departure on January 1, with a new Martina administration thereupon being formed.

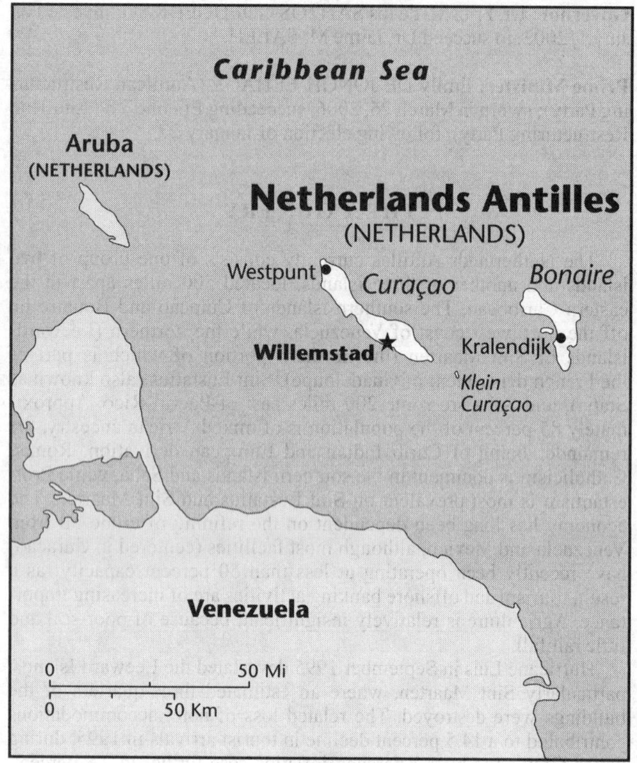

In December 1987 Claude WATHEY, leader of the Democratic Party of Sint Maarten (*Demokratiko Partido–Sint Maarten*—DP-StM), resigned from the government over the issue of island independence, and two months later the two remaining DP-StM members also departed, leaving Martina with a 1-seat legislative majority in the *Staten*. In March 1988 a representative of the Workers' Liberation Front (*Fronte Obero de Liberashon*—FOL) withdrew his support because of a proposed layoff of 1,400 public-sector employees, and the prime minister was again forced from office in favor of Liberia-Peters, who returned on May 17 as head of a new coalition that claimed the support of 13 of 22 *Staten* members.

Following a failed referendum on autonomy for Curaçao in 1993 (see Constitution and government, below), two of the PNP's non-Curaçao partners withdrew from the government coalition, reducing the latter's *Staten* representation to nine and forcing Liberia-Peters's resignation on November 25. On November 26 the justice minister, Suzanne CAMELIA-RÖMER, took over as acting prime minister. On December 28 Alejandro Felippe PAULA, a professor of sociology at the University of the Netherlands Antilles, was in turn named Camelia-Römer's interim successor, pending a general election on February 25, 1994. In the February poll, the recently organized Antillean Restructuring Party (*Partido Antiá Restrukturá*—PAR), led by Miguel POURIER, secured an eight-member plurality of *Staten* seats and on March 31 formed a broad-based coalition government.

Although the PAR maintained a plurality in the balloting for a new *Staten* on January 31, 1998, it lost four of its eight seats on a vote share that fell from nearly 40 percent to less than 19 percent. Pourier was invited by the governor on March 19 to form a new government but was unable to attract the necessary support from the ten other groups that had secured legislative representation. Consequently, while Pourier and his government continued in a caretaker capacity, lengthy negotiations were launched on a variety of alternatives, which on June 1 yielded a six-party coalition headed by the PNP's Camelia-Römer.

The Camelia-Römer government collapsed in October 1999 amid a dispute concerning a national recovery plan introduced a year earlier that would have entailed substantial civil service cuts, and Pourier formed a new coalition government on November 8. In view of continued economic difficulties, the FOL led all groups in the *Staten* balloting on January 18, 2002, winning 5 seats. However, the six-party cabinet that was finally installed on June 3 under the leadership of Etienne YS of the PAR did not include the FOL.

Prime Minister Ys resigned in late May 2003 to permit the formation of a new government that would include the FOL. However, the FOL leader, Anthony GODETT, could not be named prime minister because he was under indictment for corruption. Ben KOMPROE was sworn in as prime minister on an acting basis on July 22; and on August 11 Mirna Luisa GODETT, Anthony's sister, was, in turn, sworn in as Komproe's acting successor.

In December 2003 Anthony Godett was convicted of forgery, bribery, and money laundering, and sentenced to 12 months of imprisonment. Two of the FOL's partners thereupon withdrew from the government, leaving the coalition temporarily without a majority in the *Staten*; however, the coalition revived shortly thereafter with the addition of the Democratic Party of Bonaire (PDB) and the National Alliance.

On April 6, 2004, the government again collapsed, when the PNP refused to continue with Komproe as justice minister. On April 11 Mirna Godett resigned, with Etienne Ys returning as prime minister on June 3.

In the election of January 27, 2006, the PAR won 5 seats and the MAN, 3, with the PAR's Emily DE JONGH-ELHAGE being sworn in as prime minister on March 26.

Constitution and government. The Dutch sovereign is titular head of the present five-member state and is represented in the Antilles by an appointed governor. Domestic affairs are the responsibility of the prime minister and other members of the Council of Ministers, appointed with the advice and approval of a unicameral *Staten* (legislature) of 22 deputies (14 from Curaçao, 3 each from Bonaire and Sint Maarten, and 1 each from Sint Eustatius and Saba). Elections to the *Staten* are held every four years, subject to dissolution. In the islands represented by more than one deputy, balloting is by proportional representation. Control of foreign affairs and defense is vested in the Council of Ministers in The Hague, with an Antillean minister plenipotentiary sitting as a voting member in matters dealing with "joint affairs of the realm." Judicial authority is exercised by a Court of Appeal in Willemstad, whose members are appointed by the queen in consultation with the Antilles government and who sit singly in island courts of first instance. Ultimate appeal is to the Supreme Court of the Netherlands in The Hague.

Each of the island territories elects an Island Council, which sits for four years and is responsible for enacting legislation regarding local affairs. A lieutenant governor is appointed by the queen for a six-year term and sits with deputies named by the elected council as an island Executive Council.

In a referendum on November 19, 1993, 73 percent of Curaçao voters rejected a government-backed proposal that the island seek special autonomy status similar to that of Aruba, with 8 percent favoring incorporation into the Netherlands and only 1 percent endorsing full independence. On October 14, 1994, voters on Sint Eustatius, Saba, and Sint Maarten endorsed the status quo by votes of 91 percent, 86 percent, and 60 percent, respectively, with Bonaire following suit on October 21 by a vote of 88 percent.

By contrast, in a referendum on April 8, 2005, 68 percent of Curaçao voters endorsed autonomous status for the island within the Kingdom of the Netherlands, while in a separate poll 76 percent of Sint Eustatius voters rejected autonomous status. As a result, under a new structure approved in December, Curaçao and Sint Maarten were slated to become separate, autonomous members of the kingdom, while Bonaire, Saba, and Sint Eustatius were slated to become "Kingdom Islands" (*Koninkrijkseilanden*) with the status of municipalities within a yet-to-be specified Dutch province. (See below for subsequent developments.)

Current issues. In November 2006 Curaçao's Island Council voted to reject the 2005 agreement, under which The Hague would retain control of defense, foreign policy, and law enforcement. As a result, the date for its implementation was advanced to December 15, 2008, to permit reevaluation of the objectionable provisions. While opposition on Sint Maarten also voiced objections, particularly in regard to banking regulations, the other four islands appeared, in general, to be satisfied with the proposed restructuring.

The Dutch government in late 2007 expressed doubt that the deadline for constitutional changes for Curaçao and Sint Maarten autonomy could be met and in April 2008 formally declared that it was no longer realistic. Although agreement on division of the islands' assets and liabilities was reportedly near, a new target of early 2010 was advanced, coincident with expiration of the Antillean legislative term.

Part of the difficulty stemmed from a report by the Dutch Ministry of Justice that detailed an "ugly picture" of crime on Sint Maarten, including human smuggling, drug trafficking, and activity by the numerous casinos in money laundering on behalf of organized crime. Indicatively, the island's police commissioner was arrested and given a four-year prison sentence in November 2007 for taking bribes to provide fraudulent entry documents to foreign workers. A month later Dutch State Secretary Ank Bijleveld-Schouten declared that autonomy for Sint Maarten would be possible only after the achievement of "a good level of law maintenance and justice."

On May 15, 2009, Curaçao voters narrowly approved a nonbinding referendum acquiescing to the retention of substantial economic control by The Hague in return for Dutch assumption of a major portion of Curaçao's foreign debt, thus clearing the way for political autonomy in 2010. *(See headnote.)*

POLITICAL PARTIES

Legislative Parties:

Restructured Antilles Party (*Partido Antía Restrukturá*—PAR). The PAR is a Curaçao-based, social-Christian formation launched in the wake of the November 1993 referendum. It became the leading party of the government coalition formed after the 1994 election, in which it won 8 of 22 *Staten* seats. It was reduced to a minority of 4 seats in 1998 and secured the same number in 2002, with 1 additional seat added in 2006.

Leaders: Emily DE JONGH-ELHAGE (Prime Minister), Etienne YS, Miguel A. POURIER (Former Prime Minister), Pedro J. ATACHO (Secretary).

New Antilles Movement (*Movishon Antiá Nobo/Movimentu Antiyas Nobo*—MAN). The MAN is a left-of-center member of the Socialist International that served as the core of the Martina administrations of 1982–1984 and 1985–1988, although holding only 4 *Staten* seats on the latter occasion. Its representation dropped to 2 seats in 1990, both of which were retained in 1994 and 1998. The party failed to gain representation in 2002 but was second-ranked with 3 seats in 2006.

Leader: Dominico F. (Don) MARTINA (Former Prime Minister).

National People's Party (*Nationale Volkspartij*—NVP/*Partido Nashonal di Pueblo*—PNP). The NVP/PNP is a right-of-center Curaçao-based party that served as the core of the governing coalition from 1988 to 1993. Its leader, Maria Liberia-Peters, was obliged to step down as a result of the November 1993 referendum result, and its *Staten* representation dropped from 7 to 3 seats in February 1994, before rising to 4 in January 1998. It secured 3 seats in 2002, one of which was lost in 2006.

Leaders: Suzanne (Suzi) CAMELIA-RÖMER, Maria Ph. LIBERIA-PETERS (Former Prime Ministers).

Bonaire Patriotic Union (*Unión Patriotiko Bonairiana/Union Patriótico Bonairiano*—UPB). The Christian-Democratic UPB won all 3 of the *Staten* seats from Bonaire in 1990, 2 of which were lost in 1994. It retained the remaining seat in 1998 and 2002, to which one more was added in 2006.

Leaders: Ramonsito T. BOOI, C. V. WINKLAAR (Secretary General).

Workers' Liberation Front of 30 May (*Frente Obrero di Liberashon 30 di Mei*—FOL). The FOL is a Marxist group based on Curaçao. For the 1990 balloting it entered into a coalition with the **Independent Social** (*Soshal Independiente*—SI), which had been formed in 1986 by a group of PNP dissidents led by George HUECK. The two groups also presented joint candidates in the January 1998 balloting (under the rubric of Social Independence–Workers Liberation Front—SIFOL), winning 2 seats. The FOL left the government coalition in mid-2001 as a result of tension between FOL leader Anthony Godett and the administration regarding budget cuts. The FOL (sometimes referenced as the SIFOL) was the top vote-getter in the 2002 balloting, winning 5 legislative seats on a vote share of 23 percent. Its leader, Anthony Godett, was precluded from installation as prime minister in 2002 because of indictment (later conviction) for bribery, fraud, and money laundering. In September 2005 the High Court in The Hague upheld a 15-month prison sentence for Godett.

The party won 2 *Staten* seats in 2006.

Leaders: Anthony GODETT, Mirna Luisa GODETT (Former Acting Prime Minister), Ben KOMPROE (Former Justice Minister).

Sint Maarten Patriotic Alliance (SPA). The SPA was launched in 1990, initially as a loose grouping in opposition to the DP-StM on Sint Maarten. Its organizing component was the Sint Maarten People's Movement (SPM), which in the 1990 *Staten* poll captured one of the three seats theretofore held by the DP-StM (below). In Island Council balloting in April 1991 the SPA doubled its representation from two of nine seats to four. On July 7 it formed an island government in coalition with the recently organized PDP (below), which, however, collapsed on August 27 when its partner withdrew. It increased its *Staten* representation to two seats in 1994, one of which was lost in 1998. For the 2002 balloting the SPA joined with the **National Progressive Party** in a **National Alliance** (NA), which secured 1 seat under the leadership of William MARLIN. In 2006 the Alliance increased its representation to 2 seats.

Leaders: Leo CHANCE (President), Vance JAMES Jr.

Upwards Curaçao (*Forsa Kòrsou*). *Forsa Kòrsou* is a recently launched Curaçao formation that won two *Staten* seats in 2006.

Leader: Nelson NAVARRO.

Democratic Party–Sint Maarten (*Demokratiko Partido–Sint Maarten/Democratische Partij–Sint Marten*—DP-StM). Technically, the DP-StM is an English-speaking branch of the DP-C (below). One of its leaders, Louis C. GUMBS, resigned from the government and the party in March 1991 to stand for an Island Council seat on Sint Maarten as a candidate of the PDP (below), which had recently been launched by a group of DP-StM dissidents. In November 1993 Gumbs was found not guilty of bribery and perjury charges that had been brought against him. One month earlier DP-StM leader Claude WATHEY had been arrested in connection with an investigation of financial irregularities on the island. The party lost 1 of its 2 *Staten* seats in 1994, its leadership passing thereafter from Wathey to Sarah Westcott-Williams (formerly of the PDP). Its representation fell from 2 seats in 2002 to 1 in 2006. Former party leader Claude Wathey died on January 9, 1998.

Leader: Sarah WESTCOTT-WILLIAMS.

Democratic Party–Statia/Democratic Party–Sint Eustatius (*Democratische Partij–Statia/Democratische Partij–Sint Eustatius*—DP-S/DP-StE). Like the DP-StM, technically a branch of the DP, the DP-S also supported the Liberia-Peters government. The party lost its single *Staten* seat in 1998 but won it back in 2002 and retained it in 2006.

Leaders: Kenneth van PUTTEN, Nora Sneek GIBBS, Julian WOODLEY.

Democratic Party–Bonaire (*Democratische Partij–Bonaire*—DPB/*Partido Democratico Bonairano*—PDB). Unrepresented in the *Staten* before the February 1994 poll, the PDB currently holds 1 seat.

Leader: Jopie ABRAHAM.

Windward Islands People's Movement (WIPM). Formerly known as the West Indian People's Movement, the WIPM won the seat from Saba in the 1985 and 1990 elections. In Island Council balloting in April 1991 the WIPM won 4 of 5 seats from the incumbent SDLM (below) but retained only 2 in May 1995. One *Staten* seat won in 1990 was retained thereafter through the 2006 elections.

Leaders: Will JOHNSTON (Chair), Ray HASSEL, Dave LEVENSTONE (Secretary General).

Other Parties:

Labor Party Popular Crusade (*Partido Laboral Krusada Popular*—PLKP). A trade union-based group launched in 1997, the PLKP won 3 seats in the January 1998 legislative elections. It joined the subsequent cabinet led by the PNP's Suzanne Camelia-Römer but withdrew from the coalition in 1999 and was not included in the PAR-led cabinet of November 1999. The PLKP rejoined the government in June 2002, having secured 12.1 percent of the vote (and 2 seats) in the January legislative poll, both of which were lost in 2006.

Leader: Errol COVA (Former Deputy Prime Minister).

Saba United Democratic Party (SUDP). The SUDP was originally known as the Saba Democratic Labour Movement (SDLM), which became Saba's ruling party on May 12, 1995, by winning 3 of 5 Island Council seats, before losing all but one in 1999.

Leader: Steve HASSELL.

Democratic Party–Curaçao (*Democratische Partij–Curaçao*—DP-C). Prior to the 1985 election the DP was primarily Curaçao-based, with a Dutch-speaking branch on Bonaire and English-speaking branches on Sint Maarten and Sint Eustatius.

Leader: Errol HERNÁNDEZ.

Progressive Democratic Party (PDP). Also referenced as the People's Democratic Party, the PDP was organized by a group of DP-StM dissidents who won 2 Sint Maarten Council seats in April 1991 and joined the SPA in forming a coalition administration two months later. The group withdrew in August, forcing the government's collapse, and subsequently entered into a ruling coalition with its parent party.

Leader: Millicent de WEEVER.

United People's Labour Party (UPLP). The UPLP was launched in March 2003 as a "working class" party to contest forthcoming local elections in Sint Maarten.

Leaders: Edwin MADURO, Bienvenido RICHARDSON.

LEGISLATURE

The unicameral **States** (*Staten*) presently consists of 22 members elected for four-year terms, subject to dissolution. In the most recent balloting on January 27, 2006, the Restructured Antilles Party won 5 seats; the New Antilles Movement, 3; the Bonaire Patriotic Union, 2; the National Alliance, 2; the National People's Party, 2; Upwards Curaçao, 2; the Worker's Liberation Front, 2; and the Democratic Party–Bonaire, the Democratic Party–Sint Eustatius, the Democratic Party–Sint Maarten, and the Windward Islands People's Movement, 1 each. The next election (expected to be the last before dissolution of the Netherlands Antilles) was scheduled for January 22, 2010.

Speaker: Pedro ATACHO.

CABINET

[as of June 1, 2009]

Prime Minister	Emily de Jongh-Elhage (PAR) [f]
Ministers	
Constitutional Affairs and the Interior	Roland E. Duncan (NA)
Economic Affairs and Employment	Burney F. Elhage (UPB)
Education, Culture, Youth, and Sports	Omayra Victoria Elisabeth Leeflang (PAR) [f]
Finance	Ersilia T. M. de Lannooy (PNP) [f]
Foreign Affairs	Emily de Jongh-Elhage (PAR) [f]
Health and Social Development	Ersilia T. M. de Lannooy [f]
Justice	David A. Dick (PAR)
Attorney-General	Dick A. Piar
Plenipotentiary to The Hague	Paul R. J. Comenencia (PAR)
State Secretaries	
Constitutional Affairs and Interior, with responsibility for the Transfer of Tasks and Authority	Hubert Martis (UPB)
Finance, with responsibility for Tax Affairs	Alex Rosaria (PNP)
Health, with responsibility for Medical Care in the Windward Isles and Bonaire	Rudolph E. Samuel (NA)
Justice, with responsibility for Police Affairs and the Penal Institution of the Windward Isles	Ernie C. Simmons (DP-S)

[f] = female

COMMUNICATIONS

Press. The following are dailies published in Willemstad, unless otherwise noted: *Extra* (23,000), in Papiamento; *La Prensa* (14,000), in Papiamento; *Nobo* (12,000), in Papiamento; *Amigoe* (10,000), in Dutch; *Beurs-en Nieuwsberichten* (9,000), in Dutch; *The News* (Sint Maarten, 7,500), in English; *Saba Herald* (Saba, 500), monthly WIPM organ, in English; *Ultimo Noticia*, in Papiamento.

News agencies. The Dutch *Algemeen Nederlands Persbureau* (ANP) and the U.S. Associated Press (AP) maintain offices in Willemstad.

Broadcasting. There are a number of privately owned radio stations in operation in Curaçao, Bonaire, Sint Maarten, and Saba; commercial television service is provided in Willemstad by Tele-Curaçao.

INTERGOVERNMENTAL REPRESENTATION

Foreign relations are for the most part conducted through the Dutch Ministry of Foreign Affairs in The Hague, although the United States maintains a Consulate General's Office on Curaçao.

IGO Membership (Non-UN): *ACS*, Interpol, WCO.

NEW ZEALAND

Aotearoa

Political Status: Constitutional democracy with Queen Elizabeth II as titular head of state; formally independent since 1947.

Area: 104,454 sq. mi. (270,534 sq. km.).

Population: 4,027,947 (2006C); 4,294,000 (2008E).

Major Urban Centers (2006C): WELLINGTON (179,466), Auckland (404,658; conurbation 1,414,700), Christchurch (348,435), Manukau City (328,968), Hamilton (129,249), Dunedin (118,683).

Official Languages: English, Maori.

Monetary Unit: New Zealand Dollar (market rate December 1, 2009: 1.37 dollars = $1US).

Sovereign: Queen ELIZABETH II.

Governor General: Sir Anand SATYANAND; named by the queen on April 3, 2006, to succeed Dame Silvia CARTWRIGHT, effective August 4.

Prime Minister: John Phillip KEY (National Party), named by the governor general to form a new government following the parliamentary election of, November 8, 2008, and sworn in on November 19, succeeding Helen CLARK (Labour Party), who had served since the election of November 27, 1999.

THE COUNTRY

Located approximately 1,200 miles southeast of Australia in the southern Pacific Ocean, New Zealand is the most physically isolated of the world's economically developed countries. The two main islands (North Island and South Island), separated by the Cook Strait, extend nearly 1,000 miles on a northeast-southwest axis. They exhibit considerable topographical diversity, ranging from fertile plains to high mountains, but enjoy for the most part a relatively temperate climate. The majority of the population is of British extraction, but the Maori, descendants of the original Polynesian settlers, constitute almost 15 percent of the total. Smaller ethnic groups include Asians (9 percent) and Pacific island peoples (7 percent). The Anglican, Roman Catholic, and Presbyterian churches predominate. Women constitute over 46 percent of the active labor force, primarily in wholesale and retail trade, health and social work, and education. Female representation in the House of Representatives elected in November 2008 totaled 39 out of 122 MPs.

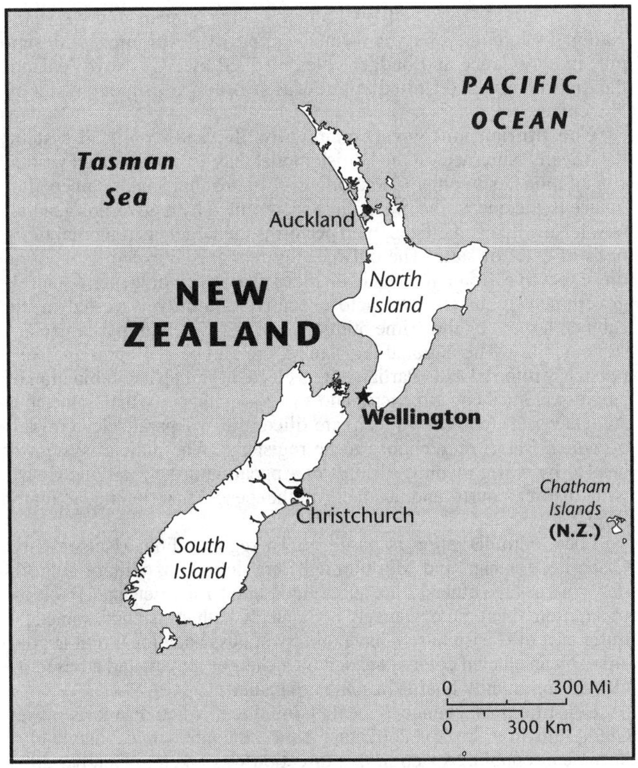

The service sector is the largest contributor to the GDP, about 70 percent in 2008, employing 64 percent of the workforce. Although the agricultural sector employs only 7 percent of the labor force, it remains the basis of the country's wealth. Dairy products, meat, forest products, fish, fruits and vegetables, wine, and wool provide about half of New Zealand's merchandise export earnings. The manufacturing sector employs 19 percent of the workforce and contributes a quarter of the GDP, with processing of foods, wood and paper products, aluminum, and chemicals ranking among the leading industries. Exports of machinery, transport and marine equipment, chemical products, and metals have become important earners. Since the mid-1970s, development efforts have focused on the exploitation of significant natural gas, oil, coal, and lignite deposits, as well as hydroelectric capacity, and by 2008 oil and mineral oil products had grown to 6,6 percent of total export earnings. Top trading partners are Australia, the United States, Japan, China, South Korea and Great Britain. In the 1990s tourism surpassed dairy exports to emerge as New Zealand's single most valuable source of foreign exchange.

New Zealand has registered positive annual GDP growth rates for the past decade except for 1998, when a severe drought and a financial crisis in East Asia contributed to a 0.2 percent decline. From 1999 through 2004 growth averaged about 4 percent annually, but the rate dropped to 2.2 percent in 2005 and 1.5 percent in 2006 due to a weakening of domestic consumption and a higher-than-usual current account deficit. Growth continued at a rate of 1.6 percent in the following year and accelerated to 3.0 percent in the year ending March 2008. But a downturn in primary production and overseas earnings and a weakening of the housing, finance, and retail markets dragged the economy into recession and the GDP shrank by nearly 2 percent in the year to November 2009.

GOVERNMENT AND POLITICS

Political background. New Zealand's link to Europe began with a landfall by the Dutch mariner Abel Tasman in 1642, but settlement by the English did not begin until the 18th century. In 1840 British sovereignty was formally accepted by Maori chieftains, who signed the Treaty of Waitangi. Recurrent disputes between the settlers and the Maori were not resolved, however, until the defeat of the latter in the land wars of the 1860s. Self-governing since 1852 and granted dominion status in 1907, New Zealand acceded to the Statute of Westminster in 1947 and became an independent member of the Commonwealth.

Through the mid-20th century both of the main political parties, National and Labour, endorsed a protected economy and extensive programs of social welfare, and the differences between them subsequently turned primarily on how such a system could best be administered. The more conservative National Party, which was in power from 1960 to 1972 under the leadership of Keith J. HOLYOAKE and then John R. MARSHALL, was defeated by Norman E. KIRK's Labour Party in 1972. Following Kirk's death in August 1974, Wallace E. ROWLING became prime minister.

In a landmark decision in 1975, the Labour government agreed to the creation of the Waitangi Tribunal, charged with investigating alleged violations of Maori land and fishing rights under the 1840 treaty. Within a decade about 70 percent of New Zealand's land area had become subject to claims filed by Maori tribes.

In the midst of growing concern over the costs of state intervention in the economy and after an aggressive "presidential-style" campaign waged by its leader Robert D. MULDOON, the Nationals won an unexpected landslide victory in November 1975 and then retained control, with shrinking majorities, for the next nine years.

Faced with intraparty defections in the wake of mounting fiscal problems and disagreements over the access policy for nuclear ships, Muldoon was forced to call an early election for July 1984 that resulted in a victory for Labour under David R. LANGE. Lange continued in charge following Labour's 1987 election win, but a year later an intraparty dispute precipitated his resignation and Geoffrey PALMER was designated as his successor. Prime Minister Palmer, whose lackluster image was credited with hastening Labour's decline in the public opinion polls, resigned in September 1990 in favor of Foreign Minister Michael (Mike) MOORE. However, the 11th-hour leadership change did not prevent defeat by the National Party under James (Jim) BOLGER by a record 40 legislative seats (68–28) in October.

Despite being weakened by the formation of the breakaway New Zealand First Party (NZ First), the National Party emerged from the November 1993 general election with a one-seat majority and formed a new government. At the same time, the voters gave final approval to the introduction of a form of proportional representation (mixed-member proportional or MMP) for the next election. Two weeks later, Prime Minister Bolger dismissed his controversial finance minister, Ruth RICHARDSON, replacing her with Bill BIRCH, a longtime conservative. Richardson responded by resigning her parliamentary seat, forcing a by-election in August 1994 that National won only narrowly. However, when National right-winger Ross MEURANT broke away in September to form the Right of Centre (subsequently Conservative) Party, both short-lived, the result was the country's first coalition government since the 1930s, in which Meurant retained his junior ministerial post.

In December 1994 the government announced a NZ$1 billion ten-year allocation for the settlement of some 400 Maori land claims filed with the Waitangi Tribunal, but most Maori leaders rejected the allocation as insufficient to meet claims valued at upward of NZ$90 billion. Protests ensued, including the violent disruption of Waitangi Day ceremonies in February 1995. Three months later Prime Minister Bolger and the Queen of the Tainui (the largest Maori federation) signed a NZ$170 million agreement in final settlement of land grievances dating back to the 1860s and the Crown expressed "profound regret and apologies." In another major settlement, in November 1997 the government agreed to turn over land and other assets valued at NZ$170 million to the Ngai Tahu Maori in the South Island, and in June 2008 a further settlement valued at over NZ$100 million was made with the Arawa *iwi* (tribe) covering disputed North Island forest resources. Parliament set September 1, 2008, as the deadline for historical Maori claims to be submitted to the Waitangi Tribunal.

The change to proportional representation had stimulated the launching of several new parties prior to the 1996 election, notably United New Zealand (United NZ), which in February 1996 became a member of the ruling coalition. The general election in October produced a fragmented House of Representatives. The National Party won only 44 seats in a legislature enlarged to 120 members, followed by Labour with 37, NZ First with 17, and the center-left five-party Alliance with 13. Protracted interparty negotiations eventually yielded the formation on December 16 of a National–NZ First coalition government with support pledged by the single United NZ member. Bolger continued as prime minister and NZ First leader Winston PETERS became deputy prime minister and treasurer.

Internal National Party disputes allowed Jennifer (Jenny) SHIPLEY in November 1997 to successfully challenge Bolger as leader. New Zealand's first female prime minister, Shipley was sworn in on December 8. Budgetary and other policy differences led her to sack Peters in August 1998. He and half of his NZ First party followers left the government, but enough remained for Shipley to win confidence votes in September 1998 and February 1999 and retain power.

Despite favorable economic trends, Shipley's coalition failed to win a majority in the November 1999 national election. However, the Labour-Alliance coalition remained 2 seats shy of a majority after the final count gave 7 seats to The Green Party of Aotearoa (the Greens). Only when the Greens agreed to extend their support on crucial votes was Labour Party leader Helen CLARK able to form a minority government. Clark was sworn in as New Zealand's first elected woman prime minister on December 10. The Alliance leader, James (Jim) ANDERTON, negotiated with Clark a novel coalition agreement permitting "public differentiation between the parties in speech and vote" when they disagreed and was rewarded with the deputy prime ministership. But in April 2002 the Alliance split over the issue of the government's and Anderton's support for the U.S.-led invasion of Afghanistan, with radical Alliance member insisting on clearer UN authorization as a precondition. The dispute obliged Prime Minister Clark to call for an early election.

In the election of July 27, 2002, Labour won 52 House seats, dealing the National Party its worst-ever defeat. With Anderton's new party, the Progressives, bringing only 2 MPs into a new coalition, Prime Minister Clark again turned for support to the Greens, but they instead joined the opposition when Clark refused to accept their demand that the government continue a total ban of importation of genetically modified crops. Clark then sought external support from the more conservative United Future party—the product of a merger in 2000 of the United NZ and Future NZ parties—whose 8 House members agreed to vote with the government on confidence motions and key legislation such as the budget. With a 2-seat working majority, a new Clark-led government assumed office on August 14.

The first major challenge to Prime Minister Clark's minority government occurred in May 2004 over a Foreshore and Seabed Bill that would ensure state ownership of New Zealand's shoreline and seabed. The legislation was adamantly opposed by most Maori leaders, who viewed it as truncating tribal rights, but polls showed a clear hardening of public opinion against accepting further indigenous claims. Although the new National Party leader, Don BRASH, had called for an end to "special privileges" for Maori, the Nationals opposed the bill as a "mess" that would damage relations with the Maori minority while giving the Maori power to delay development. Shortly before the opening of floor debate on the bill, the associate minister for Maori affairs, Tariana TURIA, announced that she would vote against the measure. As a result, Turia was dismissed from the government. She then quit Labour, resigned from parliament to force a by-election in her district, won back her seat in July, and established a new Maori Party.

On May 4, 2004, the Clark government survived a no-confidence motion by 4 votes and then secured the support of Winston Peters's 13 NZ First MPs. Despite opposition by the National, United Future, and Maori parties, and in the face of public controversy and Maori *hikoi* (prolonged protest walks), the Foreshore and Seabed Bill was enacted into law in November.

The election of September 17, 2005, saw substantial gains for the National Party, but Labour managed to retain a 2-vote plurality in the House, sufficient for Prime Minister Clark to remain in office at the head of a multiparty governing arrangement. Clark was able to secure the support of Winston Peters's NZ First (7 seats) and Peter DUNNE's United Future (3 seats) that produced a bare majority of 61 in the 121-member House. In return, Peters was named foreign minister, and Dunne took over as minister of revenue, although both remained outside the cabinet. And their parties agreed to support the government on confidence and budget votes although they could vote as they saw fit on other matters.

Uninspiring leadership, alleged contact with a religious sect, and admitted marital infidelity by Don Brash hampered the National Party until a new leader, John Phillip KEY, was chosen in November 2006, whereupon National began a steady rise in the polls, overtaking Labour and opening up a 25 percent lead by July 2008. Labour leader Helen Clark responded by shuffling her cabinet in October 2007 and persuading a half-dozen MPs to resign at the end of their term in 2008.

In the general election of November 8, 2008, the National Party won 44.9 percent of the popular vote and 58 seats in the House of Representatives, followed by Labour's 34.0 percent and 43 seats. National's John Key, having formed a minority government with support in confidence and budget votes pledged by ACT New Zealand, the Maori Party, and United Future was sworn in as prime minister on November 19.

Constitution and government. New Zealand's political system, historically patterned on the British model, has no consolidated written constitution. As in other Commonwealth states that have retained allegiance to the queen, the monarch is represented by a governor general, now a New Zealand citizen, who performs the largely ceremonial functions of chief of state. The only legally recognized executive body is the Executive Council, which includes the governor general and all government ministers. De facto executive authority is vested in the cabinet, headed by the prime minister, under a system of parliamentary responsibility. The national legislature, the House of Representatives, popularly referred to as Parliament, is elected through a combination of single-seat local constituencies and a nation-wide party list. Some constituency seats (currently seven) are filled from a separate electoral roll on which Maori may choose to be registered. The judicial system is headed by a High Court, a Court of Appeal, and the Supreme Court, with district courts and justices of the peace functioning at lower levels.

Local administration is based on 16 regions. Four (Nelson City, Gisborne, Tasman, and Marlborough) are defined as unitary authorities, whereas the other 12 are subdivided into 57 districts and 16 cities. In addition, the remote, sparsely populated Chatham Islands, some 500 miles east of Christchurch, have unitary status. Each local unit is governed by an elected council headed by a chair or mayor, and advised by elected community boards in some urban areas.

Constitutional change appeared imminent when Prime Minister Clark said in February 2002 that New Zealand would "inevitably" become a republic. A step in that direction was taken in October 2003 when the House of Representatives, over opposition by National, passed a bill ending the right of final legal appeal to the Privy Council in London and creating a Supreme Court, which began hearing cases in July 2004. The government also discontinued awarding knighthoods to deserving citizens, opting instead for non-monarchical honors.

Foreign relations. As a small nation distant from major economic centers, New Zealand has traditionally maintained preferential trading and military relations with its nearest neighbor, Australia, and has supported collective security through the United Nations, the ANZUS treaty with Australia and the United States, and the Five Power Defense Arrangements with Australia, Malaysia, Singapore, and the United Kingdom. Wellington has also engaged in regional security consultations in the Association of Southeast Asian Nations Regional Forum (ARF). New Zealand is an active member of the Commonwealth, of which former foreign minister Don McKINNON was secretary general from 2000 to 2008.

In February 1985 the Lange administration refused entry to a U.S. Navy warship alleged to be capable of carrying nuclear weapons, which Washington refused to confirm or deny. Wishing to deter similar ship visit bans by other allies, the Ronald Reagan administration retaliated by canceling ANZUS military exercises planned for March and discontinuing bilateral exercises, intelligence sharing, and cabinet-level diplomatic intercourse. In June 1987 New Zealand's parliament approved a Nuclear Free Zone, Disarmament, and Arms Control Act that legally prohibited the entry of nuclear-armed or nuclear-powered ships into New Zealand waters, whereupon Secretary of State George Schultz suspended U.S. security commitments to New Zealand. A decade of cool relations followed.

In September 1999 U.S. president Bill Clinton, to prepare for the UN-backed peacekeeping mission in East Timor, to which New Zealand committed some 800 troops, announced that the U.S. ban on military exercises with New Zealand would be waived for this and other multilateral operations. In 2001 the Clark government strongly endorsed the U.S.-led "war on terrorism," and in March 2002 Prime Minister Clark was invited to meet with U.S. president George W. Bush, the first consultation with a Labour leader since the mid-1980s. The Clark government refused to participate in the 2003 invasion of Iraq because it failed to gain UN authorization. But troop contributions to peacekeeping in Afghanistan, counterterrorism patrols in the Persian Gulf, assistance in negotiations with North Korea, and participation in the U.S.-led Proliferation Security Initiative earned goodwill in Washington, and Secretary of State Condoleezza Rice paid an official visit in July 2008, signaling that the unresolved nuclear ship disagreement would no longer impede warm working relations. The new

National-led government pledged to further cultivate the bilateral relationship and, following two meetings with President Obama, Key in August 2009 announced the deployment of 70 Special Air Service combat troops to Afghanistan, augmenting the 140 NZ Defence Force personnel and civilian specialists serving in a reconstruction mission there. He also welcomed indications by Assistant Secretary of State Kurt Campbell that training opportunities for New Zealand troops with their American counterparts were to be expanded, and extended invitations to Hilary Clinton and Barack Obama to visit in 2010.

New Zealand has played an active part in South Pacific development and Asia-Pacific economic and political cooperation. Recent initiatives included successful mediation of the Bougainville separatist conflict in Papua New Guinea in 1996 and dispatch of troops and police to support the elected government of the Solomon Islands in 2003. Wellington was quick to impose sanctions on the military junta of Fiji following the December 2006 coup, as it had done in response to coups in 1987 and 2000. New Zealand diplomats negotiated free-trade agreements with Singapore, then with Chile and Brunei, which culminated in July 2005 with the signing of a Trans-Pacific Strategic Economic Partnership agreement (TTP). President Obama in November 2009 announced the U.S. would undertake negotiations to accede to the agreement, which could include also Australia, Vietnam, and Peru. New Zealand's free-trade negotiations with China came to fruition in the New Zealand–China Free Trade Agreement signed April 7, 2008, China's first with a developed country. Agreements with Malaysia and the Association of Southeast Asian Nations (ASEAN) followed. Further trade agreements are under negotiation or study with Hong Kong, South Korea, India, and the Gulf Cooperation Council. Since 1989 New Zealand has been active in the 21-nation Asia-Pacific Economic Cooperation (APEC) forum and from 2006 New Zealand has participated in the East Asian Summit meetings, which proponents hope will evolve into a 16-nation Asia-wide trade liberalization pact.

In November 2009 New Zealand was named by Transparency International (Berlin) as the world's least corrupt country.

Current issues. Although opinion polls in the mid-2000s had spotlighted public concerns over Maori privileges and attendant race relations and immigration issues, by 2008 the economy (jobs, taxes, property values) rose to the top of the list of public worries. The economy in 2006 and 2007 had grown on the strength of high agricultural export earnings and a strong dollar, but it turned downward in 2008 as energy and food import prices rose, the dollar and property values weakened, and credit tightened. Over 25 finance companies failed or suspended payouts in the period July 2007 to August 2008. Labour got the blame despite prudent financial management, accumulation of a budget surplus, and partial repayment of overseas debt. Helen Clark, long regarded by the public as their preferred prime minister, was replaced at the top of the polls by John Key.

Campaign finance also erupted as an issue in 2007 when Labour accused National of getting illicit support from the Exclusive Brethren, a right-wing Christian group, and introduced legislation to limit electoral spending and curb advertisements during an election year by nonparty organizations. The resulting Electoral Finance Act was passed on December 18 by a narrow margin, 63–57. The National Party and other parties of the right opposed it as stifling free speech by individuals and interest groups and implicitly hindering opposition parties. Since then almost every party, including Labour, has been found in breach of the act.

The media also revealed that Winston Peters, long a vigorous critic of alleged secret donations to National by wealthy business interests, had received three such donations. By August 2008 Peters was under investigation by the Serious Fraud Office and the Parliamentary Privileges Committee, and faced a police complaint by a donor, property magnate Bob JONES. At month's end the prime minister suspended Peters from his ministerial portfolios and assumed the role of acting minister of foreign affairs. Parliament passed a motion of censure three weeks later, but Peters was cleared by the Serious Fraud Office and no charges were filed by the police.

Two other contentious issues of 2007–2008 were "anti-smacking" legislation (an amendment to the Crimes Act) and the Emissions Trading Act. The anti-smacking legislation was criticized for criminalizing parents who employed corporal punishment of any kind. The bill was a concession by Labour in return for support by the Greens and was roundly condemned by parties of the right and members of fundamentalist religious groups. A citizens' petition movement led by the new Kiwi Party and supported by fundamentalist churches succeeded by August 2008 in obtaining over 320,000 signatures to compel a referendum. Prime Minister Clark declined to include it on the ballot in the 2008 general election but proposed a postal ballot for the following year. The Emissions Trading Act, promoted by Clark to make New Zealand a leader in reducing greenhouse gas emissions, was opposed by National, ACT, United Future, and the Maori Party on grounds of its cost and marginal effectiveness. Labour persuaded the Greens and New Zealand First to support the bill by making concessions, such as subsidizing home insulation and clean energy technology research and giving households a rebate to cover higher electricity charges. National pledged to amend the act to reduce its economic impact.

The general election of November 8, 2008, concluded with neither the National Party nor Labour commanding a majority of seats. The third-ranked party, the Greens, won 6.7 percent of the vote and 9 seats, but that, when combined with Labor's 43 seats, was insufficient to overcome National's 58 seats. In the end, ACT New Zealand (5 seats), the Maori Party (5 seats), and United Future New Zealand (1 seat) pledged their support to a minority National government in confidence and budget votes. The new government comprised 23 ministers in cabinet, all National MPs, and 8 ministers outside the cabinet, including 3 from National, 2 from ACT, 2 from Maori, and 1 from United Future. On election night Helen Clark announced her resignation as party leader. Phil GOFF was subsequently chosen by Labour as Clark's successor, thereby becoming leader of the opposition in the House. Clark resigned her Mount Albert parliamentary seat in April 2009 to take up the post of administrator of the United Nations Development Program.

In 2009 the new National-led government began implementing the findings of a Labour-appointed royal commission on the governance of the Auckland region, which recommended a comprehensive amalgamation of seven existing local bodies into one "supercity" with a single elected mayor. In August it conducted a referendum on the "anti-smacking" act which found 88 percent of voters condemning the law criminalizing "responsible parental correction", Key opted not to amend the act but rather to recommend that the Police and courts "interpret" it sensibly. The government in November amended the Emissions Trading Act to soften its economic impact and began consideration of how to amend the Foreshore and Seabed Act to restore court access for Maori claims. It also restored the Queen's birthday honors practice of naming prominent New Zealanders as knights or dames.

In response to the recession the Labour-led government in October 2008 had guaranteed bank and savings institutions deposits. Unlike counterparts in Australia and the United States, the new National-led government in its April 2009 budget declined to initiate an economic stimulus package, choosing instead to accelerate infrastructure projects and implement promised tax cuts, and to make up the deficit by borrowing from abroad. Public criticism of abuse by parliamentarians of their housing and travel allowances erupted in mid-2009, obliging several MPs, including leaders of the National, ACT, and Green parties. to repay excess claims and inducing the prime minister to counsel his ministers to exercise spending restraint.

POLITICAL PARTIES

The equivalent of a two-party system has long characterized New Zealand politics, traditional conservative and liberal roles being played by the National and Labour parties, respectively. Differences between the two narrowed considerably after World War II, and even more so with the initiation of policies by the Labour Party after its election in 1984 that introduced liberalization and deregulation reforms similar to those of Britain's Margaret Thatcher, modifying New Zealand's long-standing protectionist and welfare state policies.

The potential for smaller parties to form and play a significant role in politics was enhanced by the adoption in 1993 of a mixed member proportional representation system (MMP) similar to Germany's. In the November 8, 2008, general election 19 parties offered party lists (up from 14 in 2002, prior to the advent of MMP), while a number of other parties or individuals competed in at least one electoral district.

As of July 2009 there were 19 parties registered with the Electoral Commission, each of which had to have at least 500 members and submit financial reports, as well as a half-dozen inactive or unregistered parties. The latter may support candidates for electoral seats but may not compete for party list seats.

Governing Constellation:

New Zealand National Party (National Party). Founded in 1936 as a union of the earlier Reform and Liberal Parties, the National Party controlled the government from 1960 to 1972, 1975 to 1984, 1990 to 1999, and 2008 to the present. A party of the center-right drawing its strength from well-off rural and suburban areas, National was traditionally committed to the support of personal initiative, private enterprise, and minimum government regulation. However, the distinction between right and left blurred as Labour shifted to free-market policies, and the 1975–1984 National government led by Sir Robert Muldoon endorsed selective state intervention in the economy, including subsidies for farmers. A dispute in late 1985 and early 1986 between Muldoon and his successor as party leader, James (Jim) McLAY (whose free-market philosophy mirrored that of the Labour government), led to McLay's resignation. The new leader, James (Jim) Bolger, endorsed the Muldoon position, although intraparty dissent continued.

In 1983 real estate millionaire Bob Jones announced the formation of a libertarian New Zealand Party (NZP) as an overt challenge to the National Party. In 1984 the NZP drew 12 percent of the vote, mainly from National supporters, but failed to obtain parliamentary representation. In 1986 the NZP formally merged with the National Party.

While Nationals won a landslide victory over Labour in the October 1990 balloting, Bolger's young populist colleague Winston Peters overtook him in popularity, and the two became rivals. Bolger dismissed Peters as Maori affairs minister in late 1991 for alleged disloyalty, and a year later excluded him from the party's parliamentary caucus. Peters responded by resigning his seat and humiliated the government by regaining it in a by-election under the banner of his newly established NZ First Party.

The National Party won a bare majority of 50 of the 99 legislative seats in the 1993 balloting on a lackluster vote share of 35 percent, but the defection of Ross Meurant in September 1994 to form the Right of Centre Party eliminated this margin, obliging Bolger to form a coalition with the new party. In the October 1996 legislative balloting the party slipped to 34 percent of the list vote but won a plurality of 44 out of 120 seats, sufficient for it to form a coalition government with NZ First, with Peters as deputy prime minister. In November 1997 Bolger was supplanted as party leader by Jenny Shipley, the leader of the party's right wing, who was named prime minister in December, the first woman to achieve this office.

NZ First left the coalition in August 1998, but the support of half its parliamentary delegation helped Shipley remain in office as leader of a minority government. In the November 1999 election the National vote share fell to 30.5 percent, and it won only 39 seats. Shipley resigned her party post in October 2001 and was succeeded by Bill ENGLISH, a former minister of health, who was then ousted in November 2003 by Don Brash, a former governor of the Reserve Bank of New Zealand who had joined the party only three years before. In the July 2002 election the party's list vote share plummeted to 20.9 percent, with only 27 seats won, a record low.

The National Party made a dramatic recovery in September 2005, winning 48 seats and 39 percent of the party list vote, but the totals were not enough to forestall another Labour-led government. On November 23, 2006, Brash, whose leadership was tarnished by public gaffes, marital infidelity, and alleged links to a secretive right-wing Christian organization, resigned as party leader and was succeeded by former international currency trader John Key.

By mid-2008 the National Party, and Key as preferred prime minister, were leading Labour and Clark in the polls. The November 8 election produced a plurality for National of 58 seats with 44.33 percent of the total vote and enabled Key to form a coalition government. In June 2009, following allegations of conflict of interest and sexual misconduct, minister of internal affairs Richard WORTH resigned from Parliament; his portfolios were taken by Nathan GUY and his seat was taken by Cam CALDER. Nevertheless polls in late 2009 found clear majorities still approving the performance of the National Party and Prime Minister Key in their first year in office.

Leaders: John KEY (Party Leader and Prime Minister), Bill ENGLISH (Deputy Leader and Deputy Prime Minister), Peter GOODFELLOW (President), Mark OLDERSHAW (General Manager).

Maori Party. Tariana Turia, a former Labour MP and associate minister for Maori affairs, established the Maori Party in June 2004. She had left Labour in May to protest the government's Foreshore and Seabed Bill, which she saw as a betrayal of Maori rights. Under the new banner of the Maori Party, Turia won a parliamentary by-election for her old seat on July 10, taking some 90 percent of the vote and generating speculation that the new party would consolidate Maori support at the expense of Labour, which previously had attracted Maori voters.

Prior to the September 2005 national election, the leading Maori party for the past generation, *Mana Maori Motuhake* (Maori Self-Determination), requested deregistration. (It had been established as the *Mana Motuhake* in 1979 by Maori leader Matiu RATA and participated in the Alliance from 1991 until after the 2002 election as the *Mana Motuhake O Aotearoa* and after October 2002 as the *Mana Maori Motuhake.*) Also deregistered in 2005 was the *Mana Maori* Movement, which had run unsuccessfully in 2002. Partly as a consequence of the demise of its rivals, the Maori Party won four Maori-roll seats in the 2005 election. Subsequent polls showed Maori voters divided between Labour and the Maori Party.

In the November 2008 election the Maori Party contested all seven Maori seats (and a number of general seats besides) and succeeded in winning five of them with 2.39 percent of the total vote. Both Labour and National, neither with a clear majority, wooed the Maori Party, and National won by offering Turia and her co-leader Pita SHARPLES ministerial portfolios (outside cabinet) and pledging to set up a commission to reexamine Labour's Foreshore and Seabed legislation.

Leaders: Tariana TURIA and Pita SHARPLES (Co-leaders), Whatarangi WINIATA (President), Helen LEAHY (National Secretary).

ACT New Zealand (ACT). Founded in 1994 as the political arm of the Association of Consumers and Taxpayers, ACT New Zealand advocates tax reform, welfare reform, school choice, health care reform, and discontinuation of Waitangi Treaty claims. One of the party's founders, Sir Roger DOUGLAS, was a former Labour finance minister who had been the architect of the deregulatory and free-market reforms introduced in the 1980s.

The party won eight seats on a 6 percent party list vote share in the October 1996 election. In August 1998 and February 1999 its support was crucial to the confidence votes won by Prime Minister Shipley's minority government. In the November 1999 election it won 7 percent of the list vote and got nine party list seats in the House.

In 2002 ACT New Zealand retained its nine seats on the basis of a 7.1 percent share of the party list vote. In February 2003, its parliamentary caucus expelled Donna AWATERE HUATA, who was subsequently convicted for misusing public funds provided to a children's reading foundation that she managed, and she lost her House seat.

With public support for ACT New Zealand falling below 3 percent, Richard PREBBLE stepped down as party leader in April 2004. A four-way battle to replace him followed, with Rodney Hide prevailing in June over Deputy Leader Ken SHIRLEY, Stephen FRANKS, and Muriel NEWMAN.

In September 2005 the party won only 1.5 percent of the party list vote but retained one electorate seat (Hide) and thus was eligible for one list seat (Heather ROY). In March 2008 Sir Roger Douglas agreed to contest the upcoming election as a list candidate, ranked third behind Hide and Roy; he was elected but not awarded a ministerial portfolio. ACT gained 3.65 percent of the vote and 5 seats, and Hide and Roy were awarded portfolios (outside cabinet) in the new National-led government.

Leaders: Rodney HIDE (Leader), Heather ROY (Deputy Leader), Michael CROZIER (President) Nick KEARNEY (Secretary).

United Future New Zealand (United Future). The United Future was formed in 2000 by the merger of United New Zealand (United NZ) and Future New Zealand (Future NZ).

United NZ had been launched in 1995 by a group of National and Labour legislators, including Peter Dunne, a former Labour MP who in 1994 had founded the moderate Future New Zealand Party. In February 1996 the United NZ concluded a formal coalition agreement with the National Party, one provision being that Dunne would be given a cabinet post. The "centre-liberal" United NZ won only one seat in the October 1996 election, its single member promising to give external support to the new National–NZ First coalition.

In September 1997 the United NZ had absorbed two parties closely allied with the immigrant population—the Ethnic Minority Party and Advance New Zealand, the latter led by England SO'ONALOLE. In April 1998 the Conservative Party (CP), led by Colin JACKSON, also merged into the United NZ, which hoped to benefit by adding the CP's rural and provincial base to its own largely urban constituency. The CP had been launched in September 1994 as the Right of Centre Party by

Ross Meurant, theretofore a National Party member and junior minister, but failed to win a seat in the October 1996 election.

Future NZ, previously known as the Christian Democratic Party (CDP) and led by Graeme LEE, was launched in November 1998. It did not describe itself as a Christian party and was considered more secular than the Christian Heritage Party (CHP; subsequently Christian Heritage NZ, which dissolved in October 2006), with which it ran in 1996 as the short-lived Christian Coalition. Future NZ was unsuccessful in the 1999 House election, whereas the United NZ retained its single seat.

The new United Future faced its first national election in July 2002. It won eight House seats, seven of them on the strength of a 6.7 percent party list vote, and two weeks later it agreed to extend external support for three years to Clark's Labour-Progressive coalition. In September 2005 the party won only 2.7 percent of the party list vote and a total of three seats. Those three seats proved crucial in Labour's effort to remain in power, as a consequence of which Dunne negotiated a "supply and confidence" agreement that won him the post of minister of revenue.

In May 2007 list MP Gordon COPELAND resigned after disagreeing with Dunne over the party's support for a bill that would outlaw parental corporal punishment, and subsequently joined the Kiwi Party that successfully petitioned for a referendum on the controversial anti-smacking bill.

In the 2008 election Dunne again won his electorate seat, but the party polled only 0.87 percent of the vote and was not entitled to additional seats. Dunne supported the National-led government and was kept on as minister of revenue (outside cabinet).

Leaders: Peter DUNNE (Party Leader and Minister of Revenue), Judy TURNER (Deputy Leader and Part President),)Frank OWEN (Secretary).

Other Parties in Parliament:

New Zealand Labour Party (Labour Party). Founded in 1916 and in power 1935–1949, 1957–1960, 1972–1975, and 1984–1990, the Labour Party originated much of the legislation that created the New Zealand welfare state. However, in a radical policy shift compelled by international economic changes, the post-1984 Labour administration of David Lange introduced free-market policies, including privatization of state enterprises, deregulation of commercial activities, and elimination of subsidies. The party nonetheless maintained its traditional antimilitarist and antinuclear postures and in 1985 prohibited a visit by a U.S. warship, precipitating a curtailment of bilateral defense relations by Washington. In 1987 Labour was reelected with a substantial legislative majority, but in 1989 the increasingly unpopular Lange resigned in favor of Geoffrey Palmer, who was in turn succeeded by Michael (Mike) Moore in 1990. The party's legislative representation fell to an all-time low of 28 seats in the October 1990 election, but it staged a recovery to 45 seats out of 99 in 1993.

In December 1993 a Labour caucus ousted Moore in favor of his deputy, Helen Clark, a leader of the party's left wing. In 1994 the party suffered a minor split leading to the creation of the Future New Zealand Party In the October general election Labour fell back to 37 seats and remained in opposition.

Labour led in the 1999 election, taking 38.7 percent of the list vote and gaining 49 seats. Clark negotiated a coalition with the Alliance (10 seats) secured and support on crucial votes from the Greens, and thus became New Zealand's first elected woman prime minister.

The collapse of the Alliance led to an early election in July 2002, in which Labour retained its plurality, winning 52 seats (including all 7 Maori roll seats) on the strength of 45 percent of the electorate votes and 41 percent of the party list votes. Clark then negotiated a coalition with the former Alliance leader Jim Anderton's new Progressives and a cooperation agreement with United Future that assured her new government a working majority. In late 2004 Labour lost the 7 Maori members, who left to form a new Maori Party. In September 2005, although its electorate vote dropped to 40 percent, Labour won a plurality of 50 seats, just ahead of the rival Nationals, formed another coalition with Jim Anderton's Progressives, and gained sufficient support from United Future and New Zealand First to form a minority government.

Labour expelled Mangere MP Taito Philip FIELD in February 2007 after he was indicted for bribery and perverting the course of justice, reducing Labour's ranks to 49 (of whom 18 were women). Clark shuffled her cabinet in October 2007 to downgrade Trevor MALLARD and move Mark BURTON to the back benches and to give portfolios to four younger MPs. Education Minister Steve MAHARY also vacated his ministerial portfolios in anticipation of taking up the vice-chancellorship of Massey University. By mid-2008 a half-dozen Labour MPs, including House Speaker Margaret WILSON, had indicated their intention not to seek reelection.

Labour contested the election of November 2008 with a new front bench and relatively unknown candidates, winning only 33.99 percent of the vote and 43 seats. On election night as the result became clear, Helen Clark unexpectedly announced her retirement as Labour leader. She subsequently retired from Parliament to take up the administratorship of the United Nations Development Program in New York. The party's nomination for the by-election for her seat was vigorously contested and eventually went to David SHEARER, a former UN official who had served in Iraq. Shearer won the by-election of June 13, 2009, with 63.31 percent of the vote. Labour's deputy leader, Michael Cullen, resigned in April 2009 to join the board of New Zealand Post . Damien O'Connor, a former MP, moved up the Labour Party's list to take Cullen's seat.

In March 2009 Phil Goff was unanimously chosen to lead the party and Annette KING became his deputy. Party president Mike WILLIAMS stepped down and union secretary Andrew LITTLE was elected in his place. General Secretary Mike Smith, who had served nearly eight years, in mid-2009 announced his intention to retire at the next party conference in September.

Leaders: Phil GOFF (Party Leader and Leader of the Opposition), Annette KING (Deputy Party Leader), Andrew LITTLE (President), Chris FLATT (General Secretary).

Green Party of Aotearoa (Greens). Founded in 1972 as the New Zealand Values Party, the country's left-oriented environmental party adopted its present name in 1988. In addition to environmental and conservation concerns, it advocates disarmament, pacifism, and devolution of power to the people and opposes free trade agreements. In 1991 the Greens entered an alliance with New Labour and other small groups, which gained three legislative seats in the 1996 balloting but in 1997 the Greens declared they would contest elections independently.

In the November 1999 election the Greens, on a recount, were credited with a 5.2 percent vote share and awarded seven seats in the House. The Labour-Alliance coalition failed to gain a majority, so the incoming Clark minority government was dependent on Green support, which it got for crucial votes, although a formal cooperation agreement was never concluded.

In the July 2002 election the Greens improved to 7.0 percent of the party list vote, giving them nine House seats. But Prime Minister Clark rejected their demand for a blanket moratorium on genetically modified organisms, and they went into opposition. In September 2005 the Greens won 5.3 percent of the party list vote for six seats. The party remained outside the new Labour-led minority government but agreed not to oppose it on confidence votes, enabling Clark to remain prime minister.

In 2008 Nandor TANCZOS resigned his seat and was replaced by Russel NORMAN, who was subsequently elected co-leader.

The Greens continued to poll around the 5 percent level throughout 2008 and surged to 6.72 percent in the November election, winning 9 seats and placing third behind National and Labour and well ahead of ACT. Labour's attempt to build a new coalition failed, and the Greens moved again to the opposition benches. The Greens' most popular activist, Jeanette FITZSIMONS, retired from co-leadership in June 2009, and the party chose Metiria Turei as the new co-leader.

Leaders: Russel NORMAN and Metiria TUREI (Co-leaders), Roland SAPSFORD and Moea ARMSTRONG (Co-conveners), Jon FIELD (General Secretary),-

Jim Anderton's Progressive Party (Progressives). When divisions over defense policy and relations with the United States split the Alliance coalition party in April–May 2002, its former leader and the sitting deputy prime minister organized his own "Jim Anderton's Progressive Coalition," which was registered by the Electoral Commission in June 2002. Included in the leftist coalition were the Democrats (see Democrats for Social Credit, below), also formerly a component of the Alliance, which then went their separate ways later in the year.

In the July 2002 election the Progressive Coalition attracted only 1.7 percent of the party list vote but claimed one proportional seat on the strength of Anderton's constituency seat victory. Anderton retained his ministerial portfolios, but not his position as deputy prime minister, in the new Clark minority government.

In April 2004 the Progressive Coalition was formally reregistered as the Progressive Party, which then adopted its current name in July 2005. In the 2005 national election Anderton retained his seat, but the party's 1.2 percent party list vote did not entitle it to another seat. In the 2008 election Anderton again won his electorate seat but his party garnered only 0.91 percent of the vote. Anderton joined Labour and the Greens in opposition.

Leaders: Jim ANDERTON (Leader), Matt ROBSON (Deputy Leader), Phil CLEARWATER (General Secretary).

Other Parties:

New Zealand First Party (NZ First). The right-wing populist NZ First was launched in July 1993 by the charismatic former Maori affairs minister, Winston Peters, who had been ejected from the National Party caucus earlier in the year. Forcing a by-election by resigning from the House, he retained his seat with a massive 11,000-vote majority in the Tauranga electorate and subsequently attracted much public approval for his campaign against corruption in the Cook Islands (see Related Territories, below). NZ First won only 2 seats in the November 1993 election on a vote share of 8 percent. It improved to 13 percent of the party list in the 1996 election, its 17 seats (including all 5 Maori roll seats) enabling it to negotiate a coalition agreement with the National Party whereby Peters was named deputy prime minister. However, the coalition agreement generated some unrest within the NZ First ranks,

On August 14, 1998, a day after calling Prime Minister Shipley "devious" and "untrustworthy" on the floor of the House, Peters was dismissed as deputy prime minister and treasurer. Peters took the NZ First out of the government four days later. Nevertheless, half the party's delegation, including its four other cabinet members, reaffirmed their support for the Shipley administration. Several of the dissidents subsequently formed the short-lived *Mauri* Pacific (Spirit of the Pacific) party, which failed to win any House seats in 1999 and was dissolved in 2001.

NZ First fared poorly in the 1999 national election, taking only 4.3 percent of the proportional vote, below the threshold for seats in the House. But Peters retained his Tauranga seat (by 63 votes) and this enabled NZ First to claim four additional party list seats. Peters then indicated that NZ First would support or oppose the government, issue by issue.

In July 2002 NZ First appealed to anticrime, anti-immigration, and anti-Maori sentiments and took 10.4 percent of the party list vote, to end up with 13 House seats. In the September 2005 election the party declined to only 7 list seats on a 5.7 percent vote share and Peters lost his Tauranga seat to a National candidate. But Peters then negotiated a "supply and confidence agreement" with Labour that made him minister of foreign affairs, although he remained outside the cabinet and able to criticize the government. In February 2008 a NZ First leader, Brian DONNELLY, left parliament to take up an appointment as high commissioner (ambassador) to the Cook Islands and was replaced by Dail JONES.

NZ First slumped in the polls in 2008 and in the November election won only 4.07 percent of the vote. Furthermore, Winston Peters lost his constituency race, so the party was excluded from the new Parliament altogether. Contributing to Peters's loss were allegations that he had accepted secret donations from wealthy business interests. In August 2008 Prime Minister Clark had suspended him as minister of foreign affairs. Parliament passed a motion of censure three weeks later, but Peters was ultimately cleared by the Serious Fraud Office.

Leaders: Winston PETERS (Leader), Peter BROWN (Deputy Leader), Anne MARTIN (Secretary).

The Alliance. The Alliance was launched in 1991 as a coalition of five parties—the NewLabour Party, the *Mana Motuhake*, the New Zealand Democratic Party, the Green Party of Aotearoa, and the Liberal Party—on a platform calling for preservation of the welfare state and an end to the free-market policies of the two major parties. It won 2 seats on an 18 percent vote share in 1993 and narrowly missed winning a by-election seat in 1994. The party offered to form an election alliance with Labour for the 1996 campaign but was rebuffed. Standing on its own, the Alliance achieved a creditable 10.1 percent of the party list vote in October and won 13 seats. However, in late 1997 the Greens left the Alliance. The Liberal Party, which had been formed in 1991 by a number of National dissidents, dissolved in January 1998.

In the November 1999 election the Alliance captured ten seats on a 7.7 percent party list vote share and in early December worked out a power-sharing arrangement with Labour that permitted separate stances on issues affecting the "distinctive political identity" of each party. The Labour-led cabinet sworn in on December 10 included four Alliance ministers and a fifth minister for consumer affairs and customs outside cabinet.

Meanwhile, the democratic-socialist NewLabour, formed in 1989 by former Labour member Jim Anderton, had given up its individual identity and merged into the Alliance. But in April 2002 a sharp division between the majority of the Alliance MPs and the formal party leadership, headed by Matt McCARTEN, led to the expulsion of Anderton and six other MPs who had supported the government's decision to participate in U.S.-led military operations in Afghanistan. All ten Alliance and former Alliance MPs indicated that they would continue to back the government until the election.

In the July 2002 election, called early because of the split, the Alliance was ousted from the House, having won only 1.3 percent of the party list vote. In December 2002 *Mana Motuhake* formally left the Alliance and dissolved in 2005. Former government minister Laila HARRÉ retired as Alliance leader in November 2003 and was succeeded by McCarten, and then followed by Andrew McKENZIE and Kay MURRAY as co-leaders.

In the 2005 election the Alliance offered a party list but won only 0.1 percent of the vote and no seats. The party remains officially registered but attracted only 0.08 percent of the vote in the 2008 election and won no seats.

Leaders: Andrew McKENZIE (Co-leader), Kay MURRAY (Co-leader and Treasurer), Paul PIESSE (President), Tom DOWIE (General Secretary).

New Zealand Democratic Party for Social Credit (Democrats for Social Credit). Established in May 1953 as the Social Credit Political League, the party campaigned largely on a platform that promoted economic sovereignty, small business, worker shareholding and participation in management, tax and banking reform, public ownership of utilities, and introduction of a "Universal Basic Income." Social Credit subsequently proposed a defense posture of "armed neutrality" and a nuclear-free zone, a position reaffirmed at its 1985 congress and subsequently.

Leader Bruce BEETHAM won a seat in the House from 1978 until 1987, but his party secured no representation for a decade until winning two seats as part of the Alliance in 1996. It retained both in 1999. When the Alliance split in 2002, the party joined Jim Anderton's Progressive Coalition but won no seats in the July 2002 House election. At a party conference three months later most of the Democrats, but not party leader Grant GILLON, opted to separate from the Progressives. The party adopted its present name in July 2005 but won only 0.1 percent of the party list vote and no seats. It remains officially registered but in the 2008 election garnered only 0.05 percent of the vote.

Leaders: Stephnie de RUYTER (Leader), John PEMBERTON (Deputy Leader), Neville AITCHISON (President), Katherine RANSOM (Vice President), Peter FERGUSON (Secretary).

Additional parties contested the 2008 election without success. The **Bill and Ben Party** (registered July 29, 2008; Ben BOYCE and Jamie LINEHAM, co-leaders, and Andrew ROBINSON, secretary), a "joke party" led by two TV satirists, won 0.56 percent of the vote. The **Kiwi Party** (registered February 15, 2008; Larry BALDOCK, leader; Gordon COPELAND, president; Kevin STITT, secretary), which successfully led the petition initiative to force the August 21, 2009, referendum on the anti-smacking bill, won 0.54 percent. The **Aotearoa Legalize Cannabis Party** (Michael APPLEBY, leader; Michael BRITNELL deputy leader; Kevin O'CONNELL, president; and Irinka BRITNELL, secretary) won 0.41 percent. **The New Zealand Pacific Party** (Philip FIELD, leader; Ropeti GAFA, interim secretary) won 0.37 percent. The **Family Party** (registered December 17, 2007; Richard LEWIS, leader; Paul ADAMS, deputy leader; Elias KANARIS, president; Anne WILLIAMSON, secretary), which won 0.35 percent of the vote, descends from two fundamentalist parties, the New Zealand Family Rights Protection Party (registered March 2005 and deregistered September 2007) and Destiny New Zealand (registered July 2003 and deregistered in October 2007)., The **Libertarianz** (Richard MCGRATH, leader; Sean

FITZPATRICK, deputy leader; Craig MILMINE, president; Robert PALMER secretary),a radical minimum-government party founded in 1996, won 0.05 percent. The **Workers Party of New Zealand** (registered October 3, 2008; Philip FERGUSON, national organiser; Daphna WHITMORE, national secretary), which won 0.04 percent, is a descendent of numerous small leftist parties, most recently the Anti-Capitalist Alliance (2002–2006)., The **RAM–Residents Action Movement** (Grant BROOKES, chair; Elaine BLADE, vice chair; Elliott BLADE, secretary) won 0.02 percent. The **Republic of New Zealand Party** (Kerry BEVIN, leader; Richard NIGHTINGALE, secretary), which won 0.01 percent, was registered in July 2005 and deregistered on June 30, 2009.

LEGISLATURE

The former bicameral General Assembly of New Zealand became a unicameral body in 1950 with the abolition of its upper chamber, the Legislative Council. Now called the **House of Representatives** (although delegates are referred to as members of Parliament or MPs), the body currently consists of 120 members elected by universal suffrage for a three-year term, subject to dissolution. Under a partially proportional system introduced in 1996, 69 members are elected from single-member constituencies by majority vote (including 7 elected by voters on a separate Maori electoral roll) and at least 51 from party lists to ensure proportional representation for those parties winning at least one constituency or obtaining at least 5 percent of the national vote.

In the election of September 17, 2005, the new Maori Party won one more electorate seat than would otherwise have been awarded on the basis of the party list vote. Under New Zealand's complicated mixed member proportional (MMP) electoral system, this "overhang" seat meant that for the length of its term the House had 121 seats (69 electorate, 52 party list). The November 8, 2008 election produced an "overhang" of two Maori seats and a House of 122 members. These were distributed as follows: National Party, 58 (constituency seats 41, party list seats 17); Labour Party, 43 (21, 22); Green Party of Aotearoa, 9 (0, 9); ACT New Zealand, 5 (1, 4); Maori Party, 5 (5, 0); Jim Anderton's Progressive Party, 1 (1, 0), United Future New Zealand, 1 (1, 0).

Speaker: Lockwood SMITH.

CABINET

[as of July 17, 2008]

Prime Minister	John Key
Deputy Prime Minister	Bill English

Ministers in Cabinet

Accident Compensation Corporation (ACC)	Nick Smith
Agriculture	David Carter
Arts, Culture, and Heritage	Christopher Finlayson
Biosecurity	David Carter
Broadcasting	Dr. Jonathan Coleman
Climate Change Issues	Nick Smith
Commerce	Simon Power
Communications and Information Technology	Steven Joyce
Conservation	Tim Groser
Corrections	Judith Collins [f]
Courts	Georgina te Heuheu [f]
Defense	Dr. Wayne Mapp
Disability Issues	Paula Bennett [f]
Disarmament and Arms Control	Georgina te Heuheu [f]
Economic Development	Gerry Brownlee
Education	Anne Tolley [f]
Energy and Resources	Gerry Brownlee
Environment	Nick Smith
Ethnic Affairs	Pansy Wong [f]
Finance	Bill English
Fisheries	Phil Heatley
Food Safety	Kate Wilson [f]
Foreign Affairs	Murray McCully
Forestry	David Carter
Health	Tony Ryall
Housing	Phil Heatley
Immigration	Dr. Jonathan Coleman
Infrastructure	Bill English
Justice	Simon Power
Labor	Kate Wilson [f]
Pacific Island Affairs	Georgina te Heuheu [f]
Police	Judith Collins [f]
Research, Science, and Technology	Dr. Wayne Mapp
Social Development and Employment	Paula Bennett [f]
Sport and Recreation	Murray McCully
State-Owned Enterprises	Simon Power
State Services	Tony Ryall
Tertiary Education	Anne Tolley [f]
Treaty of Waitangi Negotiations	Christopher Finlayson
Tourism	John Key
Trade	Tim Groser
Transport	Stephen Joyce
Veterans' Affairs	Judith Collins [f]
Women's Affairs	Pansy Wong [f]
Youth Affairs	Paula Bennett [f]

Ministers Outside Cabinet

Building and Construction	Maurice Williamson
Civil Defense	John Carter
Customs	Maurice Williamson
Internal Affairs	Nathan Guy
Land Information	Nathan Guy
Racing	John Carter
Senior Citizens	John Carter
Statistics	Maurice Williamson

Support Party Ministers

Community and Voluntary Sector	Tariana Turia (Maori Party) [f]
Consumer Affairs	Heather Roy (ACT) [f]
Local Government	Rodney Hide (ACT)
Māori Affairs	Dr. Pita Sharples (Maori Party)
Regulatory Reform	Rodney Hide (ACT)
Revenue	Peter Dunne (United Future)

[f] = female

Note: Unless otherwise noted, all ministers belong to the National Party.

COMMUNICATIONS

Complete freedom of the press prevails, except for legal stipulations regarding libel.

Press. Except as indicated, the following are dailies: *New Zealand Herald* (Auckland, 260,309), the only national paper; *Sunday Star-Times* (Auckland, 203,901), weekly; *Christchurch Star* (Christchurch, 110,154), twice weekly; *Sunday News* (Auckland, 110,136), weekly; *Dominion-Post* (Wellington, 98,251), established in 2002 by merger of *The Dominion* and *The Evening Post; The Press* (Christchurch, 92,465), *Otago Daily Times* (Dunedin, 43,240).

News agencies. The New Zealand Press Association (NZPA) is a cooperative, nonprofit organization established in 1879 to provide both local and international news to all New Zealand papers. Other agencies in Wellington include a number of foreign bureaus and stringers.

Broadcasting and computing. The state-owned Radio New Zealand operates public, noncommercial radio broadcasting, and Television New Zealand operates two national networks. Commercial and special interest television and radio broadcasting, including Maori, Pacific Island, Chinese, educational and religious television channels and radio networks, are also well established. Television stations were estimated to total over 40 and radio stations over 400.

As of 2008 there were 720.3 Internet users per 1,000 inhabitants.

INTERGOVERNMENTAL REPRESENTATION

Ambassador to the U.S.: Roy FERGUSON.

U.S. Ambassador to New Zealand: David HUEBNER.

Permanent Representative to the UN: Jim McLAY.

IGO Memberships (Non-UN): ADB, APEC, BIS, CWTH, EBRD, IEA, Interpol, IOM, OECD, PC, PCA, PIF, WCO, WTO.

RELATED TERRITORIES

New Zealand has two self-governing territories, the Cook Islands and Niue, and two dependent territories, Ross Dependency and Tokelau.

Cook Islands. Located some 1,700 miles northeast of New Zealand and administered by that country since 1901, the Cook Islands have a land area of 90 square miles (234 sq. km.) and are divided between a smaller, poorer, northern group and a larger, more fertile, southern group. By far the most populous island, Roratonga, is the site of the capital, Avarua. The islands' total resident population of 21,750 (2007E) consists almost entirely of Polynesians who are New Zealand citizens. In 2006, 58,011 Cook Islanders resided in New Zealand, with another 15,000 in Australia, and remittances are a significant source of income for the territory. Leading exports include fish, pearls, tropical fruits, and handicrafts, while tourism is the main source of foreign earnings. Offshore banking and the sale of fishing licenses to foreign ships also contribute income. Future prospects include mining of undersea mineral nodules. Internationally, the Cook Islands is a member of the Pacific Community, the Smaller Island States subgroup (with Kiribati, Nauru, Niue, and Tuvalu) within the Pacific Islands Forum, various UN agencies, and the Asian Development Bank.

In June 2000 the Cook Islands was named by the Organization for Economic Cooperation and Development (OECD) as 1 of 35 uncooperative tax havens and by the international Financial Action Task Force on Money Laundering (FATF) as 1 of 15 noncooperative countries and territories. In 2002 the Cook government committed to remedial action and in 2005 was removed from the FATF list, having satisfied demands for tighter controls.

Internal self-government with an elected Legislative Assembly (commonly called the Parliament) and a premier (prime minister, since 1981) was instituted in 1965, with New Zealand continuing to oversee external and defense affairs. A hereditary House of Ariki, with up to 15 members, serves as an upper legislative chamber, advising on customary matters and land use.

Over the past 25 years political power has most often swung between the **Cook Islands Party** (CIP), which dates from 1965, and the **Democratic Party** (DP), founded in 1971 and named the Democratic Alliance Party (DAP) until 2003.

The CIP, under Sir Geoffrey HENRY, governed during much of the post-independence period, but not without controversy. In 1987 he was found guilty of electoral corruption for chartering an airline flight to bring voters from New Zealand. The CIP won the election of March 1994 despite a judicial inquiry into allegations of tax fraud by New Zealand–registered firms operating in collusion with the Cook Islands government. The allegations, made by Winston Peters of the New Zealand First Party, strained relations between the Cook Islands and New Zealand governments. In August 1997, however, a special commission reported that there was no basis for the claims, a decision that was upheld by the New Zealand High Court in 1999.

Meanwhile, alleged local corruption, economic mismanagement, and a bloated government payroll (accounting for one in three of the adult population) contributed to a financial crisis in mid-1996 and erosion of support for the CIP government. In the June 1999 election the CIP attracted only 39.8 percent of the vote compared to the DAP's 44.5 percent but held on to a 1-seat plurality in the assembly. With the CIP holding 11 seats and the DAP holding 10, the balance of power lay with former Democrat Norman GEORGE, then of the New Alliance Party (NAP), who controlled the remaining 4 seats and who threw his support to the incumbent, Sir Geoffrey. In July, however, 3 CIP legislators defected to the opposition, and only by offering the prime ministership to one of the defectors, Dr. Joe WILLIAMS, did the CIP retain power.

The Williams administration proved short-lived. In September 1999 the DAP won a by-election victory and negotiated a coalition agreement with the NAP's George. When parliament reconvened, Williams lost a vote of no confidence 14–11, and on November 18 Terepai MAOATE was sworn in as the head of a new cabinet with George as deputy prime minister.

By mid-2001 dissatisfaction with Maoate's leadership had surfaced, resulting in the replacement of George by Robert WOONTON of the DAP. In February 2002 Maoate lost a no-confidence motion and was replaced as prime minister by Woonton, who had the support of the CIP as well as the NAP. Both Sir Geoffrey, as deputy prime minister, and Norman George returned to the cabinet. In May George's NAP merged with Woonton's DAP faction, leaving former prime minister Maoate as head of a competing Democratic faction as well as leader of the opposition.

The fifth coalition since the 1999 election, encompassing the DAP and the CIP, was formed in November 2002. George, having once again been dropped from the cabinet, became the sole opposition member of parliament. However, the DAP-CIP partnership lasted only until January 31, 2003, at which time Terepai Maoate replaced Sir Geoffrey as deputy prime minister under Woonton. Reunited, Woonton's DAP and Maoate's Democrats agreed to restore their organization's original name, Democratic Party (DP or Demo).

The rift between Woonton and Maoate reappeared in November 2003 and Maoate was forced out, to be replaced by Ngamau MUNOKOA ("Aunty Mau"), who became the first woman to hold the post of deputy prime minister. Meanwhile, Norman George had taken on the role of senior adviser to the prime minister.

With the next legislative election scheduled for 2004, and with the public increasingly jaundiced by the machinations of leading politicians, demands for political reform mounted. In early 2004 parliament voted to drop the overseas seat, reduce the size of the legislature to 24, and shorten the legislative term to four years.

The September 2004 election gave the DP (the renamed DAP) 14 seats to 9 for the CIP after vote-counting disputes were resolved. On November 14 Prime Minister Woonton announced a DP-CIP "unity" government. But when Munokoa's and Woonton's opponents seized control of the DP, the prime minister and his supporters formed a new *Demo Tumu* party. In mid-December, however, Woonton resigned as prime minister when a hearing determined that the race for his parliamentary seat had ended in a tie and that a by-election was required. On December 14 parliament elected as prime minister Jim Marurai of the *Demo Tumu,* which subsequently adopted the name Cook Islands First (CIF).

According to a prior agreement, Marurai was to exchange positions with Deputy Prime Minister Geoffrey Henry after two years, but in September 2005 Marurai dismissed Henry and then two other CIP ministers. Terepai Maoate, the new deputy prime minister, brought the DP back into the government, which also continued to include the CIP's Wilkie RASMUSSEN.

With the opposition CIP having won a July 2006 by-election and George siding with the opposition, Prime Minister Marurai was obliged to call for the dissolution of parliament and a snap election. The election of September 26 (and a November by-election to resolve a tie vote) concluded with the DP holding 15 seats; the CIP, 8; and a CIP-aligned independent, 1. The CIP's Tom MARSTERS became leader of the opposition. Marurai was reinstated as prime minister, with Maoate as his deputy and Rasmussen as minister of foreign affairs, and the government entered a period of relative stability.

In July 2009 Marurai hosted a visit by Prime Minister John Key and the two announced completion of a tax information exchange agreement, thus dispelling allegations of tax evasion. A similar agreement is being negotiated with Australia. Cook Islands in April petitioned the UN Commission on the Limits of the Continental Shelf (CLCS) to extend its Exclusive Economic Zone by 400,000 sq. km.

New Zealand High Commissioner: vacant.

Prime Minister: Jim MARURAI.

Niue. An island of 100 square miles (259 sq. km.), Niue is the largest and westernmost of the Cook Islands but has been governed separately since 1903. The territory obtained internal self-government in

1974, with a premier heading a 4-member cabinet and a Legislative Assembly (*Fono*) of 20 members, 6 elected from a common roll and 14 chosen by villages, serving three-year terms. The capital is Alofi. The resident population has declined almost continuously from 5,194 in 1966 to 1,740 in 2006 and an estimated 1,444 in 2008.

In 2006, 22,473 Niueans resided in New Zealand, and overseas remittances constitute a major source of income. Other economic resources include annual budgetary and project aid from New Zealand; export sales of noni juice, fish, taro, honey, and vanilla; and a small tourism industry that attracted some 1,400 tourists in 2003 but little more than half that in 2004 because of cyclone damage. Tourist visits recovered to nearly 3,000 subsequently but remain low due to limited hotel facilities and airline flights. Recent efforts to increase the island's income have included leasing its telephone area code for sex-related and other services, selling its postal code ("NU") for Internet domain addresses, and investigating prospects for commercial fishing. Internationally, Niue participates in the Pacific Community, the Smaller Island States subgroup (with the Cook Islands, Kiribati, Nauru, and Tuvalu) within the Pacific Islands Forum, and several UN agencies, but its efforts to join the Asian Development Bank have not yet succeeded.

Niue's first and longest-serving premier Sir Robert R. REX died in December 1992, and a Legislative Assembly election in February 1993 brought Frank LUI to the premiership. The period 1994–1996 saw an evenly divided assembly and a series of inconclusive no-confidence motions. Nevertheless, the *Fono* reelected Lui as premier by two votes over the Niue People's Party (NPP) nominee, Robert REX Jr., son of the former premier.

In the March 1999 election Premier Lui lost his seat, and the *Fono* elected NPP leader Sani LAKATANI by a 14–6 vote over a former government minister, O'Love JACOBSEN. In late December, by a 10–10 vote, Lakatani survived a no-confidence motion over allegedly questionable procedures in his attempt to bring more international airline flights to the island. Less than six months later the assembly split evenly again, voting 9–9 on a nonbinding call for him to step down; this followed disclosure that Lakatani had negotiated with the Niue Development Bank for a loan to help him pay a personal debt and forestall bankruptcy, which would have disqualified him from office.

Following the election of April 20, 2002, a majority within the NPP backed Young VIVIAN to replace Lakatani as leader, and on May 1 Vivian was elected premier over Hunukitama HUNUKI of the Alliance of Independents, an opposition "team" that had been formed in late 2001 by Frank Lui and O'Love Jacobsen, among others. Although Lakatani was named deputy premier, in August he was dismissed after crossing the aisle and voting against an unsuccessful budget proposal. The office of deputy was subsequently filled by independent Toke Talagi.

In June 2002 the legislature repealed a controversial 1994 act that had permitted the licensing of offshore banks. Never as lucrative as hoped, this banking legislation had contributed to Niue's designation in 2000 by the international FATF as noncompliant in fighting money laundering. Collaterally, the OECD had labeled Niue as 1 of 35 jurisdictions considered to be an "uncooperative" tax haven. By the end of 2002 Niue had taken sufficient corrective actions to warrant removal from both lists.

In early January 2004 Niue was devastated by Cyclone Heta, which killed 2, left some 200 homeless, destroyed the island's hospital as well as a fish processing plant that was under construction, and damaged or destroyed an estimated 95 percent of tourist accommodations. Although some observers immediately questioned Niue's economic viability, the extensive damage drew wide international attention to the island and generated an influx of aid that permitted the government not only to begin a recovery effort but also to contemplate a comprehensive review of economic, social, and environmental policies. Fish processing and noni juice plants opened in October 2004.

With the NPP having dissolved in 2003, all candidates in the election of April 2005 ran as independents. Young Vivian retained the premiership. In early March 2007 he easily survived a no-confidence motion, 12–7, despite a financial crisis that had necessitated a cut in civil service pay as well as other major spending reductions. Following the 2008 general election in June 2008 Toke Talagi secured 14 assembly votes to Vivian's 5 to take the premiership.

In August 2008 Niue was the host of the annual summit of the Pacific Islands Forum, over which Premier Talagi presided. In July 2009 Talagi hosted a visit by Prime Minister John Key, at which time he urged speedier release of earmarked tourism aid for Niue and hinted that he was prepared to talk with China if New Zealand did not look after the island's needs.

New Zealand High Commissioner: Brian SMYTHE.

Premier: Toke TALAGI.

Ross Dependency. A large, wedge-shaped portion of the Antarctic Continent, the Ross Dependency extends from 160 degrees east to 150 degrees west longitude and has an estimated area of 160,000 square miles (414,400 sq. km.). It includes the Ross Ice Shelf, the Balleny Islands, and Scott Island. Although the Ross Dependency has been administered by New Zealand since 1923, the Antarctic Treaty of 1959 puts New Zealand's claim, and all other states' claims as well, in abeyance. Nevertheless New Zealand criminal law and conservation laws and other legislation are recognized as valid in the territory, which in 1977 was extended 200 nautical miles into the Southern Ocean by the Territorial Sea and Exclusive Economic Zone Act. A permit is required from the Ministry of Foreign Affairs and Trade to visit the territory or from the Ministry of Fisheries to conduct fishing activities. In accordance with the Antarctica (Environmental Protection) Act 1994, mineral prospecting and mining is prohibited. The territory, in accordance with the Antarctic Treaty, is a conventional and nuclear weapons-free zone. New Zealand maintains a permanent scientific research station in the territory called Scott Base, serviced by Royal New Zealand Air Force aircraft, and cooperates with the U.S. National Science Foundation, which maintains the McMurdo scientific station nearby. In 1988, in an effort to stop illegal fishing in the Ross Sea, Wellington announced that it would step up surveillance of the area, and since then patrols have been undertaken periodically by Air Force planes and Navy vessels.

Tokelau. A group of three atolls (Atafu, Fakaofo, and Nukunonu) north of Samoa with an area of 4 square miles (10.4 sq. km.), Tokelau has a resident population of 1,449 (2007E), but 6,819 Tokelauans reside in New Zealand (2006C) and others in Sydney, Samoa, and Hawaii. International affiliations include membership in the Pacific Community and associate membership in the World Health Organization. All the islands of the Tokelau group were claimed by the United States in the Guano Islands Act 1856 but have been administered by Great Britain and, since 1923, New Zealand, and were included within New Zealand's territorial boundaries by legislation enacted in 1948. The United States ceded claims to the three main atolls in 1979 but incorporated Swain's Island (Olohega) into American Samoa, leaving potential for dispute if Tokelau becomes independent in the future. The islands have limited economic viability, the principal income sources being annual budget and project aid from New Zealand; remittances from Tokelauans working overseas; the export of coconut, copra, and tuna; the sale of stamps, handicrafts, and souvenir coins; and the sale of fishing licenses to foreign fleets.

Each of the atolls elects for a three-year term a *faipule,* whose duties include executive and judicial responsibilities. As each atoll's highest elected official, the *faipule* advises the territory's appointed administrator, who represents the crown and is responsible to New Zealand's Ministry of Foreign Affairs and Trade. Each atoll also has a Council of Elders (*Taupulega*) and an elected mayor (*pulenuku*), and together the *faipule* and the mayors constitute the Council for the Ongoing Government. The government is chaired for a one-year term by the *Ulu-O-Tokelau,* the titular head of the territory, which rotates among the three *faipule.* In June 2004 the administrator assigned to the three atoll councils a range of public service responsibilities. In 1992 the island leaders and the New Zealand government agreed to begin the process of decolonization, and on August 1, 1996, the Tokelau Amendment Act came into effect, conferring general legislative powers on a body called the General *Fono.* The 23 members of the *Fono,* which includes the *faipule* and the *pulenuku,* are elected for three-year terms, most recently in January 2008.

In 2003 the General *Fono* unanimously voted to explore the possibility of self-government in free association with New Zealand. In February 2006, however, voters failed to give the necessary two-thirds majority to a draft treaty of free association with only a simple majority of 349 in favor to 232 opposed. A repeat referendum in October 2007 also narrowly missed passing. Despite assurances from the Clark government, many opponents expressed doubts that New Zealand would sustain its present financial commitment and extension of citizenship if Tokelau changed its status.

Administrator: David PAYTON.

Faipule (Titular Head of Tokelau): Foua TOLOA (Fakaofo), Kuresa NASAU (Atafu), Pio TUIA (Nukunonu).

NICARAGUA

Republic of Nicaragua
República de Nicaragua

Political Status: Independence originally proclaimed 1821; separate republic established 1838; provisional junta installed July 19, 1979; present constitution adopted November 19, 1986, in effect from January 9, 1987.

Area: 50,193 sq. mi. (130,000 sq. km.).

Population: 5,142,098 (2005C); 5,404,000 (2008E).

Major Urban Center (2005E): MANAGUA (1,166,000).

Official Language: Spanish.

Monetary Unit: Córdoba Oro (principal rate December 1, 2009: 20.75 córdobas = $1US).

President: José Daniel ORTEGA Saavedra (Sandinist National Liberation Front); served as president 1985–1990; reelected on November 5, 2006, and inaugurated for a five-year term on January 10, 2007, succeeding Enrique BOLAÑOS Geyer (Grand Liberal Union).

Vice President: Jaime MORALES Carazo (Sandinist National Liberation Front); elected on November 5, 2006, and inaugurated for a term concurrent with that of the president on January 10, 2007, succeeding Alfredo GÓMEZ Urcuyo (nonparty).

THE COUNTRY

Bounded by Honduras on the north and west and by Costa Rica on the south, Nicaragua is the largest but, apart from Belize, the least densely populated of the Central American states. Its numerous mountains are interspersed with extensive lowlands that make it a potential site for an interoceanic canal. The population is predominantly (69 percent) mestizo (mixed Indian and European), with smaller groups of whites (17 percent), blacks (9 percent), and Indians (5 percent). Although freedom of worship is constitutionally recognized, 72.9 percent of the inhabitants adhere to Roman Catholicism.

There are approximately 2.2 million people in the Nicaraguan labor force midway through the decade, 30 percent of whom were women. Women are concentrated in domestic service, teaching, and market vending; in recent years, female participation has greatly increased, particularly in agriculture (under the sandinista regime women also constituted 30 percent of the armed forces and nearly half of the civil militia). As of mid-2008, 17 percent of the country's legislators and 40 percent of its cabinet members were women.

About one-third of Nicaragua's GDP continues to be agricultural, with coffee and seafood constituting the leading exports. The extraction of mineral resources (including silver, gold, lead, gypsum, and zinc) is also important, while efforts to promote economic growth have centered on agricultural diversification and the stimulation of industries supporting agriculture and making use of local raw materials.

The Nicaraguan economy has been battered by numerous natural and human-inflicted disasters in the past decades, including a disastrous earthquake that struck Managua in December 1972. The final phase of the anti-Somoza rebellion in 1978–1979 also severely disrupted development, as did the U.S. economic blockade of the sandinista regime and support of the anti-government rebels throughout the 1980s.

Economic recovery in the 1990s was halted by Hurricane Mitch in October 1998, which left more than 4,000 people dead and destroyed or damaged about 36,000 homes. Nine years later Hurricane Felix, which hit the impoverished Atlantic Coast on September 4, 2007, destroyed or damaged more than 19,000 homes.

As the poorest country in Central America, Nicaragua received help from international organizations and foreign governments in 2007 and 2008. The largest donation was from the International Development Bank, which forgave $984 million in loans.

Growth dropped off to 4.3 percent in 2000, rose to 10.7 percent in 2001, then receded to an annual average of 3.9 percent in 2002–2006. Annual growth remained steady in 2007–2008, averaging 3.3 percent. The annual rate of growth in 2009 was expected to contract to about 1 percent, owing in large part to decreases in remittances and demand for Nicaraguan exports as a consequence of the global economic downturn. On a more positive note, in September the government announced budgetary reforms and reductions in spending aimed at improving the economy in accordance with IMF poverty-reduction policies.

GOVERNMENT AND POLITICS

Political background. Nicaraguan politics following the country's liberation from Spanish rule in 1821 was long dominated by a power struggle between leaders of the Liberal and Conservative parties, punctuated by periods of U.S. intervention, which was virtually continuous during 1912–1925 and 1927–1933. A Liberal Party victory in a U.S.-supervised election in 1928 paved the way for the assumption of power by Gen. Anastasio SOMOZA García, who ruled the country as president from 1937 until his assassination in September 1956.

Political power remained in the hands of the Somoza family under the Liberal Party presidencies of Luis SOMOZA Debayle, the dictator's elder son (1956–1963); René SCHICK Gutiérrez (1963–1966); Lorenzo GUERRERO Gutiérrez (1966–1967); and Gen. Anastasio SOMOZA Debayle (1967–1972), the younger son of the late dictator. Constitutionally barred from a second term, Somoza Debayle arranged an interim collegial executive (consisting of two members of the Liberal Party and one member of the Conservative Party) that oversaw the promulgation of a new constitution and administered the nation until the election of September 1, 1974, when he was formally returned to office by an overwhelming margin.

The stability of the Somoza regime was shaken by the Sandinist National Liberation Front (*Frente Sandinista de Liberación Nacional*—FSLN or "sandinista"), which launched a series of coordinated attacks throughout the country in October 1977 in an effort to instigate a general uprising. While the immediate effort failed, far more serious disturbances erupted in 1978, including occupation of the National Palace in Managua by FSLN rebels on August 22 and a major escalation of the insurgency in early September. During the first half of 1979 the tide turned decisively in favor of the sandinistas, who by the end of June controlled most of the major towns as well as the slum district of the capital. Despite 12 days of intense bombardment of FSLN positions within Managua, government forces were unable to regain the initiative, and on July 17 General Somoza left the country after resigning in favor of an interim president, Dr. Francisco URCUYO Maliaños. Confronted with a bid by Urcuyo to remain in office until the expiration of his predecessor's term in 1981, three members of the FSLN provisional junta flew from Costa Rica to León on July 18 and, amid some confusion, accepted the unconditional surrender of the National Guard commander in Managua the following day.

Daniel ORTEGA Saavedra, the leader of the five-man junta and of the FSLN's nine-member Directorate, announced in August 1980 that the FSLN would remain in power until 1985, with electoral activity to resume in 1984. In addition to Ortega, the original junta included Violeta Barrios de CHAMORRO, Moisés HASSAN Morales, Sergio RAMÍREZ Mercado, and Alfonso ROBELO Callejas. On May 18, 1980, Rafael CORDOVA Rivas and Arturo José CRUZ Porras were named to succeed Chamorro and Robelo, who had resigned on April 19 and 22, respectively. On March 4, 1981, Hassan and Cruz also resigned, Ortega being named coordinator of the remaining three-member group.

On September 17, 1980, former president Somoza was assassinated in a bazooka attack on his limousine in central Asunción, Paraguay. (In early 1999 the former chief of state security during the sandinista regime reportedly acknowledged his agency's responsibility for the attack.)

In early 1984, under diplomatic pressure from Western countries and military pressure from U.S.-backed insurgent (contra) forces, the junta adjusted its electoral timetable to permit both presidential and legislative balloting the following November. Although attempts by the regime to reach procedural agreement with the opposition failed (most

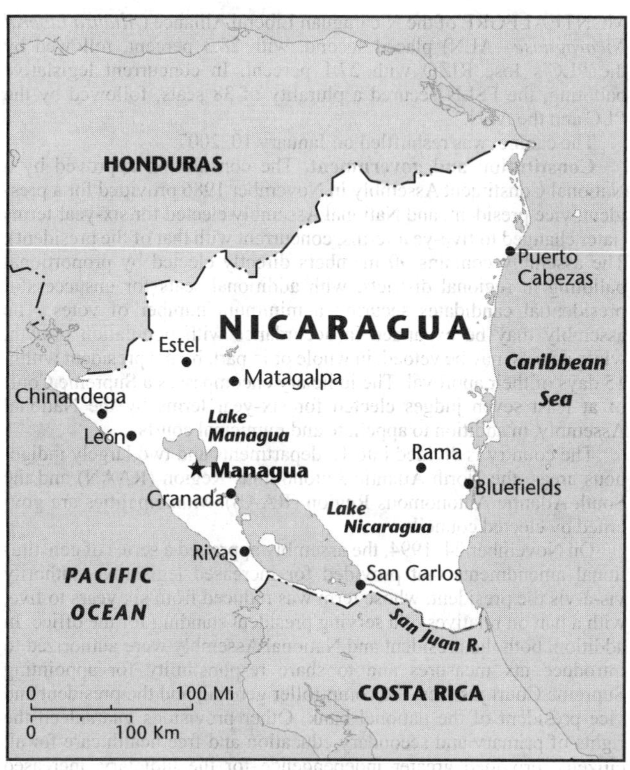

of the latter's larger parties withdrawing from the campaign), the November 4 election was contested by a number of small non-sandinista groups. In balloting described as exemplary by international observers (who nonetheless objected to preelection censorship and harassment of opposition candidates), Ortega won 67 percent of the presidential vote, while the FSLN gained a similar percentage of seats in a National Constituent Assembly, which approved a new basic law on November 19, 1986.

After extensive negotiations, a preliminary peace agreement for the region, based in part on proposals advanced by President Oscar Arias Sánchez of Costa Rica, was approved by the five Central American chief executives in Guatemala, on August 7, 1987. In accordance with the agreement, talks between the sandinista government and contra leaders were initiated in January 1988 that failed to yield a definitive cease-fire agreement, although most of the rebel forces had quit Nicaragua for Honduras by mid-August because of a failure to secure further military aid from the United States. Subsequently, the Central American presidents, during a meeting in El Salvador, on February 13–14, 1989, agreed on a program of Nicaraguan electoral reform that would permit opposition parties unimpeded access to nationwide balloting no later than February 25, 1990, while the U.S. Congress in mid-April approved a $49.7 million package of nonlethal aid for the contras over the ensuing 10 months.

Although public opinion polls had suggested that the FSLN enjoyed a substantial lead in the 1990 elections, Chamorro, heading a National Opposition Union (UNO) coalition, defeated Ortega by a 15 percent margin in the February presidential poll, with the UNO capturing 51 of 92 assembly seats. Following her inauguration in April, President Chamorro was confronted with a perilously weak economy reeling from numerous clashes between peasants who had benefited from the sandinista land policies and demobilized contras pressing for promised land and monetary compensation. Chamorro responded by naming a number of influential contras to government positions, while retaining her predecessor's brother, Cdr. (thereafter Gen.) Humberto ORTEGA Saavedra as chief of the armed forces. These actions, in addition to continuance of a social pact (*concertación*) with the FSLN led Vice President Virgilio GODOY Reyes' conservative UNO bloc to adopt a posture of de facto opposition. The complexity of the new alignment was evidenced by the January 1991 balloting for president of the National Assembly: former contra leader and presidential adviser Alfredo CESAR Aguirre, with the backing of both sandinista and moderate UNO members, defeated incumbent Míriam ARGUELLO Morales, a conservative hard-liner from the UNO party supported by Godoy.

On January 9, 1993, a cabinet reshuffle was announced that for the first time awarded a portfolio (tourism) to a sandinista, while a new assembly, dominated by sandinistas and an ex-UNO Center Group, was convened, which proceeded to elect Gustavo TABLADA Zelaya, a former communist, as its presiding officer. By now the breach between Chamorro and her former coalition supporters was such that some UNO leaders called for shortening her term of office, and in late February General Ortega charged Vice President Godoy and former assembly president César with encouraging a resurgence of contra activity in the north to create sufficient unrest to cause the government's collapse. The UNO hardliners responded by organizing a series of mass demonstrations against the president's "cogovernment" with her former adversaries.

Following an abortive effort by Chamorro to launch a national dialogue on the issues dividing the country, a remarkable series of tit-for-tat military actions erupted. On July 21–22, 1993, nearly 50 people were killed when a group of 150 demobilized *contras,* known as *recompas,* seized control of the northern town of Estelí, plundering three local banks before being routed by government troops. On August 19 right-wing recontras took 42 hostages in an attack on another northern town, El Zúngana; in retaliation a *recompas* unit stormed the Managua offices of the UNO, taking captive an equal number of individuals, including Godoy and César. All of the hostages were released within days, following intervention by the Organization of American States (OAS).

On September 2, 1993, President Chamorro angered her FSLN supporters by announcing that General Ortega would be removed as military chief in 1994; the pledge did not, however, mollify her UNO critics, who called for his immediate dismissal. During the following week General Ortega and Vice President Godoy held two private meetings that led to an unprecedented series of talks between FSLN and UNO representatives in October and November on proposals for constitutional reform.

By early 1994 a new legislative majority had emerged in the form of a working alliance between the FSLN, the Center Group, and the Christian Democratic Union (UDC), which advanced the process of constitutional revision by lifting a requirement that amendments be approved by two successive assembly sessions. Subsequently, General Ortega, in response to continuing pressure to step down, indicated that he would not do so until a new military statute had been enacted that placed nomination to his office in the hands of a Military Council (*Consejo Militar*). On May 18 President Chamorro stated that Ortega would retire on February 21, 1995. The announcement came one day before submitting to the assembly her proposals for military reform, which did not call for subordination of the military to civilian control and did not provide for a ministry of defense.

Meanwhile, the FSLN had encountered an identity crisis because of General Ortega's continuing governmental role. The sandinista dilemma became clear after the general had presented the armed forces' highest award, the "Camilio Ortega" gold medal to the U.S. embassy's defense attaché on January 21, 1993, "in recognition of his outstanding work in strengthening professional relations between the Nicaraguan and U.S. armed forces." The fact that Ortega was seen as moving to the right in a possible bid to gain the presidency in 1996 led to the formation of a centrist faction within the FSLN National Directorate that, while distancing itself from a hard-line leftist minority, sought "a basic reordering of the economy" along genuinely social-democratic lines. Disarray within the sandinista leadership was also seen in a growing cleavage between Ortega and the party's relatively moderate legislative leader, former vice president Sergio Ramírez. Significantly, one of the constitutional reforms endorsed by Ramírez would restrict a president to a single term, which would deny the former chief executive an opportunity to vindicate himself for his 1989 loss to Chamorro. Ortega subsequently repositioned himself to the left of his party's mainstream, urging opposition to economic restructuring and occasionally endorsing violence to oppose privatization by the Chamorro administration. His new hard-line posture won the day at an extraordinary FSLN congress in May 1994 and secured the dismissal of Ramírez as FSLN legislative leader in September. However, Ortega was unable to prevent the election of another moderate, Dora María TÉLLEZ, as Ramírez's Assembly bloc successor.

On September 2, 1994, a new military code was approved that limited the armed forces chief to a single five-year term and prohibited appointment of relatives of the president to the post. On the other hand, the military would continue to nominate its commander. Subsequently, the Military Council proposed Maj. Gen. Joaquín CUADRA Lacayo to succeed Gen. Humberto Ortega on February 21, 1995.

In November 1994 the National Assembly approved a lengthy series of constitutional amendments (see Constitution and government, below), significantly altering the distribution of power between the executive and legislative branches in favor of the latter. The changes were strongly opposed by President Chamorro and by the orthodox wing of the sandinistas, which supported a new effort by Míriam Argüello to recapture the assembly presidency in January 1995. Argüello was, however, unable to deny reelection to the reformist Luis Humberto GUZMÁN, and on February 17 the assembly published the constitutional revisions after Chamorro had refused to do so. The conflict intensified further on April 6, when the legislature named 5 new Supreme Court justices (2 to replace members whose terms had expired and 3 to expand the size of the Court from 9 to 12 under a provision of the amended basic law). On May 8, following presidential repudiation of the appointments, the court, without ruling on the substance of the constitutional changes, declared the amendments null and void in the absence of executive promulgation. However, on June 15, in the wake of mediation by Cardinal Miguel OBANDO y Bravo, then the archbishop of Managua, the lengthy impasse was broken with Chamorro's acceptance of the constitutional reform package, which was promulgated on July 4. An agreement on the new Supreme Court justices followed on July 21.

By early 1995 campaigning for the 1996 election by Nicaragua's more than two dozen parties was effectively under way. One of the leading candidates, Presidency Minister Antonio LACAYO Oyanguren, indicated that he might divorce his wife, Cristiana CHAMORRO, so as to comply with the new constitutional requirement that blood and marriage relatives serving heads of state be disqualified. Other likely contenders were Daniel Ortega and Sergio Ramírez of the deeply divided FSLN and, on the right, Managua Mayor Arnaldo ALEMÁN Lacayo, representing the largely reunited Liberals. On December 6, 1995, legislative passage of a new general election law included a provision for a presidential runoff if no candidate gained at least 45 percent of the vote.

On July 6, 1996, the Supreme Electoral Council (*Consejo Supremo Electoral*—CSE) formally declared Antonio Lacayo ineligible for the presidency; the council also disqualified Alvaro ROBELO of the conservative Nicaraguan Alliance (AN) and Edén PASTORA Gómez of the Democratic Action Party (PAD) for having acquired, respectively, Italian and Costa Rican citizenship.

In the balloting of October 10, 1996, Alemán Lacayo emerged as the clear victor in the presidential race, although the FSLN insisted that his official tally of 51 percent was fraudulently inflated. The legislative outcome was far less simple, Alemán's Liberal coalition being held to a plurality of 42 seats, while the runner-up FSLN gained 36.

With Alemán ineligible for reelection in 2001, Enrique BOLAÑOS Geyer, who had resigned as vice president in October 2000 to qualify as a presidential candidate, won the Constitutionalist Liberal Party (*Partido Liberal Constitucionalista*—PLC) nomination and garnered 56.1 percent of the vote to defeat Daniel Ortega in the FSLN leader's third nationwide effort on November 4. Alemán supporters subsequently secured his election as president of the National Assembly, a post that he was obliged to relinquish on September 19, 2002, amid mounting evidence of corruption during his tenure as chief executive. On December 7, 2003, Alemán was convicted of fraud, money laundering, and the theft of state funds and received a 20-year sentence.

In late 2003 Alemán, who continued as Liberal leader despite his imprisonment, joined forces with Ortega, thus splitting the party into pro- and anti-Bolaños factions. The president responded by forming a new party, the Grand Liberal Union (GUL), which joined with five minor groups in an Alliance for the Republic (APRE, under Political Parties, below) to contest the November 2004 municipal elections.

The FSLN swept the November 7, 2004, local balloting, winning more than 90 of 152 mayoralties, including 15 of 17 capitals, on a 45 percent vote share. The PLC won 41 mayoralties and only 1 capital, while the APRE took 5 mayoralties and 1 capital. Following the election, the FSLN and PLC concluded a power-sharing pact under which the two would alternate the presidency, beginning with whomever won the next election, with guarantees to the other of a share of high-level government positions.

Ortega made a comeback with his election as president for the fourth time on November 5, 2006, with 38 percent of the vote. Eduardo MONTEALEGRE of the Nicaraguan Liberal Alliance (*Alianza Liberal Nicaragünse*—ALN) placed second, with 28.3 percent, followed by the PLC's José RIZO with 27.1 percent. In concurrent legislative balloting, the FSLN secured a plurality of 38 seats, followed by the PLC and the ALN.

The cabinet was reshuffled on January 10, 2007.

Constitution and government. The constitution approved by a National Constituent Assembly in November 1986 provided for a president, vice president, and National Assembly elected for six-year terms (later changed to five-year terms, concurrent with that of the president). The assembly contains 90 members directly elected by proportional balloting in regional districts, with additional seats for unsuccessful presidential candidates securing a minimum number of votes. The assembly may be expanded in accordance with population growth, while its acts may be vetoed, in whole or in part, by the president within 15 days of their approval. The judiciary encompasses a Supreme Court of at least seven judges elected for six-year terms by the National Assembly, in addition to appellate and municipal courts.

The country is divided into 15 departments and two largely indigenous areas, the North Atlantic Autonomous Region (RAAN) and the South Atlantic Autonomous Region (RAAS). Municipalities are governed by elected councils.

On November 24, 1994, the assembly approved a series of constitutional amendments that provided for increased legislative authority vis-à-vis the president, whose term was reduced from six years to five, with a ban on relatives of a serving president standing for the office. In addition, both the president and National Assembly were authorized to introduce tax measures and to share responsibility for appointing Supreme Court justices, the comptroller general, and the president and vice president of the national bank. Other provisions guaranteed the rights of primary and secondary education and free health care for all citizens, provided greater independence for the judiciary, increased civilian control over the military, eliminated conscription, and recognized the rights of indigenous populations on both the east and west coasts.

In late January 2000 President Alemán signed into law another round of constitutional changes, including a reduction from 45 to 35 percent in the vote share required for presidential election; legislative life tenure for himself, with a two-thirds vote required for removal of immunity from prosecution; the appointment of five permanent members of the State Comptroller's Office from a list approved by the president and the assembly; an increase in the number of Supreme Court justices to 16 from 12; an increase in the membership of the Supreme Electoral Council to seven from five; and the deregistration of political parties securing less than 4 percent of the vote. In addition, President Alemán advocated holding a constitutional assembly election in place of the presidential poll scheduled for 2001, but he failed to secure sufficient legislative support for the proposal.

In late 2004 the National Assembly approved a new package of constitutional reforms that included legislative ratification of ministerial and ambassadorial appointments and lowered to a simple majority (from two-thirds) the vote needed to overturn a presidential veto. The package was struck down by the Central American Court of Justice on March 29, 2005, on the ground that it should have been submitted to a constituent assembly. However, Nicaragua's Supreme Court of Justice (CSJ) approved the changes on March 30, arguing that the regional court lacked jurisdiction because of a protocol approved by the Central American presidents in December that banned it from intervening in intrapower disputes in member states.

Foreign relations. The conservative and generally pro-U.S. outlook of the Somoza regime was reflected in a favorable attitude toward North American investment and a strongly pro-Western, anticommunist position in the UN, OAS, and other international bodies. The United States, for its part, did not publicly call for the resignation of General Somoza until June 20, 1979, and subsequently appealed for an OAS peacekeeping presence to ensure that a successor government would include moderate representatives from what it deemed acceptable to "all major elements of Nicaraguan society." Although the idea was rejected by both the OAS and the FSLN, the United States played a key role in the events leading to Somoza's departure, and the administration of President Jimmy Carter extended reconstruction aid to the new Managua government in October 1980. By contrast, President Ronald Reagan was deeply committed to support of the largely Honduran-based rebel contras, despite a conspicuous lack of enthusiasm for such a policy by many U.S. members of Congress.

Regional attitudes toward the contra insurgency were mixed, most South American countries professing neutrality, although Managua-Quito relations were broken in 1985 after (then) Ecuadorian president Febres Cordero called Nicaragua "a bonfire in Central America." Subsequently, members of the Contadora Group (Colombia, Mexico, Panama, Venezuela) and the Lima Group (Argentina, Brazil, Peru, Uruguay) met intermittently with Central American leaders in an effort to broker the conflict, although neither bloc directly influenced the accords of August 1987 and February 1989.

In April 1991 President Chamorro became the first Nicaraguan head of state in more than 50 years to make an official visit to Washington, D.C., where she was warmly received and addressed a joint session of the U.S. Congress. In sharp contrast, an August 1992 report issued by a top aide of U.S. senator Jesse Helms charged the Chamorro government with being controlled by "communists, terrorists, thugs, robbers and assassins" and recommended the discontinuance of aid to Nicaragua pending a number of changes, including the replacement of all sandinista army and police personnel by former contras and the return of properties belonging to Nicaraguans living in the United States (many of whom were supporters of the former Somoza regime). The report, which also contained the erroneous charge that Nicaragua was "the most heavily militarized state in Central America," was dismissed by Managua as "ludicrous."

Regionally, Nicaragua called in May 1991 for deferment on formal admission to the new Central American Parliament (Parlacen) on the ground that it lacked the resources for an early referendum on the matter. In October 1992 Nicaraguan authorities accused Costa Rica of contaminating the San Juan River by sanctioning the use of highly toxic pesticides on its banana plantations. A month later, in the first such meeting since the end of the sandinista-contra war, General Ortega traveled to Honduras, where he conferred with his counterpart, Gen. Luis Alonso Discua Elvir, on collaborative efforts to limit the use of their countries "for illegal drug, arms, cattle, or fish trafficking."

During a summit meeting in Managua on April 22, 1993, Nicaragua joined its three northern neighbors (El Salvador, Guatemala, and Honduras), which had previously undertaken a *Triángulo Norte* free trade initiative, in launching the *Grupo América Central 4* (AC-4), which was viewed as paving the way for a free trade zone throughout the isthmus. The process was further advanced during a five-member regional summit in Guatemala City on October 27–29, 1993, following inauguration of the headquarters of the Central American Integration System (SICA, under the Central American Common Market—CACM).

A long-dormant territorial dispute with Colombia was rekindled in April 1995 with Nicaragua's seizure of two Colombian fishing vessels and the alleged violation of its airspace by three Colombian aircraft. At issue was Nicaragua's 1980 revocation of a 1928 treaty, by which Nicaragua, under reported U.S. pressure, ceded ownership of certain Caribbean islands to its neighbor in compensation for construction of the interoceanic canal through Panama.

In November 1995 Nicaragua and Costa Rica agreed to regularize the status of 50,000 Nicaraguans working illegally in Costa Rica. Under the accord, the workers would be given special Nicaraguan passports, while work permits would be issued by Costa Rican authorities once worker employment had been certified.

Relations with Honduras, complicated during the 1980s by the presence of several thousand mainly former Somoza supporters, exiled in Honduran border camps, were exacerbated in early 1995 by the eruption of a "shrimp war" in the Gulf of Fonseca. Tensions were reignited in May and August 1997 following the Nicaraguan navy's seizure of numerous Honduran fishing boats that had reportedly strayed into Nicaraguan waters.

In August 1998 Nicaragua rescinded an agreement that had been concluded only a month earlier with Costa Rica for free navigation, including police patrols, along the San Juan River because of opposition claimed that it had ceded sovereignty to its neighbor. (The dispute was eventually abated by a new agreement in mid-2000 that restored Costa Rica's right to the patrols as long as Nicaragua received prior notification of their movements.)

A crisis with Honduras erupted in November 1999, following ratification by the Honduran legislature of a 1986 maritime border treaty with Colombia that involved 50,000 square miles of coastal waters, portions of which were alleged to have been forcibly ceded to Colombia during the U.S. occupation of Nicaragua in the 1920s. In reprisal, Nicaragua imposed a 35 percent duty on all goods imported from Honduras. In January 2000 the parties agreed to submit the dispute to a ruling by the ICJ; however, less than a month later peace in the Gulf of Fonseca was again threatened by an exchange between Nicaraguan and Honduran patrol boats, each side claiming that it had been attacked by the other. In February 2001 Nicaragua accused Honduras of not living up to an agreement on demilitarizing their land border. A March meeting in Washington, D.C., eased tensions, and in June the two countries accepted an OAS-brokered pact that allowed OAS observers to monitor activities along both land and marine borders. However, friction continued into 2002, with periodic seizures of Honduran boats in alleged Nicaraguan waters and Nicaragua authorizing oil prospecting in the region. In March 2003 the Nicaraguan assembly suspended the 35-percent tariff.

Relations with the United States warmed in 2004 when President Bolaños announced that all surface-to-air missiles remaining in Nicaragua from its conflict with U.S.-backed rebels would be destroyed. He destroyed about 1,000 of the missiles. (In 2008 President Ortega refused to destroy all of the missiles, despite ongoing pressure from the United States.)

In 2005 Nicaragua, Costa Rica, El Salvador, Guatemala, Honduras, and the Dominican Republic signed a wide-ranging free trade agreement known as CAFTA-DR with the United States.

In 2006 Ortega signed a treaty incorporating Nicaragua into the Bolivarian Alternative for the Americas (ALBA), Venezuelan President Hugo Chávez's alternative to U.S.-led free trade agreements. Nicaragua and Venezuela signed a number of other accords, including one that canceled Nicaragua's $38 million debt with Venezuela, and one that allowed Venezuela to build a $2.5 billion oil refinery in Nicaragua. Ortega also reestablished relations with Cuba and Iran.

Nicaragua and Costa Rica in recent years have disputed a 170-square-mile strip of poorly demarcated swampland on the southern shore of Lake Nicaragua. The 5,000 impoverished residents of the area have rejected the claims of both governments, seeking instead an independent "Republic of Airrecú." Tensions with Costa Rica heightened in June 2008, when Costa Rica rejected a request from Nicaragua that it halt development of an open-pit gold mine several miles from the San Juan River.

Relations with the United States cooled through mid-2008, as President Ortega criticized a loan from the U.S. Agency for International Development (USAID) to 16 nongovernmental organizations to promote citizen participation in the November municipal elections.

In the midst of a regional dispute in March 2008 prompted by a Colombian raid inside Ecuador against guerilla fighters, Nicaragua briefly suspended diplomatic relations with Colombia.

In 2009 President Ortega sided with Venezuelan president Hugo Chávez in refusing to attend a meeting of regional leaders with U.S. vice president Joseph Biden prior to the Summit of the Americas. Ortega created further tension in the region by threatening to withdraw from economic talks between Central America and the European Union.

In mid-2009 Nicaragua, like most of its neighbors, supported ousted Honduran president Manuel Zelaya and his efforts to negotiate his return to power from Nicaragua. Nicaragua further refuses to allow the use of its airspace by de facto Honduran leader Roberto Micheletti. The presence of Zelaya in Nicaragua spurred tensions between the FSLN and its opponents, and threatened long-standing bilateral agreements between Nicaragua and Honduras.

Relations with the United States and the European Union deteriorated in mid-2009 amid accusations of fraud regarding municipal elections, resulting in both major donors indefinitely suspending millions of dollars in aid to Nicaragua.

Current issues. Political infighting and tensions dominated the government in 2007, when the PLC and the ALN formed an electoral alliance in July, in direct opposition to a similar effort between the FSLN and the PLC. Subsequently, however, the PLC-ALN alliance fell apart ahead of the 2008 municipal elections because the PLC refused to break with the FSLN. This resulted in a rift in the ALN, with the party dismissing Eduardo Montealegre, its unsuccessful 2006 presidential candidate. Montealegre quickly regrouped, forming his own party, Let's Go with Eduardo (*Vamos con Eduardo*—VCE), which aligned with the PLC, the small Independent Liberal Party (*Partido Liberal Independiente*—PLI), and the Central American Unity Party (*Partido Unidad de Central America*—PUCA). Subsequently, Montealegre was named the candidate of his former party, the PLC, to run for mayor of Managua in the November 2008 municipal elections. However, Montealegre faced legal battles stemming from criminal charges related to the collapse of four banks when Montealegre was finance minister years earlier. (Montealegre filed a claim of parliamentary immunity from prosecution.) Following his unsuccessful bid, Montealegre alleged fraud and vote-rigging in the election, for which the government had refused to invite monitors. Several days of violent anti-sandinista protests followed. A recount, which was not monitored by outside observers, also drew heavy criticism, including from the United States. The results gave a narrow victory (51.3 percent) to world boxing champion and FSLN candidate Alex ARGÜELLO. (Argüello reportedly committed suicide in 2009, though some questioned the circumstances of his death, since Argüello was said to be ready to leave the FSLN.)

Meanwhile, the principal opposition parties in the National Assembly staged several walkouts in 2008 to protest Ortega's governing style. Opponents called their coalition the "Block against the Dictatorship" and criticized Ortega's increasingly hostile reaction toward the United States and excessively close ties to Venezuela and Iran.

Domestic attention has been dominated in recent years by such issues as an ongoing energy shortage, a high inflation rate, and the rising cost of living, particularly the price of food. The Civil Society Coordinating Committee, composed of numerous nongovernmental organizations, demonstrated against Ortega on July 17, 2008, the first major protest since he took office. The FSLN responded two days later, on the 29th anniversary of the sandinista revolution, with a progovernment demonstration by tens of thousands of people, including Venezuelan president Chávez and Paraguay's president-elect, Fernando Lugo.

High food prices continued to be a major challenge for the government in 2009, as poverty has affected thousands more Nicaraguans. The government sought international donor aid and initiated a "Zero Hunger Program" in March in efforts to mitigate effects from the global financial crisis. Meanwhile, President Ortega proposed constitutional reforms that included, among other things, the elimination of presidential term limits and the possibility of a recall referendum on elected officials.

POLITICAL PARTIES AND GROUPS

Historically, the Liberal and Conservative parties dominated Nicaraguan politics in what was essentially a two-party system. During most of the Somoza era (1936–1974), the heir to the liberal tradition, the Nationalist Liberal Party (*Partido Liberal Nacionalista de Nicaragua*—PLN), enjoyed a monopoly of power, while in mid-1978 the Nicaraguan Conservative Party (*Partido Conservador Nicaragüense*—PCN) joined other opposition groups in a Broad Opposition Front (*Frente Amplio de Oposición*—FAO) that called for the president's resignation and the creation of a government of national unity. In addition to the PCN, the FAO included the Independent Liberal and Nicaraguan Social Christian parties (see below); the Democratic Liberation Union (*Unión Democrática de Liberación*—Udel), organized in 1977 by former PCN leader and newspaper editor Pedro Joaquín Chamorro Cardenal, who was assassinated in January 1978; and the Group of 12 (*Movimiento de los Doce*), a pro-sandinista organization of businesspeople, academics, and priests that withdrew from the FAO in October 1978 because of a proposal to include members of the PLN in a future coalition government.

Following the sandinista victory, the principal internal groupings were the FSLN-led Patriotic Front for the Revolution (*Frente Patriótico para la Revolución*—FPR) and the opposition Nicaraguan Democratic Coordination (*Coordinadora Democrática Nicaragüense*—CDN). However, by 1984 the Patriotic Front had effectively dissolved, most of its non-FSLN components having chosen to contest the November balloting as separate entities, while the *Coordinadora,* technically reduced to the status of a "citizens' association" because of its electoral boycott, was declared to have become "inoperative" in 1985 after several of its leaders had entered into agreements with contra units that included appeals for a "national dialogue."

The 14-member National Opposition Union (*Unión Nacional Opositora*—UNO) was formally registered as a political coalition in September 1989 with Violeta Barrios de Chamorro, who declined to affiliate with any specific party, as its presidential candidate for the February 1990 election. Thereafter, coalition members tended to divide on many issues between a dominant faction loyal to the president, who sought to cultivate linkages with the FSLN, and a conservative group (PLI, see below) led by Vice President Godoy Reyes; by early 1992 most UNO legislators had shifted their allegiance to Godoy, although the government retained a legislative majority in the form of a de facto alignment between sandinista and UNO "centrist" deputies. In early 1993 the latter, after formally organizing as the Center Group (*Grupo de Centro*—GC), were expelled from the UNO, which proceeded to change its name to the Opposition Political Alliance (*Alianza Politica Opositora*—APO). In the wake of further cleavages the APO was reduced to only four members by mid-1994, while the FSLN was subjected to an internal rift that was far from resolved by the victory of Daniel Ortega's "orthodox" faction at the party's May 1994 congress.

The major contenders in the 1996 election were the FSLN and a coalition styled the Liberal Alliance (*Alianza Liberal*—AL). In 2001, the principal contestants were the FSLN and the PLC, while those in 2006 were the FSLN, the PLC, and the ALN.

Government Party:

Sandinist National Liberation Front (*Frente Sandinista de Liberación Nacional*—FSLN). The FSLN was established in 1961 as a Castroite guerrilla group named after Augusto César Sandino, a prominent rebel during the U.S. occupation of the 1920s. The FSLN displayed a remarkable capacity for survival, despite numerous eradication campaigns during the later years of the Somoza regime, in the course of which much of its original leadership was killed. In 1975 it split into three "tendencies": two small Marxist groupings, the Protracted People's War (*Guerra Popular Prolongada*—GPP) and the Proletarian Tendency (*Tendencia Proletaria*), and a larger, less extreme Third Party (*Terceristas*), a nonideological, anti-Somoza formation supported by peasants, students, and upper-class intellectuals. The three groups coordinated their activities during the 1978 offensive and were equally represented in the nine-member Joint National Directorate. Although the July 1979 junta was largely *tercerista* dominated, the subsequent withdrawal of a number of moderates yielded a more distinctly leftist thrust to the party leadership, hard-liner Bayardo ARCE reportedly characterizing the November 1984 balloting as "a bother." In an August 1985 reorganization of the Directorate, its Political Commission was replaced by a five-member Executive Commission, chaired by Daniel Ortega, with Arce as his deputy.

Following the unexpected sandinista defeat in February 1990, Ortega pledged to "obey the popular mandate" and participated in the inauguration of Violeta Barrios de Chamorro on April 25. In conformity with a post-electoral agreement precluding the holding of party office by military personnel, his brother Gen. Humberto Ortega withdrew as a member of the FSLN Executive after being redesignated armed forces commander by the new president.

The 581 delegates to the first FSLN congress on July 19–21, 1991, reaffirmed the Front's commitment to socialism, while confessing to a variety of mistakes during its period of rule. Former president Ortega was elected to the new post of general secretary, while seven former *comandantes* of the previous leadership were elected to a new nine-member National Directorate that also included former Nicaraguan vice president Sergio Ramírez Mercado.

A pronounced intraparty split emerged before an extraordinary FSLN congress on May 20–22, 1994, the reflection primarily of an "orthodox" faction headed by Ortega and a moderate "renewalist" faction headed by Ramírez, with party treasurer Henry RUIZ Hernández leading an avowedly "centrist" unity grouping. The Ortega faction emerged victorious at the congress, gaining eight seats on an expanded Directorate, against four for the renewalists and three for the centrists. However, public opinion polls had shown Ramírez to be much stronger than Ortega as a potential presidential candidate.

Ramírez served in the National Assembly as Ortega's alternate; thus, in September 1994, the former president was able to oust him as legislative bloc leader by reclaiming the seat. However the FSLN delegation proceeded to elect a moderate, Dora María Téllez, as its new leader rather than Ortega, thus formalizing a cleavage between the Front's legislative members and its National Directorate. In early 1995 Ramírez, Téllez, and approximately three-quarters of the sandinista legislative delegation withdrew from the FSLN to form the MRS (below).

In November 1995 Ortega surprised observers by announcing that he would seek his party's nomination for reelection to the post that he had lost to Chamorro five-and-a-half years earlier. In the October 1996 balloting he lost to the AL's Alemán Lacayo by more than 13 percent of the popular vote.

Ortega was reelected FSLN general secretary at a party congress in May 1998, and on January 21, 2001, defeated two other candidates, Alejandro MARTINEZ Cuenca and Víctor HUGO Tinoco, for the party's 2001 presidential endorsement.

Defeated in his third presidential bid on November 4, 2001, Ortega nonetheless retained leadership of the FSLN at its third congress in March 2002, during which the group's 205-member assembly was supplanted by a 40-member Board of Directors headed by an 8-member Executive Commission. The move was seen as concentrating power among Ortega supporters, thus limiting intraparty dissent.

In late 2004 the FSLN concluded a power-sharing pact with the PLC (see Political background, above). However, the prospect of an FSLN victory in the 2006 balloting was seemingly diminished by the expulsion from the party in February 2005 of Ortega's leading rival, former Managua mayor Herty Lewites, who had been leading Ortega in the opinion polls (see MRS, below).

His critics notwithstanding, Ortega was returned to the presidency after a 16-year hiatus on November 6, 2006. Ortega's close win and the FSLN's plurality in the National Assembly have forced the FSLN to continue its agreement, commonly referred to as "the pact," with the PLC. In the 2008 municipal elections the party was accused of widespread fraud which resulted in successful bids for more than 40 mayoral seats.

Leaders: Daniel ORTEGA Saavedra (President of the Republic and General Secretary of the Party), Jacinto SUÁREZ (Deputy General Secretary).

Other Legislative Parties:

Constitutionalist Liberal Party (*Partido Liberal Constitucionalista*—PLC). The PLC originated in 1968 as a spin-off of the Somoza-era PLN. It was subsequently affiliated with the UNO and in 1996 constituted the core of the AL.

Although retaining the presidency and securing a majority of legislative seats in 2001, the party became deeply divided between supporters of President Bolaños and former president Alemán, as a result of which Bolaños launched a separate grouping, the Grand Liberal Union (GUL) in early 2004.

Following his imprisonment in late 2003, Alemán delegated the party presidency to his wife, María Fernánda Flores. Reacting to the move, three members of the party directorate, including National Secretary René HERRERA, resigned in protest.

In January 2005 Eduardo Montealegre Rivas (see ALN, below) was expelled from the party for refusing to resign his cabinet post as secretary to the presidency after President Bolaños had endorsed corruption proceedings against his predecessor.

The PLC's José RIZO placed third in the 2006 presidential balloting with 27.1 percent of the vote. In concurrent legislative elections, the PLC won 25 seats, the second-largest number behind the FSLN.

The party supported the FSLN on key issues in 2008 but formed an alliance with several small parties to field candidates in the 2008 municipal elections. The PLC endorsed Montealegre's candidacy for the mayorship of Managua after he lost a leadership battle in the ALN.

In January 2009 the Supreme Court overturned former president Alemán's conviction on charges of fraud, money laundering and corruption. Alemán had been sentenced to 20 years in prison in December 2003 for stealing more than $35 million of state money for personal use.

Leaders: Dr. Arnoldo ALEMÁN Lacayo (Honorary Chair of the Party and Former President of the Republic), José RIZO Castellón (2006 presidential candidate), Wilfredo Navarro (Vice Chair), Maximino RODRÍGUEZ, Leonel TELLER (Spokesperson).

Nicaraguan Liberal Alliance (*Alianza Liberal Nicaragünse*—ALN). The ALN was formed under the leadership of Eduard Montealegre Rivas after his departure from the PLC in 2005. Montealegre placed second in the 2006 presidential poll, with 29 percent of the vote, and the party secured 24 legislative seats, including one for Montealegre, and one for outgoing president Bolaños.

In the 2006 presidential election, the ALN backed runner-up Eduardo Montealegre, who was subsequently ousted from the party following a dispute with Jamileth Bonilla, a legislator and former PLC member.

Tensions heightened between the FSLN and the ALN in June 2009 when ALN president Eliseo NÚÑEZ refused to meet with FSLN legislators to discuss cooperation on a legislative agenda. The party subsequently dismissed Núñez and named Alejandro Mejía Ferreti as chair. The move prompted observers to speculate about the possibility of an alliance between the new party president and the FSLN to facilitate major constitutional reforms.

Leaders: Alejandro Mejía FERRETI (Chair), Carlos GARCÍA (National Secretary).

Sandinista Renewal Movement (*Movimiento de Renovación Sandinista*—MRS). The MRS was launched in January 1995 by former sandinista legislative leader Sergio RAMIREZ Mercado and the renewalist majority of the FSLN National Assembly delegation. Members of the MRS strongly opposed Chamorro's efforts to secure an enhanced role for the presidency in the 1995 constitutional reforms. Ramírez Mercado, the party's 1996 presidential candidate, subsequently withdrew from an active role in partisan politics and was highly critical of a 2001 electoral alliance with the FSLN. In early 2006 the MRS announced FSLN dissident Herty LEWITES as its candidate for the upcoming presidential election. However, Lewites, considered one of the top three presidential contenders, died in early July. The MRS was barred from running in the 2008 elections after the Supreme Electoral Council revoked its registration in June 2008 on a technicality.

Leaders: Enrique SAENZ (President), Edmundo JARQUÍN Calderón (General Coordinator and 2006 presidential candidate), Rep. Víctor Hugo TINOCO (Vice President), Rommel MARTÍNEZ (Vice President), Monica BALTODANO.

Other Party That Participated in the 2006 Elections:

Alternative for Change (*Alternativa por el Cambio*—AC). Founded by Olando TARDENCILLA, a Christian party dissident, the party fielded Edén PASTORA Gómez as its 2006 presidential candidate. Pastora won just 0.27 percent of the vote, and the party subsequently lost its legal status.

Other Parties:

Conservative Party of Nicaragua (*Partido Conservador de Nicaragua*—PCN). Formed in emulation of Nicaragua's historic Conservative Party, the current PCN resulted from a 1992 merger of the Democratic Conservative Party (*Partido Conservador Demócrata*—PCD) with two smaller formations, the Conservative Social Party (*Partido Social Conservador*—PSC) and the Conservative Party of Labor (*Partido Conservador Laborista*—PCL).

Launched in 1979 by supporters of the traditional PCN, the PCD had long been deeply divided, with one of its leaders, Rafael Cordova Rives, joining the junta in May 1980 while most others were in exile. The party was a surprising first runner-up in the 1984 balloting, winning 14 legislative seats and a 14 percent vote share for its presidential candidate; rent by further defection, including formation of the PANC, the party secured no representation in 1990 but won three seats on a fifth-place finish in 1996.

The Conservatives, who have undergone several changes in their top leadership, including the February 2001 resignation of Pedro SOLORZANO Castillo as president, saw their poll numbers diminish in the run-up to the November 2001 elections when their presidential nominee, Noel VIDAURRE Argüello, and his running mate, Carlos TUNNERMAN Bernheim, withdrew on July 18 because of policy differences with other party leaders. Earlier in the year, the PCN's initial choice for the vice presidency, former defense minister José Antonio ALVARADO, had withdrawn because of continuing controversy over his citizenship. On July 31 the party announced a new ticket headed by Alberto Saborío Morales, whose standing in the polls fell below 5 percent in September. He won only 1.4 percent of the vote on November 4, while the party's legislative representation dropped from three to two.

For the 2006 campaign, the PCN joined in supporting the presidential candidacy of PLC dissident Eduardo Montealegre Rivas under a grouping styled the Liberal Nicaraguan–Conservative Party Alliance (*Alianza Liberal Nicaragüense–Partido Conservador*—ALN-PC). The PCN lost is registration as a valid party in June 2008 for failing to meet the threshold for candidates in municipal elections.

Leader: Alzalea AVILES.

Independent Liberal Party (*Partido Liberal Independiente*—PLI). Organized in 1944 by a non-*somocista* group calling for a return to the traditional principles of the PLN, the PLI participated in the Broad Opposition Front before the 1979 coup. Subsequently led by post-coup labor minister Virgilio Godoy Reyes, it was a member of the

Patriotic Front, but following *Coordinadora*'s withdrawal became the most vocal opposition formation of the 1984 campaign. The party was a founding member of the UNO in 1989, Godoy Reyes becoming its most conspicuous leader. Having endorsed Godoy Reyes as its 1996 presidential candidate, the PLI was the only Liberal group not to have joined the ALN before the October poll. The PLI entered into an alliance with the PLC and Let's Go with Eduardo, the movement formed by Eduardo Montealegre, to field Managua for a mayoral post in November 2008.

Leaders: Julia MENA (President of the Party and Former Vice President of the Republic), Virgilio GODOY Reyes (Former Vice President of the Republic and General Secretary).

Christian Democratic Union (*Unión Demócrata Cristiana*—UDC). The UDC was formed in early 1993 by merger of two former UNO members, the Social Christian Popular Party (*Partido Popular Social-Cristiano*—PPSC) and the Democratic Party of National Confidence (*Partido Demócrata de Confianza Nacional*—PDCN), both of which had been formed (in 1976 and 1988, respectively) by dissidents from the PSCN. The UDC joined with the FSLN in a new coalition, United Nicaragua Triumphs (*Unidad Nicaragua Triunfa*—UNT), to contest the 2008 municipal elections.

Leader: Augustín JARQUIN Anaya.

Nicaraguan Socialist Party (*Partido Socialista Nicaragüense*—PSN). The PSN was organized in 1937 as a Moscow-oriented Communist party that subsequently shifted to a social-democratic posture. The PSN joined with the MRS to run candidates in the 2008 municipal elections. It was deregistered as a party and asked to submit a new application for registration in June 2008 as a result of forming a coalition with the MRS.

Leaders: Domingo SÁNCHEZ Salgado, Luis SÁNCHEZ Sancho, Dr. Gustavo TABLADA Zelaya (General Secretary).

There are a number of small indigenously-based political parties in the Atlantic Coast region, including: **Misatán**, a pro-sandinista Indian movement led by Rufino Lucas WILFRED; the northern-based **Yátama**, a member of the FSLN's electoral coalition for the 2008 municipal elections, and a former contra group led by Brooklyn RIVERA Bryan, who was named by President Chamorro as cabinet-level head of a new Institute for the Development of the Autonomous Regions of the Caribbean Coast; the right-wing **Coastal Democratic Alliance,** led by RAAS coordinator Alvin GUTHRIE; the **Multiethnic Indigenous Party** (*Partido Indigenista Multiétnico*—PIM), led by Carla WHITE Hodgson; the **Central American Unity Party** (*Partido Unidad de Central America*—PUCA); the **Multiethnic Party for Caribbean Coastal Unity** (PAMUC); the **Union of Nicaraguan Coastal Indians** (KISAN), led by Roger GERMAN; the **Coastal Authentic Autonomy Movement;** and the Corn Island–based **Island Youth Movement**. The PAMUC and the PIM were disqualified by the Supreme Electoral Council in June 2008 for failing to field candidates in at least 80 percent of electoral districts

For a list of groups active prior to the 2006 elections, see the 2006 *Handbook*.

LEGISLATURE

The previously bicameral Congress (*Congreso*) was dissolved following installation of the provisional junta in July 1979. A 47-member Council of State (*Consejo de Estado*), representing various sandinista, labor, and other organizations, was sworn in May 4, 1980, to serve in a quasi-legislative capacity.

Under the constitution promulgated in 1987 and amended in 1994, a National Assembly was established, with 90 members popularly elected for five-year terms on a proportional representation basis from party lists, 20 from a nationwide constituency and 70 from multi-member constituencies. Two additional seats are reserved for the outgoing president of the republic and the second-place finisher in the most recent election.

In the most recent election on November 6, 2006, the seat distribution was as follows: the Sandinista National Liberation Front, 38; Constitutionalist Liberal Party, 25; Nicaraguan Liberal Alliance (ALN), 22; and Sandinista Renewal Movement, 5.. (One seat each was reserved for outgoing president Enrique Bolaños and 2006 runner-up presidential candidate Eduardo Montealegre, both of the ALN.)

President: René NÚÑEZ Téllez.

CABINET

[as of November 1, 2009]

President	Daniel Ortega Saavedra
Vice President	Jaime Morales Carazo
Ministers	
Agriculture and Forestry	Ariel Bucardo Rocha
Communication	Rosario Murillo Zambrana [f]
Development, Industry, and Commerce	Orlando Solórzano Delgadillo
Education, Culture, and Sports	Miguel de Castilla Urbina
Energy and Hydrocarbon	Emilio Rappaccioli
Environment and Natural Resources	Juana Argeñal Sandoval [f]
Family, Youth, and Children	Meyling Calero [f]
Finance and Public Credit	Alberto José Guevara Obregón
Foreign Affairs	Samuel Santos López
Government	Ana Isabel Morales Mazon [f]
Health	Guillermo González
Labor	Jeannette Chávez Gómez [f]
Secretary General of Defense	Ruth EsperanzaTapia Roa [f]
Transportation and Infrastructure	Pablo Fernández Martínez Espinosa

[f] = female

COMMUNICATIONS

The Somoza regime severely constricted the media, particularly *La Prensa,* whose former principal editor, Pedro Joaquín CHAMORRO Cardenal, had received international recognition for his opposition to government policies before his assassination on January 10, 1978. Not surprisingly, *La Prensa* was the first Somoza-era daily to reemerge under the junta, while the extreme leftist *El Pueblo* was suspended by the new government in late July after accusing the sandinistas of "selling out the revolution" to "bourgeois groups," and in January 1980 was closed down permanently. Despite its anti-Somoza record, *La Prensa* was banned from June 1986 to October 1987, when it resumed publication after receiving government assurances that it would not have to submit to prior censorship.

Press. Acceding to opposition demands, a press law stipulating that all printed matter must reflect "legitimate concern for the defense of the conquests of the revolution" was rescinded before President Ortega's departure from office. The following are published daily in Managua: *El Nuevo Diario* (40,000), founded 1980 by a pro-sandinista group of former *La Prensa* employees; *La Prensa* (35,000), pro-Liberal; *Avance* (10,000), leftist organ. In March 2000 *Barricada,* a former FSLN organ that declared bankruptcy and ceased publication in 1998, was revived as a weekly with a circulation of 20,000.

News agencies. An official *Agencia Nicaragüense de Noticias* (ANN) was launched in September 1979; in addition, a number of foreign bureaus maintain offices in Managua.

Broadcasting and computing. There are more than 50 radio stations, including the government-controlled *Radio Nicaragua* and the church-controlled *Radio Católica*, which was shut down twice between 1986 and 1988. *Sistema Nacional de Television,* one of seven TV groups, operates three regional channels. As of 2008 there were 32.6 Internet users per 1,000 inhabitants.

INTERGOVERNMENTAL REPRESENTATION

Ambassador to the U.S.: (Vacant).

U.S. Ambassador to Nicaragua: Robert J. CALLAHAN.

Permanent Representative to the UN: María RUBIALES DE CHAMORRO.

IGO Memberships (Non-UN): ACS, BCIE, IADB, Interpol, IOM, NAM, OAS, OPANAL, PCA, SELA, SICA, WCO, WTO.

NIGER

Republic of Niger
République du Niger

Note: A new constitution was promulgated on August 18, 2009, following a referendum on August 4 that was approved by 92.5 percent of voters. The opposition boycotted the disputed referendum. Under the new constitution, the president was granted an extension beyond his second five-year term (ending in December 2009) and the right to seek unlimited reelection. In National Assembly elections on October 20, the governing National Movement for a Developing Society–Victory won 76 of 113 seats. For the first time independents were elected to parliament, securing a total of 11 seats. One seat was subsequently annulled.

Political Status: Former French dependency; independence declared August 3, 1960; military regime established April 15, 1974; constitution of September 1989, providing for single-party military/civilian government, suspended on August 4, 1991, by a National Consultative Conference that had declared itself a sovereign body on July 30; multiparty constitution of December 27, 1992, suspended by military coup on January 27, 1996; new constitution adopted on May 22, 1996, following approval by national referendum on May 12; constitution suspended by the military-based National Reconciliation Council on April 11, 1999; new multiparty constitution providing for return of civilian government approved by national referendum on July 18, 1999, and promulgated on August 9. (*See headnote.*)

Area: 489,189 sq. mi. (1,267,000 sq. km.).

Population: 11,060,291 (2001C); 13,921,000 (2008E).

Major Urban Center (2005E): NIAMEY (including suburbs, 991,000).

Official Language: French.

Monetary Unit: CFA Franc (official rate December 1, 2009: 434.59 CFA francs = $1US). The CFA franc, formerly pegged to the French franc, is now permanently pegged to the euro at 655.975 CFA francs = 1 euro.

President: (*See headnote.*) Mamadou TANDJA (National Movement for a Developing Society—Victory); elected in second-round balloting on November 24, 1999, and sworn in for a five-year term on December 22; reelected in second-round balloting on December 4, 2004, and sworn in for a second five-year term on December 21.

Prime Minister: Seini OUMAROU (National Movement for a Developing Society—Victory); appointed by the president on June 3, 2007, and sworn in on June 7 to succeed Hama AMADOU (National Movement for a Developing Society—Victory), who had resigned on June 1; formed new government on June 9.

THE COUNTRY

A vast landlocked country on the southern border of the Sahara, Niger is largely desert in the north and arable savanna in the more populous southland, which extends from the Niger River to Lake Chad. The population includes numerous tribes of two main ethnic groups: Sudanese Negroes and Hamites. About 75 percent of the population is classified as Sudanese Negro, with Hausa being the predominant subgroup (56 percent); Hamites, found in the north, include the nomadic Tuareg, Toubou, and Peulh subgroups. The population is largely (85 percent) Muslim, with smaller groups of animists and Christians. While French is the official language, Hausa is the language of trade and commerce and is constitutionally classified, along with Arabic and five other tribal languages, as a "national" language. Women constitute a minority of the labor force, excluding unpaid family workers.

Agriculture and stock raising occupy 90 percent of the work force, the chief products being millet and sorghum for domestic consumption and peanuts, vegetables, and live cattle for export. The country's major exports are cotton and uranium, of which Niger is one of the world's top five producers. Coal, phosphates, iron ore, gold, and petroleum have also been discovered, but their exploitation awaits development of a more adequate transportation and communication infrastructure. Niger's economy declined in the 1980s, with agriculture suffering from both floods and drought. Also, a decrease during the decade in uranium demand contributed to a severe trade imbalance and mounting foreign debt. The introduction of austerity measures, while generating substantial social unrest, yielded assistance from the International Monetary Fund (IMF) and debt rescheduling from the Paris Club. In June 1996 the IMF approved a new three-year loan to facilitate further structural adjustments.

The government's economic policies in 1996–1998, which focused on privatization of state-run enterprises, were described as "broadly satisfactory," with GDP growth rising from 2.8 percent in 1997 to 10.4 percent in 1998. However, political turmoil and an eight-month imposition of military rule following the assassination of President Maïnassara halted economic progress, as some external financing was frozen and domestic arrears (including the payment of civil service salaries) accumulated. GDP consequently contracted by 0.6 percent in 1999, although a degree of fiscal stability returned after a democratically elected civilian government was installed late in the year. GDP grew by an average of about 1.5 percent per year between 2001 and 2003 in view of returned support from the IMF and World Bank, which have endorsed the new government's commitment to structural reform and financial transparency. Drought and widespread devastation by locusts in 2004 weakened the economy and resulted in a lack of trade and subsequent GDP growth of less than 1 percent. Because of progress the country made in economic reforms, however, the IMF provided substantial debt relief at the end of 2005, noting that Niger remains one of the poorest countries in the world. Though annual GDP growth contracted from 6.8 percent to 3.2 percent in 2007, the IMF noted strong performance in the mining sector and stable growth in the agriculture sector. The United States approved $1.4 million in poverty reduction assistance in 2007, and additional international debt relief was reported by the IMF to be "yielding results," particularly in health and education services and in the rural sector. Annual GDP growth averaged 3.5 percent in 2008-2009, owing in large part to greater mining production and an increase in investments in mining, oil, and infrastructure, as well as a strong yield in the agriculture sector. Inflation in 2009 was forecast to fall to 3.2 percent (from 11.3 percent in 2008), as a result of a decrease in food and energy prices due to the global economic downturn. Meanwhile, the IMF in 2009 approved further poverty-reduction funds for Niger, totaling $15 million.

GOVERNMENT AND POLITICS

Political background. An object of centuries-old contention among different African peoples, Niger was first exposed to French contact in the late 19th century. Military conquest of the area began prior to 1900 but, because of stiff resistance, was not completed until 1922, when Niger became a French colony. Political evolution began under a constitution granted by France in 1946, with Niger becoming a self-governing republic within the French Community in 1958 and attaining full independence in August 1960. Although its membership in the community subsequently lapsed, Niger has retained close economic and political ties with its former colonial ruler.

The banning of the Marxist-oriented *Sawaba* (Freedom) Party in 1959 converted Niger into a one-party state under the Niger Progressive Party (*Parti Progressiste Nigérien*—PPN), headed by President Hamani DIORI, a member of the Djerma tribe. Thereafter, Djibo BAKARY led *Sawaba* elements to continue their opposition activity from abroad, with terrorist incursions in 1964 and 1965 that included an attempt on the president's life. The Diori government, carefully balanced to represent ethnic and regional groupings, was reelected in 1965 and 1970 by overwhelming majorities but proved incapable of coping with the effects of the prolonged Sahelian drought of 1968–1974. As a result, Diori was overthrown on April 15, 1974, by a military coup led by Gen. Seyni KOUNTCHÉ and Maj. Sani Souna SIDO, who then established themselves as president and vice president, respectively, of a Supreme Military Council (*Conseil Militaire Suprême*—CMS). On August 2, 1975, Kountché announced that Sido and a number of others, including Bakary, had been arrested for attempting to organize a second coup.

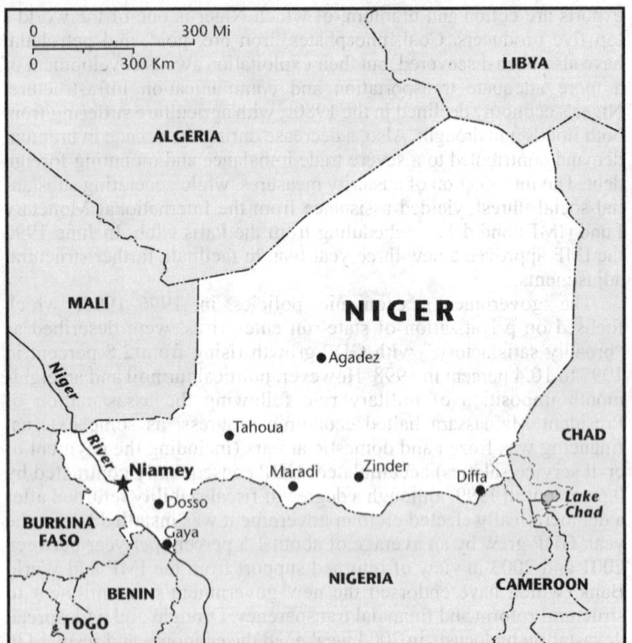

A National Development Council (*Conseil National pour le Développement*—CND), initially established in July 1974 with an appointive membership, was assigned quasi-leadership status in August 1983, following indirect election of 150 delegates. Earlier, on January 24, Oumarou MAMANE had been appointed to the newly created post of prime minister; on August 3 he was named president of the reconstituted CND. Hamid ALGABID replaced him as prime minister on November 14.

President Kountché died in a Paris hospital on November 10, 1987, after a lengthy illness. He was immediately succeeded by the army chief of staff, Col. Ali SAIBOU. After being formally invested by the CMS on November 14, the new president named Algabid to head an otherwise substantially new government.

On August 2, 1988, following a July 15 cabinet reorganization that included the return of Mamane as prime minister, Saibou announced the formation of a National Movement for a Developing Society (*Mouvement National pour une Société de Développement*—MNSD) as the "final step in normalization of Niger's politics." The CND, whose constituent functions had been reaffirmed by Saibou in December 1987, was given the task of further defining the role of the MNSD.

Adding to the complexity of the restructuring process was General Saibou's declaration on January 1, 1989, that the initial congress of the MNSD would elect the membership of a Supreme Council of National Orientation (*Conseil Suprême de la Orientation Nationale*—CSON) to replace the CMS, while the CND would become an advisory Economic and Social Council (*Conseil Economique et Social*—CES). On May 17 Saibou was elected president of the CSON, thereby becoming, under a new constitution approved in September, the sole candidate for election as head of state on December 10. Saibou was credited with more than 99 percent of the votes, as was the single list of 93 MNSD candidates concurrently elected to the new National Assembly.

The post of prime minister was eliminated upon the formation of a new government on December 20, 1989. However, it was reestablished in a March 2, 1990, reshuffle precipitated by student-government confrontations in Niamey; Aliou MAHAMIDOU, a government industrial executive, was named to the position. Three months later, the CSON committed itself to "political pluralism," and in mid-November, after encountering further dissatisfaction with his policies, Saibou announced that a National Consultative Conference would convene to consider constitutional reform.

The conference opened on July 29, 1991, with delegates from 24 political groups and 69 mass organizations in attendance. After declaring its sovereignty and electing André SALIFOU as chair, the conference suspended the constitution on August 9 and transferred all but ceremonial presidential powers from Saibou to Salifou. It was decided at the time that Prime Minister Mahamidou would remain in office. However, on November 1, in the wake of an inquiry into the May 1990 massacre of Tuareg nomads by government troops, Amadou CHEIFFOU was named to succeed Mahamidou for a 15-month transition to multiparty balloting scheduled for January 31, 1993. On November 2 the conference appointed a 15-member High Council of the Republic (*Haut Conseil de la République*—HCR), chaired by Salifou, to serve as a constituent assembly and provisional legislature for the duration of the transitional period. The following day the conference voted to disband the HCR in favor of another form of transitional government.

Cheiffou announced the creation of a transitional government on November 4, 1991, which was then dissolved on March 23, 1992, in the wake of a failed military coup on February 28; a new cabinet was named on March 27. In early July Cheiffou survived a nonconfidence motion triggered by a mid-June decision to recognize Taiwan in exchange for an economic aid package, an arrangement that the HCR branded as contravening National Conference resolutions. The split between Cheiffou and the HCR proved short-lived, as the two agreed at an August 7 meeting to reconcile their differences. Meanwhile, preparations for a constitutional referendum and multiparty election proceeded haltingly. The new constitution was finally approved on December 26 by 89 percent of referendum voters, despite observations that the polling was marred by irregularities.

In late December 1992 the government admitted it had lost control over troops assigned to the northeastern Tuareg region where the insurgent Front for the Liberation of Air and Azaouad (FLAA) had resumed activity, further complicating the transitional process. Seven months earlier, the government had responded to the FLAA capture of some 28 military personnel and two officials of the recently restyled MNSD-*Nassara* by giving the army control of security in the region, a decision criticized by local Tuareg officials as equivalent to imposing a state of emergency. Frustrated by the rebels' unwillingness to release their prisoners, the army, apparently without government approval, arrested 186 alleged FLAA rebels and supporters, including a number of prominent Tuareg members of the transitional administration. Tuareg officials denounced a subsequent soldiers-for-civilians exchange offer and appealed to the UN for assistance. A Niamey offer to create a "forum for national reconciliation" in November was rebuffed by the Tuaregs, who questioned the government's ability to provide for their safety.

Following a National Assembly election on February 14, 1993, the MNSD-*Nassara,* with a plurality of 29 seats, appeared likely to form a coalition with one or more of its competitors, as a means of retaining control of the government. However, two days later, nine opposition parties, decrying the possibility of MNSD-*Nassara* controlling 50 assembly seats and continuing its rule, formed a majoritarian Alliance of Forces of Change (AFC). In the first round of presidential balloting on February 27 MNSD-*Nassara* candidate Mamadou TANDJA led the eight-candidate field with 34.22 percent of the vote, followed by Mahamane OUSMANE of the Democratic and Social Convention-*Rahama* (CDS-*Rahama*), with 26.59 percent. However, in the second round on March 27, Ousmane was able to surpass Tandja with 54.42 percent of the vote, thanks to solid AFC backing; he was sworn in for a five-year term on April 16. The next day Mahamadou ISSOUFOU, leader of the Nigerien Party for Democracy and Socialism–*Tarayya* (PNDS-*Tarayya*), was appointed prime minister. Issoufou named a cabinet on May 23.

In early 1994 opposition legislators launched a boycott against the assembly, but all 33 were arrested for advocating civil disobedience following violent antigovernment demonstrations on April 16–17. Among those incarcerated for their roles in the unrest were Tandja and the leaders of two theretofore AFC parties, André Salifou of the Union of Democratic Patriots and Progressives–*Chamoua* (UPDP-*Chamoua*) and Issoufou ASSOUMANE of the Democratic Union of Progressive Forces–*Sawaba* (UDFP-*Sawaba*). Their defection lent credence to reports of discord within the AFC, apparently stemming from the president's poorly received efforts to seize Mahamadou Issoufou's prime ministerial powers.

The AFC lost its assembly majority on September 25, 1994, when the PNDS-*Tarayya* broke with the coalition, complaining it had been marginalized by the CDS-*Rahama*. Prime Minister Issoufou resigned on September 28, and Ousmane named CDS-*Rahama* cabinet minister Abdoulaye SOULEY as the new head of government the same day. However, on October 16, two days after the MNDS-*Nassara* and PNDS-*Tarayya* had successfully orchestrated an assembly nonconfidence vote, the 11-day-old Souley government was forced to dissolve. The following day Ousmane reappointed Souley, who proffered the same cabinet. A second nonconfidence vote ensued and, faced with the choice of appointing a prime minister from the new parliamentary majority or dissolving the National Assembly and holding a new legislative election, Ousmane chose the latter.

On January 9, 1995, three days before the election, the MNSD-*Nassara* coalition threatened a boycott due to alleged voter registration fraud and the assassination of an opposition candidate, Seydou Dan DJOUMA. Nevertheless, the coalition participated in the poll and captured 43 legislative seats; AFC-affiliated groups secured the remaining 40. Ousmane ignored MNSD-*Nassara*'s request that he name Hama AMADOU as prime minister, despite the party's assembly majority, and instead appointed another MNSD-*Nassara* member, Amadou Boubacar CISSÉ, on February 8. Two days later the MNSD-*Nassara* expelled Cissé, and on February 20 the assembly voted to censure the new prime minister. The following day Ousmane dismissed Cissé and appointed Amadou, who subsequently formed a cabinet drawn from supporters of the new governing coalition.

Despite differences within the Tuareg leadership, a final peace accord was signed on April 25, 1995. On June 12, the National Assembly unanimously decided to grant full amnesty to all participants of the civil war. Meanwhile, political turmoil continued in Niamey as the AFC, which had earlier accused the MNSD-*Nassara* and its partners of "monstrous irregularities" during the January polling, criticized Prime Minister Amadou's new government for failing to represent "half of the population." Ousmane refused Amadou's call for a cabinet meeting on July 6, in an apparent attempt to avert a vote on his own non-cabinet appointments. Amadou contended that Ousmane lacked the authority to name government officials and responded by ordering riot police to prevent Ousmane-appointed administrators from entering their offices. Despite subsequent negotiations, Amadou dismissed the officials in question on August 1; however, a Niamey court immediately reinstated them. On August 4 the prime minister held a cabinet meeting without Ousmane, who promptly declared all cabinet decisions "null and void."

In early October 1995 opposition parliamentarians aligned with Ousmane declared that the prime minister had deliberately violated the constitution by convening the cabinet without presidential approval and called for his censure. However, their attempt to pass a nonconfidence motion on October 8 failed (in part because some members boycotted the vote to protest the absence of the assembly speaker). In November international mediators met with the president and prime minister in what was described as a successful attempt to end the constitutional impasse, although the question of who controlled government appointments remained unresolved.

On January 27, 1996, at least ten people were killed in a military coup directed by Army Chief of Staff Col. Ibrahim Baré MAÏNASSARA, who claimed that he had acted to end the "absurd, irrational, and personalized crisis" gripping the Nigerien government. Following seizure of the presidential palace and assembly building, Maïnassara announced the "dismissal" of the president and prime minister (both of whom had been arrested), the dissolution of the assembly, suspension of political party activity, and his own installation as chair of the National Salvation Council (*Conseil pour le Salut National*—CSN), an 11-member military body organized to govern until a civilian government could be reestablished. On January 30 the CSN designated Boukari ADJI, vice governor of the Central Bank of West African States (BCEAO), as prime minister.

In February 1996 Maïnassara appointed a 100-member Committee of Wisemen to act as an advisory council and a 32-member Coordinating Committee for the Democratic Renewal to supervise the restoration of a democratic government and draft a new constitution. At a meeting chaired by Maïnassara on February 12, Ousmane and Amadou publicly acknowledged the "constitutional problems" that had prompted the coup and endorsed the CSN's early governing efforts.

On February 17, 1996, the CSN announced a timetable for the return to a democratically elected government, which called for a constitutional referendum in September and presidential and legislative elections by the end of the year. However, under pressure from France, which on March 6 became the first international donor to renew ties with the junta, the CSN released a revised timetable that moved the schedule up by three months. On March 27 the regime established a transitional legislature, the National Forum for Democratic Renewal, consisting of members from the Committee of Wisemen and the Coordinating Committee, as well as former National Assemblymen. The National Forum met for the first time on April 1 and six days later it approved a draft constitution that included provisions for a second legislative body (a Senate), as well as a government wherein the prime minister would be accountable to the president. On April 19 the National Forum released yet another transitional timetable, rescheduling the constitutional referendum to May 12, presidential balloting to July 7, and legislative elections to September 22.

The constitutional referendum was approved on May 12, 1996, by 92 percent of the voters—though the election was poorly attended. Maïnassara revoked the ban on political parties May 19, and lifted the state of emergency four days later. Meanwhile, a clash between government forces and rebels near Lake Chad was reportedly the first such incident since early March, when Tuareg and Toubou leaders had agreed to implement a unilateral cease-fire as a sign of support for the military regime.

In balloting July 7–8, 1996, Brig. Gen. Maïnassara (who was promoted on May 14) captured the presidency, securing 52 percent of the vote, according to government figures. However, the election was marred by the junta's termination of the Independent National Electoral Commission (CENI) on the second day of voting and installation of a National Electoral Commission (CNE) filled with Maïnassara's supporters. Dismissing the regime's claim that it had dissolved the CENI to end the "corruption" of ballots by opposition activists, Maïnassara's top three challengers (former president Ousmane, MNSD-*Nassara* chair Mamadou Tandja, and former National Assembly president Mahamadou Issoufou) filed a petition to have the results overturned. (Ousmane had been credited with 19.75 percent of the vote, Tandja 15.65 percent, and Issoufou 7.6 percent. The fifth candidate, Moumouni DJERMAKOYE of the ANDP-*Zaman Lahiya,* secured 4.77 of the vote; he did not formally contest the results.) The Supreme Court officially validated Maïnassara's electoral victory July 21, and on August 23 the new president named a cabinet, again led by Prime Minister Adji, which included no military officials.

Following his inauguration on August 7, 1996, President Maïnassara attempted to negotiate an agreement that would prompt angry opposition groups to participate in upcoming legislative elections. Among other things, he dissolved the CNE on August 30 and announced the formation of a new electoral commission. However, the opposition, most of which coalesced in September as the Front for the Restoration and Defense of Democracy (FRDD), demanded that the members of the CENI be reappointed and that other measures be taken to ensure fair elections. Unconvinced of the regime's democratic intentions, the FRDD ultimately boycotted the balloting for a new National Assembly held on November 23, paving the way for the National Union of Independents for Democratic Renewal (UNIRD), which had recently been established by supporters of resident Maïnassara, to win 59 of the 83 seats. Declaring the transition to civilian government complete, Maïnassara dissolved the CSN on December 12. On December 21 he appointed a new government, headed, ironically, by Amadou Cissé, whose attempted appointment to the premiership in February 1995 had triggered the constitutional crisis leading up to the January 1996 coup.

Antigovernment sentiment culminated in large-scale demonstrations in the capital in early January 1997. Maïnassara responded with a crackdown that resulted in the arrest of the FRDD leaders; however, the detainees were released after ten days, regional leaders having apparently persuaded the president to adopt a less harsh approach.

On March 31, 1997, Maïnassara dissolved the Cissé government in response to the opposition's agreement to set aside its preconditions for entering into negotiations (i.e. dissolution of the assembly and organization of fresh elections) and accept cabinet postings. However, talks between the two sides quickly broke down, and no opposition members were included in the government named on June 13. The opposition rejected subsequent government entreaties, and unrest was reported throughout the country. Consequently, on November 24 Maïnassara again dismissed the Cissé government, accusing it of "incompetency" and failing to ease political tensions.

On November 27, 1997, Ibrahim Assane MAYAKI was named to replace Cissé, and on December 1 a new government was appointed. Despite Maïnassara's pledge to include opposition figures in the new cabinet, only one minister, Tuareg leader Rhissa ag BOULA, came from outside the pro-presidential coalition of parties. Moreover, a number of Cissé ministers were reappointed.

Opposition candidates captured a majority of the contested seats in local, municipal, and regional balloting on February 7, 1999. Heightened government-opposition tension was consequently reported in Niamey after the Supreme Court (acting, according to the opposition, under pressure from the administration) ordered extensive repolling in early April.

On April 9 President Maïnassara was assassinated at the Niamey airport upon returning from a trip to Mecca, reportedly by members of the presidential guard. Troops immediately took control of the capital, and Prime Minister Mayaki dissolved the assembly, suspended political party activities, and asserted that he and his cabinet would continue governing until a "unity" government was formed. After two days of uncertainty, however, junior army officers announced on April 11 that they had assumed power and formed a National Reconciliation Council (*Conseil de Réconciliation Nationale*—CRN), whose chair, Maj. Daouda Malam WANKÉ (theretofore commander of the presidential guard), was also named head of state. The junta suspended the constitution and formally dissolved the government and Supreme Court. In addition, the results of the February elections were annulled. At the same time, the military announced a nine-month transitional plan that would culminate in the inauguration of an elected president. On April 16, 1999, the CRN named an interim government that included Wanké as the head of government, Mayaki in a diminished prime ministerial role, and a number of FRDD ministers.

A new constitution, designed, among other things, to resolve the presidential/prime-ministerial power-sharing confusion of the early to mid-1990s, was approved by 90 percent of the vote in a national referendum on July 18, 1999, although turnout was estimated at only 32 percent. Seven candidates ran in the presidential election on October 17, and in runoff balloting on November 24 Mamadou Tandja of MNSD-*Nassara* defeated Mahamdou Issoufou of PNDS-*Tarayya*, 60 percent to 40 percent. The MNSD-*Nassara* also secured a plurality in new assembly balloting on November 24, and in coalition with the CDS-*Rahama* controlled a comfortable majority of 55 legislative seats. Tandja was inaugurated on December 22 and, upon the recommendation of the assembly, named fellow party member Hama AMADOU as prime minister on December 31. In addition to the MNSD-*Nassara* and CDS-*Rahama*, the new cabinet announced on January 5, 2000, included representatives of two small, nonlegislative parties—the UFPDP-*Sawaba* and PUND-*Salama*—as well as two leaders of former Tuareg rebel organizations. However, in a reshuffle on September 17, 2001, the ministers from the UFPDP-*Sawaba* and PUND-*Salama* were dropped from the cabinet.

The country's first municipal elections, postponed from May 4, 2004, were successfully held on July 24, 2004, with councilors elected to represent 206 communities.

Tandja was reelected in 2004, after winning the first round of balloting on November 16 and easily defeating Issoufou in second-round balloting on December 4 with 65.5 percent of the vote. He named a new cabinet on December 30, which included five women and retained Amadou as prime minister. The assembly, also elected on December 4, seated seven members from a new party formed earlier in the year by former transitional leader Cheiffou: the Rally for Social Democracy (RSD). In the wake of the dismissal of two cabinet ministers in 2006 in connection with a corruption scandal, the parliament backed a no-confidence vote on May 31, 2007, that dissolved the government and forced the resignation of Prime Minister Amadou on June 1. President Tandja's appointment of equipment minister Seini OUMAROU as prime minister on June 3 was initially rejected by the parliament, and the opposition refused to participate in a proposed unity government. However, Oumarou was sworn in on June 7 and a new government was installed on June 9, comprising members of the MNSD-*Nassara*, the CDS-*Rahama*, and the Democratic Rally of the People–Jamaa (*Rassemblement Démocratique du Peuple–Jamaa*—RDP-*Jamaa*). The cabinet included eight women and a former Tuareg rebel leader, Issad KATO.

In 2008 the president extended a state of emergency that had been effect since August 2007 in response to the continuing conflict with Taureg rebels in the north. The measure enhanced the powers of the armed forces in the region. In May 2009 a presidential decree extended the state of emergency for another three months.

The cabinet was reshuffled on May 14, 2009, when the president dismissed ministers from two parties that opposed his plan for a constitutional referendum—the RDP-*Jamaa* and the ANDP-*Zaman Lahiya*—and replaced them with members of the MNSD. He also replaced the justice minister without explanation. On May 26 the president dissolved parliament following a Constitutional Court ruling the previous day rejecting his proposal for a referendum that, if approved, would change the constitution to allow him to seek a third five-year term. The president subsequently set August 4 as the date for the national referendum, circumventing both the court and the National Assembly. (*See headnote.*)

Constitution and government. In January 1984 President Kountché created a National Charter Commission, largely comprised of CND members, to develop a constitutional framework that was ultimately endorsed in a national referendum on June 14, 1987. On December 17 of the same year, General Saibou announced the formation of a national "reflection committee" to finalize guidelines for the new basic law, which was approved by popular referendum on September 24, 1989. Capping the government structure was the CSON, whose 67 civilian and military members (14 serving as a National Executive Bureau) were elected by the MNSD and whose president became sole candidate for election to the presidency of the republic. The 1989 document, which also provided for a National Assembly of 93 MNSD-approved members and for a judiciary headed by a presidentially appointed Supreme Court, was suspended by the National Conference on August 9, 1991.

By mid-1992 the presidency had been reduced to an essentially symbolic institution, as true executive power was exercised by the prime minister who until early 1993 answered to a quasi-legislative High Council of the Republic (HCR). One of the functions of the HCR was to oversee the drafting of the new basic law, which was approved by national referendum on December 27, 1993. The document provided for a directly elected president to serve a once-renewable five-year term. A presidentially nominated prime minister is responsible to a unicameral National Assembly whose members are also elected for five-year terms.

Upon its ascension to power in early 1996 the CSN military regime suspended the 1993 document and appointed a commission to draft a new charter. The new constitution, which was approved by national referendum on May 12, 1996, featured an executive branch headed by a powerful president, thus clearly distinguishing itself from its predecessors. Meanwhile, in early June the regime created a ten-member High Court of Justice and granted it sole authority to prosecute the president and government members.

The 1996 basic law was suspended by the CRN on April 11, 1999, and an interim Consultative Council (*Conseil Consultative*—CC) was appointed in May by the new military head of state, Maj. Daouda Malam Wanké, to draft yet another constitution. As approved in a national referendum on July 18, the new basic law accorded strong power to the president to prevent a reoccurrence of the difficulties experienced in interpreting the 1993 document with regard to the authority of the prime minister versus the president. (*See headnote.*)

Foreign relations. Prior to the 1974 coup Niger pursued a moderate line in foreign affairs, avoiding involvement in East-West issues and generally maintaining friendly relations with neighboring states. The Kountché government established diplomatic links with a number of communist states, including China and the Soviet Union, and adopted a conservative posture in regional affairs, including a diplomatic rupture with Libya from January 1981 to March 1982. Tripoli was periodically charged thereafter with backing anti-Niamey forces, including those involved in a late 1983 coup attempt and northern Tuareg rebel activity in 1985 and 1990. However, a bilateral security agreement in December 1990 eased tensions between Niger and Libya.

Niamey's relations with neighboring Algeria and Mali have been complicated since October 1991 by the resurgence of militant Tuareg activities across their shared borders. In March 1992 a meeting between Prime Minister Cheiffou and Tuareg officials in Algeria yielded a two-week truce. However, the truce was allowed to lapse, and in February 1993 Nigerien and Malian troops clashed, after reportedly mistaking each other for Tuareg units. The January 1996 military coup in Niger drew condemnation from both regional and international observers, with France, the European Union, and the United States suspending aid payments. Although Paris resumed cooperation in March 1996, Washington reiterated its stance following the controversial July presidential elections.

A number of regional and other international capitals condemned the military takeover in April 1999; France, for example, promptly broke off its relations with Niger and suspended all aid. Such pressure was considered influential in the subsequent quick return to civilian rule, after which normal international relations were reestablished and external financial assistance was resumed.

In May 2000 a long-standing dispute between Niger and Benin over ownership of Lete Island and a number of smaller islands in the Niger River resurfaced. After mediation by the Organization of African Unity (OAU, subsequently the African Union—AU) failed to produce successful border delineation, the case was submitted to the International Court of Justice (ICJ). In 2005 the ICJ ruled that 16 of the 25 disputed islands, including Lete, belonged to Niger. In 2007 Niger officially took ownership of Lete Island. In 2007 Benin officially took possession of nine other islands it was awarded by the ICJ's ruling.

Longtime tensions between Niger and Burkina Faso escalated in 2007, each accusing the other's security forces of crossing the border to rob villagers. Local officials called for a jointly controlled buffer zone, and the two countries agreed to ask the ICJ to mediate the dispute.

Relations with France were strained in 2007 following the deportation of a French journalist from Niger after his imprisonment for filming a documentary on Tuareg rebels. Questions about the role of French uranium-mining company Areva also played a part in the deterioration of ties with France (see Current issues, below).

China, meanwhile, maintained warm relations with Niger in 2007, the former having opened what was described as a "vast new embassy" in Niamey and having secured a number of uranium prospecting licenses. In September 2007 President Tandja and officials of the Chinese Communist Party met in Niger and agreed to foster cooperation between the two governments. In 2009 China loaned Niger $95 million for a uranium mining project owned in partnership between the two countries.

Current issues. Although the events of April 1999 had, in the opinion of many observers, all the earmarks of a military coup d'état, CRN Chair Wanké did not acknowledge any involvement in the killing of President Maïnassara. Instead, he argued that the junta had assumed power only as a result of the chaos that ensued following the "tragic accident." In any event, the general populace and political party leaders seemed primarily concerned with the junta's plans for return to civilian government—which, to the surprise of some analysts, was accomplished rather smoothly by the end of the year. (Wanké died on September 15, 2004, at age 58.) Both the presidential and legislative polls were described as fairly conducted by international observers, and the results were accepted in most domestic quarters. The administration of President Tandja, who had campaigned on a platform calling for national unity, was widely credited by the international financial community for having stabilized the economy. However, the newly formed opposition group known as the Coordination of Democratic Forces (*Coordination des Forces Démocratiques*—CFD) criticized the government for "ruling by edict" in order to accommodate the IMF and other lenders. The CFD organized street protests and presented several censure motions in the assembly, which were ultimately unsuccessful. Eyebrows were also raised by the decision to grant amnesty to everyone involved in the 1996 coup and the events of April 1999. Also, the government faced pressure from student protesters and Islamic organizations, some of whom had been banned in November 2000 for "disturbing the peace." On a positive note, most former rebel groups were officially disarmed as of mid-2000.

Slavery continued to be a major part of the culture, though legislation outlawing it was adopted in 2003. In March 2005 some 3,000 people in the capital protested the detention of anti-slavery activists. The government has continued to deny that slavery exists. (In 2008 a former slave sued the government for allegedly legitimizing slavery through customary law. A regional court in October issued a landmark ruling ordering the government to pay damages to the woman.)

In October 2006 the government came under severe criticism from neighboring countries after announcing plans to deport 10,000 Mahamid Arabs to Chad, their country of origin. The nomadic herders, who had been living in the Diffa area for decades and had gained wealth and influence, reportedly were planning on backing a challenger to President Tandja in the 2009 elections. Following an outcry from the Arab community in Niger and elsewhere, the government suspended the plan. The Arabs were advised to relocate to an area where there was more water, an issue that was a source of contention for local residents.

A corruption scandal involving two ministers accused of embezzling more than $1 million in 2006 led to a parliamentary vote of no confidence on May 31, 2007, based on delegates' allegations of Prime Minister Amadou's complicity. Several members of the MNSD-*Nassara* and its allies joined the 25 opposition members, resulting in 62 of 113 delegates backing the no-confidence vote. Amadou, for his part, denied any wrongdoing. After the prime minister resigned on June 1, parliament submitted a list of three nominees for his successor to President Tandja, who selected Seini Oumarou despite objections from those who claimed the MNSD-*Nassara* member was too closely associated with Amadou. However, Oumarou's appointment stood, with observers pointing out that the ethnic balance in the top political positions had been maintained. Oumarou, like Amadou, is a member of the western Djerma tribe, while the president is from the eastern region. The new government named on June 9 reportedly did not include any members of the opposition. The immediate issue of concern in the wake of the government shake-up was the renewed violence in the north by a new Tuareg rebel group, the Movement of Nigeriens for Justice (*Mouvement des Nigériens pour la Justice*—MNJ), which had emerged in February 2007 (see Rebel Groups, below). The group claimed responsibility for a series of attacks that resulted in the death or capture of numerous soldiers and the kidnapping of a Chinese uranium company executive (who was later released), among other acts of violence. The government refused to acknowledge the MNJ's existence, instead referring to the rebels as "bandits" and "drug dealers." In June the government moved 4,000 troops to the northern region to confront the rebels, who were demanding that the government use more of the country's uranium profits to improve the living conditions in the north and that the president fulfill the terms of the 1995 peace agreement.

The conflict escalated throughout 2007 and 2008, with reports of landmines laid by rebels and accusations against a French-owned uranium mining company, Areva, of fomenting instability in the north—seen as a means of discouraging other international companies from vying for a stake in the lucrative mining industry—and similar claims against Libya's president Muammar al-Qadhafi, who had offered to mediate the dispute. Additionally, international human rights groups reported that the government had carried out illegal executions, torture, and revenge attacks against Tuareg rebels, all of which the administration denied. Meanwhile, thousands of people, a majority of them said to be MNSD members, demonstrated in the capital in support of the army's efforts. Still adverse to negotiations, the government in August declared a three-month state of emergency in the north after rebels killed 50 soldiers; the decree also barred journalists from entering the region, reportedly facilitated the arrests of civilians, and, according to observers, enhanced the army's ability to crack down on the rebels in the absence of public reporting. Meanwhile, President Tandja was facing growing unrest among the populace due to food shortages and a lack of jobs, the latter making it difficult for him to pledge preferential treatment for residents in the north when thousands of recent graduates in the capital were unable to find work. The conflict also was reported to have heightened tensions between the MNSD and its ally, the CDS-*Rahama*, particularly after former prime minister Amadou proposed that the government recognize the MNJ, a public pronouncement that reportedly "annoyed" the president. In November the president renewed the state of emergency for another three months.

Fighting continued in 2008, with the first landmine explosion in the capital in January and threats from MNJ leader Mohamed ACHARIF that the group would begin attacking uranium mines and oil projects in the north unless the government agreed to negotiate. President Tandja steadfastly refused to acknowledge the rebels, who were now said to have widened their base of support to include the Toubou and some Tuaregs from neighboring Mali. Meanwhile, international human rights groups reported that a crisis was developing, as some 20,000 people had been displaced by the fighting, including the entire population of several thousand from the town of Iferouane. While the MNJ had released dozens of captured soldiers, the group remained insistent that the government give half of all uranium-rights revenues to Tuaregs. In June the rebels kidnapped four French employees of a nuclear power company, releasing them days later. The rebels announced that their reason for such actions was to pressure the governments of Niger and France to enter negotiations to end the conflict. That same month, news reports surfaced that MNJ leader Acharif had been killed by government forces. In August the rebels rejected disarmament, and fighting continued throughout the year.

Meanwhile, political turmoil was also mounting, following the arrest in June 2008 of former prime minister Amadou on corruption charges. Widely viewed as Tandja's likely successor, Amadou denied that he had embezzled state funds, claiming he was being targeted to prevent him from seeking the presidency in 2009. His supporters were banned from holding a mass demonstration in October calling for his release. Among the protesters were members of the MNDS, of which Amadou remained chair, though a rift developed in the party between that faction and those who backed President Tandja. Amadou, for his part, said he would run for president despite being in prison.

In the run-up to the 2009 elections, scheduled for November-December, President Tandja said in March that he would not seek a third term (which he could do only if the constitution were amended), but he changed his mind in early May, insisting his supporters had requested that his term be extended so that he could complete projects and to enhance the stability of the country. Earlier, the country's judges had balked at the president's requirement that they must divulge their religion in order to vie for chair of the national elections commission, so the president made his own appointment. With several parties voicing their opposition to Tandja's proposed constitutional revision allowing him to seek a third term, the president removed several cabinet members whose parties objected to the referendum. Days later the Constitutional Court, having taken up the issue after it was referred by parliament, ruled that the president "cannot undertake to change the constitution without violating his oath of office." The next day, Tandja dissolved parliament, a move observers said meant he could avoid having to appear before the High Court of Justice on charges of high treason. The high court judge, Moumouni Adamou DJERMAKOYE of the pro-government ANDP-*Zaman Lahiya*, had recently warned that the proposed referendum would divide the country into two separate factions. The president's plan drew international protests as well, the United States calling the proposed referendum "a setback for democracy," and the Economic Community of West African States (ECOWAS) threatening sanctions. Tandja, however, rejected the criticism and set August 4 as the date for the referendum. In June groups of protesters led by Mahamadou ISSOUFOU of the PNDS-*Tarayya* announced they would defy the government ban on demonstrations against the referendum. More than 230 parties and groups under the umbrella Front for Defense of Democracy (FDD) planned a series of protests to counter what they said was the president's plan to "install absolute power." (*See headnote.*)

Meanwhile, developments in the north led to the rebels' continued overtures for negotiations, urging that any talks be moderated by Libyan president Qadhafi, who in March 2009 had called on the rebels to disarm. In May it was reported that the MNJ had released its last hostage and that President Tandja had, for the first time, agreed to meet with the group's representatives. Observers noted that the president's "radical change in policy" coincided with a major deal between the government and a French mining company to develop a large uranium mine in northern Niger.

POLITICAL PARTIES

Political parties were not permitted in Niger during the more than 13 years of the Kountché regime. The National Movement for a Developing Society (MNSD, below) was established as a government formation in 1988, and some 15 parties received provisional recognition in the five months following President Saibou's November 1990 acceptance of a multiparty system. All party activity was suspended in the wake of the January 1996 coup, but the ban was soon lifted on May 19. However, the new standards guiding party formations and activities were described as restrictive. Nevertheless, numerous coalitions were formed in 1996–1998, though alliances continued changing. Most notably, the once powerful Alliance of Forces of Change (*Alliance des Forces de Changement*—AFC) appeared to have collapsed by the late 1990s. (For further information on the AFC, see p. 680 of the 1998 *Handbook.*)

Political party activity was suspended immediately following the April 1999 military takeover; however, within days of President Maïnassara's death the leading opposition groups announced their intention to cooperate with the military junta, and the suspension was lifted.

In March 2000 the PNDS-*Tarayya,* RDP-*Jamaa,* ANDP-*Zaman Lahiya,* and a number of smaller parties formed a loose antigovernment coalition called the Coordination of Democratic Forces (*Coordination des Forces Démocratiques*—CFD). In response the MNDS-*Nassara* and several allies, including the CDS-*Rahama,* announced the creation of an Alliance of Democratic Forces (*Alliance des Forces Démocratiques*—AFD) in July. The ANDP-*Zaman Lahia* joined the AFD coalition on July 8, 2002.

The following year the CFD protested President Tandja's coalition approval of a new law eliminating the requirement that ministers seeking elected office must first resign from their government position. The CFD members were angry that they had not been consulted, as electoral changes were usually made by consensus in the past.

Prior to the 2004 legislative elections, the PNDS-*Tarayya* formed electoral coalitions with several parties: the PPN/RDA and the PNA-*Al Ouma;* the UNI/UDR-*Tabbat;* and the PPN/RDA.

Government Party:

National Movement for a Developing Society–Victory (*Mouvement National pour une Societé de Développement Nassara*—MNSD-*Nassara*). General Saibou announced the formation of the MNSD on August 2, 1988. Rejecting calls for a multiparty system, he claimed that the new group would allow for the "plural expression of opinions and ideological sensibilities," while paving the way for a normalization of politics in Niger.

General Saibou was reelected MNSD chair at a party congress on March 12–18, 1991, during which a transition to multipartism was formally endorsed. The military also announced its withdrawal from politics, and the MNSD added the Hausa word *Nassara* (Victory) to its name. On July 12, just as the party prepared to enter the competitive arena, Saibou resigned his chairmanship, citing a need to serve in a nonpartisan capacity.

In legislative balloting on February 14, 1993, the MNSD-*Nassara* secured 29 seats, 7 more than its nearest competitor; however, the subsequent formation of the AFC coalition relegated the then-ruling party to minority status. Accusing the new group of procedural irregularities, the MNSD-*Nassara* refused to promote a candidate for the National Assembly presidency in April; thereafter, it spearheaded numerous protests against the government's alleged "constitutional violations." In October ten party members were sentenced to prison for engaging in violent clashes with security forces, and in March 1994 Mamadou Tandja, the MNSD-*Nassara*'s leader and former 1993 presidential candidate, was arrested for his alleged role in an antigovernment demonstration in Niamey.

The MNSD-*Nassara* again captured 29 seats in legislative balloting in January 1995, thus retaining its position as the dominant partner in the parliamentary coalition it had led since late 1994. Tandja secured 15.65 percent of the vote during presidential balloting in July 1996. Tandja and his fellow PNDS-*Tarayya* and CDS-*Rahama* presidential competitors (below) subsequently sought to have the elections nullified, claiming "massive fraud," but the Supreme Court promptly dismissed their petitions.

In September 1996 the MNSD-*Nassara* joined the PNDS-*Tarayya,* CDS-*Rahama,* and several other small groups in launching the Front for the Restoration and Defense of Democracy (*Front pour la Restauration et la Défense de la Démocratie*—FRDD), which immediately became the primary opposition to the Maïnassara regime. The leaders of the front demanded the restoration of the "original" Independent National Commission (CENI), equal access to the media, and supervision of the balloting by the Organization of African Unity and/or the United Nations as preconditions for FRDD participation in the upcoming national elections. Despite some apparent compromise on the part of the government, the FRDD ultimately called for a boycott of the legislative balloting.

Following prodemocracy demonstrations in Niamey in early January 1997, the leaders of the three main FRDD components were arrested and reportedly threatened with prosecution by a tribunal especially created for that purpose by President Maïnassara. However, the party leaders and 60 other detainees were released ten days later and immediately urged the resumption of antigovernment demonstrations.

Each of three main FRDD components presented its own presidential candidate in the first round of balloting in 1999, and Mamadou Tandja led with 32.3 percent. Thanks in part to the support of former president Mahamane Ousmane of the CDS-*Rahama,* Tandja was elected with 59.9 percent of the vote in the second round. For the November 1999 legislative balloting the MNSD-*Nassara* was portrayed as still aligned with the CDS-*Rahama,* but no longer with the PNDS-*Tarayya.*

Tandja again took the lead in the presidential elections of 2004, taking 40.7 percent of the vote in the first round of balloting on November 16. He retained his post in the second round of balloting on December 4 with a resounding victory (65.5 percent of the vote) by striking alliances with ANDP-*Zaman Lahiya* candidate Moumouni Djermakoye (who was fifth in first-round balloting) and Amadou Cheiffou of the Rally for Social Democracy-*Gaskiya,* who ran as an independent (fourth in the first round), and gaining the support of the CDS's Ousmane, who garnered just 24.6 percent of votes in the first round, and Hamid ALGABID of the Democratic Rally of the People-*Jamaa* (sixth place in the first round). The MNSD-*Nassara* captured 47 legislative seats, a gain of 9 from the previous elections, though it failed to gain an absolute majority of the expanded 113-member assembly (see Legislature, below). The legislative election coincided with the second round of the presidential elections on December 4.

In 2008 former prime minister and party chair Hama Amadou was arrested on charges of corruption and subsequently imprisoned, galvanizing his supporters in the party and creating a rift with backers of President Tandja. The Amadou faction, who viewed him as Tandja's likely successor, also denounced the violence that they alleged had been used against them. Meanwhile, tensions were exacerbated when, at a special congress in February 2009, Amadou was replaced as party chair by Prime Minister Oumarou, and later in the year after Tandja pushed forth a constitutional referendum in an effort to allow him to run for a third term in balloting at the end of the year. (*See headnote.*)

Leaders: Col. (Ret.) Mamadou TANDJA (President of the Republic), Seini OUMAROU (Prime Minister and Party Chair), Salissou Mamadou HADI (Secretary General).

Other Legislative Parties:

Democratic and Social Convention–Rahama (*Convention Démocrate et Sociale–Rahama*—CDS-*Rahama*). In the legislative balloting of February 1993 CDS-*Rahama* captured 22 seats, the most of any opposition party. Its candidate, Mahamane Ousmane, who had finished second in the first round of balloting, captured the presidency with 54.42 percent of the vote in the second round of presidential balloting on March 27. In January 1995 the party increased its assembly representation to 24 seats. Ousmane was ousted from office in the January 1996 coup; his bid to regain the presidency in the July balloting fell short as he came in second (at least according to government tallies) with 19.75 percent of the vote. He finished a close third in the first round of presidential balloting in 1999 with 22.5 percent of the vote. The CDS-*Rahama* subsequently threw its support behind Mamadou Tandja of the MNSD-*Nassara* for the second round. In the 2004 presidential balloting, Ousmane was again third in the first round of voting, and again threw his support behind Tandja in the second round. CDS-*Rahama* won 22 seats in the assembly balloting of 2004.

Though the party had been supportive of President Tandja, in 2009 it opposed his plan for a constitutional referendum, saying Niger's "political and institutional stability" would be threatened. The CDS-*Rahama* agreed with the court ruling that the referendum was unconstitutional.

Leaders: Maïdagi ALLAMBEY, Mahamane OUSMANE (Speaker of the National Assembly and Former President of the Republic), Nabram ISSOUFOU.

Nigerien Alliance for Democracy and Progress–Zaman Lahiya (*Alliance Nigérienne pour la Démocratie et le Progrès–Zaman Lahiya*—ANDP-*Zaman Lahiya*). On August 28, 1992, ANDP-*Zaman Lahiya* vice president Birgi Raffini, a former Saibou government official, was arrested during an army crackdown on suspected FLAA rebels and sympathizers. He was released in early 1993, and his party won 11 seats in legislative balloting that February. ANDP-*Zaman Lahiya's* candidate, Moumouni Adamou Djermakoye, secured only 15 percent of the vote in the first round of presidential balloting, but his support for the CDS-*Rahama*'s Ousmane was described as pivotal to Ousmane's presidential victory. In April Djermakoye was named National Assembly president. The party's legislative representation fell to 9 seats in January 1995.

In the July 1996 presidential balloting Djermakoye received only 4.77 percent of the vote, finishing last in the five-candidate field. The ANDP-*Zaman Lahiya* was the only major party not to boycott the November 1996 elections, in which it secured eight seats.

In 1998 the ANDP-*Zaman Lahiya* joined the PUND-*Salama* and the PNA (see below) to form a pro-Maïnassara group called the Alliance of Democratic Social Forces (*Alliance des Forces Démocratiques et Sociales*—AFDS). Djermakoye won 7.7 percent of the votes in the first round of presidential balloting in 1999 and endorsed Mahamadou Issoufou of the PNDS-*Tarayya* in the second round. The ANDP- *Zaman Lahiya* agreed to join the progovernment Alliance of Democratic Forces in 2002.

In 2004, presidential candidate Djermakoye received only 6.1 percent of the vote in the first round of balloting, the fifth of six candidates. Since his party belonged to the ruling coalition, his support in the second round likely went to Tandja. ANDP-Zaman Lahiya won five seats in the assembly election of 2004.

Djermakoye warned in 2009 that the country "will be split in two" if the president's proposed constitutional referendum were approved, despite his support for the president in the past.

Leaders: Moumouni Adamou DJERMAKOYE (Party President, 1999 and 2004 presidential candidate, and Former National Assembly President), Birgi RAFFINI (Vice President).

Rally for Social Democracy–Gaskiya (*Rassemblement pour Sociale Democrate*—RSD-*Gaskiya*). The RSD-Gaskiya split off from CDS in January 2004. Amadou Cheiffou, a former transitional prime minister from 1991 to 1993 and party leader, ran as an independent presidential candidate in 2004, receiving only 6.3 percent of the vote in the first round of balloting. However, the new party did win seven seats in the assembly and subsequent representation in the cabinet of President Tandje.

Leader and founder: Amadou CHEIFFOU (Former Prime Minister and 2004 presidential candidate).

Democratic Rally of the People–Jamaa (*Rassemblement Démocratique du Peuple–Jamaa*—RDP-*Jamaa*). The RDP-*Jamaa* held its inaugural congress on August 14–19, 1997, and was the party of then-President Maïnassara. Thereafter, the party emerged as the leader of a loose coalition of parties that supported the president. At local and municipal polling in early 1999, the RDP-*Jamaa* reportedly captured the largest number of seats; however, the military junta that came to power in April nullified the balloting.

Intraparty fighting erupted over the choice of a 1999 presidential nominee, leading former Prime Minister Amadou Boubacar Cissé and his supporters to leave the party. Meanwhile, Hamid Algabid of the RDP-*Jamaa* won 10.9 percent of the vote in the first round of presidential balloting and supported Mahamadou Issoufou of the PNDS-*Tarayya* in the second round. In the first round of presidential elections in 2004, Algabid won only 4.9 percent of the vote, finishing in last place. He supported Tandja in the second round. The party won only six seats in the assembly elections of 2004.

The party opposed the president's proposed constitutional referendum in 2009 unless it also included a measure that would abolish the amnesty for those who had been involved in the assassination of President Maïnassara.

Leaders: Hamid ALGABID (Chair and 1999 and 2004 presidential candidate), Abdourahamane SEYDOU (Secretary General).

Nigerien Party for Democracy and Socialism–Tarayya (*Parti Nigerien pour la Démocratie et le Socialism–Tarayya*—PNDS-*Tarayya*). In the legislative election of February 1993 the PNDS-*Tarayya*, then affiliated with the AFC, won 13 seats. Having gained only a 16 percent vote share in the first round of 1993 presidential balloting, party leader and presidential candidate Mahamadou Issoufou was eliminated from the runoff election; he was subsequently named prime minister.

On September 25, 1994, the PNDS-*Tarayya* withdrew from the AFC, claiming that it had been "betrayed" by its coalition partners, and three days later Issoufou resigned his prime ministerial post. In mid-October the PNDS-*Tarayya* joined with the MNSD-*Nassara* in a successful nonconfidence motion against the Souley government. In the January 1995 legislative poll the party won 12 seats; Issoufou was then elected National Assembly president. He captured 7.6 percent of the vote as the party's standard-bearer in the July 1996 presidential elections. He fared significantly better in 1999, finishing second in the first round with 22.8 percent of the vote before losing the runoff with 40.1 percent. Once aligned with the MNSD-*Nassara* and the CDR-*Rahama* in the FRDD, the PNDS-*Tarayya* competed against those parties in the 1999 legislative balloting in alliance with the RDP-*Jamaa* and ANDR-*Zaman Lahiya.*

Issoufou faced a runoff with incumbent President Tandja in 2004, after winning 24.6 percent of the votes in first-round balloting. In the second round, Tandja handily defeated his rival with 65.5 percent of the vote. However, the PNDS-*Tarayya* ran in coalition with a number of small parties and won 17 seats in the 2004 legislative election (see Legislature, below).

In 2007 the party's secretary general, Alou Bozari, joined numerous parties in the northern region in calling for an immediate cease-fire between government troops and Tuareg rebels.

The party opposed the president's constitutional referendum in 2009 and organized a massive, peaceful protest in May that included civil rights groups, trade unions, students, and supporters of former prime minister Amadou.

Leaders: Kalla ANKOURAO, Mahamadou ISSOUFOU (Former National Assembly President and 1999 and 2004 presidential candidate), Mohammed BAZOUM, Hassoumi MASSAOUDOU, Alou BOZARI (Secretary General).

Nigerien Democratic Front–Mutunci (*Front Démocratique Nigerien–Mutunci*—FDN-*Mutunci*). The launching of the FDN-*Mutunci* in late January 1995 represented a redefinition of the Nigerien Progressive Party (*Parti Progressiste Nigerien*—PPN), which had previously operated as the local section of the African Democratic Rally (*Rassemblement Démocratique Africaine*—RDA) under the PPN/RDA rubric. The new name was adopted shortly after the group withdrew from the AFC, as it was being increasingly dominated by CDS-*Rahama*. The platform advanced by the FDN-*Mutunci* calls for the "preservation" of Niger's sovereignty and the "strengthening of national cohesion." The party won one seat in the January 1995 balloting and none in November 1996.

Ide Oumarou was elected chair of FDN-*Mutunci* at a party congress in October 1998. Thereafter, he announced that the group (still widely referred to as the PPN/RDA) would align itself with parties supporting President Maïnassara. It ran in coalition with smaller parties for the 2004 assembly elections (see Legislature, below).

Former party chair Ide Oumarou died in February 2002. At the time of his death he had been vying with RDA leader Abdoulaye Diori Hamani, son of the country's first president, for chairmanship of the party. In 2004 the PPN/RDA contested the assembly elections in separate alliances with the PNDS-*Tarayya* and with the PNDS-*Tarayya* and the PNA-*Al Ouma*.

Leaders: Abdoulaye DIORI Hamani (Chair), Dan Dicko DANKOLODO (Former Chair), Oumarou Garba YOUSSOUFOU (1993 presidential candidate), Léopold KAZIENDE.

Niger Party for Self-Management (*Parti Nigérien pour l'Autogestion–Al Ouma*—PNA-*Al Ouma*). Former CDS vice chair Sanoussi Jackou formed the PNA in early 1997. It supported Mamadou Tandja in the 1999 presidential balloting despite its previous affiliation with the AFDS. Chair Jackou received a four-month suspended prison sentence in May 2002 after he was accused of slander and inciting racial hatred. In January 2005 he was released after serving a one-month prison sentence for insulting an ethnic group during a radio broadcast.

In the 2004 legislative elections the PNA was allied in various coalitions along with PNDS-*Tarayya* (see Legislature, below).

Leader: Sanoussi JACKOU.

Nigerien Social Democratic Party–Alheri (*Parti Social Démocrate du Niger–Alheri*—PSDN-*Alhéri*). In the January 1995 legislative balloting, the PSDN-*Alhéri* increased its representation from one seat to two. The group did not appear to participate in the November 1996 balloting, but it returned in 2004 to regain one seat.

Leaders: Gagara GREIMA, Malam Adji WAZIRI, Katzelma Omar Mahaman TAYA (1993 presidential candidate).

Other legislative parties are the **Union of Independent Nigeriens** (UNI), led by Amadou Djibo ALI; and the **Union for Democracy and the Republic–Tabbat** (UDR-*Tabbat*), founded in 1999 by former prime minister Amadou Boubacar CISSÈ, formerly of the RDP-*Jamaa*.

Other Parties:

Union of Popular Forces for Democracy and Progress–Sawaba (*Union des Forces Populaires pour la Démocratie et le Progrès–Sawaba*—UFPDP-*Sawaba*). The UFPDP-*Sawaba* is an offshoot of the UDN-*Sawaba*. It was led by Djibo Bakary, a 74-year-old former prime minister and former opponent of President Diori, from May 1957 to December 1958. He was unanimously elected party president in February 1992. Running on a platform calling for national unity and increased dialogue with the Tuareg rebels, Bakary captured 1.68 percent of the presidential vote in February 1993. The party lost both of its former legislative seats in January 1995 and was equally unsuccessful in the November 1996 balloting. Bakary died in 1998.

The UFPDP-*Sawaba* supported Mamadou Tandja in the 1999 presidential poll and was rewarded with a cabinet seat in the January 2000 government. However, the UFPDP-*Sawaba* minister, Issoufou Assoumane, was not reappointed in the September 2001 reshuffle; he formed a new political party, the USN, in October.

Party for National Unity and Development–Salama (*Parti pour l'Unité Nationale et la Développement–Salama*—PUND-*Salama*). Previously unknown, the pro-Tuareg PUND-*Salama* won three assembly seats in January 1995, including two seats in non-Tuareg districts, but was unsuccessful in the November 1996 balloting.

Although aligned with the ANDP-*Zaman Lahiya* in the pro-Maïnassara AFDS (launched in 1998), the PUND-*Salama* supported Mamadou Tandja of the MNSD-*Nassara* in the 1999 presidential campaign. The PUND-*Salama* was accorded a seat in the January 2000 cabinet but lost the post in the September 2001 reshuffle.

Leaders: Pascal MAMADOU, Akoli DAOUEL.

Union for Democracy and Social Progress–Amana (*Union pour la Démocratie et le Progrès Social–Amana*—UDPS-*Amana*). On August 28, 1992, (then) UDPS-*Amana* leader Akoli Daouel was imprisoned during the army's crackdown on suspected Tuareg dissidents. He was released in 1993 and later joined the PUND-*Salama*.

A deadly grenade attack on a UDPS-*Amana* meeting at Agades in October 1994 was blamed on Tuaregs angered by ongoing negotiations with the government. Thereafter, in the legislative balloting of January 1995, the party doubled its parliamentary representation to two seats.

Although technically an opposition grouping, the UDPS-*Amana* was awarded a cabinet portfolio by Prime Minister Amadou in February 1995. However, under pressure from opposition allies, who termed the appointment "regrettable," the minister was expelled from the party. The UDPS-*Amana* won three seats in the November 1996 assembly elections. Rhissa ag Boula, formerly with the ORA, joined the UDPS-*Amana* in August 2005. President Tandja met with Boula a few times in 2006 to discuss ways to prevent the Tuareg uprisings in neighboring Mali from spilling over into Niger. In a televised debate in 2007 Rhissa ag Boula expressed concerns over what he described as the "increasing anti-Tuareg xenophobia" and the government's failures to follow through on all aspects of the 1995 peace agreement.

Leaders: Almoctar ICHA, Mohamed ABDULLAHI, Mohamed MOUSSAL, Rhissa ag BOULA.

Other parties and groups include the radical Islamist **Alliance for Democracy and Progress** (*Alliance pour la Démocratie et le Progrès–Zumunci*—ADP-*Zumunci*), led by Issoufou BACHAR; the **Democratic and Socialist Renewal Union** (*Union Démocratique et Socialiste du Renouveau*—UDSR), led by Ibrahim Abdou GAUGE; the **Nigerien Party for Socialism** (*Parti Nigérien pour le Socialisme–Imani*—PNS-*Imani*), led by Boukari Maman SANI; the **Party for Democracy and Renewal** (*Parti pour la Démocratie et le Redressement*—PRD), led by Moumouni YACOUBA; the **Party of Consultation and Peace** (*Parti de la Concertation et de la Paix–Chawara*—PCP-*Chawara*), led by Katzelma Oumar TAYA; the **Patriotic Movement for Solidarity and Progress** (*Mouvement Patriotique pour la Solidarité et le Progrès–Anoura*—MPSP-*Anoura*), led by Moussa OUMAROU; the **Popular Front of National Liberation** (*Front Populaire de Libération Nationale–Chamsya*—FPLN-*Chamsya*), led by Jamboy Sabo DIALLO; the **Rally for a Green Sahel** (*Rassemblement pour un Sahel Vert–Niima*—RSV-*Niima*), led by Adamou GARBA; the **Republican Party for Liberties and the Progress of Niger** (*Parti Républicain pour les Libertés et le Progrès de Niger–Nakowa*—PRLPN-*Nakowa*), led by Alka ALMOU; the **Revolutionary Organization for the Defense of Democracy** (*Organisation Révolutionnaire pour la Défense de la Démocratie*—ORDD), led by Mama SUNI; the **Revolutionary Organization for the New Democracy** (*Organisation Révolutionnaire pour la Démocratie Nouvelle–Tarmamoua*—ORDN-*Tarmamoua*), led by Maman Sadi ADAMOU; the **Union for the Republic** (*Union pour la République*—UPR), led by Karimou MAMAN; the **Union of Independent Democrats** (*Union des Démocrates Indépendants*—UDI), led by Ali Sirfi MAÏGA; the **Union of Nigerien Socialists** (*Union des Socialistes Nigérien*—USN), a splinter from the UFDPD-*Sawaba* formed in October 2001 by Issoufou ASSOUMANE, who was the minister of environment and desertification in Hama Amadou's cabinet until September 17, 2001.

Former Rebel Groups:

Organization of the Armed Resistance (*Organisation de la Résistance Armée*—ORA). ORA emerged in March 1995 upon the temporary demise of the CRA when the FLAA withdrew from the coalition (see below). Successful implementation of a final peace agreement, signed by Rhissa ag Boula on behalf of the ORA on April 25, 1995, was viewed as depending on the resolution of differences between the FLAA and CRA chair Mano Dayak. In June the ORA denounced the inclusion of the so-called "self-defense" groups in the proposed amnesty, arguing that the groups were responsible for attacks on Tuareg civilians.

At the end of 1996 the FPLS and the ARLN reportedly left ORA to join the new UFRA (below) in an attempt to "rationalize" the Tuareg leadership situation. At that point it was not clear if Boula's FLAA would maintain the ORA structure, as FLAA appeared to be the dominant, and perhaps only, component in the ORA. Furthermore, the FLAA also appeared to have distanced itself from the 1995 accord. Such concerns were at least temporarily eased in September 1996 when the ORA reportedly integrated a number of its fighters into the government's newly formed "peacekeeping detachment." (In 1998 the ORA and the CRA turned in their weapons when parliament granted amnesty to the rebel groups in March.) In 1997 Boula was named to the Mayaki government. He remained in the new governments announced in January 2000 and September 2001, but was dismissed from his post as tourism minister in the Tandja government on February 13, 2004. Boula was then arrested and jailed for his alleged involvement in the assassination of a militant member of the ruling party, MNSD-*Nassara,* in January (see FLAA, below). He was released in March 2005, allegedly after his brother, rebel leader Mohamed ag Boula (see below), claimed he would not release four kidnapped soldiers until his brother was freed. (The hostages returned home in February 2005 after Libya helped secure their release.) Rhissa ag Boula left the ORA in August 2005 and became a leader of the UDPS-*Amana*; he was reported to be living in exile in France. In 2008 he was sentenced to death in absentia by a Nigerien court for the alleged assassination plot dating to 2004.

Leader: Attaher ABDOULMOUMINE.

Front for the Liberation of Air and Azaouad (*Front de Libération de l'Aïr et l'Azaouad*—FLAA). The Nigerien FLAA is a 400–1,000 member military wing of the greater Tuareg nomadic movement also active in Algeria and Mali. The FLAA "blue people," so-called because of the staining of their skin by their traditional blue cloth robes, are based in the Aïr mountains approximately 600 miles northeast of Niamey. The FLAA insurgency began in 1990 in response to the "exploitation and persecution" of the Tuareg nomads and sought the withdrawal of government forces and a broader distribution of the region's uranium ore wealth—although the Nigerien government denied the existence of any armed Tuareg group until early 1992.

FLAA activity increased dramatically in October 1991, as Tuareg officials criticized the recently concluded National Conference for failing to respect their "needs." Niamey responded to Tuareg demands for a troop withdrawal and greater autonomy in early 1992 by declaring its readiness to enter into formal negotiations with the insurgents. In mid-March the government reported that it had met with FLAA leaders, and on May 12 Niamey announced a truce, which Algeria and France would help mediate. Two weeks later, however, it accused the FLAA of violating the accord and authorized the army to take responsibility for security in the north. On August 27 Nigerien troops, later described as renegades by Niamey, launched a crackdown on alleged FLAA dissidents and sympathizers and arrested 186 people, including prominent Tuareg officials in the transitional government. The FLAA declared war and launched a series of offensives in early September. On September 14 FLAA representatives in Paris called on the United Nations to help end the "arbitrary treatment and terror imposed on the Tuareg civilian community."

Although the government claimed to have released 57 of the Tuareg detainees by late December 1992, the FLAA issued an ultimatum on December 31, threatening an even deeper crisis if all Tuareg prisoners were not immediately released. On January 9, 1993, nine MNSD-*Nassara* negotiators were killed and 20 FLAA fighters were killed or wounded when the FLAA launched an attack on the venue of negotiations with traditional Tuareg chiefs. In mid-March the FLAA, responding to MNSD-*Nassara* electoral losses, announced a truce as a peace offering to the new government; in April it released 26 prisoners of war and agreed to extend the truce as a goodwill gesture to President Ousmane. However, by midyear the party was buffeted by the defection of a number of top officials, led by Mano Dayak.

After the arrest of Rhissa ag Boula (see ORA, above), a leftist publication reported that resistance fighters had met in April 2004 and agreed to reestablish FLAA. In October 2004, combatants claiming to be members of FLAA clashed with government troops in the Aïr Mountains. Mohamed ag BOULA, brother of FLAA founder Rhissa ag Boula, claimed responsibility for the attack. In August 2005 it was reported that several hundred former FLAA members had joined the Libyan army (some analysts said Tripoli was suspected of financing the Tuareg rebellion in 1991). In October 2005 it was reported that the government had begun a program of economic aid to former rebels in the north and that the FLAA had disbanded.

Leaders: Mohamed ag BOULA, Mohammed EWANGAI.

Popular Front for the Liberation of the Sahara (*Front Populaire pour la Libération de la Sahara*—FPLS). The FPLS was launched on January 28, 1994, by Mohamed Anako and Issad Kato, who pledged to cooperate with existing Tuareg groups. In April 1999, Anako was reportedly appointed minister without portfolio and special adviser to head of state Maj. Daouda Wanké, a move some observers said was meant to avert further violence following Wanké's ascension after the assassination of President Maïnassara. Issad Kato, who had reestablished relations with the government, was named animal resources minister in 2007. Mohamed Anako in 2007 headed the Nigerien Commission for Peace, which called for dialogue with the Tuareg rebels, and was said to be an adviser to President Tandja.

Coordination of Armed Resistance (*Coordination de la Résistance Armée*—CRA). Originally formed in January 1994 by the FLAA, FPLS, ARLN, and FLT (below), the CRA met in Tenere in early February to elect an executive bureau and draft a platform calling for the creation of an autonomous Tuareg territory and Tuareg representation in the armed forces, government, and National Assembly. The coalition participated in talks with the government in Ouagadougou, Burkina Faso, in late February and in Paris in June, which ultimately resulted in a preliminary peace accord on October 9.

The CRA splintered in March 1995 following a disagreement between FLAA leader Boula and CRA chair Mano Dayak over the latter's approach to renewed peace negotiations. Immediately thereafter, Boula reorganized the CRA members, including the Dayak-led FLT, under the ORA banner; however, in June the FLT withdrew from the coalition. In July Dayak announced that he had revived the CRA; he would no longer respect the peace agreement and further negotiations would have to include his new Toubou and Arab allies (below).

In October 1995 FLT militants were accused of violating the peace accord; however, Dayak continued to negotiate with the government, and CRA officials pledged to proceed with peace talks following his death in a plane crash in December. Thereafter, at a summit of the leaders of the Tuareg and Toubou fronts in Kawar on March 8, 1996, the CRA agreed to recognize the 1995 peace accord and joined the others in declaring a unilateral cease-fire as a sign of support for the military regime. Consequently, the junta offered to include the CRA in its "application" of the treaty, and the group signed the accord on April 2.

A split between the CRA and the ORA was reported in November 1996, with the emergence of the new UFRA. Included in the "new" CRA were a number of Toubou and Arab autonomous movements based in the southeast who had complained of being ignored by the peace process.

Leaders: Mohamed AOUTCHEKI Kriska (FLT), Mohammed AKOTE.

Front for the Liberation of Tamoust (*Front pour la Libération de Tamoust*—FLT). The FLT was launched in July 1993 by Mano Dayak, previously one of the FLAA's chief negotiators, and a number of other former FLAA officials who sought continuation of the truce agreement reached with Niamey in March. (Dayak died in December 1995.) The FLT was the only Tuareg group to renew the accord in September; a month later its status was bolstered by the addition of another FLAA defector, Mohamed Aoutcheki Kriska.

FLT officials reportedly welcomed the 1996 coup, asserting that the military could "settle certain questions which could not be settled during the period of democracy," and on February 22 Aoutcheki was named as a special adviser to CSN Chair Maïnassara.

Leaders: Mohamed AOUTCHEKI Kriska, Mohammed EKIJI (Secretary General).

Democratic Renewal Front (*Front Démocratique pour le Renouvellement*—FDR). The FDR surfaced in May 1994 in the Lake Chad region under the leadership of Cpl. Ahmed Mohammed, a Nigerien who had served in the Libyan army. A militant group of members from the Arab Choa, Toubou, and Kanouri ethnic groups (who Mohammed claimed had been excluded from the greater Tuareg movement), the FDR professed dedication to "conducting the political and military battle" necessary to bring about the "annihilation" of the present governing system. The FDR's platform also advocated the division of Niger into federal states with boundaries conforming to "geographical and social reality."

In the first half of 1995 the FDR's clashes with government and Tuareg forces reportedly left over 40 people dead. At the same time, the group called attempts to implement the April 1995 peace accord the "facade of democracy" and urged Niamey to recognize their demands for autonomy. FDR/government clashes continued throughout 1996 and 1997.

In August 1998 the FDR signed a peace accord with the government, and party spokesperson Issa Lamine was named to the cabinet in January 2000.

Leaders: Cpl. Ahmed MOHAMMED, Mamane KODELAMI Ali, Goukouni ZENE, Issa LAMINE (Spokesperson).

Rebel Groups:

Armed Revolutionary Forces of the Sahara (*Forces Armées Révolutionnaires de la Sahara*—FARS). The primarily Toubou and Arab FARS gained international attention in February 1997 for kidnapping a Canadian aid worker and three Nigerien security officials in an effort to dramatize demands for an inquiry into the death of 14 FARS fighters in a clash with government forces the month before. Following peaceful resolution of that crisis, the FARS signed a cease-fire agreement with the government in June; however, that accord proved short-lived, and the FARS was subsequently reported to have formed an alliance with the UFRA before the latter grouping disarmed in 1998. In September 2001 the government launched a major crackdown that, among other things, resulted in the death of a FARS leader, Chahayi BARKAYE. In an effort to establish peace, France agreed to help finance the reintegration of some 250 FARS rebels into the northern region of Bilma.

FARS reemerged in 2006 when the group kidnapped and later released 11 tourists in protest against what the group claimed was the ongoing marginalization of the Toubous.

Leader: Barka OUARDOUGOU.

Movement of Nigeriens for Justice (*Mouvement des Nigériens pour la Justice*—MNJ). The Tuareg rebel group was not widely known until after it launched an attack against an army post near the northern town of Iferouane in February 2007. Following a series of attacks over the next several months against army installations, uranium mining sites, Red Cross convoys, and a northern airport, for which the MNJ claimed responsibility, the government refused to acknowledge the group's existence, instead blaming "bandits" and "drug traffickers." The MNJ accused the government of not upholding the tenets of the 1995 peace agreement with the Tuaregs, and called for more economic development in the north, including more equitable distribution of uranium profits; greater representation of Tuaregs in the government, the army, and the police; and government recognition of the MNJ (see Current issues, above). The MNJ reported in mid-2007 that some 700 army deserters had joined its group, including one high-ranking officer. It also claimed to have drawn support from Arabs, Fulani, and Toubou, as well as Tuaregs in Mali, the latter forming a group called the Niger-Mali Tuareg Alliance. In 2008 MNJ leaders stepped up their attacks, including strikes against uranium and oil interests. In June it was reported that MNJ vice president Mohamed Acharif had been killed by Nigerien soldiers. Throughout the year, the group continued to engage in fighting with government forces, rejecting a bid in August to disarm.

Leaders: Agali ag ALAMBO (President), Moktar ROMAN (Spokesperson).

LEGISLATURE

The unicameral **National Assembly** (*Assemblée Nationale*) was enlarged from 83 to 113 members in 2003, based on an increase of nearly 3 million in the country's population between 1998 and 2001. Members are directly elected for five-year terms: 105 from 8 multi-member constituencies using a proportional representation system, and the remainder from single-member constituencies using a first-past-the-post system.

The assembly elected in January 1995 was dissolved by the National Salvation Council on January 27, 1996, and replaced on March 27 by a 600-member transitional body known as the National Forum for Democratic Renewal, which included former assemblymen as well as members of various advisory groups supportive of the new military regime. Balloting for a new assembly was held on November 23, though it was boycotted by most major opposition groups.

On April 10, 1999, Prime Minister Mayaki suspended the assembly in the wake of the assassination of President Maïnassara. Balloting to refill the body was held on November 24, 1999, with the National Movement for a Developing Society–Victory securing 38 seats; the Democratic and Social Convention–*Rahama,* 17; the Nigerien Party for Democracy and Socialism–*Tarayya,* 16; the Democratic Rally of the People–*Jamaa,* 8; and the Nigerien Alliance for Democracy and Progress–*Zaman Lahiya,* 4.

In the most recent balloting on December 4, 2004, the seat distribution was as follows: The National Movement for a Developing Society–Victory, 47; the Nigerien Party for Democracy and Socialism–*Tarayya* (PNDS-*Tarayya*) and its allies, 25 (the PNDS-*Tarayya*, 17; the coalition of the PNDS-*Tarayya*, the Niger Progressive Party/African Democratic Rally [PPN/RDA], and the Niger Party for Self-Management-*Al Ouma*, 4; the coalition of the PNDS-*Tarayya*, the Union of Independent Nigeriens, and the Union for Democracy and the Republic-*Tabbat*, 2; and the coalition of the PNDS-*Tarayya*, the PPN/RDA, 2); the Democratic and Social Convention-*Rahama*, 22; the Rally for Social Democracy-*Gaskiya*, 7; the Democratic Rally of the People–*Jamaa*, 6; the Nigerien Alliance for Democracy and Progress–*Zaman Lahiya*, 5; and Nigerien Social Democratic Party–*Alheri*, 1. (*See headnote.*)

Speaker: Mahamane OUSMANE.

CABINET

[as of June 1, 2009]

Prime Minister	Seini Oumarou
Ministers	
African Integration	Saidou Hachimou
Agricultural Development	Mahaman Moussa
Animal Resources	Issad Kato
Basic Education and Literacy	Ousmane Samba Mamadou
Civil Service and Labor	Kanda Siptey [f]
Communications	Mohamed Ben Omar
Competition and the Fight Against the High Cost of Living	Vacant
Culture and Arts	Oumarou Hadary
Environment and the Fight Against Desertification	Mohamed Akotey
Equipment	Lamido Moumouni Harouna
Finance and Economy	Ali Lamine Zeine
Foreign Affairs and Cooperation	Aïchatou Mindaoudou [f]
Government Spokesman	Mohamed Ben Omar
Handicrafts and Tourism	Sanou Morou Fatouma [f]
Justice and Keeper of the Seals	Garba Lompo
Mines and Energy	Mohamed Abdoulahi
National Defense	Djida Hamadou
Niger Citizens Abroad	Saidou Hachimou
Population and Social Development	Boukari Zila Mahamadou [f]
Professional and Technical Training	Dagara Mamadou [f]
Promotion of Women and Protection of Children	Barry Bibata [f]
Promotion of Young Entrepreneurs	Maizama Hadiza [f]
Public Health and the Fight Against Endemic Diseases	Issa Lamine
Regional Planning and Community Development	Saade Souley [f]
Reform of Public Enterprises	Maizama Hadiza [f]
Relations with Institutions	Salifou Madou Kelzou
Religious Issues and Humanitarian Aid	Labo Issaka
Secondary and Higher Education, Research, and Technology	Sidikou Oumarou
Trade, Industry, and Normalization	Halidou Baque
Transport and Civil Aviation	Col. Issa Mazou
Urban Affairs and Housing	Diallo Aïssa Abdoulaye [f]
Water Resources	Tassiou Aminoiu
Youth and Sport	Salo Gobi
Minister of State	
Interior and Decentralization	Albade Abouba

[f] = female

COMMUNICATIONS

While press freedom in Niger have remained relatively stable, according to the international watchdog group Reporters Without Borders, journalists have been periodically arrested and detained on charges of defamation and "inciting ethnic hatred." According to Africa News, government authorities in 2007 "continued to use censorship and criminal defamation laws to silence the private press in response to accusations of corruption or mismanagement of public resources." Promises by President Mamadou Tandja to decriminalize media offenses have yet to come to fruition.

As the conflict with Tuareg rebels escalated in 2007–2008, several journalists were arrested and imprisoned on charges of breaching national security (for interviewing rebels), and the privately owned radio station Sahara FM, which operated in a northern city, was shut down for reporting alleged abuses by soldiers. Journalists were barred by the government from entering the northern region to report on the fighting and its consequences, and at least one journalist was killed in 2008 when the vehicle he was riding in hit a landmine in a suburb of the capital. It was unclear whether it was a targeted attack. In July a judge dismissed a case against a French journalist who had been imprisoned for 10 months for alleged contacts with the rebel group Movement of Nigeriens for Justice (*Mouvement des Nigériens pour la Justice*—MNJ).

Also in 2008, the managing editor of the independent weekly *L'Eveil Plus* was sentenced to one month in prison after being convicted on a charge of contempt of justice in connection with an article about embezzlement cases, and the founder and managing editor of *L'Enquêteur* were each sentenced to a month in prison on libel charges. The government subsequently imposed a media blackout in the north and banned journalists from the area of conflict.

Press. The following are published in French in Niamey: *Le Sahel* (5,000), daily news bulletin of the government Information Service; *Le Sahel Dimanche* (4,000), weekly publication of the government Information Service. An independent monthly, *La Marche,* was introduced in August 1989, while an independent weekly, *Le Républicain* (3,000), commenced publication in 1991. Other publications include *Le Tribune du Peuple* (3,000), daily in French, and the weekly, *Le Démocrate.* There are a number of other small newspapers, some of which were subjected in 2000 to government crackdowns, which, in turn, led journalists to charge that the administration was intent on "silencing" the independent press. In 2006 two journalists from *Le Républicain* were sentenced to 18 months in jail and a large fine for allegedly writing an editorial critical of former prime minister Hama Amadou, and a journalist from the private bimonthly *L'Enquêteur* received a six-month sentence after the government claimed he had published false information. The bimonthly *Air Info,* published in Agadez, was shut down for three months in mid-2007 following government allegations that it had printed articles "undermining the morale of troops" in the wake of fighting with Tuareg rebels. *Air Info* had published articles critical of government security forces and had called for the resignation of an army chief. The government also cracked down on a radio station and three weeklies, issuing warnings to *Le Démocrate, L'Evénement,* and *Opinion* for "directly reproducing news taken from rebel websites, without any professional treatment."

News agency: The government launched *Agence Nigérienne de Press* (ANP) in late 1986.

Broadcasting and computing. The Office de Radiodiffusion-*Télévision du Niger* (ORTN) operates *La Voix du Sahel,* a government radio service broadcasting in French, English, and indigenous languages, and also services nine television stations. Private stations include Anfani FM, Tambara FM, Horizon FM, Sahara FM, Tenere FM and television, R&M radio, and Telestar television. As of 2008 there were 5.4 Internet users per 1,000 inhabitants.

INTERGOVERNMENTAL REPRESENTATION

Ambassador to the U.S.: Aminata Maiga DJIBRILLA.

U.S. Ambassador to Niger: Bernadette Mary ALLEN.

Permanent Representative to the UN: Aboubacar Ibrahim ABANI.

IGO Memberships (Non-UN): AfDB, AU, BADEA, BOAD, CENT, CILSS, ECOWAS, IDB, Interpol, IOM, NAM, OIC, OIF, UEMOA, WCO, WTO.

NIGERIA

Federal Republic of Nigeria

Political Status: Independent member of the Commonwealth since 1960; republic established in 1963; civilian government suspended as the result of military coups in January and July 1966; executive presidential system established under constitution effective October 1, 1979; under military rule following successive coups of December 31, 1983, and August 27, 1985; constitution of Third Republic promulgated May 3, 1989; existing state organs dissolved following military takeover of November 17, 1993; 1979 constitution restored and Provisional Ruling Council established on November 21, 1993; current constitution entered into effect May 29, 1999, with installation of new civilian government.

Area: 356,667 sq. mi. (923,768 sq. km.).

Population: 140,003,542 (2006C); 153,754,000 (2008E). The 1991 census was undertaken with far greater care than a 1973 predecessor, the results of which were officially repudiated as being grossly inflated insofar as the northern count was concerned. On the other hand, estimates in 1988 ranged as high as 105 million, raising the possibility that the 1991 figure (88,992,220) might be unrealistically low. The suspicion was enhanced in November 1994 by the Constitutional Convention's "rejection" of the 1991 results. The 2006 figure is provisional.

Major Urban Centers (1991C): ABUJA (107,069), Lagos (5,195,247), Kano (2,166,554), Ibadan (1,835,300), Kaduna (933,642), Benin City (762,719), Port Harcourt (703,421), Maiduguri (618,278), Zaria (612,257), Ilorin (532,089), Jos (512,300). The 1991 figure for Lagos was unquestionably conservative, a UN estimate for mid-2000 being 10,103,000. Other 2000 estimates: Kano (2,763,000), Ibadan (2,284,000), Kaduna (1,273,000).

Official Language: English (the leading indigenous languages are Hausa, Igbo, and Yoruba).

Monetary Unit: Naira (official rate December 1, 2009: 146.50 naira = $1US).

President: Umaru Musa YAR'ADUA (People's Democratic Party); popularly elected on April 21, 2007, and inaugurated for a four-year term on May 29 in succession to Gen. (Ret.) Olusegun OBASANJO (People's Democratic Party).

Vice President: Goodluck JONATHAN (People's Democratic Party); elected on April 21, 2007, and inaugurated for a term concurrent with the president on May 29 in succession to Atiku ABUBAKAR (elected as a member of People's Democratic Party but subsequently [in 2007] a member of Action Congress).

THE COUNTRY

The most populous country in Africa and one of the most richly endowed in natural resources, Nigeria extends from the inner corner of the Gulf of Guinea to the border of Niger in the north and to Lake Chad in the northeast. Included within its boundaries is the northern section of the former United Nations Trust Territory of British Cameroons, whose inhabitants voted to join Nigeria in a United Nations–sponsored plebiscite in 1961. Nigeria's topography ranges from swampy lowland along the coast, through tropical rain forest and open plateau country, to semidesert conditions in the far north. The ethnic pattern is similarly varied, with tribal groups speaking more than 250 languages. The Hausa, Fulani, and other Islamic peoples in the north, the mixed Christian and Islamic Yoruba in the west, and the predominantly Christian Ibo in the east are the most populous groups. In the absence of reliable information (ethnic identification being excluded from the 1991 census), it has been estimated that nearly half the population is Muslim,

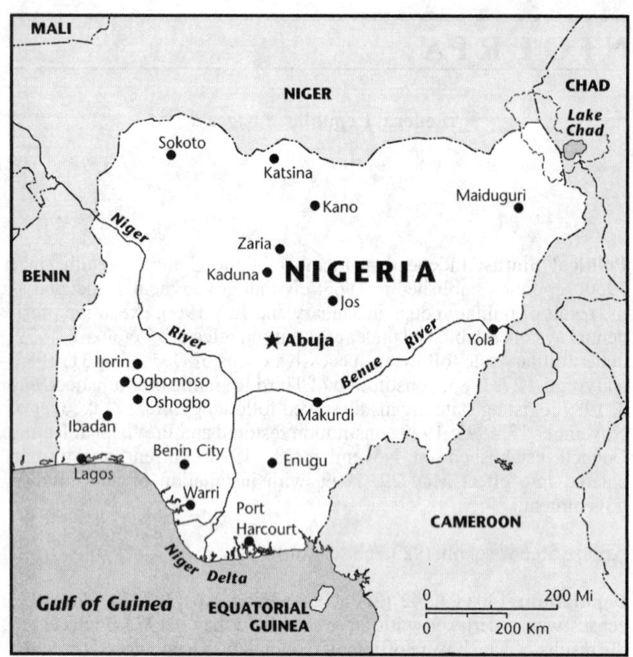

with 35 percent being Christian and the remainder adhering to traditional religious practices. Numerous traditional rulers retain considerable influence, particularly in rural areas. Women are responsible for the bulk of subsistence farming, and their participation in the paid work force (about 36 percent) is concentrated in sales and crafts.

Nigeria's natural resources include petroleum and natural gas, hydroelectric power, and commercially exploitable deposits of tin, coal, and columbite. Oil production of 2.2 million barrels per day accounts for an estimated 90 percent of exports and provides 80 percent of the government's revenue; some 60–90 percent of Nigerian crude, considered ideal for gasoline production, is exported to the United States. The leading cash crops are cocoa, peanuts, palm products, and cotton, with timber and fish also important.

The oil boom of the 1970s produced rapid industrial expansion led by consumer nondurables, vehicle assembly, aluminum smelting, and steel production. However, a world glut reduced oil revenue from $26 billion in 1980 to $5.6 billion in 1986, precipitating industrial contraction and cutbacks in government and personal spending, with per capita income dipping by more than half (from $670 to $300) during 1979–1988. Thus, a structural adjustment program launched in 1986 was actually more stringent than a number of International Monetary Fund (IMF) austerity plans that Lagos had previously been unwilling to adopt. It focused on reviving non-oil exports, achieving a realistic naira exchange rate, and discouraging the purchase of luxury goods. Not surprisingly, nationwide protests against the program were reported in 1987 and 1988, with particularly violent confrontations erupting in May–June 1989.

In January 1994 the Abacha government presented a budget that abandoned virtually all of the 1986 reforms. Subsequently, in the wake of sharp criticism from international lenders, the January 1995 budget revived free-market policies. The economy nonetheless remained severely distressed under the influence of rampant governmental corruption, external debt of more than $33 billion, and ongoing concern over the nation's political future. Abacha's successor, Gen. Abdulsalam Abubakar, moved quickly in 1998 to mend relations with the World Bank and the IMF, pledging to speed up the privatization of state-run industries and combat corruption. Moreover, in January 1999 the government abolished the heavily criticized dual-rate system of foreign exchange (which had allowed officials and favored segments of the business community to purchase U.S. dollars at one-fourth the market rate), and Lagos announced the end of its ten-year rift with the IMF, with which it had begun new negotiations on easing its huge debt burden. Although the IMF approved new lending in August 2001, it continued to criticize the government's economic management.

Increased federal and state spending subsequently undermined the government's efforts to secure foreign assistance for debt relief. The World Bank also reduced its lending program to Nigeria by half in 2003. In an effort to spur long-term growth, the government implemented a new program to repair decaying infrastructure such as roads and pipelines. Meanwhile, a broad effort was initiated to recover part of the estimated $2.2 billion that was reportedly funneled out of the country during the tenure of President Abacha.

High oil prices provided significant additional resources in 2004–2005 for the government, which, among other things, established a $6 billion "emergency fund." Satisfied with the government's recent reform efforts, the IMF in 2005 announced new aid. Late in the year, the Paris Club of creditor nations accepted an agreement under which Nigeria could fulfill its obligation to them by paying only $12 billion of the $30 billion owed. In April 2006 the government announced that it had made its final payment to the Paris Club members.

GDP rose by 6.0 percent in 2006 and 6.3 percent in 2007 (primarily as a result of higher oil prices and significant growth in the non-oil sector), while inflation declined dramatically to 5.4 percent in 2007. A modest increase in foreign investment also contributed to the improved economic outlook, as did significant advances in the telecommunication and financial sectors. However, intensified antigovernment activity in the oil-rich Niger Delta subsequently continued to constrain oil production, while most analysts concluded that corruption remained entrenched throughout all levels of government and business, hampering efforts to reduce the 55 percent poverty level. In 2008 the government began to implement IMF—recommended reforms to the banking and fuel sectors. In November 2008, Nigeria agreed to reduce its oil output by 113,000 barrels per day as part of an effort to stabilize world oil prices. In spite of the reduction and the concurrent global recession, GDP rose by 5.3 percent that year and official unemployment remained low at 5.5 percent, however, inflation spiked to 11.6 percent. In its 2009 Doing Business survey, the World Bank ranked Nigeria 125 out of 183 countries in terms of ease of conducting commerce.

GOVERNMENT AND POLITICS

Political background. Brought under British control during the 19th century, Nigeria was organized as a British colony and protectorate in 1914, became a self-governing federation in 1954, and achieved independence within the Commonwealth on October 1, 1960. Under the guidance of its first prime minister, Sir Abubaker Tafawa BALEWA, Nigeria became a republic three years later, with the former governor general, Dr. Nnamdi AZIKIWE of the Ibo tribe, as president. The original federation consisted of three regions (northern, western, and eastern); a fourth region (the midwestern) was created in 1963.

Though initially regarded as one of the most potentially viable of the new African states, independent Nigeria experienced underlying tensions resulting from ethnic, religious, and regional cleavages. Weakened by strife and tainted by corruption, the federal government was overthrown on January 15, 1966, in a coup that cost the lives of Prime Minister Balewa and other northern political leaders and resulted in the establishment of a Supreme Military Council (SMC) headed by Maj. Gen. Johnson T.U. AGUIYI-IRONSI, the Ibo commander of the army. Resentment on the part of northern Muslims toward the predominantly Ibo leadership and its subsequent attempt to establish a unitary state resulted on July 29 in a second coup, led by a northerner, Col. (later Gen.) Yakubu GOWON. Events surrounding the first coup had already raised ethnic hostility to the boiling point, and thousands of Ibo who had settled in the north were massacred before and after the second coup, while hundreds of thousands began a mass flight back to their homeland at the urging of eastern leaders.

Subsequent plans for a constitutional revision that would calm Ibo apprehensions while preserving the unity of the country were blocked by the refusal of the Eastern Region's military governor, Lt. Col. Odumegwu OJUKWU, to accept anything less than complete regional autonomy. Attempts at conciliation having failed, Colonel Gowon, as head of the federal military government, announced his assumption of emergency powers and the reorganization of Nigeria's 4 regions into 12 states on May 28, 1967. Intended to equalize treatment of various areas and ethnic groups throughout the country, the move was also designed to increase the influence of the Eastern Region's non-Ibo inhabitants. The Eastern Region responded on May 30 by declaring independence as the Republic of Biafra, with Ojukwu as head of state. Refusing to recognize the secession, the federal government initiated hostilities against Biafra on July 6. Peace plans were subsequently proposed by London, the Commonwealth, and the Organization of African Unity (OAU, subsequently the African Union—AU). However, Ojukwu rejected them repeatedly on the ground that they failed to guarantee Biafra's future as a "sovereign and independent state." Limited external support, mainly from France, began to arrive in late 1968 and enabled Biafra to continue fighting despite the loss of most non-Ibo territory, massive casualties, and a growing threat of mass starvation. A series of military defeats in late 1969 and early 1970 finally resulted in surrender of the rebel forces on January 15, 1970.

The immediate postwar period was one of remarkable reconciliation, as General Gowon moved to reintegrate Ibo elements into Nigerian life. Not only were Ibo brought back into the civil service and the military, but the federal government also launched a major reconstruction of the devastated eastern area. Normal political life remained suspended, however, and on July 29, 1975, while Gowon was attending an OAU meeting in Kampala, Uganda, his government was overthrown in a bloodless coup led by Brig. (later Gen.) Murtala Ramat MUHAMMAD. In October the SMC charged a 50-member committee with drafting a new constitution that would embrace an "executive presidential system."

General Muhammad was assassinated on February 13, 1976, during an abortive coup apparently provoked by his campaign to wipe out widespread government corruption. He was succeeded as head of state and chair of the SMC by Lt. Gen. (later Gen.) Olusegun OBASANJO, who had been chief of staff of the armed forces since the 1975 coup.

A National Constituent Assembly met in 1977 to consider the constitution proposed by the committee established two years earlier. The assembly endorsed a draft on June 5, 1978, although the SMC made a number of changes before the new basic law was promulgated on September 21, at which time Nigeria's 12-year-old state of emergency was terminated and the ban on political parties was lifted.

Elections were contested in mid-1979 by five parties that had been approved by the Federal Electoral Commission (Fedeco) as being sufficiently national in representation. Balloting commenced on July 7 for the election of federal senators and continued, on successive weekends, with the election of federal representatives, state legislators, and state governors, culminating on August 11 with the election of Alhaji Shehu SHAGARI and Dr. Alex EKWUEME of the National Party of Nigeria (NPN) as federal president and vice president, respectively. Following judicial resolution of a complaint that the NPN candidates had not obtained a required 25 percent of the vote in 13 of the 19 states, the two leaders were inaugurated on October 1.

By 1983 public confidence in the civilian regime had waned in the face of sharply diminished oil income, massive government overspending, and widespread evidence of official corruption. Nonetheless, the personally popular Shagari easily won reelection in the presidential balloting of August 4. Subsequent rounds of the five-week election process, marred by evidence of electoral fraud and by rioting in Oyo and Ondo states, left the ruling NPN in control of 13 state houses, 13 governorships, and both houses of the National Constituent Assembly. However, the economy continued to decline after the balloting, with an austerity budget adopted in November further deepening public discontent. On December 31 a group of senior military officers (most of whom had served under Obasanjo) seized power. On January 3, 1984, Maj. Gen. Muhammadu BUHARI, formerly Obasanjo's oil minister, was sworn in as chair of a new SMC, which launched a "war against indiscipline," reintroduced the death penalty, and established several special tribunals that moved vigorously in convicting numerous individuals, including leading politicians, of embezzlement and other offenses.

In the wake of increasing political repression and a steadily worsening economy, Major General Buhari and his armed forces chief of staff, Maj. Gen. Tunde IDIAGBON, were deposed by senior members of the SMC on August 27, 1985. The ensuing administration, headed by Maj. Gen. (later Gen.) Ibrahim BABANGIDA as chair of a new Armed Forces Ruling Council (AFRC), abolished a number of decrees limiting press freedom, released numerous political detainees, and initially adopted a more open style of government that included the solicitation of public opinion on future political development. However, there was a countercoup attempt late in the year by a group of disgruntled officers, several of whom were executed in March 1986.

In September 1987, the Babangida regime announced a five-year transition to civilian government, including the promulgation of a new constitution, lifting of the ban on political parties in 1989, gubernatorial and state legislative elections in 1990, and federal legislative and presidential elections in 1992. To guard against tribal and religious fractionalization, the AFRC adopted the recommendation of a university-dominated "Political Bureau" that only two political parties be sanctioned. Late in 1987 Babangida announced that most former and current leaders, including himself and the rest of the AFRC, would be barred from running in forthcoming elections. Local nonparty elections were held on December 12, 1987; however, many of the results from that poll were invalidated, and further balloting was conducted on March 26, 1988.

In May 1989 General Babangida lifted the ban on party politics, calling on parties to register with the National Electoral Commission (NEC) and announcing details of a draft constitution that had been presented to him in April by the National Constituent Assembly. Although more than 50 parties were reportedly interested in securing recognition, a short enrollment period and a complex application process limited the number of actual petitioners to 13, 6 of which were subsequently recommended to the AFRC for further reduction to 2. However, on October 7, amid reports of the arrest of members of "illegal" parties, Babangida cited "factionalism" and "failing marks" on preregistration examinations as reasons for dissolving all 13 parties and substituting in their place the regime-sponsored Social Democratic Party (SDP) and National Republican Convention (NRC).

In January 1990 General Babangida canceled state visits to Italy and the United States in the wake of widespread unrest provoked by a December 29 reshuffle of senior military and civilian officials. The tension culminated in a coup attempt on April 22 in Lagos by middle-ranked army officers, with at least 30 persons being killed in heavy fighting. On August 30 General Babangida announced another extensive cabinet reshuffle and the appointment of Vice Admiral Augustus AIKHOMU to the newly created position of vice president of the republic. Shortly thereafter, in furtherance of General Babangida's plan to "demilitarize" politics, Aikhomu and a number of other senior government leaders retired from military service, while ten military state governors were replaced by civilian deputies pending the upcoming gubernatorial elections. Meanwhile, organization of the SDP and NRC continued under stringent government supervision, with two-party local elections being held on December 8.

Neither of the parties secured a clear advantage in the 1990 local poll or in gubernatorial and state assembly elections in December 1991, although the SDP won control of both the Senate and House of Representatives in National Constituent Assembly balloting on July 4, 1992. Party presidential primaries (on August 7 and again on September 12, 19, and 26) were invalidated on grounds of widespread irregularities, with presidential balloting originally slated for December 5 being rescheduled to June 1993. Concurrently, General Babangida announced that the AFRC would be replaced by a National Defense and Security Council (NDSC) and that the existing Council of Ministers would be abolished in favor of a civilian Transitional Council to pave the way for the planned installation of a new government in August 1993. On December 15, 1992, Chief Ernest Adegunle SHONEKAN was named to chair the Transitional Council, which, along with the NDSC, was formally installed on January 4, 1993.

The long-delayed presidential balloting was held on June 12, 1993, with the SDP candidate, reputed billionaire Moshood Kashimawo Olawale ("MKO") ABIOLA, appearing to be the winner over the NRC's Bashir Othma TOFA. However, on June 16 the NEC bowed to a court order restraining it from announcing the outcome. The two parties thereupon agreed to form an interim coalition government if General Babangida would authorize a return to civilian rule by the previously agreed upon date of August 27. The general's response being negative, serious rioting erupted in Lagos on July 5, followed by the announcement that a new election, from which the earlier candidates would be excluded, would take place on July 31. Not surprisingly, this plan was scuttled, with Babangida naming Shonekan as head of an Interim National Government (ING) before stepping down as president on August 26. On September 19 the NEC announced that new presidential and local elections would be held on February 19, 1994. However, on November 10 the Federal High Court unexpectedly pronounced the ING unconstitutional, and on November 17 Shonekan resigned in favor of a new military administration headed by Defense Minister Sani ABACHA, who had long been viewed as the "power behind the throne" of both the Babangida and Shonekan governments. Subsequently, Abacha formally dissolved both the ING and the National Constituent Assembly, banned the SDP and NRC, and, on November 24, announced the formation of a Provisional Ruling Council (PRC) comprised of senior military figures and several members of a new cabinet-level Federal Executive Council (FEC).

On April 22, 1994, the Abacha regime outlined the first phase of a political transition program that called for the convening of a constitutional conference to prepare a draft basic law for approval by the PRC.

Elections were held nationwide in May to select the conference participants, although the balloting was boycotted by a number of prodemocracy groups as well as organizations representing southern interests. On June 22, 1994, Moshood Abiola, who, based on the 1993 poll, had declared himself president 11 days earlier, emerged from hiding to address a rally in Lagos; he was arrested the following day for treason. On June 27 General Abacha opened a National Constitutional Conference (NCC), which was promptly adjourned for two weeks because of "logistical problems." Subsequently a large number of strikes erupted to protest Abiola's arrest and resumption of the NCC. The most serious of the stoppages was by the oil unions, whose resistance crumbled in late August after the PRC had replaced their leaders with military-appointed administrators. On September 6, 1994, the PRC issued several new decrees that restricted the media and precluded legal challenges to action taken by the regime in regard to "the maintenance of law and order." Further underscoring the regime's hard-line approach, the new 25-member PRC formed on September 27 contained only military officers, even though 4 of the 11 members on the previous council had been civilians. Meanwhile, NCC sessions continued, and in October the conference gave its preliminary endorsement to a draft constitution (see Constitution and government, below). In addition, the NCC in December formally notified the military that the conference expected the transition to a civilian government to be accomplished by January 1, 1996. Initially appearing to support that schedule, the PRC dissolved the FEC on February 8, 1995, so that members of the council could "prepare for their upcoming political careers." However, the new FEC, which was appointed on March 20, reportedly favored an extension of military control, the apparent policy change being attributed to turbulence surrounding the recent arrest of a group of military officers and civilians in connection with an alleged coup plot. Consequently, on April 25 the NCC reversed its earlier decision regarding the deadline for a return to civilian government and approved a new resolution granting the Abacha regime what amounted to an open-ended tenure. As a result, the final NCC report, submitted to Abacha on June 27, contained the draft of a new basic law but no proposed timetable for its implementation.

The international criticism prompted by the apparent retrenchment on democratization (see Current issues in the Nigeria article in the 2007 *Handbook* for details) intensified sharply when minority rights activist Kenule SARO-WIWA and other members of the Movement for the Survival of the Ogoni People (MOSOP) were hung on November 10, 1995, soon after their conviction on what were perceived outside the government to be highly dubious murder charges. However, the regime angrily rejected what it termed external meddling in its domestic affairs and refused to reevaluate its proposed timetable, which called for the government to turn authority over to an elected civilian government on October 1, 1998.

Consequently, Nigeria entered 1996 regarded internationally as a "pariah state," and developments over the next year did little to alter that situation. The government refused to permit Commonwealth representatives into the country until November and, even then, blocked access to prisoners such as former president Obasanjo (jailed since March 1995 on what most analysts considered spurious coup plot charges) and Mobiola. In addition, following a fact-finding mission to Nigeria in March, the UN Human Rights Committee accused the government, already considered one of the most repressive in Nigeria's history, of a wide range of abuses.

Local elections were held on March 16, 1996, although political parties remained proscribed. The campaign period was limited to only five days, and balloting was conducted by having voters line up behind their preferred candidate, a practice long criticized by prodemocracy activists. Facing ongoing internal and external pressure, the government in June issued regulations for the proposed legalization of a limited number of political parties, five of which were recognized in September, although the initiative elicited only scorn from prodemocracy groups. Six new states were established on October 1, and the government announced that 183 additional municipalities would be created for the next local elections, with balloting to be conducted on a limited multiparty basis.

Two bomb attacks in Lagos killed several soldiers and wounded more than 30 other people in January and February 1997; no groups claimed responsibility. The government subsequently intensified its crackdown on opposition groups, among other things charging Nobel Prize winner Wole SOYINKA (in self-imposed exile) and 14 other dissidents with treason in March. Spokespersons for the regime linked several subsequent attacks to the National Democratic Coalition (NADECO), although impartial observers strongly questioned any such connection and suggested the government was merely attempting to silence some of its more effective critics. Harassment was also reported of journalists who questioned the regime. New local elections were held on March 15, 1997, followed by balloting for state assemblies on December 6. Meanwhile, on November 17 President Abacha announced that the cabinet had been dissolved, a number of incumbent senior ministers being left out of the new government appointed on December 18.

In national legislative elections on April 25, 1998, the United Nigeria Congress Party (UNCP) reportedly captured the majority of the seats. Voter turnout was described as scant (as little as 10 percent in some areas), with many Nigerians apparently heeding the opposition's call for a boycott of the contest. Meanwhile, Abacha was reportedly named as the candidate of all the legal parties for the upcoming presidential election. On June 8 Abacha died of an apparent heart attack, and the following day Gen. Abdulsalam ABUBAKAR was sworn in as his replacement. Opposition militants derided Abubakar's inaugural pledge to adhere to his predecessor's transitional program, and in mid-June government troops forcibly broke up an opposition demonstration. Thereafter, Abubakar approved the release of dozens of political prisoners, and in early July UN Secretary General Kofi Annan announced that the regime was preparing to release all political prisoners, including Abiola, who had reportedly agreed to relinquish his claim to the presidency. However, on July 7 (the eve of his release) Abiola fell ill during a meeting with a high-level U.S. mission and died. On July 8, General Abubakar dissolved the five legal parties as well as the government that had been named by General Abacha. Two weeks later Abubakar called for the creation of an "unfettered" democracy and announced that he would soon release all political prisoners and allow the free formation of political parties. To that end, in early August the regime appointed a 14-member electoral commission, the Independent National Electoral Commission (INEC), which it charged with overseeing a transitional schedule expected to culminate in the return to civilian rule in May 1999. On August 21 Abubakar named a new cabinet, which included only five holdovers from the Abacha government. Four days later, the INEC released an electoral timetable calling for local elections in December, gubernatorial polling in January 1999, and legislative and presidential balloting on February 20 and 27, respectively. Twenty-five political groups applied for provisional legal status between August 27 and September 5, and nine were subsequently registered. However, in local elections in December only three of those parties—the People's Democratic Party (PDP), the All People's Party (APP), and the Alliance for Democracy (AD)—secured the minimum vote tally (at least 5 percent in 24 of the 36 states) required to maintain their legal status and continue on to the next electoral stages. The PDP, under the leadership of General Obasanjo, led all parties in the local balloting with approximately 60 percent of the vote.

In gubernatorial elections held January 9–30, 1999, the PDP once again overwhelmed its competitors, capturing 21 of the 36 state houses (unrest in the state of Bayelsa had forced officials to postpone balloting there from January 9 to January 30). Seeking to prevent further PDP domination, the APP and AD subsequently announced their intention to form an electoral alliance and forward a joint candidate for president. On February 5 the INEC ruled that such an alliance would be illegal; however, faced with an APP/AD threat to boycott further elections, the commission subsequently reversed itself, although it precluded the two groups from using a single symbol on ballot papers.

The PDP won approximately two-thirds of the seats in both the Senate and House of Representatives in poorly attended legislative polling on February 20, 1999. In presidential balloting on February 27, General Obasanjo completed the sweep for the PDP, capturing 62.8 percent of the vote and easily defeating Samuel Oluyemisi ("Olu") FALAE, the APP/AD candidate. International observers asserted that the elections "generally" reflected the "will of the people" but refused to describe them as free and fair because both sides appeared to have tried to rig the balloting. Obasanjo was sworn in on May 29, and on the same day the new constitution (signed by General Abubakar on May 5) also came into effect. On June 28 Obasanjo swore in a new 47-member cabinet, claiming the large size was necessary to represent Nigeria's ethnic and regional diversity. The government included representatives from all 36 states as well as ministers from all three registered parties.

The incoming Obasanjo administration and PDP-dominated legislature confronted economic, political, and social problems of immense proportions in 1999. Among the most pressing issues awaiting the new government were violent political and social unrest in the economically critical oil-producing regions, a decayed infrastructure, and a treasury depleted by corruption. As a first step in his anticorruption program, Obasanjo in June expelled 60 senior military officers and suspended all contracts negotiated by the Abacha government.

Ethnic tensions in the oil-producing Niger Delta escalated throughout the fall of 1999, resulting in the deployment of 2,000 government troops to the state of Bayelsa. Political discord increased significantly in June 2001 when religious and ethnic conflict between Christians and Muslims in the northern state of Bauchi left 1,000 dead. Another 1,000 were killed in continuing violence in the region before the end of the year. One area of dispute involved Muslim efforts to implement sharia (Islamic religious law) in the region. (A dozen northern states instituted sharia, despite opposition from the federal government.) In addition, a series of general strikes by oil workers threatened to disrupt production.

The registration of political parties having begun in 2002, multiparty legislative and presidential elections were held on April 12, 2003. The PDP again won a commanding majority in both the House of Representatives and the Senate, its strongest opposition coming from the All Nigeria People's Party (ANPP), the successor to the APP. Gubernatorial races were also held on April 19, and the PDP secured 29 of the 36 governorships. In addition, the PDP also won about two-thirds of the total seats in the state assemblies in elections held May 3.

President Obasanjo was reelected with 62 percent of the vote in balloting on April 19, 2003, that was contested by 20 candidates. His closest rival was former SMC chair Buhari, with 32 percent; no other candidate received more than 3.5 percent of the vote. Buhari challenged the results, but the federal Court of Appeal ruled in favor of Obasanjo, who was inaugurated on May 29. However, it was not until July 17 that Obasanjo was able to form a new federal government.

President Obasanjo's second term was initially marked by efforts at economic reform and a broad range of anticorruption campaigns, but strikes and other problems in the petroleum sector continued to constrain the government's efforts. On May 18, 2004, because of the escalating violence between Christians and Muslims in the region, Obasanjo declared a state of emergency for Plateau State and ordered the federal government to take control from the state governor and assembly, the first time that the federal government had taken over a state since 1962. A similar state of emergency was also declared in Ekiti in October 2006.

In January 2007 President Obasanjo announced a major cabinet reshuffle in which a number of ministries were eliminated. The initiative was presented as a means of streamlining the government and reducing corruption, with a view toward enhancing the ruling party's domestic approval in advance of the 2007 elections.

The PDP dominated the elections for governorships and state assemblies on April 14, 2007, as well as the federal balloting for the Senate and House of Representatives on April 21. Also on April 21, Umaru Musa YAR'ADUA, nominated by the PDP after efforts to revise the constitution to permit President Obasanjo to run for a third term were blocked, handily won the presidential poll, securing more than 70 percent of the vote. Following his inauguration on May 29, the new president formed what he described as a new "government of national unity" on July 26. Although dominated by the PDP, the new cabinet was noteworthy for the inclusion of independents and members of the ANNP and several other new small parties.

Yar'Adua initiated a major cabinet reshuffle in October 2008 and finalized the new government in December. Another, minor, reshuffle occurred in July 2009, as part of a broader anti-corruption campaign by the government that included a program to spend more than $2 billion to reform the federal security forces (see Current issues, below).

Constitution and government. Before General Muhammad's assassination in February 1976, he had announced that the 12 states created in 1967 would be expanded to 19 to alleviate the domination of subunits by traditional ethnic and religious groups, thus helping "to erase memories of past political ties and emotional attachments." A decree establishing the new states was subsequently promulgated by General Obasanjo. A centrally located area of some 3,000 square miles was also designated as a federal capital territory, with the federal administration to be transferred (a process declared completed in late 1991) from Lagos to the new capital of Abuja.

In September 1987 two new states, Katsina and Akwa Ibom, were created out of territory formerly in Kaduna and Cross River, respectively. President Babangida subsequently announced that his administration would not consider additional changes. However, in August 1991 he reversed himself with a decision to further increase the number of states to 30 based on "social justice, the principle of development, and the principle of a balanced federation." On October 1, 1996, President Abacha announced the creation of six more states, one in each region, arguing that the expansion would serve the "decentralization" process. It was also announced that 183 new municipalities would be established, bringing the total to 776.

Region (Pre-1967)	*State (1967)*	*State (1987)*	*State and Capital (1996)*
Northern	Benue Plateau	Benue	Benue (Makurdi)
			† Kogi (Lokoja)*
		Plateau	Plateau (Jos)
			‡ Nassatawa (Lafia)
	Kano	Kano	Kano (Kano)
			† Jigawa (Dutse)
	Kwara	Kwara	Kwara (Ilorin)
	North-Central	Kaduna	Kaduna (Kaduna)
		Katsina	Katsina (Katsina)
	North-Eastern	Bauchi	Bauchi (Bauchi)
			‡ Gombe (Gombe)
		Borno	Borno (Maiduguri)
			† Yobe (Damaturu)
		Gongola	† Adamawa (Yola)
			† Taraba (Jalingo)
	North-Western	Niger	Niger (Minna)
		Sokoto	Sokoto (Sokoto)
			‡ Kebbi (Birnin Kebbi)
			‡ Zamfara (Gusau)
Eastern	East-Central	Anambra	Anambra (Akwa)
			† Enugu (Enugu)
		Imo	Imo (Owerri)
			† Abia (Umuahia)
			‡ Ebonyi (Abakaliki)**
	Rivers	Rivers	Rivers (Port Harcourt)
			‡ Bayelsa (Yenagoa)
	South-Eastern	Cross River	Cross River (Calabar)
		Akwa Ibom	Akwa Ibom (Uyo)
Mid-Western	Mid-Western	Bendel	† Delta (Asaba)
			† Edo (Benin)
Western	Lagos	Lagos	Lagos (Ikeja)
	Western	Ogun	Ogun (Abeokuta)
		Ondo	Ondo (Akure)
			‡ Ekiti (Ado-Ekiti)
		Oyo	Oyo (Ibadan)
			† Osun (Oshogbo)

Note: † created in 1991

‡ created in 1996

*also includes territory from Kwara

**also includes territory from Enugu

The 1979 constitution established a U.S.-style federal system with powers divided among three federal branches (executive, legislative, and judicial) and between federal and state governments. Executive authority at the national level was vested in a president and vice president who ran on a joint ticket and served four-year terms. To be declared the victor on a first ballot, a presidential candidate was required to win a plurality of the national popular vote and at least one-quarter of the vote in two-thirds of the (then) 19 states. Legislative power was invested in a bicameral National Assembly comprising a 95-member Senate and a 449-member House of Representatives.

Upon assuming power on December 31, 1983, the Supreme Military Council (SMC) suspended those portions of the constitution "relating to all elective and appointive offices and representative institutions." A constitutional modification decree issued in January 1984 established a Federal Military Government encompassing the SMC; a National Council of States, headed by the chair of the SMC and including the military governors of the 19 states, the chief of staff of the armed forces, the inspector-general of police, and the attorney general; and a cabinet-level Federal Executive Council (FEC). The decree also provided for state executive councils headed by the military governors. Following the coup of August 1985, the SMC was renamed the Armed Forces Ruling Council (AFRC), and the FEC was renamed the National Council of Ministers. The chair of the AFRC was empowered to serve as both the head of state and chief executive. However, responsibility for "civilian political affairs" was delegated to a chief of general staff. Following the AFRC's announcement in September 1987 of a five-year schedule for return to civilian government, a 46-member Constitution Review Committee was created to prepare a revision of the 1979 basic law.

In May 1988 a 567-member Constituent Assembly was established to complete the work of the Constitution Review Committee. The most controversial issue faced by the assembly was the proposed institution of sharia, which was not favored by Muslim president Babangida or the Christian population. Unable to reach agreement, the assembly provided two separate and divergent submissions on the matter, which the president stated the AFRC would review in the context of "the national interest."

The draft constitution of the "Third Republic," presented to the AFRC by the Constituent Assembly in April 1989, mirrored the 1979 basic law with the notable addition of anticorruption measures and extension of the presidential term to six years. The document took no position on sharia, as Babangida claimed the issue would constrain debate on other provisions and should be addressed separately at a future time. The existing judiciary was left largely intact, although it was enjoined from challenging or interpreting "this or any other decree" of the AFRC.

A new National Assembly was elected on July 4, 1992, and convened on December 5. Presidential balloting was, however, deferred until June 12, 1993, with a return to constitutional government scheduled for the following August 27. In the meantime, a Transitional Council, with a chair as nominal head of government, was designated to serve in a quasi-executive capacity. The system nonetheless remained tutelary, since both legislative and executive actions were subject to review by the president and the military-civilian National Defense and Security Council (NDSC). Coincident with President Babangida's resignation in 1993, the Transitional Council was abolished, not in favor of a constitutional government but of an Interim National Government (ING), which was in turn superseded by the Provisional Ruling Council (PRC)/Federal Executive Council (FEC) in November.

The 369 participants in the constitutional conference that convened on June 27, 1994, had been selected in widely boycotted balloting on May 23 and 28 from a list of PRC-approved candidates. The conference's recommendations were formally submitted to the PRC on June 27, 1995, and the provisions in the new proposed basic law called for a presidency that would rotate between the north and the south, the election of three vice presidents, the creation of several new states, and the installation of a transition civilian government pending new national elections. However, many of the 1995 document's provisions were not included in the draft charter released by the Abubakar regime for comments in September 1998. The new draft more resembled the 1979 constitution, providing for a strong, executive president responsible for nominating a cabinet subject to senate approval. At the state level, power was vested in a popularly elected governor and the state legislature. In early 1999 the regime announced that it had agreed on details of the new constitution, which was promulgated into law in May. The 1999 document codified a federal system comprising 36 states and the federal capital territory. The states were divided into 776 local government districts and municipalities. The term of office for the president and the two-house legislature (both elected by universal suffrage) was set at four years, renewable only once for the president.

Foreign relations. As a member of the United Nations, the Commonwealth, and the OAU following independence, Nigeria adhered to a policy of nonalignment, opposition to colonialism, and support for liberation movements in all white-dominated African territories. It maintained relations with both Eastern and Western governments, establishing strong economic ties with Britain, Canada, the Soviet Union, and the People's Republic of China. It also actively participated in OAU committees and negotiations directed toward settling the war in Chad, the Western Saharan conflict, and disputes in the Horn of Africa. At the regional level, Nigeria was the prime mover in negotiations leading to the establishment in 1975 of the Economic Community of West African States (ECOWAS) and spearheaded the ECOWAS military and political involvement in Liberia in 1990 and Sierra Leone in 1998.

Benin and Cameroon have challenged Nigerian territorial claims along the Benin-Nigeria border and in offshore waters, respectively. In 1989 President Babangida sought to repair relations that had been strained by expulsion of illegal aliens by the Shagira regime, primarily by providing Benin with financial assistance. Cameroon and Nigeria continued to assert rival claims to the Bakassi Peninsula, several deaths having been reported during military clashes in 1994 in that oil-rich region. Briefs in the case were submitted to the International Court of Justice (ICJ) during the first half of 1995, but tension stemming from the dispute subsequently remained high. Seeking to repair relations even as legal wrangling over the region continued, president-elect Obasanjo visited Cameroon in early 1999.

In 2002 the ICJ ruled in favor of Cameroon in the border dispute. The governments of both Cameroon and Nigeria subsequently entered into the UN-brokered talks to implement the decision. By 2003 Nigeria had turned over more than 30 small villages to Cameroon in exchange for control of a small area. A second round of territorial exchange occurred in July 2004, and diplomatic relations were also restored between the two countries. However, in September the Obasanjo administration refused to participate in a third round of land exchange, which led to a new UN mediation effort (see article on Cameroon). (In 2006 Obasanjo signed a UN-brokered agreement regarding a final settlement.)

Relations with Benin were also strengthened in the early 2000s. Joint border patrols were initiated in 2002 between the two states, which subsequently agreed to redraw their borders. Three areas claimed by Nigeria were turned over to Nigeria in return for its release of seven areas claimed by Benin. In addition, in May 2003 Nigeria and Benin agreed, along with Ghana and Togo, to the construction of a 1,000-kilometer pipeline to transship oil. In 2006 Obasango signed a UN-brokered agreement regarding a final settlement.

Relations between Nigeria and the United Kingdom, weakened by the flight to Britain of a number of political associates of former president Shagari, were formally suspended in mid-1984, when British police arrested a Nigerian diplomat and expelled two others for the attempted kidnapping of former transport minister Umaru DIKKO, who was under indictment in Nigeria for diversion of public funds. Full relations with the United Kingdom resumed in February 1986, with Dikko being denied asylum in early 1989.

Despite Nigeria's reported admission to full membership in the Organization of the Islamic Conference (OIC) in 1986, intense Christian opposition yielded the appointment of a commission to evaluate the implications of the move. As a result, the country formally repudiated its links to the conference in 1991, although the OIC continued to list Nigeria as one of its members. Muslims objected strenuously to the 1991 reversal of an 18-year lapse in relations with Israel, although the Babangida regime two years earlier had recognized the Palestinian claim to statehood.

In April 1994 the U.S. State Department accused Nigerian government officials of complicity in a global drug-trafficking network that supplied upward of 40 percent of the heroin entering the United States. However, the United States stopped short of imposing economic sanctions because of "vital national interests." (The United States was Nigeria's leading export partner.)

In February 1998 Nigerian troops were at the vanguard of the ECOWAS Monitoring Group (Ecomog) that invaded Freetown, Sierra Leone, in an effort to restore to power the democratically elected government of Ahmed Tejan Kabbah. (Kabbah had been forced into exile in the aftermath of the military coup [see article on Sierra Leone for further details].) In March 1999 Nigerian president-elect Obasanjo reiterated his country's commitment to restoring peace in Sierra Leone and pledged to keep Nigerian troops there as long as necessary.

The Obasanjo administration was also active in international efforts to resolve the Liberian civil war. In 2003 Liberian leader Charles Taylor accepted a Nigerian proposal whereby he would receive asylum in Nigeria in exchange for surrendering power. Taylor left Liberia for Nigeria in August 2003 and settled in Calabar. Nigeria then contributed 1,500 troops to the UN-sponsored peacekeeping mission to Liberia in October 2003.

The new civilian regime installed in 1999 received much international praise for its attempt to eliminate widespread corruption and its commitment to democratic practices. Among other things, the United States restored military ties and announced that Nigeria would receive $10 million in military aid. In addition, a U.S.-Nigerian committee was established in 2005 to address regional security issues as well as to combat violence in Nigeria's oil-producing areas.

Reports surfaced in 2006 that Nigeria was pursuing negotiations with China toward an agreement whereby Chinese companies would be granted oil licenses in return for as much as $4 billion in infrastructure grants. Nigeria also reportedly agreed to purchase military aircraft from China. In March former Liberian leader Taylor tried to flee from Nigeria when it became apparent that President Obasanjo planned to extradite him. However, Taylor was captured and turned over to a special UN court for trial on charges of having committed war crimes. In June Nigeria withdrew its citizens from the Bakassi Peninsula as part of an additional UN-sponsored border agreement with Cameroon. Nigeria also relocated 13 villages located along its border with Niger to move them from disputed territory. In November Nigeria finalized an agreement under which South Korea agreed to spend $10 billion on Nigerian railways in return for preferential treatment in regard to future oil contracts. In February 2007 Nigeria, Benin, and Togo signed an agreement to increase security and economic cooperation, in part through the proposed creation of a three-state common market.

Nigeria formally handed over the Bakassi Peninsula to Cameroon in August 2008, although the Nigerian government acknowledged it was "painful" to acquiesce to the transfer. (Some 100,000 of the approximately 300,000 residents on the peninsula [most of whom consider themselves Nigerian] had reportedly already relocated to Nigeria proper.) Nigerian officials were more sanguine about the recent demarcation of the maritime border with Cameroon, under which the two countries agreed to work together to develop what were expected to be rich offshore oilfields. Meanwhile, Nigeria reportedly was considering offers from both Russia and the European Union to support construction of a proposed pipeline to carry Nigerian gas northward. China was also involved in Nigeria's energy picture, having reportedly offered large loans for infrastructure improvements in Nigeria in return for oil exploration rights.

In May 2009 the U.S. firm Halliburton revealed that it had paid several million dollars in bribes to Nigerian officials in exchange for lucrative energy contracts worth more than $6 billion. The revelations prompted the government to establish investigations in several large agreements with foreign firms. Nigeria and Russia signed a joint agreement in June, worth $2.5 billion, to expand Nigeria's gas production capabilities. Also in June, China and Nigeria finalized a broad accord to improve the quality and safety of products imported from China. In July the EU pledged more than $110 million in development aid to the Niger Delta.

Current issues. The government convened a National Political Reforms Conference (NPRC) in February 2005 in an effort to ease tensions among the regions. After contentious debate, the conference in April issued a report that called for increased oil revenues to be allocated to southern and eastern regions and rejected the proposed revision of the constitution to permit Obasanjo to run for a third term. The latter issue was permanently put to rest in May 2006 when the Senate blocked an amendment presented by supporters of a third term. (Obasanjo agreed to abide by that ruling.) In June Obasanjo signed a new electoral law designed to reduce fraud in the 2007 elections by, among other things, limiting donations to campaigns and strengthening the authority of the election commission.

The other dominant issue in late 2005 and early 2006 was sustained severe discord in the oil-rich Niger Delta region. Two groups—the Niger Delta's People's Volunteer Force (NDPVF) and the Movement for the Emancipation of the Niger Delta (MEND)—claimed responsibility for a number of attacks on pipelines and kidnappings designed to disrupt production. Their goals were greater autonomy for the region and compensation for environmental damage done by oil companies in the state of Bayelsa. In June 2006 MEND declared a "cease-fire" after a Nigerian court ordered Shell (the country's largest oil-producer) to pay $1.5 billion for environmental "reparations." However, MEND conducted new attacks in August. (See MEND under Political Parties and Groups, below, for subsequent developments.) In response to the continued unrest, federal security forces launched an offensive in the region that led to more than 100 arrests but did not substantially reduce the level of violence.

A political feud between President Obasanjo and Vice President Atiku ABUBAKAR over control of the PDP led the president in September 2006 to ask the Senate to impeach Abubakar on corruption charges. Most analysts concluded that the conflict had arisen from Abubakar's open pursuit of the PDP nomination for the 2007 presidential poll, despite Obasanjo's apparent interest in handpicking his presidential successor. (Abubakar had also opposed Obasanjo's bid to amend the constitution to permit him a third term.) The High Court in November blocked the impeachment effort, thereby apparently permitting Abubakar to become a candidate. However, the PDP subsequently nominated Umar Yar'Adua, a relative unknown within the party, fueling speculation that Obasanjo had orchestrated the nomination. (Abubakar subsequently left the PDP to stand as the candidate of a new small party called Action Congress.)

Corruption allegations subsequently continued to color the political scene, as a special commission reported in February 2007 that more than 130 candidates for the upcoming National Assembly elections and some 31 incumbent governors had either been convicted of malfeasance or were under investigation. In addition, the campaign for the April elections was again marred by violence, with both pro- and anti-government candidates being attacked.

International and domestic observers strongly criticized the 2007 elections as severely compromised by fraud at the local, state, and national levels. The courts subsequently ordered new balloting for a number of governorships and other offices, but a special tribunal in February 2008 upheld the presidential results.

The new government's first year in office was marked by an anti-corruption campaign that snared a number of officials from the Obasanjo administration, which reportedly contributed to a sharp deterioration in the relationship between Yar'Adua and Obasanjo. In addition, Yar'Adua overhauled the military leadership and directed his technocrat-oriented administration to pursue policies that would provide greater benefits for the poor from oil and gas revenues. The president also asked for international assistance in dealing with the problem he characterized as "blood oil," i.e., the massive theft and smuggling of oil, particularly from the Delta region. In that regard, Yar'Adua in mid-2008 proposed a "peace summit" with MEND and other militant groups, but in September the level of violence in the Delta reached its highest level in several years. In November religious strife between Christians and Muslims in Jos, left more than 400 dead.

On February 17, 2009 an appeals court nullified the 2007 election of PDP candidate Olesegun ONI as governor of the state of Ekiti. New elections were held in April, in which Oni again placed first amidst opposition charges of widespread voter fraud. A goverment offensive against MEND fighters left hundreds dead, including civilians, and led MEND to launch retaliatory strikes against oil facilities. On June 8 Royal Dutch Shell consented to pay $15.5 million to people along the Niger delta to settle court cases brought against the energy giant. Also in June, Yar'Adua announced an amnesty program and 60-day cease-fire for MEND fighters (see Political parties, below). Meanwhile fighting in July between government forces and an Islamic militant group alternatively known as *Al Sunna Wal Jamma* or *Boko Haram* left more than 700 dead and thousands displaced. Police captured group's leader Mohammad Yusuf, who subsequently died in custody. Audits in August revealed widespread corruption in the financial sector and led the Central Bank to replace the heads of five of the nation's largest banks. The investigations were in response to bad loans and other problems that caused the Nigerian stock market to lose 65 percent of its value between March 2008 and March 2009.

POLITICAL PARTIES AND GROUPS

Upon assuming power in December 1983, the Supreme Military Council (SMC) banned all political parties, arrested many of their leaders, and confiscated their assets. The ban was lifted in May 1989, and 13 parties were legalized, 2 of which were to be selected to contest upcoming elections. However, the government, having become dissatisfied with that process, subsequently dissolved the existing parties and, on October 7, 1989, 2 new parties—the Social Democratic Party (SDP) and the National Republican Convention (NRC)—were created by presidential decree. The political platforms of the new groups were dictated by the regime, which also provided financial support until January 1991 when it declared the parties to be "on their own." The SDP and the NRC were dismantled when all party activity was banned by the Abacha regime on November 18, 1993.

In June 1995 General Abacha announced that the ban on "political activity" had been lifted, although "rallies and campaigns" remained restricted and other constraints continued as a consequence of the country's severe political turmoil. A year later the National Electoral Commission of Nigeria (NECON) announced the regulations for registration of parties, which were required, among other things, to secure the signature of 40,000 voters from each region and to forswear accepting money from external sources. The regulations promised public financing for the recognized groups. Some 23 political associations reportedly purchased the registration forms, but only 15 completed them within the 30-day limit imposed by the NECON. In September 1996 the NECON announced that 5 parties had been recognized; the other aspirants were ordered to dissolve immediately. Although the NECON argued that the selections had been based on an unbiased "point system," opposition leaders called the process a "sham." Observers generally supported the opposition assessment that the newly recognized parties all shared a "conservative" point of view, which meant tacit support of the current military regime and its proposed transition schedule. Meanwhile, no opponents of the Abacha government appeared to have gained a legal foothold.

In April 1998 all 5 legal parties nominated Abacha to be their presidential candidate in balloting then scheduled for August. However, following Abacha's death in June, his successor, General Abubakar, dissolved the 5 parties and called on political associations to register with the newly created Independent National Electoral Commission (INEC). Between August 27 and September 9, 25 political groups applied to the INEC for provisional legal status. Only 9 of the applicants met the baseline qualifications, including maintaining functional offices in 24 states. In local elections in December only 3 of those groups—the People's Democratic Party (PDP), the All People's Party (APP), and the Alliance for Democracy (AD)—secured the voting tally necessary to maintain their legal status and move on to legislative and presidential elections. The other 6 groups were reportedly deregistered. Three new parties (the NDP, UNPP, and APGA) were registered in June 2002, and by 2006 some 35 parties had been legalized. It was reported that 37 parties participated in the 2007 state and federal elections. Opposition parties were subsequently described as having formed a Conference of Nigerian Political Parties (CNPP).

Legislative Parties:

People's Democratic Party (PDP). The PDP was formed in Lagos in August 1998 as an umbrella for more than 60 organizations, including many from the so-called Group of 34, which registered among its leaders traditional chiefs, businesspeople, academicians, and a strong contingent of retired generals. Alex EKWUEME, a former national vice president, and Jerry GANA emerged from the PDP's inaugural meetings as the group's chair and second in command, respectively. The party presented a platform that reflected its broad political base, advocating the "guided" deregulation of the economy, respect for human rights, and improved funding for health care and education.

In late October 1998 Gen. Olesegun Obasanjo, the military head of state between 1976 and 1979, joined the PDP. With Obasanjo at the helm, the party subsequently swept local and gubernatorial elections, won a majority in the assembly, and in February 1999 captured the national presidency.

In January 2003 the PDP elected Obasanjo as its presidential candidate for the upcoming elections, which he won with 62 percent of the vote. The PDP also retained its majorities in the federal Senate and House of Representatives and among state governors and state assemblies.

A feud developed in 2005 between President Obasanjo and Vice President Atiku Abubakar over the proposed constitutional amendment to permit Obasanjo to seek a third term (see Current issues, above). The split also appeared to reflect the schism between the party's founding members ("concerned elders") led by Abubakar and the "progressive faction" led by Obasanjo. A party congress elected Ahmadu Ali as the PDP chair, and Obasanjo's supporters blamed Ali for the defeat of the constitutional amendment that would have allowed Obasanjo a third term. Subsequently, a PDP faction led by Solomon LAR declared itself the real leadership of the party and sued for access to the PDP assets.

Abubakar was suspended from the PDP in September 2006 for "antiparty activities," and he subsequently joined the new Action Congress (below). In December a PDP congress chose Umaru Yar'Adua as its presidential candidate. He easily secured the presidency (with more than 70 percent of the vote) in the April 2007 balloting, while the PDP also dominated the federal legislative polls and secured 27 of 36 state governorships.

Although Yar'Adua had been characterized as Obasanjo's handpicked successor, significant infighting was subsequently reported between supporters of the two leaders, particularly because the new government's anticorruption campaign focused on many officials from Obasanjo's administration. Obasanjo backed Sam EGWU to be the new PDP leader, but Egwu was defeated for the post by Vincent Ogbulafor at the PDP convention in March 2008. Ogbulafor, a former PDP general secretary, was considered a compromise candidate who reportedly faced a difficult task in reunifying the party. Between 2007 and 2009, a number of members of the All Nigeria People's Party defected to the PDP, including two sitting governors, Aliyu Mahmud SHINKAFI of Zamfara and Isa YUGUDA of Bauchi.

Leaders: Umaru Musa YAR'ADUA (President of the Republic), Goodluck JONATHAN (Vice President of the Republic), Gen. Olesegun OBASANJO (Chair of the PDP Board of Trustees and Former President of the Republic), Vincent OGBULAFOR (Chair), Alhaji Abubakar Kawu BARAJE (General Secretary).

All Nigeria People's Party (ANPP). The ANPP is a successor to the All People's Party (APP), a center-right grouping established in September 1998 by some 14 Ibo and Hausa-Fulani political associations. Within the APP's ranks were some former members of the five parties dissolved in July 1998, as well as so many associates of former president Abacha that APP detractors derisively labeled the group the "Abacha's People's Party." The APP forwarded its own candidates for local, gubernatorial, and national legislative balloting in late 1998 and early 1999, capturing one-quarter of the governorships and representation in both assembly bodies. On the other hand, prior to the 1999 presidential balloting, the APP formed an electoral alliance with the AD (below). After the AD's standard-bearer, Samuel Oluyemisi Falae, outpolled the APP's proposed candidate, Oghonnaya ONU, in intra-alliance balloting, the APP backed Falae's presidential bid.

Membership in the APP having initially come largely from the northern region, the party in 2000 claimed to have reorganized in an attempt to widen membership to the southeast, with particular focus on the Igbo tribe. As part of the APP's reorganization, the party set up a monitoring mechanism to ensure that the party's elected officials lived up to the party platform, which included support for the implementation of sharia in northern states.

In May 2002 the APP announced its intention to change its name to the ANPP in anticipation of a planned merger with the then-unrecognized UNPP (below). However, both parties subsequently suffered internal factionalization over the proposed merger, with one APP faction demanding retention of the party's original rubric. In November a special APP national convention ratified the name change, although only a portion of the UNPP membership joined the group.

In the 2003 elections Muhammadu Buhari ran as the ANPP's presidential candidate and received 32 percent of the vote. In the legislative elections, the ANPP secured 96 seats in the House and 27 in the Senate, making it the largest opposition party. Buhari finished second in the April 2007 presidential poll with 18.7 percent of the vote, while the ANPP won 22 seats in the Senate, 64 seats in the House of Representatives, and 5 state governorships. Following the elections, two members of the ANPP joined the new national unity government, although ANPP leaders continued to refer to the party as a member of the opposition, and Buhari pressed for an annulment of the presidential poll.

In 2009 an internal struggle divided that party as a faction loyal to Buhari sought to replace party chair Edwin Ume-Ezeoke with former governor Abubakar AUDU, ahead of the 2011 elections. Meanwhile reports indicated that the ANPP and the AC would combine in an electoral coalition in the 2011 polling.

Leaders: Edwin UME-EZEOKE (Chair), Etubon ASUQUO (National Secretary), Muhammadu BUHARI (2003 and 2007 presidential candidate).

Progressive People's Alliance (PPA). The PPA was formed in 2003, and the party's candidate—Orji Uzor KALU (a former PDP member)—won the gubernatorial election in Abia that year. Kalu served until 2007 but was indicted after he left office on charges of corruption. In 2007 the PPA won the gubernatorial elections in Abia and Imo. After the 2007 legislative elections, the PPA joined the PDP-led national unity government. In 2009 the governor and deputy governor of Imo, both members of the PPA, defected to the PDP leading the PPA to launch a legal challenge against the right of the former members to remain in office.

Leaders: Clement EBRI (Chair), Sam NKIRE (National Secretary).

Action Congress (AC). The AC was formed in 2006 by dissidents from the AD, Justice Party, ACD, and other smaller parties. Vice President of the Republic and former PDP member Atiku Abubakar was the 2007 AC candidate for the presidency, having left the PDP. He placed third in the balloting with 7.25 percent of the vote. On the eve of the April election, an AC gubernatorial candidate, Femi PEDRO, defected and joined the Labour Party, along with a number of other

AC members. The AC went on to win 1 governorship, 6 seats in the Senate, and 32 seats in the House of Representatives, making it the third largest party in both chambers. The AC was subsequently invited to join the PDP national unity government but declined, leading to the resignation of the party's national secretary, Bashir DALHATU who had strenuously supported participation. In 2009 Atiku led talks with the ANPP that reportedly resulted in an electoral alliance for the 2011 elections.

Leaders: Bisi AKANDE Hassan ZURMI (Chair), Usman BUGAJI (National Secretary), Atiku ABUBAKAR (Former Vice President of the Republic and 2007 presidential candidate), Lai MOHAMMED (Spokesperson).

Accord. Formed in 2006 by Ikra Bilbis, a former member of the PDP, Accord maintained close ties with the PDP, and President Obasanjo appointed Bilbis to a cabinet post in 2006. Accord supported PDP candidate Yar'Adua in the 2007 presidential election.. Reports in 2009 indicated that many members of Accord had joined the PDP.

Leaders: Muhammad Lawal NALABO (Chair), Longers ANYANWU (National Secretary).

Alliance for Democracy (AD). The Yoruba-dominated AD draws on a long tradition of leftist, nationalist politics that originated before independence under the guidance of Chief Obafemi AWOLOWO and continued more recently in the National Democratic Coalition (NADECO, below). The AD called for greater regional autonomy and constitutional reform, and AD candidates sought office in late 1998 and 1999 on a platform promising privatization of state-run enterprises, reduction of Nigeria's debt burden, and free education and health care. In early 1999 the AD formed an electoral alliance with the APP in preparation for presidential balloting, and an AD moderate, Samuel Oluyemisi ("Olu") Falae, subsequently captured the right to head the alliance ticket.

Falae finished a distant second in the February 1999 elections, which he decried as rigged in favor of the PDP. Subsequently, he petitioned the Court of Appeals to overturn the election results; however, when the court rejected his bid in early April, he reportedly abandoned his legal challenge.

In late 1999 the party factionalized over a leadership dispute. Yusuf MAMMAN, who became chair in December, was accused of misconduct for neglecting to call a party convention. The northern faction then suspended his position on December 20 and elected Adamu SONG as pro tem chair. Both men claimed the leadership post in the spring of 2000. Because of the split, the AD did not field a candidate in the 2003 presidential election. In the 2003 legislative elections, the AD won 34 seats in the House of Representatives and 6 in the Senate. AD presidential candidate Christopher Pere Ajuwa won less than 1 percent of the vote in 2007. The AD subsequently declined to join the PDP-led national unity government.

From late 2008 into 2009, the AD has divided by a leadership struggle. A party congress in December 2008 elected Michael KOLEOSHO chair, replacing Mojisoluwa AKINFEWA. However, a rival congress in January 2009, elected Rasheed Adewale SHITTA-BEY chair. In March the national electoral commission ruled that Koleosho was the legitimate leader of the AD, but the ruling was immediately challenged in court.

Leaders: Michael KOLEOSHO (Chair), Dominique ABUBAKAR (Secretary), Christopher Pere AJUWA (2007 presidential candidate).

Other Parties that Participated in the 2007 Elections:

National Democratic Party (NDP). Described as a "pan-Yoruba" party, the NDP was launched in 2001 as a merger of several groups in pursuit of "true federalism." Ike NWACHUKWU, the NDP candidate in the 2003 presidential election, received less than 1 percent of the vote. In legislative balloting, the NDP secured 2 percent of the vote in the house and gained one seat. It received less than 2 percent of the vote in Senate elections and no seats.

In April 2006 the NDP announced plans to present former president Ibrahim Babangida as the party's candidate in the 2007 presidential election. However, party leader Aliyu Habu Faru ultimately served as the NDP candidate (after Babangida withdrew to "avert a crisis"); Faru received less than 1 percent of vote. In January 2008 a faction of the NDP led by Kassim AFEGBUA declared that Faru was no longer the leader of the party, while a rival group led by Faru and 2007 vice presidential candidate Prince Chudi CHUKWUANI, ordered Afegbua expelled from the party. Chukwuani emerged from the dispute as the new chair of the NDP.

Leaders: Chudi CHUKWUANI (Chair), Aliyu Habu FARU (2007 presidential candidate), Prince Ademola AYOADE (National Secretary).

United Nigeria People's Party (UNPP). The UNPP is a successor to the United Nigeria Democratic Party (UNDP), which was launched in August 2001 by, among others, former members of the PDP and supporters of former president Babangida. The UNDP changed its name to the UNPP in May 2002 to avoid confusion with the UN Development Program (also UNDP). The UNPP subsequently was splintered by a proposed merger with the APP; although some UNPP members joined the new ANPP, a rump UNPP continued to operate. Jim NWOBODO, the UNPP candidate in the 2003 presidential poll, secured 0.43 percent of the vote. In the concurrent legislative balloting, the UNPP secured 2.72 percent of the vote in the Senate (but no seats) and 2.8 percent of the vote and two seats in the house.

In 2006, it was reported that many members of the UNPP had defected to the newly formed Movement for Restoration and Defense of Democracy (MRDD, below).

Leaders: Mallem Salek JAMBO (Chair), Ukeje NWOKEFORO (National Secretary).

All Progressive Grand Alliance (APGA). Launched in April 2002, the APGA is led by a prominent chief of the Southern Igbo ethnic group, Chekwas Okorie. However, its founders criticized those who branded the APGA as an "Igbo party," arguing instead that it intended to represent "all the marginalized people of Nigeria." Okorie came in third in presidential balloting in 2003 with 3.29 percent of the vote. The party also gained two seats in the House but none in the Senate in 2003.

A faction of the party led by Chief Victor UMEH claimed to be the legitimate leadership of the APGA in 2005–2006, and the INEC recognized the claim in 2007. However, Okorie challenged the INEC decision in the courts, but his suit was rejected in 2008. The APGA won one governorship in 2007. At a gathering in 2009, Okorie's faction reelected him as chair and expelled Umeh, along with governor Peter OBI. However, the faction led by Umeh and Obi refused to recognize the authority of the convention.

Leaders: Chief Chekwas OKORIE, Chief Victor UMEH, Sani SHINKAFI (National Secretary).

People's Redemption Party (PRP). The PRP was formed in 2002 under the leadership of Balarabe Musa, who was also the party's unsuccessful presidential candidate in 2003. The PRP won one seat in the house in 2003 but failed to gain representation in 2007. The PRP launched a series of efforts to form an electoral coalition with parties such as the PPA ahead of the 2011 elections.

Leaders: Balarabe MUSA (Chair), Dr. Ngozi OKAFOR (National Secretary).

Advanced Congress of Democrats (ACD). The ACD was formed in April 2005 to oppose President Obasanjo's bid for a third presidential term. The party attracted a number of elected officials at the state and national level, including members of the House and Senate, as well as senior PDP figures, including a former chair of the PDP, Audu OGBEH. The party mainly comprises northerners and is essentially an anti-PDP formation. After Obasanjo announced that he would not stand for a third term, the party announced a progressive platform that emphasized honesty in politics. The ACD reportedly attracted members from other parties, principally the AD, but failed to gain representation in the 2007 federal elections. In 2008 the ACD expelled its national secretary Keneth KALU after reports surfaced that he had been involved in unethical behavior.

Leaders: Alexis ANIGLO (Chair), Umar KABIRAT (National Secretary), Lawal KAITA (Former Governor of Kaduna), Ghali Umar NA'ABA (Former President of the House of Representatives), Abubakar RIMI (Former Governor of Kano).

Movement for Restoration and Defense of Democracy (MRDD). The MRDD was formed in February 2006 by disaffected members of the UNPP and PRP. The MRDD opposed President Obasanjo's bid for a third term.

Leaders: Mohammadu GAMBO (National Chair), Emmanuel UDE-OGO (National Secretary).

Other parties participating in the 2007 elections included (all received less than 1 percent of the vote and no representation in the legislature): the **People's Salvation Party** (PSP), created in 2002 and led by Lawal MAITURARE; the **National Conscience Party** (NCP), formed in October 1994 by Gani FAWEHINMI, an attorney and political activist who was arrested in mid-1995, and currently led by Osagie OBAYUWANA; the **Justice Party** (JP), led by former NADECO member Ralph OBIOHA and former NDP member Chris OKOTIE (2003 presidential candidate); the **Movement for Democracy and Justice** (MDJ), led by J.O. OSULA and Mohammed Dikko YUSUF (2003 presidential candidate); the **Progressive Action Congress** (PAC), led by A.C. NWODO; the **People's Mandate Party** (PMP), led by Arthur NWANKWO (who was also the party's 2003 presidential candidate) and Edward OPARAOJI; the **All Peoples' Liberation Party** (APLP), led by E. O. OKEREKE; the **New Nigeria Peoples' Party** (NNPP), chaired by B.O. ANIEBONAM; the **United Democratic Party** (UDP), formed in 1998 and led by Umaru DIKKO; the **Democratic Party Alliance** (DPA), a "progressive" party formed in November 2006 by Ulu FALAYE; the **Nigeria People's Congress** (NPC), led by Ngozi EMIONA and Brimmy Asekharuagbom OLAGHERE (2007 presidential candidate); the **Democratic Alternative** (DA), led by Alao AKA-BASHORUM, the attorney for detained 1993 presidential candidate Moshood Abiola; the **National Conscience Party**, formed in October 1994 by attorney and political activist Gani FAWEHINMI; the **African Democratic Congress** (ADC), formed in 2006 by Chief Okewo OSUI; and the **French Democrats**, established in 2006 under the leadership of Chris Okotie (2007 presidential candidate).

Other Groups:

National Democratic Coalition (NADECO). Organized in May 1994 by a group of former politicians, retired military officers, and human rights activists, NADECO demanded that the Abacha regime yield to an interim government led by Moshood Abiola, the apparent winner in the aborted 1993 presidential election. As in the case of other prominent antigovernment figures, several NADECO leaders were temporarily detained, including the revered 87-year-old ex-governor of Ondo, Michael AJASIN. NADECO unsuccessfully supported a People's Progressive Party for recognition in 1996, and Ajasin angrily denounced the failure of the regime to legalize opposition groupings.

Wole Soyinka, the prominent exiled critic of the government who was involved in the reported formation of several external groups (see the National Liberation Council of Nigeria in the 2007 *Handbook*), was identified as a NADECO leader in 1997. Soyinka (in absentia) and other NADECO supporters were charged with treason in March 1997 for their antiregime activities. In early May 1998 NADECO's secretary general, Ayo Opadokum, was among 20 opposition activists arrested when a rally in Ibadan turned violent.

Beginning in mid-1998 the Abubakar regime released a number of opposition figures and was reportedly preparing to release Moshood Abiola when Abiola died. In October Soyinka, who had been a leading advocate for Abiola's release, returned from exile, where most recently he had been calling for the formation of a South African–style human rights tribunal to investigate the alleged abuses of Nigeria's military regimes. Subsequently, NADECO Chair Ndubuisi Kanu stated that the organization would resume its role as unofficial opposition, although it would not assume the status of political party. In 2009 a NADECO convention endorse a call for a new constitution that emphasized regional autonomy.

Leaders: Commodore Ndubuisi KANU (Chair), Bolaji AKINYEMI, Wole SOYINKA, Ayo OPADOKUM (Secretary General).

Movement for the Survival of the Ogoni People (MOSOP). MOSOP pressed the government for years on the rights of the indigenous Ogoni ethnic group in oil-rich southwestern Nigeria. Having previously suggested that a self-determination referendum would be appropriate, MOSOP has more recently concentrated on forcing the government to share the oil wealth more equitably with the local population.

Kenule SARO-WIWA (a well-known author, minority rights activist, and longtime MOSOP leader) was arrested in 1994 on murder charges involving the death of four progovernment Ogoni leaders. Saro-Wiwa vehemently denied the charges, calling them a blatant attempt by the Abacha regime to silence his criticism. Most internal and external observers remained extremely skeptical of Saro-Wiwa's guilt, and Western and African capitals urged his release. However, Saro-Wiwa and eight others were found guilty by a special military tribunal in late October 1996 and, following ratification of the sentences by the PRC, were hanged on November 10. The executions prompted an international outcry that contributed significantly to the government's sustained isolation in 1996–1998. MOSOP subsequently attempted to change the constitution so that the presidency would rotate on a regional basis. In 2009 MOSOP was divided by a leadership crisis in which one faction supported Ledum Mitee and another Goodluck DIIGBO, following a December 2008 congress in which Mitee was reelected chair.

Leader: Ledum MITEE.

Arewa People's Congress (APC). The APC is a northern nationalist group that formed as a counter to the militant nationalist Yoruba OPC (see below). It has pledged to protect "northerners" in the southwest region.

Movement for the Actualization of the Sovereign State of Biafra (MASSOB). An Ibo group formed by lawyer and activist Ralph Uwazurike in 1999, MASSOB advocates the secession of Biafra and is opposed to the introduction of sharia in northern states. In October 2005 Uwazurike and six members of MASSOB were arrested on charges of treason and organizing an illegal organization. In 2009 MASSOB announced that after years of boycotting elections, it would participate in regional balloting in 2010 and support APGA candidates.

Leader: Ralph UWAZURIKE.

O'odua People's Congress (OPC). The OPC is a militant organization that advocates secession for the Yoruba ethnic group. It was allegedly behind a November 1999 dispute between Yoruba and Hausa merchants in the Lagos market that killed dozens. In addition, the OPC was blamed for several attacks in early 2000, including the murder of a Banga police officer. Some members of the OPC reportedly support the spread of sharia in northern states in the hope that the issue will further divide the country and thereby make Yoruba secession easier to obtain. Attacks by OPC members in October 2008 left six dead and more than a score injured.

United Democratic Forum (UDF). The UDF was launched by a group of moderate northerners and so-called Middle-Belters who opposed the implementation of sharia as well as the northern nationalist APC. The UDF was formed by Suleman TAKUMA, a Nuper from the Niger state.

Other groups mentioned in news reports in the past 15 years include the **Eastern Mandate Union,** formed by tribal leaders and politicians from southeastern Nigeria under the leadership of Patrick Dele COLE and Chuba OKADIGBO; the **Liberal Democrats** (LD), formed in August 1998 in Abuja and led by Baghir TOFA; the **Movement for National Reconciliation,** led by Anthony ENAHARO; the **National Democratic Movement** (NDM), led by Emmanuel OSAMOR; the **New Democratic Party** (NDP); the **Nigerian People's Movement,** which represents the interests of the Igbo ethnic group in eastern Nigeria; the **Northern Elders' Forum,** a conservative group; the **People's Democratic Congress** (PDC), which was launched in August 1998 in Enugu by Chief Emeka OJUKWU, who had been active in the Biafra independence movement; the **People's Liberation Party** (PLP), a coalition of youth organizations formed in Abuja in September 1998 under the leadership of Goodnews Guben ABBE; the **United Action for Democracy** (UAD), which organized anti-Abacha rallies in early May 1998; the **United Democratic Congress,** led by Alhaji Usman ABATEMI; and **"Vision '99.**"

Groups formed after 2000 include the **Fourth Dimension**, formed in 2001 by former military officers and led by Adm. (Ret.) Augustus AIKHOMU; **National Frontier,** created in 2001 by several former governors and senior military officers and led by Edwin Ume EZEOKE; **IBB Vision 2003,** established in 2002 as a political front for former president Ibrahim Babangida; and the **National Solidarity Party** (NSP), formed in 2001 by ex-military officers.

In addition, the following groups have been linked to unrest in the Niger Delta area: the **Ijaw Youth Organization,** which is composed of radical elements of the ethnic Ijaw tribe who have asserted their desire for a role in Nigerian political life and greater benefits from the oil removed from their territory; the **Federated Niger Delta Izon Communities** (FNDIC), which warned foreign oil workers to leave the region in late 1998 because their safety could "no longer be guaranteed"; and the Ijaw-dominated **Rivers' States Coalition.**

In 2005 a new insurgent group—the **South-South Liberation Movement**—was launched with the goal of creation of a Niger Delta Republic. The movement was reportedly led by a former Nigerian

Army warrant officer, John ADIE. Meanwhile, the **Niger Delta's People's Volunteer Force** (NDPVF), led by Mujahid DOKUBO-ASARI, was reported to have undertaken a number of attacks on oil production facilities. Dokubo-Asari was arrested for treason in September 2005, an appeals court rejecting bail for the jailed leader in June 2006. NDPVF members repeatedly warned of new attacks if Dokubo-Asari was not released. Although jailed, Dokubo-Asari reportedly negotiated the release of foreign hostages on several occasions. In June 2007 Dokubo-Asari was released from prison as part of new president Yar'Adua's reconciliation efforts, and he was subsequently described as supportive of a dialogue with the government toward a negotiated settlement of the Delta dispute.

The most active and militant of the Niger Delta groups has been the **Movement for the Emancipation of the Niger Delta** (MEND), which emerged in early 2006 when it conducted a series of attacks on oil production facilities. MEND was subsequently believed responsible for the kidnapping of a number of foreign oil workers. It demanded compensation from foreign oil companies for environmental damage done in the Niger Delta as well as more equitable distribution of oil revenue to the Delta inhabitants. MEND reportedly finances its operations through large-scale bunkering of oil.

In May 2007 MEND announced a cease-fire after new president Yar'Adua pledged to develop a revenue-sharing plan and to accord greater autonomy to the Niger Delta. The reconciliation was reportedly facilitated by new vice president Jonathan, who, like many MEND members, is a member of the Ijaw ethnic group. Although federal military forces were deployed into the region to confront other rebel forces, the MEND cease-fire appeared to hold into September. However, MEND subsequently resumed its attacks on oil facilities and kidnapping of oil workers after MEND leader Henry OKAH (who reportedly also uses the nom de guerre of Jomo Gbomo) was arrested in Angola on gun-running charges and was extradited to Nigeria to face trial for treason, terrorism, and arms smuggling. (A Nigerian court in May 2008 ruled that Okah's trial would be conducted in secret.) After a series of deadly incidents, MEND, reportedly interested in improving its image and differentiating itself from the numerous militias (described by some as "criminal gangs") operating in the Delta, announced another cease-fire in late June. However, hostilities erupted again in September, rebel attacks on deepwater oil platforms (previously considered safe) having prompted significant production shutdowns. In spite of a two-month government amnesty program in April 2009, MEND launched a series of new attacks on oil facilities and pipelines in the region causing more than $60 million in damage and reducing oil output by 20 percent. In July Okah accepted a government pardon and was freed from custody. Meanwhile a new rebel leader, Government EKPEMUPOLO ("Tompolo"), emerged as one of the main MEND leaders and was the subject of a government manhunt and offensive through the summer.

LEGISLATURE

The **National Assembly,** encompassing a Senate and a House of Representatives, was dissolved in December 1983. It was revived under the 1989 constitution, with an election of members to four-year terms in both houses on July 4, 1992. However, the new body did not convene until December 5 and was again dissolved in the wake of the November 1993 coup.

Five parties approved by the Abacha regime were permitted to contest the balloting for a new assembly on April 25, 1998. According to preliminary results, the United Nigeria Congress Party captured a comfortable majority of the seats; however, the election results were annulled, and the five parties were dissolved following Abacha's death in June. New elections were held on February 20, 1999, among the three parties that had achieved the required electoral threshold in the December 1998 local elections (see Political background, above).

Senate. The upper chamber consists of 109 seats: 3 from each state and 1 from the Federal Capital Territory of Abuja. Members serve four-year terms. Following the balloting of April 14, 2007, the seats were distributed as follows: the People's Democratic Party, 78; the All Nigeria People's Party, 22; the Action Congress, 6; and the Alliance for Democracy, the Progressive People's Alliance, and Accord, 1 each.

President: David MARK.

House of Representatives. The lower house consists of 360 seats, with the number of seats per state being apportioned on the basis of population. Members serve four-year terms. Following the balloting of April 21, 2007, the seats were distributed as follows: the People's Democratic Party, 258; the All Nigeria People's Party, 64; the Action Congress, 32; Progressive People's Alliance, 3; and the Labour Party and the Alliance for Democracy, 1 each; vacant.

President: Bankole DIMEJI.

CABINET

[as of October 1, 2009]

President	Umaru Musa Yar'Adua
Vice President	Goodluck Jonathan
Federal Executive Councilors	
Agriculture and Water Resources	Abba Sayyadi Ruma
Aviation	Babatunde Omotoba
Commerce and Industry	Achike Udenwa
Communications and Information	Dora Akunyili [f]
Culture and Tourism	BelloJibril Gada
Defense	Maj. Gen (Ret.) Godwin Abbe
Environment	John Odey
Federal Capital Territory	Muhammad Adamu Aliero
Finance	Mansur Muhtar
Foreign Affairs	Ojo Maduekwe
Health	Babatunde Osotimehin
Internal Affairs	Shettima Mustapha
Justice and Attorney General	Michael Kaase Aondoakaa
Labor	Adetokunbo Kayode
Mines and Steel Development	Diezani Alison-Madueke [f]
National Planning	Shamsudeen Usman [f]
Niger Delta Region	Ufot Ekaette
Petroleum	Rilwanu Lukman
Police Affairs	Ibrahim Lame
Power	Lanre Babalola
Science and Technology	Alhassan Bako Zaku
Special Duties	Ibrahim Musa Kazaure
Sports Commission	Sani Ndanusa
Transport	Ibrahim Isa Bio
Women Affairs	Salamatu Sulaiman [f]
Works and Housing	Hassan Lawal
Youth Development	Akinlabi Olasunkanmi
Ministers of State	
Agriculture and Water Resources	Fidelia Akuabata Njeze [f]
Commerce and Industry	Humphrey Aba
Communication and Information	Aliyu Bilbis
Defense	Abdulrahman Adamu
Education	Aishatu Jibril Dukku [f]
Federal Capital Territory	Chuka Odom
Finance	Aderemi Babalola
Foreign Affairs	Bagudu Hirse
	Jibril Maigari
Health	Aliyu Idi Hong
Internal Affairs	Ademola Seriki
Niger Delta Affairs	Goday Orubebe
Petroleum	Odein Ajumogobia
Power	Nuhu Somo Wyo
Works and Housing	Grace Ekpiwhre [f]

[f] = female

COMMUNICATIONS

The Nigerian media returned to their position among the freest and most active in Africa following the coup of 1985, although subsequent governments temporarily closed major publications several times over the next decade.

More recently, Nigerian journalists have been significantly affected by the violence that pervades political life, suffering, according to watchdog organizations, beatings and arrests at the hands of local, regional, and national officials who operate for the most part with impunity. "Abusive judicial procedures" are also often initiated against journalists for articles that have irked authorities, according to Reporters Without Borders, which has characterized the State Security Service as a "press freedom predator." The group ranked Nigeria 131 out of 173 countries in terms of freedom of the press in 2008.

Press. The following are published daily in Lagos, unless otherwise noted: *Daily Times* (400,000), government owned; *Nigerian Tribune* (Ibadan, 109,000), independent; *Nigerian Observer* (Benin City, 150,000), privately owned; *Nigerian Standard* (Jos, 100,000), state owned; *New Nigerian* (Kaduna, 80,000), federal-state owned; *Nigerian Chronicle* (Calabar, 50,000 daily), privately owned; *New Nigerian* (Kaduna South, 80,000), government owned; *Sketch* (Ibadan, 64,000), government owned; *The Renaissance* (Enugu, 50,000); the *Daily Independent*, privately owned; *This Day*, privately owned; *The Punch* (150,000), privately owned; *Ebonyi Voice*, privately owned; *The Democrat* (Kaduna South, 100,000); *The Guardian* (80,000), independent; *National Concord* (200,000); *Nigerian Tribune* (Ibadan, 110,000); *Leadership*, independent; the *Abuja Inquirer*, independent; and *Vanguard*, independent.

News agencies. The official News Agency of Nigeria (NAN) was established in 1978. A number of foreign agencies maintain offices in Lagos.

Broadcasting and computing. In November 1975 the government assumed control of all radio and television broadcasting facilities, placing them under a newly created National Broadcasting Corporation that was itself superseded in 1978 by the nominally independent Federal Radio Corporation of Nigeria (FRCN) and Nigerian Television Authority (NTV). Subsequently, numerous regional and state broadcast facilities were launched, as were a number of private radio and television broadcasters, one of the most prominent of which is Africa Independent TV (AIT). As of 2008 there were 158.6 Internet users per 1,000 inhabitants.

INTERGOVERNMENTAL REPRESENTATION

Ambassador to the U.S.: (Vacant).

U.S. Ambassador to Nigeria: Robin R. SANDERS.

Permanent Representative to the UN: U. Joy OGWU.

IGO Memberships (Non-UN): AfDB, AU, BADEA, CWTH, ECOWAS, Interpol, IOC, IOM, NAM, OPEC, PCA, WCO, WTO.

NORWAY

Kingdom of Norway
Kongeriket Norge

Political Status: Constitutional monarchy established in 1905; under multiparty parliamentary system.

Area: 149,282 sq. mi. (386,641 sq. km.), including Svalbard and Jan Mayen (see Related Territories).

Population: 4,520,947 (2001C); 4,791,000 (2008E).

Major Urban Centers (2005E): OSLO (528,000), Bergen (240,000), Trondheim (156,000), Stavanger (113,000).

Official Language: Norwegian.

Monetary Unit: Krone (official rate December 1, 2009: 5.62 kroner = $1US).

Sovereign: King HARALD V; succeeded to the throne January 17, 1991, upon the death of his father, King OLAV V.

Heir to the Throne: Crown Prince HAAKON Magnus, son of the king.

Prime Minister: Jens STOLTENBERG (Norwegian Labor Party); appointed by the king on October 17, 2005, to succeed Kjell Magne BONDEVIK (Christian People's Party), who had submitted his resignation on the same day, following the election of September 12; formed new government on October 20, 2009, following the election of September 14.

THE COUNTRY

A land of fjords and rugged mountains bisected by the Arctic Circle, Norway is the fifth-largest country in Western Europe but the second-lowest in population density, after Iceland. In addition to borders with its two Scandinavian neighbors, Sweden and Finland, Norway has also had a common border in the far north with the Soviet Union/Russia since 1944. Three-fourths of the land area is unsuitable for cultivation or habitation, and the population, homogeneous except for asylum-seekers and foreign workers in the south and a small Sámi (Lapp) minority of some 40,000 in the north, is heavily concentrated in the southern sector and along the Atlantic seaboard. For historical reasons the Norwegian language exists in two forms: the Danish-inspired *Bokmål* as well as *Nynorsk,* a traditional spoken tongue with a comparatively recent written form; in addition, the Sámi speak their own language, a member of the Finno-Ugrian group. The state-supported Evangelical Lutheran Church commands the allegiance of 88 percent of the population, although a recent survey concluded that only 10 percent of those members attend religious services or other church-related activities more than once a month. (In April 2008 government and opposition parties agreed to a proposal to amend the constitution to loosen the ties between the government and the Lutheran Church and to eliminate the Lutheran faith's status as the official state religion.)

Women constitute 47 percent of the active labor force, concentrated in the health and social services sector, wholesale and retail trade, and education. Slightly over one-third of the national legislators elected in 2005 were women, and no Norwegian government has been formed since 1986 with less than 40 percent women. Both the World Economic Forum and the United Nations (UN) Development Program rank Norway second in terms of economic and political gender equality. In 2006 legislation went into effect requiring publicly owned companies to staff their boards of directors with at least 40 percent women within two years.

The Norwegian merchant fleet is one of the world's ten largest (by country of owner) and, prior to the discovery of North Sea oil, was the country's leading foreign-exchange earner. Norway continues to export considerable amounts of such traditional commodities as fish and forest products, although the agricultural sector as a whole (including fishing and forestry) now contributes only 2 percent of GDP, compared to 39 percent for industry and 59 percent for services. In 2005 Norway was the world's third-largest net oil exporter, after Saudi Arabia and Russia, and the country has Western Europe's largest petroleum reserves, located in the Norwegian and Barents Seas as well as the North Sea. In addition, the development of hydroelectric power in recent decades has made Norway one of the largest exporters of aluminum and nitrogen products in Western Europe. Since exports and foreign services, including shipping, account for roughly 40 percent of the GNP, the economy is heavily influenced by fluctuations in the world market, although oil and natural gas production have made Norway, with a per capita gross national income of $40,420 in 2005 (in terms of cross-national purchasing power parity), one of the world's most affluent countries. GDP grew by an annual average of 2.7–3.9 percent in 2004–2007, but growth slipped to 2.1 percent in 2008. Under the effects of the global recession, GDP contraction of nearly 2 percent was forecast for 2009.

GOVERNMENT AND POLITICS

Political background. Although independent in its early period, Norway came under Danish rule in 1380. A period of de facto independence began in January 1814 but ended nine months later, when the legislature (*Storting*) accepted the Swedish monarch as king of

Norway. Norway remained a territory under the Swedish Crown until 1905, when the union was peacefully dissolved and the Norwegians elected a sovereign from the Danish royal house. Though Norway avoided involvement in World War I, it was occupied from 1940 to 1945 by Nazi Germany, which sponsored the infamous puppet regime of Vidkun QUISLING, while the legitimate government functioned in exile in London.

Norway's first postwar election continued the prewar ascendancy of the Norwegian Labor Party (*Det Norske Arbeiderparti*—DNA), and a government was formed in 1945 under Prime Minister Einar GERHARDSEN. Labor continued in the majority until 1961 and then maintained a minority government until 1965, when a coalition of nonsocialist parties took control under Per BORTEN, leader of the Center Party (*Senterpartiet*—Sp). The Borten government was forced to resign in 1971, following disclosure that the prime minister had deliberately leaked information on negotiations for entering the European Community (EC, later the European Union—EU). A Labor government under Trygve BRATTELI subsequently came to power but was forced from office in September 1972, when EC membership was rejected in a national referendum by 53.5 to 46.5 percent of participants. However, when a coalition government under Lars KORVALD of the Christian People's Party (*Kristelig Folkeparti*—KrF) failed to win the September 1973 general election, Bratteli returned as head of a minority government. Upon stepping down, Bratteli was succeeded in January 1976 by Labor's Odvar NORDLI. In the election of September 1977, Labor and its ally, the Socialist Left Party (*Sosialistisk Venstreparti*—SV), obtained a combined majority of one seat over four nonsocialist parties, enabling Nordli to continue in office.

Prime Minister Nordli resigned for health reasons in February 1981 and was succeeded by Gro Harlem BRUNDTLAND, the country's first female chief executive. However, in September her first minority government fell in the wake of a 10-seat loss at the polls by Labor, and in October Kåre WILLOCH formed a minority administration led by the Conservative Party (*Høyre*) with the legislative support of the KrF and the Sp. Partly because of the recessionary effects of Willoch's economic policies, in the September 1985 elections the voters nearly unseated the government; the three ruling parties obtained a total of 78 seats, as opposed to 77 for Labor and the SV, so that the right-wing Progress Party (*Fremskrittspartiet*—Frp), although winning only 2 seats, held the balance of power.

In April 1986 the Willoch government lost a confidence vote on a proposed gas tax increase when the anti-tax Frp voted with the opposition. In the first change in power without an intervening election in 23 years, Brundtland returned as head of another minority Labor administration. In the parliamentary poll of September 1989 the Labor and Conservative parties both lost ground, with the Conservatives, under Jan P. SYSE, forming a new minority administration in coalition with the KrF and Sp. However, in October 1990 the Sp deserted the coalition over the issue of foreign financial interests in Norway and then agreed to support Labor's return to power under Brundtland in December.

The resignation of the Syse government in late 1990 was forced by the Center Party's objection to the proposed signing of a European Economic Area (EEA) agreement (see article on the European Free Trade Association—EFTA) that would have necessitated revision of Norwegian laws restricting foreign ownership of industrial and financial institutions. Herself dependent on Center Party support, Prime Minister Brundtland declared that her new government would "work for a result that secures national regulation of natural resources and economic activity . . . without locking its position to demands that discriminate [against] citizens of other countries." Thus, Norway joined with other EFTA countries and the 12 EC states in signing the EEA Treaty in May 1992, after securing the addition of clauses designed to meet its concerns.

Controversy over Norway's renewed application for EC/EU membership, approved by the *Storting* in November 1992, dominated the general election of September 1993. The Labor and Conservative Parties favored accession (although the former was deeply divided over the issue), whereas the Center, Socialist Left, Christian People's, and Progress Parties were opposed. The results were far from definitive: Labor and the Center Party gained seats, while the other parties lost ground. Brundtland subsequently formed another Labor minority government, although the anti-EU parties had sufficient collective strength to deny the government the three-quarters majority required for approval of formal accession. Thus, the question was put to a referendum at which voters had to weigh whether accession provisions had sufficiently resolved questions regarding such key issues as the future of Norway's oil and gas reserves, access to Norway's fisheries, and safeguards for Norwegian farmers (among the most heavily subsidized in the world). On November 28, 1994, the Norwegian electorate again rejected EU membership, this time by a margin of 52.2 to 47.8 percent. Having acknowledged the outcome as a major defeat, Prime Minister Brundtland set as a new priority negotiating appropriate changes to the EEA Treaty that would continue to apply to Norway as a non-EU member.

With Brundtland having stepped down in October 1996, Labor entered the September 1997 election under the leadership of Thorbjørn JAGLAND, who had promised during the campaign to resign if his party polled less than the 36.9 percent of the vote it had received in 1993. Although Labor won 65 seats, compared to 25 each for the KrF and the Frp and 23 for the Conservatives, Jagland narrowly failed to meet his self-imposed target and submitted his resignation in October. KrF leader Kjell Magne BONDEVIK subsequently formed a new government, despite the fact that the parties in the new coalition—the KrF, the Sp, and the Liberal Party (*Venstre*–V)—controlled only 42 seats in the *Storting*. Bondevik submitted his resignation in March 2000 after losing a vote of confidence triggered by the government's objections to proposed construction of two gas-fired power stations. Labor's Jens STOLTENBERG was subsequently named head of an all-Labor, minority government.

The election of September 10, 2001, saw Labor narrowly retain its plurality, but with only 43 seats—its worst election returns in nearly a century. As a result, Kjell Bondevik returned to office at the head of a center-right minority coalition of the KrF, the Conservatives, and the Liberals. Controlling only 62 of the *Storting*'s 165 seats, the government required external support from the Frp, which had won 26 seats in the election.

In a dramatic reversal, Labor rebounded in the election of September 12, 2005, capturing 61 seats and, in partnership with the Socialist Left (15 seats) and Center (11 seats) parties, establishing a red-green majority of 87 seats. On October 17 Jens Stoltenberg was reinstalled as prime minister at the head of Norway's first majority government in two decades. Poor performance by the Socialist Left in the September 2007 local elections and scandals involving alleged favoritism to and by individual Labor and Center party ministers led to a series of cabinet resignations and reshuffles in late 2007 and throughout 2008; none, however, threatened the government's survival. The red-green alliance maintained its majority following the election of September 15, 2009, leaving the Stoltenberg government in place to lead the country for another four years.

Constitution and government. The Eidsvold Convention, one of the oldest written constitutions in Europe, was adopted by Norway on May 17, 1814. Executive power is exercised on behalf of the sovereign by a Council of State (*Statsråd*), which is headed by a prime minister and is responsible to the *Storting*. Should the cabinet resign on a vote of no confidence, the chair of the party holding the largest number of seats (exclusive of the defeated party) is asked to form a new government.

The members of the *Storting* are elected by universal suffrage and proportional representation for four-year terms. There are no by-elections, and the body is not subject to dissolution. Until October 1, 2009, the *Storting* operated as a modified bicameral assembly by electing one-fourth of its members to serve as an upper chamber (*Lagting*), while the remainder served as a lower chamber (*Odelsting*). Legislative proposals were considered separately by the two, but most other matters were dealt with by the *Storting* as a whole. The division proved largely meaningless in recent years as the party division in the chambers was the same, and legislation approved by the *Odelsting* was routinely rubber-stamped by the *Lagting*. In February 2007 the *Storting* approved a constitutional amendment, by a vote of 159–1, to dissolve the *Lagting* following the 2009 election.

The judicial system consists of district courts (*tingrett*), courts of appeal (*lagmannsrettene*), and a Supreme Court of Justice (*Høyesterett*). Judges are appointed by the king on advice from the Ministry of Justice. In addition to the regular courts, there are three special judicial institutions: a High Court of the Realm (*Riksrett*), consisting of the members of the Supreme Court and lay justices, which adjudicates charges against senior government officials; a Labor Relations Court (*Arbeidsretten*), which handles all matters concerning relations between employer and employee in both private and public sectors; and, in each community, a Conciliation Council (*Forliksråd*), to which most civil disputes are brought prior to formal legal action.

Local government is based on 19 counties (*fylker*), with Oslo, the capital, serving as one of the counties; in each county, the central government is represented by an appointed governor (*fylkesmann*). The County Council (*Fylkestinget*), which elects a board and a chair, is the representative institution at the county level. The basic units of local government are urban municipalities and rural communes, each of which is administered by an elected council (*Kommunestyre*), a board, and a mayor.

In 1987, following nearly a decade of agitation by the country's then approximately 20,000 Laplanders, agreement was reached on the establishment of a Sámi Parliament (*Sámediggi*) as replacement for the former Norwegian Sámi Council, which had been viewed as an inadequate defender of Sámi interests. The 43-member legislature has been granted authority in certain areas, such as the future of the Sámi language, the preservation of Sámi culture, and the determination of land use in Sámi-populated areas. It also has advisory functions in such areas as regional control of natural resources. Elections are held in tandem with balloting for the *Storting*.

Foreign relations. A founding member of the UN and the homeland of its first secretary general, Trygve LIE, Norway was also one of the original members of the North Atlantic Treaty Organization (NATO) and has been a leader in Western cooperation through such organizations as the Council of Europe and the Organization for Economic Cooperation and Development. Norway participated in the establishment of EFTA but, in national referendums held in 1972 and 1994, rejected membership in the EC/EU. Regional cooperation, mainly through the Nordic Council and the Nordic Council of Ministers, has also been a major element in its foreign policy.

A long-standing concern has been a dispute with what is now the Russian Federation regarding ocean-bed claims in the Barents Sea. At issue is a 60,000-square-mile area of potentially oil-rich continental shelf claimed by Norway on the basis of a median line between each country's territorial coasts and by its neighbor on the basis of a sector line extending northward from a point just east of their mainland border. A collateral disagreement has centered on fishing rights in a southern "grey zone" of the disputed area, where 200-mile limits overlap. A 1977 provisional agreement governing joint fishing in an area slightly larger than the "grey zone" proper has subsequently been renewed on an annual basis pending resolution of the larger controversy.

In 1992 Norway attracted international criticism by withdrawing from the International Whaling Commission (IWC) rather than accept an IWC ban on commercial whaling; a month later it joined with Iceland, the Faroe Islands, and Greenland to establish the pro-whaling North Atlantic Marine Mammals Commission. In 1993 foreign disapproval grew when Norwegian vessels resumed commercial whaling despite U.S. threats of trade sanctions and EU warnings that whaling was incompatible with membership.

Seeking to promote peaceful regional cooperation in the post-Soviet era, Norway became a founding member of the ten-nation Council of the Baltic Sea States in 1992 and also joined the Barents Euro-Arctic Council set up in 1993 by the five Nordic countries and Russia. Meanwhile, Norway had not only endorsed the EEA Treaty but had also, in 1992, accepted associate membership of the Western European Union (WEU), thereby seeking to demonstrate the pro-European axis of its foreign policy. Norway has also actively promoted peace in the wider international sphere, most dramatically through its participation in the negotiations that concluded with the 1993 Oslo Accord between Israel and the Palestinians.

Norway became enmeshed in an acrimonious fisheries dispute with Iceland in 1994, arising mainly from the latter's determination to fish in the waters around the Norwegian Svalbard islands. In November 1997 Norway concluded an agreement with Iceland and Denmark (on behalf of Greenland) establishing fishing limits in the region.

Norway's commitment to NATO has included deploying troops in peacekeeping operations in Bosnia, Kosovo, and Afghanistan. However, bilateral relations between Norway and the United States have been strained since the U.S. invasion of Iraq in 2003. Although Norway initially pledged $74 million to aid the reconstruction of Iraq and sent 150 troops to support peacekeeping efforts there, Prime Minister Bondevik described the Iraq war as "regrettable and sad." Rebuffing entreaties from Washington for additional support, the government in 2004 announced that Norway "would give priority to other nations rather than Iraq." Norway also irritated the United States and some of its European neighbors with the passage of an ethical code for investments by the country's Government Pension Fund. By law, the fund, pooled from more than $300 billion in oil exports, must be invested outside Norway. The ethical code requires investments to be made only in "socially responsible" companies. From the beginning, such U.S. companies as General Dynamics, Boeing, Lockheed Martin, and Northrop Grumman were blacklisted. Immediately after winning the 2005 election, Prime Minister Stoltenberg informed President George W. Bush that he would be removing the remaining contingent of Norwegian troops from Iraq.

Tensions between Russia and Norway increased as a result of Moscow's decision in October 2006 to forbid Norway, along with other countries, from developing Russia's natural gas fields in the Barents Sea. Norway's Statoil (later StatoilHydro) was one of a handful of companies bidding for a stake in Russia's Shtokman field, one of the world's largest. However, Norway was among the European countries expressing concern over Russia's willingness to use its control of energy reserves for political purposes. In November 2007 Helge Lund, StatoilHydro's chief executive, announced his desire to find a framework for cooperation between Norway and Russia in exploration in the Norwegian and Barents seas. At a meeting in Greenland in May 2008, Norway and Russia joined Canada, Denmark, and the United States in agreeing to use existing international laws to resolve Arctic disputes.

Current issues. The Labor Party's promise to increase welfare spending and reverse the tax reforms and other conservative policies initiated by former prime minister Bondevik resonated with voters and led to Labor's dramatic victory in the September 2005 election. The election also marked a shift on the right, with the Progress Party becoming the principal opposition party by outpolling the Conservatives, 38 seats to 28.

As expected, Prime Minister Stoltenberg subsequently drew upon the country's immense oil wealth to increase spending on education, health, and welfare, and in general to swing the domestic agenda to the left. Regarding the ongoing question of EU membership, the government rejected calls for another referendum despite public opinion polls that indicated approximately 50 percent support for accession. (Both the Center Party and the Socialist Left had long opposed membership, with the latter also favoring withdrawal from NATO.) Given the divergence of opinion on these and other matters, some analysts questioned how long the three-party government coalition would survive. That concern was reinforced by the September 2007 municipal and county elections. Although Labor improved on its 2003 performance and the Center Party basically held even, the Socialist Left took a drubbing, losing nearly half its support. The Frp's vote share also dropped from 22 percent in the 2005 national election to under 18 percent in the 2007 balloting, while the Conservatives staged a comeback, climbing from 14 to 19 percent.

In June 2007 the *Storting* approved a major consolidation within the domestic oil industry—the purchase by Statoil of the oil and gas operations of Norsk Hydro, the petroleum and aluminum giant. The $30 billion deal will make the renamed StatoilHydro, of which the state was slated to ultimately own a 67 percent interest, the world's largest offshore oil producer.

Meanwhile, the impetus to utilize petroleum profits for social welfare programs took on an international aspect, as the government initiated a campaign to work with other petroleum-exporting countries to use oil revenues more effectively in meeting national priorities. Working with countries such as Bolivia, Norway sought to export its domestic model of more equitable distribution of oil wealth.

In early 2009 the Stoltenberg government announced plans to increase public spending by using a larger than normal percentage of the country's oil revenues. These measures were credited with mitigating the economic downturn, and by August 2009 Norway looked to be on the road to recovery. The ability of Stoltenberg to shield the country from the most severe effects of the global financial crisis became a major story line leading up to the *Storting* balloting on September 15. The main challenge to the government came from the Frp, which campaigned on a platform calling for tax cuts, privatization, and tighter immigration controls. Although the election results marked a new electoral high for the Frp in votes and seats, a right-center government had effectively been ruled out prior to the election due to the unwillingness of minor center-right parties to join a Frp-led coalition. Meanwhile, the relatively stable economy, coupled with Stoltenberg's personal popularity, resulted in an increase of three seats for the DNA. The red-green DNA-led coalition claimed 86 of the 169 seats, marking the first time in 16 years that an incumbent government won reelection and the first time since 1969 that a government maintained a majority after an election.

In response to his 2009 electoral victory, Stoltenberg pledged to tackle the issues of employment, schooling, elderly care, and climate change over the next four years. In addition, by mid-October it was clear that the additional DNA seats were strengthening Stoltenberg's hand during government negotiations as the coalition announced that it would pursue his plan to reduce the number of asylum seekers coming to the country, despite the SV's desire to maintain a more liberal policy. The administration also said it continued to entertain the possibility of opening offshore oil exploration off the Lofoten archipelago, despite the SV's strongly stated opposition.

POLITICAL PARTIES

Government Parties:

Norwegian Labor Party (*Det Norske Arbeiderparti*—DNA). Organized in 1887, Labor has been the strongest party in Norway since 1927. Its program of democratic socialism resembles those of other Scandinavian Social Democratic parties. Its longest-serving post–World War II prime ministers have been Einar Gerhardsen, who served three times (for a total of over 17 years), between 1945 and 1965, and Gro Harlem Brundtland, who also served three times (for some 10 years), between 1981 and 1996.

In June 1994 a special Labor conference decided by a 2–1 majority to back EU accession in the November referendum, although substantial rank-and-file Labor opposition to membership contributed to the eventual "no" vote. When Brundtland decided to retire as prime minister in 1996, she handed over leadership to Thorbjørn Jagland. During this period, despite its close links to labor unions, the party leadership seemed open to finding private sector solutions for the problems of the welfare state, alienating some of its more left-wing supporters. Labor also remained a firm backer of NATO.

Having failed to meet his self-imposed goal of at least matching Labor's 36.9 percent vote share in 1993, Jagland resigned as prime minister after the 1997 legislative election, even though Labor had won a plurality of 65 seats. Labor's vote share also declined in municipal balloting in September 1999 and February 2000, but the fall of the Bondevik coalition government in March 2000 led to formation of a Labor minority government under Jens Stoltenberg. After Labor won a dismal 43 *Storting* seats in the September 2001 election, Stoltenberg resigned as prime minister, although he was elected party chair, replacing Jagland, in November 2002.

Under Stoltenberg's leadership Labor's fortunes turned. Building on positive results in the September 2003 local elections, Stoltenberg negotiated a red-green alliance with the Center and Socialist Left Parties that, led by Labor's 61 seats at the September 2005 election, permitted Stoltenberg to reclaim the office of prime minister. In the September 2007 local elections Labor increased its vote share over 2003 by about 2 percent, to 30 percent of the total. Even more impressive was Labor's 35.4 percent vote share in the September 2009 general election. Its 64 seats allowed the Stoltenberg-headed, Labor-led coalition to continue its majority status.

Leaders: Jens STOLTENBERG (Prime Minister and Party Leader), Helga Pedersen (Deputy Leader), Raymond JOHANSEN (General Secretary), Kathrine RAADIM (International Secretary).

Socialist Left Party (*Sosialistisk Venstreparti*—SV). Organized prior to the 1973 election as the Socialist Electoral Association (*Sosialistisk Valgforbund*), the SV was until late 1975 a coalition of the Norwegian Communist Party (below), the Socialist People's Party (*Sosialistisk Folkeparti*—SF), and the Democratic Socialist/Labor Movement Information Committee against Norwegian Membership in the Common Market (*Demokratiske Sosialister/Arbeiderbevegelsens Informasjonskomite mot Norsk Medlemskap i EF*—DS/AIK). At a congress held in Trondheim in March 1975, the members of the coalition committed themselves to the formation of the new party, although dissolution of the constituent parties was not to be considered mandatory until the end of 1976. In November 1975 the Communist Party decided against dissolution, and in the September 1977 election the SV, damaged in August when two of its deputies leaked a secret parliamentary report on defense negotiations with the United States, retained only 2 of the 16 seats formerly held by the Socialist alliance. The party nonetheless provided the Nordli government with the crucial support needed to maintain a slim parliamentary majority prior to the 1981 balloting, in which it won 2 additional seats. In 1989 the party raised its parliamentary representation from 6 to 17 seats before slipping back to 13 in 1993.

The SV played a prominent role in the successful campaign against EU accession in the November 1994 referendum, thereafter intensifying its opposition to the minority Labor government. In April 1996 SV leader Erik SOLHEIM accused Labor and its Center parliamentary allies of "Americanizing" Norway by a combination of tax cuts for the rich and welfare benefit cuts for the poor. The SV faltered in the 1997 election, dropping from 13 seats to 9. It has toned down its anti-NATO rhetoric in recent years and is now a strong advocate for Norway's "international responsibilities," including foreign aid. The SV more than doubled its representation in the September 2001 election, winning 23 seats.

Looking to build upon its 2001 success, the SV continued to move toward more centrist positions and joined Labor and the Center Party to form the red-green alliance in the September 2005 election. As a requirement for joining the alliance, the SV agreed to set aside its long-standing demand that Norway withdraw from NATO and muted much of its anti-U.S. rhetoric. However, it retained only 15 seats. Some SV members criticized party leader Kristin Halvorsen for moderating the party's anti-U.S. stance. In 2006–2007 the SV grew more critical of the government's environmental policies and the country's continuing presence in Afghanistan. In the September 2007 local elections the SV won only 6 percent of the vote, about half of its 2003 share. Its electoral fortunes also fell in the 2009 parliamentary balloting, in which it won only 6.2 percent of the vote and 11 seats. The SV subsequently kept its minor coalition partner role in government, but only after agreeing to the Labor Party positions on tightening restrictions on asylum seekers and keeping open the possibility of more off-shore oil exploration.

Leaders: Kristin HALVORSEN (Party Chair); Audun LYSBAKKEN and Bård Vegar SOLHJELL (Deputy Chairs); Inge RYAN (Parliamentary Leader); Edle DAASVAND (Secretary General); Lene Aure HANSEN (International Secretary).

Center Party (*Senterpartiet*—Sp). Formed in 1920 to promote the interests of agriculture and forestry, the Sp was originally known as the Agrarian Party. In the late 1980s it began to take steps to broaden its appeal, changing its name, stressing ecological issues, and advocating reduced workdays for families with small children. Not surprisingly, it also championed the post-1975 government policy of bringing farmers' incomes up to the level of industrial workers, although it remained conservative on some economic, social, and religious matters.

Campaigning on a strongly anti-EU ticket, the Sp made major gains in the September 1993 election, increasing its representation from 11 to 32 seats. In the new *Storting* Sp backing was often forthcoming for the minority Labor government, although in June 1996 the party issued a joint statement with Christian People's and Liberal Parties envisaging a nonsocialist coalition after the 1997 election. In 1997, when EU membership was no longer an issue, the Sp dropped back to 11 seats, although its vision of a center-liberal coalition government became a reality the following month.

Anne Enger LAHNSTEIN, Sp chair for 16 years, resigned her party post (but not her cabinet position) in March 1999 and was succeeded by Odd Roger ENOKSEN. In the 2001 election the party won ten *Storting* seats, remaining in opposition. Åslaug HAGA assumed the party's leadership in 2005 and entered into the red-green alliance with the Labor and Center Parties. By doing so, she further moved the party to a centrist position, supporting, for example, oil production in the Barents Sea (under strict environmental standards) and further participation in the global markets. Some members of the party charged that Haga abandoned farmers and the party's traditional agricultural values. In the September 2007 local elections the Sp won about 8 percent of the total vote, as it had in 2003.

After receiving fierce criticism over allegations that she had obtained illegal building permits for her family's homes, Haga resigned her party leadership and ministerial positions in mid-June 2008, citing personal health concerns. She was replaced on a temporary basis by Deputy Leader Lars Peder Brekk until the party elected Liv Signe Navarsete as its new leader in September. Under Navarsete's leadership the Sp held onto its 11 seats (on a vote share of 6.2 percent) in the September 2009 election, which allowed it to continue as a junior partner in the Labor-led majority coalition, despite misgivings about Labor's intention to keep open the possibility of more off-shore oil exploration.

Leaders: Liv Signe NAVARSETE (Party Leader); Lars Peder BREKK, Erling SANDE (Deputy Leaders); Trygue Magnus Slagsvold VEDUM (Parliamentary Leader); Ivar EGEBERG (Secretary General).

Other Parliamentary Parties:

Progress Party (*Fremskrittspartiet*—Frp). A libertarian group founded by Anders LANGE in 1974, the anti-EU Progress Party was known until 1977 as Anders Lange's Party for a Strong Reduction in Taxes, Rates, and Public Intervention (*Anders Langes Parti til Sterk Nedsettelse av Skatter, Avgifter, og Offentlige Inngrep*). Although it lost two of its four seats in the 1985 balloting, the Frp was subsequently invited to join the ruling coalition to offset the Conservatives' losses. Declining to do so, the party held a subsequent balance of power in the *Storting* and provided the crucial votes needed to defeat the Willoch government in April 1986. In the 1989 parliamentary poll the Frp emerged as the third largest party, with 22 *Storting* seats, but in 1993 it suffered a major reverse, winning only 10. In 1997 the Frp regained its strength by winning 25 seats and a 15.3 percent share of the vote, second only to Labour. The Frp has favored dismantling the welfare state and has opposed subsidies to such sectors as fishing and agriculture. It takes a restrictive stand on immigration issues and favors tough anticrime measures.

Less than a year before the September 2001 election, polls showed the Frp as the country's most popular party, but it quickly lost ground, most dramatically because of the resignation in February 2001 of its second most influential leader, Terje SÖVIKNES, following a sex scandal in which other party figures were also implicated. Meanwhile, the party was also being torn by sharp differences between its more moderate elements, on the one hand, and its more overtly fascistic and racist wing, on the other. In the end, the party registered a modest loss in vote share, to 14.7 percent, and won 26 seats. Carl I. HAGEN, the chair since 1978, extended the party's conditional support to the new Bondevik three-party coalition, thereby enabling it to take office in October.

Entering the September 2005 election, the Frp positioned itself as an outside party and campaigned both in defense of a strong welfare state and for radical tax cuts. It was rewarded with 22 percent of the vote and 38 seats, supplanting the Conservatives as the leading opposition party. In May 2006 Siv Jensen—the first woman to lead the party—was elected chair. Under her leadership the party has moved closer to the Conservative Party.

In the September 2007 local elections the Frp registered a modest improvement over its 2003 totals, winning about 18 percent of the vote, below its 2005 vote share and a percentage point behind the Conservatives. The Frp continued to make electoral progress in the September 2009 balloting, increasing its vote share to a best-ever 22.9 percent and winning 41 seats. However, the party's fate to remain an opposition party had been sealed before the vote when the Christian Democrats and Liberals said they would decline to participate in an Frp-led coalition, due in large part to the Frp's anti-immigration stand.

Leaders: Siv JENSEN (Chair), Per SANDBERG and Per Arne OLSEN (Vice Chairs), Geir MO (Secretary General).

Conservative Party (*Høyre*—H). The oldest of the contemporary Norwegian parties (founded in 1884), the *Høyre* (literally "Right") advocates a "modern, progressive conservatism" emphasizing private investment, elimination of government control in the semipublic industries, lower taxes, and a revised tax structure that would benefit business. It has long favored a strong defense policy.

Although the party's parliamentary representation declined from 50 seats in 1985 to 37 in 1989, it succeeded in forming a short-lived minority coalition administration under Jan Syse—the party's sole prime minister Kåre Willoch left office in 1986. In the September 1993 election the pro-EU Conservatives slumped from 37 seats to 28. Subsequent moves by some Conservative branches to establish local alliances with the populist Progress Party caused considerable internal dissension, as the national leadership frequently gave parliamentary backing to the minority Labor government, particularly on budgetary matters. In 1997 the party decline continued as it won only 23 seats. In 2001 it resurged, winning 38 seats, but its chair, Jan PETERSEN, yielded to KrF insistence that Kjell Bondevik be prime minister of any KrF-Conservative-Liberal government.

Although the party captured only 23 seats in the 2005 election, in 2006 it opted to maintain its leadership, reelecting Erna Solberg as chair. Solberg pledged to refocus the party on the September 2007 municipal and county elections, in which it won 19 percent of the vote, slightly more than Solberg's goal. Solberg has expressed a desire to offer a four-party center-right coalition—along with the Progress Party, the Liberals, and the Christian Democrats—in the next general election, but the Liberals and Christian Democrats said in the run-up to the September 2009 balloting that they would not take part in such a government. The Conservative vote share rebounded to 17.2 percent in 2009, increasing the party's seat total by 7, to 30, but still leaving it some distance behind the Frp as the major opposition. Perhaps out of frustration among conservatives in the electorate over the inability to elect a Center-right government, public opinion polling a month after the election showed the Conservatives pulling ahead of the Frp for the first time in several years.

Leaders: Erna SOLBERG (Chair), Per-Kristian FOSS and Jan Tore SANNER (Vice Chairs), Knut JAHR (Secretary General).

Christian People's Party (*Kristelig Folkeparti*—KrF or KFp). Also known as the Christian Democratic Party, the KrF was created in 1933 with the primary objective of maintaining the principles of Christianity in public life. In addition to support for most Conservative policies, the KrF's agenda subsequently centered on introduction of anti-abortion legislation and increased trade with developing countries. In the 1989 election its legislative strength dropped from 16 to 14 seats, falling further by 1 seat in 1993, when it campaigned against EU membership. The party nearly doubled its representation in September 1997, going up to 25 seats. Joining with the Liberal and Center Parties to form a minority coalition government in October, the KrF was permitted to select the new prime minister—former deputy prime minister and foreign affairs minister Kjell Bondevik—because it held the largest deputy bloc of the three. Bondevik resigned as prime minister in March 2000 following defeat of a government bill in the *Storting*. Although the party finished with only 22 seats after the September 2001 election, Bondevik returned to the prime ministership. Following a poor performance by the KrF in the September 2003 local elections, Valgerd Svarstad HAUGLAND resigned after nearly nine years as KrF chair; she was succeeded in 2004 by Health Minister Dagfinn Høybråten, a strong opponent of EU membership.

Under Bondevik, Norway enjoyed strong economic growth, with personal incomes rising and the stock market almost tripling. Moreover, inflation remained largely in check while interest rates declined sharply. Despite these gains, Bondevik fell out of favor. His insistence on a conservative fiscal policy and tax cuts seemed out of step with the general public, which favored higher levels of public sector spending. In 2005 the KrF won less than 7 percent of the votes cast and 11 seats. Bondevik announced his retirement from politics shortly after the election. In the September 2009 parliamentary balloting the KrF vote share fell back to 5.5 percent (good for 10 seats), its worst showing since shortly after the party was formed in the 1930s.

Leaders: Dagfinn HØYBRÅTEN (Chair); Dagun ERIKSEN and Hansen Ingen LISE (Deputy Chairs); Inger Helene VENÅS (Secretary General); Per Kristian NIELSEN (International Secretary).

Liberal Party (*Venstre*—V). Formed in 1884, the Liberal Party (*venstre* means "left"), like the Sp, currently stresses ecological issues, while in economic policy it stands between the Conservative and Labor Parties. Having suffered defections to splinter groups, the Liberals lost their two remaining parliamentary seats in 1985. In June 1988 the Liberal People's Party (*Det Liberale Folkepartiet*—DLF), which had been formed in 1972 by Liberal dissidents who favored Norway's entrance into the EC and had lost its only parliamentary seat in 1977, rejoined the parent party. After failing to regain *Storting* representation in 1989, the Liberals won one seat in 1993 and took six seats in 1997, joining the subsequent KrF-led coalition government until its dissolution in March 2000. *Venstre* won only two seats in 2001 but again joined Prime Minister Bondevik's governing coalition. In the September 2005 elections the party made its best showing since 1972, winning almost 6 percent of the vote and capturing 10 seats, but the success was short-lived. In the September 2009 the party's vote share, 3.9 percent, and seats, 2, fell back to the 2001 levels.

Leaders: Lars SPONHEIM (Leader); Trine Skei GRADE and Ola ELVESTUEN (Deputy Leaders); Terje BREIVIK (Secretary General).

Other Parties Contesting the 2009 Elections:

Coastal Party (*Kystpartiet*). The Coastal Party was organized by Steinar BASTESEN, a spokesperson for whaling interests in the fishing towns of the north who was elected to the *Storting* in September 1997 and assumed his seat as a member of the Nonpartisan Representatives (*Tverrpolitisk Folkevalgte*—TvF). In 1999 the party name was given as the Nonpartisan Coastal and Regional Party (*Tverrpolitisk Kyst og Distriktspartiet*). An internal dispute forced Bastesen to step down as chair in March 2005, and in September he lost his *Storting* seat as support for the party declined to 0.8 percent of the vote. Four years later, in the September 2009 election, the party fortunes slipped again as it won just 0.2 percent of the vote and no seats.

Leaders: Kjell Ivar VESTÅ (Chair), Roy WAAGE (Deputy Chair).

Norwegian Communist Party (*Norges Kommunistiske Parti*—NKP). The NKP held 11 *Storting* seats in 1945 but lost all of them by 1961. In March 1975 it participated in the initial formation of the Socialist Left Party, but the following November it voted at an extraordinary congress against its own dissolution. Prior to the 1989 election it joined with the Red Electoral Alliance (see Red, below) to form the Local List for Environment and Solidarity (*Fylkeslistene for Miljø og Solidaritet*—FMS), which failed to secure representation. The party chose not to contest the 1993 election and obtained only 0.1 percent of the vote or less in 1997, 2001, 2005, and 2009.

Leaders: Zafer GÖZET (Leader), Svend Haakon JACOBSEN (Deputy Leader).

Red (*Rødt*). Red was formed in March 2007 by merger of the Red Electoral Alliance (*Rød Valgallianse*—RV) and the Workers' Communist Party (*Arbeidernes Kommunistparti*—AKP). The RV had been formed in 1973 as an electoral front for the Maoist AKP but subsequently grew to include a substantial number of self-described "independent socialists." Prior to the 1989 elections the RV joined with the Norwegian Communist Party (NKP, above) in the FMS. Returning to a separate status, in 1993 the RV won 1.1 percent of the vote and one *Storting* seat, which it lost in 1997. In 2005 the RV won only 1.2 percent of the vote and again failed to capture any seats. Torstein Dahle was reelected party president in 2005 and then leader of the newly formed Red. He was able to lead the party to a slight increase in vote support in the September 2009 balloting, but the RV's 1.4 percent of the vote entitled it to no seats.

Leaders: Torstein DAHLE (Leader), Ana Lopez TAYLOR and Ingrid BALTZERSEN (Deputy Leaders), Beth HARTMANN (Secretary).

Another unsuccessful party in the 2005 and 2009 legislative elections was the **Pensioners' Party** (*Pensjonistpartiet*—Pp), which won 0.5 percent of the vote in 2005 and 0.4 percent in 2009. The only other parties to achieve at least 0.1 percent in 2009 were the **Environment Party The Greens** (*Miljopartiet De Grønne*) with 0.3 percent and the conservative **Christian Unity Party** (*Kristent Samlingparti*) with 0.2 percent

LEGISLATURE

The ***Stortinget*** (also frequently rendered as *Storting*) is a unicameral parliament whose members are elected to four-year terms by universal suffrage and party-list proportional representation from 19 multimember (3 to 16 seats each) constituencies (corresponding to the 19 counties). (Of the 169 members, 150 are elected based solely on results within each constituency. The other 19 sears [one in each constituency] serve as "top up" or compensatory seats and are distributed according to nationwide vote percentages for parties.) From 1814 through mid-2009 it divided itself for certain purposes into two chambers by electing one-fourth of its members to an upper chamber (*Lagting*), while the remaining members constituted a lower chamber (*Odelsting*). Each *ting* named its own president; the president of the *Storting* served for the duration of its term, and the presidents of the two chambers were chosen annually. The *Lagting* sat for the last time in June 2009, and the dual chamber structure was officially dissolved on October 1.

In the most recent election on September 14, 2009, the Norwegian Labor Party won 64 seats; the Progress Party, 41; the Conservative Party, 30; the Socialist Left Party, 11; the Center Party, 11; the Christian People's Party, 10; and the Liberal Party 2.

President of the Storting: Dag Terje ANDERSEN.

CABINET

[as of October 20, 2009]

Prime Minister	Jens Stoltenberg (DNA)
Ministers	
Agriculture and Food	Lars Peder Brekk (Sp)
Children and Equality	Audun Lysbakken (SV)
Culture and Church Affairs	Anniken Huitfeldt (DNA) [f]
Defense	Grete Faremo (DNA) [f]
Education	Kristin Halvorsen (SV) [f]
Environment and International Development	Erik Solheim (SV)
Finance	Sigbjørn Johnsen (DNA)
Fisheries and Coastal Affairs	Lisbeth Berg-Hansen (DNA) [f]
Foreign Affairs	Jonas Gahr Støre (DNA)
Government Administration and Reform	Rigmor Aasrud (DNA) [f]
Health and Care Services	Anne-Grete Strøm-Erichsen (DNA) [f]
Immigration	Knut Storberget (DNA)
Justice and the Police	Knut Storberget (DNA)
Labor and Social Inclusion	Rigmor Aasrud (DNA) [f]
Local Government and Regional Development	Liv Signe Navarsete (Sp) [f]
Nordic Cooperation	Rigmor Aasrud (DNA) [f]
Office of the Prime Minister	Karl Eirik Schjøtt-Pedersen (DNA)
Petroleum and Energy	Terje Riis-Johanson (Sp)
Research and Higher Education	Tora Aasland (SV) [f]
Trade and Industry	Trond Giske (DNA)
Transport and Communications	Magnhild Meltveit Kleppa (Sp) [f]

[f] = female

Note: Three revamped ministries were scheduled to be established on January 1, 2010, with Hanne Bjurstrøm (DNA) being named minister of labor and Rigmor Aasrud (DNA) being named minister of reform and church affairs. In addition, the ministry of children and equality was scheduled to become the ministry of children, equality, and social inclusion.

COMMUNICATIONS

Freedom of the press is constitutionally guaranteed. As in many other countries, media ownership has become more concentrated, which prompted the *Storting* to enact checks in 1998. At present, three companies account for more than half of total newspaper circulation.

Press. Most papers, which tend to be openly partisan, are privately owned by individuals, families, corporations, and political parties. A 1919 ban on Sunday publication was lifted in 1990. The government, which has subsidized the press for decades to promote competition, also continues to exempt newspapers from the national value-added tax (VAT). The following are published daily in Oslo unless otherwise noted: *Verdens Gang* (340,000), independent centrist; *Aftenposten* (245,000 morning; 140,000 evening), independent conservative; *Dagbladet* (160,000), independent; *Bergens Tidende* (Bergen, 90,000), independent liberal; *Adresseavisen* (Trondheim, 85,000), Conservative; *Stavanger Aftenblad* (Stavanger, 70,000), independent; *Dagens Næringsliu* (65,000); *Fædrelandsvennen* (Kristiansand, 45,000), independent; *Drammens Tidende og Buskeruds Blad* (Drammen, 45,000), independent conservative; *Dagsavisen* (formerly *Arbeiderbladet,* 40,000), formerly a Labor Party organ.

News agencies. The major domestic facility is the Norwegian News Agency (*Norsk Telegrambyrå*—NTB), which is jointly owned by the leading newspapers; in addition, numerous foreign bureaus maintain offices in Oslo.

Broadcasting and computing. A state company, *Norsk Rikskringkasting* (NRK), held a monopoly of all broadcasting until 1982, when the first private local radio stations were authorized, while its television dominance ended in 1991 when the *Storting* approved licensing of a new commercial channel. Cable and satellite service, providing a wide variety of television channels, is now common, and digital transmission is expanding. In addition, British, Danish, Finnish, Swedish, and Russian television are received in some border and coastal areas.

As of 2008 there were 825.5 Internet users per 1,000 inhabitants.

INTERGOVERNMENTAL REPRESENTATION

Ambassador to the U.S.: Wegger Christian STROMMEN.

U.S. Ambassador to Norway: Barry B. WHITE.

Permanent Representative to the UN: Morten WETLAND.

IGO Memberships (Non-UN): AC, ADB, AfDB, BIS, CBSS, CERN, CEUR, EBRD, EFTA, ESA, Eurocontrol, IADB, IEA, Interpol, IOM, NATO, NC, NIB, OECD, OSCE, PCA, WCO, *WEU,* WTO.

RELATED TERRITORIES

Norway's principal overseas territories are the islands of the Svalbard group and Jan Mayen, both of which are legally incorporated into the Norwegian state. In addition, Norway has two dependencies in southern waters, Bouvet Island and Peter I Island, and claims a sector of Antarctica.

Svalbard. Svalbard is the group name given to all the islands in the Arctic Ocean between 74° and 81° north latitude and 10° and 35° east longitude, Spitzbergen being the most important island in the group. Svalbard has a land area of 23,957 square miles (62,049 sq. km.); its resident population is approximately 2,600 (2006E), of whom some 1,600 are Norwegians, most of the remainder being Russians.

The islands were placed under Norwegian sovereignty by the 1920 Svalbard Treaty, the 39 signatories of which are entitled to exploit Svalbard's natural resources, although only Norwegian and Soviet/Russian companies have done so. Coal mining is the major activity in the area; oil and gas exploration began in the late 1980s. In 1993 the government and four Norwegian universities established at the largest settlement, Longyearbyen, the University Center in Svalbard, which hosts domestic and international researchers and students. More recently, tourism has been gaining in importance.

In 2007 construction began on the Svalbard International Seed Vault on Spitzbergen. The vault, positioned 120 meters inside a mountain, will store seeds from all known varieties of food crops as protection against their loss.

Governor: Per SEFLAND.

Jan Mayen. Jan Mayen is an island of 144 square miles (373 sq. km.) located in the Norwegian Sea, 555 nautical miles from Tromsø. It was incorporated as part of the Kingdom of Norway in 1930. A meteorological station was established on the island during World War II, with navigational and radio facilities added thereafter. There are no permanent inhabitants.

Bouvet Island (*Bouvetøya*). Located in the South Atlantic, Bouvet Island has an area of 22 square miles (58 sq. km.) and is uninhabited. It became a Norwegian dependency in 1930 and was declared to be a nature reserve in 1971.

Peter I Island (*Peter I Øy*). Situated some 250 miles off the Antarctic continent in the Bellingshausen Sea, Peter I Island has an area of 96 square miles (249 sq. km.) and became a Norwegian dependency in 1933. It is uninhabited.

Queen Maud Land (*Dronning Maud Land*). The Norwegian-claimed sector of Antarctica, Queen Maud Land, extends from 20° west longitude to 45° east longitude. Its legal status has been placed in suspense under terms of the 1959 Antarctic Treaty.

OMAN

Sultanate of Oman
Sultanat Uman

Political Status: Independent sultanate recognized December 20, 1951; present regime instituted July 23, 1970; new "basic law" decreed on November 6, 1996.

Area: 119,500 sq. mi. (309,500 sq. km.).

Population: 2,340,815 (2003C); 2,614,000 (2008E). Both figures include non-Omanis (559,257 in 2003).

Major Urban Center (2005E): MUSCAT (urban area, 640,000).

Official Language: Arabic.

Monetary Unit: Oman Rial (official rate December 1 ,2009: 1 rial = $2.60US).

Head of State and Government: Sultan Qabus ibn Said Al SAID; assumed power July 23, 1970, in a coup d'état that deposed his father, Sultan Said ibn Taymur Al SAID.

THE COUNTRY

The Sultanate of Oman (known prior to August 1970 as Muscat and Oman), which occupies the southeast portion of the Arabian Peninsula and a number of offshore islands, is bounded by the United Arab Emirates on the northwest, Saudi Arabia on the west, and Yemen on the extreme southwest. A small, noncontiguous area at the tip of the Musandam Peninsula extends northward into the Strait of Hormuz, through which much of the world's ocean-shipped oil passes. Although the Omani population is predominantly Arab (divided into an estimated 200 tribes), small communities of Iranians, Baluchis, Indians, East Africans, and Pakistanis are also found. Ibadhi Muslims constitute up to 75 percent of the population; most of the remainder are Wahhabis of the Sunni branch, although there is a small Shiite population. In addition to Arabic, English, Farsi, and Urdu, several Indian dialects are spoken.

Prior to 1970 the Sultanate was an isolated, essentially medieval state without roads, electricity, or significant educational and health facilities; social behavior was dictated by a repressive and reclusive sultan. However, following his overthrow in 1970, the country underwent rapid modernization, fueled by soaring oil revenue. Oman currently provides free medical facilities, housing assistance for most of its citizens, and schools for more than 550,000 students. Economic growth has been concentrated in the coastal cities with an accompanying construction boom relying on a large foreign workforce. However, under a government program designed to reduce migration to urban areas, services have been extended to most of the vast rural interior. It has been estimated that about half of the population still engages in farming, herding, or fishing, with a large percentage of the country's women working as unpaid agricultural laborers on family landholdings. Growing access to education (more than 40 percent of Omani students are female) has reduced the once high illiteracy rate among women. Women have visible roles in both private and public sectors in part because of the relatively moderate (in regional terms) stance of the sultan.

Although much of the labor force works in agriculture, most food must be imported; dates, nuts, limes, and fish are exported. Cattle are bred extensively in the southern province of Dhofar, and Omani camels are prized throughout Arabia. Since petroleum production began in 1967, the Sultanate has become heavily dependent on oil revenue, which, at a production rate of more than 700,000 barrels per day, accounts for more than 70 percent of government revenue and 40 percent of GDP. However, liquefied natural gas continues to be a rapidly growing segment of the economy. In a further effort to offset the nation's dependence on oil, the government has launched a program of economic diversification, intended to encourage foreign investment, promote small-scale private industry, and enhance the fledgling tourism sector. Recent initiatives include changes in investment law to permit Omani companies to be owned by non-nationals. The government of Oman has undertaken a number of large infrastructure projects, including the construction of the giant maritime trans-shipment terminal at the port of Mina Raysut, and development of gas exports.

GDP growth of 3.5 percent was recorded in 2004, rising annually to an average of 6.4 percent in 2005–2007. The International Monetary Fund (IMF) in recent years has commended Oman's sound economic policies, including diversification and the reduction of public debt. These policies, in combination with high crude oil prices, rising consumption and investment, and increasing non-oil revenue, have contributed to the positive economic forecast. Oman's decision in 2008 to continue its monetary peg to the U.S. dollar, rather than join a monetary union with the Gulf Cooperation Council (GCC), was commended by fund managers, though they acknowledged that the peg was among the chief reasons for rising inflation in the sultanate. Nevertheless, annual GDP growth remained robust at 7.4 percent in 2008, even as oil reserves (and output) declined. Plans were under way to tap several new oil fields, invest heavily in liquefied natural gas, and participate in projects with the private sector aimed at significantly increasing tourism. Economic growth was expected to contract somewhat in 2009–2010, averaging about 6 percent, as oil prices fell during the global economic downturn.

GOVERNMENT AND POLITICS

Political background. Conquered by the Portuguese in 1508, the Omanis successfully revolted in 1650 and subsequently extended their domain as far south as Zanzibar. A brief period of Iranian intrusion (1741–1743) was followed in 1798 by the establishment of a treaty of friendship with Great Britain; thereafter, the British played a protective role, although formally recognizing the Sultanate's independence in 1951.

Oman is home of the Ibadhi sect, centered in Nazwa, which evolved from the egalitarian Kharijite movement of early Islam. During much of the twentieth century, Omani politics centered on an intrasect rivalry between imams, who controlled the interior, and sultans of the Said dynasty, who ruled over the coastal cities of Muscat and Muttrah, although the Treaty of Sib, concluded in 1920, acknowledged the nation's indivisibility. On the death of the incumbent imam in 1954, Sultan Said ibn Taymur Al SAID attempted, without success, to secure election as his successor. However, revolts against the sultan by the new imam's followers were ended with British help in 1959, thus cementing the sultan's authority over the entire country. The foreign presence having become the subject of a number of UN debates, the remaining British bases were closed in 1977, although a number of British officers remained attached to the Omani armed forces.

The conservative and isolationist Sultan Said was ousted on July 23, 1970, by his son, Qabus ibn Said Al SAID. The former sultan fled to London, where he died in 1972. Qabus, whose takeover was supported by the British, soon began efforts to modernize the country, but his request for cooperation from rebel groups who had opposed his father evoked little positive response. In 1971–1972 two left-wing guerrilla groups merged to form the Popular Front for the Liberation of Oman and the Arabian Gulf (renamed in July 1974 as the Popular Front for the Liberation of Oman—PFLO), which continued resistance to the sultan's regime, primarily from bases in the (then) People's Democratic Republic of Yemen (South Yemen). Qabus maintained his superiority with military assistance from Saudi Arabia, Jordan, Iran, and Pakistan, and in December 1975 he asserted that the rebellion had been crushed, with a formal cease-fire being announced in March 1976.

Although the sultan subsequently stated his desire to introduce democratic reforms, a Consultative Assembly established in 1981 consisted entirely of appointed members, and Oman remained for all practical purposes an absolute monarchy. In November 1990 the sultan announced plans for a Consultative Council of regional representatives in an effort to provide for more citizen participation.

By the mid-1990s the Consultative Council had become the forum for rigorous questioning of government ministers, as well as sporadic grumbling over alleged corruption on the part of members of the ruling elite.

On November 6, 1996, Sultan Qabus issued "The Basic Law of the Sultanate of Oman," the nation's first quasi-constitutional document. Although it confirmed the final authority of the sultan in all government matters, it also codified the responsibilities of the Council of Ministers and provided for a second consultative body, the Council of State

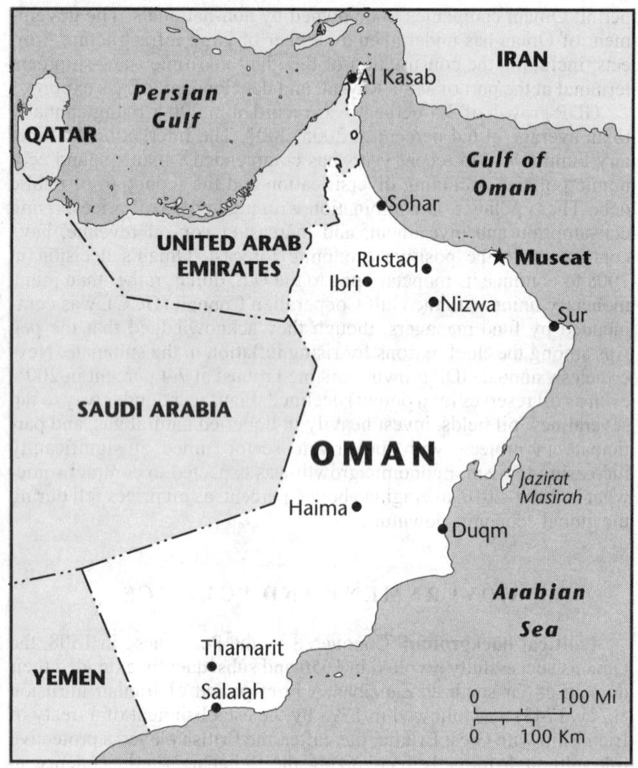

(see Legislature, below). Subsequently, following preliminary balloting for a new Consultative Council on October 16, 1997, Sultan Qabus reshuffled his cabinet on December 16, designating several "young technocrats" as new ministers.

New elections to the Consultative Council were held on September 14, 2000, successful candidates for the first time not being subject to approval by the sultan. Elections were next held on October 4, 2003, with women continuing to hold two seats. Members were elected to four-year terms in the first balloting open to all citizens (see Current issues and Legislature, below). In the October 27, 2007, Consultative Council elections, no women won seats, and the two women who had held seats were not reelected, marking the first time in many years that the assembly was without female representation. The cabinet was reshuffled on September 9, 2007, and the manpower minister was replaced in September 2008.

Constitution and government. Lagging behind most other Arab states in this regard, Oman until recently had no constitution or other fundamental law, absolute power resting with the sultan, who ruled by decree. However, on November 6, 1996, Sultan Qabus issued "The Basic Law of the Sultanate of Oman," formally confirming the government's status as a hereditary Sultanate—an "independent, Arab, Islamic, fully sovereign state" for which sharia (Islamic religious law) is the "basis for legislation." Total authority for the issuance of legislation remains with the sultan, designated as head of state and commander in chief of the armed forces. The "ruling family council" is authorized to appoint a successor should the position of sultan become vacant. The sultan rules with the assistance of a Council of Ministers, whose members he appoints. The first woman was appointed to the cabinet in 2004. The sultan may appoint a prime minister but is not so required. Consultation is also provided by the Oman Council, comprising a new Council of State and the Consultative Council (see Legislature, below). Among other things, the basic law provides for freedom of opinion, expression, and association "within the limits of the law." The basic law can be revised only by decree of the sultan.

The judicial system is also based on sharia and is administered by judges (*qadis*) appointed by the minister of justice. Appeals are heard in Muscat. In remote areas the law is based on tribal custom. Administratively, the country is divided into nine regions in the north and one province in the south (Dhofar). Governors (*walis*) posted in the country's 59 *wilayahs* (administrative districts) work largely through tribal authorities and are responsible for maintaining local security, settling minor disputes, and collecting taxes. Municipal councils are presently being established in the larger towns as instruments of local government.

Foreign relations. Reversing the isolationist policy of his father, Sultan Qabus has fostered diplomatic relations with most Arab and industrialized countries. Britain has been deeply involved in Omani affairs since 1798, while the United States and the Sultanate signed their first treaty of friendship and navigation in 1833. In recent years Japan has also become a major trading partner. Diplomatic relations were established with the People's Republic of China in 1978 and with the Soviet Union in September 1985. In June 1989 the Sultanate signed a military cooperation agreement with France.

Relations with the more radical Arab states, already cool, were not improved by Sultan Qabus's endorsement of the Egyptian-Israeli peace treaty of March 1979. However, Oman broke off relations with Israel in the wake of the intifada. Long-standing tension with the (then) People's Democratic Republic of Yemen, occasioned largely by that country's support of the sultan's opponents in Dhofar, moderated substantially at an October 1982 "reconciliation" summit, which was followed by an exchange of ambassadors in late 1983. In October 1988 the steady improvement in relations yielded a cooperation pact between the two regimes, and in 1997 Oman concluded a formal border agreement with the Republic of Yemen.

In June 1980, after statements by Sultan Qabus opposing what he viewed as Soviet efforts to destabilize the Middle East, Washington and Muscat concluded an agreement granting the United States access to Omani air and naval facilities in return for economic and security assistance. Since that time, and despite a May 1988 rebuff in regard to the purchase of Stinger missiles, Oman has become a base for U.S. military activities in the Persian Gulf.

Sultan Qabus strongly supported the Saudi decision to invite U.S. forces to defend the Gulf in the wake of Iraq's invasion of Kuwait in August 1990, and Oman subsequently contributed troops to Operation Desert Storm. Following the end of the war, Sultan Qabus proposed that a 100,000-member regional army be established to combat future security threats; however, the plan was eventually rejected by Oman's partners in the GCC.

Oman's already warm relations with Washington further improved after the September 11, 2001, terrorist attacks in the United States. Oman and Saudi Arabia issued a joint statement calling for greater cooperation in combating terrorism, and Oman was subsequently described as highly cooperative in the U.S.-led "war on terrorism." In 2006 the United States signed a free trade agreement with Oman.

The sultan also favors stronger ties with Iran as a means of promoting long-term stability in the region. For a similar reason, Oman has held to the moderate Arab position concerning a possible peace settlement with Israel and an independent Palestinian state. (Oman did not send a representative to an Arab League meeting called in May 2006 to discuss a trade boycott against Israel.) In 2007 Oman was the first country to respond to Washington's invitation to attend the U.S.-sponsored Middle East peace summit in Annapolis, Maryland, held in November. Oman continued to reinforce bilateral cooperation in meetings with Jordan and Iran. Oman considers Iran's nuclear power an asset to the region inasmuch as there is a peaceful application of the technology. In March 2008 U.S. Vice President Dick Cheney visited Oman to discuss Iran's nuclear program, an issue of heightened international concern and of particular significance for Oman, given its "guardianship" with Iran over the Strait of Hormuz.

Despite its importance as an oil-producing state, Oman is not a member of either the Organization of Petroleum Exporting Countries (OPEC) or the Organization of Arab Petroleum Exporting Countries (OAPEC). However, since the late 1980s it has cooperated with OPEC regarding production quotas.

In January 2009 Oman, along with several other Arab nations, sent tons of food and medical supplies to Gaza during the fighting between Israel and Hamas (see article on Palestinian Authority/Palestine Liberation Organization for details). In February, Oman entered into discussions with Russia regarding the expansion of bilateral ties.

Current issues. The balloting for the Consultative Council in September 2000 attracted significant international attention because only one other GCC member (Kuwait) had conducted such a nationwide election and because no other member had extended the franchise in national elections to women. (Qatar in 1999 permitted women to participate in municipal elections.) The Omani government continued to pursue "quiet progress" toward political liberalization by mandating that 30 percent of the electors in the electoral college be women. As it turned out, only two women candidates were successful then and in the October 4, 2003, elections, the first time that all citizens could participate. Voters appeared to favor fellow tribesmen, as in the previous election, making it less likely that women would be elected.

Significantly, of the hundreds arrested in early 2005 for allegedly attempting "to form an organization to tamper with national security," those convicted were neither jihadists linked to al-Qaida nor Shiites loyal to Iran or Iraq. The 31 people convicted by a state security court of plotting to overthrow the government and membership in a banned organization were Islamists who belonged to an Ibadhi sect that seeks to restore the Imamate, or leadership by an imam. There is reportedly a long history of conflict between the interior-dwelling Ibadhi sect and the authorities of the coastal region. Moreover, the Ibadhi sect believes the community leader should not be designated by heredity but decided by popular vote. In June the sultan pardoned the 31 Islamists. It was also reported that another, similar trial followed in July, resulting in the conviction of 43 Islamists, all of whom were also pardoned. Western news sources noted that the sultan's conciliatory moves and the presence of the moderate Ibadhi sect may have spared Oman from the kind of terrorist attacks experienced by other countries in the region.

A severe water shortage occurred in June 2007 in the aftermath of a cyclone that caused significant damage in the capital and eastern provinces. Following its recovery from that event, Oman's attention turned to the Consultative Council elections in October (see Legislature, below). In the run-up to the balloting, the government for the first time allowed candidates to conduct advertising campaigns on billboards, posters, banners, and in newspapers. Voter registration was reported to be at an all-time high of more than 388,000 citizens. In 2008 domestic concerns were focused on economic development. In February the sultan ordered pay raises of as much as 43 percent for public sector workers and an increase in food subsidies to help offset rising prices for housing and commodities. In the wake of the global economic crisis in 2009, the government said it would increase spending by 11 percent to help offset declining oil revenues (see Country, above), and efforts were undertaken to reduce an unemployment rate of 9 percent by expanding job training, particularly for youth.

POLITICAL PARTIES

There are no political parties in Oman. Most opposition elements previously were represented by the Popular Front for the Liberation of Oman (PFLO), although there has been no reference to PFLO activity for many years. (See the 1999 edition of the *Handbook* for a history of the PFLO.)

LEGISLATURE

The basic law decreed by the sultan in November 1996 provided for a consultative **Oman Council,** consisting of a new, appointed Council of State and the existing Consultative Council.

Council of State (*Majlis al-Dawlah*). Considered roughly the equivalent of an upper house in a bicameral legislature, the Council of State was expected to debate policy issues at the request of the sultan, although the extent of its authority and its relationship to the Consultative Council remained unclear. On December 16, 1997, Sultan Qabus appointed 41 members (including four women) from among prominent regional figures to the first Council of State. In 2006 the council had 59 members, 9 of whom were women, all serving four-year terms. On November 4, 2007, a total of 70 members, including 14 women, were appointed by royal decree.

President: Yahya bin Mafouz al-MUNTHERI.

Consultative Council (*Majlis al-Shura*). The former Consultative Assembly, established in 1981, was replaced on December 21, 1991, by the Consultative Council, an advisory body appointed by the sultan (or his designee) from candidates presented by local "dignitaries" and "people of valued opinion and experience." The council is authorized to propose legislation to the government but has no formal lawmaking role. The initial council consisted of 59 regular members (one from each *wilayah*) and a speaker who served three-year terms. In 1994 the council was expanded to 80 regular members (two from each *wilayah* with a population over 30,000 and one from each of the other *wilayahs*) and a president. For the first time women were allowed to stand as candidates (albeit only from six constituencies in or around Muscat), and two women were among those seated at the new council's inaugural session on December 26, 1994. The council was expanded to 82 members in 1997, and women from all of Oman were allowed to stand as candidates and participate in the preliminary balloting for the new council on October 16. An "electoral college" of 51,000 people (all approved by the government, primarily based on literacy requirements) elected 164 potential council members from among 736 candidates (also all approved by the government). Final selections were made in December by the sultan, who had essentially been presented with two candidates from which to choose for each seat.

On October 4, 2003, an expanded council of 83 members was elected to serve a four-year term. This was the first ballot open to all citizens. The president of the council, appointed by the sultan, serves as the 84th member. In the most recent balloting on October 27, 2007, those elected were reported by the government to have strong tribal connections or were prominent businesspeople.

President: Sheikh Ahmed bin Mohammad al-ISAI.

CABINET

[as of April 1, 2009]

Prime Minister	Sultan Qabus ibn Said al-Said
Deputy Prime Minister for Cabinet Affairs	Said Fahd ibn Mahmud al-Said
Secretary General of the Cabinet	Said Khalid bin Hilal al-Busaidi
Ministers	
Agriculture	Sheikh Salim ibn Hilal al-Khalili
Civil Service	Sheikh Muhammad ibn Abdallah ibn Isa al-Harthi
Commerce and Industry	Maqbul ibn Ali Sultan
Defense	Said Badr ibn Saud ibn Hareb al-Busaidi
Diwan of Royal Court	Said Ali ibn Hamud al-Busaidi
Education	Yahya ibn Saud al-Sulaimi
Environment and Climate Affairs	Said Hamud bin Faisal al-Busaidi
Fisheries	Sheikh Muhammad ibn Ali al-Qatabi
Foreign Affairs	Yusuf ibn Alawi ibn Abdallah
Health	Dr. Ali ibn Muhammad ibn Musa
Heritage and Culture	Said Haitham bin Tariq al-Said
Higher Education	Rawya bint Saud al-Busaidi [f]
Housing	Saif al-Shabibi
Information	Hamid ibn Muhammad al-Rashdi
Interior	Said Saud ibn Ibrahim al-Busaidi
Justice	Sheikh Muhammad ibn Abdallah ibn Zahir al-Hinai
Legal Affairs	Muhammad ibn Ali ibn Nasir al-Alawi
Manpower	Abdullah bin Nasser bin Abdullah al-Bakri
National Economy	Ahmed ibn Abd al-Nabi al-Makki
Palace Office Affairs	Gen. Ali ibn Majid Mamari
Personal Representative of the Sultan	Said Thuwainy bin Shihab al-Said
Petroleum and Gas	Muhammad ibn Saif al-Rumhi
Regional Municipalities and Water	Sheikh Abdallah ibn Salim al-Ruwas
Religious Trusts (*Awqaf*) and Islamic Affairs	Sheikh Abdallah ibn Muhammad al-Salimi
Social Development	Dr. Sharifa bint Khalfan bin Nasir al-Yahya [f]
Sports	Ali bin Masoud bin Ali al-Sunaidy

Tourism	Rajihah bint Abdallah Amir [f]
Transportation and Communications	Khamis ibn Mubarak Isa al-Alawi
Ministers of State	
Governor of the Capital	Said al-Mutasim ibn Hamud al-Busaidi
Governor of Dhofar	Sheikh Muhammad al-Maamri

[f] = female

COMMUNICATIONS

Strict press censorship is maintained. In 2005 a poet and journalist was jailed for criticizing human rights violations, and in 2009 a journalist faced a possible three-year jail sentence for posting on the Internet criticism of the country's main telecommunications company, according to the watchdog group Reporters Without Borders.

Press. The following are published in Muscat: *al-Watan* (32,500), Arabic daily; *Uman* (15,000), daily government publication, in Arabic; *Times of Oman* (15,000), English weekly; *Oman Daily Observer* (22,000), in English.

News agency. There is an official Oman News Agency (*Wakalat al-Anba al-Umaniyah*) located in the capital.

Broadcasting and computing. Radio Oman transmits from Muscat in Arabic and English, and Radio Salalah from Salalah in Arabic and Dhofari; both are government controlled. The BBC Eastern Relay on Masirah Island transmits Arabic, Hindi, Persian, and Urdu programming. A private radio station, Hala FM, began broadcasting in 2007. Color television was initiated in Muscat in 1974 and in Salalah in 1975. As of 2008 there were 200 Internet users per 1,000 inhabitants.

INTERGOVERNMENTAL REPRESENTATION

Ambassador to the U.S.: Hunaina Sultan Ahmed al-MUGHAIRY.

U.S. Ambassador to Oman: Richard J. SCHMIERER.

Permanent Representative to the UN: Fuad al-HINAI.

IGO Memberships (Non-UN): AFESD, AMF, BADEA, GCC, IDB, Interpol, IOR-ARC, LAS, NAM, OIC, WCO, WTO.

PAKISTAN

Islamic Republic of Pakistan
Islami Jamhuria-e-Pakistan

Political Status: Formally became independent on August 15, 1947; republic established on March 23, 1956; national territory confined to former West Pakistan with de facto independence of Bangladesh (former East Pakistan) on December 16, 1971; independence of Bangladesh formally recognized on February 22, 1974; martial law regime instituted following military coup of July 5, 1977; modified version of 1973 constitution introduced on March 2, 1985; martial law officially lifted December 30, 1985; constitution suspended and state of emergency imposed on October 14, 1999, following military coup of October 12; constitution restored on November 16, 2002, as amended by Legal Framework Order (LFO) promulgated on August 21; 17th constitutional amendment, containing many of the LFO provisions, approved by Parliament on December 29–30, 2003, and signed by the president on December 31; constitution most recently suspended under state of emergency declared on November 3, 2007, but lifted on December 15.

Area: 310,402 sq. mi. (803,943 sq. km.), excluding Jammu and Kashmir, of which approximately 32,200 sq. mi. (83,400 sq. km.) are presently administered by Pakistan.

Population: 130,579,571 (1998C), excluding population of Pakistani-controlled portion of Jammu and Kashmir (see Related Territories); 163,419,000 (2008E).

Major Urban Centers (2005E): ISLAMABAD (974,000), Karachi (11,767,000), Lahore (6,317,000), Faisalabad (2,514,000), Rawalpindi (1,778,000), Gujranwala (1,460,000), Multan (1,436,000), Hyderabad (1,374,000), Peshawar (1,241,000). Opponents of the 1998 census, claiming widespread urban underenumeration, estimated the population of Karachi at close to 15 million.

National Language: Urdu. The 1973 constitution identified Urdu as the "national language" but added that "arrangements shall be made for its being used for official and other purposes within fifteen years from the commencing day." In the meantime, English "may be used for official purposes." As of 2009 the clause requiring adoption of Urdu as an official language had not yet been implemented. Each province may also identify and promote its own "provincial language," and all have done so.

Monetary Unit: Rupee (market rate December 1, 2009: 83.57 rupees = $1US).

President: Asif Ali ZARDARI (Pakistan People's Party); elected for a five-year term by combined votes of Parliament and the four provincial assemblies on September 6, 2008, and sworn in on September 9, succeeding Pervez MUSHARRAF, who had resigned on August 18 to avoid impeachment proceedings.

Prime Minister: Yusuf Raza GILANI (Pakistan People's Party); elected by the National Assembly on March 24, 2008, following the general election of February 18; sworn in March 25, succeeding Caretaker Prime Minister Mohammadmian SOOMRO, who had served in that capacity since November 16, 2007, a day after the expiry of the 2002–2007 National Assembly term and the collateral dissolution of the cabinet headed by Prime Minister Shaukat AZIZ (Pakistan Muslim League–*Qaid-i-Azam*).

THE COUNTRY

Located in the northwest of the Indian subcontinent, Pakistan extends from the Arabian Sea a thousand miles northward across eastern plains to the Hindu Kush and the foothills of the Himalayas. The racial stock is primarily Aryan, with traces of Dravidian. The dominant language is Punjabi (50 percent), followed by Pushtu, Sindhi, Saraiki, Urdu, Gujarati, and Baluchi. In addition, English is widely spoken in business and government. Islam, the state religion, is professed by over 95 percent of the people; Christians and Hindus constitute most of the balance. Women make up only 21 percent of the active labor force, but many others participate in unpaid agricultural work. In addition, women are often engaged in home-based or cottage industry. Female participation in government has been constrained by Islamic precepts, although Benazir BHUTTO was the Muslim world's first woman prime minister (1988–1990, 1993–1996). Only about half the adult population is literate—less in the case of women.

Much of the country consists of mountains and deserts, but some of the most fertile and best-irrigated land in the subcontinent is provided by the Indus River system. Agriculture continues to employ 44 percent of the active labor force, the principal crops being cotton, wheat, rice, sugarcane, and maize. In addition, the western province of Baluchistan supplies a rich crop of fruits and dates. The agricultural sector contributes about 22 percent of GDP, while industry accounts for 27 percent of GDP and 21 percent of employment. Though not heavily endowed in mineral resources, the country extracts petroleum, natural gas, iron, limestone, rock salt, gypsum, and coal. Manufacturing includes production of cotton and other textile yarns and fabrics, clothing and accessories, cement, and sugar and other foodstuffs. Pakistan's exports also include fruits, seafood, carpets, and handicrafts.

Overall, the economy registered an average growth rate of 6–7 percent during the 1980s, with remittances from Pakistanis employed in the Arabian Gulf largely offsetting a substantial trade imbalance. Annual GDP growth averaged about 4 percent in the 1990s.

In the first quarter of 2000 the newly installed government moved forward on privatizing nonstrategic state-owned enterprises, improving tax collection, and cutting nonessential spending as components of an economic program partly designed to secure additional assistance from the International Monetary Fund. Fueled in large part by some $5.5 billion in U.S. aid since late 2001, by fiscal year 2003–2004 the growth rate had risen to 7.5 percent and then reached 9.0 percent in the following year—the highest growth rate in two decades—before dropping back to 6.6 percent in 2005–2006. For FY 2006–2007 the government reported growth of 6.2 percent, followed by 5.8 percent in 2007–2008. Growth for the next fiscal year was expected to remain positive, but the projected drop to 2.0 percent reflected the impact of the ongoing international financial crisis and recession. In addition to lower export earnings, Pakistan's economy was being slowed by depreciation of the rupee, double-digit inflation as the cost of food and imported fuels rose, and a diminution of foreign currency reserves. In November 2008 the IMF approved $7.6 billion in stabilization funding, which was raised in August 2009 to $11.3 billion.

GOVERNMENT AND POLITICS

Political background. Subjected to strong Islamic influences from the 7th century onward, the area that comprises the present state of Pakistan and former East Pakistan (now Bangladesh) became part of British India during the 18th and 19th centuries and contained most of India's Muslim population. First articulated in the early 1930s, the idea of a separate Muslim state was endorsed in 1940 by the All-India Muslim League, the major Muslim political party. After the league swept the 1946–1947 election, the British accepted partition and Parliament passed the Indian Independence Act, which incorporated the principle of a separate Pakistan. Transfer of power occurred on August 14, 1947, with the new state formally coming into existence at the stroke of midnight, August 15. Mohammad Ali JINNAH, head of the All-India Muslim League, became independent Pakistan's first governor general.

India's Muslim-majority provinces and princely states were given the option of remaining in India or joining Pakistan. Sindh, the North-West Frontier Province (NWFP), Baluchistan, and three-fifths of the Punjab accordingly combined to form what became West Pakistan, while a part of Assam and two-thirds of Bengal became East Pakistan. The Hindu maharaja of the predominantly Muslim state of Jammu and Kashmir subsequently acceded to India, but Pakistan challenged the action by sending troops into the territory; resultant fighting between Indian and Pakistani forces was halted by a UN cease-fire on January 1, 1949, leaving Pakistan in control of territory west and north of the cease-fire line. Communal rioting and population movements stemming from partition caused further embitterment between the two countries.

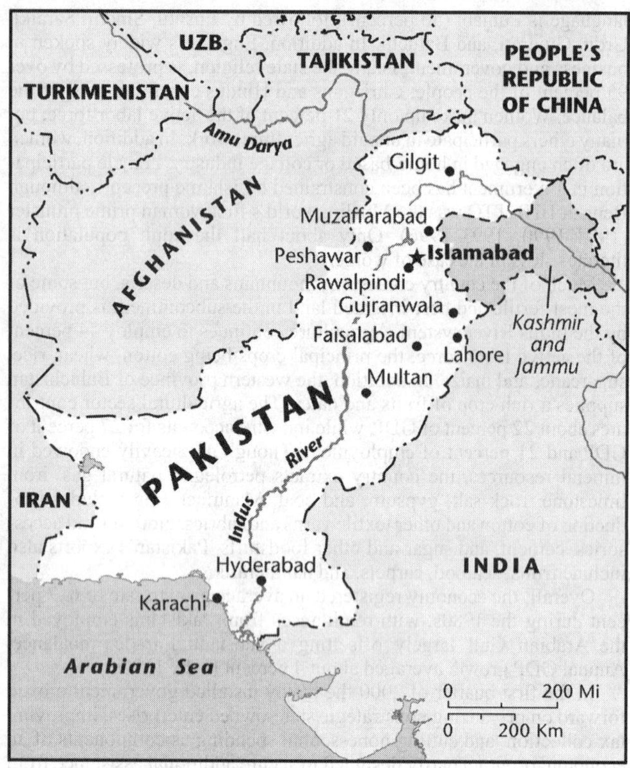

In March 1956 the tie to the British Crown was broken with implementation of a republican constitution, under which Iskander Ali MIRZA served as Pakistan's first president. In October 1958, however, Mirza abrogated the constitution, declared martial law, dismissed the national and provincial governments, and dissolved all political parties. Field Marshal Mohammad Ayub KHAN, appointed supreme commander of the armed forces and chief martial law administrator, took over the presidency from Mirza and was confirmed in office by a national referendum of "basic democrats" in February 1960.

Constitutional government, under a presidential system based on indirect election, was restored in June 1962, with Ayub Khan continuing to rule until March 1969, when, in the context of mounting political and economic disorder, he resigned. Gen. Agha Mohammad Yahya KHAN, army commander in chief, thereupon assumed authority as chief martial law administrator, suspended the constitution, dismissed the national and provincial assemblies, and took office as president.

Normal political activity resumed in 1970, the major unresolved issue being East Pakistani complaints of underrepresentation in the central government and an inadequate share of central revenues. In preparing for the nation's first direct election on the basis of universal suffrage (ultimately held in December 1970 and January 1971), efforts were made to assuage the long-standing political discontent in the more populous East Pakistan by allotting it majority representation in the new assembly, rather than, as in the previous legislature, mere parity with West Pakistan. Of the 300 seats up for direct election (162 from East Pakistan, 138 from West Pakistan), Sheikh Mujibur RAHMAN's East Pakistani Awami League won 160 and the Pakistan People's Party (PPP), 82.

After repeated postponements of the assembly opening, originally scheduled to take place in Dacca (East Pakistan) in March 1971, the government banned the Awami League and announced in August the disqualification of 79 of its representatives. By-elections to the vacated seats, scheduled for December, were prevented by the outbreak of war between Pakistan and India in late November and the occupation of East Pakistan by Bengali guerrilla and Indian military forces. Following the surrender of some 90,000 of its troops, Pakistan on December 17 agreed to a cease-fire on the western front. Yahya Khan stepped down as president three days later and was replaced by Zulfikar Ali BHUTTO as president and chief martial law administrator. In July 1972 President Bhutto and India's prime minister, Indira Gandhi, met in Simla, India, and agreed to negotiate outstanding differences. As a result, all occupied areas along the western border were exchanged, except in Kashmir, where a new Line of Control (LoC) was drawn. In July 1973 the National Assembly granted Bhutto the authority to recognize Bangladesh, and in August a new constitution was adopted. The speaker of the assembly, Fazal Elahi CHAUDHRY, was elected president of Pakistan, and Bhutto was designated prime minister.

A general election held in March 1977 resulted in an overwhelming victory for the ruling PPP; however, the opposition Pakistan National Alliance (PNA) denounced the returns as fraudulent and initiated a series of strikes and demonstrations that led to outbreaks of violence throughout the country. Faced with impending civil war, the army mounted a coup on July 5 that resulted in the arrest of many leading politicians, including Prime Minister Bhutto, and the imposition of martial law under Gen. Mohammad ZIA ul-Haq. Shortly after President Chaudhry's term expired in August 1978, General Zia assumed the presidency, announcing that he would yield to a regularly elected successor following a legislative election in 1979.

In April 1979, despite worldwide appeals for clemency, former prime minister Bhutto was hanged. Riots immediately erupted in most of the country's urban areas, and PNA representatives withdrew from the government. Later in the year, Zia postponed elections, banned all forms of party activity, and imposed strict censorship on the communications media.

An interim constitution promulgated in March 1981 provided for the eventual restoration of representative institutions "in conformity with Islam," while the formation the same year of the PPP-led Movement for the Restoration of Democracy (MRD) created a force against both the regime and right-wing Islamic parties. In late 1984 the president announced a referendum on an "Islamization" program, endorsement of which would also grant him an additional five-year presidential term. In the wake of an MRD call for a referendum boycott, the size of the turnout was hotly disputed, estimates ranging from as low as 15 percent to as high as 65 percent. Nevertheless, citing an overwhelming margin of approval, Zia scheduled parliamentary elections on a nonparty basis for February 1985. Despite another opposition call for a boycott, five incumbent ministers and a number of others associated with the martial law regime lost their bids for parliamentary seats. As a result, the president dissolved the cabinet and designated Mohammad Khan JUNEJO, of the center-right Pakistan Muslim League (PML), as the country's first prime minister in eight years. In the absence of legal parties, the assembly divided into two camps—a government-supportive Official Parliamentary Group (OPG) and an opposition Independent Parliamentary Group (IPG).

In October 1985 the assembly approved a political parties law despite objections by President Zia, who continued to view a multiparty system as "un-Islamic." Dissent immediately ensued within the MRD; some components—including the PML and the moderate *Jamaat-e-Islami,* which controlled the OPG and IPG, respectively—announced their intention to register, while others termed the entire exercise fraudulent and continued to press for fresh elections under a fully restored 1973 constitution. Without responding to the pressure, Zia proceeded with the scheduled termination of martial law on December 30.

In what was dubbed a "constitutional coup," in May 1988 President Zia abruptly dismissed the Junejo government because of alleged corruption. He also dissolved the National Assembly, the provincial assemblies, and local governments. In June he appointed a PML-dominated caretaker administration headed by himself and in July announced that "free, fair, and independent" elections to the national and provincial assemblies would be held on November 16 and 19, respectively.

On August 17, 1988, General Zia, the U.S. ambassador, and a number of senior military officers were killed in a plane crash in southeastern Punjab. Immediately afterward the Senate chair, Ghulam Ishaq KHAN, was sworn in as acting president and announced the formation of a caretaker Emergency National Council to rule the country pending the November elections. Intense political maneuvering followed, with the PPP securing a substantial plurality in the National Assembly poll but achieving only second place in three of the four provincial elections. Nonetheless, in what some viewed as a political "deal," on December 1 Ishaq Khan formally appointed as prime minister Benazir BHUTTO, daughter of the executed prime minister, and was himself elected to a five-year term as president on December 12.

By 1990 relations between the president and the prime minister were becoming increasingly strained. Accusing her government of corruption, abuse of power, and various other unconstitutional and illegal acts, President Khan dismissed Bhutto on August 6, 1990, appointing as her interim successor Ghulam Mustafa JATOI, leader of the Islamic Democratic Alliance (IDA), a somewhat disparate coalition of conservative

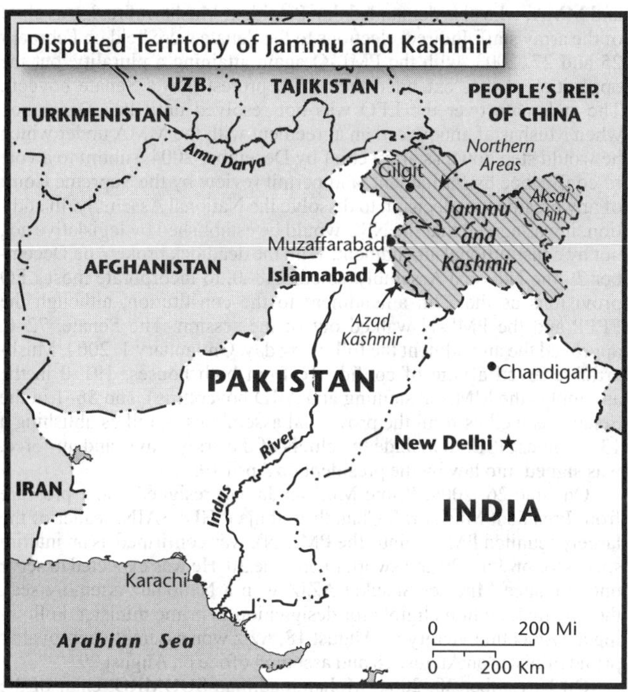

anti-Bhutto groups that had been organized two years earlier. Two months later the PPP was decisively defeated in national and provincial elections, including a loss in its traditional stronghold of Sindh. On November 6 the IDA's Mian Mohammad Nawaz SHARIF was sworn in as Pakistan's first Punjabi prime minister.

On April 18, 1993, in the wake of a failed effort by Nawaz Sharif to curtail the president's constitutional power, Ishaq Khan dismissed the Sharif government, naming Balkh Sher MAZARI, a dissident member of Sharif's PML, as acting prime minister. In May, however, the Supreme Court reinstated Sharif, thereby canceling a general election that had been scheduled for July. The action failed to resolve the widening split within the PML, and on July 18, following intervention by the recently appointed army chief of staff, Gen. Abdul WAHEED, both the president and prime minister stepped down. Ishaq Khan was succeeded, on an acting basis, by Senate chair Wasim SAJJAD. A relatively unknown former World Bank vice president, Moeenuddin Ahmad QURESHI, succeeded Nawaz Sharif.

Nawaz Sharif attempted to regain power as leader of the PML's largest faction, the PML-Nawaz (PML-N). Although the PML-N outpolled the PPP 41–38 percent in the National Assembly election of October 1993, the latter gained a plurality of seats (86, as opposed to 72 for Sharif supporters), and Bhutto was returned to office. In electoral college balloting for president in November, the PPP's Sardar Farooq Ahmad Khan LEGHARI defeated the acting incumbent.

In July 1996, in the wake of increased tension with India over Kashmir and heightened domestic unrest on the part of Islamic fundamentalists and activists of the *Muhajir Qaumi* Movement (MQM), 13 opposition parties announced an alliance to topple Bhutto. On July 31 the prime minister greatly enlarged her cabinet. Among 14 new appointees was her controversial husband, Asif Ali ZARDARI, who, in his first ministerial assignment, was named to head an investment portfolio. In September the prime minister's estranged brother, Murtaza BHUTTO, was one of seven breakaway PPP faction members killed in a gunfight outside Murtaza's Karachi home.

Citing evidence of corruption, intimidation of the judiciary, misdirection of the economy, and failure to maintain law and order, President Leghari on November 5, 1996, dismissed Prime Minister Bhutto, naming Malek Meraj KHALID, a former legislative speaker and long-estranged Bhutto confidant, as her successor in a caretaker capacity pending election of a new National Assembly in February 1997. In the interim, President Leghari announced formation of a Council for Defense and National Security (CDNS) comprising himself, the prime minister, several cabinet ministers, and the heads of the branches of the armed forces.

Voter turnout was low for the February 1997 legislative election, in which the PML-N swept to power by securing 134 of the 207 seats, compared to 19 seats for Bhutto's PPP. The PML-N subsequently invited a number of smaller parties to join the governing coalition, giving it more than the two-thirds majority required for constitutional amendment. Following the installation of a new cabinet on February 26, Prime Minister Sharif quickly oversaw the abolition of the CDNS and directed constitutional revision that, among other things, removed the president's authority to dismiss the prime minister and assembly at will and to appoint military leaders.

In the wake of renewed violence in Karachi (much of it perpetrated by rival MQM factions) as well as conflict between minority Shiite and majority Sunni Muslim militants in Punjab, a new antiterrorism bill was adopted in August 1997, granting sweeping new powers to security forces and establishing special courts to try terrorism cases. The collateral usurpation of power from traditional courts served to exacerbate tension between the government and the judiciary. On December 2, calling Sharif an "elected dictator," President Leghari resigned rather than comply with the prime minister's order to swear in a new acting chief justice. On December 31 a Sharif ally, Mohammad Rafiq TARAR, was elected president by an overwhelming majority of electors.

Throughout 1998 the upsurge in religious, ethnic, and political violence resisted resolution. In August the Sharif administration's failure to contain the violence led the principal MQM faction to withdraw its support for the government, which in February had already lost a leading ally when the Awami National Party (ANP) left the cabinet because of the prime minister's reluctance to endorse renaming the North-West Frontier Province (NWFP) as Pakhtoonkhwa (Land of the Pakhtoon). Demands for greater provincial autonomy also continued to gather momentum in the NWFP and elsewhere.

A deeply divided society came together briefly in late May 1998 when Pakistan exploded six nuclear weapons beneath the Chagai Hills of the Baluchistan desert. The tests on May 28 and 30 came in response to similar explosions conducted earlier in the month by India. Pakistan's Muslim fundamentalists were particularly jubilant, welcoming the tests as confirmation that Islamabad had developed the first "Islamic bomb."

To the surprise of many observers, on October 7, 1998, Gen. Jehangir KARAMAT, chair of the joint chiefs of staff, resigned, two days after calling for greater military participation in the government and criticizing the prime minister for his administration's economic shortcomings and its inability to stem domestic disorder. On April 9, 1999, Prime Minister Sharif named Karamat's replacement as army chief of staff, Gen. Pervez MUSHARRAF, to the chair of the Joint Chiefs of Staff Committee.

Although relations with India had improved following the May 1998 nuclear weapons tests, culminating in a meeting between Prime Ministers Sharif and Atal Vajpayee in Lahore in February 1999 (see Foreign relations, below), renewed conflict in Kashmir once again disrupted diplomatic progress. In early May 1999 India discovered that militant Islamic separatists, backed by Pakistani forces, had crossed the LoC into the mountainous Kargil area. For two months heavy shellings and clashes ensued, with India gradually gaining the upper hand. Military commanders from both sides met in July and agreed to a timetable for withdrawal, which was completed late in the month, but sporadic fighting continued as the government's perceived retreat was widely denounced within Pakistan, particularly by Islamic groups.

On October 12, 1999, while attending a conference in Sri Lanka, General Musharraf was alerted by supporters within the army that Prime Minister Sharif was replacing him. Musharraf immediately flew back to Pakistan on a commercial flight, but, on the prime minister's order, his plane was denied permission to land in Karachi, whereupon the army moved in and secured the airport. At the same time, the military arrested Prime Minister Sharif and his cabinet. On October 14 Musharraf proclaimed a state of emergency (but not martial law), suspended the constitution, and named himself "chief executive" of Pakistan. President Tarar continued in office. Addressing the nation on October 17, Musharraf identified his priorities as preventing economic collapse, pursuing corruption, and paving the way for "true democracy." He also announced that he had ordered troop reductions along the Indian border, but not the LoC. On October 25 the chief executive named the initial civilian members of a governing National Security Council (NSC), which also included, ex officio, the naval and air force chiefs. The civilian members of the NSC and a nonparty cabinet were sworn in by President Tarar on November 6.

Ruling unanimously on May 12, 2000, the Supreme Court legitimized the October 1999 coup as justified and necessary to end political corruption and lawlessness, despite being "extra-constitutional." It also ruled that democratic national and provincial assembly elections should be held no later than October 2002. On August 15 the NSC was reconstituted to include four civilian ministers, and the cabinet was expanded.

On April 6, 2000, an antiterrorism court had sentenced Nawaz Sharif to life imprisonment following his conviction for hijacking and terrorism in connection with his refusal to let General Musharraf's plane land. The terrorism conviction was ultimately overturned on appeal, and on December 10, 2000, Musharraf granted a pardon to Nawaz Sharif, who flew into exile.

On June 20, 2001, General Musharraf dismissed President Tarar, assumed the presidency himself, dissolved both houses of Parliament, and also disbanded all provincial legislatures. In an apparent effort to legitimize his standing, General Musharraf called an April 30, 2002, referendum in which voters were asked to extend his presidency for another five years, to support a crackdown against Islamic extremists, and to support economic reforms. Although 97.7 percent of those casting ballots reportedly voted "yes," the referendum was replete with irregularities, and the outcome was rejected by the boycotting Alliance for the Restoration of Democracy (ARD), an umbrella grouping of more than a dozen opposition parties, including the PPP and the PML-N.

In August–December 2001, searching for domestic stability as well as increased international legitimacy following the September 11 al-Qaida attacks on the United States, Musharraf had begun freezing assets and detaining the leaders of some militant Islamic groups. On January 12, 2002, in what was widely regarded as a landmark speech, Musharraf rejected the "intolerance and hatred" of extreme sectarianism; banned a number of militant Islamic political parties and groups (see Banned Organizations, below); stated that all fundamentalist Islamic schools (madrasas) would be brought under government supervision to ensure that they adopted adequate educational goals; and called for creation of a modern, progressive Islamic society based on the "true teachings of Islam."

On August 21, 2002, President Musharraf promulgated a controversial Legal Framework Order (LFO) that incorporated 29 constitutional amendments, including the creation of a permanent NSC to institutionalize a governmental role for the military leadership. The LFO also enlarged both houses of Parliament and gave the president sweeping powers, including the right to dismiss the cabinet, dissolve the National Assembly, appoint provincial governors if he saw fit, name Supreme Court judges, and unilaterally increase his term of office.

An election for the 272 directly elective seats in Pakistan's reconfigured, 342-seat National Assembly took place on October 10, 2002, with the Musharraf-supportive *Qaid-i-Azam* faction of the PML (PML-Q) finishing ahead of the newly registered PPP Parliamentarians (PPPP) and the *Muttahida Majlis-e-Amal* (MMA), an Islamic coalition. Most international observers regarded the electoral process as seriously deficient in meeting democratic standards. When the 60 seats reserved for women and 10 seats reserved for religious minorities were distributed at the end of the month, the PML-Q held a plurality of 118 seats, followed by the PPPP with 81 and the MMA with 60.

In simultaneous provincial assembly elections, the PML-Q won in Punjab and the MMA assumed control in the NWFP, with the two parties forming coalition administrations in Baluchistan and, in conjunction with smaller parties, in Sindh. Immediately upon assuming power in the NWFP, the MMA government announced that it would impose Islamic law in the province. The MMA's success in the NWFP was also viewed as a setback for efforts by Musharraf and the United States to track down members of the al-Qaida terrorist network and the deposed Taliban regime in neighboring Afghanistan. The MMA opposed both Islamabad's participation in the U.S.-led "war on terrorism" and the consequent presence of U.S. forces on Pakistani soil.

At the central level, over the next several weeks the PML-Q and PPPP jockeyed for MMA support in an effort to establish a governing coalition, but neither succeeded. The process culminated on November 21, 2002, when the National Assembly confirmed Zafarullah Khan JAMALI of the PML-Q as prime minister after he had secured the backing of several small parties and of ten dissenters within the PPPP, who organized as the PPP-Patriots. Runner-up in the voting was the MMA's Fazlur RAHMAN, followed by the PPPP's Shah Mahmood QURESHI.

During the following year the National Assembly was unable to overcome the obstructive tactics of LFO opponents, including the PPPP and MMA, who also demanded that President Musharraf resign as chief of the army staff. Indirect elections to the Senate were held on February 25 and 27, 2003, with the PML-Q again attaining a plurality, but the opposition parties extended their LFO protest into a Senate boycott. The stalemate over the LFO was not resolved until late December, when Musharraf announced an agreement with the MMA under which he would step down as army chief by December 2004, submit to a vote of confidence by Parliament, and permit review by the Supreme Court of any presidential decision to dissolve the National Assembly. In addition, it was agreed that the NSC would be established by legislative act, not by constitutional amendment. With the deadlock broken, on December 29 the National Assembly voted, 248–0, to incorporate most LFO provisions as the 17th amendment to the constitution, although the PPPP and the PML-N walked out of the session. The Senate, 72–0, approved the amendment the following day. On January 1, 2004, Musharraf received a vote of confidence from both houses, 191–0 in the assembly (the MMA abstaining and ARD boycotting), and 56–1 in the Senate, as well as from the provincial assemblies. A bill establishing a 13-member NSC, to include the chiefs of the army, navy, and air force, was signed into law by the president on April 19.

On June 26, 2004, Prime Minister Jamali resigned under pressure from President Musharraf. Chaudhry Shujaat HUSSAIN, leader of the largely reunited PML (minus the PML-N), was confirmed as an interim successor on June 29 and sworn in on June 30. He was expected to serve until Finance Minister Shaukat AZIZ won a National Assembly seat, thereby making him eligible for designation as prime minister. Following a by-election victory on August 18, Aziz won assembly approval as prime minister on August 28 and assumed office on August 29.

On November 30, 2004, Mohammadmian SOOMRO, chair of the Senate and acting president during a trip abroad by General Musharraf, signed into law a bill permitting Musharraf to continue as both army chief of staff and president. The new law, which proponents justified as necessary to maintain stability in the face of terrorism and subversion, was attacked by the MMA as a betrayal of its December 2003 pact with Musharraf.

On May 14, 2006, meeting in London, former prime ministers Benazir Bhutto and Nawaz Sharif signed a Charter of Democracy, which decried "the erosion of the federation's unity" and "the military's subordination of all state institutions." The charter called for repealing the LFO and the 17th constitutional amendment, establishing a Federal Constitutional Court to resolve constitutional issues, providing for minority representation in the Senate, releasing all political prisoners and permitting the return of political exiles, installing neutral caretaker governments prior to national elections, and creating a Defense Cabinet Committee (in place of the NSC) that would exert control over the military and its nuclear capability.

In September 2006 the government concluded an agreement with tribal leaders in the Federally Administered Tribal Area (FATA) of North Waziristan that tacitly acknowledged the failure of the military and security agencies to bring the region under its control despite years of efforts. In effect, the government turned control of the agency over to tribal leaders. Modeled on a pact that Musharraf had concluded in February 2005 in South Waziristan, the agreement called for Islamabad to withdraw an estimated 70,000 troops, release prisoners, and provide amnesty to Taliban and tribal militants, in return for which the tribal leaders agreed to end attacks against army and law enforcement personnel, to prevent the Taliban from launching attacks into Afghanistan, and to expel foreigners who failed to honor the agreement.

On March 8, 2007, President Musharraf set off a political firestorm by suspending Chief Justice Iftikhar Mohammed CHAUDHRY on grounds of misconduct and abuse of authority. With the presidential term set to expire in November, Musharraf apparently perceived Chaudhry as an obstacle to his reelection. Musharraf wanted the sitting national and provincial legislators—the same ones who had confirmed him in January 2004—to authorize another term, and without his first stepping down as army chief. The opposition, arguing that any such procedure would be antidemocratic and unconstitutional, pledged to appeal to the Supreme Court, which, under Chaudhry, had previously demonstrated its independence. In response to Chaudhry's dismissal, dozens of judges tendered their resignations, while the opposition and the legal establishment condemned the action as an attack on judicial independence. The crisis widened on May 12–13, when members of the government-supportive MQM clashed with Chaudhry supporters in the streets of Karachi, leaving more than 40 individuals dead. On July 20 Chaudhry was reinstated by the Supreme Court, which unanimously ruled Musharraf's action illegal.

Less than a week earlier, tribal militants in North Waziristan, responding to the storming by security forces of Islamabad's Red Mosque (*Lal Masjid*), had canceled the September 2006 agreement with the government. The Red Mosque assault concluded a July 3–11, 2007, siege that had been precipitated by clashes with militant students, who for six months had been aggressively promoting Islamization in the capital, sometimes by attacking noncompliant civilians. Following unsuccessful negotiations with the students and their clerical mentors, military personnel cleared the mosque and adjacent madrasas in a prolonged assault that cost more than 100 lives. Among those killed in the fighting was the radical cleric Abdul Rashid GHAZI. Although President Musharraf's decision to storm the mosque won considerable praise in the West and from domestic secularists, Islamists vowed retaliation, which led to an upsurge in suicide bombings, ambushes, and other attacks.

On August 23, 2007, the Supreme Court ruled that former prime minister Nawaz Sharif could not be prevented "from returning to his motherland." Nevertheless, when he flew into Islamabad on September 10, the government detained him at the airport and then deported him to Saudi Arabia within hours. Four days later, Benazir Bhutto, in the context of negotiations with Musharraf on power-sharing arrangements, announced that she planned to return to Pakistan in October.

With Chief Justice Chaudhry having recused himself, the Supreme Court ruled 6–3 on September 28, 2007, that President Musharraf could stand for reelection while still serving as army chief. Although Musharraf had stated that, should he win reelection, he would resign from the military before inauguration, most of the opposition declared that it would boycott the presidential voting. On October 6 an electoral college of Parliament and the four provincial assemblies reelected Musharraf to a five-year term by a margin of 671–8 against token opposition from a former judge, Wajihuadin AHMAD. A day earlier, however, the Supreme Court had announced that the results could not be declared official until it had ruled on opposition challenges.

Although power-sharing discussions with former prime minister Bhutto remained incomplete, on October 5, 2007, President Musharraf promulgated a National Reconciliation Ordinance (NRO) that quashed corruption charges—including 11, involving some $1.5 billion, against Bhutto and her husband, Asif Ali Zardari—targeting politicians for illegalities allegedly committed during 1986–1999. On October 18 Bhutto ended eight years in exile, returning to Karachi. The triumphal occasion turned grim, however, when suicide bombers attacked her motorcade from the airport, killing 145 and wounding more than 200 others.

On November 3, 2007, citing the need to combat rising Islamic extremism, President Musharraf, in his capacity as chief of the army staff, suspended the constitution and declared a state of emergency. Chief Justice Chaudhry was immediately dismissed, while most of his fellow justices resigned or refused to take a new oath under a provisional constitutional order. The emergency declaration provoked demonstrations by many of those associated with the July protests. More than 5,000 activists were temporarily jailed in the following days, and Bhutto was twice placed under house arrest.

On November 16, 2007, a day after the completion of the 2002–2007 legislative term, Musharraf swore in a caretaker government headed by Senate Chair Mohammadmian Soomro, an ally. On November 22 the Supreme Court, now packed with Musharraf supporters, dismissed the last of four opposition petitions challenging Musharraf's reelection, which paved the way for his stepping down as chief of the army staff on November 28 and his taking the presidential oath of office as a civilian on November 29. Shortly before, he had designated Gen. Ashfaq KAYANI, a former head of the Inter-Services Intelligence (ISI) agency, as his military successor.

On November 25, 2007, opposition demands for restoration of the constitution had been further strengthened by the successful return to Pakistan of Nawaz Sharif, following intervention on his behalf by the king of Saudi Arabia. Nevertheless, it appeared unlikely that the courts would lift the prohibition against his directly participating in the legislative election that had been scheduled for January 8, 2008.

Former prime minister Benazir Bhutto was assassinated by Islamist extremists while leaving a campaign rally in Rawalpindi on December 27, 2007. Shortly after, her 19-year-old son, Bilawal Bhutto ZARDARI, a college student in the United Kingdom, was named titular head of the PPP, while her husband, Asif Ali Zardari, was given responsibility for running day-to-day party operations. On January 2, 2008, citing the violent disturbances that had followed Bhutto's death, the Pakistan Election Commission briefly postponed the National Assembly election.. The PPP, the PML-N, and other opposition parties objected to the decision.

Voters went to the polls instead on February 18, 2008, and gave the PPP (still technically running as the PPPP) a plurality of 124 seats. The PML-N finished second, with 91 seats, while the PML-Q (officially listed on the ballot simply as the PML) came in a distant third, with 54 seats. On March 25 a PPP vice chair, Yusuf Raza GILANI, was sworn in as prime minister of a multiparty government led by the PPP and PML-N. One provision of their coalition agreement called for reinstating the dismissed judges, but the government's failure to do so led Nawaz Sharif to announce the withdrawal of the PML-N ministers on May 12.

Facing pending impeachment over allegedly unconstitutional acts, including the 1999 coup and the November 2007 state of emergency, President Musharraf resigned on August 18, 2008. A week later Nawaz Sharif took the PML-N into opposition because the PPP had not reinstated 63 dismissed judges and had proposed Zardari, rather than a nonpartisan, as Musharraf's successor. Most parties nevertheless coalesced around Zardari, who was elected president on September 6 with 482 of 700 possible electoral college votes, easily defeating retired chief justice Saeeduzzaman SIDDIQUI, who was the PML-N candidate, and Mushahid HUSSAIN Sayed, the PML-Q candidate. Zardari took the oath of office on September 9. On November 3 Prime Minister Gilani not only filled the cabinet posts that had been vacated by the PML-N withdrawal but announced one of the largest cabinets in the country's history, which was further expanded when the MQM joined the government in January 2009.

Meanwhile, in the wake of the Red Mosque siege in July 2007 and the failed peace agreements in North and South Waziristan, a dozen or more militant Islamic groups had come together under the framework of the *Tehrik-e-Taliban* Pakistan (TTP), led by Baitullah MEHSUD. Although the TTP operated throughout the FATA and the NWFP, in 2008 the Swat valley in the NWFP's Malakand division emerged as a focus of militant activity. In an effort to disrupt the government and inculcate strict adherence to Islamic law, the TTP executed dozens of opponents and alleged government collaborators, destroyed more than 180 schools (most of which had been educating girls), and by early 2009 controlled up to 90 percent of the valley. On February 13 the NWFP government and the leader of the pro-Taliban *Tehrik-e-Nifaz-e-Shariat-e-Muhammadi* (TNSM), cleric Sufi MOHAMMED, signed an agreement on adoption of sharia throughout Malakand that was approved by the National Assembly and then signed into law by President Zardari on April 13, despite protests from the MQM. By then, up to 1,500 people, many of them bystanders, had been killed in the conflict.

On March 17, 2009, the Gilani government reinstated Chief Justice Chaudhry, four other Supreme Court judges, and six provincial high court judges. The move, spurred by a Karachi-to-Islamabad protest caravan by lawyers and other activists, was seen as a victory for Nawaz Sharif. Furthermore, on May 26 the Supreme Court overturned a February ruling that, citing earlier criminal convictions, had barred Nawaz Sharif from seeking office and had forced his brother, Mian Mohammad Shahbaz SHARIF, to step down temporarily as chief minister of Punjab.

By May 2009 it had already become apparent that the February peace agreement in the NWFP was illusory, as the TTP, led locally by Maulana FAZULLAH, a son-in-law of Sufi Mohammad, continued to extend its reach beyond Swat. As a consequence, the Pakistani military, which was already fighting for control in the FATA's Bajaur Agency and elsewhere, launched a concerted effort to end the Taliban threat in Malakand. By late June most of Swat had been secured and impressive gains had been registered in other districts, in part with the cooperation of local militias.

On August 5, 2009, a U.S. missile launched from an unmanned drone mortally injured Baitullah Mehsud in South Waziristan. His death prompted retaliatory attacks against civilian as well as government and military targets, including in Islamabad and other major cities, even before the military undertook a long-anticipated ground campaign against the TTP in South Waziristan on October 17, 2009.

Constitution and government. Between 1947 and 1973 Pakistan adopted three permanent and four interim constitutions. In August 1973 a presidential system introduced by Ayub Khan was replaced by a parliamentary form of government. Following General Zia's assumption of power in 1977, a series of martial law decrees and an interim constitution promulgated in March 1981 progressively increased the powers of the president, as did various revisions accompanying official restoration of the 1973 document in March 1985. Constitutional changes introduced in April 1997 revoked major provisions of the 1985 revisions, reducing the president to little more than a figurehead.

On October 15, 1999, General Musharraf, who had suspended the constitution and assumed the title of chief executive the previous day, issued Provisional Constitution Order No. 1 of 1999, which specified that Pakistan would continue to be governed, "as nearly as may be," in accordance with the constitution. The order also restricted the president to acting on the advice of the chief executive and mandated the continued functioning of the existing court system, with the proviso that no court could act against the chief executive, his orders, or his appointees. The order left intact all fundamental constitutional rights, such as freedom of the press, not in conflict with the state of emergency.

The LFO instituted by General Musharraf in August 2002, effective from October 12, incorporated 29 constitutional changes, enhancing presidential power, enlarging both houses of Parliament, and creating as a permanent body a civilian-military National Security Council (NSC) that would include the president, the prime minister, the speaker of the National Assembly, the chair of the Senate, the leader of the parliamentary opposition, the four provincial governors, the chair of the joint chiefs of staff, and the chiefs of staff of the army, navy, and air force. The LFO also disqualified convicted criminals from running for the legislature, thereby ensuring that neither Benazir Bhutto nor Nawaz Sharif could stand in the October 2002 election. Opposition to promulgation of the LFO ultimately led to a December 2003 compromise under which most of the LFO provisions were enacted as the 17th amendment to the constitution. The NSC provision was removed, however, and enacted by law in April 2004.

The president, who serves a five-year term, is chosen by vote of the Parliament and the four provincial assemblies sitting jointly as an electoral college. The bicameral Parliament includes an indirectly elected Senate and a popularly elected National Assembly; the latter includes reserved seats for women and religious minorities, and it has sole jurisdiction over money bills. Sitting in joint session, the Parliament may by a simple majority enact bills that have been returned to it by the president. The prime minister, who must be a member of the National Assembly, may be removed by a majority vote of the house's total membership; the president may be removed by a two-thirds vote of the full Parliament.

The judicial system includes a Supreme Court, a Federal Shariat Court to examine the conformity of laws with Islam, high courts in each of the four provinces (Baluchistan, North-West Frontier, Punjab, and Sindh), and a number of antiterrorism courts authorized by legislation in 1997. The assembly approved measures in 1991 that called for formal appeal to the Koran as the country's supreme law and mandated the death penalty for blasphemy.

Centrally appointed governors head provincial administrations. Each province also has an elected Provincial Assembly and a Council of Ministers led by a prime minister, the latter named by the governor. The Federally Administered Tribal Areas (FATA), located between the NWFP and Afghanistan, and the Federal Capital Territory are governed by central appointees. The seven FATA agencies, roughly from north to south, are Bajaur, Mahmand, Khyber, Orakzai, Kurram, North Waziristan, and South Waziristan. Pakistan also administers part of disputed Kashmir (see Related Territories, below).

A Federal Legislative List defines the exclusive authority of the center; there also is a Concurrent Legislative List, with residual authority assigned to the provinces. To safeguard provincial rights, a Council of Common Interests is mandated, comprising the chief ministers of the four provinces plus four federal ministers.

In November 2006 the NWFP legislature passed an Islamic accountability law, but President Musharraf successfully petitioned the Supreme Court for a stay. In August the court had thrown out 20 subsections of a previous law authorizing clerics to oversee media content and social behavior, including interactions between the sexes. The central government had argued that the law overstepped constitutional bounds. A collateral debate focused on a national Protection of Women Bill, which was ultimately signed into law on December 1 despite fierce opposition from all but the most moderate Islamic organizations. Under the new law rape cases were assigned to civil rather than religious courts and for the first time permitted conviction on the basis of forensic and circumstantial evidence rather than on the testimony of male witnesses.

Foreign relations. Relations between India and Pakistan reflect a centuries-old rivalry based on mutual suspicion between Hindus and Muslims. The British withdrawal in 1947 was accompanied by widespread communal rioting and competing claims to Jammu and Kashmir. A start toward improved relations was made in 1960 with an agreement on joint use of the waters of the Indus River basin, but continuing conflict over Kashmir and the Rann of Kutch on the Indian Ocean involved the two countries in armed hostilities in 1965, followed by a withdrawal to previous positions, in conformity with the Tashkent Agreement negotiated with Soviet assistance in January 1966. After another period of somewhat improved relations, the internal crisis in East Pakistan, accompanied by India's open support of the Bengali cause, led to further hostilities in 1971.

Following recognition by Pakistan of independent Bangladesh, bilateral negotiations with India were renewed, and a number of major issues were resolved by the return of prisoners of war, a mutual withdrawal from occupied territory, and the demarcation of a new LoC in Kashmir. Further steps toward normalization were partially offset by Pakistani concern over India's detonation of a nuclear device in May 1974, and formal diplomatic ties were not resumed until July 1976.

A rapprochement followed General Zia's death in August 1988 but abruptly ended in early 1990 as Kashmir became the scene of escalating violence on the part of Muslim separatists. By April thousands of residents had fled to Pakistan from the Indian-controlled Kashmir valley.

On April 6, 1998, Pakistan test fired its first domestically produced medium-range surface-to-surface missile, which provoked immediate criticism from India's recently installed Vajpayee administration. Then on May 11 and 13 India exploded five nuclear weapons in underground testing, prompting Pakistan to respond on May 28 and 30 with six nuclear tests of its own. The international community quickly condemned the tests, and a number of countries imposed economic sanctions against both governments. Shortly after, however, Prime Ministers Sharif and Vajpayee adopted less belligerent stances, meeting during the July session of the South Asian Association for Regional Cooperation (SAARC) in Colombo, Sri Lanka, and again in September in New York, where they announced renewed talks on Kashmir and other matters.

Although the Kashmir talks produced no tangible results, the prime ministers met again in February 1999 in Lahore. The resulting Lahore Declaration included pledges by both administrations to reduce the possibility of accidental nuclear war. Diplomatic moves, both public and behind the scenes, stalled in May 1999 because of renewed fighting in Kashmir.

In October 1999 India reacted cautiously to Prime Minister Sharif's overthrow. General Musharraf met for the first time with Prime Minister Vajpayee in Agra, India, in July 2001. Although the two sides agreed to further meetings, they remained far apart, with Pakistan insisting on the primacy of Kashmir and with India unsuccessfully attempting to broaden the discussion to such other concerns as trade and cultural relations. On October 1 militants carried out an assault on the state assembly building in Srinagar, the summer capital of the Indian State of Jammu and Kashmir, resulting in nearly 40 deaths. Charging that Pakistan had failed to stop terrorist infiltrators, India ordered additional troops to Kashmir, with Pakistan responding in kind. On December 13 terrorists attacked India's Parliament, leaving 14 dead, including the terrorists, and by May 2002, when three gunmen stormed a Kashmiri army base and left nearly three dozen dead, India and Pakistan had a combined million troops or more stationed along the LoC. Diplomatic intervention, led by the United States, ultimately helped to diffuse the immediate situation.

When Prime Minister Vajpayee called on April 18, 2003, for "open dialogue" with Pakistan, Islamabad announced its willingness to cooperate, which led to a mutual upgrading of diplomatic relations. On November 26 the two governments instituted a cease-fire, the first in 14 years, between Pakistani and Indian forces in the disputed border region. The cease-fire was followed by an announcement at the January 4–6, 2004, SAARC session that the two governments would undertake "composite talks" on bilateral issues, and in late June 2005 Prime Minister Aziz described the peace process as "irreversible." Nevertheless, scant progress was made in the following four years, in large part because of terrorist attacks within India by Islamist groups having Pakistani connections (see Current issues, below).

Relations with Bangladesh have improved considerably in recent years, although no formula has yet been found for relocating some 300,000 Biharis, most of whom have been living in over 100 camps in the former East Pakistan since the 1972 breakup. An agreement in August 1992 led to the airlifting of an initial contingent to Lahore in early 1993, but the Bhutto government suspended the program later in the year. Although Pakistan recommitted itself in early 1998 to resettling the Biharis, no substantive move toward that goal had been achieved by May 2008, when the Bangladeshi High Court approved offering citizenship to some 150,000 Biharis who were minors in 1971 as well as all those born since then.

Although Pakistan and Afghanistan had long been at odds over the latter's commitment to the creation of an independent Pushtunistan out of a major part of Pakistan's NWFP, Islamabad reacted strongly to the Soviet invasion of its neighbor in 1979, providing Muslim rebel groups (mujahidin) with weapons and supplies for continued operations against the Soviet-backed regime. Support for the rebels occasionally provoked bombing raids in the area of Peshawar, the NWFP capital, and the presence of more than 3.5 million Afghan refugees proved economically burdensome.

Following the Soviet departure, which was completed in early 1989, Pakistan supported the installation of an interim coalition government in Kabul, and by late 1992 some 1.5 million of the displaced Afghans were reported to have returned home. Kabul later accused Islamabad of supporting the fundamentalist Taliban militia, which Pakistan in fact recognized as Afghanistan's government shortly after it took power in September 1996.

Following the U.S.-led ouster of the Taliban in 2001, relations with Kabul have been complicated by the fact that Islamic fundamentalists, having been permitted to establish education and training camps in the Peshawar area during the Afghan revolution, became increasingly active within Pakistan itself, particularly in FATA and the NWFP as well as within the divided Kashmir. Relations with Afghanistan took a downturn from early 2006 when President Hamid Karzai accused Pakistan of failing to secure Pakistan's side of the border and of not curbing Pakistani-based al-Qaida and Taliban militants.

From the mid-1990s U.S.-Pakistani relations were dominated by concerns over terrorism. In February 1995 the government permitted U.S. agents to join in the apprehension of Ramzi Ahmed YOUSEF, the suspected mastermind of the 1993 World Trade Center bombing in New York, and then approved his prompt extradition. In the wake of the March 1995 killing by Pakistani gunmen of two U.S. consular officials, Prime Minister Bhutto appealed for foreign assistance in closing down Muslim schools and other facilities used as fronts for international terrorism. In 1997 agents of the U.S. Federal Bureau of Investigation apprehended in Pakistan Mir Aimal KASI, who in January 1993 had shot five people, killing two of them, outside the Virginia headquarters of the U.S. Central Intelligence Agency. Kasi, who described his assault as a protest against U.S. involvement in Islamic countries, was sentenced to death in January 1998 by a Virginia court and executed in November 2002. In addition, in August 1997 Pakistan arrested three suspects in the bombing of U.S. embassies in Kenya and Tanzania.

Following the September 11, 2001, assaults on the United States, relations with the new U.S. administration were significantly strengthened by Pakistan's assistance against al-Qaida and, ultimately, the Taliban. In early 2002 the Musharraf regime reacted swiftly to the murder of American journalist Daniel Pearl in Pakistan. The principal suspect, Ahmad Omar SHAIKH, a UK national, was captured in February and later sentenced to death. Three codefendants received life in prison. Another leading suspect, Amjad Hussain FAROOQI, allegedly a member of the outlawed militant group *Lashkar-i-Jhangvi,* was killed in a shootout with police in September 2004.

Despite Pakistan's decision not to back the 2003 U.S. invasion of Iraq, the Bush administration continued to praise and support Musharraf. Not even a February 2004 public admission by Abdul Qadeer KHAN, the former head of Pakistan's nuclear weapons program, that he had passed nuclear secrets to Iran, Libya, and North Korea damaged the U.S.-Pakistani relationship. Musharraf immediately pardoned Khan, a national hero, without protest from Washington. (The International Atomic Energy Agency subsequently speculated that Khan's revelations were merely the "tip of the iceberg" in an operation that also involved the sale of nuclear components in a number of countries.) In March U.S. Secretary of State Colin Powell, making his fourth visit to Pakistan, announced that Pakistan was regarded as a "major non-NATO ally," and a week later U.S. President Bush lifted the few remaining sanctions imposed after the 1998 nuclear tests and the 1999 coup. As of mid-2005 Pakistan had reportedly handed over to the United States some 700 al-Qaida suspects since September 2001, including key operatives. Pakistan's armed forces had also launched major offensives against tribal Islamists, al-Qaida, and Taliban elements in the NWFP and especially in FATA, where Islamabad has never had firm control.

Current issues. In September 2008, with Nawaz Sharif's PML-N having joined the opposition, newly elected President Zardari and Prime Minister Gilani were immediately confronted by the need to shore up legislative support for what was now a minority government. The November cabinet shuffle added the Baluchistan National Party–Awami (BNP-A) and the Pakistan Muslim League–Functional (PML-F) to the existing mix of the PPP, ANP, and *Jamiat-e-Ulema-e-Islami* Fazlur Rahman Group (JUI-F), but the only remaining potential partner with sufficient seats to make a difference was the MQM, which finally agreed to join the governing coalition in January 2009.

Although the six-party coalition now commanded a slim majority in the National Assembly, former prime minister Nawaz Sharif still exerted considerable influence, especially in Punjab, and he continued to insist that Chief Justice Chaudhry and the other the judges who had been dismissed by President Musharraf be reinstated. President Zardari apparently feared that the resurrected Chaudhry Supreme Court would weaken or invalidate presidential powers and throw out the NRO, leaving Zardari vulnerable to the numerous corruption charges that had been quashed by the ordinance. Nevertheless, in March public pressure forced Zardari to yield, and the Supreme Court judges were reinstated. As of November, the NRO remained in effect. In addition, the legislature had yet to determine if it would repeal or revise the 17th amendment, an action that could have a significant impact on the presidency.

Meanwhile, the security situation, especially in the NWFP and FATA, has commanded the most international scrutiny and ratcheted up the domestic anxiety level. According to government figures, in the 15 months up to March 2009, Pakistan saw nearly 1,850 terrorist attacks, including a September 2008 blast at a Marriott Hotel in Islamabad that killed more than 50 people and injured over 260. After Baitullah Mehsud's death in August 2009 the Taliban raised the number and scope of its attacks, which included assassinating a brigadier on the streets of the capital, unleashing suicide bombers on Islamabad's International Islamic University, launching assaults against police compounds in Lahore, staging an audacious raid against military headquarters in Rawalpindi, and targeting UN aid and development workers in Islamabad as well as in the NWFP, and detonating on October 28 a car bomb in a women's market area of Peshawar that killed upwards of 100. Deaths surpassed 300 in October alone.

It has become increasingly difficult to disentangle domestic terrorism, the activities of militant Kashmiri separatists, and the broader "war on terrorism." As 2008 progressed, the number of unmanned NATO drones launching missiles into Pakistan against Taliban and al-Qaida targets rose, as did the number of reported civilian casualties. There was additional evidence that U.S./NATO special forces based in Afghanistan had undertaken missions inside Pakistan. Zardari and other politicians condemned the crossborder attacks and demanded that they stop, but some analysts suspected that the Pakistani government had at least tacitly agreed to the military actions, even though Prime Minister Gilani asserted that NATO actions were undermining his efforts to reach agreements with local leaders on opposing the militants. Visiting Pakistan in late October 2009, U.S. Secretary of State Hillary Clinton acknowledged Pakistani concerns about U.S. tactics and intentions, but she also commented to Pakistani journalists that Americans find it "hard to believe that nobody in your government knows where [al-Qaida's leaders] are and couldn't get them if they really wanted to."

In March 2009 the new Barack Obama administration in the United States had announced a revised Afghan strategy intended "to disrupt, dismantle, and defeat al-Qaida in Pakistan and Afghanistan." The strategy acknowledged that stemming the flow of militants back and forth across the Afghan-Pakistani border required Pakistan's active participation. As an incentive, President Obama proposed a five-year civilian aid package of $7.5 billion. When the aid bill was passed by the U.S. Congress, however, it met fierce criticism from some Pakistanis, who claimed that it would permit U.S. interference in Pakistan's civilian and military affairs. The bill requires the secretary of state to certify that Pakistan is participating in counterterrorism, maintaining civilian authority over the military, safeguarding its nuclear arsenal, and meeting international nonproliferation standards. The $7.5 billion, targeted for such projects as building roads, schools, and power stations, was in addition to $2.3 billion in military assistance included in a defense appropriations bill signed by President Obama in late October.

The activities of jihadist groups have also continued to complicate relations with India, which has repeatedly responded to attacks on its soil by accusing Pakistan of failing to take adequate preventive measures. The most dramatic recent instance occurred on November 26–29, 2008, when a 10-person assault team attacked predetermined targets in Mumbai, leaving 163 people dead and another 300 hurt. All of the assailants, including the lone survivor, Ajmal Amir AMIN (a.k.a. Ajmal Kasab), were ultimately shown to have Pakistani addresses. On February 12, 2009, Islamabad admitted that "some part of the conspiracy" had been hatched in Pakistan. Attention focused on the *Lashkar-i-Taiba* (LiT), whose chief of operations, Zaki-ur-Rehman LAKHVI, was alleged to be the mastermind behind the Mumbai attack. On November 19 a special antiterrorism court indicted Lakhvi and six others.

POLITICAL PARTIES AND GROUPS

Political activity has often been restricted in independent Pakistan. Banned in 1958, parties were permitted to resume activity in 1962. The Pakistan Muslim League (PML), successor to Mohammad Ali Jinnah's All-India Muslim League, continued its dominance during Ayub Khan's tenure. Opposition parties, though numerous, were essentially regional in character and largely ineffectual. The military government of Yahya Khan did not ban political formations as such, but the lack of opportunity for overt activity restricted their growth.

The election of December 1970 provided a major impetus to the reemergence of parties. The PML's supremacy ended with the rise of Zulfikar Ali Bhutto's Pakistan People's Party (PPP) in West Pakistan and the Awami League in East Pakistan (now Bangladesh). In the election of March 1977, the PPP faced a coalition of opposition parties organized as the Pakistan National Alliance (PNA). Although formal party activity was suspended following the coup of July 5, the ban was subsequently relaxed, and the PNA, with but minor defection from its ranks, became a de facto government party until withdrawing in 1979. In October all formal party activity was again proscribed.

In February 1981 nine parties agreed to form a joint Movement for the Restoration of Democracy (MRD), of which the most important component was the PPP under the leadership of Begum Nusrat Bhutto and her daughter, Benazir Bhutto. The composition of the alliance changed several times thereafter, although it remained the largest opposition grouping for the balance of the Zia era. Despite the president's denunciation of parties as "non-Islamic" and the fact that the 1985 assembly election was on a nonparty basis, some political leaders subsequently organized informal legislative coalitions. Legislation proposed immediately before the lifting of martial law permitted legalization of parties under highly controlled circumstances. While most MRD participants declined to register under the new law, the PML, led by Prime Minister Mohammad Khan Junejo, did so in February 1986, thus becoming the de facto ruling party.

Following the legislative dissolution of May 1988, all of the leading parties agreed to participate in the upcoming national and provincial elections. As the result of disagreement with the PPP over electoral strategy, the other MRD parties decided in October to campaign separately in a loose coalition of their own, the MRD becoming, for all practical purposes, moribund. Concurrently, two factions within the PML, which had split after Zia's death in August, reunited and joined a number of other groups, including the *Muhajir Qaumi* Movement (MQM), the National People's Party (NPP), and the *Jamaat-e-Islami* Pakistan (JIP), to form the Islamic Democratic Alliance—IDA (*Islam-e-Jamhoori Ittehad*). The IDA routed the PPP in the October 1990 election but fell into disarray thereafter. The PPP recovered to defeat the PML's Nawaz Group (PML-N) in a basically two-party contest in October 1993.

In February 1997 the PML-N scored a smashing victory over Benazir Bhutto's PPP. Although initially governing with the support of several smaller parties, including the Awami National Party (ANP) and the principal faction of the MQM, by late 1998 the PML-N was essentially governing on its own. Meanwhile, as in the past, various groups were attempting to coordinate their policies through loose multiparty alliances, the principal ones being the Islamic *Milli Yakjehti* Council—MYC (National Unity Council), spearheaded by the *Jamaat-e-Islami;* the largely secular Pakistan National Conference (PNC), formed in June 1997 by 12 opposition parties; and the Pakistan *Awami Ittehad* (PAI), an amalgam of 15 secular, religious, and regional opposition groups, including the PPP and two anti-Nawaz PML factions. In early 1999 some 16 mostly regional parties, several of them with concurrent connections to the PAI, were still in the process of formally establishing another alliance, the **Pakistan Oppressed Nations' Movement** (PONM), which had been announced in October 1998 at a conference called to advance the cause of autonomy for Sindhis, Pushtoons, Baluchs, and Seraikis within a federal system. Some party leaders had already raised the possibility that the PAI-PONM interconnections might lead to formation of a "grand alliance," but the PONM remained aloof from the anti-Nawaz Grand Democratic Alliance (GDA) formed in September 1999, by the PAI, the MQM, the ANP, and the *Tehrik-e-Insaaf.* Of these alliances, all are now defunct except the PONM, which reportedly encompasses some 30 parties.

In mid-April 2000 the GDA and the PML-N began discussions on forming a "political front" devoted to restoring democracy. Despite the objections of some party leaders, the PML-N allied with the PPP and over a dozen other parties in November 2000. Subsequently named the **Alliance for the Restoration of Democracy** (ARD), the grouping selected veteran politician Nawabzada Nasrullah Khan of the Pakistan Democratic Party (PDP) as its first president.

A total of 73 parties and alliances contested the October 2002 election. In addition to the ARD, whose constituent parties ran independently, the principal alliances were the recently formed Islamic *Muttahida Majlis-e-Amal* (MMA) and the government-supportive National Alliance (NA). The MMA included as its principal parties the *Jamiat-Ulema-e-Islam* Fazlur Rahman Group (JUI-F) and the *Jamaat-e-Islami Pakistan* (JIP), along with the *Jamiat-Ulema-e-Islam* Sami ul-Haq Group (JUI-S), the *Jamiat Ulema-e-Pakistan* (JUP), the *Islami Tehrik-i-Pakistan* (TiP), and the *Markazi Jamiat-e-Ahle Hadith* (MJAH). The NA included the Millat Party (MP), National Awami Party (NAP), NPP, Sindh Democratic Alliance (SDA), and Sindh National Front (SNF). A looser Grand National Alliance encompassed the PML's dominant *Qaid-i-Azam* faction and the NA plus the ANP, the MQM, the PPP (Sherpao), and a number of other progovernment, predominantly regional groups, all running independently. In 2004 some of the NA parties merged with the substantially reunited PML.

On July 11, 2007, following the conclusion of an All Parties Conference held in London and attended by Nawaz Sharif, some 30 parties, led by the PML-N, the MMA, and members of the PONM, announced formation of the anti-Musharraf **All Parties Democratic Movement** (APDM). Creation of the APDM marked a split in the ARD: Benazir Bhutto's PPP and a handful of small allied parties, more accommodating toward Musharraf and more willing to negotiate a power-sharing arrangement, remained aloof.

Prior to the February 2008 election, Pakistan had 110 registered parties and coalitions. Most of the APDM parties chose to boycott the February 2008 election, the most notable exception being the PML-N. In all, 46 parties contested the election, as did the MMA coalition, although the only MMA party to actually participate was the JUI-F. In April 2009 leaders of the six MMA parties met in an effort to revive the coalition, but they failed to reach agreement.

Government Parties:

Pakistan People's Party (PPP). An Islamic socialist party founded in 1967 by Zulfikar Ali Bhutto, the PPP held a majority of seats in the National Assembly truncated by the independence of Bangladesh in 1971. Officially credited with winning 155 of 200 assembly seats in the election of March 1977, it was the primary target of a postcoup decree in October that banned all groups whose ideology could be construed as prejudicial to national security.

Bhutto was executed in April 1979, the party leadership being assumed by his widow and daughter Benazir, both of whom, after being under house arrest for several years, went into exile in London. After having briefly returned to Pakistan in July 1985 to preside over the burial of her brother, Shahnawaz, Benazir Bhutto again returned in April 1986. The PPP won a sizable plurality (92 of 205 contested seats) in the National Assembly election of November 1988, and Bhutto became prime minister. She remained in office until dismissed in August 1990. The party's legislative strength was then cut by more than half in the October general election (for which it joined with a number of smaller groups to campaign as the People's Democratic Alliance—PDA). It regained its plurality in 1993, with Ms. Bhutto being reinstalled as prime minister.

In December 1993 the PPP's Executive Council ousted Prime Minister Bhutto's mother, Begum Nusrat BHUTTO, as party cochair. The action was the product of estrangement between the two over the political role of Benazir's brother, Murtaza Bhutto, who had returned from exile in November to take up a seat in the Sindh provincial legislature. In March 1995 he announced the formation of a breakaway faction of the PPP, but he died in a firefight with gunmen in September 1996. Following the ouster of Prime Minister Bhutto in November, her husband, Asif Ali Zardari, was charged with complicity in the killing. The new PML-led government formed an "accountability" department to investigate the allegations and corruption in general, a principal target being the PPP leadership. Meanwhile, Benazir Bhutto was meeting with leaders of smaller opposition parties, which ultimately led to the formation of the PAI alliance in February 1998.

Earlier, at the end of 1996, allegations about the death of Murtaza Bhutto had led his widow, Ghinwa BHUTTO, to form the **Pakistan People's Party (Shaheed Bhutto),** or PPP-SB, to challenge Benazir Bhutto's hold on the party. The subsequent national legislative campaign in early 1997 contained an added element of personal hostility between the two women, although both suffered disastrous defeats in the election.

During 1998–1999 new corruption allegations or charges were repeatedly brought against Benazir Bhutto and her husband: kickbacks involving gold transactions, commissions from foreign defense manufacturers, abuse of power in making political appointments, and use of Swiss bank accounts to launder money. Bhutto's political viability suffered a major blow in April 1999 when a Lahore court sentenced her and her husband to five years in prison, disqualified them from public office for five years, and fined them $8.6 million for corruption and abuse of power. Bhutto asserted from England that she would appeal the conviction to the Supreme Court, which in April 2001 threw out the decision and ordered a retrial because of apparent government involvement in the verdict.

In March 1999 the party leadership elected the former prime minister chair for life, a decision reiterated by a party convention in September 2000 in defiance of the government's August announcement that convicted criminals could not hold party offices. Bhutto remained in self-imposed exile, the Musharraf regime having refused to lift outstanding arrest warrants.

In July 2002 Bhutto was again convicted, in absentia, of corruption, as was her husband in September. He had been imprisoned since 1986. Other cases against the two were pending in Switzerland, the United States, and the United Kingdom as well as Pakistan. In September 2004 Zardari's corruption conviction was overturned, and on November 22 he was released on bail. He later left the country.

To get around a proscription against the electoral participation of any party having a convicted criminal as an officeholder, the PPP organized the legally separate **Pakistan People's Party Parliamentarians** (PPPP) in August 2002. Two months after its formation, the PPPP won 81 National Assembly seats, but in November it suffered the defection of 10 representatives who supported the installation of the Jamali government. (The move was possible because the antidefection clause of the constitution remained suspended.) The defectors then organized under Rao Sikander IQBAL as the Pakistan People's Party (Patriots), which merged with the PPP (Sherpao), a 1999 splinter (see the separate write-up, below), in June 2004. The new organization was then registered by the Election Commission as the "official" PPP. Bhutto's PPP immediately appealed the Election Commission's decision on the grounds that use of the PPP name by another party would deceive and defraud the electorate. Iqbal and his supporters joined the PML-Q before the 2008 general election, for which the PPP (Sherpao) was separately registered.

On July 27, 2007, President Musharraf and Benazir Bhutto met in Abu Dhabi in the context of ongoing discussions between the government and her representatives on a power-sharing arrangement. Bhutto returned to Pakistan on October 18, following Musharraf's promulgation of a National Reconciliation Ordinance (NRO) that freed her from prosecution, but the imposition in November of a state of emergency resulted in her calling, while under house arrest, for Musharraf's resignation. Following Bhutto's assassination on December 27, she was succeeded as party chair by a teenaged son, Bilawal, with Asif Zardari handling the party's day-to-day affairs.

In the February 2008 election the PPP, running as the still-registered PPPP, won 30.6 percent of the vote and a plurality of 124 seats. (Zardari was prevented from running by earlier corruption convictions.) It then forged a coalition agreement with the PML-N and several smaller parties, after which the PPP vice chair, Yusuf Raza Gilani, was elected as prime minister. Following President Musharraf's August resignation, Zardari emerged as the leading candidate for the presidency, even though the PML-N had withdrawn from the coalition. Zardari was elected president on September 6. In the March 2009 election for one-half of the Senate, the PPP claimed nearly half the seats and thereby surpassed the PML-Q as the plurality party in the upper house.

Leaders: Bilawal BHUTTO Zardari (Chair), Asif Ali ZARDARI (President of Pakistan and Cochair of the PPP), Yusuf Raza GILANI (Prime Minister and PPP Vice Chair), Makhdoom Amin FAHIM (Vice Chair), Syed Nayyer Hussain BOKHARI (Senate Leader), Jehangir BADER (Secretary General), Mian Raza RABBANI (Deputy Secretary General).

Muttahida Qaumi Movement (MQM). Organized in 1981 as the *Muhajir* National Movement, at that time the MQM (Nationalist People's Movement) was primarily concerned with the rights of postpartition migrants to Pakistan, whom it wanted to see recognized as constituting a "fifth nationality." Originally backed by Zia ul-Haq as a counter to Zulfikar Bhutto's Sindh-based PPP, the party became the third-largest National Assembly grouping, with 13 seats, after the 1988 election. It was subsequently allied, at different times, with both the PPP and the PML.

The assassination of party chair Azim Ahmad TARIQ in May 1993 exacerbated a violent cleavage that had emerged within the group the year before, the principal leaders being Altaf Hussain (MQM-Altaf), who is now a citizen of the United Kingdom, and Afaq Ahmed of the MQM-*Haqiqi* (below). Although the party boycotted the National Assembly election in 1993, it was runner-up to the PPP in the Sindh provincial elections. In 1994 Altaf Hussain and two of his senior associates were sentenced in absentia to 27-year prison terms for terrorism, but in 1997 the convictions were quashed.

In February 1997 the MQM-Altaf, under the banner of the **Haq Parast Group,** won 12 National Assembly seats, all from Sindh, and thereafter entered a governing alliance with the PML-N at both provincial and national levels. Also in 1997, the party changed its named from *"Muhajir"* to *"Muttahida"* to indicate that its interests had broadened to encompass Pakistanis in general rather than only the Muslim migrants from India.

In August 1998 the MQM announced its intention to withdraw from the governing coalitions, in part because the Nawaz Sharif administration had not done enough to stem increasingly violent clashes in Karachi between the MQM-Altaf and the MQM-*Haqiqi,* the latter of which was functioning primarily as a collection of urban street fighters. When Islamabad responded to the violence by dismissing the Sindh provincial government and imposing federal rule, Altaf Hussain loyalists accused the Nawaz Sharif government of trying to take away the party's power base. In 1999 a number of party leaders broke with Hussain and threatened to form a separate party unless he adopted a stronger stance toward autonomy for Sindh.

In the 2002 National Assembly election, the MQM won 17 seats, after which it joined the Jamali government. In July 2006, however, it threatened to pull its ministers from the cabinet and to leave the Sindh government because President Musharraf would not fire the Sindh chief minister. The crisis was resolved a week later, and the MQM remained in the government.

In the February 2008 election the MQM-Altaf won 7.4 percent of the vote and a total of 25 National Assembly seats. Expectations to the contrary, the MQM did not immediately join the Gilani cabinet, reportedly because the party demanded more posts than were offered. It eventually joined the government in January 2009.

Leaders: Altaf HUSSAIN (President), Babar GHAURI (Minister of Ports and Shipping), Farooq SATTAR (Minister of Overseas Pakistanis).

Awami National Party (ANP). The ANP was formed in July 1986 by four left-of-center groups: the National Democratic Party (NDP), a group of Pakistan National Party (PNP) dissidents led by Latif AFRIDI, elements of the *Awami Tehrik* (PAT, below), and the *Mazdoor Kissan* Party (MKP). As originally constituted under the direction of Pushtoon leader Khan Abdul WALI KHAN, the ANP was unusual in that each of its constituent groups drew its primary support from a different province.

The NDP had been organized in 1975 upon proscription of the National Awami Party, a remnant of the National Awami Party of Bangladesh that, under the leadership of Wali Khan, was allegedly involved in terrorist activity aimed at secession of Baluchistan and the NWFP. A founding component of the PNA, the NDP withdrew in 1978, and in 1979 a group of dissidents left to form the PNP.

The ANP won three assembly seats in October 1993 and ten seats—all from the NWFP—in February 1997. A year later the ANP terminated its alliance with the governing PML-N because of the latter's refusal to support the redesignation of the NWFP as Pakhtoonkhwa, the area's precolonial name. Later in 1998 the ANP was a prime mover in formation of the PONM opposition alliance, but it parted ways in 1999 with what it considered the PONM's unrealistic goals for national reconfiguration.

The ANP failed to win representation in the National Assembly election of 2002 but won two Senate seats in February 2003. The party's founder, Khan Abdul Wali Khan, died in January 2006.

In June 2006 the central party leadership endorsed the Charter of Democracy proposed by former prime ministers Bhutto and Nawaz Sharif. In the same month, the National Awami Party (NAP), a 2000 offshoot led by Arbab Ayub JAN and Sharif KHATTAK, reunited with the parent party.

In February 2008 the ANP won 13 National Assembly seats and also won control of the NWFP legislature. It then joined the PPP, PML-N, and JUI-F in forming a central government. In March 2009 it won 5 Senate seats, for a total of 6.

A prominent NWFP legislator, Alamzeb KHAN, was killed by a roadside bomb in Peshawar in February 2009.

Leaders: Asfandyar WALI KHAN (President), Haji Muhammad ADIL (Senior Vice President), Amir Haider Khan HOTI (Chief Minister of NWFP), Ihsan WAYN (Secretary General).

Jamiat-Ulema-e-Islam Fazlur Rahman Group (JUI-F). The *Jamiat-Ulema-e-Islam* (Assembly of Islamic Clergy) was founded in 1950 as a progressive formation committed to constitutional government guided by Sunni Islamic principles. In 1988 the JUI's Darkhwasty Group withdrew from the IDA to reunite with the parent formation, although a faction headed by Maulana Sami ul-Haq remained within the government coalition until November 1991. Factionalization subsequently remained a problem, with Sami ul-Haq heading one group, the JUI-S (below), and Fazlur Rahman heading another, the JUI-F. The latter, which won two National Assembly seats from Baluchistan in 1997, emerged as the dominant faction. Fazlur Rahman supported Afghanistan's Taliban and, following the 1999 coup, condemned ousted prime minister Sharif's "lust for unlimited powers." He was placed under house arrest in October 2001, at the opening of the U.S.-led military campaign in Afghanistan.

In the 2002 National Assembly election the JUI-F claimed the most MMA seats. The *Muttahida Majlis-e-Amal* (United Council for Action), organized in June 2001 by the JUI-F and five other Islamic parties, campaigned on a platform that included restoration of the constitution, creation of an Islamic state, and resolution of the Kashmir issue through negotiation. All of the constituent parties opposed General Musharraf's decision to join the U.S.-led "war on terrorism" and to permit U.S. forces to operate from Pakistani soil. Having won 60 seats in the National Assembly, the MMA was courted by both the PML-Q and the PPPP (with which it had little in common ideologically) to form a coalition government, but it rejected both. Its firm opposition to the 2002 Legal Framework Order was largely responsible for the yearlong stalemate in the National Assembly, until an agreement was reached with President Musharraf in December 2003.

Although the MMA was chaired from its inception by the moderate Maulana Shah Ahmad Noorani Siddiqui of the JUP (below) until his death in December 2003, the leaders of the two largest member parties—the JUI-F's Fazlur Rahman and Qazi Hussain Ahmad of the JIP (below)—exerted more influence. One contentious issue was the JIP's objections to participation in President Musharraf's National Security Council. As leader of the opposition, the JUI-F's Fazlur Rahman held a seat on the council, as did JUI-F member Akram Khan Durrani, who was at that time the chief minister of the NWFP.

In July 2007 the MMA participated in the anti-Musharraf All Parties Conference and joined in forming the APDM, but the alliance subsequently split over whether to boycott the February 2008 election. The JUI-F chose to contest the election, in which it ran under the MMA banner, taking 2.2 percent of the vote, winning 7 seats, and then joining the PPP-led government. At the same time, however, it was soundly defeated in the NWFP legislative election, winning only 14 of 124 seats. Following the 2009 Senate election, it held 10 seats in the upper house.

Leaders: Maulana Fazlur RAHMAN, Akram Khan DURRANI (Former Chief Minister of NWFP), Hafiz Hussein AHMAD.

Pakistan Muslim League (Functional)—PML-F. The PML-F was established by longtime PML leader Pir Sahib Pagaro, who broke from the PML in mid-1992. In 2002 the PML-F won five National Assembly seats and one in the Senate.

Although Pagaro initially appeared willing to participate in the reunification of the various PML parties with the dominant PML-Q in 2004, he soon retreated from that position. In 2005 the largely reunited PML indicated that it regarded the PML-F as a separate, allied party. In February 2008 the PML-F won five National Assembly seats, and two months later Pagaro indicated that he was considering unification with the PML-Q. Nevertheless, in November 2008 the PML-F joined the cabinet.

Leaders: Pir Sahib PAGARO, Abdul Razzak THAHEEM (Minister of Local Government and Rural Development), Jehangir Khan TAREEN.

Baluchistan National Party–Awami (BNP-A). One of several rival political formations in Baluchistan, the BNP was formed by the 1997 merger of the Baluchistan National Movement (Mengal Group) and the Pakistan National Party of Mir Ghaus Baksh BIZENJO. It won three National Assembly seats that year and initially backed the Nawaz Sharif government, but it later withdrew its support. The party soon split into factions. In the 2002 National Assembly election the BNP-Mengal (below) won one seat; in the 2003 Senate election the BNP-Mengal and the BNP-A each won one. Also in 2003, another BNP faction led by Hayee Baloch joined in forming the National Party (NP, below).

In the February 2008 National Assembly election the BNP-A won one seat. In July it won a second Senate seat in a by-election necessitated by the resignation of the BNP-Mengal senator. The BNP-A joined the government in November 2008 and added a third Senate seat in 2009.

Leaders: Sen. Mir Israrullah Khan ZEHRI (President), Sen. Kalsoom PERVEEN, Sen. Muhammad Ali RIND, Yaqoob BIZANJO (Member of National Assembly).

Other Parties Represented in the National Assembly:

Pakistan Muslim League (Nawaz)—PML-N. Under the leadership of former Punjab chief minister and then Prime Minister Mohammad Nawaz Sharif, the PML-N emerged from the PML-Junejo Group in 1993 and quickly established itself as the dominant PML grouping. In 1997 the PML-N won a parliamentary majority under Nawaz Sharif. Following the October 1999 coup the PML-N established a 15-member Coordination Committee to consider party reorganization. It did not, however, call for the immediate restoration of the Sharif government, having concluded that directly confronting the military would be inadvisable.

As a condition of his release from prison in December 2000, Sharif agreed to abandon politics for at least two decades, although he continued to exert considerable influence from exile. In May 2004 his brother, Shahbaz, having received a favorable ruling from the Supreme Court on his right to return, attempted to end his four-year exile but was immediately ushered back out of the country by officials.

At the October 2002 National Assembly election the PML-N ran as part of ARD, winning 19 seats. A year later the party's acting president, Javed Hashmi, was arrested for distributing a letter, allegedly written by army officers, that was critical of President Musharraf. Despite widespread expressions of outrage from ARD and other elements of the opposition, Hashmi was convicted in April 2004 of treason, mutiny, and forgery. In August he was put forward as the opposition candidate for prime minister.

In August 2007 Hashmi was freed on bail by the Supreme Court after nearly four years' incarceration. Late in the same month, the justices also ruled that Nawaz Sharif could return from exile, but his attempt to do so on September 10 was thwarted by the government, which ordered him detained at the airport, served him an arrest warrant for corruption and money-laundering, and immediately deported him to Saudi Arabia. Nawaz Sharif returned again on November 25, following the intervention of Saudi Arabia's king, and was greeted by thousands of supporters.

In the February 2008 National Assembly election PML-N candidates won 91 seats, the vast majority from Punjab. Nawaz Sharif was prevented from running by earlier corruption convictions. Afterward, the PML-N formed a governing coalition with the PPP, but it withdrew its ministers in May, primarily because of differences with the PPP over reinstatement of the Supreme Court justices and other judges that had been dismissed by President Musharraf. The PML-N nevertheless continued to support the government in Parliament until joining the opposition in August. Its candidate for president, Saeeduzzaman Siddiqui, finished second in September 2008.

Leaders: Mohammad Nawaz SHARIF (Leader), Mian Mohammad Shahbaz SHARIF (President of the Party and Chief Minister of Punjab),

Makhdoom Javed HASHMI (Senior Vice President), Raja Muhammad ZAFAR-UL-HAQ (Chair), Iqbal Zafar JHAGRA (Secretary General).

Pakistan Muslim League (PML). Officially registered in 2004 as the PML, the current party continues to be interchangeably identified as the **Pakistan Muslim League–Qaid-i-Azam** ("Father of the Nation," a reference to Mohammad Ali Jinnah), or PML-Q.

The complicated history of the PML began in 1962, when it was launched as successor to the pre-independence All-India Muslim League. Long riven by essentially personalist factions, it split over participation in the February 1985 election. A "Chatta Group," led by Kawaja KHAIRUDDIN, joined the MRD's boycott call, while the mainstream, led by Pir Sahib Pagaro, participated in the election "under protest" and won 27 seats. Mohammad Khan Junejo, a longtime party member, became prime minister.

In the absence of a party-based legislature, the PML served as the core of the government-backed Official Parliamentary Group (OPG) and was the first to register as a legal party following the lifting of martial law in 1986. Later in the year a cleavage emerged between grassroots party loyalists, led by Pagaro, and officeholders (many with no previous party affiliation), led by Junejo. The PML split again in August 1988, an army-supported faction of Zia loyalists (the PML-Fida) emerging under Fida Mohammad KHAN. The party reunited as a component of the IDA prior to the November balloting, in which the IDA routed the PPP, Mohammad Nawaz Sharif of the PML thereupon being named prime minister. Pagaro formed his own party, the PML-Functional (PML-F, above), in mid-1992.

In May 1993, two months after Junejo's death, the Junejo group split into a majority (Nawaz, or PML-N) faction headed by Nawaz Sharif and a rump (Junejo, or PML-J) faction led by Hamid Nasir CHATTA. The latter joined the Bhutto government following the October 1993 election, while the PML-N became the core of the parliamentary opposition.

Following the elections of February 1997, in which it won a majority of the assembly seats, the PML-N took power. The party remained prone to factionalism, however, with the PML-J and a Qasim Group (PML-Qasim) joining the opposition PAI alliance upon its formation in 1998. Following the October 1999 coup another faction, the PML-Q, was formed with the tacit support of the military and became the party most closely associated with President Musharraf.

Entering the 2002 election, the PML-Q was allied with the National Alliance (NA) in the Grand National Alliance. The PML-N ran as part of the ARD. The PML-J, although still separate, appeared to be drawing closer to the PML-Q. Also running independently were the PML-F; the PML–Zia ul-Haq (PML-Z), which had been formed by the son of the late president in August 2002; and the PML-Jinnah, which had been established in 1998 following a factional dispute within the PML-J. Electoral results gave the PML-Q 118 seats; the PML-F, 5; the PML-J, 3; and the PML-Z, 1.

With the PML-Q in the ascendancy, holding a plurality of seats in both houses of Parliament and dominating the government, efforts to unite the PML factions gathered strength in 2003, leading to the announcement in May 2004 of a "united PML," excluding only the PML-N. In August, however, objecting in particular to the leadership of Chaudhry Shujaat Hussain, Pir Sahib Pagaro declared that he intended to restore the PML-F's separate standing.

Days after the formation of the "united PML," the NA parties, which had won 16 seats in the October 2002 election, announced that they were merging with the PML. (One of the founding NA parties, the Sindh National Front, had already withdrawn from the alliance.) The Sindh Democratic Alliance (SDA), led by Arbab Ghulam RAHIM (chief minister of Sindh since June 2004), had been launched in September–October 2001 and had already established a working relationship at the provincial level with the PML-Q. The Millat Party (MP) had been launched in August 1998 by former president Sardar Farooq Ahmad Khan Leghari. There was, however, opposition to the merger within the other NA parties. In the end, the National People's Party (NPP, below) and the National Awami Party (see the ANP, above) retained separate identities.

In mid-June 2004 the Election Commission approved the merger of the PML-F, PML-J, PML-Jinnah, PML-Z, and SDA into the PML-Q and the redesignation of the latter as, simply, the PML, although the PML-Q designation is still commonly used (in part, to distinguish it from the PML-N) Formal incorporation of the MP followed.

In 2005 vocal opposition surfaced to the continued leadership of the party president, Shujaat Hussain, and to the prominent role of the Punjab chief minister, Chaudhry Pervez Elahi, who allegedly ignored the recommendations of National Assembly representatives in choosing candidates for local council elections. The "forward bloc" dissident group, numbering about 30 members of the National Assembly, was led by Mian Riaz Hussain PIRZADA, Farooq Amjad MIR, and Mazhan QURESHI. In May 2006 President Musharraf, looking toward the next general election, asked Shujaat Hussain to form a dispute resolution board to resolve the differences. Nevertheless, Pirzada, in particular, continued to object to many of President Musharraf's decisions, including the dismissal of the Supreme Court judges and the imposition of a state of emergency in November 2007.

In the February 2008 National Assembly election the PML finished third, with 23 percent of the vote and a total of 54 seats. Those defeated for reelection included Shujaat Hussain. In March the PML candidate for prime minister, Pervez Elahi, finished a distant second, with 42 votes. In May former senior vice president Mian Manzoor Ahmad WATTOO (previously leader of the PML-Jinnah) joined the PPP.

At the same time, dissatisfaction with the continued dominance of Shujaat Hussein and Pervez Elahi led a group of dissidents to form a **Like-Minded Bloc** within the PML. In October 2008 the bloc called for new party elections, charging that Shujaat Hussain failed to consult with the party's executive and working committees and that his failure of leadership had left the PML out of the Baluchistan provincial government despite its having won a legislative plurality. With Shujaat Hussain virtually guaranteed reelection, the bloc then boycotted the July 2009 party election. Two months later it announced its own leadership as Hamid Nasir Chatta, chair; Salim SAIFULLAH, president; and Humayan Akhtar KHAN, secretary general.

Leaders: Chaudhry Shujaat HUSSAIN (President); Muhammad Ijaz ul-HAQ (Senior Vice President of the Party and Former Leader of the PML-Z); Asad Ali Khan JUNEJO and Owais Ahmad Khan LEGHARI (Senior Vice Presidents); Wasim SAJJAD (Leader of the Opposition in the Senate), Chaudhry Pervez ELAHI, Mushahid HUSSAIN Syed (2008 presidential candidate and Secretary General).

Jamiat Ulema-e-Pakistan (JUP). Founded in 1968, the JUP (Assembly of Pakistani Clergy) is a popular Islamic group that withdrew from the PNA in 1978. It joined the MRD in February 1981, severed its membership the following March, then rejoined in August 1983 at the commencement of the civil disobedience campaign. Its president, Maulana Shah Ahmed NOORANI, was among those failing to secure an assembly slot in 1988; its secretary general, Maulana Abdul Sattar Khan NIAZI, quit the Nawaz Sharif cabinet in 1991 after being criticized by the prime minister for not supporting government policies on the Gulf war against Iraq. The party subsequently split into four factions, including those led by Noorani and Niazi. Niazi died in May 2001 and Noorani, in December 2003.

In the 2002 election the JUP's Fazal Kareem was elected on the PML-N list, but he resigned from the National Assembly in December 2006 because he regarded the legislature's passage of the Protection of Women Bill as contrary to Islam. He nevertheless ran successfully for the assembly in 2008 on the PML-N ticket.

In May 2006 the JUP (Niazi), which supported the ARD, indicated that it would sign the Charter of Democracy that had been drafted by former prime ministers Bhutto and Nawaz Sharif. In March 2008 the president of the JUP (Noorani), Muhammad Anas Noorani, announced that he was stepping down. His successor, Abu al-Khair Zubair, later led an unsuccessful effort to reconcile the leaders of the JUI-F and JIP in the hope of revitalizing the MMA.

In May 2009 the JUP joined in forming the **Sunni Ittehad Council** (SIC), a group of eight moderate Sunni parties that strongly opposed the Taliban but also called for the withdrawal of U.S. forces from Afghanistan and an end to missile attacks from unmanned drones. The JUP's Fazal Kareem was named SIC chair. Another SIC founder, cleric and religious scholar Sarfraz Ahmed NAEEMI, was assassinated by a Taliban suicide bomber in June.

Leaders: Abu al-Khair Muhammad ZUBAIR (President, JUP-Noorani), Muhammad Anas NOORANI (JUP-Noorani), Pir Syed Anis HAIDER Shah (President, JUP-Niazi), Muhammad Fazal KAREEM (President, JUP-FK), Saleem Ullah KHAN (President, JUP-*Nifaz-i-Shariat*).

National People's Party (NPP). The NPP was formed in 1986 by a group of PPP moderates led by former Sindh chief minister Ghulam Mustafa Jatoi, who accused Benazir Bhutto of "authoritarian tendencies" prior to being removed as provincial PPP president. Jatoi served as interim prime minister following the dismissal of Bhutto in 1990. The NPP entered the first Sharif government coalition but was expelled in 1992 because of alleged collusion with the PPP. The NPP turned to the PPP (Shaheed Bhutto) for an electoral alliance in 1997, winning one seat.

The NPP became a founding member of the National Alliance in May 2002. Two years later, following the announcement that some alliance parties were merging with the PML, Ghulam Mustafa Jatoi stated that although the party's parliamentary group may have decided to join the PML, he had not. The NPP has since maintained its independence and won one National Assembly seat in 2008. Jatoi died in November 2009.

Leader: Asif JATOI.

Pakistan People's Party (Sherpao)—PPP(S). The PPP (S) was established by Aftab Ahmad Khan Sherpao following Benazir Bhutto's 1999 decision to dismiss him as PPP senior vice president for breaking party discipline over political developments involving the NWFP government. In the 2002 general election the PPP (Sherpao) won two seats in the Senate and two in the National Assembly. A June 2004 merger with the progovernment PPP (Patriots) resulted in a decision by the Election Commission to assign the unified party the PPP designation—Benazir Bhutto's PPP had been deregistered—but the issue of who held title to the name became moot after Bhutto's return to Pakistan in 2007 and the decision of the PPP (Patriots) leaders to join the PML-Q.

In April and again in December 2007 Aftab Sherpao was the apparent intended target of suicide bombings that killed a total of some 80 people. The PPP(S) ran independently in the 2008 National Assembly election, retaining one assembly seat.

Leader: Aftab Ahmad Khan SHERPAO.

Additional Parties with Seats in the Senate:

Jamaat-e-Islami Pakistan (JIP). Organized in 1941, the *Jamaat-e-Islami* (Islamic Assembly) is a right-wing fundamentalist group that has called for an Islamic state based on a national rather than a purely communalistic consensus. Members of the party ran as individuals in the 1985 assembly election, and ten were elected; subsequently, although party leaders agreed to legislative coordination with the PML, the *Jamaat-e-Islami* dominated the Independent Parliamentary Group (IPG) and, despite its unregistered status, functioned as the largest legislative opposition party.

The group participated in formation of the IDA in 1988 but withdrew in 1992, in part because the coalition had failed to implement a promised Islamization program. In 1993 it was instrumental in launching a Pakistan Islamic Front (PIF), which won only three seats in the October legislative poll. Although the JIP held no national legislative seats following the 1997 election, it remained politically influential. It welcomed the October 1999 coup but called for setting up a caretaker civilian government.

One of the two largest parties in the MMA, the JIP increasingly differed with the JUI-F (above) after the 2002 general election, threatening the MMA's effectiveness. One contentious issue was the JIP's objections to the JUI-F's participation in President Musharraf's National Security Council. In 2008 the JIP boycotted the general election.

In March 2009 the JIP elected its secretary general, Syed Munawwar Hassan, to a five-year term as chair.

Officially a branch of the *Jamiat-e-Islami* in Pakistan but so independent that it might well be considered a separate movement, the **Jammu and Kashmir Jamiat-e-Islami** was active in electoral politics by 1970 and even participated to a limited degree in Indian *Lok Sabha* and provincial elections. In 1997 the party denied that it was the political wing of the militant *Hizb-ul-Mujaheddin*, and in October 40 of its members challenged the militant campaign as not contributing to the goal of an independent Kashmir.

Leaders: Syed Munawwar HASSAN (Chair), Qazi Hussain AHMAD (Former Chair), Liaqat BALOCH (Secretary General).

National Party (NP). The NP was formed in 2003 by merger of the leading faction of the **Baluchistan National Movement** (BNM), led by Abdul Hayee Baloch, and the **Baluchistan National Democratic Party** (BNDP), led by Hasil Bizenjo and Sardar Sanaullah ZEHRI. Competing primarily against supporters of the BNP, the NP has had little electoral success at the national level. It currently holds two Senate seats.

As a member of the APDM, the NP chose to boycott the February 2008 National Assembly election, but Senior Vice President Zehri objected, formed a **National Party Parliamentarians** (NPP) group, and won a seat in the Baluchistan Assembly.

In April 2009 Ghulam Muhammad BALOCH, president of the BNM and secretary general of the eight-party **Baluchistan National Front** (BNF), was killed along with another BNM leader and the head of the **Baloch Republican Party** (BRP), Sher Mohammad BALOCH. The execution-style deaths led to rioting and antigovernment demonstrations in Baluchistan, although it was unclear who was responsible for the murders.

Leaders: Abdul HAYEE Baloch, Sen. Abdul MALIK (President), Sen. Mir Hasil BIZENJO (Secretary General).

Jamhoori Watan Party (JWP). A successor to the Baluchistan National Alliance (BNA), the JWP (Republican National Party) is active at both provincial and national levels. The JWP, which was formed in 1990 by Nawab Akbar BUGTI, won two seats from Baluchistan in the 1997 National Assembly election and as of early 1999 held five Senate seats. Although initially extending support to the Nawaz Sharif government, the JWP later moved into opposition but without joining either the PNC or PAI alliance. As a participant in the ARD, the JWP won one lower house seat in 2002 and one Senate seat in 2003.

The death of the JWP's prominent founder in an August 2006 military operation precipitated widespread rioting, and the first anniversary of his death was observed by a general strike across Baluchistan. By then, the party had split into two factions, the more radical of which was led by a grandson of Akbar Bugti, Baramdagh BUGTI, who is also a leader of the separatist Baluchistan Republican Army.

The JWP boycotted the 2008 National Assembly election.

Leaders: Nawabzada Talal Akbar BUGTI (President), Sen. Shahid Hassan BUGTI, Shah Zain BUGTI.

Markazi Jamiat-e-Ahle Hadith (MJAH). A militant Sunni group with a number of factions, the MJAH has close ties to former prime minister Nawaz Sharif. Originally a component of the MMA, it withdrew when the latter decided to function as an electoral alliance for the 2002 National Assembly election, although it later returned. The leader of the most prominent faction, Sajid Mir, was reelected in 2009 to a Punjab technocrat seat in the Senate with the endorsement of the PML-N.

Leader: Sajid MIR.

Pakhtoonkhwa Milli Awami Party (PkMAP). Drawing its support mainly from the Pakhtoon ethnic group in the NWFP, the PkMAP has campaigned for greater regional autonomy. It elected three National Assembly members in 1993 but none in 1997. In 1998 it participated in formation of the PONM opposition alliance.

In the 2002 National Assembly election the PkMAP won one seat; in 2003 it won two Senate seats, picking up a third in 2006. The party's chair, Mahmood Khan Achakzai, was elected president of the PONM in June 2006 and then became convener of the APDM. He has used that platform to demand a separate province for Pukhtuns. After the March 2009 Senate election, the PkMAP held only one seat in the upper house.

Leaders: Mahmood Khan ACHAKZAI (Chair), Sen. Abdul Rahim Khan MANDOKHEL.

Other Parties:

Awami Qiadat Party (AQP). Formed in 1995, the AQP (People's Leadership Party) serves primarily as a personal vehicle for Aslam Beg, a retired general. Linked to Pakhtoon issues, the party also supports the military. Although committed to democratic procedures, General Beg has argued for a stronger response to civil disorder and sectarian violence. Prior to the 2002 National Assembly election he chastised the secular opposition parties for failing to unite. In May 2006 he called on Benazir Bhutto and Nawaz Sharif to join forces and mobilize the opposition to President Musharraf.

Leader: Gen. (Ret.) Mirza Aslam BEG (Chair).

Baluchistan National Party–Mengal (BNP-M). The present BNP-M, which is officially registered simply as the BNP, traces its origin to the Baluchistan National Movement (Mengal Group), which in 1997 merged with the Pakistan National Party to form the BNP. The

BNP soon split into several factions, however. In the 2002 National Assembly election the BNP-M won one seat; in the 2003 Senate election the BNP-M and the BNP-Awami (above) each won one. In June 2006 party chief Sardar Ataullah Mengal resigned as head of the PONM, which he had helped found.

In December 2006 the BNP-M president and a former chief minister of Baluchistan, Sardar Akhbar Mengal (son of Sardar Ataullah), was detained in connection with the kidnapping and torture of intelligence personnel. Charges were dismissed in April 2008, and he was released in May.

The BNP-M did not contest the February 2008 National Assembly election, and its senator resigned his seat shortly thereafter. Sardar Akhbar Mengal was reelected party president in June 2009.

Leaders: Sardar Akhbar MENGAL (President), Sardar Ataullah MENGAL, Jahanzeb JAMALDINI (Vice President), Habib Jalib BALOCH (General Secretary).

Jamiat-Ulema-e-Islam Sami ul-Haq Group (JUI-S). The JUI-S began as a faction of the parent JUI. Under the leadership of Sami ul-Haq, the JUI-S adopted a more conservative course than the "modernist" JUI-F (above), promoting fundamentalist Islam causes but also outwardly opposing terrorism despite vocal objections to U.S. intervention in the region.

Sami ul-Haq was prominent in the MYC alliance and participated in formation of the MMA. In the 2002 National Assembly election the JUI-S finished third among the MMA parties. Relations with the MMA became increasingly tenuous, however, leading to repeated reports that the JUI-S was separating from the alliance or that Sami ul-Haq had been expelled from the leadership, in part because of his alleged ties to the ruling coalition. In December 2005 the MMA recognized Pir Abdul Rahim NAQSHBANDI as leader of the JUI-S.

In June 2007 ul-Haq, criticizing the dominance of the JUI-F and the JIP, characterized the MMA as defunct. For the February 2008 election Haq's JUI-S registered separately but failed to win any seats.

Leader: Sami ul-HAQ.

Khaksar Tehrik. A right-wing Islamic organization advocating universal military training, the *Khaksar Tehrik* (Service Movement) is also known as *Bailcha Bardar* (Shovel Carriers) because the group's founder, Inayatullah Khan MASHRIQI, adopted the spade as a symbol of self-reliance. Following the 1999 coup, which the party leader termed a "blessing," the party called for an anticorruption drive. It subsequently opposed the Musharraf government, however, supporting restoration of the constitution and democracy and endorsing the 2006 Bhutto–Nawaz Sharif Charter of Democracy.

In September 2008 the *Khaksar Tehrik* protested against continuing U.S.-NATO strikes targeting terrorists in Pakistani tribal areas. The organization called on the government to end support for NATO forces in Afghanistan.

Leader: Hameeduddin al-MASHRIQI.

Muhajir Qaumi Movement–Haqiqi (MQM-*Haqiqi*). The MQM-*Haqiqi* (MQM-Real) resulted from a 1992 rupture within the MQM. Violent clashes between the current MQM and the MQM-*Haqiqi* have periodically flared into open warfare in Karachi. Although the MQM-*Haqiqi* has been unrepresented at the national level since the April 2003 death of its sole National Assembly representative, members continue to hold elective office in Sindh.

In December 2004 the party's secretary general, Amir Khan, was sentenced to ten years in prison in connection with the murder of two rival MQM members. Three other MQM-*Haqiqi* members were given life sentences. In August 2009 the Sindh High Court granted the defendants bail, pending completion of their appeals.

Leaders: Amir KHAN (Chair), Iqbal QURESHI and Younas KHAN (Vice Chairs), Sharif KHAN (Secretary General).

Pakistan Awami Tehrik (PAT). The *Awami Tehrik* (People's Movement) originally served as a Sindh-based Maoist youth group. Its leader, Rasul Bakhsk PALEJO, was released from prison in 1986, having been held without trial since 1979, and later served as secretary general of the ANP. Party leader Tahir ul-Qadri left the leadership of the PAI alliance in 1999, apparently because of policy differences with the PPP and the ANP, but the PAT subsequently joined the GDA. In August 2000, however, the GDA expelled Qadri.

In May 2002 PAT was a founding member of the National Alliance, but it withdrew a month later and contested the October 2002 National Assembly election independently, winning one seat. In December 2004 Qadri resigned the seat after passage of a bill permitting President Musharraf to remain in uniform.

The PAT did not compete in the 2008 National Assembly election.

Leaders: Muhammad Tahir ul-QADRI (Chair), Miskin Faiz-ur-Rahman DURANI (Central President), Anwar AKHTAR (Secretary General).

Pakistan Democratic Party (PDP). A former component of the PNA and the MRD, the PDP is a strongly Islamic party organized in 1969. Its president, Nawabzada Nasrullah KHAN, joined with the PPP and a number of smaller parties to launch the PAI opposition alliance in early 1998 and the GDA in September 1999. Khan later assumed the leadership of the postcoup ARD. He died in September 2003 and was succeeded as PDP leader by his son, who was reelected in February 2007. The party has participated in the APDM.

Leader: Nawabzada Mansoor Ahmad KHAN (President).

Pakistan Tehrik-e-Insaaf (PTI). The *Tehrik-e-Insaaf* (Justice Movement) was launched in 1996 by former national cricket captain Imran Khan, who announced that the new group's objective was to work for change in a country "on the brink of disaster" by "demanding justice, honesty, decency and self-respect." Despite high expectations, Khan failed to attract voter support in the February 1997 national election, and the party won no assembly seats. In August 2000 Imran Khan was expelled from the GDA for "undemocratic" comments.

The party won one assembly seat in October 2002. More recently, Khan voiced opposition to President Musharraf and his close ties to the United States. In July 2007 he played a significant role in forming the APDM, and he was one of the most vocal critics of the state of emergency imposed in November, during which he was placed under house arrest. Khan was later charged with violating antiterrorism laws.

The PTI boycotted the February 2008 National Assembly election. More recently, he has called for the repeal of the NRO and for the prosecution of former president Musharraf.

Leaders: Imran KHAN (Chair), Arif ALVI (Secretary General).

Sindh National Front (SNF). Mumtaz Ali Bhutto, an uncle of the former prime minister, launched the SNF following the dissolution in 1989 of the Sindh-Baluch-Pushtoon Front (SBPF), of which Bhutto had been a leader. Like the SBPF, the SNF called for a confederation of Pakistan's four provinces, with each free to establish its own domestic and foreign policies. Although a founder of the National Alliance in preparation for the 2002 general election, the SNF later withdrew.

In 2008 Bhutto opposed the election of Asif Ali Zardari for president because of corruption accusations.

Leader: Mumtaz Ali BHUTTO (Chair).

Tehrik-e-Istiqlal Pakistan. The *Tehrik-e-Istiqlal* (Solidarity Movement) is a democratic Islamic group that was a founding member of the PNA, from which it withdrew in November 1977. One of its leaders, Air Mar. (Ret.) Mohammad Asghar Khan, was a leading proponent of election boycotts, stating that "there can be no compromise" under martial law; however, following the lifting of martial law, the party broke ranks with its coalition partners by announcing its intention to register as a legal party. It was a leading component of the MRD until September 1986, when most of its leadership withdrew in opposition to Benazir Bhutto's domination of the alliance.

In October 1988 *Tehrik-e-Istiqlal* formed an electoral alliance with the JUP (above) for the November legislative balloting, although agreeing not to contest seats for which the IDA was presenting candidates. Asghar Khan resigned from the presidency of *Tehrik-e-Istiqlal* in December in the wake of poor results in the November poll. The party was subsequently a member of the PPP-led PDA in 1990.

Following the 1997 national elections, which the *Tehrik-e-Istiqlal* boycotted, Asghar Khan returned as head of the party and became a major figure in the development of the PNC opposition alliance. In January 2002 his son, Omar Asghar KHAN, formed a new **Qaumi Jamhoori Party** (QJP), but he died five months later under disputed circumstances that the authorities labeled a suicide. Asghar Khan thereupon assumed leadership of the QJP.

More recently, Asghar Khan has campaigned for a peaceful settlement of the Kashmir dispute, a reduced role for the military in government, and an end to the funding of politicians by the Inter-Services Intelligence agency.

Rehmat Khan WARDAG heads a competing *Tehrik-e-Istiqlal.*

Leaders: Muhammad Ikram NAGRA (President), Mohammad Asghar KHAN.

Banned and Other Extremist Organizations:

Tehrik-e-Taliban Pakistan (TTP). The TTP is an umbrella for radical groups that support strict adherence to sharia, oppose the presence of Western forces in Afghanistan, and have conducted attacks directed against the Pakistani military, police, and civilian government. Although Afghanistan's Taliban government had adherents and supporters in Pakistan's FATA and NWFP even before the United States launched its attack on Afghanistan in October 2001, the TTP as it currently functions probably dates from late 2007, when Baitullah Mehsud convinced a dozen or so jihadist and Islamist organizations to accept a degree of central coordination. Based in South Waziristan, Mehsud's home base, the TTP is directly linked to **al-Qaida** (see the article on Afghanistan). Al-Qaida was banned by Pakistan in 2003, as was the TTP in August 2008.

With Mehsud as its most vocal presence, the TTP quickly extended its reach in the FATA, but its greatest impact occurred in the NWFP's Swat valley, where its violent actions included bombings, assassinations, and the burning of girls' schools. In an effort to end the violence, in February 2009 the NWFP government agreed to the adoption of sharia in the Malakand division. The central government accepted the pact in April, by which time the TTP was reportedly already establishing its own sharia courts. In June militia leader Qari ZAINUDDIN, who had broken from Mehsud in 2008 and later rejected the use of suicide bombers, was assassinated. By then, the government, responding to continuing TTP violence, had already discarded the February pact and was engaged in a new military offensive.

Meanwhile, in March 2009 the United States had placed a $5 million bounty on Mehsud, who was described as a "key al-Qaida facilitator" and who was believed to have directed the assassination of former prime minister Bhutto. On August 5 a missile launched from an unmanned NATO drone mortally wounded Mehsud, who succumbed later in the month and was succeeded by Hakimullah Mehsud and Waliur Rehman. Hakimullah is believed to have close ties to *Sipah-i-Sahaba* and *Lashkar-i-Jhangvi* (below) as well as al-Qaida.

Maulana FAZLULLAH, a son-in-law of Sufi Muhammad of the TNSM (below) and a leader of the TTP in Swat, was arrested in early September 2009 during the continuing military offensive. The Pakistani government later announced a $5 million bounty for information leading to the capture or death of Hakimullah.

Leaders: Hakimullah MEHSUD, Waliur REHMAN, Maulvi OMAR.

Lashkar-i-Taiba (LiT). LiT (Army of the Pure) was established in 1993 by Hafiz Muhammad Sayeed and Zafar IQBAL as the military wing of an above-ground religious group, the *Markaz ad-Dawa Wal Irshad* (Center for Religious Learning and Propagation), which was formed in 1986 to organize Pakistani Sunni militants participating in the Afghan revolution. The *Markaz* was officially dissolved in December 2001 and all its assets transferred to the new **Jamaat-ud-Dawa**—JuD (Party for Religious Propagation) in an effort to avoid proscription. The LiT was banned by Pakistan in January 2002. The JuD was placed on a "watch list" by the Pakistani government in November 2003 and banned in December 2008 because of links to terrorists who had carried out attacks in Mumbai, India, a month earlier.

The LiT, which may be the largest Pakistan-based militant group seeking separation of Jammu and Kashmir from India, with bases in Azad Kashmir and near the LoC, has claimed responsibility for and been implicated in innumerable attacks within Kashmir and elsewhere. Following a series of transport blasts that killed several hundred people in Mumbai, India, in July 2006, the Indian government placed suspicion on LiT, which denied involvement. LiT has also been active in a number of other conflict areas, including Bosnia and Herzegovina, Chechnya, Iraq, and Southeast Asia.

Following a massive earthquake that struck the NWFP and Azad Kashmir on October 8, 2005, several reports from the stricken region particularly credited the rescue and recovery work performed by the LiT and JuD.

The LiT chief of operations, Zaki-ur-Rehman Lakhvi, has been described as the mastermind of the November 2008 Mumbai assault, which was carried out by Pakistani nationals linked to the LiT. In December Lakhvi, Sayeed, and dozens of other leaders of the LiT and the JuD were detained, but in June 2009 the Lahore High Court ordered Sayeed's release from house arrest on the grounds that his detention was without constitutional grounds. In October the court dismissed the case. Lakhvi and six others were indicted by an antiterrorism court on November 25.

In an effort to circumvent its proscription, the JuD has reportedly reorganized as the **Tehrik-e-Tahafuz Qibla Awal** (Movement for the Safeguarding of the First Center of Prayer).

Leaders: Hafiz Mohammed SAYEED, Zaki-ur-Rehman LAKHVI (Chief of Operations), Haji Muhammad ASHRAF (Chief of Finance).

Islami Tehrik-i-Pakistan (TiP). The TiP is successor to the banned **Tehrik-e-Jafariya-e-Pakistan**—TJP (Pakistan Jafari Movement), which was itself an offshoot of the **Tehrik-e-Nifaz Fiqh Jafariya**—TNFJ (Movement for the Implementation of Shia Jurisprudence). The TNFJ, formed in 1979 following the Islamic revolution in Iran, represented Pakistan's Shia minority and was also known as the **Tehrik-i-Islami Pakistan** (TIP). It launched a campaign in 1980 against the government's Islamization campaign, insisting that it was entirely Sunni based. An electoral ally of the PPP in 1990, it was frequently a target of Sunni violence.

The TJP was closely associated with the extremist Shiite **Sipah-i-Muhammad,** which was formed in 1993 to counter the extremist Sunni *Sipah-i-Sahaba* (below) and has been a major participant in Pakistan's ongoing sectarian warfare. The *Sipah-i-Muhammad* was banned in August 2001, as was the TJP and the TIP in 2002. In an effort to get around the ban, the TJP assumed the TiP designation, but the TiP was itself banned in November 2003. Its leader, Sajid Naqvi, was arrested in the same month in connection with the assassination of Maulana Azam Tariq of the *Sipah-i-Sahaba*, but he was acquitted in November 2004. Despite its being banned, the TiP was part of the now-defunct MMA.

Leaders: Allama Sajid Ali NAQVI, Abdul Jalil NAQVI.

Jaish-e-Muhammad Mujaheddin-e-Tanzeem (JMMT or JeM). Formation of the *Jaish-e-Muhammad* (Movement of the Army of the Holy Warriors of Muhammad) was announced on February 4, 2000, by Masood Azhar. He was previously a founding member of the *Harkat-ul-Ansar*—subsequently renamed the *Harkat-ul-Mujaheddin* (Islamic Freedom Fighters)—which had been organized in the mid-1980s, with the backing of Pakistan, to oppose the Soviet occupation of Afghanistan. Azhar was detained by India from 1994 until late December 1999, when the hijackers of an Indian Airlines jet demanded his release before freeing their hostages. Azhar has called for a holy war against India as part of the effort to establish an independent, Islamic Kashmir. He was detained in December 2001 but released three months later. Since then, Azhar has repeatedly been listed by India among suspected terrorists that it wants Pakistan to extradite. In 2009 he reportedly went into hiding.

Having been banned in January 2002, the JeM restyled itself as the **Khudam-ul-Islam** (Servants of Islam), which was then banned in November 2003 along with the **Jamaat-al-Ansar** (Party of Helpers), the new designation of the *Harkat-ul-Mujaheddin,* led by Fazlur Rehman KHALIL. In 2002 another JeM surrogate, the **Jamaat-ul-Furqan** (JuF), had been established by Abdul JABBAR; the JuF was also banned in November 2003. Jabbar, who was imprisoned for involvement in a December 2003 assassination attempt against President Musharraf, was released in October 2006.

The JeM and the *Harkat-ul-Mujaheddin* are both regarded by the United States as terrorist organizations. Reports in 2007 indicated that the *Jamaat-al-Ansar,* now led by Maulana Badar MUNIR, and JuF may have merged. Fazlur Rehman Khalil, who has been linked to two other banned groups, al-Qaida and the *Tehrik-e-Taliban* (above), reportedly served as a negotiator in an unsuccessful effort by the government to diffuse the 2007 Red Mosque crisis.

Leaders: Maulana Masood AZHAR, Abdul RAUF.

Sipah-i-Sahaba (SiS). The SiS (Guardians of the Friends of the Prophet) is a militant Sunni group founded in 1982 as a JUI breakaway by Maulana Haq Nawaz JHANGVI, who was later murdered. It has close connections to the extremist **Lashkar-i-Jhangvi** (LiJ) and the equally militant TNSM (below), both of which have been involved in sectarian bloodshed.

In February 2000 the SiS announced that it was prepared to give nearly 100,000 workers to Masood Azhar's newly organized JMMT (above) to aid in holy war (jihad). Both were banned in January 2002, as the LiJ had been in August 2001. The LiJ's leader, Riaz BASRA, was killed by Indian police in May 2002. Another leader, Asif RAMZI, who had been linked to the kidnapping and murder of American journalist Daniel Pearl, was killed in a bomb explosion in December 2002. ATTAULLAH, an alleged LiJ leader, was sentenced to death in September 2003. Another alleged LiJ member was also sentenced to death in June 2005 for his involvement in the bombing of Shia mosques that killed 45 in May 2004.

In October 2003 SiS leader Muhammad Azam TARIQ, who had won election to the National Assembly a year earlier as an independent while still in prison, was assassinated, allegedly by members of the Shiite TJP (see TiP, above). Earlier, the SiS had been renamed the **Millat-i-Islamia Pakistan** (MIP) to circumvent a government ban, but the MIP was then proscribed in November 2003. The United States has placed both SiS and the LiJ on its list of terrorist organizations; both have direct links to al-Qaida. The Musharraf government reportedly considered allowing MIP to operate legally but with restrictions, although it remains on the list of proscribed organizations.

Leader: Maulana Muhammad Ahmad LUDHIANVI.

Tehrik-e-Nifaz-e-Shariat-e-Mohammadi (TNSM). The TNSM (Mohammedan Movement for the Enforcement of Islamic Law), a fundamentalist group established in 1992 by Sufi Muhammad, was blamed by the government for the deaths of 11 persons in May 1994 and of 10 more the following November as the result of tribal demands in the northern Malakand division for the introduction of Islamic law. The TNSM responded to the August 1998 U.S. missile attack against terrorist camps in Afghanistan by organizing a rally in Peshawar at which it threatened to lay siege to U.S. property and kidnap Americans. In response to the 2001 onset of U.S.-led efforts to oust al-Qaida and the Taliban from Afghanistan, the TNSM helped recruit thousands of activists to fight the Western forces. The TNSM was then banned in January 2002.

After six years in prison, Sufi Muhammad was released in April 2008, which also saw the TNSM and the recently installed ANP-led NWFP government reach a peace agreement. A further agreement in February 2009 permitted the application of sharia in Malakand division, including Swat. The agreement was signed by President Zardari on April 13, after adoption by National Assembly. Nevertheless, continuing militant activity in the region led in May to a renewed effort by the Pakistani military to recover control of Malakand, with Sufi Muhammad and his three sons being among those detained in July.

Leader: Sufi MUHAMMAD.

Baluchistan Liberation Army (BLA). The BLA advocates independence for Baluchistan. In April 2006 the government banned it as a terrorist organization. In the preceding year the BLA had been blamed for a number of separatist attacks within Baluchistan, although its very existence as an organization remained in question. A Baluchistan government minister asserted that the BLA was in fact just a name that provided "an excuse for anti-state activities."

Leader: Brahamdagh Khan BUGTI.

Harkat-ul-Mujaheddin al-Alami (HMA). A splinter from the **Hizb-ul-Mujaheddin** (HuM; see the article on India), the HMA was implicated in an April 2002 assassination attempt against President Musharraf and a June 2002 bombing at the U.S. consulate in Karachi that killed 12. (In 2006 most related convictions were set aside by the Sindh High Court.) Some of its members were previously associated with the **Harkat-ul-Jihad-i-Islami** (HJI), one of whose alleged founders, Qari Saifullah AKHTAR, was released in June 2008 after having been arrested in February on suspicion of involvement in the October 2007 suicide bombing that killed some 140 people in Karachi but missed its primary target, Benazir Bhutto. The HMA, HJI, and LiJ are believed to be linked in the **313 Brigade.**

Hizb-ut-Tahrir. Founded in 1952 in Jerusalem and based in London, England, the Sunni *Hizb-ut-Tahrir* maintains a presence in several dozen countries. Its overarching goal is the creation of a caliphate uniting all Muslim countries. It was banned by the Pakistani government in November 2003. It has ostensibly disavowed terrorism but is believed to have links to many jihadist groups around the world.

In September 2009 Rehman MALIK, the minister of the interior, told Parliament that 25 groups had been banned under the Anti-Terrorism Act 1997, including most of those discussed above. Other organizations on the proscribed list included **Lashkar-e-Islam** (LeI), formed in 2004 by Munir SHAKIRA and presently led by Mangal BAGH Afridi, and **Ansar-ul-Islam** (AuI), established by Saifullah SAIFI. Both are based in the Khyber and Bajaur agencies of the FATA, and both have links to the *Tehrik-e-Taliban* but have frequently clashed with each other, employing shootings and bombings in an effort to assert their authority. Their other activities have included kidnappings for ransom. Both were banned in 2008 and have been targeted by recent offensives conducted by the Pakistani military. In April 2008 the LeI branch in Bajaur Agency, led by Wali REHMAN, reportedly changed its name to **Jaish-e-Islami,** while Mengal Bagh stated in August 2009 that he had renamed the LeI as the **Tehrik Lashkar-e-Islam**.

Pakistan has also recently banned the **Al Akhtar Trust** and the **Al Rasheed Trust,** both based in Karachi and involved in financing terrorist groups. Both have also engaged in relief and social welfare activities, such as operating medical clinics and providing support for the families of Islamic activists.

LEGISLATURE

The **Parliament** (*Majlis-e-Shoora*), also known as the Federal Legislature, is a bicameral body consisting of the president, an indirectly elected Senate, and a directly elected National Assembly. Both were suspended by proclamation of Chief Executive Musharraf on October 15, 1999, and dissolved by him on June 20, 2001. Elections to expanded lower and upper houses were held in October 2002 and February 2003, respectively.

Senate. The current upper house comprises 100 members: 22 elected by each of the four provincial legislatures (14 general seats, 4 reserved for women, and 4 reserved for technocrats/*ulema*), plus 8 from the Federally Administered Tribal Areas (FATA) and 4 from the Federal Capital (2 general, 1 woman, 1 technocrat/*aalim*). FATA and Federal Capital senators are chosen by the National Assembly members of their respective jurisdictions. Senatorial terms are six years, with one-half of the body retiring every three years, although the election of February 24 and 27, 2003, was for the full, reconfigured house. The most recent election was held March 4, 2009, for 19 contested seats; the other 31 had been filled unopposed. After the election the Pakistan People's Party Parliamentarians held 27 seats; Pakistan Muslim League, 21; *Jamiat-Ulema-e-Islam* Fazlur Rahman Group, 10; Pakistan Muslim League–Nawaz, 7 (including 1 held by the leader of the *Markazi Jamiat-e-Ahle Hadith*); Awami National Party, 6; *Muttahida Qaumi* Movement, 6; Baluchistan National Party–Awami, 3; *Jamaat-e-Islami Pakistan,* 3; National Party, 2; *Jamhoori Watan* Party, *Pakhtoonkhwa Milli Awami* Party, Pakistan Muslim League–Functional, and Pakistan People's Party–Sherpao, 1 each; independents, 11. The 8 FATA senators are all considered to be independents bur have typically had ties to Islamic parties..

Chair: Farooq Hamid NAEK.

National Assembly. Serving a five-year term, subject to premature dissolution, the current National Assembly has 342 seats: 272 directly elected in single-member constituencies; 60 seats reserved for women, distributed proportionally according to party seats won in provincial assemblies; and 10 seats designated for members of religious minorities (4 Christian; 4 Hindu; 1 Sikh, Buddhist, or Parsi; 1 Qadiani), distributed proportionally to parties based on the directly elected National Assembly seat totals. The most recent election for the directly elected seats took place on February 18, 2008. A handful of seats required by-elections, while 2 FATA seats were not filled. The final results were as follows: the Pakistan People's Party Parliamentarians won 124 seats (97 directly elected, 23 seats reserved for women, 4 seats reserved for minorities); Pakistan Muslim League–Nawaz, 91 (71, 17, 3), including 1 won by a leader of the *Jamiat Ulema-e-Pakistan* who ran with a PML-N endorsement; Pakistan Muslim League, 54 (42, 10, 2); *Muttahida Qaumi* Movement, 25 (19, 5, 1); Awami National Party, 13 (10, 3, 0); *Muttahida Majlis-i-Amal*, 7 (6, 1, 0), all won by the *Jamiat-Ulema-e-Islam* Fazlur Rahman Group; Pakistan Muslim League–Functional, 5 (4, 1, 0); Baluchistan National Party–Awami, National People's Party, Pakistan People's Party–Sherpao, 1 elected seat each; independents, 18. All 10 representatives elected from FATA are categorized as independents, but in the past the majority have supported Islamic parties.

Speaker: Fehmida MIRZA.

CABINET

[as of December 1, 2009]

Prime Minister	Yusuf Raza Gilani (PPP)
Senior Minister	Makhdoom Amin Fahim (PPP)
Ministers	
Commerce	Makhdoom Amin Fahim (PPP)

Communications	Arbab Alamgir Khan (PPP)
Defense	Chaudhry Ahmed Mukhtar (PPP)
Defense Production	Abdul Qayyum Khan Jatoi (PPP)
Education	Mir Hazar Khan Bijrani (PPP)
Environment	Hameed Ulah Jan Afridi (FATA/ind.)
Food and Agriculture	Nazar Muhammad Gondal (PPP)
Foreign Affairs	Shah Mehmood Qureshi (PPP)
Health	Mir Ejaz Hussain Jakhrani (PPP)
Housing and Works	Rehmat Ullah Kakar (JUI-F)
Human Rights, Law, and Justice	Syed Mumtaz Alam Gilani (PPP)
Industries and Production	Mian Manzoor Ahmad Wattoo (PPP)
Information and Broadcasting	Qamar Zaman Kaira (PPP)
Information Technology	Yusuf Raza Gilani (PPP)
Interior	Rehman Malik (PPP)
Interprovincial Coordination	(Vacant)
Investment	Waqar Ahmed Khan (ind.)
Kashmir Affairs and Gilgit-Baltistan	Qamar Zaman Kaira (PPP)
Labor and Manpower	Syed Khursheed Ahmed Shah (PPP)
Livestock and Dairy Development	Humayun Aziz Kurd (PPP)
Local Government and Rural Development	Abdul Razzaq Thaheem (PML-F)
Minorities' Affairs	Shahbaz Bhatti (PPP)
Narcotics Control	(Vacant)
Overseas Pakistanis	Farooq Sattar (MQM)
Parliamentary Affairs	Zaheeruddin Babar Awan (PPP)
Petroleum and Natural Resources	Syed Naveed Qamar (PPP)
Planning and Development	Makhdoom Shahabuddin (PPP)
Population Welfare	Firdous Ashiq Awan (PPP) [f]
Ports and Shipping	Babar Ghauri (MQM)
Postal Services	Mir Israrullah Khan Zehri (BNP-A)
Privatization	Syed Naveed Qamar (PPP)
Railways	Ghulam Ahmad Bilour (ANP)
Religious Affairs	Hamid Saeed Kazmi (PPP)
Science and Technology	Mohammad Azam Khan Swati (JUI-F)
Social Welfare and Special Education	Samina Khalid Ghurki (PPP) [f]
Special Initiatives	Lal Muhammad Khan (PPP)
Sports	Pir Aftab Hussain Shah Gilani (PPP)
States and Frontier Regions	Najamuddin Khan (PPP)
Textile Industries	Rana Muhammad Farooq Saeed Khan (PPP)
Tourism	Attaur Rehman (JUI-F)
Water and Power Resources	Raja Pervaiz Ashraf (PPP)
Youth Affairs	Shahid Hussain Bhutto (PPP)
Zakat and *Ushr* (Islamic Welfare)	Noorul Haq Qadri (FATA/ind.)
Adviser on Finance and Revenue and on Economic Affairs and Statistics	Shaukat Fayyaz Tareen (ind.)

[f] = female

COMMUNICATIONS

The constitution guarantees press freedom, but formal censorship has been imposed during periods of martial law and states of emergency. In July 2003 a court in the NWFP, where Islamic law was imposed in 2002, sentenced an editor of the *Frontier Post* to life in prison for blasphemy. In June 2007, in the context of ongoing public protests against the March dismissal of the country's chief justice, a presidential decree gave the Pakistan Electronic Media Regulatory Authority (PEMRA) increased powers to close broadcast facilities, halt transmissions, and impose fines. The decree was quickly rescinded, however, in response to domestic and international criticism. In April Human Rights Watch had accused the government of systematically subjecting journalists to harassment, arbitrary arrests, torture, and other violations of press freedoms. Media restrictions were reimposed under the state of emergency declared in November. Although most had been lifted by the end of the month, journalists were required to accept a code of conduct regarding governmental affairs. In March 2008 Prime Minister Gilani announced that press freedoms would be restored and PEMRA reformed.

Press. The following are among the more than 400 daily Pakistani newspapers: *Daily Jang* (Karachi, Lahore, Quetta, and Rawalpindi, 750,000), in Urdu, independent; *Nawa-i-Waqt* (Voice of the Time, Karachi, Lahore, Multan, and Islamabad, 560,000), in Urdu and English, conservative; *Dawn* (Karachi, Islamabad, and Lahore, 110,000 daily; 125,000 Sunday), in English and Gujarati; *Jasarat* (Karachi, 50,000), in Urdu, conservative; *The Nation* (Lahore, 50,000), in English; *Frontier Post* (Peshawar and Lahore), in English, leftist.

News agencies. There are three principal domestic news agencies: the government-owned Associated Press of Pakistan (APP) and the privately owned Pakistan Press International (PPI) and News Network International (NNI). A number of foreign agencies also maintain offices in leading cities.

Broadcasting and computing. The government-owned Pakistan Broadcasting Corporation (PBC) offers regional, national, and international radio programming. Private radio stations are prohibited from broadcasting news. In addition to broadcasts by the public Pakistan Television Corporation (PTC), private cable and satellite service is available.

As of 2008 there were 104.5 Internet users per 1,000 inhabitants.

INTERGOVERNMENTAL REPRESENTATION

Ambassador to the U.S.: Husain HAQQANI.

U.S. Ambassador to Pakistan: Anne Woods PATTERSON.

Permanent Representative to the UN: Abdullah Hussain HAROON.

IGO Memberships (Non-UN): ADB, CWTH, ECO, IDB, Interpol, IOM, NAM, OIC, PCA, SAARC, *SCO*, WCO, WTO.

RELATED TERRITORIES

The precise status of predominantly Muslim Jammu and Kashmir has remained unresolved since the 1949 cease-fire, which divided the territory into Indian- and Pakistani-administered sectors. While India has claimed the entire area as a state of the Indian Union, Pakistan has never regarded the portion under its control as an integral part of Pakistan. Rather, it has administered Azad Kashmir and the Gilgit-Baltistan (known as the Northern Areas until September 2009) as de facto dependencies for whose defense and foreign affairs it is responsible.

Azad Kashmir. Formally called Azad (Free) Jammu and Kashmir, the smaller (4,200 sq. mi.) but more populous (estimated at 3,623,000 in 2006) of the Jammu and Kashmir regions administered by Pakistan is a narrow strip of territory lying along the northeastern border adjacent to Rawalpindi and Islamabad. It is divided into eight districts (Bagh, Bhimber, Kotli, Mirpur, Muzaffarabad, Neelum, Poonch, and Sudhnoti). Muzaffarabad City serves as the territory's capital. An Interim Constitution Act of 1974 provided for a Legislative Assembly, now comprising 49 members—41 directly elected plus 5 women and single representatives for technocrats, overseas Kashmiris, and *mashaikh* (Muslim spiritual leaders), all named by those directly elected. The principal executive body is the Azad Kashmir Council, which is chaired by the prime minister of Pakistan and also includes the president of Azad Kashmir as vice chair, the prime minister of Azad Kashmir or his designee, six members elected by the Legislative Assembly, and five federal ministers.

In the June 1996 Legislative Assembly election the governing **All Jammu and Kashmir Muslim Conference** (also known simply as the Muslim Conference—MC) suffered an unprecedented drubbing by candidates from the Azad Kashmir affiliate of the PPP, and on July 30 Sultan MAHMOOD CHAUDHRY, president of the Azad Kashmir PPP, was sworn in as prime minister, replacing the MC's Sardar

Abdul QAYYUM Khan. Except for a brief period in 1990, the MC had been in power for 13 years. On August 12 President Sikander HAYAT Khan, also of the MC, lost a no-confidence motion in the assembly, in which the PPP now controlled more than three-fourths of the seats. On August 25 Mohammad IBRAHIM Khan was sworn in as his successor. The transition marked the fourth time the octogenarian Ibrahim had assumed the presidency.

The MC turned the tables on the PPP in the July 5, 2001, election, winning 25 out of 40 directly elected seats to the PPP's 8 and then picking up 5 more of the reserved seats. The PPP ended up with a total of 9 seats and the PML, 8. When the new legislature convened, Sikander Hayat defeated the incumbent by a vote of 30–17 and thereby returned as prime minister.

Seventeen parties contested the legislative election of July 11, 2006, in which the MC won 22 of 41 elective seats (after a revote in one district) and quickly gained the support of several independents. The PPP Azad Kashmir, led by Sahibzada Ishaq ZAFAR, won 7 seats; a PML alliance, 4; the MQM, 2; and Sardar Khalid IBRAHIM Khan's **Jammu and Kashmir People's Party,** 1. Immediately after the election the MMA, which had fielded a large slate of unsuccessful candidates, led a chorus of opposition parties in accusing the central government of vote-rigging, particularly in refugee camps set up in the wake of a devastating October 8, 2005, earthquake, which affected some 2,800 villages in Azad Kashmir and the NWFP, killed more than 73,000 people, and left 3.3 million homeless. On July 22 the MC added 6 of the 8 reserved seats to its total, with the others going to the PPP and the JUI.

With Sikander Hayat having chosen not to seek reelection to the Legislative Assembly, the MC proposed Sardar ATTIQUE AHMED Khan, son of Sardar Abdul Qayyum, as prime minister, and he was sworn in on July 24, 2006. Three days later, the new legislature elected the MC's Raja Zulqarnain Khan as president by a vote of 40–8 over the PPP Azad Kashmir candidate, Sardar QAMAR-U-ZAMAN.

A September 2006 report by Human Rights Watch labeled the Azad Kashmir government a "façade" dominated by Islamabad, the military, and the intelligence services. The report further alleged that free expression has been routinely curtailed and torture allowed. Open advocates of Kashmiri independence are not allowed to seek public office and often face persecution.

In the following two years a split within the MC widened. An anti-Attique Ahmed faction, the Forward Bloc, accused the prime minister of nepotism, mismanagement, malfeasance, and a lack of transparency. On January 6, 2009, a combination of the Forward Bloc, led by Raja FAROOQ HAIDER Khan, and the opposition passed a no-confidence motion against Attique Ahmed and endorsed as his successor Sardar Muhammad YAQOOB Khan, who had been elected in 2006 as an independent. The rift in the MC was subsequently repaired, however, and on October 14 Yaqoob Khan resigned rather than face a no-confidence vote in the Legislative Assembly. On October 22 Farooq Haider, by a vote of 29–19, defeated Yaqoob Khan and was sworn in as prime minister. Yaqoob Khan had been backed by a four-party alliance of the Azad Kashmir PPP, the MQM, Sultan Mahmood Chaudhry's **Jammu and Kashmir People's Muslim League,** and a so-called Friends Group of dissident MC members.

President: Raja ZULQARNAIN Khan.

Prime Minister: Raja FAROOQ HAIDER Khan.

Gilgit-Baltistan. Gilgit-Baltistan, which was called the Northern Areas from 1970 until September 2009, encompasses approximately 28,000 square miles, with a population (2006E) of 970,000. The region has served as the principal conduit for supplying troops and matériel to the Line of Control, facing Indian Kashmir. Pakistan's overland route to China, the Karakoram Highway, also traverses the region, which currently comprises seven districts: Astore, Diamir, Ghanche, Ghizar, Gilgit, Hunza-Nagar, and Skardu. Approximately half the population is Shiite, with the other half divided between Sunnis and Ismailis. The region has frequently seen outbreaks of sectarian violence involving Sunni and Shiite groups.

In May 1999 Pakistan's Supreme Court ruled that the Northern Areas Legal Framework Order 1994, under which Islamabad had introduced a number of governmental reforms, failed to provide adequate institutions and safeguards to residents of the Northern Areas. The court said that residents were entitled to full constitutional rights, including an elected legislature and an independent judiciary, and it gave the government six months to institute the changes. In early October the Sharif administration announced that party-based elections would be held on November 3 for a Northern Areas Legislative Council having the same powers as provincial assemblies. The announcement marked a significant departure in that the government had previously argued that no permanent institutions could be established until the fate of the entire Jammu and Kashmir was determined through a UN-sponsored plebiscite.

Although the October 1999 military coup in Islamabad intervened, the November election took place as scheduled. Of the leading parties, the PML won 6 seats (5 more than it had previously held); the PPP, 6; and the *Tehrik-e-Jafariya-e-Pakistan* (TJP), 6. Voter turnout was very low, which analysts attributed in part to the council's severely limited role. After the 5 seats reserved for women were finally filled nearly nine months later, a PML-TJP alliance controlled 19 of the 29 seats. As a result, the PML's Sahib KHAN was elected speaker of the council and the TJP's Fida Muhammad NASHAD became deputy chief executive, second in the governmental hierarchy to the federal minister for Kashmir and the Northern Areas.

At the Northern Areas Legislative Council election of October 12, 2004, the PML-Q and PPP Parliamentarians (PPPP) each won 6 of the 24 directly elective seats, and the PML-N won 2, the balance being claimed by independents, 8 of whom then aligned with the PML-Q. When the 12 reserved seats (including 6 for women), all chosen by the elected members, were finally filled on March 22, 2006, the PML-Q picked up 10 of them, with independents claiming the remaining 2. The PPPP immediately protested that the election had been rigged and argued that seats should have been assigned on a proportional basis.

In October 2007 President Musharraf announced a Northern Areas reform package that called for creation of a seventh district (Hunza-Nagar); conversion of the Northern Areas Legislative Council to the Northern Areas Legislative Assembly (NALA), to be chaired by the minister of Kashmir and Northern Areas affairs; and elevation of the office of deputy chief executive to that of chief executive. A new chief executive, Ghazanfar ALI KHAN (PPP), with enhanced administrative powers, was sworn in on January 4, 2008.

Following the national legislative election held in February 2008, members of the PML-Q–dominated NALA expressed concern that the assembly would be dissolved prematurely by the central government, which was now controlled by the PPP and PML-N. In April they were assured by Minister Qazar Zaman Kaira that the NALA would be permitted to complete its term.

On September 7, 2009, President Zardari signed the Gilgit-Baltistan (Empowerment and Self-Government) Order 2009, which had been passed by Parliament in late August. The order, in addition to changing the region's name, provided for a level of autonomy comparable to that of Azad Kashmir, which prompted some Kashmiri activists to charge that Islamabad was making Gilgit-Baltistan a de facto province of Pakistan. Under the order, Islamabad's principal representative is a governor appointed by the president of Pakistan on the advice of the prime minister. The territory's Legislative Assembly comprises 33 members—24 directly elected plus 9 named to reserved seats (6 women and 3 professionals). A chief minister and his cabinet is responsible to the Legislative Assembly, which has significantly expanded powers. An executive Gilgit-Baltistan Council is chaired by the prime minister of Pakistan, with the governor as vice chair. Also sitting on the council are the chief minister of Gilgit-Baltistan, 6 members elected from the Legislative Assembly, and 6 representatives of the central government (ministers or members of Parliament). A Supreme Appellate Court is to sit at the apex of the independent judicial system.

The first election for the new Legislative Assembly was held on November 12, 2009. The PPP was initially credited with winning 11 seats; the PML-N, 2; the PML-Q, 2; the JUI-F, 1; the MQM, 1, and independents, 4. (Polling in one district was postponed due to the death of a candidate, and disruptions at some polling stations in two other districts necessitated partial revotes.) The PML-N and other parties immediately rejected the results as the product of irregularities and of favoritism on the part of the acting governor, PPP minister Qamar Zaman Qaira. By late November, however, the PPP claimed the support of 17 legislators, including 3 of the independents and the JUI-F member, and anticipated gaining additional seats when the 9 nonelected members were chosen. The PPP's nominee for chief minister, party chair Syed Mehdi Shah, was expected to be confirmed when the full Legislative Assembly convened.

Among the groups attacking the 2009 Gilgit-Baltistan Order was the **Balawaristan National Front** (BNF), chaired by Abdul Hamid KHAN. The BNF has called for self-rule and elections to a constituent assembly that would then draft a constitution.

Governor (Acting): Qamar Zaman QAIRA. (Minister of Kashmir and Gilgit-Baltistan).

Chief Minister: Syed Mehdi SHAH (PPP nominee).

PALAU

Republic of Palau
Belu'u era Belau

Political Status: Former U.S. Trust Territory; became sovereign state in free association with the United States on October 1, 1994.

Land Area: 178 sq. mi. (461 sq. km.).

Population: 19,907 (2005C); 20,500 (2008E). Approximately 6,000 residents are nonnationals.

Major Urban Center (2005C): Koror (10,743), MELEKEOK (250). Melekeok, located on the largely undeveloped northern island of Babeldaob, replaced Koror as Palau's capital in October 2006.

Official Languages: English, Palauan.

Monetary Unit: U.S. Dollar (see U.S. article for principal exchange rates).

President: Johnson TORIBIONG (nonparty); elected on November 4, 2008, and inaugurated for a four-year term on January 15, 2009, succeeding Thomas (Tommy) REMENGESAU Jr. (nonparty), who was ineligible for reelection.

Vice President: Kerai MARIUR (nonparty); elected on November 4, 2008, for a term concurrent with that of the president, succeeding Elias Camsek CHIN (nonparty).

THE COUNTRY

Palau encompasses a chain of more than 200 Pacific islands and islets at the western extremity of the Carolines, some 720 miles southwest of Guam and 500 miles east of the Philippines. The population in 2006 was 83 percent Palauan, 12 percent Filipino, and 5 percent other. Both Palauan and English are spoken, and Roman Catholicism is the principal religion. The climate is tropical with quite heavy rainfall. Fishing and tourism are the leading economic sectors, with the United States pledging approximately $500 million in aid over a 15-year period as part of a trusteeship settlement that became effective on October 1, 1994. Because of the aid, Palau's nominal GDP grew by 24.3 percent in fiscal year 1994–1995 but declined sharply thereafter. After averaging just over 2 percent growth in 1996–1998, it dropped by 5.4 percent in the next fiscal year. For 2000–2008, GDP growth, despite some vacillation, registered about 2.2 percent annually, while the average household income on the country's largest state, Koror, was reported to be $20,000 in 2006.

GOVERNMENT AND POLITICS

Political background. Purchased by Germany from Spain in 1889, the Palau group was among the insular territories seized by Japan in 1914 and retained as part of the mandate awarded by the League of Nations in 1920. The islands were occupied by U.S. forces near the end of World War II and became part of the U.S. Trust Territory of the Pacific in 1947. A republican constitution was adopted by referendum in October 1979, and on January 1, 1981, Haruo I. REMELIK was inaugurated as the country's first president. On November 30, 1984, Remelik was elected to a second four-year term on a platform that called for early implementation of a 1980 Compact of Free Association with the United States. Remelik was assassinated on June 30, 1985, and in a special election on August 28 Lazarus SALII defeated Acting President Alfonso OITERONG in balloting for Remelik's successor.

The Palauan Compact, including provision for substantial U.S. aid, required that the republic provide facilities for U.S. conventional and nuclear forces. It was approved by 60 percent of the voters in a 1983 plebiscite, but with only 50 percent agreeing to a crucial accompanying proposal to override a constitutional ban on the entry, storage, or disposal of nuclear, chemical, or biological weapons and waste. A second plebiscite on September 4, 1984, also failed to secure the 75 percent majority needed for the override. A third plebiscite, held on February 21, 1986, in the wake of an enhanced U.S. aid commitment, yielded a favorable vote of 72 percent. President Salii, who had received assurances that Washington would not "use, test, store, or dispose of nuclear, toxic, chemical, gas, or biological weapons on the islands," then suggested that only a simple majority was needed for approval of the compact. His position was challenged by the islands' ranking chief, who obtained a favorable appellate ruling by the Palauan Supreme Court on September 17. Congressional endorsement of the compact immediately prior to the decision notwithstanding, the U.S. government responded by declaring that it would "respect the judicial process of Belau," and the agreement was not implemented.

Subsequent plebiscites on December 2 and June 30, 1987, yielded approval by 66 percent and 68 percent, respectively. A referendum on amending the constitution to suspend the applicability of its antinuclear clause to the compact was then held on August 4, which resulted in 71 percent approval, with majorities in 14 of the 16 states. The vote was hailed by the government, which contended that amending (as distinguished from overriding a constitutional proscription) required only a simple majority overall, coupled with majorities in at least 12 states. The constitutional issue seemingly having been resolved, a sixth plebiscite (yielding 73 percent approval) was held on August 21, with the Palauan legislature voting on August 27 to approve the compact. Meanwhile, a suit had been filed contending that constitutional revision could occur only in conjunction with a presidential election but was withdrawn (apparently as the result of duress) on the day of the plebiscite.

On March 28, 1988, the U.S. Senate endorsed the compact, although strong opposition continued to block action in the House of Representatives. On April 22, acting on a refiled opposition suit, the islands' Supreme Court trial division ruled that the August 4 referendum was invalid. U.S. President Ronald Reagan responded by urging the House to proceed with its vote on the grounds that the legislation contained safeguards that would preclude implementation of the pact until the court's decision had been appealed. However, intense debate continued in the House subcommittee on the issue, with Democratic leaders insisting that a public auditor's office and a special prosecutor's position be established in Palau to investigate allegations of drug smuggling, fiscal mismanagement, and government corruption.

On August 20, 1988, President Salii was found dead in his office from an apparently self-inflicted gunshot wound, and Vice President Thomas REMENGESAU was subsequently sworn in to serve for the rest of the year, pending the results of November's regularly scheduled presidential election. Shortly thereafter, the appellate division of the Supreme Court upheld the April decision invalidating the 1987 compact voting. While ruling that a special referendum on constitutional revision could be called at any time, the court declared that the proposed amendment must first be approved by 75 percent majorities in both houses of parliament or be requested by a petition signed by at least 25 percent of the electorate.

In balloting on November 2 Ngiratkel ETPISON, who appeared to enjoy the backing of many former Salii supporters, was elected president from among seven candidates. Etpison received 26.5 percent of the votes, surpassing his closest rival, Roman TMETUCHL, by less than 40 votes, with Remengesau finishing third.

A seventh compact vote on February 6, 1990, yielded an even lower approval rate (68.7 percent) than in 1987, with an Associated Press correspondent reporting that the islanders appeared to be "comfortable under the trusteeship arrangement and uncertain as to whether they are ready to take control of their destiny."

In September 1991 the Palau Senate refused to endorse a House measure that would have subjected the constitution's antinuclear clause to another referendum, and in October the government indicated that it would seek reduction of the constitutional amendment threshold from three-quarters to a simple majority if Washington would reduce the duration of the compact from 50 to 15 years and maintain a $70 million trust fund over the shorter period. The overture drew an immediate rejection from the George H. W. Bush administration. President Etpison thereupon called for a threshold vote on July 13 but was again rebuffed by the court, which ruled that prior congressional approval was required. In August the legislators responded by placing the matter on the ballot for the general election of November 4.

For the 1992 presidential balloting Etpison was defeated in a primary that resulted from abandonment of the earlier first-past-the-post

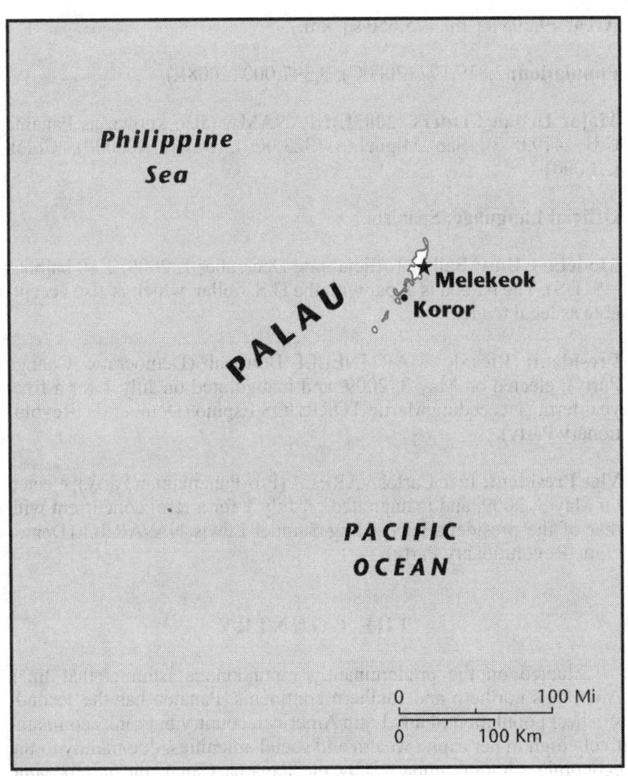

system, and on November 3 the incumbent vice president, Kuniwo NAKAMURA, moved up in edging out Johnson TORIBIONG by a slim 50.7 percent majority. More important, the amendment to reduce the threshold required to alter the antinuclear provision of the constitution was approved by the voters. This cleared the way for approval of the compact by 64 percent of the participants on November 9, 1993. In September 1994 the Palauan Supreme Court dismissed an appeal challenging the validity of the 1993 vote, and on October 1, 1994, independence was formally proclaimed.

Benefiting from an economic upswing based on the infusion of U.S. compact funds, in addition to a "look north" policy that had attracted significant Japanese, Filipino, and Taiwanese investment, President Nakamura won reelection on November 6, 1996, easily defeating the mayor of Koror, Paramount Chief Ibedul Yutaka GIBBONS, by a 2–1 margin. Earlier, Toribiong, second-ranked in preelection polling, had withdrawn from the race because of the incumbent's seemingly insurmountable lead.

Nakamura's reelection was preceded on September 26, 1996, by the collapse of a recently renovated bridge (the world's largest of its type) between Koror and Babeldaob. The collapse was a major economic disaster, as it cut off the smaller, more densely populated capital region from the country's only airport and electrical supplier. Although Nakamura secured legislative funding for construction of a temporary span, a sharp decline in tourist arrivals and curtailment of development prospects for the northern island were among the immediate consequences.

In the national election of November 7, 2000, Vice President Tommy REMENGESAU Jr. captured the presidency, winning 52 percent of the vote against Sen. Peter SUGIYAMA. Running separately, Sen. Sandra PIERANTOZZI defeated her nephew, Alan REID, for the vice presidency even though Reid had been endorsed by outgoing President Nakamura.

President Remengesau was accorded a second term in the election of November 2, 2004, although Vice President Pierantozzi was defeated by Elias Camsek CHIN. The vice-presidential outcome led to a constitutional amendment (approved in 2004) that the president and vice president thereafter be elected as a team.

At the most recent balloting of November 4, 2008, Johnson Toribiong defeated Chin with a presidential vote share of 51.2 percent.

Constitution and government. Under the Compact of Free Association, Palau is a fully sovereign state, save with regard to defense, which was to remain a U.S. responsibility for at least a 15-year period; it was also obligated to "consult" with Washington regarding major foreign policy matters. For the first decade of independence, its constitution provided for a president and vice president elected on separate tickets for four-year terms after having been selected (since 1992) by primaries replacing a first-past-the-post system. The somewhat unusual procedure was replaced in 2004 by a requirement that the two offices be filled on a single ticket. The bicameral National Congress consists of a Senate currently composed of 14 members elected on a population basis (9 from Koror, 4 from the northern islands, 1 from the southern islands), and a House of Delegates, encompassing one representative from each of the republic's 16 states (a proposal to abandon bicameralism in favor of a unicameral legislature was rejected by voters in 2004). There is also a 16-member Council of Chiefs to advise the government on matters of tribal laws and customs. The judicial system consists of a Supreme Court (including both Trial and Appellate Divisions), a National Court, and a Court of Common Pleas. In late 2007 a senate bill was introduced that would create a court to deal with land, property, and other issues governed by traditional principles.

Each of the states (Aimeliik, Airai, Angaur, Kayangel, Koror, Melekeok, Ngaraard, Ngardmau, Ngaremlengui, Ngatpang, Ngchesar, Ngerchelong, Ngiwal, Peleliu, Sonsorol, and Tobi) elects its own governor and legislature. With the addition of municipal and traditional structures, Palauans, on a per capita basis, have been termed "the most governed people on earth."

In addition to the measures referenced above, three constitutional amendments were approved in 2004: the holding of dual U.S.-Palau citizenship, a limitation of three four-year terms for legislators, and a cap on congressional salaries.

Foreign relations. Palau was admitted to the United Nations on December 15, 1994. It participates in the Pacific Islands Forum and a number of other intergovernmental organizations. Following independence, the government opened embassies in Tokyo and Washington. In 2004, on the other hand, President Remengesau announced that Palau was withdrawing from the G-77 group of developing countries (which it had joined two years before) on the grounds that it had been ineffective in lobbying on environmental issues, such as global warming.

In 1999 diplomatic relations were established with Taiwan, a linkage that critics subsequently urged the Remengesau administration to abandon in favor of ties with the People's Republic of China. However, the switch would entail an economic penalty: since 2003 Taiwan has provided Palau (whose current president served earlier as ambassador to Taiwan) with its largest group of tourists, generating some $40 million in annual revenue.

The establishment of diplomatic relations with Russia in late 2006 was followed by an upsurge in tourists that prompted an increase in Russian-speaking staff by resort owners.

Current issues. In April 2007 President Remengesau asked U.S. president George W. Bush to initiate the review process for a new Compact of Free Association to replace the one expiring in September 2009. Subsequently, a Compact Review Commission was named to meet with U.S. officials. However, a State Department official declared in mid-2008 that there was no basis for renegotiation and that, in any event, the United States was not prepared to extend the financial assistance provisions of the existing compact or commit itself to any new ones.

In February 2009, with the value of Palau's Trust Fund having lost approximately 40 percent of its value because of the U.S. recession, President Toribiong also called for renegotiation of the Compact's funding provisions, but no agreement was reached by midyear. Ironically, while the existing Compact yielded $13 million in annual subsidies and grants, Washington was reported to have offered up to $200 million in long-term budget support and other assistance if Korer agreed to accept 17 Chinese Muslims detailed at Guantánamo Bay. Although many of the detainees rejected the transfer because of Palau's proximity to mainland China, 6 arrived in Palau in November. Although officials denied any connection, a one-year extension of U.S. financial assistance was negotiated for October 2009–October 2010, and progress was subsequently reported toward finalization of funding arrangements through 2024.

POLITICAL PARTIES

Traditionally there were no formal parties in Palau. However, an antinuclear Coalition for Open, Honest, and Just Government emerged to oppose the Compact of Free Association, which was defended by a Ta Belau Party, led by Kuniwo Nakamura. Subsequently, a Palau National Party was launched by (then) opposition leader Johnson Toribiong. However, there is no indication that any of them currently exists.

LEGISLATURE

The **Palau National Congress** (*Olbiil Era Kelulau,* which translates literally as "House of Whispered Decisions") is a bicameral body, both of whose chambers have four-year mandates (there is a three-term limit). Balloting was last held on November 4, 2008.

Senate. The upper house currently consists of 14 members representing geographic districts that may be reapportioned every eight years.
President: Mlib TIMETUCHL.

House of Delegates. The lower house contains 16 members, one from each of Palau's states.
Speaker: Noah IDECHONG.

CABINET

[as of July 1, 2009]

President	Johnson Toribiong
Vice President	Kerai Mariur
Ministers	
Chief Negotiator for Compact of Free Association with the United States	Joshua Koshiba
Community and Cultural Affairs	Faustina K. Rehuher-Marugg [f]
Education	Masa-Aki Emesiochel
Finance	Kerai Mariur
Health	Dr. Stevenson Kuartei
Justice	Johnny Gibbons
Natural Resources, Environment, and Tourism	Harry Fritz
Public Infrastructure, Industries, and Commerce	Jackson Ngiraingas
Special Prosecutor	Michael Copeland
State	Sandra S. Pierantozzi [f]

[f] = female

COMMUNICATIONS

Press. The *Palau Gazette* is issued in Koror on a twice-weekly basis; there is also a *Belau News*.

Broadcasting. The Palau National Communications Corporation operates one radio station and one television station in Koror. There is also a privately operated cable television system in the capital. There were approximately 14,800 television receivers in 2003. As of 2008 there were 269.7 Internet users per 1,000 inhabitants.

INTERGOVERNMENTAL REPRESENTATION

Ambassador to the U.S.: Hersey KYOTA.

U.S. Ambassador to Palau: (Vacant).

Permanent Representative to the UN: Stuart J. BECK.

IGO Memberships (Non-UN): ADB, PC, PIF.

PANAMA

Republic of Panama
República de Panamá

Political Status: Became independent of Spain as part of Colombia (New Granada) in 1819; independent republic proclaimed on November 3, 1903; present constitution, adopted on September 13, 1972, substantially revised on April 24, 1983.

Area: 29,208 sq. mi. (75,650 sq. km.).

Population: 2,839,177 (2000C); 3,397,000 (2008E).

Major Urban Centers (2005E): PANAMA (also known as Panama City, 419,000), San Miguelito (323,000), David (83,000), Colón (23,000).

Official Language: Spanish.

Monetary Unit: Balboa (official rate December 1, 2009: 1.00 balboas = $1US). The balboa is at par with the U.S. dollar, which is also acceptable as legal tender.

President: Ricardo MARTINELLI Berrocal (Democratic Change Party); elected on May 3, 2009, and inaugurated on July 1 for a five-year term, succeeding Martín TORRIJOS Espino (Democratic Revolutionary Party).

Vice President: Juan Carlos VARELA (Pro-Panamanian Party); elected on May 3, 2009, and inaugurated on July 1 for a term concurrent with that of the president, succeeding Samuel Lewis NAVARRO (Democratic Revolutionary Party).

THE COUNTRY

Situated on the predominantly mountainous isthmus that links America's northern and southern continents, Panama has the second-smallest population of any Latin American country but ranks comparatively high in per capita wealth and social amenities, due mainly to the economic stimulus imparted by the Panama Canal, the interoceanic canal built in 1904–1914 that cuts across its waist. Population density is not high, although nearly one-fourth of the people live in Panama City and Colón. About 70 percent of the populace is of mixed Caucasian, Indian, and African derivation; pure Caucasian is estimated at 9 percent and pure African at 14 percent, the balance being of Indian and other origins. Roman Catholicism is professed by approximately 85 percent of the people, but other faiths are permitted. In 2005, 45.5 percent of adult women worked outside the home; female participation in government has traditionally been minimal, although the president in 1999–2004 was a woman (the first in the nation's history). In 2009, 3 of the 15 cabinet ministers were women. Law 22, passed on July 14, 1997, required that 30 percent of candidates nominated by parties be women. There also were 6 women in the 71-member National Assembly in 2009.

Panama's shipping fleet is the largest in the world by virtue of flag-of-convenience registrations; not surprisingly, it is one of the world's most important centers of entrepôt activity, its economy being heavily dependent on international commerce and transit trade. Since 1970, when a new banking law went into effect, it has also become a leading Spanish-language and offshore banking center. The service sector now accounts for 80 percent of GDP and employs more than 60 percent of the workforce. Bananas remain the most important export, followed by shrimp and other seafood, clothing, sugar, and coffee.

The GDP was reported to have shrunk by at least 20 percent in 1988 as a result of the political crisis that began in mid-1987, yielding a suspension of U.S. aid, a court order freezing all government funds on deposit in U.S. banks, massive capital flight, and a surge in unemployment to more than 25 percent from 10.2 percent in late 1986. Even greater adversity, in at least the short term, resulted from the U.S. invasion of December 1989, which yielded extensive property damage and widespread looting. Signs of recovery were evident in 1990 with a substantial GDP increase of 3.4 percent, although unemployment remained high at 18.1 percent.

Economic performance was mixed throughout the 1990s and the first half of this decade, following trends seen throughout most of Latin America. Conditions began changing in 2005, when GDP grew by 6 percent.

Robust annual GDP growth of 8.1 percent in 2006 was attributed almost entirely to the service sector, with little improvement in agriculture, fishing, or industry. Furthermore, economic indicators obscured the extreme disparities in wealth, as more than 95 percent of the indigenous population and 40 percent of the overall population were impoverished.

In 2007 Panama's economy outpaced that of its regional counterparts, with annual GDP growth of 11.2 percent, owing in large part to

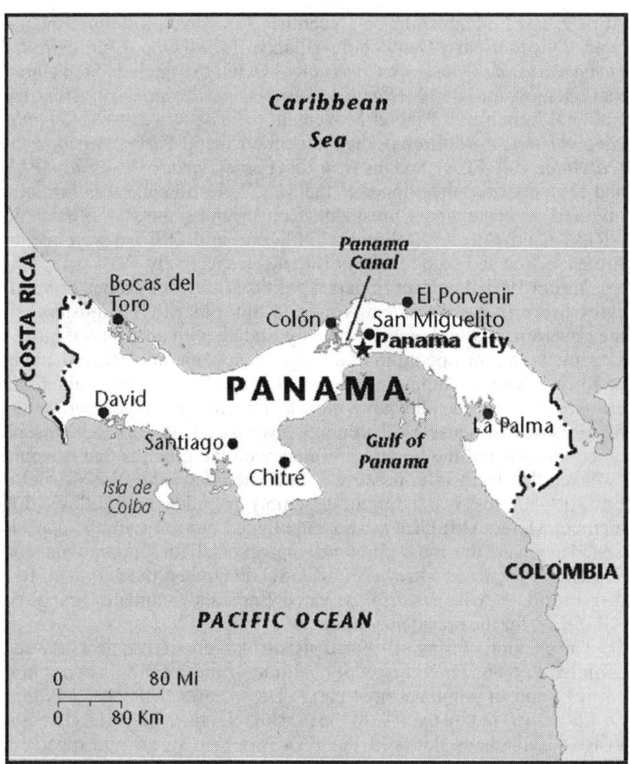

one of the highest rates of direct foreign investment in Latin America. Annual growth continued to be strong at 9.2 percent in 2008, but the global financial downturn adversely affected the economy thereafter, as trade decreased and credit tightened, according to the International Monetary Fund (IMF). Growth in 2009 was expected to slow to 3 percent, but fund managers said the country's banking system "has weathered the global financial crisis relatively well." The IMF also commended the government for reigning in public debt while still supporting social programs aimed at alleviating poverty.

GOVERNMENT AND POLITICS

Political background. Although renouncing Spanish rule in 1821, Panama remained a part of Colombia until 1903, when a U.S.-supported revolt resulted in the proclamation of an independent republic. Shortly thereafter, Panama and the United States signed a treaty in which the latter guaranteed the independence of Panama while obtaining "in perpetuity" the use, occupation, and control of a zone for the construction, operation, and protection of an interoceanic canal. Panama also received a down payment of $10 million and subsequent annual payments of $250,000.

In the absence of strongly rooted political institutions, governmental authority was exercised in the ensuing decades by a few leading families engaged in shifting alliances and cliques. Following World War II, however, Panamanian politics were increasingly dominated by nationalist discontent growing out of continued U.S. control of the canal and the exclusive jurisdiction exercised by the United States in the Canal Zone. Despite increases in U.S. annuity payments and piecemeal efforts to meet other Panamanian complaints, serious riots within the zone in January 1964 yielded a temporary rupture in diplomatic relations with Washington. Following their restoration in April, the two countries agreed to renegotiate the treaty relationship, but progress was impeded by internal unrest in Panama as well as by political opposition within the United States.

In early 1968 the outgoing president, Marco A. ROBLES, became involved in a major constitutional conflict with the National Assembly over his attempt to designate an administrative candidate, David SAMUDIO, for the presidential election of May 12. Samudio was defeated in the voting by Arnulfo ARIAS Madrid, a veteran politician who had already been twice elected and twice deposed (in 1941 and 1951). Inaugurated for the third time on October 1, Arias initiated a shake-up of the National Guard, a body that served both as an army and police force, and he was again overthrown on October 11–12 by guard officers who felt threatened by his policies. Col. José María PINILLA and Col. Bolívar URRUTIA Parilla were installed at the head of a Provisional Junta Government, which suspended vital parts of the constitution and normal political processes, promised a cleanup of political life, and indicated that a new election would be held without military participation in 1970. Real power, however, was exercised by the high command of the National Guard under the leadership of then colonel Omar TORRIJOS Herrera and Col. Boris N. MARTÍNEZ, his chief of staff. Martínez was relieved of his command and exiled in February 1969, leaving Torrijos in undisputed control of the military. In December 1969 Pinilla and Urrutia attempted to purge Torrijos; they failed, however, and were subsequently replaced by two civilians, Demetrio Rasilio LAKAS Bahas and Arturo SUCRE Pereira, as president and vice president. On July 15, 1975, Sucre resigned for health reasons and was succeeded by Gerardo GONZÁLEZ Vernaza, the former minister of agricultural and livestock development.

Politics in the wake of the 1968 coup focused primarily on two issues: renegotiation of the Canal Zone treaty and the long-promised reactivation of normal political processes. Nationalist sentiments put increasing pressure on the United States to relinquish control over the Canal Zone, while a partial return to normalcy occurred in 1972 with the nonpartisan election of an Assembly of Community Representatives. The assembly's primary function was to legitimize existing arrangements, and one of its first acts was the formal designation of General Torrijos as "Supreme Leader of the Panamanian Revolution."

Following a legislative election on August 6, 1978, General Torrijos announced that he would withdraw as head of government and would refrain from seeking the presidency for the 1978–1984 term. On October 11 the National Assembly designated two of his supporters, Arístides ROYO and Ricardo de la ESPRIELLA, as president and vice president, respectively.

During 1979 political parties were authorized to apply for official recognition, although the leading opposition party and a number of smaller groups refused to participate in balloting on September 28, 1980, to elect one-third of an expanded Legislative Council (theretofore primarily identifiable as a nonsessional committee of the National Assembly).

General Torrijos was killed in a plane crash on July 31, 1981, and on August 1 was succeeded as National Guard commander by Col. Florencio FLORES Aguilar. On March 3, 1982, Colonel Flores retired in favor of Gen. Rubén Darío PAREDES, who was widely regarded as a leading presidential contender and who was due to retire from the military on September 11. Under pressure from Paredes, President Royo resigned on July 30, allegedly for health reasons, in favor of Vice President de la Espriella, who reaffirmed an earlier pledge that "clean and honest" elections would be held in 1984. On September 6 it was announced that Paredes had acceded to requests from the president and the military high command to remain in his post beyond the mandated retirement date.

On April 24, 1983, a series of constitutional amendments (see below) were approved in a national referendum, paving the way for a return to full civilian rule, and on August 12 General Paredes retired as military commander in favor of Gen. Manuel Antonio NORIEGA Morena to accept presidential nomination by the *torrijista* Democratic Revolutionary Party (*Partido Revolucionario Democrático*—PRD). Because of widespread opposition to his candidacy, he was, however, forced to step down as PRD standard-bearer in September.

On February 13, 1984, following designation of Nicolás ARDITO Barletta as the nominee of a PRD-backed electoral coalition called the National Democratic Union (*Unión Nacional Democrática*—Unade), President de la Espriella was obliged to resign in a second "constitutional coup." He was succeeded by Vice President Jorge ILLUECA, who was identified with more leftist elements within the PRD.

On May 6, 1984, Panama conducted its first direct presidential balloting in 15 years. From a field of seven candidates, Unade's Ardito Barletta narrowly defeated former president Arias Madrid amid outbreaks of violence and allegations of vote rigging. The new chief executive assumed office on October 11, pledging to alleviate the country's ailing economy, expose corruption, and keep the military out of politics. The legislative election, held concurrently with the presidential poll, also yielded victory for the six-party Unade coalition, which took 40 of the 67 National Assembly seats.

In the second such action in 18 months Ardito Barletta resigned on September 27, 1985, being succeeded the following day by First Vice

President Eric Arturo DELVALLE Henríquez. The move was reportedly dictated by General Noriega, who had warned a month earlier that the country's political situation was "out of control and anarchic." During his year in office, Ardito had drawn criticism for a series of economic austerity measures, although the more proximate cause of his downfall appeared to be an effort by the military to deflect attention from the "Spadafora scandal," involving the death of former health minister Hugo SPADAFORA, whose decapitated body had been found near the Costa Rican border on September 14. After leaving the government in 1978, Spadafora had joined the *sandinista* forces opposing Nicaraguan dictator Anastasio Somoza but subsequently shifted his allegiance to the *contra* group led by Edén Pastora. Spadafora had publicly accused General Noriega of involvement in the drug trade, and opposition groups charged that the president's resignation had been forced in the wake of a decision to appoint an independent investigative committee to examine the circumstances surrounding the murder.

In June 1986 the *New York Times* published a series of reports that charged General Noriega with electoral fraud, money-laundering, drug trafficking, clandestine arms trading, and the sale of high-technology equipment to Cuba. Noriega vehemently denied the charges and insisted that they were part of a campaign aimed at blocking Panama's assumption of control of the Panama Canal in the year 1999. A year later, in apparent retaliation for his forced retirement as military chief of staff, Col. Roberto DÍAZ Herrera issued a barrage of accusations in support of the *Times* allegations, in addition to charging his superior with complicity in the 1981 aircraft death of General Torrijos. The action prompted widespread popular unrest generated, in part, by the National Antimilitarist Crusade (*Cruzada Civilista Nacional*—CCN), a newly formed middle-class group with opposition party and church support. In July Vice President Roderick ESQUIVEL joined in an opposition call for an independent commission to investigate Díaz's claims. Although Díaz issued a retraction late in the year, a U.S. federal grand jury handed down indictments on February 4, 1988, charging Noriega and 14 others with drug trafficking. On February 25 President Delvalle, who had previously supported Noriega, announced his intention to dismiss the general, but the following day, based on the grounds that he had exceeded his constitutional authority, he was himself dismissed by the National Assembly, which named Education Minister Manuel SOLIS Palma as his acting successor. Delvalle, whom the United States and a number of Latin American countries continued to recognize as chief executive, escaped from house arrest, went into hiding, and announced that he would continue to struggle against the Noriega "puppet regime." Subsequently, Panamanian assets in U.S. banks were frozen, further exacerbating a financial crisis stemming from the fact that the U.S. dollar was, for all practical purposes, the only circulating currency. On March 16 Noriega's forces put down a coup attempt by midlevel dissident officers, while a general strike called by the CCN five days later collapsed following the arrest of numerous opposition leaders and journalists on March 29.

Despite internal political resistance and continued economic pressure by the United States, Noriega clung to power during the ensuing year, amid preparations for national elections on May 7, 1989, in which, contrary to expectations, the general did not run. In the wake of the balloting, despite evidence of massive government fraud, it became clear that the regime's nominee, Carlos DUQUE Jaén, had been substantially outpolled by the opposition candidate, Guillermo ENDARA Galimany (Arias Madrid having died the previous August), and on May 10 the Electoral Commission nullified the results because of "obstruction by foreigners" and a "lack of voting sheets [that] made it impossible to proclaim winners."

On September 1, 1989, when Delvalle's term would have ended, Francisco RODRÍGUEZ, a longtime associate of General Noriega, was sworn in as president after designation by the Council of State, a body composed of senior military and civilian officials. Little more than a month later, on October 3 Noriega put down a violent coup attempt led by Maj. Moisés GIROLDI Vega, who, with a number of fellow conspirators, was summarily executed. On December 15 a revived National Assembly of Community Representatives elevated Noriega to the all-inclusive title conferred earlier on General Torrijos and accorded him sweeping powers to deal with what was termed "a state of war" with the United States. Washington responded on December 20 with U.S. troops attacking Panamanian Defense Forces in Panama City and elsewhere, forcing Noriega to take refuge in the Vatican Embassy, from which he voluntarily emerged on January 3, 1990. Immediately taken into custody, he was flown to the United States for trial on drug trafficking and other charges for which he was ultimately convicted on April 9, 1992. Meanwhile, on December 21, 1989, Guillermo Endara, head of the four-party Democratic Alliance of Civil Opposition (*Alianza Democrática de Oposición Civilista*—ADOC) that included the Christian Democratic Party (*Partido Demócrata Cristiano*—PDC), the National Republican Liberal Movement (*Movimento Liberal Republicano Nacional*—Molirena), the Authentic Liberal Party (*Partido Liberal Autenico*—PLA), and his Arnulfist Party (*Partido Arnufista*—PA), had been declared the winner of the May 7 election and was formally invested as Panamanian president. Concurrently, the PDC's Ricardo ARIAS Calderón and Molirena's Guillermo FORD Boyd were reconfirmed as first and second vice presidents, respectively.

During 1991 President Endara's political influence eroded dramatically. In April Vice President Arias and four other PDC ministers left the government after being charged by Endara with a variety of hostile acts, including the operation of a domestic spy operation with the help of former Noriega supporters. Subsequently, Arias (who retained his elective post) branded the government's increasingly unpopular austerity measures as "senseless," although he refused to endorse a plebiscite on continuance of the Endara presidency on the grounds that it would "weaken the democratic process." On September 1 the PLA's Arnulfo ESCALONA lost a bid for the assembly presidency to fellow PLA member Marco AMEGLIO, who had aligned himself with the opposition. However, the most embarrassing reversal for Endara came on September 30, when Mireya MOSCOSO de Gruber, the widow of former President Arias Madrid, defeated Endara's candidate, Francisco ARTOLA, for the presidency of the PA.

The election of May 8, 1994, consisted largely of a contest between a United People (*Pueblo Unido*) coalition of the PRD plus two minor parties, and a similar three-party Democratic Alliance (*Alianza Democrática*) led by the PA. In the presidential race the PRD's Ernesto PÉREZ Balladares defeated the PA's Moscoso by an unexpectedly close vote margin of 3.7 percent, while the PRD won a plurality of 31 assembly seats to the PA's 15. The new president's cabinet, sworn in with Pérez on September 1, was PRD-dominated but included a number of independents and opposition figures in accordance with a campaign pledge to form a coalition administration.

With President Pérez excluded from seeking a second term, Martín TORRIJOS Espino, Gen. Omar Torrijos's son, won a PRD presidential primary on October 25, 1998, but he was defeated on May 2, 1999, by Moscoso at the head of an *Arnulfista*-led populist coalition that included Molirena, the National Renovation Movement (*Movimiento de Renovación Nacional*—Morena), and the recently registered Democratic Change (*Cambio Democrático*—CD). The PA-led alliance failed, however, to capture a majority in simultaneous balloting for the assembly, in which the PRD-led New Nation coalition won 41 seats. Thus, Moscoso courted additional support from the PDC and two erstwhile New Nation organizations, the Solidarity Party (*Partido Solidaridad*—PS) and the National Liberal Party (*Partido Liberal Nacional*—PLN). By her September 1 inauguration she had cobbled together a working parliamentary majority of 1 seat, but it lasted only until August 2000, when the PRD and the PDC (subsequently renamed the Popular Party) agreed to cooperate in the assembly. With the further addition of two PS legislators, the opposition controlled 38 seats by September 2001.

The PRD's Martín Torrijos was elected president with 47.4 percent of the votes on May 2, 2004. The PRD-led New Nation also secured a substantial legislative majority, while the PRD won control of most municipalities (including the country's five largest) and an overwhelming majority of communal assemblies. The most surprising result of the presidential poll was the second-place finish (30.9 percent) by the PS candidate, former president Endara, who had left the PA in the wake of Moscoso's ascendancy. By contrast, the PA candidate, José Miguel ALEMÁN, captured only 16.4 percent of the vote. Following constitutional revisions approved in 2004 that abolished the post of second vice president (see Constitution and Government, below), the PRD's Rubén AROSEMENA was the last to hold the post. He subsequently was named minister of the presidency.

In the run-up to the 2009 elections, President Torrijos reshuffled the cabinet in May 2008, as ministers resigned in advance of presidential and legislative balloting, and others were dismissed because of involvement in a scandal. Meanwhile, three days before the May 3, 2009, presidential elections, the Supreme Court overturned rules barring independent candidates from running. However, the ruling came too late to have any effect on the outcome, in which businessman Ricardo Martinelli, a CD member backed by the Alliance for Change (*Alianza por el Cambio*—AC) coalition, won a landslide victory, becoming the first presidential candidate in modern Panamanian history to win an absolute majority of the votes (59.97). His closest challenger was the PRD's Balbina HERRERA, with 37.7 percent. Former president Guillermo Endara of the Moral Vanguard of the Homeland (*Vanguardia Moral de la Patria*—VM), won just 2.3 percent. In concurrent legislative elections, the AC won a majority of seats, while the PRD lost 15 seats. The PRD also lost the mayorship of Panama City to the Pro-Panamanian Party (*Partido Panameñista*—PP), though it won 62 of 75 mayoralties and more than half of municipal council seats nationwide in 2009.

President Martinelli named a new government, dominated by CD and PP members, on May 10, 2009. Independents and one PRD dissident were also given ministry posts.

Constitution and government. The constitutional arrangements of 1972 called for executive authority to be vested in a president and vice president designated by a popularly elected Assembly of Community Representatives for terms concurrent with the latter's six-year span. Under a series of amendments approved by national referendum on April 24, 1983, the 1972 document was substantially revised. The major changes included direct election of the president for a five-year term, the creation of a second vice presidency, a ban on political activity by members of the National Guard, and abolition of the National Assembly of Community Representatives in favor of a more compact National Assembly (see Legislature, below). Under an earlier amendment introduced by General Paredes in October 1982, provincial governors and mayors, all theretofore presidential appointees, were made subject to popular election.

Headed by a nine-member Supreme Court, the judicial system embraces Superior District tribunals and Circuit and Municipal courts. The country is divided into nine provinces and one special (Indian) territory, the smallest administrative units, *corregimientos,* forming the basis of the electoral system.

A Public Force that encompassed the National Police, National Air Service, and National Maritime Service was supplemented in early 1991 by the Technical Judicial Police. In 1992 the National Assembly endorsed the constitutional abolition of an armed defense force, an action that was reversed by popular referendum on November 15, but revived by President Endara in August 1994 and accorded formal ratification by the post-Endara assembly on October 4.

A package of constitutional reforms backed by President-elect Torrijos was approved by the legislature in mid-2004. Among the changes were a two-month limit on the transitional period between governments; establishment of a Constituent Assembly to consider constitutional revisions; reduction of the National Assembly from 78 to 71 seats; and abolition of the position of second vice-president.

Foreign relations. Panama is a member of the United Nations and many of its specialized agencies, as well as of the Organization of American States (OAS) and other regional bodies. Though not a member of the now-moribund Organization of Central American States (ODECA), Panama was active in some of the organization's affiliated institutions and participated in a number of regional peace initiatives in the 1980s sponsored by the Contadora Group, of which it was a founding member. However, the government, expressing an interest in joining the North American Free Trade Agreement, in the early 1990s did not pursue economic integration with its Central American neighbors with enthusiasm.

The country's principal external problems have traditionally centered on the Canal Zone and its complex and sensitive relationship with the United States because of the latter's presence in the zone (see Panama Canal Zone, below). This relationship, which eased on conclusion of the canal treaties, was again strained in 1987 as the administration of Ronald Reagan committed itself to the support of Noriega's domestic opponents—a policy complicated by evidence that the general had previously been associated with the U.S. Central Intelligence Agency (CIA) in a variety of clandestine operations. The United States refused to recognize the appointment of Solís Palma as acting president in February 1988 or of Rodríguez in September 1989 and intervened militarily to oust Noriega the following December (see Political background, above). Subsequently, the United States strongly supported the reconstruction efforts of the Endara administration, although the U.S. aid package of $420 million was estimated to be substantially less than half of the loss attributable to the invasion. As a result, an OAS body, the Inter-American Human Rights Commission (IAHRC), agreed in October 1993 to look into compensation claims of $1.2 billion advanced by 285 Panamanian families. However, the action was complicated by the fact that the United States, while a member of the OAS, had not ratified the IAHRC accord and hence remained technically outside its jurisdiction.

During 1996 Panama became increasingly concerned about an influx of Colombians, including left-wing guerrillas and right-wing paramilitaries, in the remote Darién region. In mid-July troops were dispatched to curb unrest in the area, which had been infiltrated by Colombian rebels and drug traffickers, in addition to serving as a sanctuary for refugees.

During 1998 extensive discussions with the United States focused on an idea, initially advanced by President Pérez more than two years earlier, for the creation of an international antidrug center at Howard Air Force Base in Panama City. Washington, however, sought a 12-year agreement (rather than the 3 years proposed by Pérez), with center personnel under U.S. control and enjoying diplomatic immunity. The talks were ultimately broken off in September, in part because of charges that the facility would be a challenge to Panamanian sovereignty. Opposition concern about Panama's international standing was again voiced following the February 2002 conclusion of an agreement authorizing U.S. participation in maritime patrols, the target being drug traffickers.

In August 2004 Cuba and Venezuela broke off relations with Panama after outgoing President Moscoso pardoned four men convicted of plotting to assassinate Cuba's president, Fidel Castro. Moscoso justified the release by saying that the men (one of whom had been convicted of counterrevolutionary activity and escaped from prison in Venezuela) would be executed if they were extradited. Subsequently, President Torrijos said that that he disagreed with his predecessor's action, and relations with Cuba were restored.

During 2007 Panama and the United States failed to reach agreement on the status of former dictator Manuel Noriega, who was scheduled for release in September. Panama wanted him returned as a prisoner of war, while Washington, believing that he would be accorded light treatment in his homeland, preferred extradition to France, where Noriega had been convicted of a number of criminal offenses. Ultimately, it was decided that Noriega would remain in a U.S. prison until all appeal routes had been exhausted.

In 2007 the United States and Panama signed a Trade Promotion Agreement (TPA), which the Panamanian government immediately approved, but the measure had not been ratified by the U.S. Congress as of mid-2009. The measure would eliminate some tariffs and further expand trade between the two countries. Meanwhile, Panama has established bilateral free trade agreements with Chile, Costa Rica, and Honduras.

In June 2008 the U.S. Congress approved $4 million for Panama's police as part of a security agreement between the United States and Mexico, known as the Mérida Initiative, to fight crime and drug trafficking in the region. In December, when the first Russian warship passed through the Panama Canal since World War II as part of joint naval exercises with Venezuela, the United States and Panama downplayed the event.

Relations with Cuba were enhanced in January 2009 when the two signed a trade agreement that would more than double Panama's exports to Cuba. In March President Torrijos traveled to Guatemala to sign another agreement in an effort to cushion both countries from the global economic slowdown and to fight drugs and crime. A Guatemala-Panama free-trade agreement was implemented in June.

Current issues. Despite strong GDP growth in 2007, the economy, particularly the rising cost of living, remained the primary concern of Panamanians in the final year of President Torrijos's tenure, as well as the most prominent issue of the subsequent presidential campaign. Union protests over the February 2008 police shooting of a construction worker prompted national demonstrations involving 40,000 people protesting stagnating salaries and soaring costs. The administration attempted to address the issue by increasing the minimum wage to $325 a month and providing one-time bonuses to workers earning less than $1,000 a month. However, those efforts were deemed insufficient in some quarters, and in August some 15,000 people organized by a civil society group protested.

Attention in 2008 focused on the campaign ahead of the May 2009 elections. Parties began nominating candidates, the PP tapping liquor magnate Juan Carlos VARELA, the CD choosing Martinelli, and the PRD naming former housing minister Balbina Herrera. Endara, the founder of his party, was nominated with no internal challengers. Meanwhile, as an increasing crime rate, drug trafficking, and violent conflicts near the Colombian border became major domestic concerns, the police commissioner resigned in May. He was replaced by Jaime RUIZ, whose appointment generated controversy since he was a veteran of Gen. Noriega's disbanded army. In an effort to address the crime problem, the legislature in June voted to give President Torrijos two months to rule by decree on security matters. Subsequently, the president's orders created new agencies for air and naval service, border security, national defense, and intelligence.

Critics argued that the new bodies—especially the border-security force—would too closely resemble Panama's army, abolished under a 1995 constitutional amendment. Meanwhile, the intelligence-gathering unit came under criticism, as some opponents claimed it was a virtual revival of General Noriega's feared G-2 intelligence service, as did the measure that allowed officers who had served under Noriega to head the security service. As a result, President Torrijos submitted approval of these new security measures to the legislature, which quickly approved them. Presidential candidates Varela and Martinelli opposed the measures and promised to revoke them if elected, while Herrera, though considered a candidate of the left, supported them. Subsequently, in October *La Prensa* newspaper published an explosive allegation about one of the measures' main backers, Interior and Justice Minister Daniel Delgado Diamante. The article claimed that in 1970 Delgado, then a lieutenant in Panama's National Guard, had shot a corporal to death at his home, in the presence of his wife. Delgado admitted to the shooting, but said it was an internal police matter and that he had been investigated and cleared. However, no record of an internal investigation appeared to exist. Delgado stepped down on October 23, and President Torrijos replaced him a month later.

As campaigning began in earnest, pre-election polls in 2009 consistently showed Martinelli with a comfortable lead, with the support of the AC. Martinelli pledged to improve the economy, fight corruption, and break the dominance of the PRD and the PP, which had shared power since 1964. The AC coalition began forming around Martinelli in December 2008, when the Molirena party broke from a brief alliance with the PP, whose candidate Varela was struggling in the polls. On January 28, 2009, Martinelli struck an agreement allowing the PP to join the broad opposition coalition, which was then given the AC name, and PP candidate Varela became Martinelli's running mate. (Just five months earlier, Martinelli had rejected a similar offer from Varela, accusing Varela of being corrupt and putting "his personal and party interests ahead of those of the people.") Meanwhile, the PRD government was enjoying relatively high approval ratings, though Martinelli dominated the issue of crime, which polling showed to be a rapidly growing domestic concern. Observers said the government's failure to curb crime and improve the economy, along with the controversial security measures, worked to Martinelli's advantage. A proposal by Martinelli for a $1 billion subway system to help relieve traffic congestion was also well received.

Candidate Herrera appeared to have lost significant electoral strength in 2009 following a statement by a jailed Colombian pyramid-scheme manager and accused money-launderer that he had contributed $3 million to Herrera's campaign and another $3 million to that of the PRD's Panama City mayoral candidate, Roberto VELÁSQUEZ. The remarks were said to have contributed to both candidates' failed bids for office.

Martinelli and the AC won a solid victory on May 3, 2009, with nearly 60 percent of the presidential vote and 42 seats in the legislature. The new government drew heavily from the business community and members of the AC coalition. Figuring most prominently were the PP's Varela as foreign minister, in addition to his post as vice president; banker Alberto VALLARINO, whom Varela had defeated for the PP presidential nomination in 2008, as minister of economy and finance; and José Raúl MULINO of the small Patriotic Union Party (*Partido Unión Patriótica*—PUP) as interior and justice minister. The new chief of police, Gustavo PÉREZ de la Ossa, was a controversial appointment, owing to his status as a former soldier and Noriega ally. During Martinelli's inaugural speech in July, the new president celebrated his defiance of the "ideological pendulum" swinging toward leftist leaders in much of Latin America. His first initiatives were a $100-per-month (more than 20 percent) salary increase for police officers, a $100-per-month stipend for the elderly, and initial steps toward construction of a Panama City subway.

POLITICAL PARTIES

Political parties in Panama have traditionally tended to be personalist rather than ideological in nature. All ten legal parties that participated in the 1968 balloting were suspended by the ruling junta in February 1969. The ban was relaxed before the 1978 election, although no candidates were allowed to run on party tickets. In late 1978 the government announced that legal recognition would be accorded parties with a minimum of 10,000 members; groups meeting this criterion were permitted to participate in the national and municipal elections of 1989. In February 1991 the government withdrew recognition from eight participants in the 1989 poll for failing to secure minimum vote shares.

Four of the 13 parties that secured legislative representation in May 1994 failed to secure the 5 percent vote shares needed to retain official status (see Libre and Pala under PRD, and PLA and UDI under *Partido Panameñista*, below). A number of other parties were also deregistered after the election. A total of 12 parties were officially recognized for the 1999 balloting and 4 (including two coalitions) in 2004.

Eight parties were legally recognized in 2009. Seven of them organized into two coalitions. The Alliance for Change (AC), which backed Ricardo Martinelli, included Democratic Change (CD), the Pro-Panamanian Party (PP), the Nationalist Republican Liberal Movement (Molirena), and the Patriotic Union Party (PUP). A Country for Everyone, which backed Balbina Herrera, included the Democratic Revolutionary Party (PRD), Popular Party, and Liberal Party (PL).

Government Parties:

Alliance for Change (*Alianza por el Cambio*—AC). The AC formed in January 2009 after the PP became the fourth—and largest—party to support Martinelli. The coalition's parties share a 42-seat majority in the legislature.

Democratic Change (*Cambio Democrático*—CD). The CD was initially registered in 1998 as a breakaway group from the PRD, its main campaign opposing corruption. Initially it ran as the Democratic Party, winning two legislative seats in 1999 as a minor party in the coalition, along with the PP and Molirena, that supported President Moscoso. As the CD, it won three seats in 2004.

In 2009 the CD won 15 seats, making it the third-largest vote-getter in the country, and its leader, Ricardo Martinelli, secured the presidency of the republic.

Leaders: Ricardo MARTINELLI Berrocal (President of the Republic and 2004 and 2009 presidential candidate), Giacomo TAMBURELLI (Secretary General).

Pro-Panamanian Party (*Partido Panameñista*—PP). The PP is the rubric adopted in 1995 by the Arnulfist Party (*Partido Arnulfista*—PA), which was legalized in 1990. The PA originated from the mainstream of the Authentic Panamanian Party (*Partido Panameñista Auténtico*—PPA), itself an outgrowth of the original *Partido Panameñista* that supported the three abortive presidencies of Arnulfo Arias Madrid. Following Arias's death in August 1988, the PPA split into factions, a minority headed by Hildebrando Nicosia seeking to achieve a "national union" with the Noriega-backed regime.

For the 1994 elections the PA formed a Democratic Alliance (*Alianza Democrática*) with two minor parties, the Authentic Liberal Party (*Partido Liberal Auténtico*—PLA) and the Independent Democratic Union (*Unión Democrática Independiente*—UDI). The PA won 15 of the alliance's 20 legislative seats, while its presidential candidate, Mireya Moscoso de Gruber, finished a close second. (The PLA and the UDI were subsequently deregistered for failing to obtain at least a 5 percent vote share in the legislative balloting.)

In mid-1996 the PA was reported to have formed a "strategic alliance" with Molirena, Morena, and the PDC to oppose what they termed was the government's lack of leadership. In September 1996 Mireya Moscoso de Gruber, the widow of former president Arias, was reelected president of the party. In 1997 the PA, Molirena, the PDC, and Morena grouping was expanded to include the PRC, the Gloria Young faction of *Papá Egoró*, and the PNP in a National Front for the Defense of Democracy (*Frente Nacional por la Defensa de Democracia*—FNDD) to oppose a reelection bid by President Peréz Balladares. PA president Moscoso de Gruber won the national presidency in 1999, but her party's candidate, José Miguel ALEMAN, ran a poor third in 2004.

In January 2005 the party dropped its PA designation in favor of the historical PP label. In March Moscoso de Gruber was forced to resign as the PP's leader, ostensibly because of the party's poor showing in the 2004 balloting but also in the wake of corruption charges having recently been brought against her.

The PP nominated Juan Carlos Varela as its presidential candidate for 2009. Varela had fallen out with the party in the late 1990s after he ran the losing primary campaign of Alberto VALLARINO against Moscoso. However, Varela returned to the party in 2003 and defeated Vallarino for the party's nod in the upcoming election. In January 2009 Varela, trailing in the polls, threw his support behind the CD's Martinelli and subsequently became Martinelli's running mate. The PP won 21 seats in the legislature with 23.4 percent of votes.

Leaders: Juan Carlos VARELA (Vice President of the Republic), Alcibiades Vasquez (First Vice President), Francisco ALEMAN (Secretary General).

Nationalist Republican Liberal Movement (*Movimiento Liberal Republicano Nacionalista*—Molirena). Molirena is a relatively small conservative grouping that was legally recognized in 1981. Its legislative representation increased from 14 to 16 as a result of the partial election of January 27, 1991, but fell to 5 in 1994 and to 3 in 1999. It won 4 seats as a member of the *Visión* coalition in 2004.

In the run-up to the 2009 elections, Molirena endorsed the PP's Juan Carlos Varela for president, but backed off in late December 2008 when Varela lagged in polls. Molirena subsequently endorsed Ricardo Martinelli in January 2009, shortly before the PP itself followed suit. In the 2009 elections, the party won 3.4 percent of the vote and 2 seats in the legislature.

Leaders: Sergio GONZÁLEZ Ruiz (President), Jorge ROSAS, Raúl COHN, Alain CEDEÑO (Vice President), Diomedes JAÉN (Vice President).

Patriotic Union Party (*Partido Unión Patriótica*—PUP). The PUP was formed as a result of the 2006 merger of the PLN and the PS (below). The PUP supported the CD's Ricardo Martinelli in the 2009 presidential election; in the concurrent legislative election, the PUP won 6.4 percent the vote and 4 seats.

Leaders: Guillermo FORD (President of the Party and Former Vice President of the Republic), Aníbal GALINDO (Vice President), Raul MULINO (Vice President), Jorge FABREGA (Secretary General).

A Country for Everyone (*Un País para Todos*). This coalition of the PRD, Popular Party, and PL resembles President Torrijos' earlier PRD-dominated coalition, New Nation (*Nueva Nación*). New Nation, also referenced as New Motherland (*Patria Nueva*—PN), was launched prior to the 1999 elections by the PRD, PS, PLN, and elements of the Motherland Movement (*Movimiento Papá Egoró*—MPE). (For additional information on the MPE, which lost its registration in 1999, see the 2008 *Handbook.*) The alliance won a majority (41 seats) in the Legislative Assembly in 1999 but failed to capture the presidency. As reconstituted for the 2004 balloting, New Nation included the PRD and the Popular Party; it won 42 legislative seats (41 for the PRD and 1 for the Popular Party). Defectors from other parties reportedly gave the PRD-led alliance control of 46 seats as of 2008.

The coalition supported the PRD's Balbina Herrera in the May 2009 presidential election, and subsequently a PRD member was given a cabinet appointment. In concurrent legislative elections, the coalition won 27 seats.

Democratic Revolutionary Party (*Partido Revolucionario Democrático*—PRD). The PRD was initially a left-of-center *torrijista* group organized as a government-supportive party in 1978. It obtained 10 of 19 elective seats in the 1980 Legislative Council balloting.

In May 1982 the PRD secretary-general, Gerardo González Vernaza, was replaced by Dr. Ernesto Pérez Balladares, a former financial adviser to General Torrijos. In November Pérez Balladares resigned in the wake of a dispute between left- and right-wing factions within the party, subsequent speculation being that General Rubén Paredes, commander of the National Guard, would be the country's 1984 presidential candidate. Paredes announced as a candidate in mid-1983 before accepting retirement from military service, and was reported to have been nominated by the party in August. In the face of opposition to his candidacy, he announced his withdrawal from politics in September but later ran as a nominee of the National People's Party (*Partido Nacionalista Popular*—PNP), which was deregistered in late 1984. The PRD named Nicolás Ardito Barletta, then World Bank regional vice president for Latin America, as its candidate after formation of the progovernment Unade coalition in February 1984. Elected chief executive in May 1984, Ardito Barletta resigned on September 27, 1985, and was succeeded by First Vice President Eric Delvalle, who was himself dismissed by the National Assembly in February 1988.

In early 1990 a new group of PRD leaders emerged, distancing themselves from Noriega, praising the country's commitment to democracy, and offering themselves as a "loyal opposition" to the Endara regime, which it nonetheless characterized as being responsible for the U.S. invasion. As the party's nominee in 1994, Pérez Balladares captured the presidency on a 33.2 percent vote share, while the PRD won a plurality of 31 legislative seats at the head of a United People (*Pueblo Unido*) coalition that also included the Republican Liberal Party (*Partido Liberal Republicano*—Libre) and the right-wing Labor Party (*Partido Laborista*—Pala), both of which were later deregistered for failing to meet a 5 percent vote threshold.

In primary balloting on October 25, 1998, the PRD named Martín Torrijos Espino, the son of Gen. Omar Torrijos, as its presidential standard-bearer in 1999. However, he gained only 38 percent of the popular vote in losing by a seven-point margin to Mireya Moscoso on May 2, 1999. Torrijos returned as the PRD candidate in 2004, winning the presidency by a substantial margin. The party won a majority of the legislature with 41 seats.

In 2008 the PRD nominated Balbina Herrera, a former mayor of San Miguelito, as its 2009 presidential candidate in a closely fought primary victory over Juan Carlos Navarro, the mayor of Panama City. Herrera ran as a left-of-center candidate, promising more social expenditure and denying any ties to the bloc of elected leftist governments led by Venezuela. A February 2009 scandal involving alleged financing from a Colombian pyramid scheme did further damage to her effort. She finished second behind Ricardo Martinelli with 37.7 percent of votes. The PRD was the largest single vote-getter in the legislative elections, with 34.6 percent of all votes. The party won 26 seats, 15 less than it won in 2004.

Leaders: Balbina HERRERA (President of the Party and 2009 presidential candidate), Martín TORRIJOS Espino (Former President of the Republic and Secretary General).

Popular Party (*Partido Popular*). The Popular Party adopted its current name in 2001, having previously been called the Christian Democratic Party (*Partido Demócrata Cristiano*—PDC). In what its leadership termed a "training exercise," the PDC participated in the 1980 balloting, winning two council seats. Named a vice-presidential candidate in 1984, PDC leader Ricardo Arias Calderón was viewed as a likely successor to Arias Madrid as principal spokesperson for the opposition and was ADOC vice-presidential candidate in 1989.

Possessing a plurality within the assembly, the PDC was estranged from its coalition partners in September 1990, when the latter joined with the opposition PRD to reject its nominees for chamber officials; despite the rebuff, the party stayed within ADOC until April 1991, when its ministerial delegation was ousted by President Endara for displaying "disloyalty and arrogance." In a move that was seen as reflecting a desire to distance himself from President Endara in the run-up to the 1994 election, Arias Calderón resigned as first vice president of the republic in December 1992. The party secured only one assembly seat in 1994.

With Alberto Vallarino, a prominent banker who had run in the 1994 presidential race again serving as its standard-bearer, the PDC contested the May 1999 elections in an Opposition Action (*Acción Opositora*) coalition that included the Civil Renovation Party (*Partido Renovación Civilista*—PRC), which secured one of the group's five seats, and the Liberal Party (*Partido Liberal*—PL) and Popular Nationalist Party (*Partido Nacionalista Popular*—PNP), neither of which won representation.

As the junior partner in Torrijos's 2004 New Nation coalition, the Popular Party obtained one assembly seat. In 2008 the party announced that it intended to remain in the coalition for the 2009 elections. Again, it won one assembly seat with 2.6 percent of the vote.

Leaders: Rene ORILLAC (President), Aníbal CULIOLIS (Secretary General).

Liberal Party (*Partido Liberal*—PL). The PL is the smallest member of the coalition headed by the PRD. The PL negotiated an alliance with the Popular Party to secure membership in the PRD-led coalition in 2009. With less than 1 percent of votes, it failed to win any legislative seats.

Leaders: Joaquin FRANCO III (President), Venus CARDENAS (Vice President), Augusto AROSEMENA (Secretary General).

Other Party That Participated in the 2009 Elections:

Moral Vanguard of the Homeland (*Vanguardia Moral de la Patria*—VM). The VM is a center-right party founded in November 2007 by former President Guillermo Endara after he broke with the PS. (He ran under the PS flag in the 2004 presidential election, finishing second to Torrijos with 30.9 percent of votes.) The VM did not participate in a coalition in 2009, and it failed to win a legislative seat. Former president Endara won 2.3 percent of the vote in the presidential election, finishing a distant third.

Leaders: Guillermo ENDARA (President of the Party and 2009 presidential candidate), Menalco SOLIS (Vice President), Ana Mae DIAZ de Endara (Secretary General).

Other Groups:

Alternative Grassroots Party (*Partido Alternativa Popular*—PAP). The PAP is a center-left party that was registered in August 2007 to compete in the 2009 election. However, its registration remained under review by the Electoral Tribunal, preventing it from participating in the 2009 poll.

Leaders: Raúl GONZÁLEZ (Sub-Secretary), Olmedo BELUCHE (Secretary General).

Vision of the Country (*Visión de País*). The *Visión* coalition backed Guillermo Endara in the 2004 elections. It included the PLN and the PS and won 24 legislative seats. The two member parties merged to form the PUP in 2006. (The PUP backed Martinelli in 2009 as part of the AC coalition.)

National Liberal Party (*Partido Liberal Nacional*—PLN). A member of the Liberal International, the PLN was formed in 1979. It won three assembly seats as a member of *Visión* in 2004.

Leaders: Raúl ARANGO Gasteazoro (1999 candidate for first vice president), Abraham WILLIAMS (Secretary General).

Solidarity Party (*Partido Solidaridad*—PS). Registered in 1993, the PS won two assembly seats in 1991 and four in 1999 as a member of New Nation. After the 1999 balloting the PS agreed to join President Moscoso's majority, but two representatives—Laurentino CORTIZO (the party's 1999 candidate for second vice president) and Alberto MAGNO Castillero—subsequently defected. The party ran independently in 2004, gaining second place in the presidential poll with former president Endara as its standard-bearer and winning nine assembly seats.

Leaders: Samuel LEWIS Galindo (Honorary President), Abraham MARTINEZ (President), Jorge Ricardo FABREGA (Secretary General).

LEGISLATURE

Before 1984 the Panamanian legislature consisted of an elected 505-member National Assembly of Community Representatives (*Asamblea Nacional de Representantes de Corregimientos*), which met on average only one month a year, and a de facto upper house, the National Legislative Council (*Consejo Nacional de Legislación*), consisting of 19 elected members and 37 appointed from the assembly. Under a constitutional revision approved in April 1983, the *Asamblea Nacional* was abolished, while the council was converted into a smaller, fully elected Legislative Assembly.

National Assembly (*Asamblea Nacional*). The present assembly consists of 71 members elected for five-year terms. The number of seats was reduced from 78 as part of a 2004 constitutional reform.

Following the most recent election on May 3, 2009, the distribution of seats was as follows: Alliance for Change, 42 (Pro-Panamanian Party, 21; Democratic Change, 15; Patriotic Union, 4; Nationalist Republican Liberal Movement, 2); A Country for Everyone, 27 (Democratic Revolutionary Party, 26; Popular Party, 1); and independents, 2.

President: Luis VARELA.

CABINET

[as of August 1, 2009]

President	Ricardo Martinelli Berrocal (CD)
Vice President	Juan Carlos Varela (PP)
Ministers	
Agriculture and Livestock Development	Víctor Manuel Perez (ind)
Canal Affairs	Rómulo Roux (ind)
Commerce and Industry	Roberto Henríquez (CD)
Economy and Finance	Alberto Vallarino Clement (PP)
Education	Lucy Molinar (CD) [f]
Foreign Relations	Juan Carlos Varela (PP)
Interior and Justice	José Raúl Mulino (PUP)
Health	Franklin Vergara (ind)
Housing	Carlos Dubois (PP)
Labor and Social Welfare	Alma Cortés (CD) [f]
Micro, Small and Medium-Sized Business	Giselle Calcagno (PRD) [f]
Presidency	Jimmy Papadimitriu (CD)
Public Works	Federico José Suárez (ind)
Social Development	Guillermo Ferrufino (CD)
Tourism	Salomon Shamah (ind)

[f] = female

COMMUNICATIONS

The constitution of Panama guarantees freedom of speech and of the press without censorship, but adds "there exist legal responsibilities when one of these media launch attacks against people's reputation or honor, or against social security or public order."

In early 1990 several papers, including the influential *La Prensa,* which had been forced to close under the Noriega regime, resumed publication. A revised penal code passed in 2007 abolished "gag laws" that had made it a criminal offense to defame or libel state officials, though it also criminalized exposing private information and documents, without a public interest exception.

In September 2008 a judge ordered the seizure of *El Periódico's* assets because it published a well-known business leader's tax records. As of mid-2009 the paper was defunct.

Press. The following are Spanish dailies published in Panama City, unless otherwise noted: *Crítica* (60,000), right-wing; *La Prensa* (50,000), independent centrist; *Diario El Siglo* (48,000), sensationalist; *El Panamá América* (30,000), right-wing; *La Estrella de Panamá* (21,000 daily, 25,000 Sunday), center-right; *Star and Herald* (11,000 daily, 14,000 Sunday), oldest English-language paper; *El Periódico*, pro-PRD; *Primera Plana,* right-wing.

News agencies. There is no domestic facility; several foreign bureaus maintain offices in Panama City.

Broadcasting and computing. There are more than 200 radio stations, most operated on a commercial basis; the most influential of the several television outlets is Canal 4. As of 2008 there were 274.9 Internet users per 1,000 inhabitants.

INTERGOVERNMENTAL REPRESENTATION

Ambassador to the U.S.: Jaime E. ALEMÁN.

U.S. Ambassador to Panama: Barbara J. STEPHENSON.

Permanent Representative to the UN: Pablo Antonio THALASSINOS.

IGO Memberships (Non-UN): ACS, ALADI, IADB, Interpol, IOM, NAM, OAS, OPANAL, PCA, SELA, SICA (observer), WCO, WTO.

PANAMA CANAL ZONE

Bisecting Panama in a southwesterly direction from the Atlantic to the Pacific, the Canal Zone served historically for the protection of the interoceanic waterway completed by the United States in 1914. Occupation, use, and control of a 553-square-mile area extending about five miles on either side of the canal were granted to the United

States in perpetuity by Panama in a treaty concluded in 1903. Following nationalist riots within the zone in 1964, the two countries in 1967 negotiated a new draft treaty that would have replaced the 1903 accord, recognized Panamanian sovereignty in the zone, and enabled Panama to participate in the management of the canal. In 1970, however, following a change in government, Panama declared the draft to be unacceptable. After further extended negotiations, U.S. and Panamanian representatives reached agreement on an amended accord that was incorporated into two treaties signed in Washington, D.C., on September 7, 1977. Endorsed by Panama in a plebiscite on October 23, the treaties were barely approved by the U.S. Senate on March 16 and April 18, 1978. Documents of ratification were subsequently exchanged during a state visit to Panama by U.S. President Jimmy Carter on June 16.

The first treaty provided for a phased assumption of control of the canal and the Canal Zone by Panama, beginning six months after ratification and concluding in the year 2000. Panama would assume general territorial jurisdiction, although until December 31, 1999, the United States would maintain control of all installations needed to operate and defend the canal. Until 1990 the canal administrator would be American, while his deputy would be Panamanian; from 1990 to 1999, the administrator would be Panamanian, with an American deputy.

The second treaty declared that "the canal, as an international transit waterway, shall be permanently neutral." It also provided that "tolls and other charges . . . shall be just, reasonable and equitable" and that "vessels of war and auxiliary vessels of all nations shall at all times be entitled to transit the canal, irrespective of their internal operation, means of propulsion, origin, destination, or armament."

Implementation of the treaties was delayed because of a U.S. Senate stipulation that ratification would not be deemed complete until the passage of enabling legislation by the Congress or until March 31, 1979, whichever came first. Thus it was not until October 1, 1979, that the American flag was lowered within the Canal Zone and administrative authority for the canal formally transferred to a binational Panama Canal Commission.

In early 1980, despite a significant increase in revenue accruing to Panama under the new arrangement, President Royo formally complained to the United States about a "unilateral" provision of the enabling legislation that effectively brought the commission under the control of the U.S. Defense Department. Subsequently, in the wake of an assessment that the existing facility, which was unable to offer transit to vessels in excess of 75,000 tons, would be obsolete by the year 2000, Royo and a group of high-level advisers visited Japan to discuss the possibility of Japanese involvement in the building of a new sea-level waterway.

During a meeting in Panama City in December 1982, the feasibility of a new waterway was further discussed by Panamanian, Japanese, and U.S. representatives. Earlier, a 9.8 percent increase in canal tolls had been agreed on to offset an anticipated shortfall of up to $5 million a month after the opening of a new trans-isthmian oil pipeline.

In mid-1984 the canal again became the focus for anti-U.S. sentiment, following U.S. reluctance to provide a major portion of the $400 to $600 million needed to widen the waterway on the grounds that it would be unlikely to recover its investment before full reversion in the year 2000. Late in the year, however, the United States and Japan agreed to a four-year program to consider canal improvements, not excluding the possibility of constructing a new facility to accommodate ships of up to 300,000 tons.

In June 1986 a tripartite commission, composed of Panamanian, Japanese, and U.S. representatives, began a projected four-year study on the feasibility of measures to upgrade or augment the existing facility, including improved pipeline, highway, and rail transport across the isthmus. The commission was also charged with undertaking an analysis of world shipping requirements in the 21st century and drafting recommendations on U.S.-Panamanian relations on expiration of the present canal treaties.

In July 1988 Panama refused to send delegates to a scheduled Canal Commission board meeting because of U.S. economic pressure against the Noriega regime and the U.S. rejection of representatives appointed by the Solis Palma administration. However, the problems were resolved by the overthrow of Noriega in December 1989 and the longtime Panamanian deputy administrator, Fernando Manfredo BERNAL became acting administrator on January 1, 1990. On April 30, during a visit by President Endara to Washington, D.C., President George H. W. Bush endorsed the appointment for a regular term of Gilberto GUARDIA Fábrega, who was formally approved by the U.S. Senate on September 11. Meanwhile, doubts arose as to the Panamanian government's ability to administer and defend the canal after December 31, 1999, then Government and Justice Minister Ricardo Arias Calderón having conceded in August that "a military defense [of the waterway] similar to the proportions of the U.S. is outside the practical and economic scope of Panama."

In early 1993 the Panamanian Legislative Assembly approved the establishment of an autonomous Interoceanic Region Authority (*Autoridad de la Regón Interoceánica*—ARI) to administer canal-related property acquired from the United States under the 1977 treaties. However, its future was clouded in late 1994 by a proposed constitutional amendment that would create a new Panama Canal Authority (*Autoridad del Canal de Panama*—ACP). Critics charged that the move was linked to a proposal before the U.S. Senate authorizing the formation of a corporation to administer the canal as a private undertaking.

In April 1995 the Pentagon announced that the U.S. Armed Forces' Southern Command would complete a withdrawal from Panama to a new site near Miami, Florida, in late 1998. The notice came after a U.S. request for extension of its military presence beyond 1999 elicited a cool response from Panamanian authorities. Thus in early September 1995 the Southern Command officially turned over two of its bases, Fort Davis and Fort Gulik, to the government of Panama. However, the Panamanian response shifted shortly afterward. On September 6 Pérez Balladares met with President Bill Clinton in Washington, D.C., to "explore" the possibility of "maintaining some degree of U.S. military presence after the year 2000." A month later, in sharp contrast to pretreaty rhetoric, an opinion poll indicated that 86 percent of Panamanians, which fell to a still high 72 percent in March 1997, wanted at least some bases to remain under U.S. control. Part of the change in attitude appeared to be economic, particularly regarding the substantial infusion of money from U.S. service personnel and their dependents.

On September 25, 1997, the U.S. Southern Command quit Panama one year early, leaving five of eight bases to be turned over to Panama (two more bases were relinquished in 1998). Meanwhile, representatives of 30 countries attended a Universal Canal Congress called by President Balladares on September 7–10. However, the United Nations withdrew promised funding, and most heads of state were absent because of the participation of Taiwanese President Lee Teng-hui.

During 1998 labor unions expressed concern over "the imminent privatization" of canal services, with attendant job losses, while opinion polls indicated that nearly three-quarters of Panamanians supported the continued presence of the U.S. military. In addition, opposition legislators charged government officials with profiting from the handover by acquiring cheap homes at a base returned to Panama in 1997. These problems notwithstanding, the United States formally handed over administration of the canal to Panama in December 1999, the last U.S. installation (Howard Air Force Base) having been vacated early in the month. Five months later, the canal administrator announced that technical proposals for constructing a new set of locks to accommodate ships up to 150,000 tons would be presented by the ACP to a canal advisory group representing 12 of the waterway's principal users. While the cost of the upgrade was estimated at $3 to $6 billion, experts insisted that by the year 2010 demand will have outstripped the capacity of the existing system.

By mid-2003 estimates of canal expansion costs had risen to $4 to $8 billion, with no decision as to which of several options might be adopted. The most viable, large-scale widening of the facility was bitterly opposed by *campesinos* on both shores, while funding sources were far from clear.

In April 2006 the government announced its intention to invest $5.2 billion, obtained largely from increased toll charges, in an eight-year project to expand the canal and construct a new set of locks 40 percent wider and 60 percent longer than the existing locks. The undertaking, approved in a national referendum on October 22, 2006, was officially launched on September 3, 2007, and was expected to be completed by 2014.

Three international consortia submitted bids in March 2009 for the largest single construction project, the $3.5 billion design and construction of two new locks.

Panama Authority Chair: Dani KUZNIECKY.

Panama Canal Administrator: Alberto ALEMÁN Zubieta.

PAPUA NEW GUINEA

Independent State of Papua New Guinea
Gau Hedinarai ai Papua-Matamata Guinea

Note: The literal translation of *Gau Hedinarai* is "entity of the people," hence the official title in Hari-Motu could be "Republic of Papua New Guinea."

Political Status: Former Australian-administered territory; achieved internal self-government on December 1, 1973, and full independence within the Commonwealth on September 16, 1975, under constitution of August 15.

Area: 178,259 sq. mi. (461,691 sq. km.).

Population: 5,190,786 (2000C); 6,463,000 (2008E).

Major Urban Centers (2009E): PORT MORESBY (metropolitan area, 254,158), Lae (78,038), Mt Hagen (27,789).

Official Languages: English, Tok Pisin, Hari-Motu.

Monetary Unit: Kina (market rate December 1, 2009: 2.59 kina = $1US).

Sovereign: Queen ELIZABETH II.

Governor General: Sir Paulias MATANE; elected by the National Parliament on May 28, 2004, and installed for a six-year term after formal appointment by the Queen, on June 29, succeeding Sir Silas ATOPARE and the interim incumbency of William (Bill) SKATE.

Prime Minister: Sir Michael SOMARE (National Alliance Party); served as prime minister from September 1975 to March 1980 and from August 1982 to November 1985; returned to office by the National Parliament on August 6, 2004, succeeding Sir Mekere MORAUTA (People's Democratic Movement); reappointed to head the government after election of June 30–July 14, 2007.

THE COUNTRY

Situated between Australia and the Equator in the southwest Pacific, Papua New Guinea (PNG) consists of the eastern half of the island of New Guinea and numerous adjacent islands, including those of the Bismarck Archipelago as well as part of the Solomon group. It shares its only land border with the Indonesian province of West Papua. The indigenous inhabitants, mainly of Melanesian ethnic origin, comprise over 1,000 tribes that speak more than 700 languages, of which English and two pidgins, Tok Pisin and Hari-Motu, have become lingua franca and accorded official status. Although animism and traditional beliefs are widespread among the predominantly rural population, Christianity, encouraged by foreign missionaries, is the dominant formal religion, with Protestant denominations in the majority. While females are reported to constitute 42 percent of the labor force, most are engaged in subsistence agriculture; female representation in formal elected bodies is minimal, but women's councils are active at both the national and provincial levels, and enjoy social status and government recognition and funding.

Much of the country's terrain consists of dense tropical forests and inland mountain ranges separated by grassland valleys. The climate is monsoonal. Roughly 70 percent of the population relies on subsistence farming and hunting and lives in primitive conditions, although some rural modernization has been achieved with government support. There are numerous mineral deposits, including gold, silver, and copper. The latter provided about 17 percent of government revenue and 40 percent of export earnings until closure of the vast Bougainville mine in 1989 because of secessionist activity. In addition, exploitation of natural gas and hydroelectric resources is under way. Major oil and gold discoveries offer the potential for new sources of revenue. Recoverable oil reserves in the southern highlands have been estimated at 500 million barrels, while gold extraction, from what were once described as the world's foremost undeveloped deposits, averaged more than 30 metric tons a year from 1987 through 1992.

Real economic growth, according to the World Bank, rose at an average rate of 5.0 percent during 1990–1996. However, by early 1998 the country was described as facing its "worse financial crisis since independence" because of falling mineral prices, lagging private investment, sagging demand from Asia, the aftermath of the Bougainville insurrection, a prolonged drought, and three severe tsunamis. The economy contracted nearly 4 percent in 1997 and again in 1998. Recovery of demand in the gas and minerals sectors helped spur a recovery to 4.2 percent growth in 1999. The subsequent record has been uneven. While commodity and energy exports brought the GDP growth rate up from 2.9 percent in 2003 to 7.2 percent in 2008, the Asian Development Bank forecast an easing to 4.0 percent in 2009 and 3.5 percent in 2010. In May 2008, the PNG government signed a deal with ExxonMobil for a liquefied natural gas project worth $15 billion in hopes of stimulating the economy. Nonetheless, distribution of wealth is uneven and unemployment remains high at some 80 percent in urban areas, the population below the poverty line is estimated at over 50 percent, malnutrition and hunger have been reported, and the UN in 2006 downgraded PNG from the developing country designation to that of "least developed country." Government corruption, urban crime, and tribal vendettas have combined to discourage international investment, entrepreneurialism, and tourism despite the country's natural wealth.

Papua New Guinea's exports, largely in the energy, mineral, and timber sectors, in 2008 went mainly to Australia (27.2 percent), Japan (9.2 percent), and China 5.1 percent. and its imports, largely machinery, vehicles, and consumer goods, came from Australia (42.6 percent), Singapore (15.6 percent), China (11 percent), and Japan (5.8 percent).

GOVERNMENT AND POLITICS

Political background. Sighted in 1526 by a Portuguese navigator who gave it the name Papua ("woolly haired"), parts of the island of New Guinea was colonized over the centuries by a succession of European and Asian nations, including Portugal, Netherlands, Great Britain, Germany, Japan, and Indonesia; the last retains the western half (now the provinces of Papua and West Papua). In 1906 the British New Guinea sector of the eastern half, renamed the Territory of Papua, was transferred to Australia. Northeast New Guinea, formerly a German colony, was assigned to Australia as a League of Nations mandate in 1920. Parts of both sectors were occupied by Japanese forces from 1942 to 1945, after which Australia reassumed control. A joint administration was introduced in 1949 and continued until the sectors were unified with the granting of independence to Papua New Guinea on September 16, 1975.

Representative government was initiated in 1964 when the House of Assembly replaced the former Legislative Council after the first common-roll election. In 1968 the territorial constitution was amended to provide for an Administrator's Executive Council, a majority of whose members were drawn from the elected members of the House of Assembly. Beginning in 1970 Papua New Guinea increasingly assumed control over its own internal affairs through the chief minister of the council, a process that was enhanced in December 1973 by redesignation of the Australian administrator as high commissioner. In March 1975 the territory acquired responsibility for its own defense, becoming independent six months later, with former chief minister Michael T. SOMARE assuming the office of prime minister. Somare was immediately confronted with a threat to national unity by secessionists on the island of Bougainville, who declared unilateral independence for the "Republic of the North Solomons," claiming that the central government had been extracting too much revenue from the copper industry. However, following an agreement in August 1976 that provided for substantial regional autonomy, secession leaders formally accepted provincial status for the island.

After the nation's first postindependence election for the National Parliament, held June 18–July 9, 1977, Somare's Papua and Niugini Union Pati (Pangu), the People's Progress Party (PPP), and a number of independents formed a coalition government, and Somare was reconfirmed as prime minister on August 9. In November 1978 the PPP went into opposition and was replaced in the ruling coalition by the United Party (UP). The Somare government collapsed in the face of a no-confidence vote on March 11, 1980, a new majority coalition being constituted two days later by Sir Julius CHAN of the PPP. Somare returned as

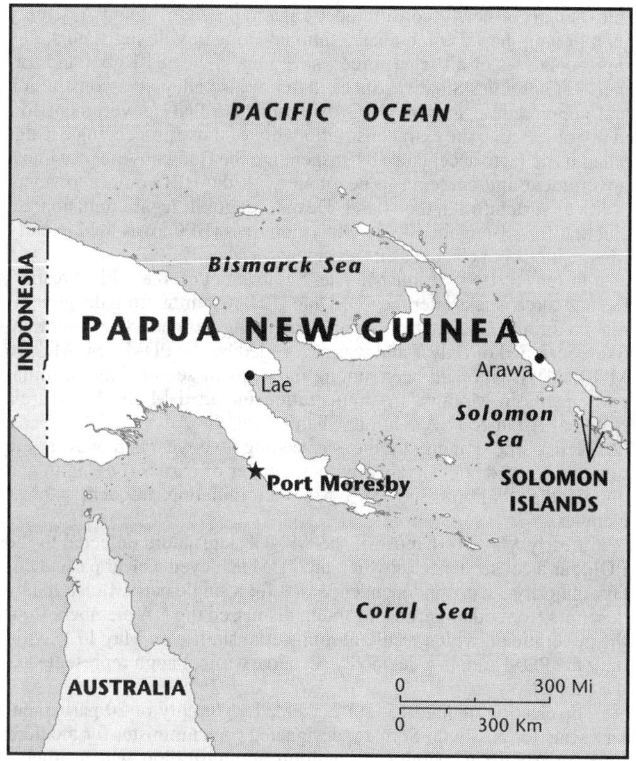

prime minister on August 2, 1982, after intense political maneuvering that followed balloting for a new parliament on June 5–26.

Somare survived a no-confidence vote on March 25, 1984, after Deputy Prime Minister Paias WINGTI and a number of his followers had withdrawn from the government; he was, however, obliged to form a new coalition on April 1 that included Pangu, the Melanesian Alliance (MA), and the National Party (NP), although the last soon returned to opposition in a dispute over the distribution of ministries. Somare survived two more no-confidence motions before succumbing to a 1986 budget vote on November 21, 1985. Opposition leader Wingti was thereupon invested as head of a coalition that included his recently organized People's Democratic Movement (PDM), the Nationalist *Papua Besena,* the NP, the PPP, and elements of UP. Contrary to expectations, Wingti retained office as the leader of a modified six-party coalition in the wake of parliamentary balloting on June 13–July 4, 1987, securing the support of a bare majority of 54 assemblymen (3 seats of 109 being vacant) at commencement of the legislative term on August 5.

On April 11, 1988, a vote on a no-confidence motion against the Wingti administration was averted by suspending legislative proceedings until June 27. Following an abortive effort to mount a "grand coalition" involving the PDM and Pangu, the Wingti administration was defeated on July 4. Four days later, Rabbie NAMALIU, who had succeeded Somare as Pangu leader, announced the formation of a six-party government that included Somare as foreign minister.

In May 1989 the Bougainville copper facility suspended operations because of mounting sabotage by local landowners who had long sought compensation for losses attributed to mining operations. By midyear the violence had escalated to a revival of full-scale secessionist activity by the Bougainville Revolutionary Army (BRA) under the leadership of a former land surveyor, Francis ONA. At the end of the year, the government yielded to rebel demands that the mine be closed, and in March 1990 it concluded a cease-fire agreement with the rebels that included the withdrawal of police and army units. Formal peace talks, which were to have been initiated on April 12, stalled over rebel demands that they be held on Bougainville, and in early May Port Moresby instituted an air and naval blockade of the island. On May 17 Ona declared Bougainville's independence, proclaiming himself president of what was styled Me'ekamui. Port Moresby responded by rejecting the declaration and tightening its blockade.

The deadlock over a venue for peace talks was eventually broken by New Zealand's offer of the use of two naval vessels, and negotiations were launched in late July 1990 between Somare and the former provincial premier of Bougainville, Joseph KABUI. On August 7 the parties signed the "Endeavor Accord" (after the vessel on which the parties met), which provided for lifting the blockade and restoring communications and other essential services; in addition, the government agreed that security forces would not return, pending a resumption of talks on September 24. However, another impasse ensued because of the occupation by the Papua New Guinea Defense Forces (PNGDF) of the small island of Buka off Bougainville's northern coast.

On January 24, 1991, a second accord, the Declaration on Peace, Reconciliation and Rehabilitation in Bougainville, was signed by Somare and Kabui in Honiara, Solomon Islands. The new agreement provided that PNG security forces would not return to the island and that BRA would surrender its arms to a multinational peace observation team. However, the pact stimulated at least as many questions as it resolved. One such issue was whether the surrender of weapons meant their "destruction." It was also unclear as to whether Ona and BRA commander Sam KAUONA had endorsed the settlement, while Kabui insisted that in approving the declaration the central government had accepted the temporary authority of the government established by the secessionists, known as the Bougainville Interim Government (BIG).

In late March 1991, after his government had called unsuccessfully for a third round of talks, Foreign Minister Somare presented the PNG cabinet with a proposal to purchase a 53.6 percent interest in the Bougainville mine from its Australian owners, the shares to be held by a new entity in which a Chicago investor would hold a 51 percent interest; the Bougainville landowners, 30 percent; and the PNG government, 19 percent. Shortly thereafter, in manifest violation of the January declaration, a PNGDF contingent landed in northern Bougainville and succeeded in bringing the region under its control. Ona and Kauona reacted by indicating their support for a multinational supervisory force, which Port Moresby now appeared to oppose. A third round of negotiations was eventually scheduled to begin on October 8 but was postponed because of disagreement as to a venue, and sporadic clashes between government and BRA units subsequently ensued. In November Prime Minister Namaliu announced that a multinational force would arrive sometime in 1992, following the establishment of six new government authorities on the island, while secessionist leader Kabui declared in December that BRA would surrender its arms if Australia and New Zealand, in addition to providing peacekeeping troops, would abide by the results of an impartially conducted referendum on the island's future.

Meanwhile, on September 27, 1991, the recently appointed governor general, Sir Vincent Serei ERI, rejected the results of a four-year inquiry that had found Deputy Prime Minister Ted DIRO guilty on 81 counts of corruption and misconduct. The unprecedented action prompted an appeal to London for Eri's ouster, as a result of which both Diro and the governor general tendered their resignations on October 1.

In legislative balloting that concluded on June 27, 1992, a record 59 (of 109) sitting parliamentarians lost their seats, including more than half of Namaliu's 28-member cabinet. At the vote for selection of a prime minister on July 17, the parliament for the first time tied 54–54, with Paias Wingti being returned to office by the tie-breaking vote of the speaker, who had himself been named by a 55–54 vote.

In what appeared to be a remarkable "political coup" made possible by a 1991 constitutional prohibition of a no-confidence vote during a government's first 18 months in office, Prime Minister Wingti tendered a surprise resignation on September 23, 1993, and accepted reappointment the following day. It seemed likely that Wingti would thereby remain in office until the general election due in mid-1997, since the constitution also prohibited a no-confidence vote during the 12 months preceding an election. However, the Supreme Court ruled in August 1994 that Wingti had failed to give a required 24-hour advance notice before calling for a new election by parliament. His status thus being construed as that of a caretaker, the court ordered a new election, which the government lost 69–32 on August 30 because of the defection of its PPP coalition partner. The latter thereupon forged a new coalition with Pangu, permitting Sir Julius Chan to return as head of a new administration installed on August 31.

On September 8, 1994, Prime Minister Chan and BRA commander Kauona concluded a new cease-fire in the Solomon Islands capital of Honiara. The agreement provided for deployment of a peacekeeping force of troops from Fiji, Tonga, and Vanuatu coincident with the launching of formal peace talks on October 10. However, the BRA representatives failed to appear for the talks on the grounds that insufficient guarantees had been given for their safety, and on October 16 the government formally abandoned the effort.

In early 1995 the parliament approved the formation of a Bougainville Transitional Government (BTG) with Theodore MIRIUNG, a former legal adviser to the secessionists, as premier. Under the terms of a subsequent peace agreement (the Waigani Communiqué), signed by Chan and Miriung on May 18, leaders of both the BTG and BRA were granted unconditional amnesties for any crimes committed against the state; however, the top three BRA figures repudiated the accord and refused to take up seats reserved for them in the 32-member provincial legislature. As a result, sporadic violence continued on the island, and on November 10 Prime Minister Chan halted government participation in talks aimed at ending the seven-year conflict. On the other hand, discussions that one observer termed "pre-peace-negotiation talks" involving BRA and BTG representatives were launched in the Australian coastal city of Cairns in mid-December. At the conclusion of the talks agreement was reached on a plan to end the lengthy rebellion, with formal peace negotiations to begin in March 1996. However, skirmishes resumed in February following the burning of the Honiara home of rebel spokesperson Martin MIRIORI, and in late March the 18-month cease-fire formally ended with a resumption of government military activity. In late June Prime Minister Chan ordered a second "Operation High Speed" designed to destroy the BRA stronghold in the vicinity of the mining complex, but the offensive was abandoned in mid-July. The situation deteriorated even further when a group of PNGDF soldiers were "massacred" under confusing circumstances in September and Miriung was assassinated on October 12. Bougainville's provincial legislature selected Gerard SINATO to succeed Miriung, the new premier pledging to continue his predecessor's efforts to facilitate a negotiated settlement to the conflict.

In late February 1997 Prime Minister Chan acknowledged that his government had contracted with Sandline International, a private British military group, to supply mercenaries against the Bougainville rebels. Brig. Gen. Jerry SINGEROK, commander of the PNGDF, reacted on March 17 by calling on Chan to resign. Although the prime minister survived a no-confidence vote on March 25, he felt obliged to step down two days later in favor of a caretaker government headed by John GIHENO, theretofore mining and petroleum minister. On April 1 a commission of inquiry was convened to look into the Sandline matter, and on June 2, upon issuance of a commission report that found "no credible evidence" of wrongdoing, Chan announced that he was resuming his post as prime minister. However, a major electoral reversal on June 14–28 included the loss of his own parliamentary seat, and on July 22 Port Moresby Mayor William (Bill) SKATE was chosen as his successor. In late November 1997 Skate himself came under intense pressure to resign because of the broadcast on Australian television of tapes allegedly showing him engaging in bribery and boasting of being the "godfather" of a Port Moresby criminal gang.

On December 2, 1997, Skate dismissed his deputy minister, Chris HAIVETA of Pangu, and Agricultural Minister Andrew BAING of the PPP, accusing them of promoting a smear campaign against him. A group of Pangu cabinet ministers immediately resigned in protest; however, the threat to the government receded when a PPP caucus voted to replace Baing as party leader with Trade and Tourist Minister Michael NALI and stay in the cabinet. Consequently, on December 15 Skate significantly reshuffled his cabinet, naming Nali as deputy prime minister, enlisting members of the newly organized United Resources Party (URP), and leaving Pangu out of the government altogether.

Meanwhile, ongoing peace negotiations with the Bougainville rebels (which had yielded a truce on October 10, 1997) achieved a peace treaty on January 23, 1998. The accord provided for the truce to become a permanent cease-fire as of April 30, 1998, as well as for phased withdrawal of the PNGDF and establishment of a regional monitoring group to oversee the settlement.

The 1998 accord envisaged the election of a Bougainville Reconciliation Government (BRG) by the end of the year, when the BTG's mandate was set to expire. However, talks proceeded slowly, and in October agreement was reached between Bougainville leaders and the national government for an interim BRG to be appointed on January 1, 1999, with elections to follow by midyear. Although the PNG opposition parties initially appeared to support the plan, most of their legislators abstained from parliamentary balloting in early December on the enabling legislation, which consequently failed to gain approval. Nevertheless, the Bougainville leaders proceeded on their own. In mid-January a newly constituted Bougainville Constituent Assembly (comprising the BTG members, national Bougainville legislators, and representatives of all rebel forces, save Ona's) elected Kabui and former BTG premier Sinato as its cochairs. It also adopted a constitution and appointed an interim BRG. Although the PNG government formally objected to the extraconstitutionality of those proceedings, it signaled its de facto acceptance by suspending the Bougainville provincial government and agreeing to negotiate with the BRG on a permanent political structure for the island. Despite ongoing legal confusion, an election for a Bougainville People's Congress (BPC) was held in early May, with Kabui elected as its president on May 27.

On June 3, 1999, Prime Minister Skate announced a cabinet reshuffle, and three weeks later the PDM and URP withdrew from the governing coalition. Confronted by an impending no-confidence motion, Skate resigned on July 7 and was succeeded by the PDM's Sir Mekere MORAUTA, who had been among those dismissed on June 3. Initial participants in Morauta's administration included Michael Somare's National Alliance (NA), Julius Chan's PPP, the Advance PNG Party (APNGP), and Pangu. In the succeeding two years, however, the line-up changed considerably, with a number of parties moving in and out of the coalition and with Morauta initiating frequent cabinet changes.

In early May 2001 most of the APNGP legislators defected to the PDM, as a consequence of which the PDM achieved a clear parliamentary majority—a postindependence first for a single party. Bolstered by deserters from other parties, Morauta dismissed the NA members from the government, with a resultant ministerial shuffle on May 17 leaving only the PDM and, in a decidedly secondary role, Pangu represented in the cabinet.

The election of June 15, 2002, yielded a plurality of 20 parliamentary seats for NA, with Somare, designated prime minister for the third time on August 6, naming a coalition administration which, after a reshuffle on August 2, 2003, encompassed NA, Melanesian Alliance Party (MAP), Pangu, People's Action Party (PAP), People's Labour Party (PLP), People's National Congress (PNC), Papua New Guinea National Party (PNGNP), PPP, UP, and URP. On May 18, 2004, the PNC members were dismissed and replaced by members of former prime minister Morauta's recently formed PNG Party (PNGP). Further changes were made in June, July, and December 2004 and in January 2005.

Meanwhile, negotiations with the BPC's Kabui had continued, leading on January 26, 2001, to acceptance of a proposal offering Bougainville greater autonomy and, for the first time, the option of independence at a referendum to be held in 10–15 years. In May 2001 the BRA and the Bougainville Resistance Force agreed to begin surrendering their arms, while autonomy talks opened later in the month. An agreement to create an autonomous Bougainville police force and restrict the PNGDF to a limited role in the province was signed on August 30 in Arawa, Bougainville, and accepted by the UN Security Council on December 20. The Bougainville interim provincial government established a Bougainville Constituent Assembly, which approved a draft constitution for the province and formally handed over power to Gov. John MOMIS on January 14, 2005. In May–June 2005 Bougainville conducted a peaceful election that brought Kabui to the presidency of the autonomous province, backed by his Bougainville People's Congress Party (BPCP) with a majority of legislative seats.

Despite his party's winning only 27 seats in the election of June–July 2007, PNG Prime Minister Somare retained leadership by forming an NA-led coalition government that also included Pangu, PDM, URP, UP, Melanesian Labour Party (MLP), MAP, PNC and two independents.

Constitution and government. Under the 1975 constitution, which can be amended by a two-thirds legislative majority, executive functions are performed by a National Executive Council that includes a governor general, nominated by the council itself to represent the Crown for a six-year term; a prime minister, appointed by the governor general on advice of the legislature; and other ministers who are designated on advice of the prime minister and must total no fewer than six and no more than one-quarter the number of legislators. The unicameral National Parliament normally sits for a five-year term, dissolution not being mandated in the wake of a no-confidence vote (which can be called by 10 percent of the members) if an alternative prime minister (previously designated by the leader of the opposition) succeeds in securing a majority. The judicial system encompasses a Supreme Court that acts as the final court of appeal, a National Court, and lesser courts (currently including district, local, warden, and children's courts) as established by the legislature.

In 1977 provision was made for replacement of the country's 20 "Australian-style" districts by 19 provinces, each with the right to an elected assembly and an executive headed by a premier, plus a National Capital District, for which a structure of partially elective government was approved in 1990. Decentralization was abandoned under a 1995 constitutional amendment that also provided for a regional assembly member from each province to become governor. Under the 2001 peace agreement, Bougainville has special status as an autonomous region. In July 2009 the National Parliament approved the upgrading of two regions, Hela and Jiwaka, to the status of provinces, bringing the total number to 21, with full provincial authority to be established by 2012. At the subprovincial level there are approximately 145 local government councils and community governments.

Foreign relations. Two issues influenced PNG foreign affairs following independence: sensitive relations with Indonesia stemming from the status of Irian Jaya (formerly West New Guinea, Papua) and a dispute with Australia regarding demarcation of a maritime boundary through the Torres Strait. Though the PNG government officially supported Jakarta's jurisdiction in Irian Jaya, advocates of a "free Papua" called on the United Nations to review the 1969 plebiscite that served as the basis of Indonesia's annexation of the mineral-rich territory. More than 10,000 refugees have entered Papua New Guinea from Irian Jaya since 1983, alleging persecution by Indonesian authorities. Attempts at even small-scale repatriation, most recently in May 2009 affecting 708 illegal migrants, have proved unsuccessful, while Jakarta has denounced the maintenance of two large border refugee camps by Port Moresby, citing the settlements as sources of aid for rebels of the Free Papua Movement, now part of a recently organized umbrella organization, the West Papua National Coalition for Liberation. On the other hand, a Status of Forces Agreement between the two countries was concluded in January 1992 to facilitate cooperation on security matters, but it stopped short of joint military operations against the insurgents. The PNG government in late 2002 ordered the refugee camps to be emptied and any separatists found therein to be arrested. In May 2008 PNG blocked a move in the Melanesian Spearhead Group to grant observer status to West Papua separatists, and in March 2009 it announced creation of a civilian Border Development Authority with a budget of $28 million to bring order to the border region. Nevertheless, armed clashes in Papua and Indonesian border incursions in pursuit of rebels, most recently by a platoon of troops in July 2008 and a police officer in June 2009, continue to disturb PNG-Indonesia relations and retard tourism and economic activity.

With regard to the Torres Strait, the PNG government attempted to negotiate a boundary equidistant between its shore and that of Australia shortly after independence. This boundary was unacceptable to Canberra because it would separate the Torres Strait islands, whose interests had been vigorously championed by the government of the state of Queensland. Thus, in June 1978 the two national governments agreed on a complex formula involving (1) a seabed line running south of a number of islands and reefs that would remain Australian enclaves, and (2) a protected zone embracing much of the waters between the two countries and to which each would have access, and ratified a treaty to that effect in February 1985. However, pressure mounted in the 1990s to renegotiate the accord on the grounds that it served to deny some islanders access to traditional fishing grounds. In 2008 the governments of Australia and Papua New Guinea agreed to extend a moratorium on drilling in the strait to protect its ecosystem.

After independence PNG conducted an uneasy relationship with the governments of both the People's Republic of China (PRC) and the Republic of China on Taiwan, initially granting formal diplomatic recognition to the PRC but also hosting a trade office sponsored by the Taiwanese. On May 22, 1995, PNG's deputy prime minister and Taiwan's foreign minister unexpectedly signed a joint "communiqué of mutual recognition." Following a strong protest by Beijing, the PNG signatory, Chris HAIVETA, clarified that the agreement represented government-to-government, rather than state-to-state, recognition, and that Beijing remained PNG's principal diplomatic partner. But four years later, on July 5, 1999, Prime Minister Skate announced PNG's formal recognition of the Republic of China on Taiwan. Beijing reacted with a threat of "serious consequences" and on July 21 Skate's successor, Sir Mekere Morauta, nullified the recognition, after which a $2 billion loan package was reportedly secured from the PRC. Prime Minister Somare paid a state visit to Beijing in April 2009 and military chief Commodore Peter HAU in June reaffirmed PNG's commitment to its military exchange program with China, which has emerged as PNG's third most valuable trading partner and a growing source of investment and aid. PNG signed a memorandum of understanding on trade, investment, and agricultural exchange with Guangdone Province in mid-2008 and Beijing approved Papua New Guinea as a "Chinese industrial zone," reflecting China's status as a significant investor in mining ventures. China's rising purchases of PNG hardwoods became controversial following revelations by international environmentalists of rapid and often illegal deforestation allegedly conducted by unscrupulous Chinese and Malaysian entrepreneurs with the connivance of corrupt PNG officials. The outcry prompted the Australian government in August 2008 to pledge more than $2 million to slow PNG's deforestation.

Relations with the neighboring Solomon Islands became tense upon the outbreak of the uprising on Bougainville in 1989 because the rebellious province is closer to the Solomons than to the PNG mainland and its people are ethnically akin to Solomon Islanders. In late 1991 Honiara's provincial affairs minister called for Bougainville's independence or its merger with the Solomons, and Solomon Islanders were reported to be smuggling supplies to the beleaguered Bougainvilleans in defiance of the PNG blockade. The peace agreement with the Bougainville leaders eased tensions between Port Moresby and Honiara, and in July 2003 the Solomon Islands National Parliament approved the participation of PNG personnel in a Pacific Islands Forum (PIF) intervention force to restore law and order in the Solomons in the wake of interisland violence. In February 2009 reports surfaced of increased illegal crossings and drug smuggling from Bougainville to the Solomon Islands' Western Province. In May 2009 PNG joined with the Solomon Islands and Federated States of Micronesia to submit to the United Nations a joint claim to the Ontong Java continental shelf, which would extend their economic zones into a pocket currently regarded as international waters.

Papua New Guinea is an active participant in a number of regional organizations. As a member of PIF, it has actively championed self-determination for French Overseas Territories, particularly New Caledonia, and in 1985 joined with Vanuatu and the Solomon Islands in a so-called "Spearhead" group within the forum to coordinate policy on regional issues with a view to possible formation of a united Melanesian state. In July 2009 PNG and other Spearhead members publicly supported Vanuatu's claim to Matthew and Hunter islands, two rocky outcrops north of New Caledonia claimed also by France.

While maintaining its status as a leading member of the Pacific Island Forum, PNG also participates in Association of Southeast Asian Nations (ASEAN) meetings as an observer, and in December 1987 was permitted to accede to ASEAN's 1976 Treaty of Amity and Cooperation. Prime Minister Somare in March 2009 sought the support of Philippines president Gloria Macapagal Arroyo for full ASEAN membership for PNG.

Relations with the United States have been continuous since independence in 1975. A dispute over tuna fishing rights was settled by negotiation in 1987 of the U.S.–Pacific Islands Multilateral Fisheries Treaty. While bilateral trade volume is small, U.S. aid is substantial, directed to education, health (particularly to combat HIV/AIDS), rural development, rehabilitation of Bougainville, and disaster relief, and the training of civil servants, police, and PNGDF personnel. U.S. based energy and mineral consortia have made major investments.

Australia continues to be a crucial partner, not only as PNG's principal trading partner but also as the largest source of aid and technical assistance. Relations are conducted within the framework of the Joint Declaration of Principles of 1987 (revised in 1992). Trade is guided by the Papua New Guinea-Australia Trade and Commercial Relations Agreement (PATCRA II), investment by the Agreement for the Promotion and Protection of Investment (APPI), and aid by the Joint Agreement on Enhanced Cooperation (July 2004). Other instruments include the Agreed Statement on Security Cooperation and the Torres Strait Treaty. Prime ministers and ministers meet regularly in the Australia-Papua New Guinea Ministerial Forum. Australian-listed investors include Oil Search Ltd, Lihir Gold Ltd (major shareholder Rio Tinto), Highlands Pacific Ltd., Coca Cola Amatil, Campbell Australia Ltd., and Nestle Australia.

From independence PNG has maintained diplomatic, trade, and aid relations with leading European governments, particularly the United Kingdom and Germany. In December 2007 it entered into an interim Economic Partnership Agreement (EPA) with the European Union, expanding on PNG participation in the prior Lomé and Cotonou agreements between the EU and more than 75 African, Caribbean, and Pacific (ACP) countries. In part, the EPA grants PNG fish exports continued preferential access to the European market and will facilitate EU aid projects. The EPA was finalized on July 30, 2009.

Current issues. The prime minister's surprise adjournment of Parliament on July 29, 2009, precipitated the desertion from the governing coalition of 14 MPs amidst accusations of bribery, threats, and dictatorship by the Somare government. This brought the number in opposition to 35 out of 107 MPs. The 56 MPs who voted for the adjournment against strong objections by the opposition parties, unions, and women's groups, were reported to have been rewarded with 2 million kina ($763,359) each to distribute through their District Support Improvement Programs (DSIP).

Ongoing corruption accusations by Transparency International and the opposition leaders were reinforced by a public "Walk Against Corruption," on June 7 inducing the prime minister to extend a Finance Commission of Inquiry that in April–July 2009 investigated fraudulent payments by the Treasury Department amounting to up to $1.3 billion between 2000 and 2006. At the same time, a rise in mayhem induced PNG's professional associations jointly to call for assistance from Australia and neighboring Pacific governments to restore law and order. Incidents have included 50 sorcery-linked murders in the highlands, police discovery in Port Moresby of counterfeit money and drugs worth $250 million, and allegations of immigration fraud, people smuggling, and human trafficking.

Recent ethnic attacks and evidence of gender discrimination have attracted international attention as well. Rioting broke out in Lae in May 2009, directed against Chinese shops and Chinese nickel miners for alleged unfair prices and discrimination in favor of Chinese workers in violation of PNG employment law. Five miners were seriously injured by mobs and the police shot six looters dead. A previous attack on Chinese took place in August 2008 at the Ramu Nico nickel mine, and another occurred in July 2009 at Popondetta, an oil palm growing center. As the Chinese embassy expressed "grave concern" about the safety of Chinese nationals and businesses, the PNG Parliament set up a bipartisan committee of inquiry into the incident and ongoing ethnic tensions. In October the chief of the General Staff of China General Chen Bingde conferred with his PNG counterpart and on November 4 Vice Premier Li Keqiang visited Port Moresby to expedite the Ramu Nico venture and other joint mineral investment projects and secure reaffirmation of PNG's "one China policy."

Earlier, following an Australian aid agency ranking of PNG at 124th out of 136 countries on the welfare and status of women, Prime Minister Somare had proposed appointing three women to Parliament to join the sole elected female MP, but in March 2009 he failed to gain a majority vote for the reform, opposition leader Morauta objecting that affirmative action had no legal grounding.

PNG's central government budget for 2009, announced in November 2008, forecast expenditures of 6.70 billion kina (US$ 2.62 billion), down from the 2008 budget due to slumping international prices of gold, copper, and gas. Although funds for rural development rose, funds to fight AIDS, of which PNG has the highest incidence in the Pacific region, declined by a quarter.

In Bougainville, effective opposition to the settlement appeared to have ceased with the death of Francis Ona in mid-2005. In the second election for the Bougainville legislature, held June 30–July 14, 2007, 77 of the 109 parliamentary seats contested saw incumbents turned out by challengers, and the rival National Alliance Party won a plurality with 27 seats. President Kabui died on June 7, 2008, and was succeeded pro tem by his vice president, John TABINAMAN. In December James TANIS was elected as the new president, taking office on January 6, 2009, to serve until provincial elections scheduled for 2010. However, Bougainville continues to pose issues for the government in Port Moresby. In October 2005 national leaders criticized a provincial legislature vote to reopen the Panguna copper mine, and in 2008 they found Bougainville's discussions with a Canadian mining company, Invincible Resources, to be premature inasmuch as the province's rights to mineral royalties and its powers to undertake international negotiations were still not legally settled by the central government.

POLITICAL PARTIES

Since independence, party loyalties have been extremely fluid, largely because the major groupings differ more over tactics than ideology. The pattern continued into 2004 with Prime Minister Somare appointing three ministers from the theretofore opposition PNG Party, led by former Prime Minister Morauta. There were 43 registered parties eligible for the June 2002 balloting. The number increased to 45 for the June–July 2007 poll, with 19 securing legislative representation.

Government Parties:

National Alliance (NA). NA was launched as an anticorruption group prior to the 1997 election by Prime Minster Somare. In December 1999 Somare formed a People's National Alliance (PNA) that also included the Bougainville-based Melanesian Alliance Party (MAP) of Fr. John Momis; the Movement for Greater Autonomy (MGA), which had been launched in May 1995 by Stephen POKAWIN and other northern premiers who opposed abolishing the provincial government system; and the People's Action Party (PAP, below), led by Ted Diro. MAP had been formed in 1978 after Momis, a former secessionist leader, was removed as minister for decentralization by Somare. In the ensuing two decades Momis moved in and out of government positions, as did another former MAP leader, Sir John KAPUTIN.

Somare entered the July 1999 Morauta cabinet as foreign minister, subsequently serving as minister for mines and Bougainville affairs before being dismissed in December 2000. The remaining NA ministers were ousted in May 2001, Morauta having accused Somare of untoward political maneuvering. Somare returned as prime minister following the election of August 2004 and continued as head of a nine-party coalition administration following the election of June–July 2007. The NA took 14 of the 25 ministerial portfolios, and one or two cabinet posts were awarded to the other eight parties and two independents, Charles ABEL and Patrick TAMMUR. Somare continues to be plagued by allegations of tax fraud and criticized for allowing corruption and immigration fraud in his government to persist.

Leader: Sir Michael Thomas SOMARE (Prime Minister).

People's Democratic Movement (PDM). The PDM was organized by former Deputy Prime Minister Paias Wingti, who broke with Pangu in March 1985. The Wingti grouping gained ground during the ensuing months by focusing on alleged government corruption and budgetary issues, with conflict over the latter leading to the formation of a PDM-led government in November. Wingti remained in office following the 1987 election but was defeated in a no-confidence vote on July 4, 1988.

In a close assembly vote, Wingti returned on July 17, 1992, as head of a coalition government that included the PPP. However, the PPP withdrew in August 1994 after the Supreme Court's invalidation of Wingti's July 1993 reappointment, forcing the defeat of the latter's chosen successor, outgoing parliamentary speaker and PNCP leader Bill Skate, on August 30. Following Skate's second ouster in July 1999, Sir Mekere Morauta was elected by the parliament to head a multiparty coalition government whose composition changed frequently over the next two years. In May 2000 most of the **Advance PNG Party** (APNGP) was absorbed by the PDM, which thereupon claimed a majority in the national legislature. After the 2007 election, the PDM joined the National Alliance coalition government. Party leader Michael OGIO was rewarded with the ministry of higher education, research, science and technology. On July 29, 2008, PDM MP John BOITO moved to the opposition benches in protest over the adjournment of parliament for four months.

Leader: Michael OGIO.

Papua and Niugini Union Pati (Pangu). The urban-based Pangu was organized in 1967 and long advocated the early achievement of independence. It was the senior component of the former National Coalition and secured the largest number of legislative seats in the 1977 election. It moved into opposition following parliamentary defeat of the Somare government in March 1980 but returned to power after the election of June 1982 and the redesignation of Somare as prime minister on August 2. Pangu was greatly weakened by the defection of Deputy Prime Minister Paias Wingti in April 1985, and Somare was ousted from power in a no-confidence vote the following November. However, the party retained a significant parliamentary bloc and secured a reduced plurality of 26 assembly seats in the election of November 1987.

Pangu suffered the worst defeat of the 1992 balloting, losing half of its 30 sitting members while picking up only 4 new seats. Following the election party leader Sir Rabbie NAMALIU announced his retirement from politics and on August 3 was succeeded as leader of the opposition by Somare, who stated that he would also step down in March 1993. Implementing the decision seven months later, Somare resigned from the party to sit as a backbench independent. His successor as leader of the opposition, Jack GENIA, died in July 1993 and was in turn succeeded by Chris Haiveta.

Following the Supreme Court's action of August 1994, Namaliu emerged from retirement to accept appointment as parliament speaker, while Pangu and the PPP revived their old partnership to form an administration led by the PPP's Sir Julius Chan, Somare indicating that he wished to continue as a backbencher. The party continued its governmental representation as part of the Skate administration until the turmoil of late 1997. It joined the Morauta government in September 1999 and continued as part of the Somare administration after the 2002 and 2007 elections. Leader Andrew Kumbakor was awarded the housing and urban development portfolio after the 2007 election.

Leaders: Andrew KUMBAKOR, Philemon EMBEL.

People's Action Party (PAP). PAP was formed on December 4, 1986, by then forestry minister Ted Diro, a staunch Wingti supporter, who was named foreign minister eight days later but denied reappointment in August 1987 following allegations of corruption in his previous post. Diro's return to the cabinet as minister without portfolio in April 1988 contributed to Wingti's defeat on July 4, while the previously independent Akoka DOI was widely viewed as a stand-in for Diro in the Namaliu administration during the PAP founder's lengthy legal struggle. PAP's founding president, Vincent ERI, was named governor general in early 1990 but resigned following Diro's conviction in September 1991. Party leader Akoka Doi was among those failing reelection in 1992. Diro served in subsequent administrations, however, including Mekere Morauta's until being dismissed as agriculture minister in December 1999. The party was accorded five cabinet posts in the 2002 Somare government. In the 2007, the party won six seats and was awarded two ministerial posts, correctional services for Tony AIMO and fisheries and marine resources for Ben SEMRI.

Leader: Gabriel KAPRIS.

People's National Congress (PNC). Launched in early 1993 by a group of largely independent ministers of parliament, the original PNC merged in April 1998 with the Christian Century Party (CCP) and a number of smaller formations to form the **PNG First Party** (PNGFP) led by Prime Minister Skate. In June 1999 the PNGFP was divided in the interest of national stability, according to Skate. Twenty-two PNG First MPs remained with the restored PNC, and 11 moved to the revived National Party (PNGNP, below), while the rump PNGFP secured one parliamentary seat in 2002. Subsequently, the PNC's ranks thinned considerably, and by mid-2001 the party held only about half a dozen seats in parliament. It won three seats in 2002 and placed three ministers in the new Somare government, all of whom were ousted in May 2004.

For reasons that were not immediately clear, Skate was expelled from the party in early 2005; he died on January 3, 2006. Meanwhile, party (and opposition) leader Peter O'Neill was arrested in August 2005 on charges of misappropriating funds from an investment account. The PNC won four legislative seats in 2007 and joined the Somare government with one cabinet post, public service, going to party leader Peter O'Neill.

Leader: Peter O'NEILL.

United Party (UP). UP is a highlands-based party organized in 1969. It favored a cautious approach to self-government and was opposed to early independence. Formerly the main opposition grouping in the House of Assembly, it entered the government in coalition with Pangu in November 1978. Technically in opposition after formation of the Chan government in March 1980, many of its members subsequently crossed the aisle to join the Chan majority. The party suffered major losses in the balloting of June 1982, after which it rejoined forces with Pangu. It returned to opposition in April 1985. Some members supported the Wingti coalition the following November, yielding another split between government and opposition.

UP won only two legislative seats at the 1997 election but subsequently saw its delegation swell to more than a dozen. Prime Minister Morauta brought the UP into his coalition, but by May 2001 its ministers had been dismissed and defections had claimed most of its MPs. It won three seats in 2002, one of which was lost in 2007. It subsequently joined the government of Somare, and leader Bob Dadae was given the defense portfolio.

Leaders: Bire KIMASOPA, Bob DADAE.

United Resources Party (URP). Organized in early December 1997 by defectors from an assortment of government and opposition parties, URP set as its principal goal obtaining a greater voice for resource owners and resource-rich provinces. After its launching it participated in the Skate administration, its withdrawal from which in June 1999 helped to precipitate the government's collapse. In December 1999 the party leaders extended their support to the Morauta government. Peter IPATAS, governor of Enga Province, defected to the PDM in April 2001. In 2007, URP won five seats and became a ruling coalition member; William DUMA was given the petroleum and energy portfolio and Benny ALLAN was made minister of environment and conservation.

Leader: William DUMA.

Melanesian Liberal Party (MLP). The MLP was formed in early 2007 by Dr Allan MARAT and in the June-July 2007 election won two seats. Marat joined Somare's NA-led coalition government and was awarded the justice portfolio.

Leader: Dr. Alan MARAT

Melanesian Alliance Party (MAP). Led by Dame Carol KIDU, the MAP (not to be confused with the earlier Bougainville-based MAP of Fr. John Momis) appeals to the urban women's vote. In the 2007 election it returned a single MP, Dame Kidu, the only women in parliament, who joined Somare's coalition government as minister of community development, religion, and sports.

Leader: Dame Carol KIDU

Opposition Parties:

Papua New Guinea Party (PNGP). Sir Mekere Morauta was ousted as PDM leader after losing the 2002 election; reinstated by court order in early 2003, he subsequently withdrew to form the PNGP. Three of PNGP's members, though not Morauta himself, joined the Somare government in May 2004. The PNGP won eight seats in the 2007 election to become the second largest party in parliament. Morauta was elected in 2007 to head the opposition government.

Leader: Sir Mekere MORAUTA (Former Prime Minister)

People's Labour Party (PLP). Launched in 2001 by Peter YAMA, the PLP won five parliamentary seats in 2002 and held the housing portfolio in the Somare administration until January 2004. The party won only two seats in the 2007 election and joined the opposition coalition led by Sir Mekere Morauta (PNGP).

Leader: Koni IGUAN.

People's Progress Party (PPP). The PPP participated in the postindependence government until 1978, when it went into opposition. It became the core component of the government that succeeded the Somare administration in March 1980. It returned to opposition after Somare was reelected prime minister in August 1982. Sir Julius Chan was involved in a number of no-confidence motions against Somare before the latter's ouster in late 1985. The party was again in opposition from July 1988 to June 1992, becoming part of the Wingti government of July 17. In the wake of the Supreme Court's August 1994 invalidation of Wingti's 1993 reappointment, the PPP withdrew from a governing coalition with the PDM and revived its earlier alliance with Pangu; Sir Julius, after 12 years, returned as prime minister on August 30. He was obliged to step down following the election of June 1997, when he lost his parliamentary seat, although PPP members continued in the cabinet. The PPP withdrew from the Skate administration in October 1998, joined the Morauta government in July 1999, but then saw party leader Michael Nali dismissed as trade and industry minister in November 2000. In 2001 Sir Julius rejoined the party leadership in preparation for the 2002 general election. The party won 9 seats and joined the Somare administration. But in 2007, Chan ran for prime minister against Somare and lost. He subsequently joined the opposition.

Leader: Sir Julius CHAN (Former Prime Minister).

Other registered groups in 2007 included the **Christian Democratic Party** (CDP), launched in January 1992; the **Economic Endeavor Party** (EEP), organized in January 2002; the **Human Rights Protection Party** (HRPP), formed in October 2001; the **Liberal Party** (LP), formed in November 1991; **Melanesian Labour Party** (MLP), established in March 1997 by Dr. Paul MONDIA; the **Melanesian People's Party** (MPP), founded in December 2001 by John TEKWIE; the **National Advance Party** (NAP); the **National Front Party** (NFP), launched in January 2001; the **National Transformation Party** (NTP), dating from July 2001; the **National Vision for Humanity Party** (NVHP), established in August 2001; the **New Generation Party** (NGP); the **One People Party** (OPP), formed in January 2002; the **Pan Melanesian Congress Party** (PMCP), incorporated in November 2001; the **Papua New Guinea Country Party** (PNGCP), the revival by Sinake GIREGIRE in 2001 of an earlier Country Party that had been absorbed by PNG First in 1998; the **Papua New Guinea Greens Party** (PNGGP), launched in November 2001; the **Papua New Guinea Integrity Party** (PNGIP), formed in January 2002; the **Papua New Guinea Labour Party** (PNGLP), organized in January 2001 by John

PASKA of the Trade Unions Congress; the **Papua New Guinea National Party** (PNGNP), led by Joe Mek TEINE; the **Papua New Guinea Revival Party** (PNGRP), launched in January 2002; the **Party for Justice and Dignity** (PJD), launched by Peter LAFANAWA in October 2001; the **People's Destiny and Development Party** (PDDP), formed by Rore RIKIS in January 2002; the **People's Development Party,** dating from November 1991; the **People's First Conservative Party** (PFCP), formed in July 2002; the **People's Freedom Party** (PFRP), organized in July 2001; the **People's Heritage Party** (PHP), formed in October 2001; the **People's Resource Awareness Party** (PRAP), launched in May 1997; the **People's Solidarity Party** (PSP), dating from March 1992; the **People's Welfare Party** (PWP), established in August 2001; the **Pipol First Pati** (PFP), formed in July 2001; the **Rural Pipols' Pati** (RPP), formed by Peter Namus in January 2002; the **Simple People's Party** (SPP), organized in November 2001; the **True People's Party** (TPP), launched in February 2002; and the **Yumi Reform Party** (YRP), formed in January 2002.

Bougainville parties include the **Bougainville Independence Movement** (BIM), led by James TANIS, now president of autonomous Bougainville; the **Bougainville Labour Party** (BLP); the **Bougainville People's Congress Party** (BPCP), led by provincial president Joseph Kabui until his death in 2008; and the **New Bougainville Party** (NBP), led by former island governor John Momis.

LEGISLATURE

The unicameral **National Parliament** was called the House of Assembly (*Bese Taubadadia Hegogo*) before independence and is sometimes still referenced as such. It currently consists of 109 members (89 from open and 20 from provincial electorates) elected to five-year terms by universal adult suffrage. Traditionally, candidates were not obligated to declare party affiliation, and postelectoral realignments were common; however, controversial legislation passed in December 2000 required future candidates to declare their affiliations and then, if elected, to maintain them or face expulsion.

The following was the distribution of seats after the balloting of June 30–July 14, 2007: National Alliance Party, 27 seats; Papua New Guinea Party, 8; People's Action Party, 6; Papua and Niugini Union Pati, 5; People's Democratic Movement, 5; United Resources Party, 5; New Generation Party, 4; People's National Congress Party, 4; People's Progress Party, 4; Rural Pipols' Pati, 4; People's Party, 3; Melanesian Liberal Party, 2; Papua New Guinea Country Party, 2; People's Labour Party, 2; United Party, 2; Melanesian Alliance Party, 1; National Advance Party, 1; Papua New Guinea Labour Party, 1; Papua New Guinea National Party, 1; People's First Conservative Party, 1; Pipol First Party, 1; independents, 19; nullified, 1.

Speaker: Jeffrey NAPE.

CABINET

[as of August 1, 2009]

Prime Minister	Sir Michael Somare (NA)
Ministers	
Agriculture and Livestock	John Hickey (NA)
Bougainville Affairs	Sir Michael Somare (NA)
Commerce and Industry	Gabriel Kapris (PAP)
Community Development, Religion, and Sports	Dame Carol Kidu [f] (MAP)
Correctional Services	Tony Aimo (PAP)
Culture and Tourism	Charles Abel (ind.)
Defense	Bob Dadae (UP)
Education	Michael Laimo (NA)
Environment and Conservation	Benny Allan (URP)
Fisheries and Marine Resources	Ben Semri (PAP)
Foreign Affairs, Trade, and Immigration	Sam Abal (NA)
Forests	Belden Namah (NA)
Health and HIV/AIDS	Sasa Zibe (NA)
Higher Education, Research, Science, and Technology	Michael Ogio (PDM)
Housing and Urban Development	Andrew Kumbakor (Pangu)
Information and Communication	Patrick Tammur (ind.)
Internal Security	Sani Rambi (NA)
Justice	Allan Marat (MLP)
Labor and Industrial Relations	Mark Maipakai (NA)
Lands and Physical Planning and Mining	Puka Temu (NA)
National Planning and District Development	Paul Tiensten (NA)
Petroleum and Energy	William Duma (URP)
Public Enterprise	Arthur Somare (NA)
Public Service	Peter O'Neill (PNC)
Treasury and Finance	Patrick Pruaitch (NA)
Works, Transport, and Civil Aviation	Don Polye (NA)

[f] = female

COMMUNICATIONS

Press. Papua New Guinea's press is considered one of the freest in the Asian Pacific area, although the Ministry of Communications called in early 1990 for curbs on excessively negative reporting. The following are published in English unless otherwise noted: *Papua New Guinea Post-Courier* (Port Moresby, 34,000), daily; *Niugini Nius* (New Guinea News, Boroko, 31,000), daily in Tok Pisin; *The National* (Boroko, 20,000), daily; *Wantok* (One Talk, Boroko, 10,000), rural weekly in Tok Pisin; *The Independent* (Boroko), launched in 1995 as weekly replacement for *The Times of Papua New Guinea;* and *Arawa Bulletin* (Arawa, 4,600), North Solomons weekly.

News agency. There is no domestic facility; the Associated Press and Australian Associated Press are used for international news.

Broadcasting and computing. Radio broadcasting is provided by the National Broadcasting Corporation of Papua New Guinea, a public agency that the government announced in early 1997 would soon be commercialized, and from the Papua New Guinea Service of Radio Australia. Television service was initiated in February 1987 by the Niugini Television Network (NTN), following a successful legal challenge to a government decision to postpone local broadcasting as potentially detrimental to the nation's culture; in July a second channel, EM TV, went on air in Port Moresby, and in March 1988 NTN was shut down, reportedly for financial reasons.

As of 2008 there were 18.2 Internet users per 1,000 inhabitants.

INTERGOVERNMENTAL REPRESENTATION

Ambassador to the U.S.: Evan Jeremy PAKI.

U.S. Ambassador to Papua New Guinea: Teddy Bernard TAYLOR.

Permanent Representative to the UN: Robert Guba AISI.

IGO Memberships (Non-UN): ADB, APEC, CWTH, Interpol, NAM, PC, PIF, WCO, WTO.

PARAGUAY

Republic of Paraguay
República del Paraguay

Political Status: Independent since 1811; under presidential rule established in 1844; present constitution promulgated on June 20, 1992.

Area: 157,047 sq. mi. (406,752 sq. km.).

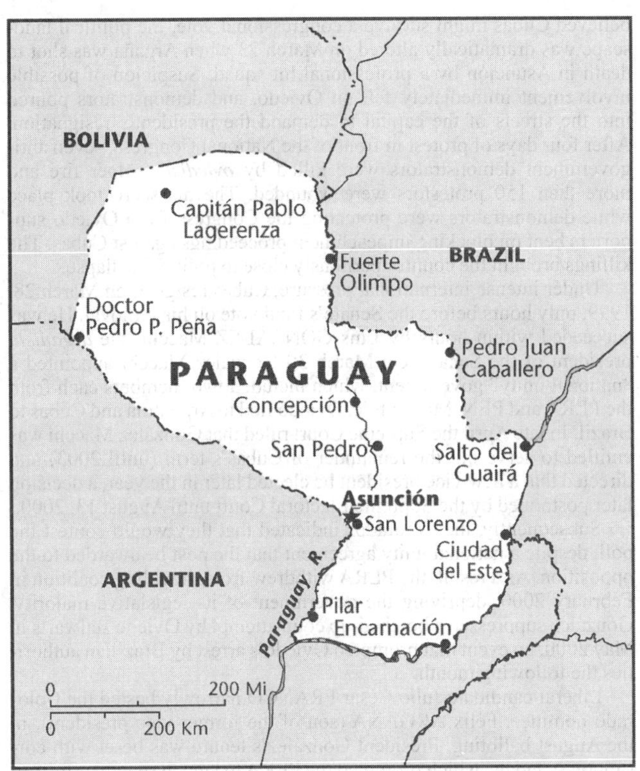

Population: 5,183,080 (2002C), excluding adjustment for underenumeration; 6,235,000 (2008E).

Major Urban Centers (2005E): ASUNCIÓN (517,000), Ciudad del Este (247,000), San Lorenzo (230,000).

Official Languages: Spanish, Guaraní.

Monetary Unit: Guaraní (market rate December 1, 2009: 4,775.00 guaraníes = $1US).

President: Fernando Armindo LUGO Méndez (Patriotic Alliance for Change); popularly elected on April 20, 2008, and sworn in on August 15 for a five-year term, succeeding Nicanor DUARTE Frutos (Colorado Party).

Vice President: Luis Federico FRANCO Gómez (Patriotic Alliance for Change/Authentic Radical Liberal Party); elected on April 20, 2008, and sworn in on August 15 for a term concurrent with that of the president. (The post had been vacant since Luis Alberto CASTIGLIONI Soria [Colorado Party] resigned on October 11, 2007, to participate in his party's upcoming presidential primary.)

THE COUNTRY

A landlocked, semitropical country wedged between Argentina, Bolivia, and Brazil, the Republic of Paraguay takes its name from the river that divides the fertile grasslands of the east ("Oriental") from the drier, less hospitable Chaco region of the west ("Occidental"). The population is 95 percent *mestizo*, mainly of Spanish and Indian origin, although successive waves of immigration have brought settlers from all parts of the globe, including Japan and Korea. Spanish is the official language; however, 90 percent of the population also speaks Guaraní, the language of most of the indigenous inhabitants. Roman Catholicism is the established religion, but other faiths are tolerated. Women constitute 39 percent of the labor force, concentrated primarily in the informal sector, manufacturing, and domestic service. Women have played a greater role in politics in recent years, but remain a minority in that sphere.

With 77 percent of the land owned by 1 percent of the population and without an adequate transportation network, Paraguayan development has long been impeded. Agriculture and cattle-raising constitute the basis of the economy; soybeans, beef, cotton, and vegetable oils are the main exports. Industry is largely confined to processing agricultural, animal, and timber products, but there is a small consumer-goods industry. The government is presently embarked on exploitation of the vast hydroelectric potential of the Paraná river. The Itaipú Dam, the world's second largest and jointly constructed with Brazil, was opened in November 1982. The Yacyretá Dam, the globe's twelfth biggest and developed together with Argentina, entered full operation in 1998. As a result, Paraguay is now one of the world's leading exporters of electricity.

The Paraguayan economy experienced significant growth between 1973 and 1981 during the construction of the Itaipú Dam. During the last years of the Alfredo Stroessner presidency, with the Itaipú construction completed and work on the even larger Yacyretá complex inhibited by fiscal adversity in Argentina, economic indicators fell off. Between 1983 and 1989 the purchasing power of the guaraní declined by nearly 50 percent, and inflation reached nearly 30 percent by the end of the period. By late 1990 the economy was responding positively to a "free-market" initiative by the Andrés Rodríguez administration, with real GDP growth increasing to a rate of 4.2 percent. Thereafter, however, growth was uneven, and unemployment in the latter half of the 1990s surged from 5 percent to double-digit levels. In the context of a major banking crisis, the rate of expansion fell to 1.3 percent in 1996. A gain of 0.5 percent in 1999 was followed by a steep decline of 4.4 percent in 2002, and an average improvement of 2.8 percent during 2003–2005. Real GDP grew by 4.3 percent in 2006 and expanded by 6.8 percent in 2007, primarily in response to the price increase of soybeans, Paraguay's main export commodity.

Paraguay is one of the world's most unequal societies in terms of income distribution. Inequities in the distribution of land, education, and wealth have fueled ongoing tensions and a climate of social mistrust. More than one-third of the Paraguayan labor force has either been unemployed or under-employed in the last decade. In 2007 one out of five Paraguayans lived in extreme poverty, while 36 percent of the population lived below the national poverty line. Health coverage in Paraguay remains one of the poorest in the Western Hemisphere. Though illiteracy has dropped to 5.4 percent of the adult population, functional illiteracy remains high. Among neighboring countries, only Bolivia's per capita GDP was below that of Paraguay's in 2007.

Paraguay's GDP rose by 5.8 percent in 2008 and unemployment was low at 5.4 percent, but was GDP expected to decline, and unemployment rise, in 2009 because of the global recession. In 2008 inflation was high at 10.2 percent. A 2008 stimulus package, combined with increased social spending, was expected to create a government deficit of around 1.5-2 percent of GDP, following a surplus equal to 2.6 percent of GDP the previous year. In September 2009 Paraguay announced that it would offer foreign bonds for the first time in its history in an effort to attract $200 million in foreign investment (foreign investment accounted for only 1.6 percent of GDP in 2008). Meanwhile, the World Bank approved $600 million in grants and loans to Paraguay to mitigate the impact of the economic downturn.

GOVERNMENT AND POLITICS

Political background. Paraguay gained independence from Spain in 1811 but was slow to assume the contours of a modern state. Its initial years of independence were marked by a succession of strong, authoritarian leaders, the most famous of whom was José Gaspar RODRIGUEZ de Francia. Known as "El Supremo," Rodriguez ruled Paraguay from 1814 until 1840, during which time he sought to isolate the country from the outside world by expelling foreigners and cutting off communications. In 1865–1870 Paraguay fought the combined forces of Argentina, Brazil, and Uruguay in the War of the Triple Alliance, which claimed the lives of approximately half of the country's population and the vast majority of its males. From 1880 to 1904 the country was ruled by a series of Colorado Party (*Partido Colorado*—PC) presidents, while the Liberals ruled for most of the period from 1904 to 1940. A three-year war against Bolivia over the Chaco territory ended in 1935, with Paraguay winning the greater part of the disputed region.

For more than half a century two men dominated the political scene: the dictatorial Gen. Higinio MORÍNIGO (1940–1947) and the equally authoritarian Gen. Alfredo STROESSNER, who came to power in 1954 through a military coup against President Federico CHÁVEZ. Initially elected to fill the balance of Chávez's unexpired term, Stroessner was subsequently reelected to successive five-year terms, the last on February 14, 1988. Stroessner was overthrown on February 3, 1989, in a coup led by Gen. Andrés RODRIGUEZ Pedotti, who was elected on May 1 to serve the balance of the existing presidential term. In simultaneous balloting, the Colorados retained their existing majorities in both houses of Congress.

At municipal balloting on May 26, 1991, the Colorados lost the race for the Asunción mayorship to the labor-backed Asunción for All (*Asunción para Todos*), while their traditional liberal opponents won in 43 other municipalities. The faction-ridden ruling party recovered to win 122 of 198 National Constituent Assembly seats on December 1. After six months of extensive debate, the assembly produced the draft of a new basic law, which became effective on its acceptance by the president on June 22, 1992.

Despite a heated challenge for the 1993 Colorado presidential nomination from Dr. Luis María ARGAÑA, Juan Carlos WASMOSY was named the party's standard-bearer at a convention in February, amid serious charges of fraud. The Colorado Party won the May 9 presidential election with overt military support and widespread use of state resources to finance its campaign. The party, however, fell short of winning a majority in either house of Congress.

In early 1995 a rift developed between President Wasmosy and the self-styled military "strongman," Gen. Lino César OVIEDO Silva. In April the general's supporters were unable to secure the election of a pro-Oviedo Supreme Court, and in mid-May Oviedo was induced to join Wasmosy in an agreement with the congressional opposition that provided for the "temporary suspension" of party memberships held by army and police personnel.

In late April 1996 General Oviedo was obliged to resign from the army for violating a constitutional ban on its members' involvement in politics. Prior to his departure, though, the general threatened to bring down the Wasmosy government. The coup attempt, however, was thwarted as a result of intense international pressure and divisions within the military. Oviedo's subsequent appointment to head the Ministry of Defense was canceled soon thereafter amid strong congressional and street opposition. The former general, as a civilian, went on to form his own Colorado Party faction (see Political Parties, below), and was spared court proceedings over charges of insurrection and insubordination by deploying various legal maneuvers.

On September 7, 1997, Oviedo outpaced Argaña and Wasmosy's candidate, Finance Minister Carlos Alberto FACETTI, to win the Colorado presidential primary, with nearly 37 percent of the vote, close to Argaña's 35 percent and well above Facetti's 22 percent. Oviedo's victory triggered fears within the political and military establishment, which prompted an alliance between Wasmosy and Argaña aimed at stopping the former general's presidential bid. Oviedo's victory was challenged in the courts following *argañista* complaints of fraud.

On October 3 Wasmosy ordered Oviedo's disciplinary arrest under military law for "insults" leveled against the president, including the charge that he was a "thief." Wasmosy's efforts to postpone the May 10, 1998, presidential elections were rebuffed at various times by the political opposition and leading foreign ambassadors, notably between December 1997 and March 1998.

On December 12 Oviedo turned himself in to serve the 30-day sentence ordered by the president. Although Oviedo on December 29 became the legally recognized Colorado standard-bearer, a special military tribunal ordered that his incarceration continue indefinitely, pending further investigation of the abortive 1996 coup.

On April 17, 1998, the Supreme Court upheld a second sentence of ten years imposed on Oviedo in March, and his registration as Colorado standard-bearer was nullified the next day. His vice-presidential running mate, Raúl CUBAS Grau, was subsequently named his successor and went on to defeat opposition candidate Domingo LAÍNO in presidential balloting on May 10.

Three days after taking power, Cubas ordered Oviedo's release on a legal technicality. The measure elicited great controversy. Under an alliance of *argañistas*, with the opposition PLRA and the National Encounter Party (PEN), the National Congress challenged Cubas's decision in the courts.

On December 2, 1998, the Supreme Court annulled Cubas's release of Oviedo and ordered that the former general be returned to jail. However, Cubas issued a statement two days later rejecting the court's decision. The court, again unsuccessfully, directed Cubas to order Oviedo back to jail in February 1999, and Congress held preliminary discussions on impeachment proceedings. Although some observers initially believed Cubas might survive a congressional vote, the political landscape was dramatically altered on March 23 when Argaña was shot to death in Asunción by a professional hit squad. Suspicion of possible involvement immediately fell on Oviedo, and demonstrators poured into the streets of the capital to demand the president's resignation. After four days of protest in front of the National Congress, seven antigovernment demonstrators were killed by *oviedista* sniper fire and more than 150 protestors were wounded. The massacre took place while demonstrators were protecting the Congress from Oviedo supporters bent on blocking impeachment proceedings against Cubas. The killings brought the country perilously close to political collapse.

Under intense international pressure, Cubas resigned on March 28, 1999, only hours before the Senate's final vote on his removal. He was succeeded within hours by Luis GONZÁLEZ Macchi, the *argañista* president of the Senate. On March 30 González Macchi appointed a "national unity" government, which included two members each from the PLRA and PEN. Meanwhile, Oviedo fled to Argentina and Cubas to Brazil. In late April the Supreme Court ruled that González Macchi was entitled to serve out the remainder of Cubas's term (until 2003) and directed that a new vice president be elected later in the year, a decision later postponed by the Supreme Electoral Court until August 13, 2000.

Subsequently, the Colorados indicated that they would contest the poll, despite a national unity agreement that the post be awarded to the opposition. As a result, the PLRA withdrew from the ruling coalition in February 2000, depriving the government of its legislative majority. González suppressed a botched-up coup attempt by Oviedo stalwarts in May 2000, an event that prompted Oviedo's arrest by Brazilian authorities the following month.

Liberal candidate Julio César FRANCO narrowly bested the Colorado nominee, Félix ARGAÑA (son of the former vice president), in the August balloting. President González's tenure was beset with corruption scandals, which prompted the PLRA to launch several efforts to impeach González, the last of which failed by a handful of votes in the Senate in February 2003.

In the election of April 27, 2003, the Colorado Party continued its 56-year domination of the presidency by electing Nicanor DUARTE Frutos on a 38.3 percent of the valid vote share. Despite the presidential victory, the Colorados secured only pluralities in the Senate (16 of 45 seats) and the Chamber of Deputies (37 of 80 seats).

Shortly after his inauguration, on August 15, 2003, President Duarte reached an agreement with the opposition to change six members of the Supreme Court. The Duarte administration stabilized Paraguay's rocky economy, after reaching a stand-by agreement with the International Monetary Fund in December 2003, and initiated various administrative and tax reforms to increase public revenue. Duarte's reformist impetus, however, began to lose traction in 2004, in the face of mounting social discontent and conflict in the countryside. That year, landless peasants occupied 74 large properties, leading to 1,156 arrests among rural activists and the assassination of five landless peasants.

In late June 2004 Oviedo returned to Paraguay and was placed under arrest in a military prison to serve the sentence issued in early 1998 for his April 1996 coup attempt. However, he was released from prison on parole in early September 2007, as result of a Supreme Court decision widely perceived as engineered by Duarte to split the broad anti-Colorado coalition formed in support a presidential bid by Fernando LUGO, a progressive Catholic bishop. On October 31 the Supreme Court annulled Oviedo's sentence for the 1996 coup attempt, which allowed him to launch his own presidential candidacy through the National Union of Ethical Citizens (*Unión Nacional de Ciudadanos Éticos*—UNACE).

Meanwhile, Lugo had become the opposition's main hope for defeating the ruling Colorado Party, after serving as the main speaker at an anti-Duarte demonstration attended by 40,000 people in late March 2006. Lugo helped to forge a broad coalition in September 2007 called the Patriotic Alliance for Change (*Alianza Patriotica para el Cambio*—APC) and, after resigning from the priesthood (the constitution forbids religious leaders from holding political office), defeated five other candidates (including Oviedo and Blanca OVELAR de Duarte of the Colorado Party) in the presidential election of April 20, 2008. The results in the concurrent congressional and gubernatorial elections were essentially split, although the Colorado Party remained small pluralities in both legislative chambers.

On April 16, 2009, Lugo conducted a minor cabinet reshuffle and replaced four ministers in an effort to enhance the popularity of the government following an inability to enact promised reforms because of legislative resistance. Later that month he reached outside of the

APC and choose Hector LACOGNATA of the Beloved Homeland Party (*Partido Patria Querida*—PPQ) to replace the foreign minister, who had resigned, in an effort to broaden his support within the Congress. He also supported the election of Miguel CARRIZOSA Galiano of the PPQ as president of the Senate. However, the effort led to the withdrawal of the PLRA from the APC (see Political parties, below). The PLRA did maintain its three cabinet positions and continued to support the government.

Constitution and government. The 1992 constitution established an important break from the 1967 constitution designed under the Stroessner regime. While maintaining the country's presidential system and a two-chamber legislature, the current constitution upholds basic democratic guarantees of association and expression, and improved the rights of women and indigenous people. The legislative branch was strengthened and various provisions included to enhance judicial independence, including a Council of Magistrates responsible for screening nominations to the Supreme Court and appointing judges to the appellate and lower courts.

The new constitution introduced the post of vice president, to be elected along with the president by simple plurality (thus denying the opposition an opportunity to join forces in a runoff), and limited the president to a single five-year term. In a rebuff to the military, the constitutional assembly prohibited the chief executive from transferring his or her powers as commander-in-chief to another and instituted elections for the governors and council members of the country's departments. Strong guarantees for private property rights were established at the expense of constitutional provisions in favor of land reform.

For administrative purposes Paraguay is divided into 17 departments (exclusive of the capital), which are subdivided into a total of 230 municipalities.

The judicial system encompasses justices of the peace, courts of the first instance, appellate courts, and, at the apex, the Supreme Court of Justice. Despite significant reforms undertaken after 1995, including the overhaul of all judges, public opinion continues to view the judiciary as a corrupt institution.

Foreign relations. A member of the United Nations, the Organization of American States, the Latin American Integration Association, and other regional organizations, Paraguay traditionally maintained a strongly anti-leftist foreign policy, including a suspension of relations with Nicaragua in 1980 following the assassination in Asunción of former Nicaraguan president Anastasio Somoza Debayle. Paraguay began to soften its approach to foreign policy with the reestablishment of diplomatic ties with Cuba in 1996. Under the Duarte administration, Paraguay maintained friendly relations with various progressive governments in the region; these are likely to intensify further under the new Lugo government.

Relations with neighboring regimes have been relatively cordial. In March 1991 Paraguay joined Brazil, Argentina, and Uruguay to establish the Southern Cone Common Market (*Mercado Común del Cono Sur*—Mercosur). Periodic disagreements with Brazil and Argentina over hydroelectric issues have flared. At the Itaipú Dam, an unfair pricing system has provoked repeated demands by successive governments to renegotiate the 1973 Itaipú treaty with Brazil.

Relations with the United States improved after Stroessner's demise. Prior to this, Paraguay had been a close ally during the Cold War, but repeated human rights violations and allegations of high-level Paraguayan involvement in narcotics trafficking strained relations between both countries, especially after 1977. The United States government played an influential role in preventing a coup against General Oviedo in 1996, and thereafter began to press Paraguay to curb illicit economic practices, notably in the realm of intellectual property violations and drug trafficking.

Following September 11, 2001, the shared border of Paraguay, Brazil, and Argentina became a leading point of concern for United States policymakers, who viewed the area as a haven for money laundering, arms and drug trafficking, and Islamist militants. In response, the United States has provided Paraguay with technical assistance, equipment, and training to strengthen counternarcotics operations and to assist in the development and implementation of legislation to counter money laundering and terrorism. In July 2003 the U.S. government suspended all military aid to Paraguay as a result of the country's refusal to grant immunity to U.S. citizens in legal cases involving the International Court of Justice in The Hague. Enhanced democratic stability in Paraguay and closer relations with neighboring leftist governments have reduced the traditional influence exercised by the United States in Paraguayan foreign policy. In 2004 Paraguay was one of twelve nations to join the newly-created Union of South American Nations (*Unión de Naciones Suramericanas*--UNASUR), designed to bring together MERCOSUR and the Andean Community.

Paraguay assumed the rotating presidency of MERCOSUR in December 2008 and in 2009, the country's foreign minister announced that the groups would sign a free trade agreement with the Gulf Cooperation Council. In July 2009 Paraguay and Brazil signed an accord that settled a long-running dispute over the operations of the bilateral Itaipu hydroelectric plant. Under the agreement, Brazil agreed to pay higher fees for the electricity produced by the plant and to cover the costs of the construction of new transmission lines. In August the government had to withdraw a bill for Venezuelan membership in MERCOSUR after opposition parties mustered the votes to defeat the measure. All members of the organization except Paraguay and Brazil, had already approved Venezuela's entry into the trade bloc. Meanwhile, Paraguay rejected participation in the U.S.-sponsored military program New Horizons 2010 which offered training and equipment to countries in the region.

Current issues. For several years, Paraguayan domestic politics have turned largely on the *oviedistas* and rivals jostling for access to presidential power amid allegations of corruption and conspiracy. In 2002 the *oviedistas* withdrew from the PC, with Oviedo announcing from Brazil, where he was then under detention, that he intended to return to Paraguay and seek the presidency in 2003. Meanwhile, opposition pressure against President González Macchi continued, fueled in part by the filing in April of formal charges against him for the diversion of about $16 million in public funds into a U.S. bank account. In addition to having immunity from prosecution while in office, the president retained enough support in the Chamber of Deputies to prevent the two-thirds vote needed to impeach him. Over the next six months, however, a series of sometimes violent antigovernment, anticorruption demonstrations took place, with supporters of González Macchi insisting that they were orchestrated by Oviedo and Vice President Franco. (In 2006 González Macchi was sentenced to eight years in prison; the ruling, though, was overturned later by the Court of Appeals.)

Following his installation in 2003, President Duarte enjoyed initial popularity, stemming in part from his opposition to the privatization of state-owned enterprises and support for land reform. In July 2005 his supporters blocked reactivation of a privatization bill that had been dormant since 2002, and in early August they approved the expropriation for redistribution of 52,000 of about 700,000 hectares of land owned by affiliates of Rev. Sun Myung Moon's Unification Church.

Disenchantment with the Duarte administration, however, increased after 2005. A series of high-profile kidnappings and street murders in early 2005 had triggered extensive concern over public security issues. The May resignation of Duarte's independent and well-reputed finance minister signaled the political limits of Duarte's promise to modernize and clean up the Paraguayan state.

In February 2006 President Duarte resumed formal leadership of the Colorados, arguing that a constitutional ban on his holding any office other than the presidency applied only to governmental posts. Concurrently, however, he indicated that he would seek a Constitutional Court ruling validating the action. In the meantime, he delegated interim leadership of the party to José Alberto ALDERETE. Three months earlier Duarte had appealed for constitutional reform in a move widely interpreted as clearing the way for a reelection bid by revoking the one-term limitation. His congressional critics, led by the PLRA, responded with a threat of impeachment, but they clearly lacked the required two-thirds majority in both chambers. However, a poll taken in late 2006 showed that only 23 percent of the population had a positive view of President Duarte, a sharp drop from the 61 percent ratings in late 2003. In May 2007 Duarte, facing pressure even within the Colorado Party, announced that he had given up on his effort to challenge the one-term limitation, therefore abandoning his plans to run in 2008.

With Duarte out of the race, Oviedo remained fixated on the presidency. On October 31, 2007, a Supreme Court ruling dismissing the sentence over his involvement in the 1996 coup attempt cleared the way for his presidential bid in 2008. Meanwhile, Duarte decided to support Blanca OVELAR de Duarte, his minister of education and culture, rebuffing Vice President Luis CASTIGLIONI Soria and the Colorado Party president Alderete, who both expected his endorsement. Castiglioni and Alderete went on to form their own movements to bid for the Colorado presidential slot.

In December 2007 Ovelar defeated Castiglioni in a heated Colorado election by less than 5,000 votes. Castiglioni and his supporters accused Duarte of masterminding an electoral fraud and refused to recognize

Ovelar's victory. However, the Colorado Party proclaimed Ovelar its standard-bearer in January 2008; she thereby became the first woman to head the presidential ticket of a major Paraguayan party. Meanwhile, the APC's Lugo, known as the "bishop of the poor," directed intense attacks against the government, calling for a "transformation" of Paraguay in economic, social, and political affairs. Oviedo also strongly criticized the government as he attempted to attract support from the same "marginalized" sector of the population that had been so receptive to Lugo.

Lugo's clear victory in the April 2008 presidential balloting ended more than 60 years of government dominance on the part of the Colorado Party, and the international community praised the peaceful balloting and unchallenged transfer of power as a sign of significant political maturity within the country. Most of the new president's campaign pledges (e.g., anticorruption initiatives, land and judicial reform, increased health spending) had been perceived as leftist. However, the PLRA (the major force within the APC) retained a centrist orientation, and Lugo appeared to face a significant challenge in keeping the disparate forces within the APC satisfied. Although the APC components had won slight pluralities in the Senate and the Chamber of Deputies, Lugo announced a desire for "pluralistic" government and, surprising some of his supporters, negotiated a legislative alliance with UNACE and Duarte's supporters in the Colorado Party. Attention also focused on the role the new administration would assume in regional affairs as Venezuelan president Hugo Chávez appeared particularly interested in attracting the support of Lugo, who pledged to support increased social spending by, among other things, raising the rates paid by Argentina and Brazil for hydroelectric power emanating from Paraguay. In December more than 50,000 farmers and agricultural workers staged protests against government inaction against a wave of violence and property destruction by landless farmers seeking to prompt land redistribution.

Lugo announced in February 2009 that he might seek to overturn the constitution's one-term limit on the presidency and seek reelection if a constitutional amendment could be adopted through a popular referendum. However, in April a series of paternity suits undermined Lugo's popularity and distracted from his reform efforts. After the president and former bishop admitted to fathering a child while he was a priest, two additional women came forward and with what reports described as "credible" paternity claims.

Lugo replaced the heads of the Army and Navy in May for permitting a Marxist youth congress to meet at military facilities. The dismissals were ostensibly because the constitution forbids the military from engagement in political activities, but reports indicated that the action was also a means for Lugo to affirm his control over the military. Meanwhile a series of kidnappings and ransoms of foreign nationals led several European countries to issue warnings to their citizens traveling to Paraguay.

POLITICAL PARTIES

Paraguay's two traditional political organizations were the now-divided Liberal Party, which was last in power in 1940, and the National Republican Association (Colorado Party), which dominated the political scene from 1947 and sponsored the successive presidential candidacies of Gen. Alfredo Stroessner. Prone to factionalism, the Colorados suffered the loss of Gen. Lino Oviedo's supporters in February 2002. In addition to these two traditional parties, Paraguay has long had a host of smaller, independent parties and political movements, ranging from right to left positions on the political spectrum. Many of these groups, however, have been of short and unstable duration.

Legislative Parties:

Patriotic Alliance for Change (*Alianza Patriotica para el Cambio*—APC). The APC is an outgrowth of the National Concertation (*Concertación Nacional*—CN), a broad coalition formed in September 2006 with the aim of ending the Colorado Party's 60-year dominance of Paraguayan politics. The CN comprised the PLRA, PPS, PEN, PPQ, and UNACE, as well as additional leftist and civil organizations, including the National Citizen Resistance (*Resistencia Ciudadana Nacional*—RCN), which had been formed earlier in the year under the leadership of Fernando Lugo, the bishop of San Pedro. Although some founders of the CN had hoped to present consensus candidates for the November 2006 municipal elections, most of the component parties presented their own candidates, thereby competing among themselves and undercutting the effectiveness of their challenge to the Colorado Party.

Dissension continued within the CN in early 2007 over the question of how to pick a candidate for the 2008 presidential elections. In February the PLRA, PPQ, UNACE, and several other parties agreed to conduct a CN-wide primary to select the CN candidates, but Lugo, considered by far the most popular opposition leader, opposed the primary system, describing it as too costly and easily manipulated. In early July the PLRA voted to name Lugo as its presidential candidate, and five smaller parties (the PPS, PEN, PDC, PRF, and the **Socialist Party** [*Partido Socialista*—PS]) followed suit shortly thereafter. However, the UNACE and PPQ (the second and third largest parties in the opposition camp) objected to the cancellation of the proposed primary system and withdrew from the CN in early September after Lugo had officially announced his candidacy.

The APC was launched on September 18, 2007, by the PRLA, PPS, PEN, PDP, PRF, PDC, MPT, the **Broad Front** (*Frente Amplio*—FA), the **Movement Towards Socialism Party** (*Partido del Movimiento al Socialismo*—P-MAS, led by Camilio SOARES), and other groups, including the influential social movement **Social and Popular Bloc** (*Bloque Social y Popular*). Lugo, whose concern for the impoverished peasantry had earned him the nickname "Red Bishop," was elected president of the republic under the APC rubric with 40.82 percent of the vote in the April 2008 election. For the most part, the APC component parties presented their own candidates in the concurrent congressional balloting, although several lists (from which two candidates were successful) were presented under the APC designation.

In July 2009 the PLRA officially withdrew from the APC (see PLRA, below).

Leader: Fernando LUGO (President of the Republic).

Authentic Radical Liberal Party (*Partido Liberal Radical Auténtico*—PLRA). Paraguay's historical Liberal Party (*Partido Liberal*—PL) was founded in 1887 and legally proscribed in 1942. The party was legally reestablished in 1961, but most of its members left in the same year to form the Radical Liberal Party (*Partido Liberal Radical*—PLR). In 1977 a majority of PL and PLR members withdrew from their organizations to form the Unified Liberal Party (*Partido Liberal Unificado*—PLU). The government, however, refused to legalize the new grouping, continuing instead to recognize a rump of the PLR. The PLRA was formed in 1978 by a group of center-left PLU dissidents, many of whom had been subjected to police harassment after the 1978 election. Although its leaders were periodically incarcerated, the PLRA subsequently grew in strength. Its president, Dr. Domingo Laíno, was permitted to return from exile in April 1987 and was runner-up to General Rodríguez in the presidential poll of May 1989, with 20 percent of the vote. In May 1990 what remained of the PL (whose vote share of 3 percent in 1988 had plunged to a minuscule 0.3 percent in 1989) and of the PLR (whose vote share had dropped from 7 percent in 1988 to 1 percent in 1989) merged with the PLRA, which ran second, with 27 percent of the vote, in the Constituent Assembly balloting of December 1, 1991. Dr. Laíno placed second in the 1993 presidential contest, with a 32.1 percent share of the vote, while the party was runner-up in both the Senate and Chamber races.

In November 1996 the PLRA's Martín BURT, running with the support of PEN (below), was elected mayor of Asunción. He subsequently heralded that outcome as an example of how cooperation between the two leading opposition parties might defeat the Colorados in 1998, and in August 1997 the PLRA joined with PEN in a Democratic Alliance (*Alianza Democrática*—AD) to contest the general election of May 1998. The PLRA was awarded two seats in the national unity government installed in March 1999. It withdrew from the González administration on February 6, 2000. In March 2002 the party's president, former foreign minister Miguel Abdón Saguier, was ousted in favor of legislator Oscar Denis.

Having won the vice presidency in August 2000, Julio César Franco resigned the office in October 2002 to meet a legal requirement that presidential candidates vacate their governmental positions six months before the scheduled balloting. With a view toward legislative elections as well as the presidential contest, the PLRA attempted to fashion an opposition Power Front 2003 (*Frente Poder 2003*) alliance that, however, did not materialize. Equally unavailing were attempts to form alliances with the *oviedista* Unace (below) and Pedro Fadul's PPQ (below). Obliged to run alone, the PLRA finished second in both the presidential and legislative races.

In October 2005 longtime party icon Domingo Laíno and a number of others were temporarily expelled from the PLRA for actions that appeared to make them de facto allies of the ruling Colorados.

After leading the formation of the CN in 2006, the PLRA in January 2007 announced plans for PLRA president Frederico Franco to serve as the PLRA's nominee in what it hoped would be a multiparty primary to determine the opposition's presidential candidate for 2008. However, in a very close vote, the PLRA in June endorsed Fernando Lugo for the CN presidential nomination over Franco. Lugo concurrently agreed that the PLRA would select his running mate. The PLRA held a heated and very close primary election for the vice-presidential slot in December. Sen. Carlos Mateo Balmelli initially rejected Franco's slim victory and charged his opponent with committing fraud but after a simmering dispute agreed to endorse Franco's candidacy. However, the party reportedly remained factionalized, and some components complained that the party was not sufficiently represented in the new government installed by Lugo in August. Tension was also reported at that time between Lugo and Franco.

The PLRA left the APC in 2009, reportedly over frustration with Lugo's efforts to reach-out to the opposition Colorados and the PPQ (including the appointment of a member of the PPQ as foreign minister).

Leaders: Federico FRANCO Gómez (Vice President of the Republic and President of the Party), Julio César ("Yoyito") FRANCO Gómez (Former Vice President of the Republic, 2003 presidential candidate, and Former President of the Party), Antonio Gustavo CARDOZA (Vice President of the Party), Sen. Blas Antonio LLANO Ramos, Carlos MATEO Balmelli (Former President of the Senate), Enrique BUZARQUIS Cáceres (President of the Chamber of Deputies).

Country in Solidarity Party (*Partido País Solidario*—PPS). The PPS was formed in 2001 by Carlos Filizzola, who had led PEN from its formation until losing a leadership election in March 1999. Earlier, he had headed the Asunción for Everybody (*Asunción para Todos*—APT), winning the capital's mayoralty in 1991, and then the Constitution for Everybody (*Constitución para Todos*—CPT), which ran third, with 11 percent of the vote, in the Constituent Assembly balloting in December 1991. A joint secretary of the labor confederation *Central Unitaria de Trabajadores,* he had been imprisoned several times by the Stroessner regime for supporting peasant land seizures. Filizzola lost the Asunción mayoral election of November 2001 despite PLRA support. The party won two Senate and two Chamber seats in 2003. However, it suffered a split in 2007 (which led to the creation of the PDP, below) and retained only one Senate seat in 2008.

Leaders: Sen. Carlos Alberto FILIZZOLA Pallarés (President), Milda RIVAROLO.

Popular Tekojoja Movement (*Movimiento Popular Tekojojá*—MPT). The MPT was established in December 2006 by left-wing social and political activists in support of Fernando Lugo's presidential candidacy. Party leader Anibal CARRILLO Iramain accepted a government post in the ministry of health as part of the Lugo government, but resigned in 2009.

Leaders: Anibal CARRILLO Iramain (President), Sen. Sixto PEREIRA.

Progressive Democratic Party (*Partido Democrata Progresista*—PDP). The PDP was founded by dissident members of the PPS in 2007. Party leader Rafael Augusto FILIZZOLA Serra accepted the post of interior minister in the Lugo government.

Leader: Rafael Augusto FILIZZOLA Serra (President and Interior Minister).

National Encounter Party (*Partido Encuentro Nacional*—PEN). PEN was organized in mid-1992 as a somewhat loose alignment of supporters of independent presidential candidate Guillermo Caballero Vargas, who consistently led in the public opinion polls until the eve of the 1993 balloting. The group, which included elements of the PRF and PDC as well as Carlos Filizzola's CPT (see PPS, above), won eight seats in each legislative house and subsequently entered into an opposition pact with the Liberals, which was reaffirmed for Asunción's mayoral contest in November 1996. In the latter balloting PEN agreed to support the PLRA candidate after public opinion polls showed him ahead of the other contenders. PEN accepted two cabinet posts in the national unity government installed in March 1999. A week earlier Filizzola had lost the party presidency to Euclides Acevedo. PEN's Diego Abente Brun ran a distant fifth in the 2003 presidential race, while none of the party's candidates won congressional representation.

Leaders: Luis Torales KENNEDY (President), Guillermo Caballero VARGAS (1993 presidential candidate), Diego ABENTE Brun (2003 presidential candidate).

Christian Democratic Party (*Partido Demócrata Cristiano*—PDC). The PDC, which was refused recognition by the Electoral Commission from 1971 through 1988, is the furthest left of the non-Communist groupings and one of the smallest of Paraguay's political parties. In March 1986 the government lifted an order under which PDC founder Luis Alfonso RESCK had been forced into exile five years earlier. The party surprised observers by winning only 1 percent of the vote in 1989. It secured one Constituent Assembly seat in 1991, none thereafter.

Leader: Dr. Luis Manuel ANDRADA Nogués (President).

February Revolutionary Party (*Partido Revolucionario Febrerista*—PRF). Initially organized by a group of Chaco War veterans, the PRF now stands substantially to the left of the Colorados in its espousal of social and agrarian reform and is affiliated with Socialist International. Although legally recognized, the party boycotted all national and local elections from 1973 through 1988. Meanwhile, a discernable ideological shift occurred within the PRF leadership, the party's 1985 congress replacing President Euclides ACEVEDO Candia with the more moderate Fernando VERA, formerly an economist for the International Monetary Fund; before the 1989 balloting, on the other hand, Acevedo returned briefly to the presidency. The party secured one seat in the Constituent Assembly balloting of December 1991 but has subsequently been unrepresented at the national level.

Leader: Nils CAMBIA.

National Republican Association–Colorado Party (*Asociación Nacional Republicana–Partido Colorado*—ANR-PC). Originating in 1887, the mainstream of the Colorado Party has long been conservative in outlook and consistently supported General Stroessner for more than three decades after his assumption of the presidency in 1954. The party has, however, been subject to factionalism (for a discussion of its shifting "currents" before 1991, see the 1990 edition of the *Handbook*).

During the run-up to municipal elections in May 1991 the principal internal groupings were three *tradicionalista* alignments: the highly conservative *Tradicionalistas Autónomos,* led by then acting party president Dr. Luis María ARGAÑA; the moderately liberal *Movimiento Tradicionalista Democrático,* led by Blás Riquelme; and the centrist *Tradicionalismo Renovador,* led by Angel Roberto Seifart. Following the municipal balloting the *democráticos* and the *renovadors* joined forces as the *Tradicionalismo Renovador Democrático* (Trardem), which commanded a majority at an extraordinary party convention on July 15–19. Subsequently, Trardem and the *autónomos* ran joint lists in Colorado balloting on October 6 to pick candidates for the forthcoming Constituent Assembly elections, winning all of the contests.

Other party factions included the *Frente Democrático* (FD), led by Waldino Ramón LOVERA; the strongly renewalist *Coloradismo Democrático* (Codem), led by Miguel Angel GONZALEZ Casabianca; and the youthful *Nueva Generación* (NG), led by Enrique RIERA Jr. In 1993 a Colorado dissident, Leandro PRIETO Yegros, attempted to campaign for the presidency under the banner of a Progressive Social Movement (*Movimiento Social Progresista*—MSP), but the electoral tribunal rejected his candidacy.

At an extraordinary Colorado convention in February 1993 the military-backed Juan Carlos Wasmosy defeated Argaña for the party's presidential nomination. Following the election, Argaña's faction, now styled the Colorado Reconciliation Movement (*Movimiento Reconciliación Colorada*—MRC), held a majority of the party's seats in the Chamber of Deputies and formed a legislative bloc with the PLRA and PEN. In late 1994, after three generals had accused Wasmosy of intraparty vote rigging, *argañistas* formally challenged the validity of the president's incumbency by calling for his impeachment. (For more information on the alliance formed between the *argañistas* and *oviedistas* in early 1995, see the 2008 *Handbook.*)

In May 1996, following his forced retirement from the army, Oviedo launched a PC faction styled the National Union of Ethical Colorados (*Unión Nacional de Colorados Éticos*—Unace). He was able to avert judicial proceedings against the charges of insurrection (see Political background, above). Meanwhile, in an April 28 election for the party leadership, Argaña secured an easy victory of 55 percent over Seifart (35 percent) and Riquelme (8 percent).

Despite his status as a coup suspect, General Oviedo was elected Colorado presidential candidate in September 1997, with runner-up Argaña accusing his opponent of fraud. Following Oviedo's preclusion from the 1998 presidential poll by the Supreme Court, he was replaced as the Colorado standard-bearer by Raúl Cubas Grau, previously the vice-presidential candidate and a close ally of Oviedo. Argaña became the vice-presidential candidate. Despite the success of the Colorado ticket, intense conflict subsequently persisted between the *argañistas* and the Cubas/Oviedo faction, particularly after Cubas ordered Oviedo's release from jail shortly after his inauguration. In mid-March the *oviedistas* took control of the Colorado headquarters in Asunción after the *argañistas* had postponed the scheduled election of new party leaders. Shortly thereafter, Argaña was assassinated, leading to the ouster of President Cubas and elevation of Luis González Macchi, an Argaña supporter, to the national presidency. González was succeeded by Nicanor Duarte Frutos in April 2003. Duarte, Argaña's running mate in the 1997 Colorado presidential primaries, became the Colorado standard-bearer after defeating Osvaldo DOMINGUEZ Dibb, a wealthy entrepreneur and president of the country's leading soccer team who contested the result of the December 22, 2002, primaries. The Colorado Party went on to win the April 27 presidential contest by a 13 percent advantage over the PLRA.

On February 19, 2006, an internal party election was held. Duarte was challenged again by Dibb, who represented the faction of the party loyal to Stroessner, but Duarte won convincingly. Alfredo Stroessner died in Brazil on August 16 of that year. His grandson, Alfredo (Goli) DOMINGUEZ Stroessner, who prefers to be known as Alfredo STROESSNER, now leads the *neostronista* faction within the Colorado Party with his uncle, Osvaldo Dominguez.

Duarte's exploration of a possible constitutional change to permit him to run for another presidential term caused further turmoil in the party. Vice President Luis Alberto Castiglioni in particular criticized Duarte and announced plans to seek the party's presidential nomination himself. In May Duarte withdrew his name from consideration and backed Education and Finance Minister Blanca Ovelar de Duarte for the nomination. Castiglioni, supported within the party by the Colorado Vanguard Movement (*Movimiento Vanguardia Colorado*—MVC), resigned as vice president in early October to contest the 2008 elections but lost a close primary vote to Ovelar in December. Castiglioni and his supporters described the vote as fraudulent and did not subsequently support the Colorado ticket with enthusiasm. When Ovelar finished second in the April 2008 presidential poll with 30.72 percent of the vote, Castiglioni promised to launch a "true" Colorado Party and demanded immediate leadership elections. However, competing claims for the party's presidency remained in a legal imbroglio through November. The party was also reportedly split by a decision by Duarte's backers to provide legislative support for the new Lugo government. (The Castiglioni camp declined Lugo's offer.) Meanwhile, Duarte, to his consternation, was seated (due to his status as a past president) as a nonvoting member of the Senate, despite the fact that he had been elected as a regular member in the April balloting. (Opposition legislators had refused to allow him to swear in as an active duty senator, claiming that the constitution forbade his Senate run.) Duarte, maintaining that his Senate bid had been approved by the Supreme Election Tribunal, pledged further legal action on the matter.

Leaders: Lilian SAMANIEGO (Party President), Nicanor DUARTE Frutos (Former President of the Republic and Leader of the *Movimiento Progresista Colorado*), Blanca OVELAR de Duarte (2008 presidential candidate), Luis Alberto CASTIGLIONI (Former Vice President of the Republic and leader of the MVC), Osvaldo DOMINGUEZ Dibb (Former President), José Alberto ALDERETE (Former President), Juan Carlos WASMOSY (Former President of the Republic), Angel Roberto SEIFART (Former Vice President of the Republic), Sen. Juan Carlos GALAVERNA.

National Union of Ethical Citizens (*Unión Nacional de Ciudadanos Éticos*—UNACE). The present UNACE (sometimes identified as the UNACE Party, or PUNACE) began as the ANR-PC's *Unión Nacional de Colorados Éticos* faction, which Lino Oviedo had launched in 1996. In March 2002, while under arrest in Brazil, Oviedo announced that he intended to sever his faction's links to the Colorados, return to Paraguay, and establish a new party as a vehicle for a presidential bid in 2003. However, the Supreme Court invalidated any candidacy by the general. His surrogate, Sen. Guillermo Sánchez Guffanti, received 13.5 percent of the popular vote. In September 2007 Oviedo was released from prison. The Supreme Court subsequently annulled his sentence for the April 2006 coup attempt, allowing him to present a presidential bid in April 2008, in which he obtained 21.98 percent of the vote. In July UNACE reached an understanding with incoming president Lugo under which UNACE agreed to support the new government in congress in return for, among other things, the Senate presidency.

Leaders: Gen. (Ret.) Lino César OVIEDO Silva (President and 2008 presidential candidate), Enrique GONZÁLEZ Quintana (Former President of the Senate and Former President of the Party), Carmelo BENITEZ Cantero (Vice President of the Party).

Beloved Homeland Party (*Partido Patria Querida*—PPQ). The PPQ was launched in early 2002 by Catholic businessman Pedro Fadul Niella, who launched an anticorruption campaign for the 2003 elections, in which he received 21.3 percent of the presidential vote, while the PPQ won nine seats in the Chamber of Deputies and seven in the Senate. Fadul subsequently initiated the abortive call for President Duarte's impeachment in November 2005.

The PPQ broke away from the CN, the broad anti-Colorado coalition, in July 2007 after Fernando Lugo agreed to have a PLRA running mate and the CN's proposed primary system was eliminated. Fadul subsequently ran as the PPQ presidential candidate in 2008, but he won only 2.37 percent of the votes. Initial returns credited the PPQ with winning four seats in the Senate and three in the Chamber of Deputies in the concurrent congressional balloting. However, the party was subsequently listed as controlling a fourth chamber seat, which had originally been listed as having been won by the list of the **Departmental Alliance of Boquerón** (*Alianza Departamental de Boquerón*—ADB), a regional political movement comprising the PPQ, PEN, and PLRA. (The successful ADB candidate, Orlando PENNER Durksen, was described as both a member of the PPQ and the president of the ADB.) In July the PPQ declined President-elect Lugo's invitation to join an APC-led legislative alliance, but PPQ member Hector LACOGNATA was appointed foreign minister in April 2009.

Leaders: Pedro FADUL Niella (President of the Party and 2003 and 2008 presidential candidate), Arsenio CAMPOS.

Other Parties Participating in the 2008 Elections:

Minor political parties and movements that participated in the 2008 elections, individually or as part of coalitions, included the **New Homeland Movement** (*Movimiento Tetã Pyahu*—MTP), whose presidential candidate, Horacio Enriqué GALEANO Perrone, won 0.16 percent of the vote; the **Tricolor Democratic Alliance** (*Alianza Democratica Tricolor*); the **Popular Unity Party** (*Partido de la Unidad Popular*); the **Hope for Social Renovation Movement** (*Movimiento Esperanza de Renovacion Social*); the **Paraguayan Humanist Party** (*Partido Humanista Paraguayo*—PHP), whose 2008 presidential candidate, Sergio MARTINEZ Estigarribia, won 0.34 percent of the vote; the **Retired People to Power Party** (*Partido Jubilados al Poder*); the **All Together Political Movement** (*Movimiento Politico Oñondivepá*); the **National Revolutionary Alliance Movement** (*Movimiento Alianza Revolucionaria Nacional*); the **Worker's Party** (*Partido de los Trabajadores*—PT), whose 2008 presidential candidate, Julio LOPEZ, won 0.13 percent of the vote; the **White Party** (*Partido Blanco*—PB); and the **Paraguayan Communist Party** (*Partido Comunista Paraguayo*—PCP). (See the 2008 *Handbook* for additional information on the PCP.)

LEGISLATURE

The bicameral **National Congress** (*Congreso Nacional*) currently consists of a Senate and a Chamber of Deputies, both elected concurrently with the president for five-year terms.

Senate (*Cámara de Senadores*). The upper house comprises 45 members who are directly elected via party-list proportional balloting in one nationwide constituency, plus former presidents of the republic, who serve as senators for life but without voting power. In the most recent election of April 20, 2008, the Colorado Party won 15 seats; the Authentic Radical Liberal Party, 14; the National Union of Ethical Citizens, 9; the Beloved Homeland Movement, 4; the Country in Solidarity Party, 1; the Popular Tekojoja Movement, 1; and the Progressive Democratic Party, 1.

President: Miguel CARRIZOSA Galiano.

Chamber of Deputies (*Cámara de Diputados*). The lower house comprises 80 members who are directly elected via party-list proportional balloting in 18 multimember constituencies (the country's 17 departments plus the capital). Following the most recent election of April 20, 2008, election officials listed the following distribution of seats: the Colorado Party, 30; the Authentic Radical Liberal Party (PLRA), 27; the National Union of Ethical Citizens, 15; the Beloved Homeland Movement (PPQ), 3; the Alliance for Patriotic Change (APC), 2; the Progressive Democratic Party, 1; the Popular Tekojoja Movement, 1; and the Departmental Alliance of Boquerón (ADB), 1. However, the chamber subsequently listed the successful APC candidates as PLRA members (giving the PLRA 29 seats) and the successful ADB candidate as a PPQ member (giving the PPQ 4 seats).

President: Enrique BUZARQUIS Cáceres.

CABINET

[as of September 1, 2009]

President	Fernando Armindo LUGO Méndez (APC)
Vice President	Luis Federico FRANCO Gómez (PLRA)
Ministers	
Agriculture and Livestock	Enzo Cardozo (PLRA)
Education and Culture	Luis Alberto Riart
Finance and Economy	Dionisio Borda (ind.)
Foreign Relations	Hector Lacognata (PPQ)
Industry and Trade	Francisco Rivas (PLRA)
Interior	Rafael Augusto Filizzola Serra (PDP)
Justice and Labor	Humberto Blasco (PLRA)
National Defense	Gen. (ret.) Luis Bareiro Spaini (ind.)
Public Health and Social Welfare	Esperanza Martínez (MPT) [f]
Public Works and Communications	Efraín Alegre Sasiain (PLRA)
Secretary General to the Presidency	Miguel López Perito (APC)
Executive Secretaries	
Children and Adolescents	Liz Cristina Torres Herrera [f]
Civil Service	Lilian Soto [f]
Culture	Ticio Escobar
Environment	Jose Luis Casaccia
Information	Augusto dos Santos
National Emergencies	Camillo Soares
Sanitation and Food Quality	Luis Llano
Social Action	Pablino Caceres
Welfare and Social Assistance	Maria Angelica Fernandez [f]
Women's Affairs	Gloria Rubin [f]

[f] = female

COMMUNICATIONS

Press. Newspapers did not enjoy complete freedom of the press, and a number ceased publication during the Stroessner era. Since the 1989 coup, however, Paraguay has enjoyed ample press freedoms. In 2008 Reporters Without Borders ranked Paraguay 90, along with Mozambique, in freedom of the press out of 173 countries. The following are published daily in Asunción: *Diario Popular* (125,000); *ABC Color* (75,000); *Última Hora* (45,000); and *La Nación* (30,000 daily).

News agencies. There is no domestic facility, although several foreign bureaus maintain offices in Asunción.

Broadcasting and computing. Broadcasting is under the supervision of the *Administración Nacional de Telecomunicaciones* (Antelco). All radio stations, with the exception of the government station, *Radio Nacional,* are commercial, one of them, *Radio Ñandutí*, being periodically shut down during 1984–1988 for broadcasting interviews with opposition politicians and reporting on differences within the ruling party. As of 2008 there were 143.4 Internet users per 1,000 inhabitants.

INTERGOVERNMENTAL REPRESENTATION

Ambassador to the U.S.: Rigoberto GAUTO.

U.S. Ambassador to Paraguay: Liliana AYALDE.

Permanent Representative to the UN: José Antonio DOS SANTOS.

IGO Memberships (Non-UN): ALADI, *CAN*, IADB, Interpol, IOM, Mercosur, OAS, OPANAL, PCA, SELA, WCO, WTO.

PERU

Republic of Peru
República del Perú

Political Status: Independent republic proclaimed 1821; military rule imposed on October 3, 1968; constitutional government restored on July 28, 1980; national emergency declared in wake of army-backed "presidential coup" on April 5, 1992; present constitution effective from December 29, 1993.

Area: 496,222 sq. mi. (1,285,216 sq. km.).

Population: 27,219,264 (2005C), including an adjustment of 3.92 percent for underenumeration; 29,159,000 (2008E).

Major Urban Center (2005E): LIMA (metropolitan area, 8,550,000).

Official Languages: Spanish, Quechua.

Monetary Unit: New Sol (market rate December 1, 2009: 2.87 new sols = $1US).

President: Alan GARCÍA Pérez (Peruvian Aprista Party); served as president 1985–1990; returned to office in second-round balloting on June 4, 2006, and sworn in for a five-year term on July 28, succeeding Alejandro TOLEDO Manrique (Peru Possible).

First Vice President: Luis GIAMPETRI Rojas (Peruvian Aprista Party); elected in second-round balloting on June 4, 2006, and sworn in on July 28 for a term concurrent with that of the president, the office having been vacant following the resignation of Raúl Diez CANSECO (Peru Possible) on January 30, 2004.

Second Vice President: Zoila Lourdes MENDOZA del Solar (Peruvian Aprista Party); elected in second-round balloting on June 4, 2006, and sworn in on July 28 for a term concurrent with that of the president, succeeding David WAISMAN (Peru Possible).

President of the Council of Ministers (Prime Minister): Jorge Alphonso Alejandro DEL CASTILLO Gálvez (Peruvian Aprista Party); appointed by the president on July 28, 2006, and sworn in the same day, succeeding Pedro Pablo KUCZYNSKI (Peru Possible).

THE COUNTRY

The third-largest country in South America and the second after Chile in the length of its Pacific coastline, Peru comprises three distinct geographical areas: a narrow coastal plain; the high sierra of the Andes; and an inland area of wooded foothills, tropical rain forests, and lowlands that includes the headwaters of the Amazon River. While it contains only 30 percent of the population, the coastal area is the

commercial and industrial center. Roman Catholicism is the state religion, and Spanish has traditionally been the official language, although Quechua (recognized as an official language in 1975) and Aymará are commonly spoken by Peruvian Indians. Of Inca descent, Indians constitute 46 percent of the population but remain largely unintegrated with the white (10 percent) and *mestizo* (44 percent) groups. Women constitute approximately 30 percent of the labor force, primarily in agriculture, with smaller groups in domestic service and the informal trading sector; female participation in government is minimal, save at the national level, where women constituted 35 of the 120 legislators elected in 2006, including the second vice president, and 3 of 17 cabinet ministers.

The Peruvian economy depends heavily on the extraction of rich and varied mineral resources, the most important being copper, silver, zinc, lead, and iron. Petroleum, which was discovered in the country's northeastern jungle region in 1971, is being extensively exploited. The agricultural sector employs approximately 40 percent of the labor force and embraces three main types of activity: commercial agriculture, subsistence agriculture, and fishing. The most important legal commodities are coffee, cotton, sugar, fish, and fishmeal, with coca production the major component of the underground economy.

Like most of its neighbors, Peru faced economic adversity in the 1980s, including flagging output in the agricultural and industrial sectors, a massive foreign debt, and inflation that reached a then record 163 percent in 1985. In August 1985 the International Monetary Fund (IMF) declared the government ineligible for further credit after it had embarked on a somewhat unorthodox recovery program that yielded a limited degree of success by late 1986 (see Political background, below). A return to fiscal difficulty in 1987 gave way to crisis conditions in 1988, with inflation (after a series of devaluations) escalating to an annualized rate of more than 3,300 percent in 1989 and 7,400 percent in 1990. In March 1993 government officials declared that the recession had bottomed out, and what was termed an economic "miracle" subsequently yielded a real GDP gain for the year of 6.8 percent. A further increase to 12.7 percent (the highest in the world) occurred in 1994. Overall, the period 1993–1997 saw an average annual gain of about 7 percent, although high unemployment and widespread poverty showed little improvement. For 1998–2001 adverse trade conditions, the slow pace of structural reform, and domestic instability combined to slow real GDP growth to only 1 percent annually. Thereafter, it rose to a region-high 5.2 percent in 2002, dipped to 4.0 percent in 2003, and then rose again to 5.1 percent in 2004, 6.8 percent in 2005, 7.7 percent in 2006, 8.9 percent in 2007, and a region-high 9.8 percent in 2008. The IMF estimated that the global economic slowdown would lower Peru's real GDP growth to 3.5 percent in 2009. Inflation has been firmly single-digit, with consumer prices rising 1.8 percent in 2007, 5.8 percent in 2008, and expected to rise 4.1 percent in 2009.

GOVERNMENT AND POLITICS

Political background. The heartland of the Inca empire conquered by Francisco Pizarro in the 16th century, Peru held a preeminent place in the Spanish colonial system until its liberation by José de SAN MARTIN and Simón BOLIVAR in 1821–1824. Its subsequent history has been marked by frequent alternations of constitutional civilian and extraconstitutional military rule.

The civilian government of José Luis BUSTAMANTE, elected in 1945, was overthrown in 1948 by Gen. Manuel A. ODRIA, who held the presidency until 1956. Manuel PRADO y Ugarteche, elected in 1956 with the backing of the left-of-center American Popular Revolutionary Alliance (APRA), presided over a democratic regime that lasted until 1962, when a new military coup blocked the choice of *Aprista* leader Víctor Raúl HAYA DE LA TORRE as president. An election in 1963 restored constitutional government under Fernando BELAÚNDE Terry of the Popular Action (AP) party. With the support of the now-defunct Christian Democratic Party (PDC), Belaúnde, although hampered by an opposition-controlled Congress and an economic crisis at the end of 1967, implemented economic and social reforms. Faced with dwindling political support, his government was ousted in October 1968 in a bloodless coup led by Div. Gen. Juan VELASCO Alvarado, who assumed the presidency, dissolved the Congress, and formed a military-dominated leftist administration committed to a participatory, cooperative-based model that was known after mid-1974 as the Inca Plan. Formally titled the Plan of the Revolutionary Government of the Armed Forces, it aimed at a "Social Proprietorship" (*Propiedad Social*) in which virtually all enterprises—industrial, commercial, and agricultural—would be either state- or worker-owned and would be managed collectively.

Amid growing evidence of discontent within the armed forces, Velasco Alvarado was himself overthrown in August 1975 by Div. Gen. Francisco MORALES BERMÚDEZ Cerruti, who had served as prime minister since the preceding February and initially pledged to continue his predecessor's policies in a "second phase of the revolution" that would make the Inca reforms "irreversible." Despite the existence of well-entrenched rightist sentiment within the military, Div. Gen. Oscar VARGAS Prieto, who had succeeded Morales Bermúdez as prime minister in September 1975, was replaced in January 1976 by a leftist, Gen. Jorge FERNÁNDEZ Maldonado, who was put forward as a figure capable of maintaining the policies of the revolution in the midst of growing economic difficulty. Under the new administration, Peru's National Planning Institute (INP) prepared a replacement for the Inca Plan known as the *Plan Túpac Amaru*. The document was, however, considered too radical by rightist elements. Its principal authors were deported as part of a move to clear the INP of "left-wing infiltrators," and Fernández Maldonado was replaced in July 1976 by the conservative Gen. Guillermo ARBULÚ Galliani, following the declaration of a state of emergency to cope with rioting occasioned by a series of austerity measures.

Gen. Oscar MOLINA Pallochia was designated to succeed Arbulú Galliani after the latter's retirement in January 1978, while on June 18, in Peru's first nationwide balloting in 15 years, a 100-member Constituent Assembly was elected to draft a new constitution. The assembly completed its work in July 1979, paving the way for presidential and congressional elections in May 1980, at which Belaúnde Terry's AP scored an impressive victory.

By 1985 economic conditions had plummeted, yielding massive inflation, underemployment estimated to encompass 60 percent of the workforce, and negative per capita GDP growth. As a result, the AP was decisively defeated in the election of April 14, Javier ALVA Orlandini running fourth behind APRA's Alan GARCÍA Pérez; Alfonso BARRANTES Lingán, the popular Marxist mayor of Lima; and Luis BEDOYA Reyes, of the recently organized Democratic Convergence (Conde). APRA fell marginally short of a majority in the presidential poll, but second-round balloting was avoided by Barrantes's withdrawal, and García was sworn in on July 28 as, at age 36, the youngest chief executive in Latin America.

In May 1986 the García administration reversed an earlier position and agreed to pay IMF arrears, but after unilaterally rolling over repayment of approximately $940 million in short-term debt, the country was cut off from further access to IMF resources. Concurrently, intense negotiations were launched with the country's more than 270 foreign creditor banks to secure 15- to 20-year refinancing on the basis of a medium-term economic program intended to reduce the country's dependence on food imports and restructure Peruvian industry, in a manner reminiscent of the Inca Plan, toward basic needs and vertical integration. The audacious effort was buoyed by short-term evidence of recovery. Aided by the upswing, APRA secured an unprecedented 53 percent of the vote at municipal elections in November 1986, winning 18 of 24 departmental capitals.

By mid-1987 the recovery had run its course, with increased inflationary pressure and a visible slackening of the 8.5 percent GDP growth registered in 1986. On June 29 García's second vice president, Luis ALVA Castro, who had served additionally as prime minister, resigned the latter post in the wake of a well-publicized rivalry with the president, leaving economic policy in the hands of the chief executive and a group styled "the bold ones" (*los audaces*), who in late July announced that the state would assume control of the country's financial system. Although bitterly condemned by the affected institutions and their right-wing political supporters, a somewhat modified version of the initial expropriation bill was promulgated in October. The action was followed by a return to triple-digit inflation, and in mid-December the government announced a currency devaluation of 39.4 percent.

During 1988 virtually all efforts by President García to reverse the country's plunge into fiscal chaos proved fruitless. An attempt at midyear to formulate an agreement (*concertación*) between business and labor (and subsequently with rightist and leftist political opponents) elicited scant response, and in September the administration introduced a "shock program" that included a 100 percent currency devaluation, a 100–200 percent increase in food prices, and a 120-day price freeze in the wake of a 150 percent increase in the minimum wage. However, the inflationary surge continued, necessitating a further 50 percent devaluation and the appointment in December of the government's fifth finance minister in less than four years. On several occasions there was evidence of García's desire to abandon the presidency, including indications that he might not be adverse to military intervention—a prospect that the armed forces, with no apparent solution to the nation's problems within their grasp, seemed unwilling to implement.

Events continued on an erratic course during 1989. The leftist alliance virtually collapsed, with the popularity of the fledgling right-wing contender, novelist Mario VARGAS Llosa, far outdistancing that of the leftist alliance's leading aspirant, Barrantes Lingán, by early May. Despite a clear lead in opinion polls for most of the year-long campaign, Vargas Llosa failed to gain a majority in presidential balloting on April 8, 1990, and was defeated in a runoff on June 10 by a late entrant, Alberto Keinya FUJIMORI, of the recently organized Change 90 (*Cambio 90*) movement.

Assuming office on July 28, 1990, Fujimori startled both domestic and foreign observers by a series of initiatives that were at once wide-ranging and controversial. He installed a supporter of Vargas Llosa, Juan Carlos HURTADO Miller, as both prime minister and finance minister, and embarked on an austerity program that was not only at variance with his campaign promises, but more severe than that advocated by his opponent. His cabinet included two active-duty army officers (appointed after the virtually unprecedented cashiering of both the air force and navy commanders), three left-wingers (one of whom resigned in late October), and a number of independents. He instituted corruption proceedings against 700 members of the judiciary, discharged 350 police officers, and publicly disagreed with the United States on antidrug policy (insisting on free-market enticement of farmers away from coca production rather than crop eradication). By mid-November his audacity had reaped visible benefits: the army appeared to be a staunch ally; triple-digit monthly inflation had eased dramatically; a near-empty treasury had been replenished with reserves of about $500 million; payment on portions of the foreign debt had been resumed; and in his attitude toward the church and judiciary, Fujimori, according to a *Washington Post* report, had "taken positions that [struck] a chord in a society long disenchanted with institutional failures."

In April 1991 the Shining Path (*Sendero Luminoso*), a guerrilla organization, launched a new wave of attacks, and Fujimori felt obliged to replace his interior minister, Gen. Adolfo ALVARADO, whose anti-insurgency policies had drawn increasing criticism. Concurrently, the administration announced that it planned a fourfold increase in the number of its rural self-defense patrols (*rondas campesinas*) while moving to establish similar units in urban areas (*rondas urbanes civiles*). In June 1991 Congress granted the president emergency powers to deal with the escalating guerrilla activity as well as drug-related terrorism, and in July Fujimori felt obliged to reverse himself and conclude an antidrug accord with the United States.

On April 5, 1992, after what appeared to have been extensive consultation with the military, Fujimori seized extraconstitutional power in a dramatic self-coup (*autogolpe*). Announcing the formation of an Emergency Government of National Reconstruction, the president dissolved Congress, launched a reorganization of the judicial and penal systems, and declared that he would take "drastic action" against both the *Sendero Luminoso* and drug traffickers.

In response to the coup a number of senior officials resigned, with Education Minister Oscar DE LA PUENTE Raygada being named prime minister. On November 13 three retired army generals who had served in the military household of the García administration mounted an unsuccessful attempt to overthrow Fujimori and hand over the presidency to First Vice President Máximo SAN ROMÁN Caceras.

With most major opposition groups as nonparticipants, Fujimori supporters captured a majority of seats in balloting on November 22, 1992, for a Democratic Constituent Congress (CCD), which was charged with drafting a new constitution. Earlier, the president had indicated that the CCD would not be superseded by a democratically constituted successor in April 1993 as initially announced, but would remain in office for the duration of his term (that is, to mid-1995). Municipal elections (postponed from October 1992) were, however, held on February 7, 1993, with both the regime and the traditional parties losing ground to locally based independent movements.

Meanwhile, on September 12, 1992, Peru's most celebrated outlaw, *Sendero Luminoso* leader Manuel Abimael GUZMÁN Reinoso, was captured in Lima after a 12-year national search. On October 17 five other members of the organization's Central Committee were also apprehended, offering hope that the antirebel campaign might be drawing to a conclusion.

Approval of the new constitution in December 1993 made it possible for Fujimori to present himself as a candidate for reelection in 1995. Given the success of his economic policies, he appeared to be an odds-on favorite before indications in early 1994 that he might be opposed by Javier PÉREZ de Cuéllar. Initially, polls showed the former UN secretary general leading Fujimori, but by not announcing his candidacy until late August, Pérez de Cuéllar gradually fell behind by about 15 percentage points.

With an ease that reportedly surprised the incumbent himself, Fujimori won nearly two-thirds of the valid votes in presidential balloting on April 9, 1995. Equally surprising was the showing of his ruling coalition (*Cambio 90–Nueva Mayoría*), which won 67 of 120 congressional seats with 51.5 percent of the vote, humbling the leading "traditional" parties, none of whom surpassed the 5 percent threshold needed to retain legal registration.

Growing concern about Peru's economic future, stemming in part from a proposed privatization of the state oil company, *Petroperú,* led to a decline in the president's popularity to 60 percent by late February 1996. On May 31 *Petroperú* was formally put up for sale, with the president's rating reportedly dropping to less than 56 percent shortly thereafter. Nevertheless, the Congress on August 23 paved the way for Fujimori to stand for a third term by voting, after a heated debate, that his initial incumbency was excluded from an existing two-term limit since it began under the previous constitution.

On December 17, 1996, about 25 members of the Túpac Amaru Revolutionary Movement (MRTA, below) stormed a reception at the Japanese embassy in Lima, taking nearly 600 guests prisoner. In the course of intense negotiations all but 83 were released by the end of the month. However, Fujimori rejected concessions in the form of economic policy changes and the release and safe passage out of the country of imprisoned MRTA members. As a result, the siege continued for 126 days, the longest in Latin American history, ending with an assault on the complex by Peruvian commandos April 22, 1997, during which all of the rebels were killed. In the wake of the crisis Fujimori's popularity, which had crested at 70 percent, plummeted to a low of 27 percent, in part because of a move by the government-controlled Congress to dismiss three members of the Constitutional Tribunal who had voted against the president's bid to seek a third term; by midyear his popularity had declined even further because of unsubstantiated charges that Fujimori had been born in Japan, rather than in Peru, as had long been alleged.

On June 4, 1998, Alberto PANDOLFI Arbulú resigned as prime minister and, somewhat surprisingly, was succeeded by Javier VALLE Riestra, a prominent defender of human rights who had publicly opposed Fujimori's reelection. Punctuated by clashes with military and governmental hard-liners, Valle Riestra's tenure lasted only two months, his predecessor, Pandolfi Arbulú, being reinvested as prime minister on August 21. Pandolfi Arbulú resigned again, on January 4, 1999, and Víctor JOY WAY Rojas, the president of Congress and a trusted Fujimori lieutenant, was named his successor. The cabinet resigned en masse on April 14 after the new labor and social promotion minister charged that corruption was rife in the customs system. Many of the ministers were reappointed the following day, although the one who made the accusations and four of his "technocrat" colleagues did not return. On October 8 Joy Way stepped down as prime minister to stand for reelection to Congress and was succeeded by Alberto BUSTAMANTE Belaúnde.

In late December 1999 the National Election Board accepted Fujimori's argument that he was not bound by the two-term limit because he had assumed office before adoption of the current constitution. In mid-March 2000, despite remarkable polling gains, the leading opposition candidate, Alejandro TOLEDO Manrique, threatened to withdraw from presidential contention because of anticipated fraud. However, he remained in the race and at first-round balloting on April 8 was officially credited with a vote share of 40.3 percent, as contrasted with 49.8 for the incumbent. Unable to secure postponement of the runoff scheduled for May 28, Toledo pulled out, urging his followers to abstain. The appeal was only partially successful: Fujimori won 50.3 percent in the "uncontested" second poll and Toledo 16.2 percent, with 32.5 percent of the ballots nullified.

The concluding months of 2000 yielded a remarkable turnabout in Peruvian politics. On September 16 a videotape surfaced that allegedly showed Fujimori's intelligence chief, Vladimiro MONTESINOS, offering a bribe to an opposition member of Congress. Two days later, Fujimori announced that he would call for a new presidential poll, at which he would not stand as a candidate. Collaterally, defections from Fujimori's Peru 2000 coalition cost him his legislative majority. On September 25 Montesinos flew to Panama, and on October 12 the government ordered that the National Intelligence Service be disbanded. On November 20 Fujimori, who had taken up residence in Japan, tendered his resignation. However, the Congress countered with a declaration that the office was vacant because the president had become "morally unfit." Meanwhile, both the first and second vice presidents had resigned, and on November 22 the recently installed congressional president, Valentín PANIAGUA Corazo, was sworn in as interim chief executive. On November 23 a new cabinet took office with Javier Pérez de Cuéllar as prime minister.

In the first-round presidential poll of April 8, 2001, Toledo again failed to secure a majority but went on to defeat former president Alan García Pérez by a narrow margin (53.1 to 46.9 percent) in a runoff on June 3. Subsequently, he named Roberto DAÑINO to head a cabinet composed, with one exception, of members from his Peru Possible grouping, which had won a plurality of 45 legislative seats in April. On July 12, 2002, with the government ministers divided over privatization policy, Toledo shuffled the cabinet, replacing Dañino with Luis SOLARI de la Fuente. Solari lasted until June 2003, after widespread public disturbances in the wake of a teachers' strike had led Toledo to proclaim a state of emergency. He was succeeded by Beatrix MERINO Lucero, a highly popular and seemingly incorruptible tax lawyer, who held office for only six months before succumbing to a whispering campaign that involved rumors of influence peddling as well as supposed homosexuality. She was followed on December 15 by Carlos FERRERO Costa, who, after having served as president of Congress, became Toledo's fourth prime minister in 30 months. In the wake of ordinances by two regional governors legalizing coca cultivation, Ferrero himself resigned on August 11, 2005, and was succeeded by Economy Minister Pedro Pablo KUCZYNSKI.

The Toledo presidency was characterized by relative social peace and higher economic growth rates than Peru had seen since the 1970s. The president himself, however, consistently rated among Latin America's least popular; Toledo spent many of his years in office with an approval rating at or below 20 percent. The president's inner circle was hit by corruption allegations, while poll respondents generally regarded Toledo as lacking a work ethic as well as an awareness of voters' priorities. Leading the list of these concerns were corruption, steadily rising crime rates, and frustration with the unequal distribution of wealth generated by recent economic growth.

Discontent was plainly visible in the 2006 presidential campaign. The candidate who most closely identified herself with Toledo's policies, conservative one-time front-runner Lourdes FLORES Nano, finished third in first-round balloting on April 9. The first-round winner was Ollanta HUMALA, an intensely nationalistic retired army officer, who led the field with 30.6 percent of the vote. Humala, however, was defeated (44.5 to 55.4 percent) by former president García in a runoff on June 4. Nonetheless, Humala's Union for Peru (UPP) won a plurality (45 of 120) of legislative seats.

Five months later, on November 19, 2006, García's Peruvian Aprista Party (PAP) was trounced in municipal and regional elections, winning only 2 (down from 12) of the country's 25 regional governments. PAP also failed to unseat Lima Mayor Luis CASTAÑEDO Lossio of the National Unity (UN) coalition. The only consolation PAP could take from the voting was that no other party fared better, including Humala's UPP/Peru Nationalist Party (PNP), which failed to win a single regional presidency. "Independent" candidates, many of them powerful local political bosses, won 20 of the regional presidencies, along with 112 of 195 provinces.

On May 13, 2008, President García created a new cabinet ministry, environment, and named Antonio BRACK Egg to head it. On October 9 of that year, in the wake of a corruption scandal (see Current issues, below), the entire cabinet tendered its resignation. García's new prime minister, leftist politician Yehude SIMON, assembled a new cabinet on October 14, keeping ten of the ministers and replacing six.

The cabinet underwent another major reshuffle on July 11, 2009, following the violent outcome of indigenous protests (see Current issues, below). Simon was replaced by the president of Congress, Javier VELÁSQUEZ Quesquén of the PAP, who retained nine ministers and replaced seven.

Constitution and government. On December 29, 1993, the "Fujimori constitution," which had been approved by a slim 52.2 percent in an October 31 referendum, came into effect. The principal departures from its 1979 predecessor were supersession of the former bicameral legislature by a unicameral body and the lifting of a ban on presidential reelection. (Although the new basic law provided for only one five-year renewal, it was subsequently argued that Fujimori's incumbency could extend to 2005, as his previous election was under the old constitution.) In addition, the president's authority was significantly enhanced, including the redesignation of control over military appointments as an executive rather than a legislative prerogative. The death penalty was restored for convicted terrorists, although assumed not to be applicable to persons currently incarcerated, while a number of social amenities were abolished, including free university education and a right to job security.

In April 2003 Congress overwhelmingly endorsed restoration of the country's two-chamber legislature, composed of a 150-member lower house and a 50-member Senate. It was argued that the lower chamber would cater to the interests of the various departments and the upper would focus on issues of national concern. The action was never implemented; in 2005 Toledo tried to restore the Senate but lacked the necessary two-thirds majority. In mid-2007 the legislature's constitutional committee approved a proposal to leave the lower house at 120 members and add a 50-member Senate. This proposal failed to pass, and the issue remains under debate.

The country's judicial system is headed by a Supreme Court and includes 18 district courts in addition to a nine-member Constitutional Court and a National Council for the judiciary. In March 1987 President García promulgated legislation that divided the country's 25 departments into 12 regions, each with an assembly of provincial mayors, popularly elected representatives, and delegates of various institutions.

Foreign relations. Peruvian foreign policy stresses protection of its sovereignty and its natural resources. After the 1968 coup the military government expanded contacts with Communist countries, including the Soviet Union, the People's Republic of China, and Cuba. Its relations with neighboring states, though troubled at times by frequent regime changes, are generally equable, apart from a traditional suspicion of Chile and a long-standing border dispute with Ecuador that yielded overt conflict in January–February 1981 and a renewed flare-up in late January 1995 when its neighbor charged Peru with "launching a massive offensive." The latter gave way to a cease-fire on February 13, after a Peruvian announcement that it had recaptured the last Ecuadorian outpost on its territory, and to another on March 1, following a brief, but intense, resumption of fighting. On July 26 the two countries agreed to demilitarize more than 200 square miles of the disputed territory, while President Fujimori attended a Rio Group (*Grupo de Rio*) summit in Quito, Ecuador, in September, during which he surprised observers by extending an unofficial invitation to Ecuadorian President Sixto Durán-Ballén to visit Peru.

A seemingly more definitive event was an agreement reached in Rio de Janeiro on January 19, 1998, on a timetable for a peace treaty. The accord called for the establishment of four commissions dealing with major aspects of the controversy, including one centering on the thorniest issue: border demarcation. The lengthy dispute was formally settled with a "global and definitive" accord signed by Fujimori and his Ecuadorian counterpart in Brasília on October 26, 1998. While the disputed territory was awarded to Peru, control (but not sovereignty) of the principal town of Tiwintza, in addition to a corridor from the border, was assigned to Ecuador, which was also granted free navigation along the Amazon and the right to establish two port facilities within Peruvian territory. Provision was also made for link-up between the two countries' electrical grids and oil pipelines. On June 1, 2007, President García met Ecuador's President Rafael Correa in the northern Peruvian town of Tumbes. García said that Peru had "no territorial or maritime claim to make with Ecuador," and Correa described relations as the "best . . . in the history of the two countries." The two countries' foreign and defense ministers met in February 2008, signing accords establishing a binational confidence-building and security commission.

Long-standing differences with Chile were largely resolved in November 1999 during a state visit by Fujimori to Santiago (the first by a Peruvian leader since the war of the Pacific in 1879–1883). However, a new flare-up occurred in early 2004 with the killing by Chilean marines of a Peruvian national after Chile had heightened border security against illegal immigrants seeking Chilean employment. Relations chilled further in November 2005, when the Peruvian Congress passed a bill claiming sovereignty over 15,000 square miles of Pacific waters controlled by Chile. The maritime border dispute went before the World Court in The Hague, which as of mid-2009 had not reached a verdict; Peru presented its arguments in March 2009, and Chile was to respond by March 2010. From the opposition, Ollanta Humala has been very vocal on this issue. In addition, since 2005 Lima had been frustrated by its inability to secure the extradition of former president Fujimori, who had been arrested in Chile in November 2005 after his return from Japan to seek recovery of the Peruvian presidency. Under house arrest, Fujimori's fate was determined by Chile's Supreme Court, which heard his case in August 2007 and extradited him to Peru on September 22, based on 7 of the original 13 charges.

Peru's relations with Venezuela have been particularly troubled since the 2006 presidential campaign, when Venezuelan President Hugo Chávez was widely accused of interference in internal affairs with his vocal endorsements of Humala. Opponents alleged that Humala's campaign was receiving financial support from Caracas, which he denied. The two countries recalled their ambassadors in April 2006, only to restore them in March 2007 amid a general relaxing of enmity. Peruvian sensitivity to perceived Venezuelan meddling has remained high, however. Strong concerns have been raised about health care programs and the opening of offices of the Venezuelan-supported ALBA movement (Bolivarian Alternative for Latin America) in several regions of Peru. The García government had been divided on the question of whether to seek its closure on grounds of trying to "destabilize" Peru. In 2008, however, it ordered an investigative commission to look into the sources of financing of dozens of such "ALBA houses" set up throughout the country. The commission released a strongly worded report in March 2009 recommending that the 148 existing "ALBA houses" be closed, characterizing them as a tool of foreign political infiltration. As of mid-2009 this step had not been taken, chiefly due to support for the program in Peru's provinces and to the political fallout of June indigenous protests that ended in violence (see Current issues, below).

Relations with neighboring Bolivia worsened significantly in 2008, as Presidents Alán García and Evo Morales—a close ally of Venezuela's Chávez—traded periodic criticisms and insults. Though the substance tended to be disagreements over free trade and Venezuelan influence, the bickering became personal. The lowest point was perhaps in June, when Morales said García was "very fat and not very anti-imperialist." Peru briefly recalled its ambassador from Bolivia.

Relations with the United States had been strained by recurrent controversies over the expropriation of U.S. businesses, the seizure of U.S. fishing boats accused of violating Peru's territorial waters, and the degree of U.S. involvement in combating the narcotics trade. The perils of the interdiction effort were vividly illustrated in April 2001 by a Peruvian jet's downing of a civilian aircraft carrying U.S. missionaries, after a CIA-contracted surveillance plane had mistakenly identified it as engaged in drug smuggling. Two of the occupants, a woman and her infant daughter, were killed in the attack. International attention had also been drawn to the case of a U.S. journalist, Lori Berenson, who was convicted in 1996 of aiding the MRTA guerrillas. Initially sentenced to prison by a secret military court, Berenson was reconvicted by a civilian court in June 2001, with an appeal rejected by the Supreme Court in February 2002.

In addition to continuing differences over the efficacy of Peru's coca eradication effort, relations with the United States were jarred in August 2003 when the U.S. Export-Import Bank refused, on environmental grounds, to issue loan guarantees for a controversial trans-Amazon natural gas pipeline; however, in September the Inter-American Development Bank, with the U.S. representative abstaining, approved a loan package for the project, which was then 70 percent completed.

Peru remains the world's second-largest producer, after Colombia, of coca, the plant used to make cocaine. Police estimate that a large number of small narcotrafficking organizations, most with ties to Mexican, Colombian, and Brazilian cartels, operate in Peru. Though U.S. and UN measurements have found coca cultivation in Peru to have increased by about one-third since 1999, Washington has generally praised Lima's commitment to eradication and interdiction. In May 2007, in part to placate the U.S. government, President García fired his agriculture minister, Juan José SALAZAR, who had taken a conciliatory attitude toward the country's organized coca growers' organizations who, like their counterparts in Bolivia, wish to see eradication replaced by assistance in marketing the leaf for legal purposes. García has pledged to increase manual eradication of coca bushes.

President García has sought to court the favor of the U.S. government, even presenting himself as a pro-American alternative to Venezuelan Chávez and his regional allies. García traveled to the United States on several occasions to urge the Democratic Party leadership in the U.S. Congress to ratify a free trade agreement that President George W. Bush and the Toledo government signed in April 2006. The agreement was ratified in December 2007, after passing the House by a 285–132 vote and the Senate by a 77–18 vote.

García's government has sought to tighten trade ties with Brazil, with a May 2008 agreement for petrochemical investments and a September 2008 offer from President García to set up "a sort of bilateral free trade agreement." Peru's trade push continued with the November 2008 hosting, in Lima, of the fifteenth meeting of the 21-member Asia-Pacific Economic Forum (APEC). During his stay in Lima, Chinese president Hu Jintao signed ten accords for new investment in Peru, while observers speculated that a Peru-China free trade accord was imminent (as of mid-2009 no such accord had been signed).

Peru's relations with Venezuela and Bolivia remained poor in 2009, due to the "ALBA houses" controversy and to Peru's decisions to offer asylum to important opposition figures from both countries. Manuel Rosales, President Hugo Chávez's main opponent in Venezuela's 2006 presidential elections, took up residence in Lima in April 2009. Peru also gave asylum in May 2009 to a top minister of the Gonzalo Sánchez de Lozada government that led Bolivia from 2002 until 2003. A month later, after Bolivian president Evo Morales expressed solidarity with indigenous protesters clashing with Peruvian police and accused the government of "genocide," the García government recalled its ambassador from La Paz.

Current issues. The return of Alan García to the Peruvian presidency was surprising, in view of the disastrous outcome of his previous incumbency. Equally surprising was the emergence of Ollanta Humala as his principal rival. Humala, who sought to emulate the success of Evo Morales, his ethnically based Bolivian counterpart, had difficulty in distancing himself from the shadow of Hugo Chávez, while García's victory would not have been possible without the support of the third-ranked contender, Lourdes Flores. Overall, García won only 9 departments, compared to his opponent's share of 15, although most of the latter were in the less densely populated, impoverished central and southern highlands, where Humala had hoped to launch his "great transformation."

Significantly, Keiko FUJIMORI, the daughter of the former president, won election to Congress in 2006, winning more votes than any other candidate. Even as the ex-president neared an extradition decision in Santiago, García's Aprista bloc entered into what some regarded to be an unofficial alliance with pro-Fujimori political movements. Fujimori's Alliance for the Future Party was the only one to join in García's failed attempt, in late 2006 and early 2007, to institute the death penalty in terrorism cases. President García's dependence on the pro-Fujimori bloc to advance his legislative agenda opened him to charges of insufficiently supporting Fujimori's prosecution for human rights crimes. Opposition politicians speculated in July that García had granted Fujimori a "golden jail" in exchange for his legislative bloc's support for PAP legislator Javier VELÁSQUEZ Quesquen's candidacy for president of the Congress.

In April 2007 García chose a hard-line response to disputes with coca farmers in the highlands, who had organized strikes and blockades to protest the forcible eradication of their crops. With much of the chamber abstaining on April 26, 2007, the Congress gave the president the authority to rule by decree on issues relating to drug trafficking, terrorism, and organized crime. Human rights defenders assailed the decrees, which included a prohibition on local officials participating in strikes and an automatic pardon for security personnel who injure or kill strikers while "fulfilling their duty."

On August 15, 2007, an 8.0 magnitude earthquake devastated a region in southern Peru centered on the city of Pisco, killing more than 500 people. President García received high marks for his personal, highly visible response to the disaster, though many voiced discontent at the confused, improvised nature of the rescue and rebuilding efforts he led.

The Fujimori trial dominated the country's political discourse during 2008. In December 2007 Fujimori was sentenced to six years in prison for illegally ordering the search and seizure of his shadowy former intelligence chief, Vladimiro Montesinos. He then went on to face human rights charges, beginning with two massacres committed by a government death squad in the early 1990s.

As the findings of a groundbreaking 2003 truth commission report continued to reverberate, human rights were a major topic of debate in 2007 and 2008. Human rights defenders argued that the PAP and pro-Fujimori political blocs wished to remove Peru from the Inter-American Human Rights Court, a body of the Organization of American States (OAS) that, on two occasions, has required the Peruvian government to pay damages to the relatives of massacred *Sendero Luminoso* guerrillas and sympathizers. In May 2008 Vice President Luis GIAMPETRI Rojas called publicly for Peru's withdrawal from the court. The PAP and pro-Fujimori blocs also collaborated in late 2006 on controversial legislation that placed strict regulations on the financing and activities of nongovernmental organizations. In May 2008, after APRODEH, one of Peru's main human rights groups, recommended that the European Union remove the nearly defunct MRTA guerrillas from its list of international terrorist groups, President García called APRODEH "traitors to the country" and ordered an investigation of its financing. That month media reports alleged that the government had set up an intelligence group, *"Comando Canela,"* to infiltrate nongovernmental human rights defenders groups and others engaged in social protest.

During his first year in office García's approval ratings consistently hovered around 50 percent, but by July 2008 they had fallen to 26 percent. Economic growth and reduced poverty levels helped the president, though good economic news was far scarcer in the impoverished regions where Humala was popular. Inflation, which was expected to reach 7 percent in 2008, was an increasing concern as higher food and fuel prices disproportionately impacted the poor. Public security became a principal complaint as citizen concerns increased about worsening crime, particularly by drug-related organizations. The García government has sought to implement a controversial policy in response, by giving the armed forces a greater internal crime-fighting role. Meanwhile, remnants of *Sendero Luminoso* and other narco-criminal gangs were responsible for sporadic acts of violence in the countryside, including ambushes that killed police and officials involved in coca leaf regulation in December 2006 and April 2007 as well as an attack on a rural police station in November 2007. About 42 Peruvian antinarcotics police or coca eradicators were killed from January 2007 to July 2009.

Social protests were frequent in 2008, including agrarian demonstrations in February, violent protests in a southern mining region in June, an anti–free-trade general strike on July 9, and a large-scale mobilization of indigenous groups in August. García government officials accused the pro-Humala political opposition of instigating the disturbances to destabilize the country. The indigenous mobilizations protested natural resource decrees that would have allowed indigenous reserves to sell concessions to foreign energy companies, an issue that the August 2008 repeal of two of the decrees failed to resolve.

Oil was at the center of an October 2008 scandal in which audiotapes revealed a top state oil-licensing official and a PAP politician discussing plans to steer contracts to a Norwegian petroleum company in exchange for bribes. The revelations triggered a major shakeup of Peru's cabinet, with Del Castillo replaced by Yehude Simon, a left-wing governor of Lambayeque province and a member of the tiny, regional **Peruvian Humanist Movement Party** (*Partido Movimiento Humanista Peruano*—PMHP) who had spent 8 years in prison during the Fujimori government on charges of "apology of terrorism."

On April 7, 2009, Peru's Supreme Court convicted 70-year-old former president Alberto Fujimori and sentenced him to 25 years in prison for his role in two massacres carried out by the Grupo Colina death squad, among other abuses. His conviction, plus a subsequent July conviction on corruption charges, left the pro-Fujimori political current with an uncertain future, though Fujimori's daughter, congresswoman Keiko FUJIMORI, continued to perform well in mid-2009 polling.

On May 16, 2009, President García declared a 30-day state of emergency in several Amazon-basin provinces, sending the armed forces to help the police deal with a growing wave of indigenous groups' protests, which had begun a month earlier and had grown to include about 30,000 people blockading roads, rivers, and pipelines. The protesters were opposing additional decrees, among a number that President García had issued in 2007, shortly before U.S. ratification of the countries' free-trade agreement, to ease foreign investment in such sectors as energy, mining, and forestry. Violence erupted in Bagua, Amazonas, on June 5, as clashes between indigenous protesters and police claimed at least 34 lives, 24 of them police officers'. Indigenous leaders claimed that their death toll was higher and that police had fired on them from helicopters.

The Congress sought a censure vote on June 30 against Prime Minister Simon and Interior Minister Mercedes CABANILLAS for their handling of the matter; the vote failed only because 11 pro-Humala legislators were under suspension for their earlier role in a raucous protest in the Congress in support of the indigenous cause. While they survived the censure vote, Simon, Cabanillas, and several other cabinet ministers were drummed out less than two weeks later, amid a cabinet shakeup that saw Simon replaced with Congressional president Velásquez of the PAP, and Cabanillas replaced with independent politician Octavio SALAZAR. Salazar became the García government's fourth interior minister in a twelve-month period.

POLITICAL PARTIES AND GROUPS

Most of the political parties active before the 1968 coup were of comparatively recent vintage, the principal exception being the Peruvian affiliate of APRA (PAP, below), which was alternately outlawed and legalized beginning in the early 1930s. While failing to capture the presidency until 1985, it contributed to the success of other candidates and was the nucleus of a powerful opposition coalition that controlled both houses of Congress during Belaúnde's 1963–1968 presidency.

During the decade after 1968, the status of the parties fluctuated, many being permitted a semilegal existence while denied an opportunity to engage in electoral activity. Most, except those of the extreme left, were allowed to register before the Constituent Assembly election of June 1978, with further relaxation occurring before the presidential and legislative balloting of May 1980, in which 20 groups participated. By contrast, only 9 groups presented candidates in 1985, with the PAP, the IU, the Democratic Convergence, and the AP collectively capturing 96.9 percent of the valid votes.

Virtually all of the major opposition parties either boycotted or failed to qualify for the Democratic Constituent Congress election of November 22, 1992, at which the regime-supportive C-90–NM won a majority of seats, with the remainder scattered among 8 other parties. Subsequent elections were held in 1995, 2000, 2001, and 2006, with 24 parties or party coalitions participating on the latter occasion.

Presidential Party:

Peruvian Aprista Party (*Partido Aprista Peruano*—PAP). The PAP was launched in 1930 as the Peruvian affiliate of the regionwide American Popular Revolutionary Alliance (*Alianza Popular*

Revolucionaria Americana—APRA), formed six years earlier in Mexico. APRA was initially a radical left-wing movement that attracted substantial mass support. Its Peruvian branch (also frequently referenced as APRA) was not legalized until 1945. Subsequently, it mellowed into a mildly left-of-center, middle-class grouping with a strong labor base. Despite long-standing antagonism between the PAP and the military, its principal figure, Víctor Raúl Haya de la Torre, was permitted to return from exile in 1969 and was designated president of the Constituent Assembly after the party had won a substantial plurality in the election of June 18, 1978. Following his death in August 1979, Haya de la Torre was succeeded as party leader by Armando VILLANUEVA del Campo. Decisively defeated in the 1980 balloting, the party subsequently split into a left-wing faction headed by Villanueva and a right-wing faction headed by second vice presidential candidate Andrés TOWNSEND Ezcurra, who was formally expelled from the party in January 1981 and later formed the Hayista Bases Movement (*Movimiento de Bases Hayista*—MBH).

While he remained an influential party figure, Villanueva's control of the organization ended in 1983, with the rise of Alan García Pérez, a centrist, who in 1985 became the first Aprista leader to assume the presidency of the republic. His widespread popularity was viewed as the principal reason for the party's unprecedented sweep of municipal elections in November 1986. Unable to resolve the country's burgeoning economic problems, García suffered a dramatic loss in popular support during 1988 and resigned the party presidency at a congress in late December, with the office itself being abolished. The delegates then voted to install his rival, former prime minister Luis Alva Castro, as general secretary. Alva Castro placed third in the 1990 presidential race.

Following the 1992 coup, former president García was granted political asylum in Colombia, which in early 1993 rejected a request by the Fujimori government that he be extradited to face charges of personal enrichment while in office. Shortly thereafter, the Aprista leadership stripped García of his position as secretary general, granting him the honorary title of "secretary general in exile." It then proceeded to name a tripartite interim secretariat consisting of an *alanista,* former prime minister Villanueva; a García opponent, Alva Castro; and an "equidistant" chair, Luis Alberto SÁNCHEZ Sánchez. However, this did not satisfy the more radical *Generación en Marcha* "renewalist" and *Nueva Generación* leaders, who pressed for a party plenum to elect new officials.

In November 1993 García announced that he had applied for Colombian citizenship, and in August 1994, following the discovery of a secret Cayman Islands bank account in the name of a fugitive businessman to whom he was linked, he reportedly resigned from the party. However, Agustin MANTILLA Campos, elected secretary general in August 1994, and Mercedes Cabanillas, the party's 1995 standard-bearer, were both *alanistas*.

By plunging to less than 5 percent of the vote in April 1995, the party faced the loss of its registration and the humiliating need to collect 100,000 signatures in support of relegalization. It responded by appointing Germán PARRA Herrera as head of an "action command" charged with reorganizing the party. He later resigned in October, claiming that other party members were refusing to recognize the gravity of the crisis. The party leadership subsequently reverted to Alva Castro, assisted by a political commission.

In early 2001 the Supreme Court revoked a sentence for corruption that had been passed against García in absentia, saying that the statute of limitations had run its course. The former president subsequently returned for a reelection bid, losing to Alejandro Toledo Manrique of Peru Possible (below) in the second-round poll of June 3.

At the first-round presidential poll of April 19, 2006, García placed second with a 24.3 percent vote share but went on to defeat Ollanta Humala of the UPP (below) in a runoff on June 4. The PAP received the second-largest vote percentage in the 2006 legislative elections, with 20.6 percent of the total valid votes cast, only 0.6 percentage points behind the UPP. Its legislators hold 36 congressional seats. The PAP fared poorly in November 2006 municipal and regional elections, but the party maintained the presidency of Peru's Congress in 2007–2009, with support from the pro-Fujimori Alliance for the Future and Humala's UPP.

Leaders: Alan Gabriel Ludwig GARCÍA Pérez (President of the Republic and President of the Party), Mauricio MULDER Bedoya (Secretary General), Mercedes CABANILLAS Bustamante (President of Political Committee).

Other Legislative Parties:

Nationalist Union Party for Peru (*Partido Nacionalista Unión por el Perú*—PNUP). The PNUP was launched by Ollanta Humala in late 2005 as a coalition of the UPP and PNP. Thereafter, it was frequently referenced as the UPP or the UPP/PNP rather than the PNUP, as the two parties maintained distinct identities. The coalition was the largest vote-getter in the 2006 legislative elections, with 21.2 percent of valid votes. Internal dissent caused two new parties, the BP and CD, to splinter from the UPP in 2008. All four parties continue to support Humala, and together, with 42 seats as of mid-2009, had the largest bloc in the Congress.

Leader: Lt. Col. (Ret.) Ollanta HUMALA Tasso (2006 presidential candidate).

Peru Nationalist Party (*Partido Nacionalista Peruano*—PNP). The PNP is the political arm of the Etnocacerista Movement (*Movimiento Etnocacerista*—ME), founded by former army major Antauro HUMALA, who participated in an abortive uprising against former President Fujimori. The ME is an openly racist, anti-white formation claiming to reflect the Incan moral code of Marshal Andrés CACERES, a hero of the nineteenth-century war with Chile. Antauro Humala is Ollanta's (UPP) younger brother. It has grown distant from the UPP, which has been more moderate in its opposition to the García government. As of mid-2009 the PNP had 23 seats in the Congress, making it the largest party in the bloc supporting Ollanta Humala.

Leader: Ollanta HUMALA Tasso.

Union for Peru (*Unión por el Perú*—UPP). The UPP was formed as a campaign vehicle for Javier Pérez de Cuéllar following the announcement by the former UN secretary general on August 18, 1994, that he would stand for the presidency in 1995. By capturing 21.8 percent of the vote on April 9 of that year, the UPP candidate ran a distant second to Fujimori. Although the party's vote share plummeted to 0.3 percent in the presidential election of April 2000, Pérez de Cuéllar was named prime minister in the Paniagua administration of November 2000.

Pérez de Cuéllar withdrew from the party following the designation of Humala as its 2006 standard-bearer. The UPP received the largest percentage of voting in the 2006 legislative elections, with 21.2 percent of the total valid votes cast.

Leaders: José VEGA Antonio (Secretary General), Eduardo ESPINOZA Ramos (President).

Popular Bloc (*Bloque Popular*—BP). On August 6, 2008, after a series of disagreements with the UPP, particularly over leading UPP members' support of PAP legislators to serve as president of the Congress, a group of eight more radical legislators split from the party and declared themselves the "Patriotic Peruvian Unity – Popular Bloc."

Leader: Antonio LEÓN (Spokesman).

Democratic Commitment (*Compromiso Democrático*—CD). Twelve days after the BP split from the UPP, another group of 3 UPP legislators followed suit, citing similar disagreements, and formed the CD.

Leader: Washington ZEBALLOS Gámez (Coordinator).

Alliance for the Future (*Alianza por el Futuro*—AF). The AF was formed in 2005 as a coalition of the two pro-Fujimori groups below, in anticipation that the former president's effort to reenter the country and seek reelection as head of his party (see *Sí Cumple,* below) would be denied. With 13.1 percent of all votes cast, the group finished fourth and won 13 legislative seats in 2006, including 1 by the former president's daughter, Keiko Fujimori, who received more votes than any other single legislative candidate. The AF bloc in the Peruvian Congress exerts power beyond its small size, as its cooperation is usually necessary to gain a majority. This power made Alberto Fujimori's extradition and trial an uncomfortable topic for Peruvian politicians whose agendas at times require AF support. An example occurred in July 2008, when *Fujimorista* support proved crucial to the election of the PAP's Javier Velásquez to the presidency of the Congress; opposition figures alleged that the vote coincided with a loosening of the conditions of Fujimori's imprisonment. Leading legislator Keiko Fujimori declared her intention in 2008 to fuse the pro-Fujimori parties into a single entity, "Fuerza 2011," to compete in the 2011 presidential and congressional elections.

Leaders: Pablo CORREA (NM), Jaime Yoshiyama TANAKA (NM), Martha Gladys CHÁVEZ Cossio (NM, 2005 presidential candidate), Keiko FUJIMORI (*Sí Cumple*), Santiago FUJIMORI (*Sí Cumple*).

New Majority (*Nueva Mayoría*—NM). The *Nueva Mayoría* was launched in 1992 by a group of independents who presented a joint list with *Cambio 90* for the 1992 and 1995 polls, participated in *Perú 2000,* and remained allied with C90 in 2001. By 2006, the C90 designation had given way to the NM.

Leader: Martha Gladys CHÁVEZ Cossio.

He Delivers (*Sí Cumple*). *Sí Cumple* was founded by former president Alberto Fujimori in 1998 as *Vamos Vecino* (Let's Go Neighbor), adopting its current name in 2005. In 2000 the party joined with C90 and the NM in a Peru 2000 Alliance to support Fujimori's reelection. In 2005 the group again joined with C90 and NM in *Aliaga Sí Cumple,* but the action was rejected by the National Jury of Elections and the other two groups contesting the 2006 poll as the Alliance for the Future (see above).

Leaders: Alberto FUJIMORI (Former President of the Republic, extradited to Peru and facing trial), Absalón VASQUEZ, Carlos ORELLANA Quintanilla (Secretary General).

Christian People's Party (*Partido Popular Cristiano*—PPC). The PPC was formed in the wake of a 1967 split in the now-defunct PDC, Luis Bedoya Reyes leading a conservative faction out of the parent group. The party was runner-up to the PAP in the Constituent Assembly election of June 1978 and placed third in the 1980 presidential and legislative races, after which it joined the Belaúnde government by accepting two ministerial appointments. For the 1985 balloting it formed an alliance with Townsend Ezcurra's MBH styled the Democratic Convergence (*Convergencia Democrática*—Conde), which secured 7 Senate and 12 Chamber seats. It participated in the 1990 campaign as a member of Fredemo, which won a plurality of one-third in each house of Congress. Initially endorsing its secretary general for the 1995 presidential race, it subsequently backed the UPP's Pérez de Cuéllar. In the congressional poll it won only 3 seats, none of which was retained in 2000.

For the 2001 campaign it served as the core of the National Unity (*Unidad Nacional*—UN) coalition, including the PPC, the PSN, RN, and *Renovación* (all below). The UN secured 15 congressional seats, while its leader, Lourdes Flores Nano, ran third, with 24 percent of the vote, in the presidential race. Led by Flores, the PPC again participated in the UN coalition in 2006, with Flores finishing third in the first round of presidential voting despite leading the preelection polls in late 2005 and early 2006. The UN finished third in voting in the 2006 legislative elections, with 15.3 percent of total valid votes cast and 17 seats. It was the only party grouping that made a strong showing in the November 2006 local elections, which heavily favored independent candidates.

Antero Flores, a top PPC leader who frequently jockeyed for position with Lourdes Flores, became the García government's defense minister in a December 2007 cabinet shake-up. Flores served in this position until July 2009. The UN political bloc effectively disbanded in August 2008, with Flores citing ideological differences with the PSN and its leader, Lima Mayor Luis Castañeda, whom she accused of being too accommodating to the García government. The UN continues to exist in name as a legislative grouping of PPC members and a handful of independent legislators, totaling 13 seats in the Congress.

Leaders: Lourdes FLORES Nano (President of the Party and 2001 and 2006 presidential candidate), Antero FLORES Aráoz (Former Minister of Defense, Former President of Congress, and Former President of the Party).

Parliamentary Alliance (*Alianza Parliamentaria—Alianza*). The *Alianza* is the successor to the Center Front (*Frente del Centro*—FC). The FC was formed before the 2006 election as a coalition of the AP, *Somos Perú,* and the CNI (see "Other parties competing in the 2006 election," below). Its candidates received 7.1 percent of votes cast in the 2006 legislative elections, finishing fifth and winning five seats. Following the election, it was joined by the two legislators from President Toledo's *Perú Posible* party, making a total of 7 seats. The coalition also included *Renovación* between 2006 and 2008. As a temporary electoral alliance, the FC was formally dissolved after the 2006 elections.

Leaders: Drago Guillermo KISIC Wagner; Victor Andrés GARCÍA Belaúnde.

Popular Action (*Acción Popular*—AP). Founded by Fernando Belaúnde Terry in 1956, the moderately rightist AP captured the presidency in 1963 and served as the government party until the 1968 coup. Democratic, nationalist, and dedicated to the extension of social services, AP sought to mobilize public energies for development on Peru's terms. After the 1968 coup the party split, a mainstream faction remaining loyal to Belaúnde and another, headed by former vice president Edgardo SEONE Corrales, collaborating with the military junta. Belaúnde was returned to office in the 1980 election, winning 45.4 percent of the votes cast, while the AP captured 98 of 180 Chamber seats and 26 of 60 seats in the Senate. However, in a massive voter reversal, the party won only one provincial city in municipal elections in November 1983 and ran fourth in the 1985 balloting, obtaining only 10 Chamber and 5 Senate seats. The party supported Vargas Llosa for the presidency in 1990 as a member of the Democratic Front. A shadow of its former self, the AP won only 4 congressional seats in 1995, while its presidential candidate, Raúl Diez CANSECO, drew a vote share of 1.6 percent. In April 2000 AP presidential candidate Víctor Andrés García Belaúnde secured a minuscule 0.4 percent of the vote, while the party's legislative representation dropped to 3 seats. It won an equal number in 2001. Former leader Terry died in June 2002. Popular Action candidates accounted for 4 of 5 seats won by the Center Front coalition in the 2006 legislative elections.

Leader: Victor Andrés GARCÍA Belaúnde (President of the Party).

Peru Possible (*Perú Posible*). *Perú Posible* leader Alejandro Toledo entered the 1995 presidential race as organizer of a group styled Possible Nation (*País Posible*) that joined with the **Democratic Coordination** (*Coordinadora Democrática*—Code) in an alignment registered as *Code–País Posible.* The renamed formation was credited with a second-place legislative finish (29 seats) in 2000, Toledo himself withdrawing from the presidential runoff of May 28 because of anticipated fraud. He secured a 53.1 percent victory at second-round balloting on June 3, 2001. A group of *Perú Posible* dissidents subsequently organized as **Peru Now** (*Perú Ahora*). Running without a coalition, the party fared poorly in the 2006 elections; it decided to run no presidential candidate, and its candidates for the legislature received only 4.1 percent of votes cast, finishing sixth and winning only 2 seats. The party made a similarly poor showing in the 2006 municipal and regional elections.

Leaders: David WAISMAN (Former Second Vice President of the Republic), Alejandro TOLEDO Manrique (Former President of the Republic), Luis SOLARI de la Fuente (Former Prime Minister and Secretary General of the Party).

We Are Peru (*Somos Perú*). *Somos Perú* is an outgrowth of the *Somos Lima* movement organized by former independent Alberto Andrade Carmona after his capture of the Lima mayorship in November 1995. The party's supporters include some former members of the defunct right-wing Solidarity and Democracy (*Solidaridad y Democracia*—Sode), which had been led by Javier SILVA Ruete. In early 1999 Andrade led public opinion polls for the 2000 presidential election but dropped to a distant third in the balloting of April 2000. For the 2001 presidential poll, it joined with the CD in supporting the candidacy of Jorge SANTISTEVAN de Noriega. Andrade is the only We Are Peru member of Peru's Congress.

Leaders: Alberto ANDRADE Carmona (2000 presidential candidate), Eduardo CARHUARICRA Meza (Secretary General).

National Alliance (*Grupo Parlamentario Alianza Nacional*—GANA). The GANA coalition formed in August 2008, after the PSN split with the PPC, effectively dissolved the UN coalition. As of mid-2009 it included 3 center-right parties and held 6 seats in the Congress. While in the opposition, it frequently adopts positions supportive of García and the PAP bloc in Congress.

Leader: Walter Ricardo MENCHOLA Vásquez (Coalition Spokesman).

National Solidarity Party (*Partido de Solidaridad Nacional*—PSN). Formally registered in early 1999, the PSN served in 2000 as the vehicle for the presidential campaign of Luís Castañeda Lossio, former head of the social security system. During the 2001 campaign, Castañeda withdrew in favor of the UN's Flores Nano. In October 2005 Castañeda announced he would not contend for the position in 2006. Later that year, he was easily reelected as mayor of Lima. Flores Nano split with the PSN in 2008, accusing Castañeda of supporting the García government in exchange for central government funding of municipal projects in Lima.

Leader: Luís CASTAÑEDA Lossio (Mayor of Lima and 2000 presidential candidate).

National Restoration (*Restauracion Nacional*—RN). The RN is a small formation led by evangelicals. Running without a coalition, it won two legislative seats in 2006, finishing seventh with 4.0 percent of votes cast. After a poor showing in 2006 local elections—during which several of the party's few winning candidates were not from an evangelical background—the party has experienced internal turmoil, expelling leader Humberto Lay Sun in early 2007. Later in the year, however, Lay reestablished himself as the party's leader.

Leader: Humberto LAY SUN.

National Renewal (*Renovación Nacional—Renovación*). This rightist party was founded by Rafael REY Rey in 1992. It formed part of the UN coalition in the 2001 and 2006 elections. It split with UN later in 2006 and spent two years as part of the Parliamentary Alliance (above) until joining the newly formed GANA in 2008. Rey has served in the García government as minister of production, ambassador to Italy (briefly in 2009), and minister of defense. He has indicated that he intends to lead *Renovación* in the 2011 elections.

Leader: Rafael REY (Current Minister of Defense).

Other Parties Participating in 2006 Election:

National Coordination of Independents (*Coordinadora Nacional de Independientes*—CNI). The CNI, a grouping of independents organized before the 2006 elections, ran as part of the Center Front coalition (see *Alianza*, above). The CNI failed to elect any of its candidates to Peru's Congress in 2006.

Leaders: Drago Guillermo KISIC Wagner, Gonzálo AGUIRRE Arriz.

Independent Moralizing Front (*Frente Independiente Moralizador*—FIM). The FIM was launched before the 1995 election by Luis Fernando Olivera Vega, a former investigator for the state prosecutor's office who had pursued a six-year crusade to bring former president Alan García to trial for alleged misdeeds while in office. The party won 6 congressional seats in 1995, 9 in 2000, and 11 in 2001. Olivera finished fourth, with 9.9 percent of the vote, in the 2001 presidential balloting. The party briefly endorsed Peru Possible candidates in 2006, then chose to run its own candidates. Olivera ultimately dropped out of the presidential balloting to focus on the legislative campaign. Neither he nor other FIM candidates won any seats.

Leader: Luis Fernando OLIVERA Vega (2001 presidential candidate).

Decentralizing Coalition (*Concertación Decentralista*—CD). The center-left CD was formed before the 2006 election as a coalition of the **Party for Social Democracy–Compromise Peru** (*Partido por la Democracia Social–Compromiso Perú*) and the **Peruvian Humanist Movement Party** (*Partido Movimiento Humanista Peruano*—PMHP). The party has since been inactive.

Leader: Susana María del Carmen VILLARÁN de la Puente (2006 presidential candidate).

Democratic Force (*Fuerza Democrática*—FA). The FA was launched in 1998 to compete at the municipal level. It won a small number of local positions in 2006, mainly in Peru's remote Amazon basin region.

Leader: Alberto BOREA.

Popular Agricultural Front of Peru (*Frente Popular Agrícola del Perú*—Frepap). In the 1995 election Frepap was known as the Peruvian Agricultural and Popular Front (*Frente Agrícola y Popular del Perú*—FAPP). It won two congressional seats in 2000 and none in 2001 or 2006.

Leader: Alfredo GÁLVEZ (2006 presidential candidate).

Country Project (*Proyecto Pais*—PP). The PP is a "law and order" group founded in 1998 by Marco Antonio Arrunategui Cevallos.

Leader: Marco Antonio ARRUNATEGUI Cevallos (2001 and 2006 presidential candidate).

Andean Renaissance (*Renacimiento Andino*—RA). The RA was launched in 2001 by Ciro Alfredo Gálvez Herrera, who won less than 1 percent of the vote that year. It withdrew from the 2006 presidential election to avoid drawing support from Lourdes Flores.

Leader: Ciro Alfredo GÁLVEZ Herrera (2001 and 2006 presidential candidate).

Socialist Party of Peru (*Partido Socialista del Perú*—PSP). The PSP is a left-wing party organized in 1979. It ran in 1995 under an Opening for a National Development–Socialist Party (*Apertura para el Desarrollo Nacional–Partido Socialista*) list but won only 0.3 percent of the legislative vote.

During the 1990s, PSP leader Javier Diez Canseco was a vigorous opponent of the Fujimori regime and, as a member of Congress, participated in investigations of alleged human rights violations by members of both the Shining Path and the Peruvian Armed Forces.

Leaders: Javier DIEZ Canseco (2006 presidential candidate), Julio Sergio CASTRO Gomez.

Also participating in the 2006 poll were the **Alliance for Progress** (*Alianza para el Progresso*—APP), led by César ACUÑA Peralta; the **National Justice Party** (*Partido Justicia Nacional*—PJN), led by Jamie SALINAS; **Advance the Country – Social Integration Party** (*Avanza País – Partido de Integración Social*—AP-PIS), led by Ulisés HUMALA, Ollanta Humala's brother; the **New Left Movement** (*Movimiento Nueva Izquierdo*—MNI), led by Alberto MORENO; the **With Force Peru** (*Con Fuerza Perú*—CFP), led by Pedro KOECHLIN Von Stein; **Peru Now** (*Perú Ahora*), led by Luis GUERRERO Figueroa; the **Democratic Reconstruction** (*Reconstrucción Democrática*—RD); the **Peruvian Resurgence** (*Resurgimiento Peruano*—RP); the **And It's Called Peru** (*Y se llama Perú*); and the **Let's Make Progress Peru** (*Progresemos Perú*—PP).

Groups Not Competing in 2006:

Land and Liberty (*Tierra y Libertad*—TL) is a new leftwing movement founded on June 30, 2009, in the wake of clashes with indigenous protesters (see Current issues, above), by Catholic priest Marco ARANA and Pedro FRANCKE.

Leaders: Marco ARANA and Pedro FRANCKE.

Change 90 (*Cambio 90*—C90). *Cambio 90* was organized before the 1990 campaign as a political vehicle for Alberto Fujimori. While Fujimori secured a majority of second-round presidential votes, C90 ran third in both upper and lower house legislative contests. Before the 1992 election it formed a coalition with the *Nueva Mayoría* (below) that won a 55 percent majority of CCD seats on a vote share of 38 percent. In 1995 Fujimori was reelected with 64.3 percent of the vote, while the ruling coalition decimated the traditional parties by securing 51.4 percent of the valid ballots. For the 2000 balloting C90 headed a coalition styled *Perú 2000,* which included *Vamos Vecino* (under *Sí Cumple,* below) and was credited with winning 52 of 120 congressional seats. It was reduced to 3 seats in 2001. By the 2006 elections C90 has largely given way to the *Nueva Mayoría* among the pro-Fujimori bloc.

Leader: Andrés REGGIARDO Sayán.

Also not competing in 2006 were two minor groups that won single legislative seats in 2001: **All for Victory** (*Todos por la Victoria*—TV), led by Ricardo Manuel NORIEGA Salaverry and Mario MOLINA Almanza, and the **Popular Solution** (Solución Popular—SP), led by Carlos BOLOÑA Behr and Alfredo GONZÁLEZ Salazar.

Guerrilla and Terrorist Organizations:

Shining Path (*Sendero Luminoso*). The *Sendero Luminoso* (also translated as Luminous Path) originated at Ayacucho University as a small Maoist group led by a former philosophy instructor Dr. Manuel Abimael Guzmán Reinoso. During 1980 it was involved in a number of bombings in Lima, Ayacucho, Cuzco, and other provincial towns in southern Peru, causing property damage only. About 170 of its followers were arrested in October 1980 and January 1981, but most were freed in a daring raid on the Ayacucho police barracks in March 1982. Thereafter, guerrilla activity in the region intensified, including the assassination of a number of local officials and alleged police informants. While the insurgency appeared to remain localized (apart from sporadic terrorist attacks in Lima), the government felt obliged to order a major sweep through the affected provinces by 1,500 military and police units at the end of the year. Subsequently, the rebellion showed no sign of diminishing, despite the imposition of military rule in the departments of Ayacucho, Apurímac, Huancavelica, Huánuco, and part of San Martín. By late 1987 more than 10,000 deaths, on both sides, had been reported since the insurgency began, and the organization, estimated to encompass at least 3,000 members, had become increasingly active in urban areas. Its reputed second-in-command, Osman MOROTE Barrionuevo, was captured by Lima police in June 1988 and subsequently sentenced to 15 years' imprisonment. The insurgency intensified during 1989 as the nation's economy approached collapse; however, its adherents were surprisingly unsuccessful in a campaign to limit participation at municipal elections in November. Guzmán himself was captured in Lima on September 12, 1992, and sentenced by a secret military tribunal to life imprisonment, while his principal deputy, Edmundo Daniel Cox Beauzeville, was apprehended in August 1993.

In January 1994 it was reported that *Sendero Luminoso* had split into two factions, one loyal to the imprisoned Guzmán and another, styled the **Red Path** (*Sendero Rojo*), committed to continuing the rebellion under the leadership of Oscar Ramírez Durand (a.k.a. "Camarada Feliciano"). By March, however, nearly 4,100 alleged *senderistas* had surrendered under a 1992 "Repentance Law," while a number of Ramírez's lieutenants were apprehended during the ensuing three months. By midyear, while 66 of the country's 155 provinces remained under a state of emergency, guerrilla activity was reported to be confined largely to three areas: some marginal districts of the capital, the highlands of Lima department, and the Huallaga valley jungle region. In August 1997 *Sendero Luminoso* guerrillas captured about 30 oil workers in a remote jungle area 200 miles east of Lima; two days later the hostages were released after their French-based employer sent supplies of food, medicine, and clothing. The deputy leader of *Sendero Rojo,* Pedro Domingo QUINTEROS Ayllón (a.k.a. "Camarada Luis"), was captured in April 1998, while the senior military leader, Juan Carlos RIOS, was arrested in December, by which time the grouping was described as "largely impotent" as the result of the government's campaign. Ramírez Durand, the formation's last major leader, was captured in July 1999 and sentenced to life imprisonment.

More recently, bomb attacks in March 2002, preceding a visit to Lima by U.S. President Bush, were attributed to a *Sendero Luminoso* faction, while renewed *Sendero* activity was reported from mid-2003 onward by what appeared to be drastically depleted guerrilla units.

In November 2004 a retrial of Guzmán and his lieutenants was launched, after a constitutional tribunal had overturned their original convictions on the grounds that they should have been tried in a civilian rather than a military court. However, the proceedings collapsed when two of the three presiding judges stepped down because of involvement in earlier rulings, with a second retrial opening in Lima in September 2005. On October 13, 2006, Guzmán and several lieutenants were sentenced to life in prison for "aggravated terrorism."

Sendero activity continued at a low but significant level in 2007 and 2008, including two ambushes that took the lives of police and civilian coca-regulation authorities as well as a November 2007 attack that destroyed a police station in Apurímac. Most analysts believe the group has less than 500 members and now depends almost entirely on the cocaine trade for its livelihood, both by protecting narco-traffickers and by engaging in the business directly.

Sendero activity increased significantly in 2008, particularly in the Upper Huallaga and Apurimac and Ene Valley (VRAE) regions, with military casualties totaling 25, the largest figure since the early 1990s. The group's VRAE faction, led by "Comrade JOSÉ," is called the Principal Regional Committee and rejects both founder Guzmán and any possibility of negotiation. "Comrade ARTEMIO," the Sendero leader in the Upper Huallaga and a member of the group since the 1980s, has made periodic offers of negotiation—the most recent in a December 2008 radio interview—which the García government has rejected.

Leaders: "Comrade JOSÉ" (Principal Regional Committee), "Comrade ARTEMIO" (Upper Huallaga region), Manuel Abimael GUZMÁN Reinoso (imprisoned), Edmundo Daniel COX Beauzeville (imprisoned), Margie Evelyn CLAVO Peralta (imprisoned), Oscar RAMÍREZ Durand (*Sendero Rojo,* imprisoned).

Túpac Amaru Revolutionary Movement (*Movimiento Revolucionario Túpac Amaru*—MRTA). Launched in 1983 by Victor Polay Campos (a former college roommate of Peru's center-left president Alan García), the Marxist MRTA took its name from Túpac Amaru, an eighteenth-century Indian rebel who was killed by the Spaniards. The group was considered responsible for a number of bomb attacks in Lima in 1984, but it suspended guerrilla activity after García's election in 1985 to give the new president an opportunity to carry out his pledges to address the needs of the nation's poor. However, the MRTA terminated the "truce" in August 1986 and subsequently was accused of several assassinations and bombings in the late 1980s, having established ties with a number of other guerrilla movements in Latin America. (Although considered "less indiscriminate" than the *Sendero Luminoso* in its attacks, the MRTA was nevertheless reported to have earned the "undying enmity" of the Peruvian military because of the assassination of Defense Minister Gen. Enrique LÓPEZ Albujar in 1989.)

As was the case with many regional guerrilla groups, the MRTA appeared to lose strength concurrent with the demise of communism in the early 1990s. Polay Campos, who had been arrested in February 1989 only to escape in a dramatic July 1990 jailbreak, was recaptured in June 1993 and sentenced to life imprisonment. The MRTA's second-in-command, Miguel Rincón Rincón, was captured in November 1995. Also attracting attention at that time was the arrest of about 20 guerrillas on charges of plotting to invade the Peruvian Congress to take hostages. Lori Helene Berenson, a U.S. citizen, was charged with assisting in the plot and was sentenced in January 1996 to life imprisonment, her case subsequently drawing international scrutiny to Peru's notorious prison conditions.

By mid-1996 some observers considered the MRTA "close to annihilation" and possibly open to a negotiated settlement that might permit it to join the legal political process. However, in December a group of Túpac Amaru rebels took control of the home of the Japanese ambassador in Lima during a formal reception, seizing more than 600 hostages. The MRTA's demands included the release of Polay, said to be confined in "tomb-like" conditions, and more than 400 other members in Peruvian jails as well as a number of rebels in Bolivian custody since the 1995 kidnapping of a Bolivian businessman. The MRTA remained in control of the ambassador's residence until government forces stormed the facility on April 22, 1997 (see Political background, above).

In September 2003 Polay Campos issued a statement conceding that the MRTA had been defeated and urging his supporters "to continue our struggle using the democratic paths." Subsequently, in March 2005 he and Rincón were sentenced in a civilian retrial of their cases to 32 years' imprisonment.

Citing inactivity, the U.S. Department of State removed the group from its list of foreign terrorist organizations in October 2001. As of mid-2009, the MRTA was reported to be defunct.

Leaders: Víctor POLAY Campos and Miguel RINCÓN Rincón (imprisoned in Peru), Juan Carlos CABALLERO Velásquez (imprisoned in Bolivia).

LEGISLATURE

The bicameral Congress (*Congreso*), established under the 1979 constitution, encompassed a Senate and a Chamber of Deputies, both elected for five-year terms by universal adult suffrage. The Congress elected in 1990 was declared by President Fujimori to have been dissolved, as of April 6, 1992. In its place a unicameral Democratic Constituent Congress (*Congreso Constituyente Democrático*—CCD) was established, elections to which were conducted on November 22, 1992. The CCD gave way, in turn, to a new unicameral Congress elected on April 9, 1995. Subsequent elections were held on April 9, 2000; on April 8, 2001 (following a premature dissolution); and on April 9, 2006.

Congress (*Congreso*). The present Congress has 120 members, who, before 2001, were selected by proportional vote from a single national list but now represent geographic constituencies. The composition of the Congress after the 2006 balloting was as follows: Union for Peru, 45 seats; Peruvian Aprista Party, 36; National Unity, 17; Alliance for the Future, 13; Center Front, 5; National Restoration, 2; Peru Possible, 2.

President: Luis ALVA Castro.

CABINET

[as of September 15, 2009]

President of Council of Ministers	Javier Velásquez Quesquén (PAP)

Ministers

Agriculture	Adolfo de Córdova Vélez (ind.)
Defense	Rafael Rey Rey (*Renovación*)
Economy and Finance	Luis Carranza (ind.)
Education and Culture	José Chang Escobedo (PAP)
Energy and Mines	Pedro Sánchez Gamarra (ind.)
Environment	Antonio Brack Egg (ind.)
Foreign Relations	José Antonio García Belaúnde (ind.)
Foreign Trade and Tourism	Martín Pérez (ind.)
Housing, Construction, and Sanitation	Juan Sarmiento (ind.)
Interior	Gen. Octavio Salazar (ind.)
Justice	Aurelio Pastor (PAP)
Labor and Employment	Manuela Esperanza García (PAP) [f]
Production	Mercedes Aráoz (ind.) [f]
Public Health	Oscar Ugarte Ubilluz (ind.)
Transport and Communications	Enrique Cornejo (PAP)
Women's Affairs and Social Development	Nidia Vílchez (PAP) [f]

[f] = female

COMMUNICATIONS

In the decade following the 1968 coup, the government assumed control of most media; it confiscated Lima's seven leading newspapers and redesignated each as a spokesperson for an "organized sector of the community." In July 1980 President Belaúnde announced return of the newspapers to their former owners, who were subsequently awarded partial compensation for their financial losses. Safety for members of the media has been a recent concern. Reporters Without Borders reported that 100 journalists had been threatened or attacked in Peru from September 2006 to September 2007, with observers charging that the government was complicit in repressing its critics. In June 2009, the government tax agency took control of the Panamericana television network, citing unpaid debts of nearly $40 million. Opposition figures charged that the takeover was politically motivated. In its 2008 annual index of press freedom, Reporters Without Borders ranked Peru 108 out of 173 countries.

Press. The following are published daily in Lima, unless otherwise noted: *Ojo* (150,000), pro-PPC conservative; *El Comercio* (120,000 daily, 220,000 Sunday), pro-PPC conservative; *Extra* (80,000), evening edition of *El Expreso*; *El Expreso* (75,000), progovernment conservative; *La República* (50,000), left-wing; *El Correo* (Arequipa, 40,000); *La Industria* (Chiclayo, 30,000); *El Peruano* (27,000), official government publication; *Unidad* (20,000), PCP weekly.

News agencies. There is a government facility, the Andean News Agency (*Agencia de Noticias Andina*); numerous foreign agencies maintain bureaus in Lima.

Broadcasting and computing. The government's *Radio y Televisión Peruana* operates several dozen radio and television stations. The overwhelming majority of the more than 1,300 radio and television outlets are, however, privately owned. There were approximately 4.7 million television receivers in Peru in 2003. As of 2008 there were 247.2 Internet users per 1,000 inhabitants.

INTERGOVERNMENTAL REPRESENTATION

Ambassador to the U.S.: Luis VALDIVIESO.

U.S. Ambassador to Peru: Peter Michael McKINLEY.

Permanent Representative to the UN: Gonzalo GUTIÉRREZ.

IGO Memberships (Non-UN): ALADI, APEC, CAN, IADB, Interpol, IOM, *Mercosur*, NAM, OAS, OPANAL, PCA, SELA, WCO, WTO.

PHILIPPINES

Republic of the Philippines
Republika ng Pilipinas

Political Status: Independent republic since July 4, 1946; currently under constitution adopted by referendum of February 2, 1987, effective from February 11.

Area: 115,830 sq. mi. (300,000 sq. km.).

Population: 88,574,614 (2007C); 89,832,000 (2008E).

Major Urban Centers (2005E): MANILA (de facto capital, 1,510,000), QUEZON CITY (designated capital, 2,375,000), Caloocan City (1,357,000), Davao (816,000), Cebu (783,000).

Official Languages: Pilipino and English.

Monetary Unit: Peso (market rate December 1, 2009: 46.85 pesos = $1US).

President: Gloria MACAPAGAL-ARROYO (*Lakas*–Christian Muslim Democrats); popularly elected as vice president on May 11, 1998, and inaugurated on June 30 for a six-year term; sworn in as president on January 20, 2001, succeeding Joseph E. ESTRADA (Party of the Filipino Masses), the Supreme Court having ruled on January 19 that the presidency was vacant; elected to a full term on May 20, 2004, and sworn in on June 30.

Vice President: Noli DE CASTRO (*Lakas*–Christian Muslim Democrats); elected for a six-year term on May 20, 2004, and sworn in on June 30, succeeding Teofisto GUINGONA (most recently an independent).

THE COUNTRY

Strategically located along the southeast rim of Asia, the Philippine archipelago embraces over 7,000 islands stretching in a north-south direction for over 1,000 miles. The largest and most important of the islands are Luzon in the north and sparsely populated Mindanao in the south. The inhabitants, predominantly of Malay stock, are 83 percent Roman Catholic, although a politically significant Muslim minority (5 percent) is concentrated in the south. The country is not linguistically unified; English and Spanish are used concurrently with local languages and dialects, although Pilipino, based on the Tagalog spoken in the Manila area, has been promoted as a national language. Women, who constitute about 38 percent of the active labor force, have been prominent in journalism and politics, though most often through their association with powerful men. Women made up 11 percent of the representatives elected to the lower house of Congress in May 2007.

Rice for domestic consumption and wood, sugar, and coconut products for export were traditionally mainstays of the economy. Although agriculture continues to employ about 35 percent of the labor force, it now accounts for only 15 percent of GDP, compared to about 32 percent for industry and 54 percent for services. Well over half of the country's exports by value are now electronics; garments, other manufactures, coconut products, sugar cane, and bananas also rank among the leading exports. The mining industry has benefited from investment in recent years. Remittances from an estimated eight million overseas workers (nearly one quarter of the country's labor force) are a leading source of foreign exchange. Since 1998, when the economy experienced a downturn of 0.6 percent that was largely caused by a regional financial crisis and a consequent sharp drop in the value of the peso, the Philippines has registered GDP growth each year, ranging from a low of 1.8 percent in 2001 to a high of 7.3 percent in 2007. However, poverty and income inequality remain persistent problems, creating an instability exacerbated by rising food prices during the global financial crisis of 2008-09. Despite rising remittance inflows, domestic consumption fell sharply in early 2009. The World Bank projected a 0.5 percent contraction of GDP

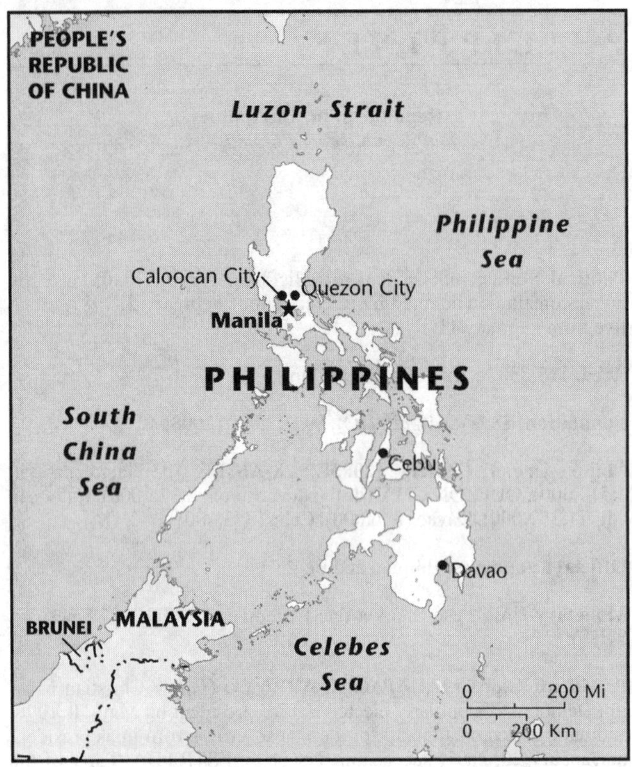

for 2009, with a decline in manufacturing exports and consequent loss of high-paying jobs in that sector. The Philippine survey group Social Weather Stations reported that 20 percent of families experienced hunger in mid-2009.

GOVERNMENT AND POLITICS

Political background. Claimed for Spain by Ferdinand Magellan in 1521 and ruled by that country until occupied by the United States during the Spanish-American War of 1898, the Philippines became a self-governing commonwealth under U.S. tutelage in 1935 and was accorded full independence on July 4, 1946. Manuel ROXAS, first president of the new republic (1946–1948), took office during the onset of an armed uprising by Communist-led Hukbalahap guerrillas in central Luzon that continued under his successor, the Liberal Elpidio QUIRINO (1948–1953). Quirino's secretary of national defense, Ramon MAGSAYSAY, initiated an effective program of military action and rural rehabilitation designed to pacify the Huks, and he was able to complete this process after his election to the presidency on the *Nacionalista* Party ticket in 1953. Magsaysay also dealt strongly with bureaucratic corruption and did much to restore popular faith in government, but his accidental death in 1957 led to a loss of reformist momentum and a revival of corruption under his *Nacionalista* successor, Carlos P. GARCIA (1957–1961). Efforts toward economic and social reform were renewed by Liberal President Diosdado MACAPAGAL (1961–1965).

The election, under *Nacionalista* auspices, of former Liberal leader Ferdinand E. MARCOS in 1965 was accompanied by pledges of support for the reform movement, but the Marcos program was hindered by congressional obstruction and a temporary renewal of the Huk insurgency. Discontent with prevailing conditions of poverty, unemployment, inflation, and corruption fostered a climate of violence that included the activities of the Maoist New People's Army (NPA), which was founded in 1969, and a persistent struggle between Muslim elements and government forces on Mindanao and in Sulu Province. In some areas Muslims sought to drive out Christian settlers from the north, but as antigovernment activities expanded under the direction of the Moro National Liberation Front (MNLF), Muslim leaders increasingly called for regional autonomy or outright independence.

In the midst of a rapidly deteriorating political situation, a Constitutional Convention began work on a new constitution in July 1971, but its deliberations were curtailed by a declaration of martial law in September 1972. Strict censorship immediately followed, as did widespread arrests of suspected subversives and political opponents of the regime, most notably Liberal Party (LP) leader Benigno S. AQUINO Jr. The new constitution, which provided for a parliamentary form of government, was declared ratified in January 1973; concurrently, Marcos assumed the additional post of prime minister and announced that the selection of an interim National Assembly called for by the constitution would be deferred.

Following talks in early 1975 between representatives of the Philippine government and the MNLF, the Muslims dropped their demand for partition of the republic, while the government agreed to an integration of rebel units into the Philippine armed forces. President Marcos ordered a suspension of military operations in the south in late 1976, following a cease-fire agreement signed in Tripoli, Libya, with representatives of the moderate MNLF faction. In accordance with the agreement, a referendum was held in April 1977 on the establishment of an autonomous Muslim region. Most Muslims boycotted the polls, however, and the proposal was defeated by an overwhelming majority of those participating. Meanwhile, in 1973 the Communist Party of the Philippines–Marxist-Leninist (CPP) and its military wing, the NPA, had joined with other leftist Marcos opponents to organize a National Democratic Front (NDF).

Amid charges of widespread voting irregularity, particularly in the Manila area, the interim National Assembly was elected in April 1978. The president's recently organized New Society Movement (*Kilusan Bagong Lipunan*—KBL) was officially credited with winning 151 of 165 elective seats.

Martial law was lifted in January 1981, prior to the April adoption by plebiscite of a series of constitutional changes that included direct presidential election. In nationwide balloting in June Marcos was overwhelmingly reelected to a six-year term, and in July Cesar E. A. VIRATA secured legislative confirmation as head of a new cabinet.

In the first full election to a unicameral National Assembly in May 1984, opposition candidates claimed approximately one-third of the seats. Despite the lifting of martial law, the Marcos regime continued to rule by decree. Opposition feeling had already been inflamed by the assassination of Benigno Aquino upon his return from the United States in August 1983, which precipitated 18 months of often violent antiregime demonstrations. In October 1984 a government commission of inquiry concluded that ultimate responsibility for Aquino's death lay with the armed forces chief of staff, Gen. Fabian VER, who was thereupon temporarily suspended from his duties. (In December 1985, having been acquitted of conspiracy in the assassination, he was reinstated.)

A year later, in the face of mounting support for Corazon AQUINO as political surrogate for her slain husband, Marcos announced that a premature presidential election would be held in early 1986 to "restore confidence" in his administration. Mrs. Aquino filed as the sole opposition candidate for the presidency, with Salvador H. LAUREL as her running mate. The election in February was conducted amid allegations by both opposition leaders and foreign observers of manifest government fraud; Aquino was named the victor by an independent citizens' watchdog group, while official figures attesting to the president's reelection were accepted by the National Assembly. With both candidates thus claiming victory, Aquino called for an expanded program of strikes, boycotts, and civil disobedience to "bring down the usurper."

The turning point came on February 22, 1986, when Defense Secretary Juan Ponce ENRILE and Lt. Gen. Fidel V. RAMOS, the leader of an anticorruption campaign within the military, declared their allegiance to Aquino. Ramos quickly joined troops loyal to him at Camp Crame, the national police headquarters. In response to an appeal from Cardinal Jaime SIN to protect the rebels, the base was surrounded by thousands of Philippine citizens in what became known as the first "People Power" rally. Subsequently, much of the media passed to opposition control, while the military, including the palace guard, experienced mass defections. On February 26, a day after the swearing in of both presidential claimants, Marcos and his immediate entourage departed for exile in Hawaii.

In March 1986 the new chief executive dissolved the National Assembly by suspending the 1973 constitution, presenting in its place an interim document "under which our battered nation can shelter."

In February 1987 more than 80 percent of those voting approved a new U.S.-style constitution, under which President Aquino and Vice

President Laurel would remain in office until 1992. In the subsequent congressional election, Aquino supporters won more than 80 percent of 200 directly elective seats in the House of Representatives and defeated opposition candidates in 22 of 24 Senate races.

In August 1987 the Aquino government barely survived a coup attempt led by Col. Gregorio HONASAN, who had been prominently involved in the military revolt that toppled President Marcos. Immediately thereafter a number of leading government officials either resigned or were removed from office. Salvador Laurel resigned as foreign minister (though retaining the vice presidency) and for all practical purposes moved into opposition by forming a de facto alliance with neo-*Nacionalista* conservatives.

The most serious of six efforts to topple the Aquino government erupted in December 1989, with the seizure by rebel troops of Manila's Fort Bonifacio army camp and the adjacent Villamar Air Force headquarters, followed by an air attack on the presidential palace. Despite U.S. air support of the government, the insurgency (which presumably included Colonel Honasan, who had escaped from prison in April 1988) was not completely crushed for ten days, in the course of which 119 persons died and more than 600 were wounded.

Seven candidates vied for the presidency in May 1992, with Aquino-endorsed Fidel Ramos turning back strong challenges by political newcomer Miriam DEFENSOR-SANTIAGO and conservative businessman Eduardo COJUANGCO of the National People's Coalition (NPC). While former House Speaker Ramon MITRA, heading the pro-Aquino Democratic Filipino Struggle (*Laban ng Demokratikong Pilipino*—LDP), had been considered by many to be the leading contender, he could salvage no better than fourth place, despite a convincing legislative victory by his party.

Nominally allied with the LDP, Ramos's People Power–National Union of Christian Democrats (*Lakas*-NUCD) emerged as the principal victor in the May 1995 legislative poll, winning approximately two-thirds of the lower house seats.

In September 1992 the MNLF had rejected an offer of amnesty until the government implemented its 1976 pledge to sanction the creation of semiautonomous political structures for the Mindanao region. In November 1993 the two sides concluded a three-month truce agreement, which was followed by the signing of a cease-fire in January 1994. In June 1996 government negotiators announced a breakthrough that called for the establishment of a three-member Southern Philippines Council for Peace and Development (SPCPD), headed by the MNLF's Nur MISUARI, to "supervise and coordinate the implementation of peace." The understanding led to a formal peace agreement on September 2, and Misuari stood unopposed on September 9 for election as governor of the Autonomous Region of Muslim Mindanao (ARMM), encompassing the four provinces—Sulu, the Tawi Tawi island group, and the mainland provinces of Maguindanao and Lanao del Sur—then controlled by the MNLF. The treaty specified that after three years a referendum would be held to determine if additional provinces referenced in the 1976 Tripoli Accord should be added to the ARMM. Meanwhile, 7,500 of the MNLF's 16,000-member military would be incorporated into the national army and police. The peace agreement was immediately rejected by the more militant Moro Islamic Liberation Front (MILF) and by hard-line MNLF splinters.

Political developments in 1997 were dominated by preparations for the 1998 presidential election. In June a Supreme Court decision scuttled a campaign by a group of President Ramos's supporters to amend the constitution so that he could run for a second term. Also in June, Vice President Joseph E. ESTRADA, a former film actor and the leading contender for the presidency, formed a three-party electoral coalition called the Struggle for the Nationalist Filipino Masses (*Laban ng Makabayang Masang Pilipino*—LAMMP), which included his own Party of the Filipino Masses (*Partido ng Masang Pilipino*—PMP), the NPC, and the LDP. In December Estrada selected the LDP's Edgardo ANGARA as his running mate. Although the ouster of NPC President Ernesto MACEDA as Senate president in December apparently forestalled LAMMP's merger into a unified party, Estrada won the May 11, 1998, presidential election with 39.9 percent of the vote in a field of ten candidates, with Gloria MACAPAGAL-ARROYO, backed by Ramos's *Lakas*-NUCD, easily winning the vice presidency over Angara. The LAMMP electoral coalition also swept to victory in the House of Representatives and won a majority of the open seats in the Senate. By inauguration day defections from the *Lakas*-NUCD, coupled with the informal merger of the LAMMP parties into the new Struggle of the Filipino Masses (*Laban ng Masang Pilipino*—LAMP), provided Estrada with a firm base of support in the Congress despite opposition from most of the business community and the Catholic hierarchy, which called him morally unfit for office. Shortly thereafter the LAMP was renamed the Party of the Philippine Masses (*Lapian ng Masang Pilipino*—LAMP).

A year into his term Estrada's popularity dropped dramatically in response to his ultimately unsuccessful effort to introduce constitutional changes that would have opened the economy to increased foreign investment. His standing was further damaged by allegations that his administration was replete with corruption, cronyism, and mismanagement. In October 2000 Luis SINGSON, governor of Ilocos Sur, charged that he had transmitted to President Estrada some $8.6 million in illegal gambling payoffs and another $2.8 million in provincial tobacco taxes. On October 12 Vice President Macapagal-Arroyo resigned from the cabinet amid opposition calls for Estrada to resign. By the end of the month the vice president was at the front of a "united opposition" that included most of the opposition political parties, led by *Lakas*-NUCD. Other prominent figures resigned from the LAMP.

On November 4, 2000, a rally organized by Cardinal Sin drew tens of thousands of anti-Estrada demonstrators into the streets of Manila. Proclaiming his innocence, Estrada asked the House to move quickly on an impeachment complaint that had been introduced in October. On November 13, arguing that more than one-third of the House membership had signed the impeachment complaint, Speaker of the House Manuel VILLAR Jr. ordered, without a formal committee vote or a floor debate, that the articles of impeachment be forwarded to the Senate for trial.

The Senate trial opened on December 7, 2000, but adjourned on January 17, 2001, a day after the Senate voted 11–10 not to admit evidence proving, according to the prosecution, that Estrada held secret bank accounts under aliases. In response, the Senate president and the House prosecutors resigned, an estimated 500,000 people took to Manila's streets in "People Power II" demonstrations, most of the cabinet joined the opposition, and the police and military withdrew their support from Estrada. On January 19 the Supreme Court, acting extraconstitutionally, ruled the presidency vacant, and Estrada abandoned the presidential palace, although he refused to resign. Macapagal-Arroyo took the oath of office as president on January 20. Her hand-picked successor as vice president, Teofisto GUINGONA of *Lakas*-NUCD, was confirmed by Congress on February 6.

On April 25, 2001, Estrada was arrested and charged with economic plunder, his immunity from prosecution having been lifted by the Supreme Court. At that time a unanimous court had also confirmed the legitimacy of the Macapagal-Arroyo presidency, asserting that Estrada "by his acts and statements" had resigned. In legislative elections held on May 14, Macapagal-Arroyo's *Lakas*-NUCD and its immediate allies won a plurality in the House of Representatives. The government also claimed a majority in the Senate until a previously supportive independent joined the opposition in June 2002, resulting in a 12–12 split.

Upon taking office Macapagal-Arroyo had moved quickly to open discussions with Communist and Muslim insurgents, with mixed results. Since 1992 the Communist-led NDF had engaged in a series of on-again, off-again talks with successive administrations, but without resolving the conflict, which was estimated to have cost 40,000–50,000 lives since the late 1960s. Negotiations were renewed in April 2001 in Oslo, Norway, but in June the government suspended the process indefinitely in response to the NPA's alleged involvement in the assassination of a congressman. At the same time, the Macapagal-Arroyo administration, having halted a military campaign against the MILF that had begun under President Estrada, opened peace talks with that organization in June in Tripoli. A preliminary peace agreement was announced two days later. On August 7, despite the condemnation of Muslim rejectionists, the MILF signed a more formal cease-fire in Kuala Lumpur, Malaysia.

In April 2001 the MNLF Central Committee had removed Governor Misuari as MNLF chair because of the ARMM government's manifest failures to improve living conditions and institute reforms. On November 19, Misuari loyalists staged an uprising on Jolo Island that led to more than 100 deaths. Misuari was arrested on November 24 while trying to enter Malaysia. Extradited to the Philippines in January 2002, the former governor was ultimately charged with inciting a rebellion. Meanwhile, in the November 26 ARMM election the MNLF's Parouk HUSSIN (Farouk HUSSEIN), with Manila's backing, had won election as Misuari's successor.

Vice President Guingona resigned his cabinet post as minister of foreign affairs effective July 15, 2002. He had been an outspoken critic of a January decision by President Macapagal-Arroyo to permit extensive U.S.-Philippine military exercises and counterinsurgency training in Mindanao's Zamboanga area and on nearby Basilan Island, stronghold of a comparatively small fundamentalist Muslim organization, the *Abu Sayyaf* Group (ASG). Since March 2000 the ASG had drawn considerable international attention through a series of frequently audacious kidnappings and ruthless hostage executions. As the six-month-long *Balikatan* (shoulder-to-shoulder) Mindanao exercises proceeded, it became increasingly clear that, despite initial denials, the U.S. contingent, peaking at about 1,000, was directly involved in largely unsuccessful efforts to root out the terrorist group.

A breakthrough with regard to the Muslim insurgency followed a statement by MILF Chair Hashim SALAMAT in June 2003 (shortly before his unexpected death) that renounced terrorism. On July 19 the government and the MILF initiated a new cease-fire that paved the way for a series of informal meetings. More formal peace talks, held in Kuala Lumpur, resumed in April 2005. Meanwhile, under the sponsorship of the Organization of the Islamic Conference (OIC), members of an International Monitoring Team from Malaysia, Brunei, and Libya had taken up their posts in Mindanao. (Japan joined the group in July 2006, in a nonmilitary advisory role.)

In December 2002 Macapagal-Arroyo had stated that she would not seek election to a full term as president because a "vindictive, vicious, and divisive" political climate was interfering with her efforts to perform her duties, but she reversed herself in October 2003, asserting that she needed a full term to implement the necessary political and economic reforms. Vice President Guingona, who had already distanced himself from the president on a number of issues, responded that she had been an ineffective leader, failing to root out corruption and to end the Muslim rebellion in the south.

With general elections approaching, in December 2003 the LDP, the Filipino Democratic Party–Laban (*Partido Demokratikong Pilipinos–*Laban—PDP-Laban), and Estrada's Force of the Filipino Masses (*Puwersa ng Masang Pilipino*—PMP, as the Party of the Filipino Masses was now known) established an opposition alliance, the Coalition of the United Filipinos (*Koalisyon ng Nagkakaisang Pilipino*—KNP). A month later the *Lakas*–Christian Muslim Democrats (*Lakas*-CMD, the reconfigured *Lakas*-NUCD) led the formation of a second major electoral alliance, the Coalition for Truth and Experience for the Future (*Koalisyon ng Katapatan at Karanasan sa Kinabukasan*—K4), which also included the NPC, the LP, and several smaller parties.

In the presidential election on May 20, 2004, Macapagal-Arroyo won 40 percent of the vote against four other candidates, chiefly the KNP's Fernando POE Jr., a film actor and friend of former president Estrada. Poe won 35.5 percent of the vote. The vice presidency was won by former news anchor Sen. Noli DE CASTRO of the *Lakas*-CMD, who defeated another former news anchor, the KNP's Sen. Loren LEGARDA. In congressional contests the K4 parties won 7 of the 12 contested Senate seats and a clear majority in the House of Representatives. Although Poe and his supporters, claiming fraud, refused to accept the presidential results, a joint session of Congress officially named Macapagal-Arroyo the winner on June 24, and she was sworn in on June 30.

Within weeks of her inauguration, differences had emerged within the *Lakas*-CMD congressional delegation over leadership posts, committee chairmanships, and party representation on key committees, precipitating a rebellion that saw more than 30 *Lakas*-CMD representatives switch their loyalties to President Macapagal-Arroyo's original party, the revitalized Alliance of Free Filipinos (*Kabalikat ng Malayang Pilipino*—Kampi), and threaten to sit with the House minority. A cabinet reshuffle in mid-August 2004 was accompanied by declaration of a "new coalesced majority" based on the *Lakas*-CMD, part of a divided NPC, the LP, and several smaller parties.

On February 11–14, 2004, Manila and the NDF had reopened peace talks in Oslo, and additional rounds were held in March–April and June. An August session was canceled by the NDF, however, in part because the government had not attempted to convince the United States, Canada, Australia, and the European Union (EU) to remove the NDF, CPP, and NPA from their lists of foreign terrorist organizations.

In July 2005 President Macapagal-Arroyo included in her annual State of the Nation address to Congress a constitutional reform proposal that called for replacing the existing "dysfunctional" presidential system with a unicameral parliamentary form of government headed by a prime minister. Such a "charter change" could, in theory, be approached in several ways, including by an elected constitutional convention or by Congress's sitting as a constituent assembly. The Senate's opposition to forming a constituent assembly led the government to begin circulating a "people's initiative" petition that, with sufficient signatures (from at least 12 percent of the voters, including a minimum of 3 percent in each congressional district) could have put the charter change proposal to the voters in a referendum. In October, however, a divided Supreme Court ruled that a plebiscite could not be employed to make such major constitutional revisions. In December, with a legislative election only six months away, charter change was shelved, at least temporarily.

On July 8–11, 2005, a dozen cabinet members and senior aides resigned and called for President Macapagal-Arroyo to do likewise over allegations of vote-rigging during the 2004 presidential election (during the vote count she had spoken with an election official) and illegal gambling payoffs to members of her immediate family. The president refused to step down and told her opponents to "take your grievances to Congress," where they could pursue impeachment. On July 20 a formal impeachment motion was introduced in the House of Representatives, where the removal effort split the LP. On August 31 the House's Justice Committee rejected the complaint 48–4, and a week later, with 79 votes needed to pursue impeachment, only 51 House members voted against accepting the committee report.

Opposition to the president nevertheless persisted, and on February 24, 2006, she declared a state of emergency in response to the discovery of an alleged coup plot by elements of the armed forces. The state of emergency was lifted on March 3, four days after charges were filed against 16 individuals. On August 24 another effort to impeach the president, citing abuse of her authority and other offenses, was ended by a 173–32 vote of the House.

The May 14, 2007, election for the House of Representatives and half the Senate saw *Lakas*-CMD and its allies, including Kampi and the NPC, win a convincing majority in the lower house. Control of the Senate swung to the opposition, now led by the LP and the NP, but candidates backed by the progovernment caucus won election as Senate president and majority leader.

On September 12, 2007, former president Estrada was convicted of plunder and sentenced to life in prison. Not long after, however, the government initiated talks with Estrada on a conditional pardon, which was granted by Macapagal-Arroyo on October 26.

General elections were scheduled for 2010 amidst widespread concern that the president would try to seek an additional term.

Constitution and government. The basic law approved on February 2, 1987, supplanting the "Freedom Constitution" of March 1986, contains broad civil rights guarantees, denies the military any form of political activity save voting, prohibits abortion, authorizes local autonomy for Muslim-dominated areas, calls for a "nuclear-free" policy (save where the national interest dictates otherwise), and requires legislative concurrence for the leasing of Filipino territory to foreign powers.

In April 2006 the Supreme Court declared unconstitutional a "calibrated preemptive response" (CPR) policy introduced "in lieu of maximum tolerance" toward rallies and public demonstrations. In its ruling the court stated that the CPR "has no place in our legal firmament and must be struck down as a darkness that shrouds freedom. It merely confuses our people and is used by some police agents to justify abuses." In the same decision the court also rejected a "no permit, no rally" policy but added that local governments could restrict permitless demonstrations to designated "freedom parks." The court further stated that officials could deny permits "only on the ground of clear and present danger to public order, public safety, public convenience, public morals or public health."

The constitution provides for a directly elected president serving a single six-year term in conjunction with a separately elected vice president; a bicameral Congress consisting of a Senate and a House of Representatives (with senators and representatives who may serve no more than two and three terms, respectively); and an independent judiciary headed by a Supreme Court. The president is specifically enjoined from imposing martial law for more than a 60-day period without legislative approval. The House of Representatives may impeach the chief executive if one-third of its membership concurs, with a two-thirds vote of the Senate then needed for conviction.

Administratively, the country encompasses 17 regions, 82 provinces, over 130 cities, 1,500 municipalities, and nearly 42,000 local authorities (*barangays*). In November 1975 an enlarged Metropolitan Manila was created by merging the city with 16 surrounding communities, including the official capital, Quezon City. The new metropolis, with a total population of more than 5 million, is governed by a Metropolitan Manila

Commission. The Autonomous Region of Muslim Mindanao (ARMM) currently includes the provinces of Basilan, Lanao del Sur, Maguindanao, Sulu, and Tawi Tawi, plus Marawi City. An agreement negotiated with Muslim rebels to expand the "ancestral domain" of Philippine Muslims was struck down by the Supreme Court in October 2008 (see Political background, above).

Foreign relations. After independence Philippine foreign policy was based on strong opposition to communism, close alliance with the United States, and active participation in the United Nations and its related agencies. The Philippines also joined various regional organizations, such as the Association of Southeast Asian Nations (ASEAN) and the Asian Development Bank (ADB). After the Vietnam War, however, uncertainty about the U.S. role in Southeast Asia spurred greater independence in foreign policy, and diplomatic and trade relations were established with several Communist states, including the People's Republic of China, the Soviet Union, and Vietnam.

A major issue for the Aquino government concerned U.S. financial assistance during the remaining years of the 1947 treaty that provided for U.S. use of six military installations, including Clark Air Base and Subic Bay Naval Station, the two largest U.S. overseas installations. Following the eruption of Mount Pinatubo in June 1991, however, the U.S. Defense Department announced that, because of the magnitude of clean-up costs, no attempt would be made to reopen Clark, which had been engulfed in volcanic ash. Negotiations to extend the Subic Bay lease ultimately broke down, with formal "disestablishment" being proclaimed in September 1992.

In January 1998, despite nationalist and leftist opposition, Manila and Washington signed a controversial Visiting Forces Agreement (VFA) that would permit large-scale joint military exercises, allow U.S. warships in Philippine waters, and accord legal standing to visiting U.S. forces. The Philippine Senate approved the pact in May 1999, one of the repercussions being the formal withdrawal of the Communist NDF from peace negotiations with the government. The first joint military exercises under the VFA were held in February 2000. In November 2002, in the context of the U.S.-led "war on terrorism," the two governments signed a Mutual Logistics Support Agreement, which permits the United States to position communications and other nonlethal equipment in the Philippines. In March 2003, during a visit by President Macapagal-Arroyo to Washington, U.S. President George W. Bush declared the Philippines to be a "major non-NATO ally." These ties were reaffirmed in August 2009 when Macapagal-Arroyo met with U.S. president Barack Obama at the White House.

In February 1994, at the conclusion of the first U.S. court case involving alleged human rights violations in another country, a federal jury in Honolulu, Hawaii, ordered the estate of the late President Marcos to pay damages of some $2.5 billion to thousands of individuals said to have suffered under his rule. To settle the claim, in February 1999 the Marcos family agreed to pay $150 million to some 10,000 victims. In July 2004 the Hawaii district court ordered $40 million in hidden assets to be paid out, but Manila appealed the decision on the grounds that "all decisions on ill-gotten wealth lie within the sovereign prerogative of the Philippines." In May 2006 a U.S. appeals court backed the Hawaii court's decision. In 1998 the Swiss Supreme Court had rejected a final appeal by Marcos family representatives that would have prevented the return to the Philippine government of $590 million from the former president's Swiss bank accounts.

Relations between Manila and its ASEAN partners have typically been stable. Nevertheless, a vexing regional issue concerns competing claims to the Spratly Islands in the South China Sea, which sit astride vital shipping lanes, support a major fishing industry, and may contain significant oil and natural gas deposits. In addition to the Philippines, the claimants include China, Taiwan, and three other members of ASEAN (Brunei, Malaysia, and Vietnam). Since 1995 China and the Philippines have had numerous clashes over fishing rights and construction on various reefs and shoals. In March 1999 the Chinese and Philippine foreign ministers, conferring in Manila, agreed to "exercise joint restraint" in the Spratlys, although China continued to oppose a Philippine proposal for international mediation. Altercations also occurred with Malaysia and Vietnam in 1999. A visit by President Estrada to China in May 2000 concluded with both countries repeating their intentions to settle the dispute peacefully. In September 2004 the Philippine and Chinese state oil companies announced that they would jointly conduct a seismic study to determine if oil and natural gas are present in the Spratlys. In March 2005 they and Vietnam's counterpart agreed to a tripartite Joint Marine Seismic Undertaking. The Philippines codified its territorial claims, including its claim to the Spratly Islands, by approving "baselines" legislation in March 2009. China protested the law and sent a military patrol boat into the area days later.

Over the past decade, Malaysia has helped broker peace talks between the Philippine government and the MILF, leading to the Memorandum of Understanding on Ancestral Domain that was invalidated by the Supreme Court in October 2008 (see Current issues). Sen. Rodolfo BIAZON of the Liberal Party, Chair of the Senate Committee on National Defense and Security, contended that Malaysia has a conflict of interest in the matter because of the Spratly Islands dispute as well as Philippine claims to another contested territory, Sabah, in eastern Malaysia. Biazon seeks to enlist Indonesia to mediate future negotiations with the rebels.

Current issues. The May 2007 election resulted in a victory for the Genuine Opposition (GO) coalition over the *Lakas*-led TEAM Unity ("Together Everyone Achieves More") in the Senate races, but the governing coalition won a solid majority in the House of Representatives. This came as no surprise, given that *Lakas*-CMD and Kampi had repaired their rift. The nation's two strongest parties agreed to merge in June 2008, and the formal merger was completed on May 28, 2009. The new Lakas Kampi CMD, the nation's largest party by far, appeared poised to make a strong run in the 2010 elections.

As the early stages of the 2010 presidential campaign unfolded, President Macapagal-Arroyo's intentions in proposing amendments to the constitution were the source of widespread anxiety. The unpopular leader continued to favor altering the constitution through a constituent assembly or charter change ("con-ass" and "cha-cha," in the lingo of the press). Many political figures worried aloud that the president's motive was to extend her tenure in office. In July 2009 six opposition candidates signed a document opposing constitutional revisions and supporting the 2010 balloting.

On August 1 former president Corazon Aquino died. More than 200,000 people lined the streets of Manila to glimpse her casket before it was laid to rest beside the grave of her husband, Benigno Aquino. The reminder of the 1986 "People Power" uprising appeared to energize the opposition to the current president and, implicitly, reject enactment of any change to the constitution.

The October 2008 Supreme Court decision nullifying the government's negotiated agreement with the MILF created a serious setback in the peace process on Mindanao. On July 16 of that year the administration announced that it had reached a peace agreement with the MILF, after three years of talks brokered by Malaysia. The Memorandum of Understanding on Ancestral Domain (MOA-AD) would create an autonomous Muslim homeland much larger than the current Autonomous Region in Muslim Mindanao (ARMM). Fearing that the pact would lead the separatists to declare an independent state, several Philippine politicians brought suit. On August 4, one day before the scheduled signing ceremony in Kuala Lumpur, the Supreme Court issued a temporary restraining order against accession to the MOA-AD. Several violent raids by MILF fighters followed; citing these incidents, the Macapagal-Arroyo administration backed away from the agreement, amid sharp criticism for failing to consult with lawmakers during the negotiations. In an 8–7 decision, on October 14 the court ruled that the administration had exceeded its constitutional authority by negotiating the document in full knowledge that it would require amending the constitution.

Numerous clashes in the succeeding months resulted in hundreds of deaths and more than a half million refugees. Despite a loss of confidence, both sides prepared to resume talks. The president ordered a suspension of military operations in July 2009, days before her final State of the Nation address, and MILF swiftly followed suit. Administration officials said the government aimed to finalize peace agreements with both the Muslim MILF rebels and the Communist forces of the NDF before the end of Macapagal-Arroyo's term, but having reneged on the previous agreement to cede a Muslim homeland, the route to a new settlement was unclear. As the new round of talks got underway, the military launched an attack on Abu Sayyaf forces on the island of Basilan on August 12, during which MILF fighters ambushed government troops. The skirmish threatened to overturn the momentum toward new negotiations.

POLITICAL PARTIES AND GROUPS

From 1946 until the imposition of martial law in 1972, political control oscillated between the *Nacionalista* Party (NP), founded in 1907, and the Liberal Party (LP), organized by slightly left-of-center elements that split from the *Nacionalistas* in 1946. Both parties concerned themselves primarily with local alliances and patronage, and their adherents readily shifted from one to the other. Powerful sugar interests, which tended to resist foreign investment in Philippine enterprises, dominated among the *Nacionalistas,* while most Liberals favored a more flexible approach to foreign capital.

In early 1978, coincident with a pro forma return to party politics, the New Society Movement (KBL) was organized as the personal vehicle of President Marcos. In February 1980 representatives of 8 opposition groups formed a loose coalition, the United Democratic Opposition (Unido), which reorganized in April 1982 as the United Nationalist Democratic Organization, a 12-party alignment that retained the Unido acronym. Participants included the *Nacionalistas,* the Liberals, and the People's Power Movement (Laban), which was under the nominal presidency of former LP leader Benigno Aquino Jr. until his assassination in August 1983.

The Aquino assassination spawned a number of cross-party alliances among the opposition, which was divided on whether to boycott the May 1984 election. In the end, most parties participated, and the opposition won about one-third of the elective National Assembly seats. In February 1986 a Unido ticket headed by Corazon Aquino challenged President Marcos, who was ultimately forced to flee the country.

A landslide in support of the Aquino government in the legislative election of May 1987 was achieved without an articulated party structure. Most pro-Aquino candidates ran under a variety of rubrics loosely joined in a Laban-centered coalition that eventually coalesced into the regime-supportive Democratic Filipino Struggle (LDP) in June 1988.

The principal contenders in the presidential and legislative balloting of May 1992 were the LDP, led by presidential candidate Ramon Mitra; the People Power–National Union of Christian Democrats (*Lakas*-NUCD), led by Fidel Ramos; the National People's Coalition (NPC) of Marcos associate Eduardo Cojuangco; and the LP, under Jovito Salonga. Although the LDP won a plurality of House seats, by mid-1993 nearly three-fourths of its delegation had aligned with President Ramos's *Lakas*-NUCD. For the 1995 legislative poll, the *Lakas*-NUCD entered into an electoral coalition with the LDP that subsequently fell into disarray.

Several electoral coalitions were formed prior to the 1998 election, the most significant being that among Vice President Joseph Estrada's Party of the Filipino Masses (PMP), the LDP, and the NPC. Under the banner of the Struggle of the Nationalist Filipino Masses (*Laban ng Makabayang Masang Pilipino*—LAMMP), the constituent parties supported Estrada for president and the LDP's Edgardo Angara for vice president. In support of its presidential candidate, Jose de Venecia, *Lakas*-NUCD joined forces with the small, Mindanao-based United Muslim Democratic Party (UMDP) and the *Kabalikat ng Mayayang Pilipino* (Kampi), whose leader, Gloria Macapagal-Arroyo, ran successfully for the vice presidency. A total of ten candidates, nine of them with party backing, competed for the presidency.

Following his victory, Estrada formed the Struggle of the Filipino Masses (*Laban ng Masang Pilipino*—LAMP), which the LDP agreed to join. Also joining the LAMP were a number of defectors from other parties, most prominently a group of some 40 *Lakas*-NUCD members led by Rep. Manuel Villar Jr. Nevertheless, the initial LAMP remained unregistered as a unified party, and in August 1999 President Estrada attempted to strengthen the alliance and give added impetus to his campaign for constitutional change by reconfiguring the "Struggle" as the Party of the Filipino Masses (*Lapian ng Masang Pilipino*—LAMP). A wave of party resignations, including those of Speaker of the House Villar and Senate President Franklin DRILON, preceded President Estrada's November 2000 impeachment. His forced departure from office in January 2001 reduced the LAMP to little more than a political artifact.

With the next legislative election scheduled for May 2001, two new coalitions quickly formed. The *Lakas*-NUCD-UMDP-Kampi group, the Liberal Party (LP), a dissenting faction of the LDP, and several smaller parties agreed to present a common senatorial candidate list as the People Power Coalition (PPC). The former LAMP participants—the PMP, LDP, and NPC—similarly formed a Democratic Filipino Struggle–Force of the Masses (*Laban ng Demokratikong Pilipino–Puwersa ng Masa*—LDP-PnM) coalition. Generally, the individual parties presented separate candidates for the House of Representatives election.

For the May 2004 national election the *Lakas*–Christian Muslim Democrats (*Lakas*-CMD, the unified and renamed *Lakas*-NUCD-UMDP) announced formation of a successor to the PPC, the Coalition for Truth and Experience for the Future (*Koalisyon ng Katapatan at Karanasan sa Kinabukasan*—K4), which also included part of the divided NPC and the LP. The LDP, Filipino Democratic Party–Laban (PDP-Laban), and the PMP (now called the Force of the Filipino Masses) agreed to form an opposition alliance, the Coalition of the United Filipinos (*Koalisyon ng Nagkakaisang Pilipino*—KNP), which proved unable to mount a successful challenge to the K4 at the ballot box.

Shortly after the election, differences within the *Lakas*-CMD led a significant number of representatives to reinvigorate Kampi. As of mid-2006, although the NPC and the LP remained part of Macapagal-Arroyo's government, each had competing pro- and antipresidential wings.

Prior to the 2007 election, parties hoping to win support for President Macapagal-Arroyo's policies, including *Lakas*-CMD, Kampi, the NPC, the LDP, and the Philippine Democratic Socialist Party (PDSP), formed **TEAM Unity** ("Together Everyone Achieves More"). Opposition groups, including the NP, the LP, the PMP, the PDP-Laban, and the KBL, formed the Grand and Broad Coalition (GBC), largely based on the **United Opposition** (UNO) that had formed in 2005 to pursue presidential impeachment. In February 2007 the GBC restyled itself as the **Genuine Opposition** (GO). For some seats, the larger parties, especially *Lakas*-CMD and Kampi, endorsed candidates jointly with small local or regional parties. In addition, a number of winning candidates also carried a UNO endorsement.

Leading Government-Supportive Parties:

Lakas–Christian Muslim Democrats—*Lakas Kampi* CMD (*Lakas-Kabalikat ng Malayang Pilipino ng Kristiyano at Muslim Demokrata*). Two of the largest Filipino parties, Lakas—CMD and Kampi, completed a merger in 2009. *Lakas*-CMD traces its origin to the People Power Party (*Partido Lakas ng Tao*—PPP) that was founded by presidential hopeful Fidel Ramos in January 1992, two months after he had left the dominant LDP because of its decision to designate Ramon Mitra as its nominee. In early February the formation was redesignated as EDSA-LDP (EDSA being an acronym for Epifanio de los Santo Avenue, the location of the first "People Power" rally in 1986). Subsequently, *Lakas ng EDSA* (EDSA Power) joined in a coalition with the National Union of Christian Democrats (NUCD), led by Raul MANGLAPUS, who had previously led the pre-1972 Christian Socialist Movement.

While *Lakas*-NUCD won only 51 of 201 lower house seats in the 1992 election, its ranks were subsequently swelled by defections from other parliamentary groups, including, most notably, the LDP. In mid-1994, by contrast, it lost a number of House supporters, most prominently its majority leader, Ronaldo Zamora (formerly of the LDP and most recently of the PMP). It captured an overwhelming majority of House seats in 1995. In June 1997 the Supreme Court ruled that Ramos could not run for reelection, and in December he backed Jose de Venecia, Speaker of the House of Representatives.

To enhance his party's chances at the polls, Ramos engineered an electoral alliance with the moderate United Muslim Democratic Party (UMDP) of Mindanao and with the Alliance of Free Filipinos (Kampi), which had been organized in 1997 to support the presidential aspirations of Gloria Macapagal-Arroyo, daughter of former president Diosdado Macapagal. Although opinion polls indicated that Macapagal-Arroyo was running second only to Joseph Estrada among presidential contenders, she agreed to unite Kampi with *Lakas*-NUCD and to serve as de Venecia's running mate.

In May 1998 de Venecia finished second, with 15.9 percent of the presidential vote, while Macapagal-Arroyo won the vice presidency with a 47 percent share and subsequently agreed to join the cabinet as secretary of social welfare and development. Following her victory, Kampi remained in existence, although most of its members were also affiliated with *Lakas*-NUCD. Although the *Lakas*-NUCD won 5 Senate seats and 50 House seats, its effectiveness as the leading opposition party was soon weakened by defections to President Estrada's LAMP. The situation was reversed following Estrada's departure from office in January 2001, and the *Lakas*-NUCD emerged from the May 2001 election with a plurality of some 85 seats (including those won by *Lakas* candidates with other endorsements).

President Macapagal-Arroyo was named chair of the party in June 2002, at which time she proposed adopting a new, consolidated name. Accordingly, in October the party leadership approved the change to *Lakas*-CMD.

In October 2003 Macapagal-Arroyo reversed a 2002 decision not to seek election to a full term in 2004, which resulted in the departure from the party of Vice President Teofisto Guingona, who had been *Lakas*-CMD's president. In the May 2004 balloting Macapagal-Arroyo won a full term, with 40 percent of the vote, against four other contenders. At the same time, the party and its K4 allies (including Kampi) captured sufficient seats to maintain a government majority in the Senate and swept to an easy victory in the House of Representatives. The K4's apparent unity subsequently suffered a significant setback in the House, however, when several dozen members, dissatisfied with the House leadership and the divvying up of key committee assignments, declared allegiance to a revitalized Kampi.

In May 2007 *Lakas*-CMD won a plurality of seats in the House of Representatives and, in partnership with second-place finisher Kampi, the NPC, and others, held a majority. De Venecia was ousted from his position as House Speaker on January 28, 2008, and from the party presidency on March 10. Prospero Nograles succeeded him in both posts.

A formal agreement on the merger of *Lakas*-CMD and Kampi was signed in Davao City on June 18, 2008, and announced by President Macapagal-Arroyo. The process of integrating the nation's two largest parties on the regional level was completed 11 months later. At a ceremony in Manila on May 28, 2009, the president assured supporters that the planned 2010 elections would take place and, she predicted, be dominated by the newly united governing party. The merger left Lakas Kampi CMD with a majority in the House of Representatives and control of more than half the nation's governorships. The party claimed more than five million members. The two leading contenders for the party's presidential nomination in 2010 were both outsiders: Vice President Noli de Castro, previously an independent, and Gilberto Teodoro, the defense minister. The youthful Teodoro left the NPC and joined Lakas Kampi CMD in July 2009. Feliciano BELMONTE, Jr., mayor of Quezon City, and Bayani FERNANDO, chairman of the Metro Manila Development Authority, also sought the party's backing.

Former speaker de Venezia petitioned the electoral commission (Comelec) to nullify the merger, claiming that it had been approved without a vote of party members at a national assembly. Party leaders castigated the ousted leader, pointing out that he himself had initiated the merger during the 1998 presidential campaign.

Leaders: Gloria MACAPAGAL-ARROYO (President of the Republic and Chair of the Party), Ronaldo PUNO (Vice Chairman), Prospero NOGRALES (Vice Chairman of the Party and Speaker of the House of Representatives), Eduardo ERMITA (President of the Party), Fidel V. RAMOS (Chair Emeritus).

Alliance of Free Filipinos (*Kabalikat ng Malayang Pilipino*—Kampi). Organized in 1997 by Jose Cojuangco and other supporters of Sen. Gloria Macapagal-Arroyo, Kampi served as the vehicle for her 1998 presidential exploration, although she ultimately opted to unite with *Lakas*-NUCD and seek the vice presidency. Following her victory, Kampi remained in existence, although most of its members were also affiliated with *Lakas*-NUCD.

In May 2004, as it had in 2001, Kampi won seats in the House of Representatives as part of a *Lakas*-led coalition. Following the 2004 election, however, disputes arose within the K4 alliance over congressional committee assignments and a reform agenda, which split the *Lakas*-CMD/Kampi partnership.

Kampi had considerable success in the 2007 House election, finishing second to *Lakas*-CMD. The long-sought merger of Kampi and Lakas-CMD took place formally on June 18, 2008, in an agreement signed in Davao City and announced by President Macapagal-Arroyo.

Leaders: Ronaldo PUNO (President of the Party), Emigdio TANJAUTCO (Secretary-General), Gloria MACAPAGAL-ARROYO (Chair Emeritus).

Nationalist People's Coalition (NPC). The NPC was formed prior to the 1992 balloting by right-wing elements of both the Liberal and *Nacionalista* parties under the leadership of President Aquino's estranged cousin and former Marcos business confidant, Eduardo Cojuangco. Although Cojuangco finished third in the 1992 presidential poll, NPC candidate Joseph Estrada won the vice presidency on a 33 percent vote share.

The NPC remained in opposition during the Ramos presidency, joining LAMMP upon its formation in June 1997. In December, however, NPC President Ernesto Maceda was ousted as Senate president and, blaming Estrada and LDP leader Edgardo Angara, apparently sidetracked a planned formal merger of the three LAMMP parties.

The NPC remained allied with President Estrada until his departure from office in January 2001, after which it agreed to cooperate with President Macapagal-Arroyo's administration. In the May 2001 lower house election the NPC finished second to *Lakas*-NUCD.

As the 2004 elections approached, the NPC was divided over support for Macapagal-Arroyo's reelection bid. As a result, some members supported her principal opponent, Fernando Poe Jr., and ran for Congress as participants in the opposition KNP alliance, while the majority participated in the K4 alliance. In the election the NPC won over 50 House seats. In 2007 it finished third, but with only 28 seats.

Senator Loren Legarda, Poe's running mate in the 2004 election, declared her 2010 presidential candidacy while traveling in the Maldives on a mission to mitigate the impact of climate change. Her fellow senator, Francis "Chiz" ESCUDERO, was a competitor for the party's nomination. Both senators, who rank highly in national polls, opposed the Macapagal-Arroyo administration. Another presidential aspirant, defense secretary Gilberto Teodoro, Jr., defected from the party and joined Lakas Kampi CMD in July 2009.

Leaders: Faustino DY Jr. (Chair), Frisco SAN JUAN (President), Eduardo COJUANGCO (Chair Emeritus).

Democratic Filipino Struggle (*Laban ng Demokratikong Pilipino*—LDP). Formally established in September 1988, the LDP constituted a merger of the Filipino Democratic Party–Laban (*Partido Demokratikong Pilipinas–Lakas ng Bayan*—PDP-Laban) and the People's Struggle (*Lakas ng Bansa*). The PDP, launched in 1982 by former members of the Mindanao Alliance, had joined with the People's Power (*Lakas ng Bayan*—Laban), nominally led by Benigno Aquino Jr. until his death in August 1983, to form the PDP-Laban. (Part of the PDP-Laban formation, led by Aquilino Pimentel, refused to enter the LDP and maintains a separate identity—see below.) The People's Struggle had been formed in 1987 by a nephew of Corazon Aquino.

Following the May 1995 election, at which the LDP was nominally allied with Lakas-NUCD, the LDP split, Edgardo Angara, the LDP chair, going into opposition after being ousted as Senate president in favor of Neptali GONZALES, also of the LDP. As a result, elements of the LDP ended up on both sides of the political aisle. In May 1996, however, the LDP severed its remaining coalition links. Five months later Gonzales, a strong supporter of President Ramos, was himself removed as Senate leader.

The LDP won 22 House seats (1 in coalition with the NPC) in the May 2001 election. Earlier in the year a faction known as the "Conscience Bloc" abandoned the party because of its support for pro-Estrada candidates. Most of the dissenters ultimately joined the *Lakas*-NUCD.

In 2004 the party was divided over the presidential contest, with supporters of party leader Edgardo Angara constituting the backbone of the KNP and backing its nominee, actor Fernando Poe Jr., who finished second, with 36.5 percent of the vote. A smaller LDP faction headed by Agapito "Butz" AQUINO supported the candidacy of Sen. Panfilo LACSON, who finished third, with 10.9 percent of the vote. (Poe died on December 14, 2004, three days after suffering a stroke.)

Angara reaffirmed his control of the party at a March 2005 national congress. Angara won reelection in 2007 and the LDP took three House seats. Angara's son, Juan Edgardo Angara, is a House member from the Aurora district. The party declined to field a presidential candidate in 2010, positioning itself as a possible swing vote.

Leaders: Sen. Edgardo ANGARA (Chair), Juan Edgardo ANGARA.

Philippine Democratic Socialist Party (*Partido Demokratiko Sosyalista ng Pilipinas*—PDSP). The PDSP dates from 1981, when it was founded by left-leaning legislators from the *Nacionalista* and other parties. Although associated with the People Power Coalition in 2001, in January 2004 the PDSP announced that it would not participate in the K4 alliance but would still support President Macapagal-Arroyo's reelection. In the May election the PDSP won two seats in the lower house, although one of the victors subsequently left the party. In 2007 it again won two seats. The party's recently appointed general secretary, Danilo YANG, was murdered in June 2009. Party leader and national security advisor Norberto Gonzales attributed the assassination to the New People's Army.

Leaders: Norberto GONZALES (National Security Adviser and Party Chair), Romeo INTENGAN (Cofounder).

Principal Opposition Parties:

Liberal Party (LP). The LP was organized in 1946 by a group of centrist *Nacionalista* dissidents. Formerly a member of Unido, its congressional delegation after the 1987 election encompassed 8 senators and 42 representatives. Subsequently, it divided into a pro-Aquino mainstream faction headed by Jovito SALONGA and a more rightist group headed by Eva KALAW. The party suffered numerous defections before and after the May 1992 elections, being reduced to little more than an echo of its former prominence.

Manila Mayor Alfredo LIM was the party's 1998 "law-and-order candidate" for president and ran with the endorsement of former president Corazon Aquino. Lim won only 8.7 percent of the vote, and the LP captured 14 House seats. The party subsequently entered a "strategic" coalition with the LAMP. In January 2000 Lim joined the Estrada cabinet.

Although the LP was also divided over the Estrada impeachment question, most of the party leadership ended up calling for the president's resignation. Secretary of Trade and Industry Manuel Roxas II resigned from the cabinet in November 2000, while the LP's president, Florencio ABAD, signed the impeachment complaint. The LP won 21 lower house seats in May 2001. It supported President Macapagal-Arroyo's reelection in 2004 and participated in the K4, winning more than two dozen seats in the House of Representatives plus 2 in the Senate.

The 2005 presidential impeachment battle effectively split the LP. In March 2006 a faction led by Manila Mayor Jose ATIENZA, supporting Macapagal-Arroyo, ousted Senate President Franklin Drilon as party leader, but the Drilon faction met shortly thereafter and expelled Atienza and cabinet member Michael DEFENSOR. Drilon subsequently asked the Commission on Elections to decide the issue. In July Drilon stepped down as Senate president. On November 26, the party's Executive Council appointed Roxas as party president. In April 2007 the Supreme Court sided with the Drilon faction. In the May election the party won 23 House seats to lead the opposition and retained 4 Senate seats.

Senator Manuel Roxas II appeared set to become the party's standard-bearer in the 2010 presidential election. The Atienza faction previously supported Roxas, but in July 2009 Atienza, environment and natural resources minister under Macapagal-Arroyo, said a national convention was necessary before the party could officially select a candidate. Ahead of the elections, the Drilon faction launched an effort to win back supporters of the current government who had left the party.

Leaders: Franklin DRILON (Chair), Sen. Manuel ROXAS II (President), Sen. Benigno C. AQUINO III (Executive Vice President).

Nacionalista Party (NP). Essentially the right wing of the Philippines' oldest party (formed in 1907), the *Nacionalistas* had been reduced by 1988 to a relatively minor formation within the Grand Alliance for Democracy (GAD), which had been organized by former defense minister Juan Ponce Enrile, prior to the 1987 congressional election as an anti-Aquino and anticommunist formation. The GAD also included the now-defunct Mindanao Alliance and the Philippine Democratic Socialist Party (PDSP, above). In February 1990 Enrile was arrested on charges of involvement in the December 1989 coup attempt, but the Supreme Court subsequently ordered the more serious charges reduced, and Enrile quickly returned to politics.

As the party's 1992 presidential candidate, Vice President Salvador Laurel ran eighth with a vote share of only 3.4 percent. In 1998 Enrile, who had been expelled from the party by Laurel in 1991, ran for president as an independent, capturing 1.4 percent of the vote. For the 1998 elections the NP was allied with the *Lakas*-NUCD and subsequently supported the removal of President Estrada.

Although allied with *Lakas*-CMD in 2004's K4 alliance, the NP ran in 2007 as part of the GO. It won ten House seats and holds four Senate seats. However, its leader, Manuel Villar Jr., was subsequently able to retain the role of Senate president only because he received the support of the pro-Macapagal-Arroyo senators. He later lost their backing and ceded the Senate presidency to Juan Ponce Enrile in November 2008. The Senate's ethics committee investigated and finally cleared Villar of corruption charges in 2009, after accusations that he had directed extra government funds to a road project traversing his own property. Despite the scandal, Villar remained atop polls in the 2010 presidential race.

Leaders: Sen. Manuel VILLAR Jr. (President of the Party), Sen. Alan Peter CAYETANO (Secretary General).

Force of the Filipino Masses (*Puwersa ng Masang Pilipino*—PMP). The PMP was founded as the Party of the Filipino Masses (*Partido ng Masang Pilipino*—PMP) in the early 1990s by Joseph Estrada, a former Liberal, to support his presidential aspirations. He ultimately ran as the vice presidential candidate of the NPC in 1992, but by 1998 the rejuvenated PMP claimed 5 million members. The PMP was virtually eliminated as an electoral force in the May 2001 election, although Estrada's wife, Luisa EJERCITO-ESTRADA, won election to the Senate as a PnM candidate.

With his trial ongoing, former president Estrada continued to hold sway over the PMP (now known as the Force of the Filipino Masses) as the 2004 elections approached. In December 2003 the PMP joined in formation with the KNP and supported presidential aspirant Fernando Poe Jr. After the May 2004 balloting the PMP claimed several House seats, while Estrada's son Jose joined his mother in the Senate. According to reports, in September 2004 the former president rejected a proposal by LDP opposition leader Edgardo Angara to merge the PMP into the LDP.

In August 2005 Juan Ponce Enrile, the chair of the party, took the unorthodox step of joining the majority in the Senate. Enrile stated at the time that former president Estrada had approved the move. In 2007 the PMP won four House seats. Shortly thereafter, Enrile and Jose Estrada were criticized by much of the opposition for joining the pro-Macapagal-Arroyo senators in supporting the NP's Manuel Villar Jr. for Senate president. The mayor of Manila, Alfredo Lim, was appointed party president in 2007, but removed from the position in August 2008.

As the 2010 presidential race heated up, Estrada repeatedly stated that he was willing to offer himself as a candidate if the opposition could not unite behind a single contender. It became increasingly clear that the former president intended to seek the office again. It was unclear, however, whether the constitution permitted him to serve as president, since he had previously held the office but failed to complete his term. Estrada unsuccessfully appealed fraud charges against him in October 2009.

Leaders: Joseph ESTRADA (Chair of the Party and Former President of the Republic), Sen. Juan Ponce ENRILE, Sen. Jose "Jinggoy" ESTRADA.

Filipino Democratic Party–Laban (*Partido Demokratikong Pilipinas–Lakas ng Bayan*—PDP-Laban). The current PDP-Laban constitutes the branch of the original PDP-Laban that refused to join in formation of the LDP (see above) in 1988. In 2004 it won two lower house seats as a component of the KNP alliance. In 2005–2006 party leader Aquilino Pimentel Jr. was one of the more outspoken voices demanding President Macapagal-Arroyo's resignation.

In the 2007 election the PDP-Laban won three House seats. Its lone senator, Pimentel, was elected minority leader in the upper house. Two PDP-Laban members entered the 2010 presidential contest: Jejomar "Jojo" Binay, mayor of Makati, and Senator Ana Consuelo "Jamby" Madrigal. The latter, a wealthy senator, appeared to have the resources to run as an independent if she failed to get the party's endorsement.

Leaders: Aquilino PIMENTEL Jr. (Senate Minority Leader), Jejomar BINAY (Mayor of Makati), Teodoro LOCSIN Jr.

Other National Congressional Parties:

New Society Movement (*Kilusan Bagong Lipunan*—KBL). Organized in 1978 as a pro-Marcos formation, the KBL was utilized by the former president's widow, Imelda MARCOS, for her own bid in 1992. Initially considered a major threat to the other contenders, Marcos captured only 10.3 percent of the vote for a fifth-place finish.

In April 1998, trailing in the polls with only a 2 percent share, Marcos withdrew from the upcoming presidential election "to save the Filipino people from the ultimate injustice of a bloody election." In 2001, 2004, and 2007 the party won one seat in the House of Representatives.

In 2007 outgoing governor of Ilocos Norte Ferdinand Marcos Jr. discredited a KBL Senate list he described as filled with "nuisance candidates" who had been put forward by "renegade members."

Leader: Ferdinand MARCOS Jr. (Member of the House).

People's Reform Party (PRP). The PRP was the nominal party vehicle for the 1992 presidential bid of political independent Miriam Defensor-Santiago, who campaigned with sufficient vigor on an anti-corruption platform to gain a 19.7 percent vote share as runner-up to

Fidel Ramos. Senator Defensor-Santiago proved less successful in 1998, winning only 3.0 percent of the presidential vote. She was one of President Estrada's strongest Senate supporters before and after his November 2000 impeachment. In May 2001 she lost her reelection bid.

Defensor-Santiago was expected to seek another Senate term in 2004 as an opposition candidate, but she ultimately gained the endorsement of the government-supportive K4. After winning, she had a falling out with the *Lakas*-CMD and declared herself an independent. Later, however, she repaired relations with the administration and spoke in favor of constitutional reform. One of the most colorful politicians in the Philippines, Defensor-Santiago was expected to run for reelection in 2010, possibly on the Nacionalista ticket.

Leader: Sen. Miriam DEFENSOR-SANTIAGO.

Local Parties Winning District Seats in 2007:

The Philippines has many small local or regional parties that are sometimes affiliated with the more established national parties. In 2007 one local party, the **Kilusang Diwa ng Taguig** (KDT), based in Taguig City, won a House seat on its own.

In 2007 single House seats were also won by candidates from the **Sarangani Reconciliation and Reformation Organization** (SARRO) and the **United Negros Alliance** (UNA), both of whom had also been endorsed by *Lakas*-CMD. The **Progressive Movement for Development of Initiatives** (PROMDI), founded by former Cebu governor and 1998 presidential candidate Emilio OSMEÑA, won one seat with the joint endorsement of *Lakas* and another Cebu party, the **Bando Osmeño–Pundok Kauswagan** (BO-PK). Another candidate endorsed by both the BO-PK and *Lakas* won a second seat from Cebu City.

Candidates from the following parties all won one seat with the joint endorsement of Kampi: the **New People Power Party of Nueva Ecija** (*Lapiang Bagong Lakas ng Nueva Ecija*—BALANE); the **One Cebu** (1-Cebu), led by Cebu's governor, Gwendolyn GARCIA; the **Padajon Surigao,** based in Surigao del Norte; and the **PTM,** from Sultan Kudarat Province.

Abante Viscaya, based in Nueva Viscaya, won one seat in partnership with the NP. **Achievers with Integrity Movement** (AIM), based in South Cotabato, won one seat with the NPC. **Ugayon,** based in Iloilo, won one with the LP.

Organizations Winning Party-List Seats in 2007:

Akbayan! Citizens' Action Party (*Akbayan*). *Akbayan* was formed in January 1998 as an electoral coalition of various leftist groups, including splinters from the Communist Party of the Philippines (CPP, below) and the KRMR (see under PMP, below). In the May 1998 election it won one party-list seat. In May 2001 it again won sufficient support for one seat, while in 2004 it captured 6.7 percent of the vote and was awarded three seats. In 2007 it held one seat. The party gained another in April 2009 following the Supreme Court's party-list reallocation (see Legislature, below). Walden Bello, an academic and well-known globalization critic, joined the lower house.

Leaders: Risa HONTIVEROS-BARAQUEL, Walden BELLO (Members of the House of Representatives).

Bayan Muna Party. The leftist *Bayan Muna* (People First), which descends from the Communist-affiliated New Nationalist Alliance (*Bagong Alyansang Makabayan*—Bayan), was the most successful of the party-list groups in 2001 and 2004, winning three House seats in both elections. In 2004 the government charged that it and two associated party-list organizations—the **Gabriela Women's Party** (GWP), led by Liza LARGOLA-MAZA, and the *Anakpawis* (Toiling Masses), previously led by the late Crispin BELTRAN—had channeled money to Communists. Party leader Satur Ocampo has also been associated with the NDF (below).

Among those arrested in connection with the alleged coup plot against Macapagal-Arroyo in February 2006 were the six party-list members from *Bayan Muna*, *Anakpawis,* and the GWP. The six, minus Beltran, who had already been arrested, initially sought sanctuary in the House complex, Batasan, and were therefore dubbed the "Batasan 5." In July 2007 the Supreme Court dismissed the charges against all six. In May, *Bayan Muna* had won two party-list seats, as had the GWP. *Anakpawis* won one. Bayan Muna and Anakpawis each gained a new representative in April 2009. In August, these groups formed the core of a new progressive coalition, Makabayan, which planned to offer Senate candidates in 2010.

Leaders: Satur OCAMPO, Teodoro CASIÑO Jr. (Members of the House of Representatives).

For a complete list of the 30 groups that held party-list seats in the House of Representatives following the reallocation of 2009, see the Legislature section, below.

Communist Groups:

National Democratic Front (NDF). The NDF was launched by the Communist Party of the Philippines (CPP) in April 1973 in an effort to unite Communist, labor, and Christian opponents of the Marcos regime, which declared it illegal. It encompasses more than a dozen "revolutionary allied organizations," most prominently the CPP and the CPP's military wing, the New People's Army (NPA). Both the NDF and the CPP were technically legalized (by repeal of the antisubversive edict under which they had been proscribed) on September 1, 1992, immediately prior to the launching of peace negotiations in the Netherlands with government representatives. The talks lasted until June 1995, when they collapsed because of the government's refusal to free imprisoned NPA leader Sotero LLAMAS, whose release had been ordered by a Manila court; the negotiations resumed a year later and continued into 1998. On March 16 in The Hague, representatives from the government and the NDF signed a Comprehensive Agreement on Respect for Human Rights and International Humanitarian Law (CARHRIHL). They also exchanged drafts of a second agreement on social and economic reforms. Two additional agreements, one on political and economic reform and another on ending hostilities, were to follow.

Shortly before leaving office in June 1998, President Ramos freed 18 Communist guerrillas as a goodwill gesture, while on August 7 President Estrada formally implemented the March human rights pact. In late February 1999, however, responding to the NPA's abduction of an army general and another officer on Mindanao, Estrada suspended negotiations. Two months later, after the release of the general and four other captives, the president expressed his willingness to reopen talks, but the NDF refused. In late May the NDF announced that it was formally ending the talks, in part because of the recently ratified Visiting Forces Agreement (VFA) with the United States, which it characterized as "treason and betrayal of national sovereignty." Talks resumed in Oslo, Norway, in April 2001 but were suspended two months later by the Macapagal-Arroyo government because of the alleged NPA assassination of a congressman.

For most of the next three years the government and the NDF took turns in proposing and rejecting cease-fires as well as the resumption of peace talks. The process was complicated by continuing clashes between NPA and government forces; by the NDF's vehement opposition to the renewed presence in the Philippines of U.S. troops to combat terrorism; and, in 2002, by the decision of both Washington (in August) and then Manila (in October) to list the NDF as a terrorist organization.

In early 2004, two new rounds of peace talks took place in Oslo, concluding with an agreement to establish a Joint Monitoring Committee to oversee implementation of the CARHRIHL. A June 22–25 session proved less productive, however, and an additional round scheduled for August was canceled by the NDF, partly because Manila had not sought removal of the Communist groups from the foreign terrorist organization lists of the United States, Canada, Australia, and the EU.

In July 2006, responding to President Macapagal-Arroyo's directive that the police join with the armed forces to pursue all-out war against the NPA, NDF leader Luis Jalandoni called for renewed peace talks. With military operations against the NPA continuing, in October 2007 the government indicated that a cease-fire would have to be established before peace talks could resume. NDF leaders expressed willingness to reopen talks, accusing the government of closing the door to further negotiations by imposing preconditions such as disarmament and demobilization.

In May 2009 the government announced the expected resumption of peace talks with the rebels. Under a restored security agreement, NDF negotiator Luis Jalandoni briefly returned from exile in July. Two detained rebel "consultants" were freed in August, but the delay in releasing more threatened to scuttle the revival of the peace process.

Leaders: Luis JALANDONI (Chair of the NDF Negotiating Panel), Fidel AGCAOILI (Spokesperson for Negotiating Panel), Jose Maria SISON (Political Consultant).

Communist Party of the Philippines–Marxist-Leninist (CPP-ML or CPP). The CPP was launched as a Maoist formation in 1968, the **New People's Army** (NPA) being added as its military wing in early 1969. Between 1986 and 1991, many of its leaders were captured by government forces, including NPA commander Romulo KINTANAR, who was released in 1992, abandoned the guerrilla movement, and was assassinated in January 2003. Jose Maria Sison (who reportedly uses the pseudonym Armando Liwanag) was reelected party chair at a Central Committee meeting in September 1992, although he had been an exile in the Netherlands since his release by the Aquino government in 1986. A number of splinter groups subsequently left the CPP (see below).

The NPA numbers some 5,000 rural-based guerrillas, down from a peak of 25,000 in 1987; it is strongest in northeast and central Luzon, in the Samar provinces of the Visayas, and in southern Mindanao, although at various times it has undertaken insurgent activity in well over three-quarters of the country's provinces. In March 1999 the NPA announced that it had established an alliance with the MILF (below). In October 2002 the government declared the CPP to be a terrorist organization.

In 2004 hard-liners attacked Sison for supporting electoral candidates through a number of party-list organizations, including the *Bayan Muna* Party. Meanwhile, the NPA and government forces continued to clash. President Macapagal-Arroyo vowed to defeat the NPA by the end of her term in 2010. In addition to stepping up military confrontation, her administration also rewarded rebels who surrendered their weapons with cash to aid in their reintegration.

Leaders: Jose Maria SISON (Chair, in exile), Benito E. TIAMZON (Vice Chair), Wilma TIAMZON (Secretary General), Gregorio ROSAL (Spokesperson).

Revolutionary Workers' Party–Philippines (*Rebolusyonaryong Partido ng Manggagawa–Pilipinas*—RPMP). The founding conference of the RPMP was held in April 1998. Many of its members were previously affiliated with the CPP but rejected its Maoist ideology in favor of a Trotskyite platform. Its military wing is the **Revolutionary Proletarian Army–Alex Boncayao Brigade** (RPA-ABB). In late December 1999 President Estrada met with four leaders of the RPMP and RPA-ABB in furtherance of his peace efforts. The four, including Arturo TABARA and Nilo de la Cruz, were immediately vilified by Jose Maria Sison of the CPP and Filemon Lagman of the KRMR. The RPMP–RPA-ABB has since been rejected by most of the left, and in September 2004 Tabara was assassinated by the NPA. Peace negotiations with the Macapagal-Arroyo government, and several development projects, are ongoing.

Leader: Nilo de la CRUZ.

Other recently active Communist splinter parties include the **Marxist-Leninist Party of the Philippines** (MLPP), which separated from the CPP in 1998 and whose members have reportedly been targeted for assassination by the CPP/NPA; the **Metro Manila Rizal Regional Party Committee,** a 1998 offshoot of the KRMR; and the **Revolutionary Worker's Party–Mindanao** (*Rebolusyonaryong Partido ng Manggagawa–Mindanao*—RPM-M), formed in 2001 as an RPMP splinter. In October 2005 the RPM-M signed a cease-fire agreement with the government, and in December 2006 the two signed additional agreements on monitoring the cease-fire and advancing the peace process. For more information on the **Filipino Workers' Party** (*Partido ng Manggagawang Pilipino*—PMP), see the 2009 *Handbook.*

Southern-Based Muslim Groups:

Moro National Liberation Front (MNLF). In separatist rebellion since 1974 on behalf of Mindanao's Muslim communities, the MNLF split in 1975 into Libyan- and Egyptian-backed factions, the latter subsequently calling itself the Moro Islamic Liberation Front (MILF, below). Originally the stronger of the two guerrilla armies, MNLF forces had dwindled by 1986 to one-third their original size, and in early 1987 the MNLF leader, Nur Misuari, tentatively agreed to drop his demands for an independent southern state in favor of autonomy. A January 1994 cease-fire and a subsequent peace agreement directly led to Misuari's election as governor of the Autonomous Region of Muslim Mindanao (ARMM) on September 9, 1996, although hard-line MNLF splinters and the MILF rejected the arrangement. In March 2000 an MNLF splinter, the **MNLF–Islamic Command Council,** currently chaired by Habib Mujahab HASHIM, announced that it intended to renew guerrilla warfare to achieve a "separate Islamic state in Mindanao," but it subsequently moderated its militancy.

In April 2001 the MNLF Central Committee voted to remove Misuari as chair, citing a lack of progress during his tenure as governor of the ARMM. He was replaced by a "Council of 15" but refused to acknowledge the decision. In August the government named the MNLF general secretary, Muslimin Sema, to replace him as head of the Southern Philippines Council for Peace and Development (SPCPD), and in October he was derecognized by the OIC. On November 19 Misuari loyalists broke the MNLF's five-year-old cease-fire in a series of attacks on Jolo Island. Arrested on November 24 while attempting to enter Malaysia, Misuari was later extradited to the Philippines to face charges of rebellion. On November 26 the MNLF's Parouk Hussin was elected to succeed Misuari as ARMM governor.

In February 2006 the MNLF elected Nur Misuari to return as chair (despite his continuing detention), only to remove him again from that position in April 2008. In June 2009, the MNLF declared it would boycott the upcoming ARMM elections to demonstrate its dissatisfaction with the implementation of the 1996 peace accord.

Leaders: Muslimin SEMA (Chair and Mayor of Cotabato City), Nur MISUARI (Former Chair), Abdul SAHRIN (Secretary General), Parouk HUSSIN.

Moro Islamic Liberation Front (MILF). The MILF was launched as a fundamentalist faction within the MNLF, with Hashim Salamat, a Cairo-trained *ulema* (Islamic religious leader), as deputy to Nur Misuari. It split from the parent group in 1978, adopting the MILF name in 1980. Estimates of the size of its military wing, the **Bangsamoro Islamic Armed Forces**, vary widely, from a Philippine government assessment of 10,000 to an MILF claim of 120,000.

In opposing the September 1996 peace agreement, the MILF indicated that it would settle for nothing less than full independence for Muslim-dominated areas. Nevertheless, the MILF, which had begun preliminary peace talks with the government a month earlier, subsequently agreed to temporarily halt hostilities. Clashes continued to occur, however, despite a series of cease-fires.

In December 1997 MILF leader Salamat returned from 20 years of exile in Libya, and in March 1998 the government and the MILF reached agreement on setting up a quick-response team to prevent future altercations from escalating. In March 1999 Hashim Salamat and the MNLF's Nur Misuari reportedly conferred for the first time in 21 years.

Intermittent formal peace talks, interrupted by suspensions and punctuated by continuing hostilities, continued into 2000. In August the MILF indefinitely suspended talks following a series of military defeats, including the loss of its headquarters at Camp Abubaker in July. Salamat responded by calling for a *"jihad"* (holy war) against the government and insisted that any further peace talks should take place abroad, in a Muslim country. Negotiations in Tripoli in June 2001 quickly led to a peace pact that was formalized in Kuala Lumpur in August. At the same time, the MILF and the MNLF concluded a "framework of unity" agreement.

Although the MILF condemned the subsequent participation of U.S. troops in the *Balikatan* military exercises, in a meeting with government representatives in Putrajaya, Malaysia, in May 2002 it agreed to assist in eliminating such criminal activities as kidnapping for ransom. The MILF also accepted responsibility for distributing funds to be provided by Manila as reparations for damages attributable to the 2000 military campaign in Mindanao.

In March 2003 the MILF and the Communist NPA announced a "tactical" alliance that stopped short of actual military cooperation. Later in the same month, the MILF agreed to resume peace negotiations with the government, but continuing military activity by the MILF led the Macapagal-Arroyo administration to cancel talks and to reject a cease-fire offer. On June 23 MILF Chair Salamat stated that the MILF renounced terrorism and denied any terrorist links, despite numerous reports that members of the regional *Jemaah Islamiah* (JI) network had infiltrated the MILF. Salamat's statement undoubtedly contributed to the government's decision to reverse itself and accept a cease-fire from July 19. Although it was not made public until August 5, 2003, Hashim

Salamat died suddenly on July 13, 2003, and was soon succeeded by the vice chair for military affairs, Murad Ebrahim.

A series of informal meetings concluded in February 2004 with an announcement that formal peace talks would open in Kuala Lumpur. The planned negotiations were ultimately postponed in response to events that included the May national elections. As the end of the year approached, a start date of early 2005 was set for the peace talks, Manila having complied with two MILF preconditions: the dropping of charges against MILF members for a series of bombings near Davao Airport and government withdrawal from a captured MILF complex in Buliok. October witnessed the deployment of some 50 Malaysian troops, the core of an International Monitoring Team offered by members of the OIC. Exploratory peace talks resumed in April–June 2005.

Negotiations with the government resulted in a Memorandum of Understanding on Ancestral Domain (MOA-AD), announced on July 16, 2008. The Philippine Supreme Court declared the agreement unconstitutional on October 14, and MILF responded by going on an offensive that led to nearly a half-million displaced people on Mindanao. The government declared a unilateral ceasefire in July 2009, and the MILF agreed to return to the negotiating table (see Current issues).

Leaders: Al-Haj MURAD Ebrahim (Chair), Ghazali JAAFAR (Vice Chair for Political Affairs), Mohaqher IQBAL (Chief Negotiator), Jun MANTAWIL (Head, Peace Panel Secretariat).

Abu Sayyaf. The most radical of the fundamentalist Muslim insurgent groups, *Abu Sayyaf* (Bearers of the Sword) has continued its activities despite an August 1994 announcement by Manila that the rebels, including their leader, Brahama SALI, had been "annihilated." Although the MILF had earlier condemned the group as a terrorist organization at odds with the precepts of Islam, *Abu Sayyaf* reportedly agreed in September 1996 to operate under MILF command in opposition to the government's accord with the MNLF. In December 1998 the authorities announced that *Abu Sayyaf*'s leader, Abdurajak Abubakar JANJALANI, had been killed by government forces. In contrast to the MILF, *Abu Sayyaf* is believed to number no more than a few hundred guerrillas.

After more than a year of relative quiescence, *Abu Sayyaf* dramatically resurfaced in March–April 2000 with the kidnapping of more than 50 Philippine hostages on the southern island of Basilan and more than 20 others from the Malaysian resort island of Sipadan, off the Borneo coast. Half a dozen of the Basilan hostages were reportedly executed, but by late July the rest had been rescued or released. Most of the Sipadan hostages were ultimately ransomed for some $17.5 million, in part through the intercession of Libya. In May–August 2001 *Abu Sayyaf* renewed its kidnapping activities, abducting dozens of people and beheading a number of them.

In May 2002 the United States offered a $5 million reward leading to the apprehension of five *Abu Sayyaf* leaders; the Philippine government already had in place its own bounty program, which had contributed in July 2001 to the capture of a principal leader, Najmi SABDULA ("Commander Global"). In December 2003 another *Abu Sayyaf* commander, Ghalib ANDANG ("Commander Robot"), was captured by government forces. The United States, noting the organization's apparent links to the Indonesian-based JI as well as al-Qaida, added *Abu Sayyaf* to its list of foreign terrorist organizations.

Through 2004 *Abu Sayyaf* continued its tactics, including deadly bombings, which most often centered on Zamboanga, a Mindanao port on the Basilan Strait, but which also included the February 2004 bombing of a Manila ferry that cost over 100 lives. In August 2004 a Basilan court sentenced 17 members to death for the 2002 kidnappings.

A failed prison break on March 14–15, 2005, resulted in over two dozen deaths. Those killed included Najmi Sabdula and Ghalib Andang. Since then, *Abu Sayyaf* has continued its bombings and kidnappings, although none on the scale evidenced earlier. At the same time, the Philippine military has stepped up its attacks, aided by intelligence data from U.S. military personnel. In September 2006 *Abu Sayyaf*'s leader, Khaddafy JANJALANI, was killed, as was another commander, Abu SULAIMAN, in January 2007. Five months later the Philippine military announced that Yasser Igasan had succeeded Janjalani. In June 2008, the group kidnapped well-known television journalist Ces Drilon and her crew, releasing them nine days later. Three workers with the International Committee of the Red Cross were kidnapped in January 2009; all three were later released, the last one in July. A military attack on Abu Sayyaf forces on Basilan left more than 50 dead on August 12.

Leader: Yasser IGASAN.

The **Rajah Solaiman Movement** (RSM) is believed to be a small radical organization with links to *Abu Sayyaf* and the JI. Led by Hilarion del Rosario SANTOS (a.k.a. Ahmad SANTOS), it may have been involved in the February 2004 Manila ferry bombing. Another militant organization, the so-called **Pentagon Group,** has been involved in kidnapping for ransom. Pentagon leader Tahir ALONTO was reportedly killed by the Philippine military in August 2004.

LEGISLATURE

The 1987 constitution provides for a bicameral **Congress of the Philippines,** encompassing a Senate and a House of Representatives.

Senate. The upper house consists of 24 at-large members who may serve no more than two six-year terms. Half of the body is elected every three years; voters may cast as many votes as there are seats to be filled.

Because of the upper house's small size, senators are often elected less by party affiliation than by personal following. (At the 2004 election, for example, the victors included three film actors with no significant political experience.) In the most recent election, held May 14, 2007, the Genuine Opposition (GO) coalition won 7 seats (Nationalist People's Coalition [NPC], 3; *Nacionalista* Party [NP], 2; and 2 who ran without other party affiliation); TEAM Unity, 3 (*Lakas*-CMD, 1; Alliance of Free Filipinos [Kampi], 1; Democratic Filipino Struggle [LDP], 1); and independents, 2 (including 1 member of the Liberal Party [LP] who chose to campaign as an independent).

Following the 2007 election the party breakdown for the Senate as a whole was as follows: LP, 4; NP, 4; *Lakas*-CMD, 3; GO, 3; NPC, 2; Force of the Filipino Masses, 2; Filipino Democratic Party–Laban, Kampi, LDP, People's Reform Party, 1 each; independent, 1; vacant, 1 (occasioned by the election of a sitting senator as mayor of Manila). Although initial news reports after the 2007 election indicated that antigovernment forces held a substantial majority, splits between pro- and antigovernment factions within some parties, coupled with what many senators have viewed as the body's historical independence, made the situation less than clear-cut.

President: Juan Ponce ENRILE.

House of Representatives. The lower house, according to the Philippine constitution, encompasses a maximum of 250 members, of whom the majority are directly elected from legislative districts. A maximum of 20 percent of the members are elected via "a party-list system of registered national, regional, and sectoral parties or organizations." Each voter may cast a ballot for both a district representative and a party-list group. For each party-list seat, an organization must receive at least 2 percent of the total party-list votes cast, but no group may exceed 3 seats. (For 2007 the Commission on Elections accredited 93 party-list organizations.) In April 2009 a Philippine Supreme Court decision (Banat vs. Comelec) changed the formula for allocating party-list seats in the House, mandating that the maximum number of party-list representatives be seated. All representatives serve for three years, with no member to be reelected more than twice.

The most recent election was held May 14, 2007, in most districts, although voter intimidation, other electoral difficulties, and violence resulted in postponement of voting or in repeat voting in 13 southern towns on May 26–27 and in additional communities in June and July. As in the past, a number of winning candidates ran with more than one party endorsement. The following totals for the 216 district seats are based on information from the House itself: *Lakas*–Christian Muslim Democrats (*Lakas*-CMD), 88 seats (total also includes *Lakas*–National Union of Christian Democrats, 1; *Lakas–Bando Osmeño-Pundok Kauswagan* [BO-PK], 1; Progressive Movement for Development of Initiatives–BO-PK–*Lakas,* 1; Sarangani Reconciliation and Reformation Organization–*Lakas*-CMD, 1); Kampi, 51 (total includes 1 representative from each of the following: Kampi-United Negros Alliance [UNA], Cebu-Kampi, Kampi-PTM, Balane-Kampi); NPC, 27 (also includes 1 representative from NPC–Achievers with Integrity Movement); Liberal Party (LP), 19 (also includes 1 representative from LP-Ugayon); NP, 10 (also includes NP/*Abante Viscaya,* 1); Democratic Filipino Struggle (LDP), 4; Force of the Filipino Masses (PMP), 4; UNO, 3; PDP-Laban, 3; PDSP, 2; *Kilusang Diwa ng Taguig* (KDT), 1; New Society Movement (KBL), 1; independents, 3.

In the May 2007 elections, 16 parties and other organizations were awarded a total of 22 party-list seats. In April 2009, following the Supreme Court's Banat decision, an additional 29 representatives were sworn in, bringing the total of party-list representatives to 51 and giving the House a total membership (counting district and party-list seats) of 267. The following parties held party-list seats as of August 1, 2009: *Buhay Hayaang Yumabong* (*Buhay*), 3; *Bayan Muna* Party, 3; Advocacy for Teacher Empowerment through Action, Cooperation and Harmony towards Educational Reforms, Inc. (A-TEACHER), 2; *Abono*, 2; Agricultural Sectoral Alliance of the Philippines, Inc. (AGAP), 2; *Akbayan!* Citizens' Action Party, 2; Alagad, 2; *Anak Mindanao* (Amin), 2; *An Waray, 2; Anakpawis*, 2; Association of Philippine Electrical Cooperatives (APEC), 2; Alliance of Rural Concerns (ARC), 2; Luzon Farmers Party (*Butil*), 2; Citizens' Battle Against Corruption (Cibac), 2; Cooperative NATCCO Network Party (Coop-NATCCO), 2; Gabriela Women's Party, 2; You Against Corruption and Poverty (YACAP), 2; and 1-United Transport Koalition (1 UTAK); *Aangat Tayo*; *lyansang Bayanihan ng mga Magsasaka; Manggagawang Bukid at Mangingisda and Adhikain at Kilusan ng Ordinaryong Tao* Coalition (ABA AKO); *Abakada Guro*; *Alyansa ng mga Batayang Sektor* (ABS); Alliance for Nationalism and Democracy (ANAD); *Ang Kassanga*; Barangay Association for Nation Advancement and Transparency (BANAT); Bantay Katarungan Foundation (BANTAY); *Kabataan*; Kapatiran ng mga Na Kulong na Walang Sala (KAKUSA); Senior Citizens/Elderly Sectoral Party of the Philippines; Trade Union Congress of the Philippines (TUCP); United Movement Against Drugs (UNI MAD); Veterans Freedom Party (VFP); 1 each.

Speaker: Prospero NOGRALES.

CABINET

[as of August 1, 2009]

President	Gloria Macapagal-Arroyo (*Lakas*-CMD)
Vice President	Noli de Castro (*Lakas*-CMD)
Secretaries	
Agriculture	Arthur Yap
Budget and Management	Rolando Andaya Jr. (LP)
Education	Jesli Lapuz (NPC)
Energy	Angelo Reyes
Environment and Natural Resources	Lito Atienza (LP)
Finance	Margarito Teves (*Lakas*-CMD)
Foreign Affairs	Alberto Romulo (*Lakas*-CMD)
Health	Francisco Duque III
Interior and Local Government	Ronaldo Puno (Kampi)
Justice	Raul Gonzalez (*Lakas*-CMD)
Labor and Employment	Marianito Roque
Land Reform	Nasser Pangandaman
National Defense	Gilberto Teodoro Jr. (*Lakas*-Kampi CMD)
Public Works and Highways	Hermogenes Ebdane Jr.
Science and Technology	Estrella Alabastro [f]
Social Welfare and Development	Esperanza Cabral [f]
Tourism	Joseph Durano (NPC)
Trade and Industry	Peter Favila
Transportation and Communications	Leandro Mendoza
Executive Secretary	Eduardo Ermita (*Lakas*-CMD)
Chair, Housing and Urban Development Coordinating Council	Noli de Castro (*Lakas*-CMD)
National Security Adviser	Norberto Gonzales (PDSP)
Director General, National Economic and Development Authority	Ralph Recto (*Lakas*-CMD)
Presidential Spokesperson	Jesus Dureza

[f] = female

Note: Ministers who have not been recorded with party affiliation are viewed as independents.

COMMUNICATIONS

Freedom of the press is guaranteed by the constitution, but in the wake of the February 2006 state of emergency the government, in an effort to reduce the incidence of negative news reports about its activities, employed pressure tactics that included, according to the *International Herald Tribune,* "warnings, watch lists, surveillance, court cases, harassment lawsuits and threats of arrest on charges of sedition." Moreover, the Communist and Islamic insurgencies have contributed to a climate of violence that has made the Philippines the second deadliest country for journalists, after Iraq.

Press. The following are English-language dailies published in Manila, unless otherwise noted: *People's Bagong Taliba* (500,000), in Pilipino; *Abante* (420,000), tabloid, in Pilipino and English; *Philippine Star* (275,000); *Manila Bulletin* (270,000); *Philippine Daily Enquirer* (250,000); *Tempo* (230,000), in English and Pilipino; *Manila Times* (200,000); *Malaya* (180,000); *Balita* (150,000), in Pilipino; *Bisaya* (90,000), weekly, in Cebu-Visayan; *Bannawag* (40,000), weekly, in Ilocano.

News agencies. The government-run facility is the Philippines News Agency (PNA); a number of foreign bureaus also maintain offices in Manila.

Broadcasting and computing. Most broadcasting is commercial. Both terrestrial and cable television are widely available. The government's Philippines Broadcasting Service, with some 30 radio stations, is a leading source of news. The government has announced its intention to privatize two state-run television channels, IBC-13 and RPN-9.

As of 2008 there were 62.2 Internet users per 1,000 inhabitants.

INTERGOVERNMENTAL REPRESENTATION

Ambassador to the U.S.: Willy Calaud GAA.

U.S. Ambassador to the Philippines: Kristie A. KENNEY.

Permanent Representative to the UN: Hilario G. DAVIDE, Jr.

IGO Memberships (Non-UN): ADB, APEC, ASEAN, BIS, Interpol, IOM, NAM, WCO, WTO.

POLAND

Polish Republic
Rzeczypospolita Polska

Political Status: Independent state reconstituted 1918; Communist-ruled People's Republic established 1947; constitution of July 22, 1952, substantially revised in accordance with intraparty agreement of April 5, 1989, with further amendments on December 29, including name change to Polish Republic; new interim "small" constitution introduced December 8, 1992; permanent "large" constitution approved by national referendum on May 25, 1997, effective October 17, 1997.

Area: 120,725 sq. mi. (312,677 sq. km.).

Population: 38,230,100 (2002C); 38,104,000 (2008E).

Major Urban Centers (2005E): WARSAW (1,697,000), Łódź (772,000), Kraków (757,000), Wrocław (635,000), Poznań (570,000), Gdańsk (458,000), Szczecin (412,000).

Official Language: Polish.

Monetary Unit: Złoty (market rate December 1, 2009: 2.72 złotys = $1US). After Poland joined the European Union in May 2004, the Polish government announced that it hoped to adopt the euro as Poland's national currency by 2007. However, that goal proved to be ambitious, and the target date was subsequently pushed back to 2010 or later.

President: Lech KACZYŃSKI (elected as a member of Law and Justice); popularly elected at second-round balloting on October 23, 2005, and inaugurated on December 23 for a five-year term succeeding Aleksander KWAŚNIEWSKI (formerly Democratic Left Alliance). (Presidents are constitutionally required to resign their party affiliations upon inauguration.)

Prime Minister: Donald TUSK (Civic Platform); nominated by the president on November 9, 2007, following the legislative elections of October 21 and inaugurated (along with his new cabinet) on November 16 to succeed Jarosław KACZYŃSKI (Law and Justice), who had remained in a caretaker capacity since announcing his resignation on November 5.

THE COUNTRY

A land of plains, rivers, and forests, Poland has been troubled throughout its history by a lack of firm natural boundaries to demarcate its territory from that of powerful neighbors of both East and West. Its present borders reflect major post–World War II adjustments that involved the loss of some 70,000 square miles of former Polish territory to the former Soviet Union and the acquisition of some 40,000 square miles of previously German territory along the country's northern and western frontiers, the latter accompanied by the expulsion of most ethnic Germans and resettlement of the area by Poles. These changes, following the Nazi liquidation of most of Poland's prewar Jewish population, left the country 96 percent Polish in ethnic composition and 90 percent Roman Catholic in religious faith.

On October 22, 1978, Cardinal Karol WOJTYŁA, archbishop of Kraków, was invested as the 264th pope of the Roman Catholic Church. The first Pole ever selected for the office, Pope JOHN PAUL II was regarded as a politically astute advocate of church independence who had worked successfully within the strictures of a Communist regime. During a June 2–10, 1979, visit by the pope to his homeland, he was greeted by crowds estimated at 6 million. In 1980 the continuing power of the church was perhaps best demonstrated by the influence exerted by Polish primate Cardinal Stefan WYSZYŃSKI in moderating the policies of the country's newly formed free labor unions while playing a key role in persuading the Communist leadership to grant them official recognition. Cardinal Wyszyński died on May 28, 1981, and he was succeeded as primate on July 7 by Archbishop Józef GLEMP, whose efforts to emulate his predecessor were jolted on December 13 by the imposition of martial law. The result was a worsening in church-state relations that continued until May 1989, when the Polish *Sejm* voted to extend legal recognition to the church for the first time since 1944. Two months later, Poland and the Holy See established diplomatic relations.

Poland's economy underwent dramatic changes in the years after World War II, including a large-scale shift of the workforce into the industrial sector. A resource base that included coal, copper, and natural gas deposits contributed to significant expansion in the fertilizer, petrochemical, machinery, electronic, and shipbuilding industries, placing Poland among the world's dozen leading industrial nations. On the other hand, attempts to collectivize agriculture proved largely unsuccessful, with 80 percent of cultivated land remaining in private hands. Most importantly the retention of traditional farming methods and the fragility of soil and climatic conditions led to periodic agricultural shortages, which, in turn, contributed to consumer unrest.

In 1987, after the external debt had risen to more than $39 billion, the United States agreed to provide assistance in loan consolidation and rescheduling with the "Paris Club" of Western creditors. The action came after Polish officials had approved limited economic and political liberalization. Far more drastic revision from late 1989 included an end to price controls, the privatization of many state-owned companies, and a variety of other measures intended to introduce a market economy. The immediate consequence was a near 20 percent GDP contraction and annual inflation of 120 percent in 1991–1992, prior to growth of 4 percent a year in 1993–1996, 6.8 percent in 1997, and 4.8 percent in 1998. Growth slowed to 4.1 percent in 1999 and 4.0 percent in 2000 but then dropped to only 1.2 percent in 2001. Inflation remained a problem, averaging 9 percent in 1998–2000 before falling under 4 percent in 2001. It subsequently increased and averaged over 6 percent in 2006 and 2007. Unemployment rose steadily from a low of about 10 percent in 1998 to a high of 20 percent in the years 2003 and 2004, but then declined to 2.6 percent in 2007.

Poland was the largest of the ten new members to join the European Union (EU) in May 2004, and a year later much of the country was reportedly content with the EU developments to date. Farmers, initially concerned that subsidies in other EU countries would undercut Polish productivity, reported increased exports and welcomed their portion of the significant EU aid provided to Poland. Foreign investment was also continuing at a brisk pace. The major economic challenge facing the Polish government over the next several years will be the transition from the złoty to the euro. The previous government had little interest in making the change, but current Finance Minister Jacek ROSTOWSKI aimed to cut the budget deficit to under the EU minimum of 3 percent for admission to the Eurozone. Poland set 2013 as the target date for adopting the euro, but that date appears to be unrealistic in face of the worldwide economic crisis. The government concedes that the deficit will rise to 5 percent of GDP for 2009, but the European Commission maintains that it will be at least 6.6 percent. If so, Poland may not be able to adopt the euro as its currency until 2015.

By 2008 Poland's economic growth slowed, expanding by only 5 percent, and it is expected to decline by 0.7 percent in 2009. Inflation was 4.2 percent in 2008. By June of that year, the unemployment rate was down to 9.4 percent, the lowest in 10 years, but the rate was expected to rise to more than 13 percent by the end of 2009. Although the economic crisis that began in 2008 caused the złoty to lose over half its value in relation to the euro, sluggish economic conditions should keep inflation down to around 2.5 percent in 2009. Membership in the EU continues to be a great success for Poland. Through 2009 Poland had the second fastest growth rate among OEDC countries, trailing only the Slovak Republic.

GOVERNMENT AND POLITICS

Political background. Tracing its origins as a Christian nation to 966 A.D., Poland became an influential kingdom in late medieval and early modern times, functioning as an elective monarchy until its liquidation by Austria, Prussia, and Russia in the successive partitions of 1772, 1793, and 1795. Its reemergence as an independent republic at the close of World War I was followed in 1926 by the establishment of a military dictatorship headed initially by Marshal Józef PIŁ SUDSKI. The first direct victim of Nazi aggression in World War II, Poland was jointly occupied by Germany and the USSR, coming under full German control with the outbreak of German-Soviet hostilities in June 1941.

After the end of the war in 1945 a Communist-controlled "Polish Committee of National Liberation," established under Soviet auspices in Lublin in 1944, merged with a splinter group of the anti-Communist Polish government-in-exile in London to form a Provisional Government of National Unity. The new government was headed by Polish Socialist Party (*Polska Partia Socjalistyczna*—PPS) leader Edward OSÓBKA-MORAWSKI, with Władysław GOMUŁKA, head of the (Communist) Polish Workers' Party (*Polska Partia Robotnicza*—PPR), and Stanisław MIKOŁAJCZYK, chair of the Polish Peasants' Party (*Partia Stronnictwo Ludowe*—PSL), as vice premiers. Communist tactics in liberated Poland prevented the holding of free elections as envisaged at the Yalta Conference in February 1945, and the election that was ultimately held in 1947 represented the final step in the establishment of control by the PPR, which forced the PPS into a 1948 merger as the Polish United Workers' Party (*Polska Zjednoczona Partia Robotnicza*—PZPR).

Poland's Communist regime was thereafter subjected to periodic crises resulting from far-ranging political and economic problems, accompanied by subservience to Moscow and the use of Stalinist methods to consolidate the regime. In 1948 Gomułka was accused of "rightist and nationalist deviations," which led to his replacement by Bolesław BIERUT and his subsequent imprisonment (1951–1954). By 1956, however, post-Stalin liberalization was generating political turmoil, precipitated by the sudden death of Bierut in Moscow and "bread and freedom" riots in Poznań, and Gomułka returned to the leadership of the PZPR as the symbol of a "Polish path to socialism." The new regime initially yielded a measure of political stability, but by the mid-1960s Gomułka was confronted with growing dissent among intellectuals in addition to factional rivalry within the party leadership. As a result, Gomułka-inspired anti-Semitic and anti-intellectual campaigns were mounted in 1967–1968, yielding the mass emigration of some 18,000 Polish Jews (out of an estimated 25,000) by 1971. Drastic price increases caused a serious outbreak of workers' riots in December 1970, which, although primarily economic in nature, provoked a political crisis that led to the replacement of Gomułka as PZPR first secretary by Edward GIEREK.

Following a parliamentary election on March 23, 1980, a new austerity program was announced that called for a reduction in imports, improved industrial efficiency, and the gradual withdrawal of food subsidies. Workers responded by demanding wage adjustments and calling strikes, which by August had assumed an overtly political character, with employees demanding that they be allowed to establish "workers' committees" to replace the PZPR-dominated, government-controlled official trade unions. Among those marshaling support for the strikers was the Committee for Social Self-Defense (*Komitet Samoobrony Społeczej*—KSS), the largest of a number of recently established dissident groups.

On August 14, 1980, the 17,000 workers at the Lenin Shipyard in Gdańsk struck, occupied the grounds, and issued a list of demands that included the right to organize independent unions. Three days later, workers from a score of industries in the area of the Baltic port presented an expanded list of 16 demands that called for recognition of the right of all workers to strike, abolition of censorship, and release of political prisoners. In an emergency session also held on August 17, the PZPR Politburo agreed to open negotiations with the strikers, eventually consenting to meet with delegates of the Gdańsk interfactory committee headed by Lech WAŁĘSA, a former shipyard worker who had helped organize the 1970 demonstrations. On August 30 strike settlements were completed, the 21-point Gdańsk Agreement being approved by the *Sejm* and signed by Wałęsa and the government on August 31. While recognizing the position of the PZPR as the "leading force" in society, the unprecedented document stated, "It has been found necessary to call up new, selfgoverning trade unions which would become authentic representatives of the working class."

Although most workers along the Baltic coast returned to their jobs on September 1, 1980, strikes continued to break out in other areas, particularly the coal- and copper-mining region of Silesia, and on September 6, First Secretary Gierek resigned in favor of Stanisław KANIA. On September 15 registration procedures to be followed by independent unions were announced, with authority to approve union statutes delegated to the Warsaw provincial court. Three days later, 250 representatives of new labor groups established a "National Committee of Solidarity" (*Solidarność*) in Gdańsk with Wałęsa as chair, and on September 24 the organization applied for registration as the Independent Self-Governing Trade Union Solidarity. The court objected, however, to its proposed governing statutes, particularly the absence of any specific reference to the PZPR as the country's leading political force. Not until November 10—two days before a threatened strike by Solidarity—did the Supreme Court, ruling in the union's favor, remove amendments imposed by the lower court, the union accepting as an annex a statement of the party's role. By December some 40 free trade unions had been registered, while on January 1, 1981, the official Central Council of Trade Unions was dissolved.

The unprecedented events of 1980 yielded sharp cleavages between Wałęsa and radical elements within Solidarity and between moderate and hard-line factions of the PZPR. Fueled by the success of the registration campaign, labor unrest increased further in early 1981, accompanied by appeals from the private agricultural sector for recognition of a "Rural Solidarity." Amid growing indications of concern by other Eastern-bloc states, the minister of defense, Gen. Wojciech JARUZELSKI, was appointed chair of the Council of Ministers on February 11. Initially welcomed in his new role by most Poles, including the moderate Solidarity leadership, Jaruzelski attempted to initiate a dialogue with nonparty groups and introduced a ten-point economic program designed to promote recovery and counter "false anarchistic paths contrary to socialism." The situation again worsened following a resumption of government action against dissident groups, although the Independent Self-Governing Trade Union for Private Farmers–Solidarity (Rural Solidarity), which claimed between 2.5 and 3.5 million members, was officially registered on May 12.

At a delayed extraordinary PZPR congress that convened on July 14, 1981, in Warsaw, more than 93 percent of those attending were new delegates selected in unprecedented secret balloting at the local level. As a consequence, very few renominations were entered for outgoing Central Committee members, while only four former members were reelected to the Politburo. Stanisław Kania was, however, retained as first secretary in the first secret, multicandidate balloting for the office in PZPR history.

Despite evidence of government displeasure at its increasingly political posture, Solidarity held its first national congress in Gdańsk on September 5–10 and September 25–October 7, 1981. After reelecting Wałęsa as its chair, the union approved numerous resolutions, including a call for wide-ranging changes in the structure of trade-union activity. Subsequently, at the conclusion of a plenary session of the PZPR Central Committee held on October 16–18, First Secretary Kania submitted his resignation and was immediately replaced by General Jaruzelski, who, on October 28, made a number of changes in the membership of both the Politburo and Secretariat. Collaterally, Jaruzelski moved to expand the role of the army in maintaining public order.

During the remaining weeks of 1981 relations between the government and Solidarity progressively worsened. On December 11 the union announced that it would conduct a national referendum on January 15, 1982, that was expected to yield an expression of nonconfidence in the Jaruzelski regime. The government responded by arresting most of the Solidarity leadership, including Wałęsa, while the Council of State on December 13 declared martial law under a Military Committee for National Salvation headed by Jaruzelski. Subsequently, a number of stringent decrees were promulgated that effectively banned all organized nongovernmental activity except for religious observances and established summary trial courts for those charged with violation of martial law regulations.

On October 8, 1982, the *Sejm* approved legislation that formally dissolved all existing trade unions and set guidelines for new government-controlled organizations to replace them. The measures were widely condemned by the Catholic Church and other groups, and Solidarity's underground leadership called for a nationwide protest strike on November 10. However, the appeal yielded only limited public support, and Wałęsa was released from detention two days later. On December 18 the *Sejm* approved a suspension (not a lifting) of martial law that voided most of its remaining overt manifestations.

On July 21, 1983, State Council Chair Henryk JABŁOŃSKY announced the formal lifting of martial law and the dissolution of the Military Committee for National Salvation, the latter body being effectively supplanted four months later by a National Defense Committee, chaired by General Jaruzelski, with overall responsibility for both defense and state security. However, these events were overshadowed by the kidnapping and murder in October 1984 of the outspoken pro-Solidarity cleric, Fr. Jerzy POPIEŁUSZKO of Warsaw, for which four state security officers were ultimately tried and convicted.

Following *Sejm* elections in October 1985, General Jaruzelski succeeded the aging Jabłońsky as head of state, relinquishing the chairship of the Council of Ministers to Zbigniew MESSNER, who entered office as part of a major realignment that substantially increased the government's technocratic thrust. Jaruzelski was reelected PZPR first secretary at the party's tenth congress in mid-1986, during which nearly three-quarters of the Central Committee's incumbents were replaced.

In October 1987 Jaruzelski presented to the PZPR Central Committee a number of proposed economic and political reforms far outstripping Mikhail Gorbachev's "restructuring" agenda for the Soviet Union. Central to their implementation, however, was a strict austerity program that included massive price increases and was bitterly opposed by the outlawed Solidarity leadership. In the wake of a remarkable referendum on November 29, at which the proposals failed to secure endorsement by a majority of eligible voters, the government indicated that it would proceed with their implementation, albeit at a slower pace than had originally been contemplated.

New work stoppages erupted in Kraków in late April 1988 and quickly spread to other cities, including Gdańsk, before being quelled by security forces. On August 22 emergency measures were formally invoked to put down a further wave of strikes, and six days later the PZPR Central Committee approved a plan for broad-based talks to address the country's economic and social ills. Although the government stated that "illegal organizations" would be excluded from such discussions, a series of meetings were held between Solidarity leader Wałęsa and Interior Minister Czesław KISZCZAK. On September 19, however, the Messner government resigned after being castigated by both party and official trade union leaders for economic mismanagement. Mieczysław RAKOWSKI, a leading author of the March 1981 economic program, was named prime minister on September 26.

In the wake of further party leadership changes on December 21, 1988, which included the removal of six Politburo hard-liners, a new round of discussions with representatives of the still-outlawed Solidarity was launched on February 6, 1989. The talks resulted in the signing on April 5 of three comprehensive agreements providing for the legalization of Solidarity and its rural counterpart; political reforms that included the right of free speech and association, democratic election to state bodies, and judicial independence; and economic liberalization. The accords paved the way for parliamentary balloting on June 4 and 18, at which Solidarity captured all of the 161 nonreserved seats in the 460-member *Sejm* and 99 of 100 seats in the newly established Senate.

On July 25, 1989, six days after being elected president of the republic by the barest of legislative margins, General Jaruzelski was rebuffed by Solidarity in an effort to secure a PZPR-dominated "grand coalition" government. On August 2 the *Sejm* approved Jaruzelski's choice of General Kiszczak to succeed Rakowski as prime minister; however, opposition agreement on a cabinet proved lacking, and Kiszczak was forced to step down in favor of Solidarity's Tadeusz MAZOWIECKI, who succeeded in forming a four-party administration on September 12 that included only four Communists (although the PZPR was, by prior agreement, awarded both the interior and defense portfolios).

On December 29, 1989, the *Sejm* approved a number of constitutional amendments, including a change in the country name from "People's Republic of Poland" to "Polish Republic," termination of the Communist Party's "leading role" in state and society, and deletion of the requirement that Poland must have a "socialist economic system." Subsequently, on January 29, 1990, formal Communist involvement in Polish politics ended when the PZPR voted to disband in favor of a new entity to be known as Social Democracy of the Republic of Poland (*Socjaldemokracja Rzeczypospolitej Polskiej*—SdRP).

In the face of widespread opposition to his status as a holdover from the Communist era, President Jaruzelski on September 19, 1990, proposed a series of constitutional amendments that would permit him to resign in favor of a popularly elected successor. At first-round balloting on November 25 Wałęsa led a field of six candidates with a 40 percent vote share; in the second round on December 9, he defeated émigré businessman Stanisław TYMIŃSKI by a near three-to-one margin, and he was sworn in for a five-year term on December 22. On January 4, 1991, the president's nominee, Jan Krzysztof BIELECKI, won parliamentary approval as prime minister, with the *Sejm* formally endorsing his ministerial slate on January 12.

In June 1991, amid mounting opposition to government economic policy, President Wałęsa twice vetoed bills calling for a form of proportional representation that he insisted would weaken Parliament by admitting a multiplicity of parties, but he was eventually defeated by legislative override on June 28. As predicted, the ensuing poll of October 27 yielded a severely fragmented lower house, with the Democratic Union (*Unia Demokratyczna*—UD) winning the most seats but no party securing more than 13 percent of the vote. A lengthy period of consultation followed. Wałęsa's offer to serve as his own prime minister was met with scant enthusiasm. Unable to secure the reappointment of Bielecki, the president was ultimately obliged to settle on a critic of his free-market strategy, Jan OLSZEWSKI, who narrowly succeeded in forming a government on December 23. Four days earlier Wałęsa had been forced to withdraw a group of proposed constitutional amendments that would have given him authority to appoint and dismiss ministers and to veto parliamentary no-confidence motions, while authorizing a simple rather than a two-thirds *Sejm* majority to enact legislation.

The government was weakened in May 1992 by the successive resignations of the economy and defense ministers, the latter in the wake of allegations he had made concerning the military's involvement in politics. Far more contentious, however, was legislative authorization on May 28 to release secret police files of individuals who had reportedly collaborated with the Communist regime. The action had long been sought by the right-of-center Olszewski government but had been resisted as a violation of human rights by the center-left parties, which insisted that many of the dossiers had been deliberately falsified by departing members of the security forces. Olszewski's subsequent publication of a list of alleged collaborators generated widespread outrage, not least from President Wałęsa, who publicly called for the prime minister's dismissal, and on June 5 the *Sejm* approved a nonconfidence motion by an overwhelming margin.

On June 6, 1992, the *Sejm* endorsed Waldemar PAWLAK, the relatively obscure leader of the PSL, as new prime minister. However, Pawlak was unable, during the ensuing month, to muster sufficient parliamentary support to form a government and was obliged to resign. On July 6 the UD's Hanna SUCHOCKA was confirmed as Poland's first woman prime minister, and five days later she secured *Sejm* approval of a new coalition administration, which included seven parties with ministerial posts and several others pledged to give it parliamentary support. Committed to speedier transition to a market economy, Suchocka's government relaunched the privatization program and secured the reactivation of International Monetary Fund (IMF) credit facilities that had been suspended since 1991. However, Suchocka's austerity policies, including a firm stand against striking coal miners and rail workers, incurred widespread opposition from Solidarity deputies, and on May 28, 1993, her government fell by one vote over a continued tight budget. President Wałęsa responded by refusing to accept the prime minister's resignation, asking Suchocka to remain in office on a caretaker basis pending a new election.

The balloting of September 19, 1993, yielded a pronounced swing to the left, with the SdRP-dominated Democratic Left Alliance (*SojuszLewicy Democratycznej*—SLD) winning 37 percent of the legislative seats and the PSL winning 29 percent. Five weeks later, on October 26, the two groups formed a coalition government headed by the PSL's Pawlak.

Conflict between the presidency and the ruling coalition intensified in October 1994, when the government rejected President Wałęsa's dismissal of the defense minister and the legislature voted by a large majority to urge the president to cease interfering in the democratic process. Wałęsa responded by denouncing the Pawlak government and calling for stronger presidential powers, the controversial defense minister being forced out the following month. The crisis deepened in January 1995 amid various policy differences between the president and his government, which yielded the resignation of Pawlak on February 7 after the president had threatened parliamentary dissolution. Collateral strains between the two coalition parties were resolved sufficiently to enable the SLD's Józef OLEKSY, a Communist-era minister, to be sworn in on March 6 as prime minister of a continued SLD-PSL coalition, albeit with half of its members new appointees.

Despite the relative failure of a 1993 effort to form a "presidential" party styled the Nonparty Bloc in Support of Reform (*Bezpartyjny Blok Wspierania Reform*—BBWR), Wałęsa in April 1995 confirmed his candidacy for a second presidential term. His main opponents among 17 other registered candidates were Aleksander KWAŚNIEWSKI of the SLD/SdRP, Jacek KUROŃ of the center-right Freedom Union

(*Unia Wolnósci*—UW), and former prime ministers Olszewski and Pawlak. In the first round of balloting on November 5 Kwaśniewski took a narrow lead, with 35.1 percent against 33.1 percent for Wałęsa. In the runoff contest on November 19 Kwaśniewski won 51.7 percent to 48.3 percent for Wałęsa, despite endorsement of the latter by most of the other first-round candidates and by most center-right parties.

Sworn in on December 22, 1995, Kwaśniewski quickly lost his prime minister, Oleksy, who was obliged to resign on January 24, 1996, over allegations (which he denied) that he had passed information to the Soviet, later Russian, intelligence service. He was replaced on February 8 by Włodzimierz CIMOSZEWICZ of the SLD, heading a further coalition of the SLD and PSL that included six independents.

In preparation for the 1997 legislative elections Solidarity in June 1996 began organizing small center-right parties into the Solidarity Electoral Action (*Akcja Wyborcza Solidarność*—AWS), which ultimately became a coalition of some 36 parties and groups. Despite President Kwaśniewski's popularity and four years of economic growth, the AWS won 201 seats against 164 for the SLD in the balloting on September 21, 1997. The AWS's success was attributed to its alignment with the Catholic Church and its appeal to lingering resentment against the ex-Communists. After protracted negotiations, the AWS signed a coalition agreement with the UW on October 20 and formed a new government on October 31, with Jerzy BUZEK of the leading AWS party, the Social Movement-Solidarity Electoral Action (*Ruch Społeczny-Akija Wyborcza Solidarność*—RS-AWS), as prime minister.

In 1998 and early 1999 Warsaw's imminent entry into the North Atlantic Treaty Organization (NATO) and its preparations for accession to the EU had far-reaching effects on both foreign and domestic policies. With Poland about to become the eastern front line of NATO and the EU, Warsaw was under pressure to tighten its eastern borders, which increased tension with Belarus and raised concerns in Ukraine. Warsaw sought to reassure its former Soviet bloc neighbors and held talks to improve relations with Germany, with whom it hoped to tie up lingering postwar issues, particularly compensation for deported Poles used by the Nazi regime as slave laborers. Poland formally entered NATO on March 12, 1999.

On the domestic front, reforms designed to prepare for EU accession created labor unrest and attendant political fallout. Privatization plans and other reforms, some of which raised the prospects of huge job losses, caused strikes in the coal mining, steel, railway, and defense industries. In trying to curb subsidies and protectionist tariffs, the government alienated farmers, who, under the leadership of radical unionist Andrzej LEPPER of the Self-Defense of the Polish Republic (*Samoobrona Rzeczypospolitej Polskiej*), blocked roads throughout the nation in a series of disruptive protests, the most serious of which began in December 1998 and extended into 1999. At the beginning of 1999 the government was also confronted by opposition to a series of health care reforms, introduction of which led to physician resignations, more strikes, and public confusion. The crisis in health care also contributed to a potential rift in the governing coalition, but the AWS managed to mollify its junior partner, the UW, in late January, in part by dismissing a deputy health minister. The UW nevertheless continued to criticize its senior partner for what it saw as half-hearted pursuit of free-market policies, particularly privatization. Meanwhile, public opinion polls registered increasing dissatisfaction with the AWS and growing support for the leftist SLD.

Policy and leadership differences within the government continued to cause persistent internal friction, and on October 11, 1999, in an effort to stabilize the situation, the AWS and the UW signed a renegotiated coalition agreement. Nevertheless, on June 6, 2000, objecting to Buzek's continuation as prime minister as well as to the inability of the AWS to exert discipline over its disparate components, the UW formally withdrew. The move left the AWS in charge of a minority government, although it continued to receive regular UW support in Parliament and survived until the legislative term ended in 2001.

On October 8, 2000, President Kwaśniewski won reelection with 53.9 percent of the vote despite the presence on the ballot of 11 other active candidates. Second place (17.3 percent) went to an independent, Andrzej OLECHOWSKI, who had previously been associated with the AWS, while Solidarity's Marian KRZAKLEWSKI, despite AWS backing, finished third (15.6 percent). Former president Wałęsa managed only 1 percent of the vote, finishing seventh.

In December 2000 Solidarity announced that it was withdrawing from active politics and turned over to Prime Minister Buzek's RS-AWS its voting rights in the AWS, which was rapidly disintegrating as its various leaders and parties sought to position themselves as the best center-right alternative to the SLD for upcoming parliamentary elections. In the *Sejm* and Senate elections on September 23, 2001, a coalition of the SLD and the much smaller Union of Labor (*Unia Pracy*—UP) claimed a plurality of 216 seats in the lower house and an overwhelming majority in the upper, while Buzek's new coalition, the Solidarity Electoral Action of the Right (*Akcja Wyborcza Solidarność Prawicy*—AWSP), failed to meet the 8 percent threshold for *Sejm* representation. The UW also lost all representation in the *Sejm* as three new formations—the Civic Platform (*Platforma Obywatelska*—PO), with 65 seats; Law and Justice (*Prawo i Sprawieliwość*—PiS), with 44; and the League of Polish Families (*Liga Polskich Rodzin*—LPR), with 38—split much of the center-right vote. Andrzej Lepper's populist *Samoobrona* entered the *Sejm,* finishing third, with 53 seats.

On October 9, 2001, the SLD/UP completed a coalition agreement with the rural PSL that permitted the SLD's Leszek MILLER, an electrician who had risen through the ranks of the PZPR and the SdRP, to become prime minister of an SLD-dominated cabinet on October 19, concurrent with the opening of the new parliamentary session.

In early March 2003 the PSL left the governing coalition following a disagreement with the SLD over a tax initiative. The government was therefore left with a minority of only 212 seats in the *Sejm,* a situation that was only partially eased by addition of the newly formed, but now-defunct, Peasant Democratic Party (*Partia Ludowe Democratyczna*—PLD) to the coalition from late March until January 2004. The government remained stressed on several fronts, and Miller announced his resignation on May 2, 2004, only one day after Poland had acceded to the EU. President Kwaśniewski immediately designated "technocrat" Marek BELKA of the SLD to succeed Miller, but Belka lost a confirmation vote on May 14 in the *Sejm,* which was then constitutionally permitted to present its own candidate. When the *Sejm* failed to act in that regard, the president reappointed Belka on June 11, and he and his SLD/UP cabinet were confirmed by the *Sejm* on June 24.

Upon his confirmation as prime minister in June 2004, Marek Belka was immediately perceived as at best a caretaker leader of a dying government. That perception was underscored by the poor performance of the SLD and UP in the June European Parliament balloting, at which right-wing and center-right parties rose in prominence.

In the legislative elections on September 25, 2005, the PiS led all parties by securing 155 seats in the *Sejm,* followed by the PO with 133 seats and *Samoobrona* with 56. The SLD was relegated to fourth place with 55 seats. On September 27 the PiS named Kazimierz MARCINKIEWICZ as its choice for prime minister and announced the goal of forming a coalition government with the PO.

The first round of presidential elections was held on October 9, 2005, with a field of 12 candidates. Donald TUSK of the PO won 36.33 percent of the vote, followed by Lech KACZYŃSKI of the PiS with 33.10 percent. On October 23, 2005, Kaczyński bested Tusk 54.04 percent to 45.96 percent to gain the presidency.

President Kwáśniewski on October 24, 2005, formally designated Marcinkiewicz to form a new government. However, the PiS/PO talks collapsed (see Current issues, below, for details), and Marcinkiewicz was sworn in as head of a minority PiS government on October 31. On November 10 the government won a vote of confidence in the 460-seat *Sejm* with 272 votes, thanks to support from *Samoobrona* and the LPR. The PiS ascendancy was completed with Kaczyński's inauguration on December 23. Subsequently, in a May 5, 2006, reshuffle, the LPR and *Samoobrona* formally joined the government, their leaders being named deputy ministers. However, following a series of disputes between Prime Minister Marcinkiewicz and President Kaczyński and his brother Jarosław KACZYŃSKI (the chair of the PiS), Marcinkiewicz resigned on July 10. President Kaczyński immediately named his brother as prime minister–designate, and Jarosław Kaczyński was sworn in as prime minister on July 14 to head an essentially unchanged cabinet. The PiS/LPR/*Samoobrona* government won a vote of confidence in the *Sejm* on July 19 with 240 votes.

On September 22, 2006, Prime Minister Kaczyński dismissed Deputy Prime Minister Andrzej Lepper of *Samoobrona* from the government following a lengthy budget dispute. After negotiations for a new government that would include only the LPR and the PLD failed, the PiS held an all-day conference with the LPR and *Samoobrona* on October 16, resulting in Lepper's reappointment to his previous posts and the return of *Samoobrona* to the coalition. However, Lepper was again dismissed on July 9, 2007, this time because of corruption allegations against him. All non-PiS ministers were sacked over the course of the next month, and the government became untenable, leading the

National Assembly to dissolve itself (by a vote of 377–54) on September 8 in advance of early elections.

Snap legislative elections on October 21, 2007, resulted in a pronounced victory for the PO, whose chair, Donald Tusk, formed a centrist government on November 16 comprising the PO and the PSL. In the *Sejm* the PO won 209 seats and its coalition partner, the PSL, won 31. The Law and Justice party took 166, while the Left and Democrats garnered only 53. In the Senate the PO obtained a clear majority, winning 60 of the 100 seats. The PiS took 39, and 1 seat went to an independent. The cabinet received a 238–204 vote of confidence in the *Sejm* on November 24. The relationship between the PO and PSL showed growing signs of strain in 2009. In July Wlademar PAWLAK, the PSL leader, gave an interview in which he was sharply critical of Tusk, whom he depicted as being driven by polls and not by a concern for the welfare of the nation. Reports indicated that Pawlak sought only to distance himself from some of Tusk's unpopular positions, but not to dissolve the government.

Constitution and government. The constitutional changes of April 1989 provided for a bicameral legislature that incorporated the existing 460-member *Sejm* as its lower chamber and added a 100-member upper chamber (Senate). For the June 1989 balloting it was specified that all of the Senate seats would be free and contested, while 65 percent (299) of the lower house seats would be reserved for the PZPR and its allies (35 on a noncontested "National List" basis). All seats at subsequent elections were to be open and contested. Initially, the combined houses were empowered to elect a state president for a six-year term; however, constitutional changes prior to the December 1990 poll provided for a popularly elected president serving a five-year term. A new "small" constitution became effective on December 8, 1992, having been signed by President Wałęsa on November 17. It redefined the powers of, and relations between, the legislature, presidency, and government. A new "large" constitution, including a charter of liberties and human rights, was approved by a popular referendum on May 25, 1997, by a vote of 56.8 percent.

Parliament sits for a four-year term, save that the *Sejm* may dissolve itself (and by such action end the Senate term) by a two-thirds majority, assuming a quorum of at least 50 percent. The president has widespread authority in foreign and defense matters, with decrees in other areas requiring countersignature by a prime minister who is nominated by the president but must be confirmed by the *Sejm*. The prime minister appoints other ministers, while the president names military leaders and high-level judges. The president may veto legislation but can be overridden by a three-fifths majority of the lower house. There is a Constitutional Tribunal, whose members are appointed by the *Sejm*, while the regular judiciary has three tiers: regional courts, provincial courts, and a Supreme Court.

As a result of constitutional and administrative reforms in 1975, the number of provinces (voivodships, or *województwa*) was increased from 22 to 49. However, in July 1998, following a contentious debate over boundaries, Parliament reduced the number to 16 (4 more than the government initially proposed). The reduction was part of a package of administrative reforms that also created a "middle tier" of 65 cities and 308 districts (*powiats*) and, in furtherance of decentralization, assigned authority for regional economic development to the voivodships. At the local level, there are nearly 2,500 communes (*gminas*). The prime minister appoints provincial governors (*wojewodowie*); provincial assemblies as well as executives and legislative organs at the lower levels are elected.

Foreign relations. During most of the postwar era, Polish foreign policy, based primarily on close alliance with the Soviet Union, supported the stationing of Soviet troops in Poland as well as Polish participation in the Warsaw Pact and the Council for Mutual Economic Assistance. The events of the second half of 1980 elicited harsh criticism from the Soviet Union, Czechoslovakia, and East Germany while prompting expressions of concern in the West that the Warsaw Pact might intervene militarily, as it had in Hungary in 1956 and in Czechoslovakia in 1968. Predictably, the Soviet Union and most Eastern-bloc countries endorsed the Polish government's crackdown of December 1981. Western disapproval was alleviated by the lifting of martial law in mid-1983, and Washington withdrew its opposition to Polish membership in the IMF at the end of 1984, facilitating the country's admission to that agency and its sister institution, the World Bank, in June 1986.

In February 1990 Prime Minister Mazowiecki traveled to Moscow for talks with President Gorbachev, reiterating Polish concern that a newly unified Germany might attempt to reclaim land ceded to Poland after World War II. These fears were allayed by the outcome of "two-plus-four" talks between the two Germanies and World War II's victorious powers in July, which yielded a treaty between Bonn and Warsaw on November 14 that confirmed Poland's western border at the Oder and Neisse rivers. Poland's other major foreign policy concern was alleviated when the last Russian military contingent withdrew on September 17, 1993.

On May 21–23, 1992, during President Wałęsa's first visit to Moscow, a friendship and cooperation treaty was concluded that subsequently generated widespread resentment in Poland for its failure to address the issue of Russian responsibility for Stalinist atrocities during World War II. In October this source of strain was reduced when Moscow, bringing to an end over 50 years of false denials, admitted that the former Communist regime had ordered the execution of some 26,000 captured Polish army personnel in Katyn forest in 1940.

On November 2, 1992, Poland's National Defense Committee adopted a new policy based on the assumption that Poland had no natural enemies and no territorial claims on neighboring states. Longer-term security was seen as lying in a Euro-Atlantic system involving Polish membership in NATO. The main thrust of Polish foreign policy, however, was toward membership in the European Community (EC, subsequently the EU). To this end, Poland was a signatory in Kraków on December 21 of the Central European Free Trade Area (CEFTA) treaty with the other "Visegrád" countries of then Czechoslovakia and Hungary. Established in 1991 to end trade barriers and establish free trade in Central Europe by 2002, CEFTA was subsequently regarded by some as a form of "training" for EU membership. By mid-1998 CEFTA had grown to include Romania, Bulgaria, and Slovenia, and the former Czechoslovakia was represented by the Czech Republic and Slovakia. Croatia joined CEFTA in January 2003, but five countries (Czech Republic, Hungary, Poland, Slovakia, and Slovenia) left the grouping in May 2004 when they joined the EU. Macedonia subsequently announced plans to join Bulgaria, Croatia, and Romania in CEFTA by the end of 2005. Meanwhile, some CEFTA leaders urged expansion of CEFTA to include all the non-EU countries of Southeastern Europe, with an eye on possible creation of a free trade area. Regionally, Poland is also a member of the Central European Initiative (CEI).

Having joined NATO's Partnership for Peace in February 1994, Poland on April 8 followed Hungary's lead in formally applying for admission to the EU. A month later, on May 9, it was one of nine former Communist states to become an "associate partner" of the Western European Union (WEU). Despite the Western thrust, which included a warm reception for U.S. President Clinton during an address to the *Sejm* on July 7, Poland also sought improved relations with Russia and the other members of the Commonwealth of Independent States (CIS). The motivation for the latter was largely economic: relatively stiff tariffs had generated a deficit in trade with the EU countries, whereas Poland had previously maintained a trade surplus with the Soviet Union. In December 1997 EU leaders agreed to open entry negotiations with Poland and five other nations, and the first formal talks were held in November 1998. Accession negotiations continued into 2002, with a referendum on admission anticipated for mid-2003.

Under an agreement signed in Paris on July 11, 1996, Poland became the third ex-Communist state (after the Czech Republic and Hungary) to gain full membership in the Organization for Economic Cooperation and Development (OECD). The signing coincided with the end of an official visit to the United States by President Kwaśniewski, during which he received assurances of U.S. support for Poland's accession to NATO. Meanwhile, Poland had assigned 700 troops to the NATO-commanded International Force (IFOR) deployed in Bosnia under the Dayton peace agreements. At the Madrid summit meeting in July 1997, NATO leaders invited Poland and two other former Warsaw Pact nations (the Czech Republic and Hungary) to join the alliance. They became members on March 12, 1999, at ceremonies celebrating NATO's 50th anniversary in Independence, Missouri.

Poland was one of the more supportive countries of the U.S./UK-led invasion of Iraq in early 2003, lending some 2,400 troops to the campaign. In a presumably related matter, Prime Minister Miller in April endorsed a plan for Poland to buy 48 U.S. fighter planes for an estimated $3.5 billion as part of a 15-year military upgrade program. (In February 2005 U.S. President George W. Bush pledged $100 million in military aid to Poland.)

On June 7–8, 2003, Polish voters endorsed their country's proposed accession to the EU by a 58.9 percent "yes" vote in a national referendum. Poland joined nine other states as new EU members on May 1.

Tensions rose between Germany and Poland in late 2004 over the issue of reparations from World War II and its aftermath. Representatives of Germans who had been deported from former German territory in 1945–1946 after the territory was incorporated into Poland renewed their campaign for compensation in 2004. In return, Poland threatened to seek reparations from Germany for damage inflicted during the war.

Some European governments had assumed that a probusiness, proforeign trade bloc (i.e., a PiS-PO government) would emerge from the 2005 elections. However, the PiS minority cabinet and the subsequent PiS-led coalition adopted a nationalistic, euroskeptic approach toward foreign policy. Among other things, other European countries reportedly objected to the new Polish administration's blockage of cross-border takeovers of Polish state-run enterprises slated for privatization. In addition, the EU specifically noted Poland in a resolution condemning perceived growing racism and ultranationalism throughout the continent. Of particular concern to the EU was the inclusion of the LPR in the Polish cabinet in 2006. The Polish legislature, in turn, issued a counter-resolution condemning the EU resolution.

Relations with the EU worsened during Germany's subsequent presidency of the EU, as the PiS coalition argued against reduced voting representation for Poland in a treaty meant to replace the EU constitution rejected by French and Dutch voters in 2005. Prime Minister Kaczyński famously asserted in a June 2007 radio interview that Poland's population-based representation would be greater if its people had not been decimated by Germany and Russia during World War II. Poland's government also charged that Germany was undermining European energy security by cooperating with Russia in the construction of a Baltic pipeline, a project that was also received coolly in Baltic capitals. Nevertheless, Poland continued to influence EU policy, particularly its relations with states outside the union. For example, in an effort to pressure Russia into lifting its ban on the importation of Polish meat and other food products, Poland vetoed a EU plan that would have allowed the EU to negotiate a partnership agreement with Russia. (Poland noted that its meat plants, which previously had caused concern in regard to sanitation standards, had recently been certified by the EU Commission as having been sufficiently upgraded.)

Given the European discord with the Kaczyński brothers, the PO victory in the October 2007 legislative balloting was met with jubilation in many of Europe's capitals. Prime Minister Donald Tusk has adopted a more europhilic stance, meeting with Angela MERKEL in Berlin in December 2007 and hosting a one-day summit with Nicolas SARKOZY in Warsaw in May 2008. In December 2007 he visited EU headquarters in Brussels and declared his will to "defend European interests." Poland and Sweden have proposed an "Eastern Partnership," a regional association under EU auspices that would work to bring Ukraine, Moldova, Georgia, Armenia, and Azerbaijan into a closer relationship with the EU. Tusk vacillated, however, about signing the EU Charter of Fundamental Rights, because it could compel Poland to recognize the claims of Germans forced from their homes following postwar border changes and because of its stance on gay rights and other social issues that are antithetical to Poland's more conservative public opinion. President Kaczyński remains hostile to the EU and refused to sign the ratification of the Lisbon Treaty, which had passed both houses of parliament in April.

While relations with the EU were occasionally tense, exchanges with the United States remained cordial. Poland allowed the United States to use its territory as a venue for incarcerating and interrogating terror suspects in 2003, though this caused it some embarrassment both at home and among its European allies. Yet Prime Minister Donald Tusk ended the mission to Iraq "in its present form" (which then consisted of 900 troops largely involved in training and humanitarian work in southeast Iraq) in October 2008. Nevertheless, Tusk continues Poland's traditional alignment with the United States, signing a long-stalled missile shield agreement on August 20, 2008, following the war between Russia and Georgia.

Russia protested the installment of missile shield components in Poland, warning that its response "would go beyond diplomacy." The rapid resolution of the agreement was spurred on by renewed concern in Poland and other former Warsaw Pact states that Russia would seek to reassert its traditional sphere of influence following the conflict, in which it destroyed Georgian infrastructure, seized strategic areas, and recognized Georgia's breakaway regions of South Ossetia and Abkhazia as independent states (see Georgia entry). Yet in June 2009 relations with Russia improved, when the Russian agreed to sell the Poles $300 million in natural gas. In September Russian president Vladimir PUTIN traveled to Poland to commemorate the start of World War II, although Russia does not mark the beginning of the war with the attack on Poland.

In 2009 Poland and Ukraine signed an agreement to make border crossings easier for people living near the frontier. Tusk has also formed closer ties with German leader Angela Merkel in spite of Polish concerns about the Nord Stream pipeline that will direct natural gas from Russia to Germany under the Baltic Sea and thus bypass Poland. Both Merkel and French president Nicolas Sarkozy supported Jerzy Buzek in his successful attempt to be president of the new European parliament.

In September 2009 the United States reversed the plan to deploy a missile shield in Poland. The decision was popular among the Polish public, but was criticized by government and foreign policy elites in the country who sought to forge a closer strategic relationship with the United States. Foreign minister Radosław SIKORSKI commented that the action created a "credibility problem" for the United States.

Current issues. Following a parliamentary term riddled with scandals, the dramatic decline of the SLD in the September 2005 legislative balloting was not unexpected. However, the plurality achieved by the rightist PiS raised eyebrows domestically as well as throughout the rest of Europe. As the PiS and the PO could not agree on the allocation of ministries, new Prime Minister Marcinkiewicz had to depend on the support of two diverse "fringe parties"—*Samoobrona* and the LPR—to maintain a legislative majority.

Although the first six months of the Marcinkiewicz government were buffeted by several ministerial resignations and firings, the prime minister himself rose in popularity, appearing to undercut President Kaczyński's political dominance. The president also reportedly considered the prime minister's approach insufficiently aggressive regarding two of Kaczyński's major goals: the cessation of the privatization programs launched by the previous government, and the campaign to remove former Communists from all levels of government. The appointment of Jarosław Kaczyński (the president's twin brother) as prime minister in July 2006 appeared to serve PiS nationalists, although analysts suggested that EU regulations would restrict dramatic action on the part of the new government. That observation was bolstered by Jarosław Kaczyński's announcement shortly after taking office that his government would not permit increased budget deficits, despite calls from the PiS's coalition partners for large welfare increases.

The gap between the goals of PiS and its coalition partners widened throughout 2006 and 2007, particularly as the Kaczyński brothers began to pursue their policies of lustration, fiscal discipline, and anticorruption more vigorously, dismissing *Samoobrona* Chair Andrzej Lepper on two occasions. *Samoobrona* was also compromised by the findings of the Central Anti-Corruption Bureau (*Centralne Biuro Antykorupcyjne*—CBA), an institution whose formation was promised in the PiS campaign platform. Critics later alleged that the CBA had focused primarily on political rivals of the ruling party. As one of its conditions for allowing allies to remain in government during the crisis of July 2007, the PiS insisted that junior coalition partners refrain from investigating the controversial agency. The combination of demands for unconditional compliance with the PiS, or "loyalty conditions," and a lack of promised evidence regarding the charges against Lepper precipitated *Samoobrona*'s break with the government. The coalition crisis endured for several weeks, prompting a PiS meeting with its rival, the center-right PO, in August, after which early elections were scheduled for the fall, two years ahead of schedule.

The early legislative poll of October 2007 resulted in a decisive victory for the europhile PO, neutralizing Prime Minister Kaczyński's bid to strengthen his power. Turnout was one of the largest in history, and the PO surge was attributed in part to its support among young voters. Tusk's first year in office went smoothly. In a June 2008 poll he was ranked as Poland's most trusted politician, while his rival Lech Kaczyński was among the least trusted. Tusk established a popular parliamentary commission to promote deregulation, which aimed to increase efficiency in health care and other sectors. However, restricted spending remained necessary to reduce the deficit, which threatened to damage his popularity and his alliance with the PSL. The roads and rail systems urgently required renovation, especially as Poland and Ukraine were due to host the European soccer championship in 2012. In December 2008 conscription was abolished.

Energy problems also provided cause for concern. Poland has the largest coal reserves in the EU and generates 95 percent of its electricity from coal. However, stringent EU carbon emission standards would raise electricity rates astronomically if Poland were forced to conform to them. Plans to build a nuclear energy plant in Lithuania have stalled, but Poland announced plans in January 2009 to build a nuclear energy plant in Poland. Stung by the reduced level of Russian natural gas delivered to Poland last winter, the government is seeking an arrangement with Qatar to supply the country with liquefied natural gas.

The PO received a vote of confidence from the Polish electorate in elections for the European Parliament that were held on June 7, 2009, winning 44.4 percent of the vote and obtaining 25 seats. The PiS gained 27.4 percent and 15 seats. A coalition of two parties of the left, the SLD and the UP, garnered 12.3 percent and 7 seats. The PO's partner in the governing coalition, the PSL, took 7 percent and 3 seats. The voter turnout was low; only about 25 percent of the voters cast a ballot. Jerzy Buzek, now a PO member, was elected president of the European parliament on July 14, 2009. He is the first Eastern European to hold this office.

Poland survived the 2008-2009 financial crisis fairly well, and it has received high marks from the IMF, which provided it with a $20.58 billion line of credit. However, a dramatic currency fluctuation in 2008, which saw the zloty first balloon against the euro and then decline by 30 to 50 percent, has wrecked havoc on the individual's buying power. Eurostat has ranked Poland among the poorest nations in Europe in terms of purchasing power.

POLITICAL PARTIES AND GROUPS

Prior to 1983, Poland's dominant Communist Party, officially known after 1948 as the Polish United Workers' Party (*Polska Zjednoczona Partia Robotnicza*—PZPR), exercised its authority through a Front of National Unity (*Front Jednośsci Narodnu*—FJN), which also included two nominally noncommunist groups, the United Peasants' Party (under PSL, below) and the Democratic Party, in addition to various trade union, Catholic, women's, youth, and other mass organizations. In 1983 the FJN was superseded by the Patriotic Movement for National Rebirth (*Patriotyczny Ruch Odrodzenia Narodowego*—PRON), but PRON was itself formally dissolved on November 8, 1989, while the PZPR was succeeded by the Social Democracy of the Polish Republic (SdRP) on January 29, 1990. The SdRP served as the core of the subsequent Democratic Left Alliance (SLD) and then dissolved in 1999, when the SLD became a party.

In the early 1980s a number of dissident organizations came into existence, the most important being the Independent Self-Governing Trade Union Solidarity (*Niezależny Samorząd Związków Zawodowych "Solidarnoùç"*—NSZZ Solidarity), in part an outgrowth of the Committee for Social Self-Defense (*Komitet Samoobrony Społeczej*—KSS). (The KSS had been formed in 1977 as successor to the Committee for the Defense of Workers [*Komitet Obrony Robotniów*—KOR], which had been organized to provide legal and financial aid to those imprisoned during price-hike demonstrations in 1976.) Launched during a conference of independent labor groups in Gdańsk on September 17–18, 1980, Solidarity had a membership estimated at 10 million workers, or some 50 percent of the Polish labor force, by mid-1981. It was officially banned upon the imposition of martial law in December 1981, although an underground "Provisional Coordinating Committee" (*Tymczasowej Komisji Koordynacyjnej*—TKK) continued to call for the restoration of independent trade union rights.

In January 1989 the PZPR Central Committee called for gradual reinstatement of Solidarity's legal status. Roundtable talks between government and union representatives began on February 6 and yielded, two months later, an agreement on political and economic reform, including opposition participation in legislative balloting in June. The Communists were decisively defeated at the June poll.

Lech Wałęsa resigned as Solidarity chair in December 1990, following his election as state president, and was succeeded by Marian Krzaklewski. Since Solidarity was technically not a political party, it participated in the national parliamentary and local elections of 1989 and 1991 through an ad hoc network of civic committees coordinated by a Central Committee appointed by Wałęsa.

Postcommunist Poland's first fully democratic election in October 1991 unleashed a profusion of parties and groupings of all conceivable orientations, several tracing their origins from the Solidarity movement. Of the more than 100 parties active in 1991, no fewer than 29 parties won representation in the 460-seat *Sejm,* none with more than 13 percent of the vote. The scene thereafter was one of constant flux in party allegiance and identity, particularly on the center-right of the political spectrum. Because of a new minimum vote threshold, only seven groups secured parliamentary representation in September 1993. As of mid-1995, however, a total of 275 distinct political parties had achieved official registration.

During the second half of the 1990s the division in Polish politics was most clearly represented by the leftist SLD coalition of President Aleksander Kwaśniewski, who had been elected in 1995, and the center-right Solidarity Electoral Action (*Akcja Wyborcza Solidarność*—AWS) coalition, which was launched in 1996 under the leadership of Solidarity in preparation for the 1997 legislative balloting. Among the other major participants in the AWS were the Conservative Peasant Party, the now-defunct Christian National Union, the Center Alliance, and the Christian Democratic Party. In all, more than 30 (mostly small) parties and groups joined the AWS, which won 33.8 percent of the vote at the 1997 legislative elections and secured a plurality of 201 seats in the *Sejm.* Its two most visible figures were Solidarity Chair Krzaklewski and the new prime minister, Jerzy Buzek.

Despite its electoral success in 1977, the AWS failed to cohere into a unified party, in part because many of the constituent organizations did not want to merge into a larger grouping that they perceived as dominated by trade unionists. Only about half of the legislators elected under the banner of the AWS coalition joined a new Solidarity-backed party, the Social Movement–Solidarity Electoral Action (see Social Movement, below), upon its formation in December 1997.

The third-place finish of Krzaklewski in the 2000 presidential race accelerated the disintegration of the unwieldy AWS, although Prime Minister Buzek managed to remain in office through the full parliamentary term. At the September 2001 legislative election, Buzek's new coalition, the Solidarity Electoral Action of the Right, failed to meet the threshold for representation in the *Sejm,* and the SLD, in coalition with the Union of Labor, easily outdistanced a handful of recently formed, post-AWS formations—chiefly, the Civic Platform (PO), Law and Justice (PiS), and the League of Polish Families. Thus, the presidency, the National Assembly, and the Council of Ministers were dominated by the heirs of Poland's Communist past, while the heirs of the Solidarity movement were scattered among a variety of center and right parties.

The 2005 elections brought a substantial change to Polish party politics, with the significant diminution of the electoral strength of the political left and the ascension of the right side of the party system. However, the presence of populist partners in the subsequent coalition government, combined with a series of contested corruption investigations, undermined the PiS goal of establishing a dominant Christian-democratic movement. This did not entirely unravel the center-right, as support remained steady for the business-friendly PO, which performed well in the 2006 regional elections, won a strong plurality in the early elections of October 2007, and went on to form a new two-party coalition government with the small Polish People's Party.

Government Parties:

Civic Platform (*Platforma Obywatelska*—PO). The PO was organized in January 2001 at the initiative of three prominent politicians: former presidential candidate Andrzej Olechowski, who, running as an independent, had finished second in the 2000 poll with 17 percent of the vote; Donald Tusk, formerly of the Freedom Union (UW, below); and former AWS leader and *Sejm* Speaker Maciej PŁAŻYŃSKI. The new formation's liberal, free-market orientation soon attracted other disparate elements, including much of the previously AWS-supportive Conservative Peasant Party (see SKL-RNP, below) and the extreme right-wing Realpolitik Union (UPR). (For additional information on the UPR, see the 2007 *Handbook.*) For the 2001 Senate campaign, the PO joined the Solidarity Electoral Action of the Right (AWSP), the UW, and Law and Justice (PiS, below) in a **Senate Bloc 2001** (*Bloc Senat 2001*) in an unsuccessful effort to prevent the SLD from gaining a majority. In the concurrent *Sejm* election the PO finished second, with 12.7 percent of the vote and 65 seats, although a number of deputies elected on its list, including eight from the SKL, chose to sit in the lower house as members of other parliamentary groups.

The PO, which had entered the 2001 elections as a "group of voters," was registered as a political party in March 2002. In April 2003 PO Chair Maciej Płażyński resigned to protest the centrist party's failure to adopt his rightist policies. The PO led all parties in the balloting for the Polish seats in the European Parliament in June 2004.

In the 2005 parliamentary elections the PO won the second largest block of seats with 133, more than doubling the 65 seats that it won in 2001. Initially, the party was thought to be in a position to partner with the PiS to form the government, but talks collapsed.

The PO's candidate, Donald Tusk, came in first in the first round of presidential polling in October 2005 but lost to the PiS candidate in the second round. Enjoying a strong 27.2 percent vote share in the 2006 regional elections, the Civic Platform secured the coveted mayorship of Warsaw and was rated the most popular party in several public opinion polls, despite being in opposition. After a meeting with the PiS in

August 2006, the PO announced support for early elections, pledging to work with the government to pass critical EU legislation before the next poll.

Early parliamentary elections in October 2007, yielded a substantial plurality for the PO in the *Sejm* (on a 41.5 percent vote share) and a three-fifths majority in the Senate. In spite of difficult economic conditions the party did extremely well in the elections for the European parliament in June 2009, gaining 44.4 percent of the vote and half of the 50 seats allotted to Poland. In order to show its commitment to Europe, a PO candidate, who subsequently won a seat in Gdańsk, debated two of his rivals in English. It is also one of the few parties that has a bilingual (English-Polish) Web site.

Leaders: Donald TUSK (Prime Minister and Party Chair); Bronslaw KOMOROWSKI, Hanna GRONKIEWICZ-WALTZ, Jacek SARYUSZ-WOLSKI, Tomasz TOMCZYKIEWICZ, Waldy DZIKOWSKI (Vice Chairs).

Polish Peasants' Party (*Polskie Stronnictwo Ludowe*—PSL). The original PSL was organized in 1945 by Stanisław Mikołajczyk after the leadership of the traditional Peasant Party (*Stronnictwo Ludowe*—SL), founded in 1895, had opted for close cooperation with the postwar Communist regime. In November 1949, following Mikołajczyk's repudiation by leftist members, the two groups merged as the United Peasants' Party (*Zjednoczone Stronnictwo Ludowe*—ZSL), which became part of the Communist-dominated FJN.

In August 1989 a group of rural activists met in Warsaw to revive the PSL on the basis of its 1946 program. (Party leaders subsequently insisted that the Polish name of the party should more appropriately be translated as Polish People's Party, a usage that has recently gained wide acceptance.) In September the ZSL was awarded four portfolios in the Solidarity-led coalition government, and in November the ZSL reorganized into two parties, the PSL-Rebirth (PSL-*Odrodzenie*—PSL-O) and the PSL-*Wilnanów* (PSL-W). Six months later, the present PSL emerged from a unification congress of the PSL-O, part of the PSL-W, and some members of the PSL-*Solidarność*, which had been formed by former Rural Solidarity members in 1989. The party was nevertheless weakened by continuing controversy between ex-ZSL activists and those who sought to have them purged. The PSL's principal support came from small farmers who opposed the introduction of large-scale agricultural enterprises on the U.S. model.

At the 1991 election the PSL was the core of a Peasant Coalition (*Sojusz Programowy*) that won 48 *Sejm* seats. Running alone, it secured 132 seats in 1993 and formed a governing coalition with the SLD. Amid frequent strains between the coalition parties, the PSL deputy president was dismissed as chair of the *Sejm*'s privatization committee in November 1994 on the grounds that he had tried to block or slow down the sell-off of state enterprises.

The PSL lost considerable ground in the 1997 balloting, dropping from 132 seats to 27 on a 7.3 percent vote share. Party leader Jarosław Kalinowski finished fourth, with 6.0 percent of the vote, in the 2000 presidential election. In September 2001 the party won 9.0 percent of the *Sejm* vote, for 42 seats, as a result of which it negotiated a governing coalition with the larger SLD/UP alliance. However, Prime Minister Miller of the SLD forced the PSL to leave the government in April 2003 after the PSL voted against its coalition partners on a contentious road tax measure.

The PSL secured only 25 seats in the 2005 *Sejm* balloting (on a vote share of 6.96 percent), but it won 13.2 percent of the vote in the 2006 regional elections. After securing 8.9 percent of the vote in the October 2007 *Sejm* balloting, the PSL moved into a surprisingly strong government position, as its 31 seats were necessary to provide the PO-led coalition cabinet with a legislative majority. Party leader Waldemar PAWLAK, who is also deputy prime minister and minister of the economy, has been a good coalition partner, but the PSL's strong commitment to social justice issues in a period of economic difficulty make some commentators skeptical that the coalition can last until the next election. The party's performance in the 2009 European parliamentary elections, where it won only 7 percent of the vote and 3 seats, has weakened their position in the coalition.

Leaders: Waldemar PAWLAK (Deputy Prime Minister and Party Chair); Jolanta FEDAK (Minister of Labor and Social Policy), Marek SAWICKI (Minister of Agriculture and Rural Development).

Opposition Parties:

Law and Justice (*Prawo i Sprawiedliwość*—PiS). Drawn primarily from conservative elements of the Christian National Union (ZChN, below), the SKL, and the Republican League (*Liga Republikańska*—LR) of Mariusz KAMIŃSKI, the PiS was organized in March 2001 under the leadership of Jarosław Kaczyński, a former editor of *Tygodnik Solidarność* (*Solidarity Weekly*) and a longtime supporter of Lech Wałęsa. In its Christian-democratic orientation the PiS resembled an earlier Kaczyński formation, the now-defunct Center Alliance (*Porozumienie Centrum*—PC; see SKL-RNP, below), which had been organized in 1991 and had then formed the core of a Center Citizens' Alliance (*Porozumienie Obywatelskie Centrum*—POC) that secured 44 *Sejm* seats the following October. In January 1998 Kaczyński resigned after eight years as PC chair because of the party's decision to remain in the AWS.

Registered as a party in June 2001, the PiS gained additional support through the presence of Kaczyński's twin brother, Lech Kaczyński, who had served in the minority AWS government following the departure of the UW but had been dismissed in July 2001 because of a disagreement with Prime Minister Buzek over the handling of a fraud investigation. Lech Kaczyński, a former justice minister, brought to the party his reputation as an anticorruption, anticrime campaigner as well as one of Poland's most popular politicians. At the September 2001 elections the PiS won 44 seats in the *Sejm,* based on 9.5 percent of the vote.

In April 2002 the PiS and the Alliance of the Right (*Przymierze Prawicy*—PP) announced their pending merger. The PP (not to be confused with the Polish Agreement [PP], below, under the LPR) had been established in March 2001 by Minister of Culture Kazimierz UJAZDOWSKI and former members of the AWS-affiliated SKL and ZChN, including the latter's ex-chair, Marian PIŁKA. Ujazdowski, a close ally of Lech Kaczyński, had headed the Conservative Coalition (*Koalicja Konserwatywna*—KK) before its merger with the SKL in early 1999. In July 2001 he resigned from the Buzek cabinet to protest Kaczyński's sacking.

The PiS consistently opposed the economic policies of the Miller administration, and the Kaczyński brothers regularly accused government officials of corruption. That stance appeared to resonate with the public, which accorded the PiS a third-place finish in the June 2004 balloting for the European Parliament.

The PiS's share of seats in the *Sejm* increased from 44 in 2001 to 155 in the 2005 elections. The party also won the presidency and a plurality of seats in the Senate. The PiS subsequently formed an unsteady coalition with two populist parties, *Samoobrona* and the LPR, hoping to establish a leading Christian-democratic conservative party by co-opting smaller factions. While the PiS performed well in regional assembly elections in 2006, taking 25.1 percent of total votes, it was eclipsed by the PO, which also took the mayorship of Warsaw from PiS control. The PiS-led coalition faced a succession of crises in 2007, as public support flowed from *Samoobrona* and the LPR to the PO. Dwindling poll numbers were exacerbated by seemingly excessive PiS-led corruption investigations of government officials, which in July 2007 resulted in the president's controversial dismissals of several cabinet ministers, including Andrzej Lepper, the agricultural minister and *Samoobrona* chair. Following a breakdown in negotiations toward continuing the current coalition, PiS leaders asserted that the *Sejm* might be dissolved and early elections held. The final blow to the coalition appeared to come with the dismissal of Interior Minister Janusz KACZMAREK on August 8 for alleged leaks that purportedly undermined ongoing investigations of Lepper. The PiS subsequently agreed with the PO to hold snap elections in the fall. Despite having hoped for a renewed mandate, the PiS was ousted from power following the October 21 poll, in which it finished second to the PO with 166 seats on a 32.1 percent vote share. Nevertheless, President Kaczyński indicated that he intended to utilize the leverage left to him in his position, exerting some control over defense, economic, and foreign affairs through his veto power. The party spent most of 2008 on the defensive but sent a representative (an invited guest) to the U.S. Democratic National Convention in Denver, who hoped to learn campaign techniques that could be applied in Poland. The PiS came in second to the PO in the European Parliament elections that were held in June 2009, electing 15 members, who plan to group with conservatives from 7 other countries to from a conservative coalition. The party remains critical of Tusk and his handling of the economic crisis.

Leaders: Lech KACZYŃSKI (President of the Republic); Jarosław KACZYŃSKI (Former Prime Minister and President of the Party); Adam LIPIŃSKI, Marek KUCHCIŃSKI, Aleksandra NATALLI-ŚWIAT, Zbigniew ZIOBRO (Vice Presidents of Party).

The Left and Democrats (*Lewica i Demokraci*—LiD). Hoping to take advantage of instability within the PiS-led government coalition, former president Aleksander Kwaśniewski announced the formation of the LiD, a center-left coalition, in September 2006. It consisted of the **Democratic Left Alliance** (*Sojusz Lewicy Demokratycznej*—SLD), the **Polish Social Democracy Party** (*Socjaldemokracja Polska*—SDPL), the **Democratic Party** (*Partia Demokratyczna*—PD, and the **Union of Labor** (*Unia Pracy*—UP). The alliance aimed to create an alternative to the PiS in the upcoming early elections and reportedly approached the PO about the possibility of creating a common ballot. Kwaśniewski, who was credited with modernizing social democracy in Poland, opposed the Kaczyński ambition of purging former communists from government. The LiD received 13.15 percent of votes in the 2007 *Sejm* elections, giving it 53 seats out of 460. The coalition was dissolved after the election.

Democratic Left Alliance (*Sojusz Lewicy Demokratycznej*—SLD). The SLD was launched prior to the 1991 election as a coalition of the Social Democracy of the Republic of Poland (*Socjaldemokracja Rzeczypospolitej Polskiej*—SdRP) and the previously Communist-dominated All Poland Trade Unions Alliance (*Ogólnopolskie Porozumienie Związków Zawodowych*—OPZZ). The SdRP had been established on January 29, 1990, upon formal dissolution of the Polish United Workers' Party (*Polska Zjednoczona Partia Robotnicza*—PZPR). Formed in 1948 by merger of the (Communist) Polish Workers' Party (*Polska Partia Robotnicza*—PPR) and the Polish Socialist Party (*Polska Partia Socjalistyczna*—PPS), the PZPR claimed approximately 3 million members prior to the events of 1980–1981, as a result of which enrollment declined by nearly 800,000.

At the December 1990 presidential poll the candidate backed by the SdRP, Włodzimierz CIMOSZEWICZ, placed fourth, with 9.2 percent of the vote; by contrast, the SLD was runner-up in the 1991 *Sejm* balloting and then became the largest *Sejm* formation in 1993 by increasing its representation from 60 to 171. Announced in May 1995, the presidential candidacy of SLD/SdRP leader Aleksander Kwaśniewski was subsequently endorsed by some 30 parties and groups, sufficient to yield a comfortable three-point margin of victory for him in the second round of the November balloting. Although the SLD improved its vote share from 1993, increasing from 20.4 to 27.1 percent, it actually won fewer seats (164) in 1997, when it was unable to withstand the pro–Catholic Church, anti-Communist campaign of the AWS. However, following the local elections of October 1998, the SLD controlled 9 of the nation's 16 provinces, having won a vote share of 32 percent.

Upon his election as president in 1995, Kwaśniewski had vacated the SdRP chairship, to which Józef Oleksy was elected in January 1996, three days after his forced resignation as prime minister. After the 1997 election the party chose Leszek Miller to replace Oleksy, who had not run for reelection. Miller's easy victory over Wiesław KACZMAREK, a former economics minister, was considered a blow to reformers who wanted further distance from the party's Communist origins.

Transformation of the SLD into a political party was announced in April 1999, after which the SdRP dissolved, and in July Miller formally took over the leadership of the SLD. Two other coalition partners, the Polish Socialist Party (PPS) and the Movement of Polish Working People (RLP), chose to remain distinct from the new party. All three parties endorsed President Kwaśniewski for reelection in 2000, and on October 8 he claimed a first-round victory against 11 other candidates, winning 53.9 percent of the vote.

In preparation for the September 2001 parliamentary elections the SLD and the Union of Labor (UP, below) forged an electoral coalition (*Koalicja Sojuszu Lewicky Demokratycznej i Unii Pracy*) that captured 41 percent of the national vote and 216 seats, 15 short of a majority. Miller thereupon negotiated a coalition with the Polish Peasants' Party (PSL) and became prime minister. The SLD/UP coalition had even greater success in the majoritarian Senate contest, winning 75 of 100 seats. However, the SLD's popularity subsequently declined amid discontent in some quarters over government austerity measures and disputes among government coalition parties. Miller resigned as SLD president in March 2004, although one of his close allies, Krzysztof JANIK, was elected to succeed him. Miller also resigned as prime minister on May 2, his replacement, Marek Belka, only achieving confirmation as a caretaker prime minister until the 2005 parliamentary balloting after pledging to undo some of the economic measures adopted by the Miller administration. The SLD (weakened by the defection of a group of legislators in March) managed only a fifth-place finish (again in alliance with the UP) in the June 2004 elections to the European Parliament. Subsequently, Janik was defeated in December in his bid for reelection as SLD leader by former prime minister Oleksy, although Oleksy came under intense scrutiny regarding allegations concerning his activities during Communist rule. The SLD was repudiated at the ballot box in 2005 when it saw its number of seats in the *Sejm* drop to 55. Oleksy was replaced as party leader by Wojciech OLEJNICZAK on May 29, 2005. The party regrouped in 2006 as part of an electoral coalition with the SDPL, UP, and PD, sharing in the collective 14.2 percent of votes taken by the coalition in the November regional elections. Along with the PiS, the SLD had its financial records for the previous cycle rejected by the State Election Commission due to the party having apparently accepted campaign donations in violation of electoral law. Its disappointing showing in the 2007 election caused the replacement of Olejniczak as party leader by Grzegorz NAPIERALSKI on May 31, 2008, but their popularity has continued to decline. Party member Marek Siwiec was elected as a vice-president of the last European parliament.

The SLD won only 7 seats in the 2009 EU elections in which the SLD ran in a coalition with UP. In that balloting, the SLD ran the first candidate of African descent, Patrick Kibangou, but the Congo-born engineer was not successful.

Leaders: Grzegorz NAPIERALSKI (Chair); Marek NAWROT (General Secretary); Katarzyna Maria PIEKARSKA, Jolanta SZMANEK-DERESZ, Jerzy SZMAJDZIŃSKI, Longin PASTUSIAK (Vice Chairs).

Polish Social Democracy Party (*Socjaldemokracja Polska*—SDPL). The SDPL was formed in March 2004 by Marek Borowski (a former Speaker of the *Sejm*) and some 22 other SLD deputies seeking to distance themselves from the administration of Prime Minister Miller. Although the SDPL declined formal coalition status in the government formed by the SLD's Marek Belka in June 2004, an SDPL member was named minister of health and the SDPL pledged to support the caretaker government in the legislature until the 2005 elections.

In 2005 the SDPL ran in coalition with the UP and failed to gain seats in the legislature. The SDLP continued to garner low returns with a 3.89 percent vote share in the 2006 regional elections. It competed in the 2009 elections for the European parliament in a coalition with the PD and the Greens, but failed to gain a seat.

Leaders: Wojciech FILEMONOWICZ (Chair); Bartisz DOMINIAK, Sylwia PUSZ (Vice Chairs).

Union of Labor (*Unia Pracy*—UP). Known as Labor Solidarity (*Solidarność Pracy*—SP) in 1991, when it won 4 *Sejm* seats as a left-wing faction of the original Solidarity movement, the UP captured 41 seats in 1993. With a 4.7 percent vote share in 1997, the UP failed to meet the 5 percent threshold and thus retained no seats. Key members, who include representatives of the Belarusan minority, subsequently were reported to have joined the UW (below) early in 1998. The UP was part of the Social Alliance in the October 1998 local elections.

Having lost most of its initial Solidarity members, the UP concluded an electoral coalition with the SLD for the 2001 legislative contests and, following the alliance's success at the polls, joined the new administration under Prime Minister Miller. Izabela JARUGA-NOWACKA was elected president of the UP at an April 2004 party congress, and she joined the new government formed by the SLD's Marek Belka in May as a deputy prime minister. The UP again presented joint candidates with the SLD in the June 2004 balloting for the European Parliament. In early 2005 it was reported that Jaruga-Nowacka had decided to resign from the UP to participate in the launching of a new left-wing political grouping.

Even running in coalition with the SDPL, the UP was unable to win a seat in the 2005 elections, after having won 16 in the 2001 contests. However, cooperation within the LiD improved the UP's prospects, and the UP coordinated platform issues such as health policy in advance of the October 2007 elections, but not a single UP candidate was elected. In 2008 the UP and the SLD signed an agreement to cooperate in attempting to collaborate to achieve a left-wing political agenda, and they ran together as a coalition in the 2009 elections for the European parliament, gaining 12.34 percent of the vote and 7 seats.

Leaders: Waldemar WITKOWSKI (President); Arkadiusz HORONZIAK, Marek PONIATOWSKI, Wieslaw NALECZ, Jaroslaw TARASIŃSKI (Vice Presidents).

Democratic Party (*Partia Demokratyczna*—PD). A promarket, pro-European grouping hoping to attract centrist support, the PD was launched in the first half of 2005 by Jerzy Hausner (former SLD deputy prime minister) and Władysław Frasyniuk of the UW (below). Hausner had recently quit the SLD after his proposal to cut the federal budget had been rejected. The PD took 2.45 percent of the vote in the 2005 parliamentary elections before joining the LiD umbrella for the 2007 balloting. Its absorption of the UW has not led to any greater success. Its coalition with the SDPL and the Greens gained only 2.44 percent of the vote in the 2009 elections for the European parliament. (The PD should not be confused with the long-standing party of the same name; see SD, below.)

Leaders: (Chair); Brygida KUZNIAK (Chair), Radosław POPIELA, (Vice Chair), Agnieszka KUNCEWICZ (Treasurer).

German Minority of Lower Silesia (*Mniejszość Niemiecka Slaska Opolskiego*—MNSO). Representing ethnic Germans in western and northern Poland, the MNSO list won seven seats in the October 1991 balloting, four of which were retained in 1993. It retained two seats in 1997, 2001, and 2005 under rules that exempt national minority parties from the 5 percent threshold. (Both deputies were from the largest German association—the German Social and Cultural Society of Opole Silesia [*Towarzystwo Spoleczno–Kulturalne Niemcówna Slasku Opolskim*—TSKN].) Ethnic rights issues having apparently faded in relevance following the recent adoption of EU legislation guaranteeing minority rights; the party won one seat in the 2007 *Sejm* balloting on a 0.2 percent vote share, which is less than the 5 percent threshold, but an exception is made for a minority party.

Leader: Henryk KROLL (Chair and Parliamentary Leader).

Other Parties:

Self-Defense of the Polish Republic Party (*Partia Samoobrona Rzeczypospolitej Polskiej*). Popularly known as *Samoobrona,* this party has its base in the agrarian trade union of the same name. Formed in 1993, the union encompassed about half a million mostly rural members, although the much smaller party initially also attracted a high percentage of businesspersons disaffected from the rest of the political establishment. Generally regarded as the most militant of Poland's three principal farmers' unions, *Samoobrona* did not become a significant parliamentary force until the 2001 national election, at which the party won 10.2 percent of the vote and 53 seats in the *Sejm*. Following *Samoobrona* success at the polls in 2001, Andrzej Lepper was named vice marshal of the lower house, but he was removed from the post in late November, partly as a consequence of provocative statements made against other national figures. Furthermore, on January 25, 2002, the house revoked his parliamentary immunity, and five days later he was fined by an appeals court for defamatory statements made against President Kwaśniewski and others in 1999. In February 2002 Lepper was charged with seven additional counts of slander. However, the charges appeared to enhance Lepper's popularity within the party as well as among segments of the general population, which seemed to be growing increasingly disenchanted with Poland's economic and political (i.e., EU membership) developments.

In 2006 *Samoobrona* (whose support fell to 5.6 percent of the vote in the 2006 regional elections) joined the PiS and the LPR to form a coalition government, with Lepper, the party's controversial chair, being named deputy prime minister. Lepper was subsequently dismissed in July 2007 in the face of corruption allegations. He was also censured by the Anti-Defamation League for accepting an honorary degree from an anti-Semitic institution. Although *Samoobrona* remained in government, it demanded elaboration of the charges brought against its chair, which included alleged manipulation of a real estate deal. The party argued that the scandal and the charges against Lepper were designed to encourage *Samoobrona* legislators to defect and join the PiS.

In the wake of their conflict with the PiS, *Samoobrona* and the LPR in July 2007 announced formation of an electoral alliance called the League and Self-Defense (*Liga i Samoobrona*—LiS) in preparation for possible early elections. The LiS pledged to challenge Poland's adoption of the euro and the new EU treaty proposed in 2007, rejecting the "loyalty conditions" endorsed by the PiS as necessary to preserve the coalition. Observers questioned the new alliance's ability to hold together over the long term, given the different objectives of the populist-agrarian *Samoobrona* and the Catholic-nationalist LPR. Those assumptions proved correct, as both parties eventually decided to contest the October balloting on their own and the LiS was disbanded. *Samoobrona* secured only 1.5 percent in the *Sejm* elections and did not win a seat. Its performance in the 2009 elections for the European parliament was equally unimpressive, winning only 1.46 percent of the vote and no seats.

Leaders: Andrzej LEPPER (Chair and Former Deputy Prime Minister), Janusz MAKSYMIUK (Director of National Bureau).

League of Polish Families (*Liga Polskich Rodzin*—LPR). Initially formed as a "group of voters," the LPR brought together an assortment of nationalist, predominantly anti-EU, Catholic groups, many of them associated with *Radio Maryja*. Registered as a party on May 30, 2001, the LPR was headed by Antoni Macierewicz, a former interior minister whose efforts to expose former Communist collaborators contributed to the fall of the Olszewski government in 1992 and who was subsequently expelled from the ZChN. In February 1993 Macierewicz launched the now-defunct right-wing Christian National Movement–Polish Action (*Ruch Chrześcijańsko-Narodowe–Akcja Polska*—RChN-AP), and in 1995 he participated in the formation of the now-defunct Movement for the Reconstruction of Poland (ROP). He broke from the ROP in late 1997 and established the Catholic National Movement for the Reconstruction of Poland, which in May 1998 shortened its name to the Catholic National Movement (*Ruch Katolicko-Narodowy*—RKN) and then joined the AWS. Another LPR founder, Jan ŁOPUSZAŃSKI of the Polish Agreement (*Porozumienie Polskie*—PP), had won 0.8 percent of the vote in the 2000 presidential race.

For the 2001 legislative elections the LPR list included not only members of the PP, but also members of the National Party (*Stronnictwo Narodowe*—SN) and the ROP. The SN dated from the December 1999 merger of Bogusław KOWALSKI'S National Democratic Party (*Stronnictwo Narodowo Demokratyczne*—SND) and an existing SN. In the 2000 presidential election campaign the SN had been a leading supporter of Gen. Tadeusz WILESKI, who won 0.2 percent of the vote.

In September 2001 the LPR won 9 percent of the vote and 38 seats in the *Sejm*. Within six months, however, significant differences had emerged within the parliamentary delegation, pitting Macierewicz's supporters against a larger group headed by Roman Giertych. In April 2002 Macierewicz and Jan Łopuszański both reportedly resigned from the party Presidium, and Macierewicz and four other disaffected LPR deputies subsequently resumed coordination under the RKN rubric. Macierewicz served as one of the main opponents to EU membership in the run-up to the 2003 referendum on the issue.

The LPR became part of the government in May 2006, but popular support for the party dwindled, as evidenced by its 4.7 percent vote share in regional elections later that year. Influential Catholic media owner Father Tadeusz RYDZYK publicly urged the coalition to continue, as LPR voters had been wooed away by the PiS's increasingly conservative stance, dampening the LPR's prospects for the next election cycle. Nevertheless, LPR Chair Giertych resigned his position as national education minister in July 2007, with *Samoobrona* and the LPR subsequently announcing plans (eventually aborted) to present candidates on a common LiS ballot in the next parliamentary poll.

Damaged by public discontent with the ruling party and a tumultuous summer, as well as isolated xenophobic incidents involving LPR members, support for the party dipped to 1.3 percent in the October 2007 parliamentary balloting. Giertych announced that he would resign as chair following the party's loss of parliamentary representation. In 2008 the party was encouraged by recent polls that showed it to have the support of 3 percent of the population. In a party meeting in August, members discussed measures to promulgate its message more effectively, but they were hardly successful. In 2009 their candidates ran as members of the Libertas party in the European parliamentary elections (see below). None were elected.

Leaders: Mirolslaw ORZECHOWSKI (Chair of Party), Anna RAŹNY (Chair of Political Council).

Conservative-Peasant Party–New Poland Movement (*Stronnictwo Konserwatywno-Ludowe–Ruch Nowej Polski*—SKL-RNP). The SKL-RNP was established in January 2002 by merger of the SKL and the Polish Party of Christian Democrats (*Porozumienie Polskich Chrześcijańskich Demokratów*—PPChD).

Founded in January 1997, the SKL united two small right-wing parties, the Conservative Party (*Partia Konserwatywna*—PK), which had been launched in December 1992 by amalgamation of the Forum of the Democratic Right (*Forum Prawicy Demokratycznej*—FPD) and others, and the Peasant-Christian Alliance (*Stronnictwo Ludowo-Chrześcijańskie*—SLCh). The SKL's founding members included ex-ministers Jan Maria ROKITA and Bronisław KOMOROWSKI, and elements of the Christian Democratic Labor Party (*Chrześcijańska Demokracja Stronnictwo Pracy*—ChDSP). (For additional information on the ChDSP, see the 2007 *Handbook*.) At the SKL party congress in late February 1998, two groups joined the SKL: the Party of Republicans (*Partia Republikanów*—PR), led by Jerzy EYSYMONTT, and the Integrative Initiative (*Inicjatywa Integracyjna*—II) faction of the Center Alliance (*Porozumienie Centrum*—PC), led by Wojciech DOBRZYŃSKI. In February 1999 the Conservative Coalition (*Koalicja Konserwatywna*—KK) of Kazimierz Ujazdowski also joined the SKL.

In September 1999 what remained of the Center Alliance, which dated from 1991, and the Christian Democratic Party (*Partia Chrześcijańskich Demokratów*—PChD) announced their merger as the PPChD under Antoni TOKARCZUK, previously the PC chair. Also joining the new formation were former members of an assortment of other small parties that had participated in the AWS. These included the 100 Movement (*Ruch 100*), which had been founded by former foreign minister Andrzej Olechowski, now of the PO; the Polish Peasants' Party–Peasant Alliance (*Polskie Stronnictwo Ludowe–Porozumienie Ludowe*—PSL-PL); and the Movement for the Republic (*Ruch dla Rzeczypospolitej*—RdR), which traced its origins to the 1992 formation of the Christian Democratic Forum (*Forum Chrześcijańsko-Demokratyczne*—FChD) by supporters of ousted prime minister Jan Olszewski. In April 2001 the PPChD added to its ranks the Electoral Solidarity (*Solidarni w Wyborach*—SwW) of Jerzy GWIŻDŻ, a longtime ally of former president Lech Wałęsa. Later in the same month the PPChD aligned itself with Prime Minister Buzek's efforts to reshape the AWS. The failure of Buzek's AWSP coalition at the September 2001 poll ultimately led the PPChD to seek a stronger alliance, which led to the 2002 merger with the SKL.

In March 2001 the SKL, theretofore a component of the AWS, had announced that it would leave the government and enter the Civic Platform (PO) in preparation for the September 2001 legislative elections. Following the balloting, however, a number of deputies who had been elected on the PO list established themselves as a separate SKL parliamentary group. In January 2002 the party split over the question of the PO affiliation. One faction, led by Jan Maria Rokita, opted to remain with the PO, and another, led by Artur BALAZS, instead approved the merger with the PPChD and the creation of the SKL-RNP. The latter was subsequently largely absorbed into the PiS but found its position there increasingly awkward, unsuccessfully pressuring the PiS-led coalition to tighten abortion laws in early 2007. The party is in a self-described "state of liquidation."

Social Movement (*Ruch Społeczny*—RS). The RS was the direct heir of the Solidarity movement, with its immediate progenitor being the AWS coalition. Formed by Prime Minister Buzek and his closest supporters as the Social Movement–Solidarity Electoral Action (*Ruch Społeczny–Akcja Wyborcza Solidarność*—RS-AWS) in December 1997, the party shortened its name to the RS at a congress in April 2002.

The initial RS-AWS chair, Marian Krzaklewski of the Solidarity trade union, had stepped down at the group's January 1999 congress in accordance with new guidelines precluding union chairs from holding formal RS-AWS positions. The same congress adopted a platform describing the party as a Christian Democratic grouping devoted to a mixed economy and support for families and social cohesion.

As the AWS coalition disintegrated following Krzaklewski's third-place finish in the October 2000 presidential election (he won only 15.6 percent of the vote), Prime Minister Buzek attempted to shore it up, taking over as leader in January 2001 and heading a newly created National Council. He also urged the remaining AWS parties to reorganize as a unified Solidarity Electoral Action of the Right (*Akcja Wyborcza Solidarność Prawicky*—AWSP), but they insisted on maintaining their independent identities. Thus, the AWSP was established on May 23, 2001, not as a party, but as an electoral coalition, by the RS-AWS, the Christian National Union (ZChN), the Polish Party of Christian Democrats (PPChD; see SKL-RNP, above), and the Movement for the Reconstruction of Poland (ROP). The ROP soon left the coalition, however, and aligned itself with the new League of Polish Families (LPR). Moreover, in May the Solidarity Union, having already announced its withdrawal from direct involvement in party politics, withdrew its support for the RS-AWS. All of the remaining AWS parties had already lost key members to other formations, and at the September *Sejm* election the AWSP won only 5.6 percent of the vote, well below the 8 percent threshold needed for a coalition to obtain representation.

Former Prime Minister Buzek stepped down as RS chair on October 21, 2001, and was succeeded by Mieczsław JANOWSKI. The latter was in turn succeeded by Sen. Krzysztof PIESIEWICZ in April 2002, at which time the renamed party attempted to reposition itself at the political center. However, Piesiewicz subsequently joined the PO, and references to the RS ceased.

Christian National Union (*Zjednoczenie Chrześcijańsko-Narodowe*—ZChN). The ideologically conservative and anti-abortion ZChN was founded in September 1989 from a number of Catholic groups and supported Lech Wałęsa in the 1990 presidential balloting. It contested the 1991 legislative election as the leading element of Catholic Electoral Action (*Wyborcza Akeja Katolicka*—WAK), which won a creditable 49 seats and participated in subsequent center-right administrations. The ZChN was weakened in 1992 when its chair, Wiesław CHRZANOWSKI (then marshal of the *Sejm*), was included on a government list of alleged Communist-era collaborators published by the ZChN interior minister, Antoni Macierewicz, who was expelled from the party and helped form the League of Polish Families (LPR). In the 1993 election the ZChN headed the Homeland (*Ojczyzna*) alliance, which also included the Peasant Alliance (*Porozumienie Ludowe*—PL) and the Conservative Party (PK; see under SKL-RNP, above), but which failed to gain representation. The ZChN was one of five right-wing groups that formed a "confederation" called the Covenant for Poland (*Przymierze dla Polski*—PdP) in May 1994. None of its members—the Center Alliance (PC), the Movement for the Republic, the ZChN, PL, and PK—had crossed the 5 percent vote-share threshold needed to secure *Sejm* representation in 1993. Chrzanowski was succeeded as party leader in March 1995 by Ryszard CZARNECKI, who himself resigned in protest at the party's decision to back Lech Wałęsa in the runoff presidential ballot of November 1995. In May 2000 the party was effectively split when Stanisław ZAJAC narrowly defeated the incumbent, Marian PIŁKA, for the party chairship. Zajac was in turn succeeded by Jerzy KROPIWNICKI in 2002. Many ZChN members subsequently joined the LPR.

Freedom Union (*Unia Wolności*—UW). The UW was organized on April 23–24, 1994, by merger of the Democratic Union (*Unia Demokratyczna*—UD) and the smaller Liberal Democratic Congress (*Kongres Liberalno-Demokratyczny*—KLD). The new formation described itself as a "strong party of the center," committed to market-oriented reforms and a democratic social order, but not insensitive to social justice.

The original UD had been launched by members of the election committees set up by the Solidarity-affiliated Citizens' Movement–Democratic Action (*Ruch Obywatelski Akcja Demokratyczna*—ROAD) to support Prime Minister Mazowiecki's 1990 bid for the presidency. At a congress in May 1991 two additional formations, the left-of-center Social Democratic Movement (*Ruch Demokratyczno Społeczny*—RDS) and the center-right Forum of the Democratic Right (*Forum Prawicy Demokratycznej*—FPD), agreed to merge into the UD. While having somewhat differing outlooks, the constituent groups shared a distrust of Wałęsa's "demagogic populism" and strongly favored a slowdown in the imposition of his free-market reform program. The UD led the *Sejm* poll in 1991, securing 62 seats, but it lost its plurality in 1992 when the FPD withdrew before participating in forming the Conservative Party (PK; see SKL-RNP, above). Although improving its representation to 74 in 1993, the UD fell to third place behind the SLD and PSL.

Launched in February 1990, the KLD was the outgrowth of a Gdańsk-based group led by journalist Donald Tusk that had been organized as the Congress of Liberals in 1988. Supported largely by white-collar and private business interests, it favored a free-market economy and the privatization of state enterprises. The KLD won 37 *Sejm* seats in 1991 but failed to reach the 5 percent threshold in 1993.

Having won 60 seats in the 1997 elections, the UW formed a ruling coalition with the AWS after protracted negotiations. UW Chair Leszek BALCEROWICZ, architect of the "shock therapy" economic reforms, was named minister of finance in the new government. At the UW's spring 1998 congress, about 20 activists from the Union of Labor (UP), including prominent Solidarity leader Zbigniew BUJAK, joined the UW.

Differences within the government caused frequent friction between the AWS leadership and the UW, and renegotiation of the coalition agreement in October 1999 only served to delay the UW's departure. On June 6, 2000, the UW formally withdrew, the party's governing council having voted on May 28 to sever its ties because of differences over the leadership of Prime Minister Buzek and the inability of the AWS to exert party discipline over its various components. The move left the AWS as a minority government, although it continued to receive UW support in Parliament.

Following the 2000 presidential election, Chair Balcerowicz was named to head the National Bank, and on December 16 former foreign minister Bronisław GEREMEK was elected to succeed him. Largely excluded from the new leadership, the party's more liberal wing, led by Donald Tusk, thereupon split from the UW and in January 2001 helped form the Civic Platform (PO). At the September 2001 *Sejm* election the UW won only 3.1 percent of the national vote, below the threshold for representation, leading to Geremek's resignation and his replacement by Solidarity stalwart Władysław Frasyniuk. However, the UW recovered somewhat in the June 2004 European Parliament balloting, securing 7.3 percent of the vote and four seats. Many former members of the UW (including Frasyniuk) were later represented in the Democratic Party (see above), an offshoot of the UW, which has absorbed it.

Christian Democratic Party of the Third Republic (*Chrześcijańska Demokracja III Rzeczypospolitej Polskiej*—ChDRP). The ChDRP was founded on December 1, 1997, by Lech Wałęsa, the former president of Poland and former leader of Solidarity. Wałęsa said the new grouping would not oppose the AWS-UW government but would be available to move toward a position of national influence should that coalition fail. The ChDRP held its first national congress in September 1998.

In July 1998 Wałęsa had announced that a ChDRP deputies team was being established within the AWS *Sejm* floor group. The team's leader, Jerzy Gwiżdż of the Electoral Solidarity (SwW), had formerly been affiliated with the now-defunct Nonparty Bloc in Support of Reform (*Bezpartyjny Blok Wspierania Reform*—BBWR), a formation initially backed by Wałęsa that had won 16 lower house seats in 1993 and then in 1996 joined the "Patriotic Camp" (*Obóz Patriotyczny*—OP) alliance with the Movement for the Republic (RdR), the PSL-PL, and part of the Confederation for an Independent Poland (KPN). The effort to advance cooperation between the ChDRP and the AWS was apparently intended, at least in part, to provide a broader base in preparation for Wałęsa's run for the presidency in 2000. After obtaining only 1 percent of the vote, Wałęsa announced his resignation as party leader in October 2000, but he continued to exert a strong influence on the party.

In the years following the 2001 legislative election there were indications that the former president might resume a more active role at the head of a new formation intended to draw together former AWS/Solidarity members who had become disenchanted with current political options. However, as of 2004 it appeared that the ChDRP had ceased to function, although Wałęsa remained active, serving, among other things, as a mediator in the Ukrainian political crisis late in the year. Wałęsa subsequently served as a vocal critic of the Kaczyński style of governance but did not appear to be interested in resurrecting the ChDRP.

Polish Socialist Party (*Polska Partia Socjalistyczna*—PPS). Founded in 1892, the PPS went underground during World War II and provided Poland's first postwar prime minister. Although only a small faction was pro-Communist, the party was formally merged with the Communist PPR in 1948 to form the PZPR. The party was revived in 1987 and in March 1990 sponsored a congress of non-Communist leftists. Weakened by internal strife, the PPS failed to secure *Sejm* representation in 1991 or 1993. In February 1996 the two main PPS factions unified under the leadership of 82-year-old Jan MULAK. He was unanimously replaced by Piotr IKONOWICZ at a party congress in April 1998. Although it had been a member of the SLD coalition, in 1999 the PPS did not enter the new SLD party. Ikonowicz won only 0.2 percent of the vote in the 2000 presidential election. In 2003 Ikonowicz formed a new party (see New Left, below), and he was succeeded as PPS chair by Andrzej Ziemski, who pledged to "moderate" the PPS to appeal to a broader range of voters. The PPS ran on a common ballot with the Polish Pensioners' Party and the Center-Left of the Republic of Poland for European parliamentary elections in 2003 and 2004. Members of the PPS were invited in 2007 to join the new LiD, which remains a group far from the mainstream of Polish politics.

Leaders: Andrzej ZIEMSKI (President); Zbigniew OLESINSKI, Janusz PRZEPOIRSKI (Vice Presidents).

Democratic Party (*Stronnictwo Demokratyczne*—SD). Recruiting its members predominantly from among professional and intellectual ranks, the SD was founded in 1939 as a non-Marxist group and was a Front party during the Communist era. In mid-1989 the party abandoned its alliance with the Communists and in September accepted three portfolios in the Solidarity-led Mazowiecki government. Thereafter, it was seemingly unable to decide what its political profile should be, securing only one *Sejm* seat in the 1991 balloting and none in 1993 or 1997. In 2001 the SD ran in conjunction with the SLD. In June 2002, at the party's 20th congress, delegates replaced Jan KLIMEK as party chair, citing the party's weak performance under his leadership. (The SD should not be confused with the PD [above] that was launched in early 2005.) In the European parliamentary elections of that year it garnered only 0.27 percent of the vote. In 2005 they formed a coalition with the SDPL, but attained only 0.17 percent. In 2009 it formed a coalition with the Greens and the SDPL called Agreement for the Future, which gained 2.4 percent of the vote in elections for the European parliament.

Leaders: Krzysztof GÓRALCZYK (Chair); Jerzy MARZECKI, Andrzej PROCHWNIK, Wlademar PRUSAK, Jerzy WÓJCIAK (Vice Chairs).

In preparation for the 2005 general election, a number of new parties emerged, including the **Center Party** (*Centrum*), a pro-EU grouping that received 0.19 percent of votes in that election and supported the PO in the 2007 election under the leadership of Dr. Zbigniew RELIGA, an internationally renowned heart surgeon; and the **New Left** (*Nowa Lewica*—NL), a left-wing "anticapitalist" grouping established in 2003 by former PPS leader Piotr IKONOWICZ, which held demonstrations against the missile shield in August 2008.

Other parties participating in the 2005 *Sejm* balloting included the **Polish National Party** (*Polska Partia Narodowa*—PPN), led by nationalist Leszek BUBEL, with 0.29 percent of votes; the **National Civic Coalition** (*Ogólnopolska Koalicja Obywatelska*—OKO), a collection of 140 social organizations and unions, with 0.14 percent of votes; the **Polish Dignity and Work Confederation** (*Polska Konfederacja-Godność i Praca*—PKGiP), with 0.07 percent of votes; the **Labor Party** (*Stronnictwa Pracy*—RS), with 0.01 percent of votes; and **Social Rescuers** (*Społeczni Ratownicy*—SR), a party in favor of expanded welfare benefits, with 0.01 percent of votes.

New parties participating in the 2007 *Sejm* elections included the socialist **Polish Labor Party** (*Polska Partia Pracy*—PPP), with 0.77 percent of votes. It did no better in the European parliamentary elections of 2009 when it also took 0.7 percent of the vote under the leadership of Bogusław Zbigniew ZIĘTEK. The year 2007 also saw the emergence of the **Women's Party** (*Komitet Wyborczy Partii Kobiet*—PK), which gained only 0.28 percent of the vote and subsequently did not compete in the 2009 elections for the European parliament.

The pan-European Libertas party, which was started by Irishman Declan GANLEY in 2009, presented candidates in Poland for the 2009 European parliamentary elections. In Poland it consisted of 3 members of the Libertas party, 57 independent candidates, and 67 members from six other parties. These consisted of **Forward Poland** (Naprzód Polsko—NP, **Polish People's Party "Piast"** (Polskie Stronnictwo Ludowe "Piast"—PSL Piast, **Party of Regions** (Partia Regionów—PR), **League of Polish Families** (Liga Polskich Rodzin—LPR), **National Polish Organization-Polish League** (Organizacja Narodu Polskiego-Liga Polska—ONP-LP), and the **Christian National Union** (Zjednoczenie Chrześcijańsko-Narodowe—ZChN). Libertas, which was organized in opposition to the Lisbon Treaty, gained only 1.14 percent of the vote and no seats. The **Greens 2004** (Zieloni 2004), a member of the European Green Party, was first registered in 2004. It ran in the 2009 European parliamentary elections in the coalition Agreement for the Future with the SD and SDPL. Other parties that participated in the 2009 EU elections included: the **Republic Right Party** *(Prawica Rzeczypospolitej*—PRP*)*, an anti-abortion party that won 1.95 percent of the vote; and the right-wing **Realpolitik Union** (*Unia Polityki* Realnej—UPR) which won 1.1 percent.

For more information on the **Peasant Democratic Party** (*Partia Ludowe Democratyczna*—PLD), the **Movement for the Reconstruction of Poland** (*Ruch Odbudowy Polski*—ROP), and smaller parties active during the 2005 balloting, see the 2008 *Handbook*.

LEGISLATURE

Under Communist rule, the 460 members of the *Sejm* (Diet or Parliament) were elected via direct universal suffrage from candidate lists strictly controlled by the Front of National Unity and its successor, the Patriotic Movement for National Rebirth. Following extensive government/Solidarity negotiations, a bicameral legislature was established in 1989 that incorporated the existing *Sejm* and added a 100-member Senate, each serving four-year terms, subject to dissolution. Only a portion of the *Sejm* seats were open to opposition candidates in the 1989 balloting, although subsequent elections have been conducted on a fully open basis. As codified in the 1997 constitution, when sitting together, the *Sejm* and the Senate constitute the **National Assembly** (*Zgromadzenie Narodowe*).

Senate (*Senat*). The upper house comprises 100 members elected under a majoritarian system from 40 multimember constituencies. The Senate cannot initiate legislation but has the power of veto over the *Sejm*, which the latter can overturn only by a two-thirds majority. Following the most recent election of October 21, 2007, the distribution of seats was as follows: Civic Platform, 60; Law and Justice, 39; and independent, 1.

Speaker: Bogdan Michał BORUSEWICZ.

Sejm. The lower house comprises 460 members elected from 41 multimember constituencies under a proportional system (revised in 2001) in which parties (save for national minority groups) must gain 5 percent of the vote and coalitions need 8 percent to qualify for lower house seats. The distribution following the election of October 21, 2007, was as follows: Civic Platform, 209; Law and Justice, 166; the Left and Democrats, 53; the Polish Peasants' Party, 31; and the German Minority of Lower Silesia, 1.

Marshal: Bronisław KOMOROWSKI.

CABINET

[as of July 1, 2009]

Prime Minister	Donald Tusk (PO)
Deputy Prime Ministers	Waldemar Pawlak (PSL)
	Grzegorz Schetyna (PO)
Ministers	
Agriculture and Rural Development	Marek Sawicki (PSL)
Culture and National Heritage	Bogdan Zdrojewski (PO)
Economy	Waldemar Pawlak (PSL)
Environment	Maciej Nowicki (ind.)
Finance	Jacek Rostowski (ind.)
Foreign Affairs	Radosław Sikorski (PO)
Health	Ewa Kopacz (PO) [f]
Infrastructure	Cezary Grabarczyk (PO)
Interior and Administration	Grzegorz Schetyna (PO)
Justice	Andrzej Czuma (ind)
Labor and Social Policy	Jolanta Fedak (PSL) [f]
National Defense	Bogdan Klich (PO)
National Education	Katarzyna Hall (ind.) [f]
Regional Development	Elżbieta Bieńkowska (ind.) [f]
Science and Higher Education	Barbara Kudrycka (PO) [f]
Sports and Tourism	Mirosław Drzewiecki (PO)
Treasury	Aleksander Grad (PO)
Without Portfolio	Michał Boni (PO)

[f] = female

COMMUNICATIONS

Press. Although the leading organs were under government control, the Polish press for most of the Communist era was livelier than in other East European countries, the regime making little effort to halt publication of "uncensored" (*samizdat*) publications, many of which were openly distributed prior to the imposition of martial law in late 1981, when strict censorship was imposed.

Hailed by Lech Wałęsa as the "first independent newspaper from the Elbe to the Pacific," the opposition daily *Gazeta Wyborcza* (Electoral Gazette) commenced publication in Warsaw in May 1989, with a press run that averaged more than 500,000 copies a day. In late 1990 nearly 200 state-controlled newspapers and magazines were privatized, with their number declining sharply thereafter because of increased production costs. There were some 50 dailies in the late 1990s. In its annual report on press freedom, Reporters Without Borders ranked Poland, along with Mauritius, Romania and South Korea, as 47th out of 173 countries.

The following Polish-language dailies are currently published in Warsaw, unless otherwise noted: *Gazeta Wyborcza* (520,000 daily, 690,000 weekends [*Gazeta Świateczna*]), independent center-left; *Rzecypospolita* (The Republic, 280,000), independent center-right; *Życie Warszawy* (Warsaw Life, 250,000 daily, 460,000 weekends), nonparty; *Trybuna Ślaska* (Silesian Tribune, Katowice, 185,000 daily, 800,000 weekends), independent successor to the SdRP's *Trybuna Robotnicza*; *Czas Krakowski* (Kraków Time, Kraków, 150,000 daily, 260,000 weekends); *Kurier Polski* (Polish Courier, 150,000 daily, 190,000 weekends); *Express Wieczorny* (Evening Express, 140,000 daily, 400,000 weekends), nonparty; *Trybuna* (Tribune, 120,000 daily, 250,000 weekends), launched by the SdRP in late 1989 as successor to *Trybuna Ludu*, the former PZPR Central Committee organ; *Zielony Sztandar* (Green Banner, 100,000), weekly PSL organ; *Gazeta Poznańska* (Poznań Gazette, Poznań, 80,000 daily, 320,000 weekends); *Tygodnik Solidarnoś* (Solidarity Weekly, 65,000), Solidarity union weekly; *Gazeta Krakowska* (Kraków Gazette, Kraków, 60,000 daily, 150,000 weekends). Several papers are also published in the languages of the national minorities (Belarusan, German, Jewish, Russian, Ukrainian).

News agencies. The Polish Press Agency (*Polska Agencja Prasowa*—PAP), with offices in numerous Polish and foreign cities, transmits information abroad in English. The Polish Information Agency (*Polska Agencja Informacyjna*—PAI), established to assist the PAP, issues foreign-language bulletins and aids foreign journalists. Numerous foreign agencies maintain bureaus in Warsaw.

Broadcasting and computing. Legislation that came into force on March 1, 1993, introduced new operating rules for public and commercial broadcasting, ending the state monopoly and creating a regulatory Polish National Radio and Television Broadcasting Council. The monolithic *Polskie Radio i Telewizja* was divided into *Polskie Radio* and *Telewizja Polska*, which operate regional as well as national stations. At present, there are both public and private national channels as well as numerous additional radio and television facilities.

In June 1994 Poland's Constitutional Tribunal upheld a broadcast law requirement that radio and TV programming "respect Christian values" by arguing that the admonition fell short of a directive to propagate such values.

As of 2008 there were 490.2 Internet users per 1,000 inhabitants.

INTERGOVERNMENTAL REPRESENTATION

Ambassador to the U.S: Robert KUPIECKI.

U.S. Ambassador to Poland: Lee Andrew FEINSTEIN.

Permanent Representative to the UN: Andrzej TOWPIK.

IGO Memberships (Non-UN): BIS, CBSS, CEI, CERN, CEUR, EBRD, EIB, EU, Eurocontrol, IEA, Interpol, IOM, NATO, OECD, OSCE, PCA, WCO, *WEU*, WTO.

PORTUGAL

Portuguese Republic
República Portuguesa

Note: In the Assembly of the Republic election held September 27, 2009, the Socialist Party (PS) won a leading 97 seats, but the loss of 24 seats from its 2005 total left it well short of a majority in the 230-seat legislature. The opposition Social Democratic Party won 78 seats; the Social Democratic Center-Popular Party, 21; the Left Bloc, 16; and the Unified Democratic Coalition, 15. Unable to attract support from the other parties, Prime Minister José Sócrates formed a minority PS government that was sworn in on October 26.

Political Status: Independent republic proclaimed on October 5, 1910; corporative constitution of March 19, 1933, suspended following military coup of April 25, 1974; present constitution promulgated on April 2, 1976, with effect from April 25.

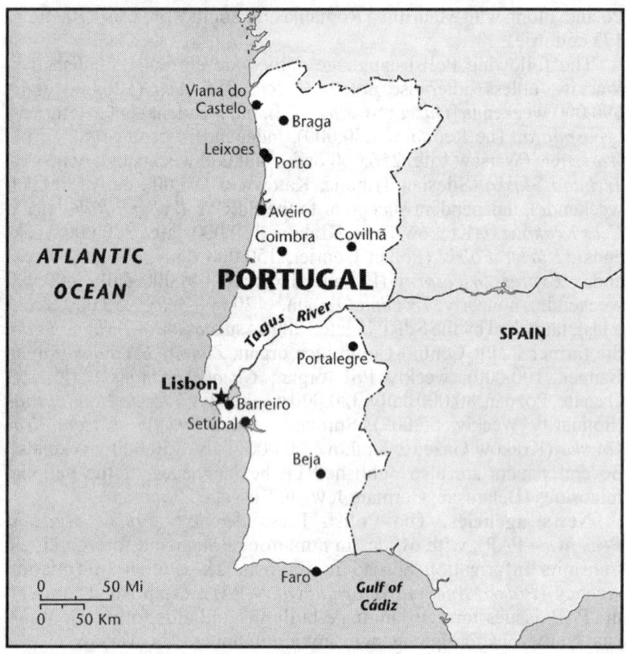

Area: 35,553 sq. mi. (92,082 sq. km.).

Population: 10,356,117 (2001C); 10,693,000 (2008E). Area and population figures include mainland Portugal plus the Azores and the Madeira Islands.

Major Urban Centers (2005E): LISBON (520,000), Porto (Oporto, 248,000).

Official Language: Portuguese.

Monetary Unit: Euro (market rate December 1, 2009: 1 euro = $1.51US).

President: Aníbal CAVACO SILVA (Social Democratic Party); popularly elected on January 22, 2006, and sworn in for a five-year term on March 9, succeeding Jorge SAMPAIO (Socialist Party).

Prime Minister: *(See headnote.)* José SÓCRATES (Socialist Party); designated by the president on February 24, 2005, and sworn in on March 12 to succeed Pedro SANTANA LOPES (Social Democratic Party).

THE COUNTRY

Known in antiquity as Lusitania, Portugal overlooks the Atlantic along the western face of the Iberian Peninsula, while including politically the Azores and the Madeira Islands in the Atlantic. Mainland Portugal is divided by the Tagus River into a mountainous northern section and a southern section of rolling plains whose geography and climate are akin to those of northern Africa. The population, a blend of ancient Celtic, Iberian, Latin, Teutonic, and Moorish elements, with a recent admixture of African and other immigrants, is culturally homogeneous and almost wholly affiliated with the Roman Catholic Church, which traditionally exercised commanding social and political influence. Portuguese, the official language, is spoken by virtually all of the population. As of 1998 women comprised 44 percent of the official labor force, concentrated in agriculture and domestic service; female representation in government and politics—despite the participation of a few prominent women, including former prime minister Maria de Lourdes PINTASILGO—averages less than 10 percent. Although the legislature recently rejected a mandate that women be allotted 25 percent of all posts in the Portuguese Assembly as well as in the Portuguese delegation to the European Parliament, all of the major parties volunteered to observe the proposed quota. (As of 2009 women held 28 percent of seats in the national legislature.)

The economy, one of the least modernized in Europe, retains a somewhat paternalistic structure characterized by limited social services and per capita GDP of only $22,000 in 2008. Although agriculture accounts for about 42 percent of the land area, it contributes only 3 percent of GDP. Industry, consisting primarily of small manufacturing firms, employs some 32 percent of the labor force and contributes 26 percent of GDP. Exports include machinery and tools as well as such traditional goods as textiles, clothing, fish products, cork, and olive oil, of which Portugal is one of the world's largest producers. The European Union (EU) accounts for three-quarters of Portugal's imports and exports. The service sector, including tourism and retail, has become Portugal's largest employer.

Unemployment, a problem in the late 1970s and early 1980s because of the influx of more than 1 million persons from former Portuguese colonies, abated substantially upon entry into the European Community (EC, subsequently the EU) on January 1, 1986, and remained well below the average for members of the Organization for Economic Cooperation and Development (OECD) in the early 1990s. EC regional development aid helped to sustain a positive annual growth rate prior to a contraction of over 1 percent a year in 1993–1994. Economic growth of 3 percent resumed in 1995–1996 and peaked at 4.2 percent in 1998. In 1998 Portugal was named to become a founding member of the EU's Economic and Monetary Union (EMU) on January 1, 1999, as Lisbon continued to direct an economic recovery program that the International Monetary Fund (IMF) described as being responsible for a "virtuous circle of lower interest rates, vigorous growth, and declining fiscal deficits." However, the economy weakened significantly in 2001, with GDP growth of about 2 percent and a government budget deficit of 4.1 percent of GDP, exceeding the limit (3 percent) set by the EU. Consequently, the new government installed in 2002 initiated a number of measures designed to reduce the deficit, including the cancellation of planned tax cuts and the intensification of the sale of state-owned enterprises to the private sector. Economic reforms yielded mixed results, with a marked reduction of the budget deficit to 2.6 percent of GDP in 2007, but continued high unemployment of 8 percent, accompanied by slow GDP growth of 1.8 percent annually. The budget deficit fell to 2.2 percent of GDP in 2008, the lowest level in 30 years. However, falling demand for goods and services, including a 20.8 percent decrease in exports, pushed Portugal's economy into negative economic growth. By mid-2009 GDP growth had contracted to negative numbers compared to the previous year. Citing hardship resulting from the global recession, the government in June reduced the income level required of immigrants to renew their residency permits. Despite its poor economic performance, Portugal was spared the worst impacts of the global recession because its banks had not invested in some of the so-called toxic assets that had undermined the economies of other Western countries. Further, the government successfully recruited investment into renewable energy industries, mainly wind and hydroelectric power, in an effort to offset Portugal's dependence on foreign sources of oil and natural gas. The government plan called for Portugal to produce more than 60 percent of its electricity from renewable sources by 2020, far more than the EU target of 20 percent. Already home to Europe's largest onshore wind farm, Portugal in February 2009 announced plans to develop the world's first floating offshore wind farm.

GOVERNMENT AND POLITICS

Political background. As one of the great European monarchies of late medieval and early modern times, Portugal initiated the age of discovery and colonization and acquired a far-flung colonial empire that was one of the last to be abandoned. Interrupted by a period of Spanish rule from 1580 to 1640, the Portuguese monarchy endured until 1910, when a bloodless revolution initiated a republican era marked by chronic instability and recurrent violence. A military revolt in 1926 prepared the way for the presidency of Marshal António CARMONA (1926–1951) and the assumption of governmental authority by António de Oliveira SALAZAR, an economics professor who became finance minister in 1928 and served as prime minister from 1932 until his replacement because of illness in 1968. Salazar, mistrustful of democratic and socialist ideologies and influenced by Italian fascism, established economic and political stability, and in 1933 he introduced a "corporative" constitution designed to serve as the basis of a new Portuguese State (*Estado Novo*). With the support of the Catholic Church, the army, and his National Union, the only authorized political movement,

Salazar completely dominated Portuguese political life and reduced the presidency to an auxiliary institution.

The later years of Salazar's regime were marked by rising, though largely ineffectual, domestic discontent and growing restiveness in the Overseas Territories. Elections were frequently boycotted by the opposition, and direct presidential elections were eliminated following a vigorous but unsuccessful opposition campaign by Gen. Humberto DELGADO in 1958. Overseas, the provinces of Goa, Damão, and Diu were seized by India in 1961; in the same year, a revolt broke out in Angola, while independence movements became active in Portuguese Guinea in 1962 and in Mozambique in 1964. Attempts to suppress the insurrections resulted in severe economic strain as well as increasing political isolation and repeated condemnation by the United Nations (UN).

The crisis created by Salazar's nearly fatal illness in September 1968 was alleviated by the selection of Marcello CAETANO, a close associate, as the new prime minister. Although he permitted a measure of cautious liberalization, including some relaxation of secret police activity and the return from exile of the Socialist Party (*Partido Socialista*—PS) leader Mário SOARES, Caetano preserved the main outlines of Salazar's policy both in metropolitan Portugal and overseas.

Prior to the parliamentary election of October 1969, opposition parties were legalized, but they were again outlawed after a campaign in which the official National Union won all 130 seats in the National Assembly. The atmosphere of repression eased again after the adoption in 1971 of constitutional legislation expanding the power of the enlarged National Assembly, granting limited autonomy to the Overseas Territories, abolishing press censorship, and permitting religious freedom. Nevertheless, in the legislative election of October 1973 the ruling Popular National Action (successor to the National Union) won all 150 seats, including 34 representing the Overseas Territories.

In a bloodless coup on April 24, 1974, a group of mainly left-wing military officers calling themselves the Armed Forces Movement (*Movimento das Forças Armadas*—MFA) seized power, ending more than 40 years of civilian dictatorship. The president and prime minister were arrested and flown to Brazil, where they were granted political asylum. The leader of the "Junta of National Salvation," Gen. António Sebastião Ribeiro de SPÍNOLA, assumed the presidency, and on May 15 a center-left cabinet was sworn in with Adelino de PALMA CARLOS as prime minister. After a dispute with the reconstituted Council of State as to the extent of his powers, Palma Carlos resigned on July 9 and was replaced by Gen. Vasco dos Santos GONÇALVES, whose administration recognized the right of the Overseas Territories to "self-determination" with all its consequences, including independence. On September 30 General Spínola also resigned, leaving power in the hands of leftist military officers and civilians. The new president, Gen. Francisco da COSTA GOMES, subsequently reappointed General Gonçalves as prime minister.

In May 1974 Costa Gomes had visited Angola, declaring upon his return that the new government was prepared to offer a cease-fire in Angola, Mozambique, and Portuguese Guinea, with the guerrilla organizations being permitted to organize political parties and participate in democratic elections. As a result of the initiative, negotiations were undertaken that led to the independence of Guinea-Bissau (formerly Portuguese Guinea) in September, while discussions with insurgent leaders in Mozambique and Sao Tome and Principe resulted in independence for both territories, as well as for Cape Verde, the following year. Although negotiations with Angolan leaders were complicated by the presence of a sizable white minority and by the existence of three major insurgent groups, the formation of a united front by the insurgents opened the way for independence. The front subsequently collapsed, but Portugal withdrew from Angola on the agreed date of November 11, 1975.

On March 11, 1975, right-wing military elements, reportedly acting at the instigation of former president Spínola, had attempted to overthrow the government. Upon failure of the coup, General Spínola flew to Brazil, and the Junta of National Salvation was dissolved in favor of a Supreme Revolutionary Council (SRC). The latter, sworn in by President Costa Gomes on March 17, was given full executive and legislative powers for the purpose of "directing and executing the revolutionary program in Portugal." Although officers constituted one-third of the cabinet announced on March 25, also included were representatives of the Communist, Socialist, and Popular Democratic parties, as well as of the Portuguese Democratic Movement.

In a Constituent Assembly election on April 25, 1975, the Socialists received 38 percent of the total vote, compared with 26 percent for the Popular Democrats and less than 13 percent for the Communists. The first session of the assembly was convened on June 2, with the Socialists holding 116 of the 250 seats. Despite their commanding legislative strength, the Socialists and Popular Democrats subsequently announced their intention to resign from the government, in part because of a Communist takeover of the Socialist newspaper *República*, and on July 31 a new, essentially nonparty cabinet was formed. However, increasing opposition to Communist influence led, on August 29, to the resignation of Prime Minister Gonçalves and the appointment of Adm. José Baptista Pinheiro de AZEVEDO as head of a new cabinet (the sixth since the 1974 coup) comprising representatives of the three leading parties, as well as of the Armed Forces Movement.

In mid-November 1975 the Communist-led labor unions mounted a general strike in Lisbon, demanding the resignation of the Azevedo government and the formation of an exclusively left-wing "revolutionary government." The strike was followed on November 26 by an uprising of leftist military units that was crushed by loyalist troops responding to government pressure to restore law and order. Although the SRC had previously rebuked Azevedo for his conduct during the strike, the coup's failure was seen as a major defeat for the Communists, and in mid-December, following designation of a new army chief of staff, the council ordered a major reorganization of the armed forces, emphasizing military discipline and the exclusion of the military from party politics.

The new constitution came into effect on April 25, 1976, and an election to the Assembly of the Republic was held the same day. The Socialists remained the largest party but again failed to win an absolute majority. On June 27 Gen. António dos Santos Ramalho EANES, a nonparty candidate supported by the Socialists, Popular Democrats, and Social Democrats, was elected to a five-year term as president. The election was a further setback for the Communists, whose candidate, Octávio PATO, finished third, behind far-left candidate Maj. Otelo SARAIVA DE CARVALHO. Three weeks later, on July 16, Soares was invested as prime minister, heading a Socialist minority government that was, however, endorsed by the other two parties in the presidential election coalition.

Having lost a crucial assembly vote on an economic austerity plan, Soares was forced to resign on December 8, 1977, though he was subsequently able to return as head of a governmental coalition with the conservative Social Democratic Center (*Centro Democrático Social*—CDS) on January 30, 1978. On July 27, however, Soares was dismissed by President Eanes after the CDS ministers had resigned over disagreements on agricultural and health policies, leaving the Socialists without a working legislative majority. His successor, Alfredo NOBRE DA COSTA, was in turn forced to resign on September 14 following legislative rejection of an essentially nonparty program. A new government, largely composed of independents, was eventually confirmed on November 22 with Dr. Carlos Alberto da MOTA PINTO, a former member of the Social Democratic Party (*Partido Social Democrata*—PSD, the renamed Popular Democratic Party), as prime minister.

Having witnessed assembly rejection of his proposed budget on three occasions since March, Prime Minister Mota Pinto resigned on June 6, 1979. On July 19 Maria de Lourdes Pintasilgo, a member of several previous post-1974 governments, was named to head a caretaker, nonparty government, pending an early legislative election. The balloting of December 2 confirmed Portugal's move toward the extremes of the political spectrum. Francisco SÁ CARNEIRO, a conservative Social Democrat who in July had formed a Democratic Alliance (*Aliança Democrática*—AD) with the Center Democrats, Monarchists, and disaffected Socialists, led his electoral coalition to a clear majority and was named on December 29 to organize a new government—the 12th since 1974—that was sworn in on January 3, 1980. The Alliance was returned to office with an increased majority at the second legislative election within a year on October 5, 1980.

Prime Minister Sá Carneiro was killed in a plane crash on December 4 and was succeeded as PSD leader and prime minister by Dr. Francisco Pinto BALSEMÃO, who proceeded to organize a new AD cabinet that was sworn in on January 5, 1981. Balsemão continued as head of a reorganized administration on September 1, 1982, prior to resigning on December 19, 1982.

In a general election on April 25, 1983, the Socialists obtained a substantial plurality, enabling Soares to form a cabinet of nine Socialists, seven Social Democrats, and one independent that assumed office on June 9. However, severe economic difficulties eroded the popularity of the Socialists, while the coalition partners disagreed on the extent of proposed austerity measures. On June 4, 1985, PSD parliamentary leader Aníbal CAVACO SILVA announced his party's withdrawal from the government, although agreeing to a postponement until the signature on June 12 of Portugal's entry accord with the EC. Two days later, Soares was named to head a caretaker administration pending a new election, while declaring himself a candidate for the forthcoming presidential poll.

The October 6, 1985, legislative balloting dealt a serious blow to the Socialists, whose representation was cut nearly in half. The largest vote share, 30 percent, went to the PSD, and Cavaco Silva formed a minority government based on his party's assembly plurality on November 6. The PSD's preferred presidential candidate, the Christian Democrat Diogo FREITAS DO AMARAL, captured nearly half the vote in the initial presidential balloting on January 23, 1986, out of a field of four candidates; however, an unusual coalition of the Socialists, the pro-Eanes Democratic Renewal Party (*Partido Renovador Democrático*—PRD), and the Communist-led United People's Alliance (*Aliança Povo Unido*—APU) succeeded in electing Soares, the remaining center-left candidate, with 51 percent of the vote in the February 16 runoff. Soares, the first civilian head of state in 60 years, was sworn in as Eanes's successor on March 9.

President Soares dissolved the assembly on April 28, 1987, following the April 3 defeat of the Cavaco Silva government on a censure motion that had charged the administration with mismanagement of the economy. In the ensuing poll of July 19, the Social Democrats became the first party in 13 years to win an absolute majority of legislative seats, permitting the incumbent prime minister to return to office on August 17 as head of an all-PSD government. Following his reconfirmation, Cavaco Silva moved to privatize state-owned firms not of "particular importance to the public service" and to reverse a number of post-1974 measures aimed at agricultural collectivization. More important, in November 1988 the two leading parties reached agreement on constitutional changes that would strip the basic law of its Marxist elements, reduce the number of legislative deputies, permit the holding of binding national referenda, and accelerate the privatization process.

On January 13, 1991, President Soares gained easy election to a second five-year term on a 70.4 percent vote share that made a runoff unnecessary, while the PSD's retention of its majority in legislative balloting on October 6 permitted Cavaco Silva to retain office at the head of a slightly modified administration on October 28.

With most economic indicators positive or stable, the government took the escudo into the broad band of the EC's exchange rate mechanism (ERM) on April 6, 1992. Five months later it was thrown off course by the European monetary crisis, which led to devaluations of the escudo by 6 percent in November and by 7 percent in May 1993. Deepening economic recession and assorted political problems resulted in a sharp decline in the government's standing, accompanied by an upsurge of "cohabitation" tensions between the president and the prime minister. In December the Socialists outpolled the PSD in local elections, winning their highest-ever share of a nationwide vote.

Continuing economic recession and rising unemployment compounded the government's unpopularity in the later months of 1994, in the face of which Cavaco Silva vacated the PSD leadership in January 1995. He nevertheless remained prime minister in the run-up to the fall general election. In balloting on October 1, the Socialists made substantial gains at the expense of the PSD, although their 112-seat tally left them just short of an overall majority. Of the two smaller parties that won seats, the center-right Social Democratic Center–Popular Party (*Centro Democrático Social–Partido Popular*—CDS-PP) trebled its representation, while the Communist-dominated Unitary Democratic Coalition (*Coligação Democrática Unitária*—CDU) lost ground. The Socialist leader, António GUTERRES, accordingly formed a minority government at the end of October that was expected to have CDU external support on most issues.

In a presidential election on January 14, 1996, the Socialist candidate and former mayor of Lisbon, Jorge SAMPAIO, scored a comfortable first-round victory, taking 53.8 percent of the vote against 46.2 percent for the PSD's Cavaco Silva. Sampaio was sworn in for a five-year term on March 9. The Socialists extended a string of electoral victories thereafter, unexpectedly adding 3 seats in the assembly election of October 10, 1999 (for a total of 115, exactly half the membership), and retaining the presidency in balloting on January 14, 2001. In the latter contest, President Sampaio won 55.8 percent of the vote, versus 34.5 percent for the PSD's candidate, Joaquim FERREIRA DO AMARAL.

The PS suffered significant losses in municipal elections on December 16, 2001, and the following day Prime Minister Guterres announced his resignation. On December 28 President Sampaio, following the unanimous advice of the Council of State, dissolved the assembly in preparation for national legislative balloting in March, the Guterres government remaining in place in a caretaker capacity.

In assembly balloting on March 17, 2002, the PSD secured 40.2 percent of the vote and 105 seats, followed by the Socialists (37.9 percent of the vote and 96 seats). On March 28 President Sampaio named José Manuel Durão BARROSO of the PSD to form a new government, and the next day Barroso signed a coalition pact with the CDS-PP, which was given three ministerial posts in the new government appointed on April 6.

Strengthened by their victory in the June 2004 European Parliament elections, the PS and other opposition parties demanded that President Sampaio call for early elections when Prime Minister Barroso resigned on July 5 to become president of the European Commission. Instead, Sampaio opted to pursue "stability" by appointing Pedro SANTANA LOPES of the PSD to succeed Barroso. The selection of Santana Lopes, who, despite being the mayor of Lisbon, was not well known in the rest of the country and had little experience at the national level, surprised many observers.

In light of the continued decline in popular support for the governing coalition, Sampaio dissolved the assembly on December 10, 2004, and directed that new elections be held on February 20, 2005, at which time the PS gained its first legislative majority (121 seats) since independence. Consequently, the new government installed on March 12 under the PS's José SÓCRATES, described as promarket and pro-European, included only PS members and a number of independents.

After months of protests against Sócrates's austerity measures, aimed at reducing government expenditures during a protracted recession, voters on January 22, 2006, elected former prime minister Cavaco Silva to a five-year term as president. Cavaco Silva, who won 50.6 percent of the vote to defeat five left and center-left opponents, including PS member Manuel ALEGRE, who ran as an independent, and former president and official PS candidate Mário Soares, became the first center-right president to serve since the restoration of democracy in 1974. Although the Socialist Sócrates supported Soares for president, Cavaco Silva declared his intention to maintain a positive "dialogue" with the Socialist government and has refrained from exercising his veto power to block government-supported bills, including a controversial law permitting abortion during the first 10 weeks of gestation.

Minor cabinet changes occurred on May 17, 2007, and on January 29 and July 2, 2008.

Constitution and government. The constitution of April 25, 1976, stemmed from a constitutional agreement concluded two months earlier by the leading parties and Costa Gomes in his capacity as chief of state and president of the SRC (subsequently the Council of the Revolution). Under the pact (which superseded an earlier agreement of April 1975), the council, while formally designated as the most important government organ after the presidency, became, in large part, a consultative body with powers of absolute veto only in regard to defense policy. The third most important organ, the Assembly of the Republic, was empowered to override the council (on nonmilitary matters) and the president by a two-thirds majority.

A series of constitutional reforms that came into effect in October 1982 abolished the Council of the Revolution and distributed its powers among a Supreme Council of National Defense, a 13-member Constitutional Tribunal, and an advisory Council of State of 16 members (plus national presidents elected since adoption of the existing basic law): five named by the president, five named by the assembly, and six ex officio (the prime minister; the national ombudsman; and the presidents of the assembly, the Supreme Court, and the regional governments of the Azores and the Madeira Islands).

The president, elected for a five-year term, serves as military chief of staff and as chair of the Council of State and appoints the prime minister, who is responsible to both the head of state and the assembly. Portugal's judicial system, based on European civil law and heavily influenced by the French model, includes, in addition to the Constitutional Tribunal, a Supreme Court, courts of appeal, and district courts as well as military courts and a Court of Audit.

Administratively, metropolitan Portugal is divided into 18 districts (each headed by a governor appointed by the minister of the interior), which are subdivided into 275 municipalities and more than 4,000 parochial authorities. The Azores and the Madeira Islands are governed separately as Autonomous Regions, each with an elected Regional Assembly and municipal subdivisions (a total of 30). In both regions the central government has been represented since March 2006 by a "representative of the republic" (previously called a minister of the republic), who is appointed by the president.

Foreign relations. Allied with England since 1373, Portugal nevertheless declared itself neutral in World War II. It currently participates in the North Atlantic Treaty Organization (NATO) and the OECD as well as in the UN and its specialized agencies. It became a member of the Council of Europe in September 1976 and, after years of negotiation, joined Spain in gaining admission to the EC on January 1, 1986.

The country's foreign policy efforts prior to the 1974 coup were directed primarily to retention of its overseas territories at a time when other European powers had largely divested themselves of colonial possessions. This policy yielded isolation in the UN and occasionally strained relations with allied governments. Nevertheless, Portugal remained a valued member of NATO and was honored by a British royal visit in June 1973 to mark the 600th anniversary of the Anglo-Portuguese alliance. Subsequent to the 1974 coup, its African problems were significantly alleviated by the independence of Guinea-Bissau (formerly Portuguese Guinea) in 1974 and of Angola, Cape Verde, Mozambique, and Sao Tome and Principe in 1975.

In late 1975 a dispute arose with Indonesia regarding the status of Portuguese Timor, the country's only remaining Asian possession except for Macao. On December 8 Indonesian Foreign Minister Adam Malik announced that pro-Indonesian parties in the Portuguese (eastern) sector of the island had set up a provisional government and that Indonesian military units had occupied Dili, the capital. Portugal promptly severed diplomatic relations with Indonesia, which had also announced the annexation of Ocussi Ambeno, a small Portuguese enclave on the northern coast of West Timor. On July 17, 1976, Jakarta proclaimed the formal incorporation of the remainder of Timor into Indonesia, although the UN continued to regard Portugal as the territory's legitimate administrative power.

Lisbon's objection to Indonesian control of East Timor was again manifested in the recall of its ambassador to Australia in August 1985, after Australian Prime Minister Bob Hawke had endorsed his predecessor's acceptance of the takeover. Relations with Canberra were further strained in 1989 when Australia concluded a treaty with Indonesia providing for the division of offshore oil resources in the Timor Gap. Claiming that Indonesia's illegal occupation of East Timor rendered the treaty invalid under international law, Portugal in 1991 took the matter to the International Court of Justice (ICJ). In June 1995, however, the ICJ ruled that it had no jurisdiction on the 1989 treaty, as it was precluded from giving a ruling on the legality of Indonesia's annexation of East Timor by Indonesia's nonrecognition of the court's jurisdiction in the matter and because Indonesia was not a party to the case brought by Portugal. UN-prompted "dialogue" between the Portuguese and Indonesian foreign ministers on the East Timor question made no substantive progress in 1995, with Portugal finding little merit in an Indonesian proposal that each side should establish "interest sections" in third-country embassies in Lisbon and Jakarta. Diplomatic relations were not restored with Indonesia until late 1999, following Jakarta's acceptance of an independence referendum in East Timor, which achieved independence as the Democratic Republic of Timor-Leste on May 20, 2002.

In early 1988 Portugal called for a "thorough overhaul" of a mutual defense treaty that permitted the United States to use Lajes air base in the Azores. Although the agreement was not due to expire until 1991, it included a provision for military aid, which the U.S. Congress had sharply reduced in approving the administration's foreign assistance budget for the year. The dispute was eventually settled in January 1989, with Washington pledging to increase levels of both military and economic compensation. An agreement granting a further extension on U.S. use of the Lajes base was signed in Lisbon on June 1, 1995.

In 1989 it was agreed that regular consultative meetings of the foreign ministers of Portugal and the five lusophone African countries would be convened to promote the latter's economic development. In 1991 the six countries plus Brazil agreed upon linguistic standardization, while plans were initiated for a common television satellite channel. Further meetings of the seven Portuguese-speaking states in the early 1990s led to the formal establishment in July 1996 of the Community of Portuguese Speaking Countries (CPLP), with a total population of some 200 million Portuguese speakers (80 percent of them in Brazil). Meanwhile, Portuguese diplomacy had scored a major success in brokering the 1991 Escuril Accord between the warring factions of postindependence Angola.

The 1991 Maastricht Treaty on the economic and political union of what became the EU was ratified by the Portuguese Assembly on December 10, 1992, by a large majority. Two days later the EU's Edinburgh summit agreed to set up a "cohesion fund" for its four poorest members, of which Portugal was one. In March 1995 Portugal participated in the inauguration of the Schengen Accord, under which most EU states undertook to remove internal border controls while strengthening their external barriers to illegal immigrants and criminals.

On July 1, 2007, Prime Minister José Sócrates took the helm of the EU presidency for a six-month term, joining former prime minister José Manuel Durão Barroso, head of the European Commission, at the EU's highest levels. Portugal, long a recipient of EU development aid, has been largely supportive of further European integration and supported Germany's rejection of an effort by Poland to allow a minority of EU states to delay EU legislation against the majority's wishes. Poland ultimately backed down, and the treaty was signed at a summit held in Lisbon on December 13. Portugal traditionally has maintained close ties with its former colonies, and Sócrates scheduled an EU-African Union (AU) summit to be held in Lisbon in December 2007 with the aim of strengthening economic ties with the continent. But tensions heightened over the inclusion of Robert Mugabe, Zimbabwe's controversial president, who had drawn international condemnation for his government's record of human rights abuses, and Britain boycotted the meeting.

Relations with the United States have been friendly, as the Barroso administration vigorously supported the U.S.-led campaign in Iraq in 2003, committing troops to the overthrow of Saddam Hussein and to subsequent security and reconstruction efforts. Responding to increasing public opposition to the war in Iraq and acting on a campaign promise, newly installed Prime Minister Sócrates withdrew Portugal's 120 troops from Iraq in February 2005. Portugal nevertheless has continued to maintain close relations with the United States, especially through its strong support of NATO and participation in NATO peacekeeping efforts in Afghanistan. In March 2009 Portugal signed an agreement with the United States to install a climate observatory on the island of Graciosa in the Azores, and in June the government agreed to accept two to three detainees from the controversial U.S. prison camp at Guantánamo Bay, Cuba.

Portugal's strong ties with China were reinforced by diplomatic meetings in 2009, though a visit in June by President Hu Jintao, which was to have included the signing of several trade deals, was postponed because of ethnic conflict in parts of China.

Current issues. Since taking office in 2005, Prime Minister Sócrates has continued to focus on improving Portugal's economy through public sector reforms. Decreased pension benefits, a reduction in the number of public sector workers, and spending cuts sparked widespread criticism. Despite unanimous opposition, in November 2006 the governing PS pushed through its austerity budget for 2007, aimed at enabling Portugal to meet the EU deadline for reducing the budget deficit from 4.6 percent of GDP to 3 percent by 2008. The government exceeded its goal, shrinking the deficit to 2.6 percent of GDP, thus ensuring Portugal's standing in the euro zone. In 2008 the government broadened its reform efforts to include education, health care, and labor. In July it won a long-sought labor agreement with employer associations and one of the two main labor unions that critics claimed eroded job security.

In May 2008 the parliament approved a controversial measure standardizing the Portuguese language among the seven Portuguese-speaking countries by adopting Brazilian spelling.

In an effort to win popular support before national elections scheduled for September 27, 2009, the PS in January issued an election platform that included a 200 euro subsidy for each child born in Portugal, mirroring similar measures introduced in other European countries that, like Portugal, have experienced falling birth rates. However, voters expressed widespread discontent with the government, especially its austerity measures amid a steep recession, by ending the PS's dominance in the Portuguese delegation to the European Parliament in elections held on June 7, 2009. The opposition PSD won 8 of 22 seats, the PS won 7, and the Left Bloc won 3, marking a shift in the parties' fortunes that analysts said prefigured a tough election campaign. Preelection tensions mounted on July 2, when Finance Minister Manuel Pinho was forced to resign after insulting a Communist deputy during a parliamentary debate.

POLITICAL PARTIES

As of June 2009 Portugal had 16 registered parties, although since the 1980s it has progressed toward a largely two-party system dominated by the center-left Socialist Party (PS) and the center-right Social Democratic Party (PSD).

Governing Party:

Socialist Party (*Partido Socialista*—PS). Organized in 1973 as heir to the former Portuguese Socialist Action (*Acção Socialista Portuguesa*—ASP), the PS won a substantial plurality (38 percent) of the vote in the election of April 1975 and 35 percent a year later, remaining in power under Mário Soares until July 1978. In the December 1979 balloting the PS lost 33 of the 107 assembly seats it had won in 1976. Its representation returned to a plurality of 101 in 1983, with Soares being redesignated prime minister on June 9 and continuing in office until forced into caretaker status by withdrawal of the Social Democrats (PSD) from the government coalition in July 1985. The party won only 57 seats in the October election, although Soares succeeded in winning the state presidency in February 1986, at which time he resigned as PS secretary general.

A party congress in June approved wide-ranging changes aimed at democratizing the party's structure and deleted all references to Marxism in its Declaration of Principles, committing the organization to an "open economy where private, public, and social institutions can coexist." Despite the changes, the party's legislative strength gained only marginally (from 57 to 60 seats) in the balloting of July 16, 1987, whereas more appreciable gains (to a total of 72 seats) were recorded in the election of October 6, 1991.

Remaining in opposition, the party elected António Guterres as its leader in February 1992 and registered its best-ever national vote in December 1993 local elections. In the general election of October 1995 the PS won 112 assembly seats, with Guterres then forming a minority government. In 1996 the PS's Jorge Sampaio captured the national presidency with a majority in the first round. In the October 1999 legislative election the PS fell just short of a legislative majority, winning 115 seats in the 230-seat chamber. President Sampaio continued the party's string of successes in January 2001, easily winning reelection. However, the PS did poorly in the December 2001 municipal elections, setting the stage for Guterres's resignation as prime minister and the PS's fall from national power in 2002. Eduardo FERRO RODRIGUES, a former minister in Guterres's 1995 cabinet, was elected in January to succeed Guterres as PS secretary general and thereby the party's candidate for prime minister. However, Rodrigues resigned the leadership in July 2004 to protest President Sampaio's decision not to call early elections following the resignation of Prime Minister Barroso. Former environment minister José Sócrates was elected as the new PS leader in late 2004, and, having attempted to move the PS "to the center," he led the party to a resounding legislative victory in February 2005.

In September 2005 Manuel ALEGRE, a member of the assembly who had lost the race for party leader to Sócrates in 2004, announced that he would seek the presidency in 2006, even though the official Socialist endorsement had gone to 81-year-old former president Soares. At the January 2006 polls Alegre finished second, with 20.7 percent of the vote, while Soares came in third, with 14.3 percent.

While in power, the PS has focused on improving economic efficiency, especially through labor market reforms, spending cuts, and a reduction in public sector employment. Despite pervasive public discontent over austerity measures that have been slow to yield tangible results, the PS led in polls ahead of the October 2009 legislative elections. However, the party's loss of five seats in the European Parliament in the June 2009 election suggested a narrowing of that support.

Leaders: António de Almeida SANTOS (President), Jorge SAMPAIO (Former President of the Republic), António GUTERRES (UN High Commissioner for Refugees and Former Prime Minister), Alberto MARTINS (Parliamentary Leader), José SÓCRATES (Prime Minister and Secretary General of the Party).

Other Legislative Parties:

Social Democratic Party (*Partido Social Democrata*—PSD). The PSD was founded in 1974 as the Popular Democratic Party (*Partido Popular Democrático*—PPD), under which name it won 26 percent of the vote for the Constituent Assembly on April 25, 1975, and 24 percent in the Assembly of the Republic election a year later. Although it initially advocated a number of left-of-center policies, including the nationalization of key sectors of the economy, a number of leftists withdrew in 1976, and the remainder of the party moved noticeably to the right.

An April 1979 disagreement over leadership opposition to the Socialist government's proposed budget led to a walkout of 40 PSD deputies prior to a final assembly vote. Shortly thereafter, 37 of the 73 PSD deputies withdrew and announced that they would sit in the assembly as the Association of Independent Social Democrats (*Associação dos Sociais Democratas Independentes*—ASDI). The party's losses were more than recouped in the December election, however, when the PSD-led Alliance won a three-seat majority, as a result of which the party president, Francisco Sá Carneiro, was named prime minister. Francisco Pinto Balsemão was designated party leader in December 1980, following Sá Carneiro's death, and became prime minister in January 1981.

In early 1983 Balsemão announced that he would not stand for another term as party leader, and, following the formal designation of a three-member leadership at a party congress in late February, he was effectively succeeded by Carlos Mota Pinto. The party was runner-up to the PS at the April election, winning 75 assembly seats. In June 1985 Aníbal Cavaco Silva, who had succeeded Mota Pinto as PSD leader the month before, led a withdrawal from the ruling coalition and formed a minority government after the party had gained a slim plurality in legislative balloting in October. Defeated in a censure vote in April 1987, the PSD became the first party since 1974 to win an absolute majority of seats in the ensuing legislative poll in July. It retained control with a slightly reduced majority of 135 of 230 seats in 1991. A subsequent slide in the PSD's standing, including losses at the 1994 election for the European Parliament, compelled Cavaco Silva to vacate the party leadership in January 1995. At the same time, he hoped to position himself for a presidential challenge.

Under the new leadership of Joaquim Fernando NOGUEIRA, the party went down to an expected defeat in the October 1995 general election, retaining only 88 seats on a 34 percent vote share. In the January 1996 presidential balloting, moreover, Cavaco Silva was defeated by the Socialist candidate in the first round. The party's response at the end of March was to elect as its new leader Marcelo REBELO DE SOUSA, a media personality on the party's liberal wing who had not held ministerial office during the period of PSD rule.

In early 1998 the PSD and CDS-PP (below) formed an electoral alliance, styled the Democratic Alliance (*Aliança Democrática*—AD), with the stated aim of presenting a single list for the upcoming European Parliament and national legislative elections. The AD Pact was formally ratified in February 1999; however, it collapsed the following month, and immediately thereafter Rebelo de Sousa resigned as leader of the PSD. His successor, José Manuel Durão Barroso, a former foreign affairs minister, led the party into the October 1999 election, but the PSD lost 7 of its 88 seats. In 2001 it failed to unseat President Sampaio, with its candidate, Joaquim Martins Ferreira do Amaral, finishing a distant second (34.5 percent of the vote).

Barroso was named prime minister following the March 2002 legislative balloting, at which the PSD won a plurality of 105 seats. He resigned as prime minister in July 2004 to become president of the European Commission. Pedro Santana Lopes succeeded Barroso as prime minister until the February 2005 legislative poll, in which the PSD fell to 75 seats. Santana Lopes resigned as PSD leader in April. In the 2006 presidential contest former prime minister Cavaco Silva won 50.6 percent of the vote, just enough to avoid a runoff. In October 2007 the party chose member of parliament Luís Filipe Menezes, a vocal critic of the government's austerity measures, to lead the PSD. Unable to mount a strong challenge to the government, Menezes resigned seven months later and was succeeded by former finance minister Manuela Ferreira Leite on May 31, 2008.

The PSD's gain of one seat in the European Parliament in June 2009 placed it slightly ahead of the PS in that body and gave the PSD a boost in anticipation of the September legislative election. It was uncertain what impact Barroso's campaign for a second term as president of the European Commission would have on the PSD's electoral fortunes, as his free-market positions came under fire during the deepening recession.

Leaders: Aníbal CAVACO SILVA (President of the Republic), Manuela Ferreira LEITE (Chair), Paulo Castro RANGEL (Parliamentary Leader), Pedro SANTANA LOPES (Former Prime Minister), José Manuel Durão BARROSO (European Commission President and Former Prime Minister).

Unified Democratic Coalition (*Coligação Democrática Unitária*—CDU). Prior to the 1979 election the Portuguese Communist Party (PCP, below) joined with the Popular Democratic Movement (*Movimento Democrático Popular*—MDP) in an electoral coalition known as the United People's Alliance (*Aliança Povo Unido*—APU). The APU won 47 legislative seats in 1979, 41 in 1980, and 38 in 1985, its constituent formations having campaigned separately in 1983. In the 1986 presidential race, the party formally endorsed the independent Maria de Lourdes Pintasilgo, with some dissidents supporting Francisco Salgado ZENHA of the now-defunct Democratic Renewal Party (*Partido Renovador Democrático*—PRD); following the elimination of both from the runoff, a special Communist Party congress on February 2, 1986, urged Alliance supporters to "hold their nose, ignore the photograph," and vote for Soares.

Apparently disturbed by allegations that it was merely a PCP front, the MDP withdrew from the Alliance in November 1986. The APU was thereupon dissolved in favor of the CDU, which embraced the PCP; a group of MDP dissidents calling themselves Democratic Intervention (*Intervenção Democrática*—ID), which effectively superseded the MDP; an environmentalist formation, The Greens (*Os Verdes*); and a number of independent leftists. The new group obtained 31 assembly seats in 1987, 7 fewer than the APU in 1985. In October 1991, having lauded the attempted hard-line coup in the Soviet Union two months earlier, the CDU's legislative representation was further reduced to 17. It slipped to 8.6 percent and 15 seats in the October 1995 legislative election but then added 2 more in 1999, when it won 9 percent of the vote. The coalition lost 2 seats in 2005, holding 14 after the elections.

Portuguese Communist Party (*Partido Comunista Português*—PCP). Founded in 1921 and historically one of the most Stalinist of the West European Communist parties, the PCP was the dominant force within both the military and the government in the year following the 1974 coup. Its influence waned during the latter half of 1975, particularly following the abortive rebellion of November 26, and its legislative strength dropped to fourth place in April 1976, prior to organization of the APU. The party made limited concessions to Soviet-style liberalization at its 12th congress in December 1988 by endorsing freedom of the press and multiparty politics. At a special congress called in May 1990, however, the PCP returned to a basically hard-line posture, although it adopted an initially accommodating attitude to the Socialist minority government that took office in October 1995. It enjoys widespread support in rural and industrial areas.

In the 1999 assembly election the PCP won 15 of the CDU's 17 seats. Its 2001 presidential candidate, António SIMÕES DE ABREU, finished third, with only 5 percent of the vote. In 2005 the party's assembly representation dropped to 12 (and later to 11 when a PCP delegate became unaffiliated in November 2007).

In 2006 presidential candidate Jerónimo Carvalho De Sousa finished fourth, with 8.6 percent of the vote.

Leaders: Albano NUNES, Bernardino SOARES (Parliamentary Leader), Carlos CARVALHAS, Jerónimo Carvalho DE SOUSA (General Secretary and 2006 presidential candidate).

Ecologist Party "The Greens" (*Partido Ecologista "Os Verdes"*—PEV). The PEV began in 1982 as the Portuguese Ecologist Movement—"The Greens" Party (*Movimento Ecologista Português—Partido "Os Verdes"*). In the October 1999 election the party won two of the CDU's legislative seats. The PEV subsequently was described as having shifted its emphasis from purely Portuguese environmental issues to broader European concerns.

In the 2005 legislative election the PEV again won two seats.

Leader: Heloísa APOLÓNIA (Parliamentary Leader).

Social Democratic Center–Popular Party (*Centro Democrático Social–Partido Popular*—CDS-PP). This right-of-center Christian democratic party was founded in 1974 as the CDS. The name was changed to the CDS-PP in 1993. The party is strongest in the northern part of the country, and a number of its members were named to key government posts following the 1979 and 1980 legislative elections. Despite the party's having lost 8 of 30 assembly seats in the October 1985 election, its presidential candidate, Diogo Freitas do Amaral, won 46 percent of the vote in first-round presidential balloting in January 1986, but he lost to former prime minister Soares (PS) in the runoff. Freitas do Amaral resigned the CDS presidency after the 1991 election, in which the party won only 5 assembly seats. Standing on an anti-EU platform, the CDS-PP gained ground in the October 1995 national election, winning 15 seats on a vote share of 9.1 percent.

Despite having repulsed a leadership challenge by Paulo Portas, Manuel MONTEIRO resigned as CDS-PP president in September 1996 in protest against internal party feuding. He subsequently agreed to return as president, although he announced he would not run again in the party congress scheduled for March 1998. As promised, Monteiro left his party post in March, and in subsequent intraparty balloting Portas finally secured the presidency. A principal architect of the 1998 PSD/CDS-PP electoral alliance, Portas nevertheless quickly grew disenchanted with the PSD leadership, and, just prior to the AD's dissolution, the PSD's Rebelo de Sousa accused Portas of publicizing confidential information. Despite a reduced vote share of 8.3 percent, the party retained its 15 assembly seats at the October 1999 election. In 2001 it endorsed President Sampaio for reelection.

Portas resigned as the CDS-PP leader in April 2005, two months after the party won only 12 assembly seats, but he regained the leadership in April 2007. The CDS-PP presence in the assembly dropped to 11 after a party member joined an unaffiliated group on December 17, 2008.

Leaders: Paulo PORTAS (President), Diogo FEIO (Parliamentary Leader), João ALMEIDA (General Secretary).

Left Bloc (*Bloco de Esquerda*—BE). The BE held its first national convention in February 1999. The alliance included the socialist **Politics XXI** (*Politica XXI*), the Trotskyite **Revolutionary Left Front** (*Frente da Esquerda Revolucionária*—FER), the Marxist-Leninist **Popular Democratic Union** (*União Democrática Popular*—UDP), and the small Trotskyite **Revolutionary Socialist Party** (*Partido Socialista Revolucionário*—PSR). The BE won 2.4 percent of the vote and two seats in the general election of October 1999. Its 2001 presidential contender, Fernando ROSAS, won 3 percent. The BE, which presents itself as a mainstream, progressive alternative to the PCP, lost two of its constituent parties with the November 2005 dissolution of the UDP and FER.

BE leader Francisco LOUÇÃ, one of six candidates in the 2006 presidential election, came in fifth with 5.3 percent of the vote. The BE tripled its presence in the Portuguese delegation to the European Parliament in the June 2009 election to that body, from 1 to 3 seats, a result that analysts attributed to public frustration over the government's austerity measures.

Leaders: Francisco LOUÇÃ (Leader of the PSR and 2006 presidential candidate), Luís FAZENDA (General Secretary and Parliamentary Leader).

Other Parties that Participated in the 2005 Elections:

Parties that contested the February 2005 assembly balloting but failed to win a seat included the **Portuguese Workers' Communist Party/Reorganizative Movement of the Party of the Proletariat** (*Partido Comunista dos Trabalhadores Portugueses/Movimento Reorganizativo do Partido do Proletariado*—PCTP/MRPP), a Maoist party led by Garcia PEREIRA; the **New Democracy Party** (*Partido da Nova Democracia*—PND), a conservative party founded in 2003 by its current leader, former CDS-PP president Manuel Monteiro; the center-left **Humanist Party** (*Partido Humanista*—PH), led by Luís Filipe GUERRA; the neo-fascist **National Renewal Party** (*Partido Nacional Renovador*—PNR), led by José PINTO-COELHO; the Trotskyite **United Socialist Workers' Party** (*Partido Operário de Unidade Socialista*—POUS), formed in 1976 and led by Aniceto BARBOSA; and the **Atlantic Democratic Party** (*Partido Democrático do Atlântico*—PDA), a grouping based in the Azores and the Madeira Islands and led by José VENTURA.

The small **People's Monarchist Party** (*Partido Popular Monárquico*—PPM), founded in 1974, has two members in the national assembly, elected on the PSD's lists, but has not won seats on its own in that body since the 1981 dissolution of the Democratic Alliance, to which it belonged. The green **Earth Party** (*Partido da Terra*—MPT), founded in 1993, also has two members in the assembly, elected on the PSD's lists.

Other Parties:

In September 2007 university professor Eduardo CORREIA founded a new centrist party, the **Merit and Society Movement** (*Movimento Mérito e Sociedade*—MMS). The party was recognized in May 2008 by the Constitutional Tribunal. The MMS advocates compulsory voting in legislative elections.

Another new centrist party, the **Hope for Portugal Movement** (*Movimento Esperança Portugal*—MEP), founded by businessman Rui MARQUES, was recognized by the Constitutional Tribunal in July 2008.

LEGISLATURE

The unicameral **Assembly of the Republic** (*Assembleia da República*) consists of 230 members elected for four-year terms (subject to dissolution) via proportional representation. (Four seats are elected by Portuguese living abroad.)

In the most recent balloting on February 20, 2005, the seat distribution was as follows: the Socialist Party, 121 seats; Social Democratic Party, 75; Unified Democratic Coalition, 14 (Portuguese Communist Party, 12; Ecologist Party "The Greens," 2); Social Democratic Center–Popular Party, 12; and Left Bloc, 8. (One Portuguese Communist Party member and one Social Democratic Center–Popular Party member have since broken away from their respective party groups to form an unaffiliated group.) The next election was scheduled for September 27, 2009. *(See headnote.)*

President: Jaime GAMA.

CABINET

[as of August 1, 2009] *(see headnote)*

Prime Minister	José Sócrates
Ministers	
Agriculture, Rural Development, and Fisheries	Jaime Silva
Culture	José António Pinto Ribeiro
Education	Maria de Lurdes Rodrigues [f]
Environment, Territorial Planning, and Regional Development	Francisco Nunes Correia
Finance and Economy and Innovation	Fernando Teixeira dos Santos
Foreign Affairs	Luís Amado
Health	Ana Maria Teodoro Jorge [f]
Interior	Rui Pereira
Justice	Alberto Costa
Labor and Social Solidarity	José António Vieira da Silva
National Defense	Nuno Severiano Teixeira
Parliamentary Affairs	Augusto Santos Silva
Presidency	Pedro Silva Pereira
Public Works, Transport, and Communications	Mário Lino
Science, Technology, and Higher Education	José Mariano Gago

[f] = female

Note: All cabinet ministers belong to the PS.

COMMUNICATIONS

Portugal's constitution guarantees freedom of the press and free speech. All newspapers are privately owned.

Press. The following newspapers are published daily in Lisbon, unless otherwise noted: *Expresso* (160,000), influential center-left weekly; *Jornal de Notícias* (Porto, 90,000), centrist; *Correio da Manhã* (85,000), centrist; *O Público* (Lisbon and Porto, 75,000), centrist; *Diário Popular* (70,000); *Jornal de O Dia* (50,000), rightist; *Diário de Notícias* (42,000), centrist; *A Capital* (40,000); *O Primeiro de Janeiro* (Porto, 32,000), centrist; *O Comércio do Porto* (Porto 30,000), rightist; *Portugal News*, *The Resident*, and *Get Real* (English language weeklies).

News agencies. The leading facility is *Agência Lusa de Informação,* formed in 1987 by merger of *Agência Noticiosa Portuguesa* (Anop) and *Notícias de Portugal* (NP); other domestic services include *Agência Europeia de Imprensa* (AEI) and *Agência de Representações Dias da Silva* (ADS). Numerous foreign agencies also maintain bureaus in Lisbon.

Broadcasting and computing. In December 1975 the government issued decrees nationalizing television, which had been only partly state owned, in addition to most major radio stations except *Rádio Renascença,* which was owned and operated by the Catholic Church under a 1940 concordat between Portugal and the Vatican. Substantial reprivatization subsequently resulted in a large number of privately owned stations, with remaining state-run radio facilities being controlled by *Radiodifusão Portuguesa* (RDP). Television broadcasting is dominated by the state-owned *Radiotelevisão Portuguesa* (RTP), which has two channels, although by mid-1994 two independent stations (*SIC* and *TVI*) had begun operations. As of 2008 there were 419.2 Internet users per 1,000 inhabitants.

INTERGOVERNMENTAL REPRESENTATION

Ambassador to the U.S.: João de VALLERA.

U.S. Ambassador to Portugal: (Vacant).

Permanent Representative to the UN: José Filipe MORAES CABRAL.

IGO Memberships (Non-UN): ADB, AfDB, BIS, CERN, CEUR, CPLP, EBRD, EIB, ESA, EU, Eurocontrol, IADB, IEA, Interpol, IOM, NATO, OECD, OSCE, PCA, WCO, WEU, WTO.

RELATED TERRITORIES

The Azores and the Madeira Islands have long been construed as insular components of metropolitan Portugal and, as such, were legally distinct from a group of Portuguese possessions whose status was changed in 1951 from that of "Colonies" to "Overseas Territories." Of the latter, the South Asian enclaves of Goa, Damão, and Diu were annexed by India in 1961; Portuguese Guinea became independent as Guinea-Bissau in 1974; and Angola, the Cape Verde Islands, Mozambique, and Sao Tome and Príncipe became independent in 1975. Portuguese Timor (East Timor) was annexed by Indonesia on July 17, 1976, but the action was never recognized by Portugal, and diplomatic relations with Jakarta were not restored until late 1999, after the Indonesian government had accepted the results of the August 1999 independence referendum in East Timor (now Timor-Leste). Macao, which had been defined as a "collective entity" (*pessoa colectiva*) under a governing statute promulgated on February 17, 1976, reverted to Chinese sovereignty in 1999 (see China article). Under the 1976 constitution, the Azores and Madeira are defined as autonomous regions.

Azores (*Açores*). The Azores comprise three distinct groups of islands located in the Atlantic Ocean about 800 miles west of mainland Portugal. The most easterly of the islands are São Miguel and Santa Maria; the most westerly and least densely populated are Corvo and Flores; Fayal, Graciosa, Pico, São Jorge, and Terceira are in the center. There are three political districts, the capitals and chief seaports of which are Ponta Delgada (São Miguel), Horta (Fayal), and Angra do Heroísmo (Terceira). The islands' total area is 890 square miles (2,305 sq. km.), and their resident population (2006E) is 244,100.

Following the 1974 coup, significant separatist sentiment emerged, particularly on Terceira, whose residents feared that the left-wing government at Lisbon might close the U.S. military base at Lajes. In August 1975 a recently organized **Azorean Liberation Front** (*Frente de Libertação dos Açores*—FLA) announced its opposition to continued rule from the mainland. Following the resignation of three appointed governors, the Portuguese government surrendered control of the islands' internal administration to local political leaders and in April 1976 provided for an elected Regional Assembly.

In March 1991 FLA leader José de ALMEIDA was acquitted of treason charges on the grounds that there was insufficient evidence of his having incited others to violence. In assembly balloting on October 11, 1992, the Social Democratic Party (PSD) regained its majority, winning 28 of 51 seats. The PSD and the Socialist Party (PS) each won 24 seats in the October 3, 1996, balloting, with the Popular Party (PP) gaining 2 seats and the Portuguese Communist Party (PCP), 1. In the election of October 15, 2000, the PS claimed a majority of 30 seats, while the PSD dropped to 18. The PP and the Unitary Democratic Coalition (the PCP and the Greens) each won 2 seats. The PS advanced to 44 of 52 seats in the assembly balloting of October 17, 2004. Three PS candidates and two PS candidates from the Azores won seats in the National Assembly in the February 2005 Portuguese election.

In October 2008 balloting the PS kept its majority in the assembly, winning 30 of 57 seats, followed by the PSD with 18; the CDS-PP, 5; the Left Bloc, 2; the PCP-PEV, 1; and the PPM, 1.

President of the Regional Government: Carlos Manuel Martins do Vale CÉSAR (PS).

Representative of the Republic: José António MESQUITA.

Madeira Islands (*Ilhas da Madeira*). The Madeira Islands consist of Madeira and Porto Santo islands and the uninhabited islets of Desertas and Salvages. Lying west of Casablanca, Morocco, some 500 miles southwest of the Portuguese mainland, they have a total area of 308 square miles (797 sq. km.) and a resident population (2006E) of 240,000. The capital is Funchal, on Madeira Island.

As in the case of the Azores, separatist sentiment exists, the **Madeira Archipelago Liberation Front** (*Frente de Libertação de Arquipélago da Madeira*—FLAM), which advocated independence from Portugal and possible federation with the Azores and the Spanish Canaries, claiming on August 29, 1975, to have established a provisional government. However, both the government that was installed on October 1, 1976, and the elected Regional Assembly that was convened on October 23 were pledged to maintain ties to the mainland.

In balloting on October 15, 2000, the Social Democratic Party (PSD) won its seventh regional election in a row, claiming 41 of the 61 seats in the assembly. The Socialist Party (PS) won only 13 seats and the Popular Party (PP), 3. Alberto João Jardim of the PSD has served as regional president for nearly a quarter of a century. The PSD won 44 of 68 assembly seats in balloting on October 17, 2004. In the February 2005 Portuguese election, three PS and three PS candidates from the Madeira Islands won seats in the National Assembly.

On Feb. 19, 2007, President Jardim resigned to protest a new, government-supported law on regional financing that would reduce aid levels from the central government to Madeira. The resignation prompted early elections on May 6, which Jardim won easily. The government rejected his call to rescind the law, but a court ruling in September forced it to do so.

Jardim presided over an Oct. 4–5, 2007, conference of presidents of the EU's "outermost regions," which include four French overseas departments (Guadeloupe, French Guiana, Martinique, and Réunion), the Spanish autonomous community of the Canary Islands, as well as Madeira and the Azores. In addition to aid for agriculture and rural development, the meeting addressed rising sea levels and other challenges posed by climate change.

President of the Regional Government: Alberto João JARDIM (PSD).

Representative of the Republic: Antero Alves MONTEIRO DINIZ.

QATAR

State of Qatar
Dawlat al-Qatar

Political Status: Traditional sheikhdom; proclaimed fully independent September 1, 1971; first permanent constitution, approved in referendum of April 29, 2003, went into effect on June 8, 2004.

Area: 4,247 sq. mi. (11,000 sq. km.).

Population: 744,029 (2004C); 958,000 (2008E), including nonnationals, who constitute more than two-thirds of the resident population.

Major Urban Centers (2005E): DOHA (al-Dawhah, 353,000), Rayyan (276,000).

Official Language: Arabic.

Monetary Unit: Qatar Riyal (official rate December 1, 2009: 3.64 riyals = $1US).

Sovereign (Emir): Sheikh Hamad ibn Khalifa Al THANI; assumed supreme power June 27, 1995, deposing his father Sheikh Khalifaibn Hamad Al THANI; also served as prime minister July 11, 1995–October 28, 1996.

Heir to the Throne: Crown Prince Sheikh Tamin ibn Hamad Al THANI, designated August 5, 2003, replacing his brother, Sheikh Jassim ibn Hamad Al THANI.

Prime Minister: Sheikh Hamad ibn Jasim ibn Jabir Al THANI, appointed by the emir on April 3, 2007, replacing Sheikh Abdallah ibn Khalifa Al THANI, who had resigned the same day.

THE COUNTRY

A flat, barren, peninsular projection into the Persian Gulf from the Saudi Arabian mainland, Qatar consists largely of sand and rock. The climate is quite warm with very little rainfall, and the lack of fresh water has led to a reliance on desalination techniques. The population is almost entirely Arab, but indigenous Qataris (mainly Sunni Muslims of the conservative Wahhabi sect) comprise substantially less than a majority, as thousands have flocked from abroad to cash in on Qatar's booming economy; the nonindigenous groups include Pakistanis, Iranians, Indians, and Palestinians. The percentage of women in the workforce grew substantially in the 1990s, and religious and governmental strictures upon women are less severe than in most other Gulf states. However, most women continue to wear veils in public, accept arranged marriages, and generally defer to the wishes of the male members of their families. Qatari culture as a whole continues to reflect the long history of "feudal tribal autocracy" and the "puritanical" (in the eyes of many Western observers) nature of Wahhabism, which is also practiced in Saudi Arabia, Qatar's influential neighbor.

The economy remains largely dependent upon revenue from oil, which has been produced for export since 1949 and under local production and marketing control since 1977. During the oil boom years of the 1970s, Qatar became one of the world's wealthiest nations. The sheikhdom was therefore able to develop a modern infrastructure, emphasizing schools, hospitals, roads, communication facilities, and water and electric plants. As a result of declining oil prices in the mid-1980s and a downturn in the economy, government investment also plummeted, leaving some projects unimplemented or incomplete. However, discoveries in oil-recovery techniques, along with soaring oil prices, have since propelled the economy, although Qatar only produces a fraction of the oil output of the Organization of the Petroleum Exporting Countries (OPEC).

Qatar is also home to the world's third-largest reserves of liquid natural gas. As domestic supplies dwindle elsewhere, other industrialized countries are poised to invest in Qatar's developing natural gas sector. The government has invested heavily in projects designed to exploit that resource. Attention has also focused on the development of new small- and medium-scale industries under joint public-private ownership. The government recently established a Qatari stock exchange partly to facilitate that process and rewrote investment laws to encourage foreign investment. In early 2005 Qatar was named the most competitive Arab economy by the World Economic Forum. Investments in new projects totaling more than $60 billion indicated growing confidence in the economy, with much of the revenue going to improve Qatar's infrastructure. Annual GDP growth averaged about 11 percent from 2004–2007, bolstered by the soaring price of crude oil.

The Qatari government has continued to emphasize diversification, announcing plans in 2008 to transform Qatar's economy from one based on oil production to one "that has knowledge as its mainstay." It has invested heavily in education, including Doha's multibillion-dollar Education City, which incorporates branches of five U.S. universities, as well as in the tourism and health sectors. The financial forecast remained positive, despite high inflation. Annual GDP growth of 16.4 percent was recorded for 2008–2009, driven by a significant expansion in the production of liquefied natural gas. The global economic downturn had less impact on the banking system in Qatar compared to other countries, according to the International Monetary Fund (IMF), and the economic forecast for 2010 remained positive.

GOVERNMENT AND POLITICS

Political background. Qatar was dominated by Bahrain until 1868 and by the Ottoman Turks from 1878 through World War I, until it entered into treaty relations with Great Britain in 1916. Under the treaty, Qatar stipulated that it would not conclude agreements with other foreign governments without British consent; in return, Britain agreed to provide for the defense of the sheikhdom. When the British government announced in 1968 that it intended to withdraw from the Persian Gulf by 1971, Qatar attempted to associate itself with Bahrain and the Trucial Sheikhdoms in a Federation of Arab Emirates. Qatar declared independence when it became apparent that agreement on the structure of the proposed federation could not be obtained; its independence was realized in 1971.

The new state was governed initially by Sheikh Ahmad ibn Ali ibn Abdallah Al THANI, who proved to be an inattentive sovereign. In February 1972 his cousin, Prime Minister Sheikh Khalifa ibn Hamad Al THANI, deposed Sheikh Ahmad in a bloodless coup approved by the royal family. Although modernist elements subsequently emerged, the sheikhdom remained a virtually absolute monarch with close relatives of the emir occupying senior government posts.

In May 1989 Sheikh Hamad ibn Khalifa Al THANI, the emir's heir apparent, was named head of the newly formed Supreme Council for Planning, which was commissioned to oversee Qatar's resource development projects. The government's economic efforts gained additional momentum on July 18 when the first cabinet reshuffling since 1978 resulted in the replacement of seven elderly ministers.

Like its Arab neighbors, Qatar faced international and domestic pressure for political reform following the 1990–1991 Gulf crisis, which focused Western attention on the dearth of democratic institutions in the region. The issue came to a head in early 1992 when 50 prominent Qataris expressed "concern and disappointment" over the ruling family's "abuse of power" and called for economic and educational reform, ultimately demanding the abolition of the Consultative Council in favor of a true legislative body. However, the government responded harshly to the criticism and briefly detained some of the petitioners, effectively muting the debate over democratization. On the other hand, reformists considered it a hopeful sign that the new cabinet, announced September 1, 1992, included men who were not members of the royal family in several key ministerial positions.

Though Qataris liked Sheikh Khalifa on a personal level, they reportedly believed he was allowing Qatar to slip behind other Gulf countries in economic and political progress. They expressed little dissent when Sheikh Hamad deposed his father on June 27, 1995, while the emir was on a private visit to Switzerland. Sheikh Hamad consolidated his authority and reorganized the cabinet on July 11, naming himself as prime minister and defense minister. (Sheikh Khalifa, who now resides in Europe, returned to Qatar on October 14, 2004, to attend his wife's funeral. It was his first visit to Qatar since he was deposed in the 1995 palace coup.)

In February 1996 the government announced that it had uncovered a coup plot, and those arrested reportedly included army and police

officers. Although Sheikh Khalifa strongly denied any involvement in the alleged plot, he argued that it indicated popular support for his reinstatement. The government concluded an out-of-court financial settlement with Sheikh Khalifa in October 1996, which permitted Sheikh Hamad to establish a sense of permanence to his reign and facilitated an at least partial reconciliation between father and son. In November 1997 some 110 people, including many military officers, were tried for alleged participation in the February 1996 coup attempt. While 85 of the defendants were acquitted in February 2000, about 30 were convicted and received sentences of either life in prison or death. An appeals court upheld their sentences in May 2001. Meanwhile, Sheikh Hamad had gained broader support from the populace and continued to promote his liberalized administration as a potential model for other countries in the region where long-standing regimes have resisted political and economic reform.

On October 22, 1996, Sheikh Hamad appointed his third son, Sheikh Jassim ibn Hamad Al THANI, as crown prince and his heir apparent. Six days later the emir appointed his younger brother, Sheikh Abdallah ibn Khalifa AL THANI, as prime minister to the government named on October 20, which included a number of younger ministers.

On March 8, 1999, the nation's first elections were held for the transitional Consultative Central Municipal Council, which the government established to introduce representative popular elections in the country. In July a committee newly appointed by the emir held its first meeting to draft a constitution that would ultimately provide for a popularly elected legislature.

In 2002 Qatar established a national human rights committee.

The crown prince relinquished his position on August 5, 2003, to his younger brother, Sheikh Tamin ibn Hamad Al THANI. In September the emir conferred the title of deputy prime minister upon two of his ministers, and the new crown prince also was named commander in chief of the armed forces. Sheikh Hamad also appointed the first woman to the Qatari cabinet, Sheikha Ahmad al-MAHMUD, in 2003 (see Cabinet, below).

The new constitution was overwhelmingly approved by voters (96.6 percent) in a national referendum on April 29, 2003, and promulgated on June 8, 2004 (see Constitution, below).

In April 2005 the emir fired two ministers and his chief of staff, reportedly because of their alleged involvement in investment fraud.

Sheikh Abdallah ibn Khalifa Al Thani resigned as prime minister on April 3, 2007, and was replaced the same day by Sheikh Hamad ibn Jasim ibn Jabir Al Thani. The new prime minister was sworn in along with a reshuffled cabinet on April 3.

The cabinet was enlarged and reshuffled on July 2, 2008, with a second woman named to a ministerial post.

Constitution and government. Qatar employs traditional patterns of authority, onto which a limited number of modern governmental institutions have been grafted. The provisional constitution of 1970 provided for a Council of Ministers, headed by an appointed prime minister, and an Advisory Council (Consultative Council) of 20 (subsequently 35) members. Three of the Advisory Council members were to be appointed and the rest elected, although national elections were not held. The judicial system embraces five secular courts (two criminal as well as civil, labor, and appeal) and religious courts, which apply Islamic law (sharia).

In November 1998 Sheikh Hamad announced that a constitutional committee would draft a new permanent basic law, one that should provide for a directly elected National Assembly to replace the Consultative Council. The emir announced that all Qataris over 18, including women, would be permitted to vote, while those over 25, also including women, would be allowed to run for the new legislative body. The new constitution, promulgated on June 8, 2004, after gaining approval in a national referendum in 2003, identifies Islam as the state religion. However, officials say Islamic law only "inspires" the new charter and is not the only source for its content. Under the new charter, the emir retains executive powers, including control over general policy and the appointment of a prime minister and cabinet. The new constitution also states that 30 of 45 members of the Consultative Council will be elected, the remainder appointed by the emir. (No elections had been scheduled as of 2008.)

Foreign relations. Until 1971 Qatar's foreign relations were administered by Britain. Since reaching independence it has pursued a policy of nonalignment in foreign affairs as a member of the United Nations (UN), the Arab League, and the Organization of Petroleum Exporting Countries (OPEC).

In 1981 Qatar joined with five other Gulf states (Bahrain, Kuwait, Oman, Saudi Arabia, and the United Arab Emirates) in establishing the Gulf Cooperation Council (GCC) and has since participated in joint military maneuvers and the formation of economic cooperation agreements. However, territorial disputes between Qatar and its neighbors have sporadically threatened GCC unity. In April 1986 fighting nearly erupted between Qatari and Bahraini troops over a small, uninhabited island, Fasht al-Dibal, that Bahrain had reclaimed from an underlying coral reef. Although Qatar subsequently acquiesced to temporary Bahraini control of the island, sovereignty remained in question. In mid-1991 Qatar asked the International Court of Justice (ICJ) to rule on Fasht al-Dibal as well as several other Bahraini-controlled islands of contested ownership. In 1997 GCC mediation produced an apparent truce under which Qatar and Bahrain agreed to open embassies in each other's capitals and await the ICJ ruling. Ultimately, in 2001 the ICJ awarded the disputed islands to Bahrain while reaffirming Qatar's sovereignty over the town of Zubara and its surrounding territory (which Bahrain had claimed as part of the case). Relations between the two countries have warmed, and in 2006 they signed a deal to begin construction of a causeway connecting them.

Another long-simmering dispute erupted in violence in late September 1992 when two Qatari border guards were killed in a confrontation along the border with Saudi Arabia. Saudi leaders dismissed the incident as an inconsequential clash among Bedouin tribes, but Qatar reacted with surprising hostility, boycotting several GCC ministerial sessions over the issue and reportedly threatening to quit the organization altogether. After years of negotiations, Qatar accepted Saudi Arabia's demands and a final agreement on land and sea border demarcation was signed in June 1999.

The sheikhdom denounced the August 1990 Iraqi invasion of Kuwait and responded further by offering its territory as a base for allied forces, expelling PLO representatives, and taking part in joint military exercises. At the GCC's December summit Qatar supported the "Doha Declaration," which called for a plan to prevent a repetition of Iraqi aggression, the departure of "friendly" forces upon the resolution of the crisis, and an Iranian role in security arrangements. In early 1991, Qatari forces (composed primarily of foreigners) participated in allied air and ground actions. Qatar remained closely aligned with the other GCC states on most security issues following the war and signed a defense agreement with the United States in June 1992 in the wake of similar U.S. pacts with Bahrain and Kuwait.

At the same time, Qatar distanced itself from the GCC majority by calling for improved relations with Iran as a means of promoting regional stability. In May 1992 Doha signed a number of agreements with Tehran (covering such matters as air traffic, customs procedure, and the possibility of supplying the sheikhdom with fresh water via a trans-Gulf pipeline); Qatar's good relations with Iran continue, with Doha calling for peaceful negotiations to resolve the Iranian nuclear issue.

Qatar has also adopted a more lenient posture than most of its GCC partners regarding Iraq. In early 1995 it called for the lifting of UN sanctions against Iraq, for humanitarian reasons. However, in the wake of the brief crisis generated by the massing of Iraqi troops near the Kuwaiti border in October 1994, Doha agreed to let the U.S. permanently store its armor in Qatar.

Qatar has recently become an important American ally in the Middle East. In mid-2000 the United States financed and built a massive staging area for its ground troops in eastern Qatar, which later became the U.S. Central Command site in the 2003 invasion of Iraq.

On another front, Qatar has faced troubled relations with Russia, dating to 1999, when Qatar harbored an exiled Chechen rebel leader. Two members of the Russian secret service were sentenced to life in prison in Qatar in 2004 for assassinating the Chechen exile. Russia denied any involvement but later detained two Qatari sports officials passing through the country. Qatar then retaliated by expelling a Russian diplomat.

On the second anniversary of the U.S.-Iraqi invasion in March 2005, a car bomb exploded in a Qatari theater frequented by Westerners. It was the first incident of its kind in Qatar; an Egyptian expatriate, allegedly linked to al-Qaida, was later blamed in the attack.

Qatar made efforts "to bring Israel into the Gulf" as a contribution to the Middle East peace process, despite contrary sentiments in the region. For example, Arab neighbors "forced" Qatar to close an Israeli trade office in 2000, but reports persisted that the office is still staffed. In May 2005 Israel agreed to Qatar's unprecedented request for support of Doha's candidacy for a rotating seat in the UN Security Council. The request marked the first time an Arab state had sought Israel's help in such a matter, and signaled the potential for increasingly positive relations between the two countries. In early 2006, however, Qatar was among 14 Arab nations attending a summit in Damascus to discuss tightening the boycott against Israel, angering the United States. Qatar allowed the governing Palestinian group, Hamas, to have an office in Doha in 2006 and pledged $50 million in aid to Hamas, despite pressure from the United States to dissuade Qatar from helping to finance the anti-Israel group. Qatar, for its part, has called for Israeli-Palestinian peace efforts.

Relations with Russia improved in 2007, evidenced by President Vladimir Putin's trip to Qatar, and in late 2008 the two countries announced that they were setting up an OPEC-style cartel, along with Iran, for natural gas. (The three countries were reported to control 60 percent of the world's gas reserves.)

Though Qatar has no diplomatic relationship with Israel, Israeli foreign minister Tzipi Livni visited Doha in April 2008, at the invitation of the emir, to lobby for Arab states' ties with Israel and for support against Iran's nuclear program. Her trip came in the wake of Qatar's offer in February to help broker a peace agreement between Israel and Hamas. Observers noted that Qatar recently has been engaging in regional mediation efforts, such as its March 2008 brokering of a peace accord between Yemen's government and an insurgent group. Following Israel's attacks on Gaza in response to Hamas's launching rockets into southern Israel in late 2008 and early 2009, Qatar closed Israel's trade office in Doha and cut off all economic and political ties with the state. However, n February Prime Minister Hamad ibn Jasim ibn Jabir Al Thani told French president Nicolas Sarkozy at a meeting in Paris that he would "intensively" engage Hamas in an effort to free a kidnapped Israel soldier upon learning that the soldier also held French citizenship.

In a move that reportedly surprised Qatari officials, Ethiopia in April 2008 suspended diplomatic relations with Qatar, claiming that media outlets in Qatar were supporting terrorism in Ethiopia and Somalia in the wake of Ethiopia's failed efforts to drive out Islamists who had gained control in Somalia.

Current issues. The constitution promulgated on June 8, 2004 (see Constitution and government, above) codified equal rights for women, as well as general rights of freedom of association, expression, and worship. The constitution also endorses a free press and independent judiciary, but does not provide for the formation of political parties. Further, Sheikh Hamad ordered a new constitutional committee to provide a draft law that would include a directly elected national legislature. The prime minister, Sheikh Abdallah ibn Khalifa Al Thani, resigned on April 3, 2007, though no reason was given. Some observers said his departure was expected in the wake of recent reports that he was "tired." The new prime minister, Hamad ibn Jasim ibn Jabir Al Thani, formerly the first deputy prime minister and minister of foreign affairs, has long been influential in the politics of Qatar, observers said.

In anticipation of legislative balloting, a training session on a code of ethics for fair elections was held in Amman, Jordan, in February 2008, covering topics such as the organization of fair elections in Qatar, legal issues, voters rights, and fair press coverage. On May 20 the Consultative Council adopted a new law establishing the direct election of two-thirds of its members. In addition, the law lowers the voting age from 24 to 18 and outlines rules for campaign funding. No elections were scheduled, and in July the emir extended council members' terms for another two years.

In 2009 attention turned to an Arab League emergency summit, held in Doha on March 30, to address, among other things, conflicts between governing Palestinian factions in the wake of Israel's recent attacks on Gaza. Qatar was described by some observers as having "upstaged" larger Arab nations by inviting the leaders of Hamas and Iran to the summit to air their views, thus angering Egypt and the Palestinians, both of whom were concerned about encouraging larger Iranian ambitions in the Arab world. Egypt, for its part, chose to be represented at the summit by a minor cabinet official instead of President Mubarak, who was said to be irritated by Qatar's having undermined Egypt's role in any reconciliation between Hamas, which governed Gaza, and Fatah, which held administrative authority in the West Bank (see article on Palestinian Authority/Palestine Liberation Organization for details). Also, despite the International Criminal Court's (ICC) appeal to Qatar to cooperate with an arrest warrant against Sudan's President Beshir for alleged war crimes, Qatari officials invited Beshir and did not detain him when he arrived. (Qatar is not a signatory to the agreement that dates to the establishment of the ICC.) Subsequently, Arab leaders in the summer rejected the ICC's arrest warrant, calling for it to be annulled.

POLITICAL PARTIES

There are no political parties in Qatar.

LEGISLATURE

The **Consultative Council** (*Majlis al-Shura*), created in 1972, was increased from 20 members to 30 in 1975 and to 35 in 1988. The present council consists exclusively of the emir's appointees, most of them named in 1972 and subsequently reappointed. Arrangements for a partially elected National Assembly are included in the new constitution that was promulgated in June 2004 (see Constitution and government, above). On June 27, 2006, the emir appointed 35 members for a term of one-year to the Consultative Council. On July 2, 2007, the emir extended the term of Consultative Council members, though the length of the new term was unclear. On July 2, 2008, another decree of the emir extended the members' terms to June 30, 2010.

Speaker: Muhammad ibn Mubarak al-KHALIFI.

CABINET

[as of September 1, 2009]

Prime Minister	Sheikh Hamad ibn Jasim ibn Jabir Al Thani
Deputy Prime Minister	Abdallah ibn Hamad al-Attiyah
Ministers	
Awqaf and Islamic Affairs	Ahmad ibn Abdullah al-Marri
Cabinet Affairs	Sheikh Nasir ibn Muhammad Al Thani
Commerce	Sheikh Fahd ibn Jasim ibn Muhammad Al Thani
Communications and Transport	Ahmad ibn Nasir Al Thani
Culture, Arts, and Heritage	Hamad ibn Abdul Azziz al-Kawari
Defense	Sheikh Hamad ibn Khalifa Al Thani
Economy and Finance	Yusuf Hussein al-Kamal
Education and Higher Education	Saad ibn Ibrahim al-Mahmud
Energy and Industry	Abdallah ibn Hamad al-Attiyah

Environment	Abdullah ibn Mubarak Aboud al-Midhadi
Foreign Affairs	Sheikh Hamad ibn Jasim ibn Jabir Al Thani
Interior	Sheikh Abdallah ibn Khalifa Al Thani
Justice	Hassan ibn Abdallah al-Ghanim
Labor	Sultan Hassan al-Dhabit al-Dousari
Public Health	Abdullah ibn Khalid al-Qahtani
Social Affairs	Nasir ibn Abdullah al-Humaydi
Municipal Affairs and Agriculture	Sheikh Abdul Raman bin Khalifa bin Abdul Azziz Al Thani
Ministers of State	
Cabinet Affairs (Acting)	Sultan Hassan al-Dhabit al-Dousari
Energy and Industrial Affairs	Muhammad Saleh al-Sada
Foreign Affairs	Ahmad Abdullah al-Mahmud
Interior Affairs	Sheikh Abdullah ibn Nasir ibn Khalifa Al Thani
International Cooperation	Khalid ibn Muhammad al-Attiyah
Without Portfolio	Sheikh Hamad ibn Abdullah bin Muhammad Al Thani
	Sheikh Hamad ibn Suhaim Al Thani

[f] = female

COMMUNICATIONS

Sheikh Hamad relaxed censorship of the press following his assumption of power in 1995. The constitution guarantees freedom of the press, and Qatari newspapers generally operate in a less restricted fashion than their counterparts in other Gulf states. In 2007 journalists were granted only limited access to courts and subsequently were required to have a judge's permission to be there, according to the watchdog group Reporters Without Borders.

Press. The following are published in Doha: *al-Watan* (The Nation, 25,000, daily), in Arabic; *al-Rayah* (The Banner, 25,000), Arabic political daily; *al-Arab* (The Arab, 25,000), Arabic daily; *al-Sharq* (The Orient, 45,000), Arabic daily; *Gulf Times* (15,000 daily), in English; *Daily News Bulletin*, in English and Arabic; the *Peninsula*, in English; and the *Qatar Tribune*, in English.

News agency. The domestic facility is the state-run Qatar News Agency (*Wakalat al-Anba al-Qatariyah*).

Broadcasting and computing. Radio programming is provided by the government-operated Qatar Broadcasting Service (QBS) and television by Qatar Television Service (QTS). In addition, the government in 1997 launched the *al-Jazira* satellite television station, which has become well known in the Gulf and elsewhere for offering "differing" and, according to many in the West, at times inaccurate views (particularly on the Iraqi conflict). The station's broadcasts gained global attention after showing videos of al-Qaida leaders in the early 2000s. The government of Qatar claimed the station was independent following criticism by the U.S. government that al-Jazira broadcasts were promoting anti-American sentiments in the region. The watchdog group, Reporters Without Borders, noted that al-Jazira does not address domestic Qatari issues. In 2006 al-Jazira launched an English-language channel.

As of 2008 there were 340.4 Internet users per 1,000 inhabitants.

INTERGOVERNMENTAL REPRESENTATION

Ambassador to the U.S.: Ali Fahad Falil Al-Shawany al-HAJRI.

U.S. Ambassador to Qatar: Joseph Evan LeBARON.

Permanent Representative to the UN: Nassir Abdulaziz al-NASSER.

IGO Memberships (Non-UN): AFESD, AMF, BADEA, GCC, IDB, Interpol, LAS, NAM, OAPEC, OIC, OPEC, PCA, WCO, WTO.

ROMANIA

România

Note: The ministers from the Social Democratic Party (PSD) resigned from the cabinet on October 1, 2009, to protest the recent dismissal of Administration and Interior Minister Dan Nica, who had reportedly speculated about the possibility of fraud in the upcoming presidential poll. Without PSD support, the government of Prime Minister Emil Boc collapsed on October 13, when it lost a confidence motion by a vote of 254–176 in the Chamber of Deputies. Independent Lucian Croitoru and Liviu Negoiță of the Democratic-Liberal Party (PD-L) successively failed to win legislative support for their proposed cabinets, and Boc on December 23 formed of a new minority government (comprising the PD-L, the Hungarian Democratic Union of Romania, and independents), which, with the support of some "rogue" members of the PSD and the National Liberal Party, had been approved by a 276–135 legislative vote. Meanwhile, President Traian Băsescu had been sworn in for another five-year term on December 21 after winning a runoff on December 6 with 50.3 percent of the vote against PSD chair Mircea Geoană.

Political Status: Independence established 1878; People's Republic proclaimed December 30, 1947; designated a Socialist Republic by constitution adopted August 21, 1965; redesignated as Romania in December 1989; presidential multiparty constitution approved in referendum of December 8, 1991.

Area: 91,699 sq. mi. (237,500 sq. km.).

Population: 21,680,974 (2002C); 21,490,000 (2008E).

Major Urban Centers (2005E): BUCHAREST (București, 1,886,000), Cluj-Napoca (315,000), Iași (314,000), Timișoara (313,000), Craiova (303,000), Constanța (299,000), Galați (291,000), Brașov (274,000).

Official Language: Romanian.

Monetary Unit: New Leu (market rate December 1, 2009: 2.81 new lei = $1US). The new leu was introduced on July 1, 2005, at the rate of 1 new leu = 10,000 old lei.

President: *(See headnote.)* Traian BĂSESCU (formerly Democratic Party, currently independent [as constitutionally required]); elected (as the candidate of the Justice and Truth Alliance) in second-round balloting on December 12, 2004, and inaugurated for a five-year term on December 20 in succession to Ion ILIESCU (elected as a member of the Social Democratic Party).

Chair of the Council of Ministers (Prime Minister): *(See headnote.)* Emil BOC (Democratic-Liberal Party); designated by the president on December 15, 2008, following the legislative elections of November 30, and inaugurated on December 22 (following approval that day by Parliament) to succeed Călin POPESCU-TĂRICEANU (National Liberal Party).

THE COUNTRY

Shaped by the geographic influence of the Carpathian Mountains and the Danube River, Romania occupies the northeastern quarter of the Balkan Peninsula. It served historically both as an outpost of Latin civilization and as a natural gateway for Russian expansion into southeastern Europe. Some 88 percent of the population is ethnically Romanian, claiming descent from the Romanized Dacians of ancient times. There are also some 1.8 million Magyars (Hungarians), the largest national minority in Europe, situated mostly in the Transylvanian lands acquired from the Austro-Hungarian Empire after World War I. A sizeable German community that totaled approximately one-half million after World War II has dwindled because of emigration under an agreement concluded in 1977 with West Germany. Traditionally, the Romanian (Eastern) Orthodox Church has been the largest religious community. While constituting approximately half of the official labor force, women are concentrated in the agricultural sector because of male urban migration; female participation in political affairs increased significantly under the former Communist regime, but the membership of Parliament in 2008 was only 11 percent women (9.5 percent in the Senate and 11.5 percent in the Chamber of Deputies).

Although one of the world's pioneer oil producers, Romania was long a predominantly agricultural country and continues to be largely self-sufficient in food production. After World War II most acreage was brought under the control of collective and state farms, while the agricultural component of the workforce dropped sharply from 65 percent in 1960 as the result of an emphasis on industrial development—particularly in metals, machinery, chemicals, and construction materials—under a series of five-year plans. Agriculture continues to account for about 13 percent of GDP and to employ about one-third of the labor force. Most farms have now been reprivatized. Leading crops include grains, potatoes, apples, and wine grapes. Industry contributes about one-third of GDP and employs a comparable share of civilian labor. Major exports include clothing, iron and steel, chemicals, and petroleum products (even though Romania is now a net importer of hydrocarbons). The leading trading partners are France, Germany, Italy, and Russia.

Following the overthrow of the Ceaușescu regime in December 1989 and the new administration's espousal of a free-market orientation, Romania suffered serious economic reversals: a 33 percent contraction of GDP from 1990 to 1993, inflation averaging 140 percent per annum, currency depreciation of 97 percent, and an increase in official unemployment to over 10 percent of the labor force. Limited improvement from 1994 to 1996 included a resumption of growth and a significant reduction in consumer price inflation (to 28 percent in 1995, rising again to 57 percent in 1996), although Romanian living standards remained among the lowest in Europe. The precarious financial situation was highlighted by an enforced 10 percent devaluation of the leu in November 1995 following a sharp fall in its value against hard currencies. In 1997, according to the government, inflation was about 150 percent and GDP declined by about 6 percent. GDP continued to fall during the next two years, dropping by 5.4 percent in 1998 and 3.2 percent in 1999, before recovering in 2000, when growth of 1.6 percent was registered. Inflation remained a problem, however, at more than 40 percent annually in that three-year period, during which disbursements of large loans from the International Monetary Fund (IMF) were often delayed by what the IMF called the country's "stop-and-go" approach to reform and macroeconomic policies. As of late 2000 some 80 percent of the large enterprises that were owned by the state at the end of the Communist era remained under government control, but in February 2001 the government announced a program to privatize 63 large state companies. However, that process was subsequently perceived to be compromised by corruption and other irregularities.

Romania achieved an average annual GDP growth rate of 5.8 percent in 2001–2006, placing it among the fastest growing economies in the region. Unemployment declined to about 5.9 percent in 2005, and inflation fell to about 8.2 percent (down from 9.6 percent in 2004). By that time the IMF reported significant privatization progress, liberalization of the electricity and gas markets, and modernization of the mining sector. GDP rose by 6 percent in 2007 and 6.1 percent in 2008, assisted by Romania's accession to the European Union (EU) at the beginning of 2007. However, rising wages and food costs pushed inflation to 6.3 percent, among the highest rates in Europe. Until recently, the main problems facing successive governments have been corruption and the large trade and budget deficits. However, those issues were overshadowed in mid-2008 by domestic economic concerns, which played a significant role in that year's legislative campaign.

GOVERNMENT AND POLITICS

Political background. Originally consisting of the twin principalities of Walachia and Moldavia, the territory that is now Romania was conquered by the Ottoman Turks in 1504. Recognized as independent at the Berlin Congress in 1878, Romania made large territorial gains as one of the victorious powers in World War I but lost substantial areas to Hungary (Northern Transylvania), to the Soviet Union (Bessarabia and Northern Bukovina), and to Bulgaria (Southern Dobruja) in 1940 under threats from its neighbors and pressure from Nazi Germany. The young King MIHAI (Michael), who took advantage of the entry of Soviet troops in 1944 to dismiss the pro-German regime and switch to the Allied side, was forced in 1945 to accept a Communist-led coalition government under Dr. Petru GROZA. Following rigged elections in 1946, the king abdicated in 1947. The Paris peace treaty in 1947 restored Northern

Transylvania to Romania, but not the other territories lost in 1940. Thereafter, the Communists proceeded to eliminate the remnants of the traditional parties, and in 1952, after a series of internal purges, Gheorghe GHEORGHIU-DEJ emerged as the unchallenged party leader.

Following a decade of rigidity, Romania embarked in the early 1960s on a policy of increased independence from the Soviet Union in both military and economic affairs. This policy was continued and intensified under Nicolae CEAUŞESCU, who succeeded to leadership of the Romanian Communist Party (*Partidul Comunist Român*—PCR) on Gheorghiu-Dej's death in 1965 and became president of the Council of State in 1967. While maintaining relatively strict controls at home, the Ceauşescu regime consistently advocated maximum autonomy in international Communist affairs. These policies were fully endorsed by PCR congresses at five-year intervals from 1969 to 1989, with Ceauşescu being reelected to the top party position on each occasion.

In March 1980 President Ceauşescu was elected to his third term as head of state by the Grand National Assembly. The next day Ilie VERDEŢ, a close associate of the president and an experienced economic planner who had succeeded Manea MĂNESCU as chair of the Council of Ministers in March 1979, presented a new cabinet that included as a first deputy Elena CEAUŞESCU, wife of the president. In the face of increasingly poor economic performance, other significant changes were subsequently made, including the replacement of Verdeţ by the relatively obscure Constantin DĂSCĂLESCU in May 1982.

In November 1989 Romania appeared impervious to the winds of change sweeping over most other East European Communist regimes. Thus, the 14th PCR congress met without incident on November 20–24, and Ceauşescu made a state visit to Iran on December 19–20. During his absence, long-simmering unrest among ethnic Hungarians in the western city of Timişoara led to a bloody confrontation between police and antigovernment demonstrators. The protests quickly spread to other cities, and on December 21 an angry crowd jeered the president during what had been planned as a progovernment rally in Bucharest. By the following day army units had joined in a full-scale revolt, with a group known as the National Salvation Front (*Frontul Salvării Naţionale*—FSN) announcing that it had formed a provisional government. Unlike other East European revolutions, Romania's overthrow of Communist rule involved fierce fighting, in Bucharest and other cities, with many civilian casualties resulting from the government's use of heavy armaments. On December 25 Ceauşescu and his wife Elena, who had been captured after fleeing the capital, were executed following a secret trial that had pronounced them guilty of genocide and the embezzlement of more than $1 billion. On December 26 Ion ILIESCU was sworn in as provisional head of state, with Petre ROMAN, a fellow member of the PCR *nomenklatura,* being named prime minister. The FSN quickly came under attack as a thinly disguised extension of the former regime, and on February 1, 1990, it agreed to share power with 29 other groups in a coalition styled the Provisional Council for National Unity (*Consiliul Provizoriu de Uniune Naţională*—CPUN).

In presidential and legislative elections (the latter involving 6,719 candidates) on May 20, 1990, Iliescu won 85.1 percent of the presidential vote, while the FSN secured 67.0 and 66.3 percent of the votes for the upper and lower houses of Parliament, respectively. The balloting went ahead despite demonstrations by opposition parties claiming that they had been accorded insufficient time to organize. The protesters were eventually evicted from Bucharest's University Square in mid-June by thousands of club-wielding coal miners summoned to the capital by the president. On June 20 Iliescu was formally invested for a two-year term as president, with Roman continuing as prime minister.

Following his reappointment, Roman declared that he would pursue a "historic transition from a supercentralized economy to a market economy," adding that the state would "abandon to the greatest possible extent its role as proprietor and manager." Leaders of the small rightist parties responded by articulating a widespread belief that the revolution had been exploited by Communists who were interested only in the overthrow of Ceauşescu. Nevertheless, Roman, who was less identified with the former regime than Iliescu, moved ahead with his reform program, declaring that only "shock therapy" could save the rapidly deteriorating economy from disaster. Thus, prices of essential goods doubled as the result of sharp cuts in state subsidies in April 1991, while a drastic revision of the foreign investment code, urged by the IMF, offered non-Romanian companies full ownership, capital protection, repatriation of profits, and multiyear tax concessions.

Despite rapidly eroding support for the government by mid-1991, the reforms continued unabated, including the enactment of legislation in August that authorized the privatization of all state enterprises except utilities. For their part, the miners responded to soaring inflation by returning to Bucharest in September for three days of violent demonstrations, and on October 1 it was announced that Theodor STOLOJAN, the nonparty finance minister, had been asked to form a new government. By December it was clear that President Iliescu and former prime minister Roman were engaged in a struggle for control of the FSN. Roman had earlier complained of having been driven from office by a "Communist-inspired coup," while the president accused Roman of having flouted an FSN campaign promise of measured conversion to a market economy. Subsequently, Iliescu supporters, formally organized from April 1992 as the Democratic National Salvation Front (*Frontul Democrat al Salvării Naţionale*—FDSN), gained parliamentary support for simultaneous legislative and presidential elections in September, at which Roman's forces were decisively routed.

At his reinvestiture on October 30 President Iliescu endorsed further progress toward pluralism and a market economy, despite having long been accused by opponents of foot-dragging on both counts. Fourteen days later, a deeply divided Parliament ended a five-week impasse by agreeing to the formation of a government led by Nicolae VĂCĂROIU, a relatively unknown tax official then without party affiliation, who proceeded to combine liberal reform with "special care" for its social consequences. In July 1993 the FDSN absorbed three other progovernment parties and adopted a new name, the Social Democracy Party of Romania (*Partidul Democraţiei Sociale din România*—PDSR), which Văcăroiu later joined.

Despite deepening economic misery, the Văcăroiu government endured, with support from the (ex-Communist) Socialist Labor Party (*Partidul Socialist al Muncii*—PSM) and far-right Greater Romania Party (*Partidul România Mare*—PRM). Amid a modest economic upturn in 1994, the government's parliamentary base was strengthened in August by the induction of the rightist Romanian National Unity Party (*Partidul Unităţii Naţionale Române*—PUNR) into coalition status. In the course of 1995, however, the PDSR's relations with all three coalition partners deteriorated sharply, with the result that the PRM and PSM left the government alliance in October, with the exit of the PUNR being finally confirmed in September 1996. Meanwhile, by now reduced to minority status at the national level, the PDSR had been outpolled by the opposition Democratic Convention of Romania (*Convenţia Democrată Română*—CDR) alliance in local elections in June.

In the first round of presidential balloting held on November 3, 1996, incumbent Iliescu (PDSR) headed the poll against 15 other candidates, winning 32.3 percent of the vote. However, he was closely followed by the CDR candidate, Emil CONSTANTINESCU, with 28.2 percent, while Petre Roman, standing for the Social Democratic Union (*Uniunea Social Democrată*—USD), came in third with 20.5 percent. The USD and most other opposition parties then swung behind the CDR candidate for the runoff polling on November 17. As a result, Constantinescu won a decisive victory over Iliescu by 53.5 percent to

46.5 percent, the incumbent having been weighed down not only by Romania's economic and social deterioration, but also by evidence of abuse of power and pervasive corruption within ruling circles, particularly in connection with the privatization of state assets. In legislative balloting also held on November 3, the CDR won pluralities in both the Senate and the Chamber of Deputies, with the USD also polling strongly as the third grouping, after the PDSR.

Interparty talks following the elections yielded the signature of an agreement on December 6, 1996, providing for Victor CIORBEA, the youthful CDR mayor of Bucharest, to head a majority coalition government with the USD and the Hungarian Democratic Union of Romania (*Uniunea Democrată a Maghiarilor din România*—UDMR), the latter representing Romania's ethnic Hungarian minority. Accorded a 316–152 endorsement by a joint session of the two legislative houses on December 11, the new administration was sworn in the following day. Among other things, the new government reinstated the citizenship of King Mihai, repealing a 1948 decree. He returned to Romania in March 1997 to a warm reception and was later appointed a diplomat at large to help make the case for Romanian membership in the North Atlantic Treaty Organization (NATO). In June the government survived the opposition's first no-confidence motion by a vote of 227 to 158.

Ciorbea's government found it difficult to implement the reforms required to resolve Romania's economic problems, which included GDP contraction, high unemployment, and inflation of about 150 percent. Coalition members, particularly the CDR's Christian and Democratic National Peasants' Party (*Partidul Național Țărănesc Creștinși Democrat*—PNȚCD) and the USD's Democratic Party (*Partidul Democrat*—PD, an FSN descendant), generally were unable to compromise. In the wake of persistent feuding and public discord, the cabinet was reshuffled in December, with a number of independents being appointed. On January 14, 1998, the PD withdrew its support from Ciorbea and threatened to quit the government if he did not resign and if no agreement was reached within the coalition on a reform program by March 31. On February 5 the PD's five cabinet ministers resigned, and a new coalition agreement was approved, the open ministerial posts going to the PNȚCD, the National Liberal Party (*Partidul Național Liberal*—PNL), and the Civic Alliance Party (*Partidul Alianța Civică*—PAC). The PD's relationship with the government remained an anomaly: though it considered itself part of the ruling coalition, the party nevertheless set up an opposition-like 17-member committee to monitor the performance of the Ciorbea cabinet. After three months of political instability, Ciorbea resigned on March 30.

On April 2, 1998, President Constantinescu named Radu VASILE, the general secretary of the PNȚCD, to replace Ciorbea; Vasile and his cabinet were sworn in on April 15. The new government included members from the PNȚCD, PD, UDMR, PNL, Romanian Social Democratic Party (*Partidul Social Democrat Român*—PSDR), and Romania's Alternative Party (*Partidul Alternativa României*—PAR). However, in October PAR quit the coalition government in protest over the slow pace of economic reform.

Himself an economist, Vasile promised to strengthen the market economy by accelerating privatization efforts, and in December 1998 he restructured the government, reducing the number of ministries to quicken the pace of reform. In early 1999, however, his plans were set back by a miners' strike in the Jiu Valley that escalated into Romania's worst civil disorder since 1991. In mid-January the government reached a compromise with the leader of the miners' union, Miron COZMA, agreeing to abandon immediate plans to close unprofitable coal mines. The agreement averted a potential armed conflict between security forces and 20,000 strikers, but in mid-February Cozma and several hundred others were arrested as he led 2,000 miners toward Bucharest in protest against his recent sentencing to 18 years in prison for his role in the September 1991 riots.

With inflation and unemployment at unacceptable levels, and with the leu having fallen by more than one-third of its value between January and mid-March 1999, general dissatisfaction with the state of the economy continued to grow. Squabbling within the governing coalition also persisted, hindering progress on reform measures, and by December Vasile had lost the support of his own PNȚCD, whose ministers, constituting the majority of the cabinet, resigned. On December 13 President Constantinescu dismissed Vasile, naming as interim prime minister the PSDR's Alexandru ATHANASIU, previously minister of labor. Initially, Vasile refused to step down, arguing that the constitution permitted such dismissals only in cases of medical incapacity. Four days later, however, Vasile resigned, thereby defusing a potential constitutional crisis. Constantinescu appointed Mugur ISĂRESCU, the governor of Romania's central bank, as the new prime minister. Isărescu and a largely unchanged Council of Ministers received the legislature's approbation on December 21.

After mid-2000, with presidential and legislative elections approaching, the political alliance behind the governing coalition gradually dissolved. In August 2000 the PNȚCD and several allied parties reconstituted the CDR as the CDR 2000, but minus one of its previous principal components, the PNL. The PD, UDMR, and PNL prepared to contest the elections independently, while in September the PSDR left the government and formed an alliance with the PDSR. The legislative election of November 26 saw the PDSR capture a large plurality in both parliamentary houses, with the xenophobic PRM rising to second place and with the enfeebled CDR 2000 failing to meet the threshold for representation. In the presidential contest, former president Iliescu of the PDSR easily defeated the PRM's Corneliu VADIM TUDOR in a two-way runoff on December 10. Iliescu assumed office on December 21. His choice for prime minister, Adrian NĂSTASE, was confirmed by the Parliament and sworn in on December 28 at the head of a minority government dominated by the PDSR, with external backing from the PNL and the UDMR. On June 16, 2001, the PDSR and the PSDR completed their merger as the Social Democratic Party (*Partidul Social Democrat*—PSD).

At legislative balloting on November 28, 2004, the PSD, and its ally in the National Union coalition, the Humanist Party of Romania (*Partidul Umanist din România*—PUR), secured a plurality of 132 seats in the Chamber of Deputies. Following closely (with 112 seats) was the Justice and Truth Alliance (*Alianța Dreptate și Adevăr*—ADA), which had been formed in 2003 by the PNL and the PD. In concurrent first-round presidential balloting, Prime Minister Năstase led 12 candidates with 41 percent of the vote. The ADA's Traian BĂSESCU finished second with 34 percent of the vote, followed by the PRM's Vadim Tudor with 12.6 percent.

In the presidential runoff on December 12, 2004, Băsescu scored a surprising victory over Năstase, securing 51.2 percent of the vote. On December 28 the Parliament, by a vote of 265–200, approved a cabinet (led by Călin POPESCU-TĂRICEANU of the PNL) comprising the PNL, PD, UDMR, and PUR (which had split from the PSD).

The Conservative Party (*Partidul Conservator*—PC, as PUR had been renamed) left the government in December 2006 after a series of disagreements within the coalition over a number of issues. (Several PC leaders were also facing corruption investigations.) The government's legislative majority was also compromised by the defections of a number of PNL deputies to a new party (the Democratic Liberal Party [*Partidul Liberal Democrat*—PLD]) formed by former prime minister Stolojan and other PNL dissidents. Nevertheless, Prime Minister Popescu-Tăriceanu declined to call new elections, in part, apparently, in an effort to maintain stability in advance of the January 1, 2007, accession to the EU.

An even stronger threat to the government arose when the ADA was dissolved and the PD withdrew from the cabinet on April 1, 2007. However, on the following day Prime Minister Popescu-Tăriceanu named a new minority government comprising the PNL and UDMR, which was easily approved by the assembled Parliament on April 5, thanks primarily to support from the PSD. Turmoil nevertheless continued as the Parliament, at the prime minister's urging, on April 19 voted 322–108 to suspend President Băsescu and conduct a referendum on his possible permanent removal from office for alleged violation of the constitution in regard to the extent of presidential authority. Nicolae VĂCĂROIU, the chair of the Senate, served as acting president until the May 19 referendum, in which nearly 75 percent of the voters rejected the proposed removal of the president, who resumed his duties on May 23.

Another national referendum was held on November 25, 2007, concerning changes in the national electoral system supported by President Băsescu, who favored decentralizing the government and making Parliament more responsive to constituents by, among other things, introducing a majoritarian element to the legislative balloting. The proposal received an 80 percent endorsement in the referendum, although the results were ruled invalid due to insufficient turnout. Nevertheless, spurred by the debate, Parliament approved new electoral arrangements in March 2008. (See Legislature, below, for details.)

In the November, 30, 2008, elections the Democratic-Liberal Party (*Partidul Democrat-Liberal*—PD-L), a recent merger of the PD and PLD, secured 115 seats in the Chamber of Deputies, compared to 114 for the alliance of the PSD and PC. The PNL won 65 seats and the UDMR 22, while the PRM failed to pass the threshold. The close results led to calls for a "Grand Coalition" between the PD-L and PSD. However, the first attempt at forming the new government was disrupted when prime minister designate Theodor Stolojan of the PD-L withdrew his name from consideration, citing the need for a "younger generation" to assume governmental responsibility. The PD-L's Emil BOC, the mayor of Cluj-Napoca, subsequently formed the coalition, which was approved by a vote of 324–115 in Parliament on December 22.

Constitution and government. Romania's third postwar constitution, adopted in 1965 and amended in 1974, declared the nation to be a "socialist republic," with an economy based on socialist ownership of the means of production. All power was ascribed to the people, but the PCR was singled out as society's leading political force. Supreme state power was nominally vested in a unicameral Grand National Assembly (which was empowered to elect the president of the republic), a Council of State serving as a legislative presidium, a Council of Ministers (cabinet), justices of the Supreme Court, and a chief public prosecutor (procurator general).

Upon assuming power in late 1989, the FSN suspended the basic law, dropped the phrase "Socialist Republic" from the country's official name, and declared its support for a multiparty system and a market economy. The balloting of May 20, 1990, was for a president and a bicameral Parliament, the latter being empowered to draft a new constitution within 18 months, with new elections to follow within 12 months. A revised basic law providing for a strong presidency, political pluralism, human rights guarantees, and a commitment to market freedom was approved by Parliament (sitting as a Constituent Assembly) on November 21, 1991, and ratified by referendum on December 8.

A national referendum held October 18–19, 2003, approved (by a 90 percent "yes" vote in a 55.7 percent turnout) a number of constitutional amendments designed for the most part to facilitate Romania's planned accession to the EU. Among other things, the changes strengthened the protection of human rights (most notably for minority groups) and property rights. In addition, the presidential term was extended from four to five years.

Administratively, Romania is divided into 41 counties plus the city of Bucharest, in addition to a large number of towns and villages. A prefect represents the central government in each county, which elects its own council. Mayors and councils are elected at the lower level.

Foreign relations. Although historically pro-Western in foreign policy, Romania during its first 15 years as a Communist state cooperated fully with the Soviet Union both in bilateral relations and as a member of the Council for Mutual Economic Assistance, the Warsaw Pact, and the United Nations. However, serious differences with Moscow arose in the early 1960s over the issue of East European economic integration, leading in 1964 to a formal rejection by Romania of all Soviet schemes of supranational planning and interference in the affairs of other Communist countries. Subsequently, Romania followed an independent line in many areas of foreign policy, refusing to participate in the 1968 Warsaw Pact intervention in Czechoslovakia, rejecting efforts to isolate Communist China, and remaining the only Soviet-bloc nation to continue diplomatic relations with both Egypt and Israel. Prior to the admission of Hungary in 1982, Romania was the only Eastern-bloc state to belong to the World Bank and the IMF.

A constant regional theme of Romania's external relations in the early 1990s was discord with Hungary over the status of Romania's substantial ethnic Hungarian minority population, concentrated in Transylvania. Tension mounted when the ultranationalist Gheorghe FUNAR, presidential candidate of the Romanian National Unity Party (*Partidul Unității Naționale Române*—PUNR), was elected mayor of Cluj-Napoca in Transylvania in February 1992, with subsequent restrictions on "anti-Romanian" public meetings. Collaterally, the central government named ethnic Romanians to replace ethnic Hungarian prefects in the two Hungarian-majority counties, the resultant outrage being only partially eased by the appointment of two prefects for each county, one Hungarian and one Romanian.

A second major preoccupation of post-Communist Romania has been the position of Moldova, once the bulk of Romanian-ruled Bessarabia and inhabited predominantly by ethnic Romanians. On September 3, 1991, the Romanian Parliament adopted a resolution endorsing an August 27 declaration of independence by Moldova (the former Soviet Republic of Moldavia), with which Bucharest had established diplomatic relations seven days earlier. On November 2, during a visit to Bucharest, Moldovan Prime Minister Valeriu Muravschi expressed the hope that intergovernmental exchanges could "speed up the process of [his country's] integration with Romania."

Romania's possible interest in uniting with Moldova had contributed to the attempted secession of the latter's Transdnestr (ethnically Russian) and Gagauz (Turkic) majority areas and the onset of armed conflict, in which Bucharest backed the Moldovan authorities, although without intervening militarily. Advancing the concept of "two republics, one nation," the Romanian and Moldovan governments took a gradualist approach to unification and from May 1992 engaged in protracted diplomatic efforts with Russia and Ukraine to bring about a lasting cessation of hostilities between the warring ethnic groups in Moldova. (On the other hand, the Moldovan election of February 1994 yielding a legislative majority for proindependence parties represented a rebuff to the reunification effort.)

Romania was a founding member of the Black Sea Economic Cooperation (BSEC) grouping launched in June 1992, and on February 1, 1993, Romania signed an association agreement with the European Community (EC, subsequently the EU). However, its continuing problems in gaining international acceptance were highlighted by the refusal of the United States to extend most-favored-nation trade status until October 1993, although Washington had joined Western European governments in applauding the overthrow of the Ceaușescu regime.

In September 1993 the Parliamentary Assembly of the Council of Europe approved the admission of Romania to the organization. Subsequently, on January 26, 1994, Romania became the first former Communist state to join NATO's Partnership for Peace program, pursuant to its aim of eventual full NATO membership as well as accession to the EU. In the latter context, Romania in mid-1994 secured an EU pledge that it would be treated on a par with the four Visegrád states (Czech Republic, Hungary, Poland, Slovakia) also seeking membership. (On June 22, 1995, Romania became the third ex-Communist state [after Hungary and Poland] to submit a formal application for EU membership, although it was not invited to open accession negotiations until December 1999 [see Current issues, below, for subsequent EU developments].)

The June 1994 advent of a Socialist government in Hungary led to an improvement in Bucharest-Budapest relations, including a visit to Hungary by the Romanian foreign minister in September. Nevertheless, difficulties continued, occasioned by such events as passage in the Romanian Parliament of legislation regulating Hungarian-language education and the display of the flag or the singing of the anthem of another state. Against this background, attempted mediation by the U.S. Carter Center in Atlanta, which Romanian and ethnic Hungarian representatives visited in February 1995, appeared to do little to bridge the ancestral divide.

In a new initiative in September 1995, the Romanian government submitted three draft documents to Hungary covering reconciliation between the two countries, bilateral cooperation, and a code of behavior on treatment of ethnic minorities. Although the response in Budapest was cool, Bucharest persisted, with the result that a 1996 bilateral treaty saw both sides make concessions on the minority question. Hungary renounced any claim to Romanian territory populated by ethnic Hungarians, and Romania undertook to guarantee ethnic minority rights within its borders. Although the treaty commanded majority support in both national legislatures, it attracted fierce criticism from nationalist parties in both Hungary and Romania.

Romanian-Hungarian relations continued to improve after the election of President Constantinescu in November 1996, and in February 1997 the defense ministers of the two countries met and agreed on the formation of a joint peacekeeping force, a move that was seen as enhancing both nations' prospects for gaining entry into NATO. In March, Prime Minister Ciorbea, in the first visit of a Romanian prime minister to Hungary since 1989, signed five agreements. The following month President Arpád Göncz became the first Hungarian head of state to visit Romania, while in June the two nations signed a friendship treaty, confirming existing borders.

Despite support from France, Italy, and Spain, Romania's request to be included in the first-round expansion of NATO was blocked in 1997 by the United States, with U.S. Defense Secretary William Cohen explaining that Washington had said "not yet" rather than simply "no." The rejection was seen as a desire by the United States to placate a nervous Russia and to delay admitting a former Communist state until democracy and free-market reforms had become irreversible. In July U.S. President Clinton, in the first visit to Romania by an American president in more than 20 years, praised the Romanians and encouraged them to stay their course.

Romania became a member of the Central European Free Trade Agreement (CEFTA) on July 1, 1997, expecting to regain access to Eastern and Central European markets as well as to enhance its prospects for NATO membership (see Poland, Foreign relations, for more on CEFTA). A month earlier, the presidents of Ukraine and Romania had signed a friendship treaty, calling existing borders "inviolable" despite earlier friction over the status of Northern Bukovina and Southern Bessarabia, both of which Romania had been compelled to cede to the USSR in June 1940. Related issues of national identity have delayed conclusion of a basic treaty with Russia, as has Romania's demand that

Russia return the state treasury that has been held in Moscow since its delivery there for safekeeping during World War I.

A trip to Romania in May 1999 by John Paul II was the first visit by a Roman Catholic pope to a country with an Orthodox majority since the Great Schism of 1054. Although restricted to Bucharest, the pope was warmly greeted by the patriarch of the Romanian Orthodox Church, TEOCTIST.

A basic treaty between Romania and Moldova was initialed on April 28, 2000, but neither country's legislature ratified the agreement. Subsequently, in November 2002, Romania and Hungary signed an agreement defining the future course of their bilateral partnership and guaranteeing each other support for EU membership.

In 2003 Romania was included in the "second wave" of candidates for membership in NATO, to which it formally acceded in March 2004 along with six other countries. Earlier, Romania had contributed a contingent of noncombat troops to the U.S./UK-led operation in Iraq. (As of mid-2008 the Romanian government was reportedly considering withdrawing its troops from Iraq by 2010.)

In October 2005 Romania and Hungary signed a number of potentially significant agreements providing for cooperation in environmental protection, law enforcement, border security, joint defense programs, and cultural and educational exchanges. The two countries also pledged to pursue common economic policies.

Tensions grew in 2007 concerning the large expatriate Romanian community in Italy. Among other things, widespread protests, including several violent attacks on Romanian immigrants, broke out in Italy when an Italian woman was allegedly assaulted and murdered by a Romanian citizen. The Italian government responded by using emergency measures to expel some Romanian citizens, drawing expressions of concern from the Romanian government. Many of those expelled were of Roma origin, highlighting problems of minority relations in both Italy and Romania.

The International Court of Justice in February 2009 resolved Romania's ongoing territorial dispute with Ukraine over the disposition of Serpents' Island (transferred at Soviet insistence in 1948) and related maritime waters. Some 9,700 square kilometers of the region were slated to be transferred to Romanian control, providing sovereignty over an area that was believed to have significant oil and gas reserves.

In campaigning for the June 2009 European Parliament elections, the PD-L and PSD both proposed changes to Romanian citizenship laws to provide citizenship to ethnic Romanians living in the Republic of Moldova. EU officials subsequently criticized such rhetoric as offering blanket Romanian citizenship (and, consequently, EU citizenship) to Moldovans, leading the Romanian foreign ministry to repudiate such proposals. The PNL subsequently called for the relaxation of visa regimes and border controls with Moldova.

Current issues. In a nationwide address in July 2000 President Constantinescu, having decided not to seek a second term as president, described Romania's current political parties as conducting "a blind struggle" for power in which "people buy and sell principles, ideologies, seats in the parliament and the cabinet, making use to that end of lies, blackmail, vulgarity, and manipulation." He also noted that his attempts to fight corruption had been held back by the complicity of high-level state institutions.

The final years of the CDR-led government were marked by political infighting and a resultant inability to establish a course that would resolve Romania's economic difficulties. At the same time, the country continued to grapple with the legacy of the Ceauşescu era. The government decided to release files held by the former secret police, the *Securitate,* and supported measures covering restitution for personal property, farmland, and forests seized under the Communists. All of these decisions proved controversial, as did government support for expanding minority-language education (although not for establishing a Hungarian-language university) and for permitting official use of minority languages in local jurisdictions having significant minority communities.

The most startling development of the 2000 election season was the increasing support accorded Vadim Tudor's Greater Romania Party (PRM), which saw its share of the legislative vote surge from under 5 percent in 1996 to roughly 20 percent. During the campaign and afterward, the PRM presidential contender showed no inclination to tone down his ultranationalist, anti-Hungarian, anti-Gypsy, anti-Semitic, populist rhetoric, asserting, for example, that Ceauşescu had been "one of the world's great statesmen" and that the IMF and the World Bank were blackmailing Romania, demanding poisonous policy changes in return for vitally needed loans and credits.

An October 2000 evaluation by the European Parliament described Romania's economy as "worrying" and cited numerous other deficiencies, including corruption, the persistent problem of abandoned children, the need for legal reform, and extensive environmental pollution. By that time, the CDR-led government had lost most of its popular support due to continued instability within the coalition (four prime ministers in four years), economic deterioration, and perceived ongoing corruption. In comparison, the PSD-led government installed in late 2000 subsequently enjoyed relative stability that contributed to a period of economic improvement. Prime Minister Adrian Năstase's administration also successfully negotiated accession to NATO and oversaw progress toward EU membership. Consequently, observers were surprised by Năstase's narrow loss in the late 2004 presidential election to Traian Băsescu of the reform-minded (in rhetorical terms, at least) ADA. Corruption apparently remained on the minds of those who voted for Băsescu, who had earned a reputation for rectitude as mayor of Bucharest. In tandem with the new coalition cabinet formed under the leadership of Călin Popescu-Tăriceanu, Băsescu promised tax reform as well as institutional change that would make Romania "a democracy in real terms." Crucial to the latter goal was judicial reform, some of which was accomplished by legislative action in the first half of 2005.

In April 2005 Romania signed an accession treaty with the EU calling for Romania to become a member in January 2007, although analysts noted that significant reform was still required. Complicating matters at midyear was reported friction between the president and the prime minister on a number of issues.

The dominant issue from mid-2005 to mid-2006 was the fight against corruption, the ADA-led government having pledged to target the major offenders regardless of their political affiliation or status. Anticorruption legislation was presented to the Parliament in late 2005 but met unexpected opposition from within both chambers. Among other things, the legislators were reportedly concerned that they would lose their own immunity from prosecution in the "clean-up" campaign and would (along with judges) be forced to make their financial assets public. Despite the initial legislative hostility, many of the new laws were ultimately approved, in part due to the efforts of Justice Minister Monica MACOVEI, an independent former human rights activist who gained substantial popular acclaim for her willingness to investigate entrenched interests. The anticorruption campaign produced its first major results in the spring of 2006 when a number of influential politicians (including legislators and cabinet members) were officially placed under investigation.

Supporters of EU integration hoped that the recent corruption investigations would facilitate Romania's EU accession, which was scheduled for January 2007. However, in April 2006 the EU postponed a decision on the question until October, indicating that Romania was "not there yet." While acknowledging Romania's recent progress, the EU urged further intensification of anticorruption measures as well as agricultural and judicial reform. Despite those concerns, the European Commission in September issued a favorable ruling regarding the admission of Romania (along with Bulgaria), although both countries were asked to make additional judicial reforms and to intensify their efforts to combat corruption and organized crime or face the loss of scheduled EU financial assistance. It was widely conceded in Romania that the ADA's much-heralded anticorruption campaign had proven largely ineffective, in part due to acrimony between Prime Minister Popescu-Tăriceanu and President Băsescu, as well as policy differences among members of the coalition government. Among other things, the turmoil precluded passage of proposed legislation meant to further reform the judiciary and boost anticorruption efforts, while also contributing to the cabinet restructurings of December 2006 and April 2007.

By mid-2007 many of the individuals under corruption probes had been brought before the courts, although decisions in most cases had been postponed. (One high-profile case involved former prime minister Adrian Năstase.) Another contentious issue in 2007 was the additional publication of files from the Communist era, which revealed that a number of members of the political elite had maintained ties with the feared secret police.

Local elections were held on June 1, 2008, with the PD-L leading with 28.4 percent of the vote, followed by the coalition of the PSD and PC (28 percent), the PNL (18.7 percent), and the UDMR (5.4 percent). The mayoral election in Bucharest received particular attention, given its previous use by Băsescu as a springboard for the presidency. Independent candidate Sorin OPRESCU (formerly of the PSD) won in the second round with 56.6 percent of the vote.

EU criticism of government corruption in Romania refocused domestic political attention on the issue. In mid-2008 the European Commission issued a report criticizing Romania for the government's limited efforts to deal with corruption. (The National Anticorruption Directorate, e.g., is allowed to pursue cases against former or current members of the cabinet only with parliamentary approval.) Both President Băsescu and Prime Minister Popescu-Tăriceanu stated that anticorruption investigations were being used unfairly by rival parties for political gain. In August EU transfers of farm aid subsidies to Romania were temporarily suspended over concerns regarding corruption in the disbursement process. However, the government subsequently chose not to renew the term of the directorate's chief prosecutor, apparently because he had been too aggressive in indicting former members of Parliament and the government.

In the campaign for the November 2008 parliamentary elections, wage levels and domestic economic concerns emerged as significant factors. The PSD and PD-L, among others, sponsored legislation before the election promising wage hikes of up to 50 percent for civil servants, subsequently promising expenditures on infrastructure to stimulate the economy and to address regional disparities in regard to development. However, Prime Minister Popescu-Tăriceanu refused to implement the proposals, arguing that the budget lacked the necessary resources. Other concerns included unemployment, continued inflation, and stagnating wage levels, all tied to the world economic crisis.

In addition to the virtual tie between the PD-L and the alliance of the PSD and PC, the November 2008 legislative elections were most noteworthy for the exclusion from Parliament of the far-right PRM. Some observers, who expected the PNL to serve as a junior partner in the new government, were surprised by the formation of the "Grand Coalition" by the PD-L and PSD. New prime minister Boc said that dealing with the economic downturn would be the administration's top priority. He also promised to pursue heavy government spending cuts and reforms in other sectors, including the judiciary. However, his description of the coalition as likely to promote "stability" seemed optimistic since the PD-L and PD appeared certain to clash on a number of issues.

European Commission President Jose Manuel Barroso in January 2009 called on Romania to show "concrete results" in fighting corruption. However, politics continued to stymie efforts to limit drug trafficking. Following arrests and formal corruption charges against leaders of the National Anticorruption Directorate (part of the ministry of justice, with its head appointed directly by the president) and the General Directorate for Intelligence and Internal Security (part of the ministry of administration and the interior, currently under a PSD minister), the PSD and PD-L issued mutual recriminations of using anticorruption efforts for political purposes.

In contrast to the 2008 parliamentary elections, the June 7, 2009, European Parliament elections continued to be determined completely by nationwide proportional representation. The alliance of the PSD and PC won a plurality of 31.1 percent of the vote and 11 of the country's 33 seats. The PD-L finished second with 29.7 percent of the vote and 10 seats, followed by the PNL with 14.5 percent of the vote and 5 seats, and the UDMR with 8.9 percent of the vote and 3 seats. The PRM won 8.65 percent of the vote and 3 seats, and independent candidate Elena BĂSESCU (President Băsescu's daughter) won a seat with 4.2 percent of the vote. Attention subsequently focused on the presidential balloting scheduled for November, president Băsescu having announced his candidacy for reelection.

POLITICAL PARTIES

Until late 1989 Romania's political system was based on the controlling position of the Romanian Communist Party (*Partidul Comunist Român*—PCR). Founded in 1921, the PCR changed its name to the Romanian Workers' Party (*Partidul Muncitoresc Român*—PMR) in 1948 after a merger with the left-wing Social Democrats, but the party reassumed its original name at the ninth party congress in 1965. Identified by the constitution as "the leading political force of the whole society," the PCR exercised its authority with the aid of the Front of Socialist Democracy and Unity (*Frontul Democrațieişi Unității Socialiste*—FDUS), which prepared the approved list of candidates for election to the Grand National Assembly and other bodies.

At the PCR congress held in Bucharest in November 1989 (only a month before his overthrow), President Ceauşescu was unanimously elected to another five-year term as PCR general secretary. Following the rebellion of December 22, the new government of Ion Iliescu declared that the question of banning the PCR would be decided by a popular referendum on January 28, 1990. However, on January 19 the ruling National Salvation Front (*Frontul Salvării Naționale*—FSN) announced that the decision to schedule the referendum had been "a political mistake," with the result that the party quickly ceased to exist as an organized force.

Eleven parties and alliances and 31 independent candidates participated in the November 2008 elections, a significant decrease from the nearly 50 parties that registered in 2004.

Government and Government-Supportive Parties (Prior to December 2009 changes *[see headnote]*):

Democratic-Liberal Party (*Partidul Democrat-Liberal*—PD-L). The PD-L was formed in January 2008 by the PD and the PLD, the merger appearing to consolidate support for President Băsescu. The new party led the June 2008 local elections with 28 percent of the vote and took (barely) the leading role in parliament with 115 seats in the Chamber of Deputies and 51 in the Senate in the November national balloting. After the PD-L's initial discussions to form a coalition with the UDMR and PNL broke down over the latter's insistence on holding the position of prime minister, a collaboration protocol between the PD-L and PSD was signed instead in December 2008, despite significant tensions between the two parties and an anticipated clash in the November 2009 presidential election between Băsescu and Mircea Geoană of the PSD.

Leaders: Emil BOC (President and Prime Minister), Theodor STOLOJAN (Vice President and Former Prime Minister), Adriean VIDEANU (Vice President), Vasile BLAGA (General Secretary).

Democratic Party (*Partidul Democrat*—PD). The PD was the direct descendant of the National Salvation Front (FSN), which was described as a "self-appointed" group that assumed governmental power following the overthrow of the Ceauşescu regime. Claiming initially to be a supraparty formation, the front reorganized as a party in February 1990 and, as such, swept the balloting of May 20. On July 6 it announced that it was further reorganizing under a social-democratic rubric. One day earlier Ion Iliescu had stepped down as FSN president in compliance with a law that prohibited the head of state from serving as the leader of a political party. Subsequently, however, he emerged as de facto leader of the Democratic National Salvation Front (FDSN), which opposed rapid economic reform.

At its first national convention held March 16–17, 1991, the FSN, despite criticism from the Iliescu faction, approved a free-market reform program entitled "A Future for Romania" that was presented by Prime Minister Petre Roman. Although Roman was obliged to step down as chief of government in October 1991, the front, at its second convention held March 27–29, 1992, reconfirmed him as its president and reiterated its support of the free-market program. With the FDSN faction having separated from the FSN, the FSN ran a distant fourth in the national presidential poll of September 1992, Roman having declined to stand as its candidate; in the legislative balloting the FSN was limited to third place behind the FDSN and CDR, winning 10 percent of the vote.

In May 1993 the FSN reconstituted itself as the Democratic Party–National Salvation Front (*Partidul Democrat–Frontul Salvării Naționale*—PD-FSN), and in October 1994 it absorbed the Democratic Party of Labor (*Partidul Democrat al Muncii*—PDM). In February 1996 Roman accepted nomination as the PD-FSN candidate in the November presidential election, proclaiming his intention to stand on a social-democratic platform. For the accompanying legislative balloting the PD-FSN not only entered into the Social Democratic Union (USD) with the PSDR, but also sought to rally other proreform groupings under its banner. These efforts yielded third place for Roman in the presidential contest, while the PD-FSN won 43 chamber and 22 Senate seats in the legislative balloting.

As part of the Ciorbea government the PD, which had dropped the FSN designation, frequently tussled with the PNȚCD (above), particularly over the forced resignation in early 1998 of PD minister of transport Traian Băsescu, who had called for more rapid economic reform. The PD briefly withdrew from the cabinet until adoption of a revised coalition protocol, and it remained at the center of governmental turmoil until Ciorbea's resignation in March 1998. The PD subsequently supported both the Vasile and Isărescu administrations, with Petre Roman becoming foreign minister in the latter. Controversy again arose when the PD minister of defense, Victor BABIUC, left the party in March 2000, Roman accusing the National Liberal Party (PLN) of encouraging his departure. Babiuc resigned from the cabinet two days later and in May joined the PNL.

In the November 2000 election the PD finished third, declining to 31 seats in the Chamber of Deputies and 13 in the Senate, and then moved into the opposition when the new Parliament convened. Among the successful senatorial candidates on the PD list was former prime minister Radu Vasile, who, having been expelled from the PNŢCD in early 2000, accepted an invitation to bring his supporters into Cornel BRAHAS's Party of the Romanian Right (*Partidul Dreapta Românească*—PDR). After overcoming a court challenge from opponents within the PDR, the expanded party then reregistered under Vasile's chairship as the **Romanian People's Party** (*Partidul Popular din România*—PPDR), which espoused authoritarianism, opposed multiculturalism, and described suspicion of foreigners as "a natural instinct." Having had little success in the June local elections, the far-right PPDR chose not to offer its own candidates in the general election in November.

Roman, who had finished the 2000 presidential race in sixth place with 3.0 percent of the vote, subsequently proposed establishing a center-right "Alternative 2004" of the PD, the Alliance for Romania (ApR), and the National Alliance (PUNR-PRN). However, at an extraordinary national convention the following May, he was replaced as chair by Traian Băsescu, recently elected as mayor of Bucharest. (In 2003 Roman formed a new party; see PFDR, below).

Between June and September 2001 the PD absorbed the National Alliance, formation of which had been announced in late July 2000 by the Romanian National Unity Party (PUNR, below) and the Romanian National Party (*Partidul Naţional Român*—PNR). In the November 2000 election the grouping—formally on the ballot as the National Alliance Party (*Partidul Alianţa Naţională* [PUNR-PNR])—won only 1.4 percent of the vote in each house, and in February 2001 the former PUNR leadership indicated its intention to reregister their organization as a separate entity.

The PNR had been founded in March 1998 by the merger of the New Romania Party (*Partidul "Noua Românie"*—PNR) of Ovidiu TRAZNEA and the Agrarian Democratic Party of Romania (*Partidul Democrat Agrar din România*—PDAR) of Mihai BERCA, with the Christian Liberal Party (*Partidul Liberal Creştin*—PLC) joining soon after. The PDAR, an agricultural workers' party launched in 1990 on a nationalist platform, later served as a governing partner of the PDSR, but it withdrew from the alliance in April 1994 in protest over a bill introducing an IMF-mandated land tax. For the 1996 presidential election the PDAR initially nominated Ion COJA, a literature professor and prominent anti-Semite who had temporarily broken with the PUNR. However, the PDAR ultimately joined the Humanist Party (PUR) and the Ecologist Movement (MER) in the unsuccessful National Union of the Center (UNC) alliance, which backed Ion Pop de POPA as its presidential candidate.

In September 1999 Viorel CATARAMĂ resigned as PNR chair, ostensibly to distance the party from a failed company that he had led. His interim replacement, Virgil MĂGUREANU, a former director of the Romanian intelligence service, was elected chair in February 2000. Cataramă ultimately joined the ApR (which merged with the PNL in 2002), while Măgureanu led the PNR into the National Alliance, and then the alliance, minus the PUNR, into the PD.

Traian Băsescu, then mayor of Bucharest and chair of the PD, became the ADA's successful presidential candidate in 2004. He was succeeded as PD chair by Emil Boc, who in 2005 convinced the delegates at a PD national convention to adopt a platform favoring promarket economic policies, a shift to the center from its former left-leaning doctrine. Boc also launched discussions with other centrist parties regarding possible unification.

After the dissolution of the ADA coalition in the spring of 2007, the PD left the government and became an opposition party to the new PNL-led cabinet.

Democratic Liberal Party (*Partidul Liberal Democrat*—PLD). The PLD was formed by former prime minister Theodor Stolojan and other PNL dissenters in December 2006. It was reported that some 30 legislators had defected from the PNL to the PLD, along with approximately 11,500 PNL members. Stolojan, an aide to President Băsescu, attacked the PNL leaders as "oil tycoons," and pledged to cooperate with the PD in reviving the ADA's center-right principles.

Social Democratic Party + Conservative Party Alliance (*Alianţa Politică Partidul Social Democrat + Partidul Conservator*—PSD+CP). In April 2008 the PSD and the PC announced the formation of a common parliamentary group and a standing electoral alliance, beginning with the June 2008 local elections and continuing through the June 2009 European Parliament elections. PSD chair Mircea Geoană characterized the initiative as a permanent "political alliance" rather than a temporary election coalition.

Social Democratic Party (*Partidul Social Democrat*—PSD). The PSD was formally established on June 6, 2001, by merger of the Social Democracy Party of Romania (*Partidul Democraţiei Sociale din România*—PDSR) and the much smaller Romanian Social Democratic Party (*Partidul Social Democrat Român*—PSDR). The two had envisaged their eventual merger in a September 2000 electoral agreement establishing the three-party **Social Democratic Pole of Romania** (*Polul Democrat-Social din România*—PDSR) in partnership with the Humanist Party of Romania (now the PC, see below).

The PDSR had been formed as the "presidential" party on July 10, 1993, by the renaming of the Democratic National Salvation Front (FDSN) and its absorption of the Romanian Socialist Democratic Party (*Partidul Socialist Democrat Român*—PSDR), the Cooperative Party (*Partidul Cooperatist*—PC), and the Republican Party (*Partidul Republican*—PR). Leess reform-oriented than their colleagues, a number of pro-Iliescu chamber deputies, styling themselves National Salvation Front–22 December (the date of Ceauşescu's overthrow in 1989), had withdrawn from the parent group in March 1992 and registered as the FDSN in April. The new formation won a plurality of seats in both houses of Parliament in the September 1992 balloting and secured the reelection of Iliescu at the second-round presidential poll of October 11. The Socialist Democrats were a leftist formation that had once been closely allied with the FSN. Their original chair, Marian CIRCIUMARU, was expelled in August 1990 for a variety of misdeeds. A centrist party favoring free enterprise, the PR was formed in 1991 by merger of an existing Republican Party and the Social Liberal Party–20 May.

Having previously headed a minority government, the PDSR in August 1994 drew the right-wing PUNR (below) into a coalition that continued to attract external support from the Greater Romania Party (PRM) and the Socialist Labor Party (PSM). However, increasing strains resulted in all three withdrawing their support from the government between October 1995 and September 1996, after which the PDSR was technically reduced to minority status in the Chamber of Deputies. Hitherto identified as a nonparty technocrat, Prime Minister Nicolae Văcăroiu announced his adhesion to the PDSR in May 1996. In local elections the following month the PDSR saw its support decline, with former tennis champion Ilie NĂSTASE failing in a bid for the Bucharest mayoralty.

In the November 1996 balloting, Iliescu suffered a second-round defeat in his presidential reelection bid, while the PDSR fell to second place in the legislature (with 21.5 percent of the lower house vote) and went into opposition, whereupon Iliescu assumed the formal party leadership. As the party attempted to regroup in 1997, tensions emerged among the leadership. At the PDSR national conference in June reformers led by former foreign minister Teodor Meleşcanu criticized Iliescu for failing to dissociate the party from corrupt elements. After the conference Meleşcanu and others resigned from the PDSR and formed the Alliance for Romania (ApR; see PNL, above). In June 1999, however, the party agreed to absorb a PUNR splinter, the Alliance for Romanians' Unity Party (PAUR; see PUNR, below).

The left-of-center PSDR descended from the historic party founded in 1893 but was forced to merge with the Communist Party in 1948. Following its re-forming in late 1989, several competing groups claimed the inheritance, a court subsequently awarding the PSDR designation to the main faction, which had Socialist International recognition. Standing on the Democratic Convention of Romania (CDR) ticket in the 1992 balloting, the PSDR won 10 chamber seats and 1 in the Senate. While maintaining its links with some CDR parties for the November 1996 elections, the PSDR established a formal electoral alliance, the Social Democratic Union (*Uniunea Social Democrată*—USD), with the Democratic Party–National Salvation Front (see PD, above), winning 10 of the USD's 53 chamber seats and 1 of its 23 Senate seats. The USD subsequently agreed to join Victor Ciorbea's CDR-led coalition government.

In July 2000 the PSDR approved a merger with the Socialist Party (*Partidul Socialist*—PS), led by unsuccessful 1996 presidential candidate Tudor MOHORA, while on September 7 it not only agreed to an alliance with the opposition PDSR for the November elections, but to join the PDSR, after the elections, in forming the

PSD. Accordingly, on September 8 it formally withdrew from the governing coalition. the agreement with the PDSR prompted long-time party leader Sergiu CUNESCU to resign, asserting that the PSDR had committed "self-enslavery" to an organization that was guilty of "confiscating the revolution" after 1990.

The Social Democratic Pole's 2000 presidential candidate, Ion Iliescu, finished first in the November 26 presidential contest, with 36.5 percent of the vote, and then defeated the Greater Romania Party's Vadim Tudor in the runoff on December 10, taking a 66.8 percent vote share. In the November legislative contests the alliance won 36.6 percent of the vote in the Chamber of Deputies, for a plurality of 155 seats, and 37.0 percent in the Senate, for a plurality of 65 seats. The minority government installed under Adrian Năstase on December 28 included one minister from the PSDR and one from PUR.

An extraordinary PDSR party conference held in January 2001 unanimously elected Prime Minister Năstase as chair, President Iliescu having resigned in accordance with a constitutional dictate. Upon formation of the PSD, Năstase remained chair.

In November 2001 the Party of Moldovans (*Partidul Moldovenilor*—PM) merged into the PSD. The PM had been organized by the mayor of Iaşi, Constantin SIMIRAD, as a vehicle for forging closer ties between Moldova and Romania. Despite discussions with the PNL in early 2000, the PM had chosen to join the CDR 2000 for the general election in November. In 2003 the PSD absorbed the Socialist Labor Party (*Partidul Socialist al Muncii*—PSM) and the National Revival Socialist Party (*Partidul Socialist al Renaşterii Naţionale*—PSRN).

The PSD participated in the 2004 UN alliance with PUR, securing a plurality of legislative seats. However, the PSD was forced into opposition when PUR and the UDMR agreed to join the ADA in a new coalition government. Adrian Năstase was narrowly defeated as the UN candidate in the 2004 presidential poll. He subsequently resigned from all party leadership posts in the wake of a corruption scandal.

Although still formally classified as an opposition party, the PSD agreed in April 2007 to support the new PNL/UDMR government in the legislature as necessary to ensure the coalition's continuation until the 2008 general elections. Although the PSD+PC won a plurality of votes in the November 2008 elections (33.1 percent in the Chamber of Deputies and 34.2 percent in the Senate), it received fewer seats (114 in the chamber, 49 in the Senate) than the PD-L. It therefore surrendered (albeit reluctantly) the lead in forming a new government to the PD-L. In December 2008 the PSD agreed to join a coalition government with the PD-L, stipulating that the new government not include the UDMR.

Leaders: Mircea GEOANĂ (Chair), Titus CORLATEANU (Vice Chair), Ion ILIESCU (Former President of Romania, Honorary Chair, and Leader in the Senate), Ecaterina ANDRONESCU (Vice President), Adrian NASTASE (President of the PSD National Council), Victor HREBENCIUC (leader of the PSD group in the Chamber of Deputies).

Conservative Party (*Partidul Conservator*—PC). The PC is a successor to the Humanist Party of Romania (*Partidul Umanist din România*—PUR), which had been formed in the early 1990s and had subsequently called for adoption of a "third way" that rejected both doctrinaire socialism and "market fundamentalism." PUR allied with the PSD in 2000 as part of the Social Democratic Pole (see PSD, above, for details). As a result, it subsequently gained legislative seats and representation in the PSD-led cabinet.

For the 2004 legislative elections, PUR again presented joint lists with the PSD through the National Union (*Uniunea Naţională*—UN). However, following that balloting, PUR deserted the PSD and the UN to join the new government led by the ADA.

In May 2005 PUR's national convention voted to adopt the PC rubric, although leaders stated that the change did not indicate a revision of what they now declared to be the party's long-standing devotion to conservative doctrine.

In February 2006 the PC merged with the **Romanian National Unity Party** (*Partidul Unităţii Naţionale Române*—PUNR). The PUNR was organized in 1990 as the political arm of the nationalist Romanian Hearth (*Vatra Românească*). It ran fifth in the 1992 parliamentary balloting on a hard-right ticket, securing 30 Chamber and 14 Senate seats on an 8 percent vote share, and was eventually co-opted into the government coalition in August 1994. Problems with coalition partners and internal dissent with party leader Gheorghe FUNAR (the mayor of Cluj-Napoca in Transylvania) weakened the PUNR. Funar was expelled as party leader in 1997, only to launch the rival **Alliance for Romanians' Unity Party** (*Partidul Alianţei pentru Unitatea Românilor*—PAUR), which subsequently joined the PDSR (Funar himself would join the PRM). In 2001 the PUNR elected Gen. (Ret.) Mircea Chelaru as chair. In the 2006 merger with the CP, Chelaru took the vice presidency of the PC (for additional information on the PUNR, see the 2008 *Handbook.*).

Gheorghe COPOS, a state minister (vice prime minister) in the ADA-led coalition government, resigned his cabinet post in June 2006 following his reported indictment on tax evasion charges. Although the PC, claiming ideological differences with the PNL, subsequently left the government, it continued to support the administration in the legislature on a case-by-case basis.

Mircea Chelaru was expelled from the CP by Chair Dan Voiculescu in April 2007, following Chelaru's criticism of Voiculescu's leadership.

In April 2008 the PC announced a political alliance with the PSD, receiving four of the alliance's seats in the Chamber of Deputies and one in the Senate in the November elections. It did not, however, receive cabinet positions in the subsequent coalition government between the PD-L and PSD.

Leaders: Daniela POPA (Chair), Dan VOICULESCU (Founding Chair), Dan Ioan POPESCU.

Opposition Parties (Prior to December 2009 changes *[see headnote]*):

National Liberal Party (*Partidul Naţional Liberal*—PNL). Founded in the mid-19th century but banned by the Communists in 1947, the PNL was reconstituted in 1990 as a right-of-center party that, in addition to supporting a free-market economy, endorsed resumption of the throne by the exiled King Mihai. (In 1992 the ex-king declined nomination as the PNL presidential candidate.) A founding member of the Democratic Convention (*Convenţia Democrată Româna*—CDR), the PNL withdrew from the alliance in April 1992. Two splinter groups, the party's Youth Wing and the PNL–Democratic Convention (*Partidul Naţional Liberal–Convenţia Democrată*—PNL-CD), the latter led by Nicolae CERVENI, refused to endorse the action and remained affiliated with the CDR. Some of the youth wing members later helped form the Liberal Party 1993 (*Partidul Liberal 1993*—PL-93), although others, grouped as the New Liberal Party (*Noul Partid Liberal*—NPL), rejoined the PNL at a February 1993 PNL "unification" congress. Ironically, the 1993 congress ultimately led to formation of a third major splinter when the election of Mircea IONESCU-QUINTUS as chair was contested by his predecessor, Radu CĂMPEANU, who went on to form the **PNL-Câmpeanu** (PNL-C).

Having failed to win any seats in the Chamber of Deputies in September 1992, the PNL later reestablished a presence in that house through absorption in May 1995 of the PL-93's Political Liberal Group (*Grupul Politic Liberal*) and the Group for Liberal Unification (*Grupul pentru Unificarea Liberală*) of the Civic Alliance Party (*Partidul Alianţa Civică*—PAC), although chamber rules to inhibit floor crossing meant that the dozen or so PNL representatives were technically classified as independents. (PAC was an outgrowth of the still active **Civic Alliance** [*Alianţa Civică*—AC], which had been organized in November 1990 by a group of trade unionists and intellectuals to provide an extraparliamentary umbrella for post-Communist opposition groups, in partial emulation of East Germany's New Forum and Czechoslovakia's Civic Forum. At its second congress in July 1991 the AC had voted to establish PAC as its electoral affiliate under the leadership of literary critic Nicolae MANOLESCU. In the 1992 general election PAC had won 13 seats in the Chamber of Deputies and 7 in the Senate as a component of the CDR.)

The PNL rejoined the CDR in time for the November 1996 election and won 25 seats in the chamber and 17 in the Senate. The PNL-CD took 5 seats in the lower house and 4 in the upper, but the PL-93, having left the CDR in 1995, won no seats as part of the National Liberal Alliance (*Alianţa Naţională Liberală*—ANL), which it had formed with PAC.

In February 1997 PNL-CD dissidents, with unofficial support from the CDR, suspended Nicolae Cerveni as chair because of his efforts to join forces with liberals outside the CDR. In June Cerveni loyalists in the PNL-CD united with the PL-93 to form the Liberal Party (*Partidul Liberal*—PL), chaired by Cerveni. Subsequently, in February 1998 PAC merged with the PNL.

In March 1998 the PL and the PNL-Câmpeanu formed an umbrella group called the Liberal Federation (*Federaţia Liberală*—FL), but differences over the PL's relationship to the PNL and the CDR soon led to a bifurcation of the PL, with Cerveni heading one faction and Dinu PATRICIU, the former PL-93 chair, and his supporters constituting another. In May the Cerveni PL was renamed the Romanian Liberal Democratic Party (*Partidul Liberal Democrat Român*—PLDR), while in July 1999 the Patriciu PL was absorbed by the PNL. At the same time, the PNL-CD and PL-93 ceased to exist. In May 1999 Cerveni agreed to merge his party with the Romanian National Party (PNR; see PD), but differences soon emerged and Cerveni competed for the presidency in November 2000 as the candidate of the PLDR, finishing last among 12 contenders. Like the PLDR, the PNL-Câmpeanu, running independently, failed to win representation in either house in 2000.

As the 2000 general election approached, the PNL, increasingly dominated by Deputy Chair Valeriu STOICA, distanced itself from the CDR, and in June 2000 it offered its own candidates in local elections, placing fourth in terms of mayoral victories. When the party formally abandoned the CDR shortly thereafter, Stoica attempted to forge ties to the Alliance for Romania (*Alianţa pentru România*—ApR), but many party members objected, Nicolae Manolescu being the most prominent member to resign as a consequence. In the 2000 presidential contest the PNL endorsed former prime minister Theodor Stolojan, but a group headed by Minister of Finance Decebal Traian REMEŞ, accusing the party of a leftward drift, denounced the selection and left to establish a new party that was registered in October as the National Liberal Party–Traditional (*Partidul Naţional Liberal–Tradiţional*—PNL-T). At the November balloting Stolojan finished third, with 11.8 percent of the vote, while the party won 30 seats in the chamber and 13 in the Senate.

A party congress in February 2001 elected Stoica as PNL chair, the octogenarian Ionescu-Quintus having decided to step down. The following November, the ApR signed a merger agreement with the PNL, and the two united under the PNL rubric on January 19, 2002.

The ApR, a center-left party founded in August 1997, had been formed by reformers who had split off from the PDSR. Led by Teodor Meleşcanu, the ApR regarded itself as a "nonconfrontational" opposition party. It claimed 13 deputies in the chamber and 2 senators upon its formation, but in the November 2000 election it failed at the polls, taking only about 4 percent of the vote for each house. Meleşcanu finished seventh in the concurrent presidential balloting, with 1.9 percent of the vote. Prior to the election the ApR had discussed an alliance with the PNL, but the overtures fell through, in part because the PNL re-fused to accept the ApR leader as its presidential candidate. Because of the ApR's dismal electoral showing, the entire leadership stepped down in early December 2000. At a party conference in March 2001, however, Meleşcanu was returned to office, and the party redefined itself as "social-liberal" (center-right) in orientation. A social democratic (center-left) faction strongly opposed the redefinition, and subsequent efforts by Meleşcanu to negotiate an alliance with the Democratic Party (DP) failed to bear fruit. However, talks with the PNL proved more fruitful, and in 2002 the ApR merged with the PNL, Meleşcanu becoming vice president of the PNL.

With the goal of reuniting all the liberal factions under one banner, in April 2002 the PNL-C absorbed the PNL-T, led by Decebal Traian Remeş. In June the Cerveni wing of the liberal movement (the PLDR) also merged into the PNL-C. At that point, there were only two major liberal groupings—the PNL and the PNL-C. Final consolidation was achieved at the end of 2003 when the PNL-C merged into the PNL. Meanwhile, by that time the Union of Rightist Forces (*Uniunea Forţelor de Dreapta*—UFD) had also merged with the PNL. (See the 2000–2002 *Handbook* for additional information on the UFD.)

In November 2003 the PNL launched the Justice and Truth Alliance (*Alianţa Dreptate şi Adevăr*–ADA) with the PD (below), with the goal of presenting a strong opposition front to the PSD-led governing coalition. The ADA pledged to combat corruption, restore the independence of the judiciary, protect property rights, pursue EU membership, and adopt promarket economic reforms. PNL chair Theodor Stolojan subsequently announced plans to seek the ADA's presidential nomination. However, he retired from the race due to health reasons, and the PNL supported the PD's Traian Băsescu, who was elected president in second- round balloting in December 2004. Subsequently, the ADA (which had finished second in the November legislative balloting to the PSD/PUR alliance) formed a coalition government with PUR and the UDMR, with PNL leader Călin Popescu-Tăriceanu as prime minister. Meanwhile, Stolojan had also resigned as PNL chair and been succeeded by Popescu-Tăriceanu.

The PNL and the PD presented separate candidate lists for the June 2004 local elections (except in Cluj and Bucharest, where joint lists were used). Analysts subsequently described the ADA as "walking a thin line" in representing the sometimes diverse aspirations of the PNL and PD while remaining sufficiently strong as an alliance. Reflecting such concerns, the ADA had copresidents (one each from the PNL and PD) and seven members from each party on its 14-member executive council.

The PNL suffered severe factionalization in the second half of 2006 when a number of prominent members, including Stolojan, strongly criticized the policies and governing approach of Prime Minister Popescu-Tăriceanu. Stolojan and others were expelled from the PNL in October and subsequently formed the PLD, taking nearly 30 PNL legislators with them.

Although there had been talk of a formal merger of the PNL and the PD, the ADA collapsed in the spring of 2007 and the PD moved into opposition. In June 2007 the PNL announced the formation with the PNŢCD and the Popular Action (*Acţiunea Populară*—AP) of a new alliance called the Center-Right Pole (*Polul de Centru-Dreapta*), dedicated to representing the interests of the middle class and supporting liberal, Christian-democratic values. In 2008 the PNL formally absorbed the AP, which had been formed in mid-2003 by supporters of former president Emil Constantinescu, who was named chair of the new party even though he had announced his retirement from politics following his 2000 presidential defeat. Upon the AP's incorporation into the PNL, Constantinescu stated that the leadership and members of the AP would correct "false attitudes" within the PNL and strengthen the party's conservative wing.

Leaders: Crin ANTONESCU (Chair), Ludovic ORBAN (Vice President), Dan Radu RUŞAN (Vice President).

Hungarian Democratic Union of Romania (*Uniunea Democrată a Maghiarilor din România*—UDMR/*Romániai Magyar Demokrata Szövetség*—RMDSz). Representing Romania's Hungarian minority, the newly organized UDMR placed second in the legislative poll of May 1990, winning 29 chamber and 12 Senate seats, despite a mere 7.2 percent vote share; it slipped to fifth in 1992 (with a slightly increased vote share), winning 27 chamber and 12 Senate seats.

Following the resignation of Géza DOMOKOS as UDMR president, the moderate Béla Marko was elected to the post in January 1993 after protestant bishop Lászlo TÖKÉS, a radical, had withdrawn his candidacy to accept appointment as honorary president. In mid-1995 the UDMR was rebuffed in efforts to establish political cooperation with other opposition parties, who claimed that it had become a party of extreme nationalism, favoring immediate local and regional autonomy for the Hungarian community. However, after the UDMR had won 25 chamber and 11 Senate seats in November 1996, it was accepted as a member of the CDR-led coalition government.

The UDMR's role in the coalition was frequently strained in subsequent years over Hungarian-language and minority education issues. The organization nevertheless remained part of the successor administrations of Radu Vasile and Mugur Isărescu. In the election of November 2000 it won 27 seats in the chamber and 12 in the Senate, while its presidential candidate, György FRUNDA, finished fifth, with 6.2 percent of the national vote. In late December the party extended its external support to the PDSR-led minority government of Prime Minister Năstase, which had indicated it would quickly move forward on legislation designed to permit wider use of ethnic languages in localities and to resolve the status of property confiscated during the Communist era.

In 2003 the UDMR suffered a potentially serious setback when several dissident groups announced their "independence" to protest what they considered the "betrayal" of party principles through continued association with the PSD. Among other things, the UDMR rebels accused party leaders of ignoring the grievances of the Hungarian community for the sake of personal gain. Bishop Tökés resigned as the UDMR's honorary president at the 2003 party congress and announced the formation of the Self-Administration of the Hungarian Community from Transylvania (*Autoadministrarea Comunităţii Maghiare din Transilvania*—ACMT), to function as an "ad-hoc parliament" within the UDMR. Another formation, calling itself the Reformist Bloc (*Blocul Reformist*—BR), also was launched at the congress under the leadership of Timis Toro TIBOR. In addition, following the congress, yet another splinter group (the Hungarian Civic Union [*Uniunea Civică Maghiară*—UCM]) was formed by UDMR members. However, the UCM was not permitted to contest subsequent local elections because the electoral commission ruled it was not an officially recognized party.

The UDMR won 22 seats in the Chamber and 10 in the Senate in November 2004, and its decision to join the ADA-led coalition in December 2004 was considered crucial to the establishment of a legislative majority for the cabinet.

The UDMR argued that the new electoral laws of 2008 would weaken the proportional voice of ethnic Hungarians in national elections. Despite these fears, the UDMR took 22 seats in the Chamber and 9 in the Senate in the November balloting. At the insistence of the PSD, the UDMR was excluded from the new ruling coalition, and the UDMR moved into the opposition for the first time since 1996.

Leaders: Béla MARKO (Chair and 2004 presidential candidate), Hunor KELEMEN (Executive President), László BORBÉLY (Vice President).

Other Legislative Parties:

Roma Party "Pro-Europe" (*Partida Romilor "Pro-Europa"*—PRPE). Representing Romania's substantial Roma (Gypsy) population, the Roma Party (*Partida Romilor*—PR) in March 1996 launched an electoral coalition with 11 other Roma groups with the aim of maximizing the impact of the Roma vote in the fall legislative elections. In 2000 the party won only 0.6 percent of the vote for the Chamber of Deputies but claimed one minority seat. The PR reportedly contested the 2004 legislative poll under the rubric of the **Social Democratic Roma Party of Romania** (*Partida Romilor Social Democrată din România*—PRSDR). Registered as the PRPE, the party was accorded the single seat in the Chamber of Deputies reserved for the Roma minority following the 2008 legislative elections.

Leaders: Nicolae PĂUN (Chair), Ivan GHEORGHE.

The 17 other parties or organizations granted one of the seats reserved for minorities in the 2008 elections to the Chamber of Deputies include the **Democratic Forum of Germany in Romania** (*Forumul Democrat al Germanilor din România*—FDGR), which also won a seat in the 2007 Romanian European Parliament elections. The FDGR, whose leaders include Klaus JOHANNIS (President), Martin BOTTESCH, and Ovidiu GANT, additionally holds several mayorships and other local offices.

Other Parties Contesting the 2008 Legislative Elections:

Christian and Democratic National Peasants' Party (*Partidul Național Țărănesc Creștin și Democrat*—PNȚCD). Founded in the prewar period and banned by the Communists, the National Peasants' Party under its veteran leader, Ion PUIU, refused to cooperate with the FSN because of the large number of former Communist officials within its ranks. Prior to the 1990 election members of the "historic" PNȚ agreed to merge with a younger group of Christian Democrats as the PNȚCD, with the leadership going to Corneliu COPOSU, another party veteran, who had spent 17 years in jail during the Communist era.

The PNȚCD was one of the core components of the Democratic Convention of Romania (*Conventia Democrata Romana*—CDR), an anti-FSN alliance launched prior to the local elections of February 1992 as a successor to the eight-party Democratic Union (*Uniunea Democrata*—UD) that had been formed in 1990. By then embracing some 18 parties and organizations, the CDR ran second to the FDSN (see PDSR) in the 1992 parliamentary balloting (winning a 20 percent vote share), while its nominee, Emil Constantinescu, was runner-up to Ion Iliescu in the presidential poll. The ethnic Hungarian UDMR was also affiliated, although it presented a separate list in the 1992 election. In June 1995 the CDR rejected the UDMR's overtures for political cooperation between the two groupings, on the grounds that the UDMR had become too nationalistic.

The PNȚCD's Coposu died in November 1995 and was succeeded in January 1996 by Ion DIACONESCU, who defeated Vice President Ion RAȚIU for the post. In the November legislative balloting the promarket PNȚCD was returned as substantially the largest CDR component party, therefore providing the prime minister in the resultant CDR-led coalition government.

Constantinescu again ran for the presidency in 1996, pledging to accelerate the privatization program and encourage domestic and foreign investment in Romania's economy. His candidacy, which had been proposed by the PNȚCD, provoked some opposition within the CDR. Nevertheless, Constantinescu was a strong second in the presidential balloting in November and comfortably defeated President Iliescu in the runoff. In simultaneous legislative elections, the CDR won pluralities in both the Senate (53 seats) and the chamber (122 seats), with vote shares of 30.7 and 30.2 percent, respectively.

At the time, the center-right CDR included the PNȚCD, the National Liberal Party (PNL), the PNL–Democratic Convention (PNL-CD), Romania's Alternative Party (PAR), the Romanian Ecologist Party (PER), and the Ecological Federation of Romania (FER). In conjunction with the UDMR and the two-party Social Democratic Union (USD), the CDR formed a majority coalition under the PNȚCD's Victor Ciorbea. The CDR remained the core of the government under his successors, Radu Vasile of the PNȚCD and then Mugur Isărescu (nonparty), but by mid-2000 the PNL was preparing to contest the upcoming presidential and legislative elections on its own. PAR had already withdrawn in October 1998.

In April 1998 Victor Ciorbea was succeeded as prime minister by the PNȚCD's Radu Vasile, who was in turn replaced in December 1999 by an independent, Mugur Isărescu. The party subsequently decided to support Isărescu's presidential candidacy in 2000, although several members left in August in support of the PNL candidate, former prime minister Theodor Stolojan. Now known as the CDR 2000, the alliance was formally reconstituted on August 31, 2000, under a protocol signed by the PNȚCD, the Union of Rightist Forces (UFD, successor to PAR), and FER. Subsequently joining were Ciorbea's new Christian Democratic National Alliance (ANCD; see below), the Traditional National Liberal Party (PNL-T), and the Party of Moldovans (PM). (The PM ultimately merged into the PSD in November 2001.)

In the November 2000 general elections the CDR 2000 was wiped out, winning barely 5 percent of the vote in each house and, as a consequence, no seats. Prime Minister Isărescu, who had received the alliance's endorsement for president, finished fourth in the contest, with 9.5 percent of the vote.

The disastrous showing of the CDR 2000 and the PNȚCD in the November 2000 election led the party's entire leadership to resign, with an interim governing board under Constantin Dudu IONESCU being elected on December 2, pending a party congress in early 2001. At the January session the party elected as chair Andrei MARGA, who defeated Ionescu on a third ballot.

In April 1999 Ciorbea had led a faction out of the PNȚCD and formed the Christian Democratic National Alliance (*Alianța Națională Creștin-Democrată*—ANCD). With neither party having won parliamentary seats in November 2000, the ANCD rejoined the parent organization in March 2001. The reunification rapidly led to yet another fissure, however, with Marga resigning as chair and being replaced by Ciorbea in early July. The opposing factions subsequently held competing extraordinary congresses, with Ciorbea being confirmed as chair by the first, on August 14. The forces loyal to Marga held their congress August 17–19 and then, on October 20, established the Popular Christian Party (PPC).

Following a poor showing by the PNȚCD in the mid-2004 local elections, Ciorbea relinquished the party leadership to Gheorghe CIUHANDU, who had just been elected mayor of Timișoara. After another dismal performance in the December 2004 legislative poll (1.85 percent of the vote in the balloting for the Chamber of Deputies), it was reported in 2005 that the PPCD was soliciting consolidation with other centrist parties. In June 2007 the party entered the Center-Right Poll alliance with the PNL and AP, subsequently electing Marian Petre Miluț as chair. In view of the PNȚCD's poor standing in public opinion polls, discussions were launched in September 2008 regarding a possible electoral alliance with the PNL for the November legislative balloting. The resulting agreement saw the PNȚCD support the PNL's parliamentary list in the 2008 elections, but without a formal political alliance in which the PNȚCD would receive a proportion of the legislative seats. Instead, several party members (including Aurelian Pavelescu) ran as candidates on the PNL list. (Pavelescu suggested that, if successful, such candidates could subsequently form an independent bloc in parliament.) Party leadership defended this approach as providing time for reorganization of the party, but the agreement, as well as broader criticism of Miluț's leadership, led to an ongoing revolt in 2009 by the regional party leadership in Cluj and Bucharest counties, including Radu SÂRBU and Gheorghe CIUHANDU, who threatened legal action to gain control over the national leadership. In June 2009 the PNȚCD participated in Romania's European Parliament elections but failed to win any seats.

Leaders: Marian PETRE MILUŢ (Chair), Aurelian PAVELESCU (First Vice Chair).

Greater Romania Party (*Partidul România Mare*—PRM). The political wing of the extreme nationalist Greater Romania movement, the PRM won a 4 percent vote share in the 1992 legislative balloting. In a speech before a congress that reelected him party chair on March 7, 1993, Corneliu Vadim Tudor praised Nicolae Ceauşescu as a Romanian patriot and portrayed his 1989 overthrow as an "armed attack" by Hungary and the former Soviet Union. From mid-1994 the PRM gave external support to the incumbent government coalition but terminated the arrangement in October 1995 amid much acrimony. Vadim Tudor was subsequently named as the PRM's candidate in the November 1996 presidential election, although by vote of the Senate in April he lost his parliamentary immunity and faced possible legal proceedings on over a dozen assorted accusations. Also in April a PRM congress adopted a "blitz strategy" to be followed if the party came to power, including the banning of the ethnic Hungarian UDMR, strict control of foreign investment, and confiscation of "illegally acquired" property.

In early September 1996 the PRM absorbed the small Romanian Party for a New Society (*Partidul Român pentru Noua Societate*—PRNS), led by Gen. Victor VOICHIŢA. It nevertheless managed only 4.5 percent of the lower house vote in the November election, for 19 chamber and 8 Senate seats. Vadim Tudor finished fifth in the presidential race, winning 4.7 percent of the vote.

In September 1997 Vadim Tudor canceled plans for an alliance with the PDSR, saying PDSR leader Ion Iliescu's unification effort was designed to return him as head of state. In February 1998 the PRM signed a protocol with Gheorghe Funar's wing of the PUNR, which envisioned the establishment of a Great Alliance for the Resurrection of the Fatherland. The alliance's agenda included a new government and outlawing of the UDMR. Subsequently, however, Funar and his supporters were forced from the PUNR, and he eventually joined the PRM leadership.

In early 1999 Vadim Tudor publicly supported the Jiu Valley miners' strike, but he subsequently expelled the miners' leader, Miron Cozma, from the PRM for bringing the party into "disrepute." Meanwhile, the Senate suspended Vadim Tudor for his having supported the strikers.

The November 2000 elections constituted a major advance for the PRM, which saw its legislative representation jump to 84 seats in the lower house and 37 in the upper, second only to the PDSR; the party's vote share of 19.5 percent in the chamber and 21.0 percent in the Senate was more than a fourfold increase over its 1996 results. In the presidential race, Vadim Tudor won 28.3 percent of the first-round vote and advanced to a runoff against the PDSR's Iliescu, who, with support from all the other leading parties, prevailed two-to-one over the PRM leader. In the following two years the party lost more than a dozen chamber deputies as well as other defectors dissatisfied with Vadim Tudor's authoritarian leadership and the party's far-right rhetoric. Principal benefactors were the joint PSD-PUR parliamentary faction (which picked up about a dozen seats), the new Socialist Party of National Revival, and the Romanian Socialist Party.

Prior to the 2004 elections Vadim Tudor expressed remorse for his past actions and recanted previous attacks on various minority groups. He subsequently finished third in the first round of presidential balloting in December, while the PRM secured 48 seats in the Chamber of Deputies.

In March 2005 Vadim Tudor issued a surprise announcement that he was stepping down as PRM leader in favor of Corneliu CIONTU, hitherto deputy chair. It was subsequently reported that the PRM had changed its name to the Popular Greater Romania Party (*Partidul Popular România Mare*—PPRM) and had adopted a more moderate centrist platform. However, the mercurial Vadim Tudor in June returned to the forefront and convinced the party's National Council to rescind the name change and return him to his leadership post. Ciontu was collaterally forced from the party, and he and a group of some 16 PRM deputies announced plans to form a new Popular Party. The PRM subsequently lost roughly half of its members to the PC. Its rump agreed in April 2007 to support the new PNL/UDMR minority government as needed in the legislature to maintain government stability.

In the 2008 legislative elections the PRM did not pass the threshold for legislative representation and failed to take any seats in the Chamber of Deputies or Senate for the first time since 1996. The defeat led to an unprecedented agreement with the PNG-CD (below) to combine electoral lists for the June 2009 balloting for Romanian delegates to the European Parliament, with Tudor taking one of the three seats won by the alliance.

Leaders: Corneliu VADIM TUDOR (Chair), Lucian BOLCAS (Vice President), Gheorghe FUNAR (Secretary General).

New Generation Party-Christian Democrat (*Partidul Noua Generaţie-Creştin Democrat*—PNG-CD). The New Generation Party (PNG) was launched in 2000 under the leadership of Virel LIS, the former mayor of Bucharest. However, Lis subsequently left the party, and the leadership mantle eventually passed to George Becali, the owner of a prominent soccer club. Campaigning on a center-right platform, Becali secured 1.8 percent of the vote in the first round of the December 2004 presidential balloting. In April 2006 the party changed its name to the PNG-CD.

The PNG-CD won less than 3 percent of the vote in the 2008 balloting for the Senate and Chamber of Deputies, failing to reach the electoral thresholds. Consequently, merger talks were launched with the PD-L in early 2009, but Becali's subsequent arrest on charges of kidnapping (allegedly, thieves who had earlier stolen his car) led to a cessation of the talks. Cooperation with the PRM in the 2009 European Parliament elections, in which Becali won a seat, reignited speculation of a merger of the two significant far-right parties.

Leader: George BECALI.

Romanian Socialist Party (*Partidul Socialist Român*—PSR). Founded in 1992, the small PSR (claiming status as the successor to various socialist parties dating back to 1872) became a parliamentary party in September 2002 with the adherence of two former Greater Romania deputies who had defected to the government earlier in the year. The party thereupon underwent a significant transformation, with one of the deputies, Sever MEŞCA, being elected party chair on October 21. The PSR failed to reach the required threshold for legislative representation in 2008.

Leaders: Ion CIUCĂ (Chair), Dan STUPARU (Executive Chair), Vasile ORLEANU (President of Supreme Council), Stefan AMUZA (Secretary General).

Romanian Ecologist Party (*Partidul Ecologist Român*—PER). The PER is an ecological group founded in 1978 in opposition to Socialist-era economic development. In 1989 it was registered as a political party with a substantially smaller membership than the Ecologist Movement of Romania (*Mişcarea Ecologistă din România*) with which it cooperated in 1992. Standing in its own right as a CDR party in 1996, it won five chamber seats and one in the Senate.

For the November 2000 parliamentary elections PER spearheaded formation of an alliance called the **Romanian Ecologist Pole** (*Polul Ecologist din România*) that also included the smaller **Green Alternative Party–Ecologists** (*Partidul Alternativa Verde–Ecologiştii*—PAVE) and the **Romanian Ecologist Convention Party** (*Partidul Convenţia Ecologistă din România*—PCER). The alliance offered a joint candidate list that polled less than 1 percent of the vote in each house. Asked before the election if he would consider an alliance with the larger **Ecological Federation of Romania** (*Federaţia Ecologistă din România*), the PER's Otto WEBER commented that he would not merge with a party of former intelligence service "informers." In early 2003 it was reported that the PER, PAVE, and PCER had merged under the PER rubric. In 2008 the PER created an electoral alliance with the Green Party to form the electoral alliance **Green Ecologist Party** (*Partidul Verde Ecologist*), which failed to reach the electoral threshold.

Leaders: Danut POP (Chair), Petre METANIE (Honorary Leader), Radu MUNTEANU (Executive Chair).

Romanian Workers' Party (*Partidul Muncitoresc Român*—PMR). The PMR was launched in March 1995 by former Communists who claimed that conditions had deteriorated in Romania since the overthrow of Ceauşescu in December 1989. The party subsequently attempted to change its name to the Romanian Communist Party (PCR), but the government refused. It won under 1 percent of the vote in the 2000 general election. In January 2001 the PMR asked that Ceauşescu's remains be exhumed to clarify the circumstances of his death. In mid-2005 it was reported that the PMR had joined with the **United Socialist Party** (*Partidul Socialist Unit*—PSU) to form the **United Left Party** (*Partidul Stângii Unite*). In April 2008 long-term chair Ilie NEACŞU retired; although he was replaced with an interim chair, party activities were halted at least temporarily and the PMR did not register for the November 2008 elections.

Leaders: Nicolae PAVELESCU (Interim Chair), Cristian NICOLAE (Vice Chair), Sever MEŞCA (Vice President).

Democratic Front of Romania Party (*Partidul Frontul Democrat din România*—PFDR). The PFDR was formed in 2003 by Petre Roman, former prime minister and former chair of the PD. Roman won 1.35 percent of the vote in the first round of the December 2004 presidential balloting.

Leader: Petre ROMAN.

Other parties participating in the 2008 legislative balloting included the **Christian Democratic National Party** (*Partidul Naţional Democrat Creştin*—PNDC); **the Popular Party for Social Protection** (*Partidul Popular şi al Protecţiei Sociale*—PPPS), formerly the **Romanian Party of Pensioners** (*Partidul Pensionarilor din România*—PPR); and **the Party of European Romania** (*Partidul României Europene*—PRE).

LEGISLATURE

The present Romanian legislature is a bicameral **Parliament** (*Parlament*) consisting of a Senate and a Chamber of Deputies, each with a four-year term. Elections from 1990 to 2004 were conducted via proportional representation on the basis of party lists. However, a complicated (and confusing to most analysts) new system (combining majoritarian and proportional elements) was adopted by Parliament in March 2008. Voters now cast a single ballot for candidates within single-member districts or "colleges," the number of districts in each of the 43 constituencies (1 constituency for each of the nation's 41 counties, 1 for Bucharest, and 1 for nonresident Romanians) varying according to population. Votes are initially tallied on a nationwide basis to determine whether parties and alliances have achieved the necessary threshold for representation (5 percent of the total national vote for single parties, 8 percent for two-party alliances, 9 percent for three-party alliances, and 10 percent for alliances of four or more parties.) Parties or alliances that win six Chamber seats or three Senate seats outright (by a candidate securing more than 50 percent of the votes in a district) are also deemed to have qualified for representation, even if they do not pass the national threshold requirements. Votes are then tallied within each of the 43 constituencies, and a proportional formula is applied to determine how many seats each party or alliance should receive in each constituency. Candidates who receive more than 50 percent of the vote in a district are elected automatically, assuming national threshold requirements have been met by their party or alliance. Unallocated seats (those from districts in which no candidate has received a majority of the vote) are then distributed on a proportional basis within the 43 constituencies. Adjustments at this point (involving, e.g., a party that received more "direct" seats than it theoretically should have received based on its proportion of the vote in a constituency) can alter the final total memberships of the two houses.

Senate (*Senat*). The upper house currently comprises 137 members elected from 137 single-member districts containing, for the most part, 160,000 inhabitants each (two seats are elected in districts, or "colleges," reserved for nonresident Romanians).

Following the elections of November 30, 2008, the Democratic Liberal Party held 51 seats; the alliance of the Social Democratic Party (PSD) and Conservative Party (PC), 49 (PSD, 48; PC, 1); the National Liberal Party, 28; and the Hungarian Democratic Union of Romania, 9.

Chair: Mircea GEOANĂ.

Chamber of Deputies (*Camera Deputaţilor*). The lower house currently comprises 334 members. Most seats are filled via voting in 315 single-member districts containing 70,000 inhabitants each (4 of the districts, or "colleges," are reserved for nonresident Romanians). Organizations representing the following 18 ethnic communities are also given seats (assuming that no members of the ethnic community had otherwise been elected): Albanians, Armenians, Bulgarians, Croats, Czechs and Slovaks, Germans, Greeks, Italians, Jews, Lipovenian Russians, Poles, Roma, Ruthenians, Serbs, Slav Macedonians, Turko-Muslim Tatars, Turks, and Ukrainians. Voting for the minority seats is via nationwide balloting for each ethnic community, the party securing a plurality of votes for each community claiming that community's seat.

Following the elections of November 30, 2008, the Democratic Liberal Party held 115 seats; the alliance of the Social Democratic Party (PSD) and Conservative Party (PC), 114 (PSD, 110; PC, 4); the National Liberal Party, 65; and the Hungarian Democratic Union of Romania, 22.

Chair: Roberta ANASTASE.

CABINET

[as of September 1, 2009] *(see headnote)*

Prime Minister	Emil Boc (PD-L)
Deputy Prime Minister	Dan Nica (PSD)
Ministers	
Administration and Interior	Dan Nica (PSD)
Agriculture and Rural Development	Ille Sărbu (PSD)
Communications and Information Technology	Gabriel Sandu (PD-L)
Culture and Religious Affairs	Theodor Paleologu (PD-L)
Development, Public Works, and Housing	Vasile Blaga (PD-L)
Economy	Adriean Videanu (PD-L)
Education, Research, and Innovation	Ecaterina Andronescu (PSD) [f]
Environment and Sustainable Development	Nicolae Nemirschi (PSD)
Finance	Gheorghe Pogea (PD-L)
Foreign Affairs	Cristian Diaconescu (PSD)
Justice	Cătălin Marian Predolu (ind.)
Labor, Social Equality, and Family	Marian Sârbu (PSD)
National Defense	Mihai Stănişoară (PD-L)
Public Health	Ion Bazac (PD-L)
Relations with Parliament	Victor Ponta (PSD)
Small- and Medium-Sized Companies, Commerce, Tourism, and Liberal Professions	Constantin Niţă (PSD)
Sport and Youth	Sorina Luminiţa Plăcintă (PD-L) [f]
Tourism	Elena Udrea (PD-L) [f]
Transport	Radu Berceanu (PD-L)

[f] = female

COMMUNICATIONS

Following the overthrow of Nicolae Ceauşescu in 1989, there was a rapid expansion in the number of mainstream news outlets as well as those devoted to "tabloid" journalism. As a whole, the Romanian media has subsequently been criticized for being too heavily influenced by political bias. Meanwhile, the criminal code has recently been revised to reduce or eliminate penalties against journalists accused of "defamation" of authorities.

Press. In 2002 there were more than 106 dailies and nearly 1,800 periodicals, although some of them have since closed due to a lack of readership and/or advertisers. *Monitorul Oficial* (the Official Monitor) is the government newspaper; it publishes laws and other formal documents that are integral to the legislative process. The leading Romanian-language newspapers published in Bucharest include *Libertatea* (Freedom, 235,000); *Jurnalul Naţional* (National Journal, 68,000), owned by prominent politician Dan Voiculescu; *Evenimentul Zilei* (Events of the Day, 53,000), a tabloid launched in 1992 that has recently begun in-depth coverage of political news; *Gândul* (Thought, 32,000), launched in 2005; *Adevărul* (The Truth, 28,000), which replaced the former Communist Party organ *Scânteia* (The Spark) in 1990; *Ziua* (The Day, 16,000); *România Liberă* (The Free Romanian, 55,000); *Curierul Naţional* (The National Courier); *Cronica Română* (The Romanian Chronicles); *Cotidianul* (The Daily); and *Realitatea Românească* (The Romanian Reality). Newspapers published in other cities include *Realitatea* (Reality), published in Timişoara; *Ziarul de Iaşi* (The Iaşi Newspaper), published in Iaşi; *Viaţa Liberă* (The Free Life), published in Galaţi; and *Clujeanul,* published in Cluj-Napoca. *Adevărul de Seară,* a free national daily, was launched in October 2008 with initial circulation of 250,000.

News agencies. The official organ is the Romanian Press Agency (*Agenția de Presă Română*—Rompres). A private news service called Media Fax was launched in 1991 and is currently reportedly used by about 90 percent of the domestic news outlets. ANSA, AP, Reuters, and *Xinhua* are among the numerous foreign agencies that maintain bureaus in Bucharest.

Broadcasting and computing. Romanian Radio and Television (*Radioteleviziunea Română*) is a state agency controlling most broadcast operations. *Radiodifuziunea Română* transmits domestic programs as well as foreign broadcasts in over a dozen languages, while *Televiziunea Română* and *Televiziunea Națională* offer domestic TV programming. Romania's first independent television station, Soti TV, was forced by financial problems to close in June 1994. Subsequently, a number of private TV stations were established, including the very successful PRO-TV, which features journalists trained in Western news operations. Government interference with Romanian Radio and Television relaxed in 1997, as promised by the Constantinescu government. As of 2008 there were 290 Internet users per 1,000 inhabitants.

INTERGOVERNMENTAL REPRESENTATION

Ambassador to the U.S.: Adrian Cosmin VIERITA.

U.S. Ambassador to Romania: Mark H. GITENSTEIN.

Permanent Representative to the UN: Simona Mirela MICULESCU.

IGO Memberships (Non-UN): BIS, BSEC, CEI, CEUR, EBRD, Eurocontrol, Interpol, IOM, NATO, OIF, OSCE, PCA, WCO, WTO.

RUSSIA

Russian Federation/Russia
Rossiiskaya Federatsiya/Rossiya

Political Status: Formerly the Russian Soviet Federative Socialist Republic (RSFSR), a constituent republic of the Union of Soviet Socialist Republics (USSR); present official designations adopted on April 17, 1992; current constitution approved by referendum of December 12, 1993.

Area: 6,592,800 sq. mi. (17,075,400 sq. km.).

Population: 145,166,731 (2002C); 140,795,000 (2008E).

Major Urban Centers (2005E): MOSCOW (10,150,000), St. Petersburg (formerly Leningrad, 4,105,000), Novosibirsk (1,406,000), Nizhny Novgorod (formerly Gorky, 1,298,000), Yekaterinburg (formerly Sverdlovsk, 1,304,000), Samara (formerly Kuibyshev, 1,152,000), Omsk (1,143,000), Rostov-na-Donu (1,058,000), Volgograd (1,033,000), Vladivostok (587,000).

Official Languages: Russian, in addition to languages recognized by the constituent republics and autonomous areas.

Monetary Unit: Ruble (official rate December 1, 2009: 29.05 rubles = $1US).

President: Dmitri MEDVEDEV; elected on March 2, 2008, and inaugurated for a four-year term on May 7, succeeding Vladimir PUTIN. (United Russia).

Chair of the Government (Prime Minister): Vladimir PUTIN (United Russia); nominated by the president on May 7, 2008, and approved by the State Duma on May 8 to succeed Viktor ZUBKOV.

THE COUNTRY

The world's largest country, with more than three-quarters of the former Soviet Union's land mass (though little more than half of its population), the Russian Federation stretches for more than 5,000 miles from the Baltic Sea in the west to the Pacific Ocean in the east. Its contiguous neighbors lie along an arc that encompasses Norway and Finland in the northwest; Estonia, Latvia, Lithuania, Poland, and Belarus in the west; Ukraine in the southwest; and Georgia, Azerbaijan, Kazakhstan, Mongolia, China, and North Korea in the south. Although there are upward of 100 nationalities, approximately 80 percent of the population is Russian. There are also many millions of ethnic Russians living in the "near abroad" of the other ex-Soviet republics. Women make up about 49 percent of the active labor force but remain underrepresented in government. About 10 percent of the 2003–2007 State Duma seats were occupied by women.

Russia possesses a highly diversified economy, including major manufacturing centers in the northwestern, central European, and Ural mountain regions; substantial hydroelectric capacity in the Volga River basin and Siberia; and widespread reserves of oil, natural gas, coal, gold, industrial diamonds, and other minerals. At present, industry contributes about 39 percent of GDP and employs 29 percent of the active workforce; agriculture, 5 percent of GDP and 11 percent of workers; and services, 56 percent of GDP and 61 percent of workers.

A commitment to radical economic reform was the centerpiece of Russian government policy following the collapse of the Soviet Union, including price liberalization, currency convertibility, privatization, and encouragement of foreign investment. Despite progress on these fronts, the transition yielded an estimated 25 percent contraction in GDP from 1992 to 1994, with further declines of 6 percent in 1995 and 5 percent in 1996. The inflation rate soared to 1,350 percent in 1992 before being reined back to 131 percent in 1995 and to 22 percent in 1996. The near-collapse of the ruble during a currency crisis in October 1994 left its value at around 4,000 to the U.S. dollar (compared with an official one-to-one rate only five years earlier), with further depreciation taking the rate above 5,500 by late 1996. Currency reform at the end of 1997 restructured the rate to about 6 rubles to the U.S. dollar.

The economy finally saw some recovery in 1997, with GDP rising by a modest 0.4 percent, but in August 1998 the economy went into a tailspin as low world oil prices, a continuing East Asian financial crisis, and Russia's unmanageable debt contributed to a rapid drop in the ruble, which had lost some 70 percent of its value by the first quarter of 1999. For 1998 as a whole, GDP dropped by 4.6 percent and inflation soared to 85 percent. In late April 1999 the International Monetary Fund (IMF), which had suspended loan disbursements to Russia the previous August, agreed to provide an additional $4.5 billion to cover part of Russia's massive debt servicing over the succeeding 18 months. In 1999, however, economic growth recovered to 5.4 percent, and inflation dropped to about 36 percent, a much better performance than initially forecast. A March 2000 report by the Organization for Economic Cooperation and Development (OECD) attributed the quick turnaround to significant progress in Russia's conversion to market economics.

GDP growth registered 8.3 percent in 2000, aided by a boom in world oil prices and the increased competitiveness of the devalued ruble. Growth in 2001 remained strong, at 5.2 percent, but consumer price inflation remained high, at over 20 percent. Inflation retreated somewhat from 2002 to 2004, with GDP growth expanding from 4.7 percent in 2002 to 7.3 percent in 2003 and holding at 7.2 percent in 2004. Annual growth for 2005–2006 averaged about 6.7 percent as hydrocarbon earnings soared. Annual growth rose to 8.1 percent in 2007, though in the second half of the year inflation rose to 12 percent. Economic growth slowed to 6 percent in 2008, owing in large part to the global financial crisis, which caused a significant decline in oil prices and thus, a dramatic decrease in government revenue. Other contributing factors were the republic's weak banking system, and the flight of some foreign investors due to the fighting in Georgia (see Current issues, below). In 2009, with economic growth expected to contract to about 3 percent as a result of the worldwide recession, the IMF recommended "urgent" reforms in the banking sector, as well as in the public sectors of health, education, and civil service. It also pressed the government to limit its $20 billion stimulus, citing concerns that the expenditure and the tax cuts that made the money available would be difficult to reverse once the recession ended. Further, the IMF said it was concerned that support for Russia's accession to the World Trade Organization (WTO) was "losing momentum." On a positive note, fund managers commended authorities' efforts to curb inflation.

GOVERNMENT AND POLITICS

Political background. Russia's early national history was that of a series of small medieval fiefs that gradually united under the leadership of the grand dukes of Moscow in the 15th and 16th centuries, expanding into a vast but unstable empire that collapsed midway through World War I. Military defeat and rising social unrest resulting from that conflict led directly to the "February" Revolution of 1917, which resulted in the abdication of Tsar NICHOLAS II (March 15, 1917, by the Western calendar), and the formation of a provisional government whose best-remembered leader was Aleksandr F. KERENSKY. Unable to cope with the country's mounting social, political, economic, and military problems, the provisional government was forcibly overthrown in the "October" Revolution of November 7, 1917, by the Bolshevik wing of the Russian Social Democratic Party under Vladimir Ilyich LENIN. The new Soviet regime—so called because it based its power on the support of newly formed workers', peasants', and soldiers' councils, or "soviets"—proceeded under Lenin's guidance to proclaim a dictatorship of the proletariat; to nationalize land, means of production, banks, and railroads; and to establish on July 10, 1918, a socialist state known as the Russian Soviet Federative Socialist Republic (RSFSR).

Draconian peace terms imposed by the Central Powers under the Brest-Litovsk Treaty of March 3, 1918, were invalidated by that alliance's eventual defeat in the west, but civil war between the Bolsheviks and the Whites, compounded by foreign intervention in Russia, lasted until 1922. Other Soviet Republics that had meanwhile been established in Ukraine, Byelorussia, and Transcaucasia joined with the RSFSR by treaty in 1922 to establish the Union of Soviet Socialist Republics (USSR), whose first constitution was adopted on July 6, 1923. The Central Asian territories of Turkmenistan and Uzbekistan became constituent republics in 1925, followed by Tajikistan in 1929 and Kazakhstan and Kyrgyzstan in 1936, at which time dissolution of the Transcaucasian SSR yielded separate union status for Armenia, Azerbaijan, and Georgia. The Estonian, Latvian, Lithuanian, and Moldavian SSRs were formally proclaimed in 1940.

Lenin's death in 1924 had been followed by struggles within the leadership of the ruling Communist Party before Joseph Vissarionovich STALIN emerged in the later 1920s as the unchallenged dictator of the party and country. There followed an era characterized by extremes: forced industrialization that began with the First Five-Year Plan in 1928; all-out collectivization in agriculture commencing 1929–1930; and far-reaching political and military purges from 1936 to 1938. The conclusion in August 1939, on the eve of World War II, of a ten-year nonaggression pact with Nazi Germany enabled Soviet military power to expand Soviet frontiers at the expense of Poland, Finland, Romania, and the Baltic states of Estonia, Latvia, and Lithuania. Nazi-Soviet collaboration came to an abrupt end when German forces attacked the USSR on June 22, 1941. The subsequent years of heavy fighting, which cost the USSR an estimated 20 million lives and left widespread devastation in European Russia, eliminated the military power of Germany and ultimately enabled the USSR to extend its influence into the heart of Europe.

Stalin's death in March 1953 initiated a new period of political maneuvering among his successors. The post of chair of the Council of Ministers, held successively by Georgy M. MALENKOV (1953–1955) and Nikolai A. BULGANIN (1955–1958), was assumed in March 1958 by Nikita S. KHRUSHCHEV, who had become first secretary of the Soviet Communist Party in September 1953. Khrushchev's denunciation of Stalin's despotism at the 20th Communist Party of the Soviet Union (CPSU) Congress in February 1956 gave impetus to a policy of "de-Stalinization" in the USSR and Eastern Europe, while emphasis in Soviet foreign policy shifted from military confrontation to "competitive coexistence," symbolized by a growing foreign aid program and by such achievements as the launching of the world's first artificial earth satellite, *Sputnik,* in 1957. Khrushchev's policies nevertheless contributed to a series of sharp crises within and beyond the Communist world. An incipient liberalization movement in Hungary was crushed by Soviet armed forces in 1956, relations with Communist China deteriorated from year to year, and recurrent challenges to the West culminated in a defeat for Soviet aims in the confrontation with the United States over Soviet missiles in Cuba in October 1962.

Khrushchev's erratic performance resulted in his dismissal in October 1964 and the substitution of collective rule, under which Leonid I. BREZHNEV became head of the CPSU and Aleksei N. KOSYGIN became chair of the Council of Ministers. In 1965 Nikolai V. PODGORNY succeeded Anastas I. MIKOYAN as chair of the Presidium of the Supreme Soviet and thereby as nominal head of state, while Brezhnev clearly emerged from the 24th party congress in 1971 as first among equals. His position as CPSU general secretary was reconfirmed at the 25th and 26th congresses in 1976 and 1981. In June 1977 the Supreme Soviet designated Secretary Brezhnev to succeed Podgorny as chair of the Presidium.

In October 1980 Kosygin asked to be relieved of his duties as chair of the Council of Ministers because of declining health, and he was replaced by First Deputy Chair Nikolai TIKHONOV. Of more far-reaching consequence was the death of Brezhnev in November 1982 and his replacement as party secretary by Yuri V. ANDROPOV, who had previously served as head of the KGB, the Soviet intelligence and internal security agency. Andropov was named chair of the Presidium in June 1983 but died in February 1984. He was succeeded as CPSU general secretary and, two months later, as head of state by Konstantin Y. CHERNENKO.

Long reputed to be in failing health and widely viewed as having been elevated to the top leadership on a "caretaker" basis, Chernenko died in March 1985. As evidence that the succession had already been agreed upon, the relatively young (54-year-old) Mikhail S. GORBACHEV was named general secretary on the following day. The Presidium chairship remained temporarily vacant.

During the ensuing four years, wide-ranging personnel changes occurred in both the party and the government. In July 1985 the long-time foreign minister, Andrei A. GROMYKO, was named Presidium chair, while Nikolai I. RYZHKOV replaced the aging Tikhonov as chair of the Council of Ministers in September. In October 1988 Secretary Gorbachev was elected to the additional post of Presidium chair, with Gromyko moving into retirement. Two months later extensive constitutional revisions introduced a new parliamentary system, competitive elections, heightened judicial independence, and other changes in keeping with Gorbachev's policies of openness (glasnost), restructuring (perestroika), and greater democracy.

In May 1989 a new, supralegislative Congress of People's Deputies elected Gorbachev to a five-year term as chair of a restructured Supreme Soviet, with Anatoly I. LUKYANOV (vice chair of the Presidium since October) redesignated as Gorbachev's deputy. Following further constitutional amendments in December 1989 and March 1990 that sanctioned a multiparty system, increased the scope of direct elections, and broadened the rights of private property and enterprise, the Congress named Gorbachev in March 1990 to the new post of Union president. Concurrently, it elected Lukyanov chair of the Supreme Soviet.

In June 1990 the Russian Federation issued a declaration asserting the primacy of the RSFSR constitution within its territorial limits. The document also asserted a right to engage in foreign relations and "freely leave the USSR" in accordance with procedures set forth in Union law.

Earlier, on the basis of constitutional reforms approved at the Union level in 1988, the Russian Federation had emulated the central USSR administration by establishing a two-tiered legislative system consisting of a Congress of People's Deputies and a bicameral Supreme Soviet elected by the Congress. On May 29, 1990, the 1,068 Congress deputies, who had been elected in competitive balloting on March 4, elected Boris YELTSIN as chair of the RSFSR Supreme Soviet, and hence, de facto president of the federation.

On July 20, 1990, Yeltsin announced a "500-day" drive toward a market economy within the federation, which subsequently became the core of an all-Union plan that secured approval in weakened form three months later. In mid-November, following a meeting with USSR President Gorbachev, Yeltsin called for a central "coalition government of national unity" as a prelude to further Union negotiations.

During the fall and winter of 1990–1991 conservative forces (principally elements of the administrative and Communist Party bureaucracies, the army, the interior police, and the KGB) ranged themselves against Gorbachev's pluralist measures. For a time, the Soviet leader appeared to offer little resistance to the backlash, but a six-month lapse into authoritarianism ended dramatically in April 1991 with a much-heralded "nine-plus-one" conference, at which the participating republics (with Armenia, Georgia, Moldova, and the Baltic states not attending) endorsed a new Union Treaty that called for extensive decentralization in social, political, and economic spheres. Under the plan, a new constitution would be drafted for a "Union of Soviet Sovereign Republics."

At a nonbinding referendum on the draft of the Union Treaty on March 17, 1991, RSFSR voters had registered 71.3 percent approval, with 69.9 percent also endorsing the creation of a directly elected RSFSR presidency. On April 5 the republican Congress voted to create the office, and on June 12 Yeltsin defeated five other candidates, including former Soviet ministerial chair Nikolai Ryzhkov, for the presidency, with Aleksandr RUTSKOI elected vice president.

During the week of August 19, 1991, a self-proclaimed State Committee for the State of Emergency (SCSE), led by Soviet Vice President Gennadi YANAYEV, responded to Gorbachev's reforms and the new Union proposal by launching an attempted coup. With RSFSR President Yeltsin in the forefront of the opposition, the coup quickly failed and USSR President Gorbachev resumed constitutional authority. By the end of the month, however, most of the republican parties had renounced the authority of the CPSU, Ukraine had declared its independence, and Yeltsin had called upon Gorbachev to recognize the independence of Estonia, Latvia, and Lithuania.

On September 6, 1991, Moscow accepted the withdrawal of the Baltic states. The remaining 12 republics, during a meeting at Alma-Ata (Almaty), Kazakhstan, held October 1–2, endorsed a plan for what Gorbachev characterized as a union of "confederal democratic states." However, in a referendum on December 1 Ukrainians overwhelmingly endorsed complete independence, and one week later in Brest, Belarus, both Russia and Belarus joined Ukraine in proclaiming the demise of the Soviet Union. On December 21 Russia and 10 of its sister republics (with Georgia not participating) proclaimed the formation of the Commonwealth of Independent States (CIS—see under Intergovernmental Organizations), and four days later Gorbachev, the last president of the USSR, resigned.

Meanwhile, in mid-July 1991 the RSFSR Congress of People's Deputies had encountered an impasse over the selection of Yeltsin's successor as chair of the Russian Supreme Soviet. When no candidate managed to muster a majority in six rounds of voting, the former deputy chair, Ruslan KHASBULATOV, who had been accused of an excessively authoritarian leadership style, was named acting chair. Two months later a dispute broke out in the Supreme Soviet over an attempt by the president to augment his executive powers, and on September 27 Ivan SILAYEV resigned as chair of the Council of Ministers. In late October Khasbulatov was confirmed as Supreme Soviet chair and Yeltsin personally took over Silayev's responsibilities, while continuing to press for enhanced capacity to move forward with his economic reforms. On November 1 the added powers were approved, as was authority to suspend the actions of the presidents of the autonomous republics within the RSFSR. On November 6 Yeltsin was formally invested as chair of the Council of Ministers. On the same day he issued a decree banning both the Union and the republican Communist parties and nationalizing their assets.

The abolition of most price controls and other "shock therapy" economic measures in 1992 intensified a clash between ministers and legislators, with Khasbulatov warning that the federation could encounter "a catastrophic decline in living standards, famine [and] social upheaval." The cabinet responded by submitting its resignation on April 12, with members withdrawing en masse from the Congress of People's Deputies. In the end, after defeating a proposal by Khasbulatov that would have stripped the president of most of his powers, the deputies adopted a declaration that permitted a resumption of governmental activity, with an architect of the Yeltsin reform program, Finance Minister Yegor GAIDAR, being named acting chair of the Council of Ministers on June 15. Yeltsin's victory was, however, less than total. He failed in a bid to further augment his executive powers and was precluded from effectively moving on land reform, most notably in regard to privatization.

During the final months of 1992 Yeltsin was forced into an increasingly defensive posture on domestic policy. In October he came under particular attack from an alliance of former Communists and Russian nationalist extremists, whose newly proclaimed National Salvation Front he felt obliged to outlaw after it had indicated a readiness to seize power. Concurrently, he ordered the disbanding of the Directorate for the Supreme Bodies of Power and Government, a 5,000-man armed formation under the personal control of Khasbulatov. Nevertheless, two months later Yeltsin was obliged to abandon Gaidar, his leading reform advocate, and accept as prime minister Viktor S. CHERNOMYRDIN, previously in charge of the state fuel-energy complex.

In early 1993 the contest between Yeltsin and Khasbulatov intensified, with the former campaigning for an April referendum on major provisions of a new constitution and the latter calling for early parliamentary and presidential elections in 1994. In mid-February the two agreed to convene an emergency session of the Congress of People's Deputies to address the issue of legislative-executive relations, although Yeltsin later indicated that he would proceed with the referendum even without the legally mandated consent of the legislature. The Presidium of the Supreme Soviet responded by approving Khasbulatov's motion to seek a declaration of emergency rule and substantial curtailment of presidential power.

On March 28, 1993, during an emergency Ninth Congress, a motion to dismiss Yeltsin secured a substantial majority, but not the two-thirds required for implementation; a similar motion to dismiss Khasbulatov, which required only a simple majority, also failed. The Congress then proceeded to authorize an April 25 referendum at which the voters simultaneously voiced support for Yeltsin and his socioeconomic policies as well as for early legislative elections.

Two days before the referendum Yeltsin had unveiled his draft constitution, which called for a strong presidency, a bicameral legislature, and an independent judiciary. Not unexpectedly, the document was rejected on May 7, 1993, by the Supreme Soviet's Constitutional Commission, which preferred a parliament with expanded powers, including the capacity to reject government appointments. Undaunted, the president on June 5 convened a 700-member constitutional conference, which approved his draft on July 12.

Yeltsin's renewed ascendancy was demonstrated on September 16, 1993, by the reappointment of Gaidar as deputy prime minister and economics minister. Moreover, in actions that were immediately repudiated by the Constitutional Court, the president on September 21 issued a decree on constitutional reform, suspended both the Congress of People's Deputies and the Supreme Soviet, called for the election of a new bicameral legislature on December 11–12, and announced that presidential balloting would take place on June 12, 1994. The Congress, assembling in an emergency session, responded by voting to impeach the president and named the conservative Rutskoi, whom Yeltsin had suspended as vice president on September 1, as his successor.

Yeltsin thereupon mounted a series of measures against his legislative opponents that culminated in the House of Soviets ("White House") being sealed off by some 2,000 troops on September 27. A number of armed clashes followed, with the anti-Yeltsin leaders surrendering on the evening of October 4 after government forces had stormed the building. Overall, the fighting cost some 140 lives, while several hundred people were injured. As the power struggle drew to a close, Yeltsin announced that the December 12 elections would be augmented to include a referendum on the new constitution. However, the proposal for an early presidential election was abandoned.

In polling for the State Duma, the lower house of the new Federal Assembly, the pro-reform Russia's Choice list won a plurality of seats but was strongly challenged by both right- and left-wing opponents. At the same time, 58.4 percent of participating voters approved the new constitution. The most startling success was that of the neofascist

Liberal Democratic Party of Russia (*Liberalno-Demokraticheskaya Partiya Rossii*—LDPR), led by Vladimir ZHIRINOVSKY, which secured the largest share (22.8 percent) in the party preference poll and finished second overall in the State Duma race, with 64 of 450 seats.

Events in early 1994 illustrated Yeltsin's increased political vulnerability as a result of the 1993 election. In January both Gaidar and the reformist finance minister, Boris FEDOROV, resigned after failing to secure a number of objectives. A month later the State Duma voted to grant amnesty not only to the leaders of the October 1993 parliamentary maneuverings but also to those involved in the August 1991 coup attempt. Yeltsin responded on April 28 by concluding a two-year Treaty on Civil Accord with 245 political and social groups. The document specified, among other things, that controversial constitutional changes would be avoided, that there would be no early elections, that local self-government would be strengthened, and that the rights of ethnic minorities would be supported. Signatories of the document included not only arch-reformer Gaidar but also Zhirinovsky, whereas some rightists, notably former vice president Rutskoi, denounced it as unconstitutional.

The Treaty on Civil Accord yielded a measure of political stability for the Chernomyrdin government, while steps were taken to reduce the potential for presidential/ministerial tension. At the same time, the slowdown in the pace of economic reform attracted growing criticism from Gaidar, whose party was renamed Russia's Democratic Choice (*Demokraticheskii Vybor Rossii*—DVR) in June 1994. In October the government was jarred by a major currency crisis that halved the external value of the ruble and led, a month later, to a major reshuffle of economic portfolios.

The Russian government made some progress in 1994 in improving relations with its more fractious constituent republics, concluding accords with Tatarstan in February and with Bashkortostan in August that provided for substantial home rule. However, the self-declared "independent" Republic of Chechnya in the Caucasus proved to be obdurate. In the wake of mounting tensions Russian forces launched a full-scale invasion of the territory on December 11 with the aim of restoring central government authority. Despite fierce Chechen resistance, the Russians finally captured the capital, Grozny, on February 6, 1995, and thereafter extended their control to other population centers.

The invasion of Chechnya dominated Russian politics in the first half of 1995. The action was strongly supported by the nationalist right but opposed by important elements of the centrist/reformist parties that had usually backed the Yeltsin administration, notably Gaidar's DVR. Ministry of Defense figures in late February 1995 put the number of dead and missing Russian soldiers at about 1,500, but independent observers estimated that some 10,000 Russians might have been killed and that Chechen civilian deaths totaled 25,000 in Grozny alone. International criticism of the action was particularly strong in the Islamic world—the Chechens being predominantly Muslim—and was heightened by Red Cross reports that Russian soldiers had massacred at least 250 civilians during an April assault on the village of Samashki in western Chechnya. Moreover, it appeared that a protracted guerrilla war was a prospect, since the self-styled Chechen "president," Gen. Dzhokhar DUDAYEV, had gone underground with a considerable military entourage. In June 1995 a band of Chechen gunmen seized a hospital in the southern Russian town of Budennovsk, holding more than 1,000 people hostage for five days until securing safe passage back to Chechnya in return for the hostages' release. At least 120 people died in the crisis, including about 30 casualties when Russian forces tried unsuccessfully to storm the hospital.

The Chechen attack was perceived as humiliating for Russia and provoked a parliamentary motion of no confidence in the government, directed mainly at the three "power" ministers of defense, interior, and security—all Yeltsin supporters—rather than at Prime Minister Chernomyrdin, who had negotiated the hostages' release. On June 21 the motion was carried by 241 votes to 72, but the result was nonbinding under the constitution unless repeated within three months. With Yeltsin's announcement that several senior ministers and officials would be dismissed, a second motion at the beginning of July failed to obtain the requisite majority. Russian and Chechen negotiators eventually signed a cease-fire agreement on July 30, but general hostilities resumed in October amid continued wrangling over the future political status of Chechnya.

Party politics from mid-1995 focused on the forthcoming legislative and presidential elections, scheduled for December 1995 and June 1996, respectively. New parties, alliances, and realignments proliferated, including the launching in May of Our Home Is Russia (*Nash Dom–Rossiya*—NDR) by Prime Minister Chernomyrdin. Several prominent figures declared their presidential candidacies, including Zhirinovsky on the far right and Gennadi ZYUGANOV of the Communist Party of the Russian Federation (*Kommunisticheskaya Partiya Rossiiskoi Federatsii*—KPRF). Despite health problems, President Yeltsin subsequently confirmed his candidacy for election to a second term.

The outcome of the State Duma election on December 17, 1995, was a significant victory for the KPRF, which won a plurality of 157 of the 450 seats with 22.3 percent of the party list vote, more than double the tally of the second-place NDR, which managed only 55 seats. In third place came the LDPR with 51 seats, while the reformist Yavlinsky-Boldyrev-Lukin Bloc (*Yabloko*), with 45 seats, was the only other list to achieve the 5 percent threshold for the allocation of proportional seats. In the constituency section, however, a total of 19 other groupings won representation.

President Yeltsin responded to the Communist/conservative electoral advance by making major government changes in January 1996. Several prominent reformers were dropped, including privatization architect Anatoly CHUBAIS as first deputy premier. Andrei KOZYREV was replaced as foreign minister by Yevgeni PRIMAKOV, hitherto chief of foreign intelligence and known to be much less pro-Western than his predecessor. These changes and a collateral slowdown in the privatization program found favor with the dominant KPRF contingent in the State Duma.

Held on June 16, 1996, the first round of the presidential balloting found Yeltsin heading the field of ten candidates with 35.3 percent of the vote, but only narrowly ahead of Zyuganov, who obtained 32.0 percent. In third place, with 14.5 percent, was Gen. (Ret.) Aleksandr LEBED, the former Russian military commander in the separatist Moldovan region of Transnistria, standing as the candidate of the nationalist Congress of Russian Communities (*Kongress Russkikh Obshchin*—KRO), while Grigori YAVLINSKY (*Yabloko*) and Zhirinovsky (LDPR) trailed. Within two days of the polling Yeltsin had forged an alliance with Lebed, who was appointed secretary of the National Security Council. With Lebed's endorsement in the run-off ballot on July 3, Yeltsin won a decisive victory over Zyuganov by a margin of 53.7 to 40.3 percent. Reinaugurated on August 9, President Yeltsin immediately reappointed Chernomyrdin as prime minister, at the head of a reshaped government in which pro-reform elements regained some of the ground lost in the January reshuffle. In addition, Anatoly Chubais assumed the key post of presidential chief of staff at a time of mounting concern about the president's health.

In Chechnya, the collapse of the cease-fire in October 1995 had been followed in January 1996 by major hostage seizures by Chechen rebels. Russian peace overtures were assisted by the death of Chechen leader Dudayev in a Russian rocket attack in April, following which his successor, Zelimkhan YANDARBIYEV, concluded a cease-fire agreement with President Yeltsin. The May cease-fire again broke down with Yeltsin's reelection, but efforts by the new presidential security adviser, General Lebed, yielded a new agreement on August 31 that provided for the withdrawal of Russian and rebel forces from Grozny. Following Yeltsin's dismissal of Lebed in October, on grounds that he had proved to be a disruptive influence, the Russian president concluded yet another peace agreement with the Chechen leadership. The November accord provided for a complete Russian military withdrawal before the holding of presidential and parliamentary elections in Chechnya on January 27, 1997.

The winner in the presidential election was the most moderate of the candidates, Aslan MASKHADOV, who nevertheless continued to favor complete independence. In May Maskhadov and Yeltsin signed a peace treaty that rejected the use of force and postponed final resolution of Chechen-Russian relations to the year 2001. The situation nevertheless remained precarious as Chechen field commanders and extralegal groups continued to engage in abductions, politically motivated murders, and skirmishes with Russian troops along the Chechen frontier.

With President Yeltsin undergoing heart bypass surgery in November 1996 and spending most of the next several months in the hospital, questions about his health dominated the political scene into 1997. Attempts at impeachment by the opposition KPRF and LDPR over the health issue failed to pass constitutional muster, however, and in March Yeltsin significantly restructured the government, bringing in two noted reformers: Anatoly Chubais as a first deputy prime minister (the position from which he had been dismissed in January 1996) and the youthful governor of Nizhny Novgorod, Boris NEMTSOV. In November 1997 Chubais was dismissed as finance minister (but retained as deputy prime minister) following revelations that he had received money for his contribution to a book on privatization in Russia, a scandal widely linked to rivalry between financial conglomerates over the spoils of privatization.

Apparently determined to end infighting within the cabinet and to forge ahead with economic reform despite such adverse signs as a falling stock market and continuing wage arrears, on March 23, 1998, Yeltsin dismissed the government and named Sergei KIRIYENKO, a young reformer, as prime minister. Facing a threat of dissolution by the president after having rejected the nomination twice, the Duma finally approved Kiriyenko on April 24. His tenure proved to be short, however, as Russia's economic plight deepened, precipitated by falling oil prices on world markets and the impact of the recent East Asian financial turmoil. The crisis led on August 17 to a major devaluation of the ruble, the suspension of foreign debt payments, and the rescheduling of domestic short-term debt. Six days later, having dismissed Kiriyenko, Yeltsin nominated a former prime minister, Viktor Chernomyrdin, as his successor. However, the Duma twice rejected the nomination and Chernomyrdin withdrew his candidacy. On September 10 Yeltsin proposed in his stead a political veteran, Foreign Minister Primakov, who, with the support of the KPRF, won easy confirmation the following day.

Primakov's accomplishments included initiating an anticorruption campaign that targeted the "oligarchs," businessmen with powerful political connections who had made fortunes since the breakup of the Soviet Union, largely through the auction of state-owned enterprises in the mid-1990s. A principal target, Boris BEREZOVSKY, had close connections to Yeltsin's entourage ("the family"), and accusations surfaced that the president himself may have been involved, at least indirectly, in illegal business dealings.

On May 12, 1999, Yeltsin dismissed the government of Prime Minister Primakov, who, at the time, had been considered the front-runner to succeed Yeltsin at the expiration of the presidential term in 2000. Primakov's replacement, First Deputy Prime Minister Sergei STEPASHIN, was confirmed by the State Duma on May 19 and thus became Russia's fourth prime minister in 14 months. Among those appointed to the new cabinet over the next month was Finance Minister Mikhail KASYANOV, who had previously served as envoy to the IMF and other multilateral financial institutions.

On August 9, 1999, Yeltsin once again dismissed his prime minister, designating as Stepashin's successor Vladimir PUTIN, theretofore head of the Federal Security Service (successor to the KGB) and secretary of the Security Council. Furthermore, Yeltsin identified Putin as his preferred presidential successor. The State Duma approved Putin's appointment as prime minister on August 16.

Speaking to the legislature before the confirmation vote, Putin not only outlined his government's economic goals, but also asserted that he would restore order to the North Caucasus and Chechnya. In early February 1999 Chechnya's President Maskhadov, under pressure from opposition field commanders, had issued a decree ordering an immediate transition to Islamic law (sharia), had curtailed the legislature's powers, and had created a commission to draft an Islamic constitution. On February 9 the field commanders set up a *Shura* (Islamic Council) and subsequently elected Shamil BASAYEV as its leader. On March 19 the instability of the entire North Caucasus region was exacerbated by a devastating bombing in Vladikavkaz, the capital of North Ossetia, which killed at least 50 and injured another 100.

In early August 1999 Chechen rebels commanded by Basayev and Jordanian-born Omar ibn al-KHATTAB invaded Dagestan, capturing several border villages and declaring an independent Islamic state. Federal and Dagestani forces began a counteroffensive and within two weeks had forced the insurgents to withdraw. On August 16 President Maskhadov declared a state of emergency in Chechnya, but the situation continued to deteriorate. When several massive bomb blasts in Moscow and elsewhere in August–September destroyed apartment blocks and killed nearly 300, suspicion immediately fell on Chechen terrorists. Additional incursions into Dagestan prompted tighter security measures, and Russian forces renewed the push into Chechnya.

By late October 1999 nearly 200,000 civilians had fled the fighting, many into neighboring Ingushetia. Emphasizing air power and artillery in an effort to minimize Russian casualties, the strong military response served to strengthen Prime Minister Putin's standing in the polls. The government asserted that its intention was to convince the entire North Caucasus region—the Republics of Karachayevo-Cherkessia and North Ossetia as well as Chechnya, Dagestan, and Ingushetia—that Moscow would exert its full force to maintain central authority and defeat terrorism.

The December 18, 1999, election to the State Duma saw the KPRF once again claim a plurality (113 seats on a 24 percent vote share), but, more significantly, the combined success of several recently formed, increasingly pro-Putin blocs secured a working majority for the government. Two of the new electoral alliances, Unity (*Edinstvo*) and the Union of Right Forces (*Soyuz Pravyh Sil*—SPS), had been endorsed by Putin. A third, the Fatherland–All Russia bloc (*Otechestvo–Vsya Rossiya*—OVR), led by former prime minister Primakov and Moscow's mayor, Yuri LUZHKOV, found itself undercut by Putin's popularity. Most of the more than 100 representatives elected as independents soon joined progovernment parliamentary factions and deputies' groups.

With Putin's standing secured, President Yeltsin unexpectedly resigned on December 31, 1999, the prime minister thereby becoming acting president pending an election to be held within three months. Putin quickly decreed immunity from prosecution for Yeltsin, although not for "family" members. (Yeltsin died of heart failure on April 23, 2007.) At the presidential contest of March 26, 2000, Putin garnered 52.9 percent of the vote; of the ten challengers, the KPRF's Zyuganov finished second, with 29.2 percent. Both former prime minister Primakov and Mayor Luzhkov of the Fatherland had declined to run in the face of Putin's certain victory. Inaugurated on May 7, Putin nominated Mikhail Kasyanov for the premiership three days later. The State Duma approved the nomination on May 17, and over the next several days confirmed a revamped cabinet that featured, most notably, major changes in the structure and leadership of economic ministries.

The newly inaugurated Putin wasted no time before initiating steps to consolidate Moscow's authority. On May 13, 2000, he issued a decree establishing seven federal "super-districts" to be funded by Moscow and headed by presidentially appointed envoys empowered to ensure regional compliance with federal law. The move was a clear effort to rein in Russia's 89 territorial units, many of which had exercised considerable autonomy in tax and other areas under Yeltsin. By August Putin had also succeeded in winning reform of the Federation Council, with regional governors and presidents to lose their ex officio seats by 2002, and had secured the authority to dismiss regional leaders for violating federal law (see Constitution and government, below).

Throughout his acting presidency Putin had continued his hard-nosed policies toward the Chechen rebels. Late in December 1999, with Grozny in ruins, federal forces had advanced into the city with the support of pro-Russian Chechen contingents. Heavy street fighting followed the advance, and it was February 6, 2000, before the government could announce that Grozny had finally been taken. The remaining Chechen rebels retreated, amid heavy casualties, to the southern mountains. At the same time charges of human rights abuses by Russian troops escalated, especially in "filtration camps" established to weed out belligerents, while on April 25 the United Nations Commission on Human Rights voted to condemn a "disproportionate and indiscriminate use of Russian military forces." By then, pro-Russian Chechen officials were increasingly being targeted for assassination by the rebels, who also continued guerrilla assaults on Russian troops. On June 8 President Putin imposed direct rule on the region, naming Mufti Akhmed KADYROV as governor four days later.

Following the September 11, 2001, terrorist attacks on the United States, public support for Putin's policies in Chechnya appeared to stiffen. On November 18 presidential regional envoy Viktor KAZANTSEV met outside Moscow with Akhmed ZAKAYEV, a representative of President Maskhadov, but the brief talks—the first since the renewed conflict began in 1999—made no progress at resolving the underlying issues or bringing hostilities to a close. In the field, Russian forces continued to take the initiative into 2002 but without obtaining a decisive victory. In April the Chechen rebels confirmed that a leading commander, Khattab, had been killed in action.

In July 2001 Unity, All Russia, and Fatherland organized an alliance that was registered in December as Unity and Fatherland–United Russia (*Edinstvo i Otechestvo–Edinaya Rossiya*), and two months later the members of all three voted to dissolve as separate entities. On the right, many of the SPS participants had also merged into a single party, while on the left the continued domination of the KPRF was called into question by factional disputes as the 2003 State Duma election approached. At the December 7 contests the Putin-supportive United Russia captured a majority of seats, while the KPRF lost support to a recently organized Motherland–People's Patriotic Union (*Rodina–Narodno-Patrioticheskii Soyuz*) electoral bloc. In a major setback, neither the SPS nor *Yabloko* met the 5 percent threshold for claiming proportional seats, while the LDPR doubled its representation to 36 seats. When the State Duma convened, the United Russia parliamentary faction surpassed the two-thirds majority needed to approve constitutional changes.

On February 24, 2004, only three weeks before a presidential election, President Putin dismissed the Kasyanov government and on March 1 named Mikhail FRADKOV, Russia's ambassador to the European Union (EU), as prime minister. Confirmed by the legislature on March 5, Fradkov completed his streamlined cabinet on March 9. Five days later Putin, running as an independent, easily won reelection, capturing 71.3 percent of the vote against five candidates, the closest of whom, KPRF nominee Nikolai KHARITONOV, managed only 13.7 percent. Required by the constitution to resign following the May 7 presidential inauguration, Fradkov was immediately reappointed by Putin and then reconfirmed on May 12.

With regard to Chechnya, frequent suicide bombings and hostage-taking continued to command international headlines. On October 23, 2002, 41 separatists seized more than 800 hostages at a Moscow theater. An attack by Russian special forces on October 26 killed all the rebels but also resulted in the deaths of some 130 hostages, all but a few of whom fell victim to a paralyzing agent that had been dispersed to disable the Chechens. Two months later suicide bombers attacked the administrative headquarters in Grozny, killing 80 and wounding 150. From May to August 2003 suicide bombers, some of them women (dubbed "black widows" in the Russian media), included in their targets a music festival in Moscow, additional government buildings and a religious festival in Chechnya, and a military hospital in North Ossetia.

On March 23, 2003, a reported 96 percent of Chechen voters endorsed a draft constitution for a self-ruling republic with an elected legislature and president. Akhmed Kadyrov won the Chechen presidential election on October 3 with more than 80 percent of the vote, his principal rivals having withdrawn from the contest, but on May 9, 2004, he was assassinated by a land mine. Prime Minister Sergei ABRAMOV, who had been in office less than two months, became acting president. On August 29 Maj. Gen. Alu ALKHANOV, theretofore the Chechen interior minister, was elected president with 74 percent of the vote. His principal rival, Chechen businessman Malik SAIDULLAYEV, had been denied a place on the ballot because of a technicality.

In the most tragic incident of the separatist struggle, on September 1, 2004, some 30 rebels, reportedly including several operatives linked to the al-Qaida network, invaded a school at Beslan, North Ossetia, and took 1,200 teachers, parents, and children hostage under conditions that rapidly deteriorated. Two days later, in a scene fraught with confusion, nearly 340 hostages died during a rescue mission.

President Putin's efforts consolidated his authority. In 2005 he had obtained the power to appoint all of the chief executives of Russia's 89 regions, republics, and autonomous areas; tightened requirements for registration of political parties; eliminated single-mandate legislative districts beginning with the 2007 State Duma election; and raised to 7 percent the vote threshold needed for parties to claim lower house seats. Putin claimed that by switching to proportional representation for legislative elections, the party system would be strengthened since there would be fewer parties in the State Duma.

Putin's consolidation of power at the center was interpreted by some observers as marking the ascendancy of the *siloviki* (roughly, the powerful), individuals with a background in the Soviet KGB or the present Russian security and military services, at the expense of former president Yeltsin's "family"—particularly some of the oligarchs who had amassed fortunes through the sale of state assets in the 1990s. Early targets had been Boris BEREZOVSKY and then Vladimir GUSINSKY, owner of Russia's largest independent media conglomerate, Media-MOST, which had angered the government with its unfavorable coverage of the war in Chechnya. Ultimately, Berezovsky was granted asylum in the United Kingdom. Gusinsky, fleeing charges of tax evasion, relocated to Israel, while Media-MOST fell under control of Gazprom, the state-owned natural gas monopoly. Mikhail KHODORKOVSKY, the chief executive officer of a leading energy company, Yukos, was convicted of tax evasion and fraud in May 2005 and sentenced to nine years in prison. Yukos, which allegedly owed tens of billions of dollars in taxes, was dismantled in 2007.

The dismantling of Yukos furthered the government's aim of regaining a controlling share of the country's natural resources and other critical industries, such as pipelines, rail transport, shipping, and nuclear energy. In what has been termed by some analysts as "statist capitalism," market forces prevail—to the extent that they benefit the Russian economy, as in the case of world oil prices—but cabinet ministers often serve simultaneously as executives or directors of companies in key industries.

The Chechen separatists suffered a significant blow on March 8, 2005, when Aslan Maskhadov died during an operation by the Federal Security Service. Two days later the separatist Chechen State Defense Committee announced that Abdul-Khalim SADULAYEV had succeeded Maskhadov as its chair. Moscow increased its control over the Chechen republic through the parliamentary elections called for November 27, 2005, which were widely criticized for irregularities and low turnout. In those elections the pro-Moscow United Russia party was declared to have won 61 percent of the vote, giving it majorities in both upper and lower chambers. In March 2006 pro-Moscow warlord Ramzan KADYROV, leader of a private army of thousands of irregular troops and son of slain president Akhmed Kadyrov, was approved as prime minister in a unanimous vote of the People's Assembly of Chechnya, succeeding Sergei Abramov, who had resigned in February. Three months later, in mid-June, Abdul-Khalim Sadulayev was killed in a Russian police operation, at which time his deputy, Doku UMAROV, assumed the separatist leadership. Then, on July 10, Shamil BASAYEV, the Chechen separatist leader who had claimed responsibility for spectacular attacks that killed hundreds of Russian civilians over the last decade, including the Beslan school massacre of 2004, died when a nearby truck carrying dynamite blew up.

In February 2007 Ramzan Kadyrov was appointed acting president of Chechnya, Alkhanov having been named federal deputy minister of justice in a cabinet reshuffle. On March 2 Kadyrov was elected president. Inaugurated on April 5, he named a cousin, Odes BAYSULTANOV, as his prime minister. By then, with the separatist leadership having been decimated, the pace and severity of separatist attacks had diminished.

In a surprise development, on September 12, 2007, Prime Minister Fradkov and the cabinet resigned, with President Putin then nominating as his successor Viktor ZUBKOV, who had been serving as first deputy finance minister and chair of the committee responsible for combating money laundering. Having been approved by the Duma on September 14, Fradkov indicated that he might seek the presidency in 2008. On October 1, speaking at a United Russia congress, President Putin not only agreed to head the party's list for the 2007 State Duma election but also stated that he would consider taking command of the party and serving as prime minister at the end of his presidential term. In the December 2, 2007, election, in which 11 parties participated, United Russia won 64.3 percent of the vote and 315 of the legislature's 450 seats. The KPRF, as expected, finished second, with 11.6 percent and 57 seats. The only other parties to surpass the 7 percent threshold for seats were the LDPR (8.1 percent, 40 seats) and Fair Russia (7.7 percent, 38 seats). Shortly after the election President Vladimir Putin gave his support for the March 2008 presidential election to First Deputy Prime Minister Dmitri Medvedev, who in turn indicated that, if elected, he intended to nominate Putin as prime minister.

Following United Russia's strong finish, Putin, barred constitutionally from seeking a third consecutive term, announced his support for First Deputy Prime Minister Dmitri MEDVEDEV for the presidency. All four pro-Kremlin parties (United Russia, Fair Russia, Agrarian Party of Russia (*Agrarnaya Partiya Rossii*—APR), and Civil Force (*Grazhdanskaya Sila*—GS) endorsed Medvedev as well. The Russian Ecological Party "The Greens" (*Rossiiskaya Ekologicheskaya Partiya "Zelenye"*—REP) also backed Medvedev. In the election on March 2, 2008, Medvedev, who officially is an independent, received 70.3 percent of the vote, well ahead of challengers Gennadi Zyuganov of the KPRF, with 19.96 percent of the vote; Vladimir Zhirinovsky of the LDPR, with 9.48 percent; and Andrei Bogdanov, of the DPR with 1.31 percent. As expected, Medvedev appointed Putin prime minister, and both were inaugurated on May 8.

Constitution and government. Under the 1993 constitution the Federation president "determine[s] guidelines for the domestic and foreign policy of the state." Directly elected for no more than two consecutive four-year terms, the president nominates the chair of government (the prime minister) as well as higher court judges; in addition, he serves as commander in chief of the armed forces, appoints and dismisses the top military commanders, and may issue decrees carrying the force of law. He may reject an initial vote of nonconfidence and upon the repassage of such a measure within three months may call for dissolution of the legislature and new elections. The current basic law makes no provision for a vice president. The president's main advisory body on security issues is the Security Council, whose powers were substantially strengthened by presidential decree in July 1996.

The bicameral Federal Assembly consists of the State Duma and, as an upper house, the Federation Council. The Duma votes on the president's nominee as government chair as well as his choices for other high positions. Legislation must first be approved by majority vote of the entire Duma; rejection by the upper house requires a two-thirds vote of the entire Duma to override. Measures vetoed by the president require approval by two-thirds of both houses. The Federation Council comprises two representatives from each of Russia's 85 territorial components (83 as of March 2008)—prior to 2002, the governing executive (governor or, in the case of republics, president) and the leader of the assembly. On August 7, 2000, however, President Putin signed into law a measure stripping regional officials of their ex officio seats and of their immunity from prosecution. With full effect from January 2002, the regional executives each appoint one member to the council (with legislative concurrence), and each territorial assembly elects a legislative representative. The Federation Council's powers include review of martial law and emergency decrees.

The judicial system includes a Constitutional Court, a Supreme Court, a Supreme Arbitration Court, and lesser federal entities as determined by law. Between 2001 and 2002 Russia introduced codes permitting the sale and private ownership of land, although the sale of agricultural land to foreigners and to companies with majority foreign ownership was prohibited. In July 2002 a new "Western-style" criminal code instituted a jury system nationwide for serious offenses, required police to obtain court warrants for arrests and searches, and set a 48-hour limit on detentions.

Local self-government is conducted through referenda, elections, and other means, with appropriate "consideration for historical and other local traditions." Mergers of territorial units have been encouraged by the central government as part of a larger plan to consolidate the federal structure, ostensibly to streamline public administration, but apparently also as a way to diminish the political authority of the often restless ethnic areas. As of late 2006 the federation encompassed 21 republics (*respubliki*), 8 territories (*kraia*), 47 regions (*oblasti*), the Jewish autonomous region (*avtonomnaya oblast*) of Birobijan, 6 autonomous areas (*avtonomnie okruga*), and 2 "cities of federal importance" (Moscow and St. Petersburg). In April 2006 voters in the Ust-Orda Buryat Autonomous *Okrug* in Siberia elected to merge with Irkutsk *Oblast*, effective January 2008. Subsequently, voters in Chita *Oblast* and the Agin-Buryat Autonomous *Okrug* elected to merge as Zabaykasky *Krai* in March 2008.

By decree, on May 13, 2000, President Putin established seven overarching federal districts—Central, Far Eastern, North Caucasus (renamed Southern by decree on June 23), Northwest, Siberian, Ural, and Volga—to oversee regional compliance with federal law. Later, in conjunction with the reform of the Federation Council, Putin signed into law two other pieces of legislation intended to restructure the federal relationship, one giving the president authority to dismiss regional heads who violate federal law and the other permitting regional executives to remove local officials for similar cause. On September 1, again by decree, President Putin established a consultative State Council of the Russian Federation, ostensibly to ensure that executives from all territorial subdivisions have an institutional voice in Moscow. Chaired by the president, the State Council has a seven-member Presidium consisting of a presidentially appointed representative from each of the "super-districts." Serving six-month terms, the appointees are chosen by rotation from among the leaders of Russia's constituent republics and regions. Legislation passed in 2004 brought an end to the election of regional governors and republican presidents, who are now appointed by the federation president with the concurrence of the legislature of the particular jurisdiction.

Foreign relations. The Russian Federation was generally accepted as successor to the Soviet Union in respect to the latter's international commitments and affiliations, including membership in the United Nations and the Conference on (later Organization for) Security and Cooperation in Europe (CSCE/OSCE). It also assumed the Soviet Union's obligations under international and bilateral treaties, such as those on arms control with the United States. In June 1992 Russia was formally admitted to membership in the IMF and the World Bank.

In the course of a highly productive summit in Washington held in June 1992, Presidents Yeltsin and George H. W. Bush concluded agreements on most-favored-nation trade status and a major extension of the 1991 Strategic Arms Reduction Treaty (START). Under the START II accord, each nation would be limited to 3,000–3,500 long-range weapons (down from 11,000–12,000 on the eve of START I), while all land-based multiple warhead missiles would be banned. In November 1992 the Supreme Soviet ratified the 1991 START I accord with the United States, although an exchange of ratification documents was deferred until Belarus, Kazakhstan, and Ukraine had signed the 1968 Nuclear Non-Proliferation Treaty (NPT) and agreement had been reached on the disposition of nuclear arms in their possession. (Under a protocol to START I signed in Lisbon in May 1992, the three ex-Soviet republics had agreed that Russia should be the sole nuclear power in the CIS.) By late 1993 Belarus and Kazakhstan had completed these procedures; Ukraine acceded to the NPT in December 1994. On April 14, 2000, the State Duma, at the urging of President-elect Vladimir Putin, ratified START II, and on April 22 approved the 1996 Comprehensive Test Ban Treaty (CTBT). On the latter day, however, the legislature also endorsed a revised military doctrine authorizing use of nuclear weapons "if the very existence of the country" were in jeopardy.

With regard to areas of the "near abroad" populated by ethnic Russian minorities, the Yeltsin administration firmly opposed the demands of right-wing nationalists that they be brought under Russian sovereignty. At the same time, it insisted that the rights of Russian minorities must be fully respected by the governments concerned. Thus, in October 1992 Yeltsin suspended the withdrawal of Russian troops from the three Baltic states, citing "profound concern over the numerous infringements of rights of the Russian-speaking population" in Latvia and Estonia, in particular. However, Western pressure and assurances on ethnic Russian rights yielded the withdrawal of Russian forces from Lithuania by August 1993 and from Estonia and Latvia a year later, subject to Russian retention of certain defense facilities for a specified period.

The rapid transformation of Russia's external relations was highlighted in June 1994 when Russia acceded in principle to the North Atlantic Treaty Organization's (NATO's) Partnership for Peace (PfP) program for former Soviet-bloc and neutral European states, and also signed a new partnership and cooperation agreement with the EU. In May 1995 Russia signed two detailed PfP agreements with NATO but repeated its opposition to any eastward expansion of the alliance.

In September 1994 President Jiang Zemin became the first senior Chinese leader to visit Moscow since 1957. Agreements signed on September 3 resolved most bilateral border demarcation disputes and committed each never to use force against the other. Further visits to Moscow by President Jiang in May 1995 and by Premier Li Peng in June continued the rapprochement, which was consolidated by President Yeltsin's April 1996 visit to Beijing. Troop reductions on the Sino-Russian border were agreed to as part of a new "strategic partnership" for the 21st century.

Similar efforts at improving ties with Japan were long stalled due to a dispute over the four southern Kurile Islands seized by the Soviet Union at the end of World War II (see the Foreign relations section of the article on Japan). In November 1997 President Yeltsin and Japanese Prime Minister Ryutaro Hashimoto pledged to sign a treaty by 2000 that would settle the dispute and normalize relations. The two leaders also concluded a fishing agreement covering the Kurile Islands and agreed to further economic cooperation. Following President Putin's inauguration in 2000, however, Russia adopted a less accommodating stance toward formal resolution of the insular question, and several meetings between Putin and successive Japanese prime ministers over the years have concluded without significant progress toward a peace treaty. In June 2009 the State Duma condemned the Japanese parliament's approval of amendments officially claiming ownership of the Kurile Islands.

The dominant foreign policy issue in 1997 was the proposed admission of former Warsaw Pact members Poland, the Czech Republic, and Hungary into an expanded NATO, despite Russian objections and its previous threat to withdraw from the 1990 Conventional Forces in Europe (CFE) treaty. Negotiations held in Moscow in May led to an accord, signed in Paris on May 27, known as the Founding Act. While Russia had sought a treaty, rather than a nonbinding accord, it accepted an agreement to strengthen the OSCE, acquiesced on the need for revisions to the CFE treaty, and received a pledge, but not a guarantee, from NATO that the Western alliance would not place nuclear weapons on the territory of any new member states. While the NATO Founding Act did not give Russia a veto over future NATO decisions, as Yeltsin had desired, a Russian-NATO joint council has afforded Russia a voice in NATO decisions. Russia also received a number of economic concessions, including enhanced status in the G-7. (In 1998 Russia became a full participant, and the G-7 officially became the G-8.) In addition,

Washington pledged to support eventual Russian accession to the World Trade Organization (WTO).

Russia's objections to the 1990 CFE treaty rested on a desire to limit NATO deployments in the former Warsaw Pact countries. Consequently, on July 23, 1997, in Vienna 16 NATO and 14 former Warsaw Pact states agreed "in principle" on a new draft accord that set national rather than bloc limitations on conventional armed forces.

Also related to the eastward expansion of NATO, Yeltsin advocated closer linkages with CIS member states, in particular regarding economic, political, and military ties between Russia and Belarus. In 1996 the two signed a Treaty on the Formation of the Community of Sovereign Republics (CSR), and in June 1997 the legislatures of both countries ratified a Charter of the Union, which set out a plan for greater integration (see article on Belarus). On December 25, 1998, Yeltsin and Belarusan President Alyaksandr Lukashenka signed several documents on setting up an integrated monetary system and customs policies and on forming a common leadership while retaining national sovereignty. Modeled on the EU, a formal Union Treaty was signed in Moscow on December 8, 1999, and unanimously ratified on December 22 by the upper houses of both countries. Adoption of a shared currency, the ruble, had been scheduled for 2006, but it subsequently appeared unlikely that currency integration would occur. Meanwhile, in September 2003 Kazakhstan and Ukraine joined Russia and Belarus in signing a treaty intended to create a Single Economic Space, which would include a free trade zone and greater coordination of economic policy. Relations with Belarus had deteriorated as of 2009, when a "bitter dispute" was revived after Lukashenka told his government the country must no longer rely on Russia. However, Putin, in an apparent attempt at appeasement, pledged to continue to provide financial support to Belarus.

Additional overtures regarding closer ties have been made toward such CIS countries as Armenia, Kazakhstan, and Kyrgyzstan. In contrast, in 2000 Russia announced its withdrawal from the 1992 Bishkek Treaty on visa-free travel among CIS members, citing threats posed by international terrorism, crime, and drug-trafficking, and adding that it preferred to regulate travel bilaterally.

In August 1992 tension between Russia and Ukraine eased in the wake of an agreement to place the former Soviet Black Sea fleet under joint command pending implementation of a June accord to divide the ships equally and jointly finance their bases. At a CIS meeting in 1994, the two countries agreed that 15–20 percent of the fleet's 800-plus ships (including auxiliary vessels) would be retained by Ukraine, with Russia "purchasing" the remainder of Ukraine's share. Agreements concluded in May 1997 permitted Russia to lease half of the Ukrainian naval base at Sevastopol for a period of 20 years and also signified Russian recognition of Crimea and Sevastopol as Ukrainian territory.

Elsewhere in the region, Russian troops remained deployed in several areas of the "near abroad" following the disintegration of the Soviet Union. When Georgia declared its independence in 1991 after the collapse of the Soviet Union, two of its regions, South Ossetia and the Abkhaz Republic, now commonly known as Abkhazia, took up arms to gain autonomy. Hundreds were killed as independence fighters engaged Georgian troops. Both breakaway regions had good relations with Moscow. In the summer of 1992, Russian peacekeepers were deployed in South Ossetia, achieving an end to the violence, but leaving the issue of sovereignty unresolved. Russian negotiators facilitated the cease-fire agreement between Georgia and the Abkhaz Republic in April 1994. Both regions have operated as de facto independent states since that time, and Russia has provided the South Ossetians and Abkhazians with peacekeeping troops, financial support, and Russian passports. Following Russian occupation of South Ossetia and Abkhazia in August 2008, Russia recognized the provinces as independent (see Current issues, below). Similarly, Transnistria declared independence from Moldova in 1991, but it was only able to maintain independence with the aid of Russian troops. As of 2009, definitive resolution of the Transnistria dispute remained elusive, and Russian troops continued to be stationed there. Meanwhile, Russia began to press Moldova for a process that would "guarantee" Russian control of the territory.

Russian contingents have participated in several peacekeeping missions, including a UN-sponsored force in Bosnia and Herzegovina and a CIS contingent in Tajikistan. Russian diplomats also attempted to exert their influence in the inspections dispute between Iraq and the UN and, in 1998 and 1999, in the confrontation between Yugoslavia and NATO over the Kosovo question. Strong ethnic ties between Russians and Yugoslavia's Serbs contributed to Moscow's pro-Belgrade stance. Despite Russian anger over the bombing campaign launched against Yugoslavia in March 1999, in the aftermath Russian troops were successfully stationed alongside NATO-led peacekeepers in Kosovo. The mission's success seemed to presage greater Russian cooperation with NATO, and a visit by U.S. President Bill Clinton to Russia in June 2000 produced a bilateral agreement on disposal of weapons-grade plutonium and on setting up an early-warning center—the first-ever permanent U.S.-Russian military operation—to reduce the risk of accidental nuclear war.

In July 2000 the government introduced a new foreign policy doctrine favoring pragmatism, cooperation with NATO, closer ties with China and India, and "active dialogue" with the United States. Moscow and Washington differed, however, over the contemplated U.S. limited missile defense plan, with Russian officials charging that the proposed warhead intercept system would violate the 1972 Anti-Ballistic Missile (ABM) Treaty.

The United States formally withdrew from the ABM Treaty in 2002, which provoked the expected outcry from Russia. For several years intervening events—especially the September 11, 2001, attacks on the United States—made the development far less significant to U.S.-Russian relations than it might otherwise have been. In the aftermath of the September attacks President Putin was quick to assert that the Chechen rebels had ties to al-Qaida, while firm Russian support for U.S. efforts to organize a broad international consensus for its "war on terrorism" apparently served to temper Washington's subsequent criticism of Moscow's Chechnya policy. Putin's intervention on behalf of the United States was also a contributing, if not a decisive, factor in the decision of the Central Asian republics to back the U.S. military campaign against al-Qaida and Afghanistan's Taliban regime.

Meeting in Moscow on May 24, 2002, Presidents Putin and George W. Bush signed the Treaty of Moscow (the Strategic Offensive Reductions Treaty—SORT), thereby committing their countries to reducing nuclear stockpiles by two-thirds over the next decade. (The Russian legislature ratified SORT in May 2003; a vote had been delayed by objections to U.S. policy toward Iraq.) Other summit concerns included improved cooperation in counterterrorism and in trade relations, particularly with regard to the energy sector. On May 28 in Rome, Italy, NATO and Russia signed the Rome Declaration, establishing a NATO-Russia Council for the purpose of discussing such crucial policy matters as nonproliferation, combating terrorism, and peacekeeping. Putin had apparently already signaled that, despite strong objections, Russia would acquiesce to additional NATO expansion into the former Soviet Baltic republics, the trade-off being closer Russian-NATO cooperation in security and political matters. On May 29, at a Russian-EU summit in Moscow, the EU recognized Russia as a market economy, a designation echoed by the United States shortly thereafter, thereby advancing Russia's efforts to enter the WTO.

In October 2004 the legislature ratified the Kyoto Protocol on global warming, which enabled the protocol to enter into effect. With the United States having refused to consider ratification, a Russian rejection would have doomed the initiative. Although President Putin had earlier expressed reservations as to whether the protocol was in Russia's best interests, ratification had become central to establishing closer relations with the EU.

In 2005 China and Russia held their first joint military exercises. China has frequently voted with Russia in the UN Security Council, thwarting U.S. initiatives such as sanctions on Iran. Near the end of 2005 Russia raised the price of gas to its immediate neighbors to more closely approximate the rates paid by EU market countries, roughly doubling the cost. Russia also insisted that Gazprom should have direct access to EU markets, a position that received some support in 2007 from French, Italian, and German gas companies. At the same time, however, several Eastern European members of the EU took a harder line toward Russia, including Lithuania, which has seen its oil supplies from Russia interrupted, and Poland, which in November 2006 vetoed proposed discussions on a new EU-Russia participation and cooperation agreement. The move was largely in retaliation for Russia's continuing ban on importation of Polish meat.

In January 2006 Gazprom cut its shipments to Ukraine, which receives more than a quarter of its natural gas from Russia. The stoppage was reportedly due to a dispute over Ukraine's debt of $1.5 billion to Gazprom, but many observers attributed it to politics. Ukraine's recent Orange Revolution had installed a pro-Western government over the incumbent favored by Moscow. Though an agreement was reached within four days, the dispute arose again in early 2008, with Russia again threatening to cut or reduce gas delivery to Ukraine. The crisis was resolved before action was taken, but political tensions remained, as the basis of the threat seemed largely attributable to Russia's opposition to the Ukraine's aim to join NATO and the EU.

Russia's relations with the United Kingdom in 2006 suffered over the bizarre murder of defector and former security agent Aleksandr LITVINENKO, a vocal critic of President Putin. In November Litvinenko died in London of poisoning by radioactive polonium-210. Russia, which refused to extradite Andrei LUGOVOI, an LDPR member and the principal target of the British investigation, attempted to implicate the exiled Boris Berezovsky in Litvinenko's poisoning.

At a Russia-EU summit in May 2007, leaders addressed key controversies, including criticism of Russia's human rights record, especially in Chechnya, and the future status of Kosovo. Russia continued to reject Kosovar independence without Serbian approval even after Kosovo declared independence in February 2008 and was recognized by many nations. Western recognition of Kosovo was viewed by some analysts as one of the provocations leading to Russia's recognition of South Ossetia and Abkhazia in Georgia, a staunch Western ally (see Current issues, below). Russia continued to struggle against U.S. plans to deploy elements of a defensive missile shield in Europe, which would include placing intercept missiles in Poland and a radar installation in the Czech Republic. Though the United States claimed that the shield would not target Russia and its purpose was to protect against "rogue" states such as Iran, Russia viewed the shield, close to its borders, as a national security threat. Putin threatened to retarget Russian missiles on Europe if the missile defense system was deployed. Further, in July 2007 Putin announced that Russia intended to suspend its participation in the CFE Treaty, partly over the proposed missile shield and partly because some NATO members had never ratified the revised treaty.

Differences between Russia and the United States persisted over Iran's efforts to develop nuclear power, which would give it the capacity to enrich uranium for weapons. Russia had been involved with Iran's nuclear development since 1995, when it took over the construction of the as yet unfinished nuclear power plant at Bushehr. In 2000, Russia abrogated the 1995 Gore-Chernomyrdin agreement, under which it pledged to limit arms sales and nuclear cooperation with Iran. In 2005 Russia sold Iran $700 million worth of missile systems, similar trade having been conducted in recent years. In 2007, when Iran reportedly violated requirements of the Non-Proliferation Treaty, the United States and other Western countries attempted to force Iran to dismantle its nuclear programs with threats of sanctions. Russia has consistently voted against sanctions against Iran in the UN Security Council, claiming that all states have a right to develop nuclear energy. Amid heightened tensions between the United States and Iran, Putin traveled to Tehran and met with President Mahmoud Ahmadinejad in October, marking the first visit by a Russian or Soviet leader to Iran since World War II.

U.S. president Barack Obama moved to "reset" relations with Russia in July 2009, when he met in Moscow with President Medvedev and Prime Minister Putin, both sides pledging cooperation that "might prove easier to translate into words than reality," according to the *International Herald Tribune*. Nonetheless, the two countries agreed to further reduce nuclear arsenals and resume military contacts that had been suspended during Russia's war with Georgia. Also, Russia agreed to open its airspace to allow U.S. troops and weapons to be transported to Afghanistan.

Current issues. Throughout 2006 observers waited to see if Putin would attempt to amend the constitution so that he could seek a third consecutive term as president. His intentions became clearer when he told delegates to the fall 2007 United Russia congress that he could foresee serving as prime minister when his presidential term expired. With United Russia assured of a major victory, and with many of the competing parties basically supportive of President Putin, the extraparliamentary opposition found itself repeatedly stymied. Among the more active anti-Putin organizations was an umbrella group, the Other Russia, led by chess champion Garry KASPAROV and former prime minister Mikhail Kasyanov. Although no one regarded the Other Russia as a serious challenge to the government, several of its demonstrations were suppressed in the first half of 2007, providing additional ammunition for critics of Russia's human rights record. Earlier, the murder of crusading journalist Anna POLITKOVSKAYA in October 2006, allegedly by former security personnel and Chechen criminal elements, was described by the Moscow Union of Journalists as "the latest encroachment on democracy, freedom of speech, and openness."

In the months preceding the State Duma election of December 2007, Putin placed his name at the head of the United Russia candidate list. A week after the party won a 315-seat majority in the lower house, Putin announced his support for Dmitri Medvedev in the presidential election of March 2008, adding that he would serve as prime minister under Medvedev and continue his work "as head of government." Medvedev was a close ally of Putin, and many observers predicted that as prime minister Putin would remain the most powerful leader in Russia. Medvedev's victory, like the earlier State Duma election, was criticized by several international groups as being fraught with irregularities. Within hours of Medvedev's inauguration in May, the new president, as expected, nominated Putin to head the new government, automatically elevating him to head of the governing party as well. It was widely acknowledged that Putin would wield the real power in the country, in concert with United Russia's control in parliament. Months later President Medvedev signed into law a measure that extended the presidential term from four years to six, effective in the next election in 2012, a measure observers said paved the way for Putin's return to the presidency. The law also extended the term of State Duma members from four years to five.

Meanwhile, with the economy in 2008 the strongest since the collapse of the Soviet Union, as high petroleum prices made Russia a powerful trader in the international market, the government began flexing its political strength as well. In April Russia announced its full support for South Ossetia and Abkazia as tensions increased markedly since the two territories broke away from Georgia. The pro-western president of Georgia, Mikheil Saakashvili, for his part, vowed to bring South Ossetia and Abkhazia under Georgian control. In early August Georgia launched a surprise air and ground assault in South Ossetia and Saakashvili ordered Georgian troops to capture Tskhinvali, the region's capital. Russia responded by sending thousands of troops into South Ossetia, engaging Georgian troops in Tskhinvali, and launching raids into Georgia from the city. Georgia declared a state of war as Russia continued its raids and deployed troops to Abkhazia, ultimately moving further into Georgia, forcing Georgian troops to retreat. On August 12, after negotiations with the president of the EU, Nicolas Sarkozy of France, Medvedev announced a cease-fire and signed a peace plan that was also later signed by Saakashvili. Russia agreed to withdraw all its troops from Georgia by mid-October, with the exception of what it called its "buffer zones" in South Ossetia and Abkhazia. Subsequently, Georgia denounced Russia's violation of its territorial integrity. Both sides agreed to have an EU observer group monitor the withdrawal.

Responding to widespread condemnation of its violation of Georgia's sovereignty, Russia claimed its intervention in South Ossetia had been necessary to protect the people of the republic, who had been granted Russian citizenship following the collapse of the Soviet Union. Russia insisted on its right to continue to protect South Ossetia and Abkhazia and on August 26, 2008, recognized the two republics as independent nations. (As of 2009 Nicaragua was the only other nation to recognize them.) In early September Russian officials announced plans to build military bases in each region and to deploy another 8,000 troops. President Medvedev warned that should Georgia attack again, there would be "catastrophe on a regional scale." The United States delivered a series of rebukes to Russia, and followed up by announcing, with Poland, completion of an agreement to base 10 U.S. missile interceptors in Poland. The United States further announced plans to give Georgia $1 billion for reconstruction. Declaring that Russia was taking too long to withdraw its troops from Georgia, the Bush administration subsequently withdrew from a pact between the United States and Russia for joint ventures involving the nuclear industry.

In response to heightened tensions with the United States, in the fall of 2008 Putin extended his model of a multipolar international system by building diplomatic and economic relations with Venezuela, Cuba, and other Latin American nations. Putin offered Venezuelan president Hugo Chávez military cooperation and $1 billion credit with which to purchase weapons. Putin and Chávez described their joint objective of limiting U.S. global power in a meeting in Moscow. In late September a fleet of Russian warships sailed to Venezuela for joint military exercises in the Caribbean Sea, nominally considered to be within the U.S. sphere of influence. Russia's recognition of South Ossetia and Abkhazia heightened some existing problems in the North Caucasus, where Russia had consistently crushed efforts at separatism. In the semiautonomous Russian republic of Ingushetia, a well-known journalist, Magomed Yevloyev, was shot in the head while in police custody on August 31, 2008. He and other opposition activists had sought independence from Russia. After his death, 1,000 activists in Ingushetia staged a rally against the Russian government; several militant attacks on Russian authorities followed in Dagestan, Kabardino-Balkaria, and Chechnya.

On April 30, 2009, Russia signed a border protection pact with South Ossetia and Abkhazia (see *Handbook* article on Georgia for details).

As attention turned to the poor state of the economy in 2009 (see Country, above), President Medvedev announced that state ownership was "inevitable" in some sectors, promising that such an arrangement would be short-lived. Meanwhile, relations with the United States garnered international attention during President Obama's visit to Moscow in July, which yielded little initial results. The United States and Russia were unlikely to come to agreement on any of the principle issues, according to Russian journalist and pundit Matvey Ganapolskiy, because the non-acceptance of Georgia and Ukraine into NATO "will certainly be linked to the annexation of Abkhazia and South Ossetia by Russia." Further, Ganapolskiy said, Russia strongly objected to Washington's failure to recognize Georgia's new borders and was "not planning to retreat on this issue."

POLITICAL PARTIES AND GROUPS

The advent of political pluralism in the Soviet Union in 1990 and the suspension of the CPSU in August 1991 stimulated the emergence of over 200 parties, most of which did not survive in the successor Russian Federation. Some three dozen formations were active in the run-up to the December 1993 legislative elections; ten ultimately gained representation in the State Duma. Thereafter, the party scene was characterized by frequent realignments and new formations, particularly among the promarket and centrist groupings broadly supportive of the Yeltsin administration. The launching in May 1995 of the center-right Our Home Is Russia (NDR) formation as the "government" party and concurrent moves to form a center-left opposition bloc were seen as an attempt by the political establishment to create a two-party system that would exclude from power the ultranationalists on the far right and the revived Communists on the reactionary left. However, both camps retained sizeable popular constituencies in the complex party maneuverings preceding the legislative balloting of December 17, 1995, at which more than 40 parties, movements, and alliances offered candidates.

As of January 1, 1999, the Ministry of Justice reported 141 registered political organizations, over 40 of which had sought official status during December 1998 to meet the eligibility deadline for the December 1999 legislative election. However, electoral laws permitted a political formation registered for less than a full year to contest the election if it constituted an alliance of at least two legally registered parties or movements. In the end, 26 organizations qualified for the election, including several alliances formed in 1999. Of the four most important groups active in September 2000, only the Communist Party of the Russian Federation (KPRF) predated 1998, the other three being the Putin-backed Unity, the left-centrist Fatherland, and the right-centrist Union of Right Forces (SPS).

At the beginning of 2001 there were 56 registered parties and 156 other political groups, but a law passed by both houses of the Federal Assembly in June and subsequently signed by President Putin rewrote registration requirements to the detriment of small parties. The law stipulated that to compete nationally parties must have at least 10,000 members, with no fewer than 100 members registered in each of 45 or more of the country's then 89 regions and republics.

The new parties law accelerated a process of political consolidation that had begun in anticipation of its passage. In May 2001, with most of its constituent groups having agreed to a formal merger, the SPS held a congress to authorize its restructuring as a unified party. A second congress in December confirmed the decision, and it was officially registered as such in March 2002. In July 2001 Unity, All Russia, and Fatherland had formed an alliance that was registered in December as the Unity and Fatherland–United Russia; its central component organizations voted to dissolve as separate entities in February 2002, by which time United Russia was already being referred to in some circles as the latest "party of power." Consolidations were also taking place among Russia's less significant parties.

For the State Duma election of December 2003 a total of 44 parties were eligible to present candidate lists for the proportional component. (Twenty public associations were also eligible, but only as members of electoral blocs.) In the end, 18 individual parties and 5 electoral blocs competed, with only 3 parties and 1 bloc meeting the 5 percent threshold for proportional seats: United Russia, the KPRF, the far-right Liberal Democratic Party of Russia (LDPR), and the Motherland–People's Patriotic Union bloc, elements of which subsequently united as the Motherland party. (For a complete discussion of parties and blocs that contested the 2003 election, see the 2005–2006 or 2007 *Political Handbook*.)

Shortly after the 2003 election, President Putin, backed by United Russia's overwhelming majority faction in the State Duma, began passing legislation intended to eliminate Russia's many medium-sized and small parties before the December 2007 election. For a party to register, it must now have at least 50,000 members, with at least 500 members in each of half the country's regions and 250 in each of the rest. Parties failing to meet the membership test must reregister as public organizations rather than parties or be disbanded by the courts. Single-mandate districts have been eliminated, and the threshold for winning proportional seats now stands at 7 percent of the total national vote. Parties and associations are no longer allowed to form electoral blocs, and members of one party are prohibited from appearing on the candidate list of another party, although individuals without a current party affiliation may be included. Except for those parties that won list seats in the preceding State Duma, parties must pay a deposit of $2.35 million (refundable for those winning at least 4 percent of the 2007 vote) or submit 200,000 supporting signatures; if more than 5 percent of a party's signatures are declared invalid, the party is disqualified. In addition, "none of the above" has been eliminated as a ballot option; it had frequently been used to cast a protest vote. Minimum turnout requirements for national elections have been eliminated, and lawmakers who switch parties after election are to be stripped of their seats.

In the run-up to the 2007 State Duma election, the Patriots of Russia (PR) formed a coalition with the Party of Russia's Rebirth (PVR). The Russian Ecological Party ("The Greens") was disqualified for allegedly faking signatures. While 11 registered parties were deemed eligible for the December election, only 4 reached the 7 percent threshold for election: United Russia, the KPRF, the LDPR, and Fair Russia.

Presidential Party:

United Russia (*Edinaya Rossiya*). In July 2001 Unity (*Edinstvo*), All Russia (*Vsya Rossiya*), and Fatherland (*Otechestvo*) organized an alliance that was registered in December as Unity and Fatherland–United Russia (*Edinstvo i Otechestvo–Edinaya Rossiya*). The members of all three then voted in February 2002 to dissolve as separate entities.

The Unity bloc, also known as the Inter-Regional Movement "Unity" (*Mezhregionalnoye Dvizhenie "Edinstvo"—Medved* [Bear]), had been announced in September 1999 by nearly three dozen leaders of regions and republics (some of whom later withdrew their support) to contest the State Duma elections in December. Backed by President Yeltsin and Prime Minister Putin as a counter to the Fatherland–All Russia bloc, Unity offered no ideological platform and was described by some commentators as a "virtual party."

Apparently benefiting from Putin's prosecution of the war in Chechnya and his accompanying rise in popularity, Unity finished second to the KPRF in the December 1999 federal election, winning 23 percent of the vote and 73 seats. In May 2000, with President Putin in attendance, Unity held its founding congress as a political party. On the same day former prime minister Viktor Chernomyrdin's Our Home Is Russia (*Nash Dom–Rossiya*—NDR), having won only 1.2 percent of the party list vote and 8 constituency seats at the most recent State Duma election, voted to disband in favor of Unity.

Little more than a year earlier, in April 1999, the organizing committee of All Russia had met in an effort to establish in the Federal Assembly a regionalist power bloc dominated by various regional governors and presidents. Two days later it allied with the Fatherland movement, which had been founded in late 1998 by Yuri Luzhkov, the mayor of Moscow. The resultant Fatherland–All Russia (*Otechestvo–Vsya Rossiya*—OVR) won 13 percent of the party list vote and 66 seats at the December State Duma election.

In April 2001 the Unity faction in the State Duma and the Fatherland–All Russia faction announced that they would work together with the goal of forming a unified party. Within days, two additional parliamentary factions, Russia's Regions and the People's Deputies, had agreed to cooperate with them on selected issues, thereby—at least on paper—creating a 234-seat majority bloc in the State Duma.

In the December 2003 parliamentary election, the unified party, now known as United Russia (sometimes translated as Unified Russia), with President Putin's backing, was the clear victor, winning 36.6 percent of the proportional vote and a slim majority of the filled seats. More important, it soon attracted additional support from independents and other parties, enabling its Duma faction to chair all committees and to surpass the two-thirds threshold for making constitutional changes.

United Russia has emerged as the vehicle for what Putin's supporters label "reform" (and his detractors, authoritarianism). It espouses "social conservatism"—a blend of market economics, promotion of the middle class, nationalism, and support for social order and stability. There has, however, been tension between the party's more rightist market forces and those committed to a more "social orientation," some of whom strongly objected to a Putin initiative that replaced guaranteed social service benefits with cash payments.

United Russia extended its political control in March 2006, winning 55 percent of the vote in eight regional and republican legislative elections. In March 2007 it took 46 percent in winning control in 13 out of 14 legislatures.

Prior to the December 2007 legislative election, United Russia continued to pick up adherents as smaller parties dissolved. Speaking at a party congress on October 1, 2007, President Putin announced that he had agreed to head the party's candidate list and would consider leading the party and serving as prime minister following the end of his presidential term in 2008. In the December election, United Russia won 64.3 percent of the vote. A month before the election, the Agrarian Party of Russia (*Agrarnaya Partiya Rossii*—APR), which had been aligned with the Communists, merged with United Russia. (See the 2009 *Handbook* for details on the APR.) Also in 2008 United Russia shortened its name by dropping the "All Russia" rubric.

Following the election of President Medvedev in 2008, Putin, as had been expected, was named prime minister. In April Putin was elected to a four-year term in the newly created post of chair of the party. The party's strength was further consolidated by its victories in most of the March 2009 mayoral elections. Following a series of televised political party debates in mid-2009, United Russia was reported to have achieved its highest-ever popularity rating of 58 percent. Earlier in the year the mayor of Smolensk was dismissed from the party allegedly because of the poor state of infrastructure in his district. However, observers said the party was backing another mayoral candidate, and when the incumbent defiantly added his name to the ballot, he was expelled. Another high-ranking party official narrowly avoided expulsion in June after he publicly criticized the country's political system.

Leaders: Vladimir PUTIN (Chair and Prime Minister), Boris GRYZLOV (Chair of the Supreme Council of United Russia and Chair of the State Duma), Yuri VOLKOV (Chair, Central Executive Committee), Yuri LUZHKOV (Co-chair and Mayor of Moscow), Mintimer SHAIMIYEV (Co-chair and President of Tatarstan), Sergei SHOIGU (Co-chair) and Minister of Civil Defense, Emergencies, and Natural Disasters), Valery BOGOMOLOV (Secretary of the General Council).

Other Leading Parties in the 2007–2011 State Duma:

Communist Party of the Russian Federation (*Kommunisticheskaya Partiya Rossiiskoi Federatsii*—KPRF). The KPRF is a late 1992 revival of the former Communist Party of the Soviet Union—CPSU (*Kommunisticheskaya Partiya Sovetskogo Soyuza*—KPSS), which was suspended in August 1991 and banned in November. The KPRF ran third in the legislative poll of December 1993 and thereafter generally opposed the Yeltsin administration, although in January 1995 a Communist was appointed justice minister. At the December State Duma election the KPRF won a plurality of 157 of the 450 seats, including 99 on a 22 percent share of the proportional vote.

KPRF leader Gennadi Zyuganov contested the mid-1996 presidential election on a platform deploring the erosion of Russia's industrial base by IMF-imposed policies and promising to restore economic sovereignty. He finished a close second to President Yeltsin in the first round on June 16, with 32 percent of the vote, but lost to the incumbent in the runoff on July 3, taking 40.3 percent of the vote. The KPRF then sought to consolidate the left-wing and conservative backing obtained by Zyuganov, initiating the formation in August of the opposition People's Patriotic Union of Russia (NPSR—see Patriots of Russia, below).

After having unsuccessfully attempted to forge a "For Victory" (*Za Pobedu*—ZP) electoral coalition of Communists, Agrarians, and others to contest the December 1999 State Duma balloting, the KPRF basically ran independently, with "For Victory" reduced to little more than a slogan. As in 1995, it won a plurality, taking 114 seats and a party list vote share of 24 percent. Three months later Zyuganov again finished second, with 29 percent of the vote, in the presidential contest.

In May 2002 the party's Central Committee expelled three leading members who refused to resign from leadership posts in the State Duma after the ascendant United Russia won committee chairs away from the KPRF. The most prominent dissenter was the chair of the Duma, Gennadi Seleznev, who subsequently built his patriotic Russia movement (*Rossiya*) into the Party of Russia's Rebirth (PVR, below).

At the December 2003 State Duma election the KPRF saw its support halved—to 12.6 percent of the proportional vote and a total of only 52 seats—in part because a significant fraction of the leftist vote was siphoned off by the new Motherland coalition. Sergei Glazyev, a former Communist who had sought an electoral alliance with the KPRF before forming the Motherland coalition, was one of several prominent leftists who had grown disenchanted with Zyuganov's continuing leadership, which led, in mid-2004, to further ruptures. In July supporters of Zyuganov and Vladimir TIKHONOV held competing congresses, with the Ministry of Justice ultimately ruling in Zyuganov's favor. Tikhonov went on to form the All-Russian Communist Party of the Future (*Vserossiiskaya Kommunisticheskaya Partiya Budushchego*—VKPB). Zyuganov also lost the support of Gennadi Semigin, chair of the NPSR, who was expelled from the KPRF and later formed the Patriots of Russia.

The KPRF's 2004 presidential candidate, Nikolai Kharitonov, finished second, with 13.7 percent of the vote.

The KPRF has subsequently led opposition to a number of President Putin's initiatives, including changes to social benefits policies. In March 2006 the KPRF came in second in six of eight regions holding legislative elections, improving its representation in five regions. The modest improvement was due in part to the fact that competing leftist party *Rodina* was excluded from the balloting in all but one of the regions. In March 2007 the KPRF received only 16 percent of the vote in 14 regional and republican legislative elections.

In the December 2007 State Duma election the KPRF received 11.6 percent of the votes. Zyuganov stood as the party's presidential candidate for the third time on March 2, 2008, finishing second with 17.8 percent of the vote.

In May 2009 reports surfaced of a rival Communist association, **Communists of Russia** (*Kommunisty Rossii*), being formed with the help of Fair Russia, to include KPRF dissidents.

Leaders: Gennadi ZYUGANOV (Chair and 2008 presidential candidate), Ivan MELNIKOV (Deputy Chair), Oleg KULIKOV (Secretary of the Central Committee).

Liberal Democratic Party of Russia (*Liberalno-Demokraticheskaya Partiya Rossii*—LDPR). The far-right LDPR was launched in Moscow in March 1990 as an all-Union grouping. Its leader, the xenophobic Vladimir Zhirinovsky, drew over 6 million votes (7.8 percent) in the 1991 presidential poll. Dubbed "the Russian Mussolini," Zhirinovsky had made a number of extravagant promises, such as providing each Russian with cheap vodka and launching a campaign to reconquer Finland. The party was officially banned in August 1992 on grounds that it had falsified its membership lists; however, it was permitted to contest the 1993 legislative poll, at which it ran second to Russia's Choice overall, while heading the party list returns with 22.8 percent of the national vote.

Although Zhirinovsky signed the April 1994 Treaty on Civil Accord between President Yeltsin and over 200 political groups, his increasingly controversial utterances caused him to be shunned by the political establishment, including his own natural allies. In the December 1995 legislative balloting the LDPR slipped to 11.4 percent of the proportional vote, coming in third place with 51 seats. In the mid-1996 presidential contest, moreover, Zhirinovsky managed only fifth place in the first round, with 5.7 percent of the vote. The LDPR continued to fare poorly in regional elections in 1997.

In October 1999 the Central Electoral Commission disqualified the LDPR party list from the December State Duma election because two of its top three candidates—one of whom was being investigated for money laundering—had not fully declared their assets. With the electoral deadline approaching, Zhirinovsky quickly cobbled together an alternative list, the Zhirinovsky Bloc (*Blok Zhirinovskogo*), based on the small affiliated Spiritual Revival of Russia Party (*Partiya Duhovnogo Vozrozhdeniya Rossii*—PDVR), led by his half-sister Lyubov ZHIRINOVSKAYA and Oleg FINKO, and the Russia Free Youth Union (*Rossiiskii Soyuz Svobodnoi Molodezhi*—RSSM), led by Yegor SOLOMATIN. The bloc won a 6.0 percent party list vote share and 17 seats at the election. In the March 2000 presidential contest Zhirinovsky polled 2.7 percent of the vote, for fifth place.

At the December 2003 State Duma election the LDPR finished with an unexpected 11.5 percent of the proportional vote and a total of 36 seats. This momentum did not last, however. Zhirinovsky, acknowledging President Putin's insurmountable lead going into the 2004 presidential election, chose not to run. The party's candidate, Oleg MALYSHKIN, finished fifth with 2.0 percent of the vote. The LDPR did not reach the threshold for winning seats in two of eight regions holding legislative elections in March 2006, and lost significant ground in the other 6. In March 2007 it won only 9 percent of the total vote in the 14 regions and republics holding elections. In the December 2007 State Duma election, the LDPR won 8 percent of the vote. In the March 2008 presidential election, Zhirinovsky finished third with 9.5 percent of the vote. Later in 2008 there was speculation that Andrei Lugovoi, a member of parliament and the main suspect in the poisoning case of former security agent and Putin critic Aleksandr Litvinenko, might replace Zhirinovsky as party chair.

In 2009 President Medvedev said though the LDPR is an opposition party, he was certain compromise and cooperation were possible.

Leader: Vladimir ZHIRINOVSKY (Deputy Speaker of the State Duma, Chair of the Party, and 2008 presidential candidate).

Just Russia–Motherland, Pensioners, Life (*Spravedlivaya Rossiya–Rodina/Persionery/Zhizn*—Fair Russia). Just Russia was established in October 2006 by merger of three parties: Motherland, the Russian Party of Life, and the Russian Party of Pensioners. Also joining, in April 2007, was the People's Party of the Russian Federation (NPRF).

Motherland (*Rodina*) had originated as the Party of Russian Regions (*Partiya Rossiiskih Regionov*—PRR), which joined the Party of National Rebirth "People's Will" (see the People's Union, below), the Socialist United Party of Russia (Spiritual Heritage) (*Sotsialisticheskaya Edinaya Partiya Rossii [Dukhovnoe Nasledie]*—SEPR), and smaller groups in forming the Motherland–People's Patriotic Union (*Rodina–Narodno-Patrioticheskii Soyuz*) electoral bloc in September 2003. Appealing to the patriotic left, the Motherland bloc surprised most observers by drawing support from the Communists and winning 9.0 percent of the proportional vote and a total of 36 State Duma seats in December.

The bloc's principal organizers, Sergei GLAZYEV and Dmitri Rogozin, had been associated with a number of political formations since the breakup of the Soviet Union, including the Congress of Russian Communities (*Kongress Russkikh Obshchin*—KRO), a moderately nationalist movement that dated from 1995. Much of the KRO's membership had followed Rogozin into the NPRF after its formation in 2001. Glazyev later became the chair of the SEPR, founded in March 2002 by merger of the Socialist Party of Russia (*Sotsialisticheskaya Partiya Rossii*—SPR) and Alexei PODBEREZKIN's Spiritual Heritage (*Dukhovnoe Nasledie*), which dated from 1996 and 1995, respectively. For the 2003 elections Glazyev had approached the KPRF about an alliance but was turned down, leading to his involvement in forming the *Rodina* alliance with Rogozin.

Soon after the unexpected success of the Motherland–People's Patriotic Union in December 2003, their ideological differences and competing political ambitions caused a rupture between Glazyev and Rogozin. In February 2004 Rogozin engineered the renaming of the PRR as the *Rodina* party, after which Glazyev, who had decided to run against President Putin, was removed from the leadership. As an independent, Glazyev finished third, with 4.1 percent of the vote, in the March 2004 balloting. Three months later his new public-political organization, For a Decent Life (*Za Dostoinuyu Zhizn*—ZDZ), based on a loyal SEPR faction and various other elements of the Motherland coalition, was denied registration by the Ministry of Justice. In March 2006 Rogozin announced his resignation from all senior party posts but remained a member of *Rodina* until formation of Just Russia. In 2007 he formed the Great Russia (VR, below) party. Glazyev, who initially supported formation of Just Russia, later announced his retirement from politics.

The Russian Party of Life (*Rossiiskaya Partiya Zhizni*—RPZh) was established in 2002 by Sergei Mironov, chair of the Federation Council. Centrist in nature, the RPZh focused on quality-of-life issues. For the 2003 State Duma election the RPZh forged an electoral bloc with the Party of Russia's Rebirth (PVR, below), but the bloc won only 1.9 percent of the proportional vote and 3 constituency seats. Mironov won less than 1 percent of the vote as a candidate for president in 2004.

The Russian Party of Pensioners (*Rossiiskaya Partiya Pensionerov*—RPP) dated from 1997. It contested the 2003 State Duma elections in a bloc with the Party of Social Justice (PSS, below), winning 3.1 percent of the vote but no seats, which contributed to the suspension of the party's chair, Sergei ATROSHENKO in January 2004. He was succeeded by Valery GARTUNG, initially in an acting capacity. In October the RPP joined in forming the Patriots of Russia coalition, but it remained separate from the subsequently organized Patriots of Russia party. In February 2005 Gartung broke with United Russia's parliamentary faction, primarily because of his opposition to President Putin's plan to replace guaranteed social service benefits with monetary payments (the so-called cash-for-benefits reform), which was widely viewed as adversely affecting pensioners. Seemingly as a direct result of this action, it was discovered that Gartung's election as party leader involved irregularities, which ultimately cost him the post that autumn.

The People's Party of the Russian Federation (*Narodnaya Partiya Rossiiskoi Federatsii*—NPRF), formed from Gennadi RAIKOV's preexisting People's Deputy group in the State Duma, was registered as a party in October 2001. At the December 2003 elections it won only 1.2 percent of the proportional vote but 17 district seats. Its deputies then elected to sit in the United Russia parliamentary faction. Citing his duties in the Duma, Raikov stepped down as party chair in April 2004 and has most recently served on the Central Electoral Commission.

At a January 2005 party congress the NPRF adopted a more social-democratic platform and criticized Putin's cash-for-benefits reform. The party leadership later threatened to pull its deputies from the United Russia deputy group, but in May the majority of the NPRF's 17 deputies instead opted to join United Russia to ensure their inclusion on the United Russia party list for the 2007 Duma election. Party chief Gennadi Gudkov later attempted to unite various leftist parties, but the effort failed and he joined Just Russia in March 2007, a month before the NPRF was deregistered by the courts.

Since its formation, Just Russia/Fair Russia has remained generally supportive of President Putin's policies while attempting to establish itself as the country's principal alternative to United Russia. Its candidate list for the 2007 State Duma election included various prominent figures whose parties had failed to meet the new stringent registration requirements, including Oleg SHEIN of the Russian Labor Party (*Rossiiskaya Partiya Truda*—RPT) and Ivan GRACHEV of the Development of Enterprise (*Razvitie Predprinimatelstva*—RP), a business-oriented party that was formed in 1998 and won 1 constituency seat in the 2003 State Duma election. Fair Russia received 7.8 percent of the vote in the December 2007 State Duma election.

In 2008 the Russian Ecological Party "The Greens" (*Rossiiskaya Ekologicheskaya Partiya "Zelenye"*—REP "The Greens") and the SEPR merged with Fair Russia, as did the Party of Social Justice (*Partiya Sotsialnoi Spravedlivosti*—PSS). (For details on these parties, see the 2009 *Handbook.*)

Leaders: Sergei MIRONOV (Chair of the Party and Chair of the Federation Council), Aleksandr BABAKOV (Former Chair of Motherland), Gennadi GUDKOV (Former NPRF Chair), Igor ZOTOV (Former NPRF Chair).

Other Parties that Participated in the 2007 State Duma Election:

Yabloko (Apple.) *Yabloko*—formally, the Russian Democratic Party *"Yabloko "* (*Rossiiskaya Demokraticheskaya Partiya "Yabloko"*)—descends from the Yavlinsky-Boldyrev-Lukin Bloc, an electoral grouping formed in October 1993 by economist Grigori Yavlinsky, scientist Yuri BOLDYREV, and former ambassador to the United States Vladimir LUKIN, who, while endorsing market reforms, opposed what they viewed as Yeltsin's "shock therapy." In December 1993 the grouping won 7.8 percent of the party list vote. Boldyrev left the party in 1994. (In 1999 he formed an electoral bloc with the KRO—see Just Russia, above.)

Yabloko finished fourth in the December 1995 legislative balloting, winning 45 seats. In the mid-1996 presidential contest Yavlinsky placed fourth in the first round, winning 7.3 percent of the vote and then giving qualified endorsement to Boris Yeltsin in the runoff balloting. Debates over the 1997 and 1998 budgets showed *Yabloko,* rather than the Communists or the nationalists, to be the most uncompromising opponent of the government's spending plans.

At the 1999 State Duma elections *Yabloko* won 21 seats. During the campaign it had been the only major party to criticize the government's conduct of the war in Chechnya, particularly the bombing of Grozny. Yavlinsky finished third, with 5.8 percent of the vote, at the March 2000 presidential election.

At the 2003 lower house election *Yabloko* won only 4.3 percent of the proportional vote and 4 seats. The poor showing of both *Yabloko* and the Union of Right Forces (SPS, below) rekindled discussions, first broached in 2000, of a merger, although Yavlinsky had significant differences with SPS leader Anatoly Chubais. In July 2004 Yavlinsky won reelection as party head over Yuri KUZNETSOV, who had advocated an alliance with the SPS. In the March 2006 regional elections *Yabloko* and the SPS, running as an electoral alliance, failed to win any legislative seats, and in June the *Yabloko* party congress voted not to pursue the merger. In the December 2007 State Duma election, Yabloko failed to reach the 7 percent threshold and lost its representation in the lower house. In a statement on election day, Yavlinsky claimed that the election had been rigged.

After 15 years as *Yabloko*'s leader, Yavlinsky stepped down on June 21, 2008, though he remained influential within the party. Sergei Metrokhin, the leader of the party's Moscow branch, took over as party chair.

In January 2009 the party protested as illegal the arrests of its members who demonstrated in memory of slain journalists and liberal public figures. Another party activist was arrested at a demonstration in April.

Leader: Sergei METROKHIN (Chair).

Union of Right Forces (*Soyuz Pravyh Sil*—SPS). The SPS emerged as a reform-minded, pro-Western electoral coalition in 1999. Initial participants were former prime minister Sergei KIRIYENKO's New Force (*Novaya Zila*—NZ), a market-oriented group that dated from late 1998; Samara governor Konstantin TITOV's federalist Voice of Russia (*Golos Rossii*—GR), a movement that was envisaged as a bloc of governors rather than as a political party upon its formation in early 1999; and Just Cause (*Pravoye Delo*—PD, also translated as Right Cause), a center-right electoral bloc formed in 1998–1999 by Yegor Gaidar, Anatoly Chubais, and a number of other prominent politicians who sought to prevent the Communists from returning to power in the December 1999 election. At a unification conference in August they were formally joined by Irina KHAKAMADA's Common Cause (*Obshchee Delo*—OD), a liberal, reformist movement that had been established in 1995 with support from a number of women's and youth groups; former deputy prime minister Boris Nemtsov's Young Russia (*Rossiya Molodaya*—RM), which had been formed in late 1998 on a platform that called for market-oriented economic reforms and an end to compulsory military service; and Gaidar's Russia's Democratic Choice (*Demokraticheskii Vybor Rossii*—DVR), which descended from the Bloc of Reformist Forces: "Choice of Russia" (*Blok Reformistkikh Sil: "Vybor Rossii"*—BRVR) and the resultant Russia's Choice (VR). In December 1993 the VR had finished first in the Duma elections. In June 1994 the VR was formally transformed into a political party, the DVR.

Along with Unity, the SPS received verbal support from Prime Minister Putin going into the December 1999 Duma election, at which it won 29 seats and an 8.5 percent proportional vote share. Although the SPS Coordinating Council announced in February 2000 that it would not endorse any candidate for the upcoming presidential election, various SPS constituent organizations went their own way. Kiriyenko's group supported Acting President Putin, Lev PONOMARYEV's Democratic Russia (*Demokraticheskaya Rossiya*—DR) component of the DVR backed Konstantin Titov, and both Nemtsov and Khakamada campaigned for *Yabloko*'s Grigori Yavlinsky. (Ponomaryev now heads the For Human Rights organization, also known as the All Russia Movement for Human Rights.)

The SPS established itself as a national organization at a congress in May 2000, at which time it passed a resolution pledging support for "any actions taken by President Putin that do not run counter to the values of liberalism, are in the interests of a free society, and contribute to the country's economic prosperity." A future merger with *Yabloko* was announced in June but was never accomplished.

At a founding congress held May 26–27, 2001, the SPS formally reorganized as a unified party, its (at that time) nine constituent parties having agreed, in the preceding weeks, to dissolve as independent entities. Support within the nine parties was not unanimous, however, and key members of the DVR, in particular, indicated that they would leave the organization. The new party's initial cochairs were Chubais, Gaidar, Khakamada, Kiriyenko, and Nemtsov. In May 2000 Kiriyenko resigned from the party to serve as President Putin's envoy to the Volga federal district.

At the December 2003 State Duma election the SPS suffered a major defeat, winning only 4.0 percent of the proportional vote and three constituency seats. As a consequence, in January 2004 the remaining cochairs resigned, with no replacements being named. In March Khakamada ran for president against Putin without the party's endorsement, finishing fourth, with less than 4 percent of the vote; she subsequently formed Our Choice (*Nash Vybor*).

At a party congress in May 2005 the SPS chose Nikita Belykh, deputy governor of Perm Oblast, as its new chair, and Leonid Gozman, a colleague of Chubais on the board of the state electricity monopoly, United Energy Systems, as his deputy. Belykh was opposed by Ivan STARIKOV, representing the party faction most opposed to President Putin's policies. In the March 2006 elections in eight regions, the SPS failed to win any legislative seats; in March 2007, however, it won 7 percent of the total vote in elections for 14 regional legislatures. In the 2007 State Duma election, the Union of Right Forces won less than 1 percent of the vote, again failing to win any seats in the lower house.

In 2008 Belykh stepped down and Deputy Chair Leonid Gozman took the party's helm. In November the party voted to dissolve and subsequently merged, along with the Civil Force and the Democratic Party of Russia, with the Right Cause (see Other Party, below).

Leaders: Leonid GOZMAN (Chair), Nikita BELYKH.

Patriots of Russia (*Patrioty Rossii*—PR). Founder and former Communist Gennadi Semigin announced formation of the PR as a unified political party in April 2005. The previous October Semigin had spearheaded formation of a PR coalition encompassing ten predominantly leftist parties and movements, including his own People's Patriotic Union of Russia (*Narodno-Patrioticheskii Soyuz Rossii*—NPSR), which had been organized in 1996 by the KPRF's Gennadi Zyuganov as a means of consolidating left-wing, nationalist parties and movements. Zyuganov had lost control of the NPSR in mid-2004, however, during the dispute over leadership of the KPRF. Other initial participants in the PR coalition included the All-Russian Communist Party of the Future (VKPB; see under KPRF, above); the Eurasian Party–Union of Russian Patriots (EP-SPR; see under VR-ES, below); the National-Patriotic Forces of the Russian Federation (*Natsionalno-Patrioticheskii Sil Rossiiskoi Federatsii*—NPSRF), led by Shmidt DZOBLAEV; the Party of Russia's Rebirth (PVR, below); the Party of Workers' Self-Government (*Partiya Samoypravleniya Trudyashchikhsya*—PST), founded in 1995 by Svyatoslav FYODOROV, who finished sixth in the 1996 presidential election; the People's Patriotic Party of Russia (NPPR); the Russian Party of Pensioners (RPP; see under Just Russia, above), a wing of the Russian Labor Party (RPT) led by Sergei KHRAMOV; and the Union of People for Education and Science (*Soyuz Liudei za Obrazovanie i Nauku*—SLON), led by Vyacheslav IGRUNOV, one of the original *Yabloko* leaders. The PR also claimed the support of some 30 public organizations.

The PR took part in five of the eight races to regional legislatures in March 2006, passing the 5 percent threshold to win seats in the parliaments of the Kaliningrad and Orenburg regions. It had scant success in the March 2007 regional elections, and received less than 0.9 percent of the vote in the December 2007 State Duma election, failing to win any legislative seats.

The Party of Russia's Rebirth (*Partiya Vozrozhdeniya Rossii*—PVR), led by Gennadi SELEZNEV, and the Party of Peace and Unity (*Partiya Mira i Edinstva*—PME), led by Sazhi UMALATOVA, merged with the PR in 2008. (See the 2009 Handbook for details on the PVR and the PME.)

Leader: Gennadi SEMIGIN (Chair).

Other Party:

Right Cause. The pro-business liberal Right Cause was formed in November 2008 by the merger of the Union of Right Forces (above), Civil Force (*Grazhdanskaya Sila*—GS), led by Mikhail BARSHCHEVSKY, and Democratic Party of Russia (*Demokraticheskaya Partiya Rossii*—DPR), led by Andrei BOGDANOV. [See the 2009 *Handbook* for details on the latter two parties.] It was officially registered on February 18, 2009, becoming only the second new party to obtain registration in recent years (Fair Russia being the other). Right Cause promotes a civil society based on democratic principles and the rule of law, and it urges political and public freedom, along with free and fair elections. Its critics, however, have accused the party of being too closely aligned with President Medvedev and Prime Minister Putin and more or less controlled by the Kremlin.

Rifts in the party over the tripartite leadership and a campaign platform were reported in 2009 in the run-up to regional elections in the fall.

Leaders: Alexei VELICHKO (Co-chair), Leonid GOZMAN (Co-chair, former leader of the Union of Right Forces), Boris TITOV (Co-chair).

Significant Parties Dissolved or Denied Registration:

Great Russia (*Velikaya Rossiya*—VR). The nationalist VR was organized in April 2007 by populist Dmitri Rogozin, who had been a principal organizer of Motherland but had decided not to join the successor party, Just Russia. Instead, he revived the Congress of Russian Communities (KRO; see Just Russia), which, along with the Movement Against Illegal Immigration, participated in formation of the VR. In July, however, the Federal Registration Service refused to register the VR for not complying with regulations. In January 2008 Rogozin became Russia's ambassador to NATO.

Leaders: Dmitri ROGOZIN, Andrei SAVELYEV, Sergei PYKHTIN.

Great Russia–Eurasian Union (*Velikaya Rossiya-Evraiskii Soyuz*—VR-ES). The VR-ES bloc was formed for the 2003 legislative election by the Eurasian Party–Union of Russian Patriots (*Evrazskaya Partiya–Soyuz Patriotov Rossii*—EP-SPR), led by Pavel Borodin, in partnership with the Russian Peace Party (*Rossiiskaya Partiya Mira*—RPM), led by Iosif Kobzon and Vladimir Medvedev, and the Citizens' Party of Russia (*Grazhdanskaya Partiya Rossii*—GPR, also translated as the Russian Civic Party), led by D. O. Serezhetdinov. The bloc won only 0.3 percent of the proportional vote and 1 constituency seat in 2003 and did not participate in the 2007 State Duma election.

Leaders: Pavel BORODIN, Iosif KOBZON, Vladimir MEDVEDEV, D. O. SEREZHETDINOV.

Liberal Russia (*Liberalnaya Rossiya*—LR). The LR, which had been formed with the support of the self-exiled oligarch Boris Berezovsky, was registered by the Ministry of Justice in October 2002—not coincidentally, shortly after Berezovsky's expulsion. Since the party's inception, differences had existed between Berezovsky's supporters, who were committed to uniting the anti-Putin opposition, and members committed first and foremost to a liberal ideology. As a consequence, the LR split in two, with both groups claiming the LR name. In April 2003, one of the party's founders, Sergei YUSHENKOV, was assassinated hours after registering the party to participate in the December parliamentary elections.

The leader of the officially registered LR, Viktor POKHMELKIN, resigned from the party in March 2004 to sit in the State Duma as an independent. At the time, he commented that "the Liberal Russia brand" had been so discredited that "it is indecent for a normal person to admit to having anything to do with it."

People's Union (*Narodnyi Soyuz*—NS). Formation of the NS was announced in March 2007 by populist Sergei Baburin. Based primarily on Baburin's Party of National Rebirth "People's Will" (*Partiya Natsionalnogo Vozrozhdeniya "Narodnaya Volya"*—PNV-NV), the new NS also brought together about a dozen other conservative, Orthodox Christian, and nationalist small parties and organizations. People's Will had emerged in 2001 from Baburin's Russian National Union (*Rossiiskii Obshenarodnyi Soyuz*—ROS, also translated as the Russian All-People's Union).

ROS had been formed in 1990 and 1991 to further a nationalist agenda that subsequently called for the restoration of the Soviet Union. ROS also advocated state ownership of land and major industries as well as strong central economic regulation. Barred from running in 1993, in 1995 it formed the core of the Power to the People (*Narodu-vlastiye*) electoral bloc, under the leadership of former Soviet premier Nikolai Ryzhkov. In 1999 ROS won 0.4 percent of the party list vote and 2 constituency seats. Joining ROS in formation of People's Will were the Union of Realists (*Soyuz Realistov*—SR), which had been established in 1995 as an alliance of some 20 centrist groupings, and Russian Revival (*Russkoye Vozrozhdeniye*), a right-wing formation committed to Russian Orthodoxy and traditional culture.

For the 2003 State Duma election People's Will joined the Motherland bloc. It subsequently decided to remain aloof from the unified Motherland party. With the December 2007 State Duma election approaching, Baburin considered other merger options but ultimately opted for transformation of the People's Will into the NS. In October 2007, the Central Electoral Commission disqualified the party for the State Duma election of December due to invalid signatures. The disqualification was upheld by the Supreme Court in November. The party backed the KPRF in the election.

Leader: Sergei BABURIN (Chair).

Republican Party of Russia (*Respublikanskaya Partiya Rossii*—RPR). A self-described "left-centrist party of the parliamentary type," the RPR was founded in 1990 by former members of the Democratic Platform within the CPSU. It subsequently helped launch the Democratic Choice bloc. In June 1995 the party announced that former minister Ella PAMFILOVA would head its list in the forthcoming elections. Called the Pamfilova-Gurov-Lysenko Bloc, the list obtained only 1.6 percent of the proportional vote and 2 constituency seats. Pamfilova subsequently formed the For Civil Dignity movement, while in November 1998 Aleksandr GUROV was named by the Interior Ministry to head an institute charged with fighting organized crime. In 2002 the party was joined by Forward, Russia! (*Vperyod Rossiya!*), led by former finance minister Boris FEDEROV. In 2003 it participated in the New Course–Automotive Russia bloc. Vladimir RYZHKOV and Vladimir LYSENKO were its leaders when it was dissolved by the Supreme Court in March 2007 for reportedly having too few members.

Russian Communist Workers' Party–Revolutionary Party of Communists (*Rossiiskaya Kommunisticheskaya Rabochaya Partiya–Revoliutsionnaya Partiya Kommunistov*—RKRP-RPK). The RKRP-RPK dated from the 2001 merger of Viktor TYULKIN's RKRP and Anatoly KRYUCHKOV's RPK. Both were among the 20-odd "old-style" communist groups grouped in the Union of Communist Parties–CPSU (*Soyuz Kommunisticheskikh Partii*—SKP-KPSS), which continued to include "Communist Party of the Soviet Union" (CPSU/KPSS) as part of its official name. For the 2003 State Duma election the KPRF had included on its list members of the RKRP-RPK and Aleksei PRIGARIN's Russian Communist Party—CPSU (*Rossiiskaya Kommunisticheskaya Partiya*—RKP-KPSS). The Supreme Court abolished it in May 2007 because its membership was 35,000, below the 50,000-member minimum. The RKRP-RPK had earlier filed an unsuccessful lawsuit, claiming that the membership requirement limited the Russian people's right to participate in the country's political processes. The group's youth organization, said to be among the most active in Russia, was led by Alexander BATOV.

Social Democratic Party of Russia (*Sotsial-Demokraticheskaya Partiya Rossii*—SDPR). The SDPR was formed in November 2001 by merger of Mikhail Gorbachev's Russian United Social Democratic Party (*Rossiiskaya Obyedinennaya Sotsial Demokraticheskaya Partiya*—ROSDP) and Konstantin Titov's Russian Party of Social Democracy (*Rossiiskaya Partiya Sotsialnoi Demokratii*—RPSD). The ROSDP had been established in March 2000 and registered in May in an attempt to organize a unified social democratic party in opposition to both Communist ideology and unrestrained free-market liberalism. The RPSD dated from February 1995, its first chair, Aleksandr YAKOVLEV, having been a leading adviser to Gorbachev at the end of the Soviet era. Titov, the governor of Samara, became chair in 2000, and for a time the party was closely associated with the SPS.

The SDPR, with Gorbachev as leader and Titov as chair, chose not to contest the 2003 State Duma election, although Titov had sought a cooperative arrangement with United Russia. For want of a viable alternative, the party backed Vladimir Putin for reelection in March 2004. Two months later Gorbachev resigned as leader, in part because of disagreements with Titov, who himself subsequently took a less active role in the party and resigned as Samara governor in 2007. The party's last chair, Vladimir KISHENIN, had previously headed the electoral list of the Russian Party of Pensioners–Party of Social Justice (RPP-PSS) bloc for the 2003 State Duma election. The SDPR was abolished by the Supreme Court in April 2007, and many of its members joined Gorbachev's new Union of Social Democrats party.

For more information on the now-defunct **New Course–Automotive Russia** (*Novyi Kurs–Avtomobilnaya Rossiya*—NK-AR), please see the 2008 *Handbook*.

Other Political Organizations:

The Other Russia (*Drugaya Rossiya*—DR). A forum organized in July 2006 by opponents of President Putin, the DR brought together a philosophically incongruous assortment of former government figures, human rights activists, communists, and nationalists. Organizers included former prime minister Mikhail Kasyanov of the **People's Democratic Union** (*Narodno-Demokraticheskii Soyuz*—NDS), a movement formed in March 2006 to unite left-wing and prodemocracy forces beneath a single banner; among the other NDS leaders were Irina Khakamada, SPS (above) founder and 2004 independent presidential candidate, and former SPS Policy Council secretary Ivan STARIKOV. Participants in the Other Russia also included former chess champion Garry Kasparov, founder in 2005 of the centrist **United Civic Front** (*Obyedinyonny Grazhdansky Front*—OGF); the writer Eduard Limonov, whose radical **National Bolshevik Party** (*Natsional-Bolshevistskaya Partiya*—NBP) had been banned as an extremist organization; and Vladimir Ryzhvov of the Republican Party of Russia (above). From December 2006 the principal DR tactic was to convene opposition rallies in major cities. The protests have often been dispersed by the police, with resultant arrests.

In September 2007 differences between Kasparov supporters and Kasyanov led Kasyanov to work outside the forum. He announced formation of **People for Democracy and Justice** (*Narod za demokratiyu i spravedlivost*—NDS) and was nominated as a candidate for the presidential election in December. He was then disqualified by the Central Election Commission, which claimed a large number of his 2 million supporting signatures were invalid. In October DR elements nominated Kasparov as their 2008 presidential candidate. Kasparov withdrew from the presidential election in December.

Leaders: Garry KASPAROV, Eduard LIMONOV.

Union of Social Democrats. On October 20, 2007, Mikhail Gorbachev announced the establishment of the Union of Social Democrats, a new political movement aimed at fighting corruption and fostering a democratic program that avoids the extremes of capitalism and socialism while blending their best principles. Gorbachev affirmed his support of President Putin's reforms and said that his new party would not run in the December 2, 2007, State Duma elections.

In September 2008 Gorbachev was reported to be planning a new, liberal party, styled the Independent Democratic Party of Russia, with business tycoon Alexander LEBEDEV.

Leader: Mikhail GORBACHEV.

LEGISLATURE

The 1993 constitution provides for a **Federal Assembly** (*Federalnoe Sobranie*) consisting of a Federation Council and a State Duma. The normal term for each is four years.

Federation Council (*Sovet Federatsii*). The upper house comprises two representatives from each of Russia's constitutionally recognized territorial units (89 units in 2003, declining to 83 in March 2008—see under Constitution and government, above). Each jurisdiction returns two members, one selected by the unit's executive and one by the unit's legislature. (Prior to January 2002, the chief executive and legislative chair of each unit had served ex officio.) Most members are designated as independents, but a majority now support United Russia.

Chair: Sergei MIRONOV.

State Duma (*Gosudarstvennaya Duma*). The lower house is a 450-member body. In the election of December 7, 2003, half of the seats were filled from single-member constituencies and half by proportional representation from party lists obtaining a minimum of 5 percent of the vote. Following repeat elections in several districts and significant realignments due to parliamentary factions, the 447 filled seats of the 2003–2007 Duma fell into bloc alignments as follows: United Russia, 306; Communist Party, 52; Motherland, 38; Liberal Democratic Party, 36; unaffiliated, 15.

In accordance with a law adopted in 2005, the State Duma elections in 2007 were conducted on a party-list proportional representation basis. Following the December 2, 2007, election, the seat distribution was as follows: United Russia, 315 seats; Communist Party of the Russian Federation, 57; Liberal Democratic Party of Russia, 40; and Just Russia, 38.

Chair: Boris GRYZLOV.

CABINET

[as of October 1, 2009]

Prime Minister	Vladimir Putin
First Deputy Prime Ministers	Viktor Zubkov
	Igor Shuvalov
Deputy Prime Ministers	Sergei Sobyanin
	Alexi Kudrin
	Aleksandr Zhukov
	Igor Sechin
	Sergei Ivanov
	Sergei Sobyanin
	Dmitri Kozak
Ministers	
Agriculture	Yelena Skrynnik [f]
Civil Defense, Emergencies, and Natural Disasters	Sergei Shoigu
Culture	Alexander Avdeyev
Defense	Anatoly Serdyukov
Director, Federal Security Services	Alexander Bortnikov
Director, Foreign Intelligence Service	Mikhail Fradkov
Economic Development and Trade	Elvira Nabiulina [f]
Education and Science	Andrei Fursenko
Energy	Sergei Shmatko
Finance	Alexei Kudrin
Foreign Affairs	Sergei Lavrov
Health and Social Policy	Tatyana Golikova [f]
Industry and Trade	Viktor Khristenko
Information Technology and Communications	Igor Shchyogolev
Interior	Rashid Nurgaliyev
Justice	Alexander Konovalov
Natural Resources	Yuri Trutnev
Regional Development	Viktor Basargin
Secretary, Security Council	Nikolai Patrushev
Sport, Youth, and Tourism	Vitaly Mutko
Transportation	Igor Levitin

COMMUNICATIONS

All mass media are licensed by the government. Most of the country's leading newspapers and broadcasting outlets are owned by companies close to the government or in which the government has majority ownership. A March 2007 presidential decree merged two agencies that had been separately responsible for protecting Russia's cultural heritage and supervising telecommunications and information technology, including the Internet. The decree was interpreted by some as a further effort by the Kremlin to control the mass media in the run-up to the December 2007 State Duma elections and the 2008 presidential contest. In September 2008 the *Nezavisimaya Gazeta* reported that it was given a warning by the governing United Russia party over an article it had published regarding personnel changes in the party.

Press. Following the demise of the USSR, many newspapers had to curtail operations because of high printing costs under free-market reforms, with average circulation falling by about 60 percent during 1992 alone. The principal organs of the USSR's central government, *Pravda* and *Izvestiya,* continue to publish, but with a mere fraction of their Soviet-era circulations. *Izvestiya* is now owned by Gazprom, while the current *Pravda* is privately owned and published in a tabloid format. The following are dailies published in Moscow, unless otherwise noted: *Argumenty i Facty* (Arguments and Facts, 2,600,000), weekly; *Moskovsky Komsomolets* (Moscow Young Communists, 800,000); *Komsomolskaya Pravda* (Young Communist Truth, 730,000), independent tabloid; *Trud* (Labor, 610,000), former trade union organ; *Rossiiskaya Gazeta* (Russian Gazette, 370,000), government organ of record; *Izvestiya* (News, 250,000); *Novaya Gazeta* (New Gazette, 100,000), twice weekly, independent; *Sankt-Peterburgskiye Vedomosti*

(St. Petersburg News, 90,000), weekly organ of St. Petersburg mayoralty; *Kommersant* (80,000), business; *Pravda* (Truth, 70,000), independent. *Nezavisimaya Gazeta* is an independent daily published by *Izvestiya*.

News agencies. In 1992 the long-dominant Telegraphic Agency of the Soviet Union (*Telegrafnoye Agentstvo Sovyetskogo Souza*—TASS) was combined with part of the former Novosti Press Agency (*Agentstvo Pechati Novosti*—APN) to form the Russian Information Telegraph Agency–Telegraphic Agency of the Sovereign Countries (*Informatsionnoye Telegrafnoye Agentstvo Rossii–Telegrafnoye Agentstvo Suverennykh Stran*—ITAR-TASS). Other facilities include a Russian Information Agency–Novosti (*Rossiyskoye Informatsionnoye Agentstvo–Novosti—RIA-Novosti*) as well as several independent agencies, most prominently Postfactum and Interfax. The leading foreign agencies maintain bureaus at Moscow.

Broadcasting and computing. In early 1991 Russia broke the Soviet government's broadcasting monopoly by establishing its own service, the All-Russian State Television and Radio Broadcasting Company (*Vserossiiskaya Gosudarstvennaya Teleradiokompaniya*—VGTRK), commonly called Russian Television and Radio (*Rossiiskoye Televideniye i Radio*—RTR). The separate Ostankino Russian State Television and Radio Broadcasting Company (*Rossiiskaya Gosudarstvennaya Teleradiokompaniya Ostankino*) was subsequently established. However, the latter was broken up in 1995, its television network becoming Russian Public Television (*Obshestvennoe Rossiiskoye Televideniye*—ORT), which was dominated by Boris Berezovsky's media empire until he sold his stake in 2001. An Independent Television (*Nezavisimoye Televideniye*—NTV) network, owned by Vladimir Gusinsky's Media-MOST, was taken over by the state-run Gazprom in 2001. As of 2008 there were 320 Internet users per 1,000 inhabitants.

INTERGOVERNMENTAL REPRESENTATION

Ambassador to the U.S.: Sergey Ivanovich KISLYAK.

U.S. Ambassador to Russia: John R. BEYRLE.

Permanent Representative to the UN: Vitaly Ivanovich CHURKIN.

IGO Memberships (Non-UN): AC, APEC, BIS, BSEC, CBSS, CEUR, CIS, EBRD, G-8, G-20, Interpol, OSCE, PCA, SCO, WCO.

RWANDA

Republic of Rwanda
République Rwandaise (French)
Republika y'u Rwanda (Kinyarwanda)

Political Status: Republic proclaimed January 28, 1961; independent since July 1, 1962; multiparty constitution adopted June 10, 1991, but full implementation blocked by ethnic-based fighting; peace agreement signed August 4, 1993, in Arusha, Tanzania, providing for transitional government and multiparty elections by 1995; twenty-two month transitional period announced January 5, 1994; new transitional government installed on July 19, 1994, by the Rwandan Patriotic Front (FPR) after taking military control in the wake of genocide of April 1994; new constitution (providing for a four-year, FPR-led transitional government but including provisions of the 1991 basic law and the 1993 Arusha peace agreement) adopted by the Transitional National Assembly on May 5, 1995; transitional period extended by the FPR for four years on June 8, 1999; new constitution providing for full transition to civilian rule adopted on June 4, 2003, following a national referendum on May 26.

Area: 10,169 sq. mi. (26,338 sq. km.).

Population: 8,128,553 (2002C); 9,902,000 (2008E). The 2002 figure remains provisional and is assumed to reflect substantial underenumeration.

Major Urban Center (1993E): KIGALI (276,000).

Official Languages: English, French, Kinyarwanda. (English was designated as an official language by the National Assembly in January 1996.)

Monetary Unit: Rwanda Franc (official rate December 1, 2009: 570.36 francs = $1US).

President: Maj. Gen. Paul KAGAME (Rwandan Patriotic Front); named interim president by the Supreme Court on March 24, 2000, following the resignation the previous day of Pasteur BIZIMUNGU (Rwandan Patriotic Front); elected in a permanent position by the combined Transitional National Assembly and cabinet on April 17, 2000, and inaugurated on April 22; reelected by popular vote on August 25, 2003, and inaugurated for a seven-year term on September 12.

Prime Minister: Bernard MAKUSA; appointed by the president on March 8, 2000, to succeed Pierre-Célestin RWIGEMA (Republican Democratic Movement), who had resigned on February 28; formed new government on March 20, 2000; reappointed by the president on October 11, 2003, and formed new government on October 19, following legislative elections on September 30; reappointed again on October 20, 2008, following legislative balloting on September 15.

THE COUNTRY

Situated in the heart of Africa (adjacent to Burundi, Tanzania, Uganda, and the Democratic Republic of the Congo), Rwanda consists mainly of grassy uplands and hills endowed with a temperate climate. The population comprises three main ethnic groups: the Hutu, or Bahutu (85 percent); the Tutsi, or Batutsi (14 percent); and the Twa, or pygmies (1 percent). There are about equal numbers of Roman Catholics and animists, with small Protestant (9 percent) and Muslim (1 percent) minorities. In addition to English, French, and Kinyarwanda (the three official languages), Kiswahili is widely spoken. Women account for about half of the labor force, primarily as unpaid agricultural workers on family plots; female representation in government and party posts is minimal, though the 2003 constitution called for increased participation by women in all levels of government, civil service, and policymaking. By 2008 the World Bank estimated that women owned 41 percent of Rwandan businesses, the highest percentage in Africa. Women also won a majority of seats in the 2008 legislative balloting (see Government and politics, below).

Economically poor, Rwanda has been hindered by high population growth (it is one of the most densely populated states in Africa), inadequate transportation facilities, distance from accessible ports, and the ravages of civil war. Over 90 percent of the people depend on agriculture for their livelihood, and goods are produced largely for local consumption. Coffee is the leading cash crop and principal source of foreign exchange, although tea cultivation is expanding. Industry is concentrated in food processing and nondurable consumer goods, but the mining of cassiterite and wolframite ore is also important. International assistance has focused on economic diversification, while recent state budgets have concentrated on agricultural and infrastructural development.

Despite the subsequent problems associated with civil war and the massive displacement and return of perhaps 2 million Rwandans, as of mid-2002 Rwanda was continuing to make considerable progress in rebuilding its economy. Due to the improved security situation, favorable weather conditions, additional foreign aid, increased food production, and the partial revival of exports, real GDP had grown by 13.8 percent in 1997, 8.9 percent in 1998, 7.6 percent in 1999, 6.0 percent in 2000, and 6.7 percent in 2001 (according to the International Monetary Fund [IMF]), while annual inflation had fallen into negative figures by the end of 2001. Reinforcing the country's economic infrastructure subsequently became the primary focus of governmental policy, which attracted substantial donor assistance. The IMF and World Bank, noting the progress in structural reform, offered debt relief, while at the same time encouraging the government to improve its revenue-collection system and intensify the privatization of state-run enterprises. A drought in 2003 cut agricultural production and caused growth to slow, while inflation rose to 9.4 percent. In addition, proposed economic reforms and privatization initiatives were slowly implemented. By 2004 only 30 of 74 state-owned enterprises scheduled for privatization

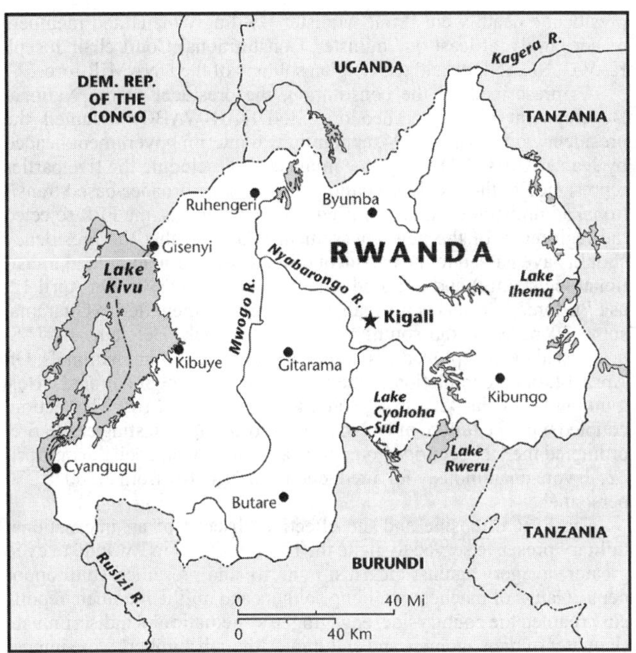

had made the transition to private ownership. The international community also closely monitored the termination of the transitional government and the return to a fully elected civilian administration (see Political background and Current issues, below).

Rwanda achieved GDP growth of 3.7 percent in 2004 and 6 percent in 2005, and the government was credited with continued liberalization of the economy and retrenchment in public spending. In 2005 the IMF and World Bank announced that Rwanda had met the requirements for large-scale debt reduction through the Heavily Indebted Poor Countries (HIPC) initiative which allowed the country to write off $1 billion of its $1.4 billion in foreign debt. For its part, the government launched programs designed to attract foreign investment, particularly in regard to an ambitious plan to make Rwanda a "high-tech hub" for central Africa by extending phone and Internet service into rural areas. GDP grew by 6 percent in 2006, while inflation declined to 6.7 percent. Subsequently, Rwanda's entry into the East African Community (EAC) in July 2007 was expected to further accelerate development by, among other things, opening neighboring markets to Rwandan goods.

In 2008 the UN ranked Rwanda 165th out of 179 countries in its Human Development Index. That year the government consolidated seven development agencies into a single body, the Rwanda Development Board, to better facilitate the disbursement of international assistance. The reform was part of a larger program designed to increase annual per capita income in Rwanda from $371 in 2008 to $900 in 2020. In addition, the country passed a milestone when its domestic government revenues exceeded foreign aid for the first time since the 1994 genocide. GDP growth was 11.2 percent, mainly due to increased agricultural production, which rose 15 percent. Approximately 90 percent of the population was employed in agriculture. Inflation remained high at 13 percent, mainly due to increased fuel and food prices. New foreign assistance allowed the government to increase its budget for 2008 to $1.2 billion. However, foreign aid declined as an overall percentage of the budget from 50 percent to 44 percent, with the government forecasting further reductions. The global economic crisis caused a decline in agricultural exports in 2009 and GDP growth for that year was expected to decline to 6 percent.

GOVERNMENT AND POLITICS

Political background. Like Burundi, Rwanda was long a feudal monarchy ruled by nobles of the Tutsi tribe. A German protectorate from 1899 to 1916, it constituted the northern half of the Belgian mandate of Ruanda-Urundi after World War I and of the Belgian-administered trust territory of the same name after World War II. Resistance to the Tutsi monarchy by the more numerous Hutus intensified in the 1950s and culminated in November 1959 in a bloody revolt that overthrew the monarchy and led to the emigration of thousands of Tutsis. The Party of the Movement for Hutu Emancipation (*Parti du Mouvement de l'Émancipation Hutu*—Parmehutu), founded by Grégoire KAYIBANDA, won an overwhelming electoral victory in 1960, and Rwanda proclaimed itself a republic on January 28, 1961, under the leadership of Dominique MBONYUMUTWA. Since the United Nations did not recognize the action, new elections were held under UN auspices in September 1961, with the Hutu party repeating its victory. Kayibanda was accordingly designated president on October 26, 1961, and trusteeship status was formally terminated on July 1, 1962. Subsequently, Tutsi émigrés invaded the country in an attempt to restore the monarchy; their defeat in December 1963 set off mass reprisals against the remaining Tutsis, resulting in 10,000–15,000 deaths and the flight of 150,000–200,000 Tutsis to neighboring countries.

The Hutu-dominated government consolidated its position in the elections of 1965 and 1969. Moreover, with President Kayibanda legally barred from seeking another term in the approaching 1973 election, the constitution was altered to assure continuance of the existing regime. The change fanned hostility between political elements from the northern region and those from the southern and central regions, the latter having dominated the government since independence. Beginning in February 1973 at the National University in Butare, renewed Hutu moves against the Tutsis spread quickly to other areas. The government did not attempt to quell the actions of the extremists, and continued instability raised the prospect of another tribal bloodbath or even war with Tutsi-ruled Burundi. In this context, a bloodless coup took place on July 5, 1973.

The new government, under Maj. Gen. Juvénal HABYARIMANA, moved quickly to dissolve the legislature, ban political organizations, and suspend portions of the constitution. A civilian-military government, composed largely of young technocrats, was subsequently installed, and it established a more centralized administrative system. A regime-supportive National Revolutionary Movement for Development (*Mouvement Républicain National pour le Développement*—MRND) was organized in mid-1976 and was accorded formal status as the sole legal party under a new constitution adopted by referendum on December 17, 1978. Subsequently, it was announced that the same poll had confirmed Habyarimana for an additional five-year term as president.

In 1980 the administration declared that it had foiled a coup attempt allegedly involving current and former government officials, including Maj. Théonaste LIZINDE, who had recently been removed as security chief after being charged with corruption. Lizinde received a death sentence, which was subsequently commuted to life imprisonment.

Single-party legislative balloting was conducted in 1981, 1983, and on December 26, 1988. Habyarimana, the sole candidate, was accorded additional five-year terms as president by means of referendums in 1983 and on December 19, 1988. In July 1990 Habyarimana called for the drafting by 1992 of a new national charter, which would separate governmental and MRND powers, reduce the size of the bureaucracy, and establish guidelines for the creation of a multiparty system. However, political reform was delayed by an October 1990 invasion from bases in Uganda of the Tutsi-dominated Rwandan Patriotic Front (*Front Patriotique Rwandais*—FPR), obliging the government to call in French, Belgian, and Zairean troops to help repel an FPR advance on Kigali. In March 1991 a cease-fire was negotiated, although fighting continued intermittently thereafter.

On April 6, 1991, a National Synthesis Commission was charged with revising the constitution, and a draft charter was completed on April 30. On June 2 the president announced the legalization of multiparty politics, and the revised constitution was adopted on June 10, one year ahead of schedule. (Earlier, plans for a national referendum were reportedly abandoned for economic reasons.) On October 12 Justice Minister Sylvestre NSANZIMANA was named to the newly created post of prime minister, and on December 30 he announced the installation of a bipartisan administration drawn from what was now termed the National Republican Movement for Democracy and Development (*Mouvement Républicain National pour la Démocratie et le Développement*—MRNDD) and the Christian Democratic Party (*Parti Démocratique Chrétien*—PDC), one of a number of newly registered formations.

In April 1992 the Social Democratic Party (*Parti Social-Démocrate*—PSD), Liberal Party (*Parti Liberal*—PL), and Republican Democratic Party (*Parti Démocratique Républicain*—MDR), which had refused to enter the government unless an opposition leader was named prime minister, agreed to join an expanded five-party administration headed by the MDR's Dismas NSENGIYAREMYE pending legislative balloting within a year. In early June the new administration's plan to expedite a debate on a national conference and then hold general elections was foiled when the FPR ejected government forces from a large area of northern Rwanda and threatened to continue its advance unless granted a role in the administration. During preliminary talks held June 5–7 in Paris, the FPR and the government agreed to revive the March 1991 cease-fire and hold a full-scale peace conference.

The first round of talks held July 10–14, 1992, in Arusha, Tanzania, with Western and regional observers in attendance, yielded a truce and a new cease-fire to take effect July 19 and 31, respectively. Thereafter, despite reports of continued fighting, negotiations continued, and on October 31 a power-sharing protocol was announced. On January 10, 1993, following two months of debate on the composition of a transitional government, a formal peace agreement was signed that would give the FPR, MDR, PDC, PL, and PSD a majority of seats in the cabinet and National Assembly. The MRNDD, which was assigned 6 cabinet seats, and a weakened presidency, denounced the agreement, saying that it categorically refused to participate in the future broad-based transitional government. By early February more than 300 people, predominantly Tutsis, had reportedly been killed in violent anti-accord demonstrations allegedly orchestrated by the MRNDD and the Coalition for the Defense of the Republic (*Coalition pour la Défense de la République*—CDR), an openly anti-Tutsi group, which had been excluded from the government. In response to continuing violence, the FPR announced that it was withdrawing from peace negotiations, and on February 8 it launched an attack on government forces in northern Rwanda near the site of a recent Tutsi massacre. However, the deployment of additional French troops (bringing their number to 600), officially to protect foreign nationals, enabled the regime to survive.

Following further negotiations with the FPR in Arusha in March 1993, Habyarimana was able in July to appoint a new coalition government of the same five internal parties, although this time with a more accommodating faction of the MDR, headed by Agathe UWILINGIYIMANA as prime minister. Renewed Arusha talks subsequently yielded a new 300-page treaty that was signed by President Habyarimana and FPR chair Alexis KANYERENGWE on August 4. Under the new accord, a Hutu prime minister acceptable to both sides would be named and the FPR would be allocated 5 of 21 cabinet posts in a government to be installed by September 10, with multiparty presidential and legislative elections to be held by mid-1995. In addition, a united military force would be formed, 40 percent of which would be Tutsi and 60 percent Hutu. Earlier, on June 22, the UN Security Council had voted to establish a UN Observer Mission Uganda–Rwanda (UNOMUR) to verify that no external military assistance was reaching the FPR. In accordance with the August agreement, the Security Council voted on October 4 to establish a UN Assistance Mission in Rwanda (UNAMIR), which was mandated to monitor the cease-fire and to contribute to security and national rehabilitation in the run-up to the planned elections.

Bickering among the Rwandan parties and delays in UNAMIR deployment made it impossible to meet a September 1993 deadline for the start of the transitional period or a revised target date of December 31. Thus, a new timetable was announced by Habyarimana when, on January 5, 1994, he assumed the presidency for a 22-month transitional period preparatory to multiparty elections in October 1995. However, intense criticism from both the FPR and the internal prodemocracy parties forced the president to postpone the designation of a transitional government and interim legislature. The assassination by unknown assailants on February 21 of PSD leader and government minister Félicien GATABAZI, a Hutu who had promoted rapprochement with the FPR, provoked a new crisis. On February 22 Habyarimana declared an indefinite extension of the transitional phase amid street clashes in which the chair of the Hutu CDR, Martin BUCYANA, was slain by a mob of PSD supporters.

Previous violence in Rwanda paled in significance compared with the wholesale slaughter that followed the death of Habyarimana on April 6, 1994. Both he and President Ntaryamira of Burundi died when their plane was shot down on approach to Kigali airport. (No official determination has been made regarding responsibility for the downing of the plane.) The reaction of Hutu militants in Rwanda, led by the Presidential Guard and CDR militia, was to embark on an orgy of killing, not only of Tutsis but also of Hutus believed to favor accommodation with the FPR. Among those murdered within hours of the president's death were Prime Minister Uwilingiyimana and members of her family, at least one minister, Constitutional Court chair Joseph KAVAUNGANDA, and ten Belgian soldiers of the UNAMIR force.

As prescribed by the constitution, the president of the National Development Council, Theodore SINDIKUBWABO, assumed the presidency on April 9, 1994, appointing an interim government headed by Jean KAMBANDA as prime minister and including the five parties represented in the previous coalition. Although a broader-based transitional administration was promised within six weeks, the FPR rejected the legitimacy of the new government (claiming that the presidency should have passed to the president of the yet-to-be-inaugurated transitional legislature) and declared a new military offensive. On April 12, as FPR forces closed in on Kigali, the new government fled to Gitarama, some 30 miles to the south. Meanwhile, French, Belgian, and U.S. troops had been deployed in Rwanda to evacuate foreign nationals. On April 14, upon completion of the transfer of the foreign nationals, Belgium withdrew its 420-strong contingent from UNAMIR. That action, coupled with the failure of UN mediators to arrange a lasting cease-fire, prompted the UN Security Council, in a controversial decision on April 22, to vote unanimously for a reduction of UNAMIR from 2,500 to 270 personnel.

The FPR offensive and the effective absence of an international military presence served to incite the Hutu militants in Rwanda to even greater savagery against the Tutsi minority and presumed Hutu opponents. Gangs of machete-wielding soldiers and militia members reportedly roamed the countryside, engaging in systematic and indiscriminate slaughter of men, women, and children. Although numbers were impossible to verify, the death toll was estimated to be at least 200,000 by late April and perhaps as high as 800,000—a scale of killing officially described by the UN as genocidal. The carnage caused a mass exodus from the country, both of surviving Tutsis and of Hutus fearing FPR vengeance. By early May some 1.5 million refugees had crossed into neighboring countries, creating one of the most severe humanitarian crises ever to afflict independent Africa.

Following widespread criticism of its April 22 decision, the UN Security Council on May 17, 1994, reversed itself by approving the creation of a UNAMIR II force of 5,500 troops, while embargoing arms supplies to the Rwandan combatants. Mainly at U.S. insistence, however, only 150 unarmed observers were initially dispatched, followed by an 800-strong Ghanaian contingent charged with securing Kigali airport. Deployment of the bulk of the force was contingent on a further report from the UN secretary general on its duration, mandate, and composition, and on the attitude of the warring factions to a heightened UN presence. The immediate reaction of the FPR to the UN decision was one of suspicion that UNAMIR II would forestall its imminent military victory. On May 30, with FPR forces controlling portions of Kigali, UN mediators succeeded in bringing about talks between government and rebel representatives. However, little of substance resulted from these and subsequent meetings, while a cease-fire agreement signed under the auspices of the Organization of African Unity (OAU, subsequently the African Union—AU) in Tunisia on June 14 was equally ineffectual. Accounts continued to emerge from Rwanda of atrocities, some allegedly committed by advancing FPR forces. Especially deplored in the West was the murder on June 9 by FPR soldiers (later described as "renegades" by the FPR leadership) of the (Hutu) archbishop of Kigali, two Hutu bishops, and ten Catholic priests.

The UN Security Council on June 9, 1994, unanimously extended the UNAMIR mandate for a six-month period and approved the speedy deployment of two further battalions, which were to protect civilians in Rwanda and facilitate the international relief effort. However, difficulties and delays in assembling and equipping the UNAMIR force (most of which was to be provided by African states) led France to propose on June 15 that it should dispatch 2,500 troops pending the arrival of the enlarged UNAMIR contingent. The Security Council endorsed the French proposal on June 22 (albeit with five members abstaining), and French troops (supported by a small Senegalese contingent) arrived in Rwanda the next day. The result was the establishment of a large "safe area" southeast of Lake Kivu for surviving Tutsis as well as for Hutus fleeing the advancing FPR forces.

The FPR leadership expressed strong opposition to the French deployment, disputing the French claim to nonpartisanship in the conflict in light of the French record of support for the Hutu-based Habyarimana regime. Moving quickly to consolidate its position, the FPR completed its capture of Kigali on July 4, 1994, and two weeks later declared itself the victor in the civil war. On July 19 the FPR installed a new transitional government, with a moderate Hutu, Pasteur

BIZIMUNGU, as president, and another Hutu, Faustin TWAGIRAMUNGU (the opposition's nominee for the post following the August 1993 agreement) as prime minister. The FPR military commander, Maj. Gen. Paul KAGAME, became vice president and defense minister, while Tutsis took most of the remaining portfolios. In addition to the FPR and MDR, the PDC, PL, and PSD were represented in the new administration, while the MRNDD and CDR were excluded.

Because of widespread reports of mass killings, the Office of the UN High Commissioner for Refugees (UNHCR) in September 1994 suspended its policy of encouraging Rwandan refugees in Zaire to return home, and on November 8 the Security Council established an International Criminal Tribunal for Rwanda (ICTR) to prosecute those responsible for genocide "and other serious violations of international humanitarian law." Subsequently, the 70-member Transitional National Assembly provided for under the 1993 Arusha agreement convened in Kigali on December 12 (see Legislature, below).

On April 22, 1995, the image of the FPR-controlled government was severely tarnished by the Tutsi-dominated army's massacre of some 2,000 Hutus in the Kibeho refugee camp near Gikongoro. The universally condemned action slowed the voluntary return of Rwandans from Zaire, in addition to setting back efforts to secure badly needed international aid. This and other atrocities by the victorious Tutsis were reportedly the reason for the resignation of Prime Minister Twagiramungu on August 28, with Pierre-Célestin RWIGEMA, the relatively obscure primary and secondary education minister, being named three days later as Twagiramungu's successor and the head of a government which included a number of new Tutsi members in posts formerly assigned to Hutus. By all accounts, however, Major General Kagame remained the most powerful figure in the administration, and on March 24, 2000, he moved into the presidency following the resignation of President Bizimungu. Earlier, on March 8, Bernard MAKUSA, a relatively unknown former ambassador to Burundi and Germany, was appointed to succeed Rwigema as prime minister.

Prime Minister Rwigema's resignation in late February 2000 was attributed to his deteriorating relationship with the Transitional National Assembly (which was investigating alleged financial improprieties on the part of government officials) as well as conflict with other MDR leaders. Likewise, an intraparty power struggle in the FPR apparently contributed to the resignation of President Bizimungu in March. The installation of Major General Kagame as president merely formalized his already de facto authority. Kagame called upon all Rwandan refugees to return home and pledged to pursue national reconciliation, although his status as the nation's first Tutsi president since independence created additional unease for those already concerned over the lack of Hutu representation in government. That worry was not alleviated by the March 2001 district elections, in which party activity was again barred and most of the successful candidates appeared to be aligned with the FPR.

In April 2003 the Transitional National Assembly approved a new draft constitution that was put before voters in a national referendum on May 26, 2003. The new basic law was approved by a 93.4 percent vote and became effective June 4. Among other provisions, the constitution created a bicameral legislature and provided for direct election of the president. In an effort to prevent further ethnic conflict, the constitution also prohibited any parties based solely on race, gender, or religion. However, some opposition parties and international human rights groups charged that this provision was enacted to reinforce the political domination of the FPR.

Prior to the presidential elections, the constitutional court ruled that the MDR and the PDC were illegal parties because of their role in the events of 1994. Consequently, the MDR candidate—former prime minister Twagiramungu—and the PDC candidate—Jean-Népomuscéne NAYINZIRA—were forced to run as independents. In the balloting on August 25, 2003, Kagame was elected with 95.1 percent of the vote, followed by Twagiramungu with 3.6 percent and Nayinzira with 1.3 percent.

Legislative balloting took place September 29–30 and October 2, 2003. Of the 53 directly contested seats, a coalition led by the FPR secured 40 seats; the PSD, 7; and the PL, 6. Makusa was reappointed prime minister and formed a new unity government on October 19. The government included representatives of all seven parties that secured representation in the Chamber of Deputies. Kagame carried out several cabinet reorganizations, including a major reshuffle on March 7, 2008, in which five new ministers were appointed, and 11 had their portfolios changed.

In balloting for the Chamber of Deputies in October 2008, women secured 45 posts, or more than 56 percent of the seats, making Rwanda the first country to have a majority female legislative chamber. Rwanda was also the first country to meet the AU's Protocol to the African Charter on the Rights of Women in Africa, which called for countries to have 50 percent of their legislature made up of women deputies. The FPR-led coalition led won the legislative balloting and Kagame subsequently reappointed Makusa as prime minister of a coalition government that included only minor alterations from the previous cabinet (see Current issues, below).

Constitution and government. Under the 1978 constitution, executive power was vested in a president elected by universal suffrage for a five-year term, the president of the MRND being the only candidate. He presided over a Council of Ministers, which he appointed, with the secretary general of the MRND being empowered to serve as interim president should the incumbent be incapacitated. A unicameral National Development Council, also elected for a five-year term, was to share legislative authority with the president and, by four-fifths vote, could censure (but not dismiss) him.

On June 10, 1991, President Habyarimana signed into law a new charter distinguished by the introduction of a multiparty system and the separation of executive, legislative, and judiciary powers. Under the 1991 constitution, executive powers were shared by the president and a presidentially appointed prime minister, who named his own cabinet. In addition, the legislature's presiding officer was empowered to serve as interim president if the incumbent left the country or became incapacitated. The constitution also stated that while political party formations could organize along ethnic and tribal lines, they had to be open to all.

On May 5, 1995, the Transitional National Assembly that had convened five months earlier adopted a new constitution incorporating the essentials of the 1991 document as well as elements of the 1993 power-sharing peace agreement. On June 8, 1999, the FPR secretary general announced that the transition period, initially scheduled to expire in 1999, would be extended to 2003.

The new constitution adopted on June 4, 2003, created a bicameral legislature and provided for a directly elected president, limited to two seven-year terms. Amendments to the constitution in October 2005 reduced the number of provinces from 12 to 5, the number of districts from 106 to 30, and the number of "sectors" (local administrative units) from 1,545 to 416. The consolidation was seen as a way to save money and streamline government. In February 2006 the language in the constitution regarding property rights was strengthened to assist returning refugees in recovering their property. In July 2008 the constitution was amended to ensure that the country's budgetary process was in accordance with requirements of the EAC. Amendments also clarified the duties of some cabinet ministers, changed the title of the country's senior military officer to chief of the defense staff, and granted perpetual immunity to former presidents of the republic.

The judiciary, headed by a Supreme Court, includes magistrates', prefectural, and appeals courts; a Court of Accounts; a Court of Cassation; and a Constitutional Court composed of the Court of Cassation and a Council of State. The president and vice president of the Supreme Court are elected by the Senate. In 2008 the tenure of judges was reduced from lifetime appointments to four-year periods, followed by a legislative review and potential reappointment. (See Current issues, below, for information on the creation of local village courts outside the regular system.)

Foreign relations. Under President Kayibanda, Rwandan foreign policy exhibited a generally pro-Western bias but did not exclude relations with a number of communist countries, including the Soviet Union and the People's Republic of China. Following the 1973 coup, however, the country took a pronounced "anti-imperialist" turn; Rwanda became the first African nation to break relations with Israel as a result of the October 1973 Arab-Israeli war, and it also contributed to the support of liberation movements in southern Africa. At the same time, President Habyarimana initiated a policy of "opening" (*l'ouverture*) with adjacent countries. Despite a tradition of ethnic conflict between Burundi's ruling Tutsis and Rwanda's ruling Hutus, a number of commercial, cultural, and economic agreements were concluded during a visit by Burundian president Michel Micombero in June 1976, while similar agreements were subsequently negotiated with Tanzania and Côte d'Ivoire. Burundi, Rwanda, and Zaire established the Economic Community of the Great Lakes Countries in 1976; two years later, Burundi, Rwanda, and Tanzania formed the Organization for the Management and Development of the Kagera River Basin.

Relations with Uganda were strained for several decades following independence by large numbers of refugees crossing the border in both directions to escape tribal-based hostilities. Following the overthrow of Ugandan president Apollo Milton Obote in 1985, some 30,000 Ugandan refugees returned from Rwanda. However, more than 200,000 Rwandan Tutsis remained in Uganda. Rwanda in 1986 urged that all the refugees be given Ugandan citizenship, but Uganda granted citizenship status only to those with ten years of official residency. Despite continued concern over the refugee issue, agreements on trade, security, and communications strengthened relations between the countries in 1986 and 1987. On the other hand, a Ugandan plan to restrict property rights of foreigners was one of the reported impulses for the invasion of northern Rwanda by Ugandan-based rebels of the FPR in October 1990. Ugandan president Lt.- Gen. Yoweri Museveni denied any prior knowledge of the attack and criticized the rebels, many of whom were recent deserters of the Ugandan military; nonetheless, relations between Uganda and Rwanda deteriorated as the FPR made military inroads in the early 1990s.

In 1995 and 1996 Rwanda's foreign relations continued to be defined by the encampment of an estimated 2 million Rwandans outside its borders. In August 1995 the UN lifted its embargo on the sale of weapons to Rwanda after months of lobbying by Rwanda, which claimed that members of the former Hutu government now exiled in Zaire were engaging in cross-border guerrilla attacks. In response to the end of the embargo, Kinshasa launched a violent and unsuccessful repatriation program, claiming that Kigali was preparing to attack the refugee camps. A subsequent repatriation attempt in February 1996 strained relations even further, and throughout the first half of 1996 the two capitals accused each other of employing "destabilization" tactics. Meanwhile, in mid-April the FPR cheered the withdrawal of the last UN peacekeepers from Rwanda. (The Tutsi regime held the UN forces responsible for both allegedly collaborating in the 1994 genocide and undermining the regime's attempts to govern.) During the second half of 1996 a stunning sequence of events in Burundi, Zaire, and Tanzania, respectively, resulted in the repatriation of approximately 650,000 refugees to Rwanda. In Burundi the military coup by Tutsi officers in late July reportedly sparked fear of reprisal attacks among the refugees, and, following the departure of 130,000 people, Bujumbura on August 27 announced the closing of the last of Burundi's camps. Thereafter, in mid-November, several hundred thousand refugees were reported to have fled back across the border from their encampments in eastern Zaire after an allegedly Kigali-funded rebellion on behalf of Zairean Tutsis, the Banyamulenge, resulted in the rout of Zairean troops and Rwandan Hutu militiamen who had been seeking to establish a "Hutuland" in the region. In December Tanzanian government forces, with the tacit and unprecedented approval of the UNHCR, forcibly repatriated over 200,000 refugees to Rwanda.

In 1997 Rwanda, along with five other nations, supported the forces of Laurent Kabila in Zaire, hoping a rebel victory there would enable Rwanda to close the rear bases of the Hutu guerrillas as well as the camps where they sought refuge. After the Kabila victory, the refugee camps along the border were closed, but guerrillas drifted across into Rwanda with returning refugees and regrouped in Rwanda. Meanwhile, Rwandan government forces who had crossed the border into the former Zaire (now known as the Democratic Republic of the Congo or DRC) remained in two provinces, North and South Kivu, in a de facto occupation apparently with Kabila's tacit approval. Relations between Kinshasa and Kigali subsequently deteriorated, as Kabila distanced himself from Tutsi influence, prompting hostility among the Banyamulenge Tutsis in the eastern portion of the DRC, as Zaire had been renamed. In July 1998 Kabila announced an end to military cooperation with Rwanda, and in August a full-fledged rebellion broke out against his administration (see article on the DRC). By November Rwanda acknowledged that its troops were allied with the anti-Kabila rebels, claiming that the DRC government was rearming the Hutus responsible for the 1994 genocide.

In an unexpected turn of events, forces from Rwanda and Uganda, previously allied in support of anti-Kabila rebels in the DRC, clashed in northeast DRC in August 1999, with underlying factors apparently including support for different anti-Kabila factions in the DRC and perhaps most importantly, rivalry regarding eventual preeminence in the region. Fighting between the Rwandan and Ugandan troops erupted again in the spring of 2000.

In November 2001, Kagame began a series of meetings with the leader of Uganda, president Museveni. Following mediation efforts by South Africa and the United Kingdom, in 2003, the two governments agreed to take stronger action to prevent rebels and dissident groups from crossing each other's borders and initiating conflicts. In addition, the two heads of state agreed on the voluntary repatriation of 26,000 Rwandans remaining in refugee camps in Uganda. In July 2002 a separate peace accord was signed in Pretoria, South Africa, between Rwanda and the DRC. By October, all 23,400 Rwandan troops had withdrawn from the DRC, and in September 2003 the two countries reestablished diplomatic relations.

In March 2005, the government offered to contribute troops to the proposed UN peacekeeping mission in Darfur, Sudan. Rwanda eventually lent 2,000 soldiers to that effort.

In May 2006 President Kagame met with U.S. president George W. Bush in Washington. The United States announced at the meeting that it was increasing its bilateral aid to Rwanda.

Burundi and Rwanda established a joint committee to resolve border issues in August 2006. Subsequently, Rwanda and Uganda agreed to increase security cooperation to suppress Hutu militias operating in the border regions of the two countries.

In November 2006, a French judge issued an international arrest warrant for nine senior Rwandan officials on charges that they had been involved in the downing of President Habyarimana's plane in 1994. All nine were close allies of Kagame. The Rwandan government adamantly rejected the charges and broke off diplomatic relations with France. Rwanda also closed its embassy in Paris and opened a new one in Sweden. Meanwhile, there were large demonstrations against France in Rwanda, including one in Kigali involving more than 25,000 people. During local trials in Rwanda, new allegations emerged that French military officers had ignored calls to help victims of the genocide. A memorandum of understanding between Rwanda and the UK led to the arrest of four genocide suspects in London in December 2006. Rwanda subsequently applied for membership in the Commonwealth as a manifestation of the country's growing ties with the UK.

China offered to provide Rwanda with $5 million in military equipment in 2007. In addition, the two countries announced that 30 Rwandan military officers would be offered advanced training in China.

In April 2007 the UN lifted the arms embargo that had been in place against Rwanda since 1994, and in July Rwanda became a member of the EAC. As part of the accession agreement, other EAC members reduced tariffs on Rwandan agricultural exports. French president Nicholas Sarkozy visited Rwanda in October in an effort to improve relations between the two countries. In November, an agreement was reached between Rwanda and the DRC to disarm the Hutu resistance group, the Democratic Forces for the Liberation of Rwanda (*Forces Démocratiques pour la Libération du Rwanda*—FDLR), and to suppress other armed groups in both countries. The agreement was followed by a DRC offensive against the FDLR. Kagame attended the meeting of heads of state of the Commonwealth in November, and the country began negotiations to join the organization. Final approval of Rwanda's membership was scheduled for November 2009.

Former British prime minister Tony Blair visited Rwanda in February 2008 to advise the government on reforms. One of his suggestions—the creation of a ministry of cabinet affairs—was implemented shortly thereafter. During the crisis in Zimbabwe (see article on Zimbabwe), Kagame emerged as one of the foremost critics of President Robert Mugabe and a proponent for new elections in that country. In March Rwanda and the UN finalized an agreement whereby those convicted by the ITCR would be allowed to serve their sentences in Rwanda. In August a commission created by the Rwandan government charged various French officials, including former president Francois Mitterrand, with complicity in the 1994 genocide. The French government rejected the accusations.

Joint Rwanda-DRC military operations against the FDLR in 2008 and 2009, resulted in a number of the rebel group's top leaders being killed or captured and allowed for the return of more than 2,000 Hutu refugees. In January 2009 it was reported that Rwanda arrested the leader of the DRC Tutsi rebel group, the National Congress for the Defense of the People (*Congrès National pour la Dèfense du Peuple*--CNDP) that had been supported by Rwanda. The CNDP had split into rival factions with one group, led by Bosco NTAGANDA, signing a ceasefire with the DRC in January. Rwanda reportedly backed the Ntaganda faction. In April Rwanda and Uganda signed an agreement to return more than 20,000 Rwandan refugees. The UNHCR pledged aid and material support to facilitate the resettlement.

Current issues. By the end of 1997 an estimated 1.5 million refugees had returned, but the FPR regime still fell short of fulfilling what it had delineated as one of the top prerequisites for national reconciliation—resolution of the judicial process for the tens of thousands of predominantly Hutu prisoners imprisoned (in reportedly subhuman conditions) for their alleged roles in the 1994 genocide. In fact, the FPR continued to be plagued by charges, largely unsubstantiated, that the Tutsi-controlled military was engaging in its own campaign of revenge killings. Meanwhile, the ICTR—26 justices assigned to more than 100,000 cases—proceeded at a glacial pace, hampered, according to a January 1998 UN internal investigation, by a mismanaged judicial system. By the end of 1997, three years after the massacres, the ICTR had not convicted a single defendant. Kigali's judicial efforts, which disposed of fewer than 300 cases in 1997, also foundered when a plea-bargaining program failed to break the logjam, causing observers to note that, barring new developments, most prisoners would die in prison long before their cases could come to trial.

Meanwhile, the toll from ethnic conflict increased in the second half of 1997 (with at least 6,000 more murders during the year, according to UN monitors) as Hutu guerrillas grew in strength and began making daylight raids, particularly in the northwest, where they had wide popular support. Although the guerrillas appeared to have no hope of a military victory, their attacks seemed aimed at making Rwanda ungovernable.

During ICTR testimony in February 1998 the former UNAMIR commander in Rwanda said he had advised the UN leadership of the impending genocide and asked for authorization (never granted) to prevent it. Similarly, a report by the Belgian parliament released in February 1998 claimed the Belgian, French, and U.S. governments also had credible advance warning of the genocide. U.S. president Bill Clinton visited Rwanda in March as part of an African tour, and he acknowledged that the United States and other Western nations had been slow to react to the developments of 1994. (In July 2000 an OAU panel strongly criticized the United States, France, Belgium, the UN, and others—including church groups—for failing to prevent or stop the genocide and called for a "significant level of reparations.")

In April 1998 Rwanda publicly executed 22 persons convicted of murders committed during 1994, and by June thousands of other prisoners had pleaded guilty, apparently to avoid death sentences. In early September the ICTR (recently expanded by the UN in response to widespread criticism) issued its first guilty verdict. Shortly thereafter, the tribunal sentenced former interim prime minister Jean Kambanda to life in prison following his conviction on genocide charges. (Kambanda had admitted his guilt earlier and had reportedly provided evidence against other officials.)

Despite the ongoing judicial quagmire, a degree of normalcy had returned to Rwanda by early 1999, as evidenced by the successful completion of nonparty local elections in March, the first balloting since 1988. At the same time, however, instability persisted near the DRC border, hundreds of thousands of civilians having moved into camps protected by government troops. International attention also remained focused on the Rwandan government's significant role in the DRC civil war (see article on the DRC). Under those circumstances, it was not surprising that the transitional government in July extended its mandate for four more years, with FPR leaders concluding that security conditions did not permit the organization of multiparty elections.

The return to normality continued with the government in December 2001 adopting a new flag, national anthem, and national seal. However, Hutu groups continued to assert periodic discrimination and retaliation by the FPR-dominated government. Domestically, hopes for Tutsi-Hutu reconciliation rested, in part, on the reestablishment in early 2002 of the traditional *gacaca* system, in which elected village judges were to adjudicate the cases of some 90,000 detainees still facing charges relating to the events of 1994. (Most of the other cases, involving those accused of ordering mass killings or participating in rapes, were to be handled by the normal court system. Meanwhile, the "masterminds" of the genocide still faced trial at the ICTR, which as of April 2002 had arrested 60 of the 75 people who had been indicted so far. Only eight convictions had been achieved by that time, although a number of high-profile cases were on the docket for the remainder of the year.)

In January 2003, the government ordered the release of 40,000 detainees, but reserved the right to arrest the released people if new evidence emerged. By the end of the year, some 25,000 had been released. Survivor groups severely criticized the measure, claiming that many involved in the genocide were being released. Meanwhile, the *gacaca* courts began to adjudicate an increasing number of cases. In August 2003, one *gacaca* court convicted 105 people in a mass two-day trial.

The passage of the new constitution and subsequent presidential and legislative elections in 2003 finalized the transition to civilian government. Defeated presidential candidate Faustin Twagiramungu protested the official results, claiming that widespread irregularities had occurred. However, the Supreme Court ruled against him, and international observers characterized the balloting as generally free and fair, despite certain significant problems.

By March 2005 the ICTR had convicted 22 defendants and acquitted 3. In addition to complaints about the continued slow pace of case resolution, criticism emanated from Rwandan Hutus over the fact that no Tutsis had been indicted by the ICTR, despite Hutu assertions that revenge killings and other atrocities had been committed by Tutsis from the FPR in 1994. Meanwhile, the *gacaca* courts faced a backlog of some 95,000 cases by the end of the year. Tension also arose from the release of documents from the Kambanda trial that appeared to support Tutsi arguments that the Hutu attacks in 1994 had been well coordinated and discussed in advance at high levels of government. On December 19 the UN Security Council passed Resolution 1855 which called upon the ICTR to have all cases completed by 2010.

Elections were held in August 2006 for local mediation councils, considered a possible alternative to the courts and a means of combining traditional conflict resolution methods with the country's legal system.

In an effort to promote national reconciliation, more than 9,000 prisoners who had been accused of participation in the 1994 genocide were released in February 2007. Although none of those released had faced charges of so-called "major crimes," genocide victims groups still criticized the action. In April former president Bizimungu was also pardoned. Meanwhile, former Maj. Gen. Laurent MUNYAKAZI became the most senior military figure to be convicted when he was found guilty of 13 counts of genocide by a Rwandan court. He was sentenced to life in prison.

A controversial family planning law was introduced in February 2007. The measure, which met with widespread opposition in the Catholic community, limited couples to three children in an effort to slow population growth. Meanwhile, the death penalty was abolished in June and replaced by life imprisonment as the country's most serious punishment.

On February 6, 2008, a Spanish judge issued international arrest warrants for 40 senior FPR military and government officials, including Kagame, for genocide in the deaths of nine Spanish citizens who were killed in Rwanda between 1994 and 2000. The Rwandan government denounced the charges, and the Chamber of Deputies passed a unanimous resolution condemning the warrants. In May Rwanda canceled a diplomatic visit by its foreign minister to Belgium when the latter refused to issue a visa to one of the members of the minister's staff who was among the 40 indicted. In May the parliament elected nine representatives, including five women, to represent Rwanda in the East African Legislative Assembly, the legislative body of the EAC. In August the Chamber of Deputies was dissolved ahead of legislative elections in September. For the balloting, the Rwandan government invited observers from the European Union and the African Union. In the balloting, the FPR again formed an electoral coalition. The grouping won 42 seats in the direct elections, while the Social Democratic Party secured 7, and the Liberal Party, 4. The main opposition groups boycotted the elections, but international observers declared the elections free and fair and noted that the National Election Commission had implemented all of the reforms recommended after the 2003 polling. In October there was a minor cabinet reorganization. The government initiated a program to change the language of instruction from French to English. Officially this was part of a broader effort to integrate into the EAC, but it also indicated the continuing tense relations between Rwanda and France.

In January 2009, Agnes NTAMABYALIRO, became the first former government minister of the 1994 Hutu cabinet to be tried and sentenced in Rwanda for her part in the 1994 genocide. In June a *gacaca* court sentenced senator Stanley SAFARI, the leader of the Prosperity and Solidarity Party (PSP), to life in prison for his role in the genocide and the PSP leader subsequently fled to Uganda to avoid detention). The Senate subsequently expelled Safari from the chamber.

POLITICAL PARTIES

A one-party state after the 1973 coup, Rwanda adopted a multiparty constitution on June 10, 1991. By mid-1993 it was reported that

17 parties, including the preexisting National Republican Movement for Democracy and Development (MRNDD), had been recognized. However, the MRNDD was not included in the government installed in July 1994 after the military victory of the FPR over the forces of the previous regime. Party candidates were not permitted in the March 1999 village elections or the March 2001 communal balloting, the government concluding that party activity might exacerbate ethnic tensions.

Under the terms of the 2003 constitution, the government has the power to ban political parties that might advocate civic unrest or exacerbate ethnic differences. Using this provision, the government banned the MDR, PDC, and several smaller parties prior to the 2003 elections (see below). Prior to the 2008 legislative elections, it was announced that the same parties that formed an FPR-led grouping in the 2003 balloting would campaign as an electoral coalition. The parties included the FPR, the PDC, the **Islamic Democratic Party** (*Parti Démocratique Islamique*—PDI), the **Rwandan Socialist Party** (*Parti Socialiste Rwandais*—PSR), and the **Rwandan People's Democratic Union** (*Union Démocratique du Peuple Rwandais*—UDPR). The **Party for Progress and Concord** (*Parti pour le Progrès et la Concorde*--PPC) and the **Prosperity and Solidarity Party** (*Parti de la Solidarité et du Progrès*--PSP) also joined the FPR-led coalition. Forty-four percent of the coalition's candidates were women.

Government and Pro-government Parties:

Rwandan Patriotic Front (*Front Patriotique Rwandais*—FPR). Currently the dominant political force in Rwanda, the FPR is a largely Tutsi formation that invaded Rwanda in October 1990 from Uganda under the command of Rwandan refugees who were formerly officers in the Ugandan armed forces. However, most of the original leadership, including FPR founder Fred RWIGYEMA, were killed in fighting with government troops in late 1990 and early 1991.

Buoyed by a series of stunning victories in early June 1992, which yielded control of much of northern Rwanda, the FPR called on the Rwandan government to integrate FPR members into both the military and the government, reduce the president's power, allow all refugees to return, and hold multiparty elections. The FPR signed the Arusha peace agreement on August 4, 1993, but implementation was subject to repeated delays. The massacres of Tutsis and moderate Hutus, which followed the death of President Habyarimana in April 1994, impelled the FPR to launch a new offensive, which brought it to power three months later. The victory was attributed largely to the military leadership of Maj. Gen. Paul Kagame, who, although designated as vice president in the new regime, was widely regarded as its preeminent figure. Kagame consolidated his power when he was elected FPR president in February 1998 and president of the republic in March 2000. Kagame was subsequently reelected president for a seven-year term in 2003. During legislative elections, the FPR led an electoral coalition that received 73.78 percent of the vote and 40 seats. (The FPR gained 33 seats alone.) The FPR conducted elections in July 2007 for local and regional party organizations. Allies of Kagame were reported to have won the majority of posts.

In 2008 the party vehemently rejected the 40 arrest warrants issued by a Spanish judge for FPR members who were currently military or government officials (see Current issues, above). In elections for the Chamber of Deputies, the FPR again led a coalition of pro-government parties. The coalition won 78.8 percent of the vote and 42 of the directly elected seats.

The FPR had to replace one of its deputies in the assembly, Beatrice NIRIERE, after she was convicted of genocide in June 2009.

Leaders: Maj. Gen. Paul KAGAME (President of the Republic and Chair of the Party), Christophe BAZIVAMO (Vice Chair), Col. Alexis KANYARENGWE (Former President of the Front), Francois NGARAMBE (Secretary General).

Christian Democratic Party/Centrist Democratic Party (*Parti Démocratique Chrétien*—PDC). The PDC accepted one cabinet post in the governments of December 1991 and April 1992. A PDC member also served in the Makusa government until March 2001. Prior to the 2003 presidential elections, the PDC was banned since the Constitution forbade religious parties. It reconstituted itself as the **Centrist Democratic Party** (*Parti Démocrate Centriste*—PDC) before legislative elections, and the reconstituted PDC joined the FPR-led coalition. It won 3 seats. Former PDC president Jean-Népomuscéne Nayinzira placed third in the national presidential polling in 2003. Party leader Alfred Mukezamfura was elected speaker of the Chamber of Deputies in 2003, but he fell ill in September 2007 and was temporarily replaced, before resuming his duties. Mukezamfura announced in August 2008 that he would not seek reelection to the Chamber of Deputies, but that the PDC would join the FPR-led electoral coalition. In June 2009 Agnes MUKABARABGA was elected chair of the PDC at a party congress.

Leaders: Agnes MUKABARABGA (Chair), Alfred MUKEZAMFURA (Former Speaker of the Chamber of Deputies).

Party for Progress and Concord (*Parti pour le Progrès et la Concorde*—PPC). The PPC was formed in 2003 after the MDR was outlawed. It is comprised mainly of Hutus. In the 2003 legislative elections, the PPC received 2.2 percent of the vote, below the 5 percent threshold needed for representation. Party leader Alivera MUKABARAMBA was the PPC's 2003 presidential candidate. She was appointed to the Senate in 2003. In February 2008 an internal split emerged in the PPC. Christian MARARA claimed to be president of the PPC after the group's leadership dismissed him and affirmed Mukabarama as party president. The PPC joined the FPR-led coalition for the 2008 assembly balloting

Leaders: Alivera MUKABARAMBA (Party President and 2003 Presidential Candidate), Etienne NIYONZIMA (Vice President).

Ideal Democratic Party (*Parti Démocratique Idéal*—PDI). Originally formed in 1992 as the **Islamic Democratic Party** (*Parti Démocratique Islamique*—PDI), the PDI changed its title in 2003 in response to a constitutional ban on religious parties and as part of a broader effort to attract voters. The PDI joined the FPR-led coalition in the 2003 and 2008 legislative elections. PDI party leader Mussa Sheikh HARERIMANA was appointed interior minister after the 2003 balloting.

Leader: Mussa Sheikh HARERIMANA (Chair).

Other members of the 2008 FPR-led electoral coalition included the **Rwandan People's Democratic Union** (*Union Démocratique du Peuple Rwandais*—UDPR), formed in 1992 and led by Adrien RANGIRA; the **Rwandan Socialist Party** (*Parti Socialiste Rwandais*—PSR), a workers' rights party launched in 1991 and led by Medard RUTIJANWA, and the **Prosperity and Solidarity Party** (*Parti de la Solidarité et du Progrès*--PSP), led by Stanley SAFARI (see Current issues, above).

Social Democratic Party (*Parti Social-Démocrate*—PSD). One of the first three opposition parties to be recognized under the 1991 constitution, the PSD was one of several prodemocracy parties that accepted cabinet posts from April 1992, and in August 1993 it was a signatory of the Arusha peace agreement. The assassination of its leader, Félicien GATABAZI, in February 1994 sparked the violence in Rwanda, which escalated to genocidal proportions from April onward. Following the death of President Habyarimana two months later, PSD president Frederic NZAMURAMBAHO and vice president Felicien NGANGO also died. The PSD's Juvénal Nksui, then Speaker of the assembly, was sacked by the legislature in March 1997 and accused of incompetence after failing to sign into law a bill passed by the assembly that would make the president accountable to it. The PSD won 6 seats in the 2003 legislative elections. Party leader Vincent Biruta was elected to the Senate and was subsequently elected Speaker of that body. The PSD participated in the subsequent Kagame unity government. Prior to the September 2008 legislative elections, the PSD announced an electoral list that included 64 candidates. It declined an invitation to join the FPR-led coalition. In the balloting, the PSD won 13.1 percent of the vote and 7 seats in the assembly.

Leaders: Vincent BIRUTA (Chair and Speaker of the Senate), Juvénal NKSUI (Former Speaker of the Assembly), Jacqueline MUHONGAYRIE.

Liberal Party (*Parti Liberal*—PL). Joining the MDR and PSD in refusing to enter the Nsanzimana government of December 1991, the PL accepted three cabinet posts under the MDR's Dismas Nsengiyaremye in April 1992 and also participated in subsequent coalitions, becoming as a consequence split into pro-government and antigovernment factions. The latter joined the government installed by the FPR following its military victory in July 1994. The PL's Joseph SEBARENZI became Speaker of the assembly when that body sacked Juvénal Nksui (see PSD, above); however, Sebarenzi resigned his speaker's position in January 2000 amid a power struggle within the party and in the face of parliamentary criticism. He was subsequently reported to have assumed self-imposed exile in the United States. Prosper Higiro became party chair in 2001. In the 2003 elections, the

PL secured 7 seats. The PL was given a cabinet post in the subsequent Kagame unity government.

Following elections for regional party officials in August 2007, the PL was divided by a power struggle. The party leadership expelled two of its parliamentarians and five other party officials after they accused senior PL officials of corruption in the party's September 2007 leadership election, which was won by Protais MITALI. The members appealed their expulsion, but on November 9 the high court rejected their appeal, and the party replaced the parliamentarians. The PL ran 62 candidates in the 2008 legislative elections. Most of the candidates were reported to be members of the Mitali-led faction of the party. The PL secured 7.5 percent of the vote and 4 seats in the assembly. Mitali was reappointed minister of youth in the subsequent FPR-led government.

Leaders: Protais MITALI (President of the Party and Minister of Youth), Prosper HIGIRO (Chair), Leopold NDORUHIRWE (General Secretary), Hirigo PROSPER (Vice President of the Senate), Esdra KAYIRANGA, Joseph MUSENGIMANA, Odette NYIRAMIRIMO.

Other Parties and Groups:

Republican Democratic Movement (*Mouvement Démocratique Républicain*—MDR). A predominantly Hutu party, which draws its support from the central Rwandan capital region, the MDR is a direct descendant of Grégoire Kayibanda's Parmehutu—MDR, which was banned in 1973. The current party was legally registered on July 31, 1991, and in November it led, along with the recently recognized PL and PSR (above), a march in Kigali in support of a national conference. From April 1992 the MDR headed successive coalition governments that included other prodemocracy parties, although the appointment of the MRD's Agathe Uwilingiyimana as prime minister in July 1993 was strongly opposed by an antiregime MDR faction. Meanwhile one of the MDR's leaders, Emmanuel GAPYISI, who had also served as president of the Forum for Peace and Democracy (a group opposed to both President Habyarimana and the FPR), had been assassinated on May 19, 1993.

The MDR was a signatory of the August 1993 Arusha peace agreement with the rebel FPR, and Faustin Twagiramungu (of the MDR antiregime wing) became the agreed nominee of the prodemocracy parties for the premiership in the envisaged transitional government. Many MDR members, including Uwilingiyimana, were killed by Hutu extremists in the bloodletting that followed President Habyarimana's death in April 1994. Early in May the antigovernment MDR faction formed an alliance called the Democratic Forces for Change (*Forces Démocratiques pour le Changement*—FDC) with the opposition faction of the PL, the PDC, and the PSD (above). The eventual military victory of the FPR resulted in Twagiramungu being appointed prime minister of a transitional government in July; he resigned in late August 1995.

The appointment of Pierre-Célestin Rwigema as Twagiramungu's prime ministerial successor exacerbated the intraparty rift between Twagiramungu's antiregime followers and the so-called "liberal" wing of the party, led by Rwigema and Anastase GASANA, the foreign affairs minister whom Twagiramungu's allies had labeled an FPR "straw man." For his part, Gasana was a vocal critic of the former prime minister, describing his government as guilty of "inaction and inefficiency." In December 1995 Twagiramungu rejected as null and void a motion forwarded by Gasana, Jean-Pierre BIZIMANA, and Laurien NGIRABANZI to force him from his party post. Subsequently, in March 1996 Twagiramungu split from the MDR to create a new anti-FPR grouping (see FRD, below).

In August 1998 the MDR's executive committee was dissolved, and party president Bonaventure UBALIJORO, who had been arrested in July, was dismissed and succeeded by Prime Minister Rwigema. In March 1999 four members of the party were expelled from the legislature, three for alleged involvement with the *Interahamwe,* the extremist Hutu militias. The fourth, Jacques MANIRAGUHA, had repeated allegations made by a local official on trial for genocide that Prime Minister Rwigema had armed the *Interahamwe* just before the genocide of 1994. In April the prime minister, on behalf of the party, asked the Rwandan people to forgive the MDR for its role in 1994. Rwigema was subsequently reported to have feuded with other MDR leaders, and the party's political bureau approved changes in MDR governing bodies (although keeping Rwigema as party president) prior to Rwigema's resignation from his prime minister's post in February 2000. Rwigema subsequently moved to the United States, Rwanda issuing an international warrant for his arrest in connection with the events of 1994. Meanwhile, the MDR, which had expelled Rwigema in August 2000, reaffirmed its support in 2001 for the "collegial" power-sharing agreement with the FPR.

Prior to the 2003 legislative elections, the National Assembly voted to dissolve the MDR under the terms of the 2003 constitution. Former MDR member Twagiramungu ran for the presidency in 2003 and placed third. Many members of the MDR joined the new Hutu-based party, the Party for Progress and Concord (*Parti pour le Progrès et la Concorde*—PPC).

Party for Democracy and Renewal (*Parti pour la Démocratie et le Renouveau*—PDR). Formed in mid-2001 by former president Pasteur Bizimungu after he had resigned his government post following an apparent disagreement with Maj. Gen. Kagame of the FPR, the PDR (also known as *Ubuyanja*, Renewal) was subsequently banned by the government on the grounds that the new grouping promoted ethnic hostility. Bizimungu, a Hutu who had served as an "icon of reconciliation" during his presidency, was arrested in mid-2002. He was convicted in 2004 on charges of embezzlement and incitement to civil disobedience and sentenced to 15 years in prison, but he was pardoned in April 2007. In April it was also reported that the PDR had been disbanded. Meanwhile, an exile group in the United States began using the name PDR-Ihumure. The opposition group was formed by Paul RUSESABAGINA, who was the subject of the film *Hotel Rwanda*, which chronicled his efforts to save Tutsis and moderate Hutus during the 1994 genocide. The PDR was reportedly still active in 2008, seeking to develop a coalition of exile groups.

Leaders: Pasteur BIZIMUNGU (Former President of the Republic), Charles NTAKIRUTINKA.

Rally for Return and Democracy (*Rassemblement pour la Démocratie et le Retour*—RDR). Based in the refugee camps of the eastern DRC, the RDR is the most prominent of the exile political groupings. The RDR has been critical of the UNHCR's compliance with FPR demands, claiming that a forced repatriation of the Hutu refugees "would mean handing over the refugees to their torturers." In January 1997 the RDR denounced the genocide trials of Hutus as a "mockery of justice," claiming, for example, that alleged murderers were falsely accused by those who wanted their property. In June the RDR reportedly decided to become a political party, while in April 2000 the grouping reacted in a conciliatory manner to President Kagame's inaugural speech in which he urged exiles to return home. The RDR was banned in 2006. However, it remained active in refugee camps in the DRC, and in January 2008 the RDR denounced the FPR for suppressing dissent.

Leaders: Charles NDEREYENE, François NZABAHIMANA.

Resistance Forces for Democracy (*Forces de Résistance pour la Démocratie*—FRD). The FRD, listed in a previous edition of the *Handbook* under its provisional name, United Political Forces, was launched by former Hutu prime minister Faustin Twagiramungu and former interior minister Seth SENDASHONGHA in Brussels on March 26, 1996, following their breaks from the MDR and FPR, respectively. Both had been sacked by the government in August 1995 after objecting to an expansion of army power, which the military claimed was necessary to hunt down perpetrators of genocide. Highlighting the new party's platform were calls for the ouster of the Tutsi regime (which the FRD cited as an unbreachable impediment to the return of Rwanda's primarily Hutu refugees) and the drafting of a new power-sharing constitution based on the 1993 Arusha peace agreement. Furthermore, the FRD accused the FPR regime of engaging in genocide against the Hutu population. Two of the party's key leaders were in exile, Twagiramungu in Brussels and Sendashongha in Nairobi, when the latter was assassinated in May 1998. Moderates had wanted Sendashongha to return to Kigali to lead reconciliation efforts. Twagiramungu strongly criticized President Kagame's call in April 2000 for exiles to return to Rwanda, charging that Kagame was attempting to cover up his "crimes against humanity." Nonetheless, Twagiramungu returned to Rwanda in June 2003 and launched a bid for the presidency as an independent. He placed second in the balloting but challenged the results. His challenge was overturned by the Supreme Court.

Leader: Faustin TWAGIRAMUNGU (Former Prime Minister).

Democratic Forces for the Liberation of Rwanda (*Forces Démocratiques pour la Libération du Rwanda*—FDLR). Described in 2004 and early 2005 as one of the last major organized resistance groups outside Rwanda, the Hutu FDLR was accused by some Western leaders of involvement in the killing of civilians in the DRC. In March 2005 the FDLR formally apologized for its role in the 1994 killings in Rwanda. In April 2005 the FDLR declared it was disarming, and the leadership announced the group's intention to return to Rwanda from the DRC and to try to establish a legal political movement.

FDLR leader Ignace MURWANASHYAKA was arrested in Germany in April 2006 on alleged immigration violations. The Rwandan government asked for his extradition, but the German government refused the request. In November 2007 the DRC and Rwanda signed an agreement to disarm the FDLR (see Foreign relations, above). In December the United States announced an effort to initiate sanctions against the FDLR through the UN. In 2008 the UN estimated that approximately 6,000 FDLR fighters remained, but more than 1,000 surrendered or were killed during a joint DRC-Rwandan offensive in December 2008 and January 2009.

Leader: Ignace MURWANASHYAKA.

It was reported in early 2002 that two exile groups in Belgium—the **African Democratic Congress** and the **Movement for Peace, Democracy, and Development**—had launched a new anti-Kagame coalition called the **Rwandan Democratic Alliance.** Another opposition coalition—the **Alliance for Democracy and National Recovery**—was reportedly launched in Brussels in April under the leadership of Valens KAJEGUHAKWA, while the Dutch-based **United Democratic Forces** (FDU-Inkingi), led by Victoire INGABIRE, announced in 2008 that it planned to field a candidate in the 2010 presidential election.

LEGISLATURE

Prior to the resumption of hostilities between the Rwandan armed forces and the Rwandan Patriotic Front in April 1994, the legislature consisted of a unicameral National Development Council (*Conseil pour le Développement National*) of 70 members elected on December 26, 1988, from 140 candidates nominated by the MRND. Under the terms of the power-sharing agreement reached by the government and FPR on January 10, 1993, and confirmed by the Arusha peace agreement of August 4, 1993, a transitional legislative body was formally launched on December 12, 1994.

Under the terms of the 2003 constitution, a bicameral **Parliament** (*Inteko Ishinga Amategeko*) was created.

Senate. The Senate (*Umutwe wa Sena*) consists of 26 indirectly elected members who serve eight-year terms. Twelve senators are elected by regional councils; 8 are appointed by the president; 4 are elected by a regulatory forum of the country's political parties; and the remaining 2 are elected by university staffs and faculty. In addition, former presidents of the republic can request to be members of the Senate. The first senators were sworn in on October 10, 2003.

President: Vincent BIRUTA.

Chamber of Deputies. The lower house (*Umutwe w'Abadepite*) consists of 80 members who serve five-year terms. Fifty-three are directly elected by a system of proportional representation in which parties must achieve a 5 percent threshold to gain representation. Two deputies are elected by the National Youth Council and 1 by the Federation of the Associations of the Disabled. The remaining 24 deputies are elected by a joint council, which includes representatives from provincial, district, and city governments, as well as members of the executive committees of women's groups at various regional levels. In balloting for the 53 directly elected members of the Chamber of Deputies on September 15, 2008, the Rwandan Patriotic Front–led coalition won 42 seats; the Social Democratic Party, 7; and the Liberal Party, 4.

Speaker: Mukantabama ROSE.

CABINET

[as of June 1, 2009]

Prime Minister	Bernard Makusa (ind.)
Ministers	
Agriculture	Christophe Bazivamo (FPR)
Defense	Maj. Gen. Marcel Gatsinzi (ind.)
East African Community	Monique Mukaruriza [f]
Education	Daphrose Gahakwa [f]
Finance and Economic Planning	James Musoni
Foreign Affairs	Rosemary Museminari [f]
Health	Richard Sezibera
Information	Louise Mushikiwabo [f]
Infrastructure	Linda Bihire [f]
Internal Affairs	Mussa Sheikh Harerimana
Justice and Attorney General	Tharcise Karugarama
Labor and Civil Service	Anastase Murekezi
Local Government	Protais Musoni
Natural Resources	Stanislas Kamanzi
President's Office	Solina Nyirahabimana [f]
President's Office in charge of Science, Technology, and Research	Romain Murenzi (PL)
Prime Minister's Office in Charge of Cabinet Affairs	Charles Murigande (FPR)
Prime Minister's Office in Charge of Gender and Women in Development	Jeanne d'Arc Mujawamariya [f]
Prime Minister's Office in Charge of Information	Louise Mushikiwabo [f]
Sports and Culture	Joseph Habineza
Trade and Industry	Monique Nsanzabaganwa (ind.) [f]
Youth	Protais Mitali (PL)
Ministers of State	
Agriculture and Animal Resources	Agnes Kalibata [f]
Community Development and Social Affairs	Christine Nyatanyi [f]
Energy	Albert Butare
Environmental Protection, Water, and Mines	Vincent Karega
Primary and Secondary Education	Theoneste Mutsindashyaka

[f] = female

COMMUNICATIONS

Press. On August 14, 1991, the legislature adopted a press law guaranteeing, with certain restrictions, a free press. Most papers stopped publishing as the result of the 1994 genocide, although the situation has since returned to normal. The press is generally considered to be supportive of the government and exercises a degree of self-censorship in that regard. In its annual index on press freedom in 2008, the journalism watchdog group Reporters Without Borders ranked Rwanda 145 out of 173 countries, up from 147 the year before. There are no daily papers; the government information office in Kigali publishes *Imvaho* (The Truth, 51,000), a weekly in Kinyarwanda, and *La Relève* (Relief, 1,700), a monthly in French. The weekly *Umuseso* is generally perceived as the most independent publication; progovernment (according to Reporters Without Frontiers) publications include *The New Times, L'Enjeu, Grand Lacs Hebdo,* and *L'Horizon.*

News agency. The official facility is *Agence Rwandaise de Presse* (ARP).

Broadcasting and computing. The government-controlled Radio Rwanda broadcasts daily in Kinyarwanda, Kiswahili, and French. Deutsche Welle Relay Kigali broadcasts in German, French, English, Hausa, Kiswahili, Portuguese, and Amharic. The government's Television Rwanda is the only television facility. As of 2008 there were 30.9 Internet users per 1,000 inhabitants.

INTERGOVERNMENTAL REPRESENTATION

Ambassador to the U.S.: James KIMONYO.

U.S. Ambassador to Rwanda: W. Stuart SYMINGTON.

Permanent Representative to the UN: Eugène-Richard GASANA.

IGO Memberships (Non-UN): AfDB, AU, BADEA, CEPGL, Comesa, CWTH, EAC, EADB, Interpol, IOM, NAM, OIF, WCO, WTO.

ST. KITTS AND NEVIS

Federation of Saint Kitts and Nevis

Federation of Saint Christopher and Nevis

Note: Both versions of the name are official, although "Federation of Saint Kitts and Nevis" is preferred.

Political Status: Former British dependency; joined West Indies Associated States in 1967; independent member of the Commonwealth since September 19, 1983.

Area: 101 sq. mi. (262 sq. km.), encompassing Saint Christopher (65 sq. mi.) and Nevis (36 sq. mi.).

Population: 45,841 (2001C); 51,800 (2008E).

Major Urban Center (2005E): BASSETERRE (Saint Christopher, 14,000).

Official Language: English.

Monetary Unit: East Caribbean Dollar (official rate December 1, 2009: 2.70 dollars = $1US).

Sovereign: Queen ELIZABETH II.

Governor General: Sir Cuthbert Montroville SEBASTIAN; took office January 1, 1996, succeeding Sir Clement Athelston ARRINDELL.

Prime Minister: Dr. Denzil Llewellyn DOUGLAS (St. Kitts-Nevis Labour Party); sworn in on July 7, 1995, succeeding Dr. Kennedy Alphonse SIMMONDS (People's Action Movement) following election of July 3; retained office following elections of March 6, 2000, and October 25, 2004.

Premier of Nevis: Joseph W. PARRY (Nevis Reformation Party); named to succeed Vance W. AMORY (Concerned Citizens' Movement) following election of July 10, 2006.

THE COUNTRY

Conventionally styled St. Kitts-Nevis, Saint Christopher and Nevis form part of the northern Leeward Islands group of the Eastern Caribbean. The population is largely of African descent and the religion primarily Anglican. The economy is dependent on tourism, with several hotels currently under construction; agriculture on the large island is devoted primarily to sugarcane and its derivatives, and on Nevis to coconuts and vegetables. Recent economic planning has focused on the promotion of small-scale local industry and agricultural diversification to reduce the islands' dependence on food imports and fluctuating sugar prices, which by 1983 had fallen to less than half the cost of local production. Subsequently, both sugar and tourist income rose substantially, with overall GDP growth from 1985 to 1992 averaging 5.3 percent per annum, then declining steadily to 2.0 percent in 1995 with higher rates of 4.8 in 1996 and 3.0 in 1997. In October 1993 Prime Minister Kennedy Simmonds reported that because of the health of its economy St. Kitts-Nevis was being "graduated" from concessionary loan financing by the World Bank, with future loans to be at commercial rates; on the other hand, the islands were dealt serious blows by Hurricane Luis in September 1995 and Hurricane George in September 1998, which caused damage estimated at $100 million and $450 million, respectively. GDP growth of 7.5 percent was reported for 2000, spurred by construction related to the tourism sector. However, the terrorist attacks in the United States in September 2001 significantly depressed the tourism sector in St. Kitts-Nevis. Real GDP, also negatively affected by problems in the sugar industry, decelerated by 0.8 percent in 2002. Thereafter, GDP growth reached 7.3 percent in 2004 before falling back to 3.2 percent in 2008, with inflation at 9.7 percent.

In July 2005 the 300-year-old sugar industry closed down because of recurring losses; however, a freefall in GDP was prevented by ongoing construction projects and activity related to the Cricket World Cup, which was held at a number of regional venues, including St. Kitts.

In late 2007, with both Brazil and the United States offering technical assistance, it was announced that the nation might resume sugar production in order to produce biofuels, including ethanol.

GOVERNMENT AND POLITICS

Political background. Although one of the smallest territories of the West Indies, St. Kitts was Britain's first colony in the region, settled in 1623. Ownership was disputed with France until 1783, when Britain acquired undisputed title in the Treaty of Versailles. The tripartite entity encompassing St. Kitts, Nevis, and the northern island of Anguilla entered the West Indies Federation in 1952 and was granted internal autonomy as a member of the West Indies Associated States in February 1967. Three months later Anguilla repudiated government from Basseterre and in 1976 was accorded a separate constitution that reconfirmed its status as a dependency of the United Kingdom (see United Kingdom: Related Territories).

The parliamentary election of February 18, 1980, yielded the first defeat of the St. Kitts Labour Party (SKLP) in nearly three decades and the formation of a government under Dr. Kennedy A. SIMMONDS of the People's Action Movement (PAM), with the support of the Nevis Reformation Party (NRP). Despite protests by the SKLP, which insisted that the coalition did not have an independence mandate, the Simmonds government issued a white paper on a proposed federal constitution in July 1982. A revised version of the document, which formed the basis of discussions in London the following December, was endorsed by the St. Kitts-Nevis House of Assembly in March 1983 and secured the approval of the British Parliament in early May. Formal independence followed on September 19.

The PAM/NRP coalition increased its legislative majority in the early election of June 21, 1984, the PAM winning six of eight seats on St. Kitts and the NRP capturing all three seats on Nevis; one of the NRP seats was lost on March 21, 1989.

The election of November 29, 1993, yielded four seats each for the PAM and SKNLP (Nevis having been added to the opposition party's name), with the NRP losing one of its remaining seats to its Nevis-based opponent, the Concerned Citizens' Movement (CCM). After the CCM had refused to form a majority coalition with either the PAM or the SKNLP, the governor general on December 1 asked Simmonds to continue as head of a PAM-NRP minority government. On December 3 SKNLP leader Denzil DOUGLAS insisted that talks between himself and Simmonds had yielded agreement on a caretaker administration for a six-month period, after which a new election would be held. However, the prime minister subsequently accused his opponent of torpedoing the negotiations by announcing an accord before its finalization.

Following an outbreak of what appeared to be drug-related crime in October 1994, political, religious, business, and labor leaders agreed at a "forum for national unity" on November 12 that all parties represented in the National Assembly would be permitted to participate in key government decisions and that the next general election would be held by November 1995, three years ahead of schedule. However, Prime Minister Simmonds scheduled the poll even earlier, on July 3, his seat being lost in a seven-to-one SKNLP victory on St. Kitts; consequently, Denzil Douglas was installed as head of a new government on July 7. Douglas retained office in an early election on March 6, 2000, the SKNLP gaining an additional legislative seat for a majority of eight.

In October 2004 Prime Minister Douglas called for early elections, and after the October 25 poll the SKNLP majority declined to seven seats. The cabinet appointed on October 30 contained most of the incumbent ministers but in reshuffled portfolios. Another major reshuffle was announced on August 8, 2008.

Constitution and government. The 1983 constitution describes St. Kitts-Nevis as a "sovereign democratic federal state" whose ceremonial head, the British monarch, is represented by a governor general of local citizenship. The governor general appoints as prime minister an individual commanding a parliamentary majority and, on the latter's advice, other ministers, all of whom, except for the attorney general, must be members of the legislature. He also appoints, on the advice of the government, a deputy governor general for the island of Nevis. Legislative matters are entrusted to a unicameral National Assembly, 11 of whose members (styled "representatives") are directly elected for

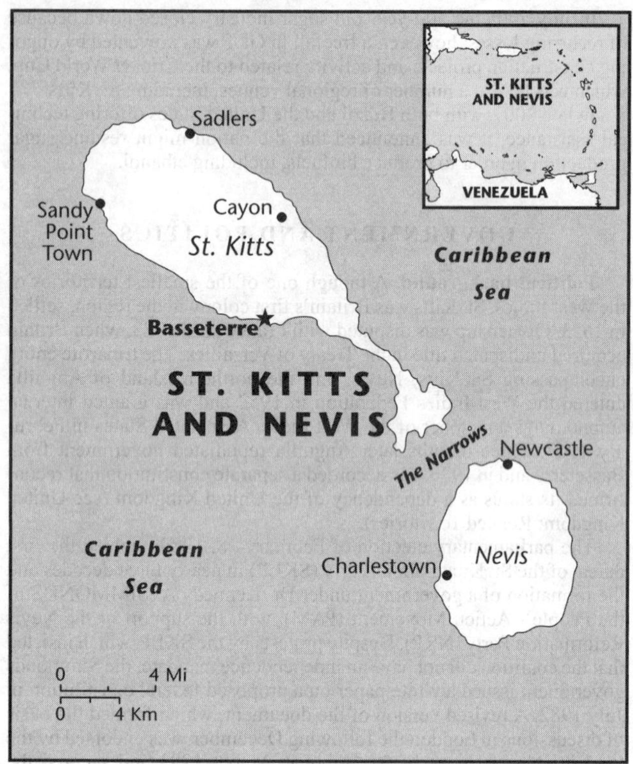

five-year terms from single-member constituencies (8 on St. Kitts and 3 on Nevis). After consulting with the prime minister and the leader of the opposition, the governor general may appoint additional members (styled "senators") who can number no more than two-thirds of the elected membership. Constitutional amendments require approval by two-thirds of the representatives, while certain entrenched provisions must also be endorsed by two-thirds of the valid votes in a national referendum. The highest court—apart from the right of appeal, in certain circumstances, to the Judicial Committee of the Privy Council in London—is the West Indies Supreme Court (based on St. Lucia), which includes a Court of Appeal and a High Court, one of whose judges resides on St. Kitts and presides over a Court of Summary Jurisdiction. District courts deal with petty offenses and minor civil actions.

Nevis is provided with an island Assembly, currently consisting of five elected and three nominated members (the latter not to exceed two-thirds of the former); in addition, the governor general appoints a premier and two other members of the Nevis Assembly to serve as a Nevis Island Administration. Most importantly, the Nevis Islanders have the right of secession from St. Kitts, if a bill to such effect is approved by two-thirds of their elected legislators and endorsed by two-thirds of those voting on the matter in an island referendum.

In late July 1995, following his installation as prime minister, Denzil Douglas announced that he intended to introduce a constitutional reform that would provide separate governments for St. Kitts and Nevis. Having discussed the matter with Nevis Premier Vance AMORY, he pledged to draw on both local and international expertise to draw up a document that would be acceptable to residents of both islands. The overture notwithstanding, Amory in June 1996 initiated secession proceedings, Douglas characterizing the action as indicating that the Nevis leader had "no other issue of note to bring to the people." Nonetheless, the inhabitants of the smaller island had long chafed at alleged policy discrimination by Basseterre. Involved were a variety of complaints ranging from slow responses to the proposed upgrading of public services to fears of exclusion from offshore banking opportunities.

Efforts by regional representatives to mediate the dispute having failed, the Nevis Assembly voted unanimously on October 13, 1997, for secession, opposition members indicating their support "on principle." The change was, however, narrowly defeated in a referendum on August 10, 1998 (see Current issues, below).

Foreign relations. At independence, St. Kitts-Nevis became an independent member of the Commonwealth and shortly thereafter was admitted to the United Nations. It joined the Organization of American States (OAS) in March 1984. Regionally, it is a member of the Association of Caribbean States (ACS), the Caribbean Community and Common Market (Caricom), and the Organization of Eastern Caribbean States (OECS). Most of its bilateral aid has come from Britain, which, at independence, provided a special grant-loan package of £10 million for capital projects and technical cooperation. The Simmonds government endorsed the U.S. intervention in Grenada in October 1983, subsequently receiving modest military assistance from the United States in support of its small voluntary defense force.

St. Kitts is one of a number of small regional countries receiving fuel under Venezuela's PetroCaribe supply initiative, and in December 2006 Prime Minister Douglas said he looked forward to deepening relations with a government whose leader displayed "unstinting efforts to alleviate poverty."

Current issues. On August 10, 1998, 61.8 percent of Nevis voters backed secession. However, the measure was defeated because it failed to gain a constitutionally required two-thirds majority. Subsequently, the Nevis administration became preoccupied with a variety of economic issues, including the island's status as an offshore financial services center, which was reportedly home to "tens of thousands of corporations," with more than 3,000 added in 2007 alone. While the activity was a major revenue source for Nevis, the Island Assembly, in response to mounting criticism by the U.S. Congress, approved legislation for the registration of international funds as of January 1, 2008.

On a more positive note, Premier Parry welcomed a discovery of significant geothermal energy on Nevis and in mid-2008 led a delegation to Iceland for talks on energy-related issues.

Meanwhile, Prime Minister Douglas had encountered a number of political problems. Under attack for failing to curb criminal activity, particularly gang violence, he announced that a former FBI associate director would advise the Ministry of National Security on coping with the situation. Earlier, he had undertaken a major cabinet reshuffle, following the resignation of National Security Minister Dwyer ASTAPHAN, who, despite 13 years of cabinet service, castigated Douglas as arriving at policy decisions unilaterally without considering the view of his ministers. For his part, Douglas refused to participate in a "war of words" and insisted that there was no "bad blood" between himself and Astaphan. Attention subsequently focused on the legislative elections scheduled for January 2010, at which the SKNLP was expected to retain its dominance.

POLITICAL PARTIES

Government Party:

St. Kitts-Nevis Labour Party (SKNLP). What was then styled the St. Kitts Labour Party (SKLP) was organized as a socialist party in 1932. Long the dominant grouping on St. Kitts, it won seven of nine Assembly seats in 1971 and retained a plurality of four in 1980 but was forced from office by the PAM/NRP coalition. The party initially opposed federal status for Nevis, claiming that it made Nevis "more equal" than St. Kitts; however, this position was reversed following the SKLP's crushing defeat in the 1984 elections, in which it lost all but two of its legislative seats, including that of opposition leader Lee L. MOORE. Subsequent changes included the ascendancy of youth leader Henry BROWNE as Moore's successor and a distancing of the party from the 40-year-old sugar workers' union. It led the 1993 popular vote, while increasing its Assembly representation from two to four; however, it was unable to persuade the CCM (below) to join it in a government coalition. The party swept to victory on July 3, 1995, winning seven of eight seats on St. Kitts. It added the eighth seat in the election of March 6, 2000, but returned to seven in 2004.

In May 2009 Prime Minister Douglas was reelected for a 21st consecutive year as Labour Party leader.

Leaders: Dr. Denzil Llewellyn DOUGLAS (Prime Minister and Leader of the Party), Timothy Sylvester HARRIS (Chair).

Other Parties:

People's Action Movement (PAM). The PAM is a moderately left-of-center party formed in 1965. It won only 3 of 9 elective seats in the 1980 preindependence balloting, but with the support of 2 members from Nevis was able to force resignation of the existing Labour government. It captured 6 of the 8 seats from St. Kitts in June 1984, thus securing an absolute majority in a new house that had been expanded to 11 elected members; it retained all 6 seats in 1989 but slipped to 4 in 1993. Although finishing second in the popular vote, the PAM, despite SKNLP objections, retained office in coalition with the NRP. It won only 1 legislative seat in the July 1995 election, which was lost in the March 2000 poll but regained in 2004.

In August 2007 the party's deputy leader, Shawn Richards, gave up his seat in the assembly after it was disclosed that he also held U.S. citizenship, thereby being among those unqualified to remain in the legislature.

Leaders: Lindsay GRANT (Party Leader), Shawn RICHARDS (Deputy Leader).

Concerned Citizens' Movement (CCM). The CCM is a Nevis-based party that in 1987 captured one local Assembly seat and in 1989 one National Assembly seat from the NRP (below). It won control of Nevis on June 1, 1992, by securing three of five Assembly seats, retaining them on February 24, 1997. It increased its National Assembly representation from one to two in 1993, retaining both in 1995, 2000, and 2004. In the balloting for the Nevis Assembly in September 2001, the CCM secured four of the five elected seats, two of which were lost in July 2006.

Leader: Vance W. AMORY (Former Premier of Nevis).

Nevis Reformation Party (NRP). Organized in 1970, the NRP had, before 1980, campaigned for Nevis's secession from St. Kitts. It won two National Assembly seats in 1980 and participated in the independence discussions that led to the formation of the federal state. It captured all three seats from Nevis in 1984, after having won all five seats to the Nevis Island Assembly in August 1983; it lost one of the latter in December 1987 and one of the former in March 1989, both to the CCM. In the Nevis election of June 1, 1992, it retained only two Assembly seats, forcing its leader to step down as island premier; its local representation was unchanged in February 1997. It lost one of two National Assembly seats in November 1993, with no change in 1995, 2000, or 2004.

Following the 1997 Nevis poll, former premier Simeon Daniel stated that he would not contest future elections, since speculation that his party favored the central government's position may have weakened its position with voters. The NRP lost one of its two seats in balloting for the Nevis Assembly in September 2001 but secured three seats (a majority) in July 2006.

Leaders: Simeon DANIEL (Former Premier of Nevis), Roberto HECTOR, Joseph W. PARRY (Premier of Nevis), Levi MORTON (Secretary).

United National Empowerment Party (UNEP). The UNEP was launched in May 2004 on a platform of constitutional reform and opposition to independence for Nevis.

Leader: Henry L. O. "Stogumber" BROWNE.

LEGISLATURE

The unicameral **National Assembly** presently consists of 11 elected members, plus no more than 7 nominated members (two-thirds by the government, one-third by the opposition). The legislative mandate is five years, subject to dissolution. In the most recent balloting of October 25, 2004, the St. Kitts-Nevis Labour Party elected 7 members; the Concerned Citizens' Movement, 2; the Nevis Reformation Party, 1; and the People's Action Movement, 1. The next election was scheduled for January 25, 2010.

President: Marcella A. LIBURD.

CABINET

[as of July 1, 2009]

Prime Minister	Denzil Llewellyn Douglas
Deputy Prime Minister	Sam Terrence Condor
Premier of Nevis	Joseph Parry
Ministers	
Cabinet Secretary	Joseph Llewellyn Edmeade
Civil Aviation and Maritime Affairs	Earl Asim Martin
Education, Youth Affairs, Social Security, Information, and Technology	Sam Terrence Condor
Finance, International Trade, Industry, Commerce, and Consumer Affairs	Timothy Sylvester Harris
Foreign Affairs	Denzil Llewellyn Douglas
Health, Social and Community Development, and Gender Affairs	Rupert Emanuel Herbert
Housing, Agriculture, and Fisheries	Cedric Roy Liburd
Immigration and Sustainable Development	Denzil Llewellyn Douglas
Legal Affairs and Attorney General	Dennis Merchant
National Security	Denzil Llewellyn Douglas
Public Works, Utilities, Transport, and Postal Affairs	Earl Asim Martin
Tourism, Culture, and Sports	Denzil Llewellyn Douglas
Ministers of State	
Prime Minister's Office with Responsibility for Education, Youth Affairs, Labour, Social Security, and Information and Technology	Nigel Alexis Carty
Prime Minister's Office with Responsibility for Tourism, Sports, and Culture	Richard Skerritt

COMMUNICATIONS

Press. The following are published in Basseterre: *The Weekend Voice* (8,000); *The Labour Spokesman* (6,000), twice-weekly organ of the St. Kitts-Nevis Trade and Labour Union; *The Democrat* (3,000), weekly PAM organ.

News agency. There is no domestic facility. International news is provided by the Caribbean News Agency (CANA).

Broadcasting and computing. Religious programming is provided by Radio Paradise and the Voice of Nevis, while the government-owned ZIZ Radio and Television broadcasts to about 12,500 TV receivers. As of 2008 there were 313.3 Internet users per 1,000 inhabitants.

INTERGOVERNMENTAL REPRESENTATION

Ambassador to the U.S.: Izben Cordinal WILLIAMS.

U.S. Ambassador to St. Kitts-Nevis: (Vacant).

Permanent Representative to the UN: Delano Frank BART.

IGO Memberships (Non-UN): ACS, Caricom, CDB, CWTH, Interpol, OAS, OECS, OPANAL, WTO.

ST. LUCIA

Saint Lucia

Political Status: Former British dependency; joined West Indies Associated States in 1967; independent member of the Commonwealth since February 22, 1979.

Area: 238 sq. mi. (616 sq. km.).

Population: 162,982 (2001C); including adjustment for underenumeration; 168,400 (2008E).

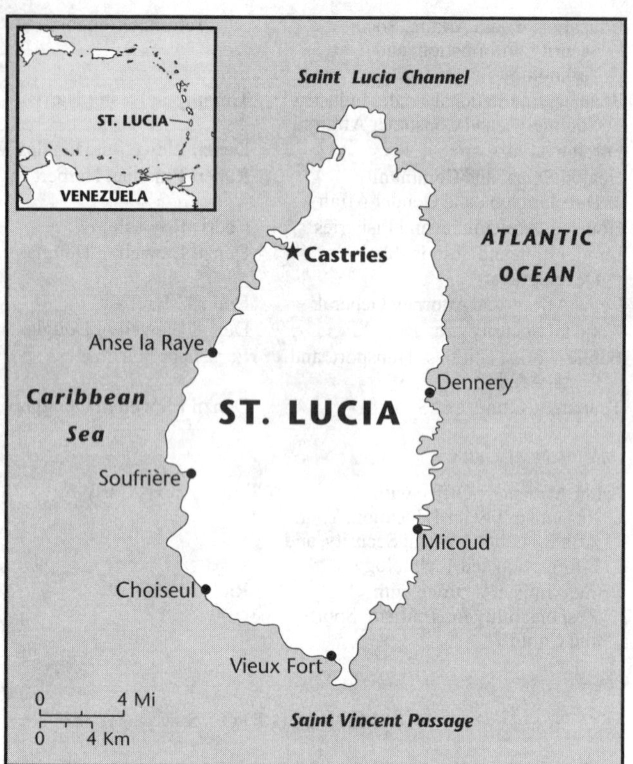

Major Urban Center (2005E): CASTRIES (14,600).

Official Language: English.

Monetary Unit: East Caribbean Dollar (official rate December 1, 2009: 2.70 dollars = $1US).

Sovereign: Queen ELIZABETH II.

Governor General: Dame Perlette LOUISY; sworn in September 17, 1997, succeeding Sir W. George MALLET.

Prime Minister: Stevenson KING (United Workers' Party); named acting prime minister on May 1, 2007, following the incapacitation of Sir John George Melvin COMPTON; inaugurated as prime minister on September 9 after Compton's death on September 7.

THE COUNTRY

The second largest of the former West Indies Associated States, St. Lucia lies between Martinique and St. Vincent in the Windward Islands chain of the eastern Caribbean. As in the case of adjacent territories, most of the inhabitants are descendants of West African slaves who were brought as plantation laborers in the 17th and 18th centuries. Following the conclusion of a treaty with the indigenous Carib Indians in 1660, France settled the island and significant traces of French culture remain despite undisputed British control after 1803. At least 80 percent of the population is Roman Catholic.

The principal economic sectors are agriculture, with bananas and coconuts as the leading export items; tourism, which has been growing rapidly in recent years; and manufacturing, which currently embraces more than 40 relatively diversified enterprises. Despite satisfactory infrastructural development and significant geothermal energy potential, the economy has been hampered by rapid population growth, which has yielded widespread unemployment (estimated at 22 percent in 1984, but with a substantial reduction to 13 percent in 1990, before rising again to 19 percent in 2001). Inflation, which rose to 7.0 percent in 1987, receded to near zero in 1997, while improvements in both tourism and banana production yielded real GNP growth of nearly 6 percent annually from 1989 to 1993, before falling to 2.5 percent in 1994 through 1998. Part of the decline was attributed to Hurricane Luis in September 1995, which destroyed about 17 percent of the banana crop. Real GDP growth of only 0.2 percent was achieved in 2000, while the economy contracted by 5.4 percent in 2001, primarily as a result of a drastic decline in tourism following the terrorist attacks in the United States on September 11. Growth gained steadily thereafter to 5.0 percent in 2006 then fell to 2.3 percent in 2008 because of a continued decline in tourism and renewed hurricane damage to banana production. Concurrently, inflation rose again to more than 7 percent.

GOVERNMENT AND POLITICS

Political background. Administered after 1833 as part of the British Leeward Islands, St. Lucia was incorporated in 1940 into the Windward Islands group, which also included Dominica, Grenada, and St. Vincent. It participated in the Federation of the West Indies from 1958 to 1962 and became one of the six internally self-governing West Indies Associated States in March 1967. As in the cases of Grenada and Dominica, St. Lucia, under Premier John G. M. COMPTON of the long-dominant United Workers' Party (UWP), applied for independence under a provision of the West Indies Act of 1966 requiring only that an Order in Council be laid before the British Parliament. The opposition St. Lucia Labour Party (SLP), led by Allan LOUISY, called initially for a referendum on the issue but subsequently participated in a constitutional conference held in London in July 1978. Following approval of the proposed constitution by the St. Lucia House of Assembly on October 24 and of a draft termination order by both houses of Parliament in December, independence within the Commonwealth was proclaimed on February 22, 1979, with Premier Compton assuming the office of prime minister. Compton was succeeded by Louisy following a landslide victory by the leftist-oriented SLP on July 2, 1979.

In the wake of mounting conflict between the prime minister and a radical SLP faction led by Foreign Minister George ODLUM, Louisy resigned on April 30, 1981, in favor of the essentially centrist Winston CENAC. Cenac, in turn, was forced to step down on January 16, 1982. The governor general subsequently named Michael PILGRIM to head an all-party administration pending a general election on May 3 in which Compton's UWP secured a decisive victory, sweeping all but three parliamentary seats. Retaining control by only one seat in the balloting of April 6, 1987, Compton called for a second election only three weeks later, which yielded the same outcome.

Buoyed by a resilient economy and campaigning on the slogan "Keep St. Lucia in good hands," Compton led the UWP to an 11–6 victory over the SLP in parliamentary balloting on April 27, 1992. He retired on March 31, 1996, and was succeeded by his recently designated party successor, Dr. Vaughan A. LEWIS, on April 2. Compton, however, returned to succeed Lewis in mid-1998.

In the election of May 23, 1997, the SLP crushed the UWP, 16–1, winning 61.3 percent of the valid votes under its new leader, Kenny D. ANTHONY. Anthony called early assembly elections for December 3, 2001, the SLP securing 14 seats compared to 3 for the UWP.

In another reversal, on December 11, 2006, the UWP regained power by winning 11 seats with the SLP taking 6, the 82-year-old Compton being invested for the fifth time as prime minister. Following Compton's death less than a year later on September 7, 2007, Stevenson KING, who had served as acting prime minister since May 1, 2006, was named prime minister.

Constitution and government. Under the 1979 constitution, the St. Lucia Parliament consists of "Her Majesty, a Senate and a House of Assembly." The queen, as titular head of state, is represented locally by a governor general whose emergency powers are subject to legislative review. Senators are appointed, serve only for the duration of a given Parliament, may not introduce money bills, and can only delay other legislation. The size of the Assembly is not fixed, although the present house has not been expanded beyond the preindependence membership of 17. The prime minister must be a member of the Assembly and command a majority therein; other ministers are appointed on the prime minister's advice from either of the two houses. Appointments to various public commissions, as well as the designation of a parliamentary ombudsman, require consultation with the leader of the opposition. The judicial system includes membership in the Eastern Caribbean Supreme Court, with appeals from its Court of Appeal transferred from the Judicial Committee of the Privy Council in London to the Caribbean Court of Justice upon the latter's launching in April 2005.

In 1985 the Compton government announced a plan to divide the island into eight regions, each with its own council and administrative services; implementation of the decentralization plan began in December 1985 and was completed the following year.

Calls for a number of constitutional changes, including abandonment of the link to the British Crown, were made to a Constitutional Reform Commission in early 2009 (see Current issues, below).

Foreign relations. During St. Lucia's independence day ceremonies, Prime Minister Compton committed his government to a "full thrust towards Caribbean integration and West Indian unity," adding, however, that the island's historic links to the West precluded diplomatic relations with Cuba. These policies were reversed under Prime Minister Louisy. In August 1979 relations were formally established with the Cuban regime of Fidel Castro, and St. Lucia was accorded observer status at the September nonaligned conference in Havana after announcing its intention to apply for full membership in the third world grouping. After returning to power in May 1982, Prime Minister Compton reaffirmed his earlier wariness of Havana while indicating that his administration would cooperate with all regional governments participating in the Organization of Eastern Caribbean States (OECS), established in June 1981. In May 1987 Compton joined with James Mitchell of St. Vincent in urging that the seven OECS members work toward the formation of a single unitary state. However, the proposal was strongly criticized as a form of neocolonialism by Prime Minister Vere C. Bird Sr. of Antigua, while drawing only modest support from other regional leaders.

Given the apparent failure of the OECS unification scheme, St. Lucia joined with its Windward Island neighbors (Dominica, Grenada, and St. Vincent and the Grenadines) in an effort to launch a less inclusive grouping. During the third meeting of a Regional Constituent Assembly in Roseau, Dominica, in September 1991, agreement was reached on a federal system with a common legislature and executive; however, opposition was also voiced to the more recent proposal, with Prime Minister Compton subsequently reported to be seeking a structure of association that would not require modification of the participants' constitutions.

On September 1, 1997, diplomatic relations were established with the People's Republic of China, three days after a severance of ties with Taiwan. Earlier, Prime Minister Anthony had offered to maintain economic and trade relations with Taiwan, its ambassador responding that his government appeared to be intent on introducing a "sort of socialist left-oriented" foreign policy. Anthony made a weeklong state visit to China in February 1999, Beijing pledging support for several projects in St. Lucia, including $4 million for a new sports complex.

Following the December 2006 election, Prime Minister Compton denied reports that his administration intended to reestablish relations with Taiwan. In early 2007, however, the government invited Taiwan to send a delegation to examine how "the interests of both parties could be advanced," and four months later, the Taiwanese flag was again raised in Castries.

Current issues. As in other Caribbean countries, there has recently been an escalation of crime in St. Lucia, the number of murders reaching record levels in 2004–2006, accompanied by a growth in drug-related crime. The failure of the Anthony administration to reverse the trend, which included a number of high-profile attacks on foreign nationals, contributed to the SLP's loss in the 2006 election.

After his inauguration in September 2007, Prime Minister King appointed a number of the UWP cabinet officials who were criticized by the opposition for having little experience in the areas assigned to them. Controversy also continued to swirl around UWP member and former external affairs minister Rufus BOUSQUET, who had been sacked earlier by Compton for discussing renewal of relations with Taiwanese officials without the prime minister's knowledge. Bousquet's situation became even more clouded with the subsequent disclosure that he had once been taken into custody by U.S. officials for applying for a passport under an assumed name; however, he was reappointed to his old post by the King administration as of January 2, 2009.

In early 2009 the renewed link with Taiwan came under stress with complaints about its subsidy of a learning center within the office of a governing party politician. Opposition leader Kenny Anthony called for expulsion of the Taiwanese ambassador, Tom CHOU, who conceded that the location of the facility had been a mistake.

In March 2009 the Constitutional Reform Commission received submissions from a large number of individuals and organizations, seeking changes in the island's basic law. Included were calls for the adoption of a republican form of government, with an elected president replacing the governor general; a fixed date for general elections; changes in the appointment and function of the Senate; and expansion of the Bill of Rights to encompass education, health, and protection of the environment.

In late May 2009 government workers mounted a demonstration in Castries, calling for the balance of a 14.5 percent pay increase promised by the government nine months earlier. The King administration, which had paid 7 percent, declared its inability to provide the remainder because of the global economic downturn.

POLITICAL PARTIES

Government Party:

United Workers' Party (UWP). The UWP was organized in 1964 by members of the former National Labour Movement and the People's Progressive Party. The party's basically moderate leader, Sir John G. M. Compton, served as chief minister from 1964 to 1967 and as premier from 1967 to 1979, becoming prime minister upon independence. Decisively defeated in July 1979, the UWP returned to power on May 3, 1982. It obtained a bare majority of one assembly seat in the election of April 6, 1987, and failed to improve its standing in a second election on April 30. By contrast, the party won a healthy margin of five seats in April 1992. In January 1996 Compton retired as party leader in favor of Dr. Vaughan Lewis, who succeeded as prime minister on April 2 before the UWP debacle in the election of May 23, 1997, in which the party secured only one seat.

Morella Joseph, a retired school principal, was elected unopposed as the UWP party leader at the October 2000 annual convention. Although Joseph was subsequently named vice president of the National Alliance (NA, below), the UWP withdrew from the formation in October 2001 and ran separately in the December elections. Despite an increase in UWP representation to three with a vote share of 36.6 percent, Joseph subsequently resigned and was replaced on an interim basis by Marius Wilson. In mid-2004 the parliamentary leader of the opposition, Marcus NICHOLS, was sacked after calling for UWP leader Lewis to resign. In March 2005 former Prime Minister Compton came out of political retirement to defeat Lewis for the UWP leadership. Compton died on September 7, 2007.

Leaders: Stephenson KING, (Party Leader and Prime Minister), Lenard Spider MONTOUTE (Deputy Party Leader).

Opposition Party:

St. Lucia Labour Party (SLP). The SLP is a left-of-center party formed in 1946. After boycotting the independence ceremonies because they were not immediately preceded by balloting for a new assembly, it won a landslide victory in the election of July 2, 1979. Party leader Allan Louisy resigned as prime minister in April 1981 because of intraparty conflict with "new Left" advocate George Odlum, who subsequently withdrew to form the Progressive Labour Party (PLP) in opposition to the government of Louisy's successor, Winston Cenac. At its 1984 annual convention, the SLP voted to assign the roles of party leader and leader of the opposition to different individuals, and, in a move interpreted as a swing to the right, named Castries businessman Julian HUNTE to the former post. Resistance from some factions to Hunte and his steadfast rejection of unity proposals from the PLP seemed to have declined by 1986, but the party was unable to secure a majority in either of the 1987 elections and secured only 6 of 17 seats in 1992. At a delegates' conference in July 1992 Hunte turned back a challenge by his former deputy, Peter JOSIE, to succeed him as party leader, and in February 1993 the party's Central Executive Committee voted to expel Josie because of his "constant criticism" of the leadership. Hunte resigned his leadership post in February 1996 because of the party's poor showing in a Castries by-election and was succeeded in March by Dr. Kenny Anthony.

Dr. Anthony led the SLP to a near sweep (16 of 17 assembly seats) in the election of May 23, 1997. George Odlum joined the subsequent cabinet as minister of foreign affairs and international trade. However, he left the government in March 2001 after announcing he would not stand as an SLP candidate in the 2002 balloting. (See National Alliance, below, for information on Odlum's subsequent activities.)

Leaders: Dr. Kenny Davis ANTHONY (Former Prime Minister and Party Leader), Allan F. L. LOUISY (Former Prime Minister), Tom WALCOTT (Chair), Oliver SCOTT (Secretary General).

Other Parties:

National Alliance (NA). The NA was launched in March 2001 as a "multiparty" grouping to challenge the SLP in the elections then scheduled for 2002. Former Prime Minister Sir John G. M. Compton was named president of the Alliance, which also listed recent SLP defector George Odlum as a leader and, apparently, the grouping's candidate for prime minister. UWP leader Morella Joseph was also listed as the vice president of the group. However, after an NA meeting in October elected Compton to head the formation, Odlum reportedly "cancelled" the meeting, thereby precipitating the breakup of the group as originally constituted. Joseph subsequently announced that the UWP was withdrawing from the NA to run independently in the upcoming elections. Odlum and his supporters retained the NA rubric, the grouping securing only 3.5 percent of the vote and no Assembly seats. Odlum died in September 2003.

Two other minor parties participated without success in the 2001 Assembly balloting: the **St. Lucia Staff Party,** a "satirical" grouping ("staff" has a drunken connotation in the local vernacular) led by television host Christopher HUNTE, and the **St. Lucia Freedom Party,** led by Martinus FRANÇOIS.

Two new formations were launched in 2004: the **Committee for Meaningful Change and Reconstruction** (CMCR) and the **National Development Movement** (NDM), which was dissolved in September 2007 when its leader, Ausbert D'AUVERGNE, accepted a cabinet post in the King administration as a member of the UWP. In 2005 the **Organization for National Empowerment** (ONE) elected as its leader Sarah FLOOD-BEAUBRUN, who had left the SLP in January 2004 following a dispute over abortion policy.

LEGISLATURE

The **Parliament** of St. Lucia consists of an appointed Senate and an elected House of Assembly, each with a normal term of five years, subject to dissolution.

Senate. The upper house encompasses 11 members, of whom 6 are appointed on the advice of the prime minister, 3 on the advice of the leader of the opposition, and 2 after consultation with religious, economic, and social groups.

President: Everistus Jn MARIE.

House of Assembly. The lower house presently consists of 17 directly elected members plus an appointed speaker. In the election of December 11, 2006, the United Workers' Party won 11 seats and the St. Lucia Labour Party, 6.

Speaker: Dr. Hilda Rose Marie HUSBANDS-MATHURIN.

CABINET

[as of July 1, 2009]

Prime Minister	Stevenson King
Ministers	
Agriculture, Land, Forestry, and Fisheries	Ezechiel Joseph
Commerce, Industry and Consumer Affairs	Sen. Charlotte Elizabeth Theresa Tessa Mangal [f]
Communications, Works, Transport, and Public Utilities	Guy Eardley Joseph
Economic Affairs, Economic Planning and National Development	Stevenson King
Education and Culture	Sen. Peter David Charlemagne
External Affairs, International Trade, and Investment	Rufus George Bousquet
Information and Broadcasting	Edmund Estephane
Finance and International Financial Services	Stevenson King
Health, Family Affairs, National Mobilization, Human Services, and Gender Development	Dr. Keith Mondesir
Home Affairs and National Security	Sen. George Guy Mayers
Housing, Physical Planning, Urban Renewal, and Local Government	Richard Frederick
Justice and Attorney General	Sen. Dr. Nicholas Frederick
Labor	Edmund Estephane
Social Transformation, Public Service, Human Resource Development, Youth, and Sports	Lenard Spider Montoute
Tourism and Civil Aviation	Sen. Allen M. Chastanet

[f] = female

COMMUNICATIONS

In July 1994 Prime Minister Compton, in a speech at the UWP's annual conference, castigated St. Lucia's broadcast and print media as "the most vicious in the entire English-speaking Caribbean." Subsequently a number of incidents, including the expulsion of a newspaper sports editor from a press conference by the sports minister, provoked opposition charges of "wholesale political censorship."

Press. The following are published in Castries: *The Star* (8,000), SLP weekly; *The Voice of St. Lucia* (8,000), independent biweekly, Sunday edition published as the *Weekend Voice* (8,000); *The Crusader* (4,000), left-wing weekly; *The Castries Catholic Chronicle* (2,500), monthly; *The Vanguard* (2,000), UWP fortnightly; *The Mirror,* weekly, launched in August 1994.

News agency. There is no domestic facility. International news is provided by the Caribbean News Agency (CANA).

Broadcasting and computing. The government-operated Radio St. Lucia, which resumed broadcasting on July 1, 1995, after a nine-month closure because of strike action and financial difficulties, provides service in English, while Radio Caribbean International (a subsidiary of CIRTES France) broadcasts in French, English, and Creole. Television is provided by the commercial Helen Television Service (HTS). As of 2008 there were 586.8 Internet users per 1,000 inhabitants.

INTERGOVERNMENTAL REPRESENTATION

Ambassador to the U.S.: Michael LOUIS.

U.S. Ambassador to St. Lucia: (Vacant).

Permanent Representative to the UN: Donatus Keith ST. AIMEE.

IGO Memberships (Non-UN): ACS, Caricom, CDB, CWTH, Interpol, NAM, OAS, OECS, OIF, OPANAL, WCO, WTO.

ST. VINCENT AND THE GRENADINES

Political Status: Former British dependency; joined West Indies Associated States in 1967; independent member of the Commonwealth since October 27, 1979.

Area: 150 sq. mi. (389 sq. km.), including the Grenadine dependencies, which encompass 17 sq. mi. (44 sq. km.).

Population: 109,202 (2001C); 129,000 (2008E). The 2001 figure remains provisional and does not accord with either prior or subsequent estimates.

Major Urban Center (2005E): KINGSTOWN (30,400, including suburbs).

Official Language: English.

Monetary Unit: East Caribbean Dollar (official rate December 1, 2009: 2.70 EC dollars = $1US).

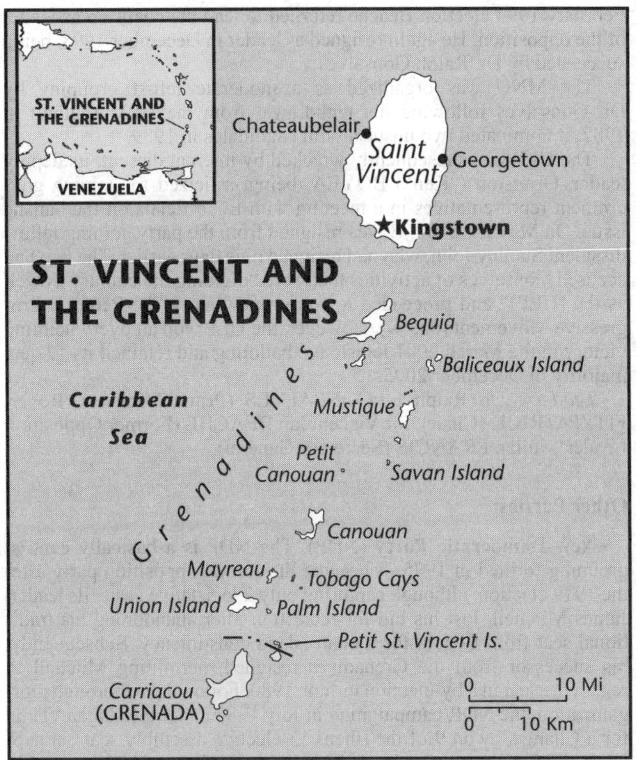

Sovereign: Queen ELIZABETH II.

Governor General: Sir Frederick Nathaniel BALLANTYNE; sworn in on September 2, 2002, after being appointed by the Queen following the death of Sir Charles James ANTROBUS on June 3. (Deputy Governor General Monica DACON had served in an acting capacity during the interim period.)

Prime Minister: Dr. Ralph E. GONSALVES (Unity Labour Party); sworn in March 29, 2001, following the election of March 28 in succession to Arnhim EUSTACE (New Democratic Party); remained in office following election of December 7, 2005.

THE COUNTRY

St. Vincent is located in the Windward group of the eastern Caribbean, south of St. Lucia and west of Barbados. Its jurisdiction encompasses the northern Grenadine islets of Beguia, Canouan, Mayreau, Mustique, Prune Island, Petit St. Vincent, and Union Island, the southern portion of the chain being part of Grenada. The population is mainly of African and mixed origin, with small numbers of Asians, Caribs, and Europeans. The economy is based almost entirely on tourism and agriculture, with bananas, arrowroot, and coconuts being the principal export commodities. An extended series of volcanic eruptions in April 1979 caused massive devastation and necessitated temporary evacuation of the northern two-thirds of the main island, although substantial recovery had been registered by early 1984. Real GDP growth for 1985–1995 averaged 3.9 percent, then dipped to 1.5 percent in 1996 and 1.0 percent in 1997 before rising to 5.7 percent in 1998 and 4.5 percent in 1999. GDP growth fell to 2 percent in 2000 and was close to zero in the ensuing two years because of declining banana exports and the negative impact on tourism of the September 2001 terrorist attacks on the United States. GDP growth then rose steadily to a vigorous 7.0 percent in 2007, before declining sharply to 1.0 percent in 2008 because of the global recession; meanwhile, inflation, which peaked at 11.6 percent in September 2008, declined marginally to 8.7 percent at year's end.

GOVERNMENT AND POLITICS

Political background. Claimed by both Great Britain and France during the 17th and 18th centuries, St. Vincent was definitively assigned to the former by the Treaty of Versailles in 1783. The islands, 50 years later, became part of the general government of Barbados and the Windward Islands and, after the separation of the two in 1885, were administered from Grenada. A founding member of the Federation of the West Indies in 1958, they joined the West Indies Associated States in 1967 as an internally self-governing territory with a right of unilateral termination, which they exercised on October 27, 1979. After the state's admission to the Commonwealth as a special member, Sir Sydney GUN-MUNRO, the former governor, assumed the titular role of governor general, while Premier Robert Milton CATO became prime minister and continued in office after balloting on December 5, in which his St. Vincent Labour Party (SVLP) captured 11 of 13 elective parliamentary seats.

In the election of July 25, 1984, the SVLP was defeated by the New Democratic Party (NDP), whose 9-member majority forced the resignation of Cato in favor of former premier James F. ("Son") MITCHELL; the NDP swept the balloting of May 20, 1989, the country being bereft of an elected opposition. It continued in office by winning 12 of 15 elective seats on February 21, 1994, those being reduced to a bare majority of 8 seats on June 18, 1998. Arnhim EUSTACE, theretofore finance minister, succeeded Mitchell as prime minister upon the latter's retirement on October 27, 2000.

In accordance with an agreement reached the previous year, early elections were held on March 28, 2001. The center-left Unity Labour Party (ULP) captured 12 elective seats to the NDP's 3. ULP leader Ralph GONSALVES was appointed prime minister on March 29 and announced a ULP cabinet on April 2, thus ending 16 years of uninterrupted NDP control. Gonsalves remained in office after the election of December 7, 2005, which yielded no change in the legislative distribution.

Constitution and government. An amended version of the 1969 document defining St. Vincent's status as an Associated State, the present constitution, adopted at independence in 1979, provides for a governor general who acts on behalf of the British Crown and who appoints as prime minister the individual best able to command a majority within the legislature. Other cabinet members are appointed on the advice of the prime minister. The unicameral House of Assembly is currently composed of 15 representatives elected by universal adult suffrage in single-member constituencies, plus six senators (four nominated by the government and two by the leader of the opposition). The highest court—apart from a right of appeal in certain circumstances to the Judicial Committee of the Privy Council in London—is the West Indies Supreme Court (based in St. Lucia), which includes a Court of Appeal and a High Court, one of whose judges is resident in St. Vincent and presides over a Court of Summary Jurisdiction. District Courts deal with petty offenses and minor civil actions. The main island of St. Vincent is divided into five local parishes (Charlotte, St. George, St. Andrew, St. David, and St. Patrick).

Foreign relations. One of the more moderate Caribbean leaders, Prime Minister Cato declared during independence ceremonies that his government would "not succumb to pressure from any power bloc" and would not seek admission to the Nonaligned Movement because such participation "is to be aligned." Although Cato assisted in establishing the U.S.-backed Regional Security System (RSS), his successor, James Mitchell, strongly opposed "militarization" of the region and in 1986 helped block the U.S. effort to upgrade the RSS to a stronger alignment that would have established a centralized military force to fight "subversion" in the Eastern Caribbean. Mitchell also canceled St. Vincent's participation in U.S.-Eastern Caribbean joint military maneuvers late in the year. In July 1996, on the other hand, he agreed to the conclusion of an extradition treaty with Washington that was aimed primarily at drug traffickers.

While opposing military enhancement, Mitchell was long viewed as the "father" of regional political integration. Following failure by the seven-member Organization of Eastern Caribbean States (OECS) to move toward a single unitary state, he advocated unification of St. Vincent with the neighboring Windward Island states of Dominica, Grenada, and St. Lucia. However, the third session of a Regional Constituent Assembly that convened in Roseau, Dominica, in September 1991 could reach agreement only on a federal system, preliminary approval for which was to be sought by referendums (not yet held) in the four nations.

In December 1991 a four-member government delegation headed by St. Vincent's ambassador to the United States, Kingsley LAYNE, was the first such group to visit Cuba. Five months later formal diplomatic relations were established with Havana. More recently, the country further distanced itself from the United States with a declaration by Prime

Minister Gonsalves in early 2009 that it would join the Bolivarian Alternative for the Americas, launched by Venezuelan president Huge Chávez as a counter to the U.S.-backed Free Trade Area of the Americas.

St. Vincent is one of about two dozen (mainly small) countries maintaining relations with Taiwan, whose foreign minister, in a discussion of financing for a variety of projects, declared in September 2006 that even a small country could speak in support of his government's bid to join international organizations. Thus, in October 2007 Prime Minister Gonsalves asserted that it was an "insult of intelligence" that Taiwan be admitted to the World Trade Organization (WTO) but not to other international bodies.

The island's principal sources of external aid, apart from Taiwan, are Great Britain, Canada, and the United States, which contribute both bilaterally and through donations to the World Bank, the United Nations Development Programme, and the Caribbean Development Bank. Admitted to the United Nations in September 1980, St. Vincent obtained full membership in the Commonwealth in June 1985.

Current issues. In January 2008 Prime Minister Gonsalves was accused of having raped a female police constable. Two months later a High Court judge upheld a decision by the public prosecutor not to pursue the matter. However, a second indecent assault charge was leveled against the prime minister shortly thereafter by a St. Vincentan woman currently residing in Canada. Opposition members in the legislature briefly boycotted the House of Assembly because of the government's failure to file charges, while Gonsalves sought damages from a local radio station for broadcasting a report of the latest allegations.

In what was considered a major setback to the ULP government, 55 percent of the voters in a national referendum on November 25, 2009, rejected a proposed new constitution that, among other things, would have replaced Queen Elizabeth II as head of state with a president chosen by the legislature and would have replaced the UK's Privy Council with the Caribbean Court of Justice as the country's final appellate court. The NDP, which had called for a no vote because it preferred that the new president be directly elected and enjoy more than ceremonial authority, described the outcome as a plebiscite on the ULP's performance and urged Prime Minister Gonsalves to call early elections.

During 2008 Gonsalves visited Taiwan and Iran, securing pledges of assistance in the construction of a $120 million international airport. Opposition leader Arnhim EUSTACE subsequently expressed concern over links to both Teheran and Caracas, stating that the country was "going to be caught up in a web of international relations."

In what was considered a major setback to the ULP government, 55 percent of the voters in a national referendum on November 25, 2009, rejected a proposed new constitution that, among other things, would have replaced Queen Elizabeth II as head of state with a president chosen by the legislature and would have replaced the UK's Privy Council with the Caribbean Court of Justice as the country's final appellate court. The NDP, which had called for a no vote because it preferred that the new president be directly elected and enjoy more than ceremonial authority, described the outcome as a plebiscite on the ULP's performance and urged Prime Minister Gonsalves to call early elections.

POLITICAL PARTIES

Government Party:

Unity Labour Party (ULP). Formed by merger of two opposition groups, the St. Vincent and Grenadines Labour Party (SVGLP) and the Movement for National Unity (MNU), the ULP held its inaugural convention on October 16, 1994. In September 1993 the SVGLP had rejected an MNU proposal to conclude an anti-NDP alliance for the next general election; however, such an alliance, formed in January 1994, won three seats in the February 21 poll.

The SVGLP was launched in 1955 as the St. Vincent Labour Party (SVLP), a moderate socialist formation that obtained 10 of 13 elective legislative seats in the preindependence balloting of 1974 and 11 seats in December 1979. It was forced into opposition after winning only 4 seats in 1984. Soon afterward, former prime minister Robert Cato, whose relatively advanced age of 69 and recent ill health were viewed as contributing factors in the election reversal, announced his retirement from politics. Hudson TANNIS was elected party leader at a special congress in January 1985. His rival for the party leadership, Sir Vincent Ian BEACHE, was later elected parliamentary opposition leader, indicating continued competition for control of the SVLP before Tannis's death in a plane crash on August 3, 1986. Beache retired in September 1992, Stanley JOHN being elected his successor. After the February 1994 election Beache returned to lead the coalition as leader of the opposition. He again resigned as leader in December 1998, being succeeded by Dr. Ralph Gonsalves.

The MNU was organized as a moderate leftist grouping by Dr. Gonsalves following his withdrawal from the UPM (below) in 1982; it nominated two unsuccessful candidates in 1989.

The ULP was subsequently wracked by internal dissent, its deputy leader, Ormiston ("Ken") BOYEA, being criticized for joining government representatives in a meeting with EC officials on the banana issue. On May 24, 2000, Boyea resigned from the party, joining fellow dissident Stanley John, who had resigned nine days earlier. The two had accused Gonsalves of activities that were "dividing the country as well as the [ULP]" and proceeded to form a new party, the People's Progressive Movement (below). However, the ULP won an overwhelming victory in the March 2001 legislative balloting and retained its 12-seat majority in December 2005.

Leaders: Dr. Ralph E. GONSALVES (Prime Minister), Robert FITZPATRICK (Chair), Sir Vincent Ian BEACHE (Former Opposition Leader), Julian FRANCIS (Secretary General).

Other Parties:

New Democratic Party (NDP). The NDP is a basically centrist grouping formed in 1975. It became the formal opposition party after the 1979 election, although capturing only 2 legislative seats. Its leader, James Mitchell, lost his bid for reelection after abandoning his traditional seat from Beguia for a main island constituency. Subsequently, his successor from the Grenadines resigned, permitting Mitchell to regain the seat in a by-election in June 1980. Following a thorough reorganization, the NDP, campaigning in July 1984 under the slogan "Time for a Change," won 9 of the (then) 13 elective assembly seats; it captured all 15 such seats in May 1989, with a vote share of 66.2 percent. In February 1994 it dropped to 12 seats on a vote share of 54.5 percent.

Mitchell resigned as prime minister in October 2000 and was succeeded by Finance Minister Arnhim Eustace, who led the party to defeat in March 2001 and December 2005.

Leaders: Arnhim Ulric EUSTACE (Former Prime Minister, President of the Party, and Leader of the Opposition), Sir James F. MITCHELL (Former Prime Minister and Former President of the Party), Daniel E. CUMMINGS (Chair), Stuart NANTON (Secretary General).

People's Progressive Movement (PPM). The PPM was launched on August 13, 2000, by former members of the ULP. It presented 11 candidates in the March 2001 balloting but won no seats, securing only 2.6 percent of the vote; it was equally unsuccessful in December 2005.

Leaders: Ormiston ("Ken") BOYEA, Stanley ("Stalley") JOHN.

United People's Movement (UPM). The UPM was organized, under the leadership of Ralph Gonsalves, as a coalition of left-wing groups before the 1979 election, in which it obtained no parliamentary representation. Gonsalves, once described as "the leading Marxist theoretician in the Caribbean," left the party in 1982 to form the MNU, his role as radical leftist advocate being assumed by Oscar Allen. The party has never secured legislative representation.

Leader: Oscar ALLEN.

St. Vincent and the Grenadines Green Party (SVGGP). Launched in January 2005, the Green Party won no seats in the December balloting.

Leader: Ivan O'NEAL.

People's Movement For Change (PMC). The PMC was launched in July 2008 as a "social-political movement" designed to "raise the consciousness of the people" by focusing on crucial national issues.

Leader: Jomo THOMAS.

Canovan People's Movement (CPM). The CPM represents inhabitants of the Grenadine islet of Canovan.

Leader: Terry BYNOE.

LEGISLATURE

The unicameral **House of Assembly** currently consists of 6 appointed senators and 15 representatives elected from single-member constituencies for five-year terms, subject to dissolution. In the most recent balloting of December 7, 2005, the Unity Labour Party won 12 of the elective seats and the New Democratic Party, 3.

Speaker: Hendrick ALEXANDER.

CABINET

[as of July 1, 2009]

Prime Minister	Dr. Ralph E. Gonsalves
Deputy Prime Minister	Sir Louis Straker
Ministers	
Agriculture, Forestry, and Fisheries	Montgomery Daniel
Education	Girlyn Miguel [f]
Finance and Economic Planning	Dr. Ralph E. Gonsalves
Foreign Affairs and International Trade	Sir Louis Straker
Grenadine Affairs	Dr. Ralph E. Gonsalves
Health and Environment	Dr. Douglas Slater
Housing, Informal Human Settlements, Physical Planning, Lands, and Surveys	Julian Francis
Legal Affairs	Dr. Ralph E. Gonsalves
National Mobilization, Social Development, NGO Relations, Family and Gender Affairs, and Persons with Disabilities	Michael Browne
National Security and Public Service	Dr. Ralph E. Gonsalves
Rural Transformation, Information, and Ecclesiastical Affairs	Selmon Walters
Telecommunications, Science, Technology, and Industry	Dr. Jerrol Thompson
Tourism, Youth, and Sports	Glen Beache
Transport and Works	Clayton Burgin
Urban Development, Labor, Culture, and Electoral Matters	René Baptiste [f]
Attorney General	Judith S. Jones-Morgan [f]
Minister of State	
Prime Minister's Office in Charge of Public Service	Conrad Sayers

[f] = female

COMMUNICATIONS

Press. The following are published in Kingstown: *The Vincentian* (6,000), independent weekly; *Justice,* UPM weekly; *The New Times,* NDP weekly; *The News,* weekly; *The Star,* ULP fortnightly; *Unity,* ULP fortnightly.

News agency. There is no domestic facility. Foreign news is provided by the Caribbean News Agency (CANA).

Broadcasting and computing. St. Vincent's National Broadcasting Corporation provides local programming as well as BBC news from Kingstown. In May 1987 the government-owned station, Radio 705, was directed not to edit official press releases and to refrain from broadcasting "opposition propaganda" without specific authorization of its manager. The order—bitterly attacked by the NDP's political adversaries as "high-handed interference" with freedom of speech—was defended as a necessary precaution against those "who would seek to cunningly exploit" the administration's commitment to democracy. Subsequently, in April 1988, a radio phone-in program was ordered off the air on the grounds that it had become a vehicle for "blatant mischief-making."

SVG Television transmits both U.S. and local programs via broadcast and cable facilities. As of 2008 there were 604.9 Internet users per 1,000 inhabitants.

INTERGOVERNMENTAL REPRESENTATION

Ambassador to the U.S.: La Celia PRINCE.

U.S. Ambassador to St. Vincent: (Vacant).

Permanent Representative to the UN: Camillo GONSALVES.

IGO Memberships (Non-UN): ACS, Caricom, CDB, CWTH, Interpol, NAM, OAS, OECS, OPANAL, WTO.

SAMOA

Independent State of Samoa
Sa 'oloto Tuto 'atasi o Samoa

Note: There is considerable confusion regarding Samoan proper names, the initial component being generally accorded benchmark status and, with some exceptions, utilized herein as such.

Political Status: Independent state since January 1, 1962; member of the Commonwealth since 1970; under mixed political system approximating a constitutional monarchy.

Area: 1,097 sq. mi. (2,842 sq. km.).

Population: 179,186 (2006C); 191,000 (2008E). The 2006 figure is provisional.

Major Urban Center (2005E): APIA (40,700).

Official Languages: English, Samoan.

Monetary Unit: Tala (official rate December 1, 2009: 2.49 tala = $1US).

Head of State: TUIATUA Tupua Tamasese Taisi Tupuola Tufuga Efi; elected by the Legislative Assembly and installed on June 20, 2007, succeeding Susuga MALIETOA Tanumafili II, who had died on May 12.

Prime Minister: TUILA'EPA Sa'ilele Malielegaoi (Human Rights Protection Party); confirmed by the Legislative Assembly on November 23, 1998, following the resignation of TOFILAU Eti Alesana (Human Rights Protection Party); continued in office following the elections of March 2, 2001, and March 31, 2006.

THE COUNTRY

What was formerly called Western Samoa consists of two volcanic islands (Savai'i and Upolu) and several minor islets located east of Fiji and west of American Samoa in the south central Pacific. The country enjoys a tropical climate and good volcanic soils, but rugged topography limits the cultivated and populated areas to the lowlands and coastal fringes. The Christian, highly literate Samoans are representatives of the second-largest ethnic group of Polynesia. They have had lengthy contact with the West but retain their traditional social structure. This structure is based on an extended family grouping known as the *aiga,* whose chief, or *matai,* serves also as the group's political representative.

The economy is largely based on subsistence agriculture and fishing, supplemented by the production of copra, coffee, and bananas for export. (Cocoa was an increasingly important cash crop in the 1980s but is currently limited primarily to domestic consumption.) Basic raw materials are lacking and the country suffers from a chronic trade deficit, part of which is offset by tourism and remittances from Samoans living in New Zealand and the United States.

Listed by the United Nations as a Least Developed Country (LDC), Samoa was ravaged by cyclones in February 1990 and December 1991 that decimated crucial banana, cocoa, and coconut plantations, leaving the economy in tatters. In 1993 leaf blight of the taro, a plant cultivated widely throughout tropical regions of Asia for its edible tuber, threatened devastation of another major crop. Nonetheless, real economic growth, led by a surge in exports, averaged over 6 percent per year in 1995 and 1996 before declining to 1.6 percent in 1997. Growth of about 3.5 percent was achieved in 1998 (primarily due to a boom in commercial tuna fishing) with inflation declining to 2.2 percent (from nearly 7 percent in 1997). Growth rose to 5.6 percent in 1999 and to an estimated 6.8 percent in 2000, with inflation averaging less than 1 percent for the two-year period. The economic improvement was attributed, in part, to government initiatives to support the private sector, which have included tax breaks for foreign investors, modernization of customs procedures, and reduction of import tariffs. The government has also privatized some state-run enterprises while promoting the fledgling

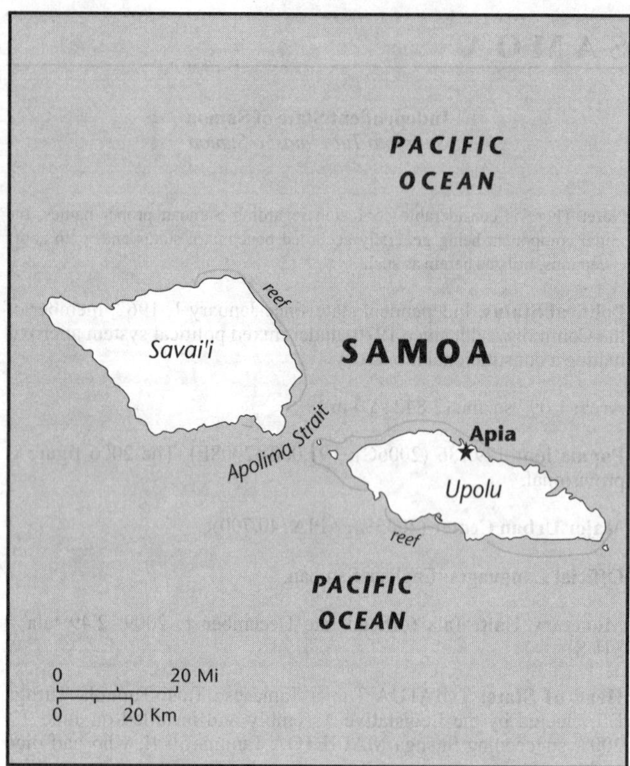

offshore banking sector. Efforts to improve oversight of offshore facilities followed criticism in June 2001 by the Organization for Economic Cooperation and Development, which included Samoa on a list of jurisdictions with questionable tax policies. Although formally deleted from the list a year later, Samoa continued to attract attention as a tax haven, most recently in early 2008.

Triggered by a widening trade deficit, the economy wavered from 2001 through 2007, GDP growth averaging 3.2 percent annually for the period. However, GDP declined by 3.4 percent in 2008 with little hope of immediate recovery because of the global recession. Meanwhile, inflation (normally close to changes in GDP) surged to an annual rate of 13.8 percent in May 2009.

GOVERNMENT AND POLITICS

Political background. An object of missionary interest since the 1830s, the Samoan Islands came under joint British, German, and American supervision in 1889 but were politically divided as a consequence of an 1899 treaty whereby the United States annexed Eastern (American) Samoa, while Western Samoa became a German protectorate. New Zealand occupied Western Samoa during World War I and acquired subsequent control of the territory under a League of Nations mandate. Opposition to the New Zealand administration resulted in the formation of a nationalist organization known as the "Mau," which was active between 1927 and 1936.

Following World War II a Samoan request for independence was rejected, and Western Samoa continued under New Zealand administration as a United Nations Trust Territory. Political evolution, however, gained momentum. Cabinet government was introduced in 1959; a new constitution, adopted in 1960, was approved by plebiscite in 1961; and the country became fully independent by agreement with New Zealand and the United Nations on January 1, 1962. The largely ceremonial position of head of state was at first held jointly by the representatives of two of the four royal lines (the Tuiaana/Tuiatua and the Malietoa), but one of the incumbents died in 1963. The other, MALIETOA Tanumafili II, continued in office until his death in May 2007.

Political life since independence has seen a number of changes as well as a series of recent challenges to certain aspects of the country's constitutional structure. The first government after independence lasted through 1970 under Prime Minister FIAME Mata'afa, when it was replaced by an administration headed by Tupua TAMASESE Lealofi IV. The Tamasese regime was in turn succeeded in 1973 by another Fiame government, although Tamasese returned as acting prime minister to serve the remainder of Fiame's term upon the latter's death in May 1975. In March 1976, following a legislative election in which over half of the incumbents lost their seats, TUPUOLA Taisi Efi became the first prime minister not a *Tama Aiga* ("Royal Son") from one of the four leading families. After balloting on February 24, 1979, that again saw over half the assembly members defeated, Tupuola was redesignated prime minister after legislative endorsement by a narrow vote of 24–23.

In the election of February 27, 1982, the islands' first formally constituted political group, the Human Rights Protection Party (HRPP), won a plurality of 22 parliamentary seats and after a lengthy period of consultation with independent members succeeded, on April 13, in organizing a government under VA'AI Kolone. However, the party lost its 1-seat majority in late June upon the ouster of a member found guilty of electoral malpractice, and on September 18 Va'ai's own seat was vacated by the Supreme Court on similar grounds. Former prime minister Tupuola was thereupon returned to office, although his attempt to form a coalition government was rebuffed by the HRPP, which argued that the court had exceeded its authority in its expulsion orders. Upon rejection of a budget bill, Tupuola was again forced to resign, and the new HRPP leader, TOFILAU Eti Alesana, succeeded him on December 30, the party having regained its majority in special elections to refill the vacated seats. In mid-1984 opposition leader Tupuola was designated a *Tama Aiga* in succession to his cousin, former prime minister Tamasese Lealofi IV, thenceforth being addressed as TUIATUA Tupua Tamasese Efi.

The HRPP captured 31 of 47 assembly seats in the election of February 22, 1985, Tofilau Eti being redesignated prime minister after former prime minister Va'ai Kolone had withdrawn a bid to recover the party leadership. Despite his party's technical majority, Tofilau was forced to resign on December 27, 1985, after members of the HRPP joined with the opposition (now including Va'ai) to defeat the 1986 budget bill on a 27–19 vote. During the following week a new coalition government headed by Va'ai was formed, the head of state having rejected a request to dissolve the assembly.

The results of the extremely close election of February 26, 1988, were not announced until the new assembly convened on April 7, at which time the HRPP was declared to have obtained a bare majority of 24 seats, with Tofilau Eti returning as prime minister. By late summer, following a number of Supreme Court rulings on electoral challenges and a series of special elections, HRPP's representation had increased to 27.

In a popular referendum on October 29, 1990, voters, by a narrow margin, indicated that they favored the adoption of universal suffrage for all persons 21 or over (albeit with only chiefs eligible as candidates), while rejecting by a 3–2 margin the establishment of an upper chamber reserved for *matai*. Under the new procedure the HRPP won an increased majority of 30 seats (1 of which was subsequently vacated) in the election of April 5, 1991, with Tofilau Eti forming a new government on May 14.

In early 1994 the introduction of a value-added tax on goods and services generated a series of demonstrations and protest marches, one of the latter being led by the head of the Catholic Church in Apia, Cardinal PIO Taofinuu, who called for the exemption of such items as food and school supplies. The HRPP responded by expelling 3 antitax members, thereby reducing its position (in the wake of several 1993 defections) to a legislative plurality of 23 seats. However, by March 1995, after special elections and other realignments, it had regained a majority of 33.

In the election of April 26, 1996, government representation declined further to 22, with a loss of 3 cabinet members and the assembly speaker. However, Tofilau Eti retained office by a 34–14 vote on May 17, with a number of independents entering the HRPP to establish its majority once more.

In early 1997 Tofilau Eti introduced a constitutional amendment, which was subsequently approved, to change the country's name from Western Samoa to Samoa. The change was bitterly opposed by American Samoans, who were, however, unable to secure a reversal.

Tofilau Eti, who had long been in ill health, resigned as prime minister in favor of his deputy, TUIA'EPA Sa'ilele Malielegaoi, on November 23, 1998, and died four months later.

Questionable practices by high-level officials were apparently involved in the bizarre murder of Public Works Minister LUAGALAU

Levaula Kamu on July 16, 1999. Eletise Leafa VITALE, the son of former Women's Affairs minister Leafa VITALE, was arrested and on August 7 sentenced to death for the crime. The elder Vitale and former Post Office and Telecommunications Minister Toi AUKUSO were subsequently charged with complicity in Luagalau's death and on April 14, 2000, were also given death sentences, which were, however, commuted by the head of state on May 12.

Prime Minister Tuila'epa was returned to office following the legislative election of March 2, 2001, although the HRPP required the adherence of independents to secure his confirmation and establish a working majority in the Legislative Assembly. He was returned with a far more commanding majority of 33 after the election of March 31, 2006.

Prior to his death on May 12, 2007, Malietoa Tanumafili II, at age 95, had been recognized as the world's oldest surviving head of state, having served since Samoa's independence in 1962. He was succeeded on May 12 by Tuiatua Tupua Tamasese Efi.

Constitution and government. As defined by the constitution of October 28, 1960, Samoa's political institutions combine the forms of British-style parliamentary democracy with elements of the traditional Samoan social structure. The head of state (*O le Ao o le Malo*) performs the duties of a constitutional sovereign. Formerly designated for life, heads of state are now elected by the Legislative Assembly (*Fono Aoao Faitulafono*) for five-year terms. The head of state appoints the prime minister and, on the latter's advice, members of the cabinet, who are drawn from the assembly and are responsible to that body. Traditionally, most members of the legislature were indirectly elected by *matai,* or family heads, whose number was increased by one-third to 16,000 in a series of controversial appointments before the 1985 balloting; direct election was limited to two special representatives chosen by universal adult suffrage of persons outside the *matai* system.

Although universal suffrage (without universal right of candidacy) was endorsed in the October 1990 referendum, the *Washington Pacific Report* noted that "only 62.4 percent [of the eligible voters] were registered, only 46.3 percent voted and only 22.9 percent actually backed . . . the measure." A similar franchise extension had been rejected by the assembly in 1981; however, with chiefly titles being created at a rate exceeding that of population growth and with some individuals holding multiple titles (each carrying an electoral vote), the *matai* system had come under mounting criticism. Given the increasingly prevalent practice of bestowing titles for political purposes, universal suffrage, ironically, came to be viewed as a means of maintaining historic Samoan values.

The judicial system is headed by a Supreme Court and includes a Court of Appeal, magistrates' courts, and a special Land and Titles Court for dealing with disputes over customary land and Samoan titles.

For the most part, local government is carried out through the *matai* system and includes the institution of the village *fono,* or council. There are some part-time government officials who operate in rural areas.

Foreign relations. Samoa has established diplomatic relations with over two dozen other countries (including the People's Republic of China), most of which conduct relations with Apia through diplomats accredited to New Zealand. Although not choosing to apply for United Nations membership until 1976, Samoa had previously joined a number of UN subsidiary agencies and other international organizations, including the World Health Organization, the International Monetary Fund, and the World Bank group, in addition to such regional organizations as the South Pacific Commission (now the Pacific Community). Its admission to the World Trade Organization was under negotiation as of mid-2009.

Relations with the country's principal trading partner, New Zealand, which had been cordial since independence, cooled in 1978 and 1979 as a result of Wellington's attempt to expel some 200 Samoan "overstayers" who had expected to be granted New Zealand citizenship. Subsequently, the Judicial Committee of the Privy Council in London ruled that all Western Samoans born between 1928 and 1949 (when New Zealand passed legislation separating its own citizenship from that of Britain), as well as their children, were entitled to such rights. However, the decision was effectively invalidated by an agreement concluded in mid-1982 by prime ministers Va'ai Kolone and Robert Muldoon whereby only the estimated 50,000 Samoans resident in New Zealand could claim citizenship. The accord was widely criticized within Samoa, then opposition leader Tupuola Efi chastising the government for abrogating "a basic tenet of the Anglo-Saxon legal heritage that the right to legal citizenship can only be surrendered by personal choice." A related issue arose in early 1989, when Wellington announced that it might terminate a special immigration quota for Samoans on the ground that the immigrants were contributing to New Zealand's high rate of unemployment. The dispute was partially resolved at midyear with a statement from Prime Minister David Lange that the quota would remain, with a stricter application of its rules. Subsequently, in September 1991, the Samoan government indicated that it would not seek amnesty from Wellington for 7,500 overstayers, following assurances by New Zealand authorities that their appeal rights would be protected. There have also been many visa overstayers in American Samoa, where it is estimated that some 37,000 of the territory's 57,000 inhabitants are nonnative. The problem is not viewed as seriously as elsewhere because of the shared cultural identity of the two island peoples; their shared identity was, however, central to American Samoa's objection to adoption of the unqualified name "Samoa" by its western neighbor. In early 1998 the lower house of the territorial legislature approved a bill that would have refused entry to anyone whose passport bore the new name; however, the measure subsequently died in the Senate.

As with a number of other financially strapped countries, accusations have been made of the illegal sale of passports to Chinese nationals. Prime Minister Tofilau Eti denied any knowledge of such a practice, although a number of individuals were formally indicted in the matter, including the former ambassador to the United States, Dr. Tuaopepe Felix WENDT.

Current issues. Claiming that the HRPP had stifled the opposition by "paternalistic and unlawful application of [legislative] Standing Orders," opposition leader ASIATA Saleimoa Va'ai published a lengthy critique of the ruling party in the *Samoa Observer* on February 17, 2009. He insisted that Samoa's governance had become that of a "one-party dictatorship," with both the prime minister and Assembly Speaker TOLOFUAIVALELEI Falemoe Leiataua engaging in a variety of alleged unconstitutional acts, particularly the SNDP's loss of parliamentary status (including voidance of Asiata's role as leader of the opposition) because defections had reduced the party's representation to less than a statutory minimum of eight members.

Joining in antigovernment protests were the recently organized People's and Tautua Samoa parties. Launched in July 2008, the People's Party campaigned initially for revocation of a controversial Road Transport Reform Bill that in September 2009 would change road driving from right to left, in accordance with the procedure in Australia and New Zealand. Formed in December 2008, the Tautua Samoa grouping consisted of nine independent legislators whose seats were declared vacant for violating Statutory Orders by establishing a new party prior to parliamentary dissolution.

POLITICAL PARTIES

Traditionally there were no political parties in Western Samoa. Following the 1979 election, the Human Rights Protection Party (HRPP) was organized by Va'ai Kolone to oppose the reconfirmation of Tupuola Efi as prime minister. Following his expulsion from the Legislative Assembly in 1982, Va'ai turned the party leadership over to Tofilau Eti Alesana and, upon his return, sat as an opposition independent before joining the Samoan National Development Party (SNDP). (Va'ai Kolone died in April 2001.)

A number of short-lived parties were formed during the 1990s. The Samoa Democratic Party was launched in 1993 by previously independent *Fono* deputy LE TAGALOA Pita, who objected to the two-year extension of the parliamentary mandate (see under Legislature, below) without submission of the issue to a popular referendum. The Samoa Liberal Party (SLP) was formed in 1994 by four deputies, including three expelled from the HRPP, who had opposed the goods and services tax. The Samoa Labour Party (SLP) was launched in 1994 by TOLEAPAIALI'I Siueva, an outspoken resort operator, who succeeded in defeating the incumbent *Fono* speaker in the 1996 election before resigning in the face of bribery charges. The Samoa All-People's Party (SAPP) was organized before the 1996 election by a previously independent deputy, MATATUMUA Maimoaga, who failed to retain her seat.

Governing Party:

Human Rights Protection Party (HRPP). One seat short of a legislative majority after its formation in 1979, the HRPP won 22 of

47 seats in the February 1982 balloting and, after protracted negotiation with independent members, secured a 1-seat majority that permitted the installation of a Va'ai Kolone government on April 13. As a result of legal actions in late June and mid-September, 2 seats, including the prime minister's, were lost, Va'ai turning the party leadership over to Tofilau Eti Alesana, who was able to form a new HRPP government at the end of the year. Tofilau subsequently led the HRPP to a landslide 31–16 victory in the election of February 22, 1985, but lost control of the government in December by defection of HRPP members to the opposition. Gaining a new term as prime minister by the barest possible legislative majority in April 1988, he described the party's program as emphasizing "electrification, sealed roads, and water supplies for the whole country." Declaring that it would be his last, the HRPP leader formed a drastically restructured government following the election of April 5, 1991. Despite a serious heart condition, he reversed himself in 1996 and won easy reelection. His party was less successful, declining to a plurality of 22 seats before regaining a majority with the conversion of independents.

Tofilau Eti's successor as prime minister, Tuila'epa Malielegaoi, carried the party to a plurality in the March 2001 election, after which the HRPP attracted enough independents to claim a majority of 28 seats when the new Legislative Assembly convened and gained 2 additional seats as a result of subsequent special elections.

The HRPP led the balloting of March 31, 2006, and with the addition of 5 members who had campaigned as independents, held a commanding majority of 33 legislative seats. After being augmented further by 2 additional former independents, its majority was returned to 33 in early 2008 by the defection of 2 members over the road driving issue (see Current issues, above).

Leaders: TUILA'EPA Sa'ilele Malielegaoi (Prime Minister), Misa TELEFONI Retzlaff (Deputy Prime Minister), Laulu Dan STANLEY (General Secretary).

Parliamentary Opposition:

Samoa Democratic United Party (SDUP). The SDUP was formed in 2003 by the merger of the Samoan National Development Party (SNDP) and the Samoan United Independent Party (SUIP) following disqualification of the SNDP for providing the Interparliamentary Union with allegedly false information about the government. The SNDP had been formed by opposition leader Tuiatua Efi after the 1988 election. The new group was reportedly backed by members of the former Christian Democratic Party (organized by Tuiatua before the 1985 balloting, in which it won 16 seats), in addition to defectors from the HRPP. It slipped to 14 seats in 1991 and to 13 in 1996. By mid-1997 SNDP representation had dropped to 8 MPs, 1 fewer than required by Samoan law to retain official recognition.

In the March 2001 general election the SNDP finished with 13 seats and proceeded to fashion a coalition with the SUIP. Before the opening of the new legislative session the coalition claimed to have sufficient support to form a new government, but it ended up 4 seats short of a majority, with 21. It therefore remained in opposition under Le MAMEA Ropati Mualia, who replaced Tuiatua Efi as leader of the party and of the opposition.

The SUIP was registered as a party before the March 2001 election, in which it initially claimed 13 seats after the balloting; however, the number fell to 7 following recounts and defections to the HRPP. After formation of an opposition coalition with the SNDP, Asiata Saleimoa Va'ai, a son of former prime minister Va'ai Kolone, was selected as leader of the opposition in the *Fono,* but he voluntarily surrendered the post to Mamea Ropati of the larger SNDP. However, in September 2006 Mamea left the party to sit as an independent, with Asiata resuming the role of opposition leader.

Leaders: ASIATA Saleimoa Va'ai (Leader of the Opposition), VELASI Tafito (Secretary).

Other Parties:

People's Party (PP). The PP was launched in July 2008 and held its first convention two months later. Its immediate objective was revocation of the law mandating left of the road driving, which it insisted would generate an increase in highway accidents.

Leader: MAPOSUA Teleafoa Punafelutu Solomona Toailoa (President).

Tautua Samoa Party (TSP). Formation of the TSP was announced in December 2008. It claimed the support of 11 *Fono* members who were, however, reported to have remained independents to avoid legislative expulsion (see Current issues, above).

Leader: LEALAILEPULE Rimoni Aiafi (Chair).

Samoan Party (SP). The SP was formed in September 2005 by Su'a Rimoni Ah Chong, who had been dismissed as auditor general in 1995 for issuing a report that criticized government corruption. The party won no seats in March 2006, and in September Rimoni was convicted of bribery during the electoral campaign.

Leader: Su'a RIMONI Ah Chong.

Samoan Christian Party (SCP). Also referenced simply as the Christian Party (CP), the SCP is primarily a women's party.

Leader: Tuala TIRESA Malietoa.

There is also a recently launched **Samoan Progressive Political Party** (SPPP) that is without legislative representation, while a number of parties that presented candidates in 2001, including the Faamatai Party (FP), the Pati Samoa Aoao (PSA), the Samoa National Party (SNP), and the Samoa United People's Party (SUPP), are now considered defunct.

LEGISLATURE

In November 1991 the term of the unicameral **Legislative Assembly** (*Fono Aoao Faitulafono*) was changed from three to five years (subject to dissolution), with 2 seats being added to the existing 47. In the most recent election of March 31, 2006, 47 *matai* were elected from territorial constituencies by universal suffrage of persons over 21, with an additional 2 members elected by and from those outside the *matai* system. After the balloting the Human Rights Protection Party held 33 seats; the Samoa Democratic United Party, 10; and independents, 6.

Speaker: TOLOFUAIVALELEI Falemoe Leiataua.

CABINET

[as of August 1, 2009]

Prime Minister	Tuila'epa Sailele Malielegaoi
Deputy Prime Minister	Misa Telefoni Retzlaff
Ministers	
Agriculture, Forests, and Fisheries	Taua Tavagokitiona Seuala
Commerce and Industry	Misa Telefoni Retzlaff
Community and Social Development	Fiame Naomi Mata'afa [f]
Education, Sports, and Culture	Toomata Alapati Poesi Toomata
Finance and National Provident Fund	Niko Lee Hang
Foreign Affairs	Tuila'epa Sailele Malielegaoi
Foreign Trade	Misa Telefoni Retzlaff
Health	Gatoloaifaana Amataga Alesana Gidlow [f]
Immigration	Tuila'epa Sailele Malielegaoi
Justice	Unasa Mesi Galo
Labor	Misa Telefoni Retzlaff
Natural Resources and Environment	Faumuina Tiatia Liuga
Parliamentary Affairs	Misa Telfoni Retzlaff
Police, Prisons, and Fire Service	Toleafoa Apulu Faafisi
Public Service Commission	Fiame Naomi Mata'afa [f]
Revenue	Tuu'u Anasi'i Leota
Telecommunications and Broadcasting	Safuneitu'uga Pa'aga Neri [f]
Tourism	Misa Telefoni Retzlaff
Women's Affairs	Fiame Naomi Mata'afa [f]
Works, Transport and Infrastructure	Tuisugaletaua Safara Aveau
Attorney General	Ming Leung Wai

[f] = female

COMMUNICATIONS

Press. Freedom of the press is constitutionally guaranteed, although instances of implicit censorship or of contempt citations against journalists are not unknown. The following are issued in Apia in English and Samoan: *Samoa News* (5,000), daily, merged with the weekly *Samoa Times* in 1994; *The Samoa Observer* (4,600), independent daily; *Samoa Weekly* (4,000); *Savali* (2,000), government fortnightly. During 1997 concern arose over threats by the government to impede publication of the *Samoa Observer,* the country's only daily. The paper faced $1.6 million in libel and defamation suits as representative of influences that "stir up trouble" but went on to become the first Pacific paper to win the 1998 Astor Award for press freedom in the Commonwealth.

Broadcasting and computing. The Samoa Broadcasting Service is a government-controlled body that provides commercial radio service in English and Samoan. Domestic television broadcasting was initiated in mid-1993, with two channels joined by a third in May 2006. The country's 40,000 television sets can also receive programming from American Samoa.

As of 2008 there were 50.3 Internet users per 1,000 inhabitants.

INTERGOVERNMENTAL REPRESENTATION

Ambassador to the U.S. and Permanent Representative to the UN: Ali'ioaiga Feturi ELISAIA.

U.S. Ambassador to Samoa: (Vacant).

IGO Memberships (Non-UN): ADB, CWTH, PC, PIF, WCO.

SAN MARINO

Most Serene Republic of San Marino
Serenissima Repubblica di San Marino

Political Status: Independent republic dating from the early Middle Ages; under multiparty parliamentary regime.

Area: 23.6 sq. mi. (61 sq. km.).

Population: 30,368 (2006C), of whom 26,432 were listed as native Sammarinese; 31,200 (2008E), not including some 13,000 Sammarinese residents abroad.

Major Urban Center (2005E): SAN MARINO (4,800).

Official Language: Italian.

Monetary Unit: Euro (market rate December 1, 2009: 1 euro = $1.51US).

Captains Regent: Massimo CENCI (New Socialist Party) and Oscar MINA (San Marino Christian Democratic Party); elected in March 2009 by the Grand and General Council for six-month terms beginning April 1, replacing Ernesto BENEDETTINI (San Marino Christian Democratic Party) and Assunta MELONI (Popular Alliance).

THE COUNTRY

An enclave within the Italian province of Emilia-Romagna, San Marino is the world's oldest and second-smallest republic (after Nauru). Its terrain is mountainous, the highest point being Mount Titano, on the western slope of which is located the city of San Marino. The Sammarinese are ethnically and culturally Italian, but their long history has created a strong sense of identity and independence. The principal economic activities are service-related industries, especially nonresident banking and financial services as well as tourism, and some light manufacturing. Agriculture now employs fewer than 2 percent of the workforce; olives and wine grapes rank with various grains as important crops. Wine, textiles, varnishes, ceramics, woolen goods, furniture, and building stone are chief exports. Traditional sources of income include the sale of coins and postage stamps and an annual budget subsidy from the Italian government. Some 3.3 million tourists visit annually.

By virtue of its economic union with Italy, San Marino became part of the European Economic Community (EEC) in the 1950s. It now has a separate customs union and cooperation agreement with the European Union (EU). Annual GDP grew steadily throughout the 1990s, averaging 7 percent annually, while the growth of the tourism industry contributed to an influx of cross-border workers (nearly one-fourth of the labor force). After stagnating early in the decade in the wake of a decline in the manufacturing sector, economic growth rose to a robust 5 percent in 2006, thanks largely to a series of regulatory reforms, spending cuts, and initiatives to boost competitiveness in services. Most economic indicators continued on a positive note at the end of 2007, with economic growth at 4.5 percent, a government budget surplus of $48 million, and unemployment at an almost negligible 2 percent. Despite a continuing budget surplus, the global recession began to take a toll on San Marino in 2008, as economic growth slowed to 2 percent and unemployment rose to 5 percent by February 2009.

GOVERNMENT AND POLITICS

Political background. Reputedly founded in 301 A.D., San Marino is the sole survivor of the numerous independent states that existed in Italy prior to unification in the 19th century. A treaty of friendship and cooperation concluded with the Kingdom of Italy in 1862 has subsequently been renewed and amended at varying intervals.

A coalition of Communists (*Partito Comunista Sammarinese*—PCS) and Socialists (*Partito Socialista Sammarinese*—PSS) controlled the government until 1957, when, because of defections from its ranks, the coalition lost its majority to the opposition Popular Alliance (composed mainly of Christian Democrats and Social Democrats). The San Marino Christian Democratic Party (*Partito Democratico Cristiano Sammarinese*—PDCS) remained the plurality party in the elections of 1959, 1964, and 1969 but required the continuing support of the San Marino Independent Social Democratic Party (*Partito Socialista Democratico Indipendente Sammarinese*—PSDIS) to cement a governing majority. The coalition split over economic policy in January 1973, enabling the Socialists to return to power in alliance with the Christian Democrats. In the September 1974 election (the first in which women were allowed to present themselves as candidates for the Grand and General Council), the Christian Democrats and the Social Democrats each lost two seats, while the Communists and the Socialists experienced small gains.

In November 1977 the Socialists withdrew from the government, accusing the Christian Democrats of being bereft of ideas for resolving the country's economic difficulties. Following a lengthy impasse marked by successive failures of the Christian Democrats, Communists, and Socialists to form a new government, a premature general election was held in May 1978, but the balance of legislative power remained virtually unchanged. Subsequently, the Christian Democrats again failed to secure a mandate, and in July a "Government of Democratic Collaboration" involving the Communists, Socialists, and the Socialist Unity Party (*Partito Socialista Unitario*—PSU, principal successor to the PSDIS) was approved by a bare parliamentary majority of 31 votes. The other PSDIS successor, the San Marino Social Democratic Party (*Partito Socialista Democratico Sammarinese*—PSDS), joined the governing coalition in 1982 but returned to opposition after the May 1983 election, in which the ruling parties gained an additional council seat. The leftist government fell in June 1986, when the Communist and Socialist Unity parties withdrew over foreign policy and other issues. In late July the council, by a 39–13 vote, approved a new program advanced by the Christian Democratic and Communist parties, the first such coalition in the country's history. The coalition was renewed in June 1988, following a general election in May in which the governing parties gained four seats at the expense of a divided Socialist

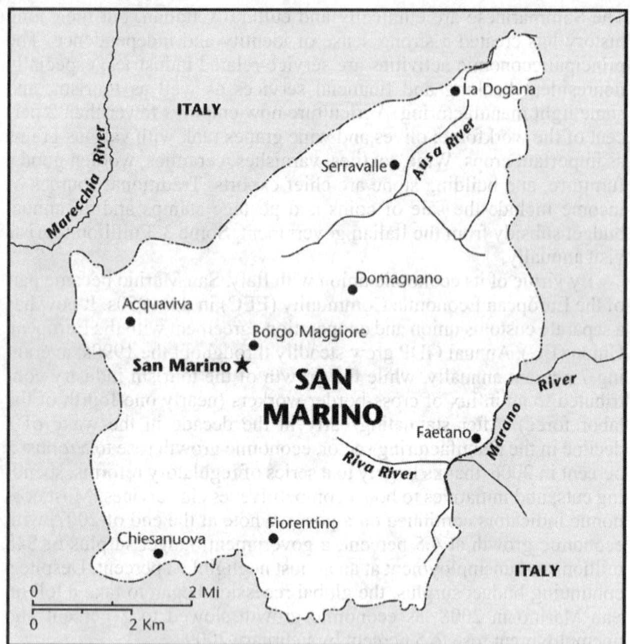

opposition. In 1990 the PCS, responding to recent events in Eastern Europe, recast itself as the San Marino Progressive Democratic Party (*Partito Progressista Democratico Sammarinese*—PPDS).

On February 24, 1992, the Christian Democrats withdrew from their coalition with the PPDS and forged a new ruling alliance with the recently reunified Socialists (see Political Parties, below). The outcome of the May 30, 1993, election was notable for the emergence of three smaller parties, although the ruling center-left coalition of the PDCS and the PSS retained a comfortable majority in the Grand and General Council. The coalition was renewed following the May 1998 legislative elections.

In February 2000 the Socialists withdrew from the government because of policy differences. The Christian Democrats then turned to the PPDS to ensure a new legislative majority, and on March 28 a government of the Christian Democrats, the Progressive Democrats, and the Socialists for Reform (*Socialisti per le Riforme*—SpR) assumed office. In February 2001, after the Christian Democrats rebuffed efforts to introduce measures aimed at tightening the country's financial and tax regulations, another crisis ensued, leading to premature dissolution of the legislature on March 11.

As in 1998, the 2001 pre-election debate raised questions about the republic's relationship with the EU, which centered on San Marino's status as a tax haven. The EU, which in November 2000 proposed an open exchange of information on nonresident investment accounts, maintained that financial secrecy creates an uneven playing field in the markets, erodes members' tax bases, and facilitates fraud. Indeed, Italian tax officials had launched raids throughout San Marino in July 1998 to snare tax evaders, estimated to cost Rome $600 million annually. The issue appeared to be largely resolved by an accord that went into effect in 2005, under which certain tax havens, including San Marino, agreed to withhold taxes on foreign deposits without disclosing confidential information on those accounts.

The legislative election held June 10, 2001, resulted in only minor changes in the makeup of the Grand and General Council. The PDCS remained in the plurality, claiming 25 seats on a vote share of 41.5 percent, while the PSS took 15 seats on 24.2 percent of the vote. Third place (20.8 percent of the vote and 12 seats) went to the newly organized Party of Democrats (*Partito dei Democratici*—PdD), successor to the PPDS, the SpR, and Ideas in Motion (*Idee in Movimento*—IM). Following the election, the PDCS, and PSS established a new coalition, but the PSS again withdrew on June 5, 2002. Subsequently, the PSS, the PdD, and the small San Marino Popular Democratic Alliance (*Alleanza Popolare dei Democratici Sammarinesi*—APDS) formed a new government that excluded the Christian Democrats. However, that government collapsed in December and was replaced with a PSS/PDCS coalition; the PdD rejoined the government in December 2003.

Following the election of June 4, 2006, a center-left coalition government was formed by the recently established Party of Socialists and Democrats (*Partito dei Socialisti e dei Democratici*—PSD), which resulted from the merger of the PSS and PdD, the Popular Alliance (*Alleanza Popolare*—AP, the renamed APDS), and the small United Left (*Sinistra Unita*—SU) alliance. On July 17 the new government presented its program, an ambitious call for broad-based political and economic reforms it claimed would enable San Marino to overcome the economic stagnation and political corruption overseen by center-right governments in the 1990s.

Shortly after taking office in 2006, the new government adopted an electoral law aimed at improving political stability by favoring the emergence of a two-party system. The new law required parties and coalitions to present their programs before elections and barred them from changing them upon gaining power. It required parties to win at least 3.5 percent of the vote to claim a seat in the council and required winning coalitions to remain intact throughout their terms in office.

The center-right returned to power following the most recent election on November 9, 2008, winning 35 seats on the council as the Pact for San Marino coalition, compared with 25 for the center-left opposition coalition, Reforms and Liberty. In March 2009 the council elected Massimo Cenci of the New Socialist Party (NPS) and Oscar Mina of the PDCS to six-month terms as captains regent, with the terms set to end on October 1.

Constitution and government. Although a document dating from 1600 is sometimes referenced as San Marino's constitution, it is perhaps more accurate to say the republic has no codified, formal constitution but rather a constitutional tradition that is hundreds of years old. Legislative power is vested in the Grand and General Council (*Consiglio Grande e Generale*) of 60 members directly elected for five-year terms, subject to dissolution. A ten-member Congress of State (*Congresso di Stato*), or cabinet, is elected by the council for the duration of its term. Two members of the council are designated for six-month terms as captains regent (*capitani reggenti*). They are the heads of state but under normal circumstances do not set policy; both have equal power. Each is eligible for reelection three years after the expiration of the term. The judicial system encompasses justices of the peace (the only level not entrusted to Italian personnel); a law commissioner and assistant law commissioner, who deal with both civil and criminal cases; a criminal judge of the Primary Court of Claims (involving penalties greater than three years); two Appeals Court judges; and a Council of Twelve (*Consiglio dei XII*), which serves as a final court of appeals in civil cases only.

Administratively, San Marino is divided into nine sectors called castles (*castelli*), each of which is directed by an elected Castle Board led by the captain of the castle, both serving five-year terms (increased from two years in 1994).

Foreign relations. On March 2, 1992, San Marino was admitted to full United Nations (UN) membership, having previously been accorded observer status with the world body, and on September 23 it became a member of the International Monetary Fund (IMF). The republic is also a member of other international organizations, including the Conference on (later Organization for) Security and Cooperation in Europe (CSCE/OSCE), in whose review sessions it has been an active participant.

The country's relations with Italy (raised to the ambassadorial level in 1979) are governed by a series of treaties and conventions establishing a customs union, regulating public-service facilities, and defining general principles of good neighborly relations. Despite its staunchly reiterated independence, the country's reliance on Italy for a variety of necessities, ranging from daily newspapers to currency, provides little evidence that it will break with a tradition of alignment with Italian social and political processes.

In May 1985 San Marino and China concluded a visa-exemption accord, the first such agreement between Beijing and a Western European state. In February 1997 Secretary of State for Foreign and Political Affairs Gabriele GATTI met with Cuban leader Fidel Castro in Havana, San Marino subsequently continuing to urge the United States to lift its embargo on Cuba.

Bilateral talks aimed at forging closer financial ties with Italy continued in 2009, prompting concern that the central Bank of Italy might gain undue influence over San Marino's domestic economic policy. At the same time, multilateral talks were held among the EU, San Marino, and four other small non-EU countries aimed at including them in the EU's tax information-sharing system.

Current issues. Under heavy criticism from the PDCS, which had been excluded from the center-left coalition despite winning a plurality of seats in the council in the June 2006 election, the government lost a confidence vote and resigned on October 29, 2007. It was replaced on November 28 by an unnamed coalition that included the previous government parties (PSD, AP, and SU) and the Center Democrats (*Democratici di Centro*—DdC), a new party founded by former Christian Democrats who had quit over the PDCS's inability to exert influence in the council. Also in 2007, another group of PDCS defectors, critical of the party's inability to attract lay moderates, founded yet another new party, Euro-Populars for San Marino (*Europopolari per San Marino*—EpS). As a result of these defections, the PDCS lost 9 of its 21 seats, 5 to the EpS and 4 to the DdC , bringing its total to just 12.

Despite the PDCS's loss of power, the center-left coalition was unable to garner enough consensus to surmount the legislative gridlock, and the coalition collapsed on July 9, 2008. After a third coalition fell apart before it could be approved by the council, the captains regent on August 5 called for early elections on November 9. A caretaker government composed of the Congress of State, the Council of XII, and state commissions conducted government business in the interim.

The November 2008 election was the first in which two broad coalitions challenged each other since the 2006 election law was implemented. Under the law, parties and coalitions were not allowed to change their programs once they were elected to government. Also, coalitions voted into office were required to remain intact throughout their terms. Following the 2008 balloting, the center-right was restored to power. The main reason for the Pact for San Marino's victory was the shift by the AP from the center-left to the center-right. Further undermining the opposition, the largest center-left party, PSD, split in July 2009.

POLITICAL PARTIES

San Marino's older political parties traditionally had close ties with and resembled corresponding parties in Italy, although recent mergers and name changes have led to more distinctive identities.

In the first contest since the 2006 election law, two coalitions were formed ahead of the November 9, 2008, election. The center-right Pact for San Marino, comprising four lists and eight parties, won 54.2 percent of the vote. The center-left opposition coalition, Reforms and Freedom, was composed of three lists, for a total of five parties; it won 45.8 percent of the vote. Reforms and Freedom lost eight seats on July 1, 2009, when defectors from the PSD formed a new opposition group on the council, the San Marino Socialist Reformist Group (GSRS).

Governing Coalition

Pact for San Marino (*Patto per San Marino*)

San Marino Christian Democratic Party (*Partito Democratico Cristiano Sammarinese*—PDCS). This list, with the same name as its principal party, won 22 seats on the council, more than any other list or single party.

San Marino Christian Democratic Party (*Partito Democratico Cristiano Sammarinese*—PDCS). Catholic and conservative in outlook, the PDCS was established on April 9, 1948, and first came to power in 1957. In recent years it has been the strongest party in the Grand and General Council, winning at least 21 seats in every election since 1974. It ruled as the senior partner in coalitions with the San Marino Socialist Party (*Partito Socialista Sammarinese*—PSS) from 1973 until the latter's withdrawal in December 1977, at which time the PDCS was unable to organize a new government majority and went into opposition. It returned to power in an unprecedented coalition with the Communist Party (subsequently the San Marino Progressive Democratic Party [*Partito Progressista Democratico Sammarinese*—PPDS]) in July 1986, from which it withdrew in February 1992 to revive the alliance with the Socialists. The party again won a plurality in the 1993 balloting, following which its coalition with the Socialists was continued.

The PDCS lost 1 of its 26 seats in the legislative election of May 1998. The subsequent collapse in 2000 of the PDCS-PSS coalition led the PDCS to reunite with the PPDS in a tripartite coalition that also included the Socialists for Reform (*Socialisti per le Reforme*—SpR). Although the PDCS retained its 25 seats in the June 2001 election, a revived PDCS-PSS coalition lasted only one year, and the PDCS was forced into opposition. In the June 2006 election the PDCS won 21 seats, more than any other party, but not enough to outweigh the combined strength of 32 seats won by the center-left governing coalition. The PDCS subsequently lost 9 council seats due to resignations from the party.

Before the November 2008 election the PDCS formed an electoral list with the breakaway Euro-Populars for San Marino (*Europopolari per San Marino*—EpS) and Arengo and Freedom (*Arengo e Libertà*—AL).

Leaders: Pasquale VALENTINI (Political Secretary), Giuseppe GUIDI (President), Luigi MAZZA (Council Leader).

Euro-Populars for San Marino (*Europopolari per San Marino*—EpS). After a new election law was approved in 2006, former PDCS political secretary Pier Marino MENICUCCI and several other prominent PDCS members resigned, citing the party's inability to adapt to the changing political climate and the need to widen its base of support to include lay moderates. On July 4, 2007, the former PDCS members launched the EpS as a centrist alternative that might draw sufficient support to gain power under the law, which promotes the emergence of a two-party system.

Leaders: Gian Marco MARCUCCI (President), Lorenzo LONFERNINI (Political Secretary).

Arengo and Freedom (*Arengo e Libertà*—AL). The center-left AL was founded in September 2008 by council members Fabio Berardi and Nadia Ottaviani, who left the PSD because they thought the party had moved too far to the left. The AL was named for the assembly (*Arengo*) that ruled San Marino during the Middle Ages.

Leaders: Fabio BERARDI, Nadia OTTAVIANI.

Popular Alliance (*Alleanza Popolare*—AP). This centrist, liberal party, formerly known as the San Marino Popular Democratic Alliance for the Republic (*Alleanza Popolare dei Democratici Sammarinesi per la Repubblica*—APDS), was formed prior to the 1993 election under the leadership of former Christian Democrats. The APDS won four Grand and General Council seats in 1993 and six seats in 1998. In 2001 it slipped to five seats.

In 2006 the party, now known as the AP, won 12.1 percent of the vote and seven seats, making it the third-largest party in the council.

Amid mounting discord with the United Left (*Sinistra Unita*—SU), one of its partners in the governing center-left coalition that collapsed in 2008, the AP joined the center-right Pact for San Marino for the November 2008 election. The AP won 11.5 percent of the vote and retained its seven council seats.

Leaders: Carlo FRANCIOSI (President), Mario VENTURINI (Coordinator), Roberto GIORGETTI (Council Leader).

Freedom List (*Lista della Libertà*—LdL). In advance of the 2008 election, the social-democratic New Socialist Party (*Nuovo Partito Socialista*—NPS) and centrist We Sammarinese (*Noi Sammarinesi*—NS) merged to form the Freedom List, which ran as part of the winning Pact for San Marino coalition. The LdL won 6.3 percent of the vote and four council seats in the November election.

New Socialist Party (*Nuovo Partito Socialista*—NPS). The social-democratic NPS was founded in November 2005 by defectors from the PSD to restore traditional socialist values for political reform and against corruption the party claimed had infiltrated government. In the 2006 election the NPS won 5.4 percent of the vote and three seats and was part of the opposition to the PSD-SU-AP governing coalition that collapsed in 2008. As a member of the LdL, the NPS became part of the governing coalition after the November election.

Leaders: Antonio Lazzaro VOLPINARI (President), Augusto CASALI (Political Secretary), Maurizio RATTINI (Council Leader).

We Sammarinese (*Noi Sammarinesi*—NS). This party, founded in 2006, defines itself as defending the republic's traditional values. It won 2.5 percent of the vote and one seat on the council in 2006. The NS joined the governing coalition in 2008.

Leader: Marco ARZILLI.

San Marino Union of Moderates (*Unione Sammarinese dei Moderati*—USDM). In an effort to reach the newly required threshold of 3.5 percent of the popular vote to win a seat on the council, the San

Marino Populars (*Popolari Sammarinesi*—PS) and the San Marino National Alliance (*Alleanza Nazionale Sammarinese*—ANS) formed this coalition on February 21, 2008. The USDM won 4.2 percent of the vote and two council seats in the November election. The PS became part of the new center-right government after the November 2008 election.

San Marino Populars (*Popolari Sammarinesi*—PS). Founded in 2003, this centrist, Catholic party won 2.4 percent of the vote and one seat on the council in 2006. PS council leader Romeo MORRI was a vocal critic of the governing coalition in 2007, calling in September for early elections to overcome what he viewed as a political stalemate caused by insurmountable tensions among the three parties. Morri's call was rebuffed in a joint statement by the coalition, which renewed its commitment to broad-based political and economic reforms in the same month. The governing coalition collapsed in 2008, and the PS joined the new government following the November election.

Leaders: Angela VENTURINI (Secretary), Antonio PUTTI (President).

San Marino National Alliance (*Alleanza Nazionale Sammarinese*—ANS). The right-wing ANS, founded in 2001 and linked to the Italian post-fascist National Alliance (*Alleanza Nazionale*), won one seat in the June 2001 council election. In 2006 it won 2.3 percent of the vote and retained its seat on the council. In 2008 it joined the San Marino Populars in a coalition to ensure its continued council voice.

Leaders: Glauco SANSOVINI (Political Secretary), Ennio Vittorio PELLANDRA (President).

Opposition Coalition:

Reforms and Freedom (*Riforme e Libertà*)

Party of Socialists and Democrats (*Partito dei Socialisti e dei Democratici*—PSD). This list comprises the party for which it was named and the small Sammarinese for Freedom (*Sammarinesi per la Libertà*—SpL). The PSD list won 32 percent of the vote and 18 seats in 2008.

Party of Socialists and Democrats (*Partito dei Socialisti e dei Democratici*—PSD). This party was founded on February 25, 2005, as a merger between the PSS and the Party of Democrats (*Partito dei Democratici*—PdD), both of which at the time participated in a governing coalition that also included the PDCS. Its Italian counterpart is the Democratic Party. The leftist PSS and the San Marino Communist Party (*Partito Comunista Sammarinese*— PCS) ruled jointly during 1945–1957. In 1973 the PSS returned to power upon forming a coalition government with the Christian Democrats that was continued after the 1974 election, in which the party won eight council seats. (It gained an additional representative when the San Marino Independent Social Democratic Party [*Partito Socialista Democratico Indipendente Sammarinese*—PSDIS], originally a right-wing splinter from the PSS, split in 1975.) In November 1977, however, it withdrew from the coalition, precipitating the fall of the PDCS-led administration. It went on to win eight council seats in 1978 and nine in 1983, entering the government on both occasions. The unprecedented PDCS-PCS coalition formed in July 1986 excluded the PSS. In 1990 the Socialist Unity Party (*Partito Socialista Unitario*—PSU), the more extreme remnant of the PSDIS, reunited with the PSS, which revived its coalition with the Christian Democrats in February 1992. In the May 1998 balloting the PSS retained its 14 legislative seats, continuing as the junior coalition partner until withdrawing from the government in February 2000. After winning 15 seats in June 2001, the PSS reentered a PDCS-led coalition. A year later it joined the PdD and APDS in a left-leaning government.

The Party of Democrats was established in March 2001 by merger of three groups: the PPDS, Ideas in Motion (*Idee in Movimento*—IM), and the Reformist Democrats and Socialists (*Riformisti Democratici e Socialisti*) led by Emma ROSSI. In the context of the political upheaval of late 1989 in Eastern Europe, the PPDS had been formally launched on April 15, 1990, as heir to the San Marino Communist Party (*Partito Comunista Sammarinese*—PCS).

The February 2000 departure of the PSS from the government enabled the PPDS to reestablish a coalition with the Christian Democrats in March, but the resultant government collapsed a year later. Meanwhile, the leftist IM had been established in 1998 by Alessandro ROSSI as principal successor to the Democratic Movement (*Movimento Democratico*—MD); following the 1998 election, the nascent IM extended its support to the newly formed PDCS-PPDS government. The MD had been formed in 1990 by members of the San Marino Social Democratic Party (*Partito Socialista Democratico Sammarinese*—PSDS), the most moderate of San Marino's several socialist parties and itself a partial successor to the San Marino Independent Social Democratic Party (*Partito Socialista Democratico Indipendente Sammarinese*—PSDIS), which had bifurcated in 1975. In the 1993 general election the MD had won three seats. Emma Rossi's reformist group was largely a continuation of the SpR, which she had formed in 1998 after quitting the PSS on the ground that it had become too closely aligned with the PDCS. After winning 12 seats in the early election of June 2001, the PdD joined the PSS and the APDS in a new coalition government in mid-2002.

In 2006 the PSD won 31.8 percent of the vote and 20 seats, 7 fewer than the total won in the previous election by its constituent parties, the former PSS and PdP, and 1 less than their former coalition partner, the PDCS. On July 12 the PSD formed a center-left governing coalition with the Popular Alliance (AP) and United Left (SU) that controlled 32 seats in the council until it fell on October 29, 2007. The PSD led a successor coalition government with the AP, the SU, and the Center Democrats (DdC) from November 28, 2007, to July 9, 2008.

Citing the need for a new entity on the council to promote traditional socialist values, PSD secretary Paride ANDREOLI and seven other PSD council members left the party and the Reforms and Liberty coalition on July 1, 2009, to form a new council group of the opposition, the GSRS (below). The move reduced the number of Reforms and Liberty seats on the council to 17 and PSD seats to 10, threw the opposition coalition into disarray, and prompted a number of other PSD members to resign.

Leader: Claudio FELICI (Council Leader).

Sammarinese for Freedom (*Sammarinesi per la Libertà*—SpL). Founded in 2002, the center-left SpL won 1.8 percent of the vote and one council seat in 2006.

Leaders: Giuseppe ROSSI (President), Monica BOLLINI.

United Left (*Sinistra Unita*—SU). The SU leftist political alliance was formed in 2005 by the San Marino Communist Refoundation (RCS) and *Zona Franca* (ZF), a PSD splinter. In 2006 the SU won 8.7 percent of the vote and five seats.

Leaders: Gastone PASOLINI (President), Alessandro ROSSI (Coordinator), Ivan FOSCHI (Council Leader), Roberto TAMAGNINI (ZF Coordinator), Angelo DELLA VALLE (RCS Secretary).

San Marino Communist Refoundation (*Rifondazione Comunista Sammarinese*—RCS). The RCS was founded in 1992 by PCS hard-liners unwilling to accept entry into the PPDS. The new formation won two legislative seats in May 1993, retaining them in the 1998 legislative contest and again in 2001.

Leaders: Natalina SAPIGNI (President), Angelo DELLA VALLE (Secretary).

Partito della Sinistra–Zona Franca (*Left Party–Free Port*—ZF). Also known as *Zona Franca,* the ZF was founded in 2005 as a social-democratic, progressive group by defectors from the newly created PSD.

Leader: Francesca MICHELOTTI.

Center Democrats (*Democratici di Centro*—DdC). A Catholic, populist movement, the DdC was founded on March 27, 2007, by four defectors from the PDCS who were frustrated by the PDCS's poor showing in the 2006 elections. The defectors, including sitting Captain Regent Rosa Zafferani, resigned from the party but not from the council, in an effort to promote the DdC as a more viable centrist party. In November the DdC joined the center-left governing coalition.

In November 2008 the DdC won 4.9 percent of the vote and two council seats.

Leaders: Orazio MASSA (President), Giovanni LONFERNINI (Coordinator), Pier Marino MULARONI (Council Leader).

San Marino Socialist Reformist Party (*Partito Socialista Riformista Sammarinese*—PSRS). Founded on July 1, 2009, by eight defectors from the PSD as a new council group of the opposition, the GSRS, the PSRS was launched as a new political party on July 15.

Leaders: Paride ANDREOLI, Germano DE BIAGI.

LEGISLATURE

The **Grand and General Council** (*Consiglio Grande e Generale*) is a unicameral body consisting of 60 members elected on a proportional basis for five-year terms by direct popular vote. The captains regent serve as presiding officers. Following the most recent election of November 9, 2008, the seat distribution was as follows: the San Marino Christian Democratic Party, 22 seats; Party of Socialists and Democrats, 18; Popular Alliance, 7; United Left, 5; Freedom List, 4; Center Democrats, 2; and San Marino Union of Moderates, 2.

Captains Regent: Massimo CENCI and Oscar MINA.

CABINET

[as of August 1, 2009]

Captains Regent	Massimo Cenci (LdL–NPS) Oscar Mina (PDCS)
Secretaries of State	
Education and Culture, the University, and Youth Policy	Romeo Morri (PS)
Finance and Budget and State Philatelic Company Relations	Gabriele Gatti (PDCS)
Foreign and Political Affairs, Telecommunications, and Transportation	Antonella Mularoni (AP) [f]
Health and Social Welfare, Social Security, Family and Social Affairs, and Equal Opportunity	Claudio Podeschi (PDCS)
Industry, Crafts, and Commerce	Marco Arzilli (NS)
Internal Affairs and Civil Defense	Valeria Ciavatta (AP) [f]
Justice, Information, Research, and Government Relations	Augusto Casalli (NPS)
Labor, Cooperation, and Postal Service Relations	Gianmarco Marcucci (EpS)
Territory, Environment, Agriculture, and State Production Company Relations	Giancarlo Venturini (PDCS)
Tourism, Sports, Economic Planning, and Public Services Relations	Fabio Berardi (AL)

[f] = female

COMMUNICATIONS

Although San Marino has no formal constitution, freedom of expression is protected by legal precedent and, more explicitly, by the Declaration of the Rights of Citizens and the Fundamental Principles of the Juridical Order of San Marino, issued by the council on July 12, 1974. The Telecommunications Act of March 18, 1988, and the Broadcasting Act of April 27, 1989, govern all the main aspects of broadcasting in San Marino.

Press. Newspapers and periodicals are published primarily by the government, by some political parties, and by the trade unions. The main publications are *San Marino Oggi* (San Marino Today), daily; *Nuovo Corriere di Informazione Sammarinese* (New Messenger of San Marino Information), daily; *Repubblica Sera* (Evening Republican), daily; *La Tribuna Sammarinese* (San Marino Tribune), daily; *Il Nuovo Titano* (The New Titano), PSS organ; and *San Marino,* PDCS organ.

News agency. There is no national facility. For foreign news the media rely primarily on the Italian news agency, ANSA.

Broadcasting. San Marino RTV (*Radiotelevisione*), which has a monopoly on public-service broadcasting in the republic, was launched in 1993. *Radio Televisione Italiano* (RAI) broadcasts a daily information bulletin about the republic under the title *Notizie di San Marino*. There is also one privately owned radio station (*Radio Titano*). As of 2008 there were 545.2 Internet users per 1,000 inhabitants.

INTERGOVERNMENTAL REPRESENTATION

Ambassador to the U.S.: Paolo RONDELLI.

U.S. Ambassador to San Marino: David H. THORNE.

Permanent Representative to the UN: Daniele D. BODINI.

IGO Memberships (Non-UN): CEUR, OSCE.

SÃO TOMÉ AND PRÍNCIPE

Democratic Republic of São Tomé and Príncipe
República Democrática de São Tomé e Príncipe

Political Status: Achieved independence from Portugal on July 12, 1975; constitution of November 5, 1975, revised in December 1982, October 1987, August 1990, and March 2003.

Area: 387 sq. mi. (1,001 sq. km.).

Population: 137,599 (2001C); 167,000 (2008E).

Major Urban Center (2008E): SÃO TOMÉ (62,500).

Official Language: Portuguese.

Monetary Unit: Dobra (market rate December 1, 2009: 15,525.00 dobras = $1US). With the support of Portugal, the dobra will be pegged to the euro beginning in January 2010.

President: Fradique de MENEZES (Independent Democratic Action); popularly elected on July 29, 2001, and sworn in for a five-year term on September 3 to succeed Miguel Anjos da Cunha Lisboa TROVOADA (Independent Democratic Action); reelected (as the candidate of the alliance of the Democratic Movement of Forces for Change and the Party of Democratic Convergence) on July 30, 2006, and inaugurated for a second five-year term on September 3.

Prime Minister: Joachim Rafael BRANCO (Movement for the Liberation of São Tomé and Príncipe—Social Democratic Party); appointed by the president on June 10, 2008, succeeding Patrice TROVOADA (Independent Democratic Action); sworn in with the new government on June 21.

THE COUNTRY

Located in the Gulf of Guinea some 125 miles off the coast of Gabon, São Tomé and Príncipe consists of a small archipelago of two main islands (after which the country is named) and four islets: Cabras, Gago Coutinho, Pedras Tinhosas, and Rôlas. Volcanic in origin, the islands exhibit numerous craters and lava flows; the climate is warm and humid most of the year. The indigenous inhabitants mainly descended from plantation laborers imported from the African mainland. The Portuguese population, estimated at more than 3,000 before independence, has reportedly declined to less than 100. Roman Catholicism is the principal religion. Women constitute about one-third of the economically active population and hold a limited number of leadership positions in politics and government.

São Tomé and Príncipe was once the world's leading producer of cocoa, although production has declined in recent years. Tourism and construction have contributed significantly to economic growth, and the government hopes that oil revenues from the Gulf of Guinea will boost its economic position. Most food is imported, often in the form of donations, with copra, coffee, palm kernels, sugar, and bananas being produced domestically. Consumables dominate the small industrial sector. Cyclical droughts, low world cocoa prices since 1980, and the flight of Portuguese managers and skilled labor at independence have taken a toll on the economy, and the country relies heavily on foreign aid. The government began moving away from a Marxist orientation in the mid-1980s and recently has emphasized economic denationalization (most importantly in the cocoa industry), foreign investment, reduction of subsidies, currency devaluation, and other liberalization measures that have won the support of the International Monetary Fund (IMF) and World Bank. In addition, it has tried to diversify its economy by developing fishing and tourism.

In 1998 the World Bank ranked São Tomé and Príncipe third on its list of the world's 40 most heavily indebted poor countries. In early 2000 the IMF agreed to a three-year support program designed to solidify the government's recent structural reforms, combat widespread poverty, and alleviate the "unsustainable" external debt burdens. Paris Club creditors subsequently approved a three-year debt reduction plan.

São Tomé and Príncipe shares with Nigeria an economic development zone believed to hold more than 10 billion barrels of crude oil. Chevron began exploratory drilling in early 2006, and many other oil companies have shown interest in developing the region, though interest has waned in recent years due to the global economic downturn and a collateral decline in the demand for oil.

Though annual GDP growth of 5.8 percent was recorded in 2008, the economy was expected to contract 4.3 percent in 2009 as a result of high inflation and an expected decrease in tourism, owing in large part to the global economic recession. In an effort to stimulate growth and curb soaring unemployment, the government in 2009 reduced the corporate tax rate from 45 percent to 25 percent. In March the IMF approved $3.8 million over three years in poverty reduction aid to support economic reforms.

GOVERNMENT AND POLITICS

Political background. Discovered by Portuguese explorers in 1471, São Tomé and Príncipe became Portuguese territories between 1522 and 1523 and, collectively, an Overseas Province of Portugal in 1951. Nationalistic sentiments became apparent in 1960 with the formation of the Committee for the Liberation of São Tomé and Príncipe (*Comité de Libertaçã de São Tomé e Príncipe*—CLSTP). In 1972 the CLSTP became the Movement for the Liberation of São Tomé and Príncipe (*Movimento de Libertaçã de São Tomé e Príncipe*—MLSTP), which quickly became the leading advocate of independence from Portugal. Based in Gabon under the leadership of Dr. Manuel Pinto da COSTA, the MLSTP carried out a variety of underground activities, particularly in support of protests by African workers against low wages.

In 1973 the Organization of African Unity (OAU, subsequently the African Union—AU) recognized the MLSTP, and Portugal granted the country local autonomy. After the 1974 military coup in Lisbon, the Portuguese government began negotiations with the MLSTP. The two agreed in November 1974 that independence would be proclaimed on July 12, 1975, and that a transitional government would be formed under MLSTP leadership until that time. Installed on December 21, 1974, the transitional government council encompassed four members appointed by the MLSTP and one by Portugal. Upon independence, da Costa assumed the presidency and promptly designated his MLSTP associate, Miguel Anjos da Cunha Lisboa TROVOADA, as prime minister. In December 1978, however, Trovoada was relieved of his duties, and in October 1979 he was arrested on charges that he had been involved in a projected coup, one of a series that da Costa claimed to have foiled with the aid of Angolan troops. The president subsequently served as both head of state and chief executive without serious domestic challenge, despite Trovoada's release in 1981. In late 1987 the government, which had already introduced many economic liberalization measures, launched a political liberalization campaign as well (see Constitution and government, below). One of the first official changes was the revival of the office of prime minister; Celestino Rocha da COSTA was appointed to the post in January 1988.

The reform process culminated in an August 1990 referendum that endorsed abandonment of the country's single-party system, and on January 20, 1991, the recently legalized Party of Democratic Convergence (*Partido da Convergência Democrática*—PCD) out-distanced the restyled MLSTP–Social Democratic Party (MLSTP–*Partido Social Democrata*—MLSPT-PSD) by winning 33 of 55 National Assembly seats. On February 8 the PCD General Secretary, Daniel Lima dos Santos DAIO, was named to head a new government, and on March 3 former prime minister Trovoada secured election as head of state. (Incumbent president da Costa had earlier announced his retirement from public life.)

Prime Minister Daio was dismissed on April 22, 1992, in favor of his finance minister, Norberto José d'Alva COSTA ALEGRE. Despite an MLSTP-PSD call for a unity government, the cabinet announced by Costa Alegre on May 16 was composed solely of PCD members.

On July 2, 1994, President Trovoada sacked Prime Minister Costa Alegre in favor of Evaristo de CARVALHO, who, although a PCD member, had long been close to the president. Four days later Carvalho was expelled from the PCD, which called for a new presidential election. Trovoada responded by appointing a Carvalho-recommended government of "presidential friends." On July 10, after the PCD had announced that it intended to introduce a motion declaring the new administration unconstitutional, Trovoada dissolved the National Assembly and called for the election of a successor.

In legislative balloting on October 2, 1994, the MLSTP-PSD returned to power with the capture of a near-majoritarian 27 seats, while the PCD and President Trovoada's recently legalized Independent Democratic Action (Acção Democrática Independente—ADI) party each secured 14. On October 25 Trovoada appointed MLSTP-PSD secretary general Carlos Alberto Dias Monteiro da GRAÇA as prime minister. Although da Graça had pledged to form a government of "national union," he named a cabinet dominated by MLSTP-PSD members on October 28.

On August 16, 1995, a group of Cuban-trained rebel soldiers led by Lt. Orlando das NEVES stormed the presidential palace, taking President Trovoada prisoner. However, Trovoada resumed his duties a week later after issuing a pardon to the officers who had seized him. Among the concessions reportedly made to secure Trovoada's release were pledges to name the long-anticipated unity government and restructure the military.

In anticipation of the formation of a multiparty government, on December 29, 1995, the MLSTP-PSD, the ADI, and the Opposition Democratic Coalition (*Coligação Democrática da Oposição*—Codo) signed a cooperation pact. Two days later, MLSTP-PSD deputy secretary general Armindo Vaz de ALMEIDA was named to replace da Graça as prime minister, and on January 5, 1996, Almeida named a cabinet that included seven members from the MLSTP-PSD, four from the ADI, and one from Codo, despite Codo's lack of legislative representation.

In delayed presidential balloting on June 30, 1996, incumbent president Trovoada led a five-man field with 40.85 percent of the vote, followed by former president da Costa (39.14 percent), the PCD's Alda BANDEIRA (14.63 percent), former prime minister da Graça, and Armindo TOMBA, an anticorruption journalist. In a second-round runoff on July 21, Trovoada defeated da Costa on a 52–48 percent split.

On September 20, 1996, an assembly nonconfidence motion reportedly orchestrated by the assembly president, Fortunato PIRES, forced the resignation of the Almeida government. Subsequent MLSTP-PSD efforts to have Pires appointed to the vacant post were blocked, however, by Trovoada and the ADI, and on November 13 Trovoada appointed the MLSTP-PSD's deputy secretary general, Raúl Bragança NETO, as prime minister. On November 28 Neto named a government that included six MLSTP-PSD ministers, three from the PCD, and one independent.

The MLSTP-PSD won 31 legislative seats in polling on November 8, 1998, with the ADI improving to 16 seats and the PCD falling to 8. The MLSTP-PSD subsequently nominated Guilherme Posser da COSTA, a former foreign minister and ambassador, to be the next prime minister, and Costa and his MLSTP-PSD government were sworn in on January 5, 1999.

In first-round presidential balloting on July 29, 2001, ADI candidate Fradique de MENEZES (56.3 percent of the vote) defeated former president Manuel Pinto da Costa (38.4 percent) and three minor candidates. Several attempts to form a "cohabitation" government failed, and Menezes, who had been inaugurated in September, consequently dismissed Prime Minister Costa and his cabinet and then named former prime minister Carvalho to head a "presidential initiative" government including members from the ADI and the PCD. Calling the minority government "unconstitutional," the MLSTP-PSD walked out of the assembly, precipitating a political crisis that prompted President Menezes to dissolve the assembly on December 7 and call for early elections. Concurrently, the leading political parties had agreed to allocate cabinet posts according to the seats won by each party in the new legislative balloting.

In the assembly poll on March 3, 2002, the MLSTP-PSD secured a one-seat plurality of 24 seats over the new electoral coalition formed by the PCD and the recently launched, pro-Menezes Democratic Movement of Forces for Change (*Movimento Democrático das Forças para da Mudunça*—MDFM). On March 26 the president appointed Gabriel COSTA (a former leader of the MLSTP-PSD but now an independent described as "close" to the MDFM) as the new prime minister. The cabinet that took office in April contained, according to the previously determined proportion, members of the MLSTP-PSD, the MDFM-PCD coalition, and the new Uê Kédadji alliance that had been formed by the ADI, Codo, and others prior to the assembly poll, and had captured third place with 8 seats.

Following a dispute between Prime Minister Costa and Defense Minister Victor MONTEIRO, President Menezes dismissed Costa and the rest of the cabinet on September 27, 2002. On October 3 the president appointed Maria das NEVES de Souza (MLSTP-PSD) as the new prime minister. On October 6 das Neves announced her new cabinet, which again included members of her own party, the coalition of the MFDM and PCD, and the Uê Kédadji alliance.

In 2003 the potential windfall from oil exploration raised concerns regarding government accountability and corruption. In June a military group briefly deposed Menezes while he was in Nigeria, but he returned to office July 23 after successful negotiations with the rebels. Parliament agreed to a deal arranged by international negotiators to grant amnesty to the junta and to the political group linked to it, the Christian Democratic Front (*Frente Democrática Cristã*—FDC). The fractious debate over energy resources, which inspired the coup, continued over the terms of a contract with the Environmental Remediation Holding Company (ERHC), a Nigerian company involved in the Joint Development Zone (JDZ).

Menezes appointed Damiao ALMEIDA as prime minister on September 17, 2003, and a reshuffled cabinet made up of the MLSTP-PSD and ADI was sworn in the next day. The minister of natural resources and environment resigned in May 2005 over delays in the allocation of oil exploration licenses. The award of five blocs of the JDZ to international oil companies on May 31, 2005, brought further disagreement. Patrice TROVOADA, an oil broker, was dismissed as oil adviser to the president, and Menezes also dismissed his chief of staff over a conflict of interest. Menezes then flew to Nigeria, where he signed off on the bloc awards, prompting the resignation of Prime Minister Almeida and the entire cabinet on June 3. Maria do Carmo SILVEIRA was named prime minister on June 7, and a new cabinet, dominated by the MLSTP-PSD, was appointed on June 8.

In legislative elections on March 26, 2006, the ADI won 11 seats, while MDFM supporters of President Menezes won 23 seats, surprising many by finishing ahead of the MLSTP-PSD, whose seat count fell to 2. Menezes subsequently named Tomé Soares da VERA CRUZ—an engineer who had previously held the position of minister of natural resources—as head of a new minority MDFM-PCD government.

On July 30, 2006, with the backing of the MDFM-PCD, Menezes was reelected in a landslide, with 60.6 percent of the vote. Menezes's main opponent, former foreign minister Patrice Trovoada, backed by the ADI and the MLSTP-PSD, received 38.8 percent of the vote. In August, in the first regional balloting since 1992, the MDFM-PCD won majorities in six of seven districts that held elections, with the MLSTP-PSD winning the other. Meanwhile, the Union for Change and Progress in Príncipe (*União para Mudança e Progresso do Príncipe*—UMPP), supported by the MDFM-PCD, won all seven seats in the regional assembly of Príncipe in concurrent balloting. José CASSANDRA, the UMPP leader, subsequently became president of the regional assembly on October 5.

Prime Minister Vera Cruz reshuffled the government in November 2006, but the ADI subsequently dropped out of the governing coalition in a dispute over several of Vera Cruz's new appointments, leaving the prime minister without a majority in the assembly.

When the parliament would not approve the 2008 budget, Vera Cruz resigned in February. President Menezes subsequently appointed former prime minister and son of former president Miguel Trovoada, Patrice Trovoada, leader of the opposition ADI, as prime minister of a new coalition government of the MDFM, the PCD, and the ADI. He named a new government on February 14. On May 20 the government lost a vote of no confidence when the PCD voted with the opposition. On June 10 Menezes appointed Joachim Rafael BRANCO (MLSTP-PSD) as prime minister. The new government sworn in on June 21 included the MDFM and the PCD, in addition to the MLSTP-PSD.

Constitution and government. The 1975 constitution, as revised in 1982, identified the MLSTP as the "directing political force" for the country, provided for an indirectly elected National Popular Assembly as the supreme organ of state, and conferred broad powers on a president, who was named by the assembly for a five-year term.

In October 1987 the MLSTP Central Committee proposed a number of constitutional changes as part of a broad democratization program. Theretofore elected by the People's District Assemblies from candidates nominated by an MLSTP-dominated Candidature Commission, legislators would now be chosen by direct and universal suffrage. Independent candidates would be permitted in addition to candidates presented by the party and "recognized organizations," such as trade unions or youth groups. The president would be elected by popular vote rather than being designated by the assembly; however, only the MLSTP president (elected by secret ballot at a party congress) could stand as a candidate. In the course of approving the reform program, the assembly provided for the restoration of a presidentially appointed prime minister.

As a consequence of the August 1990 referendum, a multiparty system was introduced, together with multicandidature and popular balloting for legislators and the president. In addition, the president was limited to two five-year terms. The National Assembly conferred local autonomy upon Príncipe in 1994, and elections were held there in March 1995 for a seven-member regional assembly and a five-member regional government (headed by a president). The new bodies were installed April 29, 1995.

In November 2002 the assembly endorsed constitutional revision designed to diminish presidential power. Despite the objections of President Menezes, the new constitution took effect in March 2003. Among other things, the new basic law eliminated the president's right to veto constitutional amendments and provided for the establishment of two new bodies—an advisory Council of State and a Constitutional Tribunal.

The judiciary is headed by a Supreme Court, whose members are designated by and responsible to the assembly. Administratively, the country is divided into two provinces (coterminous with each of the main islands) and 12 counties (11 of which are located on São Tomé).

Foreign relations. Despite the exodus of much of the country's Portuguese population from 1974 to 1975, São Tomé and Príncipe continued to maintain an active commercial trade with the former colonial power. Following independence, diplomatic relations were established with the Soviet Union and the Eastern-bloc countries as well as the major western states and other former Portuguese dependencies in Africa, particularly Angola; in 1978 some 1,000 troops from Angola, augmented by a small contingent from Guinea-Bissau, were dispatched to São Tomé to guard against what President da Costa claimed to be a series of coup plots by expatriates in Angola, Gabon, and Portugal. However, most of the troops were withdrawn by the mid-1980s as part of a rapprochement with the west.

Growing ties with nearby Francophone nations underscored France's position as the country's leading trade partner. The county also enjoyed significant aid from Taiwan, which São Tomé and Príncipe recognized in 1997.

In November 1999 the country joined six of its Gulf of Guinea neighbors in agreeing to establish the Gulf of Guinea Commission (GGC) to coordinate "cooperation and development" in the oil- and fish-rich region. In early 2001 São Tomé and Príncipe reached an accord with Nigeria to establish the JDZ in disputed waters in the Gulf of Guinea; however, in May 2005 tensions arose between the countries over operating rights in the zone. Cooperation subsequently appeared back on track, and in 2007 São Tomé and Príncipe and Nigeria created a joint military commission to enhance bilateral security cooperation. Nigeria has also supported São Tomé and Príncipe by selling the country subsidized oil and providing a $30 million credit line. (In May 2009 the Nigerian legislature approved a $10 million interest-free loan for São Tomé and Príncipe to be paid back over six years with revenue from the JDZ.)

In recent years the government has sought closer ties with Angola to counterbalance Nigeria's influence over the island nation and to help develop its economic resources.

The United States has provided training to local security forces and has assisted in numerous infrastructure projects in the islands. The two countries conducted a joint military training exercise in March 2007, and in May 2007 the United States announced that it would assist São Tomé and Príncipe in coastal security to protect oil shipments passing through the Gulf of Guinea.

In recent years São Tomé and Príncipe have sought to increase ties with Brazil, which began shipping food to the islands in April 2009 using a $5 million credit line it had previously extended to the government.

In 2009 São Tomé and Estonia established diplomatic relations.

Current issues. In October 2007 the national paramilitary police force known as the Ninjas mutinied against the government. The officers seized control of the national police headquarters, prompting violent conflict with the army when the latter recaptured the building after negotiations failed. Prime Minister Vera Cruz reshuffled the government in November, but the ADI subsequently dropped out of the ruling coalition over several of Vera Cruz's new appointments, leaving the prime minister with a minority stake in the National Assembly.

The government of São Tomé and Príncipe foiled another coup attempt on February 11, 2009. Some 38 people were arrested, including the accused leader, Arlécio COSTA, and three other members of his small, radical opposition Christian Democratic Front (FDC), which was also implicated in the 2003 coup attempt against Menezes. Costa claimed his group was merely planning a campaign of civil disobedience and had no plans to violently overthrow Menezes's government. Subsequently, officials reported finding a cache of weapons at Costa's house.

Meanwhile, the government continued to struggle with rifts in its unwieldy coalition, promoting its fledgling petroleum sector, and managing the economy in the wake of the global financial downturn. Consequently, municipal and regional elections, scheduled for August 2009, were postponed in May because of funding constraints, angering the government of Príncipe led by José Cassandra, which threatened to resign if elections were not held as planned. In late June Prime Minister Branco proposed either November 29, 2009, or February 15, 2010, arguing that the additional time would allow the legislature to complete revisions to the electoral law and administrative boundaries. (No consensus had been reached by midyear.)

The Saõtoméan government continued to struggle with ongoing corruption scandal. In March 2009 a judge handed down the first convictions in two cases involving the misappropriation of approximately $4 million of donor funds by the former government agency charged with administering foreign aid. The former agency director and treasurer were convicted of mishandling approximately $1 million of the total. Former prime minister das Neves and her commerce secretary, who had been implicated when the investigations began in 2005, were subsequently cleared of all charges due to lack of evidence. In May the director of a new agency charged with administering foreign aid was investigated for allegedly misappropriating Italian food aid, further undermining public and foreign donors' confidence in the government's handling of such aid. Meanwhile, Prime Minister Branco and the National Assembly were engaged in a dispute with the head of the national audit office, who had accused them of colluding to undermine his authority and creating the opportunity for further corruption.

In recent years much attention has been focused on the potential for petroleum wealth because bonuses paid to the government by licensed oil exploration companies have amounted to hundreds of millions of dollars. However, oil companies' plans have been delayed due to the steep decline in oil prices as a result of the worldwide recession, leaving the government with significantly reduced revenue from its oil sector. On a positive note, in May 2009 it was announced that four additional blocs in the JDZ would be auctioned over the next few years, and the government planned to license blocs in the country's Exclusive Economic Zone by year's end.

On the recommendation of the IMF in 2009, Portugal and São Tomé and Príncipe signed an economic cooperation agreement in which the Central Bank of Portugal agreed to support a credit line to its former colony, allowing it to peg its currency, the dobra, to the euro. This was seen as an effort to help reduce inflation and encourage foreign direct investment in the republic. The agreement was scheduled to go into effect in January 2010.

POLITICAL PARTIES

Government Parties:

Movement for the Liberation of São Tomé and Príncipe–Social Democratic Party (*Movimento de Libertaçã de São Tomé e Príncipe–Partido Social Democrata*—MLSTP-PSD). The outcome of an earlier Committee for the Liberation of São Tomé and Príncipe (*Comité de Libertação de São Tomé e Príncipe*—CLSTP), the MLSTP was founded in 1972 and became the leading force in the campaign for independence from Portugal. At its first congress in 1978, the movement defined itself as a "revolutionary front of democratic, anti-neocolonialist, and anti-imperialist forces"; however, it did not formally adopt Marxism-Leninism. The MLSTP was the country's only authorized political group until the adoption of a multiparty system in August 1990. Two months later, President da Costa retired from leadership of what had been redesignated the MLSTP-PSD.

Da Costa returned to party activity in 1998 to run for president in July 2001 but was defeated by Fradique de Menezes of the ADI, and the MLSTP-PSD was excluded from the new government. In February 2005 former prime minister and party vice president Guilherme Posser da Costa replaced Manuel Pinto da Costa as the party's president. In June 2005 the MLSTP-PSD threatened to resign from the government, but after negotiations, agreed to form a new government to avoid early elections. Party member Maria do Carmo Silveira became the new prime minister and finance minister.

In the March 2006 legislative elections, the party won 20 seats, finishing second behind the MDFM-PCD. In the July presidential election, the MLSTP-PSD chose not to field its own candidate and instead supported the ADI's Trovoada. In regional balloting in August 2006, the MLSTP-PSD won a majority in only one of seven districts. Following the defeat, party president da Costa resigned and was replaced in February 2007 by Joaquim Rafael Branco, a party veteran who promised to rebuild the base before the next legislative elections in 2010. During negotiations among the main political parties following the collapse of Trovoada's government in May 2008, Branco emerged as the president's choice to form a new coalition government.

Leaders: Joaquim Rafael BRANCO (Prime Minister and President of the Party), Carlos Alberto Dias Monteiro da GRAÇA (Former Prime Minister and 1996 presidential candidate), Guilherme Posser da COSTA (Former Prime Minister), Armindo Vaz de ALMEIDA (Former Prime Minister), José VIEGAS (Secretary General).

Democratic Movement of Forces for Change (*Movimento Democrático das Forças para da Mudança*—MDFM). The MDFM was formed in late 2001 by former members of the ADI (below) close to President Menezes and later established an electoral alliance with the

PCD (below) for legislative balloting in 2002. That alliance won the largest number of seats (23) in the March 2006 legislative election and went on to win the majorities in six of seven districts in regional voting in August. In July Menezes easily won reelection with more than 60 percent of the vote in the first round.

Leaders: Fradique de MENEZES (President of the Republic), Tomé Soares da VERA CRUZ (Secretary General).

Party of Democratic Convergence (*Partido da Convergência Democrática*—PCD). The PCD was launched in 1987, initially as an underground movement styled after the Reflection Group (*Grupo de Reflexão*—GR), which surfaced as an open opposition formation following the introduction of multiparty politics in August 1990.

In early 1996 the PCD refused to participate in the new government. Subsequently, it named party president Alda Bandeira de Conceicão as its presidential candidate; following his third-place finish in the first round of presidential polling in June, the PCD switched its support to Miguel Trovoada.

In the November 1998 legislative polling, the PCD's representation fell from 14 to 8 seats. The PCD supported the ADI's candidate in the 2001 presidential election, and it was given posts in the new cabinet in September 2001. However, in 2002 and again in 2006, the PCD entered into an electoral alliance with the MDFM.

Leaders: Daniel Lima dos Santos DAIO (Former Prime Minister), Alda BANDEIRA (1996 presidential candidate), Delfim NEVES (Secretary General).

Opposition Parties:

Independent Democratic Action (*Acção Democrática Independente*—ADI). The ADI was formed in 1992 under the leadership of President Trovoada's political advisor, Gabriel Costa, and participated in municipal elections that year as an "independent group." It was legally registered in early 1994. The ADI won 14 seats in the 1994 assembly balloting and 16 in 1998, claiming irregularities in the latter poll. In 2000 the ADI formed an electoral alliance with the PCD, Codo, UNDP, and PPP called the "Democratic Platform." It backed ADI candidate Fradique de Menezes in the 2001 presidential election, and subsequently, the ADI formed a coalition government with the PCD. However, Menezes subsequently fell into disagreement with pro-Trovoada factions within the ADI, and his allies later formed the MDFM (above).

The ADI participated in the UK coalition (below) from late 2001 until early 2006. The party won 11 seats on its own in the March 2006 legislative election but failed to gain any seats in regional balloting in August. Party secretary Trovoada became prime minster for a short time in the first half of 2008 but was unable to hold the fledgling coalition together. Calling for fresh legislative elections, the ADI rejected the negotiations that brought about Prime Minister Branco's coalition government in June 2008. The ADI has maintained the position that the government as of 2009 is unconstitutional.

Leaders: Patrice TROVOADA (Chair), Evaristo DE CARVALHO (Secretary General).

New Way Movement *(Movimento Novo Rumo*—NR*)*. The NR won one seat in the March 2006 legislative elections in the Autonomous Region of Príncipe but did not join the new coalition government.

Leader: João GOMES.

Other Parties and Groups:

Uê Kédadji (UK). The UK was established in late 2001 as an alliance of the ADI (above); Codo; the **National Union for Democracy and Progress** (*União Nacional para a Democracia e Progresso*—UNDP), led by Manuel Paixao LIMA; the **People's Progress Party** (*Partida Progresso do Povo*—PPP), led by Francisco SILVA; and the **Democratic Renovation Party** (*Partido da Renovaçáo Democrática*—PRD), led by Armindo GRAÇA. The UNDP and the PPP were recognized in September 1998 and were part of the Democratic Platform that supported the ADI candidate in the 2001 presidential balloting. After the 2002 balloting, the UK held eight seats in the legislature. The ADI left the alliance in early 2006, and in February 2006, the **Social Renovation Party** (*Partido Social Renovado*—PSR), led by Hamilton Vaz, joined the coalition. The UK failed to win any seats in the 2006 legislative elections.

Opposition Democratic Coalition (*Coligação Democrática da Oposição*—Codo). Codo was launched in March 1986 as an alliance of two Lisbon-based opposition groups—the **Independent Democratic Union of São Tomé and Príncipe** (*União Democrática Independente de São Tomé e Príncipe*—UDISTP) and the **São Tomé and Príncipe National Resistance Front** (*Frente da Resistência Nacional de São Tomé e Príncipe*—FRNSTP)—to combat what they called the "totalitarianism" of the da Costa government. Although the UDISTP previously had stated that it would reach its goals through "peaceful means," its association with the FRNSTP, generally considered a more radical group, led to a Codo posture that did not rule out "recourse to armed struggle."

Leader: Manuel Neves e SILVA.

Union for Change and Progress in Príncipe (*União para Mudança e Progresso do Príncipe*—UMPP). The UMPP was founded by José Cassandra, an ally of former prime minister Vera Cruz. The UMPP won control of the regional assembly in Príncipe in the 2006 balloting, and Cassandra was subsequently elected president of the assembly, promising to increase development of the island and to decrease its dependence on the island of São Tomé. Cassandra and other party leaders have threatened to resign from the regional assembly if the central government on São Tomé does not reverse its decision to delay municipal and regional elections originally scheduled for August 2009.

Leader: José CASSANDRA.

Christian Democratic Front (Frente Democrática Cristã—FDC). The government arrested six members of this party, including its four most senior members, in February 2009 for allegedly trying to overthrow the government. The party's leader, Arlécio Costa, has become known for his role in fighting for the apartheid government in South Africa in the 1980s as commander of the military's Buffalo Battalion. FDC members were also implicated in a coup attempt in 2003 and have since maintained an uneasy relationship with Menezes's government.

Leader: Arlécio COSTA.

Among the other groups active as of 2007 were the **São Tomé Workers' Party** (*Partido Trabalhista São Tomense*—PTS), led by Anacleto ROLIM; the **Democratic Alliance for the Development of Príncipe** (*Aliança Democrática para Desenvolvimento do Príncipe*—ADDP), a regional party in Príncipe supported by the MLSTP-PSD; and the **Renaissance Movement of Agua Grande,** which won two seats in regional elections in Príncipe in August 2006.

LEGISLATURE

Formerly an indirectly elected National Popular Assembly (*Assembleia Popular Nacional*) of 40 members, the current **National Assembly** (*Assembleia Nacional*) is a unicameral body of 55 members directly elected for five-year terms.

Following the most recent balloting of March 26, 2006 (and reruns in 18 districts on April 2), the seat distribution was as follows: the electoral alliance of the Democratic Movement of Forces for Change and the Party of Democratic Convergence, 23 seats; Movement for the Liberation of São Tomé and Príncipe–Social Democratic Party, 20; Independent Democratic Action, 11; and New Way Movement, 1.

President: Francisco DA SILVA.

CABINET

[as of August 1, 2009]

Prime Minister	Joachim Rafael Branco (MLSTP-PSD)
Ministers	
Agriculture, Fishing, and Rural Development	José Luís Xavier Mendes (PCD)
Commerce, Industry, and Tourism	Celestino Da Graca Andrade (PCD)
Defense	Elsa Texeira De Barros Pinto (MLSTP-PSD) [f]
Education and Culture	Jorge de Bom Jesus (MLSTP-PSD)

Foreign Affairs and Co-operation	Carlos Alberto Pires Tiny (MLSTP-PSD)
Health	Arlindo de Carvalho (PCD)
Internal and Territorial Administration, and Civil Protection	Raúl Antonio Da Costa Cravid (MDFM)
Justice, Public Administration, and Parliamentary Affairs	Justino Veiga (MDFM)
Labor, Solidarity, and Family	Maria Tomé De Araujo (MDFM) [f]
Natural Resources, Energy, and the Environment	Cristina Dias (MDFM) [f]
Planning and Finance	Ângela Viegas Santiago (MLSTP-PSD) [f]
Public Works, Transport, and Communication	Benjamin Vera Cruz (PCD)
Social Communication, Youth, and Sport	Maria De Cristo Da Costa Carvalho (PCD) [f]

[f] = female

COMMUNICATIONS

São Tomé and Príncipe's constitution protects free speech and freedom of the press. Among other things, opposition groups and parties are guaranteed access to state-controlled radio and television. In July 2007 the Higher Social Communication Council resumed its oversight of media and broadcasting after being dormant for three years.

Press. These newspapers are published occasionally in São Tomé: *Diário da República*, government weekly; *Notícias*; *Nova República*; *O País Hoje* (Country Today); *O Parvo; Tribuna*, as well as several internet newspapers, such as the *Téla Nón* and the *Jornal de São Tomé e Príncipe*.

News Agency. In mid-1985 the Angolan News Agency, ANGOP, joined with São Tomé's national radio station in establishing STP-Press.

Broadcasting and computing. Radio programming is transmitted by the official *Rádio Nacional de São Tomé e Príncipe* (RNSTP). Voice of America, Radio International Portugal, and Radio France International are all rebroadcast through state-controlled radio. There are also three private radio stations. *Televisão Santomense* (TVS), which began broadcasting on a limited basis in 1992, today services some 68,000 sets. As of 2008 there were 154.8 Internet users per 1,000 inhabitants.

INTERGOVERNMENTAL REPRESENTATION

Ambassador to the U.S. and Permanent Representative to the UN: Ovidio Manuel Barbosa PEQUENO.

U.S. Ambassador to São Tomé and Príncipe: Eunice S. REDDICK.

IGO Memberships (Non-UN): AfDB, AU, BADEA, CEEAC, CPLP, Interpol, NAM, OIF.

SAUDI ARABIA

Kingdom of Saudi Arabia
al-Mamlakah al-Arabiyah al-Saudiyah

Political Status: Unified kingdom established September 23, 1932; under absolute monarchical system; Basic Law of Government based on Islamic law promulgated by royal decree on March 1, 1992.

Area: 829,995 sq. mi. (2,149,690 sq. km.).

Population: 22,678,262 (2004C); 24,820,000 (2008E). Foreign nationals constitute approximately one quarter of both figures.

Major Urban Centers (2005E): RIYADH (royal capital, 5,126,000), Jiddah (administrative capital, 3,557,000), Makkah (Mecca, 1,446,000).

Official Language: Arabic.

Monetary Unit: Riyal (official rate December 1, 2009: 3.75 riyals = $1US).

Ruler and Prime Minister: King Abdallah ibn Abd al-Aziz Al SAUD; confirmed on August 1, 2005, by the royal court upon the death of King Fahd ibn Abd al-Aziz Al SAUD.

Heir Apparent: Crown Prince Sultan ibn Abd al-Aziz Al SAUD; appointed crown prince and heir to the throne on August 1, 2005.

THE COUNTRY

A vast, largely desert country occupying the greater part of the Arabian Peninsula, the Kingdom of Saudi Arabia exhibits both traditional and contemporary lifestyles. Frontiers were poorly defined for many years, and no census was undertaken prior to 1974. Some 85 percent of the indigenous inhabitants, who have traditionally adhered to patriarchal forms of social organization, are Sunni Muslim of the conservative Wahhabi sect. The Shiite population (15 percent) is located primarily in the east. A strict interpretation of Islam has limited female participation in the paid labor force to about 5 percent, though they have made gains under recent reforms. Mecca and Medina, the two holiest cities of Islam and the goals of an annual pilgrimage by Muslims from all over the world, lie within the western region known as the Hijaz, where the commercial and administrative center of Jiddah is also located.

Saudi Arabia is the leading exporter of oil and possesses the largest known petroleum reserves (estimated at upward of 200 billion barrels), which have made it one of the world's richest nations. The government acquired full interest in the Arabian-American Oil Company (Aramco) in 1980. Dramatic surges in oil revenue permitted heightened expenditures after 1973 that focused on the development of airports, seaports, and roads, as well as the modernization of medical, educational, and telecommunications systems. In addition, large-scale irrigation projects and heavy price subsidies yielded agricultural self-sufficiency in a country that once produced only 10 percent of its food needs. Vast sums were also committed to armaments, particularly modern fighter planes, missiles, and air defense systems.

Because of a reversal in oil prices and substantial support to Iraq in its eight-year war with Iran, the Saudis experienced a major recession in the early 1980s. An economic revival was sparked in the early 1990s, however, by increased oil production as an offshoot of Iraq's invasion of Kuwait in 1991. Subsequently, concern over falling cash reserves and growing external debt prompted substantial budgetary retrenchment, including reductions in the traditionally high subsidies upon which Saudis had come to rely. The government also introduced programs designed to help move Saudis into private-sector jobs, which are held primarily by foreign workers.

Generally higher oil prices in 1996 and 1997 permitted a return to moderately expansive budgets, with emphasis being placed on infrastructure designed to promote private-sector development. However, financial difficulties returned in 1998 as the result of a sharp drop in oil prices and the effects of the Asian economic crisis. In July 2003 the government bolstered its "Saudization" effort to help reduce unemployment, most significantly by replacing 17,800 foreign white-collar workers with Saudis. Unemployment, widely estimated at nearly 30 percent (though the government says it is in the single digits), has been a particular problem among those under age 20, a group that constitutes more than half the population.

As a result of the U.S. war in Iraq since 2003, Saudi oil prices and production have increased significantly. In September 2003 Russia and Saudi Arabia agreed to a landmark deal paving the way for a multibillion-dollar Saudi investment in the Russian oil industry, thus ensuring long-term capacity. As a result of surging economic growth, the kingdom has improved roads, schools, and hospitals. It has also continued to move ahead with privatization efforts and in 2006 opened its stock market to foreign investors. GDP growth was 6.6 percent in 2006, according to the International Monetary Fund (IMF), owing in large

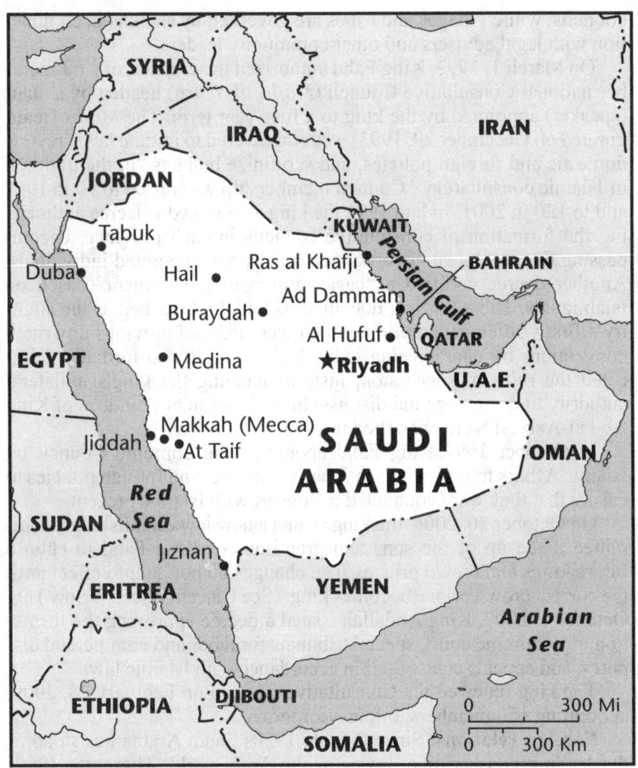

part to the global demand for oil. The IMF encouraged Saudi Arabia to sustain its broad-based expansion of the non-oil sector and to use its substantial oil revenue to promote private sector growth. Annual GDP growth averaged 3.8 percent in 2007–2008 but was expected to contract to about 1 percent in 2009 due to a dramatic decline in the price of oil during the global economic crisis. Inflation was expected to decline to about 3 percent, down from 9 percent a year earlier, as a result of a 15 percent wage increase (through 2011), food subsidies, and a mortgage law aimed at bolstering the housing sector. Meanwhile, authorities drew from the country's $400 billion reserves to fund key projects and maintain growth in the wake of the worldwide financial turmoil.

GOVERNMENT AND POLITICS

Political background. Founded in 1932, the Kingdom of Saudi Arabia was largely the creation of King Abd al-Aziz Al SAUD (Ibn Saud), who devoted 30 years to reestablishing the power his ancestors had held in the 18th and 19th centuries. Oil concessions were granted in the 1930s to what later became Aramco, but large-scale production did not begin until the late 1940s.

Ibn Saud was succeeded in 1953 by an ineffectual son, Saud ibn Abd al-Aziz Al SAUD, who was persuaded by family influence in 1958 to delegate control to his younger brother, Crown Prince Faysal (Faisal) ibn Abd al-Aziz Al SAUD. Faysal began a modernization program, abolished slavery, curbed royal extravagance, adopted sound fiscal policies, and personally assumed the functions of prime minister prior to the formal deposition of King Saud on November 2, 1964. Faysal was assassinated by one of his nephews, Prince Faysal ibn Musaid ibn Abd al-Aziz Al SAUD, while holding court in Riyadh on March 25, 1975, and was immediately succeeded by his brother, Crown Prince Khalid ibn Abd al-Aziz Al SAUD.

Despite a number of coup attempts, the most important occurring in mid-1969 following the discovery of a widespread conspiracy involving civilian and military elements, internal stability has tended to prevail under the monarchy. The regime was visibly shaken, however, in late 1979 when several hundred Muslim extremists seized the Grand Mosque in Mecca during the annual pilgrimage. Under the leadership of a *mahdi* (messiah), the men involved in the takeover called for an end to corruption and monarchical rule, and for a return to strict Islamic precepts. They held parts of the complex for two weeks; several hundred casualties resulted among the insurgents, hostages, and government forces. Citizens of several other predominantly Muslim countries, including Egypt and South Yemen, were among the 63 participants publicly beheaded on January 9, 1980, for their role in the seizure. Collaterally, the Shiite minority initiated antigovernment demonstrations in eastern areas of the kingdom.

King Khalid died on June 13, 1982, and was immediately succeeded as monarch and prime minister by his half-brother and heir, Crown Prince Fahd ibn Abd al-Aziz Al SAUD. On the same day, Prince Abdallah ibn Abd al-Aziz Al SAUD was designated heir to the throne and first deputy prime minister. King Fahd's rule subsequently encountered potential instability, with declining oil revenues threatening social programs, and a radical Islamic movement, supported by Iran, attempting to undermine the regime diplomatically and militarily.

King Fahd's decision in August 1990 to request Western, as well as regional, assistance in defending Saudi Arabia's border against the possibility of an Iraqi invasion was widely supported within the kingdom. However, the presence of Western forces and media resulted in intense scrutiny of Saudi government and society, raising questions about the nation's inability to defend itself despite massive defense expenditures; generating calls for modernization of the political system, which the king answered by promising reforms; and eliciting signs of dissent, including a quickly suppressed, but highly publicized protest by Saudi women for greater personal liberties. The government also faced growing pressure from Islamists, even though the regime was already considered one of the most conservative in the Arab world because of its active enforcement of Islamic interdictions. In May 1991 Islamist leaders sent a highly publicized letter to King Fahd demanding 12 reforms, including extended implementation of sharia and creation of an independent consultative council that would be responsible for domestic and foreign policy.

In a partial response to Islamists as well as to "liberals," King Fahd issued royal decrees on March 1, 1992, creating Saudi Arabia's first written rules of governance and providing for the formation of a national Consultative Council. At the same time, he rejected the notion that "the prevailing democratic system in the world" was suitable for Saudi Arabia and insisted that no elections would be in the offing. In September 1992 Islamist leaders again formally challenged government policy, this time in a "memorandum" to religious leaders that was viewed as "more defiant and bolder" than the 1991 document. The action was followed in May 1993 by the establishment of a Committee for the Defense of Legitimate Rights (CDLR; see Political Groups, below). However, the government quickly declared the organization illegal, with King Fahd warning the Islamists to cease distributing antigovernment material and using mosques as "political pulpits."

The most conspicuous result of a July 1993 cabinet reshuffle was the creation of a new Ministry of Islamic Guidance, which was seen as an attempt to buttress the kingdom's "religious establishment" against Islamist pressure within the Shiite and Sunni populations. The following month the king appointed the members of the national Consultative Council.

The council consisted entirely of men, none drawn from the royal family, representing a broad social spectrum. Although the government heralded the inauguration of the council in December 1993 as a major advance, some observers derided it as a "public relations exercise," noting that council sessions would not be open to the public and that topics for debate required advance approval by the king.

Questions also surrounded the king's October 1994 appointment of the new Supreme Council on Islamic Affairs, which was dominated by members of the royal family and technocrats owing their livelihood to the government. The new body was viewed as a further effort by the monarchy to undercut the appeal of the Islamists, who had been pressing for further Islamization of government policy and a curtailment of Western ties since the 1990–1991 Gulf crisis and war.

On August 2, 1995, in the most sweeping ministerial shakeup in two decades, no less than 13 portfolios, including those of finance, industry, and petroleum, changed hands, with many political veterans being succeeded by younger, Western-educated technocrats. While members of the royal family were left in charge of several key ministries (notably defense, interior, and foreign affairs), the obvious intent was to improve efficiency by bringing in a new generation of officials.

King Fahd was hospitalized in early November 1995, suffering from what was widely reported but never officially confirmed to be a stroke. On January 1, 1996, he formally transferred responsibility for "affairs of state" to Crown Prince Abdallah. Although that decision had been expected by many observers to lead to a permanent succession, King Fahd formally reassumed full authority on February 22.

An explosion near a U.S. Air Force building, the Khobar Towers, in Dhahran in June 1996 killed 19 U.S. servicemen and wounded 350, prompting the transfer of American forces to more secure desert bases. Meanwhile, in what was seen as a related development, the Saudi government launched a crackdown on Shiite dissidents in the east, where antimonarchical and anti-Western sentiment appeared to be the strongest. Members of a pro-Iran Shiite group were later accused by the United States of being responsible for the attack (see Political Groups, below).

A cabinet reshuffle was announced on June 6, 1999, with members of the ruling family retaining six key posts. A Supreme Economic Council was established in August to oversee proposed reform in non-oil sectors, and a Supreme Council for Petroleum and Mineral Affairs was created in January 2000. By 2003 major reforms had begun to take shape. In an unprecedented move in January of that year, Crown Prince Abdallah met with reformists, some of whom the government had jailed in the 1990s for advocating reforms. Government representatives also met for the first time on Saudi soil with a UN human rights group, and in October, for the first time a woman was named dean at a major university. The most stunning news, however, came on October 13, 2003, when the government announced that it would hold nationwide elections for municipal councils in 2004 (postponed to 2005), to be followed by elections for city councilors and, ultimately, members of the Consultative Council. The announcement coincided with the country's first human rights conference, held in Riyadh, October 13–15.

Further, King Fahd granted greater legislative powers to the Consultative Council in November 2003, effectively shifting some influence from the cabinet to the legislative body. The reforms followed in the wake of increasing pressure from "liberals," but more significantly after an attack in May 2003 on a luxury residential compound that killed 35 and wounded hundreds (see Foreign relations, below). The government, which came under increasing pressure from the United States since the September 11, 2001, attacks to undertake social and political reforms, in 2003 approved direct elections for half of the seats of the 178 municipal councils, though women were not allowed to vote. The first municipal elections in more than 30 years were held February 10–April 21, 2005. Islamists won the vast majority of seats.

King Fahd died on August 1, 2005, at age 82 after an extended illness and a 23-year reign. He was immediately succeeded by 82-year-old Crown Prince Abdallah, his half-brother. Sultan ibn Abd al-Aziz Al SAUD, the longtime defense minister, replaced Abdallah as crown prince (while continuing to hold the defense portfolio and several other positions).

In his first major cabinet reshuffle, King Abdallah appointed several reformers and dismissed "reactionaries," according to news reports, in new appointments announced February 14, 2009. The king also appointed the first female cabinet member, naming her to the post of deputy minister for girls' education. In March the king postponed the country's second local elections for at least two years, stating that more time was needed to change the laws in order to "expand the participation of citizens in the management of local affairs." On March 28 Prince Nayif ibn Abd al-Aziz AL SAUD was sworn in as second deputy prime minister, placing him third in line for the throne behind the king and the crown prince.

Constitution and government. Saudi Arabia is a traditional monarchy with all power ultimately vested in the king, who is also the country's supreme religious leader. The kingdom held its first national municipal elections in some 30 years in 2005, though women continued to be disenfranchised. There are no political parties in Saudi Arabia, and legislation is by royal decree, though in 2004 King Fahd granted a greater legislative role to the Consultative Council, shifting some influence from the cabinet. In recent years an attempt was made to modernize the machinery of government by creating ministries to manage affairs of state. However, the king serves additionally as prime minister, and many sensitive cabinet posts are held by members of the royal family, often for long periods of time. The judicial system, encompassing summary and general courts, a Court of Cassation, and a Supreme Council of Justice, is largely based on Islamic religious law (sharia), but tribal and customary law are also applied. Sweeping judicial reforms were announced on April 3, 2005, including establishment of a supreme court and appeals courts in the 13 provinces.

For administrative purposes Saudi Arabia is divided into 13 provinces or regions, each headed by a governor appointed by the king. In April 1994 the provinces were subdivided into 103 governorates. The principal urban areas have half-elected, half-appointed municipal councils, while villages and tribes are governed by sheikhs in conjunction with legal advisers and other community leaders.

On March 1, 1992, King Fahd authorized the creation of a 60-member national Consultative Council (*Majlis al-Shura*) headed by a chair (speaker) appointed by the king to a four-year term. The *Majlis* (inaugurated on December 29, 1993) was empowered to initiate laws, review domestic and foreign policies, and scrutinize budgets "in the tradition of Islamic consultation." Council membership was raised to 90 in 1997 and to 120 in 2001. In late 1993 the king also issued a decree authorizing the formation of consultative councils in each province, encompassing the provincial governor and at least ten appointed individuals. Another decree codified a "basic system of government" based on Islamic law. The 83-article document is widely described as the country's first written constitution, which went beyond previous unwritten conventions by guaranteeing individual rights. It also formally delineated the rules of succession, institutionalizing the king's unilateral authority to designate (and dismiss) his heir, a son or grandson of King Abd al-Aziz Al Saud, who died in 1953.

In October 1994 King Fahd appointed the Supreme Council on Islamic Affairs to review educational, economic, and foreign policies to ensure that they were conducted in concert with Islamic precepts.

On October 20, 2006, the king issued a new law establishing a committee made up of the sons and grandsons of King Fahd to choose future kings and crown princes. The changes do not go into effect until the current crown prince becomes king. (See Current issues, below.) On October 1, 2007, King Abdallah issued a decree approving the formation of a supreme court, special tribunals for labor and commercial disputes, and appeals courts—all in accordance with Islamic law.

The king renewed the Consultative Council on February 28, 2009, appointing 150 members to four-year terms.

Foreign relations. Since the late 1950s Saudi Arabia has stood as the leading conservative power in the Arab world. The early 1960s were marked by hostility toward Egypt over North Yemen, with Riyadh supporting the royalists and Cairo backing the ultimately victorious republicans during the civil war that broke out in 1962. By 1969, however, Saudi Arabia had become a prime mover behind the pan-Islamic movement and subsequently sought to mediate such disputes as the Lebanese conflict in 1976 and the Iran-Iraq war. An influential member of the Organization of the Petroleum Exporting Countries (OPEC), the kingdom was long a restraining influence on oil price increases. Since the U.S.-led invasion of Iraq in 2003, Saudi Arabia, a swing producer, has been authorized by OPEC to continue to boost production to meet global demand.

The Saudis provided financial support for other Arab countries involved in the 1967 and 1973 Arab-Israeli conflicts and broke diplomatic relations with Cairo in April 1979 to oppose the Egyptian-Israeli peace treaty. Otherwise, the kingdom has been generally allied with the United States. The outbreak of war between Iraq and Iran in September 1980 prompted the Carter administration, which earlier in the year had rejected a Saudi request for assistance in upgrading its military capability, to announce the "temporary deployment" of four Airborne Warning and Control Systems (AWAC aircraft). An additional factor was the strong support given by Riyadh to Washington's plan, introduced following the Soviet intervention in Afghanistan in 1979, to increase the U.S. military presence throughout the Gulf region. Subsequently, despite vehement Israeli objections, the Reagan administration secured Senate approval in October 1981 of a major package of arms sales to Saudi Arabia that included five of the surveillance aircraft, although delivery did not commence until mid-1986 because of controversy over U.S. supervisory rights. Earlier, in an effort to win congressional support for their arms purchases, the Saudis had indicated a willingness to allow American use of bases in the kingdom in the event of Soviet military action in the Gulf. As the U.S. Iran-contra scandal unfolded in late 1986 and 1987, it was alleged that the Saudis had agreed to aid anti-communist resistance groups around the world as part of the AWAC purchase deal, ultimately making some $32 million available to the Nicaraguan rebels between July 1984 and March 1985 after U.S. funding for the *contra* cause had been suspended by Congress. Subsequently, plans announced by the White House in May 1987 to sell more than a billion dollars' worth of planes and missiles to Saudi Arabia were delayed by congressional hearings into the Iran-contra affair. In July 1988 relations were further strained when Riyadh, citing congressional delays and other "embarrassments" caused by Washington's criticism of Chinese missile imports, purchased $25 billion of British armaments, thus undercutting reliance on the United States as its leading military supplier.

During 1987 and 1988 the Iran-Iraq war yielded continued political tension between revolutionary Tehran and pro-Western Riyadh. In July 1987 the seizure of Mecca's Grand Mosque by Muslim extremists resulted in the death of an estimated 400 Iranian pilgrims; subsequently, Iranian officials called for the immediate "uprooting" of the Saudi royal family, while King Fahd, supported by most of the Arab states, vowed to continue as "custodian" of Islam's holy shrines. In April 1988, citing the Mecca riot and increasing Iranian attacks on its shipping vessels, Saudi Arabia became the first member of the Gulf Cooperation Council (GCC) to sever diplomatic relations with Tehran. The Khomeini regime's subsequent decision to forbid its citizens from participating in the 1988 pilgrimage was seen as an attempt to discredit Saudi administration of the holy cities. (However, the subsequent rise of a more moderate leadership in Iran paved the way for a restoration of diplomatic relations in March 1991.)

In late 1982 Foreign Minister Saud al-Faisal became the first representative of the monarchy known to have traveled to the Soviet Union in several decades. Remarks by the prince that Moscow could play a role in Middle East negotiations gave rise to speculation that relations between the two countries, which had been suspended in 1938, might improve. But it was not until Moscow's 1988 announcement that it would withdraw from Afghanistan (Riyadh long having been a highly vocal supporter of the rebel president-in-exile, Sibgahatullah Mojaddidi) that the 50-year-old impasse appeared capable of resolution. Diplomatic relations were restored in 1990. In return for the Soviet Union's support during the Gulf crisis, Saudi Arabia provided some $2 billion in previously pledged emergency economic aid to Moscow. Saudi Arabia also established diplomatic ties with China in 1990. In 1992 the kingdom moved quickly to establish ties with the Commonwealth of Independent States (CIS), offering economic aid and pursuing private-sector ties. Particular attention was given to the Central Asian republics, where the Saudis were expected to vie with Turkey and Iran for influence.

In March 1989 Iraqi and Saudi officials signed a mutual noninterference pact. However, in the wake of Iraq's invasion of Kuwait on August 2, 1990, and amid reports that Iraqi troops were massing on the Saudi border, the Saudi government shed its traditional role as regional consensus builder, criticized the invasion as "vile aggression," and called for international assistance to prevent further Iraqi gains. The ensuing buildup of Western and regional forces along the Saudi border with Kuwait caused a rupture in relations with pro-Iraqi leaders of Yemen, Jordan, and the Palestine Liberation Organization (PLO). On September 19 Riyadh rescinded special privileges for Yemeni and PLO workers, prompting repatriation of more than half of the 1.5 million Yemeni citizens in the kingdom. Shortly thereafter oil deliveries to Jordan were suspended, Jordanian diplomats were expelled, and the Saudi ambassador to Amman was recalled. Meanwhile, the Saudi government moved to reimburse and reward its allies, particularly Egypt and Syria. The kingdom's most dramatic Gulf crisis decision, however, was to acknowledge its effective alliance with the United States, which responded by promising to sell the Saudis $20 billion in armaments. Saudi Arabia's pivotal role in the U.S.-led anti-Iraqi coalition during the 1991 war included participation in 6,500 air sorties, the eviction of Iraqi forces from Khafji, and the liberation of Kuwait City.

The stationing of U.S. forces in Saudi Arabia became a sensitive matter after the Gulf war. The Saudi government allowed U.S. troops to remain in the kingdom—the birthplace of Islam and home to its most sacred places—angering many, including Osama bin Laden and his supporters. During the buildup to the 2003 U.S. invasion of Iraq, King Fahd announced that the kingdom would not participate in a war against Iraq, and he proposed that Iraqi leader Saddam Hussein go into exile to avert a war. However, U.S. forces were eventually allowed to deploy to Saudi Arabia prior to the war. After the May 12, 2003, suicide bombings of a compound in Riyadh that killed 35 and wounded hundreds, Riyadh became more attuned to the U.S. war on terror, with the government declaring its own such war in August 2003.

The kingdom strengthened its relationship with the United States in 2004 when the two countries joined in asking the United Nations to crack down on one of the kingdom's largest charities, which reportedly helped fund al-Qaida. In June 2005 some 57 Islamic nations—Saudi Arabia among them—met in Yemen and agreed to fight terrorism, now a defining issue in the Middle East. Among the concerns for Riyadh, analysts said, was that sectarian violence between Sunnis and Shiites in Iraq might eventually make its way into Saudi Arabia if armed militants crossed the border and gained support from Shiite hardliners in the kingdom.

Saudi Arabia's relations with North Yemen and South Yemen and, since 1990, the unified Republic of Yemen have often been strained, particularly regarding border demarcations. In March 2005 the two countries signed a border agreement, influenced heavily by their increasing desire to halt the flow of weapons and drug smuggling and an increasing number of terrorist suspects, and the following month Yemen and Saudi Arabia held their first joint military exercise.

Saudi Arabia has played a role in supporting a negotiated settlement between Israel and the Palestinians, at times acceding to foreign pressure. In early 1993 the Saudis responded favorably to a U.S. request for resumption of aid to the PLO as an inducement to the Palestinians to rejoin stalled peace talks with Israel. Riyadh also underscored its backing for the regional peace process the following September, when it convinced the GCC countries to end their long-standing boycott of companies doing business with Israel (see Arab League article for details). In 2003 Crown Prince Abdallah presented the Arab League with an initiative for peace with Israel in return for its withdrawal from occupied territories. (The following day, however, Israel launched a massive invasion to reoccupy the West Bank.) When Saudi Arabia was granted membership in the World Trade Organization (WTO) in December 2005, the kingdom granted assurances that it had ended its trade boycott against Israel. Subsequently, however, Saudi Arabia acknowledged that it had lifted only "certain aspects" of the boycott. In February 2006 Riyadh joined other Arab countries in rejecting a U.S. request that they cut off aid to Hamas (which won election to the new Palestinian government a month earlier). The kingdom has continued to support what it has described as the legitimate rights of Palestinians.

Though in 2006 Saudi Arabia and Iran were working toward developing cordial relations, capped by a visit to Tehran by the Saudi foreign minister, Saudi Arabia remained uneasy in the wake of reports about Iran's nuclear program and its growing influence in Iraq and Lebanon.

In February 2007 Saudi Arabia invited the leaders of Hamas and Fatah to a summit in Mecca, where the warring Palestinian factions agreed to form a unity government (which subsequently failed). Shortly after the Mecca meeting, Riyadh hosted an Arab League summit that renewed the peace initiative, offering Israel normalized ties with Arab states if it would agree to return to its pre-1967 borders. Following the collapse of the peace deal and a visit in August by U.S. secretary of state Condoleezza Rice and U.S. defense secretary Robert Gates, Saudi Arabia agreed to send its foreign minister to the U.S.-sponsored Middle East peace conference in Annapolis, Maryland, in November—its participation seen as bolstering President George W. Bush's initiative at a time when U.S. standing in the region was regarded as being at a low point.

Relations with Syria deteriorated in 2008, with Saudi Arabia ultimately joining Egypt, Jordan, and Lebanon in boycotting an Arab summit in Damascus following Syria's failure to help facilitate the election of a new government in Lebanon. Riyadh grew increasingly concerned over the tumultuous events in Beirut (see article on Lebanon), calling on "all regional sides to respect the sovereignty and independence of Lebanon," with particular references to Syria and Iran. Tensions with Iran heightened following Saudi Arabia's describing Hezbollah's military attacks in Lebanon as a "coup" backed by Iran, highlighting Saudi Arabia's efforts to counter Iran's growing Shiite influence in the region. Meanwhile, the kingdom moved to strengthen ties with the United States, signing agreements with the latter in May to broaden counterterrorism efforts and bolster peaceful nuclear cooperation, among other things. In addition, President Bush pledged to push for a $20 billion arms deal for Saudi Arabia, despite the objections of Israel and some members of the U.S. Congress. Bush contended that the weapons deal was needed to counter a perceived security threat from Iran. In 2009 Iran's foreign minister made a surprise visit to Saudi Arabia as tensions heightened between Iran and the Arab nations. Saudi Arabia, for its part, strongly recommended that Iran refrain from getting involved in internal Arab disputes, particularly in Lebanon and among the Palestinians. Meanwhile, relations with Syria warmed somewhat following a visit by President Bashar al-Assad to Saudi Arabia in March.

Agreements on security issues were strengthened with Yemen in 2009 as a result of that country's crackdown in particular on al- Qaida terrorists, who were reported to be using Yemen as a staging ground for radical Islamist activities.

Current issues. In 2000 and 2001 Crown Prince Abdallah, considered the primary architect of 1999 OPEC production cutbacks that triggered a dramatic surge in oil prices, continued to emphasize the economic reform program he launched in 1998, courting foreign investment with tax reductions and easing of land ownership restrictions while the kingdom pursued membership in the WTO. The government also invited Western companies to help develop largely untapped natural gas resources and participate in related applications of the gas sector within Saudi Arabia. Domestic political reform proceeded at a slower pace, however, in view of the heavy influence of religious conservatives as well as other "vested interests" in government. Meanwhile, the international community intensified its criticism of alleged human rights violations and discrimination against women in Saudi Arabia. Responding to external pressure and perhaps to criticism by reformists, the kingdom on March 9, 2004, established the National Human Rights Association, composed of 41 members, including 10 women.

The al-Qaida attacks on the United States in September 2001 put an unwelcome spotlight on Saudi Arabia since 15 of the 19 hijackers were Saudi citizens, while Osama bin Laden, the presumed mastermind behind the plot, is a member of one of the wealthiest Saudi families. (For complete information on bin Laden, who was stripped of his Saudi citizenship in 1995, and al-Qaida, see the article on Afghanistan.) After the U.S. invasion of Iraq in 2003, with al-Qaida–linked organizations targeting Westerners with increasing frequency and ferocity, Riyadh launched a major crackdown on Islamic extremists and Islamic religious leaders preaching violence. It also attempted to overcome criticism of previous years for its support of Islamic extremists by implementing laws to combat the financing of terrorism. Concurrently, reformists renewed their efforts to push the royal family toward more democratic elections and allowing women to vote. Progress was notable in social and political reforms, with changes to the judicial system (see Constitution and government, above), and in April 2005 the grand mufti, Sheikh Abd al-Aziz al-ASHAIKH, issued an edict opposing the practice of forcing women to marry against their will. (In an unprecedented series of events in 2005, a new labor law gave women the right to maternity leave, and women were allowed to campaign openly for seats on Jiddah's Chamber of Commerce, with two women subsequently securing seats.) Meanwhile, thousands of alleged terror suspects were arrested or killed (including a top al-Qaida leader) by security forces within the country and at the border with Yemen, and three Saudi dissidents were sentenced for up to nine years after petitioning for a constitutional monarchy.

As expected, Islamists dominated in Riyadh, Mecca, and Medina, in the municipal elections of 2005, the first such balloting in more than three decades. Shiites secured representation in the eastern provinces, while a few independents were elected in the Red Sea area. Turnout was low in the major cities, and there were accusations that, in violation of election laws, some Islamists had formed coalitions to garner votes.

Joining the WTO in 2005 was called a "key achievement" for King Abdallah after more than a decade of negotiations, reflecting Saudi Arabia's progress in economic reforms and bilateral relations. However, the kingdom came under increasing criticism from the United States in 2006 for its alleged mistreatment of foreign workers, depriving women of the right to vote, arresting dissidents, restricting religious freedom, and lagging in progress toward democratization. On a more positive note, the high price of oil continued to boost revenue by billions of dollars, increasing GDP and bolstering the government's efforts to employ more Saudis. Plans were also announced for what was described as the kingdom's single largest private sector investment, the $26 billion King Abdallah Economic City project on the Red Sea near Jiddah, which aimed to create 1 million jobs for Saudi citizens.

In a move observers hailed as "the most important reform since King Abdallah ascended the throne," according to the *Financial Times*, the king set up a committee of heirs of King Fahd, empowering them to vote by secret ballot on the eligibility of future kings and crown princes. The measure was designed to ward off power struggles within the Al Saud family and ensure that consensus candidates would be chosen by giving different branches of the ruling family a voice in the selection process, observers said.

Turmoil in the region in 2006 inevitably affected Saudi Arabia, whose ambassador to the United States, Prince Turki al-FAISAL, abruptly resigned in December, reportedly because he backed the idea of U.S. talks with Iran as a way of helping to resolve the war in Iraq. The Saudi government, which supports the Sunnis in Iraq, became increasingly concerned that if the United States were to accede to mounting pressure in Washington to withdraw its forces from Iraq, the minority Sunni population would be targeted by Shiite militias. Meanwhile, with sectarian tensions between Sunnis and Shiites on the rise in the Middle East, Shiites in Saudi Arabia reportedly were worried that they would have to give up significant gains they had made in recent years. In March Iranian president Mahmoud Ahmadinejad made his first visit to Saudi Arabia. The leaders of both countries agreed to try to ease Sunni-Shiite tensions in the region, but those efforts subsequently collapsed (see Foreign Relations, above).

In February 2007 ten men were arrested on charges of financing terrorism. It was later reported that three of the men were well-known reformists who had been circulating petitions seeking political change in the kingdom. In April 172 Islamist militants were accused of planning attacks on public figures, military areas, and oil facilities in Saudi Arabia and other Gulf states, according to the government. Also in April, the government announced a program of re-education and rehabilitation as part of an intensive effort to counter the "radicalization" of Islamist militants. The government said it would help the reformed militants find jobs and wives and would help their families financially. In other moves toward reform, the government took steps toward the establishment of the first co-ed, public university in the kingdom, and Saudi authorities reportedly held secret talks with the Vatican regarding the opening of the first Roman Catholic church in the kingdom, which historically has banned all Christian denominations. The talks followed an unprecedented visit to the Vatican by King Abdallah in November 2007. Subsequently, in March 2008 the king initiated an interfaith dialogue that included representatives of all monotheistic religions.

Countering terrorism continued to be of major concern in 2008, the government announcing that it had dismantled a new terrorist organization that reportedly received its instructions from al-Qaida's deputy leader, Ayman al-ZAWAHIRI, and that it had also arrested 28 militants linked to al-Qaida who were preparing to "launch a terror campaign" in the kingdom. Authorities also enacted new laws to combat Internet-related crimes, particularly those in support of terrorism.

As global demands for oil continued to rise, Saudi Arabia was at the forefront of Western pressures in 2008, most significantly in regard to requests by the United States for greater production to help offset rising U.S. prices. In January and again in May, President Bush appealed for an increase; both times King Abdallah "politely" refused. The king pointed out that just prior to Bush's request in May, Saudi Arabia had authorized a "modest increase" of 300,000 barrels per day to help bolster supplies to some 50 countries around the world, including the United States, following cutbacks by Venezuela and Mexico.

In 2009 attention turned to what was described by observers as "a sweeping shake-up" by the king, who replaced four key cabinet ministers, most notably those in education and justice, and appointed new leaders to almost all justice-related bodies. All of these changes, including the king's appointment of a woman as deputy education minister—making her the kingdom's highest-ranking female political figure ever—were seen as significant moves toward reform. The deputy minister's appointments were seen as particularly important in the religious-based education system, which had been viewed as fostering extremism, and in the effort to codify sharia law. Some analysts said the king's most far-reaching change was his reconfiguration of the Grand Ulema Council, the country's premier religious body, to include more moderates. Further, the king appointed as head of the Supreme Judicial Council the former chair of the Consultative Council, Salih ibn HUMAYD, who was seen as more likely to advance the king's reforms than his predecessor. In addition, the king replaced the head of the "notoriously strict" religious police with a more moderate figure, according to published reports. Commenting on the broad efforts toward reform, *The New York Times* noted that King Abdallah "may finally be ready to lead his country toward greater tolerance and modernity." Meanwhile, in a move that observers said was expected, the king delayed the next municipal elections for at least two years in an effort to grant more power to the local councils and to expand the electoral process. The government explained the postponement as having "extended the mandate" of the sitting councils by two years while necessary changes to the law were prepared.

POLITICAL GROUPS

There are no political parties, as such, in Saudi Arabia.

Committee for the Defense of Legitimate Rights (CDLR). The CDLR was formed in May 1993 by several prominent Islamists who described the grouping as the kingdom's first human rights organization. However, the government charged that the CDLR was in reality a vehicle for extending fundamentalist criticism of the monarchy, which had been on the rise since the Gulf crisis. Consequently, the CDLR was ordered to disband only two weeks after its creation; in addition, CDLR leader Muhammad al-MASARI and some 1,000 followers were arrested, and a number of CDLR supporters were fired from their government positions. After his release the following November, al-Masari moved to London, where the CDLR was reestablished in April 1994 as an exile organization. The committee subsequently issued numerous communiqués criticizing the Saudi regime's human rights and economic policies. Although accused by Riyadh of attempting to promote "destabilization" so as to facilitate elimination of the monarchy in favor of a fundamentalist regime, CDLR leaders took no official antimonarchical stance and steadfastly avowed a policy of nonviolence. However, the CDLR remained critical of what it alleged to be widespread corruption within the ruling family and direct in its call for imposition of strict Islamic rule in the kingdom. (In 1998 the Saudi government released Sheikh Sulaymah al-RUSHUDI, reportedly one of the founders of the CDLR.)

In 1996 a conflict was reported between CDLR leaders Muhammad al-Masari and Saad al-FAQIH, with the latter forming a breakaway grouping called the **Movement for Islamic Reform in Arabia** (MIRA). Subsequent activity has been minimal on the part of both groups, although in 2003 MIRA led an unprecedented demonstration in Riyadh, coinciding with the opening of the kingdom's first human rights conference. MIRA's antigovernment Web site in March 2005 posted an audiotape purporting to represent the new al-Qaida leader in Saudi Arabia. According to MIRA, he was killed in April 2005. A year later, Abd al Aziz al SHANBARI, a former Saudi dissident who had been affiliated with MIRA, denounced the group during a meeting with King Abdallah. Al Shanbari returned to Saudi Arabia after two years in exile in London, reportedly having made some sort of private arrangement with the king. MIRA reportedly operates out of London.

MIRA's Web site in 2006 addressed the new succession law issued by the king, claiming that the real aim of the law was to exclude Prince Nayif ibn Abd al-Aziz Al SAUD, the interior minister and a brother of King Fahd, from ascending the throne. The reported reasons for excluding Nayif were his alleged defiance of many of the king's orders and pressure from U.S. officials who were said to be dissatisfied with the level of cooperation from Nayif. In 2007 MIRA had its own television station, broadcasting from London.

Leader: Muhammad al-MASARI.

Reform Movement. A loosely organized Shiite grouping, the Reform Movement (also referenced as the Islamic Revolutionary Organization in the Arabian Peninsula) originally operated out of London and Damascus, its activities including publication of the *Arabian Peninsula,* a newsletter critical of, among other things, the Saudi government's human rights record. In late 1993 the movement's leaders agreed to discontinue its attacks on the government in return for the release of Shiite dissidents from prison and permission for Shiite expatriates to return to Saudi Arabia. However, some members reportedly remained in "revolutionary" mode and opposed to the proposed reconciliation pact. A number of Shiites were arrested in the government crackdown that followed the 1996 bombing in Dhahran, prompting observers to suggest that the agreement with the Reform Movement had collapsed. However, little formal activity was subsequently reported on behalf of the movement, though it continues to press for change and its members are routinely arrested, convicted, and jailed. The leader, Sheikh Hassan al-Safar, was reportedly living in exile in Damascus in 1993. At some point al-Safar, a cleric, returned to the Shiite-dominated area of eastern Saudi Arabia. In 2003 al-Safar was among those invited to participate in the king's "national dialogue" in Mecca, where measures to counter extremism were among the topics. It was reported to be the first such gathering in the country to include Shiites and Sunnis, and observers made note of the fact that leaders from the two main religious branches were seen together on television.

Leader: Sheikh Hassan al-SAFAR.

LEGISLATURE

On March 1, 1992, King Fahd decreed that a **Consultative Council** (*Majlis al-Shura*) of 60 members (plus a speaker) would be appointed within six months. In accordance with the decree, a speaker was named the following September. Other members were not appointed until August 20, 1993, and the council convened on December 29. Upon the expiration of the first term of the council in July 1997, King Fahd increased its membership to 90 for the subsequent four-year term. Membership increased to 120 for the new council appointed on May 24, 2001, and the council was renewed on April 11, 2005. The king appointed an expanded 150-member council on February 28, 2009.

Chair: Abdullah Al ASHAIKH.

CABINET

[as of May 1, 2009]

Prime Minister	King Abdallah ibn Abd al-Aziz Al Saud
Deputy Prime Minister	Prince Sultan ibn Abd al-Aziz Al Saud
Second Deputy Prime Minister	Prince Nayif ibn Abd al-Aziz Al Saud
Ministers	
Agriculture	Fahd ibn Abd al-Rahman ibn Sulayman Balqhanaim
Civil Service	Muhammad ibn Ali al-Fayiz
Commerce and Industry	Abdallah bin Ahmed Yosef Zainal Alireza
Communications and Information Technology	Muhammad ibn Jamil ibn Ahmad Mulla
Culture and Information	Abd al-Aziz ibn Mohieddin Khoja
Defense and Aviation	Prince Sultan ibn Abd al-Aziz Al Saud
Economy and Planning	Khalid ibn Muhammad al-Qusaibi
Education	Prince Faisal ibn Abdullah Muhammad Al Saud
Finance	Ibrahim ibn Abd al-Aziz al-Assaf
Foreign Affairs	Prince Saud al-Faisal ibn Abd al-Aziz Al Saud
Health	Abdullah ibn Abd al-Aziz al-Rabiah
Higher Education	Khalid ibn Muhammad al-Anqari
Interior	Prince Nayif ibn Abd al-Aziz Al Saud
Islamic Affairs, Endowments, Call, and Guidance	Salih ibn Abd al-Aziz al-Ashaikh
Justice	Mohammad ibn Abdulkarim ibn Abd al-Aziz al-Issa
Labor	Ghazi ibn Abd al-Rahman al-Qusaibi
Municipal and Rural Affairs	Prince Mitib ibn Abd al-Aziz Al Saud
Petroleum and Mineral Resources	Ali ibn Ibrahim al-Naimi
Pilgrimage	Fuad ibn Abd al-Salaam ibn Muhammad al-Farsi
Social Affairs	Yusuf ibn Ahmed al-Othaimeen
Transport	Jubarah ibn Ayd al-Suraysiri
Water and Electricity	Abdallah ibn Abd al-Rahman al-Husayn
Ministers of State	
Cabinet Affairs	Prince Abd al-Aziz ibn Fahd ibn Abd al-Aziz Al Saud
Foreign Affairs	Nizar Ubayd Madani
Shura Affairs	Saud bin Said al-Methami
Without Portfolio	Musaid ibn Muhammad al-Ayban
	Abd al-Aziz ibn Abdallah al-Khuwaytir
	Mutlaab ibn Abdallah al-Nafissa

COMMUNICATIONS

Most newspapers and periodicals are published by privately (but not individually) owned national press institutions. The government also publishes a number of periodicals. Although censorship was formally abolished in 1961, criticism of the king and government policy is dealt with harshly by the government, and a genuinely free flow of ideas from the outside world is discouraged. In May 2003 the editor of the liberal daily *al-Watan* was removed after criticizing Wahhabi Islam as extremism. However, earlier in 2003 the government allowed journalists to organize and form their own association. In 2006 two journalists were dismissed by the government for reporting on topics outside the strict limits set by the authorities. In 2007 the watchdog group Reporters Without Borders said, "The Saudi regime maintains very tight control of all news and self-censorship is pervasive. Enterprising journalists pay dearly for the slightest criticism of the authorities or the policies of 'brother Arab' countries." In December 2007 the author of a blog on social and political issues was arrested on charges of violating "non-security" laws. Because Saudi Arabia had no law dealing specifically with the Internet, all media were required to obtain official permission. (New laws regarding Internet-related crimes were enacted in 2008.) The blogger was freed in April 2008.

The government also blocks access to a wide range of Internet sites it believes are offensive. Reporters Without Borders has estimated that Saudi Arabia "has created one of the world's biggest Internet filtering systems," blocking access to 400,000 Web pages.

Press. The following papers are Arabic dailies published in Jiddah, unless otherwise noted: *al-Asharq al-Awsat* (224,992); *Okaz* (107,614); *Urdu News* (30,000); *Riyadh Daily* (Riyadh, 50,000) in English; *al-Hayat*; *al-Massaiyah*; *al-Riyadh* (Riyadh, 150,000); *Ukaz* (110,200); *al-Jazirah* (Riyadh, 94,000); *al-Bilad* (66,200); *Arab News* (110,000), in English; *al-Yaum* (Dammam, 50,000); *Saudi Gazette* (50,000), in English; *al-Madinah* (46,370); *al-Nadwah* (Mecca, 35,000); *al-Watan* (Abha); *al-Sharq al-Awsat.*

News agency. The Saudi Press Agency (*Wakalat al-Anba al-Saudiyah*—SPA) is located in Riyadh.

Broadcasting and computing. The Broadcasting Service of the Kingdom of Saudi Arabia (*Idhaat al-Mamlakat al-Arabiyat al-Saudiyah*), a government facility in charge of all broadcasting in the country, operates a number of radio stations broadcasting in both Arabic and English, while Aramco Radio broadcasts from Dhahran in English. Television is transmitted from a dozen locations, including Riyadh, Jiddah, and Medina. On January 11, 2004, a state-owned all-news satellite television channel was launched, with the country's first female news presenter. Also, *al-Jazirah* began airing television broadcasts from its base in Qatar. Founded in Riyadh in September 1991, Middle East Broadcasting Center (MBC), now based in Dubai, transmits Western-style news and entertainment shows throughout the region. The MBC operates with the king's tacit approval. As of 2008 there were 308 Internet users per 1,000 inhabitants.

INTERGOVERNMENTAL REPRESENTATION

Ambassador to the U.S.: Adel bin Ahmed al-JUBEIR.

U.S. Ambassador to Saudi Arabia: James B. SMITH.

Permanent Representative to the UN: Khalid Abdalrazaq AL NAFISEE.

IGO Memberships (Non-UN): AfDB, AFESD, AMF, BADEA, BIS, GCC, G-20, IDB, Interpol, LAS, NAM, OAPEC, OIC, OPEC, PCA, WCO, WTO.

SENEGAL

Republic of Senegal
République du Sénégal

Political Status: Former French dependency, independent since August 20, 1960; presidential system established under constitution promulgated March 7, 1963; Senegalese-Gambian Confederation of Senegambia, formed with effect from February 1, 1982, dissolved as of September 30, 1989.

Area: 75,750 sq. mi. (196,192 sq. km.).

Population: 9,855,338 (2002C); 12,694,000 (2008E).

Major Urban Center (2005E): DAKAR (2,167,000).

Official Language: French.

Monetary Unit: CFA Franc (official rate December 1, 2009: 434.59 francs = $1US). The CFA franc, previously pegged to the French franc, is now permanently pegged to the euro at 655.957 francs = 1 euro.

President: Abdoulaye WADE (Senegalese Democratic Party); elected in second-round balloting on March 19, 2000, and inaugurated for a seven-year term on April 1 in succession to Abdou DIOUF (Socialist Party); reelected in the first round of balloting on February 25, 2007, and inaugurated for a five-year term on April 3.

Prime Minister: Souleymane Ndéné Ndiaye (Senegalese Democratic Party); appointed by the president on April 30, 2009, to succeed Cheikh Hadjibou SOUMARÉ (nonparty), who had resigned earlier that day following local elections on March 22.

THE COUNTRY

Senegal is situated on the bulge of West Africa between Mauritania on the north, Mali on the east, and Guinea and Guinea-Bissau on the south. Gambia forms an enclave extending into Senegal's territory for 200 miles along one of the area's four major rivers. The predominantly flat or rolling savanna country in Senegal has a population of varied ethnic backgrounds, with the Wolof, whose language is widely used commercially, being the largest group. French, the official language, is spoken only by a literate minority. In the 1988 census, 94 percent of the population was identified as Muslim, the remainder being animist or Christian. Islamic "brotherhoods" exercise significant economic and political influence throughout the country, most of them espousing what Western observers would describe as a moderate version of Islam. One such group is the Mouride brotherhood, said to represent as many as two million Sufi Muslims around the city of Touba. The illiteracy rate, while declining in recent years, remains above 60 percent, somewhat higher than for the continent as a whole. In addition, it is estimated that about 57 percent of the population lives in poverty. In 2008 the UN Human Development Index ranked Senegal 153 out of 179 nations.

About 70 percent of the population is employed in agriculture; peanuts, the principal crop, once accounted for one-third of export earnings, but production has declined. Cotton, sugar, and rice (most supplies of which have traditionally been imported) have become the focus of agricultural diversification efforts, while fishing, phosphate mining, oil refining, and tourism have grown in importance.

Economic difficulties, as exemplified by rising prices and high urban unemployment, have been addressed since 1977 by a series of adjustment programs that have reduced the role of the state in most sectors, liberalized trade measures, and limited government spending. These programs earned Senegal a high level of foreign aid, generous terms in rescheduling its more than $4.2 billion external debt, and support from the International Monetary Fund (IMF). However, overall economic improvement was minimal in the early 1990s, and in 1994 the IMF extended additional credit to Dakar to support programs designed to offset the devaluation of the CFA franc, including a reduction of customs tariffs and a "moderate wage policy." GDP grew by an average of more than 5 percent annually from 1996 to 2000, earning praise from the IMF and World Bank. At the same time, Senegal entered the new millennium with an economy that remained peasant-based and stressed by unequal distribution of wealth, high unemployment, an external debt of $3.5 billion, and deteriorating social services. Nonetheless, Senegal subsequently experienced steady, if modest, economic growth, which was accompanied by low inflation. As a result of sound fiscal policy, the government was also able to lower deficits and increase tax revenue.

In April 2003 Senegal was granted $33 million from the IMF for economic restructuring in 2003–2005. A year later, the IMF declared that Senegal had completed the necessary steps under the Heavily Indebted Poor Countries (HIPC) initiative. As a result, Senegal was accorded nearly $500 million in debt relief.

In 2006 the World Bank announced that Senegal had qualified for additional debt relief under the Multilateral Debt Relief Initiative.

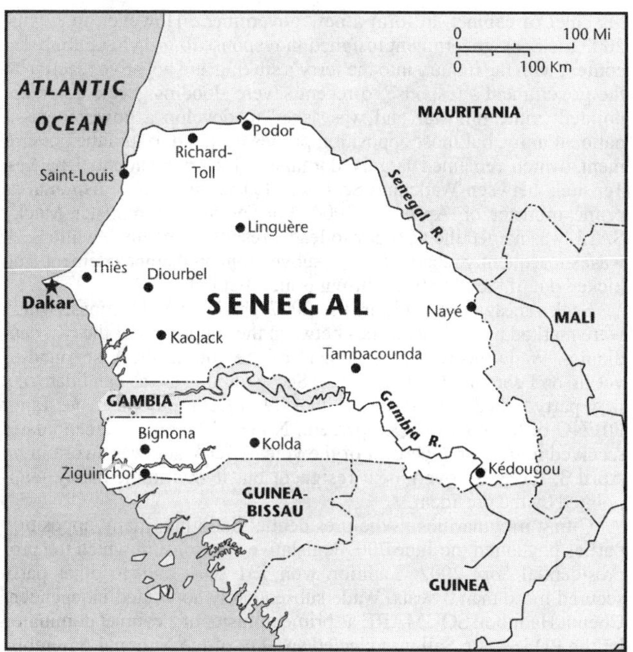

Spain announced in February 2008 that it would cancel Senegal's $75 million debt. GDP grew by 5.1 percent in 2008, while inflation was 5.4 percent and unemployment was 25 percent. The global economic crisis caused Senegal's economy to slow in 2009 because of declines in commodity exports and decreases in remittances. The IMF estimated that GDP growth would be 3 percent for the year. In December the IMF granted Senegal $75.6 million in emergency assistance to help offset the impact of rising energy and food costs, however, it also criticized the government for delays in implementing economic reforms. In addition, China extended a $57 million loan to Senegal to improve public transportation and information technology. France also announced a $174.7 million emergency loan to pay-off the country's domestic debt after ending a boycott of aid to the country (see Foreign relations, below).

GOVERNMENT AND POLITICS

Political background. Under French influence since the 17th century, Senegal became a French colony in 1920 and a self-governing member of the French Community in November 1958. In January 1959 it joined with the adjacent French Soudan (now Mali) to form the Federation of Mali, which became fully independent within the Community on June 20, 1960. Two months later Senegal seceded from the federation, and the separate Republic of Senegal was proclaimed on September 5. President Léopold Sédar SENGHOR, a well-known poet and the leader of Senegal's strongest political party, the Senegalese Progressive Union (*Union Progressiste Sénégalaise*—UPS), governed initially under a parliamentary system in which political rival Mamadou DIA was prime minister. An unsuccessful coup in December 1962 resulted in Dia's arrest and imprisonment (until his release in 1974) and the establishment by Senghor of a presidential form of government under his exclusive direction. In an election held under violent conditions on December 1, 1963, Senghor retained the presidency, and his party won all of the seats in the National Assembly, as it also did in the elections of 1968 and 1973.

In response to demands for political and constitutional reform, Senghor in early 1970 reinstituted the post of prime minister, while a constitutional amendment adopted in 1976 sanctioned three political parties, the ideology of each being prescribed by law. In early 1979 a fourth, essentially conservative, party was also accorded recognition. Additional parties were legalized under legislation enacted in April 1981.

Although he had been overwhelmingly reelected to a fourth five-year term on February 26, 1978, President Senghor resigned on December 31, 1980, and, as prescribed by the constitution, he was succeeded by Prime Minister Abdou DIOUF. The new administration extended the process of political liberalization, most restrictions on political party activity being lifted in April 1981. Coalitions were proscribed, however; thus the opposition did not present a serious threat to the ruling Socialist Party (*Parti Socialiste*—PS) in the presidential and legislative balloting of February 27, 1983, Diouf winning reelection with 83 percent of the vote and the PS capturing 111 of 120 assembly seats. In the subsequent poll of February 28, 1988, Diouf was reelected by a reported 73 percent of the vote, with the PS being awarded 103 assembly seats. However, controversy surrounding this election, and its aftermath tarnished Senegal's long-standing democratic reputation.

While the major opposition parties boycotted local elections in November 1990, a number of their leaders, including Abdoulaye WADE, Diouf's principal opponent in the 1982 and 1988 presidential campaigns, were named to a government headed by Habib THIAM on April 7, 1991. However, in October 1992 Wade and three other cabinet members from Wade's Senegalese Democratic Party (*Parti Démocratique Sénégalais*—PDS) resigned from the government, claiming they had been marginalized by their PS colleagues and included in only "trivial" decision making.

In first-round balloting on February 21, 1993, President Diouf was credited with winning 58 percent of the valid vote, thus eliminating the need for a second round. Wade was runner-up with a vote share of 32 percent. In the legislative poll of May 9, the PS won a reduced majority of 84 assembly seats, with the PDS securing 27 seats.

On May 15, 1993, the Constitutional Council's vice president, Babacar SEYE, was assassinated by a group identifying themselves as the People's Army. On May 16 Wade and a number of his PDS colleagues were detained after one of the alleged conspirators, Cledor SENE, claimed to be acting on their orders. On June 7 Sene recanted his story and publicly apologized to Wade for attempting to "decapitate" the PDS. Thereafter, relations between the government and the opposition grew increasingly acrimonious, as two PDS deputies, Mody SY and Samuel SARR, remained imprisoned for alleged involvement in the assassination, and the PDS mounted a demonstration in late July on behalf of their release. On August 24 the National Assembly further aggravated the situation by approving an emergency economic austerity plan that called for cuts in civil service salaries. Implementation of the measure was subsequently temporarily suspended following a general strike on September 2. In early October Wade and his wife, Viviane WADE, who had previously been released, were rearrested for their alleged involvement in Seye's assassination, and on November 5 more than 130 opposition activists were arrested for participating in an anti-government rally organized by the PDS and the African Party for Democracy and Socialism/And Jëf (*Parti Africain pour la Démocratie et le Socialisme/And Jëf*—PADS/AJ). Violent clashes erupted during a demonstration against the effects of the mid-January 1994 CFA devaluation, and the government moved quickly to indict Abdoulaye Wade and Landing SAVANE, leader of the PADS/AJ, for "breach against the state security," a charge for which 73 others were also being detained. However, on May 26 the Wades and their fellow PDS members were cleared of involvement in the Seye assassination, and at midyear Sy and Sarr were released after launching hunger strikes. In August Wade and Savane were acquitted of the February charges. In October three people were sentenced for their roles in Seye's assassination, although no motive was revealed.

In March 1995 the Diouf administration scored what appeared to be a major political victory when Wade accepted a cabinet-level post. As a result, the government contained three of the four leading groups previously aligned as regime opponents. In addition, although Wade had previously refused to enter the government unless the PDS was given half the posts in a 20-member cabinet, he now agreed to accept only 5 portfolios in a 33-member cabinet.

Amid reports of increasing violations of a two-year-old cease-fire between the government and secessionist Casamance rebels in southern Senegal, security forces in May 1995 arrested Fr. Augustin DIAMACOUNE Senghor, leader of the Movement of Democratic Forces of Casamance (*Mouvement des Forces Démocratiques de la Casamance*—MFDC). Full-scale fighting erupted following Diamacoune's detention, and in mid-June the cease-fire was formally abandoned. In September the government attempted to start peace talks in Ziguinchor, but fighting continued as MFDC militants refused to negotiate until Diamacoune, who had been placed under house arrest, was freed. In response to the release of a number of his associates in early December, Diamacoune called for an end to the uprising, and on December 30 charges against him were dropped. The following day Diouf announced the creation of a parliamentary upper house, a Senate, which he described as the first step in an effort to decentralize power through a process of "regionalization."

In early 1996 the Diouf administration announced that independent candidates would be prohibited from participating in the rural, regional, and municipal elections scheduled for November. Grassroots groups and small opposition parties then accused Diouf of retreating from his pledge to decentralize power. Meanwhile, electoral preparations were threatened by the renewal of Casamance rebel activity, and in May the president's party rebuffed proposals to form an independent electoral commission. In balloting on November 24 the PS won what was described as a landslide victory, although voter turnout was reported at only about 50 percent and opposition parties criticized some aspects of the way the elections were conducted.

In March 1997 President Diouf convened a conference to review the 1996 elections with the purported aim of improving polling procedures. However, 19 opposition parties accused the PS of attempting to dominate the proceedings and withdrew from the conference in May. In August the Diouf administration, in an abrupt about-face, announced that it would establish an independent electoral commission, the National Elections Observatory (*Observatoire National des Elections*—ONEL) and published a draft electoral reform document that opposition leaders described as meeting "80 percent" of their demands.

In legislative balloting on May 25, 1998, PS candidates dominated an 18-party field, winning 93 seats in the expanded 140-member assembly; the PS's nearest two competitors, the PDS and the newly formed Union for Democratic Renewal (*Union pour le Renouveau Démocratique*—URD), secured 23 and 11 seats, respectively. Although the PDS, URD, and four other parties petitioned to have the polling results overturned because of alleged fraudulent tallying, the ONEL and international observers described the elections as generally free and fair. On July 3 Diouf named Mamadou Lamine LOUM to replace Thiam as prime minister, and the following day a new cabinet that included only one non-PS member was announced.

In August 1998 the PS-dominated assembly voted 93–1 to abolish the limit on presidential terms, thereby permitting the Diouf presidency to continue past 2000. All but two opposition legislators boycotted the session, and the following day all of the leading opposition politicians condemned the assembly vote at an unprecedented joint news conference.

Elections to fill the legislature's newly formed upper house, or Senate, were held on January 24, 1999, candidates affiliated with the PS winning all 45 elective seats. Eight candidates contested the first round of presidential balloting on February 27, 2000, with Diouf securing 43 percent of the vote and Wade 30 percent. Most of the other candidates threw their support to Wade in the second round, which he won, 58.7 to 41.3 percent. Following his inauguration on April 1, Wade appointed Moustapha NIASSE of the Alliance of Forces for Progress (*Alliance des Forces pour le Progrès*—AFP) as prime minister to head a coalition cabinet that also included the PADS/AJ, the Independence and Labor Party (*Parti de l'Indépendance et du Travail*—PIT), and the Democratic League–Labor Party Movement (*Ligue Démocratique–Mouvement pour le Parti du Travail*—LD-MPT).

As promised during the 2000 presidential campaign, the PDS and its allies presented a number of constitutional amendments for a national referendum on January 7, 2001. The measures, which abolished the presidentially appointed Senate and otherwise reduced the president's authority, were approved by 94 percent of the voters in a reported 66 percent turnout.

Invoking a provision in the new basic law that authorized the president to call for new legislative elections after the most recently elected assembly had served for at least two years, Wade dissolved the assembly on February 15, 2001, and ordered new elections for April 29. Meanwhile, friction grew between Wade and Niasse, and the prime minister left his post (having either resigned or been dismissed, depending on whose account was accurate) on March 3. He was succeeded by Mame Madiou BOYE, an independent who had been serving as justice minister; Boye thereby became Senegal's first female prime minister.

The PDS-led *Sopi* (Wolof for "change") Coalition (see Political Parties, below) dominated the April 29, 2001, assembly balloting, despite the defection of the AFP and the PIT from the government. The new government named by Boye on May 12 was again led by the PDS and several of its smaller electoral partners.

On November 4, 2002, President Wade dismissed Prime Minister Boye in the wake of a ferry disaster that claimed 1,200 lives and attracted intense international scrutiny. Wade appointed Idrissa SECK, his chief of cabinet, to form a new government. However, in August 2003 the Seck government resigned in response to growing public discontent with the inquiry into the ferry's sinking and negative reaction to the government's response to recent severe flooding. Seck was reappointed prime minister and was asked to develop a government of national unity, but most opposition parties declined to join the government, which remained largely dominated by propresidential parties. Tensions between Wade and Seck resulted in the latter's dismissal as prime minister on April 21, 2004. Former interior minister Macky SALL was named the next day to lead a reshuffled cabinet, while Seck was subsequently charged with subversion and embezzlement and kicked out of the PDS (see Current issues, below).

Seck ran against Wade in the 2007 presidential elections, which were marked by violent clashes between the supporters of the two candidates. Wade received 55.9 percent of the vote in the first round of voting on February 25, followed by Seck (running as the candidate of a new party called The Nation) with 14.9 percent and Ousmane Tanor DIENG of the PS with 13.6 percent. None of the other 12 candidates received more than 6 percent of the vote. After Wade was sworn in on April 3, the Sall government resigned, but it was immediately reappointed by the president.

Citing irregularities in the presidential balloting, many opposition parties boycotted the June 2007 legislative elections, in which the propresidential *Sopi* 2007 Coalition won 131 seats and no other party secured more than 3 seats. Wade subsequently appointed independent Cheikh Hadjibou SOUMARÉ as prime minister of a cabinet dominated by the PDS, while Sall was elected speaker of the National Assembly. In balloting for the Senate in August the PDS won 34 of the elected seats, while the African Party for Democracy and Socialism/And Jëf won one. The remaining 65 seats were appointed by Wade in September. Wade ally and mayor of Dakar Pape Diop was subsequently elected speaker of the Senate. There was a major cabinet reshuffle in December that reduced the number of members from 38 to 28 in an effort to streamline the government. Wade faced significant criticism as 8 of the dismissed ministers were women.

The PS and other opposition groups announced that they would participate in local and regional elections scheduled for May 18, 2008. However, the assembly postponed the balloting until March 2009. The action led to protests by the opposition, especially after the assembly enacted legislation in May 2008 to consolidate the number of local and regional offices. In October the terms of office of speaker in both the Senate and Assembly were reduced from five years to one year.

There were a series of cabinet reshuffles in late 2008 and early 2009 as part of an effort to enhance the popularity of the government. Nonetheless, in balloting for local and municipal offices on March 22, opposition parties won the majority of posts (see Current issues, below), including a number of seats in areas that were strongholds for the ruling *Sopi* Coalition. The defeat was the first broad electoral loss for Wade's coalition since 2000. Following the losses, Wade replaced Soumaré as prime minister on April 30 with a close political ally, Souleymane Ndéné NDIAYE, a former presidential spokesperson and the current minister of fisheries. Ndiaye reshuffled the cabinet and formed a new government on May 1.

Constitution and government. Senegal is administratively divided into eleven regions, each headed by a presidentially appointed governor who is assisted by an elected Regional Assembly; the regions are divided into departments. The constitution provides for a president elected by direct universal suffrage, with runoff balloting for the two top contenders if none secures an absolute majority. Under amendments approved in 1991, presidents were limited to two terms, although the incumbent (Abdou Diouf), already elected twice, was permitted to stand one more time. An amendment in 1993 extended presidential terms to seven years. The two-term restriction was formally abandoned in 1998, thereby permitting Diouf to contest the 2000 balloting as well. Amendments in 2001 reimposed the two-term limit and returned the length of the term to five years. The president appoints the prime minister (the office having been abolished in 1983 and revived in 1991), who in turn appoints the Council of Ministers in consultation with the president. Legislative power was vested in a unicameral National Assembly until December 31, 1995, when President Diouf announced the creation of a Senate to act as an upper house. The first Senate was elected in January 1999, but that body was abolished in the 2001 constitutional amendments. Under initial procedures, half of the assembly members were elected from Senegal's departments on a "first past the post" basis, the other half by proportional representation from a national list. However, electoral changes adopted in 1989 provided that national lists would be dropped from future elections, with all members being chosen on a departmental basis. Only parties registered at least four months before an election were allowed to participate; neither independent candidacies nor opposition coalitions were permitted. However, the combination of departmental and national lists was reestablished for the April 2001 assembly election in accordance with the January constitutional revisions. Party restrictions were also lifted as were barriers to electoral coalitions. The principal judicial organs, under a system revised in 1992, include a Constitutional Council, one of whose functions is to rule on electoral issues; a Council of State; a Court of Cassation; and a Court of Appeal; with magistrate courts at the local level. In addition, a High Court of Justice, chosen by the assembly from among its own membership, is responsible for impeachment proceedings. Elections for municipal and rural community councilors were held in May 2002.

In January 2007 the National Assembly voted to reinstate the Senate, and elections for the chamber were held in August. In 2008 the presidential term of office was extended from five to seven years (see Current issues, below).

Foreign relations. Formally nonaligned, Senegal has retained especially close political, cultural, and economic ties with France. An active advocate of West African cooperation, it has participated in such regional groupings as the Economic Community of West African States, the Permanent Inter-State Committee on Drought Control in the Sahel, and the Organization for the Development of the Senegal River. (The members of the latter are Mali and Mauritania.) Regional relations improved substantially as the result of a "reconciliation" pact signed in Monrovia, Liberia, in March 1978, ending five years of friction with Guinea and Côte d'Ivoire.

Under President Senghor, Senegal maintained a generally conservative posture in African affairs, refusing to recognize Angola because of the presence of Cuban troops there, supporting Morocco against the claims of the insurgent Polisario Front in the Western Sahara, and breaking relations with Libya in mid-1980 because of that country's alleged efforts to destabilize the governments of Chad, Mali, and Niger, as well as Senegal. Reflecting the "spirit of our new diplomacy"—essentially an effort to introduce greater flexibility in its relations with other African governments—Dakar announced in February 1982 that it would reverse its long-standing support of the Angolan resistance movement and recognize the Mouvement Populaire de Libération de l'Azawad (MPLA) government in Luanda. Ties with Algeria were strengthened in the course of reciprocal visits by the respective heads of state in 1984 and 1985; relations with Libya eased as the result of a visit by Colonel Qadhafi in December 1985 and were formally restored in November 1988.

In light of the unusual geographic relationship between the two countries, one of Senegal's most prominent regional concerns has been its association with Gambia. A 1967 treaty provided for cooperation in foreign affairs, development of the Gambia River basin, and, most important, defense. Consequently, Senegalese troops were dispatched to Banjul, Gambia, in October 1980 amid rumors of Libyan involvement in a projected coup and again in July 1981 when an uprising threatened to topple the Jawara administration (see article on Gambia). The latter incident was followed by an agreement to establish a Confederation of Senegambia, completed on February 1, 1982. Although the component states remained politically independent entities, the Confederation agreement called for the integration of security forces, the establishment of an economic and monetary union, and the coordination of policies in foreign affairs, internal communications, and other areas. A joint Council of Ministers and an appointed Confederal Assembly were established, and it was agreed that the presidents of Senegal and Gambia would serve as president and vice president, respectively, of the confederation. In practical terms, however, little progress was made in actualizing the confederation, Gambia in particular appearing to procrastinate in the endeavor. Many Gambians criticized what was perceived as an unequal relationship, while Gambian government and business leaders questioned the wisdom of their country's proposed entrance into the franc zone. Economic union was also hindered by the fact that Gambia had long favored liberal trade policies in contrast to Senegal's imposition of high protective tariffs. In August 1989 Senegal unilaterally withdrew some of its troops from Gambia, and President Diouf declared that the confederation, having "failed in its purpose," should be "frozen." Gambian President Jawara responded by suggesting it be terminated completely, and a protocol was quickly negotiated formally dissolving the grouping as of September 30. Despite a presidential summit in December 1989, relations remained cool through 1990 as Senegal enacted trade sanctions aimed at stemming the importation of foreign goods via its relatively duty-free neighbor. In January 1991 the two countries moved to reestablish bilateral links by the conclusion of a treaty of friendship and cooperation. As finalized in June, the treaty provided for annual summits and the establishment of joint commissions to ensure implementation of summit agreements.

In May 1989 the third conference of francophone heads of state met in Dakar amid deepening hostility between Senegal and Mauritania that had been triggered by a dispute on April 9 over farming rights along their border. Rioting in both Dakar and Nouakchott ensued, causing death or injury to several hundred people and the cross-repatriation of an estimated 150,000–300,000, including a substantial number of Moors, who had dominated the crucial small-business retail sector in the Senegalese capital. The situation continued in crisis for the balance of the year. Relations remained broken, with a continuing exodus (forced, according to Senegalese charges) of blacks from Mauritania to Senegal; Nouakchott announced preparations for a possible war. In January 1990 border forces exchanged artillery fire across the Senegal River, but diplomatic efforts, led by Organization of African Unity (OAU, subsequently the African Union—AU) president Hosni Mubarak, helped avert additional violence. By early 1991 relations had again deteriorated, as Nouackchott accused Senegal of aiding antigovernment rebels and Dakar charged Mauritania with arming Casamance separatists with Iraqi weapons. Meanwhile, relations with Guinea-Bissau, already strained by Bissau's refusal to recognize a July 1989 international court decision favoring Senegal in their maritime border dispute, were exacerbated by a clash in May 1991 that left 17 dead and by reports that Bissau was also supporting the Casamance rebels.

A May 1991 rapprochement between Dakar and the Casamance insurgents had a positive effect on relations with both Guinea-Bissau and Mauritania. The choice of the former as the site for the signing of a cease-fire agreement signaled a further lessening of tensions, and on July 18 an agreement to reopen the Senegalese-Mauritanian border paved the way for restoration of diplomatic relations on April 23, 1992. However, on December 12 tension again flared with the bombing by Senegalese forces of alleged Casamance bases in northern Guinea-Bissau. Four days later the Senegalese government offered its apologies after Bissau had protested the violation of its border, and on December 22 it was reported that Casamance leader Diamacoune had been expelled from Guinea-Bissau.

In May 1994 Dakar demanded the withdrawal of Iran's ambassador, accusing Tehran of supporting the activities of the Islamic fundamentalist movement in Senegal. Fear of the spread of Islamic fundamentalism also dominated a meeting among Senegal, Mali, and Mauritania in January 1995, with the three agreeing to "combat fanaticism in all its forms." On February 10 Senegalese aircraft bombed a suspected Casamance rebel base in Guinea-Bissau, Dakar ignoring Bissau's subsequent demand for an explanation of the attack. However, in September Dakar and Bissau signed a security cooperation pact, and in December the prospect of closer relations improved markedly when Bissau agreed to withdraw its earlier objections to the 1989 court ruling on their shared maritime border. In 1996 Senegal continued to enjoy improved relations with its neighbors, signing cooperation agreements with Guinea, Guinea-Bissau, Mali, and Mauritania. On a less positive note, efforts to repatriate the Mauritanian refugees residing in Senegal since 1989 were only haltingly successful.

In June 1998 President Diouf deployed troops to Guinea-Bissau to shore up the embattled government there, underlining Dakar's concern that the Casamance region in Senegal would erupt in violence if the pro-Casamance Bissaun rebels secured power in Guinea-Bissau (see article on Guinea-Bissau). The administration's military strategy initially drew widespread support; however, by August opposition leaders had begun to question the effort. In March 1999 the last of the Senegalese troops were withdrawn. In 2001 armed forces from Guinea-Bissau destroyed the main Casamance rebel bases in that country. In 2002 separatist groups launched a new round of negotiations with the Senegalese government following the appointment of a new government peace commission. The government committed to a number of infrastructure programs in the province and released some government-held rebels on bail. In response the rebels adopted a cease-fire, although rebels opposed to the negotiations continued to launch minor attacks.

Wade enhanced the international status and influence of Senegal during the early 2000s by, among other things, condemning antidemocratic tendencies among African leaders. Senegal also served as an active force for regional peace by contributing peacekeeping troops to operations in the Democratic Republic of the Congo, Côte d'Ivoire, and Liberia.

Wade maintained close ties with France but also reached out to other major powers. In February 2002 he hosted Tony Blair, the first British prime minister to visit Senegal. During the meeting Blair pledged support for the New Partnership for Africa's Development (NEPAD), an organization launched through the OAU in October 2001 to promote socioeconomic recovery in Africa. In April 2002 Wade hosted the first major NEPAD conference. Wade also worked to improve relations with the United States and met with U.S. President George W. Bush in Senegal in July 2003. In addition, Senegal pledged to cooperate with the United States in the global war on terrorism. In 2003 Wade angered France by his refusal to condemn the U.S.-led war in Iraq.

On December 30, 2004, the government and the main rebel group in Casamance, the MFDC, signed a comprehensive peace settlement, although some minor rebel factions continued to fight the central government. (In March 2006, fighting between competing factions of the MFDC displaced 5,000 civilians along the border between Senegal and Guinea-Bissau.)

Tensions emerged in 2005 over a Gambian decision to double the tariff on ferry traffic on the Gambia River, which prompted Wade to close border crossings. The dispute was later resolved with a 15 percent reduction in the tariffs.

In October 2005 Senegal reestablished diplomatic relations with the People's Republic of China, ending Senegal's long-standing recognition of Taiwan. Economic relations between Dakar and Beijing were the main reason for the action, as trade between the two countries had increased by 25 percent per year since 2003.

Renewed fighting in Casamance between rival wings of the MFDC in September 2006 created 15,000 refugees, and at least 5,000 people fled across the border into Gambia. In December, Senegal and Gambia launched new talks to resolve tensions over the presence of Senegalese rebel bases in Gambia. In July 2007 the government announced that it would try former Chadian President Hisséne Habré (see article on Chad), in custody in Senegal, on charges of murder and torture following a request for such a trial from the AU. In April 2008 the National Assembly amended the constitution to allow Habré's trial on retroactive charges of crimes against humanity.

In 2006 Senegal and Spain agreed to joint patrols of Senegalese waters in order to deter illegal immigration to the Canary Islands. Senegal also reached an immigration agreement with France that eased restrictions on Senegalese immigrating to France but also simplified repatriation for illegal immigrants.

France announced in October 2007 that it would resume development loans to Senegal for the first time in 17 years. The initial loan was expected to be about $64 million. Senegal agreed in November to a governance program sponsored by the IMF. Under the terms of the initiative, the IMF provided technical advice and assistance on monetary and fiscal policy. In December Morocco recalled its ambassador to Senegal over remarks made by a member of the assembly that supported independence for the Western Sahara. Diplomatic ties were restored the following month.

In March 2008 Wade helped negotiate a non-aggression pact between Sudan and Chad. Also in March Senegal hosted the meeting of the Organization of Islamic States (OIC) in Dakar. South Africa and Senegal signed a bilateral trade agreement in April in what was reported to be a sign of growing ties between the two nations. In November Senegal deployed troops along its border with Guinea Bissau in response to an attempted coup.

In February 2009 Belgium filed a motion before the International Court of Justice in an effort to force Senegal to try former Chadian president Habré. Senegal had reportedly delayed prosecution because of the costs associated with a trial. During a visit to Senegal by Chinese president Hu Jintao, a number of new bilateral economic agreements were signed, including new accords to facilitate Chinese investment in the country. In April a crisis over Air Senegal strained relations between Senegal and Morocco. The Moroccan company Royal Air Maroc owned the largest number of shares in Senegal's national air carrier, and the Senegalese government sought to acquire a majority stake in the airline. Service was halted and more than 500 people were stranded until negotiations in May resulted in an agreement for Royal Air Maroc to withdraw and for Senegal to form a new national carrier. Also in May, Wade helped negotiate an agreement to allow elections in Mauritania in July 2009, following a 2008 coup.

Current issues. The peaceful transfer of presidential power from the PS to the PDS in 2000 was widely hailed as a triumph for the constitutional process in a continent more often known for violent changeovers. Despite having served as chief executive since 1981, President Diouf conceded gracefully. For 75-year-old Abdoulaye Wade the victory was a testament to perseverance (the campaign was his fifth) and to growing support for his long-time populist message. The new president quickly launched a number of ambitious projects designed to promote agro-industry, with particular emphasis on private-sector development. In the April 2001 legislative balloting, the public appeared still to be in the mood for a change, giving Wade a nearly two-thirds majority to work with in the assembly. By mid-2002, however, some analysts suggested that economic realities were beginning to impinge on the new administration's honeymoon, while the PS and other opposition parties were reportedly achieving more effective coordination.

In 2004 the government announced plans to build a new capital city some 150 kilometers from Dakar, which would allow for a centralized and modern government center and would facilitate economic development through new construction and the renovation of existing government facilities for private development. In July 2005 the assembly passed a measure that changed the location of the proposed capital to a new site near Kebemer.

Public opposition was provoked in January 2005 by a law designed to pardon those responsible for political crimes or acts committed since 1983 and to help promote the peace settlement in Casamance. Opposition groups asserted that the law was an attempt to cover up past crimes by former government officials and asked the Constitutional Council to examine the measure.

On July 15, 2005, former prime minister Seck was arrested on charges of embezzlement and later with endangering national security. In August the assembly voted to strip Seck of immunity and forced him to appear before a special anticorruption court. The court dismissed the embezzlement and subversion charges, and the former prime minister was released from prison in February 2006. Seck continued to face a minor charge of overspending government funds; however, his release allowed him to launch his 2007 presidential campaign.

In late 2005 legislative elections scheduled for May 2006 were postponed until June 2007, ostensibly to save money by combining the polling with presidential elections. Wade redirected the $13 million allocated for the 2006 balloting to help relocate Senegalese displaced by flooding. Opposition leaders met in Dakar in December 2005 and issued a joint statement condemning the postponement. Several opposition parties also launched discussions about the formation of electoral alliances prior to the 2007 balloting. Meanwhile, in spite of his age, Wade announced his intention to campaign for reelection.

Preelection violence in January 2007 left at least 20 dead as supporters of President Wade battled supporters of former prime minister Seck in street demonstrations in Dakar. Seck, apparently drawing support from disaffected members of the PDS and other nominally progovernment parties, won nearly 15 percent of its vote in the February poll. In the aftermath of the poll, opposition parties accused the government of widespread fraud and voter intimidation. However, international observers characterized the balloting as generally free and fair, and the country's highest court confirmed the results in March. Many opposition parties subsequently boycotted the June assembly poll and the August balloting for the reestablished Senate, which allowed the ruling propresidential coalition to secure an overwhelming majority in both houses.

A proposal to cut government salaries by 30 percent led to protests and the threat of a strike by unions in November 2007. The government instead reduced the president's salary by 30 percent, cabinet ministers' and senators' salaries by 25 percent, and assembly deputies' salaries by 20 percent. A government effort to crack down on unlicensed vendors in Dakar led to rioting and protests on November 21–22.

Rising fuel costs led to shortages throughout Senegal in the summer of 2008. One result was a series of blackouts and power shortages in June. In August Budget Minister Ibrahima Starr was dismissed after an audit revealed more than $240 million in improper and undocumented expenses. In July the assembly enacted a bill that would extend the presidential term from five years to seven years. The measure would go into effect after Wade left office in 2012 and was reported to be done for the benefit of Wade's likely successor, his son Karim. In August thousands joined a demonstration to protest the beatings of several journalists at the conclusion of a sporting event. On August 29 Civil Aviation Minister Farba SENGHOR was dismissed after he was linked to raids on two independent media organizations (see Communications, below).

In January 2009 Diadji DIOUF, a well-known gay rights activist, and eight others were tried and convicted of homosexuality. They were each sentenced to eight years in prison. International and domestic human rights groups condemned the trial and sentence. The deteriorating economy and rising costs were reportedly responsible for electoral losses by the *Sopi* Coalition in the March local elections. *Sopi* faced a coalition of opposition groups, United to Boost Senegal (see Political parties, below). Wade's coalition even lost control of the governing council of Dakar, and opposition leader Khalifa SALL was elected mayor of the capital city. Following the loss, Wade replaced the prime minister. Wade's son Karim was subsequently appointed to a cabinet post, leading to further reports that he was being groomed to succeed his father. In June the Assembly approved the creation of the post of vice president.

POLITICAL PARTIES

In March 1976 the National Assembly approved a constitutional amendment authorizing three political parties, each reflecting a specific ideological "current" that President Senghor had declared to exist in Senegalese society. Senghor's own Socialist Party (PS) adopted the centrist position of "democratic socialism," while the two other legal parties, the Senegalese Democratic Party (PDS) and the African Independence Party, were assigned "liberal democratic" and "Marxist-Leninist" postures, respectively. In early 1979 the amendment was altered to permit the legal establishment of a fourth, essentially right-wing, party—the Senegalese Republican Movement. The process of liberalization reached a conclusion in April 1981, when the assembly removed most remaining restrictions on party activity. More than 60 groups currently enjoy legal status.

A number of opposition parties including the PDS, the PADS/AJ, and the MSU operated in a loose coalition called Uniting to Change Senegal until that grouping's demise following the PDS's decision to join the government in 1995. After the PDS withdrew from the government in March 1998, it spearheaded the formation of an Alliance of Forces for Change (*Alliance des Forces pour le Changement*—AFC), which also included the PADS/AJ, the CDP, and the PIT. The AFC was superseded in late 1999 by the formation of an opposition coalition known as Alternance 2000 to challenge the PS in the 2000 presidential balloting. The new coalition, which endorsed Abdoulaye Wade of the PDS in the first round of the presidential election, was dominated by the PDS but also included the LD-MPT, PADS/AJ, MSU, PIT, UDF, ADN, and FAR/Yoon Wi. In early 2000, Alternance 2000 joined with a number of other opposition groupings, including the AFP, CDP, and URD, to form the Front for Fair and Transparent Elections (*Front pour la Régularité et la Transparence des Elections*—FRTE) to combat what the members perceived to be efforts by the PS to sabotage the election. The FRTE was not an electoral coalition; several members, including Alternance 2000, the AFP, CDP, and URD, presented their own presidential candidates in the first round.

Following the first round of presidential balloting on February 27, 2000, a number of groups previously aligned in the FRTE (including Alternance 2000, the AFP, CDP, and FSD-JB) formed the Front for Change (*Front pour l'Alternance*—FAL) to support Wade in the second round after the PDS/Alternance 2000 leader promised that his victory would be followed by installation of a coalition government. Meanwhile President Diouf of the PS was also endorsed in his reelection bid by a coalition called the Patriotic Convergence (*Convergence Patriotique*—CP), which included the PDS-R, BGC, and others.

The FAL essentially collapsed when Moustapha Niasse of the AFP resigned as prime minister in early March 2001 and the AFP cabinet members also left the government. Consequently, the PDS organized the *Sopi* Coalition, which ultimately included upwards of 40 smaller groups (including the LD-MPT, CDP, UDFP, ADN, and PSR), to contest the April 29 assembly balloting. Meanwhile, the AFP, PIT, PPS, and a number of other opposition parties formed a loose preelection coalition called the Front for Defense of Democracy (*Front pour la Défence de la Démocratie*—FDD), under the leadership of the PIT's Amath DANSOKHO. The *Sopi* Coalition was credited with winning 89 of the legislative seats. Subsequently, opposition parties (including the PS, AFP, URD, and PIT) organized a Permanent Framework for Consultation (*Cadre Permanent de Concertation*—CPC) to work against the policies of the PDS-led government. In response, the PDS organized a grouping known as the Convergence of Actions around the President for the 21st Century (*Convergence des Actions autour du Président en Perspective du 21ème Siècle*—CAP-21). The CAP-21, which included the PADS/AJ, the LD-MPT, and some 20 other smaller groups, contested the May 2002 municipal balloting as an electoral coalition, as did the CPC. For the 2007 presidential and legislative elections, propresidential parties ran as the *Sopi* 2007 Coalition. Leading opposition parties boycotted the legislative balloting under the *Siggil Sénégal Front,* while a number of other parties formed coalitions for the polling. Seventy-nine parties were registered for the 2009 local elections. A new opposition coalition, United to Boost Senegal (*Benno Siggil Senegaal*—BSS), brought together 35 opposition parties prior to the municipal balloting. The BSS was led by former PS parliamentarian, Khalifa Sall, and it included a number of parties that had boycotted the 2007 legislative elections, including the PS, the PIT, and the PPS. The BSS won a number of key constituencies in the elections.

Government and Government-Supportive Parties:

Senegalese Democratic Party (*Parti Démocratique Sénégalais*—PDS). The PDS was launched in October 1974 as a youth-oriented opposition group to implement the pluralistic democracy guaranteed by the Senegalese constitution. Although standing to the left of President Senghor on certain issues, it was required by the constitutional amendment of March 1976 to adopt a formal position to the right of the government party. Having charged fraud in both the 1980 and 1983 legislative elections (although the PDS was one of two opposition parties to gain representation on the latter occasion), PDS leaders participated in the 1984 municipal boycott and asserted their regret at having campaigned in 1983. Following the return from abroad of party leader Abdoulaye Wade in early 1985, the PDS led a number of mass prayer demonstrations for radical change, with Wade calling for "a transitional government of national unity."

As the major force in Senegal's growing opposition movement, the PDS appeared to pose a genuine threat to the PS in the 1988 legislative and presidential campaigns, partly as a result of its alliance with the LD-MPT and the PIT (below). Although presidential candidate Wade was officially credited with 26 percent of the vote, widespread indications of electoral abuse suggested that his actual total may have been higher.

In 1991 Wade attributed his acceptance of a cabinet post to fears that continued opposition activity would destabilize the country. However, Wade resigned from the government in October 1992 in what was viewed as an attempt to recapture the allegiance of PDS members estranged by his alliance with Diouf. Shortly thereafter Wade announced that the party would present candidates at the forthcoming legislative poll and entered the presidential contest in which he ran second to the incumbent, with a 32.03 percent share of the vote.

In July 1993 the PDS, ignoring a government ban, organized a demonstration for the release of jailed party deputies Mody Sy and Samuel Sarr, both of whom had been held since mid-May for their alleged involvement in the assassination of the Constitutional Council's vice president. On October 1 Wade, who had himself been detained for two days after the assassination, was arrested along with his wife for their alleged roles in the killing. Within days a number of other prominent PDS leaders, including Abdoulaye FAYE and Ousmane NGOM, were also implicated in the assassination.

On November 5, 1993, a number of party members were arrested for leading antigovernment demonstrations, and on February 18, 1994, Wade was reimprisoned for his participation in rioting, which erupted following the devaluation of the CFA franc. At a perfunctory military trial on February 24 Wade was convicted of a "breach against state security." However, on May 26 charges against him and his associates in connection with the 1993 assassination were dropped. Wade was one of five PDS leaders to accept cabinet portfolios in August 1995.

In March 1998 the PDS withdrew from the government and legislature after the PS legislators increased the size of the latter. At the same time Wade reportedly predicted that the PDS would win as many as 80 seats in the May polling. However, the party fell far short of such expectations, securing just 23 seats. In July Wade resigned his assembly post, saying that he would focus his efforts on resolving the PDS's intraparty disputes.

Wade finished second with 30.97 percent of the vote in the first round of presidential balloting in February 2000. However, after securing the support of most of the other first-round runners-up, Wade went on to defeat President Diouf in the second round in March with 58.7 percent of the vote, setting the stage, in conjunction with the

PDS legislative victory in April 2001, for one of the continent's most remarkably peaceful shifts in political power.

In April 2002 it was reported that the **Party for Progress and Citizenship** (*Parti pour le Progrès et la Citoyenneté*—PPC) had agreed to merge with the PDS. The PPC, formed in 2001 by Mbaye Jacques DIOP after he quit the PS, had secured one seat in the 2001 legislative balloting. A similar decision to merge with the PDS was also reported on the part of the **Senegalese Democratic Party–Renewal** (*Parti Démocratique Sénégalais–Rénovation*—PDS-R), which had been organized in June 1987 by an anti-Wade faction within the PDS that announced as its goal the establishment of a "truly secular and pluralist democracy." PDS-R candidates secured minuscule legislative vote shares in the 1988 and 1993 elections, while supporting Diouf for president on both occasions. Serigne Lamine DIOP, the PDS-R secretary general, was named minister of justice and keeper of the seals in the Loum government formed in July 1998, the party having secured one seat in the May legislative balloting. In 2003 the **Senegalese Liberal Party** (*Parti Libéral Sénégalais*—PLS) merged with the PDS. The PLS had been formed in June 1998 by Ousmane Ngom and a number of other party leaders who left the PDS after they failed to gain central committee posts in their former party. At the group's founding meeting, Ngom described the PLS as a vehicle of "liberalism" and denounced Wade's rule of the PDS as monarchical.

In April 2005, 14 PDS members of parliament announced their intention to leave the party and form a new group, the Forces of Change. After it was ruled that the 14 would have to resign their seats and campaign in special elections, they returned to the PDS. In May the Convention of Democrats and Patriots (*Convention des Démocrates et des Patriotes*—CDP) merged with the PDS. Also known as *Garab-Gi* ("The Cure"), the CDP was founded in May 1992 by Iba Der THIAM, a former education minister and UNESCO Executive Council member. In December 1994 the CDP and the RND (below) issued a joint statement rejecting the Uniting to Change coalition's call for the drafting of a national consensus program, describing it as a self-serving PDS maneuver. However, after Thiam secured 1.2 percent of the vote in the first round of the 2000 presidential poll, he threw his support behind Wade in the second round, becoming the coordinator of the FAL. The CDP, noted for its antipoverty platform and, more recently, an increasingly Islamic orientation, secured one seat as a member of the *Sopi* Coalition in the 2001 legislative balloting before joining the PDS.

Wade's main political rival within the PDS, Idrissa Seck, was dismissed as prime minister in April 2004. In August Seck was also dismissed from his post as PDS executive secretary, and he and several of his supporters were expelled from the party. In November 2007 former prime minister Macky SALL, and then speaker of the Assembly, was dismissed from his post as a deputy secretary general of the party, reportedly because he was perceived to be a threat to plans for Wade's son to be the future leader of the party. In November 2008 Sall was voted out of the speakership by the PDS. Sall subsequently formed a new political party, **Alliance for the Republic—Hope** (*Allaince pour le Republique—Yaakar*—APR-Yaakar), which joined the BSS opposition coalition in the 2009 local elections. Reports indicated that three factions had emerged within the party: the first led by Karim WADE, the second supportive of Pape Dion, and the third under former presidential advisor Moustapha DIAKHATE.

Wade reconciled with Seck in an effort to consolidate the party ahead of municipal elections in 2009, but the party suffered significant losses, including the defeat of .Senate Speaker Pape Diop in his reelection bid as mayor of Dakar.

Leaders: Abdoulaye WADE (President of the Republic and Secretary General), Souleymane Ndéné NDIAYE (Prime Minister), Mamadou SECK (Speaker of the National Assembly), Pape DIOP (Speaker of the Senate).

Action for National Development (*Action pour le Développement National*—ADN). Organized in mid-1996 under the leadership of Mamadou Moustapha Diop, the ADN participated in the *Sopi* Coalition in the 2001 and 2007 legislative balloting, and the 2009 municipal elections.

Leader: Mamadou Moustapha DIOP.

Senegalese Republican Party (*Parti Sénégalais Républicain*—PSR). In the first round of the 2000 presidential election the PSR's Ousseymou Fall secured 1.12 percent of the vote. Subsequently, the party joined the *Sopi* Coalition for the 2001 and 2007 legislative polls.

Leaders: Ousseymou FALL (2000 presidential candidate), Ely Madiodo FALL (Secretary General).

Union for Democratic Renewal (*Union pour le Renouveau Démocratique*—URD). The URD, originally styled the Democratic Renewal (*Renouveau Démocratique*—RD), was formed by former interior minister Djibo Ka in November 1997 to act as a reform group within the PS; however, in December Ka and ten of his dissident colleagues were suspended from the PS for three months. Subsequently, Ka declared his intention to forward an independent list of candidates for legislative balloting in May 1998. In March 1998 the PS rejected Ka's list, and on April 1 he resigned from the group and formally launched the URD. Having emerged from the 1998 legislative polling with 11 seats, the URD presented Ka as its candidate in the first round of the 2000 presidential election. He finished fourth with 7.08 percent of the vote and somewhat surprisingly threw his support to Abdou Diouf in the second round. A split in the URD regarding that decision (one faction joined the *Sopi* Coalition) apparently contributed to the URD's decline to three seats following the 2001 legislative poll.

Ka was appointed minister of state for fisheries in the Sall government and reappointed to the post in the Soumaré cabinet. Following a 2007 cabinet reshuffle, Ka became minister of state for the environment and protection of nature, reservoirs and artificial lakes. He retained that post in the new government formed after the 2009 municipal elections.

Leader: Djibo KA (Secretary General and 2000 presidential candidate).

Other pro-Wade formations include the **Senegalese Democratic Rally** (*Rassemblement Démocratique Sénégalais*—RDS), led by Abdou Latif GUEYE; the **Union of Senegalese Patriots**; the **Popular Democratic Rally** (*Rassemblement Démocratique Populaire*—RDP), formed by Ibrahim Masseck DIOP; the **Democratic Union for Federalism/ Mboloomi** (*Union Démocratique pour le Fédéralisme/Mboloomi*—UDF/Mboloomi), which broke with the *Sopi* Coalition and joined the opposition BSS coalition in the 2009 municipal balloting; and the **Union for Democratic Renewal/Front for Change** (*Union pour le Renouveau Démocratique/Front pour l'Alternance*—URD/FAL), a breakaway faction from the URD (above) that joined the *Sopi* Coalition for the 2001 and 2007 legislative balloting under the leadership of Mahmout SALEH.

Other Legislative Parties:

Engagement and Reconstruction of Senegal Coalition (*Takku Defaraat Sénégal*). This grouping was founded by Robert Sagna in 2006 as a broad-based coalition of leftists. Sagna, still officially a member of the PS, ran as the coalition's candidate in the 2007 presidential balloting, finishing fifth. The *Takku Defaraat* secured 3 seats in the 2007 legislative balloting. For the 2009 local elections *Takku Defaraat* initially formed a bilateral grouping with the **Alliance of Forces for Progress,** and then joined the opposition BSS coalition. In the balloting, Sagna was defeated in his reelection bid as mayor of Ziguinchor (a post he had held for 25 years).

Leaders: Robert SAGNA (2007 presidential candidate), El Hadj Amath CISSE, Mouhamed DIEDHIOU.

The Field (*Waar Wi*). Formed by former environment minister Modou Diagne Fada, the *Waar Wi* is made up primarily of disaffected members of the PS who opposed boycotting the 2007 legislative elections. The grouping finished tied for second in legislative balloting with three seats. In 2008 Fada announced a reconciliation with Wade and the PDS. He was subsequently elected vice president of the Assembly and reports in 2009 indicated that Fada had joined the PDS.

Leaders: Modou Diagne FADA (Chair), Jamil Ababacar Diop BA.

African Party for Democracy and Socialism/And Jëf (*Parti Africain pour la Démocratie et le Socialisme/And Jëf*—PADS/AJ). The PADS/AJ was formed in 1991 by merger of the Revolutionary Movement for the New Democracy (*Mouvement Révolutionnaire pour la Démocratie Nouvelle*—MRDN) and two other left-wing groups, the People's Democratic Union (*Union pour la Démocratie Populaire*—UDP) and the Socialist Workers' Organization (*Organisation Socialist des Travailleurs*—OST).

Also known as *And Jë*, a Wolof expression meaning "to unite for a purpose," the MRDN was a populist southern party of the extreme left that included former socialists and Maoists. It was permitted to register in June 1981 but joined the 1983 and 1984 election boycotts. In 1988 one of its leaders, Landing Savane, won 0.25 percent of the vote as a presidential candidate. The UDP was organized in 1981 by a pro-Albanian MRDN splinter group, while the OST was a small Marxist-Leninist formation launched in 1982.

Landing Savane ran a distant third as the 1993 presidential nominee of the PADS/AJ. For the May legislative balloting the party participated with the RND (below) in a **Let Us Unite** (*Jappoo Liggeeyal*) **Senegal** coalition that won three assembly seats. In November Savane was arrested for organizing a demonstration against the Diouf administration's economic austerity program. Given a suspended sentence for the incident, the PADS leader was rearrested in February 1994 and, along with Wade, he was subsequently convicted of provoking antigovernment riots.

The PADS/AJ captured four seats in the 1998 legislative balloting; subsequently it cooperated with the PIT and PLS to run a joint slate of candidates in the January 1999 Senate elections under the banner of *"And Fippu."* After supporting Abdoulaye Wade of the PDS in the 2000 presidential campaign, the PADS/AJ secured two seats in the 2001 legislative poll (on 4.1 percent of the vote) and subsequently joined the PDS-led parliamentary faction. Savane and Mamadou Diop were given posts in subsequent PDS-led governments.

Savane was the PADS/AJ candidate in the 2007 presidential election, in which he secured just over 2 percent of the vote. The PADS/AJ was the main component of the **Build Senegal Together** (*And Defar Sénégal*) coalition that secured three seats in the assembly in 2007. In 2007 divisions within the party emerged between the supporters of Savane and a group led by Madièye MBODJ that criticized the leadership for abandoning the core principles of the party. PADS/AJ won one senate seat in the 2007 direct balloting for the chamber. In 2008 party official Mamadou Diop was appointed commerce minister in the national government. Following the 2009 municipal elections Diop lost his position during a cabinet reshuffle.

Leaders: Landing SAVANE (Secretary General and 1993 and 2007 presidential candidate), Mamadou DIOP.

Front for Socialism and Democracy–Unite and Correct (*Front pour le Socialisme et la Démocratie–Benno Jubël*—FSD-JB). Launched under the direction of a prominent Muslim leader, Cheikh Abdoulaye Dieye, the FSD-JB captured one seat in the 1998 legislative balloting on a platform emphasizing care for the elderly and women. Dieye captured 0.97 percent of the first-round vote in the 2000 presidential election, and the FSD-JB subsequently joined the FAL. Cheikh Bamba DIEYE succeeded his father as party leader following the former's death in 2002.

The younger Dieye received less than 1 percent of the vote in the 2007 presidential balloting, while the party gained one seat in the assembly in 2007. The FSD-JB participated in the opposition BSS coalition in the 2009 municipal elections, in which party leader Dieye was elected mayor of Saint-Louis.

Leader: Cheikh Bamba DIEYE (2007 presidential candidate).

Alliance Jëf Jël. Formerly known as the Alliance for Progress and Justice/Jëf Jël, this grouping adopted its current name at a party congress in June 2000. Party leader Talla Sylla placed eighth in the 2007 presidential balloting, but was the sole party member elected to the National Assembly. He subsequently announced his intention to retire as party president in June for health reasons but has remained at the helm of the party. The party joined the BSS coalition for the 2009 local elections.

Leaders: Talla SYLLA (President), Moussa TINE.

Other parties that gained seats in the 2007 election include the **Rally for the People** (*Rassemblement pour le Peuple*—RP); the **Reform Movement for Social Development** (*Mouvement de la Réforme pour le Développement Social*—MRDS), led by Mbaye NIANG, which initially joined the BSS in the 2009 municipal balloting, but withdrew from the coalition prior to the elections because of differences with the PS; **Convergence for Renewal and Citizenship** (*La Convergence pour le Renouveau et la Citoyenneté*—CRC), led by Aliou DIA; the **Authentic Socialist Party** (*Parti Socialiste–Authentique*—PS-A), led by Souty TOURÉ; the **National Patriotic Union** (*Union Nationale Patriotique*—UNP), led by Me Ndèye FATOU TOURÉ; the **Rally of Ecologists of Senegal** (*Rassemblement des Écologists du Sénégal*—RES), led by Ousmane Sow HUCHARD; and the **Social Democrat Party–The Sun** (*Parti Social-Démocrate–Jant Bi*—PSD-JB), led by Mamour CISSE.

Other Parties Contesting the 2007 Legislative Elections:

Senegalese Patriotic Rally (*Rassemblement Patriotique Sénégalais–Jammi Rewmi*—RPS-JR). Founded by Ely Madiodo Fall Fall, the RPS-JR, which had been part of the *Sopi* Coalition in the 2001 legislative elections, unsuccessfully contested the 2007 balloting as an independent grouping, securing just 0.4 percent of the vote.

Leader: Ely Madiodo FALL FALL.

Other Parties and Groups:

Socialist Party (*Parti Socialiste*—PS). Known until December 1976 as the Senegalese Progressive Union (*Union Progressiste Sénégalaise*—UPS), the PS consistently held a preponderance of seats in the National Assembly until 2001. A moderate Francophile party long identified with the cause of Senegalese independence, the UPS was founded by Léopold Senghor in 1949 in a secession from the dominant local branch of the French Socialist Party. From 1963 to 1974 it was the only legal party in Senegal; it absorbed the only significant opposition grouping, the leftist *Parti de Regroupement Africain-Sénégal* (PRA) in 1966 in furtherance of Senghor's "national reconciliation" policy. In early 1981, following his resignation of the presidency, Senghor withdrew as party secretary general. During an extraordinary conference in March 1989, the PS voted to assign internal authority to a ten-member Executive Committee that was directed to recruit new members and assist in "rejuvenation" of the party. At the PS congress in 1990, Abdou Diouf was reappointed secretary general and given unchecked control of a restructured, "non-hierarchical," 30-member Politburo.

The PS experienced unprecedented levels of intraparty violence prior to its 1996 congress, spurring a call from Diouf for "reconciliation." Meanwhile Diouf and Ousmane Tanor Dieng were elected to the newly created party presidency and executive secretaryship, respectively, with the latter assuming administrative responsibilities previously assigned to the secretary general.

In March 1998 a PS faction, led by Djibo KA, broke off from the party and formed the URD (above). Among the reasons cited for Ka's decision was Diouf's reported elevation of Dieng to the status of heir apparent.

Another prominent PS member, Moustapha Niasse, left the PS after 40 years to form the AFP (below), the recent departures contributing to Diouf's failure in his 2000 reelection bid. Although Diouf was reconfirmed as the PS leader at an October 2000 congress, he subsequently announced plans to retire from politics.

The PS led the opposition to the 2006 postponement of legislative elections and tried to rally opposition parties. It was also reportedly active in unsuccessful efforts to form an opposition electoral coalition ahead of the 2007 balloting. Dieng was the party's candidate in the presidential polling, placing third. The PS boycotted the 2007 legislative balloting. Dieng was formally elected party leader in October. The PS agreed to participate in local and regional elections in 2008, in which it gained mayoral posts and majorities on councils in a number of areas. The PS was instrumental in the creation of the opposition BSS coalition and sought to use the grouping as a potential base for an alliance ahead of future legislative balloting.

Leaders: Ousmane Tanor DIENG (Chair), Abdou DIOUF (Former President of the Republic), Mamadou Lamine LOUM (Former Prime Minister), Cheikh Abdoul Khadre CISSOKHO (Former National Assembly President).

Democratic League–Labor Party Movement (*Ligue Démocratique–Mouvement pour le Parti du Travail*—LD-MPT). A self-proclaimed independent Marxist group with links to Senegal's leading teachers' union, the LD-MPT contested both the 1983 and 1984 elections. At its second congress in December 1986, the League's secretary general, Abdoulaye Bathily, called for "disorganized alliances" between opposition parties and advanced an economic "alternative to the recipes of the International Monetary Fund and the World Bank" as a means of establishing a socialist society. The party supported PDS candidate Abdoulaye Wade in the 1988 presidential poll but presented its own legislative candidates, securing no seats on a 1.4 percent vote share.

In April 1988 LD-MPT Secretary General Bathily was given a suspended sentence for having organized an illegal antigovernment demonstration, while five other party activists were indicted on similar charges late in the year. In 1990 Bathily intensified his criticism of the Diouf administration's policies and called for a non-Diouf "unity" government. Thereafter, despite the co-option of a number of opposition colleagues, Bathily initially refused Diouf's offer of a cabinet portfolio, citing Dakar's repressive policies in Casamance. However, Bathily ultimately agreed to become environment minister in June 1993, with the party being awarded a second portfolio in August 1995. Following the May 1998 legislative poll (in which it won three seats), the LD-MPT declined to participate in the next government. Instead it proposed the formation of a unified opposition front against the PS and President Diouf. Six of the 89 successful candidates from the *Sopi* Coalition in the 2001 legislative balloting were identified as LD-MPT members. Two LD-MPT deputies briefly served in the government in 2005, before disputes with Wade led to their dismissal during a cabinet reshuffle.

Bathily was the LD-MPT's presidential candidate in 2007 (he received 2.2 percent of the vote). The LD-MPT boycotted the 2007 legislative election. The LD-MPT participated in the postponed 2009 local and regional elections as a member of the PS-led opposition BSS grouping.

Leader: Dr. Abdoulaye BATHILY (1993 and 2007 presidential candidate and Secretary General).

Independence and Labor Party (*Parti de l'Indépendance et du Travail*—PIT). Organized by a group of PAI dissidents and permitted to register in 1981, the PIT was recognized by Moscow as Senegal's "official" Communist Party. It contested both the 1983 and 1984 elections but won no assembly or town council seats. The party joined the LD-MPT in supporting PDS presidential candidate Wade in 1988, while its legislative candidates won only 0.8 percent of the vote and no seats. The PIT secretary general was among those arrested after the elections, but the charges were later dismissed. In mid-1989 the PIT entered into negotiations with the ruling Socialist Party, and the party was awarded two portfolios in the cabinet reshuffle of August 1995. However, both ministers were ousted a month later in the wake of a PIT Central Committee statement critical of the Diouf administration.

The PIT was a member of Alternance 2000 in support of the 2000 presidential bid of Abdoulaye Wade, and the party's secretary general, Amath Dansokho, served in the first Wade cabinet. However, the two leaders subsequently quarreled and Dansokho resigned from the government in early 2001. Dansokho was briefly arrested in July 2005 for making antigovernment statements. The PIT participated in the 2007 boycott of legislative elections but took part in the local elections that were postponed until 2009. The PIT was a member of the BSS coalition during the balloting.

Leader: Amath DANSOKHO (Secretary General).

Movement for Socialism and Unity (*Mouvement pour le Socialisme et l'Unité*—MSU). The MSU was registered in 1981 as the People's Democratic Movement (*Mouvement Démocratique Populaire*—MDP), which, led by longtime Senghor opponent Mamadou Dia, called for a program of socialist self-management of the economy. Dia was one of the few prominent Senegalese political figures to oppose establishment of the Senegambian Confederation. The MDP contested the 1983 general election but boycotted subsequent balloting.

The MSU was listed as a member of Alternance 2000, and official government sources indicated that one MSU member was elected in the 2001 legislative balloting as a member of the *Sopi* Coalition. However, perhaps indicating a split within the party, news reports described the MSU, under the leadership of Sheikh Tidiane BA, as aligning with the PIT for the assembly elections. As of 2002 Ba was still being described as an opponent of the Wade government. In 2008 the MSU executive council was reported to be based in France. The MSU was part of the BSS coalition in the 2009 municipal balloting.

Leaders: Mamadou DIA (Former Prime Minister), Mouhamadou N'DIAYE (National Coordinator).

Alliance of Forces for Progress (*Alliance des Forces pour le Progrès*—AFP). Formed by Moustapha Niasse in the fall of 1999 after he had left the PS, the AFP supported Abdoulaye Wade in the second round of the 2000 presidential election after Niasse had finished third in the first round with 16.76 percent. Under an apparent electoral agreement with Wade, Niasse was named prime minister in Wade's first cabinet, but he subsequently quit that post in early 2001. The AFP, some of whose support comes from the Tidjane Islamic Brotherhood, competed alone in the 2001 legislative elections, finishing second to the *Sopi* Coalition.

Niasse was the AFP's 2007 presidential candidate and placed fourth in the balloting. The AFP joined the opposition boycott of that year's legislative polling. In 2008 Niasse led a failed effort by opposition parties to replace the national election commission, seen as being dominated by the PDS, with an independent agency. The AFP joined the BSS coalition for the 2009 local elections.

Leader: Moustapha NIASSE (former Prime Minister).

National Democratic Rally (*Rassemblement National Démocratique*—RND). Established in February 1976, the RND described itself as a "party of the masses." It applied, without success, for recognition in September 1977, and two years later its founder, Cheikh Anta DIOP (who died in 1986), was ordered to stand trial for engaging in unauthorized party activity. The RND was legalized in June 1981; it subsequently repeatedly criticized the government for its position on Chad and for its "systematic alignment with the positions of France and the United States." Evincing an anti-Wade orientation, the RND retained its single legislative seat in 2001, although it garnered only 0.7 percent of the vote. In June 2006 the party's sole deputy in the assembly resigned in protest over the postponement of legislative elections. The party boycotted the 2007 elections. After the boycott, Diouf was reported to have announced his retirement from politics. The RND was a member of the BSS coalition in the 2009 balloting.

Leader: Madior DIOUF (Secretary General).

Senegalese Democratic Union–Renewal (*Union Démocratique Sénégalais–Rénovation*—UDS-R). Organized in February 1985 and legally recognized in July, the UDS-R was led by Mamadou Fall, a well-known trade-union leader and former deputy, who was expelled from the PDS while in the assembly for "divisive activities." Fall described himself as a "progressive nationalist" seeking to promote the "unification of healthy forces." The party presented no candidates in 1988. It secured one legislative seat in May 1993, which it retained in 1998, but failed to gain subsequent representation. After the death of Fall in 2007, reports indicated that the party was no longer active.

African Independence Party (*Parti Africain de l'Indépendance*—PAI). Founded in 1957 and composed mainly of intellectuals in southern Senegal, the PAI was legally dissolved in 1960 but was subsequently recognized as the "Marxist-Leninist" party called for by the 1976 constitutional amendment. Claiming to be the "real PAI," a clandestine wing of the party denounced recognition as a self-serving maneuver by the Senghor government. In March 1980 two leaders of the splinter faction, Amath Dansokho and Maguette THIAM, were charged with inciting workers to strike, but in 1981 they were permitted to register the group as a distinct party (see PIT, above). Having unsuccessfully contested the 1983 election, the PAI joined the November 1984 boycott. In early 1987 the formation of a front uniting the PAI with the MDP (see under MSU, above) and the former Communist Workers' League (*Ligue Communiste des Travailleurs*—LCT) was announced, although no legislative candidates were presented by any of the three in 1988.

The PAI supported Abdou Diouf in the 2000 presidential campaign and presented its own candidates (unsuccessfully) in the 2001 legislative poll. The PAI boycotted the 2007 legislative elections.

Leaders: Majhemouth DIOP (President), Balla N'DIAYE (Vice President), Bara GOUDIABY (Secretary General).

Senegalese Republican Movement (*Mouvement Républicain Sénégalais*—MRS). The MRS is a self-styled "right-wing" party organized by former National Assembly vice president Boubacar GUÉYE. In August 1977 the party applied for legal recognition, which was not granted until February 1979. It supports human rights, free enterprise, and private property. At the domestic political level, it has urged parliamentary election of the president; regionally, it has proposed the introduction of a common currency for OAU member countries. The party failed to gain representation in the assembly in the 1998, 2001 and 2007 elections.

Leader: Demba BA (Secretary General).

Party for the African Renaissance (*Parti pour la Renaissance Africaine*—PARENA). Devoted primarily to the issues of women's rights and the "lack of transparency" in governmental affairs, PARENA attempted to present its leader, Mariame Ly Wane, as a presidential candidate in 2000 but she was disqualified on technical grounds. The party did not gain seats in the 2001 or 2007 legislative polling.

Leader: Mariame Ly WANE.

Senegalese People's Party (*Parti Populaire Sénégalais*—PPS). Legalized in December 1981, the PPS was also organized by a number of PAI adherents, who did not immediately delineate its program, indicating only that they supported the "restructuring of Senegalese society on new and scientific bases." Some of its members have been involved in demonstrations led by Casamance separatists (see MFDC, below). The party received only 0.2 percent of the vote in the 1983 legislative and presidential elections and did not participate in 1988 or 1993. The PPS was part of the BSS coalition in the 2009 local elections.

Leader: Dr. Oumar WANE (Secretary General).

Other parties include the **Party of Renewal and Citizenship** (*Partide la Renaissance et de la Citoyenneté*—PRC); the **Assembly of African Workers–Senegal** (*Rassemblement des Travailleurs Africains–Sénégal*—RTA-S), a social-democratic party recognized in March 1997 and a member of the BSS coalition in 2009; the **Movement for Democracy and Socialism/Naxx Jarinu** (*Mouvement pour la Démocratie et le Socialisme/Naxx Jarinu*—MDS/NJ); the **Union for the Republic** (*Union pour la République*—UPR); the **Social Democratic Party/Jant-Bi**; the **Democratic Union of Progressive Patriotic Forces** (*Union Démocratique des Forces Progressistes Patriotiques*—UDFP); the **Citizens' Movement for a Democracy of Development** (*Mouvement des Citoyens pour une Démocratie de Développement*); the **Action Front for Renewal/The Way** (*Front d'Action pour le Renouveav/Yoon Wi*—FAR/Yoon Wi), led by Bathie SECK; the **Gainde Centrist Bloc** (*Bloc des Gainde Centristes*—BGC), which captured a single seat in the May 1998 legislative balloting under the leadership of PDS dissident Jean-Paul DIAS, who was arrested in April 2006 for antigovernment remarks and sentenced to 12 months in prison (with nine months suspended); the **Reform Party** (*Parti de la Réforme*—PR), whose leader, Abdourahim AGNE, was arrested in May 2005 for sedition but was given a cabinet appointment in 2008; the **Rally for Unity and Peace** (*Rassemblement pour l'Unité et la Paix*—RUP), a Louga-based grouping headed by Moctar N'DIAYE; and **The Nation** (*Rewmi*), formed by former Prime Minister Idrissa SECK, who placed second in national polling as the party's 2007 presidential candidate (*Rewmi* boycotted the 2007 legislative elections).

Illegal Groups:

Movement of Democratic Forces of Casamance (*Mouvement des Forces Démocratiques de la Casamance*—MFDC). The MFDC was launched as a clandestine grouping advocating the secession of the Casamance region of southern Senegal. Many supporters, including MFDC leader Fr. Augustin Diamacoune Senghor, were jailed following demonstrations in the provincial capital of Ziguinchor in the early 1980s, and another 152 people were arrested in 1986 for allegedly attending a secret MFDC meeting. Diamacoune and most of the other detainees were subsequently released, the government being perceived as having adopted a more conciliatory approach in dealing with the separatist issue. However, new MFDC-army clashes were reported in late 1988.

In a series of actions that commenced in mid-1990, Diamacoune and most other MFDC civilian leaders were arrested or forced into exile following a resurgence of separatist violence spearheaded by *Attika* ("Fighter"), the MFDC's military wing. The uprising, which the separatists claimed was the result of their being economically and socially marginalized, continued through late 1990. However, in May 1991, following a series of secret meetings with ethnic Diola parliamentarians negotiating on Diouf's behalf, MFDC leaders agreed to a cease-fire and disarmament. Reports of the negotiations supported observers' suspicions that the separatists encompassed a limited number (300–500) of ethnic Diolas.

In April and May 1992 renewed separatist activity was attributed to a militant MFDC splinter and despite an escalating verbal confrontation between Dakar and the MFDC leadership over the military's allegedly heavy-handed response to the violence, the Diouf administration, as late as September, absolved the MFDC leadership of blame for the cease-fire breakdown.

On July 8, 1993, the MFDC signed a cease-fire agreement with the government that included provisions for further negotiations, a bilateral prisoner release, the deployment of French military observers, and the establishment of a refugee repatriation program. However, renewed clashes were reported three days later, and open fighting resumed following the government's killing of an MFDC activist in September. Thereafter, no serious cease-fire violations were reported until January 1995, when a pro-independence faction led by Léopold SANIA rejected the peace accord and resumed guerrilla activities. Following a government air attack on an alleged MFDC base in Guinea-Bissau in February, the rebels denied having personnel there.

In April 1995 the government deployed an additional 1,000 troops in the Casamance region in response to persistent breaches of the cease-fire, including the disappearance of four French tourists who were assumed to have been kidnapped by the MFDC. In late April the government announced the arrest of some 50 suspected activists, including Father Diamacoune, and in mid-July the separatists formally abandoned the cease-fire. While Diamacoune's imprisonment served as a rallying point for MFDC faithful during the 1995 crisis, his influence with party militants reportedly had already begun to wane. Subsequently, despite his declaration of a unilateral cease-fire in January 1996, rebel attacks continued throughout the first half of the year.

After a year of relative calm in the region, fierce fighting broke out in August 1997 as the government responded to renewed rebel activity with a massive offensive, and by late September over 100 people were reported dead. Meanwhile, the fighting widened the split in the MFDC between the hard-line northern wing, led by Mamadou Sane, and Diamacoune's predominantly southern followers, who were described as prepared to abandon their demand for independence in return for a government promise to speed development of the region. In early 1998 the two factions were reported to be in open conflict. Furthermore, troops from Guinea-Bissau were reportedly laying siege to Sane's longtime safe havens within Bissau's border.

In March 1998 the government claimed to have killed 50 MFDC fighters preparing to attack a village near Ziguinchor. Thereafter, fighting was reported throughout the region during the run-up to legislative polling; however, the government deployed a large number of forces to the area for the balloting period, and few incidents were reported.

Amid reports that the MFDC was preparing to enter into negotiations with the Diouf administration, the group's military and political leaders met in Banjul, Gambia, in April 1999. However, on April 30, 17 people were reported killed in a clash between the rebels and government forces, thus underscoring continued reports that the movement was splintered.

Some MFDC fighters were reported to have disarmed in mid-1999, and another questionable cease-fire was announced late in the year. However, the leadership dispute within the MFDC continued, as did the low-level war between rebels and government troops. Additional negotiations were launched in December 2000, new Senegalese President Abdoulaye Wade having declared resolution of the conflict a top priority for his government. A peace pact was again announced in March 2001, ostensibly providing for a cease-fire, release of prisoners, return of refugees and displaced persons, and infrastructure rehabilitation, particularly road repairs. It also appeared that Diamacoune and his supporters had renounced their secessionist stance and instead had agreed to pursue greater autonomy for the region while remaining a part of Senegal. The accord was greeted hopefully by many observers, especially following a face-to-face meeting between Wade and Diamacoune and the MFDC's call for fighters to lay down their guns for the April national legislative balloting. Banditry and sporadic killings continued, however, precluding finalization of a permanent settlement.

At a mid-2001 MFDC congress, Diamacoune was moved to the group's presidency, a role considered more ceremonial in nature than his previous post. Meanwhile, Sidi Badji, a hard-liner perceived as a rival to Diamacoune, was reportedly named head of military affairs. Badji subsequently claimed the secretary general's position, and the power struggle between his "radical" faction (which also included military commander Salif SADIO) and Diamacoune's "peacemaking" faction continued into mid-2002. On September 19, 2004, Diamacoune became honorary president, while Biagui became the effective leader of the MFDC. Meanwhile, continuing violence barred much rehabilitation of the poverty-stricken region.

The MFDC signed a peace agreement with the government on December 30, 2004, and it announced plans to reestablish itself as a legitimate political party and contest legislative elections in 2007. However, in March 2006 the Sadio-led faction of the MFDC initiated attacks against other MFDC groupings. In response, security forces from Guinea-Bissau launched an offensive against MFDC positions in an attempt to end the factional fighting.

On January 14, 2007, Diamacoune died of natural causes in a Paris hospital, creating an as of yet unresolved internal struggle over the leadership of the MFDC. In December a faction of the MFDC assassinated a presidential envoy during negotiations over Casamance. The attack was condemned by most of the leadership of the MFDC. There was sporadic fighting between the MFDC and government forces in May 2008. During the summer of 2009 there was a significant increase in violence in the region, which reports attributed to younger members of the MFDC who opposed a settlement with the government.

Leaders: Mamadou SANE, Sidi BADJI, Jean-Marie BIAGUI (Secretary General).

LEGISLATURE

The **Parliament** consists of a National Assembly, which was established in 1963, and a Senate, which was established in 1999, abolished in 2001, and reestablished in 2007.

Senate. According to legislation adopted by the assembly in January 2007 mandating the reestablishment of the upper house, the Senate comprises 100 members serving five-year terms. Thirty-five of the senators (one from each district) are indirectly elected for five-year terms by members of regional, rural, and municipal councils. The remaining 65 senators are appointed by the president.

In balloting (boycotted by most of the main opposition parties) for the 35 elected senators on August 19, 2007, the Senegalese Democratic Party (PDS) won 34 seats, and the African Party for Democracy and Socialism/And Jëf won 1. President Wade appointed the remaining 65 members on September 21; most were members of the PDS, although the appointees reportedly included members of opposition parties and a number of independents.

President: Pape DIOP.

National Assembly. The assembly currently consists of 150 members, 90 elected on a majoritarian basis at the department level and 60 elected on a proportional basis from national party lists. (The assembly voted in November 2006 to increase its size from 120 to 150 members.) Members serve five-year terms, although the assembly is subject to presidential dissolution after two years.

In the most recent balloting of June 3, 2007, the *Sopi* 2007 Coalition (led by the Senegalese Democratic Party) won 131 seats (90 majoritarian, 41 proportional); the Engagement and Reconstruction of Senegal Coalition, 3 (all proportional); The Field coalition, 3 (all proportional); the Build Senegal Together coalition (led by the African Party for Democracy and Socialism/And Jëf), 3 (all proportional); the Rally for the People, 2 (all proportional); and the Front for Socialism and Democracy–Unite and Correct, the Reform Movement for Social Justice, the Convergence for Renewal and Citizenship, the Authentic Socialist Party, the Alliance Jëf Jël, the National Patriotic Union, the Rally of Ecologists of Senegal, and the Social Democrat Party–The Sun, 1 each (all proportional).

President: Mamadou SECK.

CABINET

[as of July 1, 2009]

Prime Minister	Souleymane Ndéné Ndiaye
Ministers of State	
Armed Forces	Bécaye Diop
Civil Service, Labor and Professional Organizations	Habib Sy
Economy and Finance	Abdoulaye Diop
Environment and Protection of Nature	Djibo Leyti Ka (URD)
Family, National Solidarity, Food Security, Microfinance, and Early Childhood	Ndeye Khady Diop [f]
Foreign Affairs	Cheikh Tidiane Gadio
Interior, Local Communities and Decentralization	Cheikh Tidiane Sy
International Cooperation, Regional Planning, Civil Aviation and Infrastructure	Karim Wade
Justice; Keeper of the Seals	Maître Madicke Niang
Urban Affairs, Housing, Urban Water Supply, Public Hygiene and Drainage	Oumar Sarr
Ministers	
Agriculture and Aquaculture	Fatou Gaye Sarr [f]
Biofuels and Energy	Samuel Amete Sarr
Commerce	Amadou Niang
Communications and Government Spokesman	Moustapha Guirassy
Culture	Serigne Modou Bousso Leye
Elementary and Secondary Education; National Languages and Francophonie	Kalidou Diallo
Food Processing	Aida Mbodj [f]
Health, Hygiene, and Medical Prevention	Therese Coumba Diop [f]
Higher Education	Moustapha Sourang
Industry, Mines, and Small- and Medium-Size Enterprises	Ibrahima Cissé [f]
Livestock	Oumou Khairy Gueye Seck [f]
Maritime Economy, Fisheries and Marine Transport	Khoureyssy Thiam
Relations with Parliament and NEPAD (New Partnership for Africa's Development)	Faustin Diatta
Scientific Research	Amadou Tidianne Ba
Senegalese Abroad	Sada Ndiaye
Sport and Leisure	Bacar Dia
Technical and Professional Education	Moussa Sakho
Telecommunications, Transport Information, Road and Rail Transport	Abdourahim Agne (PR)
Tourism and Relations with the Private Sector	Thierno Lo
Youth, Sport and Leisure	Mamadou Lamine Keita
Ministers Delegate	
Economy and Finance, in Charge of Budget	Abdoulaye Diop
Interior, Local Communications, and Decentralization, in Charge of Local Communities and Decentralization	Alioune Sow
Agriculture and Aquaculture, in Charge of Relations with Local Organizations and Syndicates	Khadim Gueye

[f] = female

COMMUNICATIONS

Newspapers are subject to government censorship and regulation, although a number of opposition papers appeared in the 1990s, some evading official registration by means of irregular publication, and restrictions have eased significantly in recent years. Prior to the 2007 elections, the government reportedly forced the closure of some private radio stations, seized editions of newspapers, and detained journalists who were critical of the regime. On August 17, 2008, the offices of two independent newspapers, *24 Heures Chrono* and *L'As,* were vandalized. A police investigation led to the arrest of nine and the sacking of Civil Aviation Minister Fabre Senghor. In September 2008 police raided the offices of *24 Heures Chrono,* seized the current edition, and arrested the paper's editor. The paper was forced to close following a news report that accused the president and his son of involvement in corruption. In its 2008 press freedom index, the media organization Reporters Without Borders ranked Senegal 86 out of 173 countries.

Press. The following, unless otherwise noted, are published daily, in French, in Dakar: *Le Soleil* (25,000), government-owned; *Sud Quotidien* (9,000), independent; *Wal Fadjiri* (The Dawn, 13,000), independent Islamic daily; *Le Matin,* independent; *Le Populaire,* independent; *L'Actuel; Tract; La Pointe; Afrique Nouvelle* (15,000), Catholic weekly; *Sénégal d'Aujourd'hui* (5,000), published monthly by the Ministry of Communications; *Nouvel Horizon,* independent weekly; *Eco Hebdo,* weekly.

News agencies. *Agence de Presse Sénégalaise* (APS) is the official facility; the Pan-African News Agency (PANA), as well as a number of foreign agencies, also maintain offices in Dakar.

Broadcasting and computing. Broadcasting is controlled by the *Radiodiffusion-Télévision du Sénégal* (RTS). In July 1994 *SUD FM*, Senegal's first private radio station, joined two radio networks, *Radio Sénégal-Inter* and *Radio Sénégal II*. On November 14, 2005, West African Democracy Radio (WADR) began broadcasting from Dakar throughout West Africa. The station was created with support from the Open Society Initiative for West Africa. A number of new independent radio stations have started broadcasting recently, their aggressive reporting having reportedly contributed to the opposition's electoral victories in 2000 and 2001. In addition to two state television channels, there are several semi-private stations. Internet access is provided mainly through the state-owned *Société Nationale des Télécommunications* (Sonatel), which has been criticized for its slow pace in expanding service. As of 2008 there were 83.5 Internet users per 1,000 inhabitants..

INTERGOVERNMENTAL REPRESENTATION

Ambassador to the U.S.: Amadou Lamine BA.

U.S. Ambassador to Senegal: Marcia Stephens Bloom BERNICAT.

Permanent Representative to the UN: Paul BADJI.

IGO Memberships (Non-UN): AfDB, AU, BADEA, BOAD, CILSS, ECOWAS, IDB, Interpol, IOM, NAM, OIC, OIF, PCA, UEMOA, WCO, WTO.

SERBIA

Republic of Serbia
Republike Srbije

Political Status: Incorporated in the Kingdom of the Serbs, Croats, and Slovenes, which was constituted as an independent monarchy on December 1, 1918, and formally renamed Yugoslavia on October 3, 1929; became constituent republic of the communist Federal People's Republic of Yugoslavia, instituted November 29, 1945, and then of the Socialist Federal Republic of Yugoslavia, proclaimed April 7, 1963; continued as constituent republic, along with Montenegro, of the Federal Republic of Yugoslavia (FRY), proclaimed April 27, 1992; included in the "state union" of Serbia and Montenegro, established February 4, 2003, under new Constitutional Charter; proclaimed as the independent Republic of Serbia on June 5, 2006, following Montenegro's declaration of independence on June 3; currently governed under new constitution approved by referendum on October 28–29, 2006, and formally adopted by the National Assembly on November 8. (Serbia's Autonomous Province of Kosovo and Metohija was placed under administration of the United Nations Interim Administrative Mission in Kosovo with effect from June 14, 1999, by authorization of United Nations Security Council Resolution 1244. The autonomous province declared independence as the Republic of Kosovo on February 17, 2008, an action unrecognized by Serbia, which labeled it as illegal and in violation of international principles of sovereignty and territorial integrity.)

Area: 34,116 sq. mi. (88,361 sq. km.). Included are the autonomous provinces of Kosovo and Metohija, 4,211 sq. mi. (10,908 sq. km.), and Vojvodina, 8,304 sq. mi. (21,506 sq. km.).

Population: 7,498.001 (2002C, excluding Kosovo); 5,386,000 (2008E), including Vojvodina but excluding Kosovo and Montenegro.

Major Urban Centers (2005E): BELGRADE (1,117,000), Novi Sad (Vojvodina, 192,000), Priština (Kosovo, 168,000).

Official Languages: Serbian. National minorities may officially use their languages in localities where they comprise at least 15 percent of the population.

Monetary Unit: Dinar (market rate December 1, 2009: 63.10 dinars = $1US).

President: Boris TADIĆ (Democratic Party); elected in second-round voting on June 27, 2004, and inaugurated for a five-year term on July 11, succeeding Milan MILUTINOVIĆ (Socialist Party of Serbia), whose term had expired on December 29, 2002. In the interim, three chairs of the National Assembly of Serbia—Nataša MIĆIĆ (from December 30, 2002; Civic Alliance of Serbia/Democratic Opposition of Serbia), Dragan MARŠIĆANIN (from February 4, 2004; Democratic Party of Serbia), and Predrag MARKOVIĆ (from March 4, 2004; G17 Plus)—had served as acting presidents, the presidential elections of October 13, 2002, December 8, 2002, and November 16, 2003, having failed to meet the required 50 percent turnout of eligible voters. Tadić was reelected in runoff voting on February 3, 2008, and sworn in for a second term on February 15.

Prime Minister: Mirko CVETKOVIĆ (Democratic Party); nominated by the president June 27, 2008, following the National Assembly election of May 11; confirmed by the National Assembly on July 7, succeeding Vojislav KOŠTUNICA (Democratic Party of Serbia), who had stayed on in a caretaker capacity following his resignation on March 8.

THE COUNTRY

The Republic of Serbia, encompassing approximately 35 percent of pre-1992 Yugoslavia's area, is a landlocked Balkan state. While it has a Serb ethnic majority of 83 percent, Serbs are unevenly distributed. There have been particularly destabilizing effects in Serbia's Kosovo and Metohija Province, over 90 percent of whose 2.2 million inhabitants are ethnic Albanians, and in the Sandžak region of western Serbia, where half the population is ethnic Albanian. Serbia's Vojvodina Province, in the north, has a notable ethnic Hungarian minority (some 4 percent of the total population). Eastern Orthodox Christianity predominates, although a large Muslim community exists among ethnic Albanians. Vojvodina has a significant Roman Catholic minority. Women constitute about 44 percent of the active labor force and 22 percent of the current National Assembly.

Mostly underdeveloped before World War II, Yugoslavia, comprising six constituent republics (Bosnia and Herzegovina, Croatia, Macedonia, Montenegro, Serbia, and Slovenia), made rapid advances after 1945 under a Communist regime that applied pragmatic and flexible methods of economic management that ultimately moved the country toward a Western-style market economy.

Political transition and the outbreak of regional conflict in mid-1991 caused the economy to deteriorate rapidly, the decline being aggravated by the imposition of economic sanctions against the new Federal Republic of Yugoslavia (FRY, encompassing the constituent republics of Serbia and Montenegro) by the United Nations from May 1992 until November 1995. Substantial currency devaluations were undertaken in early 1992, with inflation soaring to a historically unprecedented rate of 1 million percent a month by December 1993. The "super dinar," introduced in January 1994, was valued at 13 million old dinars and had the effect of ending hyperinflation. The GDP of Serbia and Montenegro declined by more than 40 percent in the period 1990–1995. For the rest of the decade, growth averaged only about 2 percent annually.

Beginning in early 1998 escalating violence in Kosovo led to a renewal of international sanctions and then to a bombing campaign conducted by the North Atlantic Treaty Organization (NATO) in March–June 1999, severely damaging Serbia's productive capacity and economic infrastructure. In late September the government claimed that the NATO air war had caused $100 billion in damage, compared to the $30–50 billion estimated by international sources. Following the cessation of hostilities, a donor conference of over 100 countries and agencies pledged some $2 billion in reconstructive, humanitarian, and administrative assistance for Kosovo. According to FRY government

figures, GDP declined by 16 percent in 1999 because of the Kosovo conflict but increased by 5 percent in 2000. (Beginning in 2000 basic economic statistics have excluded Kosovo.) Output nevertheless stood at only half of its 1989 level, and 30 percent of the labor force was unemployed.

In 2008 Serbia's agricultural sector accounted for about 13 percent of GDP and employed about 22 percent of the active labor force. Leading crops include maize, wheat, and sugar beets. Industry contributed about 26 percent of GDP and engaged 26 percent of workers. Coal, lead, and zinc were mined in significant quantities, particularly in Kosovo. Major exports have included basic manufactures, machinery and transport equipment, and agricultural products.

In 2006 the Serbian GDP grew at a rate of 5.2 percent. Growth for 2007 was 6.9 percent, accompanied by 10 percent inflation. In 2008 Serbia began to feel the impact of the international financial crisis, and growth slowed to 5.4 percent. For 2009 the GDP was expected to fall by 4 percent due to reductions in trade, consumer demand, output, and fiscal revenues. Growth of about 1.5 percent was anticipated for 2010.

GOVERNMENT AND POLITICS

Political background. Following centuries of national struggle in the Balkans against the Turkish and Hapsburg empires, a unified state, the Kingdom of the Serbs, Croats, and Slovenes, was formed on December 1, 1918, under the Serbian House of Karadjordjević. Uniting the former independent kingdoms of Serbia and Montenegro with the Croatian, Dalmatian, and Bosnian and Herzegovinian territories previously ruled by Austria-Hungary, the new entity (formally renamed Yugoslavia on October 3, 1929) was ruled between World Wars I and II as a highly centralized, Serb-dominated state in which the Croats became an increasingly disaffected minority. The Serb-Croat antagonism, which caused many Croats to sympathize with Nazi Germany and fascist Italy, continued even after the two Axis powers attacked and occupied the country in April 1941 and set up a pro-Axis puppet state of Croatia that included most of Bosnia and Herzegovina.

Wartime resistance to the Axis was led by two rival groups, the proroyalist Chetniks, under Gen. Draža MIHAILOVIĆ, and the Communist-inspired Partisans, led by Marshal Josip Broz TITO, a Croat who sought to enlist all the country's national groups in the liberation struggle. The Partisans' greater effectiveness in opposing the occupation forces and securing Allied aid paved the way for their assumption of power at the end of the war. In March 1945 Tito became prime minister in a government of national unity; eight months later, on November 29, the monarchy was abolished and a Federal People's Republic of Yugoslavia, based on the equality of the country's principal national groups, was proclaimed. On January 14, 1953, under a new constitution, Tito was elected president of the republic.

Yugoslavia developed along orthodox Communist lines until 1948, when its refusal to submit to Soviet directives led to its expulsion from the Communist bloc and the imposition of a political and economic blockade by the Soviet Union and its East European allies. Aided by Western arms and economic support, Yugoslavia maintained its autonomy throughout the Stalin era and by the late 1950s had achieved a partial reconciliation with the Soviet-led Warsaw Pact states, although it still insisted on complete independence and the right to find its own "road to socialism." Internally, Yugoslavia had become the first East European country to evolve institutions that moderated the harsher features of Communist rule and encouraged the development of a democratic form of communism based on new interpretations of Marxism. A federal constitution promulgated in 1963 consolidated the system of "social self-management" by attempting to draw the people into economic and administrative decision-making at all levels; it also expanded the independence of the judiciary, increased the responsibilities of the federal legislature and those of the country's six constituent republics and two autonomous provinces (Kosovo and Metohija, and Vojvodina), and widened freedom of choice in elections.

In May 1980 Marshal Tito, president for life of the republic and of the League of Communists of Yugoslavia (*Savez Komunista Jugoslavija*—SKJ), died at the age of 87. The leadership of state and party thereupon passed to collegial executives—the eight-member State Presidency and the eight-member Presidium of the SKJ Central Committee. Yugoslavia's six republics and two autonomous provinces were equally represented in both. Through the 1980s the president of the State Presidency and the president of the Presidium rotated on an annual basis.

During 1990 both the federal government and the SKJ experienced acute crises as economic ills exacerbated long-standing political animosities. An SKJ congress that convened in January 1990 was forced to adjourn because of a split over introduction of a multiparty system and did not reassemble prior to a brief concluding session in May. Meanwhile, both Croatia and Slovenia had conducted open legislative elections in which the SKJ's republic-level affiliates were defeated. The situation was further aggravated in May when the hard-line Borisav JOVIĆ of Serbia became president of the State Presidency.

In July 1990 Slovenia and Macedonia declared their "full sovereignty" within Yugoslavia, while Croatia approved constitutional changes having much the same effect. In Serbia, a majority of voters endorsed a new Serbian constitution that, contrary to the federal document, effectively stripped the provinces of Kosovo and Vojvodina of autonomous status. Concurrently, ethnic Albanian delegates to the Kosovo Assembly declared their province independent of Serbia and a constituent republic of the Yugoslav federation. Serbia responded three days later by dissolving the Kosovo legislature. In a series of multiparty elections during November and December, former Communists won overwhelmingly in Serbia and Montenegro but were decisively defeated in Bosnia and Herzegovina.

The elections occurred at a time of mounting confrontation between the government of Croatia and the Serb-dominated Yugoslav National Army (*Jugoslovenske Narodne Armije*—JNA). In January 1991 Croatia and Slovenia concluded a mutual defense pact. In February the Slovene Assembly voted for phased secession from the federation. Shortly thereafter, the Serb-populated regions of Croatia opted for effective secession from that republic, prior to proclaiming at year's end a self-styled "Republic of Serbian Krajina."

In June 1991 the presidents of the six constituent republics were reported to have agreed to a plan whereby the republics would retain sovereignty within Yugoslavia but would not seek international recognition as independent states. However, the relatively prosperous Slovenes subsequently indicated their unwillingness to continue financial support for the less-developed republics, while Croatia feared that its sizable Serbian minority would force geographic dismemberment if it remained in the federation. As a result, the two western republics declared their independence on June 25.

That the federation had in fact expired was quickly apparent in the failure of the JNA to mount real opposition to Slovenia's secession, while JNA engagement in Croatia was mainly directed to backing local Serbs against Croatian government forces. By late August 1991 the conflict had cost Croatia nearly one-third of its territory, although some was later retaken. On September 8 Macedonians voted overwhelmingly in favor of establishing a sovereign and independent Macedonia.

Bosnia and Herzegovina followed suit, issuing a declaration of sovereignty on October 15. On December 5 Croatia's Stjepan MESIĆ resigned as president of the State Presidency, stating, "Yugoslavia no longer exists." The Croatian Assembly backdated the action to October 8, when its declaration of independence formally came into effect.

On January 15, 1992, one day after the advance contingent of a UN peacekeeping force had arrived in Yugoslavia, the European Community (EC, subsequently the European Union—EU) recognized the independence of Croatia and Slovenia. In contrast, on February 12 Serbia and Montenegro agreed to join in upholding "the principles of a common state which would be a continuation of Yugoslavia." In a referendum held February 29–March 1, Bosnia and Herzegovina opted for independence, and on March 26 Macedonia moved in the same direction by securing the withdrawal of JNA forces from its territory.

On April 27, 1992, a rump Federal Assembly adopted the constitution of a new Federal Republic of Yugoslavia (FRY), under which elections for a successor assembly were held in Serbia and Montenegro in May. The Socialist Party of Serbia (*Socijalistička Partija Srbije*—SPS), led by the president of Serbia, Slobodan MILOŠEVIĆ, won a slim majority in the new lower house, the Chamber of Citizens, in part because opposition elements, including the new Democratic Movement of Serbia coalition (*Demokratska Pokret Srbije*—Depos) boycotted the balloting. On June 15 the assembly elected Dobrica ĆOSIĆ, a well-known writer and political independent, as federal president. Under the new basic law, Ćosić, a Serb, was obligated to name a Montenegrin to the post of prime minister; however, in an unusual move apparently instigated by Milošević in the hope of currying favor in Washington, Ćosić nominated Milan PANIĆ, a wealthy U.S. citizen born in Serbia, who was formally confirmed by the assembly in July.

Milošević soon became increasingly critical of Panić, who, despite his questionable residential qualifications, then ran against Milošević in the Serbian presidential election in December 1992 but was soundly defeated. In the simultaneous legislative election Milošević's SPS maintained its dominance of the Serbian National Assembly. Although the SPS lost ground in the FRY's Federal Assembly, the hard-liners and anti-Panić forces were sufficiently strong to secure the overwhelming passage of a nonconfidence motion against the prime minister.

Amid uncertainty stemming from Panić's refusal to resign, his deputy, Radoje KONTIĆ of Montenegro, was named prime minister in February 1993. Thereafter, as the FRY's international isolation increased because of its involvement in the worsening ethnic conflict in Bosnia and Herzegovina, the ire of the Serbian hard-liners focused on the nonparty federal president, Ćosić, who was considered a moderate in Serbian terms even though he had drafted the intellectual blueprint for a "greater Serbia." The outcome was another success for the hard-liners: SPS legislators joined with those of the ultranationalist Serbian Radical Party (*Srpska Radikalna Stranka*—SRS) to pass motions in both federal chambers asserting that the president had breached the constitution, thus paving the way for his replacement in June by the chair of the Serbian legislature, Zoran LILIĆ.

Thereafter, Milošević was increasingly aligned with the "greater Serbia" school, although international pressure had obliged him in early May 1993 to accept the Vance-Owen plan for the cantonization of Bosnia and Herzegovina. Milošević was bitterly denounced for his action by the SRS leader, Vojislav ŠEŠELJ, whose call for a nonconfidence vote forced dissolution of the Serbian National Assembly in October. In the resultant December election, the SPS increased its strength in the 250-member body from 101 to 123 seats, while SRS representation declined from 73 to 39 in a contest that nevertheless saw a marked shift to right-wing nationalist attitudes among the opposition parties. Post-election negotiations led to the formation in March 1994 of a Serbian "cabinet of economists" that was headed by Mirko MARJANOVIĆ (SPS) and also included representation for the New Democracy (*Nova Demokratija*—ND) party.

In 1995 a major offensive by Croatian government forces had recovered most of the "Republic of Serbian Krajina" by early August (see Croatia article). In Yugoslavia, this provoked a storm of criticism directed against Milošević by hard-line Serb leaders. Political difficulties were compounded by the flight of some 200,000 Serbian refugees from Krajina, most of them into Yugoslavia, where many supported opposition demands for the government's ouster. Milošević's muted response to the Croat successes (and to subsequent advances by allied Muslim and Croat forces in Bosnia) was widely seen as in line with his recent policy of distancing the Belgrade government from the Croatian and Bosnian Serbs, in part to secure a settlement that would fully lift UN sanctions on Yugoslavia (see Foreign relations, below).

Serbian relations with the province of Kosovo remained in a state of crisis in 1995 and 1996 as ethnic Albanians, resisting Serbian attempts to impose political, social, and educational control, established their own underground administration. Elections to the Kosovo Assembly in May 1992, won by the pro-independence Democratic League of Kosovo (*Lidhja Demokratike e Kosovës*—LDK), had been condemned as illegal by Belgrade, which had officially dissolved the body in 1990. Nevertheless, the LDK leader, Ibrahim RUGOVA, was proclaimed president of a self-declared "Republic of Kosovo," which secured international recognition only from Albania. The local situation deteriorated in December 1994 when Serbian security forces carried out the most sweeping wave of arrests since 1990 in an effort to eliminate the unauthorized police force created by the ethnic Albanians. Tension intensified further in mid-1995 when the Belgrade government announced that Serb refugees from Krajina would be resettled in Kosovo with the aim of redressing the province's ethnic imbalance.

Elections in November 1996 took place amid increasing voter dissatisfaction with government mismanagement, crime, and corruption, as well as with the lack of economic improvement following the suspension a year earlier of UN sanctions. In the election for the federal Chamber of Citizens an SPS-led alliance won 64 of the 138 seats, with the government-aligned Democratic Party of Socialists of Montenegro (*Demokratska Partija Socijalista Crne Gore*—DPSCG) adding another 20 seats. SRS representation fell to 16, while the Together (*Zajedno*) coalition of moderate opposition parties obtained a disappointing 22 seats in the federal contest. In contrast, in mid-November, following a second-round election for local assemblies, the opposition parties claimed victory in most of Serbia's cities, including Belgrade. The SPS-controlled courts and electoral commissions quickly annulled the municipal results, alleging irregularities. In response, the opposition parties, joined by students and later the Serbian Orthodox Church and teachers, staged mass demonstrations of up to 250,000 people in the streets of Belgrade. After 88 days of marches, Milošević, in February 1997, finally felt compelled to have the Serbian National Assembly confirm the opposition victories.

Once in office, however, the opposition found its hands tied, the pro-Milošević bureaucracy having collaborated with departing SPS politicians in the mass transfer of government property from localities to the SPS-dominated Serbian republic. Moreover, by summer the *Zajedno* coalition had collapsed, its constituent parties having failed to agree on a common candidate to oppose Milošević for the presidency of Yugoslavia. (He was constitutionally barred from running for a third term as president of Serbia.) Thus, in July 1997 the federal legislature elected an unopposed Milošević as federal president. Two months later, in Serbia's parliamentary elections, Milošević's SPS and allies won a plurality of seats but were faced with having to rely on either the second-place SRS or the third-place opposition Serbian Renewal Movement (*Srpski Pokret Obnove*—SPO) for a parliamentary majority. After months of negotiations, in March 1998 the SPS and an ally, the Yugoslav Left (*Jugoslovenska Levica*—JUL), formed a government with the SRS under the continued leadership of Prime Minister Marjanović.

In the first round of the Serbian presidential election (held in tandem with the September 1997 parliamentary election), no candidate had won an absolute majority, forcing a runoff between Milošević's hand-picked SPS candidate, Zoran Lilić, and SRS leader Vojislav Šešelj. The results of the October 1997 second round favored Šešelj but were annulled by law as turnout had fallen below 50 percent. New first-round elections were held in early December, with Šešelj facing six candidates, including the SPS's Milan MILUTINOVIĆ. In the runoff two weeks later, Milutinović handily defeated Šešelj with 59 percent of the vote. The election was subsequently characterized as "fundamentally flawed" by the Conference on (later Organization for) Security and Cooperation in Europe (CSCE/OSCE).

Having fallen out of favor with President Milošević, in May 1998 the federal prime minister, Radoje Kontić, after more than five years in office, lost a confidence vote in the upper chamber of the Federal Assembly and was succeeded by Milošević ally and former Montenegrin president Momir BULATOVIĆ of the recently organized Socialist People's Party of Montenegro (*Socijalistička Narodna Partija Crne Gore*—SNPCG). In October 1997 Bulatović had lost a close bid for reelection as Montenegro's president, largely because of a split between pro- and anti-Milošević forces in his previous party, the DPSCG.

By this point, tensions had worsened in Kosovo, which Serbians considered their historic homeland. Following the murder of four Serbian policemen in February 1998 by members of the separatist Kosovo Liberation Army (KLA), a retaliatory security operation killed 24 ethnic Albanian villagers, many apparently by summary execution. Despite a series of diplomatic missions to Belgrade and Kosovo's capital, Priština, the Serbian crackdown continued, provoking demonstrations and calls by regional neighbors and the six-member international Contact Group on former Yugoslavia (see Foreign relations, below) for restraint and the opening of talks on Kosovar autonomy. Later in March, ethnic Albanians, in addition to casting ballots for the shadow "Republic of Kosovo" legislature, reelected the LDK's Ibrahim Rugova as shadow president.

With daily demonstrations continuing in the province, U.S. diplomats succeeded in convincing Milošević and Rugova to meet for the first time in May 1998. Although both sides agreed to initiate weekly talks in Priština, the violence in Kosovo continued to escalate as Serbian army and paramilitary security forces, sweeping through Kosovar villages, met strong resistance from the rapidly expanding KLA. Reports of civilian massacres, torture, and other human rights violations committed by Serbian contingents were regularly surfacing. In October, facing the threat of imminent NATO air strikes, Milošević agreed to begin withdrawing military and security forces from Kosovo and to allow entry of 2,000 international observers supervised by the OSCE. Although fighting intensified again in mid-December, late in the month both sides accepted a local cease-fire brokered by the head of the OSCE mission. In January 1999, however, despite renewed threats from NATO, widespread hostilities resumed. The worst atrocity of the conflict to date occurred when Serbian forces executed 45 civilians from the village of Račak.

In February 1999 peace talks between Serbian officials and ethnic Albanians—including KLA representatives—opened in Rambouillet, France. Cosponsored by France and the United States, the negotiations were aimed at winning approval of a proposal by the Contact Group that, while acknowledging Serbian sovereignty in Kosovo, envisaged almost complete administrative autonomy for the province, the withdrawal of all but 1,500 Serbian border troops, the rapid disbanding of the KLA, and formation of a new, ethnically balanced police force. The plan would also require Serbia to accept the stationing of NATO troops on its soil, which had become the major sticking point for the Milošević regime. In March the Kosovar delegation signed the pact, but the Serbian delegation continued to reject the presence of NATO peacekeepers. U.S. negotiator Richard Holbrooke met with Milošević in Belgrade March 22–23 in a final, futile diplomatic effort to avoid war.

On March 24, 1999, NATO forces from eight countries initiated Operation Allied Force, the most extensive air campaign in Europe since the close of World War II. In the following weeks allied bombing extended throughout Yugoslavia in an effort to force the Milošević regime to accept the Rambouillet agreement. Amid increasing allegations of massacres and other war crimes in Kosovo, Serbian forces stepped up a widespread campaign of "ethnic cleansing" that saw the entire Albanian population forced from some cities and villages, creating an immediate refugee crisis at the borders of Albania and Macedonia. By the end of April the refugee exodus was swelling toward 750,000, with additional hundreds of thousands displaced within the province itself.

The main Serbian opposition parties, a number of which had earlier joined various nongovernmental organizations in an umbrella grouping, the Alliance for Change (*Savez za Promene*—SZP), were largely silenced by the country's war footing. The loudest dissenting voice was that of Deputy Prime Minister Vuk DRAŠKOVIĆ of the SPO. Having joined the government in January in a show of national solidarity, he was dismissed in late April for having stated that the populace should be told, contrary to government contentions, "that NATO is not facing a breakdown, that Russia will not help Yugoslavia militarily, and that world public opinion is against us." In Montenegro, President Milo DJUKANOVIĆ (Bulatović's successor) continued his efforts to distance his administration from federal policies. Even though Montenegro was not exempt from the NATO air campaign, and despite rumors that the Serbian military was preparing to depose him, Djukanović rejected orders that the Montenegrin police be placed under the command of the army. Djukanović accused Milošević of using "the pretext of the defense of the country" to displace the civil government.

On May 6, 1999, the Group of Seven countries plus Russia (G-8) proposed a peace plan providing for "deployment in Kosovo of effective international civil and security presences" and formation of an interim provincial administration under the UN Security Council. On June 3 President Milošević accepted the terms of an amended peace agreement offered by President Martii Ahtisaari of Finland and Russia's Viktor Chernomyrdin, including the deployment in Kosovo—but not in the rest of Serbia—of a UN-sponsored, NATO-dominated peacekeeping contingent (Kosovo Force, or KFOR) expected to number some 50,000 troops. The agreement also called for the complete withdrawal of the Serb army, police, and paramilitary forces from Kosovo.

On June 10, 1999, NATO suspended its bombing campaign and the UN Security Council adopted Resolution 1244, authorizing international troop deployment and the establishment of an interim civilian administration in Kosovo. The resolution also reaffirmed Yugoslavia's "sovereignty and territorial integrity" but echoed previous calls for "substantial autonomy and meaningful self-administration in Kosovo." The agreement was widely, though often reluctantly, accepted by most of the opposition, including Serbian nationalists, the principal exception being the SRS, which protested by announcing its withdrawal from the coalition government in Serbia. (The withdrawal was technically prohibited by Serbian President Milutinović because of the state of war.) Meanwhile, on May 27 the International Criminal Tribunal for the former Yugoslavia (ICTY) had indicted President Milošević and four others, including the interior minister and army chief of staff, for crimes against humanity related to events in Kosovo.

On June 14, 1999, the UN Security Council received a plan for the civil Kosovo administration that included a new UN Interim Administration in Kosovo (UNMIK). On June 20, with the Yugoslav army having completely withdrawn from Kosovo, NATO formally concluded its bombing campaign. On the same day NATO and the KLA signed an agreement providing for KLA demilitarization. Most of the 1 million or more Kosovo Albanian refugees and displaced persons were already returning to their homes, contributing to the collateral flight from the province of ethnic Serbs, many of whom feared reprisals.

In December 1999 UNMIK announced formation of an Interim Administrative Council (IAC) of Rugova, the KLA's Hashim THAÇI, and Rexhep QOSJA of the United Democratic Movement (*Lëvizja Bashimit Demokratike*—LBD); a fourth seat on the IAC was reserved for a representative of the Serb community, which refused to participate. By then, forensic specialists from the international war crimes tribunal had already exhumed thousands of Albanian bodies from mass graves in Kosovo. (Late in the year, the Albanian death toll was estimated at 4,000–5,000, considerably less than originally projected.)

A federal cabinet reshuffle in August 1999 saw the addition of SRS ministers to the Bulatović administration in an effort to shore up support for Milošević. Political opposition to Milošević nevertheless continued to mount. In January 2000 the SPO's Drašković joined his principal opposition rival, Zoran DJINDJIĆ of the Democratic Party (*Demokratska Stranka*—DS), in forging a unified strategy that was signed by 16 opposition parties.

On April 18, 2000, the Eurocorps, with troop contingents from Germany, Spain, France, Belgium, and Luxembourg, took over control of the Kosovo peacekeeping effort from NATO, but KFOR was encountering increasing difficulty in preventing violent clashes between Albanian and Serb communities. The climate of violence was not, however, limited to Kosovo: in February the Yugoslav defense minister, Pavle BULATOVIĆ, had been assassinated in Belgrade, and in June the SPO's Drašković was wounded in Montenegro.

In a gambit designed to maintain Milošević's hold on power, on July 6, 2000, the SPS pushed through the Federal Assembly constitutional changes authorizing direct election of the president and of the upper legislative house. With most of the opposition continuing a boycott of parliament, the proposals easily received the necessary two-thirds support. The changes, in addition to permitting the incumbent to serve two additional four-year terms, put organization of elections under the FRY instead of the individual republics. On July 8 the Montenegrin assembly described the changes as illegal and "a gross violation of the constitutional rights of the Republic of Montenegro."

On July 27, 2000, Milošević called elections for September, even though his presidential term would not expire until July 2001. The governing coalition in Montenegro quickly announced that it would boycott the balloting. On August 7 the Democratic Opposition of Serbia (*Demokratske Opozicije Srbije*—DOS), ultimately encompassing some 18 parties and a trade union association, nominated Vojislav KOŠTUNICA, leader of the Democratic Party of Serbia (*Demokratska Stranka Srbije*—DSS), as their joint presidential candidate. The SPO, running independently, nominated the mayor of Belgrade, Vojislav MIHAJLOVIĆ, raising the prospect of a split in the opposition vote.

Despite allegations of vote rigging and other irregularities committed by Milošević's supporters, Koštunica emerged from the September 24, 2000, presidential election as the likely leader, although the SPS initially claimed otherwise. In the legislative contests, the DOS won a plurality in the lower house, but the electoral boycott by Montenegro's governing parties left the balance of power in the hands of the pro-Milošević SNPCG. On September 26 the government-controlled election commission admitted that Koštunica held the lead in the presidential tally, but with less than the 50 percent needed to avoid a runoff with Milošević. Rejecting the commission's count, Koštunica refused to participate in a second round of voting scheduled for October 8.

In the following days massive street demonstrations called for Milošević to step down, the Serb Orthodox Church began referring to Koštunica as the president, the Yugoslav army made it clear that it would not intervene, and ultranationalist SRS leader Vojislav Šešelj announced that he, too, would support Koštunica's claim to the presidency. On October 4, 2000, the Constitutional Court annulled the presidential poll, but two days later, with the country in the grip of a general strike and with pro-DOS demonstrators in Belgrade having burned the Federal Assembly and other buildings, the court reversed itself and declared that Koštunica had won 50.2 percent of the vote (some sources put the total at 55–56 percent). On the same day Milošević conceded, and the new president took office on October 7.

Faced with mounting opposition, the SPS-led government of Serbia resigned on October 21, 2000. The SPS's Milomir MINIĆ assumed office as prime minister on October 24 at the head of a transitional cabinet of the SPS, DOS, and SPO, pending a Serbian National Assembly election set for December 23. On November 4 the Federal Assembly confirmed the nomination of Zoran ŽIŽIĆ of the SNPCG as federal prime minister, Momir Bulatović having resigned on October 9. The Žižić cabinet included an equal number of ministers from the SNPCG and the DOS, plus two reform-oriented, nominally unaffiliated economists with strong ties to the DOS.

At the Serbian republican election in December 2000, the DOS handily defeated Milošević's SPS, winning 176 of the National Assembly's 250 seats, with 64 percent of the vote. On January 25, 2001, Zoran Djindjić of the DS took office as prime minister of Serbia, heading a new DOS-dominated Serbian cabinet that also included independents and members of the DOS-supportive G17 Plus economic think tank.

On April 1, 2001, after a violent standoff outside the former president's villa, Serbian police arrested Slobodan Milošević on charges of corruption and abuse of power. A debate continued over where he should be tried. Some members of the federal administration called for surrendering him to the ICTY, even though President Koštunica opposed any such action in the absence of legislation or a constitutional change authorizing extradition. In the Federal Assembly, efforts to pass extradition legislation were repeatedly stymied by the SNPCG. As a consequence, on June 23 the majority of the federal cabinet—minus the absent Prime Minister Žižić and all but one SNPCG minister—issued a decree on cooperation with the war crimes tribunal. On June 28 the FRY Constitutional Court stayed the decree pending determination of its constitutionality, but Serbian Prime Minister Djindjić and his cabinet, meeting in an emergency session and in near unanimity, discredited the court and refused to accept the stay. Justifying their action under a provision of the Serbian constitution that allowed the Serbian government to act unilaterally and temporarily on behalf of the whole country if federal authorities were unable to do so, the Serbian authorities immediately surrendered Milošević to UN representatives, who flew him to the Netherlands. (On March 11, 2006, 444 days into his trial before the ICTY, Slobodan Milošević would be found dead of a heart attack in his cell.) In reaction, FRY Prime Minister Žižić resigned on June 29, although he remained in a caretaker capacity until the confirmation on July 17 of Dragiša PEŠIĆ, also of the SNPCG.

In the context of a growing rivalry between Federal president Koštunica and Serbian prime minister Djindjić, Koštunica's DSS withdrew from the Serbian coalition government on August 17, 2001, ostensibly over the government's inaction in fighting organized crime. The increasing distance between the DSS and the DOS culminated on June 12, 2002, when the DSS withdrew from the Serbian legislature in protest of a government effort to replace 21 DSS deputies for absenteeism and to distribute some of their seats to other parties.

On March 14, 2002, the governments of Serbia, Montenegro, and the FRY announced an "agreement in principle" that would replace Yugoslavia with a "state union" to be called Serbia and Montenegro. Over the objections of parties that wanted a separate and independent Serbia, the Serbian legislature ratified the accord 149–79 on April 9. The same day, the Montenegrin legislature voted in favor of the agreement 58–11, but dissatisfaction on the part of proindependence parties soon cost the Montenegrin government its majority. On May 31, both chambers of the Federal Assembly approved the state union agreement by wide margins.

In August 2002, with the federal presidency certain to be replaced by a much weaker union presidency, federal president Koštunica entered the race for the Serbian presidency. In the September 29 election he won a leading 31 percent of the vote. Second place, with 27 percent, went to Miroljub LABUS, the federal deputy prime minister and the hand-picked candidate of Serbian prime minister Djindjić. In a runoff election on October 13 Koštunica took about 67 percent of the vote, but the turnout fell under 50 percent, invalidating the results. A repeat election on December 8, which pitted Koštunica against the SRS's Vojislav Šešelj and one other candidate, met the same fate, leaving Serbia without an elected president when Milutinović's term expired near the end of the month.

On January 27 and 29, 2003, the Serbian and then the Montenegrin assemblies approved a Constitutional Charter for the state union of Serbia and Montenegro. The Federal Assembly concurred on February 4 (by votes of 26–7 in the upper chamber and 84–31 in the lower), thereby excising Yugoslavia from the political map. Under the charter a new state union Assembly of Serbia and Montenegro was elected by and from among the members of the FRY, Serbian, and Montenegrin legislatures, and on March 7 the new assembly in turn elected the DPSCG's Svetozar MAROVIĆ, the only candidate, as state union president and chair of the Council of Ministers.

Five days later Serbian prime minister Zoran Djindjić was assassinated by an organized Belgrade criminal gang, the Zemun Clan, many of whose members had served in Slobodan Milošević's Special Operations Unit, the so-called Red Berets. (In May 2007 a dozen defendants were convicted in connection with the assassination and sentenced to prison terms of between 8 and 37 years.) Djindjić was succeeded in an acting capacity by Deputy Prime Minister Nebojša ČOVIĆ of the DOS-affiliated Democratic Alternative (*Demokratska Alternativa*—DA), with the Serbian legislature then confirming the DS's Zoran ŽIVKOVIĆ as the new prime minister on March 18, 2003.

Later in 2003, the DOS-led government of the Serbian Republic lost its legislative majority, precipitating an early National Assembly election on December 28. With the DOS alliance having dissolved, the ultranationalist SRS won a plurality of 82 seats but was unable to form a government. Thus, Vojislav Koštunica, who had stepped down as the last president of the FRY on March 3, 2003, was named Serbian prime minister-designate on February 20, 2004, by Dragan MARŠIĆANIN—the second of three acting Serbian presidents following the expiration of Milutinović's term in 2002. On March 3, 2004, the newly elected Serbian legislature confirmed Koštunica as the head of a minority government that included his DSS, the allied SPO and New Serbia (*Nova Srbija*—NS), and the G17 Plus. Because of its minority status, the new government depended on parliamentary support from the SPS.

In February 2004, three months after another invalidated Serbian presidential election, the Serbian Assembly eliminated the 50 percent turnout requirement. In a fresh election on June 13 Tomislav NIKOLIĆ of the ultranationalist SRS finished first, with 31 percent of the vote, against a dozen other candidates, including the DS's Boris TADIĆ (28 percent) and independent businessman Bogoljub KARIĆ (18 percent). In runoff balloting on June 27, however, Tadić, having gained the support of most mainstream parties, won 54 percent to Nikolić's 46 percent, and he was inaugurated as Serbian president on July 11.

Under their 2003 EU-backed state union agreement, both Serbia and Montenegro had the right to vote on the question of independence in three years. On May 21, 2006, by a half a percentage point above the EU-set threshold of 55 percent for approval, Montenegro's voters chose separation from Serbia, and on June 3 the Montenegrin Assembly passed a declaration of independence. Although many Serbians were unhappy with what they viewed as an abrupt divorce, on June 5 the Serbian National Assembly declared Serbia to be the independent successor state to the state union, as had been agreed upon under the charter, and thereby extinguished the last remnants of the former Yugoslavia. The two new countries then began the process of disentangling their institutions.

Independent Serbia's adoption of a new constitution, which was approved by 96.6 percent of those voting in a referendum on October 28–29, 2006, prepared the way for election of a new National Assembly on January 21, 2007. The SRS again won a plurality, 81 of 250 seats, but protracted negotiations among the other leading parties led to formation of a coalition by the DS, DSS, NS (now allied with the DSS), and the G17 Plus, which together commanded 130 seats. The new government, once again headed by Prime Minister Koštunica, took office on May 15.

Meanwhile, Kosovo, still under UNMIK administration, continued to press for independence from Serbia. Under a May 2001 Constitutional Framework for Provisional Self-Government, UNMIK had created "provisional institutions of self-government," lending legitimacy to Kosovo's presidency, government, and assembly. Following President Rugova's death from cancer on February 10, 2006, the Kosovar legislature elected the LDK's Fatmir SEJDIU as president, with Agim ÇEKU then being named prime minister in an effort to provide stronger leadership during UN-mediated negotiations over Kosovo's future political status.

On March 26, 2007, having abandoned futile efforts to achieve a compromise between the Serbian and Kosovar governments, UN Special Envoy Martii Ahtisaari submitted to the UN Security Council his plan for Kosovo's "supervised independence." The Ahtisaari plan gave considerable attention to the status of the minority Serb population. (Only a fraction of the estimated 200,000 Serbs who had fled Kosovo since 1999 had returned.) Serbs would be granted broad governmental powers in six municipalities, each of which could receive direct aid from Serbia. In addition, Serbs and other minorities would be guaranteed seats in the legislature. Although the Kosovo assembly voted its approval of the Ahtisaari plan in early April 2007, Serbia rejected it.

Given a December 2007 deadline for reaching a final decision on Kosovo's future, representatives of Serbia and Kosovo, including both presidents and both prime ministers, met in New York on September 28 for face-to-face discussions. Between then and November 26 five additional negotiating rounds were held. Serbia's final offer of self-government except in foreign relations, defense, and border control was rejected by Kosovo, the only significant point of agreement being that both would avoid threats and violence.

On November 17, 2007, the PDK won a plurality in an election for the Assembly of Kosovo. On January 9, 2008, the new legislature reelected Fatmir Sejdiu as president and then endorsed Hashim Thaçi as prime minister of a coalition cabinet comprising ministers from the PDK and the LDK, as well as two Serbs and a Turk.

In a reprise of Serbia's last presidential election, on January 20, 2008, the SRS's Tomislav Nikolić led in the first round of voting, winning 40.0 percent in a nine-way contest. The incumbent, Boris Tadić, finished second, with 35.4 percent, but went on to win reelection in the February 3 runoff, with 50.3 percent versus Nikolić's 48.0 percent. Prime Minister Koštunica, taking a harder line than the president on Kosovar independence and EU integration, had refused to support Tadić.

On February 17, 2008, Prime Minister Thaçi declared Kosovo to be "proud, independent, and free" as a "democratic, multiethnic state moving rapidly toward EU and Euro-Atlantic integration." The unilateral declaration was immediately condemned as illegal by Serbia. Addressing the UN Security Council on February 18, President Tadić asserted that Kosovo's action violated guarantees of sovereignty and territorial integrity contained in the UN charter. Protests by ethnic Serbs on both sides of the Kosovo border erupted, and in Belgrade tens of thousands of sometimes-violent demonstrators took to the streets on February 21. Among their targets were the embassies of Bosnia and Herzegovina, the United Kingdom, and the United States, all among the countries that had quickly recognized Kosovo's independence.

On March 8, 2008, having vowed that he would not support further negotiations with the EU until it accepted that Kosovo remained part of Serbia, Prime Minister Koštunica announced that the government coalition had collapsed, and five days later President Tadić dissolved the National Assembly. The resultant May 11 election saw Tadić's For a European Serbia (*Za Evropsku Srbiju*—ZES) coalition, led by the DS and G17 Plus, win 102 seats, to 78 for the SRS and 30 for Koštunica's coalition of the DSS and NS. Negotiations on forming a new coalition government concluded on June 26 with the announcement that the ZES would be joined by the SPS and several smaller parties. On July 7 the National Assembly confirmed a new cabinet headed by the DS's Mirko CVETKOVIĆ, theretofore the minister of finance.

Constitution and government. Yugoslavia under successive postwar constitutions remained a Communist one-party state until the emergence of a variety of opposition groups at the republican level in early 1990. The constitution of the Federal Republic of Yugoslavia, adopted in 1992, provided for a bicameral Federal Assembly, encompassing a Chamber of Republics (with equal representation for Serbia and Montenegro) and a Chamber of Citizens apportioned on the basis of population. The federal president was elected to a four-year term by the assembly until July 2000, when constitutional changes instituted direct elections for the presidency as well as for the Chamber of Republics. The president was expected to nominate a prime minister from the other constituent republic.

The Constitutional Charter of the state union of Serbia and Montenegro (including Serbia's Autonomous Province of Vojvodina and Autonomous Province of Kosovo and Metohija) was formally adopted in February 2003 and lasted until both countries chose independence in 2006. It established a presidency with circumscribed powers, although the head of state also served as chair of the Council of Ministers. The president was elected for a single four-year term by the unicameral legislature, the Assembly of Serbia and Montenegro, comprising 91 Serbian and 35 Montenegrin deputies. Each of the constituent republics had a popularly elected president and unicameral assembly, with a prime minister nominated by the former and confirmed by the latter.

Serbia's 2006 constitution retains a mixed presidential-parliamentary system. The president, elected by majority vote, serves a five-year, once-renewable term. The National Assembly, elected by proportional representation, also serves a five-year term, subject to dissolution. The president proposes a prime minister, who is approved by the legislature along with a cabinet. The president may return legislation to the National Assembly for reconsideration but, following repeat passage by a majority of the whole legislature, must then promulgate the resultant law. The president may also dissolve the National Assembly "upon the elaborated proposal of the Government."

A Supreme Court of Cassation sits at the apex of the judicial system. The National Assembly elects the president of the Supreme Court (for a nonrenewable five-year term) and first-time judges (for terms of three years). The latter may then be given permanent tenure by a High Judicial Council, an autonomous body elected by the National Assembly. There is also an autonomous Constitutional Court, whose authority extends to such matters as the constitutionality of laws, intergovernmental disputes, and compatibility of ratified treaties with the constitution. Local jurisdictions include 29 districts (5 in Kosovo), municipalities, towns, and the capital of Belgrade.

The constitution begins by affirming the "equality of all citizens and ethnic communities in Serbia" and adds that Kosovo and Metohija is "an integral part of the territory of Serbia," albeit with "substantial autonomy." Vojvodina is also recognized as an autonomous province. Despite Kosovo's February 2008 unilateral declaration of independence, the mainly northern, Serb-dominated areas of Kosovo participated in the May Serbian national and municipal elections. Although UNMIK branded the municipal elections as illegal, on June 28, the anniversary of the culturally important Ottoman victory over Serbian forces at the 1389 battle of Kosovo Polje, the Serb representatives from 26 municipalities convened in Mitrovica as a 45-member Assembly of the Community of the Municipalities of the Autonomous Province of Kosovo and Metohija. Self-declared competencies of the body include directing and coordinating activities of participating municipalities; proposing relevant legislation to Serbia's National Assembly; adopting "declarations, resolutions, and proposals"; and taking positions with regard to national authorities operating in the province.

Foreign relations. Following the 1948 break with Moscow, Yugoslavian foreign policy concentrated on maintaining the country's independence from both major power blocs. Though highly critical of U.S. policy in Vietnam and the Middle East, Belgrade was equally critical of the Warsaw Pact intervention in Czechoslovakia in 1968, the Moscow-supported Vietnamese invasion of Kampuchea (Cambodia) in 1978–1979, and the Soviet intervention in Afghanistan in December 1979. The Tito regime consistently advocated peace, disarmament, détente, and aid to anticolonial and developmental struggles of third world countries. Along with Egypt's Nasser and India's Nehru, Tito was considered a founder of the Nonaligned Movement.

Federal Yugoslavia was ostracized by much of the international community because of military action in support of Serbs in Croatia and in Bosnia and Herzegovina, although Belgrade insisted in early 1992 that all its troops had been withdrawn from both republics. Because of the Bosnian conflict, the UN Security Council on May 30 imposed comprehensive sanctions that included barriers to trade, a freezing of Yugoslavia's foreign assets, severance of air links, a reduction in diplomatic relations, and suspension of sporting, cultural, and technical exchanges. The EC ordered a trade embargo, and in November military units from NATO and the Western European Union were detailed to enforce both the UN and EC sanctions. On September 22 the UN General Assembly voted to exclude the FRY from its proceedings and insisted that it apply for UN membership rather than directly succeed to the seat held by its predecessor. In a subsequent "clarification," a Russian spokesperson insisted that the action referred only to the General Assembly, leaving truncated Yugoslavia as the successor state in all other UN bodies. By the end of 1992, however, Yugoslavia had also been suspended from the International Monetary Fund (IMF), as well as from the OSCE and the Central European Initiative. Nevertheless, Belgrade was not entirely without external supporters: Greece (an EC/EU member) saw the rump state as a natural ally in its disputes with Macedonia and Albania, while religious and ethnic ties contributed to significant Russian sympathy and diplomatic support for the Serb cause.

Intensified UN sanctions on the FRY compelled the Belgrade government to take an overtly stronger line with the Bosnian Serbs following the tabling of new peace proposals—the so-called Stoltenberg-Owen plan—in July 1994 by the Contact Group (of Britain, France, Germany, Russia, and the United States, together with the UN and EU). When the Bosnian Serbs rejected the plan, Belgrade's response was to announce the severance of all political and economic ties with the Bosnian Serbs and to agree to the deployment of international observers on the Yugoslav-Bosnian border to monitor compliance with the official blockade.

Belgrade's reward was UN Security Council approval on September 24, 1994, of a selective suspension of sanctions, including the resumption of international flights to Yugoslavia and the reopening of the Montenegrin port of Bar on the Adriatic. Following the intensification of NATO aerial attacks in late August 1995, the Bosnian and Croatian Serb leaders were pressured into accepting the primary role of the Serbian president Milošević in peace negotiations. As a result, after three weeks of intense negotiations between the protagonists conducted under U.S. sponsorship in Dayton, Ohio, a peace agreement was concluded on November 21, 1995 (see Bosnia and Herzegovina article), and initialed on behalf of Yugoslavia and the Bosnian Serbs by Milošević. Suspended the following day, UN sanctions against Belgrade were formally lifted by a unanimous Security Council vote on October 1, 1996 (although FRY assets remained frozen because of disputes and claims from other Yugoslav successor states).

Beginning in February 1998, however, Serbian police and military actions in Kosovo again put Yugoslavia at odds with much of the rest of the world, and on March 31 the UN Security Council imposed an arms embargo on Yugoslavia. From April to June the Contact Group, which now included Italy, met several times, with only Russia dissenting from the imposition of various economic sanctions. A September UN Security Council called for a cease-fire and condemned the "excessive and indiscriminate use of force" by the Serb military and security units. In November Belgrade barred members of the UN war crimes tribunal from entering Kosovo to investigate allegations of extrajudicial killings, prompting the U.S. president of the tribunal to brand Yugoslavia as a "rogue state, one that holds the international rule of law in contempt."

Although Yugoslavia stated during the February 1999 peace talks in Rambouillet, France, that it was prepared to consider regional autonomy for Kosovo, it continued to reject a NATO presence on its soil. Immediately following the start of the NATO bombing campaign on March 24, 1999, Belgrade declared a state of war and broke diplomatic relations with France, Germany, the United Kingdom, and the United States. Relations with all four were restored in November 2000 as Yugoslavia, now headed by Vojislav Koštunica, moved broadly to reestablish its international linkages. The FRY was formally reintegrated into the UN on November 1 and into the OSCE on November 27. On May 25, 2001, meeting in Vienna, the FRY and the other four Yugoslav successor states reached agreement on the division of assets from the former Yugoslavia. In April 2003 the FRY joined the Council of Europe.

A 2004 report by the government acknowledged Serbian involvement in the 1995 massacre of some 8,000 Muslim men and boys outside Srebrenica, Bosnia and Herzegovina. In June 2005 a state-run television channel for the first time broadcast videotape showing Serbian paramilitaries executing victims. (In April 2007 a Serbian war crime tribunal sentenced four members of the "Scorpions" paramilitary to prison for the crime.) Although the general public responded with shock and outrage, it remained divided on the overarching issue of societal responsibility. During a visit to Bosnia and Herzegovina in December 2004 President Tadić drew considerable international attention by apologizing "to all against whom a crime was committed in the name of the Serbian people."

On February 26, 2007, the International Court of Justice (ICJ), ruling in a case brought against the Federal Republic of Yugoslavia in 1993, concluded that Serbia was not responsible for genocide committed in Bosnia and Herzegovina during that country's conflict and did not owe reparations. The court severely criticized Serbia, however, for neglecting its obligations under the Convention on the Prevention and Punishment of the Crime of Genocide, both by failing to prevent the 1995 Srebrenica massacre in Bosnia and by failing to cooperate fully with the ICTY.

Prior to Montenegro's declaration of independence, the state union's ambitions to join the EU were complicated by the differences between the Serbian and Montenegrin currency, customs, and market regimes. Negotiations with the EU on a Stabilization and Association Agreement (SAA) as a precursor to EU membership primarily stalled, however, because of Serbia's testy relationship with the ICTY and the unresolved status of Kosovo. At the ICTY, the trial of former Serbian president Milan Milutinović began in July 2006, while that of SRS ultranationalist leader Vojislav Šešelj began in November 2007. Milutinović and Šešelj had surrendered to the ICTY in January and February 2003, respectively, to defend themselves against charges that included crimes against humanity and violations of the conventions of war. Although a number of once-prominent Serbian military leaders had also voluntarily surrendered to the ICTY in 2004 and 2005, the prosecutors in The Hague continued to insist that Belgrade had not rigorously pursued Radovan KARADŽIĆ and Ratko MLADIĆ, the most notorious Bosnian Serb commanders. Some human rights advocates charged that Serbia was actively protecting the two, who were under indictment for genocide, crimes against humanity, and war crimes. The Serbian government denied the accusations, even though Prime Minister Koštunica consistently argued that Serbians suspected of criminal acts during the Croatian, Bosnian, and Kosovar conflicts should be tried by a Serbian war crimes court.

The matter of cooperation with the ICTY had also delayed consideration by NATO of Serbia's participation in its Partnership for Peace (PfP) program. PfP membership was eventually offered by NATO in November 2006.

In December 2007, despite negotiations led by a troika of mediators representing the EU, Russia, and the United States, the deadline passed for Serbia and Kosovo to reach an accommodation on Kosovo's future status. Kosovo's February 2008 unilateral declaration of independence was quickly recognized by France, Germany, the United Kingdom, and the United States, among other countries, prompting some Serb nationalists to call for breaking off diplomatic relations with those states and to withdraw from an SAA with the EU that had been initialed on November 7, 2007. Nevertheless, the SAA was signed on April 29, 2008, two weeks before the legislative election that President Tadić described as setting out a "clear European path for Serbia." As of October 2009, 62 countries and Taiwan had recognized the Republic of Kosovo.

Current issues. The two principal issues that continue to face Serbia are the status of Kosovo and the country's relationship with the EU. None of the major Serbian parties, let alone the government, has dared characterize Kosovo's independence as a fait accompli, but entry into the EU undoubtedly depends on how the Kosovo question is resolved. On August 15, 2008, Foreign Minister Vuk JEREMIĆ announced that the Tadić government had asked the ICJ for an advisory ruling on Kosovo's unilateral declaration of independence. He added that the current government would "accept any opinion that comes from the ICJ," although a ruling against Serbia's claim could easily lead to a governmental crisis and new elections. In early October the UN General Assembly approved the referral to the ICJ, which then offered all UN members six months to submit written statements on the question, followed by a three-month period for submission of rebuttals. At the end of July 2009 the ICJ announced that it planned to open public hearings on the matter in December.

The issue is not clear cut. On the one hand, Serbia has a strong case that Kosovo's action violated international principles of sovereignty and territorial integrity. On the other hand, Serbian military personnel, militias, and civilians, with the backing of the Milošević government, committed genocide and other crimes against ethnic Albanians in Kosovo. Human rights advocates therefore argue that the Kosovars have not only the moral right but also the legal standing to separate unilaterally from the parent country.

Meanwhile, the camp of ardent Serbian nationalists has been torn over whether Serbia should remain closely allied with Russia and break off negotiations with the EU, as advocated by Vojislav Šešelj's SRS, or continue on the westward path toward European integration, as advocated by President Tadić. In September 2008 the SRS ruptured, primarily over that issue, with 2008 presidential candidate (and, until then, Šešelj surrogate) Tomislav Nikolić and his supporters being expelled for backing engagement with the EU. The SRS quickly lost a quarter of its National Assembly delegation to Nikolić's group, which organized as the Serbian Progressive Party (*Srpska Napredna Stranka*—SNS).

The intertwined issues of Kosovo and European integration also provided the backdrop for a May 20, 2009, trip to Serbia by U.S. vice president Joe Biden. Anticipating protests by nationalists, the government banned anti-U.S. demonstrations during the visit. Acknowledging the two countries' opposing positions on Kosovar independence, Biden encouraged a search for "pragmatic solutions" and stated that U.S. support for Serbian admission to the EU did not hinge on Belgrade's recognition of Kosovo.

As a further step toward preparing for EU membership, in 2009 the National Assembly passed a regionalization bill that calls for drawing up boundaries that would consolidate the country's 29 districts into 7 regions based on EU standards. Three of the regions would presumably be Belgrade, Vojvodina, and Kosovo-Metohija, but concerns about further ethnic partition and strife contributed to opposition from the SRS and other nationalist parties. The government reassured critics that regional boundaries would be determined on a statistical basis and would avoid ethnic homogeneity.

On July 21, 2008, a Serbian security team arrested Radovan Karadžić in a Belgrade suburb, and on the following day a judge ordered his transfer to The Hague to stand trial. Only two ethnic Serbian fugitives from ICTY indictments remain to be captured: Ratko Mladić and Goran HADŽIĆ, a Croatian Serb who acted as president of the "Republic of Serbian Krajina." Meanwhile, the ICTY has continued its activities. The trial of former Yugoslav army chief of staff Momčilo PERIŠIĆ, who had surrendered to the ICTY in 2005, opened in October 2008. Perišić faced 13 charges related to war crimes and crimes against humanity committed in 1993–1995 in Bosnia and Croatia. On February 26, 2009, former Serbian president Milan Milutinović was acquitted, although five codefendants were found guilty and sentenced to between 15 and 22 years in prison for offenses that included crimes against humanity and ethnic cleansing. The trial of SRS leader Vojislav Šešelj was interrupted in February 2009 when prosecutors alleged that witnesses were being intimidated. In July Šešelj was found guilty of contempt of court and sentenced to 15 months in prison for having revealed the names of three protected witnesses.

War crimes trials conducted by Serbia itself also continued. In March 2009 13 former soldiers, having been convicted of executing some 200 Croat prisoners in late 1991, received prison sentences of between 5 and 20 years.

POLITICAL PARTIES

For four-and-a-half decades after World War II, Yugoslavia's only authorized political party was the Communist Party, which was redesignated as the League of Communists of Yugoslavia (*Savez Komunista Jugoslavija*—SKJ) in 1952. Political control was also exercised by its "front" organization, the Socialist Alliance of the Working People of Yugoslavia (*Socijalistički Savez Radnog Naroda Jugoslavije*—SSRNJ). The collapse of Communist rule in 1989–1990 led to the formation of a large number of successor and other parties, including several "federal" groupings that sought, without success, to preserve the Yugoslav federation (see the 1994–1995 edition of the *Handbook*, p. 991).

Until late 2000 the dominant party in Serbia and at the federal level was Slobodan Milošević's Socialist Party of Serbia (SPS). Beginning in 1992 a number of opposition coalitions attempted to dislodge the SPS and its allies. The Democratic Movement of Serbia (*Demokratska Pokret Srbije*—Depos) was formed in May 1992 as an alliance whose principal members were the Serbian Renewal Movement (SPO), New Democracy (ND, subsequently the Serbian Liberals), and, following its separation from the Democratic Party (DS), Vojislav Koštunica's Democratic Party of Serbia (DSS). Depos quickly fractured, however, although the SPO and the ND, joined by the Civic Alliance of Serbia (GSS; see the Liberal Democratic Party, below), attempted to rejuvenate the alliance (dubbed Depos II) prior to the December 1993 Serbian Assembly election, in which it won 45 seats. In February 1994 the ND decided to support the Serbian government, and that, coupled with a move to the right by the SPO, brought an end to Depos.

In early 1996 the Together (*Zajedno*) coalition was established by the SPO, DS, and GSS, which were later joined by the Democratic Center (DC; see the DS, below) and, at the federal level, the DSS. The alliance captured a disappointing 22 seats in the federal poll of November 1996 but was far more successful in municipal elections later in the month, although the federal government did not acknowledge the victories for several months. Thereafter, with Serbian legislative elections approaching, relations between the SPO and its partners turned acrimonious, and in mid-1997 *Zajedno* collapsed.

A more inclusive Alliance for Change (*Savez za Promene*—SZP) originated in a June 1998 agreement by half a dozen parties to adopt a uniform opposition strategy. Among the initial participants were the DS, the GSS, and the Christian Democratic Party of Serbia (DHSS). Organizations joining later included the DC, the Democratic Party of Vojvodina Hungarians (DSVM), the New Serbia (NS), the Association of Free and Independent Trade Unions (*Asocijacija Slobodnih i Nezavisnih Sindikata*—ASNS), some 20 smaller parties, and various civic groups.

A smaller opposition grouping, the Alliance of Democratic Parties (*Savez Demokratskih Partija*—SDP), had been organized in October 1997 by the Alliance of Vojvodina Hungarians (SVM), the League of Vojvodina Social Democrats (LSV), the Reformist Democratic Party of Vojvodina (RDSV, subsequently the RVSP—see the Vojvodina Party, below), the Sandžak Coalition (KS), the Social Democratic Union (SDU), and the Šumadija Coalition (*Koalicija Šumadija*—KŠ).

The SZP and SDP, often in conjunction with the SPO, organized or participated in a number of anti-Milošević demonstrations and, beginning in September 1999, a series of opposition roundtables. These led to a January 10, 2000, meeting at which 16 opposition party leaders, spearheaded by the SPO's Vuk Drašković and the DS's Zoran Djindjić, committed their organizations to a joint strategy for forcing early elections. Following the July adoption by the Milošević-controlled Federal Assembly of constitutional changes permitting direct election of the president and the upper house, the opposition prepared for the September 24 federal elections by attempting to forge a comprehensive electoral alliance. Although the SPO and many less-influential parties ultimately chose to remain independent, the unification effort culminated in formation of the Democratic Opposition of Serbia (*Demokratske Opozicije Srbije*—DOS), which nominated the DSS's Koštunica for the presidency. By the time of the September balloting the DOS encompassed 18 parties (plus the ASNS), among them the DS, DSS, GSS, NS, and the 6 SDP parties. The DOS followed up its federal victories in September by winning 176 of the 250 seats in the December Serbian National Assembly election. By the time of the December 2003 Serbian election, however, the cumbersome DOS had dissolved.

For the May 2008 Serbian national election, 22 parties and coalitions offered party lists, up from 20 in January 2007. The leading coalition, **For a European Serbia** (*Za Evropsku Srbiju*—ZES), included as principal participants President Tadić's DS and the G17 Plus. Another significant coalition was formed by the DSS and NS, and a third by the SPS, United Pensioners of Serbia (PUPS), and United Serbia (JS). A 5 percent threshold for seats continued in effect except for ethnic minority parties, which needed only 0.4 percent of the vote to obtain a seat. Three such parties or coalitions won a total of 7 seats. A plethora of other minor organizations exist, many with a predominantly regional or ethnic character.

Government Parties:

Democratic Party (*Demokratska Stranka*—DS). The descendant of a post–World War I governing democratic party, the DS was revived in December 1989 and held a constituent convention in February 1990, with Dragoljub MIĆUNOVIĆ being elected as the party's first president. A centrist party committed to a democratic multiparty system, human rights, and a free press, the DS boycotted the May 1992 Federal Assembly election. Its reluctance to join the opposition coalition Depos in 1992 resulted in a party split, with the departing faction, the DSS, joining the alliance. Building on its modest success in the December 1992 balloting, the DS won 29 Serbian Assembly seats a year later as the party's turn toward nationalism won it surreptitious support from the Milošević-run media. At the head of the nationalist faction was Zoran Djindjić, who led the electoral campaign and in 1994 was elected party president in what was essentially a leadership coup against Mićunović, who subsequently formed the Democratic Center (*Demokratska Centar*—DC).

The party returned to active opposition in 1996 by joining *Zajedno*. The SPO's withdrawal in mid-1977 meant the demise of *Zajedno*, and the DS boycotted the 1997 Serbian elections. In 1998 Djindjić joined a number of other opposition politicians in announcing formation of the Alliance for Change (SZP). In 2000 Djindjić was a leading participant in the formation of the DOS as well as coordinator of the SZP. As prime minister of Serbia, he led the more reform-minded majority within the DOS, often in opposition to his chief rival, Vojislav Koštunica of the DSS. Djindjić was assassinated on March 12, 2003. A week later Zoran Živković was confirmed as prime minister.

Following the breakup of the DOS, the DS ran independently in the Serbian legislative election of December 2003, although various candidates from other parties, including the Civic Alliance of Serbia (GSS, below) and the DC, were included on the DS electoral list. The DS's Boris Tadić was elected president of Serbia in June 2004.

In January 2005 the DC merged into the DS. Following its formation in 1995, the DC had participated in both the Depos and the *Zajedno* opposition alliances before forming the DAN Coalition (*Koalicija DAN*) in late 1999 with New Democracy (*Nova Demokratija*—ND; renamed the Serbian Liberals [*Liberali Srbije*—LS] in 2003) and the Democratic Alternative (DA; see the SDP, below). All three DAN parties then joined the DOS in 2000. The DC's Mićunović ran as the DOS candidate in the invalidated Serbian presidential election of November 2003, finishing second. In the 2003 Serbian National Assembly election five DC candidates on the DS electoral list were awarded seats.

Following the separation of Serbia and Montenegro, and with an eye toward the growing popularity of the SRS, Tadić backed a call for early elections. In the January 2007 election the DS list won 64 seats, including 3 awarded to the Sandžak Democratic Party and 1 to the Democratic Alliance of Croats in Vojvodina (both below). It then formed a coalition government with the DSS, the NS, and G17 Plus. Tadić later confirmed his intention to seek reelection as president in January 2008. Although he finished second to the SRS candidate in the first round, with 35.4 percent of the vote, he won the February runoff, with 50.3 percent.

Following the withdrawal of the DSS from the government in March 2008 and the consequent dissolution of the National Assembly, the DS formed the ZES coalition to contest the May legislative election, in which its list won 64 of the alliance's 102 seats.

Leaders: Boris TADIĆ (President of the Republic and of the Party); Mirko CVETKOVIĆ (Prime Minister); Dušan PETROVIĆ (Deputy President); Vida OGNJENOVIĆ, Bojan PAJTIĆ, and Dragan ŠUTANOVAC (Vice Presidents); Tamara TRIPIĆ (Secretary).

G17 Plus. The G17 Plus originated in a think tank of reform-minded, nonparty economists that participated in the FRY and Serbian cabinets following the ouster of Slobodan Milošević. It was established as a political party in December 2002 under the leadership of Miroljub Labus, former FRY deputy prime minister and presidential candidate of the DS. In the December 2003 election for the Serbian National Assembly the G17 Plus electoral list finished fourth, with 11.5 percent of the vote and 34 seats, including 3 that went to members of the Social Democratic Party (SDP, below). The G17 Plus then joined the minority Koštunica government.

After the EU, dissatisfied with Belgrade's failure to capture war crimes suspects, suspended negotiations on a preaccession agreement, G17 Plus leader and Deputy Prime Minister Mladjan Dinkić protested the government's inaction by withdrawing his party from the government on October 1, 2006, although the G17 Plus ministers remained in place pending a new election. In the January 2007 voting the party saw a steep decline in its support, winning only 6.8 percent of the vote and 19 seats. In May 2008, as part of the ZES, it took 21 seats.

The G17 floor group in the National Assembly includes three additional deputies who were elected on the ZES list: one nonparty member and two members of the **Together for Šumadija** (*Zajedno za Šumadiju*—ZZS), a regional party led by Veroljub STEVANOVIĆ, the mayor of Kragujevac and a former copresident of the Serbian Democratic Renewal Movement (SDPO). The ZZS members had been associated with the Together for Kragujevac (*Zajedno za Kragujevac*—ZZK) civic movement until formation of the ZZS in May 2009.

Leaders: Mladjan DINKIĆ (Minister of Economy and Regional Development and President of the Party); Suzana GRUBJEŠIĆ (Leader of Deputy Group and Vice President of the Party); Ivana DULIĆ-MARKOVIĆ, Verica KALANOVIĆ, and Tomica MILOSAVLJEVIĆ (Vice Presidents).

Socialist Party of Serbia (*Socijalistička Partija Srbije*—SPS). The SPS was formed in July 1990 by consolidation of the former League of Communists of Serbia and its associated Socialist Alliance. The party won 194 of 250 seats in the Serbian Assembly in December 1990, while its leader, Slobodan Milošević, defeated 30 other candidates in retaining the Serbian presidency with a 65 percent vote share. The SPS won a narrow majority (73 of 138 seats) in the federal Chamber of Citizens in May 1992. Following the imposition of UN sanctions on May 30, anti-Milošević social democrats within the party formed several splinter groups; however, Milošević remained firmly in charge and was reelected in December, when the party also retained its pluralities in both the federal and the republican assemblies.

Thereafter, the SPS moved closer to the ultranationalist SRS (below), with which it cooperated to oust President Ćosić from the FRY presidency in June 1993. Four months later the SRS terminated the relationship, prior to the Serbian legislative poll in December, in which the SPS won 123 seats. In late 1995 Milošević dismissed several hard-line nationalists in the SPS leadership who were critical of the Dayton peace accord and supportive of militant factions among the Bosnian Serbs. Subsequently, an SPS-led electoral alliance, the Joint List, dominated federal parliamentary elections in November 1996 as well as the September 1997 presidential and legislative elections in Serbia. The Joint List also included the ND and the Yugoslav Left (*Jugoslovenska Levica*—JUL), an umbrella grouping of some two dozen communist and other leftist organizations led by Mirjana MARKOVIĆ, Milošević's wife.

At the federal presidential election of September 2000 President Milošević finished second, with some 35–37 percent of the vote, although he refused to acknowledge his loss to the DOS's Koštunica until early October. In simultaneous parliamentary elections, the SPS-JUL alliance saw its seat total in the lower house drop to 44, while it won only 7 of Serbia's 20 seats in the newly elective upper house. Although the SPS continued to control the republican government and legislature in Serbia, the success of the DOS precipitated a premature dissolution of the Serbian National Assembly in late October and the swearing in of an interim coalition government of the SPS, DOS, and SPO, pending an election in late December. In the meantime, a defiant Milošević was reelected party chair at a party congress in November.

The erosion of public support for the SPS continued in the December 2000 Serbian Assembly balloting. The SPS won only 37 seats, in contrast to the 86 won in 1997 as part of the Joint List with the JUL and ND. In the December 2003 election it won only 7.7 percent of the votes, good for 22 seats. Milošević, despite being on trial in The Hague, remained the SPS chair until his death in 2006.

Struggles over leadership of the SPS began after Milošević's death. The infighting undermined party unity in the assembly; this threatened the government, which depended on SPS support. In December 2006 the party elected Ivica Dačić over Milorad VUČELIĆ as successor to the late president. In the January 2007 election the SPS won just 5.6 percent of the vote and 16 seats. A year later, its presidential candidate, Milutin Mrkonjić, finished fourth, with 6.0 percent of the vote in the first round.

In the May 2008 legislative election the SPS ran in coalition with the **Party of United Pensioners of Serbia** (*Partija Ujedinjenih Penzionera Srbije*—PUPS) and the **United Serbia** (*Jedinstvena Srbija*—JS), winning 12 of the alliance's 20 seats. The PUPS, led by Jovan KRKOBABIĆ (Deputy Prime Minister), won 5 seats and then established its own deputy group, led by Momo ČOLAKOVIĆ, in the National Assembly. The JS, led by Dragan MARKOVIĆ and Jasmina MILOŠEVIĆ, won 3 seats, while 1 seat went to an SPS electoral partner, the **Movement of Veterans of Serbia** (*Pokret Veterana Srbije*—PVS), led by Saša DUJOVIĆ and Željko VASILJEVIĆ.

Leaders: Ivica DAČIĆ (Deputy Prime Minister and President of the Party), Slavica DJUKIĆ-DEJANOVIĆ (President of the National Assembly), Milutin MRKONJIĆ (Minister of Infrastructure), Žarko OBRADOVIĆ (Minister of Education), Branko RUŽIĆ (Chair, Executive Committee).

Serbian Renewal Movement (*Srpski Pokret Obnove*—SPO). The SPO was founded in March 1990 as a merger of four parties, most notably those led by Vojislav Šešelj and Vuk Drašković. In less than three months, however, internal squabbling led to the departure of Šešelj to found a new party, the SRS (below). Without Šešelj the SPO moderated its extreme nationalism and participated in the Depos coalitions in 1992 and 1993. During this time, Drašković spoke out loudly against war crimes and as a result, with his wife Danica, was arrested and allegedly beaten by Serbian police. Following the disappointing showing of

Zajedno in the 1996 federal election, the SPO was the sole opposition party to contest the 1997 Serbian elections for both parliament and the presidency, finishing third in both contests.

In January 1999 Drašković joined Prime Minister Bulatović's government as a deputy prime minister, but his show of national solidarity ended three months later when comments made contrary to policy led to his dismissal. The other three SPO ministers immediately resigned.

In 2000 the SPO remained aloof from the DOS alliance—a move that Drašković subsequently acknowledged as a mistake. In the September elections the SPO won only one upper house seat, while its presidential candidate, Vojislav Mihajlović, the mayor of Belgrade, took only 3 percent of the vote. In the December election for the Serbian assembly, the SPO won less than 4 percent of the vote and no seats. Drašković subsequently voiced support for reestablishing Serbia as a constitutional parliamentary monarchy.

For the 2003 Serbian legislative election the SPO joined forces with New Serbia, winning 13 of the coalition's 22 seats (based on a 7.7 percent vote share). Intraparty differences led in 2005 to formation of the Serbian Democratic Renewal Movement (SDPO, below) by 9 of the SPO's deputies. In 2007 the SPO list, which included members of the Serbian Liberals and the People's Peasant Party (below), won only 3.3 percent of the vote and thus no National Assembly seats. In the May 2008 election, the SPO ran as part of the ZES and was awarded 4 seats.

Leader: Vuk DRAŠKOVIĆ (Chair).

Social Democratic Party of Serbia (*Socijaldemokratska Partija Srbije*—SDPS). Formation of the SDPS was announced in August 2009 by Rasim Ljajić, minister of labor and social policy. Ljajić stated that the SDPS was an effort to unite various social democratic parties, including his own Sandžak Democratic Party, the Social Democratic Party (SDP) of Nebojša Čović, and the Independent Social Democrats (*Nezavisni Socijaldemokrata*—NSD), led by Zoran DRAGIŠIĆ. The SDPS was registered in October.

The SDP had been established in April 2002 by merger of one wing of Social Democracy (*Socijaldemokratija*—SD), led by Slobodan ORLIĆ, and the Social Democratic Union (SDU, below), led by Žarko Korać. The SD-SDU merger proved short-lived: In March 2003 the SDU was reestablished as a separate party, with the rump group retaining the SDP name. (In June 2002 the SD wing loyal to party founder Vuk OBRADOVIĆ had won title to the SD name in the courts.)

In October 2003 the SDP withdrew its support for the DOS-led Serbian government, which contributed to the collapse of the government and accelerated the alliance's disintegration. In the December 2003 parliamentary election the SDP candidates joined the G17 Plus electoral list, winning three seats.

In September 2004 Nebojša Čović's Democratic Alternative (*Demokratska Alternativa*—DA) merged into the SDP. The DA, dating from 1997, had participated in the Alliance for Change but departed and formed the DAN Coalition with the New Democracy and the Democratic Center (see DS, above) in late 1999 before joining the DOS in 2000. In the December 2003 Serbian legislative election, the DA won only 2.2 percent of the vote and no seats.

In August 2005 Prime Minister Koštunica asked the SDP to leave the government after two of its three assembly members voted against privatization of the state oil and gas company. Party chair Čović, who had been serving as head of the Serbia and Montenegro Coordination Center for Kosovo, was then dismissed, and the party formally entered the opposition. Minister of Labor Slobodan LALOVIĆ sided with the government and left the party. In 2007 the SDP joined forces with the PUPS (see under SPS, above), but the coalition won only 3.1 percent of the vote and therefore failed to meet the threshold for representation.

The NSD was established by Zoran Dragišić, a security analyst, in January 2008. The new party drew most of its members from what remained of the SD, then led by Nanad VUKASOVIĆ.

Although the Sandžak Democratic Party joined in forming the SDPS, it was expected to retain a separate identity at the regional level (see below, under Leading Sandžak Parties.) In 2008 it had won four seats in the National Assembly on the ZES list.

Leader: Rasim LJAJIĆ (Chair).

Other regional parties that won seats on the ZES list were the **League of Social Democrats in Vojvodina** (LSV), with 5 seats, and the **Democratic League of Croats in Vojvodina** (DSHV), with 1 seat (see under Leading Vojvodina Parties, below).

Other Parliamentary Parties:

Serbian Radical Party (*Srpska Radikalna Stranka*—SRS). Founded in 1991 and runner-up to the SPS in the federal lower house elections of May and December 1992, the SRS is a quasi-fascist advocate of "Greater Serbia" that emphasizes the importance of its "leader" (*vodj*). It withdrew its support of the SPS at both the republican and federal levels in September 1993 and mounted a campaign to undercut the ruling party in the run-up to the 1993 legislative election, in which, however, its representation dropped from 73 to 39 seats.

In 1994 the SRS abolished its paramilitary wing, the Serbian Chetnik Movement (formed in July 1990 as the revival of a World War II army of the same name), following charges that it was guilty of war crimes in Croatia during 1991 and 1992. It was also implicated in the Bosnia and Herzegovina conflict. Party leader Vojislav Šešelj was given a suspended prison sentence in September 1994 for violence in the assembly but committed the same offense a week later, for which he received an actual four-month sentence. In opposition to his continuing leadership, party dissidents left to form a new party, the Radical Party of the Left Nikola Pašić (*Radikolna Stranka Levice Nikola Pašić*—RSLNP), named after a 19th-century founder of an SRS precursor. The RSLNP had no success in the polls.

In the November 1996 federal election SRS lower house representation slipped further, to 16 seats. In the first runoff of the 1997 Serbian presidential election, Šešelj appeared to have beaten SPS candidate Zoran Lilić, but due to a low turnout the election was invalidated. Šešelj ultimately lost to new SPS candidate Milan Milutinović in December, though the official count and turnout levels were questionable. In the parliamentary election, the SRS, attacking Milošević as the cause of Serbia's woes, finished a strong second with 82 seats. As a result, the SPS approached the SRS about joining the Serbian government, with Šešelj being named a deputy prime minister in March 1998. The SRS was the only prominent Serb party to reject the June 1999 Kosovo peace plan.

At the federal level, the SRS 2000 presidential candidate, Tomislav Nikolić, finished third, with 6 percent of the vote, while the party captured only 5 seats in the lower house and 2 in the upper. In the December 2000 Serbian National Assembly election the SRS finished third, with 23 seats, a loss of 59.

In February 2003 Vojislav Šešelj surrendered to ICTY authorities to face charges that included crimes against humanity from 1991 to 1995. In December, with the DOS having dissolved, the SRS won a leading 27.6 percent of the vote and 82 seats in the National Assembly, far outdistancing the second-place DSS. Although the victory also gave the SRS a plurality of 30 indirectly elected seats in the new state union assembly, the party was unable to muster enough additional support to form a government in Serbia. Nikolić finished first in the June 2004 first-round voting for president of Serbia but was defeated in the second round, winning 46 percent of the vote.

In November 2006, in the midst of a four-week hunger strike, Vojislav Šešelj refused to appear at the opening of his trial in The Hague. A month earlier, the SRS had reelected him as leader. In January 2007 the SRS again emerged from the legislative election with a plurality, 81 seats based on a 28.6 percent vote share.

In late December 2007 the SRS absorbed the Serbian Unity Party (*Stranka Srpskog Jedinstva*—SSJ), an ultranationalist group launched prior to the December 1992 election, with the reported support of President Milošević, as a counter to the SRS. Its leader, Željko RAŽNJATOVIĆ ("Arkan"), a commander of the paramilitary Tigers group, had been linked in press reports to a variety of atrocities in Bosnia and Croatia. In March 1999 the ICTY announced that it had sent Belgrade a warrant for Arkan, who was killed by masked gunmen in January 2000. The hard-line stance of the SSJ won it 14 seats in the December 2000 Serbian Assembly election. In 2003 it ran under the banner of the unsuccessful ZNJ electoral list (see People's Peasant Party, below). Its chair, Borislav PELEVIĆ, ran for president in 2004.

In the January 2008 presidential race, Nikolić again led after the first round but lost in the runoff, with 48 percent of the vote. In the May National Assembly election, the SRS increased its vote share to 29.5 percent but won 3 fewer seats, finishing second to the ZES coalition. Four months later the party split over the issue of EU integration. Nikolić and others who supported eventual EU membership were expelled from the SRS, having been branded by Šešelj as traitors and "Western puppets." The departure of Nikolić and his supporters, including the SRS's general secretary, Aleksandar Vučić, reduced the

SRS contingent in the National Assembly to 57 seats. In late September Nikolić formed the Serbian Progressive Party (SNS, below).

In July 2009 the ICTY sentenced Vojislav Šešelj to 15 months in jail for contempt of court after he revealed the identities of three protected witnesses. As of December his trial for crimes against humanity had not concluded.

Leaders: Vojislav ŠEŠELJ, Dragan TODOROVIĆ (Acting Chair), Gordana POP-LAZIĆ.

Democratic Party of Serbia (*Demokratska Stranka Srbije*—DSS). The DSS was established shortly before the December 1992 election by a dissident faction of the Democratic Party that wished to join the Depos opposition bloc in that contest. Under Vojislav Koštunica it later swung further to the right than its parent.

Standing on its own in the December 1993 Serbian Assembly election, the DSS won seven seats. Although a constituent of the *Zajedno* alliance in the November 1996 election, in which it won four seats, the DSS ran separately in some municipalities in the subsequent local balloting. Like the DS, it boycotted the 1997 Serbian elections.

In August 2000 Koštunica emerged as the consensus DOS presidential candidate to oppose Slobodan Milošević, and he was declared the winner of the September election in early October. Subsequently, the conservative Koštunica had differences with the DOS majority, not least over the handling of Slobodan Milošević.

In August 2001 the DSS withdrew from the Serbian government, which it accused of failing to address the problem of organized crime. Relations with the DOS and, more specifically, the DS continued to worsen thereafter, and in December the DSS's Dragan Maršićanin was forced out as speaker of the Serbian National Assembly after being accused of vote rigging. With the rivalry between DS leader Djindjić and Koštunica heating up, the DSS in effect withdrew from the DOS.

Koštunica was denied the Serbian presidency in 2002 when a low voter turnout invalidated elections in October and December. Having led the DSS to a second-place finish, with 17.7 percent of the vote and 53 seats, in the Serbian legislative election of December 2003, he was confirmed as the head of a minority government in March 2004. For the December election the DSS had included on its electoral list a handful of candidates from several small parties, including the People's Democratic Party (*Narodna Demokratska Stranka*—NDS), led by Slobodan VUKSANOVIĆ, which then merged into the DSS in October 2004.

In November 2006, looking toward the January 2007 general election, the DSS formed an alliance with New Serbia (below). The coalition won 47 seats, including the DSS's 33 and the NS's 10. Also awarded 2 seats each on the DSS-NS list were the Serbian Democratic Renewal Movement (SDPO, below) and the United Serbia (see SPS, above).

For the January 2008 presidential contest the DSS supported Velimir Ilić of the NS. In May 2008 a coalition of the DSS and the NS won 30 seats (21 for the DSS) on an 11.6 percent vote share. The DSS, adamantly opposed to Kosovo's independence and its recognition by the majority of EU members, joined the opposition.

Leaders: Vojislav KOŠTUNICA (Former Prime Minister of Serbia and President of the Party), Miloš ALIGRUDIĆ (National Assembly Leader).

Serbian Progressive Party (*Srpska Napredna Stranka*—SNS). The SNS was formed in September 2008 by a group of SRS members, including about 20 members of the National Assembly, who broke with party policy because they supported greater European integration, including EU membership. The dissenters, led by former SRS presidential candidate Tomislav Nikolić, were expelled by the SRS leadership, prompting formation of a separate faction in the National Assembly, the Go, Serbia! (*Napred Srbijo*) floor group, and confirmation of their intention to establish a new "radical" party. Apart from the issue of closer ties to Western Europe, the SNS remains ideologically nationalistic, supporting the integrity of the state and rejecting independence for Kosovo. It also advocates military neutrality and support for ethnic Serbs throughout the former Yugoslavia.

Leaders: Tomislav NIKOLIĆ (Leader), Aleksandar VUČIĆ (Deputy Leader).

Liberal Democratic Party (*Liberalno Demokratska Partija*—LDP). The LDP was formed in 2005 by a dissenting faction of the DS following the ouster from the leadership of the LDP's founder, Čedomir Jovanović. It ran in the 2007 legislative election in coalition with the Civic Alliance of Serbia (*Gradjanski Savez Srbije*—GSS), the Social Democratic Union (SDU, below), and the League of Social Democrats of Vojvodina (LSV, below). The coalition won 15 seats, 5 of which were assigned to the LDP. In April 2007 the GSS merged into the LDP, adding 4 additional seats.

The GSS, founded in 1992 by internationally known antiwar activist Dr. Vesna PEŠIĆ, never achieved notable success in the polls despite participating in Depos, *Zajedno,* the Alliance for Change, and the DOS. In December 2003 GSS candidates for the Serbian legislature ran on the DS electoral list, ending up with five seats. In the following year a number of GSS leaders, including the party's president, Goran SVILANOVIĆ, resigned and joined the DS.

In the 2008 presidential election Jovanović finished with 5.3 percent of the vote. In May the LDP list won 5.2 percent of the National Assembly vote, for 13 seats, including 1 for the SDU and 1 for the Christian Democratic Party of Serbia (below).

Leaders: Čedomir JOVANOVIĆ (President); Nenad MILIĆ (Deputy President); Nastaša MIĆIĆ, Judita POPOVIĆ, and Nebojša RANDJELOVIĆ (Vice Presidents).

New Serbia (*Nova Srbija*—NS). The NS was organized following the expulsion of Čačak's controversial mayor, Velimir Ilić, from the SPO in 1998 and his subsequent departure from Serbia-Together (*Srbija-Zajedno*), an SPO offshoot. The NS joined the Alliance for Change and then the DOS. In November 2003 Ilić ran third in the invalidated Serbian presidential election. A month later the NS and the SPO ran as a coalition in balloting for the Serbian legislature, with the NS being awarded nine seats.

In November 2006 the NS allied with the DSS in preparation for the 2007 National Assembly election, in which the NS won 10 seats. Ilić finished third, with 7.4 percent of the vote, in the first round of the 2008 presidential contest. In May it won 9 National Assembly seats and then formed its own floor group.

Leader: Velimir ILIĆ (President).

Christian Democratic Party of Serbia (*Demohrišćanska Stranka Srbije*—DHSS). The DHSS dates from 1997, when a dispute with Vojislav Koštunica led a number of DSS members to leave the party under the former DSS vice president, Vladan Batić. He subsequently served as coordinator of the Alliance for Change and as a principal leader of the DOS.

At the December 2003 Serbian legislative election the DHSS headed the Independent Serbia *(Samostalna Srbija)* list, which won 1.1 percent of the vote. In 2007 DHSS candidates were included on the coalition list headed by the LDP and GSS; the DHSS was awarded one seat.

In February 2008 the DHSS blamed the Koštunica government for instigating the Belgrade riots ("an act of state terrorism") that followed Kosovo's unilateral declaration of independence. In May the party again ran on the LDP list, with Batić claiming the party's sole seat.

Leader: Vladan BATIĆ (President).

Social Democratic Union (*Socijaldemokratska Unija*—SDU). The SDU was formed by a University of Belgrade psychologist and former associate of the Civic Alliance, Žarko Korać. He was also linked to the student-led Resistance (*Otpor*), which repeatedly took to the streets in opposition to the Milošević regime. The SDU participated in the DOS alliance in 2000.

Following an abortive merger with a wing of Social Democracy in 2002, the SDU reemerged as a separate party in March 2003. In the December 2003 Serbian National Assembly election its candidates ran on the DS electoral list, ending up with one seat. In 2007 it competed in coalition with the LDP, GSS, and LSV and was awarded one seat. In 2008, once again allied with the LDP, it again received one seat.

Leader: Žarko KORAĆ (President).

In addition to those already mentioned above, four ethnic minority parties won seats in the May 2008 legislative election. They included the Alliance of Vojvodina Hungarians (SVM; see below, under Vojvodina Parties), 4 seats; the Bosniac Democratic Party of Sandžak (BDSS; see under SDA Sandžak, below), 1 seat; and the Social Liberal Party of Sandžak (SLSS; also under SDA Sandžak), 1 seat. Also winning 1 seat was the **Coalition of Albanians from the Preševo Valley** (*Koalicija Albanaca Preševske Doline*—KAPD), which had been formed by two ethnic parties based in the southern localities of Preševo, Bujanovac, and Medvedja: the **Democratic Action Party** (*Partija za Demokratskoe Delovanje/Partia për Veprim Demokratik*—PDD/PVD), led by Riza HALIMI, and the **Democratic Union of the Valley** (*Demokratske Unije Doline*—DUD), led by Skender DESTANI. In 2007 the two were the first ethnic Albanian parties to contest a national election since 1993. Halimi sits as part of the National Minorities Group in the National Assembly.

Other National Parties:

People's Peasant Party (*Narodna Seljačka Stranka*—NSS). In 2003 the NSS ran for the National Assembly as part of For National Unity–Prof. Borislav Pelević and Marijan Rističević (*Za Narodno Jedinstvo–Prof. Borislav Pelević i Marijan Rističević*—ZNJ), an electoral list that also included the Serbian Unity Party (see SPS, above), the People's Party (*Narodna Stranka*), Serbia Our Home (*Naš Dom Srbija*—NDS), and the Serb Party (*Srpska Stranka*—SS). The ZNJ won only 1.7 percent of the vote. The NSS's Marijan Rističević had finished fourth, with 3 percent of the vote, in the invalidated November 2003 Serbian presidential election. In 2007 NSS candidates ran for the National Assembly on the SPO list.

In January 2008 Rističević won 0.5 percent in the presidential race. In May, running under the banner "If It Were up to the Village," the NSS won only 0.3 percent of the vote.

Leader: Marijan RISTIČEVIĆ (President).

Serbian Democratic Renewal Movement (*Srpski Demokratski Pokret Obnove*—SDPO). The conservative SDPO was formed in May 2005 by nine National Assembly members who left the Serbian Renewal Movement (SPO, above), largely because of differences with the SPO leader, Vuk Drašković. The nine assemblymen then formed a joint legislative caucus with the nine members from the New Serbia party, which had previously been close to the SPO.

At the 2007 National Assembly election the SDPO ran on the DSS list and was awarded two seats. The party subsequently split, however, resulting in formation of the Together for Kragujevac (ZZK; see under G17 Plus) by former copresident Veroljub Stevanović.

Leader: Vojislav MIHAILOVIĆ (President).

Other unsuccessful parties/electoral lists contesting the May 2008 election included the **My Serbia Movement** (*Pokret Moja Srbija*), led by Branislav LEČIĆ; the **Patriotic Party of the Diaspora** (*Patriotska Stranka Dijaspore*), led by Zoran MILINKOVIĆ; the **People's Movement for Serbia** (*Narodni Pokret za Srbiju*), led by Milan PAROŠKI; Bogoljub KARIĆ's **"Strength of Serbia" Movement** (*Pokret "Snaga Srbije"*); and the **Reformist Party** (*Reformistička Stranka*—RS) of Aleksandar VIŠNJIĆ and Jugoslav DOBRIČANIN. Dobričanin finished last in the 2008 presidential race.

Leading Sandžak Parties:

Party of Democratic Action Sandžak (*Stranka Demokratske Akcije Sandžaka*—SDA Sandžak). Linked to the Party of Democratic Action in Bosnia and Herzegovina, the ethnically Bosniac SDA has distinct organizations based in the Albanian/Muslim communities of the Sandžak region (in southwestern Serbia, adjacent to Montenegro), Montenegro, Preševo, and Kosovo. A leading advocate of autonomy for Sandžak, the SDA saw 45 of its members convicted of plotting armed insurgency in 1994, although all were pardoned or had their convictions vacated in 1996.

In 1995 the chair of the SDA Sandžak, Sulejman Ugljanin, came under challenge from party elements who objected to his residence in Turkey and who also wanted to establish closer ties to the Serbian opposition. Led by the party's secretary general, Rasim Ljajić, Ugljanin's opponents held their own party congress and succeeded in reregistering the party under Ljajić. Before long, five similarly named Sandžak parties had emerged. Having returned from exile in 1996, Ugljanin continued at the head of what he deemed the "true" SDA Sandžak and organized a three-party coalition, the Sandžak List Dr. Sulejman Ugljanin (*Koalicija "Lista za Sandžak Dr. Sulejman Ugljanin"*—LZS), which won a seat in the November election for the federal legislature and three seats in the Serbian Assembly in 1997. In 2000 Ljajić's SDA Sandžak adopted the name Sandžak Democratic Party (SDP, below), which remains the principal regional rival of Ugljanin's SDA.

For the 2003 Serbian election various participants in the Sandžak List, including the **Bosniac Democratic Party of Sandžak** (*Bošnjačke Demokratske Stranke Sandžaka*—BDSS), led by Esad DŽUDŽEVIĆ, and Bajram OMERAGIĆ's **Social Liberal Party of Sandžak** (*Socijal-no-Liberalna Stranka Sandžaka*—SLSS), were included on the DS party list. In 2007 the Sandžak List, which won two National Assembly seats, also included the **Sandžak Reformists** (*Reformisti Sandžaka*—RS). In 2008 the LZS was renamed the **Bosniac List for a European Sandžak** (*Bošnjačka Lista za Evropski Sandžak*), which again won two seats, one for the BDSS and one for the SLSS.

Ugljanin, who accepted appointment to the Cvetković cabinet after the 2008 election, has also chaired the Bosniac National Council of Sandžak (*Bošnjačko Nacionalno Vijeće Sandžaka*—BNVS), which claims to be the highest representative body of Bosniacs in the region.

Leader: Sulejman UGLJANIN (President).

Sandžak Democratic Party (*Sandžačka Demokratska Partija*—SDP). The SDP began as the Sandžak SDA faction led by Rasim Ljajić after the ouster of Sulejman Ugljanin in 1995 (see SDA Sandžak, above). Ljajić was also serving as chair of the Sandžak Coalition (*Koalicija Sandžak*—KS), which joined the DOS alliance in 2000 despite reservations regarding Vojislav Koštunica's nationalist views. Following the September 2000 election, Ljajić was named to the federal cabinet over the objections of pro-Ugljanin Bosniacs. In October he announced that his SDA would reregister as the SDP.

Prior to the December 2003 Serbian legislative election the SDP joined the Alliance of Vojvodina Hungarians (SVM, below) and the League of Vojvodina Social Democrats (LSV, below) in forming the Together for Tolerance–Čanak, Kasa, Ljajić (*Zajedno za Toleranciju*), which drew additional support from several other minority groupings. Together, the coalition parties won 4.2 percent of the vote, short of the 5 percent threshold for seats.

Following the termination of the state union in June 2006, Serbia took over the federal-level Ministry of Human Rights and Minorities, with Ljajić retaining the portfolio. That ministry was subsequently eliminated, although Ljajić remained in the cabinet.

In 2007, running on the DS list, the SDP was awarded three National Assembly seats. It received four in 2008 as part of the ZES. In August 2008 Ljajić established the Social Democratic Party of Serbia (SDPS, above) in an effort to unify the country's social democratic formations. The SDP supported that effort but was expected to retain a separate identity at the regional level.

Leader: Rasim LJAJIĆ (Minister of Labor and Social Policy, and President of the Party).

Leading Vojvodina Parties:

League of Vojvodina Social Democrats (*Liga Socijaldemokrata Vojvodine*—LSV). The moderate left-wing LSV was a founding member of the Vojvodina Coalition (see the Vojvodina Party, below) and continues to support autonomy for the region. At a party congress in 2000 its chair launched a campaign for creation of a "Vojvodina Republic" within Yugoslavia. The party competed in the September election as part of the DOS alliance.

In 2004 the LSV led formation of the **Coalition "Together for Vojvodina"** (*Koalicija "Zajedno za Vojvodinu"*), which won seven seats in that year's Vojvodina Assembly election. After the election the LSV joined the DS-led provincial government. For the 2007 National Assembly election the LSV ran in coalition with the LDP, GSS, and SDU and claimed four seats.

For the May 2008 National Assembly election the LSV ran as part of the ZES, winning five seats. For the provincial election, however, it again led a Together for Vojvodina Coalition, which won six seats.

Leaders: Nenad ČANAK (Chair), Bojan KOSTRES (Deputy Chair).

Alliance of Vojvodina Hungarians (*Savez Vojvodjanskih Madjara/Vajdasági Magyar Szövetség*—SVM/VMSZ). Founded in 1994 as an offshoot of the DZVM (below), this minority party won 3 seats in the 1996 federal election and 4 in the 1997 Serbian election. It joined the DOS in 2000 but nevertheless offered a separate candidate list in several constituencies, winning 1 lower house seat in the September federal election and, in conjunction with the DOS, an overwhelming majority of seats in the Vojvodina Assembly election of September–October. In the 2004 provincial election the SVM finished third, with 11 seats, far behind the DS's 38 and the SRS's 35. It suffered similar losses in local council elections but joined in forming a DS-led provincial government.

In the 2007 national election the SVM won three seats. In May 2008 the party ran at the national and provincial levels as part of the **Hungarian Coalition** (*Madjarska Koalicija*—MK) along with the DZVM and the DSVM (below). The MK won 4 National Assembly seats and 9 in the 120-member Vojvodina Assembly, where the ZES won a majority. In January the SVM's chair, István Pásztor, had won 2.3 percent of the first-round vote for president.

Leaders: Jósef KASZA (Honorary President), István PÁSZTOR (President), Károly PÁL (Executive Vice President), Bálint PÁSZTOR (Leader in National Assembly).

Democratic Community of Vojvodina Hungarians (*Demokratska Zajednica Vojvodjanskih Madjara/Vajdasági Magyarok Demokratikus Közössége*—DZVM/VMDK). The DZVM was formed in 1990 to represent the interests of the ethnic Hungarian population of Vojvodina. It obtained three federal and nine republican assembly seats in the December 1992 election but lost four of the nine in December 1993. On the latter occasion the DZVM leader, Andraš Agošton, disclosed that proautonomy Hungarian organizations in Vojvodina had been financed from Hungary. The party subsequently became divided between those favoring autonomy for Vojvodina and those advocating cooperation with Belgrade. Agošton was replaced as chair in 1996 and organized the DSVM (below) in 1997. Remaining aloof from the DOS, the party failed to win any seats in the Vojvodina Assembly election in September–October 2000.

For the 2007 national election the DZVM joined forces with the DSVM in the Coalition of Hungarian Unity (*Koalicija Madjarska Sloga*—KMS), which won less than the 0.4 percent threshold for minority parties. In May 2008 it competed as part of the MK.

Leader: Sándor PÁL (Chair).

Democratic Party of Vojvodina Hungarians (*Demokratska Stranka Vojvodjanskih Madjara/Vajdasági Magyar Demokrata Párt*—DSVM/VMDP). The DSVM was formed in 1997 by András Ágoston, former chair of the DZVM. The party did not join the DOS in 2000. It won one Vojvodina Assembly seat in 2004. It joined the DZVM in 2007's KMS alliance and in 2008 participated in the MK.

Leader: András ÁGOSTON.

Democratic Alliance of Croats in Vojvodina (*Demokratski Savez Hrvata u Vojvodini*—DSHV). Founded in 1990, the DSHV represents the small ethnic Croat minority in Vojvodina. For the 2004 Vojvodina election it cooperated with the SVM. In the January 2007 National Assembly election its candidates ran on the DS list and received one seat. In 2008, running with the ZES, it again claimed one seat.

Leader: Petar KUNTIĆ (Chair).

Vojvodina Party (*Vojvodjanska Partija*—VP). Formation of the Vojvodina Party was accomplished in June 2005 by the merger of half a dozen small parties, including the Reformists of Vojvodina–Social Democratic Party (*Reformisti Vojvodine–Socijaldemokratska Partija*—RVSP), the Vojvodina Civic Movement (*Vojvodjanski Gradjanski Pokret*—VGP), and the Vojvodina Coalition (*Koalicija Vojvodina*—KV). A principal goal of the new formation was full autonomy for the province.

At the 2007 National Assembly election the VP headed a Coalition "Vojvodina Parties" (*Koalicija "Vojvodjanske Partije"*) that failed to win representation. In 2008, running independently, it took only 0.1 percent of the vote.

Leader: Igor KURJAČKI.

Kosovo Parties:

Ethnic Albanian parties in Kosovo have uniformly refused to participate in national elections, and most ethnic Serb parties in Kosovo have boycotted Kosovar elections. The Kosovo parliamentary and local elections held on November 17, 2007, saw 25 parties, 2 coalitions, and 36 "citizens' initiatives" competing, including an assortment of Serb and other minority parties vying for reserved minority seats. The **Democratic Party of Kosovo**, led by former Kosovo Liberation Army head Hashim THAÇI, won a plurality of 37 seats in the Assembly of Kosovo. The **Democratic League of Kosovo,** led by President Fatmir SEJDIU, finished second, with 25 seats, a net loss of 22 from its previous total. The only other parties passing the 5 percent minimum threshold for proportional seats were the **New Kosovo Alliance,** which claimed 13; the alliance of the **Democratic League of Dardania** and the **Albanian Christian Democratic Party of Kosovo,** 11; and the **Alliance for the Future of Kosovo,** 10. Six ethnic Serb parties split the 10 seats set aside for Serbians. Seven other minority parties won a total of 14 seats, including the 10 set aside for Bosniaks (3); Gorani (1); Romani, Ashkali, and Egyptians (4); and Turks (2).

For a full discussion of these and other parties, see the separate article on Kosovo.

Other Ethnic or Regional Parties:

In the 2007 National Assembly election the **Roma Party** (*Romska Partija*—RP), led by Šajn SRDJAN, and the **Union of Roma in Serbia** (*Unija Roma Srbije*—URS), led by Rajko DJURIĆ, each one 1 seat. Neither, however, was successful in May 2008. Other ethnic groups that competed in 2008 were the **Alliance of Bački Bungevci** (*Savez Baćkih Bunjevaca*—SBB), led by Mirko BAJIĆ; the **Civic Initiative of Gorani** (*Gradjanska Inicijativa Goranaca*—GIG), led by Predrag BALAŠEVIĆ; the **Montenegrin Party** (*Crnogorska Partija*—CP), led by Nenad SATEVOVIĆ; **Roma for Roma** (*Romi za Roma*—RZR), led by Miloš PAUNKOVIĆ; and the **United Vlachs of Serbia** (*Ujedinjeni Vlasi Srbije*—UVS). None won more than 0.2 percent of the vote.

LEGISLATURE

The **Serbian National Assembly** (*Narodna Skupština Srbije*) comprises 250 members elected to four-year terms by proportional representation. In general, party lists must meet a 5 percent threshold to qualify for seats, except that minority parties are awarded a seat for each 0.4 percent of the vote they receive. In the most recent election, held May 11, 2008, the For a European Serbia coalition won 102 seats (Democratic Party, 64; G17 Plus, 21; League of Vojvodina Social Democrats, 5; Sandžak Democratic Party, 4; Serbian Renewal Movement, 4; Together for Kragujevac, 2; Democratic Alliance of Croats in Vojvodina; 1; nonparty [a G17 Plus ally], 1); the Serbian Radical Party (SRS), 78; a coalition of the Democratic Party of Serbia (DS) and New Serbia (NS), 30 (DS, 21; NS, 9); a coalition of the Socialist Party of Serbia (SPS), the Party of United Pensioners of Serbia (PUPS), and the United Serbia (JS), 20 (SPS, 12 [including 1 assigned to the Movement of Veterans of Serbia]; PUPS, 5; JS, 3); the Liberal Democratic Party, 13 (including 1 assigned to the Social Democratic Union and 1 to the Christian Democratic Party of Serbia); the Hungarian Coalition, 4 (all won by the Alliance of Vojvodina Hungarians); the Bosniac List for a European Sandžak, 2 (Bosniac Democratic Party of Sandžak, 1; Social Liberal Party of Sandžak, 1); the Coalition of Albanians from the Preševo Valley, 1 (Democratic Action Party).

In September 2008 the SRS split over the issue of European integration, with a new Serbian Progressive Party (SNS) being formed by dissident members. As a consequence, the SRS deputy group fell to 57 members. The SNS formed its own deputy group with 21 members.

President: Slavica DJUKIĆ-DEJANOVIĆ.

CABINET

[as of December 15, 2009]

Prime Minister	Mirko Cvetković (DS)
Deputy Prime Ministers	Ivica Dačać (SPS)
	Mladjan Dinkić (G17 Plus)
	Jovan Krkobabić (PUPS)
Deputy Prime Minister for European Integration	Božidar Djelić (DS)
Ministers	
Agriculture, Forestry, and Water Management	Saša Dragin (DS)
Culture	Nebojša Bradić (G17 Plus)
Defense	Dragan Šutanovac (DS)
Diaspora	Srdjan Srećković (SPO)
Economy and Regional Development	Mladjan Dinkić (G17 Plus)

Education	Žarko Obradović (SPS)
Energy and Mining	Petar Škundrić (SPS)
Environment and Spatial Planning	Oliver Dulić (DS)
Finance	Diana Dragutinović (DS) [f]
Foreign Affairs	Vuk Jeremić (DS)
Health	Tomica Milosavljević (G17 Plus)
Human and Minority Rights	Svetozar Čiplić (DS)
Infrastructure	Milutin Mrkonjić (SPS)
Interior Affairs	Ivica Dačić (SPS)
Justice	Snežana Malović (DS) [f]
Kosovo-Metohija	Goran Bogdanović (DS)
Labor and Social Policy	Rasim Ljajić (SDP)
National Investment Plan	Verica Kalanović (G17 Plus) [f]
Public Administration and Local Self-Government	Milan Marković (DS)
Religious Affairs	Bogoljub Šijaković (DS)
Science and Technological Development	Bozidar Djelić (DS)
Telecommunications and Information Society	Jasna Matić (G17 Plus) [f]
Trade and Services	Slobodan Milosavljević (DS)
Youth and Sports	Snežana Samardžić-Marković (G17 Plus) [f]
Without Portfolio	Sulejman Ugljanin (SDA)

[f] = female

COMMUNICATIONS

Historically, news media in Serbia were government controlled or strictly supervised. After Slobodan Milošević's fall from power, greater freedom prevailed. The 2006 Serbian constitution prohibits censorship except where a court has deemed it necessary "to prevent inciting to violent overthrow of the system established by the Constitution or to prevent violation of territorial integrity of the Republic of Serbia, to prevent propagation of war or instigation to direct violence, or to prevent advocacy of racial, ethnic, or religious hatred enticing discrimination, hostility, or violence."

In August 2009 the National Assembly adopted controversial amendments to the Public Information Law that established heavy fines on journalists and media outlets for publishing false or libelous information. Media associations and watchdogs criticized the changes as likely to result in self-censorship and the closure of electronic and print outlets that are found in violation.

Press. The following are dailies published in Belgrade in Serbo-Croatian, unless otherwise noted: *Večernje Novosti* (270,000), evening paper; *Blic* (230,000), independent tabloid; *Politika* (130,000), founded in 1901; *Danas,* independent; *Glas Javnosti,* independent; *Dnevnik* (Novi Sad), state run; *Magyar Szó* (Novi Sad), state run, in Hungarian.

News agencies. The leading domestic facility is the state-owned Tanjug News Agency (*Novinska Agencija Tanjug*). In addition, the major foreign agencies have bureaus in Belgrade.

Broadcasting and computing. Direct state control of Serbia's leading broadcasting service *Radio-Televizija Srbije,* ended in 2006, when it began a transition to a public broadcasting company. Private television and radio stations, licensed in increasing numbers since 2000, now total over 750, but most reach only local audiences.

As of 2008 there were 335.4 Internet users per 1,000 inhabitants.

INTERGOVERNMENTAL REPRESENTATION

Ambassador to the U.S.: Vladimir PETROVIĆ.

U.S. Ambassador to Serbia: (Vacant).

Ambassador to the UN: Feodor STARČEVIĆ.

IGO Memberships (Non-UN): BIS, BSEC, CEI, CEUR, EBRD, Eurocontrol, Interpol, IOM, OSCE, PCA, WCO.

SEYCHELLES

Republic of Seychelles
Repiblik Sesel (Creole)
République des Seychelles (French)

Political Status: Independent member of the Commonwealth since June 29, 1976; present constitution approved by referendum of June 18, 1993.

Area: 171 sq. mi. (429 sq. km.).

Resident Population: 75,876 (1997C); 87,000(2008E). Some 30,000 Seychellois live abroad, mainly in Australia and the United Kingdom.

Major Urban Center (2005E): VICTORIA (25,100).

National Languages: Creole, English, French.

Monetary Unit: Seychelles Rupee (official rate December 1, 2009: 10.98 rupees = $1US).

President: James Alix MICHEL (Seychelles People's Progressive Front); elevated (from vice president) to the presidency on April 14, 2004, following the retirement of France Albert RENÉ (Seychelles People's Progressive Front); directly elected in balloting of July 28–30, 2006, and sworn in for a five-year term on August 1.

Vice President: Joseph BELMONT (Seychelles People's Progressive Front); nominated by President James Michel on April 15, 2004, and confirmed by the National Assembly on April 16 to succeed Michel as vice president following Michel's elevation to the presidency on April 14; elected in balloting of July 28–30, 2006, and sworn in for a five-year term on August 1.

THE COUNTRY

The Seychelles archipelago consists of some 115 islands in the Indian Ocean about 600 miles northeast of Madagascar. More than 85 percent of the population is concentrated on the largest island, Mahé, which has an area of approximately 55 square miles (142 sq. km.); most of the remainder is distributed between the two northern islands of Praslin and La Digue. Most Seychellois are of mixed French-African descent and adhere to Roman Catholicism. There are small minority groups of Indians and Chinese. Nearly 98 percent of adult women are classified as "economically active," largely in subsistence agriculture; women are more likely than men to be literate.

Tourism is a significant source of national income and employs about 30 percent of the labor force. Small-scale industries provide about one-quarter of GDP, while the fishing sector produces about 30 percent of export earnings. The export of copra has declined sharply in recent years, and other cash crops are limited in scope. The economy is also underpinned by a growing offshore banking sector. (Hopes that oil would deliver economic salvation receded in October 1995 when a British company abandoned exploratory drilling south of the islands, though renewed optimism was evidenced when a U.S. firm was awarded a similar bid in 2005.)

GDP growth of 4.8 percent was recorded in 2000, but the economy subsequently slumped, with real GDP declining significantly to negative numbers in the ensuing four years. The government continued to promote the offshore banking sector, despite the fact that the Seychelles had been placed on the list of questionable "tax havens" by the Organization for Economic Cooperation and Development (OECD). In 2001 the Seychelles agreed to make changes and was added to the list of OECD countries committed to eliminating harmful tax practices.

Following the Indian Ocean tsunami in December 2004, the Paris Club canceled the Seychelles' debt. The government began soliciting foreign investment for the tourism sector and promoted the Seychelles

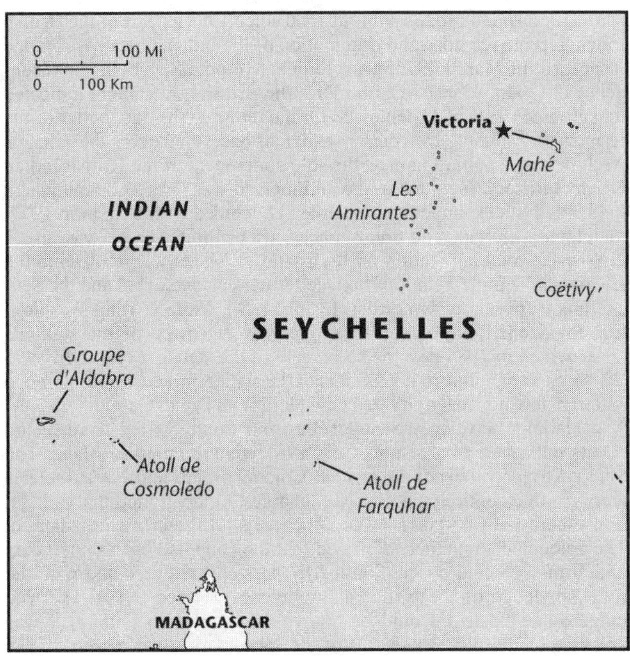

as a provider of offshore financial services. However, the International Monetary Fund (IMF) reported there was little such activity in the latter area because of the lack of financial supervision in the Seychelles. The IMF cited an "urgent" need for banking reforms and legislation that would criminalize the financing of terrorism.

Although the country continued to experience negative growth in 2005–2006, the IMF said, "the economic situation is improving," largely due to increased tourism and construction activity. The IMF commended the government for implementing policy reforms after the July 2006 elections and for its efforts toward structural reforms. Economic growth in 2007 was robust, with annual GDP of 5 percent recorded, owing in large part to foreign investment in the tourism sector, according to the IMF, which also noted that unemployment was at a historic low. Growth slowed to 2.5 percent in 2008 due to increasing international oil prices, among other factors. The IMF reiterated its emphasis on structural reforms, commending the government's progress in reducing subsidies and removing price controls on imports. In early 2009 the IMF, citing the government's progress in economic reforms, approved $1.3 million to further those efforts. Annual growth in 2009 was expected to contract by 0.5 percent, owing in large part to the global financial crisis and a related decline in tourism.

GOVERNMENT AND POLITICS

Political background. Following a half-century of French rule, the Seychelles became a British possession under the Treaty of Paris in 1814. Originally administered from Mauritius, it became a Crown Colony in 1903. A partially elected governing council was established in 1967, and limited self-government under a chief minister was introduced in 1970. Following a constitutional conference in London in March 1975, the legislative assembly established in 1970 was increased from 15 to 25 members, the 10 new members being nominated by the two parties in the government coalition. Concurrent with the achievement of independence on June 29, 1976, the former chief minister, James R. MANCHAM, was designated president, and the former leader of the opposition, France Albert RENÉ, became prime minister.

On June 5, 1977, while the president was attending a Commonwealth conference in London, the government was overthrown in a near-bloodless coup that installed René as the new head of state. In balloting on June 23–26, 1979, conducted under a single-party socialist constitution adopted on March 26, René was confirmed in office for a five-year term.

After assuming power, President René encountered a series of external and internal challenges to his authority. In November 1979 he announced the discovery of an antigovernment plot "sponsored from abroad" that allegedly involved ousted president Mancham and a force of mercenaries based in Durban, South Africa. Among the 85–100 people arrested in the wake of the allegations were the head of the country's immigration service, a former minister of finance, and a French citizen who had been advising the Seychelles police force. A potentially more serious threat was averted in November 1981 with the detection at Mahé's Pointe Larue airport of a group of mercenaries led by the celebrated Col. Michael ("Mad Mike") Hoare, an Irishman who had been involved in a number of African destabilization efforts during the previous two decades. In the course of a pitched battle with units of the Seychelles People's Defence Force (SPDF), some 45 of the invaders commandeered an Air India Boeing 707 and ordered the pilot to fly them to Durban, where they eventually surrendered to South African police. Released on bail in early December, the mercenaries were rearrested on January 5, 1982, in the wake of mounting international criticism. Most were given modest jail sentences under the South African Civil Aviation Offenses Act, Colonel Hoare ultimately being released in May 1985.

In August 1982 some 150 lower-ranked members of the SPDF seized key installations on Mahé in an abortive protest against alleged ill-treatment by senior military officials, while in September 1986 a number of army officers loyal to the minister of defense, Col. Ogilvy BERLOUIS, were charged with plotting to assassinate the president. In London, the exiled Seychelles National Movement (*Mouvement National Seychellois*—MNS) claimed knowledge of the 1986 plot, saying that the principals had been divided as to its implementation; subsequently, Colonel Berlouis resigned his post and left the country for Britain.

Despite exile opposition calls for a boycott, President René was reelected by a reported 92.6 percent of the vote on June 17, 1984, after having announced that those failing to participate would lose their right to public assistance. The National Assembly was subsequently replenished in single-party balloting on December 5, 1987, while the president was accorded a third term on June 9–11, 1989. In early 1990 President René declared that recent developments in Eastern Europe were of no concern to his administration, and at midyear he insisted that the Seychelles would "continue on the same path" with no acceptance of political change. However, in November he adopted a somewhat different posture by commenting favorably on the possibility of a reform referendum, although with reference only to the conduct of intraparty affairs. In March 1991 he was further reported to favor limited administrative decentralization through the reestablishment of district councils, whose members would, however, have to be supporters of the ruling Seychelles People's Progressive Front (SPPF).

On September 12, 1991, the assembly approved a Local Government Bill that provided for the multiple candidature, one-party election of local councils, whose heads were to meet with the Central Committee of the SPPF to rule on the desirability of a referendum on constitutional revision. However, in a remarkable turnabout on December 3, an extraordinary SPPF congress (meeting with the council heads elected two days earlier and identified as constituting a new assembly) voted unanimously to endorse an unexpected proposal by René to introduce a pluralist system. Under the plan (formally approved by the assembly on December 27), opposition parties would be permitted to register by January 1992 and a Constituent Committee would be elected by proportional representation in July to draft a new constitution. Earlier, the president had called on all political exiles, including his predecessor, to return to the Seychelles, provided that they retract their "accusations" against his regime.

In the Constituent Committee balloting on July 26, 1992, the SPPF won 14 seats on the basis of a 58.4 percent vote share, while the Democratic Party (DP) of former president Mancham was awarded 8 seats on the basis of a 33.7 percent share; no other groups secured representation. On September 18 the DP delegation withdrew from the constitutional talks, charging the SPPF with "bulldozer tactics" in attempting to meet a presidential deadline for a referendum on the document in November and a general election in December. Six days later Mancham announced a DP boycott of the proceedings, with the SPPF delegation (which constituted a quorum) indicating that it would continue alone. On October 6 opposition objectives became more specific: (1) separation of the overlapping roles of district councilors and local party officials; (2) termination of links between the SPPF and the armed forces; (3) a halt to state funding for the SPPF; (4) unhindered access to the media, including autonomy for the Seychelles Broadcasting Company;

and (5) deletion of an electoral provision that would allocate nondirectly elective legislative seats in accordance with the distribution of the presidential vote.

In the face of opposition criticism, the draft constitution secured the approval of only 53.7 percent of the votes cast (60 percent being needed for acceptance) at the referendum of November 15, 1992. The DP thereupon returned to the Constituent Committee and participated in the approval on May 7, 1993, of a revised draft that received popular endorsement by 73.6 percent of participating voters on June 18. In a general election under the new basic law on July 23, President René retained his office on the basis of a 60 percent vote share, while the SPPF was victorious in all but one of the directly elective constituencies.

New presidential and assembly elections were held on March 20–22, 1998, with President René and the SPPF again winning by convincing margins. René was reelected with 67 percent of the vote, 7 points higher than he had scored in the 1993 election; in addition, James MICHEL, whom René had appointed as vice president the previous year, was elected as René's running mate. René's nearest competitor was Rev. Wavel RAMKALAWAN, leader of the United Opposition (UO), who secured 20 percent of the vote, while former president Mancham of the DP finished with 14 percent. The DP also fared poorly in the assembly balloting, winning only one seat (down from the five they had held previously). Meanwhile, the SPPF, with 30 legislative seats, improved its total by 3 from 1993; the UO became the main opposition party, such as it was, with 3 assembly seats.

Following the approval by the National Assembly in 2000 of a constitutional amendment allowing the president to call presidential elections separately from legislative elections, René called for an early presidential poll on August 31–September 2, 2001. Once again facing Ramkalawan (representing the Seychelles National Party [SNP], as the UO had been renamed), René was reelected with 54.19 percent of the vote. Ramkalawan, however, significantly improved his vote share to 44.95 percent, partly because of Mancham's decision not to run. The cabinet announced by René on September 5 included reshuffled assignments but no new members.

In October 2002 the assembly voted to dissolve and hold new legislative balloting on December 4–6. Although the SPPF retained its majority (23 of 34 seats on a 54 percent vote share), the SNP improved from 3 to 11 seats (on a 40 percent vote share).

President René, citing the fact that he was "getting older," resigned the presidency on March 31, 2004, and Michel was inaugurated as his successor on April 14. Joseph BELMONT, a cabinet member since 1982, was confirmed as vice president by the assembly on April 16. An opposition (SNP) motion to dissolve the assembly to allow for parliamentary elections at the same time as presidential balloting in 2006—a year ahead of schedule—was rejected by the full body in May 2006. Presidential elections subsequently were held July 28–30, 2006, in which the incumbent Michel and running mate Vice President Belmont garnered 53.73 percent of the votes, defeating the SNP's Ramkalawan and running mate Annette GEORGES (45.71 percent of the vote), and independent Philippe BOULLÉ (0.56 percent). A reshuffled cabinet was sworn in on August 9, 2006.

President Michel dissolved the parliament on March 20, 2007, following a five-month boycott by opposition legislators, and called for early elections on May 10-12. The ruling SPPF retained its 23-seat majority with a 57 percent vote share; the coalition of the SNP and the DP won 11 seats on a vote share of 43 percent. The president reshuffled the cabinet on July 3.

Constitution and government. The 1993 constitution provides for a multiparty presidential system, under which the chief executive is elected for a thrice-renewable five-year term. Legislative authority is vested in a unicameral National Assembly. Constitutional amendments introduced in July 1996, following their adoption by an SPPF congress in late May, created the post of vice president and also increased the number of directly elective seats in the assembly from 22 to 25, while reducing the proportional seats to a maximum of 10 subject to a threshold of 10 percent of the vote.

The judiciary encompasses a Court of Appeal, a Supreme Court (part of which sits as a Constitutional Court), an Industrial Court, and magistrates' courts. Local government, seemingly necessary for geographic reasons, was abolished in 1971 following problems growing out of a district council system that had been introduced in 1948. However, the councils were revived in 1991.

Foreign relations. The main objectives of the Seychelles' foreign policy following independence were the "return" of a number of small islands and island groups administered since 1965 as part of the British Indian Ocean Territory and designation of the Indian Ocean as a "zone of peace." In March 1976, prior to debate on the Seychelles independence bill in the House of Commons, the British government indicated that arrangements had been made for the return to the Seychelles of the islands of Aldabra, Desroches, and Farquhar; however, the Chagos Archipelago would remain as the sole component of the British Indian Ocean Territory. Included in the archipelago was Diego Garcia, where the United States, under an agreement concluded with Britain in 1972, maintained military and communications facilities. There was also a U.S. space-tracking station on the island of Mahé, where, despite the Diego Garcia issue, relations between American personnel and the Seychellois were relatively cordial. In July 1989, while visiting Washington, President René agreed to a five-year extension of the station's lease, which in 1984 provided 5 percent of the state's revenue. In 1995 Washington announced it was closing the station in a cost-cutting move and transferring its activity to a new facility on Diego Garcia.

Relations between the Seychelles and South Africa were by no means enhanced as a result of the 1981 coup attempt on Mahé. The South African proceedings against Colonel Hoare and his associates were confined entirely to air piracy charges on the ground that judicial notice could not be taken of activities beyond Pretoria's jurisdiction. The defendants nonetheless argued that the coup had been undertaken with arms supplied by the South African Defence Force and with the full knowledge of the National Intelligence Service (NIS). The trial judge agreed that it would be "naive" to assume that the NIS was unaware of the plot, since one of the mercenaries was a former NIS agent. This finding was not disputed by Prime Minister P. W. Botha, who nevertheless argued that "neither the South African Government, the Cabinet nor the State Security Council" had been informed and that "no authorization was therefore given for any action." Significantly, 34 of the mercenaries convicted on the air piracy charges were given time off for good behavior and released on November 27, 1982, after spending only four months in prison. By early 1992 relations between the two countries had noticeably warmed, permitting the establishment of consular and trade (though not ambassadorial) relations.

In mid-1988 the Seychelles established formal diplomatic relations with the neighboring island states of Mauritius and the Comoros. The three, along with Madagascar and France (representing Réunion), are members of the Indian Ocean Commission (IOC) set up in 1982 to promote regional cooperation and economic development.

Relations with the United States cooled in 1996 following the closure of the U.S. embassy in Victoria (responsibility for the Seychelles transferring to the U.S. ambassador to Mauritius). In addition, a U.S. State Department report in March criticized the Seychelles' human rights record, referring to the ruling party's "pervasive system of political patronage and control over government jobs, contracts, and resources." (Similar criticisms were included also in the department's 2001 report.) In the wake of increasing global terrorist attacks, the United States in 2005 pledged continued support to the Seychelles military (see Current issues, below).

Although the Seychelles agreed to a regional free trade pact with the European Union (EU) in 2007, it was one of several African countries that in 2008 rejected participation in a free trade zone and a customs union as proposed by the Common Market for Eastern and Southern Africa (Comesa).

In 2009 China pledged to enhance its relationship with the Seychelles.

Current issues. President René's call for early presidential elections in 2001 was viewed by some observers as an attempt to show the world, particularly foreign investors, that his government had not lost popular support. It was also noted that a convincing victory might permit René to implement the austerity measures being demanded by the international financial community. However, the president's 54 percent vote share in the balloting was widely perceived as surprisingly narrow and unlikely to empower the government to launch any bold economic initiatives. In addition, runner-up Wavel Ramkalawan accused the government of voter intimidation and other electoral abuses, and he and his SNP boycotted René's inaugural. (International observers, though divided on whether the elections were free and fair, generally conceded that the alleged violations were not sufficient to alter the final outcome.)

René in March 2002 rejected the reforms outlined by the IMF on the grounds that they would "cripple the economy." However, following the SPPF's decline in the early assembly elections in December, dialogue was reopened with the IMF and several requested reforms were enacted. Subsequently, the European Parliament in 2003 questioned the status of human rights in the Seychelles following a crackdown on SNP supporters. In addition, in early 2004 opposition leaders argued that the René administration was attempting to limit their voice in the assembly and decrease the authority of the assembly overall. Consequently, René's decision to relinquish the rest of his presidential term to his longtime ally James Michel in April 2004 was not a complete surprise. René, 68, said he was retiring because he wanted to turn power over to a "younger person" who would nevertheless continue the policies pursued by René since the 1977 coup. (René's 27-year tenure was one of the longest ever for an African head of state.)

The Indian Ocean tsunami of December 2004 produced few casualties in the Seychelles but caused some $30 million in damage. Significantly, considering earlier tension (see Foreign relations, above) the United States promised reconstruction aid. Among other things, U.S. officials said that the United States and the Seychelles had developed a good "military-to-military relationship." Washington reportedly viewed the Seychelles as important geographically as a transit area for visiting U.S. ships. There were also concerns that the Seychelles could be used as a transfer point by terrorists seeking access to Africa.

The SNP initially demanded early presidential elections upon René's resignation, claiming the SPPF was simply attempting to provide Michel with a "training ground" for the 2006 election. (Michel's elevation to the presidency was constitutionally authorized.) However, SNP leader Ramkalawan subsequently accepted Michel's presidency, Michel reportedly having made reconciliation overtures to long-standing René opponents. For his part, Michel pledged to concentrate on improving the economy, with emphasis on dialogue with the private sector (a potentially significant policy shift). Meanwhile, René continued to serve as the leader of the SPPF and retained significant political influence in general. In mid-2006, Ramkalawan was unsuccessful in his bid to dissolve the assembly so that concurrent elections could be held with presidential balloting (see Political background, above). While all 11 legislators of the SNP voted in favor of the motion, all 23 members of the SPPF voted against, the majority party contending that the minority party lacked the authority to call for dissolution of the assembly.

Following a violent confrontation with police in October 2006 over a law banning political parties and religious groups from owning radio stations, the 11 opposition legislators began a boycott of parliament. Their five-month absence prompted President Michel to dissolve the National Assembly in March 2007, setting the stage for early legislative elections in May. The SNP initially called for a boycott of the balloting—regularly scheduled for October 2007—because of their concerns that three days of voting would allow too much time for fraud. However, the SNP soon decided to participate, and on March 27 it formed an electoral alliance with the DP. The latter's legal challenge to the early elections was struck down in April by an appeals court, which ruled that the president had the authority to dismiss parliament before the end of its full five-year term. Following the May assembly balloting, in which the SPPF and the SNP-DP alliance each fielded 25 candidates, the ruling party did not increase its representation, as Michel had hoped.

A review of the constitution was under way in 2008, and though officials sought public comments for the review, they indicated that any amendments would be approved by the National Assembly rather than made subject to a popular referendum. The review committee was chaired by Vice President Belmont. Another issue of concern—human rights—was addressed by the government's launching of a two-year program to improve awareness, based on a 2006 agreement with the EU and UN.

Attention turned in 2009 to the growing problem of piracy, the Seychelles having arrested more than a dozen suspected pirates early in the year. President Michel cut short a trip to Japan in April to deal with the problem, and Indian and European naval forces joined the Seychelles's coast guard in antipiracy efforts in the Indian Ocean. The Seychelles deployed troops to one area of the country where a boat carrying tourists was hijacked.

POLITICAL PARTIES

Prior to the 1977 coup, government was shared by the centrist Seychelles Democratic Party (SDP), led by President James R. Mancham, and the left-of-center Seychelles People's United Party (SPUP), headed by Prime Minister France René. Following the coup, René stated that the SDP "has not been banned, it has simply disappeared." The government-supportive Seychelles People's Progressive Front (SPPF) was the sole legal party from June 1978 until January 1991, following which other parties, including Mancham's Democratic Party, were recognized. Provision was also made for the financial support of parties from public funds.

Government Party:

Seychelles People's Progressive Front—SPPF (*Front Populaire Progressiste des Seychelles*—FPPS). The SPPF was organized in early 1978 as successor to the SPUP. Like its predecessor, it advocated a broad spectrum of "progressive" policies while attempting to cultivate relations with Catholic clergy sympathetic to its approach to social issues. Upon the retirement of Secretary General Guy SINON in May 1984, President René was named to succeed him as head of an expanded secretariat of 13 members, René's former position as party president being abolished.

Delegates to the party's congress in 1991 approved a Central Committee declaration that "the SPPF believes in the one-party system and in the socialist option" but left open the possibility of a future referendum on multipartyism. It also endorsed revival of an earlier system of party-controlled elective district councils, prior to approving a return to political pluralism at an extraordinary congress in December (see Political background, above). Most of the previous members were retained in the Central Committee elected at the May 1998 SPPF congress. René was reelected as party chair during the annual SPPF conference on April 3, 2005, even though many observers had expected him to vacate the post following his resignation as president of the republic in 2004.

Leaders: Joseph BELMONT (Vice President of the Republic), France Albert RENÉ (Former President of the Republic and Chair of the Party), Daniel FAURE, James Alix MICHEL (President of the Republic, 2006 presidential candidate, and Secretary General of the Party).

Opposition Parties:

Seychelles National Party (SNP). The SNP is the successor to the United Opposition (UO), which changed its name at a July 1998 congress. The UO had been formed by the three parties immediately below to oppose the 1993 constitution in both its original and final forms. Its candidate, Philippe BOULLÉ, ran a distant third in the presidential balloting of July 23, while its legislative success was limited to a single proportionally allocated seat. Boulle announced his retirement from politics in September 1995 (see National Alliance Party, below) during the party's first convention, at which its member of parliament, Rev. Wavel Ramkalawan, defeated Gabriel Hoareau of the MNS for the party presidency. Ramkalawan finished second in the 1998 presidential election with 20 percent of the vote. The UO won three seats in parliament to become the leading opposition group, and Ramkalawan (who was reelected as party leader during the July 1998 congress at which the SNP rubric was adopted) subsequently attracted substantial press coverage for his "fierce" criticism of the René administration. While relations between Ramkalawan and René appeared to improve during the 2002 elections, government forces launched a crackdown on an SNP demonstration in July 2003. The SNP subsequently won 11 seats in the December 2002 legislative elections.

In October 2006 Ramkalawan reportedly was among those arrested during a demonstration protesting a law banning political parties and religious groups from owning radio stations. In March 2007 the SNP and the DP formed an electoral alliance with the DP for the May legislative elections, the coalition retaining 11 opposition seats.

Following published attacks on SNP leaders, the party's secretary general Roger Mancienne, who owned a printing company, stopped printing the DP's newspaper, *Le Nouveau Seychelles Weekly*, which he said his company had agreed to publish "in support of freedom of expression and the work of the opposition." The newspaper's editor responded that those involved in politics should be ready to accept criticism.

Leaders: Rev. Wavel RAMKALAWAN (President of the Party and 1998, 2001, and 2006 presidential candidate), Annette GEORGES (Treasurer and Ramkalawan's 2006 running mate), Roger MANCIENNE (Secretary General).

Seychelles Party (*Parti Seselwa*—PS). Led by Jean-François Ferrari, son of Maxime FERRARI (former foreign minister and leader of the RPSD, see below), and formerly referenced most frequently by its French rubric, *Parti Seychellois,* the free enterprise-oriented PS was, prior to its legalization, the domestic clandestine affiliate of the RPSD/UDF (see below). The younger Ferrari remained party leader upon the return of his father, who occupied himself primarily with the launching of a new *Institut Seychellois pour la Démocratie.* Jean-François Ferrari, publisher of the opposition weekly *Regar,* was among those arrested in the July 2003 crackdown.

Leaders: Rev. Wavel RAMKALAWAN, Jean-François FERRARI (Secretary).

Seychelles National Movement (*Mouvement National Seychellois*—MNS). The MNS was originally formed in Brussels in 1984 as an affiliate of the MPR (below).

Leaders: Gabriel (Gaby) HOAREAU (President), Robert FRICHOT (Vice President), Terry SANDAPIN (Secretary).

National Alliance Party (NAP). The NAP was organized in early 1992 by Philippe Boullé and Kathleen Pillay, a former UDF (see below) leader. (Boulle later ran as the UO's presidential candidate in balloting in 1993 and announced his retirement in 1995 from active politics. However, he ran as an independent candidate in presidential balloting in 2001, securing only 0.86 percent of the vote, and again in 2006, winning a mere 0.56 percent.)

Leader: Kathleen PILLAY (Secretary).

Democratic Party (DP). The DP was legalized in March 1992 as a revival of the former SDP. Its leader, Sir James Mancham, returned from exile on April 12, 1992. Subsequently, the DP and the SPPF were viewed as the country's two principal political "currents."

Mancham was reelected party leader at an extraordinary party congress on March 18, 1995, from which his intraparty opponents were excluded. (DP dissident Christopher GILL, one of those expelled from the congress for complaining about Mancham's "tightfisted" control, subsequently announced the formation of a New Democratic Party. Gill, the only DP member to gain a directly elected legislative seat in 1993, was reported in late 1997 to have crossed over to the SPPF, despite his previous extremely negative analysis of the René government.) The DP was beaten badly in the 1998 elections, securing only one parliamentary seat, while Mancham won only 14 percent of the vote in the presidential balloting. Mancham declined to run in the 2001 presidential election. The DP polled only 3.1 percent in the 2002 elections, thereby losing its seat in the assembly. Mancham retired as party leader in January 2005, although he subsequently was reportedly involved in planning a conference of opposition leaders designed to promote "reconciliation."

In 2006 the DP supported the SNP's Ramkalawan in the presidential election (DP members being assured of several ministerial posts if Ramkalawan were elected). In a related move in March 2006, the DP replaced interim leader Nichol Gabriel—who observers said was reluctant to consider the alliance—with Paul Chow, reportedly of the party's "old guard" who gave his full backing to the SNP alliance. Gabriel assumed the post of party secretary. In 2007 the DP contested the National Assembly elections in a coalition with the SNP, winning 11 seats.

In March 2009 it was reported that Ralph Voicere was elected party president following the resignation of Paul CHOW.

Leaders: Ralph VOICERE (President), Bernard ELIZABETH, Sir James R. MANCHAM (Former President of the Republic), Nichol GABRIEL (Secretary).

Other Parties and Groups:

The only other party to present candidates in the 2002 assembly balloting was the **Social Democratic Alliance**, which fielded one candidate. However, several independent candidates contested the elections.

A British-based organization known simply as the **Resistance Movement** (*Mouvement pour la Résistance*—MPR) appeared to have been implicated in the November 1981 coup attempt, while a South African-based **Seychelles Popular Anti-Marxist Front** (SPAMF) announced late in the year that it had known of the mercenary effort but had declined to participate on the ground that it was unworkable. A third group, the **Seychelles Liberation Committee** (*Comité de la Libération Seychelles*—CLS) was launched in Paris in 1979. In November 1985 MPR leader Gérard HOAREAU was assassinated outside his London residence by an unknown assailant. Former president Mancham charged the René government with the killing, which was vehemently denied by a spokesman for the Seychelles embassy. A month earlier David JOUBERT, a former Mancham cabinet official, had announced the revival of the SDP as a London-based exile formation, although Mancham, who had become a British citizen, dissociated himself from the action.

During a speech before a House of Commons committee in February 1990 Mancham invited all of the exile groups to join him in a **Crusade for Democracy in Seychelles** (CDS) and subsequently called for the formation of an opposition **United Democratic Front** (UDF). A less conservative London exile, former foreign minister Maxime Ferrari, displayed ambivalence toward the Mancham overture and in December 1990 launched a **Rally of the Seychelles People for Democracy** (*Rassemblement du Peuple Seychellois pour la Démocratie*—RPSD) that, somewhat unrealistically, appeared to seek common ground between Mancham and René. Ferrari returned to the Seychelles in 1991.

LEGISLATURE

The unicameral **National Assembly** (*Assemblée Nationale*) has 25 directly contested seats from 25 single-member constituencies, plus up to 10 seats allocated on a proportional basis to parties winning at least 10 percent of the vote. (A party gets one proportional seat for each 10 percent of the vote it receives in the balloting for the directly contested seats.) The term of office is five years. The results of the most recent elections on May 10–12, 2007, were as follows: Seychelles People's Progressive Front, 23 (18 directly contested, 5 proportional); and the coalition of the Seychelles National Party and the Democratic Party, 11 (7 directly contested, 4 proportional).

Speaker: Patrick HERMINIE.

CABINET

[as of December 1, 2009]

President	James Alix Michel
Vice President	Joseph Belmont
Ministers	
Community Development, Youth, Sports, and Culture	Vincent Meriton
Defense	James Alix Michel
Education	Bernard Shamlaye
Employment and Human Resources Development	MacSuzy Mondon [f]
Environment, Natural Resources, and Transport	Joel Morgan
Finance	Daniel Faure
Foreign Affairs	Patrick Pillay
Information and Public Relations	James Alix Michel
Internal Affairs	Joseph Belmont
Legal Affairs	James Alix Michel
National Development	Jacquelin Dugasse
Police	James Alix Michel
Public Administration	Joseph Belmont
Risk and Disaster Management	James Alix Michel
Social Development and Health	Marie-Pierre Lloyd [f]
Tourism	Joseph Belmont

[f] = female

COMMUNICATIONS

The U.S. State Department's 2001 report on human rights in Seychelles expressed concern over the potential effects on press freedom of a new broadcasting and telecommunications bill, which had been approved in early 2000. In 2002 the watchdog group Reporters Without Borders protested what it described as the government's "harassment" of the weekly newsletter *Regar* through heavy financial penalties resulting from libel lawsuits filed by some top government officials.

(*Regar* ceased publishing in 2007 following a costly libel suit.) Government opponents also criticized the high registration fees required to launch private radio and television stations. Reporters Without Borders stated in its 2006 annual report that in the Seychelles, "defamation or publishing false news are considered to be crimes." According to the BBC, expensive licensing fees have discouraged the start-up of privately owned media.

Press. The following are published in Victoria in Creole, English, and French: *The Seychelles Nation* (3,500), daily government organ; *Seychelles Today,* monthly published by the Ministry of Finance; *L'Echo des Îles* (2,900), pro-SPPF Catholic weekly; *The People* (1,000), SPPF weekly; *Seychelles Review,* DP monthly; *Le Nouveau Seychelles Weekly*, the newspaper of the Democratic Party, published online; and *Vizyon,* the SNP's English-language biweekly newsletter. Another nongovernmental organ, the *Independent,* was advised by the state-owned printing facility in mid-1995 that its stories would thenceforth be vetted before publication because of complaints by opposition leader Mancham of "irresponsible and provocative" reporting of the DP's internal problems.

News agency. The official facility is the *Seychelles Agence Presse* (SAP).

Broadcasting and computing. In early 1992 President René announced that the government-controlled Radio-Television Seychelles (RTS) would be granted autonomous status equivalent to that of the British Broadcasting Corporation (BBC), and in early May its name was changed to the Seychelles Broadcasting Corporation (SBC). The system broadcasts locally from Victoria in English, French, and Creole. A missionary facility, the Far East Broadcasting Association (FEBA), services several domestic radio stations and transmits in a wide variety of languages to other Indian Ocean islands, South Asia, the Middle East, and Eastern and Southern Africa; in September 1995, however, FEBA announced that it was cutting back some of its operations because of "high operating costs." As of 2008 there were 404.4 Internet users per 1,000 inhabitants.

INTERGOVERNMENTAL REPRESENTATION

Ambassador to the U.S. and Permanent Representative to the UN: Ronald Jean JUMEAU.

U.S. Ambassador to the Seychelles: (Vacant).

IGO Memberships (Non-UN): AfDB, AU, BADEA, Comesa, CWTH, Interpol, IOC, NAM, OIF, WCO, WTO.

SIERRA LEONE

Republic of Sierra Leone

Political Status: Independent member of the Commonwealth since April 27, 1961; republic proclaimed April 19, 1971; one-party constitution adopted June 1978; multiparty constitution approved by popular referendum on August 23–30, 1991, with effect from September 24; government overthrown in military coup of April 29, 1992; ruling military council overthrown and replaced by "reconstituted" military council on January 16, 1996; democratically elected president inaugurated on March 29, 1996; government overthrown in military coup of May 25, 1997; ruling military council forcibly removed by regional forces on February 13, 1998; previously elected government reinstalled on March 10, 1998; July 1999 Lomé peace accord and UN peacekeepers unable to halt ongoing violence; cease-fire agreed between government and insurgents on May 16, 2001; previously elected president and majority party won elections of May 14, 2002.

Area: 27,699 sq. mi. (71,740 sq. km.).

Population: 4,963,000 (2004C), the 2004 figure is provisional and assumed to reflect substantial underenumerating; 5,992,000 (2008E).

Major Urban Center (2005E): FREETOWN (824,000, including suburbs).

Official Language: English.

Monetary Unit: Leone (market rate December 1, 2009: 3,908.27 leones = $1US).

President: Ernest Bai KOROMA (All People's Congress), elected in second-round balloting on September 8, 2007, and sworn in for a five-year term on September 17 to succeed Ahmad Tejan KABBAH (Sierra Leone People's Party).

Vice President: Sahr SAM-SUMANA (All People's Congress), elected on September 8, 2007, and sworn in on September 17 for a term concurrent with the president's in succession to Solomon BEREWA (Sierra Leone People's Party).

THE COUNTRY

Facing the South Atlantic and nearly surrounded by the Republic of Guinea on the northwest, north, and east, Sierra Leone ("lion mountain") encompasses three geographic regions: a peninsula in the west; a western coastal region, which consists of mangrove swamps and a coastal plain; and a plateau in the east and northeast. The indigenous inhabitants range over 12 principal tribal groups, the most important being the Mende in the south and the Temne in the north. There are also numerous Creole descendants of freed slaves. A variety of tribal languages are spoken, with Krio, a form of pidgin English, serving as a lingua franca. Traditional religions predominate, but there are many Muslims in the north and Christians in the west.

The agricultural sector of the economy employs about two-thirds of the work force. Rice is the main subsistence crop, while cocoa, coffee, and palm kernels are the leading agricultural exports. Gold, bauxite, and rutile are among the minerals extracted, with a rapidly dwindling diamond reserve providing approximately 20 percent of export earnings in 1992 (down from 60 percent in 1980). The International Monetary Fund (IMF), the World Bank group, and the European Community/Union (EC/EU) have been among the international agencies extending recent aid in support of efforts to revive an economy that has deteriorated markedly since the mid-1970s. Until quite recently, the assistance proved largely ineffectual, inflation rising to nearly 110 percent in 1990, with the balance of payments severely weakened by declining rice production and commodity smuggling. Upon assuming power in April 1992 the STRASSER regime stressed its intent to honor Sierra Leone's international obligations. Subsequently, the regime's first budget was highlighted by a three-year public investment plan formulated with World Bank assistance, and inflation for the year declined sharply to 36 percent. In March 1994 the IMF rewarded Freetown's restructuring efforts by reopening credit lines that had been frozen since 1988. Economic activity reportedly ground to a virtual standstill during the military's control of power from May 1997 to February 1998. A blockade of the Freetown harbor was lifted in late February 1998, thus allowing commercial activity to resume.

In late 1998 observers reported that mining and agriculture sectors in the north and east had been decimated by fighting. Furthermore, the subsequent return to full-scale civil war effectively dashed hopes for economic growth in 1998 and 1999. In December 1999 the IMF approved emergency assistance for the country, and a cease-fire in 2001 fostered the resumption of normal activity.

Diamond mining, the country's third largest employer, has been a prime beneficiary of the cessation of hostilities. The smuggling of "blood diamonds," a key feature of the civil war, was curbed somewhat by a United Nations diamond embargo on Sierra Leone in 2000 and a subsequent diamond-certification scheme known as the Kimberley process. Since then, the government has regained partial control over the diamond trade, enabling it to raise $126 million in tax revenues on the industry in 2004 alone. However, smuggling continued to be a problem.

Economic growth improved in 2005–2006, with a decline in inflation (to 9.5 percent) and increased foreign investment in oil and mining. The IMF approved a new three-year poverty reduction program for Sierra Leone, citing the government's "considerable progress" toward economic stability and addressing widespread poverty. (The IMF noted that 80 percent of the population lives on less than $1US per day.) The

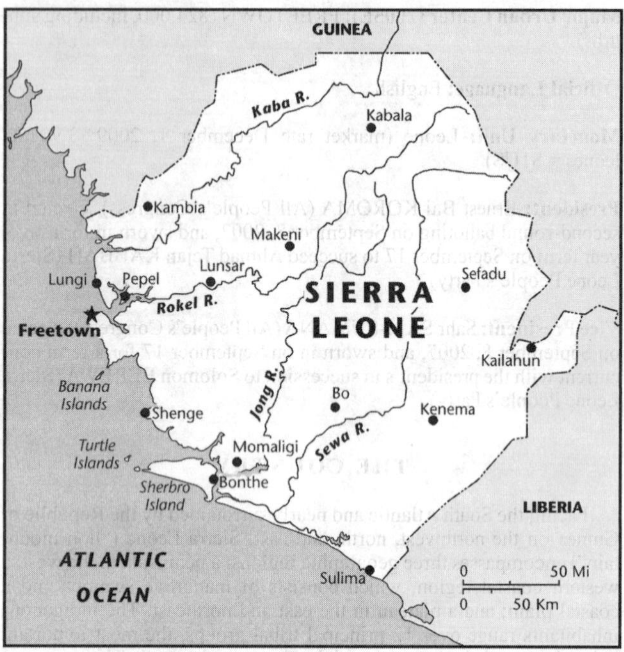

fund urged the government to enforce tax regulations, accelerate privatization efforts, and diversify and expand exports to bolster revenue. Real GDP growth in 2006 was 7.4 percent, and Sierra Leone qualified for $994 million in debt relief under the Heavily Indebted Poor Countries (HIPC) initiative.

In 2007 the IMF commended the government's commitment to structural reforms "in light of the public perception of widespread corruption," while at the same time encouraging authorities to accelerate efforts to enhance transparency and accountability. The return of "peace and stability" to Sierra Leone contributed to robust economic growth of about 6.5 annually in 2007–2008, according to the IMF, which continued to press for increased spending to help relieve pervasive poverty and for the acceleration of structural reforms. Annual growth was forecast to contract to about 2 percent in 2009, owing in large part to the global economic recession's effects on the customs and mining sectors. Also, unemployment and inflation rates remained high. On a positive note, Sierra Leone qualified in June for an additional $16.8 million in poverty-reduction assistance from the IMF, bringing the three-year total to $50.3 million. Fund managers commended the government for its efforts to broaden the tax base to generate more money for poverty relief.

GOVERNMENT AND POLITICS

Political background. Growing out of a coastal settlement established by English interests in the 18th century as a haven for freed slaves, Sierra Leone became independent within the Commonwealth in 1961. Political leadership from 1961 to 1967 was exercised exclusively through the Sierra Leone People's Party (SLPP), a predominantly Mende grouping led successively by Sir Milton MARGAI and his half-brother, Sir Albert M. MARGAI. Attempts to establish a one-party system under the SLPP were successfully resisted by the opposition All People's Congress (APC), a predominantly Temne formation headed by Dr. Siaka P. STEVENS, a militant trade-union leader belonging to the smaller Limba tribe.

Following an unexpectedly strong showing by the APC in the election of 1967, Stevens was appointed prime minister, but he was prevented from taking office by Brig. David LANSANA's declaration of martial law on March 21. Two days later, Lt. Col. Andrew JUXON-SMITH assumed the leadership of a National Reformation Council (NRC) that suspended the constitution, dissolved the parties, and ruled for the ensuing 13 months. The NRC was itself overthrown in April 1968 by a group of noncommissioned officers, the Anti-Corruption Revolutionary Movement, which restored civilian government with Stevens as prime minister.

The ensuing decade was marked by a series of coup attempts and government harassment of political opponents. In 1973 official intimidation contributed to an SLPP boycott of the general election, with the APC winning all but one of the seats in the House of Representatives. In 1975 six civilians and two soldiers were executed in Freetown after being convicted of an attempt to assassinate (then) Finance Minister Christian KAMARA-TAYLOR and take over the government. Under a new constitution adopted by referendum in June 1978, Sierra Leone became a one-party state; President Stevens was reinvested for a seven-year term on June 14.

In early 1985 the president announced his intention to retire, naming army commander Maj. Gen. Joseph Saidu MOMOH as his successor. The new president was confirmed in single-party balloting on October 1; Stevens transferred power to him on November 28, although formal swearing-in ceremonies were not held until January 26, 1986. The House of Representatives was renewed in a multicandidate, one-party poll held on May 29–30, a year prior to expiry of its normal term.

Momoh's accession was greeted with enthusiasm that subsided when a campaign to "instill military discipline" in fighting corruption and managing the economy failed to yield tangible results. By mid-1990 the Momoh regime's inability to check inflation, generate the funds for civil service salary payments, or maintain basic services had provoked widespread civil unrest and calls for the adoption of a new, multiparty constitution. Consequently, at an extraordinary APC meeting in August, President Momoh named economist Peter TUCKER to head a National Constitution Review Commission to explore government reorganization along "democratic lines." (At the same time, Momoh described multiparty activity as incompatible with Sierra Leone's tribal structures and widespread illiteracy.)

In late March 1991, less than a week after having reiterated his opposition to the idea, Momoh announced that he welcomed the introduction of a multiparty system. Two months later, the Tucker Commission submitted its report, and in early June the life of the existing House of Representatives was extended to enable it to approve a pluralistic basic law. On July 2, following intense debate both within and outside the government, the House of Representatives ratified the new constitution, and on August 23–30 the document was approved by popular referendum; over 60 percent of the 2.5 million participants reportedly favored its enactment. On September 23 President Momoh named a transitional government to rule until multiparty elections, tentatively scheduled for late 1992. One day later the constitution was promulgated, and on September 30 the ban on political parties was officially lifted.

On April 29, 1992, army units, angered at a lack of pay and the failure of the government to provide them equipment to end a 13-week rebellion in eastern Sierra Leone, ousted President Momoh, who flew to exile in Guinea. On May 1 Capt. Valentine Strasser and (then) Lt. Solomon Anthony James MUSA were named chair and vice chair, respectively, of a National Provisional Ruling Council (NPRC), which suspended the constitution and ruled by decree. On May 2 the NPRC appointed a 19-member government, which included several members of the NPRC and six civilians. Two days later the NPRC dissolved the legislature and suspended political activity. On July 14 Captain Strasser announced that the NPRC would thenceforth be known as the Supreme Council of State (SCS) and would no longer be involved in day-to-day administration. Concurrently, ministers were redesignated as secretaries of state, with Musa serving in the quasi-prime ministerial post of chief secretary. In October a 15-member advisory council was established with a mandate to work out a return to multipartyism, with an emphasis on involving citizens in the democratization process.

In mid-December 1992 the regime established a special military tribunal "in the interest of maintaining peace, security, and public order" and to assure that criminals were "rapidly punished." On December 28 government troops violently repulsed an alleged coup attempt by the so-called Anti-Corruption Revolutionary Movement (ACRM), a grouping of pro-Momoh civilians and military personnel (some of whom were already incarcerated). On December 30, following a summary military trial, 26 people (9 ACRM members and 17 others who had been convicted of high treason for their involvement in an earlier incident) were executed. The executions drew international condemnation; several Western donors announced suspension of aid payments.

On April 29, 1993, amid reports of widespread disillusionment with the one-year-old "revolution," Strasser announced the commencement of a three-year transition period to culminate in multiparty elections. In addition, the chair promised to launch an inquiry into the special military tribunal's activities and to ease some security measures.

In a government reshuffle on July 5, 1993, Capt. Julius Maada BIO replaced Musa as SCS vice chair and chief secretary. Musa's dismissal came amid reports that he had clashed with Strasser about the return to multipartyism and that he harbored his own presidential ambitions. In December Dr. James JONAH was appointed chair of the newly established Interim National Electoral Commission (INEC), which had been charged with preparing for presidential and legislative elections tentatively scheduled for 1995.

In 1994 the Strasser regime's credibility was impaired by the alleged complicity of government troops in widespread banditry and its inability to suppress the military activities of the Revolutionary United Front (RUF, below), a Sierra Leonean offshoot of Charles Taylor's National Patriotic Front of Liberia (NPFL, see Liberia article) led by Foday Savannah SANKOH; the Strasser regime claimed the RUF had been organized to punish Sierra Leone for its peacekeeping role in Liberia. By midyear RUF-related violence was reportedly responsible for the deaths of hundreds of individuals and the dislocation of thousands. Consequently, in July the State Advisory Council, noting that "local people must be collaborating" with the insurgents, announced the creation of a National Security Council charged with ending the hostilities. Thereafter, despite reports that most of the country was "lawless," the government released a draft constitution in October, which included provisions for a return to civilian rule by 1996.

On November 12, 1994, the junta executed 12 soldiers in an apparent attempt to intimidate the so-called "sobels" (soldiers during the day, rebels at night) whom observers described as increasingly beyond Freetown's control. On November 25, bolstered by reports that an offensive had severely weakened the rebels, the Strasser government called on the RUF to begin negotiations on a peace accord and cease-fire, pledging that they would be allowed to form a political party in preparation for multiparty elections. The RUF, which had gained international attention two weeks earlier when it kidnapped two British citizens, initially rejected the offer but on December 4 met with government negotiators for discussions, which were described as "frank." However, the rebels' kidnapping campaign continued into 1995; they reportedly seized an additional 15 foreigners by February. (All of the hostages were eventually handed over to International Red Cross representatives on April 20.)

On March 31, 1995, Captain Strasser announced a major government restructuring, under which Health and Social Services Secretary Lt. Col. Akim GIBRIL would become chief secretary in place of Bio, who remained SCS vice chair while assuming the position of chief of the defense staff "to provide additional mettle" to the armed forces in their campaign against the RUF. On April 27 Strasser promised to lift the ban on political parties and relinquish power to a democratically elected president in January 1996. He also offered the RUF a truce to negotiate an end to the conflict that had claimed some 5,000 lives since 1991. On May 18 he asked the Economic Community of West African States (ECOWAS) to broker negotiations with the rebels; however, the RUF rejected the initiative, calling instead for Strasser to convene a sovereign national conference to decide the future of the country.

On June 21, 1995, the regime lifted the ban on political parties, but two days later it issued a list of 57 people, headed by former president Momoh, who were ineligible to compete in the upcoming balloting. On August 18 the government convened a National Consultative Conference; however, despite its earlier entreaties, the RUF refused to attend. Among the rulings adopted by the conference were the postponement of balloting until February 1996 and the organization of simultaneous presidential and legislative polling.

On October 3, 1995, a coup attempt led by at least eight senior military officers was quashed by troops loyal to Strasser, who was out of the country. The failed uprising highlighted the growing chasm in the SCS between those who opposed the return to a civilian government and its advocates, purportedly led by Strasser.

On January 16, 1996, Strasser was overthrown by his second-in-command, Brigadier General Bio, who claimed that Strasser had been scheming to retain the presidency; Bio announced that he would lead a "Reconstituted" Supreme Council of the State (RSCS). At his inauguration the following day, Bio promised to continue preparations for "transparent, free, and fair" elections and urged the RUF to begin peace talks. In response, the RUF announced a one-week, unconditional cease-fire and called for postponement of the elections, saying it would not negotiate with a civilian government. Subsequently, Bio expressed interest in rescheduling the balloting; however, following a meeting with the leaders from a number of the newly recognized political groups on January 24, he reiterated his intent to adhere to the pre-coup electoral schedule.

In the first round of legislative and presidential balloting on February 26–27, 1996, held under provisions of the 1991 constitution, the SLPP captured 36.1 percent of the vote, easily outpacing the United People's Party (UNPP, below), which finished second with 21.6 percent, and 11 other parties. Meanwhile, SLPP presidential candidate Ahmad Tejan KABBAH and UNPP leader John KARIFA-SMART finished first and second, respectively, in their 12-candidate race. However, because neither captured a majority, a second round of balloting was held on March 15, with Kabbah winning with 59.49 percent of the vote.

The Kabbah administration moved quickly to build on the peace initiative its predecessor had begun with the RUF, and on April 23, 1996, agreement was reached between Kabbah and Sankoh on a "definitive" cease-fire and the establishment of committees to draft disarmament and peace accords. On May 30 Freetown announced that it had reached agreement with the RUF on 26 of 28 articles in a proposed peace plan, leaving unresolved only the timetable for the withdrawal of foreign troops and the establishment of a national debt commission. However, the rebels continued to refuse to recognize the Kabbah government publicly and insisted that the cease-fire was only provisional. At the same time, the administration's announced intention to reduce the military ranks from 18,000 to approximately 4,000 added the threat of yet another military coup to a domestic security landscape already populated by RUF dissidents, "sobels," and escaped prisoners.

On September 8, 1996, at least six soldiers were arrested after senior military officials were alerted to their alleged plans to overthrow the government, and within a week 150 more soldiers were purged in response to an executive order demanding the dismissal of suspected dissidents. Meanwhile, a series of clashes between government forces and rebels in the east threatened the six-month-old cease-fire. However, when government troops reportedly gained the upper hand on the battlefield, President Kabbah and RUF leader Sankoh signed a peace treaty in Abidjan, Côte d'Ivoire, on November 30. Highlighting the accord were provisions for the immediate end to hostilities, the demobilization and disarmament of the RUF, and the integration of rebel soldiers into the national army. Furthermore, the agreement entitled the RUF to transform itself into a legal political party.

Sporadic fighting was reported throughout late 1996 and early 1997; the RUF and government accused each other of violating the peace accord. In addition, clashes were reported between alleged "sobels" and ethnic Kamajor militiamen allied with the president. On March 12 the RUF's Sankoh was detained in Nigeria, and on March 15 he was dismissed from the RUF by senior party officials who accused him of blocking implementation of the peace accord. Subsequently, Sankoh's supporters threatened to attack Freetown unless he was returned from Lagos.

On May 25, 1997, junior army officers fighting alongside RUF militants overran the prison where the defendants in the September 1996 coup plot were being held. Subsequently, under the leadership of one of the freed prisoners, Maj. Johnny Paul KOROMA, the combined forces took control of Freetown and overthrew the government (with Kabbah fleeing to Guinea). On May 28 the military junta abolished the constitution and banned political parties. Meanwhile, 300,000 people reportedly fled the country amid heavy fighting between the junta's forces and Nigerian-led ECOWAS troops, who had launched a countercoup offensive. On June 1 the junta established a 20-member Armed Forces Revolutionary Council (AFRC) and named Koroma its chair. Unable to dislodge the rebel soldiers, the Economic Community of West African States Monitoring Group (Ecomog) announced a cease-fire on June 2. Nevertheless, regional and international observers vowed not to let the coup stand and refused to recognize the Koroma regime.

On June 17, 1997, Major Koroma was sworn in as the leader of the AFRC, and he subsequently agreed to participate in internationally mediated negotiations. However, the talks were promptly abandoned after the junta leader demanded a four-year term. Frustrated with Koroma's intransigence, ECOWAS officials tightened sanctions against the AFRC in late August, and on September 2 Ecomog forces bombed Freetown in an effort to enforce an embargo on imported goods. Furthermore, on October 8 the UN Security Council adopted a resolution empowering Ecomog forces to enforce oil and arms sanctions against the regime. On October 24, under pressure of heavy shelling, AFRC negotiators agreed to a peace plan that included provisions for a disarmament process (beginning December 1), Kabbah's reinstallment on

April 22, 1998, immunity for the junta's forces, and a future government role for RUF leader Sankoh. Despite the accord, clashes continued between the AFRC and Ecomog forces, and in mid-December 1997 Koroma asserted that the timetable for implementing the pact would be delayed.

Following a week of particularly intense fighting, Ecomog forces captured Freetown on February 13, 1998. On February 17 ECOWAS announced the formation of an interim "special supervision committee," headed by Vice President Albert DEMBY and the Nigerian leader of the Ecomog forces, Col. Maxwell Khobe. On February 20, 25 of the AFRC leaders were captured as they attempted to escape into Liberia (Johnny Paul Koroma is widely believed to be dead) President Kabbah was officially reinstated on March 10 and promptly named a 15-member cabinet.

As of March 1998 Ecomog-directed, pro-presidential forces reportedly controlled 90 percent of Sierra Leone. In addition to attempting to wrest control of the remainder of the country from the remnants of the combined AFRC-RUF forces, the reinstalled Kabbah government faced a myriad of other challenges, including resurrecting a devastated economy; reintegrating tens of thousands of dislocated and homeless citizens; and reestablishing relations with Sankoh and the RUF, many of whose fighters reportedly had hidden their weapons when confronted by the Ecomog offensive. Meanwhile, the Kabbah administration pressed ahead with legal actions against former Koroma coup members and their alleged collaborators. In October Freetown ignored observers' calls for leniency and executed 24 people for treasonous acts, including Koroma's brother, Brig. Gen. Samuel KOROMA. On October 23 Sankoh, who had been returned for trial from Nigeria in July, was sentenced to death for similar offenses. (Collaterally, on November 5 former president Momoh received a ten-year jail term for his ties to Koroma, who remained a fugitive.) Following Sankoh's sentencing, a dramatic upsurge in rebel attacks against civilians was reported; thousands subsequently fled to the capital to escape a campaign marked by atrocities. Despite initial depictions of the violence as being the rebels' last gasp, the RUF and its AFRC military allies advanced to within striking distance of Freetown by December.

In late December 1998 RUF commander Sam BOCKARIE rejected calls for a cease-fire, and on January 6, 1999, the rebels invaded the capital. Approximately 5,000 people were killed before Ecomog troops regained control of the city in mid-month. Thereafter, President Kabbah agreed to let Sankoh participate in cease-fire negotiations; however, apparently emboldened by reports of Ecomog gains elsewhere in the country, Kabbah insisted that the rebels respect the dictates of the 1996 peace accord. Consequently, negotiations proceeded fitfully through February and early March. On March 16 Bockarie broke off talks, reportedly suspecting the government of employing delaying tactics while it won back territory. Subsequently, the Kabbah administration came under pressure from its two largest military backers, the United Kingdom and Nigeria, to seek a negotiated end to its "unwinnable" war.

On May 18, 1999, President Kabbah and rebel leader Sankoh signed an agreement in Togo calling for a cease-fire effective May 25, and a formal peace accord was signed in July. The agreement promised to give the RUF and the AFRC four key government posts and extended total amnesty to RUF and AFRC leaders, including Sankoh, as well as former head of state Momoh, who had been charged with collaborating with the AFRC junta. Amid reports of internal divisions, the RUF and the AFRC agreed to demobilize and disarm and also dropped their demands for an immediate withdrawal of Ecomog troops. The AFRC wing that accepted Koroma's call to stop violence immediately was then reincorporated into the political arena. In October the UN Security Council authorized the United Nations Mission in Sierra Leone (UNAMSIL) to replace the Ecomog troops gradually. In November Sankoh was given powers equivalent to those of vice president, and the RUF and the AFRC were allocated non-senior cabinet posts. Concurrently, the RUF decided to transform itself into a registered political party, adopting the rubric Revolutionary United Front Party (RUFP). However, the issues of demobilization and disarmament created problems during much of early 2000, and in May the peace agreement broke down as UNAMSIL was moving to replace the Ecomog troops. RUF fighters and some renegade AFRC militia (linked with Eddie KANNEH's wing, which was uneasy with Koroma's call to stop the violence) attacked UNAMSIL detachments, and 19 civilians were killed by Sankoh's bodyguards during a demonstration in front of his residence. Although Sankoh fled the country following the incident, he was apprehended in Nigeria on May 17. Due to advances by UNAMSIL, the pro-government Kamajor militia (styled as the Civil Defense Force [CDF]), Guinean forces opposed to the RUF, and renegade AFRC forces, the rebels were on the defensive for much of the year. In November the RUF agreed once again to commit itself to the peace process and to disarm its troops and relinquish most of its territory to government and UNAMSIL control. In February 2001 Kabbah asked the National Assembly to postpone the presidential and legislative elections due to be held in February and March because of the "uncertain security situation." He also reshuffled his cabinet to include some opposition figures.

As Liberian President Charles Taylor tried to distance himself from the RUF in an effort to clean up his country's image as a protector of the rebels, the RUF signed a peace agreement in May 2001 and another cease-fire was implemented. In August it was announced that elections were expected to be held in June 2002 under a "constituency electoral system," although in September the National Electoral Commission advised the assembly to adopt a proportional representation system instead. Despite criticism from the opposition that Kabbah was trying to eliminate his potential rivals in the coming elections, as well as fears that some RUF forces might resume fighting, the country appeared to be moving toward some form of normalization.

At a dramatic weapons-burning ceremony on January 18, 2002, which marked the completion of the disarmament process, President Kabbah declared the "war is over," and the four-year state of emergency was formally lifted on March 1. (An estimated 50,000 people died as a result of the conflict.) In presidential balloting on May 14, President Kabbah was elected to another four-year term by securing more than 70 percent of the vote against eight opponents. (Kabbah's running-mate, Solomon BEREWA, the sitting minister of justice and attorney general and also from the SLPP, was elected to the vice presidency in succession to Albert Joe Demby, who had been dropped from the ticket at the SLPP congress in March.) In concurrent voting for the National Assembly, which had been expanded to 112 members elected on a proportional basis, the SLPP secured the majority of seats, followed by the All People's Congress (APC). A small number of seats were won by the Peace and Liberation Party (PLP); the RUF failed to win any seats. A new cabinet of the SLPP and two independents was sworn in on July 9, the independents subsequently joining the SLPP.

After the elections, international troops who had overseen the cease-fire ending Sierra Leone's civil war began to withdraw. In 2005 UNAMSIL forces were replaced by a small contingent of military advisers—the United Nations Integrated Office in Sierra Leone (UNIOSL)—charged with monitoring the security situation and guarding the war crimes tribunal (see Current issues, below).

The cabinet was reshuffled on September 6, 2005, all ministers representing the SLPP.

The APC was victorious in the parliamentary and presidential elections of 2007, unseating the governing SLPP, as the APC secured 40.73 percent of the seats in first-past-the-post legislative elections on August 11, followed by the SLPP with 39.54 percent and the newly formed People's Movement for Democratic Change (PMDC), an SLPP breakaway party, with 15.39 percent. Among the 572 candidates vying for 112 parliamentary seats, none was chosen from four other parties contesting the elections, nor were any independent candidates successful. In the first round of presidential balloting on August 11, APC chair Ernest Bai Koroma's vote share of 44.34 percent and Solomon Berewa's 38.28 percent as the SLPP candidate led five other contenders (from the PMDC, the Convention People's Party—CPP, the NDA, PLP, and UNPP). Since neither Koroma nor Berewa secured the 55 percent required for election, a runoff was held on September 8, in which Koroma won 54.62 percent to Berewa's 45.38 percent. President Koroma and his running mate, Sahr SAM-SUMANA, were sworn in on September 17. The president named a new APC-dominated cabinet, which included four members of the PMDC but none from the SLPP, on October 8 and October 16.

The cabinet was reshuffled on February 27, 2009, including, most notably, the appointment of the former central bank governor as finance minister. Observers said the appointment was significant as the government struggled to deal with the slumping economy. Further, analysts said, the reshuffle was necessary in the wake of corruption scandals in the ministries of mines, energy, and transport.

Constitution and government. The 1991 constitution provided for a popularly elected executive president who could serve for no more than two five-year terms; a parliament whose members could not serve simultaneously as ministers; and a State Advisory Council composed of 12 paramount chiefs (one from each local district) and ten "emergent citizens" nominated by the president. There was no limit on the number of political parties, provided they met basic requirements. The judicial system included a Supreme Court and a Court of Appeal, as well as a lower tier of high, magistrates', and native courts.

Following the establishment of the NPRC in 1992, the constitution was suspended, and on July 14 the Supreme Council of State (as the NPRC was subsequently named) called for the designation of three SCS members as "principal liaison officers," each of whom would oversee a number of government departments (successors to the former ministries). The department heads were to be styled secretaries of state under a chief who would report to the SCS. Meanwhile, the SCS had assumed a quasi-legislative function by the issuance of decrees. In 1993 the Strasser regime named a national advisory council to prepare a draft document as the basis for a new constitution (with the aim of holding a referendum in 1995). The draft, published in September 1994, included stipulations that future presidents be at least 40 years old and native-born Sierra Leoneans. It also included provisions for restoring basic human rights, guaranteeing freedom of expression, establishing a unicameral legislature, and empowering parliament to remove a president who became mentally or physically incapacitated, or who was dishonest.

On February 7, 2002, the constitution was amended in accordance with the Electoral Laws Act of 2002 adopted by parliament to provide for a party-list proportional voting system for the National Assembly. In October 2006 the government established the Constitutional Review Committee to consider changes to the charter (see Current issues, below). The constitution was amended in 2007 in accordance with the Electoral Laws Act of 2002 to provide for a first-past-the-post voting system for the National Assembly.

Sierra Leone is administratively divided into three provinces (Northern, Eastern, Southern), in addition to a Western Region that includes Freetown. The provinces are subdivided into 12 districts and 147 chiefdoms.

Foreign relations. Sierra Leone has long subscribed to a generally pro-Western foreign policy, while maintaining diplomatic relations with the former Soviet Union, several East European countries, the People's Republic of China, and North Korea. Regionally, it has been an active participant in the Organization of African Unity (OAU, subsequently the African Union—AU) and a long-standing member of OAU committees established to resolve the disputes in Chad and the Western Sahara. Traditionally cordial relations with bordering states were strained by the overthrow of civilian governments in Liberia and Guinea; however, the three countries signed a security agreement in September 1986 and revived the Mano River Union plan for economic cooperation. In early 1989 continuing efforts by Freetown to "intensify existing friendly relations" with regional neighbors led to the establishment of joint economic and social commissions with Nigeria and Togo.

Civil war in neighboring Liberia topped Freetown's foreign policy agenda in 1990 as ECOWAS's peacekeeping forces, including Sierra Leonean troops, were dispatched from Freetown. In November Momoh described the influx of Liberian refugees as "stretching thin" his government's resources and characterized Liberian rebel leader Charles Taylor, who had threatened retaliation for Sierra Leone's involvement, as "ungrateful." In March 1991 Taylor, angered by Freetown's participation in the ECOWAS operation, began launching raids into Sierra Leone, and Nigeria and Guinea were reported in mid-April to have dispatched troops to aid in repulsing the intruders. Meanwhile, Freetown also accused Libya, Burkina Faso, and Côte d'Ivoire of aiding the rebels.

By early November 1991 the government and its allies claimed to have routed the guerrillas, and Guinean forces began their withdrawal. However, a cease-fire signed earlier in Côte d'Ivoire proved short-lived; in December Taylor charged Freetown with backing incursions by the Liberian United Movement for Freedom and Democracy (ULIMO), a group linked to the deposed Doe regime. ULIMO admitted to having engaged Taylor's forces but denied being based in Sierra Leone.

During the second half of 1992 Captain Strasser reportedly developed close ties with Nigerian military leader General Babangida, who in early 1993 agreed to provide Sierra Leone with military advisers. Subsequently, Sierra Leone and ULIMO forces were reported to have participated in joint operations against RUF rebels.

In March 1994 the Strasser government pressed Ecomog commanders to establish a buffer zone along its shared border with Liberia, citing increased rebel activity as well as the volatility of Liberia's disarmament process. One month later, the Strasser government expelled Germany's ambassador to Freetown, claiming that his "undiplomatic" behavior, including meetings with Liberia's Taylor, were undermining Sierra Leone's interests and threatening relations between the two countries. However, other reports linked the German's ouster to his defense of a Sierra Leonean journalist who had been arrested for criticizing Strasser. In September 1995 seven Guinean soldiers, stationed in Sierra Leone to fulfill a defense pact between the two nations, were killed during a clash with the RUF.

In mid-1998 the UN Security Council announced the establishment of a United Nations Observer Mission in Sierra Leone (UNOMSIL) which it charged with overseeing peacekeeping efforts. In February 1999 UNOMSIL personnel accused Nigerian members of Ecomog of executing civilians suspected of aiding the antigovernment insurgents. Subsequently, observers in Lagos reported that support for continued involvement in Sierra Leone had reached a new low. Meanwhile, Liberia, Libya, and Burkina Faso were alleged to be supplying the rebels with armaments and refuge. Following the agreement reached between the Sierra Leonean government and the RUF in May 1999 there were signs of a thaw in relations with Liberia and Libya. In October the Liberian border was reopened, and in December Sierra Leone and Liberia established a joint security committee.

However, with the breakdown of the agreement and the resumption of violence in May 2000, Sierra Leone's relations with all three countries suspected of helping the RUF deteriorated once again. Although the Mano River Union summit held in May and attended by Sierra Leone, Liberia, Guinea, and Mali "deplored the attacks by the RUF," Kabbah's government and much of the international community continued to charge Liberia with assisting the rebels. With the RUF rebels crossing into the Guinean territory, and the Guinean President Lasana Conté accusing Sierra Leonean and Liberian refugees in his country of assisting the rebels, the Mano River region became a crisis zone and the scene of a severe refugee tragedy.

After the fighting in Liberia's Lofa county intensified in early 2001, Liberian President Charles Taylor renewed his claim that the Sierra Leonean and Guinean authorities were assisting the Liberian rebels. In March the ambassadors of Sierra Leone and Guinea were expelled from Liberia.

There were some signs of thaw, however, after the Sierra Leonean government and the RUF signed a new peace agreement in May 2001.

In January 2006 representatives from Sierra Leone, Liberia, and Guinea met to discuss ways to restore peace in the Mano River basin. Also in 2006, Sierra Leone became a full member of the Community of Sahel and Saharan States (CEN-SAD). On June 4, 2007, Sierra Leone and Liberia reached a border agreement, culminating in the reopening on June 7 of the Mano River bridge connecting the two countries. Peace talks continued at another Mano River Union summit in July.

In May 2008, during a summit in Monrovia, Sierra Leone and Guinea joined with their Liberian host in pledging that the Mano River Union, soon to include Côte d'Ivoire, would sustain peace and security in the region. Also in 2008 relations with China were strengthened as the two countries signed a cooperation agreement following China's granting of interest-free loans to Sierra Leone to help rebuild its war-torn economy. The leaders of China and Sierra Leone agreed in 2009 to enhance bilateral relations.

In April 2009 former British prime minister Tony Blair visited Sierra Leone on a trip designed to promote tourism in the country, and the U.K. promised aid of nearly $71 million in 2010.

Current issues. In accordance with the Lomé Accord, a Truth and Reconciliation Commission (TRC), based on the South African model, was established in 2002 as a forum to enable Sierra Leoneans on both sides of the conflict to relate their wartime experiences. Amputations, rape, and mass killings were common human rights violations during the decade-long conflict. The same year, at the government's request, the United Nations helped establish a special court in Freetown to try the most serious cases of war crimes. In March 2003 the court issued indictments against Foday Sankoh, Sam Bockarie, Johnny Paul Koroma, and former internal affairs minister Sam HINGA NORMAN. Bockarie, a notoriously brutal RUF field commander, and Koroma, then minister of the interior and former head of the Civil Defense Force (CDF), fled to neighboring Liberia. On May 5 Bockarie was killed, allegedly on orders of Liberian President Charles Taylor, who also was indicted in connection with his role in the war but continued to live in exile in Nigeria. On June 29, 2003, the chronically ill Sankoh—the RUF's former leader—died, reportedly of a heart attack, in a Freetown prison. By mid-2005, the court had indicted 13 people, of whom three had died, two had eluded arrest, and nine were in custody. (Hinga Norman died in February 2007; subsequently, Johnny Paul Koroma was also reported to have died.) Taylor was captured in March 2006 (reportedly "on the run" with bags of cash) and jailed in Sierra Leone on 11 charges related to war crimes. In June he was transferred to The Hague to stand trial after Britain agreed to imprison Taylor there if he was convicted. (The UN had asked the International Court of Justice [ICJ] in the Netherlands to hold the trial to avoid potential security problems in the region if the trial were held in Africa; the court agreed on condition that Taylor be jailed in another country if convicted.) After several delays Taylor's trial resumed in July 2007. (In 2009 the special court refused a request to acquit Taylor.) Also, the special court sentenced three former rebel leaders of the AFRC to between 45 and 50 years in prison, marking the first punishments handed down by the court.

Meanwhile, the government faced increasing criticism by war victims and human rights organizations for delays in implementing the TRC's recommendations, although some groups described the recommendations as "vague and noncommittal."

In preparation for the next parliamentary elections, the National Electoral Commission redrew constituency boundaries in 2006 to reflect changes in the population, increasing by 16 the number of constituencies in the western region, which was dominated by the APC. The SLPP, which had strongholds in the south and east, opposed the new boundaries, claiming that the number of constituencies allocated to the Western Area was disproportionate when compared to others across the country.

In the run-up to parliamentary and presidential elections in 2007, originally scheduled for July 28, a proposed constitutional referendum to be held concurrently became the focus of debate, some observers saying that President Kabbah, barred by the constitution from running for a third term, wanted to push through controversial amendments that included granting immunity from criminal charges to all presidents and vice presidents. (Opponents of Kabbah and Vice President Berewa accused them of diamond smuggling and corruption, allegations both of them denied.) Other proposed changes included provisions for a bicameral legislature made up of the elected assembly and a Senate comprised of tribal chiefs and members appointed by the president; elimination of laws that discriminate against women; abolition of the death penalty in certain cases; and broader criteria for citizenship. The UN and other groups had urged a separate date for the referendum to allow for the "unimpeded conduct" of presidential and parliamentary elections. Ultimately, the committee established to recommend proposed constitutional changes determined that more time would be needed, and the referendum was postponed indefinitely. The general election was rescheduled for August 11, the new date prompting criticism from many groups because of potential problems with mobilizing voters during the rainy season.

Meanwhile, campaigning began in earnest in mid-2007, marked by heated rhetoric from the opposition APC's Ernest Bai Koroma and from Charles MARGAI of the People's Movement for Democratic Change (PMDC, below), who had split from the ruling SLPP to form the new party with a mantra of change. Koroma was reported as saying that his party would create havoc if he lost, because that would mean the elections were rigged, while Margi alleged that the SLPP had targeted him with a "bounty." The SLPP, widely regarded as likely to maintain its political dominance, claimed that the PMDC was lining up "thugs" to disrupt the elections. Meanwhile, the RUF, which failed to put together the financial support to contest the 2007 elections, reportedly threw its support behind the APC, though observers described the RUF's role as an "insignificant" electoral force. Following the first round of balloting, in an upset for the APC over the governing SLPP, Koroma led all candidates, with Vice President Solomon Berewa, heretofore considered to be Kabbah's most likely successor, trailing in second place by 6 percentage points. Meanwhile, the APC secured the greatest number of seats in parliament, again providing a stunning victory over the previously dominant SLPP. Prior to the presidential runoff, PMDC candidate Charles Margai, who had finished third in the first round with only 13.89 percent of the vote, threw his support behind Koroma. Meanwhile, the NDA and the PLP, each of whose candidates received less than 1 percent of the vote in the first round, backed Berewa in the second round. Ethnic divisions, generally recognized as separating the Muslim-Temne north from the Christian-Mende south, were reported to be in play in the election, as the northern and western regions overwhelmingly supported the APC (Koroma is from the northern Temne group), while the southern and eastern regions backed the SLPP and the PMDC (Berewa and Margai are Christian Mendes). Though the elections were generally deemed fair, international accolades for the first round were toned down to praise for mere orderliness in the second round, in which the elections commission annulled results from 477 of 6,157 polling stations because of vote-rigging and fraud allegations. A brief but violent looting spree occurred while Koroma was being sworn in, resulting in the deaths of two people and the arrests of numerous others as hundreds ransacked the SLPP's headquarters in Freetown.

Koroma's victory was seen by observers as a significant step forward for democracy, as well as a mandate by voters disillusioned with the fractured SLPP's progress in addressing post-war reconstruction, poverty, and corruption. Koroma, who rose to prominence in the insurance industry before gaining the top post in the APC, was seen as using his leadership skills to run the country in much the same way as a successful business. Among his first acts as president were the invocation of a "certificate of emergency," granting him the authority to push laws through the National Assembly, most notably one giving prosecutorial powers to the Anti-Corruption Commission (ACC). In addition to his pronounced "zero tolerance" for corruption, he also pledged to restore electricity, available in short, sporadic supply only through private generators, in Freetown and the provincial capitals. To this end, he replaced the top tier at the National Power Authority, which had been accused of selling diesel fuel on the black market. Though Britain had withdrawn its significant financial support for Sierra Leone following a poor performance by the ACC, it pledged more than $71 million in early 2008, most of which was designated to increase the supply of electricity and to bolster the government's tax-collection efforts. Collaterally, other regional investors, as well as China, also stepped up their financial commitments. The monetary support closely followed the president's early trips to Vienna, Austria, to promote restarting the Mano River Union talks (see Foreign relations, above) with UN involvement, in addition to including Liberia and Guinea, which he also visited. Further, Western leaders were buoyed by President Koroma's decision to break with tradition and relinquish control of the defense ministry. His choice of cabinet members, overwhelmingly from the APC, included four newly elected members of parliament, forcing subsequent by-elections in those constituencies. Four members of the PMDC were also named to the new government.

Progress in human rights was also reported in 2007, with legislation approved granting unprecedented rights to women. New laws made domestic violence a crime, allowed women to inherit property, and protected young women against forced marriage. Other new laws prohibited exploitative labor practices and set up national agencies to protect the rights of children.

In 2008 attention turned to local elections, held without incident on July 5, the first such balloting since the country's civil war ended. In a further sign of peace and stability, the UN's Integrated Office in Sierra Leone (UNIOSIL), was established as a follow-up to UN peacekeepers, and began working on issues related to governance and human rights.

Effects of the global economic recession were noticeable in late 2008, particularly in the diamond sector, and further undermined what observers said were President Koroma's feeble efforts to improve the economy. Corruption scandals led to the dismissals of three ministers and a cabinet reshuffle in February 2009, which analysts said was meant to bolster the president's standing in advance of the APC's congress to elect new leadership. Meanwhile, the transport minister who had resigned amid suspicions surrounding a cocaine-smuggling case, was endorsed as a regional APC chair. (Subsequently, Koroma was reelected APC president, having garnered a broad base of support.)

Attention in early 2009 quickly turned to what was reported as the worst political violence in the country since 2007, when supporters of the APC and the SLPP attacked each other over a period of five days in March. Thousands of youthful fighters took to the streets; the SLPP's headquarters were ransacked, and women were reported to have been sexually assaulted inside the headquarters building. More than 20 women's groups sought to hold a protest demonstration but were turned down by police for security reasons. Two radio stations accused of inflaming tensions were indefinitely suspended by the government. Meanwhile, the APC was angered by the reappearance in the SLPP leadership of former NPRC members, including its secretary general, John BENJAMIN, and both the SLPP and the APC reportedly used "youth protection squads" that included former fighters. The fragility of the political situation prompted intercession by the UN, which mediated a peace agreement between the two parties in April.

A long-standing trial of war criminals concluded in April 2009 when the special court in Sierra Leone convicted three RUF leaders (see Political Parties, below) and imposed lengthy sentences. Of added significance, the court also determined that it was the AFRC that was responsible for a February 1999 invasion of Freetown in which 6,000 people died. In that case, the court determined that the RUF was not involved in the atrocities, according to *Africa Confidential.* The court made a point of highlighting that the AFRC and army dissidents had a major role in war crimes, not just the RUF as many believed. Further, the court set forth five new violations of international humanitarian law: forced marriage, sexual slavery, enlisting child soldiers under the age of 15, attacks on peacekeepers, and acts of terrorism against civilians.

Drug trafficking, in conjunction with corruption and a high unemployment rate among youth, was described in 2009 as the "main destabilizing force" in the country, as well as in neighboring West African nations, as they became transit points for the smuggling of cocaine from South America to Europe. Three people, including one U.S. citizen, had recently been transferred to the United States following their convictions on drug charges in Sierra Leone. On a positive note, the government's Anti-Corruption Act, adopted in 2008, granted more powers to the Anti-Corruption Commission (ACC) to review ministries, among other things. Subsequently, irregularities and corruption were found in two ministries, and the lawyer charged with investigating and prosecuting such cases said he had the backing of President Koroma.

POLITICAL PARTIES

During Sierra Leone's first 17 years of independence, the principal political groupings were the Sierra Leone People's Party (SLPP), strongest in the Mende area of the south, and the All People's Congress (APC), based in the Temne region of the north. The SLPP dominated from 1961 to 1967 and the APC from 1967 to 1978, when it was accorded monopoly status. Following adoption of the 1991 constitution, a number of new parties emerged, most of which were accorded legal recognition prior to the suspension of political activity in May 1992.

By late 1992 the regime had released the majority of the political figures detained in the aftermath of the coup, the most prominent of whom included SLPP leader Salia JUSU-SHERRIFF and National Action Party (NAP) co-founder Dr. Sheka KANU.

The ban on political party activity was rescinded on June 21, 1995, in preparation for elections promised by early 1996. In August the Interim National Electoral Commission granted provisional registration certificates to approximately 15 groups, 11 of which were granted permission in November to participate in the upcoming elections.

Political parties were banned by the Koroma military junta upon its seizure of power in May 1997. Following his reinstallation in March 1998, President Kabbah authorized parties to resume their activities. His decision to include representatives from only four groups in his reshuffled government was criticized by his opponents, who had expected a more inclusive cabinet.

Following the July 1999 peace and power-sharing agreement, Kabbah reshuffled his cabinet in November, and the rebels (the RUF and AFRC) were given four non-senior posts. After the resumption of fighting in May 2000, however, three rebel ministers were jailed. In March 2001 Kabbah reshuffled his cabinet to replace retiring and jailed rebel ministers. In an effort described as "forming a more inclusive national unity government" but criticized by opponents as "trying to silence and co-opt" his rivals, Kabbah appointed four new ministers. Three came from the opposition National Unity Party (NUP), People's Democratic Party (PDP), and UNPP to supplement Kabbah's SLPP-dominated government (which had also included civilians); one minister came from the Democratic Center Party (DCP). The latter party, chaired by Aiah Abu KOROMA, reportedly dissolved in 2002 after pledging its support to Kabbah. However, the UNPP, NUP, and PDP announced they were not supporting Kabbah's rule by joining the government but were merely trying to help the country in difficult times. (In 2003, however, NUP leader John BENJAMIN joined the SLPP, following the party's former chair, Dr. John KARIMU, who had defected in 2001.) Indeed, the APC, People's Democratic Alliance (PDA), People's National Convention (PNC), People's Progressive Party (PPP), PDP, and UNPP had formed an opposition alliance styled as the Grand Alliance (GA) in August 2000. A number of smaller parties reportedly joined the GA later. Although the GA members announced they would "unite under a single political party in due course," by mid-2001 various internal rifts seemed to have rendered that aim difficult to achieve. The APC and UNPP subsequently left the alliance.

In the May 14, 2002, balloting, 11 parties presented candidates for the presidency, and 12 parties were represented in the legislative contest.

Seven political parties (see below) participated in the 2007 parliamentary and presidential elections.

Following violent confrontations between APC and SLPP members in early 2009, the two parties signed a peace agreement on April 2, pledging to prevent further attacks. The SLPP acknowledged the "overall authority" of the APC government and the president, while the APC recognized "the special responsibility of the state in providing adequate security to the opposition parties…"

Government Parties:

All People's Congress (APC). Leftist and republican in outlook, the APC was formed in 1960 by Dr. Siaka Probyn Stevens in a split with a dissident group headed at that time by Albert M. Margai. Although strongest in Temne territory, the party was not exclusively tribal in character, drawing its support from wage-earning and lower-middle-class elements in both Temne and non-Temne areas. The APC won all but one of the legislative seats in the 1973 election, which was boycotted by the opposition SLPP; it won all but 15 seats in 1977 and was constitutionally unopposed in 1982 and 1986. At the conclusion of an APC conference in August 1985, despite strong support for (then) first vice president Sorie KOROMA, Maj. Gen. Joseph Momoh was nominated as the sole candidate to succeed Stevens as president of the republic. While yielding the post of secretary general to Momoh, Stevens retained the title of chair, as well as the primary loyalty of much of the party's membership, until his death in June 1988. Momoh was reelected unopposed to the party's top post at the tenth APC conference in January 1989, which also yielded abandonment of the positions of chair and vice chair and adoption of a demanding "Code of Conduct" for political leaders and public servants.

At an APC Central Committee and Governing Council joint session on August 17–20, 1990, President Momoh, pressured by calls for political reform, proposed an "overhauling" of Sierra Leone's political system. However, his support in March 1991 for the adoption of a multiparty constitution generated deep fissures within the party. In mid-July two of its leaders resigned their posts, and ten others were suspended for criticizing the document that was approved in late August. In early 1992 the party further redefined its policies and principles, and, by providing for rank-and-file balloting, underwent sweeping personnel changes.

APC presidential candidate Edward Mohammed Turay captured just 5.1 percent of the vote in 1996 balloting, while the party finished fourth in the legislative contest. In March 2002, Ernest Bai Koroma was elected party president and chosen as the party's candidate for president in the 2002 elections. Koroma won 22.3 percent of the vote, and the party finished second in the legislative election, winning 27 seats, including a seat won by Koroma. Rifts in the party resulted in Koroma's losing the top party post in June 2005, but he was reinstated in September and subsequently ran unopposed for the party leadership. Tensions within the party eased as Koroma was tapped to represent the APC in the 2007 presidential election, securing his victory in two rounds of voting. His win came as a surprise to observers, who had forecast victory by Koroma's main challenger, Vice President Berewa of the long-governing SLPP. But Koroma's leadership in the party reportedly helped it to regain support in the north, its traditional stronghold, and the APC also benefited from newfound support in the south in the runoff, with backing from the PMDC (below), which split the SLPP's support in that region. Also adding to Koroma's popularity, according to *Africa Confidential*, was the fact that "voters seem to think that since he already made so much money (in insurance), he would be less corrupt in power."

In May 2008 the party was said to have lost favor with some members in the wake of reports that the government had shut down the radio station of the SLPP. Soon thereafter, the station was cleared of four charges of misconduct.

Following the peace agreement between the APC and the SLPP in April 2009, SLPP leader John Benjamin, in a show of support for stability, spoke at the APC congress shortly thereafter. President Koroma, having consolidated his party base, according to *Africa Confidential,* was reelected party leader, as well as its 2012 presidential candidate.

Leaders: Ernest Bai KOROMA (President of the Republic and Party Leader and 2002, 2007, and 2012 presidential candidate), Chukuma JOHNSON (Deputy Party Leader), Edward Mohammed TURAY (1996 presidential candidate), Alpha KANU (Spokesperson), Victor FOH (Secretary General).

People's Movement for Democratic Change (PMDC). Registered by the government in April 2006, the PMDC was founded by Charles Margai, who left the SLPP after he lost his bid for the chairship, to promote a civilian, democratic government. Margai was arrested in 2006 on a variety of charges related to disorderly behavior against the government and was later released on bail. Several student members reportedly defected to the SLPP in mid-2007, and in midyear Margai was slated as the PMDC's presidential candidate. His defection from the SLPP caused the former governing party to lose a significant number of votes in 2007 in the south and southeast regions of the country, particularly among younger voters, who make up 56 percent of the electorate.

Following the first-round balloting in the 2007 presidential election, in which Margai secured just 13.89 percent of the vote, he backed Ernest Bai Koroma in the runoff. The new president subsequently named four PMDC members to his cabinet, including party co-founder Moses Moisa-Kapu. In the concurrent parliamentary elections, the PMDC secured a small number of seats, trailing the APC and the SLPP.

Rifts reportedly began developing between the PMDC and the APC in early 2008 when Margai accused the new APC government of "chronic tribalism." Merger talks with the SLPP later in the year did not come to fruition at a time when the PMDC was widely reported to be in disarray. Subsequently, in 2009 the national women's leader of the party blamed Margai for bringing about the "disintegration" of the PMDC. However, in February President Koroma included PMDC members in his reshuffled cabinet. Meanwhile, the party postponed its leadership election until 2011, as regional officials and the communications and youth leaders reportedly quit the party.

Leaders: Charles MARGAI (President of the Party and 2007 presidential candidate), Moses MOISA-KAPU, Ansu LANSANA (Secretary General).

Opposition Party:

Sierra Leone People's Party (SLPP). Led by former second vice president Salia JUSU-SHERIFF, whose identification with the Momoh regime was viewed as a political liability, the SLPP was launched as a revival of the party outlawed in 1978.

Ahmad Tejan Kabbah, a 64-year-old veteran politician and former UN development worker, emerged as the SLPP's presidential candidate after an intraparty contest with Charles Margai in early 1996. Subsequently, in the February 1996 parliamentary balloting, the SLPP secured ten more seats than its nearest competitor while its allies (the PDP, APC, NUP, and DCP) gained an additional 24 seats.

In mid-1998 Kabbah reportedly signaled that he would not seek another term in office. Among those cited by observers as potential successors were Margai, cabinet member Harry WILL, and Sam Hinga Norman, whose command of Kamajor militias had won him wide acclaim. Kabbah reversed his previous announcement, however, during a period of peace, which was followed by a resumption of violence and another time of peace from 1999 to 2001, when he won enough support to ensure another election victory for himself and his party in 2002. Former military leader Julius Bio returned to Sierra Leone in 2004 after ten years in exile and reportedly stated his interest in party leadership while condemning the current regime for its alleged corruption and incompetence. Margai left the party in 2005 after losing the leadership post—and, thus, the opportunity to be the party's presidential candidate—to Solomon Berewa, who *Africa Confidential* said was "generally referred to as President Number Two" because Kabbah delegated many official duties to him. Margai then formed the PMDC (above) with other SLPP defectors. Bio, for his part, announced he would not follow Margai and reiterated his support for the SLPP.

Kabbah, who observers said was increasingly unpopular at home and abroad, was barred by the constitution from seeking a third term as president, paving the way for the nomination of Vice President Berewa as the party's standard-bearer in the 2007 election. Berewa chose as his running mate Momodu KOROMA, the minister of foreign affairs, widely known as a Kabbah loyalist. Observers explained Berewa's selection as one of demographics: since Berewa is from the southeast, it was important for him to choose a running mate from the north, where the APC's Ernest Koroma had a stronghold. Though Momodu Koroma was born in the south, his father is a northerner like Kabbah. Party stalwarts reportedly opposed the selection of Koroma, based on his ties to Kabbah and on speculation that Berewa, 67 and in ill health, might not survive a first term.

Though Berewa, described as a shrewd politician, was seen by many as the near-certain successor to Kabbah, the 2007 presidential election proved to be an upset victory for the APC's candidate, bolstered in large part by support from Margai's SLPP-breakaway PMDC, which split the vote in the south. Berewa, who observers said symbolized continuity (versus the change promised by the APC's Koroma), lost in the runoff with 45.38 percent versus Koroma's 54.62 percent. Berewa subsequently resigned as party leader, the post being assumed by U.N.S. JAH.

In 2008 tensions heightened between the SLPP and the APC in advance of local elections in July, with the SLPP threatening to boycott the balloting unless ECOWAS replaced the elections commission as organizer of the poll. (The SLPP had accused the commission of improper conduct during the 2007 elections.) The SLPP ultimately participated, but it faired poorly, leading to discord within the ranks. In early 2009 party veteran John Benjamin was elected chair, and the party began to formulate its strategy ahead of the 2012 general elections. In April the party signed a peace agreement with the APC in the wake of violent confrontations involving both parties in March (see Current issues, above).

Leaders: John BENJAMIN (Chair), Kadie SESAY (Deputy Chair), Solomon BEREWA (Former Vice President of the Republic, and 2007 presidential candidate), Ahmad Tejan KABBAH (Former President of the Republic), Victor REIDER (Spokesperson), Jacob Jusu SAFFA (Secretary General).

Other Parties that Participated in the 2007 Elections:

Convention People's Party (CPP). Little has been reported about the CPP, which promotes democratic pluralism, according to its manifesto released in August 2007. It also promotes human rights, equality, and a free press, among other democratic principles. The party's leader, Andrew Turay, came in fourth in the first round of the 2007 presidential election, securing 1.56 percent of the vote. Turay had also run for president in 2002 under the banner of the Young People's Party and in 1996 as a candidate of the **National People's Party** (NPP).

In 2008 the party was declared ineligible for the upcoming local elections, the ruling usually applied to parties determined to be no longer functioning.

Leaders: Andrew TURAY (2007 presidential candidate), Lansana CONTEH.

National Democratic Alliance (NDA). The NDA fielded candidates for the legislature but not the presidency in 2002. The party reconvened in 2005 after having been inactive for several years.

In 2007 the NDA formed an alliance with the PLP to back Vice President Solomon Berewa of the SLPP in the presidential runoff election. The NDA's candidate, Amadu Jalloh, finished fifth, with 0.96 percent of the vote, in the first round of balloting.

Leaders: Ansu MASSAQUOI (Acting Chair), Amadu JALLOH (2007 presidential candidate), Abdul BAH, Margaret SEDIKIE, Francis BAWOH (Secretary General).

Peace and Liberation Party (PLP). Established in 2001, the PLP was led by the former AFRC leader Johnny Paul Koroma. It was linked with the Grassroots Awareness movement, one of many peace promotion organizations. In the May 2002 elections, Koroma came in third in the presidential race, while the party won 3.6 percent of the vote—and two seats—in the legislative contest. Though Koroma was indicted in 2003, he remained the party's leader, the party spokesman said in 2007. However, it was later reported that Koroma was dead.

In the 2007 presidential election, Kandeh Baba Conteh came in sixth in the first round, with 0.57 percent of the vote.

The PLP was ruled ineligible to participate in the 2008 local elections. The status of the party remained unclear.

Leaders: Kandeh Baba CONTEH (2007 presidential candidate), Darlington MORRISON (Chair), Bai MORROW, Amadu BAH (Spokesperson).

United National People's Party (UNPP). The UNPP secured 17 seats behind a 21 percent vote tally in the February 1996 balloting. Meanwhile, its leader, banker John KARIFA-SMART, placed second in concurrent presidential balloting. In March 1997 Karifa-Smart was charged with contempt and suspended from the assembly. He also unsuccessfully attempted in April 2001 to expel some legislators from the party due to differences on certain policies. Karifa-Smart came in last, with 1 percent of the vote, in the May 2002 presidential election, and the UNPP failed to win any seats in the legislative contest, with 1.3 percent of the vote. Following the election, a cabinet minister who had been a member of the UNPP joined the SLPP. In May 2005 the UNPP joined in coalition with the National Unity Movement (NUM, below) in advance of the next presidential elections. It backed out of a so-called merger with the RUF after some of the latter's leaders were charged with war crimes.

Karifa-Smart retired from politics in 2006, and Abdul Kadi Karim was elected as party leader and 2007 presidential candidate. He came in last with 0.39 percent of votes.

In 2008 the party was one of three ruled ineligible to take part in local elections in March.

Leaders: Abdul Kadi KARIM (Party Leader and 2007 presidential candidate), Osman CONTEH (Secretary General).

Other Parties that Participated in Recent Elections:

People's Democratic Party (PDP). The PDP was characterized by *West Africa* as the "loudest" of the new parties, whose "main handicap is the uncharismatic quality" of its leader, former information minister Thaimu BANGURA. In September 1991 Bangura had been named chair of a United Front of Political Movements (UNIFORM), a six-party opposition formation that was subsequently dissolved.

In the February 1996 balloting, Bangura placed third in the presidential contest, with 16.1 percent of the vote, and the party won 12 seats. Subsequently, as an apparent reward for supporting Kabbah in the second round of presidential balloting, the PDP secured three cabinet portfolios.

Bangura died in March 1999. Following infighting between Osman Kamara and former NPRC member Abdul Rahman KAMARA to replace Bangura, Osman Kamara was elected chair. Abdul Rahman Kamara quit the party to form his own organization, the **People's Democratic Alliance** (PDA) in November. In a cabinet reshuffle in March 2001, Osman Kamara was given the post of the trade and industry minister, although he claimed that the PDP was still an opposition party. He was subsequently replaced. The PDP, with 1 percent of the vote, failed to win a seat in the legislative election of May 2002. Following the election, one cabinet member affiliated with the PDP subsequently joined the SLPP. The party did not present a presidential candidate but came out in support of Kabbah. Several party officials were expelled in 2006 for alleged financial malfeasance. The party did not participate in the 2007 elections.

In May 2009 there was speculation that former APC minister of transport and aviation, Kemoh SESAY, was planning to revive and lead the PDP. Sesay was dismissed in the cabinet reshuffle of February 2009 because of suspicions related to a cocaine deal.

Leaders: Abdulai BANGURA, Osman KAMARA (Secretary General).

Revolutionary United Front (RUF). The Revolutionary United Front (RUF) surfaced in early 1991 as a group of Sierra Leone dissidents who had joined forces with Liberian guerrillas loyal to Charles Taylor along the Sierra Leone–Liberia border, where diamond smuggling had been estimated to yield some $100 million annually. In July 1992 the rebels rejected an appeal by the Strasser regime to surrender and negotiate a resolution of their estrangement from Freetown, demanding instead a national interim government and free democratic elections.

In August 1993 the RUF was described as "unorganized" amid indications that attempts had been made to oust its leader, Foday Sankannah Sankoh (who earlier was rumored to have died). On December 30 Sankoh's personal bodyguards surrendered when government troops overran Pujehin, and in early 1994 the RUF leader was reported to have barely escaped arrest during fighting at Kailahun, which resulted in the further capture of elite rebel troops.

Thereafter, although estimates of the actual number of RUF members fluctuated between 100 and 1,000, the group, which had reportedly broken into four units, was credited with orchestrating military activities in over two-thirds of the country. By October 1994 some observers suggested that the government's war with the rebels was nearly concluded. However, in early November the RUF appeared to be invigorated when its seizure of two British nationals drew international attention, and on November 28 the rebels rejected Freetown's cease-fire entreaties, saying it would only negotiate with the British government.

On January 18–20, 1995, the RUF captured two of the country's most important mines; however, the rebels suffered numerous casualties in a government counter-offensive that dislodged the insurgents. Subsequently, the RUF requested that the International Committee of the Red Cross act as a mediator in the conflict.

Confronted with a reorganized Sierra Leonean Army and near starvation conditions in areas under their control, RUF political leaders in September 1995 reportedly sought a dialogue with Freetown. However, rebel military activities continued unabated, underscoring the reported split between RUF moderates and militants.

Following the overthrow of the Strasser regime in mid-January 1996, the RUF announced a one-week unconditional cease-fire, and on February 25 the rebels held their first direct talks with the new government in Côte d'Ivoire, where they unsuccessfully sought a delay in nationwide elections. Subsequently, the rebels were blamed for disrupting polling in a number of regions. At a meeting with Brigadier General Bio on March 24, Sankoh agreed to a cease-fire but refused to recognize the civilian government-elect. Thereafter, the Kabbah government expressed "cautious optimism" following a meeting between Sankoh and the new president on April 22–23, which yielded a "definitive" cease-fire. The final accord signed on November 30 permitted the RUF to begin functioning as a political movement immediately, with the understanding that it would apply for formal party recognition within 30 days.

Subsequently, implementation of the peace pact stalled because Sankoh refused to meet with officials seeking to finalize the scheduling of the RUF's disarmament and reintegration, and in early 1997 the government accused Sankoh of failing to meet his responsibilities as dictated by the accord. Following a meeting with Nigerian officials, Sankoh was arrested in Lagos on March 12. Three days later, a senior RUF official, Philip Sylvester PALMER, announced that Sankoh had been dismissed from the RUF for "thwarting the peace process." The arrest and ouster of Sankoh (an "international conspiracy" according to his followers) sparked fierce internecine fighting between his loyalists and opponents.

RUF militants played a major role in the fighting, which led to President Kabbah's overthrow in May 1997, and in June at least three RUF representatives were included in the AFRC. Moreover, the AFRC's exhaustive diplomatic efforts to win Sankoh's freedom from detention in Nigeria fueled reports that the RUF was steering the junta's activities. During negotiations with the AFRC in late 1997, representatives of the Kabbah administration agreed to find a role for Sankoh upon their proposed reinstallation in Freetown. Meanwhile, RUF fighters who had aligned with rebel soldiers were being targeted by Ecomog troops.

Following the peace agreement with the government in July 1999, the RUF was promised cabinet posts, and Sankoh was given powers equivalent to those of vice president. In the meantime, the RUF decided to transform itself into a registered political party (the RUFP). However, after the breakdown of the agreement and the resumption of fighting in May 2000, Sankoh was jailed, and Issa Sesay replaced him as the interim leader. In June the government asked the UN to set up a special court to try Sankoh and other RUF officials for "war crimes."

Before and after the RUF's announcement of commitment to the peace process once again in May 2001, there were signs of a split within the organization. Reportedly, the faction for continuing the war, represented by an uneasy coalition of Sam Bockarie and Dennis Superman Mingo, was in conflict with the official leadership of Sesay and the faction committed to the peace process.

The RUFP's presidential candidate, Alimamy Pallo BANGURA, came in fourth, with 1.7 percent of the vote, in May 2002, while the party won 2.2 percent of the vote—and no seats—in the legislative contest.

Sesay, who had been indicted by the special court on war crimes charges, was replaced as interim leader in January 2005 by Peter VANDY. The following month, however, Vandy resigned from the party and joined the SLPP, declaring his belief in the SLPP as the party of reconciliation and multiparty democracy. In early 2006 Sesay was in detention on war crimes charges. Meanwhile, party official Omrie Golley was charged in 2006 with plotting to overthrow the government. Former presidential candidate Bangura resigned from the party in 2006.

In 2007 Secretary General Jonathan Kposova said the party would not contest the upcoming presidential and parliamentary elections because of a lack of financial support.

The war crimes trial of Sesay and other RUF leaders, which began in mid-2008, concluded in March 2009 with the convictions of Sesay, Morris KALLON, and Augustine GBAO on 14–16 charges of war crimes and crimes against humanity. Sesay was sentenced in April to 52 years in prison, Kallon received a 40-year sentence, and Gbao received 25 years. (The court did not have the authority to impose life sentences.)

Leaders: Samuel Gbessay KAMU (Acting Leader), Issa SESAY (in detention), Gibril MASSAQUOI (Spokesperson), Dennis Superman MINGO, Omrie GOLLEY (Peace and Political Council Chair; in detention), Jonathan KPOSOVA (Secretary General).

Movement for Progress (MOP). Formed in 2002 to promote "good governance and positive change," the MOP supported the creation of the special war crimes court and presented the only female candidate in 2002, longtime political activist Zainab BANGURA. She garnered less than 1 percent of the vote. Bangura, who had been a co-worker with Ernest Bai Koroma at an insurance company, subsequently joined the APC and in 2007 was named to the post of foreign minister in President Koroma's new cabinet.

Citizens United for Peace and Progress (CUPP). Founded in 2001 by Sierra Leoneans in the United States, the CUPP advocates "justice for victims" of the decade-long civil war. The party presented a presidential candidate in 2002, Washington lawyer Raymond Bamidele THOMPSON (who received 0.4 percent of the vote), but no legislative candidate.

Other Parties and Groups:

Other groups include the **People's Progressive Party** (PPP), led by former ECOWAS executive secretary Dr. Abass BUNDU who was a 1996 presidential candidate but in 2007 was said to be in the SLPP camp; the **People's National Convention** (PNC), led by 1996 presidential candidate Edward KARGBO, reported in 2002 to be retired; the **National Unity Movement** (NUM), led by Sam LEIGH, which formed a political alliance with the UNPP in 2005; the **National Alliance Democratic Party** (NADP), an opposition party based in the United States and led by Mohamed Yahya SILLAH; the **Sierra Leoneans Advocate for Progress** (SLAP), led by Christian JOHNSON and Jon KANU; and the **Liberal Democratic Party** (LDP) and the **Sierra Leone Socialist Party** (SLSP), both organized in 2000.

LEGISLATURE

The Sierra Leone **National Assembly** is a 124-member unicameral body. In accordance with the Electoral Laws Act of 2002, a constitutional amendment was enacted on February 7, 2002, providing for 112 assembly members to be elected on a party-list proportional basis (5 percent threshold required) from 12 multimember constituencies for five-year terms. In addition, 12 seats are filled by paramount chiefs, representing the 12 provincial districts.

Under a 2007 amendment to the Electoral Laws Act, the first-past-the-post system was re-established. Voters chose candidates rather than political parties in single-member districts.

In the most recent election of August 11, 2007, the All People's Congress won 59 seats; the Sierra Leone People's Party, 43; and the People's Movement for Democratic Change, 10. The 12 seats for paramount chiefs were filled on September 25.

Speaker: Abel N. STRONG.

CABINET

[as of December 1, 2009]

President	Ernest Bai Koroma
Vice President	Sahr Sam-Sumana
Ministers	
Agriculture, Food Security, and Forestry	Sam Sesay (APC)
Defense	Maj. (ret.) Paolo Conteh
Education, Youth, and Sports	Minkailu Bah
Energy and Water Resources	Ogunlade Davidson
Finance and Development	Samura Kamara
Foreign Affairs	Zainab Hawa Bangura (APC) [f]
Health	Sahr Sam-Sumana (APC)
Information and Communications	I.B. Kargbo (APC)
Internal Affairs and Local Government	Dauda Sulaiman Kamara (APC)
Justice and Attorney General	Abdul Serry-Kemal (APC)
Labor and Social Security	Minkailu Mansaray (APC)
Lands, Country Planning, and Environment	Dennis Sandi (PMDC)
Marine Resources	Afsatu Kabba (APC) [f]
Mineral Resources	Alpha Kanu (APC)
Presidential and Public Affairs	Joseph Koroma
Resident Minister, East	William Juana Smith (APC)
Resident Minister, North	Alie Kamara
Resident Minister, South	Musa Tarawali (APC)
Social Welfare, Gender, and Children's Affairs	Soccoh Kabia (PMDC)
Tourism and Cultural Affairs	Hindolo Trye (APC)
Trade and Industry	David Carew (APC)
Transport and Aviation	Capt. Allieu Pat Sowe
Works and Housing and Infrastructural Development	Alimamy P. Koroma (APC)
Minister of State	
Office of the Vice President	Komba Kono

[f] = female

COMMUNICATIONS

A variety of media rights conferred by the 1991 constitution were effectively abrogated by the post-coup military government, which issued a series of decrees limiting freedom of the press, introducing prior censorship, and severely curtailing private speech. One such enactment outlawed reports "likely to cause alarm, despondency or be prejudicial to the public safety, public tranquility and the maintenance of public order," while another declared illegal any attempt to influence public opinion "orally or otherwise." On March 30, 1994, new press guidelines set minimum financial and educational standards for publishers and journalists, respectively, and on May 10 seven newspapers were registered in accordance with the new guidelines. In 2005 the founder of *For Di People*, an independent daily, was released after spending 14 months in jail for publishing an article regarding issues surrounding a 1968 conviction of Ahmad Tejan Kabbah (long before he became president). Press freedom under the Kabbah government was more favorable than under previous regimes, according to international media organizations.

In the run-up to the 2007 presidential elections, various journalists were allegedly attacked by supporters of the Sierra Leone People's Party (SLPP) and those of the All People's Congress (APC), according to the watchdog group Reporters Without Borders. In February 2008, according to the same group, the editor of the weekly *Independent Observer* was prosecuted for reporting on alleged corruption by a government official. Reporters Without Borders said the transportation and aviation minister, about whom the article was written, used a repressive law, which his government had pledged to change.

In the wake of violence between the governing APC and the opposition SLPP in March 2009, authorities suspended indefinitely two radio stations, one aligned with each party, accusing them of inflaming tensions.

Press. Among the nation's daily newspapers are the government-controlled *Daily Mail* (Freetown, 10,000) and the independent *Standard Times* and *For Di People;* weekly organs include *The Weekend Spark* (20,000), *Progress* (7,000), *The New Globe, The New Breed,* the independent *Weekly Democrat,* and the pro-APC *We Yone.* The independent *Concord Times* is published three times a week; *The New Shaft* (10,000), twice weekly, and the *Independent Observer* (Freetown), weekly. *Awoko* is an online newspaper.

News agencies. The domestic facility is the Sierra Leone News Agency (Slena), established in 1980 after President Stevens complained about "the image given to Third World countries by the press in developed countries." Reuters, TASS, *Xinhua,* and *Agence France-Presse* are among the foreign agencies that maintain bureaus in Freetown.

Broadcasting and computing. The government-owned Sierra Leone Broadcasting Service (SLBS) operates a number of radio stations broadcasting in English, Krio, Limba, Mende, and Temne; it also provides limited commercial television service. ABC TV is a private television network. Radio stations include Radio Democracy, a pro-government station originally set up as the voice of the Kabbah government in exile; Radio UNAMSIL, the UN network; Believers Broadcasting Network, a Freetown Christian station; Voice of the Handicapped, founded to serve Sierra Leone's victims of mass amputations carried out during the civil war; and private stations KISS FM (Bo) and SKYY FM (Freetown). ABC-TV is a private network. As of 2008 there were 2.5 Internet users per 1,000 inhabitants.

INTERGOVERNMENTAL REPRESENTATION

Ambassador to the U.S.: Bockari K. STEVENS.

U.S. Ambassador to Sierra Leone: June Carter PERRY.

Permanent Representative to the UN: Shekou M. TOURAY.

IGO Memberships (Non-UN): AfDB, AU, BADEA, CWTH, ECOWAS, IDB, Interpol, IOM, MRU, NAM, OIC, WCO, WTO.

SINGAPORE

Republic of Singapore
Xinjiapo Gongheguo (Chinese)
Republik Singapura (Malay)
Singapur Kutiyarasu (Tamil)

Political Status: Attained self-rule within the British Commonwealth June 3, 1959; joined in formation of Malaysia on September 16, 1963; independent republic since August 9, 1965.

Area: 246 sq. mi. (636 sq. km.), including adjacent islets that encompass some 15 sq. mi. (39 sq. km.).

Population: 4,017,733 (2000C); 4,887,000 (2008E). Both figures include nonresidents, who totaled 754,524 in 2000.

Major Urban Center (2005E): SINGAPORE (urban area, 4,296,000).

Official Languages: Chinese (Mandarin is the preferred form), English, Malay, Tamil.

Monetary Unit: Singapore Dollar (market rate December 1, 2009: 1.38 dollars = $1US).

President: Sellapan Ramanathan NATHAN; declared president-elect on August 18, 1999, by Presidential Elections Commission, which had ruled other potential nominees ineligible; inaugurated on September 1 for a six-year term, succeeding ONG Teng Cheong; declared president for a second term on August 17, 2005, by the Presidential Elections Commission, which had again ruled other potential nominees ineligible.

Prime Minister: LEE Hsien Loong (People's Action Party); sworn in on August 12, 2004, upon the resignation of GOH Chok Tong (People's Action Party); continued in office following the election of May 6, 2006.

THE COUNTRY

Joined to the southern tip of the Malay Peninsula by a three-quarter-mile-long causeway, Singapore consists of a single large island, on which the city of Singapore is located, and some 50 adjacent islets. Situated at the crossroads of Southeast Asian trade routes, the country is one of the world's most densely populated, with some two-thirds of the population—about 77 percent ethnic Chinese, 14 percent Malay, and 7 percent Indian and Pakistani—residing in Singapore City. Religious divisions follow ethnic divisions: the Malays and Pakistanis are overwhelmingly Muslim, the Indians are Hindu, and the Chinese include Buddhists, Christians, Taoists, and Confucianists. Women constitute 43 percent of the active labor force and 24 percent of the 94 members of Parliament.

The economy has traditionally been geared to the entrepôt trade, with a heavy emphasis on the processing and transshipment of petroleum, rubber, timber, and other regional products, and on related banking, shipping, insurance, and storage services. Services still account for 71 percent of GDP and employ 75 percent of the labor force. In the 1980s, however, the government promoted the growth of sophisticated, capital-intensive manufacturing: computers and electronic instruments, machinery, automobile parts, and precision tools. At the same time, mandated wage increases effectively forced the relocation of labor-intensive, low-valued-added enterprises to other countries and decreased the city-state's dependence on foreign workers. Thus, in addition to ranking as a leading oil refining hub and as a "global operations center" for over 3,500 multinational firms, Singapore is now a major producer of computer-related electronics as well as pharmaceuticals. Manufacturing as a whole contributes 29 percent of GDP. Tourism is also a significant source of earnings.

GDP growth in 1990–1998 averaged 8 percent annually, despite a gain of only 1.5 percent in 1998 as a regional financial crisis continued and the world market for electronics softened. A faster-than-expected recovery ended in 2001, however, as a slump in export demand led to the country's worst recession since the mid-1960s, with GDP down 2.3 percent. A recovery in 2002 produced 4.2 percent growth, while the regional Sudden Acute Respiratory Syndrome (SARS) outbreak in the first half of 2003 contributed to a major setback in the second quarter and annual growth of only 3.1 percent. The economy soared in the following year, however, growing at a rate of 8.8 percent. For 2005–2007 average annual growth was 7.8 percent, but the rate dropped to 1.1 percent in 2008 as Singapore fell into recession as a consequence of the global financial crisis. Following a record downturn of 11.5 percent in the first quarter of 2009, the government projected that GDP for the year would fall by about 9 percent.

GOVERNMENT AND POLITICS

Political background. Established as a trading station by Sir Stamford RAFFLES in 1819, purchased by Great Britain in 1824, and subsequently organized as part of the Straits Settlements (with Penang and Malacca), Singapore became a crown colony in 1867. It was occupied by the Japanese in World War II and governed after its liberation as a separate entity, achieving internal self-rule within the Commonwealth on June 3, 1959. Led by LEE Kuan Yew of the People's Action Party (PAP), it joined in 1963 with the Federation of Malaya, Sarawak, and Sabah to form Malaysia. Malay opinion subsequently became alarmed by the efforts of Lee and his largely Chinese party to extend their influence into other parts of Malaysia, and Singapore was consequently excluded on August 9, 1965.

As a fully independent state, Singapore adopted a republican form of government. The PAP, which had been seriously challenged in the early 1960s by the more radical Socialist Front (*Barisan Sosialis*), subsequently consolidated its position, obtaining a monopoly of all legislative seats in the four elections from 1968 through 1980 and then losing no more than two seats through 1988. By then, Prime Minister Lee had made a strong effort to bring "second-liners" (second-generation leaders) into government and the PAP hierarchy.

In October 1989, Lee, having become the world's longest-serving prime minister, confirmed reports that he planned to step down as prime minister. In November 1990 GOH Chok Tong formally succeeded Lee, who nevertheless retained backstage power in the post of senior minister and, until 1992, as PAP secretary general.

Although retaining its political dominance, the PAP was jolted by the outcome of an early election called by Goh for August 1991: the opposition captured four seats while the ruling party's popular support fell to a 23-year low of 61 percent. In response, the prime minister undertook a September cabinet shakeup that dispensed with most of his second-generation colleagues in favor of a third-generation cohort, including his predecessor's son, LEE Hsien Loong. Conscious that the anti-PAP vote had secured inadequate representation, and in an apparent effort to undermine by-election campaigns by the opposition, the government approved a 1992 parliamentary recommendation that six nonelected persons should become MPs, as allowed under a 1990 constitutional amendment.

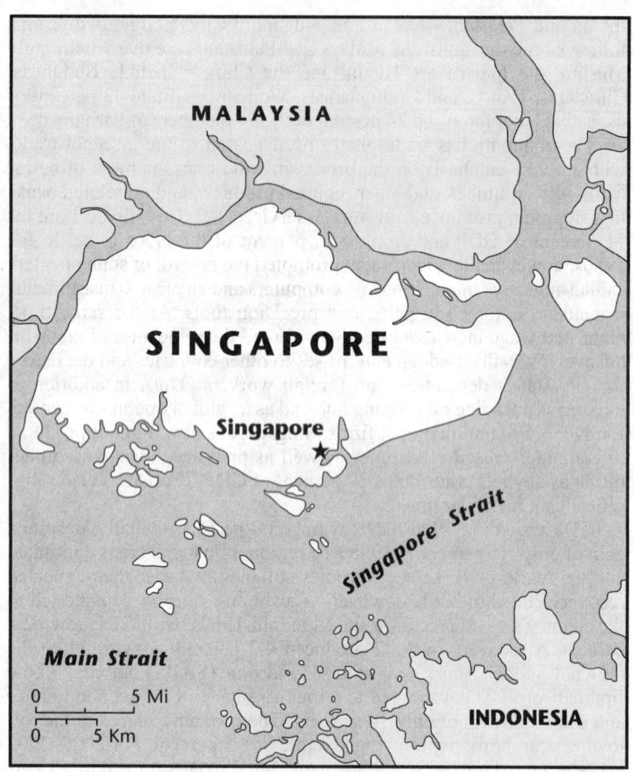

In the legislative election of January 1997, the PAP won 81 of 83 seats with about 65 percent of the popular vote. The following May J. B. JEYARETNAM, secretary general of the Workers' Party (WP) and a longtime opponent of Lee Kuan Yew and the PAP, was awarded a nonconstituency seat to bring the opposition total up to the constitutionally mandated minimum of three.

In July 1999, ONG Teng Cheong, who had been installed in 1993 as Singapore's first popularly elected president, announced that he would not seek reelection. Ong detailed "a long list of problems" he had faced during his tenure—principally, difficulty in obtaining information from his own government about the extent of Singapore's financial reserves, for which the president is responsible. S. R. NATHAN, a former military intelligence official and ambassador to the United States, was designated president-elect on August 18 by the Presidential Elections Commission, which had declared that the two other potential nominees did not meet the standards for office. On September 1 Nathan took the oath of office.

Hoping to forestall negative political consequences of an economic downturn, in October 2001 Prime Minister Goh announced an early legislative election for November 3. Earlier, four opposition parties had organized a Singapore Democratic Alliance (SDA), but the PAP nevertheless retained its stranglehold on Parliament, winning 82 elective seats, compared to 1 for the SDA and 1 for the WP.

On August 17, 2003, Prime Minister Goh confirmed what had long been anticipated when he announced that he planned to step aside in favor of Deputy Prime Minister Lee Hsien Loong. The transfer of power took place a year later, on August 12, 2004.

On April 20, 2006, Parliament was dissolved and an early election called for May 6. Although the PAP experienced a drop in overall support (67 percent of the vote, down from 75 percent in 2001), it again won 82 seats. Prime Minister Lee then reshuffled his cabinet on May 22.

Constitution and government. Singapore's current basic law has evolved since 1959, with amendments necessitated by its temporary Malaysian affiliation and the subsequent adoption of republican status. The executive branch is headed by a president with limited powers and a presidentially designated prime minister, who must command a parliamentary majority and who selects a cabinet that is collectively responsible to the Parliament. The unicameral legislature is elected by universal suffrage and compulsory voting for a maximum term of five years. A Presidential Council for Minority Rights reviews legislation (except money bills or security-related legislation) to ensure racial and religious nondiscrimination.

Originally, the president was selected by Parliament and served a largely ceremonial role, but a 1991 constitutional amendment provided for a directly elected head of state with enhanced fiscal, national security, and appointive powers. By contrast, a 1996 amendment limited presidential authority, particularly with regard to the veto, as a result of which the head of state's principal role is now to safeguard the country's financial reserves. A Presidential Elections Commission is responsible for vetting presidential nominees, who must have sufficient governmental or corporate experience and be able to demonstrate "good integrity, character, and reputation."

Under a 1984 constitutional amendment, up to six nonconstituency seats may be awarded to ensure opposition representation in Parliament, with the precise minimum number of opposition seats (currently three) determined by electoral law. Should fewer than three members of the opposition win election, the requisite number of nonconstituency seats are awarded to the opposition candidate(s) who came closest to winning. Such nonelected members are not permitted, however, to vote on key measures, such as money bills, nonconfidence motions, and constitutional amendments. In addition, a 1990 constitutional amendment authorized the president, based on recommendations from a Special Select Committee of Parliament, to name up to six similarly constrained "nonpolitical Singaporeans." A 1997 amendment raised the number of nonpolitical MPs to nine. In May 2009 Prime Minister Lee proposed that the number of nonconstituency members of Parliament (NCMPs) be increased to nine, effective the next election (see Current issues, below).

Singapore's Supreme Court encompasses a High Court and a Court of Appeal. Since 1994 the Court of Appeal has served as the highest appellate court, replacing in that capacity the Judicial Committee of the UK Privy Council. Subordinate courts include district and magistrate's courts.

Even before independence, Singapore was administered as a unified city-state, local government bodies having been absorbed by departments of the central government in 1959. In 1960 Parliament created a People's Association (PA), a statutory board chaired by the prime minister and led by a chief executive director. Its goals have included achieving multiracial harmony, advancing social cohesion, and organizing community work. As such, it has sponsored residential committees, a Social Development Service, volunteer and grassroots organizations, community clubs, and youth programs, among other bodies and activities. The PA is also responsible for appointing members of Community Development Councils (CDCs). In 2000 Prime Minister Goh stated that the government planned to give the CDCs greater authority, responsibilities, and funding, in order to decentralize delivery of various services and other government functions. At present, the country's 23 electoral constituencies are grouped into five districts, each of which has an appointed mayor (a member of Parliament) and a CDC of roughly 12–80 councilors drawn from among community leaders, administrators, and professionals.

Foreign relations. Singapore joined the United Nations in 1965 and in 1967 helped found the Association of Southeast Asian Nations (ASEAN). Upon the departure of most British defense forces in 1971, Singapore became a member of the Five Power Defense Arrangement (along with Britain, Australia, New Zealand, and Malaysia), a regional security system that calls for the maintenance of Commonwealth forces in Singapore.

Following independence, Singapore's relations with its immediate neighbors were frequently tense, but they later stabilized. In 1989 Malaysia and Singapore held their first joint military exercises since 1965, and the Lee government signed defense agreements with both Malaysia and Indonesia. In early 1992, however, Singapore-Malaysia relations were strained when a visit to Singapore by U.S. President George H. W. Bush produced an agreement on relocating a U.S. naval logistical command headquarters from Subic Bay, Philippines, to Singapore.

In 1997 Singapore's relations with Malaysia took a downturn once again after Lee Kuan Yew described the Malaysian state of Johore as "notorious for shootings, muggings and carjackings." Lee ultimately apologized for the remark, and in 1998 the two countries moved in concert to combat the regional economic crisis. In the same year the two states agreed to submit to the International Court of Justice (ICJ) competing claims to the islet of Pedra Blanca (Pulau Batu Putih), although a formal agreement to that effect was not signed until February 2003. Eight months later the International Tribunal for the Law of the Sea ruled against Malaysia and in favor of Singapore's right to conduct land reclamation on Pulau Tekong island. In January 2005 the neighbors reached a "mutually acceptable and beneficial solution" to the dispute.

In May 2008 the ICJ ruled in favor of Singapore's claim to Pedra Blanca but gave the nearby Middle Rocks to Malaysia.

In September 2001 Singapore and Malaysia signed an agreement on settling their differences over water supplies, transport links, the right of Singapore's aircraft to enter Malaysian airspace, and other matters. The accord took some 15 years to negotiate but failed to achieve quick results because of Singapore's insistence on resolving all issues as a package. In December 2004 the two countries began new talks, which also focused on releasing Malaysian workers' pension funds held by Singapore and on building a bridge to replace the outdated causeway that connects Singapore to the mainland. In April 2006, however, Malaysia scrapped plans for the bridge, construction of which Singapore continued to link to restoration of full airspace rights as well as to a 20-year commitment from Malaysia for 1 billion cubic meters of sand for reclamation.

With regard to other regional countries, Singapore's staunch anticommunist posture precluded close ties with China and Vietnam until the early 1990s. In October 1990 China announced that long-severed diplomatic links to Singapore had been resumed. Subsequently, in the wake of the October 1991 pact to end hostilities in Cambodia, Singapore and Vietnam agreed to upgrade their relations to the ambassadorial level.

In 1997–1998 Singapore responded to the economic crisis in Indonesia by offering humanitarian aid, loan guarantees, and credits, but an influx of Indonesian refugees in May 1998, preceding the resignation of President Suharto, caused considerable concern. Tenuous relations with the successor B. J. Habibie government were not helped when the new Indonesian president later characterized Singapore as a "dot" on the map. In November, however, newly elected Indonesian President Abdurrahman Wahid made Singapore the first stop on his first overseas trip and garnered a pledge of support from the Goh administration.

In 2006 Singapore and Indonesia signed an agreement on establishing special economic zones on three nearby Indonesian islands, the principal purpose being to attract investment capital from Singapore. In February 2007 the two signed a joint defense cooperation agreement and Singapore agreed to an extradition treaty, although opposition in the Indonesian legislature forced President Susilo Yudhoyono's government to postpone ratification efforts. In March 2009 Indonesia's minister of defense described the defense agreement and the treaty as "frozen" but assigned responsibility for the impasse to Singapore, which, he said, was concerned that the extradition pact might require the return of not only fugitives but also their funds. At the same time, some members of Singapore's government called for changes to implementing arrangements before instituting defense cooperation.

The government's support for the U.S.-led invasion of Iraq in March 2003 met with considerable disapproval, not exclusively from Muslims. Singapore committed a landing ship (LST) and a handful of support aircraft, but no combat troops, to the multinational operation.

Current issues. Criticism of the government remains circumscribed by legal impediments, including the country's severe slander laws and the Internal Security Act (ISA). Moreover, the PAP continues to use lawsuits and the threat of consequent bankruptcy against opponents. A frequent target has been CHEE Soon Juan, leader of the small Singapore Democratic Party (SDP) and an advocate for free speech who has been jailed half a dozen times in recent years. On June 2, 2008, Chee was sentenced to 12 days for contempt of court because he repeatedly ignored court instructions while questioning Prime Minister Lee and Lee Kuan Yew during a May hearing to determine damages in a successful defamation suit they had brought against him. In an unrelated case, on May 30 he had been fined S$5,000 for failing to obtain a permit to speak in public during the 2006 election campaign.

The ISA has also been used to detain suspected terrorists, including members of the *Jemaah Islamiah* (JI), the Indonesian-based terrorist network that has called for creation of a regional Muslim state. In September 2008 Singapore released five suspected JI members, two of whom had been detained since 2002, on the grounds that they accepted rehabilitation. At that time, there were reported to be 23 other individuals being held under the ISA. In a related development, in May 2008 Malaysia arrested Mas Salamat KASTARI, who has been described as the leader of the JI in Singapore. Kastari had escaped from prison in February 2008.

In May 2009 Prime Minister Lee opened up the debate on whether Parliament should have greater representation for the opposition. He proposed that the number of nonconstituency representatives be raised to 9 from the current 3 and that the present scheme for adding nonpolitical nominated members be made permanent. In an effort to further increase the prospects for opposition members winning seats outright, he also proposed that the size of some group representation constituencies (GRCs) be reduced and that the number of single-member constituencies be increased by 3, to 12 seats. Lee argued that the proposed changes could raise the level of parliamentary debates and lead to a more thoughtful policy formulation. Although some opposition politicians welcomed the proposed changes, others were skeptical that they would have a significant impact on the PAP's stranglehold.

Because of its heavy dependence on trade, Singapore's economy entered into recession earlier in 2008 than was true for most countries hit by the international financial crisis. The government reported a drop in GDP of 5.7 percent for the second quarter of the year, followed by an even steeper decline of 7.7 percent in the third quarter. In October, to maintain confidence in the banking system, the government and the Monetary Authority of Singapore offered guarantees until 2010 for local and foreign currency depositors. In January 2009 the budget for the next fiscal year was dubbed a Resilience Package. It offered a scheme for creating jobs, credit assistance for medium-sized businesses, tax cuts and rebates, and additional spending for infrastructure, education, and healthcare. To support the package, for the first time in the country's history funds would be drawn from the country's financial reserves.

POLITICAL PARTIES

Since Singapore achieved self-rule in 1959, the People's Action Party (PAP) has never been out of power. Although roughly two dozen legal parties have been registered in recent years, most have had minuscule memberships. In May 2006 the three leading opposition formations—the Workers' Party (WP), the Singapore Democratic Alliance (SDA), and the Singapore Democratic Party (SDP)—contested 47 of 84 elective seats in Parliament but won only 2.

Governing Party:

People's Action Party (PAP). Organized as a radical socialist party in 1954, the PAP has been Singapore's ruling party since 1959. Some of its more militant leaders were arrested by the British in 1957, and other radicals split off in 1961 to form the Socialist Front (see under WP, below). What remained was the more moderate, anti-Communist wing of the original party, which has supported a pragmatic program emphasizing social welfare and economic development.

Despite its legislative dominance, the party's share of the total vote declined steadily from 78 percent in 1980 to 61 percent in 1991. It rebounded to a 65 percent share in January 1997, when the PAP won 81 of 83 parliamentary seats, and to nearly 75 percent in 2001, when it won 82 of 84 seats. Prime Minister Goh soon announced that a "People's Action Forum" of 20 MPs would be set up as an internal opposition to encourage debate within the PAP.

Under the leadership of Goh's successor, Lee Hsien Loong, the PAP won 67 percent of the vote and 82 elective seats in the May 2006 election.

Leaders: LEE Hsien Loong (Prime Minister and Secretary General of the Party), LEE Kuan Yew (Minister Mentor), GOH Chok Tong (Senior Minister), LIM Boon Heng (Chair), YAACOB Ibrahim (Vice Chair).

Parliamentary Opposition:

Workers' Party—WP (*Parti Pekerja*). Founded in 1957 and reorganized in 1971, the WP long advocated a more democratic constitution and closer relations with Malaysia. In its early years a number of WP leaders were arrested for alleged pro-Communist activities, and in 1978 its secretary general, Joshua Benjamin Jeyaretnam, was convicted of having committed "a very grave slander" against Prime Minister Lee. In a by-election in October 1981, the Sri Lankan–born Jeyaretnam became the first opposition member of Parliament since 1968. Despite having previously been acquitted of making a false declaration about party finances, Jeyaretnam and the party chair, WONG Hong Toy, were retried in September 1985. Jeyaretnam was fined and imprisoned for one month in late 1986, which cost him his legislative seat.

Prior to the 1988 election, the Socialist Front (*Barisan Sosialis*) and the Singapore United Front—SUF (*Barisan Bersatu Singapura*) merged with the WP. Formed in 1961 by a group of pro-Beijing PAP militants under the leadership of trade unionist LIM Chin Siong, the *Barisan Sosialis* was the leading opposition party until 1966, when 11 members resigned their seats and 2 went underground. The SUF, organized in 1973, ran third in 1984 but won no legislative seats. In 1989 Singapore's most celebrated political prisoner, former *Barisan Socialis* leader CHIA Thye Poh, was released after 23 years' detention. Remaining restrictions imposed on Chia's political activity were finally lifted in November 1998.

The WP elected one MP in 1991 and again in January 1997. In May 1997 Secretary General Jeyaretnam was awarded a nonconstituency seat, even though he and fellow WP candidate TANG Liang Hong had been sued by Prime Minister Goh and other PAP members for defaming them during the election campaign. Claiming his life had been threatened, Tang fled abroad, and in March he was found guilty in absentia and ordered to pay heavy damages. Late in 1997 the government issued a warrant for his arrest on tax evasion charges. Jeyaretnam also lost his case, and in July 1998 a court not only dismissed his appeal but also raised the damage award. A subsequent report indicated that Jeyaretnam had agreed to pay some $61,500 in installments to avoid bankruptcy and forfeiture of his seat in Parliament.

In May 1999 the Court of Appeal dismissed a request by the WP to throw out a defamation award of over $150,000 won by a group called the Tamil Language Committee, which had sued over an article in the party newsletter. The septuagenarian Jeyaretnam himself lost an appeal of a bankruptcy order in July 2001 and was thereby forced to vacate his parliamentary seat. Citing lack of support for his case, he resigned from the WP before the November 2001 election, at which the party again won one seat. In April 2002 Jeyaretnam publicly apologized for his 1997 remarks, in return for which the government dropped seven other lawsuits against him.

In 2003 Sylvia Lim was elected to chair the party, thereby becoming the first woman to assume that role. In the 2006 election the WP won one seat. Lim claimed a second, nonconstituency seat. In June 2008 she was reelected chair.

Leaders: Sylvia LIM Swee Lian (Chair), Mohammed RAHIZAN Yaacob (Vice Chair), LOW Thia Khiang (Secretary General and Leader of the Opposition).

Singapore Democratic Alliance (SDA). Formation of the four-party SDA was announced on July 28, 2001. In the November 2001 election it won only one seat but was later awarded an additional nonconstituency seat. In May 2006 it retained only its electoral seat. Afterward, the SDA's lack of success led to calls from some quarters for a change of leadership and the merger of the participating parties.

In January 2007 the National Solidarity Party (NSP, below) withdrew from the SDA, which now comprises the Singapore People's Party (SPP), the Singapore Malay National Organization (PKMS), and the Singpore Justice Party (SJP). The SDA's Executive Council was most recently elected in January 2009.

Leaders: CHIAM See Tong (Chair), Ali ASJADI (Vice Chair), LIM Bak Chuan Desmond (Desmond LIM, Secretary General).

Singapore People's Party (SPP). A moderate breakaway faction of the SDP (below), the SPP was registered in November 1994. In December 1996 it joined most of the other active opposition parties, including the SDP, NSP, SJP, DPP, and SNF (all discussed below), in efforts to avoid competing against each other in the upcoming national election. In January 1997 the party won one seat, tying the WP for opposition representation in the Parliament. Currently, the SPP's sole MP is Chiam See Tong, a longtime legislator who joined the party in late 1996 after losing a power struggle in the SDP.

Leaders: SIN Kek Tong (Chair), Thompson CHUA Chee Hean (Vice Chair), CHIAM See Tong (Secretary General and Member of Parliament), LIM Bak Chuan Desmond (Secretary General).

Singapore Malay National Organization (*Pertubuhan Kebangsaan Melayu Singapura*—PKMS). Originally an affiliate of the United Malays National Organization in Malaysia, the PKMS assumed its present name in 1967. It supports Malay interests, racial harmony, national unity, and "the advancement of Islam without interfering in the affairs of other religions." In 1999 it called for government creation of a "supervisory council" charged with eliminating racial discrimination.

In recent years the party has suffered from a number of intraparty disputes. In September 2006 the party's sitting president and vice president, BORHAN Ariffin and MUHAMMAD ALI Aman, were ousted in a party election but then challenged the results. In January 2007 the courts ruled that a new election should be held by the following September. That election concluded with the apparent reelection of the unopposed sitting president, Osman Hassan, and other officers. Borhan's supporters again challenged the results, however, with the Registrar of Societies refusing to recognize the outcome of the election until its validity was examined by the courts.

The factional dispute continued into 2008, when an extraordinary general meeting in November elected a new slate of officers, led by Borhan. The Osman Hassan faction refused, however, to acknowledge the legitimacy of the election, and in September 2009, when a group of Borhan supporters attempted to enter the party headquarters, a riot ensued. The police arrested 21 individuals. Each side has accused the other of misusing party funds and violating the party constitution.

Osman Faction Leaders: OSMAN Hassan (President), ALI Asjadi (Deputy President), MALIK Ismail (Secretary General).

Borhan Faction Leaders: BORHAN Ariffin (President), NOR LELLA Mohamed (Deputy President), RAMLI Mohamed.

Singapore Justice Party (SJP). The SJP is a small group organized in 1972. It has contested only a handful of parliamentary seats, none since 1991.

Leaders: Habibi binte JOHARI (Chair), AMINUDDIN Ami (Secretary General).

Other Opposition Parties:

National Solidarity Party (NSP). According to the *Far Eastern Economic Review,* the NSP was conceived in April 1986 by a group of former SDP and SUF leaders to appeal to "young professionals [seeking] to preserve the one-man-one-vote system [while paying] more attention to the feelings of the people." It had never gained legislative representation until Steve Chia Kiah Hong was named a nonconstituency member after the 2001 election. In December 2003 Chia resigned as NSP secretary general because of admitted sexual peccadilloes, but he was reelected to the vacant post in July 2005 and continues to serve on the party's governing council.

A founding member of the SDA, the NSP left the alliance in January 2007. The "amicable parting" was intended to afford the party room to "maneuver, reengineer, and rebuild."

Leaders: Sebastian TEO (President), Christopher NEO Ting Wei (Vice President), Steve CHIA Kiah Hong (Assistant Treasurer), Ken SUN (Secretary General).

Reform Party (RP). The RP was launched in early 2008 by Ng Teck Siong and longtime Workers' Party stalwart J.B. Jeyaretnam, who had recently emerged from bankruptcy, on a platform that included abolition of the death penalty and of the ISA. One of the government's staunchest critics as well as an advocate for multiparty democracy, Jeyaretnam, 82, died on September 30. In April 2009 a son, Kenneth, took on a leadership role, and in September 2009 the party elected a new Central Executive Committee.

The RP has engaged in discussions with the SDA about joining the alliance.

Leaders: NG Teck Siong (Chair), Kenneth JEYARETNAM (Secretary General), James TEO (Treasurer).

Singapore Democratic Party (SDP). Organized in 1980 by Chiam See Tong, the SDP attracted liberal-minded Singaporeans seeking a degree of formal opposition to the PAP. Chiam won one of the two seats lost by the PAP in 1984; the seat was retained in 1988. The party won three parliamentary seats in 1991, but in June 1993 Chiam resigned as the SDP secretary general and later joined the SPP.

Having been targeted by the PAP, the SDP lost all its seats in the 1997 parliamentary elections. Four years later, despite attracting about 8 percent of the vote, the SDP failed to win any seats. It had campaigned on a "Singaporeans First" platform that blamed foreign workers for rising unemployment.

Since 1999 party leader Chee Soon Juan has been repeatedly fined and jailed for offenses that have included making unlicensed public policy speeches, illegally selling a book he had written, and defaming government officials, including the current prime minister and his two predecessors. Forced into bankruptcy in 2006, Chee was thereby disqualified to run for Parliament in May. In November he was jailed for five weeks for refusing to pay a fine of S$5,000 imposed for speaking in public without a permit during the parliamentary election campaign. Also sentenced to jail were party leaders Ghandi Ambalam and YAP

Keng Ho. Earlier in the year, longtime party leader Wong Hong Toy resigned as assistant secretary general because of policy differences with Chee.

Chee has since been charged with additional offenses, including leading an illegal march in September 2007, attempting in October 2007 to deliver to the prime minister's office a petition regarding Singapore's relationship with Myanmar's ruling junta, and holding an illegal assembly outside Parliament in March 2008 to protest rising prices. In June 2008 he and his sister, CHEE Siok Chin, served 12- and 10-day sentences, respectively, for contempt of court during a defamation proceeding.

Leaders: GANDHI Ambalam (Chair), Francis YONG (Vice Chair), CHEE Soon Juan (Secretary General), John L. TAN (Assistant Secretary General).

Other recently active parties include the **Democratic Progressive Party** (DPP), led by MANSOR Abdul Rahman, and the **Singapore National Front** (SNF), a Malay party established in 1991 by former members of the PKMS.

LEGISLATURE

The unicameral **Parliament** currently includes 84 members directly elected (from a mix of group representation and single-member constituencies) for five-year terms, subject to dissolution. In the early general election of May 6, 2006, the People's Action Party won 82 seats and the Singapore Democratic Alliance and the Workers' Party (WP), 1 each. In accordance with a constitutional provision that the Parliament must provide for a minimum number of opposition seats, a second WP representative was later named to the body. President Nathan then appointed 9 nonpolitical (unaffiliated) members, with limited powers, for terms of two and a half years, thereby bringing the total membership to 94.

Speaker: Abdullah TARMUGI.

CABINET

[as of December 1, 2009]

Prime Minister	Lee Hsien Loong
Senior Minister	Goh Chok Tong
Minister Mentor	Lee Kuan Yew
Senior Minister and Coordinating Minister for National Security	Shanmugam Jayakumar
Deputy Prime Ministers	Rear Adm. (Res.) Teo Cheen Hean
	Wong Kan Seng
Ministers	
Community Development, and Youth and Sports	Vivian Balakrishnan
Defense	Rear Adm. (Res.) Teo Chee Hean
Education and Second Minister for Defense	Ng Eng Heng
Environment and Water Resources	Yaacob Ibrahim
Finance	Tharman Shanmugaratnam
Foreign Affairs	George Yong-Boon Yeo
Health	Khaw Boon Wan
Home Affairs	Wong Kan Seng
Information, Communications, and the Arts (Acting)	Lui Tuck Yew
Law and Second Minister for Home Affairs	K. Shanmugam
Manpower	Gan Kim Yong
Muslim Affairs	Yaacob Ibrahim
National Development	Mah Bow Tan
Prime Minister's Office	Lim Boon Heng
	Lim Swee Say
Prime Minister's Office, Second Minister for Finance, and Second Minister for Trade	Lim Hwee Hua [f]
Trade and Industry	Lim Hng Kiang
Transport and Second Minister for Foreign Affairs	Raymond Lim Siang Keat

[f] = female

COMMUNICATIONS

The domestic press has long been free in principle although restrained in practice by continuous government monitoring and periodic crackdowns for exceeding official perceptions of acceptable criticism. In addition, the government has taken strong exception to stories in a number of foreign publications distributed in Singapore, including the *Economist, FinanceAsia,* and the *International Herald Tribune.* At various times and for various offenses, all have been forced to apologize for articles and to make civil payments to government officials over charges of nepotism or inappropriate financial dealings.

Effective competition between major newspapers ended in 1984 with the merger of Singapore's three largest publishers into the government-controlled Singapore Press Holdings (SPH). In 2000 the government announced it was ending the newspaper and broadcasting monopolies of SPH and state-owned MediaCorp, respectively, by licensing both to compete against each other in print and over the airwaves. In 2005, however, the two merged some of their operations.

Press. Many daily newspapers also publish Sunday editions: *The Straits Times* (390,000 daily, 390,000 Sunday), in English, Chinese, Malay, and Tamil; *Lianhe Zaobao* (200,000), in Chinese; *Lianhe Wanbao* (130,000), in Chinese; *The New Paper* (120,000), in English; *Shin Min Daily News* (120,000), in Chinese; *Berita Harian/Minggu* (70,000 daily, 70,000 Sunday), in Malay; *Business Times* (35,000), in English, Chinese, and Malay; *Tamil Murasu* (15,000 daily, 20,000 Sunday), in Tamil. There are a number of opposition newsletters.

News agencies. There is no domestic facility; the numerous foreign agencies include AP, UPI, Reuters, and *Agence France-Presse.*

Broadcasting and computing. The Media Development Authority (MDA, formerly the Singapore Broadcasting Authority) regulates all radio and television services. In 1998 the government banned political parties from making videos and buying television time so that, according to the minister for information and the arts, political debates would not "become like the selling of soap." Internet sites that include political or religious content must also register with the MDA.

As of 2008 there were 730.2 Internet users per 1,000 inhabitants.

INTERGOVERNMENTAL REPRESENTATION

Ambassador to the U.S.: Heng-Chee CHAN.

U.S. Ambassador to Singapore: (Vacant).

Permanent Representative to the UN: Vanu Gopala MENON.

IGO Memberships (Non-UN): ADB, APEC, ASEAN, BIS, CWTH, Interpol, IOR-ARC, NAM, PCA, WCO, WTO.

SLOVAKIA

Slovak Republic
Slovenská Republika

Political Status: Slovak Republic proclaimed upon separation of the constituent components of the Czech and Slovak Federative Republic (see article on Czech Republic) on January 1, 1993.

Area: 18,933 sq. mi. (49,035 sq. km.).

Population: 5,379,455 (2001C); 5,397,000 (2008E).

Major Urban Centers (2005E): BRATISLAVA (423,000), Košice (234,000), Prešov (92,000).

Official Language: Slovak.

Monetary Unit: Euro (market rate December 1, 2009: 1 euro = $1.51US). The monetary unit was the koruna until Slovakia adopted the euro on January 1, 2009, at an exchange rate of 30.1260 koruny = 1 euro. (The official rate of the koruna on December 31, 2008, was 21.45 koruny = $1US.)

President: Ivan GAŠPAROVIČ; popularly elected (as the candidate of the People's Union–Movement for Democracy) in runoff balloting on April 17, 2004, and inaugurated on June 15 for a five-year term, succeeding Rudolf SCHUSTER (Party of Civic Understanding); reelected (officially as an independent candidate but with the support of Direction–Social Democracy and other parties) in runoff balloting on April 4, 2009, and inaugurated on June 15 for a second five-year term.

Prime Minister: Robert FICO (Direction–Social Democracy); designated by the president on June 20, 2006, to form a new government following the legislative elections of June 17 and formally appointed by the president on July 4 to head a new coalition government in succession to Mikuláš DZURINDA (Slovak Democratic and Christian Union).

THE COUNTRY

Situated in the geographical center of Europe, Slovakia consists of some 40 percent of the area of the former Czechoslovak federation. It is bounded by the Czech Republic to the west, Poland to the north, Ukraine to the east, Hungary to the south, and Austria to the southwest. A former province of the Hungarian-ruled part of the Austro-Hungarian Empire, the country has a population that is 86 percent Slovak and 10 percent Hungarian (Magyar), with small minorities of Czechs, Roma (Gypsies), Ruthenes, and Ukrainians. Nearly 70 percent of the population is Roman Catholic, the other main Christian denominations being Protestant (9 percent) and Greek-Catholic (Orthodox-rite Christians who acknowledge the hierarchy of the Catholic Church; 4 percent).

A substantial proportion of former Czechoslovakia's heavy industry is located in Slovakia. Industry as a whole accounted for 33.5 percent of GDP in 2007, an increase of around 2 percent on the stable figure for the previous four years. The principal manufactures include machinery, chemicals, plastics, and processed foods; Slovakia is also the world's biggest per capita car producer. The agricultural sector contributes fewer than 3 percent of GDP; its leading crops are wheat, other grains, and sugar beets. Leading trade partners include Germany, the Czech Republic, Russia, Italy, and Poland.

Long less affluent than Bohemia and Moravia, Slovakia felt that its reform efforts in the immediate post-Communist period accentuated economic differences with the Czech Republic, fueling pressure in Slovakia for the political separation that was eventually implemented on January 1, 1993. State control and central planning were much more entrenched in the Slovak bureaucracy, which continued to be dominated by officials who had prospered under the previous regime. In 1993 Slovakia's estimated per capita GNP was only $1,500, as contrasted with $2,500 in the Czech lands, with Slovak GDP falling by an estimated 5 percent during the year; at the same time, unemployment and inflation in Slovakia rose well above Czech levels, to 15 percent and around 25 percent, respectively. Real GDP growth averaged over 6.6 percent annually in 1995–1997 before dropping to 4.4 percent in 1998 and then to 1.9 percent in 1999, despite rapid export growth. Unemployment, a persistent problem, exceeded 19 percent in December 1999, while consumer price inflation climbed to 10.7 percent for the year.

The lackluster economic performance was widely attributed to the authoritarian policies of the postseparation government, which favored a slow transfer to the free market and retained significant elements of the bloated Communist bureaucracy. Among other things, conditions impeded foreign investment and appeared to threaten the proposed accession of Slovakia to the European Union (EU) and the North Atlantic Treaty Organization (NATO). However, the situation improved in the wake of the installation in 1998 of a center-right administration that implemented numerous belt-tightening measures, including the privatization of state-owned banks and other enterprises. Reform (lower corporate taxes, paring of welfare and pension benefits, and more privatization) intensified even further when the government retained control in the 2002 general election. GDP growth averaged well over 4 percent annually in 2002–2004, with inflation falling to about 7.5 percent by the end of that period. Although unemployment remained high (about 15 percent), Slovakia was otherwise described as one of Central Europe's brightest economic performers upon its accession to the EU in 2004.

Slovakia joined the European Exchange Rate Mechanism II agreement on November 28, 2005, a key step toward the adoption of the euro and entry into the Eurozone. Although growth of 8.3 percent was achieved in 2006, concerns over inflation (4.5 percent) and unemployment (9.4 percent) were considered factors in the June 2006 legislative loss by the center-right government. Inflation and the government budget deficit remained outside of the EU's specified target range in 2007, although GDP growth, fueled by domestic demand and foreign investment, set a record of 10.4 percent for the year, Growth of 7.0 percent was registered in 2008, while the unemployment rate fell to 7.4 percent under the new left-wing government. However, those figures hid large regional disparities, with an overstretched labor market in the fast-growing west and continuing depression in the east.

The country achieved a long-standing objective by adopting the euro in January 2009. However, that success was partially overshadowed by the impact of the global financial crisis, with unemployment surpassing 10 percent by midyear. The government projected GDP growth in 2009 of less than 1 percent.

GOVERNMENT AND POLITICS

Political background. Founded in 1918, Czechoslovakia was considered to be the most politically mature and democratically governed of the new states of Eastern Europe, but it was dismembered following the 1938 Munich agreement. The preponderant role of Soviet military forces in liberating the country at the close of World War II enabled the Communists to gain a leading position in the postwar cabinet headed by strongly pro-Soviet Premier Zdeněk FIERLINGER, although President Eduard BENEŠ was perceived as nonaligned. Communist control was consolidated in February 1948, and, under Marxist-Leninist precepts, Czech-Slovak differences officially ceased to exist, the two ethnic groups being charged with building socialism in amity and cooperation. (For subsequent political developments during the Communist era, see the article on the Czech Republic.)

As elsewhere in Eastern Europe, the edifice of Communist power in Czechoslovakia crumbled in late 1989. On November 20, one day after formation of the opposition Civic Forum (*Občanské Fórum*—OF),

250,000 antiregime demonstrators marched in Prague, and 24 hours later government leaders held initial discussions with Forum representatives. On November 22 the widely admired Alexander DUBČEK (who had attempted to introduce "socialism with a human face" while serving as leader of the Czechoslovakian Communist Party in the "Prague Spring" of 1968) returned to the limelight with an address before an enthusiastic rally in Bratislava. Following a nationwide strike on November 28 (preceded by a three-day rally of 500,000 in Prague), the regime accepted loss of its monopoly status, and on December 7 Prime Minister Ladislav ADAMEC quit in favor of the little-known Marián ČALFA. On December 10 President Gustáv HUSÁK resigned after swearing in the first non–Communist-dominated government in 41 years, with the Federal Assembly naming Václav HAVEL as his successor on December 29. The Civic Forum and its Slovak counterpart, Public Against Violence (*Verejnost Proti Násili*—VPN), won a majority of federal legislative seats in nationwide balloting on June 8 and 9, 1990, with Čalfa (who had resigned from the Communist Party on January 18) forming a new government on June 27 and Havel being elected to a regular two-year term as president on July 5.

During 1991 the anti-Communist coalition, its major objective achieved, crumbled into less inclusive party formations. The Civic Forum gave rise to two Czech groups in February, while in Slovakia the VPN assumed a new identity, the Civic Democratic Union–Public Against Violence (*Občanská Demokratická Únie–Verejnost Proti Násili*—ODU-VPN), in October after having been substantially weakened by the defection of a Slovak separatist faction, the Movement for a Democratic Slovakia (*Hnutie za Demokratické Slovensko*—HZDS). In November negotiations between federal and republican leaders over the country's future political status collapsed, with the Federal Assembly becoming deadlocked over the issue of a referendum on separate Czech and Slovak states.

On March 3, 1992, the Federal Assembly presidium scheduled a general election (coinciding with elections to the Czech and Slovak National Councils) for June 5–6, and on April 14 Havel announced that he would seek a further term as president. By then, however, a contest between Czech Finance Minister Václav KLAUS and former Slovak prime minister Vladimír MEČIAR had emerged as the major determinant of federal politics, Klaus favoring a right-of-center liberal economic policy with rapid privatization and Mečiar preferring a slower transition to capitalism. The two remained in firm control of their respective regions in the election of June 5–6, after which Mečiar returned to the post of Slovak prime minister, from which he had been dismissed in April 1991. Paralleling their differing economic outlooks, the Czech and Slovak leaders entertained divergent views as to the federation's political future. Klaus insisted that Czechoslovakia should remain a state with strong central authority or divide into separate entities, while Mečiar favored a weakened central government with most powers assigned to the individual republics. In the end, the death knell of the combined state was sounded by successful Slovak opposition in the assembly to the reelection of Havel as federal president on July 3. Thereafter, events moved quickly toward formal dissolution, with agreement being reached between the two governments by the end of August and the Slovak National Council adopting an independent constitution on September 1. Ironically, public opinion in both regions opposed separation. Thus, Klaus and Mečiar were obliged to act through the Federal Assembly, 183 of whose deputies (3 more than the required minimum) on November 25 endorsed the breakup with effect from January 1, 1993.

The Mečiar government of independent Slovakia quickly came under criticism for its alleged dictatorial tendencies and its reluctance to tackle the entrenched position of former Communists in the state bureaucracy. The election of Michal KOVÁČ as president on February 15, 1993, added to the divisions in the ruling HZDS. Although Kováč, a former reform Communist, was then backed by Mečiar, his postelection offer to resign from the HZDS highlighted an internal rift between the prime minister and leading cabinet colleagues. In a cabinet reshuffle in March, Mečiar ejected his main HZDS opponent, Foreign Minister and Deputy Prime Minister Milan KŇAŽKO, who promptly defected from the party to found a new group, the Alliance of Democrats of the Slovak Republic (*Aliancia Demokratov Slovenskej Republiky*—ADSR). Mečiar also insisted on appointing a former Communist military officer, Imrich ANDREJČÁK, as defense minister. The one ministerial representative of the Slovak National Party (*Slovenská Národná Strana*—SNS) thereupon resigned in protest, although the SNS, a strongly nationalistic formation with an anti-Hungarian orientation, announced that it would continue to support the government.

Mečiar governed the country for the next seven months as head of a minority government, failing during this period to entice the (ex-Communist) Party of the Democratic Left (*Strana Demokratickej L'avice*—SDL'; see *Smer,* below) to join his administration. In October 1993 the HZDS-SNS coalition was formally revived, this time with the junior partner holding several key portfolios. However, divisions within both ruling parties became uncontainable in early 1994, and damaging defections led to Mečiar's defeat in a parliamentary nonconfidence vote on March 11. Mečiar resigned three days later and was replaced as prime minister on March 16 by Jozef MORAVČÍK, who had resigned as foreign minister the previous month and had set up a new party opposed to the HZDS. He formed a center-left coalition, headed by his own Democratic Union of Slovakia (*Demokratická Únia Slovenska*—DÚS) and including the SDL', which was to hold office pending an early general election.

The ouster of the Mečiar government, described as a "parliamentary putsch" by the former prime minister, served to enflame political antagonisms in the run-up to the election. Particularly venomous were relations between Mečiar and President Kováč, whose open criticism of the HZDS leader had been a major cause of the government's collapse. Nevertheless, in legislative balloting on September 30–October 1, 1994, Mečiar and the HZDS won a plurality, campaigning on a populist platform that appealed to the large rural population. Despite an economic upturn under the Moravčík government, the new DÚS could manage only fifth place, being outpolled by the center-left Common Choice bloc (headed by the SDL'), the Hungarian Coalition (*Mad'arská Koalícia*—MK), and the Christian Democratic Movement (*Křest'ansko-demokratické Hnutie*—KDH). Six weeks later, on December 13, Mečiar embarked upon his third term as prime minister, heading a "red-brown" coalition of the HZDS, the far-right SNS, and the now-defunct leftist Association of Workers of Slovakia (*Združenie Robotníkov Slovenska*—ZRS) that commanded 83 of the 150 legislative seats (for more background on the ZRS, see the 2007 *Handbook*).

In March 1995 tensions between Mečiar and President Kováč flared when the latter delayed a bill transferring overall control of the national intelligence agency, the Slovak Information Service (*Slovenská Informačna Služba*—SIS), from the presidency to the government. Although the president signed the bill on April 8, following its readoption by the legislature, the National Council on May 5 passed a motion censuring him for mismanagement of the SIS. The 80-vote tally in favor was below the two-thirds majority required to remove the president; nevertheless, Mečiar backed an HZDS executive call for Kováč's resignation and urged his expulsion from the party. The following month the prime minister called for a national referendum to decide whether Kováč should continue in office, while on June 23 the National Council voted to strip the president of his duties as commander in chief and to transfer them to the government.

On August 31, 1995, the president's 34-year-old son, Michal KOVÁČ Jr., was kidnapped, transported to the Austrian border, and arrested by Austrian police under a 1994 German warrant charging him with fraud (which he denied). Although responsibility for the abduction was unclear, Slovak opposition spokespersons and independent commentators saw a connection between the episode and the continuing constitutional deadlock between the president and prime minister. On September 6 the government majority in the National Council blocked a move to establish an inquiry into the affair.

Early in 1997 the opposition completed a petition drive to hold a referendum on instituting direct presidential elections, but the government suspended the referendum on April 22, claiming that the constitution could only be changed by the parliament. On May 22 the Constitutional Court ruled that the referendum would be legal, but the government asserted that the result would not be binding and, therefore, should not appear on the same ballot as a separate referendum on whether the Slovak Republic should join NATO. On the eve of the referendum the interior minister, Gustáv KRAJČÍ, ordered new ballots to be printed without the presidential question, creating voter confusion and provoking a boycott. As a result, the turnout was less than 10 percent, invalidating the results.

As was widely expected, in early 1998 the legislature failed to elect a new president, no candidate being able to command the required three-fifths majority. When President Kováč's term expired on March 2, the constitution authorized Prime Minister Mečiar to assume various presidential powers. He quickly dismissed nearly half of the government's overseas ambassadors and canceled further referendums on NATO membership and direct presidential elections. By then, Mečiar had already been attacked for alleged intimidation of the media, abuse of police powers, and the apparent enrichment of cronies through the sale of state-run enterprises. Popular support for his administration continued to decline as the HZDS repeatedly blocked the National Council from selecting a new president and also, in May, changed the electoral law to make it more difficult for small parties to win seats in the legislature (see Constitution and government, below).

In the National Council election of September 25–26, 1998, the HZDS secured only 27 percent of the vote. Although it retained a slim plurality of seats (43, down from 61 in 1994), its only potential coalition partner was the SNS, with 15 seats, the ZRS having failed to achieve representation. Consequently, the newly formed Slovak Democratic Coalition (*Slovenská Demokratická Koalícia*—SDK) allied with the SDL', the Party of the Hungarian Coalition (*Strana Mad'arskej Koalície*—SMK), and the Party of Civic Understanding (*Strana Občianskeho Porozumenia*—SOP) to form a new government on October 30 under the leadership of the SDK's Mikuláš Dzurinda. Dzurinda quickly pledged to repair the nation's international image in order to attract foreign investment and enhance chances for EU and NATO accession. Domestic reform included curtailment of strictures on the media and unions as well as the appointment of an ethnic Hungarian to the newly created post of deputy prime minister for human and minority rights.

In January 1999 the new legislature resolved the presidential impasse by approving the long-delayed constitutional amendment to provide for the direct election of the president. The governing coalition nominated SOP leader Rudolf SCHUSTER, the mayor of Košice (and a former prominent member of the Czechoslovakian Communist Party), as its candidate for the May 15 presidential election. Schuster was initially expected to face the strongest opposition from former president Kováč and actress and former ambassador Magda VÁŠÁRYOVÁ, both of whom ran as nonparty, or "civic," candidates. However, in early April former prime minister Mečiar, who had left the public arena following his regime's 1998 loss, reappeared to announce that he had accepted the nomination of the HZDS for the post, immediately positioning himself as Schuster's primary opponent. On May 15 Schuster garnered 47.4 percent of the vote, shy of the 50 percent needed for an outright victory despite Kováč's late withdrawal in his favor. In runoff balloting on May 29 against Mečiar, who had claimed second place with 37.2 percent support, Schuster won 57.2 percent and was therefore inaugurated on June 15.

The apparent stability of the multiparty Dzurinda government during its first two years in office belied the tensions in the underlying political party structure. In January 2000, acknowledging that the SDK would not outlive the current legislative term, Dzurinda announced that he planned to organize a new party, the Slovak Democratic and Christian Union (*Slovenská Demokratická Kresťanská Únia*—SDKÚ), in preparation for the 2002 election. By the end of the year the Christian Democrats and others had formally withdrawn from the SDK (see discussion in Political Parties, below), although not from the government.

The HZDS led all parties with a plurality of 36 seats in the September 20–21, 2002, legislative balloting followed by the SDKÚ with 28 and the recently formed Direction (*Smer*). Despite the HZDS's plurality, Dzurinda was subsequently able to form a new government comprised of the SDKÚ, SMK, KDH, and the recently formed New Citizen's Alliance (*Alliancia Nového Občana*—ANO). The coalition fell to minority status in September 2003 when seven SDKÚ legislators left the party.

The first round of new presidential balloting was held on April 3, 2004, with Mečiar leading all candidates with 32.7 percent of the vote, followed by Ivan GAŠPAROVIČ of the new People's Union–Movement for Democracy (*L'udová Únia–Hnutie za Demokraciu*—L'U-HZD) with 22.3 percent and the SDKÚ's Eduard KUKAN with 22.1 percent. In the runoff election on April 17, Gašparovič defeated Mečiar with a 59.1 to 40.1 percent vote share.

Dzurinda's minority coalition government collapsed in February 2006 upon the KDH's decision to quit the cabinet in a dispute over abortion policy. (The KDH had unsuccessfully promoted legislation that would have allowed hospital workers to decline to assist in abortions because of their religious beliefs.)

Early legislative elections were held on June 17, 2006, with Direction–Social Democracy *(Smer–Sociálna Demokracia,* formed in 2005 via the merger *of Smer,* the SDL', and several other parties) leading all parties with 50 seats after campaigning on a populist platform of reduced taxes, increased social spending, ending privatization of state-run enterprises, and withdrawal from Iraq. *Smer* leader Robert FICO on July 4 formed a coalition government comprised of *Smer,* the far-right SNS, and the renamed People's Party–HZDS (*L'udová Strana–HZDS*—L'S-HZDS). The coalition government maintained a comfortable majority in the National Council, with 85 of the 150 seats. A strong economy allowed Fico to maintain high approval ratings, mixing populist slogans with modest reform, such as eliminating a nominal but unpopular fee for accessing the healthcare system, while generally not reversing the Dzurinda reforms.

Presidential elections were held on March 21, 2009, with Gašparovič (supported by *Smer,* the SNS, and the Movement for Democracy [*Hnutie za Demokarciu*—HZD]) leading all candidates with 46.7 percent of the vote. He was followed by Iveta RADIČOVÁ of the SDKÚ–Democratic Party (SDKÚ–*Demokratická Strana*—SDKÚ-DS, formed in 2006 when the SDKÚ merged with the DS) with 38.1 percent. (Radičová was also supported by the SMK, KDH, and the small Civic Conservative Party [*Občianska Konzervativna Strana*—OKS].) Five other candidates received support in the single digits. In the runoff balloting on April 4, Gašparovič defeated Radičová with a 55.5 to 44.5 percent vote share.

Constitution and government. The constitution of the Slovak Republic came into effect on January 1, 1993, on dissolution of the Czechoslovak federation. It defines Slovakia as a unitary state with a unicameral legislature, the 150-member National Council of the Slovak Republic, which sits for a maximum term of four years. Elections are by proportional representation. Prior to passage of a May 1998 electoral reform, individual parties were required to obtain at least 5 percent of the national vote to claim council seats, while alliances of two or three parties needed at least 7 percent, and alliances of four or more parties, at least 10 percent. Under the amended law, however, all parties, regardless of their participation in coalitions, are required to meet a 5 percent threshold, as a result of which numerous previously allied organizations merged before the September 1998 election (see Political Parties and Groups).

In another major change, a January 1999 constitutional amendment introduced direct presidential elections. Previously, the National Council chose the president by secret ballot, a three-fifths majority being required for election. The president serves a five-year term and performs a largely ceremonial role, although legislation and treaties require presidential approval and the president may dissolve the National Council and declare a state of emergency. In addition, the president appoints the prime minister and, on the latter's recommendation, other government ministers, who are collectively responsible to the legislature. A set of amendments were passed in 2001 to address prerequisites required for membership in NATO and the EU (see Current issues, below).

Under legislation enacted in 1996, Slovakia is divided into eight regions (Bratislava, Trnava, Nitra, Trenčín, Žilina, Banská Bystrica, Prešov, and Košice), which are themselves divided into 79 districts. Regional officials were nominated at the federal level until 2002 (see Current issues, below); district officials are elected.

A feature of the Slovak constitution is its guarantee of the rights of ethnic minorities, including freedom to choose national identity and prohibition of enforced assimilation and discrimination. Under associated legislation, use of minority languages in dealings with public authorities is guaranteed in administrative areas where a minority forms 20 percent or more of the total population.

Earlier, the National Council had decreed that Czechoslovak federal law would continue to apply in Slovakia but that, in cases of conflict between Slovak and federal law, the former would prevail. In addition, following the deletion from the Czechoslovak constitution in December 1989 of the guarantee of Communist power, a systematic revision of legal codes had been initiated to reestablish "fundamental legal norms." A revision of the criminal law included abolition of the death penalty and provision of a full guarantee of judicial review, while a law on judicial rehabilitation facilitated the quashing of nearly all of the political trials of the Communist era. Commercial and civil law revisions established the supremacy of the courts in making decisions relating to rights, and property rights were reinstituted.

Foreign relations. On December 21, 1992, the "Visegrád" countries (Poland, Hungary, and Czechoslovakia) concluded a Central European Free Trade Agreement (CEFTA), to which the Czech and Slovak republics were deemed to have acceded at their attainment of separate sovereignty on January 1, 1993. (For additional information on CEFTA, see Foreign relations in the Poland entry.) On December 30 the International Monetary Fund (IMF) decided to admit both the Czech and Slovak republics as full members, effective January 1. On January 19, 1993, the UN General Assembly admitted the two republics to membership, dividing between them their seats on various subsidiary organs held by the former Czechoslovakia. The two states also became separate members of the Council of Europe, the Conference on (later Organization for) Security and Cooperation in Europe (CSCE/OSCE), and the European Bank for Reconstruction and Development (EBRD), sovereign Slovakia having declared its intention to honor and fulfill all the international treaties and obligations entered into by the Czechoslovak federation. In October 1993 agreements were signed with the EU transferring the latter's 1991 association agreement with Czechoslovakia to the two successor states in renegotiated form. (For foreign relations of the former federative republic prior to December 31, 1992, see entry under the Czech Republic article.)

As part of its orientation toward the West, Slovakia in February 1994 joined NATO's Partnership for Peace program for former Communist and neutral states, becoming in addition an associate partner of the Western European Union (WEU) in May. Shortly thereafter, it signed military cooperation agreements with Germany and France, receiving from both countries assurances of support for eventual Slovakian membership in NATO and the EU.

Following the breakup of Czechoslovakia, the Slovak government applied itself to the implementation of some 30 treaties and agreements designed to regulate relations with the Czech Republic, but some aspects of the separation (including the division of federal property, debt settlement, and border arrangements) proved difficult to finalize. A temporary currency union between the two states was terminated on February 8, 1993, accompanied by a dramatic slump in bilateral trade despite the commitment of both sides to a customs union. In 1994 Slovak-Czech trade began to recover, while the Moravčík government upon assuming office in March sought improved relations by moving quickly to conclude an agreement with Prague on police and customs arrangements.

The Czech government's unilateral decision in June 1995 to terminate the payments clearance system operating with Slovakia drew strong condemnation from Bratislava, where Czech charges of Slovak noncompliance with its rules were rejected. The premiers of the two countries met at a CEFTA summit in Brno, Czech Republic, on September 11, when a mutual desire to preserve the Czech-Slovak customs union was expressed. In January 1996 Bratislava and Prague signed a treaty defining the 155-mile Slovak-Czech border and involving land exchanges totaling some 6,000 acres in resolution of outstanding claims. Remaining property and debt disputes were resolved at prime ministerial meetings in November 1999 and May 2000.

Slovakia's relations with neighboring Hungary have long been colored by the presence of a 600,000-strong ethnic Hungarian minority: allegations of official discrimination against it inevitably draw the attention of the Budapest government, which regards itself as the protector of Magyars beyond its borders. Under the 1992–1994 Mečiar government, the influence of the nationalist SNS contributed to a worsening of relations with the ethnic Hungarian community. The Moravčík government took a more conciliatory line and also sought to improve relations with Budapest later in 1994. On Mečiar's return to office in December, rapprochement with Hungary continued to be a government aim.

A long-negotiated treaty of friendship and cooperation was signed in Paris on March 19, 1995, by the Slovak and Hungarian prime ministers that recognized the rights of national minorities and enjoined their protection, while declaring the Slovakian-Hungarian border to be "inviolable." The treaty was ratified by the Slovak legislature on March 27, 1996. A remaining disagreement involves the controversial Gabčíkovo-Nagymaros dam being built by Slovakia on the Danube. In early 1999 tentative agreement was reportedly reached for joint operation of the dam and the discontinuation of plans to build another on the Danube, but no final resolution followed. In September 2000 UN Secretary General Kofi Annan apparently offered to mediate the dispute, but Prime Minister Dzurinda rejected the offer as unnecessary.

On June 27, 1995, Slovakia formally submitted an application for full EU membership, and it subsequently expressed its desire to join NATO. However, in July 1997 the Madrid summit of NATO leaders did not include Slovakia among the three former Warsaw Pact nations, including the Czech Republic, invited to join the alliance. Neither was Slovakia numbered in December among the six nations invited to begin formal membership discussions with the EU, though it remained one of five East European countries expected to participate in a "second wave" of expansion. The decisions were reportedly based on political grounds, including the perceived lack of democratic reforms in Slovakia and its treatment of ethnic Hungarians. The change of government in the fall of 1998 improved Slovakia's prospects for EU and NATO accession, as new Prime Minister Dzurinda indicated his desire to redirect the nation's focus away from Russia and Ukraine (his predecessor's favored direction) and toward the West. Slovakia's standing with regard to NATO admission was also improved by the government's support for the 1999 air campaign against Yugoslavia.

Despite initial objections from the United States, Slovakia was invited on July 28, 2000, to join the Organization for Economic Cooperation and Development (OECD), which the Dzurinda government viewed as further recognition of the country's readiness for full integration with Western institutions. A favorable progress report in November from the European Commission offered additional encouragement that the goal of EU accession might be achieved by 2004, although the status of Slovakia's large Roma (Gypsy) minority remained a concern.

Slovakia was formally invited in November 2002 to begin membership negotiations with NATO. In what was seen as a related development, Slovakia and a group of other Eastern European countries publicly endorsed the stance of U.S. president George W. Bush regarding Iraq in early 2003. On April 10 the National Council approved NATO accession by a vote of 124–11, and in June Slovakia sent some 100 military engineers to support the U.S.-led coalition in Iraq (despite the fact that polls indicated that 75 percent of Slovakia's population opposed the war). Slovakia officially joined NATO with six other new members on March 29, 2004. EU accession followed on May 1, a national referendum on May 16–17, 2003, having approved EU membership by a 94 percent "yes" vote, albeit with a modest turnout of only 52 percent.

Prime Minister Dzurinda's defeat in the legislative balloting of June 2006 was initially seen as a possible setback in the country's goal of adopting the euro on January 1, 2009. However, in July new Prime Minister Robert Fico announced that he would support the 2009 schedule. Twelve months later the EU ratified Slovakia's entry into the euro area on the existing schedule, despite the European Central Bank's "considerable concerns" voiced in May 2008 that Slovak inflation could rise more than the euro average. On December 21, 2007, Slovakia was one of nine new countries incorporated into the Schengen Agreement, Europe's free movement zone.

Following his alliance with the HZDS (led by the former authoritarian Vladimír Mečiar) and the SNS (led by Ján SLOTA, a politician known for his xenophobic rhetoric), Fico's *Smer* party found itself excluded from the Party of European Socialists (PES), the social democratic grouping in the European Parliament. In November 2007 PES head Hannes Swoboda visited Slovakia to monitor minority issues and concluded that Slota's inflammatory statements against ethnic Hungarians caused real damage to Slovakia's international standing. *Smer* was reinstated by the PES in early 2008 after Fico and Slota reaffirmed their commitment to human rights. But in April the Slovak government further tarnished its image in Europe by approving a controversial media law (see Current issues), despite objections from the Organization for Security and Cooperation in Europe (OSCE).

Tensions with Hungary took another turn for the worse in September 2007, when the Slovak parliament approved a declaration on the inviolability of the Beneš decrees. Enacted in the 1940s by the Czechoslovak government-in-exile, this series of laws forced thousands of ethnic Hungarians out of the country following the second World War. In September 2008 Hungarian Prime Minister Ferenc Gyurcsány agreed to an official visit to Slovakia to help ease bilateral tensions, having refused a similar invitation in October 2007. However, Fico's coalition arrangement with the nationalist SNS continued to strain relations, while anxiety about Hungarian irredentism has prevented the Slovak government from recognizing the unilateral declaration of independence by Kosovo, with Fico maintaining his country's position that "international law has not been respected."

Under Fico, Slovakia has recast its bilateral relationships with both the United States and Russia. In a break with the pro-American stance of his predecessor, the prime minister withdrew the majority of Slovakia's small contingent in Iraq in early 2007 and made visits to Libya, Venezuela, and the Cuban embassy in Bratislava. Responding to U.S. plans to install a radar system in the Czech Republic and an antimissile base in Poland, Fico remarked, "We are not happy with rockets and radars in Europe." Meanwhile, in anticipation of the renegotiation of its gas supply contract with Russian gas monopoly Gazprom at the end of 2008, Slovakia increased the volume of its signals in support of Russia. "We consider [Russia] a reliable partner," said Slovak Foreign Minister Ján Kubiš. In an apparent contradiction of the official Slovak line on

Kosovar independence, the official reaction to the August 2008 conflict between Russia and Georgia over South Ossetia set Slovakia apart from the pro-Georgian stances taken by its neighbors Poland and the Czech Republic, with Deputy Prime Minister Dušan Čaplovič declaring that South Ossetia should be allowed a chance at independence.

Tension between Slovakia and Hungary has worsened recently, and the European Commission in November 2008 expressed concern over the nature of political discourse in both countries. The Slovak State Language Act of June 2009 (see Current issues, below) was criticized by Hungarian government officials. In turn, Hungarian president László Sólyom was denied permission to enter Slovakia in August to participate in a celebration of St. Stephen's Day, the Hungarian national holiday. Such issues continued to inflame the nationalist rhetoric of far-right parties in both countries.

Current issues. Following the 2006 elections, Prime Minister Fico criticized the country's media for a lack of professionalism in reporting, claiming it showed bias in favor of opposition parties and special interests. A new "Right of Reply" media law proposed in April 2007 required media to allow interested parties to respond to published material (whether true or not) and promised the Ministry of Culture powers to sanction publishers. The proposal drew domestic and international allegations that the government sought merely to limit media criticism and that the law fell out of line with Western European practices. In a move to prevent the law from passing, opposition parties—the SDKU, KDS, and KDH—tied their support of the EU Lisbon treaty to revisions to the new law, drawing moral authority and their specific recommendations from criticisms of the law supplied by the OSCE (see Foreign relations). In April 2008, however, Fico broke the opposition alliance against the media bill, pushing through the controversial proposal by drawing KDH support for the governing coalition's position on the Lisbon treaty. This KDH "betrayal" was symptomatic of a general fragmentation of Slovak center-right politics in 2008, a consequence of which was the formation in July of a new political party, the Conservative Democrats of Slovakia (*Konzervatívni Demokrati Slovenska*—KDS), by four former KDH deputies (see Political Parties, below).

The fragmentation of the opposition followed a major test of the fractiousness of the ruling coalition. In November 2007 it emerged that Branislav BRIZA, deputy director of a Ministry of Agriculture agency—the Slovak Land Fund (SPF)—and an HZDS appointee, had authorized a cut-price land sale to a company alleged to be close to Vladimír Mečiar. Fico responded by calling for the resignations of Briza and Miroslav JURENA, agriculture minister and deputy leader of the HZDS. Meanwhile, Mečiar not only backed Jurena, but also called for the director of the SPF, a *Smer* appointee, to resign. The situation finally deescalated when Mečiar consented to Jurena's replacement by another deputy from his own party. While his statements at the time suggested that Mečiar was considering suspending the coalition upon the EU's approval of Slovakia's euro bid, the coalition remained steady even following the euro assessment. The coalition weathered several other major cabinet resignations and reshuffles in 2008.

The opening of Communist-era secret police files, including the public display on the Internet of 2,927 names of former agents and informants, triggered several scandals. These included revelations regarding Slovak politicians' past work for the Secret Service (*Štátna Bezpečnosú*—ŠtB), notably a former defense minister, Miroslav VACEK, and a former interior minister, Richard SACHER. Public speculation about former prime minister Vladimír Mečiar's alleged past collaboration was fueled by the discovery that relevant files were missing or destroyed. In January 2007 it was revealed that Archbishop Jan SOKOL had worked for the ŠtB. Earlier that month, he had praised the wartime pro-German government of Archbishop Jozef Tiso, drawing protests from Slovakia's Jewish community.

Slovakia's European Parliament election on June 6, 2009, was widely seen as a barometer for the 2010 parliamentary elections, despite low turnout. The results demonstrated *Smer*'s continued popularity and roughly paralleled the 2006 parliamentary elections. The 13 seats were distributed as follows: *Smer,* 5; SDKÚ-DS, 2; SMK, 2; KDH, 2; L'S-HZDS, 1; and SNS, 1.

In late June 2009 amendments to Slovakia's State Language Act were passed to formalize the use of Slovak in official communication. The SMK criticized the law as restricting the use of the Hungarian language and discriminating against the ethnic Hungarian minority. Analysts noted that although the practical implication of the law may be minor, it has served to create populist platforms for its sponsors in government ahead of the 2010 parliamentary campaigns.

POLITICAL PARTIES AND GROUPS

From 1948 to 1989 Czechoslovakia displayed the façade of a multiparty system through the National Front of the Czechoslovak Socialist Republic (*Národní Fronta*—ČSR), which was controlled by the Communist Party. The Front became moribund in late 1989, as most popular sentiment coalesced behind the recently organized coalition of the Civic Forum (*Občanské Fórum*—OF) in the Czech lands and its Slovak counterpart, the Public Against Violence (*Verejnost Proti Násili*—VPN), which swept the legislative balloting of June 8–9, 1990. In February 1991 the Slovak prime minister, Vladimír Mečiar, accused the VPN leadership of not defending the interests of Slovakia and announced the formation of a minority faction that on June 22 organized separately as the Movement for a Democratic Slovakia (HZDS).

During the first half of 1992 the regional parties became far more influential than those attempting to maintain federal constituencies, thus setting the stage for the breakup of the federation following the June general election, at which the HZDS emerged as the largest party in Slovakia. On the establishment of independent Slovakia on January 1, 1993, those parties that had theretofore claimed a federal identity ceased to do so.

A controversial May 1998 electoral law revision mandated that individual parties, even those in coalitions, would claim National Council seats only if they obtained 5 percent of the national vote. As a direct result, a number of small parties merged with larger formations—principally the HZDS and the Slovak National Party (SNS)—while the principal opposition alliances, the Slovak Democratic Coalition (SDK) and the Hungarian Coalition (MK), technically transformed themselves into unified parties in preparation for the September 1998 election. Both participated in the formation of the multiparty Dzurinda government that took office a month later. In less than a year the diverse SDK began to fracture, leading Prime Minister Dzurinda to announce on January 17, 2000, his intention to organize a Slovak Democratic and Christian Union (SDKÚ), which held a founding congress the following November. By then it had become apparent that the SDK would survive only until the 2002 election campaign, if that long, Dzurinda having announced that he would remain its chair while advancing the SDKÚ as a leading contender for 2002. The SDKÚ congress was soon followed by the withdrawal of the Christian Democratic Movement (KDH) and much of the Democratic Party (DS) from the SDK's parliamentary organization, although both pledged continued support for the government.

Government Parties:

Direction–Social Democracy (*Smer–Sociálna Demokracia*—*Smer*). Following the Communist defeat in late 1989, elements of the Communist Party of Slovakia (*Komunistická Strana Slovenska*—KSS) reestablished themselves as the Party of the Democratic Left (*Strana Demokratickej L'avice*—SDL') in 1990. By 1994 the party had emerged as the strongest component of a new center-left coalition, but was unable to transform this into electoral success. Disputes over whether or not to join the HZDS in a coalition divided the party, resulting in the emergence of Jozeph MIGAŠ as the party's chair, with several factions breaking away to form new parties.

Smer was formally established on December 11, 1999, by former members of the SDL', and quickly emerged as a potentially significant force for the 2002 election, due to the strength of its leader's popularity. Robert Fico, previously an SDL' deputy chair, organized *Smer* as a center-left "third way" party supporting EU accession, political reform, and caution with regard to majority foreign ownership of key industries. In late 2000 opinion polls ranked Fico as the country's most trustworthy and popular politician.

Smer won 13.5 percent of the vote and 25 seats in the September 2002 general election and subsequently served as one of the strongest left-leaning opponents of the Dzurinda government. *Smer* supported Ivan Gašparovič of the HZDS in his successful run for president in 2004.

In early 2005 *Smer* merged with the SDL', the Social Democratic Party of Slovakia (*Sociálnodemokratická Strana Slovenska*—SDSS), and the Social Democratic Alternative (*Sociálnodemokratická Alternatíva*—SDA), a small party formed by former SDL' ministers that had competed unsuccessfully in the 2002 legislative poll. (For information on the historically significant SDSS, see the 2006 *Handbook.*) The SDL' had been heir to the Communist Party of Slovakia

(*Komunistická Strana Slovenska*—KSS), originally formed in 1939 but subsequently absorbed by the Communist Party of Czechoslovakia. The SDL' was reestablished in 1989, and in October 1990 its majority wing renamed itself the Communist Party of Slovakia–Party of the Democratic Left, which became simply Party of the Democratic Left later in the year.

The SDL' ran third in Slovakian local elections in November 1990 and second in the June 1992 general election. In 1993 it resisted overtures from the then-ruling HZDS to join the government, and in March 1994 it became the strongest component of a new center-left coalition. For the general election in fall 1994, it headed the Common Choice (SV) alliance, which won 18 seats (13 filled by members of the SDL', which had won 29 seats in 1992). The failure of the SDL' to emulate the recent electoral success of other East European ex-Communist parties was attributed in part to the preference of the old Slovak *nomenklatura* for Mečiar's HZDS.

From 1995 the SDL' experienced internal strife over whether to join the coalition government, as proposed by the HZDS. The election of compromise candidate Jozef Migaš as party leader in April 1996 (in succession to Peter WEISS) failed to end the dissension, which intensified when the SDL' leadership gave qualified external support to the government during a midyear cabinet crisis. Having finished third in the 1998 legislative election with 23 seats, the SDL' signed a coalition agreement under which it accepted six ministerial portfolios, compared with nine for the SDK, three for the SMK, and two for the SOP. Migaš was reelected chair at a July 2000 party conference despite considerable dissension over antigovernment statements, including his support for a no-confidence motion in April. On December 16, 2000, the SDL' minister of defense, Pavol KANIS, announced that he would shortly leave the cabinet, primarily over allegations concerning the financing of a luxury villa he had built.

The new 2005 grouping, which also reportedly attracted former members of the SOP, adopted the Direction–Social Democracy rubric, although it continued to be routinely referenced as simply *Smer.* The party secured a plurality of 29.1 percent of the legislative vote in 2006 and formed a government in coalition with two junior parties, the SNS and the HZDS. Since his election in 2006, Fico has consolidated his position within *Smer,* displacing rivals such as Monika FLAŠIKOVÁ-BEŇOVÁ (who was demoted from a deputy chair position in August 2006 after criticizing the coalition agreement with the SNS).

Polls in mid-2009 suggested that approximately 50 percent of the electorate would support *Smer* in an election. This popularity has been a factor in maintaining the stability of *Smer*'s coalition partnerships, with the two junior parties aware that a collapse of the government and an early election could lead to a drop in their parliamentary representation. *Smer* backed Ivan Gašparovič in his 2009 reelection bid, with the president going so far at some rallies as to identify his campaign with *Smer*'s political future.

Leaders: Robert FICO (Chair and Prime Minister); Robert KALIŇÁK, Dušan ČAPLOVIČ, Pavol PAŠKA, Marek MAD'ARIČ, Vladimir MAŇKA, Igor FEDERIČ (Deputy Chairs).

People's Party–Movement for a Democratic Slovakia (*L'udová Strana–Hnutie za Demokratické Slovensko*—L'S-HZDS). The L'S-HZDS originated (as the HZDS) in an early 1991 split within the prodemocracy Public Against Violence (VPN) that turned on a dispute between the mainstream leadership and Prime Minister Mečiar, who favored a diluted form of federalism offering greater protection for Slovak economic and political interests. Thus, Mečiar issued an essentially nationalist appeal "For a Democratic Slovakia" prior to his dismissal in April 1991 and the formation of the new party in late June. Subsequently, the HZDS became Slovakia's leading party. Returning to power as a result of the HZDS's victory in the June 1992 elections, Mečiar led Slovakia to its separation from the Czech Republic on January 1, 1993, and governed on the basis of an alliance with the right-wing SNS. Thereafter, the party was weakened by breakaways of centrist elements critical of the prime minister's approach, culminating in Mečiar's ouster in March 1994. In opposition, the HZDS remained the country's strongest party. It formed a populist alliance with the smaller RSS (see next paragraph) for the fall national election that headed the returns with 34.9 percent of the vote and thereafter became the dominant party in a "red-brown" coalition with the SNS and the left-wing ZRS.

In July 1998 the HZDS approved the incorporation into its ranks of three groups with which it had previously cooperated: the Party of Entrepreneurs and Tradesmen (*Strana Podnikatel'ov a Živnostnikov*—SPŽ), led by Ivan SYKORA; the New Agrarian Party (*Nová Agrárná Strana*—NAS), which had been formed in November 1997 by union of the opposition Farmers' Movement of Slovakia (*Hnutie Pol'nohospodárov Slovenska*—HPS) and the progovernment Agrarian Party of Slovakia (*Rol'nícka Strana Slovenska*—RSS); and the Social Democracy (*Sociálna Demokracia*—SD), a minor party based in Žilina. In the September 1998 national election the HZDS again finished first, but with a bare plurality of 1 seat over the SDK's 42 seats. In April 1999 Mečiar was reelected party chair and unexpectedly announced his candidacy for president, immediately rising to second place in opinion polls on the strength of his rural base. In runoff balloting on May 29 he lost to the SOP's Rudolf Schuster.

The HZDS held a "transformation" congress in March 2000 in an effort to redefine itself as a center-right "people's party." Mečiar was unanimously reelected chair, and he remained one of the country's most popular public figures. The HZDS led all parties in the 2002 legislative balloting, but 11 of its legislators resigned from the party in May 2003 to launch the People's Union (see L'U-HZD, below). A party congress in June 2003 changed the name of the party to the L'S-HZDS, although the older name remains in occasional use within the country. Mečiar led all candidates in the first round of the April 2004 presidential poll with 32.7 percent of the vote, but was defeated in the second round with only 40.1 percent of the vote. The L'S-HZDS secured 8.8 percent of the vote in the 2006 legislative poll and received two seats in the government. Mečiar was reelected chair in June 2007.

In 2006 the L'S-HZDS joined *Smer* and the SNS in Fico's center-left governing coalition. Relations between Fico and Mečiar were tense, notably over the dismissal of L'S-HZDS deputy Miroslav Jureňa from his post as agriculture minister (see Current issues), but not destructive to the partnership.

In June 2008, weakened by a series of parliamentary defections and trying to expand its ageing support base, the L'S-HZDS endeavored to gain the initiative over *Smer* on a series of social measures, including childbirth contributions. However, analysts suggested that Mečiar's party faced difficulty in attracting new voters in competition with the younger and the less controversial leadership of Fico. This likely contributed to the restructuring of the leadership during an October extraordinary party congress at which new deputy chairs, all under the age of 35, were appointed.

In the 2009 presidential election the L'S-HZDS broke with its coalition partners to support independent candidate Milan MELNIK. Melnik won 2.5 percent of the ballot in the first round.

Leaders: Vladimír MEČIAR (Chair and 1999 and 2004 presidential candidate); Josef HABÁNIK, Peter SIKA, Barbora STRAKOVÁ (Deputy Chairs); Ivana KAPRÁLIKOVÁ (Secretary).

Slovak National Party (*Slovenská Národná Strana*—SNS). Founded in December 1989, the SNS is an intensely nationalist and anti-Hungarian formation defining itself as Christian, national, and social. In the 1990 National Council balloting it received 13.9 percent of the vote but took only 7.9 percent in June 1992, after which it entered into a coalition with the HZDS. It continued to support the government after the resignation of its sole minister in March 1993 and in October resumed formal coalition status, obtaining several key ministries. Its moderate wing, led by Chair L'udovit Černák, broke away in February 1994 (see NDS-NA, under SDKÚ, below), and the SNS went into opposition after the fall of the Mečiar government in March. In May the SNS Central Council decided that only ethnic Slovaks could be members of the party, which was awarded two portfolios in the coalition formed in December 1994 after winning 9 seats in the preceding election. The party advocated a "no" vote on the NATO referendum of May 1997 and joined the ZRS in backing President Mečiar's proposal for a "voluntary exchange of minorities" between Slovakia and Hungary. Its legislative representation rose to 14 in 1998 after securing 9 percent of votes.

On June 27, 1998, the Slovak Green Alternative (*Slovenská Zelených Alternatíva*—SZA), led by Zora LAZAROVÁ, merged into the SNS. (For the 1994 election the SZA had participated in a joint list with the HZDS, drawing some environmental support away from the SZS.) On the same day the Christian Social Union (*Křest'anská Socialná Únia*—KSÚ) ratified a merger agreement signed in May by the SNS's Ján Slota and the KSÚ Chair Viliam OBERHAUSER.

In the 1999 presidential election Slota drew only 2.5 percent of the popular vote, in fifth place, and at a party congress in September he lost his chairship. In March 2000 the SNS renewed its alliance with the HZDS, the two parties agreeing to work together in parliament and in an effort to force an early election. Unlike the HZDS, the SNS opposed NATO membership.

In September 2000 the National Council stripped an SNS MP, Vít'azoslav MORIC, of parliamentary immunity, and in early October he was charged with inciting ethnic and racial hatred for having proposed that "unadaptable Gypsies" be sent to "reservations." The charges were subsequently dropped.

Slota and a number of his supporters were expelled from the SNS in late 2001. They subsequently announced the establishment of a "Real SNS," although the selection of that name was challenged by the SNS proper. The Real SNS was credited with 3.7 percent of the legislative vote in 2002, while the SNS was credited with 3.3 percent. The two factions reunited in April 2005, restoring Slota as leader. The SNS was surprisingly successful in the 2006 legislative poll, securing 20 seats on a vote share of 11.7 percent. However, in a political upset on December 2, 2006, Slota's reelection as mayor of Žilina failed, despite its status as a political stronghold of the SNS. Subsequent polls revealed public frustration with Slota for his perceived failure to establish transparency in decision making.

In 2006 SNS joined *Smer* and the L'S-HZDS in Fico's center-left governing coalition, a move that increased tensions with Hungary and contributed to a rift between the Slovak government and the social democratic faction of the European Parliament (see Foreign relations). The SNS demonstrated its role as a generally pliant coalition partner by accepting three successive requests from Fico in 2008 and 2009 that SNS environment ministers resign after criticism was raised regarding the disbursement of environmental-related government contracts. Fico subsequently withdrew the ministry of the environment from the purview of the SNS. The SNS joined *Smer* in supporting President Gašparovič's 2009 reelection bid.

Leaders: Ján SLOTA (Chair); Anna BELOUSOVOVÁ (First Deputy Chair); Rudolf PUČÍK, Dušan ŠVANTNER, Valentín ŠVIDROŇ, Jaroslav PAŠKA (Deputy Chairs); Viera KRÁLIČEKOVÁ (Secretary).

Opposition Parties:

Slovak Democratic and Christian Union–Democratic Party (*Slovenská Demokratická Krest'anská Únia–Demokratická Strana*—SDKÚ-DS). Officially registered as a party on February 14, 2000, by Prime Minister Dzurinda (formerly of the KDH), the SDKÚ held its initial congress on November 18–19, 2000. Some 19 deputies and numerous government ministers affiliated with the Slovak Democratic Coalition (*Slovenská Demokratická Koalicia*—SDK) had pledged allegiance to it by the end of the year. The SDK had emerged in 1997 as a loose, philosophically diverse coalition of opposition parties, including the SDSS; the SZS; the DÚ, which dissolved in favor of the SDKÚ; and the KDH and DS, both of which withdrew in late 2000. In February 1998 the SDK evolved into an electoral alliance, and four months later it officially registered as a unified party in order to ensure that none of its constituent organizations would fail to meet the new 5 percent threshold for claiming National Council seats. As a result, the SDK secured 42 seats in the September 1998 legislative balloting (on 26 percent of the votes) and led the subsequent coalition government. Following the withdrawal of the KDH and DS in late 2000, the SDK deputies numbered 27, including those who had announced support for the new SDKÚ and 2 (including former DÚ deputy chair and "Velvet Revolution" leader Ján BUDAJ) who had recently formed the Liberal Democratic Union (*Liberálno-demokratická Únia*—LDÚ).

On August 26, 2000, the Democratic Union (*Demokratická Únia*—DÚ), one of the founding members of the SDK, officially dissolved to join the SDKÚ, as did the minor Slovak Union of Small Tradesmen, Entrepreneurs, and Farmers (*Únie Živnostníkov, Podnikatel'ov a Rolníkov*—ÚŽPR) on June 30. (The ÚŽPR, led by Pavol PROKOPOVIĆ, had cooperated with the SDK in the 1998 election, contributing 1 seat to the alliance.) The DÚ had been founded at a Bratislava congress on April 23, 1994, as a merger of two components of the coalition government that came to power the previous month: the Democratic Union of Slovakia (DÚS), led by Prime Minister Jozef Moravčík, which had originated in February as a breakaway group of the then-ruling HZDS called the Alternative of Political Realism; and the Alliance of Democrats of the Slovak Republic (*Aliancia Demokratov Slovenské Republiky*—ADSR), another HZDS splinter group formed in June 1993 by Milan Kňažko, who had been ousted as foreign minister three months earlier. Commanding the support of 18 members of the National Council at the time of the merger, the DÚS adopted a centrist orientation and sought to build an alliance of similar formations for the fall 1994 general election. It largely failed to do so, attracting only the National Democratic Party–New Alternative (*Národná Demokratická Strana–Nová Alternatíva*—NDS-NA) onto its list, which polled 8.6 percent vote share and won 15 seats. Founded in March 1994 by a moderate faction of the SNS and led by L'udovit ČERNÁK, the NDS-NA was formally absorbed by the DÚS in early 1995. In 1998 the DÚS won 12 of the SDK's 42 National Council seats.

The SDK officially dissolved in 2001; some core components formally transferred their allegiance to the SKDÚ, while the DS, SDSS, SZS, and KDH continued as independent parties. Following the 2002 legislative balloting (in which the SDKÚ finished second to the HZDS with 28 seats and 19 percent vote share), Prime Minister Dzurinda was again asked to head a coalition government.

Following his dismissal as defense minister in September 2003, SDKÚ legislator Ivan Šimko launched the Free Forum (below), the defections throwing the SDKÚ coalition into the status of a minority government. Continuing the SDKÚ slide, Eduard Kukan finished third (with 22.1 percent of the vote) as the party's candidate in the first round of presidential balloting in April 2004.

In January 2006 the SDKÚ merged with the Democratic Party (*Demokraticka Strana*—DS), the new grouping adopting the SDKÚ-DS rubric. (For information on the DS, see the 2005–2006 *Handbook*.) In the legislative election of June 2006, Prime Minister Dzurinda and the SDKÚ-DS lost to Robert Fico's *Smer,* 29.1 percent to 18.4 percent. Dzurinda said that his reforms "should continue," a rather unlikely prospect as they were one of the main causes of the voters' desire for a change in government. Opinion polls in August 2007 continued to list Dzurinda as one of the least popular political figures in the country, while Deputy Chair Iveta Radičová polled as the third "most trusted" politician.

The SDKÚ-DS declined by 1,300 members in 2007, a 15 percent loss, and in March 2008 the party ejected 14 members for challenging the leadership of Dzurinda. In July 2008 Radičová called for a "restructuring" of the party and its communications strategy.

Despite divisions on several issues, in May 2008 the SDKÚ and KDH announced a common strategy for the 2010 parliamentary election, an agreement that initially excluded the SMK following its disloyalty in supporting the ratification of the EU treaty in April (see Current issues). Dzurinda, however, suggested that the SMK partnership would eventually resume, specifically in the three parties' backing (along with the OKS, below) of a single candidate, Iveta Radičová, to challenge popular incumbent Ivan Gašparovič in the 2009 presidential election. Radičová won 38.1 percent of the vote in the first round of balloting on March 21 and 44.5 percent in the second round on April 4. Despite her loss, analysts characterized her performance as a substantial personal victory, and there was widespread speculation she might emerge as leader of the party, although she chose not to challenge Dzurinda for leadership in party primaries in May.

Leaders: Mikuláš DZURINDA (Former Prime Minister and Chair of the Party); Iveta RADIČOVÁ (2009 presidential candidate); Eduard KUKAN (Deputy Chair, Former Foreign Minister, and 2004 presidential candidate); Ivan MIKLOŠ (Deputy Chair and Former Deputy Prime Minister); Milan HORT, Pavol KUBOVIČ, Iveta RADIČOVÁ (Deputy Chairs); Štefan HUDEC (Secretary).

Christian Democratic Movement (*Křest'ansko-demokratické Hnutie*—KDH). Previously a partner of the Czech Christian Democrats, the KDH presented its own list in Slovakia for the 1990 poll. Its chair, Ján Čarnogurský, served as Slovakian prime minister following Mečiar's dismissal in April 1991. The party went into opposition after the June 1992 election but returned to government in the center-left coalition formed in March 1994. Polling a creditable 10.1 percent and winning 17 seats in the fall election, the KDH again went into opposition and subsequently rejected cooperation overtures from the ruling HZDS. In late 1996 the KDH joined with the DÚS and DS to form the Blue opposition alliance, named after the color of the EU flag to demonstrate the participants' pro-Europeanism.

Following the 1998 election the KDH strongly argued for maintaining its separate identity within the SDK. In response to the formation of the SDKÚ (an obvious rival for Christian Democratic support), the KDH withdrew from the SDK in November 2000, taking with it nine members of the National Council. Late in the month, however, it officially joined the governing coalition. A month earlier Čarnogurský had resigned the party chairship after ten years in office.

The KDH secured 8.3 percent of the votes in the 2002 legislative poll, while its presidential candidate, legislator František MIKLOŠKO, won 6.5 percent of the votes in the first round of balloting in April 2004. In February 2006 the party left the government coalition due to objections to an international treaty signed between Slovakia and the Holy See. The KDH won 8.3 percent of the vote in the 2006 legislative poll.

On February 21, 2008, four prominent members of the KDH left the party, citing dissatisfaction with its deviation from Christian Democratic ideals. On July 15 the four members submitted a successful petition to the Interior Ministry to form a new party, the Conservative Democrats of Slovakia (see below).

In the 2009 presidential elections, the KDH supported SDKÚ-DS candidate Iveta Radičová as part of a broader strategy of cooperation with other opposition parties. In September 2009 the party elected a new leader, Ján Figel', who pledged to reverse the party's declining fortunes.

Leaders: Ján FIGEL' (Chair, Former EU Commissioner); Július DOLEJS, Anton MARCINCIN, Jana ŽITŇANSKÁ, Daniel LIPŠIC, Mária SABOLOVÁ, Pavol TARCALA (Deputy Chairs); Ján ČARNOGURSKÝ (Former Prime Minister and Member of the Presidency of the Party); Pavol HRUŠOVSKÝ (Former Chair and Former Speaker of the National Council).

Party of the Hungarian Coalition (*Strana Mad'arskej Koalície—*SMK/*Magyar Koalíció Partja*—MKP). The SMK was established in June 1998 as an outgrowth of the Hungarian Coalition (*Mad'arská Koalícia*—MK). Based in Slovakia's 600,000-strong ethnic Hungarian population, the MK had been formed for the 1994 national election by three parties, of which the first two had presented a joint list in the 1990 and 1992 elections, winning 7.4 percent of the vote on the latter occasion. In the 1994 balloting the three-party alliance came in third place with 17 seats on a 10.2 percent vote share. The ethnic Hungarian parties were the only groups in favor of across-the-board support of NATO in the 1997 referendum, endorsing membership as well as the deployment of nuclear weapons and placement of foreign military bases in Slovakia. In September they called upon Prime Minister Mečiar to resign over his suggestion that Hungary and Slovakia "exchange" minorities, which had reminded them of the postwar deportations 50 years ago. The SMK captured 15 National Council seats in the September 1998 election, in which it won 9.1 percent of the vote.

In August 2000 the party called for establishment of a self-governing region in the south, threatening to withdraw its support for the Dzurinda government. The call came in the context of national plans to establish new local administrative boundaries, creating 12 regions from the current 8. Ethnic Hungarians objected, in particular, to division of the Komárno region, fearing a dilution of their political power.

The SMK secured 11.7 percent of the vote in the 2006 legislative balloting. New party elections in March 31, 2007, ousted Béla Bugár from the chair in favor of former deputy prime minister Pál Csáky.

In the 2009 presidential election, the SMK supported SDKÚ candidate Iveta Radičová.

Leaders: Pál CSÁKY (Chair); József BERÉNYI (First Deputy Chair); István ZACHARIÁS, Pál FARKAS, László MIKLÓS, Miklós DURAY, László SZIGETI, Ágnes BÍRÓ, Klára SÁRKÖZY, Imre HUGYIVÁR (Deputy Chairs); Gyula BÁRDOS (Parliamentary Leader).

Other Parties Participating in the 2006 Elections:

Free Forum (*Slobodné Fórum*—SF). The SF was formed in November 2003 by seven SDKÚ legislators under the leadership of former defense minister Ivan ŠIMKO. The new grouping subsequently opposed the SDKÚ on most issues, but a March 2004 party conference narrowly elected Zuzana Martináková as chair over Šimko. Reports also surfaced of negotiations for an SF-SDKÚ alliance in future elections. In June 2005 it was reported that Šimko and his supporters had launched a new "neo-conservative, pro-European" party called **New Christian Democracy**. Internal disagreements weakened the SF prior to the 2006 elections, in which it won 3.5 percent of the legislative vote, failing to obtain seats in parliament. In October 2007 the party launched a new Web site touting a revitalized program following Zuzana Martináková's reelection as chair on October 13. In the March 2009 presidential elections Martináková ran in the first round, winning approximately 5 percent of the vote and coming in fourth.

Leader: Zuzana MARTINÁKOVÁ.

New Citizens' Alliance (*Alliancia Nového Občana*—ANO). Launched in April 2001 by Pavol RUSKO, former director of one of the nation's most important private television stations, the ANO described itself as a centrist party. The ANO secured 8 percent of the vote and 15 seats in the 2002 general election, although it was subsequently reported that five legislators had left the party to protest the conservative stance of other parties in the coalition government. Lubo ROMO, the ANO candidate in the first round of the April 2004 presidential balloting, received only 0.1 percent of the vote. Several ANO legislators subsequently quit the party. The ANO won 1.4 percent of the legislative vote in 2006. Its popularity fell back to 0.4 percent in early 2007. Pavol Rusko, the party chair, retired from politics on September 27, 2007.

In mid-July reports surfaced that former economy minister and new ANO head Robert Nemcsics intended to set up a new center-right party, one option being to revitalize the ANO.

Leader: Robert NEMCSICS.

Communist Party of Slovakia (*Komunistická Strana Slovenska*—KSS). Descended from the original Slovak Communist Party founded in 1939, the present KSS consists of the Marxist-Leninist minority that rejected transitioning to the democratic socialist SDL' in 1990. The party won a 2.7 percent vote share in the 1994 legislative balloting and 2.8 percent in 1998. In 1999 its candidate for president attracted only 0.5 percent of the vote. The KSS improved to 6.3 percent of the vote (and 11 seats) in the 2002 legislative poll. However, it failed to secure representation in 2006 on a vote share of 3.9 percent.

On August 12, 2008, an unaffiliated candidate, Milan SIDOR began collecting signatures in preparation for a presidential bid with the support of the KSS. Earlier, in April, KSS member and former MP Dagmara BOLLOVÁ left the party in order to launch an independent run for the presidency. Bollová took 1.13 percent and Sidor 1.11 percent of the vote in the first round of balloting in March 2009.

Leader: Jozef HRDLIČKA (Chair).

Movement for Democracy (*Hnutie za Demokraciu*—HZD). The HZD was launched in 2002 by Ivan Gašparovič, a former supporter of HZDS leader and former prime minister Vladimír Mečiar. The defection was attributed to Gašparovič's anger at being left off the HZDS candidate list for the September 2002 National Council balloting. The HZD secured 3.3 percent of the vote in the legislative poll. In January 2004 the HZD merged its candidate lists with the People's Union (*L'udová únia*—L'U; see Liberal Party, below). In the presidential elections the group nominated Ivan Gašparovič, a former speaker of the National Council, as the presidential candidate of an L'U-HZD-led Confederation of the National Forces of Slovakia that also included the SNS (above) and another small grouping called **Slovak National Unity** (*Slovenská Národná Jednota*—SNJ). Gašparovič surprised most observers by finishing second in the first round of balloting with 22.3 percent of the vote and then handily defeating his former mentor Mečiar in the runoff. Following the election, Gašparovič resigned his post as chair of the HZD so as not to appear beholden to any single party, although honorary ties to the party are often ascribed to him. In the 2009 presidential elections the HZD supported Gašparovič's reelection bid, although he ran as an independent candidate.

Polls in early 2009 suggested that only 1 percent of the electorate would support the HZD in a parliamentary election. Party leader Joseph Grapa subsequently outlined plans at midyear to compete in the local elections scheduled for November, proposing an electoral coalition with *Smer* that would strengthen the position of the HZD.

Leaders: Josef GRAPA (Chair), Ivan GAŠPAROVIČ (President of the Republic and Honorary Chair of the Party).

Liberal Party (*Liberálna Strana*—LS). In May 2003, 11 legislators quit the HZDS to form the People's Union (*L'udová Únia*—L'Ú) under the leadership of former deputy prime minister Vojtecha TKÁČA. In January 2004 the party merged its candidate lists with those of the HZD but stopped presenting joint lists after disappointing results in the 2006 elections. On March 26, 2007, the party filed to change its name to the Liberal Party.

Leaders: Gustav KRAJČI (Chair and Former Minister of the Interior); Vladimír HRICKO, Ján GABRIEL (Deputy Chairs).

Small parties that contested the 2006 legislative poll unsuccessfully included the **Agrarian Party of the Provinces** (*Agrárna Strana Vidieka*—ASV); the **Civic Conservative Party** (*Občianska Konzervatívna Strana*—OKS), which is led by Peter TATÁR and which supported Iveta Radičová in the 2009 presidential elections; **Hope** (*Nádej*); the **Left Bloc** (*L'avicový Blok*—L'B); **Mission 21–New Christian Democracy** (*Misia 21–Nová Kresť anská Demokracia—Misia* 21); the **Party of Civil Solidarity** (*Strana Občianskej Solidarity*—S.O.S.); **Slovak Prosperity** (*Prosperita Slovenska*—PS); the **Slovak National Coalition–Slovak Mutuality** (*Slovenská Národná Koalícia–Slovenská Vzájomnosť*—SLNKO); and the **Slovak People's Party** (*Slovenská L'udova Strana*—SL'S).

Other Parties:

Conservative Democrats of Slovakia (*Konzervatívni Demokrati Slovenska*—KDS). In February 2008 four MPs left the KDH over disagreements with its leader about the potential for forming a coalition with *Smer* and dissatisfaction with the party's ideological direction. The KDS described itself at its founding as based on conservative, national, and Christian principles. One of its founders, former speaker František Mikloško, contested the 2009 presidential election. He came in third in the first round of balloting, winning 5.4 percent of the vote.

Leaders: Vladimír PALKO (Leader), František MIKLOŠKO (2009 presidential candidate).

Party of Civic Understanding (*Strana Občianskeho Porozumenia*—SOP). Founded in February 1998 by former foreign minister Juraj HAMŽÍK and populist Košice Mayor Rudolf Schuster, the SOP supports a "civil society" and an "orientation toward North Atlantic structures." Schuster, a member of the small Carpathian-German minority, served as speaker of the parliament during and shortly after the Velvet Revolution of 1989. Upon his inauguration as president of Slovakia in June 1999, Schuster resigned as SOP chair; he was succeeded by Pavol Hamžík on June 26.

The SOP apparently did not present candidates in the 2002 legislative elections, and it was reported in 2003 that the party had aligned with *Smer*. When Schuster failed to garner *Smer*'s support for his presidential reelection campaign, he ran as an independent, securing 7.9 percent of the vote. Schuster subsequently announced his retirement from politics, and the SOP was described as defunct, its members reportedly having been absorbed into *Smer.*

Green Party (*Strana Zelených*—SZ). Founded in December 1989 as the Green Party in Slovakia (*Strana Zelených na Slovensku*—SZS), the SZ failed to secure federal parliamentary representation in 1990 but obtained six seats in the Slovak National Council. Having lost all six in the 1992 balloting, the party regained two seats in 1994 as part of the Common Choice coalition. In 1998 the Greens won three SDK seats, agreeing in late 2000 to work with the newly formed LDÚ on leftist concerns. The SZ adopted its current designation in January 2006.

In a move that was widely seen as a means for *Smer* to improve its environmental credentials, in March 2008 the SZ signed an agreement with *Smer,* pledging to cooperate on drawing up environment legislation. However, Fico and (then) SZ Chair Pavel PETRIK denied that the agreement was a step on the road to a merger. The SZ won 2.1 percent of the vote in the 2009 European Parliament elections.

Leaders: Peter PILINSKÝ (Chair), Ivan HIRLÄNDER (Deputy Chair), Martin JÓNA (Secretary).

Freedom and Solidarity (*Sloboda a Solidarita*—SaS). Founded in February 2009 by economist Richard Sulík, the SaS called for economic and social liberalism. It won 4.7 percent of the vote in the June European Parliament elections.

Leader: Richard SULIK (Chair).

Most–Híd (*Most–Híd*—MH). This party was founded in June 2009 by Béla Bugár, the former president of the SMK. The party's name, which translates as "bridge" in both Hungarian and Slovak, is symbolic of its platform. Bugár described the MH as a moderate formation representing the interests of the ethnic Hungarian minority in cooperation with Slovak parties.

Leaders: Béla BUGÁR (President), Rudolf CHMEL (Vice President).

There are 90 or more specifically Romany (Gypsy) parties and nongovernmental organizations in Slovakia. Over the years numerous efforts have been made to form a more unified coalition. In October 2000, 14 parties and 29 civic groups announced that they would present a uniform platform to contest the general election scheduled for 2002 and that candidates would run under the banner of the oldest and largest of the Romany parties, the **Romany Civic Initiative** (*Rómska Občanská Iniciatíva*—ROI), founded in 1990 and led by Gejza ADAM. (Adam was dismissed as the ROI chair in March 2001; he was replaced by Milan MIZIC.) On October 23 another leading Romany party, the **Romany Initiative of Slovakia** (*Rómska Iniciatíva Slovenska*—RIS), led by Alexander PATKOLÓ, announced a cooperation agreement with the HZDS, the Romany party having withdrawn in July from a similar agreement with the SDK, which it had accused of failing to keep commitments. Until a February 2000 congress the RIS had been known as the Romany Intelligentsia for Coexistence (*Rómska Inteligencia za Spolunažívanie*—RIZS). A leadership dispute between Patkoló and the party's previous chair, Ladislav FÍZIK, had led to a major rupture in the organization. Adam claimed the support of Fízik for the ROI-led 2002 electoral initiative.

LEGISLATURE

The unicameral **National Council of the Slovak Republic** (*Národná Rada Slovenské Republiky*) consists of 150 members directly elected via proportional representation in one countrywide constituency for four-year terms. Parties must secure at least 5 percent of the vote to achieve representation. Following the most recent balloting of June 17, 2006, the seats were distributed as follows: Direction–Social Democracy, 50; the Slovak Democratic and Christian Union–Democratic Party, 31; the Slovak National Party, 20; the Party of the Hungarian Coalition, 20; the People's Party–Movement for a Democratic Slovakia, 15; and the Christian Democratic Movement, 14.

Speaker: Pavol PAŠKA (*Smer*).

CABINET

[as of October 1, 2009]

Prime Minister	Robert Fico (*Smer*)
Deputy Prime Ministers	Dušan Čaplovič (*Smer*)
	Robert Kaliňák (*Smer*)
	Viera Petríková (L'S-HDZS)
	Ján Mikolaj (SNS)
Ministers	
Agriculture	Vladimír Chovan (L'S-HDZS)
Construction and Regional Development	Igor Štefanov (SNS)
Culture	Marek Maďarič (*Smer*)
Defense	Jaroslav Baška (*Smer*)
Economy	L'ubomír Jahnátek (*Smer*)
Education	Ján Mikolaj (SNS)
Environment (Acting)	Dúsan Čapolovič (*Smer*)
European Affairs, Human Rights, and Minorities	Dúsan Čapolovič (*Smer*)
Finance	Ján Počiatek (*Smer*)
Foreign Affairs	Miroslav Lajčák (*Smer*)
Health	Richard Raši (*Smer*)
Interior	Robert Kaliňák (*Smer*)
Justice	Viera Petríková (L'S-HDZS)
Labor, Social Affairs, and Family	Viera Tomanová (*Smer*) [f]
Transport, Posts, and Telecommunications	L'ubomir Vážny (*Smer*)

[f] = female

COMMUNICATIONS

Press. The following dailies are published in Slovak in Bratislava, unless otherwise noted: *Nový Čas* (New Time, 150,000), German-owned independent; *Pravda* (Truth, 65,000), former Communist Party organ, now independent; *Slovenská Republika* (80,000), right-wing; *SME* (We Are, 95,000); *Uj Szó* (New Word, 28,000), in Hungarian;

Hospodárske Noviny (Economic News, 22,000); *Národná Obroda* (National Renewal, 21,000), independent; *Večerník* (Evening Paper, 30,000); *Slovenský Východ* (Slovak East, Košice, 30,000); *Košický Večer* (Košice Evening, 25,000); *Hlas L'udu* (Voice of the People, 20,000).

News agencies. Before independence the state-owned Czechoslovak News Agency (*Československá Tisková Kanceláø*—ČTK, or *Četeka*) was divided into separate Czech and Slovak concerns, with the latter being renamed the News Agency of the Slovak Republic (*Tlačová Agentúra Slovenskej Republiky*—TASR) in November 1992. A private Slovak News Agency (*Slovenská Tlačová Agentúra*—SITA) has also operated since 1997. A number of foreign agencies also maintain offices in Bratislava.

Broadcasting and computing. The former federal broadcasting structure ended on January 1, 1993, when the state-funded Slovak Radio (*Slovenský Rozhlas*), with two national networks, and Slovak Television (*Slovenská Televízia*), with two channels, assumed full responsibility in Slovakia. The strict government control of the Communist era had ended in 1991, when the supervision of broadcasting was transferred to authorities approved by the respective parliaments, which subsequently authorized the licensing of independent radio and television stations.

As of 2008 there were 660.5 Internet users per 1,000 inhabitants.

INTERGOVERNMENTAL REPRESENTATION

Ambassador to the U.S.: Peter BURIAN.

U.S. Ambassador to the Slovak Republic: (Vacant).

Permanent Representative to the UN: Miloš KOTEREC.

IGO Memberships (Non-UN): BIS, CEI, CERN, CEUR, EBRD, EIB, EU, Eurocontrol, ICC, Interpol, IOM, NATO, OECD, OSCE, PCA, WCO, WTO.

SLOVENIA

Republic of Slovenia
Republika Slovenija

Political Status: Former constituent republic of the Socialist Federal Republic of Yugoslavia; independence declared June 25, 1991, on the basis of a referendum held December 23, 1990; present constitution adopted December 23, 1991.

Area: 7,818 sq. mi. (20,251 sq. km.).

Population: 1,964,036 (2002C); 2,033,000 (2008E).

Major Urban Centers (2005E): LJUBLJANA (256,000), Maribor (92,000).

Official Language: Slovene.

Monetary Unit: Euro (market rate December 1, 2009: 1 euro = $1.51US). Slovenia adopted the euro as its official currency on January 1, 2007. Its former currency was the tolar.

President: Danilo TÜRK (nonparty); directly elected in balloting of October 21 and November 11, 2007, and inaugurated for a five-year term on December 22, succeeding Janez DRNOVŠEK (elected as a member of Liberal Democracy of Slovenia).

President of the Executive Council (Prime Minister): Borut PAHOR (Social Democrats); nominated by the president on November 3, 2008, following the legislative election of September 21 and sworn in on November 7 (following approval the same day by the National Assembly) to succeed Janez JANŠA (Slovenian Democratic Party); formed new coalition government on November 24 following approval by the National Assembly on November 21.

THE COUNTRY

Located in the extreme northwest of post-World War II Yugoslavia, with a short Adriatic coastline south of Trieste, Slovenia is bordered on the west by Italy, on the south and east by Croatia, on the northeast by Hungary, and on the north by Austria. The population is predominantly Slovene (90.5 percent), with small Croat, Serb, Magyar (Hungarian), and Italian minorities. About 82 percent of the population is declared Roman Catholic. Women and men are equal participants in the labor force.

While many of its people were engaged in farming and animal husbandry, Slovenia was the most industrialized and economically advanced of the former Yugoslav republics, with substantial output of iron, steel, automotive products, cement, and sulfuric acid. It produced over 20 percent of Yugoslavia's GDP, despite having only 8 percent of the federation's population, and had a per capita GDP double that of Yugoslavia as a whole. Agriculture continues to account for 5 percent of GDP, compared to 39 percent for industry. Leading manufactures include transport equipment, textiles, and chemicals and pharmaceuticals. Tourism is another significant contributor to the economy. The European Union (EU) now accounts for about two-thirds of trade, with Germany and Italy in the lead.

Slovenia's industrial production declined by 21 percent in 1991 (to its 1975 level), while GDP fell by 9 percent and inflation soared to over 200 percent. However, its economy recovered more quickly than the other independent republics of the former Yugoslavia. GDP growth was steady throughout most of the 1990s, averaging close to 4 percent in 1995–1998 and reaching 4.9 percent in 1999. GDP growth was 3.5 percent in 2004. Consumer price inflation has remained under 10 percent annually since 1996, even after the introduction of a value-added tax in 1999, while unemployment has declined. In 2003 unemployment was 7.2 percent, while inflation was 3.5 percent. As one of the "fast track" Eastern European candidates for EU membership, Slovenia liberalized foreign investment regulations and privatized state enterprises such as banking, insurance, and telecommunications. In 2002 Slovenia removed all remaining restrictions on foreign investment in the country.

In March 2003 Slovenian voters approved a referendum on EU membership, and the country formally joined the organization on May 1, 2004. In 2005 the government announced new privatization initiatives and further economic reforms to prepare for the adoption of the euro as Slovenia's currency in 2007. Slovenia is the most prosperous country to emerge from the former Yugoslavia. GDP grew by 3.9 percent in 2005, while inflation was a low 1 percent, and healthy growth has been forecast by the Slovenian Central Bank into 2008. Additionally, in May 2006 unemployment hit its lowest level since independence, at 6.3 percent. In January 2007 Slovenia became the first Eastern or Central European state to adopt the euro as its currency. Slovenia's economy continued to expand through 2007. GDP growth was 6.1 percent, while inflation remained low at 3.8 percent and unemployment was 4.9 percent; however, GDP growth declined to 3.5 percent in 2008, unemployment was 4.4 percent, and inflation was 5.7 percent. In its *Doing Business* 2009 report, the World Bank ranked Slovenia 54 out of 181 countries for ease of doing business. The economy went into recession in the last quarter of 2008, and the Central Bank forecast that GDP would decline by 4 percent in 2009 because of the global economic slowdown. Meanwhile, the deficit was expected to expand in 2008 because of lower tax revenues and increased public spending.

GOVERNMENT AND POLITICS

Political background. Previously consisting of a number of Austrian crown lands, modern Slovenia was included in the Kingdom of the Serbs, Croats, and Slovenes, which was officially renamed Yugoslavia in October 1929. During World War II it was divided between Germany, Hungary, and Italy, and in 1945 it became a constituent republic of the Yugoslavian federation.

After 45 years of Communist one-party rule, a six-party Democratic Opposition of Slovenia (*Demokratične Opozicije Slovenije*—Demos) obtained a majority of legislative seats in the tricameral Slovenian Assembly in balloting on April 8 and 22, 1990, with Demos leader Lojze PETERLE being named president of the Executive Council (prime minister) on May 16. However, in the contest for president of the republic the former Communist leader, Milan KUČAN, outpolled three competitors by winning 44.5 percent of the vote in the first round and defeated the runner-up, Demos candidate Jože PUČNIK, with a 58.7 percent vote share in the second. On July 2 the assembly issued a declaration of full sovereignty for the Slovene Republic, and in a referendum on December 23 an overwhelming majority of voters opted for independence.

On February 20, 1991, the assembly approved a resolution announcing the phased "dissociation of Slovenia from Yugoslavia," and on June 25 Slovenia joined neighboring Croatia in issuing a formal declaration of independence. A brief war ensued with federal Yugoslav forces, resulting in the withdrawal of the latter after ten days of relatively minor skirmishing. Having achieved its primary objective, the Demos coalition proved unstable and was formally dissolved in December 1991. This left what became the Party of Democratic Reform (*Stranka Demokratične Prenove*—SDP) and the Liberal Democratic Party (*Liberalna Demokratična Slovenije*—LDS)—with the former having descended from the League of Communists and the latter from the former Communist youth organization—more strongly represented than any other grouping. Even so, Peterle, leader of the conservative Slovenian Christian Democrats (*Slovenski Krščanski Demokrati*—SKD), remained premier.

In early 1992 the government encountered criticism for the slow pace of economic reform, and on April 22 Peterle was obliged to resign upon passage of a parliamentary vote of no confidence. The assembly thereupon named Janez DRNOVŠEK of the LDS to form a new government, which, after being installed on May 14, announced a program that included reducing inflation and unemployment, privatizing the economy, and establishing linkages with international financial institutions.

Despite major problems arising from economic restructuring, the LDS became the strongest parliamentary party in the first post-independence general election, held on December 6, 1992, with the SKD taking second place. In simultaneous presidential balloting, Kučan, abandoning his party affiliation, was returned for a five-year term by 63.8 percent of the vote against seven other candidates. The governmental outcome was the formation of a new center-left coalition under the continued incumbency of Drnovšek, with Peterle as deputy premier and foreign minister.

The new Drnovšek government reaffirmed its commitment to the "Economic Policy Program" aimed at galvanizing the private sector, reforming fiscal legislation, restructuring the banking system, and rehabilitating state-owned enterprises. However, in the face of considerable opposition to any dramatic break with past practices, it took a cautious line in its economic reform, preferring to adapt existing structures rather than abolish them. Observers noted that the center-left cabinet included former Communists in all the key economic portfolios. Moreover, President Kučan, once Slovenia's Communist leader, retained considerable personal influence (and public popularity), even though the 1991 constitution reduced the presidency to a largely symbolic role.

In June 1993 the president and various ministers became involved in a major arms-trading scandal when some 120 tons of weaponry were discovered at Ljubljana's Maribor airport, apparently en route from Saudi Arabia to the Bosnian Muslims in contravention of a United Nations (UN) embargo. Amid conflicting allegations as to who had instigated the shipment, the affair became a power struggle between Defense Minister Janez JANŠA of the Social Democratic Party of Slovenia (*Socialdemokratična Stranka Slovenije*—SDS) and President Kučan, with the former depicting the episode as characteristic of the corrupt practices surrounding the ex-Communist ruling clique. The confrontation persisted until March 1994, when reported misconduct by military police under the defense minister's authority prompted the prime minister to dismiss Janša from the government, whereupon the SDS joined the opposition.

The transfer to opposition of the SDS was not seen as affecting survival of the Drnovšek government, which continued to command a parliamentary majority. Indeed, prior to the ouster Drnovšek had consolidated his assembly support by restructuring the LDS, now called the Liberal Democracy of Slovenia (*Liberalna Demokracija Slovenije*—LDS), to include elements of three smaller parties, two with parliamentary representation.

The SKD's participation in the ruling coalition became strained in 1994, culminating in the resignation of Peterle from his government posts in September to protest the selection of an LDS deputy to be the new president of the National Assembly. Other Christian Democrats continued to hold important portfolios, however, and the government remained secure in the National Assembly. More ominous for the LDS was the withdrawal of the United List of Social Democrats (*Združena Lista Socialnih Demokratov*—ZLSD) from the coalition in January 1996 (in protest against the prime minister's move to dismiss a ZLSD minister), while in May a parliamentary nonconfidence vote against the foreign minister, Zoran THALER, obliged Drnovšek to make a new appointment to the post.

In assembly balloting on November 10, 1996, the LDS remained the largest single party but fell back to 25 seats out of 90, while a center-right Slovenian Spring (*Slovenije Pomladi*—SP) alliance of the Slovenian People's Party (*Slovenska Ljudska Stranka*—SLS), the SDS, and the SKD won a combined total of 45 seats. Drnovšek was asked to remain as head of a caretaker government, and he immediately announced his intention to form a new government comprised of the LDS and the other non-SP parties. However, the 45–45 parliamentary split between the SP and the LDS-allied parties delayed not only the quick formation of a new government, but also the election of a permanent prime minister. The latter stalemate was finally broken in early January 1997 when an SKD deputy announced support for Drnovšek, who was reelected on January 9 by a vote of 46–44. Nevertheless, wrangling over the formation of a new cabinet continued for some seven weeks until the SLS broke with the SP to participate with the LDS and the small Slovenian Democratic Party of Pensioners (*Demokratična Stranka Upokojencev Slovenije*—DeSUS) in a government approved on February 27. Subsequently, President Kučan easily won reelection to a second five-year term on November 23, 1997, taking 55 percent of the vote in a field of eight candidates in the first-round balloting, thereby avoiding a runoff.

Drnovšek survived two nonconfidence votes in May and December 1998, both relating to claims by opposition leader Janša that the prime minister knew about a secret 1995 security agreement with Israel and failed in his constitutional duty to make it public. In the December election the opposition could muster only 24 votes in the 90-seat National Assembly.

On March 15, 2000, nine SLS ministers announced that they would leave the government on April 15, at which time the SLS and the SKD would merge in preparation for an autumn general election. With the SLS controlling 19 of the government's 49 seats in the National Assembly, Prime Minister Drnovšek faced the imminent demise of his government. On April 3 he proposed adding eight nonparty experts to the cabinet, but lack of support forced his resignation on April 8. The unified center-right SLS+SKD Slovenian People's Party (*SLS+SKD Slovenska Ljudska Stranka*—SLS+SKD) put forward Andrej BAJUK as his successor, but Bajuk, an economist with the Inter-American Development Bank who had spent all but a fraction of his life abroad, twice failed to win majority support in the legislature, obtaining 44 votes on April 20—2 shy of the required 46—and then 43 on April 26. Following negotiation of a coalition agreement with the SDS, Bajuk won confirmation, 46–44, on May 3, although on May 23 the legislature split evenly on his proposed cabinet, which did not win approval until June 7, also by a 46–44 vote. The new government included eight SLS+SKD ministers, five SDS ministers, and five independents.

The government suffered a serious rupture in late July 2000 when the majority of the SLS+SKD, but not Prime Minister Bajuk, reversed course and joined the LDS in backing retention of proportional representation in the National Assembly. (In a 1996 binding referendum the public had endorsed a majoritarian system, but the legislature had failed to enact the change because of opposition from the left.) As a result, the SDS ended its agreement with the SLS+SKD, and on July 27 President Kučan called an election for October. In the interim, Prime Minister Bajuk left the SLS+SKD and formed the New Slovenia–Christian People's Party (*Nova Slovenija–Krščanska Ljudska Stranka*—NSi), which quickly formed an electoral coalition with the SDS.

In the October 15, 2000, balloting the LDS won a plurality of 34 seats, thereby permitting Prime Minister Drnovšek's return to power in November as the head of a four-party coalition that also included the ZLSD, the SLS+SKD, and the DeSUS. Easily confirmed by the National Assembly on November 17, Drnovšek fashioned a restructured cabinet comprised of nine LDS ministers and three each from the ZLSD and the SLS+SKD. In addition, the ZLSD chair, Borut PAHOR, took over as president of the legislature.

In runoff balloting on December 1, 2002, Prime Minister Drnovšek won the presidency of Slovenia, capturing about 56.5 percent of the vote against Barbara BREZIGAR, a state prosecutor. Drnovšek resigned as prime minister the next day, and on December 6 President Kučan (who had been barred from seeking a third term) nominated Finance Minister Anton ROP (LDS) as the new prime minister. Confirmed by the National Assembly on December 19, Rop and his cabinet took office on December 20. President Drnovšek was sworn in on December 22 and assumed his duties the following day.

The main priorities of the new president and government were finalizing Slovenia's entry into both the North Atlantic Treaty Organization (NATO) and the EU. In November 2002 Slovenia was invited to join NATO along with six other countries, and in December 2002 Slovenia was one of ten countries that were offered EU membership. At a national referendum on March 23, 2003, voters approved entry into both organizations. EU membership was approved by 89.6 percent of the voters, while NATO membership was supported by 66.1 percent. On March 29, 2004, Slovenia joined NATO, and on May 1 it became a member of the EU.

In 2004 the assembly enacted controversial legislation to grant Slovenian citizenship to refugees from the former Yugoslavia (see Current issues, below). Opposition groups argued against the measure, which undermined public support for the LDS-led government and prompted the SLS (the SLS+SKD having returned to the SLS rubric) to withdraw from the government on April 7, 2004. The issue was also prominent in European parliamentary elections on June 13, 2004, in which the opposition NSi received 23.5 percent of the vote and two seats, while an alliance of the LDS and the DeSUS secured 21.9 percent and two seats; the SDS, 17.7 percent and two seats; and the ZLSD, 14.2 percent and one seat. Previously, on February 26, 2004, the National Assembly had approved legislation that required 40 percent of party candidates for the EU seats to be female.

In addition to the unpopular citizenship policy, the ruling coalition faced problems over internal strife surrounding the 2004 legislative elections. On June 24 Rop requested that the assembly approve a no-confidence vote for Foreign Minister Dimitrij RUPEL, whom the prime minister accused of cooperating with the opposition. The assembly removed Rupel through such a vote on July 5 (Rupel subsequently joined the SDS).

In the legislative elections on October 3, 2004, the SDS became the largest party in the legislature when it received 29.1 percent of the vote and 29 seats in the assembly, while the LDS only secured 22.8 percent and 23 seats. SDS leader Janez Janša was subsequently nominated by the president to form a government, and his new cabinet, which included the SDS, NSi, DeSUS, and SLS, was approved by the assembly on December 3.

Incumbent President Drnovšek announced that he would not seek reelection due to ill health in February 2007. (Drnovšek died on February 23, 2008, of cancer.) Seven candidates contested the first round of presidential balloting on October 21. Former prime minister Lojze Peterle, an independent supported by the SDS, the SLS, and the NSi, placed first with 28.73 percent of the vote. Independent Danilo TÜRK came in second with 24.47 percent of the vote. Türk was endorsed by the SD, DeSUS, Active Slovenia (*Aktivna Slovenia*—AS), and For Real (*Zares*). In the second round of polling on November 11, Türk won with 68.03 percent of the vote to Peterle's 31.97 percent. He assumed office on December 22. Meanwhile, the endorsement of Türk by the DeSUS, a member of the SDS-led government, led Janša to call for a confidence vote after the election. On November 19 the Janša government won the confidence vote by a margin of 51 to 33 votes as the DeSUS continued to support the government. The prime minister and new president subsequently pledged to work together as Slovenia assumed the rotating presidency of the EU (see Current issues, below).

In balloting for the National Assembly on September 21, 2008, the SD received 30.45 percent of the vote and 29 seats, followed by the ruling SDS with 29.26 percent and 28 seats (see Current issues, below). SD leader Borut PAHOR in November formed a coalition government that included the SD, DeSUS, LDS, and *Zares*. Meanwhile, on October 15, Pavel GANTAR of *Zares* was elected president of the National Assembly with support from the SD.

Constitution and government. The Slovenian elections of April 1990 were the first to be freely contested in former Yugoslavia in 51 years. The current constitution was adopted on December 23, 1991, and was amended by the Constitutional Act of July 14, 1997, and the Constitutional Act of July 25, 2000.

The head of state is the president, who is directly elected for a five-year term but has a largely ceremonial role. The principal executive officer is the prime minister, who is designated (and may be removed) by the National Assembly.

The 1991 document endorses basic human rights on the European model, one of the aims of the drafters having been to demonstrate Slovenia's suitability for admittance into European democratic organizations. The judiciary includes district and regional courts, with a Supreme Court at the apex. Administratively, Slovenia encompasses 210 municipalities, each consisting of 1 or more of the country's approximately 2,700 cadastral communities. Municipalities may choose to form larger districts (*upravne enote*), of which there are currently 58. Eleven large municipalities have been granted "urban status," which allows them greater autonomy. On June 22, 2008, Slovenians voted in favor of the creation of 13 regions in a nonbinding referendum that was marred by low voter turnout of 10.9 percent.

Foreign relations. The European Community (EC, later the EU) recognized the independence of both Croatia and Slovenia on January 15, 1992, with the two countries establishing diplomatic relations on February 17. (Relations with Yugoslavia were not normalized until December 8, 2000.) On May 23 Slovenia joined Croatia and Bosnia and Herzegovina in gaining admission to the UN, having two months earlier become a member of the Conference on (later Organization for) Security and Cooperation in Europe (CSCE/OSCE).

In March 1992 Slovenia was admitted to membership of the Central European Initiative (CEI), becoming active in efforts to revive the Slovenian and Italian Adriatic ports as entrepôts for the CEI countries. Slovenian officials recalled that the Trieste-Vienna railway, running through Slovenia, had been one of the first built in continental Europe and saw the CEI as a framework for recreating the economic links of the imperial era. In the longer term, Slovenia aspired to membership in the EC/EU, as did the other non-EU CEI states. On January 15, 1993, it became a member of the International Monetary Fund (IMF), and in May it was admitted to membership of the Council of Europe. In February 1994 Slovenia joined the Partnership for Peace program launched by NATO the previous month for former Communist and neutral states.

Slovenia contributed troops to the international peacekeeping mission in Bosnia. In addition, Slovenia was instrumental in creating the International Fund for Demining and Mine Victims' Assistance to support demining operations in Bosnia. In March 2004 Slovenia deployed troops and equipment to Afghanistan as part of the UN-led peacekeeping operation. In August firefighting units were also sent to Kabul, Afghanistan, to train locals.

Unresolved border disputes have strained Slovenia's postindependence relations with Croatia. The issue flared up in October 1994 when the Slovenian Assembly adopted local boundary changes that assigned territory claimed by Croatia to the Slovenian municipality of Piran. Although the Slovenian government quickly called for revision of the measure, Croatia lodged an official protest. Talks at the prime ministerial level in June 1995 were reported to have yielded agreement on "98 percent" of land and maritime border issues. However, relations cooled in December 1997 when Croatia amended its constitution, dropping Slovenes from a list of recognized ethnic minorities and raising suspicions about Zagreb's intentions.

Notwithstanding their bilateral territorial dispute, Slovenia and Croatia remained in agreement on the need to resist any revival of irredentism on the part of Italy, which had long pressed the issue of compensation for Italians whose property in Istria had been appropriated following post–World War II border changes that favored Yugoslavia. The pressure on Slovenia intensified with the advent of the right-wing Berlusconi government in Italy in May 1994, with Rome making it clear that it would block Slovenia's EU membership aspirations until it obtained satisfaction. However, following the fall of Berlusconi in December, the new nonparty Italian government lifted the veto on March 4, 1995, enabling Slovenia to commence associate membership talks with the EU, which were assisted by Spanish mediation on the dispute with Italy. Following the resolution of most outstanding issues, Slovenia signed an association agreement with the EU in June 1996, also lodging an application for full EU membership. In the same month Slovenia became an "associate partner" of the Western European Union (WEU), seeing such status as a necessary precursor to the goal of NATO membership. Subsequently, in February 1998, Slovenia agreed to compensate 21,000 ethnic Italians for property they left behind when they fled to Italy at the end of World War II.

At the NATO Summit Meeting in Prague, on November 21–22, 2002, with formal notification following a few days later, Slovenia was invited to begin accession talks for NATO membership along with six other countries: Bulgaria, Estonia, Latvia, Lithuania, Romania, and Slovakia. On March 29, 2004, Slovenia became a member of NATO, and on May 1 it joined the EU. The assembly approved the proposed EU Constitution on February 2, 2005.

Once in office in December 2004, the Janša government announced its intention to maintain close ties with the United States. (Tension between the two countries over the International Criminal Court had strained what had previously been very good relations.) The administration also pursued deeper ties with Romania, actively working to aid Romania's successful quest to join the EU.

In response to complaints from Slovenia and other new EU members, the European Central Bank called in February 2007 for countries such as Germany and France to remove restrictions on the migration of workers from the Central and Eastern European states. Subsequently, in April, Slovenia and Greece signed three bilateral agreements on maritime transport, coordination of oceanographic services, and tourism.

On January 1, 2008, Slovenia assumed the rotating presidency of the EU. The country's priorities during its presidency were ratification of the Lisbon Treaty by the EU member states, increased economic integration, and addressing climate change. Slovenia ratified the Lisbon Treaty on January 29. Slovenia also championed EU membership for Macedonia but was unable to secure an agreement to open accession discussions because of opposition from Greece (see article on Greece). In December the new government announced its opposition to EU membership for Croatia because of the continuing border dispute between the two countries. However, the assembly approved NATO membership for Croatia in February 2009. In May the two countries agreed to accept EU arbitration to settle the boundary controversy.

By 2009 Slovenia had become the largest foreign investor in Kosovo. In February Slovenia extended its participation in the NATO-led peacekeeping mission in Kosovo for an additional year, and in July Slovenia announced the donation of $794,000 to Kosovo for infrastructure programs as part of an ongoing aid initiative. In April the Pahor government approved the continuation of the nation's participation in the NATO mission in Afghanistan.

Current issues. Relations with neighboring Croatia took a step forward after the death of Croatian President Franjo Tudjman in December 1999 and the election of a new president, Stipe Mesič, two months later. Following talks with President Kučan during a March visit to Ljubljana, Mesič described bilateral issues as "solvable with just a little stronger will on both sides." Border concerns, including Slovenian access to Piran Bay, were largely resolved in July 2001, as was a disagreement over management of the jointly owned nuclear power plant in Krško, Slovenia. Austria also expressed concern about the safety of the nuclear facility, but a more contentious issue for Vienna and Ljubljana involved Austrian calls, particularly from the right, for Slovenia to renounce the World War II–era decrees under which the partisan-led Antifascist Council for the National Liberation of Yugoslavia (*Antifašističko Vee Narodnog Oslobodjenja Jugoslavije*—AVNOJ) expelled the German minority from Yugoslavia and confiscated German property. Although former foreign minister Dimitrij Rupel described the AVNOJ decrees as "a historic fact that cannot be changed," the two governments have been working on an agreement that would clarify the rights of the Slovene minority in Austria as well as those of ethnic Germans in Slovenia.

In 2004 the assembly passed legislation, requested by the Supreme Court, which granted citizenship to residents of Slovenia who had immigrated from other areas of the former Yugoslavia and who had lost their legal status because they failed to apply for citizenship within a six-month grace period following Slovenian independence. (This group became known as the "erased" since they were struck from the census records and therefore were ineligible for government benefits and services.) Conservative and opposition parties forced a national referendum on the issue, and on April 4, 2004, voters overwhelmingly rejected the citizenship law with 94 percent voting against amnesty. The government and LDS had urged citizens to boycott the referendum and turnout was low at 31 percent. Interior Minister Rado BOHINC vowed to continue registering the erased, and the Supreme Court subsequently ruled that the referendum was illegal.

Ongoing disputes with Croatia over the border continued in 2005–2006, with the most recent issue being that of demarking fishing areas in the Adriatic Sea (the talks over that issue also included Italy). Additionally, the two countries maintain overlapping claims in the Bay of Piran, Slovenia's only deepwater access to the Adriatic. On the energy front, negotiations continued with Russia's Gazprom to construct a natural gas pipeline through Slovenia into Italy. Talks were also under consideration with the United States concerning the possible construction of an oil pipeline between the Black Sea and the Adriatic Sea through Slovenia.

Further integration into Europe is a major goal of the current administration, as is general expansion of trade opportunities globally. Among other things, Slovenia is seeking to capitalize upon its location as a natural crossroads between Eastern and Western Europe.

One long-term economic problem that Slovenia shares with other EU members is growing pension and retirement spending. In 2003, 500,000 Slovenians, or one-quarter of the population, were pensioners. In that year pension expenditures accounted for 13 percent of GDP, a figure that is projected to rise to 18 percent by 2020. In 2006 the government indexed pensions to inflation, thereby creating automatic increases in payments and adding an additional financial strain on the system.

In November 2006 villagers forced a number of Roma from their homes in the village of Ambrus, and the Roma were resettled in refugee centers. A controversial plan was subsequently announced to relocate more than 600 Roma. The EU and human rights groups denounced the initiative.

Prime Minister Janša's government initiated a range of economic reforms, including tax reductions, following its installation in 2004. However, its privatization program subsequently stalled, and the government faced calls from the EU and the IMF to reduce state involvement in the banking and financial sectors. Nevertheless, when Slovenia adopted the euro as its currency in 2007, the EU roundly praised the government's management of the changeover.

A dispute between President Drnovšek and Prime Minister Janša prevented the election of a new central bank governor for more than three months in 2007. Tensions between the president and prime minister also led Drnovšek to skip the country's official independence day celebrations on June 24. Drnovšek subsequently announced that he would not be a candidate in the presidential balloting scheduled for October 21 for health reasons.

In the summer of 2008 bribery allegations emerged against Janša over a defense agreement between Slovenia and Finland. Janša was accused by Finnish reporters of accepting cash payments to approve the procurement deal which, at $402 million, was the largest in Slovenian history. Janša strongly denied the charges. In September the National Assembly debated the allegations and conducted a confidence vote, which the government won with 41 votes in favor and 11 opposed. The charges emerged as a significant factor in the campaign for the assembly election on September 21. The SD won one more seat in the balloting than the ruling SDS; however, the SD did not secure a majority and negotiations continued until November 3, when SD leader Pahor was nominated as prime minister of an SD-led coalition government supported by 50 deputies in the assembly. In December President Türk rejected 7 of 13 ambassadorial appointments that had been made by the previous SDS government.

In April 2009 the Pahor government announced deep cuts in defense spending in order to shift resources to social programs as a recession cut government revenues. In elections for the European Parliament on June 7, the SDS retained its two seats, while the SD gained one to bring its total to two. The NSi, the LDS and *Zares* each secured one seat in the balloting, which saw a voter turnout rate of 28.33 percent and reflected the continuing division of public sentiment between parties of the left and right.

POLITICAL PARTIES

For four-and-a-half decades after World War II, the only authorized political party in Yugoslavia was the Communist Party, which was redesignated in 1952 as the League of Communists of Yugoslavia (*Savez Komunista Jugoslavija*—SKJ). In 1989 noncommunist groups began to emerge in the republics, and in early 1990 the SKJ approved the introduction of a multiparty system, thereby effectively triggering its own demise. The most important initial outgrowth of liberalization was the creation of the Democratic Opposition of Slovenia (*Demokratične Opozicije Slovenije*—Demos), an electoral alliance that included the Liberal Democratic Party (LDS), the Slovenian Christian Democrats (SKD, see SLS+SKD), the Slovenian Peasant League (SKZ, forerunner of the Slovenian People's Party—SLS), the Slovenian Democratic League (SDZ; see under DS), the Social Democratic League of Slovenia (SDZS; see SDS), and the Greens of Slovenia (ZS). Demos won 47 of 80 seats in the balloting for the Slovenian Socio-Political Chamber in the spring of 1990, but the coalition collapsed following independence at the end of 1991. Meanwhile, in Slovenia the SKJ's local branch was succeeded by what became the Party of Democratic Reform (*Stranka Demokratične Prenove*—SDP), whose modest electoral performance in 1992 was partly attributable to the fact that many former Communist leaders had switched to other parties. The SDP joined the new United List (ZL) electoral alliance in November 1992 but declined to join in formation of the United List of Social Democrats (ZLSD) in May 1993. (The SDP is now defunct.)

From the first postindependence general election in December 1992, no single party has been able to command a legislative majority, resulting in coalition governments of shifting membership, all headed by Prime Minister Janez Drnovšek of the LDS except for an interregnum under Andrej Bajuk (initially of the newly merged SLS–SKD Slovenian People's Party) in April–November 2000. Prior to the November 1996 election the SLS, SKD, and SDS had formed a center-right electoral alliance, Slovenian Spring (*Slovenije Pomladi*—SP), that won 45 of the National Assembly's 90 seats on a platform that advocated speedier transition to a market economy while, like the LDS, strongly favoring NATO and EU membership. Despite its near-majority, however, the SP was unable to prevent Drnovšek's reconfirmation as prime minister in January 1997, and the coalition was crippled when the SLS agreed to join the new government in late February 1997. Following the October 2000 election Drnovšek succeeded in fashioning a new 58-seat coalition headed by his LDS and also including the ZLSD, the SLS+SKD, and the Slovenian Democratic Party of Pensioners (DeSUS). The 2004 elections saw the end of LDS-dominated governments. Instead, SDS leader Janez Janša created a 49-seat coalition that included the SDS, NSi, DeSUS, and SLS+SKD.

Ahead of the September 2008 National Assembly balloting Slovenia's election commission reported that one-third of the candidates were women among the 19 parties that registered for the voting. In the balloting, the SMS and the SLS presented a joint list of candidates.

Government Parties:

Social Democrats (*Socialni Demokrati*—SD). The SD was known as the **United List of Social Democrats** (*Združena Lista Socialnih Demokratov*—ZLSD) until 2005. The ZLSD was originally formed prior to the December 1992 election as a United List (ZL) of groups deriving from the Communist era, winning 14 seats and joining a coalition headed by the LDS. The original components were the SDP, the Social Democratic Union (*Socialdemokratska Unija*—SDU), the Workers' Party of Slovenia (*Delavska Stranka Slovenije*—DSS), and the DeSUS. Of these, the SDR declined to join a formal merger creating the ZLSD in 1993, while the DeSUS reverted to independent status after the ZLSD left the government in January 1996. Advocating neutrality as an alternative to NATO membership (but favoring EU accession), the ZLSD won 9 lower house seats on a 9 percent vote share in the November balloting. In the October 2000 election it won 12 percent of the vote and 11 seats, after which it agreed to join Prime Minister Drnovšek's new government. The ZLSD secured 14.2 percent of the vote and 1 seat in the June 2004 European parliamentary elections. In the October 2004 legislative elections the ZLSD received 10.2 percent of the vote and 10 seats. Former prime minister Anton Rop and three other LDS members of parliament left the LDS to join the SD in March 2007, making the SD the largest opposition group. Party leader Borut Pahor was expected to be the SD presidential candidate in 2007, but the party instead endorsed the independent candidate Danilo Türk, who eventually won the balloting.

The SD won the legislative balloting in 2008, and party leader Pahor was named prime minister of an SD-led coalition government. Pahor was reelected party leader at a Congress in March 2009. In protest of the party opposition to Croatian entry into the EU, SD member of the EU Parliament Aurelio JURI resigned from the party in June 2009.

Leaders: Borut PAHOR (Prime Minister and Party President), Alenka KOVŠCA, Madja POTRATA, Miran POTRČ, Patrick VLAČIČ (Vice Presidents), Uroš JAUŠEVEC (General Secretary).

For Real (*Zares*). *Zares* was formed in 2007 by dissidents from the ZLSD, led by Minister of the Economy Matej Lahovnik. Six deputies of the assembly joined Lahovnik in forming the new center-left grouping, which promised a new approach to politics. **Active Slovenia** (*Aktivna Slovenia*—AS), led by Franci KEK and which won 2.97 percent of the vote in the 2004 balloting, merged with *Zares* in 2007. *Zares* supported Danilo Türk in the 2007 presidential balloting. *Zares* placed third in the assembly elections in September 2008 and secured nine seats. It subsequently joined the SD-led coalition government and was given four cabinet posts.

Leaders: Gregor GOLOBIČ, Pavel GANTAR (President of the National Assembly).

Slovenian Democratic Party of Pensioners (*Demokratična Stranka Upokojencev Slovenije*—DeSUS). Also known as the Grey Panthers, the DeSUS was a component of the leftist ZLSD (below) until opting to contest the November 1996 election in its own right, winning five seats and 4.3 percent of the vote. The party's decision to join the government in February 1997 was crucial in providing the coalition with a slim majority in the assembly. The DeSUS saw its vote share rise to 5.2 percent in 2000, but it won only four seats. It agreed to accept junior status in the subsequent LDS-led government. The DeSUS gained 4.0 percent of the vote and four seats in the 2004 elections. It joined the SDS-led coalition government. The DeSUS split with its government coalition partners and backed Danilo Türk in the 2007 presidential polling. However, the party continued to support the SDS-led coalition government. It secured seven seats in the 2008 assembly balloting and joined the SD-led coalition government. Party leader Karl Erjavec was appointed minister of the environment and physical planning.

Leaders: Karl ERJAVEC (President), Franc ŽNIDARŠIČ (Parliamentary Leader), Pavel BRGLEZ (General Secretary).

Liberal Democracy of Slovenia (*Liberalna Demokracija Slovenije*—LDS). The LDS was formed in March 1994 as a merger of the main government formation, the Liberal Democratic Party (*Liberalna Demokratična Stranka*—LDS), led by Prime Minister Drnovšek, and three small groupings: a faction of the Democratic Party (see DS, below), including three of its six deputies; all five Green deputies (see ZS, below); and the Socialist Party of Slovenia (*Socialistična Stranka Slovenije*—SSS), led by Viktor ŽAKELJ. In total the new LDS had the support of 30 deputies in the 90-member assembly, with only the SSS (descended from the front organization of the Communist era) being without legislative seats.

Descended from the former Federation of Socialist Youth of Slovenia (*Zveza Socialistična Mladina Slovenije*—ZSMS) and initially styled the ZSMS-*Liberalna Stranka,* the old LDS was formally launched in November 1990. Unlike most communist youth organizations, the ZSMS had been a substantially independent formation in support of liberal values of individual rights and freedoms since the early 1980s. Having been among the runners-up in the 1990 election, the old LDS became the strongest parliamentary party in the 1992 balloting, with its leader being named prime minister. The new LDS retained this status in November 1996 despite falling to 25 lower house seats on a 27 percent vote share.

Prime Minister Janez Drnovšek was narrowly reelected in January 1997 and subsequently succeeded in establishing a coalition government with the SLS and the DeSUS (both above). However, Bogomir KOVAČ, the LDS candidate for president in November 1997, won only 2.7 percent of the vote, putting him next to last in the eight-man field. The April 2000 departure of the SLS led to Drnovšek's resignation, although he returned to office following the October 2000 election, the LDS having won a plurality of 34 seats with 36.3 percent of the vote.

In balloting on November 10 and December 1, 2002, Drnovšek was elected president of the republic. He nominated Anton Rop as prime minister, and Rop was confirmed on December 19. In February 2003 Rop was elected president of the party.

The LDS participated in the 2004 EU elections in an alliance with the DeSUS, but the alliance performed poorly, securing 21.9 percent of the vote and 2 seats. The LDS subsequently fell to second place in the October legislative elections with 22.8 percent of the vote and 23 seats. Rop was replaced as party leader by Jelko KACIN, but the new leader was unable to overcome the deep divisions that had emerged within the party.

In January 2007 Drnovšek left the LDS, and he subsequently announced that he would not seek reelection as president of the republic. Rop and a number of other LDS members left the party in March 2007 to join the ZLSD. Other LDS desertions dropped the party's parliamentary grouping from 23 to 11. Six former ZLSD parliamentary members formed the grouping **For Real** (*Zares*) (see above), while others became independents. On June 30 Katerina Kresal was elected as the LDS president, becoming the first woman to lead a Slovenian political party. In the 2007 presidential balloting the LDS supported Mitja GASPARI, who placed third, with 24.09 percent of the vote, in the first round of balloting and therefore was excluded from the second round of voting.

The LDS secured five seats in the assembly in the 2008 legislative balloting and joined the SD-led coalition government. Kresal was appointed interior minister.

Leaders: Katerina KRESAL (President), Slavko ZIHERI (Vice President).

Other Parliamentary Parties:

Slovenian Democratic Party (*Slovenska Demokratska Stranka*—SDS). Founded in 1989 as the Social Democratic League of Slovenia (*Socialdemokratska Zevza Slovenije*—SDZS), one of the Demos participants, the SDS has described itself as a "social-democratic party in the traditions of European democracy and the social state." However, the party has adopted center-right policies and aligned itself with Christian Democrat parties and the European People's Party (EPP) in the European Parliament.

Although its presidential candidate in 1992 registered only 0.6 percent of the vote, the party won 3.3 percent and four seats in the legislative election, subsequently participating in the LDS-led coalition government. On the dismissal of party leader Janez Janša as defense minister in March 1994, the SDS joined the parliamentary opposition. In May 1995 it absorbed the National Democrats (*Narodnimi Demokrati*—ND), which had separated from the Slovenian Democratic League (SDZ) in 1991.

As part of the SP in the November 1996 balloting, the party took third place with 16 seats on a 16.1 percent vote share. It remained in opposition until formation of the SLS+SKD-led government of Andrej Bajuk in April 2000. Holding five ministerial portfolios, the SDS remained in the cabinet despite termination of the coalition agreement in July. For the October 2000 election the party concluded a cooperation pact, "Coalition Slovenia" (*Koalicija Slovenija*), with the new NSi (below), and went on to win 15.8 percent of the vote and 14 National Assembly seats.

In September 2003 the party changed its name from the Social Democratic Party of Slovenia (*Socialdemokratična Stranka Slovenije*) to the Slovenian Democratic Party (*Slovenska Demokratska Stranka*) but kept the initials SDS. The change was designed to align the party with center-right groups in the European Parliament, including the EPP. In the European parliamentary elections of June 2004, the SDS secured 17.7 percent of the vote and 2 seats. In the October legislative elections, the SDS became the largest parliamentary group after it won the elections with 29.1 percent of the vote and 29 seats. Party leader Janez Janša was subsequently nominated as prime minister and formed a coalition government on December 3. On May 15, 2005, Janša was reelected as party president at the Eighth SDS Congress.

In June 2007 the SDS endorsed Lojze Peterle for the 2007 presidential balloting. Despite bribery allegations (see Current issues), Janša continued to enjoy strong backing from the SDS ahead of the 2008 legislative elections. The SDS placed second in the assembly balloting with 28 seats and became the largest opposition party.

Leaders: Janez JANŠA (Former Prime Minister and Party President); Romana Jordan CIZELJ, Miha BREJC, and Milan ZVER (Vice Presidents); Jože TANKO (Parliamentary Leader); Dušan STRNAD (Secretary-General).

Slovenian National Party (*Slovenska Narodna Stranka*—SNS). The SNS is an extreme right-wing grouping that stands for a militarily strong and sovereign Slovenia, the family as the basic unit of society, and preservation and restoration of the country's cultural heritage. It won 9.9 percent of the vote and 12 lower house seats in December 1992 but entered a divisive phase in 1993 after party leader Zmago Jelinčič was named as a federal Yugoslav agent. Also contributing to party disunity were disclosures that prominent members were listed in police files as informers in the Communist era. As a result, five of its assemblymen formed an Independent SNS Deputy Group, three others launched a breakaway Slovenian National Right (*Slovenska Nacionala Desnica*—SND), and one withdrew to sit as an independent.

In the 1996 election the SNS won four seats with 3.2 percent of the vote. It again won four seats in October 2000, on a 4.4 percent vote share. In the 2004 assembly elections the SNS increased its vote share to 6.3 percent and secured six seats. Jelinčič announced his presidential candidacy in May 2007. He placed fourth in the first round of polling with 19.16 percent of the vote. In 2008 SNS Vice President Sašo PEČE led a number of members out of the SNS to form a new party, Lipa (see below). The SNS secured five seats in the 2008 assembly balloting.

Leaders: Zmago JELINČIČ (President and Parliamentary Leader), Srečko PRIJATELJ (Deputy Parliamentary Leader).

Slovenian People's Party (*Slovenska Ljudska Stranka*—SLS). The SLS is the current rubric of the party that had been named the SLS+SKD Slovenian People's Party (SLS+SKD) in April 2000 upon the merger of the longstanding SLS and the Slovenian Christian Democrats (*Slovenski Krščanski Demokrati*—SKD). The 2000 merger had occurred following the decision by nine SLS ministers to leave the government.

Claiming descent from a prewar SLS, the People's Party was founded in May 1988 as a nonpolitical Slovenian Peasant League (*Slovenska Kmečka Zveza*—SKZ), which registered as a party in January 1990. It won 11 assembly seats in 1990 as a member of Demos and adopted the SLS designation in 1991. In 1992 it won 10 legislative seats on an 8.7 percent vote share, advancing strongly to 19 seats and 19.4 percent in November 1996 as part of the Slovenian Spring (SP) alliance. The SLS's defection from the alliance in February 1997 was decisive in the formation of a new coalition government led by Prime Minister Drnovšek. SLS President Marjan PODOBNIK ran a distant second in the November 1997 presidential election with 18.4 percent of the vote.

The SKD was founded in March 1990 by a group of "non-clerical Catholic intellectuals." It was the largest component of Demos, having won 11 assembly seats in the 1990 balloting, after which Lojze Peterle became head of the government that took Slovenia to independence. He remained prime minister following the disintegration of Demos in late 1991, resigning in April 1992 after losing a nonconfidence vote on government economic policy. The SKD became the second strongest parliamentary party in the December 1992 election, winning 15 seats and joining a center-left coalition headed by the LDS, with Peterle as deputy premier. Increasing strains in 1994 yielded Peterle's resignation from the government in September, although other SKD ministers remained in office. In the November 1996 election, as part of the SP, the party slipped to fourth place, winning 10 seats and 9.6 percent of the vote. The defection of SKD deputy Ciril PUCKO broke a deadlock in January 1997, allowing Janez Drnovšek of the LDS to be reelected prime minister. In the 1997 presidential election the party's Jože BERNIK finished third with 9.4 percent of the vote.

At the congress that formally approved the merger into the SLS+SKD in 2000, Franc ZAGOŽEN, the SLS parliamentary leader, was elected party president; his deputies included Peterle and Andrej Bajuk. The new party immediately claimed a plurality of 28 seats in the 90-seat National Assembly, and on April 28 it renewed its coalition with its former SP partner, the SDS. That agreement produced assembly approval of Bajuk as prime minister on May 3, although it took until June 7 for the legislature to approve an SLS+SKD-led cabinet. The coalition soon began unraveling, however, over the issue of whether to adopt a majoritarian electoral system. On July 25 most of the SLS—but not Bajuk and Peterle—sided with the LDS and other opposition parties in supporting retention of proportional representation. A day later the SLS+SKD and SDS announced the end of their coalition agreement, although they agreed to remain in a caretaker government pending legislative elections in October. On August 4 Bajuk and Peterle established the New Slovenia–Christian People's Party (NSi, below).

In the October 2000 election the SLS+SKD won only nine seats, on a 9.5 vote share. It subsequently agreed to accept three ministries in a reconstituted LDS-led government. In 2002 the SLS+SKD decided to readopt the SLS rubric. At a party congress in November 2003, Janez Podobnik was elected party president. The SLS withdrew from the LDS-led government in April 2004 over the unpopular citizenship law (see Political background, above). In the October 2004 legislative elections the SLS received 6.8 percent of the vote and secured seven seats in the assembly. It subsequently joined the SDS-led coalition government. The party announced in June 2007 that it would support Lojze Peterle in the upcoming presidential election. Bojan ŠROTwas elected party president in November 2007. In August 2008 Šrot received the endorsement of the SLS executive committee and party members as president of the party following a challenge by Ales PRIMC who accused Šrot of corruption. The SLS campaigned in a coalition with the SMS in the 2008 assembly balloting, and the grouping won five seats (all were SLS candidates). Šrot resigned as SLS leader in March. At a May 2009 party congress Radovan Žerjav was elected party president.

Leaders: Radovan ŽERJAV (President); Olga FRANCA, Franc BOGOVIČ (Vice Presidents); Jakob PRESEČNIK (Parliamentary Leader).

Other Parties:

New Slovenia–Christian People's Party (*Nova Slovenija–Krščanska Ljudska Stranka*—NSi). The NSi was established on August 4, 2000, following a split within the SLS+SKD over the issue of adopting a majoritarian electoral system for the National Assembly, as favored by then Prime Minister Bajuk. Like its predecessor, the SKD, the NSi is a conservative, Christian democratic formation supporting deregulation, privatization, a market economy, and membership in both the EU and NATO. For the October 2000 election it concluded a cooperation agreement with the SDS and won eight seats on an 8.8 percent vote share. The NSi received the highest number of votes in the June 2004 European parliamentary elections with 23.5 percent and two seats. The NSi won 9.0 percent of the vote and nine seats in the 2004 National Assembly elections. The party subsequently joined the SDS-led coalition government, and Bajuk was appointed finance minister.

Lojze Peterle, a member of the European Parliament from the NSi, was chosen as the party's presidential candidate for the 2007 balloting. He ran as an independent and was subsequently endorsed by all of the members of the governing coalition. Peterle placed second in the presidential polling. A group of conservative members of the party, led by Janez DROBNIC, defected to form the Christian Democratic Party (KDS) in August 2008. The NSi received 3.4 percent of the vote in the 2008 assembly elections, and therefore, no seats in the chamber. Following the balloting Bajuk resigned. Ljudmila Novak was appointed acting party president. The NSi did gain one seat in the EU parliamentary elections in June 2009.

Leaders: Ljudmila NOVAK (Acting President), Alojz PETERLE (2007 presidential candidate).

Lipa (Linden Tree). Formed in 2007 by SNS former party vice president Sašo Peče, Lipa is a nationalist, right-wing party. Its name is a reference to the linden tree, which is a national symbol for Slovenia. Defections from the SNS gave Lipa three seats in the assembly. In the 2008 assembly elections Lipa received 1.81 percent of the vote.

Leader: Sašo PEČE (President).

Christian Democratic Party (*Krščanski Demokrati Stranka*—KDS). The KDS was formed in July 2008 by Joze Duhovnik. The new center-right party emphasized family and education and sought to appeal to Slovenia's growing middle class. It attracted dissidents from the NSi, which party leaders identified as the main rival of the KDS and former members of the SKD. The KDS secured less than 1 percent of the vote in the 2008 elections.

Leaders: Joze DUHOVNIK (President), Marko STROVS (General Secretary), Janez DROBNIC.

Youth Party of Slovenia (*Stranka Mladih Slovenije*—SMS). The SMS was organized in July 2000 by former members of youth groups at the universities of Maribor and Ljubljana. Claiming no firm ideology, but emphasizing youth-oriented issues, the party won a surprising four seats in the October 2000 National Assembly election on a vote share of 4.3 percent. It subsequently agreed to support the return of Janez Drnovšek as prime minister. The SMS secured 2.1 percent of the vote in the 2004 assembly election and therefore did not gain any seats in the legislature. In April 2007 party leader Darko Krajnc was chosen as the SMS candidate for the upcoming presidential elections. He placed fifth in the first round of balloting with 2.18 percent of the vote and failed to qualify to advance to the second round. The SMS joined the SLS in an electoral coalition in the 2008 balloting, but none of its candidates were elected to office. Krajnc was reelected as party leader in June 2009.

Leaders: Darko KRAJNC (President); Vanja REŽONJA, Uroš BREŽAN (Vice Presidents); Jože VOZELJ (Secretary General).

Greens of Slovenia (*Zeleni Slovenije*—ZS). The ZS was formally launched in June 1989, although it had been active as a nonpolitical environmentalist group for a number of years earlier. It was an active participant in Demos, and in the 1992 assembly balloting it won five seats, with all of the occupants having participated in the postelection coalition. As the ZS-Eco-Social Party, the grouping joined the restructured LDS in 1994. Since then, the parent group has not had parliamentary representation.

For the October 2000 election the ZS joined the **Green Alternative of Slovenia** (*Zelena Alternativa Slovenije*—ZAS), led by Metka FILIPIČ, in a united **Green List** (*Zdreženi Zeleni–Zeleni Slovenije in Zelena Alternativa*) that secured only 0.9 percent of the national vote. In the 2004 assembly election the ZS received 0.69 percent of the vote. The ZS and the ZAS again agreed to run a joint candidate list ahead of the 2008 legislative elections. In the balloting the grouping received 0.51 percent of the vote.

Leaders: Vlado ČUŠ (President); Žare LIPUŠČGK, Branimir BAJDE, Andrej ŽELE (Vice Presidents).

Other parties that contested the 2008 assembly elections included (unless indicated, the parties received less than 1 percent of the vote): the **List for Justice and Development** (*Lista za Pravičnost in Razvoj*—LPR), led by Stojan AUER; the **Party of the Slovenian Nation** (*Stranka Slovenskega Naroda*—SSN), led by Borut KORUN; the **Go, Slovenia!** (*Naprez Slovenija*—NPS), headed by Blaž SVETEK; the **List for Clear Drinking Water** (*Lista za Čisto Pitno Vodo*—LZČPV); the **Green Coalition: Green Party and Green Progress** (*Zelena Koalicija: Zelena Stranke in Zeleni Progres*—ZP); and **Acacias** (*Akacije*), a regional grouping.

Other parties that contested the 2004 assembly elections included **Our Slovenia** (*Slovenija je Naša*—SJN), headed by Boris POPOVIČ, 2.6 percent; the **June List** (*Junijska Lista*), with 55 percent female candidates; the **Party of Ecological Movements** (*Stranka Ekoloških Gibanj*—SEG), led by Glorija MARINOVIČ; a coalition of the **Women's Voice Slovenia** (*Glas Žensk Slovenije*—GŽS), led by Monika PIBERL, who subsequently became her party's candidate for the October 2007 presidential elections (she finished seventh with less than 1 percent of the vote); the **Association for Primorsko** (*Zveza Za Primorsko*—ZZP); the **Union of Independents of Slovenia** (*Zveza Neodvisnih Slovenije*—ZNS); and the **New Democracy of Slovenia** (*Nova Demokracija Slovenije*—NDS).

LEGISLATURE

Prior to implementation of the 1991 constitution, the Slovene Assembly (*Zbòr*) was a directly elected tricameral body consisting of a Socio-Political Chamber, a Chamber of Associated Labor, and a Chamber of Communes. On December 6, 1992, the first elections were held for a National Assembly and a portion of a National Council.

National Council (*Državni Svet*). The 40 members of the council, who serve five-year terms, are chosen by electoral colleges of local (22 seats) and functional (18 seats) interest groups. The breakdown is as follows: 4 seats for employer groups; 4 for employee groups; 4 for farmers, tradespeople, and professions; 6 for noncommercial activities; and 22 for local interests. The council is able to propose new laws, require the holding of referendums relating to legislation, call for a parliamentary inquiry, request the Constitutional Court to review the constitutionality and legality of legislative acts, and direct the National Assembly to reconsider newly passed legislation. The last election for the National Council was conducted on November 21–22, 2007.

President: Blaž KAVČIČ.

National Assembly (*Državni Zbor*). The 90 members of the assembly are elected for four-year terms. Eighty-eight of the members are elected in eight electoral districts by proportional representation. Lists must receive a minimum of 4 percent of the national vote to achieve representation. The remaining 2 seats are reserved for Hungarian and Italian ethnic minorities, with 1 seat going to each group and with each elected in a special nationwide electoral district. The balloting on September 21, 2008, resulted in the following seat distribution: Social Democrats, 29; Slovenian Democratic Party, 28; For Real, 9; Slovenian Democratic Party of Pensioners, 7; Slovenian People's Party, 5; Slovenian National Party, 5; Liberal Democracy of Slovenia, 5; minority representatives, 2.

President: Pavel GANTAR.

CABINET

[as of July 1, 2009]

Prime Minister	Borut Pahor (SD)
Ministers	
Agriculture, Forestry, and Food	Milan Pogačnik (SD)
Culture	Majda Širca (*Zares*) [f]
Defense	Ljubica Jelušič (SD) [f]
Economic Affairs	Dr. Matej Lahovnik (*Zares*)
Education and Sports	Igor Lukšič (SD)
Environment and Physical Planning	Karl Erjavec (DeSUS)
Finance	Dr. Franc Križanič (SD)
Foreign Affairs	Samuel Žbogar (ind.)
Health	Borut Miklavčič (ind.)
Higher Education, Science, and Technology	Gregor Golobič (*Zares*)
Interior	Katarina Kresal (LDS) [f]
Justice	Aleš Zalar (LDS)
Labor, Family, and Social Affairs	Dr. Ivan Svetlik (ind.)
Public Administration	Irma Pavlinič-Krebs (*Zares*)
Transport	Dr. Patrick Vlačič (SD)
Without Portfolio, Responsible for Development and European Affairs	Mitja Gaspari (SD)
Without Portfolio, Responsible for Local Self-Government and Regional Development	Zlata Ploštajner (ind.)
Without Portfolio, Responsible for Slovenes Abroad	Dr. Boštjan Žekš (SD)

[f] = female

COMMUNICATIONS

Slovenia is considered to have a free and open press. In its 2008 annual index the media watch dog group Reporters Without Borders ranked Slovenia at 30 out of 173 countries in terms of freedom of the press.

Press. Unless otherwise noted, the following are dailies published in Ljubljana in Slovene: *Delo* (Work, 280,000); *Slovenske Novice* (Slovene News, 360,000); *Večer* (Evening, Maribor, 200,000); *Dnevnik* (Journal, 196,000).

News agency. The principal facility is the Slovenian Press Agency (*Slovenska Tiskovna Agencija*—STA), headquartered in Ljubljana.

Broadcasting and computing. Slovenian Radio-Television (*Radiotelevizija Slovenija*) offers national programming in Slovene, Hungarian, and Italian. About 50 radio stations broadcast regionally or locally, and cable television is increasingly common. As of 2008 there were 558.6 Internet users per 1,000 inhabitants.

INTERGOVERNMENTAL REPRESENTATION

Ambassador to the U.S.: Roman KIRN.

U.S. Ambassador to Slovenia: (Vacant).

Permanent Representative to the UN: Sanja ŠTIGLIC.

IGO Memberships (Non-UN): BIS, CEI, CEUR, EBRD, EIB, EU, Eurocontrol, IADB, Interpol, IOM, NATO, OSCE, PCA, WCO, WTO.

SOLOMON ISLANDS

Political Status: Former British-administered territory; achieved internal self-government on January 2, 1976, and full independence within the Commonwealth on July 7, 1978.

Area: 10,639 sq. mi. (27,556 sq. km.).

Population: 409,042 (1999C); 518,000 (2008E).

Major Urban Center (2005E): HONIARA (61,000).

Official Language: English (Solomons Pidgin is the effective lingua franca).

Monetary Unit: Solomon Dollar (official rate December 1, 2009: 7.84 dollars = $1US).

Sovereign: Queen ELIZABETH II.

Governor General: Frank Ofagioro KABUI; elected by the National Parliament on June 15, 2009, and sworn in on July 7 for a five-year term, succeeding Sir Nathaniel WAENA.

Prime Minister: Dr. Derek SIKUA (Coalition for National Unity and Rural Advancement); elected by the National Parliament on December 20, 2007, succeeding Manasseh Damukana SOGAVARE (Solomon Islands Social Credit Party), who had failed a nonconfidence vote on December 13.

THE COUNTRY

The Solomons comprise a twin chain of 922 Pacific islands stretching nearly 900 miles in a southeasterly direction from the Papua New Guinean territory of Bougainville to the northern New Hebrides. The 6 largest islands are Guadalcanal (on which the capital, Honiara, is located), Choiseul, Malaita, New Georgia, San Cristobal, and Santa Isabel. Approximately 93 percent of the inhabitants are Melanesian, with smaller groups of Polynesians (4 percent), Micronesians (1.5 percent), Europeans (0.7 percent), and Chinese (0.3 percent). Anglicans are the most numerous among the largely Christian population, followed by Roman Catholics and adherents of a variety of evangelical sects. An estimated 85 percent of the population is rural, with women bearing much of the responsibility for subsistence agriculture. No women serve in the current legislature or cabinet, although the present government has pledged action to improve their status.

Over 90 percent of the land is governed by customary land-ownership practices, creating, in combination with the strong influence of tribal nationalism, some barriers to recent development efforts. The principal traditional export commodities are copra, timber, fish, and

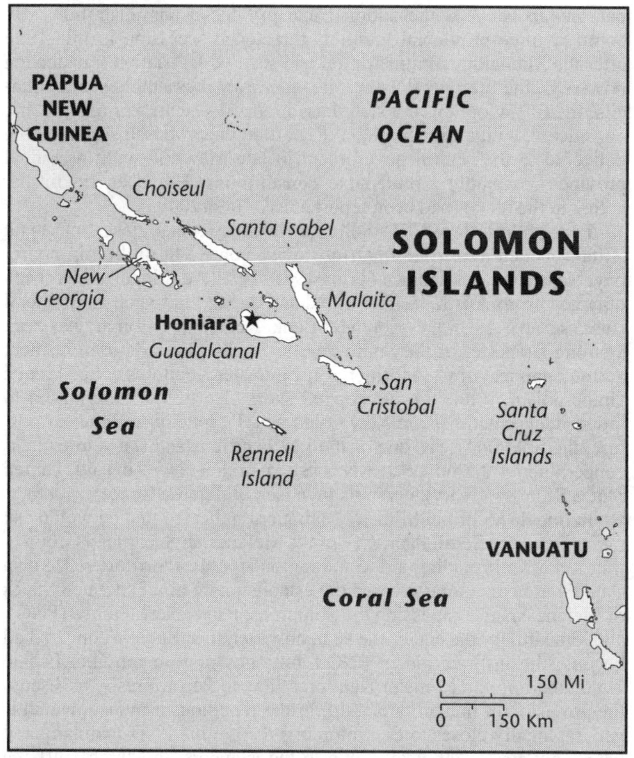

palm oil; to encourage development of a processing industry, the government in 1999 moved toward ending copra exports. Since the late 1990s gold has also been exported. Untapped resources include lead, zinc, and bauxite.

The economy has encountered severe difficulty in past years, with timber resources (the second most important source of foreign earnings) rapidly dwindling and real GNP per capita gaining an average of only 1.0 percent annually during 1990–1998. Civil unrest in 1999–2000, coupled with major shortfalls in export earnings from copra, palm oil, and fish, brought the economy to the verge of collapse. GDP fell by 3.5 percent in 1999 and by 14 percent in 2000, with soaring unemployment and investment capital in flight. Recovery thereafter yielded a rise in GDP to an annual average in 2003–2008 of 7.2 percent, a figure that appeared unlikely to be maintained in 2009–2010 because of the global recession, coupled with declining copra and lumber sales. Meanwhile, cost-of-living increases have recently outstripped those of GDP by about 2–1.

GOVERNMENT AND POLITICS

Political background. Originally named on the basis of rumors that the 16th-century Spanish explorer Alvaro de Mendana had discovered the source of the riches of King Solomon, the islands became the object of European labor "blackbirding" in the 1870s. The excesses of the indenture trade prompted Britain to declare a protectorate over the southern islands in 1893, the remaining territory being added between 1898 and 1900. Occupied by the Japanese in 1941, some of the most bitter fighting of the Pacific war occurred near Guadalcanal and in the adjacent Coral Sea during 1942–1943. After the war, a number of changes in British administration were introduced in response to a series of indigenous political and evangelical movements. In 1960 the resident commissioner's Advisory Council was replaced by separate legislative and executive councils which, under a constitution adopted in 1970, were combined into a high commissioner's Governing Council of both elected and nominated members. Four years later, the high commissioner assumed the title of governor and the Governing Council was supplanted by an elected Legislative Council led by a chief minister, who was empowered to designate his own cabinet. The territory became internally self-governing in January 1976, following the official abandonment in 1975 of its status as a protectorate. After lengthy constitutional discussions in London in 1977, full independence was achieved on July 7, 1978, former chief minister Peter KENILOREA being designated as prime minister.

Kenilorea was redesignated following a legislative election on August 6, 1980, but was defeated 20–17 in intraparliamentary balloting on August 31, 1981, and obliged to yield office to Solomon MAMALONI, who had served briefly as chief minister during the transition period immediately preceding independence.

Neither of the leading parties gained an absolute majority in the election of October 24, 1984, Kenilorea eventually being empowered by a 21–17 legislative vote on November 19 to form a coalition government that included members of his United Party and the recently organized *Solomone Agu Sogufenua,* in addition to a number of independents.

Although the opposition charged the ruling coalition with inefficiency and "inexplicable delays" in presenting a national development plan, Kenilorea survived a nonconfidence vote on September 6, 1985. However, he was obliged to resign on November 14, 1986, because of controversy surrounding the allocation of aid in the wake of a severe cyclone, Deputy Prime Minister Ezekiel ALEBUA being approved by the National Parliament as his successor on December 1.

While the opposition People's Alliance Party (PAP) obtained a plurality of only 11 legislative seats in the election of February 22, 1989, its leader, former Prime Minister Mamaloni, benefiting from crossover and independent support, was returned to office with 21 of 38 MP votes on March 28. In May the High Court ruled the 1988 appointment of Sir George LEPPING as governor general unconstitutional on the ground that he had not taken a leave of absence from a civil service position. At the same time, the Court rejected an opposition challenge to the legality of the Mamaloni government, which technically had been appointed by Lepping. The government's reappointment of Lepping in June also drew criticism because a new parliamentary vote had not been taken.

In a startling move on October 9, 1990, shortly before he was to face a leadership challenge at the ruling party's annual convention, Mamaloni resigned from the PAP to form a government of "national unity" that included a number of theretofore opposition parliamentarians and was designed to be broadly representative of the country's principal islands in terms of both geography and population. The action was later formalized by the launching of a Group for National Unity and Reconciliation (GNUR), which won 21 of 47 parliamentary seats in legislative balloting on May 26, 1993. However, the GNUR was unable to attract sufficient additional support to ensure the incumbent's retention of office on June 18. By a one-vote margin, the National Coalition Partners (NCP), an alliance of six anti-Mamaloni groups, elected Francis Billy HILLY, an independent who had not participated in national politics for eight years, as the new prime minister. Mamaloni immediately charged that Hilly's 24–23 victory did not meet the constitution's definition of an absolute majority as "at least one half of all the members plus one." Eventually both the governor general and the Court of Appeal ruled against the contention, although the issue was rendered moot in November, when three government ministers joined the opposition and one opposition MP joined the government, presumably giving Mamaloni the capacity to defeat Hilly on a 25–22 vote. However, a further shift in the fragile balance yielded approval of the government's budget on a 25–21 vote late in the year.

The defection of two ministers during a legislative adjournment in early October 1994 again reduced the Hilly coalition to a minority, and on October 13 Governor General Moses PITAKAKA dismissed the prime minister. A government crisis ensued, with Hilly refusing to stand down and the Court of Appeal upholding the action of the governor general, who proceeded to swear in Mamaloni on a caretaker basis on October 24. Two days later the judiciary reversed itself by agreeing with Hilly that dismissal required a legislative vote of nonconfidence, but added that the governor general was not obligated to take advice from a minority administration. As a result, Hilly resigned on October 31 and Mamaloni, buttressed by additional NCP defections, was formally confirmed as his successor by a 29–18 vote on November 7.

In the face of a growing financial crisis, Mamaloni called for an election on August 6, 1997. While it appeared that his National Unity group had won a plurality, Mamaloni was unable to command a legislative majority, and on August 27 Bartholomew ULUFA'ALU of the Solomon Islands Liberal Party (SILP) was elected as his successor.

Soon after assuming office, Ulufa'alu became embroiled in a long-standing ethnic dispute between the indigenous (Isatambu) inhabitants of Guadalcanal and those of the adjacent island of Malaita, many of whom had migrated to Honiara, an urban area that had emerged from the World War II American base at Henderson Field as the nation's capital. In early 1999 leaders of the Guadalcanal Revolutionary Army (GRA) demanded $4 million annual rent for accommodating the capital, eventually accepting $103,000 as a "temporary goodwill gesture." Hostilities continued, however, between the GRA, restyled as the Isatambu Freedom Movement (IFM), and the so-called Malaita Eagles Force (MEF), despite the formal signing of a peace accord on June 28. A second accord was concluded on August 12, while a third, cosigned by Fiji, Papua New Guinea, and Vanuatu on October 23, paved the way for a multinational peace-monitoring group that began arriving two days later.

On April 10, 2000, following a series of riots in Honiara, further peace talks were postponed, and on June 5 the MEF mounted a coup that included the kidnapping of Prime Minister Ulufa'alu, who, although himself a Malaitan, was charged with failure to resolve the conflict. Ulufa'alu was released on June 9 and resigned under pressure four days later, former Finance Minister Manasseh SOGAVARE being elected his successor on June 30.

Another cease-fire agreement between the IFM and MEF was concluded under Australian auspices on August 3, 2000, while additional peace talks were conducted on September 7–13 on a New Zealand frigate before the conclusion on October 15 in Townsville, Queensland, of a peace agreement that included provision for Australia and New Zealand to provide peace monitors. Forces on both sides nevertheless remained reluctant to turn in their weapons, as called for in the Townsville Peace Agreement, and by the initial deadline of December 15 only about half of the anticipated weapons—and virtually none of the more modern ones—had been surrendered. Four days later Parliament passed a bill granting amnesty to the militias for crimes committed during the civil uprising. On February 7, 2001, the IFM and another group, the Marau Eagles Force from east Guadalcanal, completed a peace agreement.

In August 2001 Parliament dissolved in preparation for a general election. In the balloting of December 5 the PAP captured a plurality of 20 seats, and on December 17 the PAP's Sir Allan KEMAKEZA was named prime minister by the National Parliament.

In May 2005 a new rebel group, the Malaita Separatist Movement (MSM), was reported to have been launched by former members of the MEF to oppose what were perceived as injustices perpetrated by the Kemakeza government and what had become known as the Regional Assistance Mission to the Solomon Islands (RAMSI).

The turmoil intensified after the April 2006 election, with rioting erupting in Honiara upon the appointment as prime minister of Snyder RINI, who was accused of being influenced by local Chinese on behalf of Taiwan, which the Solomon Islands recognized rather than the People's Republic of China (PRC). In the wake of widespread looting of Chinese businesses, Rini resigned and was replaced on May 4 by former prime minister Sogavare. Sogavare was again obliged to step down in the wake of an adverse nonconfidence vote on December 13, 2007, and was succeeded on December 30 by Dr. Derek SIKUA.

Constitution and government. The independence agreement negotiated in September 1977 provided for a constitutional monarchy with the queen represented by a governor general of local nationality, who is appointed for a five-year term on the advice of Parliament. Upon independence, the unicameral Legislative Assembly, which had been increased to 38 members in April 1976, became the National Parliament, with the authority to elect a prime minister from among its membership (subsequently increased to 47 and then to 50 legislators). The cabinet, which is appointed by the governor general on advice of the prime minister, is responsible to the Parliament. In addition, the independence agreement called for devolution of authority to local government units, within which the traditional chiefs retain formal status. The most seriously contested issue yielded a provision that nonindigenous Solomon Islanders (mainly Gilbertese, Chinese, and European expatriates) would be granted automatic citizenship upon application within two years of independence. The judicial system includes a Court of Appeal, a High Court, magistrates' courts, and local courts whose jurisdiction encompasses cases dealing with customary land titles. Ultimate appeal, as in certain other nonrepublican Commonwealth nations, is to the Judicial Committee of the Privy Council in London.

For administrative purposes the islands are currently divided into nine provinces, each headed by a premier.

In August 1991 Parliament began debate on proposed constitutional amendments, including conversion to republican status. No progress was subsequently reported, although Prime Minister Hilly informed the provincial premiers in mid-1994 that he was committed to a responsible partnership between the national and provincial administrations. By contrast, three provincial premiers threatened secession in mid-1996 after the Mamaloni administration had secured legislation transferring powers of the provincial assemblies to 75 local assemblies and councils. In 2001 adoption of a state-based federal system was again being considered, with a Constitutional Report on the proposed system being delivered to the central government in late May and with individual provinces assembling draft state constitutions. However, no further action in the matter had been reported as of mid-2009.

Foreign relations. The Solomon Islands retains close links with Britain, which agreed in 1977 to provide some $43 million in nonrepayable financial assistance during 1978–1982. Additional aid has been obtained from Australia, New Zealand, Japan, and such multilateral sources as the Asian Development Bank. Regionally, Honiara has been a strong supporter of the South Pacific Nuclear Free Zone movement and an opponent of what former prime minister Kenilorea called French "imperialism," although he stopped short of offering material aid to independence activists on New Caledonia. Despite its antinuclear posture, the Solomons was one of the few Pacific island states to express concern about the future of ANZUS (Australia, New Zealand, United States Security Treaty), given its own lack of defense forces.

In mid-1986 Prime Minister Mamaloni indicated that he would ask members of the South Pacific Forum's Melanesian Spearhead Group to join forces in providing aid to the region's poorest territories. He also stated that he had long favored the establishment of a Federated States of Melanesia, encompassing the Solomons, Papua New Guinea (PNG), and Vanuatu. By the end of the year, however, the principal concern had become the insurrection in PNG's province of Bougainville. In late 1990 then Foreign Minister Kenilorea flew to Port Moresby to discuss the provision of humanitarian aid for the rebellious province, which is geographically closer to the Solomons than to the PNG mainland and whose people are ethnically akin to the islanders. In March 1991 the government reiterated an earlier position that Bougainville was an integral part of PNG and that the rebellion was an internal PNG matter. However, relations between Honiara and Port Moresby worsened thereafter, with the Namaliu government charging in August that the Bougainville rebels were using the Solomons as both a safe haven and a conduit for arms.

The strain between the two Melanesian governments was exacerbated in April 1992, when PNG military units on two occasions crossed into Solomons territory on search-and-destroy missions. A third incursion in mid-September, during which two Solomon Islanders were killed and a third abducted, further strained relations, despite PNG acceptance of full responsibility for what its prime minister termed an "atrocious act." For its part, the Solomons government used the occasion to reiterate an earlier complaint that Papua's continuance of the antirebel struggle was sustained by military aid from Australia, which, it alleged, was acting in defense of Australian mining interests. Subsequently, Prime Minister Mamaloni was accused of meddling in PNG internal affairs upon publication of a confidential letter to a Papuan provincial premier that seemed to support secession if PNG Prime Minister Wingti abolished the regional government system. Subsequently, tension between the two governments eased somewhat, with a series of ministerial-level meetings in early 1993 yielding tentative agreement on rules for "hot pursuit" in border areas affected by the insurrection, although it was not until early 1996 that talks were launched on a comprehensive border treaty. Signed in July 1997, the resultant Basic Border Agreement recognized Bougainville as part of PNG, endorsed cooperation in security matters, and acknowledged the rights of indigenous peoples in the border area.

In July 2006 Prime Minister Sogavare announced a one-year extension of the Australian-led RAMSI, which had been augmented to include personnel from 14 countries, indicating that after three years it was still needed to suppress ethnic violence and secure law and order. In mid-September, however, Australia's high commissioner, Patrick Cole, was declared persona non grata in the Solomons, apparently because he had criticized Sogavare's handling of an inquiry into the riots that followed the April election. In late September relations deteriorated further because of Sogavare's refusal to permit the extradition to Australia of his recently appointed attorney general, Julian MOTI, who had been charged with an underage sex offense in Vanuatu. Thereafter, the deportation of an Australian national accused of complicity in a plot to assassinate Sogavare contributed to a thaw, and in March 2007 the prime minister agreed to accept the credentials of a new high commissioner.

On September 5, 2007, Sogavare's police minister reiterated the government's refusal to turn Moti over to Australian authorities, labeling their effort "nothing more than a political witchhunt." Two weeks later, Sogavare called for a review of RAMSI operations, stating that he did not oppose the force but that it had "grossly undermined" the country's laws and institutions. However, his successor, Derek Sikua, promised renewed support for RAMSI and on December 27 ordered Moti's deportation.

Current issues. By mid-2008 tension over RAMSI had subsided to a point that permitted its Participating Police Force (PPF) to organize local communities to stage a variety of citizen activities, including children's games and sporting events, throughout the country. Subsequently, RAMSI pledged to support an Anti-Corruption Task Force, and in late April 2009 the Nobel Peace Price winner Archbishop Desmond Tutu presided at the launching of a Solomon Islands Truth and Reconciliation Commission. However, these events were by no means welcomed by the parliamentary opposition, former prime minister Sogavare arguing that the government had become a "puppet of Australia." Earlier, Sogavare had called for a number of constitutional changes, including the popular election of the prime minister and the proscription of independent legislators.

POLITICAL PARTIES

As in neighboring Papua New Guinea, party affiliations tend to be transient and based more on personality than ideology. The People's Alliance Party (PAP) government formed by Prime Minister Mamaloni in 1989 was the first single-party administration since independence; in 1990, by contrast, Mamaloni withdrew from the PAP to form a "national unity" government that included a number of theretofore opposition figures and became the basis of the Group for National Unity and Reconciliation (GNUR). In June 1993 the five anti-Mamaloni parliamentary parties, led by Francis Billy Hilly, joined with Christian Fellowship and independent members to form a government alliance called the National Coalition Partners (NCP), which lost its slim legislative majority and became effectively moribund in October 1994. The GNUR, having regrouped after the 1997 election, had faded from the political scene by the 2001 balloting.

The government grouping during the Sogavare administration was styled the Grand Coalition for Change, while the opposition, in early December 2007, announced formation of a Coalition for National Unity and Rural Advancement (CNURA), led by theretofore independent Derek Sikua, that was victorious in the December 20 balloting.

Solomon Islands Alliance for Change Coalition (SIACC). The SIACC evolved in 2001 from the Solomon Islands Alliance for Change (SIAC), which had contested the 1997 election and saw its leader, Bartholomew Ulufa'alu, form a government on August 30. (As a consequence of its origins and name, the group has frequently been referenced simply as the SIAC.) Ulufa'alu was forced to resign in June 2000 but a year later filed a constitutional challenge to the action and the election of Prime Minister Sogavare of the People's Progressive Party (PPP). In November 2001 the High Court dismissed Ulufa'alu's case.

Like the SIACC, the SIAC had been formed as a grouping of smaller parties and independents, a principal component being Ulufa'alu's **Solomon Islands Liberal Party** (SILP), which had begun in 1976 as the National Democratic Party (Nadepa). The only formal party to contest the 1976 election, Nadepa won five legislative seats. It joined the first Mamaloni government in 1981 but lost three of its four seats in 1984. Having returned to four seats in 1989 (three years after redefining itself as the SILP), the party joined a number of smaller groups and independents in a parliamentary formation called the Coalition for National Unity. In the course of the 1990 realignment, Mamaloni persuaded SILP leader Ulufa'alu to resign from Parliament and accept appointment as a government consultant.

Joining Ulufa'alu in formation of the SIACC in 2001 was former prime minister Francis Billy Hilly, Fred Fono, and Patteson Oti. In the December parliamentary election it won 12 seats. Shortly thereafter Ulufa'alu decided to seek the prime ministership despite the party's endorsement of Oti. Oti ultimately finished second to the PAP's Kemakeza, with 13 votes, while Ulufa'alu won only 3. Although a member of the SIACC, Fono served in the Kemakeza cabinet. Ulufa'alu died on May 25, 2007.

Also participating in the alliance were the **National Party** (NP), led by Warren Paia, who replaced former prime minister Francis Billy Hilly as party president in August 2006, and by Ezekiel ALEBU, former prime minister and former head of the Solomon Islands United Party (Siupa); the **Solomon Islands Party for Rural Advancement** (SIPRA), led by former deputy prime minister Job Dudley TAUSINGA; and the **Solomon Islands Social Credit Party** (Socred), launched in July 2005 by former prime minister Manasseh Damukana Sogavare. (Sogavare had previously headed the now defunct PPP that had been founded and led, through a number of changes, by former prime minister Mamaloni before his death in January 2000.)

Leaders: Manasseh Damukana SOGAVARE (Leader of the Opposition and Former Prime Minister), Warren PAIA (NP President), Patteson OTI (Former Foreign Minister).

People's Alliance Party (PAP). Also called the Solomon Islands People Alliance (SIPA), the PAP was formed in late 1979 by merger of the People's Progressive Party (PPP), led by former chief minister Solomon Mamaloni, and the Rural Alliance Party (RAP), led by David KAUSIMAE. Mamaloni had urged a more cautious approach to independence than had Peter Kenilorea of Siupa (see under SIUDP, below). Chosen to succeed Kenilorea as prime minister in August 1981, Mamaloni was forced into opposition after the election of October 1984, but returned to the office on March 28, 1989. He resigned from the PAP in October 1990 to head a coalition administration that included a revived PPP, thus effectively splitting the alliance. In January 1992 PAP leader Kausimae announced the expulsion from the party of ten MPs who were serving in the second Mamaloni government.

Despite participating in the first Sogavare government, the PAP strongly opposed extension of the 1997–2001 legislative term by a year. Party leader Allan Kemakeza served as deputy prime minister under Sogavare until his dismissal in August 2001 for alleged mishandling of compensation funds related to the recent civil disruptions. With the PAP having achieved a plurality of 20 seats in the December parliamentary election, Kemakeza, with independent support, was elected prime minister, continuing in office until after the April 2006 election. The PAP has called for adoption of a federal republic headed by a president.

Leaders: Sir Allan KEMAKEZA (Former Prime Minister), Edward KINGMELE (General Secretary).

Solomon Islands Democratic Party (SIDP). The SIDP was formed in October 2005 to offer the country an "alternative leadership." It won three legislative seats in April 2006.

Leaders: Gabriel SURI (President), Sir John Ini LAPLI (Former Governor General and Former Vice President of the Party), Matthew WALE (Parliamentary Leader).

Solomon Islands Labour Party (SILP). The SILP, organized by the Solomon Islands Council of Trade Unions in 1988, won two legislative seats in 1989. A firm advocate of a federal system, party head Joses Tuhanuku retained his parliamentary seat in 2001 but lost it in 2006.

Leaders: Joses TUHANUKU (President), Tony KAGOVAI (General Secretary).

Solomon Islands United Democratic Party (SIUDP). The SIUDP adopted its current name before the 2001 election. It traced its origins to the Solomon Islands United Party (Siupa), an outgrowth of the Civil Servants' Association that placed ten members in the legislature in 1973 but saw its president, former chief minister Peter Kenilorea, defeated in his bid to sit for Honiara. Kenilorea entered the assembly in 1976 and served as prime minister from independence until supplanted by Solomon Mamaloni in 1981. He returned to office in 1984–1986 and continued thereafter to play a central role in Solomon politics, serving as chair of the Peace Monitoring Council and, after the December 2001 election, as speaker of Parliament, a post to which he was reelected in 2006.

Leaders: Sir Peter KENILOREA (Speaker of Parliament and Former Prime Minister), John MAETIA Kaluae.

Association of Independent Members of Parliament (AIMP). Not a party in the strict sense of the word, since it is composed of independents (some of whom are party aligned), the AIMP secured 13 seats in 2001 and 30 in 2006.

Leader: Snyder RINI (Finance Minister and Former Prime Minister).

Lafari Party (LP). The LP stresses the function of the tribal chiefs.
Leader: John Martin GARO (Former Minister of State).

LEGISLATURE

The unicameral **National Parliament** currently consists of 50 members elected for four-year terms. Results of the most recent balloting on April 5, 2006, gave the Solomon Islands Alliance for Change Coalition 12 seats (the National Party, 4; the Solomon Islands Party for Rural Advancement, 4; the Solomon Islands Liberal Party, 2; the Solomon Islands Social Credit Party, 2); the People's Alliance Party, 3; the Solomon Islands Democratic Party, 3; the Lafari Party, 2; and independents (grouped as the Association of Independent Members of Parliament), 30.

Speaker: Sir Peter KENILOREA.

CABINET

[as of August 9, 2009]

Prime Minister	Dr. Derek Sikua
Deputy Prime Minister	Fred Fono
Ministers	
Agriculture and Livestock	Selwyn Riumana
Commerce, Industry, and Employment	Francis Billy Hilly
Communication and Aviation	Varian Longoamei
Culture and Tourism	Seth Gukuna
Development Planning and Aid Coordination	Steve Abana
Education and Human Resource Development	Matthew Walli
Energy, Mines, and Rural Electrification	David Dei Pacha
Environment, Conservation, and Meteorology	Gordon Darcy Lilo
Finance and Treasury	Synder Rini
Fisheries and Marine Resources	Nollen Leni
Foreign Affairs and Trade Relations	William Haomae
Forestry	Sir Alan Kemakeza
Health and Medical Services	Martin Magga
Home Affairs	Peter Tom
Infrastructure Development	Stanley Festus Sofu
Justice and Legal Affairs	Laurie Chan
Lands, Housing, and Surveys	Samuel Manetoali
National Peace and Reconciliation	Sam Iduri
Police, National Security, and Correctional Services	James Tora
Provincial Government	Manasseh Maelanga
Public Service	Milner Tozaka
Women, Youth, and Children's Affairs	Johnson Koli
Attorney General	Gabriel Suri

COMMUNICATIONS

Press. The following weeklies are published in Honiara: *Solomons Voice* (10,000); *Solomon Star* (4,000), in English and Pidgin; and *Solomon Times*.

News agency. There is no national facility. The regional Pacnews moved to Honiara in 1990 after its staff was expelled from Fiji.

Broadcasting and computing. The Solomon Islands Broadcasting Corporation (SIBC) provides daily radio service in Pidgin and English. Until establishment of a Christian-oriented private station in 2002, there was no broadcast television service, although some television sets were available for videotaped programs.

As of 2008 there were 19.6 Internet users per 1,000 inhabitants.

INTERGOVERNMENTAL REPRESENTATION

Ambassador to the U.S. and Permanent Representative to the UN: Collin David BECK.

U.S. Ambassador to the Solomon Islands: Teddy Bernard TAYLOR.

IGO Memberships (Non-UN): ADB, CWTH, PC, PIF, WTO.

SOMALIA

Somali Republic
Jamhuuriyada Soomaaliyeed

Note: On May 18, 1991, the president of the Somali National Movement (SNM), Abdurahman Ahmed Ali ("Taur"), announced that northwestern Somalia (British Somaliland prior to its incorporation into Somalia in July 1960) had seceded to form an independent Republic of Somaliland. Although the self-proclaimed entity had received no international recognition as of 2007, it is accorded a separate write-up following the present article. An "autonomous region" was declared in the northeastern area of Puntland in 1998; information on that region is contained in this article.

Political Status: Independent republic established July 1, 1960; revolutionary military regime installed October 21, 1969; one-party state proclaimed July 1, 1976; multiparty system authorized on December 25, 1990, but unimplemented prior to the assumption of power by rebel forces on January 27, 1991; national charter providing for three-year transitional national government adopted by Somali National Peace Conference July 16, 2000, in Arta, Djibouti; Transitional Federal Charter approved January 29, 2004, providing for a four-year transitional government.

Area: 246,199 sq. mi. (637,657 sq. km.), including Somaliland (68,000 sq. mi.; 176,120 sq. km.).

Population: 7,114,431 (1986C); 8,331,000 (2008E). These figures, which include Somaliland, may reflect substantial underenumeration.

Major Urban Center (2005E): MOGADISHU (1,257,000, preliminary, including suburbs).

Principal Language: Somali.

Monetary Unit: Somali Shilling. Conditions in Somalia in recent years have rendered attempts to determine a genuine national currency rate essentially futile. Although a number of sources quoted an official rate as of December 1, 2009, of 1,400.00 shillings = $1US, that rate clearly bore little resemblance to reality. The United Nations reported an operational rate as of 2007 of 14,406 shillings = $1US. News stories in late 2008, however, reported that the government was using an exchange rate of approximately 22,000 shillings = $1US, while the black market rate had reached approximately 35,000 shillings = $1US.

President: Sheikh Sharif AHMED (Alliance for the Liberation and Reconstruction of Somalia); elected by the Transitional Federal Parliament on January 31, 2009, and inaugurated the same day to succeed acting President Sheikh Adan MADOBE, who assumed office on December 29, 2008, following the resignation of President Abdullahi YUSUF AHMED.

Prime Minister: Omar Abdirashid Ali SHERMARKE; appointed prime minister by the president on February 13, 2009, and confirmed by the Transitional Federal Parliament the following day, succeeding Nur Hassan HUSSEIN ("Nur Adde").

THE COUNTRY

The easternmost country in Africa, Somalia (including Somaliland) encompasses a broad band of desert and semidesert territory extending eastward along the Gulf of Aden and continuing southwestward to a point just south of the equator. The Somalis, a people of nomadic and pastoral traditions, share a common religion (Islam) and a common language (Somali). However, interclan rivalry has generated numerous economic and political cleavages, particularly between northern and southern groups. Nonindigenous inhabitants include Arabs, Ethiopians, Italians, Indians, and Pakistanis.

The economy is largely undeveloped, virtually no growth having been achieved in the last three decades, and the country remains one of the world's poorest with annual per capita GNP falling below $110 in the early 2000s. Agriculture accounts for two-thirds of economic

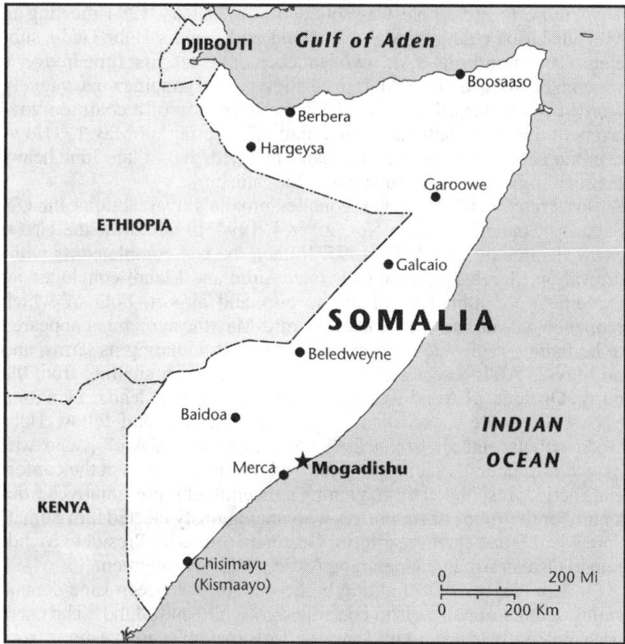

activity, although it is compromised by irregular rainfall. The country possesses some mineral deposits that thus far have not been commercially exploited. Although fishing, textile, and food processing industries have been established, much of the country's foreign exchange is derived from livestock and livestock-related products. In addition, Somalia has long been the world's largest producer of myrrh, an incense that is widely used in the Gulf region, China, and France. Development projects, including the construction of a dam for hydroelectric and irrigation purposes across the Juba River in the south, came to a virtual halt following the collapse of the central government in 1991. Meanwhile, inflation, drought, inefficiency in state enterprises, bureaucratic corruption, the presence of refugees from neighboring Ethiopia, and disruptions occasioned by civil war and interclan hostilities subsequently contributed to an overall state of destitution so severe that three-quarters of the population was estimated in mid-1992 to be at risk of starvation. The situation was only partially alleviated by the United Nations and other relief suppliers in 1993–1994. As of 1999 Somalia remained at the bottom of the UN development index, with ongoing interclan violence in the south constraining the ability of the international community to deliver aid. The interim national government (unrecognized in several key regions) that was installed in 2000 declared infrastructure development to be second only to security among its priorities. However, Somalia subsequently remained what one UN official described as a "black hole of anarchy" that lacked sufficient institutional structure to process foreign aid that could assist in addressing the dearth of health, educational, and security services. As momentum developed toward the resolution of the long-standing hostilities, the World Bank relaunched some of its aid programs to Somalia in 2003. The European Union (EU) subsequently pledged humanitarian and reconstruction aid, while UN agencies and other aid organizations launched food-distribution initiatives in the drought-affected south. However, the resumption of conflict in the spring of 2006 (see Current issues, below) prompted many aid groups to withdraw personnel and suspend assistance. Most economic activity continued to be in the informal sectors of the economy or based on remittances or expanding international assistance. However, the 2008 global economic downturn led to decreased remittances. GDP did grow by an estimated 2 percent in 2008, partly as the result of an estimated $120 million in ransoms paid by international shippers for hijacked vessels (see Foreign relations, below). Annual GDP per capita in 2008 was approximately $600.

GOVERNMENT AND POLITICS

Political background. Divided into British, French, and Italian sectors at the end of the 19th century, Somalia was partially reunited in 1960 when British Somaliland in the north and the Italian-administered Trust Territory in the south achieved their independence and promptly merged to form the United Republic of Somalia. Large numbers of Somalis remained in Ethiopia, Kenya, and the French Territory of the Afars and the Issas (subsequently Djibouti), and the new Somali regime announced that their inclusion in a "Greater Somalia" was a leading political objective.

The Somali Youth league (SYL) was the country's principal political party at independence and formed the republic's initial governments. During the late 1950s and early 1960s Somalia pursued a strongly irredentist policy toward Ethiopia and Kenya, relying increasingly on aid from the Soviet Union and other communist states. A change of policy occurred in 1967 with the presidential election of Abdirashid Ali SHERMARKE and his appointment of Mohamed Haji Ibrahim EGAL as prime minister. Under Egal's leadership, Somalia maintained its demand for self-determination for all Somalis but emphasized reduced dependence on the communist world, conciliation with neighboring states, and the cultivation of friendly relations with Western countries.

The Egal regime was ousted by military units under the command of Maj. Gen. Mohamed SIAD BARRE on October 21, 1969, in an action that included the assassination of President Shermarke. Pledging to reduce tribalism and corruption, the new military government launched a restructuring along socialist lines of what was now termed the Somali Democratic Republic. Although briefly interrupted by antigovernment plots in 1970 and 1971, the program moved forward at a deliberate pace. In 1970 foreign banks and other foreign-controlled enterprises were nationalized, and in October 1972 local government reorganization was begun. On July 1, 1976, the Supreme Revolutionary Council (SRC) that had been established in the wake of the 1969 coup was abolished, and its powers were transferred to a newly created Somali Revolutionary Socialist Party (SRSP) of which Siad Barre was named secretary general. Civilian government was nominally reinstituted following popular approval of a new constitution on August 25, 1979, the one-party election of a People's Assembly on December 30, and the assembly's election of General Siad Barre as president on January 26, 1980.

A state of emergency was declared on October 21, 1980, following a resurgence of conflict with Ethiopia (for a discussion of earlier hostilities, see Foreign relations, below). Radio Mogadishu announced two days later that the SRC had been reconstituted. The emergency decree was rescinded on March 1, 1982, despite reports of a northern army mutiny in mid-February and sporadic border incidents that persisted thereafter. In the legislative election of December 31, 1984, 99.8 percent of the voters were reported to have cast ballots, with less than 1 percent opposing the SRSP's nominees.

In May 1986 Siad Barre suffered severe injuries in an automobile accident, and First Vice President Lt. Gen. Mohamed Ali SAMATAR served as de facto chief executive for several months. Although Siad Barre recovered sufficiently to be the sole candidate for reelection to a seven-year presidential term on December 23, 1986 (in the country's first direct balloting for the position), his poor health and advanced age generated intense speculation as to a successor. Samatar appeared to be a leading candidate, particularly after being additionally named to the new post of prime minister in January 1987. However, in the wake of a government reshuffle in December, all references to his vice presidential role ceased. Given the constitutional significance of the office in regard to succession, the change was interpreted as reflecting Siad Barre's desire to be succeeded either by a family member or an individual from his Marehan clan, to which Samatar did not belong.

During 1988 the Somali National Movement (SNM), a northwestern rebel group that had joined Ethiopian units in a cross-border assault the year before, mounted a broad offensive that eventually succeeded in driving government forces from most of the region's rural areas by mid-1989. President Siad Barre thereupon announced the appointment of a constitutional review committee charged with laying the groundwork for a multiparty system that would permit the SNM to engage in electoral activity, provided it did "not solely seek to satisfy tribal interests." Meanwhile, other clan-based groups had taken up arms, including the United Somali Congress (USC) in the center and the Somali Patriotic Movement (SPM) in the south.

On September 3, 1990, in the wake of heightened rebel activity, Prime Minister Samatar was dismissed in favor of Mohamed HAWADIE MADAR. On January 20, 1991, as USC forces converged on the capital, Umar ARTEH GHALIB, a former foreign minister who had only recently been released from house arrest, was asked to form an essentially transitional government, and six days later Siad Barre departed for exile in Kenya. (He died in Nigeria on January 2, 1995.) On January 28, one day after assuming control in Mogadishu, the USC appointed its principal financial backer, Ali MAHDI MOHAMED, to the post of interim president. Mahdi, in turn, named Arteh Ghalib to head a reconstituted administration on January 29. However, neither appointment proved acceptable to the SNM, which, after rejecting two invitations to attend "national reconciliation" meetings with its erstwhile allies, announced the secession of the former British Somaliland on May 18 (see article on Somaliland). Subsequently, Gen. Mohamed Farah AIDID was elected USC chair at the party's third congress held July 4–5, provoking a bitter dispute with President Mahdi because the two came from different Hawiye subclans. In early September at least 300 people were killed in a clash between the two factions in Mogadishu, while more intense fighting, which erupted in mid-November, resulted in the slaughter of at least 4,000 civilians by the end of the year, with some 100,000 having fled the city.

In early February 1992 General Aidid was dismissed as USC chair, formalizing the cleavage between the group's pro- and anti-Mahdi factions. The action came after the announcement by UN Secretary General Boutros Boutros-Ghali of the first of a number of cease-fires, none of which proved effective. On April 24, in response to the team's recommendations, the Security Council authorized the creation of a United Nations Operation in Somalia (UNOSOM). Meanwhile, General Aidid launched a new opposition grouping called the Somali National Alliance (SNA).

On June 6, 1992, representatives of 11 Somali factions, meeting in Bahr Dar in northwest Ethiopia, agreed to support a UN-implemented cease-fire and convene a "comprehensive and joint conference" to "smooth the way" for the establishment of a provisional government in Somalia within three months. However, by late August, with reports that some 2,000 people were perishing daily from starvation, arrangements were made for the deployment of a 500-member UN peacekeeping force to guard relief supplies. In mid-September, responding to heightened evidence of famine, U.S. president George H. W. Bush ordered four warships with 2,400 marines to the Somali coast. On October 1 the United Nations announced that it was increasing its peacekeeping body to 1,200, despite protests from General Aidid, whose forces claimed control of two-thirds of the capital and most of southern Somalia. On November 27 Washington offered to provide 30,000 troops as part of a UN military intervention effort to thwart the theft of food aid. General Aidid thereupon reversed himself and hailed the U.S. overture as a way to "solve our political, economic, and social problems." On December 4 President Bush ordered the U.S. forces to Somalia as part of a projected multinational United Task Force (UNITAF) of some 35,000 soldiers.

Despite the breakdown of peace talks among 14 warring Somali factions in early January 1993, agreement was subsequently reached on a cease-fire and the appointment of a seven-member committee to lay the groundwork for a national reconciliation conference in mid-March. Meanwhile, the U.S. forces committed to "Operation Restore Hope" commenced a withdrawal, preparatory to handing peacekeeping operations over to a new 28,000-member UN Operation in Somalia (UNOSOM II) in early May.

Intense fighting erupted in the southern port city of Kismayu in mid-March 1993 between forces commanded by Siad Barre's son-in-law, Gen. Mohamed SAID HERSI, and Col. Ahmed UMAR JESS, an ally of General Aidid. However, at the conclusion of the conference in Addis Ababa, Ethiopia, on March 27, 1993, it was announced that agreement had been reached on a Transitional National Council for Somalia, which was given a mandate to lead the country to elections within two years.

On May 4, 1993, the UN formally assumed control of the multinational relief effort led since December by a U.S. commander. Unlike previous peacekeeping missions, however, the UN troops were provided with rules of engagement that permitted them to use offensive force to disarm Somali clans. This mandate was invoked on June 11 in retaliation against General Aidid, whose faction was accused of ambushing and killing 23 Pakistani peacekeepers on June 5. The action, which commenced with an attack by U.S. helicopter gunships on Aidid's Mogadishu compound, concluded on June 17 with a ground assault that failed to curb the general's military capability, Aidid himself evading capture. On November 16 the UN Security Council revoked its warrant for the arrest of Aidid, who nonetheless boycotted a further UN-sponsored peace conference in Addis Ababa in November.

A more positive note was sounded at a January 1994 meeting in Mogadishu of elders of Mahdi's Abgal and Aidid's Habr Gedir subclans. Two months later, the two leaders met for the first time in over a year in Nairobi, and on March 24 they signed a somewhat vaguely worded peace accord that called for the formation of a coalition government during a "national reconciliation" meeting on May 15. However, no action was taken on the date specified, and in late June heavy factional fighting again broke out in Mogadishu.

Frustrated in its efforts to reconcile Somalia's rival factions, the UN Security Council voted on November 4, 1994, to withdraw the UNOSOM II force by March 31, 1995. In fact, the UN completed its withdrawal on March 1. Eleven days later Aidid and Mahdi concluded an agreement for joint control of the port and airport, both of which reopened on March 14. However, by mid-May the agreement appeared to be fading, each side charging the other with violating its terms, and on May 25 Aidid's sector of Mogadishu came under shelling from the north. On June 12 Aidid was formally ousted as SNA leader by a joint SNA-USC conference called by his longtime ally and fellow Habr Gedir subclansman, Osman HASAN ALI ("Osman Ato"), who was named the general's successor. Aidid, who refused to accept the conference action, responded by convening a meeting of representatives from a number of groups of supporters who unanimously elected him Somali "president" for a three-year term. On June 16 Interim President Mahdi joined Osman Ato in condemning Aidid's "self-appointment."

In late August 1995 fighting broke out along a Green Line demarcating sectors of Mogadishu controlled by Aidid and Mahdi. The clash was apparently triggered by Aidid's efforts to confiscate weapons from civilians as part of a "rehabilitation and disarmament" drive, which followed the failure of a "reconciliation" conference launched by Osman Ato in Nairobi with the support of the Organization of the Islamic Conference (OIC). In September Aidid's forces captured the important town of Baidoa, some 90 miles northwest of the capital.

Aidid and his militiamen continued their offensive through early 1996, scoring a number of victories outside of the capital, including the capture of at least two more towns, before being slowed by the Mahdi-allied Rahanweyn Resistance Army (RRA). Subsequently, theretofore low-level hostilities erupted into widespread fighting following the collapse of peace talks in April. Particularly intense clashes were reported in Mogadishu, where, in July, the warring factions were reported to be preparing for an all-out battle for control of the capital. However, on August 1, 1996, General Aidid died from wounds reportedly suffered one week earlier in a battle against Ato's forces in the Medina neighborhood of Mogadishu. Calling Aidid's death an opportunity to launch fresh peace negotiations, Mahdi and Ato immediately announced a cease-fire.

Optimism was quickly dampened, however, by the SNA's election of Aidid's son, Hussein Mohamed Farah AIDID, as "interim president of Somalia." At his "inauguration" on August 4, 1996, Aidid, a U.S.-educated former Marine who had returned to Somalia a year earlier, pledged to gain revenge on his father's killers and renewed fighting was subsequently reported in Mogadishu. Meanwhile, international observers had persuaded Aidid, Mahdi, and Ato to accept the establishment of a commission to prepare for reconciliation negotiations, and in Nairobi on October 15 the three agreed to begin a cease-fire, remove roadblocks between the areas under their control, and facilitate the distribution of humanitarian aid. The cease-fire proved short-lived, however, with fighting beginning anew in late October.

In mid-November 1996 representatives of 26 groups, including nearly all of the major factions (with the notable exception of Aidid's), convened in Sodere, Ethiopia, for peace talks sponsored by the Organization of African Unity (OAU, subsequently the African Union—AU). On January 3, 1997, the participants announced the creation of a 41-member National Salvation Council (NSC) under the leadership of five faction leaders (including Mahdi and Ato), as well as an 11-member National Executive Committee (NEC). The NSC was charged with organizing a national reconciliation conference (then scheduled for June 1997) at which a transitional government would be formed. For his part, Aidid rejected the NSC's entreaties to participate, reasserting that he was already the "legitimate leader of all Somalia."

Aidid actively sought to resuscitate the October 1996 accord, meeting and signing new pacts with Ato and Mahdi in Cairo, Egypt, in early and late May, respectively. In June the NSC rescheduled the proposed reconciliation conference to November; however, in October the conference was postponed indefinitely, ostensibly because of a lack of international funding. On the other hand, Egypt continued its efforts to provide an alternative to the now-stalemated Sodere plan, and in early

December Aidid and leaders of other factions signed an accord in Cairo that included provisions for a "government of national union." The NSC ratified the accord in early January 1998 and scheduled a national reconciliation conference for February 15 to select a transitional president, a prime minister, a 13-member Presidential Council, and a 189-member Council of Deputies. However, the conference was postponed, and, despite subsequent efforts to resuscitate the pact, Somalia remained without a national governing authority. (On March 20 Aidid had reportedly renounced his claim to the presidency and, restyling himself "co-president," had pledged to cooperate with nominal president Mahdi.)

On July 23, 1998, a conference of some 300 leaders from the northeast region of Puntland declared the establishment of an autonomous government under the presidency of Col. Abdullahi YUSUF AHMED, a longtime military and political leader (see Somali Salvation Democratic Front under Political Parties and Groups, below). Although the conference also established a 66-member House of Representatives (appointed by local leaders, essentially on a subclan basis), a charter endorsed by the house (as well as an informal council of traditional leaders) in September rejected secession for the region, calling instead for eventual establishment of a federal system in which regional governments would enjoy extensive autonomy. A transitional government of three years' duration was initially envisioned for Puntland.

On May 2, 2000, in Arta, Djibouti, Ismail Omar Guelleh, the new president of Djibouti, convened a Somali National Peace Conference (SNPC) of prominent Somali figures representing a wide range of constituencies, including religious groups, the business community, traditional elders, intellectuals, women's organizations, and clans. (The conference was endorsed by the UN, OAU, and the Inter-Governmental Authority on Development [IGAD].) On July 16 the SNPC approved a national charter providing for a three-year Transitional National Government (TNG) to be led by a Transitional National Assembly (TNA, appointed on a clan basis) and a president (elected by the TNA). The TNA convened for the first time in Arta on August 13, and on August 27 it elected Abdiqassim SALAD HASSAN, a former deputy prime minister and interior minister in the Siad Barre regime, as president. On October 2 Salad Hassan appointed Ali Khalif GALAYDH, a professor and prominent businessman, as prime minister. Galaydh announced his first ministerial appointments, carefully balanced among clans, on October 20. Although the fledgling interim central government subsequently moved to Mogadishu, its potential effectiveness remained in serious question because it had not received the endorsement of Somaliland, the regional administration established in Puntland, or most factional militia leaders. Of the prominent Somali "warlords," only Mahdi had attended the SNPC. He was subsequently appointed to the new assembly and pledged his support to the TNG.

In February 2001 Prime Minister Galaydh announced a cabinet reshuffle, with the pro-Mahdi faction of the USC formally joining the government. However, Galaydh's government, apparently being blamed by the public for the lack of progress in negotiations with the recalcitrant warlords, lost a confidence motion in the assembly by a reported vote of 141–29 on October 28. President Salad Hassan on November 12 named Hasan Abshir FARAH, a former cabinet member, to replace Galaydh. Following the successful negotiation of a power-sharing agreement with several minor warlords in late December, Farah announced a new cabinet on February 16, 2002.

Meanwhile, political affairs in Puntland also remained complicated. As the conclusion neared of the three-year mandate accorded the transitional government of Yusuf Ahmed in 1998, it was announced in late June 2001 that the Puntland House of Representatives and clan elders had extended the government's authority for another three years, the Puntland administration continuing to reject the legitimacy of the TNG. However, Puntland Chief Justice Yusuf Haji NUR in early July declared the extension "unconstitutional" and announced he had assumed authority as "acting president" pending new regional elections. Yusuf Ahmed rejected Nur's dictate, and fighting was reported in August between Yusuf Ahmed's forces (reportedly supported by Ethiopia) and those of Nur's (believed to have the support of the TNG and, according to charges from Yusuf Ahmed, the Islamic Union [see Political Parties and Groups, below].) With Yusuf Ahmed now "ruling" from the city of Galkacyo and Nur controlling the regional capital of Garowe, a controversial congress of clan elders opened in Garowe in late August. On November 14 the congress, deemed "illegal and destabilizing" by Yusuf Ahmed, elected Jama Ali JAMA, a former army colonel who had been imprisoned during the Siad Barre regime's tenure, as the new president of Puntland from among 12 candidates. Although Jama was inaugurated on November 19, Yusuf Ahmed's forces by May 2002 had effectively regained control of the region. The TNG subsequently continued to reference Jama as the "legitimate" president, but Yusuf Ahmed was still exercising full authority as the year ended.

On April 1, 2002, the self-described State of Southwestern Somalia, the third such breakaway administration (the others being Somaliland and Puntland) was formed. Although internal dissension was reported on the matter, the new regional government was launched under the umbrella of the Somali Reconciliation and Reconstruction Council (SRRC), a loose coalition of southern factions that had been launched in 2001 in opposition to the TNG (see Somali National Alliance under Political Parties and Groups, below, for additional information on the SRRC). Col. Hassan Mohammed NUR ("Shatigadud") of the RRA was named president of the new administration, also slated to include a cabinet and 145-member legislature.

The warring factions resumed negotiations in October 2002 in Kenya, although Somaliland declined to attend. On July 5, 2003, the parties appeared to agree on a transitional peace plan, but Salad Hassan rejected the proposal, claiming that Prime Minister Farah had exceeded his authority by agreeing to allow too much power to remain at the regional level under the tentative agreement. On August 9 Salad Hassan dismissed Farah as prime minister, naming Osman JAMA ALI (former deputy prime minister) to the post. However, Jama Ali resigned on November 28, reportedly due to conflict with the president. He was succeeded on December 8 by Mohamed Abdi YUSUF, the deputy speaker of the TNA, which subsequently endorsed a new 37-member cabinet. Meanwhile, in Puntland, Yusuf Ahmed had initiated peace talks with rival groups in May 2003 that had yielded an agreement under which he was fully recognized as president while former opponents were named to the new Puntland cabinet.

In January 2004 several hitherto reluctant rebel and opposition groups (including the RRA) joined the peace negotiations in Kenya, and on January 29 some 42 factions and warlords signed a potentially historic comprehensive accord based on a Transitional Federal Charter (TFC) that provided for a transitional legislature that would elect a president and confirm a new transitional government. The TNA approved the settlement on February 9, and the new legislature (the Transitional Federal Parliament—TFP) was filled by clan and subclan appointees by early August.

In the third round of balloting for a national president in the TFP on October 10, 2004, Yusuf Ahmed was elected by a vote of 189–79. (Eleven candidates had contended the first round.) On November 3 the new president appointed Ali Mohammed GHEDI as prime minister, but the TFP on December 11 voted down his first proposed cabinet, apparently because a number of clans were not happy with their representation. However, an expanded and revised Transitional Federal Government (TFG) won TFP approval on January 7, 2005, all activity occurring in Kenya due to continued unsettled conditions in Somalia. Somaliland remained divorced from the new institutions, although the breakaway status of the State of Southwestern Somalia appeared resolved by Colonel Shatigadud's inclusion in the new national government.

Tensions over where the government should locate subsequently constrained the TFG's effectiveness, as did reported clan rivalries within the cabinet. Consequently, plans for the demobilization of clan militias in favor of a unified national army failed to produce significant results. Underscoring the fragility of the situation, a bomb exploded following an address by Prime Minister Ghedi in May 2005 in Mogadishu, killing more than 15 people. Ghedi, the cabinet, and some legislators then settled in Jowhar, while other legislators attempted to operate out of Mogadishu. Ghedi survived another assassination attempt during a trip to Mogadishu in November, an event that triggered a new round of fighting in the capital. At the same time it was reported that Islamic fighters were filtering into Mogadishu to support the Islamic Courts Union (ICU, see Political Parties and Groups, below).

The ICU took control of Mogadishu in June 2006 and held control until December, when they were ousted by TNG-allied militias with the support of Ethiopian troops, which maintain a controversial and precarious presence in Mogidishu to the present day. During the capital's period under ICU control, general security in the south improved and the number of piracy attacks in Somali waters decreased, spiking again after the ICU was driven from Mogadishu in January 2007 (see Foreign relations, Current issues, below). The TNG and Ethiopian forces continue to battle the Islamist militias for control of the city, which hundreds of thousands of Somalis have fled since the fighting broke out in December 2006.

The TNG faced numerous internal challenges in addition to its struggle with the ICU. While Ghedi retained his post during a reorganization of the cabinet in February 2007, he resigned under intense pressure on October 29, 2007, for his inability to pacify the capital and for his support for Ethiopian troops stationed in Somalia. He was replaced by an interim prime minister, Salim Aliyow IBROW, on October 30. Tensions between Ibrow and the president led Yusuf Ahmed to name a new prime minister, Nur Hassan HUSSEIN ("Nur Adde"), on November 22. Nur Adde was confirmed by the TFP two days later. On December 2 Nur Adde named a new cabinet, but that government was dismissed and a new one formed on January 5, 2008. It was confirmed by the TFP on January 10. On June 9 a peace agreement was signed by the TNG and the main opposition (see Current issues, below). Ten ministers resigned on August 2 in protest over an effort by Nur Adde to dismiss the mayor of Mogadishu, an ally of Yusuf Ahmed. A new, smaller cabinet, with six vacancies, was named on August 3. Tensions between Nur Adde and the president led Yusuf Ahmed to attempt to dismiss the prime minister on December 14. However, the legislature voted to block the president's action, even as Ahmed tried to appoint former minister of internal affairs Mohammed Mahmud GULED as prime minister. Unable to remove Nur Adde, the president resigned on December 29 and was replaced on an interim basis by the speaker of the legislature, Sheikh Adan MADOBE.

On January 8, 2009, Abdirahman Mohamed MOHAMUD (also known as "Farole") was elected president of Puntland. Mohamud campaigned as a reformer and promised to improve security and economic development. Once in office, the new president undertook steps to improve cooperation with other powers to repress pirates in the region. The Puntland parliament ratified a new constitution on June 30 that introduced a multiparty political system.

Meanwhile, on January 30 Sheikh Sharif AHMED of the Islamist group the Alliance for the Liberation and Reconstruction of Somalia (ALRS) was elected president of the Somali TNG by the transitional assembly. During the second round of run-off balloting, Ahmed received 293 votes to 126 for Gen. Maslah Mohammed SIYAD, a son of the former dictator. Ahmed was a leader of the moderate faction of the ALRS (known as the "Djibouti wing"), so members of the TNG and the international community hoped his election would ease the Islamic insurgency in Somalia. The new president appointed as prime minister Omar Abdirashid Ali SHERMARKE, the son of former president Shermarke and a Western-educated diplomat. His appointment was seen as an effort to gain the backing of both the Darod clan and the Somali expatriate community for the new government. Shermanke formed a government of national unity that was approved by the TFP on February 22. The new cabinet initially met in Djibouti, then transitioned to Mogadishu before being forced to withdraw (see Current issues, below).

Constitution and government. For the decade after the October 1969 coup, supreme power was vested in the Central Committee of the SRSP, whose secretary general served as head of state and chief executive. For all practical purposes these arrangements were continued under a constitution approved in 1979, which provided additionally for a People's Assembly of 177 members, 171 of whom were nominated by the party and 6 by the president. The president was popularly elected for a seven-year term after having been nominated by the SRSP as the sole candidate. These and other provisions of the 1979 basic law were effectively suspended with the collapse of the Siad Barre regime in January 1991, following which the independent republic of Somaliland was declared in May in the northwest (see separate article for details on the administration in Somaliland).

In part with the goal of encouraging eventual participation by the administrations already established in Somaliland and Puntland, the national charter adopted by the SNPC in July 2000 called for a federal system with strong regional governments. Pending formal establishment of such a system under a new constitution, the SNPC authorized a three-year TNG, with legislative responsibility delegated to an appointed House of Representatives. The charter also promised an independent judiciary, protection of the freedom of expression and other human rights, and support for multiparty activity. (For details of transitional institutions established through the Transitional Federal Charter of January 2004, see Political background, above.) In March 2009 the cabinet voted to impose sharia law throughout Somalia.

Administratively, the country is divided into 15 regions, which are subdivided into 70 districts, plus the city of Mogadishu.

Foreign relations. Although a member of the United Nations, the AU, and the Arab League, Somalia has been chiefly concerned with the problems of its own immediate area, where seasonal migrations by Somali herdsmen have long strained relations with neighboring states. The most serious disputes have been with Ethiopia. Somali claims to the Ogaden desert region precipitated conflicts beginning in 1963 that escalated into a full-scale war in 1977–1978 when government troops entered the region, eventually to be driven back by an Ethiopian counteroffensive. The war had international implications, producing a reversal of roles for the Soviet Union and the United States in the Horn of Africa. Ethiopia, previously dependent on the United States for military support, was the recipient of a massive influx of arms and advisers from the Soviet Union and Cuba. Collaterally, Somalia, which had developed an extensive network of relations with communist countries, broke with Moscow and Havana in favor of reliance on the West, eventually agreeing in 1980 to make port facilities available to the U.S. Rapid Deployment Force for the Middle East in return for American arms. Somalia normalized relations with the USSR in 1986 and Cuba in 1989 but continued to receive substantial military aid from the United States.

Although the 1979 constitution called for "the liberation of Somali territories under colonial occupation"—implicitly referencing Somali-populated areas of Kenya as well as of Ethiopia—the Somalis promised that they would not intervene militarily in support of external dissidents. Tense relations and occasional border hostilities continued, however, with Ethiopia supporting the major Somali opposition groups in guerrilla operations. In January 1986 President Siad Barre and Ethiopian leader Mengistu Haile Mariam established a joint ministerial commission to resolve the Ogaden question, but no results were achieved during the ensuing year, with Somalia condemning Ethiopia for a cross-border attack in February 1987. Following major Ethiopian reverses at the hands of Eritrean secessionists in the north, Siad Barre and Mengistu conferred during a drought conference in Djibouti in March 1988 and agreed to peace talks in Mogadishu in early April. The discussions yielded a communiqué that pledged a military "disengagement and separation," an exchange of prisoners, the reestablishment of diplomatic relations, and the joint cessation of support for opposition groups.

In early August 1996 Ethiopian forces attacked three towns in Somalia's Gedo region in an apparent attempt to squash the activities of the Islamic Union (see Political Parties and Groups, below), which had claimed credit for bombings and assassination attempts in Ethiopia as part of its campaign for the Ogaden region's independence. The offensive continued into 1997, and by early February Ethiopian troops had reportedly overrun the Islamic fighters' last base in the region. Ethiopia's military advances proved costly on the diplomatic front, however, as a number of Somalian faction leaders, most important the SNA's Aidid, condemned the "occupation" and refused to participate in the peace process launched in November 1996 in Sodere, Ethiopia. Thereafter, Aidid's efforts to revive the short-lived Nairobi accord of October 1996 were actively supported by Kenya and Egypt. The latter championed the establishment of a unified and centrally governed Somalia as opposed to an Ethiopian diplomatic advance, which one analyst labeled "divisive." Much of southern Somalia subsequently came under Ethiopian influence as the result of Ethiopian initiatives relating to its war with Eritrea in 1998–2000. The TNG in Somalia subsequently accused Ethiopia of supplying weapons to anti-TNG warlords in Somalia. Meanwhile, the activities of the Islamic Union also attracted the interest of the United States because of the latter's "war on terrorism" following the terrorist attacks in September 2001.

Many African states recognized the TFG established in late 2004 and early 2005 to govern Somalia, and the AU authorized a contingency peacekeeping force for possible deployment in Somalia. Meanwhile, the European Union pledged financial and technical aid for the new administration, but the United States had developed only "informal ties" with the TFG as of mid-2005. However, responding to the risk of potential Islamic terrorist activity in the region, the US government has tacitly supported the TFG in its battles against Islamist militias and was directly involved in at least one air-strike against al-Qaida targets near the Somali-Kenyan border in January 2007 (see Current issues, below). Negotiations over the proposed AU peacekeeping force continued through 2006. The UN authorized the deployment of the AU force, the African Union Mission in Somalia (AMISOM), in February 2007. Although AMISOM was designated to have up to 8,000 troops, only 2,600 peacekeepers were dispatched, mainly from Uganda and Burundi. AMISOM was deployed only in Mogadishu. The lack of forces constrained the effectiveness of AMISOM and led to calls for a larger UN operation to supersede the AU mission.

In April 2006 Prime Minister Ghedi gave the United States permission to patrol the waters off the coast of Somalia to suppress piracy.

Somalia's coastal waters witnessed the third-highest rate of pirate attacks in the world, burdening international shipping companies and aid groups trying to import relief supplies to the east African coast. Reports had also previously surfaced that U.S. marines and special forces had undertaken several covert antiterrorist operations in Somalia, prompting minor rioting and protests in some cities. During 2007 the United States launched at least four airstrikes against suspected terrorist targets. More than 40 pirate attacks occurred in Somali waters during 2007 and early 2008, including an attack on a Spanish fishing boat with a crew of 26 that was captured in April 2008 and released only after a ransom of $1.2 million was paid. In response to these attacks, the UN Security Council on June 2 authorized countries that had prior agreements with the TNG to enter Somalian waters to interdict or apprehend pirates, based on the existing model between the United States and Somalia. After a Ukrainian vessel carrying 33 tanks en route to Kenya was hijacked in September, Russia deployed naval forces to the region. In April Somali pirates captured a U.S. vessel, the *Maersk Alabama.* The crew recaptured the vessel, and U.S. naval forces killed three pirates while rescuing the ship's captain on April 12. Meanwhile, a hostage was killed when French forces recaptured the *Tanit*. In December the EU initiated a joint naval deployment to suppress pirates in Somali waters. The mission was undertaken following a UN Security Council Resolution that granted member states expanded authority to take steps to counter piracy in the region, including pursuing pirates on land.

In November 2008 Ethiopia announced the withdrawal of all its forces from Somalia. The last Ethiopian troops departed in January 2009, but reports in June indicated that Ethiopian forces had again crossed the border. Meanwhile, on January 16 the UN Security Council authorized the deployment of a UN peacekeeping force to replace AMISOM, but no formal steps had been taken to deploy a force by the summer of 2009. By January 2009 pirates had possession of at least 14 vessels captured in Somali waters. In April international donors pledged more than $250 million in economic and security aid for the TNG..

Current issues. The peace talks launched in Kenya in October 2002 were attended by a number of regional leaders as well as representatives of Somalia's civil society. The addition of holdout rebel groups to the negotiations in January 2004 appeared to break the long-standing impasse and offer the best chance to date of ending the national nightmare. However, underscoring the continued fragility of the security situation, the Transitional Federal Government (TFG) established in late 2004 remained in Kenya until April 2005. Fighting led Prime Minister Ghedi to shift most government operations to more stable cities in the south. Meanwhile, it was unclear how the new national government would ultimately affect the autonomous government in Puntland (where Mohamed Muse HERSI had been elected president in January), and there was no indication of possible reconciliation from Somaliland.

The full TNA met for the first time in Baidoa in February 2006. However, it remained clear that the TFG lacked the military means to confront the warlords who had controlled Mogadishu. Following severe rioting in February, prompted by the publication of cartoons in Denmark deemed offensive to Muslims, fighting intensified in Mogadishu between the ICU militias and the warlords, who had formed the Alliance for the Restoration of Peace and Counter-Terrorism (ARPCT), supported by the United States. These battles culminated in the Islamists taking control of Mogadishu and surrounding areas in June. The ICU subsequently established a Council of the Islamic Courts to govern the capital.

Much of the population in Mogadishu reportedly welcomed the ICU victory as representing relief from the violence and anarchy that had marked the reign of the warlords. Concern was voiced over the imposition of extreme religious strictures. Meanwhile, hard-liners in the group reportedly called for an Islamic state that would also include parts of Ethiopia, Kenya, and Djibouti. The international community urged negotiations between the TFG (located in Baidoa) and the Islamists toward creation of a government of national unity. However, talks stalled. The ICU was then ousted after an assault on Mogadishu by an interim government militia backed by Ethiopian troops in December 2006 and January 2007, with the interim government subsequently imposing a three-month state of emergency. An AU peacekeeping force started to deploy in March in Baidoa amid signs of a guerilla-style insurgency by Islamists in the capital. Earlier in the year, the AU had promised to send 8,000 troops to replace the Ethiopian contingent and then hand authority over to a UN mission later in 2007. However, the Ethiopian troops remain in the country despite widespread anger at their presence, which fueled additional violence. As a result, the government of Uganda was the only AU country to fulfill its commitment to the mission, sending 1,600 troops that protect installations in Mogadishu. The interim government, as well as Ethiopian and Ugandan troops, continue to be targeted by the ICU insurgency's bomb, grenade, and sniper attacks.

On the heels of the crisis, the cabinet was reconstituted in February 2007 in response TFP dissatisfaction with cabinet members' attendance and work ethic. In September 2007, at a congress of opposition groups in Eritrea, a new coalition, the Alliance for the Liberation and Reconstruction of Somalia (ALRS), alternatively known as the Alliance for the Reliberation of Somalia (ARS), was created. The ALRS hoped to coordinate political and military efforts against the TNG (see Political parties, below). Meanwhile, the TFG was hampered by infighting between President Ahmed and Prime Minister Ghedi, who were at odds over the handling of the Islamist insurgency. Ghedi resigned on October 29, 2007, following immense pressure from Ahmed and the transitional parliament. President Ahmed designated Deputy Prime Minister Salim Aliyow Ibrow as interim prime minister on October 30. (The president is required to appoint a permanent replacement within 30 days.) Nur Hassan Hussein ("Nur Adde") was appointed prime minister on November 22. However, conflicts quickly emerged between Yusuf Ahmed and Nur Adde over the insurgency.

Ongoing territorial disagreements between Puntland and neighboring Somaliland continued to complicate relations in the Horn of Africa in 2007. Fighting subsequently broke out between the neighbors in early October 2007 in one of the contested cities, Sool, which itself is split between sub-clans calling for Sool's independence, or backing either Somaliland or Puntland in the dispute (see Somaliland entry).

In March 2008 renewed violence in the capital killed scores of people and prompted an estimated 20,000 to flee Mogadishu. Then in May massive food riots in Mogadishu over rising prices led to a new wave of refugees. On June 9 an 11-point peace agreement was signed between the TNG and the ALRS following negotiations sponsored by the UN. However, hard-line factions within the ALRS rejected the agreement and vowed to continue fighting until Ethiopian troops were withdrawn. The factions rejected a new round of negotiations between the TNG and the ALRS in August in Djibouti. Osman Ali Ahmed, the head of the UN's development program in Somalia, was killed by gunmen on July 6. Renewed fighting in Mogadishu in September left at least 100 dead and prompted a new wave of refugees. In addition, 30 trucks of the World Food Program were looted by hungry crowds on September 25.

Islamic fighters formed a new group, *al-Shabab*, in late 2008. *Al-Shabab* opposed both the TNG and the ICU and as Ethiopian troops withdrew in 2009 was able to capture large areas of Somalia, including Baidoa, the interim site of the nominal government. In February 2009 *al-Shabab* forces killed 11 AMISOM troops in a battle in Mogadishu and subsequently launched a series of targeted assassinations and suicide-bombings. The group claimed responsibility for a suicide-bombing that killed Security Minister Omar HASHI on June 18 and a subsequent failed assassination attempt on the interior minster. Fighting forced the TNG to again withdraw from Mogadishu. By the end of July renewed fighting in and around Mogadishu was estimated to have killed 200 civilians and displaced more than 100,000.

POLITICAL PARTIES AND GROUPS

From the time of its inaugural congress in June 1976 to the nominal authorization of a multiparty system in December 1990, the Somali Revolutionary Socialist Party (SRSP) was the country's only authorized political formation. The SRSP virtually ceased to exist with the collapse of the Siad Barre regime in January 1991, at which time a large number of additional groups, almost all of them clan-based, emerged from clandestine or insurrectionary activity. The most important of the new formations was the United Somali Congress (USC), organized in January 1989. Subsequently, in November 1993, several components of the USC helped to launch the **Somali Salvation Alliance** (SSA), a loose coalition that also included components of the SDM, SAMO, SPM, SSDF, SNA, and SSNM, as well as the **Somali Democratic Front,** led by Ali MOHAMED HAMED; the **Somali National Democratic Union** (SNDU); and the **Somali National Union** (SNU), led by Mohamed RAJIS MOHAMED. The SSA was supportive of Ali MAHDI MOHAMED (who had become the nominal president of Somalia in 1991 following the ouster of Gen. Siad Barre) in his leadership fight with Gen. Mohamed Farah Aidid and, after 1996, General Aidid's son, Hussein Mohamed Farah Aidid. Both Aidids were supported by the Somali National Alliance (SNA, see below);

consequently, other groups routinely added SSA or SNA to their names to indicate their positions regarding the leadership fights.

Severe splintering continued in the SSA in the second half of the 1990s, some factions accusing Mahdi of pursuing a self-serving agenda. Mahdi attended the Somali National Peace Conference (SNPC) in Djibouti in 2000, was chosen as a member of the new Transitional National Assembly, and subsequently fully supported the interim central government led by President Salad Hassan. Although references continued in early 2001 to Mahdi's leadership of the SSA, he by that time faced a challenge from antigovernment dissidents for use of the SSA rubric (see USC-SSA, below). Mahdi's supporters reportedly considered a "revival" of the SSA in mid-2002, but the initiative did not subsequently maintain momentum.

Alliance for the Liberation and Restoration of Somalia (ALRS). The ALRS was a loose coalition of opposition groups formed following a congress in Asmara, Eritrea, in September 2007. The coalition was an effort by Islamic resistance groups, such as the **Islamic Courts Union** (ICU), to reach out to secular and other opposition parties. Sheikh Sharif Ahmed of the ICU was named chairman of the group, while Sheikh Hassan Dahir AWEYS of the ICU emerged as the main leader of the ALRS's central committee. By late 2008 the ALRS was divided into two broad camps, the moderate Djibouti faction, which sought reconciliation with the TNG, and the hard-line Asmara wing, led by Aweys, which refused to negotiate with the interim government. The ALRS signed a new peace accord with the TNG in October 2008. Although the agreement was rejected by the Asmara faction, the accord paved the way for the expansion of the TFP to include ALRS deputies and the election of Ahmed as the president of the TNG. The new cabinet included a number of ALRS ministers.

Leaders: Sheikh Sharif AHMED (President of the Transitional National Government and Leader of the Djibouti Faction), Sheikh Yusuf Mohammad SIYAD ("Indha Adde"), Sheikh Hassan Dahir AWEYS (Leader of the Asmara Faction).

Islamic Courts Union (ICU). A fundamentalist movement devoted to the creation of an Islamic state in Somalia governed by sharia (Islamic religious law), the ICU was formed in 2004 by about five of the Islamic courts that had arisen in and around Mogadishu since the mid-1990s and had become the capital's de facto judiciary. Dominated by the Hawiye clan, the ICU created its own militia to protect the courts and help to enforce the courts' decisions. Following the example of successful fundamentalist movements elsewhere in the world, the Union also set up schools and hospitals in Mogadishu, reportedly gaining popular support for these and other services.

By late 2005 the ICU had grown to include 11 courts, bolstered by a militia force of at least 1,500 Somalis as well as, reportedly, a number of militant Islamists from other countries. In early 2006 the Ifka Halam court. led by Sheikh Hassan Dahir Aweys (a hard-line former leader of the Islamic Union currently on the U.S. list of terrorism suspects), launched a campaign to drive the warlord militias out of Mogadishu, which it achieved in June 2006. The ICU subsequently announced the establishment of an 88-member Council of the Islamic Courts to govern Mogadishu, imposed sharia law, and threatened to seize Ogaden, a Somali-speaking region of Ethiopia. Aweys was selected as leader of the new council, while Sheikh Sharif Ahmed, the moderate chair of the ICU, was named head of the council's executive committee. The ICU was routed from Mogadishu in January 2007 by interim government-backed militias supported by Ethiopian troops. ICU fighters continued to fight, using guerilla tactics. The military wing of the ICU, "the Youth" (*al-Shabab*), founded in 2003, launched a campaign of terrorist attacks against the government, foreign peacekeepers, and aid workers in 2007. Aden Hashi AYRO, the leader of *al-Shabab* and the head of al-Qaida in Somalia, was killed in U.S. air strikes on May 1, 2008 (see Current issues, above). Aweys was one of the principal groups behind the creation of the ALRS, but the ICU leadership split over the June 2008 peace agreement with the TNG. Aweys endeavored to replace Ahmed with an ally, Zakaria Mohamed Haji ABDI, in June following the ALRS-Ethiopian accord. Many senior figures in the ICU also rejected the October peace accord between the ALRS and the TNG. A new coalition of Islamic groups, the **Party of Islam** (*Hizbul Islam*) was formed by ICU leaders to counter the ALRS. The new body brought together various groups that had been part of the ICU, including the **Islamic Front** (*Jabhat al-*Islamiya), led by Abdulqader KUMANDOS; the **Islamic Resistance** (*al-Muqawama Islamiya*), formed by Hassan TURKI; and the **Anole Camp** (*Mu'askar Anole*). In March 2009 Aweys was named leader of *Hizbul Islam* while the former leader of the group Sheikh Yusuf Mohammad SIYAD ("Indha Adde") became associated with the Djibouti wing of the ALRS. *Hizbul Islam* fighters fought alongside *al-Shabab* insurgents in antigovernment operations throughout 2009, although there was also interclan strife between the two groups.

Leaders: Sheikh Hassan Dahir AWEYS (Leader of the Council of the Islamic Courts), Sheikh Abdulqadir Ali UMAR.

United Somali Congress (USC). Organized in January 1989 by members of the Hawiye clan of central Somalia, the USC was instrumental in the ouster of President Siad Barre in 1991, and the grouping's principal financial backer, Ali Mahdi Mohamed, was shortly thereafter named interim president of the republic. However, at the party's third congress held July 4–5, Gen. Mohamed Farah Aidid was elected USC chair, provoking a bitter dispute with Mahdi and clashes between their respective factions in the autumn that produced widespread death and dislocation in Mogadishu. The USC subsequently remained split between pro-Mahdi and pro-Aidid factions referenced as the USC-SSA and USC-SNA, respectively. Further splintering occurred in June 1995 when Osman Hasan Ali ("Osman Ato"), a longtime ally of Aidid's, turned against the general and was named chair of a dissident USC-SNA. The USC-SNA later became the core of the Somali Reconciliation and Reconstruction Council (SRRC).

In February 2001 Muhammad Qanyarsh AFRAH, a USC leader, was named to the cabinet. However, a major USC-SSA faction, under the leadership of Musa Sudi YALLAHOW (who had challenged Mahdi for the SSA leadership in 1999) and Umar Muhammad MAHMUD ("Umar Finish"), continued to reject participation in the government. Further splintering occurred in December when Umar Finish and his supporters signed the proposed expanded power-sharing agreement, while Yallahow opposed the pact. Fighters loyal to Yallahow engaged TNG troops routinely throughout 2002, and his faction remained an integral part of the SRRC and joined in the launching of the breakaway autonomous administration in the southwest (see Political background, above). Some factions joined in the negotiations, which resulted in the 2004 TFC, and Osman Ato and Yallahow joined the 2004 transitional government. No longer a united front, factions of the party support the different warlords, such as Ato and Yallahow, and continue to support the TNG. However, other faction leaders opposed the presidency of Yusuf Ahmed. Most of the former USC factions are united in their opposition to the ICU and other fundamentalist Islamic groups.

Somali National Alliance (SNA). The SNA was launched by Gen. Mohamed Farah Aidid following the leadership conflict in 1992 in the USC (see above). The SNA claimed the support of some two dozen affiliates, including factions of the USC, SDM, SPM, SSDF, and SSNM.

In October 1994 General Aidid, responding to the announcement by his adversary, Ali Mahdi Mohamed, of a Group of Twelve alliance, announced a G-12 of his own that encompassed Aidid supporters from the previous five formations; a number of SSA dissidents; the **National Democratic Union** (NDU); an SNU faction led by Umar MUNGANI AWEYS; a SAMO faction led by Sheikh JAMA HUSSEIN; a faction of the **Somali National Democratic Union** (SNDU) led by Ali ISMAIL ABDI and Ahmad MAHMUD ATO; and a United Somalia Party (USP) faction led by Hasan Haji UMAR AMI. The other two places on Aidid's G-12 list were assigned to a northwestern clan grouping, the Somali Democratic Alliance (SDA), and Somaliland's Somali National Movement (SNM), which Abdurahmane Ahmed Ali insisted that he still led (see the Somaliland article for both groups).

In May 1995, Osman Hasan Ali ("Osman Ato"), a longtime adviser to General Aidid, broke with Aidid and announced he had assumed the leadership of the SNA. Osman Ato and his supporters were subsequently referenced as representing a dissident branch of the USC-SNA.

Several additional groups reportedly supported General Aidid at the time of his presidential self-proclamation in June 1995, including the **Somali Democratic Movement–Original** (SDM–*Asalow*), led by Dr. Yusuf ALI YUSUF, and an SPM faction led by Barreh UGAS GEDI.

Following the death of General Aidid in August 1996, his son, Hussein Mohamed Farah Aidid, an American-educated former U.S. Marine, was elected "president" and SNA leader in a three-day, two-part electoral process that reportedly split the clan along generational lines. Subsequently, although there was widespread speculation that the younger Aidid would only serve as a figurehead for the SNA's militia, he immediately pursued reconciliation pacts with a number of SNA clan leaders whom his father had alienated.

In April 1997 approximately 800 SNA militants broke off from the grouping, accusing the Farah Aidid "government" of corruption and complaining that they had not been given the respect due a national army. SNA militiamen subsequently battled with forces from the RRA (below) for control of Baidoa.

Aidid, whose militia continued to control portions of Mogadishu and surrounding areas, declined to participate in the SNPC, held in Arta, Djibouti, in 2000, and rejected the resultant transitional government. In early 2001 Aidid, still referring to himself as chair of the SNA, was announced as chair of the Somali Reconciliation and Reconstruction Council (SRRC), a new grouping of some 21 southern faction leaders committed to establishing their own interim central government as an alternative to the "Arta" plan.

Other prominent SRRC members included the RRA, SSNM, and a main faction of the SPM. Aidid was elected as the first SRRC chair, while Mawlid MA'ANE MAGMUD was named as the group's general secretary. However, Ma'ane Magmud, described as the leader of the Bantu community in Somalia, broke from the SRRC and endorsed the December 2001 power-sharing agreement between the TNG and several warlords and faction leaders. The SRRC subsequently continued to serve as the primary challenge to the TNG's authority, and in April 2002 it announced the formation of a breakaway state in southern Somalia. Farah Aidid supported the 2004 TFC and was appointed a deputy prime minister and the internal affairs minister in the December transitional government. Aidid's portfolio was then shifted to minister of public works and housing during the cabinet reshuffle of February 2007. In May 2007, PM Ghedi sacked him from the cabinet completely, though he maintains a parliamentary seat in the TFP and is a vocal opponent of the Ethiopian troop presence in the country. Reports in 2008 indicated that Aidid and his followers had joined the ALRS and had established a base of operations in Asmara, Eritrea.

Leader: Hussein Mohamed FARAH AIDID (Chair).

Rahanweyn Resistance Army (RRA). Assisted by troops from Ethiopia, the RRA in 1999 seized control of much of south-central Somalia (home to the Digil and Mirifle clans) and expelled Ethiopian rebel groups from the region. The RRA was a core component of the Somali Peace Alliance (SPA), established in August 1999 to promote the "rebuilding" of a central government through the initial establishment of a number of autonomous regional governments. (The SPA was led by Col. Abdullahi Yusuf Ahmed of Puntland and also included the pro-Ethiopian wing of the SNF.) In December 2000 the leader of the RRA, Col. Hassan Mohammed Nur ("Shatigadud"), rejected the authority of the TNG, and the RRA subsequently indicated plans to set up its own regional administration. In January 2001 the SPA appeared to have been superseded by a National Restoration Council (NRC), itself a precursor, in part at least, to the SRRC (see SNA, above). Colonel Shatigadud was elected president of the Southwestern Regional Government announced in April 2002, although some RRA members, led by Muhammad Ibrahim HABSADE and Sheikh Adan MADOBE, opposed that initiative. Fierce fighting was subsequently reported between the two RRA factions. Shatigadud was appointed agriculture minister in December 2004 and changed his portfolio to finance minister in 2005, but resigned from the government in December 2007 after being appointed minister of national security. Madobe was appointed minister of justice in the transitional government and became speaker of parliament in January 2007. He briefly served as interim president of the TNG following the resignation of Ahmed in 2008 and was instrumental in the negotiations that led to the reconciliation between the government and the ALRS in January 2009.

Leaders: Col. Hassan Mohammed NUR ("Shatigadud"), Sheikh Adan MADOBE (Speaker of the Transnational Federal Parliament), Mohamed Ali Adeh QALINLEH.

Somali National Front (SNF). The SNF was launched in 1991 by Darod clan interests in southern Somalia as a guerrilla force seeking the return to power of Siad Barre. Led by the former dictator's son-in-law, Gen. Mohamed Said Hersi ("Morgan"), the group was described as a "fair-weather-ally of Mahdi Mohamed."

In 1997 SNF militants clashed with Islamic Union fighters fleeing invading Ethiopian troops. Clashes between the SNF and Islamic militants continued into 1998, with the SNF allegedly receiving funding from Ethiopia. In addition, fighting between the SNF and SSDF was reported in the south. Moreover, beginning in April, the SNF suffered from intraparty battles in Kismayu, where General Morgan attempted to fend off attacks by fighters loyal to Omar HAJI MASALEH. (Haji Masaleh and his militiamen were reportedly supported by Mogadishu warlords Farah Aidid and Ali Mahdi.) Severe splintering continued into 2002; by that time General Morgan was no longer referenced as an SNF leader. The progovernment, anti-Ethiopian SNF faction reportedly led by Col. Abdouzarak Issak BINI and the main pro-Ethiopian faction joined the NRC and SRRC, led by Mohamad Sayyid ADEN. The SNF no longer exists as a united force.

Leader: Omar HAJI MASALEH.

Somali Patriotic Movement (SPM). The SPM surfaced in 1989 on behalf of Ogadeni soldiers of the southern Darod clan who formerly supported Siad Barre but had initiated antigovernment attacks in the area between the Juba River and the Kenyan border in an effort to gain autonomy for the region.

The SPM's leader, Gen. Adan Abdullahi Noor ("Gabio"), was one of five NSC cochairs appointed in early 1997. By that time the SPM was split into at least two main factions—one led by Noor and General Morgan (formerly of the SNF, above) and one led by Col. Umar Jess, who had once partnered with the SNM in Somaliland before joining the SPM in alliance with General Aidid in 1992. Fighting between the two factions for control of the rich agricultural region of the Juba Valley was subsequently reported, as were skirmishes between SPM fighters and those from the rival Juba Valley Alliance (see below). Neither faction reaching an agreement with the TNG, Noor and his supporters participated in the launch of the SRRC. Morgan was one of the few major warlords who did not participate in the negotiations over the TFC. He later agreed to support the TFP but opposed the election of Yusuf Ahmed as president. Morgan survived an assassination attempt in September 2008. The SPM has ceased to function in its original composition.

Leaders: Gen. Adan Abdullahi NOOR ("Gabio"), Gen. Mohamed Said HERSI ("Morgan"), Col. Ahmed Umar JESS.

Islamic Union (*Al-Itihad al-Islami*). The Islamic Union was initially described by the *New York Times* as a "faction made up of fervently religious people, mostly from the Ogadeni clan of Somalia," dedicated to gaining independence for the Ogaden region. Throughout the first half of 1996 the Union claimed responsibility for a number of terrorist attacks in Addis Ababa, Ethiopia, including the attempted assassination of a cabinet member. In August Ethiopian forces attacked three Union-controlled towns in the Gedo region of Somalia and claimed to have killed over 200 Islamic fighters before withdrawing. Consequently, Union leader Sheikh Hassan Dahir Aweys declared a "holy war" against Ethiopia and accused Ethiopia of harboring plans to occupy Somalian territory.

In late 1996 Hussein Farah Aidid reportedly sought to establish a dialogue with the Union, and in early 1997 the latter announced its interest in attaining legal party status. However, such concerns were subsequently overshadowed when an Ethiopian offensive into Somalia drove Union fighters from their last remaining military base in the Gedo region. Compounding the Union's military woes, SNF forces were reported to be attacking Union fighters retreating from the border region. In 1998 the Union accused Ethiopia of orchestrating assassination attempts against its leaders.

The United States expressed concern in the early 2000s about possible links between the Islamic Union and al-Qaida, although Union leaders have steadfastly denied any connection to terrorist activities or proclivities. However, the Union has supported the growing influence of Islamic courts in Somalia. Meanwhile, Col. Yusuf Ahmed, the leader of Puntland, accused the Islamic Union of being behind efforts by Jama Ali Jama to secure power in that autonomous region (see Political background, above, for details). However, some analysts have described reports of Union influence in Somalia as "overblown." In 2005 Yusuf Ahmed reported that the Union had ceased any major operations in Somalia, and it is now considered defunct. Many of the fighters of the Islamic Union were subsequently reported to have joined the Islamic Courts Union (above).

Somali Salvation Democratic Front (SSDF). The SSDF was initially organized in 1982 as the Democratic Front for the Salvation of Somalia (DFSS) by merger of three dissident groups: the Somali Salvation Front (SSF), the Democratic Front for the Liberation of Somalia (DFLS), and the Somali Workers' Party (SWP). The SSF (also known as Sosaf) had been formed in 1976 as the Somali Democratic Action Front (Sodaf), with headquarters in Rome, Italy, the change of name and relocation to Addis Ababa occurring in early 1979. Its leader at the launching of the DFSS was Col. Abdullahi Yusuf Ahmed, who had defected from Somalia with a group of army officers in 1978 following an abortive coup attempt. Most SSF members were drawn from the secessionist-oriented Mijarteyn tribe of northeastern Somalia, some of whom were executed after the coup had failed.

The DFLS, another Ethiopian-backed group, was led at the time of the merger by Abderahman AIDID AHMED, reportedly a former chair of the SRSP Ideological Bureau. The SWP, a Soviet-supported movement headquartered in South Yemen, was led by Hussein SAID JAMA, a former member of the SRSP's Central Committee.

At the inauguration of the DFSS, Yusuf Ahmed was named chair, Said Jama vice president, and Aidid Ahmed secretary general. A party congress in March 1983 elected a 21-member central committee and a nine-member executive committee and adopted a constitution and a political program that called for the overthrow of the Siad Barre regime, the removal of U.S. bases from Somalia, and the establishment of "genuine peace and cooperation based on the brotherhood of the Horn of Africa." However, some DFLS and SWP members reportedly were excluded from the new formation at the 1983 congress, and Said Jama and Aidid Ahmed were removed from their leadership positions the following November. In January 1984 it was reported that a number of DFSS members opposed to Yusuf Ahmed's leadership had accepted government amnesty, as had about 200 guerrillas in May. In July 1985 Said Jama was reported to have founded a splinter group, the **Somali Patriotic Liberation Front** (SPLF), based, like its SWP predecessor, in Aden, South Yemen. In October 1985 Yusuf Ahmed, who had been criticized for his attempts to lessen Ethiopian influence over the DFSS and for his unwillingness to facilitate further merger of Somali opposition movements, was arrested in Ethiopia and replaced as chair by Gen. Mohamed ABSHIR MUSSE.

In 1989 the DFSS leadership announced that the organization was no longer pursuing military confrontation with the government but was hoping for legal recognition as a political party should proposed political liberalization measures be implemented. What had been restyled as the SSDF split in May 1993, with Yusuf Ahmed concluding an accord with General Aidid, while the rump group under Abshir Musse became a member of the G-12 grouping led by Ali Mahdi. In 2000 the SSDF was referenced as supporting the TNG, an initiative opposed by Yusuf Ahmed, then the leader of the autonomous administration in Puntland. There subsequently was little reference to the SSDF.

Southern Somali National Movement (SSNM). A south coastal formation, the SSNM is led by Abdi Warsame ISSAQ, who withdrew from the SNA in August 1993 to enter the pro-Mahdi G-12. In August 1997 one faction of the SSNM rejoined the pro-Aidid wing of the SNA. The SSNM-SNA, now under the leadership of Abdullahi Sheikh ISMAIL, participated in the formation of the SRRC in 2001 and the subsequent negotiations over the TFC. Ismail was appointed foreign minister in the transitional government installed in late 2004. He served as deputy prime minister but left the government in 2007.

Leader: Abdullahi Sheikh ISMAIL.

Other groups include the **Juba Valley Alliance** (JVA), which, under the leadership of Col. Barre Aden SHIRE ("Hirale"), confronted the RRA and "Ethiopian influence" in the Juba Valley, but which reports indicated had dissolved after the Ethiopian invasion; the **Muslim Youth Party,** formed in late 2002 under the leadership of Ibrahim Muhammad HASSAN; the **Peace and Development Party,** organized in 2002 under the leadership of Gedi Shadron ABDULLAHI and Abdullahi Hassan AFRAH; the **Somali African Muki Organization** (SAMO), an ally of the RRA; the **Somali Democratic Party,** originally formed in 1993 in the Gedo region and reportedly relaunched in 2002 under the leadership of Abdi Barre ABDI and Omar Ibrahim MOHAMOUD; the **Somali Islamic Party** (SIP), which in 2002 called for a foreign peacekeeping force to be deployed in Somalia; the **Somali Peace Loving Party,** whose chair, Khalid Umar ALI, was reportedly involved in efforts to mediate between the TNG and opposition factions; the **Somali Solidarity Party** (SSP), formed in Mogadishu under the leadership of Abdulrahman Musa MUHAMMED and Muhammad UTHMAN; the **Somali Unification Party,** a small grouping led by warlord Hussein Haji BOD, who ultimately endorsed the 2000 reconciliation initiative with the TNG; the **Unity for the Somali Republic Party** (USRP), launched in 1999 under the leadership of Abdi Nur DARMAN; the **National Democratic League**, formed in 2003 and led by Abdiwahid Abdulle ABDI; the **Mujahideen Youth Movement**, an extremist group formed in 2007 with links to al-Qaida; and *al-Shabab*, a fundamentalist Islamic movement led by Sheikh Muktar Abdirahman GODANE, which captured large areas of Somalia in 2009 in an alliance with *Hizbul Islam*. *Al-Shabab* was reported to have received substantial financial and military support from Saudi Arabia.

LEGISLATURE

The former People's Assembly was dissolved after the overthrow of the SRSP government in January 1991. On August 13, 2000, a Transitional National Assembly (TNA) was inaugurated in accordance with the national charter adopted by the Somali National Peace Conference meeting in Arta, Djibouti. The TNA comprised 245 members appointed for a three-year term pending national elections. Each of four major clan groupings (Darod, Hawiye, Dir, and Digil-Mirifleh) was allowed to appoint 44 members, while 24 seats went to smaller clans and subclans. In addition, 25 seats (also reportedly allocated on a clan basis) were designated specifically for women, while Djibouti's President Ismail Omar Guelleh was given 20 appointments. The TNA began formal legislative sessions in October 2000 in Mogadishu, although many members reportedly stayed away due to security concerns. Meanwhile, the government of Somaliland, the administration of the self-declared autonomous region of Puntland, and a number of major faction leaders in and around Mogadishu did not accept the authority of the TNA.

In January 2004 most of the parties involved in the political and military conflict in Somalia agreed to a comprehensive agreement that included provision for the creation of an appointed **Transitional Federal Parliament** (TFP) to serve for four years, after which direct elections were to be held for a permanent legislature. The TFP, sworn in on August 29, 2004, comprised 275 deputies; each of the four major clans (Hawiye, Rahanweyn, Dir, and Darod) appointed 61 members, while 31 seats were allocated to smaller clans and subclans. On January 26, 2009, the TFP voted to expand to 550 members, including 200 deputies from the ALRS and an additional 75 members from civil society groups.

Speaker: Sheikh Adan Madobe.

CABINET

[as of August 1, 2009]

Prime Minister	Omar Abdirashid Ali Shermarke
Deputy Prime Ministers	Sharif Hassan Sheikh Aden (ALRS)
	Abdiwahid Ilmi Gonjeh
	Abdirahman Haji Adan Ibbi (ALRS)
Ministers	
Agriculture	Hassan Mohammad Nur
Air and Land Transport	Ali Ahmed Jama Jangali
Commerce	Abdirahman Mohammed Iro
Constitution and Federal Affairs	Madobe Nunow Mohammed
Culture and Higher Education	Ibrahim Nassan Adow (ALRS)
Defense	Mohammed Abdi Gandi (ALRS)
Education	Ahmad Abdullahi Wayel
Endowment and Religious Affairs	Sheikh Nur Adan Ali
Energy	Abdiwahid Ilmi Gonjeh
Environment and Conservation of Trees	Bur'I Mohammed Hamzi
Finance	Sharif Hassan Sheikh Aden (ALRS)
Fisheries and Marine Resources	Abdirahman Haji Adan Ibbi (ALRS)
Foreign Affairs	Mohammed Abdullahi Omar
Gender Development and Family Affairs	Fowsiya Mohammed Sheikh Hassan [f]
Health	Qamar Adan Ali [f]
Humanitarian Assistance	Mohammed Abdi Ibrahim
Industry	Abdirahman Jama Abdalla
Information	Farhan Ali Mahmud
Interior Affairs	Abdulkadir Ali Omar (ALRS)
Internal Security	(Vacant)
Justice and Religious Affairs	Abdiahman Mohamud Farah Janagow (ALRS)
Labor	Mohammed Abdi Hayir Mareye
Livestock Development	Abukar Ali Usman
Minerals and Water	Abdalla Bos Ahmad

National Heritage	Mohammed Mursal
National Planning and International Cooperation	Abdirahman Abdishakur Warsame (ALRS)
Ports and Sea Transportation	Mohammed Ibrahim Habsade
Posts and Communications	Abdirizak Osman Jurile
Reconstruction	Husayn Elabe Fahiye
Rehabilitation and the Disabled	Mohammed Ali Ibrahim
Research and Technology	Mohammed Ali Haga
Rural Development	Khadija Mohammed Diriye [f]
Somalis in Diaspora	Abdullahi Ahmad Abdulle
Sports and Youth	Suleyman Olad Roble (ALRS)
Tourism and Wildlife	Mohammed Husayn Sa'id
Works and Housing	Mohammed Abdi Yusuf (ALRS)

[f] = female

COMMUNICATIONS

Press. The press is undeveloped and circulation is low as the literacy rate is low and few people can afford to buy newspapers. Both the ICU and the interim government have reportedly repressed the independent press, and journalists are habitually harassed and assassinated. During the Siad Barre era, the only daily was the government's *Xiddigta Oktobar* (October Star), which ceased publication after the former president's overthrow. Current periodicals published in Mogadishu include *Ayaamaha,* described as supportive of Hussein Farah Aidid; *Qaran* (Nation, 2,000), daily; *Xog-Ogaal,* daily; the *Mogadishu Times;* and *Sooyal.* The newspaper *Sahan* is published in the Puntland region.

News agencies. The domestic agency is the Somali National News Agency (Sonna). The privately-owned Somali Broadcasting Corporation (SBC) is based in Puntland.

Broadcasting and computing. The previously government-owned Somali Broadcasting Service, now controlled by General Aidid's faction, operates Radio Mogadishu. Several other local stations service Mogadishu. The BBC Somali service is broadcasted from London. Puntland has one radio station called Radio Gaalkayco. Radio Kismayu broadcasts in Kismayu and started in 2000. As of 2008 there were 11.4 Internet users per 1,000 inhabitants.

INTERGOVERNMENTAL REPRESENTATION

Ambassador to the U.S.: [the Washington embassy closed on May 8, 1991].

U.S. Ambassador to Somalia: (Vacant).

Permanent Representative to the UN: Elmi Ahmed DUALE.

IGO Memberships (Non-UN): AfDB, AFESD, AMF, AU, CAEU, IDB, IGAD, Interpol, IOM, LAS, NAM, OIC.

SOMALILAND

Republic of Somaliland

Political Status: Former British Somaliland Protectorate; joined with (Italian) Trust Territory of Somalia on July 1, 1960, to form Somali Republic; announced secession as independent state on May 18, 1991; constitution endorsing independence and providing for multiparty activity approved by national referendum on May 31, 2001.

Area: 68,000 sq. mi. (176,120 sq. km.)

Population: 5,303,000 (2008E).

Major Urban Centers (2004E): HARGEISA (500,000), Berbera (35,000).

Principal Language: Somali.

Monetary Unit: Somaliland shilling, which became Somaliland's sole legal tender on January 31, 1995, with an initial value of 100 Somali shillings = $1US. Due to the lack of international recognition of Somaliland's self-declared independent status, the exchange value of the shilling is not reported in regular currency listings. However, it reportedly has recently averaged 6,500-7,000 Somaliland shillings = $1US.

President: Dahir Riyale KAHIN (United and Democratic People's Alliance); sworn in (based on his position as vice president and thereby the constitutionally authorized presidential successor) on May 3, 2002, following the death of Mohamed Haji Ibrahim EGAL (initially Somali National Movement, subsequently United and Democratic People's Alliance) the same day; popularly elected on April 14, 2003, and sworn in for a five-year term on May 16; term extended to September 29, 2009.

Vice President: Ahmad Yusuf YASIN (United and Democratic People's Alliance); named by the president on May 16, 2002, and approved by the legislature on May 21; popularly elected on April 14, 2003, and sworn in on May 16 for a five-year term; term extended to March 29, 2010.

THE COUNTRY

The northwest portion of the Somali Republic as constituted in 1960, Somaliland extends some 400 miles eastward from Djibouti along the Gulf of Aden (see map). Most of the terrain is desert or semidesert, and it is estimated that nomadic animal-herders still constitute about one-half of the population. While sharing, as throughout Somalia, a common religion (Islam) and a common language (Somali), the people are divided into numerous clans and subclans, which contributed to the 1991 break with the south as well as subsequent difficulty in forging a wholly unified regime in the north.

Largely stable and peaceful since 1997, Somaliland has nevertheless failed to achieve international recognition for its independence as the result of concern, particularly among African leaders, that the "Balkanization" of Somalia would embolden secessionists throughout the continent. Consequently, international aid has been constrained, and the economy has depended primarily on remittances from workers abroad (an estimated $312 million in 2008). About 60 percent of the population reportedly relies on agriculture, including livestock, for a living, and annual GDP per capita is currently estimated at only $290. To attract the interest of the international private sector, the government has adopted a free-market orientation, including liberal investment policies. Development plans focus on expanding the production of frankincense and myrrh, exploiting rich coastal fishing grounds, and exploring the potentially lucrative gem sector. It has been estimated that up to two-thirds of the $51 million (2008) budget goes to military spending, much of it in the form of what are essentially "bribes" to former clan militiamen who have agreed to stop fighting each other in return for employment in the police force. Few resources are therefore available for educational, health, or infrastructure purposes. However, a degree of economic progress (particularly around Hargeisa and the port of Berbera) has been reported in recent years, lending support, in the opinion of some analysts, to the contention of the government that Somaliland would best be served by remaining outside the political and economic "maelstrom" of Somalia proper. Perhaps significantly, the European Union (EU) pledged in 2006 to increase its aid to Somaliland, and has continued to assess potential areas of cooperation in 2008. However, international donors have threatened to suspend aid if presidential elections continue to be postponed (see Current issues, below). Meanwhile, oil companies from South Africa, Malaysia, India, and the United Kingdom were authorized by the Somaliland administration to pursue offshore oil exploration. However, the people of Somaliland continue to rely overwhelmingly on livestock, a trade suppressed in recent years by bans in countries in the Arabian Peninsula on livestock imports from the territory. This ban was lifted in Saudi Arabia in early 2007, leading to new contracts with Saudi businesses to export

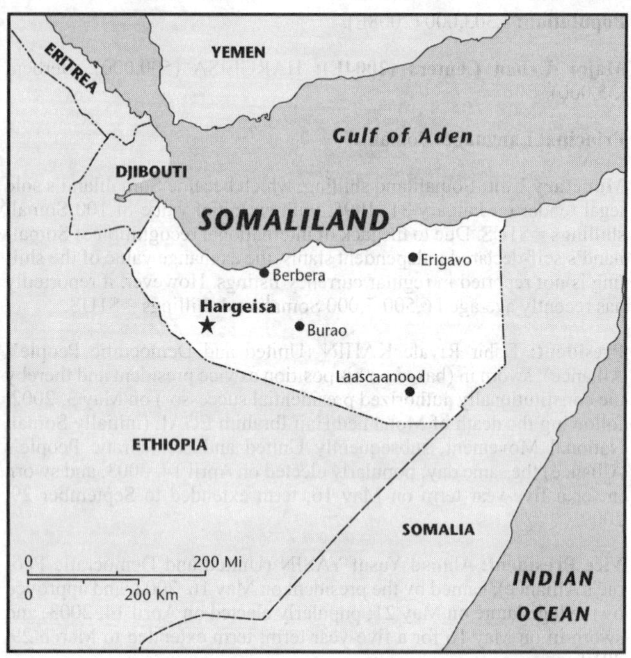

more than two million head of cattle, camels, and goats per year. A prolonged drought was estimated to have affected up to 40 percent of the population, and the government issued a call for expanded international food aid in 2009.

GOVERNMENT AND POLITICS

Political background. A British protectorate since 1887, Somaliland was overrun by Italian forces at the outbreak of World War II but was recaptured by Britain in 1941. The protectorate was terminated on June 26, 1960, and on July 1 Somaliland joined its theretofore Italian-administered counterpart in the south to form what was styled the United Republic of Somalia, prior to its redesignation as the Somali Democratic Republic in 1969.

In 1988 the Somali National Movement (SNM), a rebel group that had joined with Ethiopian units in a cross-border assault the year before, mounted a broad-gauged offensive that succeeded in driving government forces from most of the northern region's rural areas by mid-1989. However, the government continued its heavy bombing campaign against Hargeisa and other towns, much of the northern population reportedly fleeing to Ethiopia to escape the "genocidal campaign" of the Siad Barre regime. Meanwhile, elsewhere in Somalia, other clan-based groups had taken up arms, most important among them the United Somali Congress (USC) in central regions and the Somali Patriotic Movement (SPM) in the south (see Political Parties and Groups in article on Somalia for details).

On January 27, 1991, USC forces assumed control in Mogadishu, the Somalia capital, and appointed their principal backer, Ali Mahdi Mohamed, to the post of interim president. Ali Mahdi attempted to convene a "conference of national reconciliation" on February 28 but was rebuked by the SNM for having taken the initiative without prior consultation. A second such effort on March 14 also failed, and on May 18 the north proclaimed its independence as the Republic of Somaliland under the presidency of Abdurahman AHMED ALI ("Taur"). Many refugees subsequently returned to Somaliland from Ethiopia, discovering that the recent fighting, which had reportedly left 40,000 dead, had also devastated the region's infrastructure.

Ahmed Ali's control proved to be somewhat tenuous, and he did not attend a grand *shir* (gathering) of leading tribal, political, and military figures in Somaliland that met for most of February 1993 to discuss clan relations and the formalization of independence. Subsequently, a "parliamentary" meeting of the SNM Central Committee was convened to implement the *shir*'s conclusions. On May 5 the same body named Mohamed Ibrahim EGAL, a former prime minister of Somalia who had been imprisoned by the Siad Barre regime for many years, to succeed Ahmed Ali as president, with Col. Abdurahman ALI, who had been sacked as education minister in February, as vice president.

During a meeting with Gen. Mohamed Farah Aidid of the Somali National Alliance (SNA) in Ethiopia in April 1994, Ahmed Ali unexpectedly called for Somaliland to rejoin Somalia. The appeal was immediately rejected by President Egal, who branded his predecessor as a traitor and termed Somaliland's independence as "irrevocable." Egal reiterated the position in late May by rejecting inclusion in a federal state. On October 15, 1994, fighting erupted in Hargeisa airport between government forces and defecting militiamen of the Issaq subclan of Eidegalla. By late November the rebels appeared to control most of the capital, despite claims by President Egal to the contrary, and by early December about three-quarters of the city's population had reportedly fled.

In January 1995, having embarked on a build-up of arms (reportedly supplied by Albania) and with an army increased to more than 3,000 men, Egal mounted an offensive that succeeded in driving the rebels from Hargeisa. On May 9 a spokesman in Nairobi announced the government's appointment of a Peace Committee, although the Mogadishu-based Ahmed Ali continued to support anti-Egal forces. Further clashes occurred in Hargeisa airport in August 1995 and along the frontier with Djibouti three months later. On the latter occasion the government blamed the Djibouti regime for providing support to dissident Issa militiamen belonging to the United Somali Front (see Political Parties, below).

On the political front, meanwhile, in May 1995 the SNM Central Committee, acting as an interim parliament, reelected Egal president. In July Egal appointed a ten-member constitutional drafting committee that he charged with writing a new basic charter within 12 months. However, immediately thereafter, the president employed a Sudanese constitutional consultant who, along with the president and a reportedly shrinking circle of presidential advisors, drew up a draft document that included provisions for a U.S.-style presidency. In response to Egal's proposed constitution, the Central Committee, many of whose members were described as "infuriated" by the president's actions, presented a rival draft highlighted by a parliamentary democracy. The constitutional deadlock continued through mid-1996, thus "forcing" Egal to continue governing by decree.

Concurrent with the expiration of its own charter, the advisory Council of Elders in October 1996 convened a 315-member National Communities Conference to which President Egal presented the two draft documents. In early 1997 the conference provisionally approved a new constitution (see Constitution and government, below), and on February 23 the delegates reelected Egal to a five-year term (the incumbent secured 223 votes in what observers described as remarkably "amicable" polling). In May Egal appointed a new government.

In December 1997 President Egal submitted his resignation to the legislature, complaining of a "lack of collaboration" from his government and other senior officials. Citing the need for stability, the legislators voted overwhelmingly to reject his request, thus compelling the incumbent to continue at his post. Meanwhile, a number of analysts attributed Egal's actions to his desire to fortify his position amid accusations of rampant corruption as well as to underline Somaliland's independence claims at the same time that Somalian faction leaders held unity talks in Cairo, Egypt.

Constitutional amendments were proposed by the government in mid-1999 with the goals of strengthening the role of the president and responding to opposition demands for greater judicial independence. Following a number of further revisions, the new constitution received a reported 97 percent endorsement from those voting in a national referendum on May 31, 2001. Among other things, the new basic law contained an article affirming Somaliland's status as an independent republic. (The Somaliland government had declined to participate in reconciliation talks launched in 2000 in Somalia proper. See article on Somalia.) The first multiparty elections under the new constitution were initially scheduled at the local level for December 2001. However, they were subsequently postponed, and in early 2002 the legislature reportedly extended Egal's term of office (as well as that of Vice President Dahir Riyale KAHIN) until February 2003, although opponents of the administration criticized that decision and demanded that another all-inclusive conference of clan elders be held to determine the presidential status.

President Egal died on May 3, 2002, and he was succeeded on the same day by Kahin, following endorsement by an emergency meeting of legislative and ministerial representatives. Kahin's administration subsequently underscored its commitment to independence by declining to participate in the conference launched in Kenya in late 2002 regarding potential power-sharing in Somalia. Local elections were conducted in December 2002, with Kahin's United and Democratic People's Alliance (*Ururka Dimuqraadiga Ummadda Bahawday*—UDUB) securing a reported 41 percent of the vote, followed by the Solidarity Party (*Hisbiga Kulmiye*) with 19 percent and the Justice and Welfare Party (*Uruka Caddaalada Iyo Daryeelka*—UCID) with 11.2 percent. Those three parties consequently qualified for legal status under new constitutional provisions (see Political Parties and Groups, below, for details).

In presidential balloting on April 14, 2003, Kahin was reelected by a razor-thin margin (42.08 percent to 42.06 percent) over Ahmed Mohamed MOHAMOUD ("Silanyo") of *Kulmiye*. A new "propresidential" government was announced on July 3.

In Somaliland's first national legislative balloting since its declaration of independence, the UDUB secured a plurality of 33 seats in the elections to the House of Representatives on September 25, 2005. However, following the elections, the UCID and *Kulmiye* announced a cooperation agreement that produced immediate results—the election of a member of the UCID as speaker.

Kahin's term was extended by the House of Elders in 2008 and 2009, a decision that was roundly criticized by the UCID and *Kulmiye*. Meanwhile, presidential balloting was postponed until September 2009 (see Current issues, below). Kahin rejected opposition calls to step down and appoint an interim government until the presidential balloting. In April 2009 the new Somali government (see Somalia entry) initiated negotiations with Somaliland on mutual recognition.

Constitution and government. The government established in the wake of the May 1991 independence proclamation encompassed a president and vice president, appointed by the SNM, initially for a two-year transitional period during which a constitution was to be drafted that would permit the holding of open, multiparty elections. On May 28 *Radio Hargeisa* announced that the SNM leadership had also approved the formation of a high court and a civil service, in addition to the appointment of an attorney general, an auditor general, and a Central Bank governor.

In early July 1995 President Egal announced that a ten-member constitutional drafting committee had been appointed and that a basic law for Somaliland would be forthcoming within the ensuing 12 months. Meanwhile, the SNM Central Committee continued to serve as an interim legislature and electoral body for the presidency. In early 1997 the National Communities Conference provisionally approved a constitution that provided for a bicameral legislature (see Legislature, below), an electoral system of direct universal suffrage, and the organization of political parties (although groups with "tribal" or religious affiliations were proscribed). Among the details to surface subsequently about the document were stipulations that future presidents and their spouses be both native Somalians and Muslims. In late 1998 the legislature reportedly approved the implementation of measures based on Islamic religious law.

The 1997 constitution was approved with the provision that it be presented to a national referendum within three years. A one-year extension was granted in February 2000 and a three-month extension in February 2001, with the referendum finally being held on May 31, 2001. The new basic law confirmed Somaliland's independence, strengthened the executive branch, confirmed Islam as the "national faith," provided for a free press, and endorsed multiparty elections at all levels of government through universal suffrage. In March 2008, legislation reconfigured Somaliland into 12 regions and 57 districts.

Foreign relations. Refusals to attend "reconciliation" conferences in Djibouti in 1991 were defended by SNM leaders on the ground that the meetings were called to address matters of domestic concern to "Southern Somalia." However, relations between Djibouti and Somaliland had been less than cordial because of conflict between the Issa community common to both countries and the Issaq grouping in Somaliland.

Despite what was described as a "flurry of meetings" designed to promote international recognition, by mid-1995 no foreign government had complied, partly because of long-standing opposition by the Organization of African Unity (OAU, subsequently the African Union—AU) to secessionist regimes and partly because of uncertainties surrounding continued anarchic conditions in the south. Significantly, while Somaliland had agreed in 1993 to the introduction of 500 UN peacekeepers to supervise the distribution of relief supplies, it rejected any deployment of U.S. troops on the ground that its claim to autonomy would thereby be jeopardized. In May 1994 President Egal threatened to expel any UN personnel advocating reintegration into Somalia.

In mid-1995 President Egal was reported to have sent a fax message to Israeli Prime Minister Yitzhak Rabin proposing the establishment of "strategic links" between their two countries. Egal spoke of the need to counter Islamic fundamentalism in the Horn of Africa, attributed with some degree of imprecision to "the growing influence of Saudi Arabia and the pro-Islamic Yemen."

Egal's efforts to gain international support bore fruit in late 1997 as Djibouti announced that it would exchange diplomatic credentials with Somalia. Italy subsequently told Egal in early 1998 that it would support an EU proposal to grant Somaliland "semi-diplomatic" recognition. For his part, Egal agreed to accept the offer of limited recognition for an interim period. Such concerns dominated Somaliland's foreign policy agenda through early 1999, with reports of Somaliland's enhanced international standing being balanced by continued calls from regional leaders for it to be included in a unified Somalia.

Relations with Djibouti deteriorated in 2000 when that country's leadership played a major role in the establishment of the transitional government in Somalia. However, Somaliland and Djibouti agreed to "normalize" their ties again in 2001. By that time it was clear that, in addition to opposing the notion of reunification with Somalia, Somaliland was in the midst of an ongoing territorial dispute with the Puntland autonomous region in Somalia.

Relations with Ethiopia improved in January 2002, when Ethiopia appointed an ambassador to Somaliland, and the Ethiopian government has since indicated that it may recognize Somaliland unilaterally if the AU refuses its membership bid. Reports indicated in 2008 that Somaliland and Ethiopia had increased military ties.

Intense lobbying efforts by officials from Somaliland to convince the UK government to recognize Somaliland's status as a fully independent nation continue to the present day. UK lawmakers visited Somaliland, and London agreed to help pay costs involved in the 2003 presidential poll. In addition, British companies reportedly began negotiations with Somaliland regarding offshore oil exploration. However, no official recognition was forthcoming, as most of the international community pressed (unsuccessfully) the Kahin administration to participate in the comprehensive Somalia peace talks. The Arab League in 2005 declined a request for membership from Somaliland, and the country's application for AU membership is still pending. Kahin traveled to six African states in 2006 to lobby for recognition, and an AU fact-finding mission concluded that Somaliland's status was "unique" and that recognition of its independence would not open a "Pandora's box" of new secessionist movements across the continent as African leaders had feared.

Somaliland has leveraged its reputation for comparative stability to court additional European support. In January and July 2007 the EU sent foreign affairs delegations to discuss future cooperation between the EU and Somaliland. The EU has also pledged to support the upcoming elections in the country. Additionally, Somaliland interacts directly with the Swedish government in aid negotiations, despite the fact that Sweden has not yet granted formal recognition to the country.

In February 2008 France announced an initiative to improve ties with Somaliland by funding French language and cultural programs. In June the United Nations provided Somaliland with vehicles for its security forces and judiciary. The UN Development Program concurrently announced that it was doubling its aid to Somaliland to $7 million per year. Beginning in September 2008, Somaliland security forces launched an aggressive antipiracy campaign that resulted in the arrest of more than 100 alleged pirates by May 2009. The effort was reportedly part of the larger campaign to gain support from the West. In May 2009, following negotiations with Puntland officials, Ethiopia offered to host discussions in an effort to mediate the dispute over the Sool region. Renewed fighting in Somalia led an estimated 26,000 Somalis to flee to Somaliland by the summer of 2009.

Current issues. In early 1999 President Egal reportedly indicated that Somaliland would be willing to consider reunification talks with Somalia, should warlords there negotiate a cease-fire and establish a permanent central government. At the same time, Egal pushed for international development aid, reportedly receiving a degree of "empathy" but little actual support from countries reluctant to appear at odds with AU and UN hopes that all of Somalia, including Somaliland, be reunified under a single federal system. For most observers, the May 2001 constitutional referendum appeared to settle the independence question.

President Egal's death in May 2002 was widely viewed as creating conditions that could lead to instability. However, incoming President

Kahin managed the transition smoothly, and the first multiparty municipal elections were conducted without incident in December.

President Kahin's reelection in April 2003 was noteworthy for his amazingly small margin of victory (80 votes out of nearly 490,000 cast). His Solidarity Party challenger initially protested the results, but following a ruling from the Constitutional Court that validated the outcome, he urged his supporters to accept the verdict. In October 2003 the government initiated a series of "antiterrorism" measures following an attack on westerners that Kahin blamed on illegal immigrants with connections to militant Islamic organizations. Among other things, foreigners without legal permits were expelled from the country.

After numerous postponements, balloting for the first elected House of Representatives was held in September 2005, as Somaliland remained absent from nascent reconciliation efforts in Somalia (see article on Somalia for details). Severe tension was reported over Somaliland's plan to include the disputed territory of Sool along the border with Puntland in the poll. (Fighting had broken out in that area between forces from Somaliland and Puntland in 2004.) However, the balloting was completed in Sool without violence.

Foreign observers described the 2005 elections as generally fair and free, further bolstering Somaliland's argument that it represented an oasis of developing democracy in an otherwise turbulent region and should be rewarded with international recognition. On a more negative note, however, conflict over the election of the speaker of the House of Representatives prompted a walkout by UDUB legislators and riots outside the parliament buildings. After securing the speaker's post, the UCID/*Kulmiye* coalition presented a legislative agenda calling, among other things, for sweeping anticorruption measures and a reduction in the president's national security powers. Meanwhile, the government announced that security forces had arrested a group of heavily-armed men accused of plotting the assassination of public officials and other terrorist acts. (The government characterized the detainees as members of al-Qaida who had been trained in Afghanistan.)

In May 2006 the House of Elders (currently appointed) announced that it had extended its term of office until October 2010 even though elections had been scheduled for October 2006. President Kahin supported the extension, and he and the House of Elders were strongly criticized by UCID and *Kulmiye* leaders for seemingly trying to hold on to a degree of legislative authority through extra-constitutional means. In response to the rise of the Union of Islamic Courts in Somalia, a debate over the role of Islam in Somaliland's public life gained prominence in late 2006, with President Kahin announcing in October that the country would be run by Islamic law (sharia). However, specifics regarding the timing and implementation of sharia remained unknown.

Controversy erupted in the capital after the formation in April 2007 of the Qaran Party, whose leaders challenged administration claims that the constitution requires politicians to join one of the existing three political parties to enter government. The QP leaders were arrested in July (see Political Parties, below). On October 8, 2007, the National Electoral Commission announced it was delaying upcoming presidential and local government polls, scheduled for December 2007 and April 2008. An agreement was reached on June 9, 2008, between the three official political parties for presidential balloting to be held on April 6, 2009, followed by legislative polling on an unspecified date.

Long-standing territorial disputes between Somaliland and neighboring Puntland deepened in 2007. Puntland claimed the Bari, Nugaal, and Mudug regions as well as the Sanaag and Sool regions, which Somaliland also claimed. Sanaag declared independence from both in July 2007, renaming itself Makhir and choosing Badhan as a capital. Somaliland Defense Minister Adan Mire Mohamed was dismissed by Kahin for failing to prevent the fighting in Sanaag in April. Fighting then broke out between the neighbors in early October 2007, as Sool was rent by conflict between sub-clans calling for Sool's independence or backing the claims of either Somaliland, which claimed Sool due to the regions' shared history under British rule, or Puntland, which asserted its rights to the region based on common Darod clan ethnicity. By the end of October, Somaliland forces had captured Las Anod, the regional capital of Sool. The strife created an estimated 20,000 refugees. Later in the month, Somaliland levied an additional tax of two percent on its inhabitants, reportedly for the purpose of providing relief to displaced residents of Sool. There was renewed fighting in the region in January 2008 and again in July. Also in January pro-independence Somaliland demonstrators in northwestern Somalia were fired upon by Somali security forces. The minister for rural development, Fuad Adan Adde, was dismissed in April after criticizing the president.

On September 29, 2008, suicide bombers attacked the presidential palace and Ethiopian embassy in Hargeisa. The attacks killed 19, including the president's secretary, and wounded more than 100. The strikes were believed to have been carried out by Islamic extremists.

Somali member of the Transitional Federal Parliament Mohamed Mohamud ("Indhohur") was arrested in Somaliland on February 27 and held for 11 days before being expelled. Indhohur had been Somaliland's deputy regional governor for Sool before defecting to join the Somali national government. On March 28 the president's term was extended through September by the House of Elders, and Kahin issued a decree setting September 27 as the date for presidential elections. Officially, continued fighting in Sool, caused the delay, but opposition parties and groups decried it and threatened to withdraw recognition of the government. Meanwhile, a new dispute arose over voter registration when the president ordered the head of an international rights group, which was overseeing a new registration drive, to leave the country. On April 6 police used force to disperse opposition-led demonstrations in Hargeisa. The government subsequently banned demonstrations in the capital until the September balloting. Opposition groups also charged that a new voter registration system was fraudulent. On July 11, 2009, negotiations resulted in an agreement between the three major parties to support presidential elections in September.

POLITICAL PARTIES AND GROUPS

The constitution endorsed by national referendum in May 2001 provided for multiparty activity, with the restriction that parties could not be based on tribal/clan or religious affiliations. It was determined that groups would be provisionally recognized prior to proposed local elections (originally scheduled for December 2001), with those gaining at least 20 percent of the vote in four of Somaliland's six regions to be granted permanent registration prior to subsequent presidential and national legislative balloting. The first parties were registered in October 2001, but the municipal elections were postponed until December 2002, at which time the first three groups below gained legal status by meeting the constitutional requirement for minimum vote shares.

Official Parties:

United and Democratic People's Alliance (*Ururka Dimuqraadiga Ummadda Bahawday*—UDUB). Launched in June 2001 by President Egal, the UDUB was subsequently routinely referenced as the "ruling" party in Somaliland. Although some observers viewed the UDUB as primarily a personal vehicle for Egal, the party was reportedly "resuscitated" by President Kahin following Egal's death in May 2002. The party went on to dominate the December 2002 municipal elections and to achieve a plurality in the 2005 legislative balloting on a vote share of 40.7 percent. The UDUB continues to rule Somaliland and opposes the registration of the new Qaran political party. Media watchdogs have become increasingly critical of the party's crackdown on journalists, and President Kahin came under fire for postponing presidential elections until September 2009. In February 2009 a party congress elected Kahin as the UDUB candidate for the upcoming presidential balloting. However, UDUB opponents of Kahin, led by Abdullahi DARAWEL, left the meeting and held a rival congress.

Leaders: Dahir Riyale KAHIN (President of the Republic), Ahmad Yusuf YASIN (Vice President of the Republic), Usman GARAD (Secretary).

Solidarity Party (*Hisbiga Kulmiye*). Established in early 2002, *Kulmiye* is led by Ahmed Mohamed Mohamoud ("Silanyo"), who was chair of the SNM from 1984–1990. Silanyo had resigned from the Egal government in 2001, indicating his desire to campaign for the presidency. *Kulmiye* finished second to the UDUB in the December 2002 municipal balloting, securing, according to the government, about 83,000 votes to UDUB's 198,000. Silanyo finished second in the very close vote for president in April 2003. Subsequently, when the Kahin government was criticized by world leaders for refusing to participate in the Somali peace negotiations, Silanyo announced that he supported Kahin in the matter.

Kulmiye finished second in the 2005 legislative balloting with 30.3 percent of the vote. Following the election, *Kulmiye* announced a cooperative agreement with the other "opposition" party—the UCID (below). The party has supported the efforts of the Qaran party to become a registered political party. Silanyo was chosen as the *Kulmiye* presidential candidate in the 2009 elections at a September 2008 party convention. A division in the party emerged over the selection of the vice presidential candidate, Mudane SAYLICI. The choice was deeply opposed by a faction led by Ahmed Ali ADAMI. Through the spring and summer of 2009, *Kulmiye* members and supporters held a series of demonstrations against the extension of the term of President Kahin.

Leaders: Ahmed Mohamed MOHAMOUD ("Silanyo"), (Chair), Muse BIHI (Deputy Chair).

Justice and Welfare Party (*Ururka Caddaalada Iyo Daryeelka*—UCID). Established as a "modern" party devoted to "good governance," the staunchly nationalist UCID was described as an outgrowth of a Social Democratic Party that had been previously organized within the diaspora. UCID leader Faisal Farah Ali ("Warabe") was one of the founders of the SNM and currently owns a private construction company. The UCID secured an estimated 50,000 votes in the December 2002 municipal elections, securing third place out of six contesting parties. Warabe placed third in the 2003 presidential election with 16 percent of the vote. The UCID secured 29 percent of the vote in the 2005 legislative elections, and after announcement of a UCID/*Kulmiye* cooperation agreement, the UCID's Abdirahman Muhammad Irro was elected speaker of the House of Representatives. The UCID choose Warabe as its presidential candidate at a party congress in 2009.

Leaders: Faisal Farah ALI ("Warabe") (Chair), Mohamed Osman FADAL (Vice Chair), Abdirahman Muhammad IRRO (Speaker of the House of Representatives).

Other Parties and Groups:

Somali National Movement (SNM). The SNM was organized in London, United Kingdom, in April 1981 by an exile group that declared its commitment to the overthrow of the existing Mogadishu regime but did not wish to ally itself with either the United States or the Soviet Union. Deriving most of its support from Somaliland's Issaq clan, the SNM long supported greater autonomy for the area, a "more equitable" distribution of resources, and political democratization. Ideologically, however, the movement suffered from a lack of cohesion, apparently counting Marxist, pro-Western, and Islamic fundamentalist groups within its ranks.

Following the Ethiopian-Somali agreement in April 1988, the SNM was left with no external source of support as its fighters were forced to leave Ethiopia. Subsequently, the SNM initiated wide-scale military activity against the government in the north and announced the capture of Hargeisa, the country's second city, in December 1989. The SNM formed an operational alliance with Somalia's other leading rebel groups in mid-1990. Reportedly, the SNM leadership was initially willing to participate in a federal system after the fall of the Siad Barre regime in January 1991, but it bowed to rank-and-file sentiment in opting for independence in May.

After being ousted from the Somaliland presidency in favor of Ibrahim Egal in May 1993, Abdurahman Ahmed Ali took up residence in London before surfacing in Mogadishu in August 1994 as a pro-Aidid opponent of secession. In September President Egal denounced a claim from Ahmed Ali that Ahmed Ali remained SNM chair. Thereafter, in early 1996 it was reported that Ahmed Ali was advising an anti-Egal rebel group in the Burao region.

Anti-Egal forces within the SNM accused the president of corruption in 1997 and threatened to launch a legal challenge against the composition of the National Communities Conference. However, such opposition reportedly failed to materialize. The SNM subsequently remained fractionalized concerning Egal's role and other issues, the president's critics also questioning his commitment to independence. Egal in 2001 formed his own political party (see the UDUB, above), with several other former SNM leaders following suit. The SNM ceased to function as a political entity after the 2001 referendum.

Qaran Party (QP). Founded in 2007, the party has met fierce resistance from the national government, which argues that the constitution requires that only three parties can exist in Somaliland. Despite this, the leaders of the Qaran Party announced its founding in April 2007. The three top officials in the party were then arrested by the Somaliland government on July 28, 2007, for engaging in unauthorized political activity. They were released in December 2007 and the charges against them dismissed; however, they were barred from seeking public office for five years. Efforts to gain official recognition of Qaran prior to the September 2009 presidential elections were unsuccessful.

Leaders: Mohammad GABOSE (Chair), Mohammad HASHI (Vice Chair), Jamal AIDID (Second Vice Chair).

United Somali Front (USF). Emphasizing the deep cleavage between Somaliland's Issaq and Issa communities, the Issa (reportedly with encouragement from Djibouti) organized the USF in early 1991. Subsequently, President Ahmed Ali approved the action and pledged that USF supporters could participate in future multiparty elections. While claiming to be neutral in the dispute over Somaliland's future, the front's leadership joined Ahmed Ali in calling for federalism rather than independence. The USF participated in peace talks in 2000. The USF subsequently became increasingly marginalized, and it did not participate in the 2002 local elections.

Leader: Abdurahman DUALEH ALI (Chair).

LEGISLATURE

Following Somaliland's declaration of independence in 1991, the Central Committee of the Somali National Movement (SNM) served as a nominal "provisional" legislature for several years, although its actual authority was limited due to the subclan conflict that left substantial territory outside SNM control. In May 1993 the SNM "parliament" endorsed the recommendation of a recently concluded grand *shir* (gathering) for the formal establishment of a two-chamber legislature, comprised of a House of Elders and a House of Representatives (initially to be appointed on a clan basis but ultimately to be filled by elections). The two chambers began to operate shortly thereafter, although some clan seats in the House of Representatives remained vacant until August 1994. The new constitution approved by national referendum in 2001 provided for a bicameral **Parliament.**

House of Elders (*Golaha Guurtida*). The upper house is authorized to review legislation passed by the House of Representatives and to approve legislation on its own in regard to religion, culture, and security. It comprises 82 members and a number of nonvoting honorary members. The first elections to the House of Elders were scheduled for October 2006, but in a controversial decision the current appointed membership decided in May 2006 to extend its mandate until October 2010.

Speaker: Saleban Muhammad ADAN.

House of Representatives (*Golaha Wakiilada*). The lower house comprises 82 members directly elected via proportional representation (in six regions) for five-year terms. In the first elections for the house on September 29, 2005, the United and Democratic People's Alliance reportedly secured 33 seats; the Solidarity Party, 28; and the Justice and Welfare Party, 21.

Speaker: Abdirahman Muhammad IRRO.

CABINET

[as of August 1, 2009]

President	Dahir Riyale Kahin
Vice President	Ahmad Yusuf Yasin
Ministers	
Agriculture	(Vacant)
Civil Aviation	Ali Mohamed Warrancadde
Commerce (Interim)	Osman Qassim Qodax
Culture and Tourism	Usman Ali Bile
Defense	Abdullahi Ali Ibrahim
Development of Rural Areas	Fuad Adan Cade
Education	Hasan Haji Mohamoud
Family Affairs and Social Development	Fadhuma Sudi Hasan [f]
Finance	Hussein Ali Duale
Fisheries and Coastlines	Mohammed Oday
Foreign Affairs	Abdillahi Mohamed Dualeh
Health and Labor	Abdillahi Hussein Iman
Information	Ahmed Haji Dahir Elmi
Interior	Abhillahi Ismail Ali
Justice	Ahmad Hasan Ali
Livestock	Idris Ibrahim Abdi

Mineral and Water Resources	Qasim Sheikh Yusuf
Parliamentary Relations	Abdi Hassan Buuni
Planning	Ahmed Haji Dahir
Post and Telecommunication	Liban Ducaleh
Presidency	Nuh Ahmad Usman
Public Works	Said Sulub
Range and Rural Development	(Vacant)
Rehabilitation, Reconstruction, and Resettlement	Hussein Haybe
Religion	Sheikh Mohamed Sheikh Mohamed
Sports	Mahmud Said Muhammad
Ministers of State	
Foreign Affairs	Said Muhammad Nuur
Interior	Aw Adan Ali Saeed
Public Works	Adan Ahmed Muhammad
Rehabilitation, Reconstruction, and Resettlement	(Vacant)

[f] = female

COMMUNICATIONS

Press. Freedom of the press was codified in the constitution approved by national referendum in 2001. However government control is still exercised over journalists and a number have been imprisoned for criticizing the regime. In October 2003 the editor of *Jamhuuriya* was briefly detained for publishing "antigovernment" stories. In December 2007, 24 exiled Somali journalists were ordered to leave Somaliland. From March through July 2009, more than 20 journalists were arrested and imprisoned for varying lengths of time. In addition, on July 29 security forces closed the offices and studios of Horn Cable TV and arrested several staff members. Newspapers published in Hargeisa include *Jamhuuriya* (The Republic, 2,500), an independent daily that was closed by the government in 1997–1998 for printing articles critical of the government; *Huuriya* (Liberty), daily; *Mandeeq*, progovernment daily; *al-Moujahid* (The Fighter), a weekly launched in 1985 by the SNM; and the *Republican*, an English-language weekly.

Broadcasting. In May 1991 the former *Radio Hargeisa* was renamed *Radio Somaliland Republic*. Radio Horyaal, a pro-opposition radio station, broadcasts throughout Somaliland. However, private radio stations are banned. The government runs the Somaliland National TV station (SLNTV).

INTERGOVERNMENTAL REPRESENTATION

As of November 2008 Somaliland was not a member of the United Nations.

IGO Memberships (Non-UN): None

SOUTH AFRICA

Republic of South Africa
Republiek van Suid-Afrika

Political Status: Fully independent state since 1934; republican regime established May 31, 1961; Interim Constitution ratified on December 22, 1993, with effect from April 27, 1994, for a five-year term; new text signed into law on December 10, 1996, effective February 4, 1997, with certain provisions implemented gradually through 1999.

Area: 470,882 sq. mi. (1,221,037 sq. km.).

Population: 44,819,770 (2001C); 48,313,000 (2008E).

Major Urban Centers (urban areas, 2005E): PRETORIA (administrative capital, 2,534,000), Cape Town (legislative capital, 3,143,000), Bloemfontein (judicial capital, 793,000), Durban (4,610,000), Johannesburg (3,974,000). Pretoria is part of the City of Tshwane Metropolitan Municipality.

Official Languages: There are 11 official languages, of which English and Afrikaans are the languages of record.

Monetary Unit: Rand (principal rate December 1, 2009: 7.33 rand = $1US).

President: Jacob Gedleyihlekisa ZUMA (African National Congress); inaugurated May 9, 2009, succeeding Kgalema Petrus MOTLANTHE (African National Congress); inaugurated September 25, 2008.

Deputy President: Kgalema Petrus Motlanthe (African National Congress); appointed by President Zuma and sworn in on May 10, 2009, succeeding Baleka MBETE (African National Congress).

THE COUNTRY

Industrially the most developed country in Africa, the Republic of South Africa is a land of rolling plateaus within a mountainous escarpment that rims its territory on the seaward side and separates the coastal cities of Cape Town and Durban from the inland centers of Johannesburg and Pretoria. The country is peopled by four separate ethnic elements as unequal in numbers as they used to be in political status. The largest and historically least favored group, comprising approximately 79 percent of the population, consists of the Xhosa, Zulu, and Sotho, who are collectively known as the Bantu. Whites comprise 9.6 percent of the population; mixed-race people, 8.9 percent; and Asians, mainly Indians living in KwaZulu-Natal Province, 2.5 percent.

Some three-fifths of the whites are "Afrikaners," who descend from the Dutch, German, and French Huguenot settlers who colonized the country beginning in the 17th century. Traditionally agrarian in their social traditions and outlook, their native language is Afrikaans, a language closely related to Dutch (although many Afrikaners also speak English). Afrikaners, predominantly affiliated with the Dutch Reformed Church, were the most resolute supporters of the policy of separation of the races (apartheid). Most other whites speak English as their first language, identify with the British tradition, and are more involved in business and industry than Afrikaners, although this pattern has changed as Afrikaners have moved to urban areas.

South Africa has become a highly urbanized country, with half of the white population, a third of the blacks, and most Asians and mixed-race people (known in South Africa as "Cape Coloureds" or simply "Coloureds") residing in and around the dozen large cities and towns. The Coloureds form a distinct group. They are frequently of mixed nonwhite and Afrikaner descent, with Afrikaner-sounding last names and Afrikaans often their first language. They are concentrated in Western Cape Province. The term "Coloured," while still in general and official use, is coming under increasing criticism.

White women work primarily in the clerical and service sectors. In predominantly white areas, black women are employed mainly as domestic servants and casual agricultural laborers. Elsewhere, traditional law restricts women's land ownership, although men's migration to white-controlled employment sites has left women largely in charge of subsistence agriculture. Women's participation in government was long limited to minor representation by white women in national and provincial legislatures; however, women of all races were prominent in the anti-apartheid movement. The award of cabinet portfolios to women in the current administration has fulfilled a pledge by former president Nelson Mandela to give women one-third of all posts at all levels.

The first African country to experience the full force of the industrial revolution, South Africa now has an advanced economy and plays an important role in international economic affairs. The world's leading gold producer, the country's mines yield nearly one-third of global output. South Africa also mines diamonds, copper, asbestos, chrome, platinum, and vanadium and is tapping recently discovered ocean reserves of oil. The country has abundant coal, which provides a large share of energy. Agriculturally, South Africa is self-sufficient (except in coffee, rice, and tea) and exports wool, maize, sugar, and fruit.

Although agriculture now contributes only about 3 percent of GDP, it continues to employ almost 10 percent of the labor force. The manufacturing sector, spurred by the government during the apartheid era to promote industrial self-sufficiency, presently accounts for approximately 25 percent of GDP; mining adds another 6 percent. Industry employs approximately 25 percent of workers. South Africa's leading trade partner is the European Union (EU). In 2000 it concluded with the EU a free-trade agreement, which should cover some 90 percent of transactions by 2012.

From the mid-1970s to the mid-1990s, GDP increased by only 1.5 percent annually, while the population grew 2.5 percent a year. Creeping poverty was exacerbated in the late 1990s by the Russian and Asian economic crises, which contributed to a trade decline and a dampening of GDP growth to only 0.7 percent in 1998. Poverty and an uneven distribution of wealth persisted after 2000.

The Mbeki administration (installed in 1999) was credited in many quarters with restoring sound fiscal management and counteracting the economic legacy of apartheid through the Black Economic Empowerment program. However, unemployment remained very high at 30–40 percent. Some of the joblessness was attributed to South Africa's belated entry into the global economy and some to administrative inefficiencies. The administration consequently put job creation at the top of its agenda, promising to halve unemployment by 2014, in part through a significantly expanded public works program. Another recent focus of attention has been HIV/AIDS; in 2009 an estimated 10 percent of the population was infected with HIV, which affects working-age adults disproportionately and may have accounted for 43 percent of all deaths in that year.

There has been a subtle shift in the direction of economic policy from market-led to state-led growth under the current administration. The country prefers public-private partnerships to large-scale privatization. (All economic sectors are required to draw up charters committing themselves to black economic empowerment.) GDP grew by 5 percent in 2006 and subsequently declined to 5.2 percent in 2007 and 3.8 percent in 2008. Annual inflation rose steadily from 1.4 percent in 2004 to 11.3 percent in 2008 in response to high global commodity prices. It fell to an average of 8 percent in May 2009. Unemployment decreased to approximately 23 percent by mid-2008, but the economy entered recession in the first quarter of 2009, with an official real jobless rate of 31.2 percent and 4.18 million people out of work.

GOVERNMENT AND POLITICS

Political background. The Republic of South Africa as it exists today is the result of a long and complicated process of interaction between indigenous peoples and the Dutch and British colonists who came to exploit the territory. The original Cape Colony was settled by the Dutch in the 17th century but fell into British hands as a result of the Napoleonic wars. Discontented Afrikaners, known as "Boers," the Afrikaans word for farmers, trekked northward in 1835–1837, commencing a half-century subjugation of the Zulu and other native peoples and establishing the independent republics of Transvaal and Orange Free State. Following the discovery of diamonds and gold in the late 19th century, the two Boer republics were conquered by Britain in the Anglo-Boer War of 1899–1902. In 1910 they were joined with the British colonies of the Cape and Natal (annexed in 1843) to form the Union of South Africa, which obtained full independence within the Commonwealth in 1931.

Although South Africa joined with Britain in both world wars, its British and Commonwealth attachments progressively weakened as the result of widespread anti-British sentiment and racial preoccupations. The National Party (*Nasionale Party*—NP), led by Daniel F. MALAN, came to power in 1948 with a program strongly reinforcing racial separation under white "guardianship." It proceeded to enact a body of openly discriminatory legislation that was further amplified under Hendrik F. VERWOERD (1958–1966). Segregation was strictly enforced, the already token political representation of nonwhites was progressively reduced, and overt opposition was severely repressed. Similar policies were applied in South West Africa, a former German territory occupied by South Africa in World War I and subsequently administered under a mandate from the League of Nations (see entry under Namibia).

Increasing institutionalization of segregation under the Verwoerd regime led to international condemnation. External opposition was intensified by the "Sharpeville incident" of March 21, 1960, during which South African police fired on black demonstrators, killing 69 of them. In view of the increasingly critical stand of other Commonwealth members, South Africa formally withdrew from the grouping and declared itself a republic on May 31, 1961.

Prime Minister Verwoerd was assassinated by a deranged white man in September 1966, but his successor, Balthazar J. VORSTER, continued Verwoerd's policies, bringing to fruition the idea of dividing the blacks into separate tribal homelands, or "Bantustans." These areas, encompassing approximately 13 percent of the country's land, were ultimately intended to house upward of three-quarters of the population. However, a series of minor concessions to the blacks brought about a challenge from the right-wing, or *verkrampte* ("unenlightened" or "ultra-Conservative"), faction of the NP under the leadership of Dr. Albert HERTZOG, who formed the Refounded National Party (*Herstigte Nasionale Party*—HNP) to compete in the 1970 election. The NP easily survived his challenge, the HNP winning no legislative seats on a 3.6 percent vote share, although the longtime opposition United Party (UP) made some gains. In the next parliamentary balloting in April 1974 the NP increased its majority, with the UP losing five seats to the other opposition group, the Progressive Party (PP), which had since 1961 held only a single seat.

The 1974 Portuguese revolution and subsequent changes in Angola and Mozambique further isolated the South African regime. Early in 1975 the government announced a policy of "ending discrimination" within South Africa and of working for détente in external affairs. The new policy was accompanied by a partial relaxation in apartheid regulations, including a repeal of "Masters and Servants" legislation, portions of which had been in existence for over a century. During the following year, however, the country experienced its worst outbreak of racial violence since the Sharpeville episode in 1960. The rioting, which began in Soweto, the huge black township next to Johannesburg, in mid-June, grew out of black student protests against the compulsory use of Afrikaans as a medium of instruction. Although the government announced in early July that it would begin phasing out Afrikaans at the primary and secondary school levels, the disturbances spread to townships around Pretoria and, in late August and early September, to the heart of Cape Town. Despite the unrest, the Vorster government gave no indication of abandoning its commitment to "separate development" of the races, with the official position being that the policy was not based on race but on the conviction that, within South Africa, blacks made up distinct "nations" to which special political and constitutional arrangements should apply. It was in accordance with this philosophy that nominal independence was granted to the territories that would become known as the black homelands: Transkei in October 1976, Bophuthatswana in December 1977, Venda in September 1979, and Ciskei in December 1981.

Rioting intensified during 1977 amid growing signs that the Vorster government had adopted a siege mentality, although its white support increased substantially. Drastic new security legislation was approved, including a Criminal Procedure Bill that substantially augmented the powers of the police while severely limiting the rights of individuals in judicial proceedings. On September 12 Steven BIKO, one of the country's most influential black leaders, died in suspicious circumstances while in police detention. On October 19 the government instituted its most drastic crackdown in two decades, closing the leading black newspaper, arresting its editor, and banning a number of protest groups, including the Black Consciousness movement founded by Biko in 1969. Apparent white endorsement of these moves was revealed in a parliamentary election on November 30, in which the NP captured 134 of 165 lower house seats.

On September 20, 1978, Prime Minister Vorster announced his intention to resign for reasons of health. Nine days later he was elected by a joint session of Parliament to the essentially titular post of president, succeeding Nicolaas J. DIEDERICHS, who had died on August 21. One day earlier the NP elected Defense Minister Pieter W. BOTHA as its new leader (hence prime minister) over Foreign Minister Roelof F. ("Pik") BOTHA and Plural Relations and Development Minister Cornelius P. MULDER. In November a long-simmering scandal involving alleged corruption and mismanagement of public funds in the Department of Information implicated a number of individuals, including Mulder, who was forced to resign from the government prior to his formal expulsion from the NP in May 1979. On June 4 President Vorster also resigned after being charged with participation in a variety of clandestine propaganda activities and of giving false evidence in an effort to conceal gross irregularities in the affair. He was immediately succeeded, on an interim basis, by Senate president Marais VILJOEN, who was elected to a full term as head of state by Parliament on June 19. Despite the scandal and increasingly vocal opposition from both the HNP and remaining *verkrampte* elements within the NP, the Botha government remained in power with a marginally reduced parliamentary majority after the election of April 29, 1981, having campaigned on a 12-point platform, first advanced in 1979, that called for constitutional power-sharing among whites, Coloureds, and Asians, with "full independence" for the black homelands.

In a referendum conducted November 2, 1982, a Constitution Bill, providing for an executive state president and a tricameral parliament excluding blacks, was endorsed by 66 percent of white voters and was approved by the House of Assembly on September 9, 1983. After balloting for delegates to the Coloured and Indian chambers in August 1984, Prime Minister Botha was unanimously elected president by an electoral college of the majority parties in each house on September 5, and he was inaugurated in Cape Town on September 14.

Faced with mounting internal unrest and near-universal foreign condemnation, the government in April 1985 abandoned two bastions of segregationist legislation: the Mixed Marriages Act and a portion of the Immorality Act that outlawed sex across the color line, while the prohibition of multiracial political movements was lifted in June. These moves, while provoking an immediate backlash by right-wing extremists, were received by black and moderate white leaders as "too little, too late." Clashes between police and demonstrators increased, yielding nearly 300 deaths (mainly of blacks) by midyear. On July 21, in the first such action in a quarter-century, a state of emergency was declared in 36 riot-stricken black districts and townships in the Johannesburg and eastern Cape regions. On August 15, in a speech in Durban, President Botha rejected demands for further racial concessions, insisting that they would constitute "a road to abdication and suicide" by white South Africans. In mid-September, however, he indicated that Parliament would be asked in early 1986 to consider modification of a leading bulwark of residential segregation, the Group Areas Act, with possible revocation of the country's pass laws. These laws required adult black South Africans, on pain of imprisonment, to carry a pass at all times. This hated document showed what, if any, white areas the holder was allowed to enter and at which times of day.

In an address at the opening of Parliament on January 31, 1986, President Botha shocked the extreme right by declaring that "We have outgrown the outdated colonial system of paternalism, as well as the outdated concept of apartheid." In late April he announced that a bill would be introduced terminating the pass laws, though the legislation would not affect segregation in schools, hospitals, and residential areas. Earlier, on March 7, the partial state of emergency imposed eight months before was rescinded; however, a nationwide state of emergency was declared on June 12 to quell anticipated violence on June 16, the anniversary of the Soweto uprising.

Although the term of the House of Assembly had been extended from 1986 to 1989 to coincide with the five-year mandates of the Coloured and Indian chambers, President Botha announced in January 1987 that an early election for a new white chamber would be held on May 6. The results of the poll reflected a distinctly rightward swing by the white voters: the NP won 123 of the 166 directly elective seats, while the far-right Conservative Party of South Africa (CPSA), with 22 seats, displaced the liberal Progressive Federal Party (PFP, a direct descendant of the PP) as the official opposition.

During the ensuing months the government increased the practice of grudgingly yielding on the substance of apartheid while severely limiting the freedom of its opponents. A variety of new press restrictions were announced in August, while the government banned the activities of numerous groups. Banned groups included labor unions; civic, educational, and youth associations; the umbrella United Democratic Front (UDF), which linked some 650 anti-apartheid organizations; and a new Committee for the Defence of Democracy (CDD), organized in Cape Town in March 1988. In September a major constitutional crisis was averted by the government's withdrawal of five bills designed to tighten residential segregation laws, upon which the two nonwhite parliamentary chambers had refused to act. Throughout the period numerous long-incarcerated regime opponents were released, while others, primarily from the "new generation" of UDF and other leaders, were arrested and convicted of treason.

On January 18, 1989, President Botha suffered a stroke, and Constitutional Development Minister J. Christiaan HEUNIS was sworn in as acting chief executive the following day. On February 2 Botha resigned as NP leader, with Education Minister Frederik W. DE KLERK being named his successor. On March 13 the party's parliamentary caucus voted unanimously that de Klerk should also become state president; Botha, however, refused to step down and on March 15 resumed the presidency, vowing to stay in office for the remainder of his term. Less than five months later Botha complained of not being advised of a proposed meeting that de Klerk and Foreign Minister "Pik" Botha had scheduled with Zambian president Kenneth Kaunda. Terming the proposed meeting "inopportune," President Botha resigned on August 14, with de Klerk succeeding him on an acting basis the following day.

At balloting for all three legislative chambers on September 6, 1989, the NP retained its overall majority in the House of Assembly, although its share of the vote fell to less than half (48.6 percent). On September 14 de Klerk was named by the parliamentary electoral college to a regular five-year term as president. In October his administration released seven prominent ANC leaders from prison, including Walter SISULU, who had been incarcerated for 26 years.

On February 2, 1990, de Klerk announced the lifting of bans against the ANC, the Pan-Africanist Congress (PAC), and the South African Communist Party (SACP), and on February 11 he freed the long-incarcerated ANC leader, Nelson Rolihlahla MANDELA. However, on April 17, two weeks before the start of talks with ANC leaders, the president flatly rejected majority rule on the ground that it would "lead to the domination and even the suppression of minorities." He also rejected a demand by right-wing whites for racially based partition of the country and proposed a system under which power would be shared by all groups and minority rights would be constitutionally guaranteed. For its part, the ANC indicated that it would not engage in full negotiations until the nearly four-year state of emergency had been rescinded (effected in three of the four provinces on June 8) and all political prisoners and exiles had been amnestied.

On June 1, 1990, the government introduced legislation to rescind the Reservation of Separate Amenities Act that had sanctioned "petty apartheid" at public locations, such as beaches, libraries, and places of entertainment. Left in place were the Group Areas Act, which provided for racially segregated residential areas; the Lands Acts of 1913 and 1936, which reserved 87 percent of the country's land for the white minority; and the Population Registration Act, which mandated the classification of South Africans by race from birth.

On June 27, 1990, de Klerk stated that he was prepared to negotiate a new constitution that would eliminate all aspects of apartheid, and on August 7, one day after his second meeting with the president, Mandela announced that the ANC was suspending its 30-year armed struggle. In early October de Klerk and the leaders of the six "self-governing" homelands agreed to scrap the Lands Acts, and on October 15 the Separate Amenities Act was formally repealed. Subsequently, in a historic move, de Klerk asked the National Party to open its rolls to all races.

On December 13 ANC President Oliver TAMBO was permitted to return from more than three decades' exile.

In January 1991 the government and the ANC agreed to convene an all-party conference on the constitutional drafting process, although Chief Mangosuthu BUTHELEZI, leader of the Zulu-based *Inkatha* Freedom Party (IFP), responded coolly, while the CPSA, the PAC, and the Azanian People's Organization (Azapo) indicated that they would not participate. Meanwhile, on January 29, the ANC's Mandela and *Inkatha*'s Buthelezi met for the first time in 30 years to defuse the bitter rivalry that had caused the death of more than 4,000 people and had split the anti-apartheid movement. However, within two days of the leaders' reconciliation renewed fighting had broken out between their followers.

The Lands Acts of 1913 and 1936, which reserved 87 percent of the country's land for the white minority, and the Group Areas Act, which provided for racially segregated residential areas, were abolished on June 5, 1991. Five days later, the Population Registration Act, which mandated the classification of South Africans by race from birth, was repealed. Revocation of the Population Act left the capacity to vote (promised by the government under the new constitution) as the major remaining obstacle to black emancipation.

The first session of the Convention for a Democratic South Africa (Codesa), held December 20–21, 1991, featured a "declaration of intent" whereby constitutional proposals would require the approval of both the ANC and the government, with the latter pledging to employ its parliamentary majority to translate Codesa's decisions into law. Meanwhile, the de Klerk administration had become embroiled in an "Inkathagate" scandal stemming from evidence that the South Africa Defence Force (SADF) had been engaged over a three-year period in providing IFP members with anti-ANC military training.

On February 20, 1992, President de Klerk announced that a "whites-only" referendum would be held March 17 to renew his mandate for negotiating with anti-apartheid organizations. The projected poll was immediately denounced by white extremist groups as well as by the leftist PAC and Azapo, which had long demanded that a new basic law be approved by a broadly based constituent assembly rather than by the existing nonblack Parliament. The result of the referendum was a triumph for the president, with 68.7 percent of the participants endorsing continuation of the reform process.

The Codesa II session held May 15–16, 1992, proved unproductive, largely because the parties were unable to resolve an impasse over the size of the majority required for interim legislative approval of key constitutional provisions. On May 27 a commission headed by Richard GOLDSTONE, a respected South African jurist, issued a six-month study on the sources of internal violence. While not completely exonerating the government, the commission found no evidence of "a sinister and secret organization orchestrating political violence on a wide front." Rather, it attributed the disturbances in the townships to "the political battle between supporters of the African National Congress (ANC) and the *Inkatha* Freedom Party." The conclusions of the commission were sorely tested on June 17, when South African police were accused of transporting a group of Zulu speakers to Boipatong township, south of Johannesburg, where a bloody massacre ensued that claimed 45 lives. After touring Boipatong, ANC Secretary General Cyril RAMAPHOSA insisted that the slaughter was a government response to the launching of an ANC mass action campaign designed to force majority rule. While the government vehemently denied the charge, Nelson Mandela declared on June 21 that negotiations were "in tatters," and the ANC Executive Committee voted two days later to withdraw from Codesa.

ANC suspicions that the Goldstone Commission had not uncovered the whole truth about township violence were confirmed when a raid on a covert operations center of military intelligence in Pretoria yielded information that impelled President de Klerk to announce on December 19, 1992, that illegal activities by senior SADF officers were under investigation. In further reports, the commission in October 1993 found strong circumstantial evidence of security force involvement in the violence. In March 1994 it cited allegations of a conspiracy among senior police officers involving a "third force" of *agents provocateurs* tasked with anti-ANC destabilization in collaboration with the IFP.

Meanwhile, a "record of understanding" drawn up in September 1992 between the ANC and the NP had given renewed impetus to constitutional talks, which were resumed in March 1993 within what was later designated the Multi-Party Negotiating Process (MPNP). The 26 parties involved included several that had boycotted Codesa, notably the PAC and the SACP, the latter being a leading component of the Concerned South Africans Group (COSAG) of apartheid-era formations, including the IFP. The MPNP came under immediate strain as a result of the assassination on April 10 of Chris HANI, SACP general secretary and an ANC executive member. However, counsels of restraint from Mandela and others prevented the violent reaction in the black townships from getting out of control.

Negotiating breakthroughs came in May and June 1993, when most of the MPNP parties agreed that nonracial elections for a five-year transitional government of national unity would take place on April 27, 1994. Also crucial was the ANC's shift from insistence on a centralized state to acceptance of a federal structure with entrenched powers for provincial governments. The concession did not prevent the IFP and the CPSA from withdrawing from the MPNP shortly before the publication on July 26 of a draft interim constitution providing for equal citizenship rights for all races and a nine-province federal structure integrating the black homelands into the new South Africa. In September the remaining MPNP parties also reached agreement on the creation of a multiracial Transitional Executive Council (TEC), which as approved by Parliament on September 23, was to operate alongside the government in the election run-up to ensure fair play and to monitor the operations of the security forces. After the package of texts had been formally adopted by the MPNP on November 18, the TEC was installed on December 7. Finally, on December 22 Parliament ratified the Constitution of the Republic of South Africa Bill by 237 votes to 45, most of those against being CPSA members.

The problem of reconciling opponents, both white and black, to the settlement remained. In May 1993 the CPSA had joined with various right-wing Afrikaner groups to form the Afrikaner People's Front (*Afrikaner Volksfront*—AVF) under the leadership of Gen. (Ret.) Constand VILJOEN, a former head of the SADF, with the central aim of achieving self-determination for Afrikaners in a separate homeland. In June tensions mounted when armed members of the Afrikaner Resistance Movement (*Afrikaner Weerstandsbeweging*—AWB), a paramilitary group led by Eugene TERRE'BLANCHE, forcibly occupied the building in Kempton Park where MPNP talks were in progress, with no resistance from police. In October the AVF, together with the IFP and other conservative black elements, launched the Freedom Alliance as successor to COSAG. Its constituent elements at first presented a united front against the constitutional settlement, although a January 1994 decision in favor of electoral participation by the Ciskei government (originally a Freedom Alliance member) was a serious setback.

The situation was transformed in March 1994 when the AWB and other Afrikaner paramilitaries, apparently sanctioned by the AVF, tried to protect the Bophuthatswana government of Chief Lucas MANGOPE (a Freedom Alliance member) from ANC-led protests against his decision to boycott the elections. Order was restored by speedy deployment of SADF troops, the Afrikaners being routed with 3 fatalities among at least 60 deaths overall and Mangope being removed from office by decision of the TEC on March 12. In light of this debacle and earlier divisions in the Freedom Alliance, Viljoen broke ranks with the AVF by forming the Freedom Front (*Vryheidsfront*—VF), which registered for the elections, whereas the CPSA and the other AVF formations maintained their nonparticipatory stance. The split marked the effective collapse of the Freedom Alliance, as confirmed by the eleventh-hour decision of the IFP on April 19 that it too would contest the forthcoming elections, despite bloody ANC-IFP clashes near the ANC's Shell House headquarters in Johannesburg on March 28 in which over 50 IFP demonstrators had been killed.

The IFP's participation ensured that South Africa's first multiracial balloting, to be held April 26–29, 1994, would be relatively free of violence. According to the Independent Electoral Commission and numerous foreign observers, the election was in the main conducted fairly. As expected, the ANC registered an overwhelming victory in the national contest, winning 252 of 400 seats in the new National Assembly, against 82 for the NP, 43 for the IFP, 9 for the VF, and 14 for three smaller parties. In simultaneous polls for new provincial assemblies, the ANC won majorities in seven provinces, losing only Western Cape (to the NP) and KwaZulu-Natal (to the IFP).

Elected president by unanimous vote of the new assembly on May 9, 1994, Nelson Mandela was sworn in the following day. Under the terms of the constitutional settlement, the ANC's Thabo MBEKI became first deputy president and de Klerk second deputy president. The new cabinet installed on May 11 contained 19 ANC representatives, 5 from the NP, and 3 from the IFP (including Chief Buthelezi as home affairs minister). The new Senate, its members designated by the newly elected provincial assemblies, convened on May 20, with the ANC holding 60 of 90 seats.

The widespread jubilation accompanying the installation of Nelson Mandela as South African president on May 10, 1994, obscured a variety of problems confronting the new administration. Far-right Afrikaners continued to press for political autonomy, although talks between Mandela and CPSA leader Ferdi HARTZENBERG in Pretoria on August 12 suggested that the AVF did not intend to resort to force. As for the IFP, while Chief Buthelezi had accepted cabinet membership, relations between his Zulu-based formation and Mandela's ANC remained tense. Intensifying post-election controversy was the disclosure on May 19 that on the eve of the election some 7.4 million acres of state land in KwaZulu, about a third of the ex-homeland's area, had been transferred to the control of the Zulu King Goodwill ZWELITHINI under legislation adopted by the outgoing KwaZulu Assembly and approved by President de Klerk, without the knowledge of the ANC. Although the new minister of land affairs, Derek HANEKOM (ANC), announced on June 15 that the transfer would stand, the affair angered many ANC members, who suspected that its purpose had been to entice the IFP into the electoral process.

A year after the advent of majority rule, the most serious political problem facing the government was the disaffection of the IFP and its Zulu supporters, centering on their demand for a degree of autonomy for KwaZulu-Natal that fell little short of independence, including a constitutionally recognized role for the Zulu monarchy. Accompanied by periodic clashes between ANC and IFP supporters, the confrontation worsened in April 1995 when IFP members withdrew from the Constituent Assembly charged with drafting a permanent constitution. Although Chief Buthelezi remained a member of the government, he asserted that his party would not accept any constitution drawn up in its absence and repeated his demand for international mediation of KwaZulu-Natal's dispute with the central authorities. ANC ministers and officials responded that a formal international role in the dispute would imply acceptance of KwaZulu-Natal's claim to separate status; they also insisted that drafting of the new constitution would proceed according to schedule, if necessary without IFP participation.

ANC-IFP relations were further aggravated by President Mandela's admission on June 1, 1995, that he had personally authorized ANC officials "to shoot to kill if necessary" during bloody clashes between the ANC and IFP on March 28, 1994, near the party's Shell House headquarters in Johannesburg, in which over 50 IFP demonstrators had died. Amid IFP calls for his impeachment over this admission, the president sought to regain the initiative by proposing on June 14 that responsibility for the pay and perquisites of tribal chiefs should be transferred from the provincial authorities to the central government. Such a change would pose a special threat to Chief Buthelezi's power base in the KwaZulu-Natal countryside, where control of the purse strings sustained the IFP's network of support among tribal chiefs. Serious IFP-ANC clashes in August 1995 were followed on December 25 by an attack by IFP supporters on the village of Shobashobane (an ANC enclave in KwaZulu-Natal) in which at least 19 people were killed, with the security forces failing to intervene.

In sharp contrast, relations between the ANC and the white minority continued to be accommodating, with occasional rifts within the transitional government being quickly resolved. The discovery by the ANC justice minister in January 1995 that the outgoing NP government had secretly granted indemnities from prosecution to over 3,500 policemen and security officials provoked a cabinet crisis in which de Klerk claimed that he and the NP had been subjected to "insulting attack." However, the possibility of an NP withdrawal receded when de Klerk and Mandela met on January 20 and agreed that a "fresh start" should be made. The president also established working relations with several Afrikaner groups that had vigorously opposed black majority rule, with a disavowal of violence by General Viljoen and the VF seen as particularly helpful. Most Afrikaner leaders welcomed an offer by Mandela on June 27 that a nonbinding referendum be held to ascertain the views of Afrikaners on the proposal for a separate Afrikaner state (*volkstaat*), the president accepting that it was the government's duty "to consider their concerns and fears in a responsible, sensitive and constructive manner."

Two days after the endorsement of the new constitution in Parliament, de Klerk announced on May 10, 1996, that the NP was withdrawing from the government of national unity with effect from June 30. He cited the diminishing influence of the NP on government policy, the refusal of the ANC to include power-sharing arrangements in the new constitution, and the need for an effective opposition. Commentators considered that the decision was motivated by a desire to assert the NP's independence well in advance of legislative elections in 1999. The party subsequently also withdrew from all provincial governments except that of Western Cape, where it was in the majority. President Mandela appointed ANC members to replace the outgoing NP ministers and abolished the post of second deputy president vacated by de Klerk.

Much domestic attention subsequently focused on the initial proceedings of the Truth and Reconciliation Commission (TRC), which had been created in July 1995 to investigate human rights abuses and political crimes of the apartheid era with the aim of consigning their legacy to history. Chaired by Archbishop Desmond TUTU (head of the Anglican Church in South Africa until his retirement in June 1996), the TRC was empowered to grant judicial amnesties to people confessing to apartheid-era crimes (depending on their gravity) if it was satisfied that full disclosure had been made and that the crime in question had been politically motivated. The TRC began a scheduled two years of hearings in April 1996, its authority to grant amnesties being upheld by the Constitutional Court in July after Azapo and the families of several murdered political activists had argued that the commission's power to protect human rights violators from prosecution and civil damages denied them the opportunity to obtain justice through the courts.

Former state president de Klerk gave evidence to the TRC on August 21, 1996. He stated that the security forces had not, to his knowledge, been authorized during the period of NP government to commit human rights abuses, although he apologized for suffering caused by the apartheid system. However, Eugene DE KOCK, a former colonel in the South African police who was convicted in the same month for murder and other crimes during the apartheid era, subsequently claimed in court that members of the former NP government had had full knowledge of a systematic campaign by the police, armed forces, and covert security units against apartheid opponents. Furthermore, in testimony to the TRC in October, several former members of the police claimed that former president P. W. Botha and two former ministers, Louis LE GRANGE and Adriaan VLOK, had ordered state violence against anti-apartheid organizations in the 1980s. In May 1997 de Klerk, in a second appearance, again denied knowledge of human rights violations. He retired from politics in August, and the NP inaugurated a new leadership under Marthinus van SCHALKWYK, by which time the party had ended its cooperation with the TRC on the grounds of political bias.

In September 1997 the deadline for submitting petitions to the TRC passed. Among those who did not file and attempted to stave off the TRC's calls to testify were former president Botha and a number of apartheid-era judicial officials. (Botha was convicted in August 1998 for refusing to appear before the TRC, although in June 1999 his appeal was upheld on technical grounds.) The ANC was the most prominent of the organizations to apply and in its petition admitted to torture, abuse, and even executions; however, the party attempted to justify such actions as being in the name of the "dirty war" fought against apartheid.

The dominant event of 1998 was the October release of a comprehensive report from the TRC. Having reviewed evidence from some 20,000 people, the TRC described apartheid as a "crime against humanity." It also declared the government responsible for a large majority of the abuses committed between 1960 and 1994, condemning the NP regime for a broad range of atrocities that included kidnappings, torture, killings, and bombings. However, the ANC and other liberation groups as well as extreme right organizations were also held accountable for violent acts. The report sparked controversy, and every major party rejected its conclusions to some degree. The report cited prominent individuals from across the entire political spectrum for human rights abuses. They included P. W. Botha, Chief Buthelezi, General Viljoen, Eugene Terre'Blanche, and President Mandela's ex-wife, Winnie MADIKIZELA-MANDELA, one of the country's most popular female politicians and an ANC leader, who was implicated in a dozen violent acts, including murder. Although the activities of two of the TRC's three committees—the Reparation and Rehabilitation Committee and the Human Rights Violations Committee—drew to a close with the release of the report, the mandate of the Amnesty Committee, with over 1,000 cases yet to review, was extended by act of Parliament "until a date determined by the President."

In December 1997 President Mandela had resigned as ANC president and was succeeded, as expected, by Thabo Mbeki, who led the ANC into the June 2, 1999, national elections. The ANC emerged from the balloting with 266 National Assembly seats, one short of the two-thirds majority needed to amend the constitution, prompting party leaders to quickly negotiate a coalition with the Minority Front (MF), an Indian party that had won a single seat. On June 14 the National Assembly unanimously elected Mbeki as president, and he took the oath of office two days later. On June 17 the new president named ANC deputy leader Jacob ZUMA as deputy president and appointed a cabinet in which Chief Buthelezi retained his position as home affairs minister.

In the June 1999 balloting the dominance of the ANC was evident not only at the national level but also in the provinces, where it retained outright majorities in seven, formed a coalition government with the IFP in KwaZulu-Natal, and won a plurality in Western Cape. In the national balloting, the Democratic Party (DP), led by Tony LEON, displaced the New National Party (NNP) as the leading opposition formation, winning 38 seats (up from 7 in 1994), while the NNP managed only 28, a net loss of 54. Facing diminished prospects, in June 2000 the NNP joined the DP in forming a Democratic Alliance (DA), the expectation being that a full merger of the parties would eventually occur. The DA surprised many observers by winning 23 percent of the national vote in the December municipal elections, but policy and leadership clashes ultimately led the NNP to part ways with the DP in October 2001. In abandoning the DA for a closer relationship with the ANC, the NNP's van Schalkwyk noted that the two erstwhile antagonists no longer had significant ideological differences. Thus, at the end of 2001 the only opposition formations with more than a handful of National Assembly members were the rump DA (the DP plus the small Federal Alliance) and the United Democratic Movement.

In June 2001 public hearings opened into a December 1999 arms deal involving the purchase of surface ships, submarines, helicopters, and jet aircraft from a number of EU countries, at a cost of $5.4 billion. Despite accusations that officials had received kickbacks and engaged in other illegalities, in November the resultant report concluded that the procurement procedure had been flawed but not corrupt, although individuals who had derived "some form of benefit from the acquisition process" could be held criminally liable. The National Assembly opposition condemned the report as a whitewash. Throughout much of the following decade, the affair led to legal troubles for Jacob Zuma.

The Truth and Reconciliation Commission intended to release the final volumes of its report in 2002, but publication was delayed when the IFP went to court in opposition to conclusions that it had been responsible for major human rights violations. The final report was presented to the president in 2003. The commission granted amnesty to 1,200 people but rejected more than 5,000 other applications. After rejecting a suggestion that a special tax be imposed on companies that had profited from apartheid, Mbeki announced that those designated as victims by the TRC would each receive a single payment worth $3,800.

In February 2004 Mbeki signed into law the controversial Restitution of Land Rights Amendment Act, which gave the state the right to expropriate land for restitution purposes without a court order or the seller's agreement. The act applied only to land from which blacks were forcibly removed under the colonial and apartheid regimes. "Just and equitable" compensation was guaranteed to farmers whose land was expropriated. The legislation was an attempt to overcome logjams under the "willing buyer, willing seller" policy, which had been marked by disputes over fair market value of land.

Simultaneous elections to the National Assembly and the provincial assemblies took place on April 14, 2004. A total of 21 parties presented candidates in the national ballot while 37 parties contested the provincial elections. The ANC emerged as the dominant party at both national and provincial levels. It gained 279 of the 400 National Assembly seats with 69.7 percent of the votes, while the DA took 50 seats with 12.4 percent of the votes cast and the IFP 28 seats with 7.0 percent. The ANC took control of seven of the nine provincial assemblies. Although it failed to win outright majorities in KwaZulu-Natal and Western Cape, the ANC nominated premiers to head all nine provincial governments. The Democratic Alliance, led by Tony Leon, remained the official opposition.

On April 23, 2004, the assembly reelected President Mbeki to serve a second term. Members of the NNP and Azapo were included in the subsequent cabinet, as were six members of the SACP. On August 7 Marthinus van Schalkwyk announced the dissolution of the NNP, asked its members to join the ANC (as van Schalkwyk and some of his colleagues had, with former president de Klerk being a notable exception), and agreed to fight all future elections under the ANC banner. In June former president Nelson Mandela officially retired from public life.

Local government elections were held on March 1, 2006. The ANC was unseated in Cape Town where Helen ZILLE of the DA became mayor of the only opposition-controlled city in the country. On September 19 the ANC made a fifth attempt to unseat the DA-led coalition in Cape Town. It informed Zille that it intended to replace her post with rule by a committee of major parties, a system which would likely benefit the ANC. The ANC presented its proposal as necessary to create a "stable government" that represented most of the electorate. Zille replied that the ANC plan would be unconstitutional, and the DA said the plan provided further evidence of the ANC's drive for power and inability to accept electoral defeat.

Constitution and government. Under the Interim Constitution adopted by the outgoing Parliament on December 22, 1993, a president, named for a five-year term by the National Assembly, exercised executive power. Legislative authority was vested in a bicameral Parliament consisting of a Senate, 10 of whose 90 members were elected from each of nine regional legislatures, and a National Assembly, half of whose 400 members were elected from national and half from regional party lists. The two houses sat jointly as a Constituent Assembly, which debated and approved a permanent constitution (see below). The Interim Constitution detailed rights of citizenship, which for the first time constituted a universal bill of rights applying equally to all races, to be safeguarded by a Constitutional Court as the supreme judicial authority. In its first major ruling on June 6, 1995, the Court decided unanimously to abolish the death penalty in South Africa.

The four historic provinces (Cape, Natal, Orange Free State, and Transvaal) were replaced by nine new provinces: Eastern Cape, Eastern Transvaal (now Mpumalanga), KwaZulu-Natal, Northern Cape, Northern Transvaal (now Limpopo), North-West, Orange Free State (now Free State), Pretoria-Witwatersrand-Vereeniging (PWV, now Gauteng), and Western Cape, each with an elected legislature. Under the new provincial structure, the four "independent" and six "self-governing" black homelands created by the previous regime were effectively abolished. (For details regarding the "independent" homelands, see the 1993 edition of the *Handbook,* pp. 762–772.) Town and city councils were established as multiracial, with white and black voters each electing 30 percent of the councilors and the remainder being selected on a nonracial basis.

In November 1995, following 18 months of work by the Constituent Assembly, the first draft of the new permanent constitution was published, with the main political parties reaching agreement on a final version on May 7, 1996, shortly before the expiry of the deadline set during the transitional period. The following day the text was approved overwhelmingly by Parliament. The NP voted in favor, despite its reservations over provisions relating to labor relations, property rights, language, and education, in order to safeguard concessions already secured from the ANC. The IFP was absent for the vote, maintaining its boycott of the Constituent Assembly, from which it had withdrawn in April 1995. Ratified in its final version on December 4 by the Constitutional Court, which had previously rejected certain draft clauses, particularly in relation to the reduction of provincial powers, the new constitution was finally signed into law on December 10 by President Mandela in a ceremony in Sharpeville. The IFP, which had briefly returned to the Constituent Assembly on October 1 before withdrawing again on October 7, accepted the legitimacy of the new document.

The new constitution took effect February 4, 1997, although some provisions (such as those concerning budget responsibilities) were not to be implemented until later in the year and the power-sharing provisions of the 1993 interim constitution were to remain in force until the 1999 general elections. The new basic law incorporated many essentials of the 1993 text, although it abandoned the principle that all parties with 5 percent of the vote should be represented in the cabinet. It also provided for a National Council of Provinces (NCOP) to replace the existing Senate, with the aim of enhancing the influence of the provinces on the policy of the central government—although it fell short of guaranteeing the provincial powers that the IFP had demanded. In addition, it enshrined an extensive bill of rights, one of the most liberal in the world. In the future, changes to the constitution would require the approval of at least two-thirds of the members of the National Assembly and at least six of the nine provinces represented in the National Council.

With regard to ordinary legislation, the powers exercised by the two houses vary. Bills affecting the republic as a whole are introduced in the National Assembly and, if passed, proceed to the NCOP, where the members, voting individually, may concur or may propose changes for consideration by the assembly. Bills affecting the provinces may be introduced in either house, but in the NCOP each of the nine provincial delegations has one vote. If the two chambers disagree on a provincial bill, an 18-member mediation committee (9 members from each chamber) attempts to reconcile the differences and return compromise legislation for a new vote in both houses. Failing that, the National Assembly may pass the bill with a two-thirds vote and send it on for presidential signature.

In early 1997 the legislature approved the creation of a National House of Traditional Leaders, aiming to provide a forum for the leaders of tribal groups and increasing communication between the legislature and the provinces. The new body was inaugurated on April 17. Members are named by provincial-level Houses of Traditional Leaders. In 2001 the Department of Justice and Constitutional Development, responding largely to requests from rural areas, announced that traditional leaders would be permitted to function as Commissioners of Oaths (with a function similar to that of a notary public). At the same time, the Department of Provincial and Local Government has begun the process of more clearly delineating the powers and functions of the traditional leadership.

Provincial governments are led by elected legislatures of 30 to 80 members. Each legislature elects a provincial premier, who heads an Executive Council. Beneath the provincial level are 284 municipalities, including 6 recently established metropolitan municipalities ("megacities," incorporating surrounding townships): Cape Town, Durban Unicity, Ekurhuleni (East Rand), Johannesburg, Nelson Mandela (Port Elizabeth), and Tshwane (Pretoria). Legislatures are elected at each municipal level. In 2000 the proportion of traditional representatives on councils was raised from 10 to 20 percent. The smaller jurisdictions are represented throughout the governmental system by the South African Local Government Association (SALGA).

The 1996 constitution had an antidefection clause prohibiting floor-crossing because it was felt that permitting representatives to change parties would interfere with the proportional electoral system. In June 2002 legislation regulated floor-crossing in national, provincial, and local government elections. Legislators wishing to change parties were required to do so within the first 15 days of the second year of a legislative term; they could form another party or merge with a party without losing their seats. The UDM and others submitted an urgent application to the Constitutional Court challenging the constitutionality of the new legislation. In October the court ruled that floor-crossing at the municipal level could proceed but indicated that the legislation for the national and provincial levels had technical deficiencies and would require redrafting. In February 2003 the constitution was amended to permit members of the National Assembly and the nine provincial legislatures to switch allegiances from one party to another, thus bringing uniformity to the three levels of government regarding defections.

Foreign relations. Although South Africa was a founding member of the United Nations, its international standing was greatly impaired as a result of the racial restrictions maintained in its own territory and, until late 1988, that of Namibia (South West Africa). In the post–World War II period its rejection of external advice and pressure resulted in an atrophy of international contacts, notably through its departure from the Commonwealth in 1961, its suspension from membership in the Economic Commission for Africa in 1963, and its withdrawal or expulsion from a number of UN Specialized Agencies. It was also denied participation in the UN General Assembly, which repeatedly condemned the policy and practice of apartheid and advocated "universally applied economic sanctions" as the only means of achieving a peaceful solution to the problem. The UN Security Council, while stopping short of economic measures, called as early as 1963 for an embargo on the sale and shipment to South Africa of military equipment and materials.

Relations with the United Nations were further aggravated by South Africa's refusal to apply economic sanctions against Rhodesia, as ordered by the Security Council in 1966, and its long-standing refusal to relinquish control over Namibia, as ordered by both the General Assembly and the Security Council. Despite its political isolation on these key issues, Pretoria refrained from quitting the world body and attempted to maintain friendly political relations and close economic ties with most Western countries. Regionally, it belonged to the Southern African Customs Union (SACU), along with Botswana, Lesotho, Swaziland, and, later, Namibia. It also cooperated closely with the Ian Smith regime in Rhodesia over economic and defense matters, assisting its neighbor in circumventing UN sanctions. However, in accordance with its policy of seeking détente with neighboring black regimes, it publicly called for a "resolution of the Rhodesian question," endorsing in 1976 the principle of black majority rule if appropriate guarantees were extended to the white minority of what became in 1980 the Republic of Zimbabwe.

For more than a decade the government mounted repeated forays into Angola in its protracted conflict with Namibian insurgents, while relations with Swaziland and Mozambique were aggravated by the presence of ANC guerrilla bases in both countries, despite the conclusion of a nonaggression pact with the former in 1982 and a similar agreement with the latter (the "Nkomati accord") in May 1984.

During 1985 Western states came under increased pressure to impose sanctions on the Botha government. U.S. president Ronald Reagan had long opposed any action that would disrupt the South African economy, but faced in mid-September with a congressional threat to act on its own, he ordered a number of distinctly modest punitive actions, with the countries of the European Community (EC, subsequently the EU) following in an equally restrained manner. The principal American prohibitions focused on bank loans and the export of nuclear technology and computers, while the Europeans imposed an oil embargo, halted most arms sales, and withdrew their military attachés. In addition, substantial corporate divestment occurred, particularly by U.S. firms. None of these sanctions presented a serious challenge to South Africa, which was, however, sufficiently aggrieved to threaten an embargo on the export of strategic metals to the United States.

Pretoria's capacity to act with impunity in regard to neighboring states was amply demonstrated during 1986. On January 1 Lesotho was effectively blockaded, and three weeks later its government was overthrown by forces more supportive of South African efforts to contain cross-border attacks by ANC guerrillas. Subsequently, on May 19, ANC targets in Botswana, Zambia, and Zimbabwe were subjected to bombing attacks by the South African Air Force, in addition to ground raids by units of the SADF. Additional forays were conducted against alleged ANC bases in Swaziland late in the year and in Zambia in early 1987.

During 1988 South Africa's regional posture softened dramatically. In September President Botha traveled to Mozambique for his first state visit to a black African country. "Fruitful and cordial" discussions were held with President Chissano on a variety of topics, including the supply of power from Mozambique's Cahora Bassa hydroelectric facility, the status of Mozambican workers in South Africa, and "reactivation and reinforcement" of the Nkomati agreement of March 1984, which promised mutual nonaggression between South Africa and Mozambique. Subsequently, Botha visited Zaire and Cóte d'Ivoire for talks with presidents Mobuto and Houphouët-Boigny, respectively. The most important development, however, concerned the Angola-Namibia conflict. During a November meeting in Geneva, Switzerland, Pretoria accepted a U.S.-mediated agreement, previously endorsed by Angola and Cuba, for the phased withdrawal of Cuban troops from Angola, accompanied by a withdrawal of all but 1,000 South African troops from Namibia and a UN-supervised election seven months thereafter in implementation of UN Security Council Resolution 435 of 1978. A protocol finalizing the agreement was signed in Brazzaville, Congo, on December 13, followed by the formal conclusion of a tripartite peace accord at UN headquarters in New York on December 22 (for details, see articles on Angola and Namibia). Not addressed by the Namibia settlement was the status of the port enclave of Walvis Bay, which, although historically South African territory, had been administered since 1977 as part of South West Africa. Preliminary discussions on the issue were launched in March 1991, but it was not until August 16, 1993, in a major decision of the multiparty forum convened to decide the future of South Africa, that the South African government delegation agreed under pressure from the ANC and other participants to transfer the Walvis Bay enclave to Namibia. Formal conveyance occurred at midnight on February 28, 1994.

In a setback for ANC efforts to increase Pretoria's diplomatic isolation, in September 1990 President de Klerk was received at the White House by U.S. president George H. W. Bush. A few days earlier Foreign Minister Botha had announced that South Africa was prepared to accede to the UN Nuclear Non-Proliferation Treaty (see International Atomic Energy Agency, under UN: Related Organizations) in furtherance of an effort to make the African continent a nuclear weapons–free zone.

The progress made in dismantling apartheid during 1991 yielded significant diplomatic gains for Pretoria globally and on the African continent. Most economic sanctions imposed by Western nations (save in regard to military items) were relaxed, and in April 1992, after a number of political exchanges with neighboring regimes, President de Klerk made a highly symbolic state visit to Nigeria for talks with the incumbent chair of the Organization of African Unity (OAU, subsequently the African Union—AU), Ibrahim Babangida. No less symbolic was South Africa's reacceptance into international sports activity.

On July 1, 1993, President de Klerk and ANC President Mandela held separate meetings in Washington with U.S. president Bill Clinton and three days later were joint recipients of Liberty Medals in Philadelphia, with President Clinton in attendance. The end of apartheid was further celebrated on October 15, when de Klerk and Mandela were jointly awarded the 1993 Nobel Peace Prize. Concurrently, most UN economic sanctions against South Africa were terminated.

During 1994 South Africa gradually reentered the international community. On June 1 it rejoined the Commonwealth after a break of 33 years; two weeks later it became the 53rd member of the OAU. On June 23, following the Security Council's lifting of its long-standing arms embargo on South Africa, the suspension of Pretoria's participation in the UN General Assembly was rescinded, thus facilitating the reactivation of South African membership in UN specialized agencies. Two months later, South Africa joined the Southern African Development Community (SADC), and in October it signed a cooperation agreement with the EU.

In November 1996 the South African government announced that it was canceling its diplomatic relations with Taiwan, one of its foremost trading partners, and establishing formal relations with the People's Republic of China with effect from the end of 1997. Although President Mandela said that South Africa wanted to maintain its links with Taiwan on the highest level short of diplomatic ties, in mid-December Taiwan recalled its ambassador for an indefinite period in protest over the South African decision.

South Africa remained a dominant force in regional affairs in 1998, one of its most striking decisions involving the deployment of troops to help restore order in Lesotho in the fall (see article on Lesotho for details). President Mandela also continued to pursue a role as Africa's most prominent peacemaker, becoming heavily involved, for example, in efforts to resolve the conflict in the Democratic Republic of the Congo. In addition, the government further exhibited the independent nature of its foreign policy by extending ties with Iraq and North Korea, despite strong objections from Washington and several EU capitals.

South Africa has emerged in recent years as the continent's most vigorous and ambitious diplomatic power. Mbeki was the leading figure behind the African Union and New Partnership for Africa's Development (NEPAD) and was instrumental in brokering peace in Burundi and the Democratic Republic of the Congo, providing 3,000 troops in the two countries as part of UN peacekeeping operations and also shouldering most of the financial burden. South African companies have struck out north with strong investment strategies. With 40 percent of sub-Saharan Africa's GDP, South Africa is the only country capable of projecting both military power and economic clout.

South Africa has consistently opposed the U.S.-led war in Iraq and has promoted relations with many countries with whom the United States is at odds. Nevertheless, the United States considers South Africa as an ally in its efforts to promote democracy in the continent.

South Africa's two-year stint as a nonpermanent member of the UN Security Council, which began in January 2007, was controversial. For example, in January South Africa voted against allowing the council to consider a resolution on human rights abuses in Myanmar. In addition, in mid-March South Africa initially said it would oppose a request to brief the council on the deteriorating situation in Zimbabwe; South Africa later changed its position, though only after trivializing the briefing as a minor event that did not belong on the council's agenda. Later in March, South Africa delayed by a week the vote to impose sanctions against Iran to impede the development of its nuclear program. (South Africa has warm relations with Iran, whose chief nuclear negotiator and foreign minister had talks with Mbeki in South Africa in early 2007.)

Current issues. Despite its predominance in government, the ANC has made halting progress toward the resolution of fundamental national problems. Criticism of its Growth, Employment, and Redistribution program was voiced not only by the opposition but also by the closely allied Congress of South African Trade Unions (COSATU) and the South African Communist Party (SACP). Both faulted the ANC's turn toward market-oriented economics, including its privatization plans for such industries as energy, transportation, and telecommunications. They objected partly on ideological grounds and partly from concern over potential job losses, the rate of unemployment having failed to move significantly lower than the 37 percent average of 1997–1999, and economic growth having remained well below the level needed for achieving real reductions in poverty. At the same time the pace of land redistribution was slow, with the Land Claims Commission and white landowners often in dispute over fair market value. By July 2000 only 3 percent of farmland had been redistributed, far from the 30 percent called for by Parliament in 1994. As a consequence, landless blacks became increasingly impatient as the government attempted to avoid the domestic turmoil and international condemnation associated with the more radical expropriation policy in neighboring Zimbabwe.

In 2000–2002 the Mbeki administration drew withering criticism for its failure to present a cohesive plan for fighting the HIV/AIDS crisis. In April 2000 President Mbeki lent support to a scientifically discredited argument attributing AIDS to causes other than HIV infection, but by October the resultant uproar had led him to temper his comments. Although the government and AIDS activists joined forces to win a patent fight against international pharmaceutical companies, more often than not they were at odds over treatment, costs, and drug distribution, particularly with regard to preventing mother-to-child transmission. In October 2002 the government reversed itself and announced that it would look into making crucial antiretroviral drugs available through the public health system. Criticism of the government's response to the problem continued, however.

In 2004 President Mbeki signed into law the controversial Restitution of Land Rights Amendment Act, which gives the state the right to expropriate land for restitution purposes without a court order or the seller's agreement. The government's goal is to transfer 30 percent of all agricultural land from white to black farmers by 2014. In June 2005 Schabir SHAIK, financial adviser to deputy president Jacob Zuma, was found guilty of two counts of corruption and one of fraud in one of the most closely watched criminal trials since the end of apartheid. On June 15, Zuma, who the judge had called "compliant" in the malfeasance, was dismissed from the office of deputy president, and two weeks later he was charged with two counts of bribery. However, in the months that followed, a groundswell of popular support developed for Zuma, a key figure in the fight against apartheid; the powerful trade union COSATU described the pending legal action as a "political trial" and called on President Mbeki to reinstate Zuma. At year's end, however, matters became further complicated when Zuma was charged with raping the 31-year-old daughter of a friend. In May 2006 a judge found Zuma not guilty of the rape charge, and within days Zuma was reinstated as ANC deputy president.

On June 1, 2007, in advance of the ANC national policy conference (held every five years), public service unions began one of the biggest and longest strikes in the country's recent history. The strike was organized by COSATU public sector affiliates and other public servants' unions in pursuit of a 12 percent wage increase and a 30 percent increase in minimum annual pay. Some 700,000 workers—professional, skilled, and unskilled—participated in the strike, with more than 300,000 additional workers who were legally forbidden to strike taking part in other forms of protest. The strike, which crippled schools, hospitals, and public transport, ended on June 28 when public sector unions voted to end the strike and accepted the government offer of a 7.5 percent increase and improvements in housing and health benefits.

In the midst of the ANC's national policy conference and the public service strike, COSATU's general secretary Zwelinzima VAVI addressed the national congress of the National Education Health and Allied Workers Union, one of the striking unions, in Pretoria on June 28, 2007. He criticized Mbeki's government for marginalizing not only COSATU and the SACP but also the ANC, and for disproportionately concentrating power in the president's office and in the hands of government "technocrats."

The ANC's alliance partners, COSATU and the SACP, became increasingly vocal critics of President Mbeki's alleged autocratic tendencies, conservative and probusiness economic policies, and failure to effectively address unemployment, poverty, and inequality.

Mbeki's prestige declined inside South Africa after he lost the ANC chair during the party's convention in 2008 (see Political Parties, below), and during 2008 Zuma and the ANC seemed to be deliberately encroaching on his position. In March 2008 Zuma declared that the ANC, rather than the government, was the main source of political power in South Africa, and in April he visited the United Kingdom, where he met with Prime Minister Gordon Brown in a manner more reminiscent of a head of government than a party leader. Together, they called for a break in the Zimbabwean electoral stalemate (see article on Zimbabwe), demanding that Zimbabwean president Robert Mugabe release the election results.

The case against Zuma proceeded slowly through much of 2008, with Zuma and his lawyers working to have it dropped. Some of Zuma's ANC supporters, particularly in the party's youth wing, went as far as to threaten bloodshed if he were ever convicted. Zuma, in his turn, promised to name names if he were ever made to give evidence. Some news reports had linked President Mbeki to the arms scandal, and it was assumed that Zuma would accuse Mbeki if necessary. After numerous postponements, the case appeared to have finally collapsed on September 12, 2008, when a High Court judge ruled that the case against Zuma could not continue. Judge Chris NICHOLSON said Zuma's constitutional rights had been denied because he had not been questioned before charges were brought. In a blow to Mbeki's reputation, Nicholson expressed suspicion that the prosecution had been politically motivated, noting that the latest round of charges against Zuma came shortly after he defeated Mbeki for the ANC presidency. Judge Nicholson criticized all parties in the case and emphasized that they were eroding South Africa's reputation for electoral freedom and an independent judiciary. (Charges against Zuma were reinstated but were thrown out of court shortly before the April 2009 elections.)

After the High Court ruling, the ANC voted on September 24 to ask Mbeki to step down as president. Mbeki agreed to honor the motion when parliament named his replacement. The ANC nominated Kgalema MOTLANTHE, its deputy leader and an ally of Jacob Zuma, as caretaker president until the 2009 presidential election, which Zuma was still expected to win. Parliament ratified the choice on September 25, and Motlanthe was sworn in. Mbeki's resignation prompted 11 cabinet resignations. Some resignations were a courtesy to the new president, as in the case of Trevor Manuel, the well-respected finance minister who resigned but was reappointed. Other ministers were unwilling to serve in the new administration. The replacement of health minister Mantombazana TSHABALALA-MSIMANG, who had advocated garlic and beetroot to combat HIV, was widely praised.

President Mbeki's forced resignation angered many within the ANC. Among the ministers resigning in protest was Defense Minister Mosiuoa LEKOTA, who led a dissident group in forming a new political party to contest the spring 2009 elections. The new party was not expected to topple the ANC from power, but many felt it might deny the ANC the two-thirds majority necessary to change the constitution. By mid-December 2008 the ANC had successfully challenged two names proposed for the new party by claiming ownership rights over each name. The new party proposed and was granted the name Congress of the People (COPE) over the ANC's objections.

Thabo Mbeki was more active abroad than in South Africa during 2008. He led the SADC and other states in efforts to resolve the Zimbabwe crisis. Mbeki visited President Mugabe several times but was criticized for achieving little through "soft" diplomacy. Many Zimbabweans had fled to South Africa because of the post-electoral violence. Zimbabwean refugees, as well as other foreigners, were attacked during the summer of 2008 by xenophobic mobs.

The 2009 election campaign was marked by intermittent violence. Critics also objected to Zuma's appeal for support from members of his tribe, the Zulus, and an apparent willingness to distribute plum positions to loyalists, arguing that tribalism and related practices were incompatible with South Africa's modern social aspirations and norms. However, despite growing poverty and persistent inequality during the period of ANC rule, Zuma remained popular with poor black voters. He also made significant efforts to court Afrikaners, addressing them as a "white tribe" implicitly superior to English-speaking whites. Middle class blacks and ANC dissidents, however, increasingly gravitated towards COPE, while the Democratic Alliance remained the party of choice for many whites and also made inroads with biracial Afrikaners. Election results showed that Zuma and the ANC won handily but fell short of the coveted two-thirds majority due to the rising profile of COPE, which considered legislative cooperation with the DA.

Upon taking office, Zuma named Motlanthe deputy president and enlarged the cabinet from 31 to 34 members. Trevor Manuel was transferred from Finance to chair the newly created National Planning Commission. Zuma also increased the number of deputy ministers, a move that prompted charges of cronyism and payback

In an early decision of the Zuma presidency, it was announced that the government would not attempt to expropriate any white-owned farms. Nevertheless, enduring social grievances were expected to shorten Zuma's honeymoon period: the country continued to be troubled by xenophobic rioting, and a shortage of electricity and other basic amenities. Meanwhile, living standards continued to stagnate in the townships inhabited by many poor black South Africans. Observers posited that the younger generation, untouched by nostalgia or a sense of obligatory loyalty to the ANC, could demand that the party begin to deliver on its objectives of reduced unemployment and improvements to infrastructure and social services in order to retain their support.

POLITICAL PARTIES

During most of the apartheid era South Africa's leading political party was the predominantly Afrikaner National Party (NP), which came to power in 1948 and steadily increased its parliamentary strength to a high of 134 (64.8 percent) of lower house seats in the November 1977 election, before falling to 94 seats (48.1 percent) in 1989. While not as extremist as the Reconstituted National Party, the Conservative Party of South Africa, or a variety of smaller formations, the National Party was long committed to the general principle of white supremacy. Parties advocating more liberal racial policies fared poorly, with only the Progressive Party winning representation in the House of Assembly in the 1974 election; in 1977, however, a successor organization, the Progressive Federal Party (PFP), became the leading opposition party with 17 seats, which were increased to 26 in 1981. In 1989 the PFP joined with two other moderate groups to form the Democratic Party, which won 33 directly elective seats in the September balloting.

In the post-apartheid election of April 26–29, 1994, the African National Congress secured 252 of 400 National Assembly seats followed by the National Party with 82 seats. The chief opposition was the *Inkatha* Freedom Party (IFP) with 43 seats. When the NP withdrew from the governing coalition in May 1996, it became the major opposition party. In the 1999 assembly elections, Tony Leon's Democratic Party became the main opposition with 38 seats to the ANC's 266 seats.

Floor-crossings (authorized effective 2003) have led to the creation of small new parties and increased the number of parties with representation in the National Assembly. Parties could consist of as little as one member. Following the 2003 floor-crossing window, five new parties were represented in the assembly: the **African Independent Movement** (AIM), the ADP, the ID, **National Action** (NA), and the **Peace and Justice Congress** (PJC).

In 2007 the Democratic Alliance (DA) was the chief opposition party, holding 50 seats while the ANC had 279 seats. The ANC claimed 293 seats following the 2005 floor-crossing. By this time AIM, the ADP, the NA, and the PJC had disappeared from the National Assembly. In 2007 the ANC began a debate on floor-crossing, which many across the political spectrum found abusive. By 2008 floor-crossing was abolished. The 2009 elections granted COPE, an ANC splinter group, the third-largest proportion of seats in Parliament.

Government Parties:

African National Congress (ANC). Organized in 1912 as the South African Native National Congress and long recognized as South Africa's leading black formation, the ANC (as it became known in 1923) was banned from 1960 to February 1990. The organization's most charismatic figure, Nelson Mandela, was released from prison in February 1990, while its president, Oliver Tambo, was permitted to return from more than three decades' exile the following December. (Tambo died in 1993.)

On May 28–31, 1992, the ANC held a policy conference in Johannesburg, during which it celebrated its evolution from a liberation movement to a political party and replaced a 1955 commitment to comprehensive nationalization with an emphasis on a mixed economy. In January 1994, prior to its assumption of power, it did, however, announce an ambitious program to end economic apartheid by redistributing land, building more than a million low-income dwellings, assuming state control of the mining industry, and breaking up white-owned conglomerates. The draft plan, known as the Reconstruction and Development Program, drew immediate criticism from the country's business leaders and yielded a caveat from Mandela that it required "a substantial amount of additional work to be anywhere near what we want it to be."

Since April 1994, the ANC has governed in a tripartite alliance with COSATU and the SACP, whose leaders appear on ANC party lists. Among those elected on the ANC ticket in the party's landslide election victory in April 1994 was Winnie Mandela, the controversial estranged wife of the new president, whose 1991 conviction for kidnapping and being an accessory to assault did not deter her appointment as a deputy minister in the new government. In a strengthening of radical elements in the party leadership, Winnie Mandela regained her position on the ANC executive at the 49th congress in December, when First Deputy President Thabo Mbeki succeeded the ailing Sisulu as ANC vice president, thus becoming President Mandela's heir apparent. Mrs. Mandela's dismissal from the government in March 1995, following her public assertions that it lacked radicalism, drew official endorsement from ANC bodies, although she retained strong rank-and-file support. The Mandelas' 38-year marriage ended in divorce in March 1996.

In November 1995 the ANC won 66.4 percent of the votes cast in South Africa's first democratic local elections. In August 1996 President Mandela formally notified the ANC executive committee that he would not seek a second presidential term in the elections due in 1999 and that he would relinquish the ANC presidency at the party's next national conference in 1997.

In April 1997 Winnie Mandela retained her position as president of the ANC's Women's League, despite the party's apparent backing of her challengers, and in September she announced her intention to campaign for the ANC's deputy presidential post. Once again the party backed her opponent, Jacob Zuma, but what ultimately derailed her aspirations was her alleged role in apartheid-era violence, and she withdrew from the deputy leadership race.

As expected, at the ANC's congress held December 16–20, 1997, Nelson Mandela announced his retirement from the party's top post and his chosen successor, Thabo Mbeki, was unopposed in the subsequent election for party president. Also unopposed in their runs for party posts were Zuma, Kgalema Motlanthe (secretary general), and Mendi MSIMANG (treasurer general). For her part, Winnie Mandela secured a seat on the National Executive Committee.

The ANC unsuccessfully tried to block release of the comprehensive TRC report in the fall of 1998, objecting to conclusions that the ANC had been responsible for human rights abuses and acts of terrorism against its opponents during the anti-apartheid campaign and prior to the 1994 balloting. Party officials, led by Mbeki, condemned the report as "scurrilous," but President Mandela, in a pointed departure from the views of his successor, acknowledged that some of the abuses reported by the TRC had occurred and chastised the other ANC leaders for their angry response. Winnie Mandela was singled out in the TRC report for her alleged role in violent acts committed by the Mandela United Football Club, described as her "private army." Nevertheless, she remained popular in the ANC and was placed high on its candidate list for the June 1999 balloting, thereby assuring her election to the assembly.

In the June 1999 elections the ANC widened its parliamentary majority to 266 seats (with a 66.4 percent vote share) and retained control of seven provincial legislatures. It joined the IFP in a coalition government in KwaZulu-Natal and then in November 2001, having negotiated a cooperation agreement with the NNP, joined in forming a new administration in the ninth province, Western Cape, where it held a plurality of council seats.

On October 18, 2001, Winnie Madikizela-Mandela was arrested and charged with fraud and theft involving some $108,000 in dozens of bank loans to fictitious members of the ANC Women's League. Earlier in the month Tony YENGENI had resigned as ANC whip following his arrest for alleged illegal acquisition of an automobile in connection with the controversial 1999 $5.4 billion arms deal with EU countries. He resigned his assembly seat in 2003 after being convicted of defrauding parliament. (After unsuccessful appeals against his four-year jail sentence, Yengeni was in prison for only five months prior to his controversial release in January 2007.)

The ANC's entrenchment as the dominant party in South African politics has been helped by the splintering of opposition parties and by its ability to woo opposition legislators and career politicians with jobs and favors. The ANC has made heavy inroads among Zulus, working-class people, Indians, and Coloureds, although it still has not won over many white voters, who generally vote for the DA or other white liberal or right-wing parties.

Jacob Zuma, suspended in December 2006 after being charged with rape, was reinstated as the ANC deputy president after being found not guilty in May 2006. In September a judge also dismissed the corruption case begun against him in July, berating the prosecution for its poor preparation.

The ANC held its five-yearly national policy conference on June 27–30, 2007, with Mbeki asserting that the conference was not about the future of ANC leadership. He also warned the SACP and COSATU not to try to dictate ANC policy. He said the ANC had never sought to prescribe to the SACP the policies it should adopt and leaders it should elect, and that it had been accepted for decades that the SACP would not confuse its "socialist revolution" with the ANC's broader campaign to redress the ills of white rule. The conference adopted a compromise on the succession issue. It was agreed that it was party "preference" but not a "principle" that the party leader and the president be the same person. To placate those who felt the party leadership had become too authoritarian, a recommendation was made to decentralize the appointment of mayors and premiers.

ANC custom makes it inappropriate for candidates to declare their interest in the party's presidential post as one is supposed to be asked to serve. Mbeki said he would be willing to continue to serve as ANC president if asked to do so. At the same time, the COSATU and SACP leadership announced their support for Zuma, in part due to his pledge to pursue a more left-wing agenda than Mbeki should he come to power.

Jacob Zuma was elected president of the ruling ANC at the party's leadership convention on December 18, 2007, easily defeating the incumbent, South African President Thabo Mbeki. Zuma, a populist who enjoyed the support of trade unions, the Communist Party of South Africa, and other left-wing elements of the ANC, consequently became the presumptive ANC candidate for the 2009 presidential election, although his status remained compromised by corruption charges that were reinstated shortly after the convention but were dropped just before his April 2009 election as president. Many Mbeki loyalists were also ousted from ANC leadership positions at the 2007 convention, and some of them eventually left the ANC to form the Congress of the People (COPE).

Leaders: Jacob ZUMA (President), Kgalema MOTLANTHE (Deputy President), Baleka MBETE (National Chair), Gwede MANTASHE (Secretary General).

South African Communist Party (SACP). The SACP was formed in 1953, following the dissolution in 1950 of the original Communist Party of South Africa (CPSA), which had been organized in 1921 but had been banned by the Suppression of Communism Bill in 1950. The SACP has long cooperated closely with the ANC, to which a number of senior SACP members have been appointed. The party's former chair, Dr. Yusef DADOO, died in 1983, while its former general secretary, Moses MABHIDA, died in Maputo, Mozambique, in March 1986. A year later, following his appointment as Mabhida's successor, Joe SLOVO resigned as chief of staff of the ANC's military wing, *Umkhonto we Sizwe.* He returned to South Africa in April 1990. The party gathered for a "relaunching"—its first public rally within South Africa in 40 years—on July 29, 1990. In a stinging opening address to the SACP's first legal congress on December 8, 1991, Slovo insisted that former Soviet President Mikhail Gorbachev had "completely lost his way" and that what was being buried in Eastern Europe was not true socialism. Subsequently, Slovo was elected party chair, with the longtime chief of *Umkhonto we Sizwe*, Chris Hani, being named his successor as general secretary. Hani was assassinated on April 10, 1993.

As members of the governing coalition, SACP members sit as ANC members in parliament, though they are identified as SACP in their cabinet biographies. Slovo was awarded the housing portfolio in the Mandela administration, but he died in January 1995. About 80 of the ANC's National Assembly representatives have SACP membership, as do a number of cabinet ministers.

At the SACP's national conference held in Port Elizabeth in July 2007, most of those elected to the Central Committee supported Jacob Zuma in his bid to become the next ANC president, while a number of pro-Mbeki cabinet members lost their committee posts. Several of the latter subsequently resigned from the party to protest the militant anti-Mbeki stance. Meanwhile, COSATU's president, Willie Madisha, was voted off the Central Committee for being perceived as pro-Mbeki. SACP General Secretary Blade Nzimande warned that the party would hold an extraordinary congress to consider a break with the ANC if Zuma was not elected as the next ANC president.

The SACP's membership has grown to over 50,000, 70 percent of whom are under 35 years old. The Young Communist League (YCL), the youth wing of the SACP, has thus become an important power broker in the SACP.

Leaders: Blade NZIMANDE (General Secretary), Gwede MANTASHE (National Chair), Jeremy CRONIN (Deputy General Secretary), Pumulo MASAULLE (National Treasurer).

Freedom Front Plus (*Vryheidsfront Plus*—VF Plus). This group was founded in 2004 by the Freedom Front (*Vryheidsfront*—VF), the CPSA, and the *Afrikaner Eenheids Beweging* to contest the upcoming national election as a single party.

The VF was launched by Gen. (Ret.) Constand Viljoen in March 1994 following a split in the Afrikaner People's Front (AVF; see discussion under CPSA, below) over the issue of participation in the April election, with the VF opting to register to present the case for a "white homeland." Several prominent members of the Conservative Party also defected to the new grouping. In late March the VF stated that its objective was a confederal South Africa based on the "inalienable and non-negotiable" right of self-determination for Afrikaners and all other groups. Subsequent to the April poll, in which it placed fourth with 2.2 percent of the vote, the Front insisted that blatant irregularities had occurred at 80 percent of the voting stations. Having achieved a measure of accommodation with the government under black majority rule, the VF welcomed President Mandela's proposal of June 1995 that a consultative referendum should be held to ascertain Afrikaners' views on the concept of a separate Afrikaner state.

In the TRC report issued in October 1998, General Viljoen was held accountable for certain acts of violence committed by right-wingers during the run-up to the 1994 balloting. Meanwhile, the VF was described as hoping to cooperate with the DP for the 1999 election, in which it won only 0.8 percent of the vote and three National Assembly seats (a loss of six). In August Viljoen was reelected party leader by one vote over Pieter Mulder, but in March 2001 he announced his retirement from active politics. On March 31 Mulder was unanimously elected as his successor.

Following the VF's legacy, the VF Plus seeks to protect and enhance Afrikaner rights and interests through the creation of autonomous regions. The VF Plus currently holds four assembly seats. In May 2008 Mulder announced that the VF Plus had established Afrikaners as a member group in the Unrepresented Nations and Peoples Organization (UNPO), an international organization, based in the Netherlands, that campaigns for the rights of minority and indigenous populations.

Following the spring 2009 elections, the VP Plus offered its support to the incoming Zuma administration, and Mulder was named deputy minister of agriculture, forestry, and fisheries, technically securing the VF Plus status as a member of the ruling coalition. The party, however, is not a significant political force and would not be considered a member of government were it not for the minor cabinet role accorded to Mulder.

Leaders: Pieter MULDER (Party Leader), Abrie OOSTHUIZEN (Chair).

Other Parliamentary Parties:

Democratic Alliance (DA). The DA was established in late June 2000 by the Democratic Party (DP); the New National Party (NNP); and the small Federal Alliance (FA), which earlier in the month had agreed to present its candidates for upcoming local elections on the DP list. Formal merger of the three was delayed, however, pending passage of legislation permitting party consolidations. Initially seen as an attempt by the principal white formations to form a united front, the DA registered considerable success in the December municipal elections, taking 23 percent of the national vote and capturing Cape Town from the ANC. However, differences within the leadership resulted in the departure of the NNP from the DA in November 2001, and local defections in October 2002 delivered control of Cape Town to an ANC-NNP coalition.

Since it had been formed especially to contest the 2000 municipal elections, the DA's legal status was initially limited to the local level. Therefore, in order to constitute itself as a party at the provincial and national levels, the DA in 2001 launched an initiative in support of floor-crossing legislation, which, with the crucial support of the ANC, was passed by parliament in 2002. In the 2004 assembly balloting the DA emerged as the principal opposition party in the national parliament with 50 seats.

Tony Leon, leader of the DP/DA since 1994, said in November 2006 that he would not seek reelection at the 2007 party congress but that he would continue to serve out his term as a member of parliament. At the DA's congress in March 2007, Helen Zille won 70 percent of the delegates' votes to replace Leon. Joe Seremane, the only black rival, won 6 percent of votes. In her acceptance speech, Zille criticized the ANC's "race-based politics," indicating that, like Leon, she would oppose affirmative action. Zille identified the biggest challenges facing the country as education, crime, and the HIV/AIDS epidemic.

Leaders: Helen ZILLE (President and Leader of the Opposition), Joe SEREMANE (Chair), Athol TROLLIP (Parliamentary Leader and Leader of the Opposition in Parliament).

Congress of the People (COPE). Congress of the People was the name finally given to the group that broke away from the ANC after Thabo Mbeki's forced resignation from the presidency in September 2008. (See Current Issues.) Led by former defense minister Mosiuoa LEKOTA, COPE was formed to contest the April 2009 elections. Its aim was to deny the ANC the two-thirds majority needed to change the constitution. In this, COPE was successful, returning 31 members and becoming the third-largest parliamentary party behind the ANC and the DA. COPE's manifesto presents an alternative to a race-based, one-party state under the ANC to "depoliticize the institutions of state" and expedite economic growth for "large-scale labor absorption."

Leaders: Mosiuoa LEKOTA (President), Mbhazima SHILOWA (First Deputy President), Lynda ODENDAAL (Second Deputy President). Charlotte Lobe (Secretary General).

***Inkatha* Freedom Party** (IFP). In response to charges of tribalism, the *Inkatha,* a predominantly Zulu organization, voted at a general conference in 1990 to transform itself into a political party that would be open to all races; however, most observers felt that the organization remained primarily a vehicle for the expression of Zulu interests in KwaZulu. Dr. Mangosuthu Buthelezi, the KwaZulu homeland leader from 1978 to 1994, was unanimously elected president of the IFP. The party shares many ANC positions, except what it considers are the rights and prerogatives of "traditional leaders," as well as its emphasis on individual responsibility.

Bitterly opposed to the ANC and frequently engaged in violence with its larger rival, *Inkatha* declared in mid-1993 that it would not participate in the 1994 election and joined in an improbable alliance with the leading right-extremist parties and representatives of nominally independent Bophuthatswana and Ciskei in a Concerned South Africans Group (COSAG) that was subsequently styled the Freedom Alliance. Following the ouster of Bophuthatswana's Lucas Mangope in March 1994, however, the Alliance disintegrated, and the IFP agreed on April 19 to abandon its boycott of the election. It placed third. The group was awarded three portfolios in the ensuing Mandela administration, including the designation of IFP leader Buthelezi as home affairs minister. It nevertheless continued its deep disagreement with the ANC over constitutional and other issues, boycotting the Constituent Assembly charged with drafting a new constitution.

The intraparty schism between those members favoring continued participation in the national government (so-called moderates) and the Buthelezi-led, anti-ANC faction widened in early 1997. At a meeting of the National Council in January, the IFP's national chair, Frank MDLALOSE, and Secretary General Ziba Jiyane resigned and were replaced by Buthelezi supporters Ben NGUBANE and Zakhele KHUMALO, respectively. Subsequently, in March, 13 IFP activists were convicted for their roles in the slaying of 19 ANC members in 1995.

The TRC accused the IFP of having caused the death of nearly 4,000 opponents in KwaZulu in 1982–1994, attributing ultimate responsibility for the violence in large part to Chief Buthelezi, who did not testify before the commission or request amnesty. Subsequently, the IFP election campaign in 1999 focused on economic issues. In the June balloting the party won 34 seats in the National Assembly on an 8.6 percent vote share. It continued as national government partner of the ANC, with which it also formed a coalition in KwaZulu-Natal.

Relations between the IFP and ANC in 2002 fell to their lowest ebb since 1994 (when the IFP had joined the government of national unity). The main arena of the quarrel between the two parties was KwaZulu-Natal, where, in late 2002, the ruling IFP ejected two ANC ministers from the provincial government and formed a partnership with the opposition Democratic Alliance. After floor-crossing in 2003, the IFP held 31 assembly seats.

The IFP suffered considerable erosion of support in the 2004 general election, in which it secured 28 seats. For the first time since 1994, the IFP subsequently had no representation in the cabinet.

At the IFP's annual conference in July 2004, Ziba Jiyane was nominated from the floor, against the leadership's wishes, to run against the incumbent national chair and former provincial premier, Lionel

MTSHALI, whom he defeated in a landslide victory. Rev. Musa Zondi was nominated for the revived position of secretary general. The IFP also launched a campaign to shed its image as an exclusively Zulu party and appeal to the broader multiracial community.

After floor-crossing in 2005, the IFP lost an additional five assembly seats, ceding four to the newly formed Nadeco and one to the DA. (In April 2006, three IFP defectors to Nadeco returned to the IFP, whose Operation *Buyela eKhaya* [Come Back Home] encouraged defectors to return to the party.) At the IFP's annual national conference in September 2005, Zondi was elected secretary general and Zanele Magwaza was unanimously elected national chair, replacing Ziba Jiyane, who had defected earlier to help form Nadeco.

Ideologically, the IFP views itself as right of the ANC. It opposed the passage of legislation in 2005 to expropriate white-owned land because of its opposition to state intervention in the market. In 2007 the IFP submitted a private member's bill calling for an end to floor-crossing, which it considers a betrayal of the electorate. The party's main support base is among Zulus in rural KwaZulu-Natal. However, the party seeks to project itself as a national party, and IFP parliamentarians have included non-Zulus.

The IFP, a regional party, estimates its membership was 1–2 million in the 1980s and 1990s, though officials concede there has been a decline since then. If the numbers are accurate, the IFP has the largest party membership in the country.

Leaders: Chief Mangosuthu (Gatsha) BUTHELEZI (President), Rev. Musa ZONDI (Secretary General), Themba C. MSIMANG (Deputy Secretary General).

African Christian Democratic Party (ACDP). The ACDP, a conservative Christian group, was organized in 1993 with the aim of representing Christians in parliament. Sixty percent of its members are black. Prior to the 1994 balloting, in which it won two seats on a 0.5 percent vote share, the ACDP also secured representation in three provincial assemblies. In 1997 the ACDP expressed outrage at the government's decision to legalize abortion. The party won six assembly seats and its first NCOP seat in the 1999 general election, securing an additional assembly seat during the floor-crossing window in 2003. The ACDP also contested the 2004 elections, in which it won 1.4 percent of the vote and six assembly seats. This seat share was reduced to three after the 2005 floor-crossing, as the party lost two to the ANC and one to the Federation of Democrats.

The ACDP was the only party in the National Assembly that voted against adoption of the 1996 constitution because of moral and "biblical" objections to clauses, including the prohibition of government discrimination on the basis of sexual orientation. In 1997 the ACDP also expressed outrage at the government's decision to legalize abortion, and in 2000 its manifesto opposed the promotion of condoms and safe sex as preventive measures against HIV transmission. The party opposed (as did the IFP) the 2006 Civil Union Bill, which legalized same-sex marriages.

Leaders: Rev. Dr. Kenneth MESHOE (President), Jo-Ann DOWNS (Deputy President), Raymond TLAELI (Secretary General), Pastor Lydia MESHOE (President of ACDP women's organization).

Independent Democrats (ID). The ID was formed during the floor-crossing window in March–April 2003 under the leadership of Patricia de Lille, a former trade unionist and a long-time member of the Pan Africanist Congress, which she left to form the ID. The party's main support area is the Cape metro area, but it is expanding. With the motto "Back to Basics," the ID's policies are fairly centrist.

The ID won seven seats in the 2004 assembly elections. To forestall defections in the 2005 floor-crossing window, the ID sacked its deputy leader and Gauteng provincial legislature member, Themba SONO. Sono obtained a temporary court order preventing the Gauteng speaker from swearing in anyone in his place until the matter was heard in court. A temporary court order was also issued to prevent the ID from filling the Western Cape legislature seat of Lennit MAX until the party heard his internal appeal against his expulsion. Despite the party's efforts to prevent defections, the ID lost two assembly seats to the ANC during the 2005 floor-crossing window.

In June 2007 the ID held its first national policy conference, followed by its inaugural national congress in July. De Lille positioned the ID as a "people-oriented" party, favoring a role for both the state and the market. She criticized the government's black economic empowerment policy for benefiting only a small elite and identified other perceived policy failures regarding crime control, HIV/AIDS prevention, and the delivery of essential services. She also called for draft legislation to regulate party funding and for the government to institute immediate temporary relief measures and an economic recovery plan for fishing communities.

Leaders: Patricia de LILLE (President), Agnes TSAMAI and Haniff HOOSEN (Deputy Presidents), Mervyn CIROTA (National Chair), Schalk LUBBE (National Treasurer), Joe MCGLUWA (National Organizer).

Pan Africanist Congress of Azania (PAC). A militant ANC offshoot that was banned in 1960, the PAC long sought to unite all black South Africans in a single national front. Based in Lusaka, Zambia, the PAC announced in May 1979 the establishment in the Sudan of a "June 16 Azania Institute" (named after the June 1976 Soweto uprising) to instruct displaced South African students in a variety of academic and artisan skills. Its underground affiliate, the Azanian People's Liberation Army (APLA), was relatively small, compared to the military wing of the rival ANC. The PAC's longtime leader, John Nyati POKELA, died in June 1985; its president, Zephania MOTHOPENG, was released from nine years' imprisonment in November 1988, while another leader, Jafta MASEMOLA, was released in October 1989. In September 1990 the PAC rejected a government invitation to participate in constitutional talks, branding the overture as "not serious or honest." In October the PAC joined the ANC and some 60 other groups (*Inkatha* being the most notable exception) in the attempted formation of a united Patriotic Front. However, the PAC subsequently broke with the Mandela-led formation in opposing Codesa, insisting that it would settle for nothing less than "a democratically elected constituent assembly." The PAC has abandoned its more radical programs and now concentrates on the plight of the poor and related issues.

The PAC announced in the early 1990s that it was abandoning armed struggle, thus permitting it to register for elections. The party won 1.2 percent of the vote and five assembly seats in the 1994 balloting. Following a protracted leadership struggle, Clarence MAKWETU stepped down as PAC president in December 1996 and was replaced by Rev. Mmutlanyane Stanley MOGOBA. Makwetu was expelled from the party in 1997.

Under Mogoba's leadership the PAC in 1997 evinced a conciliatory attitude toward whites, while party leaders also expressed an interest in opening a dialogue with the ANC, the PAC's longtime rival. Subsequently, in January 1999, it was announced that the APLA had been officially disbanded, and the PAC was registered to contest the June national elections, in which it won three seats on a 0.7 percent vote share. In July 2001 the PAC, responding to delays in land distribution and government housing construction, began helping thousands of homeless people occupy a wasteland near Johannesburg. The government quickly evicted them.

In the 2003 floor-crossing, Patricia de Lille left the PAC to form the ID, thus leaving the PAC with only two assembly seats. The PAC deputy president, Dr. Motsoko PHEKO, was elected president on June 15, replacing Mogoba, who had continued as president after the dispute over 2002 party congress results. In February 2004, Mogoba resigned from parliament to give his seat to the deputy president of the party, Themba Godi. After the April 2004 national election, the PAC again had three assembly seats. In 2006 the PAC congress elected a new president, Letlapa Mphahlele. At the September 2007 floor-crossing, two members left to form the **African People's Convention.** The party has since experienced severe factional infighting, with supporters of Pheko and MPHAHLELE each claiming to be the "real PAC." Mphahlele was elected to Parliament in place of Pheko in April 2009.

Leader: Letlapa MPHAHLELE (President)

African People's Convention (APC). The APC was founded at the September 2007 floor-crossing by the defection of Themba Godi and Mofihli Dikotsi from the Pan Africanist Congress. After the April 2009 election Godi was the only APC member remaining in the National Assembly.

Leader: Themba GODI (President).

United Christian Democratic Party (UCDP). The UCDP was founded by Chief Lucas Mangope, former president of the Bophuthatswana homeland. The conservative formation includes in its platform support for the authority of traditional leaders. Despite reports that Mangope considered merging the UCDP with the newly formed UDM in 1997, it contested the 1999 elections independently, winning three seats in the National Assembly on a 0.8 percent vote share. In

2004 it retained its three seats but in 2009 was reduced to two. The main UCDP power base is in the North West province.

Leaders: Chief Lucas MANGOPE (Leader), Paul DITSHETELO (Deputy Leader), Isaac Sipho MFUNDISI (National Chair).

United Democratic Movement (UDM). The UDM was launched on September 27, 1997, by former NP secretary general Roelf MEYER and former ANC deputy minister Bantu Holomisa, also a former Transkei homeland leader. The new grouping, which promoted a moderate and nonracial platform, was reportedly immediately bolstered by the enrollment of a number of young, liberal NP defectors. Its first secretary general, Sifiso NKABINDE, was murdered in January 1999. Like Holomisa, Nkabinde had been expelled from the ANC.

The UDM subsequently was reported to be gaining popular support, and it competed in the 1999 assembly campaign on a pledge to narrow the gap between rich and poor without imperiling the wealth of the financial elite. The party won 14 seats on a 3.4 percent vote share. In January 2000 Meyer announced his retirement from politics, and on August 31, 2007, he joined the ANC. The second National Congress in December 2001 confirmed Holomisa as president.

The UDM is identified with Xhosa interests in Eastern Cape province. It supported the ANC during the latter's bitter struggle with the IFP for control of the KwaZulu-Natal legislature. In the 2003 floor-crossing window, nine UDM assembly members defected, including deputy president Dr. Gerhard KOORNHOF, who joined the ANC, and Mogoboya Nelson RAMODIKE, the former Lebowa homeland minister, who formed his own party, the **Alliance for Democracy and Prosperity** (ADP). (In February 2007 Ramodike joined the ANC, appearing to signal the end of the ADP.) The September 1–15, 2005, floor-crossing window led to further UDM defections. The UDM suspended eight of its parliamentary and provincial legislature representatives in August 2007, suspecting them of planning to defect in the upcoming floor-crossing. Six of the suspended senior members, including Deputy President Malizole DIKO, had their suspensions reversed on August 30 by a Cape High Court that ruled that the party had violated its constitutional procedures for suspending members. On August 31 the UDM expelled the six members, saying they had failed to follow constitutional procedures for dealing with internal disputes. During the floor-crossing window in September, Diko formed a new party, the United Independent Front (below).

Leaders: Bantu HOLOMISA (President), Hamphrey NOBONGZA (General Secretary).

Azanian People's Organization (Azapo). Azapo was founded in April 1978 to carry on the work of the black consciousness movement that was banned in October 1977; however, its founders were immediately detained, and it did not hold its first congress until September 1979. Although never a mass party, it enjoyed the support of black intellectuals. Avowedly nonviolent, it adopted a hard line on the possibility of negotiating with the white government and was strongly anti-Codesa. In early 1994 Azapo declared its opposition to the forthcoming all-party election and announced that it would intensify its struggle until land had been returned to the country's blacks. Although Azapo had boycotted the 1994 balloting, it was registered for the 1999 elections, in which it won 0.2 percent of the vote and one National Assembly seat. Some Azapo members had defected to join the **Socialist Party of Azania** (SOPA), which was formed on March 21, 1998, allegedly because Azapo had abandoned its socialist principles and its leadership was undemocratic. In January 2001 the Azapo leader, Mosibudi Mangena, was named deputy minister of education, prompting mass resignations by Azapo members who accused him of betrayal for participating in the ANC's nonsocialist and multiracial government.

In the cabinet announced after the 2004 election, Azapo leader Mangena was appointed minister of science and technology, again generating criticism that Azapo should not be in the ANC government. The May 2009 cabinet contained no Azapo members.

Leaders: Mosibudi MANGENA (President), Pandelani NEFOLOVHODWE (Deputy President), Zithulele N. A. CINDI (National Chair), Strike THOKOANE (Secretary General).

Minority Front (MF). The MF represents the rights of Indians in South Africa; it participated without success in the 1994 balloting but won one National Assembly seat in 1999 on a vote share of 0.3 percent. It then formed an alliance with the ANC, giving the latter the 267 votes needed to amend the constitution. In 2004 the MF won two assembly seats. The MF manifesto supports increased subsidies for education and housing, job creation, improving social grants and pensions, fighting unfair implementation of affirmative action, and protecting minority rights.

Leader: Amichand RAJBANSI (Leader).

Other Parties and Groups:

United Independent Front (UIF). The UIF was formed in September 2005 by a group of UDM defectors, including much of the UDM provincial executive committee leadership. The UIF's leader, Malizole Diko, said the UIF would not accept cabinet positions because it sought to be an opposition party.

Diko died in July 2006; he was succeeded in an acting capacity by Ike Kekana. However, in mid-2007, Kekana and Nomakhaya Mdaka were each reported to be claiming leadership of the UIF. Court cases were expected to resolve the dispute, including who should fill Diko's still-vacant assembly seat. After the September 2007 floor-crossing, the UIF lost its representation in the National Assembly.

Leaders: Mzwandile MANJIYA (President), Neville HENDRICKS (Deputy President).

New National Party (NNP). The NNP was the name adopted by the National Party (*Nasionale Party*—NP) at a December 1998 congress in an effort to reshape its image from that of the party that had promoted apartheid. A product of a number of splits and mergers extending back to the period before World War II, the NP had come to power under the leadership of Daniel F. MALAN in 1948, and in 1951 it absorbed the Afrikaner Party. Supported by the great majority of Afrikaners and by a growing number of English-speaking South Africans, the NP became the majority party in 1953. For many years the party's official doctrine stressed rigorous anticommunism and separate racial development, as well as the evolution of the Bantu homelands into so-called independent states. The so-called *verligte* ("enlightened") faction under former prime minister Balthazar Vorster sought to reconcile these policies with the promotion of white immigration, solidarity among all white South Africans, and the pursuit of friendly relations with the outside world, including black African states. The opposing *verkrampte* ("unenlightened") faction tended to regard the party as a vehicle of specifically Afrikaner nationalism and opposed the inclusion of English speakers in the membership. The dismissal of *verkrampte* leader Dr. Albert Hertzog in the course of a cabinet reorganization in 1968 was generally interpreted as establishing the predominance of the Vorster faction. Hertzog and other conservative elements withdrew in 1969 to form the Refounded National Party (below). Vorster's influence within the party eroded sharply following the eruption of a Watergate-type scandal that forced his resignation as state president in mid-1979.

President Pieter Botha resigned as party leader at the party's annual caucus on February 2, 1989, with F. W. de Klerk being elected his successor in a contested vote. In the general election of September 6, the NP retained control of the House of Assembly by a substantially reduced majority. Four months earlier, in a parliamentary speech, de Klerk had asserted that although South Africans should anticipate "drastic changes," the NP was committed to "a constitutional dispensation which will not be conducive to majority rule," since such a condition would be "unjust to minorities." On August 31, however, he announced that the party would thenceforth be open to members of all races.

Following the March 1992 referendum on constitutional revision, de Klerk announced that South Africa's whites had "closed the book on apartheid" and reiterated an earlier pledge that the NP would utilize its parliamentary majority to implement decisions that called for admission of all South Africans to the political process. The NP emerged from the election of April 1994 as the second-ranked party, with de Klerk being named second deputy president in the Mandela administration. A feature of the party scene thereafter was an increasing number of defections from the NP to the ANC, including those of some senior figures.

In February 1996 the NP minister of provincial affairs and constitutional development, Roelf Meyer, announced his resignation from the government to assume the new post of NP secretary general. While remaining a member of the National Assembly and taking over the party's parliamentary leadership, Meyer was charged with charting a new future and image for the NP in the post-apartheid era. To that end, de Klerk announced in May 1996 that the NP was withdrawing from the government of national unity in order to form the parliamentary opposition and to redefine itself as a distinctive political force.

Subsequently, the NP was stunned when Meyer resigned from the party in May 1997 and announced the formation of a new grouping (see UDM, above). In June, de Klerk reportedly reached agreement with Freedom Front leader Constand Viljoen to increase the level of cooperation between their two groups. However, de Klerk announced his intention to resign from politics in August. The former national president had been the target of withering criticism from the TRC after he had testified in May that he knew nothing about human rights abuses during his years in leadership positions. Following a reportedly bruising intraparty battle between the party's conservative and moderate wings, Marthinus van Schalkwyk, a relative unknown, was elected party president.

The TRC strongly condemned former president Botha for the violence, including murder and torture, committed by government security forces during his tenure as prime minister (1978–1984) and president (1984–1989). For his part the unrepentant Botha accused the TRC of "witch hunts" and refused to testify, earning a conviction for contempt that was later overturned on technical grounds.

For the June 1999 balloting the NNP reportedly sought an electoral alliance with the IFP or the DP, but neither overture succeeded. In the national election the party saw its vote share drop to 6.9 percent; as a consequence its National Assembly representation fell to 28 seats, down from 82 in 1994. In the provinces, it won enough Western Cape Council seats to form a coalition government with the DP.

On June 25, 2000, the DP and NNP announced that they would merge as the DA, with van Schalkwyk becoming the new formation's deputy chair under the DP's Tony Leon. Policy and personal disputes between the two leaders subsequently surfaced, however, and on October 21, 2001, the NNP withdrew from the DA and announced that it was prepared to seek closer ties to the ANC, with which it no longer had prohibitive policy differences. In November the ANC and NNP announced a cooperative pact, the most immediate consequence being formation of a new ANC-NNP administration in Western Cape. Looking further ahead, the NNP leadership anticipated greater participation throughout government, including at the cabinet level.

In August 2004 the NNP asked its members to join the ANC and agreed to fight all future elections under the ANC banner. The decision sounded the death knell for South Africa's second-oldest party, founded in 1914, two years after the formation of the ANC. Van Schalkwyk said that he was applying for ANC membership and advised his colleagues to do likewise. However, many hard-core NNP voters shifted their allegiance to the DA. After the September 2005 floor-crossing window, defections of the NNP's National Assembly members had reduced its parliamentary representation to zero. In August 2008 three former local government officials re-registered the old National Party with the Independent Electoral Commission. They proposed to represent the interests of whites and Coloureds, and claimed they had received the blessing of former president F. W. de Klerk. De Klerk denied this, saying he no longer took part in politics. In April 2009 this revived party contested seats on the provincial but not the national level.

Federation of Democrats (FD). The FD was formed during the September 2005 floor-crossing by ACDP parliamentarian Rhoda SOUTHGATE (the FD's only legislator) and her husband, Kevin SOUTHGATE, a member of a provincial legislature. Louis GREEN, who had served as an ADCP deputy leader and the party's chief whip, defected to the FD because he disapproved of the ACDP leadership's treatment of the Southgates. In mid-2007 the FD and several small regional parties formed a broader Christian Democratic Alliance. By 2008 the only FD representative was Louis MICHAEL, who lost his seat in the April 2009 election.

Leaders: Louis GREEN (Leader), Kevin SOUTHGATE (National Party Chair).

National Democratic Convention (Nadeco). Nadeco was formed during the floor-crossing window in September 2005 by Ziba Jiyane, the incumbent IFP national chair. Nadeco was the major beneficiary of the window, gaining four national parliamentarians and four provincial legislature members, with all but one joining at the expense of the IFP. Nadeco, which supports the restoration of family values, contested the March 2006 local elections and was a kingmaker in various local authorities in KwaZulu-Natal. However, the party has been bedeviled by internal leadership disputes between Jiyane and Rev. Hawu Mbatha, who defected from the African Christian Democratic Party (ACDP, below) in September 2005. After the first annual Nadeco conference in September 2006 failed to elect a leadership group, another conference held in Durban in October elected Rev. Mbatha to lead the new national executive committee. In November 2006 the Pietermaritzburg High Court declared that the national executive led by Rev. Mbatha represented the legitimate Nadeco leadership. Jiyane appealed that decision.

Leaders: Rev. Hawu MBATHA (President), Makhosazana MDLALOSE (Deputy President), Ziba JIYANE, Vincent NGEMA (Secretary General), Themba MBUTHU (Chair).

Afrikaner Resistance Movement (*Afrikaner Weerstandsbeweging*—AWB). Founded in 1973, the extreme right-wing AWB became the most visible of the Afrikaner paramilitary formations opposed to majority rule. In June 1993 armed AWB members invaded the Johannesburg building where constitutional talks were in progress, meeting no resistance from the police on duty. Having been convicted and fined in October for electoral violence in 1991, controversial AWB leader Eugene Terre'Blanche in November urged whites to arm themselves for "inevitable" civil war. In March 1994, however, the failure of AWB and other Afrikaner paramilitaries to preserve the Bophuthatswana regime contributed to the collapse of the broad Freedom Alliance of conservative forces. In April 1996 ten AWB members were imprisoned for their part in a bombing campaign aimed at disrupting the 1994 election.

Further arrests of AWB activists were reported in early 1997. Moreover, in June Terre'Blanche was sentenced to prison for six years for allegedly attempting to murder a black laborer. (In March 2001 he lost his final appeal and began serving his sentence.) He was released in 2004. He was also condemned by the TRC for his role in the 1993–1994 violence. In March 2008 Terre'Blanche announced that he was re-founding the movement, which had become defunct. Subsequently, the AWB was accused of using deceptive tactics to recruit young members through Facebook, the online social network.

Leader: Eugene TERRE'BLANCHE.

Refounded National Party (*Herstigte Nasionale Party*—HNP). The HNP is a right-wing Calvinist party organized by Dr. Albert Hertzog following his dismissal from the government in 1968. The party, which adopted the racist doctrine that blacks are genetically inferior to whites, competed in four subsequent elections without securing parliamentary representation. Dr. Hertzog (son of original National Party founder J. B. M. Hertzog) relinquished the HNP leadership in May 1977. In March 1979 the NP-dominated Parliament, by amendment to a 1978 electoral act, refused to register the HNP as a political party, although it was permitted to contest most constituencies (none successfully) in 1981 by producing 300 signatures in support of each nomination. It secured its first parliamentary seat, previously held by the NP, in a by-election in October 1985 but was unable to retain it in 1987. Although the HNP withdrew from the AVF shortly after its formation in May 1993, it nevertheless joined the AVF in boycotting the April 1994 election.

The HNP's attempts to reach a broader constituency were reportedly hindered in 1997 by its well-publicized conflicts with other Afrikaner groups, most notably the VF. It was reported in 1998 that the HNP was hoping to contest the 1999 balloting, but it did not appear on the final list of approved parties. Longtime leader Jaap MARAIS died in August 2000 and was officially succeeded by Willem Marais at a March 2001 party congress. Marais died in 2007 and was replaced as leader by Japie Theart.

Leaders: Japie THEART (Chair), L. J. van der SCHYFF (General Secretary).

LEGISLATURE

Prior to 1981 the South African **Parliament** was a bicameral body consisting of a Senate and a House of Assembly, from which blacks and Coloureds lost their previous limited indirect representation in 1959 and 1968, respectively. The Senate (consisting largely of members designated by the provincial assemblies) was abolished, effective January 1, 1981, some of its duties being assumed by a newly created President's Council of nominated members.

The 1983 document provided for a tricameral body encompassing a House of Assembly, a continuation of the former lower house; a House of Representatives, representing Coloured voters; and a House of Delegates, representing Indian voters. Each was empowered to legislate in regard to "its own" affairs, while the assent of all was required in regard to collective issues.

The interim constitution, which was in effect from April 27, 1994, to February 4, 1997, was the first to be based on the one-man, one-vote principle. It provided for a Senate of indirectly elected members and a directly elected National Assembly, both with five-year mandates. The two bodies sat jointly as the Constituent Assembly that drafted the permanent basic law, which entered into effect on February 4, 1997, and, among other things, replaced the Senate with a National Council of Provinces.

National Council of Provinces. The National Council replaced the Senate on February 6, 1997, at which time 54 permanent elected members (6 from each of the nine provinces) and 36 special delegates (4 from each province) were inaugurated. Members are elected by each provincial legislature from among its own ranks. Each delegation is headed by the provincial premier who is one of the special delegates.

Delegations are required to reflect the party makeup of the provincial legislatures. Following the September 2005 floor-crossing, the breakdown of the 54 permanent representatives was as follows: the African National Congress, 35; the Democratic Alliance, 10; COPE, 7; the *Inkatha* Freedom Party, 1; and the Independent Democrats, 1.

Chair: Mninwa MAHLANGU.

National Assembly. The lower house contains 400 members, 200 of whom are elected by proportional representation from national party lists and 200 from regional lists. All serve a five-year term. In the election of April 22, 2009, the African National Congress (ANC) won 264 seats; the Democratic Alliance (DA), 67; the Congress of the People (COPE), 30; the *Inkatha* Freedom Party (IFP), 18; the United Democratic Movement (UDM), 4; Independent Democrats, 4; the Freedom Front Plus (VF Plus), 4; the African Christian Democratic Party (ACDP), 3; the United Christian Democratic Party (UCDP), 2; the Pan Africanist Congress of Azania (PAC), 1; the Minority Front (MF), 2; and the Azanian People's Organization (Azapo), 1.

Speaker: M.V. Sisulu

CABINET

[as of August 1, 2009]

President	Jacob Gedleyihlekisa Zuma
Deputy President	Kgalema Petrus Motlanthe
Ministers	
Agriculture, Forestry, and Fisheries	Tina Joemat-Pettersson [f]
Arts and Culture	Lulama Xingwana [f]
Basic Education	Matsie Angelina Motshekga [f]
Communications	Siphiwe Nyanda
Co-operative Governance and Traditional Affairs	Sicelo Shiceka
Correctional Services	Nosiviwe Noluthando Mapisa-Nqakula [f]
Defence and Military Veterans	Lindiwe Nonceba Sisulu [f]
Economic Development	Ebrahim Patel
Energy	Elizabeth Dipuo Peters [f]
Finance	Pravin Jamnadas Gordhan
Health	Dr Aaron Motsoaledi
Higher Education and Training	Bonginkosi Emmanuel (Blade) Nzimande (SACP)
Home Affairs	Nkosazana Clarice Dlamini Dlamini Zuma [f]
Human Settlements	Tokyo Mosima Sexwale
International Relations and Cooperation	Maite Nkoana-Mashabane [f]
Justice and Constitutional Development	Jeffrey Thamsanqa Radebe (SACP)
Labour	Membathisi Mphumzi Shepherd Mdladlana
Mineral Resources	Susan Shabangu [f]
Police	Nathi Mthethwa
Public Enterprises	Barbara Hogan [f]
Public Service and Administration	Richard Masenyani Baloyi
Public Works	Geoffrey Quinton Michael Doidge
Rural Development and Land Reform	Gugile Nkwinti
Science and Technology	Grace Naledi Mandisa Pandor [f]
Social Development	Edna Molewa [f]
Sport and Recreation	Makhenkesi Arnold Stofile
State Security	Siyabonga Cyprian Cwele
National Planning Commission	Trevor Andrew Manuel
Performance Monitoring and Evaluation & Administration in the Presidency	Ohm Collins Chabane
Tourism	Marthinus van Schalkwyk
Trade and Industry	Rob Davies (SACP)
Transport	Joel Sibusiso Ndebele
Water and Environmental Affairs	Buyelwa Patience Sonjica [f]
Women, Children and People with Disabilities	Noluthando Mayende-Sibiya [f]

[f] = female

Note: Except as otherwise stated, all ministers are members of the African National Congress (ANC). Ministers designated as SACP are also members of the ANC.

COMMUNICATIONS

Press. Newspapers are published in Afrikaans and English, the English-language press having by far the larger circulation because its readership among nonwhites outweighs the numerical preponderance of Afrikaners in the white population. After years of restrictions and censorship under the white minority government, the 1993 majority-rule constitution guaranteed freedom of expression in the media. Print media reaches only 20 percent of the population because of the high rates of illiteracy. The majority of the population receives news through radio and television.

Conglomerates own all newspapers. One of the four major press groups, Johnnic Publishing, controls the daily newspaper with the largest circulation, *Daily Sun* (301,800). The following are English dailies, published in Johannesburg unless otherwise noted: *Sunday Times* (504,500); *Rapport* (325,800, Sunday), in Afrikaans; *The Sowetan* (118,300), leading African-oriented daily; *The Star* (171,500 weekdays, 143,800 Saturday); *The Citizen* (91,000 weekdays, 110,000 Saturday), tabloid; *City Press* (183,100), African-oriented weekly; *Sunday Tribune* (Greyville, 113,600); *Ilanga* (Durban, 100,900), twice weekly, in Zulu; *Beeld* (105,700), in Afrikaans; *Cape Argus* (Cape Town, 75,500); *Die Burger* (Cape Town, 109,500), in Afrikaans; *Daily News* (Greyville, 56,250); *UmAfrica* (Mariannhill, Natal, 33,000), independent weekly in Zulu and English; *The Mercury* (Durban, 40,500); *Die Transvaler* (40,000), in Afrikaans; *Business Day* (42,300); *Financial Mail* (25,330), weekly; *Mail and Guardian* (48,300), leading independent; and *Pretoria News* (Pretoria, 28,000).

News agencies. The South African Press Association (SAPA), an independent agency cooperatively owned by the country's major newspapers, provides domestic service; a number of foreign bureaus maintain offices in Johannesburg or elsewhere.

Broadcasting and computing. The government-owned South African Broadcasting Corporation (SABC) owns and controls the majority of radio and television outlets. It is managed by black executives and broadcasts news in all the main languages of South Africa. SABC-TV comprises three national channels and two pay-television channels. SABC-radio has 15 public broadcast stations and three commercial radio stations as well as an external radio service. In June 2009 the entire SABC board resigned in a scandal over corruption and incompetence. The only free-to-air commercial television station is e.tv, which is received by 75 percent of the population. A black economic empowerment consortium owns the station. There is one private-pay television service, M-Net. As a result of radio ownership diversification, there are now 12 private radio stations and more than 90 community radio stations. There is some self-censorship as a result of official sensitivity to criticism. Black journalists who criticize the government can be accused of disloyalty, and white journalists of racism. As of 2008 there were 84.3 Internet users per 1,000 inhabitants.

INTERGOVERNMENTAL REPRESENTATION

Ambassador to the U.S.: Welile NHLAPO.

U.S. Ambassador to South Africa: Donald Henry GIPS.

Permanent Representative to the UN: Baso SANGQU.

IGO Memberships (non-UN): AfDB, AU, BIS-BIZ, CWTH, G-20, Interpol, IOM, IOR-ARC, NAM, PCA, SADC, WCO, WTO.

SPAIN

Kingdom of Spain
Reino de España

Political Status: Formerly under a system of personal rule instituted in 1936; monarchy reestablished November 22, 1975, in accordance with the Law of Succession of July 26, 1947, as amended in 1969 and 1971; parliamentary monarchy confirmed by constitution effective December 29, 1978.

Area: 194,896 sq. mi. (504,782 sq. km.).

Population: 40,847,371 (2001C); 45,695,000 (2008E).

Major Urban Areas (2005E): MADRID (3,192,000), Barcelona (1,621,000), Valencia (798,000), Seville (703,000), Zaragoza (648,000), Málaga (543,000), Bilbao (352,000).

Official Languages: Spanish and regional languages (principally Basque, Catalan, Galician, and Valencian).

Monetary Unit: Euro (market rate December 1, 2009: 1 euro = $1.51US).

Monarch: JUAN CARLOS I de Borbón y Borbón; invested before the Spanish Legislative Assembly in 1969; sworn in as king on November 22, 1975, following the death of the former chief of state and president of government, Gen. Francisco FRANCO Bahamonde, on November 20. *Heir to the Throne:* Prince FELIPE; sworn in as heir apparent on January 30, 1986.

President of Government (Prime Minister): José Luis Rodríguez ZAPATERO (Spanish Socialist Workers' Party); nominated by the king on April 7, 2004, following the parliamentary election of March 14, elected by the Congress of Deputies on April 16, sworn in on April 18 for a four-year term, and reelected on April 11, 2008, following elections of March 9; succeeding José María AZNAR López (Popular Party).

THE COUNTRY

Occupying more than four-fifths of the Iberian peninsula (which it shares with Portugal), Spain is separated by the Pyrenees from France and the rest of Europe and includes within its national territory the Balearic Islands in the Mediterranean, the Canary Islands in the Atlantic, and some small North African enclaves, including the *presidios* of Ceuta and Melilla. Continental Spain, a region of varied topography and climate, has been noted more for its beautiful landscape than for wealth of resources, but possesses valuable deposits of slate, iron, coal, and other minerals, as well as petroleum. The Spanish are a mixture of the original mainly Iberian population with later invading peoples. The population includes several cultural/linguistic groups: Castilians, Galicians, Andalusians, Catalans, and Basques (who claim distinct ethnicity). Regional feelings remain strong, particularly in the Basque and Catalan areas in the north and east, and various local languages and dialects are used in addition to the long-dominant Castilian Spanish and are increasingly taught in schools. The population is almost entirely Roman Catholic, although religious liberty is formally guaranteed. Spain's current prime minister in 2006 was publicly noted for his dilution of longstanding ties between the state and the Roman Catholic Church and for his emphasis on women's rights. Female participation in government is rising, and several parties have adopted quota systems to ensure female access to senior party posts. Following the 2008 elections, for the first time in the country's history the national cabinet contained more women ministers than men.

Annual per capita GDP is currently estimated at nearly $34,700. Industry accounts for approximately 18 percent of GDP, with principal goods including processed foods, textiles, footwear, petrochemicals, steel, automobiles, consumer goods, and electronics. Meanwhile, tourism has grown to approximately 10 percent of GDP. Agriculture and fisheries, traditional mainstays of the economy, have seen their share of GDP decline to less that 3 percent. Important agricultural products include grain, vegetables, citrus and deciduous fruits, wine, olives and olive oil, sunflowers, and livestock. Roughly 70 percent of Spain's exports go to European Union (EU) member states, and Morocco remains an important trading partner.

The Spanish economy was transformed between 1960 and 1972 by mass tourism, with GNP increasing almost fivefold. However, high inflation, unemployment consistently in excess of 15 percent, and substantial balance-of-payments problems curtailed subsequent growth rates. In January 1986, Spain entered the European Community (EC, subsequently the EU), which provided significant economic stimulus. Nevertheless, the economy experienced severe recession in the early 1990s, and its unemployment rate, which was approximately 25 percent of the labor force in early 1995, was the EU's highest.

GDP grew by 3.4 percent in 1997, and unemployment, while still high, fell to about 20 percent as Madrid implemented a strict reform program. Unemployment fell to 18 percent in 1998, and in 1999 Spain was permitted to participate in the launching of the EU's Economic and Monetary Union (EMU), propelled by continued GDP growth (3.8 percent in real terms in 1998) and declining inflation. The economy continued to expand to a rate of 4.2 percent in 1999–2000, above the average for the other states in the Organization for Economic Cooperation and Development (OECD). Growth dropped to 2.0 percent in 2002 but edged upward thereafter, reaching 2.8 percent in 2004, 3.4 percent in 2005, and 3.9 percent in 2006. Part of the improvement was credited to Spanish construction and engineering groups having raced to Eastern Europe to sell their services in connection with the EU grant labyrinth as well as to Spanish companies having developed a more global outlook. Domestic consumption has also fueled growth, falling unemployment, and increased labor productivity, while Spain's absorption of immigrants has kept wage inflation down.

More than a decade of uninterrupted growth has transformed Spain from a backward economy with high unemployment, public deficits, and high inflation to a modern, dynamic economy with fiscal surpluses, low inflation, a strong currency, and low interest rates. However, its trade deficit in 2006 was 8.3 percent of its GDP, one of the largest such deficits in the world. Analysts have suggested that to maintain growth, Spain will have to invest more resources in education, expand research and development, and attract additional foreign investment. However, the lumbering federal bureaucracy and its legal system continue to act as disincentives, while the recent devolution of powers to the regions has added new levels of bureaucracy. Basque terrorism also remains a concern to potential foreign investors.

The global economic slowdown beginning in late 2007 hit Spain particularly hard. After fueling high growth, the country's real estate and construction industries faced one of the worst slowdowns in Europe stemming from the global credit crunch. In July 2008 Economy Minister Pedro SOLBES called the situation the "most complex crisis" ever and announced the government could see a budget deficit that year, its first since 2004. In August Spain recorded the steepest decline in mining and manufacturing output since 1993, while sales of houses and apartments fell by 34 percent from the previous year. By the second quarter of 2008 the country was in recession. Meanwhile, unemployment rose to 11 percent, the highest in the Eurozone.

Economic conditions continued to deteriorate in 2009, with GDP dropping in the first quarter at its fastest rate since 1970. With tax revenue falling and the government's passage of fiscal stimulus measures, the IMF expected Spain's budget deficit to widen from 3.8 percent in

2008 to 7.5 percent of GDP in 2009. The IMF warned that Spain needed to reform its labor laws and develop a new model for growth, switching from residential construction and private consumption to more reliance on its industrial and services sectors.

GOVERNMENT AND POLITICS

Political background. Conquered in the 8th century by North African Moors (Arabs and Berbers), who established a flourishing Islamic civilization in the south of the peninsula, Christian Spain completed its self-liberation in 1492 and went on to found a world empire that reached its apogee in the 16th century and then gradually disintegrated. Monarchical rule under the House of Bourbon continued into the 20th century, surviving the dictatorship of Miguel PRIMO de Rivera in 1923–1930 but giving way in 1931 to a multiparty republic that became increasingly subject to leftist influences, leading to the electoral victory of a Popular Front coalition in 1936. The leftist success provoked a military uprising led by Gen. Francisco FRANCO Bahamonde, precipitating the three-year civil war in which the republican forces, although assisted by Soviet and other foreign volunteers, were ultimately defeated with aid from Fascist Italy and Nazi Germany. A fascist regime was then established, Franco ruling as leader (*caudillo*) and chief of state with the support of the armed forces; the Catholic Church; and commercial, financial, and landed interests.

Having preserved its neutrality throughout World War II and suffered a period of ostracism thereafter by the United Nations (UN), Spain was gradually readmitted to international society. The political structure was modified in 1947 with the adoption of a Law of Succession, which declared Spain to be a monarchy (although without a monarch), and again in 1967 by an Organic Law confirming Franco's position as chief of state, defining the structure of other government bodies, and providing for strictly limited public participation in elections to the legislature (*Cortes*). Political and administrative controls in effect since the Civil War were considerably relaxed during the early 1960s, but subsequent demands for change generated increasing instability. In December 1973 Prime Minister Luis CARRERO Blanco was assassinated by Basque separatists and was succeeded by Carlos ARIAS Navarro.

Franco became terminally ill on October 17, 1975, and on October 30 Prince JUAN CARLOS I de Borbón y Borbón, who had previously been designated as heir to the Spanish throne, assumed the powers of provisional chief of state and head of government. Franco died on November 20, and two days later Juan Carlos was sworn in as king, in accordance with the 1947 Law of Succession.

On July 1, 1976, Arias Navarro resigned as prime minister—reportedly at the king's request—following criticism of his somewhat cautious approach to promised reform of the political system. His successor, Adolfo SUÁREZ González, moved energetically to advance the reform program, securing its approval by the National Council of the National (Francoist) Movement on October 8, by the *Cortes* on November 10, and by the public in a referendum conducted on December 15. The National Movement was abolished by cabinet decree on April 1, 1977, and on June 15 balloting took place for a new, bicameral *Cortes*, with Prime Minister Suárez's Union of the Democratic Center (*Unión de Centro Democrático*—UCD) obtaining a substantial plurality in both houses. A new constitution went into force on December 29, 1978, following overwhelming approval by the *Cortes* on October 31, endorsement in a referendum on December 6, and ratification by King Juan Carlos on December 27. Suárez was formally reappointed on April 2, 1979, a general election on March 1 having yielded no substantial party realignment within the legislature.

During 1979–1980 an increase in terrorist activity, particularly in the Basque region, gave rise to manifest uneasiness within military circles, while the UCD experienced internal dissension following the introduction of a liberal divorce bill that the Catholic Church and most right-wing elements bitterly opposed. On January 29, 1981, Suárez unexpectedly resigned. Before his designated successor had been confirmed, a group of Civil Guards, led by Lt. Col. Antonio TEJERO Molina, seized control of the Congress of Deputies chamber in an attempted coup on February 23. Due largely to the prompt intervention of King Juan Carlos, the rebellion failed, with Leopoldo CALVO Sotelo i Bustelo, the UCD secretary general, being sworn in as prime minister on February 26. However, the fissures between moderate and rightist elements within the UCD continued to deepen, with a number of new parties being spawned during late 1981 and the first half of 1982. As a result, lower house UCD representation plummeted to a mere dozen deputies at an election held October 12, when the Spanish Socialist Workers' Party (*Partido Socialista Obrero Español*—PSOE) obtained a comfortable majority (202 to 106 seats) over the Popular Alliance (*Alianza Popular*—AP), an emergent right-wing group that had previously held only a handful of seats. On December 2, PSOE leader Felipe GONZÁLEZ Márquez was inaugurated as the first left-wing head of government since the 1930s. González was sworn in for a second term on July 24, 1986, following an early election on June 22 at which the PSOE, despite marginally declining strength, retained majority control of both houses of the *Cortes*.

In the election of October 29, 1989, the PSOE lost majority control of the Congress of Deputies by one seat. Nonetheless, González continued in office, and on April 5, 1990, he survived a confidence vote because of the absence of four Basque deputies whose attempt to alter the wording of the oath of allegiance had been denied. During 1991 Prime Minister González approached his tenth year in office amid little evidence of declining popularity. With the conservative Popular Party (*Partido Popular*—PP, successor to the AP) engaged in a process of ideological self-examination and with the Communist Party (despite having been an early exponent of "Eurocommunism") reeling from events in Eastern Europe, the Socialists and their leader continued to dominate.

The PSOE government experienced a sharp drop in its popularity in 1992 amid disclosures of financial corruption in ruling party circles. Further corruption disclosures in early 1993, combined with continuing economic problems, persuaded González to call a general election four months before constitutionally required. At the balloting of June 6 the PSOE unexpectedly avoided defeat. Although reduced to a plurality of 159 seats in the 350-member Congress of Deputies, the Socialists were able to retain power as a minority government (with a third of the cabinet posts going to independents) by obtaining the parliamentary support of regional parties. In a confidence vote on July 9, the main Catalan (*Convergéncia i Unió*—CiU) and Basque nationalist (*Partido Nacionalista Vasco*—PNV) parties voted with the PSOE, giving the minority government a 181-seat majority. The immediate price of CiU support was a government commitment to transfer 15 percent of taxes raised in Catalonia to the regional Catalan government, with the CiU in February 1994 adding a demand for "real" autonomy for Catalonia.

In April 1994 González secured all-party approval for new anticorruption measures, including the creation of a special prosecutor's office. Although González prevented a new parliamentary committee from investigating past PSOE fund-raising activities, evidence of financial malpractice by the ruling party and the state administration mounted inexorably. The PP leader, José María AZNAR López, obtained considerable political benefit from the scandals, and he led his party to a crushing victory over the PSOE in the European Parliament balloting on June 12.

A further PSOE setback in Basque regional balloting on October 24, 1994, highlighted the government's political and economic difficulties, amid continuing allegations of official wrongdoing and corruption. Two months later, three former senior security officers were arrested in the wake of reports that they had run a secret "death squad" operation against Basque terrorists in the mid-1980s. Centering on the activities of the so-called Antiterrorist Groups of Liberation" (*Grupos Antiterroristas de Liberación*—GAL), the case took on additional momentum when 14 former political and security officials were indicted in April 1995 on charges ranging from attempted murder to misuse of public funds.

To add to the government's problems, the Basque *Euzkadi ta Azkatasuna* (ETA), which had been engaged in a violent separatist campaign since the 1960s, launched a new wave of terrorist attacks in 1995, including an attempt to assassinate PP leader Aznar in a Madrid car bomb attack on April 19. The episode bolstered Aznar's popular standing, as evidenced by his party's advances in regional elections on May 28.

PSOE hopes of a government revival appeared to be dashed by a sensational press disclosure in mid-June 1995 that a military intelligence unit had intercepted the mobile telephone calls of leading politicians and businesspeople, including those of King Juan Carlos. Accepting political responsibility for the operation, Defense Minister Julián GARCÍA Vargas and his immediate predecessor, Narcís SERRA i Serra, resigned from the government. Moreover, the episode brought to a head deepening strains between the PSOE and the Catalan CiU, which on July 17 formally withdrew its parliamentary support for the minority government. Meanwhile, judicial investigations into the GAL affair gathered pace, leading in January 1996 to serious criminal charges against José BARRIONUEVO, who had been interior minister in 1982–1988.

In early parliamentary balloting held on March 3, 1996, the PP won 156 lower house seats, compared to 141 for the PSOE. After protracted negotiations with the main regional parties, PP leader Aznar succeeded in forming a minority government, which secured parliamentary approval on May 4 and was sworn in two days later. The PP's parliamentary margin (186 to 166 seats) relied on external support from Basque (PNV), Catalan (CiU), and Canarian (*Coalición Canaria*—CC) regionalist parties, which won concessions that included a doubling (to 30 percent) of the proportion of income tax revenues accruing to the autonomous regions.

In the succeeding two years public resentment against ETA grew in response to an increase in civilian deaths. As part of a government crackdown, the entire 23-member national committee of the political wing of ETA, the *Herri Batasuna* (HB), was placed on trial. All were found guilty and sentenced to a minimum of seven years, although the Constitutional Court ultimately ordered their release in July 1999.

In September 1998 ETA announced a unilateral cease-fire, and in October an unofficially affiliated political "platform," the "We the Basque Citizens" (*Euskal Herritarrok*—EH), finished third in the regional elections. In December the EH participated in the formation of a Basque regional government—a first for an ETA-linked group—with the PNV and the Basque Solidarity (*Eusko Alkartasuna*—EA).

In June 1999 Prime Minister Aznar revealed that government and ETA representatives had initiated direct talks under the 1998 cease-fire, but little was achieved in succeeding months. ETA continued to insist on the withdrawal of security forces from the Basque region, the release of some 450 jailed comrades (or, at the very least, their transfer to prisons in Basque Country), and an independence referendum. On November 28, citing the lack of progress toward any of its goals, ETA announced that it would end its cease-fire as of December 3. Collaterally, the PNV ended its regional governing alliance with the EH.

At the general election of March 12, 2000, Prime Minister Aznar's PP surpassed expectations, winning an outright majority in both houses of the *Cortes,* including 183 seats in the Congress of Deputies. Reelected prime minister by the lower house on April 26, with external support from the CiU and the CC, Aznar was sworn in for a second term on April 27 at the head of a revamped and expanded cabinet. A ministerial reshuffle announced on July 9, 2002, was highlighted by the selection of Spain's first woman foreign minister, Ana PALACIO Vallelersundi, who was sworn in the following day.

On March 11, 2004, in the worst peacetime attack on Spanish civilians since the Civil War of the 1930s, a series of bombs exploded on four Madrid commuter trains, killing 191 and injuring another 1,400. The bombings had clearly been timed to affect the general election scheduled for March 14. Although the Aznar government immediately focused blame on ETA, it soon emerged that the coordinated assault had been perpetrated by militants associated with the al-Qaida terrorist network.

Prior to the March 2004 terrorist bombings in Madrid, the PP appeared on its way to a comfortable victory in the March 14 election. The Aznar government had weathered a number of difficulties, including a mishandling of the environmental crisis caused by the sinking of the Greek oil tanker *Prestige* off the coast of Galacia in November 2002. It had also overcome an 80 percent public disapproval rating of Spain's military involvement in Iraq.

Fearing adverse repercussions from the Madrid bombings, the government argued that a defeat at the polls would constitute a victory for the bombers, but by election day many Spaniards believed that the government had tried to manipulate the flow of information for political reasons, and voters displayed their anger through the ballot.

A week earlier opinion polls had given the incumbent PP, now led by Aznar's designated successor, Mariano RAJOY Brey, a lead of 5–9 percent in the contest for the Congress of Deputies, but on March 14 the voters gave the PSOE 42.6 percent of the vote, good for 164 seats, versus 37.6 percent and 148 seats for the PP. The rapid reversal of the PP's fortunes was generally attributed to the bombings, the government's misplaced blame, and underlying public opposition to Spain's military involvement in Iraq. With support from the IU and a handful of regional parties, the PSOE's José Luis Rodríguez ZAPATERO was confirmed as prime minister on April 16 and took office at the head of a 16-member cabinet, half of them women.

On December 20, 2007, Zapatero called a general election for March 9. Analysts predicted a tight race against the PP, stemming from public discontent over the ruling party's perceived leniency toward ETA and uneasiness over Spain's economic slowdown after more than a decade of expansion. However, the PSOE secured 169 seats in the balloting, falling 7 short of an absolute majority, while the PP won 153 seats. Both parties expanded their seat shares at the expense of smaller parties.

Zapatero was victorious in second-round balloting in the legislature on April 11, 2008, and was sworn into office the following day. A newly created cabinet, Spain's first with a female majority, included two new ministries: science and innovation as well as equality. The latter was headed by Bibiana AÍDO, who at 31 became Spain's youngest-ever cabinet minister.

In February 2009 justice minister Mariano Fernández BERMEJO resigned following a judges' strike and a scandal involving a hunting trip he took with a prominent judge. He was replaced by Francisco CAAMAÑO Domínguez. In early April, only a year after the start of his second term, Zapatero announced a major cabinet reshuffle to boost public confidence in the PSOE, which had soured as the economic recession deepened. He made six ministerial changes, including the replacement of economics minister Petro Solbes, a former European commissioner, with the less economically experienced Elena SALGADO, the then public administration minister. The health, education, culture, and development ministers were also replaced, and Zapatero created a new Ministry for Regional Cooperation, which was tasked with overseeing central government relations with the regions.

Constitution and government. The 169-article Spanish constitution of 1978, the seventh since 1812, abrogated the "fundamental principles" and organic legislation under which General Franco had ruled as chief of state (*jefe del estado*) until his death in 1975. The document defines the Spanish state as a parliamentary monarchy and guarantees a variety of basic rights, including those of speech and press, association, and collective bargaining. "Bordering provinces" and "island territories and provinces" with common characteristics and/or historic regional status may, under prescribed circumstances, form "autonomous communities," but no federation of such communities is to be permitted. Roman Catholicism was disestablished as the state religion, although authorities were directed to "keep in mind the religious beliefs of Spanish society." Torture was outlawed, the death penalty abolished, and "a more equitable distribution of regional and personal incomes" enjoined.

The powers of the king include nominating a candidate for the post of prime minister, after consulting the parties in the *Cortes*; dissolving the house and calling fresh elections if such approval is not forthcoming; serving as commander in chief of the armed forces, which are specifically recognized as guardians of the constitutional order; and calling referenda. The prime minister, who is empowered to dissolve the *Cortes* and call an election at any time, is assisted by a cabinet that is collectively responsible to the lower house.

Legislative authority is exercised by the bicameral *Cortes,* consisting of a 264-member Senate (208 directly elected territorial representatives plus 56 indirectly chosen by the assemblies of the autonomous regions and representing one senator for every million inhabitants) and a Congress of Deputies of 300–400 (currently 350) members elected on the basis of universal adult suffrage and proportional representation. Both houses serve four-year terms, barring dissolution; each can initiate legislation, although the upper house can only delay measures approved by the lower.

The judicial system is headed by a Supreme Tribunal (*Tribunal Supremo*) and includes territorial courts, provincial courts, regional courts, courts of the first instance, and municipal courts. An independent General Council of Judicial Power (*Consejo General del Poder Judicial*) oversees the judiciary.

The country is divided into 19 regions containing 50 administrative provinces, including the island provinces of Baleares, Las Palmas, and Santa Cruz de Tenerife. Although it was envisaged in 1978 that devolution to the regions would involve only a limited range of powers, such as alteration of municipal boundaries, control of health and tourism, instruction in regional languages, and the establishment of local police agencies, the tendency has been to delegate ever more functions to regional governments.

In October 1979 devolution statutes presented for the Basque and Catalan regions were overwhelmingly approved in regional referenda. In March 1980 elections for regional Legislative Assemblies were held in the Basque provinces of Alava, Guipúzcoa, and Vizcaya, and in the Catalan provinces of Barcelona, Gerona, Lérida, and Tarragona. Similar elections were held in Galicia in October 1981 and in Andalucía in May 1982. By February 1983 autonomy statutes had been approved for the (then) remaining 13 regions, with balloting in each being conducted in May. In 1994 the African enclaves of Ceuta and Melilla were also accorded the status of autonomous regions, bringing the total to 19. A referendum in Catalonia in 2006 on a proposal already approved by the Spanish parliament endorsed even greater autonomy for Catalonia, giving the regional parliament more powers on taxation and judicial affairs.

Known as one of the most decentralized countries in Europe, Spain has struggled to respect regional allegiances while fulfilling the essential obligations of the central government. Spain's electoral system of proportional representation is structured around provincial constituencies and is partly responsible for regional parties gaining more seats in parliament than parties that compete nationwide.

The presidents of government of the autonomous regions are elected by the regional legislatures.

Autonomous Region	*President of Government* [as of August 1, 2009]
Andalucía	Jose Antonio Grinan (PSOE)
Aragón	Marcelino Iglesias Ricou (PSOE)
Asturias	Vicente Álvarez Areces (PSOE)
Baleares (Balearic Islands)	Francesc Antich i Oliver (PSOE)
Canarias (Canary Islands)	Paulino Rivero Baute (CC)
Cantábria	Miguel Ángel Revilla Roiz (PRC)
Castilla y León	Juan Vicente Herrera Campo (PP)
Castilla–La Mancha	José María Barreda Fontes (PSOE)
Catalunya (Catalonia)	Jose Montilla Aquilera (PSC-PSOE)
Ceuta	Juan Jesús Vivas Lara (PP)
Euzkadi/País Vasco (Basque Country)	Patxi Lopez (PSE-PSOE)
Extremadura	Guillermo Fernández Vara (PSOE)
Galicia	Alberto Núñez Feijóo (PP)
Madrid	Esperanza Aquirre y Gil de Biedma (PP) [f]
Melilla	Juan José Imbroda Ortiz (UPM)
Murcia	Ramón Luis Valcarel Siso (PP)
Navarra	Miguel Sánz Sesma (UPN)
La Rioja	Pedro María Sánz Alonso (PP)
Valencia	Francisco Enrique Camps Ortiz (PP)

[f] = female

Foreign relations. Neutral in both world wars, Spain sided with the anti-communist powers after World War II but under Franco was prevented by certain democratic governments from becoming a member of the North Atlantic Treaty Organization (NATO), the European Community (EC, subsequently the European Union—EU), and other Western organizations. It was, however, admitted to the UN in 1955 and, in due course, to all of the latter's specialized agencies. The 1970s and early 1980s saw a strengthening of relations with Portugal, France, and West Germany. There also was a reduction of tension with Britain over Gibraltar (see article on United Kingdom: Related Territories), which resulted in reopening of the border in early 1985 and a British commitment to talks from which the sovereignty question was not excluded. Relations with the United States remained cordial following the conclusion in 1970 of an Agreement of Friendship and Cooperation to replace the original U.S.-Spanish defense agreement of 1953. Following the restoration of democracy in 1975–1976, Spain was admitted to the Council of Europe in 1977 and to NATO in 1982, with membership in the EC following on January 1, 1986.

In February 1976 Spain yielded control of its North African territory of Spanish (Western) Sahara to Morocco and Mauritania. The action was taken despite strong protests by Algeria and the passage of a resolution by the UN General Assembly's Committee on Trust and Non-Self-Governing Territories in December 1975 that called for a UN-sponsored plebiscite to permit the Saharans to exercise their right to self-determination. Formerly cordial relations with the Saharan representative group Polisario (see article on Morocco) were broken and its envoys expelled following a late 1985 Polisario attack on two Spanish vessels off the coast near Mauritania.

A major foreign affairs issue in the late 1980s was the U.S. military presence, which in the course of a NATO referendum campaign in 1986, Prime Minister González promised to reduce. In May voters endorsed NATO membership, but on condition that Spain remain outside the alliance's command structure, ban nuclear weapons from Spanish territory, and reduce the number of U.S. forces in Spain. Subsequent negotiations yielded an agreement in principle on January 15, 1988, whereby the United States would, within three years, withdraw from the Torrejón facility outside Madrid and transfer its 72 F-16 jet fighters to a new base in Italy. The accord, as finalized at UN headquarters in September, contained no provision for continued military or economic assistance to Spain, while permitting U.S. military activity at a number of bases, including naval operations at Rota (near Cadiz). Most importantly, it allowed both sides to maintain their positions on nuclear arms, Spain reaffirming its opposition to the presence of such weapons but agreeing not to ask for compliance by inspection of U.S. vessels. In September 1990 González defied Spanish public opinion by contributing three warships to the buildup of allied forces in response to Iraq's August invasion of Kuwait.

In the early 1990s Spain signed a series of agreements placing some of its forces under NATO's "operational control" (the wording being used in deference to the 1986 referendum decision proscribing participation in NATO's command structure). The government sought to deflect criticism of this policy by urging greater defense cooperation between Western European states, favoring the Western European Union (WEU) as the appropriate vehicle.

A perennial obstacle to Spain's participation in such moves, however, was its refusal to join in any military activity that appeared to endorse British rule in Gibraltar. The installation of a conservative government in May 1996 was followed by a parliamentary vote in November to permit full participation in NATO (which then had a Spanish secretary general). A number of administrative accommodations regarding control of Gibraltar were achieved in 2000. In June 2006 the United Kingdom, Gibraltar, and Spain concluded talks in Cordoba, Spain, concerning several issues affecting the Rock and the Campo de Gibraltar, removing many of the restrictions imposed by Spain. The agreement allowed improved traffic flow at the frontier, direct flights between Gibraltar Airport and Madrid-Baraja, and recognition of the "350" telephone code. In March 2007 participants at the ministerial meeting in Cordoba resumed their talks with an agenda that included work on cooperation on environmental issues, financial services and tax issues, judicial and law enforcement cooperation, education, maritime communications, and Schengen visa issues.

All-party support for the process of European integration was reflected in the Spanish Parliament's near-unanimous approval of the EC's Maastricht Treaty in October–November 1992. Subsequently, at the EC's Edinburgh summit in December, Spain, together with Portugal, scored a diplomatic success by securing agreement on the creation of a "cohesion fund" for the four poorer members, including itself. Spain was also due to benefit from a similar fund established under the European Economic Area (EEA) agreement signed between the EC and five countries of the European Free Trade Association in March 1993. In 2003 Spain's government was concerned about the loss of EU funds that would occur as a result of the increase in membership in the EU. Funds would be and have been channeled to new, less developed members in Central and Eastern Europe. However, Zapatero did win from the EU the continuation of EU structural and cohesion funds for Spain in the EU's 2007–2013 budget. Spain will continue to be a net recipient of funds, but the bulk of funds will be channeled to newer members. In February 2005 Spanish voters overwhelmingly endorsed the proposed EU constitution, which had the support of both the PSOE and the PP.

A frequent source of tension in Spain's external relations has been the activities of its 18,000-vessel fishing fleet (the EU's largest), whose crews combined a determination to protect home waters with a desire to exploit distant fishing grounds, often in alleged contravention of conservation and other international agreements. In mid-1994 serious clashes occurred in the Bay of Biscay between Spanish vessels and boats from Britain, France, and Ireland in exercise of their right under EU fisheries policy to catch tuna in Spanish waters. In March 1995 a bitter dispute broke out with Canada over fishing rights and practices in the Northwest Atlantic (see Canada article), which was resolved only after the EU had accepted, with reluctant Spanish concurrence, a sharply reduced catch quota in the area. In the acrimonious exchanges preceding the April settlement, there was widespread outrage in Spain when the UK government, responding to overwhelmingly pro-Canadian public opinion in Britain, vetoed Spanish attempts to invoke EU sanctions against Canada. In December Spain's endorsement of the admission of three new EU members was only granted after it had secured additional fishing access to Irish and UK waters. More recently, fishing rights in the Bay of Biscay have again been an issue. The EU's imposition of restrictions on anchovy fishing until the summer of 2008, which nearly amounted to a complete ban, led to French accusations that Spanish fishermen had provoked the fishing restrictions.

In early 2003, despite wide public opposition, the Aznar government strongly endorsed the U.S.-led ouster of Saddam Hussein's regime in Iraq and then, in the aftermath, dispatched Spanish forces to aid in peacekeeping and humanitarian efforts. A pledge by PSOE candidate Zapatero to withdraw Spanish troops from Iraq contributed to the March 2004 Socialist victory at the polls. By late May all 1,300 troops had returned home, beginning three years of frosty relations between the two NATO allies. U.S. secretary of state Condoleezza Rice said in 2007 that it was "not that [Spain] exited Iraq, but how [Spain] exited Iraq" that fractured the bilateral relationship.

Zapatero was one of the few European leaders not invited to the George W. Bush White House during Bush's first term in office. Zapatero openly supported John Kerry, incumbent President Bush's challenger, in the 2004 U.S. elections. As head of the Socialist Party in opposition, Zapatero would not stand when U.S. troops marched past a VIP stand during Spain's 2003 National Day parade. An additional source of tension with the United States arose in November 2005, when EADS-CASA, the Spanish subsidiary of the European aerospace consortium, began negotiating the sale of military aircraft to the Venezuelan government of Hugo Chávez. In June 2006 the United States officially blocked the sale because the planes in question contained U.S. technology.

In June 2007 U.S. secretary of state Rice visited Spain. While the trip was billed as an opportunity to improve bilateral relations, Rice expressed displeasure that Spanish foreign minister Miguel Angel MORANTIS would not visit with Cuban dissident groups during his April 2007 visit to Cuba, arguing that Spain's willingness to engage Castro would not aid democratization in Cuba. Spain has a policy of "constructive engagement" with Cuba, following a 2007 agreement that improved relations by aiding Cuban businesses and social programs in exchange for human rights reforms and the release of political prisoners. Spain supported Castro's decision to hand over power to his brother, Raul, saying the move would advance political reforms. In June 2008 Spain urged an easing of international sanctions against Cuba because of progress made in reforms.

Faced with its own troubles with separatist movements, Spain in February 2008 became one of the few European countries not to recognize Kosovo's declaration of independence. Meanwhile, the government faced considerable domestic criticism over its deployment of nearly 600 troops in the NATO peacekeeping operation in Kosovo.

Upon winning a second term, Zapatero said he would seek a "new chapter" in relations with the United States based on "mutual respect." The election of Barack Obama to the U.S. presidency in November 2008 brought renewed commitments in Spanish support for U.S. military operations. In December Spain lifted a 3,000-troop ceiling on the number of soldiers that may be deployed overseas, thereby clearing the way for a troop increase in Afghanistan, and in February 2009 expressed a willingness to accept detainees from the U.S. military camp at Guantanamo on a case-by-case basis.

Angered at not being invited to a European meeting on the financial crisis in October 2008, Zapatero lobbied heavily to attend a Group of 20 summit in Washington in November on the grounds that, as the world's eighth largest economy, Spain deserved a seat at the table. Spain eventually prevailed when France ceded one of its two seats. Subsequently, Zapatero called for a permanent seat at the Group of 20, while analysts saw the incident as an effort to enlarge Spain's international standing. In further such efforts, Zapatero interjected in a violent flare-up in the Gaza Strip in late 2008 by approving $1.5 million in medical aid to the Palestinians and offering his services in brokering peace. Opposition politicians accused Zapatero of trying to revive the antiwar sentiment that helped bring him to power.

In December 2008 Spain and Morocco sought to patch up lingering resentments over the 2007 visit of Spanish King Juan Carlos and Queen Sofia to Ceuta and Melilla by hosting a bilateral summit in Madrid. Moroccan Prime Minister Abbas El Fassi attended the summit in which Spain pledged $730 million to finance "projects of common interest" in Morocco with the aim to strengthen the two countries' economic ties (see Related territories, below). Zapatero also expressed his interest in Spain hosting the first summit between the EU and Morocco in the first half of 2010, when Spain will hold the EU's rotating presidency, and the two leaders reportedly also discussed construction of a tunnel under the Straits of Gibraltar.

To advance Spanish business prospects, Spanish King Juan Carlos visited Libyan President Muammar Gadhafi in early 2009 to finalize an investment pact that would boost Spanish oil and construction interests there. In March Spain hosted Russian President Dmitry Medvedev and signed an energy agreement that allows Spanish oil companies to help develop Russia's vast Shtokman gas field and to partake in joint energy sector projects with Russia around the globe. The agreement came following a controversial debate in Spain over the possibility of a Russian oil firm purchasing a large stake in Spain's major energy supplier, Repsol SA.

Revelations in January 2009 that Gibraltan authorities were extending into Spanish territorial waters by reclaiming land for building projects aroused the PP, which threatened to seek a European Commission investigation into the matter and demanded Zapatero take a stance against an official visit to Gibraltar in March by Britain's Princess Anne. In July foreign minister Miguel Moratinos went to Gibraltar to sign agreements on judicial, environmental, security, and customs measures, while the PP argued that the visit validated the territory as a sovereign state.

During a visit to Spain by Serbia's president Boris Tadic in early March 2009, Zapatero announced he would back Serbia's bid for membership in the EU in the first half of 2010, when Spain will hold the EU's six-month rotating presidency. Soon after, Spain angered NATO allies with an unexpected decision to withdraw all peacekeeping forces from Kosovo by the autumn of 2009, saying that postwar operations there no longer needed outside support. U.S. officials complained that Spain made its decision without coordinating with other NATO members.

In response to growing tensions with foreign governments, the Congress of Deputies in June 2009 voted to restrict judges' ability to investigate crimes against humanity around the world to cases only involving Spanish citizens. Spain first used the principal of "universal jurisdiction" in an unsuccessful attempt to extradite Chilean dictator Augustus Pinochet in 1998. The Spanish judge in that case, Baltasar GARZÓN Real, also invoked the principle in May 2009 against six former White House officials who he alleged provided the legal cover for torture at the U.S. prison at Guantanamo, and to investigate a deadly Israeli incursion into Gaza in 2002. At the time of the lower house vote, the Spanish High Court was investigating 13 crimes against humanity around the world involving both Spanish and non-Spanish victims.

Current issues. Some dozen seats short of a majority in the Chamber of Deputies, the Zapatero government came into office in 2004 through the support of a number of small regional parties, including the Catalan Republican Left (*Esquerra Republicana de Catalunya*—ERC), the Canarian Coalition, and the Galician Nationalist Bloc (*Bloque Nacionalista Galego*—BNG). In addition to quickly fulfilling a campaign pledge to withdraw from Iraq, Prime Minister Zapatero advanced a social agenda that included recognition of gay marriages (approved by both houses of the *Cortes* in 2005), streamlined divorce proceedings, allowed scientific research on embryonic stem cells, and reduced the role of religion in state schools. However, the policy changes provoked a backlash by conservatives, led by the Roman Catholic Church. The government maintained that advancing secular values was key to the modernization of Spain.

Zapatero also ran on a platform of more liberal treatment of illegal immigrant workers. Spain has been a magnet for immigrants with its strong economic growth, its proximity to North Africa, and its historic ties to Latin America. By 2008 Spain's immigrant population had swelled to nearly 5 million people, or 10 percent of the population, largely from South America, Eastern Europe, and North Africa. Zapatero approved an amnesty in 2005 that legalized some 600,000 illegal immigrants, to the dismay of EU leaders seeking greater immigration controls in the border-free block. In 2008 the Zapatero administration announced plans to allow immigrants to vote in local elections and offered financial incentives for unemployed immigrants to return home. In July 2008 the government announced it expected about 100,000 immigrants to leave the country under that program.

Despite immigrants' contributions to economic growth, immigration has provoked debates about the impact of new arrivals on Spanish culture. For instance, Spain's Muslim population of approximately 1 million has met public resistance in its efforts to build new mosques. In recent years some Spanish towns moderated their festivals celebrating the expulsion of the country's Muslim rulers, provoking conservative politicians to defend the tradition, which dates back three hundred years. The elaborate festivals of Christians and Moors had included destruction of effigies of Mohammed in some cases. The PP has adopted a harder stance on integration, unveiling proposals during the 2008 elections that required immigrants to renew residency permits, sign a pledge to learn Spanish, and respect Spanish customs. The PP also supported a ban on Muslim headscarves from public schools.

Since the Madrid train bombings on March 11 2004, the government has initiated proactive measures to reduce the threat of terrorism. By early 2005, authorities had rounded up some 70 suspects in the Madrid bombings, many of them from Morocco or elsewhere in North Africa. In October 2007, following a trial against 28 defendants, 21 were convicted of charges ranging from forgery to murder. Meanwhile, in September 2005, in Europe's largest trial of Islamic militants, a Spanish court convicted 18 of 24 defendants of belonging to al-Qaida, including the alleged leader of al-Qaida in Spain. Further arrests in 2008 and 2009 were aimed at stopping a suspected attack against Barcelona's transport system and disrupting terrorism financing networks.

Nevertheless in September 2008, the attorney general's office stated that Spain faces a "high risk" of another terrorist attack by Islamic extremists because of its proximity to Algeria and Morocco. He also cited repeated threats made against Spain by al-Qaida, which considers the Muslim enclaves of Ceuta and Melilla under Spanish "occupation." To counter threats emanating from North Africa in February 2009, Spain signed a comprehensive security agreement with Algeria on antiterrorism intelligence, training, and technology cooperation. In June, a similar accord was struck with Morocco, although Spain continued to deny extradition to Morocco for anyone who would face the death penalty or life imprisonment.

Since the rise of Islamic terrorism, public tolerance for violent Basque separatists has waned considerably, although the issue of nationhood for the Basque County remains unresolved. Under Prime Minister Aznar, Spain had clamped down on groups associated with ETA, most significantly the Unity (*Batasuna*) party. The Supreme Court outlawed *Batasuna* in 2003, and consistently ruled against new political formations, disqualifying some 1,500 candidates in the 2003 local elections. The Zapatero administration sought a more conciliatory approach with ETA, brokering a peace deal in March 2006 which was to be a prelude to direct negotiations. The peace deal ended 15 months later when a faction of ETA detonated a bomb in a parking structure at the Madrid airport. Since then, the government has taken a zero-tolerance approach towards ETA and has rebuffed any talk of a second peace deal. Instead the government arrested ETA leaders and initiated efforts to ban political parties that are suspected fronts. ETA has responded with frequent and bold attacks, although with extreme nationalist ideas losing political ground in recent years, some analysts see its tactics as signs of desperation (see Illegal Groups, below).

Spain's tendencies toward devolution took another significant step forward in June 2006, when voters in Catalonia overwhelmingly approved a referendum giving their region greater autonomy, including retention of a higher percentage of tax collections and greater authority over judicial appointments, immigration, licensing, and mass transportation. It also recognized Catalan as the "preferential" language over Castilian Spanish and acknowledged that Catalonia considers itself a distinct nation. Prime Minister Zapatero supported the Catalan referendum and said other regions were free to propose their own such referenda. In contrast, the opposition PP expressed concern that the Catalonia referendum would produce a cascade of similar referenda from the rest of the country's regions, leaving the national government with little authority or financial resources.

In February 2007 Andalusia voters overwhelmingly approved a referendum that expanded that region's autonomy, especially in the area of fiscal management. However, a continued effort by the **Basque Nationalist Party** (*Partido Nacionalista Vasco*—PNV/*Euzko Alderdi Jeltzalea*—EAJ) to hold a referendum on self-determination was blocked by the central government in October 2007 on grounds it was unconstitutional. The referendum also sought approval for a negotiated peace accord with ETA. The Basque party continued to press forward on the referendum into 2008, setting an October 25 date for a nonbinding vote. However, in September Spain's constitutional court blocked the referendum. Seeking to diffuse tensions, in May 2008 the PSOE offered a proposal, similar to the Catalonian referendum, to cede more autonomy to the Basque region.

In October 2007 the government passed the controversial "Law of Historical Memory" to wipe out remaining monuments to Franco's dictatorship and compensate the families of victims of the regime and the Spanish Civil War. Debate became personal because Zapatero's grandfather and political predecessors had been killed by Franco's forces. Conservative parties, which in some cases had not explicitly renounced the fascist era, argued that the law was socially divisive and did not address the suffering inflicted by leftist Republican forces on Catholics and other groups. The Catholic Church, which opposed the law, won a concession to keep memorials of fascist-era symbols on church property so long as there were "artistic-religious" reasons to keep them. In November right-wing supporters honored Franco for the last time at his tomb at the Valle de los Caidos monument outside Madrid before the new law, which banned such public homage to fascist icons, took effect.

In 2008 criminal court judge Garzón began investigating whether "crimes against humanity" had occurred under Franco and 34 of his former generals. However, his orders to open mass graves and identify missing persons were appealed by state prosecutors, who argued that a 1977 amnesty law prevented new trials be opened on political questions. Garzón later dropped the investigation, and the National Court ordered the exhumations to be suspended. In October the Spanish parliament approved decrees under the historical memory law that compensated victims' families, cleared victims' names, and extended Spanish citizenship to the children and grandchildren of Spaniards who fled the country during the civil war. Approximately 150,000 Mexicans were expected to qualify for citizenship under the new provision.

Two days before the March 9, 2008, legislative elections, campaigning was abruptly suspended with the deadly shooting of PSOE councilor Isaias CARRASCO by a suspected ETA gunman. The shooting spurred a voter turnout of more than 75 percent, which helped the PSOE secure an additional five seats in the Congress of Deputies, with 43.6 percent of the vote. The PP also garnered five new seats in the Congress, winning 40.1 percent of the vote; both leading parties expanded at the expense of smaller, regional parties such as the United Left and the Catalan Republican Left, which suffered a steep drop in support.

With 169 seats, the PSOE was 7 short of an absolute majority. Nevertheless, after the election Zapatero said he had a "sufficient majority" to carry out his agenda. Feeling confident with the extra seats, PSOE shunned a coalition arrangement with minor parties, opting instead to negotiate with them on legislation on a case-by-case basis. In response, the minor parties in the legislature withheld votes granting the prime minister a second term on April 9.

To win support for a second term, Zapatero promised to make economic growth the centerpiece of his agenda. On April 18 he announced a two-year, US$28.5 billion stimulus plan to support the real estate sector and small- to medium-sized businesses. The Zapatero administration estimated the plan would boost GDP growth by 0.2 to 0.3 percent in 2008. Additionally, to nullify PP complaints about renewed violence by ETA, Zapatero swore off all negotiations with the Basque separatist group and called for a cross-party strategy to combat ETA. In July 2008 Spain's Senate approved the EU's Lisbon Treaty after Irish voters' rejection of it undermined the treaty's legal status.

In the autumn of 2008 the Zapatero administration introduced emergency measures to stem a rapidly deteriorating economy. In October the government raised guarantees on bank deposits and new debt and announced an $87 billion fund to buy state shares of healthy financial institutions to inject liquidity into the market. A stimulus package was directed toward job creation in the public works and automobile industries. Zapatero also targeted immigrants as a means to free up more jobs for Spaniards by offering financial incentives for the unemployed to return to their home countries, halted a program to recruit immigrants from abroad, and enacted harsher penalties on illegal immigration. As a result, the number of immigrants arriving on Spanish shores was expected to drop by 40 percent between 2008 and 2010.

Nevertheless, Zapatero was criticized for reacting too slowly to the economic crisis and faced considerable opposition by the PP, which argued for tax cuts, limits on government spending, and more deregulation. For his part, Zapatero swore to maintain levels of social spending in the 2009 budget.

To cobble together enough support for the 2009 budget, Zapatero won key votes from nationalist parties in the Basque Country and Galicia with an agreement to provide the two regions with $283 million in infrastructure and research funds. However, in order to make the budget numbers work, Zapatero inserted a 1 percent growth forecast for 2009, an amount the PP called "legal fraud." Even the economy minister Pedro Solbes deemed the growth forecast unrealistic. In February 2009 the European Commission listed Spain as one of six EU states exceeding the EU budget deficit cap, although it deferred proceedings against the country because of extraordinary circumstances.

In early 2009 debates on how to handle a worsening economic outlook began to cause fractures within the Zapatero administration. Solbes openly rejected a proposal by Zapatero for a second stimulus package in March, saying there was "no room" for further spending. With public support flagging under an 11 percent unemployment rate, Zapatero in April announced a new cabinet. Solbes, who had been brought in to add weight to the PSOE's election bid in 2008, was held personally responsible for failing to rein in the construction boom and quell a sharp rise in private-sector debt, and was consequently blamed for the delay in stimulus measures. His replacement with the lesser experienced Elena Salgado and that of other ministers with PSOE stalwarts were seen by analysts as efforts by Zapatero to cement loyalty in his cabinet.

Basque regional elections on March 1, 2009, terminated the three-decades-old reign of the Basque Nationalist Party, which failed to gain an absolute majority and was thereby defeated in a governing agreement led by the PSE-EE, a PSOE affiliate. Analysts saw the results as a blow to the radical left and a sign that voters valued Zapatero's efforts, however unsuccessful, toward a negotiated peace. However, the PSOE's success was tempered by an upset in Galicia, where the PP ousted the PSOE-led coalition in a vote of 39 for the PP and 24 for the PSOE in the 75-seat regional assembly. Analysts blamed voter discontent with the coalition on the PSOE's response to the severe economic recession, although clashes over requirements that the regional language, Galician, be taught in schools also featured prominently in the election. The PSOE was defeated in the June 7 European Parliament election, in which the PP won 42 percent of the vote compared to the PSOE's 39 percent. Analysts saw the PSEO's loss of 5 percentage points from the previous election as a reflection of the poor economy and not necessarily a lengthy move away from the party.

In July 2009 the Zapatero administration signed a deal on a new financing mechanism for the regions, following two years of tense negotiations that were heavily promoted by the autonomous government of Catalonia. The agreement allows regional governments to keep more tax revenue without reducing net transfers to poorer regions in Spain. Critics complained that the result significantly increased the central government's contribution to the system by about 1 percent of GDP, money that the central government was short on at the time owing to the economic recession.

POLITICAL PARTIES

The only authorized political formation during most of the Franco era was the Spanish Falange (*Falange Española Tradicionalista y de las Juntas de Ofensiva Nacional-Sindicalista*—FET y JONS), subsequently referred to as "The National Movement." In January 1975, prior to Franco's death, a law permitting the establishment of noncommunist and nonseparatist "political associations" went into effect, and during the next two years a large number of parties, both legal and illegal, proceeded to organize. In March 1976 the Democratic Coordination (*Coordinación Democrática*—CD) was launched as a unified front embracing all strands of the opposition, from communists to liberal monarchists.

Following a December 1976 referendum on political reform and the subsequent enactment of legislation simplifying the registration of political parties, the CD broke up. Most of its moderate members joined with a number of non-CD parties in establishing the Union of the Democratic Center (UCD), which won the June 1977 election and controlled the government for the ensuing five years. Following a disastrous showing against the PSOE in the October 1982 election, the UCD leadership voted in February 1983 to dissolve the party. By then what was to become the Popular Party had emerged as the main conservative alternative to the PSOE. Although 92.8 percent of the 1996 congressional vote was shared by just five parties (with no other party securing even 1 percent), the development of a straight two-party system was qualified by a diversity of regional parties and continuing support for left-wing groups. There are presently over 2,000 registered national, regional, and local parties.

Government Party:

Spanish Socialist Workers' Party (*Partido Socialista Obrero Español*—PSOE). Founded in 1879 and a member of the Socialist International, the PSOE, under the young and dynamic Felipe González Márquez, held its first legal congress in 44 years in December 1976, and in 1979 the PSOE became the second-strongest party in the *Cortes,* winning 121 seats in the Congress of Deputies and 68 seats in the Senate at the election of March 1, in conjunction with a regional ally, the Party of Socialists of Catalonia (PSC, below). In April 1978 the Popular Socialist Party (*Partido Socialista Popular*—PSP), which had contested the 1977 election as part of the Socialist Union (*Unidad Socialista*—US), formally merged with the PSOE.

At a centennial congress in May 1979, González unexpectedly stepped down as party leader after a majority of delegates refused to abandon a doctrinal commitment to Marxism. His control was reestablished during a special congress in late September, the hard-liners being defeated by a vote of more than ten to one. In the 1982 election the PSOE/PSC won an absolute majority in both the Congress and Senate, González being invested as prime minister on December 2. In the following year the PSOE absorbed the centrist Democratic Action Party (*Partido de Acción Democrática*—PAD). Subsequently, the PSOE experienced internal strain as a result of the government's pro-NATO posture, which ran counter to the party's long-standing rejection of participation in any military alliance. The issue was resolved in favor of qualified NATO membership by the March 1986 referendum, held shortly after the PSOE government had taken Spain into the EC.

The PSOE held power with a reduced majority in 1986. Its retention of only 175 lower house seats in the 1989 balloting was blamed, in part, on the emergence in September of a dissident internal faction, Socialist Democracy (*Democracia Socialista*—DS), and the subsequent defection of party members to the IU (below). Thereafter, the PSOE's standing was adversely affected by a series of financial scandals involving prominent party figures, although at an early election in June 1993 the party retained a narrow plurality of 159 seats, sufficient for González to form a minority government with regional party support.

Continuing financial and security scandals led to the defeat of the PSOE in the election of March 1996, which left it with 141 seats in the lower house on a vote share of 35.5 percent. González declined to run for reelection as PSOE general secretary in 1997 and was succeeded by Joaquín Almunia Amann.

In 1999–2000 the PSOE suffered a series of setbacks. On May 14, 1999, Josep BORRELL Fontelles, the party's candidate for prime minister in the next election, withdrew because of a financial scandal involving two former associates. Ten days later the man who had served as the PSOE's president for over 20 years, Ramón RUBIAL

Cavia, died. On June 13, at local and regional elections, the PSOE saw its vote share increase, largely at the expense of the IU, but succeeded in gaining control of only one regional government, in Asturias. In the May 2000 national balloting, the party and its affiliates lost ground to the PP, losing 16 of their 141 seats in the lower house and prompting its prime ministerial candidate, Almunia, to immediately resign from the leadership.

Almunia's successor as secretary general, José Luis Rodríguez Zapatero, was elected by a party conference on July 23, 2000, narrowly defeating José BONO Martínez, the heavily favored president of Castilla–La Mancha. Rodríguez Zapatero, whose supporters compared him to the UK's Tony Blair, soon made wholesale changes in the party's hierarchy in the interest of "modernization" and a "New Way" (*Nueva Via*).

In July 2001 the Democratic Party of the New Left (*Partido Democrático de la Nueva Izquierda*—PDNI), which had been organized in 1996 by former members of the United Left, principally Cristina ALMEIDA and Diego LÓPEZ Garrido, merged with the PSOE. The PDNI had been allied with the PSOE in recent elections.

In the general election of March 2004 the PSOE won an unexpected victory, taking 42.6 percent of the vote and 164 seats (including those won by regional affiliates). With the support of the IU and several small regional parties allowing the party a majority, Zapatero was confirmed as prime minister in April. The PSOE then reversed some of the reforms implemented by the Anzar government, countering a strengthened role for private education and focusing primarily on social, as opposed to economic, concerns.

Since forming the government in 2004, the PSOE has decreased in popularity, due in part to its response to the Basque problem. The PSOE publicly condemned the arrest of the Batasuna party members in October 2007 (see Current issues, above) and endorsed engagement with ETA, in contrast to the opposition PP position. The PSOE also supports increased autonomy for Spain's regions.

At a congress on October 21, 2007, Juan Fernando López Aguilar was named the new PSOE general secretary, succeeding Prime Minister Zapatero with 92.97 percent of delegates' votes.

The PSOE performed better than expected in the March 9, 2008, election, winning the largest majority in both legislative houses and slightly boosting its membership. In the Congress of Deputies, the number of seats increased from 164 to 169 and in the Senate increased from 100 to 101. However, the PSOE's minority status meant the small regional parties would continue to hold the balance of power. At the July party convention, Zapatero won the position of secretary general a second time with 98.5 percent of the vote.

The 2008 elections led to significant policy shifts in the party. Among them was a renunciation of negotiations with ETA following the murder of a PSOE local politician two days prior to the poll, as well as muted support for further concessions on regional autonomy, particularly concerning the Basque Country.

However, the PSOE refused to back down on its liberal social policies after drawing ire from leaders of the Catholic Church, which joined hands with the PP to condemn the PSOE for policies that legalized same-sex marriage, instituted fast-track divorce, and introduced a new civics course for students as an alternative to religious studies. The party's policies stoked deep divisions within Spain. Particularly controversial was a plan to ease restrictions on abortions that the PSOE introduced in early 2009, which the Vatican denounced on a state visit to Spain in February.

Opposition to the PSOE's sweeping social policies was compounded by the onset of the severe economic recession, which battered the party's popularity in public polls and in the June 7, 2009, European Parliament election.

Ironically, the PSOE's victory in regional elections in the Basque Country on March 1 served to further isolate the party in parliament. The Basque Nationalist Party, a crucial legislative ally, said it would no longer support Zapatero's government after it lost governing power in the Basque parliament. However, a regional financing agreement passed in July helped shore up support among Catalan nationalist parties for an autumn debate over the 2010 budget, which was expected to be especially contentious.

In addition to the PSC, regional parties affiliated with the PSOE include the Basque Socialist Party–Basque Left (PSE-EE, below), the Party of Galician Socialists (PSdeG, below), the **Madrid Socialist Federation** (*Federación Socialista Madrileña*—FSM), the **Socialist Party of Navarra** (*Partido Socialista de Navarra*—PSN), and the **Socialist Party of the Valencian Country** (*Partido Socialista del País Valenciano*—PSPV).

Leaders: José Luis Rodríguez ZAPATERO (Prime Minister and General Secretary), José BLANCO (Vice General Secretary), Manuel CHAVES González (President), María del Carmen SILVA REGO (Parliamentary Spokesperson).

Other National Parties:

Popular Party (*Partido Popular*—PP). The PP was known until January 1989 as the Popular Alliance (*Alianza Popular*—AP), which emerged in 1976 as a right-wing challenger to the Union of the Democratic Center (UCD). Following the UCD victory in 1977, most AP deputies in late 1978 joined with representatives of a number of other rightist parties in an alliance that contested the 1979 election as the Democratic Coalition (*Coalición Democrática*—CD), winning nine lower house seats. Despite its Francoist image, the AP opposed the 1981 coup attempt. Prior to the 1982 poll, the UCD national executive, by a narrow margin, rejected a proposal to form an alliance with the AP, although a constituent group, the Popular Democratic Party (*Partido Demócrata Popular*—PDP), formerly the Christian Democracy (*Democracia Cristiana*—DC), elected to do so. In the October voting the AP/PDP coalition, benefiting from the effective demise of the UCD, garnered 106 congressional seats, thus becoming the second-ranked group in the lower house. Although pro-NATO, the AP urged a boycott of the March 1986 referendum on the NATO membership issue in an effort to undermine the González government.

The AP contested the June 1986 election as part of the Popular Coalition (*Coalición Popular*—CP), which included the PDP and secured 105 congressional seats. Describing the outcome as "unsatisfactory," the PDP (with 21 deputies and 11 senators) broke with the Coalition upon convening of the new *Cortes* on July 15, while four members of the AP also defected in opposition to Manuel FRAGA Iribarne's CP/AP leadership. Further disintegration of the CP at the regional level prompted Fraga's resignation as AP president on December 2, 1986. Antonio HERNÁNDEZ Mancha was named AP president (and leader of what remained of the CP) in February 1987.

At a party congress held January 20–22, 1989, the formation undertook a number of moves, including the change of name, to reorient itself toward the center as a moderate conservative alternative to the PSOE. In the same year, it absorbed the Liberal Party (*Partido Liberal*—PL), which nevertheless elected to retain its legal identity. The PP also has, from time to time, had local and regional pacts with a variety of other parties.

The PP retained its second-ranked standing in the October 1989 poll (albeit with a gain of only 1 lower house seat, for a total of 106), and on December 17 won an absolute majority in the Galician Parliament. Recently reinstated party chief Fraga was thereupon installed as regional president, being succeeded as PP leader by José María Aznar.

The party was able to mount an impressive opposition threat in the run-up to the June 1993 parliamentary balloting, in which it won 141 congressional and 107 senatorial seats on a vote share of 34.8 percent, less than four points behind the PSOE. Having overtaken the PSOE in the June 1994 European Parliament balloting, the PP solidified its standing as the largest party in the March 1996 national balloting, winning 156 seats and 38.9 percent of the vote, enabling Aznar to form a minority government supported by three regionalist groupings: Catalonia's Convergence and Union (CiU), the Canarian Coalition (CC), and the Basque Nationalist Party (PNV).

At a party congress in January 1999, Aznar's handpicked candidate, Javier ARENAS Bocanegra, was chosen to succeed Francisco ÁLVAREZ Cascos as secretary general. Bocanegra's ascendancy reportedly underlined the prime minister's professed desire to foster the image of a more centrist PP as well as his increasing control over the party.

In March 2000 the PP won 183 seats on an unexpectedly high vote share of 46.6 percent, but the PP's quest for a third term in office failed in March 2004, when its results fell to 37.6 percent and 148 seats. In September 2003 Aznar had confirmed his decision to pass the party reins to his deputy prime minister, Mariano Rajoy.

After the PP's surprise loss in the 2004 elections following terrorist attacks in March, the PP became the lead opposition party, shifting further to the right. The PP rejected PSOE social policies and the Law of Historical Memory providing reparations to Franco's victims, as the PP argued that the assessment of the era, as well as the targeted pensions, could undermine societal unity. The PP supports a strong central government, countering PSOE initiatives in regional devolution.

In the 2008 elections Rajoy led a campaign against Zapatero that centered on tax cuts, a tough stance on terrorism with no engagement with ETA, tough immigration laws, and the promotion of "family values" as a counterweight to the PSOE's radical social policies.

PP leadership votes in June 2008 resulted in naming Maria Dolores de Cospedal as the first female general secretary of the party, replacing Ángel ACEBES Paniagua. The move was seen as a way to renew leadership following a second defeat at the polls and to reduce public support for the PSOE, which had appointed a cabinet with a majority of women. Rajoy was reelected with 84 percent of the vote at a party congress in November, which did little to mask emerging fractures within the party and with PP allies. A longstanding partner in Navarre, the UPN, split from the PP in October.

The PP was beset by a series of corruption scandals and political infighting in 2009. Several top Madrid officials accused PP rivals of using a regional government agency to spy on them during an internal battle for power within the party. A judge subsequently charged 37 members of the PP with corruption related to a network that allegedly ran building permits and lucrative contracts in Madrid, Valencies, and other regions. The highest ranking officials implicated were the PP's national treasurer, Luis BÁRCENAS, and the president of Valencia's regional government, Francisco CAMPS. Rajoy reacted by accusing state prosecutors of acting in concert with the PSOE to smear the party's name and influence regional elections. Despite the scandal, regional elections on March 1 in Rajoy's home region of Galicia handed the PP a victory, while the June 7 European parliamentary elections resulted in the party's first victory in European elections.

In July Bárcenas quit his post as his case came before the Supreme Court. In August the Supreme Court dropped bribery charges against Camps and two other Valancian party members. Meanwhile, the PP secretary general Maria Dolores De Cospedal accused the government of using law enforcement to spy on PP members.

Leaders: Mariano RAJOY Brey (President), José María AZNAR López (Honorary President), Maria Dolores DE COSPEDAL (Secretary General), Soraya Saenz DE SANTAMARIA (Parliamentary Spokesperson).

United Left (*Izquierda Unida*—IU). The IU was formed in April 1986 as an anti-NATO electoral coalition that principally included the Spanish Communist Party (PCE, below), the **Republican Left** (*Izquierda Republicana*—IR), the **Socialist Action Party** (*Partido de Acción Socialista*—Pasoc), the **Progressive Federation** (*Federación Progresista*—FP), the left-wing liberal **Carlist Party** (*Partido Carlista*—PC), and the libertarian **Humanist Party** (*Partido Humanista*—PH). It won a total of seven congressional seats at the June 1986 election.

The PCE's Julio ANGUITA González resigned as IU general coordinator in November 1991, after opposing suggestions by members of several groups, including the PCE, that the coalition members dissolve as separate entities to form a single party; subsequently, however, he resumed the position. The IU made only marginal headway in the June 1993 election, winning 18 lower house seats with 9.6 percent of the vote. It retained third place in the 1996 national election, winning 21 lower house seats on a 10.6 percent vote share, but thereafter experienced a marked decline. In the June 1999 local elections its vote share fell from 11.7 to 6.5 percent, and in the March 2000 national election it won only 8 congressional seats. In March 2004 the IU won 5.0 percent of the vote and 5 lower house seats.

In 2007 the communist-led IU supported the PSOE-sponsored Law of Historical Memory, condemning the Franco regime, which had executed many of its political forebears. The IU was also the only parliamentary party to vote against the deployment of an additional 52 Spanish troops to Afghanistan in September. In November, IU leader Gaspar LLAMAZARES Trigo won reelection with 62 percent of the vote under a pledge to form a coalition of all "forces of the left," including the **Greens** (*Los Verdes*) and nationalist groups. His rival, Marga SANZ, was backed by a PCE faction whose criticism of Llamazares led Llamazares supporters to oust three PCE members from the executive board in December. The ousting included PCE leader Francisco Frutose and was meant to unify the party going into the 2008 election. However, continued infighting was partially to blame for the IU's dismal performance in the March 9, 2008, election, in which the IU lost one-quarter of its voters to the PSOE and two of the party's five seats in Congress.

Afterward, Llamazares announced he would not be standing for reelection in November, complaining of a "bipartisan tsunami" that was limiting political diversity. The IU's ninth party convention met in November and elected a new national committee but failed to agree on a new leader. Still stinging from losses in the March election, it approved a document stating that the IU must change because "it has reached the end of a political era" and "needs to return a sense of credibility and urgency to its leftist, anti-capitalist, alternative and transformational agenda." In December the party settled on a PCE leader, Cayo Lara Moyo, as general coordinator of the IU in a vote of 55 percent. Lara threatened to call a general strike if the PSOE did not change its response to the economic crisis by doing more to support workers.

In April 2009 the IU's only remaining city mayor left her post to become part of the PSOE government in Andalusia. However, the IU kept its two seats in the European Parliament following the June 7 election.

Other closely linked organizations include the **Ezker Batua** (EB-also translated as **United Left**) in Basque Country and Navarre, the **United Left of the Balearic Islands** (*Esquerra Unida de los Illes Balears*—EU), the **United Left of Valencia** (*Esquerra Unida del País Valenciá*—EUPV), and the Catalan **United and Alternative Left** (*Esquerra Unida i Alternativa*—EUiA). The IU has frequently formed coalitions with other small parties to contest regional elections.

Leaders: Cayo LARA Moyo (General Coordinator), Ramón LUQUE (Parliamentary Group Coordinator), Montserrat MUÑOZ DE DIEGO (Institutional Relations), Antonio CORTÉS (Secretary of Finance and Administration).

Spanish Communist Party (*Partido Comunista de España*—PCE). Founded in 1920 but soon banned, the PCE was legalized in April 1977, following the release from detention in December 1976 of its secretary general, Santiago CARRILLO Solares. On April 19–23, 1977, in Madrid, it held its first legal congress in 45 years, while on May 13 the PCE's most celebrated figure, Dolores IBÁRRURI Gómez ("La Pasionaria"), returned to Spain after 38 years in exile. The PCE and its regional ally, the **Unified Socialist Party of Catalonia** (*Partit Socialista Unificat de Catalunya*—PSUC), secured 20 seats in the Congress of Deputies and 12 seats in the Senate in the June 1977 election. In March 1979, with Ibarruri having declined to seek legislative reelection for reasons of health and age, it placed three additional deputies in the lower house but lost all of its upper house seats. In the context of sharp differences between pro-Soviet and "Eurocommunist" factions, its congressional representation declined sharply in 1982 to only four members, with the result that Carrillo, the only survivor of the Civil War still to lead a major party, was forced to step down in November. Carrillo's influence was eroded still further by the decision of new party leaders, who favored nonalignment, to adopt internal reforms and work for a "convergence of progressive forces" with other leftist groups, both elective and nonelective; in April 1985 Carrillo and 18 supporters were expelled following an emergency national congress in March, subsequently forming the Spanish Workers' Party–Communist Unity (*Partido de los Trabajadores de España–Unidad Comunista*—PTE-UC), which joined the PSOE in February 1991.

Immediately prior to the 1986 election a pro-Soviet splinter group, the Spanish Communist Workers' Party (*Partido Comunista Obrero Español*—PCOE), led by Enrique LISTER, voted to disband and rejoin the PCE. Subsequently, in February 1987, a PCE delegation visited Moscow, pledging a strengthening of relations with the Soviet Communists. A second pro-Soviet splinter, the Communist Party of the Peoples of Spain (*Partido Comunista de los Pueblos de España*—PCPE), rejoined the party at a congress of unity in January 1989. The PCPE, led by Ignacio GALLEGO, had broken from the party in 1984 because of the "politico-ideological degeneration . . . which introduced Eurocommunism."

At a party congress in December 1998, the PCE elected Francisco Frutos as its new secretary general. In 2007 the PCE endorsed Marga SANZ for IU communications secretary and sought to build collaboration between European leftists to counter the influence of new center-right formations such as the Sarkozy government in France (see article on France). The PCE is the largest member organization of the IU.

In April 2009 the PCE brought a suit to the Supreme Court against former prime minister José Maria Aznar and his former ministers of defense and foreign affairs, alleging that the March

2004 train bombings were a result of Spain's involvement in the U.S.-led invasion of Iraq.

Leaders: Francisco FRUTOS Gras (Secretary General), Felipe ALCARAZ (Executive President of the Federal Committee), Francisco MARTÍNEZ (Secretary of Finance).

The Greens (*Los Verdes*). Long a somewhat disparate movement of pacifists, feminists, and ecologists, the Spanish Greens established the Spanish Green Party (*Partido Verde Español*—PVE) in June 1984 and convened its first congress in February 1985. However, a number of the constituent organizations disavowed the action as having been taken without appropriate consultation. In the 1986 election the Green Alternative (*Alternativa Verde*) list fared poorly, and the Greens made little headway thereafter until a congress held at Grenada in 1993 resulted in formation of a Green Confederation. At present, some two dozen regional organizations belong to or have observer status in the Confederation, including the **Basque People's Greens** (*Euskal Herriko Berdeak*—EHB) and the **Initiative for Catalonia–Greens** (below).

In January 2004 the Greens and the PSOE forged an alliance for the March national election and the June balloting for the European Parliament. The Catalonian branch of the party is represented in the Senate and Congress of Deputies. The Greens boast a youth party and several smaller regional party franchises, collaborating with European Greens within the EU's European Parliament. The party held its first conference on animal rights in October 2007, supporting various initiatives to limit toxic and nuclear waste in the same year. In the March 9, 2008, election the Greens failed to win any seats, taking 0.16 percent of the vote for Congress.

In September David Hammerstein Mintz, an EU parliament representative for the Greens, led an effort to block the legal approval of houses that were built in Valencia without approval from regional water authorities.

Leaders: Margalida ROSSELLO Pons (President), David HAMMERSTEIN Mintz (Secretary for International Relations).

Spain has a long history of right-wing formations, many of them descendants of the Franco-era **Spanish Falange**. Reduced to little more than a shadow of its former significance, the Falange joined with a number of other neo-fascist groups in forming a National Union (*Unión Nacional*) that secured one legislative seat in 1979. It did not contest the 1982 election to avoid divisiveness within "the forces opposing Marxism." Subsequently, it appeared to have been largely superseded by the formation in October 1984 of a new right-wing grouping, the Spanish Integration Committees (*Juntas Españolas de Integración*), which in 1993 was absorbed by the **National Front** (*Frente Nacional*—FN). Formation of the far-right FN was announced in October 1986 by Blas PIÑAR López, former secretary general of the New Force (*Fuerza Nueva*), which had been dissolved in 1982. The FN has not contested recent elections, but some of its supporters participated in the **Alliance for National Unity** (*Alianza por la Unidad Nacional*—AUN), with little impact in the 1996 election. With its leader, Ricardo SAENZ de Ynestrillas, in prison for attempted murder, the AUN did not contest the 2000 national election. In the 1996 national election the rump Falange, which had split into "Authentic" and "Independent" wings, secured less than 0.1 percent of the vote. In 2000 a new four-party far-right electoral alliance, **Spain 2000** (*España 2000*), suffered a similar fate. The four constituent groups in the alliance were the **National Democracy** (*Democracia Nacional*—DN) of Francisco PEREZ Corrales, the **National Workers' Party** (*Partido Nacional de los Trabajadores*—PNT), the **Republican Social Movement** (*Movimiento Social Republicano*—MSR), and the **Spanish Social Apex** (*Vértice Social Español*—VSE). In late 2005 National Democracy, the Falange, and **Spanish Alternative** (*Alternativa Española*) began negotiations to form a new electoral coalition in anticipation of municipal elections in 2007 and general elections in 2008. The Spanish Alternative won 0.12 percent of the vote in the June 7, 2009, European Parliament election.

In November 2007, the Falange won a controversial court case to hold a rally to commemorate the killing of Falange founder Jose Antonio PRIMO de Rivera in 1936 by leftist forces during the Spanish Civil War. Madrid's regional government had initially banned the rally out of fear it would provoke clashes with leftist groups, a problem that had occurred earlier and continued at a number of right-wing rallies in 2008. Falange's symbol, the arrow and yoke, was banned in Spain under the Law of Historical Memory (see Current issues, above). Falange ran candidates but failed to win any seats in the March 9, 2008, election.

Regional Parties:

There are hundreds of regional parties in addition to the local affiliates of the PP, PSOE, and IU/PCE. Grouped by alphabetical order of region, the parties discussed below are represented in the *Cortes* or regional assemblies.

Andalusian Party (*Partido Andalucista*—PA). Known until 1984 as the Andalusian Socialist Party (*Partido Socialista de Andalucía*—PSA), the PA won 1 seat in the Congress of Deputies in 2000 and none in 2004. At the regional level, the PA won 5 of 109 seats in the Andalusian elections in 2000 and 2004. The PA collaborated with a previously unknown grouping, Andalusian Platform (*Plataforma Andaluces*) to push for separate elections for Andalusia, emphasizing its distinct sense of nationhood.

PA returns for regional elections held May 27, 2007, were as follows: Almería, 4.3 percent; Cádiz, 9.05 percent; Córdoba, 6.5 percent; Granada, 3.12 percent; Huelva, 7.27 percent; Jaén, 4.55 percent; Málaga, 4.76 percent; Sevilla, 7.98 percent.

After its loss of five seats in the March 9, 2008, regional election, the party failed to enter the regional parliament for the first time in its history.

Leaders: Julián ÁLVAREZ Ortega (Secretary General), Manuel LÓPEZ López (National Secretary for Organization), Antonia AGUDO González (Vice Secretary for Societal Relations).

Aragonese Party (*Partido Aragonés*—PAR). Called the Aragonese Regionalist Party (*Partido Aragonés Regionalista*—PAR) until February 1990, the PAR is a center-right grouping that retains its predecessor's initials. Although the party did not contest the 1996 national congressional election in its own right, it won three Senate seats on the strength of an alliance with the PP. In the May 2003 regional election it won eight seats and then joined a governing coalition as junior partner to the PSOE, as it had in 1999. In the 2004 national election it failed to win any seats but continued to hold one designated Senate seat.

PAR returns for regional elections held in May 2007 were as follows: Huesca, 15 percent; Teruel, 22 percent; Zaragoza, 12.24 percent.

On September 19, 2007, the PAR National Committee elected Alfredo Boné Pueyo as secretary general, succeeding Juan Carlos TRILLO Baigorri. An Executive Commission meeting on November 30 finalized candidate lists for the 2008 general elections.

In the March 9, 2008, election the PAR failed to win any seats, registering 0.16 percent of the vote for Congress. In 2009 PAR president José Ángel Biel was reportedly behind a controversial project to build a casino resort complex in Aragon.

Leaders: José Ángel BIEL Rivera (President), Alfredo BONÉ Pueyo (Secretary General).

Aragonese Junta (*Chunta Aragonesista*—ChA). The ChA won five seats in the regional *Cortes* in 1999 and nine in the 2003 election, after which it joined the PSOE in forming a government. Nationally, it won one seat in the 2000 and 2004 congressional polls.

ChA regional vote shares on May 27, 2007, were as follows: Huesca, 8.24 percent; Teruel, 5.64 percent; Zaragoza, 9.35 percent. In the March 9, 2008, national election, the party won no seats, registering 0.15 percent of the vote for Congress.

Leaders: Nieves IBEAS Vuelta (President), Augustín RUIZ (General Secretary).

Majorcan Union (*Unió Mallorquina*—UM). The centrist UM, although previously aligned with the PP, joined the PSOE-led government alliance following the June 1999 regional election, at which it had won three seats. In 2003 it again won three.

In the local elections of May 2007 the UM took a 7.45 percent vote share in Illes Balears.

Leaders: Miquel Ángel FLAQUER Terrasa (President), Damià Nicolau FERRÀ (General Secretary).

PSM–Nationalist Union of Majorca (PSM–*Entesa Nacionalista de Mallorca*—PSM-EN). The PSM-EN traces its origins to 1976, when the Socialist Party of the Islands (*Partit Socialist de les Illes*—PSI) was established. In December 1977 the party changed its name to the Socialist Party of Majorca (*Partit Socialista de Mallorca*—PSM), to which the Nationalist Left (*Esquerra Nacionalista*—EN) was added in 1984. Between then and 1990, when the PSM-EN restyled itself as the PSM–Majorca Nationalists (*PSM–Nacionalistes de Mallorca*), the party contested regional, national, and European elections in a number of alliances with other left-oriented formations. In November 1998 the organization assumed its current name.

Following the June 1999 regional election the PSOE negotiated an anti-PP governing alliance that was joined by the PSM-EN, which had won 5 of the 59 legislative seats. In May 2003 the PSM-EN retained 4 seats, but the PP returned to power. Nationally, the party contested the March 2004 lower house elections as part of a coalition, the **Balearic Islands Progressives** (*Progressistes per les Illes Balears*—PIB), that also included the IU-affiliated United Left of the Balearic Islands (EU), the regional Greens, and the Catalan Republican Left (ERC, below).

Initiatives in 2007 included motions to protect Mediterranean coral and ensure protections for minority languages under the European Charter for Regional and Minority Languages, first passed in 1992. The PSM-EN received 6.76 percent of votes in Illes Balears during the May 2007 regional elections.

Leaders: Joana Llüisa MASCARÓ Melià (President), Gabriel BARCELÓ Milta (General Secretary).

In addition to the IU-linked EU, other organizations winning seats in the Balearic legislature in May 2003 were the **Progressive Pact** (*Pacte Progressista*), a leftist coalition that claimed five seats, and the **Independent People's Group of Formentera** (*Agrupació Independent Popular de Formentera*), which won one. The two groups failed to win seats in the May 2007 regional election.

Aralar. Named for a Basque mountain range, *Aralar* is a recent leftist-nationalist splinter from the now-outlawed *Batasuna* (below). Advocating nonviolence, the party won four seats in the Navarre legislature in May 2003 and one in the Basque regional election in April 2005. For the 2004 national election *Aralar* joined with the Basque Nationalist Party (PNV), the Basque Solidarity (EA), and another nationalist Basque party, **Batzarro**, in the **Navarre Yes** (*Naffaroa Bai*—Na-Bai) coalition, which won one seat in the Chamber of Deputies.

Aralar received 6.22 percent of votes in Vizvaya in the 2007 regional elections. In May 2008 party members and Basque separatist lawmakers helped pass a motion in the regional parliament accusing the Spanish government of being complicit in police use of torture tactics following an investigation into the alleged torture of a suspected ETA member. The group also voiced support for Kosovo's declaration of independence in February 2008.

Analysts say the party is increasingly seen as a viable alternative to *Batasuna* because its stance on nonviolence allows it to remain legal while supporting similar objectives.

In September 2008 Aralar joined the Basque Nationalist Party to continue pressing for a referendum on Basque self-determination, despite a block by the Constitutional Court.

During the Basque regional elections on March 1, 2009, Aralar boosted its seats in the regional parliament from one to four, winning 6 percent of the vote. Its success was taken as a sign that voters had rejected more extremist parties. Following the election, Aralar asserted that it would only consider working with *Batasuna* if it used "exclusively political means" to try to achieve its goals.

Leaders: Patxi ZABALETA (General Coordinator).

Basque Nationalist Party (*Partido Nacionalista Vasco*—PNV/ *Euzko Alderdi Jeltzalea*—EAJ). A moderate party that has campaigned for Basque autonomy since 1895, the PNV obtained a plurality in the 1980 Basque election and formed a regional government headed by Carlos GARAICOETXEA Urizza. After the 1984 regional election a dispute regarding devolution of power to individual Basque provinces led to Garaicoetxea's replacement as premier and party leader by José Antonio ARDANZA in January 1985, with the PNV eventually concluding a legislative pact with the PSOE's local affiliate, the Basque Socialist Party (see PSE-EE, below), while Garaicoetxea joined Basque Solidarity (EA, below).

In 1989 the PNV organized mass demonstrations in Bilbao to pressure separatist militants to end their armed struggle. However, subsequent efforts to form an electoral coalition with the EA and the Basque Left (see PSE-EE, below) failed, and in October 1989 the PNV's representation in the Spanish Congress and Senate fell to five and six seats, respectively. One of the latter was lost in the 1993 balloting, after which the PNV gave intermittent support to the PSOE minority government. In the March 1996 national balloting it retained five lower house seats, whereupon it agreed to support a minority PP government in return for more devolution. However, it later withdrew that support.

In balloting for the Basque regional legislature in October 1998, the PNV led all the parties, but its lack of a majority led it to form a coalition government with "We the Basque Citizens" (EH, the restyled political arm of the ETA) and the EA. In January–February 2000, following a renewal of ETA violence, the PNV ended its alliance with the EH. In the national election of March 2000 the PNV picked up 2 seats in the Congress of Deputies, for a total of 7, while at an early regional election on May 13, 2001, it registered its biggest success in a quarter-century, winning 33 seats (a gain of 6) on a 43 percent vote share.

Having retained seven seats in the March 2004 election, the PNV entered the April 2005 regional election seeking support for the "Plan Ibarretxe," a proposal for increased autonomy that had been put forward by PNV leader and Euzkadi President Juan José Ibarretxe. The plan, which included establishment of a union with French Basque areas as well as Basque representation in the EU, had been described by Prime Minister Zapatero as secessionist and unconstitutional and then rejected by the *Cortes* earlier in the year. At the polls, the PNV lost four seats, and Ibarretxe managed to retain the presidency by only one vote when the regional legislature met in June.

The PNV received 38.76 percent of votes in the province of Vizcaya during the 2007 regional elections. The PNV's moderate president, Josu Jon IMAZ, later resigned, citing the growing influence of separatists. He was replaced in November 2007 by Iñigo Uukullu, who condemned ETA violence but nonetheless announced he would meet with all the political forces in the Basque region, including the banned *Batasuna*. The power shift prompted the party to call for a referendum on self-determination, a move swiftly rejected by Zapatero, to preempt further PP criticism of his line on the Basque question.

In July 2008 the party's efforts to conduct the referendum in October 2008 were suspended by a Spanish court pending a review of its legality. The referendum was to be part of a "new model," announced by the PNV earlier in the year, for political relations between Basque Country and the federal government based on the "free accession of its nations."

In the March 9, 2008, election the PNV won 27 percent of the vote in the Basque region, granting the party six seats in the Congress. However, voter turnout was a low 35 percent in the region, owing to a call by separatists to boycott the election to protest "oppression" by the Spanish state. Analysts said that despite ideological differences, the minority-led PSOE would need coalition support from the PNV to advance its agenda. In October the PNV secured $114 million from the PSOE for research and development projects in the region in exchange for supporting the 2009 budget.

In early 2009 the PNV announced that regional elections would be held in March despite signs that the party's political position had not improved since national elections the previous year. On March 1 the PNV captured 38 percent of the vote, winning 30 seats, but was 8 short of an absolute majority. In the following days Ibarretxe scrambled to maintain control by attempting to cobble together support from minority parties and offering a "stability agreement" with the PSE-EE. The PSE-EE instead formed a governing agreement with the PP, forcing the PNV to enter opposition status for the first time since 1980. In May Ibarretxe announced he would be retiring from politics.

Leaders: Iñigo URKULLU (President), Juan José IBARRETXE Markuartu (Former Basque President), Josune ARISTONDO Akarregi (Secretary), Josu ERKOREKA (Parliamentary Spokesperson).

Basque Socialist Party–Basque Left (*Partido Socialista de Euzkadi–Euzkadiko Ezkerra*—PSE-EE). The PSE-EE was formed in March 1993 by merger of the PSOE-affiliated Basque Socialist Party, led by Ramón JÁUREGUI, and the smaller, more radical Basque Left, led by Juan María BANDRÉS and Jon LARRINAGA. In the May 2001 regional election the PSE-EE finished third, winning 13 of 75 seats, a relatively weak performance that contributed to the resignation of the party's secretary general, Nicolás REDONDO Terreros, in December. In the balloting of April 2005 the party finished second, with 18 seats. Despite the support of the PP, the new PSE-EE leader, Paxti López, lost the contest for regional president to the incumbent, the PNV's Ibarretxe, by one vote. The PSE-EE took a 23 percent vote share during the 2007 regional poll in the Vizcaya province.

The PSE-EE performed well in the March 9, 2008, election, capturing 38 percent of the vote in the Basque region. In April 2008 ETA set off a bomb in front of the group's offices in Bilbao, injuring seven police officers and causing extensive property damage.

In October 2007 a Spanish High Court opened proceedings against PSE-EE leaders Patxi López and Rodolfo ARES, as well as Ibarretxe of the Basque Nationalist Party, under allegations that they conducted meetings with *Batasuna* after the group's cease-fire was announced to discuss the political future of the Basque Country. However, in January 2009 the court threw out the case after state prosecutors asked that it be dropped.

Basque regional elections on March 1, 2009, handed the PSE-EE/PSOE 25 seats, an increase of 18. The PSE's success catapulted López to the premiership after nearly a month of tense negotiations with non-nationalist parties. On March 30 the PSE-EE and the PP, which held 13 seats, announced a coalition agreement. On May 5 López was elected as the first non-nationalist president of the Basque parliament with the support of the PP and the sole representative of the UPyD party. Upon taking office, López announced his "priority task" was to fight ETA. He said he would also halt a program that made Basque the main language in schools. ETA responded by announcing that the López government would be its "priority target" (see ETA, below).

Leaders: Juan OTERMIN (President), Patxi LÓPEZ (Secretary General and Basque President).

Basque Solidarity (*Eusko Alkartasuna*—EA). The EA was formed in September 1986 as the Basque Patriots (*Eusko Abertzaleak*) by a group of PNV dissidents, subsequently joined by former Basque premier Carlos Garaicoetxea Urriza. A left-wing nationalist group opposed to political violence, it currently holds one seat in the national Chamber of Deputies. It contested the 1996 election in alliance with the now-defunct Basque Left (*Euskal Ezkerra*—EuE), which had separated from the *Euskadiko Ezkerra* (also translated as Basque Left) in 1993.

In late 1998 the EA agreed to participate in the formation of a Basque regional coalition government with the PNV and EH, and in the May 2001 and April 2005 elections it remained allied with the PNV. The party received 5.4 percent of votes during Basque local elections in 2007. In the March 1, 2009, regional election, the EA won 3.6 percent of the vote, taking one seat.

Leader: Pello URIZAR Karetxe (President).

Canarian Coalition (*Coalición Canaria*—CC). The CC was formed prior to the 1993 general election as a regional alliance that included the **Canarian Independent Groupings** (*Agrupaciones Independientes de Canarias*—AIC); the socialist **Canarian Initiative** (*Iniciativa Canaria*—ICAN); and the left-wing **Mazorca Assembly** (*Asamblea Majorera*—AM). Also initially part of the alliance were the **Canarian Nationalist Party** (*Partido Nacionalista Canario*—PNC) and the **Canarian Independent Center** (*Centro Canario Independiente*—CCI), predecessor of the current **Canarian Nationalist Center** (*Centro Canario Nacionalista*—CCN). More recently, the CC was joined by the **Lanzarote Nationalist Party** (*Partido Nacionalista de Lanzarote*—PNL).

The AIC, consisting principally of the **Tenerife Independents Group** (*Agrupación Tinerfeña de Independientes*—ATI) and the **Las Palmas Independent Group** (*Agrupación Palmera de Independientes*—API), had captured one congressional seat in the 1989 general election and was subsequently the only non-PSOE party to support Prime Minister González's reelection; in the 1991 regional balloting it took second place behind the PSOE in the Canaries, and the AIC nominee, ATI leader Manuel HERMOSO Rojas, secured the island presidency.

In the 1993 general election the CC returned four deputies and six senators, proceeding thereafter to give qualified support to the minority PSOE government. In September 1994 the CC-led regional government lost its narrow majority when the PNC withdrew from the coalition. The coalition won a plurality of 21 regional assembly seats in 1995, so Hermoso remained in office. Its four national deputies, reelected in 1996, backed the formation of a PP government in exchange for various concessions. The CC won 25 seats in the June 1999 Canarian election and continued to rule, with PP support. In the May 2000 national balloting the coalition won four Chamber and five Senate seats.

Following the May 2003 regional election, in which the CC won a plurality of 22 seats, the CC and the PP formed a coalition government. Nationally, the CC won 3 lower house seats in 2004 and then voted to approve the PSOE's Zapatero as prime minister. During the 2007 regional elections, the CC ran a joint ballot with a former ally, the previously unknown Canarian Nationalist Party (*Partido Nacionalista Canario*—PNC), with whom it championed Canarian identity, taking 9.54 percent of votes in Las Palmas and 37.7 percent in Santa Cruz de Tenerife.

In the March 9, 2008, election the CC-PNC won 17.5 percent of the vote for the Congress in the region, taking two seats in the lower house and one in the Senate. In January 2009 the CC was reportedly debating whether to give the federal government control over underage migrants, hundreds of whom have arrived on the island in recent years on boats from sub-Saharan Africa. The debate was significant because it represented an unusual decision to cede regional authority to the central government.

Leaders: Claudina MORALES Rodríguez (President), María del Mar JULIOS Reyes (Secretary General).

Party of Independents from Lanzarote (*Partido de Independientes de Lanzarote*—PIL). Based on the Canarian island of Lanzarote, the PIL held one seat in the previous Spanish Senate. In March 2001, having been sentenced to a three-year prison term for bribery, Dimas Martín Martín, the PIL president and senator, announced his resignation from both posts. In 2003 the PIL won three seats in the regional legislature as part of the **Canarian Nationalist Federation** (*Federación Nacionalista Canaria*—FNC). The PIL received a 1.82 percent vote share during the 2007 local elections in Las Palmas.

In May 2009 police arrested Dimas Martín and several members of the PIL as part of a round-up of 11 suspects on charges of operating a corruption ring in Lanzarote. Martín was charged with embezzlement and social security fraud. Subsequently, the PSOE broke its pact with the PIL and suspended two PSOE party officials who were also caught up in the sweep.

Leaders: Celso BETANCOR Delgado (President), Dimas MARTÍN Martín (Founder).

Cantabrian Regionalist Party (*Partido Regionalista Cántabro*—PRC). The PRC is a moderate conservative party that won 6 seats out of 39 in the 1995 and 1999 Cantabrian regional assembly elections.

Following the 2003 election, at which it won eight seats, the PRC held the balance of power and negotiated formation of a governing coalition with the PSOE. In 2007 the PRC received 21.46 percent of votes in Cantabria's local balloting. A PP/PRC/PSOE coalition government was installed in Cantábria following the 2007 regional elections.

Leader: Miguel Ángel REVILLA Roiz (President of the Cantabria Government).

León People's Union (*Unión del Pueblo Leónes*—UPL). The UPL won three seats in the *Cortes* of Castilla y León in 1999 and 2003. The party continues to support autonomous status for the León region, where it received 10.68 percent of votes during the 2007 regional elections.

Leaders: Javier CHAMORRO Rodríguez (President), Melchor MORENO de la Torre (Secretary General)

Catalan Republican Left (*Esquerra Republicana de Catalunya*—ERC). Founded in 1931, the ERC was one of two Catalan republican parties, the other being the Democratic Spanish Republican Action (*Acció Republicana Democrática Española*—ARDE), granted legal recognition in August 1977. In July 1991 the Catalan radical separatist Free Land (*Terre Lliure*) announced that it was dissolving, with its members being accepted into the ERC. In December 1991 the ERC abandoned its call for federalism, appealing instead for Catalan independence.

The ERC split in late 1996, with its national senator and deputy, together with 4 of its 13 regional deputies, defecting to the Catalan Independence Party (*Partido per la Independencia*—PI), which dissolved in September 1999.

Following the November 2003 regional election, which saw the ERC nearly double its representation to 23 seats, the ERC joined with the PSOE-affiliated PSC in forming a new regional government. In January 2004, however, party leader Josep Carod-Rovira was forced to resign as head of the government following revelations that he had secretly met with ETA leaders in what he described as an effort to convince them to renounce violence.

In the 2004 national election the ERC won eight seats in the Congress of Deputies, seven more than it had previously held. For the Senate it campaigned as part of the PSC-led Catalan Accord for Progress (ECP; see under the PSC, below). No individual regional returns for 2007 were registered with the electoral records of the Interior Ministry. In the March 9, 2008, election the ERC sustained further losses and dropped from five seats in Congress to three. The losses prompted president Joan Puigcercós to announce his intent to resign from his post in the Catalan regional government to devote his efforts full time to party building.

In December 2008 the ERC in concert with the CiU voted against Zapatero's 2009 budget because it did not provide sufficient funding for the Catalan region under the 2006 autonomy statute. In November the ERC joined forces with the IU to press for revisions to the Law of Historical Memory that would declare null and void all sentences issued under Franco, a step that would potentially open the state up to compensation claims by victims and their families. In December ERC congress member Joan TARDÀ provoked outrage when he ended a speech at festivities marking the 30th anniversary of the Spanish constitution by declaring "death to the Bourbon," a reference to the royal dynasty of King Juan Carlos.

A new regional financing deal was finally passed in July 2009, shortly before 2010 budget negotiations were to be launched in September. The deal allowed Catalonia to retain a greater share of its tax revenue, rather than collect and redistribute it to poorer regions, effectively boosting regional coffers by $5 billion.

Leaders: Joan PUIGCERCÓS (President), Joan RIDAO (Secretary General).

Convergence and Union (*Convergència i Unió*—CiU). The center-left CiU was formed in November 1978 as a coalition of the **Democratic Convergence of Catalonia** (*Convergència Democrática de Catalunya*—CDC) and the **Democratic Union of Catalonia** (*Unió Democrática de Catalunya*—UDC). In its first federal elections (1979) the CiU elected eight deputies and one senator. In the first elections to the Parliament of Catalonia in 1980, the CiU won 43 seats, allowing CDC President Jordi Pujol i Soley to be elected President of Catalonia. The CiU won a majority of seats in the Catalan legislative election of March 1992, and at the national level the CiU secured 17 congressional and 14 senatorial seats in June 1993, after which it gave qualified support to the PSOE minority government. Having initially made greater tax transfers to Catalonia its quid pro quo for supporting the PSOE government, the CiU in February 1994 lodged a demand for full Catalan autonomy and moved into opposition in mid-1995.

The CiU lost seats but retained power in the November 1995 Catalan election, not winning an absolute majority for the first time since 1984. The 16 lower house seats it secured in the March 1996 national balloting enabled it to extract tax and other concessions in return for backing the new PP government. It retained a slim plurality in the October 1999 Catalan election and at the May 2000 national election won 8 Senate and 15 congressional seats.

In the regional election of November 2003 the CiU won a plurality of seats but surrendered the government to a coalition led by the PSC (below) and ERC. Nationally, the party won four directly elected Senate seats and ten Chamber seats in March 2004. For the European Parliament election of June 2004 the CiU joined the PNV, the BNG (below), and others in the **Galeuca** (for Galician, Euskadi, and Catalonia) coalition. In the 2007 local elections the CiU took 22.32 percent of votes in Barcelona; 33.19 percent in Girona; 32.8 percent in Lleida; and 31.2 percent in Tarragona, underscoring its position as a favored party for nationally minded Catalonian voters.

In December 2007 the CiU faction in the Senate led a veto of the government's 2008 budget under claims that the spending proposals did not provide the amount of funding called for under the Catalan charter that was approved the previous year.

In the March 9, 2008, election the CiU gained the third highest number of votes, or 21 percent of the electorate, in Catalonia and boosted its number of deputies in Congress by 1 to a total of 11. The party was considered a key potential coalition partner for Zapatero, a situation that deepened in 2009 when he lost needed support from the Basque Nationalist Party after an upset in Basque regional elections on March 1. Shortly after the vote, CiU president Artur Mas warned Zapatero that the CiU would not be a "lifeboat" for him in Madrid.

Leaders: Jordi PUJOL i Soley (Founding President of the CiU and President of the CDC), Artur MAS i Gavarró (Secretary General), Ramon ESPADALER i Parcerisas (UDC President).

Initiative for Catalonia–Greens (*Iniciativa per Catalunya–Verds*—IC-V). Initially an alliance headed by the PCE-affiliated Unified Socialist Party of Catalonia (PSUC), the IC was established in 1987 and became, in effect, the Catalonian branch of the United Left. Other initial participants in the IC were the Party of Communists of Catalonia (*Partit dels Communistes de Catalunya*—PCC) and the Accord of Left Nationalists (*Entesa Nacionalistas d'Esquerra*—ENE). In 1990 the grouping evolved into a party that then became increasingly close to the Catalan branch of the Greens (*Els Verds*—EV), and together they won 11 seats in the November 1995 regional election. The coalition was formalized as the IC-V in 1998. In the 1999 regional election it won only 3 seats while cooperating with the PSOE-affiliated Party of Socialists of Catalonia (PSC). Nationally, the IC-V won 2 seats in the Congress at the March 2000 election.

In 2003 the IC-V and the allied EUiA (see the IU, above) won nine seats in the regional legislature. In the 2004 national balloting, the IC-V/EUiA won two seats. As participants in a coalition ballot with the EUiA again in 2007, the IC-V added candidates from the obscure EPM party to its candidate lists. The IC-V–EUiA–EPM list took 10.45 percent of votes in Barcelona; 6.97 percent in Girona; 4.08 percent in Lleida; and 4.43 percent in Tarragona.

The party has since favored various redistribution schemes and advocated the legalization and regulation of prostitution. With the introduction of the Law of Historical Memory, the IC-V organized a conference at the Frankfurt Fair with its German counterparts to identify best practices for acknowledging dark chapters in the history of their respective countries.

In 2008 the party advocated for immigrant rights by taking a stand against government policies to expand the amount of time illegal immigrants could be held in detention. IC-V also supported giving immigrants the right to vote in local elections.

Leaders: Joan SAURA Laporta (President), Joan HERRERA Torres (Secretary General).

Party of Socialists of Catalonia (*Partit dels Socialistes de Catalunya*—PSC). The regional affiliate of the PSOE, the PSC dates from the late 1970s, when several like-minded leftist parties merged. At the national level, it remains a major contributor to the PSOE's success. In March 2004 it won 18 seats in the lower house. In addition it won 8 in the Senate as part of the **Catalan Accord for Progress** (*Entesa Catalana de Progrés*—ECP), an alliance forged with the ERC, the IC-V, and the United and Alternative Left (EUiA; see under the IU, above).

In the October 1999 Catalan election the PSC, led by Pasqual Maragall, finished a close second to the CiU, winning more votes but ending up with four fewer seats. The PSC had contested the election in alliance with the IC-V. In November 2003 the PSC again finished second in regional balloting but then joined with the ERC to form a government headed by Maragall.

The PSC again performed strongly in 2007 regional elections, taking a 33.64 percent vote share in Barcelona; 25.6 percent in Girona; 31.06 percent in Lleida; and 30.19 in Tarragona. In the March 9, 2008, elections it again performed well and was responsible for four of the five additional seats won by the PSOE, thereby outperforming its regional rival, the ERC. With 25 of the PSOE's 169 seats in Congress, it brought a strong Catalonian voice to the government.

Leaders: Isidre MOLAS i Barllori (President), José MONTILLA Aguilera (First Secretary).

Galician Nationalist Bloc (*Bloque Nacionalista Galego*—BNG). Founded in 1983, the BNG is a left-wing group that came in third in the 1989 regional election, winning 5 seats out of 75. In the October 1993 balloting in Galicia it more than doubled its vote (to 18.7 percent) and won 13 seats out of 75. In late 1991 it had been joined by the Galician National Party (*Partido Nacionalista Galego*—PNG), which had split from the (now defunct) Galician Coalition (*Coalición Galega*—CG) in 1986. In 2000 the BNG won 3 seats in the national lower house, 1 less than in 2000. In the regional election of June 19, 2005, it won 13 seats, 4 fewer than in 2001, but sufficient to form a coalition government with the PSOE-affiliated PSdeG (below), thereby ousting the PP from power for the first time in a quarter-century. In the 2007 local balloting the BNG received 19.32 percent of votes in A Coruña; 16.53 percent in Lugo; 18.77 percent in Ourense; and 20.25 percent in Pontevedra. Following the coalition's defeat to the PP in regional elections in March 2009 (see Current events, above), party leader Anxo QUINTANA González resigned and said he had failed to create a "coalition culture" with the PSdeG. At a party congress in May Guillerme Vázquez Vázquez was elected national spokesperson.

Leaders: Guillerme VÁZQUEZ Vázquez (National Spokesperson), Teresa TÁBOAS Veleiro (Executive Coordinator).

Party of Galician Socialists (*Partido dos Socialistas de Galicia*—PSdeG). As the regional affiliate of the PSOE, in June 2005 the PSdeG won 25 seats in the Galician election, 8 more than in 2001. It then formed a coalition with the Galician Nationalist Bloc that ousted the PP from power for the first time in a quarter-century. In regional elections in March 2009, the coalition was defeated by the PP. The secretary general of the PSdeG, Emilio PÉREZ Touriño, subsequently resigned from party leadership. In April Manuel Vázquez Fernández was elected to the post in an extraordinary party congress.

Leader: Manuel VÁZQUEZ Fernández (Secretary General of the Party).

Convergence of Navarran Democrats (*Convergencia de Demócratas Navarros*—CDN). The CDN was launched in 1995 by a group that split from the PP-affiliated UPN. It won 10 of 50 regional assembly seats in 1995 but only 3 in 1999 and 4 in 2003. The CDN achieved a small return in 2007, taking 2.29 percent of regional votes. During the party's fourth congress in May 2008, Vice President José Andrés Burguete Torres was elected president.

Leaders: José Andrés BURGUETE Torres (President), Juan Cruz ALLI Aranguren (Former President of Navarra and Former CDN President), Luis Angel FORTUN Moral (Secretary General).

Union of the Navarran People (*Unión del Pueblo Navarro*—UPN). A conservative grouping allied with the PP and firmly opposed to the Basque nationalist goal of reincorporating Navarra in Euzkadi, the UPN was formed in 1979 and governed the province from 1991 to 1995, when it went into opposition (although remaining the largest party). In the June 1999 election it won 22 of the 50 legislative seats and recaptured the presidency. It increased its representation by 1 in 2003 and then in 2004 won 2 seats in the national lower house. Although it failed to achieve a majority in the 2007 regional elections, the UPN continued to govern Navarra in minority status, taking 22 seats, the largest proportion attributed to a single party with 33.08 percent of votes.

Inconclusive results in the May 2007 parliament election in Navarra resulted in a protracted struggle for power between the UPN and the PSOE's Socialist Party of Navarra, the latter of which gave up the effort after ending negotiations to form a governing coalition with Nafarroa Bai, whose members include former *Batasuna* members. As part of the power-sharing arrangement, UPN president Miguel Sanz was reelected to the regional premiership August 13 as four Socialists resigned and others abstained from the vote.

In October 2008 the UPN ended its 17-year alliance with the PP following a conflict concerning the UPN's autonomy to direct its members' votes on the 2009 federal budget. The PP announced it would begin establishing a party presence in Navarra and invited UPN politicians to join the PP.

Nevertheless, in June 2009 the UPN joined hands with the PP and other conservative forces to vocally oppose a PSOE-led abortion reform bill.

Leaders: Miguel SANZ Sesma (President of Navarra), Yolanda BARCINA Angulo (President), Carlos GARCIA Adanero (Secretary General).

Rioja Party (*Partido Riojano*—PR). A center-left formation in Spain's main wine-growing area, the PR won one seat in the 1993 general election and two in the 1995 regional contest. Although subsequently unsuccessful at the national level, it retained its regional seats in 1999 and 2003. In the regional poll of May 2007 it received 6.46 percent of votes.

Leaders: Miguel GONZÁLEZ de Legarra (President), Javier SAENZ-TORRE Merino (Secretary General).

Valencia Entesa (*Entesa pel País Valencià*). The leftist *Entesa* ("Accord" or "Agreement") coalition was established in Valencia in June 2002 by the United Left of Valencia (EUPV; see under the IU), the Valencian Greens, and the **Valencian Left** (*Esquerra Valenciana*—EV). The EUPV and the Greens had previously contested local elections together, winning a high of ten seats in the regional assembly in 1995. In the 2003 regional elections *Entesa* won five assembly seats. In March 2004 it won one seat in the national Chamber of Deputies, where its representative sits with the IU group. The *Entesa* list received 0.29 percent of votes in the May 2007 regional poll.

Leaders: Isaura NAVARRO (EUPV), Joan RIBÓ i Canut (EUPV).

Illegal Groups:

Basque Homeland and Liberty (*Euzkadi ta Azkatasuna*—ETA). Founded in 1959, ETA has long engaged in a violent separatist campaign directed primarily at police and government targets, although in recent years journalists and anti-ETA civilians have increasingly been targeted as well. By 2001 the number of deaths attributed to ETA attacks approached 800.

In 1978 ETA's political wing was indirectly involved in formation of the United People (HB; see Unity, below). More recently, the HB was the driving force behind the "We the Basque Citizens" (*Euskal Herritarrok*—EH) coalition, which contested the 1998 regional election. The EH participated in the resultant governing alliance until the end of a unilateral ETA cease-fire (September 1998–December 1999) that led to the EH's expulsion. In June 2001 elements of the EH established a unified party, Unity. In its more than three decades of operations ETA has demonstrated considerable resiliency despite the arrests or deaths of numerous leaders. In September 2000 French authorities captured the reputed ETA chief, Ignacio GRACIA Arregui (also known as Iñaki de RENTERÍA), for whom a French arrest warrant had been issued in 1987. The French also arrested the suspected ETA military commander, Francisco Xabier GARCÍA Gaztelu, in February 2001 and the alleged head of logistics, Asier OIARZABAL Txapartogi, in September 2001. In September 2002 senior leaders Juan Antonio OLARRA Guridi and Ainhoa MUGIKA Goni were arrested in Bordeaux, France, while in December Ibón FERNÁNDEZ Iradi and half a dozen other ETA leaders were arrested near Bayonne. Fernández Iradi escaped from custody two days later but was recaptured by the French in December 2003. By then, increased French-Spanish cooperation against ETA was severely hampering the organization's activities, with nearly four dozen suspected operatives having been arrested in October–November 2003 alone. Key suspects arrested in April 2004 included Félix Alberto LÓPEZ de la Calle, a military commander, and Félix Ignacio ESPARZA Luri, a logistics chief; in December alleged political leader Mikel ALBIZU Iriarte and Soledad IPARRAGUIRRE Genetxea, a suspected military commander, were also captured. In response to overtures from the Zapatero government for peace talks, ETA offered a partial truce in June 2005, involving a commitment not to attack elected officials, an offer that was deemed as insufficient by the government to begin talks. On March 22, 2006, the group announced a permanent cease-fire. The Zapatero government began to directly negotiate with the group. Unfortunately, the group itself was splintered and a part of it took responsibility for the bombing of a parking structure in the Madrid airport in December 2006. The cease-fire was officially called off by ETA in June 2007, following the attack of the previous year. In September the ETA released a statement blaming the breakup of the peace accord on the government's failure to set the "minimum conditions" for a negotiated solution and vowed to "open all its fronts" to further the creation of a Basque state.

In the aftermath of the failed peace process, ETA announced its intentions to replace would-be moderates who had been open to negotiations, implementing a stricter hierarchy of control over related groups to ensure sufficient militancy. This was confirmed by the dismissal of Rafael DÍEZ Usabiaga, who in October 2007 was replaced as secretary general of the ETA-affiliated Union of Patriotic Workers (*Langile Abertzale Sozialista*—LAB) by Ainhoa ETXAIDE Amorrortu, who represents ETA's radical wing.

In 2008 Spanish authorities made a series of arrests of prominent ETA suspects and shut down several active cells. Nevetheless, the group's violent campaign continued into the summer tourist season with a series of bomb attacks on seaside resorts.

In late July Spanish authorities reportedly stepped up security measures in the Basque region after issuing an unusual warning that a huge attack by ETA would take place. In an effort to enhance secrecy and prevent more arrests, ETA leaders reportedly removed members in prison from the group's national committee and appointed a new set of leaders and sent them underground.

In August 2008 the release of ETA member De Juana CHAOS, who served 20 years of a 3,000-year sentence for a bomb blast that killed 25 people, provoked considerable public outrage. Further attacks in northern Spain later in the month were found to be staged from France, where ETA members had apparently reorganized their logistical base. Prosecutors launched more arrests and indictments on ETA supporters into the fall, including 24 people who were charged in October with extorting money from businesses in the Basque region in the form of a "revolutionary tax." The suspected military chief of ETA was arrested in southwestern France in November, delivering what Zapatero described as a "decisive blow" against the organization.

ETA was reportedly responsible for the December killing of a businessman whose construction company had been working on a high-speed rail project in the Basque Country. In January 2009 ETA marked its 50th anniversary by vowing to continue fighting for Basque independence and warning that it would target Spanish media outlets and those involved in the construction of the rail line.

In advance of the March 1, 2009, regional elections in Basque Country, ETA issued a statement calling the elections "anti-democratic" because of bans of two far-left independence parties and urged voters to support those parties. ETA reportedly set off a bomb in front of the PSOE headquarters in the Basque Country in late February, causing extensive damage but no injuries. Nevertheless, election results demonstrated ETA's waning support in the region, according to analysts. The number of spoilt ballot papers, a common sign of ETA's support within the population, dropped by a third from previous polls to about 10 percent of the vote. Furthermore, Aralar, a new leftist independence party that is against violence, boosted its number of seats in the regional parliament from one to four. At the end of March police arrested eight members of an ETA-affiliated youth group, following the group's alleged planned attacks on the high-speed rail line project.

The election of the new Basque Country premier, Paxi López of the PSE-EE, in May ushered in a tougher stance against ETA activity. Efforts were directed at minimizing the legitimacy of a separate Basque state, including removal of pro-independence posters and other material from public buildings and the refusal to give permits to pro-ETA demonstrators. ETA stepped up attacks over the summer, which resulted in the death of a police investigator of ETA, nearly three dozen injuries in a Civil Guard barracks attack in the northern city of Burgos, and the deaths of two police officers on the resort island of Mallorca. A second explosion on Mallorca in August at a restaurant, in which no one was harmed, called into question government claims that ETA had been seriously weakened by the surge in arrests.

As of July 2009 there were nearly 1,000 ETA members jailed in Spain and France. ETA has been blamed for 828 deaths in its campaign for independence.

Communist Party of the Basque Lands (*Partido Comunista de las Tierras Vascas*—PCTV/*Euskal Herrialdeetako Alderi Komunista*—EHAK). The PCTV/EHAK was established by former members of *Batasuna* after that party was banned in March 2003. In the April 2005 regional election it unexpectedly won nine legislative seats. The subsequent support of two PCTV legislators enabled the PNV's Ibarretxe to retain the regional presidency. The PCTV did not record its 2007 regional vote share with the Interior Ministry. In February 2008 a Spanish judge barred the PCTV/EHAK and the Basque Nationalist Action from participating in the March 9 election and suspended all their activities for three years due to connections to ETA. In September the Spanish Supreme Court banned the PCTV on grounds that it was affiliated with *Batasuna,* although the party was allowed to continue to hold its nine seats in the Basque parliament. In late 2008 the court ordered the liquidation of all OCTV assets and froze its bank accounts. The PCTV was not allowed to run candidates in the March 1, 2009, regional election. In April PCTV members were among 44 charged as terrorists by constitutional court judge Baltasar Garzón. He accused them of plotting to revive ETA's political activities. In August Garzón announced he would put on trial PCTV leader Juan Carlos Ramos and two treasurers, Jesus Maria Aguirre and Sonia Jacinto, for being members of ETA.

Leaders: Juan Carlos RAMOS Sánchez, Aritz BLÁZQUEZ Díez, Javier RAMOS Sánchez, Juan Manuel RODRÍGUEZ Hernández.

Unity (*Batasuna*). *Batasuna* descends from the United People (*Herri Batasuna*—HB), which was founded in 1978. Linked with the political wing of the terrorist ETA, the Marxist HB coalition was runner-up in the Basque parliamentary election of March 1980 and obtained 2 lower house *Cortes* seats in 1982. A decision by the Interior Ministry to withdraw legal recognition from the party was overturned by court action in January 1984. In October 1989 the HB lost 1 congressional seat but surprised observers by announcing that it would occupy its 4 remaining seats, ending a decade-long boycott of elected office above municipal level. However, on November 20, the eve of the *Cortes* opening, HB congressman-elect Josu MUGURUZA was killed and another HB leader, Iñaki ESNAOLA, was wounded in an attack by alleged right-wing terrorists. Subsequently, the remaining HB deputies were expelled for refusing to pledge allegiance to the constitution. The HB won 2 congressional seats and 1 senatorial seat in the 1993 national election; it won 11 regional seats in 1994 but lost its Senate seat in 1996.

Karlos RODRÍGUEZ, an HB leader, compared the party to *Sinn Féin,* the political wing of the Irish Republican Army, in 1997, as ETA supporters staged counter-demonstrations against massive anti-violence protests across Spain. On December 1, 1997, the entire 23-member National Committee was convicted of supporting terrorism, and each member was sentenced to at least seven years in prison. On July 20, 1999, however, the Constitutional Court threw out the convictions.

In September 1998 the HB announced that it would be competing in Basque regional elections the following month as part of a leftist coalition, or "platform," styled We the Basque Citizens (*Euskal Herritarrok*—EH). The EH finished third in the October polling, with 14 seats, and subsequently agreed not only to recognize the legitimacy of the regional legislature, but also to participate in a regional coalition government with the PNV and EA. An ETA decision in November 1999 to end its 14-month cease-fire led directly to the EH's ouster from the PNV-led administration, and in the May 2001 regional election it saw its representation halved and its vote share drop 8 percentage points, to 10 percent. On June 23, 2001, the EH joined in forming the unified *Batasuna* party.

Amid an upsurge in ETA attacks, on April 30, 2002, police detained 11 *Batasuna* members who were suspected of channeling funds to ETA or laundering "taxes" collected by ETA. In August a judge suspended the organization's activities for three years and ordered its offices closed, citing its relationship with ETA. In the same month the national legislature supported a government request that the Supreme Court ban *Batasuna* altogether, and on March 17, 2003, the court concurred. The ban, which extended to the HB and EH designations, was the first of its kind since the Franco era. Subsequent efforts by *Batasuna* members to register other organizations, most prominently an *Autodeterminaziorako Bilgunea* (AuB) coalition, were rejected.

In May 2003 the United States added *Batasuna* to its list of terrorist organizations, and the United Kingdom followed suit in June. In November 2004 *Batasuna* called for peaceful dialogue among all sides to end the decades of violence. Despite this and other peace initiatives the ban on party activity was extended for two more years by a Spanish court on January 17, 2006, just days before *Batasuna* was to hold a large meeting to outline its political plans. The extension of the ban was supported by the conservative PP but was considered a blow to the Zapatero government, which saw *Batasuna* as an important participant in peace talks. On March 22, 2006, ETA announced a permanent cease-fire. The Zapatero government began direct negotiations with ETA. However, in December 2006 the truce was broken by an ETA attack at Barajas, the Madrid airport, revealing splinters within ETA that undermined *Batasuna*'s leverage.

In October 2007 Spanish police arrested 22 senior *Batasuna* members, nearly the entire leadership, in a raid on an important meeting that government officials believed was held to transfer power to a new cadre of leaders.

In late August 2008 *Batasuna* leader Arnaldo Otegi, who was reportedly instrumental in brokering the 2006 peace negotiation with ETA, was released from jail after serving a 15-month sentence for glorifying terrorism. After his release Otegi served as the group's de facto spokesperson and called for renewed peace talks, although his power within the organization had diminished following the decision of new ETA leaders to resume violence. A series of bomb attacks that month by ETA prompted *Batasuna* to call the violence an "obstacle" to the Basque independence movement and to begin promoting a clean list of candidates with no criminal records for the regional elections in March 2009.

In January 2009 Spanish authorities carried out raids on two new entities, Askatasuna and 3DM (Democracy 3,000,000) for suspected links to *Batasuna* and later banned the groups from participating in the March regional election.

Following the defeat of the Basque Nationalist Party in the Basque regional elections, Otegi called on separatist parties to renew efforts to create an independent state. Later in the month, a Spanish judge charged 44 individuals with membership in ETA, including the mayor of one northern Basque town; they were all active in *Batasuna,* the PCTV, or the PNV.

The Supreme Court in mid-May banned the *Iniciativa Internacionalista II* from taking part in the June 7 European Parliament election on the grounds that it was a front for *Batasuna.* However, weeks later the Constitutional Court reversed the decision because of insufficient evidence. Otegi then endorsed the group and said, "It is not our party but holds our opinions," and urged the *Iniciativa* to secure Europe's involvement in a "democratic and peaceful solution to the Basque conflict." The *Iniciativa* won 1.12 percent of the vote but failed to take a seat.

Also in June, the European Court of Human Rights upheld the Spanish court's ban on *Batasuna* on the grounds that it is a front for ETA. In early August a ban on a demonstration in support of ETA prisoners in San Sebastian resulted in clashes with police, while authorities blocked Otegi from going to France out of suspicion he was seeking to raise support for ETA there.

De Facto Leader: Arnaldo OTEGI.

LEGISLATURE

Traditionally designated as the *Cortes* (Courts), the Spanish legislature was revived by General Franco in 1942 as a unicameral body with strictly limited powers and officially named *Las Cortes Españolas*. Initially, it had no directly elected members, but provision was made in 1967 for the election of 198 "family representatives." The essentially corporative character of the body was retained in 1971, when several new categories of indirectly elected and appointed members were added.

In November 1976 the *Cortes* approved a long-debated Political Reform Bill, which, calling for a largely elected bicameral assembly, secured overwhelming public endorsement in a referendum held on December 15. The new **Cortes Generales**, consisting of a Senate and a Congress of Deputies, held its inaugural session in July 1977. Both houses serve four-year terms, subject to dissolution.

Senate (*Senado*). The upper house currently has 264 members, of whom 208 were directly elected in 2008: 4 from each of the 47 mainland provinces; 6 from Santa Cruz de Tenerife (3 from Tenerife and 1 each from La Gomera, La Palma, and Hierro); 5 from the Balearic Islands (3 from Mallorca and 1 each from Menorca and Ibiza-Formentera); 5 from Las Palmas (3 from Gran Canaria and 1 each from Fuerteventura and Lanzarote); and 2 each from the North African enclaves of Ceuta and Melilla. The remaining 56 members are designated at varying times (depending on regional elections) by 17 autonomous regional legislatures (Ceuta and Melilla being excluded). Each designates at least 1 senator, with the more populous regions entitled to an additional senator for each million inhabitants. The current distribution is Andalucía, 9; Aragón, 2; Asturias, 2; Balearic Islands, 2; Basque Country, 3; Canary Islands, 3; Cantábria, 1; Castilla y León, 3; Castilla–La Mancha, 2; Catalonia, 8; Extremadura, 2; Galicia, 3; Madrid, 7; Murcia, 2; Navarra, 1; La Rioja, 1; and Valencia, 5.

The overall party distribution after the elections of March 9, 2008, was as follows (directly elected members in parentheses): Popular Party, 125 (101); Spanish Socialist Workers' Party, 104 (88); Catalan Accord for Progress, 16 (12) (including 4 [3] for the Catalan Republican Left, 10 [8] for the Socialist Party of Catalonia, 1 [1] for the Initiative for Catalonia Greens, and 1 [0] for the United and Alternative Left); Aragonese Party, 1 (0); Basque Nationalist Party, 4 (2); Basque Socialist Party-Basque Left, 1 (0); Canary Islands Coalition, 2 (1); Convergence of Catalonian Democrats, 1 (0); Convergence and Union, 5 (4); Democratic Union of Catalonia, 1 (0); Independent, 1 (0); Galacian Nationalist Bloc, 1 (0); Party of Galacian Socialists, 1 (0); PSM–Nationalist Union of Majorca, 1 (0).

Speaker: Javier ROJO García.

Congress of Deputies (*Congreso de los Diputados*). The lower house currently consists of 350 deputies elected on block lists by proportional representation. Each province is entitled to a minimum of 3 deputies, with 1 deputy each from the African enclaves of Ceuta and Melilla.

The balloting on March 9, 2008, produced the following seat distribution: Spanish Socialist Workers' Party, 169; Popular Party, 153; Convergence and Union, 11; Basque Nationalist Party, 6; Catalan Republican Left, 3; United Left, 2; Galacian Nationalist Bloc, 2; Canary Islands Coalition, 2; Union Progress and Democracy, 1; Navarre Yes, 1.

President: Jose BONO Martinez.

CABINET

[as of August 1, 2009]

Prime Minister	José Luis Rodríguez Zapatero
First Deputy Prime Minister	María Teresa Fernández de la Vega Sanz [f]
Second Deputy Prime Minister	Elena Salgado Mendez [f]
Third Deputy Prime Minister	Manuel Chavez González
Ministers	
Culture	Ángeles González-Sinde [f]
Defense	Carmen Chacon Piqueras [f]
Development	José Blanco
Economy and Finance	Elena Salgado Mendez [f]
Education and Universities	Angel Gabilondo Pujol [f]
Environment, Rural Affairs, and Fisheries	Elena Espinosa Mangana [f]
Equality	Bibiana Aído Almagro [f]
Foreign Affairs and Cooperation	Miguel Ángel Moratinos
Health and Social Affairs	Trinidad Jimenez Garcia-Herrera [f]
Housing	Beatriz Corredor Sierra [f]
Industry, Commerce, and Tourism	Miguel Sebastian Gascon
Interior	Alfredo Pérez Rubalcaba
Justice	Francisco Caamaño Domínguez
Labor and Immigration	Celestino Corbacho Chaves
Science and Innovation	Cristina Garmendia Mendizabal [f]
Sport	José Luis Rodríguez Zapatero
Regional Cooperation	Manuel Chavez González

[f] = female

COMMUNICATIONS

Under the 1978 constitution, the right to disseminate true information is guaranteed and prior censorship is outlawed. The most significant restriction is a 1979 law that limits the practice of journalism to those possessing a university degree in the subject. In its 2008 report on press freedom, Reporters Without Borders ranked Spain, along with five other countries, including the United States and Taiwan, 36th out of 173 countries.

Spanish newspaper circulation dropped 4 percent between 2005 and 2006, but remains the only country in Europe, other than Ireland, where newspaper sales rose between 1996 and 2005, in Spain's case by 1.3 percent. Broadband access is below the West European norm.

Press. The following are dailies published in Madrid, unless otherwise noted: *El País* (580,000 daily, 1,040,000 Sunday), progressive; *ABC* (330,000 daily, 760,000 Sunday), monarchist; *El Mundo* (300,000 daily, 360,000 Sunday), center-left; *El Periódico* (Barcelona, 210,000 daily, 380,000 Sunday); *La Vanguardia* (Barcelona, 210,000 daily, 340,000 Sunday), conservative; *El Correo Español y el Pueblo Vasco* (Bilbao, 130,000), independent; *La Voz de Galicia* (La Coruña, 130,000 daily, 160,000 Sunday), Galician regional; *El Diario Vasco* (San Sebastián, 100,000 daily, 120,000 weekend), Basque Country regional; *El País* (Barcelona, 80,000 daily, 140,000 Sunday); *Diario de Navarra* (Pamplona, 60,000), regional; *Heraldo de Aragón* (Zaragoza, 60,000), regional; *Las Provincias* (Valencia, 60,000 daily, 85,000 Sunday), conservative regional; *La Nueva España* (Oviedo, 60,000). In February 2003 the leading Basque-language newspaper, *Euskaldunon Egunkari,* was closed because of alleged links to ETA.

News agencies. Domestic agencies include *Agencia EFE,* in which the government is the majority shareholder; *Colpisa*; and *Europa Press*. Numerous foreign agencies maintain bureaus in Madrid.

Broadcasting and computing. (*Grupo Radio Televisión*) *Española* (RTVE) is the national public broadcasting service. Its radio arm, with five principal domestic networks, is *Radio Nacional de España* (RNE), while *Televisión Española* (TVE) broadcasts internationally as well as domestically. There also are regional public radio and TV services. Private broadcasting was authorized in 1988. The largest private radio service, with over 200 stations, is the *Sociedad Española de Radiodifusión*. As of 2008 there were 567.4 Internet users per 1,000 inhabitants.

INTERGOVERNMENTAL REPRESENTATION

Ambassador to the U.S.: Jorge Dezcallar de MAZARREDO.

U.S. Ambassador to Spain: (Vacant).

Permanent Representative to the UN: Juan Antonio YÁÑEZ-BARNUEVO.

IGO Memberships (Non-UN): ADB, AfDB, BIS, CERN, CEUR, EBRD, EIB, ESA, EU, Eurocontrol, IADB, IEA, Interpol, IOM, NATO, OECD, OSCE, PCA, WCO, WEU, WTO.

RELATED TERRITORIES

Virtually nothing remains of Spain's former colonial empire, the bulk of which was lost with the independence of the American colonies in the early 19th century. Cuba, Puerto Rico, and the Philippines were acquired by the United States in 1898. More recently, the West African territories of Río Muni and Fernando Pó became independent in 1968 as the state of Equatorial Guinea; Ifní was ceded to Morocco in 1969; and the Western (Spanish) Sahara was divided between Morocco and Mauritania in February 1976 (the latter subsequently renouncing its claim on August 5, 1979). Thereafter, the only remaining European possessions in the African continent were the small Spanish enclaves discussed below.

Places of Sovereignty in North Africa (*Plazas de Soberanía del Norte de Africa*). These Spanish outposts on the Mediterranean coast of Morocco, dating from the 15th century, encompass the two enclaves of Ceuta and Melilla, officially referred to as *presidios,* or garrison towns, and three "Minor Places" (*Plazas Menores*): the tiny, volcanic Chafarinas and Alhucemas islands, and Peñón de Vélez de la Gomera, an arid garrison spot on the north Moroccan coast. Ceuta, with an area of 7.6 square miles (19.7 sq. km.) and a population of 70,400 (2007E), and Melila, with an area of 4.8 square miles (12.5 sq. km.) and a population of 67,700 (2007E), are considered parts of metropolitan Spain, and before being accorded the status of autonomous regions in September 1994, they were organized as municipalities of the provinces of Cádiz and Málaga, respectively. The Minor Places, with military garrisons of about one hundred each, are under the jurisdiction of Málaga. In 1985 intense controversy was generated by Madrid's promulgation of a new alien residence law, which required all foreigners living in Spain to reapply for residence or face expulsion; the law, which was directed mainly at fugitives who had entered Spain prior to the conclusion of extradition treaties with a number of European countries, raised serious questions regarding the status of ethnic Moroccan Muslims, who have lived in the enclaves for generations.

In February 1986 government and Muslim representatives agreed to form a commission to conduct a census while examining "ways to integrate Muslims fully into Spanish society." A general strike by Muslims in November, in support of a demand for immediate Spanish nationality, led to violent clashes between Muslims and Europeans. The internal crisis was defused when Prime Minister González announced in February 1987 that citizenship would "normally" be granted to Muslim residents. But Spain continued to oppose the Moroccan claim to the enclaves, resolutely rejecting any parallel with its own claim to British-ruled Gibraltar.

During a state visit to Morocco in July 1991 by King Juan Carlos, the Spanish and Moroccan prime ministers signed a friendship treaty (the first between Spain and an Arab country) providing in particular for the peaceful settlement of disputes between the two countries. Madrid had long felt that any attempt to alter the status of the enclaves would be interpreted by Rabat as an "annexation" of "occupied territory." Thus, it had branded as "unconstitutional" a unilateral pronouncement by Melilla's mayor in early 1993 that the city was an "autonomous community" within Spain. On September 2, 1994, however, the Spanish government approved statutes of autonomy, effective from March 13, 1995, that upgraded the status of the enclaves by authorizing the replacement of their local councils by 25-member assemblies, to which an executive and president would be responsible. The Moroccan government responded by launching a major diplomatic offensive against Spanish possession of the enclaves, contending that the forthcoming reversion of Hong Kong and Macao to China provided an example that Spain should follow. Madrid rejected such arguments, and in 1998 Spanish officials refused a Moroccan invitation to take part in a panel discussion on granting residents of the enclaves dual citizenship.

In the elections of June 13, 1999, the recently formed Independent Liberal Group (*Grupo Independiente Liberal*—GIL), led by a mainland mayor, Jesús GIL, won pluralities in the 25-seat assemblies of both Ceuta and Melilla, but in both jurisdictions anti-GIL coalitions prevailed in forming governments. In Ceuta, the GIL won 12 seats but was bested by an alliance of the PP, with 8 seats; the **Democratic and Social Party of Ceuta** (*Partido Democrático y Social de Ceuta*—PDSC), with 3; and the PSOE, with 2. Greater confusion reigned in Melilla, where six parties split the vote: the GIL won 7 seats; the PP, 5; the **Coalition for Melilla** (*Coalición por Melilla*—CpM), 5; the **Independent Party of Melilla** (*Partido Independiente de Melilla*—PIM), 3; the **Union of the Melilla People** (*Unión del Pueblo Melillense*—UPM), 3; and the PSOE, 2. Initially, the CpM leader, Mustafa ABERCHAN Hamed, assumed the presidency, but he soon fell victim to shifts in the governing alliance, losing a censure motion and being replaced in August 1999 by the UPM's Juan José IMBRODA Ortiz.

Tensions with Morocco flared again in July 2002 when Moroccan police set up camp on the offshore islet of Perejil (also known as Tourah or Leila), five miles west of Ceuta, ostensibly to combat smuggling and drug trafficking. In response, Spain dispatched members of its armed forces to Perejil. In an effort to mediate the dispute, then U.S. Secretary of State Colin Powell proposed that the islet be returned to its pre-July status. Both Spain and Morocco agreed, although Morocco subsequently voiced objection to the presence of a Spanish naval vessel near another islet, Nekor. On July 30 Morocco's King Mohamed VI reasserted his country's claims to Ceuta, Melilla, and the offshore islands and stated that Spain should end its "occupation."

The balloting on May 25, 2003, was more definitive. In Ceuta the PP won an overwhelming majority, taking 19 seats; the second-place **Cueta Democratic Union** (*Unión Demócrata Ceuti*—UDCE), a Muslim formation led by Muhammad MUHAMMAD Ali, won 3, while the PSOE and PDSC each won 1. In Melilla, Imbroda Ortiz's UPM took 15 seats, followed by the CpM with 7 and the PSOE with 3. In 2004, as in 2000, all six representatives elected to the *Cortes Generales* from the enclaves ran as PP candidates or chose to sit with the PP parliamentary group.

On September 29, 2005, five Africans were shot to death and dozens of others were injured when hundreds of individuals tried to scale the fence separating Morocco from Ceuta. The fatal shots reportedly came from the Moroccan side of the border. On the same day Madrid announced that it would deploy some 500 troops to Melilla and Ceuta in an effort to prevent such attempts, which had claimed nine lives in the preceding two months. The incidents led directly to a decision by 60 African and European countries to meet in Rabat, Morocco, in July 2006, in an effort to formulate a strategy that would stem the flow of illegal immigrants into EU countries.

In regional elections in May 2007 the PP retained its absolute majorities in Ceuta and Melilla. In Ceuta, the PP won 19 seats; the PSOE, 4; and the UDCE-IU, 2. In Melilla, the PP won 15 seats, with the PSOE and the CPM winning 4 and 5 seats, respectively.

In August a series of protests in Melilla concerning alleged mistreatment of Moroccans by Spanish police shut down the border for days and triggered supply problems. The protestors claimed that police were preventing Moroccans, particularly pregnant women, from crossing the border to prevent births that would lead to Spanish citizenship. Morocco temporarily recalled its ambassador to Spain in protest of the first official visit to Ceuta and Melilla in November 2007 by Spain's King Juan Carlos and Queen Sofia.

In the March 9, 2008, national election the PP won the seats representing Ceuta and Melilla in the congress and senate. In a July visit to Morocco, Zapatero was reportedly pressed by his Moroccan counterpart, Abbas El Fassi, about the return of Ceuta and Melilla to Moroccan sovereignty.

After the storming of a border fence by a large group of African migrants in June 2008, Spain's Defense Minister Carme Chacón announced she would station 100 extra troops in Ceuta and 250 extra in Melilla. However, the additional troops failed to quell violence in subsequent incidents. In November about 200 African migrants in Melilla stormed the border in a series of clashes with security forces. In January

2009 troops in Melilla opened fire on a group of about 80 migrants, killing one man, who were attempting to cross illegally, prompting calls by human rights groups for an investigation. Meanwhile, a stampede at a border crossing near Ceuta in May resulted in the deaths of two women and brought attention to the high amount of trade, including contraband business, between the two sides.

SRI LANKA

Democratic Socialist Republic of Sri Lanka
Sri Lanka Prajatantrika Samajawadi Janarajaya (Sinhala)
Llankais Sananayaka Socialisak Kutiyarasa (Tamil)

Political Status: Independent since February 4, 1948; present constitution adopted on August 6, 1978, effective September 7.

Area: 25,332 sq. mi. (65,610 sq. km.).

Population: 16,864,544 (2001C); 20,405,000 (2008E). The census figure is provisional and lacks results from several districts where security concerns prohibited enumeration.

Major Urban Centers (2005E): SRI JAYEWARDENEPURA (Kotte, administrative capital, 119,000), Colombo (Kolamba, commercial capital, 650,000), Dehiwala–Mount Lavinia (219,000), Jaffna (154,000), Kandy (Maha Nuwara, 111,000).

Official Languages: Sinhala, Tamil. English is recognized as a link language.

Monetary Unit: Rupee (market rate December 1, 2009: 114.41 rupees = $1US).

President: Mahinda RAJAPAKSE (United People's Freedom Alliance); served as prime minister from April 6, 2004; elected president on November 17, 2005, and sworn in November 19 for a six-year term, succeeding Chandrika Bandaranaike KUMARATUNGA (United People's Freedom Alliance).

Prime Minister: Ratnasiri WICKREMANAYAKE (United People's Freedom Alliance); previously served as prime minister August 2000–December 2001; most recently designated by the president and sworn in on November 21, 2005; succeeding Mahinda RAJAPAKSE (United People's Freedom Alliance).

THE COUNTRY

The insular location of Sri Lanka (formerly Ceylon) off the coast of southeast India has not prevented the development of an ethnic and religious diversity comparable to that of other parts of southern Asia. Approximately 74 percent of the people are of Sinhalese extraction, descended from Aryan stock of northern India, while 18 percent are Tamil, akin to the Dravidian population of southern India, and 7 percent are Moors; small minority groups include Europeans, Burghers (Eurasians), and Veddah aborigines. Roughly 70 percent of the inhabitants are Buddhist, while about 15 percent are Hindu, 8 percent Christian, and 8 percent Muslim.

The country's major ethnic problem has long centered on the Tamil population, which is divided into two groups: "Ceylon Tamils," whose ancestors have lived in Sri Lanka for many generations, and "Indian Tamils," whose forebears were brought to the island late in the 19th century as plantation laborers. The former, numbering nearly 2 million, predominate in the north and constitute about 40 percent of the population in the east. The latter, numbering about 900,000, are concentrated on the central tea plantations and, thus far, have not been prominently involved in the Tamil *eelam* (homeland) movement.

Women constitute 33 percent of the active labor force. Even though they have occupied both the presidency and the prime ministership, they make up only 5 percent of the parliament.

About 31 percent of the labor force is engaged in agriculture, which contributes about 17 percent of GDP and a comparable share of export earnings. Sri Lanka ranks with Kenya as the world's leading exporter of tea; other traditional exports include rubber, coconuts, and coconut products, with cinnamon being a leader among the specialized export crops promoted by a government-sponsored diversification program. Although a deficiency of natural resources limits the potential for heavy industry, small-scale manufacturing has advanced significantly, with garments and textiles now accounting for over 40 percent of export earnings and industry as a whole contributing 27 percent of GDP and employing 20 percent of the active workforce.

In the early 1980s Sri Lanka possessed one of Asia's most promising economies because of its advanced educational system, high literacy rate, workforce potential, and expectations of a tourist boom. However, falling commodity prices, drought, extreme Sinhalese militancy in the south (1987–1989), and widespread Tamil unrest in the north and east (since 1983) have held back growth. The complex, at times fratricidal, maelstrom of violence has left more than 100,000 dead, with some 1 million individuals being displaced during the Tamil conflict. It also has contributed to infrastructure decay (particularly in the Tamil areas), economic dislocation, lagging tourist arrivals, and long-term university closings. Nevertheless, GDP growth averaged 5 percent annually in 1987–1998. Growth was 4.3 percent in 1999 and 6.0 percent in 2000, but in 2001 the economy suffered a 1.5 percent decline—the first since independence—because of a fall in the export markets for clothing and textiles, a drought, and the economic repercussions of political uncertainties. Growth resumed in 2002, reaching 4.0 percent in that year, 6.0 percent in 2003, and 5.4 percent in 2004.

In late December 2004 the Indian Ocean tsunami disaster, in addition to killing more than 35,000 Sri Lankans and displacing hundreds of thousands, caused an estimated $1 billion in physical damage along the eastern coast. Fishing and tourism were particularly hard hit. Nevertheless, the economy grew by 6 percent in 2005 and approached a 7 percent rate in 2006.

Economic expansion continued in 2007 with GDP growth of 6.1 percent, but rising fuel and food prices caused inflation to increase dramatically to 17 percent. High inflation led the government to impose price controls on rice in April 2008; however, inflation continued to spike, rising to 28.2 percent in June, before moderating and falling to 7.6 percent in early 2009. GDP growth for 2008 was 6 percent and unemployment 6.2 percent.

GOVERNMENT AND POLITICS

Political background. After nearly four and a half centuries of foreign domination, beginning with the arrival of the Portuguese in 1505, followed by the Dutch (1658–1815) and the British (1815–1948), Sri Lanka (then Ceylon) became an independent state within the Commonwealth on February 4, 1948. Since the country's first parliamentary election in 1947, political power has oscillated between the moderate and generally pro-Western United National Party (UNP) and the Sri Lanka Freedom Party (SLFP), which has emphasized Buddhism, nationalism, "democratic socialism," and nonalignment in international affairs. Until 1956 the country was governed by the UNP, led successively by D. S. SENANAYAKE, his son Dudley SENANAYAKE, and Sir John KOTELAWALA. The SLFP, led by S. W. R. D. BANDARANAIKE, came to power in the 1956 election with an aggressively Sinhalese program reflecting the emergence of a nationalist, Sinhala-educated professional class, but a series of disorders culminated in the prime minister's assassination in 1959. The UNP formed a shaky minority government following the March 1960 general election but was unable to withstand a no-confidence vote shortly thereafter.

In July 1960 the SLFP, under the leadership of Sirimavo R. D. BANDARANAIKE, wife of the former prime minister, won a near-majority in the legislature and organized an all-SLFP government. Ceylonese policy under her leadership acquired an increasingly anti-Western character, accompanied by allegations of rightist plots and attempted coups. The UNP, however, regained a leading position in the 1965 election and organized a coalition government under the premiership of Dudley Senanayake. Subsequently, political power shifted back to the SLFP under Mrs. Bandaranaike, the UNP winning a bare 17 seats in a house of 157 members in 1970.

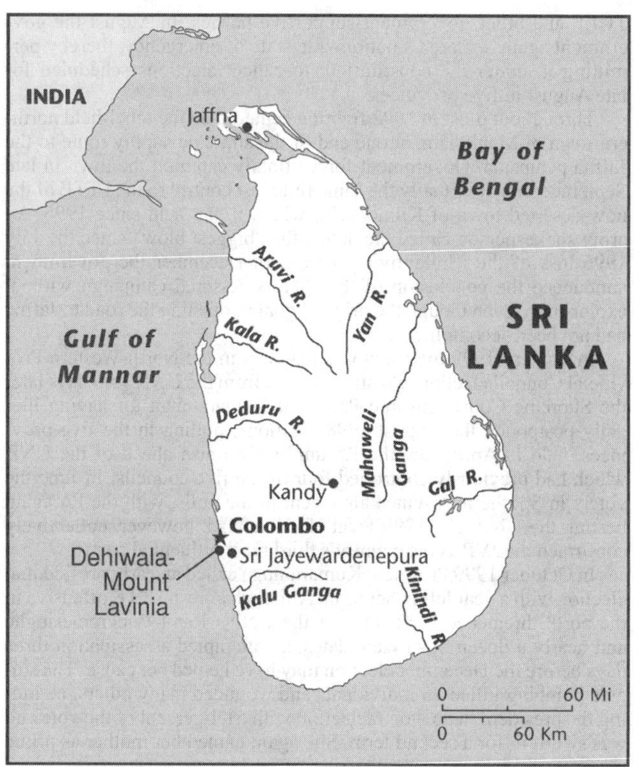

Sri Lanka's democratic tradition received a serious setback in 1971 when a radical Sinhalese group with Maoist underpinnings, the People's Liberation Front (*Janatha Vimukthi Peramuna*—JVP), attempted to overthrow the government. Most Ceylonese, however, declined to support the insurgents, and order was restored (at the cost of an estimated 20,000 deaths) within a few weeks even though the underlying cause of the uprising, a deteriorating rural economy accompanied by a high unemployment rate, persisted.

An extremely bitter election campaign culminated in July 1977 in an unprecedented victory for the UNP, which, led by J. R. JAYEWARDENE, obtained 142 of the 168 legislative seats. SLFP representation plummeted from 91 to 8. Following adoption by the National State Assembly of a constitutional amendment providing for a French-style executive system, Jayewardene assumed the presidency in February 1978 and named Ranasinghe PREMADASA prime minister.

Having secured passage of a constitutional revision permitting the president to call an election after a minimum of four years in office, Jayewardene was reelected for a second six-year term in October 1982 (effective from February 1983). In November, by a near-unanimous vote, the Parliament endorsed a government proposal that its own term be extended by six years to August 1989, subject to approval in a popular referendum. In December, under a state of emergency, 54.7 percent of the participating voters reportedly approved the measure.

In July 1983 the killing of 13 soldiers near the northern city of Jaffna set off a wave of anti-Tamil rioting that did not cease until early August. Over 400 people, mainly Tamils, died in the disturbances. In addition to proscribing three leftist parties, President Jayewardene secured passage of a constitutional amendment banning all separatist activity and requiring MPs to take loyalty oaths. The 16 MPs of the Tamil United Liberation Front (TULF) responded by withdrawing from Parliament and were subsequently declared to have forfeited their seats.

As the violence momentarily subsided, Indian Prime Minister Indira Gandhi sent an envoy to mediate between the Jayewardene government and the Tamil militants; however, most opposition leaders boycotted projected multiparty talks in October 1983. It was not until late December that the president agreed to invite the TULF to attend, without preconditions, a roundtable conference scheduled for January 1984. A series of "amity talks" ensued, with Tamil representatives advancing, as a minimal demand, the creation of an autonomous regional council encompassing the northern and eastern regions of the country. At midyear Jayewardene countered with a proposal for a second legislative chamber consisting of district representatives plus spokespersons for special interests. The overture was quickly rejected by the TULF.

During 1985 the level of violence intensified. Four of five exile groups based in Madras (now Chennai), India, announced in mid-April that they had formed a coalition to facilitate "armed revolutionary struggle for national independence." Meanwhile, the new Indian prime minister, Rajiv Gandhi, retreated somewhat from the overtly pro-Tamil posture of his recently assassinated mother. He declared his opposition to any attempt by the Tamils to establish an autonomous regime in Sri Lanka but sponsored a series of ultimately inconclusive talks between the rebels and Sri Lankan officials in Thimphu, Bhutan.

In December 1986 the government cut off essential northern services. Two months later, it mounted a major offensive against the rebels that recaptured most of the Jaffna peninsula by late May. The Indian government, under strong domestic pressure to take action on the insurgents' behalf, responded by airlifting humanitarian supplies to the north in early June, which drew a sharp diplomatic protest from Colombo. Subsequently, high-level discussions between the two governments produced an India–Sri Lanka Accord (ISLA) that brought Indian troops to Sri Lanka in support of a cease-fire and the establishment by an elected provincial council of an integrated northeastern government. On July 30, the day after conclusion of the ISLA, a 3,000-man Indian Peacekeeping Force (IPKF) arrived in Jaffna to assist in disarming the Tamils. However, the IPKF found itself in a major confrontation with the Liberation Tigers of Tamil Eelam (LTTE), the largest of the guerrilla groups. While the IPKF, augmented to a force of some 30,000, eventually gained control of much of the contested area, heavy fighting resumed in October. The LTTE failed to respond to an Indian call to surrender during a unilateral cease-fire in late November, and by early 1988 it was reported that IPKF troop strength had risen to 70,000.

In the south, the extremist JVP experienced a considerable resurgence because of its insistence that the ISLA conceded too much ultimate power to the Tamil minority. From mid-1987 the JVP engaged in a widespread assassination campaign against political figures and on August 18 almost succeeded in killing President Jayawardene in a grenade attack in the Parliament building. The government nonetheless proceeded to enact legislation that provided for elected provincial councils patterned after the Indian state legislatures.

The UNP swept a series of provincial council elections in non-Tamil areas during April and June 1988. With the SLFP refusing to participate because of alleged UNP concessions to the northern rebels, most of the remaining seats were won by the recently organized United Socialist Alliance (USA) which, although a leftist formation, had supported the mid-1987 pact with India. On September 8 Jayawardene signed a proclamation merging the Northern and Eastern Provinces. However, both the LTTE and the TULF declared a boycott of the subsequent provincial council election. Consequently, the Eelam People's Revolutionary Liberation Front (EPRLF) and the Eelam National Democratic Liberation Front (ENDLF) filled the council seats from the north without an election, while in the east the EPRLF and the Sri Lanka Muslim Congress (SLMC) each won 17 seats, compared to 1 for the UNP, in November.

In December 1988 Prime Minister Premadasa was elected to succeed the aging President Jayawardene, barely avoiding the necessity of a runoff by capturing 50.4 percent of the vote; Mrs. Bandaranaike received 44.9 percent, while USA candidate Ossie ABEYGUNASEKERA ran a distant third, with 4.6 percent. Parliament was immediately dissolved, and in the resultant legislative election in February 1989 the UNP won 125 of 225 seats. The SLFP, benefiting from the introduction of proportional representation, won 67 seats.

In March 1989 Premadasa selected former finance minister Dingiri Banda WIJETUNGE as prime minister. A month later he offered amnesty to Tamil guerrillas in the north and JVP militants in the south if they would renounce violence and join the political process. As an inducement he offered them 29 of the UNP's legislative seats. Although the LTTE agreed to negotiations, the JVP responded with a fresh wave of bombings and killings. The subsequent average daily death toll of 35–40 led to the June reimposition of a nationwide state of emergency.

In an apparent effort to neutralize one of the JVP's most popular positions, Premadasa, never a supporter of the 1987 accord with New Delhi, requested in mid-1989 that the Indian troops in Sri Lanka (then estimated at 50,000) leave immediately. An international crisis loomed over the issue until an agreement was reached in September for complete withdrawal by the end of the year. Fighting among Tamil groups broke out again, however, and the new Indian government announced in December that the deadline would be extended into 1990.

Meanwhile, bombings and assassinations continued in the south despite the killing of all known JVP leaders during an intensified anti-insurgency campaign that apparently included the use of shadowy "death squads."

India completed its withdrawal from Sri Lanka on March 24, 1990, leaving the LTTE in virtual control of the northern region. Three weeks earlier, the North-East Provincial Council had approved a resolution proclaiming the area to be an independent state of Eelam. The action was repudiated by New Delhi and seen as a "last gesture" by the council's chief minister, Annamalai Varatharaja PERUMAL, who, with numerous EPRLF associates, subsequently sought refuge in South India from the advancing LTTE.

In June 1990 President Premadasa agreed to dissolve the North-East Provincial Council and hold fresh elections, but the LTTE launched a new wave of insurgent activity and the elections were indefinitely postponed. In mid-1992 the government mounted a new offensive in the north that produced widely divergent casualty estimates. The LTTE responded in August–November with a series of assassinations and terrorist attacks on both military and civilian targets. In April 1993 opposition leader Lalith ATHULATHMUDALI of the Democratic United National Front (DUNF, subsequently the United Lalith Front) was killed by an LTTE suicide attack, as was President Premadasa on May 1. Prime Minister Wijetunge, who immediately succeeded Premadasa on an acting basis, was elected by parliament on May 7 to serve the balance of his predecessor's term, with Ranil WICKREMESINGHE filling the prime ministerial vacancy.

In the parliamentary election of August 1994, an SLFP-led People's Alliance (PA), in coalition with the SLMC, won 112 of 225 seats and obtained sufficient support from minor groups to provide a solid majority for PA leader Chandrika Bandaranaike KUMARATUNGA, who became the third member of her family to serve as prime minister. Concurrently, most mainstream Tamil parliamentarians extended their support to the new administration.

In October 1994 the UNP presidential candidate, Gamini DISSANAYAKE, and a number of his associates were assassinated in a suicide bomb attack at an election rally in Colombo. The UNP named as Gamini's replacement his widow, Srima DISSANAYAKE, who failed to prevent Kumaratunga from winning with a record-setting 62.2 percent of the vote. Following her inauguration in November, the new president not only reappointed her mother, Sirimavo Bandaranaike, to her former post as prime minister but also pledged to abolish the executive presidency by July 1995—a pledge she proved unable to keep.

In December 1994 President Kumaratunga announced that a government proposal for a cease-fire had been accepted by the LTTE, and talks aimed at ending the conflict opened in Jaffna in January 1995. The talks collapsed in April with a resumption of attacks by the rebels. Tiring of the search for a negotiated solution, in October the government launched a major military offensive, code-named *Rivirasa* (Sunshine), aimed at capturing the rebel stronghold of Jaffna. Government forces encountered fierce LTTE resistance and terrorist counteractions. Nevertheless, in December the city of Jaffna finally came under government control.

In January 1996 the financial center of Colombo was devastated by a huge LTTE truck bomb, killing over 90 people and injuring more than 1,400. With heavy fighting continuing, the government declared an extended nationwide emergency that secured parliamentary approval in April despite opposition objections, and a week later the military launched operation *Rivirasa* II to capture the areas around the city of Jaffna. On May 17 the government claimed that its forces were in control of the whole of the Jaffna peninsula, but its assertions that the LTTE had been effectively destroyed as a fighting force were disproved in mid-July when Tamil guerrillas overran the army garrison in Mullaittivu, southeast of Jaffna, inflicting the heaviest defeat on government forces since 1993. The military responded by launching another offensive in the north, during which an estimated 200,000 refugees fled.

In April 1997 Sri Lanka's two leading political parties agreed to a pact, brokered by the United Kingdom, by which they would cooperate in an effort to end the civil war. In May the military launched operation *Jaya Sikuru* (Victory Assured) in an effort to establish a stable overland supply route to Jaffna. Efforts by the government to restore normalcy to the Jaffna region included holding local elections in January 1998. Most of the leading Tamil parties participated despite threats from the LTTE, which the government had formally outlawed in response to the bombing of the country's most sacred Buddhist site, the Temple of Tooth in Kandy. Thereafter the LTTE undertook a bombing and assassination campaign to eliminate key leaders of the TULF and other government-supportive parties. In August the government again declared a nationwide state of emergency, thereby permitting it, under the constitution, to cancel elections scheduled for late August in five provinces.

Throughout most of 1998 fighting centered on the rebel-held northern town of Mankulam, at one end of the strategic supply route to the Jaffna peninsula. Government forces finally captured the town in late September but at virtually the same time lost control to the LTTE of the now-deserted town of Kilinochchi, which it had held since 1996. An army spokesperson called the defeat the "biggest blow" since the July 1996 loss of the Mullaittivu garrison. In December the government announced the conclusion of the Victory Assured campaign without explanation, even though the original goal of opening the road to Jaffna had not been accomplished.

In January 1999 the PA won a majority in the North-Western Provincial Council election, wresting control from the UNP. Two days later the Supreme Court censured President Kumaratunga for having illegally postponed the August 1998 elections; polling in the five provinces, held in April, saw the PA uniformly finish ahead of the UNP, which had previously controlled four of the five councils. In June the voters in Southern Province also went to the polls, with the PA again besting the UNP. The 1999 local elections had, however, collectively confirmed the JVP as the country's third most influential party.

In October 1999 President Kumaratunga called an early presidential election with a year left in her term. Although a fresh LTTE offensive in the north threatened her lead over the UNP's Ranil Wickremesinghe and nearly a dozen other candidates, an attempted assassination three days before the December election may have helped her cause. The suicide bombing killed 26 individuals and wounded many others, including the president, who won reelection with 51.1 percent of the vote and was sworn in for a second term. She again named her mother as prime minister.

In early November 1999 the LTTE had initiated its latest military campaign, "Unceasing Waves III," which within five days had cost the government ten towns, including, once again, Mankulam. The offensive constituted the most sustained operation ever by the insurgents. In April 2000 the LTTE forced some 17,000 government troops to retreat northward from the strategic causeway at Elephant Pass, severing the army's land connection to the south. On May 3 President Kumaratunga invoked, for the first time in the country's history, the Public Security Ordinance, which placed the country on a war footing. She also banned strikes and political demonstrations and imposed strict media censorship. Although the LTTE moved to within several kilometers of Jaffna city and also launched an assault in the east, around Batticaloa, the offensive stalled in June.

In February 2000 the government had confirmed that Norway was prepared to act as a mediator in direct talks with the LTTE. The Tamil Tigers insisted, however, on several preconditions, principally that government forces be withdrawn from the north and east and restricted to barracks during the discussions. The government refused. Meanwhile, the resurgent JVP questioned Norway's neutrality and demonstrated against its involvement in the peace process. Staunch Sinhalese Buddhists, including hundreds of monks, also were taking to the streets, demanding that the government achieve a military victory over the separatists and accusing Norway of giving LTTE leaders a safe haven.

In August 2000, with the legislative term nearing its end, the government introduced a long-delayed, controversial constitutional reform bill in Parliament, even though the proposal had already been rejected by the UNP and all the main Tamil parties. The bill's provisions included devolving powers to seven elected provincial councils and establishing an interim appointed council for a North-East region, with the final status of the latter jurisdiction dependent on whether the multiethnic population in the east approved a future referendum on union with the north. The government quickly acknowledged, however, that it could not marshal the needed two-thirds parliamentary majority to pass the 31-chapter bill and therefore withdrew it. Ten days later President Kumaratunga dissolved Parliament in preparation for a general election.

Octogenarian Prime Minister Bandaranaike resigned for health reasons on August 10, 2000, and was replaced by the minister for public administration and home affairs, Ratnasiri WICKREMANAYAKE. The retired prime minister died shortly after casting her ballot in the general election of October 10, which saw the PA capture 107 seats in the 225-member Parliament. Six seats short of a majority, the PA quickly negotiated a coalition with the National Unity Alliance (an affiliate of the PA-supportive SLMC), the Tamil-based Eelam People's

Democratic Party (EPDP), and an independent deputy, which permitted Prime Minister Wickremanayake to remain in office.

On November 27, 2000, the LTTE leader, Velupillai PRABHAKARAN, reversed his stance and called for unconditional peace talks. In December the LTTE initiated a month-long unilateral cease-fire but the government rejected the overture. Despite cease-fire extensions into April 2001, as well as the efforts of Norwegian negotiator Erik Solheim, at midyear the two sides appeared no closer to peace negotiations.

On June 20, 2001, President Kumaratunga dismissed SLMC leader Rauff HAKEEM from the cabinet, leading Hakeem and 6 other MPs from the SLMC to defect to the opposition. The loss cost the PA-led coalition its parliamentary majority and left the president's administration subject to a vote of no confidence. On July 10 the president suspended Parliament until September to avoid that consequence, and then on September 5 the PA announced a formal agreement with the JVP that restored the government majority's to 119 parliamentary seats. Although the JVP remained outside the reshuffled cabinet, it won a number of policy concessions, including an end to further moves toward Tamil autonomy, a halt to privatizations, a major reduction in the size of the cabinet, and loan relief for farmers. The pact was severely criticized by the TULF and other Tamil parties and ultimately served only to postpone the government's collapse.

On October 10, 2001, 13 PA legislators, including S. B. DISSANAYAKE, secretary general of the president's own SLFP, defected to the opposition. With a no-confidence motion looming, Kumaratunga dissolved Parliament and called a general election for December 5, only 14 months after the previous election. This latest setback also brought to an end the president's effort to hold a referendum on a new constitution, which had been scheduled for mid-October. Meanwhile, in a daring raid on July 24 an LTTE assault team had attacked the country's principal international airport and an adjoining military air base, causing an estimated $400 million in damages. Although all 13 LTTE assailants were killed, the attack constituted a major blow to the administration and also harmed an ailing economy.

With much of the public having turned against President Kumaratunga's increasingly hard-line stance toward negotiating with the LTTE, the UNP surged ahead during a violence-plagued campaign, and in the December 2001 parliamentary election it captured a plurality of 109 seats, compared to the PA's 77. As a consequence, Prime Minister Wickremanayake handed in his resignation, and Kumaratunga was forced to turn to her longtime foe, the UNP's Wickremesinghe, to form a new cabinet. The UNP leader quickly established a majority coalition, dubbed the United National Front (UNF), with the SLMC, which had won 5 seats, and also secured the external support of the TULF-led Tamil National Alliance (TNA). The bulk of the new cabinet was sworn in on December 12, with most remaining appointments then being made in February 2002. The president was forced to surrender the defense and finance portfolios she had held in the preceding cabinet.

Although the LTTE had launched a series of attacks to coincide with induction of the Wickremesinghe cabinet, it declared a unilateral cease-fire from December 24. The government reciprocated, reiterating, over the president's objections, its intention to open negotiations with the LTTE. Wide public relief, if not unanimous acclaim, greeted the announcement on February 22, 2002, of an indefinite cease-fire. The first direct government-LTTE talks in seven years were launched on September 16–18 in Thailand under Norwegian sponsorship, with the principals quickly reaching agreement on formation of a joint committee on security and a joint task force on reconstruction. An estimated 65,000 people had been killed since the beginning of the Tamil conflict.

Through early February 2003 four additional negotiating sessions were held at various locations, but on April 21 the LTTE announced its withdrawal from further talks, citing the government's unwillingness to put establishment of an interim administration for Tamil areas at the top of the agenda. It also complained of too little progress on reconstruction and rehabilitation. Meanwhile, President Kumaratunga continued to assert that Prime Minister Wickremesinghe was conceding too much to the LTTE; she insisted that a political settlement should be concluded only after the LTTE disarmed—a proposition that the LTTE labeled as "suicidal." She further insisted that the LTTE disband the Black Tigers squad of suicide bombers and fulfill its pledge to end the induction of child soldiers.

On November 4, 2003, during a visit by Prime Minister Wickremesinghe to Washington, President Kumaratunga suspended Parliament for two weeks and dismissed three key ministers, taking over the defense, interior, and mass communications portfolios herself. In response to the resultant governmental crisis, on November 14 Norway withdrew from its role as mediator of the peace process, although it left its Sri Lanka Monitoring Mission in place to continue supervising the cease-fire.

In January 2004 the SLFP and the JVP concluded an alliance, and on February 7 Kumaratunga dissolved Parliament and called an election for April 2. The multiparty United People's Freedom Alliance (UPFA, successor to the PA) won 105 seats to 82 for the UNP, and on April 6 the popular SLFP parliamentary leader, Mahinda RAJAPAKSE, was sworn in as prime minister. Although the UPFA remained 8 seats short of a parliamentary majority, Rajapakse won the external support of the newly organized Buddhist National Heritage Party (*Jathika Hela Urumaya*—JHU), which had won an unexpected 9 seats. It took the UPFA government until September 10, 2004, to cement a legislative majority, by bringing in an erstwhile UNP ally, the Ceylon Workers' Congress (CWC). Earlier, an MP from the SLMC had defected to the government, and in late October three additional members of the SLMC joined the government as noncabinet ministers.

The coalition government lost its legislative majority on June 15, 2005, when the JVP withdrew in opposition to the inclusion of Tamil separatist organizations in the distribution of international aid following the 2004 Indian Ocean tsunami. In a further blow to the UPFA, Foreign Minister Lakshman KADIRGAMAR, the government's senior ethnic Tamil, was assassinated by an unidentified gunman on August 12, 2005. The Supreme Court ruled on August 26, 2005, that President Kumaratunga's second term would expire in December 2005—not a year later to compensate for the year lost by the early election of December 1999. With the incumbent prohibited from seeking a third term, the presidential election was contested by Prime Minister Rajapakse, the UNP's Ranil Wickremesinghe, and 11 other minor candidates, several of whom withdrew at the last minute. Rajapakse had won the endorsement of the JVP and JHU by agreeing to support a unitary state rather than broad provincial or regional autonomy, to end privatization of state-run companies, and to renegotiate the terms of the cease-fire with the LTTE. On November 17 Rajapakse won 50.3 percent of the vote versus 48.4 percent for Wickremesinghe, who almost certainly lost because of a low voter turnout among Tamils following an expression of "disinterest" in the outcome by the LTTE and its political partner, the TNA. Sworn in as president on November 19, Rajapakse quickly named Ratnasiri Wickremanayake to resume his former role as prime minister.

The JVP's external support remained vital to the Rajapakse administration until late January 2007, when 18 UNP legislators crossed the aisle. In the interim, the CWC and the Up-Country People's Front (UCPF) had joined the government. On January 28 President Rajapakse announced a greatly expanded cabinet, which included 10 new UNP ministers as well as the leader of the SLMC. Two days later, the JHU agreed to accept its first cabinet post. In December, however, the SLMC withdrew because of what it considered lack of progress on Muslim issues.

In balloting for the Eastern Province regional council in May 2008, the Tamil People's Liberation Party (*Tamileela Makkal Viduthalai Pulikal*—TMVP), a progovernment Tamil group that is part of the UPFA, won 20 of the council's 37 seats. The government claimed the victory was a rejection of the LTTE and a mandate for its policies.

In January 2009 government forces captured most of the remaining LTTE strongholds and forced the rebels into a remote region of the northeast. In February 2009 the UPFA swept provincial elections in the North-Western and Central provinces. The UPFA continued its electoral success in April when it won elections for the Western Province. Government forces defeated the last significant LTTE units in May 2009 and killed Prabhakaran, effectively ending the organized Tamil insurgency (see Current issues, below).

Constitution and government. In May 1972, under the country's second constitution since independence, Ceylon was redesignated the Republic of Sri Lanka. Under the present constitution (adopted August 16, 1978, as a codification and enlargement of a series of constitutional amendments approved October 20, 1977), the name was further changed to Democratic Socialist Republic of Sri Lanka, and a British-style parliamentary structure was abandoned in favor of a "Gaullist" presidential-parliamentary system. The most visible feature of the present system is the concentration of powers in a "strong" president who may serve no more than two six-year terms. The president appoints a prime minister and, in consultation with the latter, other senior administrative officials, the only restriction being that all ministers and deputy ministers must hold legislative seats. Should Parliament reject an appropriations bill or approve a no-confidence motion, the president may appoint a new government.

The legislative term is six years, subject to presidential dissolution, although the life of the body elected in 1977 was extended by an additional six years in 1982. A constitutional amendment passed in August 1983 requires all members of parliament to take an oath of loyalty to the unified state of Sri Lanka and bans all activity advocating "the division of the state."

Judges of the Supreme Court and the Court of Appeal are appointed by the president. Courts of first instance include a High Court, which tries criminal cases, and district courts. A presidentially appointed parliamentary commissioner for administration (ombudsman) investigates complaints of wrongdoing by public officials.

In September 2001 parliament passed legislation authorizing creation of a Constitutional Council that has as part of its mandate naming independent commissions with responsibilities over police, the judiciary, public servants, and elections.

Prior to 1988 the country was divided into nine provinces, each with an appointed governor and elected Development Council. In November 1987 a constitutional amendment provided for the election of substantially more autonomous provincial councils, each headed by a chief minister. The amendment also authorized the president to merge the Northern and Eastern Provinces, a long-sought objective of their Tamil inhabitants. President Jayawardene implemented the change in September 1988. A North-East provincial government was temporarily installed, but the continuing civil strife rendered the merger moot by the early 1990s. (In October 2006 the Supreme Court ruled the merger unconstitutional.) Further devolutionary measures, approved in January 1988, called for a network of district councils (*pradeshiya sabhas*) throughout the country. Municipalities have urban or town councils, while rural areas are administered by elected village councils.

Foreign relations. Sri Lanka has long maintained a nonaligned position in world politics despite its membership in the Commonwealth and a mutual defense agreement that grants the United Kingdom the right to maintain naval and air bases, as well as land forces, on its territory. While the Jayawardene government stressed Sri Lanka's economic similarity and cultural affinity with Southeast Asia, the country's application for admission to the Association of Southeast Asian Nations (ASEAN) was rejected in 1982 on geographical grounds. The action helped to precipitate the 1985 launching of the South Asian Association for Regional Cooperation (SAARC), of which Sri Lanka was a founding member.

The island state's major foreign policy problems since independence have involved relations with India. Conflicting claims to Kachchativu Island in the Palk Strait, which separates the two countries, were resolved in 1974; India yielded its claim, and Sri Lanka agreed to permit Indian fishermen and pilgrims easy access to the island. The Palk Strait accord was supplemented in 1976 by a general agreement on maritime economic zones. At the end of 1998 New Delhi and Colombo signed a trade agreement designed to phase out most tariffs and to facilitate trade, investment, and development.

Much more explosive has been the situation involving Sri Lanka's Tamil dissidents, who have strong ties to some 50 million Tamils in southern India. As ethnic violence on the island escalated, relations between Colombo and New Delhi became strained, largely because of the use of Indian territory as a refuge and staging area by Tamil guerrilla groups. By 1986 local authorities in the Indian state of Tamil Nadu were becoming increasingly disenchanted with the LTTE presence, and the rebels transferred most of their operations to Sri Lanka's Jaffna area. In addition, New Delhi and Colombo concluded a treaty in mid-1987 under which Indian troops attempted a peacekeeping role in Sri Lanka, although the accord ultimately became a political liability for both governments, and the troops were withdrawn in March 1990 (see Political background). In 1995 the Indian government again attempted to come to its neighbor's aid by setting up the equivalent of a naval quarantine around Sri Lanka's northern coast, thereby depriving the rebels of easy access to supply bases in Tamil Nadu. Since then, Indian support has been less direct. The breakdown of the cease-fire in 2006–2007 generated renewed interest on the part of many Sri Lankans, including many Tamils, for Indian mediation.

In 1997 the United States announced that it had added the LTTE to its list of terrorist organizations. The European Union (EU) did likewise in May 2006, which prompted the LTTE to demand the removal of the 37 Danish, Finnish, and Swedish members of the five-country, 57-person Sri Lanka Monitoring Mission (SLMM), which had been established in 2002 to assist with the cease-fire.

In 2007 Brazil announced that it was reopening its mission to Sri Lanka after a 40-year absence. The move was seen as a reflection of increasing commercial ties between the two countries.

In 2008 the government announced the purchase of 10,000 rocket-launched missiles from Slovakia. In April Sri Lanka signed six new commercial agreements with Iran, including an arrangement whereby Iran pledged $1.9 billion in loans and grants to increase Sri Lanka's energy output. Through the year, the government continued to reject calls for the establishment of a UN human rights office in the country.

A continuing government offensive in 2009 was condemned by a number of foreign governments, including the United States, members of the EU, and India. International offers to mediate the conflict were rebuffed by both the government and the LTTE, which refused to lay down its weapons as a precondition to negotiations. International actors also criticized the government's policy of detaining an estimated 300,000 ethnic Tamil refugees in 15 camps and the conditions at the facilities. The United States and other governments subsequently suspended military aid and sales to Sri Lanka.

Current issues. In May 2006 Swedish negotiator Ulf Henricsson described the four-year-old cease-fire between the government and the LTTE as having become a "low-intensity war," and by August 21, when the SLMM withdrew from Jaffna and Trincomalee to Colombo, no objective observer could characterize what was happening—ground assaults, sea battles, air strikes, suicide bombings—as anything remotely resembling a cease-fire. LTTE and government representatives had met in Geneva, Switzerland, on February 22–23, 2006, to discuss the escalation in cease-fire violations, but a second round of talks scheduled for April 24–25 was canceled because the Sri Lankan navy had denied sea access to eastern LTTE leaders. In early August both sides accused the other of responsibility for the latest atrocity in the conflict: the execution in Muttur of 17 Tamils who were working for the French aid agency Action Against Hunger (*Action Contre le Faim*). Later in the month, an air strike by government forces killed some 60 Tamil schoolgirls, while in mid-October an LTTE suicide bomber attacked a military convoy and killed nearly 100 people. A further effort on October 28–29 to restart peace talks concluded without an agreement. Also in October, President Rajapakse and the UNP's Wickremesinghe signed a memorandum of understanding that called for cooperation on a range of issues, including the LTTE, electoral reform, and good governance. The agreement proved to be short-lived after 18 UNP legislators defected to the government in January 2007.

The Tamil conflict continued unabated into 2007. In March the LTTE used at least one light aircraft to launch its first-ever bombing run (against an airport), but the Sri Lankan Army was gradually gaining ground. In July the army claimed to have full control of the east and was pressing ahead in the north. At the same time, reports continued to surface about what Human Rights Watch termed "shocking abuses" of human rights by the military.

The government ended a 2002 ceasefire and launched a major offensive against the LTTE in January 2008. By November, 172 security forces had been killed and 1,122 wounded, and losses among the LTTE were reported to be close to 2,000 killed or wounded. Meanwhile, on April 6 the minister for highway and road development was killed by a suicide bomber affiliated with LTTE near Colombo. The attack also killed 12 others and wounded more than 100. Three weeks later, another suicide bomber killed 24 and injured 40 on a bus in Colombo; subsequent attacks continued through the spring and summer. In June security forces began the forced mass relocation of Tamils living in Colombo. At least 370 ethnic Tamils were removed by security forces before a court order halted the deportations. The renewed fighting left an estimated 300,000 civilians displaced and at least 250,000 trapped in the combat zone. Meanwhile, the UN reported that at least 6,000 civilians had been killed and 14,000 wounded since the offensive began. Also in June, heavy monsoons killed at least 20 and displaced more than 350,000.

In May 2009 government forces captured the last remaining LTTE stronghold in the Mullaitavu district. On May 19 government forces announced that Prabhakaran; his son and heir, Charles Anthony; and other senior LTTE leaders were killed in the final fighting. Even after the formal defeat of the LTTE, sporadic attacks continued against government figures and facilities by Tamil separatist groups. Also in May, the government revealed a plan to resettle up to 80 percent of the 200,000 Tamils held in refugee camps by the end of the year and announced that it would fully implement the Thirteenth Amendment to the country's constitution, which devolves political power to local and regional governments.

POLITICAL PARTIES AND GROUPS

In the April 2004 election 24 parties and alliances contested at least one district, and 7 won at least one seat. The present government is based on the **United People's Freedom Alliance** (UPFA), which was formed for the April 2004 parliamentary election primarily by the Sri Lanka Freedom Party (SLFP) and the People's Liberation Front (JVP). The UPFA was an expansion of the **People's Alliance** (PA; *Bahejana Nidasa Pakshaya*), formed as an SLFP-dominated coalition prior to the 1993 provincial elections. A number of the PA parties, but not the SLFP, had theretofore operated under the banner of the opposition United Socialist Alliance (USA), formed by Chandrika Kumaratunga in 1988 on the basis of her Sri Lanka People's Party (SLMP). In the 1993 elections the PA defeated the United National Party (UNP) in Western Province (including Colombo) while limiting the ruling party's majorities elsewhere. In August 1994 a broader coalition formed with the Sri Lanka Muslim Congress (SLMC) produced, with the support of minor parties, a parliamentary majority of one seat.

In the first half of 1999 the PA claimed victories in all seven provincial council elections, winning clear majorities in two, exactly half the seats in two others, and pluralities in three. In the October 10, 2000, parliamentary election the PA won 45 percent of the vote and 107 seats, 6 short of a majority, although President Kumaratunga quickly picked up sufficient support from the National Unity Alliance (NUA), the Tamil Eelam People's Democratic Party (EPDP), and an independent to form a governing coalition. In the December 2001 election the PA won only 37 percent of the national vote and 77 parliamentary seats.

Formation of the UPFA was announced in January 2004 by the SLFP and the JVP. On February 3 the National Liberation People's Party (DVJP), the NUA, the People's United Front (MEP), and the Sri Lanka People's Party (SLMP) announced their participation, as did the Lanka Equal Society Party (LSSP) and the Sri Lanka Communist Party (SLCP) two weeks later.

The participation of the JVP, which won 39 of the alliance's 105 seats, propelled the UPFA to 45.6 percent of the vote and a near-majority in the April 2004 parliamentary election. In July the UPFA also won victories in all six provinces that held elections. Sharp differences between the staunchly leftist JVP and other alliance parties persisted, however, especially over the terms of peace negotiations with the LTTE. In August President Kumaratunga resigned as alliance leader, reportedly because of differences with the JVP.

In June 2005 the JVP withdrew from the government, although it continued to provide external support. By late January 2007, however, President Mahinda Rajapakse had brought several additional parties, including the Ceylon Workers' Congress (CWC) and the SLMC, plus defectors from the UNP, into the governing coalition and was therefore no longer dependent on JVP support. Despite the departure of the JVP, the UPFA remains in existence, and the Rajapakse administration continues to be commonly referenced as the "UPFA government," even though it now includes parties that are allied with but not part of the UPFA.

In April 2006 the SLCP joined several other leftist parties in announcing formation of a Socialist People's Alliance (SPA). Other initial participants were identified as the LSSP, SLMP, the Democratic Left Front (DLF), and the National Liberation People's Party (DVJP). However, reports in 2008 indicated that the SPA was no longer active.

As of 2009 Sri Lanka had 55 registered parties.

UPFA Government:

Sri Lanka Freedom Party—SLFP (*Sri Lanka Nidahas Pakshaya*). Founded in 1951 and a leading advocate of republican status prior to adoption of the 1972 constitution, the SLFP initially advocated a neutralist foreign policy and the progressive nationalization of industry. Although winning a clear majority of seats in the House of Representatives in the election of 1970, it governed in coalition with the *Lanka Sama Samaja* and communist parties until September 1975. Its legislative representation plummeted from 90 seats to 8 in the election of July 1977.

In October 1980 former prime minister Sirimavo Bandaranaike was deprived of her civil rights for a seven-year period for alleged corruption while in office. She nevertheless remained active in party affairs, causing a split between her supporters and those of the nominal president, Maithripala SENANAYAKE. Mrs. Bandaranaike's rights were restored by means of a presidential "free pardon" issued on January 1, 1986, and she immediately launched a campaign for early general elections. In August the SLFP joined with some 20 groups, as well as prominent Buddhist leaders, in establishing the Movement for the Defense of the Nation (MDN) to oppose government policy that "conceded too much" on the Tamil question.

The party boycotted the 1988 provincial council elections but provided the main challenge to the United National Party (UNP) in subsequent presidential and legislative balloting. Mrs. Bandaranaike won nearly 45 percent of the December presidential vote, while the SLFP secured 67 parliamentary seats in February 1989.

In October 1993, Anura Bandaranaike, the former prime minister's son and theretofore leader of the opposition, withdrew from the party amid reports of a family power struggle, and subsequently joined the first Wickremesinghe administration. His departure opened the way for Mrs. Bandaranaike's younger daughter, Chandrika Kumaratunga, to assume a leading role in the SLFP-led PA and to become prime minister after the PA's electoral victory in August 1994. (Anura rejoined the SLFP prior to the December 2001 election.)

In October 2001 the SLFP general secretary, S. B. Dissanayake, was among the 13 PA defectors to the opposition, which precipitated the dissolution of Parliament. Following the PA's election loss in December, former prime minister Ratnasiri Wickremanayake, under pressure, resigned as leader of the opposition. In December 2004 Dissanayake was sentenced to two years in prison for defaming Supreme Court judges while he was SLFP general secretary.

In June 2006 President Rajapakse was elected party president, replacing former president Kumaratunga, who was resident in the United Kingdom. A year later, former foreign minister Mangala SAMARAWEERA, who had been removed from the cabinet in January 2007 after voicing policy differences with the president, announced formation of a breakaway **Sri Lanka Freedom Party–Mahagana** (SLFP-M), which quickly formed an alliance with the UNP.

In June 2008, it was reported that as many as 1,000 former members of the UNP and the JVP had defected and joined the SLFP due to dissatisfaction with their respective parties' electoral strategy. The SLFP led the UPFA coalition to 15 consecutive local and regional electoral victories from 2007 to 2009, through campaigns that emphasized the government's success in suppressing the LTTE.

Leaders: Mahinda RAJAPAKSE (President of the Republic and of the Party), Chandrika Bandaranaike KUMARATUNGA (Patron), Ratnasiri WICKREMANAYAKE (Prime Minister), Nimal DE SILVA (Minister of Healthcare and Nutrition), D. M. JAYARATNE (Minister of Plantation Industries), Maithiripala SIRISENA (General Secretary).

Ceylon Workers' Congress (CWC). Arising as part of the labor union movement in 1939, the CWC is a Tamil group that participated in formation of the Tamil United Liberation Front (TULF, below) in 1976. It regards itself as the main spokesperson for the Indian Tamils who work primarily as laborers on centrally located tea plantations. It has attempted to prevent their forging links with the Tamil insurgents in the north and east.

In 1994 the CWC elected seven members of parliament on the UNP list, but they subsequently withdrew to sit as a group of progovernment independents. In the April 1999 provincial elections, the party campaigned under the banner of the National Union of Workers (NUW) because of a legal dispute over use of the party symbol. In three provinces the NUW's support was sufficient to give the PA a working legislative majority.

The CWC's longtime president, Sauvmiamoothy THONDAMAN, died in 1999. He was succeeded as minister of livestock development and estate infrastructure by his grandson Arumugam.

In late August 2000 five MPs broke from the CWC over a leadership dispute and announced their support for the UNP. In September 2001 the party severed its ties to the PA and then negotiated an electoral pact with the UNP, but not before the original dissidents rejoined the PA as the Ceylon Workers' Alliance. Following the December 2001 election, Thondaman joined the new UNP-led cabinet.

In 2004 the CWC ran as the UNP's partner in the United National Front (UNF), winning eight parliamentary seats. Following the election, the CWC was courted by the UPFA, which needed eight seats to claim a majority. In early June the CWC leadership rejected joining the minority government, but in early September it offered its "unconditional full support," thereby giving the UPFA a parliamentary majority and earning a cabinet post. Less than a year later, however, in February 2005, the CWC threatened to resign from the government, which it accused of neglecting the needs of its Tamil constituency. Differences were patched up late in the month and the CWC remained in the government, but in October the party announced that it would support the UNP's Wickremesinghe for the presidency.

In August 2006 the CWC rejoined the government, which it had supported in the March 2006 local elections. It left again in August 2007 but returned in October. In regional balloting through the summer of 2008, the CWC did poorly and failed to win seats in previously secure districts. In April 2009 public officials in the CWC agreed to donate one month's salary to relief efforts among Tamils displaced by fighting between the government and the LTTE.

Leaders: Arumugam THONDAMAN (General Secretary of the Party and Minister of Youth Empowerment and Socioeconomic Development), Muthu SIVALINGAM.

Eelam People's Democratic Party (EPDP). The EPDP was formed in the late 1980s by Douglas Devananda, a founding member of the EROS (see EDF, below) in the 1970s and of the EPRLF (below) in the 1980s. Having abandoned armed conflict, Devananda joined the political mainstream following the India–Sri Lanka Accord.

In the 1994 legislative election EPDP members won nine "independent" seats from Jaffna, while in January 1998, defying LTTE threats and the deaths of at least two of its candidates, the party claimed victories in a majority of the 17 local council elections in the region. Nadarajah ATAPUTHARAJAH, an influential EPDP MP and editor of a widely read Tamil weekly, was assassinated in 1999.

The party backed President Kumaratunga's reelection in December 1999. Following the October 2000 general election, in which the party won four seats, it agreed to support the PA government. Its leader was awarded a cabinet post. In December 2001 the EPDP won two parliamentary seats on a vote share of 0.8 percent. In April 2004 it won only 0.3 percent and one seat. Devananda was then named to the Rajapakse cabinet, and he continues to serve under Prime Minister Wikremanayake. A close aide, Maha KANAPATHIPILLAI, was assassinated in July 2006. In 2008 Tharmalingam ELANGAKUMARAN, a regional EPDP leader, was arrested on criminal charges, including kidnapping and murder, and the party's office in Chenkaladi was reportedly closed by authorities. In 2009 the EPDP campaigned against the UPFA in local balloting in Jaffna and Vavuniya.

Leader: Douglas DEVANANDA (General Secretary of the Party and Minister of Social Services and Social Welfare).

Lanka Equal Society Party (*Lanka Sama Samaja Pakshaya*—LSSP). Established in 1935 as a Trotskyite formation named the Ceylon Equal Society Party, the LSSP first entered into a coalition with Mrs. Bandaranaike's SLFP in 1964. The party, which went into opposition in September 1975, lost all 19 of its legislative seats as a component of the ULF in the election of July 1977. Subsequently, it joined the SLMP and the SLCP in supporting measures to negotiate a settlement with Tamil activists.

In 1994 Vasudeva Nanayakkara rejoined the party. A presidential candidate in 1982, the outspoken Nanayakkara had led the NSSP (below) during his hiatus from the LSSP. In 1999 he was expelled from party membership for crossing to the parliamentary opposition, thereby technically depriving the PA of its one-vote majority. Nanayakkara ran as the candidate of the Left and Democratic Alliance in the presidential balloting of December 1999.

The party's Wimalasiri de Mel was minister of science and technology under Prime Minister Wickremanayake, having joined the cabinet in January 1998 as a replacement for recently deceased party leader Bernard SOYSA. A year later the party leadership openly criticized the government for its failure to contain the violence that preceded the January 25, 1999, North-Western Provincial Council election. It subsequently threatened to leave the PA unless the government moved forward with abolition of the executive presidency and a return to the Westminster model.

In February 2004, despite some initial objections to the SLFP-JVP alliance, the LSSP decided to join the UPFA for the April parliamentary election and party leader de Mel won the LSSP's lone seat in Parliament. Shortly after the election, longtime LSSP Secretary Batty WEERAKOON resigned. LSSP member and constitutional advisor to the government, Jayampathy WICKRAMARATNE, resigned in protest over what he described as a lack of commitment on the part of the SLFP-led government on Tamil issues. The LSSP participated in regional elections in 2008 as a member of the SPA.

Leaders: Wimalasiri de MEL (Secretary to the Central Committee), Tissa VITHARANA (Minister of Science and Technology).

National Congress (NC). The NC, initially called the National Muslim Congress, was formed in 2004 by A. L. M. Athaullah, who had previously been a leader in the SLMC and a noncabinet minister under Prime Minister Wickremesinghe. In 2003, having criticized the government for favoring the LTTE and not addressing the needs of the eastern Muslim community, Athaullah and S. SUBAIRDEEN broke away from the SLMC and established the Ashraff Congress. In February 2004 Athaullah left the Ashraff Congress and allied himself with the UPFA, joining the cabinet under Prime Minister Rajapakse. The party adopted its present name in September 2005. Shortly thereafter, some of its original members, dissatisfied with the UPFA government, returned to the SLMC. However, reports in 2009 indicated that a number of SLMC members continued to defect to the NC.

Leader: Ahamed Lebbe Marikkan ATHAULLAH (Minister of Water Supply and Drainage).

National Heritage Party (*Jathika Hela Urumaya*—JHU). Launched in March 2004 with a platform that called for protecting Buddhism as the state religion, rooting out government corruption, and rejecting concessions to the Tamil Tigers, the JHU grew out of the strongly nationalist **Sinhalese Heritage** (*Sihala Urumaya*—SU). The SU was established in April 2000 on a similar platform that opposed concessions to Tamil militants, including any movement toward a federal state. In the October 2000 election the party won only one national list seat. An intraparty dispute over who should occupy the parliamentary seat led the SU president, S. L. GUNESEKARA, to resign and form the **Sinhala National Front** (*Sinhala Jathika Sangamaya*—SJS). In December 2001 the SU won under 0.6 percent of the vote and no seats in Parliament.

In the April 2004 election the Buddhist JHU won an unexpected nine seats with 6.0 percent of the vote, after which it gave its external support to Prime Minister Rajapakse. Differences subsequently surfaced over whether the organization should abandon any future electoral role. The JHU supported Rajapakse in the 2005 presidential election, following his commitment to maintaining a unitary state and renegotiating the LTTE cease-fire. The JHU agreed to accept its first-ever cabinet post in January 2007.

In June 2008 the JHU announced a boycott of the All Party Representative Committee (APRC), a group formed to promote dialogue among the country's political parties. The JHU returned to the talks in August. The JHU was highly critical of international efforts to mediate the Tamil insurgency, and the party organized a series of protests outside of Western embassies in 2009.

Leaders: Katapola AMARAKITHTHI Thera (Chair), Ellawala MEDHANANDA Thera, Patali Champika RANAWAKA (Minister of Environment and Natural Resources), Athuraliye RATHANA (Parliamentary Leader).

National Liberation People's Party (*Desha Vimukthi Janatha Pakshaya*—DVJP). Active nationally since 1988, the DVJP is a leftist group often linked to the SLCP, SLMP, and LSSP. The DVJP endeavored to broaden the UPFA and was one of the founding members of the SPA.

Leader: G. M. PODIAPPUHAMI (General Secretary).

National Unity Alliance (NUA). The NUA was formed prior to the October 2000 election by the Sri Lankan Muslim Congress (SLMC, below) as a vehicle for expanding its influence beyond its Muslim base. Although the NUA took four seats in the balloting, the death of the SLMC's Mohamed H. M. Ashraff in September 2000 ultimately led to a power struggle between Rauff Hakeem and Ashraff's widow, Ferial, with the former assuming control of the SLMC and Mrs. Ashraff being relegated to the NUA. A further rupture between the two leaders occurred following Hakeem's removal from the cabinet in June 2001. Mrs. Ashraff ultimately remained loyal to the PA and in early July was affirmed by the courts as NUA leader, despite Hakeem's objections. She was named to the Rajapakse cabinet in April 2004 but threatened to leave the government because she was not consulted about tsunami aid negotiations. The potential rift was repaired in June 2005, and she continued to serve under Prime Minister Wickremanayake. The NUA's support continued to decline, and the party did poorly in regional elections in 2008.

Leader: Ferial ASHRAFF (President of the Party and Minister of Housing and Construction).

People's United Front (*Mahajana Eksath Peramuna*—MEP). The MEP, a left-wing party formed in 1956, was formerly allied with the JVP. Strongly Sinhalese and Buddhist, it long advocated the nationalization of foreign estates. In April 1999 it captured three legislative seats in Western Province and subsequently backed President Kumaratunga's reelection. Although it later protested against the government's proposed constitutional changes, the MEP joined the PA for the October 2000 general election. Its president was named transport minister in the reshuffled Wickremanayake cabinet.

In 2004 the MEP won two seats in the legislative balloting, and Dinesh Gunawardena was appointed to the Rajapakse cabinet, a status he retained under Prime Minister Wickremanayake. The MEP campaigned for the UPFA during regional balloting in 2008. However, it joined the JHU in boycotting all-party talks during the summer of 2008.

Leaders: Dinesh GUNAWARDENA (President of the Party and Minister of Urban Development and Sacred Area Development), Piyasena DISSANAYAKE (General Secretary).

Sri Lanka Communist Party (SLCP). Founded in 1943, Sri Lanka's official Communist party consistently urged the nationalization of all banks, estates, and factories and the use of national languages rather than English. Initially, differences within the party membership prevented it from taking a clear position on Sino-Soviet relations, but subsequent trends yielded a strongly pro-Soviet posture. During 1976 the SLCP proposed a United Socialist Front with what it called the "centralized Left" in the SLFP. The initiative resulted in the formation in April 1977 of the United Left Front (ULF), comprising the SLCP, the LSSP, and the now-defunct People's Democratic Party (PDP); however, the ULF obtained no national state assembly seats in the July election. Briefly banned in 1983, the SLCP joined the SLFP in forming the USA in 1988 and then the PA in 1993. Longtime party leader Pieter KEUNEMAN died in 1997.

In May 2004, following the UPFA's victory at the polls, the SLCP secretary general, D. E. W. Gunasekera, was named minister for constitutional reforms. In April, despite President Kumaratunga's backing, he had lost the race for speaker of Parliament by one vote. The SLCP helped create the SPA in 2006 and ran with the coalition in regional polling that year.

Leaders: D. E. W. GUNASEKERA (Secretary General of the Party and Minister of Constitutional Affairs), Raja COLLURE.

Sri Lanka People's Party (*Sri Lanka Mahajana Pakshaya*—SLMP). The socialist SLMP was formed in 1984 by Vijaya KUMARATUNGA, a popular film star, and his wife, Chandrika Kumaratunga, who had left the SLMP because of policy differences and the leadership style of her brother, Anura Bandaranaike. Vijaya was assassinated in February 1988, apparently as part of a campaign by the JVP (below) to suppress support of the 1987 India–Sri Lanka Accord. After several years abroad, Chandrika returned to Sri Lanka, organized the USA, and ultimately assumed leadership of the SLFP.

The party's general secretary and USA presidential candidate in 1988, Ossie Abeygunasekera, was among those killed in the October 1994 bomb attack that also took the life of UNP presidential nominee Gamini Dissanayake. The SLMP participated in regional balloting in 2008 as part of the SPA. In 2009, after the defeat of the LTTE, the SLMP endeavored unsuccessfully to convince the remaining Tamil separatist groups to participate in a government-sponsored cease-fire.

Leader: Ranjith NAWARATNE (General Secretary).

Up-Country People's Front (UCPF). Representing Indian Tamil plantation workers, the UCPF was organized as an alternative to the CWC by former CWC member P. Chandrasekaran, who was elected to parliament as an independent in 1994 but aligned with the PA. The party won two seats on the Central Provincial Council in April 1999, but on December 7 Chandrasekaran resigned as President Kumaratunga's deputy minister for estate housing and threw his support to the opposition UNP, which he described as "offering more benefits to the estate Tamils." In December 2001 he was named to the incoming UNP-led cabinet.

In 2004 the UCPF won one parliamentary seat. It backed the UNP's Wickremesinghe for president in 2005 but shifted its support to the Rajapakse government in 2006. The party's leader has proposed the direct participation of India in settling the Tamil question, a call that Chandrasekaran repeated in 2008.

Leaders: Periyasamy CHANDRASEKARAN (Minister of Community Development and Social Inequity Eradication), P. RADHAKRISHNAN.

Tamil People's Liberation Party (*Tamileela Makkal Viduthalai Pulikal*—TMVP). Formation of the TMVP was announced in October 2004 by Colonel Karuna, the former LTTE eastern commander who broke with the LTTE in March 2004 and quickly saw his forces, numbering some 6,000, bear the brunt of an LTTE offensive. Later in October, Karuna and the leaders of the long-dormant ENDLF announced formation of the TIVM front "to achieve the cherished rights and the reasonable aspirations" of Sri Lanka's Tamils. Since then, the Karuna breakaway group has continued to engage in open hostilities with the LTTE, amid indications that it was cooperating with the Sri Lankan military. In 2007 Karuna announced that the TMVP was prepared to enter parliamentary politics. The TMVP campaigned as part of the UPFA in provincial balloting in 2008 and won 20 of 37 seats in the Eastern regional council elections. Karuna was appointed minister of national reconciliation and integration in March 2009. In 2009 it was reported that many TMVP members had defected to join the SLFP.

Leader: Colonel KARUNA (Vinayagamurthi MURALITHARAN).

National Freedom Front (NFF). The NFF was formed in June 2008 and subsequently expanded by attracting officials and members of other political parties, including the JVP. The NFF signed a memorandum of understanding with the UPFA in December 2008. Party secretary Nandana GUNATHILAKE was subsequently appointed minister of tourism in the UPFA government.

Leaders: Wimal WEERAWANSA (President), Nandana GUNATHILAKE (General Secretary).

Other Parliamentary Parties:

United National Party—UNP (*Ekshat Jathika Pakshaya*). A democratic-socialist party founded in 1946, the UNP advocates a moderate line and the avoidance of a narrowly "communal" posture. Having survived virtual annihilation as a legislative force in 1970, the party swept 142 of 168 assembly seats in 1977 and remained in power by subsequent extension of the parliamentary term to 1989. While losing the two-thirds majority required for constitutional revision, it won 125 of 225 seats in the 1989 election. From 1978 until 1989 the UNP's Junius R. Jayewardene served as executive president of Sri Lanka.

The UNP finished second in 1994 with 94 of 225 seats, including 7 won by members of the CWC, who ran on the UNP ticket but subsequently announced that they would sit as progovernment independents. The party's initial choice as 1994 presidential candidate, Gamini Dissanayake, was assassinated less than three weeks before the November election, in which his widow, Srima, won 35.9 percent of the vote as his replacement. In the first half of 1999 the UNP uniformly finished second to the PA in elections for seven provincial councils, despite having won majorities in five of them in the previous provincial elections.

In November 1999 five members of parliament and two dozen or so other elected officials announced their break from the UNP leadership over the party's lack of support for constitutional reform. The MPs indicated that they would remain within the party but function independently. They also threatened a judicial challenge if the leadership formally expelled them, which it did. Two of the five were named to President Kumaratunga's cabinet as "special assignment" ministers.

UNP presidential candidate Ranil Wickremesinghe finished second in December 1999, with 42.6 percent of the vote. In the October 2000 parliamentary election the UNP won 89 seats on a 40 percent vote share. Three UNP dissidents received cabinet portfolios in the subsequent Wickremanayake government.

In the run-up to the December 2001 election Wickremesinghe negotiated electoral alliances with the Sri Lanka Muslim Congress (SLMC), the recently formed four-party Tamil National Alliance (TNA, below), and the CWC. With the UNP having won 109 seats and 46 percent of the vote, Wickremesinghe formed a governing coalition with the SLMC, also brought the CWC leader into the cabinet, and obtained external support from the TNA.

In April 2004 the UNP and the CWC, running together as the **United National Front** (UNF), won 37.8 percent of the vote and 82 seats (74 claimed by the UNP). In November 2005 former prime minister Wickremesinghe once again lost the presidency, this time by only 2 percent of the vote.

The first half of 2006 saw several MPs defect to the UPFA, in return for which they were given government posts. At the same time, some party members voiced dissatisfaction with Wickremesinghe's continuing leadership. In January 2007 the UNP saw another 18 MPs, led by former deputy leader Karu JAYASURIYA, cross the aisle, with 10 being named to the cabinet and the others assuming lesser ministerial posts. The UNP immediately threatened disciplinary action. Jayisuriya subsequently indicated that he intended to form a **Democratic Group** party. In 2008 the leader of the UNP's women's wing, Chandra WANNIARACHCHI, led an estimated 500 members of the UNP in a mass defection to the SLFP. Regional UNP leaders increasingly criticized party leaders and called for a reorganization to make the grouping more competitive. In July 2009 a court issued an order preventing the UNP from expelling party members that joined the UPFA government.

Leaders: Ranil WICKREMESINGHE (Former Prime Minister), Rukman SENANAYAKE (Chair), Tissa ATTANAYAKE (General Secretary).

People's Liberation Front (*Janatha Vimukthi Peramuna*—JVP). The Sinhalese JVP (not to be confused with the Tamil National Liberation Front—JVP, under TULF, below) was formed as a legal Maoist party in the mid-1960s. It led an attempt to overthrow the government in 1971, and a variety of ensuing clandestine groups were presumed to be made up of JVP members disguising their connection with the earlier uprising. The front regained legal status in 1977 and emerged as the third-ranked party in Colombo as the result of local elections in 1979. It was again proscribed after the July 1983 riots, reemerging in 1987 as a major threat to the government through a campaign of killing and terror in the south directed at government targets and Sinhalese supporters of the India–Sri Lanka Accord. In an attempt to win the JVP over to conventional politics, the government again legalized the party in 1988, but JVP leaders renounced the offer and remained underground.

Exploiting growing anti-Indian nationalistic sentiment among some Sinhalese, the JVP subsequently expanded its guerrilla campaign in the south, apparently operating through a military wing called the Patriotic People's Movement (*Deshapriya Janatha Viyaparaya*—DJV). Having disrupted provincial, presidential, and legislative elections in 1988 and early 1989, the front again rejected government overtures in September 1989. Subsequently, JVP founder and leader Rohana WIJEWEERA, General Secretary Upatissa GAANAYAKE, and other senior JVP members were killed by security forces under questionable circumstances. In all, the armed struggle in the south may have cost 50,000 lives or more.

Having disavowed violence in the mid-1990s, the JVP gathered strength late in the decade as a "third force" in opposition to the PA and the UNP, sometimes releasing joint statements with other leftist formations, including the NSSP (below) and various smaller parties. In 1999 it presented candidates for all seven provincial council elections, capturing at least one seat at each. In Western and Southern Provinces, where neither the PA nor the UNP secured a majority, the JVP held the balance of power, although JVP leaders stated that they had no intention of entering either provincial government. Its December 1999 presidential candidate, Nandana GUNATHILAKE, finished third, with 4.1 percent of the vote, having campaigned on a platform that included abolition of the executive presidency and rejection of World Bank and International Monetary Fund (IMF) prescriptions for economic reform. In October 2000 the party won 6 percent of the vote and ten seats in parliament.

In September 2001 the JVP's Gunathilake and President Kumaratunga signed a 28-point agreement that guaranteed the JVP's support to the PA government, in return for which the JVP obtained key policy concessions. Parliament was nevertheless dissolved in October, and in the December election the JVP picked up an additional 6 seats on a 9 percent vote share. In 2004 the JVP was credited with 39 of the UPFA's seats. Despite participating in the Rajapakse cabinet, the JVP continued to press its own agenda, including an end to privatization, noncooperation with World Bank and IMF economic prescriptions, and opposition to broad autonomy for Tamil areas.

Despite having left the Rajapakse government in June 2005, the JVP lent its support to Rajapakse's presidential candidacy later in the year in return for his commitment to key elements of the JVP's agenda, including renegotiation of the cease-fire agreement with the LTTE. The JVP nevertheless remained outside the subsequent Wickremanayake government and reconfirmed its decision in July 2006, when it rebuffed overtures from the UPFA and demanded the expulsion of the Sri Lanka Monitoring Mission.

In 2008 the JVP called for a boycott of Indian goods and declared that reducing Indian influence in Sri Lanka would henceforth be one of the planks in its party platform. It was reported that a large number of JVP stalwarts defected from the party to the SLFP. In April 2009 the JVP experienced its worst electoral defeat, losing regional balloting in its political base in the Western Provincial Council elections. Its representation dropped from 23 to 3 seats.

Leaders: Somawansa AMARASINGHE (Chair), Wimal WEERAWANSA (Parliamentary Leader), M. Tilvin SILVA (General Secretary).

Tamil National Alliance (TNA). The TNA was established on October 18, 2001, by the four parties listed below, in preparation for the December general election, in which it ran under the symbol of the TULF, the "rising sun." The TNA, strongly supportive of a negotiated settlement with the Tamil Tigers (LTTE, below), soon concluded an electoral pact with the opposition UNP and went on to win 15 parliamentary seats on a vote share of 3.9 percent. Following the election, it extended its external support to the United National Front government.

In the April 2004 election the TNA appeared on the ballot under the house symbol of the **Sri Lanka Tamil Government Party** (*Ilankai Tamil Arasu Kachchi*—ITAK), an original component of the TULF that had been revived because of a split in the TULF. (Organized in the 1940s, the ITAK, also known as the Federal Party, had not directly competed in a national election since 1970.) For the first time the TNA explicitly served as the proxy of the LTTE, winning 22 seats in the north and east.

In November 2005 the LTTE and TNA indicated their "disinterest" in the outcome of the presidential election, which probably contributed to a low voter turnout in Tamil areas and a resultant loss for UNP candidate Wickremesinghe. The TNA officially boycotted regional balloting in 2008 to protest the manner in which district lines were drawn. Between 2005 and 2008, three TNA legislators were killed in attacks. In February 2009 the TNA was invited to rejoin all-party negotiations. After the defeat of the LTTE in 2009, the TNA launched an initiative to develop closer ties with India and seek that country's assistance in protecting the Tamil minority.

Leaders: Rajavarothiyam SAMPANTHAN (Parliamentary Leader), Mavai S. SENATHIRAJAH (ITAK).

Tamil United Liberation Front—TULF (*Tamil Vimuktasi Peramuna*). The TULF was initially organized as the Tamil Liberation Front (*Tamil Vimukthi Peramuna*—TVP) in 1976 by a number of Tamil groups, including the CWC, the All Ceylon Tamil Congress (ACTC), the ITAK, the National Liberation Front (*Jatika Vimukthi Peramuna*—JVP), and the Muslim United Front.

The TULF stated in its 1977 election manifesto that its successful candidates would serve as the constituent assembly of a proposed Tamil state (Tamil Eelam). In the July election the front obtained 16 seats in the Northern and Eastern Provinces, becoming the largest opposition group in the National Assembly. Having previously declared their intention to resign from Parliament to protest the extension of the existing body beyond its normal term, the TULF MPs failed to appear for an oath renouncing separatism in August 1983, and their seats were thereupon declared constitutionally vacant.

Despite pressure from militants, the TULF maintained an essentially moderate posture, engaging in talks with the government and supporting the 1987 India–Sri Lanka Accord. Under pressure from the LTTE, the TULF boycotted the North-East Provincial Council balloting of November 1988; however, it won ten seats in the February 1989 parliamentary poll, its candidates reportedly having been supported by other proaccord Tamil groups. The TULF secretary general, Appapillai AMIRTHALINGAM, was killed and the party president seriously wounded in a July 1989 attack attributed by some reports to a "rogue cell" of the LTTE.

The TULF won five seats in Parliament in the 1994 election, after which it agreed to support the PA. In January 1998 the TULF won a majority of seats on the Jaffna Municipal Council, but in March the party president was quoted as saying that his organization would step aside in favor of the LTTE if the PA and the UNP would reopen talks with the group and accept it as the legitimate representative of the Tamils. In May the newly elected TULF mayor of Jaffna, Sarojini YOGESWARAN, was assassinated by a group claiming allegiance to the LTTE. Four months later her successor, Ponnuthurai SIVAPALAN, was also killed, and in December a party secretary, Ponnathurai MATHIMUGARAJAH, was assassinated at a public rally. The well-respected party vice president, Neelan TIRUCHELVAM, was killed by an LTTE suicide bomber in July 1999.

Because of intraparty differences, the TULF did not officially endorse a presidential candidate in December 1999. In October

2000 it won five seats in Parliament. In 2001 it was a prime mover in forming the TNA in opposition to President Kumaratunga.

Technically, the TULF did not contest the April 2004 parliamentary election because of a leadership dispute that remained in the courts. The TNA-supportive wing of the party, led by R. Sampanthan, backed the LTTE as the sole representative of the Tamil people, while the other wing refused to accept the LTTE's contention. The latter wing, led by V. Anandasangaree, offered a slate of independent candidates but won no seats.

In December 2005 party leader and TNA legislator Joseph PARARAJASINGHAM was assassinated. The government blamed the LTTE; the LTTE blamed government-backed paramilitaries. In January 2006 the Anandasangaree wing, the anti-LTTE faction of the Eelam People's Revolutionary Liberation Front (EPRLF, below), and the People's Liberation Organization of Tamil Eelam (PLOTE, below) formed a new Tamil electoral alliance, the Tamil Democratic National Alliance, to compete in regional elections. However, reports in 2009 indicated that Anandasangaree had reconciled with the mainline TULF leaders.

Leaders: Veerasingham ANANDASANGAREE, Rajavarothiyam SAMPANTHAN.

All Ceylon Tamil Congress—ACTC (*Akila Ilankai* Tamil Congress). Organized in 1944 and generally regarded as the founder of the movement for Tamil statehood, the ACTC participated in formation of the TULF in 1976 but subsequently reregistered as a separate party.

On January 5, 2000, its leader, Kumar PONNAMBALAM, was assassinated. An anti-LTTE group calling itself the National Front Against Tigers later claimed responsibility. The party won one seat in the 2000 and 2004 parliament elections.

Leaders: Gajendrakumar PONNAMBALAM (General Secretary), Kumar PONNAMBALAM.

Eelam People's Revolutionary Liberation Front (EPRLF). Founded in 1980, the EPRLF conducted guerrilla activity in Tamil areas in the first half of the 1980s before being decimated by a full-scale LTTE offensive in late 1986. In the wake of the 1987 accord that brought Indian troops to the region, the EPRLF was rebuilt, with New Delhi's support, to serve as a vehicle for the assumption by moderate Tamils of local political autonomy. In November 1988 the EPRLF gained 40 of 71 seats in the newly created North-East Provincial Council: It won 17 of 35 seats in the east and, under an agreement with the Eelam National Democratic Liberation Front (ENDLF, below), filled 23 seats in the uncontested north. In addition, an EPRLF leader was appointed chief minister of the province, and an EPRLF-dominated militia, the Tamil National Army, was formed. Upon completion of the Indian withdrawal in March 1990, however, the Tamil army proved to be no match for the LTTE, and many of its members joined most of the EPRLF leadership in fleeing to India. Party leader K. PATHMANABA was assassinated in 1990.

The party failed to win control of any of the local bodies in the January 1998 Jaffna balloting. A year later former party chief and North-East chief minister Annamalai Varatharaja Perumal returned from exile, reportedly to rebuild the EPRLF, but in January 2000 he was expelled by the party's central committee for "antiparty" activities. Two months earlier he had stated that he no longer considered Tamil independence realistic. Perumal and his dissident supporters contested the October 2000 elections on independent district lists while voicing support for the PA at the national level.

In June 2003 the leader of Perumal's faction, Thambirajah SUBATHIRAN, was assassinated, apparently by the LTTE. The party remained divided through 2004, with the faction loyal to Suresh Premachandran continuing its participation with the TNA. The Perumal faction, led by T. Sritharan, backed the presidential candidacy of Prime Minister Rajapakse in 2005. In 2008, a faction of the EPRLF joined with the TULF in the Tamil Democratic National Alliance. The grouping, led by G. SRITHARAN, declared its intention to elect a Tamil as the chief minister of the regional council. In June 2009 EPRLF fighters engaged in a series of gun battles in Jaffna with LTTE guerillas, which left an estimated 75 dead and scores wounded. Reports indicated that a large number of EPRLF members surrendered and subsequently joined the LTTE.

Faction Leaders: Suresh K. PREMACHANDRAN, Annamalai Varatharaja PERUMAL, Thirunavakkarasu SRITHARAN.

Tamil Eelam Liberation Organization (TELO). The TELO resulted from the merger, in Madras, India, in 1984, of a preexisting group of the same name with the Eelam Revolutionary Organization (EROS; see under EDF, below) and the Eelam People's Revolutionary Front (EPRF). The organization was reported to have been "virtually eliminated" in battles with the LTTE in 1986, with its principal leader, Mohan Sri SABARATNAM, among the estimated 300 casualties.

The TELO had little success in the Jaffna area elections of January 1998, winning control of only one village council. Reports in 1999 stated that the TELO and the PLOTE (below) had clashed over control of Vavuniya, the major northern railhead. In the 2000 and 2004 national elections the party won three seats in parliament. In 2007 and 2008 a number of TELO regional officials were attacked or killed by the LTTE, which rejected TELO's political accommodation with establishment parties. In some local elections in 2009, TELO candidates campaigned jointly with the UPFA.

Leaders: Selvam ADAIKALANATHAN (President), M. K. SHIVAJILINGAM, Indrakumar PRASANNA (General Secretary).

Sri Lanka Muslim Congress (SLMC). Formed in 1980, the SLMC declared itself a political party at a conference convened in 1986 to represent Muslim interests in the negotiations for a political settlement of the Tamil question. The party won 17 seats in the North-East Provincial Council balloting in November 1988 and supported Mrs. Bandaranaike's bid for the presidency in December 1988. It obtained 3 legislative seats in 1989, adding 4 more as a coalition partner of the PA in 1994.

In August 2000 comments by SLFP minister A. H. M. FOWZIE belittling the SLMC's importance to the PA led President Mohamed H. M. ASHRAFF to submit his resignation as ports minister, but the rift was patched at the end of the month. At the same time, the SLMC agreed to remain partnered with the PA for the October general election, although it decided to contest four districts separately. To broaden its appeal beyond its Muslim constituency, the party also decided to campaign as the National Unity Alliance (NUA, above). In the balloting the NUA won four seats in addition to those won under the PA banner.

Party founder Ashraff died in September 2000 in a helicopter crash. His widow, Ferial, was named to the cabinet announced after the October election, as was her party coleader, Rauff Hakeem. Hakeem soon supplanted Mrs. Ashraff within the SLMC, although she became the NUA leader.

In June 2001 President Kumaratunga removed Hakeem from the cabinet, at which time he and six other SLMC members of parliament abandoned the government, thereby costing it its legislative majority. Ashraff initially resigned her cabinet post but continued her support for the government. She resumed her ministerial position in early July, leaving the SLMC/NUA asunder. Following the December 2001 election, in which the SLMC won five seats, Hakeem negotiated a coalition agreement with the UNP and joined the new cabinet. Mrs. Ashraff's NUA had remained with the PA. Subsequent efforts to resolve their differences did not succeed. In 2002–2003 the party splintered further, largely over the perception of a faction led by A. L. M. Athaullah that the UNP government was favoring the LTTE at the expense of eastern Muslims (see NC, above).

For the April 2004 general election the SLMC ran independently, capturing five parliamentary seats. In May one SLMC MP defected to the UPFA, and three others did likewise in October, for which the three were named noncabinet ministers responsible for rehabilitation and district development in three Tamil districts. The SLMC leadership attempted to expel the three but was overruled by the Supreme Court.

The SLMC supported the UNP's Ranil Wickremesinghe in the 2005 presidential contest. In 2006, however, it announced that it would extend issue-based support to the government, and in January 2007 Hakeem brought the SLMC back into the government, only to withdraw on December 12 because of insufficient progress on Muslim-related issues. In 2008 a faction of the party, led by M. Lalith GUNARATNE, announced that they would support the government at the local and regional level and rejected Hakeem's call for noncooperation. In 2009 several leading SLMC figures were reported to have left the party and joined the NC.

Leaders: Rauff HAKEEM (Former Minister of Posts and Telecommunications), Basheer Cego DAWOOD (Chair), Hasan ALI (General Secretary).

Other National or Sinhalese Parties:

Liberal Party (LP). The LP began as the Council for Liberal Democracy, founded in 1981 by UNP member Chanaka AMARATUNGA, who ultimately formed the LP in 1987. It won two Western Province council seats in 1988 and ran on the SLFP ticket in 1989. In August 1996 Amaratunga, who had helped draft the revolutionary constitutional amendments favored by the Kumaratunga administration, died in an automobile accident.

The LP won no provincial council seats in 1999 despite offering candidates in six provinces. Its current leader ran for president in December 1999 but attracted little support, and in December 2001 and April 2004 the LP won only a handful of votes. Party leader Rajiva Wijesinha was appointed secretary general of the peace group, the Secretariat for Coordinating the Peace Process (SCOPP) in 2007. He was replaced by Kamal Nissanka, who was elected general secretary at a party congress.

Leaders: Kamal NISSANKA (General Secretary), Swarma AMARATUNGA (Honorary President).

Muslim National Alliance (MNA). The MNA was established in May 2005 by three parties: the **Democratic Unity Alliance** (DUA); **the Sri Lanka Muslim Kachchi** (SLMK), led by Abdul RASOOL; and the **United Muslim People's Alliance** (UMPA), led by Nizar MOULANA. Although the DUA's Nazeer Ahamed initially intended to enter the 2005 presidential contest, the alliance decided to back the UNP's Wickremesinghe. In October 2005, however, it switched its allegiance to Prime Minister Rajapakse of the UPFA. Other organizations joining the MNA included the Ashraff Congress (see NC, above) and the **Muslim United Liberation Front** (MULF). Reports indicated that the MNA was no longer active in 2009.

Leader: Hafiz Nazeer AHAMED.

New Equal Society Party (*Nawa Sama Samaja Pakshaya*—NSSP). A 1977 splinter of the LSSP, the NSSP was one of the leftist parties briefly banned for alleged seditious activity in 1983. Despite its general support for the Kumaratunga administration, in 1996 its offices were raided by the police following government allegations that it was involved in a strike against the state-owned Ceylon Electricity Board. For the December 1999 presidential race it was allied with the JVP.

Leading up to President Kumaratunga's February 2004 decision to call a snap national election, the NSSP had drawn closer to Prime Minister Wickremesinghe, who was viewed as the lesser of two evils because of his peace efforts. Immediately after the dissolution of Parliament the NSSP joined with Vasudeva Nanayakkara's **Democratic Left Front** (DLF) and a small LSSP splinter, Chandra KUMARAGE's **Alternative Group**, to announce a **New Left Front** (NLF) to contest the April election, in which it won only 0.1 percent of the vote. (A previous incarnation of the NLF had been organized in 1998 by the NSSP, eight other minor leftist parties, and the MULF; in the 2001 election it had won 0.5 percent of the vote.)

Nanayakkara, a former LSSP parliamentary deputy, had run for president in 1999 as the candidate of a Left and Democratic Alliance. His DLF won less than 0.1 percent of the vote in December 2001. He has subsequently served as an adviser to President Rajapakse, although in 2007 he unsuccessfully petitioned against an agreement with the United States permitting the transfer and exchange of logistical military supplies.

Leaders: Wickramabahu Bandara KARUNARATNE, Chamil JAYANETHTHI (2005 presidential candidate), Vasudeva NANAYAKKARA (NLF).

Sons of the Soil Party (*Sinhalaye Mahasammatha Bhoomiputra Pakshaya*—SMBP). Strongly nationalist, Sinhalese, and Buddhist, the SMBP was founded by Wijetamuni Rohana De SILVA, who attempted to assassinate Rajiv Gandhi in July 1987. In August 1997 the SMBP, blaming India for the country's civil strife, asserted that New Delhi should pay compensation because of its alleged support for the Tamil insurgents. It contested council seats in two provinces in April 1999 but won no seats. Party leader Harischandra Wijetunge ran for president in 1999, as he had in 1994, but secured less than 1 percent of the vote. In December 2001 and April 2004 the SMBP won few votes. The SMBP reportedly joined the UPFA in 2007 for subsequent regional and local elections.

Leader: Harischandra WIJETUNGE (President).

Sri Lanka Progressive Front (SLPF). The SLPF, which was formed in the late 1980s by former SLFP leader Ariya BULEGODA, won one seat in the 1994 balloting for Parliament. Its 1994 presidential candidate, Nihal Galappathy, won only 0.3 percent of the vote; Galappathy later joined the JVP. The SLPF failed to secure provincial council representation in balloting in 1999. In the 2000, 2001, and 2004 general elections it won little support. Bulegoda died in April 2004. The party's 2005 presidential candidate, Nelson PERERA, withdrew at the last minute in favor of Prime Minister Rajapakse.

Leader: Rohan JAYATUNGA (Secretary).

United Lalith Front (ULF). The ULF was launched in January 1992 as the Democratic United National Front (DUNF) by a group of eight politicians who had been expelled from the UNP for supporting the impeachment of President Premadasa. The DUNF's principal leader, Lalith ATHULATHMUDALI, was assassinated while addressing a rally in Colombo in April 1993. Subsequently, the group secured about 15 percent of the overall vote in the May provincial council balloting as an ally of the People's Alliance. The DUNF leadership passed to Athulathmudali's widow, Srimani Lalith ATHULATHMUDALI, who became a minister in the government appointed in August 1994.

In March 1997 the DUNF did not cooperate with the PA in local elections, and in June Srimani Athulathmudali lost her cabinet posting. The party subsequently adopted the ULF designation. It maintained a tenuous relationship with the PA until withdrawing from it entirely in late August 2000, apparently because the PA did not offer Athulathmudali a place on its national list for the October election. The ULF won no seats then, in December 2001, or in April 2004, when it took only 0.04 percent of the vote. Srimani Athulathmudali died in December 2004.

Leaders: Anura de SILVA (2005 presidential candidate), T. M. S. NANAYAKKARA (General Secretary).

Additional parties contesting the 2004 election (none obtaining more than 0.2 percent of the vote) included the **Ceylon Democratic Unity Alliance** (CDUA), led by S. SATHASIVAM; the rump of the **Democratic United National Front** (DUNF; see the ULF, above), led by Ariyawansha DISSANAYAKE; the **Jathika Sangwardhena Peramuna** (JSP), led by 2005 presidential candidate Achala Ashoka SURAWEERA; the **National People's Party** (NPP), led by Mudhitha KARUNAMANI; the **Ruhuna Janatha Party** (RJP), led by Aruna SOYZA; the **Socialist Equality Party** (SEP), led by 2005 presidential candidate Wije DIAS; the **Sri Lanka National Front** (SLNF), led by Wimal GEEGANAGE, who withdrew from the 2005 presidential race to back Prime Minister Rajapakse; the **Swarajya** (SR), led by Naweendra Lal GUNARATNE; and the **United Socialist Party** (USP), a splinter from the NSSP that participated in formation of the New Left Front in 1998 but ran on its own in 2001 and 2004. The USP's leader, Siritunga JAYASURIYA, finished third, with 0.4 percent of the vote, in the 2005 presidential election.

Other Tamil Parties and Groups:

Liberation Tigers of Tamil Eelam (LTTE). Founded in 1972 as the Tamil New Tigers, the LTTE is the largest and most hard-line of the militant Tamil groups. It has proposed a socialist Tamil homeland, although ideology has recently been overshadowed by military considerations. In 1985 the Tigers joined the EPRLF, EROS (see under EDF, below), and TELO in an antigovernment coalition, the Eelam National Liberation Front (ENLF), to fight for a separate Tamil state. However, the LTTE was soon engaged in a bloody campaign against some of its former allies, assuming effective control of much of northern Sri Lanka, especially the Jaffna peninsula. The Tigers also conducted extensive guerrilla activity against the Indian troops brought into the region as peacekeepers under the 1987 accord between Colombo and New Delhi. The LTTE boycotted and partially sabotaged the provincial elections in November 1988 and the presidential elections in December.

In 1989 the LTTE agreed to peace negotiations with the government, announced a temporary cease-fire, and vowed to renounce violence if the other militant Tamil groups did likewise. It also launched the People's Front of Liberation Tigers (PFLT) as a "democratic socialist" political party. However, fighting was reported at year's end between the LTTE and the EPRLF, the Tigers' primary opposition in the struggle for Tamil dominance. Completion of the Indian withdrawal in March 1990 left the LTTE in virtual control in the north. Amid periodic hostilities and an ongoing LTTE terrorist campaign against civilian targets, various peace initiatives in the 1990s failed to yield a durable settlement. The government consistently rejected LTTE demands for third-party mediation of the conflict.

In January 1998, in response to the bombing of the country's holiest Buddhist shrine in Kandy, the government officially banned the LTTE. In November the High Court ruled that party members could be tried in absentia on charges related to the January 1996 Colombo financial center bombing that killed nearly 100 and injured another 1,400. Near the end of the year, for the second time since 1995, the LTTE reportedly responded to a revolt in its ranks with a crackdown against dissident troops.

A major LTTE offensive begun in November 1999 continued into 2000, reversing many of the losses suffered in the preceding 18 months and threatening government control of Jaffna. Meanwhile, a series of LTTE-sponsored assassinations and suicide bombings continued unabated. The targets included leaders of the government-supportive Tamil parties as well as President Kumaratunga, who narrowly escaped assassination in December 1999. In the two years following the January 1998 local elections in the north, the LTTE killed at least 25 councilors.

In March–April 2000 the LTTE appeared to be inching closer to talks with the government, with Norway to serve as mediator, although the Kumaratunga administration steadfastly rejected an LTTE demand that government forces be confined to barracks during any such negotiations. A breakthrough finally occurred in the wake of the December 2001 parliamentary election, and in February 2002 the LTTE and the new UNP-led government concluded an indefinite cease-fire agreement, with formal negotiations then opening in September. In April 2003, after four additional rounds of negotiations, the LTTE called a halt to the peace process, citing lack of progress with regard to autonomy, rehabilitation, and reconstruction.

On October 31, 2003, the LTTE published its proposal for an Interim Self-Governing Authority (ISGA) for the northeast. The plan called for Tamils to exert complete control over the region for five years, after which an election would be held.

The most significant challenge to the LTTE leadership of Velupillai Prabhakaran was launched in March 2004 by the commander of forces in the east, Colonel Karuna, who led an estimated 6,000 troops (out of the LTTE's total of 15,000) in a revolt against northern domination. The rebellion was largely suppressed in April, however, and Karuna went underground. In October he announced formation of the Tamil People's Liberation Party (TMVP, below). By early 2005 his forces were again challenging the LTTE, which accused the Sri Lanka Army and Karuna of cooperating in a "secret war" against the LTTE.

The LTTE and the Rajapakse government met in February 2006 in Switzerland to discuss increasingly frequent cease-fire violations, but the severity of the clashes continued to escalate. Talks scheduled for April were canceled, and in May the EU labeled the LTTE a terrorist organization, threatening its main fund-raising activities. (In 2007 the United States, France, and the United Kingdom all arrested LTTE representatives for criminal fundraising.) An attempt to renew peace talks in October 2006 proved unsuccessful. In December the LTTE's chief negotiator, Anton BALASINGHAM, died in London of cancer.

On March 26, 2007, the LTTE, using one or two light aircraft, conducted its first air attack, but the additional capability did nothing to halt the Sri Lankan army's progress. By mid-July the army had claimed control in the east and continued on the offensive in the north. On November 2 the LTTE's political leader, S. P. THAMISELVAN, was killed in an air attack.

A new government offensive begun in January 2008 reduced the amount of territory under the control of LTTE from about 15,000 square kilometers to 4,000 square kilometers. However, Prabhakaran pledged not to negotiate with the government but to continue LTTE's armed struggle. Into 2009 government forces continued to advance, and Prabhakaran and other senior LTTE leaders were killed in fighting in May as the last rebel stronghold was captured by security forces. Although organized military resistance ceased, an estimated 5,000–7,000 fighters continued to wage a guerilla campaign against the government and progovernment Tamil groups. Selvarasa Pathmanathan was named as Prabhakaran's replacement in July by the LTTE's central committee, but the new leader was captured by authorities on August 5.

Leader: Selvarasa PATHMANATHAN.

Eelam National Democratic Liberation Front (ENDLF). Initially a strong ally of the EPRLF and a supporter of the India–Sri Lanka Accord of 1987, the ENDLF filled 13 uncontested seats from the north in the creation of the North-East Provincial Council in November 1988. Since the withdrawal of Indian troops from Sri Lanka, the ENDLF has operated primarily in India. In October 2004, however, it announced formation of the **Tamil Eelam United Liberation Front** (*Tamileela Iykkiya Viduthalai Munnani*—TIVM) with the TMVP, the new party of ex-LTTE commander Karuna. In 2008 ENDLF leader G. Gnanasekaran called for military intervention by India to end the conflict between the government and the LTTE and to protect the Tamil minority.

Leaders: G. GNANASEKARAN, Parathan RAJAN (TIVM Coleader), R. RAJARATTINAM (General Secretary).

Eelavar Democratic Front (EDF). The EDF emerged in 1988 from reorganization of the Eelam Revolutionary Organization of Students (EROS, but also known as the Eelam Revolutionary Organization), which had been organized in London in the mid-1970s. Although not legally registered, the EDF presented a slate of independent candidates (with the reported tacit approval of the LTTE) in the February 1989 parliamentary balloting, securing 13 seats and becoming the third largest legislative block. EDF representatives boycotted subsequent parliamentary sessions, calling for repudiation of the 1987 India–Sri Lanka Accord, immediate withdrawal of Indian troops, and the release of all Tamil prisoners. Two of its parliamentary members resigned their seats in early 1990, while the remaining 11 followed suit in July, saying they did "not want to be dormant spectators who witness the torment of our people." The EDF has contested a number of subsequent elections without notable success. It did not present a slate of candidates for the 2004 general election.

In mid-2007 the EROS reemerged as the **Eelam Revolutionary Organization** under the leadership of Nesan Shankar Raji (son of an original EROS founder), who described the revived EROS as a democratic Tamil front committed to a federal secular state. The EDF participated in regional and local balloting in 2008, but its candidates faced attacks and intimidation from other Tamil groups, and two were killed.

Leaders: Nesan Shankar RAJI (Nesan THIRUNESAN), Rajanathan PRABAHARAN (Secretary General).

People's Liberation Organization of Tamil Eelam (PLOTE). The PLOTE was the most important of the separatist groups not involved in the May 1985 coalition (see LTTE, above). Attempts were made on the lives of a number of its leaders in Madras in March 1985, apparently by the LTTE, which severely curtailed PLOTE rebel activity in 1986. PLOTE General Secretary Uma WAHESWARAN, who along with other PLOTE members had been implicated in an attempted coup in the Maldives in late 1988, was reportedly assassinated in Colombo in July 1989.

Since 1988 the PLOTE's political wing has been the **Democratic People's Liberation Front** (DPLF), which won three parliamentary seats in 1994 and extended its support to the PA (even though the leader of a progovernment faction, N. S. K. Uma PRAKASH, had been assassinated early in the year). The DPLF's vice president, Karavai KANDASAMY, was assassinated in December 1994.

Like the TULF, the EPDP, and the TELO, the DPLF chose to contest the January 1998 local elections in Jaffna, but it won control only of two urban and two village councils. The PLOTE, running under its own banner, had even less success, achieving no majorities. In September 1999 the PLOTE military commander, Thasan MANIKKADASAN, and a deputy were killed by a suspected LTTE suicide bomber. The party backed President Kumaratunga's reelection two months later.

In the December 2001 general election the DPLF won under 0.2 percent of the vote but one seat in parliament. It failed to hold the seat in 2004, attracting less than 0.1 percent of the vote. In 2008 it joined with other Tamil parties to form the Tamil Democratic National Alliance in regional balloting. In June 2009 the PLOTE joined discussions with the TNA in developing a common platform on Tamil issues.

Leaders: Dharmalingam SIDDHARTHAN (President), S. SATHANANTHAN (DPLF).

LEGISLATURE

Under the 1978 constitution the National State Assembly was redesignated as the **Parliament.** In December 1982 the life of the existing parliament was extended by referendum for an additional six years to August 1989 (although dissolution was decreed on December 20, 1988). The current 225-member body serves a six-year term, subject to dissolution.

In the early election of April 2, 2004, 196 members were chosen by proportional representation at the district level, while 29 members were elected on the basis of nationwide vote totals. Following the balloting, the United People's Freedom Alliance held 105 seats (92 district, 13 national); the United National Front, 82 (71, 11); the Tamil National Alliance, 22 (20, 2); the National Heritage Party, 9 (7, 2); the Sri Lanka Muslim Congress, 5 (4, 1); the Up-Country People's Front, 1 (1, 0); the Eelam People's Democratic Party, 1 (1, 0).

Speaker: W. J. M. LOKKUBANDARA.

CABINET

[as of September 1, 2009]

Prime Minister	Ratnasiri Wickremanayake
Ministers	
Agricultural Development and Agrarian Services Development	Maithripala Sirisena
Child Development and Women's Empowerment	Sumedha Jayasena [f]
Community Development and Social Inequity Eradication	P. Chandresekeran (UCPF)
Constitutional Affairs	D. E. W. Gunasekera (SLCP)
Construction and Engineering Services	Rajitha Senaratne (UNP)
Cultural Affairs	Mahinda Yapa Abeywardena
Defense, Public Security, and Law and Order	Mahinda Rajapakse
Disaster Management and Human Rights	Mahinda Samarasinghe (UNP)
Education	Susil Premajayanth
Enterprise Development and Investment Promotion	Anura Priyadharsana Yapa
Environment and Natural Resources	Patali Champika Ranawaka (JHU)
Export Development and International Trade	G. L. Peiris (UNP)
Finance and Planning	Mahinda Rajapakse
Fisheries and Aquatic Resources	Felix Perera
Foreign Affairs	Rohotha Bogollagama (UNP)
Foreign Employment and Welfare	Keheliya Rambukwelle (UNP)
Healthcare and Nutrition	Nimal Siripala de Silva
Higher Education	Wiswa Warnapala
Highways and Road Development	Mahinda Rajapakse
Housing and Construction Industry	Ferial Ashraff (NUA) [f]
Indigenous Medicine	Tissa Karaliyadde
Industrial Development	Kumara Welgama
Internal Administration	Ratnasiri Wickremanayake
Irrigation and Water Management	Chamal Rajapakse
Justice and Law Reforms	Milinda Moragoda (UNP)
Labor Relations and Manpower	Athauda Seneviratne
Land and Land Development	Jeewan Kumaratunga
Livestock Development	C. B. Rathnayake
Local Government and Provincial Councils	Janaka Bandara Tennakoon
Mass Media and Information	Mahinda Rajapakse
National Reconciliation and Integration	Vinayagamoorthy Muralidharan (Col. Karuna)
Parliamentary Affairs	M. H. Mohamed (UNP)
Petroleum and Petroleum Resource Development	A. H. M. Fowzie
Plan Implementation	P. Dayaratne (UNP)
Plantation Industries	D. M. Jayaratne
Ports and Aviation	Chamal Rajapakse
Posts and Telecommunication	Mahinda Wijesekera (UNP)
Power and Energy	John Seneviratne
Public Administration and Home Affairs	Sarath Amunugama
Public Estate Management and Development	Milroy Fernando
Religious Affairs and Moral Upliftment	Mahinda Rajapakse
Resettlement and Disaster Relief Services	Abdul Risath Bathiyutheen (UNP)
Rural Industries and Self-Employment Promotion	S. B. Nawinne
Science and Technology	Tissa Vitharana (LSSP)
Social Services and Social Welfare	Douglas Devananda (EPDP)
Special Projects	Mahinda Wijesekera (UNP)
Sports and Public Recreation	Gamini Lokuge (UNP)
Supplementary Crops Development	R. M. Dharmadasa Banda (UNP)
Tourism	Nandana Gunathilaka (NFF)
Trade, Marketing Development, Cooperatives, and Consumer Affairs	Bandula Gunawardena (UNP)
Transport	Dullas Alahapperuma
Urban Development and Sacred Area Development	Dinesh Gunawardena (MEP)
Vocational and Technical Training	Piyasena Gamage
Water Supply and Drainage	A. L. M. Athaullah (NC)
Youth Affairs	Pavithra Wanniarachchi [f]
Youth Empowerment and Socioeconomic Development	Arumugam Thondaman (CWC)

[f] = female

Note: Except as noted, ministers are affiliated with the UPFA. Those identified as UNP members belonged to that party at the time they joined the cabinet.

COMMUNICATIONS

The 1978 constitution guarantees free speech and publication, but these and other rights are "subject to such restrictions as may be presented by law." Justifications have included maintaining racial and religious harmony, national security, and public order and welfare. As a consequence, varying degrees of censorship and other forms of media control often prevail. In particular, the government has periodically banned news coverage of military operations against the Tamil Tigers and in 2009 warned foreign journalists that they would be expelled if they demonstrated "bias" toward the LTTE.

From 2006 to 2009 both international media organizations and human rights groups expressed concern over the deaths of at least 14 media personnel, particularly Tamils. The media watchdog group Reporters Without Borders charged that half a dozen killings in 2006 had occurred with "total impunity" and in 2008 ranked Sri Lanka 165 out of 173 countries in terms of freedom of the press. In January 2009 Lasantha Wickrematunga, the editor of the independent *The Sunday Leader,* was assassinated. Colleagues published a posthumous editorial written by the journalist in which he predicted his death and blamed the government. In February the BBC stopped providing its radio service to the Sri Lankan national broadcaster in response to continuing censorship.

Press. The leading publishing groups are the government-owned Associated Newspapers of Ceylon Ltd., which was nationalized in 1973; the privately held Upali Newspapers Ltd.; and the private Wijeya Newspapers Ltd. The last two have close connections to the two leading political parties. Sri Lankan newspapers do not typically reveal their circulation figures, and those given below are estimates.

The following are Sinhalese dailies published in Colombo, unless otherwise noted: *Silumina* (260,000), weekly; *Lankadeepa* (140,000 daily, 325,000 Sunday, published as *Irida Lankadeepa*), in Sinhala and English; *Divaina* (130,000 daily, 310,000 Sunday, published as *Divaina Irida Sangrahaya*); *Sunday Times* (100,000), weekly, in English and Sinhala; *Daily News* (75,000), government owned, in English; *Dinamina* (60,000), government owned; *The Island* (50,000 daily, 40,000 Sunday), in English; *Virakesari* (50,000 daily, 70,000 Sunday, published as *Virakesari Vara Veliyeedu*), in Tamil; *Observer* (19,000 daily, 90,000 Sunday), in English.

News agencies. The principal domestic facility is the National News Agency of Sri Lanka (*Lankapuvath*); TamilNet provides domestic and international coverage of Tamil affairs. A number of foreign bureaus maintain offices in Colombo.

Broadcasting and computing. The public Sri Lanka Broadcasting Corporation (SLBC) dominates radio services, although private broadcasting is permitted. The Sri Lanka Rupavahini Corporation (SLRC) provides daily telecasts, as do half a dozen private channels and the state-run Independent Television Network.

As of 2008 there were 58 Internet users per 1,000 inhabitants.

INTERGOVERNMENTAL REPRESENTATION

Ambassador to the U.S.: Jaliya WICKRAMASURIYA.

U.S. Ambassador to Sri Lanka: Patricia A. BUTENIS.

Permanent Representative to the UN: Palitha T.B. KOHONA.

IGO Memberships (Non-UN): ADB, CWTH, Interpol, IOM, IOR-ARC, NAM, PCA, SAARC, WCO, WTO.

SUDAN

Republic of the Sudan
al-Jumhuriya al-Sudan

Political Status: Independent republic established in 1956; revolutionary military regime instituted in 1969; one-party system established in 1971; constitution of May 8, 1973, suspended following military coup of April 6, 1985; military regime reinstituted on June 30, 1989; ruling military council dissolved and nominal civilian government reinstated on October 16, 1993; nonparty presidential and legislative elections held on March 6–17, 1996; new constitution providing for limited multiparty system signed into law on June 30, 1998; peace agreement signed between the government of Sudan and the Sudanese People's Liberation Movement on January 9, 2005, effectively ending a civil war between the north and the south; six-year power-sharing period initiated on July 9, 2005, with the signing of an interim constitution; peace agreement signed on October 14, 2006, between the government of Sudan and the Eastern Front, effectively ending the rebellion by eastern rebel groups.

Area: 967,494 sq. mi. (2,505,813 sq. km.).

Population: 24,940,683 (1993C); 39,432,000 (2008E). The 1993 figure does not include an adjustment for underenumeration.

Major Urban Centers (Population in 2000 based on the 1993 Census): KHARTOUM (925,000), Omdurman (229,000), Port Sudan (305,000), Kassala (234,000), El Obeid (228,000), Wad Medani (219,000), Gedaref (189,000), Juba (115,000).

Official Language: Arabic (English has been designated the "principal" language in the southern region).

Monetary Unit: Sudanese Pound (market rate December 1, 2009: 2.31 pounds = $1US). The Sudanese pound was introduced in 2007 to replace the dinar, the official currency since 1992, at a rate of 1 pound = 100 dinars.

President and Prime Minister: Umar Hassan Ahmad al-BASHIR (National Congress); installed as chair of the Revolutionary Command Council for National Salvation (RCC) following overthrow of the government of Prime Minister Sadiq al-MAHDI (Umma Party) on June 30, 1989, succeeding the former chair of the Supreme Council, Ahmad al-MIRGHANI (Democratic Unionist Party); assumed title of prime minister upon formation of government of July 9, 1989; named president by the RCC on October 16, 1993; elected to a five-year term as president in nonparty multicandidate balloting on March 6–17, 1996, and inaugurated on April 1; formed new government on April 21, 1996; reelected on December 13–20, 2000, and inaugurated for a second five-year presidential term on February 13, 2001; formed new government on February 23, 2001.

First Vice President: Salva KIIR Mayardit (Sudan People's Liberation Movement); appointed on August 11, 2005, to succeed John GARANG (Sudan People's Liberation Movement), who died in a helicopter crash on July 30, 2005.

Second Vice President: Ali Uthman Muhammad TAHA (National Congress) appointed on February 17, 1998, to succeed Maj. Gen. al-Zubayr Muhammad SALIH, who died in a plane crash on February 12, 1998.

THE COUNTRY

The largest country in Africa, Sudan borders on nine neighboring states as well as the Red Sea and forms part of the transitional zone between the continent's largely desert north and its densely forested, subtropical south. The White Nile flows north for almost 2,500 miles, from the Ugandan border, past the river's union with the Blue Nile near Khartoum, to Egypt above Aswan. Approximately 70 percent of the population is Arab and/or Muslim and occupies the northern two-thirds of the country, while the largely black south is a mix of Christian and animist. The geographic, ethnic, and religious cleavages have yielded political discord marked by prolonged periods of southern rebellion.

The economy is predominantly agricultural, although only a small part of the arable land is cultivated. Cotton is the most important cash crop, followed by gum arabic, of which Sudan produces four-fifths of the world supply. Other crops include sesame seeds, peanuts, castor beans, sorghum, wheat, and sugarcane. The country has major livestock-producing potential, and large numbers of camels and sheep are raised for export. Industry is largely limited to the processing of agricultural products and the manufacture of light consumer goods.

Sudan was plagued in the 1980s and 1990s by persistent drought and starvation, leading to the death of more than 200,000 people in 1985 and 1988. Fighting in the south impeded relief efforts and dislocated large segments of the population. In 1999 it was estimated that as many as 1.5 million Sudanese had died in the previous 16 years as the result of famine and war, while more than 2 million were in danger of starving as a result of the most recent drought. The situation was further exacerbated by a twofold refugee crisis: An estimated 1 million people, fleeing both the southern insurgency and drought conditions, sought refuge in Khartoum or in neighboring countries while, ironically, large numbers of civilians poured into Sudan to escape fighting in adjacent lands.

Economic distress resulted in more than $15 billion of external debt. The foreign aid, provided largely by the United States, West Germany, Britain, and Saudi Arabia, was decreased sharply in the 1990s due to Khartoum's human rights abuses and its failure to pursue democratization. The International Monetary Fund (IMF) in 1990 declared Sudan to be a "noncooperating" state, and Sudan's IMF voting rights were suspended in August 1993 because of an accumulation of arrears. However, in 1998 the IMF described Sudan as having made "substantial progress" in the implementation of economic reform and austerity measures, although these had prompted antiregime protests while failing to curb the estimated 100 percent annual rate of inflation. In August 1999 the IMF lifted its Declaration of Noncooperation from Sudan. Nevertheless, the civil war continued to drain resources in all regions and create instability. The fighting in Darfur compounded the instability, starting in early 2003, with an estimated 113,000 villagers fleeing to Chad by January 2004 and a death toll leading U.S. officials to declare the killing a genocide (see Current issues, below).

By 2005 the economic outlook for Sudan had become more positive, owing primarily to higher revenues from oil and other sectors. In 2006 it was reported that oil production had doubled since 2004, due in part to new investments by Indian and Chinese energy firms. In 2006 oil growth was estimated at 11 percent and non-oil growth at 10 percent, and in 2007 both oil and non-oil growth declined to 10 percent and 8 percent, respectively. IMF analysts cautioned, however, that progress in resolving Sudan's $15 billion debt hinged on resolution of the Darfur crisis and successful implementation of the peace agreement with the Sudanese People's Liberation Movement (SPLM) as well as IMF adjustment policies and economic reforms. The economy continues to be hampered by ongoing conflict, with 18.7 percent of the

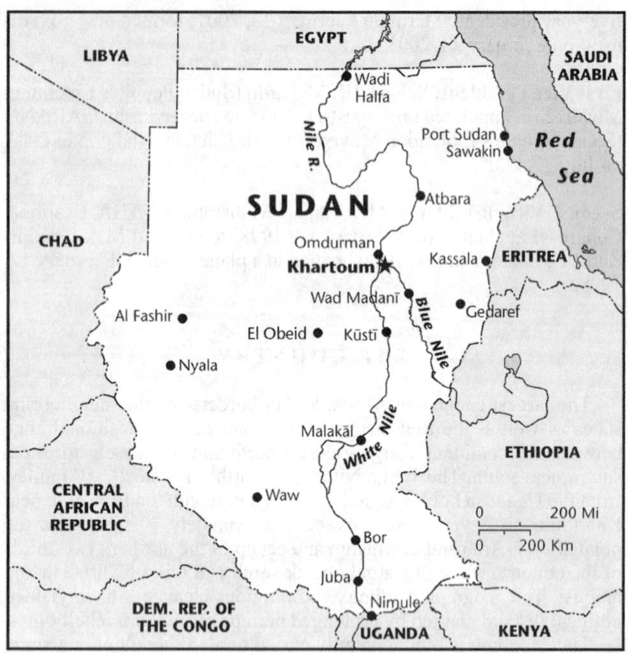

population unemployed and 40 percent below the poverty line. The government has pledged to create a Poverty Reduction Strategy Paper (PRSP) by the end of 2008.

Real GDP growth surpassed 9.5 percent in 2006 and 10 percent in 2007, yet debt estimates show an increase of external debt by $8 billion since 2000. Sudan's external debt has grown and totals just under $30 billion in 2008. The Sudanese government under the fiscal management of Awad al-JAZ issued a letter of intent to the IMF for debt servicing and macroeconomic fiscal management. In 2007 Sudan repaid $50.6 million to the IMF and made another payment of $50 million in 2008.

On January 8, 2007, as part of the Comprehensive Peace Agreement (CPA) mandate, the Central Bank of Sudan (CBS) introduced its new currency, the Sudanese pound, valued at US$2 = S£1. The pound replaced the dinar, which was seen, especially in the south, as a symbol of Islamization and Arabization. Sudan implemented a number of tax reforms, including reducing the number of tax holidays in 2008. For the year, GDP growth slowed to a still respectable 8.5 percent as international fuel prices declined. Rising food costs led inflation to rise to 14 percent. In its 2007/2008 Human Development Index, the UN ranked Sudan 147 out of 177 countries.

GOVERNMENT AND POLITICS

Political background. Historically known as the land of Kush, Sudan was conquered and unified by Egypt in 1820–1821. Under the leadership of Muhammad Ahmad, the MAHDI ("awaited religious leader"), opposition to Egyptian administration broke into open revolt in 1881; the insurrection had succeeded by 1885, and the Mahdist state controlled the region until its reconquest by an Anglo-Egyptian force in 1896–1898. Thereafter, Sudan was governed by an Anglo-Egyptian condominium, becoming self-governing in 1954 and fully independent on January 1, 1956, under a transitional constitution that provided for a democratic parliamentary regime. A civilian government, led successively by Ismail al-AZHARI and Abdallah KHALIL, was overthrown in November 1958 by Lt. Gen. Ibrahim ABBUD, whose military regime was itself dislodged following protest demonstrations in October and November 1964. The restored constitutional regime, headed in turn by Sir al-Khatim KHALIFA, Muhammad Ahmad MAHGUB, and Dr. Sadiq al-MAHDI (a descendant of the 19th century religious leader), was weakened both by political party instability and by revolt in the southern provinces.

Beginning in 1955 as a protest against Arab-Muslim domination, the southern insurgency rapidly assumed the proportions of a civil war. Led by the *Anyanya* (scorpion) movement under the command of Joseph LAGU, the revolt prompted military reprisals and the flight of thousands of refugees to neighboring countries. While moderate southern parties continued to seek regional autonomy within the framework of a united Sudan, exile groups worked for complete independence, and a so-called Provisional Government of Southern Sudan was established in January 1967 under the leadership of Agrev JADEN, a prominent exile leader.

The stability of the new Mahgub government was interrupted in May 1969 by a military coup organized by a group of nationalist, left-wing officers led by Col. Jafar Muhammad NUMAYRI. In response to Numayri's ten-man Revolutionary Council, a former chief justice, Abu-Bakr AWADALLA, formed a civilian administration of communists and extreme leftists. Revolutionary activity continued, however, including successive communist attempts in 1969 and 1971 to overthrow the Numayri regime. The latter effort succeeded for three days, after which Numayri regained power with Egyptian and Libyan help and instituted reprisals that included the execution of Abd al-Khaliq MAHGUB, the Communist Party's secretary general.

Subsequent to a temporary constitution in August 1971, Numayri was elected to the presidency in September. A month later, in an effort to consolidate his position, Numayri dissolved the Revolutionary Council and established the Sudanese Socialist Union (SSU) as the only recognized political party. Of equal significance was the ratification in April 1973 of a negotiated settlement that temporarily brought the southern rebellion to an end. The terms of the agreement, which provided for an autonomous Southern Sudan, were included in a new national constitution that became effective May 8, 1973. In November the Southern Region voted for a Regional People's Assembly, while the first national election under the new basic law took place in May 1974 for a 250-member National People's Assembly.

In September 1975 rebel army personnel led by a paratroop officer, Lt. Col. Hassan Husayn USMAN, seized the government radio station in Omdurman in an attempted coup. President Numayri subsequently blamed Libya for instigating the uprising, which was quickly suppressed. The attack had been preceded by an army mutiny in Akobo on the Ethiopian border in March and was followed by an uprising in Khartoum in July 1976 that reportedly claimed 300 lives. At a news conference in London on August 4, former prime minister Mahdi, on behalf of the outlawed Sudanese National Front (SNF), a coalition of former centrist and rightist parties that had been organized in late 1969, accepted responsibility for having organized the July rebellion but denied that it had involved foreign mercenaries. President Numayri attempted to accommodate the dissidents. In July 1977 a number of SNF leaders, including Dr. Mahdi, returned from abroad and were immediately appointed to the Central Committee of the SSU. A year later the Rev. Philip Abbas GHABUSH, titular president of the SNF, expressed his conviction that the government was committed to the building of "a genuine democracy in Sudan" and ordered the dissolution of both the internal and external wings of the Front.

In early 1980 the north was divided into five new regions to provide for more effective local self-government, and in October 1981 the president dissolved the National Assembly and the Southern Regional Assembly to decentralize legislative power to new regional bodies. He appointed Gen. Gasmallah Abdallah RASSA, a southern Muslim, as interim president of the Southern Region's High Executive Council (HEC) in place of Abel ALIER, who continued as second vice president of the republic. Immediately thereafter a plan was advanced to divide the south into three regions based on the historic provinces of Bahr al-Ghazal, Equatoria, and Upper Nile.

The projected redivision of the south yielded three regional blocs: a "unity" group led by Vice President Alier of the numerically dominant Dinka tribe, who branded the scheme a repudiation of the 1973 agreement; a "divisionist" group led by former rebel commander Joseph Lagu of the Wahdi tribe of eastern Equatoria; and a "compromise" group, led by Clement MBORO and Samuel ARU Bol, which styled itself "Change Two" (C2) after an earlier "Wind for Change Alliance" that had opposed Alier's election to the HEC presidency. None of the three obtained a majority in an April 1982 election to the Southern Regional Assembly, and on June 23 a divisionist, Joseph James TOMBURA, was designated by the assembly as regional president with C2 backing (the alliance being styled "C3"). Six days later President Numayri named General Lagu to succeed Alier as second vice president of the republic. Earlier, on April 11, Maj. Gen. Umar Muhammad al-TAYYIB (who had been designated third vice president in October 1981) was named to the first vice presidency in succession to Lt. Gen. Abd al-Majid Hamid KHALIL, who had been dismissed on January 25.

As expected, President Numayri was nominated for a third term by an SSU congress in February 1983 and reelected by a national plebiscite held April 15–26. In June 1983 the tripartite division of the south was formally implemented, with both the HEC and the southern assembly being abolished.

In the face of renewed rebellion in the south and rapidly deteriorating economic conditions, which prompted food riots and the launching of a general strike in Khartoum, a group of army officers, led by Gen. Abd al-Rahman SIWAR al-DAHAB, seized power on April 6, 1985, while the president was returning from the United States. Numayri's ouster was attributed in part to opposition by southerners and some urban northerners and to the adoption of Islamic religious law (sharia) in September 1983.

On April 9, 1985, after inconclusive discussions between a civilian National Alliance for the Salvation of the Country (NASC), General Siwar al-Dahab formed a 14-member Transitional Military Council (TMC), with himself as chair and Gen. Taq al-Din Abdallah FADUL as his deputy. After further consultation with NASC leaders, Dr. al-Gizouli DAFALLAH, who had played a prominent role in organizing the pre-coup demonstrations, was named head of an interim Council of Ministers on April 22. On May 25 a seven-member southern cabinet that included representatives of the three historic areas (henceforth to be known as "administrative regions") was appointed. Concurrently, the Sudanese People's Liberation Army (SPLA), which had become the primary rebel force in the south under the leadership of Col. John GARANG, resumed antigovernment military activity.

Adhering to its promise to hold a national election within a year, the TMC sponsored legislative balloting on April 1–12, 1986, despite continued insurgent activity that precluded polling in 41 southern districts. The new body, serving as both a Constituent and Legislative Assembly, convened on April 26 but disagreed on the composition of a Supreme (Presidential) Council and the designation of a prime minister until May 6, with a coalition government being formed under former prime minister Mahdi of the Umma Party (UP) on May 15. The UP's principal partner was the Democratic Unionist Party (DUP), which had finished second in the assembly balloting. Although several southern parties were awarded cabinet posts, most "African bloc" deputies boycotted assembly activity because of alleged lack of representation and unsatisfactory progress towards repealing sharia.

The Council of Ministers was dissolved on May 13, 1987, primarily because of a split within the DUP that weakened the government's capacity to implement policy. A new government was formed on June 3 with little change in personnel. On August 22, while cooperating with the UP, the DUP formally withdrew from the coalition because of a dispute over an appointment to the Supreme Council. Eight months later the DUP rejected a proposal by Mahdi to form a more broadly based administration that would include the opposition National Islamic Front (NIF). Undaunted, the prime minister resigned on April 16, 1988, to make way for a government of "national reconciliation." Reappointed on April 27, he issued an appeal for all of the parties to join in a proposed national constitutional conference to decide the role of Islam in a future state structure. Mahdi formed a new administration that included the DUP and NIF on May 14. In July 1988 the DUP joined the fundamentalists in calling for a legislative vote on the introduction of sharia prior to the constitutional conference. On September 19, following the government's introduction of a sharia-based penal code, the southern deputies withdrew from the assembly. In mid-November, purportedly with the prime minister's approval, DUP representatives met with SPLA leader Garang in the Ethiopian capital of Addis Ababa to negotiate a peace treaty that entailed abandoning sharia legislation, lifting the state of emergency, and convening of a national constitutional conference. However, rioting subsequently broke out in Khartoum, and on December 20, in the wake of a reported coup attempt and suspension of parliamentary debate on policy toward the south, Prime Minister Mahdi declared another state of emergency. On December 28 the DUP withdrew from the government in response to Mahdi's failure to recognize the agreement with the SPLA, the DUP ministerial posts being refilled by NIF representatives. On February 27, 1989, after another cabinet reshuffle in which the DUP did not participate, Mahdi threatened to resign if the army refused him the latitude to negotiate peace with the rebels. On March 5 some 48 parties and trade unions indicated their general acceptance of the November peace accord, and on March 22 a new governing coalition was announced composed of the UP, the DUP, and representatives of the unions and southern parties, with the NIF in opposition.

In May 1989, complaining that Khartoum had "done absolutely nothing" to advance peace, Colonel Garang announced a cease-fire in the south. A month later he met with northern representatives in Addis Ababa for peace talks mediated by former U.S. president Jimmy Carter. Shortly thereafter, Khartoum agreed to implement the November 1988 accords and schedule a September constitutional conference. The plan was nullified on June 30, when the Madhi regime was overthrown by a military coup led by Brig. Gen. Umar Hassan Ahmad al-BASHIR, who assumed the chair of a Revolution Command Council for National Salvation (RCC) and ultimately rejected the November 1988 treaty. The RCC immediately suspended the constitution, dissolved the Constituent Assembly, imposed emergency rule, and freed military leaders arrested on June 18 for allegedly plotting an earlier coup. Claiming that factionalism and corruption had led to economic malaise and an ineffective war effort, the military regime banned all political parties and arrested senior government and party leaders. On July 9 Bashir assumed the additional office of prime minister, heading a 21-member cabinet composed primarily of career bureaucrats drawn from the NIF and supporters of former president Numayri.

Despite claims that "peace through negotiation" was its first priority, the new government rejected the November 1988 treaty, suggesting instead that the sharia issue be decided by national referendum. However, the SPLA, which sought suspension of sharia while negotiations continued, resumed military activities in October.

A major cabinet reshuffle on April 10, 1990, was viewed as a consolidation of Islamic fundamentalist influence, and on April 24 a total of 31 army and police officers were executed in the wake of an alleged coup attempt the day before. Another reshuffle in January 1991 was followed by the introduction of a nine-state federal system (see Constitution and government, below), and on March 22 a new sharia-based penal code was instituted in the six northern states, prompting a strong protest from the SPLA.

In the wake of heavy fighting between his supporters and several SPLA breakaway factions in the south, Garang announced a unilateral cease-fire in late March 1993 in the conflict with government troops. Khartoum endorsed the cease-fire several days later, and peace talks with Garang representatives resumed in Abuja in late April. The government also initiated parallel negotiations in Nairobi, Kenya, with the SPLA dissidents, who had recently coalesced as the SPLA-United. However, both sets of talks were subsequently suspended when fighting between government forces and Garang's SPLA faction resumed near the Ugandan border by midyear.

On July 8, 1993, Prime Minister Bashir announced a cabinet reshuffle that was described as an "overt increase in NIF involvement." Subsequently, in a surprise, albeit essentially cosmetic, return to civilian control, the RCC dissolved itself on October 16 after declaring Bashir president and granting him wide authority to direct a transitional government. Bashir announced his administration's commitment to an undefined democratization program that would lead to national elections by the end of 1995. Nevertheless, the new cabinet, announced on October 30, appeared to further solidify NIF control and support the opposition's charges that the military-fundamentalist alliance had no true intention of loosening its stranglehold on political power.

In September 1993 the Inter-Governmental Authority on Drought and Development (IGADD, later the Inter-Governmental Authority on Development—IGAD), composed of representatives from Ethiopia, Eritrea, Kenya, and Uganda was established to mediate the Sudanese conflict. However, the talks ended in deadlock in late 1994 after the two sides had "adopted irreconcilable positions on southern self-determination and the relationship between state and religion."

On March 27, 1995, Bashir announced a unilateral two-month cease-fire to facilitate another peace initiative launched by former U.S. president Jimmy Carter. While the leading southern factions cautiously supported the truce, no progress was reported in resolving the conflict, despite a two-month extension of the cease-fire on May 25.

Widespread rioting broke out in several locations, including Khartoum and Port Sudan, in September 1995, bolstering observations of a weakened northern regime. The outbreaks, which appeared to be spontaneous, involved both student protesters and conservative elements angered by low salaries and food shortages. Further violence erupted in Khartoum in early January 1996 between police and Muslim fundamentalists calling for conversion of the country's Christians and animists to Islam.

In January 1996 the regime announced that elections would be held in March for president and a new National Assembly. However, that balloting (conducted March 6–17) was boycotted by nearly all the major opposition groups, most of whom had coalesced under the banner of the National Democratic Alliance (NDA). Some 40 independent candidates contested the presidential balloting, with Bashir being elected to a five-year term on the strength of a reported 75.7 percent share of the vote. Bashir was sworn in on April 1, and on the same day the new assembly convened and unanimously elected the NIF's Hassan Abdallah al-TURABI (long considered the dominant political leader in the country) as its president. On April 21 Bashir appointed a new cabinet, which excluded the signatories of a recent peace accord, the SPLA-United and the Southern Sudan Independence Movement (SSIM).

In January 1997 a major rebel offensive was reportedly launched by a more cohesive and potent NDA. In April the regime reached another agreement with the SSIM, the SPLA-United, and four SPLA breakaway groups, calling for suspension of sharia in the south and southern autonomy. With both the government and the SPLA claiming military success, IGAD proposed a "framework of principles" for a resumption of peace talks in July aimed to secure a self-determination plebiscite in the south. However, negotiations were quickly suspended until April 1998 and fighting continued.

Elections were held for ten southern gubernatorial posts in November 1997, and on December 1 the SSIM's Riak MACHAR was named head of a new Southern States' Coordination Council (SSCC) and given a four-year mandate to govern the south pending a decision on its permanent political status. However, the exercise was widely viewed as futile, considering Colonel Garang's depiction of the SSCC as a "sham."

A plane crash on February 12, 1998, killed First Vice President Maj. Gen. al-Zubayr Muhammad SALIH (one of the president's oldest and most trusted associates) and a number of other government officials. On March 8 Bashir finally settled on Ali Uthman Muhammad TAHA, considered second in authority in the NIF, to succeed Salih. In addition, the NIF had an enhanced presence in the extensively reshuffled cabinet, which also included dissident Umma members and representatives of southern rebels who had aligned with Khartoum.

In the face of heavy international pressure for political reform, the assembly, on March 28, 1998, approved the government's proposed new constitution, which authorized the legalization of political associations. The new basic law was endorsed by a reported 96.7 percent "yes" vote in a national referendum in late May and signed into law by President Bashir on June 30, 1998. On November 23 the assembly approved the Political Association Act, which established legal governance of party activity and registration of parties from January 1999.

As conflict rapidly escalated between Bashir and Turabi, Turabi proposed a series of constitutional amendments in November 1999 to curb Bashir's power. Bashir responded by announcing a three-month state of emergency and dissolving the National Assembly on December 12, 1999 (effective December 13). Bashir's declaration occurred a mere 48 hours prior to the scheduled National Assembly vote regarding Turabi's proposed amendments. The cabinet responded by formally issuing its resignation on January 1, 2000. Bashir appointed a new cabinet on January 25, retaining his backers in some ministry posts. The power struggle continued, however, because Turabi, while holding no official position, remained secretary general of the National Congress (NC), the successor to the NIF. Meanwhile, the government also was buffeted in February by the departure of Machar and his supporters due to the perceived failure of Bashir to implement the 1997 accord.

On March 12, 2000, the cabinet extended the state of emergency until the end of the year. Bashir consolidated power by removing Turabi as secretary general of the NC and replacing him with Ibrahim Ahmed OMAR.

Despite seemingly positive negotiations between the government and the UP (see UP under Political Parties and Groups, below), the UP led an opposition boycott of assembly and presidential elections on December 13–23, 2000. Consequently, the NC secured 355 of the 360 contested assembly seats, while Bashir was elected to a second five-year term with a reported 86.5 percent of the vote. (After returning from 14 years in exile in May 1999, former president Numayri, as the candidate of the Popular Working Forces Alliance, finished second with 9.6 percent of the vote in the presidential poll.) DUP dissidents were included in the new cabinet named on February 23, 2001, as were UP dissidents in the reshuffle of August 19, 2002. Two DUP dissidents were also among those named to the cabinet in a reshuffle on November 30, 2002.

Although elections were scheduled to occur in 2004, continued conflict between north and south and an unwillingness to relinquish power by the Bashir regime impeded the electoral process. In 2005 the peace agreement between north and south stipulated the occurrence of elections in 2009 and a southern referendum in 2011. Following the signing of the peace agreement in January 2005 between the government and the SPLM (see Current issues, below), a new 30-member power-sharing cabinet was announced on September 22, 2005. Fifteen posts went to the NC, 9 to the SPLM, and 6 to northern and southern opposition groups. On October 21, the first cabinet of the Government of South Sudan was appointed. The 22-member southern unity cabinet included 16 seats designated for the SPLM, 3 for the NC, and 3 for other south Sudan opposition groups. Conflict between the leadership of the SPLM and the NC resulted in a cabinet reshuffle in October 2007, with a number of new appointments (see Political Parties and Groups). In December the two parties reached an agreement that allowed the SPLM members to rejoin the cabinet.

There were minor cabinet reshuffles in February and May 2008. In September a more substantial rearrangement accompanied the dismissal of Pagan AMUM of the SPLM, who had been minister of cabinet affairs, following Amum's highly public criticism of the government and the NC.

On February 17, 2009, the government and JEM signed a preliminary agreement on several areas of cooperation and an eventual cease-fire. The accord was brokered by the UN, AU, Arab League, and Qatar. In March Bashir was indicted by the ICC for his role in Sudan's ethnic conflict (see Current issues, below). Following the expulsion of international aid groups in response to Bashir's indictment (see Foreign relations, below), the JEM suspended further talks with the government.

Constitution and government. The 1973 constitution provided for a strong presidential form of government. Nominated by the Sudanese Socialist Union for a six-year term, the president appointed all other executive officials and served as supreme commander of the People's Armed Forces. Legislative authority was vested in the National People's Assembly, a unicameral body that was partially elected and partially appointed.

The Southern Sudan Regional Constitution, abrogated by the June 1983 redivision, provided for a single autonomous region governed, in nonreserved areas, by the president of a High Executive Council (cabinet) responsible to a Regional People's Assembly. Each of the three subsequent regions in the south, like the five in the north, was administered by a centrally appointed governor, acting on the advice of a local People's Assembly. In a move that intensified southern dissent, President Numayri announced in June 1984 the incorporation into the north of a new province (*Wahdah*), encompassing territory theretofore part of the Upper Nile region, where oil reserves had been discovered.

Upon assuming power in 1985, the Transitional Military Committee (TMC) suspended the 1973 basic law, dissolved the central and regional assemblies, appointed a cabinet composed largely of civilians, and assigned military personnel to replace regional governors and their ministers. An interim constitution was approved by the TMC in October 1985 to provide a framework for assembly elections. The assembly members chosen in April 1986 were mandated to draft a new basic law, although many southern districts were unrepresented because of rebel activity. The assembly's charge to act as a constituent body appeared to have ceased with Prime Minister Mahdi's call in April 1988 for the convening of a national constitutional conference.

In January 1987 the government announced the formation of a new Administrative Council for the South, comprising representatives of six southern political parties and the governors of each of the three previously established regions. The council, although formally empowered with only "transitional" authority, was repudiated by both the "unity" and "divisionist" groups. Subsequently, following the signing of a pro-pluralism "Transitional Charter" on January 10, 1988, to serve as an interim basic law, the council was suspended, and the administration of the southern provinces was assigned to the regional governors.

During negotiations between the Mahdi regime and southern rebels in early June 1989, an agreement was reached to open a constitutional conference in September. However, the Bashir junta rejected the June agreement and suspended the Transitional Charter. Subsequently, a national "political orientation" conference, held April 29–May 2, 1991, in Khartoum, endorsed the establishment of a pyramidal governmental structure involving the direct popular election of local councils followed by the successive indirect election of provincial, state, and national lawmaking bodies. On February 13, 1992, Prime Minister Bashir appointed a 300-member Transitional National Assembly, and he was named president on October 16, 1993, by the RCC, which then dissolved itself. Elections were held on March 6–17, 1996, to a new National Assembly, with concurrent nonparty balloting for president.

On February 5, 1991, the RCC announced the establishment of a new federal system comprising nine states—six (Central, Darfur, Eastern, Khartoum, Kordofan, and Northern) in the north and three (Bahr al-Ghazal, Equatoria, and Upper Nile) in the south—that were subdivided into 66 provinces and 281 local government districts. The states, each administered by a federally appointed governor, deputy governor, and cabinet of ministers, were given responsibility for local administration and some tax collection, although control over most major sectors remained with the central government. In early February 1994 President Bashir announced that the number of states had been increased from 9 to 26, new governors being appointed later in the month. A Southern States Coordination Council was named in December 1997 to govern the south pending final determination of the region's status, but authority of the new body remained severely compromised by the opposition of the main rebel group, the SPLA. The 26 state administrative structure is still in use, though the southern state of Bahr al Jabal was renamed Central Equatoria in 2005 by the Government of Southern Sudan (GOSS).

On March 22, 1991, a new penal code based on sharia went into effect in the north, the government announcing that the issue would be "open" in regard to the south, pending the outcome of peace negotiations. The new constitution, which went into effect on June 30, 1998, annulled most previous decrees by the Bashir regime, thereby permitting the reintroduction of a multiparty system. The new basic law described Islam as "the religion of the majority," while noting the "considerable number of Christians and animists" in the country and guaranteeing freedom of religion. The controversial issue of sharia, particularly as it might apply to the south, was skirted, the constitution stating only that the "religion, customs, and consensus of the Nation shall be the sources of legislation."

Following the peace agreement reached on January 9, 2005, between the government and the SPLM, an interim constitution was signed on July 9, 2005, allowing for power sharing during a six-year transitional period. Whether the south would continue under Khartoum's rule was to be determined by a referendum in 2011. The south was given a large degree of autonomy, with Garang being named president of the south, as well as first vice president of Sudan. (Salva KIIR Mayardit replaced Garang as president of the south and first vice president of Sudan on August 11, 2005, following the latter's death on July 30.)

Subsequent peace agreements in 2006 and 2007 failed to staunch bloodletting in the remaining restive provinces, with rebel groups fearing government retaliation and responding skeptically to proposed solutions. In turn, the Sudanese government agreed in principle to arrangements while delaying implementation with disputes over logistics. In July 2007 the UN Security Council passed a resolution that included provisions for a joint AU-UN peacekeeping mission. Despite Khartoum's formal acceptance of the resolution, controversy over the size, troop competence, source countries, and command structure of the force delayed full deployment into 2008, while conflict continued unabated. However, in a gesture of cooperation, the government rescinded the old, "Islamist" currency, the dinar, in favor of the new Sudanese pound (see Current issues, below). The UN-AU mandate of operations in Sudan was scheduled to expire in June of 2008, but the ongoing conflict resulted in extensions of operations through April 2010.

In July 2009 the Permanent Court of Arbitration in the Netherlands granted control over most of the disputed oil-rich region of Abyei to the national government in Khartoum. The ruling was a defeat for the SPLM, which argued that the area should be part of the region included in the south's planned 2011 independence referendum.

Foreign relations. During much of the Cold War Sudan pursued a policy of nonalignment, modified in practice by changing international circumstances, while focusing its attention on regional matters. Prior to the 1974 coup in Ethiopia, relations with that country were especially cordial due to the prominent role Ethiopian Emperor Haile Selassie had played in bringing about a settlement in the initial southern rebellion. However, Addis Ababa later accused Khartoum of providing covert support to Eritrean rebels, while Sudanese leaders charged that SPLA camps were flourishing in Ethiopia with the approval of the Mengistu regime. Not surprisingly, relations between the two countries improved dramatically following the May 1991 rebel victory in Ethiopia; the presumed SPLA contingents were forced back into Sudan by Ethiopian troops and the Bashir regime became a vocal supporter of the new leadership in Addis Ababa. By contrast, the secular administration in Eritrea charged in early 1994 that Sudan was fomenting fundamentalist antigovernment activity in the new nation of Eritrea, and in December it severed relations with Khartoum. After a period of improved relations, recent tension arose over border demarcation disputes between Sudan, Ethiopia, and Eritrea, where Sudanese troops are occupying Ethiopian lands to the north. Relations have since improved, as the Eritrean government played a significant role in mediating a peace agreement between Khartoum and eastern rebel groups (see Current issues, below).

Soon after taking power in 1969 Prime Minister Numayri forged close ties with Egyptian president Gamal Abdel Nasser within a federation scheme encompassing Sudan, Egypt, and the newly established Libyan regime of Colonel Muammar Qadhafi. Although failing to promote integration, the federation yielded joint Egyptian-Libyan military support for Numayri in defeating the communist insurgency of June 1971. However, Numayri was reluctant to join a second unity scheme—the abortive 1972 Federation of Arab Republics—because of Libyan-inspired conspiracies and opposition from the non-Arab peoples of southern Sudan. President Sadat's own estrangement from Qadhafi during 1973 led to the signing of a Sudanese-Egyptian agreement on political and economic coordination in February 1974. In subsequent years Sadat pledged to support Numayri against continued Libyan attempts at subversion, and Sudan followed Egypt into close alignment with the United States. While rejecting the Egyptian-Israeli peace treaty of 1979, Sudan was one of the few Arab states that did not break diplomatically with Cairo. Egypt's main strategic interest in Sudan focuses on water supplied from the Nile River via Sudan, which is currently governed by a 1959 treaty granting Egypt generous access to the Nile. Cairo supports the Comprehensive Peace Agreement CPA (see Current issues, below) but remains ambivalent towards the prospect of southern autonomy, which would require renegotiation of the water treaty.

In October 1988 Prime Minister Mahdi, reportedly desperate for arms, signed a unity proposal with Colonel Qadhafi that was denounced by the DUP and in January 1989 labeled "inappropriate" by the United States following reports that Libyan forces had used chemical weapons in attacks on SPLA forces. Concurrently, Washington, whose nonintervention policy had drawn criticism from international aid groups, announced its intention to supply aid directly to drought victims in areas under SPLA control rather than through allegedly corrupt government channels. Four months later Washington cut off all nonfamine relief support because of Khartoum's failure to service its foreign debt, lack of democratic commitment, and human rights record. Later in the year relations with the United States deteriorated even further when Sudan refused to join the UN coalition against Iraq, a decision that also cost Sudan financial support from Saudi Arabia and Egypt. In addition, many Arab states subsequently expressed concern over the growing influence of Islamic fundamentalism under the Bashir regime. However, Iran, anxious to support the fundamentalist cause, funded Sudanese economic and, according to some reports, military aid.

In August 1994 authorities in Khartoum seized terrorist Ilich Ramírez Sanchez (a.k.a. "Carlos"), who was flown to Paris for trial on charges stemming from a 1983 attack in the French capital. In return, France was reported to have persuaded the Central African Republic (CAR) to provide Sudanese military transit through CAR territory. In addition, Khartoum sought French assistance in restoring its relations with the United States following unexpectedly low aid grants from Iran.

Meanwhile, relations with other neighboring states had deteriorated sharply. In September 1994 Egypt was accused of moving troops into Sudan's northern Halaib region, which was believed to contain substantial oil deposits, and relations deteriorated further in mid-1995 after President Mubarak had intimated that the NIF might have been involved in the failed attempt on his life in Addis Ababa on June 26. In the south, Uganda canceled a 1990 agreement providing for a military monitoring team on its side of their border, and in April 1995 it broke relations because of the alleged bombing of a Ugandan village by Sudanese government forces; however, relations were restored in mid-June as the result of talks between presidents Bashir and Museveni that were brokered by Malawian president Bakili Muluzi.

By late 1995 Sudan had come under widespread criticism for its alleged sponsorship of international terrorism, including possible involvement in the Mubarak assassination attempt. On December 19 foreign ministers of states belonging to the Organization of African Unity (OAU, subsequently the African Union—AU), met in Addis Ababa and called on Khartoum to extradite three Egyptians wanted for questioning in the Mubarak affair. On January 31, 1996, the UN Security Council instituted sanctions and adopted a unanimous resolution to the same effect. Earlier, as an expression of its displeasure, Ethiopia had ordered a reduction in Sudan's embassy staff to four, the closure of a Sudanese consulate, and a ban on nongovernmental organizations linked to the Sudanese regime.

In 1997 and early 1998, Eritrea, Ethiopia, and Uganda cooperated to restrict the spread of militant fundamentalism in the Horn of Africa, further straining relations with Sudan, which accused the other governments of supporting the SPLM and NDA. (Relations with Ethiopia subsequently improved, however, in conjunction with the outbreak of hostilities between that nation and Eritrea, which Khartoum charged was still backing Sudanese rebels.) Meanwhile, South African president Nelson MANDELA played a prominent role in efforts to bring the Bashir regime and its opponents together for peace talks under the aegis of IGAD.

Bashir's "charm offensive" improved regional and international relations in 1999 and 2000. Sudan reestablished diplomatic relations with the United Kingdom, Kuwait, Ethiopia, Eritrea, Egypt, and Tunisia, and later requested that the UN Security Council lift the 1996 sanctions. The Security Council unanimously approved the request in September 2001.

Throughout 2004 and early 2005, the international response to human rights abuses in Darfur materialized slowly (see Current issues, below). In April 2005 the UN Security Council voted to refer 51 Sudanese—many of them said to be high-ranking NIF officials—for International Criminal Court (ICC) prosecution for crimes against humanity in Darfur. That same month, Western countries pledged $4.5 billion in urgent food aid for southerners displaced by the civil war. In response to food shortages, the Arab Authority for Agriculture and the Abu Dhabi Fund for Development in 2008 worked in conjunction with the Sudanese government to develop a large-scale agricultural program to mitigate food insecurity in Sudan by providing 28,000 hectares of free land for crop production.

In response to continuing attacks on Uganda by the Lords Resistance Army (LRA) from bases in Sudan, the newly installed Government of South Sudan signed a security protocol with Uganda in October 2005 calling for joint efforts to suppress the LRA. Recent reports indicate that despite a December 1999 accord, violence continued to occur as the LRA accused Sudanese troops of attacks by their forces on the Congo border, preventing peace meetings.

Relations with Chad worsened in 2005 as Chadian rebels launched a series of attacks from bases in Sudan. By December 2005 Chadian president Idriss Déby described the two countries as being in a state of "belligerency." In April 2007 Chad severed diplomatic ties with Sudan after a rebel movement springing from Darfur attacked N'Djamena (see entry on Chad). Through 2008 rebel activity by both Chadian rebels and Darfur rebels continued on the Sudan-Darfur frontier. On March 13, 2008, the two governments signed a non-aggression accord in Dakar, Senegal, but the rebels dismissed the accord and continued armed activity.

As an economic and military partner, China has been Sudan's closest ally and has done the most to protect the regime from UN sanctions. China is Sudan's largest trade partner and the largest investor in Sudan's oil industry, with almost 68 percent of Sudan's total export portfolio and 60 percent of Sudan's oil exports accounted for by trade with China since 2004. China has also supplied the Sudanese government with small arms, anti-personnel mines, howitzers, tanks, helicopters, and ammunition, in addition to constructing three arms factories in Sudan, despite a UN-sanctioned arms embargo on the region. The government also ordered new fighter jets from China in late 2005.

In 2006 China placed limited pressure on Khartoum to relieve international criticism before the 2008 Beijing Olympic Games. China voted in favor of the October 2006 resolution for a UN force in Darfur and sent a special envoy to Sudan in May 2007 after meeting with Sudanese officials in March 2007. Nonetheless, China continued to affirm strong bilateral ties with Sudan, and Sudan offered political support as well as disaster relief after the earthquake that struck China in May of 2008. An NC delegation met with Chinese officials in July 2008 to promote the relationship. The October revelation that a hijacked freighter bound for South Sudan was carrying tanks and other weaponry with Kenyan licenses strained relations between Khartoum and Nairobi.

U.S. president George W. Bush authorized the transfer of vehicles and equipment for UNAMID in January 2009. In March Sudan expelled 13 international aid agencies in retaliation for the ICC indictment of Bashir (see Current issues, below). The agencies were allowed to return in June. Unidentified aerial forces attacked a Sudanese weapons convoy en route to Egypt. The attack was reportedly conducted by Israeli forces to prevent the arms and munitions from being smuggled into Gaza. Sudan and Chad signed an agreement to normalize relations on May 3, following negotiations brokered by Qatar and Libya. Nonetheless, reports indicated that the JEM was establishing new bases in Chad for operations against the government in Khartoum. Meanwhile, reports throughout the year indicated that the Bashir government was buying an increasing number of arms and munitions from Iran. An international effort to convince firms to divest from Sudan secured a growing number of companies in 2009, including the large U.S. investment firm TIAA-CREF, which not only withdrew its funds, but also threatened to sell the stock of international firms that remained invested in Sudan.

Current issues. Running counter to the liberalization taking place throughout much of Africa, the Bashir regime and its fundamentalist supporters were charged with widespread abuse (including torture and execution) of political opponents and mistreatment of non-Muslim groups in the 1990s. In November 1997 Washington accused the Bashir government of supporting international terrorism and human rights abuses and imposed economic sanctions against Sudan. The friction between the United States and Sudan after a meeting between U.S. secretary of state Madeleine Albright, Colonel Garang, and other NDA leaders in Uganda subsequently intensified when U.S. missiles destroyed a pharmaceutical plant in Khartoum on August 20, 1998, in response to the bomb attacks on the U.S. embassies in Kenya and Tanzania on August 7. Despite inconclusive evidence, Washington claimed the Sudanese facility was producing nerve gas chemicals in connection with the "terrorist network" of militant Islamic fundamentalist Osama bin Laden. The government in Khartoum, which had expelled bin Laden from the country in 1996 under U.S. pressure, strongly denied the U.S. accusations and branded U.S. president Clinton a "war criminal." Ironically, the episode generated a degree of sympathy on the international stage for Sudan.

As part of an overall effort to enhance his regime's image, President Bashir announced an amnesty for his opponents in June 2000. The SPLM, NDA, and most other opposition groups remained skeptical of the offer, however, and the political climate deteriorated when the state of emergency was again extended in January 2001 and former NIF strongman Turabi and several of his associates were arrested in February after Turabi's Popular National Congress (PNC) had signed an accord with the SPLA to "resist" the government. (Most of the PNC members were released by presidential order in October, but Turabi remained under house arrest until October 2003. He was rearrested on March 31, 2004, along with ten military officers and seven PNC members for what government officials said was a plot to stage a coup. Some reports claimed that those arrested had links to rebels in the western province of Darfur [see below]. Turabi was released on June 30, 2005, when Bashir announced the release of all political detainees.)

Following the al-Qaida attacks in the United States in September 2001, the Sudanese government came under additional international scrutiny. One apparent outgrowth of that increased attention was significant progress toward resolution of the southern conflict, which had led to the death of more than 1 million people (as casualties of either the fighting or related food shortages) and the dislocation of an additional 4 million. A tentative cease-fire was negotiated under U.S. mediation in January 2002. Although there was sporadic fighting in the first half of the year, with the NIF reportedly bombing civilians, a potentially historic accord was signed in Kenya on July 20 by representatives of the government and the SPLM. The agreement, mediated by the IGAD, envisioned the establishment of a joint, six-year transitional administration for the south to be followed by a self-determination referendum in the region. The government also reportedly agreed that sharia would not be imposed in the south. The two sides signed a Comprehensive Peace Agreement (CPA) on January 9, 2005, in Nairobi, bringing to an end the 21-year war in the south and, ironically, making former enemies Garang and Bashir partners in a new government.

The agreement called for national elections within four years and a referendum on independence for the south to be held in six years. It also stipulated the sharing of power and a 50–50 split of oil profits between the north and the south. In addition, it called for a six-month "preinterim" period to draft a new constitution; a transitional government in Khartoum under Bashir; a separate administration in the south headed by a first vice president; a national assembly to be appointed within two weeks of the drafting of the interim constitution, with members divided roughly 70–30 north-south, with full legislative authority by 2011; and shared governance by the NC and SPLM of Kordofan and Blue Nile. The SPLM was authorized to keep its army in the south but agreed to withdraw from the east, while the regime agreed to withdraw its troops from the south by July 2007. Despite Bashir's insistence that 85 percent of troops had withdrawn form the region, in late August 2007 observers charged that 10,000 northern troops remained in the south, largely concentrated around the oil installations, and by January 2008 at least 18,000 northern troops still occupied the south. On May 20, 2008, conflict between northern and southern troops prompted a new deadline for northern withdrawal of June 2008. That deadline was also missed and northern troops continue to occupy the oil-rich regions of the south. As of October 2008, the UN planned to deploy more peacekeepers to the region. Critics of the regime argued that this constituted a small part of a general pattern of government backsliding on some terms of the CPA.

Meanwhile, despite the far-reaching agreement between north and south, bloody struggle in the western region of Darfur continued unabated as Khartoum refused to grant the western regions self-rule. The war, which erupted in February 2003, had been preceded by years of tribal clashes. Escalation occurred when the Darfur Liberation Front claimed in February 2003 to have seized control of Gulu, and government forces were sent to retake the village in early March. The conflict, fueled by the scarcity of water and grazing land, became an increasingly fierce rivalry between Arab tribesmen who raised cattle and needed the land, and black African farmers who relied on the water. The fighting intensified in 2004, as black Africans accused the government in Khartoum of using the mounted, Arab *Janjaweed* militias, sometimes accompanied by fighters in Sudanese military uniforms, to force people from their land.

While some 113,000 refugees fled across the border into Chad and fighting intensified, U.S. president George W. Bush called on the parties to negotiate. The insurgent groups—the Sudan Liberation Movement/Army (SLM/A) and the Justice and Equality Movement (JEM)—claimed that the government had neglected the impoverished areas for years. The UN High Commissioner for Refugees decried the "scorched-earth" tactics used by the government and militias in response to the rebellion in Darfur and appealed for serious efforts to resolve the conflict.

In 2004 human rights workers charged that the government had used the *Janjaweed* to implement a policy resembling ethnic cleansing. Peace talks began in mid-July, as demanded by U.S. secretary of state Colin POWELL, but soon dissolved when Khartoum rejected the rebels' conditions, including a time frame for disarming the militias. On July 29 the UN Security Council threatened to enact punitive measures short of sanctions. In response, 100,000 people reportedly protested against a Security Council resolution in Khartoum, prompting rebel groups and government authorities to agree to meet in Nigeria for peace talks starting on August 23, 2004. However, the talks had broken down completely by August 8. The government refused to agree to stop aerial bombardment in Darfur and to disarm the *Janjaweed* militias, and the rebel groups refused to move into AU-designated confinement sites, arguing they would be too vulnerable to government attack. Powell declared on September 10 that the United States considered the killing, rape, and destruction in Darfur to be genocide and asked for urgent action by the Security Council.

On November 9, 2004, the government agreed to ban military flights over Darfur and signed two deals with the rebels after two weeks of talks in Nigeria. However, no agreement was reached on a long-term resolution to the fighting, and violence resumed within weeks. On March 23, 2005, the Security Council unanimously approved a resolution calling for 10,000 peacekeepers for Darfur and southern Sudan. However, resistance from the Sudanese government to a UN mission led to the continuation of the AU mission in Sudan. In May 2005 NATO agreed to assist the AU-led mission in Darfur with transport and other logistical aid, and Rwanda and Nigeria sent peacekeeping forces into Darfur in July. The AU force eventually numbered some 7,000. By September estimates of those killed in the conflict ranged from 70,000 to 300,000, and 2 to 3 million people were believed to have been displaced.

On another unsettling front, a tense military situation in eastern Sudan in the states of Kassala and the Red Sea Hills began to escalate in 2005 led by a group called the Eastern Front. This group came out of an alliance between the Beja Congress and the Rashaida Free Lions, which had also long complained about the government ignoring them. The conflict was widely resolved in late 2006 with aid from the Eritrean government, which mediated talks that led to the signing of the Eastern Sudan Peace Agreement (ESPA) on October 14, 2006. The agreement granted the eastern states more representation in the national government and established the Eastern Sudan Reconstruction and Development Fund (see Political Parties and Groups, below).

On July 10, 2005, Bashir ended the national state of emergency in all but three of Sudan's provinces: Darfur, Kasala, and Red Sea Hills. Bashir also ordered the release of hundreds of political prisoners, including Turabi. The SLM/A subsequently launched a new offensive in Darfur, and the AU initiated a new round of peace talks between the government and the SLM/A and the JEM in Abuja, Nigeria. The AU developed a comprehensive peace plan, which the Sudanese government accepted on April 30, 2006. On May 5, 2006, the Darfur Peace Agreement was created as a result of the peace talks in Abuja, Nigeria. The document was signed by a faction of the SLM/A as well as the Government of National Unity (GNU), which was the result of the 2005 CPA, but the primary rebel forces, a large faction of the SLM/A and JEM, did not sign the agreement. The plan called for the disarmament of the *Janjaweed* militias, elections within three years, and the provision of $500 million for the establishment and operation of an autonomous regional authority. Meanwhile, Sudan rejected a proposal from UN Secretary General Kofi Annan in April 2006 to replace the AU mission with a more expansive UN-led operation that would have included European and, possibly, U.S. forces.

Unfortunately, the April 2006 peace agreement heightened tensions in Darfur, as rival rebel groups clashed and the government stepped up military offensives against the SLA/A and JEM. On October 20, 2006, the Sudanese government threw out the UN Special Envoy Jan Pronk, accusing him of undermining Sudan's armed forces and of trying to force the government to accept an August 2006 Security Council Resolution calling for 20,000 UN peacekeeping troops in Darfur. In December 2006 a proposal presented at the AU's Joint Ceasefire Commission in Addis Ababa called for a beefed up AU mission that would include only African troops with support staff of other nationalities. Bashir initially agreed in principle to the plan, but negotiation regarding details, such as the force's size, purpose, and command structure, were all subject to controversy, allowing the Sudanese government to stall the process.

In January 2007 Bill Richardson, governor of the U.S. state of New Mexico, brokered a short-lived 60-day cease-fire agreement between the government and the main rebel groups, including the JEM and the SLA/A. In February 2007 the ICC formally accused two Sudanese of war crimes and crimes against humanity during the Darfur crisis, the first potential prosecutions since the UN Security Council referred cases to the ICC in April 2005. Formal indictments were made by June 2008, when arrest warrants issued on May 2, 2007, were pending against Ali Kushayb and Ahmad Haroun. In the same month, Luis Moreno-Ocampo, chief ICC prosecutor, complained of non-cooperation with the ICC by the Sudanese government; ICC investigations found "no trace of Sudanese proceedings in relation to crimes in Darfur during the last three years. The Government itself has clarified that there were none." The ICC presented an application for the arrest of President Bashir for war crimes on July 14, 2008, but over two-thirds of council members were in favor of deferring the decision to arrest Bashir for one year. Nations such as China, Libya, and South Africa, as well as members of the Sudanese government and the AU, fear that Bashir's arrest would damage any progress made during the peace process. The Arab League has recommended that Sudan surrender the two Sudanese already indicted, and create a domestic court for judicial proceedings related to Darfur under the supervision of international bodies. The GOS has not responded positively to this alternative, and the decision on the indictment of Bashir has been delayed until at least October 2008.

In 2007 the conflict was exacerbated by floods and resulting epidemics. A Security Council resolution passed in July 2007 authorized special envoys with the maximum authorized strength of approximately 26,000 military troops and police forces. The Sudanese government announced its formal acceptance of the plan, which outlines a joint AU-UN mission, with the majority of troops to come from African countries with logistical support from other UN member countries. Disagreement with the Sudanese government over the makeup of the mission slowed the implementation, with UN claims that many of the African troops that volunteered to take part in the mission did not meet UN peacekeeping standards in terms of training and equipment and needed to be supplemented with troops from other parts of the world. The government of Sudan and some AU leaders resisted this and argued that the African troops were capable of carrying out the UN mandate. Rebel leaders, government representatives, and international ministers and mediators prepared for peace talks in Tripoli, Libya. Talks began on October 27, 2007, and quickly collapsed. As of April 30, 2008, the AU and the UN had deployed 7,393 troops, 128 observers, and 1,716 police. The African Union/United Nations Hybrid Operation in Darfur (UNAMID) forces primarily come from Nigeria, Rwanda, South Africa, and Senegal.

By late 2007 the conflict in Darfur was attracting so much attention that the SPLM withdrew from the National Legislature, arguing that the concerns of south Sudan were being ignored. The SPLM withdrawal, announced by the party's secretary general, Pagan Amum, threatened to reignite the civil war between north and south Sudan. Peace between north and south was threatened by border disputes, which dictate oil revenue allocations between the two regions, and southern complaints that the NC did not adhere to the terms of the CPA. As a result of the SPLM withdrawal, Bashir reorganized the cabinet in December 2007 to appease the SPLM opposition.

In September 2008 the *New York Times* reported that an estimated 2.5 million people had been uprooted by the conflict in Darfur and that at least 200,000 had died. In October the government arrested the leader of a progovernment militia in Darfur, Ali Muhammad Ali ABD-AL-RAHMAN (Ali KUSHAYB), whom the ICC had indicted for war crimes. Although the government placed Kushayb in custody, it refused to turn him over to the ICC, and reports were that his arrest was a preventative measure designed to forestall his arrest by peacekeeping forces.

The ICC indicted Bashir on war crimes and crimes against humanity on March 4, 2009, and issued an international warrant for his arrest. The warrant was the first by the ICC for a sitting head of state. The government rejected the warrant and accused the court of "colonialism." In addition, African and Arab states refused calls to arrest Bashir, who openly made trips to Eritrea and Saudi Arabia and attended the Arab League Summit in Qatar. In April the National Election Commission announced that balloting would be held in February 2010 with 75 percent of the posts chosen by national balloting and the remaining 25 percent selected by state legislatures in indirect elections. The following month, fighting left at least 20 government soldiers and 40 JEM rebels dead in Darfur. Renewed fighting in South Sudan in June killed more than 1,000 and created more than 135,000 displaced persons. The strife originated in long-standing disputes among tribes over water rights and cattle-grazing areas. Opposition groups criticized the government census in August, arguing that the population count underestimated the inhabitants of southern Sudan.

POLITICAL PARTIES AND GROUPS

Following the 1969 coup, all political parties, except the Sudanese Communist Party (SCP), were outlawed. After the failure of the SCP coup in July 1971, the party was driven underground and its leaders were arrested. The following October, President Numayri attempted to supplant the existing parties by launching the Sudanese Socialist Union, modeled after the Arab Socialist Union of Egypt, the country's only recognized political group until its suspension by the TMC in April 1985. In 1986 the Union of Sudan African Parties (USAP) was formed with six parties representing the south of Sudan and the Nuba mountain region and won 36 seats in the assembly in 1986. The USAP was a founding member of the **National Democratic Alliance** (NDA), a loose antigovernment coalition. More than 40 parties were reported to have participated in the post-Numayri balloting of April 1986, although only the Umma Party (UP), Democratic Unionist Party (DUP), and National Islamic Front (NIF) obtained substantial legislative representation.

In July 1989 the newly installed military regime, led by Bashir, imposed a new ban on political groups and arrested numerous party leaders. Despite the eventual release of detainees, the ban continued, with Bashir announcing in late 1990 that a multiparty system would not be reestablished.

To counter the unofficial power that the NIF had begun to wield, a number of the other parties (including the DUP, UP, and SCP), the SPLM, trade union and university organizations, and some disaffected military leaders formed the NDA. An NDA summit, held in London January 26–February 3, 1992, called for the establishment of a transitional government in Sudan and a new constitution that would create a multiparty democracy, ensure human rights, and preserve Sudan's religious and ethnic "diversity." A second NDA summit in London in February 1994 demonstrated, according to *Middle East International,* that the Alliance "exists only on paper," as no consensus was reached on the pivotal questions of proposed self-determination for the south and the role of sharia in the state envisioned by the NDA. By contrast, a third summit in Asmara, Eritrea, on June 15–23, 1995, yielded agreement that, if and when the opposition gained power, "religion should be separate from politics," and that a referendum should be held in the south on its secession from the republic. The NDA called for a boycott of the March 1996 presidential and general elections, describing them as a "farce" that imposed "religious fanaticism" on Sudan. A joint NDA military command was established in October under the direction of the SPLM's Col. John Garang.

The NDA suffered after the UP withdrew from the Alliance in March 2000 due to a preliminary agreement between Bashir and UP leader Sadiq al-Mahdi (see UP, below, for additional information). Speculations suggest Mahdi's discomfort with the authority of DUP leader and NDA, Chair Usman al-Mirghani, as well as the SPLM's military dominance within the Alliance. In May 2001 the UP declined an invitation to rejoin the NDA, although Mahdi and Mirghani subsequently met to devise a comprehensive peace plan. The UP and DUP tentatively endorsed the proposed accords between Khartoum and the SPLM in 2002, but the NDA was not officially included in negotiations. A January 2005 agreement between the government and the NDA made in Cairo reintegrated the NDA into politics. The following December, two NDA members took up cabinet posts and 20 seats in the National Assembly.

The new constitution signed into law in June 1998 authorized the formation of political "associations" under the Political Association Act approved by the assembly in November 1998. Wide latitude was given to a government-appointed registrar of political associations to rule on applications; among other things, groups could be denied legal status if their activity was deemed incompatible with the country's "cultural course," an apparent reference to the government's Islamization campaign. The March 2000 Political Organizations Act for the Year 2000 amended the 1998 act to allow the formation of parties opposed to the government; however, it maintained government power to close down any party. Unregistered parties were not permitted to participate in elections. Subsequently, in August 2002, President Bashir called for a lifting of the ban on parties that had been represented in the legislature at the time of his assumption of power.

In January 2007 the National Assembly passed the Political Parties Bill, a controversial bill criticized by the SPLA and the NDA, who withdrew from the vote in parliament in protest on January 22. The controversial bill allows for the suspension or dissolution of any political party that the government deems to be carrying out activities contrary to the terms of the CPA, including preventing parties from participating in elections. The bill also prevents any member of security forces, the police, diplomats, civil service heads, and judges from joining any political party with the exception of President Bashir and Vice President Kiir, who are both military commanders, until the end of the CPA's transitional period. The NDA and SPLM argued that the bill was an assault on democracy and would be used by the NC to repress its political opponents.

Following the announcement that elections would be held in February 2010, 37 new parties were registered by the government, bringing the total number of official parties in Sudan to 69. Some opposition groups called for a boycott of the balloting, asserting that the electoral process would be fraudulent.

Legislative Parties:

National Congress (NC). The NC is a partial successor to the National Islamic Front (*al-Jabhah al-Watani al-Islami*—NIF), which was organized prior to the April 1986 balloting by the leader of the fundamentalist Muslim Brotherhood, Dr. Hassan Abdallah al-Turabi, who as attorney general had been largely responsible for the harsh enforcement of sharia law under the Numayri government. The NIF won 51 legislative seats but refused to enter the government until May 1988 because of the UP commitment to revise the sharia system, which the NIF wanted to strengthen. The NIF gained a number of ministerial seats vacated by the DUP in December 1988, but withdrew from the coalition upon the latter's return in March 1989. Although Turabi was arrested in July 1989, along with the leaders of many other parties, he was released in December and soon became one of the new regime's most influential supporters. As it became more and more identified with fundamentalism, the Bashir government appointed numerous NIF adherents to key government posts, most observers agreeing that the Front had become a de facto government party. NIF/Muslim Brotherhood supporters also were reported to be directing the Islamic "security groups," which had assumed growing authority since 1990.

Turabi, one of the world's leading Islamic fundamentalist theoreticians, was routinely described as the country's most powerful political figure. A follower of Iran's late Ayatollah Khomeini, he called for the creation of Islamic regimes in all Arab nations, a position that concerned several nearby states (particularly Egypt) and major Western capitals. The NIF's "number two," Ali Uthman Muhammad Taha, was named foreign minister in February 1995 and first vice president in early 1998.

It was reported in 1996 that Turabi had directed that the NIF be renamed the National Congress (NC), to reflect a broader umbrella political organization open to all citizens, and to act as a quasi-institutional governing body. Subsequent news reports appeared to use the two names interchangeably, with the NIF rubric predominating. In January 1999 it was announced that a National Congress had been officially registered as a political party, while reports in March indicated similar status had been accorded to a National Islamic Front Party. It was not immediately clear what relationship, if any, the two groupings had to each other or the traditional NIF. Meanwhile, reports (officially denied) surfaced of friction between Turabi and party reformists as well as between Turabi and Sudanese President Bashir, who was named chair of the recently established NIF advisory council. Tensions between Turabi and Bashir resulted in the removal of Turabi as general secretary in May. Turabi subsequently formed a new party, the Popular National Congress (PNC, below), and Bashir's supporters formally used the NC rubric in the December 2000 elections.

The party planned a general congress in October 2009 to determine candidates ahead of the 2010 elections. Although the ICC had indicted Bashir for his role in the country's genocide, he was expected to be the NC presidential candidate in the balloting.

Leaders: Umar Hassan Ahmad al-BASHIR (President of the Republic and Chair of the Party's *Shura* [Council]), Ibrahim Ahmed OMAR (Secretary General), Ahmad Abder RAHMAN, Ali Uthman Muhammad TAHA (First Vice President of the Republic), Ali al-Haj MUHAMMAD, Muhammad Ahmad SALIM (Registrar of Political Associations).

Sudanese People's Liberation Movement/Army (SPLM/A). The SPLM and its military wing, the Sudanese People's Liberation Army (SPLA), were formed in 1983 by Col. John Garang, until then an officer in the Sudanese army. Sent by the Numayri administration to negotiate with mutinous soldiers in southern garrisons, Colonel Garang joined the mutineers and, under his leadership, the SPLA became the dominant southern rebel force. The SPLM and SPLA were supported by Libya prior to Numayri's ouster, when Tripoli endorsed the new regime in Khartoum. The SPLA called a cease-fire immediately following the coup but thereafter initiated military action against the Khartoum government after failing to win concessions on the southern question. Relying on an estimated 20,000 to 25,000 troops the SPLA subsequently gained control of most of the non-urban south; sporadic negotiations with various northern representatives yielded several temporary cease-fires but no permanent solution to the conflict.

In 1986 the SPLM downplayed its Marxist-Leninist policies and supported a unified Sudan in which the south would be granted a larger voice in national affairs and a greater share of the nation's economic development programs. However, secessionist groups and SPLM's leaders in 1992 reportedly endorsed a division of Sudan into two autonomous, yet confederated, states, with the south operating under secular law and the north under sharia.

In August 1991 the SPLM was severely splintered when a group of second-tier leaders headquartered in the eastern town of Nasir announced their intention to wrest SPLA control from Garang, whom they accused of perpetrating a "dictatorial reign of terror." Long-standing tribal animosity also contributed to a split in the SPLA, where support for Nasir came primarily from the Nuer ethnic group, which has had a stormy relationship with Garang's Dinka supporters since the creation of the SPLA. Several months of fighting between the two factions left thousands dead, with Garang's supporters charging the dissidents with the "massacre" of Dinka civilians in January 1992. Although a temporary reconciliation between the SPLA factions was achieved at the Abuja peace talks with the government in June, sporadic fighting resumed later in the summer.

In September 1992 William Nyuon BANY conducted negotiations with the splinter group on behalf of Garang, but defected to form his own faction, which in April 1993 coalesced with other anti-Garang groups as the SPLA-United (below). In early 1994 negotiations between the SPLA and the SPLA-United yielded a tentative cease-fire agreement in which Garang reportedly agreed to support southern self-determination. Despite possible reunification of southern forces, there was ongoing friction between Garang and the SPLA-United's Riak Machar.

In April 1994 some 500 delegates attended the first SPLA-SPLM conference since 1983. The conference was reportedly called to shore up Garang's authority in the face of competition from the SPLA-United. The SPLM leader was put in charge of the joint military command announced by the NDA in October 1996 after the SPLA-United and Machar's SSIM signed a peace accord with the Bashir government. (See Current issues.)

In late 2004 rumors of "revolt" against Garang by secessionist SPLA officers who wanted Salva Kiir Mayardit to replace Garang as head of the SPLA surfaced, but Kiir feared a repeat of the 1991 uprising against Garang. On July 30, 2005, Garang died in a helicopter crash, an event that ignited rioting that led to the death of more than 100 people. He was succeeded as SPLM leader by his deputy, Kiir. Kiir appointed Machar as vice president of the Government of Southern Sudan in August 2005.

Factions of the Southern Sudan Defense Force (SSDF) signed the Juba Declaration in 2006 in collaboration with the SPLA, but a splinter group of the SSDF still remains loyal to Gordon Kong and rejects the Juba Declaration and the CPA. The SPLM continues to lead southern Sudan in disputes, particularly in relation to the contested oil rich Abyei region. In the anticipated 2011 referendum that will determine the south's political status, Abyei will also hold a referendum to determine if it will join the north or the south. The SPLM has announced that it will participate in the forthcoming elections in 2010.

Throughout 2009 the SPLM endeavored to unite southern opposition groups under a single grouping in order to contest the 2010 elections. This effort was complicated by the emergence of a new rival party, the **SPLM-Democratic Change** (see the **Sudanese People's Liberation Army—United**, below).

Leaders: Salva KIIR Mayardit (First Vice President of the Republic, President of South Sudan, and Party Chair), Riak MACHAR (Vice President of South Sudan), Yasser ARMAN.

Sudanese People's Liberation Army–United (SPLA-United). The formation of the SPLA-United was announced in early April 1993 in Nairobi, Kenya, by SPLA dissidents who opposed the "one-man rule" of longtime SPLA leader John Garang. Included in the grouping was the Nasir faction (see SPLM, above); William Nyuon Bany's self-styled **Forces of Unity;** the so-called **Kerubino Group**, formed in February by Kerubino Kwanyin Bol; and several other dissidents who had escaped from a Garang prison in the fall of 1992.

Early in 1994 the SPLA-United faced heavy domestic and international pressure to reconcile with the SPLA, as fighting resulted in civilian casualties and exacerbated famine conditions in the south. Simultaneously, the SPLA-United's independence advocates gained widespread support. In 1995 the Nasir faction split from SPLA-United, where Riak Machar formed the Southern Sudan Independence Movement (SSIM). Concurrently, Nyuon Bany was expelled from the SPLA-United after being accused of collaboration with Khartoum, despite 1996 reports of alliances with the north and Nyuon Bany resuming a pro-Garang posture within the SSIM. In April 1997 the SPLA-United and the SSIM signed an agreement with the government endorsing the preservation of Sudan's "known boundaries," thus relinquishing their drive for independence.

The SPLA-United, under Lam Akol, subsequently gained strength through a merger with the SSDF led by Machar. As a result, Machar was named head of the new Southern States Coordination Council (SSCC, see Political background, above). However, Machar later pulled out of the government, accusing President Bashir of failing to consult with him regarding governmental appointments. Machar subsequently became the USDF leader. Meanwhile, Akol served in Bashir's cabinet until August 2002, when he was dismissed for announcing that he intended to leave the NC and form a new party. By that time, Machar and his supporters had reintegrated into the SPLA and presented a unified front during peace negotiations. SPLA leader Akol was subsequently appointed foreign minister in the 2005 government of national unity. In October 2007 the SPLM, the political wing of the SPLA, withdrew from the National Legislature, demanding that the NC abide by the terms of the CPA and Akol be removed from government due to questionable loyalties, as Akol was developing closer ties with the NC. Bashir removed Akol from his position as foreign minister and appointed SPLM member Deng Alor Kol in his place. By December of 2007 SPLM legislature members were reappointed to their posts. In June 2009 Akol formed a new grouping, the **Sudan Peoples' Liberation Movement—Democratic Change,** to challenge the SPLM in the 2010 balloting.

Leaders: Lam AKOL (Commander in Chief), Deng ALOR Kol (Spokesperson), Pagan AMUM (Secretary General).

United Democratic Salvation Front (UDSF). The USDF is an outgrowth of the SSIM and was composed of southern Sudanese political figures and dissidents from the SPLA under the leadership of Riak Machar. The UDSF included representatives of rebel groups who had signed the 1997 peace accord with the government in Khartoum and was seen as a progovernment grouping that advocated a peaceful resolution of the north-south conflict. By 1999 the USDF was fully operational, and in January 2000 Machar resigned as chair; he rejoined the SPLA in 2002. He was replaced by Elijah HON at a party congress. In September 2001, the party's general secretary, Ibrahim al-TAWIL, led a large group of UDSF members in a defection to the NC. In October 2001, in an effort to unify the party, new leadership elections were conducted, and Eng Joseph Malwal was chosen chair. In March 2003 the USDF signed a cooperation agreement with the NC and was subsequently included in successive cabinets, including the 2005 unity government. The UDSF continues to hold a cabinet post, the minister of tourism, and takes part in the GOSS. At a party congress in April 2009, the UDSF elected Gabriel Changson CHANG as its new leader. Chang subsequently pledged to work with the SPLM to develop a united front in the 2010 elections.

Leaders: Gabriel Changson CHANG (Chair), Maj. Gen. (ret.) Albino Akol AKOL (General Secretary).

Government Supportive Parties and Groups:

Democratic Unionist Party (*al-Hizb al-Ittihadi al-Dimuqrati*—DUP). Also right of center, the DUP draws its principal strength from the Khatmiya Muslims of northern and eastern Sudan and is one of the parties that comprise the NDA. Based on its second-place showing at the 1986 poll, the DUP was the UP's junior partner in subsequent government coalitions, although internal divisions prevented the formulation of a clearly defined outlook. The faction led by party chair Usman al-Mirghani included pro-Egyptian traditionalists once linked to the Numayri regime, who were reluctant to repeal sharia until an alternative code was formulated. Younger members, on the other hand, urged that the party abandon its "semi-feudal" orientation and become a secular, centrist formation capable of attracting nationwide support. In early 1986 the DUP reunited with an offshoot group, the Democratic People's Party (DPP), and subsequently appeared to have absorbed the small National Unionist Party (NUP), which had drawn most of its support from the Khartoum business community.

In 1988 Mirghani conceded that compromises in the sharia had to be made if the civil war was to end, and thus met with Garang to negotiate peace. The party withdrew from government participation in late December 1988 because of failure to implement a southern peace accord that it had negotiated, with the prime minister's approval, a month earlier; it rejoined the coalition on March 22, 1989. Party leaders Usman and Ahmad al-Mirghani were arrested following the June 1989 coup, but they were released at the end of the year and subsequently went into exile in Egypt.

Despite significant divisions, the DUP was described by *Middle East International* in early 1994 as still officially opposed to independence for the south and "not adverse to some form of Islamic state" for Sudan. The latter issue apparently had contributed to the defection in 1993 of the DUP faction led by former deputy prime minister Sharif Zein al-Abidin al-HINDI, who advocated the separation of church and state despite his position as a religious leader. A possible change in the DUP's stance toward fundamentalism and southern secession may have been signaled by the party's participation in subsequent NDA summits.

DUP Chair Mirghani described the guidelines adopted in late 1998 for legalization of parties as too restrictive, and his supporters did not submit a request for registration, although a splinter group reportedly sought recognition under the DUP rubric. Ahmad al-Mirghani returned from exile in November 2001, but Usman al-Mirghani, who had been elected chair of the NDA in September 2000, remained outside the country. Meanwhile, a DUP splinter faction, calling itself the DUP–General Secretariat, had accepted cabinet posts in the government in February 2001 and in the 2005 unity government. The mainstream DUP has since refused to take part in the unity government. The deputy secretary general of the party, Ali Mahmoud Hassanein, was arrested in July 2007 at gunpoint with 27 other opposition politicians and charged with plotting to overthrow the government. The General Secretariat splinter faction, represented by Sharif Zein al-Abidin al-Hindi until his death in 2006, is now led by the minister of industry, Jalal Yusuf Mohammed Digair. The General Secretariat DUP continues to take part in the GNU government, in contrast to the Mirghani faction. Chair Mirghani's faction requested official representation in the cabinet but was rejected by the SPLM. The DUP suffered from a number of defections in 2008 and 2009. In 2009 party leaders dismissed reports that the DUP had reached a secret agreement to back Bashir in the 2010 presidential election.

Leaders: Usman al-MIRGHANI (Symbolic Chair), Dr. Ahmad al-Sayid HAMAD (Former DDP Leader), Ali Ahmed al-SAYYED, Ali Mahmoud HASSANEIN.

Sudanese National Party (*al-Hizb al-Watani al-Sudani*—SNP). The SNP is a Khartoum-based party that draws most of its support from the Nuba tribes of southern Kordofan. The SNP deputies joined the 1986 assembly boycotts on the grounds that "African bloc" interests were underrepresented in the cabinet. In November 1987 the party's leader, Rev. Philip Ghabush, was branded a "dictator" by dissidents.

The SNP officially registered in April 1999 and Ghabush announced his support for the new constitution and laws regarding party formation. Father Ghabush and his party remained outside of government and critical of the CPA, which they claim did not benefit the people of the Nuba Mountains despite the destruction they faced during the civil war. They seek unity in Sudan, but will call for self-determination if Southern Sudan votes to succeed from Sudan in 2011. Ghabush died in 2008, and subsequent reports indicated that most SNP members had joined other parties and factions.

Islamic Umma Party (*Hizb al-Umma al-Islamiya*—IUP). This small party split off from the mainstream Umma Party (see below) in 1985. In applying for recognition in early 1999, the IUP announced it would advocate sharia as the sole source of law while promoting "Mahdist" ideology and a nonaligned foreign policy. The IUP was officially registered in April 1999 and convened its first general congress with delegates from all parts of Sudan the same month. The IUP officially supports the government. Reports were that the IUP would support the NC in the 2010 balloting.

Leader: Wali al-Din al-Hadi al-MAHDI.

Groups Cooperating with Government:

Umma (People's) Party (*Hizb al-Umma*—UP). A moderate right-of-center formation, the UP has long been led by former prime minister Mahdi. Founded in 1945, UP receives its strongest support from Ansar Muslims of the White Nile and western Darfur and Kordofan provinces. It obtained a plurality of 100 seats at the 1986 assembly balloting. Members traditionally advocated the repeal of sharia law and were wary of NIF fundamentalism. Despite a historically pro-Libyan, anti-Egyptian posture, the party cultivated good relations with Western countries based, in part, on Mahdi's personal ties to Britain.

Prime Minister Mahdi and Idriss al-Banna were arrested shortly after the military coup in June 1989 (the latter being sentenced to 40 years in jail for corruption; Mahdi was released from prison and placed under house arrest in January 1990), amid rumors that the UP was considering some form of cooperation with the new regime. In light of growing fundamentalist influence within the Bashir government, the UP announced an alliance with the SPLM (see Other Groups, below) dedicated to overthrowing the government; ending the civil war; and reintroducing multiparty, secular democracy. The southern liaison notwithstanding, the UP membership was reported to be deeply divided following Mahdi's release from house arrest in May 1991. With southern groups tending more and more to support independence for their region, the UP in early 1994 was described as "open" on the question. Mahdi was rearrested in June 1994 on charges of plotting against the government and again in May 1995 for a three-month period. He was reportedly invited by the Bashir regime to join the new government formed in April 1996 but declined and eventually fled to Asmara, Eritrea, in December.

The UP was one of the first groups to seek recognition in early 1999, the pro-negotiation faction having apparently gained ascendancy. For his part, Mahdi in November concluded an agreement with Bashir known as the "Call of the Homeland Accord," which proposed a new, pluralistic constitution for Sudan and a four-year transitional period that would conclude with a self-determination referendum for the south. Consequently, in March 2000 Mahdi announced that the UP had withdrawn from the NDA, which he criticized for refusing to negotiate with the government, and directed the *Umma* militia to honor a cease-fire. Mahdi returned to the Sudan in November after four years of exile in Egypt, but the UP nonetheless boycotted the December legislative and presidential elections, arguing that the balloting should be postponed pending comprehensive "national reconciliation." The UP also declined Bashir's invitation to join the cabinet in February 2001, again on the premise that a "bilateral" agreement was not appropriate while other opposition groups remained in conflict with the government. Subsequent to leaving the NDA in 2000, the Umma Party split into several factions: the Umma Reform and Renewal faction led by Mubarak al-Fadil al-MAHDI; the Umma General Leadership faction led by Dr. as-Sadiq al-HADI; and the Federal Umma Party led by Ahmed Babiker NAHAR. The UP General Leadership splinter faction, led by Mubarak al-Fadil al-Mahdi, accepted ministerial posts in August 2002 and in the 2005 unity government. The party officially favors the deployment of a hybrid AU-UN peacekeeping force in Darfur. The party remains active but outside of the unity government. It complains that the CPA served to solidify the NC's hold on power, leaving little room for northern opposition parties to contest Bashir's power. The current head of the Umma Party General Leadership, Mubarak al-Fadil al-MAHDI, was arrested in July 2007, together with 27 other opposition leaders, and was charged with plotting to overthrow the government, although he was subsequently released. In 2009 several prominent UP members defected to the newly formed SPLM-DC. In July the UP and the JEM signed an agreement of principles, which was criticized by the government and NC.

Leaders: Dr. Sadiq al-MAHDI (Former Prime Minister), Idris al-BANNA, Mubarak Abdullah al-MAHDI, Mubarak al-Fadil al-MAHDI (Assistant to the President of the Republic and dissident faction leader), Sarrah NAGDALLA, Umar Nur al-DAIM (Secretary General), Ahmed Babiker NAHAR (Federal Umma Party Leader).

Regional Interests, Opposition Parties, and Rebel Groups:

Baath Party (*Hizb al Ba'ath as-Sudan*—BP). The BP is a small party that has struggled for recognition in the Sudan. Its main platform has been integration and unification with Egypt or Libya in support of forming a "Pan-Arab Nation," and it has been supported by the Baath Party of Iraq. In 1990 Bashir targeted the party and several arrests of party members were made, but with the onset of the Gulf War, specific targeting of the Baath Party of Sudan receded as the Sudanese government took an official stance of support for Iraq. After the fall of the regime of Saddam Hussein, the BP cut ties with the Iraqi Baath party.

Leader: Mohammed Ali JADIN (General Secretary)

Progressive People's Party (PPP). The PPP is one of the two major "Equatorial" parties representing Sudanese living near the Zairian and Ugandan borders. Both the PPP and SAPC, unlike the SSPA, are "pro-divisionist," calling for strong provincial governments within a weak regional administration for the south. The PPP's leader, Elioba Surur, is considered a leader in southern Sudan and is a member of the GOSS.

Leader: Elioba SURUR.

Sudan African National Union (SANU). Founded in 1963, the SANU is a small southern party based in Malakal. The SANU (adopting the same name as a pre-Numayri party) supports the division of the south into separate regions for administration. The SANU remains an active party in the south and is participating in writing a constitution for Southern Sudan. At a party congress in April 2009, party leader Toby MADOUT Parek was reelected to a second five-year term.

Leaders: Toby MADOUT Parek (Chair), Lino Juma MARCELLINO.

Popular (People's) National Congress (PNC). The PNC is an Islamic fundamentalist organization that was formed by the Turabi faction of the NIF/NC. Turabi had earlier accused President Bashir of betraying the NC's Islamist tenets. Thus, Turabi claimed he was merely adding "Popular" to the original party's name and expelling members who had produced the crisis. Nevertheless, the PNC officially registered as a distinct party in July 2000. Turabi described the PNC as a "comprehensive *shura* organization," which indicated it would be outside the government. The PNC has few policy differences with the NC.

Turabi and several of his PNC supporters were arrested in February 2001 (see Current issues, above). Turabi was released in October 2003 and rearrested on March 31, 2004. The registrar of political parties issued a decree on April 1, 2004, to suspend the PNC's activities, following Turabi's arrest. Turabi was released as part of the general amnesty issued by Bashir in July 2005. Turabi has since refused to take part in the unity government and called for a popular uprising against the ruling party. He was arrested in January 2009 after he called on Bashir to surrender himself to the ICC. Turabi was released in March.

Leaders: Hassan Abdallah al-TURABI, Ali al-Hajj MUHAMMAD (Secretary General).

Sudanese Communist Party (*al-Hizb al-Shuyui al-Sudani*—SCP). Founded in 1944 and a leading force in the struggle for independence, the SCP was banned under the Abbud regime and supported the 1969 Numayri coup, becoming thereafter the sole legal party until the abortive 1971 uprising, when it was again outlawed. During the 1970s the SCP was persecuted by the Numayri government with a series of quick trials that resulted in several executions of SCP members. The SCP resurfaced in the mid 1980s and campaigned as a recognized party in 1986, calling for opposition to Islamic fundamentalism; repeal of sharia; and the adoption of a secular, democratic constitution. It won 3 seats in the 1986 elections. The party displayed no interest in joining the government coalition in 1988 but accepted one cabinet portfolio in March 1989. Secretary General Muhammad Ibrahim Nugud Mansur was arrested following the June 1989 coup, and in September four more party members were detained for alleged involvement in an antigovernment protest. Nugud was released from prison in February 1990 but was placed under house arrest until May 1991, at which time he was freed under what the government described as a blanket amnesty for all remaining political detainees. The SCP, operating primarily from exile, subsequently remained active in the anti-NIF opposition; with some NDA members complaining in late 1992 that the SCP's influence continued at a higher level than was warranted in view of communism's worldwide decline. SCP reformers have recently urged the party to shed its communist orientation in favor of a more moderate left-of-center posture that would attract wider popular participation, but the group's "older generation of leaders" has thus far resisted such a move. The party leadership was reportedly critical in late 1998 and early 1999 of the closer ties apparently being established by UP leader Sadiq al-Mahdi with the NIF government. The SCP is currently led by Muhammad Ibrahim Nugud and plays only a marginal role in the national political scene. Officially, it supports a return to democratic rule and opposes the succession of Southern Sudan from the federation. Reports were that Nugud would be the SCP's candidate in the 2010 presidential elections.

Leaders: Muhammad Ibrahim NUGUD Mansur (Secretary General), Ali al-Tijani al-TAYYIB Babikar (Deputy Secretary General).

Legitimate Command. The Command is a Cairo-based group of former Sudanese officers opposed to the Bashir regime that claims the support of "democratic" officers in the Sudanese army. The Command has participated in NDA summits in recent years, some observers going so far as to describe it as the NDA's "military wing."

Leader: Fathi Ahmad ALI.

Sudan Liberation Movement/Army (SLM/A). This group is a successor of sorts to the Darfur Liberation Front, a rebel group organized to combat repressive conditions in Darfur. The SLM/A was the main force for the 2003 Darfur based rebellion against the Sudanese government. The rebels split into two groups in 2004, as the SLM/A vehemently opposed Khalil Ibrahim, a radical opponent of Khartoum (see JEM, below). The SLM/A claimed to represent the region's black African farmers, who were angry over alleged government support for Arab militias. One faction of the SLM/A, known as the *Mani Arkoi* and led by Minni Minawi, was a non-government group that signed the AU-backed 2006 Darfur peace accord, but the main SLM/A body, led by party chair Abdallah Wahid Mohamed Ahmad Nur, rejected the agreement. After the signing in 2006, the SLM/A split further, with some factions joining the National Redemption Front and others joining with the JEM to form the Alliance of Revolutionary Force of West Sudan (ARFWS), though the ARFWS unification quickly ended after its formation in 2006. In August 2009 six factions of the SLM agreed to a unity accord ahead of the 2010 elections, although one group, led by Khamis Abdullah ABAKR, refused to reconcile.

Leaders: Abdallah Wahid Mohamed Ahmad NUR (Chair), Mustafa TIRAB (General Secretary), Minni MINAWAI (Leader of the *Mani Arkoi* faction).

National Redemption Front (NRF). This is a coalition of rebel groups operating in Darfur that did not sign the May 2006 peace agreement with the Sudanese government. It was founded in June of 2006 in Asmara, Eritrea. NRF has come to symbolize opposition to the peace agreement and to the National Conference. Member groups include the Sudan Federal Democratic Alliance (SFDA) and the Justice and Equality Movement (JEM).

Leaders: Khalil Ibrahim MOHAMED (JEM), Ahmed Ibrahim DIRAIGE, Sharif HARIR (SFDA), Khamis Abdalla ABAKAR.

Justice and Equality Movement (JEM). The JEM was founded in 2002 and commenced operations in 2003 after its split from the SLM in mid-2004. This split further complicated peace negotiations with Khartoum, with each of the groups at odds with the others based on tribal rivalries. It is reportedly supported by Islamists close to Hassan Abdallah al-Turabi. Many JEM adherents reside in the Sudanese-Chad frontier region and the JEM also reportedly has the support of the Chadian government. In May 2006 the JEM refused to sign the AU-supported Darfur peace plan and is a member of the National Redemption Front (NRF) alliance due to the party's call for the government to focus on the causes of the conflict and protect the people of Darfur, rather than seeking blanket solutions through peace talks. The JEM supported the recent move by the ICC to arrest President Bashir for genocide, along with the SPLM. The JEM remains an active rebel group and as of mid-September 2007 planned to attend the peace talks scheduled for late October in Libya. Shortly before the expected talks, the JEM announced that they would not attend. The JEM attacked a Chinese oil-field on October 23, 2007, and kidnapped five Chinese workers with the intent of driving out foreign ownership. On May 10, 2008, the JEM carried out an attack on the Omdurman capital region of Sudan, demonstrating to the people of Darfur that the Sudanese government was potentially vulnerable to rebel reprisals. Meanwhile Bahar Idriss Abu GARDA, who was under indictment by the ICC for crimes against humanity, broke with the JEM and founded a new opposition grouping, the **United Resistance Front.**

Leader: Khalil IBRAHIM Mohamed.

Nobility Movement (*al-Shahamah*). This is a rebel group reportedly formed in October 2004 in West Kordofan state by a former leader of the progovernment paramilitary Popular Defense Forces. The leader, Musa Ali Muhammadayn (also a former governor of al-Rashad province), was dismissed from that post when he decided to remain loyal to Turabi in the latter's confrontations with Bashir. This group now forms part of JEM, having joined it in October 2004.

Leader: Musa Ali MUHAMMADAYN.

Sudan Federal Democratic Alliance (SFDA). The SFDA was launched in London in February 1994 under the chair of Ahmed Dreige, a former Numayri cabinet member. The group has deemed "all means to be legitimate" in securing an end to the Bashir regime and has proposed a substantially decentralized federal structure for the Sudan in which the traditional parties would play no role. The SFDA has been absorbed by the NRF.

Leaders: Ahmed DREIGE (Former Chair), Sherif HARIR, Suleiman RAHAL.

Eastern Front. Formed on February 1, 2005, this group, which operated in the east, was composed of two rebel groups: the Rashaida Free Lions Association, whose members are Rashaida tribesmen, and the Beja Congress, which represents the non-Arab, nomadic Beja tribes. Unrest in the impoverished area of eastern Sudan, long ignored by the government, began as a grassroots movement in the 1990s and gained strength with the return of Umar Muhammad TAHIR, the exiled Beja Congress leader, in November 2003. The Congress was banned by the government in October 2003 for its use of violence. With Eritrean mediation, the Eastern Front and the government signed the Eastern Sudan Peace Agreement (ESPA) on October 14, 2006, which granted the east greater representation in the national government and established the Eastern Sudan Reconstruction and Development Fund. On August 31, 2007, Chair Ahmed was sworn in as a presidential advisor to President Bashir, and Secretary General Mubarak was given the post of minister of state in the ministry of transport. The Eastern Front also was given several parliamentary seats in the national government. By 2009 an estimated 1,750 former Eastern Front soldiers had been demobilized and reintegrated into civil society under a program funded by international donors. In May former members of the Eastern Front formed a new political party, the **East Democratic Party**, under Amna DIRAR and Idris NUR.

Leaders: Musa Muhamed AHMED (Chair), Mubarak MUBARAK (Secretary General).

Sudan Alliances Forces (SAF). The SAF is a rebel group operating in eastern Sudan, reportedly from bases in Ethiopia and Eritrea. In late 1996 it was described as a participant in the NDA, although its fighters were not believed to be under the direct command of the SPLA's Colonel Garang. The SAF currently engages in anti-fundamentalist activities from their offices outside of the Sudan, primarily in Poland. By 2009 the SAF was estimated to have 300 to 500 fighters. More than 40 fighters and 60 civilians were killed in combat between the SAF and SPLA in April and May 2009.

Leader: Brig. Gen. Abd al-Aziz Khalid OSMAN.

Other Groups:

Other groups that have applied for, or been granted, recognition prior to the 2010 balloting include the **Alliance for People's Working Forces**, led by Kamal al-Din Muhammad ABDULLAH and former president Numayri; **Party of God** (*Hizb Allah* or *Hezbollah*), led by Sulayman Hasan KHALIL; **Future Party** (*Hizb al-Mustaqbal*), led by Abd al-Mutal Abd al-RAHMAN; **Islamic–Christian Solidarity,** launched under the leadership of Hatim Abdullah al-Zaki HUSAYN on a platform of religious harmony and increased attention to social problems; the **Islamic Path Party,** led by Hasab al-RASUL; the **Islamic Revival Movement,** led by Siddiq al-Haj al-SIDDIQ; the **Islamic Socialist Party,** led by Sabah al-MUSBAN; the **Liberalization Party;** the **Moderate Trend Party,** led by Mahmud JINA; the **Muslim Brothers,** led by Sheikh Sadiq Abdallah Abd al-MAJID; the **National Popular Front,** led by Umar Hasan SHALABI and devoted to pan-Arab and pan-Islamic unity; the **National Salvation Party;** the **New Forces Association,** led by Abd al-Rahman Ismail KIBAYDAH; the **Popular Masses' Alliance,** founded by Faysal Muhammad HUSAYN in support of policies designed to assist the poor; the **Socialist Popular Party,** led by Sayyid Khalifah Idris HABANI; the **Sudanese Central Movement,** led by Muhammad Abu al-Qasim Haji HAMAD; the **Sudan Federal Party,** launched by Ahmed DIRAIGE (a leader of the Fur ethnic group) in support of a federal system; the **Sudan Green Party,** led by Zakaraia Bashir IMAN; the **Sudanese Initiative Party,** led by Jafar KARAR; the **Union of Sudan African Parties** (USAP), led by Joseph UKELLO; the **Sudan Labor Party**, led by James ANDERIA; the **South Sudan Democratic Front** (SSDF), led by Gordon BUAY; the **Covenant Democratic Party**, under Benjamin OCHAN; and the **United Democratic Front,** led by Peter Abdrhaman SULE. In February 2006 the formation of a **National Democratic Party** (NDP) was reported to be a merger of several small groupings with leftist or nationalist orientations. Attempts at reigniting the Sudanese Socialist Union have been reported. On March 10, 2007, the formation of the **Socialist Union Party,** under the leadership of Fatimah Abd-al-MAHMOUD, was announced.

For more information on the now-defunct **National Movement for Reform and Development in Darfur**—NMRD, please see the 2008 *Handbook*.

LEGISLATURE

The National Legislature currently comprises the National Assembly and the Council of States. The National Assembly is composed of 450 appointed seats and the Council comprises 50 indirectly elected members. Under Numayri, the size and composition of the unicameral National People's Assembly changed several times, the assembly elected in 1974 being the only one to complete its full constitutional term of four years. All existing legislative bodies were dissolved by the TNC in April 1985.

On April 1–12, 1986, balloting was held for 260 members of a 301-member Constituent Assembly, voting being postponed in many southern districts because of rebel activity. The assembly was dissolved by the Bashir regime in July 1989.

On February 13, 1992, Prime Minister Bashir announced the appointment of a 300-member Transitional National Assembly, which met for the first time on February 24. Included in the assembly were all members of the Revolution Command Council for National Salvation (RCC); a number of RCC advisors; all cabinet ministers and state governors; and representatives of the army, trade unions, and former political parties. The prime minister decreed that the assembly would sit for an indeterminate period, pending the selection of a permanent body as the final step of the new pyramidal legislative structure envisioned by the government.

Elections to a new 400-member **National Assembly** were conducted on March 6–17, 1996, all candidates running as independents because political parties remained banned. Most of the 275 elected assembly members were selected during that balloting, although in October President Bashir appointed eight legislators from constituencies in the south, where the civil war made voting impossible. When the assembly convened on April 1, the elected legislators were joined by 125 legislators who had been selected in January by representatives of local and state councils and numerous professional associations.

In the most recent balloting, held December 13–23, 2000, the National Congress won 355 of 360 contested seats, the remaining 5 being secured by independents. (Most major opposition groups boycotted the balloting, and elections were not held in three southern provinces due to the civil war.) On December 20, 2004, the National Assembly amended the constitution to extend the term of the sitting legislature for one year, where members served four-year terms. Currently, legislators serve six-year terms.

The speaker of the National Assembly, Ahmed Ibrahim El Tahir, is committed to the advancement of the Comprehensive Peace Agreement signed January 9, 2005. The CPA marked the end of the Sudanese civil war in 2005 and the commencement of the interim transitional constitution, stipulating that seats in the legislature be divided based on a power-sharing quota. The NC holds 52 percent of the seats; the SPLM, 28 percent; northern opposition parties, 14 percent; and southern opposition parties, 6 percent. The south established its own assembly, the South Sudan Transitional Legislative Assembly, which convened for the first time on September 29, 2005. The 450-member "national unity" assembly—appointed by decree by Bashir—convened for the first time on August 31, 2005. Members were scheduled to continue to serve their six-year terms until the national election in 2010.

President: Ahmed Ibrahim al-TAHIR.

CABINET

[as of September 1, 2009]

President and Prime Minister	Umar Hassan Ahmad al-Bashir (NC)
First Vice President	Salva Kiir Mayardit (SPLM)
Second Vice President	Ali Uthman Muhammad Taha (NC)
Ministers	
Agriculture and Forestry	Abdul Haleem Ismail Al-Mutafee
Cabinet Affairs/Council of Ministers	Kosta Manibi (SPLM)
Culture, Youth and Sports	Mohammed Youssef Abdullah (NC)
Defense	Lt. Gen. Abdel-Rahim Hussein (NC)
Education	Hamid Mohamed Ibrahim (NDA)
Energy and Mining	Al-Zubayr Ahmed al-Hasan (NDA)
Environment and Urban Planning	Ahmed Babakr Nahar (NC)
Federal Governance	Lt. Gen. Abd Al-Rahman Sa'id (NC)
Finance	Awad Ahmad al-Jaz (NC)
Foreign Affairs	Deng Alor Kol (SPLM)
Foreign Trade	James Kok Reyu (SPLM)
Health	Tabita Boutros Sokaya (SPLM) [f]
Higher Education and Scientific Research	Peter Adoc Niapa (SPLM)
Humanitarian Affairs	Harun Ron Lual (SPLM)
Industry	Jalal Yusuf Mohammed Digair (DUP)
Information and Communications	El-Zahawi Ibrahim Malik (UP)
Interior	Ibrahim Mahmud Hamid (NC)
International Cooperation	Etigani Saleh Al-Tijani (NC)
Investment	George Boreng Niyami (SPLM)
Irrigation and Water Resources	Kamal Ali Mohammed (NC)
Justice	Abdel-Basit Sabdarat (NC)
Labor, Public Service, and Human Resources	Maj. Gen. (ret.) Alison Manani Makaya (NC)
Livestock and Fishery	Faysal Hasan Ibrahim
Parliamentary Affairs	Joseph Okello Abango (SPLM)
Presidency	Maj. Gen. Bakri Hassan Salih (NC)
Religious Guidance and Endowments	Azhari al-Taji Awad al-Sayyed (NC)
Science and Technology	Ibrahim Ahmad Umar (NC)
Tourism	Joseph Malwal (UDSF)
Transport and Roads	Philip Thon Lik (SPLM)
Welfare and Social Development	Samia Ahmed Mohammed (NC)
Attorney General	Ali Mohamed Osman Yassin
Governor, Central Bank of Sudan	Muhammad al-Hasan Sabir

[f] = female

COMMUNICATIONS

Press. The Bashir government banned all newspapers and magazines with the exception of the weekly military paper, *al-Guwat al-Musallaha* (Armed Forces), in June 1989. The following September two new dailies were issued under government auspices, *al-Engaz al-Watani* and *al-Sudan al-Hadith.* In May 1990 a new English-language weekly, *New Horizon,* was launched. In April 1993 it was reported that *al-Khartoum* resumed publication from exile in Cairo, Egypt. Two months later the government announced a relaxation of its press monopoly; however, in April 1994 the country's sole privately owned paper, *al-Sudan al-Dawli,* was closed for criticizing the NIF's continued support of the regime.

On May 10, 2003, the *Khartoum Monitor,* Sudan's only English-language daily, was banned. On August 12, 2003, President Bashir issued a decree to end press censorship, yet despite an increase of daily papers and online press, state media maintains control and censorship is evident. In 2008 it was reported that the government had quietly reinstituted media censorship. The SPLM has its own newspapers in the south, and there are at least six print news resources, such as the *Juba Post* and *Akhbar Al-Youm,* and eight online resources. In its annual report on press freedom, Reporters Without Borders ranked Sudan out 135 out of 173 countries.

News agencies. The domestic facility is the Sudan News Agency (SUNA) (*Wakalat al-Anba al-Sudan*). A number of foreign agencies maintain bureaus in Khartoum.

Broadcasting and computing. Republic of Sudan Broadcasting (*Idhaat al-Jumhuriyah al-Sudan*) is a government facility transmitting in Arabic, Amharic, Somali, and Tigrinya as well as in English and French. Television service is provided by the commercial State Television Service. As of 2008 there were 101.6 Internet users per 1,000 inhabitants.

INTERGOVERNMENTAL REPRESENTATION

Ambassador to the U.S.: (Vacant).

U.S. Ambassador to Sudan: Robert E. WHITEHEAD.

Permanent Representative to the UN: Abdalmahmood Abdalhaleem MOHAMAD.

IGO Memberships (Non-UN): AfDB, AFESD, AMF, AU, BADEA, CAEU, Comesa, IDB, IGAD, Interpol, IOM, LAS, NAM, OIC, PCA, WCO, IFC, IMF.

SURINAME

Republic of Suriname
Republiek Suriname

Political Status: Former Netherlands dependency; granted internal autonomy on December 29, 1954, and complete independence on November 25, 1975; constitution of November 21, 1975, suspended on August 15, 1980, following military coup of February 25; present constitution approved by referendum of September 30, 1987.

Area: 63,036 sq. mi. (163,265 sq. km.).

Population: 492, 829 (2004C), 515,000 (2008E).

Major Urban Center (2005E): PARAMARIBO (urban area, 252,000).

Official Language: Linguistically, Suriname is exceptionally diverse. The official language is Dutch, but English, Hindi, Javanese, Chinese, and Sranan Tongo (*Taki-Taki*), a Creole lingua franca, are widely spoken, while Spanish has been adopted as a working language to facilitate communication with Latin American neighbors. In the interior, a number of indigenous languages are also spoken.

Monetary Unit: Suriname Dollar (market rate December 1, 2009: 2.74 dollars = $1US). The Suriname Dollar replaced the Suriname Guilder in January 2004.

President: Ronald (Runaldo) VENETIAAN (Suriname National Party); served as president 1991–1996; elected to a second five-year term by the National Assembly on August 4, 2000, succeeding Jules Albert WIJDENBOSCH (formerly National Democratic Party); reelected by United People's Assembly on August 3, 2005, and inaugurated for a third five-year term on August 12.

Vice President and Chair of the Council of Ministers: Ramdien (Ram) SARDJOE (Progressive Reform Party); elected by the United People's Assembly on August 3, 2005, and inaugurated on August 12 for a term concurrent with that of the President, succeeding Jules R. AJODHIA (Progressive Reform Party).

THE COUNTRY

Formerly known as Dutch Guiana, Suriname lies on the north-central coast of South America and is bordered by Guyana on the west, French Guiana on the east, and Brazil on the south. Because of the early importation of slave labor from Africa and contract labor from Asia, its society is one of the most ethnically varied in the world. The largest groups are Hindustanis (39 percent) and Creoles (31 percent), followed by Javanese (15 percent), black Africans, Amerindians, Chinese, and various European minorities. Freedom of worship has traditionally prevailed among equally diverse religious groups, which adhere to Protestant (primarily Dutch Reform, Lutheran, and Moravian), Roman Catholic, Hindu, Muslim, and Confucian faiths.

The greater part of the land area is covered with virgin forest, although the coastal region is both flat and fertile. The tropical climate yields a wide range of agricultural products that include rice, various fruits, sugar, and coffee. Suriname ranks among the world's leading producers of alumina and bauxite that, together with aluminum, account for nearly 80 percent of the country's exports; however, the Australian-based BHP-Billiton, reportedly the world's largest bauxite mining company, announced in late 2008 that it would discontinue mining activities in Suriname by 2010 because of exhaustion of deposits at its three principal mines.

Although long enjoying a higher standard of living than many of its neighbors, the country has experienced economic difficulty since 1980, due largely to reduced world demand for bauxite and the suspension of Dutch and U.S. aid in reaction to a wave of official killings in December 1982. By 1986 Suriname faced what its administration termed an "economic emergency" featuring large budget deficits, mounting inflation, 25 percent unemployment, a flourishing parallel market, and disruption by rebel activity in the eastern and southern parts of the country. In early 1988, following installation of the first elected government in eight years, the country's major donors indicated that they were prepared to resume aid, agreement with the Netherlands being reached in August for the disbursement of more than $700 million over a seven-to-eight-year period. However, the aid program was suspended in mid-1993 after the disbursement of only $53 million because of the lack of an economic adjustment strategy acceptable to the International Monetary Fund and the unwillingness of the European Community to act as an external monitor for other donors. According to the World Bank, GNP per capita was $870 in 1994, a decline of nearly 20 percent from the previous year, although by 1998 it had recovered and grown to $1,660. Economic deterioration was the focus of the May 2000 legislative balloting, which led to the installation of a reformist government. GDP, in constant terms, declined by 0.1 percent in 2000 but rose thereafter by an average of 6.3 percent for 2003–2008. During the same period inflation dropped sharply from 80.4 percent to 9.5 percent.

GOVERNMENT AND POLITICS

Political background. First acquired by the Netherlands from Great Britain in 1667 in exchange for Manhattan Island, the territory now known as Suriname passed among Britain, France, and the Netherlands several times before Dutch authority was formally confirmed by the Congress of Vienna in 1815. It remained a dependency of the Netherlands until enactment of a Statute of the Realm in December 1954 that provided the country with a parliamentary form of government and the right of local constitutional revision, thereby according it full equality with the Netherlands and the Netherlands Antilles.

A substantial portion of Suriname's Hindustani population, which accounted for the bulk of the country's skilled labor force, opposed independence, fearing economic and political repression by the Creole-dominated government of Henck ARRON, who had become prime minister in 1973. More than 40,000 Surinamese, most of them Hindustanis, subsequently emigrated, the majority settling in the Netherlands. Their relocation created a number of social and economic problems for the Netherlands while leaving Suriname with a formidable gap in such areas as commerce, medicine, and teaching. Because of the émigré problem, provisions guaranteeing certain Hindustani rights were incorporated into the independence constitution of 1975, although the government for the most part failed in its efforts to convince the expatriates to return.

Prime Minister Arron was reconfirmed following a parliamentary election in October 1977 but was ousted in an armed rebellion of 300 noncommissioned officers on February 25, 1980, following government refusal to sanction trade union activity within the armed forces. On March 15 the leaders of the revolt, organized as a National Military Council (NMC), designated the politically moderate Dr. Henk CHIN A Sen as prime minister while permitting the essentially titular president, Dr. Johan H. E. FERRIER, to retain his office. On August 15 the constitution was suspended, with Ferrier being dismissed and Chin being named as his acting successor while continuing as prime minister. On December 3 Chin was confirmed as president, the office of prime minister being abolished.

During 1981 differences arose between President Chin, who had called for a return to democratic rule, and Lt. Col. (formerly Sgt. Maj.) Dési BOUTERSE, who had emerged as the strongman of the NMC. As a result, Chin resigned on February 4, 1982, being replaced four days later, on an acting basis, by Lachmipersad F. RAMDAT-MISIER. In the wake of an unsuccessful uprising by right-wing military elements on March 10–11, martial law was declared, while in apparent response to foreign pressure, a new government headed by Henry N. NEYHORST in the reactivated post of prime minister was announced on March 31. Following the reported discovery of a new antigovernment conspiracy on December 8, Neyhorst also resigned, and the NMC ordered the execution of 15 leaders of a political group called the Association for Democratic Action, claiming that they had scheduled a coup for Christmas day. On February 26, 1983, Dr. Errol ALIBUX of the leftist Progressive Workers' and Farm Laborers' Union (PALU) was chosen to head a new cabinet dominated by PALU members. Austerity measures, necessitated by the withdrawal of Dutch and U.S. aid, provoked a strike in

December by bauxite workers, who were joined by electricity workers in early January 1984. The action forced the revocation of retroactive increases in income taxes, and on January 8 Colonel Bouterse announced the dismissal of the Alibux government. On February 3 an interim administration led by former Arron aide Willem (Wim) UDENHOUT was sworn in, pending "the formation of new democratic institutions." In December the government announced a 27-month program for a "return to democracy" that included the establishment, on January 1, 1985, of an appointive 31-member National Assembly charged with the drafting of a new constitution.

On August 2, 1985, the Assembly formally designated Colonel Bouterse as "head of government," while reconfirming Ramdat-Misier as acting president. In early September it was announced that the Assembly had appointed a commission, structured on an essentially corporative basis (including representatives of the major unions and the Association of Surinamese Manufacturers), to draft a new basic law. Subsequently, a number of party leaders accepted an invitation from Colonel Bouterse to join the NMC in forming a Supreme Council (*Topberaad*) that would serve as the country's highest political organ. The new body approved the installation of a government headed by Pretaapnarain RADHAKISHUN on July 17, 1986, following the resignation of Prime Minister Udenhout on June 23. Radhakishun was in turn succeeded by Jules Albert WIJDENBOSCH on February 13, 1987.

Despite an earlier announcement that a general election would not be held until March 1988, Colonel Bouterse stated on March 31, 1987, that the balloting would be advanced to independence day, November 25, 1987, preceded by a September 30 referendum on the new constitution. The election yielded a landslide victory for the Front for Democracy and Development (FDO), a coalition of the three leading opposition parties, with Bouterse's recently organized National Democratic Party (NDP) winning only 3 of 51 legislative seats. On January 12, 1988, the new Assembly unanimously elected former agriculture minister Ramsewak SHANKAR to a five-year term as president, with former prime minister Arron designated as vice president and prime minister. Bouterse, however, remained commander in chief of the army and, because of a lack of constitutional specificity in regard to both the membership and functions of a revamped Military Council and a nonelective Council of State, appeared to have lost little capacity for the exercise of decisive political influence.

Of more immediate concern was the continued activity of a rebel Surinamese Liberation Army (SLA), led by former Bouterse aide Ronnie BRUNSWIJK, which, with apparent support from bushnegro (*bosneger*) villagers, had severely disrupted bauxite mining in the eastern region before a government counteroffensive that had driven it back to the border with French Guiana. In June 1988 the government reversed its long-standing position and announced that it would begin talks with the rebels, which did not, however, commence until late October. Following a number of clashes between elements of the "Jungle Commando" and government militia units, the National Assembly approved an amnesty for the rebels on June 1, 1989, and ratified a formal agreement for terminating the conflict on August 8. Subsequently, however, the accord was strongly condemned by Amerindian representatives as conceding too much to the *bosneger* population, while the army branded one of its key provisions as unconstitutional.

The four-year rebellion took a somewhat surprising turn on June 18, 1990, when Brunswijk appeared in Cayenne, French Guiana, stating that he had tired of the struggle and wished to seek asylum in the Netherlands. He then departed for Paris, leadership of the rebel group seemingly having been assumed by his deputy, Johan "Castro" WALLY. However, it soon appeared that the action had been a ruse to facilitate what proved to be unproductive talks with Dutch officials, followed by Brunswijk's return to Suriname in July.

A series of discussions between army and rebel representatives in October and November culminated in a request by Colonel Bouterse that the government withdraw a number of arrest warrants dating from the period of military rule. Shortly thereafter Bouterse was angered by the president's failure to offer assistance during a period of detention by Dutch authorities while on a European trip, and on December 22 the colonel resigned as military commander. His successor, Cdr. Iwan GRAANOOGST, promptly mounted a Christmas Eve coup, which yielded Bouterse's reinstatement following the December 30 replacement, on an acting basis, of President Shankar by Johannes Samuel KRAAG and of Vice President and Prime Minister Arron by former prime minister Wijdenbosch. (Arron died in December 2000 in the Netherlands, to which he had withdrawn in self-imposed exile.)

In legislative balloting on May 25, 1991, what was now termed the New Front for Democracy and Development (NFDD) won 30 of 51 seats (10 less than in 1987 and 4 short of the two-thirds needed to elect a president), while the army-backed NDP increased its representation from 3 seats to 10. After a lengthy impasse, during which no candidate was able to secure a presidential majority, a special United People's Assembly was convened (see Constitution and government, below) that on September 7 elected NFDD nominee Ronald (Runaldo) R. VENETIAAN as the new head of state; ten days later a cabinet headed by the vice president and prime minister, Jules R. AJODHIA, was announced.

On March 25, 1992, the National Assembly approved a number of constitutional amendments including, most importantly, abolition of the political role of the army, which would thenceforth be limited to national defense and combating "organized subversion." On May 5 Brunswijk's SLA and another leading guerrilla group, the Amerindian *Tucayana Amazonicas,* agreed to suspend hostilities, and on August 8 signed a revised peace treaty with the government that included revival of the 1989 amnesty. Under the accord, members of the rebel groups would be permitted to join the police force for the interior, while the government was to give the region priority in economic development and social welfare programs.

On November 20, 1992, Colonel Bouterse, buffeted by reports that he had become the country's richest man by corrupt means, again resigned as army commander. However, on October 4, 1993, he returned to the limelight as leader of a mass demonstration in Paramaribo against austerity measures recently mandated by the government and by mid-1995 appeared poised to reenter politics as NDP leader.

In an inconclusive general election on May 23, 1996, a four-party New Front (NF) coalition led by President Venetiaan's Suriname National Party (NPS) won 24 seats, as contrasted with the NDP's second-place showing of 16. Thereafter, a series of failed efforts by Venetiaan to forge a majority with smaller parties prompted defections from the NF (see Political Parties, below) that yielded a bloc of 28 legislators supporting the NDP. However, the NDP's augmented strength fell short of the two-thirds needed to elect a president. A new United People's Assembly was therefore convened, which on September 5 named NDP Vice Chair Wijdenbosch to the presidency on a 437–407 vote. While Bouterse's party was thus restored to power, the former dictator was himself barred from office at the insistence of the NDP's allies. Named as vice president and prime minister was Pretaapnarian (Pretaap) RADHAKISHUN, who had first served as cabinet head a decade earlier.

By late 1997, a number of party realignments had taken place, although the Wijdenbosch administration retained a parliamentary majority. Also jeopardized by several defections in early 1998, the government succeeded in securing the support of 26 of the 51 legislators by late March.

The situation worsened sharply in 1999. On May 28 President Wijdenbosch dismissed his entire cabinet in the wake of an economic collapse that had triggered widespread popular demonstrations. On June 1 the National Assembly voted to remove the president from office, but he refused to comply on the grounds that such action required a two-thirds majority. Six weeks later, on July 16, a Dutch court sentenced Bouterse in absentia to 11 years' imprisonment and a $2.18 million fine for participating in smuggling drugs into the Netherlands between 1989 and 1997. Additional charges, alleging the torture and killing of dissidents in 1982, were filed by the Dutch attorney general in January 2000 (see NDP, below).

Before the election of May 25, 2000, Wijdenbosch left the NDP to form a group called the Democratic National Platform 2000. However, the new formation ran a poor third behind Venetiaan's New Front, which captured 47 percent of the vote, and an NDP-led Millennium Combination, which secured 15 percent. After lengthy interparty discussions, Venetiaan succeeded in securing a new mandate on August 4 and assumed office on August 12, with Ajodhia returning as vice president and prime minister.

In inconclusive balloting on May 25, 2005, the New Front lost a third of its National Assembly representation and failed to secure a necessary two-thirds majority for Venetiaan's reelection in two legislative ballots in July. Subsequently, the party concluded an alliance with the A-Combination, a recently formed Maroon-based coalition that yielded a third term for Venetiaan in a United People's Assembly poll on August 3.

Constitution and government. In the immediate wake of the 1990 coup, Commander Graanoogst promised an early return to civilian rule, a pledge that yielded the election of May 25, 1991. The 1987 constitution, under which the polling took place, sets forth a complex system of government within which the intended distribution of power is by no means clearly defined. A 51-member National Assembly, elected for a five-year term, selects a president and vice president for terms of the same duration; however, the action must be by a two-thirds majority, lacking which the choice is made by a simple majority of a United People's Assembly (*Vereinigde Volksvergadering*), comprised of the National Assembly members plus 289 local and regional councilors. The selection must be deferred until 30 days after the election to accommodate any disputed legislative contests. The president serves as chair of a nonelective State Council whose composition is "regulated by law" and whose purpose is to advise the government on public policy, ensuring that its actions are in conformity with the basic law; the president also chairs a Security Council, which is empowered to assume governmental authority in the event of "war, state of siege, or exceptional circumstances to be determined by law." The Assembly may amend the constitution by a two-thirds majority or, lacking such a majority, by convening the equivalent of a presidential assembly. For electoral purposes the country is divided into ten districts.

In early 1992 the Assembly began debate on a variety of constitutional amendments, only one of which, a ban on political activity by the army, was subsequently approved. Other proposed changes would have limited the State Council to a purely advisory role, with no capacity to veto government decisions, and given the president the power of legislative dissolution, while permitting a two-thirds majority of the assembly to dismiss the president.

Foreign relations. Before the 1980 coup Suriname's foreign relations turned on two main issues: long-standing border disputes with neighboring Guyana and French Guiana and the status of development assistance from the Netherlands. The border disputes resulted from Guyana's claim to a 6,000-square-mile tract reputedly rich in bauxite deposits and from France's claim to a 780-square-mile tract believed to contain deposits of gold; neither controversy has yet been resolved, although Suriname and Guyana agreed in mid-1995 to open negotiations on their dispute within the framework of a joint commission. The Dutch aid, exceeding $1.5 billion, was to have been disbursed over a period of 10–15 years to ensure the opposition's support for independence, raise the standard of living for the Surinamese people, and compensate for termination of the preindependence right of emigration from Suriname to the Netherlands.

Considerable uncertainty followed in the wake of the first Arron overthrow, the coup itself being largely unplanned, with no clear foreign policy overtones. However, a distinctly leftward thrust had become apparent by the time of President Chin's resignation, the increasingly dominant Bouterse faction within the NMC having adopted a pro-Cuban posture in regional affairs, leading to a sizable increase in the flight of Surinamese to the Netherlands (despite the expiration of automatic entitlement to entry visas) and the recall of the Dutch ambassador in March 1982. The subsequent withdrawal of Dutch aid (which had been the principal source of Suriname's relatively high standard of living) was a severe blow to the country's economy. In early 1983 it appeared that the fiscal shortfall might be alleviated by commitments from Cuba and Libya. However, on June 1, coincident with reports that the administration of U.S. president Ronald Reagan had considered a Central Intelligence Agency (CIA) plan to infiltrate and destabilize the self-proclaimed "socialist" regime, a substantial military and trade agreement was concluded with Brazil. Two weeks later, amid Dutch reports that Brazil had threatened to invade Suriname if efforts were not taken to curb Cuban influence, Colonel Bouterse announced that Sgt. Maj. Badressein SITAL, one of the most pro-Cuban members of the NMC, had been dismissed from both his Council and ministerial positions. In mid-October Bouterse visited the United States and later in the month, following the Grenada action, asked Cuba to withdraw its ambassador and sharply reduce its remaining diplomatic staff in Paramaribo.

In early 1984 the regime lodged official protests with the French and Netherlands governments over their alleged complicity in an invasion plot, and in March 1985 Suriname threatened to take the Netherlands to the International Court of Justice (ICJ) for discontinuance of its aid program under the 1975 independence accord. The latter pronouncement came in the wake of an adverse UN Human Rights Commission report on the 1982 killings that dissuaded The Hague from reconsideration of its aid posture. On the other hand, an announcement by the government that it would proceed with ICJ action appeared to be rendered moot by The Hague's positive response in 1988 to the balloting of the previous November. Subsequently, at the conclusion of a three-day visit to the Hague by President Venetiaan in June 1992, the Netherlands and Suriname signed a cooperation treaty that formally ended their lengthy estrangement, although Dutch financial assistance was again suspended in mid-1993 (see The Country, above).

The aid issue was further exacerbated in September 1997 by a Dutch request that Interpol issue an international warrant for the arrest and extradition of Dési Bouterse on drug-trafficking and money-laundering charges. In a similar vein, the Netherlands appealed unsuccessfully for the arrest of Bouterse while the former dictator was on a private visit to Trinidad and Tobago in mid-1998. Bouterse went on trial in absentia in a Dutch court in March 1999 and four months later was convicted of the charge against him. Development aid from the Netherlands was again suspended in June 1999 before being resumed in early 2001, partly in response to the positive reaction of the Netherlands to the 2000 elections. Relations improved further in September 2001 when the Netherlands formally apologized for the practice of slavery in Dutch Guiana.

A new dispute with Guyana erupted in 2000 involving an offshore oil concession by Guyana to a Canadian oil exploration company. In June a Surinamese gunboat forced the company to move a rig from territory claimed by Paramaribo. The bitter dispute was at the center of discussions at the July summit of the Caribbean Community and Common Market (Caricom), to which Suriname had been admitted in 1995. With no resolution forthcoming, Guyana referred the matter to arbitration under the UN Convention on the Law of the Sea (UNCLOS) in February 2004. Suriname promptly filed a counterclaim, and in June a UN tribunal was formed in Germany to hear the case, which in September 2007 issued a ruling in favor of Guyana.

In early 2007 Suriname concluded an agreement allowing Venezuelan nationals to fish in its waters, if all of the catches were delivered to Paramaribo. However, the Surinamese government cited payment concerns in taking no immediate action to join PetroCaribe, under which Venezuela supplies oil and its byproducts to Caribbean countries on preferential terms.

A member of the UN and other international and regional organizations, Suriname was admitted to the Caricom in February 1995.

Current issues. In June 2007 a Paramaribo court ruled that former dictator Bouterse could be prosecuted for the 1982 killings, although the proceedings were suspended until early 2009 on technical grounds. Meanwhile, Bouterse was expelled from the National Assembly for failing to participate in parliamentary sessions. (The military trial for Bouterse and 24 codefendants continued through the end of 2009.)

Regionally, disputes with both eastern and western neighbors continued. Paramaribo was reported in May 2008 to have complained that efforts to rid French Guiana of illegal gold miners had resulted in many crossing the open border into Suriname; in October, the long-simmering issue over navigation on the Corentyne River included the seizure of a Guyanese vessel for "trespassing" into Surinamese territory.

POLITICAL PARTIES

An intense rivalry between Creole and Hindustani groups characterized the party structure of Suriname in the years following independence. The Creole-dominated National Party Alliance (*Nationale Partij Komibnatie*—NPK), organized in advance of the 1977 election with the Suriname National Party (NPS) as its core, controlled a bare majority in the *Staten* before the coup of February 25, 1980. Most of the leading opposition parties were grouped into the United Democratic Parties (*Verenigde Democratische Partijen*—VDP), a predominantly Hindu coalition dominated by the leftist Progressive Reform Party (VHP).

While traditional party activity was suspended following the 1980 coup, two leftist groups, the now-defunct Revolutionary People's Party (*Revolutionaire Volkspartij*—RVP) and the Progressive Workers' and Farm Laborers' Union (PALU, below), were represented in postcoup governments, initially as elements of a regime-supportive Revolutionary Front established in November 1981. The Front became moribund after the establishment of the February 25 Movement, which was itself supplanted by the army-backed National Democratic Party before the 1987 election. Earlier, following relaxation of the party ban in the fall of 1985, the VHP, the NPS, and the Party of National Unity and Solidarity were invited to participate in the government, their leaders joining the Supreme Council in November.

On August 2, 1987, leaders of the three leading opposition groups formed an electoral alliance, the Front for Democracy and Development, which swept the November balloting by winning 40 of 51 legislative seats. Before the 1991 election the Suriname Labor Party joined the Front, whose representation nonetheless dropped to a simple majority. Numerous changes in alliances occurred before and after the 1996, 2000, and 2005 elections, as indicated below.

Government Groups:

New Front for Democracy and Development (*Nieuw Front voor Democratie en Ontwikkeling*—NF). Initially a three-member coalition of traditional ethnic parties (NPS, VHP, SPA, below) styled the Front for Democracy and Development (*Front noor Democratie en Ontwikkeling*—FDO), the NF, augmented by the KTPI, (see under VVV, below), gained 30 of 51 National Assembly seats in 1991, as contrasted with 40 won by the FDO in 1987. Its representation dropped to 24 after the election of May 23, 1996, and was reduced thereafter as a result of KTPI withdrawal and defections by VHP members in support of the Wijdenbosch presidency. The New Front recovered its majority in the May 2000 elections, the *Pertjajah Luhur* having joined the coalition to once again bring its membership to four parties.

Leader: Ronald (Runaldo) VENETIAAN (President of the Republic).

Suriname National Party (*Nationale Partij Suriname*—NPS). A Creole grouping founded in 1946, the NPS was the leading advocate of independence from the Netherlands and the core party of the National Party Alliance before the 1980 coup. Its leader served as president from 1991 to 1996 and was returned to the office in 2000, when the NPS won 14 of the NF's 33 National Assembly seats, and again in 2005, despite reduction of the NF to a plurality of 23 seats.

Leaders: Ronald (Runaldo) VENETIAAN (President of the Republic), Rufus NOOITMEER (Former NF Parliamentary Leader), Willem (Wim) Alfred UDENHOUT, Otmar Roel RODGERS (Secretary).

Progressive Reform Party (*Vooruitstrvende Hervormde Partij*—VHP). Initially called the United Reform Party (*Verenigde Hervormings Partij*—VHP), and long the leading Hindu party, the left-of-center VHP originally opposed independence because of anticipated repression by the Creole-dominated Alliance. The VHP's legislative representation of 16 seats in 1987 dropped to 9 in 1991, all of which were retained in 1996 before the defection of a group styled the Movement for Freedom and Democracy (see BVD, under VVV, below).

Leader: Ram SARDJOE (Vice President and Prime Minister of the Republic).

Suriname Labor Party (*Surinaamse Partij van de Arbeid*—SPA). The SPA is a social democratic formation affiliated with the Centrale 47 trade union. It withdrew as a member of the New Front in July 2005 but subsequently returned, with its leader, Sigfried Gilds, being named minister of trade and industry. Gilds resigned his ministerial post in January 2006 after being accused of complicity in a money-laundering operation for which a nephew had been convicted. In early 2009 he was convicted and sentenced to a 12-month jail term.

Leader: Sigfried F. GILDS (Chair).

Full Confidence Party (*Pertjajah Luhur*—PL). A splinter from *Pendawa Lima* (below), the *Pertjajah Luhur* joined the New Front before the 2000 legislative balloting. Its leader, Paul Somohardjo, is currently president of the National Assembly.

Leader: Paul Slamet SOMOHARDJO.

A-Combination (*A-Combinatie*—AC or A-Com). The AC was formed before the 2005 election as an alliance that included the **General Liberation and Development Party** (*Algemene Bevrijdings en Ontwikkelings Partij*—ABOP), led by former SLA leader Ronnie Brunswijk, and the **Brotherhood and Unity in Politics** (*Broederschap en Eenheid in Politiek*—BEP), led by Caprino Allendy.

An alliance with the NF in mid-2005 yielded the majority supporting Venetiaan's retention of the presidency.

Leaders: Ronnie BRUNSWIJK (ABOP), Caprino ALLENDY (BEP).

Other Parliamentary Groups:

National Democratic Party (*Nationale Democratische Partij*—NDP). The NDP was formed before the 1987 election as a political vehicle for the supporters of Colonel Bouterse. As such, it succeeded the February 25 Movement, styled *Stanvaste* ("Steadfast") in Dutch, which had been characterized as a "movement, not a party" at its launching in 1984. Contrary to expectations, the NDP secured only three Assembly seats in 1987, two of which were subject to challenge and represented constituencies that had not been contested by Front nominees; the party's representation rose to 12 in 1991 and to 16 in May 1996.

Tension was reported in early 1999 between the rank-and-file of the NDP, described as supportive of Bouterse, and supporters (said to include most NDP legislators) of President Wijdenbosch. The president dismissed Bouterse as a presidential adviser in early April, Wijdenbosch subsequently forming the DNP 2000 (see under VVV, below).

An international arrest warrant was issued by a court in the Netherlands for Bouterse in 1997 on charges involving his alleged involvement in the smuggling of cocaine from Suriname to Europe. In June 2000 the Netherlands' court sentenced Bouterse in absentia to 11 years in prison in the case; however, Bouterse remained free in Suriname under protection of the Surinamese constitution, which prohibits extradition of nationals. (President Venetiaan has proposed revision of the basic law to permit, among other things, extradition in cases such as Bouterse's.) Meanwhile, prosecutors in the Netherlands in 2000 also attempted to pursue a case against Bouterse in connection with the execution of 15 political opponents in Suriname in 1982. The Netherlands High Court dismissed the charges in September 2001 on the ground that Netherlands had no jurisdiction in the case. However, similar charges were levied in Suriname (see Current issues, above).

For the 2000 campaign, the NDP served as the core component of an alliance styled the Millennium Combination (*Millenium Combatie*—MC) that included the KTPI (under VVV, below) and the DA'91 (under A1, below).

Leaders: Lt. Col. Désiré (Dési) BOUTERSE (Former Army Commander and NDP Chair), Col. Harvey NAARENDORP (Former *Stanvaste* Secretary General).

People's Alliance for Progress (*Volksalliante Voor Vooruitgang*—VVV). The VVV was formed before the 2005 campaign by former president Jules Wijdenbosch as a grouping of his DNP 2000, plus the other two parties listed below. It won five National Assembly seats in 2005.

Leader: Jules WIJDENBOSCH (Former President of the Republic).

Democratic National Platform 2000 (*Democratisch Nationaal Platform 2000*—DNP 2000). The DNP 2000 was launched by Jules Wijdenbosch following his break with Colonel Bouterse in 1999. Closely affiliated with the group for the 2000 elections were **D21** (under A1, below) and the **Democratic Party** (*Democratische Partij*—DP), led by Frank PLAYFAIR. For the 1996 election the DP had joined the HPP (below) in forming the Alliance.

In the 2000 balloting the DNP 2000 list won three National Assembly seats, one of which was taken up by Playfair.

Leaders: Jules Albert WIJDENBOSCH, Liakat Ali Errol ALIBUX.

Basic Party for Renewal and Democracy (*Basispartij voor Vernieuwing en Democratie*—BVD). Initially called the Movement for Freedom and Democracy (*Beweging voor Vriheid en Democratie*—BVD), the BVD is a Hindu party formed by a group of VHP dissidents in 1996. The movement participated in formation of the Wijdenbosch government in September and was subsequently registered as a party under its current name. Its former chair, Motilal MUNGRA, was dismissed as finance minister in August 1997 after accusing the president of extravagant expenditure, although the party retained its other cabinet posts. The BVD's Pretaapnarain RADHAKISHUN served as vice president and prime minister from 1996 until 2000. He died shortly after leaving office.

In the 2000 election the BVD won 3.2 percent of the National Assembly vote but no seats.

Leader: Dr. Tjanrikapersad (Tjan) GOBARDHAN (Chair).

Party of National Unity and Solidarity (*Kerukunan Tulodo Pranatan Inggil*—KTPI). Formerly known as the Indonesian Peasants' Party (*Kaum-Tani Persuatan Indonesia*), the KTPI is a small, predominantly Javanese rural party founded in 1947. It joined the National Party Alliance before the 1977 election but withdrew in December 1978. As a participant in the New Front, it won seven seats in 1991 and five in 1996 before withdrawing to enter the Wijdenbosch government. It contested the 2000 balloting as part of the Millennium Coalition.

Leader: Willy SOEMITA.

A1. A1 was formed before the 2005 balloting as a coalition that included the three groups below.

Democratic Alternative '91 (*Democratisch Alternatief '91*—DA'91). The DA'91 was launched before the 1991 election by Gerard BRUNINGS, an airline executive who urged a constitutional amendment precluding political activity by both labor and the military. At its inception the formation was a coalition of Brunings's **Alternative Forum** (*Alternatief Forum*—AF), which is now led by Ricardo (Rick) Otto van RAVENSWAAY; the Bushnegro Unity Party (*Bosneger Eenheids Partij*—BEP, see under AC, above), and two groups that withdrew before the 1996 election: the *Pendawa Lima* and the HPP (both below). The coalition won nine legislative seats in 1991, four in 1996, and two in 2000.

Leader: Djagendre RAMICHELAWAN.

Democrats of the 21st Century (*Democraten van de 21ste Eeuw*—D21). Organized in 1986, D21 was affiliated with DNP 2000 for the 2000 poll.

Leader: Soewarto MUSTADJA.

Political Wing of the Federation of Farmers and Farm Workers (*Politieke Vleugel van de Federatie van Agrariërs en Landarbeiders*—PVF, or Political Wing of the FAL). The PVF was organized in the late 1990s to advance the agenda of the FAL trade union, which opposed the Wijdenbosch government. In the 2000 National Assembly election it won two seats.

Leaders: Jiwan SITAL (Chair), Soedichand JAIRAM.

Other Parties:

Progressive Workers' and Farmers' Union (*Progressieve Arbeiders en Landbouwers Unie*—PALU). The only trade union to have retained a public role after many labor leaders were killed in December 1982, the left-wing PALU dominated the Alibux cabinet but was not represented in subsequent administrations. It won four Assembly seats from "war zone" constituencies in 1987, none in 1991 or 1996, and one in 2000.

Leaders: Jim K. HOK (Chair), Henk RAMNANDANLAL (Vice Chair).

Reformed Progressive Party (*Hernieuwde Progressieve Partij*—HPP). Formerly a member of the DA'91, the HPP is a predominantly Hindu social democratic formation that split from the VHP in 1975 and later participated in the pre-1980 National Party Alliance. For the 1996 election it joined the Democratic Party in forming The Alliance (*De Alliantie*), which secured three National Assembly seats. Also subsequently associated with the Alliance was the Christian democratic **Progressive People's Party of Suriname** (*Progressieve Surinaamse Volkspartij*—PSV) of W. WONG Loi Sing. In 2000 the HPP and the PSV registered separately.

Leader: Harry KISOENSINGH (Chair).

Pendawa Lima. A predominantly Javanese party dating from 1975, the *Pendawa Lima* ("Five Sons of King Pandu") joined DA '91 in 1991, thereafter winning four parliamentary seats in its own right in 1996. Before the 2000 legislative poll, the *Pendawa Lima* split into two factions, with theretofore *Pendawa Lima* Chair Paul Somohardjo leading his faction into the New Front and subsequent government as the *Pertjajah Luhur.* (Both the rump *Pendawa Lima* and *Pertjajah Luhur* use the abbreviation "PL," causing confusion in some news reports.)

Leader: Raymond SAPOEN.

Other parties are the **National Party for Leadership and Development** (*Nationale Partij voor Leiderschap en Ontwikkeling*—NPLO), led by Oesman WANGSABESARIE; the **National Reform Party** (*Nationale Hervormings Partij*—NHP), led by Kenneth MOENNE; **New Choice** (*Naya Kadam*—NK), led by Waldo RAMDHAL; the **Party for Democracy through Unity and Development** (*Partij voor Demokratie en Ontwikkeling in Eenheid*—DOE); and the **Suriname Amazon Party** (*Amazone Partij Suriname*—APS), led by Kenneth VAN GENDEREN.

Exile Group:

In January 1983 a Movement for the Liberation of Suriname was formed by exiles in the Netherlands under the leadership of former president Chin and former deputy prime minister André HAAKMAT. However, the Dutch government refused to recognize the group as a government in exile, and both subsequently declared their support for the Surinamese Liberation Army (SLA, below).

Guerrilla Groups:

Surinamese Liberation Army (SLA). The largely *bosneger* SLA was formed in early 1986 by former army private Ronnie Brunswijk with the avowed aim of overthrowing Colonel Bouterse and "[restoring] the constitutional state" through free elections. The government charged Surinamese émigrés in the Netherlands with supporting the SLA, whose approximately 2,000 members launched a guerrilla campaign in the country's eastern and southern regions that appeared to have been largely contained by mid-1987. In the wake of the November election, the SLA's "Jungle Commando" was reported to have declared an unconditional truce, effective January 1, 1988. Sporadic conflict, interspersed by talks with government and army representatives, nonetheless continued, before the conclusion of a preliminary peace accord in a ceremony attended by Bouterse and Brunswijk on March 26, 1991, which was followed by a suspension of hostilities on May 5 and the conclusion of a formal peace treaty on August 1, 1992. The General Liberation and Development Party, led by Brunswijk, competed unsuccessfully in the 1996 and 2000 elections. Brunswijk was sentenced in absentia to eight years in prison by a court in the Netherlands in April 1999 following his conviction on charges of cocaine trafficking. He now heads the ABOP (under AC, above), the present status of the SLA being unclear.

Other guerrilla formations have included the **Union for Liberation and Democracy,** a radical derivative of the SLA led by Kofi AJONGPONG; the Saramaccaner *bosneger* **Angula** movement, led by Carlos

MAASSI; the **Mandela Bushnegro Liberation Movement,** led by Leendert ADAMS ("Biko"); the Amerindian **Tucayana Amazonica,** led by Alex JUBITANA and Thomas SABAJO, which participated in the 1992 peace accords; and the previously unknown **Suriname Liberation Front,** led by Cornelius MAISI, which was routed by the army after a hostage seizure at a hydroelectric facility south of Paramaribo in March 1994.

LEGISLATURE

The former unicameral Parliament (*Staten*) was abolished on August 15, 1980. A constituent National Assembly (*Volksvergadering*) of 31 nominated members was established on January 1, 1985, as part of the government's "return to democracy" program. Balloting for the successor **National Assembly** (*Nationale Assemblee*) occurred on November 25, 1987, and, in the wake of the 1990 coup, on May 25, 1991. The most recent election for 51 members on May 25, 2005, yielded a distribution as follows: New Front for Democracy and Development, 23; National Democratic Party, 15; People's Alliance for Progress, 5; A-Combination, 5; Alternative-1, 3. The next election was scheduled for May 25, 2010.

President: Salam Paul SOMOHARDJO.

CABINET

[as of July 1, 2009]

Chair	Ramdien (Ram) Sardjoe (VHP)
Ministers	
Agriculture, Livestock, and Fisheries	Keremchend (Stanley) Ragoebarsingh (VHP)
Defense	Ivan Christian Fernald (NPS)
Education and Community Development	Edwin Toekidjan Wolf (PL)
Finance	Humphrey Hildenberg (NPS)
Foreign Affairs	Lygia Louise Irene Kraag-Keteldijk (NPS) [f]
Internal Affairs	Maurits Safdar Hassankhan (VHP)
Justice and Police	Chandrikapersad Santokhi (VHP)
Labor, Technological Development, and the Environment	Joyce D. Amarello-Williams (SPA) [f]
Natural Resources and Energy	Gregory Allan Rusland (NPS)
Planning and Development Cooperation	Ricardo Otto van Ravenswaay (AF)
Public Health	Celcius Waldo Waterberg (AC)
Public Works	Ganeshkoemar Kandhai (VHP)
Regional Development	Michel Felisie (AC)
Social Affairs and Public Housing	Hendrik Soerat Setrowidjojo (PL)
Trade and Industry	Clifford Marcia (SPA)
Transport, Communication, and Tourism	Richel Apensa (AC) [f]
Urban Planning and Land and Forestry Management	Michael Pierre Jong Tjîen Fa (PL)

[f] = female

COMMUNICATIONS

All nongovernmental organs of public information were closed down in December 1982, although some were subsequently permitted to resume activity.

Press. The principal newspaper is the independent daily *De Ware Tidj* published in Dutch and Sranan Tongo; others include *De West* (15,000), in Dutch, and several Chinese-language publications.

News agency. The official facility is the Suriname News Agency (*Surinaams Nieuws Agentschap*—SNA), which issues daily bulletins in Dutch and English.

Broadcasting and computing. There are a number of small commercial radio stations in addition to the government-owned *Stichting Radio-omroep Suriname* (SRS) and *Surinaamse Televisie Stichting* (STVS), each of which broadcasts in all local languages. As of 2008 there were 97.1 Internet users per 1,000 inhabitants.

INTERGOVERNMENTAL REPRESENTATION

Ambassador to the U.S.: Jacques Ruben Constantjin KROSS.

U.S. Ambassador to Suriname: John R. NAY.

Permanent Representative to the UN: Henry L. MAC-DONALD.

IGO Memberships (Non-UN): ACS, Caricom, IADB, IDB, Interpol, NAM, OAS, OIC, OPANAL, PCA, SELA, WTO.

SWAZILAND

Kingdom of Swaziland

Political Status: Independent monarchy within the Commonwealth since September 6, 1968.

Area: 6,703 sq. mi. (17,363 sq. km.).

Population: 929,718 (1997C); 1,164,000 (2008E).

Major Urban Centers (2005E): MBABANE (administrative capital, 78,000), Lobamba (royal and legislative capital, 11,000), Manzini (33,000).

Official Languages: English, siSwati.

Monetary Unit: Lilangeni (official rate December 1, 2009: 7.33 emalangeni = $1US). The lilangeni is at par with the South African rand, although under a Tripartite Monetary Area agreement concluded among Swaziland, Lesotho, and South Africa on July 1, 1986, the rand ceased to be legal tender in Swaziland.

Sovereign: King MSWATI III; installed on April 25, 1986, succeeding (as Head of State) Queen Regent Ntombi THWALA.

Prime Minister: Sibusiso Barnabas DLAMINI; appointed by the king on October 16, 2008, to succeed Absalom Themba DLAMINI; sworn in on October 23 and formed new government on October 24.

THE COUNTRY

Bordered on the north, west, and south by South Africa and on the east by Mozambique, Swaziland is the smallest of the three former British High Commission territories in southern Africa. The country comprises a mountainous western region (Highveld), a middle region of moderate altitude (Middleveld), an eastern lowland area (Lowveld), and the so-called Lubombo plateau on the eastern border. About 97 percent of the population is Swazi African, the remainder being of European and Eurafrican (mixed) stock. English is an official language, but siSwati (akin to Zulu) prevails among the indigenous population; Afrikaans is common among the Europeans, many of whom are of South African origin. Christianity is the religion of approximately half the people; there are a few Muslims, the remainder adhering to traditional beliefs. Women constitute about 37 percent of the workforce; female participation in government, with the exception of the former queens regent, has been minimal.

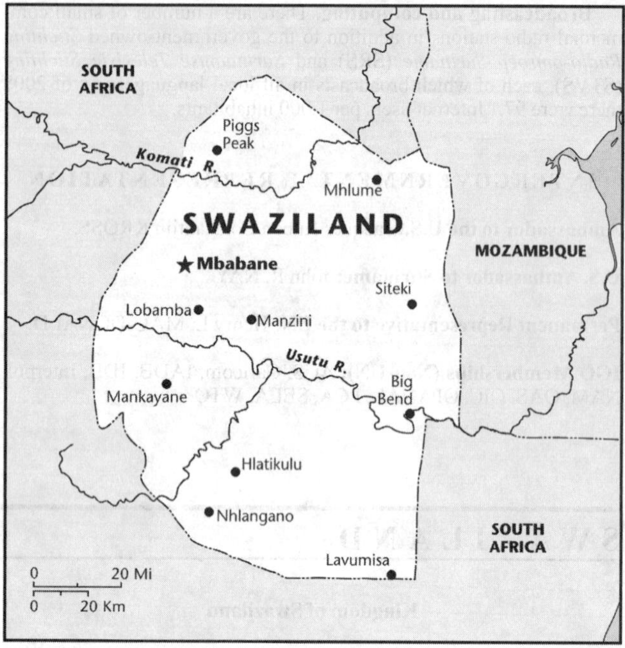

The economy is quite diversified given the country's small land area and population, although its composition, particularly in the mining sector, is changing. Production of iron ore, which accounted for 25 percent of export earnings in 1967, had virtually ceased by the end of the 1970s, while asbestos reserves, after 40 years of extraction, were also approaching depletion. Coal mining, on the other hand, underwent rapid development, while other minerals, such as tin, barites, and silica, were found in commercially exploitable quantities. Under normal conditions, water supplies are sufficient not only to support agriculture, which yields sugar, forest products, and livestock, but also to provide a potential hydroelectric power base. Swaziland experienced real GDP growth of 3.6 percent in 1996 and 3.7 percent in 1997, partially as the result of the government's implementation of economic reforms suggested by the International Monetary Fund (IMF) and the World Bank. Growth declined to about 2 percent in 1998 due to deteriorating economic conditions in South Africa and the effects of the Asian financial crisis.

Growth of 3.5 percent was achieved in 2002, mainly due to expansion of the textile industry, which took advantage of reduced U.S. tariffs and quotas designed to assist developing African nations. However, the economy subsequently continued to suffer from high unemployment, persistent poverty, localized food shortages and, according to some international donors, irresponsible spending on the part of the royal family. In addition, Swaziland faced one of the highest rates of HIV/AIDS infection in the world; UN officials estimated in 2004 that 39 percent of adults were infected. After many years of seeming failure to implement a plan to combat the pandemic, the government in 2004 declared a national emergency regarding the issue and solicited international assistance in trying to halt the spread of the disease. (In 2005 the infection rate among one age group of teens declined for the first time.) The economy experienced a downward trend, from 2.1 percent annual growth in 2004 to 1.8 percent in 2005. Little progress was made in reducing poverty, according to the IMF, which cited, among other reasons, the high rate of HIV/AIDS infection, a prolonged drought, and the removal of textile quotas in other countries, resulting in factory closings that contributed to Swaziland's 30 percent unemployment rate. The IMF urged the government to reduce its budget deficit and increase privatization in order to attract investors. Little changed from to 2006 to 2008, with annual average GDP growth of 2.5 percent and escalating poverty due to increasing unemployment, food shortages, and the HIV/AIDS pandemic. The IMF has pressed for decisive and immediate action by the government on structural reforms, which Fund managers said were "urgently needed" to improve productivity and the business climate. Tax reform was also urged. On a more positive note, the IMF commended the government's enactment of an anticorruption act and its efforts toward better supervision of commercial banks. As the economic downturn spread across the globe, Swaziland's annual GDP growth was expected to contract to 0.3 percent in 2009, far short of the 3.6 percent the IMF deemed necessary to prevent worsening poverty. The IMF reported that Swaziland was well on its way to becoming a "no man's country," mainly due to the high rate of HIV, which caused nearly a quarter of the work force to be "continually absent" from work.

GOVERNMENT AND POLITICS

Political background. Swaziland came under British control in the mid-19th century when a Swazi ruler requested protection from his people's traditional enemies, the Zulu. Kept intact when the Union of South Africa was formed in 1910, the territory was subsequently administered under native rulers by the British high commissioner for South Africa. Preparations for independence began after World War II and culminated in the promulgation of internal self-government in 1967 and the achievement of full independence within the Commonwealth in 1968 under King SOBHUZA II, who subsequently exercised firm control of the country's political institutions. Following small gains by the semiradical Ngwane National Liberation Congress (NNLC) in a 1972 parliamentary election and frustration of his attempts to have an opposition MP deported, the king in April 1973 repealed the constitution, abolished the legislature, introduced a detention act, and banned all opposition political activity. On August 21, 1982, King Sobhuza died, having technically reigned from the age of one in 1899, although he had not been formally enthroned until 1921 and had not been recognized as paramount ruler by the British until 1966. He was succeeded as head of state by Queen Mother Dzeliwe SHONGWE, authorized to act as regent until a successor king was designated and reached maturity.

The naming of Prince Bhekimpi DLAMINI to succeed Prince Mabandla Fred DLAMINI as prime minister in March 1983 seemed to mark the ascendancy of conservative elements within the royal house. In August Queen Regent Dzeliwe also was ousted from power, reportedly because she differed over the interpretation of her role with traditionalists within the *Liqoqo,* historically an advisory council of royal family members that had been elevated to the status of Supreme Council of State shortly before Sobhuza's death. Queen Regent Dzeliwe was replaced by Ntombi THWALA, the mother of Prince Makhosetive, who was named successor to the former sovereign on August 10. Two months later, however, Prince Mfanasibili DLAMINI and Dr. George MSIBI, who were prominently involved in the palace coup that installed Queen Regent Ntombi, were dismissed from the *Liqoqo.*

On April 25, 1986, two years earlier than originally planned, Prince Makhosetive assumed the title of King MSWATI III in an apparent effort to halt the power struggle that had followed his father's death. The 19-year-old king, the world's youngest monarch, moved quickly to consolidate his control, formally disbanding the *Liqoqo* in June and appointing Prince Sotsha DLAMINI, a relatively obscure former police official, as prime minister on October 6.

After authorizing the arrest in May 1987 of 12 people allegedly involved in the palace intrigue of recent years, the king dissolved parliament in September, one year early. Assembly elections were held in November, and the government was extensively reorganized at the end of the month. Although the king's bold action at the outset of his reign surprised some observers, most Swazis appeared to support his exercise of monarchical prerogative as a means of preserving stability.

The king formally assumed full executive authority at age 21 on April 19, 1989. Three months later he dismissed Prince Sotsha as prime minister, replacing him with Obed Mfanyana DLAMINI. The new prime minister was the founder and former secretary general of the Swaziland Federation of Trade Unions (SFTU), a background that appeared to strengthen the government's capacity to deal with a growing number of labor disputes.

On October 9, 1992, one month before the expiration of its term, the king dissolved parliament and declared that, with the assistance of his cabinet (which would be restyled a Council of Ministers and act as a caretaker government), he would rule by decree until the adoption of a new constitution and the holding of elections. Balloting scheduled for November was postponed until 1993 to allow for the redefinition of constituencies and compilation of a voters' register. The monarch's action followed his approval of a draft charter that called for retention of the monarchy and the revival of multipartyism (banned in 1973 by King Sobhuza II).

Fearing a conservative backlash if the reform movement outpaced the prerogatives of the royal court and powerful traditional chiefs, the constitutional commission recommended that decisions regarding political parties be deferred. Consequently, candidates for the House of Assembly elections on September 18 and October 11, 1993, competed on a nonparty basis; nonetheless, the polling marked the first time that legislators had been popularly elected and royal family members had been prohibited from participating. Underscoring the change, Prime Minister Obed Dlamini and all but three cabinet ministers lost their seats. As a result, on October 25 King Mswati named Andreas FAKUDZE as interim prime minister with responsibility for all 16 ministries. Ten days later the king appointed Prince Jameson Mblini DLAMINI, a conservative, to succeed Fakudze. Traditionalists hailed the monarch's choice, although the government named by Dlamini on November 10 included several reformists.

A follow-up round to the 1993 balloting was held on October 2, 1994, with voters selecting secretaries for the country's 55 regions (*Inkundla*). The new officials were described as links between legislators and their constituents, as well as coordinators of development activities in their areas.

The SFTU called a general strike (the most comprehensive in recent years) on March 13–14, 1995, to secure acceptance of a variety of demands, including the reinstatement of summarily dismissed state employees. The action was called off after the government appointed a select committee to consider the grievances. Subsequently, the SFTU called for another strike on July 17, which was called off after the House of Assembly imposed severe penalties for work stoppages. In mid-August the Senate endorsed a statement by King Mswati that Swazis did not want multiparty politics. Three months later, a well-attended opposition conference rejected the royal assessment.

On January 22–29, 1996, the SFTU organized a widely observed general strike, which was abandoned only after the king ordered the strikers back to work, threatening "to go to war" if necessary to end the action. Although some observers described the SFTU as "tarnished" by its capitulation to the monarch's threat, on February 16, three days before a scheduled resumption of the strike, King Mswati promised to reform the constitution and consider lifting the political party ban. Subsequently, the union suspended plans for renewed action; however, prodemocracy rallies continued.

On May 8, 1996, the king dismissed Prime Minister Dlamini, promising "concrete democratic changes." Subsequently, the king named Deputy Prime Minister Sishayi NXUMALO as acting prime minister, but Nxumalo immediately asserted that the Swazi people were not ready for political parties, which he described as ill-suited for the "close-knit, non-ethnic, traditional society." Nevertheless, on July 26 the king announced the creation of a 29-member Constitutional Reform Commission (CRC) with responsibility for drafting a new constitution and named former finance minister and IMF executive director Dr. Sibusiso Barnabas DLAMINI as the new prime minister. The cabinet was reshuffled on November 13, the king pledging emphasis on economic development and the pursuit of foreign investment and trade.

In April 1998 the king once again reshuffled the government, most notably replacing Deputy Prime Minister Nxumalo with Arthur KHOZA and naming the former to head the Swaziland Investment Promotion Authority (SIPA). Thereafter, in an apparent effort to quell increasingly vocal calls for reform from prodemocracy activists, the king abruptly dissolved the House of Assembly in August in anticipation of balloting in October.

As in 1993, in elections on October 16 and 24, 1998, candidates for the House of Assembly competed on a nonparty basis. Observers attributed the low voter turnout to voter apathy and the prodemocracy forces' call for an electoral boycott; in addition, union activists reportedly threatened would-be voters. On November 13 the king reappointed Dlamini as prime minister, and on November 20 a new government was sworn in.

On May 31, 2003, the king dissolved the assembly and appointed a special council to act as a caretaker government until elections were held. Paul SHABANGU was appointed as the interim prime minister, although no other cabinet posts were filled. The nonparty elections, which were boycotted by most of the major opposition groups, were conducted on September 20 and October 18. The king appointed five women to the assembly (there had been no women in the previous assembly). Following the elections, the king dismissed Shabangu and appointed Absalom Themba DLAMINI as prime minister on November 14. The cabinet was reshuffled on February 23, 2006, and one minister was replaced on May 24. Deputy Prime Minister Albert SHABANGU died in September 2006 at age 67 and was succeeded by Education Minister Constance Simelane, who was appointed along with a reshuffled cabinet on October 26.

The first National Assembly elections since the promulgation of the new constitution in 2006 were held on September 2008, with turnout of 57 percent reported. Following the nonparty elections, the king named Sibusiso Barnabas DLAMINI as prime minister (Dlamini, described as a royalist, had served as prime minister from 1996 until his dismissal by the king in 2003.) Dlamini named a new government on October 24.

Constitution and government. For some years after independence, King Sobhuza was reported to have been working on a revised Western-style constitution. However, in March 1977 he announced that he had abandoned the effort in favor of a form of traditional government based on tribal councils (*Tinkhundla*), which was formally introduced in October 1978. Under the *Tinkhundla* electoral system, which was voided by decree on October 9, 1992, polling was held without political campaigns or electoral rolls for an 80-member electoral college charged with naming four-fifths of a 50-member House of Assembly, which in turn named half of a 20-member Senate. Ten members of each were designated by the monarch, who also named the prime minister and other cabinet officials.

On February 14, 1992, a royal constitutional commission appointed by the king in late 1991 presented a draft charter for a multiparty electoral system, which was given preliminary approval by the monarch in October. The proposal called for a two-stage balloting process beginning with polling in the 210 *Tinkhundla* for local representatives from among candidates chosen by the chiefs. In the second round of the secret balloting, first round victors from four to six *Tinkhundla* were to compete against one another in *Inkhundla* elections for berths in an expanded House of Assembly and Senate of 55 and 20 members, respectively (the monarch having the right to appoint 10 additional members to each). The plan, while serving as a partial blueprint for the 1993 and 1998 polls, lacked formal approval, and its status remained distinctly uncertain. A Constitutional Reform Committee (CRC) formed in 1996 proceeded haltingly. In January 2001 a draft constitution report from the CRC was criticized by the opposition and human rights groups as a "doctored document" and "not a truly representative report because group submissions were denied." The long-awaited new draft constitution was presented to the king in November 2003 but he did not sign it into law until July 26, 2005, after ordering the legislature to amend sections regarding religion and taxing the royal family. The new constitution promulgated on February 8, 2006, has no specific language to legalize political parties (and stipulates that candidates for election must run as individuals). Though the constitution contains a bill of rights guaranteeing limited freedoms, the king retains ultimate authority (see Current issues, below).

The judiciary, whose members are appointed by the king, encompasses a High Court, a Court of Appeal, and district courts. There are also 17 Swazi courts for tribal and customary issues. Swaziland is divided for administrative purposes into four districts, each headed by a commissioner appointed by the central government.

Foreign relations. Swaziland is a member of the United Nations (UN), the Commonwealth, and the African Union (AU, formerly the Organization of African Unity—OAU). It maintains close relations with South Africa as a result of geographic proximity, administrative tradition, and economic dependency (more than 80 percent of the Kingdom's imports are from South Africa, and a substantial portion of its national income consists of remittances from Swazis employed in the neighboring state). Despite OAU strictures, Swaziland concluded a secret nonaggression pact with Pretoria in 1982 and subsequently strove to contain African National Congress (ANC) activity within its territory.

A series of major raids on purported ANC strongholds by South African security forces in 1986 led to vehement protests by the Swazi government and a December visit by South African Foreign Minister Roelof "Pik" Botha, who reaffirmed his government's commitment to the 1982 pact and pledged that the incursions would cease. However, in July 1987 two top ANC officials and a Mozambican woman companion were killed in Mbabane. Two additional killings by alleged South African agents in August brought the total number of ANC deaths in 1987 to 11.

Despite its ties to South Africa, Swaziland established diplomatic relations with Mozambique during 1976. The action was prompted by a need to facilitate the movement of goods through the Mozambique port of Maputo. The Mozambique Embassy in Mbabane was Swaziland's first resident mission from independent Africa, and a security accord was concluded between the two countries in mid-1984.

In September 1989 it was reported that Swaziland and South Africa had agreed on a border adjustment that would bring the largely Swazi-populated South African homeland of KaNgwane within the kingdom. However, no date was given for the formal transfer. (In 1994 KaNgwane was reintegrated into Transvaal in northern South Africa; Swaziland has continued to lay claim to the territory.)

In late 1997 relations between Swaziland and Mozambique were strained after it was reported that a Swazi prince leading a committee studying their shared border had asserted that Swazi territory legally encompassed all of Mozambique's Maputo Province. (The claim was dismissed by Maputo, which declared that it had never been formally contacted by Swaziland.) In 1998–1999, relations between the two turned on repatriation issues. In 1999 Swaziland relocated 500 Mozambicans and began a program to force Mozambicans living in Swaziland to register for military service.

In March 2005 the king and South African president Thebo Mbeki were scheduled to hold a summit, which activists had hoped Mbeki would use to push for reforms, but the meeting was postponed indefinitely. South African activists continued their efforts in support of democratization in Swaziland by staging a border blockade in 2006. Eight people were shot and wounded on the South African side of the border. In May 2006 officials from Swaziland, Mozambique, and South Africa opened the Lubombo Tourism Route in what was described as "part of the ongoing cross-border initiatives" among the three countries.

Swaziland, an ally of Taiwan, refused (along with several other African countries) an invitation by China in 2006 to participate in a conference meant to seek African support for the "one China" policy.

In March 2009 Swaziland granted refuge to the ousted president of Madagascar, Marc Ravalomanana.

Current issues. In 2000 opposition pressure for political reforms continued, but the government exhibited little concession. In November a general strike called by the SFTU led to the arrests of a number of prominent trade union and opposition leaders. The king's perceived heavy-handed approach to the prodemocracy movement was criticized by the opposition through 2001 and into 2002. Several neighboring countries (notably South Africa) and other international observers also questioned the regime's policies, particularly following a royal decree in June 2002 permitting the king to overturn court rulings, ban newspapers, and impose penalties on those charged with "ridiculing" royal authority or the government. Events surrounding the drafting of a new constitution also appeared to dampen prospects for liberalization. In August 2001 the CRC had in fact proposed enlarging the king's authority and maintaining the ban on political parties.

The draft constitution was formally presented to the king in November 2003. As expected, the document did not call for the legalization of parties and appeared to many observers to strengthen, rather than weaken, the monarch's authority. Among other things, the proposed new basic law reaffirmed the king's power to appoint the prime minister, cabinet, judges, and other government officials. It also authorized the king to dissolve the assembly and veto any legislation. Although reference was made to rights for women, freedom of expression, and other issues generally addressed by modern constitutions, the opposition immediately dismissed the draft as unacceptable. Leading the campaign against approval was the Coalition of Concerned Civil Organizations (CCCO), launched by business, professional, and legal organizations. Unions, religious groups, and the banned political parties subsequently joined the CCCO in trying to force revision of the draft. However, their efforts were fruitless, as the king signed the new constitution into law in July 2005. The constitution maintains the power of the monarchy and includes a provision that a ruler who does not perform can be removed, his authority then being assumed by the Queen Mother. A bill of rights within the constitution guarantees equality under the law and freedom of religion, speech, and assembly, though the king may suspend certain rights if he finds them to be in conflict with the (undefined) public interest. Observers questioned the commitment to women's rights, citing the fact that women historically have been grouped with minors under the law, and given that the king still has the authority to "claim" and marry underage girls. The CCCO noted that under the constitution the king enjoys legal immunity and protection against investigation by the Swaziland Human Rights Commission.

Perhaps a positive note for prodemocracy activists was that the government issued guidelines for the creation and registration of nongovernmental organizations—a move some said could be a precursor to legal political activity. Opposition leader Obed Dlamini of the NNLC vowed to challenge the constitution by attempting to register his party. The king, for his part, said in 2006 that the country was not ready for political parties and criticized foreign countries that pushed for reforms in Swaziland. Meanwhile, the government blocked a protest rally organized by the People's United Democratic Movement (Pudemo) and banned a women's group from registering as an organization. More than 20 people were arrested on the border with South Africa in April 2006 at a prodemocracy rally that drew 500 people. The rally was organized by the Congress of South African Trade Unions (Cosatu) and the South African Communist Party in solidarity with Swazi union members. Tensions in the country were heightened by reports that the king had built several lavish palaces for his wives, bought them luxury cars, and otherwise continued to spend large amounts of money, while two-thirds of the population lived on less than $1 per day. On a more positive note, after tough new anticorruption laws were approved in 2006, the king held the country's first summit to address the major problem of graft.

In 2007 thousands of trade union workers and others staged a two-day strike and a march in Manzini (after failing to get authorization to conduct their demonstration in Mbabane) to press for a multiparty democracy and to protest high unemployment and deficiencies in health care and education. The event was reported as being predominantly peaceful. In March 2008 more than 16,000 textile workers went on strike for better pay and working conditions, this demonstration having received the approval of the country's mediation commission in light of the impasse with employers. Attention soon turned to the assembly elections scheduled for September, with several groups announcing they would boycott the polls (see Political Groups, below). In April the deputy leader of Pudemo was shot to death in South Africa, where he was living in exile. Also in April, in an unprecedented move, King Mswati announced that Swaziland would allow monitors to observe the elections in an effort to improve transparency. However, political parties were not allowed to participate; all candidates were required to be unaffiliated. In the run-up to the elections, "unprecedented" protests were reported, as thousands demonstrated for political reforms and multiparty balloting. Protesters from various political groups tried to block the borders to Swaziland, a move that had the potential to inflict great economic hardship. (The elections were held just weeks after the government spent $12 million on what was described as a lavish party marking the king's 40th birthday and the 40th anniversary of the kingdom's independence.) During the election, police guarded the polling stations after prodemocracy protesters attempted to hold gatherings at the sites. Among those arrested were Pudemo members, including the group's leader, Mario Masuku, and Jan Sithole, secretary general of the SFTU. The prime minister subsequently denounced those calling for democratic reforms as "a threat to the stability of the country." Commonwealth elections observers stated that they could not declare the results "credible" because political parties were denied participation and members of parliament had "severely restricted powers." In October the government banned civil rights groups from meeting. Later that month, a bomb exploded near the royal palace.

On a more positive note for the citizenry, in March 2009 the high court ordered the government to provide free primary education as a result of a lawsuit brought by one of the unions. In April it was reported that Swaziland, in addition to its high prevalence of HIV, was facing a tuberculosis epidemic, which the government was taking steps to address. Meanwhile, the king continued to take measures to retain his absolute power, ordering a crackdown in May on trade unions and other reform-minded groups. Police reportedly confiscated any materials (including T-shirts) that called for an end to the monarchy.

POLITICAL GROUPS

During 1994 a number of parties, including Pudemo (below), joined with human rights and other groups to form a Confederation for Full Democracy in Swaziland (CFDS). During a visit to Johannesburg in September, CFDS representative Sabelo DLAMINI termed the 1993 nonpartisan poll a "pseudo election" and warned of civil war that might spill over into South Africa if Swaziland's "undemocratic government" did not agree to free elections. On November 13, 1995, the CFDS sponsored a conference of political and labor groups that called on King Mswati to go into voluntary exile "until we have sorted our political problems out."

In early 1996 the CFDS appeared to have been superseded by the **Swaziland Democratic Alliance** (SDA), a coalition that included

Pudemo; the Swaziland Federation of Trade Unions (SFTU), an 80,000 member grouping led by Jan SITHOLE; and representatives of the Institute for Democracy and Leadership (Ideal), led by Dr. Jerry GULE. Organized to "try to force change," the alliance led a march on the prime minister's office and parliamentary building, which was noteworthy mainly for the paltry number of activists who participated. In early 1999 the SDA was bolstered by the addition of the NNLC (below) to its ranks, and in April the NNLC's Obed Mfanyan Dlamini was elected, along with Pudemo's Jerry NXUMALO and Sithole, to lead the reorganized alliance. In 2003 Obed Dlamini was elected to parliament, and a year later the NNLC reportedly had decided to participate in national elections, which, observers said, would most likely mean the end of the SDA, as other alliance members opposed such participation.

Despite analysts' speculation about the freedom of association clause in the revised constitution allowing for the legal registration of political parties, in 2007 King Mswati declared that political parties remained banned. That pronouncement was reiterated in 2008 by the elections commissioner, and political parties were not allowed to participate in the September assembly elections.

Former Government Party:

Imbokodvo National Movement (INM). The *Imbokodvo* ("Grindstone") Movement dominated the political scene during the late 1960s and was the only political group permitted to function openly after 1973. The leadership of the party has been vacant since the dismissal of Prince Mabandla Dlamini as prime minister in March 1983. Two royalist groups, formed as "cultural organizations" in 1996, were the *Sive Siyinqaba*, an offshoot of the INM led by Isaac SHABANGU and Zibuse SIMELANE, and the *Sibahle Sinje*, led by former assembly speaker Marwick KHUMALO. In 2000 the *Sive Siyinqaba* called on the king to lift the ban on political parties; the *Sibahle Sinje* backs the no-party system.

Illegal Opposition and External Groups:

African United Democratic Party (AUDP). References to the AUDP first appeared in 2006 in reports that it was taking its fight for registration to the courts. It was subsequently reported that the high court had ordered the government to register the AUDP, in accordance with the revised constitution's freedom of association clause. However, King Mswati soon after confirmed that political parties are illegal.

Leaders: Stanley MAUNDZISA (President), Sibusiso DLAMINI (Secretary General).

People's United Democratic Movement (PUDM or Pudemo). Initial reports about Pudemo surfaced in 1989 when the government accused the group of illegally circulating political pamphlets. In mid-1990 it was reported that after a period of inactivity, the group had resumed actively campaigning for electoral reform, multiparty democracy, and an end to corruption. The party unilaterally proclaimed its "legality" in February 1992.

In August 1993 party president Kislon SHONGWE reportedly requested refuge at the UK's high commission in Mbabane after he was listed among opposition figures being sought for distributing "seditious pamphlets." A month later Pudemo officials countered international praise for the government's electoral preparations, contending that the balloting could not be considered democratic if the 20-year-old state of emergency remained in place and political parties were not able to participate.

On January 1, 1996, Pudemo threatened to make the country "ungovernable" if the monarch failed to adopt a multiparty democratic system of government. Subsequently, it called for the establishment of an interim government to oversee a transition to democratic rule. Underscoring its more militant stance, Pudemo subsequently replaced Shongwe, who was described as "uncombative," and Secretary General Dominic MNGOMEZULU with Mario Masuku and Bonginkhosi Dlamini, respectively. Masuku was named to the constitutional review commission established in May but later resigned on the ground that it had become apparent that the king had no intention of lifting the political party ban. In November 2000, Pudemo was among the forces of opposition to join the general strike called by the SFTU, during which Masuku was arrested along with other opposition leaders. Masuku was acquitted of sedition charges in August 2002.

In 2005 the king accused 13 Pudemo members of firebombing homes and offices of government officials; all were released, but one member was fined $800 after pleading guilty to treason and testifying that Pudemo was behind the attacks. The government cracked down on a Pudemo rally in March 2006, arresting several party members, including Masuku (who was released the same day), and Bonginkhosi Dlamini (who was charged with high treason but reportedly released later). Party leaders said they staged the protest to test the constitution's provision regarding political freedom. In August members of the party's youth wing, the **Swaziland Youth Congress**—SWAYOCO, formerly led by Mamba MDUDUZI (subsequently led by Wandile DLAMINI and Thabile ZWANE), were routed by police as the prodemocracy group marched near the capital.

During a demonstration in April 2007 at the Mananga border crossing between Swaziland and South Africa, 16 Pudemo members were arrested for allegedly carrying "seditious" pamphlets. In 2008 Pudemo called the assembly elections "a sham" and vowed to continue to press for political reforms. Party leader Mario Masuku was charged in November under the country's new anti-terrorism law and was sent to a maximum security prison. His arrest came in the wake of the prime minister's announcement that four political groups, including Pudemo and SWAYOCO, were deemed terrorist organizations and were therefore banned.

Leaders: Mario MASUKU (President), Jerry NXUMALO, Kislon SHONGWE, Bonginkhosi DLAMINI (Secretary General).

Ngwane National Liberation Congress (NNLC). The NNLC was at the forefront of opposition activities in the 1970s but thereafter was reported to have become defunct. At a meeting of the resuscitated body in December 1998, former prime minister Obed Mfanyana Dlamini was elected president of the congress, and in April 1999 he reportedly agreed to enter into the SDA. In the 2003 legislative elections, Dlamini was elected to the assembly after campaigning as a nonpartisan. In 2005 party member Jimmy HLOPHE, running as an unaffiliated individual, won an assembly seat in a special election following the death of a member of parliament. Earlier in 2005 requests to the high court by the NNLC and Pudemo to be involved in the constitutional review process were denied "because in terms of the law they are non-existent," the judge said. The NNLC was among several political groups that protested the 2008 assembly elections.

Leader: Obed Mfanyana DLAMINI (President of the Party and Former Prime Minister).

Swaziland Communist Party (SWACOPA). Founded in 1994, the SWACOPA was reported to have been suppressed by the government.

Leaders: Mphandlana SHONGWE, Zakhe GENINDZA.

Swaziland National Progressive Party (SNPP). This banned party was referenced in 2000 as being affiliated with the SDA. In 2009 the SNPP condemned the prime minister's "attitude" following his remarks that those who were critical of the king's remarks at the opening session of parliament could be charged with sedition.

Leader: Magadeyiwile MDLULI (President).

Swaziland National Front (Swanafro). Swanafro is a small Manzini- based formation.

Leaders: Elmond SHONGWE (President), Glenrose DLAMINI (Secretary General).

Swaziland Solidarity Network (SSN). Based in South Africa and led by a South African, Solly Mapaila, the SSN is a "pressure group" that has been critical of the Swaziland regime's alleged efforts to squelch prodemocracy activity. In October 1997 Mapaila, who was himself banned from the kingdom for allegedly fomenting unrest, accused the monarch of maintaining a list of ANC officials it sought to ban from entering the country. The SSN launched a campaign in 2000 calling for the international community to "isolate" Swaziland until political reforms are enacted. It renewed its calls for international action in 2005, citing the king's reported extravagant spending while most of the population lived in extreme poverty.

In 2008 the SSN backed the election boycott organized by Pudemo and called for a South Africa border blockade. Following the election, the SSN was among four political groups listed as "terrorist organizations" and banned by the prime minister. The SSN's response was that it was impossible for the government to ban the group because it was based in South Africa.

Leaders: Solly MAPAILA (Chair), Lucky LUKHELE (Spokesperson).

Other political groups are the **Inhlava Party**, founded in 2006 by Mfomfo NKHAMBULE, and the **Ngwane Socialist Revolutionary Party,** led by Thomas Vabula MAGAGULA. A group known as the **Swaziland People's Liberation Army** (*Umbane*), whose leadership remained "faceless," was reported in 2009 to be receiving financial backing and training for its members from the Sudanese People's Liberation Army. The group was declared a terrorist organization by the prime minister.

LEGISLATURE

On October 9, 1992, King Mswati dissolved the bicameral **Parliament** (*Libandla*) in preparation for new elections scheduled to follow the adoption of a new multiparty constitution in 1993. However, further deliberation on the draft charter was suspended, and the 1993 and 1998 elections were held on a nonparty basis.

Senate. The Senate is composed of 30 members, 20 chosen by the monarch plus 10 elected by the House of Assembly from within its own ranks. The current upper house was appointed on October 10 and 17, 2008. Twelve seats were held by women.

President: Chief Gelani ZWANE.

House of Assembly. Enlarged by 15 seats since the 1992 elections, the assembly consists of 65 members, 55 popularly elected (1 for each district) and 10 monarchial appointees. In the most recent elections on September 19, 2008, seven women were among the 55 popularly elected members. The king appointed 10 members on October 7, including two women.

Speaker: Prince Guduza DLAMINI.

CABINET

[as of May 1, 2009]

Prime Minister	Sibusiso Barnabas Dlamini
Deputy Prime Minister	Themba Masuku
Ministers	
Agriculture	Clement Dlamini
Commerce and Trade	Jabulile Mashwama [f]
Economic Planning and Development	Prince Hlangusemphi
Education and Training	Wilson Ntshangase
Finance	Majozi Sithole
Foreign Affairs	Lutfo Dlamini
Health	Benedict Xaba
Home Affairs	Chief Mgwagwa Gamedze
Housing and Local Government	Pastor Lindiwe Gwebu Dlamini [f]
Information, Communications, and Technology	Pastor Nelisiwe Shongwe [f]
Justice and Constitutional Affairs	Ndumiso Mamba
Labor and Social Security	Magwebetane Mamba
Natural Resources and Energy	Princess Tsandzile [f]
Public Service	Mtiti Fakudze
Public Works and Transport	Ntuthuko Dlamini
Sports, Culture, and Youth Affairs	Hlobisile Ndlovu [f]
Tinkhundia Administration and Development	Prince Gcokoma
Tourism and Environment	Macford Sibandze

[f] = female

COMMUNICATIONS

In October 1997 the government established the Swaziland Media Council, a seven-member regulatory body. The government severely restricts press freedoms, and it controls almost all broadcasting. The international watchdog group Reporters Without Borders calls freedom of the press in Swaziland "a fantasy."

In November 2008 the attorney general warned that anyone who criticized the government could face arrest under the country's new anti-terrorism law and face a sentence of up to 25 years in prison. In January 2009 Mfomfo Nkhambule, leader of the Inhlava Party and a columnist for the *Times of Swaziland*, apologized to the king (following reported harassment by state police) for articles critical of the king and his leadership style. The same month, political groups, trade unions, and civic organizations petitioned the prime minister, demanding access to state media for all citizens.

Press. The following are published in Mbabane in English: *Times of Swaziland* (18,000), independent daily; *Swaziland Observer* (11,000), independent daily; *The Swazi News* (7,000), independent weekly. Publication of the *Swaziland Observer* was suspended from February 2000–January 2001 due to pressure from the government. In May 2001 the government banned two independent publications (*The Guardian of Swaziland* newspaper, and weekly magazine *The Nation*) for "operating illegally."

In 2006 the *Times of Swaziland*, in what was termed a landmark case, won (on appeal to the High Court) a defamation case for which it had been fined $116,000.

Broadcasting and computing. The nation's radio sets receive commercial programs from the government-controlled Swaziland Broadcasting and Information Service and the privately owned Swaziland Commercial Radio, in addition to religious programs from Trans World Radio. The state-owned Swaziland Television Broadcasting Corporation (STBC) transmits to about 130,000 receivers. As of 2008 there were 68.5 Internet users per 1,000 inhabitants.

INTERGOVERNMENTAL REPRESENTATION

Ambassador to the U.S.: Ephraim M. HLOPHE.

U.S. Ambassador to Swaziland: Earl Michael IRVING.

Permanent Representative to the UN: Joel Musa NHLEKO.

IGO Memberships (Non-UN): AfDB, AU, BADEA, Comesa, CWTH, Interpol, NAM, PCA, SADC, WCO, WTO.

SWEDEN

Kingdom of Sweden
Konungariket Sverige

Political Status: Constitutional monarchy established on June 6, 1809; under revised constitution effective January 1, 1975.

Area: 173,731 sq. mi. (449,964 sq. km.).

Population: 8,587,353 (1990C); 9,246,000 (2008E).

Major Urban Centers (2007C): STOCKHOLM (788,000), Göteborg (490,000), Malmö (278,000), Uppsala (185,000).

Official Language: Swedish.

Monetary Unit: Krona (official rate December 1, 2009: 6.91 kronor = $1US).

Sovereign: King CARL XVI GUSTAF; succeeded to the throne September 19, 1973, following the death of his grandfather, King GUSTAF VI ADOLF.

Heir Apparent: Crown Princess VICTORIA Ingrid Alice Désirée, daughter of the king.

Prime Minister: Fredrik REINFELDT (Moderate Coalition Party); elected by the *Riksdag* on October 5, 2006, to succeed Göran PERSSON (Swedish Social Democratic Party); formed new government on October 6, 2006.

THE COUNTRY

Situated on the Baltic side of the Scandinavian Peninsula and projecting north of the Arctic Circle, Sweden is the largest and most populous of the Scandinavian countries. The indigenous population, about 80 percent of whom belong to the Evangelical Lutheran Church, is homogeneous except for some 400,000 Finns spread over the country and a Sámi (Lapp) minority in the north. In addition, there are more than 1 million resident aliens who have arrived since World War II. Early on, they came mainly from Greece, Turkey and Yugoslavia. Since Sweden joined the European Union in 1995, people from various member countries have immigrated, lately in particular from Poland and Denmark. Sweden has also granted permanent residencies to an increasing number of asylum-seeking refugees from Africa and Asia. Since 2003 the biggest group has come from Iraq.

In 2007 more than 78 percent of women ages 25–64 were in the labor force, compared with close to 85 percent of men. Women won 47 percent of the seats in the *Riksdag,* making it one of the most gender-balanced parliaments in the world.

Although only 7 percent of the land is cultivated and agriculture, forestry, and fishing contribute only 2 percent of the GDP, Sweden is almost self-sufficient in foodstuffs, while its wealth of resources has enabled it to assume an important position among the world's industrial nations. A big country with a sparse population, its need to find markets outside the national borders has always been significant. A major producer and exporter of wood, paper products, and iron ore, Sweden also is a leading vehicle manufacturer. Electrical and telecom equipment as well as pharmaceuticals have become important export goods. The creative sector, with design, music, fashion, and gastronomy as well as the art industry, is increasingly contributing to a healthy export income. The country's principal exports in 2007 were machinery and transport equipment, manufactured goods, and chemicals, with the largest trading partners being Germany, Norway, and Denmark.

Despite socialist leadership throughout most of the postwar period, the private sector accounts for 80 percent of Sweden's output. Companies run by public owners are included in this sector. Thirty percent of the labor force is found in the public sector. Government expenditures amounted to 26 percent of the country's GDP in 2007, primarily in the areas of education, health care, and "social protection." An estimated 48 percent of the average worker's labor costs is deducted in taxes, placing Sweden on the higher end of the European tax scales.

Heavily export driven, Sweden's economy was particularly hard hit by the global financial crisis in 2008, as exports weakened and investment declined significantly, leading to a contraction in annual GDP growth from 2.6 percent in 2007 to less than 1 percent in 2008, according to the International Monetary Fund (IMF). Inflation reached a 15-year-high annual rate of 4 percent, owing in large part to rising food and energy prices. In late 2008 the government approved a $2.4 billion cut in income taxes, $205 billion in aid to banks, a three-year $3 billion stimulus package, and $3.5 billion to shore up faltering auto companies. Nevertheless, annual growth declined to –6 percent in 2009, and unemployment of 9 percent was recorded. On a positive note, the IMF endorsed the government's "significant" stimulus spending, as well as measures to bolster the central bank, among other "prompt and appropriate policy responses" to help ensure financial stability.

GOVERNMENT AND POLITICS

Political background. A major European power in the 17th century, Sweden later declined in relative importance but nevertheless retained an important regional position, strengthening links with Norway in a union under the Swedish crown from 1814 to 1905. Finland was a part of Sweden from the Middle Ages until 1809, when the two countries peacefully separated. Swedish is still one of two official languages in Finland, though it is considered the mother tongue to only 6 percent of Finland's population. Neutrality in both world wars enabled Sweden to concentrate on its industrial development and the perfection of a welfare state under the auspices of the Swedish Social Democratic Party *(Sveriges Socialdemokratiska Arbetareparti*—s), which was in power almost continuously from 1932 to 1976, either alone or in coalition with other parties.

In the *Riksdag* election of 1968 the Social Democrats under Tage ERLANDER won an absolute majority for the first time in 22 years. Having led the party and the country since 1946, Erlander was succeeded as party chair and prime minister by Olof PALME in October 1969. Although diminished support for the Social Democrats was reflected in the parliamentary elections of 1970 and 1973, the party maintained control until September 1976, when voters, disturbed by a climate of increasing labor unrest and inflation as well as declining economic growth, awarded a combined majority of 180 legislative seats to the Center Party (*Centerpartiet*—c), the Moderate Coalition Party (*Moderata Samlingspartiet*—m), and the Liberal People's Party (*Folkpartiet Liberalerna*—fp). On October 8 a coalition government was formed under c leader Thorbjörn FÄLLDIN. However, policy differences between the antinuclear c and the pronuclear m and fp parties forced the government to resign in October 1978, providing the opportunity for Ola ULLSTEN to form a minority fp government.

Following the election of September 16, 1979, a center-right c-m-fp coalition with a one-seat majority was formed under Prime Minister Fälldin, but on May 4, 1981, m withdrew in a dispute over tax reform. However, m tacitly agreed to support the two-party government to avoid an early election and the likely return of the Social Democrats. Fälldin continued in office until the election of September 19, 1982, in which the Social Democrats obtained a three-seat plurality over nonsocialists, permitting Palme to return as head of an s minority administration supported in Parliament by the Left Party-Communists (*Vänsterpartiet-Kommunisterna*—vpk).

On February 28, 1986, Palme was assassinated in Stockholm by an unidentified gunman, the first postwar West European head of government to be killed while in office. Deputy Prime Minister Ingvar CARLSSON assumed interim control of the government and was confirmed as Palme's successor on March 12. The Social Democrats retained their dominant position in the election of September 18, 1988, with the conservatives losing ground and the Green Ecology Party (*Miljöpartiet de Gröna*—mp) entering the *Riksdag* for the first time with 20 seats.

Carlsson resigned on February 15, 1990, after losing a key vote on an economic austerity plan that would have placed upper-middle-income taxpayers in a 72 percent bracket while freezing both prices and wages through 1991. He was returned to office 11 days later after accepting a substantially watered-down tax schedule that left most of the country's budgetary problems unresolved. As a result, the Social Democrats experienced their most serious setback since 1928 at triennial legislative balloting on September 15, 1991, falling to 138 seats out of 349; concurrently, the aggregate strength of the four traditional "bourgeois" parties—the c, m, fp, and Christian Democratic Community Party (*Kristdemokratiska Samhällspartiet*—kds)—rose to 170 seats, due mainly to gains by m and the kds. While the Left Party (v, formerly the vpk) lost ground and the Greens disappeared from the *Riksdag,* the populist New Democracy (nyd) party won a startling 25 seats in its first parliamentary race. The result was the installation of a four-party center-right administration under m's Carl BILDT that was 6 seats short of an assured parliamentary majority and therefore dependent on nyd external support.

Faced with the country's worst postwar economic crisis, Prime Minister Bildt and opposition Social Democratic leader Carlsson on September 20, 1992, concluded an unprecedented economic pact that called for tax increases and major public spending cuts over five years. However, the new cooperative spirit was badly dented in November, when s declined to support specific austerity measures, obliging the Swedish authorities to allow the krona to float and thereby to depreciate by 9 percent. Further welfare spending cuts mandated by the 1993–1994 budget ended the already frayed consensus.

Through 1993 the government relied on the nyd in critical parliamentary divisions, but in late March 1994 the nyd withdrew its support following the resignation the previous month of its leader, Count Ian WACHMEISTER. In the campaigning for the fall legislative election the ruling coalition derived some benefit from a modest economic upturn, but the continuing high unemployment and uncertainty about the future of the welfare state gave the opposition Social Democrats powerful ammunition. Overhanging the campaign was the issue of Sweden's projected membership in the European Union (EU, formerly the European Community—EC) from January 1995, on which negotiations had been successfully concluded on March 1.

The outcome of the balloting on September 18, 1994, was a decisive swing to the left, with the Social Democrats and the ex-Communist v both gaining ground sharply and the left-oriented Greens reentering the *Riksdag* after a three-year absence. Of the outgoing coalition parties, m held its vote, but the other three all lost seats, while the nyd disappeared from parliament altogether. Having rejected an fp offer of a majority center-left coalition, the Social Democrats proceeded to form a minority one-party government headed by Carlsson, with qualified pledges of external support from v and the Greens.

Attention then turned to the EU referendum set for November 13, 1994, with the pro-accession center-right parties, Social Democratic leadership, and business community countering a lively anti-EU coalition of v, the Greens, and many rank-and-file Social Democrats. The result, in a turnout of 82.4 percent, was a 52.2 to 46.9 percent vote in favor of accession.

On August 18, 1995, Prime Minister Carlsson unexpectedly announced that he would retire in March 1996, more than two years before the expiration of his government's mandate. Deputy Premier Mona SAHLIN was an early favorite successor until she was forced to exit due to allegations of misusing an official credit card. After much initial hesitation, Finance Minister Göran PERSSON of the Swedish Social Democratic Party was persuaded to become a candidate. After he was elected as chair of the ruling party, Persson was sworn in as prime minister on March 17, 1996, to head a substantially reshuffled cabinet.

In the general election of September 20, 1998, the Social Democratic legislative representation fell from 161 to 131 seats on a vote share of 36.6 percent, with m finishing second with 22.9 percent of the vote and 82 seats.

The poor performance by s in the elections was largely a result of voter dissatisfaction with the government's fiscally conservative policies and its willingness to make cuts in the welfare system.

In 2002 Prime Minister Persson was reelected for a third term, thanks to his party's strong showing in the September 15 parliamentary election. The Social Democrats benefited from an economic upturn, capturing 39.8 percent of the vote, improving on its 36.4 percent showing in 1998. Shortly before the election, Persson had promised to increase spending on welfare. The conservative m was dealt the greatest loss among the parties . Running on a platform of tax cuts, including abolition of wealth and real estate taxes, the party won only 15.2 percent of the vote, many Swedes having regarded m's policies as endangering their social benefits. The Liberal Party made surprising gains, with a vote share of 13.3 percent, compared to 4.7 percent in the 1998 election. Analysts attributed the increase, at least in part, to the party's call for a language test for citizenship, among other measures.

Persson immediately ruled out giving government positions to either the Left Party or the Green Party—both coalition partners—because of their opposition to adoption of the euro. Meanwhile, the Social Democrats secured parliamentary support from v and mp to form a minority government. Analysts speculated that the v and mp agreement was based on an understanding that the government would press for reductions in defense spending and a moratorium on cod fishing in the Baltic Sea. On September 10, 2003, Foreign Minister Anna LINDH, a key proponent in the pro-euro campaign, was assassinated in a Stockholm department store. On September 14, Swedish voters rejected adoption of the euro by 56 percent to 42 percent, despite the measure's strong backing by Prime Minister Persson and Lindh.

In February 2004 a new party, the June List (*Junilistan*), was formed to contest the European Parliament election in June. Its founders were a group of economists and a former head of the Central Bank, Nils LUNDGREN. A cofounder, Lars WOHLIN, said that while the party opposed joining the Economic and Monetary Union (EMU), it was not against membership in the EU.

The June List surprised analysts by winning 14.4 percent of the vote on June 10 and securing 3 of Sweden's 19 seats. The ruling s drew a record-low 24.7 percent of the vote, which analysts attributed to Swedish voters' uncertainties about closer integration with the EU.

Prime Minister Persson announced a broad cabinet reshuffle on October 21, 2004, including the appointment of Social Democrat Mona Sahlin to head a new ministry of environment and community development. Persson also named the first immigrant to hold a cabinet post, Ibrahim BAYLAN as minister of education and culture.

The Social Democrats suffered a setback in March 2006 when Foreign Minister Laila FREIVALDS resigned amid accusations that she had lied about her involvement in shutting down an Internet website launched by the Sweden Democrats and linked to a highly controversial cartoon portraying the prophet Mohammed. The cartoon angered many Muslims, prompting protests worldwide. Freivalds had also been criticized for a slow response to the Asian tsunami in 2004 in which more than 500 Swedes died.

In the 2006 parliamentary election the Swedish Social Democratic Party won a plurality of seats (130), with 34.99 percent of the vote, but lost power to the Alliance for Sweden, whose member parties won a combined 178 seats. The Moderate Coalition Party, calling itself the new Moderates (*nya Moderaterna*), won 97 seats on a vote share of 26.23 percent, its highest since 1928. The Moderates chair, Fredrik REINFELDT, who was endorsed by all parties in the Alliance, was appointed prime minister on October 5. His new center-right coalition government named on October 6 included the Center Party, the Liberal Party, and the Christian Democrats, in addition to the Moderates. Two ministers resigned within ten days over allegations that they had failed to pay taxes. Less than a year later Defense Minister Mikael ODENBERG resigned in protest of a scheduled reduction in spending for the armed forces.

Constitution and government. The present Swedish constitution retains the general form of the old governmental structure, but the king is now a figurehead (formerly, as nominal head of government, he appointed the prime minister and served as commander in chief of the armed forces). In 1979 the *Riksdag* took final action on making women eligible for succession; thus the present king's daughter, VICTORIA, born in 1977, has become the heir apparent. Any proposed amendment of the constitution must be approved twice by the *Riksdag* in successive legislative terms, requiring that a general election occur between the first approval and the second.

The chief executive officer, the prime minister, is nominated by the speaker of the *Riksdag* and confirmed by the whole house. The prime minister appoints other members of the cabinet, which functions as a policy-drafting body. Routine administration is carried out largely by independent administrative boards (*centrala ämbetsverk*). Legislative authority is vested in the *Riksdag,* which has been a unicameral body since 1971. Since 1994, parliamentary elections are held every four years. The judicial system is headed by the Supreme Court (*Högsta Domstolen*) and includes 6 courts of appeal (*hovrätt*) and 100 district courts (*tingsrätt*). There is a parallel system of administrative courts, while the *Riksdag* appoints four *justitieombudsmen* to maintain general oversight of both legislative and executive actions.

Sweden is administratively divided into 24 counties (including Stockholm) with appointed governors and elected councils and into 289 urban and rural communes with elected councils. The 20,000-strong Sámi (Lapp) community in the north has its own local assembly.

Under legislation approved in 1996, the Evangelical Lutheran Church was effectively disestablished as the Church of Sweden on January 1, 2000, terminating a legal and financial relationship between church and state that dated from the 16th century.

Foreign relations. Sweden has not participated in any war nor joined any military alliance since 1814. Unlike Denmark, Iceland, and Norway, it declined to enter the North Atlantic Treaty Organization (NATO) in 1949, while its determination to safeguard its neutrality is backed by a defense system that is now being considerably diminished.

A strong supporter of international cooperation, Sweden participates in the United Nations (UN) and all its related agencies; in 1975 it became the first industrial nation to meet a standard set by the Organization for Economic Cooperation and Development (OECD), allocating a full 1 percent of its GNP to aid for developing countries.

Sweden also attaches importance to regional cooperation through the Nordic Council, while in 1960 it was a founding member of the European Free Trade Association (EFTA), although its membership in that body ceased upon its accession to the EU in 1995.

Stockholm's traditionally good relations with Moscow were strained during the 1980s and early 1990s by numerous incidents involving Soviet submarines in Swedish waters and intrusions of Russian planes into the country's airspace. However, during an official visit to Moscow by Prime Minister Carl Bildt from February 4–7, 1993, the long-standing controversy appeared to end when the Russians for the first time formally admitted to violations of Swedish territorial waters.

Citing the end of the Cold War and the need to improve its economy by means of increased trade, Sweden applied for membership in the EC on July 1, 1991. To pave the way, it became a signatory of the European Economic Area (EEA) treaty between the EC and certain EFTA countries on May 2, 1992. It also placed emphasis on post-Soviet regional cooperation, becoming a founding member of the ten-nation Council of the Baltic Sea States in March 1992 and of the Barents Euro-Arctic Council (of the five Nordic countries and Russia) in January 1993. Two months later Sweden modified its tradition of neutrality by agreeing to join a NATO military maneuver in August, and in May 1994 it enrolled in NATO's Partnership for Peace program for the neutral and former communist states of Europe and the ex-USSR.

Sweden has been involved in Afghanistan since 2002 as a member of the International Security Assistance Force (ISAF), focusing primarily on humanitarian support. Meanwhile, since the U.S. invasion of Iraq in 2003, thousands of Iraqi refugees have immigrated to Sweden, and Sweden has had a prominent role in efforts to rebuild Iraq.

Sweden's position regarding NATO softened in 2008, when Defense Minister Sten TOLGFERS said that joining the organization was a "natural step in the long term." Meanwhile, Sweden deployed personnel to the NATO peacekeeping mission in Kosovo.

Also in 2008 Sweden dropped plans to send a joint engineering unit with Norway to the UN peacekeeping force in Darfur in the wake of objections by the Sudanese president, who singled out Scandinavian countries because of the 2007 controversial cartoon depiction of the prophet Mohammed that ran in newspapers. Sweden instead increased its humanitarian aid to the region.

In May 2008 Denmark, Finland, Iceland, Norway, and Sweden met to discuss greater Nordic cooperation on defense matters, specifically agreements on a joint response to emergencies, as well as cooperation in defense procurement and coast guard activities. The arrangement was meant to respect each country's differing obligations to NATO and EU membership. Concern over Russia's conduct of foreign policy manners and its heavy use of the Baltic Sea for shipping prompted the talks.

Tensions heightened with Russia in the wake of the latter's military intervention in Georgia in August 2008. Sweden suspended all military cooperation with Russia (the two countries periodically had conducted joint military maneuvers) and demanded an immediate cease-fire. In October Sweden hosted Georgian president Mikheil Saakashvili, who asked that Sweden represent its interests in Russia. Sweden has since endorsed EU monitoring of Georgia

In 2009 Sweden negotiated with NATO, Norway, and Finland to collaborate on a Nordic air control operation (which Baltic states could later join) as a defense measure for the participating nations.

In May Sweden withdrew its support for Liechtenstein to join the EU's borderless Schengen zone because of Liechtenstein's status as a tax haven, effectively blocking Liechtenstein's application.

On July 1, 2009, Sweden took the helm of the rotating EU presidency for six months. Prime Minister Reinfeldt's agenda included brokering a global agreement on climate change in Copenhagen, setting new regulations for financial markets, steering the EU toward federal budget restraints, and supporting further talks with Croatia and Turkey on EU membership. One of his first acts in office was to broker a free trade deal between the EU and South Korea.

Current issues. Though public support for Sweden's social welfare system has continued in the wake of economic challenges, its system of socialism changed following the 2006 election, when the conservative Alliance for Sweden came to power, promising to reform the economy.

Tax cuts have been a cornerstone of the governing coalition, despite socialist concerns that the tax base supporting the welfare state would be eroded, creating a greater divide between rich and poor. Among the first steps taken by the new administration were a series of tax cuts directed at people of low to middle income and the abolishment of federal real estate taxes and the so-called "wealth tax" on individual assets.

The Alliance also embarked on a widespread effort to privatize state-owned assets by selling shares in some 50 publicly owned companies to raise revenue to pay down the public debt as well as to help create more jobs and foreign investment. In May 2007 the first state assets were sold from the telecommunications company for $3 billion.

Economic policy has also addressed an aging work force, resulting in greater reliance on immigrant labor in certain sectors. (More than 1 million of Sweden's 9 million residents were born outside the country.) Increasing immigration has raised concerns about the potential strain on social services and to a small degree about security. Following the immigration of thousands of refugees from Iraq, the government in 2007 tightened its policy, ruling that, in the case of asylum seekers from Afghanistan, Iraq, and Somalia, Sweden could legally deport immigrants unless it was proved that they would be threatened. Additionally, the *Rikstag* approved legislation that denies publicly funded health care to illegal immigrants. Meanwhile, relations with the Muslim community were deeply strained by the publication in 2007 of a controversial cartoon depicting the prophet Mohammed by Swedish artist Lars VILKS. Vilks claimed he did not intend to provoke Muslims but rather meant to test the boundaries of speech and press freedoms in Sweden. Prime Minister Reinfeldt took the stance that Swedish laws prohibit the government from censoring media. Earlier, the foreign minister resigned after shutting down a website linked to the controversial cartoon.

As a result of the new asylum policy, the number of Iraqi immigrants declined by a third in 2008, though the number of immigrants overall reached a record 100,000. Collaterally, there has been a growing push for changes to the Swedish for Immigrants program, including compulsory national testing, time limits on completion of studies, and a performance bonus to those who complete the program within a specific time frame. Additionally, services to help immigrants find employment have been expanded.

Amid mounting concerns over potential terrorist attacks, the *Riksdag* in June 2008 narrowly passed one of the most comprehensive—and divisive—government surveillance laws in Europe. The law, effective January 1, 2009, allows the defense department to scan all cross-border phone calls, e-mails, and faxes without a court order. The new law provoked outrage from the youth wings of the governing coalition parties, as well as from journalists, who are not exempt from possible surveillance. The Social Democrat's chair, Mona Sahlin, said she would move to annul the law if her party regains power in 2010. Meanwhile, the public backlash prompted the *Riksdag*, spurred by the Alliance, to adopt amendments in September regarding judicial oversight of the electronic surveillance. Meanwhile, though Sweden's military budget was cut significantly, the government dropped plans to disband several military units in the wake of security concerns related to Russia's military attacks in Georgia. Liberal Party leader Jan Björklund endorsed the move, saying the country's proximity to Russia could present a "direct threat."

The government in recent years has made a strong commitment to address environmental issues, though officials initially balked at EU climate change requirements, which imposed some of the heaviest mandates on Sweden. In 2009 the government stepped up its goals to reduce greenhouse gas emissions by 40 percent by 2020, compared to 1990 levels, and called for vehicles to run entirely without fossil fuels by 2030. In an effort to achieve these ends, a combination of taxes on carbon dioxide and incentives for renewable energy were approved. In February the government announced it would scrap a planned phase-out of nuclear power by 2020. Though opposition parties objected to the move, observers reported a subsequent shift toward greater public approval, signaling a dramatic change since a 1980 referendum required a phase-out of Sweden's nuclear reactors.

In March 2009 the government announced a major restructuring of the military starting in 2010. The plan will end the century-old practice of universal conscription in favor of a professional army within five years, as well as increase the number of Swedish troops by 50 percent, to 50,000, to be ready for deployment, as needed, within a week. Social Democrats criticized the plan, saying they didn't believe the military could meet its goals by voluntary conscription.

Following government approval of a second economic stimulus package in April 2009 to help local governments affected by the global economic downturn, Prime Minister Reinfeldt was reported to have gained support in public opinion polls. Meanwhile, the opposition criticized the stimulus spending as too little.

In June Reinfeldt rejected the idea of additional stimulus, saying he preferred to pursue further income tax cuts if his party retained power in the 2010 parliamentary election.

POLITICAL PARTIES

In advance of the 2006 general election the Moderate Coalition Party (m), the Center Party (c), the Liberal People's Party (fp), and the Christian Democratic Party (kd) formed the Alliance for Sweden (*Allians för Sverige*). The parties in the Alliance fielded their own candidates in the election but backed a single candidate, Fredrik Reinfeldt, for prime minister.

Government Parties:

Moderate Coalition Party (*Moderaterna*—m). Known as the Conservative Party until after the 1968 election and commonly referred to in recent years as the Moderates, m officially changed its designation to the Moderate Party in September 2007.

The party was originally organized as a vehicle for the financial and business communities and advocated tax cuts and reduced governmental interference in the economy. It has long favored a robust defense policy and strongly supported Sweden's accession to the EU. The party joined a center-left coalition government in 1976 but withdrew in 1981 after disagreeing with a tax reform plan. Its *Riksdag* representation dropped from 86 seats in 1982 to 66 in 1988 but rose again to 80 in 1991, when it formed a center-right coalition with fp, c, and the Christian Democrats (below) under the premiership of Carl Bildt. The Moderates retained 80 seats in the 1994 national balloting (on a slightly higher vote share of 22.4 percent), but an overall swing to the left returned the party to opposition. The party was unable to improve its position substantially in the September 1998 *Riksdag* election (82 seats and a 22.9 vote share), thwarting Bildt's determined campaign to return to the prime ministership. Bildt, a prominent EU/UN negotiator in Yugoslavia since 1995, resigned as m chair in mid-1999 and was succeeded by Bo LUNDGREN, a former minister of finance.

In the 2002 general election, the party's vote share dropped to 15.2 percent. As a result, Lundgren announced his resignation as party chair. Fredrik Reinfeldt replaced him in October 2003 and spearheaded the formation of the Alliance for Sweden (*Allians för Sverige*), a coalition with fp, c, and kd in August 2004.

In a bid to capture the middle ground of Swedish politics prior to the 2006 election, the party dropped its call for radical tax cuts, instead emphasizing support for public services. It won 26.2 percent of the vote, in addition to the appointment of Fredrik Reinfeldt as prime minister. The Moderate-led Alliance has embarked on a plan to liberalize the economy through the privatization of state-owned assets and reform of the welfare system, including a reduction in employers' social security contributions, restrictions on access to unemployment and sick benefits, and efforts to boost employment. Public support for these changes began to waver as the economy contracted during the global economic downturn. Meanwhile, several senior staff members in the Reinfeldt administration resigned in the wake of allegations of tax evasion and other improprieties.

The Reinfeldt administration gained public support in 2009 for its handling of the economic crisis.

Leaders: Fredrik REINFELDT (Chair), Lars LINDBLAD (Parliamentary Leader), Per SCHLINGMANN (Secretary General).

Liberal Party (*Folkpartiet Liberalerna*—fp). Originally formed as a parliamentary group in 1895, the first *Folkpartiet* merged with the Liberal Coalition Party in 1900. The two split in 1923 over alcohol issues and reunited in 1934 in today's form as fp. (The grouping has since often been referred to as the Liberal Party.) The party draws support from rural free-church movements as well as from professionals and intellectuals. Favoring socially progressive policies that also strive to acknowledge individual responsibility, fp has sought the cooperation of the Center Party (below) on many issues, promoting "knowledge, work, and security" in its party platform. It lost half of its parliamentary representation in the 1982 general election, and in July 1984 former prime minister Ola Ullsten resigned as chair "to make way for more dynamic influences."

In the September 1985 balloting, the fp gained 30 additional *Riksdag* seats for a total of 51 but lost representation in the next two ballots; it nevertheless entered a four-party center-right coalition in 1991.

After another electoral setback in 1994, to 26 seats on a 7.2 percent vote share, the Liberals reverted to opposition status, with Bengt WESTERBERG standing down as party chair. He was succeeded by Lars LEIJONBORG. In June 1996 the fp announced a relaunch as a "bourgeois left" party emphasizing the fight against unemployment and ethnic separation. The party lost 9 of its 26 seats in the September 1998 general election.

The party made dramatic gains in the 2002 election, winning 13.3 percent of the vote and 48 seats in the *Riksdag*.

As a member of the Alliance for Sweden in the 2006 election, the fp received just 7.5 percent of the vote, prompting veteran Leijonborg to step down as party chair. However, he was appointed to the cabinet.

Education Minister Jan Björklund took over as party chair in September 2007. The cabinet appointment of Nyamko Sabuni, who immigrated to Sweden from Burundi in 1981, provoked fierce debate and was opposed by Muslim groups because of Sabuni's position on integration, including a ban on veils for girls under 15, and her stance against female circumcision and arranged marriages.

Since gaining power in the Alliance, the Liberal Party has focused on diminishing religious influences in the classroom by removing exemptions from gym and sexual education classes for Muslim students.

In November 2008 the Liberals announced their preference for a new referendum by 2011 on Sweden joining the Eurozone.

The Liberals have sought to restrict the power of the Swedish Migration Board from appointing legal representation to asylum seekers since the board also determines whether the immigrants may stay in the country. However, evidence of the migration board policing itself surfaced in July with reports that the board had fired one of the lawyers it contracted with because of anti-Islam comments he published online.

Leaders: Jan BJÖRKLUND (Chair), Johan PEHRSON (Parliamentary Leader), Nyamko SABUNI, Erik ULLENHAG (Secretary General).

Center Party (*Centerpartiet*—c). Farmers' representatives first began breaking away from other parties to promote rural rights in 1910, and in 1922 formally launched the Agrarian Party (the precursor to c). In return for agricultural subsidies, the party began to support the Social Democrats in the 1930s, occasionally serving as a junior partner in coalition with s. Since adopting its present name in 1958, the party has developed nationwide strength, including support from the larger urban centers. It has long campaigned for decentralization of government and industry and for reduced impact of government on the lives of individuals, whereas in the 1970s opposition to nuclear power became its main issue. A major advance to 86 seats in the 1976 election enabled c to head a center-right coalition until 1978 under Thorbjörn Fälldin, who returned to the premiership in 1979 despite his party's 22-seat decline in that year's election. In opposition after a further slump of 8 seats in 1982, it continued to lose ground in 1985, 1988, and 1991 (when its tally stood at 31). At a party congress in June 1986, Karin SÖDER was elected to succeed Fälldin, who had resigned six months earlier because of his party's poor showing in the 1985 election. However, Söder (Sweden's first female party leader) was forced to step down in March 1987 for health reasons. The party's participation in the center-right coalition formed in 1991 was shaken by the resignation in June 1994 of Party Chair Olof Johansson as environment minister, in opposition to the Öresund bridge project. In the September election c was reduced to 27 seats (on a vote share of 7.7 percent) and again went into opposition.

Johansson resigned as party chair in April 1998 and was succeeded in June by Lennart DALÉUS, a staunch opponent of nuclear power who had led c's successful 1980 referendum on decommissioning nuclear plants. He promptly announced that the party would no longer cooperate with s and also voiced reservations about m. He hoped to be part of a centrist government following the September general election, but c lost 9 of its 27 seats on a vote share of 5.1 percent.

Daléus was replaced as party leader by Maud Olofsson in 2001. In the 2002 general election the party won 6.2 percent of the vote and 22 seats. As a member of the Alliance for Sweden, c won 7.8 percent of the vote in 2006 and Maud Olofsson was appointed enterprise and energy minister and deputy prime minister. Olofsson was criticized in April by the pronuclear camp for reportedly blocking state-owned power company Vattenfall from acquiring British nuclear operator British Energy; doing so would have expanded Sweden's nuclear assets, which are limited domestically by a moratorium.

With pressure mounting from coalition partners, Maud Olofsson led the Center Party in February 2009 to reverse its long-standing position against nuclear power. Olofsson said that though she does not like nuclear power, she respected the position of the coalition partners.

Leaders: Maud OLOFSSON (Chair), Roger TIEFENSEE (Parliamentary Leader), Anders FLANKING (Secretary General).

Christian Democratic Party (*Kristdemokraterna*—kd). Formed in 1964 as the Christian Democratic Coalition (*Kristen Demokratisk Samling*—kds) to promote Christian values in politics, the kds adopted the name Christian Democratic Community Party (*Kristdemokratiska Samhällspartiet*—kds) in 1987. The group claims a membership of more than 25,000 but for two decades was unable to secure *Riksdag* representation, although it secured a growing number of local and state seats. In September 1984 it entered into an electoral pact with the Center Party, thereby securing its first legislative seat in 1985 despite a marginal 2.6 percent vote share. Excluded completely in 1988, the kds won 26 legislative seats in 1991 and joined a center-right coalition. Reduced to 15 seats (and 4.1 percent of the vote) in the 1994 balloting, it went into opposition. In 1996 the party was renamed again, to the Christian Democratic Party (kd). Opposing adoption of the euro and stressing "cleaner politics," kd ran the most successful campaign in its history for the general election of September 1998, winning 42 seats (a gain of 27) on a vote share of 11.8 percent.

Göran Hägglund was elected party leader on April 3, 2004, succeeding Alf SVENSSON, who had been Sweden's longest-serving party leader, with 31 years in the post. The party won 9.1 percent of the vote in 2002 but lost significant support in 2004. In the 2006 election it received 6.5 percent of the vote and 24 seats.

Following the Alliance's announcement of increased fuel taxes in September 2007 in an effort to reduce greenhouse gases from emissions, the Christian Democrats were accused of betraying campaign promises to lower fuel prices. This criticism was spearheaded by their base of voters in rural areas, which had less access to public transportation.

Distancing his party from the growing popularity of the Sweden Democrats, Hägglund criticized the right-wing group in 2008, accusing the party of being xenophobic and spreading Nazi ideology.

In April 2009 the Christian Democratic Party was the only party in parliament to dissent on a bill that legalized same-sex marriage. The Christian Democrats received 4.7 percent of the vote in the June European parliamentary election, thereby retaining one seat. However, with such low support, political analysts predicted that kds might not achieve the 4 percent voting threshold in the 2010 federal election to remain a party in parliament.

Leaders: Göran HÄGGLUND (Chair), Stefan ATTEFALL (Parliamentary Leader), Lennart SJÖGREN (Secretary General).

Opposition Parties:

Swedish Social Democratic Party (*Sveriges Socialdemokratiska Arbetareparti*—s). Formed in the 1880s and long a dominant force in Swedish politics, s has a "pragmatic" socialist outlook. During more than four decades of virtually uninterrupted power from 1932, it refrained from nationalizing major industries but gradually increased government economic planning and control over the business sector. When its representation in the *Riksdag* dropped to 152 seats in 1976, s was forced, despite its sizable plurality, to move into opposition. It regained control of the government in 1982 and, despite a further reduction, maintained control in 1985 and 1988 with the aid of vpk (see v, below). There were few, if any, changes in party ideology and practice following the assassination of Olof Palme and the accession of his deputy, Ingvar Carlsson, to the prime ministership in March 1986. The group was again forced into opposition in the legislative poll of September 1991, when its seat tally fell from 156 to 138. It staged a comeback in 1994, winning 161 seats and 45.3 percent of the vote.

Carlsson's surprise announcement in August 1995 of his impending departure as party leader and prime minister, combined with rapid public disenchantment with the EU, yielded a dramatic slump in s support to only 28.1 percent in the September European Parliament balloting, when three of the seven Social Democrats elected were critical of EU membership. The party was further damaged in November by the enforced exit from politics of Carlsson's deputy and presumed successor, Mona Sahlin, after press disclosures about her financial affairs. The mantle accordingly passed to the finance minister, Göran Persson, who ran unopposed for the s chair, securing the position on March 15, 1996, two days before he was appointed prime minister.

Persson led the party to a strong showing in the September 2002 general elections, with the Social Democrats winning 39.8 percent of the vote. The party was later thrown into confusion by the assassination of Foreign Minister Anna Lindh, who was considered by many to be the natural successor to Prime Minister Persson.

The party also has been split over support for the EMU. While the party officially was in favor of the EMU in 2004, several prominent party members, including Margot WALLSTRÖM, vice president of the European commission, openly declared that they were against adoption of the euro. A majority of the population voted against exchanging the krona for the euro in the 2004 referendum, and party opinion since then has followed public opinion on the subject.

Despite the healthy state of the Swedish economy, the Social Democrats did not win control of the parliament in the 2006 election, though it held the most seats (130 seats) of any single party, on a vote share of 34.9 percent. Following the election, Göran Persson stepped down as party leader, and subsequently, Mona Sahlin was elected party chair, becoming the first woman to hold that position in the party. Recently, eroding membership, especially among urbanites, has been cause for serious concern within the party. Sahlin reportedly told a labor organization in April 2008 that if "developments continue, this party won't exist in 10 to 15 years." Party membership has reportedly been reduced by half since the 1990s.

Social Democrats objected to, but have taken few steps to stop, center-right Alliance efforts to pare back the social welfare system and privatize state-owned assets. A rift in the party developed in October 2008 over Sahlin's decision to sideline the Left because of disagreements over the Left's refusal to accept rules governing the budget and state finances in favor of an alliance with the Greens. The decision prompted fierce criticism from trade unions and the more left-leaning wing of the party. Subsequently, Sahlin reopened negotiations with the Left, and by December key differences over economic policy had been resolved, with all sides agreeing to a common economic proposal. The proposal included the Left's dropping its opposition to the maintenance of a state budget surplus and spending ceiling and the independence of the *Riksbank*. However, each party maintained that it would campaign independently.

In March 2009 support for the Social Democrats declined over pension and bonus payouts to executives overseeing one of Sweden's largest trade union pension fund. While serving on the pension board, Social Democratic party leader and trade union president Wanja Lundby-WEDIN allegedly approved a lavish pension package for a former pension CEO,at the same time that payments to pensioners were cut as a result of the decline in the stock market.

Leaders: Mona SAHLIN (Party Leader), Sven-Erik ÖSTERBERG (Parliamentary Leader), Ibrahim BAYLAN (Secretary General).

Left Party (*Vänsterpartiet*—v). Originally formed in 1917 as the Left Social Democratic Party (*Vänster Socialdemokratiska Partiet*—vsdp), the party was renamed the Communist Party (*Kommunistiska Partiet*) in 1921 and the Left Party-Communists (*Vänsterpartiet-Kommunisterna*) in 1967. In May 1990 the party adopted its present name. Long before the decline of communism in Eastern Europe, the party pursued a "revisionist," or "Eurocommunist," policy based on distinctive Swedish conditions. This posture provoked considerable dissent within the party before the withdrawal of a pro-Moscow faction in early 1977. Following the 1982 election, the party agreed to support a new s government; its voting strength became crucial following the s losses in 1985 and 1988. Having won 16 seats in the 1991 general election, v went into full opposition to the new center-right coalition government. In the 1994 balloting the party achieved its best result since 1948, winning 22 seats on a 6.2 percent vote share.

Having unsuccessfully opposed Sweden's accession to the EU, v advanced in the September 1995 European balloting, returning three representatives with 12.9 percent of the vote, and nearly doubled its parliamentary representation in the September 1998 elections, winning 43 seats on a vote share of 12 percent, its best showing since its formation. Its legislative support subsequently remained crucial in the continuation of the s minority government.

Gudrun SCHYMAN was leader of the party between 1993 and 2003, promoting feminism as well as socialism. She resigned on

January 26, 2003, when discrepancies in her tax returns were made public. Lars Ohly replaced Schyman in a party election on February 20, 2004.

Ohly's appointment highlighted a division between modernist and traditional wings of the party, with Ohly, a former railroad worker, representing the traditionalist wing. The party faced a possible split in January 2005, largely caused by Ohly's insistence on calling himself a communist. He has since retracted this. On January 29 more than 150 members met to decide if they should leave the party or work to reform it.

In the 2006 election v won 5.8 percent of the vote.

Efforts to modernize the party and address its communist past failed following an unsuccessful challenge to Ohly's leadership in June 2008 by Staffan NORBERG. In December the Left Party entered into its first coalition with the Social Democrats and the Greens ahead of the 2010 national election. Meanwhile, in the June 2009 European parliamentary election the party won 5.7 percent of the vote, retaining one seat. In the wake of the global economic recession, v advocated an increase in state ownership and control of Swedish banks, including the launch of a new state-owned investment bank.

Leaders: Lars OHLY (Chair), Alice ÅSTRÖM (Parliamentary Leader), Anki AHLSTEN (Secretary General).

Green Party (*Miljöpartiet de Gröna*). Established in 1981, the Greens benefited in the 1988 election from an upsurge of popular interest in environmental issues. It has advocated tax reduction for low-income wage earners, increased charges for energy use, and heightened penalties for pollution by commercial establishments and motor vehicle operators. It also has called for the phasing out of nuclear-generated electricity and curtailed highway construction. The party's parliamentary representation plummeted from 20 seats in 1988 to none in 1991 but recovered to 18 seats (on 5.0 percent of the vote) in 1994.

The Greens opposed EU membership, which was approved in the November 1994 referendum. In the September 1995 European Parliament balloting, the Greens won four seats and 17.2 percent of the national vote.

The party lost two seats in the 1998 general election on a vote share of 4.5 percent but agreed to continue to support the s minority government on confidence motions. The party participated in negotiations with center-right parties after the election before deciding to renew its agreement with s. In the 2006 election the Greens won 5.2 percent of the vote.

In 2008 the Green Party was reevaluating its position against EU membership because of successful strides the bloc had taken on that advanced major environmental policies. In the run-up to the 2010 national parliamentary election, the Greens were expected to join in an alliance with the Social Democrats and the Left.

Leaders: Maria WETTERSTRAND and Peter ERIKSSON (Spokespersons), Ulf HOLM and Mikaela VALTERSSON (Parliamentary Leaders), Agneta BÖRJESSON (Secretary General).

Other Parties that Participated in the 2006 Elections:

Sweden Democrats (*Sverigedemokraterna*). The Sweden Democrats is a far-right, nationalist party that was established in 1988. In the 2006 election it won 2.9 percent of the vote, failing to meet the 4 percent threshold for election to parliament. Efforts by the Moderates in the southern town of Karlskrona to cooperate with the Democrats led to a sharp rebuke by national party leaders, whose policy opposes any alliance with the Democrats. Other leading parties have similar policies because of the Democrats' links to Nazi ideology. Its party platform includes encouraging higher birthrates, stopping the development of a "multicultural society," promoting a robust national defense, and advocating harsher prison sentences. At its annual congress in May 2008 the Sweden Democrats called for an end to the special status rights of Sami herders.

In the June 2009 European parliamentary election, the party won 3 percent of the vote.

Leader: Jimmie ÅKESSON.

Feminist Initiative (*Feministiskt initiativ*—fi). The fi was established in 2005, by, among others, former v leader Gudrun Schyman, Ebba WITT-BRATTSTRÖM, and Stina SUNDBERG. (Witt-Brattström later became a vocal critic of the party, saying it was too far to the left and thus excluded some women.) The fi, which won close to 0.7 percent of the vote in the 2006 election, aims to achieve economic and social justice for women and eliminate societal complacency regarding violence against women. After the election the fi decided to function as a feminist organization rather than a political party in order to accept state grant money for gender equality projects (Swedish law prohibits political parties from receiving state grants).

However, in early 2008, the fi announced that it would reestablish itself as a political party to field candidates in upcoming local and general elections. The party won 2 percent of the vote in the June 2009 European parliamentary election on a campaign that called for abortion to be a human right.

Leaders: Gudrun SCHYMAN, Devrim MAVI, Sofia KARLSSON.

Pirate Party (*Piratpartiet*—pp). The party was founded by Rickard Falkvinge in early 2006 to advocate for an open information society in relation to the popular Internet-based file-sharing site Pirate Bay, which had brought criticism to Sweden as a safe haven for online piracy. Despite a rapidly growing membership, the pp gained just over 0.6 percent of the vote in the 2006 election. Its party program mainly focuses on fundamental reforms of copyright and patent laws and ensuring that citizens' rights to privacy are respected. In 2008 it took on a new calling as a vocal opponent of the controversial far-reaching surveillance law. The party surged in popularity in reaction to parliament's passage of an anti-file-sharing law in February 2009 and to the April convictions of the three founders and a financier of Pirate Bay for copyright infringement.

The party won 7 percent of the vote and one of Sweden's 18 seats in the European parliamentary election in June 2009, its support largely from males under age 30. The party subsequently joined the Greens/European Free Alliance parliamentary group.

Leader: Rickard FALKVINGE.

Swedish Pensioners' Interest Party (*Sveriges Pensionärers Intresseparti*—spi). Founded in 1987, the spi seeks to secure higher social and financial status for retired people. The party won just over 0.5 percent of the vote in the 2006 election. The party remains active on the regional level.

Leader: Pelle HÖGLUND.

The June List (*Junilistan*). *Junilistan* was founded in 2003 by a group of mild euroskeptics led by Nils Lundgren. The party won 14.4 percent of the vote in the European parliamentary elections on June 10, 2004.

In 2006 the party won 1 of Sweden's 19 seats in the European Parliament. The June List advocates membership in the EU but rejects the idea of a European supra-state, arguing that Sweden should retain control over Swedish national issues. In March 2008 Lundgren stepped down as party chair. He was succeeded in July by Sören Wibe. The party won 3.6 percent of the vote in the European parliamentary elections in June 2009, losing all 3 seats. Analysts cited increasing public sentiment against euroskeptics after the financial crisis resulted in the krona's losing value against the euro.

Leader: Sören WIBE.

Health Care Party (*Sjukvårdspartiet*). Established in December 2005 by a merger of six local parties, the Health Care Party focuses on people's need for appropriate health care. It gained only 0.2 percent of the vote in the 2006 parliamentary election but showed a strong regional following, in particular in the sparsely populated northern areas of Sweden. Following the 2006 elections the local Stockholm Health Party joined the national party organization.

Leader: Kenneth BACKGÅRD.

LEGISLATURE

The unicameral *Riksdag* consists of 349 members serving four-year terms. (Before the 1994 election the term was three years.) Of the total, 310 are elected by proportional representation in 28 constituencies; the remaining 39 are selected from a national pool designed to give absolute proportionality to all parties receiving at least 4 percent of the vote.

In the most recent election on September 17, 2006, the seat distribution was as follows: the Swedish Social Democratic Party, 130; Moderates, 97; Center Party, 29; Liberal Party, 28; Christian Democratic Party, 24; Left Party, 22; and Green Party, 19.

Speaker: Per WESTERBERG.

CABINET

[as of September 1, 2009]

Prime Minister	Fredrik Reinfeldt (m)
Deputy Prime Minister	Maud Olofsson (fp) [f]
Ministers	
Agriculture	Eskil Erlandsson (c)
Communications	Åsa Torstensson (c) [f]
Culture	Lena Adelsohn Liljeroth (ind) [f]
Defense	Sten Tolgfors (m)
Education	Jan Björkland (fp)
Elderly Care and Public Health	Maria Larsson (kd) [f]
Employment	Sven Otto Littorin (m)
Enterprise and Energy	Maud Olofsson (fp) [f]
Environment	Andreas Carlgren (c)
European Union Affairs	Cecilia Malmström (fp) [f]
European Affairs	Cecilia Malmström [f]
Finance	Anders Borg (m)
Foreign Affairs	Carl Bildt (m)
Foreign Trade	Ewa Björling (m) [f]
Health and Social Affairs	Göran Hägglund (kd)
Higher Education and Research	Tobias Krantz
Integration and Gender Equality	Nyamko Ana Sabuni (fp) [f]
International Development Cooperation	Gunilla Carlsson (m) [f]
Justice	Beatrice Ask (m) [f]
Local Government and Financial Markets	Mats Odell (kd)
Migration and Asylum Policy	Tobias Billström (m)
Social Security	Cristina Husmark Pehrsson (m) [f]

[f] = female

COMMUNICATIONS

Under Sweden's Mass Media Act, which was implemented in January 1977, principles of noninterference dating to the mid-1700s and embodied in the Freedom of the Press Act of 1949 were extended to all media.

Press. Most papers are politically oriented, and many are owned by political parties. The Press Subsidies Bill of 1966 granted state funds to political parties for distribution of their papers in case of financial difficulties. The following are published in Stockholm, unless otherwise noted: *Aftonbladet* (416,000 daily, 475,000 Sunday), independent Social Democratic; *Expressen* (326,000), liberal; *Dagens Nyheter* (347,000), independent; *Göteborgs Posten* (Göteborg, 242,000), liberal; *Svenska Dagbladet* (193,000), independent conservative; *Sydsvenska Dagbladet* (Malmö, 123,000), independent liberal; *Dagens Industri* (117,000), business; *Nya Wermlands-Tidningen* (Karlstad, 56,000), moderate conservative. The introduction of newspapers distributed for free has resulted in many of the big traditional dailies losing parts of their readership. The biggest of the new free publications is *Metro* (independent), which started in Stockholm in 1995. Since then, editions in Göteborg and Malmö have been added, giving it a total readership of more than 1.5 million people nationwide. *Metro* is now represented in 21 countries around the world.

News agencies. The principal domestic facility is the Newspapers' Telegraph Agency (*Tidningarnas Telegrambyrå*—TT), which is owned by the country's newspapers and other media groups. There are also smaller agencies, such as the Swedish International Press Bureau (*Svensk Internationella Pressbyrån*—SIP), and services run by the leading parties, such as the Swedish Conservative Press Agency (*Svenska Nyhetsbyrån*). In addition, numerous foreign agencies maintain offices in Stockholm.

Broadcasting and computing. Broadcasting services were long provided only by nonprofit, government-regulated companies: *Sveriges Radio, Sveriges Television* (SVT), and *Sveriges Utbildningsradio,* the last of which presents educational programming. Privately owned TV4 started in 1990 as a partly commercial station but was subject to regulations similar to the main public service company, SVT. SVT1 (one of two SVT channels) and TV4 attract equally large audiences. Other, fully commercial, stations also transmit widely. TV3 and Kanal 5 are the biggest ones. As of 2008 there were 878.4 Internet users per 1,000 inhabitants.

INTERGOVERNMENTAL REPRESENTATION

Ambassador to the U.S.: Jonas HAFSTRÖM.

U.S. Ambassador to Sweden: Matthew Winthrop BARZUN.

Permanent Representative to the UN: Anders LIDÉN.

IGO Memberships (Non-UN): AC, ADB, AfDB, BIS, CBSS, CERN, CEUR, EBRD, EIB, ESA, EU, Eurocontrol, G-10, IADB, IEA, Interpol, IOM, NC, NIB, OECD, OSCE, PCA, WCO, WTO.

SWITZERLAND

Swiss Confederation
Schweizerische Eidgenossenschaft (German)
Confédération Suisse (French)
Confederazione Svizzera (Italian)
Confederaziun Svizra (Romansch)

Political Status: Neutral confederation since 1291; equivalent of federal system embodied in constitution of May 29, 1874. A new constitution, which revised and reformed that of 1874, went into effect on January 1, 2000 (as adopted April 18, 1999).

Area: 15,943 sq. mi. (41,293 sq. km.).

Population: 7,288,010 (2000C); 7,593,000 (2008E); figures reference resident population, including noncitizens.

Major Urban Centers (2005E): BERN (118,000), Zürich (327,000), Geneva (177,000), Basel (163,000), Lausanne (109,000).

Official Languages: German, French, Italian. Romansch is recognized as a national language but without full official status.

Monetary Unit: Swiss Franc (market rate December 1, 2009: 0.99 francs = $1US).

President: Hans-Rudolf MERZ (FDP-The Liberals), elected by the Federal Assembly on December 10, 2008, to succeed Pascal COUCHEPIN (FDP-The Liberals) for a one-year term beginning January 1, 2009.

Vice President: Doris LEUTHARD (Christian Democratic People's Party), elected by the Federal Assembly on December 10, 2008, to succeed Hans-Rudolf MERZ (FDP-The Liberals) for a term concurrent with that of the president.

THE COUNTRY

Situated in the mountainous heart of Western Europe, Switzerland has traditionally set an example of peaceful coexistence among different indigenous ethnic and cultural groups, although a postwar increase in the country's "foreign" population was somewhat less than harmonious. The well-educated, politically sophisticated Swiss generally speak one of four languages: German (63.7 percent), French (20.4 percent), Italian (6.5 percent), and Romansch (0.5 percent). Roman Catholics account for 42 percent of the population, Protestants 33 percent, and Muslims 4 percent, while 11 percent assume no religious

affiliation (as of 2008). The influx of foreign workers has ebbed in recent years, although in relation to total population they constitute the highest proportion (20 percent) of any European country except Liechtenstein and Luxembourg. Women made up 45 percent of the registered labor force in 2003.

Switzerland's durable goods output is largely based on the production of precision-engineered items, pharmaceuticals, and special quality products that are not readily mass produced. Tourism, international banking, and insurance are other major contributors to the economy. Raising livestock is the principal agricultural activity, and the chief crops are wheat and potatoes. The country relies heavily on external transactions; foreign exchange earned from exports of goods and services, mostly to the EU, constitutes more than a third of the total national income. Switzerland's GDP of $67,385 per capita makes it one of the world's richest countries.

Switzerland enjoyed a decade of consistent growth following a 1982 recession. However, this period was followed by a new recession that yielded record unemployment (up to 5.1 percent in late 1993) and GDP contraction in 1992–1993. Growth resumed in 1994–1995 (at 2.3 percent a year) and was slow but steady from 1997 to 1999, averaging less than 2 percent annually. Recent economic performance has fluctuated, falling from 3.6 percent in 2000 to 0.4 percent in 2003, then rising from 1.9 percent in 2005 to 3.2 percent in 2006 and 3.1 percent in 2007. According to the Organization for Economic Cooperation and Development, unemployment has been on the rise during the early 21st century, going from 2.6 percent in 2001 to 4.5 percent in 2005 before falling slightly to 3.5 percent in 2008. Inflation during this period was quite low, with the annual growth rate in consumer prices averaging only 0.9 percent for the period of 1999–2003, rising to 2.4 percent in 2008.

In 2009 the global recession began to affect Switzerland significantly, though it was less severe than downturns in many EU countries. While exports of pharmaceuticals remained strong, the country's prominent financial sector, led by banking giants Credit Suisse and UBS, suffered from the international financial crisis, threatening to push Switzerland into deeper recession.

GOVERNMENT AND POLITICS

Political background. The origins of the Swiss Confederation date back to 1291, when the cantons of Uri, Schwyz, and Unterwalden signed an "eternal alliance" against the Hapsburgs. The league continued to expand until 1648, when it became formally independent of the Holy Roman Empire at the Peace of Westphalia. Following French conquest and reorganization during the Napoleonic era, Switzerland's boundaries were fixed by the Congress of Vienna in 1815, when its perpetual neutrality was guaranteed by the principal European powers. The present constitution, adopted on May 29, 1874, superseded an earlier document of 1848 and increased the powers conferred on the central government by the cantons. The 1874 constitution was revised by referendum on April 18, 1999, and a new constitution was put into legal force on January 1, 2000. The changes were primarily aimed at modernizing and updating the 1874 charter, which had been altered 140 times since it was written. The new constitution was approved by 59 percent of the vote; however, only 35 percent of eligible voters participated in the referendum. In addition to modernizing the document's language, the new constitution included new provisions pertaining to labor rights and equal opportunity for people with disabilities.

Women have had the right to vote in federal elections since 1971. The Federal Supreme Court ruled in November 1990 that the half-canton of Appenzell-Innerrhoden could no longer serve as Europe's last bastion of all-male suffrage. Despite this, women were denied participation in the Federal Council until quite recently. In February 1984 the Social Democrats nearly withdrew from the government coalition over the issue. The Federal Assembly subsequently reversed itself and approved the Radical Democratic nomination of Elisabeth KOPP, mayor of the Zürich suburb of Zumikon, as a member of the executive body in October of that year. In so doing, the assembly appeared to have ensured that because of the principle of presidential rotation, the position of nominal head of state would eventually fall to Kopp. However, she was obliged to resign her council post in December 1988 because of advice she improperly gave her husband while a formal money-laundering inquiry was being conducted on a company where he was an officer. On January 1, 1999, Ruth DREIFUSS of the Social Democratic Party became the first woman to hold the presidency of the confederation.

In June 1986 the Federal Assembly approved a series of measures aimed at curbing a refugee influx that included a considerable number of Turks, Sri Lankan Tamils, Ugandans, and Zairians. In an April 1987 referendum Swiss voters endorsed proposals restricting immigration and making political asylum more difficult to obtain; additional restrictions (largely procedural in nature) were enacted in October 1988.

In November 1989 Swiss voters rejected a constitutional amendment that would have abolished the country's army by the year 2000, in the highest turnout (69 percent) for a referendum since the women's franchise poll of 1971.

In a September 1990 referendum voters narrowly rejected a proposal to close the country's five nuclear power stations. However, they did approve a ten-year moratorium on the construction of additional nuclear generation facilities, demonstrating their growing concerns in the wake of the 1986 Chernobyl disaster (although controversial plans to develop deep-buried nuclear waste storage sites were not affected).

In August 1991 the country observed the 700th anniversary of the signing of its initial federal charter (the oldest such document known to exist) with minimal fanfare. Interestingly, immigration was the only issue to have a measurable impact on the 1991 election. The ruling coalition pursued what was described as a "lackluster" campaign that largely avoided the pan-Europe issue, even though the balloting came on the eve of linkage discussions between the European Community (EC, subsequently the European Union—EU) and the much looser European Free Trade Association (EFTA). Four months earlier, in a partial measure of public sentiment, Swiss voters had rejected a package of reforms designed to bring the country's fiscal system into line with those of other European countries. Swiss politics were again dominated by external policy questions in 1992, notably Switzerland's application to join the EC and its signing of the EFTA-EC European Economic Area (EEA) treaty; the Swiss citizenry's rejection of the latter by referendum in December was a serious blow to the government (see Foreign relations, below).

Reeling from the collapse of its European policy, the government stumbled into a political crisis in early 1993 when the Social Democratic Party nominated a woman for federal councilor (that is, minister). Although the tradition of exclusively male representation had ended in 1984, misogynist tendencies remained strong in the predominantly male Federal Assembly. The first Social Democratic candidate was Christiane BRUNNER, a French-speaking lawyer and trade union official from Geneva whose colorful lifestyle and feminist views caused the assembly to reject her nomination on March 3. The Social Democrats then proceeded to nominate another woman, Ruth Dreifuss, and threatened to leave the government if she were rejected. The assembly elected Dreifuss on March 10 to head the federal interior department.

The issue of Switzerland's military role resurfaced in 1993, following the government's purchase of 34 fighter jets from the United States. This decision prompted the Group for Switzerland Without an Army (GSOA) to launch another popular initiative, not only for the cancellation of the purchase but also for a constitutional amendment to ban all new military aircraft acquisitions until 2000. However, voters rejected both proposals in June 6 referendums by majorities of 57 and 55 percent, respectively. Other referendum outcomes in 1993 demonstrated an unusual degree of popular support for government-proposed economic measures.

Unemployment remained relatively high in 1994 despite an economic upturn, and the government came under strong pressure to adopt tougher policies on immigration and crime. The National Council voted on March 16, 1994, to give the police increased powers to search and detain foreigners who lacked appropriate identification. The following month the government was embarrassed by an Amnesty International report asserting that some Swiss police officers were using unwarranted force against persons in custody, especially foreigners. As a result, government legislation that criminalized racial discrimination and racist propaganda was approved by referendum on September 25 (which enabled Switzerland to ratify the United Nations Convention Against Racial Discrimination). More indicative of the popular mood, however, was another referendum, on December 4, which yielded 73 percent endorsement for tougher action against drug dealers and illegal immigrants.

The issue of accession to the EU dominated a federal lower house election on October 22, 1995, but the result was far from conclusive. The pro-EU Social Democrats achieved their best result ever, winning an extra 12 National Council seats, mainly in the urban areas of Zürich, Basel, and Geneva. However, rural voters favored the strongly anti-EU Swiss People's Party (SVP), which gained 4 seats. The question of accession was deferred as both parties wished to preserve the four-party coalition that had ruled the country since 1959.

Switzerland has long been considered an ideal example of what political scientist Arend Lijphart calls "consensus democracy," wherein institutional arrangements are such that they maximize the democratic participation of the population. Further, it demonstrates a system wherein a society with significant social cleavages (in this case primarily linguistic but also religious) can establish adequate representation for all groups. It has a multiparty system based on proportional representation (introduced in 1919) and has been governed almost continually since 1959 by a coalition of four major parties that controls the legislature and determines the composition of the collegial executive body (see Current issues, below).

Switzerland's ability to ensure sufficient representation is exemplified by its collegial executive, the seven-member Federal Council. The positions of president and vice president rotate among those seven on an annual basis. The seats on the council are allocated among the four largest political parties by what has been dubbed the "Magic Formula." From 1959 to 2003 the Magic Formula granted two seats apiece to the Christian Democratic People's Party (CVP), the Radical Democratic Party (FDP), and the Social Democratic Party, with the final slot going to the SVP.

The SVP's rising influence has undermined the formula in recent years. The party's substantial electoral success in 2003 led to an adjustment of distribution of power, which resulted in an SVP gain of one seat and the loss of one for the CVP. Indeed, the SVP had threatened to go into outright opposition if it were not awarded the additional seat. The party went from 14.9 percent of the vote for the lower house in 1995 to 22.5 percent in 1999 to 29 percent in 2007 (the largest overall share of the votes). The growth in stature of the SVP has come primarily at the expense of the center-right parties (the CVP and the FDP).

Constitution and government. Under the constitution of 1999, Switzerland is (despite the retention of "confederation" in its official name) a federal republic of 23 cantons, 3 of which are subdivided into half-cantons. The areas of central jurisdiction are largely detailed in the various articles of Title III, Chapter 1, of the 1999 charter. The cantons retain autonomy over a range of local concerns but lack the right to nullify national legislation. Responsibility for the latter is vested in a bicameral parliament, the Federal Assembly, both houses of which have equal authority. The upper house, the 46-member Council of States, is made up of 2 representatives from each undivided canton and 1 from each half-canton; election methods vary from one canton to another. The lower house, the 200-member National Council, is directly elected for a four-year term by universal adult suffrage under a proportional representation system. Legislation passed by the two chambers may not be vetoed by the executive nor reviewed by the judiciary. In addition to normal legislative processes, the Swiss constitution provides for the use of initiatives to amend the constitution and referendums to ratify or reject federal legislation. To go forward, the two require petitions bearing 100,000 and 50,000 signatures, respectively.

Executive authority is exercised on a collegial basis by the Federal Council, whose seven members are elected by the entire Federal Assembly. Each December the assembly elects two of the seven to serve for the following year as president of the confederation (in effect head of state) and vice president of the Federal Council (equivalent to deputy head of state). The president has limited prerogatives and serves as a first among equals. Although the Federal Council is responsible to the legislature, it has increasingly become a nonpolitical body of experts from the leading political parties. Its members are usually reelected as long as they are willing to serve.

The Swiss judicial system functions primarily at the cantonal level; the only regular federal court is the 26-member Federal Supreme Court, which has the authority to review cantonal court decisions involving federal law. Each canton has civil and criminal courts, a Court of Appeal, and a Court of Cassation.

Local government exists on two basic levels: the cantons and the approximately 3,000 communes (municipalities). In some of the larger cantons the communes are grouped into districts, which are headed by commissioners. There are two basic governing organs at the cantonal and communal levels, much like the federal system: a unicameral legislature and a collegial executive. In five cantons and half-cantons (as well as in numerous smaller units) the entire voting population functions as the legislature, while in the others the legislature is elected. As at the federal level, initiatives and referendums may be used to propose, amend, or annul legislation within a canton.

After 30 years of separatist strife in the largely French-speaking, Roman Catholic region of Jura, Swiss voters approved cantonal status for most of the area in September 1978. The creation of the 23rd canton, the first to be formed since 1815, was approved by over 82 percent of those voting in the national referendum. Jura's full membership in the confederation took effect on January 1, 1979. Southern Jura, predominantly Protestant and German-speaking, remained part of Bern. The small German-speaking district of Laufental, having been cut off geographically from Bern by the creation of the Jura canton, voted on September 26, 1993, to be transferred from the Bern canton to the half-canton of Basel-Land.

In a constitutional referendum on March 10, 1996, 76.1 percent of voters supported official recognition of Romansch, the 2,000-year-old language used, in five dialects, by approximately 50,000 inhabitants of the eastern canton of Graübunden (or Grisons). The measure enhanced the "national" status accorded by a 1938 referendum, obliging federal authorities to provide services to Romansch speakers in their own language. However, it did not grant Romansch the same "official" status given to German, French, and Italian; the law requires that all federal documents be issued in those languages.

Canton and Capital	*Area (sq. mi.)*	*Population (2007E)*
Aargau/Argovie (Aarau)	542	569,000
Appenzell		
Ausserrhoden (Herisau)	94	53,000
Innerrhoden (Appenzell)	66	15,000
Basel/Bâle		
Basel-Land (Liestal)	165	265,000
Basel-Stadt (Basel)	14	189,000
Bern/Berne (Bern)	2,336	1,092,000
Fribourg (Fribourg)	645	254,000
Genéve/Geneva (Genève)	109	431,000
Glarus (Glarus)	264	38,000
Graübunden/Grisons (Chur)	2,744	184,000
Jura (Delémont)	323	69,000
Luzern/Lucerne (Luzern)	576	353,000
Neuchâtel (Neuchâtel)	308	168,000
St. Gallen/St. Gall (St. Gallen)	778	451,000
Schaffhausen/Schaffhouse (Schaffhausen)	115	74,000
Schwyz (Schwyz)	351	138,000

Solothurn/Soleure (Solothurn)	305	249,000
Thurgau/Thurgovie (Frauenfeld)	391	231,000
Ticino/Tessin (Bellinzona)	1,085	328,000
Unterwalden		
Nidwalden (Stans)	106	43,000
Obwalden (Sarnen)	189	33,000
Uri (Altdorf)	416	35,000
Valais (Sion)	2,018	292,000
Vaud (Lausanne)	1,243	651,000
Zug/Zoug (Zug)	92	109,000
Zürich (Zürich)	667	1,276,000

Foreign relations. Swiss foreign policy has historically stressed neutrality and scrupulous avoidance of membership in military alliances. In the interest of maintaining that neutrality, Switzerland chose to remain outside the UN through the Cold War era, although it was accredited as a permanent observer to the organization, was a party to the statute of the International Court of Justice, and belonged to many UN specialized agencies. In 1984 both the National Council and the Council of States approved a government proposal that the country apply for UN membership; however, voters overwhelmingly rejected the action in a referendum on March 16, 1986. Switzerland eventually joined the UN in September 2002 following public endorsement in a March 2002 referendum.

By contrast, the electorate readily approved joining the International Monetary Fund (IMF) and World Bank in a referendum of May 17, 1992. The following day the government announced that it would apply for EC membership, having signed a treaty providing for the creation of the EEA between the EC and EFTA earlier that month. The EEA treaty generated considerable public debate, culminating in a national referendum on December 6, 1992, in which 50.3 percent of those voting (and 16 of 23 cantons) rejected ratification, despite having been urged to vote in favor by three of the four government parties, the centrist opposition parties, employers, trade unions, and the powerful banking sector. Opposing the measure were the smallest government formation, the Swiss People's Party, and an uneasy coalition of ecologists and rightists. The voter turnout of 78.3 percent was the highest for any referendum since 1947; analysis showed that, whereas the French-speaking Swiss voted overwhelmingly in favor of the EEA, German and Italian speakers were decisively against it.

The Swiss government reiterated its goal of joining the EU in its fall 1993 foreign policy report; however, the December 1992 referendum verdict on the EEA and divisions within the ruling coalition prevented any progress from being made in that direction. There was general agreement that Swiss policy should be concentrated on limiting the negative effects of remaining outside the EU/EEA, to which end negotiations were initiated with the European Commission. The government's strategy received a boost on May 1, 1995, when Liechtenstein acceded to the EEA while retaining its 70-year-old economic and monetary union with Switzerland. This meant that Swiss exporters with outlets in Liechtenstein also could benefit from the tariff concessions available under the EEA. The federal government continued its legislative program to bring Swiss law into line with EEA/EU practice, although it was hindered by voters' rejection of attempts to ease existing restrictions on foreign ownership of property in Switzerland in a referendum on June 25, 1995. In late 1998, after four years of negotiations, Switzerland completed a trade agreement with the EU; a national referendum endorsed the measure in May 2000. The government has maintained its stance in favor of eventual accession to the EU, although 76.7 percent of voters rejected a referendum proposal to immediately apply for membership on March 4, 2001, with recent electoral gains by the anti-EU Swiss People's Party weakening prospects for accession. Swiss-EU relations soured somewhat after the EU complained in December 2005 that low corporate tax rates in Switzerland violated the terms of their trade agreement. The Swiss government rebuffed the charge as an unjustified attack on Swiss sovereignty. The issue resurfaced in February 2007. Switzerland conducts affairs with the EU through a series of bilateral agreements. There were signs in 1995–1996 of a softening in Switzerland's stance of armed neutrality (usually referenced as dating from 1515 but formalized three centuries later by the Congress of Vienna). On June 3, 1996, Flavio COTTI became the first Swiss foreign minister to address a meeting of the North Atlantic Treaty Organization (NATO); the Swiss government appointed a military attaché to an observer role in NATO soon thereafter. Despite opposition from conservative parties, the government announced on October 30 its plans to enter the NATO Partnership for Peace (PfP) program, while stressing that it had no intention of joining NATO itself. The government also pledged that it would abide by the June 1994 referendum decision precluding any armed participation in PfP peacekeeping exercises, although since December 1995 Switzerland had permitted NATO to fly over its territory and use its railways to supply peacekeeping operations in Bosnia. In a referendum held on June 10, 2001, Swiss voters narrowly approved (by 50.9 percent) permitting armed Swiss troops to participate in international peacekeeping missions. The vote also authorized training with NATO forces, although opponents of the proposal argued that Switzerland's traditional neutrality would be jeopardized.

It was officially confirmed on May 22, 1996, that despite signing the Nuclear Non-Proliferation Treaty (NPT) in 1969, Switzerland had in the same year established a federal commission to develop and maintain a capability to construct nuclear weapons. To that end it had kept a stock of nonenriched uranium (acquired in the 1950s) until 1981; the commission was not disbanded until 1988. In confirming this history, government spokespersons contended that Switzerland was now honoring its commitments under the NPT.

Contemporary Swiss foreign policy has been strongly influenced by the principle of "solidarity," which holds that a neutral state is morally obligated to undertake social, economic, and humanitarian activities contributing to world peace and prosperity. Partly for this reason, Switzerland joined the Inter-American Development Bank in July 1976 as a nonregional member and subsequently agreed to convert assorted debts owed by various developing nations into grants.

The international image of Switzerland as a bastion of banking probity and humanitarian values was damaged in 1995–1997, particularly in the United States and Israel, when new developments emerged in the 50-year-old dispute over the assets of Holocaust victims. In late 1996 releases of archival materials in Switzerland and the former Allied countries stimulated domestic and international criticism of Swiss dealings with Nazi Germany and its victims during World War II. The controversy centered on allegations that Swiss banks had knowingly accepted gold from the Nazis that had either been looted from the central banks of occupied countries or plundered from victims of the Holocaust. (U.S. officials argued that Germany had relied heavily on the sale of the gold to prolong its war effort.) Holocaust survivors and their heirs demanded a new investigation into the thousands of long-dormant Swiss bank accounts that they suspected contained Nazi victims' assets.

The Swiss commercial banks initially assumed an extremely conservative position on the inquiries, concentrating solely on dormant accounts for which complete documentation was available. By late 1997 they had identified some 16,000 such accounts, valued at about $54 million. It was agreed that the unclaimed money would be released through an independent panel; the banks also contributed to a government-sponsored voluntary fund of some $200 million that had been established to assist needy elderly survivors of the Holocaust. However, those measures failed to address the central question of looted gold, and pressure intensified on behalf of the plaintiffs in class-action suits against the banks. Much of the international community criticized the Swiss government for its perceived foot-dragging on the issue.

In early 1998 an independent Swiss commission reported that some $450 million in Nazi gold had been received in Switzerland during the war, about 80 percent having been handled by the Swiss Central Bank and the remainder by private banks. (It was estimated that the gold would be valued at about $4 billion in today's market, without interest.) Another commission concluded shortly thereafter that officials of the Central Bank had been aware that some of the gold had come from the Central Banks of countries overrun by the Germans. Now that a degree of Swiss liability had been conclusively established in their minds, Jewish organizations demanded a settlement, without which a number of U.S. states threatened to discontinue their substantial dealings with Swiss financial institutions.

In April the three major Swiss commercial banks reversed themselves and announced they would pursue a "global settlement" of the claims. Some Jewish leaders described their initial offer in June of $600 million as "humiliating," but a $1.25 billion settlement was eventually reached in August. Most of the money (to be paid out in four installments over three years) was to be used to compensate victims (or their families) of the Holocaust for whom specific claims could not be documented—the so-called "rough justice" approach. The Swiss Central Bank notably refused to participate in the settlement, as the government argued that none of its actions as a neutral state during the war had been improper. That position partly reflected the sentiment of a growing segment of the population, which lashed out against the intense international scrutiny. (In November 1998 a government commission reported that the Holocaust debate had drawn attention to a degree of "latent Swiss anti-Semitism," creating "a political crisis concerning Switzerland's self-image.") In February 2001 the government identified the names on 21,000 accounts considered likely owned by Holocaust victims between 1933 and 1945. Some 100,000 claims were expected to be filed for the dormant accounts.

Swiss banks also faced international scrutiny on several other fronts: for their role in providing services for apartheid South Africa during the international embargo; for their reluctance to disclose and freeze the money held by former Zairian president Mobutu Sese Seko; for their alleged involvement in money laundering by organized crime syndicates in Russia; and for "serious shortcomings," according to a September 2000 report by the Federal Banking Commission, in accepting an estimated $500 million in deposits from Nigerian dictator Sani Abacha and his family. An investigation into money laundering via Swiss banks by former Argentine president Carlos Menem began in 2003, but the Swiss suspended the investigation in 2004.

U.S. objections to Switzerland's policy of strict bank secrecy resurfaced in 2008, when the Internal Revenue Service (IRS) sued Swiss banking giant UBS for helping wealthy American account holders evade taxes. In February 2009 UBS admitted to helping U.S. taxpayers hide their accounts from the IRS and agreed to provide the U.S. government with the names and account information for certain bank customers. The suit was settled on August 12, 2009, following an agreement in principle reached between the two countries on July 31. On September 25, Switzerland was removed from the "grey list" of tax havens published by the Organization for Economic Cooperation and Development after making the required reforms. Relations with the EU and Germany remained strained, however, over Switzerland's retention of generous corporate tax breaks.

Current issues. A key development in Swiss politics in recent years has been the increased popularity (and electoral success) of the nationalistic, right-wing Swiss People's Party (SVP). The party, including Christopher BLOCHER, who was elected to the Federal Council in December 2003, proffers a populist, anti-immigration, anti-asylum message. The SVP has long been a central player in national politics, with one seat on the Federal Council. However, its ability to achieve the single highest vote totals in the 2003 election (almost 27 percent) led to the acquisition of a second seat. The popularity of the SVP in some sectors underscores a profound debate taking place in Switzerland over the country's appropriate role in international politics, specifically in Europe. Concerns about the influx of foreigners into Switzerland (who now constitute roughly 20 percent of the population) have taken on increasing political significance as many Swiss fear the loss of what they view as their unique culture.

While Switzerland did take the historical step of joining the UN on March 2, 2002 (by a vote of 54.1 percent), at the same time it demonstrated linguistic cleavages among the population. The French-speaking areas of the country supported the move, while the German-speaking areas generally disagreed. As such, it is not surprising that the SVP draws a great deal of support from German speakers. This linguistic division eroded in 2003 and 2007, when the SVP drew much of its support from French-speaking cantons.

The tensions within the populace over these topics were reflected in many recent votes. In November 2002 voters defeated a measure (offered up by the SVP) to restrict the country's asylum laws by a historically thin margin (4,208 votes, or 0.2 percent). However, on September 26, 2004, provisions that would make it easier for foreigners to become Swiss citizens were defeated. A proposal to ease procedures for citizenship for second-generation immigrants failed 56.8 percent to 43.2 percent, and a provision that would have guaranteed Swiss citizenship for third-generation immigrants at birth failed 51.6 percent to 48.4 percent.

However, in a referendum held on June 5, 2005, 54.6 percent of voters agreed to join the Schengen agreement, which provides for closer security cooperation with the EU and allows persons from other Schengen countries (that is, most of Europe) to enter Switzerland without passports beginning on June 1, 2007. It also allows for the sharing of information among signatories to the agreement, such as whether an asylum seeker has sought refuge in more than one country. In a separate referendum, held on September 25, 2005, 56 percent of voters approved a government-sponsored proposal to allow citizens of the ten new EU member states to live and work in Switzerland, provided they had jobs and could support themselves. On December 12, 2008, Switzerland became the 25th country to join the Schengen zone. In a referendum backed by the anti-immigrant SVP and held on February 8, 2009, 59.6 percent of the electorate rejected a proposal to exclude Romanian and Bulgarians from the arrangement. Another crucial issue in the past several years has been whether Swiss banks would collect taxes on monies deposited in their banks on behalf of the EU. An agreement, 15 years in the making, was installed starting in July 2005 wherein withholding taxes would be extracted from the accounts in question. In 2006 the new system yielded more than $500 million in tax revenue, three-quarters of which was handed over to EU countries whose residents held Swiss bank accounts.

Switzerland's tradition of mediated political discourse eroded during the campaign leading up to the general election on October 21, 2007. On October 6 violence erupted at a Berne rally of the SVP, which displayed an anti-immigrant banner featuring three white sheep kicking a black sheep off the Swiss flag. Critics, including President CALMY-REY, decried the banner as racist, while SVP officials claimed it depicted the party's support for a controversial proposal to expel foreigners convicted of crimes. The party also called for a ban on the construction of minarets at Muslim places of worship, a proposal that further polarized the Swiss electorate.

Despite its controversial positions, the SVP made further gains in the election held on October 21, 2007, winning 29 percent of the vote and 62 seats in the lower house. When coalition members voted out SVP justice minister Christoph Blocher in favor of the more moderate SVP parliamentarian Eveline WIDMER-SCHLUMPF, however, the SVP threatened to overturn Switzerland's four-party coalition formula, unchanged since 1959, by declaring that it would act as an opposition party. Despite winning more assembly seats than any other party in 2007, the SVP could not form a majority, even in coalition with other nongovernment parties, and it was largely unsuccessful in disrupting the historic consensus. The SVP appeared to abandon its opposition ambitions when party member Ueli Maurer was elected to replace Samuel Schmid, a moderate dissident who was expelled from the SVP, as defense minister on December 10, 2008, granting the SVP a government portfolio.

Despite the SVP's apparent return to the coalition, there was lingering uncertainty about the government's ability to overcome political tensions at a time of deepening recession. On June 12, 2009, interior minister and former president Pascal Couchepin, an FDP member and frequent critic of the SVP's Blocher, announced his resignation from government office effective October 31, a move broadly interpreted as a harbinger of further political strains in Switzerland's historically stable governing structure.

POLITICAL PARTIES

Until 2008, the Swiss political scene was characterized by a multiplicity of political parties but was dominated by a four-party coalition that controlled the majority of seats in both houses of the Federal Assembly. The Swiss People's Party's decision to move to the opposition occasioned the creation of a new government party, the **Conservative Democratic Party** (*Bürgerlich-Demokratische Partei*—BDP/*Parti Bourgeois Démocratique*—PBD/*Partito Borghese Democratico*—PBD/*Partida Burgais Democratica*—PBD), founded by more-moderate former SVP members, including justice minister Eveline Widmer-Schlumpf and former defense minister Samuel Schmid.

Government Parties:

Swiss People's Party (*Schweizerische Volkspartei*—SVP/*Union Démocratique du Centre*—UDC/*Unione Democratica di Centro*—UDC/*Partida Populara Svizra*—PPS). Formed in 1971 by a merger of the former Farmers, Artisans, and Citizens' Party with the Democratic Party, the SVP is a populist, right-wing party holding strong agrarian and socially conservative positions, traditionally based in German-speaking cantons. It advocates a strong national defense as well as the protection of agriculture and small industry. The party appeared to be on the wane around 1990, but its electoral fortunes began to reverse in 1991. The SVP was the only government party to participate in the successful popular opposition to the EEA accord in 1992. In 1995 the

SVP increased its electoral support to 14.9 percent, yielding 29 lower house seats—a gain of 4 over 1991—and came within 0.08 percent of the first-place SP (see below) in 1999. Its ability to capture 26.6 percent of the vote in 2003, largely in French-speaking Switzerland, for a plurality (55) of lower house seats led the Swiss government to alter the formula used to assign seats to the Federal Council. The SVP now has 2 seats on the Council, making it one of the four main governing parties. During the 2007 campaign Cristoph Blocher, a billionaire chemicals magnate and justice minister, led the party's controversial calls to crack down on crimes committed by foreigners and prohibit the construction of minarets. The SVP won 29 percent of the vote, more than any party since 1919, and 62 seats in the National Council, making it Switzerland's strongest party. In an unprecedented move, Blocher critics nominated moderate SVP member of parliament Eveline Widmer-Schlumpf to run for Blocher's Council seat. When she won, the SVP parliamentary group voted to exclude her and the other SVP council member, Samuel SCHMID, from the group and threatened to act as an opposition party. Widmer-Schlumpf and Schmid subsequently affiliated themselves with a new SVP spinoff, the Conservative Democratic Party of Switzerland (see BDP, below). Opinion polls showed waning support for the SVP after it declared it was moving to the opposition in 2008. Business owners who were traditionally SVP supporters criticized Blocher's call for capping executive pay at troubled Swiss banks Credit Suisse and UBS and opposed SVP-backed efforts to curb the free movement of workers from EU countries. The party's apparent return to the government in 2009, with the election of former SVP leader Ueli Maurer, who replaced Schmid as defense minister, was seen as a victory for SVP moderates (see Current issues, above).

Leaders: Toni BRUNNER (President), Caspar BAADER (Leader of Parliamentary Group), Martin BALTISSER (General Secretary), Cristoph BLOCHER.

Social Democratic Party (*Sozialdemokratische Partei der Schweiz—SP/Parti Socialiste Suisse—PS/Partito Socialista Svizzero—PS/Partida Socialdemocrata da la Svizra—PS*). Frequently referenced as the Socialist Party, the SP, which organized in 1888, is the most left-leaning governing party and advocates direct federal taxation, a degree of state intervention in the economy, and accession to the EU. Although it adopted an essentially reformist social democratic program in 1982, the party also has been influenced by the ecologist and feminist movements. In 1984 it came close to withdrawing from the government after its coalition partners rejected a female SP nominee for the Federal Council; it secured their acceptance of an alternative female candidate in 1993, after a similar crisis. Since 1992 the former *Partito Socialista Unitario* (PSU), now led by Ilario LODI, has operated as an autonomous section of the national party, the *Partito Socialista, Sezione Ticinese del PS,* in the Italian-speaking canton of Ticino.

In the 2007 lower house election the SP won 43 seats on a 19.5 percent vote share, a loss of 9 seats from 2003, though it remained the second largest in the chamber behind the SVP.

Leaders: Christian LEVRAT (President), Ursula WYSS (Leader of Parliamentary Group), Thomas CHRISTEN (Secretary General).

FDP.The Liberals (*FDP.Die Liberalen/PLR. Les Libéraux-Radicaux/PLR.I Liberali/*PLD.Ils Liberals). The current FDP was founded on February 28, 2009, upon the merger of the **Radical Democratic Party** (*Freisinnig-Demokratische Partei der Schweiz*—FDP/Parti Radical-Démocratique Suisse—PRD) and the **Liberal Party** (*Liberale Partei der Schweiz—LPS/Parti Libéral Suisse—PLS/Partito Liberale Svizzero—PLS/Partida Liberal-conservativa Svizra—PLC*). Leader of the historic movement that gave rise to the federated state, the FDP/PRD was liberal in outlook and advocated free-market policies and closer ties with the EU. The LPS/PLS was led by Pierre WEISS and had a political base among Protestants in the French-speaking part of the country. The merger followed a coalition between the two parties in June 2005, the "Radical and Liberal Union," which aimed to strengthen their united front in parliament. The FDP/PRD lost ground in 2007, winning 31 seats (15.8 percent of the vote) in the lower house, down from 36 in 2003, and 12 in the upper house, down from 14. Following its poor showing, the FDP/PRD again joined forces with the Liberal Party, this time bringing the Liberals into the party's ranks in an effort to beef up popular support and adding the Liberals' four lower house seats into the FDP.

Leaders: Fulvio PELLI (President), Gabi HUBER (Leader of Parliamentary Group), Stefan BRUPBACHER (General Secretary).

Christian Democratic People's Party (*Christlich Demokratische Volkspartei—CVP/Parti Démocrate-Chrétien—PDC/Partito Popolare Democratico—PPD/Partida Cristiandemocratica—PCD*). The CVP formed in 1912 as the Swiss Conservative Party by elements long opposed to the centralization of national power; it adopted its present name in 1970. Appealing primarily to Catholics, it traditionally advocated cantonal control over religious education and taxes on alcohol and tobacco while opposing direct taxation by the federal government. Its lower house representation had declined gradually since 1979, falling to 28 seats in 2003 on a vote share of 14.4 percent. As a result, the CVP lost 1 of its 2 seats on the Federal Council to the SVP. In recent years, as its Catholic base dwindled, the CVP has gained strength in Protestant areas by promoting less-conservative social policies and defining itself as a centrist party. In 2007 the party strengthened slightly, winning 31 seats in the lower house. However, the CVP still holds the largest number of seats (15 out of 46) in the upper house.

Leaders: Chrisophe DARBELLAY (President), Urs SCHWALLER (Leader of Parliamentary Group), Tim FREY (General Secretary).

Conservative Democratic Party (*Bürgerlich-Demokratische Partei—BDP/Parti Bourgeois Démocratique—PBD/Partito Borghese Democratico—PBD/Partida Burgais Democratica—PBD*). The BDP was founded on November 1, 2008, by more-moderate members of the SVP, including Eveline Widmer-Schlumpf, who is the current justice minister, and Samuel Schmid, who was defense minister. Both politicians were elected in 2007 under the SVP banner but were subsequently expelled from the party after they opposed the re-election of former justice minister and SVP firebrand Christoph Blocher. The BDP held one seat in the upper house and five in the lower house, but lost one of its two representatives in the cabinet when Schmid stepped down on November 12, 2008. Unlike its parent party, the BDP supports closer ties with the EU and international organizations such as the UN. However, it echoes the SVP in strictly defending Switzerland's neutrality.

Leader: Hans GRUNDER (President).

Other Parliamentary Parties:

Green Party of Switzerland–The Greens (Grüne Partei der Schweiz–Die Grüne/Parti Ecologiste Suisse–Les Verts/Partito Ecologista Svizzero–I Verdi/Partida Ecologica Svizra–La Verda). The Swiss Federation of Green/Ecology Parties was founded in May 1983 by nine groupings, including two that had gained representation at the cantonal level in Zürich and Luzern the previous month and one that had elected an MP in 1979. The Federation obtained 3 seats in the October 1983 Nationalrat election and adopted its present name in 1993. The 9 lower house seats won in 1987 grew to 14 in 1991 but fell back to 9 in 1995 when it received only 5 percent of the vote. The party sustained both its vote share and number of seats in the 1999 lower house elections, in which it worked jointly with the **Green Alliance** (Grünes Bündnis/Alliance Verte), an ecologist feminist group, which has since merged with The Greens. The party increased its seat share in the lower house to 13 in 2003 and 20 in 2007, when it also won 2 seats in the upper house.

Leaders: Ueli LEUENBERGER (President), Maya GRAF (Leader of Parliamentary Group), Herbert ZURKINDEN (General Secretary).

Green Liberal Party (*Grünliberale Parteiz—GLP/Parti Vert-Libéral—PVL/Partito Verde-Liberale—PVL/Partida Verda-Liberala—PVL*). This centrist party, founded on July 19, 2007, by four canton-level parties of the same name, calls for measures to combat climate change and other threats to the environment. In its first electoral test the GLP won three seats in the National Council and one in the Council of State.

Leaders: Martin BÄUMLE (President), Jan FLÜCKIGER (General Secretary).

Evangelical People's Party (*Evangelische Volkspartei der Schweiz—EVP/Parti Evangélique Suisse—PEV/Partito Evangelico Svizzero—PEV/Partida Evangelica de la Svizra—PEV*). Established in 1919, the EVP is committed to a program that advocates conservative Protestant positions on abortion and other social issues while adopting a more centrist approach to economic policy, supporting center-left goals on environmental protection and immigration. It retained its three existing lower house seats in 1991 and formed a parliamentary group with the Independents' Alliance. In 1995 it slipped to two seats, with 1.8 percent of the vote, and maintained its parliamentary alliance.

It increased its lower house representation to three seats in 1999, retaining all three in the 2003 elections, but slipped back to two in 2007.

Leaders: Heiner STUDER (President), Joel BLUNIER (General Secretary), Ruedi AESCHBACHER and Walter DONZÉ (Leaders of Parliamentary Group).

Federal Democratic Union (*Eidgenössisch-Demokratische Union*—EDU/*Union Démocratique Fédérale*—UDF/*Unione Democratica Federale*—UDF/*Uniun Democrata Federala*—UDF). The EDU/UDF is a fundamentalist Protestant, anti-immigration party founded in 1975. It retained its single seat in the 1995 lower house election and again in 1999, when the party got 1.25 percent of the vote. In 2003 a vote share of 1.3 percent garnered two seats for the party, while the same vote share won one seat for the party in 2007.

Leader: Hans MOSER (President).

Swiss Labor Party (*Partei der Arbeit der Schweiz*—PdAd/*Parti Suisse du Travail-Parti Ouvrier et Populaire*—PST-POP/*Partito Comunista*—PC/*Partida Svizra de la Lavur*—PSdL). Organized in 1921 as the Swiss Communist Party, outlawed in 1940, and reorganized under its present name in 1944, the PST is primarily urban based and has long maintained a pro-Moscow position. In September 1991 the party removed all references to "communism" and "democratic centralism" from its statutes and the following month increased its *Nationalrat* representation from one to three seats. It retained those seats in the 1995 balloting, after which its deputies affiliated with the Social Democratic parliamentary group. In the 1999 lower house elections, the PST gained 0.9 percent of the vote and won two seats, which it kept in 2003 with 0.7 percent of the vote. On September 16, 2007, the affiliated *Partito del Lavoro,* based in the largely Italian-speaking canton of Ticino, changed its name to the Communist Party. The party secured one seat in 2007.

Leader: Nelly BUNTSCHU (President).

Christian Social Party (*Christlich-soziale Partei*—CSP/*Parti Chrétien-Social*—PCS/*Partito Cristiano Sociale*—PCS/*Partida Cristian-Sociala*—PCS). A small center-left party, the CSP contested several National Council elections without success until it was able to secure one seat in 1995. The party kept that seat with a vote share of 0.4 percent in 1999, 2003, and 2007.

Leaders: Monika BLOCH SÜSS (President), Marlies SCHAFER-JUNGO (General Secretary).

Ticino League (*Lega dei Ticinesi*). The Ticino League, founded in 1991, is a right-wing formation that advocates greater autonomy for Ticino. It won two lower house seats in the 1991 balloting, after which it formed a parliamentary group with the Swiss Democrats. It held only one seat in 1995 and two seats after the 1999 lower house elections, and was back down to one in 2003 and 2007.

Leader: Giuliano BIGNASCA (President).

Other Parties:

Freedom Party of Switzerland (Freiheits-Partei der Schweiz—FPS/Parti Suisse de la Liberté—PSL/Partito Svizzero della Libertà—PSL/Partida Svizra da la Libertad—PSL). Launched in 1985 as the Swiss Automobile Party (Schweizer Auto-Partei), a motorists' pressure group based in German-speaking Switzerland, the Freedom Party is still referred to by that name despite adopting its present rubric in 1994. Having secured two Nationalrat seats in 1987, in March 1989 the formation won 12 council seats in the canton of Aargau and a month later won 7 seats in Solothurn. Its representation at the federal level rose to 8 seats in 1991 after it had added an anti-immigration component to its manifesto. It fell back to 7 seats in the 1995 balloting on a 4 percent vote share. The lower house elections in 1999 proved disastrous for the FPS, when its vote share fell under 1 percent and it failed to secure representation. It did not improve its standing in 2003 and 2007.

Leaders: Peter COMMARMOT (President), Walter MÜLLER (Secretary).

Swiss Democrats (*Schweizer Demokraten*—SD/*Démocrates Suisses*—DS/*Democratici Svizzeri*—DS/*Democrats Svizers*—DS). This far-right party emerged in 1961 as the National Action against Foreign Infiltration of People and Homeland (*National Aktion gegen Überfremdung von Volk und Heimat/Action Nationale contre l'Emprise et la Surpopulation Etrangéres*) and as of 1977 was known as the National Action for People and Homeland (*National Aktion für Volk und Heimat*—NA/*Action National*—AN). The SD adopted its present name prior to the 1991 balloting. It has sought to reduce the number of resident foreign workers as well as the number of naturalizations, although both proposals were overwhelmingly defeated in referendums held in October 1974 and March 1977, respectively. On the other hand, a 1981 law relaxing restrictions on foreign workers, against which the NA had campaigned vigorously, was narrowly overturned by a referendum in June 1982. The party secured three *Nationalrat* seats in 1987 and five in 1991, after which it formed a parliamentary group with the Ticino League (above). In 1995 the party's lower house representation fell to three seats on a vote share of 3.1 percent, then in 1999 to one seat with 1.8 percent of the vote. In 2003 the party won 1.0 percent of the vote and one seat in the lower house, but lost that seat in 2007 as former supporters voted for the SVP.

Leader: Bernhard HESS (President).

Alternative List (*Alternative Liste*—AL). Founded in Zug in 1986, AL is a loose coalition, without major leaders, that aligns with The Greens in parliament and won its first seat in the lower house in 2003. It currently holds seats in two canton councils and three city councils.

Solidarities (*Solidarités*). The Solidarities is a leftist party based in French-speaking portions of Switzerland. Founded in 1992, it first ran as a party in 2003, winning one seat with 0.5 percent of the vote but lost that seat in 2007.

I Liberisti (*Liberisti*). This nonaligned, libertarian party first ran for election in 2007, but it failed to win any seats.

Leader: Rivo CORTONESI.

The Swiss Pirate Party (*Piratenpartei Schweiz*—PPS/*Parti Pirate Suisse*—PPS/*Partito Pirata Svizzero*—PPS/*Partida da Pirats Svizra*—PPS). Based on the Swedish Pirate Party, that country's third-largest party, the PPS was founded on July 12, 2009, by mostly young advocates of freedom of information and elimination of patents and copyrights to improve public access to information.

Leader: Denis SIMONET (President).

Minor far-right formations have included the anti-immigrant, Valais-based **Conservative and Liberal Movement** (*Mouvement Conservateur et Libéral*—MCH), launched in 1986; the **National Socialist Party** (*Nationalsozialistische Partei*—NSP), organized in Zürich by a former National Action vice president in 1986; and the Geneva-based **Vigilance Party** (*Parti Vigilance*—PV). Minor center-left parties include the **Humanist Party** (*Humanistische Partei*—HP), a member of Humanist International.

Minor left-extremist parties have included the **Socialist Workers' Party** (*Sozialistiche Arbeiterpartei*—SAP/*Parti Socialiste Ouvriére*—PSO), established in 1969 as the Marxist Revolutionary League (*Marxistische Revolutionäre Liga/Ligue Marxiste Révolutionnaire*) by dissident Trotskyite members of the PST, and the Maoist **Communist Party of Switzerland–Marxist-Leninist** (*Kommunistische Partei der Schweiz–Marxistische-Leninistiche/Parti Communiste Suisse–Marxiste-Léniniste*), founded in 1972.

There are also a number of small parties representing special interest groups, including the **Catholic People's Party of Switzerland** (*Katholische Volkspartei Schweiz*—KVP) and the following autonomist groupings in the French-speaking Jura region: the **Jura Alliance** (*Alliance Jurassienne*—AJU) and the **Southern Jura Christian Democratic Party** (*Parti Démocrate-Chrétien du Jura-Sud*—PDCJS).

LEGISLATURE

The bicameral **Federal Assembly** (*Bundesversammlung/Assemblée Fédérale/Assemblea Federale*) consists of a Council of States elected by the various cantons and a National Council elected by a uniform procedure throughout the country. As a result of this dual system, the Council of States is more conservative than the National Council, which more closely reflects the relative strength of the political parties within the country.

Council of States (*Ständerat/Conseil des Etats/Consiglio degli Stati*). The upper house consists of 46 members, 2 elected from each of the 20 cantons and 1 from each of the 6 half-cantons. Electoral procedures vary from canton to canton, but the majority of them hold direct elections based on the same franchise as for the National Council. Following the elections of October 21, 2007, the Christian Democratic People's Party held 15 seats; the Radical Democratic Party, 12; the

Social Democratic Party, 9; the Swiss People's Party, 7; the Green Party, 2; and the Green Liberal Party, 1.

President: Alain BERSET.

National Council (*Nationalrat/Conseil National/Consiglio Nazionale*). The lower house consists of 200 members elected for four-year terms by direct popular vote within each canton on a proportional representation basis. The seat distribution resulting from balloting on October 21, 2007, was as follows: Swiss People's Party, 62; Social Democratic Party, 43; Radical Democratic Party, 31; Christian Democratic People's Party, 31; Green Party, 20; Liberal Party, 4; Green Liberal Party, 3; Evangelical People's Party, 2; Federal Democratic Union, 1; Swiss Labor Party, 1; Ticino League, 1; and Christian Social Party, 1.

President: Chiara SIMONESCHI-CORTESI.

FEDERAL COUNCIL

[as of August 1, 2009]

President	Hans-Rudolf Merz (FDP/PLR)
Vice President	Doris Leuthard (CVP/PDC) [f]
Federal Chancellor	Corina Casanova (FDP) [f]
Department Heads	
Defense, Civil Protection, and Sports	Ueli Maurer (SVP/UDC)
Economic Affairs	Doris Leuthard (CVP/PDC) [f]
Environment, Transportation, Communications, and Energy	Moritz Leuenberger (SP/PS)
Finance	Hans-Rudolf Merz (FDP/PLR)
Foreign Affairs	Micheline Calmy-Rey (SP/PS) [f]
Interior	Pascal Couchepin (FDP/PLR)
Justice and Police	Eveline Widmer-Schlumpf (BDP/PBD) [f]

[f] = female

COMMUNICATIONS

Press. The Swiss press is privately owned and free from governmental influence, although editors are accustomed to using discretion in handling national security information. The three most widely read German-language newspapers are *20 Minuten* (782,000), *Blick* (Zürich, 736,000), and *Tages-Anzeige* (Zürich, 573,000). The top three French-language newspapers are *Le Matin* (Lausanne, 331,000), *24 Heures* (Lausanne, 245,000), and *Tribune de Genève* (Geneva, 187,000). In Italian the three leading newspapers are *Corriere del Ticino* (Lugano, 113,000), *La Regione Ticino* (94,000), and *Giornale del Popolo* (Lugano, 63,000).

News agencies. The domestic facility is the Swiss Telegraph Agency (*Schweizerische Depeschenagentur/Agence Télégraphique Suisse*); in addition, numerous foreign agencies maintain bureaus in Geneva.

Broadcasting and computing. Broadcasting services are primarily funded by licensing fees, with multilingual programming provided by the Swiss Radio and Television Broadcasting Society (*Schweizerische Radio und Fernsehgesellschaft/Société Suisse de Radiodiffusion et Télévision*). There are over 115 radio stations and 115 television stations in Switzerland. As of 2008 there were 770 Internet users per 1,000 inhabitants.

INTERGOVERNMENTAL REPRESENTATION

Ambassador to the U.S.: Urs J. ZISWILER.

U.S. Ambassador to Switzerland: Donald Sternoff BEYER, Jr.

Permanent Representative to the UN: Peter MAURER.

IGO Memberships (Non-UN): ADB, AfDB, BIS, CERN, CEUR, EBRD, EFTA, ESA, Eurocontrol, G-10, IADB, IEA, Interpol, IOM, OECD, OIF, OSCE, PCA, WCO, WTO.

SYRIA

Syrian Arab Republic
al-Jumhuriyah al-Arabiyah al-Suriyah

Political Status: Republic proclaimed in 1941; became independent on April 17, 1946; under military regime since March 8, 1963.

Area: 71,586 sq. mi. (185,408 sq. km.).

Population: 13,782,315 (1994C); 20,773,000 (2008E). Both figures include Palestinian refugees, numbering approximately 400,000.

Major Urban Centers (2005E, including suburbs): DAMASCUS (2,314,000), Aleppo (2,560,000), Homs (1,102,000).

Official Language: Arabic.

Monetary Unit: Syrian Pound (official rate December 1, 2009: 45.30 pounds = $1US). The Syrian pound, formerly pegged to the U.S. dollar, has been pegged to a basket of currencies since 2007.

President: Dr./Lt. Gen. Bashar al-ASSAD (Baath Party); sworn in for a seven-year term on July 17, 2000, and endorsed for a second seven-year term by a referendum held on May 27, 2007.

Vice Presidents: Farouk al-SHARAA (Baath Party); appointed by President Bashar al-ASSAD on February 11, 2006. Najah al-ATTAR (ind.); appointed by the president on March 23, 2006.

Prime Minister: Muhammad Naji al-UTRI; appointed by the president on September 10, 2003, following the resignation of Muhammad Mustafa MIRO.

THE COUNTRY

The Syrian Arab Republic is flanked by Turkey on the north; the Mediterranean Sea, Lebanon, and Israel on the west; Jordan on the south; and Iraq on the east. Its terrain is distinguished by the Anti-Lebanon and Alawite mountains running parallel to the Mediterranean, the Jabal al-Druze Mountains in the south, and a semidesert plateau in the southeast, while the economically important Euphrates River Valley traverses the country from north to southeast. Ninety percent of the population is Arab; the most important minorities are Kurds, Armenians, and Turks. Islam is professed by 87 percent of the people, most of whom belong to the Sunni sect, which dominated the region for some 1,400 years prior to the assumption of power in 1970 by Hafiz al-Assad, an Alawite. About 13.5 percent of the population is Alawite, a Shiite offshoot that also draws on some Christian traditions and is viewed as "non-Muslim" by many Sunnis. Alawites have dominated governmental affairs under the regimes of Hafiz al-Assad and, more recently, his son, Bashar al-Assad. Arabic is the official language, but French and English are spoken in government and business circles.

Syria is one of the few Arab countries with adequate arable land. One-fifth of the workforce is engaged in agriculture (more than half of the women work as unpaid family workers on rural estates). However, a lack of proper irrigation facilities makes agricultural production dependent on variations in rainfall. An agrarian reform law, promulgated in 1958 and modified in 1963, limits the size of individual holdings. Wheat, barley, and cotton are the principal crops, while Syria is one of the world's leading producers of olive oil.

Major Syrian industries have been nationalized, the most important of which are food processing, tobacco, and textiles. Industrial growth has been rapid since the 1950s, with petroleum, Syria's most valuable natural resource, providing an investment base. Increased agricultural production and oil transit revenues contributed to a sharp increase in the GNP, which expanded by an average annual rate of 10 percent in the early 1980s. After a downturn in the economy resulting from military expenditures, closure of the Iraqi pipeline at the outset of the Iran-Iraq war, a drop in oil prices, and a growing debt burden, the early 1990s

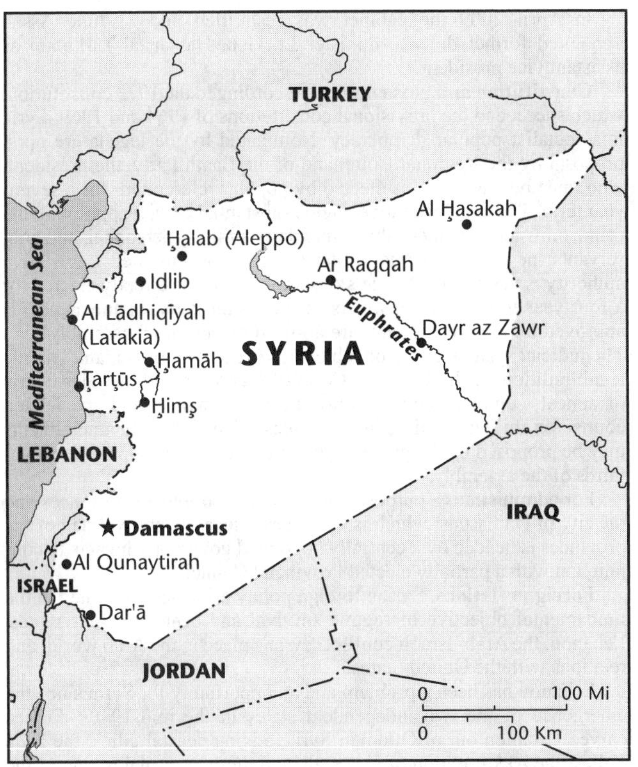

saw a rebound due to increased oil exports and aid payments from Gulf Arab states grateful for Syrian support against Iraq in the 1990–1991 Gulf war. Subsequent efforts to increase capital investment included liberal benefits for expatriate and regional investors, a new tax law, and an easing of foreign exchange restrictions. On the other hand, inefficient centralized planning remained a barrier to progress in the non-oil sectors. Consequently, in late 1994 the government announced that state-owned enterprises would be afforded greater autonomy and promised additional reforms concerning banking and exchange rate mechanisms. However, progress on those fronts was slow, with observers suggesting that the regime of President Hafiz al-Assad was reluctant to relinquish his extensive political control. Pressure for liberalization has continued, particularly from the European Union (EU), which receives 65 percent of all Syrian exports.

In 1998 further liberalization efforts allowed foreign investors to own or rent land and permitted foreign banks to open branches. In 2003 six foreign banks were granted licenses to operate. Trade negotiations with the EU are ongoing and have been complicated by the fallout from the assassination of Rafiq al-Hariri, the former Lebanese prime minister. The influx of 1.5 million Iraqi refugees into Syria has placed pressure on the Syrian economy, driving real estate prices higher while straining government services and subsidies. Nevertheless, the economy expanded by an average of 5.1 percent between 2004 and 2008. Oil made up 40 percent of the country's export receipts and agriculture, 20 percent in 2008. Per capita income in 2008 was $2,090. Inflation reached 15.5 percent in December 2008; nevertheless, the worldwide economic recession of 2008–2009 was not expected to severely affect the Syrian economy because of continued strong growth in the non-oil, industrial sectors. Economic sustainability, however, is in question because oil production is expected to decline in coming years. A stock exchange opened in March 2009 after years of delay.

GOVERNMENT AND POLITICS

Political background. Seat of the brilliant Umayyad Empire in early Islamic times before being conquered by the Mongols in 1400, Syria was absorbed by the Ottoman Turks in 1517 and became a French-mandated territory under the League of Nations in 1920. A republican government, formed under wartime conditions in 1941, secured the evacuation of French forces in April 1945 and declared the country fully independent on April 17, 1946. Political development was subsequently marked by alternating weak parliamentary governments and unstable military regimes. Syria merged with Egypt on February 1, 1958, to form the United Arab Republic but seceded on September 29, 1961, to reestablish itself as the independent Syrian Arab Republic.

On March 8, 1963, the Baath Arab Socialist Party assumed power through a military-backed coup, with Gen. Amin al-HAFIZ becoming the dominant figure until February 1966 when a second coup led by Maj. Gen. Salah al-JADID resulted in the flight of Hafiz and the installation of Nur al-Din al-ATASSI as president. With Jadid's backing, the Atassi government survived the war with Israel and the loss of the Golan Heights in 1967, but governmental cohesion was weakened by crises within the Baath Party that were precipitated by conflicts between the civilian and doctrinaire Marxist "progressive" faction that was led by Jadid and Atassi and the more pragmatic and military nationalist faction under Lt. Gen. Hafiz al-ASSAD. In November 1970 the struggle culminated in a coup by nationalist elements, with General Assad becoming president and subsequently being elected to the post of secretary general of the party. The new regime established a legislature—the first since 1966—and following a national referendum in September 1971, joined with Egypt and Libya in a short-lived Federation of Arab Republics. The first national election in 11 years was held in 1973, with the National Progressive Front (NPF), consisting of the Baath Party and its allies, winning an overwhelming majority of seats in the People's Assembly. In 1977 the Front won 159 of 195 seats, with 36 awarded to independents, while all of the seats were distributed among Front members in 1981.

General Assad's assumption of the presidency marked the growing political and economic prominence of the Alawite sect of northwestern Syria. The Alawite background of Assad and some of his top associates triggered opposition among the country's predominantly urban Sunni majority, which had experienced economic adversity as a result of the regime's socialist policies. This opposition turned into a rebellion led by the Muslim Brotherhood (see Political Parties, below) after Syria's 1976 intervention on the Maronite side in the Lebanese civil war. The incidents perpetrated by the fundamentalists included the murder of 63 Alawite military cadets in Aleppo in June 1979; another 40 deaths in Latakia in August of the same year; a series of bombings that resulted in several hundred casualties in Damascus in 1981; and numerous clashes between the dissidents and the regime's special forces led by the president's brother, Col. Rifat al-ASSAD. The struggle reached its climax in a three-week uprising in the northern city of Hama in February 1982, which was suppressed with great bloodshed (estimates of the number killed range as high as 10,000). By 1983 the seven-year insurgency had been decisively crushed, along with the Muslim Brotherhood's stated aim of establishing a fundamentalist Islamic state.

In late 1983 President Assad suffered a serious illness (widely rumored to have been a heart attack), and a committee that included Abd al-Halim KHADDAM and Muhammad Zuhayr MASHARIQA was established within the Baath Party national command to coordinate government policy. In March 1984 Khaddam and Mashariqa were named vice presidents, as was Rifat al-Assad, a move that was interpreted as an attempt to curb the latter's ambitions as successor to the president by assigning him more carefully circumscribed responsibilities than he had theretofore exercised as commander of the Damascus-based Defense Forces. In addition, Rifat was temporarily exiled, along with two adversaries, as apparent punishment for employing confrontationist tactics in the power struggle during his brother's illness. He returned in November to resume responsibility for military and national security affairs. However, soon after the president's reelection to a third term in February 1985, Rifat al-Assad again went into exile and in April 1988 was reported to have relinquished all official responsibilities. The economic recovery in 1988 was attributed to the policies of Prime Minister Mahmud al-ZUBI, who had been appointed in November 1987 to replace Abd al-Rauf al-KASM.

President Assad was the sole presidential nominee in November 1991 and in a referendum on December 2 secured his fourth term with the reported support of 99.98 percent of the voters. In early 1992 Assad announced plans to adopt an economic liberalization program and hold a conference to discuss political reform and the formation of new national parties. However, the president rejected the possibility of an immediate transition to a democratic government, saying that a democracy would be appropriate only when the income of the individual in Syria reached that of the Western states.

The Zubi government resigned en masse on June 24, 1992, but the prime minister was requested by the president to form a new cabinet which, when announced on June 29, contained many former ministers in their old posts. Later in the year, Rifat al-Assad returned to Syria from exile, once again prompting speculation regarding a successor to the president, about whom rumors of ill health had recently resurfaced. The succession question became the focus of even greater attention in early 1994 following the death in an automobile accident of President Assad's oldest son, Maj. Basel al-ASSAD, who had been assigned a growing number of official responsibilities in recent years. President Assad's next oldest son, Bashar al-ASSAD, was subsequently viewed as having assumed a role similar to that of his late brother.

More than 7,000 candidates reportedly contested the assembly balloting on August 24, 1994, with some 158 new members being elected. However, the Baath Party and its NPF partners retained solid control, securing 167 seats to 83 for independent candidates.

In December 1996 President Assad reportedly exiled his younger brother, Jamil al-ASSAD, to France in the wake of allegations concerning Jamil's business dealings. The delicate nature of the Assad family relationships—and their significance regarding succession—was further illustrated in February 1998 when the president formally dismissed Rifat al-Assad from his vice presidential post. Although no official reason was given for the decision, some observers suggested that Rifat's moderate advocacy of political pluralism and opposition to Syrian involvement in Lebanon had upset his brother.

The NPF remained in control of 167 legislative seats—all that it contested—in balloting on November 30–December 1, 1998, while President Assad, as the only candidate, was reelected to a seven-year term in a national referendum on February 10, 1999.

Reportedly under heavy pressure from President Assad and Bashar al-Assad, who had launched a highly publicized anticorruption campaign, Prime Minister Zubi and his cabinet resigned on March 7, 2000. President Assad invited Muhammad Mustafa MIRO, the governor of the city of Aleppo, with a reputation for honesty, to form a new government, which as sworn in on March 14, contained 22 newcomers among its 36 members.

After nearly 30 years in power, President Assad died on June 10, 2000. Vice President Khaddam assumed the position of acting president, although it was immediately apparent that careful plans had been laid for the swift succession of Bashar al-Assad to the presidency. After a constitutional amendment quickly approved by the assembly reduced the minimum age of the president from 40 to 34 (Bashar's age), the Baath Party Regional Command confirmed Bashar as its presidential nominee. Endorsement by a full Baath Party congress ensued within days. The assembly nominated Bashar for the presidency by acclaim on June 27, and a "yes or no" national referendum on the question on July 10 yielded a reported 97.3 percent "yes" vote.

Prime Minister Miro and his cabinet resigned on December 10, 2001, after which President Assad reappointed Miro to head a new government, which was formed on December 13. This move was widely attributed to the new president's pursuit of economic liberalization, as a number of independent and reform-minded new ministers were appointed. The retention of the prime minister and the defense and foreign ministers, however, implied the continued influence of the "old guard." As reform efforts seemed to founder and relations with the United States worsened, on September 10, 2003, President Assad appointed Muhammad Naji al-UTRI as the new prime minister and assigned him the task of picking up the pace of reform. Utri's government remained, however, effectively hamstrung on the reform front, as Syria's national security challenges multiplied with insurrection in Iraq, anti-Syrian ferment in Lebanon, and worsening relations with the United States.

The Baath Party Regional Congress in June 2005 appeared to accord the government more freedom of action in designing and implementing economic reform measures, but it also seemed to fall far short of expectations in terms of political liberalization. Following the Congress Vice President Abdul Halim Khaddam resigned and went into exile, and in December 2005 he announced that Syrian officials had threatened former Lebanese prime minister Rafik Hariri, who had been assassinated earlier that year in February 2005. Khaddam has formed a government-in-exile even though the Syrian government remains secure. In February 2006 former Syrian ambassador to the United States Walid al-MUALLEM became foreign minister, succeeding Farouk al-Sharaa, who became vice president, in a cabinet reshuffle. On April 22 the Baath-dominated National Progressive Front predictably won 172 seats in the People's Assembly (*Majlis al-Shaab*), with independents winning 78. Turnout for the poll was just over 56 percent. President Assad was endorsed for a second seven-year term by a national referendum on May 27, 2007, with a "yes" vote of 97.62 percent.

In April 2009 the cabinet was reshuffled and in June Assad appointed former defense minister Lt. Gen. Hassan al-Turkmani as assistant vice president.

Constitution and government. According to the 1973 constitution, which succeeded the provisional constitutions of 1964 and 1969, Syria is a socialist popular democracy. Nominated by the legislature upon proposal by the Regional Command of the Baath Party, the president, who must be a Muslim, is elected by popular referendum for a seven-year term. The chief executive wields substantial power, appointing the prime minister and other cabinet members, military personnel, and civil servants; he also serves as military commander-in-chief. Legislative authority is vested in a People's Assembly, which is directly elected for a four-year term. Only members of the Baath Party, or independents approved by the government, are allowed to run for an assembly seat. The judicial system, based on a blend of French, Ottoman, and Islamic legal traditions, is headed by a Court of Cassation and includes courts of appeal, summary courts, courts of first instance, and specialized courts for military and religious issues. Constitutional amendments may be proposed by the president but must secure the approval of two-thirds of the assembly.

For administrative purposes Syria is divided into 13 provinces and the city of Damascus, which is treated as a separate entity. Each of the provinces is headed by a centrally appointed governor who acts in conjunction with a partially elected Provincial Council.

Foreign relations. Syrian foreign policy priorities are rooted in the fundamental objective of regime survival and center on four issues: Lebanon, the Arab–Israeli conflict, Syria's place in the Arab world, and relations with the United States.

Lebanon has been a problem and an opportunity for Syria since the emergence of the two independent states in the mid-1940s. France carved Lebanon out of Ottoman Syria, adding coastal cities, the Biqa Valley, the Akkar region of the north, and the Jabal Amal region of the south to Mount Lebanon to create a state containing a small Christian majority. From the standpoint of successive Syrian governments dating back some 50 years, a real "red line" issue is the specter of Lebanon falling altogether out of Syria's orbit and becoming a national security threat to the Damascus regime.

This possibility became manifest in two ways during Lebanon's 1975–1990 civil war. In 1975 a rambunctious alliance of non-Christian Lebanese organizations and the Lebanon-based Palestinian resistance movement threatened to overthrow Lebanon's system of political "confessionalism" (involving set-asides for various religious groups) and to plunge Syria into an unwanted war with an alarmed Israel. With tacit U.S. and Israeli blessing, Syrian forces entered Lebanon in 1976, under the official auspices of the Arab League, to neutralize the Lebanese Muslim/Druze-Palestinian alliance, to preserve the system (buttressing Christian primacy), and to dampen the prospects of armed confrontation with Israel. Syria succeeded, but it then found itself faced with Christian militias resentful of its presence and influence and eager to make common cause with Israel against Syria, the Palestinians, and the Lebanese Muslim and Druze factions.

This volatile situation boiled over in June 1982, when Israel invaded Lebanon, and Israeli and Syrian forces clashed. It appeared at first that Lebanon might be detached from Syria's orbit—with Israeli forces in control—but Damascus took action, supporting the rise of the anti-Israeli, anti-U.S. Hezbollah and arming its erstwhile Lebanese Druze and Muslim foes. The resistance resulted in the withdrawal from Lebanon of U.S. and French peacekeeping forces, the redeployment of Israeli forces to the south of Lebanon, and the abrogation of a Lebanese-Israeli security pact. In 1990 Syrian suzerainty over Lebanon, except for the Israeli-occupied south, was solidified when Syrian forces ousted and exiled Michel Aoun, the Christian general who headed a rival government in East Beirut. Syrian suzerainty spread to the entire country in May 2000, with the evacuation of the Israeli forces from southern Lebanon.

In the summer of 2004, Syria aimed to further to strengthen its position in Lebanon by compelling the Lebanese parliament to adopt a constitutional amendment extending the term of President Emile Lahoud. By doing so, however, it fueled Lebanese resentment and drew international condemnation. The UN Security Council passed Resolution 1559, calling for, among other things, the withdrawal of Syrian military and intelligence personnel from Lebanon and the holding of free elections there. Rafik Hariri, the former prime minister, emerged as the focal point of opposition to Syria and was assassinated on February 14, 2005, prompting intensified international pressure and massive Lebanese protests against Syria, as Damascus topped the list of suspects. Syrian military forces withdrew from Lebanon in April 2005, and Lebanese elections in June produced a majority in parliament supportive of ending Syrian suzerainty. The Syrian government has since relied on indirect avenues of control, such as negotiation, intimidation, and violence against political adversaries. Key Lebanese Shiite parties (Hezbollah and Amal) remain in Syria's camp, while former general Michel Aoun, an enemy of Damascus, cooperated tactically with the Assad regime in opposition to Lebanese prime minister Fouad Siniora and his government. In November 2007 Lahoud stepped down as president of Lebanon; however, not until an agreement was reached with Hezbollah was another president, Gen. Michel Sulieman, elected in May 2008. On October 15 a formal agreement was signed in which Syria recognized Lebanon's sovereignty for the first time. Syria established an embassy in Beirut in December. Some observers suggested that Hezbollah's veto power in the Lebanese National Assembly made Syria more comfortable establishing formal relations with Lebanon.

Syria's hard-line policy toward Israel dates back to the first Arab-Israeli war in 1948. At the war's end, Syria alone among the Arab participants was in possession of land allotted to the Jewish state in the UN partition plan. Successive Syrian governments have employed anti-Zionist policies—including wars in 1967, 1973, and 1982—as an essential element of legitimacy within the country. Syrians have traditionally found the dispossession of the Palestinians, the occupation of the Golan Heights, and the willingness of other Arab states to make formal peace with Israel unacceptable and unjust. Yet Syrian policy has not been one of unremitting hostility toward Israel. Since 1974 Damascus has ensured that the cease-fire line on the Golan Heights has remained quiet, even as it supported attacks by others from Lebanese territory to remind Israel of unresolved grievances. More important, however, since the mid-1990s—after the Palestinians embarked on their own peace process with Israel—Syria indicated its desire for a "strategic decision" for peace with Israel provided that Israel agree to withdraw from the Golan Heights to the "line of June 4, 1967"—the line in the Jordan River valley separating Syrian and Israeli forces on the eve of war in 1967. Syria under President Hafiz al-Assad and Israel under Prime Minister Yitzhak Rabin had reportedly agreed to a full Israeli withdrawal in return for peace. Rabin, however, was assassinated before a deal could be formalized.

Just prior to Israel's withdrawal from Lebanon in May 2000 there was reason to believe that Syria and Israel—with U.S. assistance—might agree on terms for peace, but Israeli Prime Minister Ehud Barak effectively scuttled peace talks being held in Shepherdstown, West Virginia, in January 2000 by leaking the substance of negotiations to the press. Later, he provided to President Bill Clinton "talking points" to deliver in Geneva to the dying President Hafiz al-Assad that clearly indicated Israel's refusal to withdraw to the line of June 4, 1967. Assad, having consistently expressed that the only deal would require a full Israeli withdrawal, dismissed Clinton's overture.

President Bashar al-Assad has publicly stated a willingness to resume negotiations. But Syria's alliance with Iran, its support of Hezbollah, and its sheltering of Hamas exiled leaders have made Israel and the United States skeptical of Damascus's motives. Indeed, Syria's arms conduit to Hezbollah was an important factor in the July–August 2006 war between Israel and the Lebanese organization. Syria would like to recover from Israel all of the territory it lost in 1967 without going to war, but only the president and his closest associates in Damascus know the regime's true willingness to normalize relations with Israel. Syria's search for a leadership role in the Arab world has likewise been an important tool for successive regimes seeking to capture the elusive quality of governing legitimacy in a "nation-state" artificially created by France. The Baath Party—which has ruled Syria since 1963 and which has been, along with the military, the vehicle for the rise of minority Alawites in Syrian politics—was founded on the notion of an Arab nation, which would transcend states with boundaries established by colonial masters. Achieving the image and reality of an Arab nationalist leadership role has traditionally been a Syrian foreign policy objective with important domestic political implications, albeit a goal that has been modified—but not abandoned—considerably in recent years.

Syria's striving and pretensions in the Arab leadership sphere have taken on many manifestations over the years. A combined fear of an internal communist takeover and devotion to Arab nationalism caused Syria's leaders to subordinate the country to Egypt in 1958 by joining in the United Arab Republic; three years later the republic would be split by Syria's secession. Syria's pre-1967 rhetorical recklessness toward Israel—punctuated occasionally by military clashes in the Jordan Valley—spurred Egypt into making catastrophic provocations in the spring of 1967. In the wake of the June 1967 war, Syria steadfastly opposed the Egyptian-Israeli peace process and treaty and became a leader among the so-called rejectionist states of the Arab world. Its rivalry with the Hashemite Kingdom of Jordan culminated in a botched invasion in 1970 that encouraged Hafiz al-Assad to seize power in a coup. The desire by Damascus to dominate the Palestinian resistance movement led to a three-decade feud with Yasir Arafat that was played out in part during Syria's intervention in the Lebanese civil war and through its support for Palestinian groups opposed to Arafat.

By the late 1970s, Syria had begun to perceive that the Arab nationalist movement characterized by Nasserism and even Baathism was running its course and that its call for a collective Arab approach toward Israel would not be heeded. Indeed, Syria's decision to support Iran during the Iran–Iraq war placed it at odds with the entire Arab world. President Hafiz al-Assad's intense dislike of Iraqi leader Saddam Hussein, the rivalry between the Syrian and Iraqi branches of the Baath Party, and fear of an emerging regional hegemony in Baghdad combined to dictate a national interests-driven break with the Arab world. This schism was eventually mended by Iraq's 1990 invasion of Kuwait. Although Syrian-Iranian relations remain cordial, Iraq is no longer the factor that brings them together. The Iran-Syria alliance is vital to both parties and has taken on added significance in the wake of the 2006 summer war between Hezbollah and Israel. Hezbollah's ability to fight Israel and avoid defeat gave the Shiite, pro-Iranian organization an image of heroism in the Sunni Arab streets of Cairo, Amman, and Riyadh, which alarmed the leaders of Egypt, Jordan, and Saudi Arabia. In their eyes, Syria had become Iran's junior partner and Tehran's tool to penetrate the Levant.

Syria's decisions to participate in the coalition that ousted Iraq from Kuwait and to join in the Arab-Israeli peace process launched at the 1991 Madrid Conference helped reconcile Damascus with Cairo and strengthened an already cordial relationship with Saudi Arabia, whose financial assistance was essential. At the same time, the PLO's closeness to Iraq under Hussein and its decision to seek a separate peace with Israel only hardened the enmity between Assad and Arafat and convinced Assad to pursue a peace process of his own.

In 1998 Turkey threatened to counter Syrian support of Kurdish nationalists with an invasion. Syria capitulated completely and eventually found common ground with Turkey over the issue of Kurdish separatism, a concern that overcame differences between the two countries over Euphrates River water and Syria's claim to the Turkish province of Hatay.

Although the cold war had permitted Syria to oppose U.S. Middle East policies under the umbrella of a close security relationship with the Soviet Union, the fall of communism changed matters drastically, contributing to President Hafiz al-Assad's decisions concerning the Persian Gulf War and the U.S.-sponsored peace process. Al-Assad apparently calculated that only the United States could help bring about a complete Israeli withdrawal from the Golan Heights, a calculation that led to a fundamental shift in Syrian policy toward the United States in the early 1990s.

Although Syria's alleged links to international terrorism (including ongoing support for rejectionist Palestinian groups and Lebanon's Hezbollah) made cordial relations with Washington impossible and landed the country on the State Department's list of countries supporting terrorism, Syrian-U.S. relations during the Clinton administration featured sporadic U.S. efforts to broker a Syrian-Israeli treaty of peace. The George W. Bush administration was significantly more hostile to Syria, especially after the al-Qaida attacks of September 11, 2001. Syria's immediate reaction to the September 11 attacks was to cooperate with U.S. intelligence in neutralizing al-Qaida operations and personnel. Its cooperation, however, was not enough to sustain a working relationship. The Bush administration saw the threat posed by terrorism as broader than al-Qaida and viewed Syria, with its support of radical Palestinian groups and Hezbollah, as a problem in this regard. Syria, in turn, saw the invasion of Iraq as a national security threat and reportedly permitted insurgents to cross into Iraq from Syria. The United States applied economic sanctions and called its ambassador home for extended consultations in February 2005. U.S.-led international pressure to terminate Syrian suzerainty in Lebanon and disarm Hezbollah opened another line of confrontation between the two states in 2004–2005.

With the publication of the Report of the Iraq Study Group in December 2006, Syria became a domestic political issue of sorts in the United States. The report recommended a U.S.-Syrian diplomatic dialogue to help stabilize Iraq and ameliorate Arab-Israeli tensions. Democratic speaker of the U.S. House of Representatives Nancy Pelosi led a delegation to Damascus to meet with President Assad in April 2007. In the following month Secretary of State Rice met with her Syrian counterpart. Despite these gestures, however, Syria's apparent determination to restore its suzerainty over Lebanon placed it very much at odds with Washington, which evaluated events in Lebanon in the context of the "global war on terrorism" and regional "democratic transformation." In February 2008 President Bush signed an executive order expanding sanctions against senior government officials in Syria. In an attempt to disrupt the militant network suspected of smuggling weapons and fighters into Iraq, U.S. forces launched an attack across the Syrian border in October 2008, killing eight people. Syrian officials protested that the strike violated international law and Syrian sovereignty.

Current issues. Notwithstanding official Syrian denials of involvement in the assassination of Rafik Hariri in Lebanon in 2005, the international community has presumed that Syrian security services, in league with Lebanese counterparts, arranged the murder and its cover-up. In 2006 the UN Security Council announced that a special tribunal would be set up to try those responsible for the assassination, a crime the UN had previously described as a terrorist act. By 2008 the tribunal was in its start-up phase, and an agreement had been signed with the Netherlands to host the special court. The International Independent Investigation Commission released its tenth report on the assassination in March 2008. The report stated that a network of individuals operating in Lebanon was behind the Hariri assassination, as well as other politically motivated murders in Lebanon. In June the commission's mandate was extended through the end of the year. After its establishment, the tribunal had potential jurisdiction over other cases of political killings tied to the Hariri assassination. It remained unclear whether Syria would release any Syrian suspects to the tribunal, which is, from the perspective of Damascus, the key issue affecting the future of the Assad regime.

On September 5, 2007, eight Israeli aircraft attacked and destroyed a facility in northern Syria believed to be conducting nuclear research. In May 2008 the United States opined that North Korea was assisting Syria with a secret nuclear program. Syria insisted the bombed site was a simple military installation. The UN International Atomic Energy Agency visited Syria in June 2008 in response to the allegations. In October Syria said that it would cease giving UN weapons inspectors access to its military sites. A leaked report from the UN International Atomic Energy agency in November 2008 stated that traces of processed uranium taken from the site suggested "some kind of nuclear link."

In May 2008 Syria and Israel confirmed that Turkey was moderating peace talks between the two countries. Key issues were the Golan Heights and Syria's support for Hezbollah and Iran. President Bashar al-Assad stated there would be no direct peace negotiations with Israel until the new U.S. administration took office in January 2009. Nevertheless, relations between Syria and the Western world began to thaw, beginning with French president Nicolas Sarkozy's visit to Syria in September 2008. Saudi Arabia hosted Bashar al-Assad in March 2009, and King Abdullah Bin Abdul Aziz visited Damascus in October 2009, signaling improving relations between Syria and its Arab neighbors.

The Obama administration, which took office in January 2009, began to engage Syria diplomatically, and some analysts suggested that efforts by Assad to reorganize the Syrian government in 2009, including foreign intelligence operations, was an attempt to improve relations with the Untied States. In March U.S. secretary of state Hillary Clinton announced two senior officials would be sent on a diplomatic mission to Damascus. The officials held talks with Syrian foreign minister Walid al-Muallem. However, the United States announced renewed sanctions against Syria in May, with U.S. president Barack Obama stating that Syria was "an unusual and extraordinary threat to the national security, foreign policy, and economy of the United States." Nevertheless, the following month the Obama administration announced it would send an ambassador to Syria after a four-year absence. U.S. envoy George Mitchell was sent to Syria in June in an effort to jump-start the Middle East peace process.

POLITICAL PARTIES

Government Parties:

National Progressive Front (NPF). The Baath Party has enjoyed de facto dominance of the Syrian political system since 1963, its long tenure being partly attributable to its influence among the military. In 1972 President Hafiz al-Assad formed the NPF, a coalition of parties that has always been heavily dominated by the Syrian Baathists. Following the death of Hafiz al-Assad in 2000, the other NPF components joined the Baath in endorsing his son, Bashar, as his presidential successor. Bashar al-Assad was elected that year. Subsequently, some previously outlawed parties were allowed to join the NPF as long as membership was not based on ethnicity or religion, including the Syrian Social Nationalist Party, which had been banned since 1955. Assad was reelected in 2007 for a second seven-year term. Minor parties that make up the remainder of the NPF are the **Arab Socialist Union Party**, **Arab Socialist Party**, **Syrian Communist Party**, **Union Socialist Party**, and **Union Socialist Democratic Party**.

Leaders: Bashar al-ASSAD (Chair), Sulayman QADDAH (Deputy Chair).

Baath Party. The Baath Party has enjoyed de facto dominance of the Syrian political system since 1963, its long tenure being partly attributable to its influence among the military. Formally known as the Baath (Renaissance) Arab Socialist Party (*Hizb al-Baath al-Arabi al-Ishtiraki*), the Baath Party is the Syrian branch of an international political movement that began in 1940. The contemporary party dates from a 1953 merger of the Arab Resurrectionist Party, founded in 1947 by Michel Aflak and Salah al-Din Bitar, and the Syrian Socialist Party, founded in 1950 by Akram al-Hawrani. The Baath Party philosophy stresses socialist ownership of the principal means of production, redistribution of agricultural land, secular political unity of the Arab world, and opposition to imperialism.

At the Baath Party's 2005 Congress younger members were elected to key committee positions, reflecting efforts by President Bashar al-Assad to give the party a more youthful look. Nevertheless, in terms of policy direction there was little substantive change from the party's core principles. Assad's regime resorted to more repressive measures after the 2005 Congress, leading to a consolidation of power before the 2007 elections.

Leaders: Bashar al-ASSAD (President of the Republic, Secretary General of the Party, and Chair of the NPF), Abdallah al-AHMAR (Assistant Secretary General).

Syrian Social Nationalist Party (SSNP). Formally banned in the 1970s, the SSNP supports creation of a "Greater Syria." The party remained active in Lebanon for most of the late-twentieth century. In 2005 the SSNP was legalized and became the first official non-Arab, non-socialist political grouping. The party secured two seats in the 2007 elections. Reports in 2009 alleged widespread dissatisfaction with party leader Asaad HARDAN among the rank-and-file members.

Leader: Asaad HARDAN (Party Chairman)

Opposition Groups:

Damascus Declaration for Democratic National Change (DDDNC). Reformists hoped that Bashar al-Assad's pledge to promote greater openness would translate into permission for new parties to form. The "Damascus Declaration," signed by members of the opposition in October 2005, declared that "the authorities' monopoly of everything for more than thirty years has established an authoritarian, totalitarian, and cliquish regime," and called for a non-violent democratic overhaul of the Syrian government. In December 2007 coalition members met to elect the leadership of the group's National Council. Forty attendees were subsequently arrested, although most were released. In October 2008 twelve activists, including Secretary General Riad Seif and chairwoman of the National Council Fida al-Hawrani, were found guilty of "weakening national feeling" and "spreading false news" and sentenced to thirty months in prison. They remained incarcerated in October 2009.

Leaders: Riad SEIF (Secretary General), Fida al-HAWRANI (Chairwoman of the National Council).

Reform Party of Syria (RPF). The Reform Party of Syria is a U.S.-based opposition party formed in 2001. It is opposed to the Baathist (and what it calls "pan-Arabist") ideology of the Syrian government. The Reform Party of Syria hopes to "rebuild Syria" with economic and political reforms that will facilitate "democracy, prosperity, freedom of expression, and human rights." It also seeks to achieve peaceful relations with Syria's neighbors, including Israel. Outgoing president Farid Ghadry joined other Muslim leaders at the Moderate Muslim Summit in Washington, D.C. in July 2009.

Leader: Marc HUSSEIN (Secretary General), Farid GHADRY (Outgoing President).

Muslim Brotherhood. Founded in the 1940s, the Brotherhood is a Sunni Islamist movement that took part in parliamentary elections in its early history, winning 10 seats in 1961. The Brotherhood was banned by the Baath Party after the 1963 coup, and since then it has maintained an active underground campaign against the Baath Party and its leadership, being charged, inter alia, with the massacres in Aleppo and Latakia in 1979 as well as the killing of a number of Soviet technicians and military advisers in 1980. In February 1982 it instigated an open insurrection in Hama that government troops quelled after three weeks of intense fighting that resulted in the devastation of one-fourth of the city and the deaths of thousands. The Brotherhood was subsequently viewed as a spent force in Syria, although it nominally participated in several domestic and expatriate opposition groupings. Brotherhood members were among political prisoners released in 2000, with the new government of Bashar al-Assad lending the impression of being more accommodating toward the Islamists and anxious to downplay any ongoing Sunni-Shiite friction. At the same time, the Brotherhood remained illegal, membership could be punishable by death, and its leadership remained in exile.

Since the election of Ali Sadr al-Din al-Bayanuni to lead the party, the Brotherhood has intermittently negotiated with the Syrian government. The Brotherhood has stopped insisting on the right to use violence, no longer calls for the introduction of sharia, and claims to support a democratic system of government. It played a key role in drafting the "Damascus Declaration." At the same time, it has not accepted responsibility for violence in the 1970s and early 1980s and has not made it clear whether it will seek retribution for past human rights abuses. In 2005 Bayanuni met with other exiled Syrian opposition figures and formed the National Salvation Front. However, because of the Brotherhood's violent history, most opposition figures distanced themselves from the new alliance. In January 2009 Bayanuni announced the Brotherhood had broken with the National Salvation Front, prompting speculation that Bayanuni was engaged in private negotiations with Assad.

Leader: Ali Sadr al-Din al-BAYANUNI.

Islamic Liberation Party (ILP). The Islamic Liberation Party believes in the political and religious union of the entire Arab world. Hundreds of ILP members were reportedly detained by security forces in late 1999 and early 2000 in connection with a crackdown that coincided with fighting between Islamist militants and the Lebanese army in northern Lebanon. The ILP also had strongly criticized the resumption of peace talks between Syria and Israel. Many of the ILP detainees were reportedly released in November 2000 under an amnesty issued by the new president, Bashar al-Assad. In 2003 five ILP members were sentenced to prison terms ranging from eight to ten years.

Syrian Democratic People's Party. This party was known as the Communist Party Politburo, and alternatively as the Communist Workers' Party, until 2005. The Syrian Democratic People's Party is an antigovernment splinter of the Syrian Communist Party, formed in opposition to the Communist Party's decision to join the NPF. A number of members, including Secretary General Riad Turk, were arrested in the 1980s after campaigning for "free elections," the government charging them with belonging to an illegal organization. Turk was released in mid-1998, and many of the remaining detainees were granted amnesty in 2000. However, Turk was again detained in mid-2001 along with several other opposition figures. He was released in November 2002 on "humanitarian grounds," reportedly due to his deteriorating health. In January 2008 a Syrian court sentenced a member of the party, Faiq al-Mir, to three years in prison. The party opposed the Damascus Declaration and allied itself loosely with other opposition groups in the Democratic National Gathering (DNG).

Leader: Riad TURK (Secretary General).

For more information on the now-defunct **Arab People's Democratic Party**, please see the 2008 *Handbook*.

LEGISLATURE

The **People's Assembly** (*Majlis al-Shaab*) is a directly elected, unicameral body presently consisting of 250 members serving four-year terms. In elections held in April 2007 the NPF (which is comprised of the Syrian Baath Party and six small parties) won 172 seats, and independents won 78 seats.

Speaker: Mahmoud al-ABRASH.

CABINET

[as of October 1, 2009]

Prime Minister	Muhammad Naji al-Utri
Deputy Prime Minister for Economic Affairs	Abdallah Abd-al-Razzaq al-Dardari
Agriculture and Agrarian Reform	Adel Safar
Communications and Technology	Imad Abdul-Ghani Sabbouni
Construction and Building	Umar Ibrahim Ghalawanji
Culture	Riyadh Nasan Agha
Defense	Lt. Gen. Ali Mohammad
Economy and Foreign Trade	Amer Housni Lutfi
Education	Ali Saad
Electricity	Ahmed Qusay Kayyali
Expatriates	Joseph Soueid
Finance	Mohammed al-Hussein
Foreign Affairs	Walid al-Muallem
Health	Rida Adman Saeed
Higher Education	Gaiyath Barakat
Industry	Fouad Issa Joni
Information	Muhsen Bilal
Interior	Maj. Gen. Saeed Sammur
Irrigation	Nader al-Bunni
Justice	Muhammad al-Ghafri
Local Administration	Tamer al-Hijeh
Petroleum and Mineral Resources	Sufian Alaw
Presidential Affairs	Mansur Azzam
Religious Trusts	Abdul-Sattar al-Sayed
Social Affairs and Labor	Dialla al-Haj Aref [f]
Tourism	Saadallah Agha al-Qalaa
Transport	Yrob Solaiman Bader
Ministers of State	
Environment	Kawkab al-Sabah Dayeh (f)
Syrian Arab Red Crescent Organization Affairs	Bashar al-Shaar
	Yussef Sulayman al-Ahmad
	Ghiyath Jaraatli
	Hussein Mahmoud Ferzat
	Hassan al-Sari

COMMUNICATIONS

Press. The press is strictly controlled, with most publications being issued by government agencies or under government license by political, religious, labor, and professional organizations. Several individuals faced trial and imprisonment in 2008 for posting blogs and articles on the Internet criticizing the Syrian government. In its 2008 index of freedom of the press, Reporters Without Borders ranked Syria 159 out of 173 countries. The following are Arabic dailies published in Damascus, unless otherwise noted: *Tishrin* (October, 75,000); *al-Thawrah* (Revolution, 40,000); *al-Baath* (Renaissance, 40,000), organ of the Baath Party; *Syria Times* (15,000), in English; *al-Jamahir al-Arabiyah* (The

Arab People, 10,000); *al-Shabab* (Youth, Aleppo, 9,000); *Barq al-Shimal* (The Northern Telegraph, Aleppo, 6,500); *al-Fida* (Redemption, Hama, 4,200). Other publications include the pro-Communist Party, *al-Nur;* the satirical newspaper, *al-Damari;* and the SNNP paper, *al-Sham.*

News agencies. The Syrian Arab News Agency (*Wakalat al-Anba al-Arabiyah al-Suriyah*—SANA) issues Syrian news summaries to foreign news agencies; several foreign bureaus also maintain offices in Damascus.

Broadcasting and computing. Broadcasting is a government monopoly and operates under the supervision of the Syrian Arab Republic Broadcasting Service (*Idhaat al-Jumhuriyah al-Arabiyah al-Suriyah*). As of 2008 there were 167.9 Internet users per 1,000 inhabitants.

INTERGOVERNMENTAL REPRESENTATION

Ambassador to the U.S.: Imad MOUSTAPHA.

U.S. Ambassador to Syria: (Vacant).

Permanent Representative to the UN: Bashar JA'AFARI.

IGO Memberships (Non-UN): AFESD, AMF, BADEA, CAEU, IDB, Interpol, LAS, NAM, OAPEC, OIC, WCO.

TAJIKISTAN

Republic of Tajikistan
Jumhurii Tojikiston

Political Status: Designated autonomous republic within the Uzbek Soviet Socialist Republic on October 27, 1924; became constituent republic of the Union of Soviet Socialist Republics (USSR) on October 16, 1929; declared independence as Republic of Tajikistan on September 9, 1991; current constitution adopted by referendum on November 6, 1994.

Area: 55,250 sq. mi. (143,100 sq. km.).

Population: 6,127,493 (2000C); 7,510,000 (2008E).

Major Urban Centers (2005E): DUSHANBE (598,000), Khujand (144,000).

Official Language: Tajik. Although the 1994 constitution accords Russian the status of a language of communication between nationalities, in March 2007 President Rakhmon stated that citizens should "return to our cultural roots" and stop using Russified name endings.

Monetary Unit: Somoni (official rate December 1, 2009: 4.35 somoni = $1US).

President: Imomali RAKHMON (Imomali RAKHMONOV; People's Democratic Party of Tajikistan); designated by the Supreme Soviet on November 19, 1992, upon the resignation of Akbarsho ISKANDAROV (Islamic Renaissance Party); reelected by popular vote on November 6, 1994, and inaugurated for a five-year term on November 16; reelected for a seven-year term in 1999 and on November 6, 2006; most recently inaugurated November 18, 2006.

Prime Minister: Oqil OQILOV (Akil AKILOV; originally identified with Communist Party of Tajikistan); appointed by presidential decree on December 20, 1999, succeeding Yakhyo AZIMOV (identified with Communist Party of Tajikistan), who, as required by the constitution after a presidential election, had resigned on November 23 but remained in office during the interim; dismissed along with the entire cabinet on November 30, 2006, following the presidential election of November 6; reappointed on December 1 and confirmed by the Supreme Assembly on December 16.

THE COUNTRY

Mountainous Tajikistan is bordered by Kyrgyzstan on the north, China on the east, Afghanistan on the south, and Uzbekistan on the west. Approximately 80 percent of the population is Tajik, 15 percent Uzbek, and only 1 percent Russian, as a consequence of a significant exodus of minorities in the 1990s. The dominant religion is Sunni Islam. Women make up about 44 percent of the labor force.

Although less than 10 percent of Tajikistan is arable, ample water supplies have helped make its farmland very productive, the leading crops being cotton, grains, vegetables, and fruits. The agricultural sector as a whole employs two-thirds of the workforce, and its contribution to the GDP is about 22 percent. The industrial sector employs only about 6 percent of the active labor force but contributed 27 percent of GDP in 2007. Fueled by the country's extensive hydroelectric capacity, industry remains concentrated in such energy-intensive ventures as ore extraction and refining. Aluminum, by far the most important industrial product, is the leading national export, followed by hydroelectricity and cotton. Other mineral resources include gold, silver, and uranium. Leading manufactures include clothing and textiles, processed foods, and carpets.

The Tajik economy, the weakest among the former Soviet republics at independence, was further disrupted by civil war: The GDP contracted by half during 1991–1996, while inflation reached over 2,000 percent in 1995. With support from the International Monetary Fund (IMF), the World Bank, and other multilateral institutions, the government undertook a reform program that included privatization of state enterprises, restructuring of the financial industry, and alleviation of poverty.

Annual growth from 2000 to 2004 averaged 10 percent but slowed to 6.5 percent in 2005. After growing by 7.0 percent in 2006, the economy expanded by 7.8 percent in 2007 and 7.9 percent in 2008, but expectations for 2009 were lowered to about 2 percent as a consequence of the international financial crisis. A key factor in the slower growth rate was a drop in remittances from the millions of Tajiks working abroad, mainly in Russia. (Remittances amounted to 47 percent of GDP in 2007.) Lower exports earnings for cotton and aluminum also contributed to the slower growth as well as depreciation of the somoni. For 2009 consumer price inflation was forecast to be about 12 percent, down from 20 percent in 2008.

GOVERNMENT AND POLITICS

Political background. Most of the Tajik lands were conquered by Russia in the 1880s and 1890s. Popular uprisings in the wake of the 1917 Bolshevik Revolution were not completely suppressed until 1921. In 1924 the region was made an autonomous republic within the Uzbek Soviet Socialist Republic and in 1929 a constituent republic of the USSR.

On February 11, 1990, rioting erupted in Dushanbe when demonstrators, initially responding to reports that Armenian refugees were to be settled there, began calling for democratic reforms. A resultant state of emergency led to the suppression of the demonstrations, in part by Soviet soldiers. On August 25, 1990, with nationalism on the rise, a sovereignty declaration was issued asserting the precedence of the republic's constitution and laws over those of the USSR, and on November 30 the republic's legislature, the Supreme Soviet, voted to replace its chair with a president as head of state.

On August 25, 1991, in the wake of the failed Moscow coup against USSR president Mikhail Gorbachev, the Supreme Soviet ordered the nationalization of the assets of the Communist Party of the Soviet Union (CPSU) within the republic. On August 29 the Communist Party of Tajikistan (CPT) voted to withdraw from the CPSU, while the words "Soviet Socialist" were dropped from the republic's name. At the same time, anticommunist opposition groups, principally the Islamic Renaissance Party (IRP), the secular and pro-Western Democratic Party of Tajikistan (DPT), and the nationalist *Rastokhez* (Rebirth) movement, continued to organize demonstrations against the government.

On September 1, 1991, after losing a nonconfidence vote, the CPT's Kakhar MAKHKAMOV resigned the presidency in favor of the Supreme Soviet chair, Kadreddin ASLONOV. On September 9 the legislature declared the independence of the Republic of Tajikistan, and on September 22 Acting President Aslonov issued a decree banning all CPT activities, despite the fact that the party had redesignated itself as the Tajik Socialist Party (TSP) the day before. On September 23 the ban was reversed and Aslonov resigned, being succeeded by former CPT first secretary Rakhman NABIYEV.

Nabiyev immediately imposed a state of emergency, but he lifted it on October 2, 1991. Opposition demonstrations continued, and on October 6 Nabiyev submitted his resignation, ostensibly to permit all candidates an opportunity to campaign on equal footing for a presidential election. On November 24, despite his reputation as a hard-line conservative, Nabiyev drew a 58 percent vote share in a field of seven candidates. Significantly, his closest competitor, Davlat KHUDONAZAROV of the DPT, received backing from the IRP, thus sealing an Islamic-prodemocracy opposition alliance that was to become a crucial factor in the unfolding civil conflict, which was based more on ethnic and regional differences than on ideology. In January 1992 Nabiyev named Akbar MIRZOYEV prime minister.

In March 1992 Maksud IKRAMOV, a prominent DPT member and chair of the Executive Committee (mayor) of Dushanbe, was arrested and charged with bribery. Coupled with an earlier dismissal of a minister from the Gorno-Badakhshan Autonomous Region, the action triggered widespread antiregime protests. Led by the IRP, the DPT, *Rastokhez,* and *Lali Badakhshan* (Badakhshan Ruby Movement, a nationalist formation organized by the Pamiri ethnic group of Gorno-Badakhshan), the demonstrators called for dissolution of the Supreme Soviet and the adoption of a new constitution. In late April, with the unrest continuing and the local army commander having indicated that

his troops would not intervene, President Nabiyev organized a series of progovernment rallies in the capital, many of the demonstrators being communists from the southern Kulyab and northern Leninabad regions. In addition, Nabiyev secured legislative approval for a six-month period of direct presidential rule, including a suspension of civil liberties. DPT leader Shodmon YUSUF responded by charging Nabiyev with an attempt "to prolong totalitarian rule" and called for an interim state council similar to one that had assumed control in Georgia.

On April 22, 1992, the hard-line Safarali KENJAYEV resigned as chair of the Supreme Soviet. His reinstatement on May 3 triggered a fresh wave of protests, including a demonstration by upward of 100,000 persons on May 5. On May 10 security forces killed a reported 20 individuals gathered in front of the National Security Committee headquarters, where negotiations were taking place between government and opposition representatives. The next day, following intervention by the Muslim spiritual leader Kazi Ali Akbar TURAJONZODA of the IRP, Vice President Narzullo DUSTOV and a number of other hard-line officials resigned, and agreement was reached on a power-sharing arrangement whereby the opposition DPT and IRP would be awarded 8 of 24 cabinet posts. It was also agreed that an interim representative Assembly (*Majlis*) would be established, pending multiparty election of a permanent successor. However, the local soviets in Leninabad and Kulyab refused to accept the accord. Fighting between supporters and opponents of the agreement broke out in Kulyab and soon spread to the adjacent region of Kurgan-Tyube, where in August clashes between progovernment Kulyabi militiamen and Islamic-prodemocracy oppositionists reportedly cost hundreds of lives.

On August 30, 1992, Prime Minister Mirzoyev resigned and was succeeded on an interim basis by his deputy, Jamshed KARIMOV, while on September 7 President Nabiyev was forced to resign by opposition elements that had seized him during a melee in the Dushanbe airport. On September 24 Nabiyev's acting successor, Supreme Soviet chair Akbarsho ISKANDAROV, named Abdumalik ABDULLOJONOV to replace Karimov as the acting head of a coalition administration. Nevertheless, the conflict continued to intensify, with the new government losing effective control of Kulyab and Kurgan-Tyube to Nabiyev supporters led by Sangak SAFAROV. In early October former Supreme Soviet chair Kenjayev, who had organized a pro-Nabiyev Popular Front, tried to seize control of the capital from Islamic-prodemocracy forces. On November 19 Supreme Soviet chair Iskandarov stepped down in favor of Imomali RAKHMON, leader of the pro-Nabiyev forces in Kulyab. Concurrent with Iskandarov's departure, the presidential system was abolished in favor of a parliamentary system, with the chair of the legislature again serving as head of state. Prime Minister Abdullojonov remained in office, but the cabinet was stripped of opposition appointees. On December 10, after a two-month blockade of the capital led by Kenjayev's militias, troops loyal to the successor government regained control of Dushanbe from Islamic-prodemocracy forces, most of which were eventually driven into the Afghan border region.

On April 3, 1993, the DPT's Maksud Ikramov was for the second time dismissed as mayor of Dushanbe, after having been reinstated to the position in late 1992. On April 11 former president Nabiyev died of an apparent heart attack, and on April 27 the Russian Supreme Soviet voted to send a peacekeeping force to Tajikistan to join contingents from Kazakhstan, Kyrgyzstan, and Uzbekistan that had been dispatched by the Commonwealth of Independent States (CIS). Two months later, on June 21, the Supreme Court banned the four leading opposition groups—the IRP, DPT, *Rastokhez,* and *Lali Badakhshan*—for engaging in assassination, kidnapping, and rebellion. By that time, the government had regained control over most of the country, and many opposition leaders, including the IRP's Turajonzoda, had gone into exile. The conflict nonetheless continued in the border region, with the Islamic forces reportedly receiving support from Afghan guerrillas.

Prime Minister Abdullojonov resigned in December 1993, at least in part because of the country's economic decline, and was succeeded by his deputy, Abdujalil Ahadovich SAMADOV. Subsequently, peace talks with opposition leaders were initiated in Moscow, despite the assassination in March 1994 of Deputy Prime Minister Mayonsho NAZARSHOYEV, who had been named to head the government delegation. The talks yielded an agreement to cooperate on aid to refugees and to seek national reconciliation through "political measures alone," but clashes continued to occur in areas along the Afghan frontier. Further UN-sponsored talks in Tehran, Iran, resulted in the signature of a cease-fire accord in September, seemingly without the government making any major concessions to the opposition. The cease-fire did little to reduce hostilities, however, with another deputy prime minister, Munavvarsho NASIRYEV, being killed by a land mine on the day of its notional implementation, October 20. Meanwhile, in July a draft constitution had been approved by the Supreme Soviet, which called for its submission to a popular referendum in conjunction with the first direct election of a state president, who would have expanded executive powers under the new constitution.

Held on November 6, 1994, the constitutional referendum and presidential election were boycotted by the Islamic opposition and the DPT, although some secular opposition parties backed the candidacy of former prime minister Abdullojonov. According to the official results, over 90 percent of the voters endorsed the constitution. In the presidential election the incumbent, Rakhmon, received 58 percent of the votes cast, against some 35 percent for Abdullojonov, who complained of vote-rigging. On December 2, having been nominated by the president and endorsed by the legislature, Jamshed Karimov returned as prime minister to preside over a government that continued to be dominated by actual or former communists.

Elections to the new 181-member Supreme Assembly, held in February–March 1995, were boycotted by most of the opposition parties, Islamic and secular. A majority of the winners had no overt party allegiance, although about a third were declared communists.

Despite the presence since December 1994 of a small UN observer mission charged with monitoring the supposed cease-fire, fighting continued unabated between government and opposition forces. In a major flare-up in Gorno-Badakhshan in April 1995, hundreds died as government and CIS forces advanced on units of the Afghanistan-based IRP armed wing operating in alliance with Badakhshan separatists. By midyear some 25,000 CIS peacekeeping troops were deployed in Tajikistan, the majority of them Russian.

Further peace talks took place in Kabul, Afghanistan, in May 1995 between President Rakhmon and the IRP leader, Sayed Abdullo NURI, but no substantive progress was made on the opposition's demand for the legalization of all political parties, press freedom, release of political prisoners, amnesty for rebel leaders, and full autonomy for Gorno-Badakhshan. In June–July 1995 the government succeeded in bringing about a split in the DPT, with one faction accepting official registration and the other remaining in full opposition. During the latter part of 1995, notwithstanding an extension of the notional cease-fire, the civil war continued in the south and along the Afghan border.

An escalation of the conflict at the beginning of 1996 impelled President Rakhmon to carry out a government reorganization in early

February, with Karimov being replaced as prime minister by Yakhyo AZIMOV and with Makhmadsaid UBAYDULLAYEV being dismissed as first deputy prime minister. The changes were reportedly made in response to demands by two rebel military leaders who had occupied the southern and western towns of Kurgan-Tyube and Tursunzade; troops loyal to one of the rebels, Col. Makhmud KHUDOBERDIYEV, an ethnic Uzbek from Leninabad, had briefly threatened the capital. Thereafter, fighting intensified in the central Garm and Tavil Dara areas.

The fall of Kabul to Taliban forces in September 1996 provided a spur to further peace efforts, and new negotiations between the government and the opposition were launched in October. At a meeting in Afghanistan on December 10–11, President Rakhmon and the IRP's Nuri agreed to another cease-fire and to open formal peace talks in Moscow later in the month. Despite violations, the cease-fire appeared to contain the fighting, and on December 23 Rakhmon and Nuri signed accords in the Russian capital providing for the establishment of a transitional National Reconciliation Commission (NRC), to be headed by a representative of the IRP-led United Tajik Opposition (UTO). The NRC would assume responsibility for overseeing reform of electoral laws and the reintegration of the opposition into normal life. Under the accords, opposition representatives were to be introduced into the structures of executive power, including central and local government and law enforcement agencies, in proportion to the representation of the parties on the NRC, taking regional balance into account. The commission would cease its work after the convocation of a new parliament and the formation of its ruling bodies.

Early in 1997 the secular National Revival movement, which had been organized in July 1996 by former prime ministers Abdullojonov, Karimov, and Samadov, staged protests against its exclusion from the peace process. At the same time, further negotiations between the government and the UTO were being overshadowed by kidnappings and battles among warlords and rogue military officers, most prominently Colonel Khudoberdiyev, who for a time controlled much of southern Tajikistan and again threatened the capital before being repulsed by government troops. Nevertheless, the cease-fire between the UTO and the government, which controlled little more than the capital region, continued to hold. When an assassination attempt on the life of President Rakhmon failed in April, the UTO joined world capitals in condemning the attack.

On June 27, 1997, Rakhmon and UTO leader Nuri signed a peace agreement in Moscow, officially ending the five-year civil war. The agreement provided for the eventual legalization of the UTO parties, the return of refugees and Afghan-based opposition forces, the integration of the latter within the regular army, and the granting to the UTO of 30 percent of government posts. The signatories also agreed that the NRC would have 26 members, 13 from the government and 13 from the UTO. Implementation of the peace was by no means assured, however, and in January 1998 the UTO briefly quit the NRC, citing government delays in meeting the terms of the agreement. Under pressure from the UTO, President Rakhmon named five UTO members to his cabinet in February. In March he added as deputy prime minister the UTO's recently repatriated Ali Akbar Turajonzoda, who, however, failed to win formal parliamentary approval until November even though the position, which had previously carried supervisory responsibilities involving the economy, defense, and the interior, had been redefined to cover only economic and trade relations with CIS countries.

Sporadic fighting continued to break out throughout 1998. The combatants included troops loyal to the government, renegade field commands, UTO contingents (sometimes against each other), and unaffiliated militias. The most serious incident occurred in the northern city of Khujand (formerly Leninabad) on November 4–7, when forces under Colonel Khudoberdiyev staged a rebellion that claimed an estimated 300 lives and injured another 650 before being put down. Among those implicated in the rebellion were former prime minister Abdullojonov; his brother, Abdughani ABDULLOJONOV, who had previously served as mayor of Khujand; and a former vice president, Narzullo Dustov.

In the second half of 1999 progress accelerated toward fulfilling the terms of the 1997 peace accords. In June Nuri and President Rakhmon had agreed to emphasize constitutional reform while continuing to decommission UTO forces, to integrate UTO troops into national military and security units, and to pursue the 30 percent target for UTO staffing of government positions. In early August Nuri announced that the military goals had been accomplished, which, under the terms of the June agreement, led the Supreme Court on August 12 to reinstate the four political groups that had been banned in 1993. In September 71.8 percent of those voting in a national referendum approved constitutional amendments that affected more than two dozen articles, included provisions permitting sectarian political parties, creating a bicameral parliament, and lengthening the presidential term to seven years. With the notable exception of President Rakhmon's People's Democratic Party of Tajikistan (PDPT) and the IRP, most political parties had campaigned against the revisions, arguing that they would increase the current president's authority over legislation, regional administration, and the courts, and that the new upper house would slow down legislation and exacerbate regional tensions.

In October 1999 the UTO suspended its participation in the NRC and announced that it would boycott the November 6 presidential election, primarily because the Central Commission for Elections and Referendums had disqualified opposition candidates (technically, for having failed to obtain sufficient signatures to get their names on the ballot). Hours before the voting began, the UTO canceled the boycott, Nuri having received assurances from Rakhmon regarding the conduct of upcoming parliamentary elections. With Rakhmon's only opponent on the ballot, Davlat USMON of the IRP, having denounced the presidential contest as a sham, Rakhmon secured 97 percent of the vote, and on November 16 he took the oath of office for another term. On November 23 Yakhyo Azimov and his cabinet resigned, as constitutionally mandated. The president named Oqil OQILOV (Akil AKILOV) as the new prime minister on December 20 and continued to make cabinet changes well into the new year.

With several of the smaller opposition parties having been declared ineligible, an election for the new lower house, the Assembly of Representatives, took place in February–March 2000. Amid accusations of campaign and voting irregularities, the PDPT and supporting parties captured more than two-thirds of the 63 seats. The Communists won only 13, and the IRP, 2. On March 23 indirect elections were held for the majority of the seats in the new upper house, the National Assembly, which was also expected to support President Rakhmon's agenda.

In the next four years, amid numerous ministerial changes, President Rakhmon consolidated his power, in part through passage in June 2003 of a referendum that removed a constitutional proscription against his seeking reelection in 2006. Similarly, the dominance of the PDPT was confirmed by the legislative elections of February–March 2005, which saw the opposition win only two seats in the National Assembly and six in the Assembly of Representatives. The Organization for Security and Cooperation in Europe (OSCE) described the elections as seriously flawed.

On November 6, 2006, President Rakhmon won reelection with 79 percent of the vote against token opponents in a contest that was again criticized by objective international observers. After the election Prime Minister Oqilov was reappointed. By-elections in three parliamentary districts in April 2007 were won overwhelmingly by PDPT candidates.

Constitution and government. The last of the ex-Soviet Central Asian republics to do so, Tajikistan adopted a post-Soviet constitution by referendum on November 6, 1994, with the new text coming into force immediately. It defines Tajikistan as a democratic, secular, and unitary state, and the people as the sole source of state power. Amendments approved by referendum in September 1999 included a provision permitting formation of sectarian political parties. In all, the referendum authorized changes to 27 articles of the basic law. Another referendum, passed on June 22, 2003, made 56 mostly minor changes (which voters had to accept or reject as a single package), with the most controversial provision being removal of a one-term limit for the presidency.

The 1999 revisions also replaced the unicameral legislature with a bicameral Supreme Assembly encompassing a National Assembly of indirectly elected and appointed members (plus former presidents of the republic) and an Assembly of Representatives, the latter directly elected from a combination of single-seat districts and national party lists. Parliamentarians serve five-year terms. The powers of the National Assembly, which must meet at least twice a year, include redefining territorial divisions and considering laws proposed by the lower house. The Assembly of Representatives, meeting in continuous session, is authorized to independently adopt the state budget and can override an upper house rejection of legislation with a two-thirds vote. The Supreme Assembly can override presidential vetoes of legislation with a two-thirds vote. Passage of constitutional amendments requires a two-thirds vote of both bodies and a three-fourths vote in the event of a presidential veto.

The president, described as the head of the executive branch and commander in chief, is now directly elected for up to two seven-year terms. His powers include appointing the prime minister and other ministers, as well as judges and other senior state and regional administrators, subject to legislative endorsement. He can also initiate referendums. The system of judicial authority is headed by a Constitutional Court and includes a Supreme Court, a Supreme Economic Court, and a Military Court.

Administratively, Tajikistan currently comprises the capital city of Dushanbe, the centrally administered Region of Republican Subordination (*Nohiyahoi Tobei Jumhurii,* formerly Karotegin), and three other regions (*viloyatho*): in the north, Sughd (formerly Leninabad); in the southwest, Khatlon, established in 1992 by the merger of the Kulyab (*Kŭlob*) and Kurgan-Tyube (*Qŭrghonteppa*) regions; and in the east, the Gorno-Badakhshan Autonomous Region (*Badakhshoni Kŭhí Viloyati Avtonomii*), which the 1994 constitution specifically defines as "an integral and indivisible part of Tajikistan." Regions, districts, and towns elect local assemblies that are chaired by presidential appointees, subject to the approval of the respective assemblies.

Foreign relations. On December 21, 1991, Tajikistan became a charter member of the post-Soviet CIS. By early 1992 it had established diplomatic relations with a number of foreign countries, including the United States, and had been admitted to the Conference on (later Organization for) Security and Cooperation in Europe (CSCE/OSCE). It joined the United Nations in March 1992, the IMF in April 1993, and the World Bank in June 1993. As a predominantly Muslim country, Tajikistan also became a member of the Organization of the Islamic Conference. In February 2002 it formally joined NATO's Partnership for Peace program.

Regionally, during a summit in Tehran, Iran, in 1992, Tajikistan and its sister republics of Azerbaijan, Kyrgyzstan, Turkmenistan, and Uzbekistan gained admission to the long-dormant Economic Cooperation Organization, which had been founded by Iran, Turkey, and Pakistan in 1963. In March 1998 Tajikistan was admitted as a candidate member to the Central Asian Economic Union—renamed the Central Asian Economic Community in July 1998 and then the Central Asian Cooperation Organization (CACO) in February 2002—which had been established four years earlier by Kazakhstan, Kyrgyzstan, and Uzbekistan. In April 1998 a Tajik application to join Russia, Belarus, Kazakhstan, and Kyrgyzstan in the CIS Customs Union was approved, and formal entry occurred in February 1999. In 2005 the CACO merged into the Eurasian Economic Community (Belarus, Kazakhstan, Kyrgyzstan, Russia, Tajikistan, and Uzbekistan).

Relations with Moscow have remained close since independence. From 1993 until the mission's end in September 2000, Russia provided the bulk of troops for the CIS peacekeeping operation, which also included contingents from Kazakhstan, Kyrgyzstan, and Uzbekistan. Primarily to deter infiltration across the Afghan and Kyrgyz borders by such extremist groups as the Islamic Movement of Uzbekistan (IMU), Russian troops remain in Tajikistan. In June 2004, after lengthy negotiations, the Rakhmon government granted Russia permission to establish a permanent military base for its troops and also agreed to permit unlimited Russian use of the Soviet-built space surveillance center in Nurek, one of the world's most sophisticated facilities for tracking satellites. In return, Russia reportedly agreed to forgo some $300 million in debt payments, to be offset by partial ownership of a hydroelectric power facility.

Postindependence relations between Tajikistan and Uzbekistan have been complicated by persecution of ethnic Tajiks in Uzbekistan and by nationalist resentment in Tajikistan over the prominence of ethnic Uzbeks in the state hierarchy. Although not espoused by the government, territorial claims by Tajik nationalists on Uzbek cities, including Samarkand and Bukhara, have also caused strains. In late 1998 President Rakhmon accused the Uzbek government of complicity in the failed November revolt in Khujand. Captured rebels later claimed that members of the Uzbek special forces had helped train them, but Uzbek President Islam Karimov denied any involvement and subsequently accused Tajik officials of drug-trafficking.

Despite such tempestuous exchanges, in January 1999 Tajik prime minister Azimov met with President Karimov in Tashkent to discuss trade and economic cooperation. (Tajikistan remains dependent on Uzbekistan for almost all overland traffic.) Three months later the presidents of both countries joined their counterparts from Kazakhstan and Kyrgyzstan in signing a mutual security agreement intended to combat terrorism, Islamic extremism, and related threats. In June 2000 Tajikistan and Uzbekistan reached agreement on a protocol for delimiting their common border and signed a treaty of friendship. Talks continue regarding the border and the removal of minefields on the Uzbek side. The border with Kyrgyzstan also awaits full delimitation.

Beginning in 1994 Tajikistan met regularly with the other members of the so-called Shanghai Five—China, Kazakhstan, Kyrgyzstan, and Russia—which focused their attention primarily on matters of regional stability and security. In 2001 Uzbekistan joined the grouping, which renamed itself the Shanghai Cooperation Organization (SCO); a formal SCO charter was signed in 2002 and a Secretariat was inaugurated in January 2004. Islamic militancy in Afghanistan and elsewhere in the region has been of particular concern.

Even before the October 2001 launch of U.S.-led strikes against al-Qaida and Afghanistan's Taliban regime, Tajikistan was believed to be aiding the anti-Taliban Northern Alliance, which was dominated by ethnic Tajiks. Special forces from the Ministry of the Interior were subsequently reported to be directly assisting the Northern Alliance in its march toward Kabul, and it was later confirmed that Tajikistan had permitted several of its air bases to be used by the United States and its allies in the campaign. In January 2002, apparently rewarding the Rakhmon government for its cooperation, the United States lifted a 1993 restriction on the transfer of military equipment to Tajikistan.

In December 2003 Tajikistan joined China, Iran, Pakistan, Turkmenistan, and Uzbekistan in pledging to respect post-Taliban Afghanistan's sovereignty and to remain aloof from its internal affairs. In August 2007 President Rakhmon and his Afghan counterpart, Hamid Karzai, inaugurated a bridge over the Pyranzh River. Built with funds from the United States, the cross-border bridge was expected to facilitate development of a major trade route. Tajikistan is also constructing a power transmission line to export hydroelectric power to Afghanistan and, eventually, Pakistan.

In July 2008 Tajik foreign minister Hamrokhon ZARIFI named Kazakhstan, Kyrgyzstan, Turkmenistan, Afghanistan, and Iran as key regional partners and Russia, China, and the United States as global partners. Zarifi particularly emphasized the Tajik-Russian, relationship, noting the countries' cultural and political similarities.

Current issues. The harsh winter of 2008 saw heavy snow and mudslides cut off remote areas from food supplies well into the spring, which, combined with severe cold and water contamination, precipitated a humanitarian crisis. A number of Tajiks froze to death during prolonged power cuts, and in February a United Nations official estimated that 50 percent of the population of Tajikistan suffered from malnutrition. In response, the UN organized a $25 million international aid package. The crisis took place against the backdrop of accusations of mismanagement by the Tajikistan government. Critics said the administration was ill equipped to deal with a social crisis and that it had ignored pressing needs to update urban and rural infrastructures.

In April 2008 the government of Tajikistan agreed to repay the IMF $47.7 million as a penalty for falsifying a loan application. Tajikistan had listed $450 million in gold and foreign currency reserves as security for the IMF loan, but an investigation revealed that actual reserves on hand totaled $115 million. Nevertheless, in April 2009 the IMF extended another loan—$117 million from its Poverty Reduction and Growth Facility—to mitigate adverse effects of the global financial crisis. Later in the month President Rakhmon appealed for all citizens to donate a month's salary toward the cost of completing a hydroelectric plant on the River Vakhsh that has been in development for over three decades. Bringing the facility at Rogun online has been seen as potentially ending domestic electricity shortages and permitting expanded energy exports.

With the next election for the lower house slated for February 2010, not even the leading opposition parties, the CPT and the IRP, anticipated making major inroads in the PDPT's dominance. Each hoped to win at least five seats, sufficient to form a bloc in the legislature. President Rakhmon publicly committed his administration to conducting free and transparent elections, but in order to accomplish that, his opponents asserted, he should step down as chair of the PDPT. They also sought changes to the electoral law, including lowering from 5 percent to 3 percent the threshold for receiving proportional seats and either eliminating or greatly reducing the mandatory per-candidate electoral deposit of about $1,500—an amount difficult for many potential candidates to risk, given that losing candidates forfeit their deposits to the government.

Outspoken critics of the Rakhmon regime have often found themselves in court or threatened with prosecution. In April 2005 Mahmadruzi ISKANDAROV, chair of the DPT, was abducted in Moscow, spirited back to Tajikistan, placed on trial, and in October sentenced to

23 years in prison for a variety of offenses that included terrorism, embezzlement, and attempted murder. In March 2006 Rahmatullo ZOIROV, leader of the Social Democratic Party of Tajikistan (SDPT), accused the government of holding some 1,000 political prisoners, including Iskandarov, which prompted the prosecutor-general to warn Zoirov that he could face charges unless he produced proof. Zoirov further asserted that evidence of involvement in terrorism had been fabricated against many incarcerated members of the *Hizb-ut-Tahrir,* a regional Islamic group that has been banned by most Central Asian states. Clashes continue to occur in the Tajik-Kyrgyz-Ukbek border area, with either the *Hizb-ut-Tahrir* or the more militant IMU typically blamed.

POLITICAL PARTIES

For most of the first decade after independence, political parties did not play a significant role in governance, although the Communist Party of Tajikistan (CPT) continued to be influential in the Supreme Assembly, and, as the 1990s drew to a close, President Rakhmon's People's Democratic Party of Tajikistan (PDPT) became increasingly important.

In the wake of the June 1997 peace agreement that ended the civil war, Tajik politics was dominated by efforts to reintegrate the United Tajik Opposition (UTO) into government and the military. Established in Afghanistan in 1993 as the Islamic Revival Movement and renamed in 1996, the UTO included most opposition paramilitary organizations and four groups banned in 1993: the Islamic Rebirth Party (IRP), whose chair, Sayed Abdullo Nuri, served as principal negotiator in peace talks with the government; the Democratic Party of Tajikistan (the so-called Almaty wing of the DPT, following a party rupture in 1995); and two social organizations, the *Lali Badakhshan* and the *Rastokhez* movements. The *Lali Badakhshan*, led by Atobek AMIRBEK, had been formed in the late 1980s as a nationalist movement of the Pamiri people, who belong to the Ismaili Muslim sect and who demanded full autonomy for Gorno-Badakhshan. *Rastokhez* (Rebirth Movement) had been founded in 1990 as a nationalist/religious organization advocating the revival of Tajik culture and traditions. As a result of the 1996–1997 accords, the UTO and the government were equally represented on the National Reconciliation Commission (NRC). The IRP, DPT (Almaty), *Lali Badakhshan,* and *Rastokhez* had their legal standing restored in 1999.

In June 1999 a loose Consultative Council of Political Parties was formed in opposition to the constitutional amendments then being considered by the NRC. Parties associated with the council during the subsequent referendum campaign included the CPT, the so-called Tehran wing of the DPT, the Congress of People's Unity, Hakim MUHABBATOV's National Movement Party, the Agrarian Party, the Party of Justice, and the Party of Justice and Development (predecessor of the current Social Democratic Party of Tajikistan—SDPT). The ideological diversity of its members precluded the council's functioning as an electoral coalition in the 2000 legislative elections.

Meanwhile, the government had begun closing political parties on technical grounds. The People's Unity Party (PUP—also identified in the English-language press by a variety of other names, including the Party of Popular Unity and Accord, the Popular Unity of Tajikistan, and the National Unity Party), founded in 1994, was in part a successor to the Party of Economic Freedom (PEF) that Abdumalik Abdullojonov had formed upon resigning as prime minister in December 1993. Drawing its main support from northern Tajikistan, it won two seats in the 1995 legislative election. At that time, it was the only legal opposition party. Despite efforts by PUP leaders to condemn the November 1998 rebellion in Khujand and to disavow any recent association with Abdullojonov, in December 1998 the Tajik Supreme Court banned the PUP and ordered its property and assets nationalized.

In March 1999 the Supreme Court suspended the Tajikistan Party of Political and Economic Renewal, which had won one seat in the 1995 election under party leader Mukhtor BOBOYEV, who was murdered in March 1996. The Agrarian Party, established in 1998 by Hikmatullo NASRIDDINOV, was closed in September 1999 on the grounds that its participation in the Consultative Council of Political Parties constituted a violation of an earlier suspension by the Supreme Court. Initially registered in 1996, the Party of Justice (*Hizb-i-Adolatkhoh*) nominated Saifuddin TURAYEV, chair of the affiliated Congress of People's Unity, for the Tajik presidency in 1999, but his candidacy was disallowed for an insufficient number of supporting signatures. In the 2000 legislative election *Adolatkhoh* won only 1.3 percent of the vote and no seats. In August 2001 the Supreme Court ruled that it had failed to correct technical deficiencies and therefore made an earlier suspension final.

In April 2004, looking toward the 2005 elections, the IRP, the SDPT, and the Socialist Party of Tajikistan (SPT) agreed to cooperate in a loose For Fair and Transparent Elections alliance, which the DPT then joined in August. Given that a party must be formally registered for at least a year to contest an election, the only other parties eligible for the February 2005 balloting were the president's PDPT and the CPT. Two additional parties were registered in November 2005, bringing the total number of officially recognized parties to eight.

Presidential Party:

People's Democratic Party of Tajikistan—PDPT (*Hizb-i-Khalq-i-Demokrati Tojikiston*). Formed in 1993 as the People's Party of Tajikistan (PPT) by a group of northern business interests centered in Khujand, the PDPT includes in its membership many former Soviet-era Communists, including President Rakhmon. Formally registered in December 1994, the PPT emerged from the 1995 Supreme Assembly election with only a handful of seats, but its representation subsequently swelled to about 90 with the addition of members who had run without declaring affiliations. The party adopted its present name in 1997.

President Rakhmon officially joined the PDPT in March 1998 and was elected chair at a party congress in April. Described by a spokesperson at the time as a party of pragmatists and technocrats, the PDPT significantly expanded its base of support throughout the country as a result of the president's membership. In the election for the new lower house of the Supreme Assembly in February–March 2000, the PDPT won 15 of 22 party list seats on a 65 percent first-round vote share. In 2005 it won 52 of the lower house's 63 seats and also claimed 29 of 34 seats in the upper house.

President Rakhmon also chairs the Central Council of a closely associated social movement, the **Movement for National Unity and Revival of Tajikistan** (frequently shortened to the National Unity Movement), which was established in 1997.

Leaders: Imomali RAKHMON (President of the Republic and Chair of the Party), Davlatali DAVLATZODA (First Deputy Chair).

Parliamentary Opposition:

Communist Party of Tajikistan—CPT (*Hizb-i-Kommunisti Tojikiston*). Primarily based in the northern industrial region of Sughd (previously Leninabad) and in other areas of high ethnic Uzbek or Russian population, the CPT was the only registered party prior to the Tajik declaration of independence. In September 1991 it was banned by the Aslonov government, one day after it had decided to reorganize as the Tajik Socialist Party (TSP). The ban was immediately overturned but reimposed in October. Again functioning legally under its original name, the CPT regained its status as the dominant political group with the outlawing of its principal opponents in June 1993. In the February–March 1995 legislative balloting, at least a third of the elected candidates were acknowledged CPT members. It continued to advocate collective ownership and revival of a Soviet-based union of republics.

Claiming that a presidential victory by a Communist candidate would anger Russia, the CPT unexpectedly supported President Rakhmon for reelection in 1999. It nevertheless remained within the opposition Consultative Council of Political Parties. The CPT won five party list seats, on a 20.6 percent vote share, in the Assembly of Representatives in the 2000 legislative election. In 2005 it won a total of four seats in the lower house and two in the upper. In 2006 its presidential candidate, Ismoil Talbakov, won 5.2 percent of the vote.

Leaders: Shodi SHABDOLOV (Chair), Ismoil TALBAKOV (Deputy Chair).

Islamic Rebirth Party—IRP (*Hizb-i-Nahzati Islom,* also translated into English as the Islamic Renaissance Party and the Islamic Revival Party). A rural-based grouping founded in June 1990, the IRP has indicated that its long-term objective is the conversion of Tajikistan into an Islamic republic, although it has rejected the label "fundamentalist." It supported the DPT's Davlat Khudonazarov for the presidency in 1991 but was banned in June 1993.

During 1992–1996 the armed Defense of the Fatherland wing of the IRP engaged in hostilities against government and CIS forces, drawing support from Tajiks who had fled to Afghanistan, from pro-Tajik Afghan mujahidin, and possibly from the Afghan government. Following the June 1997 peace agreement, the IRP remained at the center of the UTO.

Relegalized in August 1999, the IRP elected UTO leader Sayed Abdullo Nuri as chair and, in the interest of national unity, gave grudging support to the constitutional referendum of September 26 despite objections to particular provisions. For the November presidential election the IRP designated as its candidate Davlat Usmon, minister of economics and foreign economic relations. In October, reversing a decision by the election commission that would have kept Usmon off the ballot, the Supreme Court ruled that a sufficient number of supporting signatures had been gathered on his behalf. However, Usmon and much of the opposition criticized the decision as an illegitimate effort to create the impression that the election offered a choice to voters. Usmon subsequently decided to boycott the election, but his name remained on the ballot and he won 2 percent of the vote.

Party and UTO deputy chair Ali Akbar Turajonzoda reportedly resigned both positions in October 1999 after being expelled from the IRP because he had broken party regulations and had described President Rakhmon as worthy of reelection.

In the first-round legislative election of February 2000, the IRP won two party list seats on a 7.3 percent vote share. In September 2003 the party's fourth conference reelected Chair Nuri, who consistently denied the existence of any IRP connections to militant Islamic groups, particularly the Islamic Movement of Uzbekistan (IMU). Nuri also charged the government with persecuting the IRP in the guise of cracking down on another regional Islamic group, the *Hizb-ut-Tahrir.*

In May 2003 IRP deputy chair Shamsiddin SHAMSIDDINOV was arrested and subsequently charged with murder, forming an armed group, and other crimes dating back to the civil war. In January 2004 he was sentenced to a lengthy term in prison, where he died of natural causes in January 2008.

In the 2005 legislative elections the IRP again won two seats. Nuri died in 2006 and was succeeded by his deputy chair, Muhiddin Kabiri. The party refused to nominate a candidate for the 2006 presidential election. Kabiri was reelected party chair in September 2007.

Leaders: Muhiddin KABIRI (Chair), Hikmotulla SAYFULLOZODA.

Other Registered Parties:

Agrarian Party of Tajikistan (APT). The APT was formed in September 2005 and officially registered two months later. (An earlier Agrarian Party was permanently suspended in 1999.) In January 2006 the APT chair, Amir Qoraqulov, denied that his party intended to form a coalition with the PDPT before the November 2006 presidential election, in which he won 5.2 percent of the vote. Some opponents have asserted that the APT is a product of government efforts to split the opposition vote.

Leader: Amir QORAQULOV (Amirkul KARAKULOV, Chair).

Democratic Party of Tajikistan (DPT). Drawing its support largely from Gorno-Badakhshan, the strongly anticommunist DPT was launched in 1990 on a platform that called for Tajik sovereignty within a framework of confederal states. It was formally outlawed in June 1993.

Divisions between moderate and hard-line DPT factions led to an open split in June 1995, when Shodmon YUSUF was ousted from the leadership but refused to recognize the election of Jumaboy NIYAZOV as his successor. Claiming to be the authentic DPT leader, Yusuf approved terms with the government under which his faction was relegalized in July as the DPT, although it was thereafter often referenced as the DPT (Tehran Platform) to distinguish it from Niyazov's DPT (Almaty Platform). The latter entered into an opposition alliance with the IRP and functioned as part of the UTO. The peace agreement of June 1997 provided for the eventual legalization of the outlawed faction, and Niyazov was later named to the NRC's political committee.

Closely associated with the DPT during the civil war was the Coordinating Center for the Democratic Forces of Tajikistan, led by Otakhon LATIFI until his return from exile in 1997. The head of the NRC legal committee, Latifi was assassinated in September 1998.

At its third congress in July 1999 the DPT (Tehran) replaced Yusuf with Azam AFZALI and in September nominated a former presidential defense adviser, Zafar IKROMOV, as its candidate for the presidential election in November. When Ikromov withdrew, citing the election commission's failure to issue the papers needed to obtain the 145,000 signatures required for a place on the ballot, the party nominated in his stead Sulton Quvvatov. Along with two other opposition candidates, Quvvatov announced in early October that he would boycott the balloting because his campaign workers were being harassed and the news media were not providing impartial campaign coverage. The boycott became moot on October 12 when the election commission disqualified Quvvatov because he had not met the deadline for obtaining the requisite signatures.

Meanwhile, in accordance with the June 1997 peace accords, the DPT (Almaty) had been legalized by the Supreme Court on August 12, 1999, although the Ministry of Justice refused to register it because of a prohibition against two parties having similar names. At its fifth congress in late September the Almaty group replaced Jumaboy Niyazov with Mahmadruzi Iskandarov. Subsequently, the Supreme Court recognized the DPT (Almaty) as the official DPT, permitting its registration in time to contest the 2000 parliamentary election. With the DPT (Tehran) officially disbanded, Afzali and Quvvatov formed the *Taraqqiyot* (below).

Iskandarov was detained by Russian authorities in December 2004 at the request of the Tajik government, which accused him of terrorism and corruption. Shortly after his April 2005 release, he was abducted and delivered to Tajikistan, where in October he was convicted of terrorism, attempted murder, embezzlement, and weapons possession. He was sentenced to 23 years in prison.

In 2006 a *Watan* (Motherland) faction within the party was organized under the leadership of Masud Sobirov. In August Sobirov's supporters held an extraordinary congress that elected him party chair. Despite claims from the Iskandarov wing that the congress had been illegal, the Justice Department recognized Sobirov as DPT leader. Subsequently, however, a party congress ousted Sobirov for inadequate performance, including a failure to get the party's presidential candidate, Tabvardi ZIYOYEV, on the November ballot. In January 2007 Acting Chair Saidjaffar Ismonov, who had previously belonged to the PDPT and then the unregistered Party of Progressive Youth of Tajikistan, was confirmed as Sobirov's successor. Reconciliation efforts have not succeeded, with the result that the DPT remains split into three wings headed by Iskandarov, Ismonov, and Sobirov. The government continues to recognize the Sobirov wing as the official DPT.

Leaders: Masud SOBIROV (Chair of Registered DPT), Saidjaffar ISMONOV (Chair of Ismonov Wing), Mahmadruzi ISKANDAROV (Chair of Iskandarov Wing, in prison), Rakhmatullo VALIYEV (Deputy Chair of Iskandarov Wing).

Party of Economic Reforms of Tajikistan (PERT). Formation of the PERT was announced in September 2005. It was officially registered on November 10. In 2006 the party's chair ran for president and finished second, with 6.2 percent of the vote. The PERT has been accused of attempting to split the opposition vote.

Leader: Olimjon BOBOYEV (Chair).

Social Democratic Party of Tajikistan (SDPT). The SDPT traces its origins to the Party of Justice and Development (*Adolat va Taraqqiyot*), formation of which was announced in April 1998 by Rahmatullo Zoirov. Initially registered in February 1999, the party subsequently added "Social Democratic Party" to its name, but shortly thereafter the Ministry of Justice indicated that it intended to seek the party's closure for violating a proscription against membership by servicemen, law enforcement personnel, and judiciary staff. As a result, its registration was annulled. Zoirov subsequently served President Rakhmon as senior adviser on legal policy from 2001 until resigning in 2003. Meanwhile, in December 2002 Zoirov had succeeded in registering the current SDPT. In 2005 he was a leading critic of how the legislative elections were conducted.

In November 2005 a deputy chair of the party, Hurinisso GHAFFORZODA, resigned from the SDPT to establish a social movement aimed at reviving cultural values. In the same month, Zoirov called for the opposition to name a joint candidate for the 2006 presidential election. When that effort failed, the SDPT chose not to contest the election.

Leaders: Rahmatullo ZOIROV (Chair), Shokirjon HAKIMOV (Deputy Chair).

Socialist Party of Tajikistan—SPT (*Hizb-i-Sotsialisti Tojikiston*). The SPT was organized in 1996 by former Supreme Soviet chair and

Popular Front leader Safarali Kenjayev. In November 1998 the party reportedly expelled former vice president Narzullo Dustov for his alleged participation, earlier in the month, in the abortive revolt in the north. (Dustov went into exile.) Kenjayev, who had been serving as the head of the Supreme Assembly's Committee on Legislation and Human Rights, was murdered by unknown gunmen in March 1999.

The SPT advocates economic and social pluralism, decentralization of power, and secularism. It supported President Rakhmon for reelection in November 1999 and won only 1.2 percent of the party list vote in the subsequent lower house election.

In August 2004 Mirhusayn NAZRIYEV was reelected chair, although he was opposed by members of a splinter group led by Abduhalim Ghafforov. In December, with both factions claiming to control the party, the Supreme Court ruled in Ghafforov's favor. In November 2006 Ghafforov won 2.8 percent of the presidential vote.

Leader: Abduhalim GHAFFOROV (Chair).

Unregistered Parties:

Progress Party (*Taraqqiyot*). Also translated into English as the Development Party, *Taraqqiyot* held its founding congress in the capital in May 2001. Virtually all of its initial membership had previously belonged to the disbanded DPT (Tehran). One of its founders, Sulton Quvvatov, was a former chair of the state tax committee and a prospective candidate for president in 1999 (see the DPT, above). Another founder, Azam Afzali, stated that the party would offer "constructive opposition" to the government.

Committed to protecting the political rights of all citizens without regard to ethnicity, religion, language, or gender, the party has repeatedly tried to register, without success. In March 2004 several members went on a brief hunger strike to call attention to the party's plight, and Quvvatov later stated that he would take his case to the International Court of Justice. The party ran into additional difficulty in August 2004 when the government filed a criminal lawsuit against Quvvatov for "insulting the honor and dignity of the president" and inciting extremism and ethnic hostility.

In July 2004 the SDPT offered to reserve places for *Taraqqiyot* members, including Quvvatov, on its party list for the 2005 legislative elections. In June 2005 party leader Rustam Fayziyev was given a six-year prison sentence for insulting the president and stirring up ethnic hatred.

Leaders: Sulton QUVVATOV (KUVVATOV, Chair), Rustam FAYZIYEV (Deputy Chair, in prison), Shodikhon KENJAYEV.

In March 2008 the Ministry of Justice, for the sixth time, rejected the registration application of the progovernment **Union Party** (*Vahdat*), led by Hikmatullo SAIDOV.

Banned Organizations:

Two banned Islamic organizations, the **Hizb-ut-Tahrir** and the **Islamic Movement of Uzbekistan** (IMU), have been active in Tajikistan. The IMU, now also known as the **Islamic Party of Turkestan,** has claimed responsibility for or been linked to numerous terrorist incidents in the Central Asian region and beyond, and both Kyrgyzstan and Uzbekistan have asserted that the group has operated from bases in Tajikistan, a charge that the government has denied. Members of the transnational *Hizb-ut-Tahrir* have been tried and sentenced to prison in Tajikistan, although the organization has not been as militant as the IMU.

LEGISLATURE

The 1994 constitution established a 181-member unicameral **Supreme Assembly** (*Majlisi Oli*). Constitutional amendments passed by referendum in September 1999 reconstituted the body as a bicameral legislature, all of whose members serve five-year terms.

National Assembly (*Majlisi Milli*). The upper chamber encompasses 25 indirectly elected members, 8 presidential appointees, and former presidents of the republic (currently one, Kakhar Makhkamov). The elected members are chosen by secret ballot of regional legislators in each of five equally weighted electoral districts: the country's four regions and Dushanbe. The most recent election was held March 24, 2005, with President Rakhmon announcing his nominees on March 25, after which the party breakdown was as follows: People's Democratic Party of Tajikistan, 29 seats; Communist Party of Tajikistan, 2; independents, 3.

Speaker: Makhmadsaid UBAYDULLAYEV.

Assembly of Representatives (*Majlisi Namoyandagon*). The lower chamber encompasses 63 members: 41 deputies directly elected on a majority basis from single-seat districts, and 22 divided proportionally among eligible parties receiving at least 5 percent of the national vote. Following the most recent election of February 27, 2005, with runoff balloting in three constituencies on March 13, the People's Democratic Party of Tajikistan held 52 seats; Communist Party of Tajikistan, 4; Islamic Rebirth Party, 2; independents, 5.

Speaker: Saydullo KHAYRULLOYEV.

CABINET

[as of November 1, 2009]

Prime Minister	Oqil Oqilov
Deputy Prime Ministers	Asadullo Ghulomov
	Ruqiya Atoyevna Qurbonova [f]
	Murodali Alimardonov
Ministers	
Agriculture and Nature Protection	Qosim Rahbarovich Qosimov
Culture	Mirzoshohrukh Asrorov
Defense	Col. Gen. Sherali Khayrulloyev
Economics and Trade	Ghulomjon Boboyev
Education	Abdujabbar Rahmonov
Emergency Situations and Civil Defense	Maj. Gen. Mirzo Zieyev
Energy and Industry	Shurali Gulov
Finance	Safarali Najmiddinov
Foreign Affairs	Hamrokhon Zarifi
Grain Products	Bekmurod Uroqov
Health	Nustratullo Fayzulloevich Salimov
Internal Affairs	Abdurahim Qahhorov
Justice	Bakhtiyor Khudoyorov
Labor and Social Welfare	Shukurjon Zuhurov
Land Reclamation and Water Resources	Said Yoqubzod
Transport and Communication	Abdurahim Ashurov
State Committee Chairs	
Environmental Protection	Khursandqul Zikirov
Investment and Management of State Property	Farrukh Mahmudovich Hamraliyev
National Security	Maj. Gen. Khayruddin Abdurahimov
Statistics	Mirgand Sharbozov

[f] = female

COMMUNICATIONS

Although the Tajik press experienced unprecedented freedoms immediately before and shortly after independence, domestically published opposition newspapers disappeared with the onset of the civil war in 1992. By 1997, 40 or more journalists had been killed. Today, much of the press remains under government control.

Press. *Narodnaya Gazeta* (People's Gazette, in Russian), *Jumhuriyat* (Republic, in Tajik), and *Khalk Ovozi* (People's Voice, in Uzbek) are government organs managed by a presidentially supervised publishing house.. The following papers are also published in Dushanbe: *Bizness i Politika* (Business and Politics), independent weekly, in Russian; *Kurer Tajikistana* (Tajikistan Courier), independent weekly, in Russian; *Minbar-i Khalk* (People's Tribune), PDPT monthly, in Tajik; *Nido-i Ranjbar/Golos Tajikistana/Tojikiston Ovozi* (Voice of the Toiler/Voice of Tajikistan), CPT weekly, in Tajik, Russian, and Uzbek. In August 2004 the government shut down a private printing firm that had been producing the IRP's weekly *Najot* (Salvation) and two independent weeklies that were also frequently critical of the government, *Ruzi Nav* (New Day) and *Nerui Sukhan* (Strength of Word). *Najot* later resumed publication.

News agencies. The principal domestic facility, *Khover*, was established in Dushanbe in 1991 as successor to the Tajik Telegraph Agency. There are several independent agencies, including Asia-Plus, which also distributes daily news summaries. *RIA-Novosti* has an office in the capital. Avesta, an online news agency, was founded in 2004.

Broadcasting and computing. An electronic broadcast law passed in 1996 requires state licensure for all facilities. To date, licenses have typically been granted to individuals and organizations with close political connections to local or national officials, although Asia-Plus and a few other private companies have recently been permitted to offer independent radio broadcasting from the capital. The state-owned Tajik Radio and Tajik Television broadcast from Dushanbe in Tajik, Russian, and Uzbek.

As of 2008 there were 87.8 Internet users per 1,000 inhabitants.

INTERGOVERNMENTAL REPRESENTATION

Ambassador to the U.S.: Abdujabbor SHIRINOV.

U.S. Ambassador to Tajikistan: Kenneth E. GROSS, JR.

Permanent Representative to the UN: Sirodjidin M. ASLOV.

IGO Memberships (Non-UN): ADB, CIS, EBRD, ECO, IDB, Interpol, IOM, OIC, OSCE, SCO, WCO.

TANZANIA

United Republic of Tanzania
Jamhuri ya Muungano wa Tanzania

Political Status: Independent member of the Commonwealth; established in its present form April 26, 1964, through union of the Republic of Tanganyika (independent 1961) and the People's Republic of Zanzibar (independent 1963); one-party constitution adopted April 25, 1977; multiparty system legalized June 17, 1992.

Area: 364,898 sq. mi. (945,087 sq. km.), encompassing Tanganyika, 363,948 sq. mi. (942,626 sq. km.) and Zanzibar 950 sq. mi. (2,461 sq. km.), the latter including Pemba (350 sq. mi., 906 sq. km.).

Population: 34,569,232 (2002C); 41,474,000 (2008E).

Major Urban Centers (2005E): DAR ES SALAAM (2,692,000), Mwanza (219,000), Zanzibar (town, 217,000), Tanga (190,000), Dodoma (169,000). The deadline for the transfer of government operations to a new capital in Dodoma has been extended numerous times. Although the National Assembly now sits in Dodoma, it remains uncertain when, or even if, full governmental relocation will occur.

Official Languages: English, Swahili.

Monetary Unit: Shilling (official rate December 1, 2009: 1,337.50 shillings = $1US).

President: Jakaya KIKWETE (Revolutionary Party of Tanzania); elected on December 14, 2005, and sworn in for a five-year term on December 21 to succeed Benjamin William MKAPA (Revolutionary Party of Tanzania).

Vice President: Ali Mohamed SHEIN (Revolutionary Party of Tanzania); nominated by the president on July 13, 2001, and sworn in on the same day following confirmation by the National Assembly to succeed Omar Ali JUMA (Revolutionary Party of Tanzania), who had died on July 4; reelected concurrently with the president on December 14, 2005, and sworn in on December 21.

Prime Minister: Mizengo PINDA (Revolutionary Party of Tanzania); appointed by the president and confirmed by the National Assembly on February 8, 2008, and sworn in on February 9, 2008, in succession to Edward LOWASSA (Revolutionary Party of Tanzania), who resigned on February 7.

President of Zanzibar: Amani Abeid KARUME (Revolutionary Party of Tanzania); elected October 29, 2000 (with a partial rerun on November 5), and sworn in for a five-year term on November 8 to succeed Dr. Salmin AMOUR Jima (Revolutionary Party of Tanzania); reelected on October 30, 2005, and sworn in for a second five-year term on November 2.

THE COUNTRY

The United Republic of Tanzania combines the large territory of Tanganyika on the East African mainland and the two islands of Zanzibar and Pemba off the East African coast. Tanzania's people are overwhelmingly African (primarily Bantu) stock, but there are significant Asian (largely Indian and Pakistani), European, and Arab minorities. In addition to the indigenous tribal languages, Swahili (Kiunguja is the Zanzibari form) serves as a lingua franca, while English and Arabic are also spoken. A majority of the population (over 60 percent on the mainland and over 90 percent on Zanzibar) is Muslim, the remainder adhering to Christianity or traditional religious beliefs. Women are estimated to comprise nearly 50 percent of the labor force, with responsibility for over 70 percent of subsistence activities; Tanzanian women have a relatively high level of literacy and are represented in most levels of government and party affairs.

The economy is primarily agricultural. The most important crops on the mainland are coffee, cotton, and sisal, which collectively account for approximately two-fifths of the country's exports. The economies of Zanzibar and Pemba are based on cloves and coconut products. Industry, which accounts for about 15 percent of the GDP, is primarily limited to the processing of agricultural products and the production of nondurable consumer goods, although there is an oil refinery that is dependent on imported crude. For many years the country benefited from few extractive resources other than diamonds, but in 2006 Tanzania became Africa's third leading producer of gold. In addition, several international mining companies have recently begun exploration for uranium in several sites. Modernization plans were enhanced by the completion in mid-1976, with Chinese financial and technical assistance, of the Tanzania-Zambia Railway (Tazara), which links Dar es Salaam and the Zambian copper belt.

In the 1980s the country encountered serious economic difficulties, exacerbated by a decline in cash-crop output and rapid population growth. Assistance from the International Monetary Fund (IMF) was suspended in 1982, necessitating severe budget cutbacks. Four years later, faced with an external debt crisis, the government acceded to IMF demands for devaluation of the Tanzanian shilling, price increases for food producers, and liberalization of export-import regulations. Additional economic reforms were pledged during 1991 negotiations with the IMF, which had expressed concern over the slow pace of privatization of state-run enterprises and apparent widespread corruption in the government bureaucracy.

In early 1993 the IMF released an analysis of Tanzanian economic reform efforts during 1986–1992, which noted progress in the previous two years but urged the government to increase its efforts in four areas: liberalizing agricultural markets and prices, privatizing parastatals and state-run industries, controlling inflation, and reducing the money supply. More overt criticism resulted from a December 1994 informal meeting of Tanzanian fund donors in Paris that focused on financial mismanagement, including the government's poor record in customs collection and its frequent issuance of tax exemptions. However, in November 1996 the IMF approved a $234 million three-year credit to assist the economic reforms endorsed by the new Mkapa administration. Thereafter, gains were reported in the mining, agriculture, and tourism sectors. In April 2000 the IMF and World Bank agreed to support a comprehensive debt relief package for Tanzania, encouraged by reduction in the size of the public sector and greater influence of the free market.

GDP growth averaged about 6 percent annually in the early 2000s, based on expansion in the manufacturing, mining, and construction

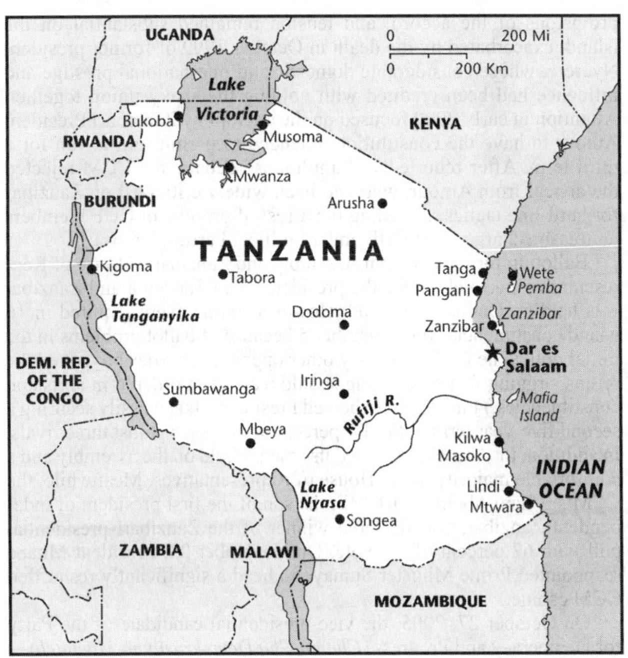

sectors. The IMF provided grants and loans under the fund's Poverty Reduction and Growth Facility (PRGF) initiative. Tanzania was also one of the countries approved for debt relief through the World Bank's Heavily Indebted Poor Country (HIPC) initiative. A series of economic reforms, including privatization initiatives and anticorruption measures, contributed to growth of 6.2 percent in 2006, while unemployment declined 11 percent. The World Bank also committed $2.3 billion in 2006 in economic development assistance over a three-year period, and Japan canceled Tanzania's $580 million debt in 2007.

Tanzania was ranked the second best place to do business in Africa in 2007 by a World Bank report, based on the country's continued strong economic performance and government programs to promote foreign investment, including the postponement of taxes for up to ten years and authorization of full foreign ownership of companies. The country's GDP grew by 7.1 percent in 2007, thanks in large part to a 30 percent increase in exports and a 15 percent increase in direct foreign investment in the country.

In 2008 the Millennium Challenge Account pledged $698 million to Tanzania for economic development. Inflation rose to 9.7 percent by March, and the central bank set a goal of reducing inflation to 6 percent by 2009. However, the global economic crisis that began in 2008 caused GDP growth to slow to 5 percent and prompted the government to initiate a $1.3 billion stimulus package. The government's deficit rose to 13.3 percent of GDP in 2009, and inflation spiked to 11 percent in the early months of the year (see Current issues, below). Meanwhile, foreign aid continued to contribute about 4 percent of the country's total GDP, and in August 2009 the EU announced more than $550 million in economic assistance for Tanzania. The IMF provided another $336 million.

GOVERNMENT AND POLITICS

Political background. The former British-ruled territories of Tanganyika and Zanzibar developed along separate lines until their union in 1964. Tanganyika, occupied by Germany in 1884, became a British-administered mandate under the League of Nations and continued under British administration as a United Nations trust territory after World War II. Led by Julius K. NYERERE of the Tanganyika African National Union (TANU), it became independent within the Commonwealth in 1961 and adopted a republican form of government with Nyerere as president in 1962.

Zanzibar and Pemba, British protectorates since 1890, became independent in 1963 as a constitutional monarchy within the Commonwealth. However, little more than a month after independence, the Arab-dominated government of Sultan Seyyid Jamshid bin Abdullah bin KHALIFA was overthrown by African nationalists, who established a People's Republic with Sheikh Abeid Amani KARUME of the Afro-Shirazi Party (ASP) as president.

Following overtures by Nyerere, the two countries combined on April 26, 1964, to form the United Republic of Tanganyika and Zanzibar, renamed the United Republic of Tanzania later in the same year. Nyerere became president of the unified state, and in September 1965 he was overwhelmingly confirmed in that position by popular vote in both sections of the country. Karume, in addition to becoming first vice president of Tanzania, continued to head the quasi-independent Zanzibar administration until April 1972, when he was assassinated. Nyerere thereupon appointed Aboud JUMBE to succeed Karume as first vice president and as leader of the ASP.

On February 5, 1977, TANU and the ASP merged to form the Revolutionary Party of Tanzania (*Chama Cha Mapinduzu*—CCM); subsequently, a new constitution was adopted on April 25, according the CCM a "dominant" role in the Tanzanian governmental system. On November 5, 1980, Prime Minister Edward SOKOINE announced his retirement for reasons of health, and two days later the president named Cleopa David MSUYA as Sokoine's successor. Sokoine returned as prime minister on February 24, 1983, but was killed in an automobile accident on April 12, 1984; he was succeeded 12 days later by Salim Ahmed SALIM. Earlier, on January 27, Vice President Jumbe had submitted his resignation in the wake of mounting secessionist agitation on Zanzibar, Ali Hassan MWINYI having been named his replacement on January 30.

Carrying out a pledge made in early 1984 to step down as head of state upon the expiration of his existing term, Nyerere withdrew from contention at the 1985 CCM congress in favor of Vice President Mwinyi, who was overwhelmingly nominated as the sole candidate for the October presidential balloting. Because of a constitutional prohibition against Zanzibaris occupying both presidential and prime ministerial offices, Prime Minister Salim was replaced following the October 27 poll by Justice Minister Joseph S. WARIOBA, who also assumed the post of first vice president; concurrently, Idris Abdul WAKIL, who had been elected president of Zanzibar on October 13, became second vice president, while Salim was named deputy prime minister and minister of defense.

Mwinyi's elevation to the presidency and his encouragement of private enterprise appeared to stem secessionist sentiment on Zanzibar. However, discord attributed to a variety of economic, religious, and political motives broke out again in late 1987. An apparent power struggle developed between Wakil and supporters of Chief Minister Seif Sharif HAMADI, a leader from the northern island of Pemba (where 90 percent of the islands' cloves are produced), after Hamadi was dropped from the CCM Central Committee. On January 23, 1988, Wakil, claiming that dissidents were plotting a coup, suspended the Zanzibari government; three days later he announced a new administration in which Hamadi was replaced by Omar Ali JUMA. In May Hamadi and six of his supporters were expelled from the CCM for alleged "antiparty" activity. Observers reported a continued "undercurrent of rebellion" on the islands, however, and Hamadi was arrested in May 1989 on charges of organizing illegal meetings, the government also accusing his supporters of forming a political group, *Bismallah* ("In the name of God"), dedicated to "breaking the union."

Mwinyi continued to consolidate his authority during 1990; in March he ousted hard-line socialist cabinet members who opposed his economic policies, and, following Nyerere's retirement on August 17, he was elected CCM chair. On October 28 the president won reelection for a second five-year term, and on November 8 he named John S. MALECELA first vice president and prime minister, replacing Warioba. Meanwhile, on October 21 Salmin AMOUR had been elected president of Zanzibar and second vice president of the republic after Wakil had declined to seek reelection to the posts.

On June 17, 1992, President Mwinyi signed a bill legalizing opposition parties. The legislation had been approved by the National Assembly on May 7 and by the Zanzibar House of Representatives on May 14, following endorsement by the CCM in February. On July 1 the CCM became the first group to be officially registered under the new law, and by the end of August, 12 of the reportedly 35 parties that had requested application forms had been granted provisional registration.

In late 1992 the government released a tentative multiparty electoral schedule, beginning with municipal and local balloting in 1993 and concluding with national elections in 1994–1995. Subsequently, the Civic United Front (CUF), a prominent opposition grouping, and four smaller parties threatened to boycott the polling, saying that the delays favored the CCM and calling instead for the convening of a constitutional conference before any elections were held.

In February 1993, Zanzibari membership in the Organization of the Islamic Conference (OIC) was categorized as "unconstitutional" and "separatist" by a Tanzanian parliamentary commission. (The membership was reportedly withdrawn in August 1993, although uncertainty on the question continued into 2000 [see Membership in OIC article].) The affair highlighted continued debate within the government over the two regions' respective roles, as well as a growing schism between Christians and Muslims, which was further evidenced by the anti-Muslim rhetoric of the increasingly popular Democratic Party leader, Rev. Christopher MTIKILA, and the militant activities of the Council for the Dissemination of the Koran in Tanzania (*Balukta*) (see under Political Parties, below).

In April 1993, at the first balloting since the introduction of multipartyism, the CCM, aided by a CUF boycott, easily won two Zanzibari municipal by-elections. However, fiscal problems, coupled with the Muslim fundamentalist issue, continued to bedevil the ruling party. By late 1994, with less than a year remaining before the next presidential poll, its leadership had fallen into disarray, with former president Nyerere criticizing President Mwinyi as a political weakling and attacking Prime Minister Malecela and CCM Secretary General Horace KOLIMBA as "hooligans" who should resign their positions. The immediate upshot was an extraordinary event: a total ministerial boycott of a cabinet meeting called by the president. Mwinyi responded on December 4 by dissolving the National Assembly, and on December 5 he named a new government headed by former prime minister Cleopa Msuya. Meanwhile, the assembly, two days before the dissolution, had approved a constitutional amendment that created a furor on Zanzibar by specifying that henceforth the island president would no longer become a union vice president unless specifically elected as the president's running mate.

In preparation for the first nationwide multiparty elections, the CCM in July 1995 elected Minister of Science Benjamin William MKAPA as its presidential nominee, President Mwinyi being ineligible for a third term. The balloting of October 29 featured more than 1,300 legislative candidates, with nine opposition parties announcing that they would form a postelectoral coalition if it would give them a parliamentary majority. However, in results that were hotly disputed, Mkapa was credited with winning 61.8 percent of the valid presidential votes, while the CCM garnered 186 of 232 elective assembly seats. Earlier, in even more contentious Zanzibari balloting on October 22, the National Electoral Commission (NEC) had announced that President Amour had been reelected on a 52 percent vote share, with the CCM having been awarded 26 of 50 elective seats in the Zanzibar House of Representatives. Mkapa subsequently named former agriculture minister Frederick Tluway SUMAYE to head a new cabinet, which contained a majority of relatively young newcomers and excluded nearly all former ministers who had been tinged by charges of corruption.

Of 13 opposition parties that contested the 1995 election, only 4 obtained legislative representation. Their disappointing capture of only 24 percent of the seats on a near 40 percent share of the vote was attributed by many to the majority electoral system and by some to widespread electoral fraud, particularly in the Zanzibari balloting, in which the opposition's Seif Hamadi was widely believed to have attracted more than the 48 percent vote share officially credited to him in the presidential poll.

Mkapa's economic and political reform efforts in 1996 drew broad praise. Such advances were overshadowed, however, by the political stalemate in Zanzibar where the CUF continued to boycott the legislature in protest over the CCM's alleged rigging of the 1995 elections. In addition, the government's anticorruption campaign was tarnished by the resignation of several ministers in late 1996 and early 1997 following bribery and abuse of power investigations, which also prompted a cabinet reshuffle in February 1997.

In January 1998 Commonwealth mediators introduced a seven-point plan to ease the tension in Zanzibar. However, both sides rejected the accord. In March the Commonwealth released another proposal that was subsequently reported to have been positively received by the CCM and CUF negotiators. The government continued its crackdown on alleged CUF militants in early 1999, but an agreement was finally signed by the CCM and the CUF providing for the return of the CUF to the National Assembly, the award of two additional assembly seats to the CUF, and the creation of an independent electoral commission to oversee the elections scheduled for October 2000. Each side subsequently charged the other with foot-dragging in implementing some provisions of the accord, and tension remained substantial on the island, exacerbated by the death in October 1999 of former president Nyerere, whose considerable domestic and international prestige and influence had been credited with holding the shaky union together. Attention in early 2000 focused on the attempt by Zanzibari President Amour to have the constitution amended to permit him to run for a third term. After reportedly "tumultuous" debate, the CCM rejected the appeal from Amour, who had been widely criticized on Zanzibar for hard-line tactics, including the arrest of prominent CUF members on treason charges (see CUF under Political Parties, below).

Balloting for the National Assembly and Zanzibar's House of Representatives, as well as for the presidencies of Tanzania and Zanzibar was held on October 29, 2000. However, reruns were required in 16 island constituencies on November 5 because of ballot problems in the initial poll. (The CUF and many other opposition parties boycotted the reruns, arguing that new voting should have been ordered in all island constituencies.) Final results showed President Mkapa easily securing a second five-year term with 71.7 percent of the vote against three rivals. In addition, the CCM maintained its stranglehold on the assembly and a comfortable majority in the House of Representatives. Meanwhile, the CCM's Amani Abeid KARUME, the son of the first president of independent Zanzibar, was declared winner of the Zanzibari presidential poll with 67 percent of the vote. On November 23, President Mkapa reappointed Prime Minister Sumaye to head a significantly reshuffled CCM cabinet.

On October 27, 2005, the vice presidential candidate of the Party for Democracy and Progress (*Chama Cha Demokrasia na Maendelo*—Chadema) died unexpectedly, and consequently, the NEC postponed presidential and legislative balloting on the mainland until December 14. However, balloting for offices in Zanzibar was allowed to go forward as planned on October 30. The Zanzibari elections were marred by electoral flaws and violence, which required a new round of voting in approximately one-third of the districts (see Current issues). Incumbent President Karume was reelected, and the CCM retained its majority in the Zanzibari legislature, although opposition parties decried the balloting and challenged the results.

The CCM candidate, Foreign Minister Jakaya KIKWETE, easily won the December 2005 presidential election in Tanzania with more than 80 percent of the vote, while the CCM increased its majority in the National Assembly. Edward LOWASSA was appointed prime minister on December 29, and a CCM cabinet was approved by the assembly on January 6, 2006. In October Kikwete conducted a major cabinet reshuffle in which ten ministers and eight deputy ministers changed positions.

In 2007 Foreign Minister Dr. Asha-Rose MIGERO was appointed as the UN's first deputy secretary general. She was succeeded as foreign minister by Bernard MEMBE.

On February 7, 2008, Lowassa resigned as prime minister following revelation of corruption charges (see Current issues, below). He was replaced by the minister of state in the prime minister's office Mizengo PINDA, who was confirmed by the assembly on February 8. A new cabinet was approved on February 12. In response to the global economic crisis and in anticipation of legislative and presidential elections in 2010, the CCM government endeavored to enact broad economic reforms in 2009 in an effort to improve the economy (see Current issues, below). In June 2009 the UN announced that it would help conduct the 2010 balloting by providing technical assistance, monitors, and $23 million in support.

Constitution and government. An "interim" document of 1965 was replaced on April 25, 1977, by a "permanent" constitution, although the system of government was essentially unaltered. A number of amendments were adopted prior to the 1985 election; significantly, however, Tanzania remained a one-party state, with controlling influence exercised by the CCM at both national and regional levels. Legislation authorizing multiparty activity was approved in 1992 (see Political background, above).

The president is elected by universal suffrage for no more than two five-year terms. Since 1995 the vice president has also been elected as part of a national president/vice president ticket. (Previously, Tanzania had two vice presidents: the president of Zanzibar [who served as first vice president if the president was from the mainland] and a presidentially appointed prime minister. The December 1994 constitutional amendment ending the automatic designation of the Zanzibar president as one of the two vice presidents left the insular region without mandated representation at the national executive level.) The prime minister is currently appointed by the president subject to confirmation by the National Assembly. Cabinet ministers are also appointed by the president.

The National Assembly, more than four-fifths of whose members are at present directly elected, sits for a five-year term, subject to presidential dissolution (in which case the president himself must stand for reelection). The judicial system on the mainland is headed by a High Court and includes local and district courts. In August 1979 a Tanzanian Court of Appeal was established to assume, inter alia, the functions of the East African Court of Appeal, which had ceased to exist with the collapse of the East African Community in 1977. All judges are appointed by the president.

Tanzania's 26 administrative regions (21 on the mainland, 3 on Zanzibar, and 2 on Pemba) are each headed by a regional commissioner appointed by the central government. Below the regional level there are 114 municipalities, town councils, and, in rural locations, area or district councils.

On October 13, 1979, a new constitution for Zanzibar was promulgated by its Revolutionary Council after having been approved by the CCM. Under the new system, designed to provide for "more democracy" without contravening the union constitution of Tanzania, the president of Zanzibar is directly elected for a five-year term and held to a maximum of two successive terms. There is also a largely elected House of Representatives endowed with the legislative authority previously exercised by the Revolutionary Council. The latter, however, has been retained as a "high executive council" of cabinet status, with members appointed by the president.

In 2000 the Thirteenth Amendment was ratified by a two-thirds majority in the National Assembly. The measure expanded presidential prerogatives to include the appointment of ten members to the National Assembly and permitted election of the president by a plurality instead of a majority of voters. The amendment also increased the percentage of seats reserved for women from 15 percent to 20 percent. In April 2002 the Zanzibari House of Representatives approved constitutional amendments that called for restructuring the national electoral commission to include opposition representation. In 2004 the Revolutionary Council on Zanzibar announced plans for a new flag, national anthem, and identity cards for the island.

In February 2005 the Fourteenth Amendment was ratified by the assembly. The measure had a number of provisions, including a section that allowed the prime minister to act as president in the absence of the president and vice president. It also loosened the rules about electoral campaigning.

In June 2009 the government announced plans to overturn laws that forbade dual citizenship and enact a new measure that would allow Tanzanians living abroad to retain, or regain, citizenship and participate in elections.

Foreign relations. Tanzania belongs to the United Nations and most of its Specialized Agencies, the Commonwealth, and the African Union. In addition, it participated with Kenya and Uganda in the East African Community (EAC) until the organization was dissolved in mid-1977. Under President Nyerere's leadership, Tanzania pursued a policy of international nonalignment and of vigorous opposition to colonialism and racial discrimination, particularly in southern Africa, maintaining no relations with Pretoria and strongly supporting the effort of the Front-Line States to avoid South African trade routes. In addition, declaring South African destabilization efforts in nearby states to be a direct threat to Tanzania, the government in 1987 sent troops to Mozambique to assist Maputo in the fight against Renamo rebels. (The troops were withdrawn in December 1988, in part, reportedly, because of the cost of their maintenance.) Tanzania also gave asylum to political refugees from African countries, and various liberation groups were headquartered in Dar es Salaam.

Relations with Britain were severed from 1965 to 1968 to protest London's Rhodesian policy. Relations with the United States have been strained at times by Tanzanian disagreement with U.S. policies on Africa and, until Washington's rapprochement with Peking, by U.S. uneasiness over Tanzanian acceptance of military and economic aid from China.

Long-standing friction with Uganda escalated into overt military conflict in late 1978 (see article on Uganda). After a six-month campaign that involved the deployment of some 40,000 Tanzanian troops, the forces of Ugandan president Idi Amin were decisively defeated, Amin fleeing to Libya. Subsequently, under an agreement signed with the government of Godfrey Binaisa, approximately 20,000 Tanzanians remained in the country to man security points pending the training of a new Ugandan army. During 1980 Kenya and Sudan were among the regional states expressing concern over the continuing presence in Uganda of the Tanzanian troops, the last of which were finally withdrawn in May–June 1981. (In 2007 Uganda paid Tanzania $67 million to retire debts that remained from the 1978 conflict.)

Relations with Kenya improved measurably upon the conclusion of a November 1983 accord among the two and Uganda on the distribution of EAC assets and liabilities. The border between Tanzania and Kenya, originally closed in 1977 to "punish" Kenya for allegedly dominating Tanzania's economy, was reopened, and the two countries reached agreement on a series of technical cooperation issues. Rapprochement was further enhanced in December, when the three former EAC members exchanged high commissioners in an effort "to facilitate expansion and consolidation in economic matters." (See Foreign relations in article on Kenya for information regarding the recent reactivation of the EAC.)

In September 1995 Prime Minister Msuya appealed to the UN High Commissioner for Refugees (UNHCR) to aid in the repatriation of more than 800,000 Burundian and Rwandan refugees living in border area camps. In January 1996 the Tanzanian Army turned back an estimated 17,000 Rwandan Hutu refugees fleeing violence in Burundi; however, three days later the government reversed itself and reopened its border. In February relations between Tanzania and Burundi were enhanced by an agreement on border security and refugee repatriation; however, in March, as fighting in Burundi spilled over Tanzania's border, Dar es Salaam rejected the appointment of a Burundian ambassador for the second time, asserting that it was "not siding with either" of the combatants in its neighbor's burgeoning civil war.

Conditions deteriorated significantly toward the end of 1996 when large numbers of Hutu refugees crossed Burundi from Zaire (where Tutsis had destroyed Hutu camps and assumed control of the eastern part of the country) into Tanzania. Burundi's president Pierre Buyoya accused Tanzania of supporting Hutu "rebels" and criticized former Tanzanian president Nyerere for spearheading the regional economic sanctions against Burundi. A number of cross-border skirmishes, substantial troop buildup on both sides, and diplomatic posturing were reported throughout 1997, and in February 1998 regional leaders, including President Mkapa, agreed to maintain the sanctions they had first imposed on Burundi in 1996. However, in early 1999 Dar es Salaam lifted its sanctions and announced that it was reestablishing diplomatic relations with Bujumbura. Subsequently, in March, Tanzania ordered the 20,000 Rwandan refugees remaining within its borders to return home, describing security conditions there as safe. However, tension continued into 2000 because of the presence in Tanzania of Rwandan and (especially) Burundian refugees and guerrillas. For example, Tanzanian security forces "arrested" over 160 Burundian Hutu "militiamen" in early 2000. By the end of 2002, the UN estimated that there were 540,000 Burundian refugees in Tanzania. However, in light of the normalization of relations between the two countries, the governments subsequently launched a broad effort to repatriate the refugees. Additional border crossings were opened, and by the end of 2003 there were 324,000 refugees left. Meanwhile, by February 2004 Tanzania had returned all identifiable Rwandan refugees; according to UN estimates, 20,000 remained in Tanzania illegally.

On August 7, 1998, 11 Tanzanians had been killed in Dar es Salaam when alleged militant Islamic fundamentalists set off simultaneous bomb blasts at U.S. embassies in Tanzania and Kenya. (For further details see articles on Kenya and Saudi Arabia, the latter containing a section on Osama bin Laden, whose terrorist network was suspected by U.S. officials of complicity in the bombings.)

The European Union (EU) provided $1.9 million in aid to support the 2001 peace accord between the government and the CUF and $14.82 million to assist Burundian refugees. Collaterally, relations between Tanzania and the United Kingdom have remained strong. The UK agreed in 2003 to provide assistance for Tanzania's refugee repatriation efforts, and in 2005 the UK announced that Tanzania would be the first African country to benefit from an initiative to write off the debt of poorer countries. Later in 2005, however, a diplomatic row occurred between the two countries when Tanzania unilaterally ended a $143.5 million water privatization project funded jointly by Britain and the World Bank. The Tanzanian government charged that the foreign companies involved in the project were not fulfilling their obligations.

In 2006 the United States granted Tanzania $11 million for an anti-corruption campaign and included the country among six other African states to receive funding from a $1.2 billion initiative to suppress malaria. The United States has also recently increased its security assistance to Tanzania for counterterrorism efforts and launched a program to train personnel from the Bank of Tanzania to interdict financing of terrorist groups.

Reports surfaced in 2007 that China had delivered a number of shipments of arms and weapons to Tanzania, provoking criticism from the assembly over the secret nature of the transactions. The revelations coincided with a scandal in which a British arms firm was discovered to have paid $12 million to Tanzanian figures to secure the sale of a radar system to the country. On more positive notes, the UK in 2007 announced that it would provide $530 million over a ten-year period to finance improvements in Tanzania's educational system, and Switzerland granted Tanzania $15.5 million for poverty-reduction programs. In April 2008 Tanzania participated in the first Africa-India summit in New Dehli as part of a broader effort to improve bilateral trade relations with India.

In March 2008 Tanzania commanded the 1,500 AU troops (750 of whom were Tanzanian) who deployed in the Comoros during a sovereignty dispute between the leader of Anjouan Island and the central government (see Comoro Islands entry). Tanzania also pledged to contribute troops to the UN peacekeeping mission in Darfur but strongly condemned the International Criminal Court's issuance of charges of genocide against Sudanese leader Umar Al-Bashir (see Sudan entry). In September Tanzania announced that it would grant citizenship to up to 76,000 Burundian refugees, many of whom had been in the country since 1972. More than 60,000 Burundians were repatriated between 2007 and 2008. The government subsequently announced the closure of most of the camps for the Burundians and threatened forcible repatriation for the remaining 36,000 refugees. In addition, an estimated 89,000 Congolese refugees remained in Tanzania in 2008. In October foreign minister Bernard Membe announced the government intended to seek membership in the Organization of the Islamic Conference (OIC). The initiative was met with criticism from the opposition and Christian groups within Tanzania. No action was taken, although the government of Zanzibar subsequently sought permission to join the OIC on its own.

The government announced in March 2009 that it would increase efforts to reduce illegal fishing off its coastline and in its waters in Lake Victoria. Tanzania also joined a multilateral effort with South Africa, Kenya, and Mozambique to patrol waters for poachers of fisheries in the Indian Ocean.

Current issues. A key factor in President Mkapa's successful reelection bid in late 2000 was the fractured nature of the opposition. International observers were generally satisfied with the conduct of the presidential and legislative balloting on the mainland but strongly criticized the situation on the islands, leading the government to agree to new voting in only 16 of 50 constituencies. The CUF and many of the other opposition parties boycotted the new elections because they wanted new voting throughout the islands. After the balloting, they refused to accept the official results and organized protests. The government banned the demonstrations and proceeded to disperse the protesters. At least 40 people were killed by police on Pemba under highly questionable circumstances. Some detainees were allegedly tortured or ill treated.

After protracted negotiations, on October 10, 2001, the CCM signed an agreement with the CUF to end the political impasse that had followed the January violence. The accord addressed a number of human rights issues and called for establishment of an independent commission of inquiry into the unrest and provision of compensation to those affected. A Zanzibar court subsequently freed two senior opposition party officials after the state dropped murder charges against them.

Politics on Zanzibar were subsequently reported to be increasingly influenced by Islamic activism, in part by supporters of the Union for Awakening and Islamic Forums (*Uamsho*), which organized several antigovernment demonstrations that led to the arrest of some top opposition leaders. There was widespread violence prior to the October 2005 elections; government and opposition groups were accused of attacks. The government reportedly launched a series of raids on the headquarters of opposition parties and arrested a number of opposition leaders. Subsequent rioting left some 14 people dead, and the administration suspended registration of new parties. Meanwhile, in April 2005, CCM offices were bombed on Zanzibar, and a party official was murdered in a separate incident. Police subsequently arrested four activists in connection with the bombing. After the polling in Zanzibar in October, CUF members and supporters rioted to protest the results, and security forces used tear gas and force to disperse the protesters. Opposition groups complained that voters in some districts had been either turned away from polling stations or had their ballots destroyed and that the CCM had sponsored groups of youths (dubbed *Janjaweed* after the Sudanese militias) who had intimidated voters. However, although international observers noted some irregularities, they described the voting as generally free and fair. Polling on the mainland was not marred by violence, according to international monitors. Following the balloting, the CCM and CUF launched talks to prevent further violence in Zanzibar. Tensions between Muslims and non-Muslims reportedly increased in February 2007 following passage of a new law that forbade women from wearing a veil while driving.

In January 2008 the head of Tanzania's central bank, Daudi BALAI, was dismissed by Kikwete because of corruption at the institution. Balai fled the country to avoid prosecution. Flooding in northern Tanzania killed more than 70 miners in March. On February 7, Prime Minister Lowassa and Energy Minister Nazir KARAMAGI resigned after reports linked them to a scandal over illicit payments to an energy company. Nine other ministers were sacked as the president attempted to restore confidence in the government. Mizengo Pinda was appointed to replace Lowassa and a new cabinet formed. On April 20 Andrew CHENGE was forced to resign as minister of infrastructure following charges of corruption involving a $40 million defense sale. Other investigations continued and revealed more than $117 million in fraudulent activity by government and business leaders through the Bank of Tanzania. By the following year, more than $46 million had been recovered and 16 Tanzanians, including a senior treasurer for the CCM Party, had been charged with fraud. In response to continuing government anticorruption efforts, a group of international donors who had withheld aid announced on November 24 that they would release more than $700 million in assistance.

In an effort to reduce the impact of the global economic slowdown and maintain the CCM's popularity ahead of elections in 2010, Kikwete announced a massive stimulus plan in July 2009. The package included tax breaks and support for sectors such as tourism and agriculture. However, unemployment continued to rise, especially in Zanzibar where unemployment in some regions reached approximately 40 percent, compared with the national average of 13 percent.

POLITICAL PARTIES

Constitutional amendments in 1992 allowed the formation of political parties other than the CCM. The first multiparty elections were held in 1995. Nonetheless, the CCM has continued to dominate the legislature and the presidency. In February 2003 opposition parties formed an electoral coalition to oppose the CCM in presidential and legislative balloting in October 2005. The coalition chose Bob Nyanga MAKANI of the Party for Democracy and Progress (*Chama Cha Demokrasia na Maendeleo*—Chadema) as its chair. Besides Chadema, the coalition included the Civic United Front (CUF), the United Democratic Party (UDP), the National Convention for Constitution and Reform–Mageuzi (NCCR-Mageuzi), the Tanzania Democratic Alliance Party (Tadea), the National Reconstruction Alliance (NRA), the Democratic Party (*Chama Cha Demokrasi*—CCD), the National League for Democracy (NLD), the United People's Democratic Party (UPDP), and the Forum for Restoration of Democracy (FORD). The only major opposition parties that did not join the alliance were the Tanzania Labor Party (TLP) and the Justice and Development Party (*Chama cha Haki na Usitawi*—Chausta). The alliance failed to present a unified candidate list for the 2005 legislative balloting and could not unite behind a single candidate in the mainland presidential polling. Some parties supported the CUF candidate, while a group of four parties rallied behind the NCCR-Mageuzi candidate.

Four opposition parties (the CUF, TLP, Chadema, and NCCR-Mageuzi) signed an agreement in May 2007 to support a single candidate in the 2010 elections and field joint electoral lists. In December a similar agreement was concluded among five smaller parties, the CCD, the NLD, the Progressive Party of Tanzania (PPT-*Maendeleo*), Sauti Ya Umma (SAU), and Demokrasia Makini (*Makini*). The grouping adopted the Patriotic Front Parties (PFP) designation.

In June 2009 12 opposition parties in Zanzibar formed an electoral alliance ahead of the 2010 balloting and agreed to support a single candidate in the island's presidential balloting. The parties included: the African Progressive Party of Tanzania (APPT-*Maendeleo*), Chadema, Jahazi Asilia, NCCR-Mageuzi, *Makini*, NLD, NRA, SAU, TLP, Tadea, the Union for Multiparty Democracy (UMD), and the UPDP. The grouping was named the Zanzibar Opposition Alliance.

Government Party:

Revolutionary Party of Tanzania (*Chama Cha Mapinduzi*—CCM). The CCM was formally launched on February 5, 1977, two weeks after a merger was authorized by a joint conference of the Tanganyika African National Union (TANU) and the Afro-Shirazi Party (ASP) of Zanzibar. During the January conference, President Nyerere had asserted that the new organization would be supreme" over the governments of both mainland Tanzania and Zanzibar. Subsequently, a National Executive Committee (NEC) was named by a process of hierarchical (indirect) election, with the NEC, in turn, appointing a smaller Central Committee, headed by President Nyerere.

Founded in 1954, TANU had been instrumental in winning Tanganyika's independence from Britain in 1961. It served after independence as the nation's leading policymaking forum, nominating the president and candidates for election to the National Assembly. Its program, as set forth in the 1967 Arusha Declaration and other pronouncements, called for the development of a democratic, socialist, one-party state.

The ASP, organized in 1956–1957 by Sheikh Abeid Amani Karume, had played a minor role in Zanzibari politics until the coup of 1964. Subsequently, it became the dominant party in Zanzibar and the leading force in the Zanzibar Revolutionary Council. Communist and Cuban models influenced its explicitly socialist program.

During the CCM's national conference in 1982, delegates approved a series of proposals advanced by the NEC to reestablish a separation of powers between party and state, particularly at the regional and local levels. Delegates to an extraordinary national party conference in February 1992 unanimously endorsed the introduction of a multiparty system. At the party's fourth national conference, held in Dodoma on December 17–20, Ali Hassan Mwinyi, who had succeeded Nyerere as state president and party chair in 1985 and 1990, respectively, was reelected chair. In addition, delegates elected (then) Prime Minister Malecela and Dr. Salmin Amour, a Zanzibari, as vice chairs.

During the first half of 1993 acrimonious debate between the party's mainland and island factions over the selection process for the vice presidency and military leadership led to the cancellation of two CCM meetings. Furthermore, the party experienced rifts over how to respond to Christopher MTIKILA, the (then) prominent leader of the CCD (below).

In July 1995 Benjamin William Mkapa, then minister of science, education, and technology, defeated two opponents in intraparty balloting for designation as the CCM presidential nominee, and he was subsequently credited with a 61.8 percent vote share in the October–November general election. Underlining his commitment to a reform-minded agenda, Mkapa named only one senior CCM party official to his technocrat-dominated cabinet. Although observers praised the new president's early initiatives, a split emerged within the party between Mkapa's supporters and old guard members aligned with former first vice president and prime minister Malecela and former party secretary general Horace Kolimba.

At party balloting on June 22, 1996, Mkapa easily captured the party chair and, bringing his reform efforts to bear on the CCM, began to replace old guard members with his supporters. In February 1997 Horace Kolimba publicly denounced the new team of CCM leaders for their lack of "vision" (a charge that was promptly seconded by the CCM's Pius MSEKWA, speaker of the assembly). Furthermore, Kolimba accused the party of abandoning its "socialist" origins. The intraparty flap and public relations imbroglio arising from Kolimba's statements quickly dissipated in March after Kolimba died of a heart attack while defending his position to party officials. At a party congress in 1997, Mkapa was reelected to the party's top post by acclamation; meanwhile, Mkapa's continued efforts to infuse fresh blood into the CCM resulted in the election of a number of new faces to top posts. On the other hand, John Malecela's retention of the vice chair was described by observers as a reminder of the continued influence (albeit waning) of the party's old guard.

In 1998 the CCM experienced further intraparty tension when, after minimal consultation, Mkapa appointed a three-member CCM team to meet with Commonwealth officials in charge of the negotiations to end the Zanzibar stalemate. Several powerful CCM leaders were subsequently reported to be considering forming a breakaway group in reaction to the CCM-CUF agreement of early 1999. However, as the October 2000 national elections approached, the CCM exhibited greater unity and discipline. A March 2000 special congress rejected an intense effort by controversial Zanzibar president Amour to have the constitution amended to permit him to run for a third term. The CCM also subsequently agreed to delay further consideration of proposed constitutional amendments that had been condemned by opposition groups on both the mainland and Zanzibar.

At a June 2000 CCM congress, President Mkapa was selected without opposition to run for a second term in the October poll. Concurrently, Amani Abeid Karume, a longtime member of the Zanzibari cabinet, was chosen as the CCM candidate for president of Zanzibar from among four candidates, including one supported by Amour. Karume was widely viewed as a strong candidate for the post based on his anticorruption image and the fact that he was the son of Abeid Amani Karume, the first president of independent Zanzibar.

Mkapa was reelected party chair at the 2002 CCM party convention. At a party congress in May, Foreign Minister Jakaya Kikwete was chosen as the party's candidate for the mainland presidency. At a party congress in June 2006, Kikwete was elected party chair. In 2007 four senior CCM figures were suspended from the party for alleged misuse of funds, while five regional officials were removed for disobeying party regulations. The disciplinary actions were reported to be part of a larger program by the CCM to improve its national reputation prior to elections in 2010. Kikwete replaced Philip MANGULA with Yusuf MAKAMBA as the CCM secretary general at the party's November 2007 congress. Makamba was a close ally of the president and his choice was reported to be part of a larger effort by Kikwete to consolidate control of the party.

In June two CUF members of Parliament defected to the CCM. In August former APPT-*Maendeleo* presidential candidate Ana SENKORO joined the CCM along with a large number of members of the small party. There was significant internal debate within the CCM over who would succeed Kikwete, with a reported 16 candidates vying to be the party's next presidential candidate. Former Zanzibar chief minister Dr. Mohamed Gharib BILAL was reported to be the front-runner.

Leaders: Jakaya KIKWETE (President of the Republic and Chair of the Party), Benjamin William MKAPA (Former President of the Republic), John MALECELA (Vice Chair, Mainland), Ali Hassan MWINYI (Former President of the Republic), Ali Mohamed SHEIN (Vice President of the Republic), Mizengo PINDA (Prime Minister), Amani Abeid KARUME (President of Zanzibar and Vice Chair, Zanzibar), Samwel SITTA (Speaker of the National Assembly), Salim Ahmed SALIM (Member of the Executive Committee and Former Secretary General of the Organization of African Unity), Yusuf MAKAMBA (Secretary General).

Opposition Parties:

Civic United Front (CUF). Also referenced as the People's Party (*Chama Cha Wananchi*—CCW), the CUF was founded in late 1991 by former NCCR-Mageuzi leader James MAPALALA, a lawyer who had also been instrumental in the February 1990 establishment of the Civil and Legal Rights Movement. Mapalala was reportedly arrested following the creation of the CUF, which was then deemed to be an illegal formation.

As in the case of other opposition groups, the CUF has been wracked by internal dissent; party chair Mapalala went so far in 1994 as to institute court action against his deputy, Seif Sharif Hamad, and Secretary General Shaaban MLOO. Although Hamad was officially declared runner-up to Salmin Amour in Zanzibar's 1995 presidential race, many observers felt he was the actual victor. Labeling the Amour government "illegal," the CUF refused to assume its Zanzibar parliamentary seats and accused the government of falsely arresting its members. Thereafter, despite a ban on its activities, CUF-directed unrest spread, with observers attributing incidents of arson and harassment to the group.

The split between the CUF's mainland and island wings widened dramatically in early 1997 when the former passed a resolution recognizing Amour's Zanzibar government. Intraparty dissension continued to plague the CUF throughout the year, and, in December, 14 members were arrested for their alleged roles in a coup plot in Zanzibar. In early 1998 further arrests of CUF dissidents were reported.

In May 1998 Mapalala broke with the CUF, announcing that he had formed a new group, the Justice and Development Party (below). Meanwhile, at Commonwealth-brokered negotiations with the Amour administration, CUF islanders agreed to participate in legislative proceedings, abandoning the position that Amour had to be removed prior to the representatives being seated.

The trial of the 18 CUF members (including four members of the House of Representatives) arrested in 1997–1998 formally opened in February 1999, the charge against them having been upgraded to treason, which carried a mandatory death sentence upon conviction. Proceedings were subsequently postponed until January 2000, when another short session resulted in further delay until at least August. Meanwhile, domestic and international human rights groups criticized the prolonged imprisonment of the defendants, whom Amnesty International described as "prisoners of conscience," and the apparent political nature of the charges.

At a general congress in early June 2000, Hamad was once again selected as the CUF candidate for president of Zanzibar in the balloting scheduled for October. The CUF candidate for president of Tanzania, Ibrahim Lipumba, finished second in the 2000 poll with 16.3 percent of the vote, while Hamad was credited with 33 percent of the vote in the controversial balloting for president of Zanzibar (see Current issues, above). Meanwhile, all of the 16 seats the CUF secured in the 2000 balloting for the Zanzibar House of Representatives came from CUF strongholds on Pemba. In the 2005 elections, Hamad was again the CUF's candidate for the presidency of Zanzibar. Hamad was defeated in controversial balloting in which he received 46.07 percent of the vote. (Only 32,000 votes separated Hamad from the winning candidate.)

In the legislative balloting in Zanzibar, the CUF increased its seats in the house to 19. Lipumba was also the CUF candidate for president of Tanzania in 2005, but he was again defeated, securing only 11.68 percent of the vote. The CUF remained the largest opposition party with 30 seats in the Tanzanian assembly.

In 2007 the CUF led efforts to create an electoral coalition of opposition parties ahead of the 2010 elections. The CUF undertook a boycott of the Zanzibar assembly in April 2008 in an effort to force the ruling CCM to create a unity government on the islands. After refusing to accept the results of the 2005 presidential balloting on Zanzibar, the CUF finally agreed in May 2008 to accept Amani Abeid Karume of the CCM as the legitimate leader of Zanzibar. Meanwhile, negotiations between the CUF and the CCM on a power-sharing arrangement in Zanzibar broke down during the summer.

The party's three top leaders, including Hamad, Lipumba, and Machano Khamis ALI, were reelected to their posts at a CUF congress in February 2009. Former CUF member of parliament and CUF deputy secretary general Wilfred LWAKATERE defected to Chadema in June, along with several hundred of his supporters after he lost his leadership position.

Leaders: Seif Sharif HAMAD (1995, 2000, and 2005 candidate for President of Zanzibar, Secretary General), Ibrahim LIPUMBA (1995, 2000, and 2005 candidate for President of Tanzania and Chair of the Party), Machano Khamis ALI (Vice Chair).

Party for Democracy and Progress (*Chama Cha Demokrasia na Maendeleo*—Chadema). Chadema was launched in 1993 by former finance minister Edwin I. M. Mtei. It was awarded three elected assembly seats in 1995.

In 1997 Chadema stunned observers when it forwarded the controversial Rev. Christopher Mtikila as a candidate at a legislative by-election contest. (Described by *Africa Confidential* as a "fiery xenophobic evangelist," Mtikila, theretofore leader of the CCD, below, had been a staunch critic of the mainland's union with Zanzibar.)

Chadema supported the CUF candidate in the 2000 presidential poll; in concurrent legislative balloting the party improved its representation to four of the elected seats. The Chadema vice presidential candidate in the 2005 mainland elections died on October 27, 2005, causing a postponement of the balloting until December 14. The party's presidential candidate, Freeman Mbowe, placed third with 5.9 percent of the vote. Chadema secured five of the elected seats in the legislative polls. Chadema refused to participate in the CUF-led parliamentary boycott in Zanzibar, but it joined the CUF in an electoral coalition ahead of the 2010 balloting.

In 2009 a number of CUF members defected to Chadema and were rewarded with leadership posts within the party. Deputy secretary general of Chadema Zitto Kabwe launched a campaign to take the party's top leadership post away from Mbowe in party elections scheduled for the fall. Chadema was instrumental in the formation of the Zanzibar Opposition Alliance in preparation for the 2010 elections.

Leaders: Freeman MBOWE (2005 presidential candidate and Chair), Edwin I. M. MTEI (2000 presidential candidate), Willbroad SLAA (Secretary General).

Tanzania Labor Party (TLP). This small party's profile grew significantly in 1999 when leading opposition figure Augustine Mrema and over 1,000 of his followers joined after leaving the NCCR-Mageuzi. Mrema won 7 percent of the vote in the 2000 presidential poll, while the TLP secured three of the elected seats in concurrent assembly elections. In mid-2001 the TLP was reportedly riven by factions devoted to Mrema and party founder Leo LWEKAMWA. The TLP opposed the opposition coalition formed for the October 2005 election and decided to contest the balloting independently. Its candidate, Mrema, placed fourth with less than 1 percent of the vote, and the TLP secured one seat in the assembly. In 2007 the TLP agreed to participate in the CUF-led electoral coalition. In October a court stripped TLP parliamentary deputy Phares KABUYE of his seat because he had defamed his rival in 2005 balloting. In 2008 many TLP members reportedly defected to other parties. The TLP joined the Zanzibar Opposition Alliance ahead of balloting in 2010.

Leaders: Augustine MREMA (2000 and 2005 presidential candidate and Chair), Rajabu TAO.

United Democratic Party (UDP). The UDP's John Cheyo ran fourth in the 1995 presidential race, with a 3.94 percent vote share; in the assembly balloting the party ran fifth, winning three elective seats. In 1997 the UDP added a fifth seat when Cheyo scored an upset victory in a by-election contest expected to be won by a NCCR-Mageuzi candidate. Cheyo secured 4.2 percent of the vote in the 2000 presidential poll. The UDP was a member of the opposition electoral coalition in the 2005 balloting and supported the CUF candidate in the presidential election. The party secured one seat in the assembly. In 2007 Cheyo emerged as one of the most vocal critics of government corruption. In June 2009 Cheyo was temporarily ejected from Parliament for his conduct during a debate on the government's response to pollution.

Leaders: John CHEYO (1995 and 2000 presidential candidate and Chair), Teddy Kassela BANTU (Secretary General).

National Convention for Constitution and Reform–Mageuzi (NCCR-Mageuzi). The NCCR-Mageuzi was formed in the first half of 1991 as an outgrowth of the Steering Committee for a Transition Towards a Multiparty System, a broad-based organization comprising leading business owners and lawyers as well as political dissidents and student activists. Its initial chair, Abdallah Said FUNDIKIRA, and vice chair, James K. Mapalala, subsequently formed splinter organizations (below), although their successors vowed to keep the committee at the forefront of the "multiparty debate" and to push for its legalization. The party was again split in 1994 when Secretary General Prince Mahinja BAGENDA and several of his supporters withdrew to form the **National Convention for Constitution and Reform–*Asili*** (the Swahili word for "original").

In April 1995 Augustine Lyatonga MREMA, who had been dismissed as minister of labor and youth development in February for "indiscipline" and who withdrew from the CCM a month later, was selected as the NCCR-Mageuzi's standard-bearer for the presidential election in October. Mrema was credited with only 27.8 percent of the vote, while his party captured only 16 of 232 elective assembly seats.

Asserting that the current constitution unfairly hampered the opposition's electoral ambitions, the NCCR-Mageuzi announced in early 1997 that its top priority for the year would be to pressure the government into organizing a constitutional conference. However, in May the party's stated agenda was overshadowed when Mabere MARANDO, the NCCR-Mageuzi's secretary general, and Masumbuko LAMWAI, a NCCR-Mageuzi parliamentarian and former CCM member, attempted to oust Mrema, who had accused Marando of acting in complicity with the CCM. During the subsequent legal and political infighting, the Central Committee reportedly aligned behind Marando and his supporters and the National Executive Committee with Mrema. The reportedly irreconcilable nature of the split was underscored by the unwillingness of the two factions (styled the NCCR-Mrema and NCCR-Marando) to cooperate on by-election campaigns, thus, according to observers, costing the group winnable legislative seats. Furthermore, in October both factions sent representatives to an opposition summit.

After sustained legal and political infighting between the two camps, in April 1999 Mrema announced that he was leaving the NCCR-Mageuzi to join the TLP (see above). Lamwai subsequently rejoined the CCM. The NCCR-Mageuzi won only one elected seat in the 2000 legislative poll, while its proposed presidential candidate, Edith LUSINA, was precluded from running for failure to secure sufficient advance signatures of support.

In the 2005 presidential election, four parties, including the FORD, NRA, UMD, and the UPDP (see below), agreed to support the NCCR-Mageuzi candidate, Sengondo Mvungi. The NCCR-Mageuzi failed to gain any seats in the assembly. In 2007 the NCCR-Mageuzi became part of the CUF-led opposition electoral coalition. In September 2008 Mvungi was injured when violence erupted at a NCCR-Mageuzi rally. The NCCR-Mageuzi blamed the incident on pro-CCM youths. The NCCR-Mageuzi led the opposition to the government initiative to join the OIC in 2008–2009 (see Foreign relations, above).

Leaders: James MBATIA (Chair), Sengondo MVUNGI (2005 presidential candidate), Hussein Mwaiseje POLISYA (Secretary General).

Other Parties Competing in the 2005 Election:

Tanzania Democratic Alliance Party (Tadea). The previously London-based Tadea was founded by Oscar Salathiel KAMBONA, a former TANU secretary general and Nyerere cabinet member who went into voluntary exile in 1967 after government authorities alleged he had been involved in a coup plot. Kambona was also one of the founders of the Tanzania Democratic Front (TDF), formed in London by a number of exile opposition groups to promote the introduction of a multiparty system. Tadea was registered in Tanzania in 1993. In 1996 Tadea was buffeted by allegations that its officials had misused publicly funded campaign finances.

The party joined the opposition alliance to contest the 2005 elections and supported the CUF mainland presidential candidate.

Leaders: John D. LIFE-CHIPAKA (Chair), Juma Ali KHATIB (Secretary General).

Union for Multiparty Democracy (UMD). The UMD was organized in late 1991 by Abdallah Said Fundikira, a well-known Tanzanian businessman, and others who had previously been involved in the NCCR. They proposed that a national conference be held to draft a new Tanzanian constitution that would permit multiparty activity. In addition, the UMD suggested that the union between the mainland and the islands of Zanzibar and Pemba be reevaluated. Following the formation of the UMD, Fundikira was arrested and released on bail after being charged with establishing an illegal organization. The UMD was nonetheless registered in 1993. The UMD supported the NCCR-Mageuzi candidate in the 2005 presidential elections and failed to gain any seats in the assembly.

Leaders: Chief Abdallah Said FUNDIKIRA (President of the Party and 1995 candidate for President of the Republic), Stephen M. KIBUGA (Vice President), Hussein Hassan YAHAYA (Secretary General).

National Reconstruction Alliance (NRA). Former industries and trade minister Kigoma Ali MALIMA resigned from the CCM on July 16 to become the NRA's 1995 presidential candidate; however, he died unexpectedly on August 5. Following the elections, the party reportedly faced an audit of its campaign financing practices amid allegations that it had misused public funds.

The NRA joined the electoral coalition that supported the NCCR-Mageuzi candidate in the 2005 elections. After being denied a permit for a demonstration in August 2008 in Zanzibar, the NRA filed a lawsuit against security forces.

Leaders: Rashid MTUTA (Chair), Maoud RATUU (Secretary General).

Forum for Restoration of Democracy (FORD). FORD was formed in April 2001 by CUF dissidents, led by Ramadhani MZEE, to oppose the CUF's bellicose stance toward the CCM. FORD supported the NCCR-Mageuzi candidate in the 2005 presidential balloting.

Leaders: Ramadhani MZEE (Chair), Natanga NYAGAWA (Secretary General).

Justice and Development Party (*Chama cha Haki na Usitawi*—Chausta). Chausta was launched in Zanzibar in May 1998 by former CUF leader James Mapalala. According to Mapalala, the new party was founded on the principle of development of the "individual." The party was officially recognized in late 2001. In August 2008 CCM youth disrupted a Chausta rally in Zanzibar.

Leaders: James MAPALALA (Chair), Joseph MKOMAGU (Secretary General).

Patriotic Front Parties (PFP). Formed in December 2007, the PFP consisted of five minor opposition parties that had competed unsuccessfully in the 2005 balloting. They coalesced for upcoming legislative and presidential elections. Most members of the PFP also joined the Zanzibar Opposition Alliance.

Leaders: Natanga NYAGAWA, Emanuel MAKAIDI.

Democratic Party (*Chama Cha Demokrasi*—CCD). The CCD was formed in late 1991 in anticipation of the introduction of a multiparty system. The CCD is sometimes referred to as the DP. Soon thereafter, the party was thrust into the national limelight by the August 1992 conviction of its leader, Christopher Mtikila, on charges of illegal assembly. The High Court subsequently dismissed the charges against Mtikila, whose nationalistic rhetoric had made him increasingly popular. However, in January 1993, Mtikila was arrested on charges of having fomented sedition and rioting by a speech in which he had accused the government of having "sold [Tanzania] to Arabs and Gabacholics [Asians]," urged Indo-Pakistanis, Arabs, Somalians, and Zanzibaris to emigrate, and warned that blood would flow if the alleged favoritism to foreigners continued. He was rearrested a number of times thereafter on a variety of charges, including the leadership of illegal demonstrations.

In 1997 Mtikila ran as a Chadema candidate in a legislative by-election, thus casting uncertainty on the future of the CCD, which had been unable to secure official recognition because of its unwillingness to accept Zanzibar as a legitimate part of the country. The CCD's candidate in the 2005 presidential election was Mtikila, who placed sixth in the balloting.

In 2008 the CCD joined with four other opposition parties in the Patriotic Front Parties coalition. Mtikila was again expected to be the party's presidential candidate in 2010.

Leaders: Christopher MTIKILA (2005 presidential candidate and Chair), Natanga NYAGAWA (Secretary General).

Other members of the PFP included the **African Progressive Party of Tanzania** (APPT-*Maendeleo*), formed in 2003 and led by Peter Kuga MZIRAY (Chair); **Jahazi Asilia**, which received less than 1 percent of the vote in the 2005 balloting and is led by Abuu Juma AMOUR (Chair); and the **Demokrasia Makini** (*Makini*), formed in 2001 and led by Godfrey HICHEKA and Georgia MTIKILA; and the **Sauti Ya Umma** (SAU), formed in 2005 and led by Paulo KYARA (2005 presidential candidate and Chair). These parties all joined the Zanzibar Opposition Alliance in June 2009.

Other Parties and Groups:

Zanzibar Organization. An offshoot of the former Zanzibar Nationalist Party, a predominantly Arab group that was influential prior to the 1964 union, the Zanzibar Organization reportedly supports full independence for Zanzibar, having recently been active within the growing Islamic fundamentalist movement on the island. Members of its leadership reportedly reside in several Gulf states. The Zanzibar Organization was reported to be establishing a radio station in 2008. The group was a staunch advocate for Zanzibari membership in the OIC (see Foreign relations, above).

Leader: Ali MOSHEN.

Other parties that were registered prior to the 2005 elections but did not participate in the balloting include the **National Democratic Union** (*Nduta*), the **Tanzania Organization for Democracy and Development** (*Topodd*), **Solidarity of United Party** (*Supa*), the **Party for Liberation of Poor People** (*Chudewama*), and the **National Democratic Party for Rehabilitation** (NDPR-*Marejesho*). The **Tanzanian People's Congress** (TPC) was registered in November 2004, but its status was revoked on May 7, 2005, after the National Electoral Commission ruled that the grouping had failed to complete required paperwork.

Banned Grouping:

Council for the Dissemination of the Koran in Tanzania (*Balukta*). *Balukta* is a militant Islamic group that was proscribed by the government in early 1993 amid rumors that it was considering reorganization as a political party. In April approximately 40 members, including leaders Yahya Hussein and Kassim bin Jumma, were arrested on charges stemming from their involvement in a campaign to forcibly close butcher shops selling pork in Muslim districts. The action was depicted by the government as part of a larger destabilization campaign, which included attacks on alcohol distributors and the recruitment of approximately 500 youths for the group's military wing, the Islamic Army, in preparation for a jihad (Holy War). In June 1993 charges against many of the *Balukta* members, including Sheikh Hussein, were dropped. Financial and military support for *Balukta* reportedly originates in Iran and is funneled through the Islamic Party of Kenya. Several figures identified with *Balukta* were active in legislative efforts to enhance the powers of Islamic courts in Zanzibar in 2008–2009.

Leaders: Sheikh Yahya HUSSEIN, Sheikh Kassim bin JUMMA.

LEGISLATURE

The Tanzania **National Assembly** (*Bunge*), also referenced as the Union Parliament, has a five-year mandate, barring dissolution. The current assembly includes 232 members directly elected in single-member constituencies (182 on the mainland and 50 on the islands). The constitution requires that women hold 20 percent of the assembly seats, an increase of 5 percent with the elections in 2000. Following every general election, parties in the assembly must nominate (according to the seats they hold) a number of women to fill any remaining seats of the 20 percent allotted them. The Zanzibar House of Representatives elects 5 of its members to the assembly, and the Tanzanian attorney general is entitled to a legislative seat. Another revision made in 2000 allows the president to appoint 10 members. At the most recent balloting of December 14, 2005, the Revolutionary Party of Tanzania (CCM) secured 206 of the directly elected seats; the Civic United Front (CUF), 19; the Party for Democracy and Progress (Chadema), 5; the United Democratic Party (UDP), 1; and the Tanzania Labor Party (TLP), 1. Following the election, the CCM was authorized to nominate an additional 58 women legislators; the CUF, 11; and Chadema, 6.

Speaker: Samwel SITTA.

The Zanzibar **House of Representatives** is a 75-member body encompassing 50 elected members, 5 regional commissioners, 10 presidential nominees, and 10 members representing women and selected organizations. At the balloting of October 30, 2005, the Revolutionary Party of Tanzania won 30 of the elected seats, and the Civic United Front won 19. (One election had to be rerun.)

Speaker: Pandu Amir KIFICHO.

CABINET

[as of September 1, 2009]

President	Jakaya Kikwete
Vice President	Ali Mohamed Shein
President of Zanzibar	Amani Abeid Karume
Prime Minister	Mizengo Pinda
Ministers of State in the President's Office	
Good Governance	Sofia Simba [f]
Public Service Management	Hawa Abdulrahman Ghasia [f]
Ministers of State in the Vice President's Office	
Environment	Batilda Burian [f]
Union Affairs	Mohammed Seif Khatibu
Ministers of State in the Prime Minister's Office	
Parliamentary Affairs	Philip Sang'ka Marmo
Regional Administration and Local Government	Celina Ompeshi Kombani [f]
Ministers	
Agriculture, Food Security, and Cooperatives	Stephen Masatu Wassira
Attorney General	Johnson Mwanyika
Community Development, Women's Affairs, and Children	Margaret Sitta [f]
Defense and National Service	Hussein Mwinyi
East African Cooperation	Diodorus Kamala
Education and Vocational Training	Jumanne Maghembe
Energy and Mineral Resources	William Ngeleja
Finance and Economic Affairs	Mustapha Mkullo
Foreign Affairs and International Cooperation	Bernard Membe
Health and Welfare Development	David Mwakyusa
Home Affairs	Lawrence Masha
Industries and Trade	Mary Nago [f]
Information, Culture, and Sport	George Mkuchika
Infrastructure Development	Shukuru Kawambwa
Justice and Constitutional Affairs	Mathias Chikawe
Labor, Youth Development, and Sports	Juma Kapuya
Lands, Housing, and Human Settlement	John Chiligati
Livestock Development	John Magufuli
Natural Resources and Tourism	Shamsa Mwangunga [f]
Public Safety and Security	Lawrence Masha
Science, Technology, and Higher Education	Peter Msola
Water and Irrigation	Mark Mwandosya

[f] = female

COMMUNICATIONS

Press. The Newspaper Ordinance of 1968 empowered the president to ban any newspaper if he considered such action to be in the "national interest," while the Newspaper Act of 1976 declared that government approval was required for the creation of any new publications. Additionally, the Zanzibar House of Representatives in September 1988 approved the imprisonment of authors of articles deemed critical of the government. Although press restrictions were eased somewhat as the country implemented its multiparty system, four newspapers, according to 1996 reports, had been temporarily suspended by the government since 1993, with a number of others having been "warned." In 2006 Reporters Without Borders declared that Tanzania had the freest press in East Africa. In 2008, the group ranked Tanzania 70, along with Benin and Malawi, out of 173 countries in freedom of the press. The following papers are published in Dar es Salaam: *Uhuru* (100,000), CCM daily, published Sunday as *Mzalendo* (116,000), in Swahili; *Mfanyakazi* (70,000 Wednesday, 120,000 Saturday), in Swahili; *Daily News* (50,000), formerly the *East African Standard,* government-owned daily, in English; *The Guardian,* independent, in English.

News agencies. The principal domestic facility has been the government-operated Tanzanian News Agency (*Shihata*), established in 1976. However, according to reports in April 2000, the National Assembly had voted to abolish it and transfer its responsibilities to the government's information department (*Maelezo*). There is also a privately owned Press Service of Tanzania.

Broadcasting and computing. The two government-owned radio stations are Radio Tanzania, which broadcasts in Swahili and English, and Radio Tanzania Zanzibar, which broadcasts in Swahili. The two stations operate transmitters on approximately 20 different frequencies. In November 1993 the archdiocese of Dar es Salaam launched Radio Tumaini (Hope) "to educate society on several social problems"; the privately owned Radio One also broadcasts from Dar es Salaam. There is a government-run, noncommercial television station on Zanzibar and a government-run and an independent station on the mainland. As of 2008 there were 12.2 Internet users per 1,000 inhabitants.

INTERGOVERNMENTAL REPRESENTATION

Ambassador to the U.S.: Ombeni Yohana SEFUE.

U.S. Ambassador to Tanzania: Alfonso E. LENHARDT.

Permanent Representative to the UN: A. Augustine MAHIGA.

IGO Memberships (Non-UN): AfDB, AU, BADEA, COMESA, CWTH, EAC, EADB, Interpol, IOM, IOR-ARC, NAM, SADC, WCO, WTO.

THAILAND

Kingdom of Thailand
Prathet Thai

Note: Considerable variation occurs in the English transliteration of Thai names. Where possible, Thai sources have been relied on, but these also present variations.

Political Status: Independent monarchy functioning under a constitution approved by popular referendum on August 19, 2007, validated by the Constitutional Drafting Assembly on August 21, and promulgated on August 24.

Area: 198,455 sq. mi. (514,000 sq. km.).

Population: 60,606,947 (2000C), excluding adjustment for underenumeration; 63,248,000 (2008E).

Major Urban Center (2008E): BANGKOK (metropolitan area, 10,100,964).

Official Language: Thai.

Monetary Unit: Baht (official rate December 1, 2009: 33.21 baht = $1US).

Sovereign: King BHUMIBOL Adulyadej (King RAMA IX); ascended the throne June 9, 1946; crowned May 5, 1950.

Heir Apparent: Crown Prince Maha VAJIRALONGKORN.

Prime Minister: ABHISIT Vejjajiva (Democrat Party), elected by the House of Representatives December 15, 2008, and endorsed by the king on December 17, replacing Acting Prime Minister CHAOVARAT Chanweerakul (People Power Party), who had assumed office on December 2 upon the disqualification by the Constitutional Court of SOMCHAI Wongsawat (People Power Party).

THE COUNTRY

The Kingdom of Thailand (known historically as Siam) is located in the heart of mainland Southeast Asia. Its immediate neighbors are Myanmar (Burma) in the west, Laos in the north and northeast, Cambodia in the southeast, and Malaysia in the deep south. Thailand is a tropical country of varied mountainous and lowland terrain. About 75 percent of its population is Thai; another 14 percent are ethnic Chinese, mostly urban residents prominent in commerce, banking, and manufacturing. Other minorities are of Malaysian, Indian, Khmer, and Vietnamese descent. Theravada Buddhism is professed by about 95 percent of the population, but religious freedom prevails and a number of other religions claim adherents. Women constitute approximately 51 percent of the labor force, primarily in agriculture; female participation in government, while increasing somewhat in recent years, remains low.

Like most countries in Southeast Asia, Thailand is predominantly rural, with nearly 50 percent of its people still engaged in agriculture. Food, especially rice, and other agricultural products traditionally accounted for the bulk of export earnings, but the growth of industrial output since the mid-1980s has raised information technology items and other manufactured goods—from garments and electrical appliances to vehicles—into the lead. Agriculture now accounts for about 11 percent of GDP, compared to 44 percent for industry and 45 percent for services. The country's mineral resources include cassiterite (tin ore), tungsten, antimony, coal, iron, lead, manganese, molybdenum, and gemstones.

Despite extreme inequality of wealth, in 1986–1995 Thailand was one of the world's most rapidly expanding economies, with average GDP growth approaching 10 percent, but in 1996 the rate of expansion dropped to 6.4 percent and export growth (goods and services) plummeted to 2.4 percent, down from 14.8 percent the previous year. At the same time, a real estate bubble burst. The boom in property values and construction had been financed in large part by short-term foreign debt, and when capital flight and currency speculation began driving the value of the baht down in 1997, more than half of the country's financial institutions faced insolvency. In addition, the central bank's initial decision to defend the baht soon cost the country the majority of its foreign-exchange reserves. The crisis not only left the country dependent on a $17.2 billion rescue plan offered by the International Monetary Fund (IMF) but also precipitated an economic downturn—widely termed the Asian Financial Crisis—that cascaded throughout Southeast and East Asia.

During 1998 the government implemented an IMF-supported recovery program that included increased taxes, budget cuts, and efforts to hold down inflation and the trade deficit. It also drafted legislation to deal with dozens of insolvent financial institutions, to transform state enterprises into limited liability companies with private shareholders, and to permit greater foreign ownership of Thai companies. Although the economy registered a 10.5 percent downturn for the year, by early 1999 the situation had stabilized. In March, with IMF backing, the government reversed course on its economic priorities, passing a stimulus package that included a temporary tax cut and an increase in the projected budget deficit. For the year as a whole, growth reached 4.4 percent—considerably higher than expected. Collaterally, foreign reserves recovered, the baht steadied, and inflation declined, although the government was left with a high debt interest burden. GDP growth for 2000 was a creditable 4.8 percent, but the World Bank termed the Thai recovery "fragile" in a September report. Growth for 2001 dropped to 2.2 percent, but subsequently surged to 5.3 percent in 2002, 6.9 percent in 2003, and 6.1 percent in 2004.

The Indian Ocean tsunami of December 26, 2004, left some 8,000 people dead or missing in Thailand—at least one-third of them foreigners (from 38 countries), most of whom were vacationing at seaside resorts. The disaster, which caused an estimated $800 million in damage to Thai property, combined with drought, a weaker electronics market, and political unrest in the southern provinces to produce a slowdown in 2005, when growth was estimated at 4.5 percent.

Despite economic policy uncertainty following a military takeover in 2006 and turbulence around the 2007 national election, Thailand's GDP grew by 5.0 percent in 2006 and 4.8 percent in 2007. Despite a trade surplus equivalent to 6.1 percent of GDP in 2007, declining public debt, and low unemployment, the GDP grew by only 3 percent in 2008 and, depressed by the global downturn, was expected to shrink by 2 percent for 2009. The Asian Development Bank forecast a modest recovery in 2010. The proportion of the Thai population living in poverty declined marginally from 11.2 percent in 2004 to 9.6 percent in 2006 but is expected to rise again.

GOVERNMENT AND POLITICS

Political background. Historical records indicate that the Thai people migrated to present-day Thailand from China's Yunnan Province about a thousand years ago. By the 14th century the seat of authority was established in Ayutthaya, a few miles from Bangkok. Toward the end of the 18th century, Burmese armies conquered the kingdom but were eventually driven out by Rama I, who founded the present ruling dynasty and moved the capital to Bangkok in 1782. Upon the conquest of Burma by the British in 1826, Rama III began the process of accommodating European colonial powers by negotiating a treaty of amity and commerce with Britain. Subsequent monarchs, Rama IV and V, demonstrated great skill, by a combination of diplomacy and governmental modernization, in avoiding colonization by European powers in the 19th and early 20th century, the only Southeast Asian country to do so.

Thailand was ruled as an absolute monarchy until 1932, when a group of military and civilian officials led by Col. (later Field Mar.) Luang PIBULSONGGRAM (PIBUL Songgram) and PRIDI Phanomyong seized power in the first of what was to be a long series of military coups. The Pibulsonggram dictatorship sided with the Japanese in World War II, but the anti-Japanese *Seri Thai* (Free Thai) movement, led by Pridi and SENI Pramoj, paved the way for reconciliation with the Allied powers at the war's end. Pridi dominated the first postwar government but was discredited and fled to China in 1947, after Pibulsonggram had again seized power. Pibulsonggram was overthrown a decade later by Field Marshal SARIT Thanarat, who appointed a constituent assembly in 1959 but continued to rule by martial law until his death in December 1963. Sarit's successor, Field Marshal THANOM Kittikachorn, likewise began his regime in authoritarian style, stressing

economic over political development and working closely with Gen. PRAPAS Charusathira, the army commander and national strongman.

Following promptings from the throne, the military regime agreed in June 1968 to promulgate a new constitution restoring limited parliamentary government. An officially sponsored political party, the United Thai People's Party (UTPP), was organized to contest a lower house election in February 1969. The opposition Democrat Party (DP), led by Seni Pramoj, won all seats in the major urban centers of Bangkok and Chon Buri, but the government, through the UTPP, mustered sufficient strength elsewhere to retain control. Subsequently the Thanom government, blaming parliamentary inefficiency, decided in November 1971 to dissolve the legislature, suspend the constitution, and ban all political parties except the government-sponsored Revolutionary Party.

However, in October 1973, as a result of widespread student demonstrations and disapproval of the king, the Thanom government fell, and the rector of Thammasat University, SANYA Dharmasakti (Thammasak), was appointed prime minister. Following the adoption of a new constitution in October 1974 and a legislative election in January 1975, DP leader Seni Pramoj formed a new government, but this lasted only into March, when it was defeated on a confidence vote. Shortly thereafter, the retiring prime minister's younger brother, KUKRIT Pramoj, succeeded in organizing a coalition government based primarily on the Thai Nation (*Chart Thai*) and Social Action (SAP) parties.

When Kukrit lost his legislative seat in an election in April 1976, Seni was reinstated as prime minister, but was ousted in October by a military coup headed by Adm. SA-NGAD Chaloryu, who was designated chair of a newly established Administrative Reform Council. Later in October King BHUMIBOL approved the formation of a military-dominated government headed by a civilian former Supreme Court justice, THANIN Kraivichien. But a year later the Thanin government was ousted by the military, which established a 23-member Revolutionary Council (subsequently the National Policy Council) virtually identical in composition to the former Administrative Reform Council. In November the council designated Gen. KRIANGSAK Chamanan, the commander of the armed forces, as prime minister. Prodded by the king and civilian elite, Kriangsak promulgated another constitution.

A legislative election held in April 1979 under the new constitution saw Kukrit's SAP secure an overwhelming plurality of the votes cast. However, Kriangsak's control of the appointive upper house permitted him to remain in office. He formed a new government in May and another in February 1980 to address an economic crisis, but to avoid a near-certain legislative vote of no confidence he resigned at the end of the month. Gen. PREM Tinsulanond was designated as his successor. A year later, in April 1981, a coup by a group of middle-ranked army officers dubbed the "Young Turks" was narrowly averted by the loyalty of senior officers and the timely intervention of the monarch.

No clear parliamentary majority emerged in the election of April 1983, and General Prem was induced to return as nonpartisan head of a four-party coalition government. In September 1985, while the prime minister and the armed forces commander, Gen. ARTHIT Kamlang-Ek, were abroad, a number of army and air force officers under the alleged leadership of Col. MANOON Roopkachorn, a former Young Turk, launched another attempted coup. Eight days later, former prime minister Kriangsak was arrested for complicity in the revolt, as were a number of senior officers.

Cleavages within the coalition's SAP weakened the government and forced General Prem to call a premature election in July 1986 in which the Democrats replaced the SAP as the dominant legislative grouping. In August a new four-party government was installed under Prem's leadership.

In April 1988, facing a nonconfidence vote, Prime Minister Prem dissolved the assembly, but no party secured an overall majority in the July election. In August Maj. Gen. CHATCHAI Choonhavan, leader of *Chart Thai,* which had won a legislative plurality, was named to head a six-party coalition administration that also included the DP, the SAP, the Citizens' Party (*Rassadorn*), the United Democratic Party, and the Mass Party (*Muan Chon*).

In August 1990, responding to mounting intragovernmental dissent and charges of corruption, Prime Minister Chatchai reshuffled his cabinet, but in early December the DP, SAP, and *Muan Chon* parties withdrew and were replaced by two groups formerly in opposition, the Solidarity (*Ekkaparb*) and Thai Citizens (*Prachakorn Thai*) parties. The realignment failed to prevent a generally accepted, if not universally applauded, coup on February 23, 1991, that installed a military National Peacekeeping Council (NPC) in power. On March 3 the NPC called upon former diplomat ANAND Panyarachun to form an interim government and 12 days later replaced the bicameral National Assembly with a wholly nominated unicameral body charged with drafting yet another constitution.

In the election of March 22, 1992, for a new 360-member House of Representatives, the leading promilitary parties (see Political Parties, below) captured a majority of seats and thereupon offered the prime ministership to the army commander, Gen. SUCHINDA Kraprayoon, who took office in April 7 after resigning his military posts. The designation of a nonelected individual as prime minister, although permissible under the 1991 constitution, triggered massive opposition demonstrations in Bangkok. Nonetheless, a new cabinet was sworn in on April 21 and the NPC was dissolved. On May 9, amid continuing popular unrest, the house speaker announced government and opposition agreement on a number of constitutional changes, including the banning of a nonelected individual as prime minister, effective upon the completion of Su-chinda's term. Extensive rioting then erupted, with security forces killing 50–100 persons on May 17–19. Five days later Suchinda resigned, and on May 25 the House of Representatives approved the first two readings of a constitutional amendment bill containing the reforms sought by the opposition. On June 10 former prime minister Anand was asked to form another interim administration, and on June 29 the house was dissolved.

In the election of September 13, 1992, four nonmilitary parties emerged with a slim 51.4 percent of legislative seats and formed a coalition that also included the conservative SAP. Ten days later DP leader CHUAN Leekpai became the first nonmilitary leader since the mid-1970s to be designated prime minister. For two years his prime ministership was rocked by shifting coalitions, party defections, military resistance to reform of the military-dominated Senate, and a land reform scandal, and on May 19, 1995, with the withdrawal of the Righteous Force (*Palang Dharma*) party, the government of the country's longest-serving elected prime minister, collapsed.

In the ensuing early election of July 2, 1995, the conservative *Chart Thai* won a plurality of lower house seats, and on July 13 its leader, BANHARN Silpa-Archa, was installed as head of a seven-party, right-wing coalition dubbed the "Thai Development Front." But again the *Palang Dharma* withdrew from the government, followed by *Prachakorn Thai,* led by SAMAK Sundaravej. Further weakened by a banking scandal, Prime Minister Banharn resigned on September 21, 1996. Six days later the House of Representatives was dissolved.

In the election of November 17, 1996, Gen. CHAOVALIT Yongchaiyut's NAP won a plurality of 125 seats, displacing Banharn's *Chart Thai,* which plunged from 92 seats to 39. On November 29 Chaovalit was installed at the head of a new six-party coalition government. When the Thai currency crisis erupted in July 1997 (see the economic discussion in the section above), the fractious Chaovalit coalition was unable to implement an effective defense. In addition, thousands of Thais took to the streets in support of a proposed new constitution that, among other things, was designed to curb political corruption. Although the government guided the new basic law through the legislature on September 27, protests continued. Withering criticism persisted as the economic crisis deepened into a major recession, finally obliging Chaovalit to announce his resignation effective November 7.

To forestall government instability the king appointed the DP's Chuan Leekpai as the new prime minister, and a DP-led multiparty coalition government took office on November 4, 1997. In October 1998, Prime Minister Chuan's position was strengthened by the addition of the *Chart Pattana* to the governing coalition, giving it an overwhelming majority in the House of Representatives. Despite the SAP's withdrawal from the government the following July in a dispute over cabinet posts, Chuan survived by reshuffling his cabinet.

On March 4, 2000, voters participated in the first direct election for the new 200-seat Senate. But the new independent Election Commission disqualified 78 of the winners because of campaign and voting irregularities, and it was late July, after four additional rounds of balloting, before the final seats were filled.

On November 9, 2000, the House of Representatives was dissolved in preparation for a January election. In balloting on January 6, 2001, the *Thai Rak Thai* (Thais Love Thais) party, competing in its first national election, won an unprecedented 248 seats in an expanded, 500-seat house. Over the next several weeks party founder THAKSIN Shinawatra, who had amassed a fortune in the telecommunications industry and was reputedly the country's wealthiest individual, negotiated a coalition with the NAP and *Chart Thai,* and on February 9 was elected prime minister by a vote of 339–127. His cabinet, dominated by ministers from his own party, was sworn in on February 18.

On August 3, 2001, the Constitutional Court, by an 8–7 vote, acquitted Thaksin of charges that he had deliberately concealed some 2.3 billion baht in assets by transferring corporate shares to household servants while he was serving in a previous administration. Had he been convicted, the prime minister would have been required to resign and to remove himself from politics for five years.

Thaksin had already consolidated his hold on the House of Representatives through *Thai Rak Thai*'s absorption in July 2001 of the *Seri Tham* party's 14 deputies. A March 2002 cabinet shuffle, which marked the addition of *Chart Pattana* to the government, was followed later in the month by completion of a much-discussed merger between *Thai Rak Thai* and the NAP. As a consequence, *Thai Rak Thai* held an unassailable legislative majority. On November 8, 2003, Thaksin shuffled his cabinet for the seventh time, dropping *Chart Pattana* but nevertheless retaining a two-thirds majority in the house. Yet another shuffle took place on March 10, 2004, amid security concerns related to Islamic militancy in the Muslim-majority southern provinces of Narathiwat, Pattani, and Yala.

Prime Minister Thaksin's popularity in rural Thailand, coupled with widespread public support for the government's comparatively well-managed response to the December 2004 tsunami disaster, carried Thaksin to an unprecedented election victory on February 6, 2005. *Thai Rak Thai* won a commanding 377 House seats, permitting Thaksin to form a one-party government. The opposition DP won only 96 seats, prompting the resignation two days later of its leader, BANYAT Bantadtan.

During the following year, opposition to the prime minister's policies and alleged authoritarianism grew, especially among middle- and upper-class political elites in Bangkok, where on February 4, 2006, an anti-Thaksin rally drew an estimated 100,000 to Royal Plaza. A direct precipitant had been the tax-free sale by Thaksin's family of its 49 percent stake in the Shin Corporation, a telecommunications company, for $1.9 billion. Immediately after the anti-Thaksin rally, leaders from some 40 nongovernmental organizations and other groups announced formation of a People's Alliance for Democracy (PAD), which demanded Thaksin's resignation and a return to political reform. The PAD brought together a broad cross-section of predominantly urban interest groups—nongovernmental organizations, academics, students, organized labor, businesses, and advocates for the poor. PAD leaders included former Thaksin mentor CHAMLONG Srimuang of the *Santi Asoke* Buddhist sect, academic SOMKIAT Pongpaiboon, labor leader SOMSAK Kosaisuk, and SURIYASAI Katasila of the Campaign for Popular Democracy. Wealthy media personality SONDHI Limthongkul, once a Thaksin supporter and subsequently one of his severest critics, had been the principal force behind the February 4, 2006, Bangkok rally. The PAD campaign, in addition to demanding Thaksin's resignation, hoped to rekindle the political reform movement that had brought down the Suchinda government in 1992. Critics of the PAD alleged, however, that it was covertly manipulated by the military and the Bangkok elite to derail the rural reforms proposed by the *Thai Rak Thai.*

Responding to the growing crisis of confidence in his administration, on February 26 Thaksin dissolved the House of Representatives and called an election for April 2. The next day, opposition leaders ABHISIT Vejjajiva of the DP, former prime minister Banharn Silpa-Archa of *Chart Thai,* and SANAN Kachornprasart of *Mahachon* announced that they would boycott the election. As a consequence, Thaksin attempted to turn the vote into a referendum on his administration, vowing to step down as prime minister unless *Thai Rak Thai* won majority support from the electorate, who had the option of casting "no vote" ballots. With 360 of 400 directly elected seats decided, including 278 where *Thai Rak Thai* candidates stood without opposition, Thaksin's party won 61 percent of the valid votes while 38 percent of voters abstained and about 12 percent of ballots were deliberately spoiled by voters. Reversing course, on April 4 Thaksin announced that he would not accept reappointment as prime minister, and the next day, stating that he was "taking some time off," he named Deputy Prime Minister CHITCHAI Wannasathit to act in his stead.

On April 25, 2006, in a nationwide address, King Bhumibol asked the nation's highest courts to solve the country's "political mess." By that time, lawsuits had been filed to nullify the April 2 results, and on May 8 the Constitutional Court did so by an 8–6 vote, primarily on grounds that voters' right to a secret ballot had been compromised by the positioning of voting booths and that the Electoral Commission had not allowed sufficient time between the late February dissolution of the sitting House of Representatives and the election date. The court by a 9–5 decision further ordered that new elections be held. On May 23 Thaksin reassumed his post as caretaker prime minister, and near the end of the month the Election Commission and the cabinet set October 15 as the new election date. But Thaksin's opponents claimed he was corrupt, arrogant, favored cronies in his numerous cabinet shuffles, surrounded himself with "yes men," tried to manage the government as if he were CEO of a private business, and used his political power to curtail media critics. In addition, the army commander-in-chief, Gen. SONTHI Boonyaratglin, a Muslim, objected to the Thaksin government's heavy-handed crackdown on the Muslim insurgency in the south.

In January 2004 the government had declared martial law in the three Muslim-majority southern provinces in response to escalating attacks that targeted not only authorities but also school teachers, civil servants, and Buddhist monks. On April 30 a coordinated series of attacks against 11 police bases was met with a lethal response from the police and military, leaving over 100 Muslims dead, 30 of them killed during the storming of a mosque. An official inquiry concluded that excessive force had been used. In October another deadly encounter ended with nearly 80 of some 1,300 detainees suffocating or dying of heat stroke while being transported in overcrowded trucks.

Although Thaksin established a National Reconciliation Commission (NRC) in March 2005 to formulate "peace-building" proposals for the south, in mid-July the cabinet approved an Emergency Powers Act that was promulgated by executive decree. The act, which was passed by both houses of the National Assembly in August, granted Thaksin authority to conduct wiretaps, ban media, conduct searches and detain suspects without warrants, censor news, and ban publications. In January 2006, with the death toll in the south having passed 1,000, Amnesty International accused the government and military of using arbitrary detentions, excessive force, and torture. In June the NRC, headed by former prime minister Anand Panyarachun, reported that the underlying issues could not be resolved militarily. Instead, it recommended that indigenous Malay be adopted as a "working language" in the south, that the application of Islamic law be permitted in some situations, that a dialog be opened with militants, that a Fund for Healing and Reconciliation be created, and that mechanisms be established to allow greater local input in cultural and governmental matters.

On September 19, 2006, with Prime Minister Thaksin in New York for the opening of the UN General Assembly, the Thai military, led by General Sonthi, seized power in a bloodless coup, imposed martial law, suspended the constitution, dissolved the National Assembly, and banned political gatherings. On September 20 King Bhumibol appointed General Sonthi head of a Council for Democratic Reform in order "to create peace in the country" while the political impasse was resolved. Sonthi promised to install a civilian government and hold legislative elections under a new constitution by the end of the year. The coup leaders subsequently reconstituted the Council of Democratic Reform as the Council of National Security to advise the interim government. SURAYUD Chulanont, a retired general, was named interim prime minister of Thailand by royal decree on October 1. With the approval of the Council of National Security and in consultation with advisers to the monarchy, Surayud named a new cabinet, which was sworn in on October 9. The new cabinet enlisted a majority of civilian experts and notables; only three ministers were serving military officers, although others had reserve rank or were retired. Martial law was lifted in most provinces on January 27, 2007.

Following the April 2006 election, the Election Commission had recommended to the attorney general that five parties—*Thai Rak Thai,* the DP, and three minor formations—be dissolved for violating the constitution and the Political Party Act. Allegations included that *Thai Rak Thai* had bankrolled small parties to offer token competition, thereby illegally circumventing a requirement that a candidate in an uncontested race had to receive at least 20 percent of the vote to claim the seat. The DP was charged with paying bribes to elicit accusations that *Thai Rak Thai* had committed electoral fraud. The cases were heard by the Constitutional Tribunal, which ruled against *Thai Rak Thai* on May 28, 2007, dissolving the party and excluding 111 of its executives, including Thaksin, from political office for five years. The DP was cleared of electoral fraud, but the other three parties were also dissolved. In June corruption charges were brought against Thaksin and his wife, and many of their bank accounts were frozen.

With regard to the southern insurgency, the Thaksin government's harsh measures had been moderated in October 2006 by General Surayud, who apologized for his predecessor's wrongs, freed a number of detainees, and urged Thai security officials to engage with the Muslim subjects. Nevertheless, the insurgency escalated, signaled by intimidation, arson, assassinations, beheadings, and ambushes of security forces. The government responded by reinforcing several local paramilitary formations, including the Ranger Force (*Thahan Phran*), the Volunteer Defense Corps (*Or Sor*), and the Village Defense Volunteers (*Chor Ror Bor*). Queen SIRIKIT sponsored a new Village Protection Force (*Or Ror Bor*). These militia were poorly trained and equipped, reported to be of dubious effectiveness save as reassurance to local Buddhists, and were allegedly implicated in extortion, beatings, and extrajudicial executions. Meanwhile, a mid-2007 report by Human Rights Watch put the number of deaths at the hands of the insurgents at 2,500, many of them victims of indiscriminate bombings and gruesome assaults.

With a new constitution having been approved in a referendum on August 19, 2007 (see Constitution and government, below), the interim government scheduled fresh elections for a reconstituted, 480-member House of Representatives on December 23, 2007. Meanwhile, on October 1 Sonthi Boonyaratglin, having retired from the military, was named deputy prime minister for security affairs.

The December 2007 legislative election gave a plurality to the People Power Party (*Pak Palang Prachachon*–PPP), which was widely seen as the successor to *Thai Rak Thai.* A dozen seats short of a majority, Samak Sundaravej, now leading the PPP, invited five of the other six parties that had won seats in the House of Representatives to join in a coalition government. The new government, with Samak as prime minster, was sworn in on February 6, 2008. The DP took up the role of opposition in the House.

Subsequently, 11 members of the PPP accused of vote-buying lost their House seats and 4 PPP ministers were obliged to resign, 2 for electoral fraud, 1 because he allegedly insulted the king, and 1 because he made an unconstitutional agreement with Cambodia over a disputed temple at their common border (see Foreign relations, below). These events, compounded by Thaksin's brief return and subsequent flight to London, and the conviction (subsequently overturned) of his wife, KHUNYING Potjaman, for corruption, undermined the PPP's credibility and fuelled the PAD's protests.

The PAD also opposed Prime Minister Samak's alleged intent to amend the constitution to restore the 111 *Thai Rak Thai* executives to political eligibility, to forestall ongoing legal challenges to the PPP's existence, and to pardon Thaksin and his wife. The protests escalated in June and culminated in mass demonstrations and the occupation of the prime minister's office grounds in August. On September 2, 2008, Samak declared a state of emergency, empowering the military and police to ban gatherings of more than five people; to prevent media reporting that "causes panic, instigates violence, or affects stability"; and to hold suspects for up to 30 days without charge. The PAD persisted with demonstrations, in which one person was killed, and the Federation of State Enterprises, encompassing more than 40 labor unions, approved strikes that would cut off power and water to government buildings and disrupt public transportation and telecommunications. PAD demonstrations in August had already closed three airports in southern Thailand, stranding thousands of tourists.

On September 9, 2008, the Constitutional Court ordered Samak's resignation, having found him guilty of a conflict of interest for taking money for participating in two chef shows on commercial television. Deputy Prime Minister SOMCHAI Wongsawat, a brother-in-law of former prime minister Thaksin, became acting prime minister on September 9, was elected prime minister in his own right by the House on September 17, and was endorsed by the king on September 18. He presented his cabinet list to the king on September 24, whereupon it was approved. The PAD threatened not to accept the new government, which was dominated by many of the same PPP figures as the previous Samak-led government, but Somchai, having complied with the constitution and received a parliamentary majority and royal assent, vowed to carry on. Violent demonstrations erupted on October 9 and were broken up by the police at the cost of several deaths and numerous injuries among the protesters.

On October 20, 2008, at the request of Prime Minister Somchai, the House set up a 120-member assembly to redraft the constitution, but the opposition DP boycotted the session and the speaker of the Senate, 40 senators, and several academics spoke out against the redrafting project, which stalled. The PAD called new demonstrations, and on November 25 its followers occupied Bangkok's recently opened Suvarnabhumi International Airport, stopping all flights and stranding 7,000 passengers for a week. The Civil Court issued an injunction and Somchai declared a limited state of emergency, but the riot police did not move against the demonstrators. The crisis ended on December 2 when the Constitutional Court dissolved the PPP, *Chart Thai,* and Neutral Democratic parties and banned Somchai from holding office. Deputy Prime Minister CHAOVARAT Chanweerakul took over as acting prime minister. Democrat Party leader Abhisit commanded only 165 votes from his own party but attracted five other parties to form a coalition government that was sworn in on December 22. Among those rallying to Abhisit were former PPP legislators who established the Friends of Newin Group within the Proud Thais Party.

Constitution and government. Thailand is a highly centralized constitutional monarchy whose governments in the modern era have been led by a prime minister and cabinet. Since 1932 the king has exercised little direct power but remains a popular symbol of national unity and identity and has played a pivotal indirect role in times of political crisis. He is advised by a Privy Council of his own appointees.

An interim constitution approved by the monarch after the 1991 coup assigned a virtually unlimited "supervisory" role to the military-led National Peacekeeping Council (NPC). A new draft constitution was subsequently endorsed by the NPC-appointed National Legislative Assembly and, after being scrutinized by an assembly-appointed review committee, was declared in effect on December 9, 1991. Bicameralism was restored, with the House of Representatives being elected but the Senate remaining appointed.

On September 14, 1996, a joint session of the two legislative houses called for the election of an assembly to draft a new constitution. The assembly's new "open government" charter elicited intense debate and drew considerable opposition, for the most part from entrenched political groups. However, in view of large public demonstrations in support of the proposal, the new basic law was approved by the National Assembly (the collective term for the House and the Senate) on September 27, 1997. Changes included the expansion of the House of Representatives to 500 members, 400 to be elected on a single-member constituency basis and 100 by proportional representation from party lists. Other provisions called for the direct election of senators; guarantees regarding human rights, freedom of the press, and the right to assembly; and establishment of increased accountability on the part of officials, "with greater governmental transparency" overall. Senatorial powers include removal of ministers, members of the House, and justices.

The 1997 constitution was set aside by the military junta and an interim charter imposed by decree on September 27, 2006. Empowered by this charter, the junta appointed a 2,000-person National Assembly, which in turn appointed 200 candidates for a Constitution Assembly, which then selected a Constitution Drafting Committee of 25. The junta chose an additional 10 members for the committee, which set about drafting a new constitution according to guidelines set out by the junta. The draft constitution was submitted to the public in a constitutional referendum, Thailand's first, on August 19, 2007. The junta encouraged officials at all levels to advocate approval but outlawed campaigning against the draft constitution. The turnout was 57 percent and the approval rate was 58 percent, both lower than expected by the junta. The Constitution Drafting Assembly endorsed the outcome on August 20, 2007, and the constitution came into force on August 24, after obtaining the king's assent.

The thrust of the new constitution was to reduce the influence of populist political parties (such as the *Thai Rak Thai*) over the selection of legislators and to restrict the powers of the prime minister. Major changes from the 1997 constitution included the appointment rather than election of senators and a reduction in their number from 200 to 150, and the adoption of an electoral system for the House of Representatives of 400 single-member constituencies plus 80 selected by proportional representation. As before, the king was to appoint the political leader commanding a majority in the House to serve as prime minister, who in turn was to nominate the ministers and other members of the cabinet, subject to approval by the House. But the role of the prime minister was to be circumscribed by new provisions, including a two-term restriction, a reduction in the number of legislators necessary to launch a no-confidence debate, and a prohibition against a prime minister's leading a caretaker administration after the legislature was dissolved—all directed at preventing the alleged abuses of the Thaksin regime. Controversial provisions included the granting of amnesty to members of the junta that staged the 2006 coup, articles forbidding legislators from overseeing the work of bureaucrats or the military, and the designation of the military as the protector of the monarchy and constitution. However, passages protecting human rights and civil liberties remained as extensive in the new constitution as in its predecessor, and the practice of electing local government officials down to the subdistrict level was reaffirmed. The 2007 constitution prescribed no fundamental changes to the judiciary or the local administrative system.

The Thai judicial system is patterned after European models. The Supreme Court, whose justices are appointed by the king, is the final court of appeal in both civil and criminal cases; an intermediate Court of Appeals hears appeals from courts of first instance located throughout the country. The constitutionality of parliamentary acts, royal decrees, and draft legislation falls under the purview of a Constitutional Court, which may also rule on the appointment and removal of public officials and political party issues.

Administratively, the country is divided into 76 provinces, including Bangkok. Provincial governors are appointed by the minister of the interior, except for Bangkok, where the governor (often referred to as the mayor) is elected. Provincial subdivisions include districts (*amphoe*), communes (*tambons*), and villages (*mubans*). The larger towns are governed by elected municipal councils. Legislation passed in March 2000 authorizes direct election of municipal mayors and most local administrators.

Foreign relations. One of the few Southeast Asian governments to depart from a neutralist posture, Thailand was firmly aligned with the United States and other Western powers after World War II and signed onto the Southeast Asia Collective Defense Treaty, which established the Southeast Asia Treaty Organization (SEATO) in Bangkok in 1954. During the period 1952–1972 Thailand received almost $1.2 billion in U.S. military aid, more than twice the value of U.S. economic assistance. The Thanom government approved the use of Thai air bases for U.S. military operations in Laos and South Vietnam, and the American buildup totaled 48,000 personnel in Thailand at its peak in 1969. The U.S. withdrawal from South Vietnam led to a corresponding reduction in Thailand, and by mid-1976, all remaining U.S. military installations were closed down. SEATO was declared inactive in 1977 and its Bangkok headquarters closed.

Various UN bodies functioning in East and Southeast Asia maintain headquarters in Bangkok, and Thailand has played a leading role in the establishment of several regional organizations, such as the Association of Southeast Asian Nations (ASEAN), of which Thailand became a charter member in 1967. More recently, Thailand has been active in the ASEAN Free Trade Agreement (AFTA), ASEAN Regional Forum (ARF), ASEAN Plus Three talks, the Asia-Pacific Economic Cooperation (APEC), and the East Asian Summit process begun in 2004. Regionally, Thailand is second only to Singapore in its pursuit of free trade agreements with governments as diverse as New Zealand, Australia, China, the United States, India, and Bahrain. In 1999 Thailand dispatched some 1,500 troops as part of the international peacekeeping force sent to East Timor (now Timor-Leste) following the territory's independence vote in August and served as cocommander with Australia; in 2009 Thailand maintained a police contribution to the UN Integrated Mission in Timor-Leste.

Relations with Cambodia have traditionally been antagonistic, although Thailand joined with other ASEAN nations in recognizing the Pol Pot regime in mid-1975 and in calling for "the immediate withdrawal of all foreign troops" following the Vietnamese invasion of December 1978. While tacitly aiding *Khmer Rouge* forces in their opposition to the Vietnamese-backed regime of Heng Samrin, Thailand encouraged the noncommunist Khmer resistance to form a united front, an effort that contributed toward the organization of the Coalition Government of Democratic Kampuchea in June 1982. Thailand was also a participant in the "Jakarta Informal Meetings" that paved the way for establishment of a quadripartite Supreme National Council for Cambodia in 1990.

As many as 250,000 Cambodians crowded refugee camps in eastern Thailand during the Pol Pot era and the ensuing occupation by Vietnamese forces, and as late as 1998 the region continued to be a refuge for those fleeing fighting between the Cambodian military and remaining *Khmer Rouge* guerrillas. Periodically, however, charges that Thailand provided sanctuary to fleeing *Khmer Rouge* strained relations with a number of countries, including the United States. Concern that arms might end up in guerrilla hands led Washington to terminate military aid and training under its 1995 Foreign Operations Act. Angered by the American action, Thailand joined Indonesia and Malaysia in opposing a request for the stationing of a "rapid response" flotilla of U.S. military supply ships in the Gulf of Thailand. Relations improved when Thailand received strong U.S. support in 1998 for its economic reforms.

In mid-2008 Thai-Cambodian relations soured over a dispute regarding ownership of land adjacent to the Preah Vihear temple. The International Court of Justice in 1962 had awarded this temple to Cambodia, but the status of surrounding land remained unresolved. Cambodia subsequently applied to register the temple and grounds with UNESCO as a World Heritage Site under Cambodian trusteeship. Thailand's minister of foreign affairs, NOPPADON Pattama, initially endorsed the application, but the Constitutional Court found that he had exceeded his authority and he was forced to resign. When UNESCO granted registration, in July 2008, Thailand moved troops onto the disputed land, and Cambodia reciprocated. Government-to-government negotiations eased the tension temporarily, but in mid-October the armed confrontation erupted into a series of sporadic fire fights that left seven soldiers dead. On August 6, 2009, foreign ministers of Thailand and Cambodia convened their joint border commission for the first time in three years to discuss the temple dispute and also an emerging dispute over waters in which each government has granted private oil and gas exploration licenses. Relations deteriorated when Thaksin visited Phnom Penh on November 10–14, 2009, at the invitation of Prime Minister Hun Sen, provoking Thailand to recall its ambassador to Cambodia and issue an extradition request. Cambodia in turn withdrew its ambassador to Thailand and rejected the extradition request, labeling it "politically motivated."

A history of uneven relations with neighboring Laos reached a low point in late 1987, when fighting broke out over disputed border territory. Despite the conflict, Bangkok subsequently adopted a conciliatory economic policy, and a "new atmosphere" of cooperation was reported to have resulted from a series of high-level governmental and military talks in late 1990, with a mutual troop withdrawal from border areas occurring in March 1991. Five months later a border security and cooperation agreement provided for the repatriation of some 60,000 Laotian refugees from Thailand over a three-year period. More than 8,000 remained in 2008. In June Thai authorities repatriated 837 Hmong refugees, prompting concern by the UN High Commissioner for Refugees (UNHCR) that they would be persecuted by the Lao authorities.

Following an initiative by Prime Minister Chatchai in 1988 to turn Indochina "from a battleground into a market place," Thai policy toward Hanoi softened. In February 1993 Thai officials met in Hanoi with representatives of Cambodia, Laos, and Vietnam to chart a new framework of cooperation for developing the resources of the lower Mekong River. Subsequently, talks were also initiated with Laos, Myanmar (Burma), and China on development of the upper Mekong, which led to completion in April 2000 of a treaty governing navigation on the waterway.

In March 1996 Banharn Silpa-Archa became the first Thai prime minister in 16 years to visit Myanmar, with whose leadership a border trade agreement was signed, while in 1998 the UN agreed to help protect some 100,000 Mon, Kayin (Karen), and other ethnic refugees from Myanmar living on the Thai side of the border. In March 1999 Myanmar's head of state, Than Shwe, joined Prime Minister Chuan for discussions on narcotics control and border tensions, but the cordiality ended on October 2 when Thai authorities freed five Myanmar dissidents who had taken 89 hostages at the Myanmar embassy in Bangkok the preceding day. Myanmar's military leadership immediately closed the Thai-Myanmar border. Bangkok, in turn, threatened to expel hundreds of thousands of illegal Myanmar migrant workers. The border remained closed until late November. A second hostage incident occurred on January 24, 2000, when members of a Myanmar ethnic minority group called God's Army occupied a hospital in Ratchaburi, near the border, taking some 700 hostages. In contrast to the October incident, the Thai forces stormed the hospital on January 25, freed all the hostages, and killed all ten rebels, some, according to eyewitnesses, by summary execution. Myanmar praised Thailand's forceful response.

On February 9–11, 2001, Thai troops engaged Myanmar forces that had reportedly pursued members of the Shan State Army across the border. The encounter led to a series of bilateral meetings, culminating in a June visit by Prime Minister Thaksin to Yangon. The two governments agreed not only to work toward resolution of remaining border issues but also to jointly fight drug production and smuggling. Nevertheless, difficulties continued into 2002, with the border being closed from May until early October. In February 2003 Thaksin again traveled to Myanmar in furtherance of improved relations, and in July he announced that all Myanmar dissidents would be moved to refugee camps near the border, of which nine had been established. The Thai government's preferred policy was voluntary repatriation, but continued political strife, ethnic warfare, and noncooperation by the authorities in Myanmar precluded this solution. In 2007 Thailand, with the help of the UNHCR, negotiated the removal of approximately 4,000 refugees, the majority from Myanmar, to third countries, led by the United States, and issued identity cards to up to 140,000 others, enabling them to work legally outside their camps. Thailand joined its ASEAN partners in urging the Myanmar junta to consult with the democratic opposition and take steps to resolve Myanmar's domestic disputes peacefully. In October Prime Minister Surayud proposed to UN special envoy Ibrahim Gambari that the UN organize regional talks including ASEAN, China, and India to address the crisis in Myanmar. Surayud also postponed the visit to Bangkok by Myanmar's new prime minister, Gen. Thein Sein, on grounds of national preoccupation with the king's 80th birthday celebrations and the December 23 general election. Relations improved in 2009 with Energy Minister WANNARAT Charnnukul's announcement on August 4 of a Thai-financed project to develop an offshore natural gas field in Myanmar waters and import 300 million cubic feet of gas per day from Myanmar starting in 2013.

In January 1998 Malaysia took a stand against the Muslim separatists of southern Thailand when it quietly arrested several alleged Muslim insurgents from a faction of the Pattani United Liberation Organization (PULO) and returned them for trial in Bangkok. Malaysia, which is predominantly Muslim, had previously been a sanctuary for the separatists, who want independence for the 2.5 million Muslims residing in Thailand's southern provinces. The change in policy was seen as evidence of a new cooperativeness at a time when both countries faced the Asian Financial Crisis. In 1997 Thailand and Malaysia established a Joint Commission on Bilateral Cooperation to facilitate border control and enhance confidence and security-building measures. In 2004 they set up a Committee on Joint Development Strategy, and by 2007 they had implemented Joint Working Groups on Education, Employment, and Entrepreneurship tasked with raising standards of living of depressed communities on both sides of the border.

Even after the September 2001 al-Qaida attacks on the United States, and despite growing Islamic militancy in Thailand's southern provinces, Thai authorities routinely discounted the possible involvement of the Indonesia-based *Jemaah Islamiah* (JI) and al-Qaida in sporadic bombings and attacks against police stations. In June 2003, however, alleged JI members were among those arrested in connection with a plot to blow up two tourist resorts and the Bangkok embassies of Australia, Germany, Singapore, the United Kingdom, and the United States. Citing the urgency of the situation, in August 2003 the government bypassed the National Assembly and issued two antiterrorism laws by decree. In the same month the U.S. Central Intelligence Agency assisted Thai authorities in capturing Riduan Isamuddin (a.k.a. Hambali), an alleged JI leader with ties to al-Qaida, who was then taken to the United States.

Thailand has warming relations with China. A free trade agreement was signed in 2004. During a visit to China in June 2005 Prime Minister Thaksin and the Chinese leadership announced that they were proceeding with an action plan to develop a "strategic partnership" in a host of areas, including trade, security, and science and technology. The interim government maintained existing links, and future administrations are expected to explore further ties, given China's cordial Olympics diplomacy and improved relations between Beijing and Taipei. But local producers remain dissatisfied by the swamping of the local market with cheap goods allowed in by the China-Thailand Free Trade Agreement.

Relations with the U.S. administration of President George W. Bush were close. Thailand assisted in the U.S.-led invasion of Iraq, although its 440 medical and engineering personnel were withdrawn in August 2004. In 2003 the U.S. government designated Thailand a "major non-NATO ally." The two governments began free trade agreement negotiations in 2004, but the talks stalled in mid-2006 over the issue of protections for U.S. pharmaceutical companies. The prospect of a free trade agreement with the United States was not welcomed by Thai farmers, small manufacturers, students, environmentalists, development-oriented nongovernmental organizations, and officials concerned with delivery of health, welfare, and local enterprise assistance. Local businesses were disturbed that U.S. investors had taken advantage of the Asian Financial Crisis to buy up Thai enterprises at devalued prices. Political turmoil and the military coup in Thailand made resumption of talks infeasible, although U.S. trade representative Susan Schwab stated in July 2007 that she hoped negotiations would start again after the December 2007 election and the installation of a new government, but the free trade agreement negotiations remained stalled in mid-2008 and were further delayed by the August–September political turmoil.

The U.S. government in 2006 and 2007 publicly urged the Thai military junta to lift martial law and restore democracy. Washington withheld over $35 million in economic aid, mainly for military training and assistance programs, but imposed no other sanctions and continued programs related to development, democracy promotion, disaster assistance, counterterrorism, counternarcotics, human trafficking, and refugee assistance valued at $34 million. Full diplomatic, economic, and military relations were restored in 2008, and Secretary of State Hillary Clinton on July 23, 2009, reiterated the Barack Obama administration's commitment to work closely with Thailand on national, regional, and global issues. State Department reports in 2008 had identified Thailand as a transit country for drug and human smuggling and as a source of human rights violations.

Current issues. On October 22, 2008, the Constitutional Court found former prime minister Thaksin guilty of corruption in a land deal case, sentenced him to two years imprisonment, and issued a warrant for his arrest. Further charges for tax evasion are pending. Thaksin and his wife, who had fled to London, relocated to Dubai when his tourist visa was revoked. (Thaksin's divorce from Khunying was announced by his spokesperson on November 16, but no details were released.) The government revoked his Thai passport in April 2009, but he continued his travels on Montenegrin and Nicaraguan passports. Meanwhile, he continued to reject the Abhisit government's validity and to incite his followers by video broadcasts and by "tweets" through the social networking and blogging service Twitter. On March 31, 20,000 of his followers under the banner of the United Front of Democracy Against Dictatorship (UDD), also known as the Democratic Alliance Against Dictatorship (DAAD), forced the cancellation of a cabinet meeting in Bangkok. Further demonstrations took place on April 8 against Gen. Prem Tinsulanand, the king's chief privy counselor, and on April 11 when 10,000 protesters forced the cancellation of an ASEAN summit in Pattaya and obliged the government to fly visiting international leaders to safety by helicopter from their hotel venue. UDD leader JATUPORN Prompan told a rally of 10,000 "red shirts" (Thaksin supporters) that a petition for a royal pardon of Thaksin with 5 million signatures would be submitted to the king's principal secretary on August 17. But Deputy Interior Minister BOONJONG Wongtrairat asserted that 2 million had signed another petition, circulated by his ministry through provincial governors and district chiefs nationwide, opposing the pardon, and that the pro-Thaksin petition would be invalid because it was not initiated by Thaksin himself. Pro-Thaksin supporters staged a major demonstration on September 19, 2009, at which Thaksin spoke by videolink, and on November 10 Thaksin visited neighboring Cambodia, further encouraging his supporters and angering the government.

Prime Minister Abhisit, in his December 2008 inaugural address, pledged to uphold the rule of law, tackle an economic downturn, and address such issues as rural poverty, healthcare, and microcredit schemes, all of which had made his predecessor Thaksin popular in the countryside. To address the economic slump the cabinet on January 13, 2009, approved an interim six-month budget of 115 billion baht (US$2.88 billion) to sustain employment and stimulate the economy. Proposals included free schooling for children up to 15 years of age and subsidies for rural infrastructure, low-income families, and small businesses. A package of tax cuts was added on January 20. The House and Senate in June authorized the government to borrow a further 400 billion baht (US$10 billion) to cover budget shortfalls.

In the south insurgent-related violence has persisted. In August 2008 two bombs in Sungai Kolok killed 2 people, including a newspaper reporter, and injured 32 others. Authorities arrested 6 suspects allegedly associated with the *Runda Kumpulan Kecil* (RKK), which operates near the border with Malaysia. In mid-September an army ranger was killed and another injured by a bomb blast in Muang, and sporadic shootings of officials and teachers continued. On September 20–21 Indonesian vice president Jusuf Kalla mediated talks in Bogor between an unofficial delegation of Thai negotiators led by former army commander KWANCHART Klaharn and representatives of the Pattani Malay Consultative Congress. A spokesperson for the Yala Provincial Islamic Committee, NIMU Kakaje, dismissed the talks as "not hopeful" because none of the negotiators had the status to make necessary changes.

Since then low-level violence has continued, including a bomb attack that wounded three paramilitary troopers on August 8, 2009, and a drive-by shooting of two Muslim village leaders the following day. October was marked by another drive-by killing of two Buddhists and a shoot-out leaving one police officer and one Muslim militant dead. Border police commander Maj. Gen. PEERA Phumphichet reported that the southern insurgency had manifested itself in nearly 10,000 violent incidents and had caused over 3,100 deaths in the period from January 2004 to August 2009.

POLITICAL PARTIES

For the quarter-century preceding the 2001 election, Thailand's civilian governments typically featured shifting multiparty coalitions, with no single party being able to emerge from national elections holding a legislative majority. Since 2001 three broad political groupings have maneuvered for power. The first was represented by the populist *Thai Rak Thai,* succeeded in 2007 by the People Power Party (PPP), which drew its support from poorer rural districts in the northeast. The second were urban civilian elites based in Bangkok, Songkhla, and other urban centers and in the southern Muslim provinces, who supported the Democrat Party. The third, a loose grouping of military officers, government officials, monarchist civilians, and business interests in central Thailand, was manifested by the *Chart Thai* party. Each was riven by factions. Numerous smaller parties formed around strong personalities or local interests, often originating in breakaway factions of the three main parties.

Although political party activity was temporarily suspended after the February 1991 coup, 15 registered parties contested the legislative election of March 1992, with 11 winning seats; the short-lived Suchinda government included the plurality legislative party, Unification Virtue (*Sammakkhi Tham*), plus the promilitary *Chart Thai, Prachakorn Thai,* Social Action Party (SAP), and *Rassadorn.* For the run-up to the September 1992 balloting, the *Chart Thai, Prachakorn Thai, Chart Pattana* (National Development Party), Unification Virtue (now defunct), and *Rassadorn* parties formed a promilitary coalition that the media dubbed "the devils"; an opposing coalition, the "angels," encompassed four prodemocracy groups: the Democrat Party (DP), New Aspiration Party (NAP), *Palang Dharma* (Righteous Force), and *Ekkaparb* (Solidarity). After the election the conservative SAP joined the four prodemocracy groups in a governing coalition led by Chuan Leekpai, but it was obliged to withdraw a year later upon the announcement of its participation in a projected "super-party" with *Prachakorn Thai, Chart Pattana,* Mass Party (*Muan Chon*), and *Rassadorn;* the SAP was replaced in the coalition by the smaller *Seri Tham* (Virtuous Freedom) party. In December 1994 the NAP also withdrew from the government but was quickly succeeded by the rightist *Chart Pattana.*

The withdrawal of *Palang Dharma* five months later precipitated the collapse of the government, and following the July 1995 election a new seven-party grouping of *Chart Thai,* NAP, *Palang Dharma,* SAP, *Prachakorn Thai, Muan Chon,* and the minor *Nam Thai* (now defunct) took office under Prime Minister Banharn Silpa-Archa. In May 1996 *Palang Dharma* withdrew from the Banharn government, and then returned, which caused *Prachakorn Thai* to briefly depart in June. In August *Palang Dharma* once again withdrew, contributing to the demise of the Banharn administration.

The six-party government formed by Gen. Chaovalit Yongchaiyut immediately after the November 1996 election included his NAP, *Chart Pattana,* the SAP, *Prachakorn Thai, Seri Tham,* and *Muan Chon,* while its successor, formed in November 1997 by returning Prime Minister Chuan, initially comprised the DP, *Chart Thai,* SAP, *Ekkaparb* (now defunct), and *Seri Tham,* plus 12 representatives from the opposition *Prachakorn Thai.* In addition, it received the backing of the *Palang Dharma* and the small Thai Party. In October 1998 the coalition was bolstered by the addition of the *Chart Pattana,* and in February 1999 most of the renegade *Prachakorn Thai* members joined the revived *Rassadorn,* the seventh member of the coalition. The SAP, however, withdrew in July 1999.

Thirty-seven parties (out of some 60 registered parties) presented lists for the proportional seats in the January 2001 election for the House of Representatives. The government announced in February that Prime Minister Thaksin was dominated by his *Thai Rak Thai* but also included *Chart Thai* and the NAP. *Palang Dharma* dissolved after failing to win any seats. In July *Seri Tham* merged with *Thai Rak Thai,* as did the NAP in March 2002. *Chart Pattana* joined the government in March 2002, was forced out in November 2003, and then returned in July 2004, after which it was absorbed by *Thai Rak Thai.* Also in July 2004, *Rassadorn* was reorganized as the Public Party (*Mahachon*). Following the February 2005 election *Thai Rak Thai* formed Thailand's first elected single-party government.

The election of April 2006 was boycotted by all the parties in the parliamentary opposition: the DP, *Chart Thai,* and *Mahachon.* Of the country's 30 registered parties, 28 were eligible for the contest, although many had minuscule memberships or existed primarily on paper; 18 ran in at least 1 district and 8 presented party lists for proportional seats. Two weeks after the April 2006 election *Muan Chon* was reregistered as the New Alternative. As of early June, with a repeat election having been scheduled for October, the number of registered parties had grown to 38.

The Constitutional Court's banning of *Thai Rak Thai* in May 2007 and the exclusion of Thaksin and 110 other party executives from political office or party leadership for five years altered the political picture substantially. The DP reemerged as the country's largest and most popular party, approved by 43 percent of Thais polled in August 2007. But many *Thai Rak Thai* members and followers regrouped in the previously minor PPP and reinvigorated it to the point where it emerged as the country's most popular party. The PPP was reported to be financed by Thaksin from exile, and its leader Samak declared his intention to continue Thaksin's populist policies.

In the election held December 23, 2007, only 7 parties out of 66 registered gained seats in the newly constituted House of Representatives, the others failing either to win any of the 400 constituency seats or to reach the 5 percent threshold for one of the 80 proportional seats. The PPP led all parties, followed by the DP. On December 2, 2008, however, the Constitutional Court dissolved the PPP, the *Chart Thai,* and the Neutral Democratic Party for vote-buying in the 2007 election and precipitated a change of government that brought a six-party, DP-led coalition to power.

Governing Coalition:

Democrat Party—DP (*Pak Prachatipat*). Organized in 1946, the DP now constitutes Thailand's oldest party. Traditionally a strong defender of the monarchy, it has derived much of its support from officials and urban professionals. It considers itself a left-of-center party. The fourth-ranked party in March 1992, with 44 seats, it secured a plurality of 79 seats the following September. It was second-ranked with 86 seats in 1995 and similarly ranked with 123 seats in 1996.

In August 2000 the Constitutional Court convicted DP Secretary General Sanan Kachornprasart of having falsified an assets declaration and banned him from politics for five years. In the January 2001 election the party actually gained a handful of seats over 1996, for a total of 128, but was far outdistanced by *Thai Rak Thai.* With former prime minister Chuan Leekpai having stepped aside as party leader, the April 2003 DP Congress chose longtime party stalwart Banyat Bantadtan as leader.

In mid-2004 supporters of former secretary general Sanan left the Democrats and joined *Mahachon* (below).

With his party having won only 96 seats in the February 2006 election, Banyat stepped down in favor of a younger leader, Abhisit Vejjajiva, who was unanimously confirmed as party leader in March. After the banning of *Thai Rak Thai,* the DP emerged as the most popular party among Bangkok residents polled in November 2007, attracting 48 percent approval. Popular support was strongest in the capital's middle-class constituencies and in the conservative southern districts of the country. In the December election the DP again came in second, with 165 seats, and chose to sit in opposition and form a shadow cabinet rather than join the coalition government led by the PPP. In December 2008 the DP formed the core of a coalition government led by Abhisit and took 15 of the 24 cabinet posts. It won 7 seats in the January 11, 2009, by-elections and, with defections from other parties, commands 173 seats in the House.

Leaders: ABHISIT Vejjajiva (Leader), KORN Chatikavanij (Deputy Leader), CHUAN Leekpai (Chief Adviser), BANYAT Bantadtan (Deputy Chief Adviser), SUTHEP Thaugsuban (Secretary General).

Proud Thais Party—PTP (*Bhum Jai Tai*) Also called the Thai Pride Party, the PTP is an offshoot of the Neutral Democratic Party (below), which was dissolved by the Constitutional Court in December 2008. The PTP was founded on November 5, 2008, and on December 15 its members in the House joined with Abhisit's Democrat Party to form the current ruling coalition government. Characterized as a populist party, it shares many values with the rural populist parties spawned by Thaksin. (The NDP had entered into a coalition with the PPP in 2008.) With over 40 seats in the House, it views itself as a possible alternative to the currently dominant Democrats. It is divided by factions, including the Friends of Newin group, a smaller Matchimathipatai group, and the Spra-at Klinpratoom splinter.

A fluid caucus numbering 22, led by banned politician NEWIN Chidchob, the Friends of Newin group emerged as influential in the DP-led government and was awarded the portfolios of interior and transport as well as two deputy ministerships. The PTP's House strength in mid-2009 stood at 32.

Leaders: CHAOVARAT Chanweerakul (Leader), BOONJONG Wongtrairat and PHAIROJ Suksamrot (Deputy Leaders), PORTIVA Nakasai (Secretary).

For the Motherland (*Puea Pan Din*—PPD). *Puea Pan Din* emerged in September 2007 in the context of an ultimately unsuccessful merger effort by *Matchima, Pracharaj,* and other post–*Thai Rak Thai* groups. Party advisers PREECHA Laoha-pongchana, SURAKIART Sathirathai, PINIJ Jarusombat, and SURANAND Vejjajiva were obliged to step aside from the party by an Electoral Commission ruling in November 2007 that, as banned executives of *Thai Rak Thai,* they could not participate in the upcoming election activity. The party won 17 constituency seats and 7 proportional seats for a total of 24, placing it fourth strongest in the new House. *Puea Pan Din* was invited by PPP leader Samak to join a six-party coalition, and for its support was awarded four cabinet and deputy ministerial posts. In late July 2008, however, Suwit Khunkitti, the party leader, announced that the PPD would withdraw from the government, which led to an internal party dispute and his eventual departure.

In the government formed by Abhisit in December 2008, PPD leaders were awarded the portfolios of industry, and information and communications technology. The party won 3 seats in the January 2009 by-elections and now occupies 32 seats in the House.

Leaders: CHARNCHAI Chairungrueng (Leader), VACHARA Phanchet (Secretary General).

Thai Nation Development Party—TNDP (*Chart Thai Pattana*). The TNDP was founded on April 18, 2008, and became the new political home for members of the *Chart Thai* Party when the latter was dissolved in December 2008. The TNDP joined the Abhisit-led coalition and was awarded a deputy prime ministership, the tourism and sports and energy ministries, and the deputy transport portfolio. The party has 25 seats in the House.

Leader: CHUMPOL Silpa-archa.

Thais United National Development Party—TUNDP (*Ruam Jai Thai Chart Pattana*). The party arose from the formation of *Ruam Jai Thai* (variously translated as United Hearts Thai and Thais United), which was announced in late June 2007 by leaders that included Pradit Phataraprasit. Although prohibited from active involvement because of his former standing in *Thai Rak Thai,* Somkid Jatusripitak, a former deputy prime minister, was a key figure behind the organization.

In September 2007 *Ruam Jai Thai* leaders announced a merger with the *Chart Pattana* (National Development) group, led by Suwat Liptapanlop, who, like Somkid, was prohibited from direct politicking. A possible merger with the *Pracharaj* and *Matchima* parties and the Bangkok 50 and *Saman Chan* groups was explored but was not consummated. The December 2007 election found the *Ruam Jai Thai* in sixth place, with nine seats. The party then joined the PPP-led coalition government and was awarded the positions of deputy finance minister and minister of energy. Following the fall of the Somchai government in December 2008, the TUNDP rallied to Abhisit's coalition, and the party's leader Wannarat Channukul was made minister for energy, and its secretary general was awarded the deputy finance portfolio in the new cabinet. It occupies nine seats in the House.

Leaders: WANNARAT Channukul (Leader), ANEK Laothammathat (Deputy Leader), PRADIT Phataraprasit (Secretary General).

Social Action Party—SAP (*Kit Sangkhom*). A 1974 offshoot of the DP, the SAP is somewhat more conservative and free-enterprise oriented than the parent group. It was the leading party in the 1983 balloting and served as the core of the Prem government coalition prior to the emergence of internal fissures that prompted the resignation of longtime party leader Kukrit Pramoj in late 1985 and necessitated the legislative dissolution of May 1986. It was runner-up to the *Chart Thai* in 1988, with Kukrit returning to the party leadership in August 1990. It won 31 legislative seats in March 1992 and entered the Suchinda government in April; however, it left the promilitary alignment in June. It secured 22 seats in the September 1992 poll. Although a participant in the ensuing Chuan coalition, its leader, MONTRI Pongpanit, was not offered a cabinet portfolio because of allegations that he had become "unusually rich."

The party went into opposition in September 1993, subsequently joining the Chaovalit coalition after the 1996 election, after which it held 20 seats, down from 22 in 1995. Kukrit Pramoj died in October 1996, and two years later Montri announced that he was stepping down as formal party leader, in part as a gesture of responsibility for a scandal that had cost the party its health portfolio.

In July 1999 the SAP withdrew from the governing coalition as a result of a dispute between Deputy Prime Minister Suwit Khunkitti and RAKKIAT Sukthana over the party's cabinet seats. In March 2000 Suwit resigned his party leadership post, and in August he led a mass defection to *Thai Rak Thai.* (He later became leader of the new *Puea Pan Din.*) With Rakkiat having joined *Seri Tham,* Montri having died in June, and Suwit having defected, the SAP's political life appeared limited, and it won one seat in the January 2001 lower house election. Nevertheless, under new leadership, the party registered for the December 2007 general election, although it won no seats. In mid-2008, however, Suwit left the PDP as a consequence of an intraparty dispute and returned to the SAP. The change of government in December 2008 and the by-election in January 2009 then offered the SAP a chance to revive by shifting its allegiance to the Democrat Party and joining Abhisit's coalition government, in which Suwit was awarded the portfolio of natural resources and environment. It occupies five seats in the House.

Leaders: SUWIT Khunkitti, THONGPHLU Diphrai.

Opposition Parties:

For Thais Party (*Phak Puea Thai*—PPT). The PPT emerged in September 20, 2008, set up by 80 PPP members of the House who deserted the party ahead of its banning in December by the Constitutional Court. Its leaders included APIWAN Wiriyachai, former vice president of the House; CHALERM Yoobamrung, a former health minister and PPP leader; and MINGKWAN Saengsuwan, formerly a minister of industry. Declining to endorse Abhisit as the new prime minister, the PPT in December called for an all-party national unity government to be led by Sanoh Thienthong of the Royalist People's Party. When that failed, the PPT called for a dissolution of the House and endorsed PRACHA Promnok as a candidate for prime minister in a possible new government, but without success. Nevertheless, the January 2009 by-election victories in five constituencies and shifting party alliances enabled the PPT's House strength to grow to 189 out of 480 seats.

Leaders: YONGYUTH Wichaidit, PRACHA Promnok.

Royalist People's Party—RPP (*Pracharaj*). RPP was registered in May 2006 under the leadership of Sanoh Thienthong, formerly of the NAP and *Thai Rak Thai*. An early supporter of Prime Minister Thaksin, Sanoh had left *Thai Rak Thai* earlier in the year, intending to retire from politics. He returned, however, to help organize the RPP, although he stated that he would serve only as interim leader. Strengthened by members from the disbanded *Thai Rak Thai*, RPP leaders in September 2007 explored a merger with *Matchima, Ruam Jai Thai*, and the Bangkok 50 and *Saman Chan* groups but could not attract a suitable leader or reach agreement on policy. In October party leaders PRACHAI Liewpairat and ANONGWAN Thepsuthin defected to *Matchima*.

The RPP managed to win five House seats in the December 2007 general election, standing on a populist platform including labor rights, free public education, public health care reform, aid to pensioners, environmental protection, and opposition to free trade agreements. It joined the PPP-led coalition government and was given the portfolio of labor minister. Upon the change of government in December 2008, the RPP refused to cooperate with the Democrat Party and moved into opposition, where, after winning four seats in the January 2009 by-elections, it now occupies eight seats in the House. The party has designated its deputy leader, Korn Dabbaransi (formerly of *Chart Pattana* and *Thai Rak Thai*), as a candidate prime minister.

Leaders: SANOH Thienthong (Leader), KORN Dabbaransi (Deputy Leader), CHIENCHUANG Kanlayanamith (Secretary General).

Other Parliamentary Party:

Citizen's Party (*Rassadorn*). Also translatable as Party of the People, *Rassadorn* was registered in May 1986 by a largely military group whose leader, Gen. TIENCHAI Sirisamphan, had played a prominent role in the countercoup operation of September 1985. It disbanded after failing to win any house seats in the November 1996 election, but on February 10, 1999, it was reregistered by VATANA Asavahame, one of the *Prachakorn Thai* rebels who had defied the party leadership by supporting the Chuan administration. Two days later the Constitutional Court ruled that the *Prachakorn Thai* "Cobras" had 30 days to find a new party or lose their house seats, and later in the month 9 of the 12 joined *Rassadorn*. On March 8 the resurrected party held a general assembly, but Vatana turned down the party chairship, which went to former *Chart Thai* leader Somboom Rahong. In April 2000 a planned merger with *Seri Tham* fell through. *Rassadorn* won only two House seats in January 2001, as a consequence of which Somboon stepped aside as party leader, to be replaced by Sanan.

In July 2004 the party adopted the name *Mahachon* (Public Party—PP) after, having been joined by followers of former DP leader Sanan Kachornprasart. Sanan and his supporters had initially intended to establish a new party but ultimately chose to transform *Rassadorn* and rename it.

In 2007 *Mahachon* claimed over 2 million members, mainly in the rural region centered on Nonthaburi district, but its prospects for the December 2007 election were considerably dimmed when Sanan and several other key leaders decided to join *Chart Thai* in late October, and it won no seats. The party was revived under the *Rassadorn* label in February 2009 by Man Pattanotai, a former minister of information and communications technology in the Samak and Somchai governments. Its ranks include defectors from *Puea Pan Din* and the DP; three House members, generally aligned with but not formally part of the governing coalition, now sit under the *Rassadorn* banner.

Leaders: MAN Pattanotai, SOMSAK Wiwatanant.

Political Parties Not Represented in the House of Representatives:

New Alternative—NA (*Thang Luak Mai*). New Alternative, formerly *Muan Chon*, was registered under its present name on April 18, 2006. The original *Muan Chon* had been formally registered in June 1985 by a group of dissidents from both government and opposition ranks. A participant in several coalition governments between then and 1997, it won only two house seats in November 1996 under the leadership of Chalerm Yoobamrung. In May 1998 the NAP absorbed the *Muan Chon*, but in late April 2002, objecting to the dissolution of the NAP and its merger into the *Thai Rak Thai*, Chalerm reregistered the revived *Muan Chon*. He then ran unsuccessfully for governor of Bangkok in 2004. In 2006 Chalerm supported the opposition boycott of the April lower house election. In November 2007 he joined the PPP as its deputy leader, leaving the New Alternative's future in doubt. The party won no seats in the 2007 election.

New Aspiration Party—NAP (*Pak Kwam Hwang Mai*). Organized by controversial former army commander Chaovalit Yongchaiyut, who had also served as General Chatchai's defense minister, the NAP was formally registered in September 1990. Characterized by its founder as an anticorruption grouping, the party claimed 300,000 adherents by early 1991.

Despite his military background, Chaovalit strongly opposed the 1991 coup and subsequently emerged as the NPC junta's most outspoken critic. The NAP was third-ranked in March 1992, winning 72 house seats, and fourth-ranked in September, with 51. The party withdrew from the ruling coalition in December 1994, after helping to defeat a government-sponsored constitutional amendment providing for direct election of local administrative bodies. It emerged from the 1995 legislative poll as the second-ranked party with 86 seats, which it increased to a narrow plurality of 125 in November 1996. Following his resignation as prime minister in November 1997, Chaovalit became leader of the opposition in the house.

In mid-April 1999 General Chaovalit and the party's entire executive board quit in a move designed to force the resignation of the party's secretary general, Sanoh Thienthong. At a party session on April 27 Chaovalit was reinstated and a new secretary general, CHATURON Chaisaeng, chosen. On March 19, 2000, Chaovalit again resigned as party leader, this time to force out the reform-minded Chaturon, who promptly resigned as secretary general. In April Chaturon and several NAP house members joined *Thai Rak Thai*, which had admitted Sanoh earlier in the month. After having won 36 seats in the January 2001 election, the NAP joined the governing coalition led by *Thai Rak Thai*.

In January 2002 the NAP leadership agreed to merge into *Thai Rak Thai*, and on March 28 the Constitutional Court approved the party's dissolution. On May 10, however, CHINGCHAI Mongkoltham, a member of the NAP's lower house delegation who had objected to the merger, reregistered the party, but without achieving electoral success in the 2007 election.

Leaders: PHANTACH Raksasuk, YONGGYUTH Rodkhlaikhlib (Secretary General).

Thai Citizens (*Prachakorn Thai*—PT). *Prachakorn Thai* was launched prior to the 1979 election by the promilitary and charismatic populist Samak Sundaravej, who succeeded in routing the Democrats in their traditional stronghold of Bangkok. From 1983 to 1986 it participated in a quadripartite governing coalition with the DP, the SAP, and the now-defunct National Democracy Party (*Chart Prachathipatai*) of former prime minister Kriangsak Chamanan, and in December 1990 it entered the reshuffled Chatchai coalition.

Although the party won only 3 house seats in September 1992, it took 18 in 1995 and again in 1996. Twelve of its MPs joined the governing coalition formed by Prime Minister Chuan in late 1997, for which they were expelled from the party in October 1998, threatening their house seats. Dubbed the "Cobras" by the party leader, the 12 appealed the decision to the Constitutional Court, which in February 1999 ruled the dismissal unconstitutional and gave the renegades 30 days to find new parties or lose their standing in the House. Nine joined the revived *Rassadorn*, 2 joined *Chart Pattana*, and 1 joined *Seri Tham*.

Samak won the Bangkok gubernatorial election in July 2000, defeating 21 other candidates, but the party failed to win any House seats in 2001 or 2005. In the April 2006 disputed election it won only 0.9 percent of the vote.

In 2007 the party put up nearly 200 candidates in the December 2007 election. In the meantime, Samak had become leader of the PPP, leaving the reigns of the allied PT in his younger brother's hands, who proved unsuccessful in winning any seats for the party in the 2007 election.

Leaders: SUMIT Sundaravej (President), SOMBOON Wesasunthornthaep (Secretary General).

Referendum Party (*Prachamati* Party—PP). Established September 25, 2007, the PP was considered close to *Matchimathipataya*. Its leader proposed that General Sonthi be named prime minister following the December election. Although the party fielded nearly 300 candidates, the PP was unsuccessful in capturing any House seats.

Leaders: PRAMUAN Ruchanaseree (Leader), WITHUN Naewphanich (Secretary General).

New Politics Party—NPP (*Karn Muang Mai*). The NPP was formally registered on June 2, 2009. An offshoot of the urban progovernment People's Alliance for Democracy, it aims to set up branches in the regions and contest the next election to offset the popularity of the rural parties and movements mobilized by Thaksin's populist appeal. Labor leader Somsak Kosaisuuk was chosen as the NPP's inaugural leader.

Leaders: SOMSAK Kosaisuuk, SURIYASAI Katasila (Secretary General).

Parties Dissolved in 2007:

Thais Love Thais (*Thai Rak Thai*—TRT). Thaksin Shinawatra, a leading figure in the telecommunications industry and a former leader of *Palang Dharma,* announced formation of *Thai Rak Thai* in July 1998. He subsequently set about positioning the party for the next general election, advocating debt relief for farmers and various measures to promote business expansion. In addition, he began recruiting senior members from virtually all of the country's other parties, including the DP, in a process that DP leaders characterized as assembling a "used car" fleet. By April 2000, however, with the standing of the NAP and other parties endangered by factionalism, Thaksin had attracted sufficient support to make *Thai Rak Thai* a leading electoral contender. In the January 2001 election the party won 248 seats, permitting Thaksin to claim the prime minister's office.

In July 2001 *Thai Rak Thai* absorbed *Seri Tham* (also known as the Liberal Democratic Party), which had been launched in 1992 by ARTHIT Urairat and which went on to win 8 seats in the 1992 election. It then entered the first Chuan government in September 1993 upon the departure of the SAP. Arthit defected to the DP before the November 1996 election, after which *Seri Tham* joined the NAP-led coalition government despite having won only 4 seats in the house (down from 11 in 1995). In the formation of the DP-led government in November 1997 the party secured one deputy ministerial position. A planned merger in 2000 with *Rassadorn* failed to materialize, and in the January 2001 election, under the leadership of former *Chart Pattana* chief adviser PRACHUAB Chaiyasarn, *Seri Tham* won 14 seats. It then supported the election of Prime Minister Thaksin, who pursued the *Seri Tham* merger in the interest of securing a *Thai Rak Thai* majority in the house. In March 2002 Chaovalit Yongchaiyut's NAP disbanded and also merged into *Thai Rak Thai.* (For a history of the NAP, which was soon reregistered by opponents of the merger, see above.)

In August 2004 *Chart Pattana* (National Development Party) merged with *Thai Rak Thai. Chart Pattana* had been launched in mid-1992 by former *Chart Thai* prime minister Chatchai Choonhavan, whose assets of some $24.5 million had been seized in mid-January as representing "unusual wealth," and who had chosen not to contest the March election. Despite its leader's liabilities, the new group captured third place with 60 lower house seats in September 1992.

Chart Pattana joined the first Chuan Leekpai government in December 1994, although General Chatchai declined a cabinet post and formally resigned as party leader to assuage DP members who disapproved of support he had given to the military junta from February 1991 to June 1992. The party came in fourth, with 53 seats, in 1995 and then took 52, for third place, in the 1996 election. Chatchai died in May 1998, and in October his successor as party leader, Korn Dabbaransi, brought the party into the governing Chuan coalition. Representation plummeted to 29 seats in the January 2001 election, after which the party was reportedly considering various merger options. None came to fruition, however, and in March 2002 *Chart Pattana* joined the government. In November 2003 it returned to the opposition upon its dismissal from the cabinet. Shortly thereafter, Korn joined *Thai Rak Thai. Chart Pattana* rejoined the government a month before the merger with *Thai Rak Thai.*

Internally, *Thai Rak Thai* was dominated by various factions loyal to Thaksin, Sudarat Keyuraphan, Suriya Jungrungreangkit, and others. The largest party constituency by far was the *Wang Nam Yom* faction. Among the leaders who resigned from the party in 2006 were Korn Dabbaransi and Sanoh Thienthong (both currently of the RPP), the latter taking with him most of his *Wang Nam Yen* faction.

Thaksin left Thailand shortly after the military takeover in September 2006, choosing to live in exile in London. He reportedly provided funding for the PPP (below) and other populist parties to which his followers transferred, although 111 former senior party members were prohibited from direct involvement in party politics for five years. Other former leaders included the following: CHAMLONG Khrutkhuntod (formerly of *Chart Pattana*), Chaturon Chaisaeng (deputy leader, formerly of NAP), Newin Chidchob (formerly of *Ekkaparb,* subsequently associated with the PPP and then the Proud Thais Party), Pinij Jarusombat (former minister of health, formerly of *Seri Tham,* now with *Puea Pan Din*), PONGPOL Adireksarn (formerly of *Chart Thai*), PRACHA Maleenont (*Wang Kang Kao* faction, former deputy interior minister), Somsak Thepsuthin (former minister of labor, *Wang Nam Yom* faction, formerly of SAP, subsequently with the Neutral Democratic Party), Sonthaya Khunplome (*Ram Nam* faction, subsequently an adviser to *Chart Thai*), SUDARAT Keyuraphan (former minister of agriculture and cooperatives, Bangkok faction, formerly of *Palang Dharma*), Suwat Liptapanlop (former deputy prime minister, *Lam Ta Kong* faction, formerly of *Chart Pattana,* now with *Ruam Jai Thai Chart Pattana*), Suwit Khunkitti (deputy leader, previously and currently with SAP), WAN Muhammad Noor Matha (*Wadah* faction, formerly of NAP), YOAWAPA Wongsawat (*Wang Bua Ban* faction), SURIYA Jungrungreangkit (former deputy prime minister, *Wang Nam Yom* faction, secretary general).

Other parties forced to dissolve in May 2007 for having committed electoral fraud were the **Pattana Chart Thai,** the **Progressive Democratic Party,** and the **Thai Ground Party.**

Parties Dissolved in 2008:

People Power Party (*Pak Palang Prachachon*—PPP). Previously a minor party established in 1998, the PPP attracted former members of the populist-welfare *Thai Rak Thai* (see below) after the latter was banned in 2007. PPP leaders were elected on August 24, 2007, led by veteran politician Samak Sundaravej, a former DP member and *Prachakorn Thai* founder. Notable new members included WICHIENCHOT Sukchotrat, a former member of the National Counter-Corruption Commission; former ambassador PHITTAYA Pukkamal; and WIKRAN Suphamongkol, nephew of former foreign minister KANTATHI Suphamongkol. Support was strongest in the poorer constituencies of the capital and in the north and northeast of the country, where former prime minister Thaksin enjoyed his greatest popularity.

The PPP was the clear winner of the December 2007 election, taking 199 out of 400 constituency seats and 34 out of 80 proportional seats. But 8 seats short of clear majority in the House of Representatives, the PPP negotiated a coalition with five other parties, for a total of 316 seats, enabling it to form a government. The new cabinet, led by PPP leader Samak, was sworn in on February 6, 2008, with the PPP taking two-thirds of the 36 portfolios. Three of the female ministers were wives of banned executives of the disbanded *Thai Rak Thai.* In May Prime Minister's Office minister JAKRAPOB Penkair resigned in the face of police charges of having insulted the king.

In July 2008 the Constitutional Court found Public Health Minister CHAIYA Sasomsup guilty of electoral reporting irregularities, ruled that Foreign Minister Noppadon Pattarna had violated the constitution in an agreement with Cambodia, and found House Speaker YONGYUTH Tiyapairat guilty of vote-buying, obliging all three to resign. Because Yongyuth was a member of the PPP executive, this conviction had the potential to disqualify the entire executive, leading to the disbandment of the party, as befell its predecessor, *Thai Rak Thai.* Samak's attempts to amend the constitution to prevent this action contributed to popular demonstrations against his government in mid-2008, led by the People's Alliance for Democracy, which had agitated successfully against Thaksin's government in 2006. PPP was dissolved on December 2, 2008, by the Constitutional Court for vote-buying in the 2007 election and its leader and executives banned from holding office for five years.

Leaders: SAMAK Sundaravej (Party Leader and Former Prime Minister), SOMCHAI Wongsawat (Former Prime Minister), CHALERM Yoobamrung (Deputy Leader), SURAPHONG Suebwonglee (Secretary General).

Thai Nation (*Chart Thai*—CT). *Chart Thai* was regarded as the principal heir of the Thanom military regime's United Thai People's

Party. In 1983 it merged with the Siam Democratic Party (*Prachatipat Siam*), a rightist monarchist group dating from 1981.

Following the 1988 election the *Chart Thai* served as the core of a governing coalition led by Gen. Chatchai Choonhavan that included the SAP, *Rassadorn, Muan Chon,* and the DP in addition to the now-dissolved United Democratic Party (*Sabha Pracha Tripathi*), with the Thai Mass (*Phangcho Chao Thai,* likewise defunct) being added in August 1990. The coalition collapsed in early December 1988, but General Chatchai formed a new coalition and remained tenuously as prime minister until 1992, whereupon he was succeeded by retired air chief marshal SOMBOON Rahong. The choice triggered popular opposition to military domination of the government, and Somboon stepped down in favor of civilian leaders. In July 1995 *Chart Thai* momentarily became the largest legislative party, its representation rising from 77 to 92, but its strength in the House declined to 39 seats in 1996 and 41 seats in the January 2001 election. In the early 2000s leadership disagreements and defections to *Thai Rak Thai*, notably by SOMPONG Amornvivat, weakened *Chart Thai*, which then decided to join in coalition with *Thai Rak Thai.*

Chart Thai won 25 seats in the 2005 election for the House of Representatives but was not invited to join Prime Minister Thaksin's new government. It boycotted the April 2006 snap election (along with the DP and *Mahachon)* and demanded Thaksin's resignation.

A November 2007 poll found *Chart Thai* to be the third most popular party among Bangkok voters, attracting 4.9 percent approval, but two of its advisers, PAVEENA Hongsakul and SONTHAYA Khunplome, were obliged by the Electoral Commission to resign because as former executives of the banned *Thai Rak Thai* they could not engage in electoral activities for five years. In the December election *Chart Thai* emerged as the third strongest party, winning 34 seats, and subsequently agreed to join the six-party coalition led by the PPP. In the new cabinet sworn in on February 6, 2008, *Chart Thai* held several positions, but in May the Electoral Commission recommended that *Chart Thai* be disbanded for electoral fraud in the December 2007 election. The Attorney General submitted the case to the Constitutional Court, which on December 2, 2008, ruled the dissolution of *Chart Thai.*

Leaders: BANHARN Silpa-Archa (Leader), SOMSAK Prisanananthakul (Deputy Leader), SANAN Kachornprasart (Chief Adviser), WIRAI Wiriyakijja, PRAPHAT Bhothasuthon (Secretary General).

Neutral Democratic Party—NDP (*Matchimathipataya*). *Matchima* was formed in 2006 by SOMSAK Thepsuthin, a former *Thai Rak Thai* cabinet minister and leader of that party's largest faction, the *Wang Nam Yom*. A populist party similar to *Thai Rak Thai, Matchima* pledged to establish 9 million ponds in rural areas, reduce the price of tickets for public transport, and guarantee agricultural product prices. In September 2007 merger talks were initiated with the *Puea Pan Din* and *Pracharaj* parties and the Bangkok 50 and Saman Chan Group on forming a "third option" between the pro- and anti-Thaksin parties, but an agreement failed to materialize. Major party leadership changes occurred in November 2007, at which time the party adopted *Matchimathipataya* as its name and THANAPORN Sriyakoon was replaced as leader by PRACHAI Leophairatana. The poor election results in December induced Prachai to resign, and on February 27, 2008, Anongwan Thepsuthin was chosen as leader.

The party emerged as fourth most popular among Bangkok residents polled in November 2007, with an approval rating of 4.6 percent, but in the December election slipped to fifth place with 7 House seats. It subsequently joined the PPP-led coalition government but was banned by the Constitutional Court on December 2, 2008.

Leaders: ANONGWAN Thepsuthin (Leader), PORNTIWA Nakasa (Secretary General).

Insurgent Groups:

For several decades the small **Pattani United Liberation Organization** (PULO) had fought for formation of an independent Islamic state carved from several southern provinces having Muslim majorities. More recently, a "New PULO" splinter was reported, as was the formation of a militant group, **Bersatu** (United), that may include members of both the PULO and the **National Revolutionary Front** (*Barisan Revolusi Nasional*—BRN). The BRN and its offshoots—the **Barisan Revolusi Nasional–Coordinasi** (BRN-C), its youth wing *Pemud,* and associated "small commando groups" known as the **Runda Kumpulan Kecil** (RKK)—have been implicated in many attacks against civilians as well as the military since 2004, including August 2008 bombs in Sungai Kolok that killed two and a beheading of a local official in early September. Also allegedly involved in carrying out escalating attacks against officials, teachers, and Buddhist leaders were the **Pattani Islamic Mujaheddin Movement** (*Gerakan Mujaheddin Islam Pattani*) and the **Patani Freedom Fighters** (*Pejuang Kemerdekaan Patani*). A recent report by Human Rights Watch put the number of attacks through July 2007 at 4,000, with deaths totaling 2,400—90 percent of them civilians.

Connections to the international al-Qaida terrorist network and to *Jemaah Islamiah* have been alleged but not confirmed. No group claimed responsibility for the rising tempo of attacks experienced in 2006 and 2007, and analysts believe they were carried out by decentralized territorial and mobile cells loosely inspired and directed by secessionist Muslim religious leaders. The widely varying locations, tactics, and weapons of the assaults suggest the absence of a central command.

LEGISLATURE

The 1991 basic law restored bicameralism in the form of a **National Assembly** (*Ratha Sapha*) encompassing an appointed Senate and an elected House of Representatives. The 1997 constitution provided for a directly elected Senate of 200 members not affiliated with political parties serving six-year terms. The House expanded to 500 seats in the January 2001 election, four-fifths directly elected from single-member constituencies and, for the first time, one-fifth chosen on a proportional basis from parties obtaining at least 5 percent of the national vote. Under the new constitution of August 2007, the legislature was to retain its two-chamber structure, but the number and method of selection of legislators were altered as described below.

Senate (*Woothi Sapha*). The first election to the new Senate was held March 4, 2000, with the successful candidates being a mix of unaffiliated political neophytes, reformers, and established figures. The Election Commission quickly disqualified 78 victors for vote-buying, fraud, and campaign offenses. All but 2 were, however, allowed to compete in a second round of balloting on April 29 for the vacated seats. Meanwhile, the term of the predecessor Senate had expired on March 21, and the Constitutional Court had ruled that the new body could not convene without the full complement of 200 senators. Sixty-six were elected on April 29, 8 in a third round on June 4, 3 in a fourth round on July 9, and the final senator in a fifth round on July 22. The new Senate convened on August 1.

The election of April 19, 2006, was once again conducted amid numerous charges that some candidates circumvented proscriptions against campaigning or were too closely connected to political parties. By late July, 180 of the 200 potential senators had been endorsed by the Election Commission, but the commission ceased to function when its three remaining members were convicted of malfeasance and forced to resign. Meanwhile, the previous Senate continued to serve in an interim capacity until suspended by the military coup of September 19, 2006.

The 2007 constitution prescribed a Senate of 150 nonpartisan members. Seventy-six senators, 1 from each province, were to be directly elected. A Senate Selection Committee of seven officials and judges chaired by the president of the Constitutional Court was to select the remaining 74 senators from among nominees of professional, academic, public sector, and private sector associations. On March 2, 2008, 55.6 percent of eligible voters cast ballots for provincial senators without incident. The new Senate was convened on March 17. In 2009 the new prime minister, Abhisit Vejjajiva, indicated his support for amending the constitution to permit senatorial candidates to declare their partisan affiliation.

Speaker: PRASOBSUK Boondech.

House of Representatives (*Sapha Poothan Rassadorn*). Following the general election of February 6, 2005, *Thai Rak Thai* held 377 seats (including 67 party-list seats); the Democrat Party, 96 (26); *Chart Thai,* 25 (7); and *Mahachon,* 2 (0).

On May 8, 2006, the Constitutional Court nullified the results of a snap election held April 2, 2006. (Reballoting had been held on April 23 in 40 districts where unopposed candidates had not won the minimum 20 percent vote on April 2; a similarly necessitated third round in 14 of the 40 constituencies had been postponed.) The Constitutional Court ruled that the voters' right to a secret ballot had been compromised and that the Electoral Commission had not allowed sufficient time between the late February dissolution of the sitting House and the election date. Had the results not been nullified, *Thai Rak Thai* would have been credited with all but a handful of the filled seats, given an election boycott by the leading opposition parties. A new election was subsequently scheduled for October 15 but was canceled by the military junta following the September coup.

The 2007 constitution prescribed a 480-member House of Representatives, of which 400 were to be elected from multimember constituencies and 80 from party lists (10 from each of eight constituencies). The general election held on December 23, 2007, resulted in the following distribution of seats: People Power Party (PPP), 233 seats (199 constituency seats, 34 proportional seats); Democrat Party (DP), 165 (132, 33); *Chart Thai,* 37 (33, 4); For the Motherland (PPD), 24 (17, 7); Thai United National Development Party, 9 (8, 1); Neutral Democratic Party, 7 (7, 0); Royalist People's Party (RPP), 5 (4, 1). The turnout was 74.5 percent of eligible voters. Subsequently, the Electoral Commission disqualified 13 winning candidates (11 from the PPP) for vote-buying and held by-elections during January 2008 to fill the vacant seats. The House convened on January 21, 2008, and the following day PPP member Yongyut Tiyapairat was elected speaker. In May Yongyut was found guilty of vote-buying and obliged to resign, to be replaced by Chai Chidchob.

The Constitutional Court on December 2, 2008, ordered the PPP, *Chart Thai,* and the Neutral Democratic Party dissolved and barred Somchai Wongsawat and 36 PPP executives from politics for five years; it also banned 15 *Chart Thai* legislators. By-elections on January 11, 2009, filled 29 empty seats, with the new Thai Nation Development Party (TNDP) winning 10, the DP winning 7, and the PPD winning 3, giving the governing coalition an additional 20. The opposition For Thais Party (practically speaking, the successor to the PPP) won 5 and the RPP, 4. As of July 2009 the ruling coalition commanded the following numbers in the House: DP, 173 seats; Proud Thais Party, 32; PPD, 32; TNDP, 25; Thais United National Development Party, 9; and the Social Action Party, 5. The opposition comprised the For Thais Party, 189 seats, and RPP, 8. *Rassadorn,* with 3 seats, generally supports the government but is not formally aligned. Three House seats remained vacant.

Speaker: CHAI Chidchob.

CABINET

[as of November 1, 2009]

Prime Minister	Abhisit Vejjajiva (DP)
Deputy Prime Ministers	Suthep Thaugsuban (DP)
	Korbsak Sabhavasu (DP)
	Maj.-Gen. Sanan Kachornprasart (TNDP)
Ministers	
Agriculture and Cooperatives	Theera Wongsamut (PTP)
Commerce	Pornthiva Nakasai (PTP) [f]
Culture	Teera Slukpetch (DP)
Defense	Gen. Prawit Wongsuwan (DP)
Education	Jurin Laksanawisit (DP)
Energy	Wannarat Channukul (TUNDP)
Finance	Korn Chatikavanij (DP)
Foreign Affairs	Kasit Piromya DP)
Industry	Charnchai Chairungrueng (PPD)
Information and Communications Technology	Ranongruk Suwunchwee (PPD) [f]
Interior	Chavarat Charnvirakul (FON)
Justice	Pirapan Salirathavibhaga DP)
Labor	Phaithoon Kaeothong (DP)
Natural Resources and Environment	Suwit Khunkitti (SAP)
Office of the Prime Minister	Satit Wongnongtaey (DP)
	Virachai Virameteekul (DP)
Public Health	Witthaya Kaewparadai (DP)
Science and Technology	Khunying Kalaya Sophonpanich (DP) [f]
Social Development and Human Security	Issara Somchai (DP)
Tourism and Sports	Chumpol Silpa-archa (TNDP)
Transport	Sopon Zarum (FON)

[f] = female

Note: FON refers to the Friends of Newin, the leading faction of the TUNDP.

COMMUNICATIONS

Immediately after the 1976 coup all newspapers were banned. Subsequently, most were permitted to resume publication under strict censorship, which was formally lifted after the coup of October 1977. The government seized all broadcast facilities in the wake of the February 1991 coup but did not impose formal censorship on the print media. The 1997 constitution protected freedom of the press, but under Prime Minister Thaksin, who made his fortune in the telecommunications industry, the government was frequently accused of interfering with opposition media. The 2007 constitution again prescribed press freedoms but during the state of emergency declared by the prime minister on September 2, 2008, the media were prohibited from any reporting that "causes panic, instigates violence, or affects stability."

Information and Communication Minister RANONGRAK Suwanchawee in January 2009 announced that websites deemed to be insulting to the monarchy were to be shut down, and in February the number closed was reported to be over 5,000. The December 4, 2008, and January 24, 2009, editions of *The Economist* were banned for similar reasons. Also in January, an Australian, Harry Nicolaides, was convicted of insulting the monarchy and sentenced to three years imprisonment, but he was subsequently deported. In March the editor of the *Prachatai* political website was arrested and charged with the same offense.

Press. The following are dailies issued in Thai in Bangkok, unless otherwise noted: *Thai Rath* (Thai Nation, 800,000), sensationalist; *Daily News* (800,000); *Naew Na* (Frontline, 200,000); *Baan Muang* (200,000); *Matichon* (180,000); *Dao Siam* (120,000); *Siam Rath* (Siam Nation, 120,000); *Tong Hua Daily News* (85,000), in Chinese; *Kia Hua Tong Huan* (80,000), in Chinese; *Krungthep Turakij* (75,000); *Sig Sian Yit Pao* (70,000), in Chinese; *Bangkok Post* (50,000), in English; *The Nation* (50,000), in English.

News agencies. The Thai News Agency is run by the government; numerous foreign bureaus maintain offices in Bangkok.

Broadcasting and computing. The National Broadcasting Commission, an independent body, is the principal regulatory agency. An estimated 595 AM, FM, and SW radio stations were broadcasting in 2007, including Radio Thailand's 100-plus stations. These included commercial, community service, and educational stations, many operating under government auspices. All radio stations were required to transmit news twice a day from the government's National Broadcasting Services of Thailand. Broadcasts are in Thai, English, French, and a number of other languages. All of the estimated 111 national television stations are controlled by the government or the military.

As of 2008 there were 238.9 Internet users per 1,000 inhabitants.

INTERGOVERNMENTAL REPRESENTATION

Ambassador to the U.S.: Don PRADMUDWINAI.

U.S. Ambassador to Thailand: Eric C. JOHN.

Permanent Representative to the UN: Norachit SINHASENI.

IGO Memberships (Non-UN): ADB, APEC, ASEAN, BIS, Interpol, IOM, IOR-ARC, NAM, PCA, WCO, WTO.

TIMOR-LESTE (EAST TIMOR)

Democratic Republic of Timor-Leste
República Democrática de Timor-Leste

Political Status: Independent republic established May 20, 2002; constitution approved by Constituent Assembly on March 22, 2002.

Area: 5,641 sq. mi. (14,609 sq. km.).

Population: 924,642 (2004C); 1,198,000 (2008E).

Major Urban Center: Dili 173,541 (2004C).

Official Languages: Portuguese, Tetum. A majority of Timorese are fluent in Bahasa Indonesia (a form of Malay); both it and English are "working languages."

Monetary Unit: U.S. Dollar (see U.S. article for principal exchange rates).

President: José RAMOS-HORTA (nonparty); elected by popular vote on May 9, 2007; sworn in for a five-year term on May 20, succeeding Kay Rala Xanana (José Alexandre) GUSMÃO (National Congress of East Timorese Reconstruction).

Prime Minister: Kay Rala Xanana (José Alexandre) GUSMÃO (National Congress of East Timorese Reconstruction); appointed by the president on August 6, 2007, and sworn in on August 8, following the legislative election of June 30, succeeding José RAMOS-HORTA (nonparty), who had stepped down before being sworn in as president. (From May 19 until August 8 Estanislau Alexio da SILVA served as acting prime minister.)

THE COUNTRY

Timor-Leste occupies the eastern half of the tropical island of Timor, near the eastern end of the Indonesian archipelago, plus the small islands of Ataúro (Pulo Cambing) and Jaco (Pulo Jako) as well as Oecussi (Ocussi Ambeno), an enclave on the northern coast of Indonesian West Timor. The landing site of the first Portuguese settlers, Oecussi was retained as part of East Timor when in 1859 Portugal and the Netherlands divided the island into East and West Timor. That north-south boundary line constitutes Timor-Leste's only land border, with Indonesia. The nearest overseas neighbor is Australia to the south across the Timor Sea. The Timorese population is primarily of Malay and Papuan descent. About three-quarters speak Bahasa Indonesia; less than one-quarter are fluent in Portuguese. Also commonly spoken is Tetum, an Austronesian language that incorporated elements of Portuguese over the centuries. The vast majority of the population is Roman Catholic, with small Protestant, Muslim, Hindu, and Buddhist minorities. Equality of the sexes is guaranteed under the 2002 constitution. Nineteen women won election to the current 65-member National Parliament.

Leading occupations continue to be subsistence agriculture and fishing, which account for 85 percent of employment and one-third of non-oil GDP (data on the oil and gas industry are imprecise). Principal crops include coffee (by far the leading export), grains, cassava, spices, coconut, vanilla, and tropical fruits. Small-scale manufacturing, accounting for less than 5 percent of non-oil GDP, involves production of processed coffee, handicrafts, cloth, and a limited range of other consumables. The industrial sector as a whole, led by construction, contributes about 13 percent of GDP. Services account for some 54 percent of non-oil GDP, led by public administration. Future development depends primarily on tapping extensive offshore hydrocarbon reserves. The International Monetary Fund (IMF) reported in 2007 that Timor-Leste's oil and gas revenues had increased from $9 million in 2002 to $342 million in 2005 and were projected to reach $882 million in 2007. The government's Petroleum Fund, in which oil and gas revenues are lodged, exceeded $4 billion in value in early 2009. Other resources include gold, manganese, and marble.

In 1999 violence perpetrated mainly by anti-independence militias, covertly supported by the Indonesian army, destroyed much of the country's infrastructure and precipitated refugee flows that were a major factor in a 35 percent economic contraction for the year. In 2000 and 2001, however, under UN administration, East Timor (subsequently Timor-Leste) registered growth rates of 15 percent and 17 percent, respectively, in its non-oil economy. In 2002, however, delays in concluding bilateral arrangements, coupled with a poorly functioning regulatory and legal structure, slowed inflows of drastically needed investment capital and donor assistance. As the international presence withdrew, output grew only by 2 percent, and that was followed in 2003 by zero growth. The economy rebounded with a GDP growth rate of 4 percent in 2004 and 5.5 percent in 2005. After a contraction of 6 percent in 2006, GDP growth rebounded to 7.8 percent in 2007 and 10 percent in 2008, and was predicted by the Asian Development Bank to continue at that level in 2009 and 2010. Exports of oil, gas, coffee, and marble produced a healthy surplus in both external trade and the domestic budget. Nevertheless, the agricultural sector, which employs 85 percent of the population, suffered a 2.2 percent decline of production in 2007 due to drought, requiring World Food Programme assistance to 30 percent of Timorese. In 2008 per capita income was estimated at $450, approximately one-half of Timorese remained below the poverty line, more than 20 percent were unemployed, and an estimated 10 percent lived in temporary camps or with host families as a result of civil unrest in 2006, although many were resettled during 2008 and 2009. Much of the population had only limited access to education and basic infrastructure. Adult literacy was under 50 percent, only half the population had safe drinking water, only one-fourth had electricity, and the infant mortality rate was 40.65 per 1,000 live births.

GOVERNMENT AND POLITICS

Political background. Even though the bulk of the Indonesian archipelago came under Dutch control in the 17th century, the eastern end of the island of Timor and the enclave of Oecussi were claimed by Portugal, whose traders first arrived there in the early 1500s. In 1859 the Netherlands and Portugal delineated the border between West and East Timor (although the resulting treaty was not ratified until 1904), and East Timor continued to be governed from Macao until reorganized as a separate colony in 1896. A local rebellion in 1910–1912 was repressed.

Following harsh Japanese occupation during World War II, East Timor returned to Portuguese control. Although Indonesia won independence from the Netherlands in 1949, a parallel struggle in East Timor failed, and in 1951 Lisbon amended the Portuguese constitution to redefine the colony as an overseas territory. After a coup in Lisbon in 1974, the new democratic government of Portugal offered to conduct a referendum on East Timor's future status. Although some organizations favored a continued relationship with Portugal or a gradual process of separation, by 1975 all the leading parties were advocating independence. Violence escalated, however, over what form of independent government should be established. On November 28 the left-wing Revolutionary Front for an Independent East Timor (*Frente Revolucionário do Timor-Leste Independente*—Fretilin) declared a "Democratic Republic," but this move was opposed by a number of anticommunist parties, including the Timorese Democratic Union (*União Democrática Timorense*—UDT) and the Timorese Democratic People's Association (*Associação Popular Democrática de Timor*—Apodeti). On December 7 Indonesian forces invaded, allegedly with tacit U.S. and Australian approval, ultimately driving Fretilin from the capital. Jakarta annexed East Timor on July 17, 1976, although Portugal and the United Nations refused to recognize the action.

The initial years of rule from Jakarta were marked by a severe humanitarian crisis that saw an estimated 100,000 East Timorese succumb to starvation or what some observers characterized as genocidal violence by Indonesian forces intent on suppressing the Fretilin-led opposition. During this period, access by the outside world was severely limited, and public expressions of dissent were routinely—often violently—suppressed.

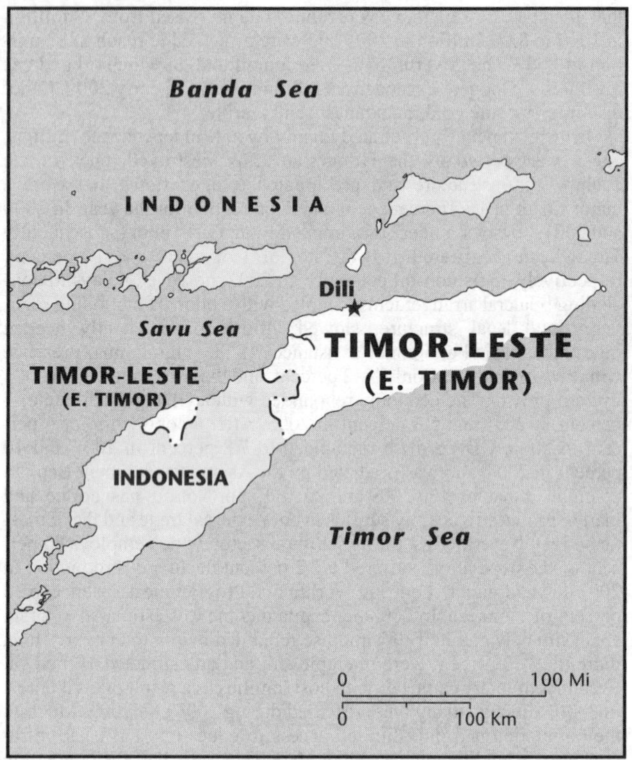

On November 12, 1991, Indonesian troops fired on an estimated 3,500 demonstrators who had assembled peacefully in a Dili cemetery to pay homage to a student killed in a clash with police two weeks earlier. Between 60 and 180 persons were shot before the troops moved in to beat up the survivors, with some 300–400 subsequently reported to have been tortured or executed. In response to worldwide condemnation, Indonesia dismissed East Timor's two principal commanders and meted out penalties to a number of other officers. The following November Fretilin's leader, Xanana GUSMÃO, was captured in a western suburb of Dili and in May 1993 was sentenced to life imprisonment (later reduced to 20 years). In November Konis SANTANA was reported to have taken over as commander of Fretilin's military wing, the *Forças Armadas de Libertação Nacional de Timor-Leste* (Falintil).

In April 1994, in the first reported public expression of dissent since the 1991 massacre, a small group of protestors calling for Gusmão's release and freedom for East Timor mounted a demonstration in Dili that was quickly dispersed by security forces. Substantially more violent confrontations occurred in Dili in July during a visit by a UN special rapporteur on human rights and in November, immediately before the opening of an Asia-Pacific Economic Cooperation (APEC) summit in Bogor, near Jakarta. On November 25 a 12-day sit-in at the U.S. embassy in Jakarta ended with 29 of the participants being permitted to leave the country for Portugal. A further protest by East Timorese youths outside the university in Dili was broken up by police and military units in January 1995.

UN-sponsored talks between Portugal and Indonesia in 1995–1996 made no substantive progress toward resolving the East Timor issue. Jakarta's policy of waiting for the East Timor question to fade from the international agenda suffered a major setback in October 1996 when two prominent Timorese proindependence campaigners were awarded the Nobel Peace Prize. In its citation for Bishop Carlos Felipe XIMENES BELO (Roman Catholic prelate of East Timor) and José RAMOS-HORTA (a former journalist and leader of Fretilin campaigning in exile against Indonesian rule), the Norwegian Nobel committee accused the Suharto government of "systematically oppressing the people" of East Timor and also referred to estimates that under Indonesian occupation "one third of the population of East Timor have lost their lives due to starvation, epidemics, war, and terror." The Indonesian government expressed its "regret" at the award, while Bishop Ximenes Belo took the opportunity to repeat his call for a referendum to decide the status of East Timor.

Sporadic unrest continued in 1997, with incidents sparked by, among other things, the installation of a new Roman Catholic bishop and by special visits by a U.S. human rights expert and a UN envoy. In June Indonesian troops reported the death of rebel leader David ALEX, his colleagues claiming he died under torture. On March 11, 1998, Falintil commander Santana died in a fall and was shortly thereafter succeeded by Taur Matan RUAK.

On April 23–27, 1998, over 200 delegates of the All-Inclusive Intra-East Timorese Dialogue (AIETD) convened in Peniche, Portugal. Most significantly, the session approved formation of a National Council of Timorese Resistance (*Conselho Nacional de Resistência Timorense*—CNRT) to better coordinate the efforts of proindependence groups, including the UDT and Fretilin. Xanana Gusmão and Ramos-Horta were named president and vice president, respectively, of the CNRT political committee.

Even more significant events were taking place in Jakarta, however. On May 21, 1998, Indonesia's longtime president, Suharto, was forced by public protests to resign. The new government quickly began showing greater flexibility toward East Timor as well as its own citizens. On June 9, less than three weeks after assuming office, President B. J. Habibie indicated that he was willing to make East Timor the country's fourth "special" region in return for UN recognition of Indonesian sovereignty. The following day the government confirmed the release of 15 Timorese political prisoners. President Habibie was reportedly prepared also to reduce troop levels in the territory, free additional prisoners, and permit greater freedom of movement for residents. Although East Timorese demonstrators and the CNRT leadership initially rejected the concept of special status, in July the CNRT stated that it might accept transitional autonomy for five years, to be followed by an independence referendum. On July 28 Habibie countered with an offer of autonomy in all policy sectors except defense, foreign relations, and economic policy. Meeting under UN auspices in New York on August 4–5, Indonesian and Portuguese representatives agreed to pursue the option of "wide-ranging autonomy."

Several setbacks occurred during the remainder of the year, including a threat by East Timor's governor, José Abilio SOARES, that civil servants would be dismissed if they failed to pledge support for Jakarta's policies. More importantly, violent clashes between proindependence and pro-Jakarta (prointegrationist) Timorese raised the specter of civil war, and in January 1999 thousands reportedly fled their homes to escape the hostilities. Late in the month, for the first time, the Habibie administration broached the possibility of eventual independence for the territory. Indonesian minister of defense Gen. Wiranto stated that the military would abide by the "will of the people" on the issue, and Foreign Minister Ali Alatas, although continuing to reject the concept of a referendum, told reporters that Jakarta would consider independence if the East Timorese rejected autonomy. On January 28 talks between Indonesia and Portugal resumed at the United Nations. The next day, the Indonesian government offered to move Xanana Gusmão from prison to house arrest, and this conciliatory gesture was carried out on February 10.

Meeting in New York on May 5, 1999, the Portuguese and Indonesian foreign ministers agreed to hold a referendum in East Timor on August 8. Two days later the agreement was supported by a UN Security Council resolution. Proindependence advocates immediately expressed concern that Indonesian forces would remain responsible for security despite increasing evidence that elements in the army were giving clandestine support to prointegrationist militias, most prominently the Red and White Iron (*Besi Merah Putih*—BMP) and the Thorn (*Aitarak*). On June 18 Gusmão and Leandro ISAAC of the CNRT, BMP head João da Silva TAVARES, and Domingos SOARES of the pro-Jakarta Forum for Democracy, Unity and Justice (*Forum Demokrasi, Persatuan dan Keadilan*—FDPK) signed a cease-fire pact and agreed to disarm before the balloting, but the agreement proved no more durable than earlier efforts. Later in the month the 4 were joined by 56 other East Timorese leaders for reconciliation talks organized by Ximenes Belo and Mgr. Basilio dos NASCIMENTO. The dialogue accomplished little, however, and by mid-July some 60,000 Timorese had sought refuge from the continuing violence by fleeing to the countryside or to West Timor.

In June 1999 and again in July the date for the referendum was pushed back because of the unstable security situation, difficulties in registering voters, and insufficient cooperation by local officials and police with the UN Assessment Mission in East Timor (UNAMET). The balloting was finally held on August 30, with UNAMET reporting a 98.6 percent voter turnout. Even before the release of official results, however, prointegrationist militia leaders stated that they would reject the outcome and refused to attend an inaugural meeting of a UN-sponsored Reconciliation Council. As soon as the results were announced on September 4—78.5 percent in favor of independence and 21.5 percent for autonomy—the militias took to the streets in violent assaults on UN workers and journalists as well as East Timorese. The Indonesian military failed to intervene, and in subsequent days attacks and murders were reported throughout the territory. Despite a declaration of martial law by President Habibie, in Dili thousands of fleeing people were driven from the compound of the International Committee of the Red Cross and the official residence of Bishop Ximenes Belo. Gusmão, released from house detention on September 7, appealed for international intervention. With Dili in ruins, the refugee total rose to 450,000, nearly half of whom fled to West Timor.

On September 9, 1999, responding to international pressure by regional leaders meeting at the APEC summit in Auckland, New Zealand, and later by the UN Security Council, President Habibie agreed to allow a peacekeeping presence in East Timor, and on September 15 the UN Security Council unanimously approved formation of the International Force East Timor (INTERFET). Led by some 4,500 Australians and commanded by Maj. Gen. Peter Cosgrove, 8,000 peacekeepers from 30 countries began deploying on September 20. Seven days later, with most of the Indonesian armed forces having withdrawn, INTERFET formally assumed control and despite sporadic clashes with militia fighters moved into the hinterlands to restore order.

On October 19, 1999, Indonesia's supreme legislature, the People's Consultative Assembly, ratified the referendum results without dissent, revoking its 1976 integration decree, and three days later Gusmão flew into Dili, receiving a hero's welcome. Shortly after, UN troops reached Oecussi, where all but a small percentage of the 57,000 population had fled into the countryside to escape prointegrationist violence, most of which was attributed to the Scorpion militia under Florentino SOARES. On October 25 the UN Security Council was able to replace INTERFET with the United Nations Transitional Administration in East Timor (UNTAET), a multipurpose body including not only troops and police but also civilian specialists. Led by Special Representative Sergio Vieira de Mello, the UNTAET was assigned the task of administering East Timor during the two- or three-year transition to independence.

Through November 1999 some 150,000 refugees remained in West Timor, primarily in 140 camps around Atambua, but they continued to suffer the depredations of the militias, which had relocated across the border. On December 1 José Ramos-Horta ended his 24-year exile, and on December 11 Vieira de Mello convened a 15-member advisory National Consultative Council (NCC), which included integrationists as well as CNRT representatives and UNTAET members. On December 12 Gusmão met at the border with the BMP's da Silva Tavares, who the following day called on his forces to lay down their arms.

On January 31, 2000, the Indonesian Commission to Investigate Human Rights Violations in East Timor asserted that members of the armed forces, the police, and the civil administration as well as the militias had conducted a postreferendum campaign of violence and destruction that it termed systematic and planned. The commission's report called for Jakarta to investigate further the actions of 33 individuals, including Wiranto and several other generals. On the same day a UN report on human rights abuses recommended creation of a war crimes tribunal, and in April the Indonesian attorney general named a 79-member investigative team to pursue the alleged "crimes against humanity."

Jorge Sampaio, the first Portuguese head of state to visit East Timor, arrived on February 12, 2000, six weeks after Jakarta and Lisbon had restored diplomatic relations. Even more significantly, on February 29, during a trip to Dili, Indonesia's new president, Abdurrahman Wahid, apologized for his country's legacy of repression, prompting Gusmão to describe him as a symbol of "peace, justice and democracy." A week earlier INTERFET, having suffered no combat casualties, handed over security responsibilities to UNTAET forces.

In May 2000 the newly organized, pro-Jakarta People's Party of Timor (*Partido do Povo de Timor*—PPT), led by Herminio da Silva da COSTA, sought recognition from the UNTAET to contest future elections. Da Costa had previously been affiliated with an anti-independence political umbrella, the Timor Warriors' Association (*Uni Timor Aswain*—Unitas), that continued to reject the referendum results. Meeting with Gusmão in mid-June, da Costa apologized for the previous year's mayhem, offered his support should Gusmão seek the presidency, and sought assurances that the thousands of prointegration refugees in West Timor would not be mistreated if they returned. The status of proindependence refugees in West Timor continued to be of greater international concern, however, because the Indonesian military remained unable or unwilling to completely disarm the militias. On September 6 a militia attack on the compound of the UN High Commissioner for Refugees in Atambua took the lives of three aid workers and prompted the temporary withdrawal of UN personnel from West Timor.

On July 12, 2000, the NCC approved formation of a transitional government comprising João CARRASCALÃO, president of the UDT; Marí ALKATIRI of Fretilin; Fr. Filomeno JACOB; Mariano LOPES, head of the Public Service Commission; and four UNTAET members. Ramos-Horta joined as foreign minister on October 19. A CNRT congress in Dili on August 21–30 elected Gusmão and Ramos-Horta as president and vice president, respectively. Carrascalão was also elected to a vice presidency.

On October 23, 2000, Gusmão was elected president of the 36-member UN-appointed interim legislature, the East Timor National Council (ETNC), but he resigned on March 28, 2001, because of dissatisfaction with the ETNC. His replacement, Ramos-Horta, was succeeded by Carrascalão on April 9. At the end of January the UN Security Council had extended the UNTAET mandate through January 31, 2002, and by midyear it was generally acknowledged that the transition to full independence could not be achieved by the end of 2001. More than 110,000 refugees remained in West Timor, although it was unclear how many wished to return to East Timor.

On August 30, 2001, East Timor democratically elected the 88 members of a Constituent Assembly, which was to supersede the ETNC and begin drafting a constitution. As expected, Fretilin dominated the election, winning 55 seats; the Democratic Party (*Partido Democrático*—PD) followed with 7 seats; the Social Democratic Party (*Partido Social Democrata*—PSD), 6; and the Timorese Social Democratic Association (*Associacão Social-Democrata Timorense*—ASDT), 6. As a result, Fretilin's secretary general, Marí Alkatiri, who had spent many years in African exile, was named chief minister of an interim East Timor Council of Ministers that included Fretilin, the PD, and a number of independents. Meanwhile, a UNTAET-sponsored court in Dili continued investigating militia-related crimes.

In October 2001 the Constituent Assembly called upon the UN to set May 20, 2002, as the date of independence. In January 2002 the assembly voted to convert itself into a National Parliament upon adoption of the constitution, which was achieved by vote of the Constituent Assembly on March 22. On April 14 Gusmão, who had severed his ties to Fretilin after the 1999 referendum, was easily elected to the presidency as an independent, capturing 82 percent of the vote against the token opposition of the ASDT's Francisco Xavier do AMARAL. Gusmão was inaugurated for a five-year term on May 20 in conjunction with the formal establishment of the Democratic Republic of Timor-Leste. On the same day Fretilin's Alkatiri was sworn in as Timor-Leste's first prime minister.

Independence day also marked the end of the UNTAET mission, which was succeeded by a United Nations Mission of Support in East Timor (UNMISET). The UN Security Council, in authorizing its formation on May 17, directed UNMISET to enhance political stability, to provide interim law enforcement while assisting the development of a domestic police service, and to help maintain external security. Although authority to secure the border with West Timor was assumed by Timor-Leste, in October 2003 continuing instability, at least some of it perpetrated by integrationists seeking to destabilize the government, resulted in decisions that extended the UNMISET mission into 2005. UNMISET was replaced in May 2005 by a scaled-down UN Office in Timor-Leste (UNOTIL) with a one-year mandate.

On April 28, 2006, demonstrations in the capital supporting soldiers who had been dismissed from the army turned violent, precipitating two months of sporadic gang violence as well as clashes between elements of the police and armed forces that left nearly 40 people dead. The roots of the civil disorder can be traced to early February, when some 400 soldiers of the Timorese army (Falintil–*Forças de Defesa de Timor-Leste*—F-FDTL), led by Lt. Gastão SINHALA, left their barracks to protest alleged discrimination. The disgruntled troops from western districts of the country (*Loromonu*), whose numbers grew to about 600 later in the month, complained of favoritism toward the majority easterners (*Lorosae*), who had been more prominent and numerous in Falintil. The F-FDTL rebels were joined early in May by Maj. Alfredo REINADO and a contingent of military police. On May 24 Foreign Minister Ramos-Horta requested international aid, and the first of some 2,500 Australian, New Zealand,

Malaysian, and Portuguese troops and police began arriving the next day as "Operation Astute," but it took two weeks for them to restore a semblance of order to Dili and its environs.

On May 29, 2006, President Gusmão convened the Council of State, which was also attended by UNOTIL representative Sukehiro Hasegawa and special UN envoy Ian Martin. The next day, Gusmão declared a 30-day state of emergency and, as commander in chief, assumed control of the F-FDTL and the Timorese police (*Policia Nacional de Timor-Leste*—PNTL), superseding the authority of Minister of the Interior Rogério LOBATO (Fretilin) and Secretary of State for National Defense Roque Félix RODRIGUES. Both cabinet members resigned on June 1, after which Ramos-Horta was assigned the defense portfolio in addition to his duties as foreign minister. On June 8 accusations surfaced that Prime Minister Alkatiri and Lobato had armed a score of civilian supporters and had directed them to eliminate Alkatiri's opponents. (Charges against Alkatiri were dismissed in February 2007, but Lobato was convicted in March 2007 and given a prison sentence of seven and a half years.)

On June 26, 2006, Prime Minister Alkatiri resigned under pressure brought to bear by supporters of the dismissed soldiers, the parliamentary opposition, and President Gusmão, who on June 22 had threatened his own resignation if Alkatiri did not step down. On July 8 Gusmão named José Ramos-Horta prime minister, and a reshuffled cabinet was sworn in on July 14.

The April–May 2006 disturbances had signaled that UNMISET's departure in 2005 had been too hasty, leaving behind fragile security institutions. The inadequately prepared PNTL had proved disorganized and indecisive during the disturbances, and many of the police had sided with the rebels against the F-FDTL. At the urging of Ramos-Horta, the UN Security Council in August 2006 set up the UN Integrated Mission in Timor (UNMIT) to succeed UNOTIL and committed it to a two-year deployment, which was later extended.

In a role reversal, Ramos-Horta was elected president for a five-year term in a two-way run-off on May 9, 2007, with 69.1 percent of votes. This followed a first round on April 9 that saw Fretilin's Francisco GUTERRES lead Ramos-Horta 27 percent to 21 percent against six other candidates, most of whose supporters opposed giving the presidency to Fretilin and therefore backed Ramos-Horta in the second round. Ramos-Horta was inaugurated on May 20. Meanwhile, on March 26 Gusmão, having chosen not to seek a second term as president, had assumed the leadership of a newly formed opposition party, the National Congress for Timorese Reconstruction (*Congresso Nacional de Reconstrução do Timor*—CNRT), and had vowed to contest Fretilin's majority in the upcoming parliamentary elections. His party won only 18 of 65 seats in the June 30 poll but was able to form a governing coalition, dubbed the Alliance of the Parliamentary Majority (*Aliança com Maioria Parlamentar*—AMP), with three other parties. President José Ramos-Horta had advocated the formation of a national unity government to include Fretilin, which had won 21 seats, but multiparty talks ultimately broke down over policy and personality differences. Weeks of wrangling followed, with Fretilin failing in its attempts to form an alternative coalition. President Ramos-Horta appointed Gusmão as prime minister on August 6, and he assumed office two days later. Disgruntled Fretilin members committed arson and rampaged in the streets in response to the formation of the AMP government. In a September 2007 report on UNMIT, UN Secretary General Ban Ki Moon stated that "the security situation in the country improved overall during the reporting period but continues to be volatile and subject to sporadic violence."

On February 11, 2008, rebels attempted to assassinate President Ramos-Horta, severely wounding him, and fired shots at Prime Minister Gusmão's motorcade. Rebel leader Reinado was killed by Ramos-Horta's guards. Parliament declared a state of emergency, Australia dispatched 350 additional troops and police, and order was restored. On April 29 Reinado's second in command, Gastão SALSINHA, and 12 followers surrendered to the government, joining 15 others who had previously surrendered. Indonesia in May 2008 apprehended and turned over 4 rebels who had fled to West Timor.

Constitution and government. The constitution drafted by the Constituent Assembly and approved in its final form on March 22, 2002, after a period of popular consultation, provides for freedom of speech and of the press, freedom of religion, the right of *habeas corpus,* and freedom of association (except that "armed, military or paramilitary associations, including organizations of a racist or xenophobic nature or that promote terrorism, shall be prohibited"). The chief executive, a popularly elected president serving a once-renewable five-year term, plays a largely ceremonial role. In the event no presidential candidate receives a majority on a first ballot, the constitution mandates a runoff between the top two contenders. Most executive power resides with the prime minister, who is appointed by the president but must command a parliamentary majority. The prime minister selects the members of the cabinet, who are then appointed by the president.

The unicameral National Parliament initially had 88 members: 13 chosen to represent single-member districts and the balance elected nationally under a proportional system based on party lists. Prior to the 2007 election the National Parliament altered the electoral law to reduce the number of representatives to 65 members. The National Parliament, which has a five-year term, may be dissolved prematurely and new elections held, but not within six months of the next scheduled election or within six months of the end of a presidential term. Among its powers, the legislature may amend the constitution on a two-thirds vote. The 2002 constitution also provides for a Council of State, an advisory body chaired by the president and encompassing all past presidents, the prime minister, the speaker of the National Parliament, five citizens selected by the legislature, and five designated by the president.

The independent judiciary is headed by a Supreme Court of Justice with authority to rule on the constitutionality of statutes and referenda and to certify "the regularity and validity of the acts of the electoral process." There is also a High Administrative, Tax, and Audit Court and provision for Military Courts. Below the national level, Timor-Leste is divided into 13 administrative districts. The constitution recognizes Oecussi as meriting a "special administrative policy and economic regime."

Foreign relations. Timor-Leste became the 191st member of the United Nations General Assembly on September 27, 2002. By the end of the year it was also a member of several UN Specialized Agencies, including the World Bank, the IMF, the International Fund for Agricultural Development, and the World Health Organization. In addition, Timor-Leste has stated its intention to seek admission to the Association of Southeast Asian Nations (ASEAN) and access to the ASEAN Free Trade Agreement. It has participated in the regional security consultation body, the ASEAN Regional Forum, since 2005.

Even before independence, Timor-Leste attempted to facilitate close relations with its immediate neighbors, Australia and Indonesia. The Australian delegation to the independence festivities was led by Prime Minister John Howard, who joined President Gusmão in signing a Timor Sea Treaty that granted Timor-Leste 90 percent of revenue from a Joint Petroleum Development Area (JPDA), the Bayu-Undan hydrocarbon field. Timor-Leste ratified the treaty in December 2002, as did Australia in March 2003, whereupon it came into force. However, the neighbors remained at odds over delineation of their maritime boundary and eligibility for royalties from further oil exploitation development rights. Consequently, in 2003 Dili sought to revise the provision of the treaty that would give Timor-Leste only 20 percent of the larger Greater Sunrise field, which lies outside the joint area in what Australia considers its territory. Dili also wanted to redraw the maritime boundary with Australia at the halfway point, but the Howard government argued for retaining the border as delineated by a 1972 agreement with Indonesia based on the continental shelf principle. Boundary talks began in November 2003, broke down in October 2004 amid charges by Dili that Australia was employing delaying tactics, and resumed in March 2005. Two months later an agreement was announced that would postpone determination of the boundary for 50 years but would give Timor-Leste 50 percent of Greater Sunrise revenues.

In January 2006 the disputants signed an agreement to that effect, the Treaty on Certain Maritime Arrangements in the Timor Sea (CMATS Treaty). Opponents in Timor-Leste's National Parliament stated that they would fight ratification, in part because the agreement did not resolve the boundary demarcation issue. Nevertheless, Prime Minister Ramos-Horta stated in late July 2006 that he intended to seek parliamentary approval of the CMATS Treaty and to make a "robust and convincing argument" in its defense. He was successful, and on February 23, 2007, Timor-Leste and Australia exchanged notes in which each government confirmed that it had ratified the agreement. The CMATS Treaty then entered into force. Exploitation of the Timor Sea oil field is expected to bring over $4 billion in royalties to Timor-Leste over the life of the project.

Australia remains Timor-Leste's main security and trading partner as well as a source of aid and foreign investment. In February 2002 Timor-Leste and Australia signed two Memorandums of Understanding (MOUs) on combating illegal immigration and people smuggling, followed in August 2003 by an MOU on Cooperation to Combat International Terrorism. The two governments also signed an MOU in October 2006 on security arrangements within the JPDA. Australia funds and staffs training programs for the Timorese armed forces and police under its Defence Cooperation Program. Canberra has granted Timorese products duty-free access to the domestic market and budgeted A$96.34 million for aid to Timor-Leste for 2008–2009 for projects ranging from rural water supply and maternal and child health to vocational training for rural youth and improved food security.

In a gesture of reconciliation, Indonesian president Megawati Sukarnoputri attended the independence ceremonies in Dili in May 2002, prompting President Gusmão to relegate decades of repression and violence under Indonesian rule to "history and the past." In early July, during a visit to Jakarta by Gusmão, Timor-Leste and Indonesia signed a joint communiqué establishing diplomatic relations. In April 2005, during a visit by Indonesian president Susilo Bambang Yudhoyono, the two countries signed a border demarcation agreement. An Indonesian team commenced a border survey to demarcate five disputed areas: Imbate, Sumkaen, Haumaeniana, Nilulat, and Tibana; the survey continued through 2009, delayed by local security concerns.

Relations with Indonesia are correct but shadowed by the issue of justice for the perpetrators and victims of the militia violence of 1999. In Jakarta, a handful of civilian and military figures were convicted of crimes against humanity by an Indonesian Ad Hoc Human Rights Court, including former governor of East Timor José Abilio Soares, former Dili military commander Lt. Col. Soedjarwo, and former army commander Brig. Gen. Noer Moeis. All three had their convictions overturned on appeal. To date, former militia leader Eurico Gutteres is the only individual to have been incarcerated in Indonesia for human rights crimes committed in East Timor, and his conviction was overturned in April 2008.

In Dili, the UN-funded Serious Crimes Unit (SCU) indicted 392 individuals between 2000 and its closure in 2005. Based on the SCU indictments, two Special Panels for Serious Crimes (SPSC), also funded by the UN, had conducted 55 trials and handed down 84 convictions and 3 acquittals. But Jakarta refused to recognize the indictments against 311 Indonesian citizens, including one against former defense minister and presidential candidate General Wiranto. The UN terminated the SCU process in May 2005. A study of the episode published by the East West Center in Honolulu, Hawaii, in July 2006 criticized the United Nations for "a massive institutional failure . . . to create a judicial enterprise worthy of the values and standards that the United Nations represents."

In November 2005 President Gusmão delivered to the National Parliament the 2,500-page final report of the appointed Commission for Reception, Truth, and Reconciliation in East Timor (*Comissão de Acolhimento, Verdade e Reconciliação de Timor-Leste*—CAVR), which had begun work in 2002. The report, which covered the period of April 1974–October 1999, put the death toll under Indonesian rule at 102,000 and attributed 85 percent of the human rights violations committed during the period to Indonesian security personnel, although the UDT and Fretilin were also blamed. The CAVR called for a renewed mandate for the SPSC to prosecute those responsible, but President Gusmão, who believed that "problems end with justice, truth, and reconciliation," was skeptical of the commissioners' "grandiose optimism."

A parallel body, the Indonesia Timor-Leste Joint Commission on Truth and Friendship, reported in July 2008, finding the Indonesian government, military, and policy responsible for murder, rape, torture, and forced displacement of Timorese in 1999. The Indonesian president expressed "deep regret" and the Indonesian military chief Gen. Djoko Santoso stated that the 1999 mayhem "has become TNI's [the Indonesian military's] responsibility." Both Indonesian leaders and the president of Timor-Leste agreed that the report was a final authoritative account of "an unfortunate chapter" and pledged to forgo further recriminations or prosecutions in order to lay a foundation for future harmonious relations, a pledge that was renewed in August 2009 on the tenth anniversary of the independence referendum. China emerged as a leading benefactor, having been among the first to recognize the new state in 2002. In 2007 China was financing the construction of the presidential palace and a hospital, building barracks and providing uniforms for the armed forces, deploying police and medical aid personnel, training civil servants and farmers, and giving scholarships to students and officials to visit China. PetroChina has won a contract to conduct a seismic survey and has expressed interest in developing offshore oil fields. In August 2008 President Ramos-Horta visited Beijing, where he was received by China's president, Hu Jintao, and in 2009 officials indicated that Timor-Leste would be purchasing two oil-fired power plants and patrol boats from China.

The United States signed an agreement in August 2009 for the U.S. Army to train Timor-Leste's marines alongside Indonesia's marines. U.S. aid focuses on technical assistance to government prosecutors, legal aid institutions, media and journalists, and civil society bodies. Other states and organizations maintaining supportive diplomatic, economic, and humanitarian relations with Timor-Leste include Portugal, Japan, New Zealand, the European Union, UN agencies, and private charities and NGOs.

Current issues. A decision by parliament in August 2008 to buy new Japanese automobiles for all its members triggered a demonstration by students demanding the money be spent instead on rice for the poor. The appointment in March 2009 of Longuinhos Montiero as commander of the faction-ridden national police also provoked controversy, voiced by the opposition party Fretilin. Nevertheless, law and order prevailed as 28 persons, including rebel deputy leader Salsinha and slain rebel leader Reinado's lover Angelita PIRES, an Australian citizen, were formally charged on March 4 with murder or accessory to murder for the failed assassination attempt of 2008; their trial began on July 13.

Urban gang violence, which flared up in 2006, has diminished. Parliament, encouraged by a peace-building project sponsored by Oxfam, Concern, Action Asia, Yayasan Hak, and NGO Forum, on July 16, 2008, passed a law to register and regulate "martial arts groups" (the core of many gangs), and in August 2008 brokered a "peace pact" between the two leading gangs, 7-7 and FSHT.

Reflecting an improved security situation, the UN in February 2009 transferred control of three Dili police posts to local police, and Australia in April announced a gradual withdrawal of 200 troops. In mid-2009 UNMIT comprised 1,559 police, 33 military liaison officers, and 357 civilian staff and 155 UN volunteers from 40 countries plus 879 local employees. These were reinforced by approximately 650 Australian Defense Force soldiers and 50 police, 150 New Zealand Defense Force troops, and contingents from 12 other states. UNMIT's mandate has been renewed to February 26, 2010, and its chief of staff, Gerard Gallucci, indicated in August that a 10 percent reduction of foreign troop strength might soon be feasible.

In October 2008 the government announced its sponsorship of a pipeline to convey oil and gas from the Greater Sunrise field to a petrochemical plant provisionally to be built in East Timor by Malaysia's national energy firm Petronas. The project was estimated to be worth up to $14 billion to the Timor-Leste government and economy. Australia's Woodside Petroleum favored a contrasting plan to run the pipeline south to a processing plant in Darwin. Because the terms of the 2006 joint development zone treaty required both governments to agree, a diplomatic impasse ensued in 2009. Meanwhile, corruption in government remained an obstacle to investment as Timor-Leste dropped from 123 to 145 in the Transparency International index during the period of 2006–2008 and Fretilin opposition leaders accused the prime minister of awarding government contracts to political associates and family members.

POLITICAL PARTIES

Timor-Leste's oldest parties date from 1974, when the question of the Portuguese territory's future status was becoming increasingly divisive, as local elites formed parties to promote or resist movement toward independence. In late 1975 vigorous debate turned into interparty violence. After the December 1975 Indonesian invasion, opposition to Indonesian annexation was led by the leftist Revolutionary Front for an Independent East Timor (Fretilin) and its military wing, Falintil. The anti-independence parties, such as the Timorese Democratic Union (UDT), accommodated the Indonesian authorities but later became disillusioned and opposed the occupation. In April 1998 Fretilin agreed to join other surviving parties in forming an umbrella National Council of Timorese Resistance (*Conselho Nacional de Resistência Timorense*—CNRT). The end of the Suharto regime in 1998 was soon followed by the emergence of a number of new parties, some of which initially sought autonomy for East Timor within Indonesia, while others, led by Fretilin, opted for total independence. The end of the Indonesian occupation saw a proliferation of new parties, most of them small, personality based, and short lived. Before Timor-Leste's first election in August 2001, 16 parties registered candidate lists; 12 won at least 1 seat in the

Constituent Assembly. In the June 2007 parliamentary election 14 parties registered their lists but only 7 won seats, the rest failing to reach the threshold of 3 percent of the popular vote. Fretilin won the most seats, 21, but the next 3 finishers formed a coalition government, the **Alliance of the Parliamentary Majority** (*Aliança com Maioria Parlamentar*—AMP), under Xanana Gusmão, the leader of the largest partner, the new National Congress for Timorese Reconstruction (also CNRT).

Governing Parties:

National Congress for Reconstruction of Timor (*Congresso Nacional de Reconstrução do Timor*—CNRT). The CNRT is an indirect descendant of the National Council for Reconstruction of Timor (*Conselho Nacional de Resistência Timorense*—CNRT) that functioned as an umbrella body for resistance to Indonesian rule. Established in 1998, it lapsed following the country's independence. The current CNRT, with a modified name but same acronym, coalesced in early 2007 from elements dissatisfied with the existing political parties. It is centrist, moderate, and pragmatic in its ideology. Its organization is based on prominent personalities rather than a formal branch structure. Outgoing president Xanana Gusmão assumed leadership of the party in March 2007 and attracted many of his followers and supporters in the electorate. The party polled well in the June 2007 parliamentary election but did not succeed in gaining a majority, winning only 24 percent of the vote and 18 seats, placing second behind Fretilin, which won 21. As neither party could command a majority, in July Gusmão negotiated an agreement with the Timorese Social Democratic Association–Social Democratic Party alliance and the Democratic Party to forge a parliamentary majority. On August 6 Ramos-Horta requested that the CNRT form a government, appointing party president Gusmão as prime minister. The current cabinet includes two CNRT ministers and a handful of independents aligned with the CNRT.

Leaders: Xanana GUSMÃO (President), Dionisio Babo SOARES (Secretary General).

Timorese Social Democratic Association (*Associação Social-Democrata Timorense*—ASDT). The current ASDT was formed in 2001 by one of the earliest Fretilin leaders, Francisco Xavier do Amaral, as a "third way" Fretilin offshoot positioned between the parent party and more conservative elements. In 1974 Nicolau dos Reis LOBATO, Xavier do Amaral, José Ramos-Horta, and others had established the original ASDT, which was soon superseded by Fretilin. During Indonesian rule, Xavier do Amaral had resided in Jakarta, and he initially returned to East Timor as a proautonomy integrationist. He has also been associated with a more radical Fretilin offshoot, the CPD-RDTL.

In the 2001 Constituent Assembly election the ASDT won 7.8 percent of the vote and six seats. Despite recognizing the inevitability of the outcome, Xavier do Amaral entered the April 2002 presidential contest as an alternative to Xanana Gusmão. He took 17.3 percent of the vote. Running again in 2007, he finished fourth, with 14.4 percent of the vote.

Prior to the June 2007 parliamentary election the ASDT negotiated an agreement with the PSD (below) to cooperate in supporting each other's electoral campaign initiatives. The ASDT-PSD won 15.7 percent of the popular vote and 11 parliamentary seats, subsequently joining the CNRT and the PD in forming a coalition government. The ASDT has one minister in the current cabinet.

Leader: Francisco Xavier do AMARAL (President).

Social Democratic Party (*Partido Social Democrata*—PSD). Founded in September 2000 as a centrist alternative to Fretilin and the Timorese Democratic Union (UDT, below), the PSD advocates consensus and formation of a national unity government. Its president had helped form the UDT in the 1970s. Its platform stresses social justice, better health care, participatory democracy, and Timor-Leste's membership in ASEAN. It would abolish the death penalty and establish a Timorese currency. In the 2001 election it won 8.1 percent of the vote and six seats.

In 2007 its presidential candidate, Lúcia LOBATO, won 8.9 percent of the vote, for fifth place. In the run-up to the June 2007 legislative election, the PSD formed an electoral alliance with the ASDT that won 11 seats and then joined in establishing the governing coalition. Three PSD leaders accepted cabinet posts.

Leaders: Mário Viegas CARRASCALÃO (President), Zacarias de COSTA (Secretary General).

Democratic Party (*Partido Democrático/Parta Demokrat*—PD). Organized in June 2001 in preparation for the August Constituent Assembly election, the centrist PD advocates participatory democracy, an independent judiciary, and a market economy with "selective intervention" by the government. The PD is influenced by student and youth movement activists and former resistance figures. Based on an 8.7 percent vote share in the balloting, in 2001 it was awarded seven assembly seats.

Party leader Fernando de Araújo finished third in the first round of the 2007 presidential election, with 19.1 percent of the vote. In the June 2007 legislative election the PD won 11 percent of the vote and eight seats. The PD holds one cabinet portfolio.

Leaders: Fernando de ARAÚJO (Speaker of the National Parliament), Joao BOAVIDA (Vice President), Mariano Sabino LOPEZ (Secretary General).

Other Parliamentary Parties:

Revolutionary Front for an Independent East Timor (*Frente Revolucionário do Timor-Leste Independente*—Fretilin). Founded in 1974 with a commitment to East Timorese independence from Portugal, the leftist Fretilin emerged from the Timorese Social Democratic Association (ASDT, above). It mounted an insurrection in 1975 and then declared formation of a Democratic Republic of East Timor on November 28. In December, however, it was forced from the capital by Indonesian forces.

Fretilin and its military wing, the Armed Forces of National Liberation of East Timor (*Forças Armadas de Libertação Nacional de Timor-Leste*—Falintil), led by Xanana Gusmão, continued to resist Indonesian annexation for more than two decades. In November 1992 Gusmão was captured by Indonesian forces, and in May 1993 he was sentenced to life in prison (subsequently reduced to 20 years, and then in 1999 to house arrest).

In the context of the UN intervention that followed the August 1999 independence referendum, Fretilin accepted a role in a UN-sponsored National Consultative Council (NCC). In July 2000 Fretilin's secretary general, Marí Alkatiri, joined a transitional government. Meanwhile, Gusmão had resigned from Fretilin after the 1999 referendum.

In the Constituent Assembly election of August 2001, Fretilin emerged with 57.3 percent of the popular vote and 55 of 88 seats, leading to Alkatiri's selection as chief minister in the second interim government and, ultimately, his assumption of the prime ministership at independence.

The April–July 2006 crisis strengthened a dissident group that sought Alkatiri's removal as party leader. In May his position was challenged at a party congress by José Luís Guterres, Timor-Leste's ambassador to the UN and the United States, who withdrew when Alkatiri engineered a change from secret ballot to a show of hands. On June 25 the Fretilin leadership backed his continuing as prime minister, but he stepped down the following day. He was replaced as president of the party by Francisco Guterres, while José Luís Guterres accepted the post of foreign minister in the Ramos-Horta cabinet. In 2007 José Luís Guterres's rebellious Fretilin *Grupo Mudança* (Reform Group) supported the CNRT in the parliamentary election and its leader was subsequently named vice prime minister, precipitating calls within the mainstream leadership to expel the Reform Group members. In March 2009 prominent member Ana Maria Pessoa Pereira da SILVA PINTO was named prosecutor-general by the CNRT-led government and resigned her Fretilin membership. Fretilin has 21 seats in the current parliament and leads the opposition.

Leaders: Francisco ("Lu'Olo") GUTERRES (President), Marí ALKATIRI (General Secretary), Aniceto GUTERRES (Parliamentary Leader), José Luís GUTERRES (Fretilin Reform Group).

National Unity Party (*Partidu Unidade Nacional*—PUN). Founded in 2006, the PUN is a Christian democratic party committed to moral and family values, basic human needs, democracy, and human rights. At its inaugural conference it claimed to have a membership base of 100,000 and the support of 426 delegates elected from 131 villages in 8 districts.

In the June 2007 parliamentary election the PUN won three seats.

Leader: Fernanda BORGES (President).

Democratic Alliance (*Aliança Democratica*—AD). The AD was formed by the Association of Timorese Heroes (KOTA, below) and the People's Party of Timor (PPT, below) as a joint electoral front for the 2007 legislative elections. The grouping secured two seats.

Association of Timorese Heroes (*Klibur Oan Timor Asuwain—*KOTA). Also known as the Sons of the Mountain Warriors, the KOTA was established in 1974 by Leão Pedro dos Reis Amaral and the late José MARTINS. The KOTA descended from the Popular Association of Monarchists of Timor (*Associação Popular Monarquia de Timor—*APMT), which represented traditional royalty. In 1975 the KOTA joined the UDT (below) and Apodeti in actively opposing Fretilin's efforts to establish a leftist government and for a time backed the Indonesian intervention. Reemerging in the late 1990s, the KOTA backed independence, joined the CNRT, and participated in the 2001 Constituent Assembly election, in which it won 2.1 percent of the vote and two seats.

Prior to the 2007 legislative election KOTA formed a coalition with the People's Party of Timor (PPT, below) called the Democratic Alliance (DA, above).

Leaders: Leão Pedro dos Reis AMARAL (President), Manuel TILMAN (Secretary General and 2007 presidential candidate).

People's Party of Timor (*Partido do Povo de Timor*—PPT). Founded in 2000 as a prointegration formation, the PPT descended from the People's Movement of East Timor (*Movimento do Povo de Timor-Leste*—MPTL). One of its founders, Herminio da Silva da Costa, was a former Apodeti leader who was subsequently closely tied to the pro-Jakarta militias, the proreferendum Forum for Democracy, Unity, and Justice (*Forum Demokrasi, Persatuan dan Keadilan*—FDPK), and its successor, the umbrella Timor Warriors' Association (*Uni Timor Aswain*—Unitas). Da Costa subsequently sought UNTAET recognition for the PPT to enter the electoral process, and in mid-June he met with Gusmão and offered his support should Gusmão seek the presidency. In the August 2001 election the PPT won 2 percent of the vote and two Constituent Assembly seats.

In the parliamentary election of June 2007 the PPT joined with the KOTA to win two seats.

Leaders: Jacob XAVIER (President), Herminio da Silva da COSTA, Francisco PINTO (Secretary General).

National Democratic Unity of Timorese Resistance (*Unidade Nacional Democrática da Resistência Timorense*—UNDERTIM). UNDERTIM split from Fretilin in early 2005 and launched itself as a new party on August 30, 2005. Its leader was a prominent resistance fighter with Falintil for 20 years. The party platform stresses better housing, health, environment, and social security. It advocates compulsory military service, traditional justice in villages, and active engagement with Australia and Indonesia.

UNDERTIM won two seats in the June 2007 election.

Leader: Cornelio GAMA (President).

Other Parties Contesting the 2007 Election:

Timorese Nationalist Party (*Partido Nacionalista Timorense/Partai Nasionalis Timor*—PNT). The PNT was established in 1999 as a proautonomy party. At one time a member of Fretilin, its leader, Abílio Araujo, had been expelled because of business links to Indonesia's Suharto family. He had also lived in exile in Portugal. In the 2001 Constituent Assembly election the PNT won two seats on a 2.2 percent vote share.

The PNT won 2.4 percent of the vote in the June 2007 election, below the threshold for claiming seats. In July it joined a loose alliance with five other small parties—the PDRT, PDC, PST, UDT, and PMD (all below)—under the name **Democratic Progressive League** (*Liga Democrética Progressiva*—LDP).

Leader: Abílio ARAUJO.

Democratic Republic of Timor-Leste Party (*Partido Democrática Republica de Timor-Leste*—PDRT). The PDRT is supported by voters in the western districts of Timor-Leste and by those who sympathized with the 594 Group comprised of dissenting soldiers led by Maj. Alfredo Reinado.

The PDRT won 1.9 percent of the popular vote in the June 2007 election.

Leaders: Gabriel FERNANDES (President), Fernando do REGO (General Secretary).

Republican Party (*Partidu Republikanu*—PR). The PR was established in December 2005 by a leading academic and member of the Council of State, Joao Mariano Saldanha, who remains the party president. The party platform advocates popular democratic participation and emphasizes security, employment, education, health, and decentralization. Reflecting its promotion of gender equality and minority rights, the PR would establish a Ministry of Gender and Minority Affairs and wants to refocus the armed forces on peacekeeping. The party advocates making Tetum the primary official language.

The PR won 1.1 percent of the popular vote in the June 2007 election.

Leader: Joao Mariano SALDANHA (President).

Christian Democratic Party (*Partido Democrata Cristão/Partai Demokrasi Kristen*—PDC/PDK). The PDC was founded in 1998 in Portugal and in August 2000 in Dili as a largely Catholic party with links to churches in Australia and Portugal and to the Indonesian Christian Democratic Party. The PDC was briefly allied with the Christian Democratic Union of Timor (*União Democrata-Cristão de Timor*—UDC). Considered somewhat more left-leaning than the UDC, it attracted both Protestants and Catholics. In the 2001 election it won 1.9 percent of the vote and two Constituent Assembly seats, whereas the UDC won one seat on a 0.6 percent vote share. In 2006 the UDC and the PDC merged under the PDC title.

The PDC advocates Christian values, social justice, and a multilateral foreign policy free from great-power domination. In the June 2007 parliamentary election the PDC won 1.0 percent of the popular vote. The PDC president, António Ximenes, studied theology in Indonesia and is currently a university lecturer in Dili. Arlindo Marçal, the secretary general, is ambassador to Indonesia.

Leaders: António XIMENES (President), Arlindo MARÇAL (Secretary General).

Socialist Party of Timor (*Partido Socialista de Timor*—PST). The PST, a Fretilin splinter, leans toward Marxist-Leninism and has a small base of support among students and labor. In August 2001 it won one legislative seat on a 1.7 percent vote share.

In June 2007 the PST received 1.0 percent of the vote. Afterward, Avelino Coelho da Silva, the party's secretary general, was named secretary of state for energy policy in the Gusmão government.

Leaders: Avelino Coelho da SILVA (Secretary General and 2007 presidential candidate), Pedro Mátires da COSTA.

Timorese Democratic Union (*União Democrática Timorense*—UDT). The conservative UDT was established in 1974 as a predominantly Catholic, anticommunist formation that was initially open to federation with Portugal. Having opted for independence, the UDT was briefly allied with Fretilin, but the two were on opposite sides of the civil war that saw Fretilin's declaration of a republic in November 1975 and the subsequent invasion by erstwhile UDT ally Indonesia.

The UDT operated primarily from exile in Portugal and Australia during the period of Indonesian rule, although it again allied itself with Fretilin in 1986. It was revived in 1997 and participated in the CNRT, the NCC, and the transitional government of October 2000 before competing in the August 2001 Constituent Assembly balloting. In the election it won 2.3 percent of the vote, for two seats.

In the June 2007 election the UDT obtained 0.9 percent of the popular vote.

Leaders: João Viegas CARRASCALÃO (President and 2007 presidential candidate), Francisco Ly Assis NICOLAU (Vice President), Domingos de OLIVEIRA (Secretary General).

Millennium Democratic Party (*Partidu Milénium Demokrátiku*—PMD). Founded November 30, 2005, the PMD base is composed of academics and students, with supporters present in all 13 of Timor-Leste's districts. The party backed the presidential bid of José Ramos-Horta. The PMD platform supports the UN's Millennium Development Goals, advocates democracy and greater participation of women and youth in public affairs, and promotes English as the official language to make Timor-Leste more globally competitive. The party has also called for creating a Reconciliation Department and a Department of Religion. The PMD president, Ermenegildo Lopes, who studied in England and continental Europe, was active in the independence struggle in Indonesia.

In the June 2007 election the PMD won 0.7 percent of the vote.

Leaders: Ermenegildo (Kupa) LOPES (President), Lettu PURN (Vice President), Melio de JESUS (Vice President).

LEGISLATURE

An 88-member Constituent Assembly (*Assembleia Constituinte*) was elected on August 30, 2001, superseding a 36-member interim body, the East Timor National Council, which had been appointed by UN administrators in October 2000. Under a transitional provision of the 2002 constitution, the assembly was reconstituted as a **National Parliament** (*Parlamento Nacional*), which now comprises 65 members elected for a five-year term on a proportional basis.

In the June 30, 2007, election the Revolutionary Front for an Independent East Timor won 21 seats; the National Congress for Timorese Reconstruction, 18; the Social Democratic Party–Timorese Social Democratic Association coalition, 11; the Democratic Party, 8; the National Unity Party, 3; the Democratic Alliance, 2; and the National Democratic Unity of Timorese Resistance, 2.

Speaker: Fernando de ARAÚJO-LASAMA.

CABINET

[as of September 1, 2009]

Prime Minister	Kay Rala Xanana Gusmão (CNRT)
Deputy Prime Minister	José Luís Guterres (Frelitin Reform Group)
Ministers	
Defense	Kay Rala Xanana Gusmão (CNRT)
Economy and Development	João Gonçalves (PSD)
Economy and Development Vice Minister	Rui Manuel Hanjam
Education	João Câncio (ind.)
Education Vice Minister	Paulo Assis Belo
Finance	Emília Pires (ind.) [f]
Foreign Affairs	Zacarias Albano da Costa (PSD)
Health	Nelson Martins (ind.)
Infrastructure	Pedro Lay da Silva (ind.)
Interior	Arcângelo Leite (ind.)
Justice	Lúcia Lobato (PSD) [f]
Tourism, Trade and Industry	Gil da Costa Alves (ASDT)
Secretaries of State	
Administrative Reform	Florindo Pereira
Agriculture and Forestry	Marcos da Cruz
Council of Ministers	Hermenegildo Pereira
Culture	Virgílio Simith
Defense	Júlio Tomás Pinto
Electricity, Water, and Urban Affairs	Januário Pereira
Energy Policy	Avelino Coelho da Silva
Natural Resources	Alfredo Pires
Professional Training and Employment	Benedito Freitas
Regional Autonomy of Oecussi	Jorge Teme
Security	Francisco Guterres
Social Security	Vítor da Costa
Tourism	Adriano do Nascimento

[f] = female

COMMUNICATIONS

Freedom of the press and of other media is guaranteed by the Timorese constitution, which requires the state to ensure the independence of the public mass media from "political and economic powers." Public broadcasting services are to be impartial and guarantee "opportunities for the expression of different lines of opinion." Media freedoms have been curtailed by occasional state of emergency decrees approved by parliament, most recently in February 2008, but promptly restored upon the return of public order.

Press. The facilities of Timor-Leste's principal newspaper, *Suara Timor Timur* (Voice of East Timor), were destroyed in 1999. The revived daily now publishes as *Suara Timor Lorisae.* The daily *Timor Post,* published in Portuguese, Tetum, Bahasa Indonesia, and English, was established in 2000. *Tais Timor,* originally published under UN auspices, served as a free national news bulletin prior to independence. It now appears as a fortnightly.

Broadcasting and computing. Beginning in 2000, the UNTAET provided radio and television services in the capital, with the facilities then being transferred to the government at independence. In addition to *Radio Nacional de Timor-Leste* and *Televisão de Timor-Leste,* there are 20 community and church radio stations. As of 2008 there were 1.6 Internet users per 1,000 inhabitants.

INTERGOVERNMENTAL REPRESENTATION

Ambassador to the U.S.: Constancio da PINTO.

U.S. Ambassador to Timor-Leste: Hans G. KLEMM.

Permanent Representative to the UN: (Vacant).

IGO Memberships (Non-UN): ADB, CPLP, Interpol, NAM, WCO.

TOGO

Republic of Togo
République Togolaise

Political Status: Independent republic since 1960; personal military rule imposed in 1967; one-party state established November 29, 1969; Third Republic proclaimed on January 13, 1980, under constitution adopted in referendum of December 30, 1979; constitution suspended by a National Conference on July 16, 1991; multiparty constitution adopted by popular referendum on September 27, 1992.

Area: 21,622 sq. mi. (56,000 sq. km.).

Population: 2,703,250 (1981C); 6,765,000 (2008E). The 1981 figure is presumed to reflect substantial underenumeration.

Major Urban Center (2005E): LOMÉ (835,000).

Official Language: French.

Monetary Unit: CFA Franc (official rate December 1, 2009: 434.59 francs = $1US). The CFA franc, previously pegged to the French franc, is now permanently pegged to the euro at 655.957 CFA francs = 1 euro.

President: Faure Essozimma GNASSINGBÉ (Rally of the Togolese People); elected on April 24, 2005, and inaugurated on May 4 following an extended constitutional crisis triggered by the death on February 5 of his father, Gen. Gnassingbé EYADÉMA (Rally of the Togolese People), who had been president since 1967.

Prime Minister: Gilbert HOUNGBO (Independent); appointed by the president on September 7, 2008, to succeed Komlan MALLY (Rally of the Togolese People), who resigned on September 5; formed new government on September 15.

THE COUNTRY

Wedged between Ghana and Benin on Africa's Guinea Coast, the small Republic of Togo extends inland from a 31-mile coastline for a distance of 360 miles. Eighteen major tribal groups are located in its hilly, hot, and humid territory, the best known being the culturally dominant Ewe in the south, whose traditional homeland extends into Ghana;

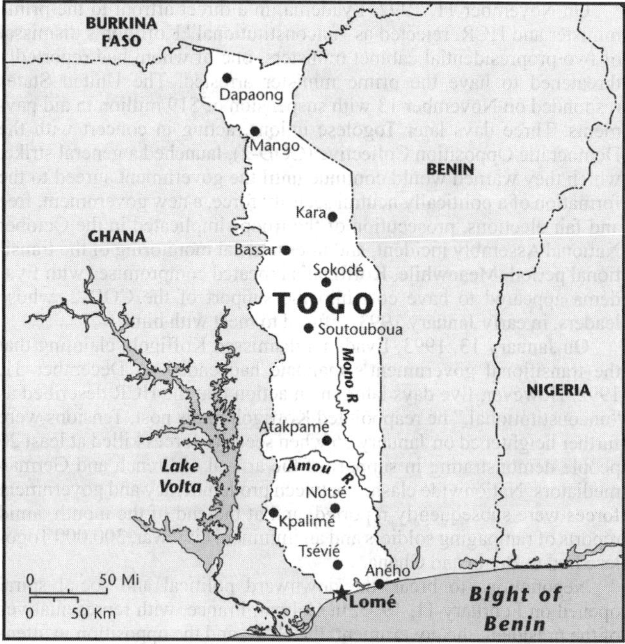

the Mina, another southern people; and the Kabiyé in the north, who staff most of the country's small army. Although French has been accorded official status, most people use indigenous languages, with Ewe being predominant in the south and Twi in the north. About 51 percent of the population adheres to traditional religious beliefs; the remainder embrace Christianity (29 percent, mainly Roman Catholicism) and Islam (20 percent). Somewhat more than half of adult women are in the work force, predominantly in the agricultural and trading sectors; however, there are few women in the government.

The economy depends primarily on subsistence agriculture, the three most important crops being cocoa, coffee, and cotton. Phosphate is the leading export, and oil refining, steel fabrication, and cement production are assuming increasing industrial importance. Smuggling has long been a source of contention with Ghana; as much as a third of Togo's cocoa exports originates in the neighboring state and are smuggled into Togo in exchange for luxury items that are much cheaper than in other parts of Africa. Development in the 1980s focused largely on tourism, agriculture, and a new free port in Lomé. The World Bank and other international institutions, encouraged by the government's commitment to budget austerity and the privatization of some state-run enterprises, supported these and other efforts to recover from the fall of commodity prices on the world market. However, the economy came to a virtual standstill in 1991, declining sharply thereafter by 8.8 percent in 1992 and by an even more calamitous 13.5 percent in 1993. In addition, foreign aid donors, most notably France and the United States, halted aid payments to protest military and presidential obstruction of democratization efforts. In September 1994 France announced its intention to renew civil and military cooperation agreements, in addition to writing off part of Togo's debt, and in early 1995 the European Union (EU) activated its aid program after a three-year suspension; however, the United States was unwilling to follow suit, reportedly citing the "lack of guarantees for the ongoing democratic process."

Togo adopted structural reforms proposed by the International Monetary Fund (IMF) in the mid-1990s, and GDP grew by an annual average of 6.9 percent in 1995–1997. However, GDP declined by about 1 percent in 1998, due to a bad harvest and a sharp increase in government spending prior to the disputed June presidential election. (The EU, which had financed much of that electoral process, subsequently suspended its aid payments after announcing it would not recognize President Eyadéma's reelection.) Meanwhile, the IMF urged the government to intensify its privatization efforts, adopt stricter banking regulations, and improve tax collection. GDP rose by 2.7 percent in 1999 but declined by 0.5 percent in 2000, the IMF attributing the economic deterioration, in part, to policy weaknesses, including the slow pace of reform in the public sector. GDP growth returned in 2001 while inflation remained low.

GDP grew by an average of 3.3 percent from 2002 to 2004, fueled by increased agricultural output and expanded phosphate production. The government's fiscal status was also improved by better tax collection procedures. However, most international donors continued to withhold assistance due to the Eyadéma regime's poor human rights record and failure to implement democratic reform. In 2004 the EU resumed aid after Togo met 22 preconditions, and in September 2005, the IMF followed suit. In April 2006 the World Bank included Togo among 11 countries that qualified for debt relief under the Heavily Indebted Poor Countries (HIPC) initiative. GDP grew by 2 percent in 2006, although prices for cotton fell significantly. Inflation remained low at about 2.5 percent for the year, despite dramatically higher energy prices, and improved tax collection measures helped the government to reduce its budget deficit.

Following the 2007 legislative elections, which were judged fair by international observers, Togo was granted additional economic aid, including $42 million from the EU and $108 million from the IMF. In 2007, GDP growth was 2.1 percent, while inflation was 1 percent. In 2008 the EU pledged an additional $190 million over a five-year period, while the World Bank agreed to write-off the arrears owed by Togo on past loans, some $135 million, and the Paris Club of creditor nations forgave $347 million in debt. In addition, the African Development Bank canceled 99 percent of Togo's $23.5 million debt to the institution. Loans from the Islamic Development Bank in the amount of $67 million were used to double phosphate production in 2008 by expanding capacity. In November the IMF announced that Togo qualified for the HIPC program, which would allow the country to write off $2.2 billion in external debt if it completed the terms of the program. Togo's GDP grew by just 0.8 percent in 2008 while inflation grew to more than 8 percent as a result of a rise in food and fuel prices caused by heavy flooding and concurrent agricultural losses. In its 2009 Doing Business survey the World Bank ranked Togo 163 out of 179 countries for ease of conducting commerce and trade.

GOVERNMENT AND POLITICS

Political background. The present Republic of Togo is the eastern section of the former German Protectorate of Togoland, which became a League of Nations mandate after World War I and was divided into separate zones of British and French administration. After World War II France and Britain continued to administer the eastern and western sections, respectively, as United Nations trust territories. Following a UN-supervised plebiscite, Western (British) Togoland became part of the new state of Ghana on the latter's accession to independence in 1957. Eastern (French) Togoland, which became a French-sponsored autonomous republic in 1956, achieved complete independence in an agreement with France and the United Nations on April 27, 1960.

Sylvanus OLYMPIO, leader of the predominantly Ewe party then known as the Togolese Unity Committee (CUT), became the country's first chief executive. Olympio's somewhat dictatorial rule, coupled with his alienation of the army by the imposition of an austerity program, contributed to his assassination in 1963. Nicolas GRUNITZKY, Olympio's chief political rival, succeeded him as president and attempted to govern on a multiparty basis with northern support. Grunitzky failed, however, to establish firm control and was deposed in 1967 by (then) Maj. Etienne EYADÉMA, a northerner who was chief of staff of the armed forces. Acting in the name of a National Reconciliation Committee (NRC), Eyadéma suspended the constitution, outlawed political activity, and instituted direct military rule. Later the same year, he dissolved the NRC and declared himself president. The Rally of the Togolese People (RPT), a regime-supportive party, was established in 1969 and, in that year and in 1971, made pro forma attempts (which were described as overruled by the "popular will") to return the nation to civilian rule.

A constitution drafted in 1969 was accepted by a reported 98 percent of the registered electorate on December 30, 1979, in balloting at which General Eyadéma (whose first name had been "Africanized" to Gnassingbé in 1974) stood as the sole candidate for a seven-year term as president. Concurrently, a unicameral General Assembly was constituted on the basis of a single list of candidates presented by the RPT.

In September 1986 the government reported that it had rebuffed a coup attempt allegedly fomented in Ghana and Burkina Faso by supporters of the exiled sons of former president Olympio. However, some external critics suggested that the seriousness of the coup attempt may have been overstated by the Eyadéma regime to shift attention away from earlier reports of torture and illegal detention of political prisoners. On December 21 President Eyadéma was unopposed in election to a further seven-year term.

In early October 1990 the imposition of lengthy jail terms on two opposition figures for alleged antigovernment activity ignited a series of protests and strikes. On October 10 President Eyadéma responded by telling a RPT Central Committee meeting that the country's "apprenticeship in democracy" was complete and preparations should be made for a multiparty system. However, the establishment of a constitutional commission and scheduling of a referendum for late 1991 failed to appease government critics, with violent protests continuing into 1991.

In March 1991 ten opposition groups formed a Front of Associations for Renewal (FAR) under the leadership of Yawovi AGBOYIBO, and four days later, after a meeting with FAR representatives, the president agreed to accelerate reforms. In mid-April he authorized the legalization of opposition parties and pledged to hold multiparty elections within a year. Nevertheless, violent demonstrations continued, fueled by the discovery of the bodies of 30 slain protestors in a Lomé lagoon. Subsequently, in the course of negotiations with opposition leaders, Eyadéma agreed to transfer power to a prime minister to be elected by a National Conference on Togo's Future, which convened in Lomé on July 8. On July 16 the opposition-dominated conference declared its sovereignty, dissolved the National Assembly, abrogated the 1980 constitution, and stripped Eyadéma of all but ceremonial powers, thus prompting a government and army withdrawal from the proceedings. On July 23 the government rejoined the conference, and, at its close on August 28, the president publicly accepted most of its findings, including a diminished presidency, the election of Joseph Kokou KOFFIGOH as prime minister, and the replacement of the RPT-dominated National Assembly with an interim High Council of the Republic (HCR). However, Eyadéma's military supporters continued to reject both the conference's sovereignty claims and the new government, in particular Koffigoh's assumption of the defense ministry. Subsequently, military coup attempts on October 1 and 8 ended only after public appeals from Eyadéma that the troops return to their barracks.

In mid-October 1991 the HCR, under pressure from newly enfranchised party leaders to establish control of the government, formally ousted Eyadéma, and on November 26 the council banned the RPT on the eve of a party congress. The following day rebel troops surrounded Koffigoh's residence, and on December 2 the troops announced that they had "reclaimed" strategic points throughout Togo and had called on Eyadéma to name a new prime minister and dissolve the HCR. On December 3 Koffigoh was seized by the rebel soldiers and brought to Eyadéma, whereupon the prime minister announced his "surrender" and agreed to Eyadéma's request that he form a national unity government, assignments to which were announced on December 30.

On January 29, 1992, the government issued a revised electoral calendar that called for a constitutional referendum and municipal balloting in early April, a legislative poll in late May, and a presidential election in June. The schedule was subsequently abandoned because of widespread violence, including the May 5 wounding of opposition leader Gilchrist OLYMPIO, son of the former president, in an attack for which Capt. Ernest GNASSINGBÉ, the president's son, was implicated two months later. On August 13 negotiations between a presidential delegation and representatives of eight opposition parties on resumption of the transitional process were suspended, and on August 23 the government, citing ongoing unrest, canceled a constitutional referendum. Meanwhile, following extensive talks between the president and prime minister, at which the latter reportedly agreed to a number of concessions reversing earlier limitations on the president's power, the transition period, scheduled to expire on August 28, was extended to December 31.

On September 27, 1992, a new constitution was endorsed in a referendum by 99.09 percent of the voters. Concurrently, a new electoral calendar was released, which called for balloting to take place between October and December. However, the democratization process was halted on October 22 with seizure of the National Assembly building by pro-Eyadéma troops, who demanded the release of frozen RPT funds in return for the release of 40 legislative hostages. The crisis was resolved the following day when the HCR agreed to release the funds; however, Koffigoh declared the HCR's action invalid because it was performed under duress, while Eyadéma, who had supported earlier efforts to free the funds, called for sanctions against the intruders. Unappeased by the government's response, the opposition organized a general strike on October 26 to protest the military's action.

On November 11, 1992, Eyadéma, in a direct affront to the prime minister and HCR, rejected as "unconstitutional" Koffigoh's dismissal of two propresidential cabinet ministers, one of whom had reportedly threatened to have the prime minister arrested. The United States responded on November 13 with suspension of $19 million in aid payments. Three days later Togolese unions, acting in concert with the Democratic Opposition Collective (COD-2), launched a general strike, which they warned would continue until the government agreed to the formation of a politically neutral security force, a new government, free and fair elections, prosecution of the troops implicated in the October National Assembly incident, and international monitoring of the transitional period. Meanwhile, Koffigoh's repeated compromises with Eyadéma appeared to have cost him the support of the COD-2, whose leaders, in early January 1993, refused to meet with him.

On January 13, 1993, Eyadéma dismissed Koffigoh, claiming that the transitional government's mandate had ended on December 31, 1992. However, five days later, in an action that the HCR described as "unconstitutional," he reappointed Koffigoh to his post. Tensions were further heightened on January 25 when security forces killed at least 20 people demonstrating in support of the arrival of French and German mediators. Nationwide clashes between prodemocracy and government forces were subsequently reported, and at the end of the month, amid reports of rampaging soldiers and an imminent civil war, 300,000 Togolese fled to Benin and Ghana.

Negotiations to break the downward political and social spiral opened on February 11, 1993, in Colmar, France, with representatives of the president, the government, the HCR, and the opposition in attendance; however, Eyadéma's delegation soon withdrew because of the opposition's demand for political neutralization of the armed forces. Three days later, following negotiations between the president and prime minister, during which the former reportedly pledged to keep troops loyal to him in their barracks, Koffigoh was named to head a "crisis government" dominated by presidential loyalists. The HCR rejected the legality of the new administration, calling it the product of a "constitutional coup d'état," and in early March COD-2 leader Olympio reportedly declared that a "short, foreign military intervention" might be necessary to break the stranglehold on the democratization process.

On March 25, 1993, Eyadéma's top military aide was among a number of military personnel reportedly killed when the president's residence came under attack from raiders who fled into Ghana. Olympio, who was accused of planning the attack, countered by charging that the incident was part of a purge of army dissidents. Lending credence to his argument, over 140 former Eyadéma troops were reported to have fled Togo by early April, claiming that a presidentially sanctioned ethnic cleansing campaign was indeed under way. Despite the unrest, an election timetable was subsequently released, which called for new presidential and legislative balloting. However, most of the opposition boycotted the long-deferred presidential poll of August 25 at which Eyadéma was credited with reelection amid increasing evidence that he had regained most of his pre-1991 powers.

In late September 1993 the COD-2 threatened to boycott legislative elections then scheduled for December unless the government agreed to provide access to state-controlled media, redefine voting constituencies, and increase the number of poll watchers. The balloting was further postponed until February following renewed fighting near Eyadéma's residence on January 5, 1994, which left more than 60 dead.

The multiparty poll, which was finally mounted on February 6 and 20, 1994, was marred by violence, with RPT militants accused of attacking opposition candidates. International observers nonetheless endorsed the results, which included a majority of 43 seats for the opposition Patriotic Front (FP) and 35 for the RPT. Subsequently, however, the Supreme Court, responding to petitions filed by the RPT, vacated three seats won by the opposition. Therefore, the FP's overall lead was imperiled, pending by-elections, which, having initially been scheduled for May, were deferred. Criticizing the Court's action, the FP's leading components (the Action Committee for Renewal—CAR and the Togolese Union for Democracy—UTD) threatened to boycott the National Assembly; however, the coalition's unanimity was sorely tested on April 22, when the president, in apparent violation of an earlier agreement, rejected CAR leader Yawovi Agboyibo as the FP's prime minister designate in favor of the UTD's Edem KODJO.

In mid-1994 a RPT characterization of the FP as a "facade of a coalition" seemed increasingly apt, as the CAR resisted UTD entreaties to join Kodjo's government. Earlier, on May 20, the CAR, which unlike the UTD had carried through on a legislative boycott, announced that it was abandoning the action, explaining that the regime's failure to mount by-elections by the legally mandated date of May 15 was tantamount to a confession that "conditions for legality, transparency, and security" had not been met. In December the CAR once again withdrew from the assembly, but in April 1995 President Eyadéma and Agboyibo reached an agreement on electoral reform, which called for equal representation for government and opposition parliamentary groups on all electoral commissions. As a result, the CAR rejoined the assembly in August; however, an alliance of RPT and UTD parliamentarians defeated the reform bill in February 1996.

Already strained relations between President Eyadéma and Prime Minister Kodjo deteriorated sharply in May 1996 when the Supreme Court supported Eyadéma's assertion that he alone controlled the appointment of senior administrative officials. For his part, Kodjo reportedly accused the president of establishing a "parallel government." Subsequently, following the RPT's capture of three assembly seats (and consequently a narrow legislative majority) in early August by-election balloting, Kodjo resigned on August 19, citing his desire to avoid the "legal war," which he described as likely to arise from the lack of an "obvious majority." The following day Eyadéma appointed Planning and Territorial Development Minister Kwassi KLUTSE as Kodjo's successor, and on August 27 the new prime minister announced the formation of a new government.

On December 3, 1996, the National Assembly voted to adopt a RPT-drafted document delineating the responsibilities of a new Constitutional Court. The poll was boycotted by the CAR, which had unsuccessfully sought to broaden the court's powers to include mediation of electoral disputes. (The new body was inaugurated in March 1997.) Thereafter, in September, the opposition boycotted an assembly vote on a new electoral code after attempts to persuade the legislature to include provisions for an independent electoral body were rebuffed. The code, approved unanimously by the propresidential legislators, provided for a nine-member commission (four from the propresidential forces and four from the opposition, in addition to an appointed chair).

Following presidential balloting on June 21, 1998, President Eyadéma was credited with a vote share of 52 percent and Gilchrist Olympio of the Union of Forces of Change (UFC) with 34 percent. The remainder of the tally was shared by four other candidates, led by Yawovi Agboyibo with 9.6 percent. However, the polling process was widely criticized by both domestic and international observers. Furthermore, two days after the polling, the chairperson of the electoral commission, Awa NANA, resigned, claiming that her efforts to prepare provisional electoral results had been blocked by "unidentified" individuals widely believed to be presidential supporters. Subsequently, the opposition, led by Olympio, who claimed that he had actually won the election with a 59 percent vote share, refused the president's offer to join a unity government and organized a number of demonstrations and work stoppages. Amid reports of mounting violence, on August 19 Prime Minister Klutse resigned; however, the president reappointed Klutse the following day, and on September 1 Klutse named a government that included a number of new members but no prominent opposition leaders.

In December 1998 government and opposition leaders announced that they had made progress in their efforts to organize a dialogue. Thereafter, however, the preparations ground to a halt as the two sides proved unable to agree on a venue for the proposed talks. Subsequently, in early 1999, the opposition announced its intention to boycott legislative polling then scheduled for early March. The Eyadéma administration rejected calls to delay the balloting until after interparty talks and proceeded with electoral preparations, albeit delaying the start of polling for two weeks.

Following legislative balloting on March 21, 1999, and two subsequent by-elections, the RPT, facing only limited competition from independent candidates and two minor parties, was credited with having won 79 of the 81 seats. On April 17 Klutse dissolved his government and offered his resignation, although he agreed to continue thereafter on a caretaker basis. On May 22 the president appointed Eugene Koffi ADOBOLI, a former official of the United Nations Conference on Trade and Development, as Klutse's successor. Facing continuing criticism for his inability to improve the economic condition, however, Adoboli resigned on August 25, 2000, one day after a vote of no-confidence against his government in the legislature. The president named Agbéyomé Messan KODJO of the RPT as Adoboli's successor on August 29.

On June 27, 2002, President Eyadéma appointed Koffi SAMA of the RPT to replace Prime Minister Kodjo. (Kodjo was subsequently expelled from the RPT for criticizing the president; he later went into exile.) Sama was sworn in on June 30, and he announced his cabinet on July 5.

The RPT dominated the October 27, 2002, assembly balloting (72 of 81 seats), in part due to a boycott by most opposition parties. Sama was reappointed as prime minister on November 13. In December the RPT-controlled assembly approved a constitutional revision that removed the limit on the number of presidential terms for one person, thereby permitting Eyadéma to seek another term in the election scheduled for 2003. The assembly also lowered the eligibility age for presidential candidates from 45 to 35, a measure apparently designed to permit the eventual succession of Eyadéma's son, Faure Essozimma GNASSINGBÉ, who was only 37 years old at the time. Moreover, the basic law was changed to require presidential candidates to have resided in Togo for one year prior to the election. That provision prevented Gilchrist Olympio, who had been in exile in France, from contesting the election; he urged supporters to vote for Emmanuel BOB-AKITANI, the vice president of the UFC.

In the presidential poll of June 1, 2003, Eyadéma was credited with 58 percent of the vote, followed by Bob-Akitani (34 percent), and four minor candidates. Prime Minister Sama and his cabinet resigned on June 23, but the president reappointed Sama on July 1. On July 29 Sama formed a new cabinet that included a few members of minor opposition parties and, notably, Faure Gnassingbé.

President Eyadéma died of a heart attack on February 5, 2005. His son, Faure Gnassingbé, backed by the military and Sama, was immediately named interim president, although the constitution required the speaker of the assembly to fill a presidential vacancy. Because the current speaker, Fambaré NATCHABA, was out of the country at the time, the assembly, on February 6, elected Gnassingbé to replace Natchaba as speaker, and Gnassingbé was sworn in as president the following day to serve until the end of his father's term in 2008. The assembly also rescinded the constitutional provision that new presidential elections be held within 60 days in case of a vacancy. However, in the wake of intense domestic and international criticism, the assembly, on February 21, voted to reverse its decisions (see Foreign relations, below). Gnassingbé resigned as speaker and interim president on February 25 and was succeeded in both positions by Abbas BONFOH (hitherto the deputy speaker) pending new elections. In highly controversial balloting on April 24, Gnassingbé was credited with 60 percent of the vote and runner-up Bob-Akitani with 38.25 percent. After the Constitutional Court validated the results on May 3, Gnassingbé was sworn in on May 4. On June 9, the president appointed Edem Kodjo of the Panafrican Patriotic Convergence (*Convergence Patriotique Panafricaine*—CPP) as prime minister in an attempt to reach out to opposition groups. Kodjo's new cabinet, formed on June 20, comprised mostly members of the RPT, although several small opposition parties agreed to join. Efforts to form a broader unity government were initially rebuffed by the major opposition parties. However, in July, nine of the leading political parties signed a Comprehensive Political Accord, which established the framework for future elections. Provisions included the creation of an independent national electoral commission and the preparation of new voter rolls (to be used in conjunction with new identification cards). The UFC initially rejected the accord but later reversed itself after the government pledged to reform the nation's security forces.

As an outgrowth of the new pact, President Gnassingbé appointed opposition leader Agboyibo of the CAR as prime minister on September 16, 2006. Four days later Agboyibo took office as head of a national unity government that included 16 new ministers. The RPT and its allies retained the majority of the ministries, but 16 posts were held by the opposition or independents, including members of the CAR, CPP, the Democratic Convention of African People, the Socialist Renewal Pact, and the Party for Democracy and Renewal.

In legislative balloting on October 14, 2007, the governing RPT won 50 seats, followed by the UFC with 27 seats and the CAR with 4 seats. Agboyibo resigned on November 13 and Komlan MALLY of the RPT was appointed prime minister on December 3. He named a cabinet composed of the RPT, with representation from some minor parties, including the Democratic Convention of African People (*Convention Démocratique des Peuples Africains*—CDPA) and independents. Both the UFC and the CAR refused to participate in the government. On September 5, 2008, Mally resigned following tensions with the president, who accused the prime minister of being ineffective. Mally was replaced two days later by Gilbert HOUNGBO, a political independent and former diplomat. Houngbo named a new cabinet on September 15 that was dominated by the RPT and did not include any members of the UFC or CAR. The size of the cabinet was increased from 22 to 26, and Mally was retained as minister of state for health. However, as part of the consolidation of power, the president's half-brother, Kpatcha, was not reappointed as minister of defense. Kpatcha was subsequently arrested for allegedly planning a coup (see Current issues, below).

Gnassingbé launched the Permanent Committee on Dialogue and Consultation (*Le Comité Permanent de Dialogue et de Concertation*—CPDC) in February 2009. The CPDC included the country's main political parties and served as a standing forum to develop concensus on issues such as elections, the constitution, and media rules. However, the CAR and the UFC initially boycotted the body. In June the CPDC allocated seats for the national electoral commission in preparation for the 2010 presidential balloting. The president replaced the minister of primary and secondary education in March and created a new post, minister of state for water resources and village water, in May to oversee internationally funded improvements to the nation's water system.

Constitution and government. The 1979 constitution provided for a highly centralized system of government headed by a strong executive presiding over a cabinet of his own selection and empowered to dissolve a single-chambered National Assembly after consulting the Political Bureau of the RPT. It detailed a judicial system headed by a Supreme Court that included a Court of Appeal and courts of the first and second instance, with special courts for administrative, labor, and internal security matters.

On July 16, 1991, the National Conference on Togo's Future abrogated the 1979 basic law, transferred all but ceremonial presidential powers to a prime minister, and dissolved the legislature, with assignment of its powers to a High Council of the Republic (HCR), pending the promulgation of a new constitution and the holding of multiparty elections.

A draft constitution accepted by the HCR on July 2, 1992, called for a semi-presidential system with the head of state elected to a once-renewable five-year term and a prime minister chosen by the president from a parliamentary majority and responsible to the legislature, which would also have a five-year mandate. Other projected institutions included a High Court of Justice and a Supreme Court, in addition to a Constitutional Court, an Accounts Court, and an Economic and Social Council. On September 27 the new basic charter was approved by 99.08 percent of the participants in a nationwide referendum. In March 1997 a seven-member Constitutional Court was appointed to serve a seven-year term.

The country is divided for administrative purposes into five provinces, which are subdivided into 30 prefectures that were formerly administered by presidentially appointed chiefs and "special delegations" (councils) but are now subject to prefectural and municipal elections on the basis of direct universal suffrage.

Foreign relations. Togo's foreign policy has long been based on nonalignment, although historical links have provided a foundation for continued financial and political support from the West. Bowing to pressure from the Arab bloc, diplomatic relations with Israel were severed from 1973 to 1987.

Although one of the smallest and poorest of the African states, Togo has played a leading role in efforts to promote regional cooperation and served as the host nation for negotiation of the Lomé conventions between the European Community (EC) and developing African, Caribbean, and Pacific (ACP) countries. It worked closely with Nigeria in organizing the Economic Community of West African States (ECOWAS) in May 1975 and, having assumed observer status earlier with the francophone West African Economic Community (CEAO), joined the CEAO states in a Non-Aggression and Defense Aid Agreement (ANAD) in 1979. Its major regional dispute concerns the status of Western Togoland, which was incorporated into Ghana in 1957. A clandestine "National Liberation Movement of Western Togoland" has been active in supporting Togo's claim to the 75-mile-wide strip of territory and has called for a new UN plebiscite on the issue. There have been numerous incidents along the Ghanaian border, and the Eyadéma and Rawlings regimes regularly accused each other of destabilization efforts, including the "harboring" of political opponents. Heated exchanges occurred with Ghana and, to a lesser degree, Burkina Faso, following the reported coup attempt in Togo in September 1986. However, Eyadéma avoided charging Accra and Ouagadougou with direct involvement in the plot, and relations were largely normalized by mid-1987, with Lomé calling for help from regional organizations to keep further enmity from developing. In December 1991 the Koffigoh administration announced that a comprehensive cooperation agreement had been reached with Ghana.

Togo's foreign affairs in 1992 and early 1993 were determined in great part by its domestic political turmoil. In early November 1992 both Benin and Ghana reported deaths of their nationals in border incidents involving Togolese security forces, although their complaints were relatively low-key in apparent support of the transitional government. On November 13 a deteriorating political situation led the United States to suspend all but humanitarian aid payments. Thereafter, in late January 1993, a French and German mediation effort was cut short when 20 prodemocracy demonstrators were killed by government forces outside the negotiation site. In mid-February, France, citing the death of the demonstrators and lack of progress toward democracy, announced restrictions on aid payments. France's decision came only weeks after its former president, Valéry Giscard D'Estaing, had written a controversial letter in support of Eyadéma.

Meanwhile, relations between Togo and Ghana continued to worsen. In March 1993 rebels who had attacked the Eyadéma compound retreated into Ghana, setting off an exchange of accusations between the two capitals. In early January 1994 Togo and Ghana were described as "close to war" after Lóme once again accused Accra of aiding alleged anti-Eyadéma insurgents in an attack on the president's residence. For its part, Ghana described the unrest in Togo as "the consequence of the government's refusal to establish a credible democratic process" and called on Lomé to resist always accusing Ghana "whenever there is an armed attack or political crisis." Such charges notwithstanding, relations between the two improved dramatically by midyear; on November 16 diplomatic ties were formally restored, and in December Eyadéma ordered the reopening of their shared border. Lomé's relations with Paris improved when France agreed to reschedule and forgive Togolese debt in May 1995.

In August 1998 the Togolese government reported that troops based near Lomé had been attacked by opposition-affiliated "terrorists" based in Ghana; however, the opposition countered that the fighters were actually government provocateurs who had attacked the headquarters and homes of UFC members. Collaterally, the incident proved to be a showcase for improved relations between Accra and Lomé (the two nations' presidents having signed cooperation agreements in Accra earlier in the year) because Ghana deployed forces to carry out a joint operation with Togolese troops pursuing the alleged "aggressors." However, conflicts over property rights were reported in 1999 along the border between Togo and Ghana, and in March 2001 Togo closed the border without explanation. The border was reopened and relations between the two sides improved dramatically with the election of John Kufuor as president of Ghana.

In 1998 Eyadéma helped mediate the conflict in Guinea-Bissau. Togolese troops also joined the international peacekeeping mission in Guinea-Bissau, and Eyadéma played a role in efforts to end the conflicts in Liberia and Sierra Leone. In addition, Togolese troops participated in the ECOWAS mission in Liberia and the UN mission in Sierra Leone. In light of Togo's importance to regional peacekeeping operations, the United States initiated joint training exercises with the Togolese military in April 2002.

France was the first country to accept Faure Gnassingbé's controversial victory in the 2005 presidential election. In February 2006 Gnassingbé traveled to China to promote increased economic interaction between the two countries. (In 2005 trade between Togo and China was worth more than $500 million.)

Togo, Benin, and Nigeria entered into a pact in February 2007 to promote peace and economic development in the region. Subsequently, Togo, Ghana, and the UN signed a tripartite agreement in April to facilitate the voluntary return of Togolese refugees, many of whom had been in Ghana since the early 1990s. In June a cooperation framework was signed between Togo and Angola in an effort to overcome tensions that have lingered from Togo's past support of the Angolan rebel movement UNITA.

In December 2007 Togo and the United Arab Emirates established full relations as part of a broader effort by Togo to improve trade and political relations with countries in the Middle East. In January 2008 Togo announced that it would contribute 800 soldiers to the AU-led peacekeeping force in Darfur. In addition, in September Togo and Belgium resumed diplomatic ties.

Togo and France signed a new defense accord in March 2009. Following meetings between Gnassingbé and German chancellor Angela Merkel in June, the Togolese president proclaimed a "new start" in relations between Togo and its former colonial power. Togo and Ghana launched an initiative in August to reduce cross-border crime, including joint border patrols. Also in August, the two governments signed an agreement in Accra whereby Ghana agreed to provide technical assistance during the 2010 elections.

Current issues. Relations between the government and the opposition remained severely strained in late 2001 and the first half of 2002. Particularly galling to the opposition was an amendment to the electoral code approved by the assembly in February 2002 that required future presidential candidates to have resided in Togo for 12 consecutive months. Critics described the new law as designed to prevent another presidential run by the UFC's Gilchrist Olympio, who remained outside the country. The opposition parties also strongly objected to the government's offer of only 5 seats on the proposed 20-member electoral commission. In view of the impasse on that membership, the government in May appointed a committee of judges to oversee the new legislative elections, which, having already been postponed from October 2001 and March 2002, were finally held in October 2002 without the participation of most opposition parties.

Critics strongly challenged the assembly's decision to permit Eyadéma to run for a third term in 2003 and described the election results as fraudulent. Although international observers accepted the poll as generally free and open, it was noted that the administration had limited the number of opposition rallies and had constrained access to the government-controlled media. Subsequently, the government appeared to soften its stance by releasing some 500 political prisoners, overturning repressive press restrictions, and promising genuine negotiations designed to bring the opposition into the political process. As part of the reform effort, Prime Minister Sama attempted to create an independent electoral commission, but the UFC, CAR, and other opposition parties refused to participate, citing what they perceived to be a continued lack of transparency in the entire election process. As a result, municipal and regional elections scheduled for December 2004 were postponed indefinitely.

President Eyadéma's death in February 2005 ended Africa's longest presidential reign (38 years) and plunged Togo into a complicated constitutional crisis (see Political background, above, for details). Faure Gnassingbé's takeover prompted numerous demonstrations that led to the death of protesters who clashed with police. In addition, regional organizations such as ECOWAS and the African Union condemned the Togolese military for attempting what was perceived as essentially a coup d'état. On February 9, the International Organization of the Francophonie suspended Togo's membership. On February 20, ECOWAS imposed a range of sanctions on Togo, including suspension of the country's membership, a travel ban on Togolese officials, and an arms embargo. Five days later, the AU endorsed sanctions by individual member states. The United States and the EU offered support for the ECOWAS and AU sanctions, apparently triggering Gnassingbé's decision to relinquish the presidency and campaign in new elections scheduled for April 24, 2005. Although opposition parties sought a postponement to give them more time to campaign, the government rejected any delay and even dismissed the interior minister on April 22 when he publicly called for additional time to prepare for the balloting.

Gnassingbé's election in April 2005 (which the opposition and international observers again described as fraudulent) triggered a new wave of violence and the flight of more than 30,000 people to neighboring countries. The UN reported that more than 500 people were killed in post-election violence, while property damage was estimated at $7 million. Turmoil continued throughout the summer, despite Gnassingbé's pledge to support new legislative elections if reconciliation could be achieved with the opposition. Gnassingbé undertook a range of actions to mollify the opposition, including the November 2005 release of 460 political prisoners.

Following the appointment of opposition leader Yawovi Agboyibo of the CAR as prime minister in September 2006, the UFC was offered four cabinet posts in the new unity government. However, the UFC declined to participate after it learned that the RPT would have the majority of posts within the government.

The EU provided $18.7 million to support legislative balloting in 2007, while France pledged an additional $4.1 million. The elections were initially set for June but were postponed several times because of delays in voter registration and cost overruns. Foreign observers certified the elections on October 14 as free and fair, but the opposition challenged the balloting. On October 20 the constitutional court rejected the challenges and certified the results in which the RPT won a reduced majority. In November Gnassingbé met with exiled opposition leader Olympio in an unsuccessful effort to convince the UFC leader to have his party participate in the subsequent government. In April 2008 Gnassingbé launched a series of public meetings as part of a national truth and reconciliation process to heal lingering divisions.

On April 16, 2009, the president's half-brother Kpatcha Gnassingbé and a number of military and civilian officials were arrested for planning a coup while the president was out of the country on a state visit to China. Five people were killed in fighting between security forces and the rebels. Gnassingbé reshuffled several senior positions within the armed forces in response in an effort to shore up his support among the security forces. Kpatcha's supporters argued that his arrest was an effort by the president to remove a political rival ahead of the 2010 presidential election. In June Togo abolished the death penalty.

POLITICAL PARTIES

Political parties were banned after the 1967 coup. Two years later, the official Rally of the Togolese People (RTP) was organized as the sole legitimate political party. However, on April 12, 1991, the Eyadéma regime, besieged by antigovernment strikes and protests, reversed the RPT's 24-year-old monopoly. Opposition activities were coordinated by a Front of Associations for Renewal (*Front des Associations pour le Renouvellement*—FAR), a coalition of human rights, prodemocracy, and student groups, which, three days after its launching on March 15, had been promised a national conference by the president if it would halt its demonstrations. In May the FAR was superseded by a Democratic Opposition Collective (*Collectif de l'Opposition Démocratique*—COD), which in turn gave way to the National Council for the Safeguard of Democracy (*Conseil National pour la Sauvegarde de la Démocratie*—CNSD) in late December. In July 1992 the CNSD was succeeded by a revived Democratic Opposition Collective (COD-2). In early 1993 the COD-2 appeared to split into two wings: a "moderate" faction aligned under the banner of the Patriotic Front (FP, below) and a "radical" component, the Union of Forces of Change (UFC, below). Although the FP joined the UFC in boycotting the 1993 presidential election, the linkage was abandoned in early 1994 as the FP ignored the UFC's call for a boycott of legislative balloting. (In July 1997 ties between the two groups were reestablished; however, a proposed electoral coalition, which would have also included the Party for Democracy and Renewal [PDR, below], collapsed following the UFC's withdrawal late in the year.)

In early 2002 a group of opposition parties formed The Front, which subsequently participated in the October launching of the Coalition of Democratic Forces (*Coalition des Forces Démocrates*—CFD) with other groups, including the Panafrican Patriotic Convergence and the UFC. The CFD sought to present a single candidate for the June 2003 election but ultimately boycotted that balloting due to perceived unwillingness on the part of the administration to permit full electoral participation by the opposition. Prior to the 2005 presidential election, six opposition parties agreed to support the candidacy of Bob-Akitani, including the UFC, the PDR, the **Action Committee for Renewal** (*Comité d'Action pour le Renouveau*—CAR), the **Democratic Convention of African People** (*Convention Démocratique des Peuples Africains*—CDPA), **Alliance of Democrats for Integrated Development** (*Alliance des Démocrates pour le Développement Intégré*—ADDI), and the **Union for Democracy and Solidarity–Togo** (*Union pour la Démocratie et la Solidarité–Togo*—UDS–Togo).

Reports in 2009 indicated that the two main opposition parties, the UFC and the CAR, were in negotiations to field a single candidate in the 2010 presidential elections.

Government Parties:

Rally of the Togolese People (*Rassemblement du Peuple Togolais*—RPT). Formed in 1969 under the sponsorship of President Eyadéma, the RPT was Togo's sole legal party until its constitutional mandate was abrogated by the National Conference in July 1991. In February 1994 the RPT captured 33 of the 57 seats decided in the first round of assembly balloting; however, the party subsequently fell short of an overall majority by winning only 2 second-round seats. The RPT's three victories in legislative by-election balloting in August 1996 left the party in control of 38 of 57 seats. It also claimed the vote of former interim prime minister Koffigoh and two former opposition legislators who held seats as independents. In November the RPT absorbed the **Union for Justice and Democracy** (*Union pour la Justice et la*

Démocratie—UJD), a small grouping that controlled 2 assembly seats. At the RPT's congress on January 9–11, 1997, the party continued its recent swing back toward a hard-line posture and away from the proreform, youth movement that had characterized a 1994 congress. Evidencing the sea change were the appointments to the Central Committee of a number of old guard stalwarts. In November the party was bolstered by the addition of another minor party, the **Movement for Social Democracy and Tolerance.** The RPT captured 79 seats in the 1999 assembly balloting and 72 in 2002.

Following the death of President Eyadéma in February 2005, his son, Faure Gnassingbé, was elected RPT president. At the party's ninth congress in December 2006, Gnassingbé was reelected as RPT leader and Solitoki Esso was selected as secretary general. In the 2007 legislative elections the RPT secured 39.4 percent of the vote and 50 seats in the National Assembly.

Following the arrest of Kpatcha Gnassingbé after an alleged coup in April 2009, reports indicated divisions within the RPT along ethnic lines (Faure's mother was Ewe, from southern Togo, and Kpatcha's mother was Kabye, from the north). Nonetheless, president Gnassingbé was expected to be the RPT candidate in the 2010 balloting.

Leaders: Faure Essozimma GNASSINGBÉ (President of the Republic and the Party), Koffi SAMA (Former Prime Minister), Solitoki ESSO (Secretary General).

Democratic Convention of African People (*Convention Démocratique des Peuples Africains*—CDPA). In December 1989 CDPA members Godwin TETE and Kuevi AKUE were arrested for distributing antigovernment leaflets. Their sentencing in October 1990 led to violent protests, which in turn were followed by the government's decision to move toward a multiparty system. The CDPA was legalized in 1991.

In September 1992 the house of CDPA leader Nguessan Ouattara was bombed during a wave of political assassination attempts allegedly orchestrated by Eyadéma supporters. In 1993 the CDPA initiated the formation of the **Panafrican Social Democrats' Group** (*Groupe des Démocrates Sociaux Panafricains*—GDSP), an opposition coalition that also included the PDR and PSPA (below). (After boycotting the 1994 legislative elections, the GDSP was subsequently dissolved.)

In August 1997 the CDPA's founder and secretary general, Léopold Gnininvi, returned from a four-year, self-imposed exile, and in presidential elections in June 1998 he captured less than 1 percent of the vote.

The CDPA joined the boycott of the 2002 legislative elections and was one of the founding parties of both the CFD and The Front. In 2003, CDPA General Secretary Léopold Gnininvi registered to run in the presidential election, but he subsequently withdrew from the race. The CDPA joined the coalition that supported Bob-Akitani's candidacy in the 2005 presidential elections. The CDPA subsequently joined the unity governments in 2006 and 2007. In the 2007 legislative balloting, the CDPA placed fifth with 1.6 percent of the vote, but no seats in the Assembly. The CDPA was part of the new government formed in 2008. However, opposition to participation in the coalition government led a number of members to publically quit the CDPA in 2008.

Leaders: Nguessan OUATTARA, Léopold GNININVI (Secretary General and 1998 and 2003 presidential candidate), Emmanuel GUKONU (First Secretary).

Opposition Parties:

Union of Forces of Change (*Union des Forces du Changement*—UFC). The UFC coalition is led by Gilchrist Olympio, who has long been linked to the MTD (below). In July 1993 the Eyadéma government issued an arrest warrant that linked Olympio to an attack on the president's residence in March, and in early August the UFC leader, who had been calling for a new electoral register, was disqualified from presidential polling for refusing to return to Togo for a medical checkup. Subsequently, the UFC spearheaded a successful boycott of the balloting by its (then) COD-2 partners; however, its calls for a boycott of assembly balloting in February 1994 were ignored. In December 1997 UFC secretary general Jean-Pierre FABRE was arrested and briefly detained after he sought to investigate the alleged murder of opposition activists by government security forces.

Although officially declared the runner-up in June 1998 presidential balloting, Olympio, who had been blocked from entering Togo from his base in Ghana during the closing days of the campaign, claimed that he had received 59 percent of the vote, not the 34 percent with which he had been credited. Subsequently, the UFC was at the forefront of the antigovernment actions that followed the polling, and in August UFC headquarters were attacked by unknown assailants. Although remaining critical of the French government's previous support of the Eyadéma regime, the UFC followed President Jacques Chirac's call for reconciliation and joined talks with the government in July 1999 along with the CAR and UTD.

The UFC helped form the antiregime CFD in 2002 but withdrew from the group in 2003. Olympio returned to contest the presidential election in 2003 but failed to meet the residency requirements. Bob-Akitani ran as his proxy and placed second in the balloting. Bob-Akitani also finished second in the disputed April 2005 presidential poll. In September 2005, UFC member Gabriel Sassouvi DOSSEH-ANYROH was dismissed from the party after he accepted a cabinet post in the Gnassingbé government. The UFC subsequently declined to participate in the 2006 unity government, but party member Amah GNASSINGBÉ agreed to serve as a minister of state on a "personal basis," not as a representative of the party.

In the 2007 legislative elections, the UFC placed second with 37 percent of the vote and 27 seats. At the UFC's 2008 congress, Olympio was unanimously reelected president of the party and chosen as the UFC's 2010 presidential candidate. Jean-Pierre Fabre was reelected secretary general and Patrick Lawson was selected as first vice president. The UFC subsequently launched discussions with other opposition parties in an effort to rally them behind Olympio in the 2010 presidential balloting.

Leaders: Gilchrist OLYMPIO (Party president and 1998 presidential candidate), Jean-Pierre FABRE (Secretary General), Emmanuel BOB-AKITANI (2005 presidential candidate and Honorary President of the Party), Patrick LAWSON (First Vice President).

Togolese Movement for Democracy (*Mouvement Togolais pour la Démocratie*—MTD). Prior to the legalization of political parties in April 1991 the MTD was a Paris-based organization, which claimed in 1980 that 34 people released from confinement on January 13 were "not real political prisoners" and that hundreds of others remained incarcerated. It disclaimed any responsibility for a series of bomb attacks in 1985, while charging that the Eyadéma regime had "unleashed a wave of repression" in their wake. In mid-1986 MTD assistant secretary general Paulin LOSSOU fled France in the face of a decision by authorities to expel him to Argentina for his "partisan struggle" against the Eyadéma regime. Several reported MTD members were imprisoned in 1986 for distributing anti-Eyadéma pamphlets, but all of their sentences were commuted by 1987.

The government accused the MTD of complicity in the September 1986 coup attempt, insisting that it planned to install Gilchrist Olympio, exiled son of the former chief executive, as president. Olympio, who was sentenced to death in absentia for his alleged role in the plot, described the charges as "preposterous," suggesting that internal dissent had generated the unrest. Olympio returned to Lomé on July 6, 1991, under an April 12 general amnesty, to participate in the National Conference. Although claiming no interest in avenging his father's death, Olympio described the existing regime as lacking "legitimacy." Subsequently, *Africa Confidential* cited his influence in Joseph Kokou Koffigoh's capture of the prime ministerial post.

In May 1992 Olympio was critically wounded in an assassination attempt which took the lives of four others, including MTD leader Eliot OHN. Following his return from rehabilitation in Europe, Olympio emerged as the opposition's most prominent spokesperson, and in early 1993 he reportedly suggested that ECOWAS establish a presence in Togo to counter the reemergence of pro-Eyadéma military factions as well as help facilitate the transitional process.

Leader: Gilchrist OLYMPIO (Party Leader).

Action Committee for Renewal (*Comité d'Action pour le Renouveau*—CAR). The CAR was one of the leaders, along with the UTD, below, in the formation in October 1992 by "moderate" COD-2 parties of the Patriotic Front (*Front Patriotique*—FP), which sought to maintain links with the government despite the objection of other coalition partners. The FP boycotted presidential balloting in August 1993. However, dismissing calls from the more militant UFC for a second boycott, the FP split from its ally and participated in the February 1994 legislative balloting. The CAR captured 36 seats (2 of which were subsequently vacated); however, despite an earlier pledge, President Eyadéma refused to appoint Yawovi Agboyibo, the CAR's leader and presidential candidate, prime minister.

At a mid-March 1994 meeting, the FP, attempting to dispel rumors that dissension would render the coalition unable to assume a governing role, issued a communiqué demanding the right to form a cabinet. On March 26 the group agreed that the next prime minister would be a CAR member, and two days later it nominated Agboyibo as its choice for the post. Consequently, on April 22 the CAR denounced the appointment of the UTD's Edem Kodjo as prime minister as a "blatant and inadmissible violation" of the March agreement, called on Kodjo to "reconsider" his position, and declared that it would not participate in a UTD-led government, thereby effectively ending the Front's existence. Nevertheless, the following day Kodjo insisted that the FP was still viable and that he controlled a parliamentary majority (albeit a tenuous one in light of a Supreme Court ruling that had invalidated three FP electoral victories).

The CAR boycotted assembly by-election balloting in August 1996, thus conceding the loss of two more seats. Meanwhile, party officials complained that they had been the victim of a RPT-orchestrated "smear campaign." In October the party's legislative seat total dropped to 32 after a deputy defected to the RPT. (Earlier, two other CAR legislators had quit the party, switching their allegiances to the Eyadéma camp.)

The CAR reportedly organized a number of antigovernment demonstrations beginning in late 1996 and continuing through 1997. Furthermore, the group spearheaded concurrent legislative boycotts. In November 1997 Agboyibo, whom *Africa Confidential* described as seeming to "seek outright confrontation with the government," was attacked after attending a function at the U.S. embassy.

Following presidential elections in June 1998, Agboyibo reportedly asserted that the UFC's Olympio was the true top vote-getter. For his part, Agboyibo finished third in the balloting with 9 percent of the tally. The CAR joined the opposition boycott of the 1999 balloting. Agboyibo was found guilty of defamation charges in August 2001. Although a court of appeal nullified a six-month sentence against him in January 2002, he was held on additional conspiracy charges. In mid-March the president ordered his release for the "sake of national reconciliation." Agboyibo ran for the presidency in 2003 and placed third with 5.2 percent of the vote. In the 2005 presidential election, CAR supported the candidacy of Bob-Akitani. Agboyibo was appointed prime minister in September 2006, but resigned in November 2007, following legislative balloting in which the CAR received 8.2 percent of the vote and 4 seats in the National Assembly.

Agboyibo resigned as party president in October 2008 and was replaced by CAR Secretary General Dodji Apevon.

Leaders: Dodji APEVON (President), Gahoun EGBOR (First Vice President), Yawovi AGBOYIBO (Former Prime Minister).

Other Parties Participating in the 2007 Legislative Elections:

Panafrican Patriotic Convergence (*Convergence Patriotique Panafricaine*—CPP). The CPP was formed in August 1999 with the formal merger of the UTD (below); the **Party of Democrats for Unity** (*Parti des Démocrates pour l'Unité*—PDU); the **Democratic Union for Solidarity** (*Union Démocratique pour la Solidarité*—UDS); and the **African Party for Democracy** (*Parti Africain pour la Démocratie*—PAD). The CPP was among the main opposition groups that continued talks with the government in 2000 and 2001 and was subsequently active in the formation of the independent electoral commission and the CFD. CPP leader Edem Kodjo was named prime minister in June 2005. He was replaced in September 2006 but was appointed minister of state in charge of the office of the presidency in the subsequent unity government. The CPP was given two other posts in the cabinet. In the 2007 balloting for the National Assembly, the CPP placed fourth with 1.9 percent of the voting, but no seats. At the CPP's 2009 congress, Kodjo initiated a reorganization of the party leadership. Kodjo also announced that he would soon retire from politics and not be a presidential candidate in 2010.

Leaders: Edem KODJO (President of the Party and Former Prime Minister), Jean-Lucien Savide TOVÉ (First Vice President), Cornelius AIDAM.

Togolese Union for Democracy (*Union Togolaise pour la Démocratie*—UTD). Aligned with the CAR, the UTD secured seven seats (one subsequently vacated) in legislative balloting in February 1994, and on April 22 its leader and former secretary general of the Organization of African Unity, Edem Kodjo, was chosen by the president to head a new government. In March 1995 the UTD temporarily withdrew from the National Assembly following a dispute with the RPT over the assignment of responsibility for two government bodies. Improved UTD-RPT relations were highlighted in November when Kodjo included a number of new RPT representatives in his enlarged cabinet. Furthermore, in February 1996 the UTD's votes were pivotal to an RPT-led assembly rejection of an opposition bid for an independent electoral commission. Thereafter, however, relations between the two deteriorated, and in August 1997 Kodjo claimed to have been attacked by government security forces. Subsequently, the UTD leader reportedly announced his intention to boycott forthcoming presidential elections, asserting that the polling would be rigged in favor of the incumbent. Nonetheless, Kodjo ran as the candidate for the CPP in the 2003 presidential election, placing fifth with just 1 percent of the vote.

Coordination of New Forces (*Coordination des Forces Nouvelles*—CFN). Formed in June 1993 by several parties, including the Union of Democrats for the Republic (*Union des Démocrates pour la République*—UDR), the Togolese Social Liberal Party (*Parti Social-Liberal Togolais*—Solito), and several professional associations, the CFN is led by former prime minister Joseph Kokou Koffigoh under a banner describing the party as "resolutely committed to an irreversible democratic process." In legislative balloting in February 1994 the CFN won one seat. In November 1995 a CFN member, Euphrem Seth DORKENOU, was named to the Kodjo government. The CFN participated (unsuccessfully) in the March 1999 legislative elections, although the party was considered pro-Eyadéma and Koffigoh was named to the cabinet formed in August 2000. The CFN also failed to win seats in the 2002 and 2007 elections.

Leaders: Joseph Kokou KOFFIGOH (Former Prime Minister), Nicolas NOMEDJI (Executive Secretary).

Rally for Support for Democracy and Development (*Rassemblement pour le Soutien pour la Démocratie et le Développement*—RSDD). The RSDD is led by Henry Octavianus Olympio, a cousin of the opposition leader Gilchrist Olympio of the UFC. Henry Olympio served in the cabinet of Kwassi Klutse and was appointed minister of democracy and promotion of the rule of law in the government formed by Prime Minister Adoboli in June 1999. However, he was dismissed from the latter post in June 2000.

Olympio was appointed minister for relations with the assembly in 2002, but he resigned in August 2003 over a dispute with the prime minister in which the RSDD leader sought a different cabinet post. Olympio secured less than 1 percent of the vote in the 2005 presidential poll. The RSDD failed to gain any seats in the 2007 National Assembly balloting. Olympio was expected to be the RSDD's candidate in the 2010 presidential polling.

Leader: Henry Octavianus OLYMPIO (2005 presidential candidate and Chair).

Socialist Renewal Pact (*Pacte Socialiste pour le Renouveau*—PSR). The PSR's 2003 presidential candidate placed fourth with 2.3 percent of the vote. The PSR was part of the six-party coalition that endorsed Bob-Akitani in the 2005 presidential polling. PSR leader Tchessa Abi broke with other opposition parties and joined the cabinet in June 2005. The PSR also participated in the 2006 unity government. The party did not gain any seats in the 2007 balloting and was not invited to join the 2008 government.

Leaders: Tchessa ABI (Party Leader).

Other parties which remained active or participated in the 2007 balloting included the **Togolese Alliance for Democracy** (*Alliance Togolaise pour la Démocratie*—ATD), led by Adani Ifé ATAKPAMEVI, who was an independent presidential candidate in 1993; the centrist **Alliance of Democrats for the Republic** (*Alliance des Démocrates pour la République*—ADR), which contested successive legislative elections beginning in August 1996; and the **Party of Action for Democracy** (*Parti d'Action pour la Démocratie*—PAD), led by Francis EKOH; the **Party for Democracy and Renewal** (*Parti pour la Démocratie et le Renouvellement*—PDR), led by Zarifou AYEWA (who joined the cabinet in June 2005 and was appointed a minister of state in the 2006 unity cabinet, but not subsequent governments) and which received 1 percent of the vote in the 2007 legislative elections;

the hard-line Marxist-Leninist **Pan-African Socialist Party** (*Parti Socialiste Panafricain*—PSPA), led by Francis AGBOBLI; the **Workers' Party** (*Parti des Travailleurs*—PT), led by Claude AMENGAVI; the **National Front** (*Front National*—FN), led by Amela AMELA VI; the **Movement of Republican Centrists** (*Mouvement des Républicains Centristes*—MRC), led by Kabou Gssokoyo ABASS; the **Party for Renewal and Redemption**, whose leader, Nicholas LAWSON, won 1 percent of the vote in the 2005 presidential poll and was a candidate for the 2010 presidential balloting; and the **Party for Renewal and Social Progress** (*Parti pour le Renouveau et le Progrès Social*—PRPS), led by Agbessi MAWOU. In 2005, the **Initiative and Development Party** was formed by Adanu Kokou KPOTUI as the country's 63rd registered party. It was followed in September by the formation of the **Democratic Alliance for the Fatherland** (*Alliance Démocratique pour la Patrie*—the Alliance) by former prime minister Agbéyomé Messan KODJO and former speaker of the assembly Maurice Dahuku PERE, formerly of the PSR.

Other newer parties include the **Alliance of Democrats for Integrated Development** (*Alliance des Démocrates pour le Développement Intégré*—ADDI), led by Nagbandja KAMPATIBE, and the **Union for Democracy and Solidarity–Togo** (*Union pour la Démocratie et la Solidarité–Togo*—UDS–Togo), led by Antoine FOLLY. Both the ADDI and the UDS–Togo were part of the coalition that supported the candidacy of Bob-Akitani in the 2005 presidential balloting. Other new parties that contested the 2007 balloting but failed to secure seats were: **The Nest** (*Le Nid*), **New Popular Dynamic** (*Nouvelle Dynamique Populaire*), and the **Regrouping of the Live Forces of Youth for Change** (*Regroupement des Forces Vives de la Jeunesse pour le Changement*). Parties formed since the 2007 balloting include **The Alliance** (*L'Alliance*), led by former national assembly speaker and RPT official Dahuku PERE, and the **Union of Socialist Democrats of Togo** (*Union des Démocrates Socialistes du Togo*) led by Agbyome KODJO.

Other Parties and Groupings:

Other parties that emerged in the early 1990s included the **Nationalist Movement for Unity** (*Mouvement Nationaliste de l'Unité*—MNU), led by Koffitse ADZRAKO; the **Togolese Democratic Party** (*Parti Démocratique Togolais*—PDT), led by Mba KABASSEMA; the **Togolese Union for Reconciliation** (*Union Togolaise pour la Réconciliation*—UTR), led by Bawa MANKOUBU; and the **Union for Labor and Justice** (*Union pour le Travail et la Justice*—UTJ), which also contested the legislative elections in 1994 and subsequent balloting; and the **Movement of October 5th** (*Mouvement du 5 Octobre*—MO5), a militant group led by Bassirou AYEWA and whose name was derived from the date of the first anti-Eyadéma demonstration. In February 1993 MO5 members were reported to have built barricades throughout Lomé to protest the late January killing of opposition demonstrators by government security forces.

For more information on the now-defunct **Coordination of Political Parties of the Constructive Opposition** (*Coordination des Partis de L'Opposition Constructive*—CPOC), see the 2008 *Handbook*.

LEGISLATURE

On July 16, 1991, the National Conference dissolved the existing National Assembly and subsequently transferred its powers to a High Council of the Republic (*Haut Conseil de la République*—HCR) for a transition period leading to multiparty elections. In early 1993 the HCR, already involved in a constitutional debate with the president over his efforts to reverse the prime minister's dismissal of two cabinet members, once again found itself in conflict with Eyadéma, who, in response to criticism of his dismissal and then reconfirmation of the prime minister, argued that the HCR's mandate had expired along with the transition period. Subsequently, after numerous postponements, Togo's first multiparty balloting took place over two rounds on February 6 and 20, 1994.

National Assembly (*Assemblée Nationale*). The National Assembly is composed of 81 members directly elected for five-year terms. In the most recent balloting on October 14, 2007, the Rally of the Togolese People won 50 seats; the Union of Forces of Change, 27; and the Action Committee for Renewal, 4.

President: Abbas BONFOH.

CABINET

[as of September 1, 2009]

Prime Minister	Gilbert Houngbo (ind.)
Ministers of State	
Health	Komlan Mally (RPT)
Industry, Handicrafts and Technological Innovation	Leopold Messan Gnininvi (CDPA)
Territorial Administration, Decentralization, Local Communities and Government Spokesman	Pascal Bodjona (RPT)
Water Resources and Village Water	Gen. Zacherie Nandja
Ministers	
Agriculture, Livestock, and Fisheries	Kossi Messan Ewovor (RPT)
Civil Service and Administration Reform	Ninsao Gnofame
Communication, Culture and Civic Education	Oulegoh Keyewo
Cooperation, Development and Regional Planning	Gilbert Bawara (RPT)
Economic Affairs, Finance and Privatization	Adji Otheth Ayassor (RPT)
Environment, Tourism and Forest Resources	Kossivi Ayikoe
Foreign Affairs and African Integration	Kofi Esaw
Higher Education and Research	Messan Adimado Aduayom (CDPA)
Human Rights, Democracy, and Reconciliation	Ykoubou Koumadjo Hamdou
Justice and Keeper of the Seals	Kokou Biossey Tozoun (RPT)
Labor, Employment and Social Security	Octave Nicoué Broohm (RPT)
Mines, Energy and Water Resources	Noupokou Dammipi (RPT)
Post and Telecommunications	Kokouvi Dogbe (RPT)
Primary and Secondary Education and Literacy	Sambiani Sankardja Lare
Relations with the Institutions of the Republic	Ninsao Gnofame
Security and Civil Protection	Col. Atcha Titikpina (RPT)
Social Affairs, the Promotion of Women, Children, and the Aged	Maimounatou Ibrahima (RPT) [f]
Technical Education and Professional Training	Henriette Kuevi Amedjogbe [f]
Tourism	Batienne Kpabre-Sylli
Urban Affairs and Housing	Issifou Okoulou-Kantchati (RPT)
Youth and Sports	Padumhekou Tchaou
Ministers Delegate	
Office of the President, Charge of Commerce, and the Promotion of the Private Sector	Guy Madje Lorenzo
Office of the Prime Minister, in Charge of Basic Development	Victorine Sidemeho-Dogbe [f]
Secretary of State in the Office of the Prime Minister, in Charge of Youth and the Employment of Young People	Nathalie Manzinewe Bitho [f]
Secretary of State at the Ministry of Co-operation, Development and Regional Planning, in Charge of Regional Planning	Bandifoh Ouro-Akondo

[f] = female

COMMUNICATIONS

For many years the media were almost exclusively government controlled. A highly restrictive press code adopted in October 1990 was significantly relaxed in early 1991; however, in June 1998 yet another, more stringent code was adopted. In early 2000 a new press bill further limited press freedom and made "defamation of the government" an offense subject to a prison sentence. In 2000 and 2001 numerous independent and pro-opposition publications came under government scrutiny. In April 2000 the director of the independent weekly *L'Exilé* was arrested, and his newspaper was suspended for six months.

A second repressive law was passed in 2002 and allowed fines of up to $7,500 and sentences of five years in prison for defaming the president. The law also imposed lesser penalties for defamation of members of the government and the assembly. However, many of the new measures were repealed in August 2004 as part of Togo's effort to restart international aid. Suppression and intimidation of opposition media continued, however, and in October 2005 there were widespread protests to denounce attacks on opposition journalists. In 2008 Reporters Without Borders ranked Togo 53, along with Montenegro and Northern Cyprus, out of 173 countries in regard to freedom of the press.

Press. The following are published in French in Lomé: *Togo Presse* (15,000), government-owned daily; *Le Combat du Peuple,* proopposition weekly; *L'Exilé, Abito, Le Regard, L'Aurore, Le Nouvel Echo,* and *Le Nouveau Journal,* all independent weeklies; *Le Nouvel Éclat*, pro-government weekly; *Le Courrier du Golfe* and *Forum-Hebdo,* independent biweeklies; *La Dépêche,* bimonthly; and *L'Echos d'Afrique,* a pro-CDPA publication.

News agencies. *Agence Togolaise de Presse* (ATOP) is the official facility; *Agence France-Presse* and *Deutsche Presse-Agentur* maintain bureaus in Lomé.

Broadcasting and computing. The government-operated *Radiodiffusion du Togo* broadcasts from Lomé in French, English, and indigenous languages. *Télévision Togolaise* began programming in Lomé in 1973; other transmitters are located in Alédjo-Kadara and Mont Agon. By the end of 2000, three private channels, *Radio Télévision Delta Santé, Radio Télévision Zion-To* (with a Christian orientation), and *Djabal Nour* (with a Muslim orientation) were still operating, while a fourth, *TV2*, was on the air in 2002. As of 2008 there were 54.2 Internet users per 1,000 inhabitants.

INTERGOVERNMENTAL REPRESENTATION

Ambassador to the U.S.: Kadanghe BARIKI.

U.S. Ambassador to Togo: Patricia McMahon HAWKINS.

Permanent Representative to the UN: Kodjo MENAN.

IGO Memberships (Non-UN): ADF, AfDB, AU, BADEA, BOAD, CENT, ECOWAS, Interpol, IOM, NAM, OIC, OIF, PCA, UEMOA, WCO, WTO.

TONGA

Kingdom of Tonga
Fakatu'i 'o Tonga

Political Status: Constitutional monarchy; independent within the Commonwealth since June 4, 1970.

Area: 289 sq. mi. (748 sq. km.).

Population: 101,991 (2006C); 103,000 (2008E).

Major Urban Center (2005E): NUKU'ALOFA (39,300).

Official Languages: Tongan, English.

Monetary Unit: Pa'anga (official rate December 1, 2009: 1.88 pa'anga = $1US).

Head of State: King SIAOSI (GEORGE) TUPOU V; succeeded to the throne on September 11, 2006, following the death of his father, King TAUFA'AHAU TUPOU IV, on September 10; coronated on August 1, 2008.

Prime Minister: Dr. Feleti (Fred) SEVELE; appointed by the king on March 31, 2006, following acting appointment to succeed Prince 'ULUKALALA Lavaka Ata, who had resigned on February 11.

THE COUNTRY

Located south of Samoa in the Pacific Ocean, Tonga (also known as the Friendly Islands) embraces some 200 islands that run north and south in two almost parallel chains. Only 45 of the islands are inhabited, the largest being Tongatapu, which is the seat of the capital and the residence of almost two-thirds of the country's population. Tongans (mainly Polynesian with a Melanesian mixture) constitute 98 percent of the whole, while Europeans and other Pacific islanders make up the remainder. The majority of the population is Christian, approximately 60 percent belonging to the Free Wesleyan Church of Tonga. The official female labor force participation rate is less than 14 percent, due in part to child-rearing demands in a society with an average of five children per family; female representation in government is virtually nonexistent, although a woman won a commoner seat in the National Assembly in a by-election in May 2006.

Primarily an agricultural country, Tonga produces coconuts and copra, bananas, vanilla, yams, taro, sweet potatoes, and tropical fruits. Pigs and poultry are raised, while beef cattle (traditionally bred by Europeans) are beginning to assume importance, thus reducing dependence on beef imports. In the early 1990s several thousand metric tons of squash pumpkins (Tonga's leading export) were shipped annually to Japan, although declining production because of drought, disease, and lower market prices led to a market collapse late in the decade. Government-sponsored diversification efforts have focused on fishing and cultivation of specialty crops, including kava and mozuku (a type of edible seaweed). With the exception of some coconut-processing plants, no significant industries exist, although exploration for oil has recently been under way. GDP growth averaged only 1–2 percent between 1994 and the first half of 1998 but was estimated at 3.5 percent in fiscal year 1998–1999 and 5.5 percent in 1999–2000. In the latter period, the economy benefited from increased remittances from some 50,000 nonresident Tongans and a surge in trade and services related to millennial celebrations. Thereafter, growth (termed "lackluster" by the International Monetary Fund [IMF]) receded to an annual average of 1.1 percent for 2002–2008. Through the same period, inflation was consistently high, averaging 10.7 percent per year. Both measures were severely affected by the prodemocracy riots of November 2006 that virtually destroyed the capital, Nuku'alofa (see Political background, below).

In 2000 Tonga was identified by the Organization for Economic Cooperation and Development (OECD) as among a number of Pacific jurisdictions with harmful tax policies permitting noncitizens to evade overseas taxes. Following passage of corrective legislation, Tonga was removed from the OECD blacklist in August 2001.

GOVERNMENT AND POLITICS

Political background. Christianized by European missionaries in the early 19th century, Tonga became a unified kingdom in 1845. British protection began in 1900 with the conclusion of a treaty of friendship and alliance whereby a British consul assumed control of the islands' financial and foreign affairs. New treaties with the United Kingdom in 1958 and 1968 gave Tonga full internal self-government in addition to limited control over its external relations, with full independence within the Commonwealth occurring on June 4, 1970.

In June 1989 the commoner (popularly elected) legislators for the first time forced rejection of a proposed government budget. Eight

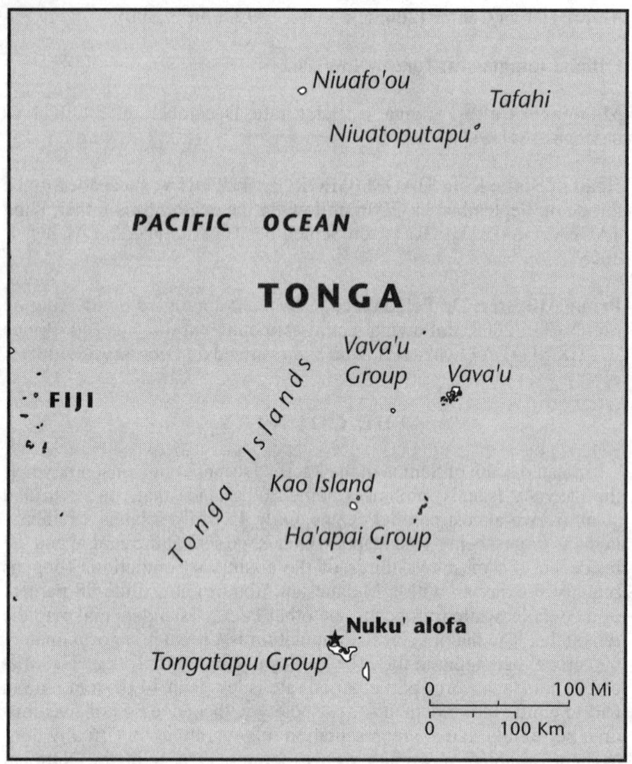

months later the country mounted its most intensely contested legislative election, with 55 candidates vying for the nine commoners' seats and 23 for the nine nobles' seats. While not organized as formal parties, two major groupings emerged: a prodemocracy movement headed by 'Akilisi POHIVA that criticized the islands' maldistribution of wealth and called for more responsible and efficient government, and a conservative group primarily concerned with economic development and the creation of new employment opportunities. Pohiva had been discharged from an education ministry post in 1985 after announcing in a radio broadcast that assemblymen had voted themselves 400 percent pay increases. Prior to the 1987 election (in which he successfully contested an assembly seat), Pohiva launched a hard-hitting opposition newsletter, *Ko'e Kele'a,* and instituted a suit for reinstatement to his former position. While the basic issue had become academic because of his assembly status, the Tongan Supreme Court handed down an unprecedented decision in mid-1988 awarding damages plus costs for unfair dismissal and a denial of free speech.

At the February 1990 poll, Pohiva's formation captured a majority of the commoner seats but remained a minority overall as the conservatives strengthened their control of the seats reserved for election by the nobles. Subsequently, the political ferment intensified, with the king of the predominantly Protestant country accusing both Pohiva and Tonga's Roman Catholic bishop of communist sympathies.

On August 21, 1991, the younger brother of King TAUFA'ANAU TUPOU IV, Prince Fatafehi TU'IPELEHAKE, stepped down after 26 years as prime minister, Deputy Prime Minister Baron VAEA being named his successor.

In November 1992 the prodemocracy movement organized a four-day public conference to indicate how the constitution could be amended to provide for greater popular participation in the political process. The government declined to participate in the conference, prevented foreign invitees from entering the country to attend its sessions, and refused to broadcast news of the event on the grounds that it was not officially sponsored. Nonetheless, the movement appeared to be growing, as evidenced by its capture of six of nine popularly elected seats in the legislative balloting of February 4, 1993, and formation of the Tonga Democratic Party (TDP, under Friendly Islands Human Rights and Democracy Movement [FIHRDM], below) in August 1994. Prodemocracy candidates retained a majority of commoner seats at the subsequent poll of January 25, 1996.

In September 1996 'Akilisi Pohiva and two *Times of Tonga* editors were jailed for contempt after publication of a story that Pohiva intended to introduce a motion of impeachment against Justice Minister Tevita TUPOU for unauthorized attendance at the Atlanta Olympic games. The 30-day sentences yielded widespread protests by international media, and after 26 days the men were freed by the Supreme Court on procedural grounds. Although Pohiva and the Human Rights and Democracy Movement in Tonga (HRDMT, a successor to the TDP) expected to increase the representation of prodemocracy advocates in the March 11, 1999, commoner balloting, only five were elected.

Crown Prince TUPOUTO'A was thought to have been the leading candidate to succeed Prime Minister Vaea upon the latter's retirement in early 2000, but he was passed over in favor of the king's youngest son, Prince 'ULUKALALA Lavaka Ata. The January 3, 2000, appointment was followed by a cabinet expansion and reorganization on January 25, 2001. In late September 2001 Justice Minister Tupou and Education Minister Tūtoatasi FAKAFANUA were forced to resign after being linked to the loss of millions in investments from the Tonga Trust Fund, into which income from the questionable sale of Tongan passports in 1983–1991 had been deposited.

In the legislative election of March 7, 2002, the HRDMT won seven of the nine popularly elected seats despite a controversy involving its recent publication in the *Times of Tonga* of a letter, possibly forged, that accused the king of holding $350 million in secret offshore accounts. On February 25 police had raided the HRDMT offices and briefly detained 'Akilisi Pohiva, who was among several politicians and journalists later charged with sedition and dealing in a forged document. Pohiva and two others were acquitted of the charges on May 19, 2003.

In the election of March 16–17, 2005, 8 of the 9 commoners were HRDMT members, and, in an unprecedented move following the poll, King Taufa'ahau named 2 commoners to an expanded 16-member cabinet, one of whom, Feleti (Fred) SEVELE, became the first commoner to serve as prime minister.

Following his death on September 10, 2006, King Taufa'ahau was succeeded by his son, Crown Prince Tupouto'a, who assumed the title King SIAOSI (GEORGE) TUPOU V.

Two months later, on November 16, a renewed prodemocracy demonstration quickly turned into a riot that destroyed some 80 percent of the capital's business district. By the end of the month, order had been restored with the help of 150 Australian and New Zealand troops, and a pledge by the government of a new election in 2008, in which a majority of legislators would be selected by popular vote. However, Prime Minister Sevele announced in mid-2007 that the constitutional changes could not be enacted in time for the 2008 election but would be in place prior to another poll in 2010.

In the election of April 23–24, 2008, the commoner representation of what was now styled the FIHRDM (see Political Parties, below) was reduced to six seats, although Pohiva's endorsement by 11,290 was more than that of any other candidate.

Constitution and government. Tonga is a hereditary constitutional monarchy whose constitution dates back to 1875. The executive branch is headed by the Privy Council, which includes the king and a cabinet that encompasses a prime minister, a deputy prime minister, other ministers, and the governors of Ha'apai and Vava'u. Meeting at least once a year, the unicameral Legislative Assembly currently includes an equal number of elected hereditary nobles' and people's representatives, plus the cabinet members sitting ex officio. When the body is not in session, the Privy Council is empowered to enact legislation, which must, however, be approved by the assembly at its next meeting. The judicial system is composed of a Supreme Court, magistrates' courts, and a Land Court. Ultimate judicial appeal is to the king, who appoints all judges.

Tonga is administratively divided into several groups of islands, the most important of which are the Tongatapu group, the Ha'apai group, and the Vava'u group.

Foreign relations. In 1900 Tonga and the United Kingdom signed a Treaty of Friendship and Protection, which provided for British control over financial and external affairs. Tonga became a member of the Commonwealth upon independence and is affiliated with the European Union under the Cotonou Agreement. It became the 188th member of the United Nations in September 1999; earlier it had joined a number of UN-related organizations, including the Food and Agriculture Organization (FAO), the World Health Organization (WHO), and the United Nations Educational, Scientific, and Cultural Organization (UNESCO). It was admitted to the IMF in September 1985. Regionally, it belongs to the Pacific Islands Forum and the Pacific Community.

Relations with the United States were initially formalized in an 1888 treaty, which was largely revoked by Tongan authorities in 1920. A successor Treaty of Amity, Commerce, and Navigation was concluded during ceremonies marking the king's 70th birthday in July 1988. The most important component of the new accord was a provision guaranteeing transit of U.S. military vessels—including nuclear-armed craft—in the Tongan archipelago. The action was seen as underscoring a "tilt toward Washington" by a government that had failed to join a majority of its neighbors in ratifying the 1985 South Pacific Nuclear Free Zone Treaty (Treaty of Rarotonga).

Earlier, in October 1986, Tonga had served as the venue for the completion of negotiations that, after 25 months, yielded agreement on a tuna treaty between the United States and members of the South Pacific Forum (subsequently Pacific Islands Forum) Fisheries Agency. The local economy was reported to have benefited substantially from the nine-day discussions, which, for approximately $60 million, permitted access by the U.S. tuna fleet to nearly 8 million square miles of prime fishing grounds over a five-year period. Tonga became the final signatory to the pact in June 1989.

In late 1998 relations with Taiwan ended after the kingdom had switched recognition to the People's Republic of China, which had promised to extend both trade and aid.

In January 2008, a Nationality Act, approved in June 2007, came into effect. The act sanctioned dual citizenship for nonresident Tongans who had lost their native citizenship by being naturalized elsewhere.

Current issues. A strike in July 2005 by public service workers (the first in Tongan history) was resolved on September 5 with government acceptance of most of the strikers' pay demands. However, it was followed on the next day by a protest march calling for democratic reforms. On October 18 the king announced that he would appoint a parliamentary commission to look into the matter, and while no action was immediately forthcoming, it was considered significant that Prime Minister Sevele's appointment in March 2006 was, for the first time, that of a commoner.

The destruction caused by the prodemocracy upheaval of November 2006 was a major setback for the already fragile Tongan economy. It did not, however, halt the move for constitutional reform. In mid-2008 a Constitution and Electoral Reform Commission, chaired by Tonga's former chief justice Gordon WARD, was formed. In June 2009 the commission recommended that the prime minister be selected by the Legislative Assembly from elected People's Representatives and that he be empowered to appoint his own ministers. No action was taken by the commission on an appeal to set aside seats for women.

POLITICAL PARTIES

Traditionally there were no political parties in Tonga, the initial equivalent of such a formation (see under FIHDRM, below) being an outgrowth of the Pro-Democracy Movement that sponsored the conference on democracy in November 1992.

Friendly Islands Human Rights and Democracy Movement (FIHRDM). The FIHRDM was styled the Human Rights and Democracy Movement in Tonga (HRDMT) from 1998 to 2005. Earlier, it was known as the People's Party (PP), which had initially been launched in August 1994 as the Tonga Democratic Party (TDP) by opposition MP 'Akilisi Pohiva. Five of the Legislative Assembly's nine commoner members were reported to have joined the group, which, while predicting a democratic Tonga by the end of the century, had pledged to retain the king as a figurehead. In January 1995 the PP claimed royal backing for the introduction of a Westminster-style system of government.

Supporters of the HRDMT captured five of the nine commoner seats in the March 1999 balloting, disappointing prodemocracy activists, who had hoped to capture at least seven (and possibly all nine) and thereby generate momentum for its petition to the king to make all assembly seats subject to election by universal suffrage. Following the election, Pohiva argued that some voters had been swayed by progovernment television broadcasts and by misinformation concerning plans for land distribution in a "fully democratic" Tonga. In August 2001 the government turned down the group's application for registration as an incorporated society.

In the March 2002 legislative election the HRDMT won seven seats. Subsequently, Pohiva was one of several persons charged with publication of a letter that accused the king of secreting some $350 million in offshore bank accounts; verdicts of acquittal were issued in May 2003. However, Pohiva was among those rearrested in early 2007 for involvement in the riot of the preceding November.

Leader: 'Akilisi POHIVA (General Secretary).

Kotoa Movement (KM). The KM was formed prior to the 2002 election to campaign in support of the monarchy.

Leader: Semisi KAILAHI (Secretary).

People's Democratic Party (PDP). The PDP was launched on April 15, 2005, by a group of HRDMT defectors with the announced goal of pursuing reform more aggressively than the parent group. On July 13 it became Tonga's first officially registered party.

Leaders: Sione Teisina FUKO (President), Clive EDWARDS (Former Minister of Police), Semisi TAPUELUELU (Secretary).

Sustainable Development of the Land Party (*Paati Langafonua Tu'uola*—PLT). The PLT was launched in August 2007 to recruit "good candidates" for the Legislative Assembly, 2 of whom were elected in 2008. It has urged a moderate approach to political reform, calling for a 27-seat parliament with 9 nobles and 9 people's representatives elected for 3 years, the remainder for 6 years.

Leader: Sione FONUA (President), Kamipeli TOFA (Secretary).

LEGISLATURE

The unicameral **Legislative Assembly** (*Fale Alea*) currently consists, apart from the speaker, of 9 nobles selected by the 33 hereditary nobles of Tonga, 9 people's representatives elected by universal suffrage, and the Privy Council, encompassing the king and his ministers. In the most recent commoner election of April 24, 2008, 6 of the available seats were won by members of the prodemocracy Friendly Islands Human Rights and Democracy Movement. Election of the legislature's 9 nobles had taken place a day earlier.

Speaker: TU'ILAKEPA.

CABINET

[as of August 1, 2009]

Prime Minister	Dr. Feleti (Fred) Sevele
Deputy Prime Minister	Dr. Viliami Tau Tangi
Ministers	
Agriculture, Food, Fisheries, and Forestry	Prince Tu'ipelehake
Civil Aviation, Marine Affairs, and Ports	Paul Karalus
Defense (Acting)	Dr. Feleti (Fred) Sevele
Disaster Relief Activities	Dr. Feleti (Fred) Sevele
Education and Culture	Dr. Tevita Hala Palefau
Environment	Tuita
Finance and National Planning	Afu'alo Matoto
Foreign Affairs	Dr. Feleti (Fred) Sevele
Health	Dr. Viliami Tau Tangi
Information and Communication	Eseta Fusitu'a
Justice (Acting)	Eseta Fusitu'a
Labor, Commerce, and Small Industries	Lisiate 'Akolo
Lands, Survey, and Natural Resources	Tuita
Police, Prisons, and Fire Services (Acting)	Dr. Viliami Tau Tangi
Public Enterprises	Afu'alo Matoto
Public Works	Nuku
Tourism	Fineasi Funaki
Training and Employment	Tu'ivakano
Women's Affairs	Dr. Tevita Hala Palefau
Youth and Sports	Tu'ivakano
Attorney General	John Cauchi
Governor of Ha'apai	Malupo
Governor of Vava'u (Acting)	Tuita

COMMUNICATIONS

Press. Tongan authorities have recently evidenced scant regard for freedom of the press. In March 1995 the editor of the independent *Times of Tonga* was deported for publishing material deemed to have offended the minister of police, while two of his colleagues were incarcerated for legislative contempt in 1996. In 2002 *Times* journalists were also charged with sedition and publishing a forged document that accused the king of holding millions of dollars in secret bank accounts. Thereafter, a lengthy contest ensued between the government and the paper that extended to 2004.

The following are published in Nuku'alofa: *Koe Taimi 'o Tonga/The Times of Tonga,* weekly, in Tongan and English (8,000); *Kalonikali Tonga/Tonga Chronicle,* government weekly in Tongan (6,000) and English (1,200); *Ko'e Kele'a/Conch Shell* (3,500), dissident news sheet, issued weekly in Tongan and English; *Matangi Tonga,* bimonthly (2,000); and *Tonga Today,* monthly. In 1990 *Tonga Nquae,* a right-wing counterpart to *Kele'a,* was launched in opposition to "any move to change the present structure of our government," while religious papers are issued monthly by the Catholic and Protestant communities. A daily, *Talanga/Speak Out,* is published in Auckland, New Zealand; aimed in part at some 25,000 expatriates, it also circulates in Tonga.

Broadcasting and computing. Radio broadcasting is the responsibility of the Tonga Broadcasting Commission (*Komisioni Fakamafolalea Tonga*—KFT), which transmits commercial programming in Tongan, English, Fijian, and Samoan. An FM outlet was inaugurated in 1986, and a Television Department was formed in 2000, which launched its second television station in 2008.

As of 2008 there were 81.1 Internet users per 1,000 inhabitants.

INTERGOVERNMENTAL REPRESENTATION

Ambassador to the U.S.: (Vacant).

U.S. Ambassador to Tonga: C. Steven McGANN (resident in Fiji).

Permanent Representative to the UN: Sonatane T. TAUMEOPEAU-TUPOU.

IGO Memberships (Non-UN): ADB, CWTH, Interpol, PC, PIF, WCO, WTO.

TRINIDAD AND TOBAGO

Republic of Trinidad and Tobago

Political Status: Independent member of the Commonwealth since August 31, 1962; republican constitution adopted August 1, 1976.

Area: 1,980 sq. mi. (5,128 sq. km.), of which Trinidad encompasses 1,864 sq. mi. (4,828 sq. km.) and Tobago 116 sq. mi. (300 sq. km.).

Population: 1,262,366 (2000C); 1,309,000 (2008E).

Major Urban Center (2000C): PORT-OF-SPAIN (49,031).

Official Language: English. On September 1, 2005, the government announced that Spanish would be adopted as an official language by 2020 to permit Trinidadians to compete more effectively in regional markets.

Monetary Unit: Trinidad and Tobago Dollar (market rate December 1, 2009: 6.34 dollars = $1US).

President: George Maxwell (Max) RICHARDS; elected by Parliament to a five-year term on February 14, 2003, and inaugurated on March 17, succeeding Arthur Napoleon Raymond ROBINSON; reelected on February 11, 2008.

Prime Minister: Patrick Augustus Mervyn MANNING (People's National Movement), appointed by the president on December 24, 2001, following general election of December 10, succeeding Basdeo PANDAY (United National Congress); reappointed on October 9, 2002, following election of October 7, and on November 7, 2007, following election of November 5.

THE COUNTRY

The English-speaking state of Trinidad and Tobago, a pair of scenic tropical islands off the northern coast of South America, forms the southern extremity of the island chain known as the Lesser Antilles. Trinidad is the larger and more highly developed of the two islands, accounting for nearly 95 percent of the country's area and population and by far the greater part of its national wealth. As in nearby Guyana, approximately 43 percent of the population are descendants of African slaves, while another 40 percent are descendants of East Indian indentured laborers brought in during the 19th century. Most of the former are presently concentrated in urban areas, while most of the latter are active as independent farmers. People of mixed ancestry, together with a few Europeans and Chinese, make up the rest of Trinidad's inhabitants, while Tobago's population is largely of African extraction. Roman Catholicism predominates, but Hinduism, Protestant Christianity, and Islam are also practiced.

The economy has traditionally been heavily dependent on refined petroleum and related products derived from both domestically extracted and imported crude oil. Although domestic reserves were thought to be approaching exhaustion in the late 1960s, natural gas and oil deposits subsequently discovered off Trinidad's southeast coast gave new impetus to the refining and petrochemical industries, which now account for more than 90 percent of export earnings. Tourism is of growing importance, while agriculture plays a relatively minor role in the islands' economy. In early 2007 the government announced plans to emulate neighboring St. Kitts by closing down its long-standing, but increasingly unprofitable, sugar industry in favor of a more balanced agricultural sector geared to domestic consumption.

Starting in 1973, soaring oil prices produced rapid growth, pushing per capita income by the early 1980s to about $7,000, the third highest in the Western Hemisphere. Between 1982 and mid-1990, on the other hand, real GDP declined by 30 percent, largely because of falling prices and markets for oil. Further economic adversity resulted from a coup attempt in August 1990, which triggered widespread violence and looting in the capital. While marginal recovery was registered in 1991, economic performance declined by an average of 1.1 percent annually during 1985–1993, before turning positive, cresting at 5.6 percent in 1998, then declining steadily to 2.7 percent in 2002. Spurred by sales of recently discovered natural gas, growth averaged 9.3 percent per year from 2003 to 2007 but declined sharply in 2008 because of the global recession. Unemployment fell from 14.6 percent in 1999 to a record low of 4.2 percent in mid-2008, while inflation rose from 5.6 percent in 2004 to a high of 14.8 percent in late 2008.

GOVERNMENT AND POLITICS

Political background. Discovered by Columbus and ruled by Spain for varying periods, Trinidad and Tobago became British possessions during the Napoleonic wars and were merged in 1888 to form a single Crown Colony. Political and social consciousness developed rapidly during the 1930s, when the trade union movement and socialism began to emerge as major influences. The People's National Movement (PNM), the country's first solidly based political party, was founded in 1956 by Dr. Eric WILLIAMS and controlled the government without interruption for the next 30 years. Following participation in the short-lived, British-sponsored Federation of the West Indies from 1958 to 1962, Trinidad and Tobago was granted full independence within the Commonwealth on August 31, 1962.

After an initial period of tranquility, "black power" demonstrations broke out, which led to the declaration of a state of emergency in April 1970 and later to an attempted coup by elements of the military.

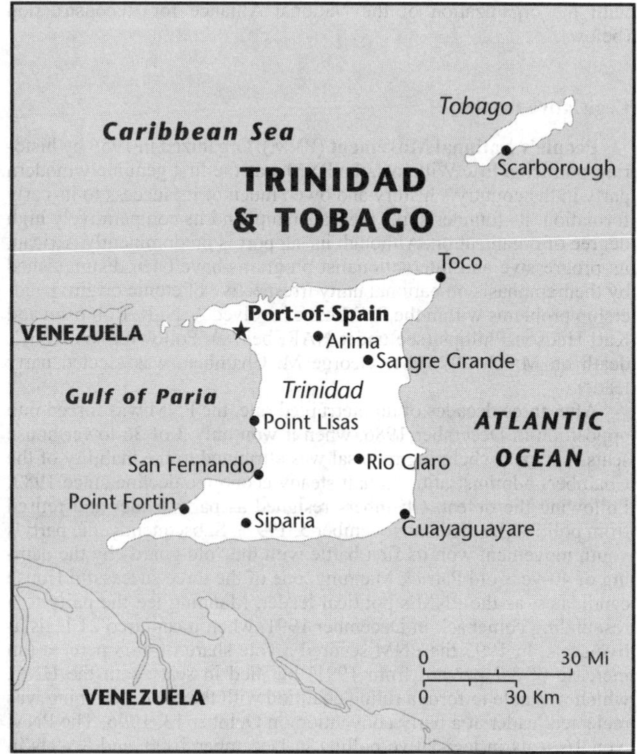

Subsequent political instability included a fresh wave of labor unrest that resulted in the reimposition of a state of emergency in October 1971.

In October 1973 Prime Minister Williams announced his intention to retire from politics, but he reversed himself two months later, ostensibly at the request of his party, until steps had been taken to implement a republican constitution. In the legislative election of September 13, 1976, the PNM won 24 of the 36 House seats. Williams died unexpectedly on March 29, 1981, and was succeeded as prime minister and party leader by George M. CHAMBERS, who led the PNM to a 26–10 victory in parliamentary balloting on November 9.

Severe economic decline and the formation for the first time of a solid coalition of opposition groups—the National Alliance for Reconstruction (NAR)—led to reversal in 1986 of the PNM's theretofore uninterrupted control of the government, with the NAR winning 33 of 36 House seats in balloting on December 15, and Arthur N. R. ROBINSON succeeding Chambers as prime minister. However, the Robinson government proved no more successful in coping with fiscal adversity than its predecessor. In April 1989 a group of dissidents under the leadership of Basdeo PANDAY, who had been expelled from the NAR seven months earlier, organized the United National Congress (UNC), which secured a stunning by-election victory over both the NAR and PNM on May 1. A far greater embarrassment to the administration was an attempted coup by members of a militant black Muslim sect, the *Jamaat-al-Muslimeen,* on July 27, 1990. The rebels succeeded in occupying Trinidad's state-run TV station and its legislative building, taking a number of hostages (including the prime minister) before agreeing to surrender on August 1.

In a forceful repudiation of Robinson's austerity program, the PNM, under the relatively youthful Patrick MANNING, won 21 house seats on December 16, 1991; only the ousted prime minister and Tobago's other representative survived the PNM landslide.

During 1995 both leading parties were overtaken by scandals that included indecent assault charges against the leader of the opposition, a storm over demotion of the PNM foreign minister, brief confinement of the speaker of the House of Representatives to house arrest, and suggestions that the police were operating a "death squad." In an effort to regain the political initiative, Prime Minister Manning called an early election for November 6, 1995, in which the PNM and the opposition UNC both won 17 seats. The UNC's Panday subsequently concluded a "partnership agreement" with the minority NAR and on November 9 was sworn in as the country's first prime minister of Indian descent. Subsequently, on February 14, 1997, Robinson was elected president of the republic in a 46–18 vote in Parliament.

The UNC secured a slim majority of 19 lower house seats in the election of December 11, 2000. However, the defection of three ministers in October 2001 forced a premature dissolution and the scheduling of a new election on December 10. The results of the polling were inconclusive (the UNC and the PNM won 18 seats each, on vote shares of 49.9 and 46.5 percent, respectively), and both Panday and Manning claimed a right to form the new cabinet. On December 17 they reportedly agreed to let the president choose who should be the next prime minister. However, when Robinson named Manning on December 24, Panday protested and declared the agreement void, claiming the president was "biased." Although Manning announced his cabinet over the next few days, Panday rejected the post of "Leader of the Opposition." In addition, his party refused to participate in the election of a speaker of the House of Representatives, which could not therefore formally convene, forcing an extended political stalemate.

On March 14, 2002, President Robinson requested that his term (expiring on March 18) be extended temporarily "in national interest," because the Parliament remained unable to elect a successor. While Panday protested the request, Manning approved the extension. On April 7, 2002, Robinson, on the advice of Manning, suspended the Parliament following yet another failed attempt to convene the House on April 5. Manning attempted to convene the house one more time in late August, but that effort also failed.

In a new election on October 7, 2002, the PNM secured a majority of 20 house seats and Prime Minister Manning was reappointed two days later. He was reelected to a third term on November 7, 2007.

Constitution and government. Under the 1976 constitution, Trinidad and Tobago became a republic, with a president (elected by a majority of both houses of Parliament) replacing the former governor general. The functions of the head of state remain limited, executive authority being exercised by a prime minister and cabinet appointed from among the members of the legislature. Parliament consists of an appointed Senate, a majority of whose members are proposed by the prime minister, and a House of Representatives elected by universal adult suffrage. The judicial system is headed by a Supreme Court, which consists of a High Court and a Court of Appeal, while district courts function at the local level. There is also an Industrial Court and a Tax Appeal Board, both serving as superior courts of record. Judges are appointed by the president on the advice of the prime minister. In a waning anomaly among former British dependencies, Trinidad retains the right of ultimate appeal to the Judicial Committee of the UK Privy Council. The provision is designed to afford litigants access to a completely disinterested final court.

Rural administration is carried out on the basis of 9 counties on Trinidad, which are subdivided into 29 electoral wards, plus 1 ward for all of Tobago. Four municipalities (Port-of-Spain, San Fernando, Arima, and Point Fortin) have elected mayors and city councils.

After three years of debate, the House of Representatives in September 1980 approved a bill establishing a 15-member House of Assembly for Tobago with primarily consultative responsibilities. In January 1987 Tobago was granted full internal self-government, its House being given control of revenue collection, economic planning, and provision of services.

In July 1993 Prime Minister Manning announced that agreement had been reached with the Tobago House of Assembly on enhanced constitutional status for the smaller island, including the creation of an Executive Council to oversee its day-to-day affairs and the appointment of a senator to represent Tobago exclusively. However, a number of changes were made in the proposed constitutional amendment before its adoption in late November 1996, with plans for additional Senate representation for Tobago being dropped altogether.

In August 2006 Manning submitted the draft of a new constitution to Parliament that would abolish the office of prime minister, whose duties would be assumed by an indirectly elected executive president, and replace the London-based Privy Council with the Caribbean Court of Justice as the country's final court of appeal. The proposal was supplemented in January 2009 by a new reform document that drew criticism from the judiciary, which claimed that the judiciary would be politicized by a provision establishing a ministry of justice, and by the opposition UNC, which preferred a unilateral legislature rather than the proposed retention of a bicameral body.

Foreign relations. In 1967 Trinidad and Tobago, which had joined the United Nations at independence, became the first Commonwealth country to be admitted to the Organization of American States (OAS). Its anticolonial but democratic and pro-Western foreign policy is oriented chiefly toward the Western Hemisphere and includes active participation in such regional organizations as the Caribbean Community and Common Market (Caricom). However, since 1983 a number of disputes with fellow Caricom members over trade restrictions have tended to hinder regional cooperation. Trinidad and Tobago's objections to the U.S.-led invasion of Grenada in October 1983 also cooled relations with a number of Eastern Caribbean states, most notably Barbados, and strained traditionally cordial relations with the United States, with Prime Minister Chambers criticizing what he perceived as U.S. president Ronald Reagan's attempt to "militarize" the region. However, efforts have since been initiated to lower the government's profile both on trade and foreign policy issues. Relations with the People's Republic of China and the Soviet Union were established in 1974, while a broad trade agreement signed in August 1984 with China was hailed as a "major leap forward in China's relations with the Commonwealth Caribbean."

No major foreign policy changes were advanced under the NAR administration, the essentially moderate Prime Minister Robinson having set as an initial priority the elimination of trade barriers within Caricom.

In February 1997 Trinidad's attorney general announced that a special intelligence unit would be established with U.S. and British assistance to monitor suspicious financial activities, including those associated with drug trafficking. In August a long-simmering dispute erupted with Venezuela over oil drilling in the straits separating the two countries, with altercations between Trinidadian riggers and Venezuelan patrol boats becoming increasingly common. Subsequently, the government signaled its intention to supply gas to nearby islands, such as Martinique and Guadalupe, via undersea pipelines, and in 2003 a feasibility study was commissioned for an 1,800-mile line to Florida.

Meanwhile, friction arose with Barbados over a 1990 treaty between Trinidad and Venezuela, which was alleged "unilaterally to appropriate to Venezuela and Trinidad and Tobago an enormous part of Barbados' and Guyana's maritime territory, as well as one-third of Guyana's land territory" (see Guyana entry). The dispute led to a ruling by the Permanent Court of Arbitration in The Hague in April 2006 that established a median line halfway between the exclusive economic zones of Barbados and Trinidad. However, the ruling allowed Barbados to exploit hydrocarbon resources up to 150 nautical miles beyond the line. On a highly contentious collateral issue, the court stated that it lacked jurisdiction to rule on the right of Barbadian fishermen to operate in Trinidadian waters.

The Manning administration has recently come under attack by fellow Caricom members for a variety of unilateral acts, including an agreement in August 2008 to pursue economic and political union with the Organization of Eastern Caribbean States (OECS).

Current issues. Both the PNM and the UMC are currently weakened by intraparty problems. In the case of the PNM, opposition allegations of corruption on the part of Finance Minister Karen NUNEZ-TESHEIRA triggered investigations by the police commissioner and the Office of Public Prosecutions, despite a declaration of support for the minister by Prime Minister Manning in February 2009. (For the UMC, see Political Parties, below.)

Meanwhile, a soaring crime rate included 544 murders in 2008. More than half were said to be gang-related, a category that has increased by nearly 900 percent in six years, with a total of 190 gangs reported by National Security Minister Martin JOSEPH to be active.

POLITICAL PARTIES

Before 1976, Trinidad and Tobago's party system was based primarily on a long-standing rivalry between the ruling People's National Movement (PNM) and the opposition Democratic Labour Party (DLP), with the PNM serving to some extent as a vehicle for African voters and the DLP mainly representing East Indians. Efforts toward a unified electoral opposition began in 1981, when the United Labour Front (ULF), which had emerged after the 1976 election as the principal opposition grouping, aligned itself with two smaller parties as the Trinidad and Tobago National Alliance; two years later, the Alliance and the Organization for National Reconstruction formed a temporary coalition (known as the "Accommodation") that gained 66 of the county council seats to the PNM's 54. The linkage was formalized in September 1985, with the organization of the National Alliance for Reconstruction (below).

Legislative Parties:

People's National Movement (PNM). Organized in 1956 by historian-politician Eric Williams, the PNM was the first genuinely modern party in the country's history and owed much of its success to its early formation, its founder's gift for leadership, and its comparatively high degree of organization. Although its support is predominantly African, its progressive and internationalist programs have been distinguished by their emphasis on national unity irrespective of ethnic origin. Leadership problems within the PNM have involved A. N. R. Robinson and Karl Hudson-Phillips (see under NAR, below). Following Williams's death on March 29, 1981, George M. Chambers was elected party leader.

After three decades of uninterrupted rule, the PNM was forced into opposition in December 1986, when it won only 3 of 36 lower house seats. The overwhelming reversal was attributed to the inability of the Chambers administration to halt steady economic decline since 1982. Following the defeat, Chambers resigned as party leader and retired from politics (he died on November 5, 1997). Subsequently, the party's youth movement won its first battle with the "old guard" by the naming of 40-year-old Patrick Manning, one of the three successful House candidates, as the PNM's political leader. Manning led the party to a resounding comeback in December 1991, when it captured 21 legislative seats. In 1995 the PNM secured a vote share of 48.8 percent (an increase of 3.7 percent from 1991) but tied in seats with the UNC, which was able to form a ruling coalition with the NAR. Manning was reelected leader at a party convention on October 13, 1996. The PNM won 16 seats in legislative polling in December 2000, and 8 seats in the Tobago House of Assembly polling in January 2001. The party increased its representation to 18 in the December 2001 legislative polling, but the result was a stalemate, since the UNC also won 18 seats. In new balloting on October 7, 2002, the PNM secured a majority of 20 seats. It increased its majority to 26 of an enlarged house of 41 members in November 2007. It retained its 8 Tobago Assembly seats in balloting on January 19, 2009.

Leaders: Patrick A. M. MANNING (Prime Minister), Kenneth VALLEY (Deputy Leader), Joan YUILLE-WILLIAMS (Deputy Leader), Franklin KHAN (Chair), Orville LONDON (Party Leader in Tobago), Martin JOSEPH (General Secretary).

United National Congress (UNC). The UNC was formally launched on April 30, 1989, by the members of Club '88 (see under NAR, below) who had been formally expelled from the NAR in October 1988 after having campaigned against Prime Minister Robinson's style of leadership. The new group drew much of its support from former ULF members opposed to Robinson's IMF-mandated austerity policies. The UNC defeated both the NAR and the PNM in a local council by-election on May 1, 1989, but, while holding six parliamentary seats to the PNM's three, did not seek appointment as the official opposition until September 1990.

A result of dissention within the party was the establishment in September 1994 of the Monday Club, an intraparty pressure group led by Hulsie Bhaggan, a member of Parliament who had been stripped of her political responsibilities two months earlier. Concurrently, three women who had been employed at UNC headquarters charged party leader Panday with rape and indecent assault. In late November, after having been arrested and released on bail, Panday lodged a suit against Attorney General Keith SOBION for alleged conspiracy to damage his reputation. Two of the indecent assault charges were dropped in mid-December, revived in January 1995, and again dismissed on March 10, after which Panday sued the government for malicious prosecution.

Although the UNC was unable to secure a plurality of seats in the 1995 balloting (it and the PNM winning 17 each), Panday was able to form a government on the basis of a "partnership agreement" with the NAR. The UNC won 19 seats in the December 2000 poll.

Relations between Prime Minister Panday and Ramesh MAHARAJ, the attorney general and UNC deputy leader, had long been strained by seeming slights, including Panday's unwillingness to name Maharaj acting prime minister while he was absent from the country. In addition, Maharaj and two other ministers had criticized Panday over corruption in state facilities and allowing business leaders excessive influence in public policy. In early October 2001, Panday dismissed his rebellious colleagues, who promptly entered into an "alliance" with the opposition PNM. Subsequently, Maharaj claimed that his faction controlled the UNC and would place candidates in all 36 constituencies in the forthcoming election. Although Panday briefly registered a new formation—the United National Party (UNP)—in case the courts allowed the Maharaj faction to use the UNC rubric, both the Elections and Boundaries Commission and the High Court ruled in November in favor of Panday, prompting the Maharaj faction to leave the party to form a group styled Team National Unity (TNU), which won only 2.5 percent of votes in the December 2001 poll, after which Maharaj returned to the UNC.

The early legislative polling of December 10, 2001, yielded a stalemate with the PNM; in the subsequent balloting of October 7, 2002, UNC representation dropped to 16.

Charges of corruption against Panday while heading the UNC administration led to his brief imprisonment in mid-2005, and in October he moved from the post of party leader to that of chair, albeit with no apparent loss of party control. His successor as party leader, Winston Dookeran, resigned in September 2006 to form a new party, the Congress of the People (below).

For the 2007 election the UNC was restyled the United National Congress–Alliance (UNC-A) as the leading component of a coalition that included the NAR, DPTT, and NDP (below).

In February 2009 Deputy Leader Jack Warner and (then) Chief Whip Ramesh Maharaj threatened to leave the UNC if Panday did not endorse internal leadership elections. A month later, Maharaj was fired as chief whip by Panday, who had warned that he would not tolerate public dissent within the party.

Leaders: Basdeo PANDAY (Former Prime Minister, Party Chair, and Leader of the Opposition), Jack WARNER (Deputy Leader of the Opposition), Kamla PERSAD-BISSESSAR (Former Leader of the Opposition).

Other Parties:

National Alliance for Reconstruction (NAR). The NAR was launched in 1984 as a coalition of the United Labour Front (ULF), the Democratic Action Congress (DAC), and the Tapia House Movement (THM); all had participated in the 1981 campaign as members of the Trinidad and Tobago National Alliance (TTNA). In September 1985 the Organization for National Reconstruction (ONR) joined the new formation, which reorganized as a unified party in February 1986.

The ULF had grown out of labor unrest in the sugar, oil, and transport industries in early 1975, and its leaders campaigned in 1976 for the nationalization of these and other major industries. Its leadership consisted primarily of a somewhat uneasy coalition of longtime opponents of the late Prime Minister Williams, including Basdeo Panday, East Indian head of the sugar workers' union; George Weekes, head of the black-dominated oil workers; and James Millette of the United National Independence Party (UNIP). The small Liberal Action Party (LAP), led by Ivan Perot, also joined the ULF before the 1976 balloting. Panday resigned as both party and union head in the wake of a poor showing by the former in the 1980 local elections, but he was subsequently returned to the posts by overwhelming majorities. The ULF obtained eight lower house seats in November 1981.

Headed by Arthur N. R. Robinson, a former PNM associate (and one-time heir apparent) of Prime Minister Williams, the DAC was a relatively conservative grouping that won the two seats from the island of Tobago in the 1976 parliamentary election, retaining both in 1981. In mid-1978 Winston Murray, one of the winners in 1976, repudiated Robinson's leadership and in 1980 withdrew from the party. Robinson himself resigned his seat to stand for reelection to the Tobago House of Assembly in 1980, subsequently being named chair of the new body.

The Tapia ("mud wall") group emerged as an offshoot of the black power movement at the University of the West Indies. It called for the nationalization of all foreign-controlled enterprises and a reconstituted, elected Senate with greater representation of ordinary citizens. In late 1974 four of its members were appointed opposition delegates to the Senate on the recommendation of Roy RICHARDSON of the now defunct United Democratic Labour Party (UDLP), who was then the sole recognized opposition member of the House of Representatives. The THM won no parliamentary seats in 1981 and many of its members, including Tapia leader Lloyd BEST, withdrew from the alliance in June 1987 after accusing the Robinson administration of "drifting as aimlessly" as its predecessor. In late 1989 the Tapia House leadership announced that it intended to withdraw from the NAR and reorganize as a separate party, although no such move was subsequently reported to have been implemented.

The moderately left-of-center ONR was founded by Karl Hudson-Phillips following his withdrawal from the PNM in April 1980. Although failing to win any legislative seats in 1981, the group ran second in the popular vote (22.3 percent) and, given the ULF's largely ethnic base among sugar workers, was called "the only real claimant, other than the PNM, to national party status." Despite his group's steadily improving position in the polls, Hudson-Phillips declared in June 1985 that he would not stand for prime minister, thereby providing indirect support for Robinson's candidacy.

The NAR's success in coalescing behind Robinson and its leader's ability to attract support from diverse ethnic and labor groups were considered major factors in the group's stunning victory in the December 1986 balloting. However, by early 1988 the alliance had encountered severe internal stress, culminating in the expulsion of a number of ULF dissidents led by Basdeo Panday, who had formed an anti-Robinson intraparty formation known as Club '88 ("Club" being an acronym for Caucus for Love, Unity, and Brotherhood). In April 1989 the Club '88 group reorganized as a separate party, the United National Congress (UNC, above).

The NAR was decimated by the December 1991 poll, retaining only its two lower house seats from Tobago. In the wake of the defeat Robinson resigned as party leader, the former minister of works, Carson Charles was named his successor at the NAR annual convention on March 29, 1992. The party retained overwhelming control of the Tobago House of Assembly on December 7, 1992, winning 11 seats to 1 for the PNM.

NAR leader Charles was replaced by Selby WILSON in early 1993, and Charles subsequently left the party to form the National Development Party (NDP). Wilson, in turn, resigned the leadership in August 1994 after having denounced a by-election alliance between the NDP and the NAR.

In the 1995 election the NAR again failed to secure representation in Trinidad. However, by keeping its 2 Tobago seats it was able to enter into a ruling alliance with the UNC. The NAR retained 10 of its 11 seats in the Tobago House of Assembly on December 9, 1996, the lost seat going to an incumbent who had resigned from the NAR in November and campaigned as an independent.

In October 1999 the NAR National Council named former party chair Anthony SMART as interim leader after "vacating of the post" by Nizam MOHAMMED, who insisted he had been dismissed and was subsequently reinstated. The NAR won one seat in the 2000 legislative election and four seats in the January 2001 Tobago House of Assembly poll. The party won no House of Representatives seats in 2001, 2002, or 2007. Carson Charles was reelected party leader on October 23, 2006.

During 2006 the NAR joined with a number of smaller parties in a series of shifting alliances. On April 20 a merger with the MND (below) and DPTT (below) was announced, which, without reference to the MND but with the addition of the DNA (below), was subsequently styled the Democratic National Alliance. However, the DNA withdrew on June 9, while in July the NDP (below) joined the grouping, which was restyled the National Democratic Alliance.

Leaders: Carson CHARLES (Leader of the Party), Christo GIFT (Chair).

Congress of the People (COP). The COP was launched on September 10, 2006, by former UNC party leader Winston Dookeran, who had been threatened with expulsion from the UNC on the basis of claims that he was maintaining a parallel political organization.

Leader: Winston DOOKERAN.

Movement for National Development (MND). The MND was launched in October 2005 with a platform of government decentralization, improving social services, and reducing the crime rate.

Leader: Garvin NICHOLAS.

Citizens Alliance (CA). The CA was launched in December 2001 by former cabinet minister Wendell Mottley to "bring a fresh voice to politics beyond the UNC-PNM polarization."

Leader: Wendell MOTTLEY.

Movement for Unity and Progress (MUP). The MUP was launched in December 1994 by Hulsie Bhaggan, who continued, however, as a member of the UNC until her formal expulsion on August 13.

Leader: Hulsie BHAGGAN.

National Joint Action Committee (NJAC). The NJAC was organized by Geddes Granger, who played a leading role in the black power disturbances of 1970 and was under detention from October 1971 to June 1972 before changing his name to Makandal Daaga. The group contested elections in 1981, when it secured 3.3 percent of the popular vote, and in 1986, when it won 1.5 percent.

Leader: Makandal DAAGA.

Republican Party (RP). The RP was launched in January 1994 by Nello Mitchell, the PNM's former general secretary, who was expelled from the party in July 1993 for "gross disrespect."

Leader: Nello MITCHELL.

National Vision Party (NVP). The NVP was formed in early 1994 by Yasin Abu Bakr, leader of the unsuccessful 1990 coup by the *Jamaat-al-Muslimeen*.

Leader: Yasin Abu BAKR.

People's Empowerment Party (PEP). The Tobago-based PEP was organized in 1999 by a group of NAR dissidents, including one of its (then) two House of Representatives members.

Leaders: Deborah MOORE-MIGGINS, Richard ALFRED (General Secretary).

Tobago Organization of the People (TAP). The TAP was launched as a coalition grouping prior to the Tobago poll of January 19, 2009, in which it won four seats.

Leader: Ashworth JACK.

Democratic National Assembly (DNA). The DNA, an outgrowth of a number of groups, including Dr. Kirk Meighoo's Committee for Transformation and Progress, was launched in March 2006 and participated briefly in the Democratic National Alliance led by the NAR.

Leader: Dr. Kirk MEIGHOO.

Trinidad's minor parties also include the **Movement for Social Transformation** (MST), led by David ABDULLAH; the **National Democratic Organization** (NDO), led by Enoch JOHN; the **United Freedom Party** (UFP), led by Ramdeo SAMPAT-MEHTA; the **West Indian National Party** (WINP), led by Ashford SINANAN; and the **Democratic Liberation Party** (DLP), a breakaway faction of the WINP, led by Bhadase S. MARAJ.

Among new parties formed in 2002 were the **Democratic Party of Trinidad and Tobago** (DPTT), led by Steve ALVAREZ; and the **National Democratic Party** (NDP), led by Robert AMAR and Michael SIMS. In early 2003 former NAR faction leader Hochoy CHARLES launched a new **Democratic Action Congress** (DAC). The move was considered significant, since the original DAC had been a founding component of the NAR; however, the party captured only one seat in the 2005 Tobago election. Another recent group, the **National Transformation Movement** (NTM), led by Lloyd ELCOCK, was formed in 2006.

LEGISLATURE

The national **Parliament** is a bicameral body consisting of an appointed Senate and an elected House of Representatives; Tobago has a unicameral **House of Assembly.**

Senate. The upper chamber consists of 31 members appointed by the president for a maximum term of five years: 16 are named on the advice of the prime minister; 6 on the advice of the leader of the opposition; and 9 at the president's discretion from religious, economic, and social groups.

President: Linda BABOOLAL.

House of Representatives. The lower chamber currently has 41 members directly elected for five-year terms, subject to dissolution. In the election of November 5, 2007, the People's National Movement won 26 seats and the United National Congress, 15.

Speaker: Barendra ("Barry") SINANAN.

Tobago House of Assembly. Tobago's legislature consists of 15 members, 12 directly elected and 3 named by the majority party; its term is four years. In a landslide victory in the most recent balloting of January 17, 2005, the People's National Movement won 11 of the elective seats and the Democratic Action Congress, 1.

Chief Secretary: Orville LONDON.

CABINET

[as of July 1, 2009]

Prime Minister	Patrick Manning
Ministers	
Agriculture, Land, and Marine Resources	Sen. Arnold Piggott
Community Development, Culture, and Gender Affairs	Marlene McDonald [f]
Education	Esther LeGendre [f]
Energy and Energy Industries	Sen. Conrad Enill
Finance	Karen Nunez-Tesheira [f]
Foreign Affairs	Paula Gopee-Scoon [f]
Health	Sen. Jerry Narace
Information	Neil Parsanial
Labor, Small and Micro-Enterprise Development	Rennie Dumas
Legal Affairs	Peter Taylor
Local Government and Community-based Environmental Protection and Enhancement	Sen. Hazel Anne Marie Manning [f]
National Security	Sen. Martin Joseph
Planning, Housing, and Environment	Sen. Dr. Emily Gaynor Dick-Forde [f]
Prime Minister's Office	Sen. Lenny Saith
Public Administration	Kennedy Swaratsingh
Public Utilities	Mustapha Abdul-Hamid
Science, Technology, and Tertiary Education	Christine Kangaloo [f]
Social Development	Amery Browne
Sports and Youth Affairs	Gary Hunt
Tourism	Joseph Ross
Trade and Industry	Mariano Brown
Works and Transport	Colm Imbert
Attorney General	Sen. Bridgette Annisette-George [f]
Ministers of State	
Community Development, Culture, and Gender Affairs	Donna Cox [f]
Planning, Housing, and the Environment	Sen. Tina Gronlund-Nunez [f]
Prime Minister's Office	Stanford Callender
Science, Technology, and Tertiary Education	Fitzgerald Jeffrey
Social Development	Alicia Hospedales [f]
Works and Transport	Roger Joseph

[f] = female

COMMUNICATIONS

Press. The following are privately owned and are published daily in Port-of-Spain: *Trinidad Guardian* (51,000 daily, 48,000 Sunday); *Trinidad and Tobago Express* (43,000 daily, 51,000 Sunday); *Newsday* (25,000), launched in September 1993. In 1997 a proposed government code of ethics that would require journalists "to highlight and promote activities of the state which aim at national unity and solidarity" was criticized as potentially limiting freedom of expression.

News agencies. There is no domestic facility. The Caribbean News Agency (CANA) is used for most international and some domestic news. A number of foreign agencies maintain offices in Port-of-Spain.

Broadcasting and computing. Radio programming is provided by the government-owned International Communications Network and by the commercial Trinidad Broadcasting Company—TBC (Radio Trinidad), which in early 1990 was purchased by a group owning the *Trinidad Guardian*. Commercial television is provided by the government-owned Trinidad and Tobago Television Company—TTT and by a Caribbean Communications Network—CCN outlet. As of 2008 there were 170.2 Internet users per 1,000 inhabitants.

INTERGOVERNMENTAL REPRESENTATION

Ambassador to the U.S.: Glenda MOREAN-PHILLIP.

U.S. Ambassador to Trinidad and Tobago: (Vacant).

Permanent Representative to the UN: Marina Annette VALERE.

IGO Memberships (Non-UN): ACS, Caricom, CDB, CWTH, IADB, Interpol, NAM, OAS, OPANAL, SELA, WCO, WTO.

TUNISIA

Republic of Tunisia
al-Jumhuriyah al-Tunisiyah

Note: Gen. Zine El-Abidine BEN ALI (Democratic Constitutional Assembly—RCD) was reelected with 89.62 percent of the vote for a fifth five-year term in multicandidate balloting on October 25, 2009. In concurrent elections for the House of Representatives, the RCD won 161 of 214 seats.

Political Status: Independent state since 1956; republic proclaimed July 25, 1957; under one-party dominant, presidential regime.

Area: 63,170 sq. mi. (163,610 sq. km.).

Population: 9,910,872 (2004C); 10,372,000 (2008E).

Major Urban Centers (2005E): TUNIS (734,000), Sfax (Safaqis, 269,000), Ariana (252,000), Ettadhamen (116,000).

Official Language: Arabic; French is widely spoken as a second language.

Monetary Unit: Dinar (market rate December 1, 2009: 1.27 dinars = $1US).

President: (*See headnnote.*) Gen. Zine El-Abidine BEN ALI (Democratic Constitutional Assembly); appointed prime minister on October 2, 1987; acceded to the presidency upon the deposition of Habib BOURGUIBA on November 7; returned to office, unopposed, in elections of April 2, 1989, and March 20, 1994; reelected in multicandidate balloting on October 24, 1999, and on October 24, 2004.

Prime Minister: Mohamed GHANNOUCHI (Democratic Constitutional Assembly); appointed by the president on November 17, 1999, to succeed Hamed KAROUI (Democratic Constitutional Assembly), who had resigned the same day; reappointed by the president following presidential balloting on October 24, 2004, and formed new government on November 10.

THE COUNTRY

Situated midway along the North African littoral between Algeria and Libya, Tunisia looks north and eastward into the Mediterranean and southward toward the Sahara Desert. Along with Algeria and Morocco, it forms the Berber-influenced part of North Africa known as the "Maghreb" (West) to distinguish it from other Middle Eastern countries, which are sometimes referred to as the "Mashreq" (East). Tunisia's terrain, well wooded and fertile in the north, gradually flattens into a coastal plain adapted to stock-raising and olive culture, and becomes semiarid in the south. The population is almost exclusively of Arab and Berber stock, Arabic in speech (save for a small Berber-speaking minority), and Sunni Muslim in religion. Although most members of the former French community departed after Tunisia gained independence in 1956, French continues as a second language, and small French, Italian, Jewish, and Maltese minorities remain. Women, who constitute approximately 31 percent of the paid labor force, are the focus of relatively progressive national policies on equal rights, educational access for girls, and family planning. In addition, by presidential decree, 20 women were elected to the national legislature in 1999 and 43 in 2004. Moreover, the current government includes female ministers and secretaries of state.

About one quarter of the working population is engaged in agriculture, which is responsible for about 13 percent of GNP; the main products are wheat, barley, olive oil, wine, and fruits. Petroleum has been a leading export, although there is also mining of phosphates, iron ore, lead, and zinc. Industry has expanded to more than 30 percent of GDP, with steel, textiles, and chemicals firmly established. Most development is concentrated in coastal areas, where tourism is the largest source of income; however, poverty is widespread in the subsistence farming and mining towns of the south. Rising oil exports underpinned rapid economic growth in the 1970s, but declining prices and reserves precipitated a tailspin in the early 1980s. Consequently, high unemployment, a large external debt, and growing budget and trade deficits led the government, with encouragement by the International Monetary Fund (IMF) and World Bank, to abandon much of its former socialist orientation in favor of economic liberalization in the second half of the decade. Led by growth in the agriculture and food processing sectors, the economy rebounded strongly in the 1990s and early 2000s as the government endorsed further privatization and measures designed to attract foreign investment. As a result, the IMF has touted Tunisia as an example of how effective adjustment programs can be in developing nations if pursued faithfully. At the same time economic advances have not been accompanied by significant democratization measures, and government at all levels remains totally dominated by the ruling party.

Strong performance in the energy sector in particular, as well as in agriculture, manufacturing, and services, contributed to average annual growth of 6 percent in 2005–2007, though unemployment remained at about 14 percent. The IMF commended Tunisia for adopting banking reform measures and praised the country's efforts toward liberalizing trade and combating money laundering and the financing of terrorism. Despite the global economic recession, annual GDP growth of 2.9 percent was forecast for 2009, owing in large part to Tunisia's lower import costs and a fully implemented free-trade agreement with the European Union. Also, the government announced plans for reforms to bolster small- and medium-size businesses in an effort to reduce unemployment.

GOVERNMENT AND POLITICS

Political background. Seat of the Carthaginian empire destroyed by Rome in 146 BC, Tunisia was successively conquered by Romans, Arabs, and Turks before being occupied by France in 1881 and becoming a French protectorate under a line of native rulers (beys) in 1883. Pressure for political reforms began after World War I and in 1934 resulted in establishment of the nationalist Neo-Destour (New Constitution) Party, which spearheaded the drive for independence under the leadership of Habib BOURGUIBA. Nationalist aspirations were further stimulated by World War II, and an initial breakdown in independence negotiations led to the outbreak of guerrilla warfare against the French in 1952. Internal autonomy was conceded by France on June 3, 1955, and on March 20, 1956, the protectorate was terminated, with the country gaining full independence.

A national constituent assembly controlled by the Neo-Destour Party voted on July 25, 1957, to abolish the monarchy and establish a republic with Bourguiba as president. A new constitution was adopted on June 1, 1959, while Bourguiba's leadership and that of the party were overwhelmingly confirmed in presidential and legislative elections in 1959 and 1964.

Bourguiba was reelected in 1969, but his failing health precipitated a struggle for succession to the presidency. One-time front-runner Bahi LADGHAM, prime minister and secretary general of the party, was apparently too successful: the attention he received as chair of the Arab Superior Commission on Jordan and as effective executive during the president's absences led to a falling-out with an eventually rejuvenated Bourguiba; he was dismissed in 1970 and replaced by Hedi NOUIRA.

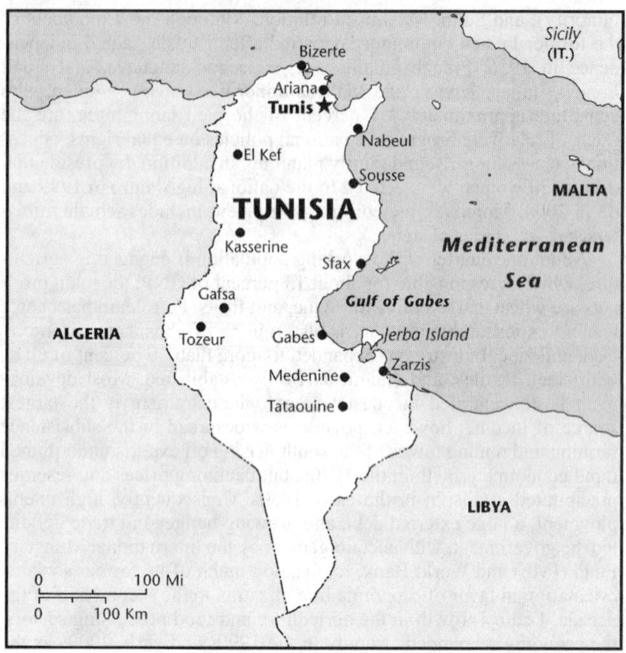

President Bourguiba encountered an additional challenge from Ahmed MESTIRI, interior minister and leader of the liberal wing of the party. The liberals succeeded in forcing democratization of the party structure during the eighth party congress in October 1971, but Bourguiba subsequently reasserted his control over the party apparatus. Mestiri was expelled from the party in January 1972 and from his seat in the National Assembly in May 1973, while Bourguiba was named president for life on November 2, 1974.

In February 1980 Prime Minister Nouira suffered a stroke, and on April 24 Mohamed MZALI, the acting prime minister, was asked to form a new government. Mzali was reappointed following a general election on November 1, 1981, in which three additional parties were allowed to participate, although none secured legislative representation. Bourguiba dismissed Mzali on July 8, 1986, replacing him with Rachid SFAR, theretofore finance minister.

Gen. Zine El-Abidine BEN ALI was named to succeed Sfar on October 2, 1987, reportedly because of presidential displeasure at recent personnel decisions. Five weeks later, after a panel of doctors had declared the aged president medically unfit, Bourguiba was forced to step down in favor of Ben Ali, who designated Hedi BACCOUCHE as his prime ministerial successor.

Although widely termed a "bloodless coup," the ouster of Bourguiba and succession of Ben Ali were in accord with relevant provisions of the Tunisian constitution. Moreover, the takeover was generally welcomed by Tunisians, who had become increasingly disturbed by Bourguiba's erratic behavior and mounting government repression of the press, trade unions, legal opposition parties, and other sources of dissent, including the growing Islamic fundamentalist movement. (Following his deposition, Bourguiba retired from public view. He died at age 97 in 2000.)

Upon assuming office the Ben Ali government announced its commitment to domestic pluralism and launched a series of wide-ranging political and economic liberalization measures, which included the legalization of some political parties, the loosening of media restrictions, and the pardoning of more than 8,000 detainees, many of them fundamentalists. Additionally, in late 1988, the new regime negotiated a "national pact" regarding the country's political, economic, and social future with a number of political and labor groups. However, the Islamic Tendency Movement (*Mouvement de la Tendance Islamique*—MTI) refused to sign the accord, foreshadowing a steady deterioration in relations between the fundamentalists and the government.

Presidential and legislative elections, originally scheduled for 1991, were moved up to April 2, 1989, Ben Ali declaring they would serve as an indication of the public's satisfaction with the recent changes. No one challenged the popular Ben Ali in the presidential poll, but the legal opposition parties and fundamentalist independent candidates contested the House of Representatives balloting, albeit without success.

On September 27, 1989, Ben Ali dismissed Baccouche and named former Justice Minister Hamed KAROUI as prime minister. The change was reportedly precipitated by disagreement over economic policy, Baccouche having voiced concern over the "social effects" of the government's austerity program. Shortly thereafter, the government announced the formation of a "higher council" to oversee implementation of the national pact, although several opposition parties and MTI followers, now operating as the Renaissance Party (*Hizb al-Nahda*—generally referenced as *Nahda*) boycotted the council's meetings. Charging that the democratic process was in reality being "blocked" by the government, the opposition also refused to contest municipal elections in June 1990 or national by-elections in October 1991. Apparently in response to criticism that the government's enthusiasm for democratization had waned as its antifundamentalist fervor had surged, electoral law changes were adopted in late 1993 to ensure opposition parties of some legislative representation in the upcoming general election (see Legislature, below). Nevertheless, the Democratic Constitutional Assembly (RCD), officially credited with nearly 98 percent of the vote, won all 144 seats for which it was eligible in the balloting for a 163-member House on March 20, 1994. On the same date, Ben Ali was reelected without challenge, two potential independent candidates being stricken from the ballot by their failure to receive the required endorsement of at least 30 national legislators or municipal council presidents.

The RCD won control of all 257 municipal councils in local elections on May 21, 1995. While opposition candidates (standing in 47 municipalities) won only 6 of 4,090 seats, it was the first time since independence that the opposition had gained any such representation at all.

Ben Ali was reelected to a third full presidential term (then the constitutional limit) in balloting on October 24, 1999, securing more than 99 percent of the vote against two candidates presented by small opposition parties. Meanwhile, the RCD again secured all the seats for which it was eligible (148) in the concurrent legislative poll. Two days after being sworn in for his new term, President Ben Ali appointed Mohamed GHANNOUCHI, theretofore the minister for international cooperation and foreign investment, as the new prime minister.

Constitutional revision in 2002 removed the limit on the number of presidential terms, thereby permitting Ben Ali on October 24, 2004, to seek a fourth term, which he won with 95 percent of the vote against three other minor candidates. On the same date the RCD won all 152 seats contested on a district basis for an expanded assembly. Ghannouchi, who was retained as prime minister, headed a new government formed on November 10.

In the municipal election of May 8, 2005, to renew 264 councils comprising 4,366 seats, the RDC garnered 93.9 percent of the vote, while 4 opposition parties and 1 independent won representation with 6.1 percent of the vote. Three opposition groups whose candidates were barred from running boycotted the election. The RDC also dominated the new House of Advisers, which was established in balloting of July 3, 2005, in accordance with provisions adopted in the 2002 constitutional revision. The cabinet was reshuffled on August 17, 2005; January 25 and September 3, 2007; and August 29, 2008.

Constitution and government. The constitution of June 1, 1959, endowed the Tunisian Republic with a presidential system backed by the dominant position of the (then) Neo-Destour Party. The president was given exceptionally broad powers, including the right to designate the prime minister and to rule by decree during legislative adjournments. In addition, the incumbent was granted life tenure under a 1975 amendment to the basic law. In the wake of President Bourguiba's ouster in 1987, the life presidency was abolished, the chief executive being limited to no more than three five-year terms.

A new constitution approved in a referendum on May 26, 2002, and promulgated on June 2, made provisions for an upper house, the House of Advisers; removed presidential term limits; and raised the age limit for a presidential candidate to 75 (from 70). The succession procedure was also altered, the president of the House of Representatives being designated to serve as head of state for 45–60 days, pending a new election, at which he could not present himself as a candidate. Other changes included reduction of the role of prime minister from leader of the government to "coordinator" of ministerial activities. Further constitutional amendments affecting the electoral code and expanding eligibility criteria for presidential candidates were promulgated on April 13, 2008 (see Current issues, below, for details).

The legislature was a unicameral body until 2005, with only a House of Representatives.

The House of Representatives (styled the National Assembly until 1981 and also referenced as the Chamber of Deputies) is elected by universal suffrage for a five-year term. Under Bourguiba it had limited authority and in practice was wholly dominated by the ruling party. Constitutional changes approved in July 1988 contained measures designed to expand the House's control and influence, although their impact has been minimal. The upper House of Advisers was seated after balloting on July 3, 2005. It comprises 126 members, 85 of whom are directly elected and 41 appointed by the president, all serving six-year terms, with half of the seats renewed every three years. Consultative bodies at the national level include a Social and Economic Council and a Higher Islamic Council. The judicial system is headed by a Court of Cassation and includes 3 courts of appeal, 13 courts of first instance, and 51 cantonal courts. Judges are appointed by the president.

Tunisia is administratively divided into 23 provinces, each headed by a governor appointed by the president. The governors are assisted by appointed government councils and 264 elected municipal councils.

Foreign relations. Tunisia assumed a nonaligned posture at independence, establishing relations with both Eastern and Western countries, although placing particular emphasis on its relations with the West and with Arab governments. It became a member of the United Nations in 1956 and is active in all the UN-related agencies. It joined the Arab League in 1958 but boycotted its meetings from 1958 to 1961 and again in 1966 as a result of disagreements with the more "revolutionary" Arab states. As a signal of its support for peace negotiations (particularly the 1993 accord between Israel and the Palestine Liberation Organization), Tunisia exchanged low-level economic representatives with Israel in October 1994 in what was considered a possible precursor to eventual establishment of full diplomatic relations. However, Tunisia recalled those representatives from Israel in 1997 as part of the broad Arab protest over a perceived intransigence on the part of the Netanyahu administration in Israel.

Beginning in 1979 a series of agreements were signed with Algeria, culminating in a March 1983 "Maghreb Fraternity and Co-Operation Treaty," to which Mauritania acceded the following December. Relations with Libya, though reestablished in 1982 after a 1980 rupture over seizure of a southern town by alleged Libyan-trained insurgents, continued to be difficult. President Bourguiba's visit to Washington in June 1985 led to a mass expulsion of Tunisian workers from Libya, as well as reported Libyan incursions into Tunisia and efforts to destabilize its government. After suspending relations with Tripoli in September 1986, Tunis resumed relations a year later following a pledge by Libya to reimburse the expelled workers. Further economic and social agreements, including provisions for the free movement of people and goods between the two countries, were announced in 1988 as Tunisia stepped up its call for regional cooperation and unity, the latter bearing fruit with the formation of the Arab Maghreb Union in February 1989 (see article under Intergovernmental Organizations). Also in 1988, relations were reestablished with Egypt after an eight-year lapse.

The Iraqi invasion of Kuwait in August 1990 appeared to precipitate a change in Tunisia's theretofore unwavering pro-Western orientation. Although critical of the Iraqi occupation, Tunis strongly condemned the subsequent deployment of U.S. troops in Saudi Arabia and the allied bombing of Iraq in early 1991. However, security forces clamped down on large-scale pro-Iraqi demonstrations during the Gulf war, apparently out of concern that the situation might be exploited by Islamic fundamentalists.

President Ben Ali welcomed the antifundamentalist stance adopted by the Algerian military in early 1992, and Tunis was subsequently in the forefront of efforts among North African capitals to coordinate an "antiterrorist" campaign against Muslim militants. In October 1991 Tunisia recalled its ambassador from Sudan, charging Khartoum with fomenting fundamentalist unrest and providing sanctuary and financial support for groups intent on overthrowing the Tunisian government.

Tunisia is prominent among those nations hoping to develop economic cooperation, and possibly a free trade area, in the Mediterranean region. "Partnership" discussions have been emphasized with the European Union (EU), the focus of an estimated 80 percent of Tunisia's trade, and Tunis signed an association agreement with the EU in 1995 that provided for the progressive reduction of tariffs (and elimination of many by 2008).

Relations with the United States warmed somewhat in 2006 when Defense Secretary Donald Rumsfeld, on a visit to Tunis, discussed strengthening military ties with Tunisia while at the same time encouraging greater political reform. (The United States provided $11 million to Tunisia for military training in 2006.)

In October 2006 Tunisia closed its embassy in Doha, Qatar, after Qatar-based *Al Jazeera* television broadcast an interview with Moncef MARZOUKI, leader of the banned Congress for the Republic and former head of the Tunisian Human Rights League, in which he criticized the government and the lack of freedom in Tunisia.

In 2009 Tunisia, unlike many countries, agreed to the return of ten Tunisian detainees being held at the U.S. military prison in Guantánamo Bay, Cuba. In May Tunisia asked the United States to turn over two men who were being held on suspicion of being Islamist militants, both of whom had been convicted in absentia in Tunisian courts.

Also in 2009 Tunisia refused entry to a Moroccan activist who had been planning to attend a conference on human rights.

Current issues. Constitutional amendments introduced in November 2001, calling for the revocation of presidential term limits and the raising of the maximum age of presidential candidates from 70 to 75, among other things, prompted sharp criticism, particularly from those who described the proposed changes as designed to permit Ben Ali, then 65, to govern for many more years. However, the revisions were approved by more than 99 percent in a national referendum on May 26, 2002, according to official reports.

Another focus of attention in 2002 was a reported increase in activity on the part of radical Islamic militants. In April the Islamic Army for the Liberation of Holy Places claimed responsibility for a bomb attack on a synagogue on the island of Djerba that killed more than 20 people. Several months later it was reported that al-Qaida had also been involved in the bombing. (Two men were sentenced to prison in Spain and one man was sentenced in Tunisia in 2006 for their involvement in the Djerba bombing.)

Despite continued criticism from human rights groups, there appeared to be little subsequent improvement in the treatment of political prisoners. In December 2003 the Ben Ali administration adopted broad new antiterrorism legislation that critics claimed could be used to apply harsh penalties to nearly any crime.

Prior to the October 2004 presidential and legislative balloting, Ben Ali pledged to "deepen the democratic exercise," but opposition parties characterized those elections as a "charade" meant to propel Ben Ali toward a "life presidency." Among other things, the opposition candidates claimed they were victims of intense harassment by the government prior to the balloting.

Controversy arose during the July 3, 2005, election for the new House of Advisers when the General Union of Tunisian Workers (*Union Générale des Traivailleurs Tunisiens*—UGTT) refused to participate. The union, which was entitled to 14 seats in the house, protested what it claimed was a lack of independence in the candidate-selection process. Though the formation of the upper body had been touted by Ben Ali as a move toward democratic reform, the president appointed 41 of the body's 126 members.

In apparent response to ongoing criticism from human rights groups, the government agreed in 2005 to change its detention policy, promising to hold prisoners in solitary confinement for no more than 10 days. (Human Rights Watch claimed Tunisia resorted to lengthy isolation terms for leaders of outlawed Islamist parties as a way of eradicating the Islamist movement.) Subsequently, in September, the Tunisian Human Rights League (*Ligue Tunisienne des Droits de l'Homme*—LTDH [see Other Groups under Political Parties, below]) was banned from holding its conference.

Syria extradited 21 suspected Tunisian Islamists in 2005, raising concerns in Tunis and Washington. Tunisia, according to observers, has been intent on reassuring its Western allies that it would not allow extremists to stir trouble abroad, concurrently intensifying the government's resolve to exclude such groups from the country's political process. In what some observers saw as a related development, the government in 2006 began a campaign against women wearing the traditional Islamic headscarf, with some offenders reportedly taken to police stations to sign a pledge that they would no longer wear them. The ban dates to a 1981 law introduced under former president Bourguiba. President Ben Ali began to clamp down on the headdress to ward against the rising influence of religiosity, which could strengthen the Islamic opposition, observers said.

From late 2006 through early 2007, security forces engaged in deadly clashes with terrorists described by the Tunisian government as Islamic extremists. Many were reported to be members of the Salafist Group for Preaching and Combat—GSPC (subsequently referred to as al-Qaida in the Islamic Maghreb), based in Algeria.

Tunisian authorities said some of those arrested carried blueprints of the British and U.S. embassies in Tunis, as well as the names of envoys, and were planning attacks. In May, 3 Tunisians were sentenced to terms of 4–11 years on terrorism charges; 30 others arrested earlier in the year faced similar charges. As the government continued its crackdown on extremists entering the country and allegedly recruiting members, the *International Herald Tribune* described Tunisia as one of the North African countries most vulnerable to terrorists "because its rigid repression of Islamists has created a well of resentment among religious youth, and its popularity with European tourists makes it an attractive target."

In December 2007 more than two dozen Salafis were sentenced in connection with a battle with security forces at the beginning of the year. Death sentences were handed down to 2 people, 8 received life sentences, and the remaining 20 received prison sentences of between 5 and 30 years. Terrorist-related activity continued in 2008, and in February al-Qaida in the Islamic Maghreb claimed responsibility for the kidnapping of two Austrian tourists in the southern desert area, prompting the U.S. State Department to issue a travel alert based on security concerns.

Continued high unemployment and a low standard of living led to demonstrations in central Tunisia in June 2008 that quickly turned violent as protesters clashed with police. One person was killed and at least eight were injured. Meanwhile, the justice minister said plans were under way to reform prison sentencing. The UN Human Rights Commission commended Tunisia for its progressive legal reforms, including its commitment to abolish the death penalty, eliminate discrimination against women, and protect the rights of children. Meanwhile, further protests erupted in the northern mining area of Gafsa, where unemployment and poverty remained high. An official of the Democratic Forum for Labor and Liberties (*Le Forum Démocratique pour le Travail et les Libertés*—FDTL) was among several people arrested during one such protest; she was charged with disturbing public order and insubordination and sentenced to eight months in jail. Some 190 people were reported to have been arrested in the region over a period of several months.

Attention in 2008 subsequently turned to the 2009 elections, as on April 24 the Chamber of Deputies approved a draft law proposing amendments to the constitution in regard to the presidential polls. The proposed law, presented by the prime minister on behalf of President Ben Ali, would allow elected political party leaders to stand as presidential candidates only if they had served in that capacity for at least two consecutive years and eliminate the requirement that the candidates' bid be presented by 30 members of parliament or chairs of municipal councils. The draft law also proposed lowering the voting age from 20 to 18. Though the government contended that the new provisions would enhance the democratic and pluralistic process, opposition groups claimed they would prevent many parties from presenting candidates. The amendments were approved by parliament in March 2009 and promulgated on April 13. Perhaps most significantly, the amendments made it possible for opposition party leaders, including those not represented in the legislature, to be eligible to run as presidential candidates since they no longer needed parliamentary votes or representation to participate. Further, the amendments increased the number of seats that opposition members would be allowed to fill in the House of Representatives by limiting the number of seats won by any electoral slate to 75 percent of total seats (thus ensuring at least 25 percent of seats go to opposition parties), regardless of the percentage of votes received in either case.

Following President Ben Ali's announcement that he would seek reelection (rejecting the opposition's call for a change in the political power structure), four parties put forth challengers for the October 2009 presidential elections: the Renewal Movement (*Harakat Ettajdid/Mouvement de la Rénovation*—MR), Unionist Democratic Union (*Union Démocratique Unioniste*—UDU), Popular Union Party (*Parti de l'Unité Populaire*—PUP, and the FDTL. Meanwhile, two parties—the Democratic Socialist Movement (*Mouvement des Démocrates Socialistes*—MDS) and the Liberal Social Party (*Parti Social Liberal*—PSL)—announced their support for President Ben Ali in the upcoming election. The president, for his part, promised to allow election monitors and greater transparency. Despite the president's pledge to allow opposition candidates access to state-run media during the campaign, however, at least one candidate accused the government of having been denied access. (*See headnote.*)

POLITICAL PARTIES

Although not constitutionally mandated, Tunisia was effectively a one-party state from the time the Tunisian Communist Party (PCT) was banned in January 1963 until its return to legal status in July 1981. In June 1981 the government had announced that recognition would be extended to all parties obtaining at least 5 percent of the valid votes in legislative balloting on November 1. On September 9 the PCT indicated that it would participate in the election after receiving official assurances that the 5 percent requirement would not be imposed in its case, and in 1983 recognition was extended to two additional opposition parties, the Popular Union Party (*Parti de l'Unité Populaire*—PUP) and the Democratic Socialist Movement (*Mouvement des Démocrates Socialistes*—MDS [below]). All three boycotted the 1986 election because of the rejection of many of their candidate lists and administrative suspension of their publications. In November 1987 the Ben Ali government endorsed the legalization of any party that would consent to certain conditions, one (advanced by the House of Representatives in April 1988) being that "no party has the right to refer, in its principles, its objectives, its activities or its programs, to religion, language, race or a regime," a stipulation that served as a barrier to the legalization of militant Islamic groups. Prior to the 1989 balloting, the government party (RCD, below) offered to head an electoral front that would have guaranteed at least minimal opposition representation in the house. However, the proposal was rejected, to the dismay of the legal opposition parties, none of which succeeded in winning more than 3 percent of the popular vote. In April 1991 the Ben Ali government agreed to provide the six legal opposition parties with moderate state financial support and limited access to government-controlled television and radio broadcasting facilities. Subsequently, in what the administration described as a further effort to strengthen the role of the opposition parties, the RCD also offered not to present candidates for the House by-elections in October. However, the opposition boycotted the balloting as a protest against the government's unwillingness to revise the electoral law or reduce the RCD's "stranglehold" on the civil service. Electoral law changes guaranteed the opposition a minimal number of seats in the March 1994 national elections, but non-RCD candidates still secured less than 3 percent of the votes even though all the legal parties participated. The government announced in 1997 that the House would be expanded for the 1999 balloting and that electoral revision would attempt to promote opposition representation of up to 20 percent. The House was expanded to 182 members for the 1999 balloting, electoral revision in 1998 having guaranteed opposition representation of at least 34 members.

In the run-up to the 2009 presidential and parliamentary elections, several small independent parties joined with the Renewal Movement (MR) and the Liberal Socialist Party in a coalition called the Democratic Initiative and nominated MR secretary general Ahmad Ibrahim as its presidential candidate.

Government Party:

Democratic Constitutional Assembly (*Rassemblement Constitutionnel Démocratique*—RCD). Founded in 1934 as the Neo-Destour Party, a splinter from the old Destour (Constitution) Party, and known from October 1964 as the Destourian Socialist Party (*Parti Socialiste Destourien*—PSD), Tunisia's ruling party was given its present name in February 1988 to provide new impetus to "the practice of democracy" within its ranks. Its moderately left-wing tendency was of less political significance than its organizational strength, derived in large part from affiliated syndicates representing labor, agriculture, artisans and merchants, students, women, and youth. Party members have filled most major government positions since independence.

At the 12th party congress in June 1986 President Bourguiba personally selected a new 90-member Central Committee and 20-member Political Bureau, ignoring party statutes calling for election by delegates. By the end of the year the PSD had ended a 1985 rift in returning to close alignment with the UGTT. A special "Congress of Salvation," held in Tunis July 29–31, 1988, endorsed the political liberalization policies of new President Ben Ali (who was reelected party chair), included a number of young party members in a new 150-member Central Committee, and named a new 12-member Political Bureau.

At a congress held July 29–31, 1993, Ben Ali was unanimously reelected party chair and designated as the RCD presidential candidate in the elections scheduled for March 1994. A new Central Committee was selected, more than half of its 200 members serving for the first time in a reflection of the RCD's "revitalization" campaign that also included enlargement of the Political Bureau to include several young cabinet ministers and the first female member. In addition, the congress reconfirmed its commitment to free-market economic policies and stated its strong opposition to Islamic fundamentalist "militancy."

Ben Ali was reelected chair at the RCD congress in 1998, and he was nominated as the party's candidate for the 1999 presidential election (which he won with more than 99 percent of the vote). In the 1999 legislative balloting, the RCD secured 92 percent of the vote; municipal elections in May 2000 and May 2005 produced similar support for the RCD.

On October 24, 2004, Ben Ali won a fourth term with 95 percent of the vote against three other minor candidates.

In July 2008 Ben Ali announced that he would seek a fifth five-year term as president in the 2009 elections. (*See headnote.*)

Leaders: Gen. Zine El-Abidine BEN ALI (President of the Republic and President of the Party), Mohamed GHANNOUCHI (Prime Minister and Second Vice President of the Party), Hamed KAROUI (First Vice President of the Party and Former Prime Minister), Abdallah KALLEL (Speaker of the House of Advisers), Ali CHAOUCH, Hédi MHENNI (Secretary General).

Other Legal Parties:

Democratic Socialist Movement (*Mouvement des Démocrates Socialistes*—MDS). Organized as the Democratic Socialist Group in October 1977 by a number of former PSD cabinet ministers who sought liberalization of the nation's political life, the MDS was refused formal recognition in 1978, although its leader, Ahmed Mestiri, had served as an intermediary between the government and the trade union leadership in attempting to resolve labor unrest. The new grouping was runner-up in the 1981 election but obtained only 3.28 percent of the vote, thus failing to secure either legislative representation or legal status. However, recognition was granted by President Bourguiba in November 1983.

Mestiri was arrested in April 1986 and sentenced to four months in prison for leading demonstrations against the U.S. bombing of Libya. The conviction automatically disqualified him from running for legislative office, the MDS thereupon becoming an early advocate of the November electoral boycott. (Under the amnesty program initiated by the Ben Ali government in late 1987, Mestiri was pardoned for the conviction.) The MDS fared poorly in the 1989 balloting, and Mestiri was criticized for rejecting the RCD's preelection offer of an electoral front with the MDS and other parties. Subsequently, Mestiri resigned as MDS secretary general, assistant secretary general Dali Jazi having earlier quit the party to join the government. Mestiri was reported to have left the party altogether in early 1992, as criticism grew of the "authoritarian" approach of its new leader, Mohamed MOUADA. Factionalization also contributed to the "suspension" by the MDS of another of its prominent leaders, Mustafa BEN JAFAAR.

The MDS supported President Ben Ali for reelection in 1994 but challenged the RCD in the national legislative balloting. Although no MDS candidates were successful on their own, ten were subsequently seated in the house under the proportional arrangement enacted to guarantee a multiparty legislature.

In October 1995 Mouada published a letter criticizing the "lack of political freedom" in Tunisia. Within days he was arrested on charges of having had illegal contacts with representatives of the Libyan government, and in February 1996 he was sentenced to 11 years in prison. Mouada dismissed the charges as "obviously politically motivated," and his conviction was widely condemned by international observers. Khemais CHAMMARI, a member of the MDS as well as the House of Representatives, was also given a five-year sentence in July for "attacking state security." Both men were released in December, although Mouada was briefly detained again one year later. Meanwhile, an MDS congress in May 1997 had elected Ismaïl Boulahia to the new leadership post of secretary general, his discussion of the future of the "new MDS" apparently reflecting a diminution of Mouada's authority. However, Boulahia was not eligible to contest the 1999 presidential election, since he had not held his MDS post the requisite five years, and he subsequently announced the MDS was supporting President Ben Ali for reelection. Meanwhile, the party secured 13 seats in the legislative balloting of 1999, again thanks solely to electoral law guarantees regarding opposition representation.

Mouada was held under house arrest for one month in late 1999 on a charge of defaming the government, and he was sent to prison in June 2001 for violations in connection with his earlier release on the 1999 charge. Two months earlier Mouada had issued a joint declaration with *Nahda* leader Rachid Ghanouchi calling for creation of a joint antigovernment front. However, apparently underscoring continued disagreement within the MDS regarding the extent of cooperation with the regime, Boulahia met with President Ben Ali in early 2001 and praised his commitment to "democratic values." In March 2002 Ben Ali pardoned Mouada. Meanwhile, Ben Jafaar joined the Democratic Forum for Labor and Liberties (below), continuing his heavy criticism of the administration.

The party supported Ben Ali in the 2004 presidential election and won representation in municipal elections of 2005. Boulahia reiterated the party's support for Ben Ali in 2008, and the party endorsed the president's reelection bid in 2009.

Leader: Ismaïl BOULAHIA (Secretary General).

Renewal Movement (*Harakat Ettajdid/Mouvement de la Rénovation*—MR). The Renewal Movement is heir to the Tunisian Communist Party (*Parti Communiste Tunisien*—PCT), which was founded in 1934 as an entity distinct from the French Communist Party. The PCT was outlawed in 1963 and regained legality in July 1981. Historically of quite limited membership, the party secured only 0.78 percent of the vote in the 1981 legislative balloting. Prior to the opposition boycott, the PCT had intended to participate in the 1986 election in alliance with the RSP (see RDP, below). Delegates to the party's 1987 congress denounced IMF-supported changes in the government's economic policies, particularly the emphasis on the private sector and free-market activity. Subsequently, the PCT supported the political reforms instituted by the Ben Ali government, before joining the MDS and MUP in boycotting the municipal elections in 1990 to protest the "failure" of democratization efforts.

The party's new name was adopted at an April 1993 congress, leaders announcing that Marxism had been dropped as official doctrine in favor of a "progressive" platform favoring "democratic pluralism." None of the MR's 93 candidates was successful in the 1994 national legislative balloting, although four MR members were subsequently seated in the House under the proportional arrangement established for opposition parties. Party leaders complained of widespread fraud in the legislative balloting and described Tunisia's slow pace of political liberalization as a national "scandal."

The MR secretary general, Mohamed HARMEL, was constitutionally prohibited from contesting the 1999 presidential election due to his age (70). The MR was accorded five seats in the legislature elected in 1999.

MR Chair Mohamed Ali el-Halouani was one of three candidates to oppose President Ben Ali in the 2004 elections. In a rare occurrence, MR supporters demonstrated in Tunis after el-Halouani complained that the party had been blocked from distributing its manifesto. El-Halouani received about 1 percent of the vote and denounced the poll as a "sham."

In August 2007 Ahmad Ibrahim was elected secretary general of the party, succeeding Mohamed Harmel, who had led the party since 1981 and who was named honorary chair.

In 2009 Ibrahim was named the presidential candidate of the Democratic Initiative coalition, a grouping of small leftist and independent parties, for the October election.

Leaders: Mohamed Ali el-HALOUANI (Chair and 2004 presidential candidate), Boujamma RMILI, Ahmad IBRAHIM (Secretary General).

Unionist Democratic Union (*Union Démocratique Unioniste*—UDU). Legalized in November 1988, the UDU was led by Abderrahmane TLILI, a former member of the RCD who had resigned from the ruling party to devote himself to the unification of various Arab nationalist tendencies in Tunisia. Tlili garnered 0.23 percent of the vote in the 1999 presidential balloting, the UDU securing seven of the seats distributed to the opposition following the concurrent legislative poll. Tlili was sentenced to nine years in prison in 2004 on embezzlement charges relating to his former government tenure. The UDU supported

President Ben Ali in the 2004 presidential election and won representation in municipal elections in 2005.

Secretary General Ahmed Inoubli was nominated as the party's candidate for the 2009 presidential election.

Leader: Ahmed INOUBLI (Secretary General).

Popular Union Party (*Parti de l'Unité Populaire*—PUP). The PUP is an outgrowth of an "internal faction" that developed within the Popular Unity Movement (MUP, below) over the issue of participation in the 1981 legislative election. Although garnering only 0.81 percent of the vote in 1981, it was officially recognized in 1983 as a legal party, subsequently operating under its current name. The PUP attempted to offer candidates for the 1986 balloting, but most were declared ineligible by the government. The party therefore withdrew three days before the election, citing the same harassment that had led to the boycott by other opposition groups. It participated in "national pact" discussions with the government in 1988, thus asserting an identity separate from that of its parent. PUP secretary general Mohamed Belhadj Amor won 0.31 percent of the vote in the 1999 presidential campaign, during which he expressed deep dismay over the failure of the so-called opposition parties to mount any effective challenge to the RCD. He subsequently resigned the PUP leadership post. His successor, Mohamed Bouchiha, received 3.8 percent of the vote in the 2004 election.

The party won representation in the 2005 municipal elections.

Bouchiha was nominated as the party's presidential candidate for the 2009 elections.

Leaders: Jalloud AZZOUNA, Mohamed Belhadj AMOR (1999 presidential candidate), Mohamed BOUCHIHA (Secretary General and 2004 presidential candidate).

Progressive Democratic Assembly (*Rassemblement Démocratique Progressiste*—RDP). The RDP had been established as the Progressive Socialist Assembly (*Rassemblement Socialiste Progressiste*—RSP) by a number of Marxist groups in 1983. The pan-Arabist RSP was tolerated by the Bourguiba government until mid-1986. It formed a "Democratic Alliance" with the PCT and planned to field candidates for the 1986 balloting. However, the coalition boycotted the election after the government disqualified some of its candidates and sentenced 14 of its members to six-month jail terms for belonging to an illegal organization. The party was officially recognized in September 1988. The RSP did not secure any of the legislative seats reserved for opposition parties in 1994 or 1999, and it called for a boycott of the municipal elections of May 2000. The RSP changed its name to the RDP in July 2001 in an effort to "broaden its ideological base." The RDP reportedly included many Marxists as well as moderate Islamists and liberals.

RDP secretary general Ahmed Chebbi was blocked from contesting the 2004 presidential election because of a recent decree by President Ben Ali that candidates could be presented only by parties with legislative representation. The RDP consequently called for a boycott of the presidential balloting and withdrew its candidates from the legislative poll.

In 2006 May Eljeribi was elected secretary general, replacing Chebbi, who had held the post for 23 years. Eljeribi became the first woman to head a political party in Tunisia. In 2007 Eljeribi went on a month-long hunger strike to protest alleged harassment against the party, specifically the party's newspaper, *al-Mawkif.* Two other party members, including Rachid KHECHANA, the paper's editor, began a hunger strike in April 2008 for the same reason.

Though the party had nominated Chebbi in early 2008 to be its 2009 presidential candidate, he was subsequently deemed ineligible under a draft law that would amend the constitution, permitting only elected party leaders who had held the post for two consecutive years to contest presidential elections.

Leaders: Maya JRIBI (Chair), Ahmed CHEBBI, May ELJERIBI (Secretary General).

Liberal Social Party (*Parti Social Liberal*—PSL). The PSL, formed to advocate liberal social and political policies and economic reforms, including the privatization of state-run enterprises, was officially recognized in September 1988 under the name of the Social Party for Progress (*Parti Social pour le Progrès*—PSP). The PSL name was adopted at the first party congress, held in Tunis on October 29–30, 1994. The PSL secured 2 of the 34 seats reserved for opposition parties in the 1999 legislative balloting. The party's president, Mounir Beji, won less than 1 percent of the vote in the 2004 presidential poll.

The name **Liberal Social Democratic Party** (*Parti Social Démocratique Liberal*—PSDL) was adopted at the party congress in April 2005, and Beji was reelected president. The party won representation in the May 2005 municipal elections. In 2007 the party called on unions to join in a "real partnership."

The party backed President Ben Ali in the 2009 elections.

Leaders: Hosni HAMMANI, Mounir BEJI (President of the Party and 2004 presidential candidate), Mondher THABET (Secretary General).

Democratic Forum for Labor and Liberties (*Le Forum Démocratique pour le Travail et les Libertés*—FDTL). Legalized in 2002, the FDTL had been active as an opposition group since it was organized in 1994. Its platform endorsed a commitment to "defending freedom, democracy, and social justice," among other things.

After the party failed to prevent passage of a constitutional amendment allowing Ben Ali to seek a fourth term in 2004, it called for a boycott of the 2004 elections and urged opposition parties to work toward cohesion. The FDTL was barred by the government from participating in the 2005 municipal elections, along with the RDP and the MR. The three groups had formed a loose alliance called the Democratic Coalition for Citizenship, which the government said did not abide by electoral regulations.

In January 2007 the group received permission to publish a weekly newspaper, *Mouwatinoun* (Citizens), which Mustafa Ben Jafaar claimed was subject to government interference that hindered its distribution.

Ben Jafaar, who was highly critical of the 2008 constitutional amendment affecting presidential candidates, in June 2009 announced his bid for the presidency in the October general elections.

Leader: Mustafa BEN JAFAAR (Secretary General).

Green Party for Progress (*Parti Verte pour le Progrès*—PVP). Authorized by the government on March 3, 2004, the PVP was the first new party to be legally established since 2002. While the party focuses on a pro-environment platform, critics claim its members are loyal to the ruling RCD. (The government had recently refused to legalize the long-standing application of another environmental group, Green Tunisia.) In the run-up to the 2009 elections, the party announced its support for President Ben Ali.

Leader: Mongi KHAMMASSI (Secretary General).

Other Groups:

Popular Unity Movement (*Mouvement de l'Unité Populaire*—MUP). The MUP was formed in 1973 by Ahmed Ben Salah, a former "super-minister" who directed the economic policies of the Bourguiba cabinet from 1962 to 1969. Ben Salah was sentenced to ten years' imprisonment in 1969 for "high treason," although the action was generally attributed to his having fallen out of favor with Bourguiba. After his escape from prison in 1973, Ben Salah directed the MUP from exile, urging the government to return to the socialist policies of the 1960s. The movement reorganized itself as a political party in June 1978 but was unable to gain legal recognition. In early 1981 friction developed within the MUP leadership after the government granted amnesty to all members theretofore subject to legal restriction, the sole exception being Ben Salah. Ben Salah subsequently declared his opposition to the group's participation in the November 1 balloting, causing a split between his supporters and an "internal" faction (see PUP, above). After maintaining a high international profile throughout his exile, Ben Salah returned to Tunisia in 1988 in the wake of Bourguiba's ouster. However, the MUP did not sign the "national pact" of late 1988, primarily to protest the government's refusal to restore Ben Salah's civil rights, a requirement for his participation in national elections. The MUP joined two legal parties (the MDS and the PCT, above) in an antigovernment coalition in 1990.

Ben Salah was one of several opposition leaders who issued a joint communiqué in London in November 1995 attacking the Tunisian government as repressive. In 1996 the MUP leader was described by *Africa Confidential* as no longer commanding a significant popular base, and he returned to Tunisia from ten years of voluntary exile in Europe in September 2000.

Leader: Ahmed BEN SALAH (General Secretary).

Renaissance Party (*Hizb al-Nahda/Parti de la Renaissance*—PR). Also known as the Renaissance Movement (*Harakat al-Nahda/Mouvement de la Renaissance*), *Nahda* was formed as the Islamic Tendency

Movement (*Mouvement de la Tendance Islamique*—MTI) in early 1981 by a group of Islamic fundamentalists inspired by the 1979 Iranian revolution. Charged with fomenting disturbances, many MTI adherents were jailed during a series of subsequent crackdowns by the Bourguiba government. However, the MTI insisted that it opposed violence or other "revolutionary activity," and the Ben Ali government pardoned most of those incarcerated, including the movement's leader, Rachid Ghanouchi, shortly after assuming power. The new regime also initiated talks that it said were designed to provide moderate MTI forces with a legitimate means of political expression in order to undercut support for the movement's radical elements. As an outgrowth of that process, the MTI adopted its new name in early 1989; however, the government subsequently denied legal status to *Nahda*, ostensibly on the grounds that it remained religion-based. Undaunted, the group quickly established itself as the government's primary opposition, its "independent" candidates collecting about 13 percent of the total popular vote (including as much as 30 percent of the vote in some urban areas) in 1989 legislative balloting.

Nahda boycotted "higher council" negotiations and municipal elections in 1990, Ghanouchi remaining in exile to protest the lack of legal recognition for the formation and the continued "harassment" of its sympathizers. Friction intensified late in the year following the arrest of three groups of what security forces described as armed extremists plotting to overthrow the government. Although the government alleged that some of those arrested had *Nahda* links, the party leadership strongly denied the charge, accusing the regime of conducting a propaganda campaign aimed at discrediting the fundamentalist movement in order to prevent it from assuming its rightful political role.

On October 15, 1991, the government announced that it had uncovered a fundamentalist plot to assassinate President Ben Ali and other government officials in order to "create a constitutional vacuum." However, *Nahda* leaders again denied any connection to violent antigovernment activity, reiterating their commitment to "peaceful methods" of protest and stressing that their vision for the "Islamization" of Tunisia was "compatible" with democracy and a pluralistic society. The disclaimers notwithstanding, the government flatly labeled *Nahda* "a terrorist organization" and intensified the campaign to "silence" it. Thousands of suspected *Nahda* sympathizers were detained, many later claiming that they had been tortured or otherwise abused in prison (a charge supported by Amnesty International). At a widely publicized trial in mid-1992 about 170 *Nahda* adherents were convicted of sedition. A number were sentenced to life imprisonment, including Ghanouchi and several other leaders who were tried in absentia. The government subsequently issued an international arrest warrant for Ghanouchi, who was living in London, but in mid-1993 the United Kingdom granted him political asylum. In 1994 Ghanouchi dismissed the recent Tunisian presidential and legislative elections as "a joke." Despite the "banned and fragmented" status of *Nahda,* Ghanouchi was described in 1996 as still the only possible "serious challenger" to Ben Ali. A number of *Nahda* adherents were released in November 1999 from long prison terms. In March 2001 Ghanouchi, in conjunction with MDS leader Mohamed Mouada, proposed establishment by *Nahda* and the legal opposition parties of a National Democratic Front to challenge the RCD, suggesting to some observers that *Nahda* hoped to return to mainstream political activity. However, *Nahda* remained relatively quiescent during the 2004 election campaign.

In March 2006 the government released 1,600 prisoners on the 50th anniversary of Tunisia's independence. Among those released were reportedly many political prisoners who had been jailed for 10 years because they were members of *Nahda*. Further, in November President Ben Ali, marking his 19th year at the helm, pardoned 55 Islamists, all said to be members of *Nahda*, including leaders Habib Ellouze and Mohamed Akrout, both of whom had received life sentences in 1992. In November 2008 Ben Ali pardoned and released another 21 PR members, some of whom had been serving life sentences. A former PR leader, Sadek CHOUROU, was arrested in 2008 on charges of maintaining an outlawed organization. In 2009 an appeals court upheld his one-year prison sentence and subsequently extended it by one year to cover time the court said he should have served in the 1990s.

Leaders: Rachid GHANOUCHI (President, in exile), Habib ELLOUZE, Mohamed AKROUT, Sahah KARKAR (in exile), Sheikh Abdelfatah MOURROU (Secretary General).

Commandos of Sacrifice (*Commandos du Sacrifice*—CS). Although the government insisted that the CS was the "military wing" of *Nahda,* the group's leader, Habib Laasoued, described it as independent and, in fact, a rival to *Nahda* for support among fundamentalists. About 100 members of the commandos were convicted in mid-1992 of planning terrorist acts, although the trials were surrounded by allegations of human rights abuses and other governmental misconduct. Laasoued, who was sentenced to life imprisonment, reportedly acknowledged that the commandos had engaged in theoretical discussions of *jihad* (Islamic holy war) but denied that any antigovernment military action had actually been endorsed.

Leader: Habib LAASOUED (imprisoned).

Party of Tunisian Communist Workers (*Parti des Ouvriers Communistes Tunisiens*—POCT). An unrecognized splinter of the former PCT, the POCT is led by Hamma Hammani, who had been the director of the banned newspaper *El Badil* (The Alternative). Hammani was sentenced to eight years in prison in early 1994 on several charges, including membership in an illegal organization, his case being prominently cited in criticism leveled at the government by human rights organizations. Hammani and another POCT member who had been imprisoned with him were pardoned by President Ben Ali in November 1995. A number of POCT members were convicted in July 1999 of belonging to an illegal association, but most were released later in the year. Hammani and several associates were charged again in absentia in 1999 for having been members of an unrecognized group. In February 2002 they were retried and committed to various prison sentences. In September, however, Hammani and some of the others were released following a hunger strike that had attracted increasing international scrutiny to their case. Hammani called for a boycott of the 2004 elections.

Leader: Hamma HAMMANI.

Congress for the Republic. Formed by activist Moncef Marzouki in July 2001, the political party was established to try to help create a democratic republic. Marzouki, who faced a year in prison (see below) for belonging to another illegal organization, lived in self-imposed exile in France for five years, returning to Tunisia in 2006 to encourage Tunisians to engage in peaceful demonstrations for human rights. Soon thereafter Marzouki was charged with "incitement to civil disobedience." He was reported to be living in exile in France.

Leader: Moncef MARZOUKI (in exile).

Several human rights groups have been prominent in the increasingly vocal opposition movement in recent years. They include the unrecognized National Council for Tunisian Freedoms (*Conseil National pour les Libertés Tunisiennes*—CNLT), founded in 1998 by, among others, Mustafa Ben Jafaar and Moncef Marzouki, who had unsuccessfully attempted to run for president in 1994. In a case that attracted wide international attention, Marzouki was sentenced in December 2000 to one year in prison for belonging to an illegal organization. Meanwhile, as of 2007 the officially sanctioned Tunisian Human Rights League (*Ligue Tunisienne des Droits de l'Homme*—LTDH) continued to be banned from repeated attempts to hold its congress since 2005. The ban was imposed after 22 members, alleged by critics to be members of the RCD, challenged the legality of the congress, claiming the LTDH refused to allow pro-government members to participate. (LTDH president Mokhtar TRIFI, who had sharply condemned the Ben Ali government after wresting control of the organization from RCD adherents, was arrested in March 2001 but subsequently released.)

In mid-1994 it was reported that a militant Islamic group had been organized among Tunisian exiles under the leadership of Mohamed Ali el-HORANI to support armed struggle against the Ben Ali government. The group, which reportedly adopted the name of Algeria's outlawed **Islamic Salvation Front** (*Front Islamique du Salut*—FIS), was described as critical of *Nahda's* official rejection of violence. References have also been made to a **Tunisian Islamic Front** (*Front Islamique Tunisien*—FIT), which reportedly has committed itself to armed struggle against the Ben Ali regime. In addition, some 14 members of a fundamentalist group called *Ansar* were sentenced to jail terms in December 2000 for belonging to an illegal organization, which the government described as having Iranian ties.

Abdallah al-HAJJI, who was reported to be affiliated with the FIT, was serving a five-year sentence in Tunis in 2007 for leading military action of the FIT; he was previously in detention in Pakistan and held by U.S. authorities in Afghanistan. In May 2008, according to the U.S. State Department, the FIT issued a warning that all foreigners in Tunisia should leave, and it also claimed responsibility for the killing of four policemen.

LEGISLATURE

House of Representatives (*Majlis al-Nuwab/Chambre des Députés*). The lower house consists of 189 members serving five-year terms. Under a new system adopted for the 1994 election, most representatives (148 in 1999 and 152 in 2004) are elected on a "winner-takes-all" basis in which the party whose list gains the most votes in a district secures all the seats for that district. (There are 25 districts comprising 2 to 10 seats each.) The remaining seats (19 in 1994, 34 in 1999, and 37 in 2004) are allocated to parties that failed to win in any districts, in proportion to the parties' national vote totals.

From the establishment of the house in 1959 until 1994, members of the ruling party (RCD) occupied all seats. Although six opposition parties were permitted to offer candidates in the 1989 balloting and a number of independent candidates sponsored by the unsanctioned Renaissance Party also ran, the RCD won all seats with a reported 80 percent of the vote. RCD candidates also won all nine seats contested in October 1991 by-elections, which were boycotted by the opposition parties. The house was enlarged from 141 members to 163 for the 1994 election and to 182 for the 1999 balloting. The membership was expanded to 189 seats for the most recent election on October 24, 2004, President Ben Ali decreeing that 43 seats be filled by women. The RCD won all 152 seats that were contested on a district basis. However, under the proportional system for distributing 37 additional seats, 5 other parties were allocated seats as follows: The Democratic Socialist Movement, 14; the Popular Union Party, 11; the Unionist Democratic Union, 7; the Renewal Movement, 3; and the Liberal Social Party, 2. (*See headnote.*)

President: Fouad MBAZAÂ.

House of Advisers (*Majlis al-Mustasharin*). A referendum on May 26, 2002, provided for several constitutional changes, the creation of the upper house among them. The House of Advisers comprises 126 members, 85 of whom are directly elected and 41 appointed by the president, all serving six-year terms (half of the members are renewed every three years). The members include 14 from each of the 3 main professional unions and federations and 43 representatives from various regions of the country. The House of Advisers was seated after balloting on July 3, 2005, with the distribution as follows: the Democratic Constitutional Assembly, 43; the Tunisian Union of the Industry, Trade, and Draft Industry, 14; and the Tunisia Union of Agriculture and Fishing, 14. The General Union of Tunisian Workers, which was entitled to 14 seats, did not participate. It was unclear whether a separate election would be held to fill those seats.

President: Abdallah KALLEL.

CABINET

[as of June 1, 2009]

Prime Minister	Mohamed Ghannouchi
Secretary General of the Government, in Charge of Relations with Parliament	Abdelhakim Bouraoui
Ministers	
Agriculture and Water Resources	Abdessalem Mansour
Communication Technologies	Haj Klaï
Communications and Relations with Parliament	Rafaâ Dekhil
Culture and Heritage Preservation	Abderraouf El Basti
Development and International Cooperation	Mohamed Nouri Jouini
Director of Presidential Cabinet	Ahmed Iyadh Ouederni
Education and Training	Hatem Ben Salem
Employment and Professional Integration of Youth	Slim Tletli
Environment and Sustainable Development	Nadhir Hamada
Equipment, Housing, and Territorial Management	Slaheddine Malouche
Finance	Mohamed Rachid Kchich
Foreign Affairs	Abdelawahab Abdallah
Governor of the Central Bank	Taoufik Baccar
Higher Education, Scientific Research, and Technology	Lazhar Bououni
Industry, Energy, and Small and Medium Enterprises	Afif Chelbi
Interior and Local Development	Rafik Belhaj Kacem
Justice and Human Rights	Béchir Tekkari
National Defense	Kamel Morjane
Prime Minister's Office	Zouhair Mdhaffer
Public Health	Mondher Zenaïdi
Religious Affairs	Boubaker El Akhzouri
Social Affairs, Solidarity, and Tunisians Abroad	Ali Chaouch
State Property and Land Affairs	Ridha Grira
Tourism	Khelil Lajimi
Trade and Handicrafts	Ridha Touiti
Transport	Abderrahim Zouari
Women, Family, Children, and Elderly Affairs	Sarra Kanoun Jarraya [f]
Youth, Sports, and Physical Education	Samir Laabidi
Minister of State	
Special Adviser to the President, and Presidential Spokesperson	Abdelaziz Ben Dhia
Secretaries of State	
Agriculture and Water Resources, in Charge of Hydraulic Resources and Fishing	Abderrazak Daâloul
Commerce, in Charge of the Craft Industry	Chokri Mamoghli
Communication Technologies, in Charge of Data Processing, the Internet, and Free Software	Lamia Chafei Seghaier [f]
Equipment and Housing, in Charge of Housing and Regional Planning	Mohamed Néjib Berriche
Development and International Cooperation, in Charge of International Cooperation and External Investment	Abdelhamid Triki
Education and Training, in Charge of Professional Training	Mongi Bédoui
Finance, in Charge of Taxation	Moncef Bouden
Foreign Affairs, in Charge of American and Asian Affairs	Saïda Chtioui [f]
Foreign Affairs, in Charge of Maghreb, Arab, and African Businesses	Abdelhafidh Harguem
Industry, Energy, and Small and Medium Enterprises, in Charge of Renewable Energy and Food	Abdelaziz Rassaâ
Interior and Local Development, in Charge of Regional Affairs and Local Communities	Mongi Chouchène
Prime Minister, in Charge of Privatization	Moncef Hergli
Public Health, in Charge of Hospitals	Najoua Miladi [f]
Social Affairs, Solidarity, and Tunisians Abroad, in Charge of Social Advancement	Naja Belkhiria Karoui [f]
Women, Family, Children, and Elderly Affairs, in Charge of Children and the Elderly	Saloua Terzi Ben Attia [f]
Youth, Sports, and Physical Education	Béchir Elouzir

[f] = female

COMMUNICATIONS

The media during most of the Bourguiba era were subject to pervasive party influence and increasingly repressive government interference. The Ben Ali government initially relaxed some of the restrictions, although the fundamentalist press remained heavily censored and mainstream publications continued to practice what was widely viewed as self-censorship, bordering on what one foreign correspondent described as "regime worship." In addition, several foreign journalists were subsequently expelled and some international publications were prevented from entering the country for printing articles critical of the government. (The French dailies *Le Monde* and *Libération* were banned from March 1994 until March 1995 because of their coverage of events prior to the national elections.) In recent years international journalists' groups have called for Western nations to apply pressure upon the Tunisian government to reduce what has been widely perceived as pervasive restraints on freedom of the press, including the arrests of journalists. In 2005 Tunisia banned the Union of Tunisian Journalists from holding a conference for independent journalists, including some from international watchdog groups.

According to the BBC, Internet use is monitored and Web sites that criticize the government are often blocked. In 2008 the watchdog group Reporters Without Borders condemned Tunisia for its censorship of a French-language Web site, Come4news. The government blocked access to the site on March 10.

In February 2009 the government reportedly banned publication of the Renewal Movement's monthly newspaper, *Al Tariq Al Jadid,* and in May the party's leader, a presidential candidate, claimed he was being denied access to the state-run media. Also in May the national journalists union accused the government of harassing journalists and restricting their access to public information. Subsequently, the watchdog Committee to Protect Journalists (CPJ) criticized the government for allegedly trying to force the ouster of the union's president, a move the CPJ said was "part of a campaign to eliminate independent media in the country." President Ben Ali, for his part, had pledged greater access to public broadcast media for opposition candidates in the run-up to the 2009 presidential and parliamentary elections.

Press. The following, unless otherwise noted, are published daily in Tunis: *As-Sabah* (The Morning, 50,000), government-influenced, in Arabic; *al-Amal* (Action, 50,000), RCD organ, in Arabic; *L'Action* (50,000), RCD organ, in French; *Le Temps* (42,000), weekly in French; *La Presse de Tunisie* (40,000), government organ, in French; *Nouvelles de Tunisie*, daily; *Le Quotidien* (The Daily, 30,000), independent, in French; *Le Renouveau* (23,000), RCD organ, in French; *La Presse-Soir,* evening; *as-Sahafa,* in Arabic; *al-Huriyya,* in Arabic; *as-Shourouq* (Sunrise), independent, in Arabic; and *Al-Horria*, an RCD organ. An opposition weekly, *al-Mawkif* (The Stance) is an organ of the Progressive Democratic Assembly. The Democratic Forum for Labor and Liberties' *Mouwatinoun* (Citizens) is published weekly in Arabic. Other opposition groups and their publications are the Popular Union Party's *Al Wahda,* the Renewal Movement's *Ettarik El Jedid,* the Liberal Social Party's *Al Oufouk,* and the Democratic Socialist Movement's *Al Mostaqbal.* The Green Party began publishing *Le Tunisien,* a weekly in French and Arabic, in 2009.

News agencies. The domestic facility is *Tunis Afrique Presse*—TAP (*Wakalah Tunis Afriqiyah al-Anba*); in addition, a number of foreign bureaus maintain offices in Tunis.

Broadcasting and computing. The *Etablissement de la Radiodiffusion-Télévision Tunisienne* (ERTT) operates a radio network broadcasting in Arabic, French, and Italian. It also operates three television channels, one of which links the country with European transmissions. The first privately owned radio station was launched in 2003, and the first private television station began broadcasting in early 2005. (Although President Ben Ali portrayed these developments as expansion of freedom of the press, thus far programming on the new stations has lacked political commentary.) As of 2008 there were 275.3 Internet users per 1,000 inhabitants.

INTERGOVERNMENTAL REPRESENTATION

Ambassador to the U.S.: Habib MANSOUR.

U.S. Ambassador to Tunisia: Gordon GRAY.

Permanent Representative to the UN: Ghazi JOMAA.

IGO Memberships (Non-UN): AfDB, AFESD, AMF, AMU, AU, BADEA, IDB, Interpol, IOM, LAS, NAM, OIC, OIF, WCO, WTO.

TURKEY

Republic of Turkey
Türkiye Cumhuriyeti

Note: On October 10, 2009, Turkey and Armenia signed a historic accord establishing diplomatic relations between the two countries for the first time. The accord, which must be ratified by the parliaments of both countries, also calls for reopening the Turkish-Armenian border, which has been closed since 1993, and paves the way for resolution of a century-old dispute regarding the deaths of many Armenians in the final days of the Ottoman Empire.

Political Status: Independent republic established in 1923; parliamentary democracy since 1946, save for military interregna from May 1960 to October 1961 and September 1980 to November 1983; present constitution approved by referendum of November 7, 1982.

Area: 300,948 sq. mi. (779,452 sq. km.).

Population: 67,803,927 (2000C); 74,827,000 (2008E).

Major Urban Centers (2007E): ANKARA (3,641,931), İstanbul (10,291,102), İzmir (2,651,568), Bursa (1,504,817), Adana (1,294,460), Gaziantep (1,136,281), Konya (932,589).

Official Language: Turkish. A 1982 law banning the use of the Kurdish language was rescinded in early 1991.

Monetary Unit: Turkish Lira (*Türk Lirası*—TL) (market rate December 1, 2009: 1.50 Turkish New Liras = $1US).

President of the Republic: Abdullah GÜL (Justice and Development Party); elected by the Grand National Assembly on August 20, 24, and 28, 2007, and sworn in for a seven-year term on the same day to succeed Ahmet Necdet SEZER (nonparty).

Prime Minister: Recep Tayyip ERDOĞAN (Justice and Development Party); appointed by the president on March 14, 2003; reappointed following early legislative elections on July 22, 2007, and formed new government on August 6; formed new government on August 29, 2007, following election of President Gül.

THE COUNTRY

Guardian of the narrow straits between the Mediterranean and Black seas, present-day Turkey occupies the compact land mass of the Anatolian Peninsula together with the partially European city of İstanbul and its Thracian hinterland. The country, which borders on Greece, Bulgaria, Georgia, Armenia, the Nakhichevan Autonomous Republic of Azerbaijan, Iran, Iraq, and Syria, has a varied topography and is subject to extreme variation in climate. It supports a largely Turkish population (more than 80 percent, in terms of language) but has a substantial Kurdish minority of approximately 12 million, plus such smaller groups as Arabs, Circassians, Greeks, Armenians, Georgians, Lazes, and Jews. Some 98 percent of the populace, including both Turks and Kurds, adheres to the Sunni branch of the Islamic faith, which maintains a strong position despite the secular emphasis of government policy since the 1920s. Sunni Muslims constitute a substantial majority, but between 10 and 20 percent of the population belong to the Alevi sect of Islam.

Women constitute approximately 36 percent of the official labor force, with large numbers serving as unpaid workers on family farms. While only 10 percent of the urban labor force is female, there is extensive participation by upper-income women in such professions as medicine, law, banking, and education, with the government being headed by a female prime minister from 1993 to 1995.

Turkey traditionally has been an agricultural country, with about 50 percent of the population still engaged in agricultural pursuits; yet the contribution of industry to GDP growth exceeds that of agriculture (9 percent and 3 percent, respectively, in 2007). Grain (most importantly wheat), tobacco, cotton, nuts, fruits, and olive oil are the chief agricultural products; sheep and cattle are raised on the Anatolian plateau, and

the country ranks among the leading producers of mohair. Natural resources include chrome, copper, iron ore, manganese, bauxite, borax, and petroleum. The most important industries are textiles, iron and steel, sugar, food processing, cement, paper, and fertilizer. State economic enterprises (SEEs) account for more than 60 percent of fixed investment, although substantial privatization has been implemented.

Economic growth during the 1960s was substantial but not enough to overcome severe balance-of-payments and inflation problems, which intensified following the oil price increases of 1973–1974. By 1975 the cost of petroleum imports had more than quadrupled and was absorbing nearly two-thirds of export earnings. A major devaluation of the lira in mid-1979 failed to resolve the country's economic difficulties, and in early 1980, with inflation exceeding 100 percent, a $1.16 billion loan package was negotiated with the Organization for Economic Cooperation and Development (OECD), followed in June by $1.65 billion in credits from the International Monetary Fund (IMF). Subsequently, aided by improving export performance and a tight curb on foreign currency transactions, the economy registered substantial recovery, with inflation being reduced to a still unsatisfactory level of 39 percent in 1987, before returning to 70 percent in 1989. High inflation rates plagued Turkey throughout the 1990s, reaching 99 percent by 1997. An economic stabilization program introduced in 1997 brought the rate down to 55 percent in 1998.

Although annual inflation had been lowered to about 35 percent in 2000 and solid GNP growth (estimated at over 6 percent) had been reestablished, a financial crisis erupted in late February 2001, forcing a currency devaluation and other intervention measures. In April 2001 the government announced it anticipated 3 percent economic contraction for the year. Among other things, resolution of the economic problems was considered a prerequisite to Turkey's long-standing goal of accession to the European Union (EU) (see Foreign relations, below, for details). The IMF approved a $15.7 billion "rescue package" in May 2001 and endorsed up to $10 billion in additional aid in November after the government pledged to intensify its efforts to reorganize the banking sector, improve tax collection, combat corruption, promote foreign investment, and accelerate the privatization program. Consequently, the government narrowly avoided defaulting on its debt repayments, much to the relief of Western capitals, for whom Turkey represents a geographic, political, and military linchpin amid the turbulence of the Middle East.

Annual GDP growth averaged 7.5 percent in 2002–2004, and the inflation rate declined to about 8 percent, owing in large part to banking reforms, privatization, and debt reduction, according to the IMF. Observers credited reform of the financial sector, including the creation of an independent agency to regulate banking, and a surplus for three consecutive years. However, the IMF cautioned against further increases in public-sector wages, which were seen as likely to fuel inflation. Meanwhile, the IMF recommended reform of the social security system, which carried a large deficit. Citing yet another year of strong growth, with GDP of about 8 percent, the IMF in 2005 approved a $10 billion loan to support Turkey's economic and financial reforms.

In April 2006 parliament approved a long-sought social security reform bill, raising the retirement age to 65 and including measures to deter abuse. Despite this measure, the IMF cautioned in May that the country needed to further rein in government spending. GDP growth slowed to an annual average of 5.4 percent in 2006–2008, partly due to a decline in consumer spending as credit rates increased. In 2009 the global economic crisis had a significant impact on the Turkish economy, most notably in the sharp drop in exports, as a result of which the unemployment rate was expected to rise to 16 percent. Meanwhile, the World Bank forecast annual GDP growth of less than 2 percent and called for social protections for the increasing number of people living in poverty.

GOVERNMENT AND POLITICS

Political background. Present-day Turkey is the surviving core of a vast empire created by Ottoman rule in late medieval and early modern times. After a period of expansion during the 15th and 16th centuries in which Ottoman domination was extended over much of central Europe, the Balkans, the Middle East, and North Africa, the empire underwent a lengthy period of contraction and fragmentation, finally dissolving in the aftermath of a disastrous alliance with Germany in World War I.

A secular nationalist republic was proclaimed on October 29, 1923, by Mustafa Kemal ATATÜRK, who launched a reform program under which Turkey abandoned much of its Ottoman and Islamic heritage. Its major components included secularization (separation of religion and state), establishment of state control of the economy, and creation of a new Turkish national identity. Following his death in 1938, Atatürk's Republican People's Party (*Cumhuriyet Halk Partisi*—CHP) continued as the only legally recognized party under his close associate, İsmet İNÖNÜ. One-party domination was not seriously contested until after World War II, when the opposition Democratic Party (*Demokrat Parti*—DP) was established by Celal BAYAR, Adnan MENDERES, and others.

Winning the country's first free election in 1950, the DP ruled Turkey for the next decade, only to be ousted in 1960 by a military coup led by Gen. Cemal GÜRSEL. The military justified the coup as a response to alleged corruption within the DP and the growing authoritarian attitudes of its leaders. Many of those so charged, including President Bayar and Prime Minister Menderes, were tried by martial courts and found guilty of violating the constitution, after which Bayar was imprisoned and Menderes and two of his ministers were executed.

Civilian government was restored under a new constitution in 1961, with Gürsel remaining as president until he suffered a stroke, and was replaced by Gen. Cevdet SUNAY in 1966. The 1961 basic law established a series of checks and balances to offset a concentration of power in the executive and prompted a diffusion of parliamentary seats among several parties. A series of coalition governments, most of them led by İnönü, functioned until 1965, when a partial reincarnation of the DP, Süleyman DEMİREL's Justice Party (*Adalet Partisi*—AP), won a sweeping legislative mandate.

Despite its victory in 1965, the Demirel regime soon became the target of popular discontent and demands for basic reform. Although surviving the election of 1969, it was subsequently caught between left-wing agitation and military insistence on the maintenance of public order, a critical issue because of mounting economic and social unrest and the growth of political terrorism. The crisis came to a head in 1971 with an ultimatum from the military that resulted in Demirel's resignation and the formation of a "nonparty" government by Nihat ERİM. The new government amended the 1961 constitution, declared martial law in eleven provinces, arrested dissident elements, and outlawed the left-wing Turkish Workers Party (*Türkiye İşçi Partisi*—TİP) and the moderate Islamist National Order Party (*Millî Nizam Partisi*—MNP). The period immediately after the fall of the Erim government in 1972 witnessed another "nonparty" administration under Ferit MELEN and the selection of a new president, Adm. (Ret.) Fahri KORUTÜRK. Political instability was heightened further by an inconclusive election in 1973 and by both foreign and domestic policy problems stemming from a rapidly deteriorating economy, substantial urban population growth, and renewed conflict on Cyprus, which led to a Turkish invasion of the island in the summer of 1974.

Bülent ECEVİT was appointed prime minister in January 1974, heading a coalition of his own moderately progressive CHP and the smaller, more religious National Salvation Party (*Millî Selâmet Partisi*—MSP). Despite securing widespread domestic acclaim for the Cyprus action and for his insistence that the island be formally divided into Greek and Turkish federal regions, Ecevit was opposed by Deputy Prime Minister Necmettin ERBAKAN, who called for outright annexation of the Turkish sector and, along with his MSP colleagues, resigned, precipitating Ecevit's own resignation in September. After both Ecevit and former prime minister Demirel failed to form new governments, Sadi IRMAK, an independent, was designated prime minister on November 17, heading an essentially nonparliamentary cabinet. Following a defeat in the National Assembly only twelve days later, Irmak also was forced to resign, although he remained in office in a caretaker capacity until Demirel succeeded in forming a Nationalist Front coalition government on April 12, 1975.

At an early general election on June 5, 1977, no party succeeded in gaining a lower house majority, and the Demirel government fell on July 13. Following Ecevit's inability to organize a majority coalition, Demirel returned as head of a tripartite administration that failed to survive a vote of confidence on December 31. Ecevit then returned to his former position, organizing a minority government.

Widespread civil and political unrest throughout 1978 prompted a declaration of martial law in 13 provinces on December 25. The security situation deteriorated further during 1979, and, faced with a number of ministerial defections, Prime Minister Ecevit was obliged to step down again on October 16, with Demirel returning as head of an AP minority government on November 12.

Divided by rising foreign debt and increasing domestic terrorism, the National Assembly failed to elect a president to succeed Fahri Korutürk, despite casting over 100 ballots. Senate President İhsan Sabri ÇAĞLAYANGİL assumed the office on an acting basis at the expiration of Korutürk's seven-year term on April 6. On August 29 Gen. Kenan EVREN, chief of the General Staff, publicly criticized the assembly for its failure both to elect a new president and to promulgate more drastic security legislation, and on September 12 he mounted a coup on behalf of a five-man National Security Council (NSC) that suspended the constitution, dissolved the assembly, proclaimed martial law in all of the country's 67 provinces, and on September 21 designated a military-civilian cabinet under Adm. (Ret.) Bülent ULUSU. The junta banned all existing political parties, detaining many of their leaders, including Ecevit and Demirel; imposed strict censorship; and arrested upwards of 40,000 persons on political charges.

In a national referendum on November 7, 1982, Turkish voters overwhelmingly approved a new constitution, under which General Evren was formally designated as president of the Republic for a seven-year term. One year later, on November 6, 1983, the recently established Motherland Party (*Anavatan Partisi*—ANAP) of former deputy prime minister Turgut ÖZAL won a majority of seats in a newly constituted unicameral Grand National Assembly. Following the election, General Evren's four colleagues on the NSC resigned their military commands, continuing as members of a Presidential Council upon dissolution of the NSC on December 6. On December 7 Özal was asked to form a government and assumed office as prime minister on December 13.

Confronted with a governing style that was viewed as increasingly arrogant and ineffective in combating inflation, Turkish voters dealt Prime Minister Özal a stinging rebuke in local elections on March 26, 1989. ANAP candidates ran a poor third overall, securing only 22 percent of the vote and losing control of the three largest cities. Özal refused, however, to call for new legislative balloting and, despite a plunge in personal popularity to 28 percent, utilized his assembly majority on October 31 to secure the presidency in succession to Evren. Following his inauguration at a parliamentary ceremony on November 9 that was boycotted by opposition members, Özal announced his choice of Assembly Speaker Yıldırım AKBULUT as the new prime minister.

Motherland's standing in the opinion polls slipped to a minuscule 14 percent in the wake of a political crisis that erupted in April 1991 over the somewhat heavy-handed installation of the president's wife, Semra Özal, as chair of the ruling party's İstanbul branch. Both Özals declared their neutrality in a leadership contest at a party congress in mid-June, but they were viewed as the principal architects of an unprecedented challenge to Prime Minister Akbulut, who was defeated for reelection as chair by former foreign minister Mesut YILMAZ.

Yılmaz called for an early election on October 20, 1991, "to refresh the people's confidence" in his government. The outcome, however, was a defeat for the ruling party, with former prime minister Demirel, now leader of the right-of-center True Path Party (*Doğru Yol Partisi*—DYP), negotiating a coalition with the left-of-center Social Democratic People's Party (*Sosyal Demokrat Halkçı Parti*—SHP) and returning to office for the seventh time on November 21, with the SHP's Erdal İNÖNÜ as his deputy.

Demirel's broad-based administration, which brought together the heirs of Turkey's two oldest and most prominent political traditions (the CHP and the DP), claimed greater popularity—50 percent voter support and more than 60 percent backing in the polls—than any government in recent decades. Thus encouraged, Demirel and İnönü launched an ambitious program to counter the problems of rampant inflation, Kurdish insurgency, and obstacles to full democratization.

On April 17, 1993, President Özal died of a heart attack, and on May 16 the Grand National Assembly elected Prime Minister Demirel head of state. The DYP's search for a new chair ended on June 13, when Tansu ÇİLLER, an economics professor, defeated two other candidates at an extraordinary party congress. On July 5 a new DYP-SHP coalition government, committed to a program of further democratization, secularization, and privatization, was accorded a vote of confidence by the assembly, and Çiller became Turkey's first female prime minister.

A major offensive against guerrillas of the Kurdistan Workers' Party (*Partîya Karkerên Kurdistan*—PKK) in northern Iraq was launched on March 20, 1995. Six weeks later the government announced that the operation had been a success and that all of its units had returned to Turkey. The popularity of the action was demonstrated in local elections on June 4, when the ruling DYP took 22 of 36 mayoralties on a 39 percent share of the vote. However, on September 20 a revived CHP, which had become the DYP's junior coalition partner after absorbing the SHP in February, withdrew its support, forcing the resignation of the Çiller government. (The SHP has since left the CHP.)

On October 2, 1995, Çiller announced the formation of a DYP minority administration that drew unlikely backing from the far-right Nationalist Action Party (*Milliyetçi Hareket Partisi*—MHP) and the center-left Democratic Left Party (*Demokratik Sol Parti*—DSP). However, the prime minister was opposed within the DYP by former National Assembly speaker Hüsamettin CİNDORUK, who resigned on October 1 and was one of ten deputies expelled from the party on October 16, one day after Çiller's defeat on a confidence motion. On October 31 President Demirel appointed Çiller to head a DYP-CHP interim government pending a premature election in December.

At the December 24, 1995, balloting the pro-Islamic Welfare Party (*Refah Partisi*—RP) emerged as the legislative leader, although its 158 seats fell far short of the 276 needed for an overall majority. Eventually, on February 28, 1996, agreement was reached on a center-right coalition that would permit the ANAP's Yılmaz to serve as prime minister until January 1, 1997, with Çiller occupying the post for the ensuing two years and Yılmaz returning for the balance of the parliamentary term, assuming no dissolution.

Formally launched on March 12, 1996, the ANAP-DYP coalition collapsed at the end of May amid renewed personal animosity between Yılmaz and Çiller over the former's unwillingness to back the DYP leader against corruption charges related to her recent premiership. The DYP then opted to become the junior partner in an alternative coalition headed by RP leader Necmettin ERBAKAN, who on June 28 became Turkey's first avowedly Islamist prime minister since the creation of the secular republic in 1923. Under the coalition agreement, Çiller was slated to take over as head of government in January 1998. However, on February 28, 1997, the military members of the National Security Council (*Milli Güvenlik Kurulu*—MGK) presented the civilian members of the council with a memorandum, reportedly expressing their concern that Erbakan's tolerance for rising religious activism would seriously threaten the country's secular tradition. After months of pressure from the military, Erbakan resigned on June 18, 1997, with the hope that a new government under the leadership of his coalition partner, Çiller, would bring the paralyzed government back to life. However, on June 20 President Demirel bypassed Çiller, whose DYP had been weakened by steady defections, and selected the ANAP's Yılmaz to return as the next prime minister. A new coalition composed of the ANAP, the DSP, and the new center-right Democratic Turkey Party (*Demokrat Türkiye Partisi*—DTP) was approved by Demirel on June 30, and Yılmaz and his cabinet were sworn in on the following day.

The new coalition government tried to reverse the Islamic influence of its predecessor and in July 1997 proposed an eight-year compulsory education plan that included the closure of Islamic secondary schools, prompting weeks of right-wing and militant Islamic demonstrations.

The Yılmaz government collapsed on November 25, 1998, when he lost a vote of confidence in the Grand National Assembly following accusations of corruption against members of his cabinet. President Demirel asked Bülent Ecevit to form a new government on December 2, thereby abandoning the long-standing tradition of designating the leader of the largest party in the legislature as prime minister. (Such action would have put Recai KUTAN's moderate Islamist Virtue Party [*Fazilet Partisi*—FP] in power, an option opposed by the military.) When Ecevit proved unable to form a government, Demirel turned to an independent, Yalım EREZ, who also failed when former prime minister Çiller rejected his proposal that her DYP be part of a new coalition. After Erez abandoned his initiative on January 6, 1999, President Demirel again invited Ecevit to form the government. This time Ecevit succeeded in forming a minority cabinet made up of the DSP and independents; the DYP and ANAP agreed to provide external support.

Ecevit's cabinet survived a crisis that erupted in mid-March 1999, when the FP threatened to topple the government and joined forces with disgruntled members of parliament from various political parties who were not nominated for reelection. In balloting on April 18, 1999, Ecevit's DSP received 22 percent of the votes and became the largest party in the assembly, with 136 seats. On May 28 Ecevit announced the formation of a coalition cabinet comprising the DSP, MHP, and ANAP. Meanwhile, on May 16 Ahmet Necdet SEZER, chief justice of the Constitutional Court, was sworn in as the new president, following the legislature's rejection of President Demirel's request for constitutional revision that would have permitted him a second term.

In October 2001, the Grand National Assembly approved several constitutional amendments aimed at easing Turkey's path into the EU. The changes provided greater protection for political freedom and civil leaders, including protection for the Kurdish minority. Moreover, the number of civilians on the National Security Council was increased from five to nine, with the military continuing to hold five seats.

In January 2002 the Constitutional Court banned Justice and Development (AKP) leader Recep Tayyip ERDOĞAN from running for the legislature because of alleged seditious activities. The court also ordered the party to remove Erdoğan from party leadership. In July Prime Minister Ecevit was forced to call early elections to the Grand National Assembly in the wake of the DSP-led coalition having lost its majority due to resignations. Subsequently, the DSP won only 1.2 percent of the vote and no seats in the November 3 election, as the AKP gained control with 34.3 percent of the vote and 363 seats. The CHP won 19.4 percent of the vote and 178 seats.

With Erdoğan prohibited from holding a seat in the assembly, the AKP's deputy leader, Abdullah GÜL, was appointed prime minister, though Erdoğan reportedly acted as de facto prime minister. Meanwhile, the AKP majority adopted constitutional changes that allowed Erdoğan to run for parliament, and in a March 9, 2003, by-election, Erdoğan won. Five days later he was appointed prime minister.

Also in March 2003, Turkey's Constitutional Court banned the People's Democracy Party (HADEP) from politics as a result of its alleged support for the PKK. In addition, 46 party members were individually banned from politics for five years The AKP further solidified its position with a strong showing in local elections on March 28, 2004, winning 42 percent of the vote, well ahead of the second-place CHP with 18 percent. Meanwhile, with AKP leadership, parliament adopted further reforms aimed at promoting Turkey's accession to the EU, including measures allowing broadcasting and education in Kurdish. Another law, enacted after an override of President Sezer's veto, allowed peaceful advocacy of an independent Kurdish state.

Political turmoil surrounded the scheduled May 2007 presidential election following Prime Minister Erdoğan's nomination of Foreign Minister Gül as the AKP candidate, prompting widespread anxiety among secular elites and the military, who claimed that Gül's Islamist leanings made him unfit for office in Turkey's secular system. While Gül's election seemed imminent given the size of the AKP's parliamentary majority, the military issued a memorandum publicly opposing Gül's candidacy. In the memorandum it was asserted that the military could not remain indifferent to the threat of an Islamist takeover. On April 27 and May 5, opposition parties boycotted presidential election votes, and Gül subsequently withdrew as a candidate. Meanwhile, the Constitutional Court ruled that a quorum of two thirds, or 367 members, was necessary for a legal presidential election. To overcome the deadlock, Erdoğan called for early general elections on July 22, a measure parliament unanimously approved. The assembly subsequently voted to amend the constitution to allow for direct popular election of the president, but the measure was vetoed by President Sezer. Another vote by parliament on June 1 produced the same result, and again Sezer rejected the measure, which would have required a national referendum to be held within 120 days. Parliament's vote to hold the constitutional referendum and then concurrent presidential and legislative elections was also vetoed by Sezer.

In the July 2007 early elections, the AKP secured a stunning victory, improving upon its 2002 return by 12 percent, with 46.7 percent of votes and 341 seats. The CHP and the MHP won 98 and 71 seats, respectively. Several smaller parties managed to circumvent the threshold and achieve small representation via coalitions or independent candidacies. Following the strong showing of the AKP, Gül, again nominated by Erdoğan, received 339 votes in parliament on August 28 to become president of the republic. Subsequently, a national referendum on the proposed constitutional changes was held in October, with 68.95 percent of voters registering approval for the amendments.

Controversy over the role of Islam in public life continued after the election, as in June 2008 the Constitutional Court annulled a constitutional amendment lifting a ban on women wearing headscarves on university campuses. A parliamentary majority had supported a constitutional amendment to lift the ban.

Following the poor performance of the AKP in the March 2009 municipal elections, Erdoğan reshuffled the cabinet on May 1. His appointments included his longtime foreign policy adviser Ahmet DAVUTOĞLU as foreign minister. Davutoğlu's appointment was seen by observers as a move toward enhancing Turkey's relations with the Middle East, among other things.

Constitution and government. The 1982 constitution provided for a unicameral 400-member Grand National Assembly elected for a five-year term (the membership being increased to 450 in 1987 and 550 in 1995). The president, elected by the assembly for a nonrenewable seven-year term, is empowered to appoint and dismiss the prime minister and other cabinet members; to dissolve the assembly and call for a new election, assuming the concurrence of two-thirds of the deputies or if faced with a government crisis of more than 30 days' duration; to declare a state of emergency, during which the government may rule by decree; and to appoint a variety of leading government officials, including senior judges and the governor of the Central Bank. Political parties may be formed if they are not based on class or ethnicity, linked to trade unions, or committed to communism, fascism, or religious fundamentalism. Strikes that exceed 60 days' duration are subject to compulsory arbitration.

In 2003 the constitution was amended to change the membership and rules of operation of the country's National Security Council (*Milli Güvenlik Kurulu*-MGK), which has served as one of the most important levers for the control of Turkish politics by the military. The amendments reduced the number of council seats reserved for the military. For the first time in its history, the MGK had a civilian majority and a civilian secretary general.

Further amendments approved in 2007 provide for the direct election of the president every four years, reducing the presidential term from seven years to five, and allowing the president to stand for a second term (see Current issues, below).

The Turkish judicial system is headed by a Court of Cassation (*Yargıtay*), which is the court of final appeal. Other judicial bodies include an administrative tribunal styled the Council of State (*Danıştay*), a Constitutional Court (*Anayasa Mahkemesi*), a Court of Accounts (*Sayıştay*), various military courts, and 12 state security courts.

The country is presently divided into 82 provinces, which are further divided into subprovinces and districts. Mayors and municipal councils have long been popularly elected, save during the period 1980–1984.

Foreign relations. Neutral until the closing months of World War II, Turkey entered that conflict in time to become a founding member of the United Nations and has since joined all of the latter's affiliated agencies. Concern for the protection of its independence, primarily against possible Soviet threats, made Turkey a firm ally of the Western powers, with one of the largest standing armies in the non-Communist world. Largely on U.S. initiative, Turkey was admitted to the North Atlantic Treaty Organization (NATO) in 1952 and in 1955 became a founding member of the Baghdad Treaty Organization, later the Central Treaty Organization (CENTO), which was officially disbanded in September 1979, following Iranian and Pakistani withdrawal.

Relations with a number of Western governments stagnated in the 1960s, partly because of a lack of support for Turkey's position on the question of Cyprus. The dispute, with the fate of the Turkish Cypriot community at its center, became critical upon the island's attainment of independence in 1960 and nearly led to war with Greece in 1967. The situation assumed major international importance in 1974 following the Greek junta coup that resulted in the temporary ouster of Cypriot president Makarios and the subsequent Turkish invasion on July 20, which yielded Turkish occupation of the northern third of the island. (For details, see the articles on Cyprus and Cyprus: Turkish Sector.)

Relations with the United States, strained by a congressional ban on military aid following the Cyprus incursion, were further undermined by a Turkish decision in July 1975 to repudiate a 1969 defense cooperation agreement and force the closure of 25 U.S. military installations. However, a new accord was concluded in March 1976 that called for reopening of the bases under Turkish rather than dual control, coupled with substantially increased American military assistance. The U.S. arms embargo was finally lifted in September 1978, with the stipulation that Turkey continue to seek a negotiated resolution of the Cyprus issue.

While the Turkish government under Evren and Özal consistently affirmed its support of NATO and its desire to gain full entry to the EC (having been an associate member of the European Economic Community since 1964), relations with western Europe deteriorated in the wake of the 1980 coup because of alleged human rights violations.

Ankara submitted a formal membership request to the EC, and in December 1989 the commission had laid down a number of stringent conditions for admission to the community, including an improved human rights record, progress toward improved relations with Greece, and less dependence on agricultural employment. Because of these concerns, Turkey remained outside the EU upon the latter's inception in November 1993, although, in an action viewed as linked to its EC bid, it had become an associate member of the Western European Union in 1992.

On March 6, 1995, Turkey and the EU agreed to a customs union, which entered into force on January 1, 1996. However, in July 1997 the EU Commission included five East European states but excluded Turkey from among those invited to join first-round enlargement negotiations scheduled for early 1998. Moreover, the commission recommended Cyprus for full membership, a decision that Turkey saw as controversial given the lack of a settlement of the Cyprus question. In light of improving Turkish/Greek relations, a December 1999 EU summit finally accepted Turkey as an official candidate for membership.

Apart from Cyprus, the principal dispute between Greece and Turkey has centered on territorial rights in the Aegean. In late 1984 Ankara rejected a proposal by Prime Minister Papandreou to assign Greek forces on Limnos to NATO, invoking a long-standing contention that militarization of the island was forbidden under the 1923 Treaty of Lausanne. The controversy revived in early 1989 with Turkey refusing to recognize insular sea and airspace limits greater than six miles on the premise that to do otherwise would convert the area into a "Greek lake." The dispute intensified in September 1994, with Greece declaring that it would formally extend its jurisdiction to 12 nautical miles upon entry into force of the UN Convention on the Law of the Sea on November 16. Turkey immediately warned that the move would be considered an "act of aggression," and on October 30 Athens announced that it would defer the introduction of what it continued to view as a "sovereign right." On June 8, 1995, the Turkish Parliament approved a declaration that an extension of Greek territorial waters in the Aegean to 12 miles would comprise a *casus belli* for Turkey, further straining bilateral relations with Greece.

Another territorial issue was addressed when Turkey concluded an agreement with Iraq in October 1984 that permitted the security forces of each government to pursue "subversive groups" (interpreted primarily as Kurdish rebels) up to a distance of five kilometers on either side of the border and to engage in follow-up operations for five days without prior notification.

The hot pursuit agreement notwithstanding, the Turkish government strongly supported UN-endorsed sanctions against Iraq in the wake of its invasion of Kuwait in August 1990. Despite considerable revenue loss, Turkey moved quickly to shut down Iraqi oil pipelines by banning ships from loading crude at offshore terminals. In September, despite opposition criticism, the legislature granted the administration special authority to dispatch troops to the Gulf and to allow foreign forces to be stationed on Turkish soil for non-NATO purposes (most important, the stationing of F-111 fighter bombers at İncirlik air base to monitor the UN-sanctioned Iraqi no-fly zone north of the 36th parallel).

Turkey's attention refocused on maritime issues in 1994 as Ankara angered Moscow by seeking to impose restrictions on shipping through the Bosporus. The issue was highly charged because of the 1936 Montreux treaty, which provided complete freedom of transit through both the Bosporus and Dardanelles during peacetime. Turkey insisted that the new regulations (including the prohibition of automatic pilots for navigation and limitations on dangerous cargo) were prompted only by technical considerations that had not existed at the time of the treaty's adoption.

In 1992, Turkey faced another dilemma, this time in regard to the conflict in Bosnia and Herzegovina. Both the Bosnians and Turkish citizens of Bosnian descent appealed for action to oppose Serbian advances in Muslim areas; however, Atatürk's secularist heirs were reluctant to move in a manner that might be seen as religiously inspired. Deeply opposed to unilateral action, Turkey launched a pro-Bosnian campaign in various international venues, including the UN, the Conference on (subsequently the Organization for) Security and Cooperation in Europe (CSCE/OSCE), NATO, the Council of Europe, and the OIC. Throughout, it urged limited military intervention by the UN and the lifting of the arms embargo for Bosnia should existing sanctions and diplomatic efforts prove ineffective.

Turkey commenced its own military action on March 20, 1995, targeting the Kurds in northern Iraq, which provoked the condemnation of most West European governments. On April 10 the EU foreign ministers, while acknowledging Turkey's "terrorism problems," called on Ankara to withdraw its troops "without delay," and on April 26 the Parliamentary Assembly of the Council of Europe approved a resolution calling for suspension of Turkey's membership if it did not leave Iraq by late June. For its part, the Turkish government reacted angrily to an announcement on April 12 that political exiles had established a Kurdish "parliament in exile" in the Netherlands, and a renewed cross-border offensive was launched by some 30,000 troops on July 5–10. In any event, no action was taken to suspend Turkey's Council of Europe membership, despite further vigorous Turkish action against the Kurdish insurgency and the forced relocation of hundreds of thousands of Kurdish villagers in southeastern Turkey. In July 1997 Turkey and the Democratic Party of Kurdistan (DPK) reached a preliminary agreement to boost security in northern Iraq. However, in August Turkish warplanes crossed the Iraqi border to bomb PKK rebel bases, drawing the condemnation of Baghdad.

A major diplomatic dispute erupted in 1998 over Syria's alleged sheltering of PKK rebels, with Ankara warning Damascus in October of possible military action unless Syrian policy changed. The crisis was also colored by Syria's concern over the recent rapprochement between Turkey and Israel, which had produced a defense agreement and a recent visit by Prime Minister Yılmaz to Israel. Following intense mediation by several Arab leaders from the region, Syria subsequently agreed that it would not allow the PKK to set up "military, logistical, or financial bases" on Syrian territory. Collaterally, PKK leader Abdullah ÖCALAN was forced to leave Syrian-controlled territory in Lebanon. Öcalan moved to Russia, which, under insistent Turkish pressure, also refused him asylum. He then entered Italy, prompting a row between Rome and Ankara. Italy rejected Turkey's extradition request on the grounds that it could not send a detainee to a country that permitted the death penalty. Italy therefore attempted to negotiate Öcalan's transfer to Germany, where he also faced terrorism charges. However, Bonn, apparently fearing violence between its own Turkish and Kurdish minorities, declined to file an extradition request. Consequently, Öcalan was released from detention in Italy in mid-December and reportedly left that country in January 1999 for an unknown destination.

In mid-February 1999 Öcalan was arrested shortly after he left the home of the Greek ambassador in Nairobi, Kenya. The incident proved to be highly embarrassing for the government in Athens. Despite the renewed animosity surrounding Öcalan's arrest, Turkish-Greek relations thawed noticeably in late 1999 when Greece lifted its veto on EU financial aid earmarked to Turkey and agreed to a European Council decision that gave Turkey the status of a candidate state for EU membership. In early 2000 the two countries agreed to establish a joint commission to "reduce military tensions" in the Aegean and to pursue cooperation in several other areas.

In 2003, Turkey's relationship with the United States faced a major challenge with Turkey's refusal to allow U.S. troops to use Turkish territory as a staging area for the invasion of Iraq in March 2003. Some observers attributed this refusal, which was an embarrassment to the Turkish government and military, to a political power struggle taking place within Turkey. While the governing Justice and Development Party (AKP) was in favor of such cooperation, many nationalistic members of the Grand National Assembly, including some AKP members, were not. Relations with the United States also cooled because the Turkish government felt that Washington was indifferent to Kurdish terrorist activity in Turkey and northern Iraq. Indeed, in November 2004, Turkish newspapers published unconfirmed reports that the Turkish government had formulated a plan to move 20,000 Turkish troops into northern Iraq to prevent Kurds from taking complete control of Kirkuk. On January 26, 2005, a senior Turkish army general said bluntly that the Turkish military was prepared to intervene if clashes erupted in northern Iraq or if Iraqi Kurds attempted to form an independent state.

Iran and Turkey signed a security agreement on July 30, 2004, to place rebels opposed to either government on each government's list of terrorist organizations.

Relations with Russia have also been further strained by Turkey's ongoing efforts to control the passage of oil tankers through the Bosporus straits. Turkey has maintained that the increased number of oil tankers represented an environmental threat to its coastline and waterways and has imposed tighter regulations on passage, which Russia said added greatly to transit time and thus to costs. In August 2004 Turkey also proposed, and offered to help fund, construction of pipelines to reduce waterborne traffic. Apart from the issue of the Bosporus strait, however, Turkish relations with Russia have been generally good. Tourism between the two countries has increased significantly, as has bilateral commerce.

Turkey's relations with the EU reached a peak on December 17, 2004, when the European Council agreed to define October 3, 2005, as the starting date of EU-Turkey accession negotiations. However, accession to the EU by the Republic of Cyprus, and the political confusion caused by popular rejection of the European Constitution, downgraded Turkish membership on the EU agenda. Negotiations followed a rather slow pace in 2005, while the reform drive that had pleasantly surprised EU entities between 1999 and 2004 seemed to have been exhausted. A rise of Turkish nationalist sentiment (see Current issues, below) made additional EU-mandated reforms even more difficult. This was complicated by the opposition of Germany and France, two of the most influential EU member states, whose political leaders objected to full EU membership for Turkey and suggested a "privileged partnership" status instead. EU representatives in recent years have cited Turkey's failure to open air and sea connections with the Republic of Cyprus as a major hurdle to membership.

Iraq resurfaced as a contentious issue between Turkey and the United States in July 2006, when Turkey again called on the United States to crack down on Kurdish rebels in northern Iraq and made veiled threats to attack rebel bases if action was not taken.

Turkey's reputation in parts of the Middle East was enhanced when it offered in May 2008 to moderate peace negotiations between Syria and Israel, the dispute over the Golan Heights considered by Turkey easier to resolve than the dispute between the Israelis and the Palestinians. In addition, a September meeting in New York between President Gül and Iraqi president Jalal Talabani further improved relations between Turkey and Iraq. A visit by Mahmoud Ahmadinejad in August, the first such visit by an Iranian president in 12 years, was seen as paving the way toward improved relations between the two countries.

The fighting between Russia and Georgia in August 2008 over the latter's sovereignty underlined the complexity of Turkish policy toward the Caucasus. As Georgia's strongest regional strategic partner, Turkey's cooperation with Georgia has focused on the construction of oil and natural gas pipelines that circumvent Russia. However, with Russia as Turkey's second biggest trade partner, bilateral relations have significantly improved in recent years. Turkey thus condemned violation of Georgia's territorial integrity and the continuation of hostilities, while at the same time Ankara tried to avoid heightened tensions with Russia by refraining from joining NATO'S most outspoken critics. In an effort to balance its Russian interests, Turkey invoked the 1936 Montreux Treaty to prohibit the immediate passage of U.S. war vessels through the Turkish straits to the Black Sea. Interestingly, a significant part of Turkey's Caucasian diaspora, which had mobilized Turkish public opinion against Russia during the Chechnya crisis, justified Russia's military intervention in 2008 by objecting to Georgia's move to restore its sovereignty over the breakaway provinces of Abkhazia and South Ossetia.

The Georgian crisis provided an opening to Armenia, which had closed its borders with Turkey in 1993 during the Armenian-Azeri war in Nagorno Karabagh. Armenia was included in Turkey's new "Caucasus Alliance" initiative, and in September President Gül accepted, despite vehement objections from the opposition, an invitation from Armenian president Serzh Sarkisyan to visit Erivan. A subsequent meeting of the foreign ministers of Turkey, Armenia, and Azerbaijan in New York raised hopes for resolution of the Nagorno Karabagh question.

Turkish-Israeli relations suffered a serious diplomatic crisis in January 2009 when Prime Minister Erdoğan quarreled with Israeli President Shimon Peres during a discussion at the annual meeting of the World Economic Forum at Davos, Switzerland. Erdoğan lashed out against Israel's Gaza operations and abandoned the forum. He was welcomed in Istanbul by jubilant crowds, who approved of his anti-Israeli stance.

The visit of U.S. president Barack Obama to Turkey in May 2009 was seen as a big boost for Turkish foreign policy, as Obama aimed to restore relations with Turkey and further promote U.S. relations with the Islamic world. Shortly before his arrival, President Obama had reiterated support for Turkey's accession to the EU, causing a clash with French president Nicolas SARKOZY, a vocal opponent of Turkey's full EU membership. While Obama's visit helped improve the image of the United States in Turkey, it failed to produce solutions for a series of long-lasting disputes, including over Armenia and the status of Kurds in northern Iraq. In April 2009 it was reported that Turkey and Armenia had signed a "road map" for rapprochement between the two countries, stating that Armenia must accept the Kars border agreement of 1921, a joint committee of historians must review Armenia's claims of genocide, and that the borders between the two countries would be reopened, among other things. (*See headnote.*)

Current issues. Four intertwined issues have dominated politics in Turkey in recent years: accession to the EU, a significant rise in nationalist sentiments among the populace, secularism and the continuing Kurdish insurgency in the southeast part of the country.

Violence from the Kurdish insurgency has been increasing in recent years. In September 2003 the Kurdish rebel group PKK announced that it was ending its five-year cease-fire with the Turkish government. In a September 2004 offensive, the largest in five years, government troops killed 11 Kurdish rebels in the southeast province of Hakkari. The government blamed Kurdish rebels for a series of bombings—including two hotel bombings and the bombing of a pop concert—in August and September. The numbers of roadside bombings in the southeastern part of the country have also increased. While a proportion of the Kurdish population remains generally loyal to the PKK, many Kurds have started to question the rebels' tactics, particularly since government reforms aimed at EU membership have resulted in a steady increase in rights for Kurds.

Improved protections were expanded on September 26, 2004, when the Turkish parliament approved major revisions to the penal code, specifically intended to bring it in line with codes prevalent in the EU. A further reform of the penal code in June 2005 provided greater protections for women and children and imposed harsher penalties for torture and "honor" killings.

In 2005 and 2006, however, European officials charged Turkey's government with backtracking on some reforms and slowing implementation of others. External observers, along with some Turks, voiced concern about the growing tensions between Islamic and secular forces inside Turkey. The rift was emphasized in May 2006, following the killing of a senior judge by gunmen who shouted Islamic slogans. Speculation arose that linked the killing to a recent court decision to uphold a ban on women's traditional Islamic headscarves in public institutions.

While the Erdoğan government attempted to reassure Europe of Turkey's status as a secular country intent on reform, some domestic policies generated concern within the military-bureaucratic establishment that Prime Minister Erdoğan, a devout Muslim, was intent on bringing Islamic values into government. Critics of the latter claimed that secular elites were more concerned with protecting their tutelary positions in Turkish politics and society, which were carefully delineated through post-coup constitutional changes.

Competition between the AKP government and the secularist bureaucracy often resulted in conflict between the AKP government and President Ahmet Necdet Sezer. In early March 2006 tensions between Islamic and secular forces were evident in President Sezer's veto of the government's nominee for central bank governor. There was speculation that the Erdoğan administration had nominated Adnan

BÜYÜKDENİZ, an economist and executive at an Islamic-style bank (which neither pays nor charges interest), in part, because of his religious convictions. The issue highlighted the distrust between the presidency, judiciary, and military on the one hand and the sitting government on the other.

As the Erdoğan government was more reticent in implementing reforms in 2005 and 2006, protests in the Kurdish sectors of the southeast increased. In 2007 there was a considerable rise in PKK activity and government operations in eastern and southeastern Turkey; on May 22 a suicide bomb in Ankara killed seven people, including the bomber, who was thought to be linked to the PKK.

Turkish nationalism has manifested itself in the unprecedented commercial success of nationalist books and films and increasing intolerance toward intellectuals and minorities. The killing of a Catholic priest in Trabzon in February 2006 preceded a series of killings of Christians, including three Protestants in the eastern city of Malatya on April 18. These were followed by the killing of an ethnic Armenian journalist in January 2007 in Istanbul; his funeral became a large demonstration in favor of Turkey's democratization and protection of minorities.

Meanwhile, the formation of a "Republican Demonstration" (*Cumhuriyet Mitingi*) in Ankara in April 2007 by a number of secularist nongovernmental organizations (NGOs) met with considerable success, drawing millions to rallies in cities throughout the country in the spring of 2007, during which cries of "No to sharia (Islamic law)" were heard. The group was highly critical of Gül's candidacy, which Erdoğan had promoted, and feared a possible Islamization of the Turkish public sphere. Attention increasingly turned to the demonstrations, including another mass rally in Izmir on May 13, as the future of secularism became the focus of public concern, and protesters demanded that the separation of religion and state be maintained.

Despite these expressions of discontent, the AKP retained power with 46.7 percent of the vote in the July 2007 parliamentary election by focusing on Turkey's economic growth, proposed constitutional amendments aimed at democratic reforms, progress toward EU accession, and removal of some Islamist candidates from its ballot. Further, the AKP enjoyed unprecedented electoral support in Kurdish regions as a result of reforms that promoted minority rights. The AKP's strong performance cleared the way for parliament's election of Gül as president of the republic, the scheduled election in May having been delayed as opposition parties boycotted the vote several times. The four-month political deadlock finally ended in August with Gül's election by 339 parliamentary votes. He assumed the office of president on August 28 and asked Erdoğan to form a new government (see Political background, above).

Meanwhile, the AKP, with the support of the Motherland Party (*Anavatan Partisi*—ANAP), in mid-2007 passed a law reducing from 120 to 45 the number of days required for holding a referendum on the AKP's amendment package, which was vehemently opposed by the military. On October 21, 69 percent of voters approved the constitutional amendments providing for the direct election of the president, reducing the presidential term from seven years to five, allowing the president to stand for a second term, holding presidential balloting every four years (instead of five), and reducing the parliamentary quorum to 184 members.

Domestic political tension continued to mount, however, following the government's decision in 2008 to press for another constitutional amendment to allow women to wear headscarves in universities. The proposal, which prompted strong secularist resistance, was nonetheless approved by a wide margin, owing to support from the AKP and the MHP. The CHP and the DSP appealed to the Constitutional Court, alleging that the amendment contravened the constitutional principle of secularism. The court overturned the amendment in June, effectively banning headscarves. Secular parties, fearing the Islamist leanings of the AKP, called for the party to be disbanded. After an indictment was issued against the party, some secular citizens were arrested. In July the Constitutional Court ruled against the banning of the AKP, though it found the party guilty of "antisecularist activities." The court also reduced by half the funds the party received from the Central Bank. While 10 of the 11 judges had accepted the charge that the party had become a center of antisecular activity, only 6 agreed with the proposed banning—one short of the number required to shut down a party (see Political parties, below). The AKP's survival prevented the collapse of the government, but conflict between the secularist bureaucracy and the AKP administration continued.

Earlier in 2008, 33 people were arrested for their alleged participation in an organization accused of destabilizing the country through assassinations and bombings attributed to Islamist or Kurdish terrorists. Named after the mythical birthplace of the Turkish nation, "Ergenekon" reportedly intended to maximize polarization, wreak havoc in Turkish society, and, thus, precipitate a military coup. Those arrested included retired generals, journalists, and other figures allegedly connected to antidemocratic constituencies within the Turkish elite. More arrests took place on March 21, including the leader of the Workers' Party, Doğu Perinçek; the former rector of the University of Istanbul; and the chief editor of the secularist daily *Cumhuriyet*. The discovery of "Ergenekon" operations by the state prosecutor reinforced allegations of planned military coups in 2003 and 2004. On July 1, 2008, a new round of arrests included three retired generals; the chair of the Ankara Chamber of Commerce, and the Ankara bureau chief of the secularist *Cumhuriyet* daily. The arrests marked the first time retired generals had been taken into custody. Further arrests followed throughout 2008 and into 2009, with court proceedings expected to last for more than a year. However, concern grew among some observers over the possible use of the Ergenekon investigation as a tool against government opposition.

The AKP suffered a blow in July 2008 when one of its most prominent members, former minister and member of parliament Abdülatif ŞENER, resigned and formed the Turkey's Party (*Türkiye Partisi*—TP) in 2009 (see Political Parties, below). Şener's alienation from the party leadership was attributed to his exclusion from the party ticket in the 2007 elections.

Despite winning most municipal elections in March 2009, the AKP lost several key cities and secured significantly fewer voters than in its landslide 2007 parliamentary victory (Its vote share was 38.9 percent, compared to 46.6 percent in the 2007 election.) The smaller showing was attributed in part to the "ongoing and deepening economic crisis." Meanwhile, four opposition parties—the CHP, MHP, DTP, and Felicity Party (*Saadet Partisi*—SP)—made gains. Observers said the results pointed to increasing sociopolitical divisions within the country, compounded by the worsening economy.

POLITICAL PARTIES

Turkey's multiparty system developed gradually out of the monopoly originally exercised by the historic Republican People's Party (*Cumhuriyet Halk Partisi*—CHP), which ruled the country without serious competition until 1950 and which, under Bülent Ecevit, was most recently in power from January 1978 to October 1979. The Democratic Party (*Demokrat Parti*—DP) of Celal Bayar and Adnan Menderes, founded by CHP dissidents in 1946, came to power in 1950 and maintained control for the next decade but was outlawed following the military coup of May 27, 1960, with many of its members subsequently entering the conservative Justice Party (*Adalet Partisi*—AP). Other formations included an Islamic group, the National Salvation Party (*Millî Selâmet Partisi*—MSP); the ultra-rightist Nationalist Action Party (*Milliyetçi Hareket Partisi*—MHP); and the leftist Turkish Labor Party (*Türkiye İşçi Partisi*—TİP). All party activity was banned by the National Security Council on September 12, 1980, while the parties themselves were formally dissolved and their assets liquidated on October 16, 1981.

Approval of the 1982 constitution ruled out any immediate likelihood that anything resembling the earlier party system would reappear. In order to qualify for the 1983 parliamentary election, new parties were required to obtain the signatures of at least 30 founding members, subject to veto by the National Security Council (NSC). Most such lists were rejected by the NSC, with only three groups (the Motherland, Populist, and Nationalist Democracy parties) being formally registered for the balloting on November 6 in an apparent effort to promote the emergence of a two-party system. Of the three, only the ruling Motherland Party remained by mid-1986: the Populist Party merged with the Social Democratic Party in November 1985 to form the Social Democratic People's Party (see under CHP, below), while the center-right Nationalist Democracy Party (*Milliyetçi Demokrasi Partisi*—MDP) dissolved itself in May 1986.

In July 1992 the government lifted bans on all of the parties closed during the military interregnum and by mid-1996 their number had risen to over 30, distributed almost equally to the right and left of the political spectrum.

Government Party:

Justice and Development Party (*Adalet ve Kalkınma Partisi*—AKP). The AKP was launched in August 2001 by the reformist wing of the FP (see below) as a moderate religious, center-right formation. Out of the former parliamentarians from the FP and other parties, 53 later joined the AKP, making it the second-largest opposition party in the assembly (after the DYP). Some analysts noted that the AKP might prove to be a strong challenger to the coalition parties in the next legislative election.

In January 2002 the electoral commission ruled that AKP president Recep Tayyip Erdoğan was ineligible to run for office due to his imprisonment in 1999 on charges of having "incited hatred on religious grounds." In the November 2002 elections, the AKP won 34.3 percent of the vote and 363 legislative seats. Erdoğan's ineligibility was overturned when parliament approved a change to the constitution that allowed Erdoğan to run in a by-election in March 2003. A few days later, he was named prime minister.

Rifts in the party appeared in February 2005 with the resignation from the government and the party of Erkan MUMCU, the minister for tourism and culture. Mumcu, a liberal and secular member considered a rising star in the party, indicated he was resigning because he felt he could no longer influence government decisions.

The elections of July 22, 2007, gave Erdoğan the chance to shift the party toward the center. More than 150 members of parliament from the party's Islamist wing were removed from AKP candidate lists. The new party lists included prominent liberal secularists, academics, and young professionals. The crushing electoral victory, in which the party improved its margin of victory by more than 12 percent over the previous election, yielded 341 seats. (This seat share was less than in 2002 due to the electoral system but, nevertheless, consolidated the party's political dominance.)

On March 14, 2007, the chief prosecutor of the Court of Cassation sought to shut down the AKP because of the party's alleged antisecular activities. However, a ruling by the Constitutional Court in 2008 upheld the party's viability (see Current issues, above).

In municipal elections in March 2009, the AKP garnered 38.83 percent of the vote and 492 municipal seats. AKP candidates were elected in the country's biggest cities, Istanbul and Ankara. However, the results were perceived as less than satisfactory compared to the AKP's performance in the 2007 parliamentary elections.

Leaders: Recep Tayyip ERDOĞAN (Prime Minister and President of the Party), Abdullah GÜL (President of the Republic), Idris Naim ŞAHIN (Secretary General).

Opposition Parties:

Republican People's Party (*Cumhuriyet Halk Partisi*—CHP). The CHP is a left-of-center party founded in 1923 by Kemal Atatürk. It was dissolved in 1981 and reactivated in 1992 by 21 MPs who resigned from the Social Democratic People's Party (*Sosyal Demokrat Halkçı Parti*—SHP) to reclaim the group's historic legacy. The CHP absorbed the SHP on February 18, 1995. (The SHP is again independent.) The CHP later absorbed the Party of Liberty and Change on June 8, 2007 (see below).

A member of the Socialist International, the SHP was formed in November 1985 by merger of the Populist Party (*Halkçı Parti*—HP), a center-left formation that secured 117 seats in the 1983 Grand National Assembly election, and the Social Democratic Party (*Sosyal Demokrat Parti*—SODEP), which was not permitted to offer candidates for the 1983 balloting. A leftist grouping that drew much of its support from former members of the CHP, SODEP had participated in the 1984 local elections, winning 10 provincial capitals. The SHP was runner-up to ANAP in November 1987, winning 99 assembly seats despite the defection in December 1986 of 20 of its deputies, most of whom joined the DSP. Its parliamentary representation was reduced to 82 upon formation of the People's Labor Party, whose candidates were, nevertheless, entered on SHP lists for the 1991 campaign. Subsequently, 18 of those so elected withdrew from the SHP, reducing its representation to 70.

On September 20, 1995, former CHP chair Deniz BAYKAL, who had been succeeded by the SHP's Hikmet CETIN at the time of the February merger, was reelected to his earlier post. Immediately thereafter he withdrew the party from the government coalition, thereby forcing Tansu Çiller's resignation as prime minister. In the resultant December election the CHP fell back to 49 seats on a 10.7 percent vote share. Baykal's CHP gave outside support to the Yılmaz-led ANAP-DSP-DTP coalition government of June 1998. However, amid accusations of corruption against various ministers, the CHP's call for a vote of no confidence against the Yılmaz cabinet brought the coalition down in November 1998. The CHP failed to surpass the 10 percent threshold in the April 18, 1999, elections, securing only 8.5 percent of the vote, and was therefore left out of the assembly. Baykal resigned from his chair's post on April 22. The CHP elected famous journalist and former tourism minister Altan ÖYMEN as its new leader on May 23; however, Baykal regained the post at an extraordinary congress in October 2000, defeating Öymen and two other minor candidates. The CHP's ranks were strengthened in 2002 by defections from the DSP.

In the November 2002 elections the CHP won 19.3 percent of the vote and 178 legislative seats, thus becoming the main opposition party. In October 2004 the New Turkey Party (*Yeni Türkiye Partisi*—YTP) merged with the CHP. (The YTP had been formed in July 2002 by former DSP cabinet ministers, including Ismail Cem, among others.)

In January 2005 Baykal's presidency was challenged at a highly explosive CHP party congress by Mustafa SARIGÜL, the popular mayor of the İstanbul district of Şişli, who eventually lost his bid but vowed to continue his opposition. A few pro-Sarigül legislators left the party following the congress to join the SHP (see below). By mid-2005, rifts had developed within the party, resulting in the resignations of numerous dissidents (including legislators).The losses were reflected in the decline in the CHP's legislative seats, down to 154 by mid-2005.

The CHP spearheaded secularist reaction against the candidacy of Abdullah Gül, culminating in several large "Republican Demonstrations" in spring 2007. The party was consequently accused of swapping its leftist identity for a nationalist platform and identifying itself with the military establishment. On June 8, 2007, the Party of Liberty and Change (*Hürriyet ve Değişim Partisi*—HÜRPARTI) decided to merge into the CHP, and its leader Yaşar OKUYAN declared that he would not be a CHP candidate.

On the eve of the 2007 parliamentary elections, the party struck an alliance with the Democratic Left Party (*Demokratik Sol Parti*—DSP), and 13 members of that party ran under the CHP ticket. The party received 20.85 percent of the vote and 112 seats, which dropped to 99 when the 13 members withdrew from the CHP parliamentary group. In the aftermath of the elections, observers and party rank-and-file members expressed concerns about the CHP's future under Baykal's leadership.

The CHP continued its opposition by appealing to the Constitutional Court against AKP parliamentary decisions, such as the proposed constitutional amendment to allow women to wear headscarves in universities. CHP's identification with the most radical elements of the bureaucracy was revealed in its fierce opposition to the "Ergenekon" investigations, which it saw as an AKP ploy to rout political opponents.

In the March 2009 municipal elections, the CHP won 23.12 percent of the vote and the municipality of Izmir.

Leaders: Deniz BAYKAL (President), Önder SAV (Secretary General).

Nationalist Action Party (*Milliyetçi Hareket Partisi*—MHP). Until 1969 the ultranationalist MHP was known as the Republican Peasant Nation Party (*Cumhuriyetçi Köylü Millet Partisi*—CKMP), formed in 1948 by conservative dissidents from the old Democratic Party. Dissolved in 1953, the grouping reformed in 1954, merging with the Turkish Villager Party in 1961 and sustaining the secession of the Nation Party in 1962.

The MHP dissolved following the 1980 military coup; in 1983 its sympathizers regrouped as the Conservative Party (*Muhafazakar Parti*—MP), which then was renamed the Nationalist Labor Party (*Milliyetçi Çalişma Partisi*—MCP) in 1985. (The MHP rubric was reassumed in 1992.) The MHP's extremist youth wing, members of which were known as the Grey Wolves (*Bozkurtlar*), remained proscribed, although similar activities were reportedly carried out under semi-official youth clubs. Holding 17 legislative seats as of September 1995, the MHP's 8.18 percent vote share on December 24 was short of the 10 percent required for continued representation. However, it subsequently acquired 2 seats from defections.

Historic MHP leader Alparslan TÜRKEŞ died in 1997. Following the election of Devlet Bahçeli as the new MHP president, members close to Türkeş's son and wife left the party to form the ATP and UBP.

The MHP won surprising support in the election of April 1999, gathering 18 percent of the votes and gaining 129 assembly seats. Some analysts noted that the party's popular support faded during its years in the coalition government from 1999 to 2002. The MHP suffered a major electoral blow in November 2002, when it received only 8.3 percent of the vote and no legislative seats. Although Devlet Bahçeli initially announced he would step down from his leadership position after the election, he ran for and won the party's presidency again in October 2003.

The party benefited from rising nationalist sentiment, which was bolstered by the Iraq crisis and deteriorating EU-Turkey relations. In the 2007 parliamentary elections, the party won 14.29 percent of the vote and 71 seats.

The MHP supported the constitutional amendment proposed by the AKP to allow women to wear headscarves in universities. This enabled the swift passage of the amendment, which was later annulled by the Constitutional Court. While the party was less opposed to the AKP and avoided siding with the radical portion of the bureaucracy in its struggle against the AKP, it maintained a nationalist stance, notably in the country's disputes with Armenia and Cyprus. The MHP and CHP vehemently objected to President Gül's unofficial visit to Armenia in September 2008.

In the 2009 municipal elections, the MHP won 16 percent of the vote. This was perceived as a success, although hardly and indicator of the party's ability to become a major political contender.

Leaders: Devlet BAHÇELI (President), M. Cihan PAÇACI (Secretary General).

Other Legislative Parties:

Members of the following parties ran as independents or on the tickets of other parties but reasserted their party affiliations after election.

Democratic Left Party (*Demokratik Sol Parti*—DSP). Formation of the DSP, a center-left populist formation, was announced in March 1984 by Rahşan Ecevit, the wife of former prime minister Bülent Ecevit, who was barred from political activity prior to the constitutional referendum of September 1987. In the October 1991 election, the party attracted sufficient social democratic support to weaken the SHP (see below), although it won only seven seats. It recovered in the December 1995 balloting, winning 76 legislative seats with 14.6 percent of the vote. The DSP became a junior partner in a Mesut Yılmaz–led coalition government, which also included the DTP (below), on June 30, 1998. After the Yılmaz–led coalition government collapsed in November 1998, Ecevit formed on January 12, 1999, a minority government, that ruled the country until the early elections of April 18. The DSP became the largest party in that balloting with 22 percent of the votes and 136 seats, and Ecevit subsequently formed a DSP-MHP-ANAP coalition cabinet.

In 2002 rifts were reported in the party, and some prominent members resigned to form the YTP. The DSP suffered a major electoral defeat in November 2002, receiving only 1.2 percent of the vote and no legislative seats. Bülent Ecevit resigned as party leader and nominated Zeki Sezer, a former cabinet minister, to replace him. Sezer was elected at the party's congress in July 2004.

The DSP struck an electoral alliance with the CHP on May 18, 2005. Thirteen DSP members of parliament, including Sezer, were elected on the CHP ticket in the 2007 parliamentary balloting. These members withdrew from the CHP during the first parliamentary session to form an independent DSP parliamentary group.

On May 18. 2009, Masum Türker defeated Sezer to become party president. In the March 2009 municipal elections, the DP garnered 2.78 percent of the vote.

Leaders: Masum TÜRKER (President), Hasan ERÇELEBİ (Secretary General).

Democratic Society Party (*Demokratik Toplum Partisi*—DTP). Formerly known as the Democratic People's Party (*Demokratik Halk Partisi*—DEHAP), which was launched in January 1999 by former members of the People's Democracy Party (*Halkin Demokrasi Partisi*—HADEP), the pro-Kurdish DTP (not to be confused with the Democratic Turkey Party [DTP], above) was initiated by former legislators Leyla ZANA, Orhan DOĞAN, Hatip DİCLE, and Selim SADAK, who had joined the Democracy Party (*Demokrasi Partisi*—DEP) in 1994. The Turkish Grand National Assembly lifted the parliamentary immunity of these four Kurdish politicians, and they were arrested and jailed from 1994–2005. Based on concerns that the DEHAP would be banned by the Constitutional Court, the DTP was launched reportedly as a preemptive "successor" on November 9, 2005. Since then, all DEHAP mayors, members, and leaders have entered the DTP. While the DEHAP decided to dissolve itself in December 2005, the Constitutional Court continued to consider banning the party and started to address the case on July 13, 2006.

In an attempt to circumvent the 10 percent electoral threshold, which had prevented it from securing legislative representation in the past, the DTP decided to abstain from the July 22, 2007, elections and support party members who would formally resign their membership to run as independent candidates. Subsequently, 22 of these candidates were elected, and 20 of them formed the DTP parliamentary group in the first parliamentary session. The presence of DTP parliamentarians presented an opportunity to reconsider Turkey's Kurdish question.

On November 16, 2007, the chief prosecutor of the Court of Cassation sought to close the DTP because it was "a focal point of activities aiming to damage the independence of the state and the indivisible integrity of its territory and nation." (The case was seen as a harbinger of the case against the AKP [see, above]. A ruling had not been handed down as of July 2009.)

As the DTP failed to draw a clear line between itself and the PKK, a rift developed between PKK sympathizers and social-democrats, who opposed terrorism. The party succeeded in restoring its electoral strength in southeastern and eastern Turkey in the March 2009 municipal elections

Leaders: Ahmet TÜRK (President), Emine AYNA (Vice President).

Great Unity Party (*Buyük Birlik Partisi*—BBP). A nationalist Islamic grouping, the BBP was launched in 1993 by a member of dissident MCP parliamentarians prior to the reactivation of the MHP in 1992. The party, whose members are known as "Turkish-Islamic Idealists" (*Türk-Islam ülkücüleri*), returned 13 deputies on the ANAP ticket in the 1995 election but subsequently opted for separate parliamentary status. The BBP won only 1.5 percent of the votes in the general election of April 1999. In November 2002 the party received 1.1 percent of the vote and no legislative seats.

While the party did not present candidates in the 2007 parliamentary elections, its leader, Muhsin YAZICIOĞLU, ran as an independent in the district of Sivas and was elected. On March 25, 2009, Yazıcıoğlu was killed in a helicopter crash near the city of Kahramanmaraş; party president Yalçın Topçu was elected as his successor.

In the 2009 municipal elections, the BBP won 2.24 percent of the vote.

Leader: Yalçın TOPÇU.

Liberty and Solidarity Party (*Özgurlük ve Dayanışma Partisi*—ÖDP). Backed by many leftist intellectuals, feminists, and human rights activists, the ODP was launched after the December 1995 election as a broad alliance of various socialist factions together with elements of the once powerful Dev-Yol movement (see Extremist Groups, below). Some of the socialist groups, notably the United Socialist Party (*Birleşik Sosyalist Parti*—BSP), had contested the balloting as part of the HADEP bloc. The BSP had been formed as a merger of various socialist factions, including the Socialist Unity Party (*Sosyalist Birlik Partisi*—SBP), itself founded in February 1991 (and represented in the 1991–1995 assembly) as in large part successor to the United Communist Party of Turkey (*Türkiye Birleşik Komünist Partisi*—TBKP), led by Haydar KUTLU and Nihat SARGIN.

The TBKP had been formed in 1988 by a merger of the Communist Party of Turkey (*Türkiye Komünist Partisi*—TKP) and the Turkish Workers Party (*Türkiye İşçi Partisi*—TİP). Proscribed since 1925, the pro-Soviet TKP had long maintained its headquarters in Eastern Europe, staffed largely by exiles and refugees who left Turkey in the 1930s and 1940s. Although remaining illegal, its activities within Turkey revived in 1983, including the reported convening of its first congress in more than 50 years. The TİP, whose longtime leader, Behice BORAN, died in October 1987, had been formally dissolved in 1971 and again in 1980 but had endorsed the merger with TKP at a congress held on the first anniversary of Boran's death. Prior to the November 1987 election, the TKP and TİP general secretaries, Kutlu and Sargin, respectively, had returned to Turkey for the prospective merger but had been promptly arrested and imprisoned.

With the Constitutional Court subsequently confirming a ban on the TBKP in early 1990, former TBKP elements were prominent in the new ÖDP. The ÖDP fared poorly in the April 1999 elections, gaining less than 1 percent of the votes. Several constituent groups reportedly left the ÖDP in 2002. In November 2002 the party won 0.34 percent of the vote and no legislative seats.

In the July 22, 2007, elections, the party won 0.15 percent of the vote. However, ÖDP leader Ufuk URAS, in order to avoid the electoral threshold requirement, resigned from the party presidency in order to run as an independent. He was elected as a representative for Istanbul and was then reinstated in the party presidency. Due to its parliamentary representation, the ÖDP was able to attract more public attention and fulfill the role of a substantial social-democratic opposition party.

Growing discord between the party's liberal and socialist wings led to the resignation of Uras from the party and the formation of a new leftist liberal group. On June 22, 2009, Alper Taş was elected party president.

In the 2009 municipal elections, the ÖDP garnered 0.16 percent of the vote.

Leader: Alper TAŞ.

Other Parties that Participated in the 2007 Elections:

Democrat Party (*Demokrat Parti*—DP). Also known as the True Path Party (*Doğru Yol Partisi*—DYP), the center-right party was organized as a successor to the Grand Turkey Party (*Büyük Türkiye Partisi*—BTP), which was banned shortly after its formation in May 1983 because of links to the former Justice Party of Süleyman Demirel. The new group was permitted to participate in the local elections of March 1984 but won control in none of the provincial capitals. By early 1987, augmented by assemblymen of the recently dissolved Citizen Party (*Vatandaş Partisi*—VP), it had become the third-ranked party in the Grand National Assembly. The DYP remained in third place by winning 59 seats in the November 1987 balloting and became the plurality party, with 178 seats, in October 1991. In November it formed a coalition government under Demirel with the SHP (see below). A second DYP-SHP government was formed by the new DYP leader, Tansu Çiller, following Demirel's assumption of the presidency in May 1993. A new coalition was formed with the CHP in March 1995, following the latter's temporary absorption of the SHP. However, a CHP leadership change in September led to the party's withdrawal and the collapse of the Çiller government.

The DYP placed second in the December 1995 election (with 19.2 percent of the vote), eventually forming a coalition government with ANAP on March 12, 1996, that featured a "rotating" leadership under which the ANAP's Mesut Yılmaz became prime minister and Çiller was to return to the top post in January 1997. However, animosity between the DYP and ANAP leaders quickly resurfaced, with Çiller calling the prime minister a "sleaze ball" (for allegedly expediting press exposés of her questionable use of official funds as prime minister) and withdrawing the DYP's support for the coalition in late May. Overcoming its previous antipathy toward the RP, the DYP the following month entered a new coalition as junior partner of the Islamist party, with Çiller becoming deputy premier and foreign minister, pending a scheduled resumption of the premiership at the beginning of 1998. By mid-January 1997 a parliamentary inquiry had cleared the DYP leader of all corruption charges relating to her tenure as premier. After the DYP-RP coalition collapsed under emphatic pressure from the military and the secular political establishment in June 1997, the DYP remained in the opposition during the Yılmaz-led ANAP-DSP-DTP coalition. By backing CHP leader Deniz Baykal's proposal for a vote of no-confidence against the Yılmaz government, the DYP facilitated its collapse in November 1998. The DYP then gave outside support to Bülent Ecevit's minority government. DYP influence waned in the April 1999 elections, as it secured only 12 percent of the votes and 85 seats.

The DYP experienced a major electoral defeat in November 2002, receiving 9.5 percent of the vote and no legislative seats. This defeat prompted Tansu Çiller to resign following the election. With defections from other parties, the party had, by mid-2005, four legislative seats. In the run-up to the 2007 parliamentary elections, party leader Mehmet AĞAR announced an electoral alliance with the ANAP. Ağar and ANAP president Erkan Mumcu named their joint party the Democrat Party (*Demokrat Parti*—DP). However, the ANAP withdrew from the alliance after barely a month, and the DP ran in the elections on its own. The DP subsequently received 5.41 percent of the vote, 4.13 percent less than in the 2002 elections. This result led Ağar to resign from the presidency of the party and call for an extraordinary congress to elect a new leader.

The party maintained the rubric of the Democrat Party (*Demokrat Parti*—DP) and in 2008 elected Süleyman SOYLU as president. "Moral politics" and "moral democracy" were Soylu's guiding principles. Nonetheless, the party did not seem to attract significant political support. On May 16, 2009, the veteran politician Hüsamettin Cindoruk was elected party president.

In the 2009 municipal elections, the DP won 3.72 percent of the vote.

Leaders: Hüsamettin CİNDORUK (President), Mahtar MAHRAMLI (Secretary General).

Party of the People's Rise (*Halkin Yükselişi Partisi*—HYP). The centrist HYP was established in February 2005 by Yaşar Nuri ÖZTÜRK, a former scholar of Islamic theology who became popular because of his "reformist" and modernist interpretations of religion. Öztürk is a former CHP legislator who left his party in April 2004 to protest Deniz Baykal's leadership style. In the 2007 parliamentary elections, the HYP collected 0.5 percent of the vote.

Leaders: Yaşar Nuri ÖZTÜRK (President), Yücel AKSOY (Secretary General).

Communist Party of Turkey (*Türkiye Komünist Partisi*—TKP). The TKP was launched in November 2001 as a merger of the Party for Socialist Power (*Sosyalist Iktidar Partisi*—SIP) and the Communist Party (*Komünist Partisi*—KP). The SIP was a continuation of the banned Party of Socialist Turkey (*Sosyalist Türkiye Partisi*—STP). The hard-line Marxist-Leninist SIP contested the 1995 election under the HADEP rubric. It secured less than 1 percent of the vote in 1999. The TKP was formed in July 2000 by former SIP members. In November 2002 the party won 0.2 percent of the vote and no legislative seats.

During 2007 legislative balloting, the party won 0.22 percent of the vote.

In the 2009 municipal elections, the BTP received 0.18 percent of the vote.

Leaders: Aydemir GÜLER (President), Kemal OKUYAN (Vice President).

Felicity Party (*Saadet Partisi*—SP). The SP was formed in July 2001 by the traditionalist core of the Virtue Party (*Fazilet Partisi*—FP), which had been shut down by the constitutional court in June. The Virtue Party had been launched in February 1998, days before a constitutional court decision banned the Islamic-oriented Welfare Party, which was in the coalition government until June 18, 1997, on charges of undermining the secular foundations of the Turkish Republic.

The Welfare Party (*Refah Partisi*—RP) had been organized in 1983 by former members of the Islamic fundamentalist MSP. It participated in the 1984 local elections, winning one provincial capital. It failed to secure assembly representation in 1987.

Having absorbed Aydın MENDERES' faction of the Democrat Party (DP), the RP attained a plurality in the December 1995 election with 21.4 percent of the vote, but at that stage was unable to recruit allies for a government. However, the speedy collapse of an alternative administration brought the RP to office for the first time in June 1996, heading a coalition with the DYP. Under intense pressure from the military and secular political establishment, Prime Minister Necmettin ERBAKAN resigned on June 18, 1997, and the RP-DYP coalition failed. On February 22, 1998, the Constitutional Court banned the RP and barred some of its founders, including Erbakan, from political activity for five years. On March 6, 2002, Erbakan was sentenced to two years and four months in jail because he had embezzled more than $3 million from the fund of the banned RP. After several appeals, his sentence was converted to house arrest due to his ailing health.

Some 135 parliamentarians of the proscribed Welfare Party joined the FP, making it the main opposition party in the parliament. Although FP leaders denied their party was a successor to the RP, Turkey's secularists did not find the denial credible. The FP assumed the role of the main opposition party to both the Yılmaz-led ANAP-DSP-DTP coalition government that ended in November 1998 and to the Ecevit-led minority DSP government that was installed in January 1999. Although some analysts initially saw the FP as a likely winner of the general elections in April, the party secured only 15 percent of the votes and 111 seats. Recai Kutan was narrowly reelected as FP chair at the party congress in May 2000, fending off a challenge from a "reformist" wing led by Recep Tayyip Erdoğan (former mayor of Istanbul) and Abdullah

Gül, which then broke away to launch its own formation, the Justice and Development Party (*Adalet ve Kalkınma Partisi*—AKP) in August 2001, following the banning of the FP in June. Further weakened by legislative defections and a marked shift of popular support to the AKP (see above), FP received an electoral setback in November 2002, winning only 2.5 percent of the vote and no legislative seats. In 2007 the party failed to provide a credible Islamist alternative to the ruling AKP and won just 2.34 percent of the vote.

On August 19, 2008, President Gül pardoned Erbakan and lifted his house detention. While AKP officials defended the decision on humanitarian grounds, secularists again became concerned about links between the AKP leadership and Islamists.

In the 2009 municipal elections, the SP garnered 5.16 percent of the vote. This was seen as a remarkable recovery from the lows of the 2007 parliamentary elections, the increase being attributed to the party's new president.

Leaders: Numan KURTULMUŞ (President), Suat PAMUKÇU (Secretary General).

Young Party (*Genç Parti*—GP). A populist, nationalist party, the GP was founded in 2002 by the controversial magnate Cem UZAN, who took control of the tiny Rebirth Party (*Yeniden Doğuş Partisi*—YDP), renaming it about two months before the November 2002 elections. His family controlled the substantial Uzan Holding, which counted a bank (İmar Bankası), a media group (Star), and Telsim, Turkey's second biggest mobile phone operator, among its assets. In the November 4, 2002, elections, the GP won 7.25 percent of the vote but secured no seats due to the 10 percent electoral threshold. Meanwhile, corruption and fraud charges against the Uzan family culminated in a lawsuit against Uzan by Motorola and Nokia, which accused him of defaulting on more than $2.5 billion worth of loans they had provided to Telsim. İmar Bankası was taken over by Turkish banking regulatory authorities, amid family complaints that the government was persecuting their businesses to neutralize Cem Uzan's political popularity. While Uzan's father, Kemal Uzan, and brother, Hakan Uzan, escaped abroad to avoid arrest, Cem Uzan remained in Turkey because he had no apparent personal involvement in corruption and fraud activities. The GP maintained its overtly populist and nationalist stance in the 2007 election campaign and won 3.03 percent of the vote.

On September 9, 2008, Uzan was convicted of insulting Prime Minister Erdoğan in a speech he gave in 2003. He was ordered by the court to enter an "anger management program" and read five books on "self development."

Leaders: Cem UZAN (President), Mehmet Ali AKGÜL (Secretary General).

Independent Turkey Party (*Bağımsız Türkiye Partisi*—BTP). An Islamist nationalist party ideologically similar to the SP, the BTP emphasizes the threat that globalization, Europeanization, and Westernization pose to Turkey's sovereignty and culture. The party platform calls for Turkey's "real independence" from foreign domination in various contexts. In the elections of November 4, 2002, the party won 0.48 percent of the vote and no legislative seats.

In the 2007 parliamentary balloting, the BTP won, taking 0.51 percent of the vote. In the 2009 municipal elections, the BTP received 0.37 percent of the vote.

Leader: Haydar BAŞ.

Workers' Party (*İşçi Partisi*—IP). The Maoist-inspired IP, founded in 1992, is the successor of the Socialist Party (*Sosyalist Parti*—SP), which was launched in February 1988 as the first overtly socialist formation since the 1980 coup. The party called for Turkey's withdrawal from NATO and nationalization of the economy. The SP was deregistered by order of the Constitutional Court in June 1992, the IP securing less than 0.5 percent of the vote in 1995. Since 2000 the IP, self-described as "national leftist," has garnered public attention due to its staunchly nationalist and anti-EU stance.

In November 2002 the party received 0.5 percent of the vote and no legislative seats. In 2007 it received 0.36 percent of the vote. On March 21, 2008, Doğu Perinçek was arrested in connection with the "Ergenekon" investigation.

In the 2009 municipal elections, the IP garnered 0.27 percent of the vote.

Leader: Doğu PERİNÇEK.

Other minor parties that participated in the 2007 elections were: the **Labor Party** (*Emek Partisi*—EMEP), led by Abdullah Levent TÜZEL; **Liberal Democrat Party** (*Liberal Demokrat Parti*—LDP), a free-market grouping led by Cem TOKER; and **Party of Luminous Turkey** (*Aydınlık Türkiye Partisi*—ATP), led by Tuğrul TÜRKEŞ.

Other Parties:

Motherland Party (*Anavatan Partisi*—ANAP). The right-of-center ANAP supports the growth of private enterprise and closer links to the Islamic world as well as the EU. It won an absolute majority of assembly seats in 1983 and obtained control of municipal councils in 55 of the country's 67 provincial capitals during the local elections of March 1984. Its ranks having been augmented by most former deputies of the Free Democratic Party (*Hür Demokrat Parti*—HDP), which was formed by a number of independents in May 1986 but dissolved the following December, ANAP won a commanding majority of 292 seats in the election of November 1987. Following the poll, Prime Minister Özal announced that he would seek a merger of ANAP and the DYP to ensure a right-wing majority of sufficient magnitude to secure constitutional amendments without resort to referendums. However, the overture was rebuffed, with DYP leader Demirel describing Özal in September 1988 as an "incompetent man" who represented "a calamity for the nation."

Following Özal's inauguration to the technically nonpartisan post of president of the Republic in November 1989, Yıldırım AKBULUT was named prime minister and party president. Upon his ouster in June 1991 he was succeeded by former foreign minister Mesut Yılmaz. In the early legislative balloting of October 20 ANAP trailed the DYP by only 3 percentage points (24 to 27), but its representation plummeted to 115, leading to the collapse of the Yılmaz administration.

ANAP was runner-up to the RP with a 19.7 vote share in the legislative poll of December 24, 1995, although placing third in representation with a seat total of 132. After considerable delay, it entered into a coalition with the DYP whereby Yılmaz would serve as prime minister for the remainder of 1996, with former prime minister Çiller slated to succeed him for a two-year period on January 1, 1997. Yılmaz had less than three months as head of government, being forced to resign in early June after the DYP had withdrawn from the coalition. ANAP then went into opposition to an RP-DYP coalition, amid much acrimony with its erstwhile government partner. Yılmaz was appointed to form a new cabinet on June 20, 1997, following RP Prime Minister Erbakan's resignation under military pressure two days earlier. Yılmaz's ANAP-DSP-DTP coalition government lasted only five months, however, after which ANAP gave parliamentary support to the Ecevit-led DSP government.

At the elections of April 18, 1999, ANAP fared poorly, securing only 13 percent of the votes and 86 seats. Although the party became a junior partner in the subsequent Ecevit-led government, ANAP's image was subsequently tarnished by press allegations of corruption among some of its members.

ANAP suffered a major electoral defeat in November 2002 and received 5.1 percent of the vote and no legislative seats. Mesut Yılmaz resigned on November 4, 2002, and the party underwent a prolonged and deep crisis. Following the short-lived presidencies of Ali Talip Özdemir and Nesrin Nas, former AKP legislator and minister of Culture and Tourism, Erkan Mumcu became the party's president in April 2005. After being joined by legislators defecting from the AKP and the CHP, the party had, by mid-2005, 21 legislative seats.

In the run-up to the 2007 parliamentary elections, the party attempted to forge an electoral alliance with the True Path Party (*Doğru Yol Partisi*—DYP). However, serious disagreements over the possible candidacy of former ANAP leader Mesut Yilmaz resulted in the dissolution of the alliance in June. The party did not participate in the elections, and several members subsequently defected. The second consecutive failure of the party to win parliamentary representation challenged Mumcu's leadership and the future of the party. The party struggled to maintain its existence amid adverse political conditions in 2008. On October 26, M. Salih Uzun was elected party president.

In the 2009 municipal elections, the DP received just 0.76 percent of the vote.

Leaders: M. Salih UZUN (President), Muharrem DOĞAN (Secretary General).

Social-Democrat People's Party (*Sosyaldemokrat Halk Partisi*—SHP). Launched by former deputy prime minister Murat Karayalçın in hopes of reclaiming the historical legacy of an earlier formation with a similar name, the SHP did not contest the November 2002 elections. The SHP was later joined by former CHP legislators who had left the party in protest of Deniz Baykal's reelection as the president over challenger Mustafa Sarigül (see above, under CHP). With these additions, by mid-2005, the SHP had four legislative seats. After the failure of negotiations with the CHP and the DSP on forging a unified leftist electoral alliance for the 2007 parliamentary balloting, party leader Murat Karayalçın announced that the SHP would not participate in the election.

Leaders: Murat KARAYALÇIN (President), Ahmet Güryüz KETENCİ (Secretary General).

Turkey's Party (*Türkiye Partisi*—TP). Founded by former AKP minister Abdülatif Şener in May 2009, the party aimed to compete against the AKP in Turkey's center-right, advocating a more conciliatory approach on issues such as secularism.

Leader: Abdülatif ŞENER.

Other nonparliamentary centrist and rightist groups include the **Justice Party** (*Adalet Partisi*—AP), which claims to be the legitimate heir of the historic AP. The extreme-right-wing ATP (see Other Parties that Participated in the 2007 Elections, above), , reportedly competes to attract former MHP dissidents. Among other parties are **My Turkey Party** (*Türkiyem Partisi*), led by Durmuş Ali EKER; and the **Party of Land** (*Yurt Partisi*—YP), an ANAP breakaway formation led by former minister Sadettin TANTAN.

Minor Marxist formations include **Revolutionary Socialist Workers' Party** (*Devrimci Sosyalist İşçi Partisi*—DSİP), led by Doğan TARKAN and Ahmet YILDIRIM; the **Turkish Socialist Workers' Party** (*Türkiye Sosyalist İşçi Partisi*—TSİP), led by Mehmet SÜMBÜL; and the **Socialist Democracy Party** (*Sosyalist Demokrasi Partisi*—SDP), a breakaway formation from ÖDP (above), led by Filiz Koçali. In late 2001 another pro-Kurdish formation, the **Party of Rights and Liberties** (*Hakve Özgürlükler Partisi*—HAK-PAR) was launched by Abdülmelik FIRAT. Other minor center-left formations include the **Equality Party** (*Eşitlik Partisi*); the **Party for Independent Republic** (*Bağımsız Cumhuriyet Partisi*), led by former foreign minister Mümtaz SOYSAL; the **Social Democrat Party** (*Sosyal Demokrat Parti*); and the **Republican Democracy Party** (*Cumhuriyetçi Demokrasi Partisi*—CDP), led by Yekta Güngör ÖZDEN.

Extremist Groups:

Pre-1980 extremist and terrorist groups included the leftist **Revolutionary Path** (*Devrimci Yol*—Dev-Yol) and its more radical offshoot, the **Revolutionary Left** (Dev-Sol, below), both derived from the **Revolutionary Youth** (*Dev Genç*), which operated in the late 1960s and early 1970s; some of its members also joined the far leftist **Turkish People's Salvation Army** (*Türkiye Halk Kurtuluş Ordusu*—THKO). The **Turkish People's Liberation Party Front** (*Türkiye Halk Kurtuluş Partisi-Cephesi*—THKP-C), the **Turkish Workers' and Peasants' Liberation Army** (*Türkiye İşçi Köylü Kurtuluş Ordusu*—TİKKO, below), and the **Kurdistan Workers' Party** (PKK, below) all experienced numerous arrests—often leading to executions—of members. In addition, Armenian guerrilla units, composed almost entirely of nonnationals, variously operated as the Secret Army for the Liberation of Armenia (ASALA), including a so-called Orly Group; the Justice Commandos for the Armenian Genocide; the Pierre Gulmian Commando; the Levon Ekmekçiyan Suicide Commando; and the Armenian Revolutionary Army. The activities of many of these groups have subsided, notable exceptions being Dev-Sol and the PKK.

Revolutionary Left (*Devrimci Sol*—Dev-Sol). Organized in 1978, Dev-Sol appeared to have retained its organizational vitality after the 1980 crackdown, although many of its subsequent activities took the form of interfactional struggle. Its founder, Dursun KARATAŞ, who had been given a death sentence in absentia that was later commuted to life imprisonment, was arrested by French authorities on September 9, 1994; subsequently, the group claimed responsibility for the murder on September 29 of a hard-line former justice minister, Mehmet TOPAÇ.

In 1993 or earlier Dev-Sol apparently split into two factions, the "Karataş" and the "Yağan" wings, with the former emerging in March 1994 as the **Revolutionary People's Liberation Party-Front** (*Devrimci Halk Kurtuluş Partisi-Cephesi*—DHKP-C). Violent clashes between the two factions have been reported in a number of European countries, and in August 1998 Germany banned both. DHKP-C militants were active in organizing the hunger strikes and prison riots since December 2000.

Other extreme left groupings include the **Communist Party of Turkey-Marxist Leninist** (*Türkiye Komünist Partisi-Marksist-Leninist*—TKP-ML) and its armed wing, the **Turkish Workers' and Peasants' Liberation Army** (*Türkiye İşçi Köylü Kurtuluş Ordusu*—TİKKO), which claimed responsibility for an attack on a police bus in İstanbul in December 2000 in retaliation for government action to break the prison hunger strikes; and the **Communist Labor Party of Turkey-Leninist** (*Türkiye Komünist Emek Partisi-Leninist*—TKEP-L).

Kurdistan Workers' Party (*Partîya Karkerén Kurdistan*—PKK). Founded in 1978, the PKK, under the leadership of Abdullah (Apo) Öcalan, was for a long time based principally in Lebanon's Bekaa Valley and northern Iraq. In southeast Anatolia, where it continues to maintain a presence, the party's 1992 call for a general uprising on March 21, the Kurdish New Year (Nevruz), was generally unheeded. Subsequently, a unilateral cease-fire declared by Öcalan under pressure from northern Iraq Kurdish leaders proved short-lived, and PKK terrorism re-escalated. In late July 1994 Turkish warplanes reportedly completely destroyed a PKK base in northern Iraq, and in mid-August a London court convicted three separatists of a number of attacks on Turkish property in the United Kingdom. Öcalan thereupon reiterated his call for a cease-fire as a prelude to the adoption of constitutional reforms that would acknowledge the "Kurdish identity." The government again failed to respond and in September charged the PKK with responsibility for the killing of a number of Turkish teachers in the southeastern province of Tunceli. Government military offensives against the Kurdish insurgents in 1995–1996 were combined with efforts to eradicate the PKK party organization.

Through 1997 and 1998 extensive Turkish military operations seriously undermined the PKK's ground forces. On April 13, 1998, the PKK's second-highest ranking commander, Şemdin SAKIK, who had left the organization a month earlier, was captured in northern Iraq by Turkish security forces. A more significant blow to the organization came with the arrest of party chair Öcalan by Turkish commandos in Nairobi, Kenya (see Foreign relations, above), in February 1999. The commander of the PKK's armed wing, the People's Liberation Army of Kurdistan (ARGK), Cemil BAYIK, had reportedly threatened Turkish authorities and foreign tourists on March 15, claiming that the whole of Anatolia "is now a battlefield." Some sources also reported a leadership struggle between Bayik and Abdullah Öcalan's brother, Osman ÖCALAN.

From February to July 1999 Kurdish militants engaged in various attacks, including suicide bombings, in response to their leader's arrest. A State Security Court accused Öcalan of being responsible for 30,000 deaths between 1984–1999. He was found guilty of treason and sentenced to death on June 29. During his defense, Öcalan argued that he could "stop the war" if the Turkish state would let him "work for peace" and spare his life. He apologized for the "sufferings PKK's actions may have caused," claiming that the "armed struggle had fulfilled its aims" and that the PKK would now "work for a democratic Turkey, where Kurds will enjoy cultural and linguistic rights." On August 2, Öcalan called on his organization to stop fighting and leave Turkish territory starting September 1. The PKK's "Presidential Council" quickly announced that it would follow its leader's commands, and during the PKK's congress in February 2000, it was announced that the party's political and armed wings would merge into a front organization called the People's Democratic Union of Kurdistan. Some analysts argued that the decision was in line with the PKK's decision to stop its armed struggle and seek Kurdish political and cultural rights within the framework of Turkey's integration with the European Union.

In 2001 a small group of renegade PKK members launched the Kurdistan Workers' Party-Revolutionary Line Fighters (*Partîya Karkarén Kurdistan-Devrimci Çizgi Savaşçıları*—PKK-DÇS) with the expressed aim to continue the armed struggle. In April 2002 the PKK decided to dissolve itself (announcing it had fulfilled its "historical mission") to launch a new organization called the Kurdistan Freedom and Democracy Congress (*Kongreya Azadî û Demokrasiya Kurdistan*—KADEK). The KADEK claimed to be against armed struggle, to have rejected fighting for an independent Kurdish homeland, and to have espoused a "political" line to press for cultural and linguistic rights for

Turkey's Kurds as "full and equal members under a democratic and united Turkey." However, in May the EU announced it still considered the PKK a "terrorist organization." The Turkish government continued to claim that the PKK's transformation into KADEK was a "tactical ploy."

In September 2003, KADEK was restyled as the Peoples' Congress of Kurdistan (*Kongra Gelê Kurdistan*—Kongra-Gel). Several high-level defections occurred in the ranks, including that of Osman Öcalan, who reportedly joined a splinter group, the Democratic Solution Party of Kurdistan (*Partiya Welatparézén Demokratén Kurdistan*—PWDK) that was established in April 2004. In June 2004, Kongra-Gel announced that the cease-fire declared by Abdullah Öcalan in September 1999 was not respected by the Republic of Turkey and that they would return to "legitimate armed defense" to counter military operations against their "units." In April 2005 it was announced that PKK was reconstituted and the new formation was styled as the PKK–Kongra-Gel. Since the announcement, numerous sporadic clashes have been reported between the Turkish security forces and PKK–Kongra-Gel's armed wing, People's Defense Forces (*Hezen Parastina Gel*—HPG).

Since March 2005, a hitherto unknown group called "Kurdistan Freedom Falcons" (*Teyrêbazên Azadiya Kurdistan*—TAK) has taken responsibility for numerous car bomb explosions and other urban terrorist acts. Although some press reports claimed that TAK was one among many breakaway wings of PKK–Kongra-Gel, the organization quickly denounced any links with the group.

In 2007 there was a considerable rise in PKK activity (see Current issues, above), with numerous Turkish security staff and PKK members killed. On October 22, a Turkish military patrol was ambushed near Dağlıca by some 200 PKK militants. Twelve Turkish soldiers were killed, 16 were wounded, and 8 were taken hostage by PKK insurgents. A DTP committee negotiated their release on November 4. However, the released soldiers were prosecuted following their return to Turkey because of their failure to obey orders that would have prevented their capture. The Dağlıca incident was the largest PKK military attack on Turkish territory in many years, shocking the Turkish public.

Following reports of rifts within the PKK, Turkish forces invaded northern Iraq on February 21, 2008, attacking a PKK outpost and headquarters. Turkish troops withdrew eight days later. In July two bombs exploded in the Istanbul suburb of Gungören, killing 17 people and wounding more than 100. While the authorities accused the PKK of having been behind the attack, the evidence apparently was inconclusive. Investigation of the "Ergenekon" affair also led to speculation about possible links between the PKK and "Ergenekon."

In May 2009, in a newspaper interview, Murat Karayılan indicated that the PKK was attempting to convey a conciliatory message. He said that the PKK had changed and was pursuing the promotion of Kurdish rights in Turkey without aiming to disrupt the unitary Turkish state. Further, he declared his readiness for armistice and dialogue with Turkey. Karayilan stressed that the solution he envisioned did not necessarily entail a federation, but greater local autonomy in accordance with a reform of the local authorities' law. The publication of this interview and other statements by Karayılan in international media raised hopes among many observers about a breakthrough in Turkey's Kurdish issue.

Leaders: Abdullah ÖCALAN (Honorary President), Zübeyir AYDAR (President), Murat KARAYILAN (Chair of the Executive Council).

On January 17, 2000, Hüseyin VELİOĞLU, reportedly a leader of the **Party of God** (*Hizbullah,* a militant Islamist Sunni group unrelated to the Lebanon-based Shiite *Hezbollah*) was killed and two of his associates were arrested in a shoot-out with police in İstanbul. The event brought attention to the group, which was believed to have been particularly active in southeast Anatolia in the early 1990s, when *Hizbullah* had reportedly launched a campaign of violence against PKK militants and pro-Kurdish lawyers, intellectuals, and human rights activists. Some unconfirmed press reports claimed that the group members were tolerated if not encouraged by the state security forces, which allegedly explained the fact that none of its members were caught until the shoot-out. During the months of January and February 2000, police arrested over 400 alleged members of *Hizbullah,* some reportedly civil servants. State security forces also found several safe-houses of the group, where they reportedly recovered mutilated bodies of dozens of victims, including famous moderate Islamic feminist Gonca KURİŞ, who was kidnapped in July 1998.

On May 7, 2000, Turkish authorities announced that they had apprehended those responsible for the murder of the former foreign minister and secularist professor, Ahmet Taner Kışlalı, killed on October 21, 1999. Turkish police claimed that those arrested were members of a hitherto unknown militant Islamist group, **Unity** (*Tevhid*), and were also responsible for the murders several years ago of famous leftist newspaper columnist Uğur Mumcu and academician Bahriye Üçok.

Following the arrest of PKK leader Abdullah Öcalan in February 1999, a shadowy far-right group, **Turkish Avenger Brigade** (*Türk İntikam Tugayı*—TİT), issued death threats against pro-Kurdish activists and politicians and claimed responsibility for attacks on various HADEP buildings. Some unconfirmed reports suggest that the group is merely a facade for occasional "agent-provocateur" activities allegedly linked to factions within the Turkish security forces. Similar activities resurfaced with the rise of nationalist sentiment after 2004. On June 13, 2007, in a shanty house in the Istanbul neighborhood of Ümraniye, police discovered large quantities of explosives, hand grenades, and other ammunition, which were allegedly intended for use in terrorist attacks against minorities and liberal Turks. The discovery marked the unraveling of the "Ergenekon" affair. The subsequent investigation sought links with the aforementioned attacks.

LEGISLATURE

The 1982 constitution replaced the former bicameral legislature with a unicameral 550-member **Turkish Grand National Assembly** (*Türkiye Büyük Millet Meclisi*) elected for a five-year term on a proportional basis (10 percent threshold).

Following the election of July 22, 2007, the seat distribution was as follows: Justice and Development Party, 341; Republican People's Party, 112; Nationalist Action Party, 71; and independents, 26. Members of the Democratic Society Party, Democratic Left Party, Liberty and Solidarity Party, and Great Unity Party ran as independents or on the tickets of other parties but reasserted their party affiliations following the assembly's first session.

Speaker: Köksal TOPTAN.

CABINET

[as of July 1, 2009]

Prime Minister	Recep Tayyip Erdoğan
Deputy Prime Ministers and State Ministers	Bülent Arınç
	Ali Babacan
	Cemil Çiçek
	Egemen Bağış
State Ministers	Mehmet Aydın
	Mehmet Zafer Çaplayan
	Faruk Çelik
	Selma Aliye Kavaf [f]
	Faruk Nafız Özak
	Hayati Yazıcı
	Cevdet Yılmaz
Ministers	
Agriculture and Village Affairs	Mehmet Mehdi Eker
Culture and Tourism	Ertuğrul Günay
Energy and Natural Resources	Taner Yıldız
Environment and Forestry	Veysel Eroğlu
Finance	Mehmet Şimşek
Foreign Affairs	Ahmet Davutoğlu
Health	Recep Akdağ
Industry and Trade	Nihat Ergün
Interior	Beşir Atalay
Justice	Sadullah Ergin

Labor and Social Security	Ömer Dinçer
National Defense	Mehmet Vecdi Gönül
National Education	Nimet Çubukçu [f]
Public Works and Housing	Mustafa Demir
Transport	Binali Yıldırım

[f] = female

Note: All ministers are members of the Justice and Development Party (AKP).

COMMUNICATIONS

Formal censorship of the media in regard to security matters was imposed in late 1979 and was expanded under the military regime installed in September 1980. A new press law promulgated in November 1982 gave public prosecutors the right to confiscate any publication prior to sale, permitted the government to ban foreign publications deemed to be "a danger to the unity of the country," and made journalists and publishers liable for the issuance of "subversive" material. However, freedom of the press was largely restored in the first half of the 1990s. On July 21, 1997, the Council of Ministers accepted a draft granting amnesty to imprisoned journalists. Under current law, however, journalists still face prosecution and imprisonment for reporting on issues deemed sensitive by the government. Article 301 of the Turkish Penal Code, which punishes those who "publicly denigrate Turkishness or the Republic of Turkey," has been repeatedly invoked to allow persecution of journalists and intellectuals who express opinions contrary to official Turkish views on a number of political issues, such as the Armenian question. Hrant Dink and Orhan Pamuk were targeted based on the code.

Concerns were raised in April 2008 over apparent government involvement in efforts to promote concentration of media ownership. Financial support of state banks to progovernment entrepreneurs to facilitate the purchase of the Sabah media group was seen as an overt government attempt to strengthen its grip over media.

The government's long-standing feud with the country's biggest media conglomerate, Dogan Media Group (*Doğan Medya Grubu*), attracted international attention following the levying of a $500 million tax fine against the group in February 2009.

Press. The following are dailies published in İstanbul: *Zaman* (Time, 781,507), conservative; *Posta* (Post, 527,084), populist; *Hürriyet* (Freedom, 465,008), nationalist centrist; *Sabah* (Morning, 345,739), centrist; *Habertürk* (Newsturk, 240,088), nationalist centrist; *Pas Fotomaç* (Pass Photomatch, 232,412), sports; *Fanatik* (Fanatic, 210,959), sports; *Vatan* (Homeland, 185,057), centrist; *Milliyet* (Nation, 175,986), centrist; *Takvim* (Calendar, 152,521), populist; *Akşam* (Evening, 147,543), conservative; *Türkiye* (Turkey, 141,287), conservative; *Sözcü* (Speaker, 127,785); nationalist sensationalist; *Güneş* (Sun, 122,593), populist; *Yeni Şafak* (New Dawn, 104,704), moderate religious, pro-AKP; *Star* (101,039), populist; *Cumhuriyet* (Republic, 60,132), nationalist secularist; *Taraf* (Side, 58,725), liberal; *Şok* (Shock, 53,125), sensationalist; *Anadolu'da Vakit* (Time in Anatolia, 52,307), radical-religious; *Efsane Fotospor* (Legend Photosport, 52,163), sports; *Yeniçağ* (New Era, 51,342), far-right nationalist; *Bugün* (Today, 50,784), conservative; *Milli Gazete* (National Newspaper, 50,015), conservative-religious, pro-SP; *Fotogol* (Photogoal, 48,9347), sports; *Radikal* (Radical, 37,938), liberal; *Yeni Asır* (New Era, 37,205), nationalist; *Halka ve Olaylara Tercüman* (Interpreter to the People and Events, 13,575), conservative; *Referans* (Reference, 11,567), finance and economics; *Yeni Asya* (New Asia, 6,643), conservative-religious; *Ortadoğu* (Middle East, 6,350), far-right, pro-MHP; *Günluk Evrensel* (Daily Global, 5,480), far-left,; *Birgün* (One Day, 5,362), left-wing; *Yeni Mesaj* (New Message, 5,388), far-right, pro-MHP; *Dünya* (World, 2,581), finance and economics; *Hürses* (Free Voice, 2,177), finance and economics.

Non-Turkish-language publications include *Jamanak* (Times) and *Nor Marmara* (New Marmara), dailies in Armenian; *Agos* (Furrow), weekly in Turkish and Armenian; *Hürriyet Daily News* (5,977), *Today's Zaman* (4,676) and *The New Anatolian*, dailies in English; *Apogevmatini* (Evening Paper) and *Iho* (Echo), dailies in Greek; *Azadiya Welat* (Free Country), bimonthly, and *Zend* (Commentary), monthly, in Kurdish; and *Şalom* (Peace), Sephardic weekly in Judeo-Spanish and Turkish.

News agencies. The leading news source is the government-owned *Anadolu Ajansı* (Anatolian News Agency—AA) followed by *İhlas Haber Ajansı* (Ihlas News Agency—İHA) and *Doğan Haber Ajansı* (Doğan News Agency—DHA). Virtually all of the leading international agencies maintain Ankara bureaus.

Broadcasting and computing. The state-controlled Turkish Radio Television Corporation (*Türkiye Radyo Televizyon Kurumu*—TRT) currently offers domestic service over several radio networks and television channels. In April 1992 a TRT International Channel (Avrasya) began broadcasting via satellite to an area from Germany to Central Asia, earning third place in international transmission after CNN International and BBC International. In July 1993 a constitutional amendment formally abolished the state broadcast monopoly. In 1994 a Higher Council of Radio and Television (*Radyo Televizyon Üst Kurulu*—RTÜK) was established to oversee all radio and television emissions and programming. The appointed body reports to the prime minister and has the authority to license and shut down radio and television stations for up to a year on the grounds of such offenses as libel and the transmission of "offensive" or "hate-inciting" programs. The council has closed down numerous radio and television stations since its inception and has been widely criticized for using vague criteria that reportedly amount to censorship. Apart from five state television channels (TRT-1, TRT-2, TRT-3, TRT-INT, TRT-AVRASYA), the most popular private television channels include KANAL D, SHOW TV, ATV, STAR, STV, KANAL7, FOX, NTV and CNN-TÜRK. As of 2008 there were 343.7 Internet users per 1,000 inhabitants.

INTERGOVERNMENTAL REPRESENTATION

Ambassador to the U.S.: Nabi ŞENSOY.

U.S. Ambassador to Turkey: James JEFFREY.

Permanent Representative to the UN: Ertuğrul APAKAN.

IGO Memberships (Non-UN): ADB, AfDB, BIS, BSEC, CEUR, EBRD, ECO, Eurocontrol, G-20, IDB, IEA, Interpol, IOM, NATO, OECD, OIC, OSCE, PCA, WCO, *WEU*, WTO.

TURKMENISTAN

Republic of Turkmenistan
Tiurkmenostan Respublikasy

Political Status: Turkmenian districts of former Bukhara and Khorezm republics added to autonomous Turkistan Soviet Socialist Republic within the Russian Soviet Federative Socialist Republic on October 27, 1924; became constituent republic of the Union of Soviet Socialist Republics (USSR) on May 12, 1925; declared independence as Republic of Turkmenistan on October 27, 1991; new constitution adopted May 18, 1992; present constitution adopted September 26, 2008.

Area: 188,456 sq. mi. (488,100 sq. km.).

Population: 4,483,251 (1995C); 5,032,000 (2008E).

Major Urban Center (2005E): ASHGABAT (Ashkhabad, 559,000).

Official Language: Turkmen.

Monetary Unit: Manat (official rate December 1, 2009: 14,215.00 manats = $1US).

President and Prime Minister: Gurbanguly BERDIMUHAMMEDOV (Democratic Party of Turkmenistan); elevated from deputy prime minister to acting president and prime minister on December 21, 2006, following the death of Gen. Saparmurad Atayevich NIYAZOV (Saparmyrat NYYAZOW; Democratic Party of Turkmenistan); elected president February 11, 2007, and sworn in February 14.

THE COUNTRY

The southernmost republic of the former Soviet Union, Turkmenistan is bordered on the northwest by Kazakhstan, on the north and northeast by Uzbekistan, on the southeast by Afghanistan, on the south by Iran, and on the west by the Caspian Sea. The Kara Kum (Garagum) Desert occupies about 80 percent of the land area. Ethnic Turkmens, who are predominantly Sunni Muslims, account for approximately 77 percent of the population, followed by Uzbeks (9 percent), Russians (7 percent), and Kazakhs (2 percent). Women constitute about 46 percent of the labor force.

Agriculture employs about 43 percent of workers but in recent years dropped from contributing more than a fifth of GDP down to 8 percent in 2008. A principal component of the country's irrigation network is a 500-mile canal that carries water from the Amu-Darya (Oxus) River, a major tributary of the Aral Sea. (The diversion has contributed to an ecological catastrophe that some have compared to the Chernobyl nuclear disaster.) Only about 4 percent of the country is arable land, and half of that land is planted with cotton. Turkmenistan normally ranks second only to Uzbekistan in regional cotton production, although output of the crop has fallen dramatically since the Soviet era. As recently as 2000 processed cotton fiber accounted for 9 percent of export earnings, but since then output has fallen further. The chief crop for domestic consumption is wheat; high-quality Persian lambs are among the country's important livestock.

Industry, which contributed about 51 percent of GDP in the first half of 2008 and employs about 12 percent of the active labor force, is dominated by hydrocarbons. Some estimates rank Turkmenistan's proven and potential natural gas reserves as the world's fourth largest. Natural gas accounts for over half of export earnings, with petrochemicals and other oil products adding another 30 percent.

The breakup of the Soviet Union caused a dramatic decline in Turkmenistan's GDP, which, according to the World Bank, declined by 30 percent in 1993–1995, 3 percent in 1996, and another 26 percent in 1997, when overall export earnings dropped by 55 percent because of regional disputes, primarily with Russia (see Foreign relations, below). During the same period, Turkmenistan experienced rampant inflation, which peaked at 1,800 percent in 1994 before declining to roughly 25 percent in 1997. Since 1998, however, growth has been constant.

The government reported a rate of expansion in excess of 10 percent each year from 1999 through 2004, including a peak of 17 percent in 2003. Reported growth remained high, at 7 percent in 2008, according to International Monetary Fund (IMF) estimates. Exports increased by 15 percent per year from 2005 to 2007, largely because of higher international oil and gas prices. Nearly half the population lives in poverty, although this is mitigated by access to free housing and utilities plus high subsidies for key foods. Despite international pressure, Turkmenistan has approached market reforms reluctantly. In 2008 the new government initiated limited economic reforms, including the redomination of the currency, reductions in state subsidies, and new incentives for foreign investment. A new natural gas pipeline to China, expected to open in late 2009, is expected to further increase GDP (see Foreign relations, below). In its 2008 corruption listing, Transparency International placed Turkmenistan among the most corrupt countries in the world and tied it with Uzbekistan and Kyrgyzstan for most corrupt country of Central Asia. Corruption remains one of the main impediments to foreign investment.

GOVERNMENT AND POLITICS

Political background. Historic Turkestan occupied a vast area extending from the Caspian Sea in the west to the border of China in the east, and from the Aral Sea watershed in the north to Persia (Iran) and Afghanistan in the south. In 1924 what had been an autonomous republic of the Russian Soviet Federative Socialist Republic was split into (western) Turkmen and (eastern) Uzbek components, both of which became constituent republics of the USSR in 1925.

Following republican elections on January 7, 1990, Saparmurad NIYAZOV, the first secretary of the Turkmen Communist Party (TCP), was named chair of the Supreme Soviet (head of state). On August 23 the Supreme Soviet issued a declaration of Turkmenistan's "independent statehood," on the basis of which the adjectives "Soviet" and "Socialist" were dropped from the republic's official name and the Turkmen constitution and laws were assigned precedence over those of the Soviet Union. In a somewhat unusual move, the declaration identified Turkmenistan as a nuclear and chemical weapons–free zone. On October 27 Niyazov was unopposed in direct election to the new post of executive president.

In April 1991 Turkmenistan overwhelmingly endorsed USSR president Mikhail Gorbachev's abortive union treaty. Four months later, with democratic activists reportedly being arrested for charging that Niyazov had supported the failed hard-liners' coup in Moscow, the president broke with the leaders of most fellow republics by not dismantling the Communist Party. Nevertheless, a referendum on independence was conducted on October 26 that yielded a 93.5 percent affirmative vote, and an implementing declaration was issued by the Supreme Soviet the following day. On December 16 the TCP was formally dissolved and immediately succeeded by the Democratic Party of Turkmenistan (DPT), which abandoned the Marxist-Leninist precepts of its predecessor while maintaining an absolute grip on power. On December 21 Turkmenistan joined the Commonwealth of Independent States (CIS).

The Supreme Soviet approved a new constitution on May 18, 1992, and on June 26 Niyazov was reinvested as president after an election five days earlier in which he was again the sole candidate. On January 15, 1994, a reported 99.5 percent of voters favored exempting the president from having to stand for an additional term, while in elections to the lower house of the new legislature, held on December 11, only 1 of 50 seats was contested, with most of the returned candidates being DPT nominees.

The first evidence of popular unrest came in July 1995 when demonstrators in Ashgabat called for new presidential elections and an end to economic hardship and shortages. Authorities swiftly removed the demonstrators, and a number of political opponents subsequently were detained in prisons or psychiatric facilities. In 1996 Turkmenistan drew criticism from the Organization for Security and Cooperation in Europe (OSCE) and other international groups for being the least politically "reconstructed" of the former Soviet republics, with no opposition parties being officially registered and dissenting political expression being effectively outlawed.

In mid-April 1998, at the urging of a visiting OSCE delegation, President Niyazov released several detainees incarcerated in connection with the July 1995 antigovernment demonstration. They included Durdymurat KHOJAMUKHAMMED, a leader of the opposition Democratic Progress Party (DPP), who had been held in a psychiatric hospital since 1996. Within days, however, exiled opposition leader and former foreign minister Avde KULIEV, having returned from Moscow, was placed under house arrest on charges that included extortion and trying to organize a coup in 1995. Kuliev was released on April 20, and he returned to Moscow on April 22. On the very same day, President Niyazov, fielding questions at the start of an official visit to the United States, denied that Turkmenistan held any political prisoners.

In December 1999 the OSCE refused to monitor the Assembly election, noting that "the legislative framework is inadequate for even a minimally democratic election." Virtually all of the 100-plus candidates were DPT nominees who had been approved by Niyazov. On December 28, as proposed by the People's Council, the newly convened Assembly amended the constitution to permit Niyazov the option of a lifetime tenure as president.

In early November 2001 it was reported that the government had issued an arrest warrant for Boris SHIKHMURADOV, a former Western-oriented foreign minister who had most recently served as ambassador to China and was then in Russia. In addition to denying allegations that he had appropriated $25 million in state property, chiefly aircraft and armaments, and then sold them, Shikhmuradov responded by announcing that he was forming an opposition group, subsequently identified as the People's Democratic Movement of Turkmenistan (PDMT), to help depose Niyazov. Subsequent rumors of a pending coup were given credence by a major shake-up of the defense and security establishment that began in March 2002 and continued into May. Those dismissed from the government included the ministers of defense and interior and the head of the National Security Committee.

On November 25, 2002, gunmen fired on a presidential motorcade. Niyazov, who was uninjured, immediately attributed the attack to a number of former government officials who had aligned with Shikhmuradov, including former deputy prime minister Khudayberdy ORAZOV and the recently resigned ambassador to Turkey, Nurmuhammet HANAMOW (Nurmukhammed KHANAMOV), who subsequently emerged as a leader of the exiled opposition. A month later Shikhmuradov, who had secretly returned to Turkmenistan, announced on an opposition Web site that he intended to surrender to authorities in an effort to prevent further persecution of government opponents. By then, over 100 individuals had reportedly been taken into custody. Within days, Shikhmuradov was arrested, tried, convicted, and sentenced to life in prison. (In a taped confession Shikhmuradov admitted stealing state property, hiring mercenaries to assassinate the president, orchestrating a coup, using illegal drugs, and various other offenses. Professing rediscovered admiration for Niyazov, Shikhmuradov praised the president as "a gift from on high to the people of Turkmenistan.") By February 2003 more than 50 individuals had been convicted of involvement in the November plot.

The Assembly election of December 19, 2004, with runoff balloting on January 9, 2005, was once again conducted without international monitoring. All candidates were members of the DPT.

On December 21, 2006, President Niyazov died unexpectedly. Although the constitution specified that the speaker of the Assembly, Ovezgeldi ATAYEV, should serve as acting president pending the election of a successor, Atayev was relieved of his duties and charged with an unrelated criminal offense. (In February 2007 he was convicted of driving a prospective daughter-in-law to suicide.) As a result, the cabinet elevated Deputy Prime Minister Gurbanguly BERDIMUHAMMEDOV to the presidency. The following day, Akja NURBERDIYEWA was appointed acting speaker of the Assembly.

In an extraordinary session on December 26, the People's Council called a presidential election for February 2007 and amended the constitution, which had previously prohibited an acting president from seeking election to the presidency. The People's Council also endorsed Berdimuhammedov and five other presidential candidates, all from the DPT. In the February 11 election Berdimuhammedov was credited with 89 percent of the vote, and he was inaugurated on February 14.

Following constitutional reforms that expanded the size of the *Mejlis* (see Constitution and government, below), new elections were held on December 14 and 28, 2008, a year earlier than required by the constitution. All 125 members elected to the Assembly were members of the Democratic Party of Turkmenistan or propresidential independents. The balloting marked the first time that foreign monitors were present as observers, although international groups criticized the elections for irregularities and because no opposition parties contested the elections (see Current issues, below).

The cabinet was reshuffled on January 15, 2009, after the Assembly elections, with further minor alterations through the year.

Constitution and government. Under the 1992 constitution Turkmenistan is led by a popularly elected strong president (head of both state and government as well as commander-in-chief) whose powers include issuing laws, save those amending the constitution or revising the criminal code. He is also empowered to appoint judges and local government administrators, who have less authority than under the former system of soviets.

Up until 2003, the country's highest representative body, the People's Council (*Khalk Maslakhaty*), typically met once a year with a mandate that included consideration of basic economic, social, and political policy; constitutional changes; ratification of intergovernmental treaties; and declarations of war and peace. The smaller Assembly (*Mejlis*) was chiefly responsible for enacting ordinary legislation. At the initiative of the president, in August 2003 the People's Council was restructured as a "fourth branch" of government, a "permanently functioning supreme representative body of popular government having the powers of supreme state authority and government." The body's membership was expanded to 2,507, encompassing executive, judicial, and legislative members as well as representatives of regional, local, civic, labor, party, and other groups.

The 1992 basic law barred the hiring of non-Turkmenians in state enterprises and dropped Russian as an official language. It also guaranteed the right of private property, despite a presidential decree of May 1992 to the contrary, and fundamental human rights, including freedom of religion.

In September 2008, the People's Council unanimously approved a new constitution touted as a step toward democracy and free market. It included guarantees of property rights, endorsed market economic principles, and limited the presidential term to five years. It also granted the president the right to appoint the nation's electoral commission and select regional governors and mayors. Meanwhile, the Assembly was expanded from 50 to 125 members in December 2008 elections. It was also granted the power to censure the president and amend the constitution, and it was given most of the powers of the People's Council, which was subsequently abolished.

The country is divided into five administrative regions, or *velayaty* (Akhal, Balkan, Dashkhovuz, Lebap, and Mary), which are subdivided into districts (*etraps*), towns, and urban settlements.

Foreign relations. By early 1992 Turkmenistan had established diplomatic relations with a number of foreign countries, including the United States. On March 2 it joined the United Nations and on September 22 was admitted to the IMF and the World Bank. As a predominantly Muslim country, it also joined the Organization of the Islamic Conference. During a summit in Tehran, Iran, in February 1992, Turkmenistan, along with its sister republics of Azerbaijan, Kyrgyzstan, Tajikistan, and Uzbekistan, gained admission to the long-dormant Economic Cooperation Organization, which had been founded by Iran, Turkey, and Pakistan in 1963. It has also attended summits of the Turkic-speaking states and in 1995 joined the Nonaligned Movement. In 1994 Turkmenistan became the first Central Asian republic to join NATO's Partnership for Peace program.

With "permanent neutrality" mandated by the 1992 constitution, the government's geopolitical priorities have focused on economic matters, particularly market access for its massive hydrocarbon reserves. In 1994 a dispute with Russia over pricing and barter arrangements led Moscow to cut off Turkmenistan's access to the sole natural gas pipeline that reached its European customers. Thereafter, Turkmenistan interrupted deliveries to Armenia, Georgia, and Ukraine because of payment arrears, while in March 1997 Russia completely stopped the flow into the regional pipeline in retaliation for Turkmenistan's decision to dissolve the financially troubled joint venture the two countries had set up to export Turkmen gas.

In February 1998 Moscow and Ashgabat resolved their major disputes, and late in the year Turkmenistan and Ukraine agreed to resume sales that were, however, stopped again in May 1999 because of nonpayment. An October 2000 visit by Ukraine president Leonid Kuchma resolved the differences over payments arrears and future gas deliveries. Meanwhile, in December 1997 President Niyazov and new Iranian president Mohammad Khatami had inaugurated a 125-mile-long pipeline carrying comparatively small quantities of natural gas to Iran.

In late 1996 the government took a more conciliatory line than neighboring republics toward the overthrow of the Afghan government by the Taliban militia, in part because the Islamic group had reportedly approved plans for a gas pipeline to Pakistan. However, the U.S. corporate sponsor of the venture withdrew following U.S. attacks in August 1998 on Afghan guerrilla bases. Following the September 2001 al-Qaida attacks on the United States and the consequent U.S.-led invasion of Afghanistan, Turkmenistan opened land and air corridors for the delivery of humanitarian aid to the Afghan people, and Niyazov indicated his support for a UN-led effort against international terrorism. He denied U.S. forces access to military facilities, however, citing his country's commitment to neutrality, but he was not averse to accepting U.S. military aid for training and equipment. In 2005 and early 2006 Ashgabat and Washington repeatedly denied reports that they were negotiating U.S. access to the Mary air base.

The overthrow of the Taliban led to a May 2002 agreement with Pakistan and the interim Afghan government to conduct a new feasibility study for the pipeline project, which was approved in December 2002 at an initial projected cost of $2–3 billion.

In April 2006, during a visit to China, President Niyazov and Chinese officials approved a framework agreement for a 4,000-kilometer natural gas pipeline to China via Uzbekistan and Kazakhstan. Construction began in August 2007. Turkmenistan has also expressed interest in a possible Trans-Caspian pipeline route that would transit Azerbaijan and Georgia and then terminate in Turkey, thereby bypassing Russia and providing a new route to European customers. At present, Turkmenistan has no gas distribution system of its own, forcing it to rely on Russia's natural gas giant, Gazprom.

Another regional issue involves national claims to the Caspian. Russia, Azerbaijan, and Kazakhstan have negotiated bilateral agreements dividing the seabed into territorial sectors, but Iran and Turkmenistan have argued for a more comprehensive approach. The presidents of the five countries conferred in Ashgabat in April 2002 but without making significant progress. A joint task force continues to meet, but the basic issue remains unresolved. The most recent littoral summit took place in Baku, Azerbaijan, in September 2008.

In late March 2000 the presidents of Turkmenistan and Uzbekistan reportedly agreed to draft a pact that would demarcate their shared border and also provide a plan for joint use of the Amu-Darya River. Following the apparent attempt to assassinate President Niyazov in November 2002, relations with Uzbekistan worsened because of alleged Uzbek involvement, which Tashkent denied. In November 2004 President Niyazov met with Uzbek president Islam Karimov in Bukhara, Uzbekistan, where they signed a declaration of friendship and pledged closer cooperation in trade and a variety of other areas.

Relations between Turkmenistan and Russia deteriorated in 2009 following an explosion at one of the pipelines carrying Turkmen gas to Europe. The Turkmenistan government blamed Gazprom for the accident. In addition, a June Sino-Turkmen agreement expanded on the 2006 accord and obligated Turkmenistan to supply China with 40 billion cubic meters of gas each year for 30 years. The agreement further alienated Moscow, which sought to control the export of Turkmen energy through its existing distribution network. Relations between the EU and Turkmenistan were normalized in April, following years of strain over the country's human rights record. Concurrently, the EU Parliament approved a new trade agreement with Turkmenistan. In May Israel opened its first embassy in Turkmenistan in Ashgabat.

Current issues. Up until his death, Turkmenistan was under the absolute control of President Niyazov, who had adopted the title *Turkmenbashi* ("leader of the Turkmen people") and who had the epithet "the Great" routinely appended to his name in government press releases. The legislature repeatedly bestowed upon him the "Hero of Turkmenistan" award, innumerable streets and structures bear his name, statues in his honor abound, and he ordered the months of the year and days of the week renamed in honor of famous Turkmen, including his mother and himself. In addition to being the country's supreme political leader, he took on the mantle of cultural protector, banning, for example, car radios, ballet, opera, and the playing of recorded music at various functions, including weddings.

His successor, Gurbanguly Berdimuhammedov, a dentist by training and a former health minister, immediately began reversing some of Niyazov's policies, advocating, for example, opening the economy to greater foreign investment and calling for educational and social reform as well as restoring pension benefits that Niyazov had cut. To reassure Russia and Western Europe, he stated that Turkmenistan would honor all existing natural gas contracts. Rather than condemn the fundamentally undemocratic process by which Berdimuhammedov assumed the presidency, the United States and other Western countries chose to view the new president's pronouncements as positive steps that merited support, particularly given the potential for improved access to Turkmenistan's hydrocarbons.

In the fall of 2007, Berdimuhammedov visited Europe and the United States. The president's tour included a speaking engagement at Columbia University, where he dismissed questions about human rights. Meanwhile, Berdimuhammedov initiated the first of eight general amnesties for prisoners, including political detainees. More than 9,000 prisoners were set free through 2009.

Following the approval of a new constitution in 2008, President Berdimuhammedov characterized the revised document as an important step in implementing his government's "New Revival," the process of democratic, economic, and cultural reform in the name of "government for the people" launched by Berdimuhammedov in January 2008. Critics abroad called it a superficial gesture toward the West. In September a group took control of a water treatment plant in Ashgabat. More than 30 were killed when security forces stormed the facility. The government described those involved as members of a criminal gang, but opposition sources claimed the figures were antigovernment rebels. Although officially allowed to do so, no opposition parties registered by the November 14, 2008, deadline for the December 14 Assembly elections. In addition, the exiled Republican Party of Turkmenistan was officially forbidden from participation. The election allowed expatriates to vote for the first time with polling stations set up in the various diplomatic missions around the world.

In May 2009 Berdimuhammedov replaced the minister of internal affairs for the latter's failure to reduce crime and corruption. The new minister, Iskander MULIKOV, was tasked to undertake a broad campaign against bribery and organized crime. Elections were held on July 26, for 6,220 seats for local councils. All candidates were members of the DPT or pro-DPT independents and members of civic associations or groups.

POLITICAL PARTIES

The Turkmen political system is dominated by the Democratic Party of Turkmenistan (DPT), which was tightly controlled by President Niyazov. A **National Movement "Revival"** (*Galkynysh*), chaired by the president, is a government-sponsored association of various associations and the DPT. Although allowed by the 1992 constitution, opposition parties have never achieved legal standing, and most political opponents currently operate from exile in Russia, Scandinavia, and Eastern Europe.

Government Party:

Democratic Party of Turkmenistan (DPT). The DPT is the successor to the Turkmen Communist Party, which was dissolved on December 16, 1991, after its 25th congress had admitted to "mistakes" during seven decades of Soviet rule. The DPT describes itself as the country's "mother party" and has been virtually unchallenged as the leading political force in the country. President Berdimuhammedov was elected chair of the party in August 2007. Following the December 2008 elections to the expanded Assembly, Akja NURBERDIYEWA was reelected speaker of the chamber.

Leader: Gurbanguly BERDIMUHAMMEDOV (President of the Republic and Chair of the Party).

Unregistered Parties:

Peasants' Party. Created in 1993 by DPT rural cadres, the Peasants' Party was often cited by the government as a first step toward a multiparty system. Nevertheless, it was never officially registered.

Unity (*Agzybirlik*). Originally formed in 1989 as a cultural and environmental forum, *Agzybirlik* was banned in 1990 and one of its founders, Shiraly NURMYRADOV, imprisoned, ostensibly for fraud. Released in 1992, Nurmyradov then relocated to Moscow. The party advocates adoption of a multiparty democracy.

In February 2000 another leader, Nurberdi NURMAMEDOV, was sentenced to five years in prison, reportedly for hooliganism and intent to murder. He had been arrested in January 2000 after criticizing the legislature's decision to permit the president more than two consecutive terms. He was released in January 2001 and attempted to run for president in 2007, but he was denied a place on the ballot.

Democratic Progress Party (DPP). Organized as a party in 1991 by *Agzybirlik* members, the DPP is sometimes identified in English as the Party of Democratic Development. One of its leaders, Durdymurat Khojamukhammed, having been incarcerated in a psychiatric institution following the July 1995 demonstration in the capital, was one of several dissidents released in April 1998. In September, however, Khojamukhammed was abducted and severely beaten by unidentified assailants. Human Rights Watch assigned responsibility for the assault to the government.

Exile opposition groups include the **Republican Party of Turkmenistan** (RPT), chaired by Nurmuhammet Hanamow, a former ambassador to Turkey, which was expressly forbidden from campaigning in the 2008 Assembly elections; the **United Democratic Opposition of Turkmenistan** (UDOT), led by former foreign minister Avde Kuliev until his death in Oslo in April 2007; and the **People's Democratic Movement of Turkmenistan** (PDMT, also identified as the National Democratic Movement of Turkmenistan), founded by former foreign minister Boris Shikhmuradov. Shikhmuradov and Hanamow were both accused of involvement in an alleged November 2002 assassination attempt against President Niyazov, and Shikhmuradov is serving a life sentence.

In October 2003 four opposition groups, all in exile, announced formation of a **Union of Democratic Forces of Turkmenistan** (UDFT). Founding members were the RPT; the UDOT; the **Socio-Political Movement *Watan*** (Motherland), now led by Hudayberdi ORAZOW (Khudaiberdy ORAZOV); and the **Socio-Political Movement "Revival,"** led by Nazar SUYUNOV. Earlier, in June 2002, various opposition formations had convened in Vienna, Austria, and had organized a "Roundtable of the Turkmen Democratic Opposition"; participants included *Agzybirlik,* the **Communist Party of Turkmenistan,** the **National Patriotic Movement of Turkmenistan,** the PDMT, Shirali NURMURADOV's **Popular Social Movement "Mertebe"** (Dignity), the **Social Democratic Party**, Turkmen communities from Russia and elsewhere, and a veterans' group.

Following President Niyazov's death, the RPT and *Watan* formed a **Democratic Coalition of Turkmenistan,** which nominated *Watan*'s Orazow as its 2007 presidential candidate. Orazow was not allowed on the ballot.

LEGISLATURE

Under the 1992 constitution, as amended, Turkmenistan has two national representative bodies: a quasi-parliamentary People's Council, which had among its powers establishing broad policy guidelines and amending the constitution, and a smaller Assembly performing ordinary legislative functions. The new constitution, approved by the People's Council in September 2008, did away with that very body and doubled the size of the Assembly, to 125 members.

Assembly (*Mejlis*). The *Mejlis* consists of 125 members elected for five-year terms from single-seat constituencies. The Supreme Soviet elected on January 7, 1990, became the *Mejlis* as of May 19, 1992. The most recent elections were held on December 14, 2008, with run-off balloting on December 28 for districts in which no candidate received more than 50 percent of the vote. One by-election was held on February 8, 2009, after an elected member declined to take his seat. All 287 candidates, including the 125 members elected to the *Mejlis,* were members of the Democratic Party of Turkmenistan or independents who ran with state backing.

Chair: Akja NURBERDIYEWA.

CABINET

[as of September 1, 2009]

Prime Minister	Gurbanguly Berdimuhammedov
First Deputy Prime Minister	Rashid Meredov
Deputy Prime Ministers	Baymyrat Hojamuhammedow
	Nazarguly Sagulyyew
	Hydyr Saparliyev
	Maysa Yazmuhammedowa [f]
	Hojamuhammet Muhammedow
	Tuvakmammed Japarov
	Myratgeldy Akmammedov
	Deryaeidi Orazow
Ministers	
Agriculture	Esenmyrat Orazgeldiyew
Communications	Owiliyaguly Jumagulyyew
Construction	Samuhammet Durdylyyew
Construction Materials Industry	Yazmyrat Hommadov
Culture and Media	Gulmyrat Hudayberdiyewic Myradow
Defense	Yaylim Berdiyew
Economic Development	Basimmyrat Hojamammedow
Finance	Annamuhammet Gocyyew
Education	Gulshat Mammedove [f]
Energy and Industry	Yazmuhammet Orazgulyyew
Foreign Affairs	Rashid Meredov
Health and Medical Industry	Ata Serdarow
Internal Affairs	Iskander Mulikov
Justice	Myrat Garryyew
Motor Transport	Gurbanmyrat Hangulyyew
National Security	Carymyrat Amanow
Natural Resources and Environmental Protection	Magtymguly Akmyradow
Oil, Gas, and Mineral Resources	Annaguly Rejepowic Deryayew
Railways	Rosymyrat Seyitgulyyew
Social Security	Bekmyrat Samyradow
Textile Industry	Hojamyrat Atamyradowic Metekov
Trade and Foreign Economic Relations	Nokerguly Hojagulyyewic Atagulyyew
Water Resources	Annageldi Yazmyradow

[f] = female

COMMUNICATIONS

All media are strictly controlled by the government. Individuals may subscribe to Russian newspapers but not to those of other foreign countries. In 2002 the OSCE stated that, in its experience, the lack of press freedom in Turkmenistan was "unprecedented." In 2008 Reporters Without Borders, in its annual World Press Freedom Index, ranked Turkmenistan 171 out of 173 countries. In 2006, a Radio Free Europe (RFE) journalist died in prison; the government ignored demands by Reporters Without Borders that a commission of inquiry be set up to investigate the case. In June 2008, another RFE correspondent in Turkmenistan was detained and allegedly tortured. Following international pressure, he was released after two weeks. In 2009 the government announced an initiative to reform its media practices, including inviting the OSCE to conduct training seminars for Turkmen journalists.

Press. The following are among the newspapers published in Ashgabat in Turkmen, unless otherwise noted: *Adalat* (Justice, 40,000), weekly; *Galkynys* (25,000), weekly DPT organ; *Watan* (Motherland, 20,000), three times a week; *Turkmenistan* (20,000), daily government organ; *Neitralnyi Turkmenistan* (Neutral Turkmenistan, 20,000), daily government organ, in Russian; *Novosti Turkmenistana* (Turkmenistan News), weekly newsletter published by the Turkmen State News Service, in Russian, English, and Turkmen.

News agency. The domestic facility is the Turkmen State News Service (TSNS), headquartered in Ashgabat.

Broadcasting. Turkmen Radio's two outlets and Turkmen Television's four stations broadcast in Turkmen and Russian. Rebroadcasts of programs from Russia are often censored, in part because of what President Niyazov described as their "indecency."

Internet access is controlled by the government's Turkmentelecom. President Berdimuhammedov has pledged to make Internet service available to all. As of 2008 there were 14.9 Internet users per 1,000 inhabitants.

INTERGOVERNMENTAL REPRESENTATION

Ambassador to the U.S.: Meret Bairamovich ORAZOV.

U.S. Ambassador to Turkmenistan: (Vacant).

Permanent Representative to the UN: Aksoltan T. ATAEVA.

IGO Memberships (Non-UN): ADB, CIS, EBRD, ECO, IDB, Interpol, NAM, OIC, OSCE, WCO.

TUVALU

Constitutional Monarchy of Tuvalu
Fakavae Aliki-Malo i Tuvalu

Political Status: Former British dependency; independent with "special membership" in the Commonwealth since October 1, 1978.

Land Area: 10 sq. mi. (26 sq. km.).

Resident Population: 9,561 (2002C); 13,000 (2008E). Both figures are exclusive of more than 3,000 Tuvaluans living overseas.

Major Urban Center (2005E): VAIAKU (Funafuti, 6,200).

Official Language: English (Tuvaluan is widely spoken).

Monetary Unit: Australian Dollar (market rate December 1, 2009: 1.08 dollars = $1US). A Tuvaluan coinage (at par with the Australian) was introduced in 1977 but is circulated largely for numismatic purposes.

Sovereign: Queen ELIZABETH II.

Governor General: Rev. Filoimea TELITO; sworn in on April 15, 2005, to succeed Faimalaga LUKA.

Prime Minister: Apisai IELEMIA; elected by parliament on August 14, 2006, to succeed Maatia TOAFA, following the election of August 3, 2006.

THE COUNTRY

Formerly known as the Ellice Islands in the Gilbert group, Tuvalu consists of nine atolls stretching over an area of 500,000 square miles north of Fiji in the western Pacific. Only eight of the islands are considered inhabited for electoral purposes; activity on the ninth is confined to a copra plantation. With a total land area of 10 square miles, Tuvalu is one of the world's smallest countries, although its population density is the highest among South Pacific island nations. Its inhabitants are predominantly Polynesian and Protestant Christian. The soil is poor, with crops subject to variable rainfall, frequent cyclones, and increasing salinization. As a consequence, agricultural activity is confined largely to the coco palm and its derivatives, yielding a dependency on imported food. Women constitute 30 percent of the paid labor force, concentrated almost entirely in the service sector; female participation in politics and government has traditionally been minimal, although a woman entered the Paeniu cabinet in 1989.

Much of the islands' revenue is derived from the sale of stamps and coins and from remittances by Tuvaluans working abroad, primarily as merchant seamen or as phosphate miners on Nauru and Kiribati's Banaba Island. In 1987 these resources were augmented by an agreement with Australia, New Zealand, and the United Kingdom for the establishment of a trust fund, worth approximately $40 million in 1999, that at that time covered approximately one-quarter of the country's annual budget. Economic development plans include the promotion of handicraft industries and the exploitation of marine resources, but neither is likely to equal the dramatic financial windfall realized through sale of the country's fortuitous Internet designation ".tv" (see Current issues, below).

GOVERNMENT AND POLITICS

Political background. Proclaimed a protectorate with the Gilbert Islands (now independent Kiribati) in 1892 and formally annexed by Britain in 1915–1916, when the Gilbert and Ellice Islands Colony was established, the Ellice Islands were separated on October 1, 1975, and renamed Tuvalu. Independence on October 1, 1978, occurred only five months after the acquisition of full internal self-government, former chief minister Toalipi LAUTI becoming prime minister and Sir Fiatau Penitala TEO being designated Crown representative. On September 17, 1981, nine days after the country's first general election since independence, Lauti, on a 5–7 parliamentary vote, was obliged to yield office to Dr. Tomasi PUAPUA. Lauti's defeat was blamed largely on his controversial decision in 1979 to invest most of the government's capital with a California business that promised assistance in obtaining a $5 million development loan; the money, plus interest, was reported to have been returned by mid-1984.

Dr. Puapua remained in office as head of a largely unchanged administration after the election of September 12, 1985, but was forced to step down in favor of Bikenibeu PAENIU because of the loss of parliamentary seats by two cabinet members in the election of September 27, 1989.

Following legislative balloting on September 2, 1993, parliament found itself in a 6–6 tie between those who wished to retain Prime Minister Paeniu and supporters of his predecessor. The deadlock remaining after a second ballot, a new election was held on November 25. Thereafter, Puapua chose not to present himself as a candidate; Kamuta LATASI, a parliamentary backbencher and former private secretary to Governor General Toalipi Lauti, was chosen over Paeniu on a 7–5 vote. Latasi himself was on the losing end of a 7–5 nonconfidence vote on December 17, 1996, and was succeeded by Paeniu on December 23.

Following a campaign of exceptional bitterness (primarily between Paeniu and Latasi), new balloting for parliament on March 26, 1998, returned Paeniu to his seat but not Latasi. Paeniu was reappointed for a new term as prime minister on April 8. However, he lost a vote of confidence by 7–4 on April 14, 1999, and the parliament on April 27 selected Ionatana IONATANA, the minister of education and culture as well as of women's and community affairs, as his successor.

Prime Minister Ionatana died unexpectedly on December 8, 2000, and was succeeded by Deputy Prime Minister Lagitupu TUILIMU, in an acting capacity. On February 23, 2001, parliament elected Faimalaga LUKA as his successor, and he was sworn in at the head of a reshuffled cabinet the following day.

On December 13, 2001, the parliament elected Koloa TALAKE, a former minister of finance, as head of government. The previous week, Prime Minister Luka had lost a no-confidence motion when four legislators, including Talake, crossed the aisle to support the motion. (Named governor general on September 9, 2003, Luka retired in April 2005 and died on August 19.)

In balloting for an expanded 15-seat parliament on July 25, 2002, Talake, three other government ministers, and the speaker of parliament all lost their seats. On August 2 Saufatu SOPOANGA defeated the other candidate for prime minister, Amasone KILEI, by a vote of 8–7 and named a completely new cabinet.

Accused of misusing government property and money (charges he heatedly denied), Sopoanga lost a no-confidence vote (8–6) on August 25, 2004, and delayed the naming of a successor by resigning his legislative seat, thus forcing a by-election. Reelected on October 7, Sopoanga was named deputy prime minister by Maatia TOAFA following his election as the new prime minister on October 11. Toafa continued in office in mid-2005 after a crucial legislative by-election in which a

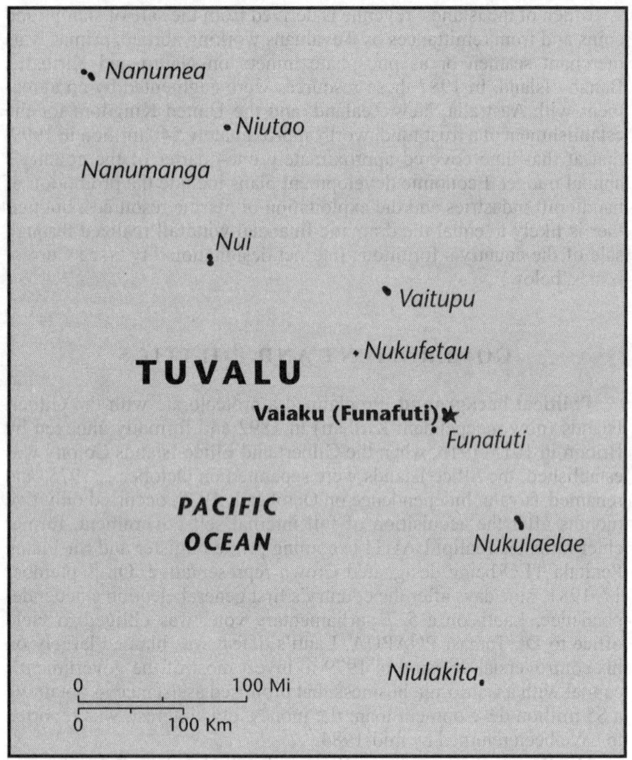

progovernment candidate was chosen to replace a member who had resigned.

On August 14, 2006, Prime Minister Toafa was succeeded by Apisai IELEMIA following a general election on August 3, in which 8 of the 15 incumbent legislators lost their seats.

Constitution and government. The 1978 constitution (a substantially revised version of a preindependence document adopted three years earlier) provides for a governor general of Tuvaluan citizenship who serves a four-year term (or until age 65) and a prime minister who is elected by a unicameral parliament of 15 members. Should the office of prime minister become vacant with parliament unable to agree on a successor, the governor general may, at his discretion, name a chief executive or call for legislative dissolution. The government is collectively responsible to parliament, whose normal term is four years. The judiciary consists of a High Court, which is empowered to hear appeals from courts of criminal and civil jurisdiction on each of the eight inhabited islands as well as from local magistrates' courts. Appeals from the High Court may be taken to the Court of Appeal in Fiji and, as last resort, to the Judicial Committee of the Privy Council in London. Island councils (most of whose members are reportedly wary of centralized government) continue to be dominant in local administration.

In accordance with the results of a 1986 public poll that rejected republican status, the government announced that the link with the Crown would be retained, although constitutional changes would be introduced that would limit the governor general to a largely ceremonial role. However, the High Court in August 2003 ruled that the governor general retained the power to convene parliament in the face of a government effort to delay recall as a means of continuing in office.

Foreign relations. Upon independence Tuvalu elected to join Nauru as a "special member" of the Commonwealth, having the right to participate in all Commonwealth affairs except heads of government meetings. It was admitted to the United Nations as the world body's 189th member on September 5, 2000. At the regional level it participates in the Pacific Islands Forum (PIF) and the Pacific Community. Most of its contacts with other states are through representatives accredited to Fiji or New Zealand, although in 1984 formal relations, backdated to 1979, were established with former colonial partner Kiribati.

In early 1979 Tuvalu and the United States signed a treaty of friendship (ratified in June 1983) that included provision for consultation in the areas of defense and marine resources, with Washington acknowledging Tuvalu's sovereignty over four islands (Funafuti, Nukufetau, Nukulaelae, and Niulakita) originally claimed by the U.S. Congress in the so-called Guano Act of 1856.

In February 1986 Tuvalu refused to sanction a "goodwill visit" by a French warship as a means of protesting continued nuclear testing in French Polynesia. Earlier, in August 1985, it had become a signatory of the Treaty of Rarotonga, which declared the South Pacific a nuclear-free zone.

In December 1998 Prime Minister Paeniu visited Taiwan, whose battle with China for diplomatic support in the South Pacific had recently intensified. Taiwanese officials pledged development aid for Tuvalu's fishing industry in return for the islands' continued "friendship." In 2001 Tuvalu joined the Marshall Islands, Nauru, Palau, and the Solomon Islands in supporting UN membership for Taiwan.

In March 2005 Tuvalu joined with Kiribati in seeking assistance from the PIF for wage arrears and repatriation of some 1,000 of their nationals who had been working for a decade as laborers in Nauru's phosphate mines. For its part, Nauru estimated that more than $2.3 million would be required for the repatriation effort.

In early 2008 Tuvalu became the 11th PIF member to ratify the Pacific Island Countries Trade Agreement (PICTA), which seeks the gradual reduction of import duties among participants. In January 2009 Tonga applied for membership in the International Monetary Fund.

Current issues. In November 1999, Idealab, a California-based firm, agreed to pay Tuvalu $50 million over the ensuing decade for use of the country's Internet suffix ".tv," which would be licensed to electronic mail and Web address customers as an alternative to the ubiquitous ".com." The government has thus far used the money, which far exceeds all other forms of revenue, for infrastructural projects in health, education, and transportation. In addition, the largess enabled the previously cash-strapped country to open a permanent mission at UN headquarters in 2001 and to purchase a controlling interest in Air Fiji, thereby ensuring improved air transport.

In early 2005 Prime Minister Toafa reopened the republican issue, declaring, over the apparent objection of his deputy, former prime minister Sopoanga, that he planned to hold a referendum on replacing Queen Elizabeth II with a president as head of state. Action in the matter was delayed, however, until April 2008, at which time a low turnout (22 percent) of the electorate rejected the change by a two to one majority.

The dominant current issue involves the consequences for low-lying Tuvalu of a continuing rise in sea level because of global warming. Overtures to New Zealand and Australia about possible resettlement have produced mixed responses for the endangered island nation, which has already experienced shore erosion and increased salinity. According to recent estimates, the land areas (most of which are little more than a meter above sea level) will be severely flooded within the next 15–20 years and will be completely submerged by the end of the century.

In early 2008 Tuvalu renewed its appeal to Australia and New Zealand for acceptance of "climate refugees," with New Zealand agreeing to accept about 17 a year, as contrasted with an official need to resettle "at least 3,000 people, and possibly [the] whole population, within the next few years." The following August it was reported that 100 Tuvaluans had resettled in the New Zealand dependency of Niue, whose premier indicated a willingness to accept more if resources could be obtained to facilitate their transfer.

POLITICAL PARTIES

Political affairs in Tuvalu are grounded in family ties and personalities, not ideology. In late 1992 it was reported that a group called the Tuvalu United Party (*Tama i Fulu a Tuvalu*) had been organized by Prime Minister Paeniu and his deputy, Dr. Alesana Kleis SELUKA, but the party has played no part in recent elections.

LEGISLATURE

Known prior to independence as the House of Assembly, the unicameral **Parliament** (*Palamente o Tuvalu*) consists of 15 members: 2

each from seven islands and 1 from the least populous inhabited island. The legislative term, subject to dissolution, is four years. In legislative balloting held on August 3, 2006, 8 new members, primarily senior civil servants, were among the 15 legislators elected.

Speaker: Kamuta LATASI.

CABINET

[as of August 1, 2009]

Prime Minister	Apisai Ielemia
Deputy Prime Minister	Taavau Teii
Ministers	
Communications, Works, and Transport	Taukelina Finikaso
Education, Sports, and Culture	Iakoba Italeli
Finance, Economic Planning, and Industry	Lotoala Metia
Foreign Affairs	Apisai Ielemia
Health	Iakoba Italeli
Home Affairs and Rural Development	Willy Telavi
Natural Resources and Environment	Taavau Teii

COMMUNICATIONS

Press. The only sources of printed news are *Tuvalu Echoes/Sikuleo o Tuvalu* (250), published fortnightly in English and Tuvaluan by the government's Broadcasting and Information Division, and a monthly religious newsletter, *Te Lama*, which includes some items of general interest.

Broadcasting. Radio Tuvalu broadcasts for about six hours daily from Funafuti to approximately 5,000 receivers. There is no television service, although an Australian engineering firm was reported in early 1995 to have been retained to install a satellite-based telecommunications network to link Funafuti with the outer islands. As of 2008 there were 429.8 Internet users per 1,000 inhabitants.

INTERGOVERNMENTAL REPRESENTATION

Ambassador to the U.S.: Tuvalu does not maintain an embassy in Washington.

U.S. Ambassador to Tuvalu: C. Steven McGANN (resident in Fiji).

Permanent Representative to the UN: Afelee F. PITA.

IGO Memeberships (Non-UN): ADB, CWTH, PC, PIF.

UGANDA

Republic of Uganda

Political Status: Independent member of the Commonwealth since October 9, 1962; republican constitution adopted on September 8, 1967; personal military rule (instituted on January 25, 1971) overthrown with establishment of provisional government on April 11, 1979; military regime installed on January 29, 1986; present constitution adopted on September 22,1995, with effect from October 8.

Area: 93,104 sq. mi. (241,139 sq. km.).

Population: 24,442,084 (2002C); 29,637,000 (2008E).

Major Urban Center (2005E): KAMPALA (metropolitan area, 1,337,000).

Official Language: English (Swahili and Luganda are widely used).

Monetary Unit: New Shilling (principal rate December 1, 2009: 1,872.50 new shillings = $1US).

President: Lt. Gen. Yoweri Kaguta MUSEVENI; sworn in on January 29, 1986, following the overthrow of Lt. Gen. Tito OKELLO Lutwa on January 27; popularly elected on May 9, 1996, and inaugurated for a five-year term on May 12; reelected for another five-year term on March 12, 2001; reelected in multiparty balloting on February 23, 2006, and inaugurated for another five-year term on May 12.

Vice President: Gilbert Balibaseka BUKENYA; appointed by the president on June 6, 2003, succeeding Dr. Speciosa Wandira KAZIBWE, who resigned; reappointed by the president on May 23, 2006.

Prime Minister: Apolo NSIBAMBI; appointed by the president on April 6, 1999, succeeding Kintu MUSOKE; reappointed on July 13, 2001; reappointed by the president following elections on February 23, 2006, and sworn in with the new cabinet on June 2, 2006.

THE COUNTRY

Landlocked Uganda, located in east-central Africa, is bounded on the east by Kenya, on the south by Tanzania and Rwanda, on the west by the Democratic Republic of the Congo (DRC), and on the north by Sudan. The country is known for its lakes (among them Lake Victoria, the source of the White Nile) and its mountains, the most celebrated of which are the Mountains of the Moon (the Ruwenzori), lying on the border with the DRC. The population embraces a number of African tribal groups, including the Baganda, Banyankore, Basoga, and Iteso. For many decades a substantial Asian (primarily Indian) minority engaged in shopkeeping, industry, and other professions. In 1972, however, the Idi Amin government decreed the expulsion of all noncitizen Asians as part of a plan to put Uganda's economy in the hands of nationals, and at present only a scattering of Asians still reside in the country. Approximately 60 percent of the population is Christian and another 15 percent is Muslim, with the remainder adhering to traditional African beliefs. Women are primarily responsible for subsistence agriculture, with most male rural labor being directed toward cash crops; women also dominate trade in rural areas, although not in the cities. The government is considered progressive regarding women's rights, with a number of seats in the current parliament being reserved for women. One-third of the seats in local councils must, by law, also go to women.

Agriculture, forestry, and fishing contribute about one-third of Uganda's gross domestic product (GDP); industry, which is growing in importance, accounts for about 21 percent of GDP. Services account for the remainder. Coffee is the principal crop (Uganda is one of Africa's leading producers), followed by cotton, tea, peanuts, and tobacco.

Beginning in the late 1960s Uganda experienced two decades of violence arising from tribal warfare, strongman governments, rebel activity, and coups that left more than 800,000 dead, many of them reportedly victims of military atrocities. The resultant drop in agricultural and industrial output, combined with heavy capital, flight led to severe economic distress. The regime installed in 1986 attempted to kindle recovery through enhanced exploitation of resources and renegotiation of the external debt in light of improved internal security. In the process, Uganda became a "major hope" of the International Monetary Fund (IMF)/World Bank approach to economic reform in sub-Saharan Africa. The success of economic reform was minimal through 1993.

In mid-1995 plans for privatization reforms were under way, calling for the abolition of government subsidies to state-owned companies, except for public utilities, where the support was to be phased out over a four-year period.

In May 2000 the IMF and World Bank announced that Uganda had qualified for $2 billion in debt service relief over the next 20 years based on the government's adherence to its comprehensive reform program and continued economic progress. By mid-2005 GDP growth of 5.4 percent was offset by one of the highest population growth rates in the world and widespread poverty. Subsequently, the IMF in 2006 cited poverty reduction as the foremost economic issue for Uganda, and it urged reforms to curb corruption. Unhappy with alleged corruption in government spending and the country's slow progress toward democratization, the UK, traditionally Uganda's biggest donor, and three other donor countries canceled millions of dollars in aid to Kampala. Despite a regional drought that continued into 2006 annual GDP growth averaged 6.1 percent from 2006–2008. The African Development Bank cited increased privatization and political stability as factors contributing to growth. In addition, with the discovery of oil in Uganda, plans were under way to produce 5,000 barrels per day by the end of 2009. Due to the global financial recession and accompanying decline in exports, annual growth was expected to contract to 5.5 percent in 2009, according to the IMF. However, strong performance in the construction and service sectors was forecast, and the government's plan for a $550 million infrastructure project was seen by the IMF as a scheme that would stimulate the economy. Meanwhile, *Africa Confidential* reported that creditors were "growing impatient over corruption and the costs of public administration," and noted that the president and his wife "live in ostentatious luxury" with a State House budget more than twice that of two large ministries combined. The IMF, for its part, reported that "the fundamentals of the Ugandan economy are strong."

GOVERNMENT AND POLITICS

Political background. Uganda became a British protectorate in 1894–1896 and began its progress toward statehood after World War II, achieving internal self-government on March 1, 1962, and full independence within the Commonwealth on October 9, 1962. A problem involving Buganda and three other traditional kingdoms was temporarily resolved by granting the kingdoms semiautonomous rule within a federal system. The arrangement enabled Buganda's representatives to participate in the national government, and the king (*kabaka*) of Buganda, Sir Edward Frederick MUTESA II, was elected president of Uganda on October 9, 1963. The issue of national unity versus Bugandan particularism led Prime Minister Apollo Milton OBOTE, leader of the Uganda People's Congress (UPC) and an advocate of centralism, to depose the president and vice president in February 1966. A constitution eliminating Buganda's autonomous status was ratified in April 1966 by the National Assembly, which consisted mainly of UPC members. Failing in an effort to mobilize effective resistance to the new government, the *kabaka* fled the country in May, and a new republican constitution, adopted in September 1967, eliminated the special status of Buganda and the other kingdoms. Earlier, on April 15, 1966, Obote had been designated president by the National Assembly for a five-year term. In December 1969 he banned all opposition political parties and established a one-party state with a socialist program known as the Common Man's Charter.

On January 25, 1971, Maj. Gen. Idi AMIN Dada, commander in chief of the army and air force, mounted a successful coup that deposed Obote while the president was abroad at a Commonwealth meeting. In addition to continuing the ban on opposition political activity, Amin suspended parts of the constitution, dissolved the National Assembly, and secured his own installation as president of the republic.

Following an invasion by Tanzanian troops and exile forces organized as the Uganda National Liberation Army (UNLA), the Amin

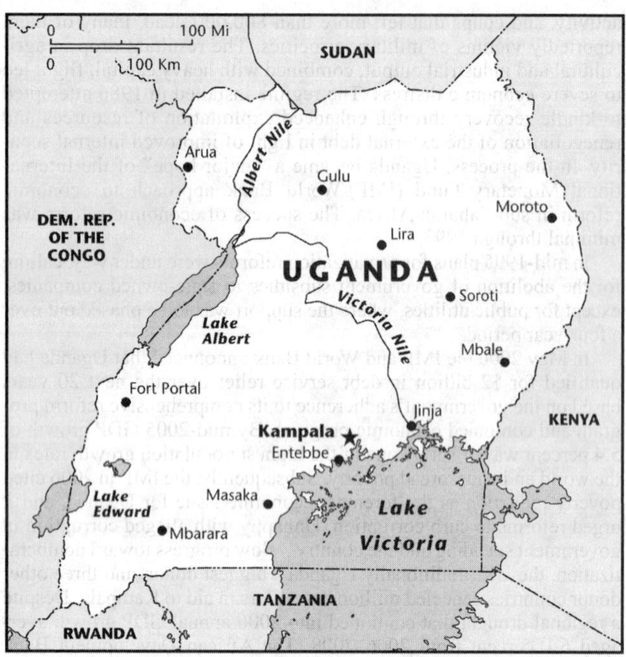

regime, which had drawn worldwide condemnation for atrocities against perceived opponents, was effectively overthrown with the fall of Kampala April 10–11, 1979, with Amin fleeing to Libya. Concurrently, the National Consultative Council (NCC) of the Uganda National Liberation Front (UNLF) designated Professor Yusuf K. LULE, former vice chancellor of Makerere University, as president of the republic and head of a provisional government. On June 20 the NCC announced that Godfrey Lukongwa BINAISA, a former attorney general under President Obote, had been named to succeed Lule in both capacities.

After a series of disagreements with both the NCC and the UNLF's Military Commission, Binaisa was relieved of his authority on May 12, 1980. On May 18 the chair of the Military Commission, Paulo MUWANGA, announced that a three-member Presidential Commission had been established to exercise executive power through a cabinet of ministers on advice of its military counterpart, pending a national election later in the year.

Former president Obote returned from Tanzania on May 27, 1980, and in mid-June agreement was reached between party and UNLF representatives on four groups that would be permitted to participate in the presidential/legislative campaign. Following balloting December 10–11, the UPC declared that it had secured a majority in the National Assembly, thus assuring Obote's reinvestiture as chief executive. Although the runner-up Democratic Party (DP) denounced the results as fraudulent, most victorious DP candidates took their legislative seats. The Uganda Patriotic Movement (UPM), led by former president Lule and his former defense minister, Yoweri MUSEVENI, refused to accept the one seat it had won. After shedding the party apparatus, Lule and Museveni formed a National Resistance Movement (NRM) and initiated a guerrilla campaign against Obote through the affiliated National Resistance Army (NRA).

During the next five years, while the UNLA achieved some success in repulsing the rebels, the NRA continued to hold the agriculturally important "Luwero triangle" north of Kampala, as well as its traditional strongholds in the Banyankore-dominated southwest. During the same period, many army actions against civilians were reported, including the harassment, wounding, or killing of DP members; by mid-1985, more than 200,000 were estimated to have died, either from army "excesses" or official counterinsurgency efforts.

On July 27, 1985, in a self-proclaimed attempt to "stop the killing," Brig. Basilio Olara OKELLO led a senior officers' coup against Obote, who had lost much international support and was again forced into exile. Two days later the constitution was suspended, and Obote's army chief of staff, Lt. Gen. Tito OKELLO Lutwa, was sworn in as chair of a ruling Military Council. On August 6 General Okello called for all guerrilla groups, including former Amin soldiers, to join his army, while naming Paulo Muwanga, who had served as Obote's vice president, as prime minister and DP leader Paul SSEMOGERERE as minister of the interior. Unlike most other resistance leaders, Museveni, the dominant NRM figure following Lule's death in January 1985, did not accede to Okello's call for "unity," citing continued abuses by army personnel who routinely failed to defer to Okello. In contrast, the NRA had a reputation for being well disciplined, relatively free of tribal rivalries, and far less brutal toward civilians.

By September 1985, when the first of a series of Kenyan- and Tanzanian-mediated peace talks began in Dar es Salaam, NRA forces had taken control of a number of strategic towns and supply routes, while another Obote associate, Abraham WALIGO, replaced Muwanga as prime minister. In November Museveni announced that "in order to provide services pending an agreement with the regime in Kampala," an "interim administration" was being established in rebel-held areas. A peace pact signed in Nairobi on December 17 gave Museveni the vice chair of the Military Council while providing for the dissolution of all existing armed units and the recruitment, under external supervision, of a new, fully representative force. However, the accord did not take effect. After failing to attend "celebrations" scheduled for January 4, 1986, Museveni, citing continuing human-rights abuses, launched a drive on Kampala, which culminated in the overthrow of the six-month-old Okello regime on January 27. Two days later, while NRA forces consolidated their control, Museveni was sworn in as president, thereafter appointing a cabinet that included as prime minister Dr. Samson KISEKKA, formerly the NRM's external spokesperson. In an attempt to prevent further civil war, Museveni also named representatives of other major political groups to his government. However, some UNLA units that had not disbanded fled to the north and the east, where they and other rebel groups continued to resist the NRA.

In mid-1986 Museveni absolved his immediate predecessor, General Okello, of atrocities committed by troops under his command. No such tender was made to former presidents Amin and Obote, with Museveni calling for their repatriation from exile in Saudi Arabia and Zambia, respectively, to face charges by a special commission of inquiry established to review the "slaughter" of Bantu southerners by their Nilotic followers. (Obote died in Zambia in October 2005.)

In February 1988 Museveni named three deputy prime ministers, including DP leader Ssemogerere, to assist the ailing Kisekka. In addition, the cabinet was reshuffled to include more representatives from the north and east, where rebel activity continued to impede national reconciliation. An even more drastic reshuffle was ordered in April 1989 coincident with conversion of the theretofore appointive National Resistance Council (see under Constitution and government, below) into a largely elective body. Six months later the council voted to extend the government's interim mandate (originally limited by President Museveni to four years) to January 1995. The action was justified by the minister of justice on the grounds that the country lacked the "essential political machinery and the logistics for the evolution of a democratic and a permanent stable government."

On January 22, 1991, Museveni appointed Kisekka to the new, largely ceremonial position of vice president, with George Cosmas ADYEBO, a 43-year-old economist, named prime minister. The government subsequently conducted a "final sweep" against rebel forces in the north and east, and in July Kampala reported that its troops had decimated the rebel forces, killing 1,500 insurgents between March and July (many, Amnesty International charged, after perfunctory military trials) and absorbing many others into the NRA. In August the government described the remaining rebels, predominantly from Joseph KONY's Uganda Democratic Christian Army, as "thugs" who had been reduced to raiding villages for food and whose earlier atrocities prevented their reintegration.

In January 1993 Museveni, who continued to reject domestic and international calls for the immediate introduction of multipartyism on the grounds that it would exacerbate religious and ethnic cleavages, announced plans for nonparty elections by the end of 1994. In February the NRC passed a constituent assembly bill that called for the delay of multiparty politics until at least the year 2000 (see Constitution and government, below).

Earlier, in what was described by critics as political repayment to the Baganda people for supporting the NRA struggle in the early 1980s, Museveni had begun negotiating with Baganda to restore its monarch. Consequently, on July 31, 1993, the son of Mutesa II, Ronald Muwenda MUTEBI, was crowned *kabaka,* an event described as a purely "ceremonial" action. Collaterally, pro forma recognition was granted to the coronation of Patrick David Matthew Olimi KABOYO II as monarch of the smaller Toro kingdom. (Kaboyo died on September 13, 1995, and was succeeded by his three-year-old son, Oyo Nyimba Kabamba IGURU IV.) On June 11, 1994, the oldest of Uganda's historic kingdoms was restored, with the crowning of Solon Iguri GAFABUSA I as king of the Bunyoro tribe. (The crowning of John BARIGYE as monarch of Uganda's Ankore kingdom was indefinitely delayed because of disputes within the clan leadership.) Meanwhile, on February 11, 1996, Henry Wako MULOKI, the Basoga's traditional leader, was reinstalled as *kyabazinga* (king) at a ceremony attended by Museveni.

On March 28, 1994, nonparty balloting was held to fill the 214-seat Constituent Assembly. As anticipated, NRM-affiliated candidates captured the majority of the seats (114), although the president's actual assembly supporters were reported as numbering only 93. In December the government announced that nonparty general elections would be held by late 1995; however, they were deferred until April–May 1996. Meanwhile, the Constituent Assembly on September 22 approved a new basic law that continued the ban on political campaigning and provided that the NRC would remain in existence for another five years. Upon promulgation of the document on October 8, the constituent body was dissolved.

At Uganda's first presidential balloting on May 9, 1996, President Museveni captured 74.2 percent of the vote, easily outpolling his two competitors, the DP's Ssemogerere (23.7 percent) and an Islamic candidate, Mohamed MAYANJA Kibirige (2.1 percent). Although Museveni controlled the media and local councils administering the polling, international observers described the polling as "fair. Thereafter, in "no-party" legislative polling staged between June 6–27, NRM candidates secured or were appointed to 271 of the 276 available posts. On July 6 Museveni named an enlarged cabinet that included only NRM members.

In early 1998 Museveni named his half-brother, Gen. Salim SALEH, as defense minister, a post held theretofore by the president himself. The appointment of Saleh, who had been credited with coordinating the government's highly successful offensives against its various rebel opponents in mid-1997, underscored Museveni's apparent dedication to a total rout of the Lord's Resistance Army (LRA—see Political Parties and Groups, below), whose call for a cease-fire in July had been rejected. (Saleh resigned in December after allegations of corrupt financial dealings were made against him.)

In May 1998 Museveni reshuffled the government and, following the retirement of Prime Minister Musoke, on April 6, 1999, the president named Apolo NSIBAMBI to head a substantially altered cabinet. In a referendum on June 29, 2000, 90 percent of the voters endorsed continuance of the no-party system.

On March 12, 2001, President Museveni was reelected to another five-year term, securing 69 percent of the vote compared to 28 percent for his nearest rival, Kizza BESIGYE, Museveni's former doctor and former military ally. Subsequently, the NRM retained its stronghold on the parliament in elections held on June 26, 2001. Although a dozen sitting cabinet members lost their legislative seats, most of them were beaten by other Museveni supporters. Following the elections, Museveni reappointed Prime Minister Nsibambi to head a significantly altered cabinet, which was sworn in on July 24. A constitutional referendum on July 28, 2005 (see Constitution and government, below), allowed for the registration of political parties, among other things, in advance of presidential and parliamentary elections on February 23, 2006. In the multiparty presidential election, Museveni defeated four challengers by garnering 59.26 percent of the vote. His nearest rival, Kizza Besigye, running as the Forum for Democratic Change (FDC) candidate, received 37.39 percent. The Democratic Party's John SSEBAANA Kizito won 1.58 percent, and the Uganda People's Congress (UPC) candidate, Miria OBOTE, widow of the former president, won less than 1 percent In parliamentary elections the same day, the NRM retained power, while five opposition parties also won representation (see Legislature, below). A reshuffled and enlarged cabinet, again led by Prime Minister Apolo Nsibambi, was sworn in on June 2, 2006.

The cabinet was reshuffled on February 16, 2009. In addition to 25 ministers, the new government named 44 ministers of state, including President Museveni's wife, Janet, as minister of state for the Karamoja region.

Constitution and government. The 1962 constitution was suspended by Prime Minister Obote in February 1966. A successor instrument adopted in April 1966 terminated the federal system but was itself replaced in September 1967 by a republican constitution that established a president as head of state, chief executive, and commander in chief of the armed forces. While he did not formally revoke the 1967 constitution when he came to power, President Amin in February 1971 assumed judicial as well as executive and legislative powers. Subsequently, though martial law was never declared, military tribunals tried both civil and criminal cases and authorized numerous public executions. With but minor modification, the 1967 constitution was reinstated by the UNLF as the basis of post-military government in 1980; it was suspended by the Military Council in mid-1985 and remained inoperative thereafter.

On February 1, 1986, while in the process of organizing an interim government dominated by members of his NRM, President Museveni announced the formation of a National Resistance Council (NRC) to serve as an appointive surrogate for the former National Assembly. The NRC was converted into a largely elective body of 278 members in February 1989.

In early 1993 a 15-member commission, appointed by President Museveni in February 1989, released a report proposing the delay of multipartyism for seven years, during which time a largely elected Constituent Assembly would draft a new constitution. (Representatives of special interest groups, including the NRA, NRC, women, youths, and unions, were subsequently added to the 214-member parliament elected in March 1994.) However, the charter that emerged in September 1995 was promulgated without submission to a promised referendum. More importantly, it continued the ban on partisan activity (save behind closed party doors). In the wake of intense criticism from U.S. and British authorities, regime opponents sought to have the ban rescinded but were told that such action could be initiated only by the legislature elected under the constitution as adopted. The "no-party" system was subsequently endorsed by national referendum in June 2000.

Local government has assumed a variety of forms since 1971, the Amin and Lule governments both having reorganized the provincial and district systems. Currently, under initiatives adopted by the Museveni administration, local affairs are handled by several tiers of elected "resistance councils" ranging from village to regional levels.

President Museveni established a Constitutional Review Commission in 2001 to examine possible adaptations to the constitution regarding political parties, federalism, the size of parliament, and voter and candidate eligibility. Opponents criticized the commission as having a pro-NRM bias, having little genuine authority, and failing to reflect the broad spectrum of Ugandan public opinion.

In January 2004 the government initiated negotiations with opposition parties on the transition to multiparty politics and the future system of government. Six months later a court ruling invalidated (on a technicality) the 2000 referendum. Subsequently, as pressure for a multiparty system continued, the parliament voted in May 2005 in favor of a national referendum on a multiparty political system, abolishing the two-term limit on the presidency, and granting the president the authority to dissolve parliament in case of a constitutional crisis. In balloting of July 28, 2005, the amendments were approved by 92.44 percent of voters.

In August 2006 parliament approved 11 new districts, creating more seats for women (99) in advance of the August 28 elections for women district representatives.

Foreign relations. From independence, Uganda based its foreign policy on anticolonialism, retaining moderate Western support from its consistently nonaligned posture. However, reacting to criticism by the Amin regime of U.S. policies in Vietnam, Cambodia, and the Middle East, Washington terminated its economic assistance program in mid-1973 and subsequently closed its embassy because of public threats against officials and other Americans residing in the country. Three years later, in an event of major international import, Israeli commandos raided the Entebbe airport during the night of July 3–4, 1976, to secure the release of passengers of an Air France airliner that had been hijacked over Greece by Palestinian Arab guerrillas and flown to Uganda via Libya. Denying allegations that he had cooperated with the hijackers, Amin protested Israel's action and accused Kenya of aiding in its implementation.

Tensions with both Kenya and Tanzania resulted not only in the collapse of the tripartite East African Community (EAC) in June 1977 but ultimately in the Tanzanian military intervention of early 1979 (see Political background, above). The latter action came in the wake of an ill-conceived incursion into northern Tanzania in October 1978 by Ugandan troops, with effective Tanzanian withdrawal from Uganda not occurring until mid-1981 due to retraining requirements of the post-Amin Ugandan army. The two neighbors were critically involved in discussions between the short-lived Okello regime and the NRA, Kenyan president Daniel arap Moi being credited with brokering the December peace agreement between Okello and Museveni. Following Museveni's takeover in January 1986, both governments were quick to recognize the new regime, as was the United States. Nevertheless, relations with Kenya were subsequently strained by a series of border incidents, mutual accusations over the harboring of political dissidents, and Nairobi's displeasure at Ugandan links with Libya, particularly as manifested in an April 1989 trade accord. During a summit of the Ugandan, Kenyan, and Tanzanian presidents in Nairobi on November 22, 1991, the three declared an interest in reactivating cooperation efforts and appointed a three-member commission to draft an agreement.

Kampala concluded a security accord with Sudan in mid-1987 but subsequently charged that Khartoum was still aiding anti-Museveni rebel forces. Border tension intensified following the June 1989 coup in Sudan, precipitating the signing of another mutual nonaggression pact in April 1990, which provided for a Sudanese monitoring team on the Ugandan side of their border after Khartoum had accused Kampala of aiding the southern Sudanese rebels. Meanwhile, the Museveni administration accused former president Obote of training soldiers in Zambia, intimating that Lusaka was turning a blind eye to the activity.

Unrest in the Sudan and Zaire/Democratic Republic of the Congo (DRC) has dominated Uganda's regional relations since the early 1990s. In October 1992 Kampala warned its northern neighbor that it would mount an "appropriate response" against Sudanese troops crossing the border in pursuit of rebels, and in January 1993 it expressed its concern that a Sudanese plot to launch an Islamic fundamentalist movement in Uganda was under way. Meanwhile, the approximately 20,000 Sudanese refugees within Uganda's borders were joined by thousands of Zaireans fleeing unrest in their country.

In October 1994 Uganda canceled the 1990 agreement with its northern neighbor and ordered Sudan to withdraw its monitoring group, accusing it of activity incompatible with its mandate. In April 1995 Kampala severed relations with Khartoum, alleging improper activity by Sudanese diplomatic personnel and the sponsorship of a cross-border rebel attack on April 20. A subsequent agreement failed to bring an end to the border hostilities, with at least a limited number of Ugandan units operating in support of Sudanese rebels and the NRA conducting raids on Ugandan rebel bases inside Sudan.

Relations were restored with Kenya in January 1996 following a border summit between the two countries' leaders. The discussions also yielded mutual pledges to revive the dormant EAC. However, the continuing fragile nature of Ugandan-Kenyan ties was subsequently underlined by Nairobi's charge that the Museveni regime was supporting Kenyan rebels.

Meanwhile, rebel-related activities along their shared border continued to buffet Ugandan-Sudanese relations in 1996, but on September 9 diplomatic representatives from the two countries signed an agreement in Khartoum that reestablished ties. In December 1999 President Museveni signed an agreement with Sudanese authorities calling for mutual elimination of support for rebel movements, but in mid-2000 Museveni complained that Sudan was not living up to its end of the bargain. Relations between Sudan and Uganda appeared to improve in 2001, as Sudan reportedly permitted Ugandan forces to conduct military action in Sudan against rebels in the LRA. However, Uganda continued to accuse Sudan of helping the LRA, and rebel attacks—some targeting aid workers—continued.

Regional observers described Uganda as playing a crucial role in Laurent Kabila's ouster of the Mobutu government in Zaire (subsequently the DRC) in 1997. Kampala denied actively supporting Kabila, although admitting that its troops had crossed the border in pursuit of Ugandan rebels. Clashes occurred in August 1999 and the spring of 2000 between previously allied Ugandan and Rwandan troops in Kisangani in north-central DRC. A UN-sponsored disengagement agreement in June 2000 brought relative peace to the area, although tensions between Ugandan and Rwandan military forces remained high. Negotiations between senior levels of the two governments under British auspices in November 2001 failed to resolve the underlying strains between the two countries.

In July 2003 a tripartite agreement was signed among Uganda, Rwanda, and the office of the UN High Commissioner on Refugees, providing for the voluntary repatriation of some 26,000 Rwandans in refugee camps in western Uganda. In February 2004 the two countries signed a bilateral agreement to strengthen cooperation in several fields. Yet Uganda still accused Rwanda of aiding the rebel People's Redemption Army (PRA), said to operate in eastern Congo and West Nile. Uganda claimed the PRA was the armed wing of the new opposition group FDC and its exiled leader, retired colonel Kizza Besigye. The FDC claimed to know nothing of the PRA and accused the government of inventing the connection to discredit the FDC. Both Uganda and Rwanda were accused of meddling in the Ituri Province of the DRC, arming rebels there in exchange for minerals. Museveni and Rwandan president Paul Kagame tried to defuse the situation. In May 2005 three Ugandan soldiers were tried for spying against Rwanda, and months later, as tensions eased, Uganda and Rwanda signed an extradition treaty to crack down on criminals crossing the borders. Meanwhile, Uganda denied UN claims that it was trading weapons for minerals with the DRC.

Tensions in the region continued into 2006 following reports that Uganda had acknowledged issuing forged passports to Hutu rebels from Rwanda. The two countries subsequently began discussions to resolve the matter. Meanwhile, Uganda asked the UN to expel the DRC for allegedly harboring rebels intent on destabilizing Uganda. Upgrades to Uganda's airstrip at its borders with the DRC and Sudan raised concerns in those countries, but Ugandan authorities said the improvements were made to prepare for the November 2007 Commonwealth summit in Kampala. Some observers said the upgrades were designed to preempt surveillance flights out of the DRC and Sudan. On a more positive note, Kenya and Uganda reached an agreement to help curb illegal arms trafficking across their shared border, and in 2007 Rwanda and Uganda undertook the first steps toward demarcating disputed areas along their border.

China in 2006 boosted its arms sales to Uganda from \$2.5 million to a contract for \$1.5 billion over the next five years and agreed to provide training to the Ugandan military. Uganda also bought \$4 million worth of weapons from Iran in 2007 for its "anti-insurgency" operation in the north.

In March 2007, in a move observers said was designed to strengthen relations with the United States, Uganda sent 1,600 peacekeeping troops to Somalia to help protect the interim government there. (The troops helped bolster U.S. efforts to prevent suspected al-Qaida terrorists from establishing a foothold in Somalia.)

In 2008 a dispute between Uganda and the DRC over an oil-rich island in Lake Albert was resolved in Uganda's favor. The dispute dated to a violent confrontation between Congolese and Ugandan forces in 2007. Another territorial dispute, this one involving Kenya, over an island on Lake Victoria was set to be resolved by a panel of experts in Britain. Uganda has maintained ownership of Migingo island, a source for deep-water fish, and has had troops stationed there since 2004. When Uganda began charging residency fees to Kenyans, tensions heightened, leading to bilateral negotiations and an agreement in 2009 to have the panel resolve the issue. However, in May 2009 Kenya asked the UN to intervene in the dispute.

For the first time since 2003, the presidents of Uganda and the DRC met face-to-face in March 2009 following the discovery of oil in the region, amounting to 1 billion barrels, to discuss regional security and disputes over land.

Current issues. Uganda, for many years, was the African darling in the eyes of Western nations, which donated millions to back President Museveni's efforts toward democratization and economic reform. Bolstered by an IMF program, the economy recorded average growth of 6 percent in the late 1990s, and inflation plummeted from 240 percent in the late 1980s to 3 percent in the 1990s. However, corruption continued to be of concern, as well as rampant poverty among Uganda's rapidly growing population.

The 20-year war with rebels in the north continued to drain the economy well into the 2000s. According to the U.S. aid agency World Vision, the conflict cost Uganda more than \$1.6 billion in lost economic development and left 1.5 million people displaced in refugee camps. The LRA's recruitment methods reportedly included abduction of children and cutting off the lips and noses of those who refused to cooperate. Peace talks collapsed in 2004, and hostilities continued, although Ugandan forces captured or killed several rebel leaders. In 2005 the International Criminal Court (ICC) took the unprecedented step of issuing arrest warrants for five LRA leaders, Joseph Kony among them, for alleged war crimes.

Key domestic issues were addressed in July 2005 with the launch of a multiparty system and extension of the president's time in office beyond the two-term limit as stated in the amended constitution. The national referendum on constitutional amendments did away with the "no-party" system in effect since Museveni took over in 1986, leaving the president's NRM to dominate government. Six opposition groups boycotted the referendum, claiming it was too costly and unnecessary, as the groups' fundamental right to political association should not be subject to a vote. Observers said the national referendum was meant to placate donor nations that had been pressing for political reforms. The referendum actually strengthened the NRM, which had advocated the multiparty system prior to balloting (ostensibly to rid the party of dissenters), and allowed Museveni to take credit for progress toward democratization. The president's power was further increased by his having secured a third elected term in multiparty balloting. Museveni's key challenger, Kizza Besigye, was arrested on rape and treason charges in Kampala shortly after he returned to Uganda in 2005 and declared he would be the FDC presidential candidate. His arrest sparked rioting in the capital city; ultimately, he was released on bail and cleared of the rape charge. Besigye, who finished a distant second to Museveni, subsequently petitioned the Supreme Court to annul the election, alleging fraud, but the court rejected his challenge. Meanwhile, Besigye's FDC party secured 37 seats in parliament—the most of any opposition party—but the NRM retained its dominance in the legislature. Given a new mandate, Museveni vowed his government would begin resettling villagers displaced by LRA rebels. However, violence repeatedly marred Museveni's third term, beginning with a national strike by judges prompted by the March 1 "invasion" of the High Court by military police, who allegedly destroyed court property and beat a lawyer representing several men charged with treason (allegedly involved with the PRA). Also early in the year, police forcibly broke up a dozen opposition rallies. Meanwhile, the president was heavily criticized for having "bloated" the bureaucracy and wasting public money by enlarging the cabinet to 69 members, many of whom were from his home area in the western part of the country. Further, the former health minister and two of his deputies were dismissed for their alleged involvement in stealing $2 million from the Global Fund to Fight AIDS, Tuberculosis, and Malaria.

President Museveni attempted to conduct peace talks with LRA leader Kony in July 2006, ultimately offering the rebel leader amnesty if Kony would agree to give up fighting. Following negotiations in August and a unilateral cease-fire called by Kony, the LRA and Museveni signed a peace treaty to be finalized on September 12. Under provisions of the agreement, the rebels were to leave Uganda and their bases in Sudan and the DRC for areas designated and protected by the government of southern Sudan. Meanwhile, the Ugandan government acceded to the ICC order that it compensate families of those killed by LRA rebels.

On March 1, 2007, in an event reminiscent of an occurrence in 2005, military police again "invaded" the high court and arrested six alleged members of the PRA who had been granted bail. The action prompted a strike by judges, followed by similar action by lawyers. The president promised to launch an investigation and met with top judiciary members on March 16.

On a more positive note, Uganda began offering free secondary education in 2007, a significant savings to families whose average annual income is $300. Beyond that, however, Museveni's popular support was deemed to be eroding, observers said, due in part to his failure to follow through on his promise to step down after two five-year terms. Meanwhile, one of Museveni's most likely successors, Brig. Noble MAYOMBO, a top intelligence officer, died in May, leading to much speculation about who might replace Museveni. Some analysts reported that Museveni's son, Maj. Muhoozi KAINERUGABA, was the inevitable choice.

Negotiations with the LRA continued fitfully throughout 2006–2008, with the LRA and the Ugandan government signing a revised truce in November 2006; and a renewed truce that expired on March 3, 2007, as both sides accused the other of violations. Meanwhile, Western donors insisted that Uganda renew stalled talks through official mediators and not directly with LRA negotiators, who had been directly issuing demands. In November 2007 reports surfaced that Kony had killed his deputy, Vincent OTTI, a month earlier, prompting an investigation by the ICC.

In March 2008, amid turmoil in the LRA, a group of rebels was reportedly ready to meet with President Museveni and had set March 28 as the date for a signing ceremony. However, the rebel group announced it would not sign any agreements until the charges brought by the ICC were dismissed. Despite promises from government negotiators that Kony would not be tried in the ICC, the LRA leader failed to show up to sign an accord on April 10. Subsequently, a large number of defections from the rebel group were reported to have occurred, in conjunction with allegations that Kony was killing members who tried to initiate a peace accord. In a further effort to resolve matters, the government set up a special war crimes court to deal with the rebels' alleged human rights violations, a move observers said was designed to get the ICC to drop its indictments against Kony and other LRA leaders. Any chance for a peace deal appeared to come to an end in June, when Kony reportedly declared he would not sign any such agreement with the government, and President Museveni vowed to "destroy" Kony. In July LRA rebels reportedly renewed attacks on forces in South Sudan, and President Museveni reinforced security along Uganda's border with the DRC to try to prevent further incursions. The following month several former LRA and Allied Democratic Forces (ADF) rebels were granted amnesty. (Some 22,000 former rebels were reported to have been granted amnesty since 2004.)

On the political front, amid considerable speculation as to whether Museveni would retire or seek a fourth term, it was reported in August 2008 that Museveni had decided to run again in 2011. Meanwhile, LRA attacks increased in northern Uganda, resulting in mass protests in September by those displaced from the DRC, who were angered by what they described as the passivity of UN troops as hundreds of civilians, including children, were abducted or killed by the rebels. Following another peace overture from Kony in November (that he again failed to show up for), a new offensive was launched against the LRA in December. Backed by the United States and with troop support from Sudan and the DRC, government and allied forces tried to track down Kony in the DRC's Garamba National Park. The operation was ultimately deemed a failure, as Kony escaped, even though "scores" of LRA rebels were killed and captured. Later that same month, the Ugandan government refused to reopen peace talks as the LRA was demanding.

With Kony still at large in 2009, and with little success other than the capture of a couple of his deputies (see Guerrilla Groups, under Political Parties and Groups, below), Ugandan troops began withdrawing from the DRC in March, a day after the LRA reportedly declared a cease fire. As thousands of civilians were displaced by the fighting, *Africa Research Bulletin* reported that the troop withdrawal "coincided with an increase in rebel attacks on villages left poorly defended by Congolese soldiers and peacekeepers from Congo's 17,000-troop strong UN mission." Meanwhile, France backed the Ugandan government's resolve against further dialogue with the LRA and said it was ready to support another military offensive against the rebels. The U.S. Senate had earlier introduced a bill calling on President Obama to support Uganda's fight against the LRA, a measure that, if adopted, could lead to a joint military operation, observers said. In June the army arrested 11 more people allegedly aligned with the rebel movement.

POLITICAL PARTIES AND GROUPS

In 1986 President Museveni ordered the suspension of political party activity pending the adoption of a new constitution, although several parties were allowed to maintain offices and small staffs. The 1989 elections were conducted on a "nonparty" basis, even though members of at least four parties (the CP, the DP, UPC, and the Uganda Patriotic Movement [UPM]) ran for office with their affiliations obvious to voters. Several others, principally political wings of military groups that had been absorbed by the NRA, had by then been effectively dissolved.

In March 1990 the government extended the formal party ban until 1995, President Museveni continuing to question the advisability of restoring a full-fledged multiparty system. Museveni's official explanation for banning political party activity was that it would cause ethnic divisions within the country. NRM officials claimed the country operated under a no-party system, although the opposition charged that the NRM operated as a party even though it claimed not to be one. Originally the ban on all party activity was to last until 2000, when the question of a multiparty system would be addressed in a referendum. The announced result of that referendum was that voters had said yes to a continued "no-party" system with the NRM in control, although the opposition questioned the legality of the election. Ultimately, a court invalidated the referendum on a technicality, but the issue of multiparty activity persisted and was addressed in a referendum on June 28, 2005, and a number of political groups emerged in Uganda to address the reforms and to contest the 2006 elections.

Originally the referendum questions of a multiparty versus a no-party system and the extension of presidential term limits were to appear on the same ballot. A "yes" vote for multiparty activity would have also meant a "yes" for term-limit extensions. In a remarkable show of independence in June 2005, parliament voted to allow citizens to vote on each issue separately. Both amendments were approved by voters, though opposition groups—styled the G6 (the FDC, UPC, DP, CP, JEEMA, and the Free Movement)—boycotted the referendum, and turnout was low (officially 47 percent, though reports from exit polls put turnout at about 20 percent). Multiparty presidential and parliamentary elections were held for the first time in 20 years in February 2006. The UPC and the DP subsequently withdrew from the G6.

In August 2006 a dozen parties and groups reportedly merged to form The Parties Platform (TPP), chaired by Emmanuel TUMUSIIME, to present a united front to try to gain power. The groups opposed a proposal by President Museveni that only the parties that held seats in parliament could participate in drafting a code of conduct for interparty cooperation. The parties of the TPP are: the Forum for Integrity in Leadership; the National Unity Party; the National Peasants Party; the Farmers Party of Uganda; the Movement for Democratic Change; the National Unity, Reconciliation, and Development Party; the Uganda People's Party; the Movement of Volunteers and Mobilizers; the Liberal Democratic Transparency; the People's United Movement; the National Convention for Democracy; and the Uganda Patriotic Movement.

Dominant Government Party:

National Resistance Movement (NRM). The NRM was formed following the controversial 1980 election by former president Yusuf K. Lule and Yoweri Museveni, the former directing the political wing from exile in London and the latter leading internal guerrilla activity through the National Resistance Army (NRA). Upon his assumption of the presidency in January 1986, Museveni declared that the NRM was a "clear-headed movement" dedicated to the restoration of democracy in Uganda. Despite the ineffectiveness of subsequent membership drives, Museveni on several occasions suggested that the NRM could become the centerpiece of a one-party or limited-party state in which wide-ranging political expression would be permitted but ethnic and religious sectarianism avoided.

In a dramatic turnaround, however, Museveni sponsored the motion in parliament in 2005 for a national referendum on a multiparty system versus a no-party system. Museveni championed multiparty political activity, observers said, to appease Western donors by assuring them of his intention to move toward a more democratic society. In addition, the multiparty ballot question was paired with a provision that would eliminate the two-term limit on the presidency, thus virtually assuring Museveni of a third five-year term.

In 2008 rifts were reported within the party between those who backed Museveni for another term and those who pressed for finding a successor, in addition to tensions resulting from Museveni's tightened control over the party. In September some 500 disaffected members of the FDC reportedly joined the NRM.

In advance of the 2011 general elections, in which Museveni said he would seek a fourth term, the NRM dominated local by-elections in 2009, winning in areas traditionally dominated by the opposition.

Leaders: Lt. Gen. Yoweri MUSEVENI (President of the Republic and Chair of the Party), Moses KIGONGO (Vice Chair), Crispus KIYUNGA (National Political Commissar), Ofwono OPONDO (Spokesperson), Dorothy HYUHA (Deputy Secretary General), Amama MBABAZI (Secretary General).

Other Legislative Parties:

Uganda People's Congress (UPC). The largely Protestant UPC was formed in 1960 with a stated commitment to "African socialism." It served as the ruling party under former president Apollo Milton Obote from independence until 1971 and again from late 1980 to 1985. Despite the inclusion of several UPC adherents in the initial Museveni administration, friction persisted between the government and Obote loyalists, particularly hardliners who launched splinters, such as the UPF, in response to the pro-Museveni posture of their former colleagues.

In February 1991 the **October 9 Movement,** an Obote-led UPC faction named after the date of Ugandan independence, was reportedly operating from a Nairobi-subsidized "training camp" along the Ugandan border in Kenya. Obote's chief of staff was identified as Lt. Col. John OGORE; also listed as movement leaders were Peter OTAI, former commander of the **Uganda People's Army** (UPA), and Peter OWILI, known as "the butcher of Nile Mansions" for the brutal interrogation methods he employed during Obote's presidency.

Despite living in exile in Zambia, Obote continued to control the UPC, and in June 1996 he ordered Assistant Secretary General Cecilia OGWAL not to participate in parliamentary elections. However, Ogwal, who had been credited with maintaining party unity after Obote's departure, defied his edict and captured a seat. Consequently, Obote dismissed her and named James RWANYARARE party spokesperson and chair of the UPC's Presidential Policy Commission (i.e., de facto party leader). For her part, Ogwal rejected Obote's authority to intervene and announced the formation of her own "task force," an act one observer described as an intraparty "coup" attempt. Her underfinanced splinter group was subsequently described as unlikely to challenge Rwanyarare, although she remained a controversial figure in the party. In 2005 Obote dismissed Rwanyarare and dissolved the Presidential Policy Commission, replacing it with a Constitutional Steering Committee. Ultimately, a court ordered the party to sort out its differences following the death of Obote in October 2005. The former president's widow, Miria Kalule Obote, was elected party leader in November 2005. She placed last in 2006 presidential balloting with less than 1 percent of the vote. (She was the first woman presidential candidate in Uganda and the first woman to lead a major political party.)

In January 2008 one faction within the party expressed its dissatisfaction with Miria Obote, but she refused to relinquish the presidency. Party veteran Joseph OTHIENO was vying to become party president in late 2009, as were numerous others, including former secretary general Peter Walubiri. Meanwhile, following an amendment to the party's constitution that reduces the president's term from seven years to five, Miria Obote said that she was ready to retire. In a subsequent move seen as Obote's way of ensuring that her son succeeded her, Obote reshuffled the party leadership in June 2009, replacing Walubiri and installing her son, Jimmy Akena, as vice chair.

Despite having considered an electoral alliance with three other parties in advance of the 2011 general election, the UPC decided to field its own presidential and legislative candidates. The move reportedly caused some friction among the other parties involved—the FDC, CP, and JEEMA. In June 2009 some members of the UPC were backing former UN diplomat, Olara OTUNNU as the UPC's presidential candidate.

Leaders: Miria Kalule OBOTE (Party Leader and 2006 presidential candidate), Jimmy AKENA (Vice Chair), Badru WEGULO (Vice President), Akhbar Adoko NEKYON, Patrick MWONDHA (Treasurer), Chris OPOKA (Secretary General).

Democratic Party (DP). An advocate of centralization and a mixed economy, the DP draws on a solid Roman Catholic base and enjoys widespread support in southern Uganda. Officially, it ran second to the UPC in the post-Amin balloting of December 1980, winning 51 of 126 legislative seats, although the results were strongly challenged. The DP subsequently was weakened by defections to the UPC and sporadic harassment, killing, or detention of its leadership by the Obote government. While DP president Paul Ssemogerere joined the Okello cabinet, most DP leaders supported Museveni's NRA in continued guerrilla fighting. Several members of the DP executive committee were included in Museveni's first cabinet, and, despite reports of some deterioration in DP–NRM relations, Ssemogerere was named second deputy prime minister and foreign minister in February 1988; he retained both posts in the cabinet reorganization of July 1991.

In mid-1992 Ssemogerere was the reported leader of a cabinet revolt against Museveni's request for extension of the ban on political party activities; however, in May 1993 he advised party activists to curtail operations in the face of a presidential decree banning theretofore implicitly acceptable activities. In June 1995 the DP leader resigned as second deputy prime minister and minister of public service to position himself for the forthcoming presidential campaign.

In early 1996 the DP and the UPC forged an unofficial alliance, the Inter-Party Coalition (IPC), on the premise that in return for its support of DP candidates in the 1996 elections the UPC would be the opposition's standard-bearer at the next national elections. Subsequently, a number of UPC leaders made campaign appearances with Ssemogerere; however, following the DP leader's overwhelming electoral defeat, the UPC's Obote reportedly denied the coalition's existence. Collaterally, observers speculated that the alliance had cost Ssemogerere the votes of the Baganda people, who had been oppressed by Obote's regime and continued to resent him. Although Ssemogerere described the presidential polling as "rigged" in favor of the incumbent and subsequently boycotted the June legislative balloting, suggestions that the party would go into opposition were greeted with skepticism by observers, who cited the DP's history of participation in NRM governments. Subsequent to the June 2000 referendum (which the DP boycotted) on political party activity, Ssemogerere announced his intention to resign the party presidency, but he stayed on until his retirement in 2005. Factions within the party clashed in advance of the 2005 constitutional referendum but reportedly reunited a month later. John Ssebaana Kizito was elected party leader in November 2005, ending Ssemogerere's 25-year reign, and faction leader Hajji Ali Sserunjogi was elected vice president. Ssebaana finished third behind Museveni in the 2006 presidential election with 1.58 percent of the vote.

Dissension in the party was reported in 2007, resulting in the formation of a breakaway group, the Social Democratic Party (see Other Groups, below), and the demotion of Secretary General Lulume Bayige to deputy secretary general. Subsequently, Bayiga served as acting secretary general until August 2008, when the party elected Mathias Nsubuga to fill the post. In September party vice president Hajji Ali Sserunjogi and chair Joseph Mukiibi were suspended because of their refusal to accept the appointment of Nsubuga. The two men disputed their suspension. Meanwhile, the party rejected a proposed electoral coalition that would have included the FDC and several other parties for the 2011 poll, as some DP members backed a regional party leader, Norbert MAO, to be the party's flagbearer.

Leaders: John SSEBAANA Kizito (President and 2006 presidential candidate), Hajji Ali SSERUNJOGI (Vice President), Joseph MUKIIBI (Chair), Lulume BAYIGA, Mathias NSUBUGA (Secretary General).

Forum for Democratic Change (FDC). This opposition group was formed in July 2004 by a merger of the Reform Agenda, the Parliamentary Advocacy Forum, and the National Democratic Forum. The FDC's leader in exile, retired colonel Kizza Besigye, had challenged Museveni in the 2001 presidential election. Several opposition members of parliament previously affiliated with the UPC and DP reportedly joined the new group, which declared its intentions of becoming "a strong, democratic, mass organization."

Besigye returned from the United States in 2005 in order to participate in 2006 elections and drew large crowds at a number of rallies in areas that traditionally had supported Museveni. In what observers said was an attempt to prevent Besigye from challenging Museveni in the 2006 elections, Besigye was arrested in Kampala for allegedly supporting the rebel PRA based in the DRC and charged with treason. He was also charged with rape in connection with a 1997 case but was cleared of that charge in March 2006. Earlier, the FDC nominated him as the group's presidential candidate, and Besigye was freed on bail a month ahead of the 2006 presidential election. He came in a distant second to Museveni. Besigye subsequently was offered a seat in parliament by a newly elected delegate who reportedly calculated that the FDC leader would wield more power as leader of the opposition. However, Besigye turned down the offer.

In 2007 Besigye said he would step down as party leader in 2010 in advance of party preparations for the 2011 elections. Regan OKUMU, a member of parliament, soon declared his intention to contest the party presidency. A rift reportedly developed in the party in July 2008 during a meeting to determine a successor to Sulaiman KIGGUNDU, the party's national chair who had died a month earlier. John Butime was named acting national chair. In February 2009, however, Besigye defeated former army commander Gregory Mugisha MUNTU to retain leadership of the party. In April the FDC challenged the country's electoral commission, seeking to delay local by-elections with legal challenges accusing the commission of being unable to conduct fair elections.

The FDC was among four parties that explored an electoral alliance ahead of the 2011 general election, but no consensus was reached. Meanwhile, Besigye's wife, Winnie BYANYIMA, indicated that she might seek the presidency in 2011.

In 2009 more than 100 NRM members defected to the FDC.

Leaders: Dr. Kizza BESIGYE (Party Leader and 2001 and 2006 presidential candidate), Ofwono OPONDO (Spokesperson), Salaami MUSUMBA (Vice President), Geoffrey EKANYA, Odongo OTTO, John BUTIME (Acting National Chair), Nuwe Amanya MUSHEGA, Alice ALASO (Secretary General).

Conservative Party (CP). The CP is a small formation whose leader, prime minister of Baganda in 1964–1966, participated in the Okello and Museveni governments. CP has adopted to some extent the positions of the **Baganda Royalist Movement,** which has long sought restoration of the traditional Kingdom of Baganda.

In early 2005 rival factions divided the group, and a lengthy dispute over leadership ensued until May, when Mayanja Nkangi, on one side, reconciled with Yusufu Nsubuga Nsombu and John Ken Lukyamuzi on the other. Lukyamuzi, who supported the DP's Ssemogerere in the 1996 presidential election over Museveni, initially supported the FDC's Besigye in 2006, then said he would run for president but did not appear on the ballot. Lukyamuzi was forced to leave parliament in 2006 for allegedly breaking the law by failing to disclose his wealth. (Lukyamuzi petitioned the High Court to review the case.) Subsequently, a dispute over his leadership of the party remained unresolved. In 2008 Lukyamuzi continued to lead one faction of the party, while Nkangi claimed leadership of the "mainstream" CP faction. According to the inspector general for government (IGG), however, Lukyamuzi was ineligible for any leadership post for five years because of his earlier failure to reveal his assets.

In August 2008 the CP was among several opposition parties that was exploring an electoral alliance ahead of the 2011 general election. In May the CP and other opposition parties called for electoral reforms, including banning representation of the army in parliament and establishing an impartial and independent electoral commission.

Leaders: John Ken LUKYAMUZI, Mayanja NKANGI, Yusufu NSUBUGA NSOMBU, Ashe James SEKAGGYA. Ssemusu MUGOBANSONGA (Secretary General).

Justice Forum (Justice, Education, Economy, Morality, African Unity—JEEMA). The Justice Forum was formed in October 1996 by Mohamed Mayanja Kibirige, who secured only 2.1 percent of the vote in the 1996 presidential election, to rally support for his candidacy in the 2001 presidential election. (Mayanja received just 1 percent of the vote in 2001.) In 2004 the group, which reportedly seeks a democratic, federal system of government, rejected a merger with the FDC.

Mayanja initially announced he would seek the presidency in 2006 but later withdrew.

JEEMA was among several parties exploring an electoral alliance in advance of the 2011 general election.

Leaders: Mohamed MAYANJA Kibirige (President and 1996 and 2001 presidential candidate), Alex OJOK (Vice President), Hussein KYANJO (Secretary General).

Other Groups:

Progressive Alliance Party (PAP). Established in April 2005 by Bernard KIBIRIGE, a former aide to Brig. Henry TUMUKUNDE, who was dismissed from his post as Uganda's military intelligence chief, the PAP has had a divisive history.

Its leaders deny that they are front men for Tumukunde, who was arrested in May 2005. (Tumukunde played a key role in Museveni's 1996 and 2001 elections, allegedly using "strong-arm" tactics and military intelligence to help the president.) Meanwhile, a rival intelligence chief and former supporter of Museveni, David Pulkol, left the FDC to join the PAP in September 2005, prompting accusations from Kibirige and other party members that Pulkol was sent by the NRM to spy on and "destroy" the party. Subsequently, however, Pulkol, who also had ties to Tumukunde, was elected party president and nominated as the party's presidential candidate for the 2006 election. Infighting in the party was blamed for his failing to meet the registration deadline, and in 2006 the group supported Kizza Besigye's FDC candidacy. A month before the election, about 100 PAP members linked to Tumukunde defected to the NRM and demanded Tumukunde's release. Reportedly, many of the defectors had been part of a "task force" organized by Tumukunde to support Museveni's 2001 bid, and they left the PAP in part because the party had no presidential candidate for 2006. Party secretary general Kibirige said in 2006 that he had quit politics to concentrate on his business.

Leaders: David PULKOL (President), Dr. Kaddu MULINDWA (Interim Chair).

Other groups include the **Freedom Movement,** part of the so-called G6 group of opposition parties that opposed the 2005 constitutional referendum; **Forces for Change,** a splinter opposition group formed in March 2005 by Nasser Ntege SSEBAGALA and David Pulkol (who later joined the PAP); the **Reform Party,** a breakaway group from the FDC, founded by Robert NDYOMUGYENYI and reportedly dissolved in 2006; the **National Peasants Party,** led by Erias WAMALA; the

Republican Women and Youth Party, led by Stella NAMBUYA; the **People's Independent Party,** led by Yahaya KAMULEGEYA and Amin SSENTONGO; **Movement for Democratic Change,** led by Paulsen KITIMBO; the **National People's Organization,** led by Abdu JAGWE; the **National Convention for Democracy,** led by Haji Jingo KAAYA; the **Farmers Party of Uganda,** led by Mudde Bombakka NSKIO; the **National Unity, Reconciliation, and Development Party,** led by Joseph NYANZI; and the **People's Progressive Party**, led by Jaberi Bidandi SSALI. In November 2007 the **Social Democratic Party** was formed by a group of dissidents from the DP, including Henry LUBOWA and Michael MABIKKE.

Guerrilla Groups:

Lord's Resistance Army (LRA). The LRA first emerged in the late 1980s as Lakwena Part Two, a small, predominantly Acholi successor group to the Holy Spirit Movement that had been led by "voodoo priestess" Alice LAKWENA from 1986 until her flight to Kenya in 1987 (Lakwena died in 2007). Under the leadership of Joseph Kony, the anti-NRA rebels remained active in northern Uganda, and in early 1991 the militants reportedly began referring to themselves as the Uganda Democratic Christian Army. Following inconclusive negotiations with government representatives in early 1994, Kony and his supporters launched a new offensive under their current name, claiming they were fighting "a holy war against foreign occupation" and seeking to install a government guided by the biblical Ten Commandments.

Casualties linked to the insurgency reached a one-month high of approximately 200 in March 1996. Observers attributed the violent upsurge to the recent arrival from Sudan of freshly armed and trained LRA fighters, many of whom were believed to have been Ugandan youths kidnapped by Kony in 1995. Kidnappings and disfigurements of uncooperative villagers have caused an international condemnation of the LRA. Several attempts at peace talks have failed. In June 1996 Museveni offered amnesty to the "ordinary fighters" affiliated with the LRA and a second group, the West Bank Nile Front (WBNF, see below), but pledged to prosecute the groups' leaders.

LRA bases in Sudan came under sustained attack by Sudanese rebel forces and the Ugandan Army beginning in April 1997, and in July LRA commanders reportedly called for a cease-fire. Subsequently, in the second half of 1997 Kony led his fighters in a series of cross-border raids, although the LRA had been forced to break into much smaller fighting cells than its usual 150–200 member units. Despite heavy casualties, according to government officials, the LRA continued to replenish its ranks by abducting teenage Ugandans and forcing them to march to Sudan for training and indoctrination.

In late 1998 a group of LRA dissidents led by Ronald Otim KOMAKECH reportedly split from the group following a dispute over the LRA's alleged targeting of civilians; subsequently, Komakech formed the **LRA–Democratic** and allied the splinter with the **Uganda National Rescue Front** (UNRF, below). The level of LRA activities actually increased after a December 1999 treaty between Sudan and Uganda ostensibly designed to end support for guerrilla groups. LRA activity subsided in 2000–2001, largely due to behind-the-scenes negotiations mediated by the U.S.-based Carter Center in Atlanta, which tried to initiate talks with LRA leader Kony and his backers, the Sudanese government. In February 2001, however, LRA rebels attacked a northern Ugandan town and abducted 40 people. In March Ugandan wildlife authorities suspended game-viewing activities in parts of the northwestern Murchison Falls National Park following an alleged LRA ambush in which at least 10 people were killed. In 2004 gains made by the Ugandan People's Defense Force (UPDF) against the rebels seemed to compel the LRA to seek a cease-fire. By mid-2005, however, talks had not made significant progress. Meanwhile, evidence of cooperation between Sudanese and Ugandan troops against the LRA raised hopes that combined pressure might force Kony's group into meaningful negotiations. In 2005 the ICC issued arrest warrants for Kony and other LRA leaders. Subsequently, the LRA leaders ensconced themselves in forested areas of the DRC and intermittently engaged in negotiations toward a permanent truce with the Ugandan government in 2006 and 2007.

Kony was reported to have executed his one-time deputy, Vincent Otti, in October 2007. Alfred James OBITA took over as leader of the LRA's negotiation team after David MATSANGA was dismissed in April 2008. Subsequently, it was reported that Matsanga had returned to replace Obita, whom Kony had dismissed. On August 4 the government granted amnesty to Obita and several other LRA and ADF rebels (see Current issues, above.) Two of Kony's top commanders, Okot ODHIAMBO (whom Kony was reported to have killed in 2008) and Dominic ONGWEN, reportedly were killed or wounded in December when their hideout was attacked by a joint military operation from which Kony escaped. Subsequently, other unconfirmed reports surfaced that Odhiambo had defected from the Kony camp in 2009 and was requesting amnesty. Another top commander, Thomas KWOYELO, was said to have been captured on March 3, 2009.

Leaders: Joseph KONY, Oti LAGONY, Willy ORYEM, Yusuf ADEK.

Allied Democratic Forces (ADF). The ADF is reportedly composed of remnants of the late Amon BAZIRA's National Movement for the Liberation of Uganda, and Islamic militant fighters, styled the *Salaaf Tabliqs,* allegedly funded by the Sudanese government. ADF activity was first reported in 1995, but the group did not achieve prominence until 1997 when its numbers were reportedly swollen by the addition of former Zairean government forces and Rwandan Hutu *Interahamwé* fighters.

A government offensive in mid-1997 decimated the ADF's fighting strength and drove a majority of its fighters deep into the mountains of the Democratic Republic of the Congo (DRC). However, ADF militants were allegedly responsible for grenade attacks in Kampala in early 1998, and thereafter the ADF launched a series of attacks that claimed dozens of civilian lives. In February 1999 the ADF was accused of orchestrating a deadly bomb attack in Kampala. A number of ADF militants were killed in subsequent government raids, while the ADF was accused of killing both civilians and soldiers in several incidents throughout the rest of the year. In April 2000 the Ugandan government pulled out 2,000 soldiers from eastern DRC, claiming that the threat of cross-border ADF incursions was greatly reduced. Ugandan authorities in July arrested 28 ADF recruits accused of undertaking bomb attacks that have killed 67 people and injured 262 others since 1997. The ADF had resorted to urban terrorism after its ground insurgency was defeated in the mountains straddling Uganda's western border with the DRC. Some ADF rebel leaders and fighters allegedly were trained in terrorist Osama bin Laden's Afghan camps, and in December 2001 the United States listed the ADF as a terrorist organization. Clashes between Ugandan forces and ADF rebels continued into 2006, with security forces arresting and killing many suspected ADF members in the western forests of Uganda. The militants reportedly were fleeing the DRC following fighting between the Congolese army and UN peacekeeping forces. In 2007, the ADF's second in command, Balaya ISIKO, was killed in fighting with DRC soldiers. The ADF in western Uganda reportedly had been defeated by the Ugandan army.

In 2008 it was reported that the ADF was seeking peace talks with the Ugandan government. News reports said that the group had not been active in recent years. However, in July the Ugandan army claimed the ADF was regrouping and recruiting in the DRC. In 2009 the group's leader, Jamir Mukulu, was reported as saying he was ready to resume fighting if the Ugandan government did not commit to a peace process.

Leaders: Jamir MUKULU, Yusuf KABANDA.

West Bank Nile Front (WBNF). The WBNF was formed during the Obote era by West Nile people who had reportedly been forced to flee to Sudan and Zaire to escape government persecution. Although President Museveni successfully integrated most of the dissident West Nile leaders into his NRM regime and facilitated the repatriation of the majority of the remaining refugees, the WBNF, allegedly funded by Sudan and Zaire, remained active through the 1990s under the leadership of Maj. Juma ORIS. Prior to the 1996 presidential elections the WBNF was reported to have penetrated close to the provincial capital of Arua before being driven back by government forces.

In early 1997 WBNF bases in Zaire were overrun by Ugandan forces, and the rebels fled into Sudan, where they suffered further heavy losses at the hands of Sudanese rebels. Oris was reportedly killed in February, and in March the group's deputy commander, Abdulatif Toya, was captured in Sudan. In August another WBNF leader, Hajji Kabeba, was arrested by government forces. In recent years WBNF activities have been extremely limited.

Leaders: Abdulatif TOYA (under arrest), Hajji KABEBA (Zairean-based Commander, under arrest), Zubair ATAMVAKU.

United Freedom Front/Army (UFF/A). The UFF/A was founded in London, United Kingdom, in February 1999 by Herman Ssemuju, former leader of the **National Freedom Party,** who had fled Uganda in 1998. (Ssemuju had run for president in 1996.) Among those in attendance at the UFF/A's launching were representatives of the LRA and ADF.

Leader: Herman SSEMUJU.

Other rebel groups have been formed in opposition to the government since Museveni's takeover in 1986, but their activities have mostly subsided or their members have been absorbed by government amnesties. In 1994 most of the *Ruwenzuru,* a 30-year-old Bakonjo autonomist group from the west, surrendered to the government, and responses to presidential amnesty continued after that. For example, the **Uganda National Rescue Front** (UNRF), led by Ali BAMUZE, began softening its stance toward the regime in 1998, and in June 2002 the government announced that a cease-fire with the UNRF had been reached. In 2007 it was reported that ten former UNFR rebels had been integrated into the Ugandan People's Defense Forces.

LEGISLATURE

The former National Assembly was dissolved following the July 1985 coup. On February 1, 1986, an appointed National Resistance Council (NRC) of 23 members was sworn in to serve as an interim legislature, its enactments being subject to presidential approval. Additional members were named in subsequent months, and in mid-1987 the NRC was expanded to include the cabinet as well as deputy and assistant ministers. In early 1989 the council was further enlarged to 278 members, of whom 210 were indirectly elected (168 on a district constituency basis, 34 as regional women's representatives, 5 representing youth organizations, and 3 representing trade unions), with the remaining 68 appointed by the president.

Balloting for a new, formally recognized **Parliament** was held on a "no-party" basis in June 1996. Government-supportive candidates captured or were appointed to 271 of the 276 available seats, while unrecognized opposition candidates reportedly secured the remaining 5 posts. Balloting was again held on a nonparty basis on June 26, 2001, for 214 chamber seats. (There were also 81 indirectly elected legislators who are selected by various interest groups, predominately the National Resistance Movement—NRM). In addition, members of the cabinet who are not already sitting legislators serve as ex-officio members of Parliament. Supporters of opposition parties were allowed to run on an individual basis, and several were elected. However, it was reported that NRM supporters secured more than 200 of the elected seats.

In multiparty balloting of February 23, 2006 (the first following the 2005 constitutional revision), 215 seats were directly elected on a constituency basis; 80 additional district seats are reserved for women and another 25 seats are reserved for representatives of youth, workers, and disabled persons (with requirements that some of these seats be reserved for women); 13 seats are filled on an ex-officio basis by cabinet ministers appointed by the president and the number may vary according to the president's wishes. The seat distribution was as follows: National Resistance Movement (NRM), 206 (141 constituency, 51 district women, 13 indirectly chosen); Forum for Democratic Change, 37 (27 constituency, 10 district women); Uganda People's Congress, 9; Democratic Party, 8; Justice Forum, 1; Conservative Party, 1; independents, 37 (28 constituency, 8 district women, 1 indirectly chosen). A by-election was held on June 30, 2006, to replace an NRM candidate who died before taking office; another NRM candidate was elected. On August 28, 2006, elections were held for women district representatives in 10 new districts, increasing the total number of seats held by women to 99.

Speaker: Edward SSEKANDI Kiwanika.

CABINET

[as of June 1, 2009]

Prime Minister	Apolo Nsibambi
First Deputy Prime Minister	Eriya Kategaya
Second Deputy Prime Minister	Henry Kajura
Third Deputy Prime Minister	Ali Kirunda Kivejinja
Office of the President	Beatrice Wabudeya [f]
Prime Minister's Office	Janat Mukwaya [f]

Ministers

Agriculture, Animal Husbandry, and Fisheries	Hope Mwesigye [f]
Defense	Crispus Kiyunga
East African Affairs	Eriya Kategaya
Education and Sports	Geraldine Bitamazire [f]
Energy and Mineral Development	Hillary Onke
Finance, Planning, and Economic Development	Sydda Bbumba [f]
Foreign Affairs	Sam Kutesa
Gender, Labor, and Social Development	Opio Gabriel
Government Chief Whip	Daudi Migereko
Health	Dr. Steven Mallinga
Information Communications Technology	Aggrey Awori
Information and National Guidance	Kabakumba L. Matsiko
Justice and Constitutional Affairs and Attorney General	Kiddu Makubuya
Lands, Housing, and Urban Development	Omara Atubo
Local Government	Adolf Mwesigye
Public Works	John Nasasira
Relief and Disaster Preparedness	Tarsis Kabwegyere
Security	Amama Mbabazi
Trade and Industry	Maj.-Gen. Kahinda Otafire [f]
Water and Environment	Maria Mutagamba [f]
Without Portfolio	Dorothy Hyuha [f]

[f] = female

COMMUNICATIONS

The press under the Amin regime was subject to very strict censorship and saw an extremely high rate of attrition. Substantial relaxation occurred after the installation of President Binaisa in June 1979. In March 1981 the Obote government banned a number of papers that had been critical of the UPC and subsequently took additional measures against both foreign and domestic journalists who had commented unfavorably on the security situation within Uganda. The press has enjoyed relative freedom under the current regime. Several private radio stations and private television stations report on local political developments. The largest newspapers and broadcasting facilities that reach rural areas remain state-owned. Governmental corruption is reported. Opposition positions are also presented, but the coverage is often not balanced. Journalists have asked parliament to enact a freedom of information act so that the public is not denied information. Intermittently journalists are arrested, but generally their cases have been handled fairly in the country's judicial system.

Nation TV, owned by the Aga Khan and his Nairobi-based media group, was shut down in February 2007 by the government which cited technical reasons and reportedly required a large fee before the station was permitted to reopen. The government reportedly defied an April parliamentary directive that allowed the station to reopen. In April 2008 the publisher of a privately owned bimonthly, *The Independent*, and two journalists affiliated with the paper were arrested for allegedly possessing seditious material. According to the watchdog Reporters Without Borders, the charges stemmed from interviews the newspaper had conducted with people who claimed to have been tortured while in government detention. The newspaper's founder earlier had received the annual International Press Freedom Award conferred by the watchdog Committee to Protect Journalists. Meanwhile, it was reported that the president was using the 2002 Suppression of Terrorism Act "to criminalize news 'likely to promote terrorism' and to compel journalists to reveal their sources in court," according to *Africa Confidential*.

In May 2009 the military detained without charge a journalist with a state-run media company who was accused of being involved with rebel activity in the country's northern region.

Press. The following, unless otherwise noted, are English-language dailies published in Kampala: *New Vision* (40,000), NRM organ launched in March 1986 as successor to the *Uganda Times,* which had ceased publication in early 1985; *The Monitor* (34,000), weekly; *Taifa*

Uganda Empya (24,000), in Luganda; *Topic* (13,000), radical weekly; *Focus* (13,000), weekly; *Ngabo* (7,000), independent, in Luganda; *Munno* (15,000), Catholic daily, in Luganda; *The Star* (5,500), independent; *The Citizen,* DP organ; *The Financial Times; Munnansi News Bulletin,* DP weekly in Luganda.

News agencies. The domestic facility is the Uganda News Agency (UNA); a number of foreign agencies maintain bureaus in Kampala.

Broadcasting and computing. The Ministry of Information and Broadcasting controls Radio Uganda, which broadcasts in 24 languages over two networks, and Uganda Television, which broadcasts primarily in English. There is also an independent television outlet broadcasting in the Kampala area. Another state-owned broadcasting company is Mega FM, based in Gulu. As of 2008 there were 79 Internet users per 1,000 inhabitants.

INTERGOVERNMENTAL REPRESENTATION

Ambassador to the U.S.: Perezi Karukubiro KAMUNANWIRE.

U.S. Ambassador to Uganda: Jerry P. LANIER.

Permanent Representative to the UN: Ruhakana RUGUNDA.

IGO Memberships (Non-UN): AfDB, AU, BADEA, Comesa, CWTH, EAC, EADB, IDB, IGAD, Interpol, IOM, NAM, OIC, PCA, WCO, WTO.

UKRAINE

Ukrayina

Note: Former prime minister Viktor Yanukovych of the Party of Regions finished first in the first round of presidential balloting on January 17, 2010, with 35 percent of the vote. Prime Minister Yulia Tymoshenko finished second with 25 percent of the vote, while incumbent president Viktor Yushchenko secured only 5 percent. A runoff between Yanukovych and Tymoshenko was scheduled for February 7.

Political Status: Formerly the Ukrainian Soviet Socialist Republic, a constituent republic of the Union of Soviet Socialist Republic; declared independence on August 24, 1991; new constitution adopted on June 28, 1996.

Area: 233,090 sq. mi. (603,700 sq. km.).

Population: 48,457,000 (2001C); 46,052,000 (2008E).

Major Urban Centers (including suburbs, 2005E): KIEV (KYÏV, 1,771,000), Donetsk (Donèc'k, 4,644,000), Dnepropetrovsk (Dniprop̀etrovsk, 3,461,000), Kharkov (Charkiv, 2,837,000), Lvov (L'viv, 2,582,000), Odessa (Odèsa, 2,407,000).

Official Language: Ukrainian (replaced Russian in 1990). The Council for Language Policy and the National Orthography Commission are currently working to restore syntax, style, and other aspects of Ukrainian to what they were before the 1930s, when Moscow ordered Ukrainian to be made more uniform with Russian.

Monetary Unit: Hryvna (official rate December 1, 2009: 8.01 hryvnas = $1US).

President: *(See headnote.)* Viktor YUSHCHENKO ("Our Ukraine" Bloc); elected in rerun second-round balloting on December 26, 2004, and sworn in for a five-year term on January 23, 2005, succeeding Leonid Danilovych KUCHMA. (The next election was scheduled for January 17, 2010.)

Prime Minister: Yulia TYMOSHENKO (Yulia Tymoshenko Bloc); inaugurated on December 18, 2007, to succeed Viktor YANUKOVYCH (Party of Regions) following the legislative elections of September 30.

THE COUNTRY

The third largest and second most populous of the former Soviet republics, Ukraine is bordered on the north by Belarus, on the east by Russia, on the south by the Black Sea, and on the west by Moldova, Romania, Hungary, Slovakia, and Poland. Approximately 71 percent of the population is Ukrainian and 22 percent Russian, with no other group greater than 1 percent. The ethnic Russian population is located primarily in southern and eastern Ukraine, where there is significant sentiment in favor of the reestablishment of greater economic, political, and military integration with Russia. The population in western Ukraine is described as strongly anticommunist and supportive of the country's orientation toward Western Europe. Most Ukrainians profess Eastern Orthodoxy, although there is a sizable Roman Catholic community and smaller numbers of Muslims and Jews.

The black-earth steppe of the south, one of the world's most productive farming regions, provided about one-quarter of the foodstuffs for the former Union of Soviet Socialist Republics (USSR). Agriculture currently accounts for about 12 percent of GDP and 15 percent of employment. The leading crop is wheat (Ukraine is one of the world's leading grain producers), followed by sugar beets, potatoes, and a wide variety of other vegetables and fruits. Natural resources, including iron, coal, bauxite, zinc, oil, and natural gas, have long supported a broad range of manufacturing activity, including metallurgy, machine building, and chemical production, which accounted for nearly a third of the Soviet Union's industrial output. Industry now contributes about 40 percent of Ukrainian GDP, primarily from mining and metallurgy, and employs some 25 percent of the labor force. Steel is the country's leading export.

The demise of the Soviet system yielded a 50 percent contraction in economic output in Ukraine in 1990–1994, accompanied by inflation that spiraled to more than 4,700 percent in 1993 before falling to 890 percent in 1994 and to under 100 percent in 1995. GDP declined by 12.2 percent in 1995, 10.0 percent in 1996, and 3.0 percent in 1997, when inflation fell to 10 percent. A modest recovery appeared possible for 1998 until the economy was rocked by the Russian financial collapse of August, which constrained trade between the two countries and prompted a significant outflow of capital. Consequently, GDP fell by another 1.9 percent for 1998, and inflation increased to 20 percent.

GDP declined by only 0.4 percent in 1999, and in 2000 the economy expanded for the first time since independence, achieving 6 percent growth. The International Monetary Fund (IMF), which had encouraged stabilization and liberalization measures, attributed the advance to exchange rate depreciation, unexpected economic resilience in Russia (Ukraine's principal trading partner), and an improved world market for Ukraine's exports, led by metals. Inflation, at nearly 26 percent, remained high in 2000, but a more fundamental problem was a lack of political consensus on what direction the economy should take. At the end of the year, virtually all the large Soviet-era state enterprises remained in government hands, while privatization and other market-oriented reforms continued to meet opposition from a Communist-Socialist-Agrarian parliamentary bloc. On the right, politically well-connected entrepreneurs, the so-called oligarchs, also opposed many reform efforts, particularly in the energy sector, where greater transparency and a sharp reduction in barter arrangements among consumers, sellers, and suppliers threatened to undermine a major source of the oligarchs' wealth. (The slow pace of reform had contributed to delayed disbursements from the IMF and other multilateral lending agencies. In 1999 the IMF had also objected to a jump in public spending shortly before the presidential election and to Ukraine's use of accounting practices that inflated foreign currency reserves. However, the IMF agreed to resume lending in December 2000 after a 14-month interruption.)

GDP rose by 9.1 percent in 2001, 4.5 percent in 2002, 9.4 percent in 2003, and 13.5 percent in 2004, led by growth in the industrial sector and strong domestic consumer demand. However, Ukraine remained heavily dependent on imported energy products, particularly from Russia. In addition, the oligarchs retained a near monopoly on the industrial and financial sectors and were perceived as blocking reform of the tax system. The World Bank and IMF pledged additional aid in response to the government's action against money laundering, but the country was still viewed as a high risk by foreign investors.

Upon taking office in early 2005, President Yushchenko pledged to pursue free-market policies and to investigate the some 3,000 non-transparent privatizations that had been completed during the Kuchma administration. Foreign investors initially welcomed the market orientation brought on by the so-called Orange Revolution but were

subsequently described as "unnerved" by the political turmoil of late 2005 and the first half of 2006. Meanwhile, the IMF reported that growth had slowed to about 3 percent in 2005, while inflation had risen to an annual rate of nearly 15 percent. On a more positive note for supporters of proposed membership in the European Union (EU) and the World Trade Organization (WTO), the United States in December 2005 formally recognized Ukraine as a market economy, with the EU following suit in February 2006.

GDP growth rebounded to 6 percent in 2006, accompanied by a decline in inflation to 9 percent. Despite significant political uncertainty, the economy remained robust in 2007 as GDP grew by 7.6 percent.

The Ukrainian economy was hit extremely hard by the global financial crisis that erupted in late 2008. In November 2008 the IMF approved $16.4 billion in emergency lending over the next two years to help stabilize the financial system, although conditions attached to the lending proved domestically controversial, causing delays in loan disbursements in 2009. Declines of more than 50 percent in the metal and chemical industries contributed to a shocking 20 percent year-on-year drop in GDP as of April 2009, with unemployment climbing to more than 9 percent and annual inflation reaching 22 percent. Most observers agreed that conditions, albeit still fragile, had improved by the end of 2009, although the IMF, demanding cuts in proposed increases in wages and pension benefits, suspended disbursements until after the January 2010 presidential elections.

GOVERNMENT AND POLITICS

Political background. Under Polish rule in the 16th century, Ukraine experienced a brief period of independence in the 17th century before coming under Russian control in the 18th century. Ukraine again proclaimed independence following the overthrow of the Russian tsarist regime in 1917, with the region becoming a battlefield of conflicting forces that eventually yielded a Red Army victory and Ukraine's incorporation into the USSR as one of its constituent republics in 1922.

On July 16, 1990, the Ukrainian Supreme Soviet, under pressure from nationalist opposition forces, issued a sovereignty declaration that asserted the "indivisibility of the republic's power on its territory," its "independence and equality in external relations," and its right to countermand the utilization of its citizens for military service beyond its boundaries. In an equivocal vein, however, it failed to claim a right of secession from the Soviet Union and explicitly provided for dual Soviet and Ukrainian citizenship. The less than clear-cut nature of the declaration prompted widespread nationalist demonstrations, led primarily by student activists. On October 23 the chair of the council of ministers, Vitaliy A. MASOL, responded by submitting his resignation; he was succeeded by Vitold FOKIN.

Ukraine endorsed Soviet President Mikhail Gorbachev's union proposal in April 1991 but, in the wake of the subsequent failed hard-line coup against Gorbachev in Moscow, issued a formal declaration of independence on August 24. On August 31 the chair of the Ukrainian Supreme Soviet, Leonid KRAVCHUK, suspended the activities of the Communist Party of Ukraine (*Komunistychna Partiya Ukrainy*—KPU), and on September 4 the leader of the KPU legislative bloc announced that the group would disband. On December 1, in a vote held simultaneously with Kravchuk's reconfirmation in direct presidential balloting, Ukrainians overwhelmingly endorsed the August independence declaration. On December 8 the republic joined Belarus and Russia in announcing the demise of the Soviet Union, and on December 21 Ukraine became a founding member of the Commonwealth of Independent States (CIS).

Fokin, who had continued as prime minister upon reorganization of the council of ministers in May 1991, survived a confidence vote on July 1, 1992, following a decision to raise food prices, but he was forced to step down on September 30 amid uncertainty over the direction and pace of the republic's economic reform program. He was succeeded, on an acting basis, by First Deputy Prime Minister Valentin SIMONENKO, who yielded the office on October 27 to Leonid D. KUCHMA, the "technocrat" director of the former Soviet Union's largest arms production complex.

Increasingly battered by conservative parliamentarians opposed to his economic reform efforts, Prime Minister Kuchma submitted his resignation for the fifth time in as many months on September 9, 1993, with the Supreme Council voting acceptance of the resignation on September 21. Kuchma's deputy, Yukhym ZVYAHILSKIY, was named acting prime minister, although President Kravchuk assumed direct control of the government by decree on September 27. (Three days earlier the Supreme Council had averted a constitutional crisis by agreeing that parliamentary and presidential elections would be held in the first half of 1994.)

In first-round presidential balloting on June 26, 1994, incumbent president Kravchuk won 37.7 percent of the vote, as contrasted with 31.3 percent for former prime minister Kuchma. However, at the runoff on July 10, Kravchuk lost to his opponent, 45.1 percent to 52.1 percent, critical factors in Kuchma's success being endorsement of his candidacy by the revived KPU and support for him in the eastern industrialized areas with a heavy ethnic Russian population. At his inauguration on July 19 the new head of state promised gradual electoral reform and closer ties to Russia. Meanwhile, in an apparent overture to his pro-Russian opponents, President Kravchuk had, on June 16, 1994, reappointed Vitaliy Masol as prime minister. Masol resigned in March 1995, reportedly over economic policy differences with President Kuchma, who was seeking more active reform. Masol was replaced by Col. Gen. Yevhen MARCHUK, theretofore a deputy premier and state security chair.

The 292–4 parliamentary passage on April 4, 1995, of a motion of nonconfidence backed by both Communist conservatives and reformers precipitated a major political crisis. President Kuchma reappointed Prime Minister Marchuk on April 8 and tabled proposals to strengthen the powers of the presidency pending the adoption of a new constitution (see Constitution and government, below). The Supreme Council's failure to ratify the changes on May 30 caused the president to threaten to call a referendum, whereupon the legislature, cognizant of the wide public support for the changes, on June 15 acceded to an interim "constitutional treaty" that granted most of the new powers sought by Kuchma. Conflict over economic reform nevertheless simmered between the legislature and the president, with Kuchma's determined pursuit of a market economy generating strains not only between the president and the KPU-led bloc but also within the mainly centrist political groups that provided the president's core support.

Prime Minister Marchuk was dismissed by President Kuchma on May 27, 1996, ostensibly for shortcomings in the conduct of economic policy, and was replaced by the first deputy prime minister, Pavlo LAZARENKO. A cabinet reshuffle following the adoption of a new constitution in June 1996 was completed in October. Kuchma also reshuffled his cabinet in February 1997 in an attempt to deal with corruption, stabilize the financial system, and press on with economic reforms. In June, Prime Minister Lazarenko was replaced on an acting basis by First Deputy Prime Minister Vasyl DURDYNETS, ostensibly because of Lazarenko's failing health. However, Lazarenko had faced serious allegations of corruption and antireform sentiment, and his ouster had reportedly been ordered by Kuchma. In July the legislature approved Kuchma's nomination of Valeriy PUSTOVOYTENKO, minister of cabinet affairs and a member of the People's Democratic Party of Ukraine (*Narodno-Demokratychna Partiya Ukrainy*—NDPU), as the new permanent prime minister.

In late 1997 a new electoral law was adopted to increase the role of political parties in legislative elections by providing for half the legislators to be selected from party lists in nationwide balloting. New Supreme Council balloting was conducted under the revised system for the first time on March 29, 1998. Thanks to a strong performance in the proportional poll, the KDU improved its representation substantially. However, the KDU-led left-wing opposition was still unable to achieve a majority, with many of the independent candidates elected in the single-member districts representing business interests supportive of President Kuchma's economic reform efforts. Consequently, Prime Minister Pustovoytenko remained in office following the election, although the cabinet was extensively reshuffled in early 1999.

Thirteen candidates contested the presidential election of October 31, 1999, including Kuchma, KPU leader Petro SYMONENKO, Oleksandr MOROZ of the Socialist Party of Ukraine (*Sotsialtstychna Partiya Ukrainy*—SPU), and former prime minister Yevhen Marchuk, who was backed by a number of smaller parties. (In August, Moroz, Marchuk, and two other candidates had agreed that they would unite behind one of their number before the election, but Marchuk's selection on October 25 immediately led Moroz to assert that he would nevertheless remain in the race. A third member of the "Kaniv Four," Oleksandr TKACHENKO, chair of the Supreme Council and leader of the Peasants' Party of Ukraine [*Selyanska Partiya Ukrainy*—SelPU], withdrew in favor of Symonenko, not Marchuk.) The first round of presidential balloting ended with Kuchma claiming 36.5 percent of the vote, necessitating a November 14 runoff against the second-place Symonenko, who had won 22.2 percent. With third-place finisher Moroz and the other leftist candidates having thrown their support to Symonenko for the second round, Kuchma wielded his presidential prerogatives in an effort to secure the victory. On November 3 he dismissed the governors of three regions that had supported either Moroz or Symonenko, and on November 10 he named Marchuk head of the National Security and Defense Council in a bid to gain the 8.1 percent support Marchuk had received as fifth-place finisher in the first round. In the runoff election Kuchma took 57.7 percent of the vote. The Parliamentary Assembly of the Council of Europe and the Organization for Security and Cooperation in Europe (OSCE) were among the observer organizations citing flaws in the conduct of the second round.

Following President Kuchma's inauguration for a second term on November 30, 1999, the cabinet resigned, as required by the constitution. Kuchma quickly renominated the incumbent prime minister, but on December 14 the Supreme Council rejected Pushtovoytenko by a vote of 206–44. Two days later Kuchma nominated reformist Viktor YUSHCHENKO, the nonparty chair of the National Bank of Ukraine, who was confirmed and sworn in on December 22. The new prime minister came into office pledging a reform program that included "open" privatization, lower inflation, a balanced budget, cuts in the size of the government bureaucracy, payment of remaining wage and pension arrears, and restructuring of the agricultural sector. (President Kuchma had proposed converting the country's 10,000 collective farms into cooperatives and joint stock companies.) Subsequent cabinet changes included the appointment by Kuchma of three new deputy prime ministers, including Yulia TYMOSHENKO, a leader of Fatherland (*Batkivshchnyna*) and a former energy industry executive, who assumed responsibility for fuel and energy policy in January 2000.

On January 13, 2000, former president Kravchuk announced formation of a government-supportive parliamentary majority by 11 center-right factions, including his own Social Democratic Party of Ukraine (United) (*Sotsial-Demokratychna Partiya Ukrainy [Obyednana]*—SDPU[O]) and a number of independent deputies. The new Supreme Council majority immediately attempted to remove the SelPU's Tkachenko as parliamentary chair, but obstruction from the left initially prevented a vote. Convening in a nearby exhibition hall, the 239-member majority voted Tkachenko out of office on January 21, and on February 1 it elected in his place Ivan PLYUSHCH, who had previously served in the same capacity. The leftist opposition continued to meet in the Supreme Council chamber despite lacking a quorum, but a week later a group of majority deputies forced its way into the building. By February 15 the leftist opposition effort had lost its momentum, and regular parliamentary sessions resumed shortly thereafter.

Despite her earlier background in the energy sector, Deputy Prime Minister Tymoshenko vowed in 2000 to fight the sector's oligarchs and to end graft, insisting, for example, that electricity contracts specify transparent cash settlements instead of the barter arrangements that had left the industry open to profiteering and abuse. However, by mid-2000 Tymoshenko was drawing fire from President Kuchma, who was particularly critical of a natural gas deal Tymoshenko had initialed with Turkmenistan to reduce reliance on Russia's Gazprom, to which several of Ukraine's oligarchs had connections. In November a report from a special ministerial commission chaired by National Security and Defense Council Chief Yevhen Marchuk created additional controversy by accusing the government of overstating fuel reserves and revenues from the energy sector while understating debt owed by energy companies to the state. Yushchenko condemned the report, and Tymoshenko charged its authors with committing politically motivated inaccuracies.

On November 28, 2000, SPU leader Moroz released to the public audiotapes implicating President Kuchma and others in a plot to "get rid of" independent journalist and presidential critic Heorhiy GONGADZE, who had gone missing in mid-September and whose headless body had been recovered near Kiev in early November. Kuchma, supported by the prosecutor general's office, insisted that the relevant recordings were fabrications, although participants in other conversations on the tapes attested to their authenticity. In response to the scandal, an anti-Kuchma National Salvation Forum (NSF) was organized in February 2001, including as a member former deputy prime minister Tymoshenko, who had been dismissed by Kuchma in January after being formally charged with corruption while head of Unified Energy Systems of Ukraine in 1996–1997.

Tymoshenko characterized her January 2001 removal from office as a reprisal carried out by Kuchma on behalf of "criminal clans of oligarchs." For its part, the prosecutor general's office justified Tymoshenko's detention in February–March by citing new evidence that she had paid nearly $80 million in bribes to former prime minister Lazarenko while he was in office. (Lazarenko, his immunity from prosecution having been lifted by the Supreme Council in 1999, also continued to face numerous charges in Ukraine, from accepting bribes to ordering contract killings. In June 2000 he was convicted in Switzerland of money laundering during his earlier tenure as governor of Dnipropetrovsk. Lazarenko, not to be outdone, charged in 2000 that Kuchma and his aides had themselves embezzled and laundered hundreds of millions of dollars, including proceeds from IMF loans that were used to purchase high-yielding Ukrainian debt.)

In early 2001 a philosophically incongruous coalition, ranging from Oleksandr Moroz's Socialist Party to the fascist Ukrainian National Assembly (*Ukrainska Natsionalna Asambleya*—UNA), continued to stage a series of militant "Ukraine Without Kuchma" rallies. Meanwhile, the NSF, led by Moroz, Tymoshenko (who had quickly donned the mantle of an anticorruption, proreform antagonist), and others, also pressed for President Kuchma's resignation or removal from office. In addition, there were indications that the loyalty of Ukraine's oligarchs, who had been among Kuchma's strongest supporters, might also be wavering. As a further complication, Kuchma and Prime Minister Yushchenko were not always in agreement, although they jointly condemned the NSF in a February 2001 statement that was also signed by Supreme Council Chair Ivan Plyushch.

The new center-right parliamentary majority having already dissipated, the country's oligarchs in early 2001 demanded formation of a new government that would better represent their interests. (The oligarchs' "fiefdoms" were being threatened by Prime Minister Yushchenko's reform policies.) From the opposite side of the political spectrum, the Communists and other leftists joined the oligarchic parties in calling for the market-oriented, centrist Yushchenko to be replaced. On April 26 Yushchenko lost a no-confidence vote in the Supreme Council, 263–69. He submitted his resignation on April 27, and a day later President Kuchma dismissed the cabinet, which remained in office in a caretaker capacity. On May 29 the Supreme Council confirmed Anatoliy KINAKH, a former first deputy prime minister, as Yushchenko's successor. Kuchma announced the final appointment to a revamped cabinet on July 10.

In the context of ongoing efforts by a frequently fractious opposition to force President Kuchma's resignation or to impeach him, Ukrainians elected a new Supreme Council on March 30, 2002. Former prime minister Yushchenko's "Our Ukraine" Bloc (*Blok Viktora Yushchenka "Nasha Ukraina"*—NU) finished with a plurality of 110 seats, followed by the pro-Kuchma "For a United Ukraine!" Electoral Bloc (*Vyborchiy Blok "Za Yedinu Ukrainu!"*—ZYU) with 101, and the KPU with 66. The NU and the KPU were joined by the Yulia Tymoshenko Bloc (*Blok Yuliyi Tymoshenko*—BYT) and the SPU as the principal opposition formations, which, despite their ideological differences, pledged to renew a joint effort to force Kuchma from office.

On November 16, 2002, President Kuchma nominated Viktor YANUKOVYCH, the governor of the Donetsk *oblast* (province) and leader of the recently formed pro-Russian Party of Regions (*Partiya Rehioniv*—PR), to be the new prime minister. The appointment was confirmed with 234 votes in the Supreme Council on November 21.

In October 2002 a senior judge opened a criminal investigation into alleged corruption and abuse of power on the part of the Kuchma administration. Although the Supreme Court subsequently ordered the investigation suspended, anti-Kuchma demonstrations were held in major cities in 2003 and 2004, the opposition claiming that inappropriate force was used by security forces to quell the protests. Consequently, Kuchma in early 2004 announced that he would not seek reelection, despite having been authorized to run by the Constitutional Court. The three major presidential contenders thereby became Prime Minister Yanukovych (Kuchma's preference as a successor), former prime minister Yushchenko, and Oleksandr Moroz of the SPU. The first round of balloting on October 31 produced a near dead heat between Yanukovych (40.20 percent of the vote) and Yushchenko (39.01 percent). Election observers reported numerous violations of fair election practices, while opposition parties claimed that the government had been involved in a conspiracy to poison Yushchenko (see Current issues). The government announced that Yanukovych won the November 21 runoff balloting with 49.46 percent of the vote, compared to 46.31 percent for Yushchenko, prompting protest demonstrations in major Ukrainian cities as well as an international outcry over perceived fraud on the government's part. The Supreme Council refused to ratify Yanukovych's victory and ordered a second runoff for December 26, at which Yushchenko, now the leader of an Orange Revolution (so named after his main campaign color) achieved a clear victory with 52 percent of the vote. Yanukovych initially refused to accept the results, but he eventually resigned as prime minister on December 31, paving the way for Yushchenko's inauguration on January 23, 2006. The following day Yushchenko named Yulia Tymoshenko, his main Orange Revolution partner, as prime minister. Her appointment was confirmed on February 4 via 457 votes in the Supreme Council.

Despite the near euphoria that greeted the installation of the new administration in early 2005, infighting soon broke out within the cabinet, and friction over policy differences developed between the president and the prime minister. Consequently, on September 8 Yushchenko dismissed Tymoshenko and her cabinet. Tymoshenko immediately announced that she and her supporters were crossing over to the opposition. On September 9 Yushchenko nominated Yuriy YEKHANUROV, the governor of the Dnepropetrovsk region and a member of the NU, to be the next prime minister. However, the appointment was able to muster only an insufficient 223 votes of support in the Supreme Council on September 20, forcing Yushchenko to offer significant concessions to Yanukovych. The PR subsequently agreed to support Yekhanurov, who was confirmed with 289 votes on September 23. The new cabinet announced on September 27–28 was dominated by the NU, although a number of posts were filled by nonparty technocrats.

Following a controversial gas deal with Russia in early January 2006 (see Current issues), the Supreme Council on January 10 passed a motion of no confidence against the Yekhanurov government. However, the government remained in place pending balloting for a new Supreme Council, which, under recent constitutional revision, would be empowered to appoint most of the new cabinet.

The March 26, 2006, legislative balloting produced a surprising plurality for the PR, with the BYT and NU splitting the Orange Revolution vote. Several attempts by the NU and BYT to form a coalition government foundered over the ensuing months, as did the PR's attempts to find enough partners to achieve a legislative majority. Consequently, conditions reached a critical point by July, with President Yushchenko facing the choice of calling for new elections or accepting an arrangement with his former arch-rival Yanukovych. Finally, on August 3 Yushchenko agreed to nominate Yanukovych to lead a new government dominated by the PR but also including members of the SPU, NU, and KPU. The proposed government was approved the following day with 271 votes in the Supreme Council. However, friction between Yushchenko and Yanukovych contributed to the resignation of four NU ministers in October and the NU's concurrent decision to officially move into opposition.

In the wake of intensifying conflict between the president and the prime minister (most notably over their authority in regard to cabinet appointments), Yushchenko in April 2007 ordered the legislature dissolved and called for new elections. Although the PR-dominated Supreme Council disputed Yushchenko's power to issue such a decree, new elections were finally held on September 30. The PR secured a plurality, but the BYT and Yushchenko's Our-Ukraine–People's Self-Defense (*Nasha Ukraina–Narodna Samooborona*—NU-NS) bloc combined for a slim majority. After extensive negotiations between the BYT and the NU-NS, Yulia Tymoshenko returned to the premiership on December 18 after being approved by the Supreme Council by the barest possible majority (226 votes in the 450-member council).

On September 3, 2008, ministers and legislators from the NU-NS announced that they were withdrawing their support for the coalition government led by Prime Minister Tymoshenko. When Tymoshenko and the BYT were subsequently unable to entice the NU-NS back into the coalition, the speaker of the Supreme Council on September 15 declared that the government had formally collapsed. Negotiations toward a new coalition government subsequently failed, and on October 8 President Yushchenko ordered the dissolution of the Supreme Council and announced that new legislative balloting would be held on December 7. However, under pressure from Tymoshenko, the Supreme Council challenged the dissolution decree and refused to approve funds for the elections, which Yushchenko subsequently postponed. On December 9 it was announced that a new majority coalition had been formed in the Supreme Council by the BYT, some 40 of the legislators from the NU-NS, and the Lytvyn Bloc, whose leader, Volodymyr LYTVYN, was elected speaker of the council with 244 votes, signaling that the coalition enjoyed sufficient legislative support to preclude immediate snap elections.

Political background (Crimea). In 1954 the Soviet leadership transferred the Crimean autonomous republic from Russian to Ukrainian administration, despite Crimea's largely ethnic Russian population. Subsequent moves to "rehabilitate" the original Crimean Tatars, who had been transported to Central Asia during World War II because of alleged collaboration with the Germans, yielded the return of some 250,000 Tatars to Crimea by the early 1990s. (It has been recently estimated that there are 1 million ethnic Russians, 600,000 Ukrainians, and 300,000 Tatars in Crimea.)

The status of Crimea became intertwined with postindependence political developments when the aspiration of the majority ethnic Russian population for union with Russia generated strains in Moscow-Kiev relations (see Foreign relations, below), with the added complication of disaffection among the peninsula's original Tatar inhabitants. Another source of friction was the long-running dispute over the ownership of the ex-Soviet Black Sea fleet based in the Crimean port of Sevastopol. In February 1992 Ukraine refused a Russian request for the retrocession of Crimea on the grounds that the CIS agreement included a commitment to accept existing borders, to which the Russian *Duma* responded in May by declaring the 1954 transfer of Crimea to Ukraine unconstitutional and void. The *Duma*'s action was in support of a declaration of independence from Ukraine by the Crimean Supreme Soviet, which the Crimeans repealed after the Ukrainians had voted to annul its content by an overwhelming margin. Subsequently, the Ukrainian foreign ministry issued a statement declaring that "the status of the Crimea is an internal Ukrainian matter which cannot be the subject of negotiation with another state."

In June 1992 an agreement in principle between President Kravchuk of Ukraine and President Boris Yeltsin of Russia provided for the Black Sea fleet of more than 800 ships, including auxiliary vessels, to be divided equally between the two countries. Differences nevertheless persisted, accompanied by periodic incidents involving naval personnel in Sevastopol and by nationalist opposition to compromise in both parliaments.

The election of Yuriy MESHKOV, leader of the secessionist Republican Movement of Crimea (*Republikanskve Dvizheniya Kryma*—RDK), as Crimean president on January 31, 1994, was seen in Kiev as a threat to the country's territorial integrity. Although he insisted that he was not calling for separation from Ukraine, Meshkov repeated an earlier call for a referendum on the establishment of "an independent Crimea in union with CIS states."

On May 19, 1994, the Crimean legislature voted to restore its proindependence constitution of May 1992, with Sevastopol declaring in August that it had "Russian legal status." The Ukrainian Supreme Council consequently adopted legislation designed to curb Crimea's autonomy, enacting a measure in November providing for the automatic invalidation of any Crimean legislation in conflict with Ukrainian law. In March 1995, moreover, the Kiev legislature annulled Crimea's constitution and effectively abolished the Crimean presidency, with

Ukrainian President Kuchma assuming direct control over the region from April 1. Meshkov denounced these actions as unconstitutional, although plans to hold a referendum on the separatist 1992 basic law were canceled at the end of May. In June 1995 Presidents Kuchma and Yeltsin reached a further accord, with Russia agreeing to buy part of the Ukrainian half of the fleet, thus increasing its share to 81 percent, and with both sides having naval bases in Sevastopol.

Kuchma rescinded his direct rule decree in August 1995, while asserting that candidates for the Crimea premiership must first be approved by him. In February 1996 the appointment of Arkady DEMYDENKO as Crimean prime minister was so confirmed.

In May 1997 Russian president Yeltsin made a state visit to Ukraine to sign a 10-year friendship treaty and to resolve remaining differences over the Black Sea fleet. By virtue of a 20-year lease, the fleet was to be based primarily in Sevastopol. Both the Russian and Ukrainian navies were to use Streletskaya Bay, but the rest of the Black Sea would be used exclusively by Ukraine. Russia also recognized Crimea and the city of Sevastopol as Ukrainian territory. In addition, the agreement settled questions about Ukraine's bilateral debts and its claims on ships the Russians "inherited" upon the dissolution of the Soviet Union. (In February 1999 the Russian *Duma* ratified the treaty, which formally recognized, for the first time, Ukraine's sovereignty within its current borders.)

On June 3, 1997, Kuchma approved the dismissal of Prime Minister Demydenko after the Crimean parliament had voted three times to sack Demydenko. Kuchma subsequently approved the appointment of Anatoli FRANCHUK, Kuchma's ally and a former Crimean premier (1994–1995), as prime minister; Franchuk's cabinet was approved by the Crimean parliament on June 19.

Elections to the Crimean Supreme Council were conducted on March 29, 1998, in conjunction with the balloting for the Ukrainian Supreme Council. Left-wing parties advanced in the Crimean Supreme Council, which elected Leonid HRACH of the Communist Party of Crimea (*Kommunisticheskaya Partiya Kryma*—KPK) as its new speaker. However, in an apparent reflection of the balance of power maintained at the national level, Kuchma named Serhiy KUNITSYN, the leader of the centrist factions in the Crimean Supreme Council, as the new Crimean prime minister on May 19. Subsequently, in January 1999 a new constitution was adopted for Crimea, which, among other things, gave the autonomous republic substantial budgetary authority. Tensions between factions loyal to Hrach and Kunitsyn continued to play out in the following two years, with Hrach repeatedly working through the legislature for Kunitsyn's dismissal. In September 2000 President Kuchma commented that he saw no need for the removal of Kunitsyn given the current balance of powers in the province, but on July 18, 2001, the Crimean legislature voted to dismiss Kunitsyn, who ultimately stepped down five days later. Kuchma then named Valeriy HORBATOV as Kunitsyn's successor. However, Kunitsyn returned to the prime minister's post in April 2002 following the March legislative elections, which were reportedly marred by numerous irregularities. (Horbatov had been elected to the Ukrainian Supreme Court.)

Tension between Crimea and the national government continued to simmer into 2004, as the Russian nationalists who dominated Crimea pressed for designation of Russian as an official language and for stronger military and political links with Russia. In the wake of the Orange Revolution at the national level in late 2004 and early 2005, Kunitsyn resigned as Crimean prime minister in April 2005, being described as the last major leader of the Kuchma era to leave office. He was succeeded by Anatoliy MATVIYENKO, a close associate of Ukrainian Prime Minister Tymoshenko and a member of the BYT. However, Matviyenko also fell victim to national politics only a few months later when Tymoshenko and President Yushchenko became estranged. Anatoliy BURDYUHOV, a member of the NU, was named in September to replace Matviyenko as head of a Crimean government that included a number of bankers (including Burdyuhov) and increased representation for the Crimean Tatars.

Prior to the March 26, 2006, balloting for the Crimean Supreme Council, the region was described as still polarized along ethnic lines and suffering economic malaise. Not surprisingly, considering the fact that ethnic Russians constituted 60 percent of the Crimean population, the pro-Russian For Yanukovych Bloc won a strong plurality of 44 seats in the new Crimean Supreme Council. With President Yushchenko's endorsement, Viktor PLAKYDA was selected in June as the new Crimean prime minister. Plakyda, the former director of the Crimean energy company, announced his intention to focus on economic development. However, political discord continued to dominate regional events as evidenced by major protests against the North Atlantic Treaty Organization (NATO) that forced cancellation of planned Ukrainian-U.S. military exercises in June as well as by ongoing calls from members of the Russian parliament (*Duma*) for the reannexation of Crimea by Russia.

International attention focused on Crimea in August 2008 following the military conflict between Russia and Georgia over South Ossetia, observers wondering if the Russian hard line might also soon extend to Crimea. (Russian leaders, at least at the national level, continued to disavow any interest in regaining sovereignty over Crimea.) Meanwhile, the Crimean Supreme Council in mid-September endorsed Russia's recognition of the independence of South Ossetia and Abkhazia.

Constitution and government. In mid-1990 the Council of Ministers was restructured as a Western-style cabinet headed by a prime minister. Coincident with his formal reinstallation as Ukrainian head of state on December 5, 1991, Leonid Kravchuk's title changed from that of Supreme Soviet chair to president of the republic. The draft of a new constitution published in October 1993 called for retention of most of the existing governmental structure, providing for a 450-seat Supreme Council with a four-year mandate and a Council of Ministers guided by a president directly elected for a five-year term.

Under the terms of the June 1995 interim "constitutional treaty," a Constitutional Commission completed work on the draft of a new constitution in March 1996. Despite some opposition to stronger presidential authority at the expense of the legislature, the Supreme Council in June adopted the new text; it granted significant new powers to the president, including the right to name the prime minister (with the concurrence of a parliamentary majority) and other officials, and recognized the right to own private property. In addition, the new basic law provided for the establishment of a National Security and Defense Council and for the holding of parliamentary and presidential elections in March 1998 and October 1999, respectively. It also specified that parliamentary deputies could not simultaneously hold government appointments. The parliament in September 1997 approved a mixed voting system for the Supreme Council, half of which was to be directly elected from single-seat constituencies; the remaining 225 seats were to be apportioned to parties that received at least 4 percent of all ballots cast in separate nationwide balloting.

In an April 2000 referendum voters overwhelmingly approved four Kuchma proposals that, if enacted, would have cut the number of legislative deputies from 450 to 300, added an appointive upper chamber to parliament to represent regional interests, limited legislators' immunity from prosecution, and given the president authority to dismiss the parliament if it went more than a month without a working majority or if it failed to pass the annual budget within three months of submission. Kuchma had lobbied for the measures as a means of furthering "the systematic and efficient work of the legislature," whereas the majority of the Supreme Council saw the referendum as Kuchma's attempt to diminish the council's authority and to install a presidential system of government. In January 2001 the Supreme Council instead passed a bill adopting a strictly proportional party-list system for the next general election, with parties having to achieve 4 percent of the vote to obtain representation. The bill obviously favored the larger parties and factions and could have dramatically altered the balance of power in the Supreme Council. Kuchma promptly vetoed the electoral bill. The debate over such fundamental structural changes continued into 2002 as much of the opposition sought controls on presidential power.

In August 2002 President Kuchma announced formation of a constitutional commission to study reforms in the hope of eliminating the administrative impasses that had characterized governance since independence. Among other things, he called for establishment of a bicameral legislature. However, his lack of a legislative majority precluded progress.

A number of constitutional revisions were negotiated as part of the resolution of the presidential crisis of late 2004. Under the changes (which went into effect on January 1, 2006), significant authority previously exercised by the president was transferred to the Supreme Council. Although the president retained the formal right to nominate the prime minister, the Supreme Council acquired de facto control of the post. The Supreme Council was also given authority over all cabinet appointments except for the defense and foreign affairs portfolios, which remained under the president's purview. In addition, the Supreme Council was authorized to dismiss the prime minister and cabinet members. The basic law revisions also decreed that all 450 members of the Supreme Council would henceforth be elected by proportional voting.

In the midst of ongoing conflict between the president and the prime minister, the Supreme Council in December 2006 adopted legislation designed to further undercut presidential prerogatives. However, President Yushchenko refused to sign the new legislation, asking for a review by the Constitutional Court. The issue of the division of authority between the president and the prime minister/legislature subsequently remained contentious, although legislation was adopted in May 2008 confirming that the foreign affairs and defense ministers were presidential nominees. Yushchenko presented his proposals to the Supreme Council in March 2009 for revision of the basic law (based on recommendations from the National Constitutional Council he had established in late 2007). However, little attention was given to his proposals (including creation of a bicameral legislature and codification of substantial presidential authority) because of his diminished legislative clout. No action on constitutional revision was expected until at least after the January 2010 presidential elections, although many analysts continued to describe the current system as dysfunctional.

A Supreme Court was installed in January 1997; there is also a Constitutional Court with members appointed by the president, legislature, and the bar association. In addition, the 2005 Code of Administrative Procedure provided for an additional court system headed by a High Administrative Court to deal with a variety of issues, including election-related cases.

Ukraine is divided into 24 provinces (*oblasts*), with Crimea administered as an autonomous republic. The metropolitan areas of Kiev and Sevastopol have special status. Local self-government functions in divisions and subdivisions.

Foreign relations. Although at the time not an independent country, Ukraine, like Byelorussia (now Belarus), was accorded founding membership in the UN in 1945 as a gesture to the USSR, which feared the world body would have an anti-Soviet bias. Theretofore not a member of the IMF or World Bank, independent Ukraine was admitted to both institutions in September 1992; earlier, it had become a member of the Conference on (subsequently Organization for) Security and Cooperation in Europe (CSCE/OSCE) following the demise of the Soviet Union and the creation of the CIS in December 1991.

Ukrainian leaders insisted following independence that they wished the country to become nuclear free, even though a substantial proportion of the former USSR's nuclear arsenal was located in Ukraine. Although Ukraine was a signatory of the 1992 Lisbon Protocol to the 1991 Strategic Arms Reduction Treaty (START I), which designated Russia as the sole nuclear power in the CIS, implementation was delayed by difficulties over the terms demanded by the Ukrainian government and the Ukrainian nationalist opposition. Not until November 1993 did the Ukrainian Supreme Council conditionally ratify START I, while indicating that it was not prepared to endorse the Nuclear Non-Proliferation Treaty (NPT) without substantial Western security guarantees, financial assistance for weapons dismantling, and compensation for nuclear devices transferred to Russia for destruction. The conditional ratification and statement of terms yielded speedy progress in January 1994 on a tripartite agreement, whereby the United States would provide assistance for the dismantling of nuclear weapons by Ukraine, with warheads being shipped to Russia for destruction. Eventually, Ukraine would also receive about $1 billion, via Russia, from the sale of reprocessed uranium from the warheads. In accordance with the agreement, Ukraine began shipping warheads to Russia in early March, and in December Ukraine formally acceded to the NPT, following parliamentary ratification the previous month. (On June 1, 1996, President Kuchma announced that Ukraine had completed the process of nuclear disarmament by transferring the last of its warheads to Russia.)

Ukraine acceded to NATO's Partnership for Peace program in February 1994, and in June it signed a partnership and cooperation agreement with the EU. An important aspect of the latter accord was the provision of EU aid for closure of the remaining nuclear reactors in Chernobyl, site of the world's worst nuclear accident in 1986. Having been formally admitted to the Council of Europe in November 1995, Ukraine became a full member of the Central European Initiative (CEI) in May 1996 and was granted observer status within the Nonaligned Movement in September. In September 1997 Ukraine tentatively agreed to a plan by which it would join the Central European Free Trade Agreement (CEFTA, see Foreign relations in article on Poland), though no firm timetable was announced (Ukraine had not joined by late 2009). A new EU economic cooperation agreement with Ukraine took effect on March 1, 1998, committing each to increased trade and investment. Ukraine concurrently indicated that it eventually intended to apply for full EU membership.

As one of the largest recipients of U.S. foreign aid, Ukraine bowed to the pressure from the United States and Israel in March 1998 and declined to sell turbines for Russia to use in nuclear reactors destined for Iran. The agreement on commercial nuclear technology removed an impediment to improved relations with Washington at a time of sharply increased contacts between Ukraine and NATO officials. Despite the prospect of reprisals by Russia, which asked Kiev not to cancel the turbine contract, Ukraine tried to maintain the momentum it had gained in July 1997 when it had signed a cooperation charter with NATO. The agreement, reportedly modeled on the Russia-NATO Founding Act of May 1997, established a special relationship (short of membership) that included the exchange of military missions and the establishment of a NATO-Ukraine Commission, through which Ukraine could consult with NATO if it came under an external threat. In March 1998, clarifying its neutrality and its relationship with the Western alliance, Kiev said it did not rule out joining NATO in the future if membership would not jeopardize its relationship with neighbors, particularly Russia. President Kuchma also endorsed the expansion of NATO in March 1999 (again contrary to Moscow's wishes), although he condemned the subsequent NATO military campaign in the former Yugoslavia.

In June 1997 the presidents of Ukraine and Romania signed a treaty, subsequently approved by their respective parliaments, confirming existing borders and protecting the rights of national minorities. Meanwhile, the informal "Union of Three" alliance of Georgia, Ukraine, and Azerbaijan became identified through the abbreviation GUAM when Moldova joined the group in October. Earlier, in the fall of 1996, those former Soviet bloc nations had begun to strengthen their economic and political relationships based on a common pro-Western orientation, suspicion of Russia, and the prospects of collaborating on the exploitation of Azerbaijan's Caspian oil reserves. GUAM expanded to the GUUAM upon the accession of Uzbekistan in April 1999. However, in May 2005 Uzbekistan withdrew from the grouping, which in May 2006 changed its name to the GUAM Organization for Democracy and Economic Development.

Having received grant and loan pledges valued in the billions of dollars from the European Bank for Reconstruction and Development (EBRD) and other multilateral agencies as well as individual countries, Ukraine officially shut down the last operating nuclear reactor in Chernobyl on December 15, 2000. The financial and technical assistance was targeted for a range of projects, including construction of a more permanent sarcophagus around the highly radioactive reactor that was destroyed by the 1986 explosion. Other priorities included building replacement power facilities, upgrading safety at remaining nuclear plants, and aiding the local population.

A decade after the demise of the Soviet Union, delineation of Ukraine's borders with Moldova and Romania remained somewhat problematic. A treaty concluded with Moldova in 1999 provided the basis for border demarcation that began in late 2003. Meanwhile, negotiations with Romania continued over areas encompassing various arms of the Danube, the adjacent delta, the Black Sea continental shelf, and the minuscule Zmiyiny (Serpent) Island in potentially oil- and gas-rich waters in the Black Sea. (The question of Serpent Island and maritime delimitation in the Black Sea was submitted in 2004 to the International Court of Justice, which in February 2009 issued a ruling that awarded partial control to both countries but appeared to favor Romania by declining to classify the islet as qualifying for maritime demarcation.) Romania has long claimed Northern Bukovina and Southern Bessarabia, which it ceded to the Soviet Union in 1940, and fervent Romanian nationalists remained committed to incorporating the two areas into a Greater Romania.

Ukraine's foreign policy under President Kuchma was driven by two contradictory goals: to maintain friendly relations with Russia on the one hand and to open the door to Europe with a possible view to membership in the EU on the other. In reference to the former, in 2003 Kuchma was elected as chair of the CIS, becoming the first non-Russian to hold the post. In addition, treaties were signed in 2003 delineating the land boundary between Russia and Ukraine as well as resolving the status of the Sea of Azov as joint territorial waters. At the same time the Kuchma administration sought to counterbalance its close relations with Russia through a policy of engagement with the United States and the EU. In pursuit of this opening to the West, Kuchma sent 1,650 troops to serve in Iraq in 2003, even though the Supreme Council had approved a motion condemning the U.S.-led intervention there. (The troops were withdrawn in 2005.)

The victory of Viktor Yushchenko in the controversial 2004 presidential race put a strain on Ukraine's relations with Russia, as Russian president Vladimir Putin had openly supported Yushchenko's main opponent, Viktor Yanukovych. However, Yushchenko's first foreign visit after his inauguration was to Moscow, where he pledged continued close relations. On the other hand, Yushchenko intensified Ukraine's efforts to join the EU and endorsed eventual membership in NATO.

In what was seen as at least a significant symbolic initiative, in November 2005 the EU sent 70 police and customs personnel to help combat smuggling along the Ukrainian-Moldovan border. The EU also recognized Ukraine as having a market economy in February 2006, an important step toward further integration. However, the EU clearly remained skeptical of further membership expansion and as of late 2007 was only offering Ukraine additional economic cooperation, with accession remaining off the negotiating table for the immediate future. By that time it was also apparent that possible NATO membership had also receded from both Ukraine's and NATO's immediate concerns. Significantly, public opinion in Ukraine reportedly opposed NATO accession, particularly in view of Russia's strong objection to such an initiative. Russia was also distressed over the passage by Ukraine's Supreme Council in mid-2007 of legislation needed to proceed with Ukraine's WTO membership request. Analysts agreed that Moscow preferred that Ukraine not join the WTO unless Russia also gained admission; however, Ukraine acceded to the WTO in May 2008, Ukrainian officials indicating that they expected the WTO membership to enhance the country's EU membership prospects.

In late March 2008 the United States and Ukraine reached agreement on "strategic priorities" and additional trade cooperation. U.S. president Bush also urged the April NATO summit to approve a Membership Action Plan (MAP) for both Ukraine and Georgia despite Russia's continued strong objections. Although no MAPs were approved (primarily due to opposition from France and Germany), the summit appeared to endorse Ukraine's and Georgia's eventual memberships. In the opinion of most analysts, the NATO issue contributed to Russia's intensifying hard line regarding regional security issues, culminating in the Georgian-Russian military conflict in August. Arguing that Crimea could be the next focus for Russia (despite Russia's insistence that it did not challenge Ukraine's current borders), President Yushchenko immediately called for Ukraine's accelerated integration into "Euro-Atlantic structures."

An acrimonious dispute erupted with Russia in January 2009 over the delivery of natural gas to Ukraine as well as the transshipment of gas through Ukraine to EU countries, several of which suffered shortages before resolution was achieved. Although the EU was critical of Ukrainian leaders (as well as those in Russia) in the matter, it nevertheless included Ukraine among the six post-Soviet countries invited in May to participate in the EU's Eastern Partnership. Subsequently, in June, new U.S. vice president Joseph Biden during a visit to Ukraine affirmed the U.S. administration's continued support for Ukraine's eventual NATO membership, despite recent U.S. efforts to improve U.S. relations with Russia. For his part, Russian president Medvedev in August accused Ukrainian president Yushchenko of pursuing "anti-Russian policies" and urged Yushchenko's defeat in the upcoming presidential poll.

Current issues. The dramatic presidential campaign of late 2004 in Ukraine was one the world's most closely watched political developments. One major focus of attention was the apparent poisoning of reformist candidate Viktor Yushchenko during the campaign. Yushchenko, who nearly died as a consequence of what was initially described as an unknown illness, later claimed that he had been poisoned during a meeting in September with leaders of the Ukrainian security forces. Tests subsequently appeared to verify that Yushchenko was suffering from dioxin poisoning, which, among other things, had left his face severely disfigured. For many observers, the "before and after" photos of Yushchenko seemed to encapsulate the essence of the presidential contest—a corrupt, perhaps criminal, entrenched administration (represented by Prime Minister Viktor Yanukovych, President Kuchma's handpicked candidate as his potential successor) versus a rising tide of reformists determined to shake off the last vestiges of a communist past. Of course, such analysis was simplistic at best, as Yanukovych enjoyed substantial genuine support in industrialized areas of eastern and southern Ukraine, where much of the population spoke Russian and continued to prefer strong ties with Russia. He also appeared generally content with the economic role of the nation's oligarchs. Meanwhile, Yushchenko campaigned on a "pro-Western" platform that called, among other things, for Ukraine's eventual membership in the EU and NATO. Underscoring Ukraine's long-standing geographic schism in that regard, Yushchenko's support was strongest in central and western areas of the country. Russian leader Putin roiled the political waters even further with his blatant endorsement of Yanukovych's candidacy during Putin's state visit to Ukraine in October.

The mass demonstrations in November and December 2004 that prompted the Supreme Court decision to permit new runoff presidential balloting were widely praised by democracy advocates around the world. Most Western capitals appeared to accept the conclusion that the initial poll had been irrevocably fraudulent. At the same time, however, concern arose that the country faced possible fragmentation, perhaps disintegration, if the results of the final runoff were not accepted by both sides. Consequently, Yanukovych's ultimate capitulation, reportedly issued under intense international pressure, was greeted with great relief. Nevertheless, critics charged the Kuchma/Yanukovych administration with one final example of corrupt government action, achieved through legal maneuvers that delayed Yushchenko's inauguration until late January 2005. Reformists argued that members of the outgoing government used the extra time before the inauguration to enrich themselves and their cohorts in several ways, particularly through additional sales of state-run enterprises at cut-rate prices. Some critics went so far as to allege that systematic "looting" of public resources had taken place.

Yushchenko's appointment of Yulia Tymoshenko as prime minister in early 2005 was not considered a surprise in view of the electoral pact they had concluded prior to the presidential poll. (Tymoshenko had eschewed presidential ambitions of her own in favor of support for Yushchenko's bid.) Tymoshenko's new cabinet contained a number of "Our Ukraine" ministers as well as representatives of the Socialist Party of Ukraine and the Party of Industrialists and Entrepreneurs of Ukraine; the legislators from the Communist Party of Ukraine provided the main opposition to her appointments. The new administration promised immediate reform in many areas, most notably in regard to combating corruption. Consequently, a number of investigations were reportedly launched into the recent spate of privatizations. The government also announced its intention to pursue EU and NATO memberships with vigor. Shortly thereafter, NATO signaled its inclination to eventually approve Ukraine's application, provided that the new government enacted the required military reforms. Meanwhile, the EU approved a three-year "action plan" designed to facilitate Ukraine's possible membership, although the commitment was reportedly not sufficiently strong for Yushchenko, who was dissatisfied with the EU's failure to set a timetable for formal accession negotiations to begin. In addition to the perceived need for major additional reforms, the EU's caution was also attributed to concern that quicker action might alienate Russia, which for many years had strongly objected to Ukraine's further integration with the West. For his part, U.S. President George W. Bush unequivocally endorsed Ukraine's applications for membership in NATO and the WTO. (During Yushchenko's visit to Washington in April 2005, Bush described the Orange Revolution as a prominent example of the "world changing for the better" through democratization, a cornerstone of Bush's stated foreign policy.)

In March 2005 the government relaunched the criminal investigation into the Gongadze case (see Political background, above), Yushchenko charging that the previous administration had covered up the facts in the matter. However, momentum toward uncovering the details of the previous privatizations (another reform goal) was subsequently reported to have slowed. It appeared that enthusiasm for the review of the privatizations had waned in part due to concern expressed by foreign investors, who reportedly feared that their interests might be compromised by such scrutiny. Consequently, the government announced new guidelines designed to convince investors that "property rights" would henceforth be protected.

Reform efforts also appeared to be compromised by growing friction between President Yushchenko and Prime Minister Tymoshenko. In April 2005, faced with gasoline prices that had soared by 30 percent, Tymoshenko imposed mandatory price caps. Perhaps in protest, Russian oil suppliers (responsible for 80 percent of Ukraine's oil needs) subsequently cut back on their distribution to Ukraine, causing significant shortages and consumer angst. Consequently, Yushchenko ordered that the price caps be removed, arguing that they ran counter to his administration's commitment to a market economy. Analysts thereafter noted additional problems, including personal rivalries, that were constraining the ability of the disparate elements behind the Orange Revolution to enact change. For example, surprisingly fractious debate was reported in July over legislation geared toward implementing economic reform required for WTO membership. Complaints also greeted Yushchenko's announcement in August of plans to revamp the nation's mining sector. Overall, the lack of effective action was seen as eroding the government's credibility both domestically and internationally only six months after the new administration had been installed amid much optimism.

Mutual allegations of corruption from the supporters of Yushchenko and Tymoshenko intensified following Tymoshenko's dismissal as prime minister in September 2005. Among other things, the president reportedly had to make several compromises, including a pledge not to prosecute the electoral fraud that had allegedly surrounded the 2004 elections, to earn the support of the PR for new prime minister Yekhanurov. The new cabinet was described as "pragmatic" and "more cautious" than the Tymoshenko government, which contributed to the apparent growing disillusionment among supporters of the Orange Revolution as the year ended.

In early January 2006 Russia reduced the flow of natural gas to Ukraine in the wake of several months of conflict over prices. An agreement was reached a few days later that permitted a resumption of full deliveries, but opponents of the accord claimed that Ukraine was being forced to double its payments as a "punishment" for the Orange Revolution. Popular discontent also was exacerbated by the lack of progress in the Gongadze case. (The trial of three police officers charged with involvement in the journalist's death was initially adjourned for the judge to assess if state secrets were involved, and trial proceedings continued slowly. The three officers were convicted in March 2008, although critics of the investigation charged that the "masterminds" of the crime remained at large.)

The NU and BYT hoped to form an electoral coalition prior to the March 2006 legislative poll, but continued friction between the leaders of the two groups prevented an agreement. Consequently, the door was opened for a remarkable comeback by former prime minister Yanukovych and his pro-Russian PR. After months of inconclusive coalition negotiations, Yushchenko ultimately "swallowed his pride" and agreed to Yanukovych's return to the premiership in August. (Analysts suggested that Yushchenko's alternative—new elections—would have produced further decline for the NU.) Although the installation of a new government resolved the immediate crisis, it was widely believed that the coalition partners would have difficulty finding lasting common ground regarding issues such as economic reform, relations with Russia, the intensity with which to pursue EU membership, and possible accession to NATO. Regarding the last, Yushchenko, in apparent deference to the anti-NATO SPU, suggested that a national referendum might be held to define Ukraine's final stance.

Conflict between President Yushchenko and Prime Minister Yanukovych subsequently continued unremittingly. In addition to disagreement on foreign policy (Yanukovych remaining much more oriented toward Russia than Yushchenko), the uncomfortable "cohabitation" was roiled by the prime minister's effort (in conjunction with the PR-dominated Supreme Council) to wrest control of the foreign and defense ministries from the president's control. Various legislative and court maneuvers resulted in a standoff, and, after the NU and the BYT had announced their "joint opposition" to Yanukovych's "anticrisis coalition" in February 2007, mass demonstrations by supporters of both camps rocked the capital at the end of March.

Charging Yanukovych with "unconstitutional behavior" in regard to the alleged "solicitation" of floor-crossing by NU legislators in order to maintain a legislative majority for the government, Yushchenko in April 2007 ordered that new legislative elections be held in late June. However, the Supreme Council continued to meet in defiance of Yushchenko's dissolution decree and refused to allocate funds for new elections. With government essentially paralyzed, 169 NU and BYT legislators resigned in June, providing the basis for Yushchenko to issue another dissolution decree on the grounds that the legislature no longer had two-thirds of its seats filled (a constitutional requirement for its continuation). Although many of the legal issues remained unresolved, a compromise was reached between the PR and the NU/BYT in late May for new legislative elections on September 30. Interestingly, the campaign focused less on international issues such as relations with Russia and NATO and more on domestic affairs. (All three leading electoral blocs [the PR, BYT, and Yushchenko's NU-NS] made what independent analysts considered unrealistic campaign pledges regarding financial assistance to the working class.) The electorate again proved deeply divided, and the new BYT/NU-NS government, with Tymoshenko again serving as prime minister, was approved in December by only one vote.

Considering the history of bickering between Yushchenko and Tymoshenko, it was not surprising that the Orange Revolution "redux" of late 2007 failed to usher in a period of political calm. Continued disputes with Russia also roiled the political scene in the first half of 2008, as did Yushchenko's insistence that the April NATO summit should approve a membership action plan for Ukraine. (Large PR-led demonstrations against the NATO initiative were conducted in several cities.) Although Tymoshenko was perceived as less vehemently anti-Russian than Yushchenko in regard to Russia's actions in Georgia in August, most independent observers concluded that the schism between the two leaders was personal, not ideological. Their mutual antipathy continued to dominate political affairs through the rest of the year, culminating in the factionalization of the NU-NS (see NU-NS under Political Parties, below), Yushchenko's efforts to force early legislative elections, and the frantic negotiations that barely saved the Tymoshenko government in December (see Political background, above). The president and prime minister also clashed (for the most part) in regard to dealings with the IMF in late 2008 and early 2009, Yushchenko's popularity in particular plummeting in the face of the nation's economic free fall (see The Country, above). Finance Minister Viktor PYNZENYK resigned in February 2009, criticizing Tymoshenko for allowing politics to interfere with sound budgetary policies. Mass protests in Kiev in April also contributed to the turmoil, as the PR objected to the conditions attached to the IMF lending.

In April 2009 the Supreme Council, which had recently forced the dismissal of Foreign Minister Volodymyr OHRYZKO (one of President Yushchenko's two cabinet appointees), called for early presidential elections to be held on October 25. However, Yushchenko challenged that initiative, and in May the Constitutional Court declared the legislative resolution invalid. The next presidential balloting was therefore scheduled for January 17, 2010. As the campaign progressed in the fall of 2009, the PR's Viktor Yanukovych enjoyed a comfortable lead in public opinion polls, although it was widely expected that he would not achieve a first-round majority and would face a runoff against Tymoshenko. (An attempt by Yanukovych and Tymoshenko to forge a BYT-PR coalition had collapsed at midyear over the long-standing issue of the division of authority between the president and the prime minister [see BYT, below, for additional information].)

POLITICAL PARTIES

As of early 2001, there were 110 officially registered parties in Ukraine. In January 2001 a reported 11 parties and 30 civic groups joined the Ukrainian Right-Wing (*Ukrainska Pravytsya*) alliance as a step toward consolidation of anti-Kuchma forces on the right. It was largely superseded, however, by formation in February of the National Salvation Front (NSF), which was organized as a "citizens' initiative," primarily by supporters of Yulia Tymoshenko. The NSF had as its goals coordinating activities with the "Ukraine Without Kuchma" movement, advancing a center-right legislative agenda, and marshaling diplomatic support for its anti-Kuchma stance. At the same time, other elements on the center-right coalesced around former prime minister Viktor Yushchenko, and in July they announced formation of an electoral bloc, "Our Ukraine." A formal accord by the initial participating parties (*Rukh*, KUN, Christian Popular Union Party [PKNS], RiP, LPU, Solidarity, Republican Christian Party [RKP], and the Youth Party of Ukraine) was signed in early October.

In July 2001 the NSF formed an electoral committee that, Tymoshenko indicated, was prepared to engage in "peaceful coexistence or cooperation" with Yushchenko, but Yushchenko ultimately rejected any alliance with Tymoshenko. In early November the NSF was renamed the Yulia Tymoshenko Bloc (*Blok Yuliyi Tymoshenko*—BYT). Parties in the BYT included Fatherland, USDP, UNP *"Sobor,"* and URP. Meanwhile, in October the pro-Kuchma forces had established the third principal electoral bloc, **"For a United Ukraine!"** (*Vyborchiy Blok "Za Yedinu Ukrainu!"*—ZYU), which was chaired by Volodymyr LYTVYN, head of presidential administration. The parties in the ZYU included the Agrarian Party of Ukraine (APU), NDPU, PPPU, PR, and TU. (The ZYU had finished second in the 2002 legislative balloting with 102 seats.) Forces on the left continued to be led by the Communist Party of Ukraine (KPU) and the Socialist Party of Ukraine (SPU).

Twenty-eight parties competed independently in the March 2006 legislative balloting, while another 50 parties participated in 17 electoral blocs, including a revamped NU and a slightly modified BYT. Under recent changes in the electoral law, parties were required to have been registered for at least one year to participate in the elections. Twenty-one parties or blocs presented candidates in the 2007 legislative poll, while some 18 registered to participate in the presidential election scheduled for January 2010.

Government Parties:

Yulia Tymoshenko Bloc (*Bloc Yuliyi Tymoshenko*—BYT). A successor to the NSF formed by supporters of Yulia Tymoshenko prior to the 2002 legislative balloting (at which it won 22 seats), the BYT for the 2006 elections (at which it secured 129 seats on a vote share of 22.3 percent) comprised the parties below plus remnants of the Ukrainian People's Party "Assembly" (*Ukrainskoho Narodnoho Partiya "Sobor"*—UNP *"Sobor."*) The UNP *"Sobor,"* an anti-Kuchma party formed in 1999, had split in 2005 after a party congress voted to align with the BYT. (See URP *"Sobor,"* below, for additional information.)

The BYT was also aided in 2006 by the inclusion of Levko LUKYANENKO and his supporters from the URP, who had been left without affiliation following a split in the URP. The BYT campaigned on a platform of support for integration with Western Europe and opposition to the recently completed natural gas deal with Russia. Tymoshenko also maintained a populist stance that promised increased welfare spending and wide-ranging corruption investigations.

Having in 2006 declared its "uncompromising opposition" to the Yanukovych government and having subsequently aligned itself with the NU, the BYT finished second in the September 2007 legislative balloting with 156 seats (on a 30.7 percent vote share). It then formed a coalition government with the NU-NS that included Tymoshenko as prime minister, although friction between her and President Yushchenko subsequently continued to dominate the political scene (see Political background and Current issues, above, for additional information).

In the first half of 2009 the BYT appeared close to reaching a coalition agreement with the Party of Regions (PR), the primary opposition party led by former prime minister Viktor Yanukovych. According to various reports, the proposed accord called for the groups to cooperate within parliament to amend the constitution to authorize parliament to elect the president (currently elected by popular vote), with Yanukovych slated to fill that position while Timoshenko continued as prime minister (with expanded powers). However, the proposed "grand coalition" collapsed in June when Yanukovich abruptly withdrew his support.

In October 2009 the BYT unanimously nominated Tymoshenko as its candidate for the January 2010 presidential election. She subsequently pledged, if elected, to pursue "warmer relations" with Russia (while also supporting additional cooperation with the EU) and to combat corruption (in part through judicial reform).

Leaders: Yulia TYMOSHENKO (Prime Minister and 2010 presidential candidate), Oleksandr TURCHYNOV (First Deputy Prime Minister), Ivan KYRYLENKO (Parliamentary Leader).

Fatherland (*Batkivshchyna*). The social-democratic Fatherland (also frequently translated as Motherland) was established as a Supreme Council faction in March 1999 by Yulia Tymoshenko and other members of the All-Ukrainian Association *"Hromada"* (below) who objected to the parent party's support for Pavlo Lazarenko. Ironically, Tymoshenko had once been a close associate of Lazarenko, who had encouraged her to enter politics. Initially numbering about two dozen deputies, the Fatherland faction soon surpassed *"Hromada,"* which ultimately fell below the 14 adherents needed for official faction status.

In late December 1999 President Kuchma named Tymoshenko to the new Yushchenko cabinet as deputy prime minister for fuel and energy, but by mid-2000 she was already drawing criticism from Kuchma for her handling of the sector. Despite continuing support from the prime minister, she was dismissed from her cabinet post by Kuchma on January 19, 2001, four days after being formally charged with gas smuggling, tax evasion, and document forgery while head of Unified Energy Systems of Ukraine in 1996–1997.

In late 2001 Fatherland absorbed Stepan KHMARA's Ukrainian Conservative Republican Party (*Ukrainska Konservatyvna Respublikanska Partiya*—UKRP). Intensely anti-Communist and anti-Russian, the UKRP had been formed in June 1992 by a radical wing of the URP (below) led by Khmara. (For additional information on the UKRP, see the section on Fatherland in the 2007 *Handbook.*)

Leaders: Yulia TYMOSHENKO (Prime Minister), Oleksandr TURCHYNOV, Stepan KHMARA.

Ukrainian Social Democratic Party (*Ukrainska Sotsial-Demokratychna Partiya*—USDP). The USDP was established in November 1998 by former justice minister Vasyl Onopenko, previously the leader of the Social Democratic Party of Ukraine (United). He finished eighth in the 1999 presidential election, with 0.5 percent of the vote.

Leader: Vasyl ONOPENKO.

Reforms and Order Party (*Reformy i Poryadok Partiya*—RiP). The previously pro-Kuchma RiP secured 3.1 percent of the national proportional vote in the 1998 legislative poll after negotiations for its inclusion in the "Forward, Ukraine!" alliance with the PKNS and Ukrainian Christian Democratic Party (UKhDP) had fallen through. In December 2000 it joined Udovenko's *Rukh* and the KUN in announcing formation of a center-right electoral bloc. The RiP supported economic reform and greater integration of Ukraine with Western Europe. The RiP participated in the NU for the 2002 legislative poll but formed an alliance called the Civil Political Bloc (*Pora*—PRP) with the reformist It Is Time (*Pora*) Party for the 2006 legislative poll, winning 1.47 percent of the vote.

The center-right RiP joined the BYT for the September 2007 legislative elections. RiP leader Viktor Pynzenyk (a noted economist) was named finance minister in the December 2007 government although he resigned the post in early 2009, saying policy initiatives were being held "hostage to politics."

Leader: Victor PYNZENYK.

Our Ukraine–People's Self-Defense (*Nasha Ukraina–Narodna Samooborona*—NU-NS). The NU-NS was formed in August 2007 as an electoral bloc in advance of the September legislative balloting. To a large extent, the NU-NS was a successor to the "Our Ukraine" Bloc (*Bloc "Nasha Ukraina"*—NU), the pro-Yushchenko grouping that had finished third in the 2006 election for the Supreme Council, securing 81 seats on a vote share of 13.95 percent. (See the NSNU, below, for additional background on "Our Ukraine.") For the 2006 electoral campaign, the NU had included the NSNU, *Rukh*, PPPU, KUN, KDS, and URP *"Sobor."*

Some members of the NU components joined the new cabinet that was installed in early August 2006, but most of them resigned as the NU formally went into opposition in October. The NU subsequently formed a pact with the BYT to coordinate their legislative activities.

After the NU-NS secured 72 seats on a vote share of 14.15 percent in the September 2007 legislative poll, Yushchenko negotiated a coalition government with the BYT. In addition to the parties indented below, the other components of the NU-NS included the **European Party of Ukraine** (*Evropeyska Partiya Ukraini*—EPU), which was organized in 2006 under the leadership of Mykola KATERYNCHAK, and the **Party of Motherland Defenders** (*Partiya Zakhisnikiv Vitchizni*—PZV), led by Yuri KARMAZIN. Some NU-NS members subsequently lobbied for the members of the electoral bloc to merge into a single party, but the initiative failed to gain momentum.

The NU-NS splintered in late 2008 when a majority of its legislators agreed to support the new BYT-led government despite objections from Yushchenko, whose relationship with Prime Minister Tymoshenko had deteriorated sharply. Some 17 NU-NS deputies, led by parliamentary leader Byacheslav Kyrylenko formed their own "For Ukraine" faction in parliament to support Yushchenko, while Arsensy YATSENYUK (sacked in December as speaker of the Supreme Council) subsequently formed a Front for Change, former defense minister Anatoliy HRYTSENKO launched a Civic Initiative, and former chief of staff Viktor BALOGA established a new party called **United Center**. Although their groups formally remained nongovernmental organizations rather than parties, Yatsenyuk and Hrytsenko registered as candidates for the January 2010 presidential elections, Yatsenyuk (only 35 years old) having attracted significant support in public opinion polls by criticizing the prevalence of personal politics among the country's leading figures. Although he had initially professed a middle-of-the-road approach to Ukraine's main issues, by late 2009 Yatsenyuk, reportedly enjoying support among the oligarchs, was campaigning on a platform that opposed NATO and EU membership. Meanwhile, Yushchenko, reduced to single-digit support in public opinion polls, registered as an independent candidate in his reelection bid.

People's Union "Our Ukraine" (*Narodni Soyus "Nasha Ukraina"*—NSNU). The propresidential, right-of-center NSNU was formed in early 2005 by supporters of President Yushchenko to, among other things, contest the 2006 legislative elections. It was considered to be a successor to "Our Ukraine," the electoral bloc that had supported Viktor Yushchenko's successful presidential campaign. Reports indicated that some 25 component groups of

"Our Ukraine" had participated in the launching of the NSNU. Described by some as the "next party of power," the NSNU nevertheless failed to attract a number of major Yushchenko allies.

Meeting in Kiev in March 2005, some 6,000 delegates to the NSNU's founding congress elected a 120-member Council and an Executive Committee. Deputy Prime Minister Roman BEZMERTNY was elected as head of the Council, while Yuriy Yekhanurov was named head of the Executive Committee. Yushchenko was named as the party's honorary chair. The NSNU's 21-member presidium included 5 cabinet members.

Like its predecessor, the NSNU advocated market-driven economics and accelerated integration with Europe. It was initially reported that the NSNU planned to contest the 2006 elections in alliance with the BYT and the APU, but the NSNU ultimately served as the core component of the NU (which did not include the BYT or APU) for the 2006 balloting and of the NU-NS for the 2007 poll. In the wake of the subsequent factionalization within the NU-NS (see above), the NSNU in late 2009 endorsed President Yushchenko for reelection in the January 2010 presidential poll, although the party was described as "bankrupt" following the withdrawal of business-sector financial support in view of Yushchenko's dismal popular standing.

Leaders: Viktor YUSHCHENKO (President of Ukraine and Honorary Chair of the Party), Vera ULIANICHENKO (Party Leader), Vyacheslav KYRYLENKO (Parliamentary Leader), Yuriy YEKHANUROV (Former Prime Minister and Head of Executive Committee), Oleh HUMENYUK (Chair of the NSNU Council).

Popular Movement of Ukraine (*Narodnyi Rukh Ukrainy—Rukh*, or NRU). *Rukh* was organized in September 1989 as the Popular Movement of the Ukraine for Restructuring (*NRU za Perebudovu*). From the outset the grouping advocated Ukrainian independence, causing its critics among the anti-Communist groups to charge it with being more nationalist than democratic. Its founding chair, the writer Ivan DRACH, appealed to his colleagues to rally behind President Kravchuk after the latter's break with the KPU. Another leader, Vyacheslav CHORNOVIL, who had secured a 25 percent vote share as the grouping's presidential candidate in 1991, insisted that *Rukh* should continue in opposition. Thereafter, the grouping remained deeply divided in regard to the president, although it agreed to fill two important positions (first deputy prime minister and economics minister) in the Kuchma administration. It was not formally registered as a party until 1993. Campaigning on a platform of market reform and opposition to CIS membership, *Rukh* won 20 seats in the 1994 legislative elections. The party called for Ukraine's integration into NATO and the EU and for other democratic and reformist parties to unite against the left.

Rukh was the second leading party in the 1998 legislative poll, being credited with about 10 percent of the vote in the nationwide proportional balloting. However, it continued to suffer from what one analyst described as a "crisis in direction," occasioned more by personality differences than policy disputes. In January 1999 Chornovil was ousted as chair in favor of Yuriy Kostenko, a former cabinet minister. Chornovil and his supporters subsequently formed a new parliamentary faction called the Popular *Rukh* of Ukraine-1, or *Rukh*-1. Chornovil died in a car accident in March, and Hennadiy UDOVENKO, a former foreign minister, was named acting chair of the new faction.

Kostenko and Udovenko both ran for president in 1999; the former, technically on the ballot as an independent, won 2.2 percent of the vote, and the latter took 1.2 percent. Following a court challenge over the use of the party name, the two factions were registered separately in January 2000, with Udovenko's party assuming the NRU designation and the Kostenko group taking the name Ukrainian Popular Movement (*Ukrainskyi Narodnyi Rukh—Rukh*, or UNR).

In November 2000, looking ahead to the next legislative election, Udovenko's NRU announced an electoral alliance with the Congress of Ukrainian Nationalists (KUN, below) and the Reforms and Order Party (RiP, above). In early 2001 it appeared that the two *Rukh* parties could well be allies for the next Supreme Council balloting and might even reunite beforehand. However, although both joined the Yushchenko bloc, they failed to resolve their differences before the March 2002 election. Afterward, both branches continued to express an interest in reuniting. In 2004 Udovenko was replaced as head of his faction by Borys Tarasyuk, while Kostenko and his supporters formed the UNP (below). Both branches participated in the NU-NS for the 2007 legislative balloting.

Leaders: Borys TARASYUK (Leader), Yaroslav MYKHAYLOVYCH.

Ukrainian People's Party (*Ukrainska Narodna Partiya—*UNP). The UNP was formed in 2004 by Yuriy Kostenko and other members of the UNR faction of *Rukh*. The UNP reportedly won several mayoral races in the 2006 local elections.

In advance of the 2006 legislative elections, the UNP participated with other center-right parties in the launching of an electoral bloc called the Ukrainian National Bloc of Kostenko and Plyushch, which won 1.87 percent of the 2006 vote. (The bloc supported the UNP's Kostenko and parliamentarian Ivan Plyushch. Other components of the bloc included the Party of Free Peasants and Entrepreneurs of Ukraine.) The UNP secured 6 of the NU-NS's 72 seats in the 2007 legislative elections. In late 2009 Kostenko, who had won 2.2 percent of the presidential vote in 1999, announced his UNP candidacy for the January 2010 presidential election.

Leaders: Yuriy KOSTENKO (Leader), Yaraslav DZHODZHYK (Deputy Leader).

Christian Democratic Union (*Khrystiyansko Demokratichnyj Soyuz—*KDS). The KDS was formed in 2003 by the centrist Christian Popular Union Party (*Partiya Khrystiyansko Noradniy Soyuz—*PKNS), the Ukrainian Christian Democratic Party, and the All Ukrainian Union of Christians. The first two of those groups had participated in the Forward, Ukraine! (*Vpered, Ukraino*!) electoral alliance that had secured 1.7 percent of the national proportional poll in the 1998 legislative balloting. (Forward, Ukraine! subsequently became a party in its own right; see below.)

Leaders: Volodymyr STRETOVYCH (Leader), Volodymyr MARUSCHENKO (Deputy Leader).

Ukrainian Republican Party "Assembly" (*Ukrainska Respublnkanska Partiya "Sobor"—*URP *"Sobor"*). The center-right URP *"Sobor"* was formed in December 2005 by former UNP *"Sobor"* leader Anatoliy Matviyenko and disaffected members of the Ukrainian Republican Party.

Leaders: Anatoliy MATVIYENKO (Leader), Oleksandr BONDAR (Deputy Leader).

Forward, Ukraine! (*Vpered, Ukraine!*). Initially formed as an electoral alliance of the PKNS and the Ukrainian Christian Democratic Party for the 1998 legislative poll, Forward, Ukraine! subsequently registered as a party in its own right and participated in the NU in the 2002 legislative poll. Running on its own, Forward, Ukraine! secured 0.02 percent of the legislative vote in 2006.

Yuriy LUTSENKO, who was dismissed under pressure from the PR as interior minister in December 2006 and subsequently became an adviser to President Yushchenko, established a civic movement called People's Self-Defense that included Forward, Ukraine! and the KDS. That movement formed an important component of the NU-NS in the 2007 legislative balloting, in which Forward, Ukraine! secured four of the NU-NS's seats.

Leaders: Oleh NOVIKOV (Acting Leader), Kateryna LUKYANOVA (Deputy Leader).

It Is Time (*Pora*). The reformist *Pora* was formed in 2005 by members of youth organizations that had supported the Orange Revolution. It participated unsuccessfully in an electoral bloc with the RiP in the 2006 legislative elections before gaining one seat in the 2007 balloting as part of the NU-NS.

Leader: Vladyslav KASKIV.

Lytvyn Bloc. This electoral bloc was formed prior to the 2006 legislative balloting by the NP, the **Peasant Democratic Party,** and the small **Party of All-Ukrainian Union of the Left "Justice"** in support of Supreme Council Speaker Volodymyr Lytvyn. The bloc secured 2.44 percent of the vote in 2006 and failed to gain representation. However, the Lytvyn Bloc, performing well in rural areas and small towns in central Ukraine, won 20 seats on a vote share of 3.96 percent in the 2007 elections, when its primary components were the NP and the Labor Party.

Volodymyr Lytvyn, the leader of the bloc, was elected speaker of the Supreme Council (a post he had held before) in December 2008 as part of the formation of a new BYT-led coalition government, announcing he hoped to serve as a "peacemaker" in the nation's frayed political affairs. In declaring his candidacy for the January 2010 presidential election, Lytvyn lobbied for support from disgruntled former SPU members.

Leader: Volodymyr LYTVYN (Speaker of the Supreme Council and 2010 presidential candidate).

People's Party (*Narodna Partiya*—NP). The NP is the recently adopted rubric of the former Agrarian Party of Ukraine (*Ahrarna Partiya Ukrainy*—APU), which was established in 1996 to support farmers and which secured 3.7 percent of the proportional vote in the 1998 legislative balloting, just missing the 4 percent threshold necessary to be allocated proportional seats. At the APU's third congress in June 1999, Mykhaylo HLADIY, then deputy prime minister for the agro-industrial complex, was elected leader over the incumbent, parliamentary deputy Kateryna Vashchuk. The APU supported President Kuchma's reelection in the October–November balloting.

The APU was renamed the People's Agrarian Party of Ukraine in 2004, with Volodymyr Lytvyn becoming its leader. The NP rubric was adopted in 2005.

Leaders: Volodymyr LYTVYN (Leader), Kateryna VASHCHUK.

Ukrainian Labor Party. This grouping, also referenced as the Working Party, was launched in September 1999 by Mykhaylo SYROTA, a member of the legislature who had been instrumental in the adoption of the new Ukrainian Constitution in 1996. (This party should not be confused with the historical Labor Party of Ukraine, which was a founding member of the PR, or with Working Ukraine, below, with which Syrota had briefly been associated.) Syrota died in a car accident in August 2008. His son, Dmytro Syrota, was subsequently elected as the party's new leader.

Leaders: Dmytro SYROTA, Mykhaylo DMYTROVYCH.

Opposition Parties:

Party of Regions (*Partiya Rehioniv*—PR). The PR held its initial congress in March 2001 as the culmination of a process that began with the signing of a merger agreement by five centrist parties in July 2000. Connected to Donetsk financial and industrial interests, the nascent PR quickly formed a new parliamentary faction, Regions of Ukraine.

Of the PR's five founding organizations, the Labor Party of Ukraine (*Partiya Pratsi Ukrainy*—PPU) dated from late 1992, when it was organized by elements descended from Soviet-era official unions. Led by Valentyn LANDYK, the PPU participated in the 1998 general elections in the "Together" electoral alliance with the LPU (below). The Party of Regional Revival of Ukraine (*Partiya Rehionalnoho Vidrodzhennya Ukrainy*—PRVU), which won 0.9 percent of the proportional vote in the 1998 legislative election, was led by Donetsk's mayor, Volodymyr RYBAK, and Yukhym ZVYAHILSKIY. The other three founding parties were the recently formed Party "For a Beautiful Ukraine" (*Partiya "Za Krasyvu Ukrainu"*—PZKU), led by Leonid CHERNOVETSKIY; the All-Ukrainian Party of Pensioners (*Vseukrainskoi Partiya Pensioneriv*—VPP), led by Andriy KAPUSTA and Hennadiy SAMOFALOV; and the Party of Solidarity of Ukraine (*Partiya Solidarnosti Ukrainy*—PSU), formed in July 2000 by the Solidarity (*Solidarnist*) parliamentary faction under Petro POROSHENKO.

In November 2000 the emerging party had adopted the unwieldy designation Party of Regional Revival "Labor Solidarity of Ukraine" (*Partiya Rehionalnoho Vidrodzhennya "Trudova Solidarnist Ukrainy"*). At the time, it was considered pro-Kuchma, while claiming to represent the interests of the regions within a unified state. At the March founding congress, Mykola AZAROV, the controversial chair of the State Tax Administration, was elected chair, although he was quoted as saying he saw the position as temporary. Poroshenko, who had reportedly sought the chair's position, continued to lead the separate Solidarity faction in the Supreme Council and ultimately established the Solidarity Party. With the next legislative election in sight, Azarov resigned as party leader in January 2002 to avoid charges of conflict of interest.

The PR was a principal forum for Viktor Yanukovych in the 2004 presidential elections. The PR was assisted in the 2006 legislative balloting by financial support from billionaire tycoon Rinat AKHMETOV, who was elected on the PR's list, along with a number of his business associates. Western campaign consultants also contributed to the PR's success (a plurality of 186 seats on a vote share of 32.1 percent). The PR advocated "strong ties" to the EU but opposed NATO membership. Yanukovych also pledged to pursue official language status for Russian and improvements in relations with Russia in general.

Yanukovych was named prime minister in the cabinet installed in August 2006, but the PR was forced into opposition status following the September 2007 legislative elections (despite having won a plurality of 175 seats on a vote share of 34.37 percent). In 2008 the PR opposed Ukraine's request for a NATO membership action plan, while in August Yanukovych endorsed Russia's recognition of the independence of South Ossetia and Abkhazia following the Georgian-Russian conflict.

The PR organized several mass protests in Kiev in April 2009 to protest government policies, particularly interaction with the IMF. (The PR blocked action on the IMF plan in the Supreme Council, forcing the government to accept IMF conditions without legislative support.)

After withdrawing from a proposed grand coalition with the BYT in June 2009 (see BYT, above), Yanukovich routinely led public opinion polls in advance of the January 2010 presidential elections. Among other things, Yanukovych, considered Russia's preferred candidate, and the PR called for increased wages and pension benefits despite strong IMF objections.

Leader: Viktor YANUKOVYCH (Party Leader, Former Prime Minister, and 2010 presidential candidate).

Communist Party of Ukraine (*Komunistychna Partiya Ukrainy*—KPU). Formerly Ukraine's ruling party, the KPU was banned in August 1991 but was allowed to reregister in October 1993 (without regaining party property of the Soviet era); Petro Symonenko was elected party leader. Standing on a traditional platform of anticapitalism and antinationalism, the KPU secured a plurality of seats in the 1994 legislative balloting and subsequently served as the core of the parliamentary opposition to the economic restructuring efforts of President Kuchma.

The KPU's plurality rose in the 1998 legislative poll, the party performing particularly well in the nationwide proportional balloting, winning about 25 percent of the votes. First Secretary Symonenko finished second in the 1999 presidential poll, winning 22.2 percent of the initial vote and 38.8 percent in a runoff against the incumbent. KPU demands of the subsequent Yushchenko government included severance of ties to NATO, designation of Russian as an official language, commitment to a socialist economy, and central planning for state enterprises.

In 2000 it was reported that the KPU had split into two factions. The first was led by Symonenko and remained decidedly antimarket, anti-American, and pro-Russian. The second adopted the name **Communist Party of Ukraine (Reformed)**; its leader was reported to be Mikhail SAVENKO, a "progressive socialist" who was a member of the Working Ukraine faction in the Supreme Council.

At the March 2002 election the KPU took 66 seats, 59 of them on the basis of winning 20 percent of the proportional vote. It secured 21 seats in 2006 on a vote share of 3.7 percent and 27 seats in 2007 on a vote share of 5.39 percent. (The KPU [Reformed] won 0.29 percent of the vote in 2007.) The KPU continued its anti-NATO campaign in 2008.

In late 2009 Symonenko was named as the candidate of a KPU-led Bloc of Left and Center-Left Forces for the January 2010 presidential elections. Other groups in the bloc included the **Justice Party**, the SDPU, and the **Union of Left Forces**.

Leader: Petro SYMONENKO (First Secretary and 2010 presidential candidate).

Other Parties Participating in the 2007 Legislative Elections:

Socialist Party of Ukraine (*Sotsialtstychna Partiya Ukrainy*—SPU). Although organized in 1991 by the former leader of the Communist legislative majority, the SPU was described as "not so much a successor to the Communist Party, as a party of economic populism." As such, it urged retention of a major state role in the economy, while favoring priority for workers in privatization. It won 15 parliamentary seats in 1994 and attracted a further 12 independent deputies into its parliamentary group. In early 1996 2 SPU deputies, Nataliya Vitrenko and Volodymyr Marchenko, were expelled from the party for criticizing the leadership for deviating from socialist ideals; they subsequently formed the PSP (below).

The SPU and the Peasants' Party of Ukraine (SelPU, below) formed an electoral bloc called "For Truth, for the People, for Ukraine" for the 1998 legislative poll, the alliance being credited with about 8 percent of the national proportional vote. SPU Chair Oleksandr Moroz, a former chair of the Supreme Council, finished third in the 1999 presidential election, taking 11.3 percent of the vote.

In November 2000 Moroz released secret tape recordings implicating President Kuchma in the disappearance of an independent journalist and then helped form the "Ukraine Without Kuchma" movement and the National Salvation Forum. At the March 2002 election the SPU won 22 seats, 20 of them on the basis of a 6.9 percent share of the proportional vote.

The SPU joined the cabinet named in January 2005. After winning 33 seats on a vote share of 5.7 percent in the March 2006 legislative poll, the party was initially perceived as a potential partner in a coalition government that would have included the NU and the BYT. However, Moroz switched allegiance to the PR, after which he was elected speaker of the Supreme Council and the SPU joined the new PR-led cabinet. The SPU suffered a dramatic reversal in the September 2007 balloting, securing only 2.86 percent of the votes and thereby losing all representation. In mid-2008 Moroz reportedly suggested that the SPU form a "leftist bloc" with other parties to compete in subsequent elections, although no progress in that regard was reported and Moroz ran as the SPU candidate in the January 2010 presidential elections.

Leader: Oleksandr MOROZ (Chair, Former Speaker of the Supreme Council, and 2010 presidential candidate).

Progressive Socialist Party (*Prohresyvna Sotsialistychna Partiya*—PSP). Formed in 1996 by legislators recently expelled from the SPU, the PSP, considered the most radical of the country's leftist groupings, secured 4 percent of the national proportional vote in the 1998 legislative poll. Labeling herself a "true Marxist," the party's 1999 presidential candidate, Nataliya Vitrenko, finished fourth in the balloting, with 11 percent of the vote.

For the 2002 election Vitrenko organized the Nataliya Vitrenko Bloc (*Blok Nataliyi Vitrenko*), which included the PSP and the **Party of Educators of Ukraine** (*Partiya Osvityan Ukrainy*—POU). The Bloc won 3.2 percent of the proportional vote but no seats.

The PSP participated in the 2006 legislative poll in a People's Opposition Bloc of Nataliya Vitrenko (*Blok Nataliyi Vitrenko Narodna Opoziciya*) with the **Rus'-Ukrainian Union Party** (*Partiya Rus'ko-Ukrainsky Soyus*—RUS). The extremely pro-Russian and anti-American grouping opposed Ukraine's proposed membership in NATO, the EU, and the WTO and called for a new union of Belarus, Russia, and Ukraine. It won 2.93 percent of the vote, narrowly missing the threshold required to gain representation. Running on its own, the PSP won 1.32 percent of the vote in the September 2007 balloting. Vitrenko subsequently announced her candidacy for the January 2010 presidential election.

Leaders: Nataliya VITRENKO (1999 and 2010 presidential candidate), Volodymyr MARCHENKO.

Green Party of Ukraine (*Partiya Zelenykh Ukrainy*—PZU). The PZU was formed in 1990 as the political wing of the Green World (*Zeleniy Svit*) movement established in 1987. The party was best known for its campaigning on the Chernobyl issue, but it remained poorly organized as an electoral force. The PZU was credited with only 1.3 percent of the nationwide proportional vote in the 2002 legislative balloting, 0.54 percent in 2006, and 0.40 percent in 2007.

Leaders: Vitaliy KONONOV (President), Serhiy KURYKIN (Chair).

Party of National Economic Development (*Partiya Natsionalno Ekonomichnoho Rozvytku Ukrainy*—PNERU). Led by banker Volodymyr Matviyenko, the PNERU won one seat in the 2002 legislative balloting but fell to a 0.23 percent vote share in the 2006 poll and 0.14 percent in 2007.

Leader: Volodymyr MATVIYENKO.

Election Bloc of Lyndmyla Suprun—Ukrainian Regional Activists. This grouping was formed for the 2007 legislative poll by the **People's Democratic Party** (led by Lyudmyla Suprun), the **Democratic Party** (led by Serhiy KOZACHENKO and Anna ANTONYEVA), and the **Republican Christian Party** (led by Volodymyr POROVSKY and Mykhaylo POROVSKY). (The People's Democratic Party and the Democratic Party had participated in the 2006 elections in a People's Democratic Party Bloc that also included the **Christian and Democratic Party** [led by the mayor of Kiev, Leonid CHERNOVETSKY].) The 2006 bloc secured 0.49 percent of the vote, and the 2007 bloc won 0.34 percent. Suprum was nominated as the candidate of the People's Democratic Party for the January 2010 presidential election.

Leader: Lyudmyla SUPRUN.

Party of Free Democrats. This center-right grouping was formerly known as *Yabluko* ("Apple"), which was formed in December 1999 to support Ukraine's capitalists and the middle class. A corresponding faction of about 14 deputies (the minimum required for recognition) formed within the Supreme Council. At the 2002 legislative election, however, *Yabluko* won only 1.2 percent of the proportional vote and no seats. The party's leader, Mykhaylo Brodskiy, announced in 2005 that *Yabluko* was merging with the BYT. However, *Yabluko* was revived in early 2007 following a rift between Brodskiy and Yulia Tymoshenko. The party adopted its new rubric in March; it secured 0.21 percent of the vote in the September legislative poll. Brodskiy was subsequently nominated by the party for the January 2010 presidential election.

Leaders: Viktor CHAIKA, Mykhaylo BRODSKIY.

Party of Industrialists and Entrepreneurs of Ukraine (*Partiya Promislovtsiv i Pidpryyemtsiv Ukrainy*—PPPU). The PPPU was established by Prime Minister Anatoliy Kinakh in late November 2001. Previously the head of the Ukrainian Union of Industrialists and Entrepreneurs, Kinakh was elected to lead the new party at its February 2002 congress. The party's probusiness platform called for such measures as a significant reduction in the value-added tax and the adoption of policies favoring investment and the development of high-tech, export-oriented industry. Kinakh was named deputy prime minister in the January 2005 cabinet.

The PPPU participated in President Yushchenko's "Our Ukraine" (NU) bloc in the March 2006 legislative poll. However, Kinakh was named economics minister in the PR-led cabinet in March 2007, and most of the PPPU legislators concurrently switched allegiance to the PR's "anticrisis coalition." (They were subsequently expelled from the NU.) Kinakh was elected to the Supreme Council in 2007 on the list of the PR, to which the PPPU had thrown its support.

Leaders: Lyudmyla DENYSYUK (Leader), Anatoliy KINAKH (Former Prime Minister).

Other parties and blocs that participated unsuccessfully in the 2007 legislative elections included the **All-Ukrainian Union "Freedom,"** a successor (also known as the Svoboda Party) to the right-wing Social-National Party of Ukraine led by Oleh TYAHNYBOK and described in mid-2008 as having "no serious rivals in the right flank"; the **Bloc of the Party of the Pensioners of Ukraine**, comprising the **Party of Pensioners of Ukraine** and the **Party for the Defense of Pensioners of Ukraine;** the **Agrarians Bloc "Agrarian Ukraine,"** which included the **Ukrainian Peasant Democratic Party** (led by Valeriy VOSHCHEVSKIY); the **Christian Bloc**, comprising the **Social Christian Party**, which had been established in 2004 under the leadership of singer Oksana BILOZIR (a supporter of Viktor Yushchenko) and had secured 0.09 percent of the vote in the 2006 elections, and the **All-Ukrainian Political Party of Ecology and Social Protection;** the **All-Ukrainian Party of People's Trust**, which, under the leadership of Andriy AZAROV, had secured 0.11 percent of the vote in the 2006 balloting; and the **Election Bloc of Political Parties "Kuchma,"** an alliance (led by Oleksandr VOLKOV) of the **Center Party** (led by Viktor HOLOVKO) and the **Union Party** (led by Lev MYRYMSKY).

Other Parties and Blocs Participating in the 2006 Legislative Elections:

Council (*Viche*). *Viche* is the recently adopted rubric of the Constitutional Democratic Party (*Konstytutsiyno-Demokratychna Partiya*—KDP), a centrist party that participated in the 1998 legislative balloting with the Interregional Reform Bloc (*Mizhrehionalny Blok Reformiv*—MBR) as part of the Social Liberal Association (*Sotsialno Liberalne Obyednannya*—SLOn), which secured 0.9 percent of the proportional vote. For the 2002 legislative poll the KDP joined the Winter Generation Team (*Komanda Ozymoho Pokolinnja*—KOP). Described by the media as appealing to the Ukrainian equivalent of the West's "Generation X," the KOP bloc won 2 percent of the proportional vote at the March 2002 election. It encompassed the KDP, USDP, LDPU, and the **Private Property Party** (*Partiya Privatnoi Vlasnosti*—PPV).

The new name for the KDP was adopted prior to the 2006 legislative balloting, at which *Viche* secured 1.74 percent of the vote. For the 2007 legislative poll, *Viche* delegates, acknowledging that the party's prospects for gaining representation on its own were poor, joined the PR electoral list.

Leader: Inna BOHOSLOVSKA.

Liberal Party of Ukraine (*Liberalna Partiya Ukrainy*—LPU). Largely based in Donetsk, the LPU was formed in 1991 by Volodymyr SHCHERBAN, who subsequently served as the governor of the Sumy *oblast,* and Yevhen SHCHERBAN, who was assassinated in 1996. The LPU contested the 1998 legislative poll in the "Together" alliance with the Labor Party of Ukraine; the alliance won 1.9 percent of the national proportional vote.

In January 2005 Shcherban left office, and he subsequently reportedly fled Ukraine after an arrest warrant was issued charging him with corruption. (The former governor insisted the charges were politically motivated.) As a result of Shcherban's status, the LPU was not permitted to participate in the NU for the 2006 legislative poll. Running on its own, the LPU won only 0.04 percent of the vote.

Leader: Petro TSYHANKO (President).

"Not Right" Bloc (*Blok "Ne Tak"—Ne Tak*). This bloc was formed in December 2005 by parties opposed to the Orange Revolution. It opposed Ukraine's proposed membership in Western organizations such as NATO and the EU. In addition to the SPDU(O), other *Ne Tak* parties included the **All-Ukrainian Political Union "Women for the Future"** (*Vseukrainske Politychne Obyednannya "Zhinky za Majbutnie"*—ZM), which won 2.1 percent of the proportional vote in the 2002 legislative elections under the leadership of Valentyna DOVZHENKO; the small, centrist **Republican Party of Ukraine,** launched in early 2005 by Yuriy BOYKO, a former head of the state gas company; and the **All-Ukrainian Union "Center."** *Ne Tak* won 1.01 percent of the vote in the 2006 legislative elections.

Social Democratic Party of Ukraine (United) (*Sotsial-Demokratychna Partiya Ukrainy [Obyednana]*—SDPU[O]). Launched in 1990 by the minority leftist faction of the Ukrainian Social Democratic Movement (*Sotsial-Demokratychna Dvizheniya Ukrainy*—SDDU), the SDPU(O) was committed to democratic socialism in the tradition of the Second International, as exemplified by the prewar Ukrainian Social Democratic Workers' Party. The party's failure to win representation in the 1994 legislative poll strengthened those within it favoring reunion with what was by then the SDPU.

Although the party included critics and prominent rivals of Kuchma, officials of the Kuchma government were also members. The SDPU(O) attempted a merger with the SDPU (below) late in 1997, but the negotiations failed. However, the SDPU(O) displayed surprising strength in the 1998 legislative election, attaining the required threshold of 4 percent to be allocated seats in the nationwide proportional voting. At the March 2002 election the SPDU(O) won 6.3 percent of the proportional vote and 24 seats.

The SPDU(O)'s Mykhaylo PAPIEV was named minister for labor and social policy in the August 2006 PR-led cabinet, and party Deputy Chair Nestor SHUFRYCH was appointed minister of emergency situations in December. Viktor MEDVEDCHUK, the SPDU(O) chair since 1998 and the head of the administration of President Kuchma in 2002–2005, resigned as party leader in July 2007. The new leaders subsequently announced that the SPDU(O) would not participate in the September legislative elections, describing them as unconstitutional. However, the party informally supported the PR in the balloting.

Leaders: Yuriy ZAHORODNIY (Chair), Ihor SHURMA (Deputy Chair).

Peasants' Party of Ukraine (*Selyanska Partiya Ukrainy*—SelPU). Organized in January 1992 as the rural counterpart of the SPU, the SelPU was committed to land collectivization and opposed to rapid economic reform. By virtue of its strong support in the Soviet-era rural bureaucracy, it won 19 seats in the 1994 legislative balloting and subsequently attracted 31 independent deputies into its parliamentary group. Following the 1998 legislative poll (in which the SelPU competed in alliance with the SPU), Chair Oleksandr TKACHENKO, a strong opponent of IMF-requested economic reform, was elected chair of the Supreme Council. However, in early 2000 he was voted out, in what was dubbed a "velvet revolution," by a pro-Kuchma majority. Since 2002 Tkachenko has been included on the KPU electoral list for national legislative balloting. The SelPU secured 0.31 percent of the vote in the 2006 legislative poll.

Ukrainian National Assembly (*Ukrainska Natsionalna Asambleya*—UNA). The UNA, an essentially fascist grouping, was formed initially as a loose alliance of right-wing parties that from June 1990 to August 1991 styled itself the Ukrainian Interparty Assembly. The UNA compared the situation in Ukraine with that of Germany under the Weimar Republic and in the fall of 1991 organized a paramilitary affiliate, **Ukrainian National Self-Defense** (*Ukrainska Narodna Samboobo-runu*—UNSO), in emulation of the interwar Nazi brown shirts. At least three candidates identified with the UNA were elected in western Ukraine in the 1994 legislative balloting, and the party also polled strongly in Kiev. It came under legal challenge in 1995 because of its alleged involvement in paramilitary activities at home and abroad and was reportedly banned by order of the Justice Ministry on September 6. However, it was permitted to contest the 1998 legislative balloting, securing 0.4 percent of the national proportional vote. Its registration was subsequently revoked again, but in early 2001 the UNA-UNSO was actively organizing the more militant "Ukraine Without Kuchma" demonstrators. The UNA won less than 0.1 percent of the proportional vote at the 2002 legislative election and 0.06 percent in 2006.

Patriots of Ukraine Bloc. Formed in advance of the 2006 legislative balloting, this bloc included the UNKP and the **Patriotic Party of Ukraine** (*Patriotychna Partiya Ukrainy*—PPU), which, under the leadership of Mykola HABER (who had won 0.1 percent of the vote in the 1999 presidential election), had organized the **Against All** bloc in the 2002 legislative poll.

Ukrainian National Conservative Party (*Ukrainska Natsionalno-Konservatyvna Partiya*—UNKP). The UNKP was formed in 1992 by merger of the former Ukrainian National Party (*Ukrainska Natsionalna Partiya*—UNP), founded in Lviv under the leadership of Hryhorii PYRKHODKO in October 1989, and the Ukrainian People's Democratic Party (*Ukrainska Narodno-Demokratychna Partiya*—UNDP), a free-market group launched in Kiev in June 1990 under the leadership of Oleksandr BONDARENKO. The UNKP participated in the KNDS coalition in the 1994 legislative balloting.

In 1999 the party dismissed Deputy Chair Viktor RODIONOV for his support of Yevhen Marchuk in the presidential race. The party instead backed President Kuchma and his proreform, pro-European integration policies, although by early 2001 it had joined other rightist groups in criticizing Kuchma for his economic failures, what was perceived as a softened stance toward Russia, and authoritarianism. In late January the UNKP was one of the more than 40 parties and civic organizations forming the Ukrainian Right-Wing alliance.

Leader: Oleh SOSKIN.

Revival Party. This group was founded in 2005 by Heorhiy Kirpa, who was a former minister of transportation. It won 0.96 percent of the vote in the 2006 legislative poll.

Leader: Heorhiy KIRPA.

State Party (*Derzhava Partiya*). Formed by former federal prosecutor Hennadiy Vasylyev, *Derzhava* led a *Derzhava*–Labor Union Bloc that included the **All-Ukrainian Party of Laborers** in the 2006 legislative elections, securing 0.14 percent of the vote.

Leader: Hennadiy VASYLYEV.

"For Union" Bloc. This bloc was formed in 2005 by the Union Party, the **Socialist Ukraine Party,** the **Homeland Party,** and the **Slavic Party.** The bloc secured 0.20 percent of the vote in the 2006 legislative poll.

Union Party (*Partiya "Soyuz"*). Essentially a Crimean grouping that advocates creation of a union of Ukraine, Belarus, and Russia, this party secured 0.7 percent of the vote in the 1998 national proportional poll. In 2002 it ran as part of a **Russian Bloc** that also included the **"For a United Russia" Party** and the **Russo-Ukrainian Union Party**.

Leader: Svitlana SAVCHENKO.

Ukrainian Conservative Party. This group is reportedly most well-known for what is perceived to be its anti-Semitic platform. It secured 0.09 percent of the vote in the 2006 legislative elections.

Leader: Heorhiy SHCHYOKIN.

Lazarenko Bloc. Supportive of former prime minister Pavlo Lazarenko (as of August 2006 facing a ten-year jail sentence in the United States on money-laundering and other charges), this bloc was formed for the 2006 legislative elections by the two parties below and the **Social Democratic Union** (*Sotsial Demokratychnyy Soyuz*—SDS). (The SDS had been a member of the Unity Bloc for the 2002 poll.) The Lazarenko Bloc secured 0.30 percent of the vote in 2006. When the election commission refused to register Lazarenko (facing additional time in prison in the United States [see *"Hromada,"* below]) as a candidate for the 2007 legislative elections, the Lazarenko Bloc refused to participate in that poll.

Leaders: Pavlo LAZARENKO (in custody in the United States), Ivan LAZARENKO, Pavlo LAZARENKO.

All-Ukrainian Association "Community" (*Vseukrainske Obyednannya "Hromada"*). Founded in September 1997, *"Hromada"* elected former prime minister Pavlo Lazarenko as its first chair and joined the KPU and other leftist groups in blocking many initiatives proposed by the Kuchma/Pustovoytenko administration. The party's legislative stance appeared less founded in ideology than in Lazarenko's enmity toward Kuchma, who had insisted on Lazarenko's ouster as prime minister in the wake of corruption allegations. *"Hromada"* was credited with about 5 percent of the nationwide proportional vote in the 1998 legislative poll.

In December 1998 Lazarenko was arrested at the border by Swiss authorities on money-laundering charges; he was subsequently released on bail of $2.6 million. Lazarenko left Ukraine for the United States in February 1999 after the Supreme Council had removed his immunity from prosecution and Ukrainian prosecutors had begun preparations to charge him with embezzlement and other malfeasance. The scandal surrounding Lazarenko split *"Hromada,"* with his supporters nominating him as the party's 1999 presidential candidate despite the corruption charges while Lazarenko's opponents coalesced in a breakaway faction called Fatherland (above) under the leadership of Yulia Tymoshenko.

Lazarenko pleaded guilty to Swiss charges in June 2000. He received an 18-month sentence in absentia, and authorities confiscated $6.6 million from his accounts for return to Ukraine. In October 2002 he remained under custody in the United States, where he faced additional money-laundering charges. (He was released on bail in 2003.) Ukraine continued to seek his extradition. In August 2006 Lazarenko was convicted by a U.S. court and sentenced to nine years in prison.

Leader: Pavlo LAZARENKO (Former Prime Minister).

Social Democratic Party of Ukraine (*Sotsial-Demokratychna Partiya Ukrainy*—SDPU). The SDPU was formed as the SDP by the majority moderate faction of the Ukrainian Social Democratic Movement, which split at its inaugural congress in May 1990. Likened to the German SPD, the party urged a complete break with Marxism but attracted only sparse support, winning two seats in 1994. In February 1995 the SDPU was reregistered following a merger with the Human Rights Party and, according to reports, the Ukrainian Party of Justice, although the latter contested the 1998 election as part of the Working Ukraine alliance. The SDPU received only 0.3 percent of the proportional vote in the 1998 legislative election. In the 2002 campaign it renewed its claim to being the only truly social democratic party in Ukraine, but it again attracted negligible vote support.

Leader: Yuriy BUZDUHAN.

Bloc of National-Democratic Parties. This bloc was formed for the 2006 legislative balloting by the parties below and others, including the **Christian Liberal Party of Ukraine** (led by Leonid CHERNOVETSKY, the mayor of Kiev) and the **Ukrainian Christian Democratic Party**. The bloc secured 0.49 percent of the 2006 vote.

Democratic Party of Ukraine (*Demokratychna Partiya Ukrainy*—DPU). Based in the intelligentsia, the DPU was organized in December 1990 by a number of former members of *Rukh*. It supported strong presidential rule, a social market economy, and withdrawal from the CIS, while placing somewhat greater emphasis on human rights than the URP. Strongly represented in the 1990–1994 legislature, the DPU slumped to two party seats and four associated independents in 1994. It contested the national proportional component of the 1998 legislative poll in an alliance with the PEVK (see Regional Parties, below) called the "Bloc of Democratic Parties—NEP (Power of People, Economy, Order)," which secured 1.2 percent of the vote. In 2002 the DPU joined the liberal **Democratic Union** (*Demokratychnyy Sojuz*—DS) of Volodymyr HORBULIN in a DPU-DS electoral bloc that won four Supreme Council seats.

Leader: Volodymyr YAVORIVSKIY.

People's Democratic Party of Ukraine (*Narodno-Demokratychna Partiya Ukrainy*—NDPU). The NDPU was registered in June 1996 as the result of a merger of centrist political forces, including the **Party for Democratic Revival of Ukraine** (*Partiya Demokratychna Vidrodzhennia Ukrainy*—PDVU), **New Wave** (*Nova Khvylia*—NK), and the **Labor Congress of Ukraine** (*Trudova Kogres Ukrainy*—TKU). The PDVU had earlier formed the core of the New Ukraine center-left alliance and had won four seats in the 1994 balloting.

The NK had been launched in 1993 by a number of centrist deputies anxious to provide a promarket alternative to reactionary nationalism. It returned four "independent" deputies from Lviv in the 1994 balloting, partly because of the high profile of Viktor Pynzenyk as the leading reformer in the government. The NDPU was credited with about 5 percent of the nationwide proportional vote in the 1998 legislative balloting.

In June 1999 Anatoliy Matviyenko, the party chair, resigned in opposition to the NDPU's endorsement of President Kuchma for reelection. Matviyenko was particularly critical of Kuchma's economic failures. Prime Minister Pustovoytenko was elected to succeed Matviyenko, who went on to form URP *"Sobor"* (above) later in the year.

Leaders: Valeriy PUSTOVOYTENKO (Chair of the Party and Former Prime Minister), Oleksandr KARPOV.

Popular Movement of Ukraine for Unity (*Narodnyi Rukh Ukrainy za Yednist*). A "third way" *Rukh* splinter that rejected participation in either Yuriy Kostenko's UNR or Hennadiy Udovenko's NRU, this party participated unsuccessfully on its own in the 2002 legislative poll. It secured 0.13 percent of the vote in 2006.

Leader: Bogdan BOIKO.

Congress of Ukrainian Nationalists (*Konhres Ukrainskykh Natsionalistiv*—KUN). The KUN was founded in October 1992 as an electoral front of the émigré Organization of Ukrainian Nationalists, which had led the struggle against Soviet communism before being finally suppressed internally in the 1950s. Advocating Ukraine's exit from the CIS but divided between procapitalists and those favoring a state economic role, the KUN won five seats in the 1994 balloting, although its leader was prevented from standing in a Lviv constituency. The KUN participated in the National Front alliance with the Ukrainian Republican Party and Ukrainian Conservative Republican Party in the 1998 legislative poll. The KUN participated in the "Our Ukraine" bloc for the 2006 legislative poll but decided not to participate in the 2007 balloting.

Leader: Oleksiy IVCHENKO.

Other Parties and Groups:

Liberal-Democratic Party of Ukraine (*Liberalno-Demokratychna Partiya Ukrainy*—LDPU). The LDPU was founded in Kiev in November 1990 on the premise that "socialism is incompatible with humanism and democracy." Its centrist orientation sharply distinguished it from the right-wing Russian Liberal Democratic Party. In the December 1991 presidential election the LDPU backed the candidacy of Volodymyr HRYNYOV. The LDPU participated in the European Choice electoral alliance with the USDP for the 1998 legislative balloting. The party was refused permission to participate in the 2006 legislative poll for technical reasons.

Leader: Andriy KOVAL.

Ukrainian Republican Party (*Ukrainska Respublikanska Partiya*—URP). The URP was launched during a congress of the Ukrainian Helsinki Union in April 1990, becoming Ukraine's first modern non-Communist party to receive official recognition. Its stated aim was the creation of a "parliamentary republic . . . [with] guaranteed freedom of activity."

In 1992 Mykhaylo HORYN, a cofounder of *Rukh,* joined the URP and was instrumental in organizing the Congress of National Democratic Forces (*Kongres Natsionalno–Demokratychnykh Syl*—KNDS), a coalition of some 20 organizations dedicated to working for national unity under President Kravchuk. In addition to the URP and the Ukrainian Christian Democratic Party, the congress included the DPU, UNKP, and USDP (all above).

The KNDS was credited with winning an aggregate of some 25 seats in the 1994 balloting, although the URP, weakened by the exit of a radical faction that became the Ukrainian Conservative Republican Party (UKRP, see Fatherland, above), won only 11 of those seats, one of its defeated candidates being Horyn. (He subsequently helped form the Republican Christian Party.) The URP led an unsuccessful effort to impeach President Kuchma in September 1997, accusing him of compromising the nation's sovereignty through the Black Sea treaty with Russia.

The URP contested the 1998 legislative election in a National Front (*Natsionalnyi Front*) alliance with the KUN (above) and the UKRP; however, the front won only 2.7 percent of the national proportional voting and therefore no proportional seats. The URP joined several other right-wing parties in supporting the 1999 presidential candidacy of former Security Service chief and prime minister Yevhen Marchuk, who won 8.1 percent of the vote, for fifth place in the October election.

In late 2001 the URP absorbed Oleksandr SERHIYENKO's Ukrainian Christian Democratic Party (*Ukrainska Khrystiyansko-Demokratychna Partiya*—UKhDP). Based in the Uniate Catholic population of Galicia, the UKhDP had been organized in April 1990 as the outgrowth of a Ukrainian Christian Democratic Front formed in 1989. Its founders hoped to emulate the success of Bavaria's Christian Social Union, before encountering a number of internal controversies that led in 1992 to the withdrawal of a moderate faction to form the Christian Democratic Party of Ukraine (*Khrystiyansko-Demokratychna Partiya Ukrainy*—KhDPU).

At an extraordinary session in October 2005, the URP split into two camps. One faction under the leadership of Levko Lukyanenko retained the URP rubric, while a larger faction formed the URP *"Sobor"* (above). The rump URP was left without legal standing for the 2006 legislative poll. Consequently, Lukyanenko and several supporters were elected to the Supreme Council as part of the BYT. Following the elections, Lukyanenko said that the URP would be relaunched.

Leader: Levko LUKYANENKO.

Unity Bloc (*Blok "Yednist"*). Led by Kiev Mayor Oleksandr Omelchenko, the Unity electoral bloc was established prior to the 2002 national election on the basis of his **Ukrainian Party "Unity"** (*Ukrainska Partiya "Yednist"*), which was joined by several other minor formations, including the **Social Democratic Union** (*Sotsial Demokratychnyy Sojuz*—SDS) of Sergei PERESUNKO, the **Young Ukraine** (*Moloda Ukraina*—MU), and the **Ukrainian Party of Justice–Union of Veterans, Invalids, and Victims of Chernobyl and the Afghan War** (*Ukrainska Partiya Spravedlivosti–Sojuz Veteraniv, Invalidiv, Chornobiltsiv, Afgantsiv*—UPS). The Unity bloc won three Supreme Council seats in 2002.

Leader: Oleksandr OMELCHENKO.

Working Ukraine (*Trudova Ukraina*—TU). Working Ukraine (frequently translated into English as Labor Ukraine) was organized in March 1999 as a parliamentary faction. A 1998 electoral bloc of the same name, encompassing the Ukrainian Party of Justice (*Ukrainska Partiya Spravedlyvosti*—UPS) and the Civil Congress of Ukraine (*Hromadyanskiy Kongres Ukrainy*—HKU), had won 3 percent of the national proportional vote and one seat, held by the UPS's Andriy DERKACH, who joined the new faction.

Established as a party in June 1999, the TU was initially led by Mykhaylo SYROTA, who was subsequently associated with the Solidarity parliamentary faction. By that time, TU leadership had passed to former economic minister Serhiy TYHYPKO, who was generally regarded as one of Ukraine's most prominent oligarchs. As of February 2001 the party's parliamentary faction comprised 48 deputies, second only to that of the KPU. Having called for formation of a coalition government, the TU subsequently campaigned to unseat Prime Minister Yushchenko.

One of the TU's stalwarts was Viktor PINCHUK, a son-in-law of former President Kuchma and representative of the powerful Dnepropetrovsk clan. The TU participated in the For a United Ukraine electoral bloc in 2002.

Tyhypko, who managed the 2004 presidential campaign of the PR's Viktor Yanukovych, resigned as the TU leader in 2005. The party ran on its own in the 2006 legislative balloting, securing only 0.09 percent of the vote. In August 2007 TU leaders announced plans for the party's merger into the PR. However, Tyhypko, a prominent banker, presented himself as an independent candidate for the January 2010 presidential election.

Leader: Valeriy KONOVALYUK.

Organization of Ukrainian Nationalists (*Orhanizatsiya Ukrainskykh Natsionalistiv*—OUN). The present OUN was established in Lviv in January 1993 by Ivan KANDYBA and elements of the historic OUN that were critical of the organization's émigré leadership for deciding to set up the Congress of Ukrainian Nationalists (KUN, above) as an electoral arm. Kandyba and his associates instead wanted to reestablish the domestic OUN, which had led opposition to Communist rule until suppressed in the 1950s. To distinguish it from the external group, the new group was initially identified as the "Organization of Ukrainian Nationalists in Ukraine."

Although the OUN and the KUN ran separately in the 1994 legislative election, the OUN was registered not as a party per se, but as a civic association. In 1999 it backed Yevhen Marchuk for the presidency, and in January 2001 it joined in formation of the anti-Kuchma Ukrainian Right-Wing.

Leader: Vitaliy TSAPOVYCH.

Regional Parties:

There are a number of active Crimean parties in addition to branches of many Ukrainian parties. The **Communist Party of Crimea** (*Kommunisticheskaya Partiya Kryma*—KPK), led by Leonid Hrach, was banned in 1991 but was permitted to reregister in 1993. The **National Movement of the Crimean Tatars** (*Natsionalyi Dvizheniya Krymskikh Tatar*—NDKT), led by Vashtiy ABDURAYIMOV, is the oldest of the Crimean Tatar groups, dating from the 1960s and formally established in April 1987. The **National Party** (*Milli Firka*—MF) is a radical Tatar group founded in August 1993 and named after the party that attempted to set up an independent Crimean Tatar republic in 1917–1918. The **Organization of the Crimean Tatar National Movement** (*Organizatsiya Krymskotatarskogo Natsionalnogo Dvizheniya*—OKND), the largest of the Crimean Tatar parties, urges exclusive jurisdiction for the Crimean parliament. The business-oriented **Party for the Economic Revival of Crimea** (*Partiya Ekonomicheskogo Vozrozhdeniya Kryma*—PEVK), which won one seat in the Ukrainian Supreme Council in 1994, has been led by Vladimir SHEVIOV (Volodymyr SHEVYOV). The secessionist **Republican Movement of Crimea** (*Republikanskoe Dvizheniya Kryma*—RDK) is led by Yuriy Meshkov, who was elected president of Crimea in January 1994. The **Russian Party of the Crimea** (*Russkoi Partiya Kryma*—RPK) was founded under the leadership of Sergei SHUVAINIKOV in September 1993 as a radical splinter of the RDK. The **For Yanukovych Bloc** was organized in Crimea in 2005 by supporters of former prime minister Viktor Yanukovych, while the **Kunitsyn Bloc** was launched by supporters of former Crimean prime minister Serhiy Kunitsyn. The former won 44 seats on a 33 percent vote share in the March 2006 balloting for the Crimean Supreme Council, while the latter secured 10 seats on a 7.6 percent vote share. The KPK finished fourth in the balloting with 9 seats. Reports in 2008 described the **Russian Bloc**, led by Vladimir TYUNIN, as the "most powerful" party in Crimea. Among other things, Tyunin called for Crimea to become part of Russia.

Other regional or ethnically based groups include the **Democratic Movement of the Donbas** (*Demokraticheskoe Dvizheniya Donbassa*—DDD); the **Union for Democratic Reforms** (*Obiednannia Demokratychnykh Peretvoren*—ODP), formed under the leadership of Serhiy USTYCH in December 1993 by former Soviet officials in the Transcarpathia region of western Ukraine; and the **Subcarpathian Republican Party** (SRP), which was established in 1992 to press for Transcarpathian autonomy. In 2008 the **Congress of the Carpathian Rusyns** called for creation of an ethnic Rusyn (or Ruthenian) state.

LEGISLATURE

Supreme Council (*Verkhovna Rada*). Formerly styled the Supreme Soviet, Ukraine's legislature is a unicameral body of 450 members. Under constitutional changes that went into effect in January 2006, all 450 members are selected via proportional representation from a single nationwide constituency. The threshold to secure representation is 3 percent (reduced in 2006 from 4 percent); the term of office is five years.

Following the most recent balloting of September 30, 2007, the seats were distributed as follows: the Party of Regions, 175; the Yulia Tymoshenko Bloc, 155 (Fatherland, 105; Reforms and Order Party, 9; Ukrainian Social Democratic Party, 8; and unaffiliated, 33); the "Our

Ukraine"–People's Self-Defense bloc, 72 (People's Union "Our Ukraine," 29; People's Movement of Ukraine, 6; Ukrainian People's Party, 6; Forward, Ukraine!, 4; European Party of Ukraine, 2; Ukrainian Republican Party "Assembly," 2; the Christian Democratic Union, 2; It Is Time, 1; Defenders of the Fatherland, 1; and unaffiliated, 19); the Communist Party of Ukraine, 27; and the Lytvyn Bloc, 20 (People's Party, 13; Ukraine Labor Party, 7).

Speaker: Vlodymyr LYTVYN.

CABINET

[as of November 1, 2009]

Prime Minister	Yulia Tymoshenko (BYT) [f]
First Deputy Prime Minister (Economic and Financial Affairs)	Oleksandr Turchynov (BYT)
Deputy Prime Minister (European and International Integration	Hryhoriy Nemyrya (BYT)
Deputy Prime Minister (Humanitarian Affairs)	Ivan Vasiunyk (NU-NS)
Ministers	
Agrarian Policy	Yuriy Melnyk (BYT)
Cabinet Affairs	Petro Krupko (BYT)
Coal Industry	Viktor Poltavets (BYT)
Culture and Tourism	Vasyl Vovkum (BYT)
Defense (Acting)	Valerii Ivashchenko
Economy	Bohdan Danylyshyn (BYT)
Education and Science	Ivan Vakarchuk (NU-NS)
Emergency Situations	Volodymyr Shandra (NU-NS)
Environmental Protection	Heorhiy Philipchuk (BYT)
Family, Youth, and Sports	Yuriy Pavlenko (NU-NS)
Finance (Acting)	Ihor Umanskyi
Foreign Affairs	Petro Poroshenko*
Fuel and Energy	Yuriy Prodan (BYT)
Health	Vasyl Knyazevych (BYT)
Housing and Communal Services	Oleksiy Kucherenko (NU-NS)
Industrial Policy	Volodymyr Novytsky (BYT)
Interior	Yuriy Lutsenko (NU-NS)
Justice	Mykola Onishchuk (NU-NS)
Labor and Social Policy	Lyudmyla Denysova (BYT) [f]
Regional Development and Construction	Vasyl Kuybida (NU-NS)
Transport and Communications (Acting)	Vasily Shevchenko

[f] = female

Note: BYT = nominated by the Yulia Tymoshenko Bloc, NU-NS = nominated by Our Ukraine–People's Self-Defense, * = nominated by President Yushchenko. (Not all ministers are necessarily formal party members.)

COMMUNICATIONS

Freedom of speech is guaranteed in the Ukrainian constitution, but prior to liberalization following the Orange Revolution, opposition publications were frequently subjected to official harassment and libel suits brought by government officials. Officials were known to limit access to licenses, newsprint, and electricity and to exert pressure on advertisers. Collaterally, domestic and international advocates for freedom of expression criticized the Ukrainian government for inadequately investigating the disappearance and murder of independent journalist Heorhiy Gongadze in 2000. The Parliamentary Assembly of the Council of Europe, for one, cited "intimidation, repeated aggressions, and murders" directed against journalists.

In 2003 Freedom House downgraded its assessment of Ukraine's media status from partially free to not free. Reporters Without Borders reported that more than 50 reporters were arrested in 2003. In addition, the Kuchma administration passed legislation in 2004 allowing the government to monitor Internet publications and e-mails, an initiative critics claimed was aimed at popular opposition websites. The hard line toward media freedom was perceived as partially responsible for the popular antigovernment sentiment that propelled the Orange Revolution in late December 2004, after which the Yushchenko administration pledged quick liberalization in favor of a Western-style media policy. The OSCE reported that the media coverage of the 2006 legislative elections was significantly improved, with parties and electoral blocs able to communicate their messages to the electorate. The media were generally perceived in 2007 as operating freely in regard to criticizing government officials, although several physical attacks on journalists have been reported subsequently, possibly as the result of corruption investigations.

Press. The newspaper sector has grown significantly since the Orange Revolution, in both size and independence. Although most papers profess neutrality, a political bias reportedly can be identified in many of them. (Such biases currently often reflect support for either President Yushchenko or for former prime minister Yanukovych, two major protagonists in recent political turmoil.)

The following are dailies published in Kiev in Ukrainian, unless otherwise noted (circulation figures, as provided by the papers, are most likely significantly inflated); *Holos Ukrainy* (Voice of Ukraine, 160,000), Supreme Council organ in Ukrainian and Russian; *Silski Visti* (Rural News, 380,000), former KPU organ; *Uradoviy Kuryer* (Official Courier, 85,000), government organ, now privately owned; *Fakty I Kommentarii* (Facts and Commentary, 700,000), in Russian; *Segodnya* (Today, 150,000), in Russian, pro-Yanukovych; *Kiyeskiye Vedomosti* (140,000), in Russian, pro-Yushchenko; *Ukrainy Moloda* (Ukraine Youth, 120,000), pro-Yushchenko; *Den* (Day, 60,000), in Russian and Ukrainian, nonpartisan; *Vecherniye Vesti* (The Evening Gazette, 28,000), in Russian, linked to Prime Minister Tymoshenko; *Gazeta Po-Kiyesvski* (Kiev Gazette, 300,000), in Russian; *Komsomolskaya Pravda v Ukraine* (140,000), in Russian; *Zerkalo Nedeli* (weekly, 46,000), in Russian and Ukrainian, pro-Yushchenko; *2000* (weekly, 60,000), in Russian, pro-Yanukovych.

News agency. The official domestic facility is the Ukrainian National News Agency (Ukrinform), headquartered in Kiev; the Ukrainian Independent Information and News Agency (*Ukrayinske Nezalezhne Informatsiyne Agentsvo Novyn*—UNIAN) is a leading independent press source. A number of foreign bureaus, including Reuters, maintain offices in the capital.

Broadcasting and computing. In February 2000 a unified State Committee for Information Policy, Television, and Radio Broadcasting (*Derzhkominform*) was established, one of its goals being to restrict national broadcasts to the Ukrainian language except in areas with substantial minority communities. There is also a National Council for Television and Radio Broadcasting, which is responsible for overall regulation and licensing. There are currently more than 300 radio stations; the state-owned station is UR1, which broadcasts in Ukrainian. The state-controlled national television channel is UT1, which also broadcasts mostly in Ukrainian. Major private stations include *Inter*, in Russian and Ukrainian; *One Plus One*, in Ukrainian; and *5 Kanal*, an all-news channel primarily in Ukrainian. As of 2008 there were 106 Internet users per 1,000 inhabitants.

INTERGOVERNMENTAL REPRESENTATION

Ambassador to the U.S.: Oleh SHAMSHUR.

U.S. Ambassador to Ukraine: John F. TEFFT.

Permanent Representative to the UN: Yuriy SERGEYEV.

IGO Memberships (Non-UN): BSEC, CEI, CEUR, CIS, EBRD, Eurocontrol, Interpol, IOM, OSCE, PCA, WCO, WTO.

UNITED ARAB EMIRATES

al-Imarat al-Arabiyah al-Muttahidah

Political Status: Federation of six former Trucial States (Abu Dhabi, Dubai, Sharjah, Fujaira, Ajman, and Umm al-Qaiwain) established December 2, 1971; the seventh, Ras al-Khaima, joined in 1972.

Area: 32,278 sq. mi. (83,600 sq. km.).

Population: 4,104,695 (2005C), embracing (2003 estimates) Abu Dhabi (1,591,000), Dubai (1,204,000), Sharjah (636,000), Ras al-Khaima (195,000), Ajman (235,000), Fujaira (118,000), and Umm al-Qaiwain (62,000); 4,203,000 (2008E). Figures include noncitizens, who in 2008 represented approximately 80 percent of the population.

Major Urban Center (2005E): ABU DHABI (606,000).

Official Language: Arabic.

Monetary Unit: Dirham (official rate December 1, 2009: 3.67 dirhams = $1US).

Supreme Council: Composed of the rulers of the seven emirates (with dates of accession): Sheikh Khalifa ibn Zayed al-NAHYAN (Abu Dhabi, 2004), Sheikh Muhammad ibn Rashid al-MAKTUM (Dubai, 2006), Sheikh Sultan ibn Muhammad al-QASIMI (Sharjah, 1972), Sheikh Saqr ibn Muhammad al-QASIMI (Ras al-Khaima, 1948), Sheikh Hamad ibn Muhammad al-SHARQI (Fujaira, 1974), Sheikh Humayd ibn Rashid al-NUAYMI (Ajman, 1981), and Sheikh Saud ibn Rashid al-MUALLA (Umm al-Qaiwain, 1981).

President: Sheikh Khalifa ibn Zayed al-NAHYAN (Ruler of Abu Dhabi); elected by the Supreme Council on November 3, 2004, to a five-year term, succeeding his father, Sheikh Zayed ibn Sultan al-NAHYAN, who died on November 2; reelected by the Supreme Council for a second five-year term on November 3, 2009.

Vice President and Prime Minister: Sheikh Muhammad ibn Rashid al-MAKTUM (Ruler of Dubai); named vice president and prime minister by the Supreme Council on January 5, 2006, succeeding his older brother, Sheikh Maktum ibn Rashid al-MAKTUM, who died on January 4.

THE COUNTRY

Formerly known as the Trucial States because of truces concluded with Britain in the 19th century, the United Arab Emirates extends some 400 miles along the Persian Gulf from the southeastern end of the Qatar peninsula to a point just short of Ras Musandam. It encompasses a barren, relatively flat territory characterized by extreme temperatures and sparse rainfall. The majority of the indigenous population is Arab and adheres to the Sunni sect of Islam; there are also significant numbers of Iranians, Indians, Pakistanis, Baluchis, and descendants of former African slaves among the noncitizen population. The UAE has one of the most open societies in the Gulf region in terms of welcoming its huge foreign population and vast numbers of tourists without strictly enforcing many of its social laws among either group. Also, the UAE encourages women to participate in public life, and women may hold jobs. The UAE Women's Federation, established in 1975, has achieved many legal rights for women as well, and 20 percent of the seats in the consultative Federal National Council are reserved for women. Although Arabic is the official language, English is becoming the most common language among the diverse population; Persian, Russian, Urdu, Tagalog, and Hindi are also spoken.

Traditionally, the area was dependent upon trading, fishing, and pearling. However, the discovery in 1958 of major oil reserves in Abu Dhabi and, subsequently, of smaller deposits in Dubai and Sharjah dramatically altered the economy. Oil wealth led to rapid infrastructural modernization, advances in education and health services, and a construction boom requiring a massive inflow of foreign labor. New industrial cities established at Jebel Ali in Dubai and Ruwais in Abu Dhabi gave rise to shipyards, cement factories, and other manufacturing sites. During the 1980s, on the other hand, the UAE experienced a slowdown in economic growth because of reduced export revenues. As a result, the government moved to streamline the petroleum industry, which continued to account for 70 percent of government income, and began developing marketing, refining, and petrochemical aspects of the oil trade.

In addition to its vast oil capacity—reserves are estimated at 97.8 billion barrels, approximately 8 percent of the world's total—the UAE possesses one of the largest reservoirs of natural gas in the world. The government controls 60 percent of the energy sector, although, unlike several of its Gulf neighbors, it has permitted partial foreign ownership, thereby maintaining links with Western companies that have provided important ongoing infrastructure support. Moreover, the nation has firmly established itself as the region's leading trading center, partly on the strength of the Jebel Ali Free Trade Zone, where more than 350 companies operate. Dubai, in particular, has been effectively promoted in recent years as the region's trading and financial hub and as a major tourist destination. Successful diversification efforts have also contributed to rapid economic growth. On a less positive note, pervasive aspects of Western culture have been criticized by conservatives, who have attempted to "preserve" Islamic traditions through stricter imposition of Islamic law (sharia) and policies designed to reduce dependence on foreign workers.

Annual GDP growth for 2005–2008 averaged more than 8 percent, bolstered by increasing oil revenues and investments in the building and manufacturing sectors, as well as government progress in public administration reforms, according to the International Monetary Fund (IMF). The fund singled out Abu Dhabi, Dubai, and Sharjah for carrying out reforms to encourage more private sector development aimed at further diversifying the economy and reducing unemployment among UAE citizens.

The international financial crisis that developed in the second half of 2008 affected the UAE significantly (see Current issues, below, for additional information). Only minimal growth was projected for 2009, with inflation remaining as high as 9 percent.

GOVERNMENT AND POLITICS

Political background. Originally controlling an area known in the West as a refuge for pirates, some sheikhs of the eastern Persian Gulf entered into agreements with the British in the early 19th century. After the failure of the initial treaty agreements of 1820 and 1835, a Perpetual Maritime Truce was signed in 1853. Relations with Britain were further strengthened by an Exclusive Agreement of 1892, whereby the sheikhs agreed not to enter into diplomatic or other foreign relations with countries other than Britain. In return, Britain guaranteed defense of the sheikhdoms against aggression by sea.

The treaty arrangements with Britain lasted until 1968, when the British announced their intention to withdraw from the Persian Gulf by 1971. An early attempt at unification, the Federation of Arab Emirates, was initiated in 1968 with British encouragement but collapsed when Bahrain and Qatar declared separate independence in 1971. Subsequently, the leaders of the Trucial States organized a new grouping, the United Arab Emirates, which was formally constituted as an independent state on December 2, 1971, with Sheikh Zayed ibn Sultan al-NAHYAN as president; Ras al-Khaima, which initially rejected membership, acceded to the UAE two months later.

Apart from the death of Sheikh Khalid ibn Muhammad al-QASIMI (ruler of Sharjah) following an attempted coup in 1972, few major political developments occurred until the spring of 1979, when a series of disputes, principally between Abu Dhabi and Dubai over the extent of federal powers, led to the April 25 resignation of Prime Minister Sheikh Maktum ibn Rashid al-MAKTUM and his replacement five days later by his father, Sheikh Rashid ibn Said al-MAKTUM, ruler of Dubai, who retained his position as vice president. In 1981 the emirs of Ajman, Sheikh Rashid ibn Humayd al-NUAYMI, and of Umm al-Qaiwain, Sheikh Ahmad ibn Rashid al-MUALLA, both of whom had ruled for more than 50 years, died and were succeeded by their sons, Sheikh Humayd ibn Rashid al-NUAYMI and Sheikh Rashid ibn Ahmad al-MUALLA, respectively.

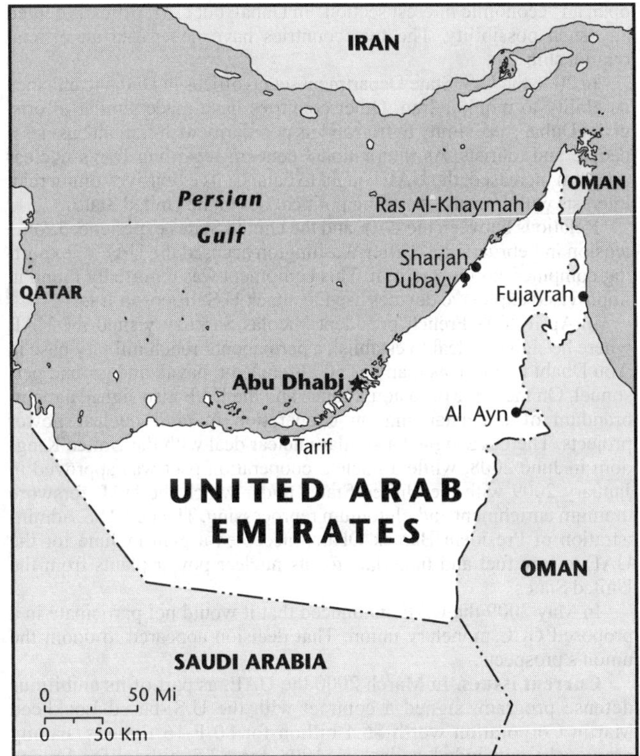

On June 17, 1987, Sheikh Abd al-Aziz al-QASIMI seized power in Sharjah, accusing his brother Sheikh Sultan ibn Muhammad al-QASIMI of fiscal mismanagement. On July 20 Sheikh Muhammad was reinstated by the Supreme Council, which decreed that Sheikh Abd al-Aziz should thenceforth hold the title of crown prince and deputy ruler; however, he was stripped of the title on February 4, 1990.

Following the death of Sheikh Rashid ibn Said al-Maktum on October 7, 1990, his son Sheikh Maktum ibn Rashid was named vice president and returned to his former position as prime minister.

In 1991 the UAE suffered a major blow to its international prestige by the collapse at midyear of the Luxembourg-chartered Bank of Credit and Commerce International (BCCI), 77 percent of whose shares were owned by President Zayed and a group of financial associates. Ultimately, it was revealed that Sheikh Zayed had provided at least $1 billion to shore up the troubled institution since 1989. (For additional information, see the 2005–2006 *Handbook.*) A plan was approved in December 1995 under which BCCI creditors would be reimbursed $1.8 billion by the bank's major shareholders, observers estimating the paybacks would cover 20 to 40 percent of most deposits. BCCI was formally liquidated by the UAE Central Bank in February 1996. (As of 2003 $5.7 billion had been authorized in paybacks to BCCI creditors, total claims having been estimated at $9 billion among some 80,000 depositors. The case, unprecedented in scope in British courts, went to trial in 2004, but liquidators dropped their case in 2005 in a move that shocked financial observers.)

The UAE cabinet submitted its resignation on March 17, 1997, and Sheikh Maktum was asked to form a new government, which was announced on March 25. The reshuffle, the first significant government change since 1990, was promoted as infusing "young blood" in the UAE policymaking process, although several important ministries remained in the hands of incumbents.

The president and vice president were reelected by the Supreme Council on December 2, 2001. The first cabinet shuffle since 1997 took place on November 1, 2004, as decreed by President Zayed one day before he died. (Among the new cabinet members was the first woman minister, a move in line with a policy to involve more women in decision making.) Sheikh Khalifa ibn Zayed al-NAHYAN succeeded his father (Sheikh Zayed) as president of the UAE and ruler of Abu Dhabi.

In 2005 President Khalifa announced plans to hold limited elections as part of a package of political reforms. He proposed allowing half of the 40 members of the Federal National Council (FNC) to be elected by citizens appointed to electoral colleges in each emirate. The remaining 20 members of the FNC would continue to be appointed by the rulers of the 7 emirates (see Constitution and government, below).

Following the death of 62-year-old Sheikh Maktum on January 4, 2006, his younger brother, Defense Minister Sheikh Muhammad ibn Rashid al-MAKTUM, was named vice president and prime minister by the Supreme Council on January 5; he also succeeded his brother as ruler of Dubai.

The first indirect elections to the FNC were held in December 2007. The cabinet was reshuffled in February 2008 and May 2009.

Constitution and government. The institutions of the UAE were superimposed upon the existing political structures of the member states, which generally maintain their monarchical character. (Effective power within the federation remains in the hands of senior members of the ruling families of the seven emirates, led by Abu Dhabi, by far the most oil-rich emirate, and, to a lesser extent, Dubai, a major business center.) Under the federal constitution adopted in 1971 (designated an "interim" basic law until 1996), the rulers of the constituent states are members of the Supreme Council, which elects a president and vice president for five-year terms. Supreme Council decrees require the approval of the rulers of Abu Dhabi and Dubai and at least three other emirates. The president appoints a prime minister and a cabinet, and there is a consultative Federal National Council (FNC) whose 40 members were all appointed by the rulers of the constituent emirates until indirect elections for 20 of the members began in December 2006 (see Legislature, below, for details). Constitutional amendment in late 2008 authorized the FNC, previously confined to domestic affairs, to make recommendations on international matters as well.

In July 1976 the FNC, following a failure to reach agreement on a new constitutional draft, voted to extend the life of the existing constitution for another five years beyond December 2. Further extensions were voted at five-year intervals thereafter until 1996, when the Supreme Council (May 20) and the FNC (June 18) approved an amendment removing "interim" from the language in the constitution, thereby effectively making it a permanent document.

Judicial functions have traditionally been performed by local courts applying Islamic law (sharia) and by individual decisions rendered by the ruling families. In June 1978 the president signed a law establishing four Primary Federal Tribunals (in Abu Dhabi, Ajman, Fujaira, and Sharjah) to handle disputes between individuals and the federation, with appeal to the federal Supreme Court. However, a later decree of February 1994 specified that a variety of crimes (including murder, theft, adultery, and juvenile and drug-related offenses) would be tried in Islamic, rather than civil, courts.

The basic administrative divisions are the constituent states, each of which retains local control over mineral rights, taxation, and police protection. Abu Dhabi effectively controls the UAE's 65,000-member federal army.

Foreign relations. The United Arab Emirates is a member of the United Nations, the Arab League, the Organization of the Petroleum Exporting Countries (OPEC), and various regional groupings. Relations have been cordial with most countries, including the United States, although there have been territorial disputes with Iran, Oman, Qatar, and Saudi Arabia.

In 1971 Iran occupied Abu Musa, a small island in the Persian Gulf, and laid claim to the Greater and Lesser Tunbs, two uninhabited but potentially strategically important islands. Soon after, an agreement was reached between Tehran and the emir of Sharjah that provided for joint administration of Abu Musa and the sharing of revenue from offshore oil wells. However, no accord was reached regarding the Tunbs (claimed by Ras al-Khaima). Following the establishment of diplomatic relations between Iran and the UAE in 1972, the issue remained relatively dormant before flaring up in 1992 (see below).

A dispute with Saudi Arabia and Oman concerned portions of Abu Dhabi, including the potentially oil-rich Buraimi Oasis, located at the juncture of the three states. Under the terms of an agreement reached in 1974, six villages of the oasis were awarded to Abu Dhabi and two to Oman; Saudi Arabia, in return for renouncing its claim, was granted a land corridor coterminous with the existing Abu Dhabi–Qatar border to the Persian Gulf port of Khor al-Adad. The border demarcation issue resurfaced in September 1992 in the form of a clash between Saudi Arabian and Qatari forces (see Qatar: Foreign relations). In June 2002 Oman and the UAE implemented an agreement to demarcate their border.

In early 1981 the UAE joined with five neighbors—Bahrain, Kuwait, Oman, Qatar, and Saudi Arabia—in establishing the Cooperative Council of the Arab Gulf States (more commonly known as the

Gulf Cooperation Council—GCC) to coordinate members' policies on security and stability in the area. Concern over the Iran-Iraq war led the UAE to participate in the GCC's annual Peninsula Shield joint military maneuvers. Although the hazards of the regional conflict did not preclude an increase in trade with Tehran, the UAE and the other GCC states became increasingly aware of their vulnerability to possible Iranian aggression and to the potentially destabilizing effects of an Iranian-inspired Islamic revolution. Thus, during a December 1987 GCC summit in Saudi Arabia, discussion centered on negotiations with Egypt for military aid and support. Meanwhile, in the wake of oilfield bombings by the Gulf combatants, including one by unidentified aircraft that killed eight people and destroyed two of five platforms in Abu Dhabi, the UAE took steps to purchase advance-warning systems from Britain, France, and the United States.

The UAE reacted nervously to Iraq's occupation of Kuwait on August 2, 1990, because it, like Kuwait, had been charged by Baghdad with overproduction of oil. On August 19, having joined with other GCC governments in calling for Iraq's withdrawal, the UAE agreed to the deployment of foreign military units on its soil. It also cooperated with coalition forces during the confrontation that concluded with Iraq's defeat in February 1991. In April it was reported that the UAE had contributed nearly $3 billion to U.S. Gulf War costs.

With Iraqi belligerence still appearing to present a challenge to regional security, the Gulf states attempted to improve relations with Iran, and the UAE in July 1991 named its first ambassador to Tehran since the latter's 1979 revolution. However, in early 1992 Iran reignited the long-dormant Gulf dispute between the two nations by expelling some 700 UAE nationals from Abu Musa and seizing complete control of the island. After the GCC demanded in September that Iran repudiate its "annexation" of Abu Musa, Tehran reasserted its claim of sovereignty over the island as well as over the Greater and Lesser Tunbs, vowing that UAE forces would have to cross a "sea of blood" to retake the territory. Although the UAE subsequently sought international mediation of the dispute, Iran rejected the proposal, and tension between the countries continued. The UAE at the same time continued to lead efforts to "rehabilitate" the regime of Saddam Hussein, in part with an eye on future economic ties with Baghdad, and in April 2000 the UAE's embassy in Baghdad was reopened. In March 2003, the UAE president offered a vague plan for Hussein's permanent exile, defying the Arab League stance on noninterference in the internal affairs of a neighboring country. After the U.S. invasion and occupation of Iraq, the UAE was among the first countries to send relief shipments. It has continued to provide humanitarian aid, as well as build a desalination plant and equip Iraqi hospitals.

In July 1994 the UAE became the fourth GCC country to conclude a military cooperation pact with the United States. The agreement, which provides for joint military exercises and the stationing of a U.S. naval task force on UAE territory, was reportedly signed because of the Emirates' vulnerability to attack by Iran and Iraq. In 2004 the commander of U.S. Central Command described U.S.-UAE military cooperation as among the strongest in the region. France's defense minister expressed similar sentiments, while the United Kingdom in 2005 announced its commitment to developing military and industrial cooperation with the UAE.

As did its GCC neighbors, the UAE expressed concern in the 1990s over the security implications of growing Islamist militancy in North Africa and the Middle East. Following the attacks on the United States in September 2001, the UAE agreed to cooperate closely with the George W. Bush administration's war on terrorism. Among other measures, the UAE severed diplomatic relations with the Taliban administration in Afghanistan after it refused to hand over Osama bin Laden. At least two senior al-Qaida operatives have been arrested in the UAE since 2002.

Following years of political violence in the region, the UAE cabinet decided in June 2005 to fight against terrorism by punishing people who organize, commit, finance, or contribute to terrorist acts. Money laundering and smuggling have long been troublesome issues in the UAE (see Current issues, below) and were among the topics addressed by GCC members in June 2005.

The UAE historically has objected to the slow pace of progress in the Middle East peace process, joining a number of other Arab countries in boycotting a regional economic development conference in 1997 to protest what it perceived as an inappropriate U.S. tilt toward Israel at the expense of the Palestinian cause. The UAE has also adopted a strongly pro-Palestinian, pro-Arab stance regarding the future status of Jerusalem, a major sticking point in the Israeli-Palestinian impasse. In May 2005 reports surfaced from Jerusalem that Israel planned to open an "economic interest section" in Dubai, but UAE officials denied any such possibility. The two countries have never had an official relationship.

In 2006 the U.S. State Department set up offices in Dubai to enhance its ability to monitor Iran. Other countries have made similar efforts, given Dubai's proximity to Iran and its popularity with Iranian businesspeople and tourists. As international concern regarding Iran's nuclear program increased, the UAE sought to balance its extensive commercial interests with Iran and its strong political ties to the United States.

Relations between the UAE and the United States experienced some tension in February 2008 after Washington accused the UAE of exporting computer circuitry to Iran. This equipment was reportedly found in improvised explosive devices used to attack U.S. troops in Iraq.

In April 2008 French president Nicolas Sarkozy visited the UAE where he signed a deal to establish a permanent French military base in Abu Dhabi to house as many as 500 French air, naval, and ground personnel. On the same occasion, France and the UAE also signed a memorandum of understanding on cooperation in civil nuclear power projects. The UAE signed a similar nuclear deal with the United Kingdom in June 2008, while a nuclear cooperation pact was approved in January 2009 with the United States under which the UAE forswore uranium enrichment and plutonium reprocessing. The new U.S. administration of President Barack Obama accepted a plan in June for the UAE to buy fuel and materials for its nuclear power plants from the United States.

In May 2009 the UAE announced that it would not participate in a proposed GCC monetary union. That decision appeared to doom the union's prospects.

Current issues. In March 2000 the UAE, as part of its ambitious defense program, signed a contract with the U.S.-based Lockheed Martin Corporation worth $6.4 billion for 80 F-16 fighters, having previously concluded a deal in 1998 for $3.5 billion for French planes. Washington had initially objected to the inclusion of certain components that had previously been shared only with members of the North Atlantic Treaty Organization (NATO). The first delivery of the U.S. planes was in 2005, with the remainder to be delivered within three years.

In March 2000 the UAE announced plans to spearhead an $8 billion regional gas network in conjunction with other GCC members as well as Western energy companies. As a first stage of the 25-year project, Abu Dhabi negotiated a $3.5 billion agreement to develop gas fields in Qatar and ship gas from there initially to the other emirates and Gulf states, such as Oman, and eventually to India and Pakistan. The project, the first such cross-border arrangement in GCC history, was considered an important element in establishing the UAE as the hub of a regional "energy security" network. At the same time, however, it brought increasing pressure from the international community on the UAE to establish procedures to ensure greater transparency and accountability in its financial sector. Critics charged that long-standing secrecy contributed to UAE banks being used for money laundering, while lack of oversight of business dealings permitted unnoticed transshipment of drugs and illegal weapons through UAE ports. The UAE's banking system and financial practices were further criticized after the September 2001 attacks in the United States when it became evident that close associates of Osama bin Laden had used the country's banks to transfer and receive money from several of the hijackers. Promising reform, the UAE in January 2002 adopted a series of policy changes to monitor banking practices and financial transactions and instituted new penalties to combat money laundering. As of April 1, 2003, the UAE Central Bank required *hawalah* (informal money transfer) operators to register and provide details of transactions. Additionally, in June 2005 the UAE joined the UN Convention Against Transnational Organized Crime, while the IMF subsequently commended the UAE for its enactment of an extensive set of laws to regulate international banking practices.

In 2006, in one of the most politically charged events of recent years, DP World, a state-owned Dubai company, sought to manage terminal operations at six U.S. ports. The company sold its interests after "an unrelenting bipartisan attack" in the U.S. Congress over security concerns, according to *The New York Times*. Ironically, observers pointed out, the Dubai company's operations originated in Jebel Ali, the port outside the United States most often visited by the U.S. Navy and known for its state-of-the-art security. Soon after the DP World controversy, the Bush administration expressed security concerns over reported shipments of sensitive military technology from Dubai ports to Iran and Syria.

On the domestic front, attention in 2006 focused on the limited elections December 16–20 for 20 members of the legislature. The rulers of the seven emirates chose those who could vote as members of an electoral college. The actual number of eligible voters was 6,689, or 0.8 percent of UAE citizens. Nevertheless, the election was seen as a first step toward political reform. The UAE, under pressure from its neighbors and from Washington, was the last of the Gulf states to initiate such changes.

The continued surge in world oil prices subsequently contributed to a real-estate boom in Dubai, as well as a boom in commerce. Dubai, attracting some 5 million tourists a year, announced plans for the world's tallest building, the world's largest shopping mall, and a Disneyland-like park. Along with the construction boom, however, came reports of public protests and strikes by migrant workers. In 2006 the government drafted a new labor law that would grant more rights to workers, the Emirates' alleged abusive treatment of migrant workers having drawn criticism from international human rights groups.

Facing major negative effects from the global financial crisis, the UAE government in late 2008 pledged to back banks and other institutions facing liquidity problems. Additionally, the regulations for corporate governance were tightened in the wake of a recent corruption investigation, while cabinet members were constitutionally precluded from participating in business deals (previously a common practice).

Having earlier made $33 billion available to prop up banks in all seven emirates, the federal government in February 2009 approved an additional $10 billion bailout for the financial sector in Dubai, where real estate prices had fallen by more than 30 percent and construction of many projects had been suspended. Many analysts characterized the action as Abu Dhabi (the location of 90 percent of the country's oil wealth) reining in its "profligate brother" (Dubai), which was forced to initiate retrenchment. Late in the year the specter of Dubai's possible default on a portion of its international debt roiled international financial markets, but Abu Dhabi offered another $10 billion bailout, which appeared to resolve the immediate crisis.

POLITICAL PARTIES

There are no political parties in the United Arab Emirates.

LEGISLATURE

Federal National Council (*Majlis al-Watani al-Itihadi*). The UAE's consultative body currently consists of 40 delegates, 20 appointed by the rulers of the constituent states and 20 elected by an electoral colleges (established in 2006) whose members are appointed by the rulers. The first elections were held in three rounds December 16–20, 2006, for 20 seats: 4 each from Abu Dhabi and Dubai, 3 each from Sharjah and Ras al-Khaima, and 2 each from the 3 other emirates. The 20 elected and 20 appointed delegates were sworn in on February 12, 2007, for a two-year term, although the term was extended to four years in late 2008.

Speaker: Abdul-Aziz Abdallah al-GHURAIR.

CABINET

[as of October 1, 2009]

Prime Minister	Sheikh Muhammad ibn Rashid al-Maktum
Deputy Prime Minister (Interior)	Maj. Gen. Sheikh Saif ibn Zayed al-Nahyan
Deputy Prime Minister (Presidential Affairs)	Sheikh Mansur ibn Zayed al-Nahyan
Ministers	
Cabinet Affairs	Mohammed Abdullah al-Gargawi
Culture, Youth, and Community Development	Abdul Rahman Muhammad al-Owais
Defense	Sheikh Muhammad ibn Rashid al-Maktum
Economy and Industry	Sultan bin Said al-Mansouri
Education	Hamaid Muhammad Obaid al-Qatami
Energy	Muhammad ibn Dhain al-Hamili
Environment and Water	Rashid Ahmad Bin-Fahd
Finance and Industry	Sheikh Hamdan ibn Rashid al-Maktum
Foreign Affairs	Sheikh Abdallah ibn Zayed al-NAYHAN
Foreign Trade	Shaikha Lubna al-Qasami [f]
Health	Hanif Hassan Ali
Higher Education and Scientific Research	Sheikh Nahyan ibn Mubarak al-Nayhan
Justice	Hadef ibn Juan al-Zaheri
Labor	Saqr Ghabbash Said Ghabbash
Public Works	Sheikh Hamdan ibn Mubarak al-Nahyan
Social Affairs	Mariam Muhammad Khalfan al-Roumi [f]
Ministers of State	
Federal National Council Affairs	Anwar Muhammad Gargash
Financial and Industrial Affairs	Ubayd Hamid al-Tayir
Foreign Affairs	Anwar Muhammad Gargash
Without portfolio	Maytha Salim al-Shamisi [f]
Without portfolio	Rim Ibrahim al-Hashimi [f]

[f] = female

COMMUNICATIONS

While the constitution of the UAE guarantees freedom of the press, the government closely monitors Arabic-language media, although English-language media receive less scrutiny, according to Reporters Without Borders. The Federal National Council in early 2009 endorsed a controversial new press law that while eliminating prison sentences for journalists, increased, according to critics, the changes for additional government restrictions on the media. UAE president Khalifa subsequently postponed signing the measure into law. Meanwhile, journalism watchdogs reported that the UAE government had blocked politically charged websites and otherwise filtered Internet use.

Press. The following are published in Arabic, unless otherwise noted: *Khalij Times* (Dubai and Abu Dhabi, 72,000), English daily; *al-Ittihad* (Abu Dhabi, Dubai, and Sharjah, 58,000), designated as the official daily of the UAE; *Gulf News* (Dubai and Abu Dhabi, 91,000), English daily; *al-Khalij* (Sharjah, 85,000), independent daily; *Emirates News* (Abu Dhabi, 2,000), English daily; *al-Wahdah* (Abu Dhabi, 20,000), independent daily; *al-Bayan*, (32,000); *al-Fajr* (Abu Dhabi and Dubai, 28,000); *Mathrubhumi* (Malayalam); *National*, government-owned English daily.

News agencies. The official Emirates News Agency (*Wikalat al-Anba al-Imarat*—WAM) was founded in 1977. Reuters maintains an office in Dubai.

Broadcasting and computing. The United Arab Emirates Broadcasting Service (*Idhaat al-Imarat al-Arabiyah al-Muttahidah*) operates radio stations in five of the seven emirates. In addition, most of the individual emirates engage in radio or television programming. CNN, BBC World, Voice of America, and Bloomberg L.P. are among the major broadcasters based in Dubai Media City. The state-controlled Abu Dhabi TV is owned by the Abu Dhabi Media Company. As of 2008 there were 651.5 Internet users per 1,000 inhabitants.

INTERGOVERNMENTAL REPRESENTATION

Ambassador to the U.S.: Yousef al OTAIBA.

U.S. Ambassador to the United Arab Emirates: Richard G. OLSEN.

Permanent Representative to the UN: Ahmed Abdulrahman al-JARMAN.

IGO Memberships (Non-UN): AFESD, AMF, BADEA, GCC, IDB, Interpol, IOR-ARC, LAS, NAM, OAPEC, OIC, OPEC, PCA, WCO, WTO.

UNITED KINGDOM

United Kingdom of Great Britain and Northern Ireland

Political Status: Constitutional monarchy, under democratic parliamentary regime.

Area: 94,249 sq. mi. (244,104 sq. km.), embracing England and Wales, 58,382 sq. mi. (151,209 sq. km.); Scotland, 30,415 sq. mi. (78,775 sq. km.); Northern Ireland, 5,452 sq. mi. (14,120 sq. km.).

Population: 58,789,194 (2001C), including England, 49,138,831; Scotland, 5,062,011; Wales, 2,903,085; Northern Ireland, 1,685,267; 62,122,000 (2008E).

Major Urban Centers (2005E): *England:* LONDON (urban area, 7,396,000), Birmingham (971,000), Liverpool (464,000), Leeds (451,000), Sheffield (443,000), Bristol (426,000), Manchester (390,000); *Wales:* CARDIFF (300,000); *Scotland:* EDINBURGH (442,000), Glasgow (619,000); *Northern Ireland:* BELFAST (276,000).

Principal Language: English (Scottish and Irish forms of Gaelic are spoken in portions of Scotland and Northern Ireland, respectively, while Welsh is spoken in northern and central Wales).

Monetary Unit: Pound Sterling (market rate December 1, 2009: 1 pound = $1.66US).

Sovereign: Queen ELIZABETH II; proclaimed queen on February 6, 1952; crowned June 2, 1953.

Heir Apparent: CHARLES Philip Arthur George; invested as Prince of Wales on July 1, 1969.

Prime Minister: James Gordon BROWN (Labour Party); appointed by the queen on June 27, 2007, to succeed Anthony (Tony) BLAIR (Labour Party), who had resigned on the same day.

THE COUNTRY

The United Kingdom of Great Britain and Northern Ireland (UK) occupies the major portion of the British Isles, the largest island group off the European coast. The individual identity of its separate regions, each with distinctive ethnic and linguistic characteristics, is reflected in the complex governmental structure of the country as a whole. England, the heart of the nation, accounts for over half the total area and 83 percent of the total population. Wales, conquered in the Middle Ages, has its own capital, Cardiff, and a national language, Welsh, with which some 30 percent of the population have familiarity. Scotland, ruled as a separate kingdom until 1707, has long had its own legal and educational systems; its capital is Edinburgh. Conquered by the English in the Middle Ages, Ireland became part of the UK in 1800 but in 1921 was partitioned into Northern Ireland, whose Protestant majority opted for retention of British status, and the predominantly Catholic Irish Republic. Varieties of the Gaelic language are spoken in both Scotland and Northern Ireland. There are two established churches, the Church of England (Episcopalian or Anglican), with some 1.5 million active members, and the Church of Scotland (Presbyterian), with some 700,000 members. Nonestablished religions include Roman Catholicism, which claims over 4 million adherents; Islam, with 1.5 million; and Methodism, with 400,000. At the 2001 census, 71.6 percent of the population identified themselves as Christians, while 23.2 percent reported no religious affiliation. Apart from a legal prohibition on the monarch (who is head of the Church of England) or the heir to the throne becoming a Roman Catholic, religious freedom prevails.

In 2004 women comprised 46 percent of the paid (including part-time) workforce, concentrated in the retail, clerical, and human services sectors. As of October 2009 women held 126 seats in the 646-member House of Commons, 147 of the 737 occupied seats in the House of Lords, and 4 cabinet posts.

Great Britain was the seat of the industrial revolution of the 18th century, and most of its urbanized and highly skilled population is engaged in manufacturing and service industries, mainly transport, commerce, and finance, with agriculture accounting for only 1 percent of GDP and employment. Machinery, basic manufactures, and agricultural products constitute the bulk of British imports. Machinery and transport equipment, basic manufactures, chemicals, and mineral fuels are the chief exports. Germany, the United States, and Japan rank as the leading trading partners.

The British economy experienced intermittent crises after World War II as the result of factors that included the wartime liquidation of most of the country's overseas assets and a lack of flexibility in management and labor practices. Emigration and immigration, featuring the "brain drain" of skilled professional personnel (mainly to the United States) and a concurrent influx of nonwhite labor from Africa, South Asia, the West Indies, and elsewhere, also produced unsettling economic and social effects, including racial tensions. The oil crisis of 1973–1974 was particularly damaging to the UK economy, but in the late 1970s fiscal constraint and increased exploitation of North Sea oil reserves yielded annual GDP increases of 2–3 percent, despite remaining structural problems. Under the post-1979 Conservative government, policies to increase productivity at first exacerbated the effects of international recession, causing unemployment to rise into the double digits and industrial output to fall. From 1983 the economy experienced something of a boom: Overall economic growth averaged over 3 percent a year from 1983 to 1989, corporate profits rose, productivity was second only to that of Japan, annual inflation fell to around 4 percent, and the government ran a budget surplus.

The "British economic miracle" foundered in the wake of the stock market crash of October 1989. Initially, the government sought recovery by increasing liquidity, but a rapid inflationary surge forced it to apply interest rates at record highs. In October 1990 the pound sterling was placed in the broad band of the European Community (EC) exchange rate mechanism (ERM), which in effect pegged it to the deutsche mark. By then, the economy had entered its deepest and longest recession since the 1930s, aggravated by similar difficulties in other industrial economies. In 1991–1992 overall output dropped by 3.6 percent and unemployment, having fallen to a ten-year low of 5.9 percent in 1989, rose to 10.5 percent by late 1992. In September 1992 massive speculation against the pound sterling forced its withdrawal from the ERM and, in effect, a 20 percent devaluation.

Clear signs of a rebound appeared in 1993, and by April 1994 the GDP had regained its preslump (1990) peak. The recovery continued in 1995–1997, with annual GDP growth averaging about 3 percent. A global slowdown held expansion to 2.2 percent in 1998 and 2.0 percent in 1999, although growth in the last three quarters of the latter year returned to an annualized rate of about 3 percent and helped vault the UK over France and into fourth place among the world's largest economies. Moreover, unemployment stood at only 4 percent, the lowest rate in a quarter of a century, while retail inflation remained below the target of 2.5 percent. Although the Labour administration that took office in 1997 had initially maintained the fiscal restraint imposed during the 18-year reign of the Conservatives, the budget for 2000–2001 proposed significant spending increases, with a focus on improving the national health system and education. According to the International Monetary Fund (IMF), GDP growth for 2000 held at 3.0 percent before dropping to 2.2 percent in 2001 and 2.0 percent in 2002, then rising to 2.5 percent in 2003 and 3.2 percent in 2004.

In its 2005 report, the IMF praised the UK for a "remarkable performance" over the past decade, marked by sustained growth, low inflation, and steadily low unemployment (4.8 percent from 2003 to 2005). However, GDP growth for 2005 fell to 1.9 percent (the lowest in 13 years), primarily as the result of reduced consumer spending. In addition, unemployment crept up to 5.3 percent in mid-2006. Meanwhile, the UK government rejected a request from the European Union (EU) that it raise taxes or cut spending in order to reduce the budget deficit. (Although the UK is not a member of the eurozone and therefore is not subject to formal EU sanctions, it has committed itself to the EU's stability and growth pact, which theoretically limits national budget deficits to 3.0 percent of GDP.)

GDP growth accelerated to 2.9 percent in 2006 and 2.6 percent in 2007. However, declining housing prices, reduced exports, tightening credit, and sagging domestic consumer demand contributed to a significant slowdown in the first quarter of 2008, which was exacerbated in the last quarter by the global financial crisis. GDP growth for 2008 was

only 0.7 percent, although the government's aggressive response to the financial crisis by means of a large stimulus to the public sector was credited with averting a systemic breakdown. Meanwhile, the budget deficit as a percent of GDP rose to 7.0 percent in 2008, and unemployment rose to 7.6 percent in 2009. It was estimated that GDP might decline by 4.2 percent in 2009, while the budget deficit might soar to more than 13.0 percent of GDP as the result of the stimulus spending and the declining employment rate.

GOVERNMENT AND POLITICS

Political background. After reaching its apogee of global influence in the closing decades of the Victorian era, the UK endured the strains of the two world wars with its political institutions unimpaired but with sharp reductions in its relative economic strength and military power. The steady erosion of the British imperial position after World War II was only partially offset by the concurrent development and expansion of the Commonwealth, a grouping that continued to reflect an underlying British philosophy but whose center of gravity shifted to newly developed and developing nations. Despite continuing differences on many issues, the three traditional parties—Conservative, Labour, and Liberal (now the Liberal Democrats)—have in some respects drawn closer together.

The Labour Party, after winning the postwar elections of 1945 and 1950 under the leadership of Clement R. ATTLEE, went into opposition for 13 years while the Conservative Party governed under prime ministers Winston CHURCHILL (1951–1955), Anthony EDEN (1955–1957), Harold MACMILLAN (1957–1963), and Alec DOUGLAS-HOME (1963–1964). A Conservative defeat in the general election of October 1964 returned Labour to power under Harold WILSON. At the election of June 1970 the tide swung back to the Conservatives, who under Edward HEATH obtained a 30-seat majority in the House of Commons. In February 1974 the Conservatives outpolled Labour but fell 3 seats short of a plurality, Wilson returning to head the first minority government since 1929. A second election eight months later gave Labour an overall majority of 3 seats. In April 1976 Wilson unexpectedly resigned and was succeeded as prime minister by Foreign Secretary James CALLAGHAN, who saw Labour's fortunes plummet in the 1978–1979 "winter of discontent" that featured damaging public sector strikes.

In May 1979 the Conservatives obtained 339 seats (a majority of 44) in the House of Commons, enabling Margaret THATCHER to become the first female prime minister in British (and European) history. Benefiting from popular response to her handling of the Falkland Islands War (see Foreign relations, below), the Conservatives surged to a 144-seat majority at the election of June 1983. They retained control of the Commons with a somewhat diminished but still comfortable majority of 102 in June 1987, Thatcher becoming the first prime minister in modern British history to win three consecutive terms.

Following the introduction of a widely disliked community charge ("poll tax") in April 1990, the Conservatives' popularity took a downward turn that was only briefly reversed by public appreciation of Thatcher's firmness in response to the Persian Gulf conflict precipitated by Iraq's invasion of Kuwait in August. Amid a damaging series of by-election defeats for the Conservatives, a sense of crisis was generated by the resignation on November 1 of the deputy prime minister, Geoffrey HOWE, over the prime minister's lack of support for enhanced British participation in the EC. On November 13 the former defense secretary, Michael HESELTINE, reversing an earlier pledge, challenged Thatcher for the party leadership, and at an intraparty poll on November 20 he won sufficient backing to deny the prime minister a first-round victory. Two days later Thatcher announced her intention to resign. In the second-round ballot on November 27 Chancellor of the Exchequer John MAJOR defeated both Heseltine and Foreign Secretary Douglas HURD. Having abandoned the poll tax and moderated other aspects of "Thatcherite" policies that had enjoyed his keen support theretofore, Major led the Conservatives to a fourth successive election victory on April 9, 1992, despite economic recession and negative forecasts from opinion pollsters. Although Labour made significant gains, the Conservatives retained a working majority of 336 seats in the 651-member House of Commons.

The Danish referendum vote in June 1992 against the Maastricht Treaty on greater EC economic and political union caused divisions to surface within the Conservative Party between pro- and anti-EC factions, the latter being dubbed "Eurosceptics." Because of the government's modest majority, anti-EC Conservative MPs were able to mount protracted resistance to parliamentary ratification of the Maastricht Treaty until after reversal of the Danish negative vote in May 1993 (see Foreign relations, below).

The opposition Labour Party displayed its own internal fissures over the EC. However, its main task was to revitalize its leadership following the resignation of Neil KINNOCK, who had suffered defeat in two successive general elections. Elected leader in July 1992, John SMITH maintained Kinnock's moderate, pro-EC stance while initiating reviews of Labour's social and constitutional policies. A rapid Labour rise in the opinion polls in late 1992 was assisted by a series of major government reverses and blunders, amid a European currency crisis that forced the pound sterling out of the EC's ERM.

The withdrawal from the ERM represented a traumatic collapse of government economic policy. In March 1993 Chancellor of the Exchequer Norman LAMONT presented a "budget for jobs" and claimed that the recession was over, but a spiraling budget deficit obliged him to introduce tax increases effective in 1994, some in breach of Conservative election pledges. Major later sought to recover the initiative by launching a "back to basics" campaign, stressing traditional Conservative values on education, law and order, and other matters.

The issuance of the joint UK-Irish Downing Street Declaration on Northern Ireland in December 1993 yielded some political credit to Major (and led eventually to the historic cease-fire announcement by the Irish Republican Army [IRA] on August 31, 1994—see Northern Ireland article). Conservative fortunes nevertheless continued their decline, and in June 1994 the party lost 16 of its 34 seats in the European Parliament. The clear victor in the balloting was the Labour Party, under the interim leadership of Margaret BECKETT following the sudden death of Smith on May 12. Subsequent Labour leadership elections, for the first time involving all individual party members, resulted in 41-year-old Tony BLAIR emerging an easy winner on July 22. Seeking to appeal to "middle England," Blair accelerated the modernization of Labour policies and structures.

Rocked by scandals, including the press revelation that certain Conservative MPs had accepted "cash for questions" (payment from outside interests for tabling parliamentary questions to ministers), the government continued to face bitter opposition from some of its own backbenchers. On November 28, 1994, eight Conservative Eurosceptics rebelled against a financing bill for the EU that the government had made an issue of confidence. The EU issue, the "sleaze factor" resulting from an unremitting flow of sex and financial scandals, and other divisions contributed to all-time low opinion-poll ratings for the Conservatives, who in local elections on May 4, 1995, suffered the party's heaviest postwar defeat.

Amid renewed speculation about his future, Prime Minister Major on June 22, 1995, announced his formal resignation from the party leadership, forcing critics to "put up or shut up" regarding his reelection. All but one cabinet minister declared support for the prime minister, the exception being John REDWOOD, who resigned as secretary for Wales in order to challenge Major on a strongly Eurosceptic platform. Major emerged the comfortable first-round victor on July 4.

Local elections in May 1996 dropped the Conservatives to third place, behind Labour and the Liberal Democrats, in terms of total local councilors. With allegations of improper financial conduct on the part of Conservative members of Parliament (including junior ministers) being supported by the Nolan Commission on Standards in Public Life, and with time running out on the five-year legislative term, the prime minister on March 17, 1997, asked for a dissolution of Parliament. The election held on May 1 resulted in one of the worst defeats for any governing party in the last century, as the Conservatives won only 165 seats, its losing candidates including 7 cabinet members. Labour swept to power by securing 418 seats on the strength of 44.4 percent of the vote. In keeping with his "centrist" stance, Blair named a mix of "old hands" and "New Labour modernizers" to the new cabinet appointed on May 7. Following the election, former prime minister Major announced his resignation as Conservative leader, with Eurosceptic William HAGUE defeating the pro-EU Kenneth Clarke in the subsequent contest to lead the party.

Carrying through on one of Labour's most prominent campaign pledges, the Blair government quickly pursued decisions in Wales and Scotland regarding devolution of regional authority. In a referendum on September 11, 1997, 74 percent of the voters in Scotland approved the proposed creation of a Scottish Parliament, while on September 18 a plan for establishment of a National Assembly was endorsed by 50.3 percent of the voters in Wales. Elections for the two bodies—the first Scottish legislature since 1707 and the first ever in Wales—were held on May 6, 1999, with Labour emerging as the plurality party in both. The Scottish Parliament and Welsh National Assembly both held opening ceremonies on July 1, with Queen Elizabeth II in attendance in Edinburgh.

The long process of negotiation and accommodation in Northern Ireland, which included the direct involvement of both British and Irish governments, led to the signing on April 10, 1998, of a multiparty peace accord, the Belfast (Good Friday) Agreement, followed on June 25 by the election of a Northern Ireland Assembly. Devolution of powers from London to the assembly and a power-sharing executive occurred on December 2, 1999. Even then, however, a lingering dispute over the disarming of the paramilitary IRA led London to reimpose direct rule on February 11, 2000. On May 30 power was again devolved, the IRA having agreed, earlier in the month, to put its arsenals under international supervision. Little progress was made in the following 16 months, despite repeated negotiating efforts by Prime Minister Blair, Irish Prime Minister Ahern, and others, as paramilitary arms decommissioning, police reform, and withdrawal of British forces continued to be at issue. On August 10, 2001, and again on September 22 London briefly suspended the assembly as a technical maneuver to avoid calling a new election. The devolved government was given new life by the IRA's October 23 announcement that it had begun decommissioning to "save the peace process," but revelations of IRA spying ultimately led London to reimpose direct rule from October 15, 2002 (see Northern Ireland article for details).

At an early election called by Prime Minister Blair for June 7, 2001, Labour was overwhelmingly returned to office with 412 seats in the House of Commons (6 fewer than in 1997). A reshuffled cabinet was announced on June 8, and on the same day Conservative leader Hague stepped down despite modest gains by his party in simultaneous local elections. (Hague was succeeded in 2001 by Iain DUNCAN SMITH and in 2003 by Michael HOWARD. See section on the Conservative Party under Political Parties for details.)

At the poll of May 5, 2005, Labour, for the first time, registered its third consecutive victory in the House of Commons, albeit with a substantially reduced majority of 355 seats. Prime Minister Blair conducted only a minor cabinet reshuffle on the following day, but his government reorganization was much more extensive on May 5, 2006, following an extremely poor performance by Labour in partial local elections the previous day.

Prior to the 2005 elections, Prime Minister Blair had announced that he would enter a third term but would not lead Labour in a fourth election bid. Following a series of negative developments (see Current issues, below, for details), Blair on September 7, 2006, announced he would step down within a year. On June 24, 2007, Gordon BROWN was elected as the new Labour leader, and he became prime minister upon Blair's resignation from that post on June 27. Brown reshuffled the cabinet on June 28.

The balloting for the Scottish Parliament on May 3, 2007, was most noteworthy for the advancement of the Scottish National Party (SNP) to a plurality status with 47 of 129 seats, compared to 46 for Labour. The SNP subsequently formed a minority government in Scotland, but the party's lack of a legislative majority was expected to preclude further movement (at least for the immediate future) toward its goal of full independence for Scotland. Meanwhile, Labour and *Plaid Cymru,* a Welsh nationalist party, formed a coalition government in Wales following the May elections to the Welsh National Assembly. Among other things, the coalition negotiations had apparently produced a pledge from Labour to support a referendum on *Plaid Cymru*'s call for the assembly to be given additional legislative authority.

Constitution and government. The UK is a constitutional monarchy that functions without a written constitution on the basis of statutes, common law, and long-standing but flexible traditions and usages, subject since 1973 to EC/EU membership and thus acceptance of the primacy of EC/EU law. Executive power is wielded on behalf of the sovereign by a cabinet of ministers drawn from the majority party in the House of Commons and, to a lesser degree, from the House of Lords. The prime minister is the leader of the majority party in the House of Commons and depends upon it for support. There is also a historically important Privy Council of government members and some 300 other individuals drawn from public life. Although superseded in importance by the cabinet, it retains an advisory role in some policy areas and continues to issue "orders in council," either under authority of the monarch, who presides over its meetings, or as authorized by Parliament. The Privy Council also reviews legislation passed by Crown dependencies (the Channel Islands and the Isle of Man).

Elected by universal adult suffrage, the House of Commons has become the main repository of legislative and sole repository of financial authority. The House of Lords retains the power to review, amend, or delay for a year legislation other than financial bills and takes a more leisurely overview of legislation, sometimes acting as a brake on the House of Commons. The lower house, which has a maximum term of five years, may be dissolved by the sovereign on recommendation of the prime minister if the latter's policies should encounter severe resistance or if the incumbent feels that new elections would increase the ruling party's majority.

Under legislation approved by the House of Lords 221–81, with Conservatives abstaining, on October 26, 1999, Labour's 1997 campaign pledge to end hereditary membership in the upper house moved forward. The bill, which received royal assent on November 11, authorized formation of an interim upper chamber to include among its members 92 hereditary peers. Meanwhile, the Wakeham Royal Commission appointed in October 1998 continued to draft proposals for a permanently restructured upper body. The final report, issued on January 20, 2000, proposed a chamber of 550 mostly appointed members but with a minority of 65, 87, or 195 to be elected through regional proportional representation. Law Lords (Lords of Appeal in Ordinary), lifetime appointees who have traditionally constituted the kingdom's highest court of appeal, would retain their seats. The existing 26 seats held by archbishops and bishops would be supplemented by 5 seats for representatives of non-Christian religions. Other life peers would be gradually phased out and replaced by a combination of appointed and elected members. A Labour white paper published in November 2001 offered an alternative proposal—abolition of all hereditary peers in a 600-member house encompassing 120 directly elected members, 120 appointees, 16 bishops, and most of the balance party nominees in proportion to vote shares in the most recent general election—but the plan was largely abandoned in May 2002, a number of party leaders insisting that a higher proportion of the upper house should be directly elected.

Following the developments of 2000–2002, the Blair administration called for abolition of the post of Lord Chancellor, the establishment of a Supreme Court, and, in the wake of devolution, absorption of the offices for Scotland and Wales by a department of constitutional affairs. Thus, in a mid-2003 cabinet reshuffle, the secretaries of state for Scotland and Wales, while retained, were assigned secondary status, with Lord FALCONER of Thoroton named secretary of state for constitutional affairs and invested as Lord Chancellor "for the transitional period."

In March 2004 the House of Lords referred the Constitutional Reform Bill to a special select committee, while the government abandoned plans for a bill to abolish the 92 seats held by remaining hereditary peers.

A year later, on March 25, 2005, royal assent was given to a revised Constitutional Reform Bill that provided for a Supreme Court separate from the House of Lords and, without abandoning the office itself, transferred the legislative functions of the Lord Chancellor to the Lord Speaker and the judicial functions to a President of the Courts for England and Wales.

In March 2007 the parliament took a series of free votes (no party obligation) on preferences for an elected House of Lords. Majorities in the House of Commons supported both an 80 and 100 percent elected composition. A majority in the House of Lords supported a wholly appointed body. Justice Secretary Jack STRAW announced in July that work on "fundamental" reform would continue. However, decisive action appeared unlikely before the next general election.

Apart from the newly established Supreme Court, which was inaugurated on October 1, 2009, the judicial system of England and Wales centers on a High Court of Justice for civil cases, with three divisions (Chancery, Family, and Queen's Bench); a Crown Court for criminal cases; and a Court of Appeal, with civil and criminal divisions. Scotland has its own High Court of Justiciary (criminal) and Court of Session (civil), both including appeal courts, while Northern Ireland has a separate Supreme Court of Judicature, comprising a (civil) High Court of Justice, a (criminal) Crown Court, and a Court of Appeal. In relevant cases, UK citizens and groups have the right of appeal against national legal rulings to the European Court of Human Rights in Strasbourg, France.

Local government in England traditionally encompassed a two-tier structure of county and district (or borough or city) councils, but in recent years dozens of unitary authorities have been established. The traditional structure largely survives in 34 county and more than 200 district councils, although some of the counties have seen unitary authorities established within their geographical boundaries. Under legislation enacted in 1994, Wales and Scotland, formerly with two tiers, moved on April 1, 1996, to a unitary system, with 22 and 32 elected councils, respectively. Northern Ireland has 26 district councils.

Since 1986, when the Greater London Council was abolished, the capital has been governed through 32 boroughs, each with its own elected council, and the Corporation of the City of London, its unique status reflecting its commercial rather than residential character. Additionally, at a referendum held on May 7, 1998, Londoners overwhelmingly approved direct election of a mayor and establishment of a 25-member London Assembly. The first mayoral and assembly elections were held in May 2000. (Subsequent mayoral and assembly elections were held in June 2004 and May 2008.)

Published on July 30, 1998, a government white paper, *Modern Local Government in Touch with the People,* heralded other changes ahead, including greater budgetary freedom for local authorities and separation of executive and legislative responsibilities. In another reform, in December 1998 the government appointed members to eight newly established Regional Development Agencies (RDAs), with a ninth added for London in 2000. Tasks mandated for the RDAs include promoting sustainable economic development, increasing efficiency and competitiveness, and encouraging investment.

The viability of the UK as a political entity has been a matter of major concern for three decades. The most intractable problem has been that of deep-rooted conflict in Northern Ireland between the majority Protestants, most of whom remain committed to the union with Great Britain, and a Catholic minority, substantial elements of which have long sought union with the Republic of Ireland. A multiparty peace accord, the Belfast (Good Friday) Agreement of April 10, 1998, was approved in Northern Ireland by referendum on May 22, with a new Northern Ireland Assembly being elected on June 25. Devolution of authority from London to the assembly and a Northern Ireland Executive occurred on December 2, 1999, although differences over the decommissioning of weapons held by the IRA resulted in reimposition of direct rule from February 11 to May 30, 2000. Upon devolution, the secretary of state for Northern Ireland retained authority in "excepted and reserved" areas, including law, criminal justice, and foreign affairs. Direct rule was again imposed for 24 hours in August and September 2001, and then for an indefinite period on October 15, 2002. In October 2006 talks involving the British government, the government of the Republic of Ireland, and all major parties in Northern Ireland produced the St. Andrews Agreement, which prompted new elections in Northern Ireland on March 7, 2007, and the restoration of the Northern Ireland Assembly on May 8 (see article on Northern Ireland for details).

Although not characterized by the violence endemic in the Irish question, a powerful separatist movement has also developed in Scotland. Alarmed by the growing influence of the Scottish National Party (SNP), which won a third of the Scottish votes in the October 1974 general election, the Labour leadership, in a 1975 government paper, proposed the establishment of elected assemblies for both Scotland and Wales. Despite Conservative criticism that the departure would prove costly and contain "the danger of a break-up of Britain," pertinent legislation was completed in mid-1978. In March 1979, however, referendums yielded rejection of devolution in Wales and approval by an insufficient majority in Scotland. Successive Conservative administrations subsequently ruled out the creation of regional assemblies, although in March 1993 the government, in what was officially described as the first major review of the England-Scotland relationship since 1707, introduced measures to give the 72 Scottish MPs a larger role in decision making.

Immediately after taking power in May 1997, the new Labour government set out plans for new Scottish and Welsh devolution referendums. On September 11 the Scottish electorate voted by a substantial majority for an elected Parliament, and on September 18 Welsh voters approved creation of a National Assembly. Under the Government of Wales Act and the Scotland Act, both passed by the UK Parliament following the referendums, elections for the two new bodies were held on May 6, 1999, with formal transfer of devolved powers occurring on July 1. Although the UK Parliament retains ultimate authority to legislate on all matters, it will not routinely do so in devolved sectors, which include education, health, culture, local government, housing, transportation, and the environment. The Scottish Parliament cannot propose independence from the union, nor can it legislate in reserved areas, which include defense and treaty obligations. Because Wales has a closer legal association with England, the Welsh assembly has a more limited scope than the Scottish Parliament, with no authority to pass primary legislation governing, for example, the legal system or taxation. Both Scotland and Wales, like Northern Ireland, continue to be represented in the UK Parliament and in the Westminster cabinet. With regard to England, the Blair administration indicated its willingness to go beyond establishing the RDAs and the London Authority (mayor plus assembly) and to devolve powers from the UK government to English regional bodies as the demand arises.

Since 1997 the Labour government has also been examining proportional representation for use in British elections. The 1999 balloting for the new Scottish and Welsh legislatures utilized, for the first time, a combination system in which each voter cast two ballots, one for a constituency representative elected under the traditional "first-past-the-post" basis and the second for a party list from which "top-up" seats were allocated, thereby assuring that the makeup of the legislatures would better reflect each party's overall vote share. A proportional scheme was also introduced for the European Parliament elections held in June 1999. However, many members of the UK House of Commons, including a substantial number of Labour MPs, have not expressed enthusiasm for converting to a basically proportional system for the House, as proposed in the report of the Jenkins Commission on electoral reform in October 1998. In March 2008 Justice Secretary Jack Straw proposed consultation on whether the centuries-old "first-past-the-post" electoral system should be replaced by an "alternative vote" system, which would allow voters to express a first and second preference for candidates running in a constituency. Straw's proposal also asked whether voting should be designated a civic duty, thereby making voting mandatory, and whether elections should be conducted over a two-day weekend. (A consultative paper in 2009 on a proposal for a bill of rights and responsibilities made no mention of mandatory voting.)

In another matter of constitutional significance, the monarchy, with the full support of the Labour government, has recently pledged initiatives to modernize its role in state and society. The decision followed widespread criticism directed at the royal family's allegedly distant demeanor following the death of DIANA, Princess of Wales, the former wife of Prince CHARLES, in an automobile accident in August 1997. In February 1998 Queen ELIZABETH II indicated that she would support abolishing primogeniture with regard to the line of succession, although Parliament has not yet formally considered such a change. The government confirmed in March 2009 that the prime minister and the monarch's representatives were discussing removing the prohibition on the monarch being married to a Roman Catholic and creating equality of succession for females and males.

Foreign relations. Reluctantly abandoning its age-long tradition of "splendid isolation," the UK became a key member of the Allied coalitions in both world wars and has remained a leader in the Western group of nations, as well as one of the world's nuclear-armed powers. Postwar British governments have sought to retain close economic and military ties with the United States while maintaining an independent British position on most international issues. Britain has continued to play an important role in the United Nations and in collective security arrangements, such as the North Atlantic Treaty Organization (NATO), although after 1957 Britain's withdrawal of most military forces from the Far East and the Persian Gulf substantially diminished its weight in the global balance of power.

The UK's participation in the work of such institutions as the IMF, the General Agreement on Tariffs and Trade/World Trade Organization (GATT/WTO), and the Organization for Economic Cooperation and Development (OECD) reflects its continued central position in international financial and economic affairs as well as its commitment to assist in the growth of less-developed countries. (Similar concerns have also become a focus of the Commonwealth, which was formally established in 1931.) Unwilling to participate in the creation of the original three EC components (the European Economic Community [EEC], European Coal and Steel Community [ECSC], and European Atomic Energy Community [Euratom]), it took the lead in establishing the European Free Trade Association (EFTA) in 1960. Subsequently, Conservative and moderate Labour leaders began to urge British entry into the EC despite anticipated problems for the UK and other Commonwealth members. France, however, vetoed the British application for admission in 1963 on the grounds that the country remained too closely tied to the United States and the Commonwealth to justify close association with the continental nations. With the abandonment of French objections after President de Gaulle's resignation in 1969, a bill sanctioning entry was approved by the House of Commons in October 1971, and Britain was formally admitted to the EC on January 1, 1973. In a referendum held in June 1975, continued membership of the EC was endorsed by a two-thirds majority of participating voters, but enthusiasm for the European venture remained low in Britain over the subsequent two decades.

In late 1979 the Thatcher government won worldwide plaudits for its resolution of the seven-year Rhodesian civil war through a lengthy process of negotiation that culminated in independence under black majority rule in April 1980 (see Zimbabwe article). In September 1981 Belize (formerly British Honduras) secured independence, as did Antigua and Barbuda in November. These were the latest territories to benefit from Britain's post-1957 imperial disengagement, which had seen 18 former possessions, protectorates, and colonies becoming independent during the 1960s, 10 in the 1970s, and 2 (including Zimbabwe) in 1980. Subsequently, St. Kitts and Nevis achieved independence in 1983, followed by Brunei in 1984.

The Falkland Islands War that erupted in April 1982 followed nearly two decades of sporadic negotiations between Britain and Argentina in a fruitless effort to resolve a dispute that had commenced in the late 18th century (see Falkland Islands under Related Territories, below). Following the Argentine defeat, the UN General Assembly renewed appeals for a negotiated solution to the sovereignty issue, and since 1984 the UN Committee on Decolonization has routinely passed Argentine-sponsored resolutions asking London to reopen negotiations on the matter. Two days of high-level talks in Madrid, Spain, in February 1990 produced a compromise settlement of conflicting claims to fishing rights and an agreement to restore a seven-year rupture in diplomatic relations, but the sovereignty issue remains unresolved.

In September 1984 Britain and China agreed that the latter would regain possession of Hong Kong in 1997, although the Conservative government continued to rebuff Spanish appeals for the reversion of Gibraltar, given manifest opposition to such a move by its inhabitants (see Special Administrative Region in China article for information on Hong Kong, and Gibraltar under Related Territories, below).

While the Thatcher government had reservations about U.S. military intervention in Grenada in 1983, its generally close foreign policy alignment with Washington was demonstrated by endorsement of the U.S. bombing of Libya in 1986, as contrasted with the prevailing view of other EC countries. UK-U.S. cooperation was also a key factor during the Gulf crisis of 1990–1991, with British forces participating in the U.S.-led coalition that expelled Iraq from Kuwait.

In December 1991 the Major government was successful in negotiating various UK opt-outs from the EC's Maastricht Treaty on European union, notably from its commitment to a single European currency and from its jobs-imperiling social policy chapter. However, not until July 23, 1993, did the government obtain final parliamentary authority for its opt-out policy. This followed a stinging attack on the treaty by former prime minister Margaret Thatcher in the House of Lords, who cast her first vote in 34 years against her party's leadership, and came about only after Major had gained the reluctant support of his Conservative opponents in the House of Commons by making the decision a confidence motion. On July 30 a British court rejected the last legal challenge to the treaty, and on August 2 instruments of UK ratification were deposited in Rome.

In October 1997 the new Labour administration signaled a slightly more pro-European position by announcing that Britain would consider joining the EU's Economic and Monetary Union (EMU), but not immediately. Earlier, in May, the incoming foreign secretary had confirmed a Labour commitment to accept the social charter of the EU. In November 1998 the queen gave her assent to legislation that incorporated into British law the 1950 European Convention on Human Rights, with effect from October 2, 2000.

During 1992 UK diplomacy became increasingly preoccupied with the conflict in former Yugoslavia. Although some 3,400 British troops were committed to the UN humanitarian effort by 1994, the government firmly opposed any direct military intervention by external powers and backed both the UN arms embargo and the Vance-Owen diplomatic effort to obtain a negotiated settlement. Following major escalation of the Bosnian crisis in March 1995, London's policy underwent a significant shift. In addition to raising its troop contingent in the former Yugoslavia to 10,000, Britain agreed to contribute an additional 7,000 soldiers to a new NATO-led rapid reaction force charged with providing "enhanced protection" to the UN peacekeeping force. Subsequently, the British government was party to a NATO decision to step up air strikes around the Bosnian capital with the twin aims of relieving pressure on its inhabitants and of forcing Bosnian Serb acceptance of the latest peace plan. Britain gave its full support to the Dayton Accords of December 1995, which brought the conflict to a swift close. British troops remained part of the continuing UN peace force.

Relations with Iran reached a nadir following the late Ayatollah Khomeini's 1989 death sentence against the naturalized British writer Salman RUSHDIE for alleged blasphemy against Islam in his novel *The Satanic Verses*. In September 1998 Iran disassociated itself from the Rushdie *fatwa,* clearing the way for London and Tehran to exchange ambassadors in May 1999.

The Blair and Brown governments have been consistent supporters of the second U.S.-led incursion into Iraq, often at their political peril. A number of Blair's key aides resigned over the issue, including parliamentary leader Robin COOK in March 2003 and International Development Secretary Claire SHORT two months later. Even greater damage came from the fallout after the apparent suicide on July 13, 2003, of David KELLY, a ministry of defense weapons expert, who had been the source for alleged reports that Downing Street had "sexed up" a 2002 dossier on Iraqi weapons of mass destruction. Despite speculation that Brown as prime minister would distance himself and the UK from American foreign policy, he continued to work closely with the George W. Bush administration.

In April 2004 Blair announced that he would call for a referendum on Britain's commitment to the EU after the next election. However, in June 2005 he said that the government would not proceed with a referendum bill, given the rejection of the EU constitution by the French and Dutch electorates. In mid-2006 the administration indicated that it might approve certain revisions in EU institutions on a "piece-by-piece" basis without a referendum. In December 2007 Prime Minister Brown signed the EU's Lisbon Treaty, which contains 96 percent of the language of the erstwhile EU constitution. The treaty, which amends rather than replaces previous EU treaties and would take effect no earlier than 2014, includes protocols and vetoes to protect UK interests in regard to security, foreign affairs, and social policy. The treaty requires UK parliamentary approval, but since Brown considers the treaty less significant than the constitution, his government is not likely to hold a referendum on the matter. In March 2008 the House of Commons voted against a Conservative Party proposal to conduct a referendum. In May, however, a high court judge granted a private individual permission to seek judicial review of the issue by ruling that the Lisbon Treaty is arguably the same as the EU Constitutional Treaty and thereby required a referendum. The UK parliament ratified the treaty in June, and, following dismissal of the related court case, the necessary ratification instruments were filed in July.

In 2009 Prime Minister Brown declared that some 9,000 UK troops would remain in Afghanistan, forming the second-largest contingent (behind that of the Untied States). The deployment remained a source of dissension within the populace, which was also focusing on the Iraq War Inquiry, which opened in November (see Current issues, below).

Current issues. In the first two years after his overwhelming victory at the polls in 1997, Prime Minister Blair moved forward on a broad range of initiatives, including reform of the House of Lords and devolution in Scotland, Wales, and Northern Ireland. Between January 1998 and May 1999, white papers, or commission reports, addressed the future makeup of local government, various proportional representation schemes, campaign finance reform, freedom of information, and social service reform. At the same time, however, the Blair government downplayed any commitments that might entail substantial increases in spending or taxation, while encroaching even further on traditional Conservative territory by promoting "family values," social responsibility, citizenship, and a hard line on street crime. The "New Labour" program also attacked "something for nothing" welfare policies and proposed pension reform, despite considerable opposition from Labour traditionalists.

One of the most contentious issues during the early years of the Blair administration was if and when to adopt the EU's euro as a replacement for the pound sterling. Although the Blair government consistently supported eventual entry into the EMU, widespread public opposition forced the administration to review its strategy and adjust its timetable.

The Conservatives cited the euro issue as but one example of what they charged was Blair's willingness to set aside principle and change his agenda based on public opinion. Such assertions contributed to a fundamental image problem that was further fueled in July 2000 by a leaked memo in which Blair called for "eye-catching initiatives" in the area of family policy and a get-tough approach to crime.

The issues of immigration and political asylum also came to the fore in the late 1990s and early 2000s. With the Conservative Party calling for tough measures to discourage "economic migrants" posing as political refugees, Home Secretary Jack Straw in March 2000 called for a complete reexamination of the 1951 UN Convention on the Status of Refugees. An Immigration and Asylum Bill, passed in November 1999 with effect from April 1, 2000, instituted a voucher system instead of cash payments to asylum seekers and also authorized their dispersal around the country, over the objections of many local authorities.

In the wake of the September 11, 2001, terrorist attacks in the United States, the Blair government stood as the most steadfast supporter of the George W. Bush administration's October decision to launch military attacks against the al-Qaida network and the Taliban regime in Afghanistan. Earlier, Blair had called for tighter domestic security and had initiated steps to freeze assets of suspected terrorist organizations, monitor bank transactions, and introduce fast-track extradition. On December 14 an Anti-Terrorism, Crime, and Security Bill was enacted, although the Conservative majority in the House of Lords had exacted a number of tempering concessions beforehand.

The May 2005 balloting for the House of Commons cut Labour's working majority in half, as both the Conservatives and Liberal Democrats achieved noteworthy gains. The results were similar in the simultaneous, partial local elections.

The terrorist threat became a reality in July 2005 with a series of London subway bombings in which 56 persons died and a subsequent second, albeit failed, series of attacks in three subway trains and a bus. The Blair government subsequently adopted a number of antiterrorist measures, including a catalog of offenses for which foreign militants could be deported. In September the government introduced new antiterrorism legislation calling, among other things, for an extension of the time a suspect could be held without charges being filed from 14 to 90 days. The following month a number of foreign-based Islamic groups were banned from operating in the UK on the government's assertion that they had ties to al-Qaida. In general, the government's antiterrorism measures appeared to gain acceptance among the population and most political parties. However, the more stringent initiatives fueled a growing debate over the extent to which civil rights and liberties should be curtailed in the name of national security.

Attention in early 2006 focused on the ongoing slide of the Labour Party (buffeted by a series of scandals and policy disputes) and the collateral emergence of the new Conservative leader, David CAMERON, as a dynamic actor on the political stage. Both appeared to contribute to the "meltdown" of Labour at the partial local elections in early May, as the government party suffered a third-place finish in vote percentage. Particularly costly (apparently) for Labour was the revelation that several wealthy businessmen who had secretly lent money to the party's 2005 campaign had been nominated by Blair for peerages, status that automatically includes appointment to the House of Lords. Popular discontent was also reported concerning the perceived lax enforcement of deportation laws for foreigners being released from prisons. Although Blair reportedly faced growing criticism from Labour backbenchers, his cabinet reshuffle (the biggest of his tenure) on the day after the May local elections indicated his intention to pursue additional reform in areas such as education, energy, pensions, and health with vigor. At the same time, Blair pledged that he would resign the premiership in sufficient time to let Gordon Brown (his presumed successor) establish himself as prime minister prior to the general election due by 2010. (In early September Blair announced that he would hand over the premiership within a year.) Meanwhile, Brown (the chancellor of the exchequer and an architect with Blair of "New Labour") began to speak out on a variety of issues outside the purview of his office, prompting some observers to suggest the Blair-Brown relationship was in effect an "undeclared shared premiership." For his part, Cameron focused on a determined effort to move the Conservatives toward the center on many topics in order to sustain the party's electoral momentum for, among other things, the elections scheduled for the spring of 2007 in Scotland and Wales.

By July 2006 public satisfaction with the way the government was running the country and with Blair as prime minister had dropped below 25 percent. An August report from the Home Office drew further attention to the simmering issue of immigration, reporting that almost 50,000 work applications from East Europeans had been approved in the second quarter of the year and that since 2004, when a number of East European countries had joined the EU, 427,000 Eastern Europeans had registered for work in the UK. Meanwhile, some cabinet ministers remained in open disagreement with Blair over his muted response to Israeli bombings in the Israeli-Lebanon war and his refusal to distance himself from Washington's pro-Israeli posture. On September 16, 8 junior aides resigned to protest Blair's refusal to set a definite date for his resignation, and an open letter from 17 Labour MPs called for Blair to step down. On the following day, Blair announced that he would leave within a year. However, Blair continued to be dogged by the "cash for peerages" scandal, in which the Labour Party received large loans from individuals later nominated for peerages. (Such loans, unlike direct donations, are not subject to strict public reporting requirements.) The suspicions of a quid pro quo got so close to Blair that he became the first prime minister interviewed by police in a criminal investigation. (In the end no one was charged with a criminal offense.) Blair also alienated members of the Labour Party in December 2006 when he urged that Britain's nuclear arms program be extended with a new generation of submarines. The March 2007 vote on the matter in the House of Commons produced the largest Labour Party rebellion since the Iraq war began; the measure passed only because of support from Conservatives.

After further losses by Labour and gains by Conservatives in May 3, 2007, local balloting and Labour's loss of plurality party status in the Scottish Parliament to the SNP on the same day, Prime Minister Blair announced on May 10 he would step down as party leader and prime minister before the end of June. When no viable challenge to the long anticipated leadership transfer to Gordon Brown emerged, Brown accepted the position as Labour leader on June 24 and as prime minister on June 27.

In his first month in office, Brown's standing in the public opinion polls showed him with a 20 point lead over Conservative Party leader Cameron, encouraging widespread discussion that Brown would call a snap election in November. After his standing began to slip in August and September, however, Brown quashed such discussion in early October when he told a reporter that he wanted to take the time to show the country his vision for change, with particular emphasis on housing, health, and education. He noted that he and Labour could stand on a platform of competence in regard to the handling of various summer crises involving foot-and-mouth disease, terrorism, floods, and sagging financial markets. However, on the heels of a renewed discussion of the party funding scandal and the report of a loss by the government of computer data on some 25 million individuals, Cameron asked during a subsequent prime minister's session if Brown "was cut out for the job" of prime minister.

Confidence in Brown's leadership waned throughout his first year in office. The depth of the financial crisis, apparent since July 2007, led the government to nationalize Northern Rock bank in February 2008, after Brown failed to find a private-sector solution to the bank's impending failure. Further complicating matters for Brown, the government was able to secure only a 28-vote margin to stave off a Conservative Party attempt to force a public inquiry into decisions leading up to the invasion of Iraq, with 12 Labour backbenchers defecting from the government's position that such an inquiry should wait until the operations had ended. By early May, on the heels of a series of Labour by-election losses and the loss of the London mayoralty, Brown had to reverse himself on his proposed increase in a starter tax rate, which would have affected over 5 million low-income taxpayers. Facing growing protests within his own party, Brown announced that the tax plan was a mistake and that the proposed higher rates would not be applied to 80 percent of those originally targeted.

In a June 2008 vote on the government's bill to extend the maximum period terrorism suspects could be held without charge from 28 to 42 days (which was whittled back from the 90-day period Blair had proposed in 2005 and on which Blair had suffered his first defeat by parliament) passed by a mere 9-vote margin, supplied by 9 members of the Democratic Unionist Party as 36 Labour backbenchers defected. In August the government's plans to build a number of nuclear power plants suffered a setback when the sale of "British Energy" to a French energy interest that was to have played a major role in nuclear plant construction fell through.

Prime Minister Brown's leadership in regard to the rescue of financial institutions in the fall of 2008 was generally well received by the public, and the double digit lead the Conservatives had earlier held over Labour in opinion polls was cut to single digits. However, in May 2009 a major scandal erupted in the House of Commons involving expense account abuses. Although legislators from other parties were also cited, Labour appeared to suffer the greatest fallout from the scandal, especially since cabinet members and other Labour leaders were involved. The speaker of the House of Commons, Michael MARTIN (originally elected on the Labour ticket), announced his resignation from the speaker's post (effective June 21) after being harshly criticized for his handling of the issue. In addition, two Labour peers were suspended from the House of Lords (the first suspensions in 350 years) and two others were rebuked for allegedly seeking money in return for adding amendments to proposed legislation. Meanwhile, the harsh realities of the ongoing effects of the economic crisis had become apparent. The country's creditworthiness was downgraded, and government debt reportedly breached the level of 40 percent GDP, which Labour for many years had set as the maximum acceptable level. (Some analysts predicted the debt might rise to 100 percent of GDP over the next four or five years, while unemployment was expected to peak in 2010 at 9.2 percent.) Consequently, Labour fell to third place in both the local elections and balloting for the European Parliament, held concurrently on June 4.

In an apparent attempt to counter anticipated challenges to his premiership, Brown reshuffled the cabinet on June 5, 2009. However, the government subsequently faced criticism on several policy fronts. In August the SNP government in Scotland returned a convicted Lockerbie bomber to Libya on compassionate grounds (the prisoner had been diagnosed with terminal cancer). Opposition parties and other critics charged that the Labour government in Westminster had been complicit in the decision and had bargained, in conjunction with the SNP, for oil and gas concessions from Libya (Brown denied that any deal had been made).

Despite polls showing that more than two-thirds of the public favored an early withdrawal of UK troops from Afghanistan, Brown declared in November 2009 that his government would not bow to the popular mood on the subject. Attention also focused on the Iraqi War Inquiry, some of whose opening witnesses in November questioned the bona fides of the intelligence on which the decision to participate in the U.S.-led invasion had been based. Others questioned the legitimacy (but not the legality) of the decision, given the lack of support from the UK populace and much of the international community. Brown and former prime minister Blair were also scheduled to testify, which was expected to add to Labour's woes as it headed into the general election due by June 3, 2010.

POLITICAL PARTIES

Government Parties:

Labour Party. An evolutionary socialist party in basic doctrine and tradition, the Labour Party (founded in 1900) has moved to the center over the past decade but continues to reflect the often conflicting views of trade unions, doctrinaire socialists, and intellectuals, while seeking to broaden its appeal to the middle class and white-collar and managerial personnel. The trade unions traditionally constituted the basis of the party's organized political strength and provided the bulk of its income, although their influence over policy formulation and candidate selection has been reduced in recent years.

After periods of prewar minority government and participation in the wartime coalition, Labour won a large parliamentary majority in 1945 under Clement Attlee and between then and 1951 proceeded to create a comprehensive welfare state, while nationalizing some of the "commanding heights" of the economy. Returning to government in 1964 under Harold Wilson, Labour was unexpectedly defeated in 1970. However, it returned to power in February 1974 as a minority government, still under Wilson, who in a further election in October 1974 won a narrow victory. In early 1977 resignations and defections deprived the government of its majority, forcing Labour to conclude a parliamentary alliance with the small Liberal Party that lasted until late 1978. Meanwhile, James Callaghan succeeded Wilson as Labour leader and prime minister in April 1976.

Defeated by the Conservatives in the May 1979 balloting, Labour swung to the left and also changed its leadership selection procedure. Designated party leader in November 1980 under the old system of election by Labour MPs, Michael FOOT, a revered representative of Labour's "old left," presided over changes that in 1981 established an electoral college of affiliated trade unions, Labour MPs, and local constituency parties for selection of the party leader and deputy leader. This change, and a mainstream antipathy to the EC, caused a small number of right-wing, pro-EC MPs to break away in March 1981 and form the Social Democratic Party (see under Liberal Democrat Party, below). Foot fought the June 1983 election on a platform of withdrawal from the EC, unilateral nuclear disarmament, and socialist economic policies. Overwhelmingly defeated, he resigned the Labour leadership and was succeeded in October 1983 by Neil Kinnock. A disciple of Foot, Kinnock contested the June 1987 election on broadly the same policies as in 1983 and also suffered defeat. Thereafter, he initiated a radical policy review, which eventually resulted in Labour's dropping its hostility to the EC and to Britain's nuclear deterrent, while supporting market economics (subject to regulation). Kinnock continued Foot's policy of expelling Trotskyites of the "Militant Tendency."

Kinnock suffered a further election defeat in April 1992, although Labour's tally of 271 seats and a 34.4 percent vote share represented a significant gain over the 1987 results. He thereupon resigned and was succeeded by John Smith, a moderate who continued the "modernizing" thrust, notably by forcing through "one member, one vote" arrangements for the selection of Labour candidates and leaders. Smith led Labour to major advances in local balloting in 1993 and 1994 but died on May 12, 1994. He was succeeded in July, under the new voting arrangements, by another "modernizing" lawyer, Tony Blair. In the interim, Labour had won a major victory in the June European Parliament elections, taking 62 of the 87 UK seats with a 42.7 percent vote share, while the "Blair factor" boosted the party's electoral resurgence in subsequent parliamentary by-elections and in local balloting in May 1995. In a symbolic change to Labour's constitution, a special party conference on April 29 agreed to drop its celebrated "clause 4" commitment to "the common ownership of the means of production, distribution and exchange" in favor of a general assertion of democratic socialist aims and values. The trend toward "modernization" of the party continued with efforts to further reduce the role of union bloc votes. Moreover, Blair moved the party to the center by co-opting Conservative issues—a strategy often compared to that used by Democratic president Bill Clinton against the Republicans in the United States.

Labour's huge victory in the May 1997 balloting for the House of Commons (418 seats) included the election of 101 female Labour MPs, the party having purposefully presented "women only" lists in a number of safe constituencies. Following his accession to the prime ministership, Blair continued to promote "New Labour" in such areas as budget constraint and welfare reform while pressing ahead with promised initiatives on devolution of regional power in Wales and Scotland.

Labour's "pro-yes" campaigns on the devolution referenda were conducted in alliance with the Liberal Democrats as well as *Plaid Cymru* in Wales and the Scottish National Party in Scotland.

In May 1998 the party's National Executive Committee (NEC) approved tightened procedures for vetting of parliamentary candidates, the main intention being to weed out those who had voted contrary to party policy or were otherwise deemed unsuitable. Six months later the NEC banned its members from leaking committee discussions and began requiring them to inform the Labour press office before making public comments on NEC matters. The measures offered opponents a further opportunity to label the Blairites as autocratic, as had a decision early in the year to expel two Labour members of the European Parliament, in part for attacking proposed welfare reforms and the leadership's control of the European Parliament candidate list.

Although failing to win a majority in either the new Scottish Parliament or the Welsh National Assembly, Labour emerged from the May 6, 1999, elections as the plurality party in both, taking 56 of 129 seats in Scotland and 28 of 60 in Wales. It entered into a coalition agreement on May 13 with the Scottish Liberal Democrats but in Wales chose to form a minority government under UK Secretary of State for Wales Alun MICHAEL. In a heated battle, Michael, relying on Prime Minister Blair's support, had defeated Rhodri MORGAN for leadership of Welsh Labour three months earlier. A year later, however, on February 9, 2000, Michael resigned as Welsh first minister shortly before the assembly passed a no-confidence motion, 31–27, largely because of his failure to distance himself from London. On February 15 the assembly confirmed Morgan as his successor. (The title of the office was subsequently changed to first secretary.)

At the European Parliament balloting of June 1999 Labour suffered its first major defeat since Blair's assumption of power, taking only 28 percent of the vote and 29 seats, a loss of 33. The defeat was largely explained by voters' opposition to Labour's pro-euro policy.

On February 20, 2000, Blair's preferred candidate for the new London mayoralty, former minister of health Frank DOBSON, won a narrow victory in a party electoral college, defeating leftist MP Ken LIVINGSTONE. The latter won 60 percent support from London party members and 72 percent from labor unions and societies, but Dobson prevailed on the strength of 86 percent support from the third, equally weighted electoral college bloc: Labor MPs, members of the European Parliament, and candidates for the Greater London Authority (GLA). To the chagrin of the party hierarchy, Livingstone ran as an independent and won the election on May 4. Despite Labour's previous strength in the capital, the party won only 9 seats on the 25-member GLA, equaling the Conservative total. In a further setback on May 4, Labour lost control of 16 of the 73 local councils it had previously held.

At the same time, intraparty disputes continued to surface over Prime Minister Blair's "command and control" managerial style (dubbed "control freakery" by opponents), his reliance on a small circle of advisers that critics dubbed "Tony's cronies," and his centrist "New Labour" programs. Peter KILFOYLE, who had resigned as under secretary of state for defense in January 2000, announced in February that he was forming a "heartlands group" of Labour MPs committed to the party's core supporters and traditional, left-of-center policies. Blair nevertheless remained firmly in control of Labour, which handily won the June 2001 House of Commons election, capturing 412 seats on a slightly reduced vote share of 42 percent.

The May 2005 poll was won by Labour with a Commons majority (55 percent) reduced for a number of reasons, including widespread disagreement over constitutional revision, Britain's role in the EU, and Blair's support of the U.S. position in Iraq. The prime minister subsequently faced growing criticism from left-wing backbenchers opposed to his ongoing reformist agenda. Following Labour's dismal performance in the May 2006 local elections (third place with only 26 percent of the vote), calls intensified for Blair to determine a timetable for his resignation in favor of Gordon Brown (the chancellor of the exchequer). At summer's end, Blair announced that he would step aside within a year. Eight months later, on the heels of another setback for Labour in the May 2007 local elections as well as in the Welsh Assembly and Scottish Parliament elections the same day, Blair said he would resign as party leader and prime minister by the end of June. By mid-May it was clear Gordon Brown would be the only leadership candidate with the required nomination support among MPs. Brown accepted the leader position unopposed at a party conference in Manchester on June 24. The same conference elected Harriet Harman as deputy leader over five others, including the odds-makers' preconference favorite and presumed Blair favorite, Alan JOHNSON. Brown was sworn in as prime minister on June 27.

The party subsequently found itself in the political doldrums. It lost a series of by-elections in early 2008, some in what had been strongly pro-Labour constituencies. The party was generally able to hold its own in the May 2008 London Assembly elections. However, its mayoralty candidate (Ken Livingstone, a two-term incumbent who had been expelled from the party in 2002 for his renegade run in 2000, only to be reinstated in the run-up to the 2004 mayoralty balloting) lost his reelection bid. By summer Labour's support had declined to 24 percent in public opinion polls, and it continued to fare poorly in by-elections. Plotting among Labour backbenchers to depose Brown as party leader subsequently became increasingly public, but the prime minister's standing rebounded in the wake of the support he received, at home and abroad, for his handling of the financial credit crisis.

Public discussion of removing Brown arose again in mid-2009 in the wake of a major scandal in the House of Commons over dubious expense account payments to MPs and the poor performance by Labour in the simultaneous balloting in June for local councils and the European Parliament. (Labour finished third in the local elections in the popular vote and won just 178 of the more than 2,300 seats on the councils, losing more than 60 percent of the seats it had previously held. The party also finished third in the European Parliament elections with 15.7 percent of the vote, good for only 13 seats [down from 22.6 percent of the vote and 19 seats in 2004].) Brown also faced the resignation of several cabinet ministers and outright revolt among some Labour members, although his leadership position remained intact at the September party conference.

Leaders: James Gordon BROWN (Prime Minister and Leader of the Party), Harriet HARMAN (Deputy Party Leader, Leader of the House of Commons, and Party Chair), Tony LLOYD (Chair of the Parliamentary Party), Alistair DARLING (Chancellor of the Exchequer).

Co-operative Party. Founded in 1917, the Co-operative Party operates largely through some 200 affiliated cooperative societies throughout Britain. Under a 1927 agreement with the Labour Party, it cosponsors candidates at local, national, and European elections.

Leaders: Gareth THOMAS (Chair), Peter HUNT (General Secretary).

Other UK Parliamentary Parties:

Conservative Party. Although in opposition during 1945–1951, 1964–1970, 1974–1979, and since 1997, the Conservative Party (formally the Conservative and Unionist Party, informally the Tory Party) dominated British politics through much of the 20th century, drawing support from business, the middle class, farmers, and a segment of the working class.

In February 1975 Margaret Thatcher, former secretary of state for education and science, was elected party leader, succeeding Edward Heath, under whom the Conservatives had lost three of the previous four elections. Following the party's return to power in May 1979, a rift developed between moderate members (derogatively styled "wets") and those supporting Thatcher's stringent monetary and economic policies; through the 1980s prominent wets were gradually dropped from the government, while others came to terms with "Thatcherism." The party's successful 1983 campaign manifesto called for, among other things, tough laws to curb illegal strikes and privatization of state-owned industry. The emphasis for the June 1987 election was on continued "positive reform" in such areas as fiscal management, control of inflation, greater financial independence for individuals, and improved health care.

Deepening divisions over European policy led in November 1990 to a leadership challenge by former cabinet minister Michael Heseltine, who obtained enough first-round votes to force Thatcher's resignation. But the succession went to the chancellor of the exchequer, John Major, who was regarded as the "Thatcherite" among the three second-round contenders but who quickly jettisoned his predecessor's more controversial policies. The Conservatives fought the April 1992 election on a platform of further privatization (including British Rail and the coal mines), financial accountability in the National Health Service, and freedom of choice in the state education sector. On a vote share of 41.9 percent, the party won its fourth consecutive term, taking 336 (out of 651) seats in the House of Commons, 40 fewer than in 1987.

Postelection difficulties caused a massive slump in the Conservatives' public standing, as evidenced by unprecedented local electoral trouncings in 1993–1994 and the concurrent loss in by-elections of several "safe" Conservative parliamentary seats to the Liberal Democrats. In June 1994 the party also fared badly in European Parliament balloting, falling from 34 to 18 seats (out of 87). Increasing intraparty criticism led Prime Minister Major to place his leadership on the line in June 1995. Reelected the following month with the support of 218 of the 329 Conservative MPs, he proceeded to elevate Heseltine to "number two" status in the Conservative hierarchy.

Additional by-election losses and several defections were followed by another rout in local elections in May 1996, even in the party's southern heartland. By the end of 1996, the government was perilously close to minority status in the House of Commons and reliant on the tactical support of Ulster Unionists to survive until the May 1997 election, at which Conservatives captured only 165 seats. The defeat was so extensive that Major resigned as party leader.

After three rounds of balloting, William Hague, former Welsh secretary, defeated former chancellor of the exchequer and EU advocate Kenneth Clarke to become (at 36) the youngest Conservative leader of the century. The EU issue flared up again later in the year when Clarke, Heseltine, and others objected to the decision by party leaders to maintain opposition to the EU's proposed single currency. Following through on a Hague commitment, in January 1998 the parliamentary delegation approved new procedures for selecting the party leader and challenging the incumbent. Under the new rules all party members, not just MPs, were empowered to vote for the leader.

At the annual party conference in October 1998, Hague reiterated his opposition to a single European currency, citing in support the results of a recently concluded referendum of party members. In February 1999 Heseltine, Clarke, and former prime minister Heath all voiced support for Prime Minister Blair's "national changeover plan" and later joined the cross-party "Britain in Europe" movement.

On December 2, 1998, Hague dismissed the party's leader in the upper house, Viscount CRANBORNE, for failing to consult with him before approving the so-called Cranborne compromise with Labour over the hereditary membership of an interim upper house of Parliament (pending full reform of the House of Lords) and over passage of a proportional representation scheme for the European Parliament elections in June 1999. Subsequently, Hague's apparent willingness to accept proportional representation for some elected bodies as well as an end to hereditary voting rights in a new upper chamber drew fire from hard-line Conservatives, as did his initial support for a statement by (then) deputy leader Peter LILLEY in April 1999 that "the free market has only a limited role in improving public services like health, education, and welfare." The right interpreted the statement as further evidence of a retreat from Thatcherism.

As expected, the party fared poorly at the May 6, 1999, elections for the new Scottish Parliament and Welsh National Assembly, although it registered significant gains in simultaneous nationwide local elections. Conservatives took only 18 seats (all of them "top-up") in the 129-member Scottish legislature and 9 (8 "top-up") in the 60-member Welsh Assembly, but, following up on modest gains made locally in 1998, the party displaced the Liberal Democrats as the second largest party at the local level. A month later Conservatives outpolled Labourites at balloting for the European Parliament, winning 36 seats, more than reversing the party's losses in 1994. The trend continued in 2000, when a March by-election victory gave the party its first directly elected seat in the Scottish Parliament, with further gains recorded in May's local council elections.

In October 1999 Hague, in a retreat from an earlier attempt to delineate a "caring" conservatism, had outlined a "common sense revolution" that marked a clear return to Thatcherism. Over the next six months Hague elaborated on his call for tax cuts; repeated his "sterling guarantee" that the party would not adopt the euro during the next Parliament; took a strong Eurosceptic stance, including support for a proposal that the founding Treaty of Rome be renegotiated to permit members to opt out of EU policies unrelated to trade; accused the Labour administration of being soft on criminals, including sexual offenders; and opposed initiatives on homosexual rights. By mid-2000 the party's standing in public opinion polls had risen dramatically. Prior to the turnaround, many observers had expected Hague's leadership to be challenged by Michael PORTILLO, a former defense secretary under John Major who had returned to the House of Commons with a November 1999 by-election win. Hague, showing new confidence, nevertheless awarded Portillo the key role of shadow chancellor of the exchequer in February 2000.

Despite successes in local council elections, the Conservatives failed to make gains against Labour at the election of June 2001, winning 166 seats and 32.7 percent of the vote in England, Scotland, and Wales. As a consequence, Hague resigned on June 8. Although Portillo was initially regarded as his likely successor, the acrimonious leadership contest ultimately narrowed to a choice between Eurosceptic Iain Duncan SMITH and Kenneth Clarke, with Smith winning a clear victory on September 13. However, dissatisfaction subsequently arose over Duncan Smith's quiet and perceived unsure leadership, and he was forced to resign on October 29, 2003, after losing a vote of confidence among Conservative MPs. He was succeeded by Michael HOWARD on November 6. Howard himself resigned following the Conservative defeat in May 2005, although the Conservatives had improved their seat total to 197 on a vote share of 32.3 percent.

David Cameron, a youthful (39-year-old) "modernizer," was elected chair of the party in December 2005 by a two-to-one margin of party member votes over David DAVIS. Cameron immediately pledged to move the Conservatives toward the center for upcoming elections, promising a "more compassionate party" that would present a much larger percentage of female candidates (only four of the party's current MPs were women) and minority candidates. The new leader also emphasized environmental issues, called upon businesses to address "social concerns," and announced that it would undermine the party's credibility to pledge tax cuts during the next general election considering the national budget situation. Although the party's right wing reportedly objected to many of Cameron's centrist policies, the immediate results of the shift to the center included resounding success for the Conservatives in the May 2006 local elections (40 percent of the vote) and continued improvement in the party's position in public opinion polls. The Conservatives also secured 40 percent of the vote in the May 2007 local balloting and improved its representation by three seats in the London Assembly in May 2008 balloting. In the London balloting its mayoral candidate, Boris JOHNSON, defeated two-term incumbent and Labour candidate Ken Livingstone.

The Conservatives gained majority control of 26 of 27 county councils on a vote share of 38 percent in the June 2009 local elections. The party also won 25 of 69 seats in simultaneous balloting for the European Parliament on a vote share of 27.7 percent. A few weeks late Conservative MP John BERCOW was elected speaker of the House of Commons.

Leaders: David CAMERON (Party Leader and Leader of the Opposition), George OSBORNE (Shadow Chancellor of the Exchequer), Sir George YOUNG (Senior Parliamentary Leader and Political Advisor), Theresa MAY (Shadow Leader of the House of Commons), Eric PICKLES (Chair), Lord ASHCROFT and John MAPLES (Deputy Chairs).

Liberal Democrat Party. A federal organization of largely autonomous English, Welsh, and Scottish parties, the Liberal Democratic Party (routinely referenced as the Liberal Democrats) formed by merger of the Liberal and Social Democratic parties, as approved at conferences of the two groups on January 23 and 31, 1988, respectively. Initially called the Social and Liberal Democratic Party (SLDP), it adopted the shorter name in October 1989.

Reduced to a minority position by the rise of Labour after World War I, the Liberal Party (founded in 1859) continued to uphold the traditional values of European liberalism and sought, without notable success, to attract dissident elements in both of the main parties by its nonsocialist and reformist principles. Despite having won only 13 seats in the election of October 1974, the party played a crucial role in 1977–1978 by entering into a parliamentary accord with Labour, thus, for the first time in nearly 50 years, permitting a major party to continue in office by means of third-party support. In September 1982 the party voted to form an electoral alliance with the Social Democratic Party (SDP), which yielded an aggregate of 23 parliamentary seats in the 1983 election and 27 in 1987.

The SDP had been formally organized on March 26, 1981, by the "gang of four" right-wing Labour dissidents (Roy JENKINS, Dr. David OWEN, William RODGERS, and Shirley WILLIAMS), who strongly objected to the party's swing to unilateralist and anti-European positions. However, after a series of by-election successes in 1981–1982, the SDP lost impetus. Objecting to the proposed merger with the Liberals after the 1987 election, Owen resigned from the SDP leadership in August 1987 and in February 1988 announced the formation of a "new" SDP, which was ultimately dissolved in June 1990.

Meanwhile, in July 1988 the merged Liberal Democrats had elected Paddy ASHDOWN as its leader.

At the April 1992 election the Liberal Democrats won 20 seats, which rose to 25 as a result of subsequent by-election victories. The May 1995 and May 1996 local elections saw the Liberal Democrats overtake the Conservatives as the second party (after Labour) in local government, its greatest strength being mainly in the south and west of England. In the May 1997 general election the party increased its representation to 46 seats, adding another with a by-election win in November. Having announced that it would cooperate with the new government, it subsequently agreed to participate in a special cabinet committee established by Prime Minister Blair for regular consultation in areas of "mutual interest."

In May 1999 the party finished fourth in balloting for the new Scottish and Welsh legislatures, but its 17 seats in the Scottish Parliament enabled it to emerge as the junior partner in a coalition administration in Scotland with Labour. As part of the agreement, David STEEL, former leader of the Liberal Democrats, was chosen to be speaker of the Scottish Parliament. In the May local council elections, Conservative gains dropped the Liberal Democrats back to third place in terms of total local seats.

On August 9, 1999, Charles KENNEDY was elected party leader, Ashdown having announced in January that he would step down following the June European Parliament elections. Under a proportional representation system, the Liberal Democrats saw their European Parliament seat total rise to ten, eight more than in 1994, despite a reduced vote share.

In March 2000 the party threatened to stop cooperating with the government if Labour reneged on its campaign pledge to pursue adoption of proportional voting for the House of Commons. The party also remained firmly committed to the EU and adoption of the euro.

In October 2000 the Liberal Democrats joined Labour in forming a coalition government in Wales. At the June 2001 election for the House of Commons, the party gained 6 seats, for a total of 52, although in local elections it lost the 2 local councils it had controlled. At the 2005 poll, the party gained 10 lower house seats for a total of 62 on a vote share of 22.1 percent.

Kennedy resigned as chair on January 7, 2006, after acknowledging an ongoing struggle with alcoholism. Walter Menzies ("Ming") CAMPBELL, a former Olympic sprinter and Scottish MP, became interim leader the same day and won the March 2 leadership contest in a three-way race. The Liberal Democrats subsequently remained opposed to British participation in the war in Iraq and expressed concern about the effect on civil rights of recent antiterrorism initiatives. The Liberal Democrats moved into second place (on a 27 percent vote share) behind the Conservatives in the May 2006 local elections.

Campbell resigned as party leader on October 15, 2007, after it became clear that new Prime Minister Brown did not intend to call for early elections. By that time, the Liberal Democrats were experiencing a decline in popularity polls, and party members had publicly expressed worries that Campbell's advanced age would be a detriment in leading the party into an election that was still two years away. Vincent Cable served as interim leader until Nick Clegg was elected as the party's new leader in December in a closely contested contest with Chris HUHNE.

The party suffered a setback in the May 2008 London Assembly elections, winning just 11.4 percent of the vote and three seats (a loss of two). Its candidate for mayor finished a distant third, with 9.6 percent of the first-preference votes. Although the party finished second in the June 2009 local elections with 28 percent of the vote, its seat total declined as it lost seats to the Conservatives. In concurrent balloting for the European Parliament, the Liberal Democrats finished fourth with 13.7 percent of the vote and 11 seats (down 1 from 2004).

Leaders: Nick CLEGG (Party Leader), Vincent CABLE (Deputy Leader), Rosalind SCOTT (President), Paul BURSTOW (Chief Whip), Lord MCNALLY (Leader in the House of Lords).

Scottish National Party (SNP). Founded in 1934, the SNP advocates Scottish independence within the EU. At the 1979 election it lost 9 of its 11 seats in the House of Commons and since then has managed to win no more than 6. The SNP aligned with Labour and the Liberal Democrats in support of a "yes" vote in the September 1997 referendum on creation of a Scottish Parliament.

As the May 6, 1999, elections for the new Parliament approached, Labour pulled away from the SNP in opinion polls, ending speculation that the nationalists could command a parliamentary majority. Although winning only 7 of 73 constituency seats despite a 28.7 percent firstvote share (second to Labour's 38.8 percent), the SNP received an additional 28 "top-up" seats, making it the leading opposition party in the legislature.

At the party's annual conference in September 1999 party leader Alex Salmond predicted that Scotland would be independent by 2007, and in March 2000 the SNP put forward an independence referendum plan that it would pursue if it won the next Scottish election. Four months later Salmond announced that he would resign as SNP leader in September, at which time the party elected John SWINNEY, his deputy, to succeed him. Swinney had been challenged on the left by Alex NEIL.

At the June 2001 UK general election the SNP retained 5 of the 6 seats it had previously held. Amid criticism for ineffective election leadership and arguably disappointing results, Swinney resigned in June 2004. Salmond returned as leader following his election on September 3. The SNP returned to a representation of 6 in the House of Commons in 2005 on a vote share of 17.7 percent of the votes cast in Scotland, and the SNP became the largest party in the 129-seat Scottish Parliament when it won 47 seats in the May 3, 2007, balloting for that body. Salmond was elected first minister of Scotland on May 16 and was sworn in as leader of a minority government the next day.

Leaders: Alex SALMOND (Party Leader and First Minister of Scotland), Nicola STURGEON (Deputy Leader), Ian HUDGHTON (President), Angus ROBERTSON (UK Parliamentary Leader).

Plaid Cymru (literally, "Party of Wales," usually referred to by its Welsh name, or informally as the Welsh Nationalist Party). Founded in 1925, *Plaid Cymru* sought full self-government for Wales as a democratic socialist republic. In May 1987 it entered into a parliamentary alliance with the SNP to work for constitutional, economic, and social reform in both regions. It elected four MPs in 1992, when it gained 8.9 percent of the Welsh vote (partly through an alliance in six constituencies with the Welsh Green Party). In 1997 the party retained the four seats, and it joined the Labour Party and the Liberal Democrats in urging passage of the September referendum regarding establishment of a Welsh regional assembly.

Plaid Cymru finished second to Labour at balloting for the Welsh National Assembly on May 6, 1999, taking a 28.4 percent first-vote share and winning a total of 17 seats (9 constituency, 8 "top-up"). Labour subsequently backed the party's nominee as speaker of the new legislature, Lord Dafydd ELIS-THOMAS. In June 1999 *Plaid Cymru* won 2 seats in the European Parliament.

In May 2000, citing health reasons, the party's president, Dafydd WIGLEY, resigned. Ieuan Wyn Jones handily won election as his successor on August 3, and at the party's September annual conference he set 2003 as the target date for supplanting Labour as the foremost party in the Welsh National Assembly. At the June 2001 election for the House of Commons, *Plaid Cymru* retained its four seats. Three months later, at its annual conference, the party formally ended its demand for Welsh independence.

At the May 1, 2003, assembly election the *Plaid Cymru* lost 5 of its 17 seats and barely kept its position as the official opposition. Jones resigned as president and assembly leader within a week of the election. Folk singer and politician Dafydd Iwan was subsequently elected party president, with Jones winning reelection as assembly leader. *Plaid Cymru*'s representation in the House of Commons dropped to 3 in 2005 on a vote share of 12.6 percent of the votes in Wales. Jones subsequently warned party members at the *Plaid Cymru* annual conference that internal squabbling was compromising electoral effectiveness.

In the May 3, 2007, balloting for the Welsh assembly, *Plaid Cymru* improved by 3 seats to a total of 15. The party joined Labour in a coalition government that was installed on May 25, after negotiations had prompted a commitment from Labour to hold a referendum on *Plaid Cymru*'s proposal for additional law-making powers to be given to the assembly.

Leaders: Dafydd IWAN (President), Ieuan Wyn JONES (Party Leader and Deputy First Minister of Scotland), Elfyn LLWYD (UK Parliamentary Leader), Jill EVANS (Vice President).

Respect–The Unity Coalition. Respect was launched in January 2004 by MP George Galloway, who had been expelled from the Labour Party in October 2003 after being found guilty of inciting UK troops in Iraq to disobey orders. Galloway was reelected in 2005 by a constituency heavily populated by immigrants.

The party allows its members to hold memberships in other parties, most notably, until late 2007, the Socialist Workers Party. A schism emerged over Galloway's charge that the party was too disorganized to be effective, which drew the counter charge that he was willing to sacrifice principle for election. In the May London Assembly elections the two factions ran on different lists, and both received less than 2.5 percent of the vote.

Leaders: Salma YAQOOB (Chair), George GALLOWAY (Founder).

UK Independence Party (UKIP). The UKIP was created in 1993 by Alan SKED and members of the Anti-Federalist League (founded 1991) to oppose what it saw as the surrender of British sovereignty implicit in the terms of the EU's Maastricht Treaty; the party urged withdrawal from the EU. It failed to win any parliamentary seats in 1997 but won 7 percent of the vote and 3 seats in the European Parliament balloting in June 1999. It fared even better in the European poll of June 2004, winning 12 of 75 seats in a third-place showing. Two members of the UKIP were elected to the London Assembly in 2004, but they subsequently defected to Veritas, a new party dedicated to the restoration of probity in public life, which had been founded in January 2005 by the UKIP's most celebrated MP, former talk show host Robert KILROY-SILK. Following the dissolution of Veritas, the two members of the assembly formed their own **One London** party. (They lost their seats in the assembly in 2008.)

In January 2007 three Conservative Party members of the House of Lords defected to the UKIP and thus gave the party its first parliamentary representation. The party claimed one seat in the House of Commons in April 2008 when Conservative member Bob SPINK declared his membership in the UKIP.

The UKIP recorded its best-ever electoral showing by finishing second (behind only the Conservatives) in the June 2009 balloting for the European Parliament, winning 13 seats on a vote share of 16.5 percent. In November Lord Pearson (Malcom Pearson) was elected as the new party leader, succeeding Nigel FARAGE, who had stepped down as party leader to concentrate on his membership in the European Parliament. Subsequently, Lord Pearson offered to keep the UKIP out of the general election due in 2010 if the Conservatives would pledge in writing that, if elected, they would hold a national referendum on the EU's Lisbon Treaty. However, Conservative leader David Cameron rejected the offer, the Czech Republic having recently become the final EU country to ratify the treaty.

Leaders: Lord PEARSON (Leader), David Campbell BANNERMAN (Deputy Leader), Paul NUTTALL (Chair).

Note: For information on the Democratic Unionist Party, *Sinn Féin,* the Social Democratic and Labour Party, and the Ulster Unionist Party (all represented in the UK House of Commons), see Political Parties and Groups in the article on United Kingdom: Northern Ireland.

Nonparliamentary Parties:

Green Party of England and Wales. Organized in 1973 as the Ecology Party, the Greens adopted their present name in 1985. (The semiautonomous Welsh branch is the **Welsh Green Party** [*Plaid Werdd Cym*].) The party addresses human rights issues in addition to problems affecting the environment.

The Greens have consistently polled less than 1 percent of the vote for the House of Commons. In June 1999, however, the Greens won two seats in the European Parliament on a 6.3 percent vote share. In November 1999 Lord BEAUMONT of Whitley, a life peer in the House of Lords, resigned from the Liberal Democrats and joined the Greens as their sole member in the UK Parliament. The party secured no lower house seats on a 1 percent vote share in 2005, and the death of Lord Beaumont in April 2008 meant the party was no longer represented in either chamber of parliament. However, the party retained its two seats in the London Assembly in 2008 and its two seats (on a vote share of 8.6 percent) in the European Parliament in 2009.

Leaders: Caroline LUCAS (Leader), Jayne FORBES (Chair), Adrian RAMSAY (Deputy Leader).

British National Party (BNP). The BNP was founded in 1982 by a breakaway faction of the fascist National Front (NF). In early 2006 BNP leader Nick Griffin was acquitted of charges of inciting racial hatred related to a speech he gave at a party conference in 2004 in which he reportedly made strongly anti-Muslim remarks. In the 2005 general election the BNP's 119 candidates secured 0.7 percent of the nationwide vote, up from 0.5 percent in 2001. The BNP doubled its seats in the local elections held in May 2006, performing well in the white working-class areas of east London, and held its own in the May 2007 local elections. The BNP claimed its first seat on the London Assembly when it won 5.4 percent of the party-list voting in the May 2008 balloting. In June 2009 the party won its first seats above the local level, securing two seats on 6.2 percent of the nationwide vote for the European Parliament. The electoral progress brought the BNP enough legitimacy for the BBC to invite Griffin to take part in a television debate it airs weekly involving representatives from Britain's major parties. The success also attracted fire from the Equality and Human Rights Commission, which sued the party for violating race relation laws for its "Whites only" membership, employment, and services policies. Griffin subsequently announced the BNP would have to change its policies because the party could not afford the legal fees to defend them.

Leaders: Nick GRIFFIN (Chair), Simon DARBY (Deputy Chair).

The 2005 general election was contested by more than 110 of the 300-plus registered parties, with only a dozen receiving 0.5 percent or more of the nationwide vote and with 66 parties fielding a candidate in but a single constituency. Covering the full political spectrum, the small parties highlighted below are among those recently active.

On the left, the **Socialist Labour Party** (SLP) was launched in 1996 by miners' union leader Arthur SCARGILL to protest the perceived rightward drift of the Labour Party. An **Independent Labour Network** (ILN) was later formed for similar reasons by European Parliament members Ken COATES and Hugh KERR following their expulsion by the Labour leadership for criticizing the party's "Tory policies." In 1999 Coates unsuccessfully sought reelection on an Alternative Labour List, while Kerr joined the Scottish Socialist Party (below). The more militant **Socialist Workers' Party** (SWP), dating from 1950, has recently withdrawn its traditional support for Labour and until recently formed part of Respect–The Unity Coalition (above); its founder, Tony CLIFF, died in April 2000. A coalition (the London Socialist Alliance) of the SWP and the **Communist Party of Britain** (CPB) supported maverick Ken Livingstone's successful campaign for the capital's mayoralty in 2000. In 1997 the **Militant Labour** (ML, originally the Militant Tendency within the Labour Party) founded the Trotskyite **Socialist Party** (SP), led by Peter TAAFFE. An ML minority, led by the group's founder, Ted GRANT, remained within Labour as the Socialist Appeal, while the ML's Scottish branch, led by Tommy SHERIDAN, helped form a Scottish Socialist Alliance that, in turn, in 1998 established the autonomous **Scottish Socialist Party** (SSP), which is led jointly by Colin FOX and Frances CURRAN. In 1999 the SSP took one seat (won by Sheridan) in the new Scottish Parliament, as did the **Scottish Green Party** (SGP), led by Eleanor SCOTT and Patrick HARVIE (co-covenors). The **Socialist Party of Great Britain** (SPGB), a non-Leninist Marxist group founded in 1904, continues to maintain branches throughout the country but did not have a candidate in the 2005 election.

On the extreme left, the CPB, currently led by Robert GRIFFITHS, split in 1988 from the historical **Communist Party of Great Britain** (CPGB) to protest the CPGB's conversion to Eurocommunism. The CPGB was founded in 1920, briefly enjoyed parliamentary representation, and was influential in the trade union movement. However, it is now defunct, most of its remaining membership having reorganized in 1992 as the moderate **Democratic Left** (DL). The DL presented itself as an association rather than a party and so did not contest elections. In 1999, under the leadership of Nina TEMPLE, the DL membership voted to reorganize as the nondoctrinaire New Times Network. Other CPBG remnants include the Marxist-Leninist **New Communist Party** (NCP), formed by dissidents in 1977, and the **Communist Party of Scotland** (CPS). (Although the CPGB continues to pursue a reforging of the original CPGB, it is not officially registered as a party. Neither is the NCP or CPS.) The **Workers' Revolutionary Party** (WRP) has also undergone extensive splintering; the faction that has retained the WRP name is led by Sheila TORRANCE. A WRP offshoot includes the Trotskyite **Socialist Equality Party** (SEP, formerly the International Communist Party), which is led by Christopher Howard MARSDEN and serves as the British branch of the International Committee of the Fourth International. Other small groups include the Trotskyite **Alliance for Workers' Liberty** (AWL), led by Cathy NUGENT; the **Revolutionary Communist Group** (RCG); and the **Revolutionary Communist Party of Great Britain** (Marxist-Leninist), led by Chris COLEMAN.

On the extreme right, the **National Front** (NF), a fascist grouping founded in 1967, won a number of local council seats in the 1970s but largely disintegrated thereafter. Most of the NF defected in 1982 to what is now the BNP (above). In 1995 most remaining NF members regrouped under Ian ANDERSON as the **National Democrats** (ND). Under the leadership of Thomas HOLMES, the rump NF contested 13 constituencies in 2005. Founded in 1990 as the **Third Way** and registered in 2006 as the **National Liberal Party–the Third Way**, the party has roots in the NF but denounced national socialism in favor of worker participation in industry, adoption of Swiss-style democratic reforms, immigration restrictions, withdrawal from the EU and other multilateral groups, and an ecological agenda. The party is currently led by Daniel KERR. Extremist groups include the violent **Combat 18**.

Other formations include the **Christian People's Alliance** (CPA), launched in May 1999 as a Christian Democratic party and chaired by Alan CRAIG; the **Liberal Party** (currently led by Rob WHEWAY), which was formed by those who opposed the conversion of the historic party into what became the Liberal Democrats; **Mebyon Kernow** (literally, "Sons of Cornwall"), a Cornish separatist group formed in 1951 and led by Dirk COLE; the **Islamic Party of Britain,** founded in 1989 and led by David Musa PIDCOCK; and the **Legalize Cannabis Alliance** (LCA), which voted in 2006 to deregister and continue as a pressure group. In addition, the anti-euro Democracy Movement, a self-described "non-party movement" led by Robin BIRLEY, was organized in 1999 as successor to the Referendum Movement, which began in 1994 as the Referendum Party of the late James GOLDSMITH.

Among the numerous British fringe groups are the **Natural Law Party** (NLP), founded in 1992 by practitioners of Transcendental Meditation and led by Dr. Geoffrey CLEMENTS (the NLP is no longer registered as a party); the **Official Monster Raving Loony Party,** led by Alan (Howling Laud) HOPE since the 1999 suicide of the party's founder, former rock singer (Screaming Lord) David SUTCH; and the **Make Politicians History Party** (led by Ronnie CARROLL), a successor to the individualist Rainbow Dream Ticket Party, which advocated abolishing Parliament and instituting government by home-based electronic referenda (the party voluntarily deregistered in 2009).

LEGISLATURE

The **Parliament** serves as legislative authority for the entire UK. Meeting in Westminster (London) with the queen as its titular head, until November 1999 it consisted of a partly hereditary, partly appointed House of Lords and an elected House of Commons (the real locus of power). Under the House of Lords Act 1999 the membership of the upper house was restructured (see below).

Following voter approval at separate devolutionary referendums held in Scotland and Wales in 1997, the UK Parliament passed legislation in 1998 that authorized creation of a Scottish Parliament and a Welsh National Assembly. Elections for both legislatures were held for the first time on May 6, 1999. Creation of a New Northern Ireland Assembly was approved by referendum on May 22, 1998, with the initial election occurring a month later, on June 25 (see the Northern Ireland article). All three of the new legislative bodies are elected for four-year terms under a proportional representation system that combines single-member constituencies and "top-up" seats drawn from party lists.

House of Lords. Before reforms were instituted in 1999, the House of Lords had 1,330 members, of whom 751 were hereditary peers, either by succession or of first creation. The remaining members included the 2 archbishops and 24 other senior bishops of the Church of England, serving and retired Lords of Appeal in Ordinary (who constituted the nation's highest body of civil and criminal appeal), and other life peers. Only about 200–300 members of the House of Lords attended sessions with any degree of regularity. The House of Lords Act 1999 abolished the hereditary component and replaced it on an interim basis, pending more comprehensive reform, by 92 ex-hereditary members: 75 elected by all the hereditaries according to a predetermined party ratio, 15 house officers elected by the full membership, and 2 appointed royal office holders (the Earl Marshall and the Lord Great Chamberlain). The 75 peers elected on October 29 on a party basis comprised 42 Conservatives, 28 "crossbenchers" (independents), 3 Liberal Democrats, and 2 Labour members. The collateral election of house officers added 9 Conservatives, 2 Labour peers, 2 Liberal Democrats, and 2 crossbenchers.

Following the reforms, the full interim chamber had 670 members. The subsequent naming of new life peers—most of them Labour supporters, in an effort by the government to achieve political parity—plus the naming in April 2001 of 15 independent "people's peers" by an appointments commission, brought the total to 715 as of July 31, 2001. As of November 2009 the total was 737: Labour Party, 212; Conservative Party, 190; crossbenchers, 183; Liberal Democrats, 71; Democratic Unionist Party, 3; Ulster Unionist Party, 3; United Kingdom Independence Party, 2; archbishops and bishops, 26; peers on leave of absence, 13; suspended, 2; and others, 32 (including 17 currently "disqualified" because of their position as senior members of the judiciary or as members of the European Parliament); suspended, 2.

On June 28, 2006, the House of Lords for the first time elected its own leader as part of broader governmental changes proposed by the prime minister in 2003. The new Lord Speaker, who may serve a maximum of two five-year terms, assumed (effective July 4) the leadership role previously exercised by the Lord Chancellor (the prime minister's appointee and a member of the cabinet). Baroness Hayman of the Labour Party was elected as the first Lord Speaker, and, following the custom of the speaker of the House of Commons, she subsequently withdrew her party affiliation. Meanwhile, in March 2007 both houses of Parliament took a series of votes on a variety of possible alternatives for a popularly elected component for the House of Lords. In July 2008 the government submitted a white paper to the House of Commons proposing an 80 to 100 percent elected upper chamber.

Lord Speaker: Baroness HAYMAN.

House of Commons. Following the general election of May 5, 2005 (and one subsequent by-election on June 23 in a constituency where initial balloting had been postponed due to the death of a candidate), the House of Commons consisted of 646 members directly elected from single-member constituencies for terms of five years, subject to earlier dissolution. The strength of the parties was as follows: Labour Party, 355 seats; Conservative Party, 198; Liberal Democrats, 62; Democratic Unionist Party, 9; Scottish National Party, 6; *Sinn Féin,* 5 (seats not taken); *Plaid Cymru,* 3; Social Democratic and Labour Party, 3; Respect–The Unity Coalition, 1; Ulster Unionist Party, 1; independents, 2; speaker (running as "The Speaker Seeking Reelection"), 1. (According to long-standing convention, the speaker serves without party affiliation and votes only in case of a tie vote. The current speaker, elected to the House of Commons on the Conservative ticket in 2005, was elected speaker on June 22, 2009, following the resignation of the previous speaker.) The next general election was due by June 2010.

Speaker: John BERCOW.

Scottish Parliament. Party strength in the 129-member Parliament after the May 3, 2007, election was as follows: Scottish National Party, 47; Labour Party, 46; Conservative Party, 17; Liberal Democrats, 16; Scottish Green Party, 2; independent, 1.

Presiding Officer: Alex FERGUSSON.

Welsh National Assembly (*Cynulliad Cenedlaethol Cymru*). Party strength in the 60-member National Assembly after the May 3, 2007, election was as follows: Labour Party, 26; *Plaid Cymru,* 15; Conservative Party, 12; Liberal Democrats, 6; independent, 1.

Presiding Officer: Lord Dafydd ELIS-THOMAS.

CABINET

[as of November 1, 2009]

Prime Minister and First Lord of the Treasury	Gordon Brown
Secretaries of State	
Business, Innovations, and Skills	Lord Mandelson
Cabinet Office	Tessa Jowell [f]
Children, Schools, and Families	Ed Balls
Communities and Local Government	John Denham
Culture, Media, and Sport	Ben Bradshaw
Defense	Bob Ainsworth
Energy and Climate Change	Ed Miliband
Environment, Food, and Rural Affairs	Hilary Benn
Foreign and Commonwealth Affairs	David Miliband
Health	Andy Burnham
Home Department	Alan Johnson
International Development	Douglas Alexander
Justice	Jack Straw
Northern Ireland	Shaun Woodward

Olympics	Tessa Jowell [f]
Scotland	Jim Murphy
Transport	Lord Adonis
Wales	Peter Hain
Work and Pensions	Yvette Cooper [f]
Chancellor of the Exchequer	Alistair Darling
Chief Secretary to the Treasury	Liam Byrne
Leader of the House of Commons	Harriet Harman [f]
Leader of the House of Lords	Baroness Royall of Blaisdon [f]
Lord Chancellor	Jack Straw
Lord President of the Council	Lord Mandelson
Lord Privy Seal	Harriet Harman [f]
Minister of the Civil Service	Gordon Brown
Minister for Women and Equality	Harriet Harman [f]

[f] = female

COMMUNICATIONS

Freedom combined with responsibility represents the British ideal in the handling of news and opinion. The press, while privately owned and free from censorship, is subject to strict libel laws and is often made aware of government preferences with regard to the handling of news reports. In late 1989, faced with the prospect of parliamentary action to curb the excesses of the more sensationalist papers, publishers adopted an ethics code that limited intrusion into private lives, offered the objects of press stories reasonable opportunity for reply, provided for appropriately prominent retraction of errors in reporting, precluded payments to known criminals, and barred irrelevant references to race, color, and religion.

A Press Complaints Commission was established by the industry in 1991. Responding to public concerns following the death of Diana, Princess of Wales, in a high-speed motor vehicle accident in August 1997, the commission in December announced a revised code of conduct that widened the definition of privacy for individuals, prohibited "persistent pursuit" by photojournalists, and offered additional protections for children. In February 1998 Prime Minister Blair offered support for continued self-regulation by the press.

A communications bill, which was first published in May 2002, replaced five current regulatory bodies for the press, television, and radio with a single Office of Communications, the first chair of which was appointed in July.

A unanimous ruling in October 2006 by the Law Lords (Britain's highest court) tightened the provisions under which the press can be sued for libel. Previously, the onus had fallen on newspapers in libel cases to defend what they had printed by affirmatively demonstrating its truth, unlike systems such as those in the United States under which libel plaintiffs are required to prove that the newspaper had printed information the newspaper knew to be wrong. The 2006 UK case involved a newspaper report that Saudi Arabia, at the request of the United States, was monitoring bank accounts of Saudi businessmen to detect possible siphoning of funds to terrorist groups. The Law Lords ruled that the newspaper was not subject to libel proceedings, even though the article's assertions were impossible to prove in open court.

Press. Per capita consumption of newspapers in the UK, once the highest in the world, has fallen off substantially in recent years. Major consolidation in ownership has occurred over the past several decades. The best known of the current chains is Rupert Murdoch's News International PLC, which includes among its newspapers the UK's largest daily tabloid, *The Sun;* the largest Sunday tabloid, *The News of the World;* and the influential *Times* and *Sunday Times*. The regional press is also highly concentrated, with 674 titles being owned (in 1996) by 10 corporations. In 2004, there were more than 2,600 regional and local newspapers.

England: The following papers are dailies published in London, unless otherwise indicated: *News of the World* (3,242,000), Sunday, usually pro-Conservative tabloid; *The Sun* (3,155,000), usually pro-Conservative tabloid; *Daily Mail* (2,242,000), pro-Conservative tabloid; *The Mail on Sunday* (2,239,000), pro-Conservative tabloid; *The Mirror* (formerly *Daily Mirror,* 1,441,000); *Sunday Mirror* (1,316,000), pro-Labour tabloid; *The Sunday Times* (1,221,000), pro-Conservative; *Sunday Express* (656,000), pro-Conservative tabloid; *The Daily Express* (739,000), pro-Conservative tabloid; *The Daily Telegraph* (851,000), Conservative; *Daily Star* (731,000), pro-Conservative tabloid; *The Sunday Telegraph* (622,000), Conservative; *The Times* (638,000), usually pro-Conservative; *The Observer* (453,000), Sunday, independent; *The Financial Times* (429,000), independent; *Evening Standard* (298,000), moderate Conservative tabloid; *The Guardian* (London and Manchester, 349,000), center-left; *The Independent on Sunday* (183,000), independent; *The Independent* (221,000), independent; *Express* and *Star* (Wolverhampton, 138,000); *Manchester Evening News* (162,000), independent; *Liverpool Echo* (103,000); *Birmingham Mail* (66,000); *Evening Chronicle* (Newcastle upon Tyne, 92,000); *Leicester Mercury* (69,000); *Shropshire Star* (Telford, 71,000), *Sunday Mercury* (Birmingham, 57,000); *Sunday Sun* (Newcastle upon Tyne, 64,000); *Yorkshire Evening Post* (Leeds, 53,000); *Nottingham Evening Post* (56,000); *Evening Standard* (Stock-on-Trent, 75,000), *The Star* (Sheffield, 50,000); *Evening Post* (Bristol, 49,000); *The News* (Portsmouth, 53,000), *Evening Telegraph* (Coventry, 62,000); *Yorkshire Post* (Leeds, 48,000).

Wales: *South Wales Echo* (Cardiff, 45,000); *South Wales Evening Post* (Swansea, 51,000); *Western Mail* (Cardiff, 37,000).

Scotland: *Sunday Mail* (Glasgow, 428,000), pro-Labour tabloid; *Sunday Post* (Dundee, 257,000), tabloid; *Daily Record* (Glasgow, 347,000), independent tabloid; *Evening Times* (Glasgow, 73,000); *The Press and Journal* (Aberdeen, 80,000); *The Herald* (Glasgow, 63,000), independent, the oldest national newspaper in the English language; *The Courier and Advertiser* (Dundee, 75,000); *Scotland on Sunday* (Edinburgh, 67,000), independent; *The Scotsman* (Edinburgh, 51,000), independent; *Evening News* (Edinburgh, 68,000); *Evening Express* (Aberdeen, 53,000).

Northern Ireland: See next article.

News agencies. Britain boasts the world's oldest news agency, Reuters, founded by the pioneer German newsgatherer Paul von Reuter, who established his headquarters in London in 1851. The company is now a worldwide service controlled by press interests in Britain, Australia, and New Zealand. The other leading agencies included the Associated Press Ltd. (a British subsidiary of the Associated Press of the United States) and the Press Association, founded in 1868.

Broadcasting and computing. Broadcasting services are provided by the British Broadcasting Corporation (BBC), founded in 1922, and various independent commercial companies. The BBC, which is publicly financed by compulsory license fees, operates two national television services, various satellite channels, five national and four regional radio services, and several dozen local stations. The commercial sector is regulated by the Independent Television Commission (ITC) and the Radio Authority (RA). Funded by paid advertising, the commercial television companies have their own national network, while the fourth national television station (Channel 4) is also financed by advertising but has statutory obligations, including a duty to broadcast a suitable proportion of its transmissions in Wales in the Welsh language. A fifth national television station (Channel 5), also commercially operated, began broadcasting in 1997. As of 2008 there were 762.4 Internet users per 1,000 inhabitants.

INTERGOVERNMENTAL REPRESENTATION

Ambassador to the U.S.: Nigel SHEINWALD.

U.S. Ambassador to the UK: Louis B. SUSMAN.

Permanent Representative to the UN: Mark Lyall GRANT.

IGO Memberships (Non-UN): ADB, AfDB, BIS, CDB, CERN, CEUR, CWTH, EBRD, EIB, ESA, EU, Eurocontrol, G-7, G-8, G-10, G-20, IADB, IEA, Interpol, IOM, NATO, OECD, OSCE, PCA, WCO, WEU, WTO.

RELATED TERRITORIES

All major, and many minor, territories of the former British Empire achieved full independence in the course of the last century, and most are now members of the Commonwealth, a voluntary association of states held together primarily by a common political and constitutional heritage and, in most cases, use of the English language (see "The Commonwealth" in Intergovernmental Organizations section). In conventional usage, the term Commonwealth also includes the territories and dependencies of the UK and other Commonwealth member countries. As of 2006 the UK retained a measure of responsibility, direct or indirect, for 3 Crown dependencies, 11 inhabited territories, 2 essentially uninhabited territories, and the so-called Sovereign Base Areas on Cyprus.

In September 1998, following up on a commitment made at the Dependent Territories Association conference in London the preceding February, the Blair government announced that it intended to introduce legislation that would supersede the 1981 British Nationality Act, which had excluded most colonial residents from British citizenship, and restore their "right of abode" in the UK, which had been revoked in 1962. The dependencies would be restyled British overseas territories. A white paper issued in March 1999 reaffirmed the government's intentions, although the government added that the Caribbean colonies would be required to introduce various criminal justice reforms—for example, abolishing the death penalty and decriminalizing consensual homosexual relations—before attaining the new status. Implementing legislation was passed in 2002, with British citizenship being conferred on citizens of all British overseas territories (except the Sovereign Base Areas) from May 21. Since 2005 many of the territories, with London's cooperation and encouragement, have been studying possible constitutional reforms.

Several of the Overseas Territories and Crown Dependencies were hit hard by the 2008 global financial crisis, prompting the UK's chancellor of the exchequer, Alistair DARLING, to commission a report on their need to improve standards of financial regulation and to find new methods for raising tax revenue. The report called upon UK related territories to put their government finances on firmer footing through more diversified tax systems, including the possible introduction of taxes on income, profits, capital gains, and sales. The report also called on territories with significant financial sectors to provide more help in tracking financial crimes. However, it went on to note the significant contributions the UK territories and dependencies play in funding UK banks and to argue that tax avoidance by UK companies conducting financial operations through institutions in those areas was lower than previously thought.

Crown Dependencies:

Though closely related to Great Britain both historically and geographically, the Channel Islands and the Isle of Man are distinct from the UK and are under the jurisdiction of the sovereign rather than the state.

Channel Islands. Located in the English Channel off the northwest coast of France, the Channel Islands have been attached to the English Crown since the Norman Conquest in 1066. The nine islands have a total area of 75 square miles (198 sq. km.) and a population (2006E) of 154,000. The two largest and most important are Jersey and Guernsey, each of which has its own parliament (the States) but is linked to the Crown through a representative who bears the title lieutenant governor and serves as commander in chief. While the Channel Islands control their own domestic affairs, defense policy and most foreign relations are administered from London. St. Helier on Jersey and St. Peter Port on Guernsey are the principal towns. Because of their mild climate and insular location, the islands are popular tourist resorts, and their low tax rate has attracted many permanent residents from the UK.

The government of Jersey is based in the "Assembly of the States," a 53-member elected body composed of 29 deputies, 12 constables (heads of parishes), and 12 senators, not counting 3 nonvoting ex officio members (attorney general, solicitor general, dean of Jersey) plus the lieutenant governor and a bailiff, who presides over the legislature. Deputies and constables serve three-year terms; senators serve six-year terms, with elections for half their number held triennially.

November 2005 marked a major change in Jersey's governmental structure. Under the States of Jersey Law 2005, the previous committee system of governance was replaced by a ten-member cabinet-style system headed by a chief minister. The other nine ministers are nominated by the chief minister from among the membership of the Assembly of the States, which then elects each minister individually. The authority of the lieutenant governor to veto resolutions of the states was abolished, and "orders in council," issued by the Privy Council in London, were henceforth to be referred to the States for review. On December 5 Sen. Frank Walker was elected chief minister by a vote of 38–14 over Senator Syvret.

Following Walker's election, the government launched two public consultations in 2007. Jersey residents were surveyed for their views on civil unions for homosexual and heterosexual couples, and also registered their preferences for alternative strategies to provide public services to an aging population in the face of a shrinking workforce. Results were scheduled for consideration in 2008.

The most recent senatorial election was held October 15, 2008, with the balloting for deputies following on November 26. All winning senatorial candidates ran as independents, although three parties had candidates on the ballot: the **Jersey Democratic Alliance** (JDA), **Time 4 Change, and Jersey 2020.** The Centre Party, which had fielded senatorial candidates in 2005, changed its name to the **Jersey Conservative Party** (JCP) in 2007 but presented no candidates in 2008. Three JDA candidates won election as deputies, with the remaining 26 deputy seats being filled by independents.

Guernsey is governed through its "States of Deliberation," which comprises 45 people's deputies elected from multi- or single-member districts every four years, 2 representatives from Alderney, 2 ex officio members (attorney general and solicitor general), and a bailiff. Prior to the election of April 21, 2004, the States had included 10 local (parish) representatives, but those seats were eliminated as part of a governmental reform process that also saw, from May 1, 2004, adoption of a ministerial administration. At that time, 43 separate committees were abolished in favor of a Policy Council, comprising a chief minister and 10 other ministers elected from and by the members of the States; 10 departments, each headed by a minister; and 5 "specialist" committees. The first Privy Council resigned en masse in February 2007 after revelations of an alleged rigged bidding process for a hospital construction project.

The small islands of Alderney, Sark, Herm, Jethou, Brecqhou, and Lihou are usually classified as dependencies of the Bailiwick of Guernsey, although Alderney and Sark have their own legislatures: the States of Alderney, encompassing a president and 10 deputies serving four-year terms (half elected every other year), and the Sark Court of Chief Pleas, comprising 40 hereditary "tenants" (landowners) and 12 deputies elected for three-year terms. Anticipating the need to dismantle the island's feudal political system in order to comply with the European Convention on Human Rights, voters in October 2006 approved the creation of a Chief Pleas Assembly, to comprise 28 elected and 2 ex officio members. The Chief Pleas approved the new law in February 2008, and elections were scheduled for the following December, pending approval from the British Privy Council.

Although the Channel Islands are not legally part of the EU, certain EU directives are deemed to apply to them, notably those relating to tariffs and agricultural policy. In February 1995 the Sark Court of Chief Pleas rejected the incorporation of relevant parts of the EU's Maastricht Treaty into Sark law. In November 1999, however, the court voted to rescind a 1611 law that had restricted property inheritance to men. In December the UK Privy Council approved the change, thereby preventing a future challenge in the European Court of Human Rights.

In November 1998 a report presented by the UK Home Office recommended that the Channel Islands and the Isle of Man, which between them have registered some 90,000 offshore businesses, require such operations to provide greater details about their ownership and activities. The report also proposed that the dependencies take additional steps to prevent money laundering and other financial offenses. The June 2000 decision of the OECD to include the Channel Islands and the Isle of Man among 35 international jurisdictions with harmful tax and investment regimes led the islands' administrations to assert that reform would be pointless unless other, larger jurisdictions, such as Switzerland and Luxembourg, also participated. In early August, however, the islands pledged to cooperate with OECD efforts to eliminate tax crimes perpetrated by offshore corporations, and in February 2002 they were removed from the blacklist.

In a February 2000 ruling with major implications for a number of UK institutions, the European Court of Human Rights determined that a Guernsey flower grower had been denied a fair trial when he appealed a planning decision denying him use of a packing shed as a residence. The original appeal had involved the bailiff of Guernsey, who held executive and legislative as well as judicial responsibilities, thereby calling into question his impartiality, according to the court. The decision increased the likelihood of future challenges against, for example, the UK's lord chancellor, particularly in cases based on policies that the chancellor helps administer.

In December 2007 an amendment to the Reform Law granting 16-year-olds the right to vote received Royal Sanction and was implemented ahead of the 2008 general election. Guernsey's "Zero-10" tax strategy was also implemented in 2008, with income tax on company profits eliminated. The strategy singled out a minority of banking activities for a uniform 10 percent tax.

Lieutenant Governor and Commander in Chief of Jersey: Andrew RIDGWAY.

Bailiff of Jersey and President of the Assembly of the States: Michael BIRT.

Chief Minister of Jersey: Terence LE SUEUR.

Lieutenant Governor and Commander in Chief of the Bailiwick of Guernsey and Its Dependencies: Vice Adm. Sir Fabian MALBON.

Bailiff of Guernsey and President of the States of Deliberation: Geoffrey Robert ROWLAND.

Chief Minister of Guernsey: Lyndon TROTT.

Isle of Man. Located in the Irish Sea midway between Northern Ireland and northern England, the Isle of Man has been historically connected to Great Britain for over 700 years but remains politically distinct. It has an area of 227 square miles (588 sq. km.) and a population of 80,058 (2006C). The principal town is Douglas, and most income is derived from offshore banking and business services.

The island's self-governing institutions include the High Court of Tynwald (the world's oldest parliament in continuous existence), encompassing a president elected by the court, the Legislative Council, and the House of Keys, which is a 24-member body popularly elected for a five-year term. The Legislative Council includes a president, the lord bishop of Sodor and Man, a nonvoting attorney general, and eight others named by the House of Keys. The British monarch serves as head of state ("Lord of Man") and is represented by a lieutenant governor, who historically functioned as head of government and presided over an Executive Council. In 1986, however, the office of chief minister was created, and in 1990 a Council of Ministers replaced the Executive Council. Concurrently, the president of the Tynwald assumed many of the responsibilities of the lieutenant governor, who nevertheless still reserves important constitutional powers, including the authority to dissolve the House of Keys. The chief minister, elected by the legislature, nominates the other ministers.

The island levies its own taxes and has a special relationship with the EU, falling within the EU customs territory but remaining fiscally independent of it. In August 2000 the Manx administration joined the Channel Islands in agreeing to work with the OECD on tax harmonization, improved financial transparency, and information exchange.

At the election of November 22, 2001, independents won 19 seats in the House of Keys. Candidates affiliated with the **Alliance for Progressive Government** (APG), an identifiable political group but not an official party, won 3 seats, and the **Manx Labour Party** (MLP) won 2. The nationalist **Mec Vannin** (Sons of Mannin), which dates from 1962 and advocates republican independence, boycotts elections.

Following the 2001 polling the incumbent chief minister, Donald GELLING, was unanimously reelected to the post, but he stepped down a year later and was succeeded by Richard CORKHILL. In December 2004 Corkhill resigned because of a financial scandal, and on December 14 Gelling was returned as chief minister. James Anthony (Tony) Brown was elected chief minister on December 14, 2006, resigning, as required by law, his position of speaker of the house. Stephen Rodan was subsequently elected speaker. The November 23, 2008, balloting for the House of Keys resulted in the election of 21 independent members (1 affiliated with the APG), with the **Liberal Vannin Party** (LVP, founded in 2006) winning 2 seats and the MLP 1.

Lieutenant Governor: Sir Paul HADDACKS.

President of the Tynwald: Noel Quayle CRINGLE.

Speaker of the House of Keys: Stephen RODAN.

Chief Minister: James Anthony BROWN.

Inhabited Overseas Territories:

The territories described below remain directly subordinate to the UK, although a number of them enjoy almost complete autonomy in internal affairs. The term "colony" or "crown colony," a historical relic without contemporary legal import, is often still used in reference to these jurisdictions.

Anguilla. One of the most northern of the Caribbean's Leeward Islands (see Antigua/Barbuda map, p. 53), Anguilla has a land area of 35 square miles (91 sq. km.), exclusive of Sombrero's 2 square miles (5 sq. km.), and a resident population (2006E) of 13,100. There is no capital city as such, apart from a centrally located sector known as The Valley. The main industries are tourism, offshore banking and finance, and construction. Overseas remittances from Anguillans living abroad are a substantial source of island revenue.

Anguilla was first settled by the British in 1632 and became part of the Territory of the Leeward Islands in 1956. Following establishment of the Associated State of St. Kitts-Nevis-Anguilla in early 1967, the Anguillans repudiated government from Basseterre, St. Kitts, and a British commissioner was installed following a landing by British security forces in March 1969. The island was subsequently placed under the direct administration of Britain, while a separate constitution that was enacted in February 1976 gave the resident commissioner (subsequently governor) authority over foreign affairs, defense, civil service, and internal security. Other executive functions are undertaken on the advice of an Executive Council that, in accordance with a 1982 constitution (amended in 1990), consists of a chief minister; three additional ministers; and the deputy governor and attorney general, ex officio. Legislative authority, save in respect of the governor's reserve powers, is the responsibility of a House of Assembly encompassing a speaker; seven elected members; two nominated members; and the deputy governor and attorney general, ex officio. An act of December 1980 formally confirmed the dependent status of the territory, which also includes the neighboring island of Sombrero.

Ronald WEBSTER, then leader of the People's Progressive Party, headed Anguilla's government after the separation from St. Kitts-Nevis in 1967 until 1977, when he was replaced by Emile GUMBS, then leader of what became the **Anguilla National Alliance** (ANA). Webster returned to power in 1980 as leader of the **Anguilla United Party** (AUP) but in 1984 was again replaced by Gumbs, who remained chief minister following the 1989 election until his retirement in February 1994 (by which time he was Sir Emile). Meanwhile, Webster had founded what became the **Anguilla Democratic Party** (ADP) but had reverted to the AUP for the 1989 election; subsequently, he formed the **Anguillans for Good Government** (AGG) party.

The March 1994 election failed to produce a clear winner, with the ANA (led by Eric REID), the ADP (led by Victor BANKS), and the AUP (led by Hubert HUGHES) each winning two seats; an independent, one; and Webster's new party, none. The outcome was an AUP-ADP coalition under the chief ministership of the AUP leader. At the election of March 4, 1999, the ANA, led by Osbourne Fleming, captured three house seats, but with the ADP and the AUP again winning two seats each, a renewal of the AUP-ADP coalition permitted Hughes to claim a second term as chief minister. Earlier, Hughes had stated that he hoped to move Anguilla closer to full internal self-government, citing Bermuda as a model and commenting that the present constitution placed ministers in "positions without power."

Within months of the election, a constitutional deadlock developed, Victor Banks having resigned as finance minister over Hughes's managerial style and his failure to consult the ADP. Banks then realigned his ADP with the ANA, and together they began a boycott of the house, leaving it without a quorum. Having failed to convince the High Court that the speaker of the house, a member of the ADP, should be forced to convene the legislature, in January 2000 Hughes asked the governor to call a new election. Held on March 3, the balloting returned all the incumbents to office, but with the **Anguilla United Front** (AUF) alliance of the ANA and the ADP controlling four seats; the AUP, two; and a former ADP member, now an independent, the seventh. On March 6 Osbourne Fleming assumed office as chief minister, with Banks again in charge of finance and economic development as well as investment and commerce.

At the election of February 21, 2005, the AUF retained its four seats; the **Anguilla National Strategic Alliance,** led by opposition leader Edison BAIRD, secured two; and Hubert Hughes's **Anguilla United Movement** won one. Also competing in the election was the **Anguillan Progressive Party** (APP), led by Brent DAVIS.

Anguilla's process for constitutional review and reform, consistent with the 1999 white paper on overseas territories, was jump-started in 2006 with the appointment of a Constitutional and Electoral Reform Commission. The commission presented its report in August of that same year. Negotiations with UK officials over proposed constitutional changes, scheduled for July 2007, were delayed by Chief Minister Fleming in order to extend the period for public consultation. The government issued a press release on July 17, 2007, stating that Anguilla planned to seek "full internal self government" status from the UK.

On April 21, 2009, Alistair Harrison assumed the governorship from Andrew GEORGE, who retired. In a May address Harrison said he considered financial regulation of the off-shore financial industry his top priority. Of particular concern was Anguilla's inclusion on the OECD's so-called grey list of countries that have stated their intention to comply with rules for sharing tax information but have not yet done so.

Governor: Alistair HARRISON.

Chief Minister: Osbourne FLEMING.

Bermuda. Named after Juan de Bermudez, a Spanish sailor who reached the islands in the early 1500s, Bermuda remained uninhabited for a century. Settled by the British and then established as a Crown colony in 1684, it consists of 150 islands and islets in the western Atlantic. It has a total land area of 21 square miles (53 sq. km.) and a population (2006E) of 64,900, concentrated on some 20 islands. Blacks make up approximately 60 percent of the total population. The capital is Hamilton, with a population of approximately 3,000. The main economic activities are offshore business services (principally insurance and reinsurance), tourism, and light manufacturing. Over 10,500 international companies are registered, but only about 300 maintain a physical presence. Customs duties constitute the principal source of government revenue.

Under a constitution approved in mid-1967 (amended, in certain particulars, in 1979), Bermuda was granted a system of internal self-government whereby the Crown-appointed governor, advised by a Governor's Council, exercises responsibility for external affairs, defense, internal security, and police. The governor appoints as premier the majority leader in the lower chamber of the Parliament, the House of Assembly, which is popularly elected for a five-year term. (Formerly consisting of 40 members from 2-member constituencies, the representation was reduced to 36 single-member constituencies prior to the 2003 election.) The 11 members of the upper house, the Senate, are appointed by the governor, including 5 on recommendation of the premier and 3 on recommendation of the leader of the opposition.

The first general election under the new constitution, held in May 1968 against a background of black rioting, resulted in a decisive victory for the moderately right-wing, multiracial **United Bermuda Party** (UBP), whose leader, Sir Henry TUCKER, became the colony's first premier. The left-wing **Progressive Labour Party** (PLP), mainly black in membership, had campaigned for independence and an end to British rule, and its unexpectedly poor showing was generally interpreted as a popular endorsement of the existing constitutional arrangements.

At the election of October 5, 1993, the UBP (led since 1981 by Sir John SWAN) returned 22 members to the House of Assembly against 18 for the PLP (led by Frederick WADE), while the **National Liberal Party** (NLP; led by Gilbert DARRELL) lost the seat it had won in 1989. In February 1994, following an announcement that U.S. and UK forces would vacate Bermuda in 1995, the new legislature voted 20–18 in favor of holding a referendum on independence. The consultation eventually took place on August 16, 1995, with traditional party lines being partially reversed in that Sir John and some other UBP leaders (although not the party as such) urged a "yes" vote and the pro-independence PLP advocated abstention. Of a 58.8 percent turnout, 73.6 percent of the voters opposed independence, whereupon Sir John resigned from the premiership and UBP leadership and was replaced by Finance Minister David SAUL. The new premier moved to heal divisions within the UBP remaining from the bruising independence referendum and a subsequent conflict in the summer of 1996 over approval of a franchise license for a fast food chain. Three members who had rebelled against party leadership on both issues were returned to cabinet portfolios in January 1997, although the moves were insufficient to save the premier. On March 27 Saul was replaced by Pamela GORDON, the new leader of the UBP. Earlier, in December 1996, Jennifer SMITH had been elected leader of the PLP following the death in August of Frederick Wade.

Premier Gordon's decision to reshuffle her cabinet in May 1998 failed to prevent a dramatic victory by the PLP at the election of November 9. The PLP won for the first time, capturing 26 house seats versus 14 for the UBP, which had been in power for three decades. The victory was even more remarkable in that the winning party had run only 34 candidates for the 40 seats. Jennifer Smith was sworn in as premier on November 10 and shortly thereafter named a cabinet of 12 additional ministers, all but 1 black.

At the election of July 24, 2003, the PLP won 22 House seats and the UBP 14. Although reinstalled as premier, Smith had drawn criticism for an alleged "arrogant and secretive" leadership style and was forced to step down on July 28 in favor of Alex SCOTT.

In December 2004 the issue of independence was reopened by Prime Minister Scott, who announced the establishment of a Bermuda Independence Commission (BIC) that was instructed to hold public hearings on the subject in early 2005. While the current government favors independence, a July 2007 opinion poll indicated that 63 percent of Bermudans opposed it, with 25 percent in favor and 12 percent undecided.

At an October 2006 PLP delegate conference Dr. Ewart Brown was elected party chair by a 107–76 vote over Alex Scott. Brown was subsequently sworn in as premier on October 30. UBP leader Wayne FURBERT stepped down on March 31, 2007, and was replaced by Michael DUNKLEY on April 2 by a unanimous vote.

The Brown government's health minister resigned from the cabinet in February 2007 amid the opening of a criminal investigation into his business activities. In June the police arrested the former minister under theft and corruption charges. A new heath minister was sworn in on June 12.

At the election of December 18, 2007, in a replay of the previous balloting, the PLP won 22 House seats and the UBP 14. New UBP leader Michael Dunkley failed to win reelection from his constituency, leaving the party in disarray.

Sir John VEREKER stepped down as governor in October 2007 and was replaced by Sir Richard GOZNEY in December.

Governor: Sir Richard GOZNEY.

Premier: Ewart BROWN.

British Indian Ocean Territory. At the time of its establishment in 1965 the British Indian Ocean Territory consisted of the Chagos Archipelago, which had previously been a dependency of Mauritius, and the islands of Aldabra, Farquhar, and Desroches, which had traditionally been administered from the Seychelles (see Mauritius map, p. 868). The territory was created to make defense facilities available to the British and U.S. governments and was legally construed as being uninhabited, although in 1967–1973 some 1,800 Chagos Islanders (Ilois) were relocated from Diego Garcia in the Chagos group to make way for the construction of U.S. air and naval installations. Upon the granting of independence to the Seychelles in June 1976, arrangements were made for the reversion of Aldabra, Farquhar, and Desroches, the territory thenceforth to consist only of the Chagos Archipelago, with its administration taken over by the Foreign and Commonwealth Office. The total land area of the archipelago, which stretches over some 21,000 square miles (54,400 sq. km.) of the central Indian Ocean, is 20 square miles (52 sq. km.). At present, the only inhabitants are some 2,000 members of the British and U.S. military plus another 1,500 civilian personnel (mainly Filipinos and Sri Lankans) providing services for the Diego Garcia naval facility.

On March 3, 1999, the UK High Court ruled that the Chagos Refugee Group, led by Louis Olivier BANCOULT, could challenge the legality of the Ilois removal. The majority of the Ilois had settled in Mauritius, from where they have long pressed unsuccessful compensation claims. Appearing in the High Court in 2000, the claimants' counselor successfully argued that the 1971 Immigration Ordinance, which barred permanent residence in the archipelago, should be overturned, in part because it violated the European Convention on Human Rights. In 2004, however, the UK Privy Council issued orders in council that again placed visits to the islands under immigration control. On May 11, 2006, the High Court overruled the orders, calling the removal of the Chagossians "repugnant" and opening the possibility of their return. In late June the UK government indicated that it would appeal the decision. Meanwhile, in late March 102 islanders had set sail from Mauritius for a 12-day visit to the archipelago, the first such excursion permitted by the UK in more than three decades.

Under the joint usage agreements between the UK and the United States, the archipelago will be ceded to Mauritius when it is no longer needed for defense purposes.

The UK government began its appeal on February 5, 2007, of the High Court's 2006 decision overturning the removal order. In March Mauritian president Sir Anerood Jugnauth revealed that Mauritius was prepared to withdraw from the Commonwealth in order to bring the UK before the International Court of Justice (IJC) on behalf of the Chagossians. On May 23, 2007, the court of appeal upheld the previous decision and ordered the UK government to pay the Chagossians' legal fees and allow resettlement of all but Diego Garcia. The government appealed the decision to the House of Lords, and in October 2008 the lower court ruling was overturned, thereby barring the return of the Chagossians and removing any obligation for the UK government to pay further compensation.

Commissioner: Colin ROBERTS (resident in United Kingdom).
Administrator: Joanne YEADON (resident in United Kingdom).

British Virgin Islands. A Caribbean group of 46 northern Leeward Islands located some 60 miles east of Puerto Rico, the British Virgin Islands have a total area of 59 square miles (153 sq. km.) and a population (2006E) of 22,465. Tourism and international business are the main industries, with the latter reportedly accounting for 90 percent of government revenue. The largest island, Tortola, is the site of the chief town and port of entry, Road Town (population 11,000 in 2002). The administration is headed by a governor. Representative institutions include a 15-member Legislative Council (13 elected members serving four-year terms; the attorney general, ex officio; and a speaker) and a 6-member Executive Council appointed and chaired by the governor. A chief minister is chosen from the legislature by the governor.

At the election of September 1986 the **Virgin Islands Party** (VIP), led by H. Lavity STOUTT, won five of nine Council seats, ousting the administration headed by independent member Cyril B. ROMNEY, who had been involved with a company undergoing investigation for money laundering. In March 1988 the deputy chief minister, Omar HODGE, was dismissed for attempting to delay the issuance of a report charging him with bribery; the following year he formed the **Independent People's Movement** (IPM). Stoutt remained in office following the balloting of November 2, 1990, at which the VIP won six seats; the IPM, one; and independents, two. The **United Party** (UP), led by Conrad MADURO, lost the two seats it had held since 1986.

In early 1994 a proposal by a UK constitutional review commission to expand the Legislative Council to 13 elective seats by adding four "at-large" members drew criticism from several islands parties. Chief Minister Stoutt led the attack on the plan, but to no avail. Balloting on February 20, 1995, for the 13 legislators yielded 6 seats for the VIP, 2 for the UP, 2 for Hodge's new **Concerned Citizen's Movement** (CCM), and 3 for independents. One of the independents sided with the VIP in return for a ministerial post, enabling Stoutt to begin a fifth successive term as chief minister. However, Stoutt died unexpectedly on May 16 and was succeeded by Deputy Chief Minister Ralph O'Neal. The opposition—numbering five members—received an unexpected boost when two supporters of the government temporarily switched sides in April 1997, coming close to bringing the government down. By June, however, the failure to unseat the government and dissatisfaction with the leadership of the UP's Maduro led three of the five opposition members to rebel, and in December 1997 Maduro was replaced as leader of the opposition by the leader of the CCM, Walwyn BREWLEY.

The VIP claimed a narrow election victory at balloting on May 17, 1999, winning seven seats in the Legislative Council to five for the recently formed **National Democratic Party** (NDP) and one for the CCM. Both the CCM and the UP took less than 10 percent of the total constituency and at-large votes, many of their previous supporters having switched allegiance to the NDP, led by Orlando SMITH.

At the election of June 16, 2003, the NDP won eight seats and the VIP five, permitting Smith to head the new government.

The Smith government won unanimous approval from the Legislative Council for its proposed draft of a new constitution in May 2007. The UK Privy Council ratified the bill and the new constitution came into force on June 15, 2007. Among the new powers of the British Virgin Islands government was the creation of a national security council.

The VIP regained control of the government at balloting on August 20, 2007, winning in a landslide with ten seats to two for the NDP, while the remaining elective seat went to an independent. Voter turnout was 66 percent. Ralph O'Neal headed the new government as First Premier under the new constitution (formerly the position was titled Chief Minister).

Governor: David PEARY.
First Premier: Ralph Telford O'NEAL.

Cayman Islands. Located in the Caribbean, northwest of Jamaica, the Cayman Islands (Grand Cayman, Little Cayman, and Cayman Brac) cover 100 square miles (259 sq. km.) and have a population (2006E) of 47,400. George Town, on Grand Cayman, is the capital. The traditional occupations of seafaring and turtle and shark fishing have largely been superseded by tourism and other services. The islands have become one of the world's half-dozen largest offshore banking centers as well as a corporate tax haven. As of January 2000, 570 banks and trust companies, more than 2,200 mutual funds, some 500 insurance companies, and 47,000 other companies were registered. In mid-1999 the territory became the first government to request certification under the newly introduced UN Offshore Initiative. Accordingly, the UN Global Programme against Money Laundering had agreed to review the islands' banking and financial systems.

Discovered by Columbus in the early 1500s, the essentially uninhabited Caymans passed from Spain to England in 1670. Governed from Jamaica from the 1860s until 1959 and then briefly a part of the Federation of the West Indies, the islands were placed in 1962 under a British administrator (later governor), who chairs an Executive Council of 8 other members, including 3 ex officio and 5 chosen by and from among the Legislative Assembly. The latter body initially consisted of a speaker, 3 ex officio members, and 12 elected members. At balloting for an enlarged assembly on November 18, 1992, a National Team of government critics won 12 of the elective 15 seats, the remaining 3 going to independents. The outcome rendered uncertain a plan to introduce ministerial government, as the National Team had campaigned against it. However, after deliberations involving the governor and London, a ministerial system was introduced under a constitutional revision implemented in February 1994. Thus, the 5 elected members of the Executive Council now have ministerial responsibilities.

At a general election on November 22, 1996, the National Team secured nine seats, while two recently formed groupings, the **Democratic Alliance** and **Team Cayman,** took two and one, respectively, with independents winning three. In 1997 W. McKeeva Bush, now of the **United Democratic Party** (UDP), was ousted from the Executive Council following allegations that a bank of which he was a director had approved more than $1 billion in fraudulent loans.

In June 2000 George Town expressed astonishment at the decision of the international Financial Action Task Force (FATF) to place the Caymans on its list of 15 jurisdictions considered noncooperative with efforts to combat money laundering. In addition to having repeatedly asked the FATF to visit the Caymans, the government had recently been praised by the UK's Foreign and Commonwealth Office for its regulatory and enforcement efforts. In June 2001 Cayman Islands was delisted.

At the election held on May 11, 2005, after a six-month postponement because of damage from Hurricane Ivan in September 2004, the **People's Progressive Movement** (PPM), led by Kurt TIBBETTS, won 9 of the 15 elective seats, while the UDP won 5 and an independent, 1.

The Caymans' constitutional review process, dubbed the Constitutional Modernization Initiative, is multistaged. In October 2007 the government hosted a roundtable discussion on including a bill of rights and launched a voter registration drive for a constitutional referendum.

A discussion paper on proposed changes was released in May 2008. A referendum on the matter was originally scheduled for July, but UDP leaders argued that the timetable provided insufficient time for debate. The government consequently postponed the referendum until the general election in May 2009, at which the draft constitution received 63 percent support. Meanwhile, the UDP won nine seats, the PPM five, and independents one in the general election.

Newly elected assembly members were sworn in on Mary 27, 2009, with Bush returning to the post of Leader of Government Business. Throughout the remainder of the year the Bush administration struggled to deal with the deeply troubling government debt crisis and a much threatened financial sector by seeking and receiving a $277 million loan from the UK government and pledging to cut spending to austerity levels. However, Bush resisted calls from the UK to impose new taxes, claiming that they would negatively alter the islands' unique economic base. The new constitution entered into force on November 6, and Bush was sworn in as premier, the territory's first, the same day.

Governor: Stuart JACK.
Premier: William McKeeva BUSH.

Falkland Islands. Situated some 480 miles northeast of Cape Horn in the South Atlantic (see Argentina map, p. 51), the Falkland Islands currently encompasses the East and West Falklands in addition to some 200 smaller islands; the South Georgia and the South Sandwich islands ceased to be governed as dependencies of the Falklands in 1985. The total area is 4,700 square miles (12,173 sq. km.), and the resident population, almost entirely of British extraction, is 2,172 (2006C), excluding civilian employees of a British military base, who numbered 534 in 2001; most inhabitants live in the capital, Stanley, on East Falkland Island. The economy, traditionally dependent on wool production, has diversified in recent years, with fishing licenses now being the main source of revenue. Tourism has also increased in importance.

Under a constitution introduced in 1985 (replacing one dating from 1977), the governor is assisted by a Legislative Council that includes eight members elected on a nonpartisan basis (most recently on November 17, 2005) and by an Executive Council, three of whose members are selected by and from the elected legislators. In addition, both bodies have two ex officio members and a chief executive and a financial secretary, who are responsible to the governor. The attorney general and the commander of British forces may also attend Executive Council sessions.

The territory is the object of a long-standing dispute between Britain and Argentina, which calls it the Malvinas Islands (*Islas Malvinas*). Argentina's claim to sovereignty is based primarily on purchase of the islands by Spain from France in 1766; Britain claims sovereignty on the basis of a 1771 treaty, although uninterrupted possession commenced only in 1833. The Argentine claim has won some support in the UN General Assembly, and the two governments engaged in a lengthy series of inconclusive talks on the future disposition of the territory prior to the Argentine invasion of April 2, 1982, and the eventual reassertion of British control ten weeks later (see Argentina article). The issue is complicated by evidence that significant oil and gas deposits may lie beneath the islands' territorial waters. In addition, Britain has taken the position that any solution must respect the wishes of the inhabitants. Thus, the current constitution refers explicitly to the islanders' right of self-determination.

In the wake of the 1982 war, Britain imposed a 150-mile protective zone, to which it added a 200-mile economic zone, effective February 1, 1987, although only a 150-mile radius was subsequently policed, principally to protect Falklands fisheries. As part of the 1990 Madrid agreement that led to the resumption of diplomatic relations with Argentina, Britain maintained its claim to a 200-mile economic zone but conceded that Argentine ships and planes could approach within 50 and 75 miles, respectively, of the islands without prior permission. In a further concession to Buenos Aires, London agreed in November 1990 to convert its 200-mile zone (exclusive of overlap with Argentina's own 200-mile limit) into an Anglo-Argentine cooperation area from which fishing fleets from other countries would be excluded.

In 1992 President Carlos Menem of Argentina pursued a dual policy of behind-the-scenes diplomacy and public assertions of the inevitability of Argentinean sovereignty over the Falklands. In November the first direct meeting between islanders' representatives and an Argentinean minister since 1982 took place in London. A major issue was Argentina's policy of reducing the cost of its fishing licenses in an attempt to lure foreign fleets into Argentinean waters and thus to deprive the Falklands government of its main source of revenue. In legislative elections on October 14, 1993, the eight elective seats were contested by 25 candidates, all independents, with those elected all rejecting unnecessary contact with Argentina until its sovereignty claim was dropped.

After the new Argentinean constitution promulgated in August 1994 repeated the claim to the islands, the UK government announced that the full 200-mile Falklands' economic zone would be policed even where it overlapped with the Argentinean zone. Talks in London in October at the foreign minister level made little progress on possible joint oil exploration in Falklands waters and other issues, while the collateral confirmation by President Menem that Argentina was prepared to pay substantial individual compensation to islanders in exchange for sovereignty did nothing to improve relations.

In October 1996 the Falklands administration issued oil exploration licenses to 13 companies, refusing only one application, from a consortium with Argentinean involvement. In a significant departure from previous policy, President Menem on December 30 suggested that sovereignty over the islands might be shared. His suggestion was immediately rejected by the UK government and by the Falkland Islands administration.

In April 1998 the UK announced that oil exploration of the Falklands coast had started, while in Argentina legislators introduced a bill to impose sanctions on commercial companies that failed to obtain Argentinean permission before operating in Falkland waters. The following October President Menem paid the first official visit to the UK by an Argentinean leader in nearly 40 years. Topics covered in a meeting with Prime Minister Blair included Falklands relations, while a subsequent letter from Menem to the islanders called for reconciliation "to heal old wounds." With secret talks reportedly under way on the territory's status, in January 1999 Buenos Aires offered to put in abeyance its sovereignty claim if the UK, in a largely symbolic gesture, would permit Argentinean flags to fly at selected locations, including the graveyard for its service-members killed during the Falklands war. Two months later Prince Charles visited both the Falklands and Argentina, where he laid a wreath at a monument to casualties of the conflict, as President Menem had done in England during his 1998 visit.

In May 1999 an Argentinean ministerial delegation met in London with members of the Falklands Legislative Council. Discussion topics included fishing and air connections. In the latter regard, in March Chile had announced a halt to Falklands flights—the only such contact between the islands and South America—to protest the continuing detention in London of former president Augusto Pinochet, pending resolution of a Spanish extradition warrant for human rights abuses during his reign. In July Buenos Aires and London agreed to permit air travel between Argentina and the islands, and Chile resumed flights with stopovers in Argentina.

In early 2004 Argentina granted its flagship airline two routes between Buenos Aires and Stanley. However, the islanders rejected the prospect of regularly scheduled flights from Argentina, and the recently installed Néstor Kirchner regime responded by denying permission for Chilean planes to fly through Argentine air space. Meanwhile, the Falkland economy, which had expanded 13-fold in the two decades after the war, was increasingly imperiled by a decline in sales of fishing licenses that was attributed to collapse in stocks of the previously abundant Ilex squid.

Relations between the UK and Argentina soured further in 2006 as President Kirchner, backed by the UN Special Committee on Decolonization and the Organization of American States, repeated his call for London to reopen negotiations on the territory's future status. Kirchner also indicated that he was considering taking a more hard-line approach on the issues of fishing rights and oil exploration. Upon his wife's investment in the presidency in 2007 (see Argentina entry), Cristina Fernández de Kirchner maintained Argentina's right to the islands. For its part, the British government reiterated that it had no intention to negotiate sovereignty in the absence of evidence that the islanders themselves sought a change.

A new constitution was announced for the islands in November 2008, effective January 1, 2009. In order to enhance internal self-government, the governor was required by the new constitution to abide by the advice of the Executive Council on most domestic policies. However, the governor retained veto power with respect to external, defense, and justice policies as well as when the governor deems the advice of the council to be contrary to the "the interests of good government." The new constitution also tightened rules for the acquisition of Falkland "status" (and thereby voting rights), installed the chief executive as head of the civil service, established a public accounts committee and a complaints commissioner in order to enhance transparency, and adopted provisions of the European Convention on Human Rights. The UK government emphasized that the constitutional revisions did not change the UK's commitment to the islands, nor the status of the islands as an overseas territory, nor the Falklanders' right to self-determination.

Governor: Alan HUCKLE. (Huckle's term was scheduled to end in September 2010, and the UK government announced that his successor would be Nigel HAYWOOD.)

Chief Executive: Tim THORGOOD.

Gibraltar. The territory of Gibraltar, a rocky promontory at the western mouth of the Mediterranean, was captured by the British in 1704 and ceded by Spain to the UK by the Treaty of Utrecht in 1713. It has an area of 2.1 square miles (5.5 sq. km.), and its population numbers 29,600 (2006E), of whom about 21,000 are native Gibraltarians. The economy was long dependent on expenditures in support of its air and naval facilities; in recent years, however, tourism and financial services have grown in importance, and special status within the EC/EU has permitted it to transship foreign goods without payment of such duties as value-added taxes. Financial services currently constitute about one-fifth of the economy, significantly more than UK defense expenditures.

British authority is represented by a governor. Substantial self-government was introduced in 1964 and further extended in 1969 by a new constitution that provided for a House of Assembly of 15 elected and 2 ex officio members (the attorney general and the financial and development secretary), plus a speaker appointed by the governor. Of the elected members, no more than 8 can represent the same party. The executive Gibraltar Council, chaired by the governor, has 4 additional ex officio members and 4 other members, including a chief minister, drawn from the elected members of the House of Assembly. The governor names as chief minister the majority leader in the assembly.

Gibraltar has been the subject of a lengthy dispute between Britain and Spain, which has pressed in the UN and elsewhere for "decolonization" of the territory and has impeded access to it by land and air. A referendum conducted by the British in 1967 showed an overwhelming preference for continuation of British rule, but Spain rejected the results and declared the referendum invalid. Spain's position was subsequently upheld by the UN General Assembly, which called in December 1968 for the ending of British administration by October 1, 1969. A month after promulgation of the 1969 constitution, which guarantees that the Gibraltarians will never have to accept Spanish rule unless the majority so desires, Spain closed its land frontier. In January 1978 Spain agreed to the restoration of telephone links to the city, but the border was not fully reopened until February 1985, following an agreement in November 1984 to provide equality of rights for Spaniards in Gibraltar and Gibraltarians in Spain; in addition, Britain agreed, for the first time, to enter into discussions on the sovereignty issue.

At the election of March 1988 the **Gibraltar Socialist Labour Party** (GSLP) won the permissible maximum of eight legislative seats, its leader, Joe BOSSANO, becoming chief minister. Upon assuming office Bossano declared that most of the residents opposed the 1984 accord with Spain. Earlier, in December 1987, the assembly had rejected a UK-Spanish agreement on cooperative administration of the territory's airport. Quite apart from the impact of exclusive British control on the sovereignty issue, Spain has argued that the isthmus to the mainland, on which the airport is located, was not covered by the 1713 treaty.

The GSLP was again victorious at the election of January 16, 1992, retaining its majority with a vote share of 73 percent; the **Gibraltar Social Democrats** (GSD), led by Peter Caruana, won seven seats and the **Gibraltar National Party** (GNP), led by Dr. Joseph GARCIA, none. Following the election, Bossano insisted that his party's campaign for greater autonomy from Britain was not anti-Spanish, but rather "a clear expression of the desire for self-determination." Declining tourism and rising unemployment in 1993 caused further strains with Britain, which Bossano accused of neglecting Gibraltar's interests at the EU level.

The December 1994 round of UK-Spanish foreign ministers' talks on Gibraltar was snagged by heightened Spanish vigilance and consequential delays at the border crossing. Part of the Spanish concern was that Gibraltarians were increasingly supplementing traditional cigarette smuggling operations with drug trafficking and money laundering. In July 1995 UK pressure led the government to table a bill designed to stop money laundering and to bring Gibraltar's offshore banking into line with British and EU standards. Meanwhile, Chief Minister Bossano maintained his refusal to participate in the UK-Spanish talks, calling instead for direct discussions with Madrid on self-determination for Gibraltar.

A more flexible stance by the center-right GSD, which held that negotiations could proceed on any issue other than sovereignty, won the support of 48 percent of voters in a general election on May 16, 1996, with the GSLP slumping to 39 percent. The GSD secured eight assembly seats against seven for the GSLP, with the GNP again failing to win representation despite taking 13 percent of the vote. GSD leader Peter Caruana was sworn in as chief minister, pledging to participate in UK-Spanish talks.

In April 1998, in a shift of strategy, Madrid offered to open bilateral talks with Chief Minister Caruana regarding its recent proposal that Britain and Spain share sovereignty during a transitional period, with Gibraltar ultimately to achieve self-governing status under Spain—a proposal that Caruana and the Blair government dismissed. Later in the year both sides demonstrated a willingness to improve cooperation with regard to overflights of Spanish territory by Royal Air Force and NATO aircraft as well as the use and development of Gibraltar's airport. In 1999, however, a continuing dispute over fishing rights off Gibraltar for Spanish trawlers led Spanish customs officials to enforce strict, time-consuming border controls in retaliation. In October Caruana labeled bilateral talks on sovereignty between London and Madrid as "inappropriate and unacceptable." Instead, he proposed a "two flags, three voices" approach—the third voice being Gibraltar—which Spain has rejected.

In January 2000 Caruana surprised the opposition by calling an election for February 10, three months ahead of schedule. At the balloting his GSD increased its vote share to 58 percent and again claimed eight seats in the House of Assembly. An alliance of Bossano's GSLP and Joseph Garcia's small **Gibraltar Liberal Party** (successor to the GNP) won the other seven elective seats.

Two months later, on April 19, 2000, Spain and Britain announced that they had resolved differences over the territory's administrative status. Madrid's refusal to accept Gibraltar as a "competent authority" had delayed a range of EU business and economic initiatives. Spain agreed to recognize the validity of various documents issued by Gibraltar, including passports and identity cards. Britain agreed to act as a "postal box," relaying communications to and from Spain, which could thereby continue to avoid direct contact with the Gibraltar government. In addition, the agreement cleared the way for Britain to accede to parts of the EU's Schengen agreement on frontier controls, and it opened the way for Gibraltar-based financial corporations to compete throughout the EU. Chief Minister Caruana responded to the announcement of the agreement by saying, "Spain, Britain, and Gibraltar have all preserved their interests; there are no winners and no losers."

For the first time since December 1997, ministerial talks between Spain and the UK resumed on July 26, 2001, and by early 2002 it was clear that the two sides were moving closer toward a joint sovereignty arrangement. However, the prospect of any such arrangement was greeted with scorn by Caruana and generated, over the ensuing months, massive demonstrations by Gibraltarians.

Madrid and London nonetheless pressed ahead and by mid-2002 had reached agreement on joint rule, though differing as to its duration. The UK clearly viewed it as more than "transitional." In addition, Britain insisted that its military bases remain under its control. Caruana, meanwhile, refused to participate in the talks, save as an equal partner. Subsequently, on November 7, Gibraltar mounted a referendum in which 98.9 percent of the participants voted against shared sovereignty. At the most recent general election of November 28, 2003, Caruana's Gibraltar Social Democrats retained its eight seats, while the GSLP-Liberal alliance again won seven.

After winning a challenge before the European Court of Human Rights to Gibraltar's exclusion from participating in elections to the European Parliament as part of the UK, Gibraltarians cast EU ballots for the first time in 2004 (as part of the South West England constituency). The UK's Conservative Party secured 69.5 percent of the vote from Gibraltar, reflecting dissatisfaction with the Labour government's joint sovereignty proposal as well as the significant attention (including an appearance by Conservative leader Michael Howard) voters in Gibraltar had received from the Conservatives.

In October 2004 Spain agreed, for the first time, to give Gibraltar a seat at the negotiating table, which led to the first three-party discussion in December. On February 10, 2005, the first session of a Trilateral Forum, with an open agenda, met in Malaga, Spain. Issues considered by the forum have included the airport and benefits for Spanish workers, but sovereignty has remained off the table.

On November 30, 2006, a referendum approved the new constitution, which was implemented on January 2, 2007. The updated constitution aimed to "modernize" relations with Britain, emphasize self-determination, and strengthen local autonomy, notably by increasing the number of legislative seats to 17, with the House of Assembly renamed the Gibraltar Parliament. The governor's veto powers were curtailed and those of the British foreign secretary were eliminated.

Workers' concerns again took prominence on January 18, 2007, as over 10,000 protested against conditions proposed in the Trade Unions and Workforce In-House Option Submission legislation, rejected by the House of Assembly two days earlier. The government then fashioned an agreement with three leading unions to improve job security within the ministry of defense.

An August 12 collision between a Danish tanker, *Torm Gertrude*, and *New Flame*, a bulk carrier, prompted official complaints that Spanish beaches were being polluted. These claims were rejected by the Gibraltar government, but the incident emphasized the importance of coordination on maritime safety between the two neighbors.

In elections held October 11, 2007, the Gibraltar Social Democrats received 49 percent of votes; the Gibraltar Socialist Labour Party-Liberal coalition, 45 percent; the **Progressive Democratic Party**, 4 percent; the Parental Support Group, 1 percent; and the **New Gibraltar Democracy Party,** 1 percent. Turnout was 84.1 percent. (The **Progressive Democratic Party** [PDP] was launched in 2006, touting itself as a "positive alternative" for voters dissatisfied with the two major parties.) Caruana remained chief minister, with 10 seats in the Gibraltar Parliament, while the GSLP-Liberal alliance claimed 7.

Voters from Gibraltar showed their continued support for the UK Conservative Party by giving it 53.3 percent of the vote in the June

2009 balloting for the European Parliament. No other party received as much as 20 percent.

Governor and Commander in Chief: Sir Adrian JOHNS.

Chief Minister: Peter CARUANA.

Montserrat. A West Indian dependency in the Leeward Island group (see Antigua/Barbuda map, p. 48) with an area of 39.4 square miles (102 sq. km.), Montserrat had a population (1996E) of 10,500 prior to large-scale evacuation (see below), which reduced the total to 4,482 in the 2001 census before recovering to an estimated 4,800 in 2006. Its principal sources of income are tourism, offshore business services, and export of machinery and transport equipment. Ministerial government was introduced in 1960, the territory currently being administered by an Executive Council comprising the chief minister, three additional elected ministers, and two ex officio members (attorney general and financial secretary) under the presidency of the London-appointed governor. The Legislative Council is composed of nine elected and the same two ex officio members. Elections are normally held every five years.

In August 1987 John OSBORNE of the **People's Liberation Movement** (PLM) was installed for a third five-year term as chief minister. In August 1989 a dispute arose between Osborne and Gov. Christopher TURNER over the latter's alleged failure to inform elected officials of police raids on banks suspected of illicit financial transactions. In late November, with most banking licenses having been canceled, the Organization of Eastern Caribbean States issued a statement condemning as "absolutely repugnant" an announcement by the UK Foreign and Commonwealth Office (FCO) that a proposed new constitution would transfer responsibility for offshore banking regulation to the governor. In return for Osborne's acceptance of the controversial change, the new basic law as implemented in February 1990 recognized Montserrat's right to self-determination and withdrew certain legislative powers formerly held by the governor.

Osborne's PLM retained only one seat in the balloting of October 8, 1991, after which a new administration was formed by the **National Progressive Party** (NPP), led by Reuben MEADE, who had accused the Osborne administration of corruption and mismanagement. Efforts by the new Legislative Council to reestablish Montserrat as an offshore banking center failed. On February 2, 1993, after an investigation by Scotland Yard, Osborne and Noel TUITT, an associate, were cleared of the corruption charges, and in March 1994 Tuitt joined the NPP government following Meade's dismissal of David BRANDT as deputy chief minister. A partial eruption of long-dormant Chance's Peak volcano on July 19, 1995, precipitated the evacuation of some 5,000 people from their homes by late August. Further disruption was caused by a hurricane and tropical storm in September.

The eruptions continued intermittently in 1996, by the end of which the entire population of the southern part of the island, including the capital, Plymouth, had been evacuated; 800 were admitted to Britain under a special exemption from normally strict immigration rules, and the rest were housed in temporary accommodation in the north, where the second town, St. Peter's, became the de facto capital. With the island administration and the UK overseas aid program disputing how emergency aid grants should be used, the NPP retained only one seat in an election that was held on November 11 even though four southern election districts were either empty or depopulated by evacuation. Two seats were won by the **Movement for National Reconstruction** (MNR), two by John Osborne's new **People's Progressive Alliance** (PPA), and two by independents. The outcome was an MNR-PPA coalition, MNR leader Bertrand OSBORNE being sworn in as chief minister on November 13.

In June 1997 the Soufrière Hills volcano erupted, claiming at least 19 lives and obliterating the capital. By the end of the year, only 3,400 of the original population were still on the island (with 500 living in temporary shelters), the remainder having either migrated to the UK or relocated to adjacent islands. The destruction slowed economic activity to a near standstill.

As aid packages were caught up in London's governmental transition in May–June 1997 and the island administration was coping with abandoning the capital, simmering discontent grew among the islanders. On August 21, 1997, after four days of continuous demonstrations and protest, Chief Minister Osborne resigned and was replaced by independent David Brandt, who received the support of the MNR and NPP. Almost immediately, the new chief minister created conflict with London, alleging that aid packages for reconstruction and personal assistance, especially for off-island relocation, were insufficient to meet the emergency and that British policy was directed at depopulating the island. The criticism led London's secretary of state for international development to assert that the island was asking for "mad money" and "golden elephants next." A November 27, 1997, report by a Commons select committee placed blame for delays and maladministration on all parties, leading to a rationalization of the aid process and a gradual cooling of tensions.

On February 14, 1998, Robin Cook became the first FCO secretary to visit Montserrat. In May the UK government announced that all Montserratians who had not resettled elsewhere would be allowed to reside in Britain, while in June a draft development plan for the northern part of the island was announced. Despite continuing periodic volcanic activity and additional damage caused by Hurricane Georges in September, residents and businesses gradually began returning to the island's central zone. In 1999 the Blair administration announced that it would pay relocation travel costs for most Montserratians who wished to return to the island from Britain or Caribbean relocation sites. At the same time, the island administration moved forward with a proposal to build a new capital at Little Bay, on the northwestern coast, a project expected to take at least ten years to complete.

With the devastation in the south having made the parliamentary constituency system unworkable, in 2000 the government introduced legislation to facilitate adoption of a nine-member, at-large system for the 2001 election. By mid-2000 the resident population numbered about 5,000.

The collapse of Chief Minister Brandt's coalition in February 2001 precipitated an early election. At balloting on April 2 John Osborne's **New People's Liberation Movement** (NPLM) won seven of the nine seats in the Legislative Council, permitting him to reclaim the title of chief minister a decade after his last term in office. The NPP won the other two council seats.

Three parties and four independents contested the May 2006 legislative election. Although Rosalind CASSELL-SEALY's recently formed **Movement for Change and Prosperity** (MCAP) won four of the nine seats, Osborne's NPLM, which won three, formed a coalition administration with independent David BRANDT and Lowell LEWIS, the head of the **Montserrat Democratic Party** (MDP) and the leading vote-getter. Lewis stated after the election that the government's priorities would be the economy, housing, use of natural resources, and discussions with London about development projects, including a safe harbor and marina at Little Bay that would attract more visitors.

Montserrat's constitutional review commissioners made their initial report in 2002. The Legislative Council reviewed this in 2005 and made recommendations to the UK government in April of that year. Four rounds of talks with Monserratian and British officials followed, with the latest held in May 2007.

In June 2009 Chief Minister Lewis removed two cabinet ministers and called an election for September 8, two years earlier than required. The balloting produced a six-seat majority for the MCAP, and its leader, Reuben Meade, was sworn in as chief minister on September 9. The three remaining seats were won by independents, including Lewis.

Governor: Peter WATERWORTH.

Chief Minister: Reuben MEADE.

Pitcairn Islands. Isolated in the eastern South Pacific and known primarily because of its settlement in 1790 by the *Bounty* mutineers, Pitcairn has been a British possession since 1838. Jurisdictionally encompassing the adjacent uninhabited islands of Ducie, Henderson, and Oeno, the dependency has a total area of 1.75 square miles (4.53 sq. km.) and a declining population, which in 2005 totaled 48 persons. The only established community is Adamstown. The largest island of the group, Henderson, is a UNESCO World Heritage Site and wildlife sanctuary.

The British high commissioner to New Zealand serves as governor. Locally, the island is administered by an Island Council that also has judicial responsibilities. It consists of ten members: an elected island mayor, who serves a three-year term; the chair of the council, ex officio; four directly elected members; one member indirectly selected by the chair and the elected members; two members nominated by the governor, including the island secretary; and a commissioner, who serves as liaison, linking the mayor, council, and governor. All but the mayor and secretary serve one-year terms. The offices of mayor and council chair were established in 1999, prior to which the duties of both were performed by an island magistrate.

The island administration is the only significant source of regular employment, although efforts to organize apiculture and dried fruit industries have begun. Other sources of income are the sale of stamps and handicrafts as well as *Bounty*-related souvenirs. Pitcairn has also begun licensing its Internet designation, "pn," an international abbreviation for "telephone." At present, the territory is accessible only by ship, but a recent privately funded feasibility study concluded that an airstrip could be built, which would make possible an air connection to Mangareve, French Polynesia, some 310 miles away. The UK Department for International Development has funded repairs to infrastructure and provision of limited television and Internet service, as well as telephone connections for each household.

In mid-2004 a scandal that had simmered for more than a decade erupted with charges of child rape, incest, and indecent assault against seven men, including the island mayor, Steve CHRISTIAN. Upon Christian's conviction in October, the Island Council designated his sister, Brenda CHRISTIAN, as interim mayor. On December 15 the islanders elected Jay WARREN, a former council chair and the only one of the seven to be acquitted, as her successor. In July 2006, hearing the final appeal of the six convicted defendants, the Privy Council quickly rejected assertions that they neither understood nor were subject to British law. In December 2007 Mike Warren defeated Jay Warren in a three-person mayoralty election.

Governor: George FERGUSSON (resident in New Zealand).
Commissioner: Leslie JAQUES (resident in New Zealand).
Island Mayor: Mike WARREN.

St. Helena. St. Helena and its dependencies, Ascension Island and the Tristan da Cunha island group, occupy widely scattered positions in the South Atlantic between the west coast of Africa and the southern tip of South America. St. Helena, the seat of government, has an area of 47 square miles (122 sq. km.) and a population (2005E) of 4,460. Its principal settlement is Jamestown. The economy currently depends on budgetary aid from the UK and on the sale of fishing licenses; small quantities of coffee are exported. Remittances from abroad also provide income, and a fish freezing facility has been established. With the final residence of the French Emperor Napoleon having been developed into a museum, St. Helena has considerable potential as a tourist destination, but it remains largely inaccessible, with no airport or safe anchorage for small vessels.

Under a 1989 constitution the territory's governor presides over an Executive Council that includes 5 committee chairs drawn from the 12 elected members of the Legislative Council, who serve four-year terms; both councils also include, as ex officio members, the government secretary, attorney general, and financial secretary. The governor, represented by island administrators, holds executive and legislative powers for the dependencies.

Issues of immigration to the UK and citizenship in the mother country, along with local resentment over decisions by Gov. David SMALLMAN, led to disturbances in April 1997. A police van was burned and the governor was jostled, islander resentment having been sparked by the governor's choice of a different social services committee chair than the nominee of the legislators. The approach of the July 9 Legislative Council elections also underscored the relatively limited power of the council compared to the reserve powers of the governor. Smallman retired in 1999.

The November 1999 breakdown of the island's only regularly scheduled cargo and passenger ship led to panic buying by Saints (as the islanders call themselves) concerned about running out of basic provisions. Although interim shipping arrangements were soon made, the temporary halt in the *St. Helena*'s bimonthly visits raised renewed concerns about the territory's isolation and led islanders to call for construction of an airport that would promote what has been termed "big earner" tourism. (Initial plans called for construction of an airport by 2010, but the UK government put the schedule on hold in light of the global recession of 2008–2009.).

In mid-2008 Gov. Andrew GURR proposed a new draft constitution for St. Helena, Ascension Island, and Tristan da Cunha that would, among other things, eliminate references to Ascension Island and Tristan da Cunha as dependencies of St. Helena, expand the authority of restructured elected councils on the islands, and incorporate a bill of rights. The new basic law was endorsed by the Legislative Council, submitted to the Queen, and came into force on September 1, 2009, prior to the general elections of November 4.

Governor: Andrew GURR.
Speaker of the Legislative Council: (An election was scheduled for November 27, 2009.)

Ascension Island. Encompassing an area of 34 square miles (88 sq. km.) and with a 2001 population (excluding Royal Air Force personnel) of 982, Ascension Island was annexed to St. Helena in 1922 and is presently the site of a major sea-turtle hatching ground, a BBC relay station, and a U.S. space-tracking station. During the Cold War it served as a signals intelligence base, and during the 1982 Falklands war it was a transit point for UK aircraft and ships. In March 1990 an Ariane telemetry reception station became operational under an agreement with the European Space Agency.

The first island government was introduced in April 2001, and an Island Council, chaired by the St. Helena governor, met for the first time in November 2002. Seven members are elected on a nonpartisan basis; two others (the attorney general and the director of financial services) serve ex officio.

In mid-2000 a government study warned that the island's social structure was in danger of collapse without private sector development that could then fund such common services as education and health care. Otherwise, the island could become a "single-person's work-camp," with severe consequences not only for the permanent residents but also for the St. Helena citizens who earn their living there.

Administrator: Ross DENNY.

Tristan da Cunha. Annexed to St. Helena in 1938, Tristan da Cunha has an area of 38 square miles (98 sq. km.), with a population in 2007 of 275. The dependency also includes the uninhabited islands of Inaccessible and Nightingale as well as Gough, a UNESCO World Heritage Site and residence of a South African meteorological team. The main island's entire population was evacuated because of a volcanic eruption in 1961 but was returned in 1963. Under the original 1985 constitution, the island administrator is advised by an Island Council of 11 members, with 8 elected for three-year terms (most recently in March 2007) and 3 appointed. The 2009 constitution reasserted the advisory role of the Island Council.

Administrator: David MORLEY.

Turks and Caicos Islands. The Turks and Caicos Islands, a southeastward extension of the Bahamas, consist of 30 small cays (8 inhabited) with a total area of 166 square miles (430 sq. km.) and a population (2005E) of 24,800. The capital is Cockburn Town on Grand Turk. The principal industries are tourism, offshore banking and finance, and fishing. As of 1997, some 14,600 offshore businesses were registered in the islands.

Linked to Britain since 1766, the Turks and Caicos became a Crown colony in 1962 following Jamaica's independence. A constitution adopted in 1976 provided for a governor and an Executive Council comprising a chief minister, 5 additional ministers chosen by the governor from among elected legislators, and 3 ex officio members (governor, attorney general, chief secretary). A 20-member Legislative Council comprises 13 elected members, the 3 ex officio members of the Executive Council, 3 members appointed by the governor, and a speaker.

The former chief minister, Norman B. SAUNDERS, was obliged to resign after his arrest on drug-trafficking charges in Miami, Florida, in March 1985, Deputy Chief Minister Nathaniel J. S. FRANCIS being elected as his successor on March 28. Francis was also forced to resign following the issuance of a commission of inquiry report on arson, corruption, and related matters. The British government decided on July 25, 1986, to suspend the constitution and impose direct rule under the governor, with assistance from a four-member advisory council. Subsequently, a three-member constitutional commission was appointed to draft revisions in the basic law to inhibit corruption and patronage and promote "fair and effective administration."

At an election marking the islands' return to constitutional rule on March 3, 1988, the **People's Democratic Movement** (PDM), previously in opposition, won 11 of the 13 elective Legislative Council seats; by contrast, at the poll of April 3, 1991, the PDM (led by Derek TAYLOR) lost 6 seats to the **Progressive National Party** (PNP), whose total of 8 permitted Charles Washington MISICK to form a new government. In an election on January 31, 1995, Taylor and the PDM regained power, winning 8 seats against 4 for the PNP and 1 for Saunders standing as an independent, while the recently formed **United Democratic Party** (UDP), led by Wendal SWANN, failed to secure representation.

Resentment remaining from the 1986 constitutional suspension, objections to the reserve powers of the governor, and alleged British indifference to the islands found a focus in hostility to Gov. Martin BOURKE in April 1996. Among other things, he was charged with favoring one island (Providenciales, the center of the booming tourist industry) over the others in development. In addition, he caused concern by alleging both police corruption and a steady flow of drugs through the island chain. A petition for his removal from the island administration to the Foreign and Commonwealth Office was rejected in April 1996 after consultations with the islands, but in September, when his term expired, he was not reappointed.

At the election of April 24, 2003, the PDM secured seven of the elective seats on the Legislative Council, while the PNP took six. Chief Minister Taylor thereby appeared to have retained office for an unprecedented third consecutive term. However, the PNP challenged the results in two closely fought constituencies and won both at by-elections on August 7. As a result, Taylor was obliged to resign in favor of Michael Misick.

A constitutional review process begun in 1999 concluded in 2006 with the adoption of a new constitution providing increased internal autonomy. The new document entered into force on August 9, at which time Misick was sworn in as the first premier of Turks and Caicos. The new constitution provides for a governor appointed by HM Queen Elizabeth II, a House of Assembly with 15 elective seats, and 6 seats appointed by the governor, including a speaker and attorney general. The cabinet consists of the governor, the premier, 6 other ministers, and the attorney general.

At the election of February 9, 2007, the PNP won a decisive majority by securing 13 of the elective seats on the Legislative Council, while the PDM, now led by Floyd SEYMOUR, took only 2.

In July 2008 (a month before leaving office), Gov. Richard TAUWHARE announced that a commission of inquiry had been launched to investigate allegations of government corruption in the islands. Premier Misick described the UK House of Commons report that had spurred the inquiry as "unbalanced" and based on false accusations.

By March 2009 the UK government had raised the possibility of temporarily suspending self-government in the islands and transferring governmental powers to the recently appointed governor, George Wetherell. The inquiry commission subsequently reported that there were strong indications of "political immorality and immaturity and of general administrative incompetence," prompting Misick to resign his premiership. Galmo WILLIAMS was sworn in as premier on March 24. Misick sought to combat the charges in British courts, but by early summer he had exhausted his appeals. On August 14, 2009, under instructions from the UK Foreign Office, the governor imposed direct rule, which he said could last two years. Meanwhile, criminal investigation in the corruption charges against Misick and four of his cabinet ministers continued.

Governor: Gordon WETHERELL.

Premier: (Office temporarily suspended).

Uninhabited Overseas Territories:

South Georgia and the South Sandwich Islands. South Georgia is an island of 1,387 square miles (3,592 sq. km.) situated approximately 800 miles east-southeast of the Falklands; it was inhabited only by a British Antarctic Survey team at the time of brief occupation by Argentine forces in April 1982. The South Sandwich Islands lie about 470 miles southeast of South Georgia and were uninhabited until occupied by a group of alleged Argentine scientists in December 1976, who were forced to leave in June 1982. Formerly considered dependencies of the Falklands, the islands were given separate status in October 1985. The governor of the Falkland Islands also serves, ex officio, as territorial commissioner.

In 1993 concern over unregulated fishing led London to impose a 200-mile maritime zone and to increase efforts to manage the territory's fisheries, with particular emphasis on Patagonian toothfish, icefish, krill, and crab. On September 18, 1998, London announced that the 15-member military presence on South Georgia would be withdrawn in 2000, with territorial security to be assumed by troops stationed in the Falkland Islands.

In March 2004, in recognition of management practices that had been introduced to maintain sustainability, the South Georgia toothfish fishery became the first southern ocean fishery to be certified by the independent Marine Stewardship Council. Increased eco-tourism has brought more traffic to the islands in recent years, with indigenous species providing the greatest attractions.

Commissioner: Alan HUCKLE (resident in the Falkland Islands). (In September 2009 the UK government announced that Nigel HAYWOOD would succeed Huckle in September 2010.)

British Antarctic Territory. Formerly the southern portion of the Falkland Islands Dependencies, the British Antarctic Territory was separately established in 1962. Encompassing that portion of Antarctica between 20 degrees and 80 degrees west longitude, it includes the South Shetland and South Orkney Islands as well as the Antarctic Peninsula. Sovereignty over the greater portion of the territory is disputed by Great Britain, Argentina, and Chile, and its legal status remains in suspense in conformity with the Antarctic Treaty of December 1, 1959. Until June 30, 1989, the responsible British authority was a high commissioner, who served as governor of the Falkland Islands; on July 1 the administration was moved to the Foreign and Commonwealth Office, London, the head of the South Atlantic and Antarctic Department being designated commissioner. The British Antarctic Survey team, based year-round at Halley and Rothera stations, numbers roughly 40–50 in winter and 150 in summer, when stations at Fossil Bluff on Alexander Island and Signy in the South Orkneys are also manned. A number of other countries also maintain research facilities in the territory.

As of 2007, Britain planned to submit to the UN claims to areas of the Antarctic seabed, believed to be rich in energy reserves, based on UK sovereignty over the territory. Chile and Argentina could register competing petitions for rights to the seabed. Critics argued that the claims would undermine the 1959 Antarctic Treaty.

Commissioner: Colin ROBERTS (resident in the United Kingdom).

Sovereign Base Areas:

Akrotiri and Dhekelia. Under the 1960 Treaty of Establishment, which recognized Cyprus as an independent republic, the UK retained sovereignty over two Sovereign Base Areas (SBAs). Akrotiri (Western Sovereign Base Area) and Dhekelia (Eastern Sovereign Base Area) are to remain sovereign British territory "until the Government of the United Kingdom, in view of changes in their military requirements, at any time decide to divest themselves of the sovereignty or effective control over the SBAs or any part thereof." Although the SBA boundaries were drawn to exclude civilian population centers, the separation of the island into predominantly ethnic Greek and ethnic Turkish sectors in the mid-1970s led to a influx of civilians, and approximately 7,000 Cypriots now live within the SBAs. The UK resident population, military and civilian, numbers some 7,800. The UK Ministry of Defense owns approximately 20 percent of the 98 square miles (254 sq. km.) that constitute the SBAs, as does the Crown, with the balance being privately held. Most of the private land is farmed.

Reporting to the Ministry of Defense rather than the Foreign and Commonwealth Office, the SBA administration, headquartered in Episkopi, is led by the commander of the British Forces Cyprus, who has executive and legislative powers comparable to those of a governor in a civilian overseas territory. Assisting the administrator are a chief officer, an attorney general, an administrative secretary, and two area officers. A Court of the Sovereign Base Areas adjudicates nonmilitary offenses.

Administrator: Maj. Gen. James GORDON.

UNITED KINGDOM: NORTHERN IRELAND

Political Status: Autonomous province of the United Kingdom under separate parliamentary regime established in 1921 but suspended March 30, 1972; coalition executive formed January 1, 1974; direct rule reimposed May 28, 1974; consultative Northern Ireland Assembly elected October 20, 1982, but dissolved by United Kingdom June 19, 1986; devolution of limited self-rule to (new) Northern Ireland Assembly and multiparty power-sharing Northern Ireland Executive effected December 2, 1999; direct rule reimposed February 11–May 30, 2000, for one day on August 11, 2001, for one day on September 22, 2001, and from October 15, 2002, until the return of limited self-rule upon the convening of a new assembly and election of a new executive on May 8, 2007, in accordance with the St. Andrews Agreement of October 2006.

Area: 5,452 sq. mi. (14,120 sq. km.).

Population: 1,685,267 (2001C); 1,762,000 (2008E).

Major Urban Center (2005E): BELFAST (276,000).

Official Language: English.

Monetary Unit: Pound Sterling (market rate December 1, 2009: 1 pound = $1.66US).

First Minister: Peter ROBINSON (Democratic Unionist Party); elected by the Northern Ireland Assembly on June 5, 2008, succeeding Ian PAISLEY (Democratic Unionist Party), who had resigned on May 31.

Deputy First Minister: Martin McGUINNESS (*Sinn Féin*); elected by the Northern Ireland Assembly on May 8, 2007; reelected June 5, 2008, on a joint ticket with First Minister Peter Robinson.

United Kingdom Secretary of State for Northern Ireland: Shaun WOODWARD; appointed on June 28, 2007, by UK Prime Minister Gordon Brown, succeeding Peter HAIN.

THE COUNTRY

Geographically an integral part of Ireland, the six northern Irish counties (collectively known as "Ulster," although excluding three counties of the historic province of that name) are politically included within the UK for reasons rooted in the ethnic and religious divisions introduced into Ireland by English and Scottish settlement in the 17th century. As a result of this colonization effort, the long-established Roman Catholic population of the northern counties came to be heavily outnumbered by Protestants, who assumed a dominant political, social, and economic position and insisted upon continued association of the territory with the UK when the rest of Ireland became independent after World War I. Although a minority, Roman Catholics are strongly represented throughout Northern Ireland and constitute a rising proportion of the total population (40.3 percent according to the 2001 UK census, compared to 45.6 percent Protestant). Catholic complaints of discrimination, especially in regard to the allocation of housing and jobs and to limitation of the franchise in local elections, were the immediate cause of the serious disturbances that commenced in Northern Ireland during 1968–1969.

Despite recurring political violence, foreign investors have been drawn to Ulster by lucrative financial incentives and its proximity to the European market. After sharing in the UK recession of the early 1990s, Northern Ireland experienced an economic upturn in 1993. The signing of the multiparty Good Friday Agreement in April 1998 served as another spur to growth. A month later London announced a new $500 million economic aid package directed toward encouraging foreign investment, developing small businesses, easing unemployment, and improving labor skills. Tourism was also targeted for growth.

For 1997–1998 Northern Ireland reported record exports, led by expanding sales of transport equipment. Other manufactures include clothing and textiles, food and beverages, and machinery, with the industrial sector accounting for about one-fourth of the GDP. Growth industries include software, telecommunications, and electronics. In 2007 the service industry accounted for 72.5 percent of jobs, while manufacturing accounted for 11.2 percent. Agriculture, which dominated the economy until recent years, now accounts for under 5 percent of GDP and employs a similarly small percentage of the workforce; principal crops are barley, wheat, and potatoes. Leading trading partners are the rest of the UK and the United States, although commerce with the Republic of Ireland has been growing.

Women made up 45.6 percent of the active labor force in 2007, and the ratio of male/female hourly wage rates was virtually at parity. Women hold 18 of 108 seats in the Northern Ireland Assembly, 4 of 12 cabinet posts, 3 of the 18 seats at Westminster, and 21 percent of local councilor elected posts.

Gross value added (GVA) per capita (the UK measure of economic prosperity) lags 19 percent behind the UK as a whole. Meanwhile, unemployment, which had improved steadily over the past decade to 4.0 percent in 2007, rose to more than 7.0 percent in 2009 as the effects of the global financial crisis took hold.

GOVERNMENT AND POLITICS

Political background. Governed as an integral part of Ireland, and therefore of the UK, throughout the 19th and early 20th centuries, Northern Ireland acquired autonomous status in 1921 as part of a general readjustment necessitated by the success of the Irish independence movement in the rest of Ireland. The Government of Ireland Act of 1920 provided for a division of Ireland as a whole into separate northern and southern sections, each with its own legislature. Enshrined in the December 1921 Anglo-Irish treaty, this arrangement was reluctantly accepted by the Irish nationalist authorities in Dublin but embraced in Northern Ireland as the best available means of continuing as an integral part of the UK. The new government of Northern Ireland was dominated from the beginning by the pro-British, Protestant interests controlling the Ulster Unionist Party (UUP), with militant elements becoming known as "loyalists." Ties with Britain were sedulously maintained, for both religious and historic reasons and because of accompanying economic benefits, including social services and agricultural subsidies. Opposition Catholic sentiment in favor of union with the Irish Republic represented a continuing but long-subdued source of tension.

Catholic-led "civil rights" demonstrations against political and social discrimination erupted in 1968, evoking counterdemonstrations by Protestant extremists and leading to increasingly serious disorders, particularly in Londonderry (known to Catholics as Derry). In November 1968 the government of Terence O'NEILL proposed a number of reform measures that failed to halt the disturbances and yielded an erosion of support for the prime minister within his own government and party. Parliament was accordingly dissolved, with a new election in February 1969 producing the usual unionist majority but failing to resolve an internal UUP conflict. In April mounting disorder and acts of sabotage led the Northern Ireland government to request that British army units be assigned to guard key installations. Although O'Neill persuaded the UUP to accept the principle of universal adult franchise at the next local government elections, he resigned as party leader on April 28 and as prime minister three days later. His successor in both offices, Maj. James D. CHICHESTER-CLARK, an advocate of moderate reform, was chosen by a 17–16 vote of the UUP over Brian FAULKNER, an opponent of the O'Neill reform program. The government promptly announced an amnesty for all persons involved in the recent disturbances and received a unanimous vote of confidence on May 7.

After renewed rioting in Belfast, Londonderry, and elsewhere during the first half of August 1969, Chichester-Clark agreed on August 19 that all security forces in Northern Ireland would be placed under British command; that Britain would assume ultimate responsibility for public order; and that steps would be taken to ensure equal treatment of all citizens in Northern Ireland in regard to voting rights, housing, and other issues. The subsequent deployment of regular British soldiers in the province was at first welcomed by the Catholic population as affording protection from Protestant incursions into their localities. However, under the influence of the Provisional Irish Republican Army (Provisional IRA or the "Provos"), many Catholics quickly came to see the British troops as an occupying force, and their alienation increased as the result of the internment without trial of several hundred Catholics in August 1971. Growing polarization was highlighted by the formation in 1971 of the ultra-loyalist Democratic Unionist Party (DUP) by a hard-line faction of the UUP led by Dr. Ian PAISLEY.

The situation turned sharply worse on "Bloody Sunday," January 30, 1972, when a prohibited Catholic civil-rights march in Londonderry was infiltrated by hooligan elements, and 14 unarmed civilians died as the result of clashes with British troops. A wave of violence and hysteria followed. Unable to act in agreement with the Belfast regime of Prime Minister Brian Faulkner, who had succeeded Chichester-Clark in March 1971, British Prime Minister Edward Heath announced that he would reimpose direct rule. The Northern Ireland Parliament was prorogued rather than dissolved, and William (subsequently Viscount) WHITELAW was designated to exercise necessary authority through the newly created office of secretary of state for Northern Ireland. With the backing of the three leading British parties, these changes were quickly approved by the British Parliament and became effective, initially for a period of one year, on March 30, 1972. The 1972 death toll from political violence reached 478, the highest annual total during the post-1969 "Troubles."

A plebiscite on the future of Northern Ireland was held on March 8, 1973, but was boycotted by the Catholic parties. An unimpressive

57.4 percent of the electorate voted for Ulster's remaining within the UK, while 0.6 percent voted for union with the Republic of Ireland and the remainder abstained. The British government subsequently organized the election on June 28 of a Northern Ireland Assembly of 80 members to serve a four-year term. This step was formalized on July 18 by passage of a parliamentary bill permitting the devolution of powers to the assembly and an executive, and on November 27 Brian Faulkner was named chief of an executive-designate that included representatives of both Protestant and Catholic factions.

In a meeting in Sunningdale, England, on December 6–9, 1973, that was attended by members of the Irish and UK governments as well as the executive-designate of Northern Ireland, agreement was reached on the establishment of a tripartite Council of Ireland to oversee changes in the relationship between the northern and southern Irish governments. On January 1, 1974, direct rule was terminated. While the (mainly Catholic) Social Democratic and Labour Party (SDLP) endorsed the agreement, the bulk of the Unionist Party rejected it, forcing Faulkner's resignation as party leader on January 7 and as chief executive on May 28, in the wake of which direct rule was again imposed.

In July 1974 the UK Parliament passed the Northern Ireland Act of 1974, which authorized the election of a Constitutional Convention. At balloting on May 1, 1975, the United Ulster Unionist Coalition (UUUC), a grouping of largely "anti-Sunningdale" parties, won 45 of 78 convention seats. On September 8 the UUUC convention members voted 37–1 against the participation of republicans in a future Northern Ireland cabinet, and on November 20 the convention concluded its sitting with a formal report that embraced only UUUC proposals. The convention was reconvened on February 3, 1976, in the hope of reaching agreement with the SDLP and other opposition parties, but it registered no further progress and was dissolved a month later.

The UUUC was itself dissolved on May 4, 1977, following the failure of a general strike called by its more intransigent loyalist components, acting in concert with the Ulster Workers' Council (UWC) and the Ulster Defense Association (UDA), the largest of the Protestant paramilitary groups. With the level of violence having declined, Secretary of State for Northern Ireland Roy MASON proposed in late November that a new attempt be made to restore local rule. The effort was abandoned, however, because of intensified violence in the first quarter of 1978, which prompted the House of Commons in late June to extend the period of direct rule for another year. In the absence of a political settlement, the order was renewed annually thereafter.

Following the failure of another attempt at constitutional talks in early 1980 and a further escalation of violence, seven republican inmates of the Maze prison near Belfast began a hunger strike on October 27 in support of a demand for "political" status. While the strike was called off on December 18 following government promises of improvement in prison conditions, the action was widely publicized and was renewed in March 1981, with ten prisoners ultimately dying, including Bobby SANDS and Kieran DOHERTY, who had won election to, respectively, the UK and Irish parliaments shortly before their deaths. The most significant diplomatic development of the year was a meeting in London on November 6 at which UK Prime Minister Margaret Thatcher and Irish Prime Minister Garret FitzGerald agreed to set up an Anglo-Irish Intergovernmental Council (AIIC) to meet on a periodic basis to discuss matters of common concern.

In early 1982 the Thatcher government secured parliamentary approval for the gradual reintroduction of home rule under a scheme dubbed "rolling devolution." The initiative assumed substantive form with balloting on October 20 for a new 78-member Northern Ireland Assembly. For the first time the Provisional *Sinn Féin* (the political wing of the Provisional IRA) participated in the process, obtaining five seats. The poll was accompanied, however, by an upsurge of terrorist activity, with both the Provisional *Sinn Féin* and the SDLP boycotting the assembly session that convened on November 11 to formulate devolution recommendations.

During a meeting in Hillsborough Castle, Northern Ireland, on November 15, 1985, Prime Ministers Thatcher and FitzGerald concluded an Anglo-Irish Agreement that established an Intergovernmental Conference (IGC) within the context of the AIIC to deal on a regular basis with political and security issues affecting the troubled region. Subsequently, in reaction to unionist maneuvering, the small nonsectarian Alliance Party joined *Sinn Féin* and the SDLP in boycotting the Northern Ireland Assembly, while the 15 unionist MPs resigned their seats in the UK House of Commons to force by-elections as a form of referendum on the Hillsborough accord. (One unionist seat fell to the SDLP.) On June 19, 1986, the UK government dissolved the assembly, which had become little more than an anti-accord forum for unionists. The dissolution, which signaled the failure of London's seventh major peace initiative in 14 years, did not, however, abolish the body, leaving open the possibility of future electoral replenishment.

In February 1989 agreement was reached on the functions and membership of another joint undertaking provided for in the Anglo-Irish accord: a British-Irish Inter-Parliamentary Body of 25 MPs from each country, including minority party representatives. The first meeting of the new group opened in London on February 26, 1990, but two seats reserved for unionist parliamentarians remained vacant because of their continued opposition to the 1985 accord.

In March 1991 continued tension in the province was momentarily eased by the announcement of agreement on new talks in three "strands": first, discussions between the Northern Ireland "constitutional" parties, focusing on devolution and power sharing, chaired by Secretary of State Peter BROOKE; second, "North-South" talks between the Northern Ireland parties and the UK and Irish governments; and third, "East-West" talks between London and Dublin on replacing the 1985 Anglo-Irish Agreement. Any agreement reached under the talks would be put to referendums in both Northern Ireland and the Republic of Ireland.

Although preliminary first-strand talks opened on schedule on April 30, 1991, the so-called Brooke initiative quickly ran into procedural and political obstacles. Not until June 17 was it possible for full first-strand discussions to begin in Belfast, marking the first formal inter-party talks in Northern Ireland in 16 years. However, it became apparent that Brooke had overestimated the willingness of the parties to seek common ground, with the unionist parties remaining resolutely opposed to any formula that appeared to give Dublin a role in Northern Ireland's affairs.

A July 1991 breakdown in the talks was followed by an escalation of sectarian violence, and by January 1992 the number of British troops assigned to the province had risen to 11,500. The conflict nonetheless continued, with the number of killings attributed to Protestant paramilitary groups, principally the Ulster Volunteer Force (UVF) and the Ulster Freedom Fighters (UFF), reportedly approaching those perpetrated by the IRA.

The talks were formally suspended by Brooke on January 27, 1992, pending the outcome of the UK election on April 9. In that contest the 17 Northern Ireland constituencies returned 13 Unionists, while the SDLP increased its representation in the House of Commons to 4 by gaining the West Belfast seat held since 1983 by the *Sinn Féin* president, Gerard (Gerry) ADAMS. In the postelection reshuffle Brooke was replaced as Northern Ireland secretary by Sir Patrick MAYHEW, who on April 17 announced his intention to resume the talks.

On June 30, 1992, representatives of the four leading Ulster formations met in London with an Irish government delegation, the first time since Ireland became independent in 1921 that hard-line unionists had met with Irish officials. On July 1 the participants agreed to undertake sustained negotiations on the North-South relationship, but deadlock soon emerged, in part over the Republic of Ireland's continuing constitutional claim to the whole of Ulster. The talks formally concluded without agreement in early November, whereupon meetings of the IGC resumed. Meanwhile, sectarian violence continued unabated. On August 10, 1992, the UK government announced the banning of the loyalist UDA, bringing the number of proscribed organizations in Northern Ireland to ten.

The advent of a *Fianna Fáil*/Labour coalition government in the Republic of Ireland in January 1993 heralded a more accommodating line by Dublin, and despite continuing IRA bombings in England, the quest for a negotiated settlement appeared to gain momentum. During April and May 1993, SDLP leader John HUME held a series of meetings with *Sinn Féin* leader Adams in what was characterized by Hume as an effort to bring about "a total cessation of all violence." On May 27 Irish President Mary Robinson conferred in London with Queen Elizabeth II in the first such meeting between the two countries' heads of state. Most significantly, on December 15, 1993, Prime Ministers John Major and Albert Reynolds issued their Downing Street Declaration. Aiming to bring about the end of hostilities in the province, the declaration acknowledged that "the people of the island of Ireland" might wish to opt for unification but reiterated that "it would be wrong to attempt to impose a united Ireland in the absence of the freely given consent of the majority of the people of Northern Ireland." The declaration thereby raised the possibility that Dublin would take steps to delete its constitutional claim to the North; it also stated that if IRA violence were brought to "a permanent end," *Sinn Féin* could expect to participate in all-party talks. Reaction to the new document was decidedly cool among the unionists, while *Sinn Féin* declined to give an immediate response, preferring instead to call for "clarifications."

The 25-year-old logjam in Northern Ireland appeared to be broken by an IRA announcement on August 31, 1994, that from midnight that day "there will be a complete cessation of military operations" by all IRA units. Noting that "an opportunity to secure a just and lasting settlement has been created," the statement called for "inclusive negotiations." Received with great rejoicing in Northern Ireland, especially among Catholics, the IRA announcement prompted London to take the position that if the cease-fire proved to be a permanent renunciation of violence, *Sinn Féin* would be invited to participate in future negotiations. In Dublin Prime Minister Reynolds took speedier action, receiving Adams on September 5 to discuss the convening of a "forum of peace and reconciliation." Unionist spokespersons, however, described the cease-fire as a public relations ploy and demanded that the IRA surrender its weapons and explosives prior to meaningful talks. On October 13 the three main loyalist paramilitary organizations also declared a cessation of hostilities but made it clear that they would not surrender their weapons until the IRA had done so.

The position of *Sinn Féin,* however, was that arms decommissioning should be dealt with at the talks rather than before and should be part of a complete "demilitarization" of Northern Ireland, including the withdrawal of British troops. This basic impasse persisted, despite the progressive upgrading of the UK government's contacts with *Sinn Féin*. The first public talks between the two sides took place in December 1994 in Belfast, while Adams and Secretary of State Mayhew finally met on May 24, 1995, on the margins of a Washington conference aimed at promoting investment in Northern Ireland.

Meanwhile, the UK and the Irish government, now headed by Prime Minister John Bruton, continued to clarify their positions. A joint "framework document" issued on February 22, 1995, envisaged the creation of a North-South council with "executive, harmonizing or consultative functions" and the restoration of self-government to Northern Ireland under a power-sharing formula. The document also recorded the Irish government's pledge to introduce a constitutional amendment deleting any territorial claim to Northern Ireland, while the UK government would propose constitutional legislation enshrining its commitment to uphold the democratic wish of the Northern majority. Reactions to the document were predictable: conditional approval from Adams, who noted that "its ethos is for one Ireland," but strong condemnation from unionist leaders, with Paisley of the DUP describing it as "Ulster's death warrant."

In early July 1995 violence resurged in conjunction with the annual "marching season," during which Protestant fraternal orders hold upward of 3,000 marches, some through Catholic neighborhoods, chiefly to mark the July 1690 defeat of the Catholic King James II by the Protestant William of Orange at the Battle of the Boyne. Amid fears that the peace process was losing momentum, on July 24 the UK and Irish prime ministers issued a three-part plan under which the disarmament of paramilitary groups would be supervised by an international commission, a target date would be set for the opening of all-party talks, and early release dates would be set for some of the 1,000 republican and loyalist paramilitaries currently serving prison sentences. The timing of decommissioning remained a sticking point, however, with London continuing to insist on paramilitary disarmament as a precondition for all-party discussions. While attempting to persuade London to modify its stance, the Dublin government went ahead with its "forum of peace and reconciliation," in which *Sinn Féin,* the SDLP, and a large number of others (but not the main unionist parties) set out their positions on the issue and the constitutional future. In September the UUP elected a new leader, David TRIMBLE, who had come to prominence in July by defying a police blockade and leading an Orange Order march through the Catholic neighborhood of Drumcree, near Portadown.

Intensive UK-Irish negotiations in October–November 1995 attempted to confront the decommissioning issue and thereby prepare the way for multiparty negotiations. As a result, on December 15 an international commission headed by former U.S. senator George Mitchell began to address the disarmament question, while a tentative date of February 1996 was set for opening interparty talks. In January 1996 the Mitchell panel proposed that all parties adhere to six principles, including the renunciation of political violence and a commitment to eventual, full decommissioning under international supervision.

Blaming what it labeled British intransigence, the IRA abruptly ended its cease-fire on February 2, when a massive bomb exploded in London, killing two men and causing damage later estimated at up to $300 million. The bombing appeared to catch even *Sinn Féin* off guard, casting doubt on the extent of its influence over the IRA. Security measures in Northern Ireland, which had been relaxed, were rapidly stepped up, and on February 28 both governments demanded an immediate and unequivocal restoration of the cease-fire, pending which *Sinn Féin* would be excluded from talks.

After individual discussions with Northern Ireland parties started in March (the uninvited *Sinn Féin* representatives being turned away), the UK government enacted legislation authorizing election of a consultative Northern Ireland Forum for Political Dialogue. Balloting took place on May 30, returning 90 members from 18 constituencies and a further 20 members from the 10 parties securing the largest shares of the popular vote. Although *Sinn Féin* participated in the election, winning 17 seats on a larger-than-expected vote share, it remained aloof from the forum. Moreover, the SDLP, with 21 seats, soon withdrew, preferring to concentrate on direct talks. Thus, the forum was left to the two main unionist parties, the UUP (30 seats) and the DUP (24 seats), and to various smaller groupings. The latter included the Ulster Democratic Party (UDP) and the Progressive Unionist Party (PUP), which were described as "close to the thinking of" the leading loyalist paramilitaries, the UDA and the UVF, respectively.

With the forum effectively sidelined by the absence of the nationalist parties, attention turned to the multiparty negotiations, which opened on June 10, 1996, in Stormont Castle, the seat of the direct-rule administration. Both governments and all of the main parties except *Sinn Féin,* whose leaders were again turned away, took part, although the proceedings were initially stalled by unionist objections to the proposal that former senator Mitchell be the chair. In July the traditional Protestant marches again provoked sectarian altercations, while the IRA and a splinter, the Continuity Army Council, or Continuity IRA, continued their attacks into the autumn and beyond. In October the UUP and the SDLP finally agreed on a full agenda for the Stormont negotiations, while in November the SDLP and *Sinn Féin* requested, among other things, a guarantee that *Sinn Féin* would be admitted to the talks if the IRA declared another cease-fire. Britain and Ireland disagreed, however, on the precise terms for *Sinn Féin*'s participation.

Talks resumed in January 1997 but were suspended in March to await the UK election of May 1, in which the UUP took 10 of Northern Ireland's 18 seats in the House of Commons, followed by the SDLP with 3, and the DUP and *Sinn Féin* with 2 each. Under Prime Minister Tony Blair the new UK Labour government moved swiftly to place Northern Ireland high on the political agenda, with Dr. Marjorie (Mo) MOWLAM assuming office as secretary of state for Northern Ireland. Despite another round of hostilities associated with the Protestant marching season, on July 19 the IRA announced a resumption of the August 1994 cease-fire, opening the way for *Sinn Féin* to join the multiparty talks when they began again in mid-September. Although *Sinn Féin* had explicitly endorsed the six Mitchell principles, which also included a commitment to abide by the terms of any negotiated peace settlement, the unionists, objecting to *Sinn Féin*'s presence, boycotted the opening session. In late September, however, in a precedent-shattering shift of policy that drew the wrath of hard-line loyalists, the UUP's Trimble agreed to rejoin the talks despite *Sinn Féin*'s presence. Thus, representatives of eight parties—the UUP, SDLP, *Sinn Féin,* UDP, PUP, the Alliance Party of Northern Ireland (APNI), the Northern Ireland Women's Coalition, and the Labour Coalition—gathered in Stormont in October, the principal absentee being Paisley's DUP. In tandem, an Independent International Commission on Decommissioning (IICD), chaired by a retired Canadian general, John de Chastelain, broached the disarmament issue.

In October 1997 Tony Blair met with Gerry Adams, the first such meeting between a UK prime minister and *Sinn Féin* in more than 70 years, while in November the new Irish prime minister, Bertie Ahern, conferred with the UUP's Trimble. Despite such confidence-building steps, little progress was achieved before the Christmas break, during which the leader of the paramilitary Loyalist Volunteer Force (LVF), Billy WRIGHT, was murdered inside the Maze prison by members of the Irish National Liberation Army (INLA). Retaliations ensued, and on January 9, in a spectacular political gambit, Secretary Mowlam met in the Maze with loyalist prisoners and earned their support for continued peace discussions.

Although provocations by paramilitaries on both sides continued, Prime Ministers Blair and Ahern issued a brief framework for peace titled "Propositions on Heads of Agreement" on January 12, 1998. The outline proposed "balanced" constitutional change by both the UK and Ireland; establishment of a directly elected Northern Ireland legislature and a North-South ministerial body; formation of British-Irish "inter-governmental machinery"; and adoption of "practical and effective measures" concerning such issues as prisoners, security, and decommissioning. The constitutional changes put forward by the prime ministers included excision of the Irish Republic's territorial claim to Northern Ireland, coupled with revision of British constitutional legislation dealing with the UK's authority over affairs in the North. *Sinn Féin* initially evinced little enthusiasm for the proposal, which fell significantly short of the party's long-standing demand for reunification with the South, while unionists expressed concern that creation of a North-South organ would in fact pave the way for reunification.

Early in 1998 the UDP and *Sinn Féin* were separately suspended from the multiparty talks because of cease-fire violations committed by their paramilitary associates, the UFF and the IRA, respectively, but in March both parties were readmitted to Stormont. On March 25 Mitchell set a 15-day deadline for the two governments and the eight participating parties to achieve a final peace plan, which was concluded on April 10 (a day late) following a marathon negotiating session. The Belfast Agreement, which quickly became better known as the Good Friday Agreement, called for the following: (Strand One) creation of a Northern Ireland Assembly with full authority to legislate "in devolved areas," an Executive Committee (Northern Ireland Executive) of ministers drawn from the legislature and headed by a first minister and a deputy first minister, a consultative Civic Forum of community and business leaders, and a continuing role for the secretary of state for Northern Ireland in matters not devolved to the new institutions; (Strand Two) creation of a North-South Ministerial Council; and (Strand Three) establishment of a British-Irish Council with representatives from Ireland and all the British isles, including devolved institutions in Scotland and Wales. In addition to requiring removal from Ireland's constitution of the claim to Northern Ireland, the agreement mandated adherence to human rights and equal opportunity, full decommissioning by May 2000, normalization of security arrangements in Northern Ireland (including the withdrawal of the roughly 17,500 British troops), and formation of an independent commission to review policing procedures. Finally, an assessment of the criminal justice system was to include "an accelerated programme for the release of prisoners" affiliated with those organizations maintaining a "complete and unequivocal" cease-fire. Accompanying the Good Friday Agreement was a new British-Irish Agreement, superseding the 1985 Anglo-Irish Agreement and committing London and Dublin to carrying through on the peace arrangements.

With an islandwide referendum—the first such vote since partition—scheduled for May 22, supporters and opponents of the Good Friday Agreement quickly began campaigning. In April David Trimble convinced the UUP as a whole to back the agreement despite vehement opposition from six of his party's ten MPs, the DUP, the small United Kingdom Unionist Party (UKUP), and the fraternal Orange Order. Meeting in Dublin on May 10, a special *Sinn Féin* conference also endorsed the agreement and authorized members to sit in the proposed Northern Ireland Assembly. In the end, the referendum passed with a 71 percent affirmative vote in the North, on a turnout of 81 percent. Balloting for the new 108-member assembly took place on June 25, with 16 parties offering candidates. The UUP obtained a plurality of 28 seats, followed by the SDLP with 24, the DUP with 20, and *Sinn Féin* with 18. In all, opposition unionists claimed 28 seats, just short of the number that would have enabled them to tie up legislation (see Constitution and government, below, for a discussion of rules governing passage of measures requiring "cross-community support").

On July 1, 1998, the new Northern Ireland Assembly elected the UUP's Trimble as first minister and the SDLP's Seamus MALLON as deputy first minister, John Hume having declined the latter nomination. Already, however, a major stumbling block to full formation of the power-sharing Executive Committee, and thus to devolution, had emerged. Whereas Trimble demanded that the IRA begin decommissioning its arms before he would allow *Sinn Féin* to take up any ministerial positions, Gerry Adams argued that the Good Friday Agreement contained no such stipulation.

Once again, the Protestant marching season brought with it a series of violent incidents, including the torching of ten Catholic churches on July 2–3, 1998. Following a ruling by an independent Parades Commission that the traditional Orange Order parade in Drumcree would not be allowed to pass through a Catholic neighborhood, more than 5,000 Orangemen protested at the barricades. A month later, on August 15, in the worst carnage since the "Troubles" began, a car bomb exploded in Omagh, killing 29 and injuring more than 200 others. A recently formed IRA splinter, the "Real IRA," claimed responsibility for the attack, which even the INLA and the Continuity IRA condemned. The bombing provoked Prime Ministers Blair and Ahern to introduce in their respective legislatures antiterrorism measures that Ahern characterized as "extremely draconian." Both parliaments passed similar bills in early September.

On September 10, 1998, for the first time, Trimble and Adams met privately in Stormont, but they made no progress on the decommissioning dispute. Trimble, responding to the announcement on October 16 that he and John Hume had won the Nobel Peace Prize for their efforts, expressed the hope that the decision had not been "premature." On October 31 the negotiators missed the deadline set by the Good Friday Agreement for creation of the "shadow" (predevolution) Executive Committee and the North-South Ministerial Council.

The stalemate appeared broken on December 18 with the announcement in Stormont of a further agreement covering formation of ten government departments and six cross-border bodies, the principal goal being British transfer of authority to the Northern Ireland Assembly and Executive Committee in February 1999. The new agreement provided for the UUP and the SDLP to head three departments each, with *Sinn Féin* and the DUP being responsible for two each. Ministerial nominations would await progress on disarmament. Although the LVF on the same day became the first paramilitary group to turn in some of its weapons, the IRA refused to reciprocate, calling the LVF action a "stunt."

In January 1999 Trimble set February 15 as the date for inaugurating the Executive Committee, while Secretary of State Mowlam established March 10 as the date for transferring powers to the assembly. However, neither deadline was met. On February 16 the assembly voted 77–26 in favor of the December power-sharing accord and also approved creation of the Civic Forum, the North-South Ministerial Council, the British-Irish Council, and the cross-border bodies. Nevertheless, the decommissioning issue remained unresolved, even after the UUP and *Sinn Féin* held their first party-to-party session the following day. Despite personal efforts by Prime Ministers Blair and Ahern, Secretary of State Mowlam announced on March 9 that she was postponing devolution again, until April 2, Good Friday.

Although all the principal paramilitary groups continued to adhere to cease-fires (despite a notable increase since late 1998 in the number of "punishment beatings" inflicted by gangs against members of their own communities), a prominent nationalist civil rights lawyer, Rosemary NELSON, was killed by a car bomb on March 15, 1999. The apparent perpetrator, the recently organized loyalist Red Hand Defenders (RHD), was quickly added by Secretary of State Mowlam to the list of banned organizations, as was another new loyalist paramilitary group, the Orange Volunteers (OV). At the end of March, Blair and Ahern made another attempt to resolve the decommissioning impasse. They proposed in the Hillsborough Declaration that the UUP, SDLP, *Sinn Féin,* and DUP nominate their members of the Executive Committee and that within one month, in a "collective act of reconciliation," the paramilitaries voluntarily "put beyond use" various arms. Upon IICD certification of the decommissioning, the assembly could confirm the nominees to the Executive Committee. The "changed security situation" would also permit "further moves on normalisation and demilitarisation." On April 13, however, *Sinn Féin* rejected the declaration, reiterating that all parties should adhere to the letter of the Good Friday Agreement, which specified only that decommissioning occur by May 2000. On April 20 Ahern and Blair met in London with UUP, SDLP, and *Sinn Féin* leaders, to no avail. In mid-May London and Dublin set a new deadline of June 30 for formation of the Executive Committee, but further attempts by Blair and Ahern to broker an agreement proved fruitless. On July 14 Trimble reaffirmed that the UUP would not sit with *Sinn Féin* in a devolved government until decommissioning had begun, prompting Deputy First Minister-elect Mallon to resign on July 15 and Blair to announce that devolution would be further postponed.

Through August 1999, unionists and *Sinn Féin* verbally skirmished over whether the IRA had broken its cease-fire. Meanwhile, former U.S. senator Mitchell had agreed to chair a review of the peace process that opened on September 6 in Belfast and moved on October 12 to London, where the newly appointed secretary of state for Northern Ireland, Peter MANDELSON, insisted that the negotiators had no alternative but to meet the terms of the Good Friday Agreement. "There is no Plan B," he asserted. "It's that or nothing." An effort by both the UUP and *Sinn Féin* to temper their rhetoric prompted Mitchell to extend negotiations beyond an October 23 deadline, and in early November he held meetings with U.S. President Clinton as well as the British and Irish prime ministers. Shortly thereafter, *Sinn Féin* reported that the IRA was prepared to establish contact with General de Chastelain. On November 15–16, in a sequence of carefully worded, coordinated statements, Mitchell, Trimble, and Adams separately endorsed the continuance of devolution and decommissioning. On November 17 the IRA confirmed that, following establishment of the institutions outlined in the Good Friday Agreement, it would name a representative to "enter into discussions" with de Chastelain. In a secret ballot on November 27, 58 percent of the UUP's governing council backed Trimble's cautious acceptance of the IRA initiative. Thus, the UUP gave up its demand that decommissioning had to begin before it would sit with *Sinn Féin* on the power-sharing Northern Ireland Executive.

On November 29, 1999, the Northern Ireland Assembly approved ten nominees to serve in the executive under Trimble and Mallon. The latter had been reaffirmed as deputy first minister by a 71–28 vote of the assembly, thereby negating his July resignation through a legally questionable maneuver that was challenged by the DUP and other hard-liners. (The stratagem circumvented having to jointly reelect Mallon and First Minister Trimble, who probably would not have secured the necessary 30 unionist votes.) On December 1 the UK Parliament authorized devolution, and on December 2 London formally transferred power to the assembly and the executive; however, the cabinet convened minus the two DUP ministers, who refused to sit with the two *Sinn Féin* ministers. On the same day, Dublin formally promulgated the constitutional changes that ended the Irish Republic's claims to the North, and on December 2–3 IRA representatives met for the first time with General de Chastelain. On December 13 the North-South Ministerial Council held its inaugural meeting, and on December 17 representatives of Ireland, the UK, the Channel Islands, the Isle of Man, and the devolved governments of Northern Ireland, Scotland, and Wales gathered in London for the first session of the Council of the Isles.

The IRA's subsequent failure to begin disarming led the UK government to reimpose direct rule on February 11, 2000. In a last-minute effort to salvage the power-sharing government, the IRA had told General de Chastelain that it was prepared to address putting its arms and explosives "beyond use," but the offer came too late to forestall the reimposition. In response, on February 15 the IRA suspended further contacts with de Chastelain.

While attending talks in Washington in mid-March 2000, Trimble indicated that he might consider reinstituting the power-sharing government prior to any actual arms decommissioning by the IRA. The statement catalyzed his opponents within the UUP, and at a March 25 session of the party's governing council he faced a leadership challenge by the Rev. Martin SMYTH. Although Trimble managed to win 57 percent of the council vote, Smyth's supporters, including the influential hard-liner Jeffrey DONALDSON, succeeded in linking restoration of the government to a highly charged symbolic issue: retaining the name of the territory's controversial police agency, the Royal Ulster Constabulary (RUC). On September 9, 1999, Chris Patten, a former UK governor of Hong Kong, had released a report on RUC reform that proposed, among a list of 175 recommendations, changing the force's name to the Police Service of Northern Ireland (PSNI). Unionists had immediately denounced the proposal as well as suggestions that the police oath and insignia be revised to remove all association with the UK. (*Sinn Féin* had responded to the report by repeating its long-held position that the RUC should be abolished.)

Despite a series of diplomatic meetings and public negotiations, little substantive progress on resolving the armaments impasse occurred until May 6, 2000, when the IRA announced that it would accept international inspection of its arms stockpiles and would "completely and verifiably" put its weapons beyond use. As inspectors it nominated Martti Ahtisaari, former president of Finland, and Cyril Ramaphosa, former secretary general of South Africa's ruling party, the African National Congress. London and Dublin quickly proposed that power-sharing be resumed on May 22, but on May 18 Trimble, fearing defeat, postponed a crucial meeting of the UUP governing council. In an effort to defuse the RUC issue, Secretary of State Mandelson agreed to amend pending legislation on RUC reform, adding, for example, mention of the RUC to the legal description of the police service. On May 27, by a vote of 459–403, Trimble again prevailed over the UUP hard-liners, despite the opposition of Deputy Leader John TAYLOR, who viewed Mandelson's concessions as inadequate.

On May 30, 2000, London returned authority to the Northern Ireland Assembly and Executive. In early June Mandelson made additional concessions to garner republican support for the RUC reform legislation, but he left the name-change issue unresolved. At the same time, the new home rule government faced differences over other symbolic issues—principally, the refusal of the *Sinn Féin* ministers to fly the Union Jack over their offices.

On June 25 the IRA stated that it had reopened discussions with de Chastelain's IICD, and on June 26 arms monitors Ahtisaari and Ramaphosa reported that they had conducted their first inspections of IRA stockpiles. In further fulfillment of the Good Friday Agreement, authorities by late July had released more than 425 paramilitary prisoners, loyalist and republican alike, from prison, although Johnny ADAIR, a former leader of the UFF, was returned to prison on August 22 following renewed feuding between loyalist paramilitary groups in July–August. Responding to the outbreak of violence, Secretary of State Mandelson ordered British troops onto the streets of Belfast.

On October 28, 2000, First Minister Trimble overcame another challenge to his leadership when the UUP governing council rejected a hard-line proposal that the party withdraw from the government if the IRA failed to actively begin disarmament by November 30. Trimble instead proposed that he prohibit the executive's two *Sinn Féin* ministers from participating in official North-South meetings until the IRA actively engaged with the IICD. Trimble's decision drew immediate criticism not only from Gerry Adams, but also from Deputy First Minister Mallon. Meanwhile, in the last week of October weapons inspectors Ahtisaari and Ramaphosa conducted their second inspection of IRA stockpiles, as a result of which they described the IRA as "serious about the peace process."

During the first half of 2001 no significant progress was made in resolving three linked issues: IRA decommissioning, as demanded by the unionists; departure of the UK military, as demanded by the republicans; and reform of the RUC, as demanded by both (though with seemingly irreconcilable goals). Renewed negotiating efforts by Prime Ministers Blair and Ahern failed, leading First Minister Trimble to announce in May 2001 that he would resign his office on July 1, in the absence of concrete action by the IRA.

As predicted by Trimble himself, hard-liners made notable gains in the general election of June 7, 2001. Whereas his UUP lost 3 of its 9 seats in the UK House of Commons (having already lost 1 to the DUP at a September 2000 by-election) and 31 of its 185 local council seats, Ian Paisley's DUP gained 2 seats in the House of Commons, for a total of 5, and 40 additional council seats, for a total of 131. The SDLP held steady, retaining its 3 parliamentary seats and losing only 3 of its 120 local council seats, while *Sinn Féin* saw its membership in the House of Commons rise from 2 to 4 and its local council representation increase from 74 to 108.

With a backdrop of renewed sectarian rioting, centered on a Roman Catholic school in a predominantly Protestant area of Belfast, Trimble, as he had threatened, resigned on July 1, 2001. His action automatically vacated the office of deputy first minister. A diplomatic scramble ensued as Ireland and the UK attempted to reinvigorate the peace process before six weeks had passed, after which a new first minister had to be elected, a Northern Ireland Assembly election called, or direct rule reimposed. On August 6 the IICD released a statement confirming that the IRA had accepted a method for putting its weapons "completely and verifiably" beyond use, but in the absence of a timetable and at least a minimal surrender of weapons, the unionists dismissed the agreement as inadequate. Nevertheless, believing that a breakthrough might be near, London decided to exploit a legal loophole and reset the six-week clock by imposing direct rule for a single day beginning at midnight on August 11. The move by Secretary of State for Northern Ireland John REID angered the IRA, however, and it withdrew from its agreement with the IICD. The situation was further complicated by the arrest in Colombia of three alleged IRA members who, according to Colombian authorities, had been assisting the principal leftist guerrilla organization, the Colombia Revolutionary Armed Forces (*Fuerzas Armadas Revolucionarias de Colombia*—FARC). (Gerry Adams subsequently denied accusations that at least one of the men was acting as a *Sinn Féin* representative.) Meanwhile, the sectarian violence in Belfast again worsened, leading Reid to announce on October 12 that the government no longer recognized the cease-fires with the UDA/UFF and the LVF.

Facing increasing international pressure following the September 11, 2001, attacks by Islamic terrorists in the United States, the IRA stated on September 20 that it would renew and accelerate its talks with the IICD. Collaterally, London heralded a breakthrough based on the decisions of the SDLP and then the UUP and DUP (but not *Sinn Féin*) to participate in the formation of a cross-community Northern Ireland Policing Board as part of a new Police Implementation Plan. (The RUC was formally renamed the PSNI on November 4.) Citing these positive developments, on September 21, with the second six-week period about to expire, London announced another direct-rule interregnum that began at midnight on September 22 and concluded 24 hours later.

On October 18, 2001, the UUP and DUP ministers withdrew from the executive after the assembly had rejected a unionist demand that the two *Sinn Féin* ministers be excluded. Shortly thereafter, Adams and his deputy, Martin McGUINNESS, for the first time explicitly called upon the IRA to begin disarming, and on October 23 both the IRA and the IICD released statements announcing that a quantity of arms had in fact been decommissioned. In response, Trimble announced that the UUP would return to the executive and that he would seek reelection as first minister.

At the assembly's first vote on November 2, two members of the UUP voted against Trimble, leaving him one vote short of the necessary unionist majority, despite unanimous nationalist support. On November 6 he achieved the necessary margin when the assembly allowed three members of the Alliance Party to temporarily redesignate themselves as unionists. However, the DUP was incensed by the maneuver, which led to scuffles outside the assembly.

An additional IRA decommissioning occurred in April 2002, but continuing sectarian violence in Belfast prompted Trimble, in early July, to threaten the withdrawal of the UUP from the assembly if authorities did not take corrective measures. Although he accused the IRA of fomenting the rioting, loyalist paramilitaries appeared to be equally culpable. The annual marching season once again led to repeated clashes, and in late July London vowed to stiffen its response to security violations. A week earlier, on July 16, the IRA had issued an unprecedented public apology to the families of its innocent victims.

On October 4, 2002, the *Sinn Féin* offices in Stormont were raided by authorities investigating alleged IRA spying, and two days later Denis DONALDSON, a *Sinn Féin* administrator, was arrested and charged with possessing some 1,200 documents of potential use to paramilitaries. The unionists immediately demanded the resignations or dismissal of the *Sinn Féin* ministers. On October 15, in an effort to forestall the collapse of the peace process, London reimposed direct rule for the fourth time.

Despite the continuation of direct rule, elections to the suspended Northern Ireland Assembly were held on November 26, 2003. The results suggested that resumption of the peace process might prove impossible. For the Protestants, Ian Paisley's DUP, which strongly opposed the 1998 Good Friday Agreement, displaced Trimble's UUP to become the largest party, with 30 seats. For the Catholics, in a similar reversal of the 1998 results, *Sinn Féin* won 24 seats, as opposed to the SDLP's 18.

Despite the 2003 electoral results, multiparty talks were resumed on February 3, 2004, with the DUP and *Sinn Féin* communicating through intermediaries. Subsequently, UK Prime Minister Blair and Irish Prime Minister Ahern held a series of meetings that yielded no consensus on power-sharing, while in December Paisley announced a hardening of the DUP position by insisting on photographic evidence of IRA arms decommissioning.

In early 2005 the peace process reached a new point of collapse with the IRA being blamed for an armed attack on Belfast's Northern Bank in December 2004 and thereafter withdrawing its offer to decommission. On April 7 *Sinn Féin* leader Adams drew no response in urging the IRA to abandon its "armed struggle," while an appeal by Blair and Ahern for the IRA to end "all paramilitary and criminal activity" was equally unproductive until late July when, in a potentially historic development, the IRA pledged to lay down its arms and oppose British rule in the future only through peaceful political involvement. Specifically, the IRA announced that it had "formally ordered an end to the armed campaign" and would pursue a "purely political and democratic program through exclusively peaceful means." Promises were also made that the IRA's massive stockpiles of arms (reportedly buried in bunkers throughout Northern Ireland) would be quickly dismantled.

The May 5, 2005, local elections reinforced the shifts in unionist and nationalist party success. The DUP gained more than 50 additional councilors; *Sinn Féin* improved by 18; the UUP dropped by 39 to fall behind the DUP in number of unionist councilors regionwide; and the SDLP dropped by 16 seats to fall behind *Sinn Féin* in number of nationalist councilors. However, a single party gained majority control in only 2 of 18 councils (the DUP in Ballymena and Castlereagh).

Prime Minister Blair labeled the IRA announcement a step of "unparalleled magnitude," and in August 2005 the UK indicated that it would cut its troop level (then 10,000) in Northern Ireland in half by 2007 in view of the improved security outlook. In addition, in September General de Chastelain said the IICD was satisfied with the decommissioning of the IRA weapons. However, DUP leader Paisley condemned the UK response as "premature," calling for the "dissolution" of the IRA. He and other Protestant leaders also accused the British and Irish governments of "disregarding" loyalist concerns. Consequently, the DUP continued to refuse to meet directly with *Sinn Féin* when Blair and Ahern relaunched negotiations toward another power-sharing government.

In February 2006 the Independent Monitoring Commission (IMC), established by the UK and Ireland in 2004 to monitor armed groups in Northern Ireland, concluded that the IRA was no longer "engaged in terrorism," while Protestant militants had been responsible for more than 20 killings in the fall of 2005. Encouraged by the IRA's "progress," Blair and Ahern subsequently appeared to focus on pressuring the DUP to adopt a more positive negotiating role. In April the two prime ministers declared a deadline of November 24 for the assembly parties to agree on formation of a new executive, without which a "new way to govern" Northern Ireland would be pursued. Analysts suggested that the deadline posed a "veiled threat" to the DUP, as it implied that the alternative to a power-sharing government could be greater control by the Irish Republic. Adams welcomed the announcement, and in May he proposed that Paisley be named as first minister of the proposed new government. However, the offer was emphatically rejected by Paisley (described as *Sinn Féin*'s "most intractable foe"), and little progress was reported through the summer, despite the establishment of a multiparty Preparation for Government Committee and the reconvening of the Northern Ireland Assembly (see Legislature, below). Blair and Ahern consequently scheduled "last-ditch" negotiations for October in Scotland.

Following the negotiation of a historic agreement in St. Andrews, Scotland, in October 2006, limited self-rule returned to Northern Ireland in May 2007. (See Recent developments, below, for details.)

Constitution and government. The Government of Ireland Act of 1920 gave Northern Ireland its own government and a Parliament empowered to act on all matters except those of "imperial concern" (e.g., finance, defense, foreign affairs) or requiring specialized technical input. The royal authority was vested in a governor appointed by the Crown and advised by ministers responsible to Parliament; in practice, the leader of the majority party was invariably designated as prime minister. Parliament consisted of a 52-member House of Commons, directly elected from single-member constituencies, and a Senate, whose 26 members (except for 2 serving ex officio) were elected by the House of Commons under a proportional representation system. Voting for local government bodies was subject to a property qualification that excluded an estimated 200,000 adults, including a disproportionate number of minority Catholics. The effective disenfranchisement of a substantial portion of the Catholic population precipitated the original disturbances in 1968–1969.

Until 1998 British efforts to bring about agreement on a form of coalition government acceptable to both Protestants and Catholics failed to bear fruit. The Northern Ireland Constitution Act of 1973 abolished the office of governor and provided for a regional assembly and executive; however, the executive functioned only in 1974, and the assembly and its successor in 1973–1974 and 1982–1986. A Constitutional Convention in 1975–1976 failed to produce agreement, and the only major constitutional developments for more than a decade thereafter involved the extension of a consultative role to the Irish government by means of various bilateral accords. Accordingly, direct rule, in effect since 1972 (save for January–May 1974), continued through the UK secretary of state for Northern Ireland. Under direct rule local government encompassed 26 elected city, district, and borough councils with very limited responsibilities for refuse collection, street cleaning, recreational facilities, environmental health, and consumer protection.

Following completion of the Belfast Agreement of April 10, 1998 (familiarly called the Good Friday Agreement but also referenced in some official documents as the Multi-Party Agreement), and pending approval of the agreement by referendum on May 22, the British Parliament passed legislation authorizing election of a New Northern Ireland Assembly, the term "New" being dropped upon formal devolution of authority to the body. Elected on June 25, the legislature comprised 108 members from 18 constituencies.

Under the terms of the Good Friday Agreement and the Northern Ireland Act of 1998, which Parliament passed in November 1998 and which repealed the Government of Ireland Act of 1920, assembly members individually defined themselves as a "designated unionist," a "designated nationalist," or "other." Decisions requiring "cross-community support"—for example, standing orders, budget allocations, and election of the assembly chair—required either majority approval, including support from a majority of both nationalists and unionists, or assent by a weighted majority of 60 percent, with affirmative votes from at least 40 percent of unionists and 40 percent of nationalists. To further protect the minority, the cross-community provision could be triggered on any other matter if 30 or more assembly members presented a "petition of concern."

Assembly members were to be elected for five-year terms, subject to early dissolution by a vote of two-thirds of the entire membership. Devolved legislative authority extended to such areas as agriculture, economic development, tourism, and education, while "excepted and reserved matters" remaining in the hands of the UK Northern Ireland secretary included international relations, defense, security, criminal justice, taxation, regulation of financial services, national insurance, and regulation of broadcast and telecommunication services. Under devolution, executive authority resided in an Executive Committee of ministers chosen from the leading assembly parties in proportion to their membership in the body. The assembly selected a first minister and a deputy first minister, who stood for election jointly and were required to secure majority support from both nationalists and unionists. In addition to heading the executive, which might have up to ten additional members, the two leaders jointly nominated ministers and junior ministers to two principal intergovernmental bodies, the North-South Ministerial Council and the British-Irish Council (also known as the Council of the Isles), both of which were established under treaties concluded by the UK and Ireland on March 8, 1999.

The North-South Ministerial Council had as its mandate bringing together "those with executive responsibilities in Northern Ireland and the Irish Government, to develop consultation, co-operation, and action within the island of Ireland," on both an islandwide and a cross-border basis. Decisions required agreement by both sides. The British-Irish Council, which was to meet at the summit level twice a year and in other formats "on a regular basis," included representatives from Scotland, Wales, the Channel Islands, and the Isle of Man in addition to Great Britain, Northern Ireland, and Ireland, the purpose being "to promote the harmonious and mutually beneficial development of the totality of relationships among the peoples of these islands." Two additional treaties signed on March 8 authorized formation of various implementing bodies and of a British-Irish Intergovernmental Conference, the latter replacing the Anglo-Irish Intergovernmental Council and the Intergovernmental Conference of 1985.

Northern Ireland is represented in the UK House of Commons, currently with 18 seats (increased from 17 in 1997). It also has 3 seats in the European Parliament.

The UK government reimposed direct rule on Northern Ireland on October 15, 2002 (see Political background, above). However, limited self-rule was restored on May 8, 2007 (see Recent developments, below).

Recent developments. The assembly voting in Northern Ireland in 2003 and the balloting in Northern Ireland in 2005 for local councils and the UK House of Commons underscored the ongoing polarization between the unionists and the nationalists/republicans. Nevertheless, Prime Ministers Blair of the UK and Ahern of Ireland managed to bring the two chief protagonists (Ian Paisley of the DUP and Gerry Adams of *Sinn Féin*) and leaders of other parties together for a series of meetings in St. Andrews, Scotland, on October 11–13, 2006. Tentative agreement was reached for the restoration of self-rule the following spring, assuming that final details were successfully negotiated for the proposed power-sharing arrangements. In addition, final approval was required from *Sinn Féin* regarding the acceptance of and support for the police force and the criminal justice system. (Theretofore, *Sinn Féin* supporters had refused to recognize the authority of the PSNI, which the nationalists believed was dominated by the unionists.)

Although neither the DUP nor *Sinn Féin* expressly endorsed the St. Andrews Agreement by the November 10, 2006, deadline, the British and Irish governments deemed the parties' statements of intent to be sufficient to continue. Consequently, on November 22 Westminster approved the enabling legislation required for the agreement to go into effect. Two days later, the Northern Ireland Assembly that had been elected in 2003 met to receive nominations from the DUP and *Sinn Féin* (expected to finish first and second, respectively, in the upcoming assembly balloting) for the two principal executive positions. Adams nominated *Sinn Féin*'s Martin McGuinness for deputy prime minister, but Paisley deferred acceptance of the post of first minister pending *Sinn Féin*'s formal agreement to participate in the police force and criminal justice system. After a *Sinn Féin* conference on January 28, 2007, Blair and Ahern announced on January 30 that new assembly elections would be held as planned.

In the assembly balloting on March 7, 2007, the DUP increased its seat representation from 30 to 36, while *Sinn Féin* advanced from 24 to 28. Paisley and Adams met on March 26 and agreed upon the nominations of Paisley and McGuinness to head the new executive. Those appointments were approved when the new assembly convened on May 8, as were the remaining cabinet appointments. (Under the unique system in Northern Ireland whereby cabinet posts are assigned according to assembly representation, the DUP was accorded 5 of the 12 cabinet posts; *Sinn Féin,* 4; the UUP, 2; and the SDLP, 1.)

Despite widespread concerns over the potential stability of the new government, it survived without major incident throughout 2007. Symbolic of the cooperative working relationship between Paisley and McGuinness was their joint visit to the United States in December, at which time President George W. Bush congratulated all parties in the decades-long dispute for having apparently put violence behind them in favor of a "more hopeful chapter."

A leading indicator that Ian Paisley's time as first minister may have been nearing its end came with his January 2008 resignation as leader of the Free Presbyterian Church. He also announced on March 4 that he would resign as DUP party leader. Although his age (82) and recent resignation of his son from a junior ministerial position likely weighed in his decision, the main impetus appeared to be dissatisfaction among church and party leaders with Paisley's facilitation of the peace process and cooperation with McGuinness.

On April 14, 2008, Peter Robinson, theretofore deputy leader of the DUP, was elected unopposed as Paisley's successor as DUP leader. Cooperation between the DUP and *Sinn Féin* was expected to diminish under Robinson's leadership, and, when Paisley officially vacated the office of first prime minister on May 31, interparty tensions reemerged. *Sinn Féin* initially threatened to prevent Robinson from replacing Paisley as first minister by refusing to renominate McGuinness on the joint ticket unless the DUP took action on the issues of policing, justice, and the Irish Language Act. However, negotiations led by UK prime minister Gordon Brown, as well as officials from the U.S. and Irish governments, were successful in getting *Sinn Féin* to lift its threat. On June 5 Robinson was elected as first minister and McGuinness was reelected as deputy first minister. The election was followed on June 9 by a shuffle of cabinet positions held by the DUP. However, three months of stalemate followed, as *Sinn Féin* blocked all efforts for the executive to meet on other business until the DUP agreed to a date for transferring policing and justice powers to local ministers. Progress in that regard was achieved in October when Paul GOGGINS, minister of state in the UK Northern Ireland office, clarified that the transfer of the related responsibilities to the Northern Ireland Assembly would not include access to sensitive national security information, such as secret files on IRA informers. Consequently, the assembly in November met for the first time since June and forged a compromise to create a justice ministry. The plan called for the justice minister to be chosen from outside the ranks of the DUP or *Sinn Féin,* although both parties would have a veto over the appointment. (It was believed that a member of the Alliance Party was likely to be named to the post.)

No firm timetable was set for inauguration of the justice ministry, and finalization appeared contingent in 2009 on a reduction in violence and resolution of fractious divisions within the DUP. In regard to the former issue, the Real IRA claimed responsibility for the March 2009 murder of two British soldiers, the first such murders in the province since 1997. Two days later members of the Continuity IRA (CIRA) claimed responsibility for the murder of a police constable in Amagh. On a more positive note, three unionist paramilitary groups (the UVF, RHC, and UDA) voluntarily decommissioned their weapons in June.

Regarding the issue of the strength of the resolve within the DUP to follow through on the power-sharing governance arrangement, two developments in 2009 portended an uncertain future. In the June balloting for the European Parliament, the newly formed Traditional Unionist Voice (TUV), created by a DUP dissident, cut substantially into the DUP's vote support while running on a platform objecting to joining in a government in which participation by *Sinn Féin* was mandated. Unionist voters also appeared upset over unseemly personal finances among DUP leaders (see DUP, below). The TUV was sufficiently buoyed by its vote support to announce its intention to contest upcoming elections in unionist strongholds. Should the TUV cut so far into DUP support that it emerges as the largest unionist party, the power-sharing arrangement might be in jeopardy. On the other hand, if the TUV and DUP split the hard-line unionist vote so that one of the more moderate unionist parties becomes the plurality winner, then the power-sharing arrangement could be strengthened. The UK parliamentary election in 2010 was expected to offer a reading of what might follow in the 2011 balloting for the Northern Ireland Assembly.

POLITICAL PARTIES AND GROUPS

Parties Represented in the Cabinet:

Democratic Unionist Party (DUP). The DUP was founded in 1971 by a hard-line loyalist faction of the UUP, attracting working-class Protestant support for its strongly anti-Catholic, anti-Dublin position. It was consistently the runner-up to the parent party, winning 21 seats in the 1982 assembly election and 3 UK House of Commons seats in June 1983, all of the latter being retained in 1987. The party was represented at the 1988 Duisburg talks by Deputy Leader Peter Robinson, who urged the creation of an alternative to the 1985 Anglo-Irish accord.

A growing schism between the DUP's older and younger members was, in part, responsible for the party leader's decision in May 1990 to agree to political negotiations. The older faction, led by Ian Paisley, had long adhered to a "no negotiation" policy, while the more youthful faction, exemplified by Robinson, advocated the creation of a political and religious dialogue. At the same time, the party mainstream was moving from an "integrationalist" to a "devolutionist" posture that favored a provincial government with relatively strong legislative and executive powers.

The DUP retained its three Westminster seats in the UK balloting of April 1992, after which the failure of yet another round of constitutional talks left the party's internal divisions unresolved. In the forum elections of May 1996 the party fell into third place, with 19 percent of the vote, and in the May 1997 UK election it lost the constituency of Mid Ulster to *Sinn Féin.*

The DUP strongly opposed *Sinn Féin*'s presence at the Stormont negotiations of 1997–1998 and refused to participate. It campaigned against the Good Friday Agreement and won 20 of the 28 seats captured by unionist oppositionists at the June Northern Ireland Assembly election. Allotted two portfolios in the Northern Ireland Executive, the DUP adopted obstructionist tactics to protest *Sinn Féin*'s presence in the body.

In a September 2000 by-election for a seat in the UK House of Commons, the DUP captured the district from the UUP, prompting Paisley to declare that First Minister Trimble "is finished, absolutely finished." In the UK general election of June 2001 the DUP won 5 seats, a gain of 2. In simultaneous local balloting the party added 40 council seats, for a total of 131.

In the Northern Ireland Assembly balloting of November 2003, the DUP outpolled the UUP for a plurality of 30 seats. The DUP also won 1 of 3 Northern Ireland seats in the June 2004 elections to the European Parliament. In the House of Commons election of May 2005, the DUP increased its representation from 5 to 9, securing 33.7 percent of the vote in Northern Ireland and consolidating its status as the dominant unionist party with a similar advance in the simultaneous local elections. The DUP remained the plurality party in the March 7, 2007, balloting for the Northern Ireland Assembly, securing 36 seats on a 30.1 percent share of first-round votes. As the largest party, the DUP was able to nominate Paisley for the position of first minister in the subsequent coalition government with *Sinn Féin.* The power-sharing coalition and Paisley's overtly friendly relationship with Deputy First Minister McGuinness subsequently created strains in party ranks. Amid controversies over power sharing and his son's property dealings, Paisley announced in March 2008 that he would resign as party leader at the end of May. His longtime adviser and confidant, Peter Robinson, won election to the party leader post in April, assumed the leadership position on May 31, and was elected first minister on June 5.

Although Robinson's subsequent approach to the DUP's power-sharing arrangements with *Sinn Féin* was less friendly and less accommodating than Paisley's, hard-line unionist elements still remained skeptical, thereby creating a possible source of a permanent fracture within the party. In addition, Robinson found himself in political trouble over reports in April 2009 that he, his wife, and other DUP members were "double dipping" on salaries and claiming large expense reimbursements. (Robinson and his wife, each of whom held positions as representatives in both the UK Parliament and the Northern Ireland Assembly, reportedly were paid more than one-half million pounds in annual salaries and expenses.)

The DUP's vote share fell to 18.1 percent in the June 2009 elections to the European Parliament, down dramatically from 32 percent in 2004. In an ominous sign for the DUP's long-term political standing, most of the defecting voters appeared to turn to the TUV (below), the new hard-line unionist alternative.

Leaders: Peter ROBINSON (First Minister of Northern Ireland and Party Leader), Nigel DODDS (Deputy Leader), James McCLURE (President), Maurice MORROW (Chair), David SIMPSON (Vice President).

Sinn Féin. The islandwide *Sinn Féin* (see also Ireland: Political Parties) serves as the legal political wing of the outlawed IRA (see Former and Current Republican Paramilitary Groups, below). In addition to advocating improved living and working conditions for its primarily Catholic, working-class constituency, throughout the 1970s and 1980s it consistently called for the disbanding of British security forces, the withdrawal of Britain from Northern Ireland's government, and the negotiation of a political settlement through an all-Ireland constitutional conference.

Its president, Gerard (Gerry) Adams, was *Sinn Féin*'s only successful candidate in the 1987 UK general election, but, as in 1983, he refused to occupy his seat in the Commons. In early 1988 the SDLP (below) attempted to forge ties with *Sinn Féin,* but its interest waned in April when *Sinn Féin* refused to "repeal its commitment to limited guerrilla warfare." A second attempt at linkage was broken off in September following the resumption of IRA bombings in downtown Belfast.

Responding to comments made by UK Secretary of State Peter Brooke, in April 1990 Adams said that the IRA might be persuaded to cease terrorist activities if London established a dialogue with *Sinn Féin.* However, *Sinn Féin*'s continued refusal to renounce IRA violence led to its exclusion from the April 1991 talks. In April 1992 Adams lost his Westminster parliamentary seat to the SDLP.

The IRA cease-fire declaration of August 31, 1994, yielded enhanced international stature and negotiating prominence for Adams and other *Sinn Féin* leaders. However, the IRA renewed hostilities in February 1996 while continuing to press for unconditional talks. Though successful in both the 1996 Forum elections (winning 15 percent of the vote) and in the May 1997 UK general elections (winning two seats), the party still chose to remain aloof from either political process. Renewal of the IRA cease-fire in July 1997 and *Sinn Féin*'s affirmation of its commitment to the six Mitchell principles, including full decommissioning and rejection of political violence, enabled Adams to join the Stormont multiparty peace talks in September. In response, a hard-line faction left the party and formed the 32 County Sovereignty Committee (below).

At a special party session convened in Dublin on May 10, 1998, and attended by a number of furloughed nationalist inmates from prisons in Northern Ireland and Britain, Adams won overwhelming endorsement of the Good Friday peace plan and permission for *Sinn Féin* members to take up seats in the new Northern Ireland Assembly. In balloting for the assembly in June, the party won 18 seats, sufficient for it to claim 2 positions on the governing Executive Committee upon devolution.

In June 2000 Cathal CRUMLEY became the first member of *Sinn Féin* to be elected mayor of a Northern city, Londonderry, since partition. Earlier in the year the UK government had introduced a bill in the House of Commons that would permit a member of any UK legislature, including the Northern Ireland Assembly, to hold simultaneously a legislative seat in the Republic of Ireland. The Disqualifications Bill, which passed Parliament on November 30, was widely regarded as a "sweetener" for *Sinn Féin* as it permitted the party's assembly members, particularly Gerry Adams, to seek election to the *Dáil.*

In the UK general election of June 2001, *Sinn Féin* doubled its representation in the House of Commons, to 4 seats. It also made gains locally, adding 34 council seats to the 74 it had previously held.

On October 4, 2002, the *Sinn Féin* offices in Stormont were raided by authorities investigating IRA spying, and two days later Denis Donaldson, the party's office administrator, was arrested and charged with possessing some 1,200 documents of potential use to paramilitaries.

The revelations ultimately contributed to London's reimposition of direct rule on October 15. (The case took a surreal turn in December 2005 when the charges against Donaldson were dropped and Donaldson acknowledged that he had in fact been a British agent for 20 years.)

The party won 24 seats in the Northern Ireland Assembly election of November 2003.

In August 2004 Adams, in an effort to counter the DUP's objection to revival of the peace talks, called publicly for the disbanding of the IRA as a paramilitary force.

Sinn Féin gained one of Northern Ireland's three seats in the 2004 European Parliament elections and secured five seats (including one by Adams) in the May 2005 UK House of Commons balloting on a share of 24.3 percent of the votes in Northern Ireland. Shortly thereafter, Adams intensified his call for the renunciation of violence, and the IRA subsequently announced its historic pledge to disarm. (Adams has never acknowledged having played a leadership role in the IRA, although many observers have ascribed such status to him.)

In January 2007 *Sinn Féin* formally endorsed the provisions for police services in the St. Andrews Agreement of the previous November, thereby permitting plans for new assembly elections to proceed in March. *Sinn Féin* won 28 seats (finishing second to the DUP) in that balloting on a 26.2 percent share of first-preference votes. The party also retained its 1 seat from Northern Ireland in the June 2009 European Parliament elections with a first-place vote total of 26.3 percent.

Leaders: Gerard (Gerry) ADAMS (President), Martin McGUINNESS (Deputy First Minister of Ireland), Declan KEARNEY (Chair), MaryLou McDONALD (Vice President), Dawn DOYLE (General Secretary).

Ulster Unionist Party (UUP). The UUP, historically Northern Ireland's dominant party, was split by the 1973 Sunningdale Agreement, the anti-Sunningdale majority becoming known as the Official Unionist Party (OUP). The formation of a "joint working party" between the OUP and the DUP (above) was announced in August 1985 to protect "Ulster's interests within the UK." Throughout 1986 the working party attempted to disrupt local government in protest of the Anglo-Irish Agreement of 1985. By contrast, joint OUP-DUP publications in 1987 called for all Northern Ireland parties to negotiate an alternative to the 1985 accord in a spirit of "friendship, cooperation, and consultation." In addition, the OUP, DUP, and the now-defunct Ulster Popular Unionist Party (UPUP) of James KILFEDDER agreed to present only one unionist candidate from each constituency in the 1987 House of Commons elections, at which they retained 13 of 14 seats. The OUP continued to issue conciliatory statements during 1988, but the party's demand that the Anglo-Irish accord be rescinded before any substantive negotiations could take place between unionists and republicans helped derail initiatives advanced at a meeting of the OUP, DUP, Alliance Party, and Social Democratic and Labour Party (SDLP, below) in October in Duisburg, West Germany.

In May 1990 OUP leaders softened their position, reportedly agreeing to tripartite talks between the province's parties and the British and Irish governments in return for "de facto" (temporary) suspension of the bilateral pact. Subsequently, in April 1991, OUP and DUP representatives attended the opening of the Ulster talks as joint unionist negotiators despite the incompatibility of the DUP's "devolutionist" position and the OUP's "integrationalist" call for increased linkage between Ulster and Britain. The Official Unionists won 9 of the 17 Northern Ireland seats in the UK election of April 1992, by which time they had officially adopted the UUP designation to signify continuity with the historic party.

Having held the party leadership since 1979, James MOLYNEAUX stood down in August 1995 and was succeeded by David Trimble, a leading UUP critic of the concessions being made to Dublin in the peace process. Two years later, in a remarkable turnaround, Trimble agreed to sit at the same negotiating table as *Sinn Féin,* and on April 10, 1998, UUP representatives signed the multiparty Good Friday Agreement. Fighting off intraparty opponents, including 6 of the party's 10 members of Parliament, Trimble secured UUP approval of the peace plan, and in the June 25 election the party won a plurality of 28 seats in the 108-seat Northern Ireland Assembly. On July 1 the assembly elected Trimble first minister of the Executive Committee, and in October 1998 he shared the Nobel Peace Prize with the SDLP's John Hume.

On October 9, 1998, a faction within the UUP formed Union First in opposition to the Good Friday Agreement and the presence of *Sinn Féin* in the government. Thereafter, criticism of Trimble continued to grow. Resentment over what hard-line unionists viewed as ill-advised concessions to *Sinn Féin* culminated in a March 25, 2000, challenge to his leadership by the Rev. Martin Smyth. Although the party's governing Ulster Unionist Council (UUC) gave Trimble 57 percent of the vote, Union First's Jeffrey Donaldson and Deputy Leader John Taylor were both considered to be likely future challengers. On May 27, having threatened to resign in the event of a negative vote, Trimble gained only 53 percent endorsement of the UUC (459–403) to accept the IRA's offer to permit international monitoring of its arms stockpiles.

On October 28, 2000, the UUC reconvened to consider a Donaldson proposal that the UUP withdraw from the government unless the IRA began decommissioning by November 30. Trimble countered by asserting that, as first minister, he would not authorize the government's two IRA ministers to participate in official North-South meetings until the IRA actively engaged with General de Chastelain's IICD. Trimble again won the council's support, 445–374.

Trimble resigned as first minister effective July 1, 2001. A month earlier the UUP had seen its support at the polls decline, costing it 3 of its 9 seats in the UK House of Commons and 31 of its 185 local council seats. Trimble was reelected first minister on November 6, 2001, although he had failed to obtain the needed majority of nationalist votes four days earlier when two UUP members, Peter WEIR and Pauline ARMITAGE, voted against him. Weir was subsequently expelled from the party and joined the DUP in April 2002; Armitage's membership was suspended.

The UUP lost its plurality to the DUP in the Northern Ireland Assembly election of November 26, 2003, and in late December Trimble's most severe intraparty critic, Jeffrey Donaldson, announced that he was quitting the UPP and aligning himself with the DUP. The UUP member of the European Parliament, Jim NICHOLSON, retained his seat in the 2004 balloting for that body, as the UUP came in third in votes (behind the DUP and *Sinn Féin*). At the UK general election of May 5, 2005, the UUP lost four of its five seats in the House of Commons, including the one held by Trimble, on a share of only 17.7 percent of the votes in Northern Ireland. The UUP also declined in the concurrent local elections, and Trimble, who had apparently suffered from the voters' perception that he and the UUP had been "too soft" regarding *Sinn Féin* and the IRA, promptly resigned as party leader. He was succeeded on June 24 by Reg Empey. While Trimble officially remained a UUP member of the suspended Northern Ireland Assembly through 2007, he was named as a member of the House of Lords in April 2006 and sat on that body as a crossbencher. In April 2007 Trimble announced he had joined the Conservative Party.

The UUP won 18 seats in the March 2007 elections for the Northern Ireland Assembly on a 14.9 percent share of first-preference votes. With 9 fewer seats than it had won in 2003, the UUP fell from second to third largest party in the assembly. Throughout 2008 UUP and UK Conservative Party leaders held discussions on reestablishing their once strong relationship, with an eye toward the UUP regaining lost support and the Conservatives broadening their geographical appeal. In November the parties announced an agreement to field candidates jointly for the June 2009 European Parliament elections and the 2010 balloting for the UK Parliament under the rubric of the **Ulster Conservative and Unionists–New Force.** The alliance finished third with 17.0 percent of the vote in the European Parliament poll, with the UUP incumbent retaining his seat.

Leaders: Reg EMPEY (Party Leader), John WHITE (President), David CAMPBELL (Chair), Terrence WRIGHT (Vice Chair).

Social Democratic and Labour Party—SDLP (*Páirtí Sóisialta Daonlathach an Lucht Oibre*). Founded in 1970 and a member of the Socialist International, the SDLP is a largely Catholic, left-of-center party that has championed the reunification of Ireland by popular consent, with Catholics being accorded full political and social rights in the interim. Its longtime leader, Gerard FITT, participated in the post-Sunningdale Faulkner government and subsequently became the only non-unionist to hold a seat in the UK House of Commons. Fitt resigned as party leader in November 1979 after the SDLP constituency representatives and executive had rejected the government's working paper for the 1980 constitutional conference on devolution. The SDLP won 14 assembly seats in 1982 but joined *Sinn Féin* in boycotting sessions. It won 3 UK House of Commons seats in 1987 on a platform that attacked the Thatcher government on employment, housing, education, and agricultural policies.

In addition to supporting the 1985 Anglo-Irish Agreement and resultant UK-Irish cooperation on Northern Ireland, the party became an enthusiastic participant in the 1991 Brooke initiative and its successor talks. Seeking a framework for peace, in April and May 1993 SDLP leader John Hume undertook an unprecedented series of meetings with *Sinn Féin* leader Gerry Adams and subsequently helped negotiate the 1994 IRA cease-fire.

The SDLP had mixed results at the polls during the 1990s, picking up 1 seat in the 1992 UK general election but returning just 3 MPs in 1997. A year earlier it had won a somewhat disappointing 21 seats in balloting for the Northern Ireland Forum. A strong supporter of the 1998 Good Friday Agreement, the party carried 24 seats, second to the UUP, in the subsequent election for the Northern Ireland Assembly. The party's deputy leader, Seamus Mallon, was elected deputy first minister of the Executive Committee, the position having been turned down by the overtaxed Hume, who served in the European Parliament as well as the UK House of Commons.

Hume received the 1998 Nobel Peace Prize, not only for his contribution to the Good Friday Agreement, but also for having been, over several decades, "the clearest and most consistent of Northern Ireland's political leaders" in the search for peace. In August 2000 Hume announced that he intended to resign his assembly seat but would retain his other positions. On September 17, 2001, however, he indicated that he would step down as party leader, and a day later Mallon made a similar announcement. At a November party conference Mark Durkan was named to replace Hume. Hume retired from public life in February 2004.

In balloting for the European Parliament in June 2004, the SDLP failed to win any of Northern Ireland's 3 seats. At the May 2005 balloting for the UK House of Commons, the SDLP retained its 3 seats with 17.5 percent of the votes in Northern Ireland. The party finished fourth in the March 7, 2007, elections for the Northern Ireland Assembly, securing 16 seats on a 15.2 percent share of first-preference votes. It also came in fourth (only 1 percent behind the UUP/Conservative alliance that won the third and final seat) in the June 2009 balloting for the European Parliament.

Leaders: Mark DURKAN (Party Leader), Alasdair McDONNELL (Deputy Leader), Gerry COSGROVE (General Secretary).

Other Parties Winning Seats in the 2007 Assembly Elections:

Alliance Party of Northern Ireland (APNI). A nonsectarian and nondoctrinaire group founded in 1970 in reaction to growing civil strife, the Alliance Party, like the SDLP, participated in the post-Sunningdale Faulkner government. It won ten assembly seats in 1982 and was the only non-unionist party to participate in that body's subsequent proceedings. For lack of alternative proposals, the party in 1987 announced continued support of the 1985 Anglo-Irish Agreement, although it called for the additional enactment of a bill of rights for Northern Ireland. It has achieved occasional success in local elections but has never won a seat in the UK House of Commons.

The Alliance was one of the four Ulster parties represented at talks between unionists and republicans in Duisburg, West Germany, in October 1988. Alliance officials attended the opening of the interparty Ulster talks on April 30, 1991, and, although sympathetic to the unionist position, indicated that they would support the SDLP.

Party leader Dr. John ALDERDICE was nominated to the House of Lords in 1996, giving the Alliance representation in the UK Parliament for the first time. It backed the Good Friday Agreement of 1998 but won only six seats at the subsequent assembly election, a performance that led Lord Alderdice to resign the party leadership. UK Secretary of State for Northern Ireland Mo Mowlam immediately named him as initial presiding officer of the assembly.

Party Leader Sean NEESON announced on September 6, 2001, his decision to step down in favor of "a fresh face," with David Ford then being elected in October as his successor. A month later, in a maneuver designed to secure David Trimble's reelection as first minister and thereby avert a collapse of the power-sharing government, Ford and two other Alliance assembly members temporarily redesignated themselves as unionists. As a result, Trimble was able to secure a bare majority of unionist votes, permitting his return to office.

The party retained its existing six seats at the 2003 assembly election. Although it improved to seven seats in 2007, that level of representation was not sufficient for it to be accorded any portfolios in the subsequent multiparty cabinet (determined by a formula that does not guarantee posts to smaller parties).

Leaders: David FORD (Party Leader), Naomi LONG (Deputy Leader), Colm CAVANAGH (President), Michael LONG (Chair), Dan McGUINNESS (Vice Chair), Gerry LYNCH (Executive Director).

Progressive Unionist Party (PUP). The PUP emerged out of the loyalist paramilitaries, in this case the Ulster Volunteer Force (UVF). The PUP's former leader, David ERVINE, served in the UVF and was imprisoned for five years for possession of explosives. The party is distinctive in that, while it is part of the unionist camp, it also champions working-class causes without regard to sect, and the party leader speaks openly of parallels in policy to British Labour. With a definition of unionism based more on the idea of citizenship than on religion, the party has appeared the most flexible in the unionist camp. It signed the 1998 Good Friday Agreement and won two seats in the June Northern Ireland Assembly election, one of which was lost in 2003.

In the wake of the renunciation of violence by the IRA in 2005, Ervine came under increasing pressure to facilitate similar action on the part of the UVF (below). Meanwhile, Ervine in May 2006 formed a controversial alliance with the UUP in the assembly in an attempt to secure an executive position for unionist forces. However, the assembly speaker ruled that the maneuver violated assembly rules.

Ervine died unexpectedly in early January 2007. He was succeeded as party leader by Dawn Purvis, who also was chosen to defend (successfully) Ervine's assembly seat in the March 2007 balloting for the Northern Ireland Assembly.

Leader: Dawn PURVIS (Party Leader).

Green Party in Northern Ireland (GPNI). A left-leaning branch of the Irish Green Party, the GPNI emphasizes environmental concerns and an integrationist perspective on the governance of Northern Ireland. In the 1998 assembly balloting the party placed last in first-preference votes, and in the 2003 assembly balloting its first-preference support was only 0.4 percent of the total votes. After the party won only three local council positions in 2005, a party conference on December 4, 2006, chose to replace its constitution by taking on the status of a regional grouping with direct association with the Irish Green Party and enhanced ties to green parties in Scotland, England, and Wales. At the same convention it elected Kelly Andrews and Brian Wilson to join in party leadership activities with John Barry.

Leaders: Kelly ANDREWS and John BARRY (Regional Co-Leaders).

Other Parties Contesting the 2007 Assembly Elections:

United Kingdom Unionist Party (UKUP). The UKUP was formed in 1995 to support the successful parliamentary by-election campaign of prominent lawyer Robert McCartney, who opposed the Anglo-Irish Agreement of 1985, the Downing Street Declaration by the British and Irish governments in 1993, and their joint framework document issued in February 1995. McCartney was the only UKUP candidate elected to a constituency seat in the 1996 forum poll, but the party gained two regional-list seats, providing a place for one of Ireland's most distinguished men of letters, Conor Cruise O'BRIEN. Like the DUP, the UKUP refused to sit at the same table as *Sinn Féin* and therefore boycotted the 1997–1998 Stormont talks. It opposed the resultant Good Friday Agreement but won five unionist seats at the June assembly election.

In October 1998 O'Brien, the party's president, withdrew from membership after he was quoted as suggesting that unionists might better negotiate with constitutional nationalists for a united Ireland instead of facing additional British concessions to extremist republicans. The party suffered another blow in January 1999 when four of its assembly members formed the Northern Ireland Unionist Party (below). In the June 2001 UK election the UKUP lost its only seat in the House of Commons, and in November 2003 it lost four of its five assembly seats.

The UKUP did not present candidates in the 2004 balloting for the European Parliament or the 2005 elections for the UK House of Commons. McCartney, the lone UKUP candidate elected to the Northern Ireland Assembly in 2003, stood for election in six different constituencies in the 2007 assembly poll but failed to win a seat. Overall, the UKUP won 1.5 percent of first-preference votes in that balloting. The party formally deregistered in September 2008.

Leader: Robert McCARTNEY.

Conservatives in Northern Ireland (Conservatives NI). This grouping is the Northern Ireland branch of the UK Conservative Party.

Its branch affiliation previously was with the UUP, which sat with the Conservatives in Westminster until disagreement over the 1973 Sunningdale Agreement split the UUP and severed the UUP's bond with the UK Conservatives. The Conservatives NI fielded candidates in the 1998, 2003, and 2007 Northern Ireland Assembly elections, its best showing being in 2007 when it won 0.5 percent of the first-preference votes. In July 2008 UK Conservative Party Leader David Cameron announced exploratory talks that could lead to recementing relations with the UUP. Among other things, Cameron promised to include a UUP MP in a ministerial post in a future Conservative government in Westminster. The Conservatives NI formed an electoral alliance with the UUP later in the year.

Leaders: Tim LEWIS (Chair).

Eight other registered parties fielded candidates in the 2007 assembly elections without success: the **Socialist Environmental Alliance,** led by Goretti HORGAN; **UK Independence,** led by Nigel FARAGE; the **Workers' Party,** led by John LOWRY; the **People Before Profit Alliance,** led by Gordon HEWITT; the **Socialist Party,** led by Peter HADDEN; **Make Politicians History,** led by Ronnie CARROLL; the **Labour Party of Northern Ireland,** led by Malachi CURRAN; and **Procapitalism,** led by Samuel SMYTH. In addition, six candidates were presented without formal party affiliation but in apparent association with **Republican** *Sinn Féin,* a group of former *Sinn Féin* members who walked out of a 1986 party conference in objection to withdrawing from the policy of abstentionism in the Republic of Ireland's Parliament. Republican *Sinn Féin* is led by Ruairi Ó BRÁDAIGH.

Other Parties and Groups:

Traditional Unionist Voice (TUV). The TUV was established in October 2007 by James (Jim) Allister, who had been elected to the European Parliament on the DUP ticket in 2004. Allister had resigned from the DUP in March 2007 in disagreement over the DUP's willingness to accept the requirement that *Sinn Féin* be included in a power-sharing arrangement. The TUV holds essentially the same positions as the DUP in regard to strong bonds with the UK and traditional family values. However, the TUV more stridently opposed putting police powers under the control of the Northern Ireland Assembly. It also completely rejects any form of devolution arrangement that requires a unionist and republican coalition. (The TUV does not formally oppose the possible formation of such a coalition but argues that it should not be mandated.)

Allister lost his seat in the European Parliament in the June 2009 balloting, as the TUV finished fifth with 13.5 percent of the vote and thereby did not qualify for any seats. However, the party appeared ready to continue to press its policy principles, having attracted many disaffected UUP voters. Allister subsequently stated his intention to contest the new UK Parliament elections (2010) and Northern Ireland Assembly balloting (2011) as a candidate in the unionist stronghold of North Antrim, Ian Paisley's constituency.

Leaders: James (Jim) ALLISTER (Leader), William ROSS (President), Ivor McCONNELL (Chair).

Northern Ireland Unionist Party (NIUP). Creation of the NIUP was announced on January 5, 1999, by four of the UKUP's five assembly members. Despite their opposition to formation of a power-sharing government with *Sinn Féin* membership, they had resigned from the UKUP in protest of Robert McCartney's order that the party withdraw from the legislature should *Sinn Féin* be permitted to join the Executive Committee prior to decommissioning. One of the four, Roger HUTCHINSON, was expelled from the party on December 2, 1999, for accepting membership on two assembly committees charged with scrutinizing executive ministries. The NIUP failed to win representation at the 2003 assembly poll and presented no candidates in 2007. It formally deregistered in March 2008.

Leader: Cedric WILSON (Leader).

United Unionist Assembly Party (UUAP). The UUAP, now formally registered as the United Unionist Alliance, was established with effect from September 21, 1998, by three unionists who had been elected to the Northern Ireland Assembly as independents. In April 2000 one of the three, Denis Watson, a leader of the Orange Order who had been expelled from the UUP for opposing the Good Friday Agreement, was reported to have joined the DUP. However, he remains listed as the UUP leader in the official party registry. The UUAP currently has two members serving as local councilors.

Leader: Denis WATSON (Leader).

Northern Ireland Women's Coalition (NIWC). The NIWC emerged in time for the forum elections of May 1996, although it won only about 1 percent of the vote. The movement was strongly nonpartisan, with candidates from a range of political persuasions, and nonsectarian. It signed the 1998 Good Friday Agreement and won two assembly seats in 1998 and none in 2003. The NIWC formally disbanded in May 2006. Its cofounder and former leader, Monica McWILLIAMS, is the current chief commissioner of the Northern Ireland Human Rights Commission.

Ulster Democratic Party (UDP). The UDP (known in 1981–1989 as the Ulster Loyalist Democratic Party—LDP) was founded in 1978 as the New Ulster Political Research Group by leaders of the Ulster Defence Association (UDA, below). The UDP had negligible electoral support but served as a channel of communication to the UDA and its supporters. Although a signatory to the 1998 Good Friday Agreement, it has never won assembly representation. The UDP was dissolved in 2001.

32 County Sovereignty Movement (32 CMA). This *Sinn Féin* splinter was formed in September 1997 as the 32 County Sovereignty Committee by ardent nationalists opposed to Gerry Adams's decision to support the Mitchell principles and join the multiparty negotiations in Stormont. One of its organizers, Bernadette SANDS-McKEVITT, is the sister of Bobby Sands, a leader of the Maze prison hunger strikes who died in 1981. The Movement is believed to be affiliated with the paramilitary Real IRA (below), which claimed responsibility for the August 1998 Omagh bombing. In June 2000 the Movement condemned the IRA's decision to permit international inspections of its arms stockpiles as "the first stop in a decommissioning surrender process." The U.S. State Department, describing the 32 CMA as an "alias" for the Real IRA, has designated the 32 CMA as a terrorist organization.

Numerous parties based in the Republic of Ireland also have branches in Northern Ireland. (See the article on Ireland for information on those parties.)

Former and Current Republican Paramilitary Groups:

Irish Republican Army (IRA). In the late 1960s arguments escalated between the dominant socialist faction in the Republican Clubs, as the (illegal) Northern Ireland section of *Sinn Féin* was then known, and traditional nationalist elements wanting to organize an armed defense of Catholic areas under attack from police and Protestant gangs. The dispute led to the creation in 1969 of a breakaway "Provisional" Army Council that set about rebuilding the IRA, which had withered away since its last terrorist campaign in 1956–1962. The "Provisional" IRA, supported by the "Provisional" *Sinn Féin,* quickly became a large and effective guerrilla organization, defining its aims as British withdrawal from Northern Ireland and the reunification of Ireland as a socialist republic. (Although in frequent use into the 1990s, the term "Provisional" had become redundant in the early 1980s, when the "Official" rump of the *Sinn Féin* became the Workers' Party—see the discussion of *Sinn Féin* in the Republic of Ireland article.)

Especially active in 1971–1976, when it carried out more than 5,000 bombings, a similar number of armed robberies, and more than 15,000 shootings, resulting in many hundreds of security-force and civilian deaths, the IRA was banned under the 1978 Emergency Provisions Act. It continued its activities in Northern Ireland, Britain, and sometimes continental Europe almost without interruption until 1994.

On August 31, 1994, following secret contacts with the British government, the IRA instituted a cease-fire with the aim of making it possible for *Sinn Féin,* which after 1981 had developed a strong electoral following, to take part in negotiations with the British and Irish governments and with regional parties. With *Sinn Féin* remaining marginalized by demands from most parties and the government that the IRA surrender its weapons, the IRA resumed its military activities in February 1996 by exploding a massive bomb in the financial district of London.

The cease-fire was renewed on July 19, 1997, which opened the way for *Sinn Féin* to join the peace negotiations in Stormont two months later. The IRA gave qualified support to the Good Friday Agreement of April 1998 but at the time refused to link decommissioning of its arms to formation of a devolved government for Northern Ireland, as demanded by the plurality UUP. In December 1998 senior IRA leaders elected a seven-member Army Council headed by hard-liner Brian KEENAN, reinforcing the possibility that the cease-fire might be rescinded were *Sinn Féin* to be excluded from the Northern Ireland Executive.

The IRA's continuing refusal to begin disarming before the inauguration of the power-sharing executive delayed devolution until December 2, 1999, shortly after the IRA had indicated that it was willing to discuss disarmament with Gen. John de Chastelain of the IICD. Nevertheless, no tangible progress was made in the following two months. On February 11, 2000, the IRA offered, in the words of a report from de Chastelain, "to consider how to put arms and explosives beyond use," but the proposal was too late to prevent London's reimposition of direct rule. On May 6, however, the IRA announced that it would accept international monitoring of its arsenals and would "completely and verifiably" put its weapons beyond use. The breakthrough and a subsequent positive UUP response led London, on May 30, to return authority to the Northern Ireland Assembly and Executive. On June 25 the IRA stated that it had reopened discussions with de Chastelain's IICD, and on June 26 arms inspectors reported that they had completed their first visits to IRA caches. Another inspection occurred in May 2001, although the IRA still refused to consider a firm timetable for decommissioning. In early August the IICD announced an agreement on how decommissioning might proceed, but a week later the IRA rescinded its approval because of the August 11 suspension of the power-sharing government. In mid-September it agreed once again to move forward on discussions with the IICD, and on October 23 the IRA announced its first confirmed decommissioning of weapons. An additional, larger decommissioning occurred in April 2002, and on July 16 the IRA issued its first public apology to the families of its innocent victims.

In October 2002 the discovery of alleged IRA spying in official offices in Stormont led to demands from UK Prime Minister Blair, among others, that the IRA reject violence and fully commit itself to peace. The reimposition of direct rule from London on October 15 led the IRA, two weeks later, to discontinue talks with the IICD.

The IRA's alleged involvement in the December 2004 robbery of Belfast's Northern Bank yielded a breakdown in what had appeared to be a promising outcome for the lengthy peace talks. However, momentum returned in mid-2005 when the IRA, following the encouragement of *Sinn Féin* leader Gerry Adams, renounced the use of violence and vowed to disarm. There have been few reports of IRA activity recently in the wake of cross-community political progress (see Recent developments, above). The Independent Monitoring Commission (IMC), a group organized by the UK and Irish governments to evaluate paramilitary activities, reported in September 2008 that the IRA leadership and terrorist structure were no longer operational and thus no longer posed a security threat.

Irish National Liberation Army (INLA). Formed in 1975 by dissident members of the "Official" IRA after that group had adopted a policy of nonviolence, the INLA was banned in 1979 after assassinating a close associate of Margaret Thatcher. A number of INLA members joined the Maze hunger strikes of 1980–1981. Other members of the INLA and its political front, the **Irish Republican Socialist Party** (see Ireland: Political Parties), were killed in internal feuds, in disputes with the IRA, or in attacks allegedly related to the involvement in the drug trade of the INLA itself and a splinter group, the **Irish People's Liberation Organization** (IPLO). The INLA declared a cease-fire on August 22, 1998, in the wake of the Omagh bombing, and reaffirmed it in early August 1999. In March 2000 the INLA stated that it had delivered to the principal loyalist paramilitary groups, the UDA and UVF, a paper on maintaining the cease-fire even in the face of political impasse. In late 2009 the INLA appeared ready to announce decommissioning of its weapons.

Continuity IRA (CIRA). Adamantly opposed to the peace process, including the IRA cease-fire announced in 1994, the CIRA (also referenced as the Continuity Army Council—CAC) in 1996 claimed responsibility for a number of attacks in Northern Ireland. Some reports characterized the CIRA as an armed wing of the Republican *Sinn Féin* (RSF) party (see Ireland: Political Parties), although the RSF denied any such linkage. Although itself responsible for bombings and killings, the CIRA condemned the August 1998 Omagh bombing as an unjustified "slaughter of the innocents." Believed to number at that time only about 30, the group may have attracted additional members following the cease-fire declared by the Real IRA (below) in September 1998. The CIRA remained the only republican group not to have declared a cease-fire, and in the first seven months of 2000 it claimed responsibility for a number of bombings in Northern Ireland and England. Some antiterrorism agencies suspected, however, that other groups, particularly the Real IRA, may have been using the CIRA as a cover name. In March 2009 the CIRA, declared a terrorist organization by the United States, claimed responsibility for the murder of a Catholic PSNI officer.

Real IRA. Apparently organized in October 1997 in opposition to the renewed IRA cease-fire and *Sinn Féin*'s participation in the Stormont peace talks, the Real IRA probably numbered no more than 100–150 members. It was believed in some quarters to be serving as the military wing of the 32 County Sovereignty Movement, whose leaders have denied any connection.

In June 1998 reports surfaced that the Real IRA, the Continuity IRA, and the INLA had held a summit in Dundalk, Ireland, and may have agreed to unify their forces. Following the August Omagh bombing, however, the Continuity IRA and the INLA distanced themselves from the attack, for which the Real IRA claimed responsibility. On August 18, three days after the car bombing, the Real IRA announced a "complete cessation of all military activity." On September 8, reportedly after its leaders received personal visits from the IRA, it declared a "permanent" cease-fire, although it was implicated in subsequent bombings, including a number in England. In May 2000 it warned that it was preparing a renewed bombing campaign. Two months later the Real IRA was implicated in a failed effort to smuggle a shipment of explosives and weapons from Croatia, and in September it was branded as the probable perpetrator of two attacks on security bases in the North. In March 2001 authorities implicated the Real IRA in a car-bomb explosion outside the West London offices of the British Broadcasting Corporation (BBC). Other bombings in May and August were also attributed to the Real IRA. In May 2002 three Real IRA members pleaded guilty to conspiracy and other charges and received 30-year sentences.

Michael McKevitt, the leader of the Real IRA, was convicted in 2003 of the charge of heading a terrorist organization; he was sentenced to a 20-year prison term. (The verdict was handed down by a nonjury Special Criminal Court authorized to adjudicate terrorism cases following the 1998 Omagh bombing.) In March 2009 the Real IRA claimed responsibility for the murder of two UK soldiers.

Leader: Michael McKEVITT (in prison).

Former and Current Loyalist Paramilitary Groups:

Ulster Defence Association (UDA). Formed in 1971 by the amalgamation of loyalist paramilitary groups, mainly in greater Belfast and Londonderry, the UDA was initially a mass-membership organization involved in street protests and rallies, including the political strike and accompanying intimidation that brought down the power-sharing administration in 1974. It became increasingly involved in sectarian violence, using such cover names as **Ulster Freedom Fighters** (UFF) and "Ulster Young Militants" to claim responsibility for several hundred killings, the vast majority being noncombatant Catholics. From the mid-1970s the UDA also became deeply enmeshed in racketeering in Northern Ireland, while in the late 1980s it obtained significant material support from the apartheid regime in South Africa.

The UFF was banned in 1973, but the UDA remained legal until 1992, when it was proscribed after a British Army intelligence agent operating in the UDA high command was convicted of conspiracy to murder. The case highlighted allegations that the loyalist paramilitaries had benefited extensively from collusion with members of the police, the army, and the intelligence services. In the interim, the UDA had established a political front, the **Ulster Democratic Party** (UDP), which remained legal.

In 1991 the UDA/UFF joined the Ulster Volunteer Force and the Red Hand Commando (below) in forming a Combined Loyalist Military Command (CLMC) to coordinate paramilitary activities. The CLMC declared a brief cease-fire in 1991 and then an indefinite cease-fire (subsequently violated) in October 1994, four months after the IRA had done so. In October 1997 conflict within the CLMC broke into the open, and the UDA announced its withdrawal, leading to reports that the joint command had disbanded. Within days sporadic intraloyalist violence was reported, without, however, threatening the cease-fire.

Cease-fire violations attributed to the UFF led to suspension of the UDP from the Stormont peace talks in January–March 1998, but on April 25 the UDA announced its support for the Good Friday Agreement. It may now number only several hundred members, although it claimed the support of as many as 40,000 at its peak in the 1970s. In September 1999 UFF leader Johnny Adair was released from prison in accordance with the peace agreement, having served 4 years of his 16-year term for terrorism.

On June 20, 2000, members of the UFF threatened to break its cease-fire, "reserving the right" to defend Protestant homes in the context of "ethnic cleansing" and "intimidation" perpetrated by nationalists. Three days later, however, it retracted its warning. Two months later, Adair's early release was suspended in the context of violent clashes between the UFF/UDA and the UVF/PUP in Belfast. Altercations continued for several more months. On December 15 the UDA, the UVF, and the Red Hand Commando agreed to a truce.

On October 12, 2001, responding to a renewed wave of violence and rioting, Secretary of State for Northern Ireland John Reid declared an end to the government's cease-fire with the UDA/UFF. Adair, having completed his sentence, was released from prison on May 15, 2002.

The UDA formally renounced violence and disbanded its armed units in November 2007 and in 2009 announced the decommissioning of its weapons.

Ulster Volunteer Force (UVF). The UVF was founded in 1966 and was quickly banned after allegedly killing two Catholics. It was restored to legal status in 1974 to encourage it to become involved in politics through the Volunteer Political Party (later reconstituted as the Progressive Unionist Party—PUP, above). Banned again after several murders in October 1975, the UVF conducted a protracted campaign of sectarian assassinations designed to put pressure on the IRA to halt its activities, the most active UVF units being based in Belfast, Armagh, and Tyrone.

In general, the UVF held to the CLMC cease-fire of 1994, despite differences with the UDA that reportedly led to the UVF's expulsion from Londonderry in November 1997. A splinter group, the Loyalist Volunteer Force (below), left the UVF in 1996, and infighting between the two persisted. In January 2000 a UVF commander, Richard JAMESON, was assassinated, with suspicion immediately falling on the LVF. The parent group may now number a few hundred members, compared to 1,500 in the 1970s.

In July and August 2000 a renewed feud with the UFF for control of loyalist territory (and possibly drug trafficking) in Belfast resulted in the redeployment of UK troops in the capital. In December 2000 the UVF joined the UDA and the Red Hand Commando in a truce.

The UK government charged that the UVF was significantly involved with "loyalist riots" that broke out in Belfast in September 2005, and the UVF was also blamed for several murders in connection with its ongoing feud with the LVF. Consequently, the UK signaled that it no longer considered the UVF to be honoring the cease-fire. In mid-2006 the UVF was pressured to disband (as the LVF had), but it refused to "clarify" its stance. However, the UVF announced in 2009 that it would decommission its arms.

Red Hand Commando (RHC). Formed in 1972 and proscribed since 1973, the small RHC was frequently linked to the UVF, with some reports describing it as nothing more than a cover name for the larger group. The RHC agreed to the December 2000 truce between the UVF and the UDA. In 2009 the RHC joined the UVF and UDA in agreeing to the decommissioning of their weapons.

Loyalist Volunteer Force (LVF). Apparently dating from about 1994, the LVF formed within the UVF around the leadership of Billy Wright, who opposed the 1994 cease-fire and any concessions to nationalists. The LVF withdrew from the UVF in 1996 and was banned a year later. On December 27, 1997, Wright was murdered in Maze prison by INLA inmates, after which the LVF was implicated in a number of apparently retaliatory sectarian killings. (Collaterally, unconfirmed reports suggested that the group was permitting UFF paramilitaries to use the LVF name as a cover.)

The LVF declared a unilateral cease-fire on May 15, 1998, but also urged a "no" vote at the May 22 referendum on the Good Friday Agreement. Three months later it called for an "absolute, utter" end to terrorism and made its cease-fire permanent, thereby qualifying its incarcerated members for early release under the peace accord. On December 18, 1998, the LVF became the first paramilitary organization to decommission some of its weapons, a gesture that the IRA labeled a "stunt."

In November 2005 it was reported that the LVF had disbanded after directing its members to discontinue all operations. The decision was described as a "direct response" to the IRA's recent decision to decommission its arms.

Orange Volunteers (OV). Reviving the name of a major loyalist paramilitary group of the 1970s, the Orange Volunteers emerged in 1998 in opposition to the Good Friday Agreement and the cease-fires declared by other loyalist organizations. It subsequently conducted a small number of sectarian attacks. Its membership, apparently numbering no more than a few dozen individuals disaffected from the UDA/UFF and the LVF, may have overlapped that of the Red Hand Defenders (below). In 2000 both groups were added to the U.S. government's annual list of organizations suspected of terrorism.

Red Hand Defenders (RHD). Like the OV, the RHD was formed in 1998 by loyalist rejectionists. In March 1999 it claimed responsibility for the car bombing that killed prominent lawyer Rosemary Nelson. Two days later, Frankie CURRY, a reputed RHD member, was killed in what some officials characterized as an ongoing conflict between loyalist groups engaged in organized crime. The RHD blamed the UVF for Curry's death but denied that he was a member. In January 2002, following the shooting of a postal worker, the RHD indicated that it was disbanding at the request of the UFF, but another shooting in April was attributed to the group. Some analysts argued that the RHD was a cover name for the UDA/UFF.

LEGISLATURE

The former bicameral Northern Ireland Parliament was replaced by a unicameral Northern Ireland Assembly under the Northern Ireland Constitution Act of July 1973. The assembly and a Northern Ireland Executive functioned in 1973–1974, while a 1982 act of Parliament led to the election of another assembly, initially with consultative powers, in November 1982. With its tasks unfulfilled, the assembly was dissolved in June 1986, although subject to legislative provision that it could be reactivated. On May 30, 1996, provincial elections were held for a 110-member Northern Ireland Forum for Political Dialogue, a nonlegislative body designed to provide a platform for discussion and to assist in choosing delegates to the coming peace talks.

A 108-member body, initially termed the New Northern Ireland Assembly, was elected for a five-year term on June 25, 1998, but was suspended upon the reintroduction of direct rule on October 15, 2002. New assembly balloting was conducted on November 25, 2003, although the body remained under suspension. The 2003 poll yielded 30 seats for the Democratic Unionist Party (DUP), 27 for the Ulster Unionist Party (UUP), 24 for *Sinn Féin,* 18 for the Social Democratic and Labour Party (SDLP), 6 for the Alliance Party of Northern Ireland, 1 for the Progressive Unionist Party (PUP), 1 for the United Kingdom Unionist Party (UKUP), and 1 for an independent. (In June 2006 it was reported that a UUP member of the assembly had defected to the UK Conservative Party.)

The assembly convened "without power" on May 15, 2006, for the first time in three-and-a-half years as part of the revived effort to resolve the governmental impasse, and assembly committees continued to meet throughout the summer. In the wake of the St. Andrews Agreement of November 2006 providing for the return of self-rule to Northern Ireland, balloting was held for a Northern Ireland Assembly on March 7, 2007, resulting in the following distribution of seats: the DUP, 36; *Sinn Féin,* 28; the UUP, 18; the SDLP, 16; the Alliance Party of Northern Ireland, 7; the Green Party in Northern Ireland, 1; the PUP, 1; and independents, 1. (The 108 members of the assembly [6 from each of 18 constituencies] are elected via universal suffrage under a single-transferable vote system for five-year terms, subject to dissolution.)

Speaker: William HAY.

CABINET

[as of November 1, 2009]

First Minister	Peter Robinson (DUP)
Deputy First Minister	Martin McGuinness (SF)

Ministers

Agriculture and Rural Development	Michelle Gilderneew (SF) [f]
Culture, Arts, and Leisure	Nelson McCausland (DUP)
Education	Caitriona Ruane (SF) [f]
Employment and Learning	Reg Empey (UUP)
Enterprise, Trade, and Investment	Arlene Foster (DUP) [f]
Environment	Edwin Poots (DUP)
Finance and Personnel	Sammy Wilson (DUP)
Health, Social Services, and Public Safety	Michael McGimpsey (UUP)
Regional Development	Conor Murphy (SF)
Social Development	Margaret Ritchie (SDLP) [f]

[f] = female

Note: DUP = Democratic Unionist Party, SF = *Sinn Féin,* UUP = Ulster Unionist Party, and SDLP = Social Democratic and Labour Party.

COMMUNICATIONS

Press, radio, and television are organized along the same lines as in Great Britain.

Press. The following newspapers are published in Belfast: *Belfast Telegraph* (76,000); pro-unionist daily; *Sunday Life* (66,800); *Irish News* (47,900), nationalist daily; *News Letter* (26,200), pro-unionist daily.

UNITED STATES

United States of America

Political Status: Independence declared on July 4, 1776; federal republic established under constitution adopted on March 4, 1789.

Area: 3,732,396 sq. mi. (9,666,532 sq. km.); includes gross area (land and water) of the 50 states, excluding Puerto Rico and other territories. These totals are somewhat higher than earlier ones because of a 1990 change in the method of calculating interior waters.

Population: 281,421,906 (2000C); 304,514,000 (2008E). In July 1991 the U.S. government conceded that the 1990 count of 248,709,873 missed about 2 percent of the population but declined to provide an official adjustment for underenumeration. The 2000 figure was advanced by the Census Bureau as being "much more robust" than anticipated.

Major Urban Centers (2008E):

City Proper	*Population*	*Metro Area*
WASHINGTON, D.C.	591,000	5,353,000
New York, N.Y.	8,299,000	18,819,000
Los Angeles, Calif.	3,849,000	12,885,000
Chicago, Ill.	2,845,000	9,592,000
Houston, Texas	2,244,000	5,751,000
Phoenix, Ariz.	1,588,000	4,315,000
Philadelphia, Pa.	1,528,000	5,845,000
San Antonio, Texas	1,363,000	2,047,000
San Diego, Calif.	1,275,000	3,002,000
Dallas, Texas	1,252,000	6,311,000
Detroit, Mich.	915,000	4,441,000
Jacksonville, Fla.	813,000	1,323,000
Indianapolis, Ind.	798,000	1,720,000
Columbus, Ohio	753,000	1,773,000
San Francisco, Calif.	774,000	4,244,000
Memphis, Tenn.	671,000	1,290,000
Baltimore, Md.	633,000	2,673,000
Seattle, Wash.	603,000	3,357,000
Boston, Mass.	602,000	4,500,000
Milwaukee, Wisc.	601,000	1,547,000
Denver, Colo.	600,000	2,519,000
Kansas City, Mo.	453,000	2,008,000
Cleveland, Ohio	433,000	2,087,000
St. Louis, Mo.	348,000	2,814,000
Pittsburgh, Pa.	308,000	2,329,000
New Orleans, La.	272,000	1,072,000

Principal Language: English. In the 2000 census approximately 82.1 percent spoke only English; 10.7 percent, Spanish; 7.2 percent, other.

Monetary Unit: Dollar (selected market rates December 1, 2009: $1US = .60 UK pounds sterling, 86.68 Japanese yen, 0.99 Swiss francs, and 0.66 euros).

President: Barack H. OBAMA (Democratic Party); elected on November 4, 2008 (technically, by the electoral college on December 15), and inaugurated on January 20, 2009, for a four-year term, succeeding George W. Bush (Republican Party).

Vice President: Joseph R. BIDEN Jr. (Democratic Party); elected on November 4, 2008, and inaugurated on January 20, 2009 , for a term concurrent with that of the president, succeeding Richard B. CHENEY (Republican Party).

THE COUNTRY

First among the nations of the world in economic output and productivity, the United States ranks third in area (behind Russia and Canada) and also third in population (after China and India). Canada and Mexico are the country's only contiguous neighbors. Most of U.S. territory ranges across the North American continent in a broad band that encompasses the Atlantic seaboard; the Appalachian Mountains; the Ohio, Mississippi, and Missouri river valleys; the Great Plains; the Rocky Mountains; the deserts of the Southwest; and the narrow, fertile coastland adjoining the Pacific. Further contrasts are found in the two noncontiguous states: Alaska, in northwestern North America, where the climate ranges from severe winters and short growing seasons in the north to equable temperatures in the south; and Hawaii, in the mid-Pacific, where trade winds produce a narrow temperature range but extreme variations in rainfall.

Regional diversity is also found in economic conditions. Industrial production is located mainly in the coastal areas and in those interior urban centers with good transportation connections, as in the Great Lakes region. Agricultural products come primarily from the far western, plains, midwestern, and southeastern states. Per capita income varies considerably from state to state, ranging in 2008 from a high of $56,248 in Connecticut to a low of $29,569 in Mississippi, with a national average of $40,398.

The nation's ethnic diversity is a product of large-scale voluntary and involuntary immigration, much of which took place before 1920. According to Census Bureau estimates, the population in 2007 was (2000 census estimates in parentheses) 73.9 (75.1) percent white, 12.4 (12.3) percent black, 4.5 (3.7) percent Asian and Pacific Islander, and 0.8 (0.9) percent American Indian and native Alaskan. In addition, Hispanic Americans (a nonexclusive category) constituted 14.8 percent in 2006 (up from 12.5 percent in 2000 and 9 percent in 1990), thereby becoming the country's largest minority group.

Religious diversity parallels, and is in part caused by, ethnic diversity. In 2009 83.1 percent of adults identified themselves as religious, of whom Protestants constituted 51.3 percent; Roman Catholics, 23.9 percent; Jews, 1.7 percent; and Orthodox Christians, 0.6 percent. Although English is the principal language, Spanish is the preferred tongue of sizable minorities in New York City (largely migrants from Puerto Rico), in Florida (primarily Caribbean expatriates), and in the Southwest and California (mainly from Mexico). Other languages are spoken among foreign-born and first-generation Americans.

In 2008 women constituted 46.5 percent of the full-time labor force and were concentrated in clerical, retail, and human service occupations. Women earned approximately 80 percent of the median male wage. As of September 2009, females held 76 nonterritorial seats (17.5 percent) in the U.S. House of Representatives (up from 62 [14.3 percent] in 2002) and 17 seats (17 percent) in the Senate (up from 13 in 2002). In addition, female governors led six states (down from eight in 2006).

Owing to a historic transfer of population from farm to city (now seemingly at an end, with migration to rural areas fluctuating close to a reversal in 1990–2000), only a small proportion of the population is engaged in agriculture, which nevertheless yields a substantial proportion of U.S. exports. As of August 2009 agriculture employed 2.1 million workers out of a total civilian labor force of 154.3 million (1.4 percent, excluding 14.9 million unemployed). By contrast, 18.6 percent of the labor force was engaged in mining, manufacturing, and construction; 14.7 percent in retail trade; and 71.6 percent in government and other service activities (excluding domestic employment). Of increasing importance to the administration of the nation's Social Security system is the aging of the population; the percentage of those of age 65 and older rose from approximately 4 percent in 1900 to 12.5 percent in 1998 but declined marginally to 12.3 percent in 2008.

The United States has experienced long-term economic growth throughout most of its history, with marked short-term fluctuations in recent years. During 1960–2005 the real per capita change in GDP averaged 3.7 percent. December 2000 marked the 127th consecutive month of economic expansion, the longest period of peacetime growth in U.S. history. Budget surpluses continued to accrue into 2001 but went into deficit thereafter.

GDP expanded by approximately 1.7 percent in 2001, the economy being described as on "fragile footing" after the terrorist attacks against the United States on September 11. However, due to the Federal Reserve Banks's lowering interest rates and collateral government tax cuts, a fairly rapid recovery followed, with average annual growth of about 3 percent reported for 2002–2005. The economy began to cool again in 2006–2007, with average annual GDP growth of 2.1 percent for that period. A significant decline of 1.9 percent was registered in 2008 following the dramatic downturn in the housing market and the stock market and the collapse of several large financial institutions, in what many observers described as a deepening recession (see Political Background, below). The government responded with varying public and private capital injections, popularly known as "stimulus" spending, and bailout plans by the end of the year. Other proposals to boost the economy were debated in Congress through 2009 as unemployment persisted.

GOVERNMENT AND POLITICS

Political background. Beginning as a group of 13 British colonies along the Atlantic seaboard, the "United States of America" declared themselves independent on July 4, 1776, gained recognition as a sovereign state at the close of the Revolutionary War in 1783, and in 1787 adopted a federal constitution that became effective March 4, 1789. George WASHINGTON took office as the first president of the United States on April 30. Westward expansion, colonization, judicious purchase, and annexation during the ensuing 100 years found the nation by 1890 in full possession of the continental territories that now make up the 48 contiguous states. Alaska, purchased from Russia in 1867, and Hawaii, annexed in 1898, became the 49th and 50th states, respectively, in 1959.

The constitutional foundation of the Union has been severely threatened only by the Civil War of 1861–1865, in which the separate confederacy established by 11 southern states was defeated and reintegrated into the Federal Union by military force. The U.S. political climate has been characterized by the alternating rule of the Republican and Democratic parties since the Civil War, which initiated a period of industrial expansion that continued without major interruptions through World War I before being temporarily checked by the Great Depression of the early 1930s.

The modern era of administrative centralization and massive federal efforts to solve economic and social problems began in 1933 with the inauguration of Democratic president Franklin D. ROOSEVELT. The onset of direct U.S. involvement in World War II on December 7, 1941, brought further governmental expansion. Following the defeat of the Axis powers, efforts supporting European reconstruction and attempting to meet the challenge posed by the rise of the Soviet Union as a world power dominated the administration of Harry S. TRUMAN, the Democratic vice president who succeeded Roosevelt upon his death on April 12, 1945, and was elected in 1948 to a full four-year term. Newly armed with atomic weapons, the United States abandoned its traditional isolation to become a founding member of the United Nations (UN) and the leader of a worldwide coalition directed against the efforts of the Soviet Union and, after 1949, the People's Republic of China, to expand their influence along the periphery of the communist world. A series of East-West confrontations over Iran, Greece, and Berlin culminated in the Korean War of 1950–1953, in which U.S. forces were committed to large-scale military action under the flag of the UN.

Dwight D. EISENHOWER, elected president on the Republican tickets of 1952 and 1956, achieved a negotiated settlement in Korea and some relaxation of tensions with the Soviet Union, but efforts to solve such basic East-West problems as the division of Germany proved unavailing. Whereas Eisenhower's attempts to restrict the role of the federal government met only limited success, his eight-year incumbency witnessed a resumption of progress toward legal equality of the races—after a lapse of 80 years—pursuant to the 1954 Supreme Court decision declaring segregation in public schools unconstitutional. An economic recession developed toward the end of Eisenhower's second term, which also saw the beginning of a substantial depletion of U.S. gold reserves. In spite of a resurgent economy, balance-of-payments problems persisted throughout the succeeding Democratic administrations of presidents John F. KENNEDY (1961–1963) and Lyndon B. JOHNSON (1963–1969).

The assassinations of President Kennedy in 1963 and civil rights advocate Martin Luther KING Jr. and Sen. Robert F. KENNEDY in 1968 provided the most dramatic evidence of a deteriorating domestic climate. To counter sharpening racial and social antagonisms and growing violence on the part of disaffected groups and individuals, Congress, at President Johnson's urging, passed laws promoting equal rights in housing, education, and voter registration and establishing programs to further equal job opportunities, urban renewal, and improved education for the disadvantaged. These efforts were in part offset by the negative domestic consequences of U.S. involvement in the Vietnam War, which had begun with limited economic and military aid to the French in the 1950s but by the mid-1960s had become direct and massive. Disagreement over Vietnam was also largely responsible for halting a trend toward improved U.S.-Soviet relations that had followed the Cuban missile crisis of 1962 and had led in 1963 to the signing of a limited nuclear test-ban treaty. Moved by increasing public criticism of the government's Vietnam policy, President Johnson on March 31, 1968, announced the cessation of bombing in most of North Vietnam as a step toward direct negotiations to end the war, and preliminary peace talks with the North Vietnamese began in Paris on May 13.

Richard M. NIXON, vice president during the Eisenhower administration and unsuccessful presidential candidate in 1960, was nominated as the 1968 Republican candidate for president, whereas Vice President Hubert H. HUMPHREY became the Democratic nominee, and former Alabama governor George C. WALLACE, a dissident Democrat, ran as the candidate of the American Independent Party, which sought to capitalize primarily on sectional and segregationist sentiments. Nixon won the election on November 5 with 43.4 percent of the national popular vote, the poorest showing by any victorious candidate since 1912. Humphrey captured 42.7 percent, and Wallace won 13.5 percent—the largest total for a third-party candidate since 1924.

Following Nixon's inauguration on January 20, 1969, the president embarked on a vigorous foreign policy campaign while selectively limiting the nation's external commitments in Southeast Asia and elsewhere. Domestically the Nixon administration became increasingly alarmed at the growing antiwar movement and reports of radical extremist activity, and in April 1970 it initiated a program of surveillance of militant left-wing groups and individuals. In May the president's decision to order Vietnamese-based U.S. troops into action in Cambodia provoked an antiwar demonstration at Kent State University, in the course of which the Ohio National Guard killed four students. Final agreement on a peace treaty in Vietnam was not obtained until January 27, 1973 (see Foreign relations, below), by which time the "youth rebellion" that had characterized the late 1960s was in pronounced decline.

Nixon was reelected in a landslide victory over an antiwar Democrat, Senator George S. McGOVERN of South Dakota, on November 7, 1972. Winning a record-breaking 60.7 percent of the popular vote, Nixon swept all major electoral units except Massachusetts and the District of Columbia, although the Democrats easily retained control of both houses of Congress. Within a year, however, the fortunes of Republican executive leaders were quickly reversed. On October 10, 1973, Spiro T. AGNEW resigned as vice president after pleading no contest to having falsified a federal income-tax return. He was succeeded on December 6 by longtime Michigan representative Gerald R. FORD, the first vice president to be chosen, under the 25th Amendment of the Constitution, by presidential nomination and congressional confirmation. On March 1, 1974, seven former White House and presidential campaign aides were charged with conspiracy in an attempted cover-up of the Watergate scandal (involving a break-in at Democratic National Committee headquarters at their Washington, D.C., building on June 17, 1972), while President Nixon, because of the same scandal, became on August 9 the first U.S. chief executive to tender his resignation. Vice President Ford, who succeeded Nixon on the same day, thus became the first U.S. president never to have participated in a national election.

In the election of November 2, 1976, the Democratic candidate, former Georgia governor Jimmy CARTER, defeated President Ford by a bare majority (50.6 percent) of the popular vote. Ford thus became the first incumbent since 1932 to fail in a bid for a second term. Carter also became a one-term president on November 4, 1980, as his Republican opponent, Ronald REAGAN, swept all but six states and the District of Columbia with a popular vote margin of 10 percent and a near ten-to-one margin in the electoral college. In congressional balloting the Republicans ended the Democrats' 28-year control of the Senate and registered substantial gains in the House of Representatives, the two bodies for the first time since 1916 being controlled by different parties.

The 1980 outcome was hailed as a "mandate for change" unparalleled since the Roosevelt landslide of 1932. Accordingly, President Reagan moved quickly to address the nation's economic problems by a combination of across-the-board fiscal retrenchment and massive tax cuts, with only the military establishment receiving significant additional funding to redress the perception of a widening gap between U.S. and Soviet tactical and strategic capabilities. An important component of what was billed as the "New Federalism" was sharply curtailed aid to the states, which were invited to accept responsibility for many social programs that had long been funded directly from Washington, D.C. While most liberals decried the new administration's commitment to economic "realism," the country made significant progress in lowering interest rates and slowing inflation.

Despite the onset of a severe economic recession that the administration sought to counter with a series of "hard-line" fiscal and monetary policies, the midterm elections of November 2, 1982, yielded no significant alteration in the domestic balance of power. The Democrats realized a net gain of 7 governorships (the resultant distribution being 34 Democratic incumbents to 16 Republican) and increased their majority in the House of Representatives by 26 seats to 269–166. However, Republican control of the Senate remained unchanged at 54–46.

On November 6, 1984, President Reagan won reelection by the second-largest electoral college margin (97.6 percent) in U.S. history, nearly equaling the record of 98.5 percent set by President Roosevelt in 1936. His Democratic opponent, Walter F. MONDALE, won only in his home state of Minnesota and in the District of Columbia. The Republicans also retained control of the Senate (53–47), while the Democrats retained control of the House with a reduced majority of 253–182. The gubernatorial balloting yielded a net gain of 1 for the Republicans, who, as in 1982, could thereafter claim incumbents in 16 states, as contrasted with 34 for the Democrats.

During the 1984 campaign Reagan promised no increase in personal income taxes, and in his inaugural address on January 21, 1985, he called for a simplified tax system and drastic limitations on federal spending, from which the military would, however, be partially exempt. Over the ensuing 18 months, sweeping changes were made in what ultimately emerged as the Tax Reform Act of 1986, particularly in a reduction in the number of tax brackets and a lowering of the top rate, with families at or below the poverty line freed of any obligation. The package was to be paid for, in part, by the elimination of many deductions and loopholes, with little measurable gain for individuals in the middle-income range. During the same period, while inflation and unemployment remained at moderate levels, the nation recorded massive trade deficits, despite steady erosion in the value of the U.S. dollar, which declined by more than 20 percent in trade-weighted terms from December 1984 to March 1986. As a result the Reagan administration, steadfastly maintaining its commitment to free trade, called for measures to counter what it perceived as a "protectionist upsurge" on the part of many of its trading partners.

In the nonpresidential balloting of November 4, 1986, the Democrats increased their margin in the House to 258–177 while regaining control of the Senate, 55–45. At the state level they suffered a net loss of 8 governorships, retaining a bare majority of 26.

On November 8, 1988, Republican George H. W. BUSH became the first sitting vice president since Martin Van Buren in 1836 to win the presidency, defeating his Democratic opponent Michael S. DUKAKIS by securing 54 percent of the popular vote and 79 percent of the electoral college vote. The Democrats, however, marginally increased their control of the House (260–175), with no change in the composition of the Senate and a net gain of 1 gubernatorial office over the 27 held immediately before the election.

Following the midterm balloting of November 6, 1990, the Democrats held 267 House seats (a net gain of 8 over the preelection distribution) and 56 Senate seats (a net gain of 1), while retaining a total of 28 governorships (a net loss of 1). One House seat in 1990 was won by Bernard SANDERS, an independent Vermont socialist, and the remaining 167 by the Republicans, who retained 44 Senate seats and 20 governorships, with 2 of the state houses being filled by independents. In the presidential poll of November 3, 1992, Arkansas governor William CLINTON denied Bush reelection by winning 43 percent of the popular and 69 percent of the electoral college votes, as contrasted with percentages of 38 percent and 31 percent for the incumbent. Business owner H. Ross PEROT, running as an independent, secured no electoral college support despite capturing 19 percent of the popular vote (the best showing by a third candidate since 1912). In congressional balloting the Democrats retained control of the Senate by an unchanged majority of 57 (including a vacancy filled on December 4); they also retained control of the House of Representatives by a reduced majority of 259 seats, 175 being won by Republicans and Sanders retaining his seat from Vermont. At the state level the Republicans gained a single governorship from the Democrats, the resultant distribution being 27–21–2. A record number of voters (more than 104 million) cast ballots in 1992, although the 55.9 percent turnout of those eligible fell short of the 60.8 percent reported in 1968.

Five days after Clinton's inauguration on January 20, 1993, the president named his wife, Hillary Rodham CLINTON, to head a task force on health care reform, for which he campaigned vigorously in the months that followed. Although most observers felt that some form of national health insurance would eventually emerge, the president's proposals were challenged as administratively burdensome and far too costly, while one of his party's most influential senators, Daniel Patrick MOYNIHAN of New York, insisted that priority should be accorded to welfare reform. Other legislative matters included a struggle (ultimately successful on November 30, 1993) to secure passage of the so-called Brady bill, requiring a waiting period for the purchase of a handgun, and a bitterly contested budget and deficit reduction plan that secured final approval by a two-vote margin in the House of Representatives on August 5 and by a vice-presidential tie-breaking vote in the Senate the following day.

By early 1994 the president's agenda was becoming increasingly hostage to the "Whitewater" scandal, involving a failed property venture (Whitewater) in which the Clintons had a substantial interest. At the president's request, a special prosecutor was appointed on January 20, 1994, to investigate the affair, which also became the subject of congressional hearings. To add to the president's troubles, Paula JONES, a former Arkansas state employee, filed a sexual harassment suit against Clinton on May 6. Despite such distractions, the president in late August finally secured congressional approval for his centerpiece crime bill, approving (but not authorizing) expenditure of $30 billion over six years on anticrime measures and banning certain categories of assault weapons.

The midterm election of November 8, 1994, yielded disastrous setbacks for the Democrats, who lost control of the Senate for the first time since 1986 by a margin of 52–48 and, far more unexpectedly, of the House for the first time since 1954 by a margin of 230–204, with Sanders again returning as an independent. Astonishingly, no Republican incumbent at either the gubernatorial or congressional levels was defeated. The day after the November poll, Alabama senator Richard C. SHELBY switched his allegiance from Democrat to Republican. Far more embarrassing to the Democrats was the defection of Colorado senator Ben Nighthorse CAMPBELL, a Native American, on March 3, 1995, leaving the Republicans with an upper house majority of 54.

A chastened President Clinton accepted responsibility for the congressional defeat and called for a "partnership" between the executive and legislative branches of government. The appeal drew a guardedly favorable response from Republican Senate leader Robert J. (Bob) DOLE, while the more flamboyant incoming House speaker, Newt GINGRICH, indicated that cooperation with the president would take second place to implementation of a ten-point "Contract with America," which called for a balanced-budget amendment to the Constitution, a presidential line-item veto of budget legislation, denial of welfare benefits to minor mothers, and the introduction of congressional term limits. The balanced-budget and term-limits amendments subsequently were defeated, while nine other proposals were approved in the House and pending in the Senate. (On May 27 the Supreme Court ruled that action by the states to impose term limits on federal legislators was unconstitutional.)

In a record of restraint unmatched by any chief executive since the Civil War, President Clinton did not cast his first veto until the 28th month of his incumbency, rejecting on June 7, 1995, a spending reduction bill for the year ending September 30. Thereafter, with the 1996 election looming, the president and opposition legislators became locked in a bitter struggle over long-term budget cuts. Meanwhile, in the aftermath of the country's worst domestic bombing attack, the destruction of a federal office complex in Oklahoma City on April 19, Congress approved several administration proposals designed to inhibit and punish terrorist attacks on U.S. property or personnel at home and abroad.

Buffeted by continuing legal problems but buoyed by public opinion polls that showed Clinton leading Republican challenger Dole by as much as 20 points, the president accepted renomination by the Democrats and went on to defeat Dole on November 5, 1996, by a popular vote margin of 49–41 percent, with third-party candidate Perot winning 8 percent. In the electoral college the race was substantially more unbalanced; Clinton secured 379 of the 538 votes, whereas Dole won 159. Despite the president's victory, the Republicans retained control of both houses of Congress by substantial margins (55 of 100 Senate and 227 of 435 House seats). The biennial congressional balloting of November 3, 1998, yielded an unchanged Senate division, but the Democrats scored an upset by gaining five seats in the House despite the president's mounting personal difficulties and conventional wisdom regarding midterm elections.

On December 19, 1998, President Clinton became the second U.S. president (after Andrew Johnson in 1868) to be impeached by the House of Representatives. The principal charges against him were perjury in testimony before a grand jury regarding a sexual relationship with a former White House intern, Monica LEWINSKY, and obstruction of justice in seeking false testimony from Lewinsky in the sexual harassment case brought by Paula Jones. On February 12, 1999, Clinton was acquitted, the Senate having failed to register the two-thirds majority needed for conviction on largely party-line votes of 45–55 and 50–50, with 10 Republicans defecting on the first count and 5 on the second.

The presidential election of November 7, 2000, was one of the most remarkable events in U.S. political history. On election night an extremely close electoral college count indicated that the outcome in Florida would be decisive. Exit polls that initially gave the state to the Democratic nominee, Vice President Al GORE, changed to favor Texas governor George W. BUSH (son of the 41st president), and then suggested a race "too close to call." Subsequently, a recount of 45,000 disputed ballots was halted by Florida's secretary of state, resumed by order of the state supreme court, suspended by the U.S. Supreme Court, and then effectively terminated by the Court on December 12. As a result Bush was declared the victor by an electoral college count of 271–266, although he trailed Gore in the popular count and won the Florida contest by only 537 votes of 6 million cast. Meanwhile the Senate was evenly split (50–50) for the first time in 120 years, while the Republican House majority fell to its narrowest since 1954: 221 against 212 for the Democrats, with 2 independents. On June 6, 2001, however, the Democrats assumed control of the Senate as a result of a decision by Sen. James JEFFORDS of Vermont, theretofore a Republican, to sit as an independent and vote with Democrats on most matters. This marked the first time in U.S. history that the balance of power in a house of Congress shifted because of a midterm change in party allegiance.

On the morning of September 11, 2001, the United States suffered the most devastating terrorist attack in its history when two hijacked commercial airliners were deliberately flown into the upper floors of the World Trade Center's twin 110-story towers in New York City. The towers collapsed shortly after impact, and about 2,800 people died in the catastrophe, which also led to the collapse or ruin of other buildings in the vicinity. On the same morning, hijackers steered a third airliner into one side of the Pentagon, the headquarters of the U.S. Department of Defense, near Washington, D.C., costing an additional 184 lives. A fourth hijacked flight crashed in rural Pennsylvania, killing the 44 passengers and crew, some of whom, having been alerted by mobile phone to the fate of the other three aircraft, had attempted to overpower the hijackers. In response to the terrorist assaults, the White House ordered all civilian flights in U.S. airspace grounded and temporarily closed the country's borders. As a further precaution, President Bush, who was in Florida at the time of the attacks, was routed by the Secret Service to secure military bases in Louisiana and Nebraska before returning to Washington, D.C., that evening.

Attention immediately focused on the al-Qaida terrorist network of Osama bin Laden, and within days the government confirmed that all 19 hijackers had connections to al-Qaida. The Bush administration subsequently demanded that the Taliban regime in Afghanistan, which had afforded safe harbor to bin Laden, hand him over and eliminate his terrorist training camps. The Taliban refused. On October 7 aerial forces from the United States and the United Kingdom, supported on the ground by the opposition Northern Alliance, launched a military assault to unseat the Taliban, capture or kill bin Laden, and destroy the al-Qaida bases. The Taliban succumbed in December, and late in the month an interim government was established in Kabul (see Afghanistan article). Military action against pockets of al-Qaida and Taliban resistance continued as the U.S. government contemplated additional steps in what it characterized as a worldwide "war on terrorism."

In late October 2001 the U.S. Congress passed the USA PATRIOT Act, a cornerstone of the Bush administration's domestic response to the terrorism threat. The act expanded the government's authority to wiretap, conduct Internet surveillance, combat money laundering, and detain foreign nationals. Additional legislation strengthened airport security, while an executive order of November 13 authorized secret military tribunals for foreign nationals. By the end of the year 1,200 individuals were being detained in connection with the September 11 events, and the government had begun "voluntary" questioning of 5,000 noncitizens.

The U.S. economy, already in a slump, also suffered significant damage from the September 11 attacks, which the hijackers, most of them Saudi nationals, had aimed at the heart of the U.S. financial and business district. The New York Stock Exchange experienced a massive, but temporary, sell-off upon reopening on September 17, consumer confidence flagged, unemployment rose, and the U.S. airline industry registered losses that threatened bankruptcy as business and tourist travel declined precipitously. The government acted quickly to shore up the airlines, supplement defense appropriations, provide tens of billions of dollars for homeland security and for relief and recovery efforts in New York City, and stimulate the economy. One consequence was a swift end to the brief era of budget surpluses recorded during the final years of the Clinton administration.

In the midterm elections of November 5, 2002, the Republican Party recaptured control of the U.S. Senate by a 51–48 margin (Senator Jeffords remained an independent) and added 6 seats in the House, its majority rising to 229. On November 25 President Bush signed legislation creating a cabinet-level Department of Homeland Security and then named Tom RIDGE, then director of the White House Office of Homeland Security, as its head. Two days later he approved the establishment of an independent ten-member commission to investigate intelligence failures leading up to the attacks of September 11, 2001.

In his State of the Union address on January 29, 2002, President Bush grouped Iraq, Iran, and North Korea in an "axis of evil" intent on developing weapons of mass destruction (WMD) and, in the case of Tehran and Baghdad, supporting international terrorism. In October Congress authorized President Bush to take preemptive military action against Iraq if all other means failed to deter the Saddam Hussein regime from an alleged buildup of WMD. Given the Bush administration's view that Hussein had not adequately complied with UN Security Council Resolution 1441 of November 8, 2002, to begin disarming, U.S. forces launched an attack (code-named Operation Iraqi Freedom) on March 20, 2003. On May 1 Bush announced that combat operations had ended, despite resistance that took on an increasingly complex character in the following three years (see the Iraq article).

In the 2004 presidential election, President Bush won a second term with 286 electoral college votes on a popular vote share of 50.7 percent, versus 252 electoral college votes for his Democratic opponent, Sen. John KERRY of Massachusetts. In the congressional poll Republicans secured a majority in both chambers (55–44 in the Senate and 232–202 in the House of Representatives). Following the election, the Republicans held 29 governorships versus the Democrats' 21. In January 2006 Bush nominated a federal court judge, Michael CHERTOFF, to succeed Ridge as secretary of Homeland Security; subsequently, Bush won congressional approval for the creation of an overarching director of the nation's 15 spy agencies, tapping former UN ambassador John D. NEGROPONTE for the post.

In late 2005 a controversy erupted over President Bush's authorization that allowed the National Security Agency (NSA) to conduct eavesdropping on telecommunications between U.S. citizens and foreign nationals. The administration argued that the monitoring was key to prosecuting the war on terror, was within the president's authority as commander in chief, and had been authorized by a congressional resolution to use "all necessary and appropriate force" in response to the September 2001 terror attacks. Critics of the policy, including the Republican chair of the Senate Judiciary Committee, Arlen SPECTER of Pennsylvania, countered that it violated the 1978 Foreign Intelligence Surveillance Act (FISA) and had not been authorized by Congress. (In August 2007, Congress passed the FISA Amendment Act, clarifying the FISA court's oversight responsibility with respect to domestic and foreign eavesdropping.)

Throughout 2006, the war in Iraq continued to dominate the political front. The rapid U.S. military ouster of Saddam Hussein and the dismantling of his Sunni regime had been followed by several years of unremitting sectarian violence, mostly between Shiite and Sunni factions, as well as attacks from diverse sources—remnants of the prior regime, militias loyal to Islamic clerics and tribal leaders, Iraqi nationalists, al-Qaida recruits, and foreign nationals—against U.S. military forces and their newly trained Iraqi counterparts. Insurgents' use of improvised explosive devices, suicide bombings, kidnappings and videotaped beheadings of those captured, and other unconventional tactics took an increasing toll on military personnel, journalists, and civilians alike.

Popular opposition to the Iraq war continued to mount and contributed to significant gains for the Democratic Party in the November 2006 midterm election. Democrats won control of the House of Representatives by a margin of 31 seats (233–202) and, somewhat unexpectedly, of the Senate, where a 49–49 tie was broken by two pro-Democratic independents. Following the November 7 poll, the Democrats also held 28 of 50 governorships, effectively reversing the Republican Party's gains in 2004. At the start of the 110th Congress in January 2007, Democrat Nancy PELOSI of California, a severe critic of the Bush administration, was elected Speaker of the House, becoming the first woman to hold that position.

Among the country's mounting problems in the second half of 2007 were economic challenges arising from spiraling energy costs; a record trade deficit; an increase in foreclosures in the housing market, accompanied by a wave of major financial institutions losing unprecedented amounts of money as fallout from a subprime mortgage-lending crisis; and a drop in the value of the dollar to its lowest level in 25 years. The housing market declined further in 2008 as house prices fell dramatically and foreclosures mounted. This trend was exacerbated by a tightening of credit as banks reported huge losses linked to the mortgage-backed securities. Several large investment firms went bankrupt or were taken over, and unemployment reached a five-year high of 5.8 percent for the year. As the wave of turmoil continued on Wall Street, Congress approved a revised version of a Bush administration proposal for a $700 billion emergency bailout to buy up "toxic" mortgage assets and stabilize the economy in response to the most serious crisis since the Great Depression. The Treasury Department announced plans to invest up to $250 billion into nine of the largest U.S. banks, a measure designed to help ease the credit crunch.

On a more positive note, Gen. David Petraeus, the Iraq war commander, reported to Congress that the U.S. troop "surge" in Iraq, which had been initiated in February 2007, was working. Petraeus further reported that the U.S. could begin withdrawing troops by early 2008. Insurgent attacks in Iraq declined significantly in 2007 and 2008; meanwhile, numerous U.S. politicians complained that the Iraqi government had failed to meet many of the "benchmarks" that had been established to measure progress.

The presidential election campaign dominated the U.S. political scene from mid-2007 through 2008, one of the longest campaign periods in U.S. history. After a protracted and spirited Democratic primary contest, Hillary CLINTON, the junior senator from New York, and Barack Obama, the junior senator from Illinois, became the front-runners. Obama, 47, claimed victory on June 3, 2008, becoming the first African-American to win the nomination of either major party, despite questions raised about his relative inexperience as a two-term senator. Meanwhile, Republican senator John McCain of Arizona, a prisoner of war during the Vietnam War, overcame a wave of Republican opposition to immigration legislation he sponsored in 2007 and emerged from a large field of primary contenders to claim victory as the party's nominee on March 4. McCain surprised political pundits and the public at large with his subsequent selection of Alaska governor Sarah PALIN as his running mate. Palin, who was virtually unknown outside of her home state, nonetheless appeared to energize the Republican Party with her conservative values. McCain's campaign focused on government reforms, national security, and the economy. His strength in foreign policy dwindled as an electoral commodity as the situation in Iraq stabilized and the market deteriorated further. Meanwhile, Obama named a veteran legislator, Senator Joseph BIDEN of Delaware, who served as chair of the Foreign Relations Committee, as his running mate. Obama, campaigning on a broad platform of change, pledged to withdraw all troops from Iraq within 16 months of taking office and to raise taxes on wealthier citizens and reduce taxes for the "middle class." Meanwhile, a surge in violence in Pakistan coincided with increased unrest in its lawless tribal regions along its border with Afghanistan, which were considered the likely stronghold of al-Qaida. These developments led both U.S. presidential candidates to support a build-up of U.S. military efforts to oust Taliban supporters of al-Qaida in the region.

In the general elections on November 4, 2008, Democrat Barack OBAMA was elected president with 365 electoral college votes and 52 percent of the popular vote, defeating Republican John McCain, who received 173 electoral votes and 46 percent of the popular vote. Democrats also substantially increased their standing in Congress.

Constitution and government. The Constitution of the United States, drafted by a Constitutional Convention in Philadelphia in 1787 and declared in effect on March 4, 1789, established a republic in which extensive powers are reserved to the states, currently 50 in number, that compose the Federal Union. The system has three distinctive characteristics. First, powers are divided among three federal branches—legislative, executive, and judicial—and between the federal and state governments, themselves each divided into three branches. Second, the power of each of the four elements of the federal government (the presidency, the Senate, the House of Representatives, and the federal judiciary) is limited by being shared with one or more of the other elements. Third, the different procedures by which the president, senators, and members of the House of Representatives are elected make each responsible to a different constituency.

Federal executive power is vested in a president who serves for a four-year term and, by the 22nd Amendment (ratified in 1951), is limited to two terms of office. The president and vice president are formally designated by the electoral college, composed of electors from each state and the District of Columbia. Selected by popular vote in numbers equal to the total congressional representation to which the various states are entitled, the electors are pledged to vote for their political parties' candidates and customarily do so. Presidents are advised by, and discharge most of their functions through, executive departments headed by officers whom they appoint but who must have Senate approval. Presidents may, if they desire, use these officers collectively as a cabinet having advisory functions. In addition, presidents serve as commanders in chief, issuing orders to the military through the secretary of defense and the Joint Chiefs of Staff of the Army, Navy, and Air Force, who also serve the chief executive collectively as an advisory body.

Legislative power is vested in the bicameral Congress: The Senate has two members from each state chosen by popular vote for six-year terms, with renewal by thirds every two years; the House of Representatives, elected by popular vote every two years, has a membership based on population, although each state is entitled to at least one representative. The two houses are further differentiated by their responsibilities: For example, money bills must originate in the House, whereas the advice and consent of the Senate is required for ratification of treaties and appointment of top government officials such as cabinet members. In practice no major legislative or financial bill is considered by either chamber until it has been reported by, or discharged from, one of many standing committees. By custom the parties share seats on the committees on a basis roughly proportional to their legislative strength. Within the parties preference in committee assignments has traditionally been accorded on the basis of seniority (continuous service in the house concerned), although departures from this rule are becoming more common. The Senate (but not the House) permits "unlimited debate," a procedure under which a determined minority may, by filibustering, bring all legislative action to a halt unless three-fifths of the full chamber elects to close debate. Failing this, a bill objectionable to the minority will eventually be withdrawn by the leadership. A presidential veto may be overridden by separate two-thirds votes of the two houses.

Congress has created the General Accountability Office (formerly the General Accounting Office) to provide legislative control over public funds and has established 66 agencies, boards, and commissions—collectively known as "independent agencies"—to perform specified administrative functions.

The federal judiciary is headed by a nine-member Supreme Court and includes courts of appeal, district courts, and various special courts, all created by Congress. Federal judges are appointed by the president, contingent upon approval by the Senate, and serve during good behavior. Federal jurisdiction is limited, applying most importantly to cases in law and equity arising under the Constitution, to U.S. laws and treaties, and to controversies arising between two or more states or between citizens of different states. Jury trial is prescribed for all federal crimes except those involving impeachment, which is voted by the House and adjudicated by the Senate.

In early July 2005 Supreme Court Justice Sandra Day O'CONNOR, the Court's first female justice, announced her retirement, providing President Bush with his first opportunity to influence the Court's direction. To replace O'Connor, who in recent years had been a prominent "swing" vote on a range of conservative-versus-liberal issues, including abortion rights, Bush selected a conservative, John ROBERTS, who was a judge on the Court of Appeals for the District of Columbia Circuit. As Senate and media investigations into Roberts's background were getting under way, the court's chief justice, William REHNQUIST, died on September 3, with Bush then nominating Roberts to succeed Rehnquist. Roberts was quickly confirmed by the Senate and sworn in on September 29. Bush's new pick to succeed O'Connor was more controversial. Samuel ALITO's opposition to abortion and his support for expanding presidential powers while serving as a judge on the Third Circuit Court of Appeals sparked considerable opposition, but not enough to block Senate confirmation. Alito was sworn in on January 31, 2006. After Justice David SOUTER, a centrist on the Court, announced his retirement in April 2009, President Obama selected Sonia SOTOMAYOR, a judge of Puerto Rican descent on the Court of Appeals for the Second Circuit, whose rulings were largely centrist, though some critics objected to their potential implications for race politics. Republican opposition centered on earlier comments she had made alluding to what she had termed the superior judicial insights of a "wise Latina woman," but the Senate confirmed Sotomayor's appointment. She was sworn in on August 6, becoming the first Hispanic justice to serve on the Supreme Court.

The federal Constitution and the institutions of the federal government serve generally as models for those of the states. Each state government is made up of a popularly elected governor and legislature (all but one bicameral) and an independent judiciary. The District of Columbia, as the seat of the national government, was traditionally administered under the direct authority of Congress; however, in May 1974 District voters approved a charter giving them the right to elect a mayor and city council, both of which took office on January 1, 1975. Earlier, under the 23rd Amendment to the Constitution (ratified in 1961), District residents had won the right to participate in presidential elections, and in 1970 they were authorized by Congress to send a nonvoting delegate to the House of Representatives. An amendment to give the District full congressional voting rights was approved by both houses of Congress in 1978 but not ratified by the requisite 38 of the 50 state legislatures.

In practice, the broad powers of the federal government, its more effective use of the taxing power, and the existence of many problems transcending the capacity of individual states have tended to make for a strongly centralized system of government. Local self-government, usually through municipalities, townships, and counties, is a well-established tradition, based generally on English models. Education is a locally administered, federally subsidized function.

State and Capital	*Area (sq. mi.)*	*Population (2008)*
Alabama (Montgomery)	51,705	4,666,000
Alaska (Juneau)	591,004	669,000
Arizona (Phoenix)	114,000	6,377,000
Arkansas (Little Rock)	53,187	2,841,000
California (Sacramento)	158,706	36,859,000
Colorado (Denver)	104,091	4,960,000
Connecticut (Hartford)	5,018	3,508,0000
Delaware (Dover)	2,045	877,000
Florida (Tallahassee)	58,664	18,445,000
Georgia (Atlanta)	58,910	9,752,000
Hawaii (Honolulu)	6,471	1,301,000
Idaho (Boise)	83,564	1,535,000
Illinois (Springfield)	56,345	12,929,000
Indiana (Indianapolis)	36,185	6,387,000
Iowa (Des Moines)	56,275	3,003,000
Kansas (Topeka)	82,277	2,796,000
Kentucky (Frankfort)	40,410	4,278,000
Louisiana (Baton Rouge)	47,752	4,344,000
Maine (Augusta)	33,265	1,319,000
Maryland (Annapolis)	10,460	5,634,000
Massachusetts (Boston)	8,284	6,426,000
Michigan (Lansing)	58,527	10,042,000
Minnesota (St. Paul)	84,402	5,241,000
Mississippi (Jackson)	47,689	2,939,000
Missouri (Jefferson City)	69,697	5,918,000
Montana (Helena)	147,046	969,000
Nebraska (Lincoln)	77,355	1,786,000
Nevada (Carson City)	110,561	2,640,000
New Hampshire (Concord)	9,279	1,320,000
New Jersey (Trenton)	7,787	8,706,000
New Mexico (Santa Fe)	121,593	1,998,000
New York (Albany)	49,108	19,314,000
North Carolina (Raleigh)	52,669	9,257,000
North Dakota (Bismarck)	70,702	643,000

Ohio (Columbus)	41,330	11,470,000
Oklahoma (Oklahoma City)	69,956	3,656,000
Oregon (Salem)	97,073	3,804,000
Pennsylvania (Harrisburg)	45,308	12,584,000
Rhode Island (Providence)	1,212	1,054,000
South Carolina (Columbia)	31,113	4,487,000
South Dakota (Pierre)	77,116	804,000
Tennessee (Nashville)	42,144	6,240,000
Texas (Austin)	266,807	24,411,000
Utah (Salt Lake City)	84,899	2,710,000
Vermont (Montpelier)	9,614	621,000
Virginia (Richmond)	40,767	7,785,000
Washington (Olympia)	68,139	6,562,000
West Virginia (Charleston)	24,232	1,815,000
Wisconsin (Madison)	56,153	5,631,000
Wyoming (Cheyenne)	97,809	533,000
Federal District		
District of Columbia	69	591,000

Foreign relations. U.S. relations with the world at large have evolved subject to the changing conditions created by the growth of the country and its international influence. An initial policy of noninvolvement in foreign affairs, which received its classical expression in President Washington's warning against "entangling alliances," gradually gave way to one of active participation in the concerns of international community. At the same time, the nation has evolved from a supporter of revolutionary movements directed against the old monarchical system into a predominantly conservative influence, with a broad commitment to the support of traditional democratic values.

U.S. policy in the Western Hemisphere, the area of most historical concern, continues to reflect the preoccupations that inspired the Monroe Doctrine (of President James Monroe) of 1823, in which the United States declared its opposition to European political involvement and further colonization in the Americas and in effect established a political guardianship over the states of Latin America. Since World War II this responsibility has become largely multilateral through such bodies as the UN and the Organization of American States (OAS), and direct U.S. intervention in Latin American affairs has typically been limited to instances in which a Central American or Caribbean country appeared in immediate danger of falling into chaos or under leftist control.

Overseas expansion during the late 19th and early 20th centuries resulted in the acquisition of American Samoa, Hawaii, and, following the Spanish-American War of 1898, the Philippines, Puerto Rico, and Guam; in addition, the United States secured a favored position in Cuba in 1902–1903, obtained exclusive rights in the Panama Canal Zone in 1903, and acquired the U.S. Virgin Islands by purchase in 1917. The country did not, however, become a colonial power in the European sense and was among the first to adopt a policy of promoting the political evolution of its dependent territories along lines desired by their inhabitants. In accordance with this policy, the Philippines became independent in 1946; Puerto Rico became a commonwealth freely associated with the United States in 1952; Hawaii became a state of the Union in 1959; measures of self-government have been introduced in the Virgin Islands, Guam, and American Samoa; and the Canal Zone was transferred to Panama on October 1, 1979, although the United States retained effective control of 40 percent of the area through 1999. Certain Japanese territories occupied during World War II were provisionally retained for strategic reasons, with those historically of Japanese sovereignty, the Bonin and Ryukyu islands, being returned in 1968 and 1972, respectively. The greater part of Micronesia (held by Japan as a League of Nations mandate after World War I) became, by agreement with the UN, the U.S. Trust Territory of the Pacific. In 1986, following the conclusion of a series of compacts of association with the Commonwealth of the Northern Mariana Islands, the Federated States of Micronesia (FSM), the Republic of the Marshall Islands, and the Republic of Palau (Belau), the UN Trusteeship Council indicated that it would be appropriate to terminate the trusteeship. This was eventually approved by the UN Security Council in December 1990 in respect of the FSM and the Marshall Islands (which became UN members in 1991) and of the Northern Marianas (which had opted for political union with the United States), whereas a lengthy internal wrangle over Palau's constitutional status was not conclusively resolved until October 1, 1994 (see entry under Palau).

Globally, U.S. participation in the defeat of the Central Powers in World War I was followed by a period of renewed isolation and attempted neutrality, which, however, was ultimately made untenable by the challenge of the Axis powers in World War II. Having played a leading role in the defeat of the Axis, the United States joined with its allies in assuming responsibility for the creation of a postwar order within the framework of the UN. However, the subsequent divergence of Soviet and Western political aims, and the resultant limitations on the effectiveness of the UN as an instrument for maintaining peace and security, impelled the United States during the late 1940s and 1950s to take the lead in creating a network of special mutual security arrangements that were ultimately to involve commitments to more than four dozen foreign governments. Some of these commitments, as in the North Atlantic Treaty Organization (NATO), the Australia, New Zealand, United States (ANZUS) Security Treaty Pact, and the Inter-American Treaty of Reciprocal Assistance (Rio Pact), are multilateral in character; others involve defense obligations toward particular governments, such as those with Thailand, the Philippines, and the Republic of Korea.

The United States also exercised leadership in international economic and financial relations through its cosponsorship of the International Monetary Fund (IMF) and World Bank, its promotion of trade liberalization efforts, and its contributions to postwar relief and rehabilitation, European economic recovery, and the economic progress of less-developed countries. Much of this activity, like parallel efforts put forward in social, legal, and cultural fields, has been carried on through the UN and its related agencies.

The United States has pursued international agreements on measures for the control and limitation of strategic armaments. The country initiated first-round strategic arms limitation treaty (SALT) talks with the Soviet Union in late 1969 that ran until May 1972, resulting in a five-year agreement to limit the number of certain offensive weapons. Although second-round talks, held from November 1972 until early 1974, produced few substantive results, President Nixon and the Soviet Union's general secretary Leonid Brezhnev agreed in July 1974 to negotiate a new five-year accord. The intention was reaffirmed during a meeting between Brezhnev and President Ford in Vladivostok in November 1974. Progress again slowed until late 1978, when President Carter and Brezhnev finally signed SALT II in Vienna on June 18, 1979. However, the treaty remained unratified following the Soviet invasion of Afghanistan on December 27. A collateral series of meetings between NATO and Warsaw Pact representatives on mutual and balanced force reductions (MBFR) in Central Europe had been initiated in 1973 but yielded little in the way of substantive agreement during the ensuing 16 years. In November 1981 U.S.-Soviet negotiations on limiting intermediate-range nuclear forces (INF) began in Geneva and were followed in June 1982 by the initiation of strategic arms reduction talks (START).

Soviet insistence during a summit in Reykjavik, Iceland, in October 1986 that limits on development of the U.S. Strategic Defense Initiative ("Star Wars") be included in any major arms agreement created an impasse in the START talks. But in the INF negotiations a precedent-setting accord, providing for the elimination of an entire category of nuclear missiles (those with a range of 300–3,400 miles, including cruise missiles), was initialed during a summit between President Reagan and Soviet leader Mikhail Gorbachev in Washington, D.C., on December 8, 1987, with formal signature following on June 1, 1988, during a reciprocal summit in Moscow.

U.S. military forces, operating under a UN mandate, actively opposed Communist-sponsored aggression in the Korean War of 1950–1953. Other U.S. forces, together with those of a number of allied powers, assisted the government of South Vietnam in combating the insurgent movement that was actively supported by North Vietnamese forces for nearly two decades. By 1965 this assistance had become a major U.S. military effort, which continued after the initiation of peace talks in 1968. The lengthy discussions, involving U.S. Secretary of State Henry A. KISSINGER and North Vietnamese diplomat Le Duc Tho as the most active participants, resulted in the conclusion of a four-way peace agreement on January 27, 1973, that called for the withdrawal of all remaining U.S. military forces from Vietnam, the repatriation of American prisoners of war, and the institution of political talks between South Vietnam and its domestic (Viet Cong) adversaries. The U.S. withdrawal was followed, however, by a breakdown in talks, renewed military operations in late 1974, and the collapse of the South Vietnamese government on April 30, 1975.

In a move of major international significance, the United States and the People's Republic of China announced on December 15, 1978, that they would establish diplomatic relations as of January 1, 1979. The normalization was essentially on Chinese terms, with the United States meeting all three of China's long-sought conditions: severance of U.S. diplomatic relations with Taipei, withdrawal of U.S. troops from Taiwan, and abrogation of the Republic of China defense treaty. On the other hand, the United States indicated that it would maintain economic, cultural, and other unofficial relations with Taiwan.

In the Middle East, Secretary Kissinger embarked on an eight-month-long exercise in "shuttle diplomacy" following the Arab-Israeli "October War" of 1973. U.S. economic interests were, for the first time, directly undermined as a result of an Arab embargo, instituted in October 1973, on all oil shipments to the United States and the Netherlands, and on some shipments to other Western European states. The embargo was terminated by all but two of the producing nations, Libya and Syria, in March 1974, following the resumption of full-scale diplomatic relations (severed since 1967) between the United States and Egypt. A first Kissinger-brokered Israeli-Egyptian disengagement agreement in January 1974 was followed by a second in September 1975. Meanwhile Kissinger brought about a limited Golan Heights disengagement between Israel and Syria in May 1974, followed a month later by a renewal of diplomatic relations between the United States and Syria (also suspended since 1967). In September 1978 President Carter, hosting a Camp David summit, was instrumental in negotiating accords that led to the signing of a peace treaty between Egypt and Israel in Washington, D.C., on March 26, 1979.

Despite a recognized danger to U.S. diplomatic personnel, the Carter administration permitted the deposed shah of Iran to enter the United States in October 1979 for medical treatment, and on November 4 militants occupied the U.S. embassy compound in Tehran, taking 66 hostages. Within days 13 blacks and women were released, with the militants, supported by Iranian leader Ayatollah Khomeini, demanding the return of the shah in exchange for the remainder. Although condemnations of the seizure were forthcoming from the UN Security Council, the General Assembly, and the World Court, neither their nor personal pleas by international diplomats were at first heeded by the Islamic Republic's leadership, which vilified the United States as "the great Satan." President Carter aborted a rescue mission by a U.S. commando force in April 1980 after early mishaps. Eventually, however, negotiations that commenced on the eve of the 1980 U.S. election culminated in the freeing of the hostages on Reagan's presidential inauguration day (January 20, 1981).

The Reagan administration was active in a wide range of foreign contexts. It viewed the conclusion of the 1988 INF treaty as the result of consistent (and largely successful) pressure on U.S. European allies to maintain a high level of military preparedness as compared with the Soviet Union. In the Middle East the Reagan administration attempted to negotiate a mutual withdrawal of Israeli and Syrian forces from Lebanon in the wake of the Israeli invasion of June 1982 and the subsequent evacuation of Palestinian Liberation Organization (PLO) forces from Beirut, for which the U.S. government provided truce supervision assistance. In 1987, despite the risk of a major confrontation with Iran, the Reagan administration mounted a significant naval presence in the Persian Gulf to protect oil tankers from seaborne mines and other threats stemming from the Iran-Iraq conflict. In Asia, the United States provided substantial military assistance to Pakistan and Thailand in response to Soviet intervention in Afghanistan and communist operations in Cambodia, respectively, while strongly supporting the post-Marcos regime in the Philippines. In the Caribbean, the United States provided the bulk of the forces that participated in the 1983 postcoup intervention in Grenada, and it welcomed the 1986 ouster of Haitian dictator François Duvalier. In Central America, the Reagan administration attempted to contain Soviet-Cuban involvement in Nicaragua and to help the Salvadoran government defeat leftist guerrilla forces. Overall, in keeping with a 1980 campaign pledge, President Reagan sought to restructure both the military and civilian components of the nation's foreign aid program so as to reward "America's friends," whatever their domestic policies, in an implicit repudiation of his predecessor's somewhat selective use of aid in support of global human-rights objectives.

Relations with Panama deteriorated sharply following the nullification of presidential balloting in May 1989. Seven months later Gen. Manuel Noriega assumed sweeping powers to deal with what was termed "a state of war" with the United States, and on December 20 the George H. W. Bush administration intervened militarily to oust the Panamanian dictator, who was flown to Miami two weeks later to face trial (and ultimate conviction) on drug-trafficking and other charges.

In 1990 the Bush administration became preoccupied with the international crisis generated by Iraq's seizure of Kuwait on August 2 and the remarkable prodemocracy upheaval in Eastern Europe that had been triggered by Gorbachev's reforms in the Soviet Union. Five days after the fall of Kuwait, the United States announced the deployment of ground units and aircraft to defend Saudi Arabia, and on November 29 the UN Security Council approved the use of "all necessary means" if Iraq did not withdraw from Kuwait by January 15, 1991. On January 12 the U.S. Congress authorized military action against Iraq, and on January 16 "Operation Desert Storm" began, yielding the liberation of Kuwait on February 26–27 by a U.S.-led multinational force.

Four decades of superpower confrontation formally ended on November 21, 1990, with the adoption of a treaty reducing conventional forces in Europe at a Paris summit of the Conference on Security and Cooperation in Europe (CSCE). Agreement eight months later on final details of the long-sought START treaty paved the way for signing by Bush and Gorbachev at a Moscow summit on July 30–31, 1991. Under the accord, 50 percent of the Soviet and 35 percent of the U.S. ballistic missile warheads were slated for destruction.

Following the Gulf War President Bush identified resolution of the Arab-Israeli dispute as the top priority of his administration. In pursuit of this objective, Secretary of State James BAKER painstakingly negotiated a conference involving Israel, Syria, Lebanon, and a joint Jordanian-Palestinian delegation, convened in Madrid, Spain, in October 1991 under the joint auspices of the United States and Soviet Union. Additional bilateral and multilateral talks were held over the ensuing months, with no substantive results.

Following the failed Moscow coup of August 1991, the United States welcomed the achievement of independence by the Baltic states, and in December, after the legal collapse of the Soviet Union, Congress moved to recognize Ukraine. President Bush and Russia's Boris Yeltsin signed an unprecedented extension of the 1991 START accord during their first formal summit on June 16–17. Under START II, each nation would be limited to 3,000–3,500 long-range weapons (down from 11,000–12,000 on the eve of START I), while all land-based multiple warhead missiles would be banned. Other summit highlights included agreement on reciprocal most-favored-nation trade status and an enthusiastically received address by President Yeltsin to a joint session of the U.S. Congress. Meanwhile, the Bush administration had recognized all of the remaining former Soviet republics, as well as the former Yugoslavian republics of Croatia, Slovenia, and Bosnia and Herzegovina, despite the ongoing ethnic conflict in the latter.

On November 24, 1992, the United States completed its military withdrawal from the Philippines (see Philippines article), ending a presence that had existed since 1898, save for three years during World War II. Ten days later, in an operation termed "Restore Hope," President Bush ordered the dispatch of 28,000 U.S. soldiers to Somalia to ensure the safe delivery of international relief supplies to the country's starving population (see Somalia article).

Trade issues occupied center stage during the waning months of the Bush administration. The North American Free Trade Agreement (NAFTA), which had been concluded on August 12, 1992, by the United States, Canada, and Mexico after 14 months of negotiation, was formally signed on December 17. It secured U.S. legislative approval in November 1993 and came into force on January 1, 1994.

Initially preoccupied with domestic issues, President Bill Clinton met with Russian President Yeltsin in Vancouver, Canada, on April 4–5, 1993, in talks that focused largely on financial aid for the economically beleaguered Russian regime.

The foreign policy highlight of Clinton's first year was the formal signing at the White House on September 13, 1993, of a historic agreement between Israel and the PLO on Palestinian self-rule in Jericho and the Gaza Strip (see Israel article and PLO article following the country listings). Other 1993–1994 concerns included a deteriorating situation in Somalia, where 18 U.S. soldiers were killed in October 1993, due in large part to the refusal by Defense Secretary Les ASPIN to provide more tanks and armored vehicles. Aspin subsequently admitted his mistake, and on December 15, President Clinton announced Aspin's resignation. On February 3, 1994, William J. PERRY was sworn in as the new defense secretary, and by March 31, 1994, all but a small number of U.S. troops were withdrawn from Somalia.

In the face of a somewhat wavering posture regarding events in Bosnia and Herzegovina, the Clinton administration in early 1994 issued a new set of guidelines for peacekeeping and related activities that would preclude U.S. military involvement short of a clear threat to international security, a major natural disaster, or a gross violation of human rights. From February 1994 the launching of UN-approved NATO air strikes against Serbian positions in Bosnia eased U.S.-European differences on how to respond to the conflict in former Yugoslavia, where deployment of U.S. ground troops continued to be confined to the UN/CSCE observer contingent in Macedonia. Thereafter, the genocidal Rwandan crisis that erupted in April elicited a substantial U.S. humanitarian effort in neighboring countries and the dispatch of 200 U.S. troops to help run Kigali airport, although participation in UN peacekeeping was ruled out. These measures, however, failed to prevent widespread bloodshed.

On June 2, 1994, the Clinton administration called for international economic sanctions against North Korea to force disclosure of that country's nuclear weapons capacity (see article on Democratic People's Republic of Korea); following the death of North Korean leader Kim Il Sung on July 8, a U.S.-North Korean agreement signed on August 12 met some of the concerns of the international community.

On June 30, 1994, the United States announced its readiness to sign the 1982 UN Law of the Sea treaty, having negotiated changes in sections deemed hostile to free enterprise. The following month U.S. Middle East diplomacy registered a major success when President Clinton on July 25 supervised the White House signing of a peace declaration between King Hussein of Jordan and Prime Minister Rabin of Israel.

During 1994 the Clinton administration also directed attention toward Haiti and efforts to implement a 1993 agreement providing for departure of the military junta and the return of exiled President Jean-Bertrand Aristide. Having initially preferred increasingly draconian UN sanctions to direct action, the U.S. government concluded by August 1994 that some form of armed intervention was required. Accordingly, on September 19 an advance contingent of 20,000 troops landed, unopposed, on Haitian soil under a UN mandate to oust the incumbent regime. On October 13 junta leader Gen. Raoul Cédras left aboard a U.S. flight to Panama, and on October 15 Aristide returned to Haiti (see Haiti article). Meanwhile, large numbers of Haitian "boat people" had been picked up and transported to the U.S. Guantánamo Bay Naval Base in Cuba, with Cuban refugees (in a change of policy) being accorded like treatment as of August 19. In another policy shift on May 2, 1995, the United States agreed to admit Cuban, but not Haitian, detainees remaining at Guantánamo, with all subsequent refugees being returned to their homeland.

In what was hailed as a significant foreign policy move, the U.S. Senate on December 1, 1994, ratified the 1993 GATT accord establishing the World Trade Organization (WTO). The action came after the new majority leader, Sen. Robert Dole, had given his support in return for creation of a review panel empowered to trigger a congressional vote on withdrawal should membership be seen as detrimental to U.S. interests.

In 1996, the Clinton administration, which for some time had indicated its displeasure with UN Secretary General Boutros Boutros-Ghali, vetoed his reelection by the Security Council. At issue was Boutros-Ghali's alleged failure to reform the world body, in response to which Congress continued to withhold dues of more than $1 billion. On December 13 a lengthy confrontation with France over Boutros-Ghali's successor ended with the selection of Kofi Annan, a Ghanaian and longtime UN civil servant who had earned high marks for directing peacekeeping operations in Bosnia.

On October 26, 1997, Jiang Zemin began a nine-day state visit to the United States, the first by a Chinese head of state since 1985, with President Clinton reciprocating in June 1998. Although the two leaders failed to resolve fundamental differences on human rights that had persisted since the violent suppression of the 1989 Tiananmen Square protest, Clinton and Zemin did reference many areas of "significant common interest," including efforts to end the proliferation of WMD. Shortly thereafter, Clinton failed to win "fast track" trade authority, a practice precluding Congress from partial amendment of trade legislation, even though it had been extended to every other president since 1974 (and would be granted to Clinton's successor, George W. Bush, in August 2002).

In 1998 President Clinton ordered cruise missile attacks on Afghanistan and Sudan in response to the August 7 terrorist bombings of U.S. embassies in Kenya and Tanzania. He also ordered air strikes against Iraq in mid-December after Baghdad had failed to honor a November 14 pledge to resume full cooperation with UN weapons inspectors.

On March 24, 1999, following a year of escalating ethnic fighting between the Kosovo Liberation Army (KLA), a group of ethnic Albanians, and Serb and Yugoslav security forces, NATO air strikes began in which the United States participated. At the same time, Clinton pledged that no U.S. ground troops would be sent to Kosovo. By June, however, Clinton said he would send as many as 7,000 ground troops to assist NATO in peacekeeping operations.

In April 1999 relations with China were sorely tested by NATO bombing of the Chinese embassy in Belgrade, Yugoslavia, which the United States attributed to a mapping error. In August the Senate, by a 51–48 vote, refused to ratify the Comprehensive (nuclear) Test Ban Treaty (CTBT), an action for which the former Joint Chiefs of Staff chairperson, Gen. John M. SHALIKASHVILI, strongly urged reconsideration in early 2001.

Talks began in Geneva in April 2000 on a START III accord, following Russian ratification of START II, while the House on May 24 approved the China trade bill, thus paving the way for Chinese admission to the WTO. On August 22 President Clinton signed a controversial measure providing upward of $1.3 billion to aid Colombia's war on drug traffickers. On October 12, 17 U.S. sailors were killed and 37 wounded in a terrorist attack on the USS *Cole,* a destroyer in the process of mooring at Aden, Yemen.

Before leaving office on January 20, 2001, President Clinton, voicing reservations, signed a treaty to establish an International Criminal Court (ICC) to succeed the ad hoc international war-crimes tribunals in The Hague (an action for which the succeeding Bush administration promptly withdrew support). Concurrently, Senator Helms, the Senate's leading critic of UN financing, agreed to the release of $582 million in back dues to the world body under a deal providing for reduction of the U.S. share in the annual $1.1 billion administrative budget to 22 percent (down from 25 percent) and of its contribution to the peacekeeping budget to 26 percent (down from 31 percent) by 2004.

The second war in the Persian Gulf, launched by President George W. Bush on March 20, 2003, proved far more divisive and much more costly than the first. While the United States expressed regret that the UN Security Council would not issue a resolution specifically authorizing military action against Iraq, it insisted that Resolution 1441 provided sufficient authority. However, the chief UN weapons inspector, Hans Blix, had, on March 7, given a decidedly mixed assessment of Iraq's compliance with the 2002 resolution, and at midyear an administration spokesperson conceded that the President Bush had relied on "incomplete and possibly inaccurate" intelligence in having declared in his January State of the Union address that Saddam Hussein had attempted to secure uranium from Africa. Subsequent evidence that Iraq apparently possessed no WMD at the outset of hostilities damaged the credibility of the administration. By early 2005 more than a dozen countries participating in the U.S.-led military coalition had decided to pull out or reduce their forces in Iraq, with more following in 2006 and 2007.

In November 2007, Arab leaders, including Syria's foreign minister, accepted an invitation by the United States to attend a broadly inclusive Middle East peace summit, organized by Secretary of State Condoleezza RICE, in Annapolis, Maryland. At the summit's end, Israeli Prime Minister Ehud Olmert and Palestinian President Mahmoud Abbas issued a statement of "joint understanding" committing to negotiating a peace agreement by the end of 2008. That deadline appeared unrealistic after Olmert, amid allegations of corruption, resigned in September, and as a five-month-old cease-fire in Gaza appeared to have collapsed in November 2008, with renewed border fighting between Israel and the Palestinians.

Tension heightened between the United States and Russia in August 2008, after the former Soviet state of Georgia sent troops into South Ossetia in a crackdown on separatists there. Russia retaliated by bombing cities throughout Georgia, prompting calls for a halt to the fighting from the United States, NATO, and the EU. Veiled threats from Russian prime minister Vladimir Putin followed the deployment of NATO ships to the Black Sea and the delivery of humanitarian aid to Georgia by the United States. In September the United States accused Russia of breaking a cease-fire agreement with Georgia. President Bush expressed his "grave concern" over what he described as Russia's "disproportionate response" to Georgia.

In October 2008 the United States removed North Korea from its list of states that sponsor terrorism, citing North Korea's recent agreement on measures to verify its nuclear program. In November President Bush, in his final days in office, called Libyan leader Col. Muammar Abu Minyar al-Qadhafi, marking the first conversation ever between the Libyan leader and a U.S. president. Bush formally acknowledged that Libya had settled a long-standing dispute over terrorist attacks, including the bombing of a commercial jet flying over Lockerbie, Scotland, in 1988. However, the August 2009 release from a Scottish prison of a terminally ill, convicted perpetrator of the attack, and his hero's welcome home in Libya, prompted a souring of U.S.-Libyan relations.

Current issues. Given voters' evident desire for change in Washington, D.C., expressed by the Democratic Party's sweep of the White House and both houses of Congress in the November 2008 elections, incoming president Obama claimed a mandate to implement his ambitious and transformational agenda. President Obama launched a series of executive orders and legislative proposals designed to reverse his predecessor's policies, to institute some of the protections common in developed social democracies, and to enable his vision of a more multilateral foreign policy.

Soon after his January 20, 2009, inauguration, President Obama issued orders that reversed the Bush administration's 2001 ban on federal funding for new embryonic stem cell research and called for the closure of the controversial Guantánamo Bay prison camp and overseas secret prisons set up by Bush for suspected terrorists. The closure of the Guantánamo prison was delayed in May when Congress refused to fund it due to fears that some of the detainees, who could not be tried because of evidence provided in their cases that could compromise covert agents, were nevertheless deemed too dangerous to be released and might be transferred to U.S. prisons. Obama reiterated his commitment to close the facility by early 2010 and convinced several allies to take a number of the prisoners. The first detainee from the camp to be transferred to U.S. soil was flown to New York City in June to stand trial on charges involving the bombing of U.S. embassies in Africa. However, it seemed unlikely that the facility could be closed in the near future. The president also modified the Bush "war on drugs" to focus more on treatment and rehabilitation than enforcement, allowing limited quantities to be legally used for medicinal purposes.

But the main thrust of the administration's early agenda focused on the economic crisis, the wars in Iraq and Afghanistan, and the president's plan to reform the nation's health care system. The recession, the deepest since the 1930s, continued to worsen in the first half of 2009, as corporations collapsed and unemployment rose. The new administration responded in February with a sweeping plan for capital injections, commonly known as a stimulus package, embodied in the American Recovery and Reinvestment bill. The bill called for government employment projects like road and bridge repair and extended unemployment benefits to help those impacted by the growing unemployment rate—which reached 10.2 percent in the fourth quarter of 2009, the highest in 26 years. Both chambers of Congress approved the final version of the $789 billion package, which Obama signed into law on February 17. Also in February, Treasury Secretary Timothy GEITHNER announced a $2.3 trillion plan to stabilize the financial sector, whose failures had precipitated the onset of the global financial crisis in September 2008, by providing further federal support of banks that passed a "stress test" to assess their financial soundness. On February 18, in response to the foreclosures on nearly a half million homeowners in 2008, Obama unveiled a $275 billion program to assist millions of homeowners obtain more affordable mortgages and millions more reduce their monthly payments.

The government's stake in failing businesses grew in March 2009, when American International Group (AIG), a major insurer of the troubled banks, announced the largest loss in U.S. corporate history, prompting the administration to provide it with $30 billion in emergency funding to stem further threats to the financial system. The government's stake in the private sector grew again in June, when it assumed shares in both General Motors and Chrysler after the two auto giants filed for bankruptcy.

Signs that the economy was gradually improving came with rising stock prices following news in June of 2009 that 10 of the country's 19 largest banks had passed the Treasury's stress test and would repay some $70 billion they had received in emergency bailout funds. However, even as Federal Reserve chair Benjamin BERNANKE heralded improved economic indicators in September, he cautioned that improvement would be slow, and experts said the economy was entering a "jobless recovery," with little hope of rising employment in the near future, or of complete repayment of taxpayer-funded investments in the distressed companies that received federal "bail-outs."

Obama also launched new departures in foreign policy early in his tenure, emphasizing a preference for diplomacy over the use or threat of military power. In February 2009 he announced that he would commit 17,000 more U.S. troops to combat a resurgent Taliban in Afghanistan but end combat operations in Iraq by August 2010, withdrawing more than half the 142,000 troops stationed there by that date. On June 4 the president addressed the Muslim world in a speech delivered in Cairo in which he promised to "personally pursue" a two-state solution to the Israeli-Palestinian conflict. President Obama also called the conflict in Afghanistan one of "necessity" to fight al-Qaida, in contrast to the U.S. incursion into Iraq, which he described as "a war of choice" that had alienated much of the Muslim world. After a prolonged debate over a request from General Stanley McCRYSTAL for more troops for Afghanistan, Obama announced on December 1 that he would send an additional 30,000 troops but would begin withdrawing U.S. forces from the country in 2011. Both the president of Afghanistan, Hamid Karzai, and his rival for the position, Abdullah Abdullah, viewed more troops as essential for stability and prevention of a resurgence of dominance by the fundamentalist Islamist Taliban.

During his first visit to Europe since becoming president, from March 31 to April 7, 2009, Obama appealed to the NATO allies to contribute more troops to the conflict in Afghanistan, with little success. On April 1, before the G-20 summit in London, he reached an agreement with Russian president Dmitri Medvedev on bilateral reductions of nuclear weapons and on negotiation of a new Strategic Arms Reduction Treaty (START) with Russia before the existing treaty expires on December 5. In September Obama announced he was abandoning the Bush administration's plan to install a missile defense system in eastern Europe, a plan that Russia had strongly opposed, causing disappointment and consternation in eastern capitals, particularly in Poland and the Czech Republic, which had been scheduled to host the shield components, viewed by some as an implicit American guarantee of the given countries' national security. Conservative critics described the move as a capitulation towards Russia, while supporters took the development as evidence of a positive move towards a more cooperative and engaged foreign policy.

As the year progressed Obama turned his attention to his plan to reform the health care system. He called on Congress to pass legislation before the end of the year extending health insurance to almost all Americans, almost 50 million of whom had no coverage, barring private insurers from refusing coverage to individuals with "preexisting conditions," and creating a new, government-sponsored health insurance plan that consumers could choose instead of private insurance. The proposal sparked a contentious debate between Democratic supporters and Republican opponents, who characterized it as "socialized medicine." Independent and conservative voters, meanwhile, focused on the plan's impact on the ballooning budget deficit, which was projected to expand by a trillion dollars in addition to existing debt over the 2010-2019 period if the plan was passed. Public support fell during the August congressional recesses, as voters engaged in heated town-hall exchanges with their representatives across the country. Nevertheless, some form of healthcare legislation was expected to pass following the Senate's approval of a draft in October 2009, at great cost in political capital: the president's approval ratings were the lowest for any first-term president in the third quarter since 1953.

Observers attributed the drop in support for the Democratic agenda to the unexpected outrage in response to health reform, which some saw as a mask for more general economic anxiety, given public confusion about the exact nature of the plan; and to the realization that no president could have satisfied the expectations inspired by President Obama's disciplined campaign and optimistic promises to right the country in a time of recession and war, ushering in a new era of bipartisan cooperation.

POLITICAL PARTIES

Although the U.S. Constitution makes no provision for political parties, the existence of two (or occasionally three) major parties at the national level has been a feature of the U.S. political system almost since its inception. The present-day Democratic Party traces its origins back to the Democratic-Republican Party led by Thomas Jefferson during George Washington's administration, whereas the contemporary Republican Party, though not formally constituted until the 1850s, regards itself as the lineal descendant of the Federalist Party led by Alexander Hamilton during the same period.

The two-party system has been perpetuated by tradition, by the practical effect of single-member constituencies as well as a single executive, and by the status accorded to the second main party as the recognized opposition in legislative bodies. The major parties do not, however, constitute disciplined doctrinal groups. Each is a coalition of autonomous state parties—themselves coalitions of county and city parties—that come together chiefly in presidential election years to formulate a general policy statement, or platform, and to nominate candidates for president and vice president. Control of funds and patronage is largely in the hands of state and local party units, a factor that weakens party discipline in Congress. Policy leadership is similarly diffuse, both parties searching for support from as many interest groups as possible and tending to operate by consensus.

For at least a quarter of a century, popular identification with the two major parties was remarkably stable. From 1960 to 1984, according to surveys by the University of Michigan, between 40 and 46 percent of the voters considered themselves Democrats, whereas 22–29 percent identified with the Republicans. During the same period, 23–35 percent viewed themselves as independents (the higher figure occurring in the mid-1970s, when younger voters tended to dissociate themselves from partisan politics). In a subsequent poll conducted in early 1995, 37 percent of respondents called themselves independents, 30 percent Republicans, and 29 percent Democrats, with nearly 60 percent of voting-age individuals voicing their preference for a tripartite system.

Since 1932 the rate of voter participation has averaged 55.7 percent in presidential elections, ranging from a high of 62.8 percent for John F. Kennedy in 1960 to a low of 49.0 percent for Bill Clinton in 1996 (the 2008 figure was 64 percent). The turnout in nonpresidential years has been substantially lower, averaging between 30 and 40 percent.

Congressional Parties:

Democratic Party. Originally known as the Democratic-Republican Party, the Democratic Party counts Thomas JEFFERSON, Andrew JACKSON, Woodrow WILSON, Franklin D. Roosevelt, John F. Kennedy, Lyndon B. Johnson, and Bill Clinton among its past presidents. Its basis has traditionally been an unstable coalition of conservative politicians in the southeastern states, more liberal political leaders in the urban centers of the Northeast and the West Coast, and populists in some towns and rural areas of the Midwest. The party was weakened in 1968 by such developments as the conservative secessionist movement of southern Democrats led by George C. Wallace and the challenge to established leadership and policies put forward by senators Eugene J. McCarthy and Robert F. Kennedy, both of whom had sought the presidential nomination ultimately captured by Hubert H. Humphrey. The party was further divided by the nomination of Sen. George S. McGovern, a strong critic of the Vietnam policies of both presidents Johnson and Nixon, as Democratic presidential candidate in 1972.

The party benefited from the circumstances surrounding the resignations of Vice President Spiro Agnew in 1973 and of President Nixon in 1974, scored impressive victories in both the House and Senate in 1974, recaptured the presidency under Jimmy Carter in 1976, and maintained its substantial congressional majorities in 1978. In 1980 it retained control of the House by a reduced majority while losing the Senate and suffering a decisive rejection of President Carter's bid for reelection. The party's strength in Congress was largely unchanged in 1984, despite the Reagan presidential landslide, and in 1986 it regained control of the Senate; it retained control of both houses, despite the defeat of its presidential candidate, Michael Dukakis, in 1988. Led by Clinton of Arkansas, the Democrats regained the White House in 1992 while preserving their congressional majorities, but, in a startling reversal, the party lost control of both houses in 1994. Although unable to regain control in 1996 or 1998, the Democrats countered expectations by registering marginal recovery in 1998. Denied the presidency in 2000, despite a popular majority for Vice President Al Gore, the party drew even with the Republicans in the Senate, whereas a ten-seat gain in the House was insufficient to win control. In June 2001, however, the Democrats assumed control of the Senate with the support of Sen. James Jeffords of Vermont, who had left the Republican Party to sit as an independent.

The disappointing results of the November 2002 balloting, in which the party was unable to win either house of Congress, were attributed by many observers to the Democrats' inability to present clear policy alternatives to the Republican agenda. Following the election, Richard A. GEPHARDT of Missouri, the House minority leader, resigned his post and was succeeded by Nancy Pelosi of California, the first woman to head either party in Congress.

In 2004 the party was even less successful than in 2000, failing to gain the White House for its standard-bearer, Sen. John Kerry of Massachusetts, and losing further ground in both the Senate and House.

On February 12, 2005, the party elected former Vermont governor Howard Dean as its national chair. A contender for the 2004 presidential nomination, Dean was a committed liberal whose widely publicized antiwar stand was considered secondary to his status as a vigorous and effective political leader.

The lengthy presidential primary campaign got under way following the midterm elections in November 2006, with candidates stumping in earnest by early 2007. Those vying for the party's nomination, in addition to Hillary Rodham Clinton, Barack Obama, and Joseph Biden, were Christopher DODD, senator from Connecticut; Mike GRAVEL, former senator from Alaska; Dennis KUCINICH, congressman from Ohio; Bill RICHARDSON, governor of New Mexico; and Tom VILSACK, former governor of Iowa. Senator Clinton had a strong showing early on, which tapered as the primary elections continued throughout 2008. Clinton did not concede the closely fought race until four days after Obama won the party's nomination on June 3. She then announced her endorsement of Obama for president.

The Democratic Party's presidential nominee, Barack Obama, secured 365 electoral college votes and 52.9 percent of the popular vote in November 2008 to become the first presidential candidate since Carter to receive more than a 50 percent vote share.

The Democrats captured significant majorities in the Senate and the House in the 2008 elections but initially fell two seats short of the 60-seat powerful majority in the upper house. On April 30, 2009, Arlen Specter of Pennsylvania, elected as a Republican in 2004, switched to the Democratic Party, and on June 30 the Minnesota Supreme Court upheld the decision of a lower court to recognize the narrow victory of Democrat Al FRANKEN over Republican incumbent Norm COLEMAN, ending the Republicans' ability to filibuster to defeat legislation. The August 25 death of Massachusetts Senator Edward. M. KENNEDY from cancer reduced the party's majority to 59 seats temporarily until the state governor appointed Paul G. KIRK Jr as his temporary replacement.

Leaders: Barack H. OBAMA (President), Joseph R. BIDEN Jr. (Vice President), Nancy PELOSI (Speaker of the House), Harry M. REID (Senate Majority Leader), Robert C. BYRD (Senate President Pro Tempore), Richard (Dick) DURBIN (Senate Majority Whip), Steny H. HOYER (House Majority Leader), James E. CLYBURN (House Majority Whip), Tim KAINE (National Chair and Governor of Virginia).

Republican Party. Known informally as the "Grand Old Party" (GOP), the present-day Republican Party was founded as an antislavery party in the 1850s and includes Abraham LINCOLN, Theodore ROOSEVELT, Dwight D. Eisenhower, Richard Nixon, and Ronald Reagan among its past presidents. Generally more conservative in outlook than the Democratic Party, the Republican Party has traditionally drawn its strength from the smaller cities and from suburban and rural areas, especially in the Midwest and parts of New England. In recent years Republicans have tended to advocate welfare and tax reforms, including a simplified tax system and revenue-sharing to relieve the burden of local property taxes; the achievement of a "workable balance between a growing economy and environmental protection;" and military preparedness sufficient to preclude the nation's becoming a "second-class power."

Following a hard-fought campaign, with results not clear until December 12, the party's presidential candidate in 2000, George W. Bush, secured a bare majority of electoral votes. The Senate was split 50–50, while the Republicans retained control of the House with a reduced majority of 221 seats. In June 2001 the Republicans lost control of the Senate when Jeffords of Vermont became an independent, but they regained it in the November 2002 election and held it for the ensuing four years.

Charged with violating Texas campaign laws, House Majority Leader Tom DeLAY stepped down in January 2006 and was replaced by John Boehner on February 2. Other changes followed the party's legislative reversal in November 2006.

In the presidential primary campaign, which began in early 2007, the following Republican candidates sought the party's nomination, in addition to John McCain: Michael D. (Mike) Huckabee; Mitt Romney; Fred THOMPSON, former senator from Tennessee; Duncan HUNTER, congressman from California; Ron PAUL, congressman from Texas; and Rudolph Giuliani. Mitt Romney was the most serious challenger to McCain until the latter's campaign surged ahead in mid-2008.

In the 2008 elections Republican representation declined by 21 House seats and 8 Senate seats. In the presidential election, Senator John McCain received 173 electoral votes and 45.7 percent of the popular vote as the Republican nominee. After Sen. Arlen Specter's defection to the Democratic Party in 2009, the Republicans also lost the ability to filibuster to defeat Democrats' proposed legislation.

Leaders: Mitch McCONNELL (Senate Minority Leader), John BOEHNER (House Minority Leader), Roy BLUNT (House Minority Whip), George W. BUSH (Former President of the United States), Dick CHENEY (Former Vice President of the United States), John McCAIN (Senator from Arizona and 2008 presidential candidate), Sarah Palin (Former Governor of Alaska and 2008 vice presidential candidate), Newt Gingrich (Former Speaker of the House), Tim PAWLENTY (Governor of Minnesota), Mitt ROMNEY (Former Governor of Massachusetts), Michael D. (Mike) HUCKABEE (Former Governor of Arkansas), Haley BARBOUR (Governor of Mississippi), Michael STEELE (National Chair and former Lieutenant Governor of Maryland).

Other Parties:

Although third parties have occasionally influenced the outcome of presidential balloting, the Republican Party in 1860 was the only such party in U.S. history to win a national election and subsequently establish itself as a major political organization. The third parties having the greatest impact have typically been those formed as largely personal vehicles by prominent Republicans or Democrats who have been denied nomination by their regular parties, such as Theodore Roosevelt's Progressive ("Bull Moose") Party of 1912 and the American Independent Party organized to support the 1968 candidacy of George C. Wallace.

The only nonparty candidates in recent history to attract significant public attention were former Democratic senator Eugene J. McCARTHY, who secured 751,728 votes (0.9 percent of the total) in 1976; former Republican representative John B. ANDERSON, who polled 5,719,722 (6.6 percent) in 1980; and Texas entrepreneur H. Ross PEROT, who won 19,237,247 (19 percent) in 1992 and whose substantial support gave rise to subsequent attempts to establish a credible third party before his **Reform Party**'s far less impressive showing of 8 percent in 1996. Thereafter, despite a 1998 Minnesota victory for the party's gubernatorial candidate, former professional wrestler Jesse VENTURA, the party declined further, winning only 0.4 percent of the vote in 2000 under longtime Republican conservative Patrick J. BUCHANAN. In a marginally more impressive showing, **Green Party** nominee Ralph NADER obtained 2.7 percent of the vote, whereas the **Natural Law Party** candidate, Harry BROWNE, secured 0.4 percent. Nader ran as an independent in 2004, winning only 0.3 percent of the vote, and in 2008. Other third-party candidates in 2008 were Rep. Ron PAUL, Texas Republican running as an independent; Reform Party nominee Ted WEILL, chair of the Mississippi Reform Party; **Libertarian Party** (LP) nominee Bob Barr, a former Republican representative from Georgia; Green Party nominee Cynthia McKINNEY, a former Democratic representative from Georgia; **Constitution Party** (CP) nominee Chuck BALDWIN, a Florida pastor and former Republican; **America's Independent Party** nominee and former ambassador Alan KEYES; **Boston Tea Party** nominee Charles JAY; **Party of Socialism and Liberation** nominee Gloria E. LARIVA; **Prohibition Party** (PP) nominee Gene AMONDSON; **Socialist Party USA** nominee Brian P. MOORE; and **Socialist Workers Party** (SWP) nominee Róger CALERO.

Other minor parties, none of national significance in recent elections, have included the **Alaskan Independence Party** (AIP), led by Lynette CLARK; the **American Beer Drinker's Party,** led by Buddy PILSNER; the **American Independent Party** (AIP), led by Markham ROBINSON; the **American Nazi Party** (ANP), led by Rocky SUHAYDA; the **Communist Party of the United States of America** (CPUSA), led by Gus HALL until his death on October 16, 2000, and currently by Sam WEBB; the **Concerned Citizens** (CC), Connecticut affiliate of the **Constitution Party**; the **Conservative Party** (CP), based in Louisiana, Massachusetts, New Jersey, and New York; the Rhode Island–based **Cool Moose Party,** led by Robert J. HEALEY Sr.; the **Corrective Action Party** (CAP), led by Bernard PALICKI; the **Democratic Socialists of America** (DSA), which is a member of the Socialist International and led by Frank LLEWELLYN; the **Expansionist Party of the United States** (XP), which seeks expansion of the United States into an eventual world union, led by L. Craig SCHOONMAKER; the **Independent Party** (IP); the **Independent American Party** (IAP); the Latino **La Raza Unida** (People United) **Party** (LRUP); the **Liberal Party** (L); the **Liberty Union Party** (LU) of Vermont; the **Light Party,** led by Da VID; the **Mountain Party** (MP) of West Virginia; the **National Democratic Policy Committee** (NDPC), which has supported dissident Democrat, Lyndon LAROCHE, as a presidential candidate; the white supremacist **National Patriot Party** (NPP), which was formally launched in April 1994, mainly by former supporters of Perot; the now-defunct **National Unity Party** (NUP), which in 1984 endorsed John Anderson for a second presidential bid; the **New Federalist Party** (NFP), organized in 1975 "to promote the principles of George Washington and the Federalist founders of this nation"; the **Pacific Party** (PP); the **Pansexual Peace Party** (PPP); the feminist and socialist **Peace and Freedom Party** (PFP), based in California; **Politicians Are Crooks** (PAC); the now-defunct **Populist Party of America** (PPA), an outgrowth of the middle-class "America First" movement of the 1930s; the **Progressive Party** (PR); the Marxist **Progressive Labor Party** (PLP); the **Right to Life Party** (RLP), based in New York; the **Social Democrats USA** (SDUSA), a member of the Socialist International; the **Socialist Labor Party** (SLP); the **Timesizing.com Party** (TCP), based in Massachusetts; the **United States Pacifist Party** (USPP); the **Vermont Grassroots Party** (VGP); the **Veterans Industrial Party** (VIP), led by Ernest Lee EASTON; the **Working Families Party** (WFP); and the **World Socialist Party of the United States** (WSPUS).

LEGISLATURE

Legislative power is vested by the Constitution in the bicameral **Congress of the United States.** Both houses are chosen by direct popular election; one-third of the Senate and the entire House of Representatives are elected every two years. Congresses are numbered consecutively, with a new Congress meeting every second year. The last election (for the 111th Congress) was held November 4, 2008.

Senate. The upper chamber consists of 100 members—2 from each state—elected on a statewide basis for six-year terms. Following the 2006 election, the Democratic and Republican parties each held 49 seats, with the Democrats controlling because of support by two independents elected in 2006—Joseph LIEBERMAN of Connecticut, who had lost a Democratic primary bid in August, and Bernard (Bernie) SANDERS of Vermont.

Of the 35 seats up for election in the most recent balloting on November 4, 2008, the Democrats won 20 and the Republicans won 15. As a result, the Democrats gained control of 59 seats (with the continued support of Lieberman and Sanders) and the Republicans 41. The balance shifted to 60 Democrats and 40 Republicans on April 30, 2009, with Arlen Specter's switch to the Democratic Party.

President: Joseph R. Biden Jr. (Vice President of the United States).

President Pro Tempore: Robert C. BYRD.

House of Representatives. The lower house consists of 435 voting representatives, with each state entitled to at least 1 representative and the actual number from each state being apportioned periodically on the basis of population. The size and shape of congressional districts are determined by the states themselves; however, the Supreme Court has ruled that such districts must be "substantially equal" in population and must be redefined when they fail to meet this requirement. Resident commissioners from the District of Columbia, Guam, Puerto Rico, and the Virgin Islands were traditionally nonvoting delegates; however, in January 1993, over unanimous Republican opposition, they were given the right to vote in the body's Committee of the Whole, though not in the (usually pro forma) final passage of legislation. The right was revoked by the new Republican majority in January 1995; Democrats restored the privilege when they retook House control following the 2006 elections. In 2009 the resident commissioner of the Northern Marianas joined the ranks of nonvoting delegates, bringing their total to six, all of whom were Democrats or pledged to caucus with the Democrats.

In the most recent elections on November 4, 2008, Democrats won 257 seats, and Republicans won 178.

Speaker: Nancy PELOSI.

CABINET

[as of September 1, 2009]

President	Barack H. Obama
Vice President	Joseph R. Biden Jr.
Secretaries	
Agriculture	Thomas J. Vilsack
Commerce	Gary F. Locke
Defense	Robert M. Gates
Education	Arne Duncan
Energy	Steven Chu
Health and Human Services	Kathleen Sebelius [f]
Homeland Security	Janet A. Napolitano [f]
Housing and Urban Development	Shaun L. S. Donovan
Interior	Kenneth L. Salazar
Labor	Hilda L. Solis [f]
State	Hillary Rodham Clinton [f]
Transportation	Raymond L. LaHood
Treasury	Timothy F. Geithner
Veteran's Affairs	Eric K. Shinseki
Attorney General	Eric H. Holder Jr.

Note: All of the above, except Republicans Gates and LaHood, are members of the Democratic Party.

Cabinet-Level Aides	
Administrator, Environmental Protection Agency	Lisa P. Jackson [f]
Director of the National Drug Control Policy	R. Gil Kerlikowske
Director of the Office of Management and Budget	Peter Orszag
President's Chief of Staff	Rahm Emanuel
United States Trade Representative	Ron Kirk

[f] = female

COMMUNICATIONS

The press and broadcasting media are privately owned and enjoy editorial freedom within the bounds of state libel laws. There is no legal ban on the ownership of broadcasting facilities by the press, and in 1950, 43 percent of the commercial television stations were so owned. The Federal Communications Commission (FCC) has, however, been under some pressure to deny relicensing under potentially monopolistic circumstances.

Press. There were 10,855 newspapers, excluding in-house and special-purpose publications, issued in the United States as of 2002. Weeklies and semiweeklies outnumbered dailies by more than five to one. Until recently only a few papers have sought national distribution, the most important of the dailies being the New York–based *Wall Street Journal,* published in four regional editions; the Boston-based *Christian Science Monitor,* published in three domestic editions plus an international edition; the *New York Times,* whose national edition is transmitted by satellite for printing in eight locations throughout the country; and *USA Today,* which, after a phased market-by-market expansion beginning in 1982, reached a nationwide circulation of 2.3 million in January 2005 (a figure relatively unchanged as of 2008). (The *Christian Science Monitor*, whose circulation had dropped to 52,000, announced in October 2008 that it would discontinue its print version as of April 2009 and rely exclusively on its online version.)

After a lengthy period of decline, due in part to the impact of television on the printed media, the number of daily newspapers appeared to have stabilized in 1979–1980 at 1,750; however, their number again declined thereafter to 1,452 in 2005, with circulation falling from 62.2 million to 53.3 million over the same period, followed by an unprecedented plunge to 43.7 million in September 2006. Significantly, some of the country's leading papers, including the *Buffalo Courier Express,* the *Cleveland Press,* the *Des Moines Tribune,* the *Minneapolis Star Tribune,* the *Philadelphia Bulletin,* the *Pittsburgh Press,* the *Richmond News Leader,* and the *Washington Star,* were among the casualties. Concurrently, an ever-growing number of formerly independent papers were brought under the control of publishing groups.

In June 1993 the *New York Times* acquired the *Boston Globe* for $1.1 billion, the most ever paid to that point for an American newspaper. In mid-2000 the Tribune Company (publisher of the *Chicago Tribune* and several smaller papers) purchased the Times Mirror Company (publisher of seven papers, including the *Los Angeles Times, Newsday,* and the *Baltimore Sun*) for $8 billion. Also in 2000 Gannett acquired Central Newspapers, Inc. (owner of six papers, including the *Arizona Republic* and the *Indianapolis Star*), for $2.6 billion. In addition Gannett announced plans to purchase a number of papers from the Thomson Corporation, a Canadian publisher that had decided to divest itself of its once formidable newspaper holdings in the United States. Overall, newspaper purchases totaling more than $15 billion were reported for 2000.

Major turnovers in newspaper ownership occurred in 2006 and 2007. On March 13, 2006, the McClatchy Company announced it had bought Knight Ridder for $6.5 billion. On April 26, 2006, McClatchy announced that the *San Jose Mercury News, Contra Costa Times, Monterey Herald,* and *St. Paul Pioneer Press* would be sold to MediaNews Group for $1 billion. In 2007 the *Chicago Tribune* and its corporate parent the Tribune Company were taken private in a transaction underwritten by real estate mogul Sam Zell. Rupert Murdoch's News Corporation acquired the *Wall Street Journal* from Dow Jones in a deal finalized on December 13, 2007. As circulation and advertising revenues declined significantly in the industry, many newspapers, including the *Chicago Tribune*, the *Los Angeles Times*, and the *Washington Post*, announced a high number of layoffs. In 2008 several newspaper companies, including McClatchy, began the process of financial restructuring, and in December the Tribune Company filed for bankruptcy protection. Meanwhile, circulation overall was down 5 percent for the year. In February 2009 the *Rocky Mountain News* folded, leaving the *Denver Post* as that city's sole daily.

The principal guides to the following selection are size of circulation and extent of foreign affairs news coverage. A few newspapers with relatively low circulation are included because of their location, special readership character, or other points of interest. The list is alphabetical according to city of publication, with city designations as components of formal names being omitted. Also omitted are Saturday editions. Circulation figures are averages for the six months ending September 31, 2008, as provided by the Audit Bureau of Circulations.

Albany, New York: *Times Union* (83,496 morning, 143,261 Sunday).

Austin, Texas: *American-Statesman* (151,520 morning, 186,219 Sunday).

Akron, Ohio: *Beacon Journal* (110,999 morning, 150,919 Sunday).

Anchorage, Alaska: *Daily News* (61,882 morning, 70,272 Sunday).

Atlanta, Georgia: *Journal-Constitution* (274,999 morning, 464,805 Sunday).

Baltimore, Maryland: *Sun* (218,923 morning, 350,640 Sunday).

Birmingham, Alabama: *News* (131,133 morning, 163,825 Sunday).

Boston, Massachusetts: *Globe* (323,983 morning, 503,659 Sunday), retains "full editorial autonomy," despite acquisition by the New York Times Company; *Herald* (167,506 morning, 100,760 Sunday); *Christian Science Monitor* (online only).

Buffalo, New York: *News* (175,984 all day, 255,369 Sunday).

Charlotte, North Carolina: *Observer* (193,577 morning, 252,300 Sunday).

Chicago, Illinois: *Tribune* (516,032 morning, 864,845 Sunday); *Sun-Times* (313,176 morning, 255,905 Sunday).

Cincinnati, Ohio: *Enquirer* (193,326 morning, 272,703 Sunday).

Cleveland, Ohio: *Plain Dealer* (305,529 morning, 411,061 Sunday).

Columbus, Ohio: *Dispatch* (195,317 daily, 331,977 Sunday).

Dallas, Texas: *Morning News* (338,933 morning, 483,841 Sunday).

Dayton, Ohio: *News* (111,855 morning, 152,937 Sunday).

Denver, Colorado: *Post* (210,585 morning, 545,442 Sunday). Although the *Post* remains editorially independent, it is published by the Denver Newspaper Agency, which is owned 50 percent by E. W. Scripps Company and 50 percent by Media News Group.

Des Moines, Iowa: *Register* (135,056 morning, 219,745 Sunday).

Detroit, Michigan: *Free Press* (298,243 morning), *News* (178,280 evening). Combined editions are published on Saturday and Sunday (605,369), as well as on holidays.

Fort Lauderdale, Florida: *South Florida Sun-Sentinel* (183,562 morning, 269,256 Sunday).

Fort Worth, Texas: *Star-Telegram* (194,257 morning, 280,447 Sunday).

Fresno, California: *Bee* (139,649 morning, 166,380 Sunday).

Grand Rapids, Michigan: *Press* (123,893 evening, 178,033 Sunday).

Hartford, Connecticut: *Courant* (164,338 morning, 234,514 Sunday).

Honolulu, Hawaii: *Advertiser* (132,894 morning, 142,401 Sunday).

Houston, Texas: *Chronicle* (448,271 morning, 584,164 Sunday).

Indianapolis, Indiana: *Star* (220,133 morning, 321,760 Sunday).

Jacksonville, Florida: *Florida Times-Union* (127,661 morning, 181,155 Sunday).

Kansas City, Missouri: *Star* (239,358 morning, 324,837 Sunday).

Little Rock, Arkansas: *Arkansas Democrat-Gazette* (176,275 morning, 270,477 Sunday).

Los Angeles, California: *Times* (739,147 morning, 1,055,076 Sunday).

Louisville, Kentucky: *Courier-Journal* (192,896 morning, 268,942 Sunday).

Memphis, Tennessee: *Commercial Appeal* (147,598 morning, 178,082 Sunday).

Miami, Florida: *Herald* (210,884 morning, 279,484 Sunday).

Milwaukee, Wisconsin: *Journal Sentinel* (212,156 morning, 375,857 Sunday).

Minneapolis, Minnesota: *Star and Tribune* (322,360 all day, 520,828 Sunday).

Nashville, Tennessee: *Tennessean* (149,686 morning, 210,277 Sunday).

New Orleans, Louisiana: *Times-Picayune* (175,530 morning, 194,248 Sunday).

New York, New York: *Daily News* (632,595 morning, 674,104 Sunday); *Newsday* (377,517 morning, 433,884 Sunday); *Post* (625,421 morning, 386,105 Sunday); *Times* (1,000,665 morning, 1,438,585 Sunday); *Wall Street Journal* (2,011,999 morning, 1,927,247 weekend).

Newark, New Jersey: *Star-Ledger* (316,280 morning, 455,699 Sunday).

Oklahoma City, Oklahoma: *Oklahoman* (179,703 morning, 243,379 Sunday).

Omaha, Nebraska: *World-Herald* (169,722 all day, 216,285 Sunday).

Orlando, Florida: *Sentinel* (206,363 morning, 307,976 Sunday).

Philadelphia, Pennsylvania: *Inquirer/Daily News* (Inquirer: 300,674 morning, 556,426 Sunday; Daily News: 97,694 morning).

Phoenix, Arizona: *Arizona Republic* (361,333 morning, 463,036 Sunday).

Pittsburgh, Pennsylvania: *Post-Gazette* (203,588 morning, 317,008 Sunday).

Portland, Oregon: *Oregonian* (283,321 all day, 344,950 Sunday).

Providence, Rhode Island: *Journal* (131,620 morning, 186,571 Sunday).

Raleigh, North Carolina: *News and Observer* (158,573 morning, 205,654 Sunday).

Richmond, Virginia: *Times-Dispatch* (160,886 morning, 196,271 Sunday).

Rochester, New York: *Democrat and Chronicle* (141,812 morning, 196,146 Sunday).

Sacramento, California: *Bee* (253,249 morning, 299,207 Sunday).

St. Louis, Missouri: *Post-Dispatch* (240,796 morning, 423,588 Sunday).

St. Petersburg, Florida: *Times* (268,965 morning, 390,289 Sunday).

Salt Lake City, Utah: *Tribune and Desert Morning News* (191,109 combined morning, 211,526 combined Sunday).

San Antonio, Texas: *Express News* (206,933 morning, 302,720 Sunday).

San Diego, California: *Union-Tribune* (269,819 morning, 342,384 Sunday).

San Francisco, California: *Chronicle* (339,430 morning, 398,116 Sunday.) In an initiative approved in 2000 following a protracted court case, Hearst Communications, Inc. sold its longtime paper, the *Examiner,* to purchase the *Chronicle.*

San Jose, California: *Mercury News* (224,199 morning, 241,518 Sunday).

Seattle, Washington: *Times* (198,741 morning); *Post-Intelligencer* (117,572 morning). Although the *Times* and the *Post-Intelligencer* remained editorially independent, they had a joint operating agreement under which the Seattle Times Company provided most noneditorial services.

Syracuse, New York: *Post-Standard* (107,272 morning, 157,759 Sunday).

Tampa, Florida: *Tribune & Times* (187,689 morning, 258,089 Sunday).

Toledo, Ohio: *Blade* (115,058 morning, 144,204 Sunday).

Washington, D.C.: *Post* (622,714 morning, 866,057 Sunday); *USA Today* ([national paper] 2,293,310 morning).

West Palm Beach, Florida: *Post* (134,350 morning, 164,363 Sunday).

Wichita, Kansas: *Eagle* (79,233 morning, 128,195 Sunday).

News agencies. The two major news agencies are the Associated Press (AP), an independent news cooperative serving more than 1,700 newspapers and 5,000 radio and television stations in the United States, and the financially plagued United Press International (UPI), which was rescued from bankruptcy by Mexican publisher Mario Vázquez Raña in 1986 and whose operating rights were sold to an investment group associated with Financial News Network in early 1988 before being sold to the London-based, Saudi-controlled Middle East Broadcasting Centre Ltd. in June 1992 and, in 2000, to News World Communications, owned by Sun Myung Moon's Unification Church. In addition, many important newspapers that maintain large staffs of foreign correspondents sell syndicated news services to other papers. Among the larger of these are the *New York Times,* the *Chicago Tribune,* the *Los Angeles Times,* and the *Washington Post.*

Broadcasting and computing. Domestic radio and television broadcasting in the United States is a private function carried on under the auspices of the Federal Communications Commission (FCC), which licenses stations on the basis of experience, financial soundness, and projected program policy. Under a "fairness doctrine" embodied in FCC rules and upheld by the Supreme Court, radio and television broadcasters are required to present both sides of important issues. However, the so-called equal time legislation, which required a broadcaster who gave free time to a political candidate to do the same for his or her opponent, was amended on September 25, 1975, by the FCC, which stated that candidates' news conferences and political debates are news events and thus are not subject to the equal-time ruling (thus in 1996 Reform Party candidate Ross Perot was barred from the presidential debates, despite having participated four years earlier). The National Association of Broadcasters (NAB) is a private body that sets operating rules for radio and television stations and networks.

Of 10,944 commercial radio stations in operation in 2006, 4,707 were AM and 6,237 were FM outlets. Approximately one-third of the total were owned by or affiliated with one of the four major commercial radio networks: American Broadcasting Company (ABC), Columbia Broadcasting System (CBS), Mutual Broadcasting System (MBS), and National Broadcasting Company (NBC). Supported primarily by paid advertising, most stations carry frequent news summaries; a few in the larger cities now devote all of their airtime to such programming. Noncommercial programming was offered by more than 1,300 additional FM outlets.

There were 1,401 commercial television stations in operation during 2006, most of them owned by or affiliated with one of three commercial television networks headquartered in New York City: American Broadcasting Company (ABC), Columbia Broadcasting System (CBS), and National Broadcasting Company (NBC), in addition to the Los Angeles–based Fox Network. Supported primarily by paid advertising, most stations present news highlights, evening news summaries, and programs of comments and analysis. There is also the nonprofit Public Broadcasting Service (PBS), which services approximately 380 affiliated noncommercial television stations. In addition, more than 8,500 commercial cable TV systems are in operation, a decline from 11,200 in 1995 because of consolidations. An early beneficiary of the advent of cable TV was the Turner Broadcasting System, which by its tenth year of operation in 1990 was widely regarded as a "fourth major network"; by 1995 more new systems had been added, some (such as Paramount and Warner) with roots in historic film companies.

Foreign radio broadcasting is conducted under governmental auspices by the Voice of America (VOA), a former division of the United States Information Agency (USIA) that is now part of the International Broadcasting Bureau (IBB). It broadcasts in English and 44 other languages throughout the world. The IBB also supports Radio Free Europe, broadcasting in Bulgarian and Romanian (transmissions in seven other Eastern European languages were dropped in mid-1993), and Radio Liberty, broadcasting to the peoples of the former Soviet Union, both of whose facilities were relocated from Munich to Prague in mid-1995. The Florida-based Radio Martí, a VOA affiliate, commenced Spanish-language transmissions to Cuba in May 1985, while a controversial counterpart, Television Martí, was subjected to electronic jamming upon its launching in March 1990. In September 1996, after lengthy congressional debate, an equally controversial Radio Free Asia was launched to "confront tyranny" in East Asia; although its Chinese-language impact from transmitters as far away as Armenia and Tajikistan appeared minimal, its sponsors nonetheless pressed ahead with a Tibetan-language program in December and scheduled future broadcasts aimed at North Korea and Vietnam.

As of 2008 there were 740 Internet users per 1,000 inhabitants..

INTERGOVERNMENTAL REPRESENTATION

The various U.S. ambassadors to foreign governments, as well as the various foreign ambassadors accredited to the United States, are given at the end of the relevant country articles.

Permanent Representative to the UN: Susan E. RICE.

IGO Memberships (Non-UN): AC, ADB, AfDB, APEC, BIS, EBRD, G-7, G-8, G-10, G-20, IADB, IEA, Interpol, IOM, NATO, OAS, OECD, OSCE, PC, PCA, WCO, WTO.

RELATED TERRITORIES

The United States never acquired a colonial empire of significant proportions. Among its principal former overseas dependencies, the Philippines became independent in 1946, Puerto Rico acquired the status of a commonwealth in free association with the United States in 1952, and Hawaii became the 50th state of the Union in 1959. In addition to Puerto Rico, the United States now exercises sovereignty in the Virgin Islands, Guam, American Samoa, the Commonwealth of the Northern Mariana Islands, and an assortment of smaller Caribbean and Pacific islands. Until October 1, 1979, the United States held administrative responsibility for the Panama Canal Zone (see Panama: Recovered Territory), while U.S. administration of the Trust Territory of the Pacific Islands was effectively terminated with the independence of Palau on October 1, 1994. (For a discussion of the Trust Territory see the 1993 edition of the *Handbook,* pp. 946–948.)

Major Caribbean Jurisdictions:

Puerto Rico. Situated in the Caribbean between the island of Hispaniola in the west and the Virgin Islands in the east, the Commonwealth of Puerto Rico is composed of the large island of Puerto Rico together with Vieques, Culebra, and many smaller islands. Its area is 3,515 square miles (9,103 sq. km.). Its estimated population in 2007 was 3,943,000. Since 1972 "reverse emigration" has largely offset relocation to the mainland. Despite a falling birth rate, population density remains among the highest in the world, amounting in 2007 to 1,122 persons per square mile (433 per sq. km.). San Juan, with a population of 421,958 (2000C), is the capital and principal city. Spanish blood and culture are dominant, with an admixture of Native American, African, and other immigrant stock, largely from Western Europe and the United States. Most Puerto Ricans are Spanish-speaking and Roman Catholic, although religious freedom prevails. Both English and Spanish served as official languages from 1902 to 1991, when a bill was approved requiring that all government proceedings take place in Spanish, with official bilingualism being reestablished in January 1993. The economy, traditionally based on sugar, tobacco, and rum, advanced dramatically after 1948 under a self-help program known as "Operation Bootstrap" that stressed diversification and the use of incentives to promote industrialization through private investment, both local and foreign. Subsequently, industry surpassed agriculture as a source of income, with per capita income more than doubling, from $1,069 to $2,222, between 1965 and 1975 and soaring thereafter to $17,741 in 2007. Despite marked economic and social gains, however, the commonwealth is burdened by inflation, high public debt, and unemployment that has ranged as high as 23 percent of the workforce since 1975, the lowest being 10.5 percent in 2001. Reflecting an extreme maldistribution of wealth, 45.4 percent of the population was listed in 2006 as below the poverty line.

Ceded by Spain to the United States under the 1898 Treaty of Paris, Puerto Rico was subsequently governed as an unincorporated U.S. territory. The inhabitants were granted U.S. citizenship in 1917, obtaining in 1947 the right to elect a chief executive. The present commonwealth status, based on a U.S. congressional enactment of 1950 approved by plebiscite in 1951, entered into effect on July 25, 1952; under its terms, Puerto Rico now exercises approximately the same control over its internal affairs as do the 50 states. Residents, though U.S. citizens, do not vote in national elections and are represented in the U.S. Congress only by a resident commissioner, whose right to vote in Committee of the Whole, conferred in January 1993, was revoked in January 1995. (In November 1997 the Puerto Rican Supreme Court recognized the existence of Puerto Rican, in addition to U.S., citizenship.) Federal taxes do not apply in Puerto Rico except by mutual consent (for example, Social Security taxes). The commonwealth constitution, modeled on that of the United States but incorporating many progressive social and political innovations, provides for a governor and a bicameral Legislative Assembly (consisting of a Senate and a House of Representatives) elected by universal suffrage for four-year terms. An appointed Supreme Court heads the independent judiciary.

Puerto Rican politics was dominated from 1940 through 1968 by the **Popular Democratic Party** (*Partido Popular Democrático*—PPD) of Governor Luis MUÑOZ Marín, the principal architect of "Operation Bootstrap" and of the commonwealth relationship with the United States. While demands for Puerto Rican independence declined sharply after 1952, a substantial movement favoring statehood continued under the leadership of Luis A. FERRÉ and others. In a 1967 plebiscite 60.4 percent opted for continued commonwealth status, 39 percent for statehood, and 0.6 percent for independence. Following shifts in party alignments in advance of the 1968 election, Ferré was elected governor as head of the pro-statehood **New Progressive Party** (*Partido Nuevo Progresista*—PNP), which also gained a small majority in the House of Representatives. Four years later the PPD, under Rafael HERNÁNDEZ Colón, regained the governorship and full control of the legislature, while the PNP, under San Juan Mayor Carlos ROMERO Barceló, returned to power in 1976.

The traditionally anti-statehood PPD officially boycotted the October 1978 primary for selection of delegates to the U.S. Democratic Party national convention, and a pro-statehood faction, styling itself the New Democratic Party, easily won. With PPD head Hernández Colón having been succeeded in July by Miguel HERNÁNDEZ Agosto, and despite octogenarian Muñoz Marín's return to politics as an advocate for continued commonwealth status, "statehooders" thus held control for the first time of both the PPD and the PNP.

In 1979 former governor Hernández Colón, leader of the procommonwealth *autonomista* wing of the PPD, was designated as his party's 1980 gubernatorial candidate. With the campaign largely focused on the issue of the island's status, the "new thesis" of the PPD called for commonwealth administration of most transferred federal funds, authority to negotiate international trade agreements, and creation of a 200-mile economic zone to ensure local control of marine resources and potential offshore petroleum deposits. Governor Romero Barceló, meanwhile, was expected to call for a 1981 plebiscite on statehood, if he won reelection. At the November 4 balloting, the PNP won the governorship by an extremely narrow margin of 0.3 percent of the votes cast, while losing the Senate to the PPD (15–12) and tying the opposition in the House (25–25). In view of the outcome, Romero Barceló announced that the plebiscite on statehood would be deferred.

At the 1984 election Romero Barceló was defeated in his bid for another term by Hernández Colón, thereby ensuring that the statehood issue would, for the moment, recede in importance. The PPD victory was attributed, in part, to an active campaign waged by the **Puerto**

Rican Renewal Party (*Partido Renovación Puertoriqueño*—PRP), a group organized by dissident PNP leader Dr. Hernán PADILLA in August 1983. By an extremely close margin (50,000 of nearly 2 million votes cast), Hernández Colón won reelection in November 1988, defeating Baltasar CORRADA del Río, the PNP mayor of San Juan.

In January 1992 Hernández Colón announced that he would not seek reelection and in February resigned as leader of the PPD. His successor in the party post, Victoria MUÑOZ Mendoza, was defeated at the November gubernatorial balloting by the PNP's Pedro ROSSELLÓ, who, upon taking office in January 1993, scheduled a new referendum on Puerto Rico's constitutional future for November, at which commonwealth sentiment plummeted to 48 percent, while supporters of statehood and independence registered 44 percent and 4 percent, respectively.

On November 5, 1996, Rosselló won reelection to a second four-year term as governor, while the PNP won 38 House seats, as contrasted with 12 for the PPD and 1 for the PIP; additional opposition seats were, however, added under a constitutional provision that mandated a majority of no more than two-thirds.

The anti-statehood PPD secured an upset victory at the election of November 7, 2000, sweeping the governorship, both legislative houses, and most city halls. Its standard-bearer, Sila María CALDERÓN, who on January 7, 2001, became the commonwealth's first female governor, obtained 49 percent of the vote and the pro-statehood PNP candidate, Carlos PESQUERA, 46 percent, with Rubén BERRÍOS Martínez of the **Puerto Rican Independence Party** (*Partido Independentista Puertoriqueño*—PIP) a distant third.

A disputed gubernatorial poll in 2004 was closer than the U.S. presidential balloting of 2000. After a recount that lasted two months, followed by a bitter court battle between the procommonwealth and pro-statehood parties, the PPD's Aníbal Acevedo-Vilá was declared the winner over former president Pedro Rosselló by 3,500 votes out of 2 million cast. In the Senate and House races, however, the pro-statehood forces secured majorities.

In 2008 Acevedo-Vilá chose to seek another term despite a federal indictment against him on corruption charges, which he insisted were politically motivated. Although he was found not guilty in early 2009, the charges contributed to his defeat in the November poll by the PNP's Luis FORTUÑO, theretofore Puerto Rico's representative in the U.S. Congress. The PNP also won majorities in both houses of the Legislative Assembly. (Nominally Republican, the PNP endorsed Barack Obama in 2008.)

A comparatively small but frequently violent independence movement has been active since the 1920s, when the radical Nationalist Party was formed by Pedro ALBIZU Campos. On November 1, 1950, a group of *nacionalistas* attempted to assassinate President Harry S. Truman, while on March 1, 1954, another group wounded five U.S. members of Congress on the floor of the House of Representatives; on September 6, 1979, President Jimmy Carter commuted the sentences of the four Puerto Ricans still serving sentences for the two attacks, despite Romero Barceló's strong objection. Currently, the separatist movement is directed by the PIP and the Marxist **Puerto Rican Socialist Party** (*Partido Socialista Puertoriqueño*—PSP), which collectively have won no more than a combined 6 percent of the vote in recent elections. The most prominent far-left organization advocating independence is the **Armed Forces for National Liberation** (*Fuerzas Armadas de Liberación Nacional*—FALN), which has engaged in terrorist activities in New York City as well as in San Juan. On December 3, 1979, three other terrorist groups—the **Volunteers of the Puerto Rican Revolution,** the **Boricua Popular Army** (*Ejército Popular Boricua,* also known as the *Macheteros*), and the **Armed Forces of Popular Resistance**—claimed joint responsibility for an attack on a busload of U.S. military personnel that killed two and left ten injured.

On August 11, 2000, President Bill Clinton offered clemency to 16 FALN members who had been convicted of terrorist acts more than two decades earlier. A month later, 11 of the prisoners were released, despite a 311–41 House vote that condemned the president's action.

Internationally, the independence movement received support in September 1978 when the UN Decolonization Committee endorsed a Cuban resolution that labeled Puerto Rico a "colony" of the United States and called for a transfer of power before any referendum on statehood. The most recent attempt to authorize a binding referendum in the matter failed to be reported out by a Senate committee in February 1991. (Apparently Republicans feared that as a state Puerto Rico would send an overwhelmingly Democratic delegation to Congress, with others concerned that Puerto Rican statehood would fuel a campaign to grant similar status to the District of Columbia.)

Following Rosselló's reelection as president of the ruling PNP on August 22, 1994, the governor promised to hold another vote on the island's status, at which time he hoped for an "absolute majority" in favor of statehood. However, in September 1996 a bill to authorize a new plebiscite was withdrawn from the U.S. House of Representatives at the request of Romero Barceló (then resident commissioner), who, while still favoring statehood, objected to a provision that would require English as the official language under such status.

On March 4, 1998, the U.S. House of Representatives voted 209 to 208 in favor of a bill authorizing the Puerto Rican government to organize a plebiscite on its future status; however, the U.S. Senate appeared unwilling to address the measure in the foreseeable future. Meanwhile, on December 13, in yet another nonbinding referendum, 50.8 percent of Puerto Ricans voted for no change in status, while 46.5 percent favored statehood, and 2.5 percent, independence.

In a November 1997 ruling, the Puerto Rican Supreme Court recognized distinct Puerto Rican citizenship, while affirming that holders thereof, even if renouncing U.S. citizenship, could vote in U.S. elections, if resident in Puerto Rico. In August 2000 a U.S. federal court agreed that Puerto Ricans had a right to vote for president and vice president. However, an appeals court overturned the decision in October.

In the wake of the 2004 election, Governor-elect Acevedo-Vilá declared, "I am not going to impose my vision on the people of Puerto Rico." He added that he would seek an appropriate means (presumably a plebiscite or constitutional convention) for settling the issue of the commonwealth's future status. In December 2005 President George W. Bush's Task Force on Puerto Rico's Status proposed that the U.S. Congress set a date for a plebiscite in which the island's voters would indicate if they wanted to change the island's status. If so, the task force further recommended that Congress should then authorize a second vote in which the choice would be between statehood and independence.

While the PNP and the PIP supported the recommendation, Governor Acevedo-Vilá, a proponent of "enhanced commonwealth" status, rejected it. In an October 2007 letter to the task force, he described the 2005 report as containing "one of the most absurd sets of conclusions I have ever read," primarily the determination that the term "commonwealth" was merely descriptive and that the U.S. Constitution, having endowed Congress with plenary authority over all nonstate territories, limited the legal options to just two: statehood or independence. Furthermore, the governor disparaged the task force for concluding that Congress was not legally required to take the will of the Puerto Rican citizens into consideration when acting on the island's status. Despite the governor's dismissive assessment, the task force reiterated its stand in a second report, delivered in December 2007.

In early 2008 Acevedo-Vilá appeared to veer somewhat from his party's procommonwealth position by calling on the UN to back Puerto Rico's right to determine its own future course. He accused Washington of failing to grant additional self-governing power in return for the retention of commonwealth status and charged President Bush with being "clumsy and partisan" in his handling of the issue. Another recent controversy involved the status of the island of Vieques, two-thirds of which had long been used as a bombing range by the U.S. Navy. The issue came to a head after the killing of a civilian security guard during a bombing run in April 1999, with numerous protests erupting in the ensuing months. In December President Clinton ordered a halt to live-fire training on the island and an end to all exercises there by 2003 unless local residents agreed to an extension. In February 2000 the Puerto Rican government agreed to a resumption of limited training as part of a deal involving up to $90 million in aid. In May federal authorities cleared protesters from the range, and in June the navy resumed shelling with inert bombs.

On June 14, 2001, President Bush announced that all exercises on Vieques would end by May 2003, but that did not satisfy Vieques residents, who on July 29 voted by a two-to-one margin for immediate closure of the naval facility. The U.S. Congress thereupon insisted that the range was needed for tests in connection with the war on terrorism. The PIP responded that it would mount a general strike and call for civil disobedience if the navy did not leave on schedule. As a result, the navy withdrew on May 1, 2003, turning about 14,500 acres over to the U.S. Fish and Wildlife Service. Since then, with oversight from the Environmental Protection Agency, contract workers have been clearing the site of unexploded munitions.

Despite apparent settlement of the Vieques dispute, controversy resurfaced in the wake of a U.S. proposal to burn nearly 100 acres of its old training ground, instead of searching for and detonating unexploded munitions. In addition, the island's more than 9,000 residents have filed claims for illnesses from pollutants released during the period of live-fire exercises.

Newspapers in Puerto Rico are free of censorship; the largest circulations are those of San Juan's *El Vocero de Puerto Rico* (259,000) and *El Nuevo Dia* (203,000 daily, 246,000 Sunday). There were 120 commercial radio stations and 15 commercial television stations in 2002. In addition, the Commonwealth Department of Education sponsors a radio and a television network, while the U.S. Armed Forces operates one radio and three television stations. There were approximately 1.2 million television receivers in 2003.

Governor: Luis G. FORTUÑO.

Virgin Islands. Situated 40 miles east of Puerto Rico and just west and south of the British Virgin Islands, the U.S. Virgin Islands (formerly known as the Danish West Indies) include the large islands of St. Croix, St. Thomas, and St. John, and about 50 smaller islands. The total area, including water surfaces, is 132 square miles (342 sq. km.); the population numbered 108,612 at the 2000 census and remained relatively constant thereafter. The capital and only substantial town is Charlotte Amalie on St. Thomas. Two-thirds of the people are of African origin, and approximately one-quarter are of Puerto Rican descent. Literacy is estimated at 90 percent, and English is the principal language, although Spanish is widely spoken. The people are highly religious, with most being either Baptist or Roman Catholic.

Purchased by the United States from Denmark in 1917, the Virgin Islands are governed as an unincorporated territory and administered under the Department of the Interior. The inhabitants were made U.S. citizens in 1927 and were granted a considerable measure of self-government in the Revised Organic Act of 1954, which authorized the creation of an elected 15-member Senate. Under a New Organic Act of 1968, executive authority was vested in a governor and a lieutenant governor, both of whom since 1970 have been popularly elected. Since 1973 the territory has sent one delegate to the U.S. House of Representatives.

There is only marginal sentiment for independence, a formal constitution for the islands having been rejected in 1964, in 1971, and in March 1979, when 56 percent of the electorate voted against a proposal that would have authorized elective local governments for each of the three main islands. Nonetheless, President Ronald Reagan in July 1981 signed into law a resolution approving a basic law for the territory, which was also rejected in a referendum the following November.

Juan F. LUIS of the **Independent Citizens' Movement** (ICM, a breakaway faction of the dominant Democratic Party) was sworn in as governor on January 2, 1978, upon the death of Gov. Cyril E. KING. Luis was elected to a full four-year term the next November and reelected to an additional term in 1982. Alexander Farrelly, a Democrat, defeated the ICM's Adelbert BRYAN at gubernatorial runoff balloting in November 1986 and defeated two independents in winning a second term in 1990.

In a referendum held October 11, 1993, 90 percent of those voting favored continued or enhanced U.S. territorial status, while the options of full integration with the United States and independence each attracted about 5 percent. Only 27.4 percent of the electorate voted, but a turnout of at least 50 percent plus one was required to validate the outcome.

On November 22, 1994, Dr. Roy SCHNEIDER, a Republican standing as an independent, was elected governor, defeating the former lieutenant governor, Derek HODGE, a Democrat. Schneider had promised a campaign against crime, the prevalence of which had been the feature of a ten-part series in the *Virgin Islands Daily News,* a local newspaper that in April 1995 was awarded a Pulitzer Prize for its efforts but subsequently went bankrupt and was purchased by a Pennsylvania-based media company in early 2008.

On November 4, 1998, retired university professor Charles TURNBULL, a Democrat, denied reelection to Schneider, who had been under attack for overspending. Turnbull was reelected on November 5, 2002. The Democratic candidate, John deJONGH Jr., was elected as his successor in a runoff poll on November 21, 2006. On November 7 Democrats won 8 senatorial seats, to 4 for the ICM; 3 independents were also elected.

On June 12, 2007, voters chose 30 delegates for a constitutional convention. (Despite four previous efforts since 1964 to draft a constitution, the islands remained an unincorporated territory.) After two years of often contentious negotiations, the convention forwarded a draft proposal to Governor deJongh in late May 2009. However, the governor refused to submit the proposal to U.S. president Barack Obama and the U.S. Congress for consideration on the grounds that some of its provisions were outside the framework of the U.S. constitution and thereby unacceptable. Among other things, the proposal failed to recognize the supremacy of the U.S. constitution and inappropriately (according to its critics) offered extra rights (including property tax exemptions) to "native" Virgin Islanders.

Governor: John deJONGH Jr.

Major Pacific Jurisdictions:

American Samoa. Located in the South Pacific just east of the independent state of Samoa, American Samoa includes the six Samoan islands (Annuu, Ofu, Olosega, Rose, Tau, Tutuila) annexed by the United States pursuant to a treaty with Great Britain and Germany in 1899 and also the privately owned Swain's Island (currently with 30 inhabitants), 200 miles to the north and west, which was annexed in 1925. The land area of 77 square miles (199 sq. km.) is inhabited by a population almost entirely of Polynesian ancestry that more than doubled from 27,159 at the 1970 census to 57,291 at the 2000 census but, reflecting a slower rate of increase, was estimated at approximately 60,000 in 2008. Pago Pago, the capital, is situated on the island of Tutuila. The social structure is based on the same *matai* (family chief) system that prevails in neighboring Samoa. Although educational levels are comparatively high, subsistence farming and fishing remain the predominant way of life. U.S. government spending, fish canning, and tourism are the main sources of income, and the government is the territory's single largest employer. About one-third of all high school graduates leave Samoa for the U.S. mainland.

Constitutionally, American Samoa is an unorganized, unincorporated territory whose indigenous inhabitants are nationals but not citizens of the United States. (Ironically, American Samoans can participate in the selection of U.S. presidential nominees by political parties but cannot vote in presidential elections.) Administered since 1951 by the Department of the Interior, the territory voted for its first elected governor in November 1977. Its bicameral legislature (*Fono*) consists of an 18-member Senate chosen by clan chiefs and subchiefs and a popularly elected, 20-member House of Representatives, exclusive of a nonvoting member from Swain's Island. The judiciary consists of five district courts and a High Court, although a Court of Appeals in San Francisco recently ruled that the U.S. District Court for Hawaii has jurisdiction over federal crimes committed in American Samoa. Appointed district governors head the territory's three political districts.

At four-way gubernatorial balloting on November 3, 1992, former governor A. P. LUTALI, a Democrat, bested the Republican incumbent, Peter Tali COLEMAN, 53–36 percent, for his first victory in four contests involving the two. Coleman had been the only person in American history to serve as governor in five different decades. In 1996 Coleman, nearing 77 and in poor health, chose not to run again, while Lutali placed third in the first round of nonpartisan voting on November 5; as a result, Lutali's lieutenant governor, Tauese P. F. SUNIA, entered a November 19 runoff against Coleman's nephew and longtime campaign manager, Sen. Leala P. REID, emerging victorious by a 51.2 to 48.8 percent margin. He was elected to a second term in November 2000, once again defeating Reid in a close contest that saw Reid unsuccessfully challenge the results in court.

The current governor, Togiola T. A. Tulafono, was elected on November 16, 2004, and sworn in January 3, 2005. He was reelected with 57 percent of the vote in runoff balloting on November 18, 2008, despite the fact that Lieutenant Governor FAOA Aitofele Sunia (reelected as Togiola's running mate) was scheduled for a federal trial in 2009 on corruption charges.

American Samoa has been alone among the U.S. insular possessions in failing to conduct a referendum on change in its territorial status. Indeed, the Samoan delegate to Congress, E. F. H. FALEOMAVAEGA, was asked by the local legislature in September 1993 to withdraw a request for establishment of a joint federal-territorial political status commission. The principal reason for resistance to a change in Samoa's status is a fear that elements of the U.S. Constitution might thereby be invoked to invalidate the territory's traditional land tenure system. Subsequently, Faleomavaega was paraphrased by the *Washington Pacific Report* as suggesting that "only the chiefs tend to speak at village meetings, demonstrating once again the classic difficulty inherent in any attempt to overlay western institutions on nonwestern societies." These considerations notwithstanding, a new constitutional review process was launched, beginning with the formation of a Future Political Status Study Commission, which submitted its final report at the end of December 2006. Its recommendations included continuation of the island's "unorganized and unincorporated" status, enactment of legislation to strengthen the *matai* system and prevent further alienation of communal land, and the imposition of new restrictions on the entry and residence of aliens. Concurrently, TUFELE Liamatua, American Samoa's first elected lieutenant governor, called for complete autonomy, noting that the United Nations had classified the territory as nonself-governing and that, despite popular election, its leading officials are subject to removal by the U.S. secretary of the interior.

In early 2009 Samoa Packing, one of two canneries upon which a reported 85 percent of the economy is based, announced that it was planning to close down, while the other, Starkist Samoa, said that it intended to lay off 250 workers. Subsequently, Governor Togiola argued that part of the problem was federal legislation that permitted fishing vessels to register American Samoa as their home port without maintaining a presence in the territory.

In late September 2009 a powerful tsunami, generated by an earthquake under the Pacific about 120 miles away, caused widespread damage and casualties in American Samoa.

Governor: TOGIOLA T. A. Tulafono.

Guam. The unincorporated U.S. territory of Guam is geographically the southernmost and largest of the Mariana Islands in the west-central Pacific. Its area of 209 square miles (541 sq. km.) supports a population that numbered 154,805 at the 2000 census, inclusive of U.S. service members and their dependents, and an estimated 175,000 in 2007. The capital, Hagåtña (formerly Agaña), has a civilian population of about 1,100. The islanders, predominantly of Chamorro (Micronesian) stock and Roman Catholic faith, have a high level of education, with a literacy rate of more than 90 percent. The economy depends largely on military spending (despite closure of the Naval Air Station in early 1995) and tourism (about 350,000 arrivals a year, almost entirely from Japan).

Originally acquired from Spain by the 1898 Treaty of Paris, the island is the responsibility of the U.S. Department of the Interior. Guamanians were made U.S. citizens by an Organic Act of 1950; although they do not vote in national elections, they have sent a delegate to the U.S. House of Representatives since 1973. Under the Guam Elective Governor Act of 1968, both the governor and lieutenant governor have, since 1970, been popularly elected for four-year terms. The legislature, reelected every two years, was reduced from 21 to 15 members in 1998. A Federal District Court heads the judicial system. Local government in 19 municipalities is headed by elected district commissioners.

At the election of November 2, 1982, the Democratic nominee, Ricardo J. BORDALLO, narrowly defeated the Republican gubernatorial incumbent, while the Republicans won control of the legislature. On September 6, 1986, Bordallo won the Democratic primary in a bid for reelection, despite having been indicted three days earlier for influence peddling, but he lost in the November balloting to the Republican candidate, Joseph F. ADA; concurrently, completing a reversal of the 1982 outcome, the Democrats, although deeply divided between pro- and anti-Bordallo factions, captured the legislature. Bordallo was ultimately convicted in February 1987, secured partial suspension of the sentence against him in October 1988, and committed suicide in Hagåtña immediately before he was to serve out the remainder of the sentence in prison in February 1990. The Republicans retained the governorship and representation in the U.S. House but fell one seat short of capturing legislative control on November 6, 1990; on November 3, 1992, the Democrats secured a substantially increased legislative majority of 14–7. On November 8, 1994, Democrat Carl GUTIERREZ overcame charges of sexual impropriety to defeat Tommy TANAKA, the Republican nominee, by a comfortable 54.6 percent majority; concurrently the Democrats also bucked a national trend by retaining legislative control with a slightly reduced majority of 13–8. In 1996, on the other hand, Republicans regained legislative control for the first time since 1980 by a razor-thin margin of 11–10. In a comeback effort, former governor Ada failed to turn back Gutierrez's reelection on November 3, 1998, while the Republicans surged to a 12–3 majority in the downsized legislature. A recall effort against the governor floundered in October 2000 when he attracted enough Republican support to keep the issue off the November ballot.

At the November 5, 2002, election Republican Felix Camacho won the governorship over Democrat Robert UNDERWOOD, taking 55.2 percent of the vote. In the legislative election, Democrats won nine seats, while Republicans took the other six. There was no shift in the legislative balance at the next election, held November 2, 2004, but on November 7, 2006, the Republicans won an eight-to-seven majority. Collaterally, Camacho won reelection by again defeating Underwood, but the margin of victory was narrow, 50.3 percent to 48.0 percent. The Democrats regained their legislative majority by securing 10 of the 15 seats in the balloting on November 4, 2008.

In 1982 voters, by a three-to-one margin, had expressed a preference for a commonwealth rather than statehood, and in an August 8, 1987, referendum, approved 10 of 12 articles of a Commonwealth Act; on November 7 the remaining articles, providing for the recognition of indigenous Chamorro rights and local control of immigration (both bitterly opposed by non-Chamorros) were also approved. In 1992 the end of protracted talks between Guam's Commission on Self-Determination, chaired by Governor Ada, and a Bush administration task force on Guam, brought a "qualified agreement" on a commonwealth bill. Although endorsed by Democratic presidential candidate Bill Clinton at the party's 1992 convention, the measure was not introduced in the U.S. Senate until November 1997; by then, President Clinton, under pressure because of congressional unwillingness to sanction a Chamorro-only franchise or line-item veto power over federal legislation, had reversed himself, and the measure did not pass. Accordingly, the Guam administration announced plans in mid-1998 to hold a new status vote, restricted to Chamorros, in November 1999 that would delete the status quo and commonwealth options and limit the choices to independence, free association, and statehood. The action came shortly after a public opinion poll of all residents had yielded a 56-percent majority in favor of the status quo, with a small minority endorsing free association and only a smattering of support for independence.

A drastic improvement in Guam's economy is expected during 2010–2015, as the United States relocates upwards of 8,000 servicemen and their families from Okinawa to Guam at an estimated cost of $15 billion. Objection to the relocation has been led by the Guam Landowners Association, which insists that the territory would suffer the loss not only of land, but also part of its identity because of the influx of military personnel. In addition, concern has been voiced about a U.S. congressional proposal that 70 percent of the projected 12,000 construction workers be U.S. citizens, which would limit the number of lower paid guest workers from other Pacific islands and the Philippines.

Governor: Felix P. CAMACHO.

Commonwealth of the Northern Mariana Islands. Located north of the Caroline Islands and west of the Marshalls in the western Pacific, the Marianas (excluding Guam) constitute an archipelago of 16 islands with a land area of 184 square miles (477 sq. km.). The population of 69,221 at the 2000 census and an estimated 82,000 in 2007 resides on six islands, including Saipan (the administrative center), Tinian, and Rota. Classed as Micronesian, the people are largely Roman Catholic.

In 1972 a Marianas Political Status Commission initiated negotiations with Washington that resulted in the 1975 signing of a covenant to establish a Commonwealth of the Northern Mariana Islands in political union with the United States. The covenant was approved by the U.S. Senate on February 24, 1976, and signed by President Gerald Ford on March 24. In December 1977 a government consisting of the commonwealth's first governor and a Northern Marianas Commonwealth Legislature was established. The bicameral legislature encompassed a 9-member Senate elected for a four-year term and a 14-member (currently 18-member) House of Representatives elected biennially. The initial legislators assumed office on January 9, 1978. Under U.S. and local law, the commonwealth ceased to be a component of the Trust Territory of the Pacific Islands on November 3, 1986, with its residents becoming U.S. citizens on the same day. (According to a census report, the percentage holding U.S. citizenship had dropped to 50.3 in 2008.) The change in status under international law came with formal removal from trusteeship by vote of the UN Security Council on December 22, 1990.

In early 1991 a question arose as to whether the commonwealth's representative in Washington, D.C., should seek a seat in Congress on a basis similar to that of delegates from Guam and the Caribbean territories. Whereas the former representative (a Democrat) felt that commonwealth interests were best served by a person with "quasi-diplomatic" status, his successor (a Republican) appeared to favor a congressional presence, in part because of the direct entrée to lawmakers, but also because the costs would be assumed by the federal government. In August 1992 six in ten respondents to a *Pacific Daily News* poll were reported to favor congressional representation, which was in abeyance because of tension between Congress and the commonwealth administration. Much of the difficulty stemmed from a flow of ill-paid foreign workers into the Marianas, which controlled its immigration and minimum wage policies and was able to ship tariff-free goods to the United States, thus underpricing mainland clothing manufacturers. In addition, Congress was unwilling to increase financial aid to the commonwealth because of a highly regressive tax structure that included substantial rebates to the rich. Partly for these reasons, the incumbent Republican governor, Lorenzo (Larry) I. De Leon GUERRERO, lost a reelection bid in November 1993 to his Democratic opponent, Froilan C. ("Lang") TENORIO, although the Republicans retained majorities in both legislative houses. However, the split-party government weakened the executive because commonwealth executive orders (unlike those issued by the U.S. president) are subject to legislative veto within 60 days of promulgation. Thus a major government reorganization plan was defeated in early 1994.

At the election of November 1, 1997, Tenorio and Lt. Gov. Jesus C. BORJA ran on separate tickets (the latter technically as an independent), thus splitting the Democratic vote and enabling two-time former Republican governor Pedro Pangelinan ("Teno") TENORIO to win with 45.6 percent of the vote. A subsequent judicial challenge to Teno's victory on the basis of a two-term limit adopted in 1986 was rejected on the grounds that the change could not be applied retroactively.

By late 1998 it was unclear when covenant-mandated consultations between Saipan and Washington, in abeyance for more than two years because of immigration and wage issues, would resume. One U.S. member of Congress termed the commonwealth a "legalized sweatshop," while the commonwealth administration insisted that the islands' garment industry would be wiped out if mainland minimum wage legislation were to be mandated. Others objected to a compromise increase of $.50 enacted in early 2008. Local leaders also complained of competition from Mexican garment factories operating under the North American Free Trade Agreement (NAFTA).

As a source of new jobs, commonwealth officials hailed the advent of casino gambling on Tinian. Designed primarily as a boon to the tourist trade, the new industry was expected to have a multiplier effect on an economy that had seen a plunge in annual per capita income from $9,151 in 2000 to $6,178 in 2004.

In May 2000 it was reported that the commonwealth representative in Washington, D.C., Juan BABAUTA, was promoting legislation for a nonvoting delegate in the House, insisting that widespread support had emerged for such a position. The effort was successful, and the first election of a nonvoting House member was held on November 4, 2008.

At the election of November 3, 2001, Babauta, a Republican, captured the governor's office with 42.8 percent of the vote, defeating Benigno Fitial of the **Covenant Party** (CP), the Democrat Borja, and Froilan Tenorio, now of the **Reform Party.** Republicans also retained control of both legislative chambers.

A four-way gubernatorial race on November 5, 2005, pitted Governor Babauta against Speaker of the House Fitial, Froilan Tenorio, and independent Heinz HOFSCHNEIDER. The contest was so close, however, that the outcome remained unclear until more than 1,200 absentee ballots were counted two weeks later. In the end, Fitial won by 99 votes over Hofschneider. In simultaneous legislative balloting, no party won a majority in either house. In the Senate, the CP and the Republicans each held three seats, compared to two for the Democratic Party and one for an independent; in the House, the CP and the Republicans each won seven seats, followed by the Democrats and independents with two each.

In contrast, Republicans dominated the November 3, 2007, election for an expanded House, winning 12 of the 20 seats. The CP won 4; the Democrats, 1; and independents, 3. Of the 3 Senate seats up for election, a member of the CP, a Democrat running as an independent, and an independent each won 1.

In August 2008 Lt. Gov. Timothy P. VILLAGOMEZ, Commerce Secretary James SANTOS, and a number of others were indicted on charges of conspiracy, wire fraud, and the theft of federal funds in connection with business deals involving the Commonwealth Utilities Corporation. Following his conviction in April 2009 Villagomez resigned and was replaced by CP Chair and Finance Secretary Elroy INOS.

One long-term prospect is that the CNMI and Guam might merge, with the resulting entity becoming the 51st state of the federal union. Advocates of such a move point out that the two had been administered jointly by Spain but were separated after the Spanish-American War in 1898. In 1969 Guam had rejected reintegration, largely because of participation by Northern Mariana Chamoros in Japan's wartime occupation. However, in May 2008 Guam Governor Camacho apologized to the CNMI for the rejection.

A more current issue stems from the CNMI's increasingly fragile economy, which yielded a prediction by Chief Justice Jose S. DELA CRUZ in early 2009 of likely bankruptcy if changes were not made in a land alienation rule that discourages foreign investment. The assessment came in the wake of a sharp decline in tourism (expected to continue because of the exclusion of Chinese and Russians from the federal visa waiver process) and U.S. congressional approval of measures to federalize labor and immigration controls that would severely affect the status of "guest workers." Under federal immigration control, according to a report commissioned by the governor, the territory's economy will lose some 60 percent of its jobs and 44 percent of its real GDP by 2015. Governor Fitial was reelected to another five-year term in runoff balloting on November 23, 2009, at which Hofschneider, running as the Republican candidate, lost by 370 votes despite having led the first-round balloting by a few votes.

Governor: Benigno R. FITIAL.

Other Insular Possessions:

Palmyra Island. A group of about 50 islets situated on a horseshoe-shaped reef about 1,000 miles south of Honolulu, Palmyra became a U.S. territory upon the annexation of Hawaii in 1898. It was placed under civil administration of the Interior Department by the Hawaii Statehood Act of 1959. Privately owned by the Fullard-Leo family of Hawaii from 1922, the atoll, covering 4 square miles (10.44 sq. km.), was occupied during World War II by the U.S. Navy, which built an airstrip subsequently used by the U.S. Air Force until 1961. In early 2000 the U.S.-based Nature Conservancy announced that it had launched a $37 million fund-raising campaign to buy the atoll, which is home to 20 bird species and has five times as many coral species as the Florida Keys. The sale was concluded in November 2000 and has led to the construction of a $1.5 million wildlife research station.

In January 2009 Palmyra was designated by President George W. Bush as part of a Pacific Remote Islands National Monument under the supervision of the U.S. Interior Department.

Wake Island. Consisting of three islets with a combined area of 3 square miles (7.8 sq. km.) with no indigenous population, Wake Island lies roughly midway between Hawaii and Guam. It was formally claimed by the United States in 1900. In 1990 congressional representatives of Guam and Hawaii introduced a bill to give Guam jurisdiction over Wake Island and Hawaii jurisdiction over Howland, Baker, and Jarvis islands, Kingman Reef, Midway, and Palmyra. At stake was a potential gain of 120,000 square miles to Guam's exclusive economic zone (EEZ) and of 300,000 square miles to Hawaii's. The move was condemned by Marshall Island leaders, who had long viewed Wake as Marshallese territory, although no claim to such effect had been included in its compact of free association with the United States. The bill died and was not reintroduced in the next Congress.

Although Wake Island falls under the jurisdiction of the Department of the Interior, activities have long been administered by the U.S. military. An air and naval station was established before World War II, during which Wake was occupied by Japanese forces. It is also the site of a U.S. Missile Defense Agency facility. In August 2006 the remaining military personnel, numbering fewer than 200, were evacuated in advance of one of the central Pacific's most powerful storms, Typhoon Ioke, which caused an estimated $88 million in damage on the island. Subsequently, upwards of 100 people, mainly civilian contractors, were engaged in restoring services. The airfield remains available for emergency landings by civilian as well as military aircraft.

In January 2009 Wake was designated by President George W. Bush as part of the new Pacific Remote Islands National Monument.

Johnston Island. Part of an atoll that also includes the Sand, Hikina, and Akau Islands, Johnston Island lies about 700 miles southwest of Hawaii. The islands have a combined area of about 0.5 square miles (1.3 sq. km.). The population of Johnston Island was 1,387 (primarily government personnel) in 1994; the other islands are uninhabited.

Annexed in 1858, the atoll has been under the joint administration of the U.S. Defense and Interior Departments since World War II.

During the first half of 1990 a number of island governments, including those of American Samoa, the Marshall Islands, and the Northern Marianas, complained to the federal government of the incineration of dangerous chemicals (including nerve gas) and armaments on Johnston Island, arguing that there was a danger of the jet stream carrying pollutants not only to their shores but "around the world." Subsequently, during an October summit meeting with Pacific leaders in Hawaii, President George H. W. Bush indicated that the Defense Department would proceed with disposal of the materials already on the island but had no plans to continue the practice thereafter. In early 1999 the U.S. Army announced that its Johnston Island Atoll Chemical Disposal System (JACADS) would be closed. It was subsequently reported that the destruction of chemical weapons on Johnson had been completed in 2004, and the U.S. Environmental Protection Agency in 2009 certified that the facility had been properly cleaned and closed. (The U.S. Fish and Wildlife Service, which in 1926 was assigned responsibility for the area as a wildlife refuge, had been reluctant to resume its role because of the contamination.)

Johnson Island was included in the Pacific Remote Islands National Monument proclaimed by President George W. Bush in January 2009, as were Howland, Baker, and Jarvis Islands, in addition to Kingman Reef (below).

Howland, Baker, and Jarvis Islands. Uninhabited, with a combined area of about 3 square miles (7.77 sq. km.), Howland, Baker, and Jarvis are widely scattered islands situated more than 1,300 miles south of Honolulu. Claimed by the United States in 1936, they are under the administration of the Department of the Interior. All three were designated National Wildlife Refuges in 1974, and in late 2007 the U.S. Fish and Wildlife Service announced the availability of a number of conservation plans for their management over the next 15 years.

In May 1999 President Teburoro Tito of Kiribati claimed that the three islands were geographically part of Kiribati and should come under its jurisdiction; there was no indication, however, that Washington was prepared to consider the claim.

Kingman Reef. The uninhabited Kingman Reef, surrounding a lagoon 1,100 miles south of Honolulu, was annexed in 1922 and is administered by the Department of the Navy. Characterized by the Scripps Institution of Oceanography in early 2008 as "one of the planet's most pristine coral reefs," Kingman has been a National Wildlife Refuge since 2001.

Midway Islands. Consisting of Eastern and Sand islands (not to be confused with Sand Island, above), the Midway Islands have a combined area of 2 square miles (5.2 sq. km.) and had a largely military population in 1994 of about 2,500, most of which was subsequently withdrawn. Located at the northwestern end of the Hawaiian chain, the Midway Islands were annexed in 1867 and are best known as the site of a major U.S. naval victory against Japan in 1942. Administered by the Department of the Navy until 1996, Midway was then taken over by the Department of the Interior.

On June 15, 2006, President George W. Bush turned a 200,000 square mile tract of ocean including the Midway Islands into the world's largest marine sanctuary, the Northwestern Hawaiian Islands Marine National Monument. Renamed the Papahanaumokuakea Marine National Monument in March 2007, it is home to approximately 7,000 wildlife species, a number of which are endangered by plastic debris. Because of the threat, particularly to nearly 2 million Laysan albatrosses (all of whom are reported to have imbibed a quantity of the toxic substance), the U.S. Fish and Wildlife Service launched an unusual program in late 2007 to admit tourists pledged to engage in a cleanup effort.

Navassa. Situated between Jamaica and Haiti and claimed by the United States in 1916, Navassa is a small island of 2 square miles (5 sq. km.) that served as the site of a lighthouse maintained by the U.S. Coast Guard until 1996. In July 1981 six U.S. Marines were temporarily deployed on Navassa to thwart a semi-official attempt by Haitians to lay claim to the island. The island is currently administered by the Department of the Interior.

Numerous other small insular territories have historically been claimed by the United States, including Christmas Island in the Indian Ocean, which passed from British to Australian administration in 1958. Quita Sueño, Roncador, Serrana, and Serranilla, a group of uninhabited islets in the western Caribbean, were turned over to Colombia under a 1972 treaty that the U.S. Senate failed to ratify until 1981 because of conflicting claims by Nicaragua.

Under the so-called Guano Act of 1856, the United States claimed jurisdiction over 58 Pacific islands ostensibly discovered by American citizens and presumed to contain extractable resources, principally phosphate. In 1979 it was reported that the United States had concluded a treaty with the newly independent state of Tuvalu whereby it renounced all claims under the act to the four southernmost of the country's nine islands. The following September the government concluded a similar treaty with Kiribati under which, in addition to surrendering Canton (subsequently Kanton) and Enderbury (theretofore under joint British and American administration), it relinquished claims, under the 1856 legislation, to the eight Phoenix Islands, the five Southern Line Islands, and Christmas (subsequently Kiritimati) Island in the Northern Line group. In June 1980 a treaty was concluded with New Zealand whereby U.S. claims to four islands in the northern Cook group were also abandoned. The treaties were ratified by the U.S. Congress in 1983 over strong conservative opposition.

URUGUAY

Oriental Republic of Uruguay
República Oriental del Uruguay

Note: On October 25, 2009, Uruguay held parliamentary and presidential elections that resulted in gains for the political left. The Broad Front (Frente Amplio), the governing coalition, won 16 of 30 seats in the Senate and 50 of 99 seats in the lower house. The Blanco Party won 9 seats in the Senate and 30 in the lower house while the Colorado Party won 5 in the Senate and 17 in the lower house. The smaller Independent Party won 2 seats in the lower house. Neither José Mujica of the Broad Front, who won 48 percent of the popular vote, nor Luis Alberto Lacalle of the Blanco Party with 29 percent of the vote won a majority of the votes necessary to avoid a runoff. On November 29 Mujica won the presidency with 52.4 percent, defeating Lacalle with 43.5 percent. Mujica was scheduled to be inaugurated on March 1, 2010.

Political Status: Independent state proclaimed in 1825; republic established in 1830; presidential-congressional system reinstated on March 1, 1985, supplanting military-controlled civilian government in power since February 1973.

Area: 68,037 sq. mi. (176,215 sq. km.).

Population: 3,241,003 (2004C); 3,326,000 (2007E). The 2004 figure excludes and the 2006 figure includes an adjustment for underenumeration.

Major Urban Center (2005E): MONTEVIDEO (1,265,000).

Official Language: Spanish.

Monetary Unit: Uruguayan Peso (market rate December 1, 2009: 19.90 pesos = $1US).

President: *(See headnote.)* Dr. Tabaré Ramón VÁZQUEZ Rosas (Progressive Encounter– Broad Front); elected on October 31, 2004, and inaugurated on March 1, 2005, for a five-year term, succeeding Jorge BATLLE Ibáñez (Colorado Party).

Vice President: Rodolfo NIN Novoa (Progressive Encounter–Broad Front); elected on October 31, 2004, and inaugurated on March 1, for a term concurrent with that of the president, succeeding Luis HIERRO López (Colorado Party).

THE COUNTRY

Second smallest of South American countries, Uruguay has historically been among the best performers in terms of education, per capita income, and social welfare. Its official designation as the Oriental

(Eastern) Republic of Uruguay derives from its position on the eastern bank of the Uruguay River, which forms its frontier with Argentina and opens into the great estuary of the Rio de la Plata, on which both Montevideo and the Argentine capital of Buenos Aires are situated. From its 120-mile Atlantic coastline, Uruguay's rolling grasslands gently climb to the Brazilian boundary in the northeast. More than half of the population, which is almost entirely of Spanish and Italian origins, is concentrated in Montevideo, the only large city. While Uruguay was once a popular destination for immigrants, the flow of people has reversed. An estimated one-fifth of the population lives abroad, mostly in Europe or the United States.

Although cattle- and sheep-raising were the traditional basis of the economy, crop farming has increased in recent years, and a sizable industrial complex (primarily food processing) has developed around the capital. Textiles, meat, wool, and leather goods are currently the leading exports, while industrial promotion and foreign investment laws instituted in the early 1980s have encouraged production of electrical equipment and minerals. The GDP rose at an average rate of 4.8 percent during 1974–1980 but was accompanied by massive inflation that ranged between 45 and 80 percent annually. After 1980, inflation fell dramatically (to a low of 19 percent in 1982) but was coupled with a severe recession induced, in part, by devaluation of the Argentine peso in 1981, followed by disruptions attributed to the Falklands war the following year. During 1987 inflation returned to more than 60 percent, although unemployment fell from upward of 30 percent in 1983 to a more acceptable 8.3 percent. By early 1988 the nation's economy, brightened by a rise in exports, showed further signs of improvement, although the external debt had grown to more than $5 billion. During 1990, on the other hand, inflation accelerated to nearly 130 percent because of adverse economic conditions in neighboring Argentina and Brazil.

GDP growth averaged 3.7 percent in 1990–1996 and then reached 5.1 percent in 1997 and 4.5 percent in 1998. In the latter year consumer price inflation finally dropped below double digits, while unemployment fell to about 10 percent. Thereafter, however, the economy entered a protracted recession, contracting by 2.8 percent in 1999, 1.4 percent in 2000, and 3.1 percent in 2001. A principal cause of the downturn was declining world commodity prices for Uruguayan exports, but in late 2001 the economy was thrown into a tailspin by the financial crisis in Argentina. The result was a GDP contraction of 11 percent in 2002, before an improvement in beef exports contributed to a 2.5 percent gain in 2003 and a surge to 12.6 percent growth in 2004. The International Monetary Fund (IMF), citing the significant economic rebound, bolstered by expanded investment and exports, recorded Uruguay's annual GDP growth as 7.4 percent in 2007. A slight decline in the price of commodities in 2008 was not expected to dampen Uruguay's robust growth, owing in part to the opening of a new paper pulp mill on the Uruguay River and, according to analysts, the government's responsible economic policy. The IMF, for its part, has commended the government for recent reforms resulting in "the significant strengthening of the regulation and supervision of the financial system."

Despite higher than expected inflation of 9.9 percent in the January of 2009, the economy grew by 2.2 percent in the first quarter of 2009, causing many economists to make upward revisions to GDP estimates for the year. The country, which has traditionally enjoyed more affluence than its neighbors, appears likely to avoid the worst of the international economic crisis, with a slight contraction expected before a return to economic growth in 2010.

GOVERNMENT AND POLITICS

Political background. Before the 20th century Uruguay's history was largely determined by the buffer-like position that made it an object of contention between Spain and Portugal and, later, between Argentina and Brazil. Uruguay proclaimed its independence in 1825 and was recognized by its two neighboring countries in 1828, but both continued to play a role in the internal struggles of Uruguay's Colorado and Blanco parties following the proclamation of a republic in 1830. The foundations of modern Uruguay were laid during the presidency of José BATLLE y Ordóñez, who took office under the Colorado banner in 1903 and initiated the extensive welfare program and governmental participation in the economy for which the nation was subsequently noted. Batlle y Ordóñez and the Colorado Party were also identified with a method of government characterized by a presidential board, or council, employed from 1917 to 1933 and again from 1951 to 1967. The Colorados, who had controlled the government continuously from 1865, were finally ousted in the election of 1958 but were returned to power in 1966, when voters also approved a constitutional amendment returning the country to a one-person presidency.

The first of the presidents under the new arrangement, Oscar Diego GESTIDO (Colorado), took office in March 1967 but died nine months later and was succeeded by Vice President Jorge PACHECO Areco (Colorado). Faced with a growing economic crisis, rising unrest among workers and students, and increasing activity by *Tupamaro* guerrillas, both presidents sought to enforce economic austerity and resorted to emergency security measures. The election of Juan María BORDABERRY Arocena (Colorado) in November 1971 did little to alleviate the country's problems. Continuing economic and political instability, combined with opposition charges of corruption, culminated in military intervention on February 8, 1973. Under the direction of Gen. César Augusto MARTÍNEZ, José PÉREZ Caldas, and Esteban CRISTI, the military presented a 19-point program that placed emphasis on economic reform, reducing corruption by officials, and greater military participation in political life. The program was accepted by President Bordaberry on February 13, with governmental reorganization commencing almost immediately. A National Security Council was created to oversee the administration, Congress was dissolved and replaced by a Council of State, and municipal and local councils were supplanted by appointed bodies. Opposition to the increasing influence of the military was met by coercion: a general strike by the National Confederation of Workers (*Confederación Nacional de Trabajadores*—CNT) resulted in the group's proscription, while several opposition political leaders were placed in temporary detention during July and August. The National University of Montevideo was closed in October, and the Communist-led *Frente Amplio,* in addition to numerous minor leftist groups, was banned in December. Subsequently, as many as 400,000 Uruguayans were reported to have fled the country.

In early 1976 a crisis shook the uneasy alliance between President Bordaberry and the armed forces. The president, whose constitutional term was due to expire, wished to remain indefinitely in office as head of a corporativist state within which normal political activity would be prohibited. The military, on the other hand, preferred a Brazilian-style "limited democracy," with the traditional parties gradually reentering the political process over the ensuing decade. On June 12 the military view prevailed: Bordaberry was deposed, and Vice President Alberto DEMICHELLI was named as his interim successor. On July 14 a newly constituted Council of the Nation (incorporating the Council of State, the three heads of the armed services, and other high-ranking officers) designated Dr. Aparicio MÉNDEZ Manfredini as president for a five-year term commencing September 1.

In August 1977 the government announced that President Méndez had accepted a recommendation by the military leadership that a general election be held in 1981, although only the Colorado and National (Blanco) parties would be permitted to participate. Subsequently, it was reported that a new constitution would be promulgated in 1980, while all parties would be permitted to resume their normal functions by 1986.

The proposed basic law, which would have given the military effective veto power within a context of "restricted democracy," was rejected by more than 57 percent of those participating in a referendum held November 30, 1980. The government promptly accepted the decision while announcing that efforts toward "democratic institutionalization" would continue "on the basis of the current regime."

Following designation by the Council of the Nation, the recently retired army commander, Lt. Gen. Gregorio Conrado ALVAREZ Armellino, assumed office on September 1, 1981, as "transition" president for a term scheduled to end upon reversion to civilian rule in March 1985. Fourteen months later, on November 28, 1982, a nationwide election was held to select delegates to conventions of three legally recognized groups, the Colorado and Blanco parties and the Civic Union, whose leaders were to participate in the drafting of a constitution to be presented to the voters in November 1984. The balloting, in which antimilitary candidates outpolled their promilitary counterparts within each party by almost five to one, was followed by a series of talks between the regime and the parties, which broke down in July 1983 over the extent of military power under the new basic law. The impasse yielded a period of instability through mid-1984, with escalating public protests (including Chilean-style "banging of the pots"), increased press censorship, and arrests of dissidents (most prominently the respected Blanco leader, Wilson FERREIRA Aldunate, upon his return from exile on June 16). Government statements that adherence to the declared electoral timetable (which called for balloting on November 25) would be "conditional" upon the cooperation of the civilian parties yielded further protests, while deteriorating economic conditions prompted a series of work stoppages.

After talks resumed in July 1984 between the army and a multiparty grouping (*Multipartidaria*) consisting of the legal parties (excluding the Blancos, who had quit the group in protest at the imprisonment of their leader) and a number of formations that were still nominally illegal, an agreement was reached on August 3 confirming the November 25 election date and establishing a transitional advisory role for the military until late 1985. The signing of the pact was followed by a relaxation of press censorship and the legalization of a number of additional parties that, in concert with the Communist Party (*Partido Comunista*—PC), which remained outlawed at the time, reactivated the 1971 Broad Front (*Frente Amplio*—FA) coalition (see Political Parties, below).

Despite the Blanco Party's condemnation of the August 1984 agreement as an "acceptance of dictatorship," the party rejoined the *Multipartidaria* after the group had initiated talks with business and union leaders on a peaceful transition to civilian rule. However, because of the continued proscription of both the Blanco leader and *Frente Amplio*'s Gen. Liber SEREGNI, the Colorado candidate, Julio María SANGUINETTI Cairolo, enjoyed a considerable advantage in the presidential race, gaining a 38.6 percent vote share at the November balloting while his party won a slim plurality in both houses. The new Congress convened on February 15, 1985, followed by Sanguinetti's inauguration on March 1. To avoid public embarrassment at the swearing-in ceremony (the president-elect having indicated an aversion to accepting the presidential sash from a military ruler), President Alvarez had resigned on February 12, Supreme Court President Rafael ADDIEGO Bruno being named his interim replacement. In further attempts to remove the legacy of the military regime, the Sanguinetti government, with broad support from the public and opposition parties, released all political prisoners, including former *Tupamaro* guerrillas, and permitted the return of an estimated 20,000 exiles. Subsequently, a 1986 decision to declare an amnesty for military members charged with human rights abuses generated strong dissent, although Uruguayan voters failed to reverse the action in a referendum conducted in April 1989.

While the Blanco right-wing candidate, Luis Alberto LACALLE Herrera, won the presidency in November 1989, the party's inability to win more than a plurality of legislative seats necessitated the formation of a National Agreement (*Coincidencia Nacional*) with the Colorados under which the latter were assigned four portfolios (later three) in the government that took office on March 1, 1990. The de facto coalition was terminated by Lacalle in the course of a cabinet reshuffle in January 1993, albeit with two right-wing Colorados being retained until mid-May 1994.

The election of November 27, 1994, returned Sanguinetti Cairolo to the presidency, but in the legislature the vote share was split nearly three ways by the Colorado, Blanco, and recently launched Progressive Encounter (*Encuentro Progresista*—EP) groupings. Earlier, in a plebiscite conducted on August 28, a number of reforms that had been expected to pass easily (including a measure that would have sanctioned "ticket-splitting") were overwhelmingly rejected. Given the Colorados's narrow legislative plurality, President Sanguinetti emulated his predecessor in organizing a coalition government with 6 of 13 cabinet posts awarded to members of three other parties: 4 from the Blancos and 1 each from two nonlegislative groups, the Civic Union (*Unión Cívica*—UC) and the People's Government Party (*Partido por el Gobierno del Pueblo*—PGP) (see Political Parties, below).

In the election of October 31, 1999, the left-wing Progressive Encounter–Broad Front (EP-FA) captured pluralities in both legislative chambers. In a presidential runoff on November 28, however, the EP-FA candidate, Tabaré VÁZQUEZ Rosas, saw his first-round lead of 38.5 percent overcome by the Colorado candidate, Jorge BATLLE Ibáñez, who had also received Blanco's backing following the third-place finish of Lacalle Herrera in the initial balloting. Installed as Sanguinetti's successor on March 1, 2000, President Batlle named a coalition cabinet of Colorados and Blancos.

In late October 2002, with Uruguay in the throes of a serious economic crisis, the five Blanco ministers announced their intention to resign, and on November 3 a party convention supported the decision, although the Blancos, despite some dissent, indicated that they would continue to work with the government in the legislature.

On October 31, 2004, Vázquez, who had been denied election five years earlier, secured a first-round presidential victory of 50.7 percent, becoming at his inauguration on March 1, 2005, the first left-wing chief executive in Uruguayan history. He was supported by narrow majorities in both houses of Congress, the most conspicuous losers in the lower body being Colorados, whose representation plummeted from 35 to 10.

The cabinet was reshuffled on March 1, 2008, when President Vázquez replaced six ministers in advance of the 2009 presidential elections; ministers with leading roles in political parties were removed to ensure that government work was not interrupted by party activities.

Constitution and government. The present governmental structure is modeled after that of the 1967 constitution. Executive power is vested in the president who appoints the cabinet, while legislative authority is lodged in a bicameral General Assembly. Both the president and the legislature were elected, before 1996, through a complex system of electoral lists that allowed political parties to present multiple candidates, with the leading candidates within each of the leading lists being declared the victors. However, on December 8, 1996, voters narrowly approved a constitutional amendment that provided for internal party elections for presidential candidates. Under the change, a runoff between the two leading candidates is required if one does not win 40 percent of the vote with a 10 percent lead over the runner-up. The judicial system includes justices of the peace, courts of first instance, courts of appeal, and a Supreme Court. Subnationally, Uruguay is divided into 19 departments, which were returned to administration by elected officials in November 1984.

In accordance with "Institutional Act No. 19" (the August 1984 agreement between the Alvarez regime and the *Multipartidaria*), the army, navy, and air force commanders participate in an advisory National Security Council (*Consejo Nacional de Seguridad*), which also includes the president, the vice president, and the defense, foreign, and interior ministers. The council's actions are subject to the approval of the General Assembly. Other provisions of the act require the president to appoint military commanders from a list presented by the armed forces, limit the scope of military justice to crimes committed by members of the armed forces, and preclude the declaration of a state of siege without congressional approval.

Foreign relations. A member of the United Nations, the Organization of American States (OAS), the Latin American Free Trade Association, Mercosur, and other Western Hemisphere organizations, Uruguay has been a consistent supporter of international and inter-American cooperation and of nonintervention in the affairs of other countries. Not surprisingly, the former military government maintained particularly cordial relations with neighboring rightist regimes, while vehemently denying accusations of human rights violations by a number of international bodies. As a result, military and economic aid was substantially reduced under U.S. President Jimmy Carter. Although marginal increases were permitted during the Ronald Reagan's first administration, a campaign led by the exiled Ferreira Aldunate tended to isolate the Méndez and Alvarez regimes internationally, while the January 1984 accession of Raúl Alfonsín in Argentina substantially inhibited relations with Buenos Aires.

Before his initial assumption of office, President Sanguinetti met with Alfonsín and other regional leaders. His inauguration, attended by 500 representatives of more than 70 countries, featured a carefully staged but largely unproductive meeting between U.S. Secretary of State George Shultz and Nicaraguan President Daniel Ortega. Diplomatic relations with Cuba, broken in 1974 at the request of the OAS, were restored in late 1985, while in an effort to stimulate economic revitalization, trade accords were negotiated with Argentina, Brazil, Mexico, Paraguay, and the Soviet Union. During a February 1988 regional summit near Colonia, Uruguay, with Presidents Alfonsín of Argentina and Sarney of Brazil, President Sanguinetti pledged his government's accession to protocols of economic integration adopted by the neighboring states in December 1986; the pledge was reaffirmed during a tripartite summit in Buenos Aires in November 1989, and on May 22, 1991, the Uruguayan Senate unanimously approved entry into what had become known as the Southern Cone Common Market (*Mercado Común del Cono Sur*—Mercosur). By early 2000, however, Uruguay had joined Paraguay in complaining of "creeping bilateralization" of Mercosur decision making, with the smaller partners being pressured to accept agreements reached between Argentina and Brazil. As a result, a number of concessions were made for the minor participants, including special rates for their imports of cars and spare parts.

Relations with Argentina have been strained since early 2006 as a consequence of the construction of two pulp mills by Spanish and Finnish firms in Uruguay across the Uruguay River from Gualeguaychú, Argentina. Environmental activists in Argentina succeeded in blockading bridges across the waterway, preventing thousands of tourists from traveling to seaside resorts in Uruguay. In July the International Court of Justice (ICJ) rejected Argentina's request that the construction work be suspended. Meanwhile, President Vázquez filed a new complaint against Argentina at the ICJ over the roadblocks. The Spanish company abandoned its plan to build on the Uruguay River and instead decided to construct a mill on the River Plate. (The Finnish mill was completed in 2007.) Both parties were seen to be moving toward concessions in 2007, but the dispute escalated in early 2008 as Argentine environmentalists, supported by the Entre Rios provincial government, pledged to block traffic twice a week. Tensions eased in July, when the Argentine and Uruguayan foreign ministers agreed to establish a binational commission to study the environmental impact, giving the panel a six-month deadline. However, protests continued. The pulp mill issue also led a number of Uruguayan politicians to revive the long-standing dispute over the value of the country's participation in Mercosur, given alleged "hegemonistic" behavior by its two largest members. The construction of the pulp mill caused tensions within the Union of South American Nations (UNASUR) in which Uruguay vetoed the nomination of former Argentine president Nestor Kirchner as president for his role in the ongoing dispute. However, the two countries cooperated in securing UNESCO protection status for tango dance and music from the UN that month.

In 2009 Uruguay provided vital support to Venezuela in its efforts to launch its first satellite in cooperation with the Chinese government. While Uruguay received some benefit, the move served primarily to demonstrate the close relations between Uruguay and Venezuela. This was underscored in August 2009 when Uruguay, along with six other South American nations, contributed to the founding of *Banco del Sur* (Bank of the South), a development bank intended to rival the power of U.S. banks in the region. Despite cooperation with Venezuela's controversial president, Hugo Chávez, Uruguay's president Vázquez joined the United States in expressing concern over the recent increase in arms purchases by Venezuela that year.

Current issues. Any doubts as to President Vasquez's social policies were resolved at his inauguration on March 1, 2005, with the announcement that he would launch a "Social Emergency Plan" (*Plan de Atención Nacional de Emergencia Social*—PANES). Inspired, perhaps, by the Peruvian president's *ProPerú* scheme, PANES (an acronym translatable as "loaves") was meant to attempt to offer "a life with dignity" to 200,000 of the country's poor by providing them with food, medicine, housing, and employment at an estimated cost of $200 million over a two-year period. Subsequently, the president made good on a campaign pledge by securing the reluctant approval of his economy minister to draft a budget that included a significant budget appropriation for education.

Early in his tenure Vázquez was the driving force behind vigorous prosecution of human rights violators. In 2005 he began the first investigation into political killings that occurred under military rule in the 1970s. Further, in November 2006, former president Bordaberry and Juan Carlos BLANCO Estradé, who had served as his foreign minister, were arrested in connection with the assassinations of two lawmakers, allegedly part of an organized operation between the military regimes of Uruguay and Argentina to remove political opponents. Bordaberry was later charged in connection with at least 10 more deaths. (His trial was to begin in 2008.)

President Vázques continued to push liberal reforms to enhance the living standards for the poor and working-class population, who made up a significant portion of the EP-FA's political base, and he succeeded in gaining parliamentary approval for his tax reform measures. In the run-up to presidential elections in October 2009, Vázques insisted he would not seek reelection, a move that would require a constitutional amendment. But in early 2008, when sectors of the *Frente Amplio* (FA) grouping advocated such reform, President Vázquez deemed it "necessary." Observers said Vázquez was likely to support the anticipated candidacy of Daniel ASTORI, his former finance minister, who stepped down from the cabinet in September and returned to the Senate to prepare for upcoming election. In the June 2009 primary elections Asotri lost to the former minister of agriculture, livestock, and fisheries José MUJICA of the Movement of Popular Participation (*Movimiento de Participación Popular*—MPP). Despite a tense primary and initial reluctance by Asotiri, the FA planned to present a Mujica-Asotiry ticket in the October 2009 elections. The main contender running against the FA ticket is former president Luis Alberto Lacalle of the Blancos. In the final months before the election analysts predicted that the Blancos would exploit the rift between the two FA candidates. Meanwhile, the FA was expected to highlight the guerrilla past of the Blanco candidate, linking him to Venezuelan president Hugo Chávez. Also competing in the elections is Pedro Bordaberry of the Colorados. Three months before the election, 7 percent of the electorate remained undecided, but polls showed the FA ahead with 42 percent; the Blancos trailing with 36 percent; and the Colorados maintaining 10 percent.

In the midst of the global economic crisis and during the lead-up to the 2009 presidential elections, President Vázques created a new high-level position to coordinate employment efforts. The new coordinator will work with various ministries and banks to monitor unemployment rates, the effects of the economic crisis, and the impact of water deficits in Uruguay. (*See headnote.*)

POLITICAL PARTIES

Uruguay's two traditional parties, the historically liberal Colorado Party and the more conservative Blanco (National) Party, take their names from flags used by their respective factions in the 1836 civil war. Before the "temporary" proscription of all party activity in June 1976, both principal parties had included innumerable factions, which were not subject to overall party discipline and were permitted to run candidates at election time. In the party delegate balloting of November 28, 1982, Colorado factions presented 45 lists of candidates and Blanco factions presented 21, although most of the votes were won by a quite limited number of groups or coalitions representing both pro- and anti-government sentiment. A third legal participant, the ultraconservative Civic Union, obtained only 1.2 percent of the vote.

The *Multipartidaria,* a grouping formed in late 1983 to mobilize and solidify opposition to the military regime, was composed of all three groups plus the proscribed Communist, Socialist, and Christian Democratic parties. The legalization of the last two in August 1984 yielded the rebirth of a 1971 coalition, the Broad Front (*Frente Amplio*), which presented a tripartisan candidate in the November 1984 election. All parties were legalized following President Sanguinetti's inauguration in March 1985.

While most opposition parties formally refused to join the Colorados in the National Unity Government proposed by Sanguinetti in late

1984 (the Blancos and Broad Front together holding more legislative seats than the Colorados), some Blanco and Civic Union members were allowed by their parties to join the cabinet as individuals.

Although the Blancos outpolled the Colorados at the 1989 balloting, their inability to secure a majority of congressional seats necessitated the formation of a coalition administration following the inauguration of President Lacalle in March 1990. The 1994 poll yielded an essentially tripartite division of vote shares among the Colorados, Blancos, and recently organized Progressive Encounter (below). In 1999 the Progressive Encounter secured a plurality in both the presidential and legislative races, but was unable to capitalize on the former because of a second-round coalition by the traditional parties. In 2004 the leftists, for the first time, won majorities in both the presidential and congressional balloting. In 2009 the Chamber of Representatives was considering a law approved by the Senate to regulate televised campaign advertisements by distributing free timeslots between parties and limiting television advertisements to those slots. If approved, the law would take effect in 2014.

Presidential Grouping:

Progressive Encounter–Broad Front (*Encuentro Progresista–Frente Amplio*—EP-FA). Encompassing a number of left-wing groups, plus a group of Blanco dissidents, the EP was launched before the 1994 election. While running third in the November poll, the alliance was only marginally eclipsed by the second-place Blancos, thus effectively terminating Uruguay's traditional two-party system. Tabaré Vázquez, the popular former mayor of Montevideo who had been the EAP standard-bearer in 1994, easily won the EP's 1999 presidential nomination, securing 82 percent of the votes in the April primary. Although winning a plurality of 38.5 percent in October 1999, he was defeated in second-round balloting by Colorado-Blanco nominee Jorge Batlle Ibáñez. However, in 2004 Vázquez received slightly more than 50 percent of the first-round vote to win election as president.

Originally a Communist-led formation of 11 members that included the PSU, PDC, and MRO (below), the FA contested the 1971 election but was subsequently proscribed by the military regime, while its presidential candidate, retired general Líber Seregni, was imprisoned and stripped of his military rank. Seregni was released in March 1984 but was banned from political activity, thus unable to serve as the November nominee of the Front, which had attracted a number of dissidents from the Colorado and Blanco parties. In the 1984 balloting, Front candidate Juan CROTTOGINI won 20.4 percent of the vote, while the coalition won 21 Chamber seats (almost as many as the Blancos) and 6 Senate seats. In early 1985 a split developed between the group's Marxist and social democratic legislators over the degree of support to be given to the Sanguinetti administration, although in May the president, in a gesture to the Front, decreed that Seregni's military rank be restored. Subsequently a noncommunist "Lista 99" faction joined with elements of the PDC and PSU in a "Triple Alliance" that contested elections in student and labor organizations, winning the leadership of the leading student federation in July.

Throughout 1986 the Front was solidly opposed to the military amnesty program, joining the call for a plebiscite to decide the issue, although it initially rejected a membership bid by the like-minded MLN (see under MPP, below). Meanwhile the "Lista 99" group became increasingly identified as the People's Government Party (PGP), which, before the 1989 balloting, joined the PDC and Civic Union in a coalition styled the New Space (*Nuevo Espacio*) (below), with the MLN subsequently becoming a Front member.

By 1992 the Socialists had displaced the long-dominant Communists as the leading component of the Front, but the Socialists failed to control the group's plenum, with the highly popular mayor of Montevideo, Vázquez, threatening in late 1993 to withdraw from the 1994 presidential race if internal party elections were not held; however, in March 1994 Vázquez was proclaimed the group's standard-bearer for the presidential campaign.

On February 5, 1996, Seregni resigned as FA president because of irreconcilable differences over electoral reform (primarily in regard to Seregni's willingness to endorse second-round presidential balloting in return for abolition of the *ley de lemas*). In late 1996, following the interim leadership of a 12-member executive, Tabaré Vázquez was elected Seregni's successor; however, he resigned in September 1997 because of opposition to his support of the privatization of a Montevideo hotel complex. Seregni died on July 31, 2004.

At the time of the 2004 election, the EP-FA (sometimes referenced as EP-FA-NM [*Nueva Mayoría*] encompassed the groups listed below. The New Space Party (*Nuevo Espacio*) joined the EP-FA following the election and the 26th of March Movement (*Movimiento 26 de Marzo*—M26M) withdrew in mid-2008 (see below). Despite president Vázquez's endorsement of Danilo Astori in the 2009 primary elections the party's seat was won by José Mujica, who was supported by the party's former guerrilla and communist factions. (*See headnote.*)

Leaders: Dr. Tabaré Ramón VÁZQUEZ Rosas (President of the Republic), José ("Pepe") MUJICA (2009 presidential candidate), Daniel ASTORI (2009 vice-presidential candidate).

New Space (*Nuevo Espacio*—NE). The NE was founded following a struggle within the *Frente Amplio* nominees for the 1989 presidential balloting. The Marxist wing wished to renominate General Seregni as the coalition's sole candidate, while social democrats within the party supported PGP leader Hugo BATALLA, or, alternatively, both contenders under an electoral law provision permitting multiple nominees. As an agreement between the factions proved impossible, the PGP and PDC withdrew from the *Frente Amplio* in March 1989, subsequently joining the Civic Union (see below) in launching *Nuevo Espacio* as a tripartite formation with Batalla as its standard-bearer.

Prior to the 1994 balloting, the PGP's Batalla agreed to campaign as a vice-presidential contender on a ticket with Sanguinetti, the Colorados' presidential candidate. The PDC joined the Progressive Encounter, and the Civic Union withdrew to campaign separately, with a rump group of PGP members remaining within a reorganized *Nuevo Espacio.* The latter ran fourth in the presidential race. After the 2004 election the party decided to join the EP-FA and was accepted in November 2005.

Leaders: Rafael MICHELINI (Founder, President of the Party), Héctor PÉREZ Piera (Former President of the Party).

Uruguayan Socialist Party (*Partido Socialista del Uruguay*—PSU). Founded in 1910, the PSU has participated in the Broad Front since its inception in 1971. At present, its most conspicuous member is Tabaré Vázquez, who in 1989 became the first left-wing mayor of the capital and subsequently, as a "renewalist" leader within the FA, became the EP-FA standard-bearer in 1999 and the country's first Socialist president in 2005. The Vázquez cabinet included the first woman to serve as Interior Minister, Daisy Tourné.

Leaders: Dr. Tabaré Ramón VÁZQUEZ Rosas (President of the Republic), Reinaldo GARGANO (President of the Party), Eduardo (Lalo) FERNANDEZ (Secretary General).

Movement of Popular Participation (*Movimiento de Participación Popular*—MPP). Commonly referred to as the Tupamaros (after Túpac Amaru, an 18th-century Inca chief who was burned at the stake by the Spaniards), the MPP is an outgrowth of the National Liberation Movement (Movimiento de Liberación Nacional—MLN), a longtime clandestine guerrilla group that used violence and charges of political corruption in an attempt to radically alter Uruguayan society. Its last recorded clash with the police was in Montevideo in April 1974; six years later, in 1980 MLN founder Raúl SENDIC Antonaccio was sentenced to 45 years' imprisonment after having been held without trial since 1972. A number of others were sentenced for "subversion" in late 1983 at the height of the antidissident campaign. Many Tupamaros were among the hundreds who returned to Uruguay at the end of 1984, while the core of the group, including Sendic, was released when all political prisoners were freed in March 1985. At the MLN's first legal convention in December 1985, an estimated 1,500 delegates established a 33-member central committee and endorsed the abandonment of armed struggle in favor of nonviolent electoral politics. Its bid to join the Broad Front was rebuffed in 1986, reportedly due to PDC objection, but approved before the 1989 poll. The MLN was one of the leading opponents of the government's controversial military amnesty program, attracting an estimated 17,000 for its first political rally in December 1986. Sendic died in Paris in April 1989, reportedly from a neurological condition occasioned by his years of imprisonment, with the Movement campaigning as a Front member during the ensuing electoral campaign.

During 1991 relations with other Front members were reported to have cooled, with the MLN's Eleuterio FERNÁNDEZ calling for General Seregni's resignation and an internal election to determine "who are the real leaders of the Uruguayan Left."

MPP candidates attracted nearly one-third of the EP-FA votes in the 2004 balloting, and its leader, José Mujica, was displeased about some of the president-elect's initial cabinet choices (particularly that of Danilo ASTARI of the basically centrist Uruguay Assembly [Asamblea Uruguay—AU] as economy minister). However, he was seemingly mollified by his subsequent appointment to head the powerful agricultural ministry. In 2009 Mujica won the presidential primary for the FA.

Leaders: José ("Pepe") MUJICA (2009 presidential candidate), Nora CASTRO (Former President of the Chamber of Representatives).

Christian Democratic Party (*Partido Demócrata Cristiano*—PDC). Currently left-democratic in orientation, the PDC was founded in 1962 by dissidents from the predecessor of the current Civic Union (below). Banned at the time of the primary balloting in November 1982, the PDC operated negatively as a "fourth party" by calling on its followers for blank ballots, 84,000 of which were cast. The ban was lifted in August 1984. Before joining the *Nuevo Espacio* in 1989 the PDC operated as the "moderate" tendency within the *Frente Amplio*. It participated in forming the Progressive Encounter before the 1994 poll. The party is a member of the Christian Democratic International. A party convention was held in October 2006, during which the PDC confirmed its complete support for the government of President Vázquez.

Leaders: Héctor LESCANO (President of the Party), Juan A. ROBALLO (Secretary General).

Workers' Party (*Partido de los Trabajadores*—PT). The PT is an extreme left-wing formation founded in 1980. It is affiliated with the Progressive Encounter-Broad Front (*Encuentro Progresista-Frente Amplio*—EP-FA). The PT received just 336 votes, or .03 percent of the vote, in the national primary election in June 2009.

Leaders: Juan Vital ANDRADE (1984 presidential candidate), Rafael FERNANDEZ (2004 presidential candidate).

Three additional EP-FA components secured cabinet posts in the Vásquez administration: the **Artiguist Source** (*Vertiente Artiguista*—VA), led by Mariano ARANA, the **Progressive Alliance** (*Alianza Progresista*—AP), led by Vice President Rodolfo NIN Novoa and Uruguayan Assembly (Asamblea Uruguay—AU), led by Danilo Astori. Also participating in the EP-FA, but without ministerial representation, were the **Blanco Popular and Progressive Movement** (*Movimiento Blanco Popular y Progresista*—MBPP); the **Communist Party** (*Partido Comunista*—PC), known when the formation was banned as the Democratic Advance Guard Party (*Partido de Democracia Avanzada*—PDA); the **Left Front of Liberation** (*Frente Izquierda de Liberación*—Fidel); the **Leftist Current** (*Corriente de Izquierda*—CI); the **Nationalist Action Movement** (*Movimiento de Acción Nacionalista*—MAN); the **Party for the Victory of the People** (*Partido por la Victoria del Pueblo*—PVP); and the **Pregon Group** (*Grupo Pregón*—GP); and the **26th of March Movement** (*Movimiento 26 de Marzo*—M26M), which announced its departure from the EP-FA in March 2008, citing ideological differences.

Other Parties:

Colorado Party (*Partido Colorado*—PC). Founded in 1836 and in power continuously from 1865 to 1958, the largely urban-based PC has emphasized liberal and progressive principles, social welfare, government participation in the economy, and inter-American cooperation.

For some years the party's leading faction, as heir to the policies of former president José Batlle y Ordóñez, was the *Unidad y Reforma,* led by a longtime opponent of the military establishment, Jorge Batlle Ibáñez. However, the group was formally headed by Dr. Julio María Sanguinetti because of the personal proscription of Batlle Ibáñez under the military regime. *Unidad y Reforma* obtained 45 percent of the vote in the November 1982 election and successfully advanced Sanguinetti as its presidential candidate in 1984. Other factions included the promilitary *Unión Colorado Batllista* (*pachequista*) group led by former president Jorge Pacheco Areco, who ran as a minority presidential candidate in 1984; the *Libertad y Cambio,* led by former vice president Enrique Tarigo; and the antimilitary *Batllismo Radical* and *Corriente Batllista Independiente.*

In 1986 the party strongly endorsed the military amnesty urged by President Sanguinetti, while continuing to promote coalition efforts with elements of the Blanco Party. Runner-up in the 1989 balloting, the PC was awarded four portfolios in the Lacalle administration of March 1990, an alliance that effectively ended in January 1993, although two Colorado ministers retained their portfolios until May 1994.

By 1992 *Unidad y Reforma* had split into two components, the *Batllismo Unido,* (subsequently *Batllismo Radical*), headed by Batlle Ibáñez, and the *Foro Batllista,* led by Sanguinetti. Also active were the *Unión Colorado Batllista* and *Cruzada 94,* led by Pablo MILLOR. Batlle Ibáñez captured 54 percent of the votes within the PC's presidential primary in April 1999, earning the nomination over Luis HIERRO López (45 percent), who had the support of President Sanguinetti. With the additional backing of the Blancos, Batlle won the November runoff against the *Frente Amplio*'s Tabaré Vásquez and took office as president in March 2000.

The party placed third in the 2004 presidential poll with only 10.3 percent of the vote, while losing two-thirds of its congressional representation. At the party's national convention in September 2009, Pedro Bordaberry, son of former president Bordaberry, was chosen as the Colorado presidential candidate for the October 2009 general elections. At the same meeting it was also decided that two former presidents, Julio María Sanguinetti and Jorge Batlle, would not participate in the National Executive Committee, breaking a forty-year tradition.

Leaders: Pedro Bordaberry (Secretary General; 2009 presidential candidate), Guillermo STIRLING (2004 presidential candidate), José Luis BATLLE (Former President of the Republic).

Blanco (Nacional) Party (*Partido Nacional*—PN). Traditionally representing conservative, rural, and clerical elements but now largely progressive in outlook, the *Partido Nacional* won the elections of 1958 and 1962, subsequently failing to win either the presidency or a legislative plurality until November 1989. Its longtime principal grouping, the centrist *Por la Patria,* was led, before his death in March 1988, by Wilson Ferreira Aldunate, who was in exile at the time of the 1982 balloting. His absence did not prevent the *ferreiristas* from obtaining 70 percent of the party vote in 1982; other antimilitary factions in 1982 included the *Consejo Nacional Herrerista (Herrismo),* heir to a grouping formed in 1954 by Luis Alberto de Herrera, and the conservative *Divisa Blanca,* led by Eduardo Pons Etcheverry.

Ferreira returned to Uruguay in June 1984 and was promptly arrested, along with his son, Juan Raúl, who had led an exile opposition group known as the Uruguayan Democratic Convergence. After officially rejecting the August "Institutional Act No. 19" and refusing to participate in the election campaign, the main faction, at Ferreira's urging, offered Alberto Zumarán as its presidential candidate. Zumarán won 32.9 percent of the vote, while the Blancos obtained 35 seats in the Chamber of Deputies and 11 Senate seats. Released from prison five days after the November poll, Ferreira was elected party president in February 1985. Although he initially criticized the reported "deal" between the military and the Colorados to thwart the initiation of human rights trials, he vowed to "let the president govern" and supported the military amnesty program in 1986. The issue split the party, however, as the left-leaning *Movimiento Nacional de Rocha* faction, led by Carlos Julio Pereyra, called for a referendum to defeat the measure. The smaller, right-leaning *Divisa Blanca* not only supported the amnesty but also reportedly urged coalition with the Colorados.

Both Pereyra and Zumarán presented themselves as Blanco candidates in the 1989 presidential poll, which was won by Luis Alberto de Herrera's grandson, Luis Alberto Lacalle, with Gonzalo Aguirre Ramírez of the *Renovación y Victoria* faction as his running mate. The coalition forged by Lacalle with the Colorados was effectively terminated as the result of a midterm cabinet reshuffle in January 1993, with the last two Colorado ministers resigning in May. At the 1994 poll, four Blancos presented themselves as presidential candidates: Aguirre Ramírez, party chair Carlos Julio Pereyra, former interior minister Juan Andrés Ramírez (favored by President Lacalle), and state power utility head Alberto Volonté.

Lacalle, the candidate of the party's right-wing, secured the Blanco nomination for the 1999 presidential election by winning 49 percent of the votes in the April primary, but he ran third in the first-round poll of October 31. To prevent a possible victory by the Left, the Blancos threw their support in the runoff of November 28 to the Colorado's Batlle Ibáñez, who then formed a coalition government in which the Colorados participated until withdrawing in November 2002.

In 2003 Cristina MAESO, leader of a *Basta y Vamos* ("Enough–Let's Go") faction, became the first woman to contend (albeit unsuccessfully) for a major party's presidential nomination.

The party ran second in the 2004 presidential race with a 34.1 percent vote share, while increasing its lower house representation from 22 to 34. The Blancos quickly presented themselves as a unified party after the June 2009 primary elections, placing great pressure on the FA to overcome internal differences or lose the election. The party continued to present itself as a unified party throughout the political campaigns, quickly criticizing the FA candidate for comments that upset Argentine leaders. (*See headnote.*)

Leaders: Dr. Luis Alberto LACALLE de HERRERA (President), Luis Alberto LACALLE Herrera (Former President of the Republic, Former Party Chair, President of *Consejo Nacional Herrerista,* and 1999 and 2009 presidential candidate), Gonzalo AGUIRRE Ramírez (Former Vice President of the Republic and leader of *Renovación y Victoria*), Jorge LARRAÑAGA (2004 presidential candidate), Alberto VOLONTE (1994 presidential candidate, *Consejo Nacional Herrerista*), Carlos Julio PEREYRA (leader of *Movimiento Nacional de Rocha,* 1994 presidential candidate and President of the Party), Juan Andrés RAMÍREZ (Former Interior Minister and 1994 presidential candidate), Carlos Alfredo CAT Vidal, Francisco UBILLES (*Consejo Nacional Herrerista*), Eduardo Pons ETCHEVERRY (*Divisa Blanca*), Alberto Sáenz de ZUMARÁN (Secretary General and leader of *Por la Patria*).

Anti-imperialist Unitary Commissions (*Comisiones Unitarias Antiimperialistas—COMUNA*). COMUNA was formed is 2008 through the unification of the Oriental Revolutionary Movement (*Movimiento Revolucionario Oriental*—MRO) and various defectors from the FA coalition. The MRO is a pro-Cuban former guerrilla group that participated in the FA's launching in 1971. It made headlines (and embarrassed other Front groups) in late 1991 by characterizing a follower who had been arrested for robbery as a "social fighter." It was expelled from the FA in 1993 after some of its leaders had urged a return to "armed revolutionary struggle for Latin America." The party received official recognition by the Electoral Council to participate in the June 2009 primary elections posing Mario Rossi Garretano as its sole candidate.

Leader: Mario ROSSI Garretano (Founder, President of the Party).

Civic Union (*Unión Cívica*—UC). The original *Unión Cívica* was a conservative Catholic action party from which the left-of-center Christian Democrats withdrew in 1962. The present party is composed of right-wing Christian Democrats who withdrew from the PDC in 1971. A distinctly minor grouping, the party obtained only 14,244 votes out of nearly 1.1 million cast in 1982 and won only two lower house seats in 1984, with 5.8 percent of the presidential vote going to its candidate, Dr. Juan Vicente CHIARINO.

Leader: Aldo Lamorte (2004 presidential candidate).

LEGISLATURE

The bicameral Congress (*Congreso*), dissolved in June 1973 and replaced under the military regime with an appointive Council of State, reconvened for the first time in 12 years on February 15, 1985, following the election of November 25, 1984. The two houses, now styled collectively as the **General Assembly** (*Asamblea General*), are elected simultaneously on a proportional basis, both for five-year terms.

Chamber of Senators (*Cámara de Senadores* o *Senado*). The upper house consists of 30 elected members and one ex-officio member (the vice president). In the October 31, 2004, election, the seat distribution was as follows: the Progressive Encounter–Broad Front, 16; National (Blanco) Party, 11; and Colorado Party, 3.

President: Rodolfo NIN Novoa.

Chamber of Representatives (*Cámara de Representantes*). The lower house comprises 99 members. Following the election of October 31, 2004, the seat distribution was as follows: the Progressive Encounter–Broad Front, 52; the National (Blanco) Party, 36; the Colorado Party, 10; and independent, 1.

President: Alberto PERDOMO Gamarra.

CABINET

[as of September 15, 2009]

President	Tabaré Vázquez Rosas (EP-FA)
Vice President	Rodolfo Nin Novoa (EP-FA)
Ministers	
Agriculture, Livestock, and Fisheries	Ernesto Agazzi Sarasola (EP-FA)
Economy and Finance	Álvaro García (PSU)
Education and Culture	Maria Simon (EP-FA) [f]
Defense	Gonzalo Fernandez (EP-FA)
Foreign Affairs	Pedro Vaz Ramela
Housing, Territorial Planning, and Environment	Carlos Colacce (EP-FA)
Industry, Energy, and Mining	Daniel Martínez (EP-FA)
Interior	Jorge Bruni (EP-FA)
Labor and Social Welfare	Eduardo Bonomi (MPP)
National Defense	Jose Bayardi (EP-FA)
Public Health	María Julia Muñoz (VA) [f]
Social Development	Marina Arismendi Dubinsky (EP-FA) [f]
Tourism and Sport	Héctor Lescano (AP)
Transport and Public Works	Víctor Rossi (AP)

[f] = female

COMMUNICATIONS

The press is privately owned and edited; broadcasting is conducted under both private and governmental auspices. Though Uruguay's long tradition of press freedom was severely curtailed during the military interregnum of 1973–1984, the country is now considered to have a free press, with attacks on journalists reported to be "rare," according to the watchdog Reporters Without Borders. Uruguay also has initiated a pioneering law on community media to encourage and support small radio stations. By granting permission to the Venezuelan government for the use of its internationally recognized frequencies and space for orbiting a satellite, Uruguay gained a 10 percent of a new satellite's transmission capacity, which will allow the government to upgrade expand internet and television communications throughout the country. (See Foreign Affairs, above.)

Press. The following dailies, all published in Montevideo, survived intermittent suspension during this period: *El Diario* (170,000), Colorado independent; *El País* (110,000 daily, 120,000 Sunday), Blanco conservative; *La Mañana* (50,000), Colorado; *El Diario Español* (20,000); *Diario Oficial,* official bulletin.

In late 1984 *El Nuevo Tiempo,* representing the Blanco *corriente popular* tendency, and the pro-Communist *Útima Hora* commenced daily publication, as did a number of weeklies, including the following: *Jaque,* independent Colorado-*batllista; Opinar,* Colorado-*Libertad y Cambio; El Correo de los Viernes* and *La Semana Uruguaya,* Colorado-*batllista; La Democracia,* Blanco-*Por la Patria; Sin Censura,* Blanco-*ferreirista; Aquí,* Christian Democratic. In 1990, on the other hand, competition from nonprint media plus increased newsprint costs forced *La Democracia* and several other weeklies to join the influential daily, *El Día,* in suspending publication, while *Última Hora* was forced to cut back to weekly issuance in early 1991.

News agencies. There is no domestic facility; numerous foreign bureaus, including AP and Reuters, maintain offices in Montevideo.

Broadcasting and computing. The *Administración Nacional de Telecomunicaciones* (Antel) and the *División Control Servicios Radio-Eléctricos* supervise radio and television transmissions, which originate under both governmental and commercial sponsorship. As of 2008 there were 400.1 Internet users per 1,000 inhabitants.

INTERGOVERNMENTAL REPRESENTATION

Ambassador to the U.S.: Carlos Alberto GIANELLI.

U.S. Ambassador to Uruguay: (Vacant).

Permanent Representative to the UN: José Luis CANCELA.

IGO Memberships (Non-UN): ALADI, *CAN,* IADB, Interpol, IOM, Mercosur, OAS, OPANAL, PCA, SELA, WCO, WTO.

UZBEKISTAN

Republic of Uzbekistan
Uzbekistan Zhumhurijati

Note: In the two-stage Legislative Chamber election held December 27, 2009, and January 10, 2010, only progovernment parties were permitted to offer candidates. The Liberal Democratic Party of Uzbekistan won 53 of the 150 seats in the expanded lower house. The People's Democratic Party of Uzbekistan won 32; the *Milli Tiklanish* Democratic Party, 31; and the Justice Social Democratic Party of Uzbekistan, 19. Fifteen reserved seats were indirectly filled by the Ecological Movement of Uzbekistan.

Political Status: Eastern portion of Turkistan Soviet Socialist Republic detached on October 27, 1924, to form Uzbek Soviet Socialist Republic within the Russian Soviet Federative Socialist Republic (RSFSR); became constituent republic of the Union of Soviet Socialist Republics (USSR) on May 12, 1925; declared independence as Republic of Uzbekistan on August 31, 1991; present constitution adopted on December 8, 1992.

Area: 172,740 sq. mi. (447,400 sq. km.).

Population: 19,810,077 (1989C); 27,579,000 (2007E).

Major Urban Centers (2005E): TASHKENT (2,167,000), Namangan (375,000), Samarkand (360,000), Andijan (323,000).

Official Language: Uzbek. Russian remains the principal everyday language.

Monetary Unit: Sum (official rate December 1, 2009: 1,507.55 sums = $1US).

President: Islam A. KARIMOV; elected to the new office of president by the Supreme Soviet on March 24, 1990; reconfirmed for a five-year term by popular election on December 29, 1991; granted three-year term extension (to December 31, 1999) by referendum of March 26, 1995; reelected on January 9, 2000; current term extended by the Supreme Assembly to 2007, in accordance with a referendum passed on January 27, 2002; reelected on December 23, 2007.

Prime Minister: Shavkat MIRZIYOEV (MIRZIYAYEV); appointed by the president and confirmed by the Supreme Assembly on December 11, 2003, succeeding Otkir SULTONOV.

THE COUNTRY

The Central Asian state of Uzbekistan—the region's most populous—is bordered on the north and west by Kazakhstan, on the northeast by Kyrgyzstan, on the southeast by Tajikistan, and on the south, save for a short frontier with Afghanistan, by Turkmenistan. The national territory also includes several small exclaves in Kyrgyzstan, the largest being the town of Sokh. The principal ethnic groups are Turkic-speaking Uzbeks (approximately 76 percent); Russians (6 percent); Tajiks (5 percent), Kazakhs (4 percent), and Tatars (2 percent). The vast majority of citizens are Sunni Muslims, but there is also a small Shiite population; Eastern Orthodoxy predominates among the Russians. Women make up slightly less than half of the workforce and constitute one-sixth of the current lower house of the Supreme Assembly.

Endowed with a basically dry climate but traversed by two of the region's major rivers—the northern Syr Darya and the southern Amu Darya, both of which flowed into the now vanishing Aral Sea—Uzbekistan developed the most extensively irrigated agricultural sector of any of the former Soviet republics. Its crops include cotton and rice (once contributing two-thirds and one-half, respectively, to total USSR output), wheat, tobacco, sugarcane, and a wide variety of vegetables and fruits. Although cotton output has dropped since 1990, the agricultural sector still contributes about 28 percent of GDP (down from 37 percent in 1991) and employs about 30 percent of workers.

Legislation passed in 1998 prohibits private ownership of land, but the breakup of collective farms and crop diversification have helped to overcome Uzbekistan's Soviet-era reputation as little more than a cotton plantation writ large—a situation that caused irreparable damage to the land and a reduction of almost a foot a year in the water level of the increasingly polluted Aral Sea. A $65 million Aral Sea restoration project has focused on the northern part of the sea, in Kazakhstan. In August 2008, the World Bank, which provided the loan, called it a partial success, with a dyke causing water levels in that area to rise some 30 percent. However, studies have shown that parts of the southern sea cannot be saved.

At present, cotton fiber still ranks among the country's leading exports, and Uzbekistan remains one of the world's top cotton exporters in spite of boycotts, including one declared by Wal-Mart in September 2008, in response to reports of widespread forced child labor. Uzbekistan produces more than a million tons of cotton fiber each year, much of which is supplied to Russia. Industry contributed 31 percent of GDP in 2009 up from 24 percent in 2007 but down from 33 percent in 1991). Uzbekistan ranks as one of the world's leading producers of gold, the leading export; other extractable resources include oil, coal, uranium, copper, molybdenum, tungsten, zinc, and natural gas. Construction of the Uzbekistan portion of the China-Central Asia natural gas pipeline began in June 2008.

A growing source of income has been remittances and other transfers (8–12 percent of GDP in 2005–2007) into Uzbekistan from some of the 5.5 million Uzbek citizens working abroad, though remittances are expected to decline in 2009 due to the worldwide economic downturn.

The end of the Soviet system led to a 15 percent contraction in Uzbekistan's GDP during 1992–1994, combined with inflation averaging over 700 percent a year. Since then, market reform has proceeded slowly. In December 1996 the International Monetary Fund (IMF) suspended assistance after the government, reacting to poor harvests and dropping world prices for both cotton and gold, imposed strict trade and foreign-exchange controls. Nevertheless, by 1997 the GDP was at more than 90 percent of its pre-independence level, a substantially better performance than nearly all other former Soviet republics. Inflation, having peaked at over 1,100 percent in 1994, was measured at 14 percent in 2008.

Government figures, which are historically unreliable and difficult to verify, put GDP growth at slightly more than 4 percent annually in 1999–2003. It then accelerated to 9 percent in 2008, driven by trade, transport, services, communications, and industry, before dropping significantly to a forecasted 2.5 percent in 2009 due to recession in export markets and a sharp decline in remittances as expatriate workers faced more challenging labor markets. Overall exports are expected to decline in 2009, while government controls prevented expansion of imports. The government carried out a financial stimulus in late 2008 to help the economy weather the global economic downturn. The stimulus consisted of a government guarantee of bank deposits, relaxed tax penalties, and increased available credit to exporters.

GOVERNMENT AND POLITICS

Political background. Astride the ancient caravan routes to the Orient, Uzbekistan is one of the world's oldest civilized regions. In the 14th century what is now its second city, Samarkand, served as the hub of Tamerlane's vast empire. In the 19th century, after a lengthy period of decay, much of its territory was conquered by Russia. In 1920 it became part of the Turkistan Soviet Socialist Republic within the Russian Soviet Federative Socialist Republic. Separated from Turkmenia in 1924, Uzbekistan entered the USSR as a constituent republic in 1925. In 1929 its eastern Tajik region was detached and also accorded the status of a Soviet republic.

On March 24, 1990, at the opening of a recently elected Uzbek Supreme Soviet, Islam A. KARIMOV was elected by secret ballot to the new post of Supreme Soviet president. Concurrently, Shakhrulla MIRSAIDOV was reelected chair of the Council of Ministers. The following November, however, a government reorganization resulted in creation of a cabinet to replace the Council of Ministers, and Mirsaidov was named vice president. In April 1991 Uzbekistan endorsed USSR president Mikhail Gorbachev's abortive union treaty proposal. On August 23, in the wake of a failed Moscow coup against Gorbachev, President Karimov opposed dissolution of the Communist Party of the Soviet Union but nonetheless resigned from its Politburo. The property of the Uzbek Communist Party (UCP) was nationalized the following day. On August 28 Uzbekistan assumed control of all

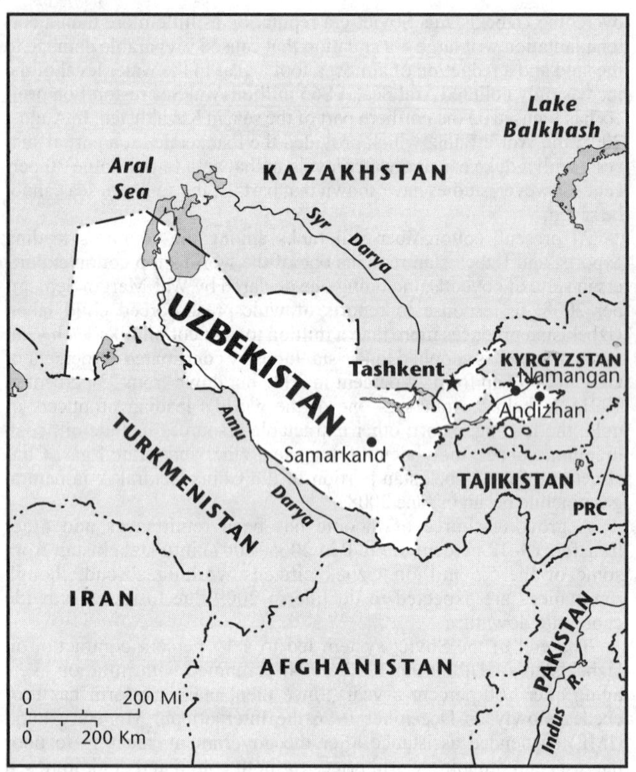

union enterprises within its territory and declared its intention to conduct its own foreign policy. Three days later the Supreme Soviet issued a declaration of independence and announced a change of name to Republic of Uzbekistan, while in November the UCP was replaced by the People's Democratic Party of Uzbekistan (PDP). On December 29 independence was endorsed, by a 98.2 percent vote, in a popular referendum.

In a parallel poll, Karimov, as the PDP candidate, won popular confirmation as president with an 86 percent share of the vote, as contrasted with the 12 percent garnered by Muhammad SALIH of the opposition Freedom (*Erk*) grouping. Following the poll, Abdulhashim MUTALOV of the PDP was named independent Uzbekistan's first prime minister. A month later, the vice presidency was abolished.

Although the 1992 constitution enshrined a commitment to multiparty democracy, Uzbekistan remained effectively a one-party state under the PDP. Genuine opposition parties, such as the nationalist Unity (*Birlik*) movement and the more moderate *Erk*, experienced systematic harassment leading to outright proscription, while the authorities encouraged the formation of new parties broadly supportive of the government.

Elections to a new 250-member legislature, held in three rounds in December 1994 and January 1995, were contested by two parties, the PDP and the government-aligned Progress of the Fatherland, with the PDP winning a large majority of the seats claimed by party nominees. In a March referendum President Karimov further consolidated power by securing 99.6 percent endorsement for a three-year extension of his existing five-year term, due to expire at the end of 1996. The referendum results were dismissed by opposition leaders as fantasy reminiscent of the Soviet era. In December, with the economy facing continuing difficulties, the Supreme Assembly confirmed the appointment of Otkir SULTONOV as prime minister in succession to the demoted Mutalov, who three months later was dismissed from the cabinet altogether.

In June 1996, on the eve of a visit by Karimov to the United States, the government granted amnesty to a few political prisoners, but critics, including former vice president Mirsaidov, continued to accuse the government of authoritarianism and one-party rule. Later in the year the legislature approved a new law that banned ethnic- and religious-based political parties. In November–December 1997 an outbreak of violence in Namangan precipitated a government crackdown against alleged Islamic activists, and between May 1998 and January 1999 several dozen were convicted of terrorism and anticonstitutional acts.

A series of at least six bomb blasts shook Tashkent on February 16, 1999, killing 15 and injuring more than 120. Hundreds of Islamic activists and government critics were arrested in succeeding weeks. Uzbekistan drew support from Russia, Ukraine, Kazakhstan, Kyrgyzstan, and other regional states in its efforts to track down Uzbek dissidents. Between June and August more than two dozen individuals were sentenced to death or lengthy prison terms on related charges that included attempted assassination of the president. Most of those arrested in the wake of the bombings were subsequently released, after months in detention.

For the Supreme Assembly elections of December 1999 nominations were permitted by local authorities, citizens' initiative groups, and five progovernment parties; *Birlik* and *Erk* were denied registration. Although the PDP again won more seats than any of its competitor parties, its predominance was challenged by the National Democratic Party "Self-Sacrificers" (*Fidokorlar*), formation of which had been announced, with President Karimov's imprimatur, in December 1998. In January 2000 Karimov, officially nominated by *Fidokorlar* but also backed by the rest of the political establishment, easily won reelection as president, capturing 92 percent of the vote against the PDP's token candidate, Abdulkhafiz JALOLOV, who stated on election day that he, too, had cast his ballot for the incumbent.

In a January 27, 2002, referendum a reported 92 percent of those voting approved extending the presidential term to seven years, while 94 percent endorsed introducing a bicameral legislature, as had been proposed by President Karimov in May 2000. The Supreme Assembly subsequently passed implementing legislation, effective from the legislative election scheduled for December 2004. On December 11, 2003, the Supreme Assembly confirmed President Karimov's selection of Shavkat MIRZIYOEV, governor of Samarkand and an agricultural specialist, as successor to Prime Minister Sultonov, who was retained as a deputy prime minister.

On March 28–April 1, 2004, a series of explosions in Bukhara and Tashkent claimed nearly 50 lives, the majority of them suspected terrorists. On July 30, three coordinated suicide bombings occurred outside the U.S. and Israeli embassies and at the prosecutor general's office. A then unknown group called the Jihad Islamic Group (JIG), a splinter group of the Islamic Movement of Uzbekistan (IMU), claimed responsibility for these attacks. Dozens of individuals were ultimately tried, convicted, and sentenced to between 3 and 18 years in prison for the spring incidents.

In the first election for the new 120-seat Legislative Chamber, held on December 26, 2004, with runoff balloting on January 9, 2005, the recently organized Liberal Democratic Party of Uzbekistan (LDP) won a plurality of seats, ahead of the PDP and *Fidokorlar.* Elected members of the new Senate were chosen indirectly by regional bodies on January 17–20.

On May 13–14, 2005, the eastern city of Andijan erupted in mass protest against civil rights abuses and widespread poverty that ended with troops reportedly firing indiscriminately into crowds of mostly unarmed civilians numbering in the low thousands. The government, which put the death toll at 187, blamed terrorists and Islamic extremists associated with the Islamic Movement of Uzbekistan (IMU) and *Hizb-ut-Tahrir.* According to some reports, protesters had occupied a government building after freeing from prison a number of alleged extremists. Human rights groups put the death toll at 500–750 and charged that many had been massacred in the streets. Hundreds fled across the Kyrgyz border. In response to Tashkent's refusal to allow an independent inquiry, as called for by the UN and others, the European Union (EU) imposed sanctions that barred the import of arms or equipment that could be used in state repression and limited international travel for government officials. In October 2008, the EU announced it was reversing its visa ban but would leave the arms embargo in place.

Despite a two-term limit on the presidency, President Karimov deftly circumvented the constitutional prohibition to seek a third term in office. The president argued that the 2002 referendum, which extended the presidential term seven years instead of five reset the clock and that his years in office prior to his reelection in 2000 therefore did not count. President Karimov, having been endorsed by the LDP and facing only token challenges from three other candidates, easily won reelection on December 23, 2007. Two of the other three presidential candidates on the ballot represented government-supportive parties, while the third, Akmal SAIDOV, nominated by a citizens' initiative group, was a legal scholar, member of the Legislative Chamber, and former ambassador. The United States and the Organization for Security and Cooperation in Europe said the elections failed to meet international standards. The Russian-led Commonwealth of Independent States (CIS) called the vote legitimate.

In late 2008, President Karimov reshuffled the positions of several regional governors and replaced the defense minister in what analysts viewed as attempts to consolidate further his power.

Constitution and government. The 1992 constitution describes Uzbekistan as a democratic presidential republic in which "there may be no official state ideology or religion." Freedom of thought and conscience and respect for human rights are guaranteed, although a 1998 law set stringent requirements governing the reregistration and activities of religious groups, which are prohibited from engaging in sectarian social movements, missionary work, proselytizing, most forms of religious education, and publication of religious materials deemed extreme, chauvinistic, or separatist.

The popularly elected head of state, who may serve no more than two consecutive terms, wields broad authority that includes naming the prime minister and cabinet (subject to parliamentary confirmation), initiating legislation, and serving as commander in chief. The bicameral Supreme Assembly comprises a directly elected 120-member Legislative Chamber and a 100-member Senate. The Senate is largely chosen by and from among regional and local councils but also includes presidential appointees. It has authority to approve certain government officials (e.g., ambassadors and Supreme Court justices) as well as limited powers to delay or block bills passed by the Legislative Chamber. According to a new law passed in December 2008 (see Legislature, below), the Legislative Chamber will include 150 members following the December 2009 elections.

At its highest level the independent judiciary includes a Constitutional Court, a Supreme Court, and a High Economic Court. Administratively, Uzbekistan encompasses 12 regions (*wiloyatlar*), the autonomous republic of Karakalpakstan (Qoraqalpoghiston), and the capital city (Tashkent). Subdivisions include more than 160 districts and over 110 cities and towns. The president appoints regional governors (*khokims*) as well as lower court judges.

Foreign relations. On December 21, 1991, Uzbekistan became a sovereign member of the CIS. By early 1992 it had established diplomatic relations with a number of Western countries, including the United States. On March 2 it was admitted to the United Nations and in September became a member of the IMF and World Bank. It joined the Conference on (later Organization for) Security and Cooperation in Europe (CSCE/OSCE) in 1992 and subscribed to the NATO-sponsored Partnership for Peace program in July 1994. In June 1996 Tashkent signed a partnership and cooperation agreement with the EU.

The Uzbek government has historically had close relations with Russia. A March 1994 economic integration agreement led in July 1995 to the signing of 15 detailed accords covering economic and military cooperation. During a visit by President Karimov to Russia in May 1998, he and President Boris Yeltsin agreed to coordinate their efforts to control the spread of fundamentalism, with President Imomali Rakhmonov of Tajikistan concurring. In October Yeltsin paid a return visit to Uzbekistan, at which time the two chiefs of state promised mutual aid in the case of an attack on either country, presumably by Afghanistan's Taliban or its allies. In February 1999 Uzbekistan announced that it would not renew its participation in the CIS Collective Security Treaty, although the government denied reports that the decision reflected its objections to military assistance provided by Russia to other regional states, particularly Armenia and Tajikistan (Uzbekistan rejoined the body in 2006). In May 2000 President Karimov, speaking to the Supreme Assembly, stated that Uzbek troops would not be deployed in external conflicts and that while Russian military-technical assistance remained desirable, Russian forces would not be stationed in Uzbekistan. Uzbekistan's relations with Russia have cooled in 2009 due to Russia's declining economic power as a result of the international recession and its efforts to increase its military activity in the region.

Regionally, during a summit in Tehran, Iran, in February 1992, Uzbekistan, along with its sister republics of Azerbaijan, Kyrgyzstan, Tajikistan, and Turkmenistan, gained admission to a long-dormant Economic Cooperation Organization (ECO), which had been founded by Iran, Turkey, and Pakistan in 1963. Two years later, in January 1994, Uzbekistan joined with Kazakhstan and Kyrgyzstan to form the Central Asian Economic Union (CAEU), which was later extended to cover defense, foreign policy, and social affairs. In July 1998, with Tajikistan having joined as a candidate member in March, the CAEU adopted the name Central Asian Economic Community, which was then reconfigured in March 2002 as the Central Asian Cooperation Organization (CACO). Russia became the fifth member in October 2004. In January 2006 Uzbekistan was admitted to the Eurasian Economic Community (Eurasec) of Belarus, Kazakhstan, Kyrgyzstan, Russia, and Tajikistan, which at the same time decided to absorb the redundant CACO. Uzbekistan has also participated in various summits of Turkic-speaking states. In November 2008, the Uzbek government confirmed its intention to withdraw from Eurasec and to pursue closer relations with non-Eurasian countries.

In June 2001 Uzbekistan joined China, Kazakhstan, Kyrgyzstan, Russia, and Tajikistan in establishing the Shanghai Cooperation Organization (SCO), which had begun as the so-called Shanghai Five in the mid-1990s. The principal mandate of the SCO is to ensure regional stability, with a particular focus on containing Islamic militancy. The SCO has also played an increasingly important role in determining oil and natural gas production development and diversification throughout the region.

Uzbekistan's overriding concern with Islamic militancy can be traced to the Afghan civil war of the 1990s, when the Uzbek government, despite its denials, was widely reported to be providing weapons and financial assistance to the anti-Taliban militia led in the north by Gen. Abdul Rashid Dostam, an ethnic Uzbek. In July 1999, as a member of the "Six-Plus-Two" contact group on Afghanistan, Uzbekistan hosted UN-sponsored peace talks between the Taliban and its principal opponents. The Tashkent meeting produced no significant progress in resolving the Afghan civil war, although the Six-Plus-Two partners (China, Iran, Pakistan, Russia, Tajikistan, Turkmenistan, and the United States as well as Uzbekistan) reaffirmed their ban on military assistance to all belligerents in the conflict. A month earlier, in an effort to reduce tensions with the Taliban regime, Uzbek Foreign Minister Abdulaziz KAMILOV conferred in Kandahar, Afghanistan, with the Taliban's leader, Mullah Mohammad Omar. Relations remained strained, however, and in late 2001 the Karimov government agreed to support the United States and its allies in the collateral effort to oust the Taliban.

In April 2000 the presidents of Kazakhstan, Kyrgyzstan, Tajikistan, and Uzbekistan signed a mutual security agreement providing for joint action against terrorism, political and religious extremism, organized crime, and other threats. The situation has been complicated, however, by strongly nationalistic, but antigovernment, sentiments among Kyrgyzstan's and Tajikistan's ethnic Uzbek minorities, most of whom are also Muslim. Disputes between Uzbekistan and the other three countries have often involved Islamic militancy and mutual borders.

In the mid-1990s Uzbek authorities displayed increasing apprehension that the Tajik civil war might spill across the border. Uzbekistan's relations with Tajikistan shifted significantly in January 1998, when Presidents Karimov and Rakhmonov signed several bilateral agreements covering, among other things, the resolution of debt issues and joint antidrug activities. The meeting also apparently indicated Karimov's grudging acceptance of proposed Islamist participation in the Tajik government. Later in the year, however, relations again grew more heated, with President Rakhmonov asserting in November that Uzbekistan had allowed leaders of a failed revolt in northern Tajikistan to enter the country and that it aimed "to take the whole of Tajikistan under its control." Shortly thereafter, captured rebels reportedly admitted that members of the Uzbek special forces had helped train them. In addition to denying the allegations, Karimov later accused Tajik officials of involvement in drug trafficking. In August 1999, in an effort to root out ethnic Uzbek militants, government aircraft bombed camps across the Tajik border. Some of the bombs hit Tajik villages, provoking an outcry from Dushanbe. In June 2000, however, Uzbekistan and Tajikistan signed a friendship treaty and agreed to demarcate their border, although the alleged persecution of ethnic Tajiks in Uzbekistan and claims by Tajik nationalists to Uzbek territory continue to cause strains.

In August 1999 fundamentalists associated with the IMU seized hostages in southern Kyrgyzstan and reaffirmed their intention to create an Islamic state in Central Asia. Uzbekistan joined Russia and Kazakhstan in providing military assistance to the Kyrgyz government, which negotiated the release of the final hostages in October. In 2000 Uzbekistan unilaterally began mining its borders with Tajikistan and Kyrgyzstan as part of its efforts to stop incursions by militants and to halt the flow of illegal drugs. The mining of the border remained a sore point into 2004, when Tashkent announced that it would remove the explosives. In 2005 Kyrgyzstan refused to extradite 29 of the more than 400 refugees who had fled across the border in May to escape the unrest in Andijan. In August 2006 Kyrgyzstan extradited five suspects despite protests that their extradition violated their rights as refugees. A terrorist bombing along the Uzbek-Kyrgyz border in May 2009 and Kyrgyzstan's agreement to host a second Russian military base potentially located near its border with Uzbekistan, have further complicated the relationship.

Relations with Kazakhstan tend to be less volatile, and in 2008 the two countries agreed to establish a free trade zone to ease movement of goods, individuals, and investment. However, tension remained as Uzbekistan periodically reduced water flow into Kazakhstan.

Water rights have long been a source of regional disputes. Tensions over water supplies erupted in a demonstration in July 1997 on the Kazakh-Uzbek border when Tashkent decided to reduce the amount of water flowing through its territory to southern Kazakhstan. Meanwhile, Kyrgyzstan debated how much to begin charging Uzbekistan and Kazakhstan for water from Kyrgyz reservoirs. In September the three nations agreed with Turkmenistan and Tajikistan to set up a fund to try to save the Aral Sea by alleviating the damage caused by overuse of the Amu-Darya and Syr-Darya rivers for irrigation. Later in March 2008, the Uzbek government held an international conference on the Aral Sea crisis, as the volume of the sea had dropped to a tenth of its 1977 levels.

Energy disputes also continued to complicate Uzbekistan's regional relationships, and the government routinely used its natural resources as a tool to influence with its weaker neighbors. Uzbekistan also significantly reduced its export of natural gas to Kyrgyzstan and Tajikistan in mid-June 2009 as the two countries fell into arrears on their energy payments.

The U.S.-led "war on terrorism" provided the Karimov regime with an opportunity to exploit its strategic location in Central Asia. Having been visited by U.S. secretary of Defense Donald Rumsfeld, in October 2001 Karimov granted U.S. forces access to the former Soviet air base in Khanabad—the largest such facility in Central Asia—as part of a "qualitatively new relationship" with the United States. Although the initial announcement indicated that the base would be used for launching search and rescue missions and for funneling humanitarian aid to the Afghani people, Khanabad was soon being used for offensive staging by U.S. and, later, NATO forces. In March 2002 Karimov met with President George W. Bush at the White House, and Karimov and U.S. Secretary of State Colin Powell signed five cooperation agreements, one of which stated that the United States would "regard with grave concern any external threat" to Uzbekistan. U.S operations in Afghanistan aimed at defeating the Taliban were also directed at IMU elements present in Afghanistan and elsewhere in the region. For its part, Uzbekistan promised to move forward with its political and economic transformation. In July 2005, however, hard U.S. criticism of the events in Andijan may have contributed to Tashkent's demand that U.S. forces vacate the Khanabad base in 180 days. The United States completed its withdrawal on November 21.

In March 2008, U.S. Ambassador Richard Norland said the United States had no plans to establish a base in Uzbekistan. Relations seemed to have warmed in late 2008 as a result of Russia's recession, which decreased its ability to provide foreign aid or exert political pressure on Uzbekistan. This was exemplified in February 2009 when Uzbek government agreed to allow U.S. supplies transit through Uzbek territory from Russia and Kazahkstan to NATO forces in Afghanistan. General David Petraeus, the head of the U.S. military's Central Command, later visited Uzbekistan in mid-August 2009 and signed a military cooperation agreement with the government.

Current issues. Opposition parties and human rights groups were mobilized by the 2005 Andijan massacre. In addition to decrying Karimov's authoritarianism, the opposition tried to call attention to the government's failure to relieve widespread poverty and its persistent human rights violations. The government was accused of arbitrary arrests, secret trials, torture, misuse of mental institutions to house political dissidents, and incarceration of religious practitioners—especially Muslims but also Protestant Christians—for not restricting their activities to officially sanctioned institutions.

The government banned Human Rights Watch (HRW) researchers from the country in July 2008, and the ban not been rescinded as of the time of writing. However, HRW continued to complain of ongoing abuses in the wake of the Andijan massacre and criticized the EU for conditionally suspending most of the sanctions it imposed in 2005 and for loosening them further in October 2008. Nevertheless, Uzbekistan was applauded by human rights groups in 2008 for its abolition of the death penalty, and the EU commended the Uzbek government for releasing four Uzbek human rights activists from prison in February of that year, while the EU continued to lobby for the release of remaining prisoners. On December 6, 2008, the government arrested ten more activists for staging a small protest in Tashkent.

The United States and EU countries have refrained from harsh criticism of Uzbekistan's human rights record because of the country's willingness to allow supplies to pass through its territory to NATO troops in Afghanistan. Germany in particular has pursued deeper engagement with Uzbekistan since the EU relaxed its sanctions, and European countries view imports of Uzbek natural gas as an alternative energy source that could reduce their dependence on Russia.

The country continues to struggle with violent Islamic extremism. On May 26, 2009, the Jihad Islamist Group (JIG), a group associated with the Islamic Movement of Uzbekistan (IMU), carried out two terrorist attacks in the country, one at a border post on the Kyrgyz border and another in Andijan. The Ferghana Valley, where Andijan is located, has experienced increasing unrest in 2009 and was believed to be the geographical epicenter of the IMU's resurgence within Uzbekistan.

The legislative elections scheduled for December 27, 2009, attracted scant media coverage or public interest, as Uzbekistan's increasingly strategic importance to the United States and EU will likely continue to preclude any external pressure for real political change. However, though government-supportive political parties were widely expected to dominate the balloting, President Karimov's hold on power was viewed by observers as less complete than at the time of the last poll. Many Uzbeks worry about Karimov's ailing health and the potential instability a succession process could inflict upon the country if he became unable to govern. Some analysts speculate that his daughter, Gulnora KARIMOVA, is being groomed to replace her father. The worsening economic outlook is creating additional uncertainty. Since the Uzbeks have few legal avenues to challenge government policy if its response to these challenges proves inadequate, the risk of renewed civil unrest is increasing.

POLITICAL PARTIES

Throughout most of the 1990s the political system was dominated by the People's Democratic Party of Uzbekistan (PDP), successor to the Soviet-era Uzbek Communist Party. Although authorities permitted a small number of other parties to form, the government routinely banned true opposition parties. All six of the progovernment parties and organizations discussed below were established with President Karimov's participation or approval.

In October 1995 a number of opposition parties, including *Birlik* and *Erk,* formed a Democratic Opposition Coordination Council (DOCC) chaired by former prime minister and vice president Shakhrulla Mirsaidov. In March 1998 Mirsaidov announced his intention to retire from politics and criticized the DOCC members for quarreling among themselves and failing to address the hardships and economic difficulties faced by most Uzbeks. In a surprising reversal, he also claimed that the government had "laid down the foundations" for establishing both a democratic state and a free-market economy. Although Mirsaidov indicated that the DOCC had in effect dissolved, a number of member organizations met a month later and called for greater harmony within the opposition, but also for improved cooperation with the government.

A new law on political parties, effective January 7, 1997, proscribed groups based on religious or ethnic lines as well as those considered subversive. Prospective parties were also required to submit evidence that they had no fewer than 5,000 members, spread over eight provinces. Although 1,010 candidates contested the December 1999 legislative election, the Ministry of Justice refused to register any opposition parties, and no declared opponents of the government were permitted to run.

In May 2004 the government reported that registration had been approved for 73 of the 76 nongovernmental organizations and political parties that had applied. Of the 73, however, only 5 were officially recognized as parties, all government supportive. The three organizations that had been denied registration were *Erk, Birlik,* and the new Free Peasants' Party (OD), making them ineligible to contest the December 2004 elections. The government alleged that all three had forged signatures on their membership lists. Since 2004, electoral regulations have required 50,000 membership signatures for a party to be registered, with no more than 8 percent of the total coming from any single administrative region.

In July 2005, meeting in Alexandria, Virginia, representatives of most major Uzbek opposition and human rights groups, including *Erk, Birlik,* and the OD, agreed to cooperative efforts toward promoting democratic change in Uzbekistan. The resultant **Congress of Democratic Uzbekistan,** chaired by Jahongir MAMATOV, an exile, was formally established the following September.

Progovernment Parties and Organizations:

Liberal Democratic Party of Uzbekistan (LDP). Aiming to attract businesses, entrepreneurs, and industrial workers, the LDP held its founding congress in November 2003, a month after receiving the imprimatur of President Karimov. The only new party to have been registered since the 1999 Supreme Assembly election, the LDP contested the December 2004–January 2005 balloting for the new lower house of the Supreme Assembly, finishing first, with 41 seats.

The party's original chair, Qobiljon TOSHMATOV, resigned in May 2004, ostensibly for health reasons, although some reports indicated that he had earned President Karimov's displeasure at a recent session of the Supreme Assembly. In February 2005 the LDP, *Fidokorlar,* and *Adolat* announced formation of a Democratic bloc in the legislature.

In November 2007 the LDP endorsed President Karimov for reelection in December.

Leaders: Islam KARIMOV (President of the Republic), Muhammadyusuf Mutalibjanovich TESHABOEW (Chair).

People's Democratic Party of Uzbekistan—PDP (*Khalk Demokratik Partiiasi*). The PDP was organized in November 1991 as successor to the former Uzbek Communist Party, whose activities had been suspended in August. Officially committed to promarket reform and multi-party democracy, the PDP has nevertheless backed the Karimov government's cautious line on both fronts. In June 1996 President Karimov resigned as party chair and PDP member. His successor, Abdulkhafiz Jalolov, contested the January 2000 presidential race, with Karimov's approval, but won only 4.2 percent of the vote and subsequently retired from politics. A month earlier the PDP had won 48 Supreme Assembly seats, down from the 69 it had claimed in the balloting of December 1994–January 1995.

In the December 2004–January 2005 election for the new lower house the PDP won 28 seats, with another 8 being captured by party members who had been nominated by independent citizens' groups. In December 2007 the party's presidential candidate, Asliddin Rustamov, finished second, with 3.27 percent of the vote.

Leaders: Latifjon GULOMOV (Central Committee Chair and First Secretary), Asliddin RUSTAMOV (2007 presidential candidate), Abdulkhafiz JALOLOV (2000 presidential candidate).

Milli Tiklanish Democratic Party (*Milli Tiklanish Demokratik Partiiasi*—MTDP). The MTDP was formed in June 2008 by the merger of the two parties below, the National Democratic Party "Self-Sacrificers" (*Fidokorlar*) and National Revival Party (*Milli Tiklanish Partiiasi*—MTP).

National Democratic Party "Self-Sacrificers" (*Fidokorlar*). Established at a congress on December 28, 1998, *Fidokorlar* (sometimes translated as "Patriots") was created in response to President Karimov's call a month earlier for a new party of uncorrupted, more youthful, future leaders. *Fidokorlar* won 34 seats in the December 1999 national election, and in January 2000 President Karimov was reelected under the party's banner.

On April 14, 2000, *Fidokorlar* and **Progress of the Fatherland** (*Vatan Tarrakiyeti*—VT) announced a merger, with the new group to retain *Fidokorlar* as its name. The VT, founded in 1992, was a promarket party broadly supportive of the Karimov government.

In the 2004–2005 national election the united *Fidokorlar* party won 18 seats, not counting 1 won by a party member nominated by an independent group of citizens. The party merged with the MTP (below) on June 20, 2008.

Leaders: Xurshi DOSTMUHAMMAD (Chair of Party, Deputy Speaker of the Legislative Chamber), Ahtam TURSUNOV (First Secretary).

National Revival Party (*Milli Tiklanish Partiiasi*—MTP). Based in the Uzbek artistic and intellectual community, the MTP held its founding congress in June 1995, declaring its intention to work for national progress and self-awareness. It won 10 Supreme Assembly seats in 1999 and 11 in 2004–2005.

The party chair, Xurshid Dostmuhammad, was nominated for the presidency in 2007, but he was kept off the ballot after failing to obtain the required number of supporting signatures (5 percent of the electorate).

Leader: Xurshid DOSTMUHAMMAD (Chair).

Justice Social Democratic Party of Uzbekistan (*Adolat*). *Adolat* was relaunched in February 1995 as a progovernment grouping, having in a previous incarnation been a grouping of Muslim dissidents that was banned shortly after its formation in 1992. Adopting a left-of-center economic and social program, the new party claimed the support of some 50 deputies in the new Supreme Assembly and subsequently obtained official registration. It won 11 Supreme Assembly seats in 1999 and 8 in the 2004–2005 election, not counting 2 seats claimed by party members nominated by independent citizens' groups.

In 2007, the party's leader at the time, Dilorom TASHMUKHAMEDOVA, became the first woman to stand for president in Uzbekistan. She finished third in the December 2007 presidential election, capturing 3.03 percent of the vote, and is the current speaker of the Legislative Chamber.

Leaders: Ismail SAIFNAZAROV (First Secretary), Dilorom TASHMUKHAMEDOVA (2007 presidential candidate).

Ecological Movement of Uzbekistan (EMU). Formed in August 2008, government sponsored the creation of the EMU, an organization focused on environmental and public health issues. Aslan MAVLYANOV, the director of the Institute of Hydrology and Geological Engineering under the State Committee on Geology leads the group, which is composed primarily of scientists and medical professionals. According to a law passed on December 5, 2008, the EMU will hold 15 seats in the Legislative Chamber following the December 2009 legislative elections.

Leader: Aslan MAVLYANOV.

Unregistered Groups:

Birlik Popular Movement Party. The *Birlik* Party, which held its founding congress in August 2003, traces its origin to the Popular Movement of Uzbekistan "Unity" (*Ozbekiston "Birlik" Xalq Harakati—Birlik*), a nationalist and secular formation launched in 1988 on a platform that urged secession from the Soviet Union. Presumed to be the strongest of the opposition groups (although weakened by the formation of *Erk,* below), it was not permitted to contest the presidential balloting of December 1991 and was banned by the Supreme Assembly for "antigovernment activities" the following year. Most of its principal leaders were subjected to beatings, imprisonment, and other forms of harassment by the Karimov regime.

Having failed to obtain reregistration as a party, *Birlik* did not contest the 1994–1995 election and held a congress in exile in Moscow in July 1995. Since again being denied party status in 1999, *Birlik* has continued as a nongovernmental social movement. Hoping to finally achieve recognition as a party, in 2003 *Birlik* members organized the *Birlik* Party, which was nevertheless equally unsuccessful in its effort to register. The organization has close ties to the *Ezgulik* human rights society headed by Vasila Inoyatova. However, while *Ezgulik* condemned the EU's decision in 2007 to ease sanctions against the Uzbek government, *Birlik* leadership supported the EU's move. *Birlik* leaders also asked the EU to demand their party be allowed to participate in the 2009 parliamentary elections.

Leaders: Abdurahim PULAT (Abdurakhim PULATOV) (Chair, in exile), Polat OKHUNOV (Deputy Chair), Vasila INOYATOVA (Secretary General).

Freedom Democratic Party (*Erk Demokratik Partiiasi*). *Erk* was organized in April 1990 by a group of *Birlik* dissidents who called for economic and political autonomy for Uzbekistan within a Soviet federation (i.e., in positive response to President Gorbachev's union proposal). Its chair, Muhammad Salih, a prominent poet, was a distant runner-up to the Islam Karimov, then representing the PDP, in the 1991 presidential poll and in July 1992 resigned from the legislature (and left the country) after being denied an opportunity to speak. At a joint meeting the same month, *Erk* and *Birlik* representatives committed themselves to common action against the Karimov regime.

In October 1993 *Erk* failed to meet a deadline for reregistration as a party because it had no address, its offices having been declared a fire risk. A brother of the *Erk* chair was reported in August 1995 to have been jailed for five years for activism in the Association of Young Democrats of Turkistan, an *Erk* affiliate.

It was reported in late 1997 that *Erk* had asked President Karimov to endorse the party's proposed reregistration and to permit the group's chair, Muhammad Salih, to return from exile. Karimov subsequently accused Salih of being behind the February 1999 bombings in Tashkent, despite an absence of convincing evidence. Salih was convicted of terrorism in November 2000 and sentenced, in absentia, to 15 years in prison.

Erk was permitted to hold its first party congress in ten years in October 2003, but it remained unregistered. An internal dispute saw a number of party members, led by Samad MUROV, argue for replacement of the party leadership—an effort that Secretary General Otanazar Oripov characterized in February 2004 as a government effort to undermine the party. In May 2006 a National Salvation Committee, newly established among exiles in Kyrgyzstan, proposed Salih as a presidential candidate for 2007. In late 2008, Salih announced his and other opposition leaders' intention to unite and carry out a bloodless coup against Karimov's regime at some point in the future.

Leaders: Muhammad SALIH (SOLIH, SOLIKH; a.k.a. Salay MADAMINOV) (Chair, in exile), Otanazar ORIPOV (Secretary General).

Free Peasants' Party (*Ozod Dehqonlar*—OD). At its founding congress in December 2003, the OD called for agricultural reform and limitations on presidential powers. The party failed to achieve legal status in 2004, and in September 2008 held a meeting in Tashkent to discuss economic issues. Among those invited were four human rights activists from the Jizakh region, who were detained at a Tashkent hotel by antiterrorism officials but released after a few hours. Other rights activists saw the arrests as an attempt to intimidate the organizers.

In April 2005 the OD announced formation of an opposition coalition called **Sunshine Uzbekistan** (*Serquyosh Ozbekistonim*). The Sunshine Coalition, as it is also known, is headed by Sanjar UMAROV, who in March 2006 was given a ten-year prison sentence for theft. After visiting him in July 2008, family members sent a letter to President Karimov pleading for his release, citing health concerns. Another of the group's leaders and sister to the general secretary, Nodira Hidoyatova, received a ten-year sentence but was released in May 2006

Leaders: Muhammadbobir MALIKOV (Chair), Olim KARIMOV (Honorary Chair), Nigora HIDOYATOVA (Nigara KHIDOYATOVA) (Secretary General), Sanjar UMAROV and Nodira HIDOYATOVA (Leaders of Sunshine Uzbekistan).

Party of Peasants and Entrepreneurs (PPE). Established in 2003, the PPE, which is also known as the Party of Agrarians and Entrepreneurs, joined several opposition forums in 2004, including an April round-table discussion organized by various parties and human rights organizations. The party leader, Marat Zohidov, also chairs the unregistered Committee for Individual Rights and serves as vice president of the Germany-based International Society for Human Rights.

Leader: Marat ZOHIDOV (ZAKHIDOV, ZAHIDOV) (Chair).

Solidarity (*Birdamlik*). *Birdamlik* is an opposition movement led from the United States and committed to nonviolent change. In March 2007 it attempted to stage small protests in Tashkent, but these were disrupted by the authorities. It later called for a peaceful demonstration on the anniversary of the 2005 Andijan protest. Its leader says the group has the support of *Birlik* and OD parties and hopes to unify all democratic Uzbek opposition parties.

Leader: Bahodyr CHORIEV.

Banned Groups:

Islamic Movement of Uzbekistan (IMU). The militant IMU, which has also been known since 2001 as the **Islamic Party of Turkestan,** advocates creation of an Islamic republic under religious law. Some of its members may have participated in the Justice (*Adolat*) Movement that was banned in 1992, but the IMU itself did not emerge until 1999. In May 2000 a U.S. State Department report labeled it as one of the world's most dangerous terrorist organizations and alleged that it had been behind the February 1999 Tashkent bombings and an August–October hostage situation in Kyrgyzstan. Later reports indicated that at least some members were moving from bases in Tajikistan to Afghanistan, where many of its members were apparently trained at al-Qaida camps.

In August 2000, two IMU incursions from across the Tajik border occurred. Operations against the 100 or so militants continued into September. Two months later, on November 17, the Supreme Court found IMU leaders Tohir Yoldoshev and Juma Namangoniy guilty, in absentia, of terrorism and imposed death sentences. In November 2001 Namangoniy was killed in Afghanistan, where IMU forces suffered heavy losses as allies of the Taliban. In May 2005 the Uzbek government assigned blame for the Andijan unrest to the IMU and *Hizb-ut-Tahrir* (below).

In January 2008, Yoldoshev, who was reportedly dead, appeared in a video, declaring jihad on the Pakistani government and its security forces. IMU adherents were implicated in killings in Waziristan, and in July, Pakistan premier Yousaf Raza Gillani complained that the IMU was behind a spike in violence in his nation's tribal areas.

Security forces in other countries clamped down on IMU and other fundamentalist elements. In January 2008, a prominent IMU member, Abdulkhai Yuldashev, was arrested in Kyrgyzstan. The Tajik Supreme Court in February sentenced an Uzbek national to 18 years in prison for membership in the IMU. In May, French, German, and Dutch police arrested ten people suspected of financing the IMU. In June, three IMU members were jailed in Tajikistan.

Leaders: Tohir YOLDOSHEV (Tahir YOLDASH), Juma NAMANGONIY.

Jihad Islamic Group (JIG, or *Jamoat* in Uzbek, a.k.a. Islamic Jihad Union). Believed to have been established in March 2002 by members of the IMU after the IMU was severely weakened by the US war in Afghanistan in the early 2000s, the JIG or *Jamoat* claimed responsibility for a series of terrorist acts in Uzbekistan in March–July 2004. The organization also took responsibility for a foiled terrorist plot against a U.S. military base in Germany in September 2007 and for two terrorist attacks on May 26, 2009, one taking place at a post along the Uzbek-Kyrgyz border, and another in Andijan.

Hizb ut-Tahrir. Originating in the 1950s in Syria, the *Hizb ut-Tahrir* (Liberation Party) is a pan-Islamic movement that has been banned in a number of countries throughout Northern Africa and the Middle East. Its Central Asian activists support establishment of an Islamic state in portions of Uzbekistan, southern Kyrgyzstan, and western Tajikistan. Some of those convicted for the February 1999 bombings in Tashkent claimed allegiance to the group, as did others rounded up by authorities following the incident.

President Karimov alleged that the organization was involved in the May 2005 Andijan incident. In March 2008, Russian officials said IMU and *Hizb ut-Tahir* members had made repeated attempts to move operations into Russia.

In June 2008, four female residents of southern Uzbekistan were given varying sentences for their involvement with the organization.

For more information on the **Islamic Renaissance Party** founded in 1990, please see the 2008 *Handbook*.

LEGISLATURE

The **Supreme Assembly** (*Oliy Majlis*) was initially established as a unicameral legislature of 250 directly elected members. Amendments to the election law passed after the 1994 balloting opened the nomination process to citizens' initiative groups in addition to political parties and local authorities. Constitutional revisions passed by referendum in February 2002 called for the establishment of a bicameral Supreme Assembly encompassing a Senate and a Legislative Chamber, with the members of both serving five-year terms. A law passed by the Supreme Assembly in December 2008 (see below) disqualifies independent candidates from contesting seats in the Legislative Chamber.

Senate. The Senate comprises 100 members: 16 presidential appointees in addition to 84 representatives (6 from each of the country's 12 regions, 6 from the capital, and 6 from the Karakalpakstan autonomous republic), chosen by and from among regional "representative bodies of state power." Elected members were most recently chosen on a nonpartisan basis on January 17–20, 2005. Named on January 24, the initial presidential appointees included several cabinet members, judges, academics, heads of civil organizations, and industrialists.

Speaker: Ilgizor SOBIROV (a.k.a. Ilgizar SABIROV).

Legislative Chamber. The lower chamber, directly elected from among nominees put forward by parties and citizens' groups, comprises 120 members. The first election to the Legislative Chamber, held December 26, 2004, with runoff balloting in 58 constituencies taking place on January 9, 2005, produced the following results: Liberal Democratic Party of Uzbekistan, 41 seats; People's Democratic Party of Uzbekistan (PDP), 28; National Democratic Party "Self-Sacrificers" (*Fidokorlar*), 18; National Revival Party, 11; Justice Social Democratic

Party of Uzbekistan (*Adolat*), 8; nominees of citizens' initiative groups, 14. Of the last 14, 8 nominees were PDP members, 2 were members of *Adolat,* and 1 belonged to *Fidokorlar.* On December 5, 2008, the Supreme Assembly at the request of the president passed a law increasing the number of deputies from 120 to 150, effective following the legislative elections scheduled for December 2009–January 2010. (*See headnote.*) Fifteen of the deputies will come from the Ecological Movement of Uzbekistan, and the other 135 deputies will be directly elected in a constituency-based system.

Speaker: Dilorom TASHMUKHAMEDOVA.

CABINET

[as of August 1, 2009]

Prime Minister	Shavkat Mirziyoev
Deputy Prime Ministers	Abdulla Aripov
	Nodirkhon Khanov
	Ergash Shaismatov
	Rustam Sadikovich Azimov
	Farida Akbarova [f]
Ministers	
Agriculture and Water Resources	Sayfiddin Ismoilov
Culture and Sports	Rustam Javdatovich Kurbonov
Defense	Kobil Berdiyev
Economy	Sunatilla Bekenov
Emergency Situations	Bakhtiyor Subanov
Finance	Rustam Sadikovich Azimov
Foreign Economic Relations, Investments, and Trade	Elyor Ganiev
Foreign Affairs	Vladimir Norov
Higher and Secondary Specialized Education	Azimzhon Parpiev
Interior	Bahodir Matlubov
Justice	Ravshan Abdulatifovich Muhiddinov
Labor and Social Security	Aktam Akhmatovich Khaitov
Public Education	Gayrat Baxromovich Shoumarov
Public Health	Adham Ikromov
Chairs of State Committees	
Architecture and Construction	Azamat Tokhtaev
Customs	Sodirkhon Nosirov
Demonopolization, Competition, and Business Support	Boymurot Suyunovich Ulashev
Geology and Mineral Resources	Nariman Ganievic Mavlyanov
Land Resources, Geodesy, Cartography, and Real Estate	Ergashali Kurbanov
Nature Protection	Bari Borisovich Alikhanov
State Property Management	Dilshod Olimjonovich Musayev
Statistics	Gafurjon Kudratov
Taxes	Botir Parpiyev

[f] = female

COMMUNICATIONS

In January 1995, a registration process completed the previous month effectively denied authorization to all independent publications, and only the organs of the state "power structures" were able to continue publishing. In May 2002 Uzbekistan ostensibly ended formal press censorship, but the government continues to dominate the media and exert overwhelming pressure on nongovernmental outlets. The international monitoring group Reporters Without Borders has repeatedly reported that journalists' rights have been seriously threatened in Uzbekistan. Both print and broadcast journalists were prohibited from reporting on the Andijan unrest in 2005.

In October 2007, Alisher Saipov, correspondent for Voice of America and editor of an Uzbek newspaper in Kyrgyzstan, was shot dead. He had written extensively about torture in Uzbek prisons. After an investigation, the International Crisis Group said in 2008 that there were "strong indications" that Uzbek security forces murdered Saipov.

In October 2008, the government held a press freedom conference. However, while some journalists were allowed to speak during the event, none were permitted to cover it. On Journalists' Day in June 2009, President Karimov issued a statement discouraging journalists from practicing self-censorship and encouraging coverage of official corruption, in keeping with the Uzbek government's pattern of promoting free expression and human rights in its rhetoric while repressing the opposition in practice.

Press. The following are published at least five times a week in Tashkent in Uzbek, unless otherwise noted: *Khalk Suzi* (People's World, 55,000), government organ, in Uzbek and Russian; *Narodnoye Slovo* (People's Word, 50,000), government organ in Russian and Uzbek; *Fidokor* (30,000), three times a week, *Fidokorlar* party organ; *Marifat* (Enlightenment, 20,000), twice weekly; *Pravda Vostoka* (Eastern Truth, 10,000), government organ in Russian.

News agencies. The domestic facility is the Uzbek National News Agency (UzA), headquartered in Tashkent. Leading American, British, French, and Russian bureaus also have offices in the capital.

Broadcasting and computing. The State Television and Radio Broadcasting Company runs Radio Tashkent International, which broadcasts in Uzbek and a dozen other languages. Uzbek Television offers local programming and relayed broadcasts from Russia and several other countries, while a joint venture with a U.S. firm provides satellite television service and relays from the United States, the United Kingdom, India, and Russia. There are a number of other private broadcasting companies. The government routinely blocks independent Web sites carrying political information about Uzbekistan.

As of 2008 there were 90.8 Internet users per 1,000 inhabitants.

INTERGOVERNMENTAL REPRESENTATION

Ambassador to the U.S.: Abdulaziz KAMILOV.

U.S. Ambassador to Uzbekistan: Richard B. NORLAND.

Permanent Representative to the UN: Murad ASKAROV.

IGO Memberships (Non-UN): ADB, CIS, EBRD, ECO, IDB, Interpol, NAM, OIC, OSCE, SCO, WCO.

VANUATU

Republic of Vanuatu
République de Vanuatu (French)
Ripablik blong Vanuatu (Bislama)

Note: Prime Minister Edward Natapei announced a major cabinet overhaul on November 17, 2009. Most notably, he dropped the ministers from the National Unity Party and the Vanuatu Republican Party, replacing them with members of the opposition, including Sato Kilman, theretofore the leader of the opposition in Parliament, who was named deputy prime minister. The new government reportedly enjoyed the support of 33 legislators, enabling Natapei to easily survive several subsequent non-confidence motions.

Political Status: Formerly the New Hebrides; became the Anglo-French Condominium of the New Hebrides in 1906; present name adopted upon becoming an independent member of the Commonwealth on July 30, 1980.

Area: 4,647 sq. mi. (12,035 sq. km.).

Population: 186,678 (1999C); 233,000 (2008E).

Major Urban Center (2005E): VILA (Port Vila, 36,600).

Official Languages: English, French, Bislama. The last, a pidgin dialect, is recognized constitutionally as the "national language," and efforts are currently under way to accord it equal status with English and French as a medium of instruction.

Monetary Unit: Vatu (official rate December 1, 2009: 98.65 vatu = $1US).

President: Iolu Johnson ABIL (Party of Our Land); elected by the electoral college on September 2, 2009, and inaugurated the same day for a five-year term in succession to Kalkot MATASKELEKELE Mauliliu, whose term of office had expired on August 16. (Maxime CARLOT Korman, the speaker of Parliament, served as acting president from August 16, 2009, to September 2.)

Prime Minister: Edward NATAPEI (Party of Our Land) elected by Parliament on September 22, 2008, to succeed Ham LINI (National United Party), following general election of September 2.

THE COUNTRY

An 800-mile-long archipelago of some 80 islands, Vanuatu is situated in the western Pacific southeast of the Solomon Islands and northeast of New Caledonia. The larger islands of the group are Espiritu Santo, Malekula, Tanna, Ambrym, Pentecost, Erromanga, Aoba, Epi, and Efaté, on which the capital, Vila, is located. Over 90 percent of the inhabitants are indigenous Melanesians; the remainder encompasses small groups of French, English, Vietnamese, Chinese, and other Pacific islanders. Approximately 85 percent are Christian, Presbyterians constituting the largest single denomination, followed by Roman Catholics and Anglicans. Approximately three-quarters of adult women have been described as "economically active," most of them in agricultural pursuits; female participation in government, on either the village or national level, is minimal.

The bulk of the population is engaged in some form of agriculture. Coconuts, taro, and yams are grown for subsistence purposes, with copra, kava, timber, cocoa, and beef constituting the principal exports. In 1981 a national airline was established, while maritime legislation was enacted to promote Vanuatu as "a flag of convenience." The country also emerged as an offshore financial center, with well over 1,000 companies (including more than 60 banks as of 2000) incorporated in Port Vila yielding close to $1.5 million annually in revenue.

Although Vanuatu was formally characterized by the United Nations as a "least developed country," tourism, forestry projects, and the discovery of promising mineral deposits, including gold and manganese, offer potential for long-term economic growth. From 1990 to 1997, however, the annual real change in GNP averaged –3.5 percent. Growth of 6 percent in 1998 was followed by another downturn (of 2.5 percent) in 1999, in part because of adverse weather. Renewed expansion of 2.8 percent occurred in 2000, with further improvement thereafter to an annual average of 6.4 percent for 2004–2008. The economic progress led the UN to announce in July 2006 that Vanuatu would likely qualify for "developing country" status by 2013, a change rejected by the Natapei administration in mid-2009, since it would entail a reduction in foreign aid.

In June 2000 Vanuatu was threatened with economic sanctions by the Organization for Economic Cooperation and Development (OECD) for "harmful" policies related to its offshore financial services. Although the government subsequently pledged its cooperation in fighting money laundering and other financial crimes, in 2001 it insisted that it had the right to set its own tax policies and would not share information about nonnational accounts with foreign tax authorities. Further action regarding Vanuatu's international tax status served as the nucleus of a dispute with Australian authorities in early 2008 (see Current issues, below).

GOVERNMENT AND POLITICS

Political background. Settled during the first half of the 19th century by a variety of British and French nationals, including a sizable contingent of missionaries, the New Hebrides subsequently became the scene of extensive labor recruitment by plantation owners in Fiji and Queensland. Following a series of unsuccessful efforts to stem the frequently inhumane practice of "blackbirding," Britain and France established a Joint Naval Commission in 1886 to safeguard order in the archipelago. Two decades later, faced with competition by German interests, the two governments agreed to form a cumbersome but reasonably serviceable condominium structure that entailed dual instruments of administration at all levels, including two police forces, two resident commissioners, and two local commissioners in each of the territory's four districts.

A 42-member Representative Assembly (replacing an Advisory Council established in 1957) convened for the first time in November 1976 but immediately became embroiled in controversy as to whether 13 members not elected by universal suffrage (4 representing tribal chiefs and 9 representing economic interests) should be required to declare party allegiance. Condemning what they termed the "present unworkable system of government," the 21 representatives of the Party of Our Land (*Vanua'aku Pati*—VP) boycotted the second assembly session in February 1977, prompting the colonial administrators to call a new election, the results of which were voided because of another VP boycott.

In the assembly election of November 14, 1979, the VP won 26 of 39 seats, and on November 29 party leader Fr. Walter Hadye LINI was designated as chief minister. Earlier, the colonial powers had agreed to independence in 1980, a constitution having been drafted in September and approved in a series of notes between London and Paris in October.

The attainment of independence on July 30, 1980, was clouded by secessionist movements on a number of islands, most importantly Espiritu Santo, whose principal town had been seized, with indirect support from the local French community, by the cultist *Na-Griamel* movement under the leadership of Jimmy Tupou Patuntun STEVENS. The Vanuatu flag was, however, raised on Santo on July 30 by an emissary of the Lini government in the presence of a contingent of British and French troops that was withdrawn on August 18 upon the arrival of a Papua New Guinean force backed by central government police. Most of the insurgents subsequently surrendered, and Stevens was sentenced on November 21 to a prison term of 14.5 years (ultimately serving 11, before being released because of poor health). The aftermath of the revolt continued well into 1981, with over 700 eventually convicted of related crimes. Stevens's trial had revealed that the insurgency was supported by both the former French resident commissioner (subsequently declared *persona non grata* by the Lini government) and the Phoenix Foundation, a right-wing group based in Carson City, Nevada. By late 1981 the security situation had improved substantially, and all of the imprisoned rebels except Stevens and his principal lieutenant, Timothy WELLES, were released.

The Lini government was returned to office in the islands' first post-independence election on November 2, 1983. Three months later, following his conviction on a charge of nonpayment of a road tax, President George Ati SOKOMANU resigned. Despite voicing his frustration with

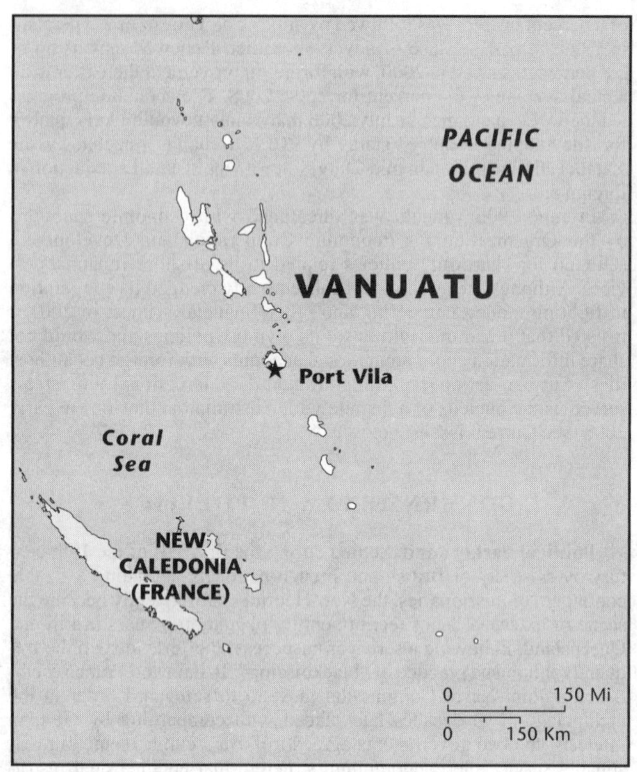

Father Lini and offering to lead a new "national unity" government as prime minister, Sokomanu was reappointed to his former post by the electoral college on March 8.

Lini was returned to office in the balloting of November 30, 1987, with the VP's vote share falling for the first time below 50 percent, while the opposition Union of Moderate Parties (*Union blong Moderet Pati*—UMP) increased its showing to 42 percent, compared with 33 percent in 1983.

Following the 1987 election a leadership dispute erupted between Lini and party ideologue Barak SOPE Ma'au Tamate, who mounted an unsuccessful bid for the prime minister position and was subsequently charged with instigating a major riot in Vila on May 16, 1988. In the wake of the disturbance, Sope was dismissed from the cabinet, stripped of his longtime post as party secretary general, and, along with four associates, expelled from the party after endorsing a no-confidence motion against the administration. On July 25 the "Gang of Five" was also ousted from parliament under a 1983 Vacation of Seats Act that precluded alteration of party affiliation by members. In response to the action, 18 members of the opposition UMP initiated a legislative boycott and on July 27 were also expelled for violating a parliamentary ban on three consecutive absences. Ironically, the Vanuatu Court of Appeal on October 21 ruled the 1983 act unconstitutional and reinstated the Sope parliamentarians (who had regrouped as the Melanesian Progressive Party—MPP) while upholding the ouster of the UMP members.

Five days after by-elections on December 13, 1988, for the vacated UMP seats, which neither the UMP nor the MPP contested, President Sokomanu attempted to dissolve parliament and name an "interim" government headed by Sope. Lini reacted by arresting Sope and his "ministers," with the Supreme Court ruling on December 19 that the president's action had been unconstitutional because it had not been undertaken with the support of two-thirds of the legislators and the advice of the prime minister. On January 12, 1989, Sokomanu was dismissed from office for "gross misconduct," and on January 30 Health Minister Fred TIMAKATA was designated by the electoral college as his successor. Subsequently, Sokomanu was convicted of incitement to mutiny and sentenced to a six-year prison term, while Sope and UMP leader Maxime CARLOT received five-year sentences for seditious conspiracy and treason. The sentences were dismissed in April by an appeals tribunal of jurists from Tonga, Papua New Guinea, and Vanuatu, although the convictions were allowed to stand.

At a party congress in April 1991 Lini was severely castigated by four ministerial associates, including the VP's secretary general, Donald KALPOKAS, for what was viewed as an increasingly autocratic and arbitrary leadership style. An ultimatum in May that the dissidents pledge their loyalty or face dismissal yielded a joint letter suggesting that the prime minister himself step down. Lini thereupon sacked the ministers, although an attempt to oust Kalpokas from his party post was rebuffed by the VP's Executive Council.

In the wake of numerous other purges of government personnel (the prime minister at one point reported to be holding more than 50 portfolios), Lini was replaced by Kalpokas as VP president at a special party congress on August 7, 1991. On September 6, after President Timakata had denied a request that parliament be dissolved, Lini was also ousted as prime minister, with Kalpokas designated his successor. Lini and a number of supporters thereupon organized the National Unity Party (NUP), which, by splitting the traditional VP vote in the election of December 2, gave a plurality to the francophone UMP. On December 16, in an action he characterized as stemming from a "pact with the devil," the UMP's Carlot (the honorific "Korman" subsequently being added to his name) formed a governing coalition with the NUP and a small regional formation, *Fren Melanesia.*

Initially withdrawing to the status of a parliamentary backbencher, Lini precipitated a government crisis in mid-1993 by reportedly demanding appointment as deputy prime minister and minister of justice. Rebuffed in the matter, Lini and five legislative colleagues withdrew their support for the government, thereby causing a rupture with a progovernment NUP faction led by Sethy John REGENVANU, which subsequently reorganized as the People's Democratic Party (PDP). The ensuing reduction in Carlot Korman's parliamentary majority to 24 of 46 seats made it impossible to reach the two-thirds majority in the electoral college needed to elect a new president at the expiration of the incumbent Timakata's term on January 31, 1994. It was not until March 2 that a compromise government nominee, Jean-Marie LEYE Lenelgau, was able to secure election through a decision by the VP, which held 9 legislative seats, to support his candidacy. As a result of its action the VP was expelled from the opposition coalition, with Barak Sope succeeding the VP's Kalpokas as leader of the opposition.

In September 1994, as the result of a Decentralisation Act approved four months earlier, the country's 11 local government councils were abolished to pave the way for elected bodies in six newly defined provinces. For the ensuing provincial council balloting of November 15, the opposition consisted, on the one hand, of Lini's NUP and, on the other, of a Unity Front (UF) coalition encompassing the VP, the MPP, the Tan Union, and a relegalized *Na-Griamel* under the leadership of its founder's son, Frankie STEVENS (although the younger Stevens was also serving as the leader of government business in parliament). The result was a three-way split, with the UMP, NUP, and UF winning two provinces each, although the UF secured an overall plurality of 41 seats, as contrasted with 34 and 20 for the UMP and NUP, respectively.

In the general election of November 30, 1995, Kalpokas's UF secured a plurality of 20 legislative seats, while Carlot's UMP won 17 and Lini's NUP, 9. Meanwhile, a deep intra-UMP split had developed between Carlot and the party president, Serge VOHOR, with the UF seeking an alliance both with the Vohor faction and with the NUP. Intense negotiation then ensued, with Vohor eventually concluding a pact with the NUP that yielded his installation as Carlot's successor on December 24.

In early February 1996 a number of Carlot's supporters joined the UF in a motion of no confidence in Vohor, whose resignation averted the need for a vote and permitted Carlot to form a new government in coalition with the UF. The dispute between Carlot and Vohor intensified in March, with Vohor convening a UMP congress (on his home island of Santo) at which Carlot and his supporters were expelled from the party. Two months later, anti-Vohor faction leader Amos ANDENG called for a retaliatory congress (in Carlot's home village of Erakor) that declared the action of the Santo meeting invalid and named Carlot to succeed Vohor as UMP president.

In mid-1996 the Carlot administration was rocked by the issuance of an ombudsman's report charging that the country faced bankruptcy because of an alleged scam involving issuance of letters of guarantee signed by Carlot and his finance minister, Barak Sope. While denying any wrongdoing, the prime minister shuffled his cabinet on August 5, reassigning Sope to the Ministry of Commerce and Trade. Having refused to accept the demotion, Sope was dismissed from the government on August 12. Concurrently, Carlot cited the MPP leader for "disloyalty" in withdrawing his party from the UF in favor of a new alliance with the Tan Union and *Fren Melanesia,* styled the MTF. The government coalition thus being effectively reduced to his UMP faction and the VP rump of the UF, Carlot succumbed to a no-confidence vote on

September 30 and was immediately succeeded by party rival Vohor, who named Sope as his deputy.

On October 12, 1996, while Vohor was visiting French Polynesia, striking members of the paramilitary Vanuatu Mobile Force (VMF) abducted President Leye and flew him to the northern island of Malekula for talks at gunpoint with Acting Prime Minister Sope, who promised that payment would be forthcoming to the VMF for long overdue arrears of $980,000. Thirteen days later Sope and three MTF ministerial colleagues were sacked in a cabinet shakeup that brought the VP into the government as a coalition partner of Vohor's UMP faction and the NUP.

In late May 1997 Vohor and Carlot were apparently reconciled, with Carlot and his UMP-Natora faction joining Vohor's UMP group, Sope's MPP, and the NUP in a new government coalition, the VP's Kalpokas again becoming leader of a one-party opposition. However, the friction between Carlot and Vohor soon resurfaced, with the former filing a no-confidence motion in November against the prime minister, whose government had been the target of numerous corruption allegations. President Leye immediately dissolved the legislature and ordered new elections, which, following a January 1998 Court of Appeal ruling upholding his decision, were held on March 6. The balloting produced no significant alteration in the party makeup of the parliament, and intense negotiations were reportedly required before the VP and the NUP, longtime rivals, agreed to form the next government. On March 30 the VP's Kalpokas returned to the prime ministerial post he had held in the early 1990s, while the NUP's Lini was named deputy prime minister.

On October 19, 1998, Kalpokas dismissed Lini and expelled his NUP from the ruling coalition because of the party's participation in drafting a no-confidence motion against the government. Kalpokas then formed a new alliance with a faction of the UMP headed by Willie JIMMY and the John Frum Movement (JFM).

Nearly two dozen candidates competed in the 1999 presidential race. Not surprisingly, no one received the required support in the first round of balloting of the electoral college in mid-March. Following apparently intense negotiations, Fr. John Bernard BANI, an Anglican minister and Kalpokas ally, was elected on March 25 with the reported support of all parties except the NUP, even though he had received only two votes on the first ballot.

The government lost its parliamentary majority in by-elections in August 1999 and, facing the loss of a no-confidence vote, Kalpokas resigned on November 25. MPP leader Barak Sope was immediately elected his successor, appointing a coalition administration that included members of the JFM, the NUP, the UMP, the Vanuatu Republican Party (VRP), and *Fren Melanesia Pati* (FMP).

Divisions within the UMP, including the departure in early 2001 of Willie Jimmy's faction, were followed in late March by Serge Vohor's decision to withdraw what was left of the UMP from the government and side with the VP, now headed by Edward NATAPEI, leader of the opposition. Without UMP support, Prime Minister Sope could no longer command a parliamentary majority, but he failed to convince President Bani to dissolve parliament and schedule a new general election. In early April, Parliament Speaker Paul Ren TARI of the NUP refused to permit legislative debate on a no-confidence motion filed by the opposition, which turned to the courts for redress. With the country's chief justice having threatened to cite Tari for contempt if he failed to let debate proceed, the no-confidence motion passed 27–18 on April 13, immediately after which Natapei was elected prime minister at the head of a VP-UMP coalition.

In the parliamentary election of May 2, 2002, Natapei's VP secured 14 seats and its coalition partner, the UMP, won 15, thereby ensuring the reelection of Natapei as prime minister when the new parliament convened on June 3. His tenure ended with the inconclusive election of July 6, 2004, that yielded the third designation of the UMP's Serge Vohor on July 29. Vohor subsequently became embroiled in a dispute over his decision in early November to establish diplomatic relations with Taiwan (see Foreign relations, below), and his government fell on December 11, followed by the election of Ham LINI as head of a nine-party coalition administration.

At the most recent election of September 2, 2008, the VP won a plurality of 11 seats, and Natapei was again designated to lead a coalition government that included Lini as his deputy.

Constitution and government. Under the independence constitution, Vanuatu's head of state is a largely titular president designated for a five-year term by an electoral college consisting of all members of the parliament and the presidents of the six provincial councils. Executive power is vested in a prime minister elected by secret legislative ballot; both the prime minister and other ministers (whom the prime minister appoints) must hold legislative seats. Members of the unicameral parliament are elected from multimember constituencies through a partially proportional system intended "to ensure fair representation of different political groups and opinions." The legislative term is four years, subject to dissolution. There is also a National Council of Chiefs, whose members are designated by peers sitting in District Councils of Chiefs. The National Council is empowered to make recommendations to the government and parliament on matters relating to indigenous custom and language. A national ombudsman is appointed by the president after consultation with the prime minister, party leaders, the president of the National Council of Chiefs, and others. The judicial system is headed by a four-member Supreme Court, the chief justice being named by the president after consultation with the prime minister and the leader of the opposition; of the other three justices, one is nominated by the speaker of parliament, one by the president of the National Council of Chiefs, and one by the six council presidents. A Court of Appeal is constituted by two or more Supreme Court justices sitting together. Parliament is authorized to establish village and island courts, as deemed appropriate.

President Kalkot MATASKELEKELE wrote a formal letter to Prime Minister Lini in June 2006 repeating a recommendation he had made earlier that Vanuatu adopt a republican system of government with a popularly elected president who would be the head of state and the head of government with the power to appoint a cabinet whose members would not necessarily be members of parliament. Lini responded by acknowledging that the country needed to engage in a review of the national constitution but stopped short of endorsing a presidential system.

The six provinces created in 1994 bear names that are acronyms of those of their principal islands. Stretching roughly from north to south they are Torba (Torres, Banks), Sama (Espiritu Santo, Malo), Penama (Pentecost, Ambae, Maéwo), Malampa (Malakula, Ambrym, Paama), Shefa (Shepherds, Epi, Efaté), and Tafea (Tanna, Anatom, Futuna, Erromango, Aniwa).

Foreign relations. Although Vanuatu was not admitted to the United Nations until the fall of 1981, it became, at independence, a member both of the Commonwealth and the *Agence de Coopération Culturelle et Technique,* an organization established in 1969 to promote cultural and technical cooperation within the French-speaking world. Regionally, it is a member of the Pacific Community and the Pacific Islands Forum (PIF), while in 1984 both the Asian Development Bank and the Economic and Social Commission for Asia and the Pacific established regional headquarters in Port Vila. Diplomatic relations were established with the Soviet Union in July 1986 and with the United States the following October, although Vanuatu maintains no embassies abroad, save for the appointment in late 2007 of an ambassador to the European Union in Brussels as part of an effort to secure enhanced development aid.

Under the francophone UMP, Vanuatu's prior policy of supporting liberation struggles and actively attacking remaining pockets of colonialism in the Pacific subsided, particularly with regard to the French territory of New Caledonia. On the other hand, President Jacques Chirac's 1995 announcement that France would launch a new series of nuclear tests at Mururoa Atoll in September posed a dilemma for Prime Minister Carlot Korman. While indicating that his government would end its intransigence and approve the Treaty of Rarotonga establishing a South Pacific Nuclear-Free Zone, he refused to join his regional colleagues in condemning the testing, insisting that it was a purely internal matter of France.

In a highly unusual move, Prime Minister Vohor announced on November 3, 2004, that Vanuatu had established relations with Taiwan, asserting that the country could continue to maintain existing relations with the People's Republic of China (a position to which the PRC took immediate exception). Vohor's own cabinet responded by voting twice against the action, and on November 16 Vohor dismissed Foreign Minister Barak Sope, who had led the opposition to it. The outcome was Vohor's ouster on December 11 and repudiation of "all agreements made by Vohor with Taiwan" by the new government's foreign minister, Sato KILMAN. Subsequently, during a visit to China in March 2005, Prime Minister Lini applauded Beijing's reunification efforts under a one-China policy.

Vanuatu is a member of the Melanesian Spearhead Group (MSG), a South Pacific island regional bloc that includes Fiji, Papua New Guinea, and the Solomon Islands. The MSG was formed in 1986 to promote economic development and sustainable growth, good government, preservation of Melanesian cultures, and regional cooperation and security among members, and in the 1990s was a force supporting decolonization movements in New Caledonia.

Membership in the PIF has increased Vanuatu's support for greater regional and international labor mobility as a means for improving the local economy, especially in regard to greater access to Australia and New Zealand labor markets for its citizens. More recently, Vanuatu in early 2008 completed domestic requirements for inclusion in the Pacific Island Countries Trade Agreement (PICTA).

Vanuatu has recently sought to formally restart talks for accession to the World Trade Organization (WTO). Talks had been suspended in 2001, in part over Vanuatu's unwillingness to expose its retail, telecommunications, and services sectors to rapid liberalization. In furtherance of its independence in trade policy, Vanuatu continued to withhold negotiation on WTO entry until April 2009, when most of its concerns had apparently been resolved.

Current issues. Few countries have displayed party alliances as tenuous as those of Vanuatu. In the late 1980s and throughout the 1990s the VP and the UMP were repeatedly split by factional disputes that ultimately saw breakaway groups form the MPP, the NUP, the VRP, and other less significant parties. Invariably, these ruptures arose as much from personality and leadership clashes as from policy differences, the nearly all-encompassing coalition formed by Ham Lini in late 2004 being more a result of the row over Vohor's seemingly impetuous Taiwan move than a sudden coalescence on government policy. By the same token, the coalition was susceptible to fracture as easily as it had been formed. Thus, the VP left the government in early 2007 but returned at midyear, following ejection of the UMP in a cabinet reshuffle. Concurrently, another coalition member, the People's Progressive Party (PPP), was forced to leave the government coalition after evidence surfaced that seven of its members had participated in the fraudulent cashing of government checks.

The situation became even more complex in mid-2009, when Maxime Carlot Korman abandoned his post as deputy opposition leader to support the Natapei administration, while Natapei's deputy, Ham Lini, expelled the parliamentary speaker, George WELLS, from the NUP for alleged involvement in negotiations to topple the coalition government.

In May 2008 Vanuatu complained of a money-laundering sting operation by the Australian Federal Police (AFP) against a local businessman who had been arrested in Perth for alleged tax fraud. The AFP argued that the action had been cleared by Vanuatu's attorney general, who insisted that the authorization had been confined to action by the Vanuatu police.

Meanwhile, dispute resurfaced regarding Vanuatu's status as a tax haven. On May 5, 2008, the head of the Vanuatu Financial Services Commission announced that the country's International Companies Act would be revised to abolish the ban on information about private client accounts. One day later, however, Finance Minister Willie Jimmy stated that such action would be a severe blow to the country's economy, and in mid-2009 Vanuatu remained one of six Pacific island countries on the OECD list of money-laundering venues.

POLITICAL PARTIES

Government Parties: (Prior to November 2009 changes *[see headnote]*):

Party of Our Land (*Vanua'aku Pati*—VP). Long at the forefront of the drive for independence and the return of indigenous lands, the VP was formed in 1972 as the New Hebrides National Party. Its boycott of a Representative Assembly election in 1977 led to cancellation of the results. It won 26 of 46 legislative seats in November 1987, a reduction, proportionally, from 24 of 39 in 1983. In an unexpected contest in December 1987, Secretary General Barak Sope challenged Fr. Walter Lini for the party leadership but was defeated by a near 2–1 vote. Sope was expelled from parliament on July 25, 1988, after having been dismissed from the cabinet and the party for reportedly instigating a riot in Vila in mid-May. He and four other former VP members responded by announcing the formation of a rival Melanesian Progressive Party (MPP, below), whose members refused to accept court-sanctioned legislative reinstatement on October 21. Subsequently, in early 1989, Sope was convicted of sedition after having been named head of the anti-Lini "interim government" by President Sokomanu in mid-December. The VP won all of the 5 vacant seats filled by special elections in 1989 because of boycotts by the MPP and UMP.

The VP split as a result of the 1991 ouster of its longtime leader, Father Lini, who subsequently formed the NUP. Prior to the November 1994 provincial elections the party joined the MPP and the Tan Union in a coalition called the Unity Front (UF), which won a plurality of 20 seats in the general election of November 1995 but became effectively moribund upon withdrawal of the MPP and Tan Union in August 1996.

The VP returned to government in October 1996, moved into opposition in May 1997, and in March 1998 joined with the NUP in forming an administration under Donald Kalpokas that lasted until November 1999. Shortly thereafter, Kalpokas was replaced as party leader by Edward Natapei, who became prime minister in April 2001 and retained the post after the May 2002 election, in which the party won 14 seats. Natapei was forced to resign after the election of June 2004, in which the VP was reduced to 8 seats, but was named Lini's deputy prime minister in July 2007. He returned as prime minister in September 2008.

Leaders: Edward NATAPEI (Prime Minister and President of the Party) Donald KALPOKAS (Former Prime Minister and Honorary President of the Party), Sela MOLISA (Secretary General).

National Unity Party (NUP). The NUP was organized by Fr. Walter Lini following his ouster as VP president on August 7, 1991, and his defeat on a parliamentary no-confidence motion on September 6. A majority (21) of the VP MPs supported Lini in the September vote, leaving his successor, Donald Kalpokas, with a bare overall majority. After winning ten seats in the December balloting, the NUP joined the coalition supporting Carlot as prime minister. However, a majority faction led by Lini withdrew its support of Carlot in August 1993. In May 1994 Deputy Prime Minister Sethy Regenvanu and two other NUP MPs who had remained in the Kalpokas cabinet in the wake of Lini's withdrawal were expelled from the party; in June they formed the People's Democratic Party (PDP). Third-ranked with nine seats, after the 1995 election, the NUP reentered the government as the UMP's junior partner. Excluded from the Carlot government of February 1996, the NUP returned as a participant in the second Vohor administration in late October 1996, although Lini did not enter the cabinet until succeeding his estranged sister, Hilda LINI, as justice minister in November.

Prior to his dismissal in October 1998, Walter Lini served as Prime Minister Kalpokas's deputy in a VP-NUP coalition. He died on February 21, 1999. Ten months later the NUP was a leading participant in formation of Barak Sope's five-party government. In the 2002 parliamentary election the NUP declined from 11 to 8 seats, but it rebounded to a plurality of 10 seats in July 2004, with Lini's brother, Ham, forming a coalition government on December 11. It retained the 8 seats, but lost its plurality to the VP in the September 2008 poll.

Leaders: Ham LINI (Deputy Prime Minister), Charles LINI (National Coordinator), Willie TITONGOA (Secretary General).

Vanuatu Republican Party—VRP (*Ripablikan Pati blong Vanuatu*). The formation of the VRP was announced in January 1998 by Carlot, who had previously led a UMP faction opposed to Prime Minister Vohor. The VRP won three seats at the May 2002 legislative election, four in 2004. A split within the party emerged in June 2009, when Carlot crossed the aisle to support the government, thereby relinquishing his position as deputy leader of the opposition. However, most VRP legislators eventually endorsed the action by Carlot, who was subsequently elected speaker of Parliament..

Leaders: Maxime CARLOT Korman (Speaker of Parliament and Former Prime Minister), Yoan MARIASUA (Secretary General).

Union of Moderate Parties (*Union des Partis Moderés*—UPM/ *Union blong Moderet Pati*—UMP). The UMP is the successor to the New Hebrides Federal Party, which was organized in early 1979 as an alliance of predominantly pro-French groups, including Jimmy Stevens's *Na-Griamel.* Following the deportation of two Federal Party MPs to New Caledonia in 1982 for involvement in the Santo rebellion, the non-secessionist elements of the party regrouped under the present label, winning 12 seats in the 1983 election and 19 seats in 1987. Party leader Vincent Boulekone was ousted from parliament in 1986 for missing meetings but was ordered reinstated by the Supreme Court, which ruled that ill health excused the absences. Following the 1987 balloting, Boulekone was replaced by Carlot.

On July 27, 1988, 18 UMP members were dismissed from parliament after having walked out in protest at Barak Sope's expulsion, the party refusing to recontest the seats in by-elections on December 13.

Carlot was among those convicted of sedition after having been named deputy prime minister in the abortive Sope government of December 18. The Tan Union, [QUERY a now-defunct breakaway UMP faction headed by Boulekone, contested the December balloting, becoming the official opposition upon winning six legislative seats.

Following the December 1991 election, in which it won a plurality of 19 seats, the UMP joined with Lini's NUP to form a coalition government under Carlot. Most of the Lini group went into opposition in mid-1993, save for a faction that later reorganized briefly as the People's Democratic Party (PDP) to continue as the UMP's junior partner. A new UMP-NUP coalition was concluded after the November 1995 balloting, although the UMP was by then divided into factions led by Carlot and Vohor. Carlot left the UMP in early 1998 to launch the VRP, and the party was further split by the decision of a faction led by Willie Jimmy to support the VP-led Kalpokas government in October. Vohor and Jimmy, rivals for the party leadership, reached a short-lived accommodation at a November 2000 party congress, but in early 2001 Jimmy announced his resignation from the UMP and eventually joined the NUP. Meanwhile, Vohor's decision to leave the Barak Sope government led to the no-confidence motion that ended Sope's tenure in April 2001, with Vohor then being appointed deputy prime minister in the Natapei VP-UMP administration. The UMP won a plurality of 15 seats at the May 2002 parliamentary election, 7 of which were lost in July 2004. Seven of the remaining seats were retained in September 2008.

Vohor's unpopular decision as prime minister to establish diplomatic relations with Taiwan in 2004 diminished his influence inside and outside the party.

Leaders: Serge VOHOR (Former Prime Minister and President of the Party), Henri TAGA (Former Speaker of Parliament).

Na-Griamel Movement. *Na-Griamel* was founded by Jimmy Stevens, whose secessionist rebellion on Espiritu Santo was crushed in 1980. Stevens was released from 11 years' imprisonment in August 1991 and died on February 28, 1994, the leadership of *Na-Griamel* passing to his son, Frankie. Elected to parliament in 1991, the younger Stevens served briefly as deputy opposition leader before defecting to the government in early 1994. *Na-Griamel* was permitted to reopen its headquarters for the first time in 14 years the following August. Despite the ambiguous role of its leader, *Na-Griamel* participated in the UF for the 1994 provincial poll before formally rejoining the government in February 1995. It secured one legislative seat in 1995, none thereafter until 2008, when it again captured one seat.

Leader: Frankie STEVENS.

Melanesian Progressive Party (MPP). The MPP was organized by Barak Sope and four other VP members after the former VP secretary general had been expelled from the party in mid-1988. In April 1989 ousted president George Sokomanu formally joined the new group after he, Sope, and two others had been released from prison by reversal of their sedition convictions.

During 1989 both the Vanuatu Independent Alliance Party (VIAP) and the National Democratic Party (NDP) merged with the MPP. The VIAP was a Santo-based group formed in June 1982 by two dismissed VP ministers, Thomas Reuben SERU and George WOREK; for the 1983 campaign it adopted a platform based on "free enterprise capitalism and anticommunism," losing all three of its existing parliamentary seats. The NDP was formed in late 1986 by John NAUPA, transport minister in the Lini government from 1980 to 1983; it was critical of the administration's handling of the economy and insisted that foreign policy should concentrate on the maintenance of good relations with Britain and France.

Following Prime Minister Sope's ouster in April 2001, it appeared likely that the MPP and the other leading opposition party, the NUP, would establish a coalition or merge. Instead, an MPP faction led by Sato Kilman split off (see PPP, below) in August. The MPP won only three seats in the 2002 election and an equal number in 2004. It declined further to one seat in 2008.

Leaders: Barak SOPE Ma'au Tamate (Former Prime Minister and Party Chair), George Ati SOKOMANU (Former President of the Republic), Georges CALO (Secretary General).

Other Parliamentary Parties:

Vanuatu Green Party (VGP). Vincent BOULEKONE and Paul TELUKLUK organized the Vanuatu Greens after leaving the UMP (below) in early 2001. Boulekone had previously helped found the Tan Union, also a splinter from the UMP, before the December 1988 election but subsequently rejoined the parent party. His 2001 departure coincided with that of Willie Jimmy and was generally regarded as reflecting leadership rather than ideological differences with the UMP's Serge Vohor faction. The Greens won three parliamentary seats in May 2002; the seats were retained in 2004 by a **Green Confederation** (GC) that included the VGP and the **Vanuatu Green Alliance** (VGA). Telukluk won a seat in the 2004 poll as leader of the *Namangi Aute* (NA), a rural group from North Malekula, which he retained in 2008.

Leader: Moana CARCASSES Kalosh (Leader of the Opposition).

People's Progressive Party (PPP). Formation of the PPP was announced in August 2001 by Sato Kilman, previously a faction leader of the MPP. Kilman indicated that the party's focus would be on development of agriculture, commerce, communications, and tourism. The party won four parliamentary seats in 2004 and participated in the Lini government until forced out in mid-2007 because of alleged involvement in a financial scandal (see Current issues, above). Its legislative representation was unchanged in 2008.

Leaders: Sato KILMAN (Leader of the Opposition, Former Deputy Prime Minister, and Former Foreign Affairs Minister), Gary MAHINA (Chair).

People's Action Party (*Parti de l'Action Populaire*—PAP). The PAP was launched prior to the 2004 election, in which it secured one seat (retained in 2008).

Leader: Peter VUTA.

Vanuatu Labour Party (VLP). A trade-union grouping launched in 1986, the VLP captured one parliamentary seat in 2008.

Leader: Kenneth SATUNGA.

Recently organized minor parties that also secured representation in 2008 included the **Shepherd's Alliance Party** (SAP), the **Vanuatu Family First Party** (VFFP), the **Vanuatu National Party** (VNP), and the **Vanuatu Progressive Republican Farmer Party** (VPRFP).

Other Parties and Groups:

Tu Vanuatu Movement (*Tu Vanuatu Kominiti*). The Tu Vanuatu Movement was launched by Fr. Walter Lini's sister, Hilda Lini, after she resigned from the NUP in November 1996. Not a political party per se, the group is dedicated to support for women's and rural issues in a context of traditional Melanesian and Christian values. The legislature lost its only female member when Lini failed to secure reelection in March 1998.

Leader: Hilda LINI.

National Community Association—NCA (*Association de la Communauté Nationale*—ACN). The NCA secured two legislative seats in 2004 and was awarded portfolios in both the Serge Vohor and initial Ham Lini administrations. It won no seats in 2008.

Regional parties include the **Efaté Laketu Party** (ELP), based on the island of Efaté; the **Fren Melanesia Pati** (FMP), which won a parliamentary seat in 1995 under the leadership of former agriculture minister Albert RAVUTIA; and the **John Frum Movement** (JFM), led by Song KEASPAI, which represents interests on the island of Tanna and won two legislative seats in 1998.

LEGISLATURE

The Vanuatu **Parliament** is a unicameral body currently consisting of 52 members elected for four-year terms, subject to dissolution. Balloting was most recently held on September 2, 2008, with results as follows: Party of Our Land, 11 seats; National Unity Party, 8 seats; Union of Moderate Parties, 7; Vanuatu Republican Party, 7; People's Progressive Party, 4; Greens Confederation, 2; Melanesian Progressive Party, *Na-Griamel* Movement, *Namangi Aute,* People's Action Party, Shepherd's Alliance Party, Vanuatu Family First Party, Vanuatu Labour Party, Vanuatu National Party, and the Vanuatu Progressive Republican Farmer Party, 1 each; independents 4.

Speaker: Maxime CARLOT Korman.

CABINET

[as of September 1, 2009]

Prime Minister	Edward Natapei (VP)
Deputy Prime Minister	Ham Lini (NUP)
Ministers	
Agriculture, Forestry, and Fisheries	Havo Molisale (*Na-Griamel*)
Education	Charlot Saluwai (UMP)
Finance and Economic Management	Sela Molisa (VP)
Foreign Affairs	Joe Natuman (VP)
Health	Moses Kahu (VP)
Justice and Social Welfare	Ham Lini (NUP)
Internal Affairs	Patrick Crowby Manarewo (NUP)
Lands, Geology, Mines, and Energy	Harry Iauko (VP)
Ni-Vanuatu Business Development	Esmon Sai (MPP)
Public Utilities and Infrastructure	Serge Vohor (UMP)
Sports and Youth	Josie Masmas (VRP)
Trade, Industry, and Tourism	James Bule (NUP)

COMMUNICATIONS

Press. The following are published in Port Vila: *Vanuatu Daily Post* (2,000), independent, in English; *Port Vila Presse* (2,000), English/French daily launched in 2000; *Vanuatu Weekly* (1,700), government organ, in English, French, and Bislama; *Viewpoints,* VP weekly. In early 1995 a presidential aide threatened the editor of the *Vanuatu Daily Post* (then known as *The Trading Post*) with deportation if he did not publish some material in French; however, President Korman repudiated the action on the ground that only the government was held to multilingual publication. *Vanuatu Post* publisher Marc Neil-Jones, an Australian, ran into additional difficulties in 2000 and 2001, when Prime Minister Sope objected to "unbalanced" reporting in the publication and pursued deportation.

Broadcasting and computing. The government-operated *Radio Vanuatu* broadcasts from Vila. *Television blong Vanuatu* began transmitting in 1993, with its first production facilities being inaugurated in mid-1995.

As of 2008 there were 72.7 Internet users per 1,000 inhabitants.

INTERGOVERNMENTAL REPRESENTATION

Ambassador to the U.S.: Vanuatu does not maintain an embassy in Washington.

U.S. Ambassador to Vanuatu: Teddy Bernard TAYLOR.

Permanent Representative to the UN: Donald KALPOKAS.

IGO Memberships (Non-UN): ADB, CWTH, NAM, OIF, PC, PIF.

VATICAN CITY STATE

Stato della Città del Vaticano

Political Status: Independent sovereign state, under papal temporal government; international status governed by the Lateran Treaty with Italy of February 11, 1929; constitution of June 7, 1929, superseded by a New Fundamental Law signed by the pope on November 26, 2000, with effect from February 22, 2001.

Area: 0.17 sq. mi. (0.44 sq. km.).

Population: 549 (2007E). There are numerous lay workers, most of them Italian citizens, who live outside the Vatican.

Official Language: Latin (Italian is the working language).

Monetary Unit: Euro (market rate December 1, 2009: 1 euro = $1.51US). On December 29, 2000, the Vatican and Italy signed an agreement permitting Vatican adoption of the euro, authorization having already been granted in principle by the European Union. Under a 1929 agreement with the Italian government, the Vatican had the right to issue papal coinage in Vatican lire at par with the Italian lira (its total value not to exceed 100 million lire, except in holy years and in the year a council is convened). Since introduction of euro notes and coins in 2002, the Vatican has been permitted to mint its own euro coins, which are issued in small quantities for collectors, as was true of Vatican lire.

Sovereign (Supreme Pontiff): Pope BENEDICT XVI (Josef RATZINGER); elected to a life term by the College of Cardinals on April 19, 2005, succeeding Pope JOHN PAUL II (Karol WOJTYŁA), who died on April 2, 2005.

Secretary of State of the Roman Curia and Papal Representative in the Civil Government of the Vatican City State: Cardinal Tarcisio BERTONE; appointed by Pope Benedict XVI on September 15, 2006, while still an archbishop, succeeding Cardinal Angelo SODANO, who had resigned on June 22, 2006; named a cardinal on January 10, 1994.

Secretary for Relations with States: Archbishop Dominique MAMBERTI; appointed by Benedict XVI on September 15, 2006, succeeding Archbishop Jean-Louis TAURAN.

President of the Governatorate of Vatican City State: Cardinal Giovanni LAJOLO; appointed by Pope Benedict XVI on September 15, 2006, succeeding Cardinal Edmund SZOKA, who had been archbishop of Detroit from 1981 to 1990. Cardinal Lajolo functions as the "mayor" of Vatican City.

THE COUNTRY

An enclave surrounding the Basilica of Saint Peter and including 13 other buildings in and around the city of Rome, the Vatican City State, the smallest independent entity in the world, derives its principal importance from its function as the world headquarters of the Roman Catholic Church and official residence of its head, the pope. The central administration of the church is customarily referred to as the Holy See (*Santa Sede*), or more informally as the Vatican. The Vatican City State is the territorial base from which the leadership of the church exercises its religious and ecclesiastical responsibilities for a worldwide Catholic population of more than 1 billion people and over 400,000 Catholic priests. The city state's population, predominantly of Italian and Swiss extraction, is limited mainly to Vatican officials and resident employees and their families. Italian is the language of common use, although Latin is employed in the official acts of the Holy See.

The Vatican's income is based on contributions from Roman Catholic congregations around the world; the sale of postage stamps and souvenirs; and substantial investments in real estate, bonds, and securities. The Administration of the Patrimony of the Apostolic See (*Amministrazione del Patrimonio della Sede Apostolica*) manages its holdings, while the Institute for Religious Works (*Istituto per le Opere di Religione*—IOR) acts as a bank for monies held by affiliated religious orders. The Vatican's financial status long remained confidential and hence the object of intense speculation. However, an unprecedented announcement in 1979 revealed that the church's operations would be $20 million in deficit for that year. By 1991 a projected deficit of more than $90 million led to a conference at Vatican City on ways to generate more revenue from local dioceses around the world. Spearheading this economic reform was an American, Cardinal Edmund SZOKA, who became the chief financial officer in 1990 and introduced the Vatican to American business practices and the widespread use of computer technology. Many observers considered Vatican finances a mystery, but Vatican officials themselves were often unclear as to their financial status. Each department used its own accounting methods, creating difficulties for administrators seeking an accurate financial picture of the institution as a whole. Szoka regularized the accounting practices and

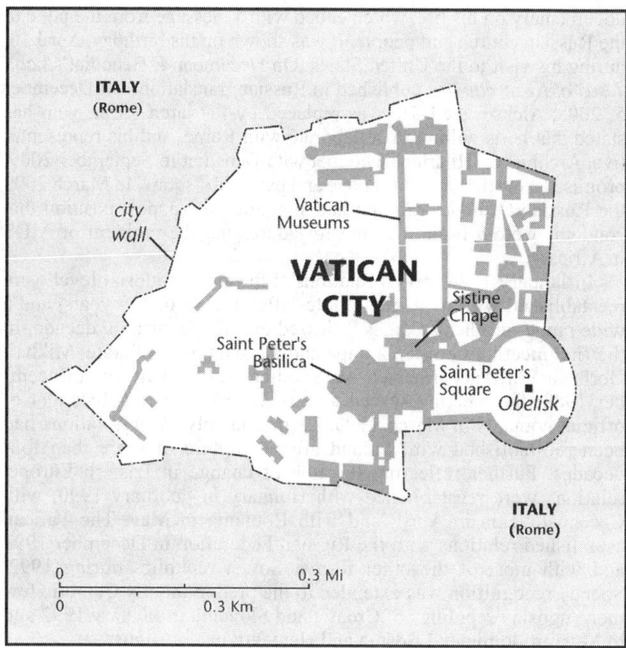

was able to assess accurately the Vatican's financial state. Szoka also made use of Canon 1271, an often- neglected provision in church law that requires bishops to support the Holy See. He called the heads of over 100 bishops' conferences from various countries around the world to remind them of their financial obligations to Rome. He was also innovative in finding ways to handle daily expenses, such as turning an unused train station on Vatican property into a department store for Vatican employees. The resultant remedial action produced a 1993 surplus (the first in more than 20 years) of $1.5 million on income totaling $169 million. Strong investment performance buoyed Vatican finances in the 1990s, but the weakening dollar marked the deficit's return in 2000. The losses continued until 2004 when the Vatican showed a surplus of $4.2 million. It greatly improved on that figure in 2005, making a profit of $13.2 million in spite of over $9 million in expenses relating to Pope JOHN PAUL II's funeral and Pope BENEDICT XVI's election. In 2006 the Vatican had a smaller surplus of $4.2 million. The sagging dollar was again responsible for the decline. Although the euro is the official currency of the Holy See, it has substantial investments in U.S. dollars and receives generous contributions from the church in the United States. In July 2008 the Vatican announced that the Holy See finished 2007 with a deficit of more than $14 million. It blamed its loss on the continuing poor performance of the U.S. dollar. Losses continued in 2008 but they were not nearly as dramatic, amounting to $1.28 million. The global financial crisis and the corresponding decline in donations were blamed for much of the decline. The Vatican also made significant investments in 2008, integrating their communications services, installing solar panels on the roof of the papal audience hall, and restoring works of art and historic churches. The annual Peter's-Pence collection, which is taken once a year in churches to help support the pope's charitable activities, was down slightly (0.05 percent). It declined from $79.8 million in 2007 to $76 million in 2008. U.S. Catholics were the most generous giving $18.7 million; Italy was next with $8.6 million. Germany donated $4 million, followed by Spain with $2.7 million.

GOVERNMENT AND POLITICS

Political background. Italy's recognition of the Vatican City State in the Lateran Treaty of 1929 terminated a bitter political controversy that had persisted since the unification of Italy in 1860–1870. Before that time the popes had exercised political sovereignty over the city of Rome and substantial portions of the Italian peninsula, where they ruled as territorial sovereigns in addition to performing spiritual and administrative functions as heads of the Catholic Church. The absorption of virtually all territorial holdings by the new Italian state and the failure of Pope PIUS IX to accept the legitimacy of the compensation offered by the Italian Parliament left the Holy See in an anomalous position that was finally regularized after a lapse of two generations. In addition to the Lateran Treaty, by which Italy recognized the independence and sovereignty of the Vatican City State, a concordat was concluded that regulated the position of the church within Italy, while a financial convention compensated the Holy See for its earlier losses. The status of the Vatican City State as established by the Lateran Treaty has since been recognized, formally or tacitly, by a great majority of the world's governments.

Cardinal Josef RATZINGER, who became pope with the title Benedict XVI in April 2005, follows one of the longest and most significant papal terms in modern history. Cardinal Karol WOJTYŁA, archbishop of Kraków, Poland, was elected as Pope John Paul II in 1978, and was the most widely traveled pope of any era. He commanded worldwide veneration, even as he moved the church away from the liberal direction of the Second Vatican Council, opened in 1962 during the papacy of Pope JOHN XXIII. Cardinal Ratzinger was a close confidant of John Paul II. From 1981 until John Paul II's death, Cardinal Ratzinger served as head of the Congregation for the Doctrine of the Faith (once known as the Holy Office of the Inquisition), the Vatican office responsible for maintaining orthodox doctrine throughout the Roman Catholic communion.

Constitution and government. On November 26, 2000, Pope John Paul II signed a new constitution intended to "harmonize in a legal manner" various governmental changes, such as abolition of the death penalty, which had been introduced since promulgation of the preceding basic law on June 7, 1929. As in the past, the Vatican City State retains the form of an absolute monarchy. Supreme legislative, executive, and judicial power is vested in the pope in his capacity as bishop of Rome; the pope, who is elected for life, serves concurrently as supreme pontiff of the Universal Church, primate of Italy, archbishop and metropolitan of the Province of Rome, and sovereign of the Vatican City State. Assisting the pope in the exercise of his varied responsibilities are the members of two major organs, the College of Cardinals and the Roman Curia (*Curia Romana*).

Members of the college, who numbered 190 as of September 1, 2009, are named by the pope and serve as his chief advisers and coadjutors during his lifetime; upon his death, those under the age of 80, of which there were 112 as of September 1, 2009, meet to elect his successor, which is their right as titular clergymen in the city of Rome. The meeting of the college to elect a pope is still referred to as a conclave from the Latin *cum clave* (with a key), which refers to the locked room where the cardinals meet. Reforms instituted by John Paul II in February 22, 1996, in an Apostolic Constitution entitled *Universi Dominici Gregis,* changed the procedures by which a pope was elected. It ended the practice of detaining the electors in a locked room until a result emerged, although strict secrecy of the voting process has been maintained. Also before 1996 a candidate for pope (usually a cardinal) normally required a majority of two-thirds (or two-thirds plus one, depending on the number of electors), But because of the 1996 reform in the event of a protracted deadlock a majority vote was able to decide to proceed to election by majority. The 1996 reform also eliminated the options of election by universal acclamation or by delegation to an electoral subcommittee. In that same year the *Domus Sanctae Marthae,* a hospitality residence named after St. Martha, opened within the precincts of Vatican City. This air-conditioned guesthouse is considerably more comfortable than accommodations available to cardinals during previous conclaves, and its existence has been seen as an inducement to older and infirm electors to take more time in coming to a decision. On June 11, 2007, Benedict XVI modified the election procedures established in *Universi Dominici Gregis*, phasing out the possibility of election by simple majority even in the case of a protracted deadlock. In future elections under any circumstances a two-thirds majority will be needed to elect a pope. While the papacy is vacant, the full college (meeting in General Congregation) or subcommittees (Particular Congregations) may deal with the ordinary government of the church and of the Vatican City State as well as with any emergency matters arising, with the strict exception of matters that would otherwise be reserved to the authority of the pope.

Apart from conclaves, the full college meets infrequently. A number of cardinals also hold positions on the various bodies that constitute the Curia, which serves as the church's central administrative organ. Political responsibilities have devolved primarily to the Secretariat of State, which in 1988 was divided into two sections, one dealing with general affairs and the other addressing relations with states. A secretary of state heads the Secretariat. The governor of the Vatican works closely with the Secretariat. The governor is currently the same person (Cardinal Giovanni LAJOLO) as the president of the Pontifical Commission for the Vatican City State, a body that seems to have reduced its activity in favor of the Governatorate. Prior to Cardinal Szoka, who was governor from 1997 to 2006, the position had been vacant since 1952.

The Vatican City State has its own security force (the Swiss Guard), postal service, coinage, utilities, department store, communication system, and local tribunal with a right of appeal to higher ecclesiastical courts. A papal edict issued in July 1995 set out "rules of conduct" for all Vatican employees, requiring them, on pain of automatic sanctions (including dismissal), to observe Catholic moral doctrines "even in the private sphere" and not to associate with organizations whose "goals are incompatible" with those of the church.

Foreign relations. The foreign relations of the Holy See are centered primarily on its international status as seat of the church, set in the context of its position as a sovereign entity. Its activities as a sovereign state continue to be governed by the Lateran Treaty and related agreements with the Italian government, which enable it to enter into international agreements and bilateral diplomatic relations in its own right. Worldwide, such diplomatic linkages now total well over 100 (supplemented by unofficial representation in other countries), while the Holy See has permanent observer status at the United Nations, with, as of July 2004, all rights of full membership except that of voting. It is also a full member of certain specialist agencies at the UN, and it participates in the Organization for Security and Cooperation in Europe (OSCE).

The Vatican's close relations with Italy were threatened in the 1980s by the revelation of links between the Institute for Religious Works (IOR), otherwise known as the Vatican bank, and Italy's Banco Ambrosiano, which collapsed in August 1982. The Vatican and the Italian government subsequently appointed a joint commission to investigate the matter, and in May 1984 the IOR agreed "in recognition of moral involvement," but without admission of culpability, to pay 109 creditor banks up to $250 million of a $406 million settlement against Banco Ambrosiano's successor institution.

Earlier, in February 1984, negotiations were concluded on a new Italian-Vatican concordat. Provisions included the abandonment of Roman Catholicism as Italy's state religion and of mandated religious instruction in public schools, although secular authorities would continue to accord automatic recognition to church marriages and full freedom to Catholic schools.

John Paul II exemplified a concerted effort to use the papal position to improve relations, not only with non-Catholic Christian entities but also with some non-Christians. Benedict XVI seems to be continuing this tradition. The historic breach with Protestant Christendom, dating to the 16th century, was partly overcome in 1982, when the Vatican established full diplomatic relations with the United Kingdom and with the Lutheran countries of Denmark, Norway, and Sweden.

In contrast, major differences with the Orthodox Christian hierarchy continue to affect the Vatican's relations with a number of countries. In 1992 the Orthodox Church severely criticized Rome for seeking converts in "Orthodox" territory, as signified by Pope John Paul II's 1991 creation of new dioceses in the former Soviet Union. The ecumenical patriarch, Bartholomew I (representing 15 churches, with 170 million adherents), made a first official visit to the Vatican in June 1995, while a trip by John Paul II to Romania in May 1999 marked the first visit in 1,000 years by a Roman Catholic pope to a country having an Orthodox majority. It was followed in May 2001 by a first visit to Greece, where the pope met with Archbishop Christodoulos of the Greek Orthodox Church. At that time John Paul II apologized for the sacking of Constantinople in 1204. The pope subsequently undertook groundbreaking visits to Ukraine (June 2001), Kazakhstan and Armenia (September 2001), and Azerbaijan and Bulgaria (May 2002). Benedict XVI continued John Paul II's outreach to the Orthodox Church by visiting with Bartholomew I during Benedict's trip to Turkey (November 2007). The patriarch of Moscow, Aleksei II, remained overtly critical of the Vatican, however, condemning its February 2002 decision to upgrade four previously "temporary" apostolic administrations in Russia to full dioceses.

Despite invitations from Russian president Vladimir Putin to visit Russia, Benedict XVI will not go (like John Paul II before him) unless he receives an invitation from the head of the Russian Orthodox Church. In 2008 Benedict received another positive sign from the Russian government when a state-run television station broadcast a flattering documentary on his life, which ended with a message from the pope to the Russian church and people. It was shown on his birthday, April 16, during his visit to the United States. On December 4, Benedict's book *Jesus of Nazareth* was published in Russian translation. On December 5, 2008, Aleksei died. He was replaced by Patriarch Kirill, who has stated that he is willing to collaborate with Rome, and his representative, Archbishop Hilarion, who met with Benedict in September 2009, promised a meeting between pope and patriarch "soon." In March 2009 the Russian Orthodox Church had supported the pope's position that condoms were a futile measure for addressing the problem of AIDS in Africa.

In January 1984 formal relations at the ambassadorial level were reestablished with the United States after a lapse of 117 years, and a wide range of other linkages followed during the ensuing decade. In the first meeting between a pope and a Soviet head of state, Mikhail Gorbachev was accorded a private audience at the Vatican in December 1989; the meeting served as a prelude to the establishment of official contacts in March 1990. Earlier, in July 1989, relations had been reestablished with Poland after a rupture of more than four decades. Further reflecting the tide of change in Eastern Europe, relations were reestablished with Hungary in February 1990, with Czechoslovakia in April, and with Romania in May. The Vatican established relations with the Russian Federation in December 1991 and with most of the other former Soviet republics during 1992. Speedy recognition was extended to the predominantly Catholic former Yugoslav republics of Croatia and Slovenia in January 1992 and to Muslim-dominated Bosnia and Herzegovina in August.

In addition, relations with Mexico (broken in 1861) were normalized in September 1992, following the deletion of anticlerical clauses from the country's 1917 constitution. As a result of the changes, the church was authorized to own property and operate schools, while priests and nuns were enfranchised and permitted to wear clerical garb in public. John Paul II had a special fondness for the country and visited it four times during his pontificate (1979, 1990, 1993, and 1999). On February 1, 1996, President Ernesto Zedillo became the first Mexican head of state to visit the Vatican. On October 18, 2001, President Vicente Fox, who was the first Mexican president to publicly confess Catholicism in 70 years, visited the Vatican. Benedict XVI also has good relations with Mexico. On June 4, 2007, he received Felipe Calderón, the president of Mexico, who has spoken out against the liberalization of Mexico's abortion laws, and who was the second president, after Vicente Fox, to address the plenary assembly of Mexican bishops. In May 2007 Benedict XVI traveled to Aparecida, Brazil, to address the Fifth General Conference of the Episcopate of Latin America and the Caribbean, where he discussed the impact of globalization and social inequality on Latin America. It also gave him the opportunity to meet with Brazilians in order to shore up the faith in a Catholic country that has seen many defections to evangelical Protestantism and New Age movements.

In 2009 antireligious sentiment grew in some countries of Latin America. On April 14 the home of Cardinal Julio Terrazas Sandoval, archbishop of Santa Cruz de la Sierra and president of the Bolivian bishops' conference, was bombed. Later in July the Bolivian president, Evo Morales, who was critical of Honduran archbishop Cardinal Oscar Rodriguez for not condemning the coup that removed President Manuel Zelaya of Honduras for power, asserted that certain bishops use prayer "as an anesthesia to put people to sleep." However, tensions subsequently relaxed, and on August 21, Bolivia and the Vatican signed the Treaty of Inter-Institutional Cooperation, which was meant to improve relations between the two states and reflect the important role the church plays in providing social services in Bolivia. Cardinal Terrazas signed the treaty on behalf of the Vatican.

The situation is Venezuela is worse; it was added to a list of counties where religious freedom is under threat, which was complied by the U.S. Commission on International Religious Freedom. A bomb had also been set off outside the apostolic nunciature (Vatican embassy) in February 2008. In November 2008 a church was covered with political slogans shortly before local elections. There was also an attempted takeover of a Catholic seminary in the state of Barinas during the campaign season. In addition, there were two tear gas attacks on the Vatican embassy within a two-week period in January and February 2009. In February 2009 supporters of President Hugo Chavez briefly occupied the archiepiscopal palace. In July a law as passed that barred religious education in schools, a practice that had been traditional in Venezuela, a predominately Catholic country. In August the Vatican replaced its apostolic nuncio (ambassador) with Archbishop Pietro PAROLIN, a diplomat with a great deal of experience, who, they hope, can cope with the difficult situation.

From March 17 to March 23, 2009 Pope Benedict visited Cameroon and Angola. He stated that he did not come as an expert on religious and economic affairs but as a man of God, a teacher, and religious educator. Throughout his visit he discussed topics that included peace, reconciliation, democracy, and human rights. Particularly noteworthy was his meeting in Llunda on women, where he lamented the adverse conditions to which women have been subjected and affirmed their right to "equal dignity." His comment that generated the most publicity, however, was made on the flight to Cameroon, when, in response to a journalist's question, he stated that AIDS "cannot be overcome by the distribution of prophylactics." This assertion created a great deal of controversy, even provoking the Belgian parliament to "condemn the unacceptable statements of the pope." The Vatican deplored the condemnation and maintained that it was an attempt to intimidate the pope from teaching the church's doctrine.

In September 1993 a senior member of the Vatican's Congregation for the Oriental Churches became the highest-ranking Catholic official to visit China since the Communist takeover in 1949. Ostensibly responding to an invitation to attend China's National Athletic Games, the emissary reportedly met with "government personalities" amid indications of a possible end to the lengthy estrangement. Further discussions took place between 1996 and 1998, but the Vatican's continuing recognition of the Taiwanese government has prevented normalization with Beijing. The Vatican has long been troubled by the existence of the Chinese Catholic Patriotic Association (CCPA), a Catholic organization that observers view as a creation of the Beijing government. Although it claims that it wants to maintain a "religious connection" with the Vatican, it rejects the pope's power to govern the Chinese Church, claiming that the Vatican's assertion of its authority in China amounts to political interference. The situation was exacerbated on November 30, 2006, when the CCPA had Father John Wang Renlei ordained bishop without Vatican approval. It was the third illicit ordination of the year. In a letter to the Chinese people dated May 27, 2007, Benedict XVI objected to ordination of bishops without the approval of the Vatican while maintaining that the Vatican had no desire to meddle in Chinese politics. On July 2, 2007, the Chinese government suppressed the letter, and mainland Catholic Web sites were ordered to remove it. In 2008 relations between the church and the Chinese government remained ambiguous. There were negotiations and hints about a papal visit to China, but nothing concrete emerged. In May the Shanghai Orchestra performed the Mozart "Requiem" at the Vatican. (Mozart is Benedict's favorite composer.) It was an event that would not have happened without the approval of the Chinese government, which in the same month forbade Chinese citizens from making pilgrimages to a Marian shrine near Shanghai on the Virgin Mary's feast day. Restrictions had not substantially loosened by 2009. In March Bishop Jia Zhiguo was arrested, for the thirteenth time, just as a Vatican commission established to study the church in China was meeting. In July the Vatican issued a summary of Benedict's 2007 letter in a question-and-answer format. It is hoped that the simplified form will make the document easier to understand. According the retired archbishop of Hong Kong, Cardinal Joseph Zen, some members of the underground church thought the letter encouraged them to come out into the open and merge with the state-approved church. The compendium was offered in both Chinese and English.

Cordial relations between the Vatican and Israel have gradually evolved during the past quarter-century. Pope John Paul II departed from tradition by strongly endorsing the Egyptian-Israeli peace treaty immediately prior to its signing in Washington in March 1979. In April 1986, in an act without recorded precedent, he was received by the chief rabbi of Rome at the city's central synagogue, where he condemned all forms of anti-Semitism and deplored the genocide inflicted on the Jewish people during World War II. In 1993 a meeting with the chief rabbi of Israel's Ashkenazi Jews—the first such event since the founding of the Jewish State in 1948—paved the way for a December 30 agreement on establishing formal Vatican-Israeli relations, effective June 15, 1994.

The Vatican had long opposed diplomatic ties because of questions regarding Israeli treatment of Palestinians, the rights of the church in the Holy Land, and the status of Jerusalem. The first of these concerns had been allayed by a September 1993 agreement between Israel and the Palestine Liberation Organization. A Vatican-Israeli agreement in 1997 granted autonomy to over 1,100 Catholic institutions and holy places while also placing them under state protection. Negotiations continue over freedom to clerics to travel to Israel and the rights of charitable and religious institutions to be exempted from Israeli taxation. Over the years the church has also shifted its position toward Jerusalem, supporting negotiation of an internationally enforceable statute to protect the city. That stance was included in a February 2000 agreement between the Vatican and the Palestinian National Authority that drew swift Israeli criticism.

In February 2000 John Paul II became the first pope to visit Egypt, and a month later he made the first pilgrimage to the Holy Land by a pope since 1964, visiting Jordan and Israel, including Palestinian-controlled Bethlehem, where he recognized the Palestinians' "natural right to a homeland." Later in the year, responding to the latest wave of Palestinian-Israeli violence, the Pontifical Council for Inter-Religious Dialogue rejected all "exclusive" claims to Jerusalem, noting that the city belongs "to the spiritual patrimony of humanity."

On May 5, 2009 Pope Benedict began an eleven-day trip to Jordan, the Palestinian territories, and Israel. The pope hoped to build better relations with Muslims and Jews, to defend the rights of Christians living in the Holy Land, and to encourage peace between Israel and her neighbors. During the trip he reiterated the Vatican's position that both Israelis and Palestinians have a right to their own states, and he also stressed that members of all three religions are children of Abraham and should show mutual respect for each other. The Vatican was pleased that King Abdullah of Jordan broke protocol to greet Benedict at the airport and also arrived unexpectedly on the banks of the Jordan River on May 10, to give the pope a tour. Prime Minister Benjamin Netanyahu also broke precedent and greeted the pontiff, along with President Shimon Peres, when Benedict arrived at the airport in Israel on May 11. Netanyahu was particularly pleased that Benedict acceded to his request to affirm Israel's right to exist in view of Iran's hostility, and was also at the airport when the pope departed on May 15. In his departing speech, the pontific alluded to an olive tree that President Peres and he planted in the garden of the presidential palace. He saw it as a metaphor for the whole trip, expressing his hope that demonstrations of mutual respect during the visit yield greater peace in the future.

In recent years the Vatican has taken an active interest in global affairs while maintaining its doctrinal opposition to "liberation theology." Pope Benedict XVI, then Cardinal Ratzinger, was considered a leader in that opposition. As head of the Congregation for the Doctrine of the Faith, Ratzinger silenced a number of well-respected liberal Catholic clergy and scholars. In early 1987, in its first attempt to address a global policy issue, the Pontifical Commission for Justice and Peace urged the rescheduling of third world debt, including total remission in "emergency situations." A subsequent wide-ranging papal encyclical deplored the widening gap between rich and poor nations and denounced the ideological rivalry between East and West as having subjected third world countries to imperialistic "structures of sin." In May 1988, during his ninth Latin American tour, John Paul II offered his "unconditional support and encouragement to the organizers of labor unions." In a May 1991 encyclical celebrating the 100th anniversary of Pope LEO XII's *Rerum Novarum,* which addressed working-class conditions at the end of the 19th century, John Paul II endorsed the free market as "the most efficient instrument for utilizing resources and effectively responding to needs." He added, however, that capitalism should be constrained by legal safeguards rooted in an "ethical and religious" conception of human freedom.

In January 1998 John Paul II made a highly publicized trip to Cuba, the only Latin American country that he had not previously visited. In addition to calling upon the government to introduce pluralism, he criticized the long-standing U.S. economic sanctions against Fidel Castro's regime as "unjust and ethically unacceptable." In early 1999, while visiting Mexico, he urged the massive throngs who attended his appearances to use their faith to battle government corruption. He also reemphasized his concern for the marginalization of the world's poor by the global effects of unfettered free-market activity.

On March 12, 2000, Pope John Paul II delivered a far-reaching but nonspecific apology for sins committed by Catholics, the church's "children," over the two preceding millennia. Without mentioning the Crusades, the Inquisition, or the Holocaust, church leaders cited such offenses as intolerance and discrimination against women, minorities, indigenous peoples, Jews, and the poor. The apology came two years after release of a long-awaited report from the Vatican on the role of the church during the Nazi era. Calling the official document an "act of repentance," the Vatican apologized for the failure of many Roman Catholics to protect Jews during the period. However, it defended the actions of Pope PIUS XII during World War II, claiming his silence regarding Nazi action was necessary to avoid further killings and permit behind-the-scenes assistance to Jews. Some Jewish leaders replied that the statement did not go far enough in addressing the perceived historic role of the church in fostering anti-Semitism.

Current issues. In his first encyclical, viewed as an inclusive and conciliatory message, issued on January 26, 2006, Pope Benedict XVI affirmed the importance of charity and love, including sexual intimacy, as fundamental expressions of Christian faith. During his first year in office, however, Benedict XVI mostly lived up to his reputation for conservatism in doctrinal matters, continuing his predecessor's affirmation of traditional teachings on such matters as papal primacy and infallibility, the exclusion of women from the priesthood (while at the same time acknowledging that the church has long marginalized and discriminated against women), and opposition to birth control and gay marriage.

From the first month of his pontificate Pope Benedict XVI spoke out forcefully against a proposed measure to legalize gay marriage in Spain, urging Catholics to work and vote against it. Nonetheless, it passed on July 30, 2005. During a trip to Spain in July 2006, the pope reiterated his stance that the marriage covenant is a "permanent bond" between a man and a woman and "a great good for all humanity." Benedict has also been very critical of the European Union's failure to mention Europe's Christian roots in its now moribund constitution. In March 2007 Benedict declared that Europe suffered from "a peculiar form of apostasy." The EU, in his opinion, describes itself as "a community of values," but it "seems to increasingly contest the existence of universal and absolute values." In the view of some Vatican pundits, the speech was "very harsh and very dark." In September 2008, the pope made a three-day visit to the Marian shrine of Lourdes and Paris. His reflection on the visit was upbeat, and he was pleased by the warm welcome he received, particularly by young people, in Paris. During the trip he encouraged the French to reflect not only on the need to protect freedom of conscience, but also on the valuable contributions that the church makes to a society. On September 17, two days after the pope's return to the Vatican, the Archbishop of Paris, Cardinal André Vingt-Trois, urged the French to consider an "open secularism," that would recognize the church's active role in society. His words seemed to echo those of French president Nicholas Sarkozy, who called for a "positive secularism" on a visit to Italy in 2007.

Since 2001 the Vatican has struggled to deal with the repercussions of a major scandal in the United States and elsewhere involving child sexual abuse by clergy and the institutional church's perceived long-standing indifference to the problem. On November 21, 2001, John Paul II voiced an apology to victims, and in January 2002 the Vatican issued new procedures for handling alleged abuse, including trying accused clergy in secret ecclesiastical courts, but without precluding civil and criminal action by secular authorities. In subsequent statements John Paul II called pedophilia "grievously evil" and, during a summit of all U.S. cardinals in Rome in April, both a crime and "appalling sin." Such statements did not, however, quell the outcry from much of the laity. Moreover, individual dioceses, which are generally responsible for their own financial affairs, faced millions of dollars in settlements to victims, and several were forced to file for bankruptcy protection. The Vatican's immunity from U.S. prosecution, under the Foreign Sovereign Immunity Act, was challenged in June 2006, when a U.S. district judge ruled that a lawsuit brought against the Vatican for allowing a priest who was a known child molester to be transferred from city to city could proceed. Pope Benedict XVI has shown ambivalence in this matter. One of his earliest acts as pope was to meet with Cardinal Bernard Francis Law, former archbishop of Boston, who had been forced to resign because of his lack of action against pedophile priests. But in May 2006 he asked the Rev. Marcial Maciel Degollado, founder of the conservative Legionaries of Christ and target of multiple molestation charges, to leave the ministry for a life of "prayer and penitence." In November 2005 Benedict XVI officially excluded from the priesthood candidates who support the "gay culture" or have "deep-seated homosexual tendencies," as well as those who are "actively homosexual." His condemnation of priests who are sexual predators has continued. On July 20, 2007, a member of the Congregation for the Doctrine of the Faith produced a pamphlet entitled "Pedophilia and the Priesthood," in which he called the abuse, "a crime against the most weak." In 2008 Benedict continued to confront the problem head-on by meeting with victims of abuse on his American visit in April and at World Youth Day in July in Sydney, Australia.

Benedict's five-day trip to Washington and New York in April 2008 was generally considered a success. His demeanor helped to soften an image that had been considered rigid, although he did not compromise his principles. He met with President George W. Bush and addressed the UN, stressing the need for religious freedom. In reviewing his trip after his return to Rome, the pope admired what he called the "healthy secularism" of the United States. He meant that religious values in the United States are not only tolerated but also understood as something fundamental to the spiritual life of the nation. The contrast with his views on religion in the EU was dramatic.

On June 10, 2009 Benedict received in audience President Barak OBAMA, who was in Italy to attend the G8 summit. The two discussed a number of issues relating to world politics and social justice. The pope gave the president a copy of his recently published encyclical, *Caritas in Vertitate* (Charity in Truth) and his pastoral letter *Dignitas Personae* (The Dignity of a Person), which discusses questions of bioethics, an area where the pope and president disagree. The director of the Vatican Press, Father Federico Lombardi declared that the presentation of the letter was "very significant." Yet the meeting seemed to have gone well, and the Vatican newspaper *L'Osservatore Romano* gave a positive assessment of the new U.S. president.

In April 2006 Pope Benedict XVI signaled a possible loosening of the Vatican's ban on all forms of artificial birth control by ordering a study of the use of condoms among people with AIDS and other infectious diseases. In November 2006 the report on condom use was submitted to the Congregation for the Doctrine of the Faith by Cardinal Javier Lozano BARRAGÁN, the president of the Pontifical Council for Health Care Ministry, who stated that the matter was now under the "special wisdom" of Benedict XVI. On May 10, 2008, however, the pope addressed an international congress convened to mark the fortieth anniversary of *Humanae Vitae*, the encyclical of PAUL VI that condemned artificial means of birth control. Benedict proclaimed, "The truth expressed in *Humanae Vitae* does not change." Responding to an advertisement calling for a change in the church's teaching that appeared in a Milan newspaper in July 2008, a Vatican spokesperson dismissed the complaints and reacted to one of the criticisms by stating, "Policies against AIDS based mainly on the distribution of condoms have largely failed."

In relations with the non-Catholic world Pope Benedict XVI has had a mixed record. He has been largely unsuccessful in improving Jewish-Catholic relations, despite the dramatic change in the church's attitude toward Jews, who have gone from being called "perfidious" in the old Good Friday service to being referred to as "our elder brothers" by John Paul II. As Cardinal Ratzinger, Benedict XVI had an important role in articulating a new theological position for the church toward Jews and other non-Catholics. However, observers depict him as a bookish scholar who lacks the political acumen of his predecessor. In May 2005 Benedict XVI met with the Israeli ambassador to the Vatican, promising to visit the main synagogue in Cologne, Germany, during his visit to the city for the August 2005 World Youth Day. Nevertheless, he was reproached for failing to mention Israel in a list of countries affected by terrorism. Benedict XVI came under further criticism from Jewish leaders when he failed to explicitly condemn anti-Semitism during a May 2006 visit to the Nazi death camp Auschwitz-Birkenau in Poland. The pope has lately shown greater sensitivity toward Jewish communities. His trip to the United States in April 2008 included a visit to the Park East synagogue in New York City.

In 2009 there was a temporary setback in Catholic-Jewish relations. Benedict lifted a ban on four bishops of Society of St. Pius X, a schismatic group that does not recognize the Second Vatican Council. But what the pope described as a "discreet gesture of mercy" soon turned into an 'unforeseen mishap for me." Unbeknownst to the pope, one of the bishops, Richard Williamson, had denied the mass murder of the Jews during World War II in an interview that he gave for Swedish television that was telecast shortly before the excommunication was lifted. Williamson's tepid apology, in which he seemed to be sorry only for offending people's sensibilities and not for factual errors, exacerbated the situation, although Williamson admitted that he is not a professional historian. The scandal strained the relationship between the Chief Rabbinate of Israel and the Vatican. Subsequently the pope denounced Holocaust deniers and wrote a letter that apologized for the errors that surrounded the event. On March 12, 2009 a delegation from the rabbinate met with the pope, and Rabbi Shear-Yashuv COHEN, the chief rabbi of Haifa, thanked the pope for "deploring Holocaust denial." In October

2008 Rabbi Cohen was invited to a synod of bishops on the Word of God. He was the first Jew to ever participate in a Catholic synod.

Papal relations with Islam have been more volatile during Benedict XVI's tenure. The most controversial event of Benedict XVI's pontificate thus far has been his speech at the University of Regensburg, given on September 13, 2006, in which he quoted a 14th-century Byzantine emperor, who claimed that Islam was "evil and inhuman." This characterization of Islam was an aside not relevant to the overarching theme of the speech, which was also highly critical of the West. However, the protest from the Islamic world was immediate and sporadically violent. The pope explained that he was only quoting a medieval source and not expressing his own opinion, but his apology did little to assuage the anger. Continued fallout from the speech threatened to sour Benedict XVI's visit to Turkey in November 2006, but he was warmly greeted by the Turkish prime minister at the airport and received favorable coverage on Turkish television. In April 2008 Benedict personally baptized a prominent Italian journalist who was born a Muslim. The Egyptian-born Magdi ALLAM, who is deputy director of the prestigious *Corriere della Sera*, was received into the church during the Easter Vigil Mass. There were no objections from Muslim dignitaries, and the incident has not generally damaged the Vatican's relations with the Islamic world

On July 7, 2009 Benedict issued a third encyclical, *Caritas in Veritate* (Charity in Truth). The first encyclical on social teaching in 20 years, it was issued to coincide with G8 summit in L'Aquila, Italy. The long encyclical is, in part, a response to the economic crisis that gripped the world for the last year. It covers wide range of economic justice issues, while also covering topics as disparate as the environment and abortion. The document is rooted in a sense of human solidarity that sees love and mutual respect as a basis for solving our individual and social predicaments, without fully endorsing capitalism or socialism. Perhaps the most controversial suggestion is its call for reforming the United Nations into a stronger institution that could protect the vulnerable nations of the developing world as well as regulate the world economic system, while recognizing national sovereignty.

THE ROMAN CURIA

[as of September 1, 2009]

Note: In addition to the bodies noted below, which have political and administrative functions relating to the Vatican as a state, there are numerous other bodies within the Curia with mainly ecclesiastical, theological, ecumenical, disciplinary, cultural, or pastoral functions, including congregations, tribunals, councils, commissions, and committees. The major bodies are referred to as dicasteries of the Roman Curia.

Secretariat of State

Secretary of State	Cardinal Tarcisio Bertone
Substitute for General Affairs	Archbishop Fernando Filoni
Secretary for Relations with States	Archbishop Dominique Mamberti
Member of the Secretariat of State	Archbishop Marco Dino Brogi
Member of the Secretariat of State	Archbishop Luigi Travaglino

Governatorate of Vatican City State

President	Cardinal Giovanni Lajolo
Secretary General	Archbishop Carlo Maria Vigano

COMMUNICATIONS

As the seat of the central organization of the Roman Catholic Church, Vatican City is also the center of a worldwide communications network and of a variety of publicity media directed to both Italian and international audiences. All publications and broadcasting are conducted under church auspices and generally reflect a clerical point of view, though with varying degrees of authority.

Press. *L'Osservatore Romano,* the semiofficial Vatican daily, and related publications are the principal media for Vatican comment on secular affairs; other publications are primarily concerned with ecclesiastical matters. In addition to *L'Osservatore Romano* (70,000), which also produces weekly editions in English, French, German, Italian, Portuguese, and Spanish, plus a monthly edition in Polish, the leading publications with secular content are the daily *Bollettino Sala Stampa della Santa Sede* (Bulletin of the Holy See Press Office) and the *Annuario Pontificio,* an official annual edited by the Central Statistics Office.

News agencies. The Vatican Information Service (VIS), of the Holy See Press Office, provides daily news in English, French, Italian, and Spanish. *Agenzia Internazionale Fides* (AIF) is a source for news of mission countries throughout the world.

Radio and television. Radio Vatican (*Radio Vaticana*), located in Vatican City and in Santa Maria di Galeria, outside Rome, broadcasts in about three-dozen modern languages and, for liturgical and related purposes, in Latin. A Vatican Television Center (*Centro Televisivo Vaticano*) was established in 1983 to produce and distribute religious programs; it also offers live broadcasts, mainly of events held at the Vatican, that are available to Catholic networks and other satellite links.

INTERGOVERNMENTAL REPRESENTATION

Apostolic Nuncio to the U.S.: Archbishop Pietro SAMBI.

U.S. Ambassador to the Holy See: Miguel Humberto DÍAZ.

Permanent Observer to the UN: Archbishop Celestino MIGLIORE.

IGO Memberships (Non-UN): Interpol, OSCE.

VENEZUELA

Bolivarian Republic of Venezuela
República Bolivariana de Venezuela

Political Status: Independence originally proclaimed in 1821 as part of Gran Colombia; independent republic established in 1830; federal constitutional system restored in 1958. Current constitution approved by referendum on December 15, 1999.

Area: 358,850 sq. mi. (916,445 sq. km.).

Population: 23,054,210 (2001C); 27,943,000 (2008E). The 2001 figure excludes an adjustment for underenumeration as well as 180,000 Amerindian jungle dwellers.

Major Urban Centers (2005E): CARACAS (2,073,768), Maracaibo (1,764,000), Valencia (1,325,000), Barquisimeto (893,000).

Official Language: Spanish.

Monetary Unit: Bolívar (official rate December 1, 2009: 2.14 bolívares fuertes = $1US).

President: Lt. Col. (Ret.) Hugo Rafael CHÁVEZ Frías (United Socialist Party of Venezuela); elected on December 6, 1998, and inaugurated on February 2, 1999, for a five-year term, succeeding Dr. Rafael CALDERA Rodríguez (National Convergence); reinaugurated by Constitutional Assembly on August 11, 1999; reelected to a new six-year term under the 1999 constitution on July 30, 2000; reelected on December 3, 2006, and reinaugurated for another six-year term on January 8, 2007.

Vice President: Col. (Ret.) Ramón CARRIZALEZ (United Socialist Party of Venezuela); appointed by the president on January 3, 2008, to succeed Jorge RODRÍGUEZ (United Socialist Party of Venezuela).

THE COUNTRY

Situated on the northern coast of South America between Colombia, Brazil, and Guyana, the Republic of Venezuela is made up of alternating mountainous and lowland territory drained, for the most part, by the Orinoco River and its tributaries. Two-thirds or more of the rapidly growing population, most of it concentrated in coastal and northern areas, is of mixed descent, the remainder being Caucasian, Negro, and Amerindian. Roman Catholicism is the dominant faith, but other religions are tolerated. Women constitute about one-third of the paid labor force, concentrated in the clerical and service sectors. Traditionally holding a small portion of elective offices, women were named to a number of high-level positions in the Pérez administration and constituted nearly one-third of appointees to the Chávez regime's Legislative Commission. In 2009, women held 29 seats in the 167-seat National Assembly, 7 out of 25 cabinet seats, the attorney general's position, and 10 of 32 Supreme Court judgeships.

One of the world's leading oil producers, Venezuela has one of the highest per capita incomes in Latin America, although national wealth is unevenly distributed. The industrial sector, which includes iron and natural gas, employs about one-fourth of the labor force and contributes 50 percent of GDP. By contrast, agriculture now accounts for only 5 percent of GDP; rice, corn, and beans are the principal subsistence crops, while coffee and cocoa are exported, along with some sugar, bananas, and cotton. Under government sponsorship Venezuela has been attempting to regain its historic position as a major stock-raising country, while diversification has become the keynote of economic planning, in part to reduce a dependence on oil sales.

During the boom years of the 1960s and 1970s Venezuelans earned a worldwide reputation for "conspicuous consumption"; subsequently, a period of negative growth (–5.3 percent from 1987 to 1989) threatened fiscal stability and necessitated stringent austerity measures that prompted widespread unrest and two attempted coups in 1992. Economic performance continued to be poor throughout the 1990s, a period during which the poverty rate reportedly rose to 80 percent, with "extreme poverty" in excess of 20 percent. GDP rose by 2.8 percent in 2001 but, amid widespread social unrest that included a petroleum workers' strike, declined by 8.9 percent in 2002 and by 9.2 percent in 2003. Then, in a remarkable reversal caused by surging oil prices and increased production in the non-oil sector, the index rose by 17.9 percent in 2004, before retreating to what remained a regional high of 9.0 percent in 2005. In 2006 the economy grew by another 10.3 percent, and 8.4 percent in 2007.

Oil has driven Venezuela's phenomenal growth rates in recent years. It accounted for about 90 percent of the country's export earnings, more than 50 percent of the central government budget revenues, and about 30 percent of GDP in 2006. Venezuela's proven oil reserves were 80 billion barrels in 2007, among the highest in the world. Production, however, has decreased from about 3.5 million barrels per day in 1999 to about 2.5 million barrels per day in 2007, according to the Organization of the Petroleum Exporting Countries (OPEC). Venezuelan oil revenues have fueled a dramatic increase in government spending, which increased 48 percent in 2006. This has resulted in a more equitable distribution of wealth, with government estimates showing the percent of population in poverty decreasing from more than 50 percent in 2003 to 33 percent in 2006. However, government spending has also aggravated inflation. Inflation was estimated at 30.4 percent in 2008, the highest rate in Latin America and the Caribbean. The IMF expected a similarly high rate of 29.4 percent in 2009. This view was bolstered by the wide disparity between official and unofficial exchange rates: as of late 2008, the exchange rate was fixed at about 2,150 bolívares to the dollar. On the black market, however, a dollar was widely reported to garner more than twice as many bolívares (5,200)—a consequence of high inflation. The Venezuelan government announced in early 2007 a plan to remove three zeroes from the currency and issue a "strong bolívar" (*bolívar fuerte*) in January 2008. This conversion was completed in 2009.

Unemployment and underemployment, meanwhile, remain stubbornly high; the government reported in March 2007 that 45 percent of the labor force continues to work in the informal sector, a figure that has not improved appreciably. GDP grew by 4.8 percent in 2008, but the IMF projected a 2 percent decline for 2009. In March 2009 reduced oil prices, combined with the effects of the global economic slowdown, forced President Chávez to announce a 6.7 percent cut in the government's budget for the year.

GOVERNMENT AND POLITICS

Political background. Homeland of Simón BOLIVAR, "the Liberator," Venezuela achieved independence from Spain in 1821 and became a separate republic in 1830. A history of political instability and lengthy periods of authoritarian rule culminated in the dictatorships of Gen. Juan Vicente GÓMEZ from 1908 to 1935 and Gen. Marcos PÉREZ Jiménez from 1952 to 1958, the interim being punctuated by unsuccessful attempts to establish democratic government. The ouster of Pérez Jiménez by a military-backed popular movement in January 1958 prepared the way for subsequent elected regimes.

The return to democratic rule was marked by the December 1958 election of Rómulo BETANCOURT, leader of the Democratic Action (AD) party and of the non-Communist Left in Latin America. Venezuela made considerable economic and political progress under the successive AD administrations of Betancourt (1959–1964) and Raúl LEONI (1964–1969), with Cuban-supported subversive efforts being successfully resisted. The election and inauguration of Dr. Rafael CALDERA Rodríguez of the Social Christian Party (COPEI) in 1969 further institutionalized the peaceful transfer of power. As the first Christian Democratic president in Venezuela and the second in Latin America (following Eduardo Frei Montalva of Chile), Caldera adhered to an independent pro-Western policy while seeking to "normalize" Venezuelan political life through such measures as legal recognition of the Communist Party, appeals to leftist guerrilla forces to lay down their arms, and the broadening of diplomatic contacts with both Communist and non-Communist regimes.

Caldera was succeeded by AD candidate Carlos Andrés PÉREZ following the election of December 1973, which was highlighted by challenges from the rightist Nationalist Civic Crusade of former dictator Pérez Jiménez and the New Force, an alliance of left-wing parties. Following his inauguration in March 1974, President Pérez focused on plans to equalize distribution of Venezuela's substantially increased petroleum revenue.

In a minor upset at the election of December 1978, COPEI presidential candidate Luis HERRERA Campíns defeated AD candidate Luis PIÑERUA Ordaz. The two parties won an identical number of elective seats in both houses of Congress, but the AD secured a one-member plurality in the Senate because of a seat constitutionally reserved for outgoing President Pérez.

Capitalizing on disillusionment with COPEI's inability to halt declining oil revenue, the AD won 50 percent of the vote in the election of December 4, 1983, COPEI polling less than 30 percent; AD presidential candidate Jaime LUSINCHI defeated former president Caldera and six other candidates and was inaugurated on February 2, 1984.

Although economic conditions steadily worsened during the ensuing five years, Carlos Pérez became, on December 4, 1988, the first Venezuelan president to be elected for a second term; the AD, on the other hand, lost its congressional majorities, winning only 23 of 49 elective seats in the Senate and 97 of 201 seats in the Chamber of Deputies.

Following his inauguration in February 1989 Pérez launched an "economic shock program" that included the elimination of price and wage controls, in addition to the deregulation of interest and exchange rates. The result was skyrocketing unemployment and inflation. On February 27, 1989, days of looting and intense street violence, known as the "*Caracazo*," erupted following a jump in transport costs; the official death toll from the mayhem was 276 but was believed to be several times higher. The violence was followed by voter apathy: in December 1989 only 30 percent of eligible voters took part in the first-ever gubernatorial and mayoral elections.

On February 4, 1992, the president escaped assassination during an abortive coup by junior officers, including a prominent paratrooper named Hugo CHÁVEZ, which included an attack on his official residence. In mid-May legislative members of both leading parties announced a draft bill to cut short Pérez's term by one year, but in early June COPEI withdrew from the effort, citing a fear that it would trigger a coup. On June 11 COPEI's two representatives resigned from the "National Unity" government they had joined only three months before, and on June 29, in accepting the resignations of 11 cabinet members, Pérez implemented a previously announced plan to slash cabinet-rank personnel by two-thirds. Despite a second major coup attempt on November 27, state and local elections were held on December 6, at which the AD lost further ground.

In March 1993 the attorney general applied to the Supreme Court for a ruling as to whether President Pérez should be charged with the embezzlement of $17 million in state funds that the chief executive said had been expended for secret security and defense purposes, but that opponents insisted had been diverted to campaign and other nonofficial uses. After the court responded in the affirmative, the Senate on May 21 suspended the president, who was constitutionally succeeded, on an interim basis, by the Senate president, Octavio LEPAGE, on May 22. On June 5 the Congress named a highly respected, pro-AD independent, Sen. Ramón José VELASQUEZ, to complete the final eight months of the Pérez presidency.

On December 5, 1993, former president Caldera, who had been expelled from COPEI in June for refusing to support its presidential candidate, Oswaldo ALVAREZ Paz, was elected to a second term as the nominee of a recently organized, 17-party National Convergence (CN) coalition. Although credited with only 30.5 percent of the vote, he was but one contender in a record field of 18.

On June 24, 1994, in the face of continued economic and political problems that had sparked rumors of a possible coup, President Caldera adopted wide-ranging powers that included a suspension of six constitutional guarantees. On July 21 Congress voted to restore five of the guarantees, leaving in place a limitation on freedom of economic activity. Among the financial difficulties was a liquidity crisis that resulted in a total of 13 banks being brought under state control by mid-August.

Although no respite from the recession was evident, President Caldera suspended his remaining emergency powers on July 6, 1995, promulgating instead a financial emergency law that authorized him to intervene in the economy without having to abrogate constitutional rights. Nonetheless, at year's end what economists termed "an honorable and reasonable agreement" for assistance from the International Monetary Fund (IMF) remained elusive.

Considerable social unrest preceded the accord finally concluded with the International Monetary Fund in April 1996, which called for accelerated privatization and flotation of the bolívar. Thereafter, on May 30, the Supreme Court handed down a guilty verdict against former president Pérez, who was, however, released from 28 months of detention on September 19 and then returned to the political arena by campaigning successfully for his old Senate seat in November 1998.

On December 8, 1998, the February 1992 coup leader, Hugo Chávez Frías, gained an impressive victory in presidential balloting over Henrique SALAS Römer, the nominee of both traditional rival parties, with former beauty queen Irene SÁEZ a distant third. Following his election, Chávez pledged to pursue constitutional revision to lay "the foundations of a new republic," and at a Constituent Assembly poll on July 25, 1999, candidates from his Patriotic Pole coalition won 121 of 128 contested seats.

The Assembly created a "judicial emergency commission" to restructure the nation's court system on August 19, 1999, and on August 30 stripped the opposition-controlled Congress of its remaining powers. The Assembly then drafted a new basic law (see below), which was approved by 71.2 percent of the participants in a December 15 referendum.

At its concluding session on January 30, 2000, the Constituent Assembly named its president, Chávez's political mentor Luis MIQUILENA, to head a transitional National Legislative Commission, pending the election of a National Assembly on May 28. However, the balloting was subsequently postponed for technical reasons until July 30, when President Chávez was elected to a new six-year term and his Fifth Republic Movement (*Movimiento Quinta República*—MVR) and its allies won a majority of the 165 seats in the new National Assembly.

In November 2000 Chávez secured legislative approval of an enabling law granting him decree powers for a year. Further enhancing his power was voter approval of rigid labor controls in a December 3 referendum. Having already alienated organized labor, Chávez exacerbated a growing rift with the military leadership in February 2001 by naming a longtime associate, José Vicente RANGEL, as Venezuela's first civilian minister of defense. In June, in an effort to consolidate his support among leftists and the poor, he authorized formation at the neighborhood level of Bolivarian Circles (*Círculos Bolivarianos*) committed to advancement of the "Bolivarian revolution."

On November 13, 2001, using his decree powers, President Chávez promulgated 49 laws involving economic, financial, infrastructural, and social policies. The most controversial measures permitted expropriation of underutilized farmland, in the name of an "agrarian revolution," and required that joint hydrocarbon ventures include majority government participation. Oil royalties were also increased. In response, the Venezuelan Federation of Chambers of Commerce and Industry (*Federación Venezolana de Cámaras y Asociaciones de Comercio y Producción—Fedecámaras*), supported by the country's largest labor union group, the Venezuelan Workers' Confederation (*Confederación de Trabajadores de Venezuela*—CTV), announced that it would mount a nationwide one-day strike in December.

In March 2002 managerial staff of the state petroleum company, *Petróleos de Venezuela* (PDVSA), with support from the industry's union, the *Federación de Trabajadores Petroleros* (*Fedepetrol*), began a job action, which was followed on April 9 by a general strike organized by the CTV and *Fedecámaras*. Two days later, with 150,000 anti-Chávez protesters massed outside the presidential palace, more than a dozen demonstrators were killed by gunfire from, apparently, members of the Bolivarian Circles.

On April 12, 2002, senior military officers, led by Gen. Luis RINCON, the armed forces commander, announced that Chávez had resigned, although it quickly became apparent that a coup had been mounted against him. With Chávez in custody, the military named Pedro CARMONA, president of *Fedecámaras*, as provisional president. Acting by decree, Carmona attempted to dissolve the National Assembly and the Supreme Court and to suspend the constitution, but wide popular support for the government takeover failed to materialize as advocates of democracy joined Chávez loyalists in the streets. Carmona subsequently resigned, and on April 13 the National Assembly elevated Vice President Diosdado CABELLO to the presidency. Cabello, in turn, returned the presidency to Chávez on April 14. (In 2009, Cabello was serving as the Chávez government's minister of public works.)

In late 2002 and early 2003 major business and labor sectors staged a general strike over several months that crippled the economy, severely reducing oil production. In the end, the strike's proponents found themselves forced to call off the action in the face of rising public anger.

In 2003 the opposition was nonetheless confident that it could remove Chávez by means of a popular referendum, campaigning for which was launched on November 21. Although surviving a court challenge to petition signatures, the recall ballot on August 26, 2004, was endorsed by only 40.7 percent of participating voters. The president and his allies were further strengthened on October 31 by winning 20 of 23 state governorships (15 of which had been held by *antichavistas*), as well as the mayoralty of Caracas. With opposition parties boycotting the election of December 4, 2005, Chávez loyalists won unanimous control of the National Assembly.

Despite the opposition's collective endorsement of Zulia state governor Manuel ROSALES under the New Time (*Un Nuevo Tiempo*—UNT) banner, Chávez nonetheless beat Rosales in December 2006 by a 62 to 37 percent margin in voting that was internationally judged to be free and fair. No other candidate received more than 0.04 percent of the vote. On January 8, 2007, just before being reinaugurated, Chávez replaced nearly every minister in his cabinet and named a new vice president, former National Electoral Council president Jorge RODRÍGUEZ, to succeed José Vicente Rangel.

Another cabinet shakeup occurred on January 3–4, 2008, with the naming of a new vice president, retired Col. Ramón CARRIZALEZ, and nine new ministers. In November 23, 2008, municipal and gubernatorial elections, candidates from President Chávez's **United Socialist Party of Venezuela** (*Partido Socialista Unido de Venezuela*—PSUV) won 17 of 23 governorships, a slightly weaker showing than 2004. The opposition won nearly 48 percent of the total votes cast, the governorships of the three most populous states, and the mayoral races in Caracas and Maracaibo.

Following President Chávez's quick triumph in a February 2009 constitutional referendum to abolish term limits (see Constitution and government, below), he reshuffled the cabinet, consolidating some ministries and giving vice president Carrizalez the additional post of defense minister. The *Washington Post* noted that President Chávez controlled "the Supreme Court, the lower courts, the state oil company, the armed forces, and all investigative and oversight agencies, including the attorney general's office." The legislative branch, due to the lopsided 2005 vote, also remained under the president's solid control.

In September 2009, Chávez restructured the Council of Ministers, giving six cabinet ministers the additional title of "vice president" with responsibility for broader policy issues. Vice President Carrizalez assumed the title of first vice president in a structure that bears resemblance to Cuba's Council of Ministers.

Constitution and government. Under its constitution of January 23, 1961, Venezuela was designated a federal republic that now encompasses 23 states (the newest, Vargas, created with effect from January 1, 1999), a Federal District, and 72 Federal Dependencies (islands in the Antilles). Executive power was vested in a president who was elected by universal suffrage for a five-year term and until mid-1992 (when a one-term ban was imposed on all future incumbents) could be reelected after a ten-year interval. The legislative body (Congress of the Republic) consisted of a Senate and a Chamber of Deputies, both elected by universal suffrage for five-year terms concurrent with that of the president. The states were administered by popularly elected governors; had their own elected, unicameral legislative assemblies; and were divided into county-type districts with popularly elected mayors and municipal councils.

Among the numerous changes introduced by the 1999 basic law, the presidential term was extended to six years with the possibility of one immediate renewal; executive authority vis-à-vis the economy was substantially enhanced; the bicameral legislature was abandoned in favor of a unicameral National Assembly; public administration was drastically reorganized; oil production was to remain vested in the state; the rights of indigenous peoples were affirmed; and the country was renamed *República Bolivariana de Venezuela* in honor of the independence hero.

In May 2004 President Chávez secured passage of a bill enlarging the Supreme Court from 20 to 32 members, a step seen by the opposition as "stacking" the court with pro-Chávez justices.

In 2007 President Chávez introduced a new package of constitutional reforms, which critics portrayed as an attempt to concentrate power in the presidency. These reforms included permitting indefinite presidential reelection, empowering the president to declare extended states of emergency, reducing the central bank's autonomy, redefining property rights, and establishing a six-hour workday, among several others. The reforms won quick approval in Venezuela's Congress, all of whose representatives come from pro-Chávez parties. In a December 2, 2007, referendum, however, Venezuelans rejected them by a margin of roughly 51 to 49 percent. The result was brought about by a 44 percent abstention rate and opposition from several leaders usually supportive of Chávez. Opposition leaders cheered the outcome, but President Chávez indicated that he would attempt to implement the measures at a later time, whether through a referendum or by other means. He began to do so in October 2008, when the National Assembly approved a bill establishing a "Geometry of Powers." This measure, among the reforms rejected in the 2007 referendum, allowed the president to appoint officials, popularly referred to as "viceroys," empowered to carry out most of the functions of elected mayors and governors, effectively supplanting them. The president soon used this measure to weaken opposition leaders of local governments.

At the president's behest, the National Assembly approved a February 15, 2009, constitutional amendment referendum to remove the two-term limit on the president, mayors, governors and National Assembly members. The measure passed by a vote of 54.9 percent in favor to 45.1 percent opposed. Venezuela now has no term limits on reelection.

State and Capital	*Area (sq. mi.)*	*Population (2010E)*
Amazonas (Puerto Ayacucho)	69,550	146,000
Anzoátegui (Barcelona)	16,720	1,503,000
Apure (San Fernando)	29,540	485,000
Aragua (Maracay)	2,710	1,689,000
Barinas (Barinas)	13,590	774,000
Bolívar (Ciudad Bolívar)	91,890	1,566,000
Carabobo (Valencia)	1,800	2,264,000
Cojedes (San Carlos)	5,710	306,000
Delta Amacuro (Tucupita)	15,520	157,000
Falcón (Coro)	9,580	919,000
Guárico (San Juan)	25,090	759,000
Lara (Barquisimeto)	7,640	1,824,000
Mérida (Mérida)	4,360	860,000
Miranda (Los Teques)	3,070	2,905,000
Monagas (Maturín)	11,160	873,000
Nueva Esparta (La Asunción)	440	444,000
Portuguesa (Guanare)	5,870	890,000
Sucre (Cumaná)	4,560	931,000
Táchira (San Cristóbal)	4,290	1,198,000
Trujillo (Trujillo)	2,860	724,000
Vargas (La Guaira)	580	335,000
Yaracuy (San Felipe)	2,740	610,000
Zulia (Maracaibo)	24,360	3,688,000
Federal District		
(Caracas)	170	2,090,000

Foreign relations. A member of the United Nations and its related agencies, the Organization of Petroleum Exporting Countries (OPEC), the Organization of American States (OAS), the Latin American Integration Association, the Union of South American Nations (UNASUR), and other hemispheric organizations, Venezuela was traditionally aligned with the West in both inter-American and world affairs. During the presidencies of Betancourt and Leoni, it was subjected by the Cuban regime of Fidel Castro to repeated propaganda attacks and armed incursions. Although it consequently took a particularly harsh line toward Cuba, it was equally critical of right-wing dictatorships in the Americas and for some years refused to maintain diplomatic relations with governments formed as a result of military coups. This policy was modified during the 1960s by the establishment of diplomatic relations with Argentina, Panama, and Peru as well as with Czechoslovakia, Hungary, the Soviet Union, and other Communist countries, while in December 1974, despite earlier differences, a normalization of relations with Cuba was announced.

A long-standing territorial claim to the section of Guyana west of the Essequibo River has caused intermittent friction with that country, Venezuela declining in June 1982 to renew a 12-year moratorium on unilateral action in the dispute and subsequently refusing to sanction submission of the controversy to the International Court of Justice. In September 1999 the issue was revived by the Venezuelan foreign minister, who rejected the century-old award to the former UK dependency.

A Venezuelan claim to tiny Bird Island (*Isla de Aves*) to the west of Dominica has periodically strained relations with Caribbean neighbors. While the island, on which Venezuela is reportedly constructing a scientific station, is of little intrinsic importance, the Organization of Eastern Caribbean States (OECS) has expressed concern that it might serve as the basis of a claim by Caracas to a 200-mile-wide exclusive economic zone.

For more than three decades Caracas has been engaged in a dispute with Colombia regarding sovereignty over the Gulf of Venezuela (Gulf of Guajira), with tension escalating to the level of high military alert following the unauthorized intrusion of a Colombian ship into Venezuelan territorial waters in August 1988. Other disagreements have arisen over the smuggling of foodstuffs, drug trafficking, and alleged attacks by Colombia's guerrilla and paramilitary groups on the Venezuelan national guard and Venezuelan citizens. Over the years the two countries have concluded a number of agreements aimed at combating drug traffickers, but an "open border" has made interdiction of drug shipments difficult.

The Chávez government's ties with the United States have deteriorated steadily, with some of the first problems brought about by an August 2000 visit by President Chávez to Iraq (the first by a head of state since the first Gulf war), a visit to Caracas by Fidel Castro in late October, the conclusion of a military cooperation treaty with Russia in May 2001, and subsequent criticism of the U.S. bombing of Afghanistan as "fighting terror with terror." Relations worsened following the failed April 2002 coup attempt, which Chávez insists occurred with strong U.S. backing and support.

In December 2004 Chávez embarked on a tour of countries viewed as potential buyers of Venezuelan oil, including the People's Republic of China. Earlier, Venezuela concluded an agreement with Cuba to supply Havana with cut-rate oil in return for a medical assistance program valued at over $750 million. Venezuela has been Cuba's closest ally during the 2000s, with President Chávez the only foreign leader routinely granted audiences with the Castro brothers.

A major rupture in Colombian-Venezuelan relations followed Colombian security forces' abduction from Caracas of Rodrigo Granda, a Colombian citizen considered to be the "foreign minister" of Colombia's largest guerrilla group, the Revolutionary Armed Forces of Colombia (FARC), in early 2005. High-level tensions continued to simmer as top Colombian officials, including Defense Minister Juan Manuel Santos, accused Venezuela of harboring and assisting Colombian guerrillas on Venezuelan territory. For his part, Chávez continued to be an ardent critic of "Plan Colombia" and other U.S. programs in the Andes. Venezuela also objected to Colombia's decision to grant asylum to Pedro Carmona, who was briefly named to Venezuela's presidency during the abortive April 2002 coup.

Venezuela's relations with Peru soured in 2006, when Chávez openly endorsed Peruvian presidential candidate Ollanta Humala. Humala did not win, in part because opponents, including the eventual victor, Alán García, portrayed him as a Chávez puppet. Relations between Chávez and García have remained rocky, as García government officials have demanded investigations into possible Venezuelan support of the Bolivarian Alternative for Latin America (ALBA) movement, a political and social-service network that has opened numerous offices throughout Peru.

A similar election-year dynamic that year damaged relations between Venezuela and Mexico, with Chávez and Mexican president Vicente Fox engaging in a series of bitter verbal exchanges. Relations with Fox's successor, Felipe Calderón, have improved somewhat, and Venezuela sent an ambassador to Mexico City in September 2007.

The Chávez government's most notable foreign policy embarrassment came in fall 2006, when it failed to win a nonpermanent seat for Venezuela on the UN Security Council. After 47 rounds of voting, neither Venezuela nor U.S.-backed Guatemala was able to win the two thirds of General Assembly votes necessary to fill the seat normally reserved for a Latin American country. The position eventually went to a compromise country, Panama.

In August and September 2007, relations with Colombia appeared to improve as President Uribe invited Chávez to facilitate possible peace and prisoner-exchange dialogues with the FARC. However, relations hit perhaps their lowest point in a century after Uribe abruptly "fired" Chávez from this role on November 22, 2007. The two leaders engaged in months of name-calling.

South America's worst security crisis in decades was triggered by a March 1, 2008, Colombian raid into Ecuadorian territory that killed Raúl Reyes, one of the FARC's most senior leaders. In response to what he viewed as a serious violation of Ecuador's sovereignty, Chávez warned Colombia that he would respond to a similar operation in Venezuela with fighter jets, and ordered his military to deploy ten tank battalions—about 9,000 troops—to Venezuela's border with Colombia. The threat of hostilities was defused by a March 7 meeting of the region's leaders in Santo Domingo, at which the leaders agreed to reinstate their ambassadors.

Tensions remained very high, however, as files recovered from Reyes' computer appeared to indicate that guerrilla leaders and high Venezuelan government officials had been discussing the possibility of material support for the FARC's cause. While Venezuela denied any wrongdoing and challenged the files' authenticity, Chávez's Colombia rhetoric toned down substantially over the following months. On June 8 Chávez surprised nearly all observers by publicly calling on the FARC to release all of their hostages and to abandon the armed struggle. Tensions with Colombia did not flare up again for the remainder of 2008.

The volume of U.S. criticism toward the Chávez government increased in 2008 as tensions grew between Venezuela and Colombia, a close U.S. ally. In March 2008 President George W. Bush said that Venezuela's "agenda amounts to little more than empty promises and a thirst for power. It has squandered its oil wealth in an effort to promote its hostile, anti-American vision." In the 2008 U.S. presidential campaign, Republican candidate John McCain repeatedly attacked his opponent, Democrat Barack Obama, for expressing willingness to meet with Chávez.

On September 11, 2008, after Bolivia expelled its U.S. ambassador, Venezuela declared U.S. Ambassador Patrick Duddy *persona non grata* in an act of "solidarity." The U.S. government responded in kind, expelling Ambassador Bernardo Álvarez. A few days later, the U.S. Treasury Department added Ramón Rodríguez Chacín, who had just vacated his post as Venezuela's interior minister, to its list of major international narcotrafficking figures, citing indications of links to Colombia's FARC that appeared on recovered guerrilla computers. In 2008, meanwhile, the U.S. Justice Department prosecuted four Venezuelan men in a Miami court for acting as unregistered agents of the Venezuelan government. The men were involved in a 2007 delivery to Buenos Aires of a suitcase containing $800,000 that, prosecutors contend, was to support the campaign of Argentine President Cristina Fernández de Kirchner.

The U.S. government has placed several sets of sanctions on Venezuela for failing to cooperate on initiatives against drugs and terrorism, and for violating religious freedom, making it impossible for Caracas to receive U.S. aid or to purchase weapons with U.S.-made components.

Despite these irritants, commercial ties between the United States and Venezuela have never been closer, thanks to the U.S. demand for oil. Trade between the United States and Venezuela increased from $40 billion in 2005 to $50 billion in 2006. In 2006 Venezuela exported 60 percent of its oil to the United States, which accounted for 11 percent of U.S. oil imports. In 2008 Venezuela was the United States' fourth-largest source of imported oil, after Canada, Saudi Arabia, and Mexico.

Venezuela has been an intense competitor with the United States for influence in the region. In August 2007 the Associated Press estimated that, in the first eight months of the year, Chávez had pledged grants and loans to the rest of the hemisphere totaling $8.8 billion. The United States, by comparison, granted and loaned about $3 billion per year to the hemisphere during the mid-2000s. Some analysts see Chávez using oil largesse to form a "bloc" of countries governed by elected leftist leaders.

In October 2008, the Venezuelan government ejected two researchers from Human Rights Watch, a prominent U.S.-based non-governmental organization, from the country. The move earned a sharp rebuke from the European Parliament. That month, the Government Accountability Office, the independent auditing arm of the U.S. Congress, issued a report criticizing Venezuela for its failure to prevent its territory from being used by narcotraffickers. The Venezuelan official reaction was one of outrage and rejection of U.S. drug policy.

Beyond Latin America, President Chávez has sought warmer relations with countries that are generally cool to the United States. A September 2008 visit to China resulted in a host of new investment agreements, including increased Chinese access to Venezuelan oil. Ties with Russia have warmed significantly, with arms purchases from Moscow totaling about $7 billion between 2005 and 2009. Russia sent two long-range strategic bombers on a visit to Venezuela in September 2008, one month after fighting erupted in Georgia. Venezuela is one of the only countries in the world to recognize the breakaway Georgian regions of Abkhazia and South Ossetia. The two countries held a joint naval exercise in the Caribbean in November 2008. In 2009, Venezuela announced still more arms purchases from Russia, including a fleet of tanks and help from the Medvedev government in establishing a nuclear energy program.

President Chávez offered more conciliatory language to incoming U.S. president Barack Obama in early 2009. The two presidents sustained cordial public exchanges when their paths crossed at the April

2009 Summit of the Americas in Trinidad and Tobago. In June, the two countries reinstated their ambassadors. This slight warming occurred despite the April release of a State Department report alleging that the Chávez government's "ideological sympathy" with Colombian guerrillas "limited Venezuelan co-operation with Colombia in combating terrorism," and despite an early July interview granted to the opposition-leaning Globovisión television network by Secretary of State Hillary Clinton.

Venezuela's already rocky relations with Peru meanwhile sank further in April 2009, as the government of Alán García granted asylum to President Chávez's chief political rival, Maracaibo mayor and former presidential opponent Manuel Rosales. Venezuelan authorities had ordered Rosales's arrest on corruption charges widely viewed as a pretext to weaken the opposition (see Current issues, below).

The first half of 2009 saw Venezuela's relations with Colombia improve. Presidents Chávez and Uribe met in January 2009, pledging greater economic cooperation to weather the global recession. In April Chávez, speaking at a joint press conference with Uribe, again called on the FARC guerrillas to negotiate and plan to disband.

Progress in relations with the United States and Colombia halted in mid-July 2009, when Colombian media revealed that Bogotá was to allow U.S. military personnel to use seven military bases on Colombian soil. Chávez responded by "freezing" relations with Colombia. The Uribe government parried by revealing that it had recovered several Swedish-made rocket launchers from the FARC that had originated in Venezuela. Arguing that the launchers had disappeared from Venezuela's arsenal before he became president, Chávez recalled his ambassador, announced plans to cut deeply Venezuela's $7 billion in annual trade with Colombia and to expropriate Colombian businesses in Venezuela, and obtained a $2.2 billion line of credit for new arms purchases from Russia. Tensions increased following the U.S.-Colombia defense agreement's October 30 signing, as Chávez instructed the Venezuelan military to "prepare for war" with Colombia.

Chávez also cultivated closer ties with Iran, a process that most visibly began when President Mahmoud Ahmadinejad visited Caracas in January and November 2007. Chávez visited Teheran in April 2009 and again in September 2009, when he became one of the first foreign leaders to visit following the Ahmadinejad government's June crackdown on protests of alleged electoral fraud. The leaders discussed sales of Venezuelan uranium for Iran's nuclear program. The September visit to Iran was part of a so-called "rogue states" tour that also took Chávez to Libya, Syria, Algeria, Turkmenistan, and Belarus, as well as Russia and Spain. Ahmadinejad paid a visit to Venezuela during a November 2009 tour that also took him to Brazil and Bolivia.

Current issues. President Chávez issued a decree in January 2005 to speed up a land reform process that had lagged since its inception in late 2001. As of early 2007, 1.9 million hectares (4.7 million acres) of land had been redistributed.

Having failed to oust Chávez in the 2004 referendum, the leading opposition parties boycotted the December 2005 legislative balloting. The result was a 75 percent abstention rate, and an Assembly with almost no opposition representation. The administration advanced proposals for a constitutional change that permitted Chávez to run, successfully, for a third term on December 3, 2006. The fractious opposition had united behind a single candidate, endorsing Manuel Rosales of the UNT. Instead of assailing the president's popular economic reform programs, Rosales attacked Chávez for weakening checks on presidential power, doing little to combat corruption, presiding over rising crime and insecurity, and failing to maintain basic infrastructure.

Following his January 2007 re-inauguration, Chávez began to take Venezuela in a markedly more radical direction toward "21st Century Socialism," obtaining from the National Assembly a second "enabling law" allowing him to rule by decree for 18 months, which the opposition derided as a "blank check." Though he suffered a setback with the December 2007 constitutional reform referendum, the president managed to push through a host of reforms through other means, including decrees and laws that easily passed the Assembly.

By May 2007, the government had increased its ownership share in the country's main telecommunications company (CANTV, which was more than one-quarter owned by U.S. telecom giant Verizon), the Caracas electricity company, and oil fields in the Orinoco basin of eastern Venezuela. Nationalizations in many sectors, from banks to energy to hotels, continued in 2008 and 2009.

In the name of increasing "participatory democracy," Chávez moved to increase the funding of "community councils," citizen groups accountable to the presidency that are increasingly taking functions away from local governments. Civil-military relations were roiled by a new requirement that soldiers salute with the slogan "fatherland, socialism, or death." An April 9, 2008, decree began the consolidation of 126 regional or municipal police forces into a single national force. Chávez meanwhile moved to eliminate "any vestige of autonomy" from Venezuela's central bank, placing monetary policy under presidential control.

The president's 18-month decree authority expired on July 31, 2008. On that day, Chávez issued 26 decrees. These included a restoration of the "Geometry of Power" proposal for central control over states and municipalities, which had been defeated in the December 2007 referendum. Also controversial was the creation of a "National Reserve" outside the military chain of command and reporting directly to the president, ostensibly to form the vanguard of resistance to invasion by a foreign power. Another decree increased the state's ability to regulate the production, distribution, import, and export of food.

Chávez has also incurred criticism for restraining independent media. On May 27, 2007, the government refused to renew the broadcast license of Venezuela's most-watched television network, Radio Caracas Television (RCTV), which had frequently criticized the president's policies. The administration justified the closure of RCTV, which inspired a week of large-scale street protests, on the grounds that the network supported the April 2002 coup attempt. The television frequency previously occupied by RCTV was given to a state-sponsored channel, TVes. As of mid-2009, only one major opposition television station remained on the air: Globovisión, a 24-hour news network. The previously critical Venevisión network toned down its coverage significantly after the 2002 coup attempt.

While the president's popularity remained high, the oil-fueled economy showed signs of overheating, as staple items disappeared from stores to be resold abroad or on the black market in response to government price controls. World oil prices, which reached $140 per barrel in July 2008, plummeted to $60 by October. The price slide, as well as the U.S. financial collapse and economic slowdown, have had an impact on Venezuela's economy and government revenue, with negative GDP growth and budget cuts both announced in mid-2009.

In February 2008 Venezuela's pro-Chávez comptroller-general, citing corruption and misuse of funds, banned 272 individuals, nearly all of them opposition politicians, from contesting municipal and state gubernatorial elections later in the year. As the November 23 election day approached, polls nonetheless indicated a close contest, with Chávez promising special development funds only to jurisdictions that elect progovernment candidates and accusing the opposition of seeking office "in order to launch a coup next year." The opposition still made small but significant gains at the polls. It owed its modest success to concerns about democratic checks and balances, shortages and inflation, and public security, which has steadily worsened as the government has failed to reduce common crime. Venezuela's murder rate has tripled since 1999, to 48 per 100,000 in 2007, the second-highest in the world after El Salvador. Kidnappings have also been on the rise, especially in states that border Colombia.

As polling for the November 2008 local elections showed the opposition gaining ground, President Chávez increased pressure on the opposition. In October he warned that if the opposition were to win Zulia, the oil-producing home state of Manuel Rosales, its capital, Maracaibo, would become the "epicenter" of a U.S.-supported insurgency, forcing him "to take action, even military," against them. Chávez also accused Rosales of financing a conspiracy to assassinate him.

Judicial and legal attacks on the opposition intensified in 2009. Rosales fled the country rather than face arrest, gaining asylum in Peru on April 28, following several days as a fugitive. On April 2 retired Gen. Raúl Isaías BADUEL, President Chávez's former defense minister and erstwhile ally turned vocal critic, was arrested at gunpoint, charged with corruption, and jailed. That month Antonio LEDEZMA, the opposition mayor of Caracas elected in November, saw most of his power and budgetary authority stripped as Chávez, using the new "Geometry of Power" authority, appointed Jacqueline FARÍA, the former head of the state-owned mobile telephone company, to head a parallel government as the central government's "viceroy" for Caracas.

Nationalizations of key industries proceeded apace in 2009, with a gas compression plant, steel and iron companies, a pasta factory, and the Bank of Venezuela passing into government hands. In May, the National Assembly approved a law giving the state dominion over all "goods and services connected to primary hydrocarbon activities."

In August 2009 the government and opposition clashed over the promulgation of a new education law making "Bolivarian Doctrine" the guiding principle of education and reducing the autonomy of universities. The law also includes punishments for media reporting that "causes terror in children, incites hatred, or attacks the Venezuelan people's values or the population's mental and physical health."

POLITICAL PARTIES

Presidential Party:

United Socialist Party of Venezuela (*Partido Socialista Unido de Venezuela*—PSUV). Before the 2000 election, a Patriotic Pole (*Polo Patriótica*—PP) of 14 pro-Chávez parties included the MVR and MAS (below). A year later, the MAS withdrew, leaving the MVR as the coalition's only major component. For the 2005 poll, the pro-Chávez group reorganized as the Block for Change (*Bloque para el Cambio*).

Following his 2006 reelection victory, President Chávez pressured all government-supportive parties to form a single party instead of, in his words, "an alphabet soup that is fooling the people." Instead of a ruling coalition of 21 groups as before, the president declared that all of his supporters must join the new party and cease to exist as independent entities, or be considered political adversaries. Following the dissolutions or mass defections from most other pro-government parties, the new party, the United Socialist Party of Venezuela (*Partido Socialista Unido de Venezuela*—PSUV), is now by far the dominant pro-Chávez force. Three coalition members—For Social Democracy (*Podemos*), Fatherland for All (PPT), and the Communist Party of Venezuela (PCV)—signaled their desire not to join the new party. The still-forming PSUV united with smaller pro-government parties to compete in the 2008 municipal and state elections as the Patriotic Alliance (*Alianza Patriótica*), a designation that by 2009 was no longer used.

The PSUV held its inaugural congress on January 12, 2008, and elected its executive committee in March. As of mid-2009 141 of the National Assembly's 167 deputies were PSUV members.

The principal founding organizations are discussed immediately below. Some subsequent reports indicated, however, that several of them, including the MEP and the UPV, have retained distinct identities within the PSUV framework.

Leaders: Lt. Col. (Ret.) Hugo CHÁVEZ Frías (President of the Republic), Cilia FLORES (First Vice President), Alberto MÜLLER Rojas (Party Coordinator).

Fifth Republic Movement (*Movimiento Quinta República*—MVR). The MVR was launched in July 1997 by presidential aspirant Hugo Chávez Frías, who had previously been associated with the outlawed Revolutionary Bolivarian Movement–200 (*Movimiento Bolivariano Revolucionario–200*—MBR-200), an intensely nationalist formation composed largely of former military figures opposed to the alleged corruption and social disparity occasioned by government economic policies. Chávez, having been arrested following the February 1992 revolt and then released from prison in March 1994 as part of a conciliatory gesture by President Caldera toward the military, had indicated that the MBR-200 would be converted into a political formation. In 2002 the MVR saw some Chávez opponents leave to form the Solidarity Party (below) and the Revolutionary Transparency Party (TR).

For the 2005 legislative poll, all MVR candidates were designated by the party's "National Tactical Command," with nearly a quarter of sitting members of the National Assembly deemed insufficiently loyal to be given an opportunity for reelection.

Unity of Electoral Victors (*Unidad de Vencedores Electorales*—UVE). The UVE was founded in 2005 as one of several pro-Chávez parties competing within the Block for Change coalition. The group appeared to be indistinguishable from the MVR, even using the same logo; critics alleged it was part of a strategy to increase the pro-government bloc's majority by adding to proportional representation. The group won four National Assembly seats in the 2005 legislative elections; immediately afterward, however, its deputies joined the MVR. The party was dormant until 2008, when it was revived as a legal entity though it ran few candidates in that year's local elections.

National Indian Council of Venezuela (*Consejo Nacional Indio de Venezuela*—CONIVE). Founded in 1989 to defend indigenous rights, this pro-Chávez party won all three National Assembly seats reserved for indigenous communities in the 2000 elections, and won two of three seats in the 2005 elections. Both CONIVE deputies since joined the PSUV.

Leader: Noeli POCATERRA.

People's Electoral Movement (*Movimiento Electoral del Pueblo*—MEP). The MEP was founded in 1967 by a left-wing faction of the Democratic Action (AD, below) that disagreed with the party's choice of a presidential candidate for the 1968 election. It won three lower house seats in 1978, none thereafter. In 1987 the party selected Edmundo CHIRINOS, rector of the Central University of Venezuela, as its 1988 presidential nominee, who, in addition to being supported by the Communist Party (below), received the endorsement of the Independent Moral Movement (*Movimiento Moral Independiente*—MMI), a small left-wing group formed in 1986. Based on nationwide polling results, the MEP was granted one seat in the Chamber of Deputies after the November 1998 election. In 2005 the MEP won 1 National Assembly seat. That legislator joined the PSUV; the MEP, refusing to dissolve, still exists without legislative representation.

Leader: Dr. Jesús Angel PAZ Galárraga (General Secretary), Wilmer NOLASCO (President).

Venezuelan Popular Unity (*Unidad Popular Venezolana*—UPV). The UPV was founded in February 2004 as a "radical and ruthless" pro-Chávez leftist party. It won 1 seat in the December 2005 National Assembly election. In 2007 its leader, Lina RON, indicated that the party would accept President Chávez's dictate that supporting parties unite as the PSUV, given that Chávez is "the messiah God sent to save the people." Chávez has criticized Ron for an excess of fervor and lack of "revolutionary discipline." She was arrested in August 2009 after leading 40 followers in a tear gas attack on the offices of the pro-opposition Globovisión television network.

Leader: Lina RON.

Several other parties and groups in the pro-Chavez coalition with no legislative representation joined the PSUV as well. They include the **Independent Solidarity Movement** (*Movimiento Solidaridad Independente*—MSI or SI), organized in early 1997 to support the interests of the middle class and led by Paciano PADRON and Luis EDUARDO Ortega; the **Union Party** (*Partido Unión*—PN), launched in May 2001 as a social democratic alternative to the AD and COPEI by Lt. Col. (Ret.) Francisco ARIAS Cárdenas; the **Agriculturalist Action** (*Acción Agropecuaria*—AA), led by Hiram GAVIRIA and Gustavo BASTIDAS; the **Emergent People** (*Gente Emergente*—GE), founded in 1991 in opposition to the "irresponsible power elite" and led by Fernando ALVAREZ Paz and Lazaro CALAZÁN; the **Independents for the National Community** (*Independientes por la Comunidad Nacional*—IPCN), which was organized by Antonio GONZÁLEZ to foster community development; the **Moral Force** (*Fuerza Moral*—FM), formed in 1998 by Hernán GRÜBER Odreman, a former rear admiral who participated in the abortive coup of November 1992 and was appointed governor of the Federal District by Chávez in January 1999; and the **New Democratic Regime** (*Nuevo Régimen Democrático*—NRD), which was launched in 1997 by Guillermo GARCÍA Ponce, Manuel ISIDRO Molina, and Pedro MIRANDA. In addition, by 1998 an **Independence Movement** (*Movimiento Independencia*—MI), headed by J. A. COVA Sosa, had evolved from The Notables (*Grupo Notables*), a group of well-known public figures who had supported the 1992 coup attempts. One of The Notables was José Vicente Rangel, the 1983 presidential candidate of the New Alternative (*Nuevo Alternative*—NA), a coalition that had included, among other groups, the pro-Moscow faction of the MIR (see MAS, below).

Other Legislative Parties:

For Social Democracy (*Por la Democracia Social—Podemos*). The center-left *Podemos* was formed in November 2002, primarily by former members of MAS (below) who remained loyal to President Chávez. In 2005 it finished a distant second to the MVR in the National Assembly election, winning 15 seats. Though it lost some deputies to the PSUV, its 6 remaining legislators have resisted joining the new party. While its deputies have often been shouted down when they attempt to speak in the legislature, they have insisted that they are more of a third option than an opposition. "We have occupied this space—not to get rid of Chávez, not to throw him out or see him die," Podemos deputy Juan José MOLINA told the *Washington Post* in February 2009. "Ours is a defense of democracy. And so we criticize." In June 2009 the party signaled its intention to compete in the 2010 legislative elections as part of the opposition Unity Table coalition (below). That month, deputies from Podemos and the FPH (below) joined in a "parliamentary opinion group" that they called the Patriotic Popular Union.

Leader: Ismael GARCÍA (Secretary General).

Fatherland for All (*Patria para Todos*—PPT). The PPT was organized in late 1997 by a dissident faction of *La Causa Radical* (below). In December 2005 it won 11 seats in the National Assembly. While it was a member of the Patriotic Alliance in the 2008 local elections, the PPT's remaining 5 deputies have been attacked for not joining the PSUV. It is expected to join in coalition with PSUV for the 2010 legislative elections.

Leader: José ALBORNOZ (Secretary General).

Humanist Popular Front (*Frente Popular Humanista*—FPH). This legislative grouping formed in January 2009. It is made up of five deputies who left the pro-Chávez bloc out of disagreement with the February 2009 referendum to change the constitution to allow the president to run for indefinite reelection. In June 2009 FPH deputies joined with Podemos in a "parliamentary opinion group" that they called the Patriotic Popular Union.

Leaders: Wilmer AZUAJE, Luis DÍAZ, Tomás SÁNCHEZ, José Ramón REGNAULT and Pastora MEDINA (National Assembly deputies).

Communist Party of Venezuela (*Partido Comunista de Venezuela*—PCV). Founded in 1931, the PCV was proscribed in 1962 but relegalized in 1969 following its renunciation of the use of force. The party lost its three seats in the Chamber of Deputies after endorsing the 1988 presidential candidacy of the MEP's Edmundo Chirinos. In 1997 it expelled its only MP, Ricardo GUTIÉRREZ, who subsequently became a leader of *Podemos*.

The PCV won eight National Assembly seats in 2005; all but three have defected to the PSUV. As it did in the 2008 local elections, it is expected to join in coalition with PSUV for the 2010 legislative elections.

Leaders: Jerónimo CARRERA (President), Oscar FIGUERA (Secretary General).

New Revolutionary Way (*Nuevo Camino Revolucionario*—NCR). This party incorporates four National Assembly deputies expelled from the PSUV in May 2008 for denouncing official corruption and defending prominent dissident Gen. Raúl Isaías Baduel, President Chávez's former defense minister (see Current issues, above). The NCR claims to support President Chávez "from a critical perspective." It held its first internal elections in February 2009.

Leaders: Luis TASCÓN (National Assembly deputy).

Venezuelan Ecological Movement (*Movimiento Ecológico Venezolano*—MOVEV). Founded in 2005, Venezuela's green party had no legislative representation until 2008, when Pedro Bastidas, a PSUV dissident, left the dominant party and joined MOVEV. Bastidas has said that the movement is centrist, supporting neither President Chávez nor the opposition and focused principally on environmental issues.

Leaders: Manuel DÍAZ (Secretary General, party founder), Pedro BASTIDAS (President, National Assembly deputy).

United Movement of Indigenous Peoples (*Movimiento Unido de Pueblos Indígenas*—MUPI). An indigenous-based party founded in 1997 and based principally in the state of Amazonas, the MUPI competed in its first national election in 2005, when it won one of three seats in the National Assembly reserved for indigenous communities. While not aligned with the PSUV, the MUPI does not support the opposition either; its formulation has been "*ni-ni*," slang for "neither one nor the other."

Leader: Julio YGARZA (National Assembly Deputy).

Other Parties:

Democratic Unity Table (*Mesa de la Unidad Democrática*—MUD). The National Unity (*Unidad Nacional*—UN) was the principal opposition coalition participating in the November 2008 regional elections. It was formed with the signing of a January 2008 agreement between leaders of its member parties. Several additional parties joined in February 2008. The coalition won five states and four out of the five Caracas mayors' offices. On June 8, 2009, all of the same major opposition parties – plus Podemos, the only coalition member with legislative representation (above) – came together to form the MUD. The coalition intended to make policy proposals and to prepare a joint challenge to the PSUV in the December 2010 legislative elections.

A New Time (*Un Nuevo Tiempo*—UNT). In 2006 a coalition of forty-four opposition groups, including all of Venezuela's dominant pre-1998 political parties, formed behind the UNT standard to support one presidential candidate to challenge Chávez. Manuel Rosales, the governor of Zulia state in western Venezuela, was unsuccessful in his bid for the presidency.

Founded in 1999, the Zulia-based UNT movement was founded by regional dissidents from the Democratic Action Party. Rosales, an outspoken Chávez opponent from a social democratic background, was a longtime member of Democratic Action. Nearly all viable opposition parties below were part of the UNT coalition. During the year after the 2006 elections, UNT ceased to play a formal leadership role in the opposition, as the coalition's member parties—many of which continue to coordinate closely—remained autonomous. As a single party, UNT was the largest of several opposition parties participating in the 2008 municipal and gubernatorial elections under the UN banner.

In April 2009 Rosales, then the mayor of Maracaibo, went into exile in Peru to avoid arrest on corruption charges he claimed were politically motivated.

Leaders: Omar Barboza (President and MUD Spokesman), Manuel ROSALES (Consultative Council), Gerardo BLYDE (General Secretary).

Democratic Action (*Acción Democrática*—AD). Founded in 1937, the AD was forced underground by the Pérez Jiménez dictatorship but regained legality in 1958 and held power for ten years thereafter. An advocate of rapid economic development, welfare policies, and Western values, it won an overwhelming victory in 1973, capturing the presidency and both houses of Congress. Although losing the presidency in 1978, it remained the largest party in the Senate and tied the Social Christians for representation in the Chamber of Deputies. In 1983 it regained the presidency and won majorities in both houses of Congress. By 1987, with its popularity waning because of continued economic crisis, the AD was deeply divided in the selection of a candidate for the 1988 presidential poll, former interior minister Octavio LEPAGE Barretto, hand-picked by President Lusinchi as his successor, ultimately being defeated in party electoral college balloting by former president Carlos Andrés Pérez, who, following his election on December 4, returned to office on February 2, 1989.

The party suffered a major setback at state and municipal balloting in December 1992, and its candidate finished second with 23.6 percent of the vote in the presidential poll of December 1993, although it won pluralities in both houses of Congress on the latter occasion.

In November 1998 presidential hopeful Luis ALFARO Ucero was expelled by the party but nevertheless pursued his quest as an independent supported by an assortment of small parties, including the URD (below). The AD, which had retained both its congressional pluralities earlier in the month, backed the PRVZL's Salas Römer in the December presidential race. (Alfaro Ucero attracted 0.4 percent of the vote, for a fourth-place finish.)

AD/ABP candidate Antonio Ledezma defeated his PSUV opponent in November 2008 elections for the mayoralty of Caracas. Shortly afterward, President Chávez moved to strip the mayor's office of most of its powers.

Leaders: Víctor BOLÍVAR (President), Henry RAMOS Allup (Secretary General), Antonio LEDEZMA (Mayor of Caracas).

"Bravo People" Alliance (*Alianza Bravo Pueblo*—ABP). Founded in 2000 as a conservative splinter of AD, the faction remains closely tied to the larger party. It is led by Caracas mayor Antonio Ledezma.

Leaders: Antonio LEDEZMA (Mayor of Caracas), Richard BLANCO (President).

Social Christian Party (*Partido Social-Cristiano/Comité de Organización Politica Electoral Independiente*—COPEI). Founded in 1946, COPEI offers a moderately conservative reflection of the social doctrines of the Roman Catholic Church. It nonetheless spans a wide range of opinion, from a clerical right wing to an ultraprogressive, youthful left wing. The party won the presidency by a narrow margin in 1968 and recaptured the office in 1978 without, however, winning control of the Congress. Although it secured 14 Senate and 61 Chamber seats in 1983, it ran a poor second to the AD at the 1984 municipal elections. Subsequently the party was torn by a bitter presidential nomination race between COPEI founder Rafael Caldera Rodríguez and his one-time protégé Eduardo Fernández, whose nearly 3–1 victory in late 1987 was termed a "patricidal" embarrassment for the veteran party leader. Fernández won 40.4 percent of the popular vote as runner-up to Pérez at the election of December 1988. The party won eight gubernatorial seats in the December 1989 balloting, despite continued friction between Fernández and former presidents Caldera and Herrera; in December 1992 it won a total of ten in alliance with the MEP (above).

In June 1993 former president Caldera Rodríguez was expelled from the party for refusing to step down as an independent presidential candidate in the wake of COPEI's nomination of Oswaldo ALVAREZ Paz, who placed third in the December poll. The party finished third in both houses of the Congress at the November 1998 election and supported the PRVZL's Salas Römer in the presidential election. In early 2000 a faction led by Alvarez Paz left COPEI, proclaiming the "death of the party."

Leaders: Luis Ignacio PLANAS (President of the Party), Luis Carlos SOLÓRZANO (Secretary General).

Justice First (*Primero Justicia*—PJ). The PJ traces its origins to a civil association formed in 1992 by a Supreme Court justice, Alirio ABREU Burelli, to promote legal reform. It was constituted as a political party in 2000 and went on to win five seats from the state of Miranda in the National Assembly election. It was the second-largest vote-getter of all 44 parties in the coalition that supported Manuel Rosales' failed 2006 opposition presidential bid.

Leaders: Julio BORGES (National Coordinator).

Project Venezuela (*Proyecto Venezuela*—PRVZL or Proven). Originating in the regional *Proyecto Carabobo,* the PRVZL was launched nationally before the 1998 elections by previously independent presidential candidate Henrique Salas Römer, who ran second to Chávez in the December 6 balloting with 40 percent of the vote. A month earlier the party had finished fourth in the lower house election. The PRVZL did not participate in the 2006 presidential elections. It is led by Salas Römer's son, Henrique SALAS Feo, who is governor of Carabobo state.

Leaders: Henrique SALAS Feo (President), Henrique SALAS Römer (Advisor).

The Radical Cause (*La Causa Radical* or *Causa R*). *Causa R* began as a far-left group whose founder, Alfredo MANEIRO, died in 1983. It retained three Chamber seats in 1988 and in December 1989 captured one governorship. In December 1992 it won the Caracas mayoralty, although the victor, Aristóbulo ISTURIZ, refused to take office until authorities agreed to investigate the alleged fraudulent election of an AD councilor, whose seat was needed for a *Causa R* majority. The party placed fourth in the December 1993 balloting with a 22.0 percent vote share and captured one governorship in December 1995. In 1997 it split into factions headed by Andrés Velasquez and Pablo Medina, with the Medina group then forming the PPT. The *Causa R* presidential candidate, Alfredo Ramos, finished sixth in 1998 with 0.1 percent of the vote. The party is strong in Bolívar state, where it narrowly lost the governorship in 2008 and retains the mayoralty of Ciudad Bolívar, the state's second-largest city.

Leaders: Andrés VELÁSQUEZ (President and 1993 presidential candidate), Daniel SANTOLO (Spokesman).

Democratic Republican Union (*Unión Republicana Democrática*—URD). Founded in 1946 and once Venezuela's second-largest party, the URD champions principles similar to those of the AD and has, in the past, supported AD governments. It won three Chamber seats in 1983, all of which were lost in 1988. For the 1988 presidential balloting the party, for the first time, put forward a woman, Ismenia Villalba, as its nominee; however, she joined a number of other candidates in obtaining less than 1 percent of the vote. Following the November 1998 legislative election, the URD was given one lower house seat. It backed the former AD secretary general, Alfaro Ucero, in the December 1998 presidential election, and UNT candidate Manuel Rosales in the 2006 election, in which the party attracted 0.7 percent of all votes.

Leaders: Rafael RODRÍGUEZ Mudarra (President), Ramón TENORIO Sifontes (Spokesman).

Movement to Socialism (*Movimiento al Socialismo*—MAS). Originating as a radical left-wing group that split from the PCV in 1971, the MAS subsequently adopted a "Eurocommunist" posture and became the dominant legislative party of the left by capturing 2 Senate and 11 Chamber seats in 1978. It supported José Vicente Rangel for the presidency in 1978 but, with the exception of a small group of dissidents, was deeply opposed to his 1983 bid as leader of the left-wing New Alternative coalition. Having responded positively to a mid-1981 appeal from AD leader Carlos Andrés Pérez for a "synchronization of the opposition," it appeared to be adopting a democratic socialist rather than a rigidly Marxist orientation. In late 1987 the majority, anti-Moscow faction of the Movement of the Revolutionary Left (*Movimiento de Izquierda Revolucionaria*—MIR), led by Moisés MOLEIRO, was reported to have merged with the MAS. (The MIR, which was founded by radical students in 1960, engaged in urban terrorism from 1961 to 1964 and thereafter conducted guerrilla operations from a rural base. Legalized in 1973, it won four Chamber seats in 1978 before splitting into two factions, the smaller being a pro-Moscow group led by party founder and 1978 presidential candidate Américo MARTIN.)

At the 1988 balloting, the MAS secured 3 Senate and 18 Chamber seats, while its nominee, former guerrilla Teodoro PETKOFF, repeated his 1983 performance by placing third in the presidential race. The party captured one governorship in December 1989. It joined COPEI (below) in a 1992 coalition that won ten state governorships, and then joined the National Convergence (*Convergencia Nacional*—CN) in supporting Rafael Caldera's presidential bid in 1993. (For more information on the now-defunct CN, see the 2008 or earlier editions of the *Handbook.*)

In March 1996 the MAS formed an alliance with the anti-Caldera legislative bloc, while insisting, somewhat incongruously, that by so doing it was asserting its independence rather than going into opposition. Teodoro Petkoff resigned from the MAS in July 1998 over its decision to support Chávez.

The party began distancing itself from the government coalition in May 2001 in the wake of reports that the president was considering a declaration of emergency that would permit him to rule by decree. Five months later Chávez stated that the MAS was "no longer an ally of the Bolivarian revolution" and called on it to leave the coalition. In late November a dissident group formed *Podemos* (above).

Leaders: Felipe MUJICA (President), José Antonio ESPAÑA and Nicolás SOSA (National Coordinators).

Red Flag (*Bandera Roja*—BR). A small Marxist guerrilla group in the 1970s and the 1980s, the BR officially demobilized in 1994 but first competed in elections as a political party in 1993, supporting the unsuccessful candidacy of its leader, Gabriel PUERTA Aponte. The BR has consistently opposed Hugo Chávez, considering him to be a "false communist" and supporting Manuel Rosales in 2006, attracting 0.16 percent of the vote. The party has run very few candidates of its own but is among those listed as a component of the MUD. In January 2009, the party's 39th anniversary celebration was broken up by a tear gas attack from a mob led by UPV leader Lina Ron.

Leader: Gabriel PUERTA Aponte.

Other opposition parties in the MUD coalition include **Democracy Renovated** (*Democracia Renovadora*—DR), led by Secretary General José Gregorio GARCÍA Urquiola; **Liberal Power** (*Fuerza Liberal*—FL), led by President Haydée DEUTSCH; **Venezuela Vision** (*Visión Venezuela*—VV), led by Secretary General Omar ÁVILA; the **Platform for Social Encounter** (*Plataforma de Encuentro Social*—PES), founded in 2008 by Globovisión television host Augusto URIBE; **Only One People** (*Un Solo Pueblo*—USP), founded in 2002 and led by Director-General Enrique ARTEAGA; **Independent Solidarity** (*Solidaridad Independiente*—SI), led by President Juan de Dios RIVAS Velásquez; and the **Republican Movement** (*Movimiento Republicano*—MR), led by President Carlos PADILLA.

Solidarity (*Solidaridad*). Solidarity was formed in mid-2002, primarily by former members of the MVR who had turned away from what they considered the corruption and confrontation that had come to characterize the Chávez administration. The party's leaders were followers of former justice minister and MVR secretary general Luis Miquilena, who had left the Chávez government early in the year and was engaged in an effort to unite the opposition. With party leader Miquilena over 90 years old, by 2009 the party was largely inactive.

Leaders: Luis MIQUILENA, José FARIAS Correa (Former Leader in the National Assembly), Alejandro ARMAS.

Democratic Left (*Izquierda Democrática*—ID). The ID was launched by a group of former Communists in early 2005 as the vehicle "for a left different than the one that is now ruling us." It claims to differ from the *chavistas* in that the latter are alleged to be basically "undemocratic." In early 2007 the ID decided to merge its membership into the UNT party, effectively ceasing to exist.

Leaders: Pompeo MARQUEZ, Luis Manuel ESCULPI.

Armed Groups:

The Pebble (*La Piedrita*). This small, far-left, Caracas-based group launched a series of tear-gas attacks on the offices of opposition political parties, media outlets and the Catholic Church in 2008 and 2009. Its leader, Valentín SANTANA, gained notoriety for publicly threatening to kill Marcel GRANIER, the head of the RCTV network that lost its broadcast license in 2007. Though the roughly 30-member group claims to be ardently pro-Chávez, the President asked the attorney-general's office to arrest Santana in February 2009. As of mid-2009, Santana was a fugitive.

Leader: Valentín SANTANA.

Bolivarian Liberation Forces (*Fuerzas Bolivarianas de Liberación*—FBL). This group, which has operated sporadically in Colombian border zones since the early 2000s, is believed to work closely with Colombia's FARC guerrillas. It has occasionally killed members of the security forces, prompting President Chávez to order that the group, which claims to support him, be fought. In June and July 2009, it appeared that at least part of the group had decided to demobilize.

Leaders: Eleazar JUÁREZ, Felipe PÉREZ, Antonio ALARCÓN.

LEGISLATURE

Under the former constitution, the Venezuelan legislature was a bicameral Congress of the Republic (*Congreso de la República*) consisting of a 46-member Senate (*Senado*) and a 189-member Chamber of Deputies (*Cámara de Diputados*), both with additional nominated members to compensate for party underrepresentation. The Congress was effectively superseded by the Constitutional Assembly elected on July 25, 1999, and was formally dissolved on January 4, 2000. On January 30, the Assembly delegated its legislative powers to a 21-member National Legislative Commission that served until the National Assembly election of July 30.

National Assembly (*Asamblea Nacional*). The current legislature is a unicameral body of 167 members, including 3 representing indigenous peoples. At the election of December 4, 2005, which was boycotted by opposition groups, the president's Movement for the Fifth Republic won 114 seats; For Social Democracy, 15; Fatherland for All, 11; Communist Party of Venezuela, 8; Unity of Electoral Victors, 4; National Indian Council of Venezuela, 2; People's Electoral Movement, 1; Venezuelan Popular Unity, 1; and 11 seats for regional parties and independents. By mid-2009, following four years of party defections and the disappearance, at President Chávez's strong urging, of all progovernment parties except the PSUV, the Assembly's makeup had changed substantially to United Socialist Party of Venezuela with 141 seats; For Social Democracy, 6; Fatherland for All, 5; Humanist Popular Front, 5; New Revolutionary Way, 4; Communist Party of Venezuela, 3; Venezuelan Ecological Movement, 1; United Movement of Indigenous Peoples, 1; and 1 independent. The legislature's makeup remained extremely fluid but overwhelmingly progovernment.

An August 2008 electoral reform law increased, from 60 to 70 percent, the number of deputies elected directly, with the number chosen by proportional representation dropping from 40 to 30 percent. The next legislative elections were scheduled for December 2010.

President: Cilia FLORES.

CABINET

[as of October 1, 2009]

President	Col. (Ret.) Hugo Rafael Chávez Frías
First Vice President	Ramón Carrizalez Rengifo
Vice President, Energy and Oil	Rafael Darío Ramírez Carreño
Vice President, Foreign Affairs	Nicolás Maduro
Vice President, Planning and Development	Jorge A. Giordani C.
Vice President, Science, Technology, and Intermediate Industries	Jesse Chacón
Vice President, Secretary of the Presidency	Luis Reyes Reyes
Ministers	
Agriculture and Lands	Elías Jaua Milano
Basic Industries and Mining	Rodolfo Sanz
Communications and Information	Blanca Eckout [f]
Culture	Héctor Soto Castellanos
Defense	Ramón Carrizalez Rengifo
Domestic Affairs and Justice	Tareck El Aissami
Economy and Finance	Ali Rodríguez Araque
Education	Héctor Augusto Navarro Díaz
Environment	Yuviri del Carmen Ortega Lovera [f]
Food	Lt. Col. (Ret.) Felix Osorio Guzmán
Health and Social Welfare	Carlos Rotondaro Cova
Higher Education	Luis Augusto Acuña Cedeño
Indigenous Peoples	Nicia Maldonado [f]
Labor and Social Security	María Cristina Iglesias [f]
Neighborhoods and Social Protection	Erica Farías [f]
Public Works and Housing	Diosdado Cabello
Sports	Victoria Mata [f]
Tourism	Pedro Morejón Carrillo
Trade	Eduardo Samán
Women and Gender Equality	María León [f]
Minister of State	
Attorney General	Luisa Ortega Díaz [f]

[f] = female

COMMUNICATIONS

The media are free in principle but subject to censorship in times of emergency. Private media remain occasionally critical of the government, though threats to revoke broadcast licenses have resulted in widespread self-censorship. In a February 2007 report, the Committee to Protect Journalists accused Chávez of seeking to silence his critics in the media. The report was strongly critical of the Radio and Television Social Responsibility Act discussed below. Reports by Human Rights Watch and the OAS Inter-American Human Rights Commission in 2008 and 2009 characterized Venezuela as a country that "abuses its broad regulatory powers to harass its critics" and "a hostile environment for political dissent."

In December 2006 the government announced that it would not renew the broadcast license of Radio Caracas Television (RCTV), the country's oldest and most-watched television network, whose news programmers were notoriously critical of the regime. RCTV went off the air on May 27, 2007. In 2009 President Chávez greatly increased pressure on Globovisión, the last opposition broadcast network, whose concession does not end until 2015. His government sought to sanction the network for "inciting violence" and, in September, for broadcasting, amid a stream of text messages from viewers, a call for a military coup. In August the government closed 32 radio stations and 2 regional television stations, nearly all of them opposition-leaning, claiming that they were broadcasting illegally. In its 2009 annual index on freedom of the press, the media watch-dog group Reporters Without Borders ranked Venezuela 124 out of 175 countries.

Press. The following are Spanish dailies published in Caracas, unless otherwise noted: *Ultimas Noticias* (200,000), independent; *El Universal* (120,000 daily, 250,000 Sunday); *Panorama* (Maracaibo, 120,000 daily, 123,000 Sunday); *El Nacional* (100,000), independent; 2001 (100,000), independent; *El Carabobeñ* (Valencia, 97,000); *El Mundo* (80,000); *El Siglo* (Maracay, 75,000); *El Globo* (68,000); *El Tiempo* (Puerto la Cruz, 65,000); *The Daily Journal* (15,300 daily, 17,200 Sunday), in English.

News agencies. The domestic agency, Venpres, is operated by the government's Central Information Office; most of the major foreign agencies maintain bureaus in Caracas.

Broadcasting and computing. Broadcasting is regulated by the *Cámara Venezolana de la Industria de Radiodifusión* and the *Cámara Venezolana de la Televisión*. Most of the country's radio stations are privately owned and commercial. The state-owned *Venezolana de la Televisión* services two national and four regional networks; half a dozen private stations, with numerous relay facilities, also broadcast.

In December 2004 President Chávez signed a Radio and Television Social Responsibility Act to prohibit programming that would expose children to depictions of undue violence or sexual activity. The legislation also prohibits any programming viewed as an incitement to anti-state violence. The law is implemented by a Directorate of Social Responsibility, 7 of whose 11 members would be regime-appointed. It would also require broadcasters to air government information material for up to 70 hours a week.

In July 2005 Telesur, a Latin American venture in which Venezuela has a controlling interest, began broadcasting "alternative news" to offset programs originating in the United States. The action prompted the U.S. House of Representatives to approve legislation authorizing transmissions to counter the facility's "anti-U.S. propaganda."

As of 2008 there were 254.9 Internet users per 1,000 inhabitants.

INTERGOVERNMENTAL REPRESENTATION

Ambassador to the U.S.: Bernardo Álvarez HERRERA.

U.S. Ambassador to Venezuela: Patrick Dennis DUDDY.

Permanent Representative to the UN: Jorge VALERO BRICEÑO

IGO Memberships (Non-UN): ACS, ALADI, CDB, IADB, Interpol, IOM, *Mercosur*, NAM, OAS, OPANAL, OPEC, PCA, SELA, WCO, WTO.

VIETNAM

Socialist Republic of Vietnam
Cộng Hòa Xã Hội Chủ Nghĩa Việt Nam

Political Status: Communist republic originally proclaimed September 2, 1945; Democratic Republic of Vietnam established in the north on July 21, 1954; Republic of Vietnam established in the south on October 26, 1955; Socialist Republic of Vietnam proclaimed on July 2, 1976, following surrender of the southern government on April 30, 1975; present constitution adopted on April 15, 1992.

Area: 128,402 sq. mi. (332,561 sq. km.).

Population: 76,323,173 (1999C); 86,471,000 (2008E).

Major Urban Centers (metropolitan areas, 2005E): HANOI (5,046,000), Ho Chi Minh City (formerly Saigon, 5,289,000), Haiphong (2,032,000), Can Tho (1,120,000), Da Nang (720,000).

Official Language: Vietnamese.

Monetary Unit: Dông (market rate December 1, 2009: 18,489.50 dông = $1US).

President: NGUYEN MINH TRIET; elected by the National Assembly on June 27, 2006, to fill the remaining year in the term of the retiring TRAN DUC LUONG; reelected for a five-year term on July 24, 2007.

Vice President: NGUYEN THI DOAN; elected by the National Assembly on July 25, 2007, succeeding TRUONG MY HOA.

Prime Minister: NGUYEN TAN DUNG; elected by the National Assembly on June 27, 2006, succeeding PHAN VAN KHAI; renominated by the president on July 24, 2007, and reelected on July 25.

General Secretary of the Vietnamese Communist Party: NONG DUC MANH; appointed by the Central Committee on April 22, 2001, succeeding LE KHA PHIEU; reappointed on April 25, 2006.

THE COUNTRY

A tropical land of varied climate and topography, Vietnam extends for roughly 1,000 miles along the eastern face of the Indochina Peninsula between the deltas of its two great rivers, the Red River in the north and the Mekong in the south. To the east, the country borders on the Gulf of Tonkin and the South China Sea; in the west, the mountains of the Annamite Chain separate it from Cambodia and Laos. A second mountainous region in the north serves as a partial barrier between Vietnam and China, which historically has exercised great influence in Vietnam and provided its name, "Land of the South."

The Vietnamese population is of mixed ethnic stock and includes numerous highland tribes as well as Chinese, Khmer, and other non-Vietnamese peoples. The Viet (Kinh) constitute some 88 percent of the population. Although religion is not encouraged by the state, most Vietnamese are nominally Buddhist—there is a state-sponsored Buddhist Church of Vietnam—or Taoist, with a significant Roman Catholic minority, particularly in the south. Vietnamese is the national language, while French was long the preferred second language. Women constitute 48 percent of the active labor force, but their participation in party and governmental affairs has traditionally been much less. Women hold 26 percent of the seats in the current National Assembly.

Northern Vietnam was traditionally a food-deficient area, dependent on supplementary rice and other provisions from the south. It developed a considerable industrial economy, however, based on substantial resources of anthracite coal, chromite, iron, phosphate, tin, and other minerals. According to statistics compiled by the Asian Development Bank, 55 percent of the country's employed labor force continues to work in the agricultural sector, which contributes about 20 percent of GDP, compared to 42 percent for industry and 38 percent for services. Manufacturing and mining account for about 12 percent of the employed workforce. As of 2006, crude oil constituted Vietnam's leading export (about one-fifth of total earnings), followed by textiles, marine products (mainly frozen seafood), and electronic goods and components. Wood and wood products, rubber, coffee, and coal have steadily increased in importance.

A key component of the reunified socialist republic's 1976–1980 Five-Year Plan was large-scale redistribution of the population, including a shift of surplus labor northward and resettlement of many residents of southern cities into "new economic zones" in rural areas. Midway through the plan the government announced that it intended to nationalize all land beyond what was needed by individual families to meet basic requirements, but the adverse impact on production led to new decrees in 1979 permitting greater freedom to cultivate reclaimed and virgin land. Since that time, food self-sufficiency has largely been achieved, in part because the government introduced a contract system whereby farmers could market their products freely after meeting state quotas. Incentives for industrial export production, foreign investment, and expansion of such nonsocialist industries as handicrafts were also initiated.

Decentralization of economic planning yielded only marginal overall growth, however, and in 1986 Vietnam enacted a political and economic "renovation" (*Đổi Mới*) program, reportedly modeled after the Soviet Union's perestroika. Radical reforms included fiscal and monetary austerity, a shift away from public sector control of the economy, and an opening of markets to international trade. The resultant turnaround was marked by a strengthened dông; a drop in overall inflation to single digits, down from the triple-digit levels that had prevailed in the 1980s; and an average annual GDP growth rate of about 9 percent for 1992–1997. Growth fell to an average of about 4 percent in 1998 and 1999, however, as Vietnam began to suffer the effects of a regional economic crisis. Other problems besetting the economy included the slow pace of reform within state-owned enterprises, widespread smuggling, and corruption, compounded, in November 1999, by the worst flooding in a century, which left an estimated 1 million or more peasants temporarily homeless.

For 2000–2006 GDP growth average about 7.5 percent annually and then peaked at 8.5 percent in 2007. The growth rate dropped to 6.2 percent in 2008 and was projected to fall further, to under 5 percent in 2009, as a consequence of the international recession. Meanwhile, consumer price inflation soared to 23 percent in 2008 due to rapidly rising commodity prices and credit growth attributable to capital inflows, but it was expected to return to about 8 percent in 2009.

GOVERNMENT AND POLITICS

Political background. Vietnam's three historic regions—Tonkin in the north, Annam in the center, and Cochin-China in the south—came under French control in 1862–1884 and were later joined with Cambodia and Laos to form the French-ruled Indochinese Union, more commonly called French Indochina. The Japanese, who occupied Indochina in World War II, permitted the establishment on September 2, 1945, of the Democratic Republic of Vietnam (DRV) under HO CHI MINH, the Communist leader of the nationalist resistance movement then known as the Vietminh (*Việt Nam Độc Lập Đồng Minh Hội*, or Vietnamese Independence League). Although the French on their return to Indochina accorded provisional recognition to the DRV, subsequent negotiations broke down, and in December 1946 the Vietminh initiated military action against French forces.

While fighting with the Vietminh continued, the French in 1949 recognized BAO DAI, former emperor of Annam, as head of state of an independent Vietnam within the French Union. Treaties conceding full Vietnamese independence in association with France were initialed in Paris on June 4, 1954; in practice, however, the jurisdiction of the Bao Dai government was limited to South Vietnam as a consequence of the military successes of the Vietminh, the major defeat suffered by French forces at Dien Bien Phu in May 1954, and the armistice and related agreements concluded in Geneva, Switzerland, July 20–21, 1954. The Geneva accord provided for a temporary division of Vietnam near the 17th parallel into two separately administered zones—Communist in the north and non-Communist in the south—pending an internationally supervised election to be held in 1956. These arrangements were rejected, however, by the Bao Dai government and by the republican regime that succeeded it in South Vietnam in 1955. Vietnam thus remained divided between a northern zone administered by the Communist-ruled DRV and a southern zone administered by the anti-Communist government of the Republic of Vietnam.

Within North Vietnam, a new constitution promulgated in 1960 consolidated the powers of the central government, and elections in 1960 and 1964 reaffirmed the preeminence of Ho Chi Minh, who continued as president of the DRV and chair of the Vietnam Workers' Party (VWP), successor in 1954 to the Indochinese Communist Party (ICP). Ho Chi Minh died in 1969, his party position remaining unfilled in deference to his memory. The political leadership passed to LE DUAN, who had been named first secretary of the VWP nine years earlier.

Communist-led subversive and terrorist activity against the government of South Vietnam resumed in the late 1950s by Vietcong (Vietnamese Communist) resistance elements in a continuation of the earlier anti-French offensive, now supported and directed from the north. Within the south, these operations were sponsored from 1960 onward by a Communist-controlled political organization called the National Front for the Liberation of South Vietnam (NLF). Despite the initiation of U.S. advisory assistance to South Vietnamese military forces in 1954, guerrilla operations by Vietcong and regular North Vietnamese units proved increasingly disruptive, and by early 1965 the Republic of Vietnam appeared threatened with military defeat. The United States therefore intensified its efforts by initiating air operations against selected military targets in the north and by ordering large contingents of its ground forces into action in the south.

Earlier, in 1961, the growth of the Communist-supported insurgency forced NGO DINH DIEM (who had assumed the South Vietnamese presidency following the ouster of Bao Dai in 1955) to assume emergency powers. Popular resentment of his increasingly repressive regime led, however, to his death in a coup d'état that was secretly supported by the United States and directed by Gen. DUONG VAN MINH ("Big Minh") on November 1, 1963. A period of unstable military rule followed. Leadership was held successively by General Minh (to January 1964), Gen. NGUYEN KHANH (to February 1965), and Gen. NGUYEN VAN THIEU, who assumed the functions of head of state in June 1965. The powerful post of prime minister went to Air Marshal NGUYEN CAO KY. In response to U.S. pressure, a new constitution was promulgated on April 1, 1967, and Thieu and Ky were elected president and vice president, respectively, on September 3.

On January 31, 1968, a holiday marking the Vietnamese lunar new year (*Tết Nguyên Đán*), Communist forces launched an audacious offensive throughout the south, including in Saigon and other urban centers. Although viewed by most historians as unsuccessful in strictly military terms, the Tet offensive had deep political consequences. In the United States it served to crystallize growing antiwar sentiment and contributed to the decision of U.S. president Lyndon Johnson not to seek reelection. On March 31 Johnson announced a cessation of bombing in all but the southern area of North Vietnam, adjacent to the demilitarized zone straddling the 17th parallel. The action proved more successful than a number of earlier bombing halts in paving the way for peace talks. Preliminary discussions between U.S. and North Vietnamese representatives were initiated in Paris on May 13, while expanded talks began in Paris on January 18, 1969. It was not until September 1972, however, following major U.S. troop withdrawals and the failure of another major Communist offensive, that Hanoi agreed to drop its insistence on imposing a Communist regime in the south and accepted a 1971 U.S. proposal for a temporary cease-fire.

A peace agreement was concluded on January 27, 1973, on the basis of extensive private discussions between U.S. secretary of state Henry

Kissinger and DRV negotiator LE DUC THO. (Although the two were jointly awarded the Nobel Peace Prize in October 1973, Le Duc Tho declined the award, stating that peace had not yet been achieved.) The agreement provided for a withdrawal of all remaining U.S. forces and for political talks between the South Vietnamese and the Vietcong aimed at the establishment of a National Council of National Reconciliation and Concord (NCNRC). The Saigon government and the Provisional Revolutionary Government of South Vietnam failed, however, to reach agreement on the council's composition. Moreover, despite the U.S. withdrawal and North Vietnam's formal support of the peace accord, it was estimated that as of May 1974 some 210,000 North Vietnamese troops were fighting in the south, as compared to 160,000 at the time of the 1972 cease-fire.

A new Communist offensive, launched in late 1974, resulted in the loss of Phuoc Long Province, 70 miles north of Saigon, in early January 1975. By late March, in the wake of a near total collapse of discipline within the South Vietnamese army, the cities of Hué and Da Nang had fallen. On March 25 President Thieu ordered Prime Minister TRAN THIEN KHIEM to organize a broadly representative government to deal with the emergency, but by early April demands were being advanced for Thieu's resignation. On April 4 the new government resigned and NGUYEN BA CAN, the speaker of the House of Representatives, was named to head another new cabinet that was installed on April 14. Seven days later, as the Communist forces neared Saigon, President Thieu announced his resignation, and Vice President TRAN VAN HUONG was sworn in as his successor. Huong himself resigned on April 28 in favor of Gen. Duong Van Minh, who called for a cease-fire and immediate negotiations with representatives of the North Vietnamese and the NLF's military wing, the People's Liberation Armed Forces (PLAF). The appeal was rejected, and on April 30 Communist forces entered Saigon to receive the surrender of the South Vietnamese government.

On June 6 the Provisional Revolutionary Government under the nominal presidency of HUYNH TAN PHAT was invested as the government of South Vietnam, although real power appeared to be exercised by PHAM HUNG, fourth-ranked member of the VWP Politburo and secretary of the party's South Vietnamese Committee. At a conference in Saigon held November 5–6, a delegation headed by Pham Hung was named to negotiate with northern representatives on an election to a common National Assembly for a reunified Vietnam.

Elected on April 25, 1976, the enlarged legislature convened for the first time in Hanoi on June 24. On July 2 it proclaimed the reunification of the country as the Socialist Republic of Vietnam. On the same day it named TON DUC THANG, the incumbent president of North Vietnam, as head of state. It also appointed two vice presidents: NGUYEN LUONG BANG, theretofore vice president of the DRV, and NGUYEN HUU THO, leader of the southern NLF. DRV Premier PHAM VAN DONG was designated to head a cabinet composed largely of former North Vietnamese ministers, with the addition of six South Vietnamese. On December 20 the VWP concluded a congress in Hanoi by changing its name to the Vietnamese Communist Party (VCP) and adopting a series of guidelines designed to realize the nation's "socialist goals."

Under a revised constitution, a new National Assembly was elected on April 26, 1981, and a five-member collective presidency (Council of State) designated on July 4. The second-ranked member of the VCP Politburo, TRUONG CHINH, was named council chair (thus becoming nominal head of state). The third-ranked Pham Van Dong continued as chair of the Council of Ministers.

Longtime party leader Le Duan died in July 1986, with the VCP Central Committee naming Truong Chinh as his successor. The designation proved temporary: In a remarkable change of leadership at the Sixth VCP Congress in December, NGUYEN VAN LINH was named general secretary, with Chinh, Dong, and Tho being among those retired from the Politburo. A major governmental reorganization ensued in February 1987, while in mid-June, following a National Assembly election in April, Gen. VO CHI CONG succeeded Chinh as chair of the Council of State, and Hung replaced Dong as chair of the Council of Ministers. Sr. Gen. VO VAN KIET, theretofore a deputy chair of the Council of Ministers, was named acting chair following Hung's death in March 1988. In an unprecedented contest in June, the nominee of the party's Central Committee, DO MUOI, was forced to stand against Vo Van Kiet for election as permanent chair, winning the office by only 64 percent of the National Assembly vote.

Another major restructuring of the party leadership occurred at the Seventh VCP Congress in June 1991, when 7 of 12 Politburo members were dropped, with Do Muoi succeeding Nguyen Van Linh as general secretary. The party shake-up was paralleled by sweeping government changes when the Eighth National Assembly met for an unusually lengthy 9th session in July and August. A new Council of State was named (albeit with Vo Chi Cong continuing as chair), as well as a new Council of Ministers under Vo Van Kiet. The legislature also initiated debate on a new constitution, the draft of which was completed at the body's 10th session in December and approved at the 11th session in April 1992.

Following its replenishment by the election of prescreened candidates on July 19, 1992, the National Assembly on September 23 named Sr. Gen. LE DUC ANH and NGUYEN THI BINH to the newly created posts of president and vice president, respectively, while reappointing Vo Van Kiet as head of government, with the new title of prime minister. In 1996 an ailing President Le Duc Anh was temporarily replaced by Vice President Nguyen Thi Binh, whose party credentials were insufficient to ensure her eligibility for permanent succession.

Significant personnel changes were recorded in the government and party leadership ranks in the second half of 1997. In September the new National Assembly, elected on July 20, chose TRAN DUC LUONG and PHAN VAN KHAI to succeed Le Duc Anh and Vo Van Kiet as president and prime minister, respectively. On December 29 the VCP Central Committee elected the decidedly more conservative Lt. Gen. LE KHA PHIEU as general secretary in place of Do Muoi.

In January 1998 Prime Minister Khai acknowledged a division within the leadership over the country's economic direction, noting that some party officials had expressed second thoughts about the *Đổi Mới* reform program. By that time the ongoing Asian economic crisis had clearly penetrated Vietnam's borders, adding weight to the debate over the pace of reform and contributing to delays in conclusion of a major trade pact with the United States that was ultimately signed, after four years of negotiations, in July 2000 and ratified in late 2001.

Meeting at its Ninth Party Congress, the VCP on April 22, 2001, replaced Le Kha Phieu with economic reformer NONG DUC MANH, a member of the northern Tay ethnic minority and theretofore chair of the National Assembly. No major changes in the government occurred until a new cabinet was installed on August 8, 2002, during the opening session of the expanded, 498-seat National Assembly, which had been elected on May 19. President Luong and Prime Minister Khai were reelected on July 24 and 25, respectively, by the legislature, which chose TRUONG MY HOA as vice president.

The Tenth Congress of the VCP, held April 18–25, 2006, marked the departure from the party leadership of President Tran Duc Luong and Prime Minister Phan Van Khai. On June 27, as expected, the National Assembly elected NGUYEN MINH TRIET as president (to complete the remaining year in Tran's term) and confirmed NGUYEN TAN DUNG as prime minister. Following the National Assembly election of May 20, 2007, the legislature reelected the president and prime minister on July 24 and 25, respectively.

Constitution and government. Upon reunification in 1976, the DRV constitution of January 1, 1960, was put into effect throughout the country pending adoption of a new basic law that on December 18, 1980, received unanimous legislative approval. The 1980 document defined the Socialist Republic as a "state of proletarian dictatorship" advancing toward socialism, and identified the Communist Party as "the only force leading the state and society." It provided for a unicameral National Assembly, elected for a five-year term by universal adult suffrage, as the highest organ of state authority. The assembly was mandated to elect, for a term corresponding to its own, a Council of State as the state's collective presidency; administrative functions were to be directed by a chair and other members of a Council of Ministers, all appointed by and responsible to the assembly.

Under the 1992 constitution the Council of State was abolished in favor of a president who is elected by and from within the assembly. The chief executive nominates a vice president, a prime minister, a chief justice of the Supreme Court, and a head of the Supreme People's Inspectorate, all of whom must be approved by the assembly. According to the current basic law, the party continues to define overall state policy but no longer conducts its day-to-day implementation.

The judicial system is headed by the Supreme People's Court and the procurator general of the Supreme People's Organ of Control. People's Courts, Military Tribunals, and People's Organs of Control operate at the local level. Economic courts to adjudicate business disputes were authorized in 1993, while the country's first comprehensive civil code was approved in 1994, effective from July 1996.

For administrative purposes the country is divided into 59 provinces and 5 centrally administered municipalities (Can Tho, Da Nang, Haiphong, Hanoi, and Ho Chi Minh City); subdivisions include districts, towns, and provincial capitals. Each administrative unit elects a People's Council, which then selects a People's Committee to serve as an executive.

In its November–December 2001 session the National Assembly approved 24 constitutional amendments, including recognition of private enterprise as a legitimate economic sector. Another change permits the National Assembly to consider no-confidence motions against government leaders.

Foreign relations. For many years prior to reunification, North Vietnamese external policy combined traditional Vietnamese nationalism with Communist ideology and tactics. Relations with most other Communist nations were close, and aid from the People's Republic of China, the Soviet Union, and Eastern Europe was essential to both the DRV's industrial development and its military campaigns in the south. Largely because of this dependence, the DRV avoided commitments to either side in the Sino-Soviet dispute, although it disregarded Beijing's objections by participating in the Paris peace talks in 1968.

Prior to the end of the Vietnam War, Hanoi had evidenced no interest in joining the United Nations. An application submitted in July 1975 was blocked by U.S. action in the Security Council, as was a second application submitted on behalf of the newly unified state in August 1976. In May 1977 the United States withdrew its objection after Hanoi agreed to provide additional information on the fate of missing U.S. servicemen, and the socialist republic was admitted to the world body on September 20.

The DRV had long been involved in the internal affairs of both Laos and Cambodia (Kampuchea), where it supported insurgent movements, partly as a means of keeping open its supply routes to South Vietnam. Following reunification, Hanoi concluded a number of mutual cooperation agreements with Laos that some observers viewed as leaving that country little more than a province of Vietnam. Collaterally, relations with the *Khmer Rouge*–led government of Democratic Kampuchea deteriorated sharply, resulting in numerous military encounters along the two countries' common frontier and a severance of diplomatic relations in December 1977. The clashes continued throughout 1978, escalating into full-scale border warfare and a Vietnamese invasion of its neighbor at the end of the year. In January 1979 Phnom Penh fell to the Vietnamese, supported by a small force of dissident Khmers styling themselves the Kampuchean National United Front for National Salvation (KNUFNS), and a pro-Vietnamese "People's Republic of Kampuchea" was proclaimed under Heng Samrin, a former member of the Kampuchean General Staff. Some 200,000 Vietnamese troops remained in the country.

In reaction to the drive into Cambodia, Chinese forces invaded northern Vietnam on February 17, 1979, and occupied a number of border towns, suffering heavy casualties before withdrawing in mid-March. The incursion was described by Beijing as a "limited operation" designed to "teach Hanoi a lesson" after failure to resolve a number of long-standing disputes—primarily, the validity of late-19th-century border agreements between France and the Chinese empire, jurisdiction over territorial waters in the Gulf of Tonkin, and sovereignty over the Paracel and Spratly islands in the South China Sea. The last island group (also claimed in whole or in part by Brunei, Malaysia, Philippines, and Taiwan) was considered particularly important because of its strategic location astride shipping lanes and the possibility (subsequently confirmed) of oil and gas reserves in its vicinity. Peace talks undertaken by Hanoi and Beijing in April 1979 were broken off by the Chinese in March 1980. Intermittent border conflicts continued thereafter. In January 1987, in the bloodiest encounter since 1979, China mounted a three-day incursion into Vietnam's Ha Tuyen Province, while a brief but pitched encounter between Chinese and Vietnamese naval units erupted in March 1988.

In January 1989 Hanoi dispatched a delegation to Beijing for the first, highly secret, high-level discussions between the two governments in eight years. Seven months earlier Vietnam had formally turned over control of the anti-insurgent campaign in Cambodia to Phnom Penh. Of even greater significance was the fact that Hanoi had participated in an unprecedented meeting of all parties to the Cambodian conflict in Bogor, Indonesia, in July 1988. On September 26, 1989, Vietnam announced that it had withdrawn all its troops from Cambodia, a claim disputed by China.

In November 1991 high-level talks resulted in normalization of Vietnam-China relations after a 20-year estrangement, although it was not until October 1993 that the two countries agreed to negotiations aimed at resolving their various territorial disputes. Meanwhile, following the Communist collapse in Eastern Europe and the dissolution of the Soviet Union (on which Vietnam had remained heavily dependent for economic assistance), regional relations with Japan, South Korea, Thailand, Brunei, and Malaysia had improved, as had relations with various European states, including France, Italy, Germany, and the United Kingdom.

In April 1992 Australia formally renewed aid to Vietnam, ending a 12-year suspension, and the United States eased its long-standing trade embargo with a statement that agricultural and medical supplies to meet basic human needs would no longer be withheld. In early November Japan ended a 14-year freeze on official developmental assistance, and in mid-December U.S. President George H. W. Bush authorized U.S. companies to initiate commercial relations with Vietnam. The U.S. decision followed progress on the issue of missing U.S. servicemen.

In July 1993 Washington indicated that it was dropping its opposition to international assistance in the repayment of $140 million in International Monetary Fund (IMF) debt obligations, and in late September, France, Japan, and 13 other countries joined as Friends of Vietnam to clear the arrears, after which the IMF, the World Bank, and the Asian Development Bank resumed lending. Subsequently, U.S. President Bill Clinton announced on February 4, 1994, an end to the 19-year U.S. economic embargo in view of "significant and tangible results" in the search for American servicemen missing in action.

The leading foreign affairs problem during the first half of 1995 turned on the status of more than 46,000 Vietnamese expatriates in numerous detention camps ringing their homeland, from Thailand to Hong Kong. In mid-March representatives of 30 countries met in Geneva and agreed that 40,000 "boat people" in Hong Kong and Southeast Asia would be returned by early 1996, triggering riots by detainees in Hong Kong, Malaysia, and the Philippines. Many of the detainees declared that they preferred death to repatriation. In the end, however, an aid program sponsored by the European Union assisted some 50,000 returnees before concluding in mid-1999.

Declaring that it was time to "bind up our own wounds," U.S. President Clinton extended full diplomatic recognition to Vietnam on July 11, 1995, 22 years after the American disengagement. (In November 2000 Clinton would become the first U.S. president to visit the unified Vietnam.) The action appeared to have been triggered by Vietnam's admission to the Association of Southeast Asian Nations (ASEAN), which was formalized a month later. In 1996 Vietnam officially applied to join the Asia-Pacific Economic Cooperation (APEC) forum, to which it was formally admitted in 1998.

In October 1998 a visit by Prime Minister Phan Van Khai to China prompted an announcement that both governments intended to resolve land and Gulf of Tonkin boundary disputes by the year 2000. The two signed a land border treaty on December 30, 1999, and a maritime agreement was concluded in December 2000, although the latter did not resolve the Spratly and Paracel disputes. (Actual demarcation of the land border was finally concluded in 2008.) On November 4, 2002, China and the ten ASEAN members signed a voluntary Declaration on the Conduct of Parties in the South China Sea that, while not a formal code of conduct, pledged to seek nonviolent solutions to the competing territorial claims. The agreement did not, however, prevent flaps over such subsequent events as Taiwan's 2004 construction of what it termed a "bird-watching stand" in the Spratlys and Vietnam's announced plans to lead a sight-seeing tour there.

In December 1998 South Korea's President Kim Dae Jung apologized for his country's having sent some 300,000 troops to supplement U.S. forces during the Vietnam War. Prime Minister Khai, noting that Vietnam required neither an apology nor reparations, called instead for a "progressive and future-oriented bilateral relationship."

In September 2000 Vietnam and Russia reached agreement on settling Soviet-era debts, with Hanoi indicating that it would repay $1.7 billion over 23 years, mostly through business concessions. In February 2001 Russian President Vladimir Putin became the first Russian head of state to visit Vietnam.

During a visit by Chinese President Hu Jintao on October 31–November 2, 2005, China and Vietnam marked an improving relationship by signing an agreement for $1 billion in Chinese loans to finance the construction of power plants, rail upgrades, and a police academy. Earlier, the neighbors agreed to conduct joint naval patrols.

In the context of recent economic liberalization and dramatic growth, Vietnam's accession to the World Trade Organization (WTO) was given the highest priority by the Communist government.

Admission was all but sealed in May 2006 when Vietnam overcame a last major hurdle: completion of a new bilateral trade and investment agreement with the United States. In addition to opening up Vietnam's banking, securities, and insurance markets to foreign companies, the pact also ended U.S. quotas on the importation of Vietnamese garments, cut Vietnamese tariffs, and cleared the way for foreigners to participate in wholesale and retail trade. At the beginning of August the U.S. Senate Finance Committee overwhelmingly voted to extend permanent normal trading relations (PNTR) status to Vietnam, but it took until December for both houses of the U.S. Congress to pass the measure. Opposition came from U.S. garment and textile manufacturers, organized labor, and some members of Congress. On November 7 the WTO voted to admit Vietnam, which ratified the accession protocol on November 28. On January 10, 2007, Vietnam officially became a member.

On June 20–22, 2007, Nguyen Minh Triet became the first president of the reunited Vietnam to visit the United States. He conferred with President George W. Bush at the White House and approved a bilateral trade and investment agreement. The preceding November President Bush had made his first visit to Hanoi in connection with the APEC meetings being held there.

Current issues. Hanoi's opponents have long attacked the government's restrictions on religion; alleged human rights abuses against the country's (largely Christian) Montagnard minority; and prosecution of dissidents for offenses that have included "violating state security," "abusing democratic rights," providing false information to "reactionary forces overseas," "sabotaging national unity and causing social disorder," and posting on the Internet information that "tarnished" the VCP and "distorted history." Although the regime has recently shown increased tolerance toward religion, it remains steadfastly opposed to political dissent. In March 2007 it imposed an eight-year prison sentence on Thaddeus NGUYEN VAN LY, a Catholic priest and longtime activist who had been imprisoned at least twice before. This time, a court had convicted him of disseminating information intended to undermine the state.

In March 2008 the government arrested two investigative newspaper reporters who had exposed a major corruption scandal as well as two senior internal security officers who were accused of leaking the stories. The security officials and the reporters, NGUYEN VIET CHIEN of *Thanh Niên* (Young People) and NGUYEN VAN HAI of *Tuổi Trẻ* (Youth), faced charges of "abusing their positions and powers while performing official duties." Their reporting concerned a corruption case involving Ministry of Transport personnel who used department money to bet on European football matches and to conceal their actions with bribes. The case was also noteworthy in that a number of party-run newspapers condemned the arrests on their front pages, which led to speculation that the VCP Politburo was split on how to handle the matter. Sentenced to two years in prison in October 2008, Nguyen Viet Chien was released in January 2009 as part of a traditional new year's amnesty. Nguyen Van Hai, who had pleaded guilty at the start of his trial, was required to participate in "reeducation" but was not jailed. In late December 2008 the editors of both *Thanh Niên* and *Tuổi Trẻ* were sacked.

During a visit to the United States by Prime Minister Nguyen Tan Dung in late June 2008, U.S. and Vietnamese delegations held wide-ranging discussions on such topics as education, the environment and climate change, food security, economic integration, and human rights. A collateral statement by the U.S. State Department noted the "deepening relations" between the two countries, encouraged Hanoi to continue making economic reforms, and announced that talks on a bilateral investment treaty would begin. In the area of human rights, however, "serious concerns remain." The State Department urged that Fr. Nguyen Van Ly and other political prisoners be released and that Vietnam stop using national security provisions "to detain dissidents for activities considered legal acts of free speech under international norms."

In October 2009 nine individuals were convicted and sentenced to between two and six years in prison for engaging in activities deemed harmful to national security—in this case, hanging prodemocracy banners, passing out leaflets, writing articles critical of the government, and posting similar material on the Internet. All were accused of participating in Bloc 8406, a prodemocracy group founded in 2006 (see Opposition Movements, in the Political Parties section, below). Another prominent dissident, LE CONG DINH, a prodemocracy and human rights lawyer, had been arrested in June 2009 on charges of colluding with other dissidents and foreigners to subvert the government.

POLITICAL PARTIES

The Communist party apparatus of North Vietnam operated for many years as the Vietnam Workers' Party—VWP (*Đảng Lao Động Việt Nam*). The VWP was formed in 1954 as successor to the Indochinese Communist Party (founded in 1930 and ostensibly dissolved in 1954) and was the controlling party of North Vietnam's National Fatherland Front (NFF). In South Vietnam, the core of the Provisional Revolutionary Government formed in 1969 was the National Liberation Front (NLF), which had been organized in 1960 by some 20 groups opposed to the policies of President Diem.

In July 1976, representatives of the NFF, the NLF, and other organizations met in Hanoi to organize an all-inclusive **Vietnam Fatherland Front**—VFF (*Mặt Trận Tổ Quốc Việt Nam*), which was formally launched during a congress held in Ho Chi Minh City January 31–February 4, 1977. In addition to the Vietnamese Communist Party (VCP), the front includes various trade union, peasants', women's, youth, and other mass organizations. Under an electoral law approved by the National Assembly in 1980, the VFF is responsible for nominating candidates in all constituencies, in consultation with local groups. PHAM THE DUYET was elected chair of the front's Central Committee Presidium at the organization's Fifth National Congress, held in August 1999. The 879 delegates to the Sixth National Congress, which met in September 2004 in Hanoi, reelected Pham, but he chose to retire in January 2008 and was succeeded by HUYNH DAM. The Seventh National Congress, which met September 28–30, 2009, named an enlarged Central Committee of 355 members and reelected Huynh Dam for a full term.

Leading Party:

Vietnamese Communist Party—VCP (*Đảng Cộng Sản Việt Nam*). The VCP is structured on traditional Communist party lines. A party Congress meets at five-year intervals to select a Central Committee, a Politburo that functions as the executive body, and an administrative Secretariat. The ruling party's present name was adopted by the VWP at its Fourth Congress in 1976. In 1996 the Eighth Party Congress created a five-member Standing Board to replace the larger Secretariat, but the Secretariat was reinstituted at the Ninth Party Congress in 2001.

At a party plenum in June 1997 the Central Committee chose Phan Van Khai to replace Vo Van Kiet as prime minister (pending assembly approval) and voted to limit local officials to two five-year terms (the appointments were previously for life). The committee members were unable, however, to decide on a replacement for President Le Duc Anh, who, along with Vo Van Kiet, had been left off the candidate list for the National Assembly elections due in July. Subsequently, despite reports that competition for the presidency had been narrowed to Foreign Minister NGUYEN MANH CAM and Defense Minister DOAN KHUE, the Committee gave the nod to Tran Duc Luong, and in September its choices were approved by the National Assembly.

In December 1997 the Central Committee elected Lt. Gen. Le Kha Phieu as the party's new general secretary, replacing Do Muoi, who joined Le Duc Ahn and Vo Van Kiet in resigning from the Politburo. All three were subsequently named advisers to the VCP Central Committee.

In January 1999 the party expelled TRAN DO, a retired general and a Central Committee member, for having advocated open elections and freedom of expression. His subsequent request to publish a newspaper was denied. He died in August 2002.

The Ninth Party Congress, held April 19–22, 2001, elected a 150-member Central Committee, a 15-member Politburo, and a 9-member Secretariat. Reportedly, the outgoing Politburo had recommended a second term for General Secretary Le Kha Phieu but was resisted by the Central Committee, which settled on the chair of the National Assembly, Nong Duc Manh. A tenth member was added to the Secretariat at the party's seventh plenum in January 2003.

Meeting April 18–25, 2006, the 1,176 delegates to the Tenth Party Congress elected a 160-member Central Committee (plus 21 alternate members), a Politburo of 14, and an 8-member Secretariat. Although Nong Duc Manh stayed on as general secretary, President Tran Duc Luong, Prime Minister Phan Van Khai, and National Assembly Chair NGUYEN VAN AN all retired from the leadership, signaling their imminent departure from government.

General Secretary: NONG DUC MANH.

Other Members of Politburo: HO DUC VIET (Chair, Central Committee Organization Commission), LE HONG ANH (Minister of Public Security), LE THANH HAI (Chair, Ho Chi Minh City People's Committee), NGUYEN MINH TRIET (State President), NGUYEN PHU TRONG (Chair, National Assembly), NGUYEN SINH HUNG (Deputy Prime Minister), NGUYEN TAN DUNG (Prime Minister), NGUYEN VAN CHI (Director, Central Committee Inspection Commission), PHAM GIA KHIEM (Deputy Prime Minister), PHAM QUANG NGHI (Chair, Hanoi People's Committee), Gen. PHUNG QUANG THANH (Minister of National Defense), TRUONG TAN SANG (Director, Central Committee Economic Commission), TRUONG VINH TRONG (Deputy Prime Minister).

Secretariat: LE VAN DUNG, NGUYEN VAN CHI, NONG DUC MANH, PHAM QUANG NGHI, TO HUY RUA, TONG THI PHONG, TRUONG TAN SANG, TRUONG VINH TRONG.

Opposition Movements:

The government actively suppresses prodemocracy movements and rigorously prosecutes their most outspoken proponents. On April 8, 2006, a total of 118 prodemocracy supporters signed a "Manifesto 2006 on Freedom and Democracy for Vietnam," which gave birth to the **Bloc 8406.** Signers included PHAN VAN LOI and Nguyen Van Ly, the Catholic priest who was imprisoned in March 2007 for distributing material deemed antigovernment by the state. In 2006 a dissident **Democratic Party of Vietnam**—DPV (*Đảng Dân chủ Việt Nam*), named after an earlier party that had been disbanded in 1988, was founded by HOANG MINH CHINH, who died in 2008. Activists associated with the DPV have also been prosecuted by the government.

Expatriate Vietnamese in the United States, Europe, and elsewhere have established numerous political groups, many of which claim insurgent or other support within Vietnam. For example, the **Vietnam Populist Party** (*Đảng Vì Dân*—DVD, also known as the For the People Party) is based in Houston, Texas, but describes itself as a grassroots organization with a number of underground chapters in Vietnam. The international **Vietnam Reform Party** (*Việt Nam Canh Tân Cách Mạng Đảng—Việt Tân*), chaired by DO HOANG DIEM, dates from 2004, when it succeeded the National United Front for the Freedom of Vietnam (NUFLV).

LEGISLATURE

The present **National Assembly** (*Quốc Hội*) is a unicameral body of 493 members serving five-year terms. For the most recent election of May 20, 2007, the Fatherland Front approved 876 candidates, including about 150 nonparty candidates and 30 described as self-nominated. The Vietnam Communist Party won 450 seats, with nonparty candidates winning 42 and self-nominees winning 1.

Chair: NGUYEN PHU TRONG.

CABINET

[as of November 15, 2009]

Prime Minister	Nguyen Tan Dung
Deputy Prime Ministers	Hoang Trung Hai
	Nguyen Sinh Hung
	Nguyen Thien Nhan
	Pham Gia Khiem
	Truong Vinh Trong
Ministers	
Agriculture and Rural Development	Cao Duc Phat
Construction	Nguyen Hong Quan
Culture, Sports, and Tourism	Hoang Tuan Anh
Education and Training	Nguyen Thien Nhan
Finance	Vu Van Ninh
Foreign Affairs	Pham Gia Khiem
Industry and Trade	Vu Huy Hoang
Information and Communication	Le Doan Hop
Internal Affairs	Tran Van Tuan
Justice	Ha Hung Cuong
Labor, War Invalids, and Social Welfare	Nguyen Thi Kim Ngan [f]
National Defense	Gen. Phung Quang Thanh
Natural Resources and Environment	Pham Khoi Nguyen
Planning and Investment	Vo Hong Phuc
Public Health	Nguyen Quoc Trieu
Public Security	Gen. Le Hong Anh
Science and Technology	Hoang Van Phong
Transport	Ho Nghia Dung
Chair, Committee of Ethnic Minorities	Giang Seo Phu
Director, Government Office	Nguyen Xuan Phuc
Governor, State Bank	Nguyen Van Giau
Inspector General	Tran Van Truyen

[f] = female

COMMUNICATIONS

All communications media are controlled and operated by the government, the Vietnamese Communist Party, or subordinate organizations. A June 2006 Decree on Cultural and Information Activities requires prepublication review of articles and sets fines for using anonymous sources, defaming unspecified "national heroes," distributing "reactionary ideology," and revealing "party secrets, state secrets, military secrets, and economic secrets." Internet access is closely monitored, and postings deemed adverse to state interests may also result in prosecution.

Press. Approximately 75 daily and 250 weekly newspapers are published in Vietnam. The following appear daily in Hanoi, unless otherwise noted: *Nhân Dân* (The People, 200,000), official VCP organ; *Sài Gòn Giải Phóng* (Liberated Saigon, Ho Chi Minh City), local VCP organ, in Vietnamese (100,000) and Chinese (14,000); *Lao Động* (Labor, 80,000), trade-union publication; *Hanoi Moi* (New Hanoi, 35,000), local VCP organ; *Việt Nam News* (25,000), English-language organ published by the Vietnam News Agency.

News agencies. The domestic facility is the Vietnam News Agency (*Thông tấn Xã Việt Nam*). A number of foreign bureaus maintain offices in Hanoi.

Broadcasting and computing. The state-owned Voice of Vietnam (*Tiếng Nói Việt Nam*) and Vietnam Television (*Đài Truyền Hình Việt Nam*) are the main broadcasting facilities. Cable television service, including some foreign channels, is available in some areas.

Internet service providers are closely monitored. As of 2008 there were 239.2 Internet users per 1,000 inhabitants.

INTERGOVERNMENTAL REPRESENTATION

Ambassador to the U.S.: LE CONG PHUNG.

U.S. Ambassador to Vietnam: Michael W. MICHALAK.

Permanent Representative to the UN: LE LUONG MINH.

IGO Memberships (Non-UN): ADB, APEC, ASEAN, CP, Interpol, IOM, NAM, OIF, WCO, WTO.

YEMEN

Republic of Yemen
al-Jumhuriyah al-Yamaniyah

Political Status: Independent Islamic Arab republic established by the merger of the former Yemen Arab Republic (North Yemen) and the People's Democratic Republic of Yemen (South Yemen) on May 22, 1990.

Area: 205,355 sq. mi. (531,869 sq. km.), encompassing 75,290 sq. mi. (130,065 sq. km.) of the former Yemen Arab Republic and 195,000 sq. mi. (336,869 sq. km.) of the former People's Democratic Republic of Yemen.

Population: 19,685,161 (2004C); 23,066,000 (2008E).

Major Urban Center (including suburbs, 2005E): SANA (1,625,000).

Official Language: Arabic.

Monetary Unit: YAR Rial (market rate December 1, 2009: 206.46 rials = $1US).

President: Fld. Mar. Ali Abdallah SALIH (General People's Congress); former president of the Yemen Arab Republic; assumed office upon the merger of North and South Yemen on May 22, 1990; elected for an anticipated five-year term by the Presidential Council on October 16, 1993; elected for a new five-year term by the House of Representatives on October 1, 1994, in accordance with constitutional amendments approved September 28; directly elected for an anticipated five-year term on September 23, 1999; current term extended from five to seven years by national referendum of February 20, 2001; reelected on September 20, 2006, and inaugurated for a seven-year term on September 27.

Vice President: Gen. Abdurabu Mansur HADI (General People's Congress); appointed by the president on October 2, 1994; reappointed by the president following elections of September 20, 2006.

Prime Minister: Ali Muhammad MAJUR (General People's Congress); appointed by the president on March 31, 2007, to succeed Abd al-Qadir Abd al-Rahman BAJAMMAL (General People's Congress); sworn in with new government on April 7.

THE COUNTRY

Located at the southern corner of the Arabian peninsula, where the Red Sea meets the Gulf of Aden, the Republic of Yemen shares a lengthy, but until recently largely undefined northern border with Saudi Arabia and a narrow eastern border with Oman (formally demarcated in 1992). Hot, semidesert terrain separates the Red Sea and Gulf coasts from a mountainous interior. The people are predominantly Arab and are divided into two Muslim religious communities: the Zaidi of the Shia sect in the north and east, and the Shaffii community of the Sunni sect in the south and southwest. Tribal influences remain strong, often taking priority over formal governmental activity outside of urban areas. The population growth rate has been estimated recently at about 3.7 percent per year, among the highest in the world.

At the time of the Iraqi invasion of Kuwait in August 1990, more than 1 million Yemeni men were employed outside the country, primarily in Saudi Arabia and other oil-rich Arab states. Their exodus partially reversed by Saudi action following the onset of the Gulf crisis, had created an internal labor shortage and increased women's responsibility for most subsistence agricultural production. In the former Yemen Arab Republic the requirements of purdah precluded any substantial participation by women outside the household; by contrast, the Marxist government of the former People's Democratic Republic emphasized women's rights. Unification brought mixed results: Women were granted suffrage in the new republic's constitution, but observers cited a "turn to the Islamic right" in Yemeni society that led, inter alia, to the legalization of polygamy and the adoption of conservative Muslim dress (already widespread in the north) by many women in the south.

As a result of topographical extremes, Yemeni farmers produce a variety of crops, including cotton (the leading export), grains, fruits, coffee, tobacco, and *qat* (a mild narcotic leaf, which is chewed daily by an estimated 90 percent of the northern population and is estimated to account for nearly 50 percent of GDP). There have been significant discoveries of water in connection with oil exploration, raising the possibility of major agricultural expansion in the future.

Although Yemen is one of the poorest Arab countries and among the poorest nations in the world, significant (and potentially dramatic) economic improvement was expected with the exploitation of extensive oil reserves, first discovered in 1984. Yemen produces nearly 450,000 barrels of oil per day and has reserves of at least 4 billion barrels. Oil revenue accounts for an estimated 70 percent of government income. Significant gas reserves have also been discovered; the Yemen Liquid Natural Gas Company signed a contract in 2005 to supply French, Swiss, and South Korean energy firms. In addition, the port of Aden, one of the world's leading oil bunkering entrepôts prior to the 1967–1975 closure of the Suez Canal, was rehabilitated and became part of the Aden Free Trade Zone.

In 1995 the government adopted a structural adjustment program recommended by the International Monetary Fund (IMF); priorities included promotion of the private sector, trade liberalization, civil service and judicial reform, subsidy reductions, support for the non-oil sector, and tax changes. In view of encouraging developments, the Paris Club of creditor nations rescheduled repayments of much of Yemen's external debt in 1997.

Annual GDP growth bolstered by high oil prices averaged 2.9 percent in 2005–2006. Progress in construction, transportation, and trade accounted for similar growth in the non-oil sector, but a high unemployment rate, reported to be around 20 percent, continued to be of concern, particularly as thousands of Somali refugees fled to Yemen looking for work. Privatization laws and a bank reform plan were put in place, and an anticorruption authority was established by parliament in 2006. However, because of Yemen's lack of progress in curbing corruption, millions of dollars in international aid have been withheld in recent years. With the prospect of declining oil production in years to come, the IMF urged Yemeni authorities to diversify, to elicit public support for reforms, and to impose a general sales tax. Meanwhile, little foreign investment was reported beyond the Aden area. On a more positive note, in 2006 and 2007 the United States and Britain pledged increased financial assistance to Yemen for several years, continuing to exert pressure on the Yemeni government to implement significant economic reforms.

Annual GDP growth of about 4 percent in 2008 was attributed to the rising global price of oil and increases in salaries and pensions to help offset the effects of double-digit inflation. Meanwhile, the IMF warned that Yemen's oil reserves could be depleted in 10 to 12 years and said the launching of a new liquefied natural gas project in 2009 would only "partly compensate for the expected decline in crude oil." The global economic recession appeared to have little effect on economic growth, forecast at 4.4 percent in 2009, with fund managers commending Yemeni authorities for progress in structural reforms and full implementation of a general sales tax. While the IMF stressed the need for Yemen to diversify its economy and expand its revenue base, it also praised the government's commitment to reducing spending, including the gradual elimination of fuel subsidies, and its establishment of an anticorruption commission.

GOVERNMENT AND POLITICS

Political background.

Yemen Arab Republic (YAR). Former site of the Kingdom of Sheba and an early center of Near Eastern civilization, the territory subsequently known as North Yemen fell under the rule of the Ottoman Turks in the 16th century. The withdrawal of Turkish forces in 1918 made it possible for Imam YAHYA Muhammad Hamid al-Din, the traditional ruler of the Zaidi religious community, to gain political supremacy. Yahya remained as theocratic ruler until 1948, when he was murdered in an attempted coup and was succeeded by his son, Saif al-ISLAM

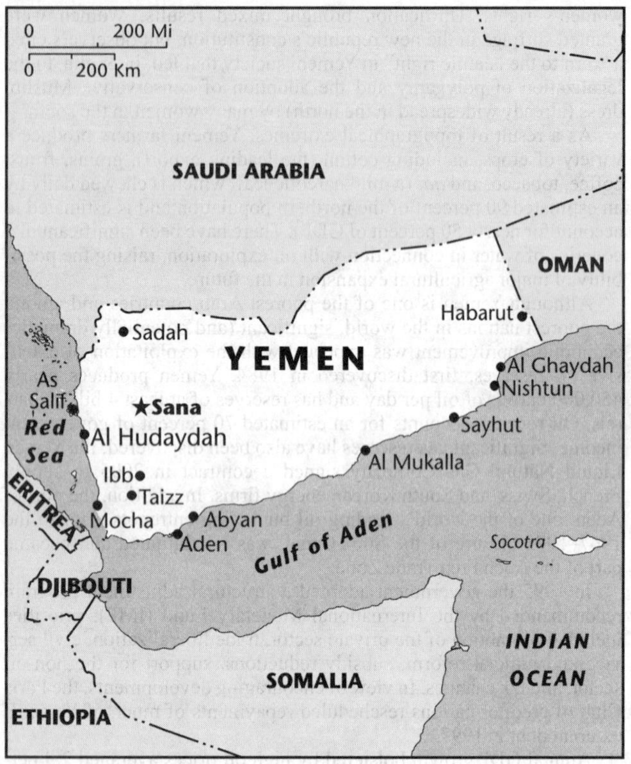

Ahmad. The new leader instituted a more outward-looking policy: Diplomatic relations were established with the Soviet Union in 1956, and in 1958 the monarchy joined with the United Arab Republic (Egypt and Syria) in a federation (the United Arab States), which was dissolved three years later.

A series of unsuccessful uprisings against the absolute and antiquated regime of the imams culminated on September 26, 1962, in the ouster of the newly installed Imam Muhammad al-BADR by a group of army officers under Col. (later Field Marshal) Abdallah al-SALAL, who established a republic with close ties to the United Arab Republic (UAR). Although the new regime was recognized by the United States and many other governments, resistance by followers of the imam precipitated a civil war that continued intermittently until early 1969.

Outside forces, including from Saudi Arabia (which supported the royalists) and Egypt (which supported the republicans), were withdrawn in late 1967 following the UAR's defeat in the June war with Israel and the conclusion of an agreement with Saudi Arabia at an Arab summit in Khartoum, Sudan. President Salal was subsequently ousted in favor of a three-man Presidential Council headed by Abd al-Rahman al-IRYANI. Internal factional rivalry continued, but in May 1970 an informal compromise was reached whereby royalist elements were assimilated into the regime. The rudiments of modern governmental institutions were established with the adoption of a new constitution in late 1970 and the election of a Consultative Council in early 1971, although political stability continued to depend on the personal success of such leaders as prime ministers Hassan al-AMRI and Muhsin Ahmad al-AYNI. On June 13, 1974, in another, apparently bloodless coup, the Iryani regime was superseded by a seven-man Military Command Council (MCC) led by Lt. Col. Ibrahim Muhammad al-HAMADI. In January 1975, Prime Minister Ayni, who had been appointed only seven months earlier, was replaced by Abd al-Aziz Abd al-GHANI.

On October 11, 1977, Colonel Hamadi was assassinated in Sana by unknown assailants, and the MCC immediately established a Presidential Council headed by Lt. Col. Ahmad Husayn al-GHASHMI, with Prime Minister Ghani and Maj. Abdallah Abd al-ALIM, commander of the paratroop forces, as the other members. Ghashmi was assassinated on June 24, 1978, by a bomb-bearing "special emissary" of the South Yemeni government. A new four-member provisional Presidential Council was thereupon organized, including Prime Minister Ghani, Constituent Assembly Speaker Abd al-Karim al-ARASHI, armed forces commander Ali al-SHIBA, and Maj. Ali Abdallah SALIH. The assembly elected Salih president of the republic on July 17 and three days later named Arashi to the newly created office of vice president. Ghani continued as prime minister.

Attempts to overthrow Salih were reported in July and October 1978. A prolonged delay in reaching agreement on constitutional issues was attributed to continuing conflict between republican and traditionalist groups. The situation was further complicated in early 1979 when South Yemeni forces crossed into North Yemen and were joined by rebels of the leftist National Democratic Front (NDF), led by Sultan Ahmad UMAR. Following mediation by the Arab League, a cease-fire was implemented on March 16, and the southern troops were withdrawn. On March 30 talks in Kuwait between President Salih and Council Chair Abd al-Fattah Ismail of the People's Democratic Republic concluded with a mutual pledge to reopen discussions on eventual unification of the two Yemens. Toward that end, a number of high-level meetings between Sana and Aden took place during the next 18 months, while on October 15, 1980, in a significant internal reorganization, Prime Minister Ghani was replaced by Abd al-Karim Ali al-IRYANI and named co-vice president. On May 22, 1983, the assembly reelected Salih for a second five-year term, while on November 12 Vice President Ghani was reappointed prime minister, with Iryani being assigned to direct the reconstruction of earthquake-damaged areas.

Balloting for 128 members of a new 159-seat Consultative Council (*Majlis al-Shura*) to replace the Constituent Assembly took place on July 5, 1988, the remaining 31 seats being filled by presidential appointment. On July 17 the council reelected Salih to a third five-year term as head of state, with Vice President Arashi being designated council speaker. On July 31 Salih reappointed Major Ghani to head a partially reorganized administration. (See Republic of Yemen, below, for information on negotiations leading to unification with the People's Democratic Republic of Yemen (and political developments from 1990 to the present.)

People's Democratic Republic of Yemen (PDRY). British control of South Yemen began with the occupation of Aden in 1839, and through treaties with numerous local rulers, was gradually extended north and eastward to include what came to be known as the Western and Eastern Protectorates. Aden was ruled as part of British India until 1937, when it became a separate Crown colony. In preparation for eventual independence, the British established the Federation of South Arabia, in which the colony of Aden was associated with 16 dependent states that had previously belonged to the protectorates. Plans for a transfer of power to the rulers of the federation were frustrated, however, by increasing nationalist agitation and resistance activity on the part of radical elements. By 1967 a power struggle among rival nationalist groups had resulted in the emergence of the left-wing National Liberation Front (NLF) as the area's strongest political organization. Control of the territory was handed over by Britain to representatives of the NLF (restyled as the National Front—NF) on November 30, 1967.

Qahtan al-SHAABI, the principal NF leader, became president and prime minister of the new People's Republic of Southern Yemen, which, though beset by grave internal problems and revolts, rapidly emerged as a center of left-wing revolutionary nationalist agitation in South Arabia. The position of the comparatively moderate Shaabi became progressively weaker, and as the result of a continuing power struggle between the moderate and radical wings of the NF, he was forced from office in June 1969; the country's name was changed in December 1970 to the People's Democratic Republic of Yemen. In August 1971 another change of government brought into power Salim Rubayi ALI and Abd al-Fattah ISMAIL, heads of the NF's pro-Chinese and pro-Soviet factions, respectively; both participated in a three-member Presidential Council, chaired by Ali as head of state.

In the course of a leadership struggle that erupted into street fighting in the capital on June 26, 1978, Ali was removed from office and executed after allegations (largely discounted by foreign observers) that he had been involved in the assassination two days earlier of President Ghashmi of North Yemen. Following Ali's ouster, Prime Minister Ali Nasir MUHAMMAD al-Hasani was designated chair of the Presidential Council, with Ismail and Defense Minister Ali Ahmad Nasir ANTAR al-Bishi as the other members. Although expanded to five members on July 1, the presidential collegium was superseded on December 27 by an 11-member presidium of the recently elected Supreme People's Council (SPC), with Ismail serving as chair. Earlier, in mid-October, the Yemeni Socialist Party (YSP) had been organized, in succession to the NF, as the country's controlling political organization.

On March 30, 1979, SPC chair Ismail and President Salih of North Yemen concluded a three-day meeting in Kuwait that had been called in the wake of renewed hostilities between their two countries. Despite obvious ideological differences between the conservative North and the Marxist-Leninist South, the leaders pledged that they would renew efforts, first broached in 1972 but suspended in 1975, to unify the two Yemens.

On April 21, 1980, Council Chair Ismail, ostensibly for reasons of ill health, resigned his government and party posts, with Prime Minister Muhammad being named by the YSP Central Committee as his successor in both capacities. Five days later, the SPC confirmed Muhammad (who retained the prime ministership) as head of state. His position was further consolidated at an extraordinary party congress held October 12–14, when a Politburo and a Secretariat dominated by his supporters were named, and at an extraordinary session of the SPC on October 16, when a revamped cabinet was approved.

At the conclusion of an SPC session on February 14, 1985, Muhammad resigned as chair of the council of ministers, while retaining his position as head of state. Concurrently, a new cabinet was approved, headed by former construction minister Haydar Abu Bakr al-ATTAS. In October Muhammad was reelected secretary general of the YSP, albeit as part of a political compromise that necessitated enlargement of the Central Committee from 47 to 77 members and the Politburo from 13 to 16. In particular, the reinstatement of former chair Ismail to the Politburo indicated that there would be increased opposition to the policies of the incumbent state and party leader.

On January 13, 1986, SPC chair Muhammad mounted a "gangland-style" massacre of YSP opponents, in the course of which Ismail and a number of others, including Defense Minister Salih Muslih QASIM, were killed. However, the chair's opponents regrouped and, after more than a week of bitter fighting in the capital, succeeded in defeating the Ali Nasir faction, with Muhammad gaining asylum in North Yemen. On January 24 ministerial chair al-Attas, who had been in India at the time of the attempted purge, was designated interim head of state. On February 6 the YSP Central Committee named Ali Salim al-BEIDH to succeed Muhammad as its secretary general, while the SPC on February 8 confirmed al-Attas as presidium chair and appointed a new government headed by Yasin Said NUMAN; both were reconfirmed on November 6, 1986, by a new council elected October 28–30.

Republic of Yemen. In the fall of 1981 unification talks between North Yemen's President Ali Abdallah Salih and his South Yemen counterpart, Ali Nasir Muhammad, culminated in an agreement signed in Aden on December 2 to establish a Yemen Council, embracing the two chief executives, and a Joint Ministerial Council to promote integration in the political, economic, and social spheres. On December 30 the Aden News Agency reported that a draft constitution of a unified Yemeni Republic would be submitted to referenda in the two states at an unspecified date. Progress toward unification slowed, however, in the wake of domestic turmoil in the south in early 1986, which resulted in Muhammad's ouster and flight to the north.

Strongly influenced by the impact of Soviet leader Mikhail Gorbachev's policy of restructuring (perestroika) on the PDRY's Marxist-oriented leadership, the Yemen and Joint Ministerial councils were revived in May 1988, while on December 1, 1989, a draft joint constitution was published that called for an integrated multiparty state headed by a five-member Presidential Council. The new basic law was implemented on May 22, 1990, after having been ratified the previous day by the constituent states' respective parliaments. On the same day, as agreed upon earlier by both parliaments, newly promoted General Salih assumed the presidency of the Republic of Yemen for what was initially proclaimed as a 30-month transitional term. The PDRY's Ali Salim al-Beidh was named vice president for a projected term of the same duration. On May 26 former South Yemeni president al-Attas was named prime minister by the transitional House of Representatives, with a joint administration being installed on May 27.

The first general elections were postponed by Salih from the original date of November 1992 (the end of the proposed 30-month transitional period) because of domestic unrest. When the voting for a new House of Representatives was finally conducted on April 27, 1993, Salih's General People's Congress (GPC) outpolled the more than 40 participating parties, followed by the conservative Yemeni Congregation for Reform (*Islah*) and the YSP. On May 30 the three leading parties announced the formation of a coalition government, again led by al-Attas and initially encompassing 15 GPC, 9 YSP, and 4 *Islah* members. However, *Islah* subsequently demanded greater representation on the basis of its electoral showing and was awarded two newly created additional cabinet posts on June 10.

On October 11, 1993, the House of Representatives elected Salih and al-Beidh to a new Presidential Council, along with former YAR prime minister Ghani of the GPC, the YSP's Salim Salih MUHAMMAD, and *Islah*'s Abd al-Maguid al-ZINDANI. Five days later the council elected Salih as its chair and thereby president of the republic, al-Beidh being renamed vice president. However, al-Beidh, who had refused to leave Aden since August because of security concerns, did not attend the induction or take the oath of office.

In February 1994 Salih and al-Beidh signed a Document of Pledge and Agreement, which had been brokered by a multiparty Committee for National Dialogue formed in November 1993 to resolve the political stalemate between the two leaders. The accord provided for many of the so-called "18-points" al-Beidh had recently issued as requirements for continued southern support for the union. They included the withdrawal of army units from the former north-south border, establishment of a new national intelligence organization, investigation into the numerous assassinations of YSP members since unification, decentralization of government authority, and a review of national economic policy.

Despite widespread internal and external relief over the signing of the peace agreement in early 1994, it quickly became apparent that no true reconciliation had been achieved, al-Beidh and Muhammad refusing to attend a March Presidential Council session in Sana. Intense international mediation notwithstanding, sporadic fighting between northern and southern military units (never unified under the 1990 arrangements) broke out in late April 1994.

As hostilities escalated into full-fledged war, Salih declared a state of emergency on May 5, 1994, and dismissed al-Beidh and Muhammad from the Presidential Council and Prime Minister al-Attas and several other YSP members from the government. Industry Minister Muhammad Said al-ATTAR, a member of the GPC, was named acting prime minister.

Heavy fighting over the next two weeks appeared to favor northern forces, which had launched a sustained offensive toward Aden. Consequently, in an apparent attempt to garner international support for his cause, al-Beidh on May 21, 1994, announced the south's secession from the union and the formation of an independent Democratic Republic of Yemen. A Presidential Council, with al-Beidh as its president, was established for the new state along with a provisional National Salvation Council, while al-Attas was named prime minister of a YSP-dominated government announced on June 2. However, no international recognition was forthcoming for the new republic, and the south's military position became increasingly precarious, several cease-fires quickly collapsing. Following a week of heavy shelling, during which most separatist leaders (including al-Beidh) fled the country, northern forces secured control of Aden on July 7, effectively ending the civil war and the short-lived secession.

On September 28, 1994, the House of Representatives approved several constitutional amendments, the most important of which eliminated the Presidential Council, whose unwieldiness had contributed to prewar friction. Three days later the house, acting as an "electoral college" on a onetime basis as provided for in the basic law revision, elected Salih by a nearly unanimous vote to a new five-year presidential term. On October 2 Salih appointed Maj. Gen. Abdurabu Mansur HADI as vice president, and on October 6 he named former YAR co-vice president Ghani to head the first postwar government. A new cabinet, announced the day of Ghani's appointment as prime minister, included 16 ministers from the GPC, 9 from *Islah,* and 1 independent, the rump YSP having gone into opposition.

President Salih subsequently adopted a conciliatory stance, issuing a general amnesty for all southerners except former vice president al-Beidh and 15 other separatist leaders. (However, Salih and al-Beidh reconciled at a May 2003 meeting in Abu Dhabi, and Salih reportedly promised that all exiled socialist officials could return.) Salih also placed the nation's military forces under a unified command and announced similar plans for the police and intelligence organizations. In addition, the government pledged to put restrictions on civilian weapons, some reports suggesting that there were as many as 50 million guns in the country (an average of more than three per person). On the political front, the constitutional changes approved in September 1994 served to consolidate power in the hands of Salih, who was declared eligible for two five-year terms in the newly strengthened presidency.

The first new legislative poll since the civil war was conducted on April 27, 1997, with the GPC securing 187 seats, followed by *Islah* with 53. (The YSP, deemed unlikely to recover from the secessionist debacle for many years, boycotted the balloting, as did several small parties.) On March 14 the president named Faraj Said ibn GHANIM, a nonparty economist from the south who had once been a member of the YSP, as the new prime minister. The cabinet appointed the following day included a relatively even mix of old and new faces but, most notably, no representatives from *Islah,* which moved into a position of formal opposition.

Despite the YSP boycott, the peaceful legislative balloting of April 1997 was broadly viewed as an important step toward cementing Yemen's image as a stable country genuinely committed to democracy. International observers described the balloting as generally free and fair, while the participation of women both as candidates and voters earned Western praise. However, the explosion of several bombs in Aden in late July underscored the ongoing fragility of the social fabric, while the subsequent arrest of more than 100 opposition figures reminded observers of the government's continued penchant for heavy-handed action.

Amid reports of growing friction between Prime Minister Ghanim and President Salih over economic issues, Ghanim offered his resignation in mid-April 1998. Salih formally accepted the resignation on April 29 and asked Deputy Prime Minister Abd al-Karim Ali al-Iryani (former prime minister of the Yemen Arab Republic) to take over the government on a caretaker basis. Salih formally appointed Iryani as prime minister on May 14, and a new (only slightly changed) government was sworn in on May 17. All ministers were affiliated with the GPC except for one independent and one member of the small Truth Party; the latter resigned four months later.

In the country's first direct presidential election on September 23, 1999, Salih was credited with 96.3 percent of the vote. (Only one challenger was sanctioned under controversial electoral regulations [see Current issues, below].) Subsequently, in another development that was strongly criticized by the government's opponents, Salih and the GPC proposed constitutional amendments extending the presidential term from five to seven years and the legislature's term from four to six years and calling for a new, enlarged Shura Council. The amendments received a reported 73 percent "yes" vote in a national referendum on February 20, 2001.

On March 31, 2001, President Salih named Abd al-Qadir Abd al-Rahman BAJAMMAL, theretofore the deputy prime minister, to replace Prime Minister Iryani. (Reports variously said that Iryani had resigned for health reasons or had been dismissed by the president in order to inject "new blood" into the government.) Bajammal on April 4 announced a new cabinet, which was inaugurated on April 7.

In legislative elections on April 27, 2003, the GPC significantly increased its majority, winning 238 seats, with some 8 million Yemenis reportedly going to the polls. In the wake of the U.S. invasion of Iraq in March, Yemeni authorities wanted to show the strength of their determined steps toward democracy. Significantly, the YSP, which had boycotted the 1997 elections, yielded some 100 candidates and negotiated with *Islah* and other constituencies to avoid splitting the antigovernment vote. However, the YSP won only 7 seats, and *Islah* 46. In a conciliatory move, President Salih appointed a prominent socialist, Salim Saleh MUHAMMAD, as his special adviser. Some accusations of vote fraud surfaced. Three people died and 15 were injured in polling-day violence. A cabinet reshuffle followed the election, with half of the 35 members being replaced. A new ministry of human rights was established a few months later, headed by a woman.

In a major cabinet reshuffle on February 11, 2006, seven months before the scheduled presidential election, President Salih replaced 16 members, resulting in a cabinet in which all ministers were members of the GPC. In the presidential election of September 20, 2006, President Salih was reelected to a third term with 77.2 percent of the vote. Next among the four other candidates was Faisal bin SHAMLAN, the nominee of the opposition Joint Meeting Parties (JMP) who was credited with 21.8 percent of the vote. Yasin Abdu SAID, who ran under the banner of the National Council of Opposition Parties (NCOP), and two independent candidates each won less than 1 percent of the vote. Salih was sworn in for a seven-year term on September 27.

On March 31, 2007, President Salih appointed Electricity Minister Ali Muhammad MAJUR of the GPC to replace Bajammal as prime minister. Majur named a new cabinet on April 4, and he was sworn in along with the new government on April 7.

The country's first election of provincial governors on March 17, 2008, resulted in the GPC winning the governorship of Sana and 16 other provinces; independents were elected in three provinces. The governors were indirectly elected by members of municipal councils in Yemen's 20 provinces. In a cabinet reshuffle on May 19 ordered by President Salih, GPC members were appointed to six key ministries in addition to other changes.

Elections scheduled for the House of Representatives on April 27, 2009, were postponed for two years in February pending proposed constitutional changes.

Constitution and government. The 1990 constitution of the Republic of Yemen provided for a five-member Presidential Council, chosen by a popularly elected House of Representatives. The council was empowered to select its own chair and vice chair, who served effectively as the republic's president and vice president. The term of office was set at five years for the Presidential Council and four years for the House of Representatives. However, in the aftermath of the civil war, the House on September 28, 1994, revised the basic law, abolishing the Presidential Council and providing for an elected chief executive with broadened powers, including the right to name the vice president and prime minister. In view of the turmoil remaining from the secessionist conflict, the house empowered itself to select the next president to serve for a five-year term, after which chief executives were to be chosen by direct popular election. In addition, future presidents were limited to two five-year terms. Following the legislative balloting of April 1997, President Salih announced the creation of a new Consultative Council, an advisory body of 59 presidentially appointed members. In the February 20, 2001, constitutional referendum, the presidential term of office was extended to seven years, and a new Shura Council was established with 111 members appointed by the president. Unlike the Consultative Council it replaced, the Shura Council was granted some decision-making responsibilities (see Legislature, below).

In a move with widespread political implications, the transitional government in 1990 appointed a commission to redraw the boundaries of local governorates, some of which had traditionally been ruled as virtual fiefdoms by tribal chiefs. On April 27, 2008, the country's local authorities law was amended to provide for the first elections for provincial governors. Previously, the governors were appointed by the president. Under the amended law, all 20 provincial governors are indirectly elected by members of municipal councils in each governorate.

The 1990 basic law stipulated that the Islamic legal code (sharia) was to be utilized as "one source" of Yemeni law; the wording was changed to "the source" in 1994.

Foreign relations. North Yemen broke out of its long, largely self-imposed isolation in the mid-1950s, when the imam's government accepted economic and military aid from the Soviet Union, the People's Republic of China, the United Arab Republic, and the United States. Diplomatic relations with Washington were broken off in June 1967 during the Arab-Israeli war, but resumed in July 1972. Subsequent foreign concerns turned primarily on relations with the country's two immediate neighbors, conservative Saudi Arabia and Marxist South Yemen. Despite the former's previous record of support for Yemen's defeated royalists, Saudi money and arms were instrumental during intermittent border warfare with South Yemen during 1971–1972 and again in February–March 1979. However, subsequent reaffirmation of the two Yemens' intention to merge (originally announced in 1972) was coolly received by Riyadh, which withheld several hundred million dollars in military supplies. In turn, North Yemen renewed its military dealings with the Soviet Union, and in October 1979 the Saudis were reported to have ended their annual budgetary supplement of $250 million. In May 1988 an unimplemented 1985 accord between the two Yemens to create an 850-square-mile "joint economic zone" straddling the poorly demarcated border between the YAR's Marib region and the PDRY's Shabwa area was reactivated. However, Saudi Arabia had previously entered a claim for much of the disputed territory on the basis of recently published maps that extended its border with North Yemen many miles to the west of the previously assumed location.

The People's Democratic Republic of Yemen professed a policy of nonalignment in foreign affairs, but its relations with other Arab countries were mixed because of its long-standing opposition to all conservative regimes and its record of close association with the Soviet Union. It voted against admission of the Persian Gulf sheikhdoms to the Arab League. Numerous border clashes resulted from tensions with Saudi Arabia and the Yemen Arab Republic. Elsewhere, as a member of the hard-line Arab "steadfastness front," Aden rejected any partial settlement of the Middle East question, particularly the 1979 Egyptian-Israeli peace treaty.

Iraq's incursion into Kuwait dominated the Republic of Yemen's foreign policy agenda throughout the second half of 1990 and early 1991. Having initially deplored the invasion, Sana was criticized for maintaining a pro-Iraqi stance by abstaining in early August from a UN Security Council vote for sanctions against Baghdad and an Arab League vote to condemn the occupation. Subsequently, the government withdrew its threat to ignore international sanctions, but its unremitting criticism of the presence of Western troops in Saudi Arabia led Riyadh on September 19 to withdraw special privileges granted to Yemeni citizens. By late November upward of 700,000 Yemeni nationals had been repatriated, with Sana claiming that Yemen should be compensated $1.7 billion for losses caused by the crisis. On November 29 Yemen (the sole Arab UN Security Council member) voted against the council's resolution to use "all necessary means to uphold and implement" its earlier resolutions concerning Iraq, calling instead for a peaceful, Arab-negotiated settlement. Consequently, in January 1991 the United States announced it would withhold $18 million of aid promised to Yemen; the Gulf states also withheld aid. Tension between Yemen and Saudi Arabia was described as being at an all-time high in mid-1992, their border conflict having taken on greater significance in view of recent oil discoveries in the region. Meanwhile, the antipathy generated in the West by Yemen's pro-Iraqi tilt during the Gulf crisis had also largely dissipated, with Western attention again focusing on oil exploration licenses being issued by Sana.

The United States endorsed unity and thereby the northern cause during the 1994 civil war. In addition, Washington reportedly pressured Saudi Arabia (which apparently preferred a divided Yemen) and several other Arab countries into forgoing plans to recognize the PDRY, thereby hastening the secessionist regime's collapse. Riyadh's "quiet" financial and military support for the southern forces exacerbated tension with Sana, and sporadic clashes were reported in late 1994 between Saudi and Yemeni troops in the contested border region. Under heavy international pressure to avoid further hostilities, however, the two countries agreed in February 1995 to negotiate, and the result was a preliminary accord that called for joint committees to demarcate the border and monitor future troop movements in the region. On June 3 Yemen and Oman completed demarcation of their frontier in accordance with a 1992 agreement.

In late 1995 a major foreign relations problem arose when Eritrean forces invaded Greater Hanish, one of nine islands in the archipelago between the two countries near the mouth of the Red Sea. Although sovereignty over the islands had never been formally established by international convention, Yemeni fisherman had operated from Greater Hanish for many years, and some 200 Yemeni soldiers had been garrisoned there to provide "security" for a new hotel construction site. Eritrea, which based its claim on a 1938 agreement between Britain and Ethiopia, assumed control of Greater Hanish in December after three days of fighting, which took some 12 lives. Yemen, which based its claim on British turnover of two lighthouses on the islands to South Yemen in 1967, subsequently agreed to submit the dispute to binding arbitration by a panel of five judges. Tension remained high in early 1999, however, as Eritrea's war with Ethiopia complicated regional affairs. However, Eritrea returned control of Greater Hanish (and nearby islands) to Yemen shortly after the international tribunal ruled in the latter's favor in December. The tribunal also demarcated the maritime border between the two countries, whose relationship was subsequently described as "normalized." Relations with Saudi Arabia, strained by significant border clashes in 1997, 1998, and early 2000, improved substantially after a border agreement was announced in June 2000. Finally, in May 2004 both sides accepted the border demarcation plans developed by a German firm. In March 2005 officials from both countries, in a small sign of warming relations, discussed bilateral cooperation. By 2006, they had established a cooperation council, and in June they signed a final border treaty, which included infrastructure, fisheries, and social affairs agreements.

In mid-2004 Yemen was invited to take part in a G-8 Summit in Georgia that focused on promoting democracy in the Middle East. Observers attributed Yemen's presence to the country's support of the U.S. "war on terror." Yemen claimed to have arrested or jailed a large number of terror suspects linked to al-Qaida, which led the United States to resume arms sales to Yemen in 2004.

In 2006 members of the Gulf Cooperation Council (GCC) agreed to provide sufficient aid to help boost Yemen's economy to the point at which the country could be considered for membership in the GCC. (In December 2008 Yemen was admitted to four new GCC bodies, and in March 2009 it was admitted to the GCC's Chambers of Commerce.)

In November 2007 Yemen sent Foreign Affairs Minister Abu-Bakr Abdallah al-QIRBI to the U.S.-sponsored Middle East peace talks in Annapolis, Maryland, which resulted in a statement of "joint understanding" by Israel and Palestine to commit to a negotiated peace accord by the end of 2008. In March 2008 President Salih brokered an agreement in Sana between representatives of Hamas and Fatah to begin reconciliation talks. In January 2009 Yemen called on Hamas and Fatah to "resume dialogue" and form a unity government.

In the early months of 2009 as many as 5,000 Somali refugees fleeing their war-torn country settled in refugee camps in Yemen.

In May 2009 the U.S. deputy director of the U.S. Central Intelligence Agency held talks in Sana with Yemeni officials regarding cooperation in the U.S. war against terrorism, the official praising Yemen's counterterrorism efforts. Earlier in the year Yemen had rejected a U.S. bid to send some of the Yemeni detainees held at the U.S. military prison at Guantánamo Bay, Cuba, to a rehabilitation program in Saudi Arabia. The Yemeni government said it would take in the men—who comprise the largest group of prisoners in Guantánamo—after building its own rehabilitation center. Subsequently, however, it was reported that the United States and Yemen were close to an agreement on sending the detainees to Saudi Arabia.

Current issues. Yemen became the focus of intense international attention in 2000 when 17 U.S. sailors died following a suicide bombing attack against the destroyer USS Cole while it was refueling in Aden harbor on October 12. (The refueling arrangement had been implemented in 1999 as part of Washington's "engagement" policy, which also included mine-clearing assistance by U.S. forces in Yemen and a White House audience in the spring of 2000 for President Salih.) Five years later, a Yemeni court commuted the sentence of one of two people and jailed four others for their role in the bombing, now considered by the United States to have been an al-Qaida attack. A year earlier, ten suspects in the Cole attack escaped from a Yemeni jail, aided by some two dozen others during a time of heightened violence by Islamic militants in the country. Many of these extremists were suspected of being linked to Osama bin Laden, who, the United States warned, might be trying to regroup in his ancestral home.

Relations with Washington improved following the al-Qaida attacks in the United States in September 2001, with Salih announcing that his government would cooperate with the subsequent U.S.-led global "war on terrorism." Among other things, the Yemeni government shut down a number of religious and educational institutions suspected of serving as recruiting grounds for Islamic militants. The initiative intensified friction with the opposition *Islah* party, which had established some of the schools. However, terrorist attacks continued to plague Yemen, with high-profile episodes such as the killing of three American missionaries at a Baptist hospital in December 2002. A member of the *Islah* party was sentenced to death in September 2003 for that crime. Earlier in 2003 "scores" of Muslim militants with suspected links to terrorism were arrested, and another *Islah* official, who claimed to be bin Laden's "spiritual leader," was captured in Germany. Government forces also attacked the Islamic Army of Aden-Abyan, said to be linked to al-Qaida, and the leader of the group was executed in 2003. In the same year, authorities began experimenting with a "re-education" program in response to complaints about the large number of arrests and detainees being held without trial. The detainees were given religious instruction about "the true meaning of jihad," and those who signed consenting documents were released to their families.

Adding to Yemen's difficulties was the uprising in 2004 led by popular Shiite cleric Husayn al-HUTHI and his Organization of Believing Youth (*al-Shabab al-Mumin*). Hundreds of al-Huthi's followers were killed, and more continued to die in violent clashes even after Yemeni army officials announced in September 2004 that al-Huthi had been killed. Confrontations in the mountainous northwest province of Saada were sustained through April 2005. Following a period of calm, President Salih announced in September an amnesty for all imprisoned supporters of al-Huthi. About the same time, a Yemeni court canceled trials for and pardoned 36 people accused in the death of al-Huthi.

With several hundred suspected al-Qaida members jailed as of March 2005, the United States praised the government's crackdown on terrorists. At the same time, analysts suggested that Salih faced a difficult job balancing cooperation with the United States with growing sentiment within the populace against Israel and the United States. To enhance its standing, Yemen created a new ministry of human rights, and Salih continued to endorse democracy publicly, although skeptics reportedly viewed his stance as "window dressing" in response to pressure by President George W. Bush for more democracy in the Middle

East. In February 2006, 23 prisoners, including 13 al-Qaida members and one of the men responsible for the USS *Cole* attack, escaped from a Yemeni military prison. Observers pointed to the escape as an example of the country's deteriorating security situation, although the government continued its crackdown on terror suspects.

On the political front, in what was described as an unprecedented move in the region, President Salih announced in 2005 that he would not seek reelection in 2006, preferring to turn leadership over to "young blood." However, he ultimately registered as a candidate in response to what he described as rallies by millions of supporters and pledged to pursue democratization. In the days leading up to the election, 51 people were killed and at least 200 were injured in a stampede at a pro-Salih rally in an overcrowded stadium. The campaign focused on curbing government corruption and advancing democracy, with Salih making broad gestures toward democratization by providing government funding for candidates and granting them free access to Yemeni television. Faisal bin Shamlan presented the president with his strongest challenge in 28 years. Shamlan had resigned as oil minister in 1995 to protest alleged corruption in the government and staged his campaign with the support of Islamic and socialist parties, among other opposition groups in the JMP coalition (see Political Parties and Groups, below). Salih's victory was bolstered by GPC success in local elections held the same day, further reinforcing his authority (along with the GPC majority already established in parliament). Though the JMP initially rejected the results of the presidential poll, claiming fraud and other irregularities, it ultimately accepted the outcome. The international community appeared to acknowledge the results as sufficiently representative of the popular will. (Five people were killed in election-day clashes, but turnout nevertheless was strong, at 65 percent.) Salih, for his part, was intent on pursuing much-needed reforms, observers said. Salih's major cabinet reshuffle in March 2007 (to include more technocrats) was seen as a response to international pressure to introduce reforms.

In 2006–2007 Yemen continued its antiterrorism efforts with a series of arrests, including two alleged suicide bombers plotting attacks on oil installations. Government forces killed at least two al-Qaida members who had escaped from prison following their conviction for a 2002 plan to attack a French oil tanker. Clashes with members of the Organization of Believing Youth escalated in 2007, resulting in numerous deaths of Yemeni security forces. President Salih called on al-Huthi's followers to disarm, but the group reportedly indicated it would broaden its insurgency outside of Sadaah province in the north and, according to a foreign Web site, it allegedly threatened Jewish families in Yemen.

In July 2007 it was reported that the government was allowing known al-Qaida members and other Islamic extremists to stay out of prison in exchange for signing an agreement with the government to obey the law. Government officials said it was a practical solution in Yemen, the ancestral home of al-Qaida leader Osama bin Laden. Meanwhile, observers said unemployment and poverty in Yemen continued to contribute to a growing number of insurgents recruited from Yemen by terrorist groups and paid to go to Iraq. Relations with the United States were strained in 2007–2008, following Sana's refusal to accede to a U.S.request to extradite Jamal al-BADAWI, a member of al-Qaida who had been found guilty of organizing the attack on the USS *Cole*, and another al-Qaida suspect.

Meanwhile, political changes were under way in 2008 with the republic holding its first elections for provincial governors on May 17. The JMP boycotted the election, nominating its candidates as independents. The GPC dominated the results, winning in 17 provinces, while independents were chosen in the remaining 3. The opposition, which favored direct, public voting, criticized as undemocratic the system of indirect balloting by members of local councils. The elections were part of a package of reforms promised by the president in April following a series of violent demonstrations in the south by army officers, activists, and unemployed citizens protesting alleged unequal treatment by the government in the north. On May 19 the cabinet was reshuffled because several ministers had been elected as governors. Most of the replacement ministers were members of the GPC, reinforcing the party's hold on the central government, in addition to its gains in the provinces. Shortly thereafter, four of the ousted ministers were accused of corruption.

While hostilities between the government and al-Huthi Shiite rebels continued to escalate in 2008, an attack in May on a mosque in Saddah that killed 18 and wounded 45 resulted in a pronounced government crackdown. Within weeks the government sentenced four al-Huthi rebels to death (though three of them were still at large) and launched missile attacks on rebels in the northwest region. Ultimately, the government offensive led to a peace agreement with al-Huthi insurgents, who on August 7 confirmed that the rebellion had ended and that the rebel group had agreed to abide by the government's terms, which included a cease-fire, disarmament, and the freeing of army hostages. In September Islamist militants attacked the U.S. embassy in Sana, using among other weapons, rocket-propelled grenades and a suicide car bomb, killing 16 people, including 6 of the attackers. None of the embassy personnel was wounded or killed. A group called the Islamic Jihad in Yemen claimed responsibility.

Political progress appeared to advance in August 2008 when the JMP agreed to proposed amendments to Yemen's electoral law. The amendments were approved by parliament and sent to a joint human rights legislative committee for further study. The president had initiated the proposed changes nearly a year earlier, recommending a reduction in the presidential term from seven years to five; shortening legislative terms from six years to four; reserving 15 percent of seats in both chambers of the legislature for women; and proposing a 15-member electoral commission. Opposition groups objected to the proposed formulation for the electoral commission, pressing for representation from political parties and criticizing the GPC for trying to dominate the commission. Opposition members of parliament boycotted the legislature for three weeks, returning after the GPC agreed to include political party representatives on the electoral commission. Subsequently, hundreds of thousands of people demonstrated in Sana and other towns against the upcoming legislative elections, protesting what they claimed were forged voter lists. Ultimately, the opposition secured a pledge from President Salih in February 2009 that he would help push through reforms and ensure fair elections. Shortly thereafter, an agreement was reached between the GPC and opposition parties, and parliament approved a two-year postponement of the House of Representatives elections, until April 2011. The postponement, pending revisions to the electoral law, appeased the opposition's concerns about vote-rigging, but despite the parliamentary agreement having been moderated by delegations from the European Union and the nonprofit U.S. National Democratic Institute, the U.S. government expressed its "deep concern and disappointment" over the delayed elections, characterizing the move as a setback to the cause of democracy in Yemen.

Following the sentencing of a Shiite rebel to death and 12 others for up to 10 years in prison early in 2009, the peace agreement between the rebels and the government unraveled as fighting resumed, resulting in several insurgent deaths and at least 25 rebels facing trial. Adding to the government's concerns were a wave of attacks in March, when four South Korean tourists were killed in a suicide bomb attack in southern Yemen, and days later a similar (but failed) attack took place against South Korean officials traveling in the area to recover the victims' bodies. An al-Qaida offshoot calling itself al-Qaida in the Arabian Peninsula claimed responsibility, citing retaliation for South Korea's support of the U.S. war on terrorism. Also in March the government arrested seven suspected al-Qaida militants, including several accused of planning attacks on oil installations, foreign targets, and tourists.

In May 2009 the *International Herald Tribune* (IHT) described a growing separatist movement in several southern provinces marked by violent demonstrations and confrontations with government forces in which eight people were killed and dozens wounded. Tensions heightened due to reported government delays in reconstruction and humanitarian aid. The situation deteriorated to the point that journalists were banned from southern Yemen, and a government crackdown on the media ensued (see Communications, below). The IHT also reported that some political figures had begun "openly demanding" independence for the south. Meanwhile, Nasir al-WAHISHI, the leader of al-Qaida in the Arabian Peninsula, was reported to have declared his group's support for the uprising. Subsequently, the government appointed a commission to examine the violence, which was seen by analysts as a major threat to Salih's power, in addition to what they described as the "festering rebellion" by the al-Huthi Shiites in the north.

Addressing another growing issue of concern in 2009, Yemen established a counterpiracy center in the southern Red Sea area and partnered with France to build an artificial harbor off Yemen's Perim Island in a further effort to thwart piracy.

POLITICAL PARTIES AND GROUPS

Under the imams, parties in North Yemen were banned, political alignments being determined largely by tribal and religious loyalties. Prior to independence, the National Liberation Front (NLF) and the Front for the Liberation of Occupied South Yemen (FLOSY) fought for control of South Yemen; adherents of the latter subsequently went into exile. In October 1975 the NLF's successor, the National Front (NF), joined with the Popular Vanguard Party (a *Baath* group) and a Marxist formation, the Popular Democratic Union (PDU), to form the United Political Organization of the National Front (UPONF). In 1978 the UPONF was supplanted by the Yemeni Socialist Party (YSP, below).

Under the liberalized constitutional provisions of the successor Republic of Yemen, some 70 groups were reportedly legalized, with about 40 presenting candidates in the April 1993 legislative balloting. In February 1995 a Democratic Opposition Coalition (DOC) was formed by 13 groups, including the YSP, the Arab Socialist *Baath* Party, the League of the Sons of Yemen, the National Democratic Front, and a number of small parties. Coordination within the DOC appeared to collapse, however, with some members choosing to participate in the April 1997 legislative elections and others supporting a boycott. Ongoing involvement of a YSP-led Opposition Coordination Council, also referenced as the National Council of Opposition Parties (NCOP), was subsequently reported, the council unsuccessfully attempting to present a candidate in the 1999 presidential balloting and opposing the constitutional amendments ratified in early 2001.

In 2006, in advance of presidential elections scheduled for September, six opposition groups formed a coalition variously styled as the Joint Gathering or the Joint Meeting Parties (JMP). The six groups were the YSP, *Islah, Baath,* NUPP, UFP, and *al-Haqq*. (The *Baath* later withdrew from the JMP following disputes on a number of policies.) The JMP's nominee for president was former oil minister Faisal bin Shamlan, the main challenger to Salih. The NCOP, an alliance of the Democratic Nasserite Party, the Liberation Front Party, the National Social Party, the Popular Liberation Unity Party, the Popular Unity Party, the UPF, and the NDF fielded a candidate in the 2006 presidential election who won less than 1 percent of the vote (see Political Background, above).

In 2008–2009 the JMP, chaired by Hasan Muhammad Zayd of *al-Haqq*, was instrumental in pressing for fair elections, ultimately resulting in the postponement of the 2009 legislative elections until 2011. The JMP had threatened to boycott the elections if they had been held as originally scheduled, claiming vote-rigging ahead of the poll.

Government Party:

General People's Congress—GPC (*Mutamar al-Shabi al-Am*). Encompassing 700 elected and 300 appointed members, the GPC was founded in 1982 in the YAR with the widespread expectation that it would assume the quasi-legislative duties of the nonelected Constituent People's Assembly. However, the latter body continued to function until replaced in 1988 by a predominately elected Consultative Assembly, the GPC essentially taking on the role of an unofficial ruling party, with delegates to its biennial sessions being selected by local congresses. Longtime YAR president Ali Abdallah Salih relinquished his position as secretary general of the GPC upon assuming the presidency of the Republic of Yemen in May 1990; however, the group continued as one of the parties (along with the YSP, below) responsible for guiding the new republic through the transitional period culminating in the 1993 legislative election.

The GPC won a plurality, 123 seats, in the April 1993 House of Representatives balloting, its support coming primarily from northern tribal areas. Although a coalition government with the YSP was announced on May 30, the two leading parties grew increasingly estranged prior to the onset of the 1994 civil war. Following that conflict, the GPC announced the formation of a new government in coalition with *Islah* (below). At its fifth congress, held June 25, 1995, the GPC reelected all incumbent party leaders, including Salih as chair.

The GPC, aided by a YSP boycott, won a majority of 187 seats in the April 1997 House balloting, and following *Islah*'s decision to join the opposition, GPC members filled all but three posts in the new government named the following month. GPC secretary general Abd al-Karim Ali al-Iryani was named prime minister in May 1998 following the resignation of Faraj Said ibn Ghanim, who was not a GPC member. Salih was reelected to another term as president of the republic in September 1999 in the nation's first direct balloting for that post.

In the balloting of April 27, 2003, the GPC won 238 seats. The opposition *Islah* negotiated, though ultimately unsuccessfully, to avoid splitting the antigovernment vote.

President Salih was reelected party president in 2005 and nominated as the party's 2006 presidential candidate. Following Salih's reelection in September coupled with the party's success in concurrent local elections, the GPC solidified its dominant position. Its stronghold was further enhanced in May 2008 when the party dominated elections for provincial governors, and six party members were named to a reshuffled cabinet.

In February 2009 the GPC reached agreement with opposition groups to postpone the April legislative elections and work on reforms to the electoral system.

Leaders: Ali Abdallah SALIH (President of the Republic and Chair of the Party), Abdurabu Mansur HADI (Vice President of the Republic), Abd al-Aziz Abd al-GHANI (Former Prime Minister and Speaker of the Shura Council), Abd al-Karim Ali al-IRYANI (Former Prime Minister and Vice Chair of the Party), Abd al-Qadir Abd al-Rahman BAJAMMAL (Former Prime Minister and Secretary General of the Party).

Other Legislative Parties:

Yemeni Congregation for Reform (*al-Tajammu al-Yamani lil-Islah*). Also referenced as the Yemeni *Islah* Party (YIP), *Islah* was launched in September 1990 under the leadership of influential northern tribal leader Sheikh Abdallah ibn Husayn al-Ahmar, formerly a consistent opponent of unification. The party subsequently campaigned against the 1990 constitution in alliance with several other groups advocating strict adherence to sharia.

Somewhat surprisingly, *Islah* finished second in the April 1993 House balloting by winning 62 seats, its success due primarily to strong support from the conservative, pro-Saudi population in northern tribal areas. Its principal leader, Sheikh al-Ahmar, was elected speaker of the new house, while its initial allocation of four cabinet posts in May was increased to six in June, with one *Islah* representative being named to the five-member Presidential Council in October. The party's influence grew further during the 1994 civil war because of its strong support for President Salih and the northern unity forces. It was given nine portfolios in the postwar coalition government with the GPC. Four of the ministerial posts were filled by members of the Muslim Brotherhood, the influential charitable and quasi-political organization with branches in many Arab nations. Observers suggested that the appointments reflected the growing strength of the Islamist tendency within the YIP at the possible expense of conservative, tribal-based elements. For the moment, a balance was seemingly maintained during *Islah*'s September 1994 congress in Sana, with Sheikh al-Ahmar being reelected party leader and "fundamentalist ideologue" Abd al-Maguid al-Zindani being elected chair of the party's 100-member governing council.

Islah's subsequent relationship with the GPC remained tenuous, the minority government partner continuing to question the GPC's handling of economic and administrative reform. At one point prior to the 1997 legislative balloting *Islah* was reportedly considering not participating in the elections. However, an arrangement was apparently concluded under which the GPC agreed not to challenge *Islah* candidates in a number of constituencies. After securing 53 seats in the new house, *Islah* declined to join the new cabinet, although Sheikh al-Ahmar was reelected house speaker. By exiting the cabinet *Islah* lost control of the education portfolio, which had accorded it authority over religion in the nation's schools. Despite remaining outside the government, *Islah* continued to support some major proposals of the Salih administration, including the constitutional amendments approved in early 2001. However, the relations between *Islah* and the government soured later in 2001 due to the government's continued efforts to take over religious schools organized by *Islah.* The party also criticized the government for its close cooperation with the United States following the al-Qaida attacks of September 2001. In the elections of April 27, 2003, *Islah* garnered 46 seats, and al-Ahmar was subsequently reelected as speaker of the House of Representatives. In 2005 some in the party reportedly agreed to allow women to participate in elections, though there was no official pronouncement on the subject.

In 2005 Yemen asked the United States to remove al-Zindani, who had been accused of working with Osama bin Laden, from its list of suspected terrorists.

Party leader Sheikh al-Ahmar, who heads the tribe of which President Salih is a member, said he personally supported Salih's reelection bid, though his preference was "not binding" on the party. "Better the devil you know than the angel you don't," al-Ahmar was quoted as saying. The party, as part of the JMP coalition (above), officially supported Faisal bin Shamlan in the 2006 presidential election.

In February 2007 the party replaced al-Zindani as its spiritual leader but urged the government to continue to press Washington to remove al-Zindani's name from its list of suspected financiers of terrorism. In March al-Ahmar was reelected party president, and al-Zindani was named to the party's supreme panel. Muhammad Ali al-Yadumi, formerly vice chair of the party, was named chair in January 2008 to succeed Sheikh al-Ahmar, who died as a result of illness in December 2007.

In May 2009 a regional YIP leader indicated his intent to form a new southern "reform" movement.

Leaders: Muhammad Ali al-YADUMI (Chair), Muhammad Ali AJILAN (Chair of *Islah* Governing Council), Sheikh Abd al-Wahab Ali al-UNSI (Secretary General).

Yemeni Socialist Party—YSP (*al-Hizb al-Ishtiraki al-Yamani*). Modeled after the Communist Party of the Soviet Union, the YSP was formed in 1978 as a Marxist-Leninist "vanguard party" for the PDRY and subsequently maintained strict one-party control of South Yemen's political affairs despite several serious leadership battles (see Political background, above). In February 1990 the YSP Central Committee announced the separation of state and party functions under a multiparty system as a means of promoting Yemeni unity. Upon unification, YSP secretary general Ali Salim al-Beidh was named vice president of the new republic.

The YSP won 56 seats in the April 1993 House of Representatives election, and party leaders announced a potential merger with the GPC. However, with substantial opposition to the plan having reportedly been voiced within the YSP's 33-member Politburo, no progress toward the union ensued, and the YSP on its own was allocated 9 cabinet seats in the government formed in May.

Personal animosity between al-Beidh and Yemeni president Salih was considered an important element in the subsequent north-south confrontation, which culminated in the 1994 civil war. However, al-Beidh and his supporters attributed the friction to the inability (or, possibly, the disinclination) of security forces to protect YSP members. An estimated 150 YSP members were assassinated between May 1990 and early 1994.

Following the collapse of the YSP-led People's Democratic Republic of Yemen in July 1994, the party appeared to be in disarray. Al-Beidh announced from exile that he was "retiring from politics," although some of the other secessionist leaders who had fled the country pledged to pursue their goal of an independent south. Meanwhile, in September the YSP rump in Yemen elected a new Politburo comprising 13 southerners and 10 northerners. Aware that a significant portion of the YSP had opposed the ill-fated independence movement, President Salih announced that the reorganized party would be allowed to keep its legal status. However, he declared al-Beidh and 15 other separatist leaders to be beyond reconciliation and subject to arrest for treason should they return to Yemen. Subsequently, when the GPC/YIP coalition government was formed in October, the YSP announced it was assuming the role of "leading opposition party." A bitter dispute was reported within the party in 1997 concerning the decision not to participate in the April house balloting, boycott supporters claiming government fraud during voter registration. Meanwhile, al-Beidh, former PDRY prime minister Haydar Abu Bakr al-Attas, and three others were sentenced to death in absentia at the conclusion of a trial in March 1998.

YSP secretary general Ali Saleh OBAD attempted to run for president of the republic in 1999 but, as was the case with nearly all of the other potential challengers, failed to achieve the required support in the legislature. The party subsequently continued to challenge the GPC's stranglehold on power, and in what was described as a "provocative" decision, al-Beidh and al-Attas were included in the next Central Committee elected at the YSP General Congress in August 2000 in Sana. Not surprisingly, the YSP strongly opposed the 2001 constitutional amendments, which extended the presidential and legislative terms of office.

In late 2002 the secretary general of the YSP, Jarallah UMAR, was assassinated by an Islamic extremist. His assassin was believed to be an associate of the man who killed the American missionaries days later (see Current issues, above).

In 2003 Salih reconciled with al-Beidh and pardoned the YSP members who had been sentenced to death. The party secured eight seats in the 2003 elections. In a move toward further cooperation, YSP leaders began talks with the GPC in 2005 to bridge the gap between them.

In May 2008 three members of the YSP went on trial in connection with violent demonstrations in the southern provinces earlier in the year. The party's members of parliament boycotted the legislative session in July to protest proposed constitutional amendments recommended by the president. YSP leaders said the amendments did not address the release of political prisoners, among other issues. Trials began in July for four senior party members for allegedly encouraging secessionist sentiments in the south. In September President Salih pardoned a number of activists, including three YSP members. However, party officials claimed that one of its high-ranking members, Hassam BAOUM, remained in jail on charges related to deadly clashes in the south earlier in the year. The government asserted that Baoum had been among those pardoned.

Leaders: Yassin Said NUMAN (Former Speaker of the House of Representatives), Ali SARARI, Ali Salih MUQBIL (Secretary General).

Arab Socialist Baath Party. Seven *Baath* Party candidates were successful in the April 1993 legislative elections, and party member Mujahid ABU SHAWARIB was subsequently named a deputy prime minister in the cabinet formed in May. However, *Baath* leaders announced that the party would sit in opposition, with Abu Shawarib serving essentially as an independent rather than a *Baath* representative. The grouping secured two seats in the 1997 house elections and two seats in the 2003 elections. In 2006 the party announced its support for President Salih in the upcoming presidential election.

In July 2008 the Baath Party, along with a grouping of opposition parties, was reported to have signed a cooperation pact with the GPC.

Leader: Abdullah al-AHMAR (Assistant Secretary General), Dr. Qasim SALAM (Secretary General).

Nasserite Unionist People's Party—NUPP (*al-Tanthim al-Wahdawi al-Shabi al-Nasri*). Formed in 1989 and reportedly the largest of the nation's Nasserite groupings, the NUPP won one seat in the 1993 legislative balloting, three in 1997, and three in 2003.

Leader: Abdul Malik al-MAKHLAFI, Sultan al-ATWANI (Secretary General).

Other Parties and Groups:

Truth Party (*al-Haqq*). Founded by Islamic religious scholars in late 1991, *al-Haqq* won two seats in the 1993 parliamentary balloting. Although *al-Haqq* had no successful candidates in the 1997 elections, party leader Ibrahim al-Wazir was named minister of justice in the new GPC-led cabinet formed in May. He was replaced after the 2003 reshuffle. Sheikh Ahmad ibn Ali Shami, the secretary general of *al-Haqq,* was named minister of religious guidance in the May 1998 reshuffle, although he left the post in September because of what he described as "interference" from other officials in carrying out his duties. In October 2004 a party official was beaten in what could well have been a politically motivated attack. The government has accused the group of backing the rebellion of cleric and former Truth leader Husayn al-Huthi (see Current issues, above). Police attacks on followers of al-Huthi reportedly continued in 2005.

Leaders: Ibrahim al-WAZIR, Sheikh Ahmad ibn Ali SHAMI, Hasan Muhammad ZAYD (Secretary General).

Yemeni Unionist Alliance (*Tajammu*). *Tajammu* was formed in 1990 by human rights proponents from the north and south, party leaders subsequently criticizing the national government for its pro-Iraqi stance during the Gulf crisis. In late 1991 a mainstream Islamic party, *al-Nahdah* (Renaissance), reportedly merged with *Tajammu,* partly in response to government efforts to get smaller parties to coalesce. However, in 1995 *al-Nahdah* was reported to have entered the Democratic Opposition Coalition (DOC) as a discrete entity.

Leaders: Omar al-JAWI, Muhammed Abd ar-RAHMAN.

League of the Sons of Yemen (*Rabibat Abna al-Yaman*). Founded in 1990 to represent tribal interests in the south, the league campaigned against the proposed constitution for the new republic because it did not stipulate sharia as the only source of Yemeni law. The party offered 92 candidates in the 1993 general elections, none of whom were successful. League leader Abd al-Rahman al-Jifri, born in Yemen but a citizen of Saudi Arabia, was named vice president of the breakaway Democratic Republic of Yemen in 1994. Following the separatists' defeat, al-Jifri moved to London, where he served as chair of the Yemeni National Opposition Front (normally referenced as MOWJ, an abbreviation derived from the transliteration of its Arabic name). Al-Jifri maintained that he was also still the leader of the League of the Sons of Yemen, but reportedly members remaining in Yemen had voted to dismiss him from his post. A small league rump participated in the 1997 elections without success.

In March 1998 al-Jifri was sentenced in absentia to ten years in prison for his role in the 1994 conflict. However, the sentence was immediately suspended, separating the MOWJ leader from the YSP separatists who had been tried at the same time. Although critical of government policies that had allegedly contributed to a deterioration in living conditions, the MOWJ Executive Committee in March 2000 called for national reconciliation through dialogue with the Salih government, and following the accord between Saudi Arabia and Yemen at midyear, the MOWJ announced that it was suspending its antigovernment activities. Al-Jifri announced in 2006 that he would return to Yemen and support Salih's reelection bid despite his political differences with the president. He said his decision was based on discussions he had with Salih about the need for political and economic reforms.

Leader: Abd al-Rahman al-JIFRI.

National Democratic Front (NDF). Formed in 1976 by an assortment of *Baathists,* Marxists, Nasserites, and disaffected Yemenis, the leftist NDF subsequently conducted a sporadic guerrilla campaign against the government of North Yemen and supported the South Yemeni army in the 1979 invasion. However, although the NDF remained an opponent of the YAR regime, its antigovernment activities were relatively unimportant during the 1980s. Four of the new members appointed to the House of Representatives upon the creation of the Republic of Yemen were identified as NDF members. No NDF candidates were successful in the 1997 legislative balloting. There was no record of this party in the 2003 elections.

Liberation Party (*Hizb al-Tahrir*). Organized in 2003 with the aim of creating an orthodox Islamic state, the Liberation Party did not participate in the elections that year. In 2004 security forces arrested a number of party members after they staged a public demonstration.

Leader: Nasir Abdu ALLAHBI (Spokesperson).

Union of Popular Forces (UPF). Little is known about this group, whose newsletter editor was sentenced to a year in prison in 2004 after being accused of aiding the rebellion of former Truth leader Husayn al-Huthi.

Leader: Muhammad al-RABOEI (Secretary General).

Other parties include the **Democratic Nasserite Party**, led by 2006 presidential candidate Yasin Abdu SAID; the **Liberation Front Party,** established in South Yemen in the 1970s by Abdul Fattah ISMAIL; the **National Social Party,** led by Abd al-Azziz al-BUKIR; the **Popular Liberation Unity Party**; and the **Popular Unity Party**.

The previously unknown **Aden-Abyan Islamic Army** claimed responsibility for the December 1998 kidnapping of 16 westerners in southern Yemen. Zein al-Abidine al-MIHDAR, described as one of the leaders of the group, reportedly called for strikes against U.S. installations and an end to U.S. "aggression" against Iraq. Mihdar and several others went on trial in April 1999. Meanwhile, U.S. and UK officials were reportedly investigating possible links between the Aden-Abyan Islamic Army (which reportedly comprised so-called Arab Afghans who moved to Yemen in the early 1990s after fighting Soviet forces in Afghanistan) and the terrorist network of Osama bin Laden. (Several of those accused in the bombings of U.S. embassies in Kenya and Tanzania in mid-1998 had carried Yemeni passports.) Mihdar was executed in October 1999 after being found guilty of terrorism in August. The reported new head of the Aden-Abyan Islamic Army, Hatim Muhsin ibn FARID, formerly of the League of the Sons of Yemen, was sentenced to seven years in prison in October 2000. In October 2002 the group claimed responsibility for an explosion on a French tanker off the Yemeni coast, and Yemeni officials subsequently arrested others in the attack who were suspected of having ties to al-Qaida. The government continued its attacks against the Aden-Abyan Islamic Army, by then widely believed to be linked to al-Qaida. In 2005 Yemeni authorities asked the UK to extradite Abu Hamza al-MASRI so they could try him for his alleged support of the Aden-Abyan Islamic Army and for his alleged involvement in terrorist activities in Yemen. However, British authorities said if al-Masri was ever released, he would be extradited to the United States on numerous terrorist charges.

In 2006 the Aden-Abyan Islamic Army claimed there had been an assassination attempt against its leader, Sheikh Khalid Abd al-NABI, by government security forces. The government denied the charge and said President Salih had pardoned Abd al-Nabi on unspecified charges. In 2007 the government released from jail 100 men described as Muslim extremists, including some members of the Aden-Abyan Islamic Army, who were each given $1,000 to help them start new lives. In March 2008 al-Nabi again accused the government of an assassination attempt. In 2008 al-Nabi was confronted by security forces, and his house was damaged by gunfire, according to a report by the BBC.

In 2009 the government arrested 10 members of the Aden-Abyan Islamic Army, four of whom were wounded in fighting with police near Aden, where police were reported to have been searching houses for members of what were termed jihadist groups.

LEGISLATURE

Shura Council (*Majlis al-Shura*). The largely advisory Shura Council was established in accordance with constitutional amendments approved in a national referendum on February 20, 2001. The president appointed all 111 members of the advisory body, including some from the opposition, on April 28. The Shura Council, which has some legislative authority, replaced the 59-member Consultative Council formed in 1997.

Speaker: Abd al-Aziz Abd al-GHANI.

The transitional **House of Representatives** (*Majlis al-Nuwwab*) installed in 1990 was a 301-member body encompassing the 159 members of the former YAR Consultative Assembly, the 111 members of the former PDRY Supreme People's Council, and 31 people named by the government (in part to represent opposition groups). A national referendum on February 20, 2001, approved a constitutional amendment increasing the legislative term of office from four to six years.

A new 301-member house was directly elected by universal suffrage on April 17, 1993. Following the most recent elections, on April 27, 2003, the seats were distributed as follows: the General People's Congress, 238; the Yemeni *Islah* Party, 46; the Yemeni Socialist Party, 8; the Nasserite Unionist People's Party, 3; the Arab Socialist *Baath* Party, 2; independents, 4.

Elections originally scheduled for 2009 were postponed for two years (see Government and Politics, above).

Speaker: Yahya ARRAI.

CABINET

[as of September 1, 2009]

Prime Minister	Ali Muhammad Majur
Deputy Prime Minister for Defense and Security	Rashad Muhammad al-Alimi
Deputy Prime Minister for Economic Affairs	Abd al-Karim al-Arhabi
Deputy Prime Minister for Interior Affairs	Sadiq Amin Abu-Rass
Ministers	
Agriculture and Irrigation	Mansour al-Houshabi
Communications and Information Technology	Kamal al-Jabri
Culture	Muhammad al-Maflahi
Defense	Muhammad Nasir Ahmad Ali
Education	Abd al-Salam al Jawfi
Electricity and Energy	Awad al-Suqatri

Expatriate Affairs	Ahmad Musaead Hussain
Finance	Numan Salih al-Suhaybi
Fisheries	Muhammad Saleh Shamlan
Foreign Affairs	Abu-Bakr Abdallah al-Qirbi
Higher Education and Scientific Research	Salih Ali Ba Surah
Human Rights	Huda Adul-Latif al-Ban [f]
Industry and Trade	Yahya al-Mutawakel
Information and Government Spokesperson	Hassan Ahmad al-Awzi
Interior	Maj. Gen. Mutahar al-Masri
Justice	Ghazi Shaif al-Aghbari
Labor and Social Affairs	Amat al-Rassaq Ali Hamad [f]
Legal Affairs	Rashad al-Rassas
Local Administration	Vacant
Local Authority Affairs	Sadiq Amin Abu-Rass
Oil and Mineral Resources	Amir al-Aidarous
Planning and International Cooperation	Abd al-Karim al-Arhabi
Public Health and Population	Abd al-Karim Rasi
Public Works and Urban Development	Umar Abdullah al-Qurshumi
Religious Guidance	Hamoud al-Hitar
Shura Council and Parliamentary Affairs	Khalid al-Sharif
Social Security and Civil Service	Yahya al-Shuaibi
Technical Education and Vocational Training	Ibrahim Hajri
Tourism	Nabil Hasan al-Faqih
Transportation	Khalid al-Wazir
Water and Environment	Abd al-Rahman Fadi al-Iryani
Youth and Sport	Hamud Ubad

Minister of State

Director of the Office of the Prime Minister	Abdul Yahy Raman Tarmoum

[f] = female

COMMUNICATIONS

Although government control of the press was strict in both North Yemen and South Yemen, unification yielded considerable liberalization. By late 1991 Yemen boasted more than 100 newspapers and other periodicals, many of them critical of the government. However, extensive censorship was reimposed at the outbreak of the 1994 civil war, ongoing restrictions prompting a demonstration in support of freedom of expression in Sana in February 1995 that was broken up by government forces. Harassment (including prosecution) of journalists by the government subsequently has been reported on a regular basis. In April 2005 the Ministry of Information drafted amendments to expand freedom of the press and free speech, and the following month President Salih asked for legislation that would not include prison or detention for journalists. However, press freedoms remained uneven, with some 11 journalists sentenced to prison for two years in early 2005 for "criminal acts" in Yemen. Though the government denies it monitors use of the Internet, the U.S. State Department says the government sometimes blocks certain Web sites.

In April 2008 the government revoked the license of *al-Wasat*, a private, independent weekly, for allegedly publishing articles that were "against national unity" and accusing it of attempting to stir a feud with Saudi Arabia. Press freedom deteriorated markedly in 2009 under a major government crackdown on journalists, particularly in regard to reporting on civil strife in southern Yemen. Eight publications critical of President Salih's administration were suspended in May, when police stopped distribution and seized all copies, including those of the main southern daily, *al-Ayyam*. A few weeks later government security forces stormed the *al-Ayyam* compound, killing two guards and a passer-by, according to the watchdog Committee to Protect Journalists (CPJ). The CPJ also reported that an Internet journalist was arrested and was being held incommunicado, and several other journalists were harassed and detained as part of the crackdown on independent media in the south. In addition, in what the CPJ described as "another disturbing development," the Yemeni High Judicial Council in May established a "special press court" to review and handle cases related to the media and publishing offenses. Meanwhile, parliament in 2009 was considering a controversial new press law that journalists contended would hinder freedom of expression.

Press. Except as noted, the following are published in Sana in Arabic: *al-Thawrah* (The Revolution, 110,000), government-owned daily; *al-Jumhuriyah* (100,000), government-controlled daily published in Taiz; *Yemen Times* (30,000), independent weekly in English; *26th September* (25,000), armed forces weekly; *al-Rabi Ashar Min Uktubar* (14th October, 20,000), government-controlled daily published in Aden; *al-Ayyam*, an independent daily published in Aden; *al-Shura* (15,000), weekly; *al-Shararah* (The Spark, 6,000), government-controlled daily published in Aden; *al-Sahwah* (Awakening), Islamist weekly; *al-Mithaq* (The Charter), GPC weekly; *al-Wahdawi,* NUPP weekly; *Yemen Observer,* independent weekly in English; *al-Bilad* (The Country), rightist weekly; *Sana,* leftist monthly.

News agency. The Saba News Agency is located in the capital. There is also an Aden News Agency.

Broadcasting and computing. At unification the northern and southern state broadcast organizations were combined to form the Broadcasting Service of the Republic of Yemen (*Idhaat al-Jumhuriyah al-Yamaniyah*), which operates radio stations in Sana, Taiz, Hodeida, and Aden as well as television services in Sana and Aden. As of 2008 there were 16.1 Internet users per 1,000 inhabitants.

INTERGOVERNMENTAL REPRESENTATION

Ambassador to the U.S.: Abdulwahab A. al-HAJJRI.

U.S. Ambassador to Yemen: Stephen A. SECHE.

Permanent Representative to the UN: Abdallah M. ALSAIDI.

IGO Memberships (Non-UN): AFESD, AMF, CAEU, IDB, Interpol, IOM, IOR-ARC, LAS, NAM, OIC, WCO.

ZAMBIA

Republic of Zambia

Political Status: Independent republic within the Commonwealth since October 24, 1964; under one-party, presidential-parliamentary system from 1972 to adoption of multiparty constitution on August 29, 1991.

Area: 290,584 sq. mi. (752,614 sq. km.).

Population: 9,885,591 (2000C); 12,152,000 (2008E).

Major Urban Center (2005E): LUSAKA (metropolitan area, 1,647,000).

Official Language: English.

Monetary Unit: Kwacha (official rate December 1, 2009: 4,680.00 kwachas = $1US).

President: Rupiah BANDA (Movement for Multiparty Democracy); popularly elected in a by-election on October 30, 2008, to fill the unexpired five-year term of Levy Patrick MWANAWASA (Movement for Multiparty Democracy), who died on August 19; inaugurated on November 2.

Vice President: George KUNDA ((Movement for Multiparty Democracy); appointed by the president on November 14, 2008.

THE COUNTRY

Landlocked Zambia, the former British protectorate of Northern Rhodesia, is bordered by the Democratic Republic of the Congo, Tanzania, and Malawi on the north and east, and by Angola, Namibia, Zimbabwe, and Mozambique on the west and south. Its terrain consists primarily of a high plateau with abundant forests and grasslands. The watershed between the Congo and Zambezi river systems crosses the northern part of the country. The bulk of the population belongs to various Bantu tribes, the most influential being the Bemba in the north and the Lozi, an offshoot of the Zulu, in the southwest. (Tribal influences remain highly influential in political affairs.) Nonindigenous groups include a small number of whites (mainly British and South African), Asians, and persons of mixed descent concentrated in the Copperbelt in the north. Nearly three-quarters of native Zambians are nominally Christian, almost equally divided between Catholics and Protestants; the remainder adheres to traditional African beliefs. The official language is English, but Afrikaans and more than 70 local languages and dialects are spoken. Women comprise approximately one-third of the labor force, not including unpaid agricultural workers. Although a number of women involved in the independence struggle achieved positions of influence in the former ruling party, female representation is minimal at local levels.

Zambia is one of the world's largest producers of copper and cobalt. The former accounts for 75 percent of export earnings, but Zambia's share of the world copper market has declined significantly in the wake of a nearly 80 percent decline in production, attributed in large part to mismanagement of state-owned mines. Zinc, coal, cement, lime, sulphur, and magnetite are among other minerals being extracted. Agriculture employs two-thirds of the labor force, with maize, peanuts, tobacco, and cotton constituting the chief commercial crops. Because of a booming copper industry, Zambia, until the early 1970s, enjoyed one of Africa's highest standards of living, with rapid development of schools, hospitals, and highways. However, a subsequent decline in copper prices yielded infrastructural decay, rising unemployment within the rapidly growing and highly urbanized population, a foreign exchange shortage, an external debt of more than $6 billion, and the erosion of social services. Although the government had exercised budgetary restraint and relaxed its control of the economy in accordance with International Monetary Fund (IMF) strictures dating to the mid-1970s, rioting over price increases in late 1986 prompted Lusaka to abandon austerity measures and break with the IMF. However, economic reform measures were reinstated in 1998, paving the way for renewal of relations with international lenders and donors. In 1992 the Chiluba government launched a privatization program; however, market reform was subsequently seen as having failed to help the nation's poor (an estimated 83 percent of the population). Funds for education and health remained severely constrained at a time when about one-fifth of the population was believed to be HIV-positive. The IMF and World Bank continued to approve loans (Western aid accounted for one-half of the government's budget), and Zambia was included on the list of countries eligible for the international community's new debt-relief program. However, donors expressed concern over the apparent pervasive nature of corruption in government affairs at all levels. Particularly disappointing to foreign observers was the decision in 2002 of South African mining giant Anglo-American to abandon the massive copper mining initiative it had launched in Zambia only two years earlier. Among other things, the economic distress contributed to the emergence of a degree of political instability that was unusual by Zambian standards.

Severe drought in 2002 caused a decline in agricultural production that left 25 percent of the population temporarily dependent on food aid. Collaterally, the pace of economic reform slowed, prompting the temporary suspension of IMF and World Bank assistance. However, real GDP growth averaged 4.8 percent a year in 2004 and 2005, in part due to soaring copper prices and the investment of $1 billion by mining companies. In addition, the Group of Eight in 2005 canceled Zambia's $2.5 billion debt. GDP growth of 6 percent was reported for 2006, bolstered by expansion in the mining sector and a recovery in agricultural production. Inflation was reduced by half, to 9 percent, partly due to stable food prices. Zambia also qualified for $3.8 billion in debt relief from the IMF. Meanwhile, the Zambian administration's program for combating HIV/AIDS, including free drugs, resulted in significantly reduced death rates in its first two years and was hailed internationally as a success.

In 2008 GDP growth of 5.8 percent was recorded, further growth said to be inhibited by investors' lack of enthusiasm for emerging markets and a decline in global commodity prices. Other troublesome issues were double-digit inflation and a decline in copper prices that observers said could offset the government's tax rate increase for mining companies under a law that went into effect in 2008. On a more positive note, about 2,000 jobs were created as two large mining projects began operations in midyear. Later in the year, however, the impact of the global economic crisis was felt as demand for copper declined dramatically, mining companies cut thousands of jobs, and inflation increased to 15.2 percent as food costs soared.

In 2009 the mining companies successfully lobbied for the abolishment of the windfall tax of 47 percent that had been approved the previous year at the height of the copper boom. In the wake of the worldwide recession, annual growth was expected to contract to 4 percent as global prices of food and fuel pushed up inflation, and the steep drop in copper prices reduced export revenue. The World Bank urged diversification and "concerted action on the part of government" to encourage growth in other sectors. On a positive note, in May the IMF approved $330 million in financial aid to help Zambia's economic recovery as part of a three-year program initiated in 2008.

GOVERNMENT AND POLITICS

Political background. Declared a British sphere of influence in 1888, Northern Rhodesia was administered jointly with Southern Rhodesia until 1923–1924, when it became a separate British protectorate. From 1953 to 1963, it was linked with Southern Rhodesia and Nyasaland (now Malawi) in the Federation of Rhodesia and Nyasaland, which was dissolved at the end of 1963 in recognition of the unwillingness of the black majority populations in Northern Rhodesia and Nyasaland to continue under the political and economic domination of white-ruled Southern Rhodesia. A drive for Northern Rhodesia's complete independence, led by Harry NKUMBULA and Kenneth D. KAUNDA, concluded on October 24, 1964, when the territory became an independent republic within the Commonwealth under the name of Zambia (after the Zambezi River). Kaunda, as leader of the majority United National Independence Party (UNIP), became head of the new state; Nkumbula, whose African National Congress (ANC)

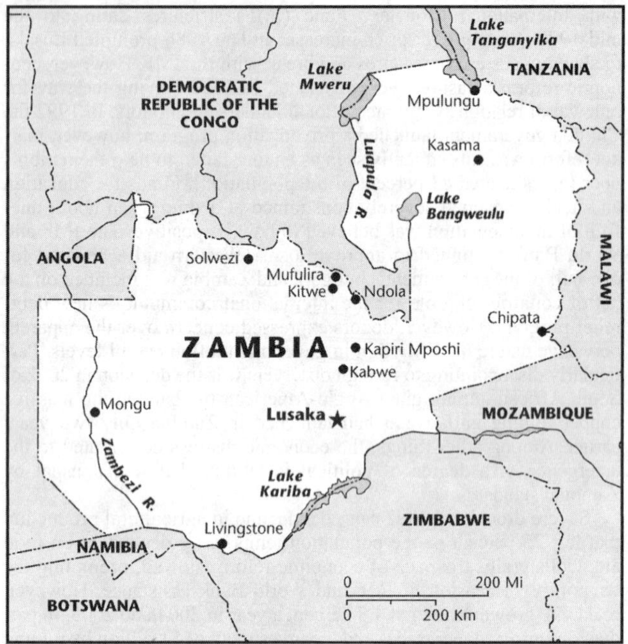

had trailed in the preindependence election of January 1964, became leader of the opposition. The political predominance of Kaunda and his party was strengthened in the general election of December 1968, Kaunda winning a second five-year term as president and the UNIP again capturing an overwhelming legislative majority. In December 1972 Kaunda promulgated a law banning all parties except the UNIP and introduced what was termed "one-party participatory democracy." In December 1978 he was reelected for a fourth term following disqualification of Nkumbula and former vice president Simon M. KAPWEPWE.

On August 27, 1983, the president dissolved the National Assembly to pave the way for an October 27 election, in which, as sole presidential candidate, he garnered 93 percent of the vote and was returned to office for a fifth five-year term. Two years later Kaunda transferred both the prime minister and the UNIP secretary general to diplomatic posts; Defense Minister Alexander Grey ZULU was chosen to head the party, while Prime Minister Nalumino MUNDIA was replaced by Minister of Education and Culture Kebby MUSOKOTWANE.

Following a UNIP restructuring that was generally interpreted as enhancing his personal control of both party and government, Kaunda, again the sole candidate, was elected for a sixth presidential term on October 26, 1988, with a reported 96 percent "yes" vote. On the other hand, eight cabinet members were defeated in assembly elections held the same day, apparently reflecting increased opposition to government policy. Shortly after the election, Kaunda reshuffled the cabinet, and on March 15, 1989, he named Gen. Malimba MASHEKE to replace the young and popular Musokotwane as prime minister; the subsequent posting of Musokotwane to a diplomatic mission lent credence to the view that he had become a political threat to Kaunda.

In early 1990 the regime rejected a number of proposals for liberalization of the Zambian political system. However, by midyear the government had grudgingly agreed to implement reforms in an attempt to appease increasingly vociferous critics, particularly among the trade and business communities. In the wake of a coup attempt in June and price riots in July, Kaunda agreed to a voter registration drive and the freeing of a number of political prisoners. In September, following a series of major prodemocracy rallies, the president announced plans for multiparty elections by October 1991. On December 4 the National Assembly legalized the formation of political parties, and on December 30 the Zambian Congress of Trade Unions (ZCTU) aligned itself with the leading opposition group, the Movement for Multiparty Democracy (MMD).

In 1991 the regime's practices, including strict control of the media, drew MMD condemnation and led to violent clashes between MMD and UNIP supporters. Nevertheless, on August 2 the National Assembly approved a new multiparty constitution, and, following its formal signing on August 29, the president dissolved the legislature and allowed the state of emergency decree to lapse for the first time since independence. On October 31, in balloting supervised by former U.S. president Jimmy Carter and representatives of the Commonwealth and the Organization of African Unity (OAU, subsequently the African Union—AU), the MMD's Frederick CHILUBA won 74 percent of the presidential vote and the movement's candidates captured 125 of 150 assembly seats.

The MMD secured a vast majority of the 1,190 local council seats contested on November 30, 1992; however, the ruling party's victories were tainted by a lack of competition in approximately 400 councils, coupled with voter apathy (less than 10 percent of eligible voters reportedly having participated). Observers attributed the apparent growing disenchantment among voters to the effects of a severe economic austerity program compounded by the perception of unmitigated governmental corruption.

On March 4, 1993, the administration's prestige was further damaged when Chiluba declared an indefinite state of emergency and 25 UNIP members, including three of former president Kaunda's sons, were arrested on charges relating to an alleged coup plot. On March 9 the president shortened the detention without trial period from 28 to 7 days, apparently seeking to combat domestic and international charges that his administration had overreacted to reports about the alleged plot, and on May 25 the state of emergency was lifted.

In August 1993, 15 prominent MMD officials resigned from the government and National Assembly because of the Chiluba administration's alleged unwillingness to investigate corruption and drug trafficking charges against powerful cabinet ministers; the MMD defectors, citing a "critical national crisis of leadership and governance," launched the National Party (NP). Chiluba dismissed the resignations as the "teething problems" of democratic reform; however, in December international aid donors meeting in Paris voted to withhold aid payments until Lusaka investigated the allegations, and on January 6, 1994, the ZCTU called on the Chiluba administration to dissolve the government. Consequently, on January 11, 1994, Chiluba reshuffled his cabinet, claiming to have ousted tainted ministers, and in March the World Bank agreed to release suspended aid payments despite opposition protestations that the president had shielded corrupt ministers while dismissing two who had sought to expose malfeasance.

On July 3, 1994, Vice President Levy MWANAWASA resigned, citing alleged irresponsibility and greed among his colleagues. On the following day Chiluba named Brig. Gen. Godfrey MIYANDA, theretofore a minister without portfolio, to replace Mwanawasa.

In October 1994 former president Kaunda officially announced that he would end his retirement to campaign for early presidential elections, saying "there is a crisis in Zambia. . . . I have accepted the call to come back." Thereafter, in February 1995, Kaunda, who had been under surveillance since August 1994 because of allegations that his return was being financed by foreign backers, was charged with attempting to hold an illegal political party meeting. Meanwhile, the MMD sought to block his presidential eligibility by pressing for a constitutional amendment that would disqualify anyone not born in Zambia of Zambian-born parents (Kaunda's parents having been born in Malawi). Such an amendment, as well as a second amendment disqualifying any person who had already been twice-elected president, were included in a draft document issued on June 16. The proposed charter was released despite the objections of an independent constitutional review commission, which had declared the amendments "rubbish" and accused the MMD of having bribed its authors.

On May 16, 1996, the National Assembly approved the Constitution of Zambia Amendment Act 1996, and 12 days later the president sanctioned the measure, thus officially banning Kaunda from future elections. Subsequent opposition efforts to have the constitutional changes suspended and the upcoming balloting held in accordance with the 1991 document were dismissed in September by the president and High Court, respectively. On the other hand, in an effort to dampen mounting opposition charges that electoral preparations were being "rigged," Chiluba agreed to provide opposition representatives with equal access to the media and oversight of vote tabulation. On October 19 Chiluba dissolved the assembly and announced that presidential and legislative elections would be held on November 18. (The opposition's subsequent charge that the government's mandate would expire on October 31 and that any of its actions thereafter would be illegal were dismissed by the regime as "immature.") On October 23 Kaunda announced that the UNIP would boycott the November elections to protest the constitutional changes and the government's alleged manipulation of the voter registration drive.

As anticipated, President Chiluba and the MMD secured landslide victories in polling on November 18, 1996, with the former capturing 69.5 percent of the vote and his party 131 of the 150 seats contested. Their victories were marred, however, by alleged electoral irregularities and by what one observer described as a "revolt of MMD voters" in high-profile contests won by independents and opposition candidates. Thereafter, amid widespread opposition calls for a campaign of civil disobedience to force the government to hold fresh elections, Chiluba put the military on alert on November 28. On December 2 Chiluba named a new cabinet that was described as "tribalist" because of the preponderance of members from the Northern and Luapula regions (Chiluba is from the latter).

Tensions remained high in Lusaka throughout the first half of 1997 as the Chiluba administration, now reportedly under the direction of MMD hard-liners, was sharply denounced by both domestic and international observers for introducing legislation that would strictly regulate both the media and nongovernmental organizations. (In March the latter law went into effect, but in April the government suspended the controversial Press Council Bill.) In early August antigovernment demonstrations in Lusaka turned into rioting, and, at an illegal opposition rally on August 23, Kaunda and Roger CHONGWE, leader of the Liberal Progressive Front, were shot and wounded in what Kaunda described as an assassination attempt.

On October 28, 1997, a group of junior military officers led by Capt. Steven LUNGU (a.k.a. "Captain Solo") took over a government radio station and declared that they had established a "National Redemption Council" and were prepared to overthrow the government. Within hours the reportedly drunken rebels were overpowered by forces loyal to the president; nevertheless, the government declared a state of emergency, and in the following weeks more than 80 mid-level officers and dozens of opposition members were detained, with a number of others reportedly fleeing the country amid reports that those arrested were being tortured.

On December 2, 1997, Chiluba demoted his vice president, Brig. Gen. Godfrey Miyanda, to the education ministry and named as his replacement Lt. Gen. Christon TEMBO. Furthermore, Chiluba drastically reshuffled both the government and the military leadership.

In late April 2001 a fractured MMD congress agreed to seek constitutional revision to permit President Chiluba to run for a third term, prompting massive protest demonstrations and significant external condemnation. Under heavy pressure, Chiluba finally declared he would not seek reelection. However, on May 4 he dissolved the cabinet, permitting him to appoint a new government on May 6 that pointedly did not include theretofore Vice President Tembo and some 11 other MMD members who had opposed the third-term initiative. Former vice president Mwanawasa became the surprise MMD candidate in the December 27, 2001, presidential balloting, securing, according to official results, a narrow victory (28.69 percent to 26.76 percent) over the second-place finisher, Anderson K. MAZOKA of the United Party for National Development (UPND). However, opposition parties charged that the balloting had been rigged and demanded a court review. (The Supreme Court launched a review of the charges but closed the case in November 2004.) Meanwhile, the MMD was also credited with pluralities in the concurrent assembly and municipal elections, the UPND easily outdistancing the other contenders to secure its position as the dominant opposition grouping. Not surprisingly, considering the electoral challenge, no opposition parties were represented in the cabinet appointed by Mwanawasa on January 7, 2002. However, Mwanawasa appointed members of the UNIP and the Forum for Democracy and Development (FDD) to junior cabinet positions in a May 28, 2003, reshuffle. He also named Nevers MUMBA, a prominent pastor and leader of the National Citizens' Coalition (NCC), as vice president. Mumba was in turn succeeded by Lupando MWAPE of the MDD on October 4, 2004, and by 2005 it was reported that the non-MDD cabinet members had been replaced by MDD stalwarts.

On April 5, 2006, the assembly adopted a controversial electoral reform bill establishing the president's authority to set election dates and requiring only a plurality in a single-round election to decide presidential balloting, among other provisions (see Current issues, below). The bill was promulgated on May 19, and on July 26 President Mwanawasa dissolved Parliament and called for early tripartite elections on September 28, 2006. President Mwanawasa won reelection with a plurality of 43 percent of the vote, defeating main challengers Michael SATA of the Patriot Front (PF) with 29 percent, and Hakainde HICHILEMA of the United Democratic Alliance (UDA) with 25 percent. Two other candidates, including former vice president Godfrey Miyanda, received less than 2 percent of the vote. In legislative balloting the MMD remained the largest parliamentary party with 73 seats, though it lacked a clear majority without the 8 presidentially appointed members. The opposition PF, however, made a stunning comeback with 43 seats (it had won 1 seat in 2001). The newly formed United Democratic Alliance (see Political Parties, below) secured 26 seats. On October 9 the president named Rupiah BANDA of the UNIP as vice president to replace Mwape, who lost his seat in the parliamentary elections. Banda and the new cabinet were sworn in on October 10. Three cabinet ministers were replaced in early 2007.

President Mwanawasa died at age 59 on August 19, 2008, following complications of a stroke weeks earlier. A by-election to choose a successor to serve the remaining three years of Mwanawasa's term was held on October 30. The acting president, Vice President Rupiah Banda (MDD), secured 40.09 percent of the vote, narrowly defeating Michael Sata of the PF, who garnered 38.13 percent. The remaining challengers, Hakainde Hichilema (UPND) and Godfrey Miyanda of the Heritage Party (HP), trailed far behind.

On November 14, 2008, President Banda appointed Legal Affairs Minister George Kunda as vice president, while still allowing Kunda to retain his cabinet post. Banda reshuffled the cabinet the same day.

A minor cabinet reshuffle was announced on March 24, 2009. The communications and transport minister, Dora SILIYA, resigned on April 21, 2009, after she was accused of wrongdoing for allegedly ignoring advice from the attorney general in a contract matter. An appeals court subsequently cleared Siliya of the charges, and on June 17 she was reappointed as education minister in a minor cabinet reshuffle.

Constitution and government. Zambia's 1964 constitution was superseded by the adoption at a UNIP conference in August 1973 of a constitution of the "second republic" that reaffirmed the introduction in 1972 of a one-party system and further provided for the sharing of authority between the party and traditional organs of government. To further emphasize the role of the UNIP, its secretary general (rather than the prime minister) was designated the nation's second-ranking official.

On August 2, 1991, the National Assembly adopted a new constitution that provided for multiparty elections, a two-tiered Parliament, abandonment of the post of prime minister in favor of a revived vice presidency, and a presidentially appointed cabinet. In 1993 President Chiluba named a 22-member commission to revise the 1991 document. Draft amendments, released in June 1995 in expectation of a constituent assembly and national referendum, were approved by the National Assembly on May 16, 1996, and by President Chiluba on May 28. The Constitution of Zambia Amendment Act 1996 limits participation in presidential polling to Zambian-born citizens whose parents were also born in Zambia and disqualifies traditional chiefs and anyone who has lived abroad during the previous 20 years. The chief executive is limited to two five-year terms.

The judiciary embraces a Supreme Court, a High Court, and various local courts. Administratively, the country is divided into nine provinces, including the city of Lusaka and its environs, which are subdivided into 55 districts.

Foreign relations. While pursuing a generally nonaligned foreign policy (an 18-year coolness with Britain having been ended by a Kaunda state visit to London in 1983), Zambia consistently opposed racial discrimination in southern Africa and provided sanctuary for numerous exile groups engaged in guerrilla operations against white-controlled territories. Prior to the constitutional changes in South Africa, Zambia's prestige among Front-Line States was pronounced. In the wake of treaties concluded by Angola and Mozambique with South Africa, Lusaka became the headquarters of the African National Congress (ANC), making it a target for bomb attacks in May 1986 by South Africa forces, which also crossed the border on a "reconnaissance mission" in April 1987 that left several persons dead. Kaunda assumed the chair of the Front-Line grouping in early 1985, vowing to promote increased mutual support among member governments. In 1986 he denounced the United States and the United Kingdom for "conspiring" to support the South African government, warning they would share responsibility for the impending anti-apartheid "explosion." Zambia was also in the forefront of a regional plan to lessen reliance on South African trade routes that included rehabilitation of the Benguela Railway in Angola and the Tanzania-Zambia (Tanzam) link to Dar es Salaam. In other regional affairs, troops were at times deployed in border clashes with Malawi and Zaire, the latter agreeing in 1986 to a joint review and demarcation of disputed territory that yielded a settlement in 1989. (Disputes continued to erupt in 2005 at the border of the renamed Democratic Republic of the Congo, reportedly notorious for illegal crossings and smuggling.) In November 1989 a joint security commission was established with Mozambique in an attempt to thwart cross-border guerrilla activity.

Since its ascension to power in October 1991, the Chiluba government's foreign policy agenda was topped by relations with international creditors. In late 1991 the government negotiated a release of the aid allocations suspended in September when the Kaunda regime had allowed debt repayment and austerity programs to lapse. The government's decision to sever diplomatic ties with Iran and Iraq for their alleged financing of coup plotters against Chiluba was described in *Africa Confidential* as owing more to "fundamentalist Christian and anti-Muslim" tendencies within the administration than to substantive evidence of foreign involvement. Furthermore, the Chiluba government experienced slow progress in establishing relations with regional neighbors, many of whom were Kaunda supporters and had expressed distrust of the new administration's criticism of the ANC as well as of its links to South African commercial interests.

The Zambian assembly's approval of a controversial constitutional amendment bill in May 1996 provoked widespread disapproval from Zambia's Western donors, and in June a number of them suspended aid payments. Regionally, however, the Southern African Development Community (SADC) was described by observers as having adopted a "passive" position after the Chiluba government rebuffed its initial intervention efforts, and South Africa, the only SADC member considered powerful enough to influence Lusaka, refused to assume a leadership role.

Aid donors remained unwilling to restart payments through the first half of 1997; however, in July the suspension was partially lifted. Negotiations on further relaxation of payment restrictions were postponed after Lusaka imposed a state of emergency from October until March 1998. In May 1998 the World Bank agreed to a new aid package contingent on Lusaka enacting economic and political reforms; in particular, the bank pressed the government to speed privatization efforts and improve its human rights record.

Zambian-Angolan relations deteriorated in early 1999 as Luanda threatened military action against Zambia if Lusaka continued its alleged support for Angolan rebels. Thereafter, in a thinly veiled reference to Luanda, the Chiluba administration blamed "external forces" for a series of bombings in Lusaka. Later agreements between Luanda and Lusaka appeared to ease the tension, however, although a large Angolan refugee population subsequently continued to create difficulties for the Zambian government, as did an influx of refugees from fighting in the Democratic Republic of the Congo (formerly Zaire). A joint UN-Zambian program to repatriate Angolan refugees subsequently had substantial success, although there continued to be sporadic raids by Congolese rebels into Zambia. In response, the government increased border patrols.

In November 2004 the Zambian military launched a series of training exercises overseen by French military experts. The operations were part of a larger regional initiative through which France hoped to promote military cooperation among Tanzania, Zambia, and Zimbabwe that could lead, among other things, to joint regional humanitarian operations.

The final repatriation of some 34,500 Angola refugees was reported to be under way in 2005, though many were still living in camps in remote areas of Zambia in 2006.

Zambian opposition leader and 2006 PF presidential candidate Michael Sata was refused entry into Malawi in March 2007, reportedly on suspicion that he intended to help former Malawi president Elson Bakili Muluzi reorganize his former ruling United Democratic Front party. Sata denied the allegations. In June the Zambian government began revoking the refugee status of some 6,000 Rwandans who fled their war-torn country in the mid-1990s. Another 10,000 refugees from the Democratic Republic of the Congo also were urged to leave.

Chinese companies stepped up their investments in copper mining in Zambia in 2007, signing multimillion-dollar deals in exchange for significant tax concessions from the government. However, tension existed in relations at the popular level. In February workers at a Chinese-based company planned a large demonstration against China's president, resulting in his visit being canceled.

In 2008 Russia stepped up its economic interest in Zambia as three firms engaged in talks with President Mwanawasa over the possibility of investing $2 billion in Zambian mining projects. If successful, according to news accounts, this would amount to the country's single largest direct investment by a foreign entity.

Current issues. Political affairs in the early 2000s were dominated by the question of whether the constitution would be revised by national referendum to permit President Chiluba to seek a third term. Civic groups strongly objected to the initiative, and public anti-Chiluba demonstrations in March 2001 prompted mass arrests and a crackdown on meetings devoted to discussion of the question. Although nearly one-third of the delegates walked out of the MMD congress in late April, Chiluba's bid received official party endorsement, prompting another wave of street protests before the campaign was abandoned. By that time, many analysts had concluded that the party wrangling, resentment over Chiluba's autocratic style, and the perception of substantial corruption in government circles had made the MMD vulnerable in advance of the December elections. However, although they had proven successful in a number of recent by-elections, some of the opposition parties appeared to be regionally or tribally based and therefore of limited national scope, while the UNIP remained in disarray. In addition, despite much negotiation on the matter, the opposition failed to coalesce behind a single presidential candidate, permitting the MMD's Levy Mwanawasa to eke out a victory in the first-past-the-post contest among 11 candidates. Second-place finisher Anderson Mazoka of the UPND and a number of the other losing candidates immediately charged that the presidential balloting had been severely tainted by, among other things, the intimidation of voters and ballot-box stuffing. International observers agreed that electoral preparations had been seriously flawed, while EU monitors concluded it would be "unsafe" to accept the official results as accurately reflecting the will of the voters. Meanwhile, the president dedicated his new government to combating corruption, a campaign that quickly appeared to place him at odds with many MMD stalwarts, including his predecessor. In July 2002 the National Assembly lifted the immunity from prosecution previously enjoyed by former president Chiluba. As a result, Chiluba was arrested in 2003 on a wide range of corruption charges. Some 150 other senior figures from the Chiluba government, including the chief of the army and the country's intelligence head, were also arrested. Initial reports estimated that tens of millions of dollars may have been embezzled during the ten years of the Chiluba administration.

The appointment of opposition legislators to the cabinet in May 2003 was seen as an effort by President Mwanawasa to deal with plummeting popular support for the MMD in the wake of the Chiluba scandals. The administration had also been recently confronted by public protests over the effects of austerity measures. Further complicating matters for the government was the decision in August 2004 to postpone the local elections scheduled for November for two years because of financial constraints. Finally, Chiluba was rearrested in September 2004 (the initial charges had been botched by the prosecution), and supporters of the former president split from the MDD to form the Party for Unity, Democracy, and Development (PUDD).

As attention in 2005 turned to the 2006 presidential and legislative polls, opposition leaders called for drafting of a new constitution that would, among other things, establish at least a degree of proportional representation in the assembly. The government's critics also demanded revision in the makeup and authority of the electoral commission to help avoid the problems experienced in 2001. However, the electoral reform law adopted by the assembly and endorsed by President Mwanawasa in 2006 rejected the electoral commission's recommendations, including the stipulation that presidential balloting be decided by majority vote. The new law gives the president the authority to set the date of elections (President Mwanawasa set the date for September), which opposition groups claimed would not give them enough time to prepare. Meanwhile, several opposition groups formed alliances in advance of the elections (see Political Parties, below), but observers said the opposition was in "disarray," as it had been assumed elections would not be held until closer to the end of the year. However, the opposition appeared to have secured victory as early results indicated a substantial lead for controversial PF leader Michael Sata, who ran strong in the Copperbelt and the cities. When the results of the rural areas and the northwestern and eastern districts were tallied, Sata's hopes and those of his supporters were dashed, as President Mwanawasa won with a plurality in turnout of 70 percent, reported to be among the highest in recent years. Though foreign observers declared the elections fair, Sata's backers rioted after the elections, clashing with police until Sata appealed for them to desist. Sata protested the results but subsequently conceded defeat in October, though he still accused the government of vote-rigging. He also had alleged that China, seeking to protect its investments in Zambia, had intervened in the elections. Meanwhile, Sata's PF secured the second-largest number of seats in parliament, while the MMD, even with its dominant representation, lacked a majority. Mwanawasa, who ran on his strong economic record, promised to pursue planning for a new constitution by 2011. In 2007 a National Constitutional Conference drew up proposals for a draft bill and political parties were invited to make submissions to the draft. Meanwhile, the government banned groups from holding planned demonstrations during the SADC summit in Lukasa in mid-August.

Following a trial in a London court in 2007, former president Chiluba was convicted of stealing $46 million in public funds from Zambia. Chiluba, who had been ill, was hospitalized shortly after the trial. President Mwanawasa offered to pardon Chiluba if he admitted wrongdoing. The case eventually went to trial (see below).

The illness of President Mwanawasa, for which he was hospitalized in Paris in mid-2008, spurred political turmoil and jostling for position among various potential candidates for succession. Meanwhile, during the president's absence, members of parliament voted themselves large salary increases, even as Vice President Banda warned that such a move was "immoral" in the face of rising prices for food and fuel. Following the death of President Mwanawasa in August, his wife revealed that the late president had recorded a videotape naming Finance Minister Ngandu MAGANDE as his preferred successor. Magande was seen by some observers as the one best suited to carry on Mwanawasa's legacy, particularly in fighting corruption. Prior to the election on October 30, former finance minister, Katele KALUMBA of the MMD, withdrew his name and threw his support behind Banda. However, the fact that Banda was a former member of the UNIP and reportedly had never joined the MMD, raised objections by many governing party stalwarts. (Party leaders later said that Banda was a member.) Ultimately, Banda ran under the MMD banner, but even before the by-election took place, the PF and the UPND were charging that a government-backed ballot-tampering plot was under way. The chair of the electoral commission subsequently called an emergency meeting with the four presidential candidates on October 10 to review accusations that extra ballots had been printed. All but Banda attended. Banda's challengers—Sata, the UPND's Hakainde Hichilema, and the HP's Godfrey Miyanda—wanted to know why extra ballots had been printed, when there had never been 100 percent turnout among voters. The electoral commission chair explained that more ballots were printed in case voters made mistakes. Meanwhile, it was reported that Banda had given Kenneth Kaunda a mansion, thereby allegedly securing the founding president's backing just after Kaunda had sought, unsuccessfully, to persuade Sata and the UPND's Hakainde Hichilema to agree on only one opposition candidate. Chiluba, still facing trial on corruption charges, also dropped his support for Sata in favor of Banda.

In September 2008 Banda officially became the presidential nominee of the MMD and was endorsed by numerous small parties. Following Sata's narrow defeat in the October by-election, 38 percent to Banda's 40 percent (the PF candidate having lost by some 35,000 votes), his supporters rioted in protest, and Sata demanded a recount in 78 of 150 constituencies. Election monitors found the balloting to be fair but the electoral commission began verifying the votes on November 6. Banda, meanwhile, pledged to fight poverty and improve the standard of living. Banda also invited the three candidates he defeated to work with him to help unite the country.

As Banda began his short-term administration, the next presidential elections having been scheduled for 2011, attention turned to the state of the economy, which had declined significantly as a result of the global financial crisis. The price of copper plunged on the international market, severely affecting Zambia's revenue base, at the same time food and fuel costs were rising. Mining companies suspended operations and cut jobs—nearly 10,000 from December 2008 to February 2009, which observers said could further hurt Banda politically. Banda, who had lost the Copperbelt in the 2008 election, also came under heavy criticism from his main challenger, Michael Sata, as the administration grappled with the effects of the downturn. The government instituted food subsidies to offset the price of maize and, in an effort toward diversification, began planning irrigation projects and providing start-up funds for small and medium-size businesses. Plans for a Copperbelt Zone were on hold due to the lack of demand, and the country's electrical system, scheduled for upgrades by 2015, were inadequate to supply all the copper mines. In June some 5,000 civil service workers went on strike over salary issues, and two weeks later scientific researchers went on strike to protest working conditions. On a positive note, the government pledged nine tons of maize to neighboring Zimbabwe, which had been suffering from several years of drought.

In what was described as a landmark trial in August 2009, former president Chiluba was acquitted on all corruption charges. His wife, who had been sentenced in March 2009 to 42 months in prison, was released on bail and later rearrested for allegedly having received money and property stolen by her husband when he was in office. Both Chiluba and his wife protested the charges.

POLITICAL PARTIES

In December 1972, the United National Independence Party (UNIP) became the country's only legal political party. During the late 1980s reformists called for a multiparty system, with President Kaunda repeatedly dismissing the idea as unworkable because of "too many tribal conflicts." However, in September 1990 he bowed to mounting pressure and agreed to termination of the UNIP monopoly. Three months later, the president signed a National Assembly bill legalizing the formation of political parties, and in August 1991 a multiparty constitution was adopted. Thereafter, on October 31 the UNIP, the Movement for Multiparty Democracy (MMD), and 12 smaller parties participated in the first multiparty balloting since 1968.

Several parties formed electoral alliances in advance of the 2006 presidential and parliamentary elections. The UPND, the UNIP, and the FDD formed the United Democratic Alliance (UDA). A coalition of smaller parties, styled the National Democratic Focus (NDF), included the ZRP, Zadeco, and the ZDDM.

Dominant Government Party:

Movement for Multiparty Democracy (MMD). Formed in mid-1990 as a loose alliance of anti-UNIP groups in support of a voter registration drive, the MMD applied for legal party status immediately following legislative approval of a multiparty system in December. Among other things, the group issued a manifesto declaring its commitment to a free-market economy.

In June 1991 the MMD denounced a proposed draft constitution on the grounds that it would advance an excessively powerful presidency; the party threatened to boycott upcoming elections if it were adopted. Consequently, President Kaunda met in July with MMD leaders to forge a compromise document. Meanwhile, violent clashes between MMD and UNIP supporters continued, and in September the MMD complained that limiting the campaign period to two months favored the incumbents. Nevertheless, in the October 31 balloting Frederick Chiluba of the MMD defeated Kaunda's bid for reelection, with the MMD also winning an overwhelming majority of National Assembly seats. Subsequently, in sparsely attended balloting in late November 1992, the party captured nearly 75 percent of 1,190 local council seats.

In early 1993 a growing interparty chasm was reported between those members urging faster governmental reform and a second, reportedly more influential faction, which was concerned less with reform and more with "strengthening the political and financial interests of the . . . commercial class." Founding member and party chair Arthur Wina was one of 14 prominent MMD officials who withdrew from the grouping in August to protest the dismissal of cabinet ministers identified as having exposed corruption and drug trafficking by their colleagues. Thereafter, more members left the party as its popularity plummeted amid allegations that top officials were sheltered from the effects of the government's economic austerity program. On the other hand, in November 1993 Enoch Kavindele, leader of the United Democratic Party, dissolved his party and joined the MMD, claiming that he and Chiluba shared similar development strategies.

Internal friction, based in part on tribal differences as well as the personal ambition of various MMD leaders, was reported throughout the rest of the 1990s, although the party retained solid political control at both the national and local levels. Fractionalization reached its apex in early 2000 when it became apparent that President Chiluba's supporters were intent on constitutional revision that would permit him a third term. Some 400 delegates walked out of the MMD congress in Lusaka at the end of April to protest the initiative; however, the remaining delegates dutifully endorsed Chiluba as the MMD candidate in the upcoming presidential race, calling for a national referendum on the proposed constitutional change. In the wake of massive protest demonstrations, Chiluba several days later announced he had decided not to seek a third term, but at the same time more than 20 senior members of the MMD (including some 11 cabinet members) were expelled from the party, some of them subsequently helping to form new opposition parties.

In August 2001 Levy Mwanawasa, a prominent attorney and former vice president of the republic, was selected as the new MMD standard-bearer. Critics initially described Mwanawasa as Chiluba's hand-picked successor, but tension was apparent between the two MMD leaders following Mwanawasa's controversial victory in the national balloting, the new president, among other things, reportedly rejecting Chiluba's suggestions for cabinet appointments. In 2002 Chiluba was forced to resign as party president, resulting in Mwanawasa becoming acting president. According to some reports, Mwanawasa subsequently was unanimously elected as party president on the understanding that he would not prosecute Chiluba. After thousands of protesters demanded that Parliament lift Chiluba's immunity, the president made the same request. Following Chiluba's arrest on corruption charges in 2003, his supporters defected from the MMD and formed the PUDD (below).

The National Citizens' Coalition (NCC), sometimes referred to as the National Christian Coalition, merged with the MDD after the MDD's leader, prominent pastor Nevers Mumba, was appointed vice president in 2003. (Mumba had run for the presidency in 2001 but had received only 2.2 percent of the vote.) In October 2004 Mumba was dismissed as vice president following his comments accusing opposition parties of taking funds from foreign sources. He was forced to leave the party in 2005 after he reportedly accused President Mwanawasa and his wife of using government money to buy party convention votes, and subsequently supported opposition candidate Michael Sata of the PF in the 2006 presidential election.

Although Mwanawasa won the party leadership by a landslide in 2005, providing him a mandate to seek a second term as president of the republic in 2006, rifts in the party were reported among rivals who campaigned against him. Following Mwanawasa's decisive victory in 2006, the party appeared to rally behind Mwanawasa and the reforms he proposed.

Former ZRP Secretary General Sylvia MASEBO, then minister of local government and housing, defected to the MMD in June 2006.

Rifts in the party reappeared in 2008 as Mwanawasa lay ill in a Paris hospital. While some in the party suggested that a search for a successor begin, the idea was soundly rejected by others. The party had no vice president to tap as a successor to Mwanawasa (the party congress having canceled an election for the seat in the wake of reports of alleged vote-buying by candidates). Additionally, some of the party's other possible contenders, specifically Michael Mabenga and Katele Kalumba, the latter a finance minister under former President Chiluba, were tainted by allegations of corruption. The party was also divided over the selection of a presidential candidate, as 19 members sought to be the standard-bearer. Ultimately, Vice President Rupiah Banda, a former member of the UNIP, who, MMD leaders claimed, had joined the MMD "a long time ago," was chosen on September 5 as the party's presidential nominee over six others, including Finance Minister Ngandu Magande.

Despite President Banda's weak victory over the PF's Michael Sata in the October 2008 by-election, in June 2009 the party endorsed Banda for reelection in the 2011 poll. Banda pledged to strengthen the party in advance of the elections.

Leaders: Rupiah BANDA (President of the Republic and Acting President of the Party), Michael MABENGA (National Chair), Lupando MWAPE (Former Vice President of the Republic), Benny TETAMASHIMBA (Spokesperson), Katele KALUMBA (National Secretary).

Other Legislative Parties:

United Democratic Alliance (UDA). In advance of the September 2006 elections, the UPND, UNIP, and FDD formed the UDA, with the leader of each party serving as co-president. Former UPND leader Anderson Mazoka had played a major role in the three parties' electoral agreement that they would equally divide the country's 150 constituencies. UPND leader Hakainde Hichilema was the UDA standard-bearer in the 2006 and 2008 presidential elections. However, in the 2008 by-election, the PF did not join in the electoral alliance, instead nominating party leader Michael Sata as its presidential candidate.

United Party for National Development (UPND). Described as representing the interests of urbanized Zambians, the UPND was launched on December 1998 under the leadership of business leader Anderson Mazoka, who had recently left the MMD. The party quickly became a major opposition grouping, winning four of the six legislative by-elections it had contested as of mid-2000. Mazoka, running with the support of the National Party, secured an official 26.76 percent of the vote in the 2001 presidential balloting, although his supporters charged he had actually won the election and challenged the results in court. Meanwhile, the UPND easily became the leading opposition party by securing 49 seats in the concurrent legislative balloting.

Following Mazoka's death in 2006, a rift developed in the party, with members from the Southern Province backing Mazoka's widow as successor while party officials approached ZCTU president Leonard HIKAUMBA over the party's acting president, Sakwiba SIKOTA. After the party's divisive and chaotic convention in July, in which Lusaka businessman (and Mazoka protégé) Hakainde Hichilema was elected president, Sikota resigned (along with party vice president Robert SICHINGA and secretary general Logan SHEMENA), and he subsequently formed the United Liberal Party (below). Sikota blamed "tribalism and violence" for the party's election upheaval, though the election was declared fair by the Foundation for Democratic Process (FODEP). Sikota's departure reportedly left the party in disarray, with party vice president for economic and political affairs Patrick Chisanga trying to mend fences. Following Hichilema's failed bid for the presidency in 2006, the UDA faced a rift with FDD leader Edith Nawakwi over whether Hichilmena would automatically be the UDA's candidate for the next presidential election in 2011.

The UPND was unsuccessful in persuading the PF's Michael Sata to participate in an electoral alliance with the UPND and back Hichilema in the 2008 by-election. Meanwhile, Hichilema caused a rift in the party as a result of his trip to China in May to sign a cooperation agreement with the Chinese Communist Party, since China was seen as being a key supporter of the MMD government.

In 2009 the UPND called on parliament to repeal a public procurement act adopted a year earlier and replace it with one that had stronger anti-corruption measures. In advance of the 2011 presidential elections, the UPND and the PF agreed in June to an electoral alliance to challenge the MMD.

Leaders: Hakainde HICHILEMA (President of the Party and 2006 and 2008 presidential candidate), Richard KAPITA (Vice President), Charles KAKOMA (Spokesperson), Tiens KAHENYA (Secretary General).

United National Independence Party (UNIP). The UNIP was formed as a result of the 1958 withdrawal of Kenneth D. Kaunda, Simon M. Kapwepwe, and others from the preindependence African National Congress (ANC), led by Harry Nkumbula. The UNIP was banned by the British in March 1959, reconstituted the following October, and ruled Zambia from independence until October 1991.

On May 29, 1990, in announcing that the National Council had approved the holding of a referendum on multipartyism, President Kaunda stated that it would be "stupid" for the party not to explain to the public that approval of such a system would be equivalent to "courting national disaster." Nevertheless, at the 25th meeting of the UNIP National Council on September 24, 1990, Kaunda announced that referendum plans would be canceled and a multiparty constitution adopted prior to the 1991 poll.

At an extraordinary party congress held August 6–7, 1991, Kaunda faced a leadership challenge from businessman Enoch Kavindele; however, under pressure from party stalwarts, Kavindele withdrew his bid, and Kaunda won unanimous reelection as party president. Thereafter, in nationwide balloting on October 31, both Kaunda and the UNIP suffered resounding defeats, the former capturing only 24 percent of the presidential vote and the latter being limited to 26 assembly seats. In the wake of his electoral defeat, Kaunda resigned as party leader on January 6, 1992, but reversed himself four months later.

Fueled by the defection of a number of party members to Kavindele's newly formed United Democratic Party (UDP) and the UNIP's poor showing in local elections in November 1992, speculation mounted in early 1993 that Kebby Musoktwane, who had been elected party president at an extraordinary congress on October 1, would be supplanted by Maj. Wezi Kaunda, head of the UNIP's military wing and son of the former president. However, Wezi Kaunda, along with his two brothers, Tilyenji Kaunda and Panji KAUNDA, were among approximately 25 people, including 7 UNIP central committee members, arrested in March 1993 on charges stemming from an alleged coup plot. For its part, the party denied charges that it had planned to overthrow the Chiluba administration, with Musoktwane insisting that he had aided the government in exposing the plot.

In June 1993 former president Kaunda resigned from the party, citing a desire to become "father" to all Zambians and complaining that he had been denied a pension by the Chiluba government. In March 1994 approximately 85 members of the now defunct UDP rejoined the UNIP. (Prior to its dissolution in late 1993 UDP membership had been dominated by UNIP defectors.) In June 1994 the UNIP was instrumental in the formation of the Zambia Opposition Front (Zofro), an opposition umbrella organization that included the **Independent Democratic Front** (IDF), led by Mike KAIRA; the **Labour Party** (LP), led by Chipeza MUFUNE; the **National Democratic Alliance** (NDA), led by Yonam PHIRI (the NDA was reportedly deregistered in 1998); the **National Party for Democracy** (NPD), led by Tenthani MWANZA; and the **Zambia Progressive Party** (ZPP).

Although Kaunda's decision in May 1995 to return to political life was coolly received by Musoktwane and his youthful supporters, the former president encountered little difficulty in being reelected to the UNIP presidency on June 28. Kaunda continued to enjoy broad party support throughout 1995 and the first half of 1996 despite intensive government efforts to discredit him. However, in June 1996 former party secretary general Benjamin Mibenge called for an extraordinary UNIP congress to elect a new leader, asserting, according to *Africa Confidential,* that it was time to break "the myth that Dr. Kaunda can forever lead the party." Meanwhile, the government arrested seven people (including Kaunda) with ties to the UNIP, charging them with complicity in a wave of bombings and bomb threats allegedly masterminded by a terrorist group called *Black Mamba,* Kaunda's nickname during Zambia's independence drive.

In early October 1996 Zofro announced it would back single candidates in the upcoming legislative balloting. Meanwhile, Kaunda declared his intention of running for president again despite the recent controversial amendment that appeared to have disqualified him. However, later in the month the UNIP announced plans to boycott the legislative balloting, citing what it described as the "mismanagement" of the voter registration drive and charging the government with manipulating the constitution. Furthermore, Kaunda asserted that the continued imprisonment of six prominent party members on treason charges had undermined the UNIP's electoral preparations. The charges were dropped on November 1. (Charges against Kaunda had been dismissed earlier.)

In April 1997 a simmering intraparty rivalry between Kaunda's supporters and members opposed to his continued domination exploded into public view as the two groups clashed at a UNIP function. Internecine concerns were subsequently overshadowed, however, by violent encounters between the UNIP and supporters of the Chiluba government. In June the UNIP and its opposition allies called for foreign intervention to ease the political and social "crisis" gripping Lusaka. Two months later Kaunda accused the government of attempting to assassinate him and Roger Chongwe, leader of the **Liberal Progressive Front** (LPF), a small party allied with the UNIP.

In January 1998 Kaunda was indicted by the government for his alleged role in the October 1997 coup attempt. The UNIP president was held under house arrest until June 1, when the government, under intense international pressure, dropped the charges. In June Kaunda said he would retire from the UNIP, although he agreed to serve as party president on an acting basis until his successor was elected. Subsequently, members of the UNIP's youth wing were reported to have rallied behind the succession ambitions of Wezi Kaunda. However, Wezi died in November 1999 after being attacked by gunmen in his driveway.

Kenneth Kaunda officially retired from the UNIP presidency at the beginning of an extraordinary congress in Ndola in May 2000. He was succeeded by Francis NKHOMA, a former central bank governor, although severe factionalization was subsequently still reported in the party, particularly in regard to the new president's positive comments about potential cooperation with the MMD, of which he had been a member from 1990 to 1994. Tilyenji Kaunda was elected to the UNIP presidency in April 2001 and won 9.96 percent of the votes in the December presidential election. In 2003 the UNIP announced it would cooperate with the ruling MMD, and UNIP legislators were appointed to junior cabinet posts. Following President Mwanawasa's reelection in 2006, he appointed former UNIP representative in Europe and former cabinet minister Rupiah Banda as vice president of the republic.

The party claimed in September 2008 that Vice President Rupiah Banda had never officially resigned from the UNIP, even though Banda was on the ballot as the MMD's candidate for president. However, Kaunda threw his support behind Banda's candidacy because, observers said, he felt Banda would be more sympathetic to the UNIP than would Sata. In mid-October the party officially announced its endorsement of Banda's candidacy.

In April 2009 the UNIP and the UPND condemned the PF's plans for a protest demonstration against job losses in the Copperbelt, arguing that the demonstration would not resolve the issue, and that it was not necessary to blame the government when the global economic downturn was the cause.

Leaders: Tilyenji KAUNDA (President and 2001 presidential candidate), Njekwa ANAMELA (Vice Chair), Rev. Alfred BANDA (Secretary General).

Forum for Democracy and Development (FDD). Reportedly enjoying support among students and other urban dwellers, the FDD was launched in 2001 by former MMD members opposed to efforts by President Chiluba to run for a third term. Party founders included Lt. Gen. Christon Tembo, who had been dismissed as vice president of the republic by Chiluba in May. Tembo finished third in the 2001 presidential balloting, securing 12.96 percent of the vote according to the official results. The FDD expelled four members in 2003 after they accepted cabinet posts in the MMD-led government. Several other FDD members subsequently left the party and joined the MMD. Former finance minister Edith Nawakwi was elected party president in 2005.

The FDD did not participate in the 2008 by-election, thus weakening Hichilema's candidacy, observers said.

Tembo died in March 2009.

Leaders: Edith NAWAKWI (President), Given LUBINDA (Spokesperson).

Patriotic Front (PF). The PF was formed in 2001 by disgruntled former MMD members, including Michael Sata, who resigned as MMD secretary general in September to protest what he described as the irregular method of selection of Levy Mwanawasa as the MMD's standard-bearer. Sata was credited with 3.35 percent of the vote in the 2001 presidential poll.

In 2005 Sata, a staunch critic of President Mwanawasa, was charged with alleged espionage for supporting striking mine workers (unresolved as of mid-2008), and in 2006 Sata and party secretary general Guy Scott were charged with defaming the president after Sata allegedly leaked a letter written by President Mwanawasa. Sata claimed the letter was a forgery and a "trap." (In 2008 the Supreme Court rejected an appeal for a stay and ordered that the case proceed.)

Sata's supporters engaged in violent protests when initial reports of his 2006 presidential victory were determined to be wrong. Riots occurred mainly in the Copperbelt, where Sata was regarded as a hero because of his battle for the rights of miners. Sata made headlines during the campaign by saying if elected he would expel Chinese investors from the mining industry in Zambia and would promote ties with Taiwan, angering Chinese officials. In December 2006 Sata was arrested on charges of "false declaration of assets" in connection with documents he had filed in his election bid. The charges were dropped a few days later.

In 2008 the Supreme Court nullified three of the PF's parliamentary seats following a ruling that the seats had not been won fairly. The PF began to organize a massive protest but subsequently agreed instead to "open a dialogue" with the government, according to *Africa Confidential.*

In the run-up to the 2008 presidential by-election, a rift in the party developed in May after Sata dismissed some 20 party members who had attended a government-sponsored conference on proposed revisions to the constitution, which the PF officially opposed. The disaffected PF members were said to have joined the camp of Peter MACHUNGWA, a former minister in the Chiluba government, who had rejoined the PF in 2006. Presidential candidate Sata ruled out a proposed electoral alliance with the UPND to back the candidacy of Hakainde Hichilema, saying the PF was strong enough to win on its own. Two days before the October 30 by-election, 300 members of the PF reportedly resigned to join the MMD.

However, in advance of the 2011 elections, the PF and the UPND in 2009 agreed to an electoral alliance to challenge the MMD.

In February 2009 Secretary General Edward MUMBI resigned from the party in the wake of what he called "weird allegations" against him leveled by Michael Sata. Following the 2008 elections, Sata had accused Mumbi of accepting a bribe to derail the PF's presidential campaign. Mumbi, for his part, said Sata failed to provide donated resources to rural areas to ensure PF success in the election, and he blamed Sata for the party's loss.

Leaders: Michael SATA (President, and 2001, 2006, and 2008 presidential candidate), Guy SCOTT (Vice President), Rosemary CHITIKA (Spokesperson), Wynter KABIMBA (Secretary General).

United Liberal Party (ULP). Former UPND acting president Sakwiba Sikota formed the United Liberal Party in July 2006 after his failed bid to become UPND president. He broke away with several other senior officials of UPND, accusing the latter party of corruption and tribalism. Many of his supporters were reported to be from his home Western Province.

The party backed Rupiah Banda in the 2008 presidential election.

Leaders: Sakwiba SIKOTA, Chrispin SHUMINA (Secretary General).

National Democratic Focus (NDF). An alliance of smaller parties, initially referenced as the National Democratic Front, was formed prior to the 2006 presidential election and included the APC, the PUDD; Zadeco, the RP, and the ZRP. The APC later withdrew over a dispute with alliance leader and former vice president of the republic Nevers Mumba; the PUDD withdrew after ZRP leader Benjamin Yorum Mwila decided not to seek the presidency; and the RP pulled out in July 2006 in protest of Mwila's election as alliance president over Mumba. The ZDDM later was reported to have joined the alliance. The NDF supported President Mwanawasa, and it won 1 seat in Parliament in the 2006 elections.

The NDF supported Rupiah Banda in the 2008 presidential election.

Leader: Benjamin Yorum MWILA.

Zambia Republican Party (ZRP). The formation of the ZRP was announced in February 2001 as a merger of the Zambia Alliance for Progress (ZAP, see below), the Republican Party (RP), and the small National Republican Party.

The RP, with support centered in the Copperbelt, had been founded in mid-2000 by wealthy businessman Ben Mwila and a number of his supporters following their expulsion from the MMD. (Mwila had incurred the wrath of other MMD leaders by indicating a desire to run for president of the republic while a possible third term for President Chiluba was still under consideration.)

Both Mwila and Dean MUNGOMBA of the ZAP announced their presidential ambitions prior to the creation of the ZRP, and friction quickly materialized between the two. Consequently, Mungomba announced that he and his supporters were withdrawing from the ZRP to resume ZAP activity, although a number of former ZAP members remained in the new grouping.

Mwila was officially credited with 4.84 percent of the vote as the ZRP candidate in the 2001 presidential poll. Among other things, the ZRP platform called for increased privatization of state-run enterprises and the extension of agricultural subsidies.

In June 2006 a faction that included about 15 members, led by party secretary general Shirley Masebo, defected to the MMD.

Leaders: Benjamin Yorum MWILA (President and 2001 presidential candidate), Ben KAPITA (Chair).

Zambia Democratic Congress (Zadeco). This party was formed in mid-1995 by several former MMD members of Parliament and more than 80 cadres from Kabwata and Kanyama constituencies who expressed their disillusionment with the parent party. Zadeco leaders reportedly alienated a number of supporters when they issued a handpicked candidate list, thus dashing expectations of intraparty polling. Thereafter, Zadeco president Dean Mungomba was described as at the "forefront" of opposition activists threatening unrest if the Chiluba government remained in office after its mandate expired on October 31, 1996. Mungomba won 12 percent of the votes in the 1996 presidential poll, while Zadeco secured two seats in the concurrent legislative balloting.

Suspected of having played a role in the abortive October 1997 coup, Mungomba was imprisoned and reportedly beaten by government security forces; meanwhile, Zadeco's secretary general, Azwell Banda, fled to Zimbabwe. Thereafter, Zadeco called for international intervention to ease the tensions gripping Lusaka.

In April 1998 a Zadeco faction led by Eden JERRY and Don CHISANDO broke from the group and formed the **Zambia Democratic Congress–Popular Front** (Zadeco–PF), which its founders asserted was based on the same principles as Zadeco, but without the "undemocratic" leadership. Meanwhile, Mungomba remained imprisoned until December 1998, when the charges against him were dropped.

In 1999 the **Zambia Alliance for Progress** (ZAP) was formally launched in June 1999 by Zadeco, the National Lima Party (NLP), and a nonparty organization called the National Pressure Group. The NLP had been launched on August 11, 1996 by Guy Scott, a former agriculture minister and MMD parliamentarian (later of the PF), and Ben Kapita, the president of the Zambian National Union of Farmers. In legislative balloting in November, NLP candidates, campaigning on a platform calling for protection of Zambian farmers from foreign competitors, secured 6.6 percent of the vote but no seats.

The first ZAP general congress in July 2000 selected Mungomba as the party's candidate for the 2001 presidential contest. However, Mungomba subsequently participated in the creation of the ZRP in February 2001, apparently with the hope of securing the new grouping's nomination. After withdrawing from the ZRP several months later, Mungomba continued to present himself as the ZAP presidential candidate before leaving the race in October. By that time critics described the rump ZAP as a "one-man show," and the party secured less than 0.2 percent of the votes in the legislative balloting.

After Mungomba's death in 2005, Zadeco secretary general Langton Sichone said the party would disband. In 2006, however, Zadeco was still active, though divided by a rift between Sichone and leader Dan Pule.

In 2008 Zadeco backed Rupiah Banda for president to ensure continuity in government and avoid "political turbulence" ahead of the regularly scheduled elections in 2011.

Leaders: Rev. Dan PULE (President), Langton SICHONE (National Chair).

Zambia Direct Democracy Movement (ZDDM). The ZDDM joined the NDF in 2006, but little is known about the party. In 2008 party leader Edwin Sakala urged a government of national unity prior to the October 30 by-election.

Leaders: Edwin SAKALA (Chair), Maurice CHOONGO (Spokesperson).

Other Parties that Participated in the 2006 Elections:

Heritage Party (HP). The HP was formed in 2001 by Brig. Gen. Godfrey Miyanda, a former MMD stalwart and former vice president of the republic, who had left the ruling party in the dispute over a proposed third term for President Chiluba. He rejected pressure to join with the FDD; subsequently, some FDD and MDD members reportedly defected to the HP in 2001. Miyanda secured 7.96 percent of the vote in the 2001 presidential balloting, according to official results, and the party gained 4 seats in the legislative balloting. In 2006 the HP and the AC entered into an alliance in which the AC agreed not present a presidential candidate and to support the candidate put forth by the HP. Also, candidates in parliamentary and local elections in 2006 ran under the HP banner, according to the agreement between the HP and the AC.

Leader: Brig. Gen. Godfrey MIYANDA (Former Vice President of the Republic and 2001, 2006, and 2008 presidential candidate).

Agenda for Change (AC). Established in 2006 by a U.S.-based professor, Henry KYAMBALESA, this small party entered into an electoral agreement with the HP in advance of the presidential and parliamentary elections. It also reportedly formed a loose alliance with the ULP.

All People's Congress (APC). Formed in 2005, the APC's stated goal was to "set the Zambian political life on a new course for the future," striving for economic progress and social justice. The APC briefly joined the NDF in March 2006 but subsequently withdrew over reported tribal differences. Some reports said that APC leader Ken Ngondo was expelled from the NDF.

Ngondo, a businessman and former member of Parliament, finished last in the 2006 presidential balloting with less than 1 percent of the vote.

The APC backed Rupiah Banda in the 2008 presidential election.

Leader: Ken NGONDO (President of the Party and 2006 presidential candidate).

New Generation Party (NGP). Former FDD youth leader Humphrey Siulapwa formed the NGP in 2003 to address issues of youth, in particular. Siulapwa registered as a presidential candidate in 2006 but subsequently withdrew because of the high entry fee required. The party fielded parliamentary candidates in 2006 but failed to win any seats.

The NGP endorsed Banda in the 2008 election.

Leader: Humphrey SIULAPWA.

Reform Party (RP). The Reform Party was founded in 2005 by supporters of former vice president of the republic Nevers Mumba after he was expelled from the MDD. (He reportedly had planned to challenge President Mwanawasa for the party presidency.) Mumba said he would be the Reform Party candidate in the 2006 presidential election but subsequently withdrew, citing as his reason the short amount of time before the balloting. Mumba then announced he would support President Mwanawasa. The RP failed to win any seats in the concurrent parliamentary elections. Some senior members reportedly resigned following the elections.

The Reform Party was dissolved in February 2007, and in 2008 its former members were urged to support former RP president, Nevers Mumba, who had filed an application to be the MMD's presidential nominee. Following the MMD's selection in September 2008 of Rupiah Banda as its presidential candidate, the former RP leaders endorsed him.

Other parties participating in the 2006 elections were the **Democratic Party** (DP), led by businessman Emmanuel MWAMBA, and the **Zambia Conservative Party** (ZCP), led by Joseph CHIPILI and Peter SIMPEMBA. In 2008 the ZCP backed Rupiah Banda.

Other Parties and Groups:

Social Democratic Party (SDP). The SDP was formed in mid-2000 under the leadership of former diplomat Gwendoline Konie with the goal of addressing issues of special importance to women and young people. Konie, one of the first women to lead a Zambian party, won 0.58 percent of the vote in the 2001 presidential poll. She retired from politics in 2005 after establishing a nongovernment organization to help women in the prevention of HIV/AIDS. The party's status was unclear as of 2006. Party leader Gwendoline KONIE, a 2001 presidential candidate, died in March 2009.

National Leadership for Development (NLD). The NLD was launched in mid-2001 by Yobert Shamapande, a former United Nations (UN) official and relative newcomer to domestic politics. Running on a platform that emphasized education, poverty reduction, gender balance in government, and better health services, Shamapande won 0.5 percent of the vote in the 2001 presidential balloting. Thereafter, Shamapande pledged his support to President Mwanawasa's policies.

Leader: Yobert SHAMAPANDE (President and 2001 presidential candidate).

Party for Unity, Democracy, and Development (PUDD). The PUDD was formed in September 2004 by former members of the MMD who supported former president Frederick Chiluba. It also attracted dissident members of the PF who opposed the party's leader, Michael Sata. Former party leader Dan Pule led a cadre of defectors to Zadeco in 2005. Subsequently, former MMD national chair Chitalu SAMPA became interim leader of PUDD. The party sought to draw disaffected political figures into a new coalition ahead of the 2006 legislative elections, and though there was speculation that Chiluba might use the new party to challenge President Mwanawasa in the 2006 presidential election, Chiluba's health and legal problems (see Current issues, above) cast doubt on his candidacy. In 2006 the PUDD withdrew from the NDF (above) prior to the presidential election.

The party backed Rupiah Banda in the 2008 by-election. Former party leader Chitalu Sampa died in April 2009. He had left the PUDD and was national chair of the PF at the time of his death.

Leaders: Isaac MUSONDA (President), Josiah CHISHALA (National Chair).

Barotse Patriotic Front (BPF). References to the BPF first appeared in 1998 in regard to calls for independence or autonomy for a portion of western Zambia that had, along with regions in what are now Namibia and Botswana, been known as Barotseland. That kingdom of Lozi-speakers had enjoyed what one journalist called "half-independence" under British colonial rule. The area in Zambia became part of that country at independence in 1964 under an autonomy agreement with the UNIP under which the tribal chieftain was to retain significant powers, particularly in regard to control of land and resources. Lozi leaders subsequently claimed that UNIP had abrogated the agreement by stripping the chief of many of his powers.

The BPF in 1999 supported the secessionist activities of the Caprivi Liberation Front, which represents Lozi-speakers in Namibia (see Illegal Groups in article on Namibia for details). The BPF also called for a self-determination vote in western Zambia, prompting the detention of BPF leader Imasiku Mutangelwa on sedition charges. The BPF has acted in concert with a Barotse Cultural Association, while a Forum for the Restoration of Barotseland in July 2001 petitioned the OAU and the UN to conduct a self-determination referendum. In 2004 the BPF renewed its call to restore the name Barotseland to the Western Province and for the constitution of Zambia to uphold the 1964 agreement. It remained unclear whether the BPF was legally registered as a political party.

Leaders: Imasiku MUTANGELWA (President), Pumulo YUSIKU (Executive Secretary).

Minor parties include the **Common Cause Democracy** (CDD), led by James MTONGA; the **New Congress Party** (NCP), led by Cosmas MWALE and Secretary General John CHIBOMA; the **Progressive Parties Alliance** (PPA), led by Paul BANDA; the **United Nationalist Party** (UNP), led by Achim NGOSA; and the **United Poor People of Zambia Freedom Party** (UPPZFP), led by Alex MULIOKELA. The **National Revolution Party** (NRP), headed by Cosmo MUMBA, formerly of the NGP, allegedly received a payoff from the MMD in 2008 in exchange for the NRP's support for Rupiah Banda. The MMD said it had made a donation to help out the smaller party.

LEGISLATURE

The current **National Assembly** is a unicameral body consisting of 150 elected members, 8 presidentially appointed members, and the speaker, who is elected by the members of the assembly from outside their membership. The term of office is five years. Prior to the 1991 election, candidates were required to be members of the United National Independence Party (UNIP) and endorsed by that party's Central Committee. In the most recent elections on September 28, 2006, the seat distribution was as follows: the Movement for Multiparty Democracy, 73; the Patriotic Front, 43; the United Democratic Alliance, 26; the United Liberal Party, 2; the National Democratic Front, 1; and independents, 3. Two seats were vacant.

Speaker: Amusaa K. MWANAMWAMBWA.

CABINET

[as of November 1, 2009]

President	Rupiah Banda
Vice President	George Kunda

Ministers

Agriculture and Cooperatives	Brig. Gen. Brian Chituwo
Commerce, Trade, and Industry	Felix Mutati
Communications and Transport	Geoffrey Lungwangwa
Community Development and Social Services	Michael Kaingu
Defense	Kalombo Mwansa
Education	Dora Siliya [f]
Energy and Water Development	Kenneth Konga
Finance and National Planning	Situmbeko Musokotwane
Foreign Affairs	Kabinge Pande
Gender and Women in Development	Sarah Sayifwanda [f]
Health	Kapembwa Simbao
Home Affairs	Lameck Mangani
Information and Broadcasting	Lt. Gen. Ronnie Shikapwasha
Labor and Social Security	Austin Liato
Lands	Peter Daka
Legal Affairs	George Kunda
Local Government and Housing	Ben Tetamashimba
Mines and Mineral Development	Maxwell Mwale
Presidential Affairs	Ronald Mukumba
Science, Technology, and Vocational Training	Gabriel Namulambe
Sport, Youth, and Child Development	Kenneth Chipungu
Tourism, Environment, and Natural Resources	Catherine Namugala f]
Without Portfolio	Bradford Michila
Works and Supply	Mike Mulongoti

[f] = female

COMMUNICATIONS

In April 1980, following publication in the *Times of Zambia* of an article critical of the government, President Kenneth D. Kaunda warned that press freedoms might be curtailed. Subsequently, on October 1, 1982, the *Times,* which had long been dominated by the UNIP, was acquired outright from the British conglomerate Lonrho. Prior to its electoral defeat in October 1991, the UNIP exercised rigid control over the news media. Since then, an essentially free press has emerged. However, in 1998 a number of *Weekly Post* staff members were arrested after their paper reported that the Zambian military would be incapable of fending off an Angolan invasion. In 2006 Reporters Without Borders said "government partisans can use unfair laws to throw any journalist in prison at whim." Criticizing the head of state, the watchdog group said, is a "high risk exercise" for journalists since defaming the president is a criminal offense.

Press. The following are English-language newspapers published in Lusaka: *National Mirror* (40,000), Catholic weekly; *Zambia Daily Mail* (40,000), government owned; *Weekly Post* (40,000), influential independent launched in July 1991; *Times of Zambia* (32,000 daily, 44,200 Sunday), government owned; *The People,* independent weekly.

News agencies. The Zambia News Agency (Zana) is the domestic facility; *Agence France-Presse, Deutsche Presse-Agentur,* and Reuters are among the foreign agencies maintaining bureaus in Lusaka.

Broadcasting and computing. The government-supervised Zambia National Broadcasting Corporation (ZNBC) controls both radio and television. Radio Zambia transmits in English and seven Zambian languages, while Television-Zambia provides programming. As of 2008 there were 55.5 Internet users per 1,000 inhabitants.

INTERGOVERNMENTAL REPRESENTATION

Ambassador to the U.S.: Inonge Mbikusita LEWANIKA.

U.S. Ambassador to Zambia: Donald BOOTH.

Permanent Representative to the UN: Lazarous KAPAMBWE.

IGO Memberships (Non-UN): AfDB, AU, BADEA, Comesa, CWTH, Interpol, IOM, NAM, PCA, SADC, WCO, WTO.

ZIMBABWE

Republic of Zimbabwe

Political Status: Became self-governing British Colony of Southern Rhodesia in October 1923; unilaterally declared independence November 11, 1965; white-dominated republican regime proclaimed March 2, 1970; biracial executive established on basis of transitional government agreement of March 3, 1978; returned to interim British rule on basis of cease-fire agreement signed December 21, 1979; achieved de jure independence as Republic of Zimbabwe on April 18, 1980.

Area: 150,803 sq. mi. (390,580 sq. km.).

Population: 11,631,657 (2002C); 13,471,000 (2008E). The 2002 figure appears to involve substantial underenumeration.

Major Urban Center (including suburbs, 2005E): HARARE (formerly Salisbury, 1,527,000).

Official Language: English (Shona and Sindebele are the principal African languages).

Monetary Unit: Zimbabwe Dollar (official rate December 1, 2009: 351.70 dollars = $1US).

President: Robert Gabriel MUGABE (Zimbabwe African National Union-Patriotic Front); sworn in as prime minister on April 18, 1980, following legislative election of February 14 and 27–29; reconfirmed following election of June 30 and July 1–2, 1985; elected president by parliament on December 30, 1987, and inaugurated for an anticipated six-year term on December 31, succeeding the former head of state, Rev. Canaan Sodindo BANANA; reelected for a six-year term, following constitutional revision, by popular vote March 28–30, 1990; reelected for another six-year term March 16–17, 1996; reelected for another six-year term March 9–11, 2002; reelected in a disputed runoff on June 27, 2008, and sworn in for a five-year term on June 29.

Vice President: Joyce MUJURU (Zimbabwe African National Union-Patriotic Front); appointed by the president on December 6, 2004, to succeed Simon MUZENDA, who died on September 20, 2003; reappointed by the president on October 13, 2008, and sworn in the same day.

Prime Minister: Morgan TSVANGIRAI (Movement for Democratic Change); sworn in February 11, 2009, as authorized by the terms of a Global Political Agreement, signed September 15, 2008, which called for the formation of an inclusive transitional government.

THE COUNTRY

Bordered by Botswana, Zambia, Mozambique, and South Africa, Zimbabwe occupies the fertile plateaus and mountain ranges between southeastern Africa's Zambezi and Limpopo rivers. The population includes approximately 11.5 million Africans, mainly Bantu in origin; some 200,000 Europeans; and smaller groups of Asians and people of mixed race. The Africans may be classified into two multitribal groupings, the Shona (about 82 percent) in the north, and the Ndebele, concentrated in the southern area of Matabeleland. Shona-Ndebele rivalry dates to the 19th century and has contributed to a pronounced north-south cleavage. The majority of the European population is Protestant, although there is a substantial Catholic minority. The Africans include both Christians and followers of traditional religions; the Asians are a mixture of Hindus and Muslims.

In 1982 a Legal Age of Majority Act significantly enhanced the legal status of women (including the right of personal choice in selecting a marital partner, the right to own property outright, and the ability to enter into business contracts); it has, however, been unevenly utilized because of its conflict with traditional law. In 1996 about

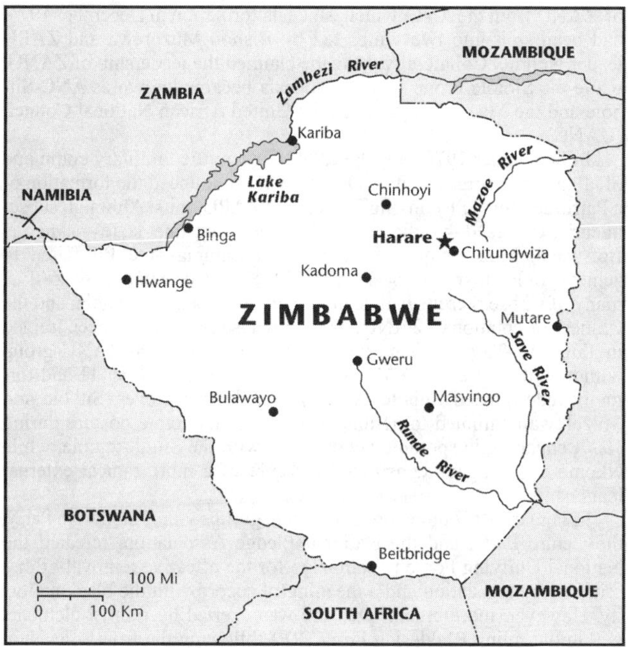

44 percent of the paid labor force was estimated to be female; black women are responsible for most subsistence agriculture (cash-crop production had been undertaken mainly by some 4,500 white farmers who at one time owned more than 70 percent of the arable land); white and Asian women are concentrated in the clerical and service sectors.

Zimbabwe was historically endowed with natural resources that yielded a relatively advanced economy oriented toward foreign trade (to which tobacco is a large contributor), exporting asbestos, chrome, copper, and other mineral products to a wide variety of foreign markets. During the country's period of agricultural self-sufficiency, Zimbabwe exported maize and other food crops to shortage-plagued neighbors. Although international trade sanctions were imposed on Zimbabwe (then Rhodesia) from 1965 to 1979, its economy prospered for much of the period because of continued access to trade routes through Mozambique (until 1976) and South Africa, which became the conduit for up to 90 percent of Rhodesian imports and exports. The lifting of sanctions at the end of 1979 further stimulated the economy, although drought and falling commodity prices subsequently contributed to fiscal difficulties, including budget deficits and persistent inflation. In addition, unemployment was aggravated by a growing pool of workers seeking better jobs as the result of rapid educational advances for blacks. The government consequently relaxed its control of the economy in favor of private business, industry, and agriculture, while an accelerated rate of disinvestment by foreign companies prompted revision of the country's investment guidelines.

In September 1995 the International Monetary Fund (IMF) announced the nonrenewal of loans for balance-of-payments support for six months in the wake of what were viewed as unacceptable projections of deficit reduction in the 1995–1996 budget. Following President Robert MUGABE's reelection in March 1996, the Zimbabwean business community lobbied the administration to enact the reforms sought by international lenders, including military and civil service budget cuts.

Zimbabwe has continued to suffer gravely from severe deterioration of economic, social, and political conditions, in part due to controversy surrounding the government's land redistribution program (see Current issues, below). The government has also been buffeted by allegations of corruption and broad mismanagement of the economy, marked by a bloated and inefficient civil service, massive budget deficits, and a soaring inflation rate. Severe poverty has remained widespread, and the rate of adults infected with HIV was 15.3 percent in 2007.

Real GDP declined by 7.2 percent in 2005, while inflation ballooned to a record 620 percent in 2004, reducing to around 400 percent by the end of 2005. In early 2006, following a payment of $9 million in arrears, Zimbabwe avoided expulsion from the IMF but lost its voting rights and access to general resources of the fund. Despite calls for reforms by the IMF and the United Nations (UN), the government refused help or intervention. By April 2006 conditions worsened further as the country's inflation rate hit 1,042.9 percent, among the highest in the world; millions of people were said to be suffering from food shortages, and the infant mortality rate was also estimated to be the highest in the world. The government devalued the currency and subsequently introduced emergency reforms, issuing new currency in August and seizing cash from citizens and businesses in an effort to curtail black-market trade.

In mid-2007 price controls were introduced in an effort to regulate the market. Meanwhile, a severe food shortage persisted and inflation was reported to be 100,000 percent. The IMF expressed its "deep concern over the deteriorating economic and social conditions" and Zimbabwe's $129 million in arrears to the fund's poverty-reduction program. The fund subsequently tabled its review to consider restoring Zimbabwe's voting rights.

Zimbabwe's economy reached its nadir in 2008. With the nation's reserve bank printing excess money without restraint to bankroll government spending, Zimbabwe posted the world's highest rates of inflation (in the trillions of percent at its peak) and debt-to-GDP ratio. Zimbabwe's GDP dramatically contracted by 14 percent in 2008, according to the IMF, capping a decade in which the nation's economy shrank by half. Severe food shortages and an epidemic of cholera that killed more than 4,000 people illustrated the breakdown in governance and services amidst the humanitarian crisis.

The government began to control hyperinflation in January 2009 when it abandoned the domestic currency in favor of the U.S. dollar and the South African rand. Under the unity government formed in February, with the finance ministry in the hands of the opposition Movement for Democratic Change, inflation slowed to nominal rates and food returned to store shelves. Bilateral development aid remained frozen due to donor concerns over economic mismanagement and persistent human rights violations. In August and September, the IMF released $500 million in reserves to Zimbabwe, the nation's first loan from the international financial institutions in nearly a decade. Finance minister Tendai BITI aimed to direct the funds to long-delayed infrastructure projects, while many observers expressed concern that the money could be diverted to the coffers of the ruling ZANU-PF party (see Current issues, below).

GOVERNMENT AND POLITICS

Political background. Originally developed and administered by the British South Africa Company, Southern Rhodesia became an internally self-governing British colony in 1923 under a system that concentrated political power in the hands of its white minority. In 1953 it joined with Northern Rhodesia (now Zambia) and Nyasaland (now Malawi) in the Federation of Rhodesia and Nyasaland. However, Southern Rhodesia reverted to separate status in 1963 when the federation was dissolved and Northern Rhodesia and Nyasaland prepared to claim their independence. A new constitution granted to Southern Rhodesia by Britain in December 1961 conferred increased powers of self-government and contained various provisions for the benefit of the African population, including a right of limited representation in the Legislative Assembly. However, the measure failed to resolve a sharpening conflict between African demands for full political equality based on the principle of "one-person, one-vote" and white Rhodesian demands for permanent white control.

In view of the refusal of Britain to agree to independence on terms that would exclude majority rule, the colonial government under Prime Minister Ian D. SMITH on November 11, 1965, issued a Unilateral Declaration of Independence purporting to make Rhodesia an independent state within the Commonwealth, loyal to the queen but free of external constraints. Britain repudiated the action, declared the colony to be in a state of rebellion, and invoked financial and economic sanctions; however, it refused to use force against the Smith regime. British Prime Minister Harold Wilson met personally with Smith in December 1966, after which UN sanctions were imposed, and again in October 1968, but no agreement was reached.

Rhodesia approved a new constitution on June 20, 1969, declaring itself a republic; subsequently, Britain suspended formal ties with the separatist regime. However, further British initiatives under Conservative leadership resulted in a set of proposals for settlement of the dispute in November 1971. These proposals were declared unacceptable by independent African leaders at the UN, and they were dropped in May 1972 after a 15-member British commission under Lord Pearce found them equally unacceptable to the majority of Rhodesia's African population.

On December 8, 1974, an agreement was concluded in Lusaka, Zambia, by Bishop Abel MUZOREWA of the African National Council (ANC), Joshua NKOMO of the Zimbabwe African People's Union (ZAPU), Ndabaningi SITHOLE of the Zimbabwe African National Union (ZANU), and James CHIKEREMA of the Front for the Liberation of Zimbabwe (Frolizi), whereby the latter three, representing groups that had been declared illegal within Rhodesia, would join an enlarged ANC executive under Bishop Muzorewa's presidency for a period of four months to prepare for negotiations with the Smith regime aimed at transferring power to the majority. Three days later Prime Minister Smith announced that, upon the receipt of assurances that insurgents within Rhodesia would observe a cease-fire, all black political prisoners would be released and a constitutional conference would be held without preconditions. On December 15, however, Smith again reiterated his government's opposition to the principle of majority rule.

In March 1975 Sithole, who had returned to Salisbury in December, was arrested by Rhodesian authorities on charges of plotting to assassinate his rivals in order to assume the ANC leadership. He was released a month later, following the intervention of Prime Minister Balthazar Johannes Vorster of South Africa. A few days earlier the Zambian government had announced that the Lusaka offices of ZANU, ZAPU, and Frolizi would be closed in accordance with its interpretation of the December 1974 agreement and the subsequent recognition of the ANC by the Organization of African Unity (OAU, subsequently the African Union—AU). ZANU spokesmen responded by charging that the presidents of Botswana, Tanzania, and Zambia had secretly agreed at the December talks to reconstitute the ANC leadership under the presidency of Nkomo without consulting Rhodesian African leaders.

During an ANC executive committee meeting in Salisbury on June 1, 1975, fighting broke out between ZANU and ZAPU representatives, and ZANU announced that it would not send delegates to an ANC congress scheduled for June 21–22. Frolizi also indicated that it would be unrepresented because the government had refused to grant its delegates an amnesty to return to Rhodesia. On June 16 Bishop Muzorewa announced that the proposed congress would not take place "due to serious administrative and other extreme difficulties."

Following an inconclusive meeting in Victoria Falls held August 25– 26, 1975, by the leaders of Rhodesia, South Africa, Zambia, and the ANC, the Nkomo faction, meeting in Salisbury on September 27–28, elected Nkomo president of the ANC within Rhodesia. On December 1 Nkomo and Prime Minister Smith concluded a series of meetings by signing a Declaration of Intention to negotiate a settlement of the Rhodesian issue. Under the agreement, which was repudiated by external ANC leader Bishop Muzorewa (then resident in Zambia) and by ZANU leader Sithole, all members of the ANC negotiating team were guaranteed freedom to enter Rhodesia to attend the projected talks.

Early 1976 witnessed an intensification of guerrilla activity by Mozambique-based insurgents under the leadership of former ZANU secretary general Robert MUGABE, the closing of the Mozambique border on March 3, and a breakdown in the talks between Nkomo and Smith on March 19. In early September it was reported that South African prime minister Vorster had agreed to a U.S.-British offer to provide upwards of \$2 billion in financial guarantees to Rhodesia's white settlers, contingent upon Salisbury's acceptance of majority rule. Prime Minister Smith subsequently announced that he had accepted a comprehensive package tendered by U.S. Secretary of State Henry Kissinger in a meeting on September 19 in Pretoria, South Africa, that called for a biracial interim government and the establishment of majority rule within two years. Britain responded to the Kissinger-Smith accord by convening a conference in Geneva between a white delegation led by Smith and a black delegation that included Nkomo, Mugabe, Muzorewa, and Sithole. However, the conference, which ran from October 28 to December 14, failed to yield a settlement, with the black leaders rejecting the essentials of the Kissinger plan by calling for an immediate transfer to majority rule and the replacement of the all-white Rhodesian army by contingents of the nationalist guerrilla forces. Alternative proposals advanced by the black leadership revealed major differences among the various factions. Mugabe and Nkomo demanded a British presence in Rhodesia (rejected by Sithole) while refusing to accept Sithole's and Muzorewa's proposals for an election prior to the transfer of power. Earlier, on September 9, Sithole had announced the withdrawal of ZANU from the ANC, which, since its formation in December 1974, had been split into two wings led by Bishop Muzorewa and ZAPU leader Nkomo. Collaterally, Mugabe claimed the leadership of ZANU, while the Sithole group within Rhodesia became known as ANC-Sithole and the Muzorewa group as the United African National Council (UANC).

In September 1976 Mugabe called for a unified military command of all guerrilla forces, and on October 9 he announced the formation of a Patriotic Front (PF) linking ZANU and ZAPU units. Although subsequently endorsed by the OAU and the front-line states—Angola, Botswana, Mozambique, Tanzania, and Zambia—the PF failed to achieve full integration because of the Soviet orientation of ZAPU, many of whose recruits had been trained by Cubans in Angola, and the Chinese orientation of ZANU, most of whose recruits had been trained in Tanzania. To complicate matters further, a dissident ZANU group withdrew its cadres from Mugabe's leadership on October 11 and formally redesignated Sithole as party president; however, Sithole and Muzorewa continued to assume a relatively moderate posture during 1977, engaging in sporadic negotiations with the Smith regime, while Nkomo and Mugabe constituted the core of a more radical external leadership.

In January 1977 three moderate white groups—the Rhodesian Party, the Centre Party, and the National Pledge Association—created the National Unifying Force to campaign for the effective removal of discriminatory legislation and a meaningful accord with the black majority. However, more crucial pressure was exerted by rightist elements within the ruling Rhodesian Front (RF) following the front's decision in March to liberalize constitutional provisions regarding land tenure. The dissidents were expelled from the RF on April 29 and organized themselves as the Rhodesian Action Party (RAP) on July 4. Since the RF thus lost the majority required for constitutional amendment, a new election was called for August 31, in which the front regained all 50 seats on the European roll.

During 1977 a number of British proposals were advanced in hopes of resolving the impasse on interim rule. In January, concurrent with an announcement that resumption of the Geneva discussions would be indefinitely postponed, Ivor Richard, British representative to the UN and chair of the Geneva Conference, called for the appointment of a British resident commissioner in Salisbury who would play a balancing role in the negotiations with "a great deal of constitutional power." He further proposed an interim Rhodesian Council including 20 blacks (5 from each of the leading nationalist factions) and 10 whites (5 British and 5 Rhodesian). The proposal was immediately rejected by Prime Minister Smith, who conveyed his government's opposition to any form of British presence. In September, however, a revised version of the proposal was endorsed by the UN Security Council. Under the new plan, a British resident commissioner (Field Marshal Lord Carver) would be appointed for a period of six months, during which arrangements would be made for a new constitution and a one-person, one-vote general election. The plan also called for the creation of a new Rhodesian army containing mixed black-white units and the appointment of a UN special representative (Indian Lt. Gen. Prem Chand, former commander of the UN Force in Cyprus, who was named to the new post on October 4). While the initial reaction from all parties was encouraging, both Nkomo and Mugabe subsequently insisted that transitional control be exercised by the PF rather than by the British commissioner. The change in attitude was occasioned largely by a dispute regarding the timing of a general election, with PF leaders insisting, because of Bishop Muzorewa's apparent widespread popularity, that the election be deferred for as long as three years after independence. Subsequently, Prime Minister Smith declared that the British settlement plan had failed and resumed discussions, based on a revision of the earlier Kissinger package, with Muzorewa and Sithole. In December Nkomo declared that front leaders would not join the "fake so-called internal settlement talks by Smith and his puppets."

Despite the intransigence of the PF, an agreement was reached on March 3, 1978, by Smith, Muzorewa, Sithole, and Mashona Chief Jeremiah S. CHIRAU of the Zimbabwe United People's Organization (ZUPO) to form a transitional government that would lead to black rule by the end of the year. Accordingly, an Executive Council comprising the four was established on March 21, while a multiracial Ministerial Council to replace the existing cabinet was designated on April 12. On May 16 the Executive Council released preliminary details of a new constitution that would feature a titular president elected by parliament sitting as an electoral college. In the face of escalating guerrilla activity, however, the existing House of Assembly voted on June 26—despite the unanimous objection of its black members—to renew the state of emergency that had been in effect since 1965 for another year. More importantly, although all racial discrimination was formally abolished on October 10, the projected national election was postponed in early November until April 1979, following the failure of a renewed effort to convene an all-party conference.

A new constitution was approved by the assembly on January 20, 1979, and endorsed by 84 percent of the white voters in a referendum on January 30. Although condemned by the UN Security Council by a 12–0 vote (with 3 abstentions) on March 8, a lower-house election was held on April 10 and 17–20 for 20 white and 72 black members, respectively, in which the UANC won 51 seats in the face of a boycott by the PF parties. Following a Senate election on May 23, Josiah GUMEDE of the UANC was elected president of Zimbabwe/Rhodesia, and on May 29 he requested Bishop Muzorewa to accept appointment as prime minister.

On June 7, 1979, U.S. President Jimmy Carter rejected an appeal for recognition of the new government, expressing doubt that the election had been either free or fair since "the black citizens . . . never had a chance to consider or to vote against the Constitution," while the white minority retained control of the police, the army, the justice system, and the civil service. Earlier, the newly appointed British prime minister, Margaret Thatcher, had stated that responsibility for deciding on the legality of the Muzorewa government lay with the UK parliament, although Foreign and Commonwealth Secretary Lord Carrington argued in the House of Lords that it would be "morally wrong to brush aside an election in which 64 percent of the people of Rhodesia cast their vote."

Following renewed guerrilla activity by PF forces in mid-1979, British and other Commonwealth leaders issued a call for talks between representatives of the Muzorewa government and the Patriotic Front. The discussions, which commenced on September 10 and ran for 14 weeks, yielded a constitutional agreement, an interim administration agreement, and a cease-fire agreement on December 5 that called for Britain to reassume full administrative authority for an interim period, during which a new and carefully monitored election would be held as a prelude to the granting of legal independence. On December 7 the terms of the agreement (which was not formally signed by the principals until December 21) were approved by parliament, and Lord SOAMES was appointed colonial governor, with Sir Anthony DUFF as his deputy. On December 12 Lord Soames arrived in Salisbury, where he was welcomed by members of the former government of Zimbabwe/Rhodesia, who, one day earlier, had approved a parliamentary bill terminating the Unilateral Declaration of Independence and transferring authority to the British administration.

White and common roll elections were held in February 1980, the Rhodesian Front winning all 20 white seats and Mugabe's ZANU-PF winning a substantial overall majority in the House of Assembly. Accordingly, Mugabe was asked by Lord Soames on March 4 to form a cabinet that included 16 members of ZANU-PF, 4 members of Nkomo's Patriotic Front–ZAPU, and 2 members of the RF. The new government was installed during independence day ceremonies on April 18 following the inauguration of Rev. Canaan Sodindo BANANA, a Mugabe supporter, as president of the republic.

The period immediately after independence was characterized by persistent conflict between armed forces of ZANU-PF and PF-ZAPU (units of Mugabe's Zimbabwe African National Liberation Army [ZANLA] and Nkomo's Zimbabwe People's Revolutionary Army [ZIPRA], respectively). To some extent the difficulties were rooted in ethnic loyalties, with most ZANLA personnel having been recruited from the northern Shona group, while ZIPRA had recruited primarily from the Ndebele people of Matabeleland. During 1981 the level of overt violence subsided, the government announcing in November that merger of the two guerrilla organizations and the former Rhodesian security force into a 50,000-man Zimbabwean national army had been completed. However, personal animosity between Mugabe and Nkomo continued, threatening the viability of the coalition regime. On February 17, 1982, Nkomo and three other ZAPU government members were dismissed in a major cabinet reorganization, Nkomo declaring that his group should thenceforth be construed as an opposition party. By 1984 violence on the part of dissident Nkomo supporters had produced major confrontations between government forces and Ndebele civilians in Matabeleland and Midlands, while defections from Ian Smith's party, renamed the Conservative Alliance of Zimbabwe (CAZ), saw its number of members in the assembly reduced to seven.

After a series of postponements attributed to a need to redraw electoral districts and prepare new voter lists, the first postindependence legislative elections were held in mid-1985. Smith's CAZ rallied to regain 15 of the 20 white seats on June 27, while in common roll balloting held July 1–4, Mugabe's ZANU-PF won all but 1 of the non-Matabeleland constituencies, raising its assembly strength to 64 as contrasted with ZAPU's 15. Although the results fell short of the mandate desired by Mugabe for introduction of a one-party state, ZAPU members, including Nkomo, responded to overtures for merger talks, which eventually yielded an agreement on December 22, 1987, whereby the two parties would merge, with Nkomo becoming one of two ZANU-PF vice presidents. Three months earlier, following expiration of a constitutionally mandated seven-year entrenchment, the white seats in both houses of parliament had been vacated and refilled on a "non-constituency" basis by the assembly. On December 31 Mugabe, having secured unanimous assembly endorsement the day before, was sworn in as executive president; concurrently, Simon MUZENDA was inaugurated as vice president, with the post of prime minister being eliminated.

The Senate was abolished prior to the balloting of March 28–30, 1990, in which Mugabe won 78 percent of the presidential vote and ZANU-PF swept all but four seats in the House of Assembly. Following the election, a second vice presidency was established by constitutional amendment, with Nkomo being named to the post.

On May 1, 1993, the government released a list of 70 farms, encompassing approximately 470,000 acres, which it planned to purchase for redistribution under authority of the 1992 Land Acquisition Act. Subsequently, the powerful Commercial Farmers' Union (CFU), representing approximately 4,000 white farmers, denounced the government for violating its pledge to buy only "derelict and underutilized" properties. Furthermore, Western donors reportedly warned the Mugabe administration that it risked suspension of aid payments if it followed through with its proposed acquisitions. In August the president responded that his government would seize the properties without compensation and expel "resistant" whites if domestic and "racist" foreign interference continued, and in September he dismissed a legal challenge to the Land Acquisition Act as futile. However, following the revelation in early 1994 that a majority of the 98 parcels appropriated under the act had been granted on cheap leases to senior government officials and civil servants, Mugabe suspended that specific program in April.

At presidential balloting held March 16–17, 1996, President Mugabe captured a third term. The president's victory was tarnished, however, by the withdrawal of his only two competitors, Sithole and Muzorewa, during the week prior to balloting. Both men complained of being harassed by government security forces, and they charged that the electoral system unfairly favored the incumbent. Furthermore, voter turnout was reported to have been only 32 percent, the first polling since independence to attract less than 50 percent of the electorate. Thus, even with an official 92 percent vote share (Sithole's and Muzorewa's names remained on the ballot, and both garnered votes), Mugabe was rumored to have secured only 28.5 percent of the potential vote, far from the mandate for which he had campaigned.

ZANU-PF reportedly won most of the seats in local elections in August 1999, although low turnout again tarnished the results. Shortly thereafter, opposition forces coalesced as the Movement for Democratic Change (MDC), which lobbied strongly against the constitutional revision proposed by the government that, among other things, would have made Mugabe president for life, given him the power to dissolve parliament, and endorsed the administration's land redistribution program. In January 2000, Mugabe added a further proposed constitutional revision that required Britain to pay compensation for all land that the government acquired compulsorily for resettlement. Underscoring growing internal discontent, 55 percent of those voting in a national referendum held on February 12–13, 2000, rejected the proposed changes in the basic law.

ZANU-PF barely withstood an electoral challenge from the MDC in new assembly balloting held June 24–25, 2000, securing 62 of the 120 elective seats. Subsequently, in presidential balloting on March 9–11, 2002, Mugabe won another term, defeating Morgan TSVANGIRAI of the MDC 56 to 42 percent, although the MDC, as it had with many of the legislative results, rejected the results as fraudulent. (A court ruling in 2006 rejected Tsvangirai's charge of voter fraud in the 2002 election.)

In the legislative elections of March 31, 2005, ZANU-PF made a strong recovery, winning 78 seats, which, coupled with its 30 appointive seats, gave the president's party a two-thirds majority. The MDC won 41 seats, and 1 seat went to an independent candidate. The president reshuffled the cabinet on April 15, 2005, moving house speaker Emmerson MNANGAGWA to a ministry post, among other changes. On August 30, 2005, the House of Assembly voted 103–29 to establish a new 66-member Senate (see Constitution and government, below), in addition to other constitutional amendments. In the first polling for 50 Senate seats on November 26, 2005, the ZANU-PF won 43 and the MDC won 7. Several other parties and independent candidates failed to win representation.

In January 2008 President Mugabe issued a proclamation that presidential elections would be held simultaneously with parliamentary elections on March 29 and by-elections for three seats on June 27. The MDC-Tsvangirai faction (MDC-T) became the largest party in the House of Assembly by a very narrow margin. In the enlarged Senate, the ZANU-PF retained its position as the largest party. In the presidential election, the results of which were not announced until May 2, Morgan Tsvangirai of the MDC won 47.9 percent of the vote to Mugabe's 43.2 percent. Two independent candidates, including Simba MAKONI, a former finance minister who was expelled from ZANU-PF ahead of the election, together received less than 10 percent of the vote. Since no candidate won at least 50 percent of the vote, a runoff was scheduled for June 27. Days before the balloting, Tsvangirai withdrew due to escalating violence against the MDC. Attempts by the UN and South African President Thabo Mbeki to broker an agreement between Mugabe and Tsvangirai failed, and the runoff was held as scheduled, with Tsvangirai's name remaining on the ballot. Mugabe was reelected with 85.5 percent of the vote, compared to 9.3 percent for Tsvangirai, and was sworn in on June 29.

Mugabe, bowing to international pressure after the discredited runoff, agreed to talks with the MDC mediated by the Southern African Development Community (SADC), resulting in a Global Political Agreement signed September 15, 2008, by Mugabe, Tsvangirai, and Arthur MUTAMBARA, head of a rival MDC faction. The pact called for the creation of a power-sharing government, but despite further mediation by Thabo Mbeki, then the president of South Africa, disputes over the allocation of ministerial authority made Tsvangirai reluctant to govern alongside Mugabe, his long-time rival. On January 30, 2009, the opposition leader finally agreed to enter an inclusive government. He was sworn in as prime minister on February 11. Under the government of national unity, ZANU-PF retained control of 15 ministries, including defense, foreign affairs, and justice; the two MDC factions together presided over 16; and the ministry of home affairs was jointly run.

Constitution and government. The constitution that issued from the 1979 London talks provided for a president designated for a six-year term by the (then) two houses of parliament sitting as an electoral college. Executive authority was vested in a cabinet headed by a prime minister, with the appointment going to the person best able to command a legislative majority. However, in late 1987 the post of prime minister was abolished in favor of an executive presidency. The (then) unicameral legislature consisted of a 150-member House of Assembly, 120 of whom were popularly elected (see Legislature, below) for five-year terms. An Advisory Council of Chiefs and an ombudsman, appointed by the president, investigate complaints against actions by political authorities. The judicial system is headed by a High Court (with both general and appellate divisions) and includes magistrate courts at the local level. A national referendum in 2000 defeated proposed changes to enhance presidential authority (see Political background, above, for details).

Since 1980, the assembly has amended the constitution numerous times. In August 2005, the assembly approved the establishment of an upper house, the Senate (see Legislature, below). Other constitutional amendments approved by the assembly in 2005 denied owners the right to appeal government expropriation of their land and empowered the government to confiscate passports in the interest of national security, with no right to appeal.

The assembly amended the constitution in September 2007, the changes promulgated on October 30. Under these amendments, the House was expanded to 210 directly elected seats, and the Senate was enlarged to 93 seats, 60 of them directly elected. The amendments also provide for simultaneous presidential and parliamentary elections; change the president's term of office from six years to five to coincide with parliamentary terms; set provisions for presidential elections within 90 days should a sitting president resign, die, or be removed from office; and establish a Human Rights Commission.

The Global Political Agreement accepted by ZANU-PF and the two MDC formations on September 15, 2008, called for a transitional power-sharing government with executive power divided between the president and prime minister. The agreement requires the inclusive government to prepare a new draft constitution for the nation within 18 months of its accession to power; this constitution is then to be offered to the public by referendum, and if adopted, to serve as a basis for new elections. The process of drafting a constitution began in April 2009 with the formation of a parliamentary select committee, but has since been deadlocked by partisan differences (see Current issues, below).

The country is currently divided into ten provinces: West, Central, and East in Mashonaland; North and South in Matabeleland; Midlands; Manicaland; Masvingo; Harare; and Bulawayo (though the latter two are cities, they have provincial status). Each is headed by a centrally appointed provincial governor and serves, additionally, as an electoral district for senate elections. Local government is conducted through town, district, and rural councils.

Foreign relations. Zimbabwe became a member of the Commonwealth upon achieving de jure independence in April 1980; it was admitted to the OAU (subsequently the African Union—AU) the following July and to the UN in August. In January 1983 it was elected to a seat on the UN Security Council, where its representatives assumed a distinctly anti-American posture. The strain in relations with the United States culminated in 1986 with Washington's withdrawal of all aid in response to strongly worded attacks from Harare on U.S. policy regarding South Africa. Despite (then) Prime Minister Mugabe's refusal to apologize for the verbal onslaughts, the aid was resumed in August 1988.

In regional affairs, Harare occupied a leading position among the front-line states bordering South Africa, concluding a mutual security pact with Mozambique in late 1980 and hosting several meetings of the Southern African Development Coordination Conference (now the SADC). It also provided active support for the Maputo government's anti-insurgency campaign, with approximately 10,000 troops being stationed in Mozambique in 1986, primarily to defend the transport corridor to Beira on the Indian Ocean, which the front-line states viewed as crucial to diminish reliance on South African trade routes. In June 1988 Zimbabwe and Mozambique signed a military cooperation agreement aimed at containing the border activities of the rebel Mozambique National Resistance (Renamo). Nonetheless, news reports in January 1990 that some 60 Zimbabwean civilians had been killed by Renamo insurgents during the preceding six months prompted Mugabe to extend state of emergency measures, which had been renewed every six months since the country achieved independence. In July Harare closed the border in an attempt to contain the unrest, while Mozambique's Chissano government engaged in peace talks with Renamo. Thereafter, in compliance with a Chissano-Renamo accord, Zimbabwe on December 28 completed the withdrawal of its troops to defensive positions along Mozambique's trade routes, ceding control of previously held territory to Mozambique government forces. In April 1993, Harare withdrew its remaining troops.

The Zimbabwean government initially declined, for the sake of its own domestic "reconciliation," to provide bases for black nationalist attacks on South Africa. However, the anti-apartheid African National Congress (ANC) continued to operate from Zimbabwean territory, its cross-border attacks yielding retaliatory incursions by South African troops into Zimbabwe.

In February 1997 Zimbabwe and South Africa signed a defense agreement; however, their ties were subsequently strained by what Harare asserted were unfair South African trade practices and Pretoria's crackdown on illegal Zimbabwean immigrants. In February 1998 Zimbabwe, South Africa, and Namibia signed an extradition treaty.

In mid-1998 President Mugabe dispatched troops to the Democratic Republic of the Congo (DRC) to shore up the presidency of Laurent Kabila, from whose administration Harare reportedly sought mining concessions. At the peak of the conflict, an estimated 12,000 Zimbabwean troops were in the DRC, President Mugabe also strongly endorsing the succession of Joseph Kabila to the DRC presidency after the death of Laurent Kabila in early 2001. The support from Zimbabwe was considered crucial to the lasting power of the DRC administration, although the economic drain on scarce Zimbabwean resources contributed to growing anti-Mugabe sentiment. The last contingent of Zimbabwean troops left the DRC in November 2002.

In December 2003, the Commonwealth Heads of Government Meeting in Abuja, Nigeria, suspended Zimbabwe, citing continued human rights violations. Zimbabwe responded by withdrawing from the organization.

In 2005 Zimbabwe was reelected to the UN Human Rights Commission, drawing sharp criticism from Western countries, among others, which cited Zimbabwe's appalling human rights record.

Zimbabwe increasingly turned to South Africa and China for financial aid as economic conditions worsened (most Western donors had frozen development aid and imposed an arms embargo after Mugabe enacted the controversial land redistribution program). South Africa loaned $470 million to bail Zimbabwe out of IMF and humanitarian crises in 2005, and China signed a $1.3 billion energy deal with the Mugabe government in 2006.

Cooperation with China slackened somewhat in 2007, as China halted aid to the country, citing the impact of hyperinflation on investment. In December tensions rose ahead of the EU-AU summit in Lisbon, Portugal, because Britain's new prime minister, Gordon Brown, refused to attend to protest the invitation of President Mugabe.

Relations with numerous countries were strained in 2008 following the disputed reelection of President Mugabe (see Current issues, below), which drew harsh rebukes from the UN Security Council, the AU, the United States, and the United Kingdom, among others. Meanwhile, Botswana, Kenya, Sierra Leone, and Zambia called for punitive action against Mugabe, but the AU ultimately pressed for power-sharing talks.

Following negotiations between ZANU-PF and the two MDC under the auspices of the SADC, components leading to the Global Political Agreement (GPA) were signed September 15, 2008. Press reports indicate that SADC pressure was instrumental in gaining MDC leader Morgan Tsvangirai's consent to form a government of national unity in February 2009. Botswana was among some neighboring governments who criticized the deal as rewarding Mugabe for suppressing the previous year's presidential runoff.

The United States and EU kept sanctions in place after the installation of the new government, citing continued violations of the rule of law. Prime Minister Tsvangirai traveled to Europe and North America in June, meeting with U.S. president Barack Obama and other leaders but failing to persuade them to restart non-humanitarian aid to the government. An EU delegation visiting Zimbabwe in September refused to consider renewing aid in the absence of full implementation of the GPA.

The Zimbabwean government defied a November 2008 order by an SADC tribunal to halt evictions of white landholders. In September 2009 the justice minister, Patrick Chinamasa of ZANU-PF, announced that Zimbabwe was pulling out of the regional organization, but Prime Minister Tsvangirai declared Chinamasa's letter null and void because the cabinet had not been consulted.

A summit of SADC leaders in Kinshasa, Democratic Republic of Congo, in September, declined to put the crisis facing Zimbabwe on its agenda. The meeting's communiqué called for the lifting of sanctions against Zimbabwe without demanding stricter adherence to the GPA, an outcome considered a diplomatic victory for Mugabe.

Current issues. A possible settlement appeared in the making in early 1999 concerning the incendiary question of land redistribution. According to the plan, the Zimbabwean government was to buy land from the dominant white farmers for use by black farmers, while the international community was to provide substantial aid for the development of infrastructure related to agriculture. However, the government's true intentions remained obscure as President Mugabe continued to threaten to expropriate the white farms, and donor countries demanded significant economic reform on the part of the administration before releasing the promised financial assistance. Consequently, Mugabe attempted to secure authority to seize white farms through proposed constitutional revision. When the national referendum in February 2000 rejected the measure, land expropriation by blacks (many from influential war veterans' groups) began. Collaterally, the administration, according to a rising chorus of domestic and international critics, launched a campaign of intimidation against opposition parties and dissidents, particularly the surging MDC, in advance of the assembly balloting scheduled for June. Attendant disorder left more than 30 people dead, as Mugabe promised additional resettlement in language described by one critic as "radical, racist rhetoric." In April 2000 parliament passed a constitutional amendment that incorporated the land clause that Mugabe had inserted into the draft constitution in January 2000. The clause allowed the regime to forcibly acquire land without paying compensation, which was made the responsibility of the British government. The Supreme Court's ruling in November 2000 that the land invasions were illegal was ignored.

Conditions continued to deteriorate following the June 2000 legislative balloting, the MDC claiming it had been fraudulently deprived of many seats. International observers were reluctant to characterize the balloting as fair, and observers subsequently warned that Zimbabwe could implode, especially when rioting broke out in October. Throughout the first half of 2001, the administration stepped up its attacks on journalists and judges who opposed the ruling party's land expropriations and electoral machinations, while white-owned businesses in the cities also became the target of "invasions." (Whites, less than 2 percent of the population, still controlled more than 50 percent of industry and most commercial agriculture.) The United Kingdom at midyear withdrew its financial support to protest the takeovers, and unrest increased in August following the "evacuation" of some white farmers.

The assembly in January 2002 approved the Public Order and Security Act banning public gatherings without police approval to undercut the MDC challenge to Mugabe in the March presidential poll. Following the Commonwealth observers' adverse report on the conduct of the election, the Commonwealth suspended Zimbabwe and imposed sanctions, including travel bans and aid restrictions, in protest of the perceived heavy-handedness of the administration. The United States, for its part, declared that Mugabe's governance was "illegitimate and irrational." Mugabe said his reelection was a "stunning blow to imperialism" and condemned the "blatant racism of the West." Zimbabwe's economy continued to contract in 2003, and by 2004 the country had stopped repaying foreign debt, resulting in the suspension of its membership from the IMF. Living standards continued to decline, and even the finance minister acknowledged that the country's economy was in a severe crisis.

In 2005 the governor of the central bank called on the government to allow some of the white farmers whose land had been seized to resume growing crops to bolster output. Reportedly, lack of expertise among black farmers who had received land, as well as drought conditions early in the year, the lack of government-subsidized inputs, and the disinterest of many of those who had acquired large commercial farms, resulted in what was described as an "economic catastrophe." Urgent requests by UNICEF to bring in food aid were rejected by government officials, who insisted the country had enough food. Ultimately, however, the government agreed to allow UN assistance, but only under strict conditions.

With no abatement of the crisis, the government allegedly used food to buy votes in the March 31, 2005, assembly elections (the vote-buying was cited by a Zimbabwe judge in October), increasing its ZANU-PF representation by 16 seats, mainly with support from poor rural areas. The MDC again alleged massive fraud, although AU observers endorsed the elections, albeit citing some concerns, and the South African Development Community (SADC) observer mission found the election to be credible. Most Western observers were not permitted into the country by the government.

The ZANU-PF won by a landslide in balloting for a newly established Senate in November 2005, though the very low turnout of 19.5 percent was seen as evidence of voter apathy. Also, the election was boycotted by the Tsvangirai faction of the MDC, the larger of the two factions into which the MDC had split in October 2005 (see Political Parties, below).

Further exacerbating the declining economic and social conditions, the government in May 2005 launched Operation Murambatsvina ("drive out rubbish") purportedly to rid urban areas of informal market traders and shantytowns. As a result, 700,000 people were displaced. The MDC charged that the program was meant to punish the urban dwellers who voted in March against the ZANU-PF. While the government said the operation was designed to "restore social order," critics claimed that by dispersing urban dwellers, the government reduced the possibility of an uprising and drove people back to rural areas in the aftermath of the economic collapse precipitated by the land redistribution program. The slum clearing continued into 2006 under another program called Operation Roundup, and the houses that were built were mostly allocated to ZANU-PF loyalists rather than to displaced persons.

In 2006 white farmers were invited to lease back their land from the government under a 99-year agreement, but the few white farmers still in Zimbabwe were reported to be largely uninterested in the offer. In August the MDC factions came together in the Save Zimbabwe

Campaign, agreeing to use nonviolent action against Mugabe's plan to postpone the presidential election until 2010 and arguing for simultaneous parliamentary and presidential elections in 2008.

Political tensions escalated beginning in early 2007 when police arrested dozens of MDC members at a series of rallies, including one in February where party leader Morgan Tsvangirai had planned to announce his intention to run for president. Tsvangirai himself was among those briefly detained. In March Tsvangirai and about 50 other MDC and civil society members were arrested and severely beaten or tortured, according to published reports. South Africa's President Mbeki continued to try to negotiate a political solution, though President Mugabe refused to negotiate on the MDC's main issue, a proposed new constitution.

The deteriorating economic situation reportedly contributed to an alleged coup attempt in June 2007. Six men, including active duty and retired army officers, were charged with treason for allegedly plotting to overthrow Mugabe's government and replace him with a government led by Housing Minister Emmerson Mnangagwa and the heads of the country's armed forces. A week after the alleged plot was exposed, the presidential guard commander who had been linked to it was killed in a car accident, leading to speculation that he had been murdered.

Adding to Mugabe's problems in mid-2007 was a warning from members of his administration that inflation was the most pressing threat to his presidency. Mugabe subsequently ordered all shops and businesses to cut their prices by half and deployed troops to monitor compliance. He also vowed to nationalize any businesses that failed to comply. By the end of July, some 8,500 shop owners and executives had been arrested. Additionally, the price-cut directive reportedly increased shortages, further fueling the black market.

In September 2007 the House of Assembly and the Senate passed constitutional amendments proposed by President Mugabe that would provide for concurrent presidential and parliamentary elections, as well as expand the size of both legislative chambers. The amendments had the backing of the MDC after the ZANU-PF agreed, in talks mediated by South Africa, to numerous changes in advance of the anticipated March election. These included amendments allowing parliament to choose a successor if a president resigned or died before the end of term, as well as amendments restoring freedom of assembly and association, the creation of a human rights commission, and reform of the electoral laws to include nominations to the Electoral Commission by the parliament rather than the president.

Passage of the 2007 Indigenization and Economic Empowerment Bill did not go smoothly because MDC lawmakers walked out in protest when the ZANU-PF pushed the bill through in November. The legislation, formally approved by Mugabe just weeks before the March 2008 elections, stipulates that foreign-owned companies and those owned by whites and Asians would be required to sell 51 percent of their shares to indigenous black Zimbabweans. Firms that did not comply would have their operating licenses rescinded.

As attention turned to the 2008 presidential elections, factionalism increased in the leading parties. The Mujuru faction of ZANU-PF supported fellow member Simba MAKONI over Mugabe, although they had initially sought the leadership of ZANU-PF member Dumiso DABENGWA. Makoni, who had earned international support by speaking out against Mugabe's economic policies, was expelled from ZANU-PF by Mugabe and subsequently ran as an independent. Meanwhile, the Tsvangirai faction of the MDC (the MDC-T) split into two more factions (see Political Parties and Groups, below.) The discord within MDC-T weakened Tsvangirai's ability to challenge Mugabe in the elections. In addition, Arthur MUTAMBARA, head of the MDC-M faction, chose to back Makoni. Another independent, Langton TOWUNGANA, emerged from a small village in the Victoria Falls regions, albeit with little support and presenting no major challenge. Violence against the opposition was reported just prior to the elections, when police allegedly beat Tsvangirai during a demonstration in Harare.

In the parliamentary elections in March, simultaneous with presidential elections for the first time, 14 parties fielded 773 candidates for 210 assembly seats. Despite party factionalism, the MDC-T secured the largest number of seats by a narrow margin, bolstering its position by one additional seat in by-elections on June 27 to fill three vacancies. In the presidential balloting, Tsvangirai won 47.9 percent of the vote to Mugabe's 43.2 percent, marking the first time since 1980 that an opposition party had secured a larger percentage of the vote than ZANU-PF. Official results were not announced until May 2, and in the meantime violence escalated between supporters of the ZANU-PF and the MDC, most observers blaming "militias" affiliated with ZANU-PF. Since neither candidate won at least 50 percent of the vote, a runoff was scheduled for June 27. Meanwhile, the MDC disputed the official results, claiming that they had won more than 50 percent of the vote according to their own tally. The elections commission stood firm with its scheduling of a runoff, prompting renewed violence against the MDC. Tsvangirai, who claimed that 86 MDC supporters were killed and thousands were displaced, took refuge in the Dutch embassy in Harare on June 23 and withdrew from the presidential runoff. The UN Security Council condemned the "campaign of violence against the political opposition" but did not go along with Britain's push to remove international recognition of the Mugabe government. (Queen Elizabeth, for her part, stripped Mugabe of an honorary knighthood he had been awarded in 1994.) Though Tsvangirai's name remained on the ballot, Mugabe was declared the winner on June 29, with 85.5 percent of the vote, compared to 9.3 percent for Tsvangirai in turnout that was described as "sparse" by the *International Herald Tribune*.

In the wake of international condemnation of his party's harassment of his opponent, Mugabe consented to a power-sharing agreement in September. However, he insisted on retaining exclusive control of the police, military, and security forces. After several months of wrangling, during which time a cholera epidemic killed thousands and hyperinflation brought the economy to a standstill, a compromise over ministerial appointments allowed the national unity government to be formed.

The new MDC ministers were sworn in on February 13, 2009 in Harare, but the appointed deputy agriculture minister, Roy BENNETT, a senior MDC official, was arrested the same day and charged with treason. On March 6, Tsvangirai was severely injured and his wife was killed in a car crash south of Harare. Opposition figures suspected an assassination attempt, and the prime minister was flown to Botswana for treatment. Tsvangirai later dismissed accusations of foul play. Bennett was released March 12 but blocked from taking office.

In the months that followed, critics charged that Mugabe and his party violated numerous commitments under the Global Political Agreement. Among the violations were harassment and arbitrary arrests of activists (including several opposition MPs); continuing to evict white commercial farmers despite an order from a SADC regional tribunal to cease farm invasions; and appointing several key officials, including Reserve Bank governor Gideon GONO, without consulting the other members of the coalition. Gono, a close Mugabe ally, was widely disparaged for exacerbating the inflation crisis by printing money. Gono and finance minister Tendai Biti (MDC-T) sparred publicly over a $510 million IMF loan in September. The rare loan to Zimbabwe's pariah government came as part of an IMF package of "special drawing rights" intended to aid states impacted by the global recession. Biti arranged for the funds to bypass the Reserve Bank of Zimbabwe, foiling Gono's endeavor to dip into the funds to repay debts from Mugabe's 2008 campaign.

A central provision of the Global Political Agreement is the drafting of a new constitution for Zimbabwe within 18 months of the inclusive government's tenure. ZANU-PF officials took the position that the "Kariba draft" was the only acceptable basis for constitutional negotiations. This document was negotiated secretly in Kariba by ZANU-PF, MDC-T and MDC-M leaders in 2007, in preparation for the 2008 elections. According to legal scholars, the Kariba draft is strongly weighted toward executive power and closely resembles the proposed constitution rejected by a national referendum in 2000. MDC leaders dismiss the draft as out of keeping with Zimbabwe's current situation, but ZANU-PF planned to campaign for the draft's adoption. Supporters of the ruling party disrupted a national constitutional conference, held in July in Harare, by dancing on tables and throwing water bottles. Subsequently, the party allegedly deployed veterans' groups known for their intimidation of political opponents.

Frustrated with what was perceived as bad faith on the part of its coalition partner, the mainstream MDC held a series of conferences in September 2009 to consider whether to withdraw from the national unity government. When Roy Bennett was imprisoned again in October, Tsvangirai announced that the MDC-T would boycott cabinet meetings and refuse to work with ZANU-PF, but stopped short of resigning from the government.

POLITICAL PARTIES

Prior to the "internal settlement" agreement of March 1978, Rhodesian parties could be broadly grouped into (1) the all-white Rhodesian Front (RF), which maintained overwhelming predominance in the elections of 1965, 1970, 1974, and 1977; (2) a number of small white opposition groups on the right and left of the ruling front; and (3) a variety of black opposition parties ranging from relatively moderate formations under such leaders as Bishop Abel Muzorewa, Reverend Ndabaningi Sithole, and Chief Jeremiah Chirau, to the more radical and insurgent groups led by Robert Mugabe and Joshua Nkomo. The principal African leaders agreed during a summit conference at Lusaka, Zambia, in December 1974 to work together under Bishop Muzorewa of the African National Council (ANC) to achieve majority rule in Rhodesia, but disagreements precluded the creation of a unified black movement. The moderate leaders thereupon joined the RF's Ian Smith in establishing a transitional government to prepare for a one-person, one-vote election originally scheduled for December 1978 but subsequently postponed to April 1979.

Mugabe and Nkomo entered into a somewhat tenuous Patriotic Front (PF) committed to the military overthrow of the biracial regime, forming a political union in 1976. However, they later failed to integrate their respective military units and were ultimately unable to effectively cooperate. Although Nkomo expressed a desire to continue the alliance, Mugabe's Zimbabwe African National Union–Patriotic Front (ZANU-PF) and Nkomo's Patriotic Front–Zimbabwe African People's Union (PF-ZAPU) contested the common roll election of February 27–29, 1980, as separate entities, with ZANU-PF winning 57 of 80 assembly seats and PF-ZAPU winning 20.

Nkomo's PF revived its earlier ZAPU designation following the government rupture of February 1982, while ZANU-PF moved toward the establishment of a one-party state that was consummated, on a de facto basis, with the signature of a merger agreement by Mugabe and Nkomo on December 22, 1987. However, on August 2, 1990, 21 of 26 ZANU-PF Politburo members voted against Mugabe's appeal for a constitutional amendment to institutionalize the one-party system.

At a convention of the Zimbabwe Congress of Trade Unions (ZCTU) in Harare in late February 1999, the ZCTU announced that it had coalesced with the anti-regime civic organization, the National Constitutional Assembly (NCA), as well as 30 other civic groups and a number of human rights, trade, and student organizations to form a political movement dedicated to pressuring the Mugabe government to enact economic, electoral, and constitutional reforms. Morgan Tsvangirai and Gibson Sibanda, leaders of both the ZCTU and the new coalition, had emerged in 1998 as point men for the anti-Mugabe forces. The NCA subsequently served as a major force in the creation of the nation's first effective opposition party, the Movement for Democratic Change (below).

By 2000 the MDC had emerged as the chief opposition party and the only one of consequence. Only one of the numerous smaller parties, ZANU-Ndonga, had been able to elect any of their members to the parliament. In August 2006, opposition leaders, including those from the two MDC factions (below), announced they would form an alliance in an effort to unseat the ZANU-PF. However, opposition unity was badly fragmented by the leading MDC bloc's decision to back the Constitutional Amendment Bill (No. 18) in 2007, which was viewed as a capitulation by more purist opposition groups.

Between 2006 and 2008 several new parties emerged, however, none posed serious opposition to the ZANU-PF or the MDC. Factions within the ZANU-PF and the MDC contributed to turmoil in advance of the 2008 elections, and both parties were divided over candidate selection. ZAPU was revived as an independent party in 2009 (see below).

Legislative Parties:

Zimbabwe African National Union–Patriotic Front (ZANU-PF). ZANU was formed in 1963 as a result of a split in the Zimbabwe African People's Union (ZAPU), an African nationalist group formed in 1961 under the leadership of Joshua Nkomo. Nkomo had in 1957 revived the dormant ANC, which was banned in 1959. He then was elected from exile as the president of a new National Democratic Party, which was declared illegal in 1961, leading to the formation and quick banning of ZAPU. ZANU, led by Ndabaningi Sithole and Robert Mugabe, was also declared illegal in 1964, and both ZANU and ZAPU initiated guerrilla activity against the Rhodesian government announced in November 1965.

In December 1974 ZANU President Sithole agreed to participate (along with ZAPU) in the enlargement of the African National Council to serve as the primary organization for negotiating with the Smith government (see Political background, above, for further information). However, Mugabe opposed such discussions and went into exile in Mozambique, from where he contested Sithole's dominance in ZANU. By late 1976 Mugabe was widely recognized as ZANU's leader, and he concluded a tactical (Patriotic Front—PF) agreement with Joshua Nkomo of ZAPU, although a minority of the ZANU membership apparently remained loyal to Sithole. The PF alliance broke down prior to the 1980 assembly election, Nkomo's group campaigning as PF-ZAPU and Mugabe's as ZANU-PF. Both parties participated in the government formed at independence, although ZANU-PF predominated with 16 of 22 ministerial appointments.

At ZANU-PF's third ordinary congress held December 19–21, 1989, the Politburo was enlarged from 15 to 26 members, the Central Committee was expanded from 90 to 150 members, a national chair was created, and ZAPU was formally incorporated into the party (despite rejection of its demands for a sole vice presidency filled by Nkomo and an expunging of the group's Marxist-Leninist tenets). Furthermore, in an apparent expression of dissatisfaction with reform-minded East European regimes, the party's socialist orientation was redefined to emphasize the Zimbabwean historical, cultural, and social experience. Ultimately, on June 22, 1991, the party agreed to delete all references to Marxism, Leninism, and scientific socialism from its constitution.

At a party congress in December 1995, Mugabe loyalists blocked efforts to open a party-wide dialogue on the question of presidential succession. At the same time, analysts predicted that party power would soon devolve to a younger generation of financially oriented technocrats and grassroots activists.

The revelation in April 1997 that senior party officials close to Mugabe had allegedly plundered the pension fund of war veterans created a rift in the party between its military and political wings. Meanwhile, analysts, and Mugabe himself, were reportedly critical of the party's senior leadership for having become preoccupied with positioning themselves for possible presidential succession. Defying both international donors and ZANU-PF moderates, the Central Committee in December urged the president to forge ahead with plans to seize white-owned properties.

Despite the schisms within ZANU-PF, Mugabe was reelected without opposition as party president in 1999. Subsequently, in controversial balloting, ZANU-PF retained a narrow majority in the assembly in June 2000, and Mugabe was reelected to another term as president in March 2002.

With the rise of factionalism within ZANU-PF, party solidarity began to disintegrate in 2004. Five party officials were arrested on espionage charges (three of the officials were later convicted of spying for South Africa), and a purge of the party targeted members who had been involved in the Tsholotsho meeting on November 18, 2004, and who opposed Mugabe's choice of Joyce Mujuru as vice president of the republic. Mujuru was appointed in December 2004 over house speaker Emmerson Mnangagwa, regarded by many as the president's likely successor until the political fallout from the failed palace coup attempt to make Mnangagwa the replacement for the late Simon Muzenda.

On April 16, 2005, Mnangagwa was moved from the powerful post of speaker of parliament to a low-profile ministry post when the president reshuffled the cabinet following the ZANU-PF's substantial victory in the March assembly election. The president also dismissed Information Minister Jonathan Moyo from the party after Moyo chose to run as an independent in the assembly balloting. At mid-year, Mugabe said he would retire upon his term's expiration in 2008 but said he intended to remain active in the party until the 2009 national congress.

In a turnabout in December 2006, Mugabe declared at the ZANU-PF congress that only "God" could remove him from office, though a constitutional amendment would be required for an extension of his term. The Mujuru and the Mnangagwa factions refused to support the motion, and no vote was taken on the resolution. Still, Mugabe maintained that he would seek to have his term extended so that he could run for office in 2010 in presidential balloting proposed to coincide with parliamentary elections. The Mujuru and Mnangagwa factions united for a brief time to oppose Mugabe's attempt to remain in power until 2010.

During a ZANU-PF Central Committee meeting on March 30, 2007, the committee decided, without a vote, that Mugabe (who had chaired the meeting) would be the party's only presidential candidate and backed a proposal for parliamentary elections, which were not due until 2010, to be held concurrently with the presidential election in 2008. The Mnangagwa faction supported Mugabe with the incentive of potential parliamentary seats that could be won in the simultaneous 2008 elections. However, the Mujuru faction (headed by Mujuru's husband Solomon MUJURU, a retired army leader) backed former ZANU-PF member, Simba Makoni, who ran as an independent presidential candidate after being expelled from the party by Mugabe.

The party's internal battle over succession intensified in 2009, as ZANU-PF lost exclusive control of Zimbabwe's government. In May, the party formed a committee, led by national chair John Nkomo, to oversee the succession issue ahead of the next party congress in December. Independent press reported that Nkomo was likely to take over the vice presidential position vacated by Joseph Msika's death in August. Nkomo, loyal to the Mnangagwa faction, reportedly had the support of seven of the nation's ten provinces. In August, finance minister Tendai Biti, an MDC-T member, publicly stated that the succession crisis in President Mugabe's party was harmful to the nation's development, and urged its swift resolution.

Leaders: Robert Gabriel MUGABE (President of the Republic and President of the Party), Joyce MUJURU (Vice President of the Republic and of the Party), Emmerson MNANGAGWA (Minister of Defense), Didymus MUTASA, John NKOMO (National Chair), Solomon MUJURU (former army commander).

Movement for Democratic Change (MDC). Launched in September 1999, the MDC was an outgrowth of the ZCTU/NCA (see above), its core components including workers, students, middle-class intellectuals, civil rights activists, and white corporate executives opposed to the perceived corruption of the ZANU-PF government as well as its management of the economy. Many of the MDC adherents were former members of the Forum Party of Zimbabwe, which had been established in 1993 under the leadership of Enoch DUMBUTSHENA (a retired chief justice) and David Coltart (see 1999 *Handbook* for details on the Forum Party).

In a rapid rise, the MDC secured 57 out of 120 elected seats in the 2000 assembly balloting. MDC leaders claimed fraud on the part of the government in some 37 of the 62 seats secured by the ZANU-PF. The MDC was the first opposition party to have broad inter-ethnic appeal and challenge the ruling party for every elected seat. Party leader Morgan Tsvangirai narrowly lost to President Mugabe in the controversial 2002 presidential election. On February 25, 2002, days before the presidential election in March, Tsvangirai was charged with treason for allegedly plotting to assassinate President Mugabe. In October 2004 he was acquitted and in February 2005 the government withdrew its appeal against his acquittal. In November 2004 he was charged with treason, this time relating to his call in 2003 for street protests to remove Mugabe. The government withdrew this charge in August 2005 before the plea without giving reasons.

Prior to the November 2005 senate election, the MDC was deeply divided over whether to participate in the election. Party leader Arthur Mutambara led the faction (MDC-M) that contested the election. Tsvangirai's faction opposed participation in the balloting, while a faction led by party Secretary General Welshman Ncube planned to field candidates. Subsequently, 26 members who had been expelled by Tsvangirai stood for election, with only 7 winning Senate seats. In October 2005 the MDC split, leaving the lawful leadership of the party in question. Tsvangirai maintained he was still in charge of the party despite dissidents claiming he had been expelled.

At the party congress of the Tsvangirai-MDC faction in March 2006, Tsvangirai was reelected president and Isaac Matongo was reelected chair. That month, government detained eight men, including two Tsvangirai-MDC faction members, for alleged links to the UK-based **Zimbabwe Freedom Movement,** which was accused of plotting to overthrow Mugabe. The Tsvangirai faction's spokesperson later asserted that the arrest was "a state plot to destabilize [the Tsvangirai-MDC faction] ahead of our congress."

Ncube's faction, styled the Pro Democracy MDC, appointed former MDC vice president Gibson Sibanda as acting president. The Ncube group held a congress in February 2006 and elected former student activist Arthur Mutambara as party president and Sibanda as vice president, with Ncube retaining the post of secretary general. The following month, however, Mutambara said it was wrong for MDC members to have contested the senate elections and he urged those who were elected to resign. Further, he proposed reconciling with Tsvangirai's faction, and in July the leaders of both factions vowed to work together to unseat the ZANU-PF. Negotiations for a working relationship began in mid-2006 and unity became an objective in September, though it remained fraught with obstacles.

After the torture and beatings of MDC members, including Tsvangirai, following the MDC's participation in a prayer meeting organized by the Save Zimbabwe Campaign (an umbrella organization of civic organizations, churches, and parties) in Harare on March 11, 2007, the factions agreed in April to contest the 2008 elections as a coalition. It was agreed that Tsvangirai would be the coalition's president and Mutambara its vice president and that the factions would respect each other's autonomy and equality. Nevertheless, at a May 19 meeting, Tsvangirai tried to install Thokozani Khupe, his deputy, as second vice president and demanded that a panel of 30 from each faction select parliamentary candidates. In July, the Mutambara faction announced it would field its own candidates in 2008 and withdrew from the Save Zimbabwe Campaign, claiming the campaign supported Tsvangirai's agenda. The two factions' failure to unite strengthened ZANU-PF's electoral prospects.

Later in 2007 the party continued to face internal conflicts, particularly when Tsvangirai dismissed the leader of the women's league, Lucia MATIBENGA, from her post. Matibenga supporters claimed that Tsvangirai's action was an infringement on the democratic rights of women. Elias MUDZURI, the former mayor of Harare, also disagreed publicly with Tsvangirai's removal of Matibenga and subsequently carried his own supporters within MDC-T. Leading up to the 2008 elections, tensions heightened within the MDC when Tsvangirai supporters attacked the Matibenga faction during a march on MDC headquarters in November. However, the high court deferred a decision on the Matibenga case to the MDC party congress, which ruled that Matibenga's dismissal was constitutional. Meanwhile, Simba Makoni, the former ZANU-PF member who announced his independent candidacy in the presidential election, received the backing of Mutambara, head of the MDC-M faction.

Before the presidential election in March and the runoff in June 2008, violence against the MDC increased, resulting in Tsvangirai's seeking shelter in the Dutch embassy in Harare. Ultimately, the MDC won the most seats in the assembly, despite weakening party alliances and alleged intimidation by ZANU-PF.

Mugabe, Tsvangirai, and Mutambara signed the Global Political Agreement (GPA) on September 15, 2008, and after months of squabbling over the details of the power-sharing arrangement, the unity government was established in February 2009. Tsvangirai and the MDC-T, junior members of an unequal partnership, struggled to rebuild the nation's devastated economy (see Current issues, above). Many of the party's leaders, including elected officials and ministerial appointees such as Roy Bennett, faced trial on what were widely deemed to be politically motivated charges. As the party celebrated its tenth anniversary in September, six months into the term of the unity government, many rank and file MDC-T members, frustrated at what they perceived as ZANU-PF's bad faith and continued use of repressive measures, advocated for the party to withdraw from the coalition. For his part, Mutambara opined that the government should remain in office for five years rather than its allotted two.

Leaders: Morgan TSVANGIRAI (President of the MDC-T faction and Prime Minister of Zimbabwe), Thokozani KHUPE (Vice President), Tendai BITI (Secretary General of the party and Minister of Finance), Arthur MUTAMBARA (President of the MDC-M faction and Deputy Prime Minister), Gibson SIBANDA (Vice President), David COLTART, Welshman NCUBE (Secretary General).

Other Parties that Participated in Recent Elections:

Zimbabwe African National Union–Ndonga (ZANU-Ndonga). Led by Ndabaningi Sithole from its formation ahead of the 1980 election until his death in December 2000, the ZANU-Ndonga's main electoral base has been the small ethnic group the Ndau, who are concentrated in Chipinge in Manicaland Province. Sithole was a vocal supporter of Mozambique's Renamo grouping, opposing the ZANU-PF government's policy of supporting the Mozambican government. He announced from exile in the United States that, despite government threats to arrest and prosecute him on treason charges, he would return to Zimbabwe during an October 1991 meeting of the Commonwealth leaders in Harare; in actuality his return was postponed until early 1992.

At least 18 of ZANU-Ndonga's members were reportedly arrested in mid-1994 after engaging in a clash with ZANU-PF supporters near the capital. Its sole parliamentary representative for Chipinge, who had been elected in 1985 and re-elected in 1990, was killed in an automobile accident in October 1994, but Sithole recaptured the seat in a by-election held December 19–20. In the 1995 election, the Chipinge constituency was divided into two electoral districts. Sithole was elected to represent Chipinge South and Wilson Khumbula, to represent Chipinge North. ZANU-Ndonga was the only opposition party to be represented in the 1995 parliament, the other opposition seat held by independent Margaret Dongo.

In October 1995 Sithole was charged with participation in a plot to assassinate President Mugabe. Shortly thereafter William NAMAKONYA, a Sithole bodyguard who allegedly confessed to being a member of the Mozambique-based Chimwenje rebel group, was found guilty of possessing illegal arms, while on December 1 Simon MHLANGA, a Sithole supporter, was found guilty of having been illegally engaged in guerrilla training.

Sithole, who had been released on bail, announced his candidacy in the 1996 presidential election but later withdrew from the race in March 1996, charging that security forces were harassing his supporters. In late 1997 he was found guilty of treason and sentenced to two years in prison. In January 1998 Sithole, who remained free while preparing an appeal, called for drafting a new constitution, asserting that amending the current document, as suggested by other political leaders, would fail to bring down the Mugabe administration. Sithole died in December 2000, his appeal of his 1997 sentence never having been heard.

In the June 2000 election, Wilson Khumbula won the only seat secured by ZANU-Ndonga. In March 2005 Khumbula lost the seat and the party failed for the first time since 1985 to have any representative in the House of Assembly. The party sought representation in the November 2005 senate election but secured only 1.81 percent of the votes.

A leading government news organ, *The Herald*, reported on September 6, 2007, that ZANU-Ndonga President Wilson Khumbula had taken two of his senior officials, Gondai Paul Vutuza and Joseph Mushonga, to court in order to prevent them from convening an extraordinary meeting. Vutuza said that Khumbula's presidency was not legitimate because the party had refused to allow him to run in the 2002 presidential election under its name and symbol; he had been obliged to run as an independent. Vutuza also said that the party had not held a congress since 1997 and that every office holder was appointed. Despite continued fighting between Khumbula's faction and a faction loyal to Ndabaningi Sithole's widow, Vesta Sithole, Khumbula has retained control of ZANU-Ndonga.

Khumbula supported Simba Makoni in the 2008 presidential election.

Leaders: Wilson KHUMBULA (President), Reketayi SEMWAYO (National Chair), Gondai Paul VUTUZA, Joseph MUSHONGA.

Zimbabwe African People's Union–Federal Party (ZAPU-FP). In 2002 this Matabeleland-based breakaway party was led by Agrippa Madhlela and Paul SIWELA, the former secretary general of the revived ZAPU. The party campaigns for federalism and full regional autonomy for Matabeleland. Siwela ran without ZAPU's endorsement in the 2002 presidential race because the party president supported the candidacy of Morgan Tsvangirai of the MDC. ZAPU-FP could not raise the funds to participate in the March 2005 election but did contest the senate election that year, securing only 0.03 percent of the vote.

In September 2007 the MDC and the ZAPU-FP, under Paul Siwela, agreed to form an alliance ahead of the 2008 elections, resulting in Siwela's expulsion from ZAPU-FP, whose members said that Siwela participated in the negotiations without their consent. Siwela subsequently formed a new party, the Federal Democratic Union (see below).

ZAPU-FP remained on the ballot in March 2008 but failed to win any parliamentary seats. Party leader Sikhumbuzo Dube challenged the use of the ZAPU name by the faction of ZANU-PF that broke from the 1987 Unity Accord to revive ZAPU as a national party (see ZAPU).

Leader: Sikhumbuzo DUBE.

Federal Democratic Union (FDU). Paul Siwela formed the FDU on February 18, 2008, after having been dismissed by the ZAPU-FP. The party, running on the issue of decentralization and the creation of a Matabeleland state, failed to win any seats in the 2008 legislative elections.

Leader: Paul SIWELA.

United People's Party (UPP). The formation of the UPP was announced in January 2006 by Daniel Shumba, a former chair of Masvingo Province and a prominent businessman, but it was not formally launched until June 2007. The UPP vowed to lead the country "from hopelessness to hope, from poverty to prosperity, from terror to well-being, from dictatorship to democracy." Shumba's application to participate in the 2008 presidential elections was denied, along with the nomination papers of Zimbabwe People's Party's (ZPP) Justin Chiota, on the grounds that he filed it too late. The UPP failed to win any seats in the 2008 parliamentary election. Shumba filed a suit challenging his party's exclusion from the negotiations that led to the 2008 Global Political Agreement, and advocated for the inclusion of minority parties and civil society representatives in the national unity government.

Leader: Daniel SHUMBA.

Zimbabwe Youth in Alliance (ZIYA). Led by Daniel MBANJE and Bernard NYIKADZINO, ZIYA was formed on September 15, 2003. Its leader, Chawaona Kanoti, a U.S. law school graduate, reportedly once worked in the president's office as an intelligence operator. The party failed to win any seats in the 2005 and 2008 parliamentary elections.

Leader: Chawaona KANOTI.

Other parties that participated in recent elections include the **Zimbabwe Progressive People's Democratic Party** (ZPPDP), formed in 2007 by Tafirenyika MUDUANHU; the **Zimbabwe Development Party** (ZDP), led by former ZANU-PF member Kisinoti MUWAZHE and Facemore MUSEZA; **Voice of the People/Vox Populi** (VP), formed in 2006 by Moreprecision MUZADZI with the support of Zimbabweans living in regions such as Botswana and South Africa; **ZURD,** led by Madechiwe COLLIAS; the **Patriotic Union of Matabeleland** (PUMA), established in 2006 by Leonard NKOLA, a former member of ZANU-PF, to unify Matabeleland and seek autonomy for the region; and the **Christian Democratic Party** (CDP), formed by William GWATA in 2008.

Other Parties:

Zimbabwe African People's Union (ZAPU). The new incarnation of ZAPU constitutes a reconfiguration of Zimbabwe's oldest political party. Originally led by Joshua Nkomo, ZAPU was formed in 1961 (predating ZANU-PF by two years) and played a leading role in the popular struggle against colonial rule in Rhodesia. The party and its Zimbabwe People's Revolutionary Army (ZIPRA) drew their strength primarily from the Ndebele people of Matabeleland and the Midlands. Conflict between ZAPU and ZANU intensified after independence was achieved, culminating in massacres perpetrated by ZANU-PF forces that claimed the lives of thousands of Ndebele civilians in 1987. In part to put a stop to these clashes, ZAPU agreed to the unity accord of December 22, 1987, whereby its party infrastructure was absorbed into that of ZANU-PF.

On December 13-14, 2008 in Bulawayo, a national conference of ZAPU members declared that the party was pulling out of the unity accord, asserting that ZANU-PF had violated the spirit of the agreement and reneged on its commitments. This meeting elected former ZANU-PF politburo member Dumiso Dabengwa the party's interim chairman. A ZAPU party congress in Bulawayo on May 16, 2009, attended by more than 1,000 delegates, ratified the withdrawal. The party's ranks swelled as thousands defected from ZANU-PF in Matabeleland and other parts of the country. In September, President Mugabe dismissed the new formation as an illegitimate endeavor by "rogue" elements within the ruling party; in response, Dabengwa claimed that ZAPU was and remained the nation's authentic liberation movement, predating the president's entrance into the political arena.

Leader: Dumiso DABENGWA (Interim Chairman).

Democratic Party (DP). Launched by Zimbabwe Unity Movement (ZUM) expellees (including Emmanuel MAGOCHE) in 1991, the DP held its inaugural congress in September 1992. In early 1996 the DP was identified as an organizer of the now-disbanded reformist MPC grouping. DP President Wurayayi Zembe had been a leading member of the NCA committee, which included parties aligned to the NCA that embraced the cause for a new democratic constitution. At the annual general meeting of the NCA held in Harare, Zembe was nominated to the NCA chair but withdrew from the race. Lovemore MADHUKU was reelected after the NCA's constitution had been amended to allow for a third term.

In July 2006, at the first public meeting between the two rival leaders of the MDC, Zembe was present along with two other opposition party leaders in what was taken to be a sign of a tentative broad alliance against ZANU-PF. On June 23, 2007, the DP's national executive committee met and criticized the SADC initiative to resolve the conflict in Zimbabwe because, among other concerns, President Mbeki's mediation was only between the MDC and ZANU-PF and excluded other parties.

The DP has claimed resource constraints have prevented the party from having held any congresses. The party has boycotted all elections since 1995 on the grounds that a new democratic constitution is necessary before free and fair elections can be held. The DP blasted the formation of a constitutional committee in parliament in April 2009, declaring the process illegitimate and proposing an inclusive constitutional conference facilitated by the UN, African Union and SADC. On April 30, 2009, as reported in the *Harare Tribune*, Zembe was arrested outside the office of the national government in Harare and forced to stand under a water tap for 15 minutes before being released.

Leader: Wurayayi ZEMBE.

Zimbabwe People's Party (ZPP). The ZPP was formed in August 2007, claiming to stand for "genuine democracy" and calling on Zimbabweans to fight poverty. There was some speculation that the ZPP was sponsored by Zimbabwe's Central Intelligence Organization to split the opposition vote in the 2008 elections, but the interim party president, Justin Chiota, denied the rumors. In 2000 Chiota was an unsuccessful candidate for the **Zimbabwe Progressive Party** in Harare North, which was won by the MDC.

In August 2008 Chiota, who was excluded from participation in elections for reportedly submitting his nomination papers past the deadline, voiced strong opposition to the March elections. Chiota went to the Supreme Court to restrain the power-sharing talks between the MDC and ZANU-PF after he was excluded from participating in them.

Leader: Justin CHIOTA (President).

United People's Movement (UPM). On July 26, 2005, Jonathan Moyo, a former ZANU-PF information minister and independent member of parliament since March 2005, announced the establishment of the UPM, characterizing the party as a "third way" between ZANU-PF autocracy and MDC inertia. Another former ZANU-PF member of parliament, Pearson MBALEKWA, resigned from ZANU-PF in July 2005 in protest against Operation Murambatsvina and joined the UPM. In November 2005 Moyo tried to claim that Emmerson Mnangagwa was the UPM's leader, but Mnangagwa denied it. The UPM did not field candidates in the November senate elections, Moyo claiming that "parliamentary elections, under the prevailing conditions, cannot lead to a change of government."

By 2006 Mbalekwa was the UPM's only other known member. Nevertheless, in April Moyo claimed that the UPM was "emerging as the next most powerful opposition in the country," drawing prominent members from the MDC, business, and ZANU-PF. In mid-2007 Mbalekwa left the UPM to join the MDC.

Moyo participated in the 2008 legislative elections as an independent candidate subsequent to an electoral agreement with the MDC's Morgan Tsvangirai, in which Tsvangirai's faction pledged not to field any candidates against Moyo. Subsequently, Moyo won an assembly seat with 0.48 percent of the vote. In 2009, Moyo applied to rejoin ZANU-PF, leaving unclear the fate of the party he founded.

Leader: Jonathan MOYO.

Multi-People's Democratic Party (MPDP). Formed on May 20, 2007, in South Africa, the MPDP was reported to have received threats from Zimbabwean intelligence operatives in South Africa. Party leader Emmanuel Moyana Muzondi condemned the MDC for voting for constitutional amendments in 2007 and promised his party would work closely with civic organizations that sought to introduce a more democratic constitution that would create a truth and reconciliation commission.

Leader: Emmanuel Moyana MUZONDI.

Zimbabwe Integrated Party (ZIP). Originally launched as the Zimbabwe Integrated Program, a nongovernmental organization devoted to promoting development projects, the ZIP was founded in 1996 by Heneri DZINOTYIWEI, a mathematics professor and businessman. It secured 0.02 percent of the legislative vote in 2000. In June 2006 Dzinotyiwei announced that he had joined Morgan Tsvangirai's faction in the MDC and said the ZIP was operating as a think tank. Dzinotyiwei became minister for science and technology in 2009.

Zimbabwe People's Democratic Party (ZPDP). The ZPDP claims to have been in existence since 1991. In the 2005 assembly elections, it contested only one seat, which it lost. Its leader, Isabel Madangure, did not seek an assembly seat, and the party did not contest the senate elections later in the year.

Leader: Isabel MADANGURE.

Other parties include the **Zimbabwe Integrated Party** (ZIP), formed in 2008 by Fanuel ZIMIDZI (a separate entity from Heneri Dzinotyiwei's ZIP, which joined the MDC on June 28, 2006), the **United Democratic People's Constitution** (UDPC), formed in February 2008 by Tasunungurwa MHURUVENGWE, and the **Zimbabwe National Congress** (ZNC), formed in 2009 by Ibbo MANDAZA and retired officer Kudzai MBUDZI. For more information on the **National Alliance for Good Governance**—NAGG or the **National Democratic Union**—NDU, see the 2009 *Handbook*.

LEGISLATURE

Zimbabwe has had six legislatures since 1980. The first two were bicameral (for details see the 1989 edition of the *Handbook*). In February 1990 the upper house (Senate) was abolished, the legislature thereupon becoming a unicameral body, the House of Assembly. A bicameral legislature was reinstituted in 2005, following a constitutional amendment approved by the house on August 30 to establish a Senate. The Constitutional Amendment Bill (No. 18), which was passed unanimously by the House on September 18, 2007, and the Senate on September 26, provides for changes in the number of house and senate members, and makes all house members directly elected by voters (see Constitution and government, above). In 2007 the House of Assembly and the Senate were enlarged, all members serving five-year terms.

Senate. The Senate comprises 93 members. All serve five-year terms. In 2008, 60 of the 93 members were directly elected, while 5 were appointed by the president. The remaining members comprise 10 provincial government representatives and 18 traditional chiefs.

In the most recent balloting on March 29, 2008, the seat distribution was as follows: The Zimbabwe African National Union–Patriotic Front 30; the Movement for Democratic Change–Tsvangirai, 24; and the Movement for Democratic Change–Mutambara, 6.

President: Edna MADZONGWE.

House of Assembly. There are currently 210 members in the House, all directly elected.

Following the most recent balloting on March 29, 2008, and by-elections on June 27 for three vacancies, the seat distribution was as follows: the Movement for Democratic Change–Tsvangirai, 100; the Zimbabwe African National Union–Patriotic Front, 99; Movement for Democratic Change–Mutambara, 10; and independent, 1.

Speaker: Lovemore MOYO.

CABINET

[as of September 1, 2009]

President	Robert Gabriel Mugabe (ZANU-PF)
Vice President	Joyce Mujuru (ZANU-PF) [f]
Prime Minister	Morgan Tsvangirai (MDC-T)
Deputy Prime Minister	Thokozani Khupe (MDC-T) [f]
Deputy Prime Minister	Arthur Mutambara (MDC-M)
Ministers	
Agriculture	Joseph Made (ZANU-PF)
Constitutional and Parliamentary Affairs	Eric Matinenga (MDC-T)
Defense	Emmerson Mnangagwa (ZANU-PF)
Economic Development	Elton Mangoma (MDC-T)
Education, Sports, and Culture	David Coltart (MDC-M)
Energy and Power Development	Elias Mudzuri (MDC-T)

Environment and Natural Resources	Francis Nhema (ZANU-PF)
Finance	Tendai Biti (MDC-T)
Foreign Affairs	Simbarashe Mumbengegwi (ZANU-PF)
Health and Child Welfare	Henry Madzorera (MDC-T)
Higher and Tertiary Education	Stanislaus Mudenge (ZANU-PF)
Home Affairs	Kembo Mohadi (ZANU-PF) and Giles Mutseyekwa (MDC-T) [joint position]
Industry and Commerce	Welshman Ncube (MDC-M)
Information and Publicity	Webster Shamu (ZANU-PF)
Information Communications Technology	Nelson Chamisa (MDC-T)
Justice,	Patrick Chinamasa (ZANU-PF)
Labor and Social Welfare	Pauline Mpariwa (MDC-T) [f]
Lands and Land Resettlement	Herbert Murerwa (ZANU-PF)
Local Government, Urban and Rural Development	Ignatius Chombo (ZANU-PF)
Mines	Obert Mpofu (ZANU-PF)
National Housing and Social Amenities	Fidelis Mhashu (MDC-T)
Public Service	Eliphas Mukonoweshuro (MDC-T)
Public Works	Theresa Makone (MDC-T) [f]
Regional Integration and International Trade	Priscilla Misihairabwi (MDC-M) [f]
Science and Technology	Henri Dzinotyiwei (MDC-T)
Small and Medium Enterprise Development	Sithembiso Nyoni (ZANU-PF) [f]
State Enterprises and Parastatals	Joel Gabuza (MDC-T)
Tourism	Walter Mzembi (ZANU-PF)
Transport and Infrastructural Development	Nicholas Goche (ZANU-PF)
Water Resources	Samuel Sipepa Nkomo (MDC-T)
Women's Affairs, Gender and Community Development	Olivia Muchena (ZANU-PF) [f]
Youth Development, Indigenization and Empowerment	Saviour Kasukuwere (ZANU-PF)
Ministers of State	
National Security (Office of the President)	Sydney Sekeramayi (ZANU-PF)
Presidential Affairs	Didymus Mutasa (ZANU-PF)
Prime Minister's Office	Gordon Moyo (MDC-T)

[f] = female

COMMUNICATIONS

In mid-1998 the government passed a bill forbidding foreign ownership of media outlets. Relations between the administration of President Robert Mugabe and the independent press subsequently deteriorated sharply, and journalists charged the government with widespread harassment and intimidation during and after the 2000 legislative campaign. Meanwhile, independent observers strongly criticized the government-controlled media for exhibiting a strongly pro–ZANU-PF bias in covering the election.

On March 15, 2002, after the presidential election, Mugabe signed into law the Access to Information and Protection of Privacy Act, which made it a crime for journalists to practice without a license, for which they must apply to a government-controlled media commission.

Following the formation of the unity government, press freedom slightly improved in 2009. The government lifted a six-year ban on the privately owned *Daily News* and allowed CNN and the BBC to return. A Zimbabwe Media Commission was formed by parliamentary statute, with nine commissioners to be named by agreement of the president and prime minister.

Press. In early 1981 the government purchased 42 percent of the shares of the (South African) Argus group, thereby acquiring control of the largest newspapers in Zimbabwe, which it subsequently published through Zimbabwe Newspapers Ltd. Current government-controlled dailies include *The Herald* (122,000), published in Harare, and *The Chronicle* (45,000), published in Bulawayo. Weeklies produced by Zimbabwe Newspapers Ltd. include *Sunday Mail* (159,000), published in Harare, and *Sunday News* (50,000), published in Bulawayo.

A number of privately owned papers now exist, the best-selling of which is the *Daily News,* published in Harare. Independent weeklies published in Harare include the *Financial Gazette* (35,000), *The Standard,* the *Zimbabwe Independent,* and the *Zimbabwe Mirror.*

News agencies. In October 1980 the South African Press Association relinquished its interest in the Salisbury-based Inter-African News Agency, the latter being reorganized as the Zimbabwe Inter-African News Agency (ZIANA). *Agence France-Presse,* AP, Reuters, and UPI are among the foreign agencies that maintain bureaus in Harare.

Broadcasting and computing. The Zimbabwe Broadcasting Corporation (ZBC) regulates radio and television stations; service is in English and a variety of African languages. Although ZBC is formally an independent statutory body, it is dependent on public funds and has been broadly criticized in recent years for a progovernment orientation the news. As of 2008 there were 114 Internet users per 1,000 inhabitants.

INTERGOVERNMENTAL REPRESENTATION

Ambassador to the U.S.: Machivenyika T. MAPURANGA.

U.S. Ambassador to Zimbabwe: Charles Aaron RAY.

Permanent Representative to the UN: Boniface G. CHIDYAUSIKU.

IGO Memberships (Non-UN): ADF, AfDB, AU, BADEA, Comesa, Interpol, IOM, NAM, PCA, SADC, WCO, WTO.

PALESTINIAN AUTHORITY/PALESTINE LIBERATION ORGANIZATION

Political Status: Declaration of Principles establishing a "Palestinian authority" to assume partial governmental responsibility in Gaza and portions of the West Bank signed by Yasir Arafat, chair of the Palestine Liberation Organization, and Israeli prime minister Yitzhak Rabin on September 13, 1993; agreement reached on May 4, 1994, between Arafat and Rabin for formal launching of the withdrawal of Israeli troops from certain occupied territories and inauguration of the first Palestinian Authority (PA, or Palestinian National Authority [PNA]) on July 5; extension of limited Palestinian self-rule to additional territory approved in Israeli-Palestinian accord on September 24, 1995; elected civilian government inaugurated February–May 1996 to govern most of Gaza and portions of the West Bank; mixed presidential–prime ministerial system adopted for Palestinian self-rule areas on March 10, 2003; Israeli settlements in Gaza dismantled and all Israeli forces withdrawn unilaterally from Gaza in August–September 2005; control of Gaza taken over in June 2007 by the Islamic Resistance Movement (Hamas), with the PNA retaining control of Palestinian self-rule territory in the West Bank.

President: Mahmoud ABBAS (Fatah/Palestine Liberation Organization); directly elected on January 9, 2005, and inaugurated for a four-year term on January 15 to succeed Yasir ARAFAT (Fatah/Palestine Liberation Organization), who had died on November 11, 2004. (President Abbas's term was subsequently extended by one year to permit simultaneous presidential and parliamentary elections in 2010.)

Prime Minister: Salim Khaled Abdallah FAYYAD; appointed by the president on June 14, 2007, to succeed Ismail HANIYEH (Islamic Resistance Movement [Hamas]), who was dismissed (along with his entire cabinet) by the president the same day in conjunction with the president's declaration of a state of emergency following the takeover of Gaza by Hamas (Haniyeh refused to accept the dismissal of his cabinet and continued to head a de facto government in Gaza); reappointed by the president on May 19, 2009.

GEOGRAPHY

Gaza Strip. The Gaza Strip consists of that part of former Palestine contiguous with Sinai that was still held by Egyptian forces at the time of the February 1949 armistice with Israel. Encompassing some 140 square miles (363 sq. km.), the territory was never annexed by Egypt and since 1948 has never been legally recognized as part of any state. In the wake of the 1967 war, nearly half of its population of 356,100 (1971E) was living in refugee camps, according to the UN Relief and Works Agency for Palestinian Refugees in the Near East (UNRWA). The population was estimated by Palestinian officials to be 934,000, prior to a census conducted in late 1997, the results of which indicated an increase to about 1,022,000.

Most of Gaza was turned over to Palestinian administration under the Israeli-Palestinian accord of May 4, 1994, with Israel retaining authority over Jewish settlements and responsibility for external defense of the territory. On February 20, 2005, the Israeli cabinet by a vote of 17 to 5 endorsed a plan for unilateral disengagement from Gaza to begin on August 15 of that year. The plan required the dismantling of all Israeli settlements in the Gaza Strip, the evacuation of 8,000 Jewish settlers, and the closure of Israeli military bases. The withdrawal was finally completed on September 12, 2005, marking the end of 38 years of Israeli rule over the territory. However, Israel retained offshore maritime control as well as control of airspace over Gaza.

West Bank. Surrounded on three sides by Israel and bounded on the east by the Jordan River and the Dead Sea, the West Bank territory encompasses what was the Jordanian portion of former Palestine between 1948 and 1967. It has an area of 2,270 sq. mi. and, according to results of the Palestinian census of late 1997, a Palestinian population of 1,873,000 (including East Jerusalem); earlier figures had also reported over 130,000 Jewish settlers.

The West Bank was occupied by Israel following the 1967 war. In July 1988 King Hussein of Jordan announced that his government would abandon its claims to the West Bank and would respect the wishes of Palestinians to establish their own independent state in the territory.

Under the Israeli-Palestinian accord of May 4, 1994 (an extension of the September 13, 1993, Oslo Agreement [see Political background, below]), the West Bank enclave of Jericho was turned over to Palestinian administration on May 13. Palestinian control was extended to six more West Bank towns (Bethlehem, Jenin, Nablus, Qalqilya, Ramallah, and Tulkarm) in late 1995 as the result of the second major "self-rule" accord, signed on September 28, 1995. Concurrently, civic authority in more than 450 villages in the West Bank was also turned over to the Palestinians, although Israeli forces remained responsible for security in those areas. In January 1997 Israeli troops withdrew from all but about 20 percent of the West Bank town of Hebron. In addition, an agreement was announced for additional redeployment of Israeli troops from other West Bank areas in three stages over the next 18 months.

It was generally expected in 1997 that the withdrawals would occur relatively quickly from most of the villages already under Palestinian civic authority, with as yet ill-defined redeployment from the rural areas in the West Bank to follow. However, none of the withdrawals had occurred by March 1998, as negotiations between Palestinian representatives and the Israeli government collapsed. A new series of withdrawals was authorized by the Wye agreement of October 1998, but only the first of those stages was implemented. An ambitious timetable for further withdrawals was endorsed by the Sharm al-Shaikh agreement of September 1999, but implementation was never achieved. The subsequent "effective state of war" between the Palestinians and Israelis precluded further resolution as Israeli forces occupied many of the areas previously turned over to Palestinian control.

In June 2002 Israel began constructing a barrier to separate the West Bank from Israel. The Israeli government stated that the construction of the barrier was necessary to prevent the flow of Palestinian suicide bombers from the West Bank. The route of the barrier was subsequently mired in controversy given that it did not completely follow the 1949 Israeli-Jordanian armistice line, also known as the Green Line, and that it encircled Palestinian communities close to the Israel–West Bank border. The barrier also diverged from the Green Line in places to incorporate large Jewish settlements in East Jerusalem and the West Bank and left some Palestinian population centers on the Israeli side of the barrier. The Israeli government subsequently approved a new route after the Israeli Supreme Court ruled that the previous route would have been disruptive to the lives of Palestinians who would have been put on the Israeli side of the barrier. As a result, the new route ran closer to Israel's boundary with the West Bank, although it still included more than 6 percent of West Bank land on the Israeli side of the barrier. Concomitant with Israeli disengagement from the Gaza Strip in August–September 2005, Israeli forces were also redeployed from some areas in the northern West Bank, including the Israeli settlements of Ganim, Kadim, Sa-Nur, and Homesh.

GOVERNMENT AND POLITICS

Political background. (For information on developments prior to November 1988, see the section on the Palestine Liberation Organization [PLO], below.) Upon convocation of the 19th session of the PLO's Palestine National Council (PNC) in Algiers in mid-November 1988, it appeared that a majority within the PLO and among Palestinians in the occupied territories favored "land for peace" negotiations with Israel. On November 15 PLO chair Yasir ARAFAT, with the endorsement of the PNC, declared the establishment of an independent Palestinian state encompassing the West Bank and Gaza Strip with the Arab sector of Jerusalem as its capital, based on the UN "two-state" proposal that had been rejected by the Arab world in 1947. The PLO Executive Committee was authorized to direct the affairs of the new state pending the establishment of a provisional government.

In conjunction with the 1988 independence declaration, the PNC adopted a new political program that included endorsement of the

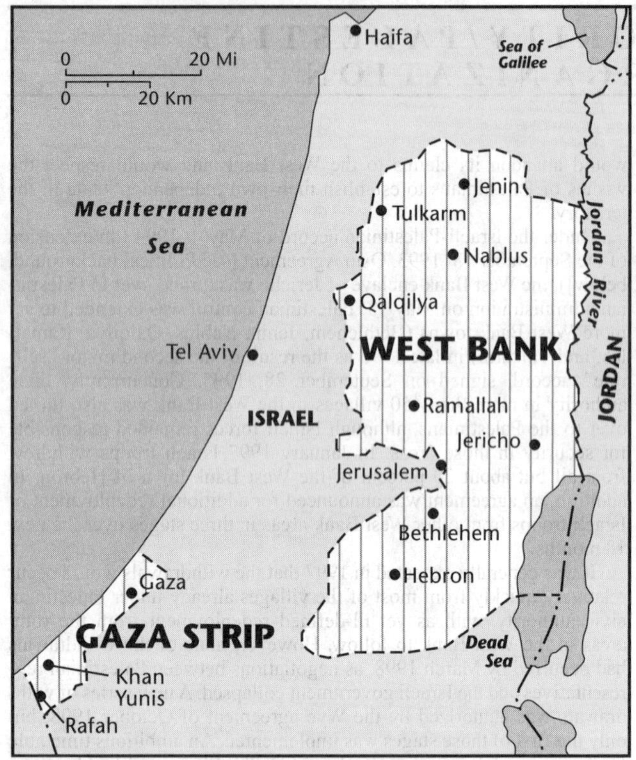

UN resolutions that implicitly acknowledged Israel's right to exist. The PNC also called for UN supervision of the occupied territories pending final resolution of the conflict through a UN-sponsored international conference. Although Israel had rejected the statehood declaration and the new PLO peace initiative in advance, many countries (over 110 as of April 1989) subsequently recognized the newly proclaimed entity. The onrush of diplomatic activity following the PNC session included a speech by Arafat in December to the UN General Assembly, which convened in Geneva for the occasion because of U.S. refusal to grant the PLO chair a visa to speak in New York. A short time later, after a 13-year lapse, the United States agreed to direct talks with the PLO, Washington announcing it was satisfied that Arafat had "without ambiguity" renounced terrorism and recognized Israel's right to exist.

On April 2, 1989, the PLO's Central Council unanimously elected Arafat president of the self-proclaimed Palestinian state and designated Faruk QADDUMI as foreign minister of the still essentially symbolic government. Israel remained adamantly opposed to direct contact with the PLO, however, proposing instead that Palestinians end the intifada in return for the opportunity to elect non-PLO representatives to peace talks.

During the rest of 1989 and early 1990, the PLO appeared to make several significant concessions, despite growing frustration among Palestinians and the Arab world in general over a perceived lack of Israeli reciprocity. Of particular note was Arafat's "conditional" acceptance in February 1990 of a U.S. plan for direct Palestinian-Israeli peace talks, theretofore opposed by the PLO in favor of the long-discussed international peace conference. However, the Israeli government, unwilling to accept even indirect PLO involvement, rejected the U.S. proposal, thus further undercutting the PLO moderates. By June the impasse had worsened, in part because of PLO protests over the growing immigration to Israel of Soviet Jews. Moreover, Washington decided to discontinue its talks with the PLO because of a lack of disciplinary action against those claiming responsibility for an attempted commando attack in Tel Aviv.

Subsequently, the PLO leadership and a growing proportion of its constituency gravitated to the hard-line, anti-Western position being advocated by Iraqi president Saddam Hussein, a stance that created serious problems for the PLO following Iraq's invasion and occupation of Kuwait in August 1990. Despite anti-Iraq resolutions approved by the majority of Arab League members, Arafat and other prominent PLO leaders openly supported President Hussein throughout the Gulf crisis. As a result, Saudi Arabia and the other Gulf states suspended their financial aid to the PLO (estimated at about $100 million annually), while Western sympathy for the Palestinian cause eroded. Following the defeat of Iraqi forces by the U.S.-led coalition in March 1991, the PLO was left, in the words of a *Christian Science Monitor* correspondent, "hamstrung by political isolation and empty coffers." Consequently, the PLO's leverage in Middle East negotiations initiated by the United States at midyear was reduced, and the 20th PNC session in Algiers in late September agreed to a joint Palestinian-Jordanian negotiating team with no official link to the PLO for the multilateral peace talks inaugurated in Madrid, Spain, in October. However, it was generally conceded that the Palestinian negotiators were handpicked by Arafat and represented a direct extension of PLO strategy.

As the peace talks moved into early 1992, Arafat and Fatah faced growing criticism that concessions had yielded little in return, and fundamentalist groups such as the Islamic Resistance Movement (Hamas) benefited from mainstream PLO defections in the West Bank and Gaza. Consequently, it was widely believed that Arafat would face yet another strong challenge at the Central Council meeting scheduled for April. However, circumstances changed after the PLO leader's plane crashed in a sandstorm in the Libyan desert on April 7, with Arafat being unaccounted for, and widely presumed dead, for 15 hours. Panic reportedly overcame many of his associates as they faced the possible disintegration of a leaderless organization. Thus, when Arafat was found to be alive, a tumultuous celebration spread throughout the Palestinian population, reconfirming his preeminence. As a result, even though the succession issue remained a deep concern, Arafat's policies, including continued participation in the peace talks, were endorsed with little opposition when the Central Council finally convened in May. Negotiations were put on hold, however, until the Israeli election in June, after which PLO leaders cautiously welcomed the victory of the Israel Labor Party as enhancing the peace process.

Although peace talks resumed in August 1992, they failed to generate any immediate progress, and criticism of Arafat's approach again intensified. In September the Democratic Front for the Liberation of Palestine (DFLP), the Popular Front for the Liberation of Palestine (PFLP), Hamas, and a number of other non-PLO groups established a coalition in Damascus to oppose any further negotiations with Israel. In addition, it was subsequently reported that Arafat's support had dwindled at the October session of the PLO's Central Council.

Israel's expulsion of some 400 Palestinians from the occupied territories to Lebanon in late December 1992 further clouded the situation, the PLO condemning the deportations and ordering the Palestinian representatives to suspend their participation in the peace negotiations. Even after the talks resumed in mid-1993, they quickly appeared deadlocked, and rancorous debate was reported within the PLO leadership on how to proceed. By that time, with Hamas's influence in the occupied territories continuing to grow, some onlookers were describing the PLO and its aging chair as "fading into oblivion" and "collapsing." However, those writing off Arafat were unaware that PLO and Israeli representatives had been meeting secretly for nearly eight months in Oslo, Norway, and other European capitals to discuss mutual recognition and the beginning of Palestinian self-rule in the occupied territories. Although initial reports of the discussions in late August were met with widespread incredulity, an exchange of letters on September 9 between Arafat and Israeli prime minister Yitzhak Rabin confirmed that the peace process had indeed taken a hopeful turn. For his part, Arafat wrote that the PLO recognized "the right of the State of Israel to exist in peace and security" and described PLO Charter statements to the contrary to be "inoperative and no longer valid." The chair also declared that the PLO renounces the "use of terrorism and other acts of violence." In return, Rabin's short letter confirmed that Israel had "decided to recognize the PLO as the representative of the Palestinian people and commence negotiations with the PLO within the Middle East peace process."

For all practical purposes the initial round of direct PLO-Israeli negotiations had already been completed, and the mutual recognition letters were quickly followed by unofficial but extensive reports of a draft Declaration of Principles regarding Palestinian autonomy. The PLO Executive Committee endorsed the draft document on September 10, 1993, although several members resigned in protest over Arafat's "sell-out," and the stage was set for a dramatic ceremony on September 13 in Washington, D.C., that concluded with the signing of the declaration by Arafat and Rabin. The Declaration of Principles authorized a "Palestinian authority" to assume governmental responsibility in what was projected to be a gradually expanding area of the occupied territories from which Israeli troops were to withdraw.

The 1993 peace accord proposed the establishment of an interim Palestinian government in the Gaza Strip and the West Bank town of Jericho and committed Israel and the PLO to negotiating a permanent settlement on all of the occupied territories within five years. However, mention of the agreement was rarely made without immediate reference to the many obstacles in its path, including strong opposition from Israel's *Likud* Party and, on the Palestinian side, from Hamas, the DFLP, and the PFLP. There was also widespread concern that militant activity could sabotage the peace agreement. In addition, many details remained to be resolved before the Declaration of Principles could be transformed into a genuine self-rule agreement. Finally, there still appeared to be a wide, and possibly unbridgeable, gulf between the Israeli and PLO positions on several issues, such as the future of Jerusalem, the status of Palestinian refugees, and whether a completely independent Palestinian state would ultimately be created. Nevertheless, the remarkable image, flashed via television to a transfixed world, of Arafat and Rabin shaking hands at the Washington ceremony seemed to persuade even the most skeptical observers that a historic corner had been turned. For the PLO chair, the agreement represented an extraordinary personal triumph, his enhanced status being reflected by a private session with U.S. president Bill Clinton after the signing ceremony and by a meeting the next day with UN secretary general Boutros Boutros-Ghali.

International donors quickly expressed their enthusiasm for the September 1993 agreement by pledging $2.4 billion to promote economic development in Gaza/Jericho over the next five years. Shortly thereafter, the PLO's Central Committee approved the accord by a reported vote of 63–8. However, the declaration's projection that Israeli troops would begin their withdrawal by mid-December 1993 proved unrealistic, and extended negotiations were required on issues such as the size of the Jericho enclave and the control of border crossings.

Amid growing international concern that the peace plan could unravel, negotiations resumed in April 1994, and, at a May 4 ceremony in Cairo, Arafat and Rabin signed a final agreement formally launching Israeli troop withdrawal and inaugurating limited Palestinian self-rule. The Israeli pullout, and concurrent assumption of police authority by PLO forces, was completed in Jericho on May 13 and in most of Gaza on May 18. (Israeli troops remained stationed in buffer zones around 19 Jewish settlements in Gaza.)

The 1994 accord provided for all government responsibilities in Gaza/Jericho (except, significantly, for external security and foreign affairs) to be turned over to the "Palestinian authority" for a five-year interim period. Negotiations were to begin immediately on the second stage of Israeli redeployment, under which additional West Bank territory was to be turned over to Palestinian control, while a final accord on the permanent status of the occupied territories was to be completed no later than May 1999.

On May 28, 1994, Arafat announced the first appointments to the Palestinian National Authority (PNA), with himself as chair of the cabinet-like body. (The PLO leader subsequently routinely referred to himself as "president" of the PNA. However, the title, and indeed the Palestinian insistence on including "National" in the PNA's name, was not sanctioned by the Israeli government, which remained officially opposed to the eventual creation of a Palestinian state. Meanwhile, the media was split on the matter, with some referencing the PNA and others the Palestinian Authority [PA].) With most PLO offices in Tunis having been closed, Arafat entered Gaza on July 1, setting foot on "Palestinian soil" for the first time in 25 years. It was initially assumed that the PNA's headquarters would be in Jericho, where the PNA, which had already held several preliminary sessions, was formally sworn in before Arafat on July 5. However, Arafat and most government officials subsequently settled in Gaza City.

Internal security initially proved to be less of a concern than anticipated within the autonomous areas, and the PNA focused primarily on efforts to revive the region's severe economic distress. The World Bank, designated to manage the disbursement of the aid pledged by international donors the previous fall, announced plans to distribute about $1.2 billion over the next three years, primarily for infrastructure projects. On the Palestinian side, coordination of such assistance fell to a recently established Palestinian Economic Council for Development and Reconstruction (PECDAR).

In late August 1994, Israeli officials announced they were turning educational responsibilities for Palestinian areas in the West Bank over to the PNA as the beginning of an "early empowerment" program. The PNA was scheduled to assume authority throughout the West Bank soon in four additional areas—health, social welfare, taxation, and tourism. On the political front, the PNA proposed that elections to a Palestinian Council be held in December. However, no consensus had been reached by September either between the PLO and Israel or among Palestinians themselves on the type, size, constituency, or mandate of the new body.

Pessimism over the future of the self-rule plan deepened in the fall of 1994 as security matters distracted attention from political and economic discussions. Under heavy pressure from Israel, the PNA authorized the detention of several hundred members of Hamas after that grouping had claimed responsibility for a gun and grenade attack in Jerusalem on October 9. Ten days later a Hamas suicide bomber blew up a bus in Tel Aviv, killing 22 people and prompting Israel to close its borders with the West Bank and Gaza and implement other new security measures. In addition, Palestinian police arrested nearly 200 members of the militant group Islamic Jihad (*al-Jihad al-Islami*) after it claimed responsibility for a bombing in Gaza in early November that left three Israeli soldiers dead. The tension culminated on November 18 in the killing of 13 people as Palestinian police exchanged gunfire with Hamas and Islamic Jihad demonstrators in Gaza, some observers suggesting that the Palestinians were on the brink of a civil war. Further complicating matters for the PLO/PNA, a meeting of the PLO Executive Committee called by Arafat in November failed to achieve a quorum when dissidents refused to attend. Among other things, the PLO chair had hoped that the committee would formally rescind the sections in the organization's National Covenant that called for the destruction of Israel.

Another Islamic Jihad suicide bombing on January 22, 1995, killed more than 20 people in the Israeli town of Netanya. Israel responded by suspending negotiations with the PNA until stronger measures were taken to prevent such attacks from the West Bank and Gaza. Consequently, Arafat authorized the creation of special military courts in February to deal with "issues of state security" and thereby permit a crackdown on militants. While the action appeared to appease Israel, it was criticized by human rights activists and non-PLO Palestinian organizations. As a result, facing yet another test of his leadership, Arafat called for a PLO Executive Committee meeting, the absence of the proposed covenant change from the agenda apparently facilitating the achievement of a quorum.

Although reportedly facing intense scrutiny from the Executive Committee, which was seen as attempting to recover some of the influence it had lost to the PNA, the PLO chair nevertheless emerged with a mandate to pursue negotiations with Israel. Following a further intensification in April of the PNA campaign against "terrorists," peace talks regained momentum, 100-member negotiating teams from each side sequestering themselves in the Egyptian resort of Taba for several months. Finally, after six consecutive days of direct negotiations between Arafat and Israeli foreign affairs minister Shimon Peres, agreement was reached on September 24, 1995, on the next phase of Israeli troop redeployment and the extension of Palestinian self-rule to much of the West Bank. Israeli troops were to start withdrawing immediately from certain towns and villages in the West Bank, with the PNA assuming control therein. Temporary joint responsibility was arranged for rural areas, while Israeli troops were to continue to guard the numerous Jewish settlements in the West Bank and Gaza. Upon completion of the Israeli redeployment, elections were to be held, under international supervision, to a new Palestinian Council. Provision was also made for a 25-member "executive authority," whose head would be elected in separate balloting. It was estimated that self-rule would initially be extended to about 30 percent of the West Bank, with additional territory (up to a 70 percent total) to be ceded following the proposed Palestinian elections. In support of the accord, Israel pledged a three-stage release of thousands of Palestinian prisoners, while the PLO agreed to revoke the anti-Israeli articles in its covenant within two years.

The Israeli-Palestinian Interim Agreement on the West Bank and Gaza (informally referred to as "Oslo II") was signed by Arafat and Prime Minister Rabin at another White House ceremony on September 28, 1995, the attendees including King Hussein of Jordan and President Husni Mubarak of Egypt. Israel and the PLO agreed that Israeli troops would begin immediately to withdraw from six more West Bank towns while negotiations continued on the contentious issue of the town of Hebron, home to a small but highly vocal group of ultrareligious Jewish settlers. The agreement also envisioned the turning over of authority to Palestinians in more than 450 additional villages in the West Bank, followed by Israeli withdrawal from most other rural areas. Although most details of the latter withdrawal were left unspecified, it was agreed that it would be conducted in three stages—6 months, 12 months, and 18 months after the election of the Palestinian Council, which was designated to succeed the PNA as the primary Palestinian governmental body. It was estimated that the council would be responsible for more than 70 percent of the West Bank following the proposed Israeli withdrawal, with Israel maintaining control of the Jewish settlements there and its numerous military installations.

Although "less mesmerizing" than its 1993 predecessor, the 1995 signing was considered no less consequential since the 400-page accord delineated in "intricate detail" most of the substantive aspects of the Israeli-Palestinian "divorce." On the other hand, very contentious issues remained to be resolved, including the rights of several million Palestinian refugees in countries such as Jordan, Lebanon, and Syria, many of whom hoped to return "home" to the West Bank and Israel. Talks were scheduled to begin in May 1996 on that question as well as the future status of Jerusalem, the eastern portion of which Palestinians claimed as their "capital." Difficult negotiations were also forecast regarding the estimated 140,000 Jewish settlers in Gaza and the West Bank, who vowed never to leave the region to which, in their opinion, "Greater Israel" had a biblically ordained right. A final agreement on these and all other outstanding issues was due no later than May 1999, at which point the Palestinian Council was scheduled to turn over authority to whatever new governmental organs had been established. It was by no means clear what the final borders of the Palestinian "entity" would be or, for that matter, what official form of government it would assume. Although Israeli officials maintained their formal opposition to an independent Palestine, Arafat described the 1995 agreement as leading to "an era in which the Palestinian people will live free and sovereign in their country." However, in a decision that was to have major repercussions, the Israeli and PLO negotiators postponed further discussions of the contentious issue of the proposed withdrawal of Israeli troops from Hebron.

Despite concerns that the assassination of Israeli Prime Minister Rabin in November 1995 would interfere with the implementation of the recent agreement, Israeli withdrawals from the six additional towns proceeded even more quickly than expected and were completed by December 30, 1995. Consequently, with the formal encouragement of the PLO Executive Committee, Arafat subsequently attempted to convince Hamas and theretofore "rejectionist" PLO factions to participate in the upcoming Palestinian elections. Although those discussions initially appeared promising, Hamas and a number of major PLO components (most notably the DFLP and the PFLP) ultimately urged their supporters to boycott the balloting on the grounds that electoral regulations were skewed in favor of Arafat's Fatah at the expense of smaller formations. Nevertheless, the elections on January 20, 1996, for the Palestinian Council and separate balloting for the head (or "president") of the council's "executive authority" were still viewed as a major milestone in the self-rule process. Only one person (Samihah Yusuf al-Qubbaj KHALIL, an opponent of the Oslo peace agreements) challenged Arafat for the latter post. The PLO chair garnered 87.1 percent of the votes in balloting that was widely construed (in conjunction with Fatah's success in the legislative poll) as confirming strong support for him personally and majority endorsement of his peace policies. Arafat was inaugurated in his new position in ceremonies in Gaza City on February 12, 1996, and on May 9 he announced the formation of a new cabinet, technically the "executive authority" of the Palestinian Council but widely referenced as the "new" PNA, which continued the semantic PNA/PA controversy. The government won a vote of confidence in the Palestinian Legislative Council (PLC, as the new body had widely become known) by 50–24 on July 27.

Militant opposition to the Oslo accords moved even further to the forefront of concerns in late February and early March 1996 when bomb attacks left some 60 Israelis dead in Jerusalem and Tel Aviv. Temporary closure of the borders of the self-rule areas by Israeli forces generated pressure upon Arafat from within the Palestinian population, while the additional security issues were seen as a substantial political problem for Israeli prime minister Shimon Peres, facing an early election in May. For his part, Arafat implemented several measures apparently designed to help Peres, including the arrest of a number of militants from Hamas and other groups and the banning of some six Palestinian "militias." In addition, the PLO chair convened the 21st session of the PNC (now reported as comprising 669 members) in Gaza City on April 22–24 to consider formal revision of the National Covenant to reflect recent understanding of the issue. The PNC session, the first to be held on "Palestinian" soil since 1966, agreed by a vote of 504–54 that all clauses in the covenant that contradicted recent PLO pledges were to be annulled. In general, the changes would recognize Israel's right to exist and renounce "terrorism and other acts of violence" on the part of the PLO. Final language on the revisions was to be included in a new charter, which the PNC directed the Central Council to draft.

The "final talks" on Palestinian autonomy officially opened on May 5, 1996, but substantive negotiations were postponed until the Israeli election of May 29. Following the surprising *Likud* victory in that balloting, resulting to some extent from security concerns within the Israeli populace arising from the recent bomb attacks, progress slowed on the Palestinian front. No agreement was quickly forthcoming regarding Hebron, which became the focus of Israeli right-wing attention, and the planned three-stage withdrawal of Israeli troops from rural areas in the West Bank was not implemented. Israeli-PLO talks resumed in late July, but no progress ensued, even after the much sought after face-to-face discussions between Arafat and new Israeli prime minister Benjamin Netanyahu in early September. International concern that the autonomy plan was deteriorating and growing criticism from moderate Arab states also seemingly failed to move the Netanyahu government (a tenuous coalition that included several ultraconservative groupings). Rising pressure finally erupted in fighting between Palestinians and Israelis in late September. U.S. president Bill Clinton quickly summoned Arafat, Netanyahu, and Jordan's King Hussein to a "crisis summit" in Washington, which appeared to reduce tensions, albeit without any apparent resolution of the underlying issues, particularly the status of Hebron, described as a "powder keg" that seemingly had assumed a psychological importance well out of proportion to its intrinsic significance.

As Netanyahu continued to resist redeployment of Israeli troops from Hebron throughout the rest of 1996, Arafat warned of the risk of the spontaneous resumption of the intifada. Finally, under apparent heavy U.S. pressure, Netanyahu accepted an agreement in early January 1997 that essentially reaffirmed the provisions of Oslo II. Among other things, the new accord (approved by the PLO Executive Committee on January 15) provided for Palestinian control to be extended to about 80 percent of Hebron, with Israeli withdrawal from additional rural West Bank areas to occur in stages from March 1997 through mid-1998. Assuming satisfactory progress on that front (not a certainty considering differing Israeli and Palestinian views on how much territory would ultimately be ceded to Palestinian rule), final talks were to be conducted on the still highly charged issues of the status of Palestinian refugees throughout the region, the nature of permanent governmental structures for the Palestinian "entity," and disposition of sovereignty claims to East Jerusalem.

Chair Arafat convened a "national dialogue" meeting in February 1997 in an effort to involve the formerly dissident PLO factions as well as non-PLO Palestinian groups in adopting a consensus on Palestinian proposals should final status talks be launched with Israel. However, with Israeli-Palestinian negotiations having collapsed, Arafat's "national unity" conference in August appeared primarily aimed not at negotiations but rather at portraying solidarity in the face of perceived Israeli intransigence. The presence of Hamas and Islamic Jihad at the session lent weight to Arafat's assertions that military resistance (including resumption of the intifada) was becoming a growing possibility. Meanwhile, the PNA itself had come under heavy domestic and international criticism, one corruption commission suggesting that more than $300 million in aid had been mishandled. The PLC demanded in late 1997 that President Arafat replace the cabinet with a new government comprising experts in their various fields rather than political appointees. It also called upon him to address allegations that Palestinian police and security forces had been responsible for widespread human rights abuses.

In February 1998 the PLO Executive Committee deferred a final decision on the proposed new PLO charter, eliciting Israeli concern that the 1996 action by the PNC remained insufficient as far as guaranteeing Israel's security was concerned. In addition, when agreement could not be reached on the extent of Israeli withdrawal, the Israeli government approved highly controversial Jewish settlement construction in East Jerusalem. Meanwhile, attention within the PLO focused on the question of a successor to Arafat, whose health was believed to be in decline. No dominant candidate had emerged, once again spotlighting the difficulties that would be faced if Arafat were unable to continue as the champion of the Palestinian cause.

The PLC threatened a no-confidence motion against the PNA in June 1998, which Arafat forestalled by indicating a major reshuffle was imminent. However, to the disappointment of the reformists, the new cabinet announced on August 5 contained many incumbents, changes focusing primarily on the addition of new ministers of state. Several incumbent ministers declined reappointment on the grounds that the reorganization failed to address Palestinian problems sufficiently, but the cabinet was approved by a vote of 55–29 in the Legislative Council on August 10.

In July 1998 Israeli and Palestinian negotiators met for the first time in over a year, and in October Netanyahu traveled to the United States to meet with Arafat and Clinton at the Wye Plantation in Maryland. After ten days of reportedly "tortuous" negotiations (capped off by a surprise visit from ailing King Hussein of Jordan), Netanyahu and Arafat signed an agreement on October 23 that proposed a three-month timetable for the next withdrawals of Israeli forces from the West Bank. Completion of the new redeployments would have left about 17 percent of the West Bank under full Palestinian control and 23 percent under joint Israeli/Palestinian authority. It was envisaged that negotiations would then begin regarding the third (and last) withdrawal phase and the other outstanding issues.

In addition to the geographic expansion of Palestinian autonomy, Israel also agreed in the 1998 Wye accords to release a number of Palestinian prisoners, permit the opening of the Gaza airport, and proceed with the establishment of a transit corridor for Palestinians from the West Bank to Gaza. For their part, Palestinian leaders pledged expanded security measures and additional repudiation of the anti-Israeli sections of the PLO Covenant. The first redeployment (centered around the northern West Bank town of Jenin) occurred on November 20, and international donors, signaling support for the resumption of progress, subsequently pledged some $3 billion in additional aid for development in the autonomous areas. However, Netanyahu faced significant opposition within his cabinet over the accord and appeared to place numerous barriers in the way of further implementation by, among other things, authorizing the expansion of Jewish settlements in the West Bank and demanding that Palestinian officials adopt a comprehensive weapons collection program, refrain from anti-Israeli "incitement," and drop their plans to unilaterally declare statehood on May 4, 1999. Clinton visited Israel and the self-rule territories on December 12–15 in an effort to reinvigorate the Wye plan, attending the session of the PNC in Gaza that endorsed the requested Covenant changes. However, the Netanyahu coalition finally collapsed in the ensuing days, and the cabinet on December 20 voted to suspend further implementation of the Wye provisions pending new Israeli national elections (later scheduled for May 1999). (Arafat subsequently defused a potentially explosive situation in late April 1999 by announcing that Palestinians would defer their unilateral declaration of statehood.)

Reacting to reformist pressure from the PLC, the PNA in January 1999 released a number of political detainees. However, a group of council members in November distributed a leaflet that charged the PNA with continued "systematic corruption" and other "abuse of power."

Following his inauguration in July 1999, new Israeli prime minister Ehud Barak called for a comprehensive peace settlement with the Palestinians, Syria, and Lebanon within 15 months. On September 4, he and Arafat signed an agreement in Sharm al-Shaikh in Egypt that provided for the "reactivation" of the 1998 Wye accord via the immediate transfer to Palestinian control of additional territory in the West Bank and the release of some Palestinians under Israeli arrest in return for the Palestinian leadership's "zero tolerance" of terrorism. So-called final status negotiations were subsequently launched on the very difficult issues of Jewish settlements in the occupied territories, the eventual status of Jerusalem (which both sides envisioned as their capital), and the future of some 3.6 million Palestinian refugees seeking a return to Israel. Little progress was achieved by the spring of 2000, however, except for some redeployment of Israeli forces in the West Bank (bringing about 43 percent of the West Bank under complete or partial Palestinian control). In April, Barak appeared to accept the eventual creation of "an independent Palestinian entity" (he avoided using the word "state") comprising Gaza and 60–70 percent of the West Bank. However, he indicated a "majority" of the Jewish settlers in the disputed areas would remain under Israeli sovereignty. Hopes for a resolution declined further in May when sporadic violence broke out in Gaza and the West Bank, fueled by Palestinian anger over the lack of progress in negotiations.

Faced with a collapsing coalition in Israel, Barak attended a "make-or-break" summit with Arafat and U.S. president Clinton at Camp David in July 2000. Although agreement appeared close on several issues, the summit ended unsuccessfully when common ground could not be found regarding the status of Jerusalem and sovereignty over holy sites there, notably Temple Mount (*Haram al-Sharif*), a sacred location for both Jews and Muslims. (Clinton criticized Arafat for being unwilling to make the "difficult decisions" required to conclude a pact.)

Serious rioting on the part of Palestinians erupted in late September 2000 following a visit by hard-line *Likud* leader Ariel Sharon to Temple Mount that was viewed as unnecessarily "provocative" by many observers. Although Barak subsequently indicated a willingness to endorse the establishment of two separate "entities" in Jerusalem, negotiations collapsed in October in the face of the "second intifada" and heavy reprisals by the Israeli military that included the use of assault helicopter and rocket attacks. By the end of December more than 350 people had been killed and 10,000 injured in the violence. In addition, Israel had banned Palestinian workers from entering Israel and had imposed other economic sanctions such as the withholding of tax payments to the PNA.

At the end of 2000, President Clinton, attempting to cap his eight-year tenure with a "last hurrah" Middle East breakthrough, proposed a settlement under which all of Gaza and some 95 percent of the West Bank would be placed under Palestinian control, although some West Bank settlements would remain Israeli. The proposed accord also reportedly called for Palestinian sovereignty over certain areas of East Jerusalem, the return of a "small number" of Palestinian refugees, and a "mutual accommodation" regarding Temple Mount. Barak reportedly approved the compromise, but Arafat in early 2001 raised a number of objections, particularly in regard to the refugee issue. (The Palestinian position—that all refugees and their descendants be permitted to return to Israel—had been rejected as an impossibility by most Western capitals and, of course, Israel, on the grounds that the Jewish Israeli electorate would be overwhelmed politically by the returnees.)

Barak's defeat by hard-liner Sharon in the February 2001 special prime ministerial balloting in Israel appeared to doom prospects for any settlement soon of the Palestinian questions, particularly in view of the fact that George W. Bush's new administration in Washington had announced it did not consider itself in any way bound by the "parameters" endorsed by Clinton. Sharon pledged that Jerusalem would remain "whole and unified" under Israeli sovereignty and that no Jewish settlements would be dismantled. Consequently, the rest of the year was marked by escalating violence that included numerous suicide bombings by Palestinian militants and massive retaliation by Israel in the form of missile attacks and tank incursions. Late in the year President Bush expressed his support for the eventual establishment of a Palestinian state and called for the withdrawal of Israeli forces from the areas previously under Palestinian control. Peace advocates also saw a glimmer of hope when Arafat, whose compound was besieged by Israeli troops, subsequently called upon all Palestinian groups to honor a cease-fire and indicated "flexibility" on the refugee question. However, suicide bombings continued unabated in early 2002, and Israel in April launched an offensive of unprecedented scale that left it in control of most West Bank towns. When that initiative failed to restrain the suicide bombers, the Sharon government announced at midyear that it would begin to construct a "security fence" around the West Bank. Positions subsequently remained hardened as Sharon called Arafat an "enemy" and demanded a change in the Palestinian leadership.

Meanwhile, criticism in Palestinian circles of Arafat's government had continued in 2000–2001, although it was muted somewhat by an apparent desire within the Palestinian community to present a unified front in the face of renewed Palestinian/Israeli violence. In mid-2002 Arafat pledged to conduct new presidential and legislative elections when Israeli forces were withdrawn from areas previously under Palestinian control. In the spring of 2002, Arafat, whose compound in Ramallah had been under siege by Israeli forces for months as part of a broad Israeli incursion into areas previously under Palestinian control, reportedly admitted "errors" in peace negotiations as well as in the administration of the PNA, and he promised significant reform efforts. However, concerned over the number of suicide bombings and other attacks on Israeli citizens, President Bush called for the "removal" of Arafat, portraying the Palestinian leader as unable or unwilling to combat terrorism. (Many analysts had concluded by that time that Arafat had little control over the attacks being claimed by Hamas and Islamic Jihad.)

Arafat trimmed his cabinet on June 9, 2002, although he was unable to convince the so-called rejectionist groups (notably Hamas, Islamic

Jihad, the PFLP, and the DFLP) to participate in the new government. Facing a possible nonconfidence vote in the PLC, Arafat again reorganized his cabinet on October 29 in preparation for proposed new elections. Arafat also promised reform in social sectors and indicated support for the eventual establishment of the post of prime minister, who would theoretically assume some of the authority heretofore exercised by Arafat.

In late 2002 Arafat declared that new elections would be postponed indefinitely due to Israel's occupation of territory formerly under Palestinian control. However, under heavy international pressure, Arafat in early 2003 formally endorsed the proposed installation of a Palestinian prime minister. The PLC on March 10 established the new position, although power-sharing arrangements vis-à-vis the president were left vague. (Among other things, Arafat retained control over peace negotiations with Israel.) Mahmoud ABBAS was nominated to the premiership, and his new cabinet was installed on April 29. Abbas promised to combat corruption, disarm militants, and pursue additional reform in Palestinian institutions. However, it quickly became clear that Abbas and Arafat were locked in a power struggle, and Abbas resigned on September 6. He was succeeded on September 10 by Ahmad QURAY, the speaker of the PLC.

At the end of April 2003, the Middle East Quartet (the European Union [EU], Russia, the UN, and the United States) presented its "road map," calling for the eventual establishment of an "independent, democratic, and viable" Palestinian state. The first steps would be an immediate and unconditional cease-fire and a freeze on new Israeli settlements. The plan also envisioned completion of a new Palestinian constitution, in the hope that Palestinian elections could be held by the end of the year. The major component of the second phase of the road map would be the convening of an international conference that would, among other things, help determine provisional borders for the new state. Final negotiations were slated for completion by the end of 2005, assuming Palestinian institutions had been "stabilized" and Palestinian security forces had proven adequate in combating attacks against Israel. Israeli prime minister Sharon offered qualified support for the road map, as did the Israeli *Knesset*, although the latter insisted that it be made clear that Palestinian refugees would not be guaranteed the right to return to their former homes in Israel.

In the wake of renewed heavy violence, the *Knesset* in September 2003 endorsed the potential expulsion from the Palestinian territories of Arafat, whom Sharon and Bush blamed for the ongoing stalemate. In February 2004 Sharon announced that he intended to order the unilateral disengagement of Israel from the Gaza Strip in light of the lack of progress regarding the road map.

Apparently in response to the growing reform tide, Arafat in mid-2004 once again acknowledged that he had "made mistakes," indicating that he was prepared to lead a renewed negotiation initiative. However, by that time it was clear that his health had failed to a point of unlikely recovery, and attention mostly focused on ensuring a smooth transition to the new PNA and PLO leaderships.

In July 2004 Prime Minister Quray threatened to resign unless the PLC granted him greater authority, particularly in regard to security. His request was partially granted, and the issue became mostly moot when Arafat died of an unknown illness at a hospital near Paris on November 11. Mahmoud Abbas was quickly named to replace Arafat as chair of the PLO executive committee, while PLC speaker Ruhi FATTUH assumed presidential authority on an acting basis.

Hamas and Islamic Jihad boycotted the presidential balloting on January 9, 2005, on the grounds that their involvement would have implied acceptance of the 1993 Oslo accords. Abbas won the presidency with 62 percent of the vote. His nearest rival (20 percent of the vote) was Moustafa BARGHOUTI, a secular independent associated with neither the PLO nor Hamas. Abbas was sworn in on January 15, and he invited Quray to form a new government. The international community welcomed the installation of a new Palestinian regime, and President Bush called Abbas "a man of courage."

Despite its boycott of the January 2005 presidential balloting, Hamas competed in the successive rounds of municipal elections held in the Palestinian territories in December 2004–January 2005 and in May and September 2005. Hamas performed strongly in all of those polls, underscoring the growing disenchantment among Palestinians with Fatah's governance.

In February 2005 President Abbas appointed a new cabinet consisting mainly of technocrats, again under the leadership of Quray. The appointments were seen as an effort to reduce the influence of the Fatah "old guard" that had been closely aligned with Yasir Arafat. Meanwhile, Ariel Sharon pushed ahead with his plan to evacuate the Gaza settlements and to disengage militarily from the Gaza Strip, overcoming opposition from within his own governing coalition. The disengagement was achieved in August–September. Although Sharon and Abbas subsequently agreed on a cease-fire, and Hamas itself declared a period of "calm," violence continued throughout 2005 as little progress was made in negotiations. Sporadic conflict also broke out between Palestinian security forces and Islamist militants. President Abbas visited Bush twice in 2005, but Abbas's positive international stature did not have much impact on Palestinian dissatisfaction with political and economic conditions.

Hamas scored a stunning victory in balloting for the PLC on January 25, 2006, securing 74 of 132 seats, compared to 45 seats for Fatah. Ismail HANIYEH of Hamas was inaugurated on March 29 to lead a new government that included only Hamas members and several independents, Fatah having declined to join the cabinet.

In light of ongoing violence between supporters of Hamas and Fatah as well as the suspension of economic aid to the PNA by Western donors opposed to Hamas (see Current issues, below), President Abbas on February 8, 2006, signed an agreement with the Hamas leadership for a new "national unity" government. Among other things, the new coalition pledged to pursue a settlement with Israel based on the 2002 "land-for-peace" proposal from King Abdullah of Saudi Arabia that had recently been reendorsed by the Arab League. Consequently, Haniyeh and his cabinet resigned on February 15, although Abbas immediately reappointed Haniyeh to form a new government. On March 17 the PLC approved the new cabinet (which included ten ministers from Hamas, six from Fatah, three from recently formed smaller groups, one from the DFLP, and five independents) by a vote of 83–3. However, Israel, still vehemently opposed to any negotiations with Hamas, called the new PNA a "step backwards" and continued its hard-line approach by arresting Hamas leaders and supporters in the West Bank.

Severe factional infighting broke out between Fatah and Hamas in May 2007 in Gaza, and in June Hamas took over complete control of Gaza. President Abbas on June 14 dissolved the PNA in light of what he called a "military coup" in Gaza and declared a one-month state of emergency. On June 17 Abbas appointed a new "emergency" government headed by Salim FAYYAD, theretofore the PNA's finance minister. The emergency cabinet resigned on July 13, but most of its members were included in the "caretaker" or "transitional" government appointed the following day. However, Haniyeh disputed the legitimacy of Abbas's actions, arguing that a new government required approval of the PLC. Consequently, Haniyeh continued to lead a five-member cabinet in Gaza that he described as the legitimate Palestinian government. Haniyeh expanded the Hamas cabinet in mid-2008.

Prime Minister Fayyad announced the resignation of his transitional cabinet on March 9, 2009, in anticipation of the formation of a Hamas-Fatah national unity government. However, when negotiations in that regard collapsed, President Abbas on May 19 appointed a new government (again led by Fayyad) that included a number of independents, several members of Fatah, and one member each from the DFLP, PFLP, and PDU.

Current issues. The United States and European states greeted the formation of the Hamas-led cabinet in March 2006 by suspending financial aid to the PNA and demanding that Hamas pledge to cease violence and recognize the state of Israel. Israel also stopped the transfer of customs tax revenues to the PNA, causing severe economic distress for a large part of the Palestinian population, especially those employed by the PNA. However, Hamas subsequently gave no indication that it would accept Israeli and Western demands (although Hamas had declared a conditional cease-fire in March 2005).

In May 2006 three people were killed when armed supporters of Hamas clashed with Abbas loyalists in Gaza. The fighting escalated over the next few weeks as Hamas deployed a militia of some 3,000 to Gaza. However, Hamas subsequently withdrew its "implementation force" from Gaza to calm tensions. Shortly thereafter, Abbas called on Hamas to endorse a national accord document that had been drawn up by prisoners detained in Israel, including Fatah leader Marwan BARGHOUTI. The plan called for acceptance of the pre-1967 boundaries for a Palestinian state (with Jerusalem as its capital), the establishment of a national unity government to include Hamas and Fatah, and PLO negotiations with Israel for a two-state solution. Furthermore, Abbas issued an ultimatum to Hamas to recognize Israel or else he would call for a referendum on the proposed accord. Hamas consented to many of the articles of the document, with the notable exception of negotiations that would lead to the recognition of Israel. However, any potential for a peace initiative was squashed after two Israeli soldiers were killed and another kidnapped by Palestinian militants who had tunneled under the border in Gaza. While rival Palestinian factions still called for a government of national unity, Abbas tabled further negotiations on the subject because of the "sensitivity" of the most recent event. Hamas demanded that Israel fully withdraw from the occupied territories, turn over tax revenues owed to the Palestinians, and immediately release all Palestinian ministers and lawmakers (including the speaker of the PLC) arrested in the months following the June abduction of the Israeli soldier.

Some analysts perceived a softening of Hamas's stance regarding potential recognition, or at least "acceptance," of the Israeli state during national unity negotiations between Fatah and Hamas in September 2006. Hamas also implied it might consider a "long-term truce" with Israel. However, Ehud Olmert (who had become prime minister of Israel in the wake of Ariel Sharon's stroke in January) authorized additional construction of Jewish settlements in the West Bank. Israel also maintained its economic "blockade" of Gaza and initiated several military offensives into Gaza in response to rocket attacks into Israel. Meanwhile, Palestinian workers went on strike in September to demand back wages, the Hamas-led government responding that it was being crippled by Israel's refusal to release tax revenues. Hamas also charged Fatah with promoting the demonstrations.

Israel withdrew its forces from Gaza in early November 2006, and a cease-fire was announced at the end of the month between Israel and most of the militant Palestinian groups. (Significantly, Islamic Jihad did not accept the agreement.) Olmert also urged "dialogue" that would lead to "an independent and viable Palestinian State," while Arab nations and Iran agreed to contribute financially to the PNA.

Factional Hamas-Fatah fighting intensified in December 2006, and President Abbas threatened to call early elections unless a national unity government could be established. Nevertheless, violence continued in January 2007, spreading from Gaza into several major cities in the West Bank. The Hamas-Fatah national unity government installed in March proved unable to achieve progress, and Israeli forces arrested a number of Palestinian militants in the West Bank cities of Jenin and Nablus in April, prompting rocket attacks from Gaza into Israel. The conflict between Hamas and Fatah deteriorated in May into what many analysts described as a civil war, and by June Fatah forces had been defeated in Gaza. Consequently, Palestinian self-rule now meant separate administration of Gaza by Hamas and of the West Bank territories by Fatah. Concurrently, Palestinian security forces in the West Bank detained a number of Hamas leaders.

Western donors immediately resumed aid to Abbas's PNA following the installation of the emergency government in the West Bank in June 2007. Also with the goal of supporting Abbas in his conflict with Hamas, Israel subsequently released tax revenues to the PNA and called for renewed peace talks. At the same time, Israel continued its daily attacks on what it called rocket-launching sites in Gaza.

In October 2007, as part of ongoing talks on the "fundamental issues," Israeli prime minister Olmert indicated that Israel might consider a division of Jerusalem as part of a potential final peace settlement. That and other initiatives were discussed at a U.S.-led peace conference in Annapolis, Maryland, at which Olmert and Abbas agreed to resume formal negotiations with the goal of reaching agreement within a year. However, Hamas called Abbas a "traitor" for participating in the conference, while Olmert faced significant opposition in Israel for his perceived concessions to the Palestinians.

Deadly conflict continued in Gaza in late 2007 and early 2008 between Hamas and Fatah and between Hamas supporters and Israeli security forces. In mid-January 2008 Israel, responding to rocket attacks from Gaza into Israel, launched a major incursion into Gaza and closed Gaza's borders. Palestinians destroyed a border fence into Egypt later in the month, permitting them to rush into Egypt to buy much-needed fuel, food, medical supplies, and other necessities constrained by the Israeli blockade.

A suicide bombing in Israel in early February 2008 (the first in more than a year) prompted another Israeli air strike in Gaza, and tit-for-tat violence intensified into the summer. Israel and Hamas finally announced a cease-fire in June, with Israel agreeing to ease its controversial blockade. Meanwhile, President Abbas called for a "national dialogue" between Fatah and Hamas with the goal of new national elections. (In the opinion of many analysts, the initiative reflected an acknowledgment that Hamas had solidified its control in Gaza by, among other things, replacing judges and prosecutors with Hamas supporters and by expanding the Hamas network of social services and business connections.) Nevertheless, Fatah-Hamas discord continued, and the prospects for a comprehensive settlement with Israel before the end of the year dimmed in the face of political chaos in Israel.

Hamas formally declared the six-month cease-fire with Israel ended as of December 19, 2008, arguing that Israel had not lived up to its agreements regarding the truce, which Hamas had also sporadically violated. (Hamas argued that Israeli had reneged on its pledge to lift the economic blockade on Gaza and had contravened the accord through the arrest of Hamas members in the West Bank.) After Hamas rocket attacks from the Gaza Strip into Israel intensified, Israel on December 27 launched a series of massive air strikes ("Operation Cast Lead') against suspected Hamas security compounds in Gaza. In the face of additional rocket and mortar attacks into southern Israel, Israeli ground forces entered the Gaza Strip on January 3 to at least neutralize, if not topple, Hamas through "all-out war" if necessary. More than 1,500 Palestinians were killed (including some 900 civilians) during the offensive, which also destroyed or damaged 21,000 houses and otherwise decimated the infrastructure in Gaza before Israel declared a cease-fire on January 17. Hamas, which had continued to fire rockets and mortars into Israel during the conflict, declared its own unilateral cease-fire the same day, although it reserved the right to resume military activity unless Israeli troops were withdrawn quickly.

Most Arab states strongly condemned the Israeli offensive in Gaza (Egyptian president Hosni Mubarak characterized it as "savage aggression"), and most Western capitals expressed concern over the intensity of the Israeli campaign. (A UN report later in the year criticized both sides in the conflict, citing the ongoing Hamas rocket attacks. However, the report's strongest language was reserved for the Israeli military, accused of a "disproportionate attack" that leveled "collective punishment" against civilians. The UN called for further investigation of possible war crimes, including Israel's alleged use of white phosphorous against mostly civilian targets and the alleged execution of Palestinian civilians. Israel, which rejected the report as biased, accused Hamas of having used civilians as human shields. Human rights groups also charged Hamas with arresting, torturing, and, in some cases, executing alleged Palestinian "collaborators" with Israel following the conflict.)

In early March 2009 international donors pledged some $4.5 billion to assist in reconstruction in Gaza over the next two years, although delivery of the aid was subsequently compromised by donor insistence that it not be used to prop up Hamas. The international community also called for Hamas and Fatah to negotiate a resolution to their political stalemate. However, what had been initially deemed as promising discussions in March collapsed in May, prompting Abbas to announce a new government that once again did not include any Hamas representatives. Meanwhile, discussions between the Abbas administration and Israel toward resumption of formal peace talks foundered when newly installed Israeli prime minister Benjamin Netanyahu, despite some conciliatory rhetoric, resisted heavy U.S. pressure to halt the construction of Jewish settlements in East Jerusalem and the West Bank.

New U.S. president Barack Obama in June 2009 described the stateless status of Palestinians as "intolerable." Netanyahu subsequently endorsed the proposed "two-state" solution to the impasse, although the conditions he attached on Palestinian sovereignty appeared to doom prospects immediately. Frustrated by the lack of progress, President Abbas, in scheduling new presidential elections for January 24, 2010, announced that he might not run for reelection. Collaterally, other Palestinian leaders called for a unilateral declaration of a Palestinian state based on the territory gained by Israel in the 1967 war. For its part, Hamas did not endorse the proposed election schedule, and in December the balloting was postponed indefinitely, with its terms for Abbas and legislators being extended until at least June 2010.

POLITICAL PARTIES AND GROUPS

Palestine Liberation Organization (PLO). Establishment of the PLO was authorized on January 17, 1964, during an Arab summit held in Cairo, Egypt. Largely through the efforts of Ahmad SHUQAIRI, the Palestinian representative to the Arab League, an assembly of Palestinians met in (East) Jerusalem the following May 28–June 2 to draft a National Covenant and General Principles of a Fundamental Law, the latter subsequently serving as the constitutional basis of a government-in-exile. Under the Fundamental Law, the assembly became a 315-member Palestinian National Council (PNC) comprised primarily of representatives of the leading *fedayeen* (guerrilla) groups, various

Palestinian mass movements and trade unions, and Palestinian communities throughout the Arab world. An Executive Committee was established as the PLO's administrative organ, while an intermediate Central Council (initially of 21 but eventually of 100 members) was created in 1973 to exercise legislative-executive responsibilities on behalf of the PNC between PNC sessions.

In its original form, the PLO was a quasi-governmental entity designed to act independently of the various Arab states in support of Palestinian interests. Its subordinate organs encompassed a variety of political, cultural, and fiscal activities as well as a Military Department, under which a Palestine Liberation Army (PLA) was established as a conventional military force of recruits stationed in Egypt, Iraq, and Syria.

In the wake of the 1967 Arab-Israeli war, the direction of the PLO underwent a significant transformation. Shuqairi resigned as chair of the Executive Committee and was replaced in December 1967 by Yahia HAMMUDA, who was in turn succeeded in February 1969 by Yasir Arafat, leader of Fatah (below). At that time the PNC adopted a posture more favorable to guerrilla activities against Israel, insisted upon greater independence from Arab governments, and for the first time called for the establishment of a Palestinian state in which Muslims, Christians, and Jews would have equal rights. In effect, the PLO thus tacitly accepted a Jewish presence in Palestine, although it remained committed to the eradication of any Zionist state in the area.

In 1970–1971 the PLO and the *fedayeen* groups were expelled from Jordan, and Lebanon became their principal base of operations. The Israeli victory in the October 1973 war, and the fear that Jordan might negotiate on behalf of Palestinians from the occupied territories, resulted in another change in the PLO's strategy: in June 1974 it formally adopted a proposal that called for the creation of a "national authority" in the West Bank and Gaza as a first step toward the "liberation" of historical Palestine. This tacit recognition of Israel precipitated a major split among the PLO's already ideologically diverse components, and on July 29 a leftist "rejection front" was formed in opposition to any partial settlement in the Middle East.

In December 1976 the PLO Central Council voiced support for establishment of an "independent state" in the West Bank and Gaza, which was widely interpreted as implying acceptance of Israel's permanent existence. Shortly thereafter, contacts were established between the PLO and the Israeli left.

On September 1, 1982, immediately after the PLO withdrawal from West Beirut (see article on Lebanon), U.S. president Ronald Reagan proposed the creation of a Palestinian "entity" in the West Bank and Gaza, to be linked with Jordan under King Hussein. The idea was bitterly attacked by pro-Syrian radicals during a PNC meeting in Algiers in February 1983, with the PNC ultimately calling for a "confederation" between Jordan and an independent Palestinian state, thus endorsing an Arab League resolution of five months earlier that implicitly entailed recognition of Israel. Over radical objections, the Algiers meeting also sanctioned a dialogue with "progressive and democratic" elements within Israel, i.e., those favoring peace with the PLO. This position, however, was also unacceptable to the group's best-known moderate, Dr. Issam SARTAWI, who resigned from the council after being denied an opportunity to deliver a speech calling for formal discussions with Israeli leaders on the possibility of a clear-cut "two-state" solution. Subsequently, in an apparent trial balloon, Fatah's deputy chair, Salah KHALAF, declared that the group would support the Reagan peace initiative if the United States were to endorse the principle of Palestinian self-determination. The meeting's final communiqué, on the other hand, dismissed the Reagan proposal as not providing "a sound basis for a just and lasting resolution of the Palestinian problem."

PLO chair Arafat met for three days in early April 1983 with King Hussein without reaching agreement on a number of key issues, including the structure of a possible confederation, representation of Palestinians in peace negotiations with Israel, and the proposed removal of PLO headquarters to Amman. As the discussions concluded, Dr. Sartawi was assassinated in Albufeira, Portugal, by a member of an extremist Fatah splinter, headed by the Damascus-based Sabry Khalil al-BANNA (also known as Abu NIDAL). A week later, amid evidence of growing restiveness among Palestinian guerrillas in eastern Lebanon, the PLO Executive Committee met in Tunis to consider means of "surmounting the obstacles" that had emerged in the discussions with Hussein.

In mid-May 1983 Arafat returned to Lebanon for the first time since the Beirut exodus to counter what had escalated into a dissident rebellion led by Musa AWAD (also known as Abu AKRAM) of the Libyan-backed Popular Front for the Liberation of Palestine–General Command (PFLP-GC), a splinter of the larger PFLP. In late June Arafat convened a Fatah meeting in Damascus to deal with the mutineers' insistence that he abandon his flirtation with the Reagan peace plan and give greater priority to military confrontation with Israel.

On June 24, 1983, Syrian president Hafiz al-Assad ordered Arafat's expulsion from Syria after the PLO leader had accused Assad of fomenting the PFLP-GC rebellion, and a month later Arafat ousted two senior commanders whose promotions had precipitated tension within the ranks of the guerrillas in Lebanon's Bekaa Valley. The fighting nonetheless continued, and in early November one of Arafat's two remaining Lebanese strongholds north of Tripoli fell to the insurgents. Late in the month the PLO leader agreed to withdraw from an increasingly untenable position within the city itself, exiting from Lebanon (for the second time) on December 20 in a Greek ferry escorted by French naval vessels.

In early 1985 Arafat strengthened and formalized his ties with Jordan's King Hussein in an accord signed by both leaders on February 11. The agreement, described as "a framework for common action towards reaching a peaceful and just settlement to the Palestine question," called for total withdrawal by Israel from the territories it had occupied in 1967 in exchange for comprehensive peace; the right of self-determination for the Palestinians within the context of a West Bank–Gaza–Jordan confederation; resolution of the Palestinian refugee problem in accordance with UN resolutions; and peace negotiations under the auspices of an international conference that would include the five permanent members of the UN Security Council and representatives of the PLO, the latter being part of a joint Jordanian-Palestinian delegation.

Arafat's peace overtures deepened divisions within the ranks of the Palestinian national movement. In reaction to the February 1985 pact with Jordan, six PLO-affiliated organizations formed a Palestine National Salvation Front (PNSF) in Damascus to oppose Arafat's policies. Differences over peace initiatives also erupted during a November meeting in Baghdad of the PNC's Central Council. Disagreement turned mainly on whether to accept UN Security Council Resolutions 242 and 338, which called for Israeli withdrawal from the occupied territories and peaceful settlement of the Palestine dispute in a manner that would imply recognition of Israel. Shortly thereafter, Arafat attempted to reinforce his image as "peacemaker" with a declaration denouncing terrorism. The "Cairo Declaration" was issued after lengthy discussions with Egyptian president Husni Mubarak on ways to speed up peace negotiations. Arafat cited a 1974 PLO decision "to condemn all outside operations and all forms of terrorism." He promised to take "all punitive measures against violators" and stated that "the PLO denounces and condemns all terrorist acts, whether those involving countries or by persons or groups, against unarmed innocent civilians in any place."

Meanwhile, relations between Arafat and Hussein had again been strained by a number of incidents that displeased the king. In October 1985 guerrillas allegedly linked to the Palestine Liberation Front (PLF) hijacked the Italian cruise ship *Achille Lauro,* which resulted in the killing of an American tourist, while talks were broken off between the British government and a joint Palestinian-Jordanian delegation because of PLO refusal to sign a statement recognizing Israel and renouncing the use of terrorism.

The PLO sustained a major setback at the hands of Shiite Amal forces that besieged two Palestinian refugee camps in Lebanon during May and June 1985. From Tunis an extraordinary session of the Arab League Council called for an end to the siege, which was accomplished by Syrian mediation in mid-June. One effect of the action was to temporarily heal the rift between pro- and anti-Arafat Palestinian factions.

By early 1986 it had become apparent that the Jordanian-PLO accord had stalled over Arafat's refusal, despite strong pressure from King Hussein and other Arab moderates, to endorse UN Resolutions 242 and 338 as the basis of a solution to the Palestinian issue. Among the PLO's objections were references to Palestinians as refugees and a failure to grant them the right of self-determination. On the latter ground, Arafat rejected a secret U.S. tender of seats for the PLO at a proposed international Middle East peace conference. In February Hussein announced that the peace effort had collapsed and encouraged West Bank and Gaza Strip Palestinians to select new leaders. He underscored the attack on Arafat during ensuing months by proposing an internationally financed, $1.3 billion development plan for the West Bank, which he hoped would win the approval of its "silent majority." The PLO denounced the plan, while describing Israeli efforts to appoint Arab mayors in the West Bank as attempts to perpetuate Israeli occupation. The rupture culminated in Hussein's ordering the closure of Fatah's Jordanian offices in July.

King Hussein's overture elicited little support from the West Bank Palestinians, and by late 1986 it was evident that Arafat still commanded the support of his most important constituency. Rather than undercutting Arafat's position, Hussein's challenge paved the way for unification talks between Fatah and other PLO factions that had opposed the accord from the outset. Following initial opposition from the PNSF in August, the reunification drive gained momentum in early 1987 with indications that Georges HABASH of the PFLP (the PNSF's largest component) might join leaders of the Democratic Front for the Liberation of Palestine (DFLP) and other groups in trying to rescue the PLO from its debilitating fractionalization. Support was also received from PLO factions in Lebanon that had recently coalesced under Fatah leadership to withstand renewed attacks by Amal forces. Indeed, Syria's inability to stem the mass return of heavily armed Fatah guerrillas to Lebanon was viewed as a major contribution to Arafat's resurgence within the PLO. Meanwhile, King Hussein also attempted to mend relations with the PLO by announcing that the Jordanian-PLO fund for West Bank and Gaza Strip Palestinians, suspended at the time of the February 1986 breach, would be reactivated. Subsequently, the fund was bolstered by new pledges totaling $14.5 million from Saudi Arabia and Kuwait.

Although hard-line factions continued to call for Arafat's ouster, the PLO leader's more militant posture opened the way for convening the long-delayed 18th session of the PNC (its membership reportedly having been expanded to 426) in Algiers on April 20–26, 1987. Confounding critics who had long predicted his political demise, Arafat emerged from the meeting with his PLO chair intact, thanks in part to a declared willingness to share the leadership with representatives of non-Fatah factions. Thus, although several Syrian-based formations boycotted the Algiers meeting, Arafat's appearance at its conclusion arm-in-arm with former rivals Habash of the PFLP and Nayif Hawatmeh of the DFLP symbolized the success of the unity campaign.

During the last half of 1987 there were reports of secret meetings between the PLO and left-wing Israeli politicians to forge an agreement based on a cessation of hostilities, a halt to Israeli settlement in the Gaza Strip and West Bank, and mutual recognition by the PLO and Israel. However, nothing of substance was achieved, and by November it appeared that interest in the issue had waned, as evidenced by the far greater attention given to the Iran-Iraq war at an Arab League summit in November.

The Palestinian question returned to the forefront of Arab concern in December 1987 with the outbreak of violence in the occupied territories. Although the disturbances were believed to have started spontaneously, the PLO, by mobilizing grassroots structures it had nurtured throughout the 1980s, helped to fuel their transformation into an ongoing intifada (uprising).

In an apparent effort to heighten PLO visibility, Arafat demanded in March 1988 that the organization be accorded full representation (rather than participation in a joint Jordanian-Palestinian delegation) at any Middle Eastern peace conference. However, the prospects for such a conference dimmed in April when the PLO's military leader, Khalil al-WAZIR (also known as Abu JIHAD), was killed, apparently by an Israeli assassination team. Whatever the motive for the killing, its most immediate impact was to enhance PLO solidarity and provide the impetus for a dramatic "reconciliation" between Arafat and Syrian president Assad. However, that rapprochement soon disintegrated, as bloody clashes broke out between Fatah and Syrian-backed Fatah dissidents (see Fatah Uprising, below) for control of the Beirut refugee camps in May. Elsewhere in the Arab world, the position of the PLO continued to improve. A special Arab League summit in June 1988 strongly endorsed the intifada and reaffirmed the PLO's role as the sole legitimate representative of the Palestinian people. In addition, a number of countries at the summit reportedly pledged financial aid to the PLO to support continuance of the uprising.

On July 31, 1988, in a move that surprised PLO leaders, King Hussein announced that Jordan would discontinue its administrative functions in the West Bank on the presumption that Palestinians in the occupied territories wished to proceed toward independence under PLO stewardship. Although Jordan subsequently agreed to partial interim provision of municipal services, the announcement triggered extensive debate within the PLO on appropriate policies for promoting a peace settlement that would yield creation of a true Palestinian government. (For information on developments from 1988 to 1998, see Political background, above).

The peace process appeared to have been relaunched by the Wye accords of October 1998. As part of the Wye agreements, the PLO Central Council met on December 10 to consider Israeli requests regarding the PLO covenant. Arafat and other Palestinian representatives had argued that no further action was required, claiming that the PLO chair's earlier letter to President Clinton had made it clear that articles in the covenant had been voided by the PNC in 1996. However, the Central Council endorsed the particulars in Arafat's letter, and on December 14 the PNC reaffirmed the covenant changes by a nearly unanimous show of hands. In addition, under heavy international pressure, the Central Council in late April 1999 endorsed Arafat's recent decision to postpone the unilateral declaration of Palestinian statehood, which had been planned for May 4, 1999. Following the Sharm al-Shaikh agreement of September 1999, the PLO Central Council extended the deadline for statehood declaration until September 2000. Meanwhile, by early 2000 the PFLP and the DFLP had resumed participation in the council's deliberations. Another positive development, at least for Palestinians, was a meeting in February 2000 between Arafat and Pope John Paul II at which the Vatican reportedly recognized the PLO as the legitimate voice of Palestinian sentiment and endorsed eventual "international status" for Jerusalem.

Prior to the "make or break" summit between Arafat and Israeli prime minister Barak (who faced growing opposition to his peace efforts within Israel) in the United States in July 2000, the PLO Central Council indicated its solid support for Arafat and authorized him to declare statehood on September 13. However, when the U.S. summit collapsed, the Central Council, under intense international pressure, agreed at a meeting on September 9–10 to postpone the declaration once again. (Arafat had traveled to some 40 countries to solicit support for the declaration. The United States, EU, and many others resisted the idea, however, in part because of the prevailing sentiment in many capitals that Arafat had missed a significant opportunity at the U.S. summit. The PLO chair had reportedly been offered substantial concessions by Barak but had ultimately rejected terms regarding the status of holy sites in Jerusalem as well as the return of Palestinian refugees and their descendants to Israel.)

Although the PLO was not one of the groups demanding the creation of the post of prime minister to share PNA responsibilities with Arafat, Fatah dutifully approved the cabinet installed under new Prime Minister Mahmoud Abbas (the secretary general of the PLO executive committee) in April 2003. Subsequently, differences within Fatah and the PLO seemed to mirror those in the PLC and PNA over the power struggles between Arafat and Abbas and between Arafat and Abbas's successor, Ahmad Quray. PLO reformists pressed for significant power sharing and implementation of genuine anticorruption measures, while Arafat's long-standing backers in the organization supported his demand for retention of the responsibility for peace negotiation and control of Palestinian security forces.

Abbas was elevated to the chair of the PLO executive committee only hours after Arafat's death on November 11, 2004. In addition, Faruk Qaddumi was named chair of the Fatah Central Council with no apparent tumult.

Following a funeral in Cairo (his birthplace), Arafat was buried in Ramallah, where he had lived under virtual Israeli siege for three years. (Israel refused Arafat's request to be buried in Jerusalem.) The Cairo ceremony was attended by many Arab leaders and dignitaries from around the world, while public demonstrations in Ramallah and elsewhere illustrated the deep grief felt by the Palestinian population at the loss of the only leader the PLO had known for 35 years. At the same time, the occasion appeared even sadder to many observers because of their belief that Arafat had missed several opportunities in the past decade to see much of his Palestinian dream accomplished prior to his death. For their part, the United States and Israel focused on the transition to new Palestinian leaders as an opportunity to revive the peace process.

Following Abbas's election as president in January 2005 and Prime Minister Quray's formation of a new cabinet, the two leaders indicated a desire to establish a clear "separation" between the "political" PLO and the "governmental" PNA. Plans were also announced to expand, restructure, and revitalize the PNC. In addition, at midyear Abbas called for negotiations with Hamas and Islamic Jihad toward their possible membership in the PLO. Moreover, Abbas launched talks with the hitherto "rejectionist" PLO factions with the goal of having them participate in a new PNA following the anticipated unilateral withdrawal of Israeli forces from Gaza in August.

Following Hamas's resounding victory in the January 2006 legislative elections, tensions increased within the PLO as Fatah lost its majority in parliament and thus its power base. Among other things, newly elected Fatah members of parliament walked out after Hamas canceled all decisions made by the outgoing PLC. Abbas, though still holding executive authority, was now part of what was described as a "two-headed administration" in a power struggle with the ruling Hamas government. (See Political background and Current issues, above, for subsequent developments.)

Executive Committee: Mahmoud ABBAS (Chair), Zakaria al-AGHA, Yasir AMR, Samir GHOSHEH, Abdallah al-HURANI, Ali ISHAQ, Mahmud ISMAIL, Emile JARJOUI, Taysir KHALID, Mahmoud ODEH, Riyad al-KHUDARY, Abd al-Rahim MALLOUGH, Muhammad Zudi al-NASHASHIBI, Yasir Abed RABBO, Dr. Assad Abd al-RAHMAN, Ghassen al-SHAKAA, Faruk QADDUMI (Secretary General).

Fatah. The term Fatah (Arabic for "opening") is a reverse acronym of *harakat al-tahrir al-watani al-filastini* (Palestine Liberation Movement). Fatah was established mainly by Gulf-based Palestinian exiles in the late 1950s. The group initially adopted a strongly nationalist but ideologically neutral posture, although violent disputes subsequently occurred between traditional (rightist) and leftist factions. While launching its first commando operations against Israel in January 1965, Fatah remained aloof from the PLO until the late 1960s, when divisiveness within the PLO, plus Fatah's staunch (though unsuccessful) defense in March 1968 of the refugee camp in Karameh, Jordan, contributed to the emergence of Yasir Arafat as a leading Palestinian spokesperson. Following Arafat's election as PLO chair in 1969, Fatah became the PLO's core component.

Commando operations in the early 1970s were a primary responsibility of *al-Asifa,* then the formation's military wing. Following expulsion of the *fedayeen* from Jordan, a wave of "external" (i.e., non–Middle Eastern) operations were conducted by "Black September" terrorists, although Fatah never acknowledged any association with such extremist acts as the September 1972 attack against Israeli athletes at the Munich Olympics. By early 1973 the number of "external" incidents had begun to diminish, and during the Lebanese civil war of 1975–1976, Fatah, unlike most other Palestinian organizations, attempted to play a mediatory role.

As the result of a Fatah leadership decision in October 1973 to support the formation of a "national authority" in any part of the West Bank it managed to "liberate," a hard-line faction supported by Syria broke from Fatah under the leadership of Sabry Khalil al-Banna (see Revolutionary Council of Fatah, below). Smaller groups defected after the defeat in Beirut in 1982.

Internal debate in 1985–1986 as to the value of diplomatic compromise was resolved in early 1987 by the adoption of an essentially hard-line posture, a decision apparently considered necessary to ensure continuance of Fatah's preeminence within the PLO. However, Fatah's negotiating posture softened progressively in 1988 as Arafat attempted to implement the PNC's new political program. Thus, Fatah's Fifth Congress, held August 3–9, 1989, in Tunis, Tunisia, strongly supported Arafat's peace efforts, despite growing disappointment over the lack of success in that regard to date. The congress, the first since 1980, also reelected 9 of 10 previous members to an expanded 18-member Central Committee and elected Arafat to the new post of Central Committee Chair.

Salah KHALAF (alias Abu Iyad), generally considered the "number two" leader within Fatah, was assassinated in Tunis in January 1991, the motivation for the attack subsequently remaining unclear. Several other prominent Fatah leaders were also assassinated in 1992, some of the killing being attributed to Fatah's continuing confrontation with hard-line PLO splinters as well as with the Islamic fundamentalist movement.

It was reported that prior to the September 1993 signing of the PLO-Israeli peace settlement, the Fatah Central Committee had endorsed its content by a vote of 12–6. As implementation of the accord proceeded in 1994, some friction was reported between formerly exiled leaders returning to Gaza/Jericho and Fatah representatives who had remained in those regions during Israeli occupation. In part to resolve such conflict, new by-laws were proposed under which Fatah "would operate more like a normal party" with numerous local branches and national committees led by elected chairs. Meanwhile, as would be expected, many of those named to the new Palestinian National Authority (PNA) and other governmental bodies were staunch Fatah supporters. Some discord was reported within Fatah during late 1994 and the first half of 1995 as progress in the gradual self-rule accord for Gaza/Jericho stalled. However, several public opinion polls showed Fatah's support within the occupied territories to be about 50 percent of the population, a figure that was significantly higher than some observers had estimated. Fatah presented 70 candidates (reportedly handpicked by Arafat) in the January 1996 Palestinian legislative elections; about 50 of these "official" Fatah candidates were successful. However, a number of Fatah dissidents ran as independents and secured seats. In concurrent balloting for president of the PNA, Arafat was elected with 87.1 percent of the vote, further cementing Fatah's dominance regarding Palestinian affairs. However, Arafat and Fatah were subsequently subjected to intense legislative scrutiny (surprisingly rigorous in the opinion of many observers) over perceived governmental inefficiency, or worse.

Following the outbreak of the second intifada (or the *al-Aqsa intifida*, a reference to a mosque on Temple Mount in Jerusalem) in 2000 and the collapse of Israeli-Palestinian peace negotiations, "deep dialogue" was reported within Fatah regarding the military and political future for Palestinians. A new guerrilla formation, the *al-Aqsa* Martyrs' Brigade, was reportedly organized as an offshoot of *Tanzim,* the grassroots Fatah militia in the West Bank. *Al-Aqsa* claimed responsibility for a number of attacks against targets within Israel in the first few months of 2002, and the United States placed the group on its list of terrorist organizations. Marwan Barghouti, the reported leader of *Tanzim* and generally considered the second most popular Palestinian leader after Arafat, was arrested by Israeli security forces in April 2002 and charged with terrorism. At about the same time, *al-Aqsa* announced it would not carry out any attacks on civilians in Israel but reserved the right to attack military targets and Jewish settlements in Gaza and the West Bank.

On the political front, a number of Fatah members were among reformists who pressured Arafat in 2002 to combat perceived corruption and mismanagement within the PNA and to appoint a prime minister to share executive authority. Fatah subsequently endorsed the appointments of Mahmoud Abbas and Ahmad Quray to the new prime ministership in March 2003 and September 2003, respectively. Meanwhile *al-Aqsa* claimed responsibility for a number of attacks on Israeli soldiers and suicide bombings in 2002–2004. (To some observers Fatah appeared at best dysfunctional at that point because some of its members were regularly perpetrating attacks, while others in the government and police forces were attempting to establish "security.")

Following Arafat's death in November 2004, Faruk Qaddumi was named to succeed Lim as chair of Fatah's Central Council. Subsequently, Fatah successfully presented Abbas as its presidential candidate in the January 2005 balloting. (Barghouti, sentenced to life in prison in mid-2004 on the terrorism charges, had initially expressed an interest in running for president from jail, observers suggesting he would have had a good chance of success. However, his supporters apparently chose unity over confrontation, and Barghouti withdrew from contention.)

In February 2005 reformist elements in Fatah reportedly blocked efforts by Fatah's old guard to retain dominance in the new Palestinian cabinet. Among other things, the reformists argued that Fatah was losing popular support to Hamas because of perceived ties of many Arafat loyalists to long-standing corruption.

Following what was described as Fatah's "stunning" defeat by Hamas in the January 2006 legislative elections, violent demonstrations in Gaza by hundreds of Fatah supporters demanded the resignation of the Fatah leadership, prompting a trip to the area by President Abbas, who called on Hamas to participate in a national unity government. However, Fatah continued to be at odds with the Hamas-led government, seeking to unify the leadership to include PLO members and pressuring the PNA to endorse a national accord document proposed by Marwan Barghouti and other Palestinians prisoners in Israel. (See Current issues, above, for information on subsequent Fatah-Hamas conflict.)

Fatah held its sixth congress (the first in 20 years and the first to be held in Palestinian-controlled territory) in August 2009 amid reports of severe generational divisions and disagreement regarding negotiations with Israel and Hamas. Abbas was reelected as Fatah's leader by a show of hands among the 2,300 delegates, although a number of reform advocates (including Marwan Barghouti) were elected to the new 18-member Central Council. The congress's final document essentially reconfirmed the movement's previous policy positions, including the right to resistance "in all its forms" to Israeli occupation. For his part, Abbas urged peaceful civil disobedience as the preferred tactic and called for an agreement with Hamas on a new national unity government.

Leaders: Mahmoud ABBAS (Chair); Mohammad GHNEIM; Faruk QADDUMI (Former Chair of Central Council); Ahmad QURAY (Former Prime Minister of the Palestinian National Authority); Marwan BARGHOUTI (imprisoned in Israel), Mohammad DAHLAN, Saeb EREKAT, Muhammed SHAHEEN, Jibril RAJOUB, Naser al-KIDWA (Members of the Central Council); Ahmad HILLIS (Secretary General).

Palestine People's Party (PPP). A Soviet-backed Palestine Communist Party (PCP) was formed in 1982 to encompass Palestinian Communists in the West Bank, Gaza Strip, Lebanon, and Jordan with the approval of parent communist organizations in those areas. Although it had no formal PLO affiliation, the PCP in 1984 joined the Democratic Alliance's campaign to negotiate a settlement among sparring PLO factions. As part of the reunification program approved in April 1987, the PNC officially embraced the PCP, granting it representation on PLO leadership bodies. The PCP, which was technically illegal but generally tolerated in the occupied territories, endorsed the creation of a Palestinian state adjacent to Israel following withdrawal of Israeli troops from occupied territories. In late 1991 the PCP changed its name to the PPP.

In September 1993 the PPP endorsed the PLO-Israeli accord on the condition that substantial "democratic reform" be implemented within the PLO. Although it was subsequently not represented in the PNA formed in 1994, the PPP was described as an "effective ally" of Fatah and PLO chair Arafat in the fledgling Palestinian self-rule process.

The PPP contested the January 1996 Palestinian legislative elections, albeit without success. However, PPP general secretary Bashir al-Barghuthi was named minister of industry in the Palestinian cabinet named in May. The PPP's presidential candidate, Bassam al-Salhi, secured 2.7 percent of the vote in the January 2005 presidential balloting. In 2006 the PPP urged a government of national unity and, along with Fatah and the PFLP, sought to have the PLO recognized as the only legitimate representative of the Palestinian people.

Leaders: Bashir al-BARGHUTHI, Bassam al-SALHI (Secretary General).

Arab Liberation Front (ALF). The ALF has long been closely associated with the Iraqi branch of the Baath party. Its history of terrorist activity included an April 1980 attack on an Israeli kibbutz. Subsequently, there were reports of fighting in Beirut between the ALF and pro-Iranian Shiites. ALF leader Ahmed ABDERRAHIM died in June 1991, and the status of the front's leadership subsequently remained unclear. Although the ALF was reported to have considered withdrawing from the PLO following the September 1993 agreement with Israel, it was apparently persuaded to remain as part of the "loyal opposition." In 1995, however, the front was reported to have split into two factions over the question. In the early 2000s, the ALF reportedly distributed Iraqi money to relatives of suicide bombers.

In 2006 the group refused to participate in legislative elections, saying there could be no democracy under occupation.

Leaders: Mahmoud ISMAEL, Rakad SALIM (Secretary General, jailed in Israel).

Democratic Front for the Liberation of Palestine (DFLP). Established in February 1969 as a splinter from the PFLP (below), the DFLP was known as the Popular Democratic Front for the Liberation of Palestine (PDFLP) until adopting its present name in 1974. A year earlier the front had become the first Palestinian group to call for the establishment of a democratic state—one encompassing both banks of the Jordan—as an intermediate step toward founding a national entity that would include all of historic Palestine. Its ultimate goal, therefore, was the elimination of both Hashemite Jordan and Zionist Israel. The DFLP advocated a form of secular nationalism rooted in Marxist-Leninist doctrine, whereas Fatah initially envisaged a state organized on the basis of coexistent religious communities. Despite their political differences, the DFLP and Fatah tended to agree on most issues after their expulsion from Jordan in 1971. However, unlike Fatah, the DFLP supported the Islamic left in the Lebanese civil war of 1975–1976.

The DFLP, which since 1984 had taken a middle position between pro- and anti-Arafat factions, played a major role in the 1987 PLO reunification. In addition, its close ties with the PFLP, reduced in 1985 when the DFLP opted not to join the PFLP-led Palestine National Salvation Front (PNSF), were reestablished during the unity campaign. The DFLP endorsed the declaration of an independent Palestinian state by the PNC in November 1988, although its leaders interpreted the new PLO political position with less moderation than PLO chair Arafat, declaring they had no intention of halting "armed struggle against the enemy." Subsequently, differences were reported between supporters of longtime DFLP leader Nayif Hawatmeh, who opposed granting any "concessions" to facilitate peace negotiations, and supporters of Yasir Abed Rabbo, a DFLP representative on the PLO Executive Committee, who called for a more "realistic" approach and became one of the leading PLO negotiators attempting to implement the PNC's proposed "two-state" settlement. In early 1990 the DFLP Political Bureau reported it was unable to resolve the internal dispute, which was symptomatic of disagreement among Palestinians as a whole. After his supporters had failed to unseat Hawatmeh at a party congress late in the year, Rabbo formed a breakaway faction in early 1991. Both factions were represented on the new PLO executive committee late in the year, although Hawatmeh continued to criticize Arafat's endorsement of the U.S.-led Middle East peace talks. He also called for formation of a "collective" PLO leadership to reduce dependence on Arafat.

Rabbo's wing subsequently continued to support Arafat, but the main DFLP faction remained dedicated to a "no negotiations" stance. Not surprisingly, Hawatmeh and his followers rejected the September 1993 peace accord with Israel, and the DFLP leader described the May 1994 Cairo Agreement as "not binding on the people of Palestine." Meanwhile, Rabbo was given the culture and arts portfolio in the new PNA, and he was subsequently described as a leader of the recently formed PDU (see below).

In January 1994 the DFLP joined with five PLO groupings (the PFLP, the PLF, the PPSF, the RPCP, and the PNSF), plus Hamas and Islamic Jihad to form a loosely knit coalition known as the Alliance of Palestinian Forces. Earlier, in October 1993, the same groups had reportedly formed a National Islamic Front, the subsequent name change appearing to reflect concern among secularist PLO factions over participation in an "Islamic" organization. In any event, the Alliance of Palestinian Forces was based on the opposition of its constituent groups to the accord negotiated by PLO chair Arafat with Israel in September 1993. The alliance pledged to "confront and resist" the Gaza/Jericho agreement and to pursue an independent Palestinian state and the return of Palestinian refugees to Israel. A 10-member Executive Committee was announced and 20 members of what was expected eventually to be a larger Central Council were appointed. Although policy coordination was envisioned, it was reportedly agreed that each component of the alliance would determine how to proceed with its own "resistance" activities. However, the alliance subsequently collapsed, apparently due to the "incompatibility" of its leftist and Islamic elements.

Several DFLP "lieutenants" were reported in mid-1995 to have relocated from Damascus to Gaza, prompting speculation that the grouping might participate in the proposed election of a Palestinian Council. Although the DFLP ultimately boycotted that balloting, it encouraged its supporters to register as voters in anticipation of municipal elections that were expected to be held following the completion of the proposed Israeli withdrawal from the West Bank. The DFLP attended Palestinian conferences chaired by Arafat in February and August 1997, indicating that it was hoping to have a say in the proposed negotiations with Israel concerning the final status of Palestinian autonomy. However, in early 1998 it was reported that a plenary session of the DFLP in Damascus had agreed to draw up new strategies, apparently out of conviction that the current peace process was moribund.

In August 1999 DFLP leaders met with Arafat for the first time since 1993, and the DFLP resumed participation in the PLO's Central Council later in the year. In October the United States dropped the DFLP from the U.S. list of terrorist organizations. However, the DFLP claimed responsibility for an attack in mid-2001 in Gaza that left three Israeli soldiers dead. The DFLP later blamed Israel for a car bombing in Gaza in February 2002 that killed several DFLP members.

The DFLP joined the PFLP in mid-2004 in denouncing the fledgling unilateral disengagement plan being considered by Israeli prime minister Sharon, and the groups announced that the "armed struggle" would continue. The DFLP participated in the January 2005 presidential elections (its candidate, Taysir Khalid, won 3.4 percent of the vote), but in 2006 the DFLP declined to participate in the PNA following the unilateral withdrawal of Israeli forces from Gaza.

Leaders: Nayif HAWATMEH (Secretary General), Taysir KHALID (2005 presidential candidate).

Popular Front for the Liberation of Palestine (PFLP). The leftist PFLP was established in 1967 by merger of three main groups: an early Palestine Liberation Front, led by Ahmad Jabril; and two small offshoots of the Arab Nationalist Movement—the Youth for Revenge and Georges Habash's Heroes of the Return. However, Jabril and some of his followers quickly split from the PFLP (see PFLP-GC, below). The PFLP favored a comprehensive settlement in the Middle East and resisted the establishment of a West Bank state as an intermediate strategy. Its ultimate goal was the formation of a Palestinian nation founded on scientific socialism, accompanied by the PFLP's own evolution into a revolutionary proletarian party.

After the failure of efforts to achieve PLO unity in 1984, the PFLP played a key role in formation of the anti-Arafat PNSF. It endorsed the 1987 reunification in light of Fatah's increased militancy, but PFLP delegates to the 1988 PNC session voted against the new PLO political program. Habash subsequently announced that his group, the second largest PLO faction, would accept the will of the majority "for the sake of unity." However, he added that he expected the peace initiatives to fail and vowed continued attacks by PFLP fighters against Israeli targets. In early 1990 Habash was described as in "open opposition" to Arafat's acceptance of a U.S. plan for direct talks between Palestinian representatives and Israel, calling instead for increased military confrontation. Habash subsequently continued to criticize Arafat's policies, particularly the PLO leader's concessions in the new Middle East peace talks. The PFLP reportedly suspended its membership in the PLO executive committee in late 1991 to protest the negotiations and was apparently considering the possible establishment of an anti-Arafat coalition with other hard-line groups. On the other hand, as of mid-1992 the PFLP continued to be viewed as part of the "loyal opposition" within the PLO, a clear break with Arafat seeming unlikely because, in part, of Habash's poor health. (The PFLP leader had been the center of an international furor earlier in the year when he went to France for emergency medical treatment, French police detaining him because of alleged PFLP terrorist involvement in the late 1970s, then permitting him to leave the country in the wake of widespread outcries from Arab leaders.)

During its Fifth Congress, held December 12–14, 1992, in Damascus, Syria, the PFLP vowed to return to "radical action" in order to "regain credibility" among Palestinians. Consequently, Habash condemned the peace accord of September 1993, urging an "intensification" of the struggle for an independent state with Jerusalem as its "capital." However, the PFLP remained represented in the new PLO executive committee named in April 1996, although several subsequent shootings of Israeli settlers (which prompted the arrest by Palestinian police of some 30 PFLP members) apparently indicated continued resistance to the current peace process on the part of at least some of the PFLP faithful. By 1997 the PFLP was described in general as interested in participating with Arafat's Fatah and other PLO factions in establishing a consensus position to present in proposed "final status talks" with Israel should the peace process develop that far. Meanwhile, in November 1997 a breakaway group reportedly formed as the Palestinian Popular Forces Party (PPFP) under the leadership of Adnan Abu NAJILAH.

The PFLP subsequently suspended its activity in the PLO's Central Council to protest the lack of progress in negotiations with Israel, although it resumed its role in that body in February 2000. In late April 2000 Habash announced his retirement; he was succeeded by his longtime deputy, Mustafa al-ZIBRI (Abu Ali Mustafa), who had returned to the West Bank in 1999 after 32 years in exile. (Habash died of a heart attack in January 2008.) Al-Zibri was killed by rockets fired at his Ramallah office by an Israeli helicopter in August 2001, thereby becoming the highest-ranking Palestinian leader to die in such an attack. The PFLP subsequently claimed responsibility for four bomb explosions in Jerusalem in September 2001 and the assassination of Israeli tourism minister Rechavam Ze'evi in October. A number of PFLP adherents, including Secretary General Ahmed Saadat, were subsequently arrested by Palestinian security forces, and the PFLP military wing was reportedly "banned" from Palestinian self-rule areas.

The PFLP claimed joint responsibility with Fatah for an attack on Israeli soldiers in February 2003. Several PFLP members were killed in subsequent Israeli reprisals. Although PFLP leaders joined other dissident PLO factions in meeting with Palestinian president Abbas in mid-2005, they reported that "no real coalition" had been formed and complained of ongoing Fatah domination of PLO affairs. By October, the PFLP was holding alliance talks with groups that included the DFLP, PPP, PDU, and the PPSF to register candidates, including eight women, under a so-called alternative list.

In 2006 the group's secretary general, Ahmed Saadat, was arrested by Israeli forces after they stormed a prison in Jericho where he and other Palestinian activists were being held. Saadat faced 19 charges in Israel, including arms dealing and inciting violence. Two PFLP members were sentenced to life imprisonment in early 2008 following their convictions on charges relating to the 2001 Ze'evi assassination. The Israeli prosecutor ruled that there was insufficient evidence against Saadat in regard to the assassination, although Saadat remained in jail on other charges.

Leaders: Ahmed SAADAT (Secretary General, jailed in Israel), Jamil MAJDALAWI, Nasser IZZAT, Mahir al-TAHER, Abdel Rahim MALOUH.

Palestine Liberation Front (PLF). The PLF emerged in 1976 as an Iraqi-backed splinter from the PFLP-GC. In the early 1980s the group itself split into two factions—a Damascus-based group led by Talaat YACOUB, which opposed PLO chair Yasir Arafat, and a Baghdad- and Tunis-based group led by Muhammad ABBAS (Abdul Abbas), who was sentenced in absentia to life imprisonment by Italian courts for his alleged role in masterminding the hijacking of the cruise ship *Achille Lauro* in 1985. Although Arafat had vowed that Abbas would be removed from his seat on the PLO Executive Committee because of the conviction, Abbas was granted "provisional" retention of the position at the 1987 PNC unity meeting, which was supported by both PLF factions.

Reconciliation within the PLF was subsequently achieved, at least nominally: Yacoub was named secretary general, while Abbas accepted a position as his deputy. However, Yacoub died in 1988, leaving control largely in Abbas's hands. In May 1990 the PLF accepted responsibility for a failed attack on Tel Aviv beaches by Palestinian commandos in speedboats, an event that precipitated a breakdown in the U.S.-PLO dialogue because of a lack of subsequent disciplinary action against Abbas. Apparently by mutual agreement, Abbas was not included in the new PLO Executive Committee selected in September 1991.

In March 2004 it was reported that Abbas had died of "natural causes" while in "unexplained U.S. custody in Iraq." New PLF secretary general Umar Shibli said he hoped to reintegrate the PLF into PNA activity. In 2006, the PLF was one of several factions that blamed Fatah and Hamas for increasing conflict in Gaza.

Leader: Umar SHIBLI (Secretary General).

Palestinian Democratic Union (PDU). The PDU (also referenced as FIDA ["sacrifice" in Arabic], which is also a reverse acronym for the group's Arabic name, *al-ittihad al-dimuqrati al-filastini*) was launched in early 1993, not as a challenge to the PLO (then headquartered in Tunis, Tunisia) but, in the words of a spokesperson, as a means of "moving the center of gravity" of the Palestinian opposition to "the occupied territories." Although some of the group's organizers were described as members of the DFLP, the PDU identified itself as nonideological and committed to the Middle East peace process. Operating under the reported leadership of Yasir Abed Rabbo (a longstanding Arafat loyalist), the PDU was one of the few non-Fatah groupings to contest the January 1996 elections to the Palestinian Legislative Council, securing one seat. In 2004 the group called on Hamas and Islamic Jihad to join the Palestinian leadership.

Leaders: Siham al-BARGHUTHI, Yasir Abed RABBO, Zuheira KAMAL, Jamil SALHUT, Saleh RAFAT (Secretary General).

Palestine Popular Struggle Front (PPSF). The PPSF broke from the PFLP while participating in the Lebanese civil war on behalf of the Islamic left. Although the PPSF was represented at the 1988 and 1991 PNC sessions, it denounced the council's political initiatives on both occasions and was not subsequently represented on the PLO Executive Committee. In 1995 it was reported that the PPSF had split into several factions, one of which had expressed support for PLO chair Arafat and the PNA.

Leaders: Anwar Abu MAWAR, Khalid Abd al-MAJID (Secretary General), Samir GHOSHEH.

Islamic Resistance Movement (Hamas). Hamas rose to prominence in 1989 as a voice for the Islamic fundamentalist movement in the occupied territories and as a proponent of heightened conflict with Israeli authorities. It subsequently confronted mainstream PLO elements, particularly Fatah, over leadership of the intifada as well as Palestinian participation in Middle East peace negotiations. Capitalizing on the initial lack of progress in those talks, Hamas scored significant victories in various municipal and professional organization elections in the occupied territories in the first half of 1992. In addition, the movement's military wing—the *Izz al-Din al-Qassam* Brigades—was believed to be involved in fighting with Fatah supporters and to be responsible for the execution of Palestinians suspected of cooperating with the Israeli authorities. Hamas founder Sheikh Ahmed YASSIN, arrested in 1989, was sentenced to life imprisonment by an Israeli court in October 1991 for ordering several such killings of alleged Palestinian "collaborators." Breaking with a long-standing insistence on the annihilation of Israel, Mousa Abu Marzouk, one of the group's leaders (then based in Syria), stated in April 1994 that peace was possible if Israel withdrew from the occupied territories.

On May 14, 1995, Sayid Abu MUSAMEH, a high-ranking Hamas official, was sentenced by an Israeli court to two years' imprisonment for publishing "seditious" articles in a Hamas newspaper, *Al-Watan*. On June 5, Israeli authorities arrested 45 Hamas militants on suspicion of plotting attacks on civilian targets, and on August 1 it took steps to secure the extradition of Marzouk, who had been detained as a suspected terrorist upon entering the United States a week earlier. (The United States in 1997 "expelled" Marzouk to Jordan, from which he again relocated to Syria after the Jordanian government ordered the closure of all Hamas offices in Jordan in late 1999.)

In 1995 and 1996 Hamas was described as deeply divided between those favoring continued violence against Israel and those believing it was time to join the peaceful political process unfolding in the Palestinian self-rule areas. Palestinian leader Yasir Arafat met with Hamas leaders in late 1995 in what was described as a determined effort to win the movement's participation in upcoming Palestinian elections. After apparently wavering on the proposal, however, Hamas announced it would boycott the balloting.

In January 1996 Yahya AYYASH, a Hamas militant known as "The Engineer" who had been blamed by Israeli officials for a number of bomb attacks, was assassinated in the Gaza Strip by a bomb that was widely attributed to Israeli security forces. Subsequently, Hamas militants calling themselves the "Yahya Ayyash Units" claimed responsibility for several suicide bombings in Israel in February and March. Following the blasts, Marzouk (in a interview from his U.S. jail) said that the Hamas political wing had little direct control over the "militias" in the occupied and previously occupied territories. Meanwhile, Arafat outlawed the *al-Qassam* Brigades but continued his political dialogue with Hamas moderates, mindful that the grouping retained significant popular support among Palestinians, built, in part, upon its network of schools, health services, and other social programs.

Sheikh Yassin was released from prison on October 1, 1997, apparently as part of the "price" Israel agreed to pay after the bungled assassination attempt of Hamas militant Khaled Meshal in Jordan the previous month. Yassin went to Jordan for medical treatment and then to his home at Gaza, where he was welcomed as a hero by ecstatic crowds. He subsequently maintained an apparently deliberately vague position on developments regarding Palestinian autonomy, at times reverting to previous fiery rhetoric exhorting holy war against Israeli forces while at other times appearing conciliatory toward Arafat and the PNA, despite the fact that an estimated 80 influential Hamas leaders remained in PNA detention.

According to some reports, Hamas was approached by Arafat about joining the Palestinian cabinet in mid-1998. Although that overture was rejected, Yassin in April 1999 attended a PLO Central Council meeting as an observer, suggesting a growing degree of "accommodation" between the two groups. On the other hand, Palestinian security forces arrested some 90 Hamas activists in Gaza in August.

In December 2000 Hamas warned of a return of a campaign of suicide bombings in view of renewed Palestinian-Israeli violence, and the grouping subsequently claimed responsibility for a number of car bomb and suicide bomb attacks in Israel, Palestinian leader Arafat criticizing Hamas's "aggression." In July 2002 a Hamas political leader in Nablus, Jamal MANSUR, was killed in an explosion attributed by Hamas to Israeli agents, while an *al-Qassam* leader was also assassinated during that month in Gaza. Yassin promised Israel would "pay a price," and Hamas claimed responsibility for several subsequent suicide bombings.

In February 2003 Yassin urged Muslims around the world to attack "Western interests" in the event of a U.S.-led invasion of Iraq. Yassin also rejected the "road map" peace proposal offered by the Middle East Quartet in April and vowed that attacks on Israeli targets would continue.

Abd al-Aziz RANTISI, a prominent Hamas figure, was wounded by an Israeli missile attack in June 2003, but Hamas pledged to pursue its "Holy War." International attention focused even more intently on Hamas when Yassin was killed by Israeli missiles in March 2004. Israeli prime minister Sharon dismissed Yassin as an "arch-terrorist," although the assassination of the blind, wheelchair-bound Hamas leader was viewed with dismay in many areas of the world. Such consternation had little effect on Israeli policy, however, and Rantisi, who had succeeded Yassin as the leader of Hamas, was himself killed in an Israeli attack in April.

Throughout 2005 Hamas slowly grew in popularity to become a formidable rival to Fatah. In successive municipal elections Hamas won the majority of seats in several local councils, including West Bank towns, such as Nablus, that had been Fatah strongholds. Meanwhile Hamas claimed that Israel's withdrawal from the Gaza Strip was the result of Hamas's armed struggle against Israeli occupation. A watershed moment for Hamas came in January 2006 when it won a clear majority of seats in the legislative elections (74 out of 132), capitalizing on Palestinian anger over corruption and poor delivery of services as well as public disillusionment with the overall process of negotiations with Israel (the withdrawal from Gaza notwithstanding). Subsequent to the election and the formation of a Hamas-dominated cabinet, the group faced immense Western pressure to commit itself to a two-state solution and to renounce violence.

Following the collapse of the unity government in mid-2007 in the wake of severe Hamas-Fatah conflict, Ismail Haniyeh insisted that his Hamas-led cabinet remained legitimate, although its de facto control was limited to Gaza. Hamas solidified its dominance in Gaza over the ensuing year as it arrested a number of Fatah leaders and otherwise suppressed opposition. (Many of the Hamas leaders in the West Bank were similarly detained by Fatah.) Egypt attempted to broker a reconciliation between Hamas and Fatah that envisioned the installation of a new joint transitional cabinet, new presidential and legislative elections in 2009, and the inclusion of Hamas and Islamic Jihad in the PLO. However, the talks were suspended indefinitely in November 2008. Meanwhile, the leaders of Hamas reiterated their willingness to "accept" (but not formally recognize) the state of Israel in return for establishment of a Palestinian state based on the 1967 borders and further negotiations regarding the rights of Palestinian refugees.

Following the devastating Israeli offensive in Gaza in December 2008–January 2009 (in which a number of Hamas leaders were killed or arrested), talks between Hamas and Fatah towards a possible national unity government opened in February 2009. However, no progress was achieved, and the relationship between the two groups reportedly remained "venomous." Subsequently, Khalil Mishal, who had been reelected as chair of the Hamas Political Bureau in May, announced that Hamas hoped to be a participant in negotiations toward a peace settlement with Israel, although he rejected official recognition of Israel, offering only a "long-term truce." Meanwhile, several reports in the fall of 2009 focused on the perceived struggle within Hamas between the current leadership and Islamic fundamentalists pushing for stricter adherence to Islamic law in Gaza.

Leaders: Khalil MISHAL (Chair of the Political Bureau, in Damascus), Ismail HANIYEH (Prime Minister of the De Facto Hamas Government in Gaza and Former Prime Minister of the Palestinian Authority), Mahmud al-ZAHAR (Foreign Affairs Minister in the Hamas Cabinet in Gaza and Former Foreign Affairs Minister for the Palestinian Authority), Abdel Aziz DUWAIK (Speaker of the Palestinian Legislative Council, released from Israeli prison in 2009), Ahmed BAHAR (Deputy Speaker of the Palestinian Legislative Council), Khalil al-HAYEH (Member of the Political Bureau), Nizar AWADALLAH (Member of the Political Bureau), Mousa Abu MARZOUK, Abu OBEIDA (Leader of the *Izz al-Din al-Qassam* Brigades).

Palestinian National Initiative (PNI). The PNI is a movement founded by Moustafa BARGHOUTI in 2002 as a democratic "third force" alternative to both the PLO and Hamas. The base of the PNI included secular, left-leaning intellectuals, many of whom, such as Barghouti, had been prominent in the Palestinian nongovernmental organization community. Barghouti finished second in the January 2005 presidential elections, winning 20 percent of the vote. In the January 2006 legislative elections, the PNI won three seats with 2.7 percent of the vote.

Islamic Jihad (*al-Jihad al-Islami*). Islamic Jihad is presumably a Palestinian extension of Egypt's Islamic Jihad which was originally launched as a splinter of Egypt's Muslim Brotherhood (see entry on Egypt). Islamic Jihad has been linked to a number of bomb attacks against Israeli soldiers both in the occupied territories and within Israel. Fathi SHAQAQI, described as the leader of Islamic Jihad was assassinated in Malta in October 1995, reportedly by Israeli secret agents. It was subsequently reported that Ramadan Abdullah Shallah, a "Gaza-born militant" who had helped form Islamic Jihad, had assumed leadership of the grouping. Like Hamas, the other leading "rejectionist" grouping in the occupied and previously occupied territories, Islamic Jihad boycotted the 1996 Palestinian elections. Following the bomb attacks in Israel in early 1996, the Islamic Jihad military wing was one of the groups formally outlawed by Palestinian leader Arafat.

Islamic Jihad boycotted the February 1997 "national dialogue" meeting convened by Arafat but, in what was seen as a potentially significant shift, attended the August unity conference, which was also chaired by the Palestinian president. Nevertheless, leaders of the group were careful to point out that Islamic Jihad had not renounced the use of violence against Israel, and Islamic Jihad claimed responsibility for some of the attacks on Israeli civilians in 2001–2005. Islamic Jihad did not participate in the January 2005 Palestinian presidential elections or the January 2006 legislative elections. Some of the rocket and mortar attacks into Israel in late 2008 and early 2009 were attributed to Islamic Jihad.

Leaders: Ramadan Abdullah SHALLAH (in Damascus), Abdallah al-SHAMI (Spokesperson), Muhammad al-HINDI, Sheikh Bassam SADI.

Popular Front for the Liberation of Palestine–General Command (PFLP-GC). Although the General Command broke from the parent front in late 1967, both organizations fought on the side of the Islamic left in the Lebanese civil war. The PFLP-GC was one of the founding members (along with the PFLP, PLF, PPSF, *al-Saiqa,* and Fatah Uprising) of the Palestine National Salvation Front (PNSF), launched in February 1985 in Damascus in opposition to the policies of PLO chair Arafat. Following the reconciliation of the PFLP and the PLF with other major PLO factions at the 1987 PNC meeting, PFLP leader Georges Habash declared that the PNSF had been dissolved; the remaining "rejectionist" groups continued to allude to the PNSF umbrella, however. The PFLP-GC, headquartered in Damascus, was reported to have influenced the uprisings in the West Bank and Gaza Strip in late 1987 and 1988, having established a clandestine radio station, the Voice of Jerusalem, that attracted numerous listeners throughout the occupied territories. In addition to refusing to participate in the 1988 PNC session, the PFLP-GC pledged to step up its guerrilla attacks against Israel. U.S. and other Western officials reportedly suspected the PFLP-GC of complicity in the December 1988 bombing of a Pan American airliner over Lockerbie, Scotland, although PFLP-GC officials vehemently denied that the group was involved. In early 1990 PFLP-GC leader Ahmad Jabril called upon Arafat to step down as PLO chair on the grounds that "concessions to Israel have achieved nothing."

In May 1991 the PNSF, by then representing only the PFLP-GC, *al-Saiqa,* and Fatah Uprising (the PPSF having attended the 1988 PNC meeting), negotiated a preliminary "unity" agreement of its own with the mainstream PLO under which each PNSF component was to be given representation in the PNC. The proposed settlement was generally perceived as an outgrowth of a desire by Syria, the primary source of support for the PNSF, to normalize relations with the PLO and thereby enhance its influence in projected Middle East peace talks. However, negotiations with Fatah ultimately proved unproductive, yielding a PNSF boycott of the 1991 PNC session.

In September 1993 PFLP-GC leader Jabril warned that Arafat had become an appropriate target for assassination because of the peace settlement with Israel. In mid-1996 the PFLP-GC was described as the primary conduit for the transfer of Syrian weapons to Hezbollah guerrillas in southern Lebanon, where Jabril's son, Jihad JABRIL, was reportedly in charge of a PFLP-GC "training center."

The PFLP-GC declined to join the PFLP in resuming activity in the PLO's Central Council in early 2000. In April 2002 the PFLP-GC claimed responsibility for rocket attacks from Lebanon into the Golan Heights and Israel, and Jihad Jabril was killed in a car bomb attack in Beirut the following month. (His father attributed the attack to Israeli agents.) In mid-2005 Ahmad Jabril announced that the PFLP-GC was not yet ready to commit to participation in the Palestinian government following the planned withdrawal of Israeli forces from Gaza, although he agreed to join negotiations on the matter. In 2006, following Hezbollah's cross-border attack from Lebanon on Israeli soldiers, Israel reportedly targeted a PFLP-GC stronghold in eastern Lebanon.

Leaders: Talal NAJI, Musa AWAD, Ahmad JABRIL (Secretary General).

Al-Saiqa. Established in 1968 under the influence of the Syrian Baath Party, *al-Saiqa* ("Thunderbolt") came into conflict with Fatah as a result of its active support for Syrian intervention during the Lebanese civil war. The group's longtime leader, Zuheir MOHSEN, who served as the PLO's chief of military operations, was assassinated in Paris in July 1979, his successor being a former Syrian air force general. Denouncing the decisions of the November 1988 PNC session, *al-Saiqa* leaders said they would attempt to get the PLO back on its original revolutionary course of "struggle."

In 2006 the group opposed President Abbas's proposed national accord referendum.

Leaders: Issam al-KADE, Mohamed KHALIFAH.

Revolutionary Palestinian Communist Party (RPCP). The existence of the RPCP was first reported in 1988, the party having apparently been formed by former PCP members who wished to support the intifada in the occupied territories but objected to the PCP's endorsement of the "two-state" peace proposal being pursued by the PNC. There has been no recent reference to the RPCP.

Leader: Abdullah AWWAD (General Secretary).

Fatah Uprising. An outgrowth of the 1983 internal PLO fighting in Lebanon, the Uprising is a Fatah splinter group that draws its membership from PLO dissidents who remained in Beirut following the departure of Yasir Arafat. One of the most steadfast of the anti-Arafat formations, it waged a bitter (and largely successful) struggle with mainstream adherents for control of Beirut's refugee camps in May–July 1988. It condemned the PNC declaration of November 1988 as a "catastrophe," and in early 1990 called for attacks on U.S. interests worldwide "because America is completely biased towards the Zionist enemy." The group also called for the assassination of Arafat in the wake of the PLO's September 1993 agreement with Israel.

In 2006 the group reportedly was smuggling arms into Lebanon and was reinforced by forces from Damascus in its clashes with the Lebanese army near the border with Syria.

Leaders: Saed MUSA (Abu MUSA), Muraghah Abu-Fadi HAMMAD (Secretary General).

Revolutionary Council of Fatah. The Revolutionary Council (also known as the Abu Nidal Group) was held responsible for more than 100 terrorist incidents in over 20 countries after it broke away from its parent group in 1974. Targets included Palestinian moderates as well as Israelis and other Jews, and the group's predilection for attacks in public places in Europe and Asia led to allegations of its involvement in the assaults on the Vienna and Rome airports in December 1985. The shadowy organization, which operated under numerous names, was formed by Sabry Khalil al-BANNA, better known as Abu Nidal, one of the first PLO guerrillas to challenge the leadership of Yasir Arafat. Nidal reportedly plotted to have Arafat killed soon after their split, prompting his trial in absentia by the PLO, which issued a death sentence. Somewhat surprisingly, the Revolutionary Council of Fatah sent representatives to the preparatory meeting for the April 1987 PNC session, although they walked out during the first day of the regular session.

After its Syrian offices were closed by President Assad in 1987, the council transferred the bulk of its military operations to Lebanon's Bekaa Valley and Muslim West Beirut, with Abu Nidal and other leaders reportedly moving to Libya. Fierce personal rivalries and disagreements over policy were subsequently reported within the group, apparently prompting Abu Nidal to order the killing of about

150 dissidents in Libya in October 1989. Consequently, several former senior commanders of the organization fled to Algiers and Tunis, where they established an "emergency leadership" faction opposed to the "blind terrorism" still espoused by Abu Nidal's supporters. The internecine fighting subsequently spread to Lebanon, where in June 1990 the dissidents were reported to have routed Nidal's supporters with the aid of fighters from Arafat's Fatah.

In July 1992 Walid KHALID, described as Abu Nidal's top aide, was assassinated in Lebanon, apparently as part of a series of "score settling" killings by rival guerrilla groups. In November 1995 Palestinian police arrested a group of reported council members in connection with an alleged plot against Arafat's life.

In mid-1998 it was reported that an ailing Abu Nidal was being detained in Egypt after having crossed the border from Libya, possibly as the result of a falling out with Libyan leader Muammar al-Qadhafi. However, Egyptian officials denied that report, and U.S. officials subsequently suggested Abu Nidal may have relocated to Iraq. In August 2002 the Iraqi security forces reported that Abu Nidal had committed suicide during their attempt to arrest him in connection with an alleged plot to overthrow the regime of Saddam Hussein. Although uncertain of the circumstances, Western analysts accepted the fact of Abu Nidal's death, noting that it presumably meant the formal end of the Revolutionary Council, for which no activity had been reported since 1996.

Army of Islam. A small faction in Gaza led by prominent clan leader Mumtaz DOGMUSH, the Army of Islam was the focus of a crackdown by Hamas in September 2008. The grouping had earlier claimed responsibility for several kidnappings reportedly conducted in association with the so-called Popular Resistance Committees, led by another branch of the Dogmush clan.

LEGISLATURE

Palestinian Legislative Council. The September 1995 Interim Agreement on the West Bank and the Gaza Strip (the second of the Palestinian "self-rule" accords between Israel and the PLO) provided for the election of a Palestinian Council to exercise legislative and executive authority in those areas of the previously occupied territories to which Palestinian autonomy had been or was about to be extended. The agreement initially established the size of the council at 82 members, but the membership was increased to 88 late in the year by mutual consent of Israeli and Palestinian representatives. Sixteen electoral districts were established in the Gaza Strip, West Bank, and East Jerusalem, and all Palestinians who were at least 18 years of age and had lived in those districts for at least three years were declared eligible to vote.

Nearly 700 candidates, including over 400 independents and some 200 representatives of small parties and political factions, reportedly contested the initial council elections conducted on January 20, 1996. However, balloting was dominated by Yasir Arafat's Fatah faction of the PLO, most other major groupings (including Hamas, Islamic Jihad, the Democratic Front for the Liberation of Palestine, the Popular Front for the Liberation of Palestine, and other PLO factions opposed to the current peace negotiations) having boycotted the election. According to *Middle East International,* Palestinian officials reported that the successful candidates included 50 of the 70 "official" Fatah nominees, 37 independents (including 16 Fatah dissidents), and 1 member of the Palestinian Democratic Union.

The council (by then routinely referenced as the Palestinian Legislative Council, or PLC) convened for the first time on March 7, 1996, in Gaza City. Ahmad Quray was elected speaker by a vote of 57–31 over Haidar Abd al-SHAFI, a critic of Arafat and the recent accords with Israel. In addition to serving as leader of the new council, the speaker was also envisioned as the person who would assume the position of head of the council's executive authority in the event of the incapacitation or death of the person in that position. Regarding such matters, the council proposed a Basic Law of Palestine, which would serve as a "constitution" until the completion of the "final talks" with Israel. The council fell into conflict with Arafat in 1997 over his failure to sign the Basic Law or to pursue other reforms the council had recommended, including the replacement of the current cabinet with a technocrat government better able to deal with the myriad Palestinian economic and development needs. Late in the year the council suspended its sessions to put pressure on the Palestinian leader, who agreed to reorganize the government.

Following the death of Arafat in November 2004 and installation of new Palestinian leadership in early 2005, new PLC elections were scheduled for July 2005. However, they were later postponed as deliberations continued on, among other things, whether a proportional representation system should be established. In preparation for the upcoming elections, the legislative council was expanded from 88 members to 132. Half the seats, or 66, would be elected through proportional representation, while the remaining 66 would be elected from 16 constituencies, whose number of seats would be determined by population. Six seats in the council were also reserved for Christians.

Hamas, running as "Change and Reform," won 74 seats in the January 25, 2006, balloting for the PLC. Fatah finished second with 45 seats. (Although Hamas scored only 3 percentage points higher than Fatah overall, it won 45 of the 66 seats elected on a constituency basis. Meanwhile, Fatah won 28 seats elected by proportional representation and 17 on a constituency basis.) Of the 13 remaining seats, the Popular Front for the Liberation of Palestine—running as the Martyr Abu Ali Mustafa List—won 3 seats; The Alternative—a coalition of the Democratic Front for the Liberation of Palestine, the Palestinian People's Party, and the Palestine Democratic Union—won 2; the Palestinian National Initiative won 2; and Third Way—founded by Hanan Ashrawi and former Palestinian finance minister Salam Fayyad—won 2. Independents won 4 seats. (In October 2009 President Abbas announced that the next election would be held on January 24, 2010, although it was subsequently postponed indefinitely.

Speaker: Abdel Aziz DUWAIK.

CABINET

[as of November 1, 2009]

Prime Minister	Salim Fayyad
Ministers	
Agriculture	Ismail Idiq
Communications and Information Technology	Mashur Mohammed Abu Daqqah
Culture	Siham al-Barghuthi [f]
Economy	Hassan Abu Libdah
Education and Higher Education	Lamis al-Alami [f]
Finance	Salim Fayyad
Foreign Affairs	Riyad al-Malki
Health	Dr. Fathi Abu Maghli
Interior	Said Abu Ali
Jerusalem Affairs	Salim Fayyad
Justice	Ali Khashaan
Labor	Ahmad Majdalani
Local Government	Khalid al-Qawasmi
Minister of State	Majdah Ghunaym
Planning and Development	Ali al-Jarbawi
Prisoner Affairs	Isa Qaraqi
Public Works and Housing	Muhammad Shtayyeh
Religious Affairs and Waqf	Sheikh Mahmud Sidqi al-Habbash
Social Affairs	Majida al-Masri [f]
Tourism and Antiquities	Khouloud Khalil Duaybas [f]
Transport	Sadi al-Kurunz
Women's Affairs	Rubayha Dhiyab [f]

[f] = female

Note: Hamas, which controls the Gaza Strip, operates its own de facto cabinet for that territory under the leadership of Prime Minister Ismail Haniyeh.

INTERGOVERNMENTAL REPRESENTATION

Ambassador to the Permanent Observer Mission of Palestine to the UN: Riyad H. MANSOUR.

INTERGOVERNMENTAL ORGANIZATIONS

AFRICAN UNION (AU)

Established: By charter of the predecessor Organization of African Unity (OAU) adopted May 25, 1963, in Addis Ababa, Ethiopia; Treaty Establishing the African Economic Community (AEC)—the Abuja Treaty—adopted June 3, 1991, by the OAU heads of state and government in Abuja, Nigeria, and entered into force May 12, 1994; Constitutive Act of the African Union (AU) adopted July 11, 2000, by the OAU heads of state and government in Lomé, Togo, and entered into force May 26, 2001. (The OAU remained in existence during a one-year transitional period ending July 8, 2002; the Abuja Treaty remains a cornerstone of the AU.)

Purpose: To "achieve greater unity and solidarity" among African states; to "accelerate the political and socio-economic integration of the continent"; to "promote and defend African common positions"; to "promote peace, security and stability"; to "promote democratic principles and institutions, popular participation and good governance"; to assist in Africa's effort "to play its rightful role in the global economy and in international negotiations"; and to "promote sustainable development at the economic, social and cultural levels."

Headquarters: Addis Ababa, Ethiopia.

Principal Organs: Assembly of Heads of State and Government; Executive Council; Peace and Security Council (15 members); Permanent Representatives Committee; Pan-African Parliament; Economic, Social, and Cultural Council; Commission.

Web site: www.africa-union.org

Chair of the Commission: Jean Ping (Gabon).

Membership (53): Algeria, Angola, Benin, Botswana, Burkina Faso, Burundi, Cameroon, Cape Verde, Central African Republic, Chad, Comoro Islands, Democratic Republic of the Congo, Republic of the Congo, Côte d'Ivoire, Djibouti, Egypt, Equatorial Guinea, Eritrea, Ethiopia, Gabon, Gambia, Ghana, Guinea, Guinea-Bissau, Kenya, Lesotho, Liberia, Libya, Madagascar, Malawi, Mali, Mauritania, Mauritius, Mozambique, Namibia, Niger, Nigeria, Rwanda, Sahrawi Arab Democratic Republic, Sao Tome and Principe, Senegal, Seychelles, Sierra Leone, Somalia, South Africa, Sudan, Swaziland, Tanzania, Togo, Tunisia, Uganda, Zambia, Zimbabwe. (Madagascar, which was suspended by the OAU in June 2002 as a consequence of a disputed change of government, remained under suspension by the AU until reinstated in July 2003.)

Working Languages: Arabic, English, French, Kiswahili, Portuguese, Spanish, and, "if possible," other African languages.

Origin and development. The OAU was the most conspicuous result of the search for unity among the emerging states of Africa, a number of whose representatives participated in the first Conference of Independent African States in April 1958 in Accra, Ghana. However, common action was seriously impaired by the division of the newly independent states into rival blocs, notably the "Casablanca group" led by Ghana and Guinea, which stressed left-wing socialism, radical anti-colonialism, and pan-Africanism; and the more moderate "Monrovia group," which favored a cautiously evolutionary and more subregional approach to African problems. In an attempt to heal this split, a 20-state summit conference of African leaders met May 22–25, 1963, in Addis Ababa at the invitation of Emperor Haile Selassie of Ethiopia and agreed to form the OAU.

Intense controversy erupted in February 1982 over the seating of a delegation from the Sahrawi Arab Democratic Republic (SADR)—the national name adopted by the Polisario Front guerrillas in the Western Sahara. The 19th Assembly of Heads of State was unable to convene in August in Tripoli, Libya, because of Moroccan-led opposition to SADR attendance. An effort was made to reconvene the meeting in November, after the SADR was induced to voluntarily and temporarily withdraw from participation; however, a new boycott resulted from Libya's refusal to admit Chadians representing the Hissein Habré government. The summit was finally convened in June 1983 in Addis Ababa with Libya's boycott still in effect and the SADR seat remaining vacant. Morocco withdrew from the organization following the return of the SADR in October 1984; in support of Morocco, Zaire suspended its membership but returned as a participant at the 1986 summit.

The OAU long functioned as a sounding board for African opinion on such problems as colonialism and racial discrimination. Thus, the Liberation Committee assisted the South West African People's Organization in the fight for Namibian independence and supported the African National Congress and the Pan-Africanist Congress in their struggle for majority rule in South Africa. At the same time, attention also focused on refugee problems, human rights issues, and the continent's deteriorating economic condition, including what the OAU called its "excruciating debt burden."

At the June 1991 meeting in Abuja, Nigeria, the assembly passed the Treaty Establishing the African Economic Community (AEC), which reflected both the OAU's mounting concern that world events were marginalizing Africa and the members' desire to reverse the continent's declining economic prospects. To be implemented in six phases over a 30-year period, the Abuja Treaty (as the AEC founding document is commonly called) sought to remove trade and travel barriers and spur development through economic integration, with the ultimate goal of creating an economic union controlled by a pan-African parliament and marked by a single African currency. A court of justice would also be established. The treaty's first phase called for the strengthening of existing regional economic bodies in anticipation of their eventual merger.

With South Africa registering progress toward a political settlement, the 1993 OAU summit in Cairo, Egypt, focused on the broader question of conflict resolution throughout the continent. In its Cairo Declaration the summit endorsed the proposed creation of an OAU mechanism to help prevent or resolve conflicts both between and within states, although the heads of state declined to authorize the establishment of an OAU peacekeeping force requested by Secretary General Salim Ahmed Salim of Tanzania.

Final arrangements for the Mechanism for Conflict Prevention, Management, and Resolution were completed at a November 1993 meeting of foreign ministers, and the OAU Peace Fund was established to help finance endeavors under the new interventionist mandate. However, concern was expressed during the 1994 summit at Tunis, Tunisia, that OAU efforts in this area were doomed to ineffectiveness unless the organization's financial status was strengthened. The Tunis summit also marked the admission of post-apartheid South Africa as the OAU's 53rd member.

The July 1996 summit in Yaoundé, Cameroon, considered the possibility of sending a peacekeeping mission to Burundi. Much of the international community, led by the United States, continued to call for the implementation of an OAU intervention mechanism using all-African forces. Although the concept had significant support within the OAU as well, the logistical problems and political ramifications associated with intervention in domestic conflicts remained a barrier to effective action.

Civil strife and its aftermath were also among the dominant themes of the OAU's annual summit in June 1997 in Harare, Zimbabwe. On one hand, the body applauded the ouster of Zairean president Mobutu Sese Seko by Laurent Kabila's rebel forces (while urging the latter to fulfill his pledge to hold elections within two years in the newly proclaimed Democratic Republic of the Congo); on the other hand, it gave its approval to the use of force to remove the military junta that seized control of Sierra Leone in late May.

In the second half of 1997, OAU energies were directed at attempting to settle the growing separatist crisis in the Comoro Islands. In August the OAU reported it had convinced the leaders of the independence movements on the Anjouan and Moheli islands to participate in reconciliation talks, and in November it dispatched an eight-member military observation force to the region.

The June 1998 summit in Ouagadougou, Burkina Faso, opened with calls for an end to the fighting between Eritrea and Ethiopia. To help mediate the conflict, summit participants agreed to send a mission to the region from the Mechanism for Conflict Prevention, Management, and Resolution. However, the mission came under criticism from South African president Nelson Mandela, who said it was ineffective. He called instead for the development of alternative means to resolve conflicts on the African continent. Mandela also recommended that the OAU abandon one of its core principles, that of nonintervention, arguing that Africans had a responsibility to protect other Africans living under oppressive regimes.

The 35th OAU summit met July 12–14, 1999, in Algiers, Algeria. Among the notable achievements were passage of the Convention on the Combating and Elimination of Terrorism, which entered into force in December 2002, and an agreement that the OAU would no longer recognize any government that came to power by unconstitutional means. Considerable attention was again devoted to the ongoing conflicts on the continent, particularly involving Ethiopia and Eritrea, the Democratic Republic of the Congo (DRC), and the Comoro Islands.

The Algiers summit also marked the return of Libya's Col. Muammar al-Qadhafi, who had not attended OAU heads of state meetings in more than 20 years and who now proposed that an extraordinary summit be held to consider establishing a "United States of Africa." As a result, on September 8–9, 1999, the heads of state and government reconvened in Sirte, Libya, and agreed to the formation of the African Union as successor to the OAU. Following subsequent negotiations, African leaders signed the Constitutive Act of the AU at the OAU summit on July 10–12, 2000, in Lomé, Togo.

At the OAU's fifth extraordinary summit, held March 1–2, 2001, in Sirte, the OAU declared the AU to be established, although the Constitutive Act did not technically enter into force until May 26, 30 days after ratification by the 36th OAU state. The OAU remained in existence for a one-year transition period, during which technical arrangements were worked out and remaining protocols for various AU organs drafted. On July 9–10, 2002, the heads of state and government, meeting in Durban, South Africa, inaugurated the AU.

Structure. The Assembly of Heads of State and Government, the supreme decision-making organ of the AU (as it was of the OAU), meets twice annually in ordinary session to define overall AU policy and to supervise the activities of the other AU organs. Substantive decisions are made by consensus or, failing that, a two-thirds majority. A simple majority suffices on procedural questions.

The Executive Council, comprising the foreign ministers or other designated representatives of all member states, meets at least twice a year to confer on preparation for meetings of the assembly, the implementation of assembly decisions, the AU budget, and matters of intra-African cooperation and general international policy. Assisting the Executive Council is the Permanent Representatives Committee, made up of ambassadors accredited to the AU. An advisory Economic, Social, and Cultural Council (ECOSOCC) was launched in March 2005.

Among the actions taken by the July 2002 inaugural summit in Durban was adoption of the Protocol Relating to the Establishment of the Peace and Security Council (PSC) of the African Union. On December 26, 2003, Nigeria became the 27th AU state to deposit its instrument of ratification, thereby bringing the protocol into force. Consisting of 15 members elected with due regard for "equitable regional representation and rotation," the PSC includes in its mandate supervision of a planned African Standby Force equipped to intervene in crisis situations (see Activities, below). Pending constitution of the PSC, the Central Organ of the OAU's Mechanism for Conflict Prevention, Management, and Resolution continued to meet.

The Pan-African Parliament, established under a protocol to the AEC treaty, is envisaged as evolving into a directly elected organ with full legislative powers. Initially, however, it comprises five representatives chosen by and from the member states' legislatures and reflecting "the diversity of political opinion in each." The inaugural parliamentary session was held on March 18–20, 2004, in Addis Ababa.

The AU Commission replaced the OAU's Secretariat. The Commission chair, who is elected by the assembly for a four-year term, is assisted by a deputy and eight elected commissioners. The commissioners separately oversee the Peace and Security Directorate; the Political Affairs Department; the Directorate of Infrastructure and Energy; the Social Affairs Directorate; the Department of Trade and Industry; the Rural Economy and Agriculture Directorate; the Department of Economic Affairs; and the Human Resources, Science and Technology Department. Also coming under the purview of the Commission are the Women, Gender, and Development Directorate; the Afro-Arab Cooperation Department; the Pan African Tsetse and Trypanosomiasis Eradication Campaign (PATTEC); the Programming, Budget, Finance, and Accounting Directorate; the Administration Department; the Office of Legal Counsel; the Policy Analysis Support Unit (PASU); and the Protocol Services Unit. In addition, the Commission services the Conference on Security, Stability, Development, and Cooperation in Africa (CSSDCA), which was established by the 2000 OAU summit in Lomé and has a primary role in regional monitoring and evaluation.

The chair of the entire AU, as distinct from the AU Commission, rotates annually, by vote of the Assembly, among the heads of state of member countries.

The Constitutive Act additionally called for the formation of eight specialized technical committees: Rural Economy and Agricultural Matters; Monetary and Financial Affairs; Trade, Customs, and Immigration Matters; Industry, Science, and Technology; Energy, Natural Resources, and the Environment; Transportation, Communication, and Tourism; Health, Labor, and Social Affairs; and Education, Culture, and Human Rights. The assembly may create additional specialized technical committees.

Three new financial institutions are also mentioned in the founding act: the African Central Bank, the African Monetary Fund, and the African Investment Bank. At the eighth Ordinary Session of the Executive Council, held January 16–17, 2006, in Addis Ababa, the first members of the African Court on Human and People's Rights were elected. Creation of this body was proposed in a protocol to the 1981 African Charter on Human and People's Rights. An organ yet to be established as of mid-2008 is the Court of Justice, which was provided for in the Abuja Treaty and supposed to be created out of the African Court on Human and People's Rights.

Related specialized agencies, all previously associated with the OAU, include the African Accounting Council, the African Civil Aviation Commission (AFCAC), the African Telecommunications Union (ATU), the Pan-African Institute of Education for Development, the Pan-African News Agency (PANA), and the Pan-African Postal Union (PAPU).

Activities. Based loosely on the model of the European Union (EU), the AU was envisaged as building on existing elements of the OAU—for example, the AEC and the Mechanism for Conflict Prevention, Management, and Resolution—but with a stronger institutional structure. It was also expected to serve as a means of achieving faster sustainable economic development and integration and as a better vehicle for representing unified African positions in international forums and organizations.

During the 2001–2002 transition year, with many AU procedures yet to be codified and key organs yet to be established, conflicts continued to occupy much of the OAU's attention. In May 2001, for example, the Mechanism for Conflict Prevention, Management, and Resolution participated in a meeting in Togo that addressed ongoing problems in Burundi, Comoro Islands, the DRC, Republic of Congo, and the Mano River region of Guinea, Liberia, and Sierra Leone.

The OAU's 37th and final full summit convened on July 9–11, 2001, in Lusaka, Zambia, at which time Amara Essy of Côte d'Ivoire was elected OAU/AU secretary general. On the economic front, the summit launched the New Africa Initiative (NAI) with the goal of ending poverty, war, and disease in Africa by 2015 through, among other things, better governance, foreign investment in a more open marketplace, and sustainable development. The NAI represented a consolidation of the Millennium Partnership for the African Recovery Program (MAP—proposed in 2000 by the presidents of Algeria, Nigeria, and South Africa) and Senegal's Omega Plan. Having attracted widespread support from the developed world and from the UN Economic Commission for Africa, the plan was renamed the New Partnership for Africa's Development (NEPAD) at an October 23, 2001, OAU meeting in Abuja, where, in the wake of the September 11 attacks against the United States, terrorism was also a principal discussion topic.

In addition to adopting the PSC's founding protocol, the inaugural AU Assembly of Heads of State and Government in Durban stressed the parallel need for a unified defense and security policy. Although the Constitutive Act continued to uphold the OAU-era principle of noninterference in members' internal affairs, it also set forth "the right of the Union to intervene in a Member State pursuant to a decision of the Assembly, in respect of grave circumstances, namely: war crimes, genocide and crimes against humanity." The document also stated, in accordance with a declaration adopted July 2000 in Lomé, that any regime coming to power through unconstitutional means could be suspended from the organization and have sanctions imposed.

The first extraordinary AU summit, meeting February 3, 2003, in Addis Ababa, approved several amendments to the Constitutive Act, making explicit, for example, that the "African Diaspora" should participate in building the organization and that the AU would ensure women's "full and effective participation" in decision making, "particularly in the political, economic and socio-cultural areas." In a significant expansion of the AU's military authority, the session also approved extending the grounds for intervention in a member state to include "a serious threat to legitimate order."

On the same day, summit attendees reconvened as the Seventh Ordinary Session of the Central Organ of the Mechanism for Conflict Prevention, Management, and Resolution at the Heads of State and Government Level. The session examined a half dozen conflict situations on the continent and expressed its "deep concern" regarding the worsening tensions over Iraq. With regard to Burundi, the Central Organ approved the deployment of troops, as agreed to by the disputants in their December 2002 cease-fire agreement. The first military contingent arrived in late April 2003. As of June 1, 2004, the African Mission in Burundi (AMIB) gave way to a UN-sponsored peacekeeping mission, which was approved unanimously by the Security Council in May. At that time, there were about 2,400 AU personnel in Burundi, including troops from Ethiopia, Mozambique, and South Africa, as well as military observers from Burkina Faso, Gabon, Mali, Togo, and Tunisia. The AMIB was generally regarded as a significant contribution to a peace process that concluded with parliamentary and presidential elections in July–August 2005.

The second ordinary session of the assembly met July 10–12, 2003, in Maputo, Mozambique, where a primary focus continued to be organizational matters. In addition to authorizing the Commission and the Executive Council to continue their preparations for getting the PSC operational as soon as possible after completion of the protocol ratification process, the assembly asked the EU to consider funding PSC missions through a Peace Support Operation Facility. The assembly also advanced toward establishment of another major AU organ by approving the Protocol of the Court of Justice of the African Union and sending it on to the individual states for ratification. The assembly did likewise with the Convention on the Prevention and Combating of Corruption and also supported efforts to draft an international code of conduct for counterterrorism. The assembly also decided to hold a 2004 Extraordinary Summit on Employment and Poverty Alleviation in Africa.

The second extraordinary session of the assembly met February 27–28, 2004, in Sirte, at which time it adopted the Common African Defense and Security Policy (CDSP), as called for in the Constitutive Act and the PSC protocol. Asserting that the causes of intrastate conflict, in particular, necessitated a new, multidimensional emphasis on "human security," the CDSP defined defense as encompassing "both the traditional, military, and state-centric notion of the use of the armed forces of the state to protect its national sovereignty and territorial integrity, as well as the less traditional, non-military aspects which relate to the protection of the people's political, cultural, social and economic values and ways of life."

By the end of 2003, the PSC protocol entered into force. One of the first tasks of the PSC was to organize the African Standby Force (ASF), planned to be fully operational by 2010. This force intends to incorporate police and civilian components, as well as military personnel, in keeping with its broad mission, which includes possible preventive deployment, peacekeeping, and post-conflict disarmament and demobilization. The Southern Africa Brigade, the first component of the ASF, was established in August 2007.

With regard to regional economic development, NEPAD has begun moving forward with support not only from the African Regional Economic Communities (RECs), but from the UN, the Group of Eight (G-8), the EU, and other international organizations. In 2002 it adopted a Declaration on Democracy, Political, Economic, and Corporate Governance and developed an African Peer Review Mechanism (APRM). The AU's 2003 Maputo summit described the intent of the APRM to foster the adoption of "policies, standards and practices leading to political stability, high economic growth, sustainable development and accelerated regional and continental economic integration." In its Declaration on the Implementation of NEPAD, the summit acknowledged the importance of integrating NEPAD and its organs into the AU structures and processes. It also called on member states and the RECs to assist NEPAD in implementing programs in such priority areas as agriculture and infrastructure and in developing detailed sectoral action plans in culture, education, environment, health, science and technology, and tourism.

At the January 30–31, 2005, summit in Abuja, the assembly decided to meet twice annually. The African Union Non-Aggression and Common Defense Pact was adopted, and by mid-2007 32 countries had signed, but only seven had ratified and deposited the agreement. (Deposit by 15 countries is required for the pact to go into effect.) The summit participants also agreed to disperse institutions geographically: the African Central Bank to a country in West Africa, the Court of Justice to East Africa, the African Monetary Fund to Central Africa, and the Pan-African Parliament to Southern Africa. (The Pan-African Parliament was since established in Midrand, South Africa.)

The fifth regular summit, held July 4–5, 2005, in Sirte, focused on economic matters. The meeting called for a full cancellation of all African countries' debts and for "the abolition of subsidies that stand as an obstacle to trade"—an issue slated for discussion at the forthcoming G-8 summit in Scotland. The final declaration also called for two permanent and five nonpermanent African seats on the UN Security Council. The AU was only able to offer small contingents for peacekeeping missions to Somalia and the Darfur region of Sudan in 2005, and the forces were generally considered not large enough to be fully effective. However, after the Somali warlords' ouster in mid-2006 by the Union of Islamic Courts and the union's subsequent overthrow by Ethiopia, a small AU peacekeeping force was able to enter Mogadishu in March 2007.

In March 2006 the AU decided, on the PSC's recommendation, to send more than 400 personnel (mostly troops and some police) to the Comoro Islands between April and June to help ensure tranquility during presidential elections and the installation of the new president. A complication to the AU's peacekeeping efforts in Darfur was Sudan's bid at the sixth AU summit (held January 23–24, 2006, in Khartoum, Sudan) to assume the organization's presidency for the year. Amid accusations of genocide over the Sudanese government's role in the Darfur conflict, Sudan withdrew in favor of the Republic of the Congo (Congo-Brazzaville), but with suggestions that it might renew its bid in 2007. The AU's 7,000-strong peacekeeping force in Darfur, funded by the United States and the EU but at odds with the Sudanese government, had little success in stopping the violence. The peacekeeping force continued to operate nonetheless, and after months of negotiation with the government of Sudan, a mid-August 2007 resolution of the UN Security Council called for the establishment of a peacekeeping force of 26,000 under joint UN and AU command, consisting only of troops from Africa. This force was in place by the end of the year.

The July 2–4, 2007, summit, held in Accra, raised once again the issue of a single government for Africa. Most participants favored stronger economic union but had no appetite for complete political union. Col. Qadhafi—who had called for the immediate establishment of a single government, foreign policy, and army for Africa—left the summit early.

Throughout 2007 and 2008, the AU was preoccupied with crises in several member states. The joint UN/AU peacekeeping force (United Nations African Union Mission in Darfur—UNAMID) began operations as scheduled on December 31, 2007, but was seriously undermanned and poorly equipped. The force was also plagued by obstructive tactics of the Sudanese government and occasional attacks by well-armed guerrillas. In August 2008 the UN Security Council extended the force's mandate for another year. Only then did Sudan promise to allow its full deployment. In April 2008 AU and UN mediators were beginning a slow process of reconciling the various Sudanese factions. On June 30 the AU and UN appointed Djibril Yipene Bassole, foreign minister of Burkina Faso, as joint chief mediator. His task was complicated by the efforts of the International Criminal Court to bring Sudanese government officials, including President Omar al-Bashir, to trial for genocide. The AU deprecated these efforts as working against the peace process and specifically asked for the charges against al-Bashir to be dropped.

The AU's response to rebellion in the Comoro Islands of Anjouan was military (see separate article on the Comoro Islands). In late February 2008 the Comoro Islands central government rejected an AU proposal of sanctions against Anjouan, peace talks broke off, and by late March AU troops arrived to assist in an attack to retake Anjouan. This operation, the AU's first offensive military operation, was successful, and in June 2008 Anjouan held an election to replace its deposed president.

The AU peacekeeping force in Somalia, sanctioned by the UN Security Council as the African Union Mission to Somalia (AMISOM), received six-month extensions to its mandate on August 20, 2007; February 20, 2008; and August 20, 2008. Like its counterpart in Darfur the Somalia mission was seriously undermanned and suffered much more from guerrilla attacks. On July 1, 2008, the AU announced that it would continue the difficult mission in its present form through the end of the year but urged the UN to take it over. The AU repeated this request later in the month. On August 19, 2008, the two main Somali factions, the Transitional Federal Government (TFG) of Somalia and the Alliance for the Re-Liberation of Somalia (ARS), signed a peace agreement under AU auspices.

The AU was most successful in mediating a resolution of the disputed December 27, 2007, presidential election in Kenya and its violent aftermath. By the end of February, AU chair Jakaya Kikwete and former UN secretary general Kofi Annan were in talks with all parties involved to ensure that a power-sharing agreement took hold. Their efforts were successful and the AU gained a great amount of prestige. The Kenyan elections caused the AU, through the PSC, to call for a review of electoral procedures throughout Africa and for AU monitors to be invited to all elections at least two months in advance.

The AU's role in the disputed March 2008 Zimbabwe elections received less praise. Jean Ping, the chair of the African Union Commission, first visited Zimbabwe in early May. Further action took the form of electoral monitoring and a vote at the July 1–2, 2008, summit disapproving of Zimbabwean president Mugabe's actions. Mugabe had rushed from his inauguration to attend this meeting, held in Sharm-el-Sheikh, Egypt, and the face-to-face rebuff that Mugabe received was unprecedented in African diplomacy. On July 22, 2008, Mugabe and Morgan Tsvangirai, his rival, signed an agreement to begin negotiations on sharing power, an agreement that the AU welcomed.

In other business at the Sharm-el-Sheikh summit, the organization endorsed the concept of an all-African government, though there was no consensus how that might be achieved. A more detailed plan was to be available for the 2009 summit. Another decision from the meeting was to merge the African Human and Peoples' Rights Court and the African Court of Justice into one body. Notably, the Rights Court, set up ten years previously, had yet to hear a case.

On August 8, 2008, a military coup overthrew the government of Mauritania. AU mediation, coupled with sanctions and with pressure from other international groups, ended in a presidential election in July 2009. This election, certified by the AU as fair, returned the coup leader, General Mohamed Ould ABDELAZIZ, to office as a civilian president.

In September 2008 Chad, long involved in an undeclared war with neighboring Sudan, signed the AU's non-aggression pact. In November the AU brokered restoration of diplomatic relations between the two countries.

The twelfth summit, held January 26–February 3, 2009, in Addis Ababa, was most notable for the Executive Council electing Muammar Qadhafi as chair, succeeding Jakaya Kikwete of Tanzania. Qadhafi i again announced that he wanted to turn the AU into a "United States of Africa," but few other African heads of state seem to have much enthusiasm for a political union. As a compromise, the group commissioned a study to consider restructuring the Commission as an "Authority." Qadhafi had previously stated that multi-party democracy in Africa led to tribalism and bloodshed, and should be replaced by one-party systems such as his own. At the June Ordinary Session of the Executive Committee, held in Sirte, Qadhafi proposed immediate dissolution of all organs of the AU, and creation of the United States of Africa. Commission chair Ping said that more urgent matters needed attention, and they should wait for the reaction of the July 1-3 session of the AU Assembly. The latter meeting adopted the notion of transforming the AU Commission into the African Union Authority. The Authority would have broader powers than the Commission, and would be responsible for creating common defense, diplomacy, and trade policies. Libyan media, perhaps too hopefully, stated that the chair of the Commission would become "Africa's first president." The change would, however, first have to be ratified by all the AU member states.

The twelfth summit also called on the International Criminal Court (ICC) to reconsider indicting Sudanese president Omar al-Bashir on charges of war crimes and crimes against humanity in Darfur. The ICC issued an arrest warrant for Bashir in March 2009. By August 2009 the commander of UNAMID forces in Sudan declared that the war was essentially over, with fighting reduced to banditry and inconsequential local disputes.

On March 17, 2009, a military coup in Madagascar forced out president Marc Ravalomanana, and installed Andry Rajoelina in his place. The AU suspended Madagascar from participation in its activities, and relocated the July summit from Madagascar to Libya. Tensions on the island grew worse throughout the summer, and the AU decided that military intervention, such as its actions in the Comoro islands, was not feasible. In August 2009 the AU assisted in brokering a power-sharing arrangement, but the cabinet named by Rajoelina in early September contained few of his opponents, and opposition parties cried foul.

In May 2009 Zimbabwean prime minister Morgan Tsvangirai urged the AU and the SADC (see article on Zimbabwe) to help make the power-sharing between President Mugabe and himself work (see separate article on Zimbabwe).

AU peacekeeping operations continued in Somalia, though without much success. At the July 2009 Summit Commission chair Ping said that the AU with its 4,000 peacekeepers had essentially abandoned Somalia to its fate. At least 8,000 were needed, he said. The heads of state agreed to look for more troops among the AU member states.

AGENCY FOR THE PROHIBITION OF NUCLEAR WEAPONS IN LATIN AMERICA AND THE CARIBBEAN (OPANAL)

Organismo para la Proscripción de las Armas Nucleares en la América Latina y el Caribe

Established: By Treaty of Tlatelolco (Mexico), signed February 14, 1967. The inaugural meeting of OPANAL's General Conference was held September 2, 1969.

Purpose: To administer the Treaty for the Prohibition of Nuclear Weapons in Latin America and the Caribbean, without prejudice to peaceful uses of atomic energy. Designed to make Latin America and the Caribbean a nuclear-free zone, the treaty prohibits all testing, manufacture, acquisition, installation, and development of nuclear weapons.

Headquarters: Mexico City, Mexico.

Principal Organs: General Conference of Contracting Parties; Council (five members); Good Offices Committee (five members); Committee on Contributions, Administrative, and Budgetary Matters (at least five members); The Ad Hoc Working Group; Secretariat.

Web site: www.opanal.org

Secretary General: None.

Deputy Secretary General: Perla Carvalho (Mexico).

Membership (33): Antigua and Barbuda, Argentina, Bahamas, Barbados, Belize, Bolivia, Brazil, Chile, Colombia, Costa Rica, Cuba, Dominica, Dominican Republic, Ecuador, El Salvador, Grenada, Guatemala, Guyana, Haiti, Honduras, Jamaica, Mexico, Nicaragua, Panama, Paraguay, Peru, St. Kitts and Nevis, St. Lucia, St. Vincent and the Grenadines, Suriname, Trinidad and Tobago, Uruguay, Venezuela.

Working Language: Spanish.

Origin and development. The idea of making Latin America a nuclear-free zone was broached in the early 1960s, with the Cuban missile crisis of October 1962 raising concern that the region could become the scene of a confrontation involving nuclear weapons. In April 1963 the presidents of Bolivia, Brazil, Chile, Ecuador, and Mexico announced they were prepared to sign a multilateral agreement to that end, and the following November their declaration gained the support of the United Nations (UN) General Assembly. During a conference November 23–27, 1965, in Mexico City, a Preparatory Commission on the Denuclearization of Latin America was created, with instructions to prepare a draft treaty. Differences regarding transit, guarantees, boundaries, and safeguards on peaceful nuclear activities were eventually resolved, and the Treaty of Tlatelolco (Mexico) was signed February 14, 1967. The treaty went into force April 25, 1969, after 11 states deposited ratifications, with OPANAL formally launching to supervise compliance with the treaty's obligations and conduct periodic consultations among the signatories.

For many years the adherence of several important states to the treaty was delayed by national ambitions and regional rivalries. Brazil signed and ratified the treaty in the late 1960s while Chile signed in 1967 and ratified in 1974. However, both countries declined to bring the treaty into force, in accord with a provision (Article 28) specifying it would not enter into effect until all regional states adhered to it. (Other signatories waived this provision, permitting the treaty to enter into force for them.) Argentina, which signed the treaty in 1967, delayed both ratification and the waiving of Article 28, citing several technical reservations while insisting Brazil implement the treaty first. Argentina and Brazil also sought assurances regarding peaceful nuclear projects planned or already under way in both countries.

Following the Falklands (Malvinas) dispute in 1982, Argentina charged that Britain violated Protocol II by operating warships equipped with nuclear weapons within the Latin American nuclear-free zone. This contention, along with the claim that the agreement hampered less developed countries' utilization of nuclear technology for peaceful purposes, led Argentina to announce in June 1984 that it did not intend to proceed toward ratification. Subsequently, however, negotiations were conducted with Buenos Aires over the use of nuclear explosions for peaceful purposes, and OPANAL in 1987 urged that an additional protocol be considered to govern such explosions "following the rules of radiological protection accepted by the international community." In a related vein, OPANAL urged members who had not yet done so to complete treaty-mandated negotiations with the International Atomic Energy Agency (IAEA) for the application of IAEA safeguards, including periodic inspections, to their nuclear activities.

An important development for OPANAL was the bilateral accord (endorsed in November 1990 and formally signed in July 1991) in which Argentina and Brazil renounced the manufacture of nuclear weapons and promised to use nuclear activity "exclusively for peaceful ends." Although neither country was known to have produced a nuclear weapon, their capacity to do so had been a long-standing international concern. In December 1991 the two countries also pledged to place all their nuclear sites under full IAEA safeguards. Furthermore, at an extraordinary session in August 1992 the General Conference passed several amendments to the Tlatelolco treaty designed to facilitate the full incorporation of Argentina, Brazil, and Chile. The changes permit special IAEA inspections (if authorized by the OPANAL Council) to investigate "any extraordinary event or circumstance" concerning treaty compliance. Consequently, Argentina and Chile (their former border tension having dissipated under recent bilateral agreements) joined OPANAL on January 18, 1994, Argentina by ratifying the Treaty of Tlatelolco and waiving Article 28, and Chile by waiving Article 28. Brazil also became a full OPANAL member May 30 when it waived Article 28. In February 1995, Argentina deposited its ratification of the treaty on the Non-Proliferation of Nuclear Weapons (see IAEA article), although Brazil did not do so until September 1998.

Continuing the momentum toward complete regional implementation of the Treaty of Tlatelolco, Belize became the 29th OPANAL member by ratifying the treaty and waiving Article 28 in November 1994. In addition, Guyana signed and ratified the treaty in January 1995 while St. Kitts and Nevis and then St. Lucia completed their ratifications in April and June 1995, respectively. Cuba, although it had stated it would withhold adherence until the United States relinquished its military base at Guantánamo, signed the treaty in March 1995. However, Cuba's intentions regarding ratification and the waiving of Article 28 remained unclear, Havana having in the past "stated clearly and repeatedly that once all the countries of Latin America enter the treaty, it will do likewise," according to OPANAL officials. In 2000, while continuing its "full support" for the precepts of the treaty, Cuba noted that its relationship with the United States "limits the possibilities" for ratification in the short term. Nevertheless, Havana ultimately ratified the treaty and waived Article 28 in October 2002, the final regional state to do so.

Structure. The General Conference, the principal political organ of OPANAL, comprises representatives of all member states who attend regular sessions every two years. The conference, which may also hold special sessions, elects the members of the Council. The latter is comprised of five members (currently Argentina, Cuba, Guatemala, Mexico, and Peru) elected for four-year terms, equitable geographic distribution a consideration. The Council functions continuously, its responsibilities including maintenance of a control system for verifying the absence of tests and manufacture of nuclear weapons in Latin America.

The Good Offices Committee has sought the adherence of nonparticipating states, including those toward which the Treaty of Tlatelolco's Additional Protocols are directed (see Activities, below). The Committee on Contributions, Administrative, and Budgetary Matters consists of five members (currently Brazil, Belize, Chile, Guatemala, and Mexico) serving four-year terms, plus other interested members as approved by the General Conference for one-year terms. The secretary general, the chief administrative officer of the agency, is elected by the conference for a maximum of two four-year terms. He may not be a national of the country in which the agency is headquartered.

Activities. OPANAL's primary functions are to ensure the absence of nuclear weapons in Latin America and to encourage peaceful uses of atomic energy. For example, it attempts to prevent the diversion of economic resources into nuclear armament technology and to guard against possible nuclear attacks. In the latter regard, OPANAL has been active in seeking ratifications of Additional Protocols I and II of the treaty. The former requires external powers controlling territories in Latin America (France, Netherlands, United Kingdom, and United States) to respect the region's "denuclearized status" in the event of war in any of those territories. The latter, open to all current or potential nuclear powers in the world, enjoins signatories from using or threatening to use nuclear weapons in the region. Protocol I went into force in August 1992 following France's long-delayed signature, while Protocol II has been ratified by France, China, Russia (as successor to the Soviet Union), the United Kingdom, and the United States.

At the 14th Regular Session of the General Conference, held March 28–30, 1995, in Viña del Mar, Chile, OPANAL Secretary General Enrique Román-Morey asked members to increase their contributions so the agency could undergo a "political revitalization." Among other things, Román-Morey, who was appointed January 1, 1994, called for increased consultation with the signatories of Protocols I and II regarding worldwide nuclear policies and with other organizations, such as the IAEA, regarding the peaceful uses of nuclear energy. OPANAL has also expressed its goal of assuming a leadership role in planning and coordinating regional nuclear energy policy, stressing the need to negotiate an agreement to prevent radioactive pollution, particularly in the marine environment.

At the 16th Regular Session of the General Conference, which convened November 30–December 1, 1999, in Lima, Peru, the attendees echoed recommendations from an Ad Hoc Working Group for the Strengthening of OPANAL, which called for cementing ties to other intergovernmental bodies and identifying further common steps that could be taken toward the prohibition of nuclear weapons. At the same time conferees called for formation of a professional group within OPANAL that would increase the group's analytical capabilities. In May 1998 the council quickly responded to weapons tests by India and then Pakistan by condemning not only those nuclear explosions, but the testing of nuclear weapons anywhere in the world.

Following the appointment of Secretary General Román-Morey as deputy secretary general for the UN's Disarmament Conference and director of the UN Disarmament Office in Geneva, Switzerland, the 15th Special Session of the General Conference on March 15, 2001, unanimously elected Edmundo Vargas Carreño of Chile as his successor, through December 2005. A preceding special session in November 2000 focused primarily on budgetary and administrative matters. Beginning in 1997 the organization undertook unprecedented belt-tightening, which by 2000 reduced the annual budget by a cumulative total of more than 50 percent. At the November meeting the secretary general appealed for those member states in arrears to fulfill their overdue commitments, which at that time amounted to more than $1 million, or more than three times the annual budget. The trend continued at the 2005 meeting, at which a $324,000 budget was approved.

The 17th Regular Session of the General Conference, held November 29–30, 2001, in Panama City, saw Secretary General Vargas call for improved safeguards to prevent terrorists from obtaining nuclear materials. Labeling the September 11 attacks against the United States a wake-up call, Vargas expressed particular concern over inadequate regulations for the transportation of radioactive materials, especially through the Panama Canal and around Cape Horn.

A year later, OPANAL finally achieved its original goal of full regional adherence to the Treaty of Tlatelolco. Addressing the UN General Assembly in September 2002, Cuba's President Castro announced that his government would at long last ratify the treaty despite the United States' continued hostility toward Havana. Accordingly, Cuba deposited its instrument of ratification on October 23, making Latin America the world's first completely nuclear-weapons-free zone

(NWFZ). The 18th Regular Session of the General Conference, held November 5–6, 2003, in Havana saw the OPANAL members sign the Declaration of Havana, which declared the region free of nuclear weapons.

The 19th Regular Session of the General Conference was held November 7–8, 2005, and resulted in the Santiago de Chile Declaration, in which the member states reiterated the organization's commitment to maintaining a nuclear-free zone in Latin America. At this conference, Chile's Edmundo Vargas Carreño was elected by acclamation to a second term, ending in June 2009.

Financial problems dominated an extraordinary meeting held on November 23, 2006. Member nations were urged to catch up and pay their dues. But in February 2007 the organization was able to celebrate 40 years of existence.

On May 14, 2007, the secretary general, Edmundo Vargas Carreño (Chile), sent a letter to the member states in which he described the dire financial plight of the organization and submitted his resignation, effective June 30, 2007. The 20th Regular Session of the General Conference, held November 22, 2007, in Mexico City, designated Perla Carvalho (Mexico) as deputy secretary general from January 1, 2008, to June 30, 2009, with the possibility of extending the mandate until the 21st Regular General Conference in November 2009. Carvalho was charged with creating a work plan that would put the organization back on a sound financial footing and restore it to effectiveness.

Since that time the organization has kept a relatively low profile. In August 2008 UN secretary general Ban Ki-Moon addressed a conference of the organization, congratulating it on its work and noting how much more needed to be done to rid the world of nuclear weapons. A special meeting of the agency's General Conference, held October 19, 2008, in Mexico City, was mostly concerned with financial matters. It adopted a zero-increase budget for fiscal 2009, and adopted various measures to encourage delinquent members to pay their dues. OPANAL continues to be active in supporting nuclear-free zones around the world. It was active at the April 27–28, 2009, meeting celebrating the establishment of such a zone in Mongolia.

ANDEAN COMMUNITY OF NATIONS (CAN)

Comunidad Andina de Naciones

Established: By Agreement of Cartagena (Colombia), dated May 26, 1969 (effective October 16, 1969), as modified by the Protocol of Lima, dated October 30, 1976; Decision 117, dated February 14–17, 1977; the Arequipa (Peru) Protocol, dated April 21, 1978; the Amending Protocol of the Cartagena Agreement (Trujillo Act), dated March 10, 1996; and the Sucre (Bolivia) Protocol, dated June 25, 1997.

Purpose: To promote trade integration, regional development, competitiveness, a common foreign policy, and political and social cooperation among members.

Headquarters: Lima, Peru.

Principal Organs: Presidential Council, Council of Foreign Ministers, Commission, Andean Parliament, Court of Justice, General Secretariat, Andean Development Council, Latin American Reserve Fund.

Web site: www.comunidadandina.org/endex.htm

Secretary General: Freddy Ehlers Zurita (Ecuador).

Membership (4): Bolivia, Colombia, Ecuador, Peru.

Associate Members (5): Argentina, Brazil, Chile, Paraguay, Uruguay.

Observers (2): Mexico, Panama.

Official Language: Spanish.

Origin and development. Officially known until 1997 as the *Junta del Acuerdo de Cartagena* after its founding instrument, the Andean Group (*Grupo Andino*) was also identified as the Andean Pact, Andean Subregional Group, or the Andean Common Market (Ancom). Under an amendment to the original agreement adopted in 1996 with effect from August 1997, the organization is now formally called the Andean Community of Nations (*Comunidad Andina de Naciones*—CAN).

The Andean Group was formed in 1969 by Bolivia, Chile, Colombia, Ecuador, and Peru to speed economic integration among those countries whose economies were more compatible with each other than with the rest of the Latin American states. Venezuela became a full member in 1973, while Mexico has considered itself a "working partner" since 1972.

The controversial Andean Foreign Investment Code (Decision 24), under which foreign-owned enterprises were required to become "mixed companies" of less than 50 percent foreign capital to benefit from the group's tariff concessions, was adopted in 1971. In 1974, Chile introduced a very liberal foreign investment law in contravention of Decision 24; after intense negotiation, it withdrew from membership in 1976 because of its partners' refusal to rescind the code. Panama became an observer in 1979.

In practical terms, the Andean Group failed to achieve most of its major long-term goals as of the early 1980s. As a result, negotiations began in 1982 to modify the original accord to reflect the group's true role more accurately and to ease the terms of Decision 24 to permit greater flow of capital to the region. After numerous disputes and delays over proposed changes, the Quito Protocol, which was signed May 12, 1987, in Quito, Ecuador, and which came into effect May 25, 1988, rescinded nearly all of Decision 24. Members became free to establish their own regulations on foreign investment, with the proviso that major ownership of enterprises be sold to local investors within 30 or 37 years, depending on the country involved. However, despite the group's new philosophy that "foreign investment is better than foreign debt," political and economic turmoil in the individual countries continued to restrain investment except in the petroleum and tourism sectors.

Participants in a 20th anniversary summit, held in May 1989 in Cartagena, acknowledged that serious obstacles to integration remained and that the Quito Protocol had produced little apparent economic benefit for the region. Consequently, a Cartagena Manifesto was issued that called, among other things, for the immediate lifting of intraregional trade barriers and compliance with tariff reduction agreements. The manifesto also endorsed linkage with non-Andean countries and intergovernmental organizations to promote development via "Latin American unity."

During a November 1990 summit in La Paz, Bolivia, the presidents of Bolivia, Colombia, Peru, and Venezuela took much greater strides toward Andean economic integration, agreeing on a preliminary timetable for the elimination of virtually all tariffs on trade among their countries, the institution of a Common External Tariff (CET) system, and the eventual establishment of a full-fledged Latin American common market. A greater sense of urgency was reported at the summit in light of the world trend toward the creation of regional economic blocs, and most of the decisions were quickly formalized in the Caracas Declaration, which was signed by the presidents of the five Andean Pact nations on May 18, 1991, in Caracas, Venezuela.

A number of contentious issues surfaced in December 1991 regarding what had been agreed on the CET. Consequently, the Andean free trade zone was formally launched January 1, 1992, without reference to the external tariff. Moreover, only Colombia and Venezuela immediately eliminated their mutual tariffs as required by the pact, although Bolivia, Ecuador, and Peru indicated a willingness to follow suit later in the year.

The Peruvian presidential coup of April 1992 threw Andean affairs into turmoil. After Venezuela's severance of relations with the Fujimori government in Peru, the group postponed a presidential summit scheduled for June. Bolivia then announced it was applying for membership in the new Southern Cone Common Market (see Mercosur entry) and, with Ecuador indicating it was not yet prepared to enter the free trade zone, the entire Andean integration scheme seemed in jeopardy.

Surprising many observers, however, the Andean Group subsequently rebounded strongly, with tension between Peru and the other members becoming less of an issue as the result of Lima's suspension of its active participation in the organization in August 1992. A subsequent Andean ministerial session appeared to resolve most of the outstanding problems with the proposed CET, with agreement also being reached to eliminate national subsidies and export incentives so as to provide more equitable conditions for producers throughout the region. With integrationist momentum reestablished, Bolivia formally joined the free trade zone in October, and Ecuador began to phase in the graduated intraregional tariff reductions approved by the other group members.

Consequently, attention in 1993 turned to the harmonization of customs procedures and finalization of the CET. Although negotiations again took longer than anticipated, a four-tiered external tariff was finally negotiated in May 1994 and signed on November 26, effective February 1, 1995. About 90 percent of the region's imports were covered by the CET. Exemptions were initially granted to Bolivia and Ecuador in some areas, while Peru, in view of its inactive status, was permitted to postpone implementation of the pact.

The group endorsed the June 1994 Group of Three accord in which Colombia and Venezuela agreed to phase out tariffs with Mexico over the ensuing decade. Support for such negotiations between Andean and non-Andean countries reflected the growing opinion among Andean nations (and most other Latin American countries as well) that regional organizations should be considered building blocks for an eventual free trade zone stretching from Mexico to Argentina. In that regard, formal Andean/Mercosur negotiations were launched in early 1995.

Some Andean representatives cautioned in the mid-1990s that free-market influence alone would not suffice in combating poverty in the region. Using the European Union (EU) as a model, the Andean Parliament urged that additional attention be given on a regional level to social issues, including the lack of adequate housing and the need for better educational and health services. Moreover, some observers called for establishment of supranational political institutions as well, citing the border conflicts between Ecuador and Peru and between Colombia and Venezuela in early 1995 as indicative of disputes that could easily sabotage fledgling Andean economic progress. Poverty and social development issues were reflected in the 2005 agreement to create a Social Humanitarian Fund.

At a summit held March 10, 1996, in Trujillo, Peru, the presidents of the Andean nations signed an Amending Protocol to the Cartagena Agreement, also known as the Trujillo Act, which provided for substantial restructuring of Andean institutions and significant expansion of the purview of the renamed Andean Community of Nations (CAN). Supporters of the proposal expressed the hope that CAN would operate in some respects similarly to the EU, while possibly facilitating creation of a broader Latin American free trade area.

On June 25, 1997, the five countries signed in Quito the Sucre Protocol, amending the Agreement of Cartagena. A new chapter on foreign relations called for establishment of a Common Foreign Policy "on matters of subregional interest," greater integration with other regional economic blocs, and creation of an associate membership category for external countries that concluded free trade treaties with the Andean countries. The Sucre Protocol entered into effect April 14, 2003, with all five CAN members having submitted their instruments of ratification.

Structure. The Trujillo Act formalized the status of a Presidential Council, comprising the presidents of all member states, as the highest CAN authority. (The Andean presidents had met regularly since 1989 to coordinate regional integration efforts.) A new Council of Foreign Ministers was also established, while the Commission, formerly the highest decision-making body, became a subordinate component, although it retained substantial responsibility for CAN coordination. The Commission, comprising a plenipotentiary member from each member state, holds regular sessions three times a year and special meetings as necessary. Also in 1997, a new General Secretariat was inaugurated to succeed the former Board (*Junta*). The secretariat is headed by a secretary general with expanded responsibilities for oversight of day-to-day CAN activities, as well as policy coordination with other organizations. The Andean Parliament, its members selected by national legislatures, was established in 1979 to make recommendations on regional policies. (The Trujillo Act called for direct election of members by 2002, but only Venezuela achieved that goal.) To address disputes among member states regarding compliance with the Cartagena Agreement, the Andean Court of Justice was established in July 1983 in Quito, although the tribunal's role was later expanded to include adjudication of disputes between members.

Over the years the Andean grouping has sponsored several associated institutions, collectively called the Andean Integration System (*Sistema Andino de Integración*—SAI). The Andean Development Corporation (*Corporación Andina de Fomento*—CAF) was launched in 1970, and in 1978 the group established the Andean Reserve Fund (FAR), which was subsequently restructured as the Latin American Reserve Fund (FLAR). Other SAI organizations include the Simón Bolívar Andean University, founded in 1985 in Sucre, Bolivia; the Andean Labor Advisory Council, which met for the first time in 1998 in Caracas; and the Andean Business Advisory Council, based in Lima since its formation in 1998.

Activities. The reconciliation with Peru permitted formal launching of the new CAN institutions, with well-known Venezuelan diplomat Sebastián Alegrett taking office August 1, 1997, as the first CAN secretary general. Alegrett immediately announced that priority would be given to discussions with Mercosur in the hope that a free trade pact with that grouping could be reached by the end of the year. A CAN-Mercosur accord would cover a population of nearly 300 million and some 13 percent of total GDP in the Americas. Promising CAN discussions were also reported with the EU, while in March 1998 CAN participated as a bloc during a preparatory meeting on how to structure negotiations for a Free Trade Area of the Americas (FTAA).

CAN and Mercosur continued their negotiations in 1998, signing the Framework Agreement for the Creation of the Free Trade Area on April 16. The accord established a schedule for further discussion leading up to a proposed free trade agreement between the two organizations by January 1, 2000. However, those talks repeatedly bogged down. In late 1998 Venezuelan president-elect Hugo Chávez warned that if the talks did not progress, Venezuela would join Mercosur but continue to be a member of the Andean Community, while in early 1999 Brazil began negotiating a trade preference pact with Colombia, Ecuador, Peru, and Venezuela on its own. A two-year Partial Economic Complementation Accord with Brazil was initiated in August, and in the same month the CAN secretary general conferred with members of the Caribbean Community (Caricom) on closer ties. In August 2000 a Complementation Accord with Argentina entered into effect.

The 12th CAN summit on June 9–10, 2000, in Lima took several significant steps toward greater integration. In addition to reaffirming the 2005 start date for the common market, an effort that has since been subsumed into a closer association with Mercosur, the member presidents encouraged ongoing efforts to develop a Common Foreign Policy and approved guidelines for macroeconomic policy coordination. During the summit the members' foreign ministers signed a protocol, the Andean Community Commitment to Democracy, which would enter into force following deposit of national ratifications. The document committed the CAN members to democracy, the rule of law, and human rights, while also reaffirming principles of national sovereignty and nonintervention in internal affairs.

On September 1, 2000, at a meeting of South American presidents in Brasília, Brazil, the participants agreed to relaunch the CAN/Mercosur talks and called for introduction of a free trade area in the "briefest term possible." The 2001 annual CAN summit, held June 24–26 in Valencia, Venezuela, reaffirmed the members' resolve to move forward on the Mercosur negotiations and also approved an Andean Cooperation Plan for the Control of Illegal Drugs and Related Offenses. CAN subsequently scheduled an extraordinary presidential summit for January 30, 2002, in Santa Cruz de la Sierra, Bolivia, to move ahead with the free trade area; the introduction of a customs union, preliminary to initiation of the CAN common market; a Common Agricultural Policy; macroeconomic harmonization; and the Common Foreign Policy. In addition, the summit endorsed the introduction of a new CET by late 2003. In September 2002, Guillermo Fernández de Soto, former foreign minister of Colombia, assumed the post of secretary general, succeeding Sebastián Alegrett, who died in early August. On January 17, 2007, Ecuadorian author and television journalist Freddy Ehlers, the present secretary general, took office.

The 14th Andean Presidential Council, held June 27–28, 2003, in Quirama, Colombia, recognized the need to prepare for a "new stage" in the integration process. Development of Common Foreign Policy guidelines were also given priority, as were continued negotiations on a new Political Dialog and Cooperation Agreement with the EU, leading to an eventual Association Agreement. The Presidential Council additionally called for strengthening ties to several other countries, including China, Russia, Japan, Canada, the United States, and Cuba. Furthermore, the Commission was encouraged to work toward completing the "finishing touches" on the CAN-Mercosur Free Trade Agreement by the end of 2003. An Economic Complementation Agreement with Mercosur was signed December 6, 2002.

On December 16, 2003, CAN and Mercosur signed the much-anticipated free trade accord in Montevideo, Uruguay, during a Mercosur summit that also saw Peru join Bolivia and Chile as associate members of the Southern Cone group. Although many details remained subject to further negotiations, the agreement called for ending all tariff barriers within 15 years. In 2004, Ecuador, Colombia, and Venezuela were admitted to Mercosur as associate members, and CAN admitted all the members of Mercosur as associate members with Decision 613 on July 7, 2005. Venezuela started the process of becoming a full member of Mercosur in late 2005.

At a May 2003 summit in Guadalajara, Mexico, CAN entered into an agreement with the EU to launch an integration process that would aid in the creation of a free trade agreement between the two organizations. This agreement was codified by CAN in Decision 595 on July 11, 2004. The talks reflect a process started with the Joint Declaration on the Political Dialog signed June 30, 1996, in Rome. Meetings have continued, including a May 2005 ministerial-level meeting in Luxembourg and a May 2006 meeting in Vienna.

The biggest challenge currently facing CAN is the political fissure created by the negotiation of free trade agreements with the United States by Colombia, Ecuador, and Peru, while Bolivia and Venezuela oppose such agreements. On April 3, 2006, Bolivian president Evo Morales called an emergency meeting of CAN "in an attempt to save the bloc," but no movement to hold such a meeting resulted from the call. On April 19, 2006, Venezuelan President Hugo Chávez announced that his country would leave CAN, declaring the organization "fatally wounded" as a result of the free trade agreements signed by Colombia, Ecuador, and Peru with the United States. On April 29, 2006, Chávez signed a three-way trade pact with Bolivia and Cuba designed to combat U.S. influence in the hemisphere.

The bloc's reaction to this discord has been to try to preserve relations with Venezuela as much as possible. In November 2006 Chile was invited to re-enter the Andean bloc, and its newly elected president, Michelle Bachelet, enthusiastically accepted. In mid-2008 Chile was listed as an associate member. The years 2006 and 2007 also saw intensive negotiations for closer relations with the EU, and in April 2007 the EU announced a large aid package for the region, to be allocated between 2007 and 2013. In May 2007 Spain separately endorsed CAN's closer ties with Europe, and announced its own plans for environmental assistance.

Evo Morales assumed presidency of the bloc in June 2006. His subsequent pronouncements were critical of regional organizations such as CAN and Mercosur, saying that while they favored business interests, they did too little to help the social advancement of their populations. In September 2007 Venezuela accepted Colombia's invitation to rejoin CAN. As of mid-2009, negotiations were ongoing.

2007 and the first half of 2008 were dominated by several critical matters: the developing relationship with the EU; the desire of some CAN members for bilateral deals with the EU; internal strife within the bloc; and the formal creation of the Union of South American Nations (UNASUR).

Talks about a free trade agreement (FTA) between CAN and the EU began in July 2007, were seriously disrupted by a diplomatic crisis between Columbia and Ecuador in April 2008, but came to a partial agreement in May 2008, with a fuller agreement expected by 2009. Meanwhile, Peru and Colombia made moves to conclude bilateral FTAs with the EU, since Bolivia and Ecuador seemed to have little enthusiasm for the enterprise. Statements to this effect began in June 2007, and took on a much more definite form in November, when the Bolivian government expressed doubt over CAN's future, because Peru, CAN's most prosperous member, was moving closer to a trade deal with the U.S. Bolivia and Ecuador were blocking this deal, by refusing Peru the right to amend its intellectual property laws as the U.S. treaty required.

The EU's position has always been to conclude FTAs with trade blocs, not with individual countries. In May 2008 Peru stated that it had no intention of leaving CAN, but at the same time signed FTAs with Canada and Singapore.

In March 2008 Colombian troops crossed the border into Ecuador to raid a camp of the Colombian rebel group FARC. Reciprocal withdrawals of ambassadors followed. There were accusations that computer hard disks seized from the rebels by the Ecuadorian raiders pointed to Venezuelan complicity with FARC, though Venezuela strenuously denied that. Interested neighbors, notably Brazil's president Luiz Inacio Lula da Silva, called for a peaceful solution and a return to normal relations.

May 2008 also saw the formal creation of the Union of South American Nations (UNASUR), when Ecuador was the last country to sign the treaty. UNASUR encompasses both the Andean Community and MERCOSUR, and has the potential of becoming a very influential continent-wide grouping. Discussions about a common currency are under way, as well as a common military policy. This last could pose problems for U.S. interests, if ever realized.

In June 2008 Panama applied to change its status from observer to associate member. Meanwhile, the trade negotiations between CAN and the EU continued to be difficult. There was sentiment within CAN to abort the talks because of the EU's new immigration law, which allowed for detaining illegal immigrants for up to 18 months before deporting them. In early July the EU canceled an upcoming round of talks, citing the lack of a united position on the part of CAN. However in late July the EU allocated nearly 10 million euros for various development projects in the region.

In August 2008 CAN allowed member states to create their own intellectual property (IP) laws. Peru had lobbied for this, allowing the tightening of its IP rules as a prerequisite to enacting the free-trade deal with the U.S., while Ecuador and Bolivia were now, as often previously, at odds with Peru's free-trade stance. Also in August Bolivia called for the dismissal of secretary general Ehlers over the IP question, but affirmed its intention to remain in CAN on receiving no support for Ehlers' removal.

In November 2008 CAN suspended trade talks (which had recently been scheduled to restart) with the EU. The EU responded by announcing that they would negotiate only with Colombia and Peru, bypassing the more left-leaning governments of Bolivia and Ecuador. Differences within CAN continued to widen, and the organization cancelled yet another meeting with EU representatives in May 2009. That month secretary general Ehlers called on CAN members to rededicate themselves to the unity of the group. He promised a "new vision," to be rolled out at the June annual meeting.

ARAB LEAGUE

al-Jami'a al-'Arabiyah

Official Name: League of Arab States.

Established: By treaty signed March 22, 1945, in Cairo, Egypt.

Purpose: To strengthen relations among member states by coordinating policies in political, cultural, economic, social, and related affairs; to mediate disputes between members or between members and third parties.

Headquarters: Cairo, Egypt. (In 1979 the league transferred its headquarters from Cairo to Tunis, Tunisia, because of Egypt's peace treaty with Israel. In early 1990 members agreed unanimously to return the headquarters to Cairo, with the relocation formally completed January 1, 1991.)

Principal Organs: Council of the League of Arab States (all members), Economic and Social Council (all adherents to the 1950 Collective Security Treaty), Joint Defense Council (all adherents to the 1950 Collective Security Treaty), Permanent Committees (all members), Arab Summit Conferences, General Secretariat.

Web site: www.arableagueonline.org (This site is in Arabic; English content said to be under construction, but not progressing.) Although not the official site of the league, www.arabji.com/ArabGovt/ArabLeague.htm provides some useful basic information in English but has not been maintained for several years.

Secretary General: Amr Mahmoud Moussa (Egypt).

Membership (22): Algeria, Bahrain, Comoro Islands, Djibouti, Egypt, Iraq, Jordan, Kuwait, Lebanon, Libya, Mauritania, Morocco, Oman, Palestine, Qatar, Saudi Arabia, Somalia, Sudan, Syria, Tunisia, United Arab Emirates, Yemen.

Official Language: Arabic.

Origin and development. A long-standing project that reached fruition late in World War II, the league was founded primarily on Egyptian initiative following a promise of British support for any Arab organization that commanded general endorsement. In its earlier years the organization focused mainly on economic, cultural, and social cooperation, but in 1950 a Convention on Joint Defense and Economic Cooperation was concluded that obligated the members in case of attack "immediately to take, individually and collectively, all steps available, including the use of armed force, to repel the aggression and restore security and peace." In 1976 the Palestine Liberation Organization (PLO), which had participated as an observer at all league conferences since September 1964, was admitted to full membership. Egypt's participation was suspended from April 1979 to May 1989 because of its peace agreement with Israel.

Structure. The principal political organ of the league is the Council of the League of Arab States, which meets in regular session twice a year, normally at the foreign ministers level. Each member has one vote in the council; decisions usually bind only those states that accept them, although a two-thirds majority vote on financial and administrative matters binds all members. The council's main functions are to supervise the execution of agreements between members, to mediate disputes, and to coordinate defense in the event of attack. There are numerous committees and other bodies attached to the council, including permanent committees dealing with finance and administration, legal affairs, and information.

The council has also established an Administrative Court, an Investment Arbitration Board, and a Higher Auditing Board. Additional ministerial councils, attended by relevant ministers or their representatives, are held in a dozen areas including transport, justice, health, telecommunications, and environmental affairs.

Three additional bodies were established by the 1950 convention: a Joint Defense Council to function in matters of collective security and to coordinate military resources; a Permanent Military Commission, comprised of representatives of the general staffs, to draw up plans for joint defense; and an Economic Council, comprised of the ministers of economic affairs, to coordinate Arab economic development. The last was restructured as an Economic and Social Council in 1977. An Arab Unified Military Command, charged with the integration of strategy for the liberation of Palestine, was formed in 1964.

The General Secretariat is responsible for internal administration and the execution of council decisions. It also administers several agencies, including the Bureau for Boycotting Israel (headquartered in Damascus, Syria).

Membership in the league generally carries with it membership in an array of specialized agencies, including the Arab Bank for Economic Development in Africa (BADEA) and the Arab Monetary Fund (AMF), as well as a variety of other bodies dealing with economic, social, and technical matters.

Many Arab Summit Conferences have been held since the first one met in 1964. Summit resolutions give direction to the work of the council and other league organs, although the organization's charter did not provide a framework for convening summits.

Activities. After many years of preoccupation with Arab-Israeli issues, the league's attention in 1987 turned to the Iraq-Iran conflict as Arab moderates sought a united front against Iran and the potential spread of militant Islamic fundamentalism. An extraordinary summit conference held November 8–11 in Amman, Jordan, condemned "the Iranian regime's intransigence, provocations, and threats to the Arab Gulf States" and called for international "pressure" to encourage Iran to accept a UN-sponsored cease-fire.

Palestinian issues quickly returned to the forefront of the league's agenda in early 1988 because of the uprising (intifada) in the Gaza Strip and West Bank. A June summit affirmed "moral, political, and diplomatic" support for the intifada while most of the members made individual financial pledges to the PLO. The major development at the May summit in Casablanca, Morocco, was the readmission of Egypt, whose president Husni Mubarak urged the other attendees to stop "wasting time and opportunities" for formulating a "vision" for peace in the Middle East.

A special summit in late May 1990 in Baghdad, Iraq, although convened at the PLO's urging to discuss the mass immigration of Soviet Jews to Israel, focused primarily on U.S. policy. In condemning Washington as bearing a "fundamental responsibility" for Israel's "aggression, terrorism, and expansionism," the league reflected growing frustration among Arabs over the lack of progress in peace negotiations.

The prospect for effective cooperation was severely compromised by Iraq's takeover of Kuwait on August 2, 1990, which split the league into two deeply divided blocs. On August 10, the majority (comprising Bahrain, Djibouti, Egypt, Kuwait, Lebanon, Morocco, Oman, Qatar, Somalia, Syria, Saudi Arabia, and the United Arab Emirates) voted to send a pan-Arab force to guard Saudi Arabia against possible Iraqi attack; several members (most notably Egypt and Syria) ultimately contributed troops to the U.S.-led liberation of Kuwait in early 1991. The minority included members overtly sympathetic to Baghdad (such as Jordan, the PLO, and Sudan) and those that, while critical of the Iraqi invasion, were adamantly opposed to U.S. military involvement.

Although both sides continued to promote an "Arab solution" throughout the Persian Gulf crisis, the schism precluded the league from playing any meaningful negotiating role.

Following the coalition victory over Iraqi forces and the restoration of the Kuwaiti government in early 1991, it appeared that Egypt, the leading Arab coalition member, had regained league dominance, although "intense animosities" reportedly remained from the Persian Gulf crisis. Evidence of Cairo's standing included the May appointment by the Arab League Council of Egypt's retiring foreign minister, Ahmad Ismat Abd al-Magid, as the next secretary general.

In September 1993 the Arab League's foreign ministers gave quick approval to the recently negotiated peace accord between Israel and the PLO. However, the league subsequently announced it would not lift the Arab economic boycott against Israel until Israeli troops withdrew from all the occupied territories. The ban, adopted at the creation of the Jewish state in 1948, precluded any direct commercial contact between Arab countries and Israel. In 1951 a secondary boycott was declared against any companies in the world that conducted business with Israel, followed by a tertiary boycott against any companies dealing with those companies already blacklisted. However, the secondary and tertiary boycotts have been widely ignored recently, and in September 1994 the members of the Gulf Cooperation Council (Bahrain, Kuwait, Oman, Qatar, Saudi Arabia, and United Arab Emirates) announced their formal abandonment.

In the wake of the victory of the right-wing Likud party of Benjamin Netanyahu in the May 1996 Israeli elections, the league held its first full summit since 1990 on June 21–23 in Cairo to address, among other things, Netanyahu's perceived retreat from previous Israeli positions regarding the Palestinian self-rule process. The summit reaffirmed its positions supporting full Israeli withdrawal from the occupied territories, Palestinian self-determination, and an end to settlement building in the West Bank. However, divisions among members on the issue were readily apparent, with moderate states such as Jordan and Egypt leading successful efforts to dilute stronger language proposed by Syria. In other activity, the summit again criticized Iraq, which was not invited to the session, for its lack of cooperation with the UN and issued a statement of support for Bahrain and the United Arab Emirates in their disputes with Iran.

The summit's final communiqué also called for greater Arab solidarity and a strengthening of the organization's institutions, although skeptics noted a "hollow ring" to the language. The prospects for institutional reform were also constrained by financial difficulties: only four members (Egypt, Jordan, Saudi Arabia, and Syria) had paid their full dues, while the remaining members were a combined $80 million in arrears. As a consequence, the league was forced to close several foreign offices and reportedly had difficulty meeting its payroll at times.

In November 1997, despite the league's financial troubles, 17 members agreed to proceed with the establishment of the Arab Free Trade Zone in 1998, with the goal of cutting customs duties by 10 percent a year until their elimination at the end of 2007. In other activity during the year, the Arab League foreign ministers, meeting in March in Cairo, recommended that members reactivate the economic boycott against Israel and cease all activity geared toward normalizing relations with that country, given the stalled peace process.

In late 1997 and early 1998 the league expressed concern over rising tension between Iraq and Western capitals. It reportedly encouraged Baghdad to adopt a more conciliatory posture while at the same time warning against "unilateral" U.S. action. An emergency summit convened in early January 1999 to address Iraq's request that the league condemn the recent U.S.-UK air assaults. However, the final statement from the summit was mild in tone.

The league began to focus on antiterrorism. An accord was signed in April 1998 by the interior and justice ministers of the league's members, who pledged to exchange evidence in terrorist investigations and extradite suspects. The Arab states also agreed not to harbor or assist groups responsible for terrorist acts against Arab nations, although an exemption was granted regarding "national liberation" groups.

In March 2000 the council addressed Israel's announcement of a pending pullout from its "security zone" in southern Lebanon by warning that renewed Palestinian attacks could result unless Israel provided for the repatriation of Palestinians from refugee camps in the region. The league basically adopted what had been the Syrian position on the matter, rejecting the pullout in the absence of a comprehensive peace agreement—clearly, an effort by Syria to interweave the issue of an Israeli pullout from the occupied Golan Heights.

Although the league subsequently cosponsored peace talks in Djibouti on the Somali conflict, from late September 2000 league concerns were largely dominated by the renewal of the Palestinian intifada, which quickly led to the first emergency summit in four years on October 20–21 in Cairo. As in the past, however, league reaction was far from unified. Libya's Colonel Qadhafi pointedly avoided the session altogether, anticipating, from his hard-line perspective, an inadequate response to the renewed hostilities. Iraq's representative called for holy war (jihad), while the majority endorsed a halt to further diplomatic normalization with Israel. (At the time, Mauritania, Morocco, Oman, Qatar, and Tunisia had representative offices in Israel.) The summit communiqué continued to call for a renewal of the peace process, while the participants agreed to set up a $1 billion fund to aid Palestinians affected by the uprising and Israeli counteractions.

The Amman summit of March 27–28, 2001, marked the first regular summit since 1990, with Iraq in attendance as a full participant. The intifada remained a principal subject, although no significant new initiatives resulted. Presummit speculation centered largely on efforts to repair the rift between Iraq and Kuwait, but only marginal progress toward that end occurred. The league ended up calling once again for an end to the sanctions against Iraq but also for Baghdad to work out its differences with the UN over inspections and related issues. In other matters, the summit advocated accelerating the movement toward free trade as well as forming a customs union and promoting cooperative development in areas such as transport, telecommunications, and information technology. Two months later on May 16, Amr Mahmoud Moussa, previously Egypt's foreign minister, began his tenure as the league's new secretary general.

At the 14th Arab League summit, held March 27–28, 2002, in Beirut, Lebanon, attention focused on Iraqi-Kuwaiti relations and on a "land-for-peace" plan offered by Saudi Arabia's Crown Prince Abdullah to settle the Arab-Israeli conflict. Although Iraq and Kuwait appeared ready to resolve their differences, positive international expectations for the Saudi plan were undercut even before the summit got under way. In the context of continuing Israeli-Palestinian violence, PLO leader Yasir Arafat decided not to attend the summit for fear the government of Israeli Prime Minister Sharon would not permit his return. Egypt's President Mubarak and Jordan's King Abdullah also chose not to attend, while several of the smaller Persian Gulf states sent less senior delegations. In addition, on the summit's opening day the Palestinian delegation withdrew over Lebanon's refusal to permit a satellite address by Arafat. As a consequence of these developments, Crown Prince Abdullah's plan failed to register as great an impact as had been anticipated, although it was endorsed by the attendees.

The Saudi plan called for normalization of relations with Israel and affirmed that state's right to security. In return, Israel was expected to withdraw from all occupied territories and recognize a Palestinian state with East Jerusalem as its capital. The summit's concluding Beirut Declaration both called for a "just solution" to the Palestinian refugee problem and rejected "all forms of Palestinian repatriation which conflict with the special circumstances of the Arab host countries."

In October 2002 Libya's Qadhafi announced he would pull his country from the organization because of its demonstrated inability to deal effectively not only with the Palestinian situation, but also the looming crisis involving Iraq and the United States. A March 1, 2003, summit in Sharm el Sheikh, Egypt, to discuss the Iraq crisis left the league divided after a heated exchange between Qadhafi, who attacked Saudi Arabia for permitting U.S. forces on its soil, and Crown Prince Abdullah. The summit concluded with condemnation of any "aggression" against Iraq but also called for Baghdad's compliance with UN weapons inspections. As late as April 2003, Libya maintained its intention to withdraw from the league, but in May, apparently at the urging of the Egyptian president, Qadhafi reversed himself.

With regard to the "road map" for peace in the Middle East that was formally introduced April 30, 2003, by the European Union, the UN, Russia, and the United States, the Arab League expressed its cautious support. The league welcomed the June decision of militant Palestinian groups to introduce a three-month cease-fire, but a league spokesman cautioned that Israel had yet to "implement its obligations" and cease assassinations, incursions, demolitions, and seizures. He further urged the United States in particular to ensure Israeli compliance with the terms of the peace initiative. On February 25, 2004, in the course of oral presentations before the International Court of Justice in The Hague, the league argued that the separation barrier being erected on Palestinian land by Israel was illegal and "an affront to international law."

In December 2003, the league sent its first official delegation to Iraq, signaling a change in attitude from its earlier criticism of the U.S. invasion in March.

A league summit scheduled for March 29, 2004, in Tunis was abruptly called off two days in advance of the opening because of divisions over peace overtures to Israel, with tensions heightened following Israel's assassination of the leader of the radical Palestinian group Hamas just days prior to the summit. The resulting outrage in the Arab world inflamed league ministers and complicated plans to relaunch the Saudi-backed peace initiative adopted at the 2002 Beirut summit. The collapse of the Tunis summit was widely reported as reflective of the turmoil in Arab ranks.

The rescheduled Tunis summit of May 22, 2004, was marred the first day by the walkout of Libya's Qadhafi, who again threatened to withdraw from the league. Qadhafi said he was "disgusted" by the treatment of Saddam Hussein and Yasir Arafat and wholly dissatisfied with the summit agenda. Furthermore, 10 of the 22 league members did not attend the two-day summit, which ultimately issued a strongly worded denunciation of abuse inflicted on Iraqi prisoners by U.S. forces, pledged further reforms to be launched in league countries, and called for an international security force for the Palestinians. The league also called for an extensive UN role in rebuilding Iraq.

An emergency session of the league was called August 8, 2004, to address ways to help Sudan resolve the humanitarian crisis in Darfur, but little was reported from that event. The issue was again addressed at a meeting specific to that purpose on May 16, 2005, producing a resolution promoting resumption of negotiations between the Sudan government in Khartoum and the Darfur rebels.

On March 22–23, 2005, only 13 of 22 leaders attended the league summit in Algiers, and the resolutions adopted "were of comparatively little significance," according to the *New York Times*. However, plans were unveiled for an Arab common market by 2015 and a regional security system. The participants also approved establishment of an interim Arab Parliament, which met for the first time on December 27, 2005, in Cairo. The Parliament has 88 representatives, 4 from each Arab League member, but has no legislative authority, leaving its responsibilities and importance unclear apart from serving as a forum on Arab issues. It was decided that this interim legislature would move to Syria, meeting twice a year with the aim of creating a permanent Arab legislature by 2011. Mohammad Jassim al-Saqr, a Kuwaiti described as a liberal, was elected its speaker.

The Arab League's response to the landslide victory of the militant group Hamas in the January 2006 Palestinian Authority elections was mixed. Secretary General Moussa said Hamas should renounce violence against Israel and recognize its right to exist if it expects to function as a legitimate government. On the other hand, at its March 28–29, 2006, summit in Khartoum, the league pledged to contribute $55 million a month toward the operation of the Palestinian Authority, at a time when some foreign funding appeared likely to be withdrawn because of Hamas's intransigence.

The 2006 summit, like its predecessor, was not attended by the heads of several member states, for reasons including poor security and Sudan's position on the Darfur crisis. In addition to its commitment to the Palestinian Authority, the league pledged $150 million to support the mission of African Union peacekeepers in Darfur. The years 2006 and 2007 saw continuing Arab League involvement in efforts to broker peace between the Hamas and Fatah factions of the Palestinian Authority. When Hamas seized control of the Gaza Strip in June 2007, however, the Arab League joined in the policy of the U.S. and Israel of supporting the rump Palestinian Authority government of the Fatah-led faction in the West Bank.

The 2007 summit, held March 28–29 in Riyadh, Saudi Arabia, produced a renewed call for Israel to negotiate on the basis of the 2002 "land for peace" proposal. In April 2007 the league set up a contact group, consisting of Jordan and Egypt (countries having diplomatic relations with Israel), to deal directly with Israel on the proposal. On July 25, 2007, the foreign ministers of those countries went to Israel and met Israeli prime minister Ehud Olmert. They described their visit as "extend[ing] the hand of peace" on behalf of the Arab League. By September 2007, however, the league began to say that Israel was not taking the dialogue seriously, regarding it only as an exercise in public relations. Arab League representatives were present at the November 27, 2007, peace conference, sponsored by the United States and held in Annapolis, Maryland. The main outcome of the conference was a statement of "joint understanding" in which Israeli prime minister Ehud Olmert and Palestinian president Mahmoud Abbas committed themselves to negotiate a peace agreement by the end of 2008. This did not happen.

The Arab League was also active in the troubles of Iraq and Lebanon. In September 2007 the league turned down a Syrian government request to establish a fund in aid of Iraqi refugees in Syria. No reason was given, except a lack of consensus on the matter. In January 2008, however, the league tried to reestablish itself as a mediator in Iraq after almost a year of absence, but with little success. Lebanon (see separate article) was in a prolonged and sometimes violent state of unrest after its president's term ended in November 2007, and parliament failed to elect a successor. Many blamed pro-Syrian factions for the stalemate, and the Iranian-backed Hezbollah movement temporarily took over much of Beirut in early May 2008. The Arab League was deeply involved in negotiations that led to a compromise, with Hezbollah's official standing much increased, and the Lebanese parliament finally elected a president on May 28, 2008.

None of this activity, and the obvious tension between Syria and the rest of the Arab League, made for an easy summit. This meeting was held in Damascus March 29–30, 2008. Several countries, including Jordan, Saudi Arabia, and Egypt, sent only low-level delegations in protest at what they called Syria's meddling in Lebanon. Although Iran is not an Arab country, an Iranian observer attended.

By mid-2008 the primary matter of concern for the Arab League was the situation in Darfur, in particular the prospect of the International Criminal Court (ICC) issuing an arrest warrant for Sudanese president Omar al-Bashir, charging him with genocide. The league's aim was to postpone or defuse the potential crisis, and in any case not to support Bashir's arrest. On July 19 it passed a resolution declaring that there was no need for an international trial, but that a Sudanese court was capable of trying Bashir. The matter dragged on until March 4, 2009, when an ICC arrest warrant was finally issued. Bashir defiantly attended the March 28–29 league summit in Doha, Qatar, and received the united support of the attendees. According to international law, Bashir should have been arrested as soon as he left Sudanese airspace. He returned without incident, and as of late 2009 has not been arrested on the several occasions when he traveled around Africa.

In late August 2008 a league representative visited Iraq, looking for ways for friendly Arab states to build their influence with the government there. In October 2008 the league supported Syria in its attempt to gain a seat on the board of the International Atomic Energy Agency (IAEA). Iran had originally been campaigning for the seat but dropped its bid in favor of its ally Syria. The seat went to the United States' nominee, Afghanistan. Also in October a league delegation visited Ankara, Turkey, with a view to improving relations with that country.

The conflict between Israel and Hamas in Gaza and the massive destruction that it caused was responsible for a serious rift between league members. In January 2009 two rival conferences were held simultaneously on the question: a meeting of Arab League foreign ministers in Kuwait and a "Pan-Arab" meeting in Doha, called by the emir of Qatar. Saudi Arabia and Egypt in particular disapproved of the Doha meeting, fearing that would undercut Egyptian attempts to broker an end to the Gaza attacks. The rift continued through the March summit in Doha, which Egyptian president Mubarak did not attend.

On April 8, 2009, president of the (Greek) Republic of Cyprus Demetris Christofias met in Cairo with Secretary General Moussa, and announced that his country would accredit an ambassador to the Arab League. Moussa declared that the Cyprus problem should be solved in accordance with UN resolutions.

ARAB MAGHREB UNION (AMU)

Established: By the Arab Maghreb Treaty, signed by the heads of state of the member countries on February 17, 1989, in Marrakesh, Morocco, effective July 1, 1989.

Purpose: "To strengthen the bonds of brotherhood which bind the member states and their peoples to each other . . . to work gradually towards the realization of the freedom of movement of [the member states'] people, goods, services, and capital . . . to safeguard the independence of every member state . . . to realize the industrial, agricultural, commercial, and social development of the member states . . . by setting up joint ventures and preparing general and specialized programs . . . to initiate cooperation with a view to developing education at various levels, to preserving the spiritual and moral values derived from the tolerant teachings of Islam, to safeguarding the Arab national identity."

Headquarters: Casablanca, Morocco.

Principal Organs: Presidential Council (heads of member states), Council of Prime Ministers, Council of Foreign Ministers, Consultative Council, Judicial Body, Follow-up Committee, Specialized Ministerial Commissions, General Secretariat.

Web site: www.maghrebarabe.org

Secretary General: Mohamed Habib Benyahya (Tunisia).

Membership (5): Algeria, Libya, Mauritania, Morocco, Tunisia.

Official Language: Arabic.

Origin and development. The idea of a unified northern Africa was first voiced by Arab nationalists in the 1920s and subsequently received widespread support during World War II and among the movements in African countries in the 1950s and early 1960s for independence from the European colonial powers. By contrast, the post-independence era yielded a variety of territorial disputes, political rivalries, and ideological differences that hindered meaningful integration efforts. However, the Maghrebian movement regained momentum following the 1987 rapprochement between Algeria and Morocco (see articles on those countries). Meeting together for the first time in June 1988 in Algiers, Algeria, the leaders of the five Maghrebian countries appointed a commission and five subcommittees to draft a treaty that would encompass the "Greater Arab Maghreb." After intensive negotiations, the treaty was signed February 17, 1989, following a two-day summit in Marrakesh, Morocco, with formal ratification following shortly thereafter.

Although the five heads of state appeared unified after the summit, reports indicated that volatile Libyan leader Muammar al-Qadhafi, upset at the rejection of his proposal that Chad, Mali, Niger, and Sudan be brought into the union, had attended only at the last minute. After the summit Qadhafi continued to push for "one invincible Arab nation" from the Atlantic to the Persian Gulf, and, apparently at his insistence, the Arab Maghreb Treaty left AMU membership open to other countries "belonging to the Arab nation or the African group."

Structure. The supreme political organ of the AMU is the Presidential Council, which is comprised of the heads of state of the member nations. The chair of the council rotates among the heads of state, who are assisted by a Council of Prime Ministers. The Council of Foreign Ministers is empowered to attend sessions of the Presidential Council and is responsible for preparing summit agendas. Reporting to the Council of Foreign Ministers is a Follow-up Committee, comprised of the members' secretaries of state for Maghreb affairs, which is mandated to oversee the implementation of integrationist measures. In addition, Specialized Ministerial Commissions have been established in five areas: interior, human resources, infrastructure, economy and finance, and food security.

The original treaty provided for a Consultative Council of 10 representatives from each member state; in 1994 the size of each delegation was increased to 30. The Consultative Council meets in ordinary session once a year and in emergency session at the request of the Presidential Council, to which it submits recommendations and draft resolutions. The treaty also calls for a "judicial body," consisting of two judges appointed by each member state, to "deal with disputes concerning the implementation of the treaty and the accords concluded within the framework of the Union." A small General Secretariat operates from Morocco, the participants having pledged to keep the union's bureaucracy to a bare minimum.

Activities. Despite economic and political differences among its members, the AMU was perceived at its formation as having the capacity to provide a significant regional response to the single internal market being planned then by the European Community (EC, now the

European Union—EU). In subsequent months preliminary agreement was reported on the establishment of a regional airline and unification of postal and telecommunications services. In addition several joint industrial projects were approved, and a campaign was launched to vaccinate children against an array of diseases. However, by early 1990, AMU proponents acknowledged that progress at integrating economic and social services had been slower than anticipated. Consequently, the AMU heads of state, during a January summit in Tunis, Tunisia, agreed to appoint a secretary general, establish a permanent headquarters, and implement other changes to strengthen AMU authority and effectiveness. It was also announced that the AMU defense and foreign ministers were asked to study ways of achieving "cooperation and coordination" in security matters. Nevertheless, several difficult political issues continued to work against regional unity, including Mauritania's displeasure over lack of support from Morocco in its border dispute with Senegal (see articles on Mauritania and Senegal), irritation among several members over positions taken by Libya's Colonel Qadhafi, and failure to resolve the Western Sahara dispute (see Morocco article).

During a July 1990 summit in Algiers, the heads of state were unable to agree on a location for the permanent AMU headquarters or to select a secretary general. Activity within the AMU was subsequently constrained by events associated with Iraq's invasion of Kuwait in August. Although Morocco adopted a solidly anti-Iraq stance and contributed troops to the U.S.-led Desert Shield operation, the other AMU members opposed the presence of U.S. troops in the Persian Gulf. As a result, the AMU summit in Ras Lanuf, Libya, in March 1991 called on the Arab League to work quickly to heal divisions created by the war so that a pan-Arab consensus could be reached on economic, political, and security issues.

During the 1991 summit the AMU heads of state (with the exception of Libya's Colonel Qadhafi, whose absence was unexplained) agreed to establish the organization's General Secretariat in Casablanca, the Maghreb Consultative Council in Algeria, the Maghreb University and Science Academy in Libya, the Maghreb Court in Mauritania, and a Maghreb Bank for Investment and External Trade (*Banque Maghrébine d'Investissement et de Commerce Extérieur*—BMICE) in Tunisia. In October Mohammed Amamou of Tunisia was selected as the AMU's first secretary general. However, most of the AMU's planned initiatives remained unimplemented as conflict among the members left the impression, in the words of the *Middle East International*, that the union was "dead, if not quite buried."

One major stumbling block to effective regional action was the imposition of limited sanctions by the United Nations (UN) against Libya in the spring of 1992. The sanctions were levied because of Tripoli's refusal to turn over two suspects in the 1988 bombing of an airliner over Lockerbie, Scotland. Despite strong protests from Colonel Qadhafi, Libya's AMU partners honored the sanctions, although the AMU summit held November 10–11 in Nouakchott, Mauritania, urged the UN to reconsider its position. The summit also issued a declaration condemning the "terrorism" stemming from militant Islamic fundamentalism in the region and called for "concerted effort" to keep it in check.

Some rhetorical commitment to union aims returned at the sixth AMU summit, held after several postponements on April 2–3, 1994, in Tunis. In addition to urging faster implementation of previous agreements, the AMU leaders called for intensified trade and security negotiations with the EU. However, the Libyan regime, which prior to the summit had bluntly labeled the AMU a "failure," reportedly remained "bitter" that the AMU members were still upholding the UN sanctions. For their part, the AMU leaders expressed "concern" over the effects of the sanctions on the Libyan people and called for a "just, honorable, and swift settlement" based on international laws, resolutions, and charters."

The next AMU summit was postponed indefinitely after Libya announced it would not assume its scheduled chair tenure because of the Lockerbie impasse. Following the apparent resolution of the sanctions issue in early 1999, observers suggested that a revival of AMU progress was at hand, but the AMU remained essentially moribund because of differences between Morocco and Algeria over the latter's support for the Polisario insurgents in the Western Sahara. The 35th session of the Follow-up Committee convened in Algiers in mid-May, ostensibly to relaunch the union, but little came out of the meeting. In August newly crowned King Mohamed of Morocco proposed to Algerian president Bouteflika that the AMU be reinvigorated, and a month later a Moroccan spokesperson described the union as "still a fundamental project in our view." Nevertheless, a summit anticipated for November never occurred, and in February 2000 Tunisian president Ben Ali, marking the union's 11th anniversary, once again urged that the AMU be revived, calling it "a strategic choice and an historical aspiration."

A March 2001 meeting of the Council of Foreign Ministers in Algiers was partly undercut by Morocco's unenthusiastic participation. Later in the year, however, it appeared that the Moroccan and Algerian leaders were attempting to work around the Western Sahara issue. The fourth session of the Consultative Council met in September in Rabat, Morocco, after a lapse of nine years. In October 2001 the AMU trade ministers announced agreement on a draft free trade area and customs union, while a meeting of foreign ministers in January 2002 was viewed as a prelude to a seventh summit in mid-2002. At the January session the ministers appointed Habib Boularès of Tunisia as successor to Secretary General Amamou.

The Council of Foreign Ministers convened January 3–4, 2003, in Algiers, where one of the concerns was the need for the AMU to adapt to the challenges posed by increasing globalization. The concluding communiqué again denounced Israeli aggression against Palestinians, called for the lifting of sanctions against Iraq as well as those remaining against Libya, and condemned terrorism (while noting the right of resistance against foreign occupation). The foreign ministers also supported continuation of the "5 + 5 dialog" on Mediterranean issues begun in 1991 with France, Italy, Spain, Portugal, and Malta.

On December 22, 2003, a day before a much-discussed AMU summit was to have been held, the AMU foreign ministers, meeting in Algiers, indefinitely postponed the meeting. The cancellation followed announcements that the king of Morocco, the president of Mauritania, and the Libyan leader had all declined to attend. Shortly before, Mauritania had accused Libya of financing a plot to overthrow Mauritania's government. After the summit's cancellation Colonel Qadhafi indicated the summit might be rescheduled following Algeria's 2004 presidential election. A subsequent attempt to hold a summit in Tripoli in May 2005 was also canceled at the last minute as the king of Morocco declined to attend because of the ongoing dispute with Algeria over Western Sahara.

The period 2006–2008 has been marked by continued efforts to revitalize the union, particularly in light of a resurgence of terrorist attacks, especially in Algeria, and a sense that radical Islamist groups might be gaining a foothold in the region. Union foreign ministers met in June 2006 to discuss these issues, but the dispute between Algeria and Morocco remained intractable.

On a more positive note, the July 2006 African Union summit, while deciding to recognize no new Regional Economic Communities (RECs) in Africa, agreed to continue recognition of several existing RECs, including the AMU. Also, in May 2007 a conference of AMU security officials reportedly agreed on a plan to improve security cooperation among member states, sharing information about militant Islamist groups in North Africa.

Interest in reinvigorating the AMU extended to citizens of its member countries. In an unusual gesture, a Tunisian blogger organized a one-day blogging campaign for June 1, 2007. Bloggers who were citizens of AMU countries posted negative or positive comments about the organization to increase its visibility.

Tunisian president Zine el Abidine Ben Ali led efforts to revive the AMU but was frustrated by the Western Sahara dispute. He held a conference on April 27–28, 2007, in Tangier, Morocco, where acrimonious debate between Moroccan and Algerian participants, as well as noisy demonstrations from the audience, destroyed any chance of the meeting ending on a positive note.

Not all the organs of the AMU have been inactive, however. In November 2007 the Consultative Council denounced any attempt by foreign countries to establish military bases on African soil—a statement presumably aimed at the United States whose newly formed Africa Command (AFRICOM) was said to be looking for a permanent base in Africa. In February 2008 U.S. president George W. Bush, on a visit to Ghana, denied having any such plans. On July 3, 2008, the AMU energy ministers met in Algiers "after 13 years of infighting and foot-dragging" to restart cooperation on energy matters. The ministers agreed to work closely together to produce renewable energy.

The August 2008, military coup in Mauritania overthrew that country's first democratically elected president. After the coup, AMU secretary general Benyahya visited Mauritania, and conferred with Gen. Mohamed Ould Abdelaziz, the head of the junta. Benyahya declared himself hopeful about the situation, and in January 2009 the junta promised elections and a constitutional referendum by the following June. The Western Sahara problem continued to fester. In September 2008 Morocco offered local autonomy for the area, declaring that such a move would help revitalize the AMU, but this proposal satisfied no one.

The member states of the AMU had been among the countries joining the new Mediterranean Union, launched by France in July 2008. The new body, which included Israel, was intended to bring peace to the area. But following the destructive conflict in Gaza, the AMU announced that its members were reconsidering their membership in the Mediterranean Union.

In February 2009 the AMU celebrated its twentieth anniversary. Tunisia has always been a leading supporter of the group, and Tunisian president Zine El Abidine Ben Ali sent a message of congratulations. He declared that the AMU was a "necessary, strategic choice," and called on all parties to make it work better. But the Moroccan and Algerian representatives chose the occasion to exchange insults. In April however, the Moroccan foreign minister, speaking at an AMU meeting, expressed his desire to normalize relations with Algeria.

ARAB MONETARY FUND (AMF)

Established: By Articles of Agreement signed April 27, 1976, in Rabat, Morocco, effective as of February 2, 1977.

Purpose: To correct disequilibria in the balance of payments of member states; to promote the stability of exchange rates among Arab currencies, rendering them mutually convertible; to promote Arab economic integration and development; to encourage the creation of a unified Arab currency; and to coordinate policies in other international monetary and economic forums.

Headquarters: Abu Dhabi, United Arab Emirates.

Principal Organs: Board of Governors (all members), Board of Executive Directors (nine members), Loan and Investments Committees.

Web site: www.amf.org. As of December 2009, the site was down for "review." The site previously had an English-language section, but many documents were available in Arabic only.

Director General: Jassim al-Mannai (Bahrain).

Membership (22): Algeria, Bahrain, Comoro Islands, Djibouti, Egypt, Iraq, Jordan, Kuwait, Lebanon, Libya, Mauritania, Morocco, Oman, Palestine, Qatar, Saudi Arabia, Somalia, Sudan, Syria, Tunisia, United Arab Emirates, Yemen. (The memberships of Iraq, Somalia, and Sudan were suspended in February 1993 because of payments arrears. Sudan reached a repayment agreement, and its membership was reactivated in April 2000. Iraq's membership was reinstated in September 2003, after the overthrow of Saddam Hussein.)

Official Language: Arabic.

Origin and development. Although a proposal to form an Arab Payments Union was made by the Arab Economic Council in the 1960s and a meeting was subsequently held for that purpose, the idea was discarded as attention was drawn to more pressing political issues. With the quadrupling of oil prices in 1974, however, concern once again focused on the issue of monetary problems. The objective was now more ambitious: an organization to deal with recycling, or investing, Arab "petrodollars" to decrease dependence on foreign handling of surplus funds. This goal is clearly implicit in the Articles of Agreement signed in April 1976. Since then the AMF has gradually expanded its mission to promote economic integration and development, aid Arab financial institutions, encourage intra-Arab trade, and assist member countries in structural financial reforms.

Structure. The Board of Governors, comprising one governor and one alternate governor from each member state, serves as the fund's general assembly and holds all administrative powers. Meeting at least once a year, the Board of Governors is responsible for capitalization, income distribution, the admission and suspension of members, and the appointment of the fund's director general. The Board of Executive Directors, consisting of the director general and eight experts elected from the member states for three-year terms, performs tasks assigned it by the Board of Governors. Subsidiary departments include the Economic and Technical Department, the Economic Policy Institute, and the Treasury and Investments Department.

Activities. One of the AMF's principal aims is to foster the economic integration of member states. Thus the fund has guaranteed loans to Arab countries to correct payment imbalances resulting from unilateral or pan-Arab development projects. It has also used its capital as a catalyst to advance Arab financial interests and has promoted the creation of a unified Arab currency. It provides technical assistance to the monetary and banking agencies of member countries, largely through training seminars in such areas as branch banking and accounting, bank supervision and internal auditing, and documentary credit. It also cooperates with other Arab and international organizations to discuss and promote areas of common interest.

In late 1987 the AMF launched a restructuring program believed to have widespread support from Arab bankers; its "fresh priorities" included the creation of a regional securities market and the strengthening of securities markets in member states to provide long-term financing for development. In September 1988 the fund endorsed further changes, such as an emphasis on "productive projects" leading directly to economic growth, rather than on the infrastructural programs of earlier years. Although not yet willing to say it would attach conditions to AMF loans, the Board of Executive Directors announced its intention to take a more active interest in how loans were used. The board also approved the creation of an Economic Policy Institute to assist member states in formulating national policies and to promote the development of financial strategies for the Arab countries as a group.

Attention subsequently shifted to the Arab Trade Financing Program (ATFP), established by the AMF and other pan-Arab financial institutions to promote trade among Arab countries. The AMF agreed to provide $250 million of the initial $500 million of authorized capital for the program and was accorded control of five of the nine seats on its board of directors. The first ATFP loan agreement was signed in January 1992 with Morocco.

As was the case with most Arab financial institutions, AMF activity was severely curtailed by the 1990–1991 Gulf War, although the AMF began to rebound in the mid-1990s. Cumulative approvals reached 718.8 million Arab Accounting Dinars (AAD) ($2.9 billion) for 103 projects as of January 1, 1998. Since then, most loans have involved a new Structural Adjustment Facility (SAF), which was set up to support reforms in the financial sector.

In March 2003 the AMF changed its general lending policy, replacing its traditional fixed-interest loans with two types of market-related variable rates on new loans and allowing member countries to choose between the two. Following the U.S.-led invasion of Iraq in the spring 2003, the fund figured in attempts to rebuild Iraqi national life. In March 2004 the AMF, in conjunction with the International Monetary Fund (IMF), organized a course on "Macroeconomic Management and Policies" for Iraqi officials from the Central Bank of Iraq and the Iraqi ministries of finance and planning. This course was held at the AMF's headquarters in Abu Dhabi. The fund declined, however, to write off Iraq's debts, but declared it would not seek repayment until the country's situation improved. At this time the fund also approved the reinstatement of Sudan, having approved an agreement to settle its arrears, estimated at nearly $93 million.

The year 2005 was characterized by the beginning of a run-up in oil prices combined with the sinking value of the U.S. dollar against other major currencies. As a result the fund's conservative management made adequate progress. Also during this period, the AMF's educational arm held several conferences and seminars for its member banks on national and international money management.

The year 2006 saw the unexpected victory of Hamas in Palestinian Authority elections. The fund announced that it would allocate 10 percent of 2005's net profits, approximately $50 million, to aid Palestinians, but none of it would go to the Hamas-led government. 2006 and 2007 were also marked by the effects of the Iraq war on the finances of the Arab countries. In December 2006 Dubai Ports World, owned by the Dubai government, was forced to sell six U.S. ports, and this action was widely seen as the result of an unreasonable fear by the United States of all things Arab. In August 2007 the fund concluded a major review of its dealings with Sudan, and reaffirmed its willingness to help the country recover from civil war through financial help and technical advice. As part of this effort, the fund forgave $60 million of Sudan's debt of $340 million. In December 2007 the fund lent Lebanon a total of $75 million, and in March 2008 it lent $900,000 to Comoro Islands to assist with that country's balance of payments deficit.

As the effects of the global credit crisis, together with a run-up in world oil and food prices, became centrally important in 2008, the U.S. dollar continued its decline in value against the euro. Diversification of the fund's foreign exchange reserves in favor of the euro came under widespread discussion, but had not yet happened as of May 2008. In fact, in February 2008 the central bank of the United Arab Emirates strongly rejected a call for diversification. The fund's director general, a strong advocate of abolishing the U.S. dollar peg, suggested the fund should instead use a basket of the currencies of the region's main trading partners. That basket would contain the euro, the yen, and the pound sterling, as well as the dollar.

In June 2008 the fund wrote off $100 million of Iraq's debt, and rescheduled the remaining $400 million over a period of 18 years. In December 2008 Lebanon secured a loan of $85 million for the purchase of oil and fuel oil. In the same month the fund lent Syria $45 million, to facilitate "structural banking and financial reform."

In April 2009, in response to the continuing worldwide financial crisis, the fund's management decided to place all loan requests on a fast track with emergency status. Likewise in April the fund granted Jordan a loan of $55 million, for infrastructural improvements, and to support the country's public debt.

ARCTIC COUNCIL

Established: By the Declaration on the Establishment of the Arctic Council, signed September 19, 1996, in Ottawa, Canada.

Purpose: To provide regular intergovernmental consultation on Arctic issues to ensure the well-being of the inhabitants of the Arctic, sustainable development, and the protection of the environment.

Principal Organs: Ministerial Meetings, Senior Arctic Officials Meetings, Secretariat.

Web site: www.arctic-council.org

Chair: Per Stig Møller (Denmark).

Membership (8): Canada, Denmark, Finland, Iceland, Norway, Russia, Sweden, United States. There are also six "Permanent Participants" representing Arctic indigenous peoples as allowed by the charter: the Aleut International Association, the Arctic Athabaskan Council, the Gwich'in Council International, the Inuit Circumpolar Conference, the Saami Council, and the Russian Association of Indigenous Peoples of the North.

Observers, permanent status (6): France, Germany, Netherlands, Poland, Spain, United Kingdom.

Observers, ad hoc status (3): China, Italy, South Korea. The latest country to gain ad hoc observer status was China in 2006. Eighteen organizations, including the Association of World Reindeer Herders and the United Nations Environment Program, also have observer status.

Origin and development. Canada first proposed the idea of the Arctic Council in 1989 when concerns about the cultural and environmental degradation of the Arctic region associated with modern development arose. In 1994 Canada resurrected the concept of a permanent forum in which diplomats, scientists, and policy analysts could coordinate their efforts toward the protection and management of the fragile Arctic domain. Preliminary discussions were held in June 1995 and August 1996 to draft the council's charter, which was formally signed September 19, 1996, in Ottawa, Canada.

Structure. After initial protest by the United States, it was decided that the Secretariat would not be given a permanent home but would instead rotate every two years, along with the position of chair, among the council members. The charter calls for decisions to be made by consensus at biannual Ministerial Meetings. Meetings of Senior Arctic Officials (SAOs) convene twice a year.

At the start of Norway's term in the chair, an agreement was reached to coordinate activities with Sweden and Denmark, the next two chair countries, and to set up a secretariat in Tromsø, Norway. The Secretariat was to remain in Tromsø at least through Sweden and Denmark's terms, that is, through 2012.

Following the fourth Ministerial Meeting on the Arctic Environmental Protection Strategy (AEPS) held June 12–13, 1997, in Alta, Norway, the Arctic Council assumed responsibility for the AEPS and the programs initiated in support of it. Advancing the related overriding goals of environmental protection and sustainable development are six working groups: the Arctic Contaminants Action Program; Arctic Monitoring and Assessment Program (AMAP); Protection of the Arctic Marine Environment (PAME); Emergency Prevention, Preparedness, and Response (EPPR); Conservation of Arctic Flora and Fauna (CAFF); and the Sustainable Development Working Group (SDWG).

Activities. The Arctic Council has drawn considerable international attention since its formation and has steadily expanded its contacts with other intergovernmental forums. For example, representatives of the European Union, the Nordic Council of Ministers, the Council of the Baltic Sea States, and the Barents Euro-Arctic Council attended the SAO session held November 18–19, 1999, in Washington, D.C. Council supporters, describing the Arctic as "an environmental early warning system for our globe," have suggested the group could serve as a model for similar endeavors in other regions.

At present, the Arctic Council has three work programs. The Regional Program of Action for the Protection of the Arctic Marine Environment from Land-Based Activities (RPA) was adopted in September 1998 at the first Ministerial Meeting, held in Iqaluit, Canada. The Arctic Climate Impact Assessment (ACIA), with a secretariat based in Fairbanks, Alaska, was formally authorized at the second ministerial session, held October 12–13, 2000, in Barrow, Alaska, as was the Arctic Council Action Plan to Eliminate Pollution of the Arctic (ACAP). The ACIA's principal purpose is "to evaluate and synthesize knowledge on climate variability, climate change and increased ultraviolet radiation and their consequences." The ACAP, which originated in a 1997 report by the AMAP on Arctic pollution, lists reducing the emission of pollutants and forging international cooperative efforts to reduce pollution risks as its primary goals.

Specific Arctic Council projects include assisting Russia in phasing out polychlorinated biphenyls (PCBs) and managing PCB waste cleanups, as well as assessment of persistent toxic substances (PTS) and radioactive contamination in the region. The SDWG, which held its first session during the May 3–6, 1999, SAO meeting in Anchorage, Alaska, has discussed wide-ranging projects covering areas such as youth health, telemedicine, regional fisheries, safety in the fishing industry, ecotourism, rural sanitation, and regional transport and transport infrastructure.

Roundtable discussions at the Barrow Ministerial Meeting focused on the ACIA, the future of Arctic cooperation, the effects of contaminants in the region, and the relationship between sustainable development and Arctic communities. At the conclusion of the meeting, the position of chair of the Arctic Council passed from the United States to Finland.

The Finnish chair tenure concluded at the third Ministerial Meeting, held October 9–10, 2002, in Inari, Finland, at which time Iceland assumed the council leadership. At the ministerial session, the AMAP presented a report titled "Arctic Pollution 2002," the CAFF outlined recommendations for preservation of regional flora and fauna, and the EPPR presented a "Circumpolar Map of Resources at Risk from Oil Spills in the Arctic."

The fourth Ministerial Meeting, held October 24, 2004, in Reykjavik, Iceland, was dominated by debate over a report from the ACIA on the accelerated pace of climate change related to global warming in the Arctic. Reports indicate the United States opposed specifying steps to take against climate change, and that conference delegates had to negotiate forcefully to produce a document that could accommodate the U.S. point of view. At the meeting the ministers also received the extensive Arctic Human Development Report (AHDR) and directed the SDWG to "make full use of the report" to prepare an action plan for sustainable development. The AHDR is the first comprehensive scientific assessment of human well-being to cover the entire Arctic region.

The fifth Ministerial Meeting was held October 26, 2006, in Salekhard, Russia, when Russia relinquished the chair to Norway. It took place amid increasingly serious reports about global warming and the deterioration of the Arctic environment. The melting of the polar ice caps, in addition to being an ecological disaster, was recognized as having geopolitical implications not necessarily favorable to the Arctic Council's peaceful mission. The melting is expected to make once unreachable oil deposits and mineral available for development. The stretch of frozen ocean that might one day become the Northwest Passage between the Atlantic and Asia is in contention between Canada and the United States. Canada claims sovereignty, while the United States maintains that the waters should be international.

During 2007 the countries with the most to gain or lose in competing territorial claims—Canada, Denmark (through Greenland), and Russia—all moved in various ways to assert their positions. Canada increased its military presence in the Arctic, and a Russian submarine planted a flag on the seabed at the North Pole on the mineral-rich Lomonosov Ridge. This topographic feature lies under much of the Arctic Ocean. In September 2007 Russia claimed the ridge as part of its continental shelf. Canada and Denmark, which conducted their own surveys, do not agree. In November 2007 Sergei Lavrov, the Russian foreign minister, declared that Russia would, nevertheless, continue to cooperate with all Arctic organizations, including the Arctic Council.

An important diplomatic outcome of these competing claims came in May 2008. Denmark invited some, but not all, members of the Arctic Council to a meeting May 27–29, 2008, in Ilulissat, Greenland. It asked Canada, Norway, Russia, and the United States, but not Iceland, Finland, or Sweden. Denmark defended the guest list, saying it had invited the countries that directly border the Arctic Ocean and that it had no intention of supplanting the Arctic Council. The meeting ended with a statement that the participants would amicably pursue their claims according to the 1982 United Nations Convention on the Law of the Sea (UNCLOS)—a convention that the United States has never ratified.

The Ilulissat meeting has variously been described as a victory for peaceful negotiation, a reaffirmation—perhaps an augmentation—of the Arctic Council's role, and "a carve-up." Environmentalists feared that only a few countries would one day manage the area and its resources. They called instead for the Arctic to be protected by a treaty similar to the one governing the Antarctic so that military activity and drilling in the region would be prohibited.

Also in May 2008 South Korea, a major shipping country, applied for its status to be upgraded to that of Permanent Observer. Italy did likewise in September. As of mid-2009, both requests were still pending. In 2009 the countries with major interests in the Arctic called for peaceful cooperation. Both Russia and Canada made this point, and in April 2009 Russia announced that it was scrapping plans to create a special force to defend its interests in the Arctic. Foreign minister Lavrov told the April 29 ministerial meeting in Tromsø that Russia would be a "reliable, transparent and predictable partner in the Arctic." Canada, the country with most potential for territorial disputes as seaways open in what was once uncontested Canadian ice, vowed to assert its sovereignty in the Arctic. Canadian prime minister Stephen Harper declared that his attitude towards the Arctic was "use it or lose it." In late April the UN approved Norway's claim to 147,000 square miles of continental shelf, extending Norway's territory to within 375 miles of the North Pole.

The April 29 meeting also deferred action on the request of the European Union (EU) for Permanent Observer status. This was in response to an anticipated EU ban on seal products. Canada in particular was opposed, the Canadian position being that seals are not endangered, and that their conditions in the Arctic are better than those of animals in European slaughterhouses.

ASIA-PACIFIC ECONOMIC COOPERATION (APEC)

Established: At a meeting of foreign and economic ministers of 12 nations November 6–7, 1989, in Canberra, Australia; objectives and principles set forth in Seoul Declaration approved during ministerial meeting November 12–14, 1991, in Seoul, South Korea; Declaration of Institutional Arrangements adopted September 10–11, 1992, in Bangkok, Thailand.

Purpose: To provide a forum for discussion on a variety of economic issues and to promote multilateral cooperation among the region's market-oriented economies.

Headquarters: Singapore.

Principal Organs: Economic Leaders' Meeting, Ministerial Meeting, Senior Officials' Meeting, Budget and Management Committee, Committee on Trade and Investment, Economic Committee, Secretariat.

Web site: www.apec.org

Executive Director: Michael Tay (Singapore, 2009), succeeding Juan Carlos Capuñay (Peru, 2008). The position has up until now been held by a national of the country that presides over the organization. Beginning in 2010 the position will be for a three-year term, open to any qualified citizen of a member country.

Membership (21): Australia, Brunei, Canada, Chile, China, Hong Kong, Indonesia, Japan, Republic of Korea, Malaysia, Mexico, New Zealand, Papua New Guinea, Peru, Philippines, Russia, Singapore, Taiwan ("Chinese Taipei"), Thailand, United States, Vietnam.

Observers: Association of Southeast Asian Nations, Pacific Economic Cooperation Council, Pacific Islands Forum.

Official Language: English.

Origin and development. In early 1989, Australian Prime Minister Robert Hawke proposed that a permanent body be established to coordinate economic relations among market-oriented nations on the Pacific Rim, with particular emphasis to be given to dialogue between Western Pacific countries and the United States. The proposal was endorsed by the Pacific Economic Cooperation Conference (PECC; a group of business, academic, and government representatives who had held informal discussions since 1980), and the first APEC meeting was held November 6–7 in Canberra, Australia. Ministers from 12 nations—Australia, Brunei, Canada, Indonesia, Japan, Republic of Korea, Malaysia, New Zealand, Philippines, Singapore, Thailand, and United States—attended the inaugural session, with debate centering on how to proceed in adopting formal APEC arrangements.

Primarily because of concern among some members of the Association of Southeast Asian Nations (ASEAN; see separate article) that they might be overwhelmed by such economic giants as Canada, Japan, and the United States if the organization moved too quickly, the Canberra session decided to keep APEC as a loosely defined, informal grouping officially committed only to an annual dialogue meeting. As regional economic cooperation gained momentum in other areas of the world, however, pressure grew within APEC for a more structured format. Consequently, the Ministerial Meeting in November 1991 in Seoul, South Korea, adopted a declaration outlining APEC's objectives; established additional organizational structure; and approved the membership of China, Hong Kong, and Taiwan.

The "institutionalization" of APEC was completed during a Ministerial Meeting September 10–11, 1992, in Bangkok, Thailand, with the decision to establish a permanent Secretariat in Singapore as of January 1, 1993. Mexico and Papua New Guinea were admitted in November 1993, while Chile's membership application was approved effective November 1994. The latter was the subject of debate within APEC, with some officials suggesting that admission of South American countries could cost the organization its focus. Consequently, a moratorium on any additional APEC members was declared until at least 1996. In 1998 another South American country, Peru, joined, along with Russia and Vietnam, but leaders also decided that no new membership requests would be considered for at least ten years.

Structure. APEC's governing body is the annual Ministerial Meeting, the chair of which rotates each year among the members. Decisions are reached by consensus. Since 1993 overall guidance has been provided by the Economic Leaders' Meeting, an informal gathering of APEC heads of state and/or government that immediately follows the yearly Ministerial Meeting. In addition, sectoral ministerial meetings have been held (some annually) regarding education, energy, environment and sustainable development, finance, human resources development, science and technology cooperation, small and medium enterprises, telecommunications and information, tourism, trade, transportation, and women's affairs. In 2002 a Marine Resources Conservation/Fisheries Working Group was added at this level.

Responsibility for policy implementation rests primarily with a Senior Officials' Meeting (SOM), which convenes as necessary. There are four standing committees: Budget and Management; Trade and Investment, which is assisted by more than a dozen subcommittees and expert groups; Economic, assisted by an Economic Outlook Task Force; and the SOM Committee on Economic and Technical Cooperation. Other organs include several topical special task groups that address concerns related to anticorruption and transparency, counterterrorism, electronic commerce, gender, health, social safety nets, and emergency preparedness. There are also 11 working groups: Agricultural Technical Cooperation, Energy, Fisheries, Human Resources Development, Industrial Science and Technology, Marine Resources Conservation, Small and Medium Enterprises, Telecommunications and Information, Tourism, Trade Promotion, and Transportation. Since 1996 an APEC Business Advisory Council, comprising up to three senior business executives from each member country, has met to discuss APEC action plans and other business issues. A small Secretariat is led by an executive director appointed for a one-year term by the nation chairing the upcoming Ministerial Meeting.

Activities. The November 1992 Ministerial Meeting directed APEC's new permanent Secretariat to establish an electronic tariff database for the region, survey members regarding investment regulations, and study ways to harmonize customs procedures and reduce impediments to "market access" among members. Additional emphasis in the telecommunications, tourism, and environmental sectors was also approved at the November 14–18, 1994, Ministerial Meeting in Seattle, Washington.

Hoping to impel integrationist sentiment in the region (which controls more than one-half of the world's economy and accounts for nearly one-half of all global trade), the APEC finance ministers met for the first time March 18–19, 1994, in Honolulu, Hawaii. Among other things, plans were endorsed to double the capital of the Asian Development Bank, to promote cross-border investment, and to study ways of facilitating finance for large infrastructure projects. The mood of the meeting was described as upbeat, although caution was still expressed about tension between the United States and Japan over the Japanese trade surplus and disagreement between Washington and several Asian capitals, particularly Beijing, over U.S. efforts to couple trade and human rights issues.

A potentially historic step was taken at the second APEC summit, held November 15, 1994, in Bogor, Indonesia, with the adoption of a "declaration of common resolve" to pursue "free and open trade and investment" over the next quarter century. The loosely worded accord called on the region's developed nations to dismantle their trade barriers by 2010, followed by similar action by developing nations by 2020. However, many observers cautioned that it would be extremely difficult to translate APEC "resolve" into action.

Differences of opinion regarding the appropriate pace and intensity for implementing the 1994 action agenda were readily apparent at the next summit, held in November 1995 in Osaka, Japan. The United States called for a concrete liberalization schedule that would strictly limit the number of exemptions made for specific sectors. Other nations resisted that approach, however, led by China, Japan, South Korea, and Taiwan, who sought substantial protection for their farmers. In addition, some of the poorer Asian countries argued against cooperation between APEC and the World Trade Organization (WTO) to protect their industrial sectors. Consequently, it was agreed that many APEC stipulations, at least for the time being, would be implemented on a voluntary basis.

A degree of momentum was maintained at the November 1996 summit, held in Subic Bay, Philippines. Among other things, the members agreed to draft individual plans specifying the various impediments they faced in reducing and/or eliminating trade barriers, along with specific proposals for addressing those areas.

The central issue of the November 1997 summit, held in Vancouver, Canada, was the Asian economic crisis, which prompted several APEC members to seek assistance from the International Monetary Fund (IMF). Japan proposed creating a separate Asian fund to help resolve the crisis, but that idea was rejected at an ASEAN meeting held earlier in November in Manila, where it was agreed that the IMF would play the central role in promoting economic stabilization. However, APEC also endorsed additional backup funding from other sources and asked for greater regional cooperation to help mitigate the crisis.

Japan's insistence that it could not reduce tariffs on fish and forest products led to an acrimonious dispute with the United States at the November 1998 APEC summit, held in Kuala Lumpur, Malaysia. The United States insisted that tariffs be lifted on all goods included in the agreement reached at the previous summit and accused Japan of attempting to bribe other members with a $30 billion assistance package in return for their support on this issue. In response, a Japanese spokeswoman said the United States was jeopardizing the region's economy by insisting on greater trade liberalization at a time when several of the members' economies were already in trouble. The two sides could not reconcile their differences, and the summit decided to send the matter to the WTO for further consideration. Despite their disagreement, the United States and Japan disclosed a $10 billion plan at the summit to provide debt relief to the region's ailing economies.

Political events in East Timor, Indonesia, provided a backdrop to the September 12–13, 1999, Economic Leaders' Meeting in Auckland, New Zealand, where the APEC foreign affairs ministers supported formation of a United Nations (UN) multinational military presence to restore order to the troubled jurisdiction. The summit noted progress toward economic recovery in Asia, approved APEC Principles to Enhance Competition and Regulatory Reform, and called for an improved "international framework" for the flow of trade and investment capital. With a WTO ministerial conference set to convene in late November in Seattle, Washington, the summit also voiced support for launching a new round of comprehensive trade negotiations, with abolition of agricultural export subsidies as a principal APEC concern.

The timing of a new round of trade negotiations proved to be a contentious topic at the November 15–16, 2000, summit, which was held in Bandar Seri Begawan, Brunei. Partly in an effort to restore momentum in the wake of the disrupted WTO talks in Seattle, the United States, Japan, and Canada pressed for a rapid start, whereas Malaysia and many of the smaller economies preferred a more deliberate pace. In its final declaration the summit opted for a carefully worded compromise in which the leaders agreed "that a balanced and sufficiently broad-based agenda that responds to the interests and concerns of all WTO members should be formulated and finalized as soon as possible in 2001 and that a round be launched in 2001." Also coming out of the summit were, among other things, an agreement to fight e-piracy, a call for increased oil supplies and petroleum price stability, a further commitment to narrow the digital divide, and a decision to invite North Korean participation in APEC committees and working groups.

The October 19–21, 2001, Economic Leaders' Meeting, held in Shanghai, China, offered general support for U.S.-led efforts to combat terrorism, including cutting off funding for terrorist groups. The summit declaration did not, however, specifically address U.S. military response to the September terrorist attacks on New York and Washington. The attendees also expressed concern over the ongoing worldwide economic downturn and the consequences for emerging economies, reaffirmed the goal of sustainable growth, highlighted the necessity of sharing the benefits of globalization and the "New Economy," and repeated their commitment to a new round of multilateral trade negotiations by the WTO.

During 2002, rather than proposing new initiatives, APEC concentrated its efforts on previously established goals, including improved business management and evaluation, peer review, structural reforms, and transparency. All were in keeping with the three emphases outlined in the 1994 Bogor Declaration, namely trade and investment liberalization, business facilitation, and economic and technical cooperation. At the October 26–27 Economic Leaders' Meeting in Cabo San Lucas, Mexico, attendees endorsed a Trade Facilitation Action Plan aimed at reducing transaction costs by 5 percent over five years; a Statement to Implement APEC Transparency Standards; several counterterrorism measures, including an APEC Energy Security Initiative and a proposal for Secure Trade in the APEC Region (STAR); and a Statement to Implement APEC Policies on Trade and the Digital Economy. The summit also urged the WTO to complete its current round of trade negotiations by January 2005; condemned the October 12 terrorist bombing in Bali, Indonesia; and called on North Korea to end its nuclear weapons program.

In the first half of 2003, planned APEC activities were overshadowed by the onset of the Severe Acute Respiratory Syndrome (SARS) outbreak. Precautions against the spread of the newly identified viral illness led to the cancellation of some 30 APEC-sponsored meetings in March–July. Meeting on June 2–3, in Khon Kaen, Thailand, the APEC Ministers Responsible for Trade, recognizing the severe economic repercussions of SARS for the region, pledged to restore business confidence in trade, investment, travel, and mobility and endorsed a plan of action that focused on the need to establish principles for health screenings, the timely exchange of information on the outbreak, and cooperation in prevention and treatment.

The 2003 Economic Leaders' Meeting, held October 19–21 in Bangkok, endorsed the SARS Action Plan and a Health Security Initiative, but with the outbreak contained, greater attention was directed toward economic matters and, at U.S. urging, international security. A principal focus was on "free and open trade and investment," including the need for bilateral, regional, and multilateral accords to be "complementary and mutually reinforcing." Along the same lines, the participants called for a renewed commitment to WTO liberalization negotiations and efforts to extend the perceived benefits of globalization to a broader spectrum of people and societies. With regard to security matters, APEC attempted to address the challenges posed by terrorism and weapons of mass destruction. North Korea's continuing effort to develop nuclear weapons was of particular concern.

A Ministerial Meeting in early June 2004 in Pucón, Chile, called for steps that would "provide a clear way forward" for renewed WTO negotiations. The ministers noted the need for "special attention" to dismantling trade barriers in agriculture, especially the elimination of export subsidies by developed countries, and for improving market access. In a similar vein, the APEC annual summit, held November 19–21 in Santiago, Chile, adopted the Santiago Initiative for Expanded Trade in APEC and also received a study from the APEC Business Advisory Council outlining the dimensions of a possible Free Trade Area of the Asia-Pacific. In addition to highlighting trade and investment liberalization as a path toward advancing development, the leaders' closing declaration stressed the importance of promoting energy security; strengthening public health systems; advancing the fight against AIDS, SARS, avian flu, and other health threats; and combating corruption and ensuring transparency.

As in 2003, U.S. President George W. Bush devoted much of his time to discussing with other heads of government North Korea's nuclear program. The summit participants also noted the need to improve security through adoption of antiterrorist conventions and implementation of measures intended, for example, to cut off terrorist financing. Some critics have asserted, however, that expanding the scope of APEC discussions to include such matters as security and good governance was a mistake in that it has diminished APEC's importance as an economic forum.

At the Ministerial Meeting on November 15–16, 2005, in Busan, Korea, APEC adopted a document called the Busan Roadmap, which outlines a strategy for reaching the organization's original goals in the light of a decade of globalization and change in world economic relationships, while maintaining sustainable development practices. The national leaders issued a separate statement in support of a successful conclusion to the WTO's sixth Ministerial Meeting in Hong Kong, China, and agreed to confront pandemic health threats and continue to fight against terrorism.

The APEC summit, held in Hanoi, Vietnam, on November 18, 2006, took place in the shadow of North Korea's recent nuclear test, but the conferees were not able to come up with a completely unified approach to the problem. The summit urged a speedy resumption of the Doha round of world trade liberalization talks. In advance of the gathering, U.S. President George W. Bush, speaking in Singapore, urged the group to give very serious consideration to the idea of a comprehensive Asia-Pacific free trade zone. Summit participants acknowledged for the first time that the APEC area contained too many bilateral trade agreements, to the point of being an impediment to free trade.

Australia became the 2007 host for APEC, and the Australian government announced initiatives to strengthen the organization. These initiatives would include increasing its budget by 30 percent and making the Secretariat stronger and more centralized, with the position of executive director not rotating each year. (As of 2008 the executive directorship continues to rotate.) The aim would be to prevent the organization's focus changing each year with a new host country.

The September 8–9, 2008, APEC summit was held in Sydney, Australia. It had been expected to move forward with India's application to join the group—a recognition of India's growing economic power, but a move that could lead to a significant shift in APEC's direction. At the event the United States and New Zealand opposed India's accession, which Australia had strongly supported. The meeting decided to extend a moratorium on admitting new members until 2010.

On environmental matters, the summit made a commitment to the "aspirational goals" of increasing energy efficiency 25 percent from 2005 levels by 2030 and increasing forest cover in the region by at least 20 million hectares (approximately 8.1 million acres) by 2020. The summit also committed its members to work toward creating a successor to the Kyoto climate accords, which expire in 2012. As with all APEC agreements, these declarations were not binding for the member countries. The summit also called, again, for a rapid conclusion to the long-stalled Doha round of trade talks. It was announced that the United States would host the summit in 2011, and Russia in 2012. Russian president Vladimir Putin had said that he felt APEC to be one of the most effective and useful international organizations, though some commentators felt that such a high-level meeting producing so few concrete results was a sign that APEC was irrelevant.

In June 2008 APEC's Business Advisory Council (ABAC) called for APEC to pay attention to the recent unprecedented rise in food prices. Also in June a meeting of APEC trade ministers in Arequipa, Peru, agreed to cut tariffs among APEC members to zero by 2020. The matters that dominated APEC in 2008 and 2009, however, were the world economic crisis and the organization's direction after the apparent failure of the Doha round of free-trade negotiations. The November 19–20, 2008, ministerial meeting, as well as the November 22 summit, both held in Lima, Peru, focused on the world financial crisis and the perceived need to avoid a return to protectionism. The meetings reaffirmed APEC's desire to complete the Doha round, and worked towards an action plan to make that happen. They also approved the change of the executive secretary's tenure from annual rotation to a three-year term. Singapore, the group's incoming chair, promised a year of renewed emphasis on regional economic integration, and the summit concluded with a declaration that the economic crisis could be overcome.

By July 2009, with the crisis far from over, APEC trade ministers were compelled to take a stand against a rising desire for protectionism. They declared that they would develop an "inclusive growth" strategy to deter protectionism during Japan's 2010 tenure in the organization's chair.

ASSOCIATION OF CARIBBEAN STATES (ACS)

Asociación de Estados del Caribe
Association des Etats de la Caraibe

Established: By convention signed July 24, 1994, in Cartagena de Indias, Colombia.

Purpose: To promote "economic integration, and the creation of an enhanced space of free trade and cooperation among the countries of the Caribbean . . . to meet the challenges and exploit the opportunities arising from the globalization of the international economy and progressive liberalization of hemispheric trade relations."

Headquarters: Port-of-Spain, Trinidad and Tobago.

Principal Organs: Heads of State/Government Meetings, Ministerial Council, Secretariat.

Web site: www.acs-aec.org

Secretary General: Luis Fernando Andrade Falla (Guatemala).

Membership (25): Antigua and Barbuda, Bahamas, Barbados, Belize, Colombia, Costa Rica, Cuba, Dominica, Dominican Republic, El Salvador, Grenada, Guatemala, Guyana, Haiti, Honduras, Jamaica, Mexico, Nicaragua, Panama, St. Kitts-Nevis, St. Lucia, St. Vincent and the Grenadines, Suriname, Trinidad and Tobago, Venezuela.

Associate Members (4): Aruba; France (on behalf of Guadeloupe, French Guiana, and Martinique); Netherlands Antilles; Turks and Caicos Islands.

Observers (18): Argentina, Brazil, Canada, Chile, Ecuador, Egypt, European Union, Finland, India, Italy, South Korea, Morocco, Netherlands, Peru, Russia, Spain, Turkey, Ukraine, United Kingdom. Founding observer organizations are the Caribbean Community, Caribbean Tourism Organization, Central American Integration System, Latin American Economic System, Permanent Secretariat of the General Agreement on Central American Economic Integration, and United Nations (UN) Economic Commission for Latin America and the Caribbean.

Official Languages: English, French, Spanish.

Origin and development. By the early 1990s, it had become evident to the various island nations and territories of the Caribbean Basin that the Caribbean Community and Common Market (Caricom) was insufficient for promoting the region's integration into the rapidly transforming global economy. Multiple problems such as bureaucratic red tape and protective trade barriers continued to impede economic interaction within the region even after the advent of Caricom. The signing of the North American Free Trade Agreement (NAFTA) by Mexico, Canada, and the United States was also of concern, alerting the Caribbean region to the vulnerability that could result from the failure to form their own broader trading bloc. Thus the Caricom members, the Group of Three (Colombia, Mexico, and Venezuela); the Central American countries; Cuba; Haiti; and the Dominican Republic envisaged an organization that might foster gradual economic, social, and even political cooperation among its members. The hope was that the new union would lead to the creation of a full-fledged free trade bloc.

The original proposal for the ACS came from the West Indian Commission during the 1992 Caricom summit, and a year later Caricom endorsed the creation of the new grouping. The Convention Establishing the Association of Caribbean States was signed July 24, 1994, during a meeting of the heads of state/government of its members in Bridgetown, Barbados. Although the ACS was initially scheduled to begin operations January 1, 1995, from its headquarters in Port-of-Spain, Trinidad and Tobago, formal approval of the convention proceeded more slowly than anticipated as national legislators grappled with the proposed budget structure. Consequently, the inaugural ACS summit was delayed until August 17–18, 1995, following receipt of the required ratification by 17 (two-thirds) of the convention's signatories. Plans also called for inviting the region's dependent territories to join the ACS as associate members.

Structure. The Ministerial Council is the primary decision-making body, and it creates special committees as needed. Current committees are Budget and Administration, Trade Development and External Economic Relations, Natural Disasters, Transport, and Sustainable Tourism. There is also a committee-level Council of National Representatives of the Special Fund. The fund, which has its own budget, was established to aid cooperative development and regional integration through projects in such sectors as tourism; trade; transportation; the environment and natural resources; small and medium enterprises; communications and information; and social, cultural, scientific, and technological development.

Administrative tasks are carried out by the Secretariat, headed by a secretary general elected for a four-year term. The size of the Secretariat has been deliberately limited to avoid creating an unwieldy bureaucracy. Overall ACS policy guidance is provided by summit meetings of the members' heads of state/government.

Activities. The hope among ACS supporters that the new grouping would be able to pursue "parity" with NAFTA was immediately compromised by its emphatic inclusion of Cuba as a member despite strong objection from the United States. Among other consequences, Puerto Rico's participation in the ACS was precluded. Nonetheless, the initial ACS summit in August 1995 in Port-of-Spain offered a broadly worded plan of action designed to promote economic integration, encourage extra-regional and intra-regional private investment, and produce a regional tourism strategy. A modest annual budget of $1.5 million was established, and Simon Molina Duarte, a Venezuelan economist and diplomat, was elected as the association's first secretary general. The summit attendees also discussed regional strategies to combat drug trafficking and denounced the U.S. decision to increase economic pressure on Cuba. Additionally, tentative approval was given to the establishment of a regional integration fund to solve problems associated with economic transition.

While there was general consensus within the ACS that the environment should be protected, in 1997 a controversy emerged regarding the shipping of nuclear material through the region. Most members wanted to ban the movement of such material in the Caribbean, but the French representative argued that specialists should decide the issue. At the November 27–28 ministerial session, held in Cartagena, Colombia, the ACS agreed to form a Sustainable Tourism Zone to promote tourism in the region; urged the international community to increase its efforts to end such practices as the U.S. Helms-Burton Law, which ordered sanctions against companies doing business with Cuba; and encouraged members to work toward reducing trade barriers in the region. Also in November the ACS signed a coordination agreement with Caricom.

The Helms-Burton Law and the U.S. embargo of Cuba came under renewed criticism at the second ACS summit, held April 16–17, 1999, in Santo Domingo, Dominican Republic. Discussions on the creation of a Caribbean tourism zone also continued at the summit, with the participants agreeing to cooperate in developing air and sea transportation. Competition for Europe's banana market led to a dispute over how to respond to a World Trade Organization (WTO) ruling overturning a European Union (EU) banana importation scheme that granted several Caribbean states preferential access to EU markets. The Caribbean states argued that the WTO decision would devastate their economies, but several Central and South American members stood to benefit from the ruling. No unified response to the matter could be reached at the summit.

The Ministerial Council session December 3–7, 1999, in Panama City, Panama, saw the election of Norman Girvan of Jamaica as the organization's new secretary general. At the meeting the ACS authorized creation of an Intergovernmental Reflection Group (IRG) to examine ways of improving regional cooperation. Meeting for the first time in July 2000, the IRG called for greater coordination among the various regional secretariats, including those of Caricom and the Latin American Economic System (see article on SELA). Central to the IRG discussion was a report by a group of high-level consultants who had been assigned the task of assessing progress on ACS aims and objectives during 1996–1999.

The October 2000 inaugural session of another affiliated body, the ACS Business Forum, was highlighted by announcement of an energy agreement between ten oil-importing ACS members and fellow member Venezuela, which agreed to help participating countries offset the cost of oil purchases. All other ACS members were also eligible for long-term, low-interest loans under the new Caracas Energy Agreement.

On December 6–8, 2000, the sixth Ministerial Council convened in San Pedro Sula, Honduras. Participants reached agreement on an Environment Strategy and on Principles for a Common Commercial Air Transport Policy. The ministers also approved a Rationalization and Prioritization of the ACS Work Program, in accordance with which the activities of several special committees were suspended and some of their activities reassigned.

On May 17–18, 2001, the ACS Secretariat hosted ten other regional groups in the Second Cooperative Meeting between the Secretariats of the Greater Caribbean. The participants approved creation of an Integrated Information System of the Greater Caribbean and, looking toward upcoming international negotiations sponsored by the WTO, discussed coordinating their trade positions.

The third ACS summit was held December 11–12, 2001, in Margarita Island, Venezuela, immediately following the seventh session of the Ministerial Council. The assembled leaders agreed to establish a Greater Caribbean Zone of Cooperation; national disasters, trade, and sustainable tourism were identified as initial foci. With regard to the tourism issue, the leaders also signed and urged member jurisdictions to ratify a new Convention for the Establishment of the Sustainable Tourism Zone of the Caribbean. As at past summits, the concluding declaration asked the United States to end the Helms-Burton proscriptions directed against Cuba.

At the eighth Ministerial Council session, held November 29, 2002, in Belize City, Belize, the ACS passed a resolution voicing support for an anti-corruption campaign under way in Nicaragua. Participants at the ninth session, held November 27, 2003, in Panama City, Panama, discussed security issues, trade, tourism, and regional integration. They also approved an Air Transport Agreement among the Member States and Associate Members of the Association of Caribbean States and the Draft Protocol to the Convention establishing the Sustainable Tourism Zone of the Caribbean (STZC). Also at this session Finland and the Ukraine were admitted as observers to the ACS, and Dr. Rubén Arturo Silié Valdez (Dominican Republic) was elected secretary general. The tenth ministerial meeting was held December 15, 2004, in Port-of-Spain, Trinidad and Tobago. There the ACS received the application of the Turks and Caicos Islands for associate member status. Formal ratification of the Turks and Caicos Islands' new status occurred at the 11th Ministerial Council meeting, also held at Port-of-Spain, on March 26–28, 2006.

The fourth ACS summit was held in Panama City, Panama, on July 29, 2005. The proceedings of the summit were dominated by discussions on how to reduce hunger in the region and improve regional response to natural disasters.

The ACS at the 12th Ordinary Meeting of the Ministerial Council, held at Port-of-Spain, Trinidad, on March 15, 2007, made a formal call for all members and associate members to sign or ratify any legal instruments on which they had not yet acted by the end of the year. The Agreement for Regional Cooperation in Natural Disasters, the Agreement for the Establishment of the Sustainable Tourism Zone of the Caribbean, the multilateral Air Transport Agreement, and the Protocol on Privileges and Immunities were all a few votes short of ratification, and the instruments were available for signature at the Colombian mission to the United Nations.

In June 2007 the ACS began the process of petitioning the United Nations to have the Caribbean Sea recognized as a "special area" in terms of sustainable development. It did this in the context of Panama's plan to widen the Panama Canal—a development that would greatly increase the amount of shipping in the area.

The 13th Ordinary Meeting of the Ministerial Council was held in Panama City on January 25, 2008. Luis Fernando Andrade Falla of Guatemala was elected to a four-year term as secretary general. The Council repeated the previous year's call for pending legal instruments to be signed or ratified. Some participants encouraged the ACS to take advantage of the wealth of some of its member states to strengthen its international impact.

In February 2008 the ACS entered into a memorandum of understanding with South Korea, affirming that country's desire to improve relations with the Caribbean region. In October 2008 the Organization of American States (OAS) and the ACS reaffirmed their commitment to working closer together in areas of common interest, notably climate change and disaster mitigation. An ACS delegation attended a January 28–30, 2009, summit in Haiti on tourism, natural disasters, and climate change. The meeting included several international organizations, including the OAS and the International Atomic Energy Agency (IAEA).

In a meeting held in Port-of-Spain, Trinidad and Tobago, April 24, 2009, the ACS tourism ministers reaffirmed their intention to develop a plan to make the Caribbean region the first Sustainable Tourism Zone in the world. On June 29, 2009, the ACS strongly condemned the previous day's military coup in Honduras.

ASSOCIATION OF SOUTHEAST ASIAN NATIONS (ASEAN)

Established: By foreign ministers of member states August 9, 1967, in Bangkok, Thailand.

Purpose: "To accelerate economic growth, social progress and cultural development in the region . . . to promote active collaboration and mutual assistance on matters of common interest in the economic, social, cultural, technical, scientific, and administrative fields . . . to collaborate more effectively for the greater utilization of [the member states'] agriculture and industries, the expansion of their trade, including the study of problems of international commodity trade, the improvement of their transport and communication facilities and raising the living standards of their people."

Headquarters: Jakarta, Indonesia.

Principal Organs: ASEAN Heads of State and Government, ASEAN Ministerial Meeting, Standing Committee.

Web site: www.aseansec.org

Secretary General: Surin Pitsuwan (Thailand) for a five-year term beginning in 2008.

Membership (10): Brunei, Cambodia, Indonesia, Laos, Malaysia, Myanmar (Burma), Philippines, Singapore, Thailand, Vietnam.

Official Language: English.

Origin and development. ASEAN was part of a continuing effort during the 1960s to create a framework for regional cooperation among the non-Communist states of Southeast Asia. Earlier efforts attempts included the Association of Southeast Asia (ASA), established in 1961 by Malaya, the Philippines, and Thailand; and the short-lived Maphilindo association, created in 1963 by Indonesia, Malaya, and the Philippines. The change of government in Indonesia in 1966 opened the way to a broader association, with plans for ASEAN broached at an August conference in Bangkok, Thailand, and implemented a year later with Indonesia, Malaysia, Philippines, Singapore, and Thailand as founding members.

The first ASEAN-sponsored regional summit conference was held February 1976 in Pattaya, Thailand. Sri Lanka was denied admission on geographic grounds in 1982, while Brunei was admitted following independence in 1984. Vietnam joined in July 1995, Laos and Myanmar in July 1997, and Cambodia in April 1999. As the association has grown, it has pursued a more global posture, in part by establishing agreements for formal consultation with a list of dialogue partners that currently includes Australia, Canada, China, the European Union (EU), India, Japan, the Republic of Korea, New Zealand, Russia, the United States, and the United Nations (UN) Development Program.

Structure. While the ASEAN Heads of State and Government is the organization's highest authority, the annual Ministerial Meeting, comprised of the foreign ministers of the member states, ordinarily sets general policy. Continuing supervision of ASEAN activities is the responsibility of the Standing Committee, which is located in the country hosting the Ministerial Meeting and includes the directors general of the ASEAN departments within each member country's foreign ministry. The foreign minister of the host country acts as chair, and the ASEAN secretary general also participates.

Sectoral ministerial meetings convene in more than a dozen fields, including agriculture and forestry, economics, energy, environment, finance, information, investment, labor, law, rural development and poverty alleviation, science and technology, transportation, and tourism. Nearly 30 committees and more than 120 working groups offer support. In addition, the heads of the ASEAN countries' diplomatic missions in various countries—Australia, Belgium, Canada, China, France, India, Japan, Republic of Korea, New Zealand, Pakistan, Russia, Switzerland, United Kingdom, and United States—meet to confer on matters of external relations. The Secretariat is headed by the secretary general, who serves a five-year term.

ASEAN has also established a number of specialized bodies, including centers for Agricultural Development Planning, Biodiversity Conservation, Earthquake Information, Energy, Management, Specialized Meteorology, Poultry Research and Training, Rural Youth Development, Timber Technology, Tourism Information, and University Network.

Activities. Although economic cooperation has long been a principal ASEAN concern, progress has been slowed by such factors as differing levels of development among member countries and similarity of exports. By contrast, the association generally demonstrated political solidarity in its early years, primarily through an anticommunist posture that yielded strong condemnation of Vietnam's 1978–1989 military involvement in Cambodia.

ASEAN convened its first summit in a decade on December 14–15, 1987. Meeting in Manila, Philippines, the heads of state called for a reduction in tariff barriers between members and a rejuvenation of regional economic projects. Observers noted that concerted action seemed more likely than in the past because of an increasingly hostile global trading environment and concern over growing Western protectionism. Another major development of the summit was an announcement by Japan that it was offering ASEAN countries $2 billion in low-interest loans and investments over the next three years to finance private sector projects.

ASEAN's dominant concern in 1988 remained the situation in Cambodia. ASEAN members met with representatives of the Vietnamese and warring Cambodian factions in July 1988 and February 1989 in Jakarta, Indonesia, in an effort to negotiate a settlement. When Vietnam withdrew its last troops in September 1989, ASEAN continued to play an important role in talks aimed at producing a permanent political resolution to the Cambodian conflict. The association also became increasingly vocal in attempts to resolve the status of the estimated 125,000 Vietnamese "boat people" who had fled to ASEAN countries to escape communism in the years following the Vietnam War.

Another major issue for ASEAN was the formation of the Asia-Pacific Economic Cooperation (APEC) forum, which now includes seven ASEAN members plus 14 other countries (see article on APEC). Apparently concerned that their interests could be slighted in a grouping involving global economic powers, the ASEAN countries were initially seen as resisting efforts to formalize the APEC, which was inaugurated in November 1989, beyond regular meetings of foreign and trade ministers. In fact, in early 1991 Malaysia proposed that an alternative economic bloc—the East Asian Economic Grouping (EAEG)—be established to include the ASEAN members, Hong Kong, Myanmar, South Korea, and possibly Japan and Vietnam, but not nations in which the non-Asian population dominates.

Concerned that economic integration in North America and Europe might negatively affect the Far East, the January 27–28, 1992, ASEAN Summit in Singapore created the ASEAN Free Trade Area (AFTA) and offered foreign investors and manufacturers simplified access to the region's increasingly affluent 330 million people. The decision to phase the agreement in over 15 years came at the urging of Indonesia and the Philippines, who reportedly feared being overwhelmed by their more rapidly expanding neighbors.

The summit participants also considered but did not approve a plan for an East Asian Economic Caucus (EAEC), a forum recommended as an alternative to the EAEG. A partial compromise was apparently reached on how the region should pursue global economic cooperation when ASEAN agreed later in the year to APEC's institutionalization. It was subsequently decided that the EAEC would operate under the "umbrella" of the APEC but would be directly coordinated by the ASEAN economic ministers. An informal ministerial session was held in July 1994 to discuss preliminary EAEC plans, but a proposed full-scale summit to formalize the caucus failed to materialize.

In July 1993 the ASEAN foreign ministers decided the association would host a regional security forum designed, among other things, to facilitate the peaceful resolution of disputes and promote regional stability. The forum—now comprising the ASEAN members, Australia, Canada, China, the EU, India, Japan, Democratic People's Republic of Korea, Republic of Korea, Mongolia, New Zealand, Pakistan, Papua New Guinea, Russia, and United States—was perceived by some as an Asian equivalent of the Conference on (later Organization for) Security and Cooperation in Europe (CSCE, OSCE), although its eventual structure and purview remained vague. It was also unclear if the new body would address human rights issues, a delicate subject for some ASEAN members.

The ASEAN Regional Forum (ARF) met for the first time July 25, 1994, during the ASEAN Ministerial Meeting in Bangkok, Thailand. Substantive talks were reported on a variety of concerns, including North Korea's nuclear posture, the region's escalating arms race, claims by a number of countries to the potentially oil-rich Spratly Islands in the South China Sea (see article on Vietnam), and the need for the other ARF members to engage China in a "genuine security dialog." However, no formal agreements were reached regarding conflict resolution mechanisms, and most attendees cautioned that they expected the ARF to proceed slowly.

Much of the attention at the August 1, 1995, session of the ARF focused on what was perceived in some quarters as Beijing's "aggressiveness," as China had recently conducted missile tests off the coast of Taiwan and constructed a military outpost on one of the Spratly Islands. Some reduction in tension was reported following the meeting in the wake of China's decision to negotiate a resolution with the other Spratly claimants based on the UN's International Law of the Sea Convention.

Meanwhile, at their annual meeting just prior to the ARF session, the ASEAN foreign ministers endorsed a proposal to move up the final implementation date for AFTA from 2003 to 2000. (The original target date of 2008 had already been changed to 2003 the previous year.) Vietnam, admitted as a full ASEAN member at the meeting, was given until 2006 to comply with the AFTA tariff reductions. Although the 2003 target date was retained at the December 1995 ASEAN summit held in Bangkok, it was agreed that attempts would be made to achieve the 2000 goal for most products.

The ASEAN foreign ministers meeting on July 20–21, 1996, appeared to be at odds with the United States and other Western nations regarding the extent to which international bodies should interfere in the domestic affairs of members. The ASEAN leaders suggested that issues such as human rights and government corruption should not be addressed by the upcoming first ministerial meeting of the World Trade Organization (WTO). The question came into even sharper focus for ASEAN two days later at the third session of the ARF, attended for the first time by India and Myanmar. The presence of the latter was the source of much discussion considering the heavy pressure Western capitals had exerted on Myanmar regarding human rights and political repression. The Myanmar controversy was also the "burning issue" at the ASEAN summit held at the end of November in Jakarta, Indonesia.

Laos and Myanmar were admitted to ASEAN on July 23, 1997, the day before the 30th annual meeting of foreign ministers was held in Kuala Lumpur, Malaysia. However, Cambodia's admission, which was to have occurred on the same day, was postponed because of renewed political turmoil there. The West, as expected, objected to Myanmar's accession, and at the July 27 meeting of the ARF the Western nations and Japan criticized Myanmar's human rights record.

The biggest problem addressed by ASEAN in 1997 was the financial crisis experienced by many of its members and other Asian countries in the latter half of the year. After some debate, in early December the ASEAN finance ministers announced they would support a leading role for the International Monetary Fund (IMF) in providing relief to regional governments in need of assistance. Later that month, the Chinese, Japanese, South Korean, and ASEAN heads of state and government, meeting in Kuala Lumpur, called for "global efforts" to help combat the fall in value of the region's currencies. The general feeling at the meeting was reportedly one of "growing dissatisfaction" with the aid offered by the IMF.

The admission of Myanmar continued to be a source of tension between ASEAN and the West in 1998, and Myanmar was excluded from the Asia-Europe Meeting (ASEM) held in London, England, in April. The primary topic of discussion at the session was the continuing Asian financial crisis. United Kingdom prime minister Tony Blair, responding to earlier criticism that the EU had not done enough to assist the ASEAN members during the recent trouble, pledged that Europe would "stick by Asia thick and thin."

At a July 1998 meeting of the ASEAN foreign ministers, a proposal from the Philippines and Thailand to include discussions on the internal affairs of members within the ASEAN framework was rejected by the other members. However, expanded dialogue was endorsed for such regional issues as forestry and piracy. The ASEAN Summit held on December 15–16 in Hanoi, Vietnam, was marked by disagreement over Cambodia's prospective membership; Hanoi, backed by Indonesia and Malaysia, pushed hard for Cambodia's immediate accession, but the other members insisted on further delay to assess the new Cambodian government's stability. (Cambodia was ultimately admitted to ASEAN at a special ceremony April 30, 1999, in Hanoi.) Prior to the summit, the ASEAN foreign and finance ministers agreed to bring AFTA's launch date forward to 2002 for the original ASEAN partners.

The 1999 annual foreign ministers' session convened July 23–24 in Singapore and was immediately followed by an ARF session. The political crisis in Indonesia and East Timor generated great concern throughout the region, but ASEAN's commitment to noninterference in members' internal affairs prevented consensus on an appropriate response. Because of the climate of violence that followed the August East Timorese independence referendum, in September the wider international community organized a peacekeeping mission led by Australia.

An informal summit held November 27–28, 1999, in Manila, overlapping meetings of the ASEAN foreign and finance ministers, again discussed developments in East Timor and also proposed a code of conduct regarding the disputed Spratly Islands, but the session was dominated by economic developments. With China, South Korea, and Japan participating, in a format dubbed "ASEAN plus three" (ASEAN +3), the session reached agreement on a nonspecific framework for East Asian economic cooperation, which was hailed as a major advance toward wider regional integration. The ASEAN leaders also advanced the target date for elimination of all import duties from 2015 to 2010 for all members except Cambodia, Laos, Myanmar, and Vietnam, which saw their target moved from 2018 to 2015.

The 33rd annual Ministerial Meeting was held July 24–25, 2000, in Bangkok, with the most notable development being a decision to establish an informal ministerial troika that would serve as a rapid response team in the event of a regional emergency. Consisting of the current ministerial chair, his predecessor, and his successor, the troika would have limited ability to act, given the noninterference principle and the need to consult all ASEAN members beforehand. The foreign ministers' meeting was once again followed by a session of the ARF, which for the first time included North Korean participation. At this meeting the EU agreed to reopen its dialogue with ASEAN three years after suspending the talks in protest of Myanmar's accession.

An informal summit November 24–25, 2000, in Singapore agreed to examine the feasibility of a free trade area that would include China, South Korea, and Japan. The summit also agreed to $1 billion in central bank support for the Chiang Mai Initiative. Final plans for implementing the swap arrangement were concluded the following May.

At the Ministerial Meeting held July 23–25, 2001, in Hanoi, Vietnam, ASEAN Secretary General Rodolfo Severino of the Philippines delivered a harsh message that summarized recent concerns over the organization's international status and its difficulties in moving forward since expansion. Describing the region as in "disarray and rudderless," Severino called for the ASEAN members to institute social and political reforms and to support more rapid economic integration.

The annual summit held November 5–6, 2001, in Bandar Seri Begawan, Brunei, was also attended by leaders of China, Japan, and South Korea. Two major developments were a commitment to oppose terrorism, despite some differences over the U.S.-led military intervention in Afghanistan, and an agreement to support a Chinese proposal for an eventual ASEAN-China free trade area (FTA). With regard to the latter, Malaysia, in particular, expressed concerns about the ability of ASEAN products to compete directly against Chinese manufacturers.

On May 20–21, 2002, the ASEAN home and security affairs ministers met in Kuala Lumpur in search of a cooperative approach toward combating terrorism and furthering regional security. At the same time, the attendees cautioned against linking terrorism to any "religion, race, culture or nationality." The annual meeting of foreign ministers, held July 29–30 in Bandar Seri Begawan, was immediately followed by an ARF session. With U.S. secretary of State Colin Powell in attendance, the ARF meeting concluded on August 1 with a declaration on fighting terrorism that specifically endorsed U.S. involvement in regional antiterrorism efforts.

The November 3–5, 2002, summit in Phnom Penh, Cambodia, was also attended by Chinese president Zhu Rongji and the Indian prime minister, Atal Bihari Vajpayee. At the meeting the ten ASEAN members signed a framework agreement on establishing an FTA by 2010, although the poorer ASEAN states—Myanmar, Cambodia, Laos, and Vietnam—were given an additional five years to eliminate specified tariff barriers. The ASEAN leaders also created a task force for drafting an FTA framework agreement with India. Significant progress was also made regarding competing territorial claims in the South China Sea, although the summit's joint declaration on the issue did not contain the formal code of conduct that ASEAN states had sought. In other business, the summit formally approved the appointment of Ong Keng Yong of Singapore as the organization's next secretary general, effective January 2003.

The second quarter of 2003 was dominated by the Asian outbreak of the new viral disease Severe Acute Respiratory Syndrome (SARS), which was most prevalent in Hong Kong and China. (Of the ASEAN states, Singapore recorded the most cases.) An emergency meeting of the ASEAN +3 health ministers on April 26 in Kuala Lumpur was quickly followed by a Special ASEAN Leaders' Meeting on SARS (and a parallel ASEAN-China session) April 29 in Bangkok. The meeting noted the outbreak's "serious adverse impact" and emphasized the importance of "strong leadership, political commitment, multisectoral collaboration and partnership" in overcoming the economic and societal consequences. By the June 11–13 meeting of the ASEAN +3 health ministers in Siem Reap, Cambodia, the crisis had passed, as the last regional case was identified May 11.

Meeting October 7–8, 2003, in Bali, Indonesia, the ASEAN leaders endorsed creation of an FTA by 2020. The Bali Concord II plan also called for greater security and social cooperation, but significant barriers remain to be overcome, including the economic disparities among members. The summit also saw various agreements signed with China, India, and Japan.

On July 2, 2004, in Jakarta, Indonesia, the ARF admitted Pakistan to its membership, following the withdrawal of Indian objections. The ARF session, which was immediately preceded by ASEAN foreign minister and ASEAN +3 meetings, covered in its discussions North Korea's nuclear weapons program, international terrorism, improved maritime security, the need to increase export controls on technology and materials that could be used in producing weapons of mass destruction (WMD), and the political situation in Myanmar. The November 27–30 summit in Vientiane, Laos, appeared to indicate a return to the principle of noninterference in members' internal matters, however, as further initiatives on Myanmar were shelved, as was the topic of Thailand's handling of an insurrection in its Muslim-dominated south. Major developments in the economic sphere included a decision to accelerate by three years the schedule for introducing the ASEAN FTA. Additionally, Brunei, Indonesia, Malaysia, Philippines, Singapore, and Thailand committed to ending internal tariffs by 2007, with Myanmar, Cambodia, Laos, and Vietnam following suit by 2012. Also at the summit, Chinese prime minister Wen Jiabao and the ASEAN leaders signed a trade agreement eliminating tariffs on many agricultural and manufactured goods by 2010.

At the foreign ministers' meeting held in Cebu, Philippines, on April 9–12, 2005, Malaysia, Philippines, and Singapore reportedly led a movement exerting pressure on Myanmar to bypass its turn to chair ASEAN. Although the Myanmar government previously resisted any such suggestion, the foreign ministers announced July 25 that Myanmar would in fact "relinquish" the chair for 2006 in favor of the Philippines, ostensibly because it wanted to maintain its focus on reconciliation and democratization at home. Meeting on July 27 the ASEAN +3 welcomed North Korea's decision to resume six-party talks (with China, Japan, Russia, South Korea, and the United States) on its nuclear program and also to resume an inter-Korean dialogue with Seoul. It was also announced that Australia, India, and New Zealand had decided to participate with the ASEAN +3 in the first East Asia Summit, scheduled for December 14, 2005, in Kuala Lumpur. Russia was also invited to participate, but the United States was not. The East Asia Summit was held jointly with the 11th ASEAN Summit on December 12–14, 2005, in Kuala Lumpur.

The early months of 2006 were marked by efforts to arrange an ASEAN fact-finding mission to Myanmar to investigate the human rights situation there. After several delays, the Myanmar government agreed to a visit by Malaysian foreign minister Syed Hamid Albar at the end of March. He made the visit, but returned one day early on March 24, apparently because he was not allowed to meet with pro-democracy leader Aung San Suu Kyi, who was under house arrest. Syed Hamid subsequently issued a statement that Myanmar's inflexibility was holding its neighbors hostage, and that ASEAN could not be expected to continue shielding Myanmar from criticism. Despite this, the July 25, 2006, foreign ministers' meeting, held in Kuala Lumpur, produced a relatively benign statement calling upon Myanmar to show progress in restoring democracy and releasing political prisoners. The meeting made little headway regarding the question of North Korea's nuclear weapons.

After a November 17, 2006, meeting in Kuala Lumpur, ASEAN promised increased cooperation with the United States in virtually all areas of mutual concern. The ASEAN summit held January 11–15, 2007, on the Philippine island of Cebu, notable for the presence of a Chinese delegation, produced an agreement to open up some service sectors of the participants' economies by July 2007. This would be a first step in creating a China-ASEAN free trade area by 2015.

During 2007 and 2008 several interrelated issues dominated ASEAN affairs. A July 20, 2007, ministerial meeting in Manila approved a draft charter for the organization. The charter, for the first time, gave legal status to ASEAN and imposed binding rules on its members. In general, the charter strengthens the secretary general's position. Among other things, it provides for a commission to monitor human rights in the region. (ASEAN has several members whose human rights records are not unblemished.) The military rulers of Myanmar came close to not signing the document charter, but the organization formally adopted the draft at its November 18–22, 2007, summit in Singapore. At the end of July 2008, at least seven member countries, including Myanmar, had ratified the charter. On October 21, 2008, Indonesia became the last country to do so, and the charter was formally launched on December 15, 2008.

Former Malaysian deputy prime minister Anwar Ibrahim, himself once a victim of human rights abuses (see Malaysia article), called the protections for democracy and human rights in the charter inadequate. Work on creating the commission was still in progress in late 2009. In general, ratification of the charter was the occasion for much comment that, while ASEAN had long talked about being an organization for its countries' peoples, it had never achieved much in that regard.

There were violently suppressed anti-government protests in Myanmar from late 2007 to early 2008. In February 2008 the ruling generals announced a referendum on a new constitution for the following May, with elections in 2010. On May 2 Cyclone Nargis devastated large parts of Myanmar, causing untold loss of life and property. Myanmar's junta initially refused outside assistance, even as thousands died from the storm's aftermath, and on May 10 it went ahead with the referendum where possible. Foreign countries were appalled by the developing tragedy, and after much wrangling ASEAN agreed to take the lead in a "coalition of mercy" to bring aid to Myanmar. The government of Myanmar grudgingly accepted medical and other assistance, but only if it came from neighboring countries.

Pitsuwan declared that ASEAN had emerged from the Myanmar disaster stronger and better able to solve regional problems as a group.

Unfortunately for ASEAN's reputation, July 2008 brought an armed standoff between Cambodian and Thai forces over the disputed site of the Preah Vihear temple. Conflict over the temple, which sits on the Cambodian-Thai border, was provoked by the UN's recent approval of Cambodia's request to classify the building as a World Heritage site. Cambodia asked ASEAN to mediate, but ASEAN foreign ministers declined, saying that the "bilateral process must be allowed to continue" between Thailand and Cambodia.

A meeting of ASEAN finance ministers was held February 26–March 1, 2009, in Thailand. This meeting was in preparation for the fourteenth ASEAN summit, originally planned for December 2008, but rescheduled for April 10–12, 2009, due to massive anti-government unrest. At the Finance Ministers' Meeting ASEAN signed a free-trade agreement with Australia and New Zealand. The meeting's main focus was on ways to mitigate damage to the group's export-dependent economies in the global economic downturn. The April 2009 summit had to be aborted. Anti-government protesters broke through police cordons at the Thai resort of Pattiya while the meeting was in progress. The ASEAN participants were airlifted to safety. Before the summit's collapse, China had offered a $10 billion investment fund to ASEAN for cooperation on infrastructure construction, energy resources, and communication.

ASEAN had always been devoted—to a fault, many said—to noninterference in its members' internal affairs. However, in August 2009, in an almost unprecedented move, ASEAN condemned Myanmar for putting the pro-democracy leader Aung San Suu Kyi on trial, after an apparently deranged American swam to the house where she was under detention.

BANK FOR INTERNATIONAL SETTLEMENTS (BIS/BIZ)

Banque des Règlements Internationaux
Bank für Internationalen Zahlungssausgleich
Banca del Regolamenti Internazionali

Established: By Agreement of Incorporation with the Swiss government dated January 20, 1930, with operations commencing March 17, 1930.

Purpose: "To promote the cooperation of central banks and to provide additional facilities for international financial operations; and to act as trustee or agent in regard to international financial settlements."

Headquarters: Basel, Switzerland. The BIS opened the Representative Office for Asia and the Pacific in Hong Kong in 1998, with a second for the Americas in Mexico City, Mexico, in November 2002.

Principal Organs: Board of Directors (16 members), General Meeting, Management.

Web site: www.bis.org

President and Chair of the Board: Guillermo Ortiz (Mexico).

Membership (55): Algeria, Argentina, Australia, Austria, Belgium, Bosnia and Herzegovina, Brazil, Bulgaria, Canada, Chile, China, Croatia, Czech Republic, Denmark, Estonia, Finland, France, Germany, Greece, Hong Kong, Hungary, Iceland, India, Indonesia, Ireland, Israel, Italy, Japan, Republic of Korea, Latvia, Lithuania, Macedonia, Malaysia, Mexico, Netherlands, New Zealand, Norway, Philippines, Poland, Portugal, Romania, Russia, Saudi Arabia, Singapore, Slovakia, Slovenia, South Africa, Spain, Sweden, Switzerland, Thailand, Turkey, United Kingdom, United States, and the European Central Bank. As of late 2009 the BIS had not yet resolved the legal consequences of the 2006 constitutional transformation of a 56th member, the Federal Republic of Yugoslavia, into Serbia and Montenegro.

Official Languages: English, French, German, Italian.

Monetary Unit: Special Drawing Right (SDR) (market rate May 30, 2007, 1.51 SDR = $1US).

Origin and development. The BIS was created to handle post–World War I reparations payments. Though the worldwide economic depression of the 1930s resulted in a moratorium on these payments, the BIS continued to function as the "central bankers' central bank." Its existence was threatened at the end of World War II, when the United States proposed its dissolution during the Bretton Woods conference, but by the 1960s the BIS had regained an important role in international monetary affairs. It became an active participant in the market and its annual reports contained valuable data on market size and fluctuations.

While the BIS was traditionally identified as a European bankers' association, the designation became less appropriate as U.S., Canadian, and Japanese banks took an increasingly active role in its policymaking. In 1970 the central bank of Canada became a member, and Japan rejoined after its membership lapsed from 1952 to 1970 as part of the World War II peace settlement. In June 1992 the status of the central banks of Estonia, Latvia, and Lithuania as BIS members was reactivated after a lapse of more than 50 years. In June 1993 the BIS agreed to divide the capital formerly held by the central bank of Czechoslovakia between the central banks of the Czech Republic and Slovakia.

On June 11, 2001, an extraordinary BIS General Meeting canceled the original shares of Yugoslavia (dating to 1931) and the provisional shares issued in June 1997 to the central banks of four of the states that succeeded the Socialist Federal Republic of Yugoslavia. The bank issued new shares to all five successor states—Bosnia and Herzegovina, Croatia, Macedonia, Slovenia, and the Federal Republic of Yugoslavia—after the five had agreed on the division of shares during April–May 2001. Yugoslavia's participation was put in abeyance in 2003 following the country's conversion to the state union of Serbia and Montenegro, each component of which has its own central bank, and the position of Serbia and Montenegro with respect to the BIS is still not settled. Other recent additions to BIS membership are the central banks of Argentina, Malaysia, and Thailand, as well as the European Central Bank, all of which were invited to join by the BIS Board of Directors in November 1999. In June 2003 similar invitations were extended to the central banks of Algeria, Chile, Indonesia, Israel, New Zealand, and the Philippines.

At an extraordinary General Meeting on January 8, 2001, the BIS amended its statutes to restrict shares to central banks and require that all privately held shares, about 14 percent of the total, be repurchased at $99.50 per share. A year later, however, representatives of small shareholders sued, claiming undervaluation by the BIS. In November 2002 the Permanent Court of Arbitration ruled in favor of the shareholders, who were to receive approximately 50 percent more per share, but still less than they had sought.

Structure. Administration is vested in three organs: the General Meeting, the Board of Directors, and the Management. The General Meeting is held annually on the second Monday in June. The Board of Directors is responsible for the conduct of the bank's operations at the highest level. The United States, although regularly represented at the bank's meetings, did not occupy the two seats to which it is entitled on the board from World War II until September 1994, at which time the chair of the Board of Governors of the U.S. Federal Reserve System and the president of the Federal Reserve Bank of New York were seated. The BIS board currently numbers 17: 6 ex officio central bankers from Belgium, France, Germany, Italy, United Kingdom, and United States; 6 named by the ex officio members; and 5 elected.

Working closely with the bank is the privately funded Group of 30, made up of leading central and commercial bankers, which meets periodically to discuss trends within the international banking community.

Activities. Although created to play a role in international settlements, the bank functions in a variety of capacities. First, it aids member central banks in managing and investing their monetary reserves. Second, it is a major research center, as evidenced by the influence of its annual report in international monetary circles and by its role in collecting and distributing statistical data on international banking and monetary trends. Third, it provides a cooperative forum for central bankers and representatives of international financial institutions. In addition, the BIS acts as (or hosts) the secretariats of the Markets Committee, formed in 1962 by the Group of 10 (G-10); the Committee on the Global Financial System (CGFS), which was set up in 1971 by the G-10 to track the functioning of financial markets; the Basel Committee on Banking Supervision (BCBS), established in 1974 by the G-10; the G-10's Committee on Payment and Settlement Systems, dating from

1990; the International Association of Insurance Supervisors (IAIS), founded in 1994; the Financial Stability Institute (FSI), established by the BCBS and the BIS in late 1998 to advance sound financial standards and practices; the Financial Stability Forum (FSF), formed in 1999; and, since May 2002, the International Association of Deposit Insurers (IADI). Since 1994 the BIS has also served as a collateral agent, holding and investing collateral for those who purchased bonds issued by Brazil as part of its debt rescheduling. The bank has since taken on a similar role with regard to Peru (1997) and Côte d'Ivoire (1998).

A recent innovation has been bimonthly global economic meetings, which are attended by central bankers from major emerging markets and from the G-10. In addition, throughout the year the BIS sponsors meetings that address such matters as financial security, information exchange, and information technology.

Another focus of recent international attention has been the deliberations of the BCBS regarding a New Capital Accord (Basel II) that would revise risk criteria for determining how much capital banks should hold. A long-awaited draft framework was issued in January 2001, but ultimately the completed Basel II accord was not released until April 2003, with implementation expected in two phases by the end of 2007. The measures set forth rigorous criteria for data collection, systems integration, and management that were expected to be expensive and challenging to meet, but implementation was expected to benefit banks by permitting them to hold less capital to cover operational, credit, and market risks. By mid-2007 national banks were rushing to meet Basel II's capital requirements.

The Annual Report issued by the BIS provides an analysis of world economic conditions and problems and summarizes the bank's activities during its fiscal year (April–March).

The 74th Annual Report (April 2003–March 2004), while noting a generally improving economic climate, warned against excessive consumer debt, particularly that fueled by the cash-out of home equity in the United States and Europe. The report also noted the extent to which the United States' current account deficit was financed by foreigners. For this and subsequent reports, the bank switched from reporting in Swiss gold francs to reporting in Special Drawing Rights (SDRs). The SDR is a valuation based on a basket of currencies, created by the International Monetary Fund (IMF) in 1969 to support the now-defunct Bretton Woods fixed exchange rate system. It has been little used in recent years, but the BIS regards it as an efficient yardstick against which to measure any currency. The 74th report showed assets of SDR million 167,934.80, as against a sum restated in SDRs as 149,619.30 for the previous year. Liabilities were SDR million 158,324.80 as against a restated 140,690.10.

The 75th Annual Report (April 2004–March 2005) noted that the world's major economies were generally growing well, with deflation no longer a concern. Competition for natural resources, however, was beginning to affect the world economy. The report encouraged the United States to get its current account debt more under control. It reported assets of SDR million 180,486.40 and liabilities of SDR million 170,223.10. In September 2005 the bank was instrumental in recovering funds of the former Nigerian dictator Sani Abacha from Swiss banks and returning them to Nigeria.

The 76th Annual Report (April 2005–March 2006) again painted a generally optimistic picture, though noting a "massive and unexpected deterioration of the US current account balance during 2005." It also warned against renewed inflation. In June 2006 the organization elected three additional central bank chairmen to its board of governors, one from Mexico, one from the European Central Bank, and the third from China. As 2006 and 2007 advanced, the U.S. dollar's position continued to weaken, and the bank reported that both China and the major oil-producing countries were beginning to diversify their foreign currency holdings away from the dollar.

The year 2008 was dominated by financial crisis, with the problems in the U.S. housing market and the worldwide and credit markets threatening economic collapse. The crisis was amply documented in the 78th Annual Report, and the BIS continued to send dire signals throughout the year. In February 2008 Malcolm Knight (Canada), the general manager of BIS, warned that the system of rating credit for financial securities needed improvement. By March the BIS was warning of inflation, even as it was calling for the world's central banks to inject liquidity into the system. By April Knight was calling the situation "probably the most serious financial turbulence in the advanced countries since the Second World War." By June the BIS believed the situation was improving a little, but Knight still called for major reforms in securitization.

Amid the turmoil, there were many complaints about financial executives losing vast amounts of money for their companies and customers, then leaving with large personal payouts. Thus Malcolm Knight's departure to manage Deutsche Bank's relations with its regulators came at an awkward time. Knight originally announced his resignation on June 20, 2008, to take effect the end of the following September. But on July 1, amid complaints about at least a perception of conflict of interest, the BIS board placed Knight on leave until his declared departure date and named Deputy General Manager Hervé Hannoun (France) to fill Knight's post on an interim basis. On November 21, 2008, the board announced the appointment of Jaime Caruana (Spain) to replace Knight as general manager. Caruana, previously counselor and director of the International Monetary Fund's Monetary and Capital Markets Department, began a five-year term on April 1, 2009.

In March 2009 the Basel Committee on Banking Supervision decided to expand its membership by inviting the participation of Australia, Brazil, China, India, Korea, Mexico, and Russia. By July the enlarged Basel Committee was in operation.

The Financial Stability Forum was an international group of financial authorities, established in 1999 to advise on and promote international financial stability. It was housed at BIS headquarters is Basel. The April 2009 London meeting of the Group of Twenty (G20, see separate article) transformed this group into a much larger Financial Stability Board, with representatives from all G20 countries, plus Spain and the European Commission. This new institution was supposed to act as a monitor and—at least in an advisory capacity—a regulator of the world's largest financial services firms. It was intended to discourage risky financial instruments, particularly the kind of derivatives that had played so large a part in the current difficulties. Like its predecessor it was to be co-located with the BIS.

By June 2009 there was some sense that the financial crisis might be easing. In this context the 2008–2009 BIS annual report caught the financial world's attention. The report warned that government spending for economic stimulus should end at the earliest possible moment to avoid serious worldwide inflation after the present crisis had passed; governments should not "mortgage the future," according to the report. More radically, the report suggested that financial products should be treated like pharmaceutical drugs, with appropriate levels of risk assigned to all products, and, on the model of over-the-counter drugs, only the safest available to everyone.

In September 2009 the bank called for a general increase in capital requirements, and Caruana stated, "It is not the right time for complacency."

BENELUX ECONOMIC UNION

Union Economique Benelux
Benelux Economische Unie

Established: Original incarnation created by Customs Convention signed September 5, 1944, in London, England; entered into force November 16, 1944, becoming fully effective January 1, 1948. Present organization created by treaty signed February 3, 1958, in The Hague, Netherlands, effective November 1, 1960.

Purpose: To develop closer economic links among member states; to ensure a coordinated policy in economic, environmental, financial, tourist, transport, and social fields; and to promote a common policy in foreign trade, particularly with regard to the exchange of goods and services with developing countries.

Headquarters: Brussels, Belgium.

Principal Organs: Committee of Ministers, Interparliamentary Consultative Council, Council of the Economic Union, Economic and Social Advisory Council, Benelux Court of Justice, General Secretariat.

Web site: www.benelux.be The site has an English-language section, but most documents are available only in French and Dutch.

Secretary General: Dr. J. P. R. M. van Laarhoven (Netherlands).

Membership (3): Belgium, Luxembourg, Netherlands.

Official Languages: French, Dutch.

Origin and development. The origins of the Benelux Economic Union can be traced to 1930 when Belgium, Luxembourg, and the Netherlands concluded a convention with Denmark, Norway, Sweden, and Finland setting forth a joint intention to reduce customs autonomy. In 1932 the Belgium-Luxembourg Economic Union (founded in 1922) and the Netherlands concluded the Convention of Ouchy, by which the three governments agreed not to increase reciprocal customs duties, to reduce import duties, and to eliminate existing commercial restrictions as soon as possible. An impasse of ten years followed, largely because of international tensions and the opposition of several countries to the loss of most-favored-nation status, but in October 1943 in London, England, the three governments in exile concluded an agreement designed to regulate payments and strengthen economic relations after the conclusion of World War II. In September 1944 in London, the same three signed the Dutch-Belgium-Luxembourg Customs Convention, which entered into force November 16, 1944, although economic disparities caused by the war delayed full implementation until January 1948. In June 1953 the governments adopted a protocol embracing social and economic policies, and an additional protocol setting forth a common commercial policy soon followed. Thus the Benelux Treaty of 1958 served primarily to codify agreements that were already concluded.

Structure. The governing body of the union is the Committee of Ministers, which comprises at least three ministers from each member state; the ministers of foreign affairs, who chair each country's delegation; and the ministers of economic affairs and finance. Meeting a minimum of once every quarter, it supervises application of the treaty and is responsible for ensuring that treaty aims are pursued. Decisions are made unanimously.

The Benelux Interparliamentary Consultative Council, often known simply as the Benelux Parliament, was established by a convention signed November 5, 1955, and predates the establishment of the present organization. The council's 49 members—21 each from Belgium and the Netherlands and 7 from Luxembourg—are chosen from the respective national parliaments. Recommendations by the council to the member states require a two-thirds majority vote; other decisions need only a simple majority.

The Council of the Economic Union, comprising senior officials from the member governments, serves as the principal administrative organ, with responsibility for ensuring implementation of decisions made by the Committee of Ministers and for recommending to the committee any proposals necessary for the functioning of the union. It also coordinates the activities of the union's numerous committees, special committees, and working parties and transmits their proposals, with its own comments, to the Committee of Ministers.

The Benelux Court of Justice was established May 11, 1974, in Brussels, Belgium. Comprised of senior judges from the member countries, it interprets common legal rules, either at the request of a national court, in which case the decisions are binding, or at the request of a member government, in which case the court serves only in a consultative capacity.

There is provision for a College of Arbitrators to settle disputes between the member states concerning the Benelux Treaty and its application, but as of mid-2008, this body had never met.

The General Secretariat is headed by a secretary general, always of Dutch nationality, and two deputy secretaries general, one from Belgium and the other from Luxembourg. It includes divisions for General Affairs, Internal Market and Economic Cooperation, Territorial Cross-Border Cooperation, Internal Affairs, and Language.

An Economic and Social Advisory Council existed prior to the new treaty of 2008 (see Activities, below). This body was designed to represent people from all walks of life. It could advance proposals on its own initiative to the Committee of Ministers and also renders advisory opinions on matters referred to it by the committee.

Activities. Benelux has facilitated the free movement of people, services, goods, and capital between member states by such measures as the abolition of passport controls and labor permits; the elimination of discrimination in regard to working conditions, social benefits, and the right to practice a profession; the removal of import duties and most quotas; and the banning of national discrimination in purchases by public bodies. It also levies uniform customs duties on products imported from non–European Union (EU) countries; acts as a single unit in concluding trade, immigration, and patent agreements with such countries; and operates as a caucus for the member countries, particularly prior to meetings of such intergovernmental economic organizations as the EU and the Organization for Economic Cooperation and Development (OECD). To further disencumber intra-Benelux trade, all internal border formalities have been conducted since 1984 through the use of a shortened form, the Single Administrative Document (SAD), which was subsequently adopted throughout the EU's predecessor, the European Community (EC).

In 1985 Benelux concluded the Schengen Agreement with France and West Germany, permitting easier border crossing for both individuals and merchandise and providing for enhanced cooperation in police and security matters. The goal was the elimination of nearly all controls at the internal borders of participating countries by 1990, although delays were encountered in that timetable as other states became signatories (see below). Coordination of the Schengen initiative was entrusted to the Benelux Secretariat.

Internally, Benelux has also focused on environmental concerns, including noise abatement, reduction in water and air pollution, and the creation of union-wide zoning maps. Cross-border cooperation between local authorities in other areas, such as fire, sewer, water, and telecommunication services, was also authorized by a convention that went into effect in 1987.

In May 1988 the Committee of Ministers endorsed a 1988–1992 work program calling for additional Schengen Accord implementation, further steps toward complete realization of the Benelux internal market, and joint action by Benelux members in larger intergovernmental organizations. Throughout 1988, discussion in Benelux organs focused on preparations for the proposed implementation of a single market by the EC on January 1, 1993, with Benelux perceiving itself as a pioneer in such integration and an important potential "motor" for the successful operation of the single market.

Another topic that joined EC integration at the top of the Benelux agenda in 1989 was the startling pace of political and economic change in Eastern Europe. In particular, the prospect of German unification contributed to a decision in late December to postpone the signing of the Schengen Accord's final convention. However, as the German picture clarified, momentum on the accord was reestablished, and a revised convention was signed June 19, 1990, by the five original signatories. Although border checks were to be lifted to provide free movement of people, the five nations agreed to tighten immigration and police controls and to establish common criteria for granting political asylum.

Italy signed the Schengen convention in November 1990, followed by Portugal and Spain in June 1991 and by Greece in November 1992. Although officials had hoped that, following ratification by the participants, the accord would be implemented on January 1, 1993, various complications arose in 1992 that made this target impossible to achieve. In part, the delay was attributable to the complexities of the ratification process of the EC's 1991 Maastricht Treaty, which provided for enhanced political and monetary union of what was styled thereafter as the EU. (The Schengen Accord was a collateral part of the Maastricht process, although Schengen cooperation would be "intergovernmental" rather than through established EU channels.) Meanwhile, Benelux pursued economic cooperation with a number of non-EU states, including the recently independent Baltic republics; the increasingly free-market-oriented Visegrád Four group (Czech Republic, Hungary, Poland, and Slovakia); and members of the Association of Southeast Asian Nations (ASEAN).

The Schengen Agreement was formally declared ready to enter into force in September 1993, even though ratification had not been completed by Italy or Greece. However, the abolition of passport controls within the bloc was subject to a series of postponements because of technical problems with the Schengen Information System (SIS). Located on a police computer in Strasbourg, France, the SIS was intended to help control immigration from non-Schengen countries, as well as assist in the fight against drug trafficking and other international crime. Several 1994 target dates proved impossible to meet, but the Schengen Accord eventually entered into force March 26, 1995, for a three-month trial period applicable to seven of the nine signatory states (the Benelux countries, France, Germany, Portugal, and Spain). The nonparticipants were Greece, in which ratification remained outstanding, and Italy, whose domestic ratification in October 1993 was not yet accepted by all other signatories. In both cases, moreover, software incompatibilities obstructed their participation in the SIS.

Austria signed the Schengen Accord on April 28, 1995, while on June 16 a framework agreement was concluded with Denmark, Finland, and Sweden, under which they would be able to join the Schengen group without jeopardizing long-established freedom of movement among all five Nordic countries (i.e., including Norway and Iceland, both non-members of the EU). Full accession by these four countries would leave Britain and Ireland as the only EU members not to be Schengen signatories, the former out of preference and the latter because of the greater importance of preserving free movement between the republic and the United Kingdom. One difficulty encountered in the April–June 1995 trial period of the Schengen Accord was the refusal of the French authorities to allow cross-border pursuit of suspected criminals in France on the grounds that the necessary domestic legislation had not been enacted. After reviewing this and other problems, a meeting of the Schengen executive committee on June 29 rejected a French request for a six-month extension of the trial period, declaring that the accord was "irrevocably in force," whereupon France invoked a clause allowing it to maintain border controls unilaterally for reasons of special national interest.

On January 1, 1997, the Nordic countries (Denmark, Finland, Iceland, Norway, and Sweden) acceded to the Schengen Accord, Iceland and Norway having concluded Cooperation Agreements that allowed them to participate despite their non-EU status. The Greek Parliament ratified the accord the following July, while Austria, Germany, and Italy announced they would implement the Schengen provisions in 1998. Meanwhile, all three Benelux countries received European Commission endorsement for participation in the launching of the EU's Economic and Monetary Union in 1999.

Responsibility for Schengen matters officially passed to the EU under the Schengen Protocol of its 1997 Treaty of Amsterdam, which entered into effect May 1, 1999. Adoption of the treaty necessitated revision of the arrangements permitting Norwegian and Icelandic participation, and on May 18 a replacement "association" agreement was concluded. Full Schengen participation by the Nordic countries was inaugurated on March 25, 2001. The United Kingdom and Ireland have been permitted to implement selected Schengen provisions, such as those involving cross-border crime and illegal immigration.

The Benelux countries have focused their attention on eliminating remaining obstacles in their combined market, chiefly those caused by lack of harmonization in national laws. Other areas of interest include coordinating Benelux implementation of new EU regulations and fostering cooperation in such areas as standardization and certification and intellectual property. Cross-border cooperation has also taken on increased importance with regard to town and country planning, the interactions of local authorities, the environment, transport and distribution, and the status and problems of trans-frontier workers.

In May 2003, with major expansion of the EU only a year away, Dutch foreign minister Jaap de Hoop Scheffer joined his Czech counterpart Cyril Svoboda in promoting close cooperation between the Benelux and the Visegrád Four countries. Their stance reflected the concern among many of the smaller current and prospective EU states that their voices would carry less weight in a future EU. Similarly, in October 2007 the Benelux foreign ministers met in Riga, Latvia, with their counterparts from Estonia, Latvia, and Lithuania. They discussed the position of smaller states within the EU and planned to continue meeting at least annually. The latest of these so-called "3+3" meetings occurred in April 2009.

April 2004 saw a series of accords designed to improve standardization and harmonize cooperation of police activity in the three Benelux countries. The provisions were to be phased in on an ad hoc basis over the next two years, with final implementation due in January 2007. On November 30, 2005, the Benelux countries renewed an expiring 1999 treaty concerning a common approach to development and the mobility of commerce in the Rhine-Scheldt estuary. This treaty will remain in force until 2011. The 2005 failure of the proposed European Constitution to be ratified caused a long-running debate about the future of the EU and the effects of eastward enlargement. In this debate, the Benelux countries stressed the importance of strengthening the EU's internal institutions before significant further growth in the community.

The original Benelux treaty was scheduled to expire in 2010. In June 2008 the three original signatories renewed the treaty, with amendments to address present-day conditions. The new treaty recognizes a Benelux Organization for Intellectual Property. The treaty strongly affirms the Benelux grouping's importance, and affirms that the three nations, when combined, can have a much stronger voice within the councils of the EU than they might have had individually.

CARIBBEAN COMMUNITY AND COMMON MARKET (CARICOM)

Established: August 1, 1973, pursuant to the July 4, 1973, Treaty of Chaguaramas (Trinidad), as successor to the Caribbean Free Trade Association.

Purpose: To deepen the integration process prevailing within the former Caribbean Free Trade Association, to enable all member states to share equitably in the benefits of integration, to operate certain subregional common services, and to coordinate the foreign policies of the member states.

Headquarters: Georgetown, Guyana.

Principal Organs: Heads of Government Conference, Heads of Government Bureau, Community Council of Ministers, Ministerial Councils, Secretariat.

Web site: www.caricom.org

Secretary General: Edwin Carrington (Trinidad and Tobago).

Membership (15): Antigua and Barbuda, Bahamas (member of the community but not the common market), Barbados, Belize, Dominica, Grenada, Guyana, Haiti, Jamaica, Montserrat, St. Kitts-Nevis, St. Lucia, St. Vincent and the Grenadines, Suriname, Trinidad and Tobago.

Associate Members (5): Anguilla, Bermuda, British Virgin Islands, Cayman Islands, Turks and Caicos Islands.

Observers (7): Aruba, Colombia, Dominican Republic, Mexico, Netherlands Antilles, Puerto Rico, Venezuela.

Official Language: English.

Origin and development. The formation of the Caribbean Free Trade Association (Carifta) in 1968 followed several earlier attempts to foster economic cooperation among the Commonwealth countries and territories of the West Indies and Caribbean. Antigua, Barbados, and Guyana signed the initial agreement December 15, 1965, in Antigua, while an amended accord was approved February 23, 1968, in Georgetown, Guyana, by those governments, Trinidad and Tobago, and the West Indies Associated States. Jamaica joined in June 1968 and was followed later in the month by the remaining British-associated islands, which had previously agreed to establish their own Eastern Caribbean Common Market. Belize was accepted for membership in June 1970.

At an eight-member conference of heads of state of the Caribbean Commonwealth countries in April 1973 in Georgetown, the decision was made to replace Carifta with a new Caribbean Community and Common Market (Caricom) that would provide additional opportunities for economic integration, with an emphasis on obtaining greater benefits for the less-developed members. The new grouping was formally established July 4, 1973, in Chaguaramas, Trinidad, by the prime ministers of Barbados, Guyana, Jamaica, and Trinidad. Although the treaty came into effect August 1, 1973, Carifta was not formally superseded until May 1, 1974, by which time all former Carifta members except Antigua and St. Kitts-Nevis-Anguilla had acceded to the new group. Antigua joined July 5, 1974, and St. Kitts-Nevis-Anguilla acceded on July 26, with St. Kitts-Nevis continuing its membership after the United Kingdom resumed responsibility for the administration of Anguilla in late 1980. After a lengthy period of close cooperation with the grouping, the Bahamas formally acceded to membership in the community (but not the common market) in July 1983. Suriname was admitted in 1995, thereby becoming the first Caricom member whose official language was not English. Haiti, a long-standing observer, was invited to join at the July 1997 Caricom summit, with final terms for full accession set two years later. Deposit of an accession instrument followed ratification by the Haitian Parliament in May 2002.

The 1973 treaty called for a common external tariff (CET) and a common protective policy vis-à-vis community trade with non-members, a scheme to harmonize fiscal incentives to industry and development planning, and a special regime for the less-developed members of the community. However, in the wake of unfavorable economic developments during the mid-1970s, progress toward economic coordination and integration stagnated. Cooperation in finance and joint development projects was virtually halted, and members resorted to developing separate, often conflicting, policies. This problem was most acute in the area of trade, in which Guyana and Jamaica adopted protectionist policies in an effort to offset severe foreign exchange shortages.

The 1984 Nassau Agreement called for the dismantling of trade barriers among Caricom members, but quick implementation proved difficult. The Eighth Conference of Heads of Government in July 1987 successfully pledged to remove all intracommunity protectionist measures by the final quarter of 1988, although the smaller Eastern Caribbean countries, who had protested that certain sectors were not sufficiently "healthy" to withstand free market pressures, were allowed to protect several industries and products at least until 1991.

As early as 1984 Caricom leaders had agreed to impose a CET on certain imports, but over the next decade deadlines for introducing a comprehensive CET were repeatedly missed. The first CET, with a 30–35 percent maximum, was finally instituted in 1993 and then lowered, in two additional phases, to 0–25 percent, although members were permitted considerable flexibility with regard to application. At the same time, Caricom moved forward on a 1989 pledge to create a unified regional market in "the shortest possible time." Goals for the market included elimination of any remaining trade barriers between members, free movement of skilled labor, abolition of passport requirements, development of regional air and sea transport systems using the resources of existing carriers, and rationalization of investment incentives throughout the community. Adoption of a single currency was also discussed. In furtherance of economic and political integration, in 1989 the heads of government established the West Indian Commission that, in 1992, proposed formation of the broader Association of Caribbean States (see separate entry on the ACS).

Recognizing the need for collateral organizational reform, in October 1992 the Caricom heads of government authorized formation of a task force whose work ultimately led to adoption in February 1997 of Protocol I amending the Treaty of Chaguaramas. The first of nine related protocols, Protocol I significantly restructured Caricom's organs, principally by creating the Community Council of Ministers as the second highest Caricom organ and authorizing formation of supportive ministerial councils. Five months later at the annual summit held in Montego Bay, Jamaica, the Caricom leaders called for establishing the Caricom Single Market and Economy (CSME) by 1999, although the goal was still unattained in 2009.

Structure. Policy decisions under the Treaty of Chaguaramas are assigned to the Heads of Government Conference, which meets annually and is the final authority for all Caricom forums. Each participating state has one vote and most decisions are taken unanimously. The chair of the conference rotates annually among the members. Until 1998 the Common Market Council dealt with operational aspects of common market activity, but, as part of the Protocol I restructuring, it was replaced by the Community Council of Ministers. The new council, the organization's second-highest organ, consists of community affairs ministers and any others designated by each member state. Its responsibilities include strategic planning and coordination of economic integration, functional cooperation, and external relations.

In 1992 the four-member Bureau of the Conference, comprised of the current conference chair, predecessor and scheduled successor, and the secretary general, was established to initiate development proposals, as well as to help bridge the gap between summit decisions and member implementation. Partly in response to criticism that the bureau would be unable to provide the necessary day-to-day oversight, the Technical Action Services Unit was established within the Secretariat in 1994. It currently helps member states implement regional decisions and also assists in preparations for initiating the CSME.

Also assisting the Conference and the Council of Ministers are four ministerial councils: Council for Finance and Planning (COFAP), Council for Foreign and Community Relations (COFCOR), Council for Human and Social Development (COHSOD), and Council for Trade and Economic Development (COTED). In addition, there are legal affairs, budget, and central bank governors committees. The Secretariat, Caricom's principal administrative organ, is headed by a secretary general and includes several administrative directorates in support of the Ministerial Councils. A deputy and various assistant secretaries general oversee numerous subsidiary offices.

The Assembly of Caribbean Community Parliamentarians (ACCP), whose creation was endorsed at the 1989 Caricom summit, was established in mid-1994 after a sufficient number of member states ratified the related agreement. A consultative body, the new assembly was designed to promote public and governmental interest in Caricom.

Caricom has established or sponsors several other community institutions, including the Caribbean Agricultural Research and Development Institute in St. Augustine, Trinidad and Tobago; the Caribbean Center for Development Administration in St. Michael, Barbados; the Caribbean Community Climate Change Center in Belmopan, Belize; the Caribbean Disaster Emergency Response Agency in St. Michael; the Caribbean Environmental Health Institute in Castries, St. Lucia; the Caribbean Food and Nutrition Institute in St. Augustine; the Caribbean Food Corporation in Port-of-Spain, Trinidad and Tobago; the Caribbean Institute for Meteorology and Hydrology in Husbands, Barbados; the Caribbean Meteorological Organization in Port-of-Spain; the Caribbean Regional Fisheries Mechanism; the Caribbean Regional Negotiating Machinery in Kingston, Jamaica; the Caribbean Regional Organization for Standards and Quality in Bridgetown, Barbados; and the Caribbean Telecommunications Union in Nassau, Bahamas. Associate institutions include the Caribbean Development Bank (CDB) in St. Michael (see separate entry on the CDB under Regional and Subregional Development Banks); the University of Guyana in Turkeyen, Guyana; the University of the West Indies in Bridgetown; the Caribbean Law Institute in Bridgetown; and the Secretariat of the Organization of Eastern Caribbean States (OECS; see separate entry) in Castries.

Activities. Regional integration and development lie at the center of Caricom's activities, but the organization has also negotiated agreements with neighboring countries and sought a common voice in various international forums, particularly those involving trade and globalization. Among the nearby countries with which Caricom has concluded trade or other agreements are Mexico, Colombia, Venezuela, and the Dominican Republic. Caricom regularly meets with the latter in the Caribbean Forum, and the two concluded a free trade agreement in May 2000 after four years of negotiations. With regard to the broader issue of positioning itself to compete in the global economy, in 1997 Caricom created a Regional Negotiating Mechanism (RNM) to outline a strategy for international trade and economic negotiations, although the RNM soon ran into "serious financial problems" because of funding shortfalls.

Relations with the United States have frequently proved frustrating, in part because of Washington's objections to Caricom's behind-the-scenes efforts to facilitate Cuba's reintegration into the Organization of American States (OAS) and other international groupings. Despite this, U.S. president Bill Clinton met with Caricom leaders May 10, 1997, in Bridgetown to discuss drug smuggling and other issues. Security agreements between the United States and Caricom members that allow U.S. law enforcement officials access to the national waters of Caribbean countries were completed. Clinton promised limited aid to overcome the effects of a recent World Trade Organization (WTO) ruling on a complaint brought by the United States protesting the European Union (EU) granting Caribbean bananas preferential access to EU markets.

Caricom has also found itself at odds with the EU. In the late 1990s, in the course of negotiations related to replacing the soon-to-expire Lomé Convention, Caricom objected to the European Commission's proposed division of the African, Caribbean, and Pacific (ACP) group by region and level of economic development, and the inclusion of human rights and good governance language in the successor to the Lomé agreement. Caricom launched a campaign to counter these proposals in March 1998, and it also urged the EU to minimize the extent of revisions to its banana import regime, fearing that drastic changes would wreak havoc on some of the economies in the region.

At the July 1998 Caricom summit, held in St. Lucia, community leaders approved plans to form the new Caribbean Court of Justice (CCJ) to function as a court of final appeal (replacing the United Kingdom's Privy Council in the case of the 12 Caricom states with historical ties to the United Kingdom) and settle disputes arising from the Treaty of Chaguaramas. The community's ongoing mediation efforts in Guyana were also discussed (see separate article on Guyana).

The 20th summit, held July 4–7, 1999, in Port-of-Spain saw further progress toward establishing the CCJ, despite objections from some who saw the proposed displacement of the UK Privy Council as an effort to reintroduce capital punishment. The Heads of Government Conference also addressed another controversy—namely, the threat of sanctions by the Organization for Economic Cooperation and

Development (OECD). The OECD included 11 Caricom members (the exceptions being Bahamas, Guyana, Suriname, and Trinidad and Tobago) on its list of jurisdictions having "harmful" tax policies. The heads of government also signed three of the last five protocols—on trade, transport, and disadvantaged sectors and countries—needed for implementation of the CSME. (Previously signed protocols, including Protocol I, covered the establishment of businesses; provision of services; movement of capital and labor; industrial policy; trade policy; and agricultural policy.) The last two protocols, covering rules of competition and consumer protection and disputes resolution, were signed at the 11th intersessional Heads of Government Meeting, which met March 13–14, 2000, in St. Kitts. At the session, also in furtherance of CSME preparation, the leaders assigned special sectoral portfolios: to Antigua and Barbuda, services, including information technology and telecommunications; Bahamas, tourism; Barbados, the CSME, including monetary union; Belize, sustainable development, including disaster management; Dominica, labor; Grenada, science and technology; Guyana, agriculture; Haiti (despite its then-provisional status), transportation; Jamaica, external relations; St. Kitts-Nevis, health; St. Lucia, justice and governance; St. Vincent, bananas; Suriname, community development and culture; and Trinidad and Tobago, security, including drug-related issues.

On July 15–16, 2000, shortly after the 2000 annual conference, Caricom convened in Castries to discuss the OECD tax policy issue and the recent report of the Group of Seven's Financial Action Task Force (FATF), which labeled Bahamas, Dominica, St. Kitts-Nevis, and St. Vincent as "uncooperative" in efforts to combat money laundering. In response, the Bureau of the Conference set up the Caribbean Association of Regulators of International Business (CARIB), which was assigned the initial task of evaluating the FATF criteria. In June 2001 the FATF removed Bahamas from its noncompliance list, although Grenada was added in September. St. Kitts was removed in June 2002, as were Dominica in October 2002, Grenada in February 2003, and St. Vincent in June 2003.

In November 2000 Caricom leaders objected to EU plans to grant, with effect from 2001, the world's 48 least-developed countries duty- and quota-free access to EU markets, which Caricom saw as having "disastrous social and economic consequences" for particular member states. In February 2001 the EU somewhat assuaged Caricom's concern by delaying full implementation of the policy until 2006 for the banana market and until 2009 for the rice and sugar markets. The banana market ultimately remained untouched, though threatened, into 2008 (see below).

In furtherance of introducing the CSME, the July 3–6, 2001, Heads of Government Conference agreed in principle to phase out remaining restrictions on the free movement of capital, goods, and services, while in August Caricom joined with the International Monetary Fund and the UN Development Programme in announcing establishment in Bridgetown of a Caribbean Regional Technical Assistance Center (Cartac) to provide technical assistance and training in economic and financial management issues; including budgeting, tax policy and administration, statistics, and financial oversight. With additional funding from Canada, the CDB, the Inter-American Development Bank, the United Kingdom, the United States, and the World Bank, Cartac opened in November.

In the wake of the September 11, 2001, terrorist attacks on the United States, an emergency summit convened October 11–12, 2001, in Nassau, Bahamas, to examine the regional economic impact. Particular concern was expressed about major losses in the tourism industry. In addition, the participants agreed to implement a Regional Task Force on Crime and Security, with its sphere of concern including money laundering and terrorism.

The July 3–5, 2002, Heads of Government Conference in Georgetown continued preparations for the CCJ, called for accelerated progress toward the CSME, and discussed ACP policies under the new Cotonou Agreement. The conference attendees also expressed concern about the decelerating regional growth rate, which was attributed to such factors as globalization and the loss of trade preferences, stiffer international requirements for offshore financial activities, and losses in the tourism industry. Illicit drug trafficking and a rise in related violent crime also drew attention at the session. More positively, the participating countries signed a collective agreement with pharmaceutical companies to reduce the cost of HIV/AIDS drugs.

Later in the year, on December 8, many of the Caricom heads of government convened in Havana, Cuba, to mark the 30th anniversary of having established diplomatic relations with the Castro government. The session's concluding declaration once again called for an end to the U.S. economic embargo of Cuba and efforts to restrict Havana's participation in multilateral forums.

Meeting July 2–5, 2003, in Montego Bay, the heads of government signed several documents required for inaugurating the CCJ, to be sited in Trinidad and Tobago, in November. They included the Protocol on the Privileges and Immunities of the Caribbean Court of Justice and the Regional Judicial and Legal Services Commission, and the Agreement Establishing the Caribbean Court of Justice Trust Fund. The latter measure permitted the CDB to begin raising some $100 million to capitalize the trust fund. In the area of external trade, the attendees discussed anticipated negotiations with the EU related to Economic Partnership Agreements under the ACP, continuing plans for the proposed Free Trade Area of the Americas (FTAA), and ongoing WTO negotiations, all of which will have significant impact on the CSME. Governance issues within the organization and the prospects for restructuring regional air transportation were among the other topics addressed at the midyear summit.

The July 4–7, 2004, summit in St. George's, Grenada, continued a review of options for administrative reform of the organization, including the possibility of establishing a commission (like the EU's) or a similar executive mechanism. The matter was referred to the ACCP, whose consultative role was also under review. In April the heads of government welcomed the start of discussions with the EU on a regional Economic Partnership Agreement, although significant differences, especially over bananas and sugar, persist. The summit agreed that a tenth special session in November would focus on the CSME.

The CCJ was inaugurated on April 16, 2005, even though only Barbados and Guyana approved its jurisdiction over civil and criminal appeals. In general, the Caricom members favored letting the court review issues related to the revised Treaty of Chaguaramas and the anticipated CSME, but most had not resolved reservations about the court's appellate status. The CCJ began hearing its first case, an appeal of a libel verdict from Barbados, in August 2005.

The 26th Heads of Government Conference convened July 3–6, 2005, in St. Lucia, and the participants agreed that the CSME would be launched at the end of the year. The Bahamas, however, opted out, fearing that its comparatively prosperous economy would attract an overwhelming number of immigrants from other Caricom states and that, with most of its trade involving non-Caricom countries, it would not significantly benefit by participating. To assuage the concern of the Eastern Caribbean member states that they would be dwarfed by Trinidad and Tobago's economy, the summit agreed to investigate establishing a regional development bank. In other matters, the summit endorsed the Management Framework for Crime and Security, which would raise national security and law enforcement to the ministerial level, and continued to express concern about political turmoil in Haiti. Haiti was suspended from active participation in Caricom after the ouster of its president, Jean-Bertrand Aristide, in February 2004.

The 10th conference of heads of state was held October 3–5, 2005, in Belize. Discussions focused on environmental matters, including the protection of biodiversity and the promotion of sustainable development. The 17th intersessional meeting of the Heads of Government Conference on February 9–10, 2006, in Port-of-Spain, was mostly concerned with a review of progress toward implementation of the CSME. Significant among the ongoing developments were the Caricom passport, currently adopted by some but not all states, and progress toward an agreement on free movement of all workers within the group. Free movement is currently confined to certain categories of skilled workers and students, and full liberalization is proving slow. Barbados prime minister Owen Arthur was quoted after the meeting as saying the way was now clear for full implementation of the CSME, which he saw happening by 2008.

After the February 26, 2006, victory of Rene Preval in the Haiti presidential elections, Caricom was quick to invite Haiti to return to full participation in the organization. President Preval was welcomed at the 11th Heads of State Conference held on July 3–6, 2006, in St. Kitts-Nevis. A September 2006 meeting in New York between Caricom foreign ministers and the U.S. secretary of state, Condoleezza Rice, was described as "very cordial." However, the organization did not waver in its (ultimately unsuccessful) support for Venezuela receiving a nonpermanent seat on the UN Security Council, and it continued its support for Cuba's reintegration into world counsels.

Much of 2008 was dominated by controversy over the Economic Partnership Agreement (EPA) between the Cariforum (Caricom plus the Dominican Republic) and the European Union (EU), originally scheduled for signing by December 31, 2007, when the Cotonou agreement expired. The EPA was duly initialed in December 2007, but its ratification by the Caricom states, first scheduled for April 2008, was postponed several times. The last date mentioned was October 31, 2008, a date specified by the EU as a deadline. The agreement was widely criticized throughout the region as exposing Caricom members to job losses and competition from EU products and services. On October 30, 2008, all Cariforum members except Guyana and Haiti signed the EPA. The president of Guyana, Bharrat Jagdeo, declared that his country would be prepared to sign a goods-only version of the EPA. Otherwise, he prophesied complete EU domination of the region within twenty years. Haiti was not ready to sign the agreement at all.

The Caribbean Regional Negotiating Machinery (CRNM) had taken the lead on EPA negotiations, and was widely criticized by Caricom members who did not favor the deal. At Caricom's intersessional Heads of Government Meeting, held March 12–13, 2009, in Belmopan, Belize, it was decided to phase out the CRNM, and integrate its functions into the Caricom secretariat. As Dean Barrow, the prime minister of Belize, said, "Nobody was quite sure how the CRNM fit into the Caricom structure, from the point of view of the treaty and what it had to say about various organs and the legal authority of the various organs." The March meeting, dominated by the world financial crisis and its implications for the region, also considered the practicalities of implementing the EPA with Europe, and the status of negotiations with Canada on a new trade agreement.

The economic crisis continued to take a toll on prospects for Caribbean unity. In May 2009 Prime Minister Ralph GONSALVES of St. Vincent declared that his fellow-citizens were being discriminated against in some Caricom countries, and that it might be better for St. Vincent to withdraw from the CSME. In May also came complaints of discrimination by the government of Antigua and Barbuda against other Caricom nationals, with stories of midnight raids and deportations. Similarly in August 2008 Guyanese citizens who had been convicted of crimes were deported from Barbados under the provisions of a new "Barbadian First" amnesty law, which allowed them to be treated differently from Barbadian nationals.

Global economic conditions cast a general malaise over Caricom. In July 2009 Jamaican prime minister Bruce GOLDING spoke in favor of creating a permanent institution, so that important community decisions need not wait for a semi-annual conference. Debate continued as to whether an unelected directorate, on the EU model, would be suitable for Caricom.

CENTRAL AFRICAN ECONOMIC AND MONETARY COMMUNITY (CEMAC)

Communauté Economique et Monétaire de l'Afrique Centrale

Established: By the Central African Customs and Economic Union (UDEAC) under a treaty signed March 15–16, 1994, in N'Djamena, Chad; formally succeeded the UDEAC in June 1999, following ratification of the treaty by the member states.

Purpose: To promote socioeconomic integration and sustainable development in Central Africa through monetary and economic unions.

Headquarters: Bangui, Central African Republic.

Principal Organs: Conference of Heads of State, Council of Ministers of the Central African Economic Union, Ministerial Council of the Central African Monetary Union, Executive Secretariat.

Web site: The site www.cemac.cf appears to be defunct.

President of the Commission: Antoine Ntsimi (Cameroon).

Membership (6): Cameroon, Central African Republic, Chad, Republic of the Congo, Equatorial Guinea, Gabon.

Official Language: French.

Origin and development. Prior to attaining independence, the Central African Republic, Chad, the Congo, and Gabon were joined in the Equatorial Customs Union (*Union Douanière Equatoriale*—UDE), which sought to harmonize the fiscal treatment of industrial investments. In June 1961 Cameroon joined the UDE, and by mid-1962 an external common tariff had been established. In 1964 the members began to practice more comprehensive economic cooperation, including coordination of development policies, especially in the fields of infrastructure and industrialization. Then on December 8 of that year, in Brazzaville, Congo, the five countries signed a treaty establishing the Central African Customs and Economic Union (*Union Douanière et Economique de l'Afrique Centrale*—UDEAC), effective January 1, 1966.

In early 1968 Chad and the Central African Republic announced their intention to withdraw from the UDEAC, but the latter reversed itself later in the year. Chad's withdrawal became effective January 1, 1969, although N'Djamena continued to participate in some activities. In December 1975 Chad was granted observer status in the Council of Heads of State and ultimately rejoined the group in December 1984. Equatorial Guinea joined the UDEAC in December 1983.

The November 1992 UDEAC summit endorsed the creation of a Central African Economic and Monetary Community (*Communauté Economique et Monétaire de l'Afrique Centrale*—CEMAC). Subsequently, in 1994, prompted in part by repercussions from the 50 percent devaluation of the CFA franc in January, a UDEAC summit on March 15–16 in N'Djamena signed a treaty creating CEMAC. Although another summit on December 21–22 in Yaoundé, Cameroon, reaffirmed the integrationist commitment, decisions were delayed on a timetable for the implementation of CEMAC provisions.

At the February 5, 1998, summit, Gabonese president Omar Bongo urged members to ratify the CEMAC treaty, stating that the establishment of the Central African Monetary Union would "mark the end of recovery and the beginning of a new dynamism." The only country to have ratified the treaty by that time was the Central African Republic, but the ratification process accelerated thereafter, and the inaugural CEMAC summit was held in June 1999, in Malabo, Equatorial Guinea.

Structure. The Conference of Heads of State meets at least once a year to coordinate the general monetary and economic policies of the participating states. The CEMAC treaty created a Monetary Union (*Union Monétaire de l'Afrique Centrale*—UMAC), which is under the direction of a Ministerial Council, and an Economic Union (*Union Economique de l'Afrique Centrale*—UEAC), directed by a Council of Ministers. Specialized institutions integrated into the UEAC are the Interstate Customs School, the Subregional Multisectoral Institute for Applied Technology, the Subregional Institute for Statistics and Applied Economics, and the Development Bank of the Central African States (*Banque de Développement des Etats de l'Afrique Centrale*—BDEAC). The UMAC incorporates the Bank of the Central African States (*Banque des Etats de l'Afrique Centrale*—BEAC) and the Banking Commission of Central Africa. The treaty also called for formation of a Community Parliament and a Community Court of Justice.

The chief administrative officer of the CEMAC is an executive secretary, who heads an Executive Secretariat with various divisions and offices responsible for administrative and financial affairs. These departments include agriculture, food security, and the environment; the common market; economic analysis; education and culture; industrial commerce and tourism; juridical and institutional affairs; and transport and telecommunications.

Activities. As forerunner of the CEMAC, the UDEAC adjusted common external customs tariffs; coordinated legislation, regulations, and investment codes; harmonized internal taxes; and developed common industrialization projects, development plans, and transport policies. In 1973 the BEAC was established as a central bank for all UDEAC members and Chad, and it continues in that capacity for the CEMAC.

In January 1978 the UDEAC heads of state adopted additional measures designed to facilitate economic unity. These included a projected common income tax, community administration of waterways between Bangui in the Central African Republic and Brazzaville, and harmonization of legislation dealing with migration and industrialization. In addition, members agreed to increase cooperation in business and civil service administration; to standardize customs procedures; and to establish common structures for scientific and technical research, transportation, communications, and tourism. Subsequently, the UDEAC played a major role in formation of the Economic Community of Central African States (*Communauté Economique des Etats de l'Afrique*

Centrale—CEEAC), an association of 11 French- and Portuguese-speaking states established in October 1983 (see separate CEEAC article).

The late 1980s saw the UDEAC make little specific headway on regional economic integration, although a declaration issued at the conclusion of the organization's 1988 summit reaffirmed the members' commitment to that goal. In light of continuing financial constraints, the December 1990 summit ordered sharp cutbacks in the UDEAC secretariat staff and deferred consideration of a regional value-added tax and/or a community integration tax.

Activity over the next several years focused on establishment of the CEMAC, which was expected to be a more effective vehicle for regional integration. CEMAC was formally inaugurated at a summit on June 25–26, 1999, in Malabo, concurrent with the summit of the CEEAC. The two organizations again held parallel summits in June 2000 in Libreville, Gabon, where the CEMAC attendees remarked positively on the ongoing development of institutional arrangements, including formation of an interparliamentary commission. They also announced their intention to revitalize the BDEAC and called attention to the challenges presented by economic globalization and the concomitant need for stronger regional and subregional integration. In May–June 2001 the CEMAC/CEEAC trade ministers met in Yaoundé to prepare for ACP (African, Caribbean, and Pacific) trade negotiations with the European Union (EU). At the second regular CEMAC summit, held in mid-December 2000 in N'Djamena, the national leaders agreed to accelerate introduction of a common passport and to establish a regional stock exchange in Libreville.

The focus of attention at an extraordinary summit held in early December 2001 in Libreville was the volatile political situation in the Central African Republic (CAR), where the armed forces chief, Gen. François Bozize, was dismissed because of his alleged involvement in a failed May 2001 coup against President Ange-Félix Patassé. The CEMAC leaders established an ad hoc commission of Presidents Bongo of Gabon, Idriss Déby of Chad, and Denis Sassou-Nguesso of the Republic of Congo to encourage the disputants to negotiate. Shortly after the December 5 conclusion of the Libreville session, the CEMAC leaders convened for a previously scheduled annual summit in Yaoundé, where plans for a joint air transport company, introduction of the common passport, and medium-term customs and tax reforms were discussed.

Beginning in early 2002 the CEMAC's attention became increasingly diverted by the deteriorating situation in the CAR. An extraordinary summit on August 15 in Brazzaville authorized dispatch of an observer team to the CAR as a consequence of escalating tensions with Chad, which gave refuge to General Bozize. Meanwhile, Bozize loyalists continued to threaten the CAR's internal security. A CEMAC crisis summit in early October 2002 was followed in late January 2003 by the fourth ordinary Conference of Heads of State, which urged the CAR government to open talks with the rebels and called on the two neighboring states to resolve their differences. By that time a CEMAC peacekeeping force was already being deployed to the CAR, replacing a contingent that Libya sent in May 2001 to protect President Patassé's government. On March 15, 2003, however, General Bozize mounted a successful coup, which led the CEMAC Conference of Heads of State, meeting June 2–3 in Libreville, to officially recognize the successor regime. The decision came following General Bozize's presentation of a plan for the rapid restoration of democracy. The conference then called for international humanitarian assistance for the CAR as well as other measures to restore the country's peace and security. Several hundred CEMAC troops from Gabon, Chad, and the Republic of the Congo remained deployed in the CAR with a mandate that included protecting the capital and provincial towns, securing transportation routes, disarming combatants, and restructuring the CAR armed forces.

Meanwhile, the CEMAC moved forward on various initiatives, including improvements in cross-border land transport and initiation of the public/private Air CEMAC. This airline, which was initially expected to begin operations by the end of 2003, encountered difficulties in starting up, and its first flight is still a matter of conjecture. In addition to their involvement in negotiating partnership agreements with the EU, the CEMAC trade ministers continued to formulate a common position for international trade forums. Other CEMAC concerns included food security and self-sufficiency, as well as sustainable use of the region's forests.

The fifth Heads of State Conference, held January 28, 2004, in Brazzaville, produced a nonaggression pact, an agreement on judicial cooperation between the member states, and an agreement on extradition. The sixth conference was held February 11, 2005, in Libreville. It encouraged peace and civic responsibility in the troubled states of the CAR, Côte d'Ivoire, and Togo, and expressed concern about the deteriorating situation in the Darfur region of Sudan.

The seventh conference, held on March 14–15, 2006, in Bata, Equatorial Guinea, was marked by the early return home of President Déby of Chad in face of an attempted coup against him; the coup failed. The conference, noting the slow progress of subregional integration, set up a task force, due to report in 2008, to see what could be done.

Jean Nkuete resigned as the organization's secretary-general to become Cameroon's minister of state for agriculture and rural development in September 2006. He was succeeded on an acting basis by his former deputy, Dieudonné Mouriri Boussougou of Gabon.

Amid criticisms that CEMAC was ego-ridden and ineffective, the proposed March 17, 2007 summit, to be held in N'Djamena, was delayed at the last minute. It finally began on April 25. This eighth summit ended with a declaration urging the CAR and Chad to pursue cordial relations with Sudan, while at the same time deploring outside efforts (that is, from Sudan) to destabilize these two countries. The meeting also decided to set up a special fund to help victims of atrocities in Chad and the CAR.

In July 2007 the Institutional Reforms Steering Committee met in Yaoundé and produced a reform plan that, among other things, replaced the Executive Secretariat with a Commission. The new structure was expected to make CEMAC more effective. The June 2008 CEMAC summit, also held in Yaoundé, endorsed the plan. Cameroonian politician Antoine Ntsimi headed the Commission.. The June summit articulated the goal of a revitalized CEMAC, together with a call for the establishment of a common CEMAC passport by 2010, cooperation with regional airline companies to make Air CEMAC a reality, and development of a regional economic plan to be ready for signature by December 2008 at an extraordinary summit of CEMAC heads of state. In December 2008 South African Airways announced a deal to operate flights under the Air CEMAC name.

The summit actually took place on January 30, 2009, in Libreville, and was dominated by the world economic crisis. The meeting's consensus was that the CEMAC area was not as badly affected by the crisis as it might have been. The most serious problem seemed to be at the Bank of Central African States (BEAC, see article on Regional and Subregional Banks) which appeared to have deposited unwise amounts in the seriously troubled Paris-based Société Generale des Banques. The summit suspended a number of BEAC transactions pending a general audit of the bank.

On April 17, 2009, finance ministers of all countries that use the CFA franc (including the West African Economic and Monetary Union (UEMOA) and CEMAC) met in Ouagadougou, Burkina Faso, to discuss the effect of the CFA franc being pegged to the euro. They hailed the recent G-20 decision (see separate G-20 article) to inject $1.1 trillion into the International Monetary Fund (IMF).

In other matters, while the CEMAC countries were expected to adopt a common CEMAC passport by 2010, Equatorial Guinea appeared to show xenophobia, particularly toward its neighbor Cameroon. During the summer of 2009 many Cameroonian nationals were expelled from Equatorial Guinea.

CENTRAL AMERICAN INTEGRATION SYSTEM (SICA)

Sistema de la Integración Centroamericana

Established: By the Protocol of Tegucigalpa to the 1962 Charter of the Organization of Central American States, signed December 13, 1991, in Tegucigalpa, Honduras, effective February 1, 1993.

Purpose: In furtherance of "the new vision of Central American development," to serve as a vehicle for coordinating political, social, economic, cultural, and environmental integration.

Headquarters: San Salvador, El Salvador.

Principal Organs: Meeting of Central American Presidents, Council of Ministers, Executive Committee, Consultative Committee, Central

American Parliament, Central American Court of Justice, General Secretariat.

Web site: www.sica.int

Secretary General: Juan Daniel Alemán Gurdián (Guatemala).

Membership (7): Belize, Costa Rica, El Salvador, Guatemala, Honduras, Nicaragua, Panama.

Associated State (1): Dominican Republic.

Observers (8): Argentina, Brazil, Chile, Republic of China (Taiwan), Germany, Italy, Mexico, Spain.

Official Language: Spanish.

Origin and development. The Central American Integration System (SICA) traces its origins to the Organization of Central American States (*Organización de Estados Centroamericana*—ODECA), which was established by charter in 1951 and revamped under a second charter in 1962. However, ODECA eventually fell into inactivity, largely as a result of domestic and regional turmoil. In the late 1980s, spurred by the formation of other regional and subregional groups, Central American leaders expressed a renewed interest in closer political, social, and economic integration on a scale beyond that offered by the Central American Common Market, which Costa Rica, El Salvador, Guatemala, Honduras, and Nicaragua formed in 1960 to promote intraregional trade and industrial development. After a decade of moderate success, the CACM's economic model proved inadequate, and it, too, lost impetus. Thus, the Central American governments returned to the 1962 ODECA charter and drafted an extensive protocol to that document through which they could provide a new framework for further integration.

Meeting in the Honduran capital in December 1991, in their 11th summit since 1986, the heads of state of the five CACM members plus Panama signed the Protocol of Tegucigalpa to the ODECA Charter, and in 1993 the General Secretariat of SICA began operations. A number of additional legal documents were required in the effort to make SICA all-encompassing, including the Statute of the Central American Court of Justice (1992), the Central American Alliance for Sustainable Development (1994), the Treaty of Central American Social Integration (1995), and the Central American Democratic Security Treaty (1995).

In November 1997 the armed forces of El Salvador, Guatemala, Honduras, and Nicaragua formed the Central American Armed Forces Conference (*Conferencia de las Fuerzas Armadas Centroamericanas*—CFAC) for the purpose of creating a joint military force to engage in United Nations (UN) peacekeeping missions and possibly pave the way for eventual integration of the region's military. Costa Rica and Panama objected to the agreement, preferring demilitarization to military cooperation.

Belize, previously an observer, deposited its instrument of adhesion in December 2000. Another observer, the Dominican Republic, later became an associated state. Current observers are Argentina, Brazil, Chile, the Republic of China (Taiwan), Germany, Italy, Mexico, and Spain. SICA's acceptance of Taiwan as an observer in February 2000 generated considerable controversy, with some critics asserting that Taipei, eager to build its international ties, bought its way into the organization by offering financial assistance.

Structure. The supreme SICA organ is the twice-yearly Meeting of Central American Presidents (including the prime minister of Belize since that country's accession), which has authority over regional decision making related to democracy, development, peace, and security. Decisions are made by consensus. The Council of Ministers of Foreign Affairs is identified as the principal organ of coordination and carries out summit decisions; it is assisted by an Executive Committee of national representatives. Other ministerial-level councils for integration, regional development, and sectoral policies also meet regularly. The Consultative Committee, comprising business, labor, academic, and other civil society representatives, offers additional input, while the General Secretariat (*Secretaría General de le Integración Centroamericana*—SG-SICA), headed by a secretary general, serves a coordinating and administrative role. The Central American Court of Justice (*Corte Centroamericana de Justicia*—CCJ) adjudicates disputes related to the 200 or so regional integration treaties, declarations, protocols, and covenants, which cover everything from social integration to combating trafficking of illegal drugs and stolen vehicles.

After its formation SICA incorporated key existing institutions within its framework, including the Central American Parliament (*Parlamento Centroamericano*—Parlacen), which was established under the CACM and convened for the first time in October 1991, and the CACM's Permanent Secretariat (*Secretaría Permanente del Tratado General de Integración Económica Centroamericana*—SIECA), based in Guatemala City, Guatemala, and responsible for administering SICA's "economic subsystem." SICA also includes various other specialized technical secretariats: the Central American Social Integration Secretariat (*Secretaría de Integración Social Centroamericana*—SISCA), located in San Salvador; the General Secretariat for Central American Educational and Cultural Coordination (*Secretaría General de la Coordinación Educativa y Cultural Centroamericana*—SG-CECC), in San José, Costa Rica; the Executive Secretariat of the Central American Commission for the Environment and Development (*Secretaría Ejecutiva de la Comisión Centroamericana de Ambiente y Desarrollo*—SE-CCAD), in San Salvador; the Executive Secretariat of the Central American Monetary Council (*Secretaría Ejecutiva del Consejo Monetario Centroamericano*—SE-CMCA), in San José; the Secretariat for Central American Tourist Integration (*Secretaría de Integración Turística Centroamericana*—SITCA), in San Salvador; the Executive Secretariat of the Central American Commission for Maritime Transport (*Secretaría Ejecutiva de la Comisión Centroamericana de Transporte Marótimo*—Secocatram), based in Managua, Nicaragua; and the Secretariat of the Central American Agricultural Council (*Secretaría del Consejo Agrícola Centroamericano*—SCAC), in San José. Some two dozen other Central American institutions, including the Central American Bank for Economic Integration (*Banco Centroamericano de Integración Económica*—BCIE), also fall within SICA's purview.

Activities. SICA encompasses four "integration subsystems"—economic, social, environmental, and political—each of which provides functional and institutional coordination among the relevant SICA organs and affiliated Central American bodies. Although the founding Protocol of Tegucigalpa explicitly assigned responsibility for economic administration to the SIECA, the 1993 Protocol of Guatemala more clearly delineated the responsibilities of various organs of the economic subsystem (e.g., the Council of Ministers for Economic Integration, SCAC, CMCA, and SITCA). Similarly, a framework for the Central American Alliance for Sustainable Development (*Alianza Centroamericana papa el Desarrollo Sostenible*—Alides) was adopted at the Guácimo, Costa Rica, summit of August 1994 and initiated at the October 1994 Managua Environment Summit. The Treaty of Central American Social Integration, signed March 30, 1995, at the presidential meeting established the legal and institutional framework for the various organs of the social subsystem. On September 2, 1997, in Managua, the national executives committed themselves to the progressive implementation of a Central American Union.

In practice, however, the plethora of SICA-related bodies, often with overlapping responsibilities, has created a bureaucratic morass and led to infighting between competing agencies. The structural problems have also been complicated by waxing and waning enthusiasm for integration within various member states' governments, with the result that SICA accomplished relatively little in the 1990s. Another impediment to closer integration has been long-standing border disputes. Honduras and Nicaragua, for example, have competing claims in the Gulf of Fonseca, Guatemala has claimed roughly half of Belize, and Nicaragua and Costa Rica have sparred over navigation on the San Juan River.

In 1997 a report issued by the UN Economic Commission for Latin America and the Caribbean (ECLAC) and the Inter-American Development Bank (IADB) castigated the wastefulness of the overlapping secretariats and also criticized payments arrears by some members, a widespread lack of technical expertise, and the financial burden created by some of the institutions. Parlacen was singled out for particular criticism because it absorbs a large percentage of the members' contributions but has no real decision-making authority. The report also asserted that the integration process had "scant public support and social participation." Among the recommendations included in the report were strengthening the coordinating role of SICA, eliminating duplication to help reduce costs, relocating the various affiliated headquarters to San Salvador, and reducing the size of both Parlacen and the CCJ.

At their July 1997 presidential summit in Panama, the Central American leaders voiced support for many of the proposals outlined in the ECLAC-IADB report and endorsed the Guidelines for the Strengthening and Rationalization of the Regional Institutions of the Central American Integration System. Nevertheless, a number of entrenched bureaucracies, facing elimination or budget cuts, showed little enthusiasm for reform, and no significant concrete actions were immediately taken. Then in October 1998, the reform impetus was brought to a virtual halt when Hurricane Mitch caused widespread damage, devastating agricultural production in Honduras and Nicaragua. In the aftermath, individual countries found themselves competing for international attention and aid. At the same time, the international financial crisis of 1988–1999 and a related drop in world prices for key Central American commodities exacerbated the underfunding caused by payments arrears. In response, some SICA institutions sought funding from external sources.

Recent summits have focused not only on such economic matters as integration and progress toward a customs union, but also on security and terrorism, measures to combat organized crime, and reform of Parlacen. A special summit held April 1, 2005, concentrated on energy costs and supply, as well as on crime. The 26th regular summit meeting, held June 29–30, 2005, included in its discussions drug trafficking, organized crime, and prospects for adoption of a Central American passport and a common visa.

Like all of the regional integration organizations in Latin America, the issue that has dominated SICA members' activities in the past year is trade negotiations with the United States. Specifically, the proposed Central American Free Trade Agreement (CAFTA) has been the most significant topic for SICA. Negotiations that resulted in CAFTA were approved at the 22nd Central American Summit on December 13, 2002, in San José.

SICA heads of state met with President Roh Moo-hyun of South Korea on September 13, 2005, to announce that South Korea would join the Central American Bank for Economic Integration. Also, at the 27th regular summit meeting held December 2–5, 2005, it was agreed that SICA should pursue a free trade agreement with the European Union (EU).

On April 27–28, 2006, a meeting of foreign ministry officials from SICA countries and the United States was held in Panama City to discuss issues such as youth gangs, drug trafficking, arms control, border security, and human trafficking. It was the first such meeting involving the United States. SICA activity in 2006 and 2007 concentrated on reaching out to other international organizations. Results included a February 2007 agreement for closer cooperation with the Caribbean Community and Common Market (Caricom), with a summit proposed between the two organizations in 2009. SICA also received a proposal from Brazilian president Luiz Inacio Lula da Silva in May 2007 for the creation of a free trade area with the South American trade bloc Mercosur and began negotiations for a new association agreement with the EU in July 2007. At a December 12, 2007, summit, SICA agreed on a framework to form a Central American customs union. Such a union is a prerequisite for any association agreement with the EU.

China's growing economic power has been felt by SICA recently, as by many other countries and regional groupings. On June 1, 2007, Costa Rica decided to break ties with Taiwan and establish relations with the Beijing government. This caused the remaining SICA countries to reaffirm that their ties were with Taiwan.

In February 2008 SICA leadership agreed to specific reforms of Parlacen, giving it binding power over "integration-related issues," the ability to create special commissions to resolve regional disputes, and the power to withdraw immunity from legislators. A seat in Parlacen had long been criticized as being a refuge from prosecution. The reform awaits ratification by SICA's members.

India actively courted SICA in 2008, much as China had already begun to do. India and SICA agreed in June 2008 to a target of more than $1 billion in mutual trade by 2011, as well as signing pacts easing visa restrictions. In June 2008 Chile became an associate member of the organization.

In October 2008 a meeting of SICA presidents in Tegucigalpa agreed that SICA countries should work together to mitigate the effects of the world economic crisis on their region. They also decided to invest $5 billion in agricultural cooperation and grain production. Also in October a SICA delegation met in Washington with representatives of the Organization of American States (OAS), to look at ways in which the two organizations were and might be cooperating.

At the January 15, 2009, summit of the organization members pledged even faster regional integration as a buffer against global economic conditions. This meeting followed a few months in which the region had been courted with offers of aid from China and Russia, in addition to SICA observer state Taiwan. The summit also named Juan Daniel Alemán Gurdián (Guatemala) as the new secretary general.

Barack Obama's election as U.S. president caused a general scramble throughout Latin America for the attention of the United States. Daniel Ortega, the left-leaning president of Nicaragua, which happened to be holding the revolving presidency of SICA, convened an extraordinary summit in early April 2009. At this meeting he declared that the United States should give the region an economic bailout.

Along with most international organizations, SICA condemned the June 28, 2009, coup in Honduras, and demanded the return of President Zelaya to power.

CENTRAL EUROPEAN INITIATIVE (CEI)

Established: By agreement signed January 28, 1992, in Vienna, Austria, pursuant to earlier regional cooperation framework inaugurated November 11, 1989, in Budapest, Hungary, and known successively as the Quadragonale, the Pentagonale, and the Hexagonale.

Purpose: To coordinate the implementation of joint projects in fields where advantage can be obtained from the regional harmonization of policies.

Headquarters: Trieste, Italy.

Principal Organs: Meeting of Heads of Government, Conference of Foreign Ministers, Committee of National Coordinators, Executive Secretariat.

Web site: www.ceinet.org

Secretary General: Pietro Ercole Ago (Italy).

Membership (18): Albania, Austria, Belarus, Bosnia and Herzegovina, Bulgaria, Croatia, Czech Republic, Hungary, Italy, Macedonia, Moldova, Montenegro, Poland, Romania, Serbia, Slovakia, Slovenia, Ukraine.

Origin and development. On the initiative of the Italian foreign minister, Gianni De Michelis, the Quadragonale grouping was created in November 1989 by Austria, Hungary, Italy, and Yugoslavia. This became the Pentagonale in May 1990 with the accession of Czechoslovakia and the Hexagonale in July 1991 with the accession of Poland. The initial aim of the grouping was to promote economic and cultural cooperation; however, the dramatic post-1989 political changes in Eastern and Central Europe gave it a new dimension as a vehicle for assisting the revival of democracy in former Communist states. It was also acknowledged, by Italy in particular, that the grouping was intended to be a counterweight to the political and economic power of a united Germany.

In January 1992 the Hexagonale countries (minus Yugoslavia) established the CEI, which later that year accepted into its ranks Croatia, Slovenia, and Bosnia and Herzegovina, followed by Macedonia in July 1993. Meanwhile, Czechoslovakia's membership had devolved to the Czech Republic and Slovakia on their establishment as separate states in January 1993. Albania, Belarus, Bulgaria, Romania, and Ukraine became CEI members in May 1996, with Moldova being admitted as the 16th member in November. The October 2000 change of government in the Federal Republic of Yugoslavia into Serbia and Montenegro led directly to Serbia's admission in November 2000. Montenegro joined as a member in its own right after its separation from Serbia in June 2006.

Structure. The annual heads of government summit and foreign ministers' conferences determine the main areas of cooperation, the chair being held by the member states in turn for a calendar year. The Committee of National Coordinators acts as the link between CEI working groups and the member states. In general, the CEI has refrained from establishing formal institutional structures; even a 1995 compromise decision to set up a Center for Information and Documentation in Trieste, Italy, met with some resistance within the membership. The November 28–29, 1997, Meeting of Heads of Government (summit) in Sarajevo, Bosnia and Herzegovina, authorized conversion of the center into the current Executive Secretariat. Much of the organization's work is conducted through various working groups including agriculture;

civil protection; combating organized crime; culture and education; energy; environment; human dimension; human resource development and training; information and media; interregional and cross-border cooperation; migration; minorities; reconstruction and development; science and technology; small- and medium-size enterprises; tourism; transport; and youth affairs.

Financing for CEI infrastructural and other projects is provided by member states and by international institutions, including the World Bank, the European Bank for Reconstruction and Development (EBRD), the European Investment Bank, and the European Union's PHARE financing program for Eastern and Central European countries. (The acronym derives from the program's initial name, Poland and Hungary: Action for the Restructuring of the Economy.) A secretariat for CEI projects operates within the EBRD in London, United Kingdom.

Activities. Yugoslavia organized the Hexagonale summit July 26–27, 1991, in Dubrovnik, Croatia, but the unfolding Yugoslav crisis resulted in the rump Yugoslav government being excluded when the grouping was reconstituted as the CEI in January 1992. Having unavailingly warned against the dangers of a breakup of the Yugoslav federation, the CEI subsequently admitted four ex-Yugoslav independent states to membership and sought to act as a forum for the resolution of regional conflicts. The July 18, 1992, CEI summit in Vienna, Austria, appealed for international assistance to cope with the flow of refugees from the former Yugoslavia into member states and urged the United Nations (UN) to defend the territorial integrity of Bosnia and Herzegovina.

A conference of CEI foreign ministers March 4–5, 1994, in Trieste witnessed clashes between Slovak and Hungarian representatives over the status of the ethnic Hungarian minority in Slovakia. At the fifth CEI summit, held July 15–16 in Trieste, foreign ministers approved a draft declaration on minority rights, intended to be binding on member states and described as going beyond the principles laid down by the Conference on Security and Cooperation in Europe (CSCE, subsequently the Organization for Security and Cooperation in Europe—OSCE) for the treatment of minorities.

A session of CEI premiers and foreign ministers in Warsaw, Poland, in October 1995 agreed in principle to expand the organization to other regional states, despite some resistance on the ground that the CEI's intended role as a stepping-stone to European Union (EU) membership would be compromised. The inclusion of five new members (Albania, Belarus, Bulgaria, Romania, and Ukraine) was duly agreed upon by CEI foreign ministers meeting in late May 1996 in Vienna, in advance of a CEI summit in Rzeszów, Poland, the following month. A further summit in November in Graz, Austria, expanded membership to 16 countries by admitting Moldova.

A CEI summit November 20–21, 1998, in Zagreb, Croatia, declared EU expansion as the most important element in establishing regional stability, particularly in the troubled Balkan region. The CEI leaders also expressed their concern over developments in Kosovo and urged Serbian officials (accused of "ethnic cleansing" by the CEI foreign ministers the previous June) and the leaders of the ethnic Albanians to accept a negotiated settlement.

The November 5–6, 1999, summit in Prague, Czech Republic, was dominated by the situation in Kosovo, with the session's final document extending support to the UN Mission in Kosovo (UNMIK) and the efforts of the associated NATO-led Kosovo Force (KFOR) to maintain peace and security in the troubled province. At the same time, the summit participants expressed interest in having the Federal Republic of Yugoslavia (FRY) ultimately join the CEI. Another major topic of discussion was the recently adopted Stability Pact for South Eastern Europe, sponsored by the EU and grouping some 40 countries interested in helping the regional states "foster peace, democracy, respect for human rights and economic prosperity in order to achieve stability in the whole region."

The November 24–25, 2000, annual summit in Budapest, Hungary, featured the formal admission of the FRY, later known as Serbia and Montenegro, and reemphasized the "fundamental importance" of European integration and EU enlargement. The summit's concluding statement also indicated the CEI's willingness to contribute toward reopening the Danube to free navigation, called for settlement of the Transdnestrian question and the withdrawal of Russian troops from that Moldovan region, supported Ukraine's decision to shut down the final Chernobyl nuclear reactor in December, and encouraged maximum attention to environmental concerns and to enhanced assistance for CEI countries "in special need."

Meeting in March 2001 in Trieste, the member states' ministers of justice adopted the Trieste Declaration on Judicial Cooperation and Legislative Harmonization as part of their efforts toward further cooperation in law enforcement and prosecution. In early 2003 preliminary efforts were under way to establish a CEI Parliamentary Assembly comprised of members of Parliament (MPs) from the member states.

The November 21–23, 2001, CEI summit, held in Trieste under heightened security, was highlighted by discussions related to international terrorism. Meeting in parallel, the associated fourth Summit Economic Forum (SEF), like its three predecessors, brought together business, economic, and political leaders from the member states as well as representatives of such multilateral institutions as the World Bank, the EBRD, and the EU's Stability Pact for a series of meetings that have taken on increasing importance. Discussions have focused on cooperation, exchanges, and investments.

The 2002 CEI summit, which convened November 13–15, in Skopje, Macedonia, emphasized the importance of further EU expansion, even beyond the anticipated May 2004 enlargement. In December 2002 the EU confirmed that the Czech Republic, Hungary, Poland, Slovakia, and Slovenia were being offered membership. (Bulgaria and Romania acceded in early 2007.) Specific topics discussed at the summit included globalization and efforts to control international terrorism, crime, and illegal migration.

The 2003 summit and SEF, held November 19–21 in Warsaw, Poland, adopted a streamlined Plan of Action for 2004–2006; denounced international terrorism, and called for closer cooperation with the EU. The summit's Final Declaration noted that, following the 2004 EU expansion, the CEI would concentrate on helping its non-EU member states join the EU. This aim was reinforced at the 2004 summit, held November 25–26 in Portoro, Slovenia; at the 2005 summit, held November 25 in Piestany, Slovakia; and at the 2006 summit, held November 24 in Tirana, Albania. Concerns were also raised that the organization was trying to do too much on a small budget. The 2006 summit authorized the creation, at the suggestion of the Italian representative, of a task force on the "repositioning" of the CEI.

The recommendations of this task force were presented and approved at the November 27, 2007, Heads of Government meeting in Sofia, Bulgaria. The working groups (described above) were to be replaced by "a network of focal points which will serve as a reservoir of experts to be consulted on questions of policy and . . . associated to the Project Implementation Groups to be convened for the implementation of concrete projects." CEI areas of activity were also to be reduced in number, and the CEI heads of government committed themselves to doubling the organization's budget. Some members stressed the importance of implementation of infrastructural projects, if the group was to remain relevant.

At the November meeting the CEI pledged to work even more closely with the EU. Macedonia obtained the CEI's support for its bid to join the EU and NATO. At the meeting Moldova took over the presidency of the organization.

A summit of CEI leaders was held May 2, 2008, in Ohrid, Macedonia. No representative from Kosovo was invited, but the status of this majority-Albanian former Serbian province was on the agenda. Macedonia, itself with a large ethnic Albanian population, said that it wanted good relations with Kosovo, but that Kosovo remained a significant problem for stability in the Balkans. The meeting concluded with a statement that the region's move toward Europe would not be irreversible until all Balkan countries, as well as Ukraine, had joined the EU.

Moldova hosted the 2008 CEI economic summit, held October 8–9 and the Heads of Government meeting, held November 28, in Chisinau, its capital. In the context of these meetings Romania reaffirmed its support for Moldova's bid to enter the EU. An EU special representative urged Moldova to work with the breakaway Dniester region to resolve their dispute, but declared that Russia must pull its troops out of the disputed area. The Serbian interior minister said his country was doing everything that it could to apprehend war criminals. The Hungarian prime minister again emphasized that the CEI's chief purpose was to assist all member states seeking EU membership. CEI Secretary General Pietro Ercole Ago made a special point of praising Moldova's work during its presidency of the group.

Romania assumed the CEI presidency for 2009. In July 2009 Franco Frattini, the Italian foreign minister, announced that Italy would offer to host a summit for the leaders of the Balkan countries to advance their entry into the EU. He made special mention of Serbia, Montenegro, Bosnia, and Albania. "Ten years after the end of war in the former Republic of Yugoslavia, the moment has arrived to tell all the governments to fulfill their responsibilities," he said. Frattini called for a relaunch of the CEI.

COMMON MARKET FOR EASTERN AND SOUTHERN AFRICA (COMESA)

Established: By treaty signed November 5, 1993, in Kampala, Uganda; effective as of December 8, 1994.

Purpose: To promote wide-ranging regional economic cooperation, particularly in the areas of agriculture, industry, transportation, and communications; to facilitate intraregional trade through the reduction or elimination of trade barriers and the establishment of regional financial institutions; to establish a common external tariff and internal free trade zone; and to pursue "economic prosperity through regional integration."

Headquarters: Lusaka, Zambia.

Principal Organs: Authority of Heads of State and Government, Council of Ministers, Committee of Governors, Intergovernmental Committee, Court of Justice, Secretariat.

Web site: www.comesa.int

Secretary General: Sindiso Ngwenya (Zimbabwe).

Membership (19): Burundi, Comoro Islands, Democratic Republic of the Congo, Djibouti, Egypt, Eritrea, Ethiopia, Kenya, Libya, Madagascar, Malawi, Mauritius, Rwanda, Seychelles, Sudan, Swaziland, Uganda, Zambia, and Zimbabwe. (In 1996 signatories Lesotho and Mozambique announced they would not ratify the Comesa treaty and were instead withdrawing from the grouping. However, in 1997 Mozambique announced it was only suspending its affiliation.)

Origin and development. The creation of a permanent organization to coordinate economic cooperation among eastern and southern African states was first proposed in the mid-1970s by the United Nations' Economic Commission for Africa and subsequently endorsed by the Organization of African Unity (OAU) in its 1980 Lagos Plan of Action for the continent's overall economic development. Despite the seeming incompatibility of some of the national economies in the region, and given that many potential members relied on the production of the same commodities, after tough negotiations the Preferential Trade Area for Eastern and Southern African States (PTA) was launched on December 21, 1981, by nine nations—the Comoro Islands, Djibouti, Ethiopia, Kenya, Malawi, Mauritius, Somalia, Uganda, and Zambia. Lesotho, Swaziland, and Zimbabwe joined in 1982, followed by Burundi and Rwanda in 1984; Tanzania in 1985; Mozambique and Sudan in 1988; Angola in 1990; and Eritrea, Madagascar, Namibia, and Seychelles in 1993. Zaire also applied for admission in the early 1990s, but consideration of its request was postponed because of its domestic turmoil.

The operational phase of the PTA began in 1984 when tariffs on some goods traded between members were reduced, and a PTA financial clearinghouse, run by the Reserve Bank of Zimbabwe, was established to permit trade based on members' national currencies. In addition, the PTA Trade and Development Bank was opened in 1986 in Bujumbura, Burundi, although it moved to Nairobi, Kenya, in 1994.

At the January 1992 PTA heads of state meeting, delegates conceded that the organization had little to show for its first ten years of existence. Many tariffs on trade between members remained high, most of the region's communications and transportation facilities were still subpar, and members' arrears continued to undercut the potential effectiveness of the PTA Secretariat. In addition, most members were preoccupied with turbulent domestic affairs to the apparent exclusion of regional concerns. Nevertheless, supporters of integration expressed the hope that spreading democratization and free market emphasis in the region would soon translate into greater economic cooperation. Toward that end, PTA officials proposed a merger with the Southern African Development Community (SADC), whose overlapping membership and objectives were producing a "parallel existence" between the two groups that was seen as counterproductive. However, the SADC, historically much more successful in attracting international financial support because of its highly visible face-off with apartheid-era South Africa, rejected the proposed union.

Many of the PTA's original tasks were expanded in the treaty establishing the Common Market for Eastern and Southern Africa (Comesa), which was signed during the PTA's 12th summit on November 5, 1993, in Kampala, Uganda. Following ratification of the Comesa treaty by enough signatories for the accord to enter into force on December 8, 1994, officials and journalists routinely began to refer to Comesa as the "successor" to the PTA, even though some PTA members—Lesotho, Mozambique, and Somalia—ultimately opted not to join Comesa, and two nonmembers of the PTA—Democratic Republic of Congo and Egypt—did join. Tanzania withdrew in September 2000. The renamed Eastern and Southern Africa Trade and Development Bank continues to be known less formally as the PTA Bank, and the autonomous *Compagnie de Réassurance de la Zone d'Echanges Préférentiels* (ZEP-RE) is similarly styled the PTA Reinsurance Company in English.

Structure. At the apex of Comesa is the Authority of Heads of State and Government, which establishes by consensus fundamental policy and directs subsidiary organs in pursuit of the common market's objectives. The Council of Ministers monitors and reviews the performance of administrators and financial managers in addition to overseeing the organization's programs and projects. The Intergovernmental Committee, comprising permanent secretaries from the member countries, develops and manages cooperative programs and action plans in all sectors except finance and monetary policy, which is the domain of the separate Committee of Governors of the members' central banks. There are also a number of technical committees and the Secretariat, which, following a recent reorganization, includes five divisions: Administration; Trade, Customs, and Monetary Harmonization; Investment and Private Sector Development; Infrastructure Development; and Information and Networking. The secretary general serves a once-renewable, five-year term. The Court of Justice is responsible for interpreting the Comesa treaty and for adjudicating related disputes between members.

The PTA Bank is the most prominent of various Comesa-established autonomous institutions, which also include the Comesa Bankers' Association (BAPTA), the Comesa Metallurgical Industries Association (Comesamia), the Comesa Telecommunications Company (Comtel), the Eastern and Southern Africa Business Association (ESABO), the Federation of National Associations of Women in Business (Femcom), the Leather and Leather Products Institute (LLPI), and the Pharmaceutical Manufacturers of Eastern and Southern Africa (Pharmesa).

Activities. The initial Comesa summit was held December 7–9, 1994, in Lilongwe, Malawi; however, whereas the treaty had 22 signatories at that point (all the PTA members except Djibouti, Seychelles, and Somalia, plus Zaire), it had only been ratified by 12 (Burundi, Comoro Islands, Eritrea, Ethiopia, Kenya, Madagascar, Malawi, Mauritius, Sudan, Tanzania, Uganda, and Zambia). Thus, although plans were discussed for eventual cooperation in the areas of customs, transportation, communications, agriculture, and industry, formal arrangements remained incomplete, partly because of uncertainties over the relationship between the PTA/Comesa and the SADC. (Most SADC members seemed to prefer distinguishable north and south zones of economic cooperation.)

The outlook for Comesa was further clouded in late 1995 when South Africa announced it did not intend to join. At the end of 1996 Mozambique and Lesotho announced their withdrawal from Comesa, and speculation arose that Namibia might follow suit. Also that year the SADC countries once again vetoed Comesa's offer to merge as a single trade zone. Kenya, Tanzania, and Uganda considered turning away from Comesa activity in favor of the proposed reactivation of their old East African Community (EAC). In fact the EAC was revived (see separate EAC article), but Kenya, Tanzania, and Uganda remained members of both groups.

In late January 1997, Secretary General Bingu Mutharika was suspended during an investigation into the recent management of funds within the Secretariat. Mutharika resigned in April (although he continued to deny any wrongdoing), and Erastus Mwencha of Kenya succeeded him in an acting capacity.

Mwencha officially replaced Mutharika at the third Comesa summit, held in mid-1998 in Kinshasa, Democratic Republic of Congo (formerly Zaire). Summit participants agreed to eliminate tariffs and the need for visas within the group by 2000 and to admit Egypt as the first North African member. Egypt officially became a member after ratifying the Comesa treaty later that year, but progress toward the removal of tariffs was slower than hoped. In other activities, the Comesa Court of Justice, established under the Comesa treaty, held its first session in September 1998, and the PTA Development Bank decided to invite countries from outside the region to become members in an effort to increase the bank's capital.

Speaking at the fourth Comesa summit May 24–25, 1999, Kenyan president Daniel arap Moi called for greater subregional cooperation, which he described as crucial for achieving high economic growth rates and attracting investment capital. Otherwise, he warned, the Comesa countries would face being marginalized by ongoing economic globalization and competition from other trading blocs. As a key step toward further integration, the summit established a committee charged with preparations to introduce a Free Trade Area (FTA). (Many Comesa members had already reduced tariffs by 60–90 percent on goods produced within the grouping.) The summit participants, acknowledging the importance of regional stability, also agreed to study setting up a mechanism for maintaining peace and security.

Arguably the most significant event in the organization's history occurred at an extraordinary summit in Lusaka, Zambia, on October 31, 2000, when nine Comesa members—Djibouti, Egypt, Kenya, Madagascar, Malawi, Mauritius, Sudan, Zambia, and Zimbabwe—inaugurated Africa's first FTA, enabling duty-free trade in goods, services, and capital and eliminating other nontariff trade barriers for the participants. Political concerns in several states, including Burundi, Rwanda, and Eritrea, delayed their participation, and Namibia's and Swaziland's membership in the Southern African Customs Union (SACU) made their entry into Comesa's FTA problematic. Moreover, in what was generally acknowledged to be a major setback, Tanzania withdrew from Comesa in September 2000, citing the need to streamline its international memberships and preferring to remain in the SADC because of the latter's emphasis on building capacity for the production of goods.

The sixth Comesa summit, held May 22–23, 2001, in Cairo, Egypt, formally endorsed moving ahead with the Common External Tariff (CET) despite problems in administering the FTA, including disputes between Zambia and Zimbabwe, Egypt and Sudan, and Egypt and Kenya. One of the major difficulties was determining how to compensate local industries damaged by the expansion of competition. At the same time, a May 22 meeting of Comesa and the SADC leaders suggested the rivalry between the two organizations had abated somewhat. In fact, they decided to form a secretariat-level task force charged with coordinating programs and activities.

The 2001 summit's final communiqué directed Comesa to move forward in such areas as gender policy, e-commerce, and food security. Later in the year Comesa launched the African Trade Insurance Agency (ATIA) in Nairobi, with funding from the World Bank group, the European Union (EU), and Japan, to protect investors against political risks. In addition, on October 29 Comesa and the United States signed a significant Trade and Investment Framework Agreement.

The May 23–24, 2002, summit in Addis Ababa, Ethiopia, saw the reappointment of Secretary General Mwencha. The attendees also authorized the return of the Comesa Trade and Development Bank to Bujumbura and signed a protocol for establishing the Fund for Cooperation, Compensation, and Development.

The organization's eighth summit, held March 17, 2003, in Khartoum, Sudan, focused on the anticipated introduction of the customs union and accompanying CET in December. Meanwhile, Secretary General Mwencha reported, intra-Comesa trade had expanded at a rate of 30 percent per year since the 2000 launch of the FTA. The summit also called for further development of basic infrastructure; discussed food security, particularly in light of recurrent crises in the Horn of Africa; and emphasized the need to strengthen regional peace and security. With regard to trade, Comesa agreed to adopt a regional approach in pursuit of an Economic Partnership Agreement with the EU. In other business, the summit received a request for membership from Libya.

Rwanda and Burundi announced in 2003 that they were preparing to join the FTA, as did Namibia and Swaziland, assuming that remaining issues involving their SACU memberships were resolved. Namibia, however, left Comesa in July 2003, intending to concentrate on its relationship with the SACU. On January 1, 2004, Burundi and Rwanda joined the FTA.

The ninth summit was held on June 7–8, 2004, in Kampala, Uganda. Trade and investments within the community were discussed, as was the plan to move to a customs union by the end of the year. For the first time a business summit ran concurrently with the heads of state and government meeting, attracting more than 600 delegates. At the tenth summit on June 2–3, 2005, in Kigali, Rwanda, Comesa admitted Libya. The eleventh summit was held November 15–16, 2006, in Djibouti, with the main theme being to strengthen the group through the projected customs union, now targeted for 2008. Also in 2006, Tanzania looked at the possibility of rejoining Comesa, but the price of entrance appeared to be Tanzania's withdrawal from SADC. In spite of pressure from Tanzanian business groups who felt that their country had suffered from leaving Comesa, a government representative stated in July that Tanzania had no plans to rejoin.

At the 12th summit, held May 22–23, 2007, in Nairobi, all Comesa states were urged to join the FTA as soon as possible. This was to facilitate launch of the customs union and the CET by December 2008. Thirteen states were members at that time. Rivalry between Comesa and SADC intensified in 2007, spurred by the World Trade Organization (WTO) rule that no country can be a member of more than one customs union. As Comesa and SADC each intended to create a customs union, member countries were forced to choose between the organizations. In August 2007 Zambia declared that, if possible, it would benefit by remaining in both trade blocs, feeling that their markets did not overlap much. By late 2007 Angola had left Comesa for the SADC. In November 2007 Comesa signed a Regional Integration Support Mechanism (RISM) with the EU, granting the bloc 78 million euros (U.S. $100 million) over five years to offset harm done to poorer member countries by the customs union.

By January 2008 several African trade blocs were showing concern about agreements with the EU. Comesa had been negotiating with the EU under the Eastern and Southern Africa (ESA) platform, but several member states had signed individual agreements with Brussels. There were complaints at the January African Union (AU) summit that the EU was adopting a "divide and rule" approach to Africa (see separate article on the African Union). In February 2008 a meeting of Comesa trade ministers endorsed a proposal for a unified FTA among Comesa, the SADC, and East African Community (EAC) states. The attitude seemed to be that membership in multiple trade blocs might, after all, be acceptable. In May 2008 it was announced that Comesa had set September 2008 as the cut-off date for member states to submit their national tariff schedules, as agreed under the CET.

At a July 2008 extraordinary summit meeting in Sharm-el-Sheikh, Egypt, Sindiso Ngwenya of Zimbabwe was chosen as secretary general in place of Erastus Mwencha, who had resigned to take a job with the African Union secretariat. Shortly thereafter Ngwenya announced that in October 2008 Uganda would convene a meeting between Comesa, SADC, and EAC representatives to discuss the harmonization of trade. On October 22 representatives of the three groups, meeting in Kampala, agreed to form a free trade zone of all their members—an area stretching along the east side of Africa from Egypt to South Africa.

At the Comesa summit held June 7-8, 2009, in Victoria Falls, Zimbabwe, presidency of the group rotated to that country. Sudanese president Omar al-Bashir attended the meeting, which called on the International Criminal Court (ICC) to suspend the arrest warrant against him. The summit approved the launch of a Comesa Customs Union. This launch was marred by Ugandan president Yoweri Museveni telling the summit that while East African Community (EAC) members in Comesa supported the concept of the customs union, they needed to reevaluate their participation, since they were close to completing a customs union of their own. Shortly thereafter, the EAC members, more than half of Comesa, opted out. The summit also voiced support for opposed Madagascan president Marc Ravalomanana.

THE COMMONWEALTH

Established: By evolutionary process and formalized December 31, 1931, in the Statute of Westminster.

Purpose: To give expression to a continuing sense of affinity and to foster cooperation among states presently or formerly owing allegiance to the British Crown.

Commonwealth Center: The Secretariat is located in Marlborough House, London, which also serves as the site of Commonwealth meetings in the United Kingdom.

Principal Organs: Meeting of Heads of Government, Secretariat.

Web site: www.thecommonwealth.org

Head of the Commonwealth: Queen Elizabeth II.

Secretary General: Kamalesh Sharma (India).

Membership (54, with years of entry)**:** Antigua and Barbuda (1981), Australia (1931), Bahamas (1973), Bangladesh (1972), Barbados (1966), Belize (1981), Botswana (1966), Brunei (1984), Cameroon (1995), Canada (1931), Cyprus (1961), Dominica (1978), Fiji (1970, reentered 1997, suspended 2009), Gambia (1965), Ghana (1957), Grenada (1974), Guyana (1966), India (1947), Jamaica (1962), Kenya (1963), Kiribati (1979), Lesotho (1966), Malawi (1964), Malaysia (1957), Maldives (1982), Malta (1964), Mauritius (1968), Mozambique (1995), Namibia (1990), Nauru (1999), New Zealand (1931), Nigeria (1960), Pakistan (1947, reentered 1989, but suspended following military coup of October 1999; readmitted on May 22, 2004), Papua New Guinea (1975), Rwanda (2009), St. Kitts-Nevis (1983), St. Lucia (1979), St. Vincent and the Grenadines (1979), Samoa (1970), Seychelles (1976), Sierra Leone (1961), Singapore (1965), Solomon Islands (1978), South Africa (1931, reentered 1994), Sri Lanka (1948), Swaziland (1968), Tanzania (1961), Tonga (1970), Trinidad and Tobago (1962), Tuvalu (2000), Uganda (1962), United Kingdom (1931), Vanuatu (1980), Zambia (1964). (Zimbabwe, a member since 1980, withdrew in 2003.)

Working Language: English.

Origin and development. A voluntary association that gradually superseded the British Empire, the Commonwealth traces its origins to the mid-1800s, when internal self-government was first introduced in the colonies of Australia, British North America (Canada), New Zealand, and part of what was to become the Union of South Africa. The increasing maturity and independence of these overseas communities, particularly after World War I, eventually created a need to redefine the mutual relationships between the United Kingdom and the self-governing "dominions" that were collectively coming to be known as the British Commonwealth of Nations. The Statute of Westminster, enacted by the British Parliament in 1931, established the principle that all members of the association were equal in status, in no way subordinate to each other, and united by allegiance to the Crown.

The original members of the Commonwealth, in addition to the United Kingdom, were Australia, Canada, the Irish Free State, Newfoundland, New Zealand, and the Union of South Africa. In 1949 the Irish Free State became the Republic of Ireland and withdrew from the Commonwealth. In the same year Newfoundland became a province of Canada. South Africa ceased to be a member upon becoming a republic in 1961 because of the opposition of the other Commonwealth countries to Pretoria's apartheid policies; however, it was readmitted June 1, 1994, following the installation of a multiracial government. Pakistan withdrew in 1972 but rejoined in 1989. Because of political instability, its status has changed or come into question several times since (see below). Likewise, Fiji's status has often been in jeopardy because of political unrest.

The ethnic, geographic, and economic composition of the Commonwealth has been modified fundamentally by the accession of former colonial territories in Asia, Africa, and the Western Hemisphere. This infusion of racially nonwhite and economically less developed states had significant political implications, including modification of the Commonwealth's unwritten constitution to accommodate the desire of many new members to renounce allegiance to the British Crown and adopt a republican form of government. In 1949 the pattern was set when Commonwealth prime ministers accepted India's formal declaration that, on becoming a republic, it would accept the Crown as a symbol of the Commonwealth association and recognize the British sovereign as head of the Commonwealth. The movement toward a multicultural identity was solidified by the Declaration of Commonwealth Principles adopted by the heads of government at their 1971 Singapore summit. In addition to acknowledging the organization's diversity, the Singapore declaration enumerated a set of common principles, including the primacy of international peace and order; individual liberty regardless of racial, ethnic, or religious background; people's "inalienable right to participate by means of free and democratic processes in framing the society in which they live"; opposition to "colonial domination and racial oppression"; and the "progressive removal" of wide disparities in wealth and living standards.

The new thrust was further evidenced by a North-South summit in October 1981, which reflected that most Commonwealth members were developing countries. Subsequently, a 1982 report, *The North-South Dialogue: Making It Work*, proposed many institutional and procedural reforms to facilitate global negotiations on development and related issues, and a 1983 document, *Towards a New Bretton Woods*, proposed short-, medium-, and long-range changes to enhance the efficiency and equity of the international trading and financial system.

A declaration in October 1987 that Fiji's Commonwealth status had lapsed followed two successive coups, abrogation of the country's constitution, and proclamation of a republic. Readmission required the unanimous consent of the Commonwealth members, and Fiji's application remained blocked until mid-1997 by India on the grounds that appropriate constitutional recognition had yet to be given to the island's Indian population. Fiji was finally readmitted effective October 1, 1997, following the adoption of a new constitution in July, but its membership was suspended in May 2000 following displacement of the elected government. Full participation was restored in late 2001, following democratic elections in August through September.

The October 1991 summit in Harare, Zimbabwe, was noteworthy for the adoption of a declaration redefining the Commonwealth's agenda. The Harare Declaration, drafted under the guidance of a ten-member High Level Appraisal Group, committed all Commonwealth countries, regardless of their political or economic conditions, to promote democracy, human rights, judicial independence, equality for women, educational opportunities, and the principles of "sound economic management."

In a departure from precedent, membership was granted on November 13, 1995, to Mozambique, even though it had never been a British colony and was not at least partly English speaking. A "unique and special" case regarding Mozambique had been presented by its Anglophone neighbors because of regional trade concerns. In 1999 Nauru became the 53rd full member of the Commonwealth after 31 years as a special member, and Tuvalu, a special member from 1978, became the 54th full member in 2000. In 2005 Nauru resumed its status as a special member, a category of membership available to very small countries.

In March 2002 Zimbabwe's participation in Commonwealth meetings was suspended as a consequence of a widely condemned presidential election earlier in the month. In response to its continued suspension, Zimbabwe withdrew effective December 7, 2003.

Structure. One of the least institutionalized intergovernmental organizations, the Commonwealth was virtually without permanent machinery until the establishment of its Secretariat in 1965. The symbolic head of the organization is the reigning British monarch, who serves concurrently as constitutional sovereign in those member states that still maintain their traditional allegiance to the British crown. Since World War II, the heads of government have held biennial meetings, and specialized consultations occur periodically among national ministers responsible for such fields as foreign affairs, defense, finance, education, agriculture, health, trade, legal affairs, science and the environment, and women's and youth affairs. National finance ministers normally convene in the nearest convenient Commonwealth site on the eve of the annual fall meetings of the International Monetary Fund and World Bank to discuss monetary and economic issues.

The Secretariat organizes meetings and conferences, collects and disseminates information on behalf of the membership, and is responsible for implementing collective decisions. The secretary general, who currently serves a four-year term, is assisted by three deputies with responsibilities for political affairs, economic and social development, and development cooperation. Since its reorganization in 2002, the Secretariat has encompassed nine divisions: Communications and Public Affairs, Corporate Services, Economic Affairs, Gender and Human Resources Development, Governance and Institutional Development, Legal and Constitutional Affairs, Political Affairs, Science and Technology, and Special Advisory Services. The organization's technical assistance program is financed primarily through the Commonwealth Fund for Technical Cooperation (CFTC).

The fund is supported by all Commonwealth countries on a voluntary basis, and its governing body includes representatives of all contributors. In addition, a Commonwealth Equity Fund, designed to encourage private sector investment in the emerging stock markets of developing countries, was launched in 1990 and was followed in 1995 by formation of a Commonwealth Private Investment Initiative (CPII). The latter was established to help geographic regions attract capital for small- and medium-size ventures and for former state enterprises that were being privatized. The first CPII investment fund, for Sub-Saharan

Africa, was established in 1996, and others followed. On the political front, a Commonwealth Ministerial Action Group (CMAG) was created in November 1995 to provide guidance toward "good governance" in countries undergoing transition to democracy.

The autonomous Commonwealth Foundation, the formation of which was authorized by the Commonwealth heads of government in 1965, supports nongovernmental organizations, professional associations, and other such bodies. Known informally as the "unofficial Commonwealth," the foundation directs its attention to "inter-country networking, training, capacity-building, and information exchange." The Commonwealth of Learning, likewise authorized by the heads of government and located in Vancouver, Canada, was established in 1987 to promote distance learning and thereby improve access to education and training. Some three dozen additional Commonwealth associations, institutes, councils, and other groups were also established over the years, largely to promote development or disseminate information in such fields as forestry, health, telecommunications, education, journalism, law, and sports. Most are based in London.

Activities. The Secretariat's divisions oversee Commonwealth activities. Among the most prominent, the Political Affairs Division participates in organizing Commonwealth Heads of Government Meetings (CHOGMs), conducts research, aids various committees in their tasks, and monitors political issues and developments of importance to Commonwealth members. Since 1990 its observer missions have also monitored election campaigns, preparations for balloting, and elections in some two dozen Commonwealth countries around the globe. In 1999 it drafted a Framework for Principles for Promoting Good Governance and Combating Corruption. The Economic Affairs Division conducts research and analysis and supports expert groups in such areas as North-South economic relations, protectionist tariffs, reform of the international financial system, debt management, and youth unemployment. Its purview also includes environmental concerns and sustainable development. In the area of technical assistance and development, CFTC provides training, expertise, and advice in the promotion of economic growth, public sector reform, poverty alleviation, infrastructural and institutional development, and capacity building. A Commonwealth Youth Program likewise funded through voluntary contributions is an effort to encourage youth participation in economic and social development. Among more recent innovations, in 1995 the heads of government endorsed a Commonwealth Plan of Action on Gender and Development.

During the 1980s and early 1990s, the Commonwealth was most prominently identified with its efforts to end apartheid in South Africa, although debate frequently raged within the organization over tactics, especially the imposition of sanctions. Accordingly, the formal readmission of South Africa at midyear was the highlight of 1994, newly elected South African president Nelson Mandela hailing the "sterling contribution" of the grouping to the installation of a nonracial government in Pretoria.

The CHOGM held November 8–13, 1995, in Auckland, New Zealand, was dominated by discussion of the excesses of Sani Abacha, the military ruler of Nigeria, who executed the internationally known author and nonviolent activist Ken Saro-Wiwa while the conference was in progress. This resulted in the suspension of Nigeria's membership and the launching of efforts (ultimately largely unsuccessful) by the Commonwealth to influence the actions of the military regime in Abuja. The governments of Gambia and Sierra Leone were also criticized for their perceived failure to support genuine democratization; the summit established CMAG in part to "guide" developing Commonwealth countries toward abiding by the principles enunciated in the 1991 Harare Declaration.

Nigeria, Gambia, and Sierra Leone were also major topics at the 1997 CHOGM held in Edinburgh, Scotland. While praising the role Nigeria played in the Liberia conflict, the summit decided to continue Nigeria's suspension because of ongoing human rights abuses and the suppression of democracy. The summit also indicated it might impose sanctions if they would help move Nigeria toward democracy. Sierra Leone was also suspended (until the restoration of President Tejan Kabbah's government in March 1998), and the summit called on Commonwealth members to support the United Nations (UN) and Economic Community of West African States (ECOWAS) sanctions imposed on that country. In contrast, the government in Gambia was praised for having made progress toward genuine democratization.

Another focus of attention at the summit was the promotion of economic prosperity. The heads of government adopted the Edinburgh Commonwealth Economic Declaration, which called for continued global economic integration with greater attention to the smaller, less developed countries that believed they were being left behind. To assist the smaller countries, the Commonwealth leaders agreed to support efforts to develop a successor to the Lomé Convention (see European Community section of European Union article), to offer duty-free access to certain markets, and to establish a Trade and Investment Access Facility (TIAF) with initial funding from Australia, Canada, New Zealand, and the United Kingdom.

In October 1998 CMAG concluded that the Nigerian government had taken enough steps toward democracy to warrant a lifting of sanctions and a resumption of Nigerian participation in some Commonwealth activities. Full participation was restored May 29, 1999, following presidential elections the previous February. In other activities during the year, a Commonwealth ministerial mission lobbied leading providers of aid and loans to developing countries on behalf of small island states, arguing they deserved special consideration because of their extreme exposure to outside political, economic, and environmental forces.

At the November 12–15, 1999, Commonwealth summit in Durban, South Africa, the organization established a ten-member High-Level Review Group (HLRG) comprising the heads of government of Australia, India, Malta, Papua New Guinea, Singapore, South Africa, Tanzania, Trinidad and Tobago, United Kingdom, and Zimbabwe. The HLRG was assigned the task of recommending how the Commonwealth could best meet the challenges of the 21st century. Issues facing the organization included what measures to take in response to corrupt governments and how to reconcile promotion of good governance with the principle of national sovereignty and noninterference in internal affairs.

Also at the Durban session, Donald McKinnon, former deputy prime minister and foreign minister of New Zealand, was elected to succeed Chief Eleazar Chukwuemea (Emeka) Anyaoku of Nigeria as secretary general, effective April 2000. The heads of government also confirmed Pakistan's suspension from Commonwealth activities in the wake of the previous month's coup in Islamabad.

Pakistan (like Fiji, Gambia, Sierra Leone, and the Solomon Islands) continued to be one of the countries on the CMAG agenda for 2001. Recent threatening events in Zimbabwe were also discussed at CMAG's March 19–20 session. At the same time, HLRG established three working groups to consider the Commonwealth's political role, including conflict prevention and the mandate of CMAG; its developmental role, including how to reduce the "digital divide"; and Commonwealth governance and structures.

The CHOGM scheduled for October 2001 was postponed in the wake of the September 11 terrorist attacks in the United States and then rescheduled for March 2–5, 2002, in Coolum, Australia. The meeting's concluding declaration called for a rationalized and streamlined organizational structure, as HLRG's report recommended. Emphasis was also given to "people-centered economic development," good governance and human rights, efforts to bridge the widening gap between rich and poor, and the elimination of terrorism. (Some African participants, however, although condemning the September 11 al-Qaida attacks, expressed concern that the definition of terrorism was too closely tied to U.S. and Western concerns and ignored, for example, that a number of present-day African leaders had themselves been branded as terrorists during the colonial and apartheid eras.)

In keeping with a summit recommendation that they pursue more active consultations, the Commonwealth foreign ministers convened for the first time in September 2002, during the opening days of the annual UN General Assembly session in New York. At that time the ministers agreed to hold annual meetings.

The next CHOGM, which was held December 5–8, 2003, in Abuja, Nigeria, was dominated by the Zimbabwe issue. Although many African states argued that the Mugabe government could best be engaged by lifting the suspension, opponents prevailed. The Commonwealth proceeded to form a balanced committee of leaders from Australia, Canada, India, Jamaica, Mozambique, and South Africa to pursue "national reconciliation" in Zimbabwe and a rapid return of that country to full participation, but Zimbabwe's governing party quickly voted to terminate membership in the Commonwealth. In acknowledging the withdrawal, Secretary General McKinnon, who was elected to a second term at the CHOGM, expressed his hope that Zimbabwe would rejoin "in due course, as have other members in the past." Also at the CHOGM, membership applications from the Palestinian Authority, Rwanda, and Yemen were rejected.

Four and a half years after the military coup that brought Gen. Pervez Musharraf to power, Commonwealth ministers decided to restore full membership to Pakistan at a May 2004 meeting in London. Ministers insisted that General Musharraf uphold his pledge to step down as chief of the army by the end of the year and expected the country to move forward with democratic reforms. Some African nations, including Nigeria and Tanzania, objected to the readmission of Pakistan because they feared that military rulers, believing that any international sanctions levied against them would eventually be reversed despite their actions, might take power in other countries.

The marriage of Prince Charles, Queen Elizabeth's son and heir to the throne, to Camilla Parker Bowles in April 2005 had implications for the Commonwealth. The British Department of Constitutional Affairs stated on March 21 that Parker Bowles would automatically become queen when Charles became king, despite Charles's declarations to the contrary, unless the parliaments of the UK and the Commonwealth countries of which the UK monarch was head of state all agreed to a change in the law. On March 23 the Commonwealth Secretariat announced that Charles would not automatically succeed Queen Elizabeth as head of the Commonwealth when he became king. Instead, the various Commonwealth heads of government would elect the next head of the Commonwealth. Appointing anyone other than the British monarch to this symbolic position would mark a substantial shift away from the organization's British and imperial roots.

The next CHOGM, which was held November 25–27, 2005, in Valletta, Malta, declared that Pakistan could remain a member in full standing as long as General Musharraf resigned from the military within two years. Ugandan president Yoweri Museveni was much criticized for the arrest on treason charges of Uganda's main opposition leader, Col. Kiza Besigye. The European Union received criticism for maintaining agricultural subsidies and for a 36 percent cut in the guaranteed price of sugar—a matter of great concern to Commonwealth Caribbean countries. The summit issued a Statement on Multilateral Trade, calling for agreement on trade subsidies at forthcoming World Trade Organization talks. In December 2006 Fiji was suspended from some privileges of Commonwealth membership following a military coup. Also in that month Rwanda formally applied to join the Commonwealth. Subsequently, Burundi also expressed an interest. When the 2007 CHOGM took place in Kampala, Uganda, November 23–25, the president of Rwanda was present as an observer, and Rwanda's application was again on the agenda. A representative also came from Burundi, saying that his country would begin the application process soon. An outcome of the meeting was a clarification of the rules, spelling out the right of countries that had never been under British rule to join the Commonwealth, if on examination they met the appropriate democratic standards. A conference on Rwanda's proposed accession was subsequently held in August 2008, in Kigali, Rwanda. Rwanda, which in October 2008 mandated English as the language of education instead of French, received widespread support for its bid. Rwanda's application was approved at the 2009 CHOGM, held in Trinidad and Tobago, November 27–29. Rwanda thus became the second Commonwealth member, along with Mozambique, that had never been part of the British Empire.

Zimbabwe was not invited to the 2007 CHOGM. In November 2007 the Commonwealth suspended Pakistan from full membership because President Musharraf had not ended the state of emergency, released political prisoners, and stepped down as army chief of staff as he had promised. The suspension was lifted in May 2008, democratic elections having been held in Pakistan, and Musharraf having resigned from the army.

That same year saw stiff competition to host the 2014 Commonwealth Games. The games were awarded to Glasgow, Scotland, which narrowly and contentiously beat out Arusha, Nigeria. Meanwhile, there was concern about India's progress in building the facilities for the 2010 games. In March 2009 the Commonwealth gave Fiji six months to make progress toward holding elections, with expulsion from the organization as the alternative. In September 2009 Fiji's suspension, though not expulsion, was reaffirmed. In March the Commonwealth also celebrated its 60th anniversary.

According to a July 2009 survey, commissioned as part of an effort to rejuvenate and "re-brand" the Commonwealth, interest in the group seemed to differ sharply among its members. Populations of the older, predominately white, members showed less interest, with Britons the least interested, and only one third of Australians and Canadians strongly opposed to leaving the Commonwealth. Members of developing countries, to the contrary, valued the Commonwealth much more highly, and South Africans thought more of the Commonwealth tie than of relations with the United States. There was also some talk in the Republic of Ireland that it might have been too hasty in leaving the Commonwealth in 1949.

COMMONWEALTH OF INDEPENDENT STATES (CIS)

Sodruzhestvo Nezavisimykh Gosudarstv

Established: During a meeting of 11 of the former constituent states of the Union of Soviet Socialist Republics in Alma-Ata (now Almaty), Kazakhstan, on December 21, 1991.

Purpose: To assist in the orderly transfer of governmental functions and treaty obligations of the former Soviet Union to its independent successor states, to promote coordinated policies in disarmament and national security, and to work toward economic unity among members.

Administrative Center: Minsk, Belarus.

Principal Organs: Council of Heads of State, Council of Heads of Government, Ministerial Councils, Interparliamentary Assembly, Joint Chiefs of Staff, Executive Committee, Secretariat.

Web site: www.cisstat.com (Site has a comprehensive English section.)

Executive Secretary: Sergei Lebedev (Russia).

Membership (12): Armenia, Azerbaijan, Belarus, Georgia, Kazakhstan, Kyrgyzstan, Moldova, Russia, Tajikistan, Ukraine, Turkmenistan, Uzbekistan. In August 2008 Georgia declared its intention to withdraw from the CIS. This decision became effective in August 2009.

Origin and development. Following acceptance on September 6, 1991, of the Baltic states' withdrawal from the Soviet Union, a proposal was advanced for the creation of an economic commonwealth of the remaining Soviet republics. The plan was endorsed by all 12 republics during a meeting on October 1–2 in Alma-Ata (now Almaty), Kazakhstan, although four states (Azerbaijan, Georgia, Moldova, and Ukraine) abstained from signing a formal treaty in Moscow on October 18. Less than a month later, on November 14, agreement was reached on the formation of the Union of Sovereign States, which its principal advocate, USSR president Mikhail Gorbachev, characterized as a "union of confederal democratic states." However, the seven republican delegations that attended a subsequent meeting November 25 decided not to initial a draft treaty, returning it to their Supreme Soviets for more consideration. Ukraine's absence from the discussions cast further doubt as to the treaty's viability.

In a referendum December 1, Ukrainians voted overwhelmingly for independence, and one week later, in a highly symbolic meeting in Brest, Belarus, the Russian Federation and Belarus joined Ukraine in proclaiming the demise of the Soviet Union and the establishment of the Commonwealth of Independent States (CIS). On December 13 the five Central Asian republics of Kazakhstan, Kyrgyzstan, Tajikistan, Turkmenistan, and Uzbekistan agreed to join the CIS, which, with the additional endorsement of Armenia, Azerbaijan, and Moldova, was formally launched in Alma-Ata on December 21.

The Azerbaijan legislature voted against ratification of the accord in October 1992 but reversed its position the following June upon a change in government in Baku. Azerbaijan's membership was formalized at the CIS summit in September. Georgia's membership was ratified by the Georgian Supreme Council in March 1994. Moldova's parliament ratified CIS membership in April 1994, reversing a negative vote on the question taken the previous August.

After the first six months of its existence, the viability of the CIS appeared in question because little effective action had been taken in economic, political, or military affairs. In seeming contradiction to their stated goal of cooperation, CIS members were preparing to introduce their own national currencies and had instituted numerous cross-border trade restrictions. The commonwealth had also proved ineffective in resolving the fighting between Armenia and Azerbaijan over Nagorno-Karabakh, ethnic conflict in Moldova, and secularist-Islamic fundamentalist disputes in Central Asian republics.

Tension remained high between Russia and Ukraine over the status of Crimea and control of the Black Sea fleet. Ukraine was one of five countries (the others being Azerbaijan, Belarus, Kyrgyzstan, and Moldova) that declined to sign a CIS collective security treaty at a May 1992 summit in Tashkent, Uzbekistan. However, a certain CIS momentum appeared to develop following the June agreement between Russia and Ukraine on the Black Sea fleet dispute (see separate article on Ukraine).

In March 1992, CIS members (except Azerbaijan, Moldova, and Ukraine) endorsed the creation of a joint CIS military command, which subsequently moved into the former Warsaw Treaty Organization headquarters in Moscow. CIS leaders also backed establishing CIS peacekeeping forces to act within and between member states, and in May most signed the Treaty on Collective Security. However, *de facto* control of both nuclear and regular forces remained in national hands. In 1993 the participating CIS defense ministers ended the joint military command, preferring less structured and, at least from the Russian perspective, less expensive efforts at military cooperation. The CIS did, however, set up an integrated air defense network in 1995 under Russian control and financing and has since continued joint exercises. In 1999 six members of the CIS Collective Security Council—Armenia, Belarus, Kazakhstan, Kyrgyzstan, Russia, and Tajikistan—renewed their commitment to collective defense for an additional five years. Meeting on April 28, 2003, the six completed arrangements for formation of the separate Collective Security Treaty Organization—CSTO (*Organizacii Dogoora o Kollektivnoi Bezopasnosti*—ODKB).

Turkmenistan downgraded its participation to associate status in 2005, while Uzbekistan restored full membership in June 2006. Georgia withdrew from the CIS Council of Defense Ministers in February 2006 with aims to join the North Atlantic Treaty Organization (NATO). Georgia later announced its complete withdrawal from the CIS on August 13, 2008 (see Activities, below).

Structure. The Council of Heads of State (the supreme CIS body) and the Council of Heads of Government are required to meet at least every six and three months, respectively, although more frequent meetings were held during the CIS start-up period. In addition, CIS discussions regarding foreign affairs, defense, transportation, energy, the environment, and other areas have been regularly conducted at the ministerial level. Preparation for the various CIS meetings is the responsibility of a permanent administrative staff located in Minsk, Belarus.

Creation of the Interparliamentary Assembly was approved by seven CIS states (Armenia, Belarus, Kazakhstan, Kyrgyzstan, Russia, Tajikistan, and Uzbekistan) in April 1992. Subsequently, Azerbaijan, Georgia, Moldova, and Ukraine joined. The assembly meets in St. Petersburg and is assisted by its own secretariat.

In April 1999 the CIS Executive Secretariat was reorganized as the Executive Committee; the executive secretary was given the collateral title of chair of the Executive Committee. Many other organs were subsumed by the new committee, including the Interstate Economic Committee.

Activities. In July 1993 Belarus, Russia, and Ukraine agreed in principle to establish their own "single economic space," reflecting an apparent acknowledgment that effective CIS activity remained a distant prospect. Central Asian states also voiced concern over the commonwealth's future, and in 1994 Kazakhstan, Kyrgyzstan, and Uzbekistan formed the Central Asian Economic Union (CAEU).

Nevertheless, negotiations continued within the CIS, and in 1994 enthusiasm for economic integration increased substantially. On September 9 the Council of Heads of Government endorsed the creation of the Interstate Economic Committee (IEC), described as the first CIS supranational executive body. Supporters of the proposal anticipated that the IEC would assume control of transnational systems (in the energy and communications sectors, for example), with the possible addition of certain industrial and financial corporations jointly owned by member states. They also projected that the new committee would coordinate an integration process that would eventually lead to a common market. However, thorny issues remained unresolved, particularly the extent to which members would be willing to turn sovereign powers over to the IEC. (Ultimately, the CIS Executive Committee absorbed the IEC.)

Supporters of genuine economic cooperation were buoyed by the signing of a customs union between Belarus and Russia during the May 1995 CIS summit in Minsk. Meeting in Moscow in November, CIS heads of government signed integration agreements covering gas supplies, external relations, and scientific research but failed to resolve CIS members' energy supply debts to Russia.

Delegates to a CIS summit in Moscow agreed in January 1996 that sanctions should be imposed on the breakaway republic of Abkhazia to compel it to accept Georgian sovereignty; it also extended the mandates of the CIS peacekeeping forces in Abkhazia and Tajikistan. On March 29 the presidents of Russia, Belarus, Kazakhstan, and Kyrgyzstan, meeting in Moscow under CIS auspices, signed a treaty to create a CIS customs union.

The CIS enterprise appeared to lose momentum later in 1996 amid mounting criticism that CIS accords were not being implemented. A heads of state summit scheduled for December 1996 to mark the fifth CIS anniversary was postponed into 1997, and a session of prime ministers in mid-January 1997 in Moscow was far from united on yet another CIS economic integration plan, which Azerbaijan, Georgia, Ukraine, and Uzbekistan declined to support as drafted.

Seeking to deflect charges that the CIS was dedicated to "paper creativity," Executive Secretary Ivan Korotchenya claimed in December 1996 that 365 of some 800 treaties and agreements signed within the CIS framework since December 1991 had been implemented, the others having encountered opposition from one or more member states.

The next CIS summit was finally held on March 28, 1997. Once again plans were endorsed by CIS members (with the exception of Georgia) for accelerated integration. The prime ministers of six CIS states also signed an agreement in early October called the Concept for the Integrated Economic Development of the CIS, but little hope for implementation was provided by the subsequent CIS summit, held October 23 in Chişinău, Moldova. A number of CIS leaders reportedly criticized Russia for failing to provide strong leadership, while Russian leaders warned that concerns over national sovereignty were preventing other members from acting effectively within the CIS. CIS supporters also wondered whether the proliferation of smaller economic groupings among CIS members was proving counterproductive to the goals of the parent grouping. Blocs included the Belarus-Russia union; the CIS Customs Union of Belarus, Kazakhstan, Kyrgyzstan, and Russia; the Central Asian Economic Community (CAEC, successor to the CAEU) of Kazakhstan, Kyrgyzstan, Tajikistan, and Uzbekistan; and the so-called GUAM grouping of Georgia, Ukraine, Azerbaijan, and Moldova. (Tajikistan joined the CIS Customs Union in February 1999. The GUAM became the GUUAM for a short time with Uzbekistan's admission in April 1999, but returned to its former name when Uzbekistan suspended membership in June 2002. In February 2002 the participants of the CAEC agreed to reshape it as the Central Asian Cooperation Organization [CACO]).

The January 20, 2000, Moscow summit voiced support for the 1972 Anti-Ballistic Missile Treaty, which CIS saw as threatened by efforts in the United States to implement a national missile defense system. At a meeting on November 30–December 1 in Minsk, CIS leaders agreed to establish an antiterrorism center in Moscow.

On October 10, 2000, the five constituent states of the CIS Customs Union signed a treaty in Astana, Kazakhstan, authorizing conversion of the organization into the Eurasian Economic Community (EAEC), effective April 2001. Initial goals of the EAEC, which is modeled on the European Economic Community, were to harmonize tariff and taxation policies, employment regulations, and visa regimes. Armenia, Moldova, and Ukraine have observer status in the EAEC. Uzbekistan joined at a January 2006 summit in St. Petersburg and the EAEC decided to absorb the CACO to eliminate institutional duplication.

Meeting in Yerevan, Armenia, May 25, 2001, the presidents of the six states of the CIS Collective Security Council agreed to move ahead on formation of a 3,000-troop rapid reaction force to be headquartered in Bishkek, the Kyrgyz capital, in response to heightening concerns over drug trafficking, organized crime, and terrorism and attendant Islamist militancy. The session was followed by a full CIS summit on May 31–June 1 in Minsk, where the focus of attention was progress toward establishment of a much-delayed free trade zone.

At an informal summit held on August 1, 2001, in Sochi, Russia, Russian president Vladimir Putin identified mutual economic concerns as "the sole basis for developing cooperation in all spheres" and described the EAEC, the GUUAM, the CAEC, and similar CIS-related offspring as complementary to the CIS and "a sort of laboratory" where various initiatives could be tested before wider introduction.

The organization's focus turned once again to terrorism in the wake of the September 11, 2001, al-Qaida attacks against the United States. Particular emphasis was given to closer coordination on counterterrorism and border security. The most significant shift in policy, however, may have been Russian acquiescence in the positioning of U.S. forces in Central Asia to root out terrorist bases in Afghanistan and oust the Taliban regime. Uzbekistan and Kyrgyzstan permitted the entry of U.S. contingents, but a number of other CIS member states objected to the U.S. military presence. In August 2005, the United States was ordered to vacate its bases in Uzbekistan.

The tenth anniversary CIS summit in Moscow on November 29–30, 2001, identified stable development and "dignified integration" into the world community as principal commonwealth goals. President Putin lent support to creation of a single economic zone and encouraged respect for minority rights (with an eye toward the millions of Russians living in the former Soviet republics).

In April 2002 the six parties to the Collective Security Treaty met in Almaty, Kazakhstan, to strengthen joint efforts against terrorism, drug smuggling, and illegal immigration. The session concluded with agreement on establishing a more formal security structure and was immediately followed by military exercises involving the Collective Rapid Reaction Forces. Plans for the new security organization were further advanced at the October 6–7, 2002, CIS summit in Chişinău, where the treaty participants signed a charter for the organization. In other business, the summit continued to emphasize efforts against terrorism and the drug trade and discussed measures to boost flagging interstate CIS trade.

Meeting on April 28, 2003, in Dushanbe, Tajikistan, the presidents of Armenia, Belarus, Kazakhstan, Kyrgyzstan, Russia, and Tajikistan formally established the Collective Security Treaty Organization with headquarters in Moscow and named Nikolai Bordyuzha of Russia as its first secretary general. One of the organization's principal assignments was identified as management of the rapid reaction forces.

A CIS summit on September 18–19, 2003, in Yalta, Ukraine, saw the presidents of Belarus, Kazakhstan, Russia, and Ukraine reach agreement on formation of a single economic space (SES) that would ultimately harmonize customs, tariff, transport, and related regimes. However, as the SES initiative moved forward in 2004, various disputes arose over the adoption of a single economic agreement for the CIS. Ultimately, the CIS decided to adopt 61 separate agreements to be reviewed at a summit in Yalta in September, at which time several were signed. Other fractious issues arose over SES members' move to try to join the World Trade Organization (WTO) as a single entity. Because of differences that could not be resolved, the members instead decided to approach the WTO separately.

The CIS heads of government met in April 2004 and supported creation of the CIS Reserve Fund, which would help member states in the event of natural disasters. The following month CIS defense ministers met in Armenia and agreed to form a CIS peacekeeping force, and in June they drafted a document that encouraged the CIS and NATO to cooperate in managing a peacekeeping force under United Nations (UN) mandate. Because of increasing concerns about terrorism and border control (and to bolster military cooperation among members), the Secretariat of Defense Ministers was increased from 10 members to 21 in August 2005.

The 38th CIS summit on September 16, 2004, in Astana, Kazakhstan, focused primarily on security and economic issues; the group issued a statement on the fight against international terrorism and vowed to step up the work of the CIS antiterrorist center. A summit on August 16, 2005, in Kazan, capital of the Republic of Tatarstan in Russia, included adoption of antiterrorism documents but also marked the departure of Turkmenistan from full membership. Turkmenistan, which expressed its preference for establishing its international neutrality, remained an associate member. Meanwhile, dramatic changes of government in the region—the "rose revolution" in Georgia in 2003, the "orange revolution" in Ukraine in 2004, and the "tulip revolution" in Kyrgyzstan in 2005—did not bode well for the organization's future. President Putin increasingly seemed to see the West as a rival rather than a partner and began to exploit politically Russia's position as a supplier of oil and natural gas. During the winter of 2005–2006, huge increases in the price of natural gas caused outrage and recrimination in the European Union (EU) and such Western-leaning CIS members as Ukraine.

In May 2006, Georgia, Moldova, and Ukraine threatened to leave the CIS as tension increased with Russia over energy prices and a Russian ban on Moldovan and Georgian wine. The relationship steadily worsened that year as Georgia demanded the withdrawal of Russian peacekeepers from secessionist South Ossetia under accusations that Russia was propping up the separatist regime. After Georgia arrested four Russian military officers on spying charges, Russia slapped transport and postal blockades on Georgia and visa restrictions on Georgian citizens. Russia's longtime ally, Belarus, also began chafing at an expected spike in Russian natural gas prices.

Tensions rendered several 2006 CIS meetings unproductive, with the commonwealth unable to serve as an effective negotiating forum. Georgian and Ukrainian presidents were conspicuously absent at a July meeting of heads of state. The CIS summit on November 28, 2006, in Minsk, Belarus, scheduled to coincide with a NATO summit meeting, produced few results. The summit was held to address "questions on the effectiveness and improvement of the Commonwealth" and to sign an agreement delimiting state borders between CIS members, thereby completing the process of turning administrative borders into national borders. Amidst continued rancor, the subject of reform was put off until the following year. Kazakh president Nursultan Nazarbayev, at the time the holder of the CIS's rotating presidency, lamented that less than one-third of the commonwealth's 1,600 agreements had been implemented.

In the meantime, alienated CIS member states continued seeking other avenues for economic, energy, and military cooperation. GUAM was formalized as an international agency committed to a "pro-European" path at a May 2006 meeting in Kiev. The member nations signed a new charter pledging to uphold democratic values and foster mutual economic development and cooperation. Its immediate goals were to reduce dependence on Russian energy and boost relations with the United States as a way to resolve conflicts in their regions. GUAM nations also signed a protocol to implement a free trade zone within member nations' borders. In the same year, member states began discussing the creation of a peacekeeping force that could work under UN mandates, potentially with the aim to replace Russian peacekeepers in the separatist regions of Georgia and Moldova.

On the pro-Russian side, EAEC members—Russia, Belarus, and Kazakhstan—signed the legal framework to establish a customs union immediately following the October 5, 2007, CIS summit in Dushanbe, Tajikistan. At the summit, CSTO members signed agreements enhancing the organization's military power by allowing member states to purchase Russian arms at lower Russian domestic prices. The CSTO also agreed to create an international peacekeeping force, although the Russian foreign minister denied that it would be used in conflicts involving the breakaway Georgian areas of Abkhazia and South Ossetia.

The 2007 CIS summit produced several outcomes. A reform plan was adopted calling for a "qualitatively new level of interaction" among member states. It included the appointment of national coordinators to monitor compliance with decisions adopted by CIS governing bodies. Georgia and Turkmenistan refused to sign and Azerbaijan did so with reservations, while Georgia's president suggested that CIS membership had done nothing to counter Russia's retaliatory trade and travel sanctions. A common migration policy for member states was also adopted, emphasizing regulation and coordination of worker's movements to ensure legal migration and greater social protections for migrants.

Additional developments in October 2007 saw Russia's head of foreign intelligence, Sergei Lebedev, become CIS executive secretary in a move viewed by observers as a Russian attempt to cement its influence over the body.

In April 2008 the president of Turkmenistan, Gurbanguly Berdymukhammedov, attended a NATO summit in Romania. Subsequently there were reports of NATO aircraft landing in Turkmenistan en route to Afghanistan, amid speculation that Turkmenistan might be moving closer to NATO, perhaps under the cover of an agreement worded to maintain its official neutrality.

In July 2008 the presidents of three of the countries in the Western-leaning GUAM group, (Georgia, Ukraine, Azerbaijan, and Moldova), held their annual summit in Batumi, Georgia. Moldova was represented by its foreign minister. The presidents of Lithuania and Poland, both NATO members, were present as observers. The group issued a statement calling for the peaceful resolution of regional disputes, specifically addressing Azerbaijan's breakaway region of Nagorno-Karabakh. The meeting also discussed a project to build an oil pipeline from Odessa, Ukraine, to Poland, which would circumvent Russia in moving Caspian oil to Europe.

The informal CIS summit in Saint Petersburg on June 6–7, 2008, served to demonstrate some CIS members' recognition of Russia's resurgence. Moldova, in particular, seemed concerned with adopting a more conciliatory approach to Russia than in the past. Between May and July 2008, Russian president Dmitry Medvedev made several pronouncements on foreign policy. These seemed at times to emphasize closer relations with such developing powers as India and China, and he called for a "strategic partnership" with the United States in July.

At a conference of CIS prime ministers in Minsk on May 16, 2008, Belarus assumed the rotating presidency of the organization. The meeting adopted a draft convention on migration. After the meeting the president of Belarus, Alexander Lukashenko, declared that it was time to address issues of integration within the CIS more seriously.

In 2008 relations between Russia and Georgia slid toward collapse, with Russia offering overt support of the breakaway Georgian regions of Abkhazia and South Ossetia. In May 2008 Russia sent peacekeeping forces into Abkhazia under CIS auspices. In the same month, a Russian fighter aircraft shot down a Georgian spy drone over Abkhazia. Georgia protested, but stopped further drone flights. In June NATO urged that Russia remove troops from Abkhazia, but on June 19 there was a standoff between Georgian and Russian forces on the border, solved only after a tense telephone conversation between the two countries' presidents. Medvedev publicly warned Georgia of the most serious consequences if it persisted in trying to join NATO, but he appeared to rule out Russian military intervention. However, on August 8 Georgian troops assaulted the South Ossetian capital of Tskhinvali, and Russia responded with a military thrust into Georgia proper. After a French-brokered cease-fire, Russian forces began slowly to withdraw from captured Georgian territory. On August 13, Georgian president Mikhail Saakashvili announced that Georgia was withdrawing from the CIS, and urged other members, particularly Ukraine, to do likewise. On August 19 the CIS Secretariat said that it had received official notice of Georgia's withdrawal, which would become effective, under the CIS constitution, one year from that date. Georgia further announced that it was withdrawing from all peacekeeping agreements with Russia, going back to 1994. Russia recognized Abkhazia and South Ossetia as independent states, and on September 12 Abkhazia applied to join the CIS. Early in September U.S. vice president Dick Cheney visited Georgia, and U.S. navy ships delivered humanitarian aid.

President Medvedev declared that one reason for Russia invading Georgia was "to respect the life and dignity of Russian citizens wherever they are"—a statement that implied Russia's right to intervene anywhere in the former Soviet Union, if not beyond. Russia's belligerent stance seemed designed to discourage Georgia and Ukraine from joining NATO, though Georgia apparently remained interested in late 2008. It was noted that not all CIS states supported Russia's action in Georgia, with Azerbaijan and Turkmenistan being chiefly interested in a stable Georgia as a safe conduit for their gas supplies. Even Belarus, once the CIS member most closely aligned with Moscow, had been at odds with Russia about gas supplies, and offered only lukewarm support to the Russian incursion into Georgia. In general, Russia's influence within the CIS seemed to be waning. At the October 10, 2008, CIS summit in Bishkek, Kyrgyzstan, the presidents of Ukraine and Azerbaijan did not attend. Georgia was told that the door was open for it to return to the CIS, though in the event it did not do so. Moldova was designated to hold the rotating presidency of all CIS organizations in 2009.

In May 2009 Medvedev said he hoped that Ukraine would abandon its increasingly pro-Western policies. He also declared that CIS countries should better coordinate their economies for mutual support. Relations with Belarus remained bad, however, and in June Kyrgyzstan announced that the NATO could use an airbase on its soil for shipment of supplies to troops in Afghanistan.

COMMUNITY OF PORTUGUESE SPEAKING COUNTRIES (CPLP)

Comunidade dos Países de Lingua Portuguesa

Established: By statutes signed July 17, 1996, in Lisbon, Portugal.

Purpose: To promote "concerted political and diplomatic action" between sovereign and equal member states in the international arena; to assist cooperation, "particularly in the economic, social, cultural, juridical, technical, and scientific fields"; to implement projects "for the promotion and diffusion of the Portuguese language."

Headquarters: Lisbon, Portugal.

Principal Organs: Conference of Heads of State and Government, Council of Ministers, Parliamentary Assembly, Standing Committee of Ambassadors, Executive Secretariat.

Web site: www.cplp.org (Mostly in Portuguese, with limited English material.)

Executive Secretary: Domingos Simões Pereira (Guinea-Bissau).

Membership (8): Angola, Brazil, Cape Verde, Guinea-Bissau, Mozambique, Portugal, São Tomé and Principe, Timor-Leste.

Associate Members (3): Equatorial Guinea, Mauritius, Senegal.

Official Language: Portuguese.

Origin and development. The idea of creating a grouping of Portuguese-speaking countries, in emulation of the English-speaking Commonwealth and the Francophonie network, was proposed following the independence of Portugal's colonies in the mid-1970s. Protracted civil war in Angola and Mozambique contributed to a delay in implementation, as did a lack of enthusiasm on the part of Brazil, in which nearly 80 percent of the world's 200 million Portuguese speakers live. Eventually, however, the regular ministerial conferences of the seven Lusophone countries yielded a decision by their foreign ministers in February 1994 that an institutional community should be established. Further instability in Angola and disagreements on funding contributed to the postponement of an intended mid-1995 launch, and it was not until July 1996 that the founding summit convened at the Portuguese capital.

The heads of state of Angola, Brazil, Cape Verde, Guinea-Bissau, Mozambique, Portugal, and São Tomé and Principe duly signed the statutes of the new community, enunciating eight principles that would govern it: sovereign equality of the member states; no interference in internal matters; respect for national identity; reciprocal treatment; upholding of peace, democracy, the rule of law, human rights, and social justice; respect for territorial integrity; promotion of development; and promotion of mutually advantageous cooperation. The community would be open to any other state with Portuguese as its official language, subject to a unanimous decision of the existing members.

Timor-Leste, the former Portuguese Asian colony of East Timor, was admitted as the eighth CPLP member at the organization's fourth summit, July 31–August 1, 2002.

Structure. The CPLP's statutes prescribe that political decisions be achieved by consensus. The highest organ is the Conference of Heads of State and Government, which meets every two years (unless two-thirds of the members request an extraordinary meeting) and is headed by a president serving a two-year term. Responsibility for the coordination and definition of CPLP activities and approval of its budget is vested in the Council of (Foreign) Ministers, which convenes at least annually and is headed by a president serving a one-year term. The Standing Committee of Ambassadors meets at least once a month, charged in particular with supervising the implementation of conference and council decisions by the Executive Secretariat, which is the main executive organ of the CPLP. The secretariat is headed by an executive secretary elected by the Conference of Heads of State and Government for a two-year term, renewable once.

Activities. The intention of the CPLP to adopt the Commonwealth model of an outward-oriented organization, rather than the metropolitan focus characteristic of the Francophonie, was highlighted by the appointment of the former Angolan prime minister, Dr. Marcolino José Carlos Moco, rather than a Portuguese national, as the organization's first executive secretary. This orientation was also apparent in the initial diplomatic tasks that the new community set for itself, namely support for Brazil's quest to become a permanent member of the United Nations (UN) Security Council and advocacy of self-determination for the inhabitants of East Timor (a former Portuguese colony annexed by Indonesia exactly 20 years before the launching of the CPLP). In 1997 the CPLP foreign ministers met for two days to discuss cooperation in the areas of security, services, and immigration.

The second Conference of Heads of State and Government was held in July 1998 in Praia, Cape Verde. The CPLP leaders called on Indonesia to conduct a self-determination referendum in East Timor, which sent an observer delegation to the summit. The summit also condemned renewed rebel activity in Angola, formed a contact group to help negotiate a settlement to the fighting in Guinea-Bissau, and reelected Secretary General Carlos Moco to a second two-year term.

In May 2000 the CPLP defense ministers met in Luanda, Angola, and agreed to establish a joint military force that would cooperate with UN missions in addition to undertaking peacekeeping and humanitarian assignments within the CPLP member countries. As a follow-up to the decision, the community conducted its first joint military maneuvers in October 2000 in Portugal.

On July 17–18, 2000, six of the seven CPLP heads of state (excluding Angola's José Eduardo dos Santos) convened in Maputo, Mozambique, for the third CPLP summit. In addition to electing Brazil's Dulce Maria Pereira as successor to Executive Secretary Carlos Moco, the participants issued a concluding declaration that acknowledged the prevention and treatment of AIDS and other diseases as a prerequisite for sustained development and security; expressed support for the ongoing reconciliation process in Guinea-Bissau; reinforced the importance of international compliance with UN sanctions against the rebel National Union for the Total Independence of Angola (UNITA); and asserted that peace, democracy, and human rights would be accorded maximum priority.

Coincident with independence festivities in May 2002 in Dili, Timor-Leste, the CPLP Council of Ministers held an extraordinary meeting, at which time the government of the world's newest state requested admission to the CPLP. As expected, the CPLP states granted formal membership at the fourth CPLP summit, held July 31–August 1 in Brasília. Timor-Leste thus became the first Asian member of the community.

The group has focused in recent years on shared security concerns, combating the spread of HIV/AIDS, and promotion of shared culture. Cultural exchange initiatives have included the establishment of a Lusophone Culture Day (*Dia da Cultura Lusófona*), the CPLP Games (last held in 2005 in Angola), and the attempt to create a CPLP soccer event sanctioned by the sport's world governing body. Additionally, the increased ease of movement of CPLP citizens was furthered by changes in visa rules and the installation of a special entry port for CPLP citizens at the Lisbon airport. The organization has also worked to aid in member state crises such as the coup in São Tomé and Principe and the election controversy in Guinea-Bissau.

A goal of the organization has been to create a CPLP parliamentary assembly. This was decided at a special session of CPLP ministers in July 2006 in Lisbon. The parliament's chair was to rotate biennially among community members. Work on this project was continuing in mid-2008. The CPLP heads of government met on July 17, 2006, in Guinea-Bisseau at a summit that commemorated the organization's ten-year anniversary. The meeting decided that the CPLP's main focus for the immediate future would be to try to implement the UN's Millennium Declaration to eliminate poverty or at least reduce it by half in member countries. This meeting also welcomed Equatorial Guinea and Mauritius as the group's first associate members. Both of these countries have Portuguese-speaking communities.

In April 2007 a group of CPLP observers joined other international teams to monitor presidential elections in Timor-Leste—the first elections in that country since independence. The elections were considered fair and peaceful. China was active among CPLP member states, and a meeting between CPLP and Chinese representatives in Maputo in May 2007 produced several preliminary memoranda of understanding about cooperation in trade matters.

In October 2007 Portugal set up a military operations center in São Tomé and Principe, aiming to facilitate military cooperation with other CPLP countries and to perhaps discourage further coup attempts. In the same month the Angolan and Portuguese defense ministers met and pledged to create a strategic partnership between the two countries.

The Portuguese language itself came under discussion at CPLP meetings in 2007 and 2008. In May 2008 the Portuguese parliament voted to modify Portuguese spelling, bringing it closer to the Brazilian practice. Opponents criticized this measure as giving way to a dominant Brazilian influence among Lusophone countries. At the July 2008 summit Senegal became the third associate member. It was noted that Croatia, Ukraine, and Venezuela were also interested in association, with strong economic growth in Angola and Brazil having increased the Lusophone group's prominence. The summit also agreed on several measures to promote the Portuguese language worldwide.

In October 2008 the CPLP announced plans to create a development bank for the group's member countries. In November a CPLP mission observed the parliamentary elections in Guinea-Bissau, and pronounced itself pleased with the way in which the elections were conducted. But in March 2009 the organization condemned the murder of Guinea-Bissau's president. In April 2009 the first session of the CPLP's parliamentary assembly opened in São Tomé.

COUNCIL OF ARAB ECONOMIC UNITY (CAEU)

Established: By resolution of the Arab Economic Council of the League of Arab States on June 3, 1957, in Cairo, Egypt, effective at its first meeting May 30, 1964.

Purpose: To provide a flexible framework for achieving economic integration of Arab states.

Headquarters: Cairo, Egypt.

Principal Organs: Council, General Secretariat.

Web site: www.caeu.org.eg/English/Intro

Secretary General: Ahmed Guweili (Egypt).

Membership (11): Egypt, Iraq, Jordan, Kuwait, Libya, Mauritania, Palestine, Somalia, Sudan, Syria, Yemen. (Egypt's membership was suspended from 1979 to 1988. Although not a de jure state, Palestine succeeded the Palestine Liberation Organization as a member following formation of the Palestinian Authority in 1994.)

Official Language: Arabic.

Origin and development. In January 1956 the Arab League agreed on the necessity for an organization that would deal specifically with the economic problems of Arab countries. As a result, on June 3, 1957, a resolution was passed creating the Council of Arab Economic Unity. The organization officially came into existence May 30, 1964.

In December 1988 the CAEU announced it was lifting a nine-year suspension of Egypt's membership that had been occasioned by Cairo's conclusion of a peace agreement with Israel.

In March 1990, Kuwait threatened to withdraw over the council's "poor performance" and the belief that CAEU objectives overlapped those of other Arab organizations. Continuing disputes over budget assessments and shortfalls, including Kuwait's back dues, also played a part in the decision. The CAEU lost its only other Gulf member when the United Arab Emirates withdrew in late November 1999, immediately after a summit of the Gulf Cooperation Council.

Structure. The Council, consisting of the economic, finance, and trade ministers of member states, meets twice a year to discuss and vote on the organization's agenda. The General Secretariat oversees implementation; it also has responsibility for drawing up work plans, which are presented to the council.

Activities. Since its inception, activities have focused on furthering economic development and encouraging economic cooperation among Arab countries. To promote these ends, the council established an Arab Common Market in 1964. Seven years later the market achieved its initial aim of abolishing all taxes and other duties levied on items of trade between Arab countries. The second part of the plan, a customs union of all members, has not yet been fully implemented. The council has also emphasized forming joint Arab companies and federations, coordinating agricultural and industrial programs, and improving road and railway networks. Industries in which joint ventures and federations or unions have been formed include textiles, processed foods, pharmaceuticals, fertilizers, building materials, iron and steel, shipping, petrochemicals, and information technology. The CAEU has also promoted harmonization of statistics and data collection.

The CAEU was thrown into disarray by the Persian Gulf crisis in August 1990. Several prominent CAEU members participated in the U.S.-led coalition that succeeded in driving Iraqi forces from Kuwait in early 1991. Subsequently, in part to restore a sense of normality to Arab affairs, as well as for humanitarian reasons, the CAEU repeatedly called on the United Nations (UN) Security Council to discontinue its sanctions against Iraq.

The CAEU continues to encounter considerable difficulty in achieving its economic goals. The planned introduction in 1998 of an Arab Free Trade Zone, which had the support of most Arab League members as well as the overlapping CAEU membership, was undermined by requests for exceptions involving nearly 3,000 commodities.

At the CAEU Council session held June 6–7, 2001, Egypt, Iraq, Libya, and Syria announced they were establishing their own free trade zone, which once again called into question the CAEU's long-term prospects.

The December 2002 CAEU Council session heard Arab League secretary general Amr Mussa warn of the political, economic, and social consequences posed by threats to the Arab world, principally U.S. antagonism toward the Iraqi government, as well as the ongoing Israeli confrontation with Palestinian militants. Also in 2002 the CAEU established a committee to encourage inter-Arab investment by redirecting some of the estimated $1 trillion in Arab funds that are invested elsewhere.

In 2004 the CAEU acceded to the 2001 Agadir (Morocco) Declaration, which was seen as a step toward creating a pan-Arab free trade zone. Initial signatories were Morocco, Jordan, Tunisia, and Egypt. The declaration also proposed launching a Mediterranean Arab Free Trade Association, bringing together various Arab countries with bilateral partnerships with the European Union (EU) and other foreign entities. The Council session that year produced a strongly negative report concerning unemployment in Arab countries. The Council stated it was finalizing details of an Arab Investment Map (AIM), a means of connecting Arab investors with prospective Arab recipients. The intent was to make it as easy for Arabs to invest inside the Arab world as it is elsewhere. The CAEU is now concentrating on the AIM. It continues to push for Arab economic self-sufficiency and to warn against domination of key economic sectors by outside entities.

In December 2006 the CAEU organized a meeting attended by Secretary General Mussa to look at ways in which Arab countries could help with Iraq's economic reconstruction. The CAEU held a similar meeting in Egypt with an Iraqi commission in March 2007. In May 2007 CAEU secretary general Ahmed Guweili, addressing a committee of the Egyptian parliament, urged that the Arab Common Market, theoretically created in 1964, be made a reality. In statements made in August 2007, Guweili said that the independent economies of the Arab countries needed to be connected by unified customs banking, financial, and monetary policies before a common Arab currency could become a reality. For these reasons, he did not anticipate a common Arab currency earlier than 2020.

The CAEU remains active as a source of statistical information about Arab economies. During 2007, 2008, and 2009 Secretary General Guweili participated in several regional conferences on matters ranging from tourism and transport in Arab countries to an exhibition of products made in Yemen. The CAEU's own meeting, held in Alexandria, Egypt, in June 2008, addressed the world food crisis, calling on Arab countries to put more land under cultivation and warning of an increasing wealth gap between those Arab countries that produce oil and those that do not. In October 2008 the organization announced a blueprint for setting up a customs union, leading to an Arab common market by the end of 2019.

In April 2009 Guweili attended a Sino-Arab trade conference in Hangzhou, China, where there was agreement that each side's banks and investment houses should be allowed a much greater presence in each other's countries. Conference participants took note that trade between China and Arab countries had jumped from $US 36.7 billion in 2004 to $US 132.8 billion in 2008.

COUNCIL OF EUROPE

Conseil de l'Europe

Established: By statute signed May 5, 1949, in London, England, effective August 3, 1949; structure defined by General Agreement signed September 2, 1949.

Purpose: To work for European unity by strengthening pluralist democracy and protecting human rights, seeking solutions to the problems facing European society, and promoting awareness of European cultural identity.

Headquarters: Strasbourg, France.

Principal Organs: Committee of Ministers, Parliamentary Assembly, Secretariat.

Web site: www.coe.int

Secretary General: Terry Davis (United Kingdom).

Membership (47): Albania, Andorra, Armenia, Austria, Azerbaijan, Belgium, Bosnia and Herzegovina, Bulgaria, Croatia, Cyprus, Czech Republic, Denmark, Estonia, Finland, France, Georgia, Germany, Greece, Hungary, Iceland, Ireland, Italy, Latvia, Liechtenstein, Lithuania, Luxembourg, Macedonia, Malta, Moldova, Monaco, Montenegro, Netherlands, Norway, Poland, Portugal, Romania, Russia, San Marino, Serbia, Slovakia, Slovenia, Spain, Sweden, Switzerland, Turkey, Ukraine, United Kingdom.

Observers to the Committee of Ministers (5): Canada, Holy See, Japan, Mexico, United States.

Observers to the Parliamentary Assembly (3): Canada, Israel, Mexico.

Official Languages: English, French. German, Italian, and Russian are also working languages in the Parliamentary Assembly.

Origin and development. In 1946 Winston Churchill put forward his plan for a "United States of Europe," and former European resistance fighters subsequently drew up an implementing program in Hertenstein, Switzerland. International groups were quickly established, and one of the most important of these, the Union of European Federalists, joined Churchill's United Europe Movement, the Economic League for European Cooperation, and the French Council for United Europe to form an International Committee of Movements for European Unity. Under the leadership of Duncan Sandys of the United Kingdom, the committee organized the first Congress of Europe in The Hague, Netherlands, in May 1948, and called for the establishment of a European Assembly and other measures to unite Western Europe. Meanwhile, the signatories of the five-power Brussels Treaty of March 17, 1948, took up the proposals at the governmental level. These combined efforts came to fruition on May 5, 1949, when the foreign ministers of Belgium, Denmark, France, Ireland, Italy, Luxembourg, Netherlands, Norway, Sweden, and the United Kingdom met in London to sign the Statute of the Council of Europe.

The organization was conceived as an instrument for promoting increased unity in Western Europe through discussion and, where appropriate, common action in the economic, social, cultural, scientific, legal, and administrative areas, and in the protection of human rights. Matters relating to national defense were specifically excluded from its scope. Greece, admitted in 1949, was obliged to withdraw in 1969 because of alleged violations of human rights by the Papadopoulos military government; it was readmitted in November 1974 after a change of government in July and the holding of parliamentary elections. Turkey's credentials were suspended in May 1981 in response to the military coup the previous September. In September 1983 the assembly also voted to bar members from the new Turkish legislature because of the unrepresentative character of their election. However, the action was rescinded in May 1985, following a report by the council's Political and Legal Affairs Committee that progress had been made over the last year in the restoration of democracy and respect for human rights.

In response to overtures from Eastern European countries, the Parliamentary Assembly in May 1989 created a Special Guest of the Assembly status, which, following the collapse of communism and the breakup of the Soviet Union and Yugoslavia, became an intermediate stage toward full membership for most ex-Communist states, although the admission of some proved contentious because of issues related to human rights and regional conflicts (see Activities, below). Hungary became a full member in 1990, followed by Czechoslovakia and Poland in 1991; Bulgaria in 1992; Romania, Estonia, Lithuania, Slovenia, the Czech Republic, and Slovakia in 1993 (the last two as successors to Czechoslovakia); Latvia, Albania, Moldova, Ukraine, and Macedonia in 1995; the Russian Federation and Croatia in 1996; Georgia in 1999; Armenia and Azerbaijan in 2001; and Serbia and Montenegro in 2003. Andorra was admitted in 1994 following its promulgation of a democratic constitution and multiparty elections in 1993.

Of the remaining nonmember European states, Belarus has applied for full membership but was suspended from special guest status in January 1997 because of its perceived undemocratic tendencies. A 1998 application for membership by Monaco was not approved because the principality's lack of a parliamentary opposition complicated its ability to guarantee a pluralist delegation. Election law changes followed by elections in February 2003 remedied the situation, and Monaco was admitted as a member on October 5, 2004. The Holy See has observer status.

Structure. The Committee of Ministers, comprised of the foreign ministers of all member states, considers all actions required to further the aims of the council. The decisions of the committee take the form either of recommendations to governments or of conventions and agreements, which bind the states that ratify them. The committee normally meets twice a year in Strasbourg. Most of its ongoing work, however, is performed by deputies who meet collectively almost weekly. Overall policy guidance has recently been provided by meetings of the heads of state and government.

The Parliamentary Assembly, the deliberative organ, can consider any matter within the purview of the council. Its conclusions, if they call for action by governments, take the form of recommendations to the Committee of Ministers. The members of the assembly are drawn from national parliaments and apportioned according to population, the states with the smallest populations having 2 seats and those with the largest, 18. (Countries granted Special Guest of the Assembly status have held seats, although without voting power.) The method of delegate selection is left to the national parliaments. Within the assembly all members participate not as state representatives but as individuals or as representatives of political groups; each delegation includes spokesmen from both the government and the opposition.

Assembly committees cover culture, science, and education; economic affairs and development; environment, agriculture, and local and regional affairs; equal opportunities for women and men; honoring of obligations and commitments by member states; legal affairs and human rights; migration, refugees, and demography; political affairs; rules of procedure and immunities; and social, health, and family affairs. In addition, a joint committee comprises, in equal numbers, members of the assembly and a representative from each member government. A standing committee comprises the chairs of national delegations, the chairs of the general assembly committees, and the Bureau of the Assembly (the assembly president, 18 vice presidents, and leaders of the political groups). The president of the assembly is elected annually for a renewable term; normally he serves a total of three years.

Part of the council's work is carried out by specialized institutions, such as the European Court of Human Rights, the European Youth Foundation, the European Center for Global Interdependence and Solidarity (the North-South Center), the Social Development Fund, and the Congress of Local and Regional Authorities of Europe.

The council's many parliamentary, ministerial, and governmental committees and subsidiary groups are serviced by a Secretariat staffed by some 1,800 recruits from all member countries. The secretary general is elected by the assembly for renewable, five-year terms from a list of candidates proposed by the Committee of Ministers.

Activities. Except for matters of national and regional defense, the Council of Europe and the Parliamentary Assembly of the Council of Europe (PACE) conduct activities in every conceivable aspect of European political, social, and cultural life. For example, deputies responsible to the Council of Ministers participate in a plethora of rapporteur groups, working parties, and committees concerned with, among other issues, human rights; democratic stability; administrative and budgetary matters; legal cooperation; social and health questions; education and culture; institutional reforms; and relations with the European Union (EU), the Organization for Security and Cooperation in Europe (OSCE), and the Organization for Economic Cooperation and Development (OECD).

Among the most significant achievements of the council are the drafting and implementation of the European Convention for the Protection of Human Rights and Fundamental Freedoms. Signed in November 1950 and entering into force in September 1953, the convention set up the European Commission of Human Rights, comprised of independent lawyers from member states, to examine alleged violations by signatories and to attempt to broker negotiated settlements between the involved parties. A European Court of Human Rights was also established to consider cases in which those negotiations fail. Under the 11th protocol to the human rights convention, on November 1, 1998, the commission was abolished, with all alleged violations proceeding directly to a new permanent court. The Council of Ministers then approved creation of the new post of commissioner for human rights in May 1999.

An additional protocol, which entered into force in November 1988, seeks to protect the rights of aliens in cases of expulsion, the right of appeal in trial cases, the right of compensation for miscarriage of justice, the right not to be tried twice for the same offense, and the equality of spouses. The most recent additions to the 1950 convention are the 12th and 13th protocols. Protocol No. 12, which was opened for signature November 4, 2000, provides a general protection against discrimination on the basis of sex; race; religion; ethnic, national, or social origin; and political or other opinions. Protocol No. 13, which extends the prohibition against capital punishment to acts committed during war, was opened for signature May 5, 2002, and entered into force on July 1, 2003. The latest country to ratify it was France, in October 2007.

Other landmark conventions include the European Cultural Convention (which entered into force in 1955); the European Convention for the Peaceful Settlement of Disputes (1958); the European Social Charter (1965); the European Convention on the Suppression of Terrorism (1978); the European Convention for the Prevention of Torture and Inhuman or Degrading Treatment or Punishment (1989); the Convention on Laundering, Search, Seizure, and Confiscation of Proceeds from Crime (1993); the Framework Convention for the Protection of National Minorities (1998); the Convention on Human Rights and Biomedicine (1999); and the European Convention on the Exercise of Children's Rights (2000).

Much of the council's attention in recent years has focused on defining its role among the continent's often overlapping organizations, particularly in regard to the former Soviet-bloc countries of Eastern Europe. It became the official coordinator of human rights issues for the Conference on Security and Cooperation in Europe (CSCE, subsequently the OSCE) following that body's institutionalization in 1990; it also assisted with the establishment of a CSCE Parliamentary Assembly in 1992, in accordance with the council's earlier proposal for an all-European representative forum. In addition, the council's program on democratic institutions has provided assistance to the emerging European democracies in the field of constitutional, legislative, and administrative reform. On the proposal of President Mitterrand of France in May 1992, the council held its first summit meeting of heads of state and government October 8–9, 1993, in Vienna, Austria, to consider structural reform of the organization.

Minority and political rights remained prominent council concerns in 1996, particularly in connection with new accessions to full membership. Opposition to Russia's admittance in the Parliamentary Assembly (over the Chechnya military operation and then the Communist victory in the December 1995 State Duma election) was eventually overcome early in 1996 on the strength of various Russian promises. The required two-thirds assembly majority was marshaled in January, with the Committee of Ministers moving swiftly to admit Russia the following month. Even more controversial was Croatia's application, which was approved by the assembly in April but, in an unprecedented move, deferred by the Committee of Ministers in light of concern about the democratic credentials of the Tudjman government and its commitment to the Dayton peace agreement for Bosnia and Herzegovina. On the basis of assurances from Zagreb, Croatia was eventually accorded formal membership in November, its admittance highlighting a recent trend away from insistence on pre-entry observance of council standards toward a policy of monitoring compliance after accession. However, the suspension of the special guest status of Belarus in January 1997 (because the new Belarus constitution adopted in November 1995 was seen as vesting excessive authority in the president) indicated that basic council standards had not been relaxed.

The second summit of the council's heads of state and government was held October 10–11, 1997, in Strasbourg to pursue the "consolidation of democracy" on the continent and to reconfirm the council's standard-setting" role in such areas as human rights. The summit's final declaration called on the Committee of Ministers to propose structural reform within the council to promote, among other things, social cohesion; cultural diversity within the context of respect for democratic values; and the security of citizens, via programs designed to combat organized crime, government corruption, and terrorism.

In January 1999, Lord Russell-Johnston, a former leader of the Scottish Liberal Democratic Party, was elected to a three-year term as president of the Parliamentary Assembly. The UK's Terry Davis was also nominated as the council's next secretary general, but in the June election he lost by two votes to Walter Schwimmer of Austria. Davis was elected secretary general in 2004.

During the first half of 2000 renewed fighting in Chechnya generated not only a decision by the Parliamentary Assembly to suspend Russia's voting rights, but also calls for Russia's suspension from the full council. Moscow, in turn, threatened to withdraw from the organization. Admission of special guests Armenia and Azerbaijan proved almost as contentious, although both were formally welcomed in early 2001 on the strength of the argument that simultaneous admission would encourage democratization and resolution of the Nagorno-Karabakh dispute. At the same time, PACE restored Russia's voting rights, although Moscow has continued to be criticized not only for its actions in Chechnya, but also for a widely perceived failure to adhere to principles of free speech and press.

On June 21–22, 2001, the council hosted the first world congress on abolition of the death penalty. The council has repeatedly criticized the United States, in particular, for executing convicted criminals, and in mid-2001 threatened both the United States and Japan with suspension of their observer status if they did not take steps toward ending capital punishment. On July 1, 2003, Protocol No. 13 to the European human rights convention entered into effect, thereby making prohibition of capital punishment absolute.

The 109th session of the Committee of Ministers convened November 7–8, 2001. Immediately following the September 11 terrorist attacks on the United States, the council had vowed its support for the fight against terrorism and indicated it would consider updating the European Convention on Suppression of Terrorism. The organization also noted it would soon open for signature a Convention on Cyber-Crime and a Second Additional Protocol to the 1959 European Convention on Mutual Assistance in Criminal Matters. On September 25, however, PACE offered a word of caution to the United States, describing the September 11 attacks as "crimes" rather than acts of war and urging Washington to seek United Nations (UN) Security Council approval before initiating reprisals. The PACE also proposed that the remit of the International Criminal Court (ICC), which the United States has not joined, be expanded to cover international terrorism.

The Convention on Cyber-Crime was opened for signature November 23, 2001, and was to enter into force after ratification by five council members. More than two-dozen member states (plus the United States, Japan, Canada, and South Africa) immediately signed the convention, which entered into force in July 2004.

Five months after the admission of Bosnia and Herzegovina on April 24, 2002, PACE voted 122–6 in favor of admitting Yugoslavia as soon as its two constituent republics had completed ratification of a new constitution. (The Socialist Federal Republic of Yugoslavia's special guest status was suspended in November 1991; the successor Federal Republic of Yugoslavia was reinstated as a guest in January 2001.) Accordingly, the new "state union" of Serbia and Montenegro was admitted April 3, 2003. (In June 2006, Montenegro declared independence, and was admitted as a separate member in May 2007.) In September 2007 Montenegro complained that Serbia was violating the council's 1997 declaration on citizenship, which prohibits discrimination on the basis of national origin or gender.

In May 2003, PACE president Peter Schieder voiced concern over ongoing efforts by the United States to convince various countries in Southeast Europe to sign bilateral agreements exempting U.S. officials, military personnel, and nationals from ICC jurisdiction. Moreover, on the agenda for the June 23–27 PACE session was a report on the rights of prisoners held by the United States in Afghanistan or at its Guantanamo Bay, Cuba, base. Other notable reports prepared for the session discussed stem cell research and trafficking in human organs. Debate at the summer session focused in part on a Convention on the Future of Europe and the Council of Europe. Also in May 2003, the anticipated amendment to the suppression of terrorism convention was opened for signature.

At its May 16–17, 2005, summit in Warsaw, Poland, the council issued a declaration strengthening its commitment to all aspects of individual freedom and justice. The council established a presence in the fight against human trafficking, corruption, and computer crime. Also in May 2005, a new Convention on the Prevention of Terrorism; a Convention on Laundering, Search, Seizure, and Confiscation of the Proceeds from Crime and on the Financing of Terrorism; and a Convention on Action Against Trafficking in Human Beings were opened.

During 2005 and 2006 the council became involved in the controversy over reports that the United States was moving people suspected of terrorism for interrogation in countries in which torture was practiced, and that some Eastern European countries were cooperating with the U.S. Central Intelligence Agency (CIA) by holding such people in secret prisons. The council's special rapporteur, Dick Marty of Switzerland, declared in a June 6, 2006, report that at least 14 European governments were to some degree cooperating with, or at least turning a blind eye to, this program of "extraordinary rendition." His report stated there was clear evidence of aircraft bearing such prisoners flying over and landing in Europe for rendition operations, with the UK, Portugal, Ireland, and Greece as "stop-off points." The report also cited evidence for suspicion that Poland and Romania were harboring secret prisons in their territory, a charge that Romania immediately rejected as "speculation," and that the Polish prime minister, Kazimierz Marcinkiewicz, called "libelous."

On May 15, 2006, Russia rotated into the six-month chair of the council's Committee of Ministers. This caused controversy as many believed Russia's record on observing human rights and the rule of law was too weak to justify this position. The Russian response was that compliance was only a matter of time, rather than political will. Russia also complained that the council was trying to impose a pro-Western position on Belarus, where a pro-Russian candidate had won a much-disputed presidential election that observers from the West declared was tainted by blatant fraud. The council's affairs in late 2006 and 2007 were marked by tensions between a pro-EU tendency and the resurgence of Russia. In October 2006 Russia objected, in the person of its Foreign Minister Sergey Lavrov, who headed the council's Committee of Ministers, to any expansion of the North Atlantic Treaty Organization (NATO) eastward. This objection was in the context of Georgia's interest in joining NATO.

On October 10, 2007, the council sponsored a Europe-wide day of action against the death penalty. This event was originally to have been sponsored by the EU, but Poland, which had some interest in reintroducing the death penalty, had threatened to veto it. The Council of Europe had previously told Poland that if it reintroduced capital punishment it would be expelled.

The former Soviet republics of the Caucasus and beyond continued to be the council's main focus in late 2007 and into 2008. Secretary General Davis visited Armenia in November 2007 to discuss the dispute with Azerbaijan over the region of Nagorno-Karabakh. He promised council involvement in the peace process, but declined to compare the region's status to that of Kosovo, which is under a UN mandate. The March 2008 presidential election in Armenia was criticized, both by council and OSCE observers, and violence followed. In April the Parliamentary Assembly adopted a resolution urging an open dialog between opposing groups, and criticized the Armenian government for its lack of response.

Council of Europe monitors denounced the December 2007 Russian presidential election as unfair, a charge that Russian election managers angrily denied, accusing Western observers of bias.

In January 2008 the council's rapporteur on Belarus recommended a measured reopening of contacts with that country. However, the council was forced to condemn Belarus in February for carrying out three executions. It has subsequently called for increased respect for freedom of speech.

The council was involved to some extent in mediating an end to the August 2008 military clash between Georgia and Russia. After a visit to the region, secretary general Davis condemned Russia's unilateral recognition of the Georgian regions of Abkhazia and South Ossetia as independent states. Other nations and international organizations joined in this condemnation.

Subsequent PACE resolutions were critical of both Russia and Georgia. In November 2008 Davis visited Moscow to help Russia "overcome any difficulties that may arise in carrying out its commitments to the Council of Europe." The main points of contention were Russia's deteriorating record on civil liberties, its frequent failure to carry out decisions of the European Court of Human Rights, and its failure to ratify the 2004 Protocol 14 to the European Convention on Human Rights, which seeks to streamline and speed up the court's work. Russia, while not signing the protocol, continues to declare support for its aims, and for the Council of Europe in general. In February 2009 the council opened a new office in the city center of Moscow, replacing a previous facility in a more remote location. In April 2009 the council declared it was ready to work with Russia on modifying its recently tightened regulations on the activities of NGOs in that country.

In December 2008 the European Court of Human Rights unanimously declared that indefinite retention of the DNA and fingerprint records of persons who have been arrested but not convicted is illegal. This ruling was expected to have a large impact in the UK, where such retention is standard practice. In September the council's commissioner for human rights, Thomas Hammarberg (Sweden), criticized new UK procedures for handling people who had requested asylum.

The June 2009 Parliamentary Assembly, meeting in Strasbourg, saw one of the most serious disagreements in the organization's history. With the term of office of the current secretary general, Terry Davis, due to expire on August 31, the assembly was presented with two candidates chosen by the Committee of Ministers. In the past the assembly had always chosen its own candidates. Declining to vote on the Committee of Ministers' nominees, the assembly struck the election of a new secretary general from its agenda, and the meeting ended with no replacement for Davis selected. At the same meeting the assembly agreed to reinstate the special guest status of Belarus, if that country agreed to a moratorium on executions.

COUNCIL OF THE BALTIC SEA STATES (CBSS)

Established: March 5, 1992, by a meeting of foreign ministers of the ten Baltic states in Copenhagen, Denmark.

Purpose: To promote cooperation and coordination among all states bordering on the Baltic Sea or its main links to the open sea; to support new democratic institutions, economic development, humanitarian aid, energy and the environment, culture and education, and transportation and communication.

Headquarters: Stockholm, Sweden.

Principal Organs: Council of Ministers, Committee of Senior Officials, Commissioner of the CBSS on Democratic Development, Secretariat.

Web site: www.cbss.org

Director of Secretariat: Gabriele Kötschau (Germany).

Membership (12): Denmark, Estonia, European Commission, Finland, Germany, Iceland, Latvia, Lithuania, Norway, Poland, Russia, Sweden.

Observers (7): Belarus, France, Italy, Netherlands, Slovakia, Ukraine, United Kingdom, United States.

Special Participants (6): Baltic Sea Parliamentary Conference, Baltic Sea Seven Islands Cooperation Network, Baltic Sea States' Subregional Cooperation, Conference of Peripheral Maritime Regions of Europe-Baltic Sea Commission, Union of the Baltic Cities, Organization for Economic Cooperation and Development.

Origin and development. The idea of an umbrella organization for cooperation among the Baltic Sea states was first raised in the fall of 1991 during a meeting of the Danish and German foreign ministers. Originally, the proposed council was viewed as a vehicle for the Nordic countries and Germany to assist Estonia, Latvia, Lithuania, Poland, and Russia in their transformation into democratic, free-market societies. However, at the March 5–6, 1992, inaugural council meeting, the foreign ministers broadened the scope of proposed cooperation to include other areas, such as the environment, transportation, and education. Military and security matters were specifically excluded from the council's mandate in order not to intrude upon other international organizations.

Structure. The Council of Ministers, comprising the foreign ministers of the member states and a commissioner of the European Commission, meets annually; the chair rotates each year, and the ministerial session takes place in the chair's country. The Council of Ministers provides policy guidance to the Committee of Senior Officials (CSO), which monitors CBSS programs and activities. Since 1996 CBSS has also held informal summit meetings, which are attended by the members' heads of government.

In May 1994 the organization established the autonomous office of Commissioner on Democratic Institutions and Human Rights, based in Copenhagen, Denmark. In 2000 the office's mandate was revised, and the title was changed to Commissioner of the Council of the Baltic Sea States on Democratic Development.

A director heads the Secretariat, which was formally inaugurated in October 1998. Its staff includes several senior advisers whose jobs include assisting various CBSS working groups such as Assistance to Democratic Institutions, Cooperation on Children at Risk, Economic Cooperation, Nuclear and Radiation Safety, Transportation Issues, and Youth Affairs. In April 2000 the Secretariat launched the Energy Unit, and in January 2001 it started the Baltic 21 Unit to promote sustainable development in accordance with the organization's Agenda 21 action program. The Children's Unit commenced work in June 2002.

In 1994 the CBSS adopted the statutes for the EuroFaculty, which assists in the reform of higher education in business administration, economics, law, and public administration at universities in Estonia, Latvia, and Lithuania. Based originally in Riga, Latvia, the EuroFaculty subsequently initiated an additional project in Kaliningrad, Russia, to integrate the exclave further into regional institutions. A Business Advisory Council was formed in 1996 to assist member countries in privatization and business restructuring and the promotion of small- and medium-size enterprises. Other CBSS bodies include the Task Force on Organized Crime in the Baltic Sea Region and the Task Force on Communicable Disease Control. Members of national and regional legislatures also meet annually at a Baltic Sea Parliamentary Conference.

Activities. Backers of the CBSS expected it to work closely with other European organizations to avoid duplication and the creation of unnecessary bureaucracy. However, because the new situation in Europe after the collapse of communism forced many of the continent's organizations to rethink their missions, the CBSS's purpose was at first unclear. Moreover, political differences within the CBSS (such as the dispute between the Baltic states and Russia over Moscow's reluctance to withdraw forces of the former Soviet military) temporarily hindered institutional progress. Nevertheless, the March 1993 session of the Council of Ministers approved numerous common guidelines for future activity; there were approximately 50 proposed CBSS initiatives by that time. Several working groups were also established to report to the CBSS Committee of Senior Officials. Over the next year, the Working Group on Economic Cooperation evaluated ways to expedite customs procedures and border crossings and urged members to support regional transportation and energy projects. Ole Espersen of Denmark became the CBSS commissioner on democratic institutions and human rights at the Council of Ministers meeting held May 25–26, 1994.

CBSS foreign ministers welcomed the withdrawal of all Russian troops from Lithuania and Poland by August 1994 and urged Russia to also leave Estonia and Latvia. At the CBSS Council of Ministers session held May 18–19, 1995, in Gdańsk, Poland, Russian officials called upon Commissioner Espersen to address what Moscow perceived to be the "continual infringement" of the civil rights of the Russian-speaking population in Estonia and Latvia. Russia also criticized a "lack of action" by the CBSS in other mandated areas.

The Council of Ministers meeting held in early July 1996 in Kalmar, Sweden, focused on strengthening ties with the European Union (EU), to which four CBSS members (Denmark, Finland, Germany, and Sweden) already belonged, and four more (Estonia, Latvia, Lithuania, and Poland) were seeking to join. The Kalmar meeting also formally endorsed three action programs concerned with participation and stable political development, economic integration and prosperity, and the environment.

In 1997 the Council of Ministers assigned the CSO the task of determining whether or not the CBSS needed a secretariat, and in February 1998 it concluded that a "small and efficient" secretariat should be established in Stockholm, Sweden. The CBSS Secretariat, with Jacek Starosciak of Poland as its director, opened the following October.

At the second meeting of CBSS prime ministers, held January 22–23, 1998, in Riga, Latvia, the heads of government praised past, and supported future, cooperation in the areas of prevention of organized crime and child molestation, economic integration, civic security, education, environment, and the adaptation and diffusion of information technology. At their seventh annual meeting, held June 22–23 in Nyborg, Denmark, the Council of Ministers adopted Agenda 21 for the Baltic States Region, an action program geared to sustainable development and coordination in agriculture, education, energy, fisheries, forestry, industry, spatial planning, transport, and tourism.

The third CBSS summit convened April 12–13, 2000, in Kolding, Denmark. The principal topic of discussion was how to restructure the organization to enhance regional integration. At the meeting's conclusion, the heads of government decided that the CBSS should encompass the full range of intergovernmental, multilateral, and cooperative efforts in the region. Two months later, on June 21–22, the Council of Ministers convened in Bergen, Norway, for its ninth session. In addition to naming Helle Degn of Denmark to succeed Commissioner Espersen, the foreign ministers voiced their support of the EU's Northern Dimension Action Plan, which focused on the environment, nuclear safety, justice and home affairs; encouraged continued regional cooperation in energy, the environment, and information technology; and discussed balanced growth.

At the fourth CBSS summit, held June 9–10, 2002, in St. Petersburg, Russia, a major topic of discussion was the anticipated impact on Kaliningrad of EU accession by Poland and Lithuania. At the time, residents of the Russian region were accorded visa-free travel across Poland and Lithuania, but when the two prospective EU members adopted the EU's Schengen rules, which allow for visa-free travel only between Schengen countries, the practice would come to an end. Russia, in particular, strongly objected. The June meeting of government leaders was preceded by a March 5–6 ministerial session in Svetlogorsk, Russia, which marked the tenth anniversary of the CBSS.

The 12th Council of Ministers session, held June 10–11, 2003, in Pori, Finland, continued the emphasis on EU-related matters—particularly the anticipated accession of Estonia, Latvia, Lithuania, and Poland to the EU in May 2004—and their broader impact on the non-EU CBSS members. The Russian foreign minister noted that it was CBSS members' "common duty" not to let regional trade ties weaken following EU expansion. The assembled ministers gave their support to the EU's Wider Europe initiative and the new Northern Dimension Action Plan for 2004–2006. On July 1, 2003, as expected, Poland and Lithuania ended visa-free travel between Kaliningrad and the rest of Russia.

The fifth CBSS summit was held on June 21, 2004, in Laulasmaa, Estonia. The final declaration expressed confidence that, with Estonia, Latvia, Lithuania, and Poland now in the EU, European interest in the Baltic region would increase. Noting a recently concluded summit between the EU and Russia, the CBSS expressed hope that its mixture of EU and non-EU countries, all belonging to or with membership pending in the World Trade Organization (WTO), would be good for the political and economic future of the region.

The sixth summit, held on June 8, 2006, in Reykjavik, Iceland, affirmed support for regional cooperation regarding energy issues (such as the laying of international gas pipelines) and the protection of the environment. The Lithuanian foreign minister stressed the group's role in encouraging democratic institutions in Ukraine and Belarus. (Ukraine is an observer at the CBSS; Belarus was not at the time.) Russia's renewed assertive stance in world affairs has caused discussion within the CBSS, and at a May 2007 meeting of CBSS trade and economy ministers in Stockholm, Russia's pending accession to the WTO was considered, with a recommendation that the EU and the Russian Federation should achieve free trade. Two topics dominated the CBSS from the second half of 2007 through its June 2008 summit meeting: the position of a reemergent Russia and reform of the CBSS organization itself.

After assuming the presidency of the organization in June 2007, Latvia called on Russia to ratify the long-delayed border treaty between the two countries. This was done on September 5, 2007. In November 2007 the Russian foreign minister repeated Russia's desire to play an active and constructive role in the CBSS, as well as with other regional organizations. In May 2008 Vladimir Putin, the Russian prime minister, announced that he would not be attending the June 3 CBSS summit (which Chancellor Angela Merkel of Germany also missed). In July 2008 Putin signed a declaration that reduced from 101 to 12 the number of international organizations allowed to operate tax-free in Russia. The CBSS was one of the remaining twelve.

CBSS meetings during the Latvian presidency stressed that the CBSS had met most of its original development goals, and could foster smoother relations between the EU; Russia; and its other non-EU members, Iceland and Norway. The June 2008 summit adopted a proposal for reform of the organization. The existing working groups were to be disbanded or transformed into committees of experts, and there would be an effort to avoid duplication of effort. The Secretariat would be restructured to improve fundraising efforts and project management. Amid speculation that the CBSS had outlived much of its usefulness, France applied for full membership, concerned, some said, about Germany's increasing influence in the organization. The CBSS, now under the presidency of Denmark, took the application of this very non-Baltic country under advisement. In the period 2008–2009 many observers felt that the CBSS was continuing to lose ground as an organization capable of proposing and mounting initiatives separate from the EU. At the 15th ministerial session, held June 4, 2009, in Copenhagen, Denmark, the chief topic under discussion, or at least in the minds of delegates, was the dispute between Russia and most CBSS European members about the proposed Nord Stream natural gas pipeline project. This pipeline would bring gas from Russia to Germany through the Baltic seabed. The Russian foreign minister, Sergei Lavrov, criticized what he called a double standard, disguising political objections as environmental concerns. The Lithuanian foreign minister had previously called for the CBSS to focus on projects that would unite, not divide, the group. At the June meeting Lithuania assumed the group's presidency, and Belarus was given observer status.

COUNCIL OF THE ENTENTE

Conseil de l'Entente

Established: May 29, 1959, in Abidjan, Côte d'Ivoire, by a convention signed by representatives from countries that were once part of French West Africa.

Purpose: To promote political, economic, and social coordination among the member states.

Headquarters: Abidjan, Côte d'Ivoire.

Principal Organs: Council, Ministerial Council, Mutual Aid and Loan Guarantee Fund, Secretariat.

Web site: None.

Secretary General: Magloire Kéké Téti (Côte d'Ivoire).

Membership (5)**:** Benin, Burkina Faso, Côte d'Ivoire, Niger, Togo.

Official Language: French.

Origin and development. The Council of the Entente was formed in 1959 by Benin (then Dahomey), Burkina Faso (then Upper Volta), Côte d'Ivoire, and Niger; Togo joined in 1966. In its early years the council was seen as a vehicle for Côte d'Ivoire, by far the most economically and politically powerful member, to promote its preeminence in West Africa.

In 1966 the council adopted a convention that established the Mutual Aid and Loan Guarantee Fund to promote economic development and regional integration; to assist in preparing specific economic projects; to obtain assistance from donor organizations; and to promote increased trade, commerce, and investment among council members and their neighbors. In 1970 an associated Economic Community of Livestock and Meat (*Communauté Economique du Bétail et de la Viande*—CEBV) was established to provide technical and financial support for the region's cattle industry.

Structure. The organization's principal organ, the Council, encompasses the members' heads of state, and the location of meetings rotates among the capitals of the members. Council sessions are preceded by meetings of the Ministerial Council, which is comprised of representatives of the five governments.

In accordance with a modified structure adopted in December 1973, a board of directors (the five heads of state) governs the Mutual Aid and Loan Guarantee Fund. Its management committee handles administrative and financial matters, such as the approval of guarantees. The council's Secretariat considers applications for guarantees, reduction of interest rates, and extension of loan repayment periods. It also provides regional centers with support for technical assistance, development, and cooperation.

Activities. The member states have established a port and harbor administration, a railway and road traffic administration, and a unified quarantine organization. Development programs have concentrated on food production, village water projects, expansion of tourism, and energy.

In the 1990s, institutional effectiveness remained marginal at best because member states, several of them beset by sustained political turmoil, failed to make their allotted financial contributions. Consequently, the members' heads of state convened for the first time in 11 years on October 31, 1994, in Kara, Togo, in an effort to "relaunch" the organization, which the participants characterized as "an irreplaceable framework for debate and solidarity."

At the August 1998 Council meeting, the heads of state denounced illegal arms trade in the region and the associated rise in crime. They also discussed ongoing conflicts in Africa and expressed concern about renewed fighting in Angola. The Council gave its support to the Economic Community of West African States (ECOWAS) and the Community of Portuguese-Speaking Countries (CPLP), which were mediating the crisis in Guinea-Bissau. Council leaders also signed agreements to establish a regional tourist visa and enhance cooperation among the members' national lotteries.

At the council summit of March 2000, the leaders of the five member states were joined by President Obasanjo of Nigeria for discussions on regional security. This was the first time the head of a nonmember state had attended a Council summit. Meeting again in mid-February 2001 in Kara, the council executives conducted wide-ranging discussions on political, economic, social, peace, security, and regional stability matters. The summit's final communiqué voiced support for the free movement of goods and people in the region, closer integration through ECOWAS and the West African Economic and Monetary Union (*Union Economique et Monétaire Ouest-Africaine*—UEMOA), and rapid adoption of the founding statute for the OAU-sponsored African Union. Five months later, in late July, the council members initiated their regional tourist visa.

In March 2002 the five members' security ministers and their counterpart from Mali met in Niamey, Niger, to discuss regional security issues, including illegal arms sales, banditry, and child trafficking. Shortly thereafter, the Council's tourism ministers met to review implementation of the regional visa and to identify possible improvements. They also discussed prospects for including Ghana and Mali in the organization.

In early July 2002 the council leaders met in Lomé, Togo, but two months later attention turned from regional cooperation to instability in Côte d'Ivoire. In September a failed coup, continuing conflict, and a resultant flow of refugees in Côte d'Ivoire complicated the already strained relations between Côte d'Ivoire and Burkina Faso, and their common border was closed as a consequence. Although France helped broker a peace agreement between the Ivorian government and rebel forces in March 2003, the border remained closed until September 2003. Burkina Faso's president did not attend an extraordinary "mini-summit," which was held in May in Lomé to promote reconciliation in Côte d'Ivoire. Subsequently, regional conflicts severely limited the organization's ability to function.

On January 17, 2008, an extraordinary meeting of the five member states' heads of state or government in Ouagadougou, Burkina Faso, relaunched the organization. Magloire Kéké Téti was nominated by Côte d'Ivoire as the organization's secretary general, the top post having been vacant since its previous incumbent's death in 2005. In May 2008 Kéké Téti reported that the organization, with 41 employees, had set a budget for the fiscal year. Since that time, however, little activity seems to have occurred.

EAST AFRICAN COMMUNITY (EAC)

Established: By Treaty for the Establishment of the East African Community, which was signed November 30, 1999, in Arusha, Tanzania, and entered into force July 7, 2000; community formally launched January 15, 2001.

Purpose: To coordinate trade, monetary, defense, and sectoral policies with a view toward establishment of a customs union, a common market, a monetary union, and, eventually, a political federation of the partner states.

Headquarters: Arusha, Tanzania.

Principal Organs: Summit, Council of Ministers, Coordination Committee, Sectoral Councils, Sectoral Committees, East African Court of Justice, East African Legislative Assembly, Secretariat.

Web site: www.eac.int

Secretary General: Juma Volter Mwapachu (Tanzania).

Membership (5)**:** Burundi, Kenya, Rwanda, Tanzania, Uganda.

Official Language: English. Kiswahili is to be developed as a lingua franca.

Origin and development. The original East African Community (EAC) of Kenya, Tanzania, and Uganda was established in 1967 but collapsed in July 1977, although its affiliated East African Development Bank (EADB), which had been established under an annex to the original treaty, was reorganized by the founding states in 1980 and continues to function. (For background on the original EAC and its collapse, see the section on foreign relations in the Kenya article.) In 1984 the former EAC members signed a Mediation Agreement to explore ways of resuming cooperation, which led in 1993 to an Agreement for the Establishment of the Permanent Tripartite Commission for East African Cooperation. A corresponding Secretariat began operations in Arusha, Tanzania, in March 1996 under Executive Director Francis Muthaura of Kenya.

The main task of the tripartite commission soon became negotiation of a new EAC treaty, the three neighboring states having confirmed in 1997 their intention to reestablish the EAC. On November 30, 1999, in Arusha, Presidents Daniel arap Moi of Kenya, Benjamin Mkapa of Tanzania, and Yoweri Musaveni of Uganda signed the new Treaty for the Establishment of the East African Community. The requisite ratifications having been completed, the treaty entered into force on July 7, 2000, with the reestablished EAC being formally launched at a meeting of the three leaders on January 15, 2001.

Structure. The Summit, consisting of the heads of state or government of the three members, provides "general direction and impetus" to the EAC. It meets annually or in extraordinary session at the request of one member state. The summit chairmanship rotates annually; decisions are reached by consensus. The Council of Ministers, which meets at least twice a year, comprises the members' ministers for regional cooperation plus any other ministers designated by the individual states. As the principal EAC policymaking organ, the council reviews and oversees the EAC's programs, establishes oversight Sectoral Councils from among its own members, and appoints working Sectoral Committees. A Coordination Committee, which also convenes at least twice a year, includes the member states' permanent secretaries responsible for regional cooperation; other permanent secretaries may also be named to it by each state. Its responsibilities include implementing council decisions and coordinating the work of the Sectoral Committees. The latter have responsibilities for such concerns as agriculture and food security; energy; education, culture, and sports; fiscal affairs; gender and community development; labor/employment, refugee management, and movement of persons; and transport, commerce, and meteorology.

The Secretariat is headed by a secretary general, who is selected by the summit for a five-year term on a rotational basis. The secretary general is assisted by two deputies, one for Projects and Programs and the other for Finance and Administration.

The treaty also provided for an East African Court of Justice to interpret and apply the treaty, although the Council of Ministers may extend the court's jurisdiction to other areas, subject to protocol approval. The East African Legislative Assembly comprises 5 ex-officio and 27 elected members; the latter are selected by the three national assemblies, but sitting deputies and government ministers are excluded.

Activities. Even before conclusion of the new EAC treaty in 1999, the three prospective member states had concluded a 1997–2000 East African Cooperative Development Plan in which they agreed to work toward harmonizing policies in key sectors, making their currencies convertible, easing border crossings, reducing bilateral tariffs, identifying needed infrastructural projects, and bringing investment incentives and codes in line with each other. The first session of the EAC council convened January 13, 2001, immediately before the first summit, which officially launched the organization. At the second EAC summit, held two months later, the heads of state agreed to move ahead with the Second Cooperative Development Strategy (2001–2005).

Looking ahead, the EAC anticipated quick completion of a Protocol on the Customs Union as well as closer coordination of monetary and fiscal policies, banking regulations, and value added tax (VAT) rates. The EAC also requested the participation of agencies and offices involved in such areas as tourism, posts and telecommunications, investment promotion, and scientific research, plus the participation of civil groups representing, for example, women, youth, professionals, and workers.

The heads of state met for a third time on November 30, 2001, to launch the Court of Justice and the Legislative Assembly and to sign a revised Memorandum of Understanding on Cooperation in Defense, updating a document that they had completed in April 1998. The possible future membership of Rwanda and Burundi was also discussed, but at an April 11, 2002, summit any such expansion was indefinitely postponed. The EAC leaders saw as their principal short-term goal not expansion, but completion of a Protocol on the Establishment of the East African Customs Union. The East African Legislative Assembly, meeting in early June, renewed a quarter-century-old debate on forming an East African political federation, but the discussion was regarded as largely symbolic at the time.

The heads of state convened again on November 30, 2002, in Arusha, Tanzania, where the topics under discussion included a common external tariff (CET), the community's road network, and development of the Lake Victoria area. In an extraordinary summit on June 20, 2003, in Nairobi, Kenya, the leaders reached tentative agreement on the CET, including a maximum rate of 25 percent (to be lowered to 20 percent five years after introduction of the customs union). The EAC also reaffirmed its commitment to antiterrorism measures but cautioned that the travel bans imposed on the region by other countries were hampering the tourism industry.

At the seventh summit of heads of state, held on April 5, 2006, in Arusha, an application from Rwanda and Burundi to join the community was passed forward for detailed negotiation. Their membership became effective July 1, 2007, giving them access to a customs union that has significantly increased trade in the area. In July 2006 the African Union decided to recognize no new Regional Economic Communities (RECs), but to continue to recognize many of those already in existence. The EAC was one of those so grandfathered.

An extraordinary meeting of the enlarged EAC's heads of state, held on August 20, 2007, in Arusha, called for the group's trade ministers to push toward negotiating with the European Union (EU) on an Economic Partnership Agreement (EPA). This meeting affirmed that the EAC would negotiate with the EU as one bloc—including the participation of Kenya, which some had doubted. The agreement had to be signed by December 31, 2007, in order to avoid losing access to EU markets under the expiring Cotonou agreement. The same August 2007 meeting called for the EAC to establish a common market and monetary union by 2012. The meeting shelved a proposal to create a complete political union, with a federal president, by 2013. Tanzania in particular opposed the idea.

In early November 2007 serious negotiations began on the formation of the EAC Common Market. By late November 2007 an interim agreement had been reached between the EAC and the EU. The agreement would allow for a gradual opening of the EAC to EU goods over a 25-year period, with approximately one-fifth of imports from the EU still subject to the current level of customs duties. There was to be some protection for EAC agricultural and industrial production, but many observers considered the deal a bad one for the EAC's poor populations, and the result of excessive pressure from the EU. Negotiations continued with the aim of putting a complete EPA into place by 2009. Negotiations were supposed to be finished by July 31, 2009, but were put on hold at the last minute because, the EAC said, the EU had introduced fresh issues.

An EAC summit scheduled for Nairobi in February 2008 was canceled because of unrest following the disputed elections in Kenya. The summit was eventually held June 26, 2008, in Kigali, Rwanda, where participants discussed the proposed common market model. In July 2008 the U.S. trade representative, Susan C. Schwab, signed a trade and investment agreement with the EAC.

The EAC's progress was impeded in 2008 and 2009 by a shortage of funds, some member states not having paid their dues. Matters came to a head in February 2008, when Secretary General Mwapachu, claiming funding had run out, canceled a session of the Legislative Assembly, perhaps improperly. On February 20 Mwapachu declared that the EAC administration would have to close down if no money was forthcoming in a few days. The Bank of Tanzania immediately injected $2 million into the organization.

Meanwhile regional and sub-regional work on integration had been progressing on multiple fronts. In October 2008 the EAC signed an agreement with Southern African Development Community (SADC) and the Common Market for Eastern and Southern Africa (Comesa), aiming to create a free trade zone encompassing every East African country. In January the EAC's Sectoral Council on Legal and Judicial Affairs began considering proposed changes to the EAC, changes designed to further integration and strengthen the position of the secretariat. In July the community appeared to be on track to establish a common market by January 1, 2010.

ECONOMIC COMMUNITY OF CENTRAL AFRICAN STATES (CEEAC)

Communauté Economique des Etats de l'Afrique Centrale

Established: By treaty signed by the heads of state of the member countries on October 18, 1983, in Libreville, Gabon.

Purpose: Initially, to end customs duties and other restrictions on trade between the member countries and establish a common market; more recently, to also promote regional integration, security, and stability.

Headquarters: Libreville, Gabon.

Principal Organs: Conference of Heads of State and Government, Council of Ministers, Secretariat.

Web site: www.ceeac-eccas.org

Secretary General: Louis-Sylvain Goma (Republic of the Congo).

Membership (10): Angola, Burundi, Cameroon, Central African Republic, Chad, Democratic Republic of the Congo, Republic of the Congo, Equatorial Guinea, Gabon, Sao Tome and Principe. (Rwanda, a founding member, left the organization in June 2007.)

Official Languages: French, Portuguese.

Origin and development. In 1977 President Mobutu Sese Seko of Zaire proposed a merger of the three-member Economic Community of the Great Lakes Countries (CEPGL) with the four-member Central African Customs and Economic Union (*Union Douanière et Economique de l'Afrique Centrale*—UDEAC) to form a francophone Central African grouping. The proposal resurfaced in 1981, yielding the UDEAC Libreville Declaration in December, which called for the establishment of a group comprising the members of the CEPGL and the UDEAC plus Angola, Chad, Equatorial Guinea, and Sao Tome and Principe. The resulting ten-member CEEAC (plus Angola as an observer) was formally inaugurated December 21, 1985, in Libreville, Gabon, in accordance with a treaty concluded October 18, 1983, in Libreville. Angola became a full member in 1999.

Structure. The principal governing body of the CEEAC is the Conference of Heads of States and Government, which meets annually. Other bodies include the Council of Ministers, the Court of Justice, the Consultative Commission, and the Secretariat.

Activities. At the formal launching of the CEEAC, Secretary General Lunda Bululu declared that the aim of the organization was to "promote and reinforce cooperation and a sustained and balanced development in all areas of both economic and social activity between member states." The 1986 summit charged the secretary general with the drafting of a program of action aimed at increasing intracommunity trade and requested that he prepare a study on community transport and communications infrastructure. In July the central bank governors of the member states met in Libreville to consider the establishment of a clearinghouse for the diverse national currencies used in the area.

At the 1988 summit, support was again voiced for customs, financial, transportation, and communications integration within the community, although there appeared to be little hope for implementation of such plans in the near future given mounting arrears in members' budget contributions—a problem that has perpetually plagued the CEEAC. The 1989 summit underscored the lack of CEEAC consensus on how to reduce trade barriers, and the summit leaders decided to extend debate on the question until at least 1991. However, a "greater sense of urgency" was reported at the 1990 summit, partly in response to challenges posed by the European Community's impending single market and the attention being given to developments in Eastern Europe, possibly to the detriment of African interests. The CEEAC leaders authorized the free circulation within the region of several categories of individuals, such as students and researchers, starting in 1991; agreed to establish a CEEAC bank in Kigali to finance intraregional trade; called for additional airline cooperation among members; and gave priority to road and bridge projects that would facilitate trade within the community. However, the group still appeared "timid" in the opinion of some observers. Addressing their critics at the 1991 summit, CEEAC leaders expressed the opinion that small regional groupings such as their own should work toward the creation of an economic community covering all of Africa to achieve international negotiating leverage. Underscoring the difficulties facing the smaller organizations, the CEEAC summit on May 17–18, 1992, in Bujumbura, Burundi, achieved little discernible progress because most member states were preoccupied throughout the year by wide-ranging political changes precipitated by the rapid spread of pro-democracy movements in the region.

The community remained in financial crisis in early 1993, and in March staff members went on strike to protest salary arrears. The staff went on strike again in May 1994, reportedly criticizing Secretary General Kasasa Mutati Chinyata for not addressing employee concerns. Subsequently, CEEAC activity was severely constrained by ongoing political turmoil within several key member states. Nonetheless, in response to the region's rapidly changing political and governmental landscape, the CEEAC members, under the auspices of the United Nations (UN), drafted a proposed mutual nonaggression pact, and defense ministers and/or military leaders from five CEEAC members (Central African Republic, Republic of the Congo, Equatorial Guinea, Gabon, and Sao Tome and Principe) initialed the accord in October 1994. Discussion also took place on the creation of a regional conflict prevention body and the designation of special peacekeeping forces within members' armed forces. The organization nevertheless remained hamstrung by continuing financial difficulties, as well as by regional and intrastate political disturbances.

Meeting in extraordinary session in February 1998 in Libreville, the community heads of state agreed on the necessity of reinvigorating the organization. Accordingly, the summit requested assistance from the UN Economic Commission for Africa in evaluating the CEEAC budget and financial structure, operations, and salaries. The following July, Louis-Sylvain Goma, a former prime minister of the Republic of the Congo, was appointed CEEAC secretary general.

The inauguration of recently reelected Gabonese president Bongo in January 1999 provided an opportunity for "mini-summit" consultations that for the first time included Angola as a full CEEAC member. A month later the member states, convening in Yaoundé, Cameroon, as the UN Standing Advisory Committee on Security Questions in Central Africa, reached agreement on establishing the Council for Peace and Security in Central Africa (Copax), which was envisaged as a political forum for consultation in the event of threats to peace and security in the region. Also included under Copax would be a nonstanding multinational force for peacekeeping, security, and humanitarian relief efforts.

In late June 1999 in Malabo, Equatorial Guinea, the CEEAC and the Central African Economic and Monetary Community (*Communauté Economique et Monétaire de l'Afrique Centrale*—CEMAC; successor to the UDEAC) met in parallel sessions to discuss regional security and economic concerns. At the summit the CEEAC leaders stated their intention to make the organization a "model of regional and subregional integration," as well as a "linch-pin within the African economic community." They also agreed to form the CEEAC Parliament, a center for human rights, and a peace and security council. A third extraordinary CEEAC summit in February 2000 in Malabo ratified the Copax agreement and a mutual assistance pact. A month earlier, eight CEEAC member states (excepting Angola, the Democratic Republic of the Congo [DRC], and Rwanda) joined eight Western countries (Belgium, France, Italy, Netherlands, Portugal, Spain, United States, United Kingdom) in military exercises designed to improve regional peacekeeping and crisis intervention capabilities. Both the UN and the Organization of African Unity (OAU, subsequently the African Union—AU) had endorsed the training activities.

Opening speakers at the tenth ordinary summit, held June 13–17, 2002, in Malabo, once again called attention to the organization's precarious financial status. Although the CEEAC was designated as one of the five regional "pillars" of the AU's African Economic Community (along with the Economic Community of West African States, the Common Market for Eastern and Southern Africa, the South African Development Community, and the Arab Maghreb Union), its financial difficulties and relative lack of integration have diminished its role. The summit called for creation of an "autonomous financing mechanism," liberalized freedom of movement for nationals of the member states, supported ongoing efforts with the UN Food and Agriculture Organization (FAO) to establish a regional food security program, and issued a directive to the Secretariat to negotiate financial assistance from the African Development Bank. In addition, with regard to peace and security issues, the attendees approved declarations supporting peace efforts in Angola, Equatorial Guinea, and the Republic of the Congo and also adopted standing orders for three Copax organs: the Defense and Security Committee, the Early Warning Mechanism of Central Africa, and the nonpermanent Multinational Force of Central Africa. (A number of CEEAC states have yet to ratify the Copax agreement.)

In July 2003 the CEEAC condemned a coup in Sao Tome and Principe and then participated in a successful mediation effort led by the Community of Portuguese-Speaking Countries (CPLP). On August 19, 2003, the CEEAC heads of state and government met in Brazzaville and established an International Monitoring Committee for Sao Tome and Principe.

CEEAC has also made some effort to address the region's instability. The military chiefs of the CEEAC countries declared, at their annual meeting held April 24–26, 2006, in Brazzaville, that they would work together to promote regional peace. In April 2006 the secretary general declared that the CEEAC was ready to send observers to the DRC to help ensure a fair outcome in the June 2006 elections in that country. In June 2006 the EU announced a grant of 4 million euros ($2.7 million) to help the CEEAC maintain peace and security in the region. Also in that month, the African Union (AU) announced that it would recognize no more regional or subregional economic groupings, but grandfathered its recognition of many already in existence, including the CEEAC. However, in June 2007 Rwanda announced that it was leaving the CEEAC. The CEEAC's internal trade remained weak, and in July 2006 it was revealed that trade within the region represented only 2 percent of all the region's trade exchanges, the majority of trade being with Organization of Economic Cooperation and Defense countries and, more recently, with China. At the 13th meeting of heads of state, held October 26, 2007, in Brazzaville, the assembled dignitaries heard a report from the secretary general stating that in terms of economic integration little had yet been achieved.

On October 31, 2007, immediately following the heads of state meeting, Angolan president José Eduardo dos Santos promised that his country would do whatever was necessary to help neighboring Mozambique (which is not a member of the CEEAC) to develop its potentially large oil fields. Mozambique is the only southern African country to belong only to one regional trade bloc—the Southern African Development Community (SADC). Dos Santos said he saw no problem with a country having multiple memberships, and predicted that the CEEAC and the SADC would one day be combined. Angola and the DRC had previously announced that they would not be joining the SADC Free Trade Area (see separate article on the SADC) when it became effective in 2008.

In February 2008 the CEEAC condemned any effort to seize power by force in Chad. After the subsequent defeat of rebel forces in a proxy war between Sudan and Chad, president Joseph Kabila of the DRC organized an emergency CEEAC summit, held March 10, 2008, in Kinshasa, DRC. The participants discussed possible steps in the event the presidents of Chad and Sudan met during the Organization of the Islamic Conference summit that month and signed a peace agreement.

In May 2009 CEEAC health ministers met in Kinshasa, to develop a joint strategy against the A/H1N1 strain of influenza. In June 2009 a meeting of CEEAC economic ministers decided to build a bridge over the Congo River between Brazzaville and Kinshasa, thus directly linking the capitals of the two Congos. A delegation from CEEAC, along with one from the African Union (AU), and the International Organization of the Francophonie (OIF) monitored the July 12, 2009, presidential election in the DRC.

ECONOMIC COMMUNITY OF THE GREAT LAKES COUNTRIES (CEPGL)

Communauté Economique des Pays des Grands Lacs

Established: By convention signed by the heads of state of the member countries on September 26, 1976, in Gisenyi, Rwanda.

Purpose: To promote regional economic integration; to increase security and welfare for the region; to facilitate political, cultural, technical, and scientific cooperation among the members; and to contribute to the strengthening of national sovereignty and African unity.

Headquarters: Gisenyi, Rwanda.

Principal Organs: Conference of Heads of States, Council of Ministers and State Commissioners, Consultative Commission, Specialized Technical Commissions, Permanent Executive Secretariat.

Web site: None.

Executive Secretary: Gabriel Toyi (Burundi)

Membership (3): Burundi, Democratic Republic of the Congo, Rwanda.

Official Language: French.

Origin and development. The first proposal for the creation of an organization concerned with the social, cultural, economic, and political problems of the Central African subregion emerged from discussions held during a 1966 summit of the heads of state of the former Belgian possessions Burundi, Rwanda, and the former Belgian Congo, today called the Democratic Republic of the Congo (DRC). On August 29, at the conclusion of their four-day meeting in Kinshasa, Congo, the three leaders signed a mutual security pact, while Burundi and the Congo signed trade and cultural agreements that contained provisions for closer policy coordination and cooperation. The Kinshasa agreement was reaffirmed during a tripartite summit in 1974 and was strengthened with the addition of clauses on refugees; undesirable aliens; and joint promotion of tourism, communication, and social security measures. In May 1975 the three states' foreign ministers met to discuss a drafted general convention on economic, technical, scientific, and cultural cooperation, the final version establishing the Economic Community of the Great Lakes Countries, which was signed by the heads of state of Burundi, Rwanda, and Zaire (as the DRC was then called) on September 26, 1976. In 1980 the Development Bank of the Great Lakes States (*Banque de Développement des Etats des Grands Lacs*—BDEGL) was inaugurated in Goma, Zaire, to finance community projects. The subsequent Economic Community of Central African States (*Communauté Economique des Etats de l'Afrique Centrale*—CEEAC) was formally launched in October 1983 by a treaty signed in Libreville, Gabon, to which all three CEPGL states were signatories. Although left open to "any country in the region which wished to join it in order to contribute to the strengthening of African unity," CEPGL's membership has remained at three.

Structure. The legal authority of CEPGL is vested in the Conference of the Heads of State, which normally meets once a year to approve the community's budget and action program. Preparation for annual summits and the implementation of CEPGL resolutions are responsibilities of the Council of Ministers and State Commissioners. The Permanent Executive Secretariat provides technical and administrative assistance for both groups. The organization's five Specialized Technical Commissions address political and juridical affairs; society and culture; planning, agriculture, industry, and natural resources; commerce, finance, immigration, and tourism; and public works, energy, and transport. As the organization rebuilds itself in 2009 and beyond, this structure may well change.

Activities. Although emerging from a mutual security pact during South Africa's apartheid era, CEPGL in its first two decades focused much of its activities on economic issues. To promote economic development and integration, the community proposed a number of projects, including development of the Ruzizi River Valley for hydroelectric power; methane gas extraction from Lake Kivu; coordination of members' transportation and communications networks; and joint cement, bottling, and agricultural materials production.

The 14th summit was delayed twice because of the civil war in Rwanda before finally being held in the nation's northeastern city of Gisenyi on August 2, 1992. The CEPGL heads of state agreed to seek resolution of border security problems through "regular official contacts." However, a resumption of full CEPGL activity was subsequently precluded by extremely unsettled conditions in the region, including the political stalemate in Zaire, the deaths of the presidents of Burundi and Rwanda in April 1994, the subsequent Hutu-Tutsi conflict in those two countries, and the genocide of Tutsis in Rwanda.

Following the installation of a government led by the Tutsi-dominated Rwandan Patriotic Front in Rwanda in 1994, the defense ministers of the CEPGL countries met June 10, 1995, in Bujumbura, Burundi, to "reactivate" the community's security arrangements. It was concluded that joint forces would patrol the community's common borders under the direction of a tripartite CEPGL subcommission. However, CEPGL intentions were subsequently overwhelmed by the massive dislocations and fighting that developed in the region in 1996 as the Hutu-Tutsi conflict crossed the borders of the three member states and precipitated extreme turmoil, including the rebel victory in Zaire in 1997 and Zaire's renaming as the Democratic Republic of the Congo. CEPGL was in limbo through 2004 due to continuing conflict and a lack of cordial bilateral relations between members. A meeting in April 2005 in Lubumbashi, DRC, with the European Union (EU) commissioner of development and humanitarian aid, Louis Michel, was said at the time to mark a new beginning for unity in the Great Lakes region. The sum of €50 million ($75 million) was promised for this purpose.

Between 2005 and 2007, CEPGL was not much involved in the jockeying for position among Africa's often competing economic organizations. In August 2005 the DRC, already a member of CEEAC and the Common Market for Eastern and Southern Africa (Comesa), announced that it was now a full member of the Southern African Development Community (SADC; see separate articles on CEEAC, Comesa, and SADC). In contrast, Rwanda announced in September 2007 that it was no longer interested in joining SADC.

The CEPGL was described as "relaunched" in a joint statement of the three governments on April 17, 2007, and on April 19 of that year the military chiefs of the three countries again pledged to take joint action against rebel groups throughout the region. In August 2007 an EU representative visited Rwanda, expressing support for the CEPGL. Statements of support also came in September 2007 and March 2008 from the presidents of Rwanda and Burundi, respectively. The DRC showed notably less enthusiasm for the CEPGL's revival.

A Web site, www.cepgl.com, came into existence, but was gone by December 2008. That aside, during 2008 and 2009 the organization showed some progress in reestablishing itself. In July 2008, there was a meeting in Gisenyi to discuss ways to improve farming in the region. However, the difficult and complicated relations between Rwanda and the DRC, stemming from the 1994 genocide, delayed the DRC's sending a formal representative or monetary contributions to the organization. It was not until December 2008 that the foreign ministers of Rwanda and the DRC met, agreeing a plan for joint action against the Hutu guerrillas, who were mostly based in the DRC, but operating across the border into Rwanda. At the December 12, 2008, CEPGL meeting in Bujumbura, Burundi, the DRC announced its intention to participate fully in the organization.

In January 2009 plans were announced to reopen a CEPGL agricultural research center, which had been dormant for ten years. During 2009 the CEPGL held various meetings to address the problem of security. On May 8, 2009, the DRC finally named a formal representative to the CEPGL. This done, the EU dispensed the promised €50 million in aid.

ECONOMIC COMMUNITY OF WEST AFRICAN STATES (ECOWAS/ CEDEAO)

Communauté Economique des Etats de l'Afrique de l'Ouest
Comunidade Economica dos Estados da Africa do Oeste

Established: By Treaty of Lagos (Nigeria), signed May 28, 1975; amended by Treaty of Cotonou (Benin), signed July 24, 1993; entry into force of the latter announced July 30, 1995.

Purpose: "To promote cooperation and integration leading to the establishment of an economic union in West Africa in order to raise the living standards of its peoples, and to maintain and enhance economic stability, foster relations among member states and contribute to the progress and development of the African Continent."

Headquarters: Abuja, Nigeria.

Principal Organs: Authority of Heads of State and Government, Council of Ministers, Community Parliament, Economic and Social Council, Specialized Technical Commissions, Community Court of Justice, ECOWAS Bank for Investment and Development, Executive Secretariat.

Web site: www.ecowas.int

President: Mohamed Ibn Chambas (Ghana).

Membership (15): Benin, Burkina Faso, Cape Verde, Côte d'Ivoire, Gambia, Ghana, Guinea, Guinea-Bissau, Liberia, Mali, Niger, Nigeria, Senegal, Sierra Leone, Togo.

Official Languages: English, French, Portuguese, and "all West African languages so designated by the Authority."

Origin and development. The Economic Community of West African States (ECOWAS) received its greatest impetus from discussions in October 1974 between Gen. Yakubu Gowon of Nigeria and President Gnassingbé Eyadéma of Togo. The two leaders advanced plans for a more comprehensive economic grouping than the purely francophone West African Economic Community (*Communauté Economique de l'Afrique de l'Ouest*—CEAO; see separate article on the West African Economic and Monetary Union [UEMOA]), which had been recently launched by Côte d'Ivoire, Dahomey (later Benin), Mali, Mauritania, Niger, Senegal, and Upper Volta (later Burkina Faso). The treaty establishing ECOWAS was signed by representatives of 15 West African states on May 28, 1975, in Lagos, Nigeria, and by the end of June had been formally ratified by enough signatories (seven) to become operative. However, it took until November 1976 for an agreement to be worked out on protocols to the treaty. The delay resulted in part from Senegal's effort to make its ratification dependent upon a broadening of the community to include Zaire and several other francophone states of Central Africa. Ultimately, it was decided that any such expansion would be unrealistic. Cape Verde joined in 1977.

In 1991 a special committee was established to propose revisions to the ECOWAS treaty. After extensive negotiation the committee's proposals were adopted in the Treaty of Cotonou, which was approved at the July 1993 ECOWAS summit. The treaty was designed to make summit decisions binding on all members and also expanded ECOWAS's political mandate. Members agreed, for example, to the peaceful settlement of interstate disputes, the protection of human rights, and the promotion of democratic systems of governance. In addition, a number of new bodies, such as the Community Parliament and the Economic and Social Council, were authorized.

At the conclusion of a summit on July 28–29, 1995, ECOWAS announced that sufficient ratifications had been received for the treaty to enter into effect, although the Community Parliament and Community Court of Justice were not inaugurated until 2000 and 2001, respectively. Meanwhile, Mauritania, apparently objecting to moves toward greater military and monetary integration, announced in December 1999 its intention to withdraw from the organization, effective December 2000.

Structure. The basic structure of ECOWAS consists of the Authority of Heads of State and Government; the Council of Ministers comprised of two representatives from each member; the Executive Secretariat, which is headed by a secretary appointed for a four-year period; the Community Court of Justice, which settles disputes arising under the treaty; the Economic and Social Council; and eight specialized technical commissions. These commissions are Administration and Finance; Food and Agriculture; Environment and Natural Resources; Human Resources, Information, and Social and Cultural Affairs; Industry, Science and Technology, and Energy; Political, Judicial, and Legal Affairs and Regional Security and Integration; Trade, Customs, Taxation, Statistics, Money, and Payments; and Transport, Communications, and Tourism. The ECOWAS Community Parliament of 120 national representatives began its inaugural session in November 2000 in Abuja. The Community Court of Justice was inaugurated in January 2001. The Council of Elders was formed in July 2001.

The Treaty of Lagos authorized creation of the Fund for Cooperation, Compensation, and Development (FCCD), supported by members' contributions, the revenues of community enterprises, and grants from non-ECOWAS countries. In addition to financing mutually approved projects, the fund, headquartered in Lomé, Togo, was established to compensate members who suffered losses due to the establishment of community enterprises or the liberalization of trade. Upon ratification of treaty changes approved by the heads of state in December 2001, the FCCD was reconfigured as the ECOWAS Bank for Investment and Development (EBID), which has the broader mission of financing private investment in infrastructure and such public sector activities as poverty reduction.

Activities. Although the May 1990 summit marked the 15th anniversary of the signing of the ECOWAS treaty, the mood was described as "far from celebratory" in light of the domestic problems facing several key members, ongoing disputes between others, and a persistent fiscal shortfall. Despite the absence of half of the heads of state and past ECOWAS difficulty in translating plans into action, several major resolutions were approved. They included creation of the Standing Mediation Committee to intervene in regional disputes, the approval of a common residency card for the community, and support for reliance on ECOWAS as the "single economic community in West Africa"—an oblique reference to "competing" organizations such as the Mano River Union and the Council of the Entente.

Purely economic concerns were pushed into the background by ECOWAS's controversial involvement in the civil war that broke out in Liberia in August 1990. The ECOWAS Monitoring Group (Ecomog) was formed and sent to Liberia to facilitate a cease-fire, organize an interim government, and oversee the holding of new national elections. However, only Gambia, Ghana, Guinea, Nigeria, and Sierra Leone supplied soldiers for the group, and a proposed special ECOWAS summit was canceled because of differences among the members. A tenuous cease-fire was finally negotiated at an extraordinary summit in late November, but the political situation in Liberia remained chaotic.

During the second half of 1991, ECOWAS endorsed the peacemaking efforts of a committee involving the heads of state of Burkina Faso, Côte d'Ivoire, Gambia, Nigeria, and Togo, which in late October yielded the so-called Yamassoukro IV peace accord. The agreement, signed by interim Liberian president Amos Sawyer and Charles Taylor, head of the National Patriotic Forces of Liberia (NPFL), directed Ecomog troops to supervise the disarmament and encampment of rebel forces throughout Liberia, establish a buffer zone along the Liberia-Sierra Leone border, and facilitate the holding of elections. However, the NPFL subsequently refused to permit implementation of the agreement. Consequently, attendees at the ECOWAS summit on July 27–29, 1992, held in Dakar, Senegal, displayed rare unanimity and agreed to impose economic sanctions against NPFL-held Liberian territory if Taylor's forces continued to undermine Ecomog efforts.

To the surprise of some observers, Ecomog began to gain the upper hand in early 1993. Subsequently, in what was seen as a remarkably successful response to the ECOWAS intervention, a peace accord (negotiated with United Nations [UN] assistance) was signed by Liberia's warring factions in July. The appearance of success produced an atmosphere of enthusiasm during the ECOWAS summit in Cotonou, Benin, on July 22–24, with *West Africa* magazine voicing the opinion that the community had become "planted much more firmly on the international map as a serious and credible organization." Hoping to capitalize on the newfound cohesion, the summit signed the Treaty of Cotonou, a revision of the original Lagos treaty. The new accord was designed to speed up implementation of a regional common market, which would include, progressively, a monetary union, an internal free trade zone (providing for the free movement of people, goods, services, and capital), and a common external tariff and trade policy. The signatories also committed themselves to "solidarity and collective self-reliance" and pledged to refrain from any aggressive action against another ECOWAS member. In general, ECOWAS was seen as trying to secure its position as the West African "pillar" of the African Economic Community fashioned by the Organization of African States (OAU, subsequently the African Union—AU).

Throughout 1996 the ECOWAS agenda remained dominated by the problems associated with the Liberian peace process. However, the situation brightened in August with the signing of the Abuja Accord, which directed ECOMOG to disarm and demobilize the warring factions by January 31, 1997.

In a change from past summits, an optimistic attitude was reported at the meetings held in Abuja on July 27–28, 1996, with only four heads of state failing to attend. Nevertheless, it was clear that problems such as high arrears were continuing to impede ECOWAS operations. In order to provide operating funds, it was agreed that a small levy on imports from nonmembers would be imposed. Introduced in July 2003, the levy amounted to 0.5 percent of customs duties.

The major topics of discussion at the summit held August 28–29, 1997, in Abuja were the July election of Charles Taylor as president of Liberia and the May coup in Sierra Leone. In recognition of the apparent resolution of the long-standing Liberian conflict, ECOWAS lifted its sanctions. However, Ecomog troops were directed to remain in the country to help "in the restructuring of Liberia's national army and police force." Meanwhile, ECOWAS responded to the overthrow of the Kabbah government in Sierra Leone by recommending a boycott and blockade of the country and the deployment of Ecomog contingents to enforce them.

At the October 1998 ECOWAS summit, most of the discussions were devoted to promoting peace and stability in the region. Toward this end, the summit participants agreed to ban the trade in, and manufacture of, small arms throughout ECOWAS and called on other parts of Africa to do the same. The summit also approved a peace accord that ECOWAS representatives had helped to negotiate in Guinea-Bissau that committed the community to providing peacekeeping forces in that country as of early 1999. In what was perhaps the boldest move at the summit, ECOWAS also endorsed a conflict resolution mechanism authorizing it to intervene in the internal affairs of its member states if the security of the region was threatened.

The December 9–10, 1999, summit in Lomé, Togo, was highlighted by approval of a draft protocol for the Permanent Mechanism for the Prevention, Management, and Settlement of Conflicts and the Maintenance of Peace in the Region. The heads of state also approved creation of the Mediation and Security Council; endorsed conversion of Ecomog into a permanent standby force capable of enforcement, peacekeeping, and humanitarian missions; and voiced continuing support for the community-wide moratorium on the manufacture, export, and import of light/break weapons.

Although ECOWAS failed to achieve a common external tariff by its target of January 2000, in April the anglophone Gambia, Ghana, Guinea, Liberia, Nigeria, and Sierra Leone, plus Portuguese-speaking Cape Verde, reached an agreement on establishing by 2003 a new West African monetary union in parallel to the francophone West African Economic and Monetary Union (*Union Economique et Monétaire Ouest-Africaine*—UEMOA). In February 2000, apparently setting aside what ECOWAS chair and president of Mali, Alpha Oumar Konare, termed the "anglophone/francophone distractions" that had long impeded economic integration, ECOWAS and the UEMOA agreed to a joint action plan that envisaged, in part, a merger of the UEMOA and the proposed second monetary union into a single zone by 2004.

Throughout 2000, developments in Guinea, Liberia, and Sierra Leone continued to generate international concern. The December 2000 summit authorized positioning Ecomog monitors along the three countries' borders, as had been previously proposed in 1999, shortly before Ecomog's Liberian mission had effectively ended. Nevertheless, neither Guinea nor Liberia signed the requisite Status of Forces Agreement. The 25th annual ECOWAS summit, which convened in Dakar, Senegal, on December 20–21, called attention to positive developments in the troubled Mano River region, but also approved sanctions against recalcitrant rebel groups in Liberia and asked the Liberian government to undertake a "national reconciliation policy." In addition, the summit took a major step toward creation of the second regional monetary zone, encompassing Gambia, Ghana, Guinea, Nigeria, and Sierra Leone. (The general view was that conditions in Liberia and Cape Verde would prevent their immediate participation.)

The 26th session of the Authority of Heads of State and Government, held in Dakar on January 26–31, 2003, focused its attention on economic and security issues. Having been designated as the West African coordinator and monitor for the AU-sponsored New Partnership for Africa's Development (NEPAD), ECOWAS reaffirmed its support for the initiative. The summit participants also praised steps taken with the UEMOA toward harmonizing trade liberalization measures, the eventual goal being a regional common market. In addition, progress was noted in the areas of community water resource management; energy coordination and development, particularly with regard to a planned West Africa gas pipeline project involving Benin, Ghana, Nigeria, and Togo; preparations for negotiating an Economic Partnership Agreement (EPA) with the European Union (EU); and funding of the EBID.

With regard to security, the session heard extensive reports on developments in Côte d'Ivoire and Liberia. In addition to expressing its support for the French-sponsored Marcoussis Accord earlier in the month, ECOWAS remained committed to deployment of a peacekeeping ECOWAS Mission in Côte d'Ivoire (ECOMICI), formation of which had been approved in December 2002. A September 2002 emergency meeting on the crisis in Côte d'Ivoire had established a contact group of Ghana, Guinea-Bissau, Mali, Niger, Nigeria, and Togo. Shortly after the summit, on February 4, 2003, the UN Security Council authorized deployment of the ECOMICI, which numbered over 1,800 troops by the end of the year. With respect to the troubled Mano River area, the January summit called upon the international community to provide additional development assistance to Sierra Leone, where peace had taken hold, but it expressed regret over renewed hostilities in Liberia between the government and rebel forces.

Issues of peace and security continued to dominate the region throughout 2003. Events in Côte d'Ivoire, Liberia, and Guinea-Bissau prompted a number of emergency summits and other meetings. In early July, following the failure of yet another negotiated cease-fire in Liberia, ECOWAS agreed to dispatch several thousand troops to Monrovia, and the resultant ECOWAS Mission in Liberia (ECOMIL) was deployed in August.

The ECOWAS summit on December 19, 2003, in Accra saw Executive Secretary Mohamed Ibn Chambas and other speakers lament that the repeated political and military crises in the region had diverted ECOWAS from its goal of furthering economic integration and regional development. Chambas also asserted that a lack of political will in some member countries had delayed integration. Nevertheless, those attending the brief summit reiterated a commitment to establishing a West African free trade area by the end of 2005 and introducing a customs union by 2008.

The ECOWAS summit on January 19, 2005, in Accra was marked by dissension over Côte d'Ivoire, whose president, Laurent Gbagbo, was forced to hear declarations that he and his country's various faction leaders must "search their hearts" about bringing peace to their country. ECOWAS peacekeeping efforts in Côte d'Ivoire had been previously handed over to the African Union (AU)—an event that some summit participants described as a failure on their organization's part. The summit postponed plans to introduce a common currency by July 1, 2005.

In March 2005 ECOWAS launched the Regional Market Systems and Traders' Organizations in West Africa in an effort to improve regional cooperation in trade, with a particular focus on agriculture. The program was seen as the first step toward development of an ECOWAS common agricultural policy. Progress was also reported in regard to the proposed common external tariff for ECOWAS, a key component of the planned free trade area. Meanwhile, on the political front, ECOWAS was active in early 2005 in helping to resolve the turmoil in Togo; the community also subsequently assisted in Liberia and Côte d'Ivoire.

At the April 12, 2006, summit, held in Niamey, Niger, the ECOWAS heads of state approved organizational changes to turn its secretariat into a commission to increase efficiency and productivity. ECOWAS leaders approved various efforts to improve members' economies and infrastructure, including moves toward a common airline and a common standard for mobile telephones. On April 12, 2006, the group's trade ministers met in Abuja to evaluate progress toward the second phase of negotiations with the EU on an Economic Partnership Agreement (EPA). This prospective agreement would lead to creation of a free trade area between the two regions. At that meeting it was also announced that India had extended a $250 million line of credit, repayable over 25 years, for development projects within the group. But, as ECOWAS celebrated 31 years of existence, some wondered about its long-term effectiveness, particularly considering the apparent split in agenda between its anglophone and francophone members, the latter group sometimes seeming to put the interests of Paris ahead of those of the African community.

At a July 2006 meeting, ECOWAS finalized plans to transform the Executive Secretariat into the Executive Commission. The group would now have a president, a vice-president, and seven commissioners, with a limited and well-defined role for each commissioner. Member states would be expected to cede some of their powers to the commission in the interest of faster decision making. The same restructuring was intended to make the Community Parliament more powerful by making its decisions binding on member states. The new arrangement came into effect in February 2007.

In other developments, ECOWAS observers were active in monitoring elections in Gambia, Senegal, and Nigeria, and the group encouraged Liberia's acceptance by the international community at the end of a long period of civil disturbance. Negotiations on the EPA with the EU moved forward. In June 2007 ECOWAS leaders met in Abuja to discuss ways of speeding up the group's transition (now long behind schedule) into a border-free zone, and the group set 2020 as a target for full regional integration. In October 2007 the group's Convergence Council commissioned a study on ways to bring about a single currency for West Africa. The previous ECOWAS summit had rejected the group's original two-track approach of first creating a common currency, the ECO, among anglophone states by 2009 and merging it with the CFA franc of the francophone states at a later date. A further meeting on the topic was held in July 2008. The ECOWAS standby force, successor to Ecomog, came into being at the end of 2007, with the appointment of a Nigerian general as chief of staff in November and the holding of maneuvers in Senegal in December.

Late 2007 and early 2008 saw controversy over ECOWAS states signing the proposed EPA with the EU. The original deadline was the end of 2007, but several member states and individual politicians objected, calling the proposed agreement a bad one for the region. They felt that the EPA, rather than helping the region's economies, would open them up to subsidized European goods. At the January 18, 2008, summit in Ouagadougou the matter was put on hold until 2009. As of late 2009 the matter was still under heated discussion.

Travel and migration between ECOWAS states was envisioned by the group as being relatively free of restriction. In 2008 the ECOWAS passport was close to full implementation, but on several occasions trouble arose between migrant groups and residents of countries. This was especially true of Nigerian shopkeepers operating in Ghana, many of whom had their stores closed by the government. The reason given was that immigrants from other ECOWAS countries must come with a sufficient amount of capital before they can trade. However, Nigeria and Ghana are in many ways rivals, and this explanation was seen by some as dubious.

In June 2008 a group of ECOWAS electoral observers visited Zimbabwe. In August 2008 it was announced that by 2010 all ECOWAS parliamentarians would be individually elected "on their own merit."

In September 2008 Aliou M. Diallo, the secretary general of the Mano River Union (MRU, see separate article) called on the ECOWAS Commission to help the MRU in its quest for lasting peace and stability. He wished for closer ties between ECOWAS and the MRU. In November ECOWAS protested against its failure to be invited to the G20 economic summit in New York.

A special summit held January 10, 2009, condemned the December coup in Guinea, and suspended that country from all ECOWAS meetings until constitutional order was restored. It appeared that discussions between ECOWAS and the Guinea regime were being fruitful. But the group's chairman-in-office, Nigerian president Umaru Musa Yar'Adua, called on member states to avoid working at cross-purposes in helping Guinea.

ECOWAS had been active in trying to maintain constitutional peace in Guinea-Bissau since the November 2008 attempted assassination of that country's president João Bernardo Vieira. Following a successful attempt on Vieira's life by renegade soldiers in March 2009, an ECOWAS mission visited Guinea-Bissau, where senior military officers assured them that the murder was not part of a coup. Chambas noted that "the lack of serious security sector reform" had long been a major problem in Guinea-Bissau, and Chambas hoped the issue would now be comprehensively addressed.

The June 21, 2009 summit, held in Abuja, was noteworthy in that it incorporated a special ECOWAS-Spain summit. Spanish prime minister Jose Luis Zapatero led a delegation to discuss strengthening cooperation between Spain and ECOWAS, a situation that would be "to the mutual benefit of both the sub-region and the Kingdom of Spain given its proximity to Africa." The ECOWAS summit otherwise called on all member states to work harder on regional economic integration. Yar'Adua also called on member states to continue pushing forward the peace process in Guinea and Guinea-Bissau. He noted that thanks to ECOWAS efforts, elections would shortly be held in Guinea-Bissau, and later, he hoped, in Guinea.

In June 2009 ECOWAS announced that a Common Mining Code for its members would be in place by the end of 2012. In August The Gambia hosted the ECOWAS sensitization campaign, designed to promote a greater appreciation of and participation in ECOWAS by its citizens. There was widespread concern within the organization that few ECOWAS citizens knew or cared much about the institution.

ECONOMIC COOPERATION ORGANIZATION (ECO)

Established: As Regional Cooperation for Development in 1962 by Iran, Pakistan, and Turkey; reactivated under present name in 1985; formally launched in 1990, following amendment of the (1977) Treaty of İzmir; membership expansion approved by heads of state summit on February 16–17, 1992; Treaty of İzmir further amended on September 14, 1996.

Purpose: To promote regional cooperation in trade, transportation, communications, tourism, cultural affairs, and economic development.

Headquarters: Tehran, Iran.

Principal Organs: Summit, Council of Ministers, Regional Planning Council, Council of Permanent Representatives, Secretariat.

Web site: www.ecosecretariat.org

Secretary General: Khurshid Anwar (Pakistan).

Membership (10): Afghanistan, Azerbaijan, Iran, Kazakhstan, Kyrgyzstan, Pakistan, Tajikistan, Turkey, Turkmenistan, Uzbekistan.
Guest: Turkish Republic of Northern Cyprus.

Origin and development. The Regional Cooperation for Development (RCD), established in 1962 by Iran, Pakistan, and Turkey, achieved little progress and was moribund after 1979 until revived and renamed the Economic Cooperation Organization in 1985. For the rest of the decade, the ECO remained of minor influence, although it established the South and West Asia Postal Union in 1988 and a joint Chamber of Commerce and Industry in 1990.

Following the breakup of the Soviet Union in 1991, the ECO assumed greater significance as a potential vehicle for regional economic cooperation that would include the new Central Asian republics. The ECO Heads of State Summit on February 16–17, 1992, in Tehran, Iran, approved membership requests from Azerbaijan, Kyrgyzstan, Tajikistan, Turkmenistan, and Uzbekistan. Afghanistan and Kazakhstan joined those nations (minus Tajikistan, whose foreign minister was unable to attend because of that nation's domestic turmoil) in formally signing the ECO charter on November 27.

The expanded ECO faced significant political problems, particularly internal crises in various member states and a perceived contest between Iran and Turkey for leadership. Stressing the Islamic identity of the members, Tehran appeared to view the ECO as a means for establishing a future Islamic common market that would promote Muslim solidarity and values; Ankara, while supportive of trade negotiations, was just as insistent that the ECO remain a secular body devoted entirely to reducing trade barriers, establishing a free market system, and developing the region's infrastructure.

Structure. Policy decisions at the highest level are made by summits of the members' heads of state or government, who convene, at a minimum, biennially. The Council of Ministers, comprising the foreign ministers of the member countries, is the ECO's principal decision-making body. Council meetings, which are held at least once a year, rotate annually from country to country. The Regional Planning Council (RPC), which also convenes annually, formulates plans and policies in line with ECO objectives and direct instructions from the council. It also reviews the work of the Secretariat and progress on the various ECO programs, and it may propose the formation of ad hoc committees. Assisting the RPC is an ambassadorial-level Council of Permanent Representatives. Under the Secretariat are seven sectoral or service directorates: Agriculture, Industry, and Health; Energy, Minerals, and Environment; Trade and Investment; Transport and Communications; Economic Research and Statistics; Project Research; and Coordination and International Relations.

The oldest of the ECO's three specialized agencies is the Tehran-based Cultural Institute, which began as an RCD organ and was revived by the March 1995 Third ECO Summit. A Science Foundation, authorized at the same summit, is to be based in Islamabad, Pakistan. In October 2007 its charter was being finalized. At the Fifth Summit, in 1998, the ECO leaders signed a charter for an ECO Educational Institute, to be located in Ankara, Turkey, but the charter has not been ratified by all member states, and, more than ten years later, the effort remains at a standstill. Functioning regional institutions are the Chamber of Commerce and Industry, the ECO Shipping Company, the Consultancy and Engineering Company, an ECO Supreme Audit Institution, and the College of Insurance. In various stages of development are the ECO Reinsurance Company and the ECO News Agency. Plans to establish a regional airline, ECO Air, were scrapped in 2001. A Trade and Development Bank, known as Ecobank, began operation in late 2007.

Activities. Discord was reported at the Fourth ECO Summit, held on May 14–16, 1996, in Ashgabat, Turkmenistan, as a number of members objected to efforts by Iran to "politicize" the grouping by criticizing Israel and the United States. Uzbekistan, Kazakhstan, and Tajikistan were described as the most irritated by Tehran's actions; Uzbek president Islam Karimov reportedly accused Iran of trying to transform the ECO into a "military-political unit." However, the summit leaders did manage to endorse a 22-point declaration pledging expanded cooperation in a number of fields, including energy, trade, transportation, and communications.

The need for oil and gas pipelines dominated the 1997 extraordinary summit, held on May 13–14 in Ashgabat. One area of particular interest was how to get oil from Azerbaijan to international markets, a principal stumbling block being the resistance of the United States to the idea of shipping Azeri oil through Iran, a route many experts consider the best. In contrast, the heads of state of Turkmenistan and Pakistan reached an agreement with U.S. and Saudi oil companies to construct a pipeline from Turkmenistan to Pakistan. Turkmenistan also came to an agreement to ship gas to Europe through Iran and Turkey. In other business, the Taliban government in Afghanistan objected to its exclusion from the summit, arguing that there was no "true and lawful" Afghan representative present. (The Afghanistan delegation seated at the summit was from the government that had fled Kabul in 1996.)

At the Fifth Summit, held on May 10, 1998, in Almaty, Kazakhstan, ECO leaders called for the establishment of several ECO institutions (see Structure, above) and urged greater cooperation in agriculture and industry. Meeting just before the summit, Iran and Kazakhstan agreed to continue negotiations over the legal status of the Caspian Sea, the two having adopted different positions on access to the sea's resources.

A leading topic at the Sixth Summit, held June 10–11, 2000, in Tehran, was prospects for accelerating sustained regional socio-economic development. The summit also called for greater cooperation in agriculture, industry, and human development; welcomed a proposal for cooperation in tourism; called attention to the growing importance of environmental issues; and praised the continuing effort to stop illegal drug production and trafficking. (The ECO-UNDCP Project on Drug Control Coordination Unit in the ECO Secretariat had opened in July 1999.)

Held in the Turkish capital on October 14, 2002, the Seventh Summit reviewed the ECO's accomplishments during its first decade of expanded membership and envisioned increased cooperation, integration, and development. Since 2000 the ECO has inaugurated ministerial-level meetings in multiple sectors, with an emphasis on infrastructure, trade and resources. The 2002 summit participants called for early conclusion of an ECO Trade Agreement (ECOTA), which would remove nontariff barriers to trade and reduce intraregional tariffs. The closing summit declaration highlighted growing cooperation with regional and international organizations, including many United Nations (UN) agencies and the World Trade Organization.

Meeting in July 2003, ECO ministers signed the ECOTA, one provision of which is the stepped reduction of internal tariffs to 15 percent within eight years. A month earlier the ECO had established a fund for economic aid to Afghanistan as part of its efforts to help the social and economic rebuilding of that member state.

The Eighth Summit was held in September 2004 in Tajikistan. Other activity in 2004–2005 included agreement to finally establish the ECO Trade and Development Bank and otherwise expand cooperation in financial affairs. Several prominent ECO members also called for the "revitalization" of the organization to, among other things, combat terrorism and drug smuggling. The Ninth Summit, held on May 5, 2006, in Baku, Azerbaijan, concluded that to continue the organization needed to reform and modernize its structure. Later that month ECO announced that Iran would become the hub of an electricity grid for member states.

In November 2006 members agreed to hold annual meetings on the ministerial level to pave the way for further cooperation on border security, combating drug trafficking, the training of police and security staffs, and exchange of criminals. In April 2007 the organization held a conference on privatization among its members. However, at a June 2007 meeting with ECO secretary general Khurshid Anwar, President Kurmanbek Bakiyev of Kyrgyzstan criticized the organization for not doing more to put its good intentions into practice. The November 2007 ministerial meeting took place in Herat, Afghanistan, focusing primarily on evaluating progress toward meeting ECO objectives in the past year. In December 2007 the ECO signed a memorandum of understanding with the Shanghai Cooperation Organization (SCO), agreeing to work more closely with the group.

Other meetings in late 2007 and the first half of 2008 addressed corruption, money laundering, and trafficking of drugs and people. In March 2008 the ECO held a joint workshop with the International Organization for Migration (IOM; see separate article) on ways to combat human trafficking. Also in March ECOTA became operational, and the first meeting of the ECOTA Cooperation Council was held in May. In June 2008 ECO announced plans to build a rail corridor connecting Turkey with China. A project was also started to build a railroad connection between Turkey and Azerbaijan, through Iran. In May 2009 a rail container link between Islamabad, Tehran, and Istanbul, was announced. This container train was expected to be operating by August 2009.

The tenth ECO summit was held in Tehran on March 11, 2009. Guest delegations from Iraq and Qatar attended. The meeting was dominated by the world economic crisis, with all member states being encouraged to move towards an ECO free trade area by 2015. The conference noted with satisfaction a recent Memorandum of Understanding with the Shanghai Cooperation Organization (SCO, see separate article). Some commentators noted, however, that the SCO was proving successful in part because it contained large powers such as Russia and China, and speculated that the ECO would work better if it included the superpowers as stakeholders in its deliberations.

EUROPEAN FREE TRADE ASSOCIATION (EFTA)

Established: By convention signed January 4, 1960, in Stockholm, Sweden, effective May 3, 1960; updated convention signed June 21, 2001, in Vaduz, Liechtenstein, with entry into force on June 1, 2002.

Purpose: Initially, to promote economic expansion, full employment, and higher standards of living through elimination of barriers to nonagricultural trade among member states; more recently, to expand trade and other cooperation relations with external countries and to further

European integration through a single European Economic Area, extending not only to free trade, but also to deregulation, removal of technical and nontariff barriers to trade, and cooperation with the European Union in the service and agricultural sectors as well as industry.

Headquarters: Geneva, Switzerland.

Principal Organs: Council, EFTA Council Committees, Consultative Committee, EFTA Surveillance Authority, EFTA Court, Secretariat.

Web site: www.efta.int

Secretary General: Kåre Bryn (Norway).

Membership (4): Iceland, Liechtenstein, Norway, Switzerland.

Working Language: English.

Origin and development. EFTA was established under British leadership in 1959–1960 as the response of Europe's so-called outer seven states (Austria, Denmark, Norway, Portugal, Sweden, Switzerland, United Kingdom) to creation of the original six-state European Economic Community (EEC). With the breakdown of negotiations to establish a single, all-European free trade area encompassing both groups, the seven decided to set up a separate organization that would enable the non-EEC states both to maintain a unified position in further bargaining with the "inner six" and to carry out a modest liberalization of trade within their own group, provided for in the establishment of the 1960 EFTA Convention (the Stockholm Convention). Finland became an associate member of EFTA in 1961; Iceland joined as the eighth full member in 1970. At the start of 1973, however, Denmark and the United Kingdom withdrew upon joining the European Community (EC).

Unlike the EEC, EFTA was not endowed with supranational features. It was not designed to establish a common market or common external tariff, but merely to eliminate internal trade barriers on nonagricultural goods. This objective was met at the end of 1966, three years ahead of schedule. A second goal, a comprehensive agreement permitting limited access to EC markets, led to completion of various trade pacts, the first of which became effective January 1, 1973, concurrent with the initial round of EC expansion.

Following enlargement of the EC, a further range of activity was unofficially added to the EFTA agenda, and cooperation was extended to more diverse economic matters than the trade concerns specified in the Stockholm Convention. Explicitly recognized by the EFTA Council at its meeting in May 1975, these concerns involved such areas as raw materials, monetary policy, inflation, and unemployment.

Organized outside EFTA's institutional framework, the first summit in 11 years convened in May 1977 in Vienna, Austria, and adopted the Vienna Declaration, which prescribed a broad framework for future activities. It included, for example, a resolution calling upon EFTA to become a "forum for joint consideration of wider European and worldwide economic problems in order to make a constructive contribution to economic cooperation in international fora." In pursuit of this goal, a multilateral free trade agreement between the EFTA countries and Spain was signed in 1979 in Madrid, while in 1982 concessions were extended to permit Portugal to expand its industrial base prior to joining the EC. Upon their accession to the EC, it was agreed that Spain and Portugal would conclude special arrangements with EFTA countries.

Cooperation between EFTA and the EC/European Union (EU) continued to grow based on general guidelines promulgated in the 1984 Luxembourg Declaration, which endorsed the development of a European Economic Space (EES) including all EFTA and EC countries. The accord called for the reduction of nontariff barriers (the last duties on most industrial trade having recently been removed); more joint research and development projects; and exploratory talks in such areas as transportation, agriculture, fishing, and energy. In an effort to reduce border formalities, EFTA reached agreement with the EC on the use of a simplified customs form, the Single Administrative Document (SAD), to cover trade within and between the two groups. The SAD convention was the first direct agreement between EFTA and the EC, previous pacts having taken the form of similar but separate agreements between each EFTA member and the EC. Both the SAD accord and a related convention on common transit procedures became effective on January 1, 1988.

Two years earlier, at the start of 1986, Portugal had left EFTA to join the EC, at which time Finland rose to full EFTA membership. Liechtenstein, which previously participated as a nonvoting associate member by virtue of its customs union with Switzerland, was admitted as a full member in May 1991.

An EFTA summit in June 1990 again strongly endorsed the EES concept, and formal EC-EFTA discussions immediately began, but the negotiations proved much more difficult than anticipated. The major sticking points were EFTA's request to exempt many of its products from EC guidelines and an inability to agree on a structure through which EFTA could influence EC decision making. Some progress, particularly in regard to the exemptions issue, was reported at a special December session called to "reinvigorate" talks on the European Economic Area (EEA), as the EES had been renamed at the EC's request. In addition, negotiations in early May 1991 resolved many of the remaining disagreements, with a preliminary accord being signed in October. However, an objection from the European Court of Justice mandated the omission of a proposed EEA legal body from the agreement, and a new pact was signed in May 1992.

The EEA was scheduled to go into effect on January 1, 1993, but its final ratification proved contentious. For EFTA the most surprising problem was the rejection of the EEA by a Swiss referendum on December 6, 1992. Despite this, the other EFTA members agreed to pursue the EEA without Switzerland. A protocol to accommodate the change was signed on March 17, 1993, in Brussels, and by late 1993 all the EC states and the remaining EFTA countries had completed their ratification procedures. (In Liechtenstein, the only other EFTA member to require a popular vote on the question, the EEA was approved by a comfortable margin a week after the Swiss balloting. However, Liechtenstein's customs and monetary union with Switzerland meant that its participation in the EEA had to be deferred.) As finally launched on January 1, 1994, the EEA provided for greatly expanded freedom of movement of goods, services, capital, and labor among the (then) 17 participating nations, home to a population of some 372 million. After negotiating amendment of its customs and monetary union with Switzerland, Liechtenstein became the 18th EEA member on May 1, 1995.

For four EFTA member states the EEA arrangement was regarded as a stepping stone to full EU membership, Austria having submitted its application as early as July 1989, with Finland, Norway, and Sweden following suit in 1991–1992. Negotiations with all four applicants were completed by early 1994, and referendums later in the year in Austria, Finland, and Sweden approved EU membership. However, Norwegian voters voted "no" on the proposal, as they had once before in 1972. Consequently, an EFTA ministerial session in December 1994 in Geneva decided that EFTA would continue to function, even though its membership was to fall as of January 1, 1995, to four countries with a total population of scarcely more than 11 million, nearly two-thirds less than before.

Meeting in June 1999 in Lillehammer, Norway, the EFTA ministers called for the Stockholm Convention to be updated in order to consolidate the EEA regime and a set of agreements between the EU and Switzerland that was about to be concluded. Switzerland had already proposed that the benefits of the new Swiss-EU accords be extended on a reciprocal basis to its EFTA partners. EFTA was also interested in seeing that a revised convention reflect recent developments with regard to its free trade partnerships and multilateral arrangements.

Work on the proposed convention revisions continued through 2000 and into 2001, with the EFTA Council signing the revised EFTA Convention during its ministerial session in Vaduz, Liechtenstein, on June 21–22, 2001. The Vaduz Convention entered into force on June 1, 2002.

Structure. The EFTA Council, the association's principal political organ, consists of one representative from each member state and normally meets two times a year at the ministerial level, twice a month at lower levels. Its responsibilities include supervising the implementation and operation of various free trade agreements and managing relations with the EU. Decisions are generally reached by consensus. Assisting the Council are various standing organs, including the Committee on Customs and Origin Matters, the Consultative Committee (comprising representatives from government and private economic organizations in the member states), the Committee on Technical Barriers to Trade, the Committee of Members of Parliament of EFTA Countries, the Committee of Trade Experts, and the Committee on Third-Country Relations. The latter two and the Council are aided by a number of Expert Groups that provide advice on state aid; public procurement; intellectual property; price compensation; trade procedures; legal issues; and services, investment, and establishment. The EFTA Secretariat opened an office in 1988 in Brussels to facilitate cooperation with the EC. In addition, an Office of the EFTA Statistical Adviser is located in Luxembourg.

EFTA also participates in various bodies in connection with the EEA. The EEA Joint Committee, which brings together EFTA, EU, and European Commission representatives, is the main EEA decision-making organ, while an EEA Council of EU and EFTA ministers offers overall direction. A Standing Committee of the EFTA States (Switzerland participates as an observer) consolidates the position of EFTA members regarding incorporation of EU laws, regulations, and procedures into the EEA. The committee is itself assisted by five subcommittees (Free Movement of Goods, Free Movement of Capital and Services, Free Movement of Persons, Flanking and Horizontal Policies, Legal and Institutional Matters) and some 40 working groups. The EEA Joint Parliamentary Committee, which serves as a forum for EEA issues, brings together 12 members from parliaments of the EEA states and 12 members of the European Parliament. The EEA Consultative Committee focuses on social matters. EFTA has also established its own Brussels-based Surveillance Authority, which monitors implementation of the EEA agreement, and an EFTA Court, sitting in Geneva, as final arbiter of legal disputes.

Activities. In addition to its focus on the EEA, EFTA has devoted considerable energy to expanding other external ties. An EFTA ministerial session in June 1995 saw representatives of the three Baltic republics (Estonia, Latvia, and Lithuania) express interest in negotiating free trade agreements, which formally entered into effect in 1996–1997. EFTA already had similar arrangements with Bulgaria, the Czech Republic, Hungary, Israel, Poland, Romania, Slovakia, Slovenia, and Turkey. Additional free trade agreements were reached with Morocco and the Palestine Liberation Organization (PLO) in 1997 and 1998, respectively, and then with Macedonia in June 2000, Mexico in November 2000, Croatia and Jordan in June 2001, Singapore in June 2002, and Chile in June 2003 (with effect from February 2004).

The agreements with Morocco, the PLO, and Jordan were noteworthy in that they marked a clear decision by the EFTA Council to expand the organization's relationships throughout the Mediterranean region, while the agreement with Mexico marked EFTA's first transatlantic venture, and that with Singapore, the first into the Far East.

Attention in 2002 and the first half of 2003 largely focused on the planned expansion of the EU to 25 members in May 2004. In the 2002 EFTA annual report, the organization's secretary general, William Rossier, had praised the move, noting the "bonding effect of reuniting the European family" and the positive impact on regional stability and security. Under the EEA Agreement, all ten new EU members (Cyprus, Czech Republic, Estonia, Hungary, Latvia, Lithuania, Malta, Poland, Slovakia, and Slovenia) were required to negotiate EEA participation. Two principal stumbling blocks quickly emerged: (1) the EU's request that the three EFTA EEA members increase their contributions toward eliminating economic and social disparities in the poorer EU countries (the ten prospective members plus Portugal, Spain, and Greece), and (2) the need to adjust tariff arrangements affecting Poland's significant fishmeal processing industry. Poland argued that a loss of tariff-free fish imports from Iceland and Norway would devastate its fishmeal industry. The EU, however, insisted that a uniform tariff regime for the entire union had to be maintained.

The EFTA and EEA councils had hoped to resolve both matters before the ten new EU states signed their accession treaties on April 16, 2003, but they fell short of this goal. As a result, the EEA signings were delayed until July 3. The final agreement called for Iceland, Liechtenstein, and Norway to provide some $1.4 billion in 2004–2009 for the poorer EU countries, down from the $3 billion that had initially been requested. Poland was forced to concede the tariff issue, and the final agreement authorized a community-wide, duty-free fish import quota significantly smaller than the previous level of Icelandic and Norwegian imports to Poland alone.

The increasingly integrated relationship between EFTA and the EU advanced in other respects in the early 2000s. For example, the EFTA EEA members joined three recently established EU-sponsored organizations—the European Maritime Safety Agency, the European Food Safety Authority, and the European Aviation Safety Agency. At the same time, EFTA ministers also have focused attention on expansion of free trade with non-EU countries. EFTA and the EU have also worked together on a "European Neighborhood Policy," designed to reach out to Eastern European and Mediterranean countries that are currently outside the EEA, and to try to prevent the formation of new barriers. The collapse of World Trade Organization (WTO) talks in late 2006, and difficulties since then in reviving them, led to an increased interest by EFTA in forming bilateral free trade agreements (FTAs) with non-European countries.

In 2008, EFTA adopted new decisions into its EEA agreement, including participation of member states into the Greenhouse Gas Emissions Trading Scheme from 2008–2012, participation in a new European Chemical Agency, and the extension of rights to EU citizens to reside in member states.

At a ministerial meeting on June 22, 2009 in Hamar, Norway, EFTA signed a free trade agreement with the Gulf Cooperation Council, which includes the oil-producing states of Saudi Arabia, Kuwait, United Arab Emirates, Oman, Dubai, Qatar, and Bahrain. The agreement covered goods, services, and government procurement. Additionally, the ministers opened FTA negotiations with Hong Kong and agreed to consider initiating talks with Vietnam and Russia, although Russia's FTA was not expected to be finalized until after WTO accession.

As of October 2009, the EFTA had concluded 18 FTAs with nations and groupings outside the EU. Besides the GCC agreement, the most recent FTAs have been with Columbia in November 2008 and Canada, whose agreement went into force in July, 2009. The Canadian pact centered primarily on exchanging goods. However, it was opposed by the Canadian shipbuilding industry, which feared competition from Norway's strong maritime sector. To cushion the impact, the agreement included a 15-year phase-out of Canadian shipbuilding duties.

Additionally, the EFTA was in talks with Albania, Algeria, India, Indonesia, Peru, Serbia, Thailand, Ukraine in 2009.

Trade talks with India were launched in 2008 and focused on liberalizing the movement of service suppliers, at India's request, and ensuring intellectual property rights for Swiss pharmaceutical companies. Although initially projected to conclude in 2009, negotiations were extended by disputes over subjecting India's low-cost generic pharmaceutical market to intellectual property restrictions. Norway withdrew from talks, reportedly in protest against Swiss insistence that India abide by stricter rules than those required by the WTO. Nevertheless, trade talks with India continued in September 2009 with a fourth round that focused on agricultural and industrial goods.

EFTA's 2009 annual status report stated that its four nations comprised the world's fifth largest provider of commercial services and the EU's third largest trading partner.

EUROPEAN ORGANIZATION FOR NUCLEAR RESEARCH (CERN)

Organisation Européenne pour la Recherche Nucléaire

Established: By convention signed July 1, 1953, in Paris, France, effective September 29, 1954.

Purpose: "To provide for collaboration among European States in subnuclear research of a pure scientific and fundamental character, and in research essentially related thereto. The Organization shall have no concern with work for military requirements and the results of its experimental and theoretical work shall be published or otherwise made generally available."

Headquarters: Geneva, Switzerland.

Principal Organs: Council, Committee of Council, Scientific Policy Committee, Finance Committee.

Web site: www.cern.ch

Director General: Rolf-Dieter Heuer (Germany).

Membership (20): Austria, Belgium, Bulgaria, Czech Republic, Denmark, Finland, France, Germany, Greece, Hungary, Italy, Netherlands,

Norway, Poland, Portugal, Slovakia, Spain, Sweden, Switzerland, United Kingdom.

Observers (8): European Commission; India; Israel; Japan; Russia; Turkey; United Nations Educational, Scientific, and Cultural Organization (UNESCO); United States.

Official Languages: English, French.

Origin and development. The European Organization for Nuclear Research was established September 29, 1954, after ratification of a convention drawn up in Paris, France, the preceding July. The convention followed the resolution of the United Nations Educational, Scientific, and Cultural Organization (UNESCO) general conference held in 1950 in Florence, Italy, and an intergovernmental conference convened by UNESCO in December 1951. The organization replaced the *Conseil Européen pour la Recherche Nucléaire* (CERN), which was established February 15, 1952, but retained its predecessor's acronym. One of the original 12 members, Yugoslavia, withdrew in 1961. Austria acceded in 1959 and Spain in 1961; the latter withdrew in 1968 but returned in 1982. CERN was subsequently joined by Portugal (1986), Finland and Poland (1991), Hungary (1992), the Czech Republic and Slovakia (1993), and Bulgaria (1999).

In 2002, India, whose scientists have participated in CERN projects since the 1960s, became the organization's eighth observer. As such, it may participate on a nonvoting basis in all Council sessions.

Additionally, CERN has signed cooperation agreements with more than a dozen countries to further research collaborations. The latest was in May 2008 with Saudi Arabia.

Structure. The Council of CERN, which normally meets four times a year, is comprised of two representatives—one from the government and one from the scientific field—for each member state. The Committee of Council, consisting of the Council president and vice presidents; one or more representatives per member state; and the chairs of the Scientific Policy Committee, the Finance Committee, and the European Committee for Future Accelerators, is a less formal forum in which members monitor operations, discuss proposals, and confidentially discuss difficult questions. The Scientific Policy Committee, comprised of some two dozen scientists from member and observer states without regard to geographical distribution, provides the Council with advice on research priorities, resource allocation, management and staffing, and scientific developments and their implications for the organization. The Finance Committee consists of one or more delegates from each member state. The director general, elected by the Council, serves as CERN's head of management, overseeing a directorate and managing various departments focused on research, accelerators and related technology, technical tasks, and administration.

Activities. CERN's experimental facilities were used more sparingly in the organization's early years, but are now utilized by 8,000 visiting scientists from more than 500 universities and research institutes. The CERN staff numbers more than 2,500. It claims to have half the world's particle physicists involved in research with the organization.

The organization's many accomplishments have included producing in 1981 the first collisions between protons and their antimatter counterparts, antiprotons; verifying the electroweak theory in 1983 that unifies the weak nuclear force and electromagnetic force; announcing in 1984 evidence of the existence of the quark; confirming in 1989 that all matter consists of only three families of subatomic particles; and synthesizing in 1995 atoms of antimatter from their antiparticles. In addition, CERN computer scientist Tim Berners-Lee was credited with inventing the World Wide Web in 1990 to provide CERN-affiliated physicists around the world with rapid access to scientific information.

The highlight of 1989 was the inauguration of the Large Electron-Positron Collider (LEP), with which CERN was generally perceived to have outdistanced U.S. rivals in the subatomic particle research race. In addition, at its December meeting the Council agreed, in light of the political developments in Eastern Europe, to provide physicists from that region immediate access to CERN facilities and services pending negotiation of formal arrangements.

In December 1991 the CERN Council unanimously supported a resolution recognizing the Large Hadron Collider (LHC) as the "right machine" for further research in the field of high-energy physics. The LHC, to be built in the same 27-kilometer tunnel housing the LEP collider, would produce head-on proton collisions at much higher energies than previously achieved, causing the protons to be shattered into smaller, very short-lived particles such as quarks. It was envisioned that it would be the most powerful high-energy particle accelerator ever built.

In 1993 attention focused on negotiations in the United States regarding its 87-kilometer Superconducting Supercollider (SSC), which the U.S. House of Representatives terminated. Consequently, the CERN Council, recognizing the organization's growing status as a "world, rather than a European laboratory," invited nonmembers, especially the United States, to contribute (both scientifically and financially) to the development of the LHC. In addition, in 1993 the CERN Council endorsed a public relations campaign to explain the valuable technical "spin-offs," in areas such as vacuums and cryogenics, from subatomic particle research.

Last-minute budget concerns on behalf of Germany and the United Kingdom delayed a vote on the LHC at the June 1994 Council session, but the project was finally approved at the December meeting after France and Switzerland agreed to provide additional support. However, the threat of German budget cuts on scientific research programs in 1996 again jeopardized the project schedule and contributed to a decision to seek financing from nonmember users, such as Japan, which acquired Council observer status in 1996. Canada, India, and Russia also agreed to contribute funds in 1996. In December 1997 the United States was granted observer status at CERN in return for contributing $531 million in money and material.

On November 8, 2000, the LEP was shut down after 11 years in operation to make way for the LHC project, which was initially targeted to come online in 2005. In preparation, an LHC computing grid (LCG) project, involving distributed computing technology, was nearing completion, and CERN began cooperation with the European Union (EU) on an Enabling Grids for E-science in Europe (EGEE) project that would establish a continent-wide grid infrastructure with the LCG the primary sight of the project's development. Additionally, the "CERN openlab" was set up as a joint venture with private industry to develop technological solutions for the massive data generated from the LHC.

CERN has also produced small, but measurable, amounts of antimatter (thousands of atoms of antihydrogen as opposed to the few atoms previously attained). Antimatter atoms, which vigorously react with and destroy atoms of normal matter when they touch them, may have a role to play in fighting cancer.

Administrative reorganization at CERN advanced under the previous director general, Robert Aymar of France, who succeeded Italy's Luciano Maiani in January 2004. Restructuring plans, based on recommendations of an External Review Committee, included reducing the size of the directorate and reorganizing the more than a dozen divisions into eight departments. Responsibility for public communications, technology transfer, and safety were brought under the director general's office.

In December 2007, it was announced that Aymar would be resigning as director general at the end of the following year. He was replaced in January 2009 by German national Rolf-Dieter Heuer, who formerly held the position of particle physics director at the Deutsches Elektronen-Synchrotron (DESY) laboratory in Hamburg, Germany.

In March 2008, CERN signed a cooperation agreement with ITER, an international fusion power research project that is supported by China, the EU, India, Japan, South Korea, and the United States and based in Cadarache, France. The five-year agreement began immediately and allows for resource and technological collaboration.

At a Council meeting on December 12, 2008, Romania was accepted as a candidate for accession, with its participation expected to be phased in progressively over a five-year period. Additionally, the Council established a body to examine enlarging CERN membership and scientific pursuits. In 2009, Cyprus, Israel, Turkey, Serbia, and Slovenia applied for membership. In May 2009, Austria announced it would withdraw from CERN, as its annual membership contribution was a disproportionate burden on the country's budget for international research. However, following protests by Austrian researchers, the government reversed the decision.

The LHC project experienced a series of delays and setbacks on it course to launch. In April 2007, the failure of one of its magnets pushed the start-up date to 2008. Meanwhile, a lawsuit filed in a U.S. district court in Hawaii in March 2008 sought to prevent the project from moving forward out of concern it might produce a black hole that would swallow the Earth. CERN officials said there had been adequate safety checks and questioned the jurisdiction of a Hawaiian-based court.

The first beam of light entered the LHC on September 10, 2008. However, hours later, a faulty electrical connection caused extensive damage and the collider shut down, costing some $37 million in repairs.

CERN announced in February 2009 that it was adding safety features to the LHC, including a new pressure valve and a detection device for the electrical system, to avert another incident. Initially expected to relaunch in April 2009, CERN has since delayed the date several times out of operational caution. As of October 2009, the latest projection was a relaunch in November at half power, which would reportedly give operators experience in running the machine safely.

The LCG was also scheduled to go live at the same time with approximately 100,000 CPUs of processing power to assist with data analysis for the LHC.

EUROPEAN ORGANIZATION FOR THE SAFETY OF AIR NAVIGATION (EUROCONTROL)

Established: By convention signed on December 13, 1960, in Brussels, Belgium, effective March 1, 1963; amended by protocol signed February 12, 1981, effective January 1, 1986. (Convention revisions signed on June 27, 1997, are still undergoing ratification.)

Purpose: To harmonize and integrate air navigation services in Europe, aiming to create a uniform air traffic management system for civil and military users in order to achieve safe, orderly, expeditious, and economic flow of traffic while minimizing adverse environmental impact.

Headquarters: Brussels, Belgium.

Principal Organs: Commission, Provisional Council, Agency.

Web site: www.eurocontrol.int

Director General: David McMillan (UK).

Membership (38): Albania, Armenia, Austria, Belgium, Bosnia and Herzegovina, Bulgaria, Croatia, Cyprus, Czech Republic, Denmark, Finland, France, Germany, Greece, Hungary, Ireland, Italy, Lithuania, Luxembourg, Macedonia, Malta, Moldova, Monaco, Montenegro, Netherlands, Norway, Poland, Portugal, Romania, Serbia, Slovakia, Slovenia, Spain, Sweden, Switzerland, Turkey, Ukraine, United Kingdom.

Official Languages: Dutch, English, French, German, Portuguese.

Origin and development. As early as 1957, governments had considered developing an air traffic control procedure that would disregard national frontiers. The growing number of aircraft traveling at ever-higher speeds and altitudes, the pace at which the aeronautical sciences were advancing, and the greater interdependence of the industrialized states of Western Europe suggested the need for such a joint venture. However, the idea was not officially discussed until January 1958 at the Fourth European Mediterranean Regional Air Navigation Convention of the International Civil Aviation Organization (ICAO) in Geneva, Switzerland. Subsequently, several meetings were held by concerned directors general of civil aviation, and on June 9, 1960, the ministers responsible for civil and military aviation in Belgium, France, the Federal Republic of Germany, Italy, Luxembourg, the Netherlands, and the United Kingdom met in Rome, Italy, to consider a draft convention. Two diplomatic conferences followed (the Italians no longer participating), and the convention was signed at the second of these in December 1960. Ireland acceded to the convention in 1965; Portugal became an associate member in 1976 and a full member in 1986. Greece joined in 1988, Turkey and Malta in 1989, Cyprus in 1991, Hungary and Switzerland in 1992, Austria in 1993, and Denmark and Norway in 1994. In 1995 Slovenia and Sweden joined, followed by the Czech Republic, Italy, and Romania in 1996; Spain, Slovakia, Croatia, Bulgaria, and Monaco in 1997; Macedonia in 1998; Moldova in 2000; Finland in 2001; Albania in 2002; Ukraine and Poland in 2004; Serbia and Montenegro in 2005; and Armenia in 2006. Most recently, Montenegro (now separated from Serbia) joined in May 2007.

Structure. Eurocontrol is currently governed through the Commission, comprised of delegates from each member state who represent the interests of civil aviation and national defense. The Commission formulates general policy and is responsible for regulatory functions, approving budgets, and appointing the director general and agency directors. The Provisional Council, comprised of civil aviation officials from the member states, meets at least three times a year and implements Commission policy and supervises agency work.

Reporting to the Council are the Performance Review Commission, the Safety Regulation Commission, the Regulatory Committee, the Civil/Military Interface Standing Committee, the Committee of Management, the Enlarged Committee for Route Charges, the Audit Board, the Standing Committee on Finance, and the Performance Review Commission. The Eurocontrol Agency, headed by the director general, serves as a secretariat and includes various groups concerned with air traffic management (ATM), training, financial arrangements, and research and development. The Safety Regulatory Oversight reports to the committee.

Upon ratification of convention revisions signed in 1997, the Commission and the Provisional Council are to become the General Assembly and the Council, respectively. The committee structure will also change, with separate standing committees, for example, overseeing the Central European Air Traffic Services (CEATS) and the Maastricht International Upper Area Control Center in the Netherlands. However, as of mid-2009 the ratification process had still not been completed, although some of the provisions had already been implemented.

Eurocontrol's central administration is financed by means of contributions from each member state assessed on the basis of the state's GNP and the value of the state's route facility cost base.

Activities. The organization is required to analyze the future needs of air traffic and develop new techniques to meet them; to establish common long-term objectives in the field of air navigation and a common medium-term plan for air traffic services; to coordinate the research and development programs of the member states; and to assist, on request, in the performance of specific air navigation tasks or in the provision and operation of air traffic services.

Specifically, when requested the organization provides air traffic control services from its Maastricht center to aircraft operating in the upper airspace of the three Benelux states and the northern part of what was formerly the Federal Republic of Germany. In addition, the CEATS is being developed to serve eight Central European countries (Austria, Bosnia and Herzegovina, Croatia, Czech Republic, Hungary, Italy, Slovakia, and Slovenia).

The organization also prepares and executes studies, tests, and trials at its Research and Development Centre in Brétigny-sur-Orge, near Paris; trains air traffic services personnel at the Institute of Air Navigation Services in Luxembourg; calculates, bills, and collects air navigation route charges at the Central Route Charges Office in Haren, near Brussels; and provides an international air traffic flow management system through its Central Flow Management Unit (CFMU) in Haren.

Despite the wide range of its activity, Eurocontrol falls far short of the common European air control system envisioned at its formation, due to the refusal of most members to surrender national prerogatives such as control of their military airspace and the allocation of lucrative air traffic control equipment contracts. However, in recent years substantial progress has been made in response to growing air traffic congestion in Europe.

In November 1988 the transportation ministers of the (then) 23-member European Civil Aviation Conference (ECAC) called for the development of common air traffic control specifications and operating procedures and asked Eurocontrol to determine the standards. The CFMU evolved as a result of this request. In April 1990 the ECAC approved the comprehensive European Air Traffic Control Harmonization and Integration Program (EATCHIP) and designated Eurocontrol to manage the project. Subsequent Eurocontrol activity included an agreement in 1994 to assist NATO's new Partnership for Peace associates from the former Soviet bloc in upgrading surveillance radar facilities.

In April 1995 Eurocontrol's CFMU assumed responsibility for air traffic flow management (not actual air traffic control) in France, and similar measures were subsequently extended within a year to all ECAC members (then numbering 41). In March 1996 Eurocontrol signed a new cooperation agreement with the International Civil Aviation Organization (ICAO) designed, among other things, to eliminate duplication of services.

In December 1996 the Eurocontrol Permanent Commission tentatively approved a far-reaching revision of the Eurocontrol Convention. The changes, which involved a major reorganization (see **Structure**, above), were expected to streamline operations and facilitate an expansion of services related to aircraft safety and safety regulations; review of airline performance; improved military/civilian cooperation; and implementation of EATCHIP's successor regime, the European Air Traffic Management Program (EATMP). The revised convention was formally signed in June 1997, and some of its provisions were implemented in 1998, prior to the still-pending formal ratification.

During the 1990s Eurocontrol also participated in the Program for Harmonized Air Traffic Management Research (PHARE), and in June 1998 it agreed to participate in development by 2010 of a European Global Navigation Satellite System (GNSS), in cooperation with the European Commission and the European Space Agency (ESA). It subsequently adopted an ATM 2000+ Strategy, which Eurocontrol described as "a blueprint for developing a seamless, pan-European ATM system."

In December 2003 Eurocontrol signed a Memorandum of Cooperation with the European Commission, ensuring a closer commitment to European integration. Additional memberships in Eurocontrol followed the expansion of the European Union (EU) to 25 states in 2004.

In October 2004 the Single European Sky concept was introduced with the goal of replacing the existing system wherein airspace is controlled by national governments with one characterized by a "single, seamless airspace within which traffic can cross national frontiers, supported by a synchronized, integrated system of air traffic management." The need for the single sky approach had become apparent because of air corridor congestion. In 2006 and 2007 Eurocontrol successfully sought to establish a data link between aircraft and air traffic control, which led to the end of pilot reliance on voice communication. In line with predictions, increased air congestion continued to plague Europe, reaching an all-time high in 2007 with an increase of 5.3 percent overall from the previous year and a 20 percent increase in some Eastern European countries. The growth was mainly attributed to the popularity of low cost carriers. Although the economic recession stemmed growth in 2008 to 0.1 percent, with predictions of a 6 percent decline in 2009, Eurocontrol asserted that growth would resume in the long term.

Out of concern over safety and airline costs, a European Commission advisory body in July 2007 urged Eurocontrol to speed up efforts on its single sky concept. The report noted that air travel in Europe was 70 percent less cost efficient than in the United States because of the fragmentation of air traffic control systems. The report further noted that the current system jeopardized safety by creating unnecessary bottlenecks in the air.

In July 2007 Eurocontrol opened a new air traffic management center to cope with the increase in traffic. The new Central Flow Management Unit is a cornerstone of the single sky initiative and is expected to specialize in trans-Atlantic and intra-European air traffic flow.

Soon after entering office in January 2008, the new director general, David McMillan, announced that Eurocontrol was working with the European Commission on a legislative package to update the single sky policy, which was released on schedule in June. The package strengthened ongoing efforts to consolidate functional airspace blocks (FABs), which are meant to maximize airspace efficiency within Europe, and named Eurocontrol as the agency that would gradually assume control over the implementation of the single sky policy and management of the EU's air traffic control network.

The framework for developing the single sky policy is known as the Single European Sky ATM Research Program (SESAR) and is governed by the SESAR Joint Undertaking, a consortium of Eurocontrol officials and air transport stakeholders. SESAR research aided in the development of a September 2008 agreement between Eurocontrol, the Civil Air Services Organization, and the International Air Transport Association that identified measures to optimize flight planning and efficiencies. In December 2008 Eurocontrol launched a $2.7 billion program to build a satellite-based air traffic control system for completion in 2020 to replace the 60-year-old radar and radio-based system.

Meanwhile, in February 2009 a new Air Navigation Services Board, comprised of industry and airport representatives, took office with the mandate to assist Eurocontrol in the development of its annual and long-term business plans. The board represented efforts to build support and collaboration with industry as Eurocontrol assumes greater authority over other elements of the Single Sky initiatives. In March EU parliament passed a revised Single Sky II package that focused on fast tracking the program through binding targets for improved performance and a 2012 deadline fort the implementation of nine FABs. Eurocontrol was expected to take the role of network manager of the FABs.

In March 2009, SESAR had finished a master plan for the next ten years. Although it had not been formally adopted, the plan defined the deployment of a new ATM system in which technology and enhanced coordination would bring about policy objectives. The 2020 objectives included a three-fold increase in capacity, improved safety performance by a factor of 10, a fuel emissions reduction of 10 percent per flight, and a 50 percent reduction in the cost of airspace use.

In June, 16 contracts worth $2.7 billion, compiled by EC, Eurocontrol, and private industry stakeholders, were awarded, initiating the execution of the SESAR program. A plan to allow for a single communications system between all European air navigation services was announced that October.

EUROPEAN SPACE AGENCY (ESA)

Established: On a de facto basis by agreement signed at a meeting of the European Space Conference July 31, 1973, in Brussels, Belgium, effective May 1, 1975; de jure establishment achieved after ratification of the ESA Convention on October 30, 1980.

Purpose: To provide for and promote, for exclusively peaceful purposes, cooperation among European states in space research and technology, with a view to their being used for scientific purposes and for operational space applications; to elaborate and implement a long-term European space policy; and progressively to "Europeanize" national space programs.

Headquarters: Paris, France.

Principal Organs: Council (all members), Directorates.

Web site: www.esa.int

Director General: Jean-Jacques Dordain (France).

Membership (18): Austria, Belgium, Czech Republic, Denmark, Finland, France, Germany, Greece, Ireland, Italy, Luxembourg, Netherlands, Norway, Portugal, Spain, Sweden, Switzerland, United Kingdom.

Cooperating States (9): Canada, Czech Republic, Hungary, Poland, Romania, Estonia, Latvia, Cyprus, and Slovenia.

Origin and development. The decision to form the ESA was made at meetings of the European Space Conference in December 1972 and July 1973, representing the culmination of 14 years of persistent effort by the Consultative Assembly of the Council of Europe to establish a single European space organization and a common European satellite and launcher program. The long gestation period was in part because of delicate negotiations over how the European Space Research Organization (ESRO) and the European Space Vehicle Launcher Development Organization (ELDO) projects would be continued after their consolidation into the ESA, and in part because of disagreement between France and the Federal Republic of Germany as to the naming of a director general. Austria and Norway, initially observers and subsequently associate members, acceded to full membership January 1, 1987. Finland was an associate member from that date until January 1, 1995, when it became a full member. The fifteenth member, Portugal, joined in December 1999.

Canada, an ESA observer during the mid-1970s, has been a "cooperating state" since 1979. In April 2003 the ESA and Hungary signed a European Cooperating State Agreement that might serve as a model for other countries seeking closer relationship with (and possibly eventual membership in) the ESA. The Czech Republic signed a similar agreement in November 2003, as did Romania in February 2006, and

Estonia, Slovenia, Latvia, and Cyprus in 2008 and 2009. In addition, cooperation agreements (as distinguished from cooperating state memberships) have been signed with several other countries.

Structure. The ESA structure is patterned essentially after that of the ESRO, with a Council as its governing body in which each member state has one vote. The management team is headed by a director general elected by the Council every four years. Assisting him are 11 directors who oversee the ESA's programs in such areas as Earth observation, industrial matters and technology, launchers, manned space flight, and technical and operational support.

The agency also has several national program facilities and five technical establishments: the European Space Research and Technology Centre (ESTEC) in Noordwijk, Netherlands; the European Space Operations Centre (ESOC) in Darmstadt, Germany; the European Space Research Institute (ESRIN) in Frascati, Italy; the European Space Astronomy Centre (ESAC) in Villafranca del Castillo, Spain; and the European Astronauts Centre (EAC) in Cologne, Germany. The Guiana Space Center (CSG) in Kourou, French Guiana has operational control over the launch and launch production facilities.

The member states finance the agency, contributing on the basis of a percentage of GNP to the general and scientific budgets, and on an ad hoc basis to other programs, such as the International Space Station. Contributions are also made by nonmember nations that participate in specific programs.

Activities. The ESA has developed or contributed to a variety of satellite programs in many fields, including telecommunications and earth and space observation, while promoting experiments related to the scientific and commercial exploitation of space. Initially a "junior partner" with the U.S. National Aeronautics and Space Administration (NASA) on several projects, the agency, through its commercial affiliate Arianespace, now competes directly with NASA in the satellite-launching business. However, ESA-NASA cooperation continues in other areas, such as the Hubble Space Telescope; Spacelab, the self-contained laboratory in which numerous experiments are conducted on U.S. space shuttle flights; and the International Space Station, which also involves Canada, Japan, and Russia.

Central to the overall ESA program is the development of a series of Ariane rockets to propel its own launches from facilities in Kourou, French Guiana. Because the ESA Convention prohibits the agency from engaging in profit-making activities, the launches are conducted by Arianespace, which was established in 1980 by European aerospace industries and banks in conjunction with the French Space Agency.

Notable ESA achievements include the Giotto probe (launched in 1985) for studying Halley's Comet; the Ulysses solar polar probe (1990); the European Remote Sensing satellites (ERS-1 and ERS-2) for gathering data on the earth's atmosphere, surface, and climate (1990 and 1995); the Infrared Space Observatory (ISO) for studying deep space (1995); the Solar Heliospheric Observatory (SOHO) for expanding knowledge of the sun (1995); the joint NASA-ESA Cassini/Huygens mission to Saturn and its moon Titan (1997), which successfully reached the region of Saturn, transmitting much new information about the planet and its moons, and whose Huygens lander safely reached Titan's surface January 14, 2005; the X-Ray Multi-Mirror (XMM) mission—the first Ariane-5 satellite launch—for studying such phenomena as neutron stars and black holes (1999); the Cluster satellite quartet for examining earth's magnetosphere (2000); and Envisat, ESA's largest and most scientifically advanced Earth observation satellite (2001). The Mars Express explorer, which reached Mars orbit in late December 2003, suffered a major failure when its lander was lost during its descent to the Martian surface.

In March 2000 Director General Antonio Rodatà of Italy appointed a committee of three "wise men" (from government, finance, and technology) to examine the ESA's role and to make recommendations for its future. In November the committee proposed, among other things, a closer relationship with the European Union (EU), thereby lending support to the view that, in an era of rapidly increasing European integration, the ESA should effectively become the EU's space agency. A week later the European Union Research Council and the ESA Council adopted a new European Strategy for Space to strengthen launch capacities and space technology, to advance scientific knowledge, and to exploit space for the benefit of industry and society. In keeping with these broad goals, the ESA redirected some of its Horizons 2000 Programme toward Small Missions for Advanced Research in Technology (SMART). (SMART-1, the first European spacecraft to orbit the moon, was launched in September 2003.) The ESA has developed closer cooperation with other institutions, including the Russian Aviation and Space Agency and the Chinese National Space Administration. The ESA now has an office in Moscow and in February 2007 began construction of facilities at its Spaceport in French Guiana to launch Russian Soyuz rockets. The ESA has also entered into a research program called Double Star with the Chinese National Space Administration, marking the first collaborative project between the two agencies. The first satellite of the two-satellite endeavor, the Double Star TC-1, returned to Earth in October 2007 after completing its mission studying the sun's effects on the Earth's environment. Subsequent collaborations began in October 2007 under the Change 1 project to send an unmanned rover to the moon to take the first ever 3-D pictures.

One of the projects in which Moscow has expressed an interest is the planned Galileo global positioning system, which appears to have vast commercial possibilities. Galileo is envisaged as challenging the monopoly of the U.S. military's current navigation and positioning system, even though the latter is made available without charge for civil uses. The ESA, the European Commission, and the European Organization for the Safety of Air Navigation (Eurocontrol) agreed in 1998 to combine efforts in developing such a global navigation satellite system (now known as Global Monitoring for Environment and Security [GMES]). In March 2002 the EU decided to allocate $3.1 billion for the Galileo project, despite questions from some EU members about its financial feasibility. The U.S. military also expressed concerns about the consequences of deployment, including the danger that NATO transmissions might be compromised, but EU-U.S. differences were resolved in February 2004. The first Galileo satellite was launched December 28, 2005, from Baikonur, Kazakhstan.

In December 2002 an enhanced Ariane-5 rocket with increased load capacity veered off course shortly after launch and blew up, a serious setback that precipitated a review of all Arianespace launch procedures and management. The most immediate consequence of the rocket's failure was a decision to postpone launch of the Rosetta probe, which was scheduled for a 2012 comet interception and was subsequently retargeted for a 2014 interception and launched in March 2004.

Five months prior to the rocket incident, in July 2002, the ESA and Eurocontrol had signed a five-year renewable agreement on the use of satellite navigation, telecommunications, and other space technology for purposes of civil aviation. In a similar vein, in December 2003 the ESA and the International Mobile Satellite Organization (Inmarsat) signed an agreement on mobile broadband communications that has as its principal goal facilitating broadband capability virtually worldwide, including for ships at sea and aircraft in flight. A low-cost solution allowing fast Internet access for ships at sea became available in April 2006.

In May 2004, the ESA and the EU implemented a framework cooperation agreement that defined two principal goals: establishing "a common basis and appropriate practical arrangements for efficient and mutually beneficial cooperation," and developing an overall European Space Policy designed to link ESA space capabilities and infrastructure with services and applications desired by the EU, and ensuring the EU's unfettered access to the space services it required. The European Space Policy was unveiled on May 22, 2007. It committed all EU and ESA members to sustainable funding for ESA initiatives, particularly the flagship GMES, which was meant to provide reliable, long-term observation services to the patchwork of national and regional level satellite systems in place. The stated objective of GMES was to monitor and better understand the environment and climate change, although service components also include use for emergency and security purposes for humanitarian aid, maritime surveillance, and border control. In 2008, GMES launched pre-operational services with the goal to be operational in 2011.

The EU and United States moved toward closer cooperation on Galileo and the U.S. military's Global Positioning System (GPS) after signing an agreement in July 2007 to make the two systems interoperable, thereby adding to the precision and coverage of the signals. In May 2008, a Galileo project satellite began transmitting the first common navigational signal for both systems. In September 2008, the Russian system, GLONASS, announced it would strive for interoperability with the two other systems as well.

It became apparent in late 2007 that the Galileo project was severely behind schedule because of cost overruns and bickering among private contractors, who were supposed to help finance the fee-for-service venture. Spain's complaints that it wasn't handed a leading role in the system complicated matters further. Only one satellite had been sent into orbit by early 2008, despite an aim to have 30 satellites launched by 2011. The delays risked Galileo's standing in an increasingly competitive global satellite market, as China and Russia were working to develop their own satellite systems. Amid concerns that the whole project might fail, EU governments in November 2007 agreed to fund the entire $3.6 billion program without private support. A second satellite, which missed a 2006 launch date, finally went into orbit in April 2008.

The ESA inaugurated the European Space Astronomy Centre in Villafranca del Castillo, Spain, in February 2008, which, at its inception, was charged with operating ten astrophysics and solar system missions. Additionally, in April 2008 the EU created an oversight panel, the Galileo Surveillance Authority, thereby giving the European Commission shared authority over the Galileo project with the ESA. EU transport commissioner Jacque Barrot said the system would be fully operational by 2013.

Meanwhile, in July 2009, the European Court of Auditors released a report on Galileo that blamed "inadequate governance" on cost overruns and project delays and recommended that the project's objectives be clarified for strategic and operational purposes. The report also raised concerns that Galileo might never be profitable. The EC was expected in 2010 to present proposals for financing mechanisms beyond 2013. In October 2009, a precursor system to Galileo, the European Geostationary Navigation Overlay Service (EGNOS), was launched using three satellites to provide free positioning over most of the 27 EU nations.

Among other missions, in February 2008 ESA made a successful connection of the Columbus space laboratory, another long delayed project, to the International Space Station. Columbus was designed to support some 500 experiments per year for 10 years, thereby significantly expanding the ESA's contribution to space science. Columbus represents ESA's single largest contribution to the ISS. In June, ESA concluded the 17-year mission of Ulysses, which explored uncharted territory around the Sun's poles.

The orbital telescopes Herschel and Planck were launched in May 2009 on separate missions, with Hershel hosting the largest mirror ever in space.

At a joint meeting in The Hague on November 25–26, 2008, EU ministers and the Council approved a 2009–2013 budget of $12.6 billion for space projects, renewing commitments for the International Space Station, whose future beyond 2014 is uncertain. A new Space Situational Awareness program was funded to protect European space systems against space debris and adverse space weather, while the ExoMars venture was scaled back with the decision to drop the Humboldt weather component. The group also agreed to streamline the agency's decision-making and procurement policies.

ESA has also sought further cooperation agreements with NASA as a way to expand resources and information. In July 2009, NASA and the ESA announced the Mars Exploration Joint Initiative (MEJI) to collaborate on exploration of Mars following delays to separate Mars missions in both agencies (ESA's ExoMars robotic mission was bogged down with design and financing problems). At a bilateral meeting in the UK, it was decided that MEJI would send its first launch in 2016 to return samples from Mars in the 2020s. Additionally, in September ESA and NASA signed a cooperation agreement to exchange technical information and personnel in the development of new space transportation systems. ESA also opened a new facility in Harwell, UK, in July to focus on climate change, robotics, and the domestic applications of space technology.

A number of Eastern European countries have expressed interested in joining ESA. The Czech Republic, formally became a member in June 2008, while Ukraine filed accession papers in June 2009 with the intent of joining as early as 2012.

THE EUROPEAN UNION (EU)

Note: The commissioners delegate for the 2010–2014 term were announced on November 27, 2009, and scheduled to take up the following positions: Joaquín Almunia, Competition and Vice President of the Commission; László Andor, Employment, Social Affairs and Inclusion; Baroness Catherine Ashton, High Representative of the Union for Foreign Affairs and Security and Vice President of the Commission; Michel Barnier, Internal Market and Services; Dacian Ciolos, Agriculture and Rural Development; John Dalli, Health and Consumer Policy; Maria Damanaki, Maritime Affairs and Fisheries; Karel De Gucht, Trade; Štefan Fule, Enlargement and European Neighborhood Policy; Johannes Hahn, Regional Policy; Connie Hedegaard Climate Action; Maire Geoghegan-Quinn, Research and Innovation; Rumiana Jeleva, International Cooperation, Humanitarian Aid and Crisis Response; Siim Kallas, Transport and Vice President of the Commission; Neelie Kroes, Digital Agenda and Vice President of the Commission; Janusz Lewandowski, Budget and Financial Programming; Cecilia Malmström, Home Affairs; Günter Oettinger, Energy; Andris Piebalgs, Development; Janez Potočnik, Environment; Viviane Reding, Justice, Fundamental Rights and Citizenship and Vice President of the Commission; Olli Rehn, Economic and Monetary Affairs; Maroš Šefčovič, Vice President of the Commission for Inter-Institutional Relations and Administration; Algirdas Šemeta, Taxation and Customs Union, Audit and Anti-Fraud; Antonio Tajani, Industry and Entrepreneurship and Vice President of the Commission; Androulla Vassiliou, Education, Culture, Multilingualism and Youth.

Established: European Coal and Steel Community (ECSC) created by treaty signed in Paris, France, April 18, 1951, effective July 24, 1952; European Economic Community (EEC) and European Atomic Energy Community (Euratom) created by Treaties of Rome, signed March 25, 1957, in Rome, Italy, effective January 1, 1958; common institutions of the three European Communities (EC) established by Merger Treaty signed April 8, 1965, in Brussels, Belgium, effective July 1, 1967; European Union (EU) created by Treaty on European Union, initialed by the heads of state and government of the 12 members of the EC on December 11, 1991, in Maastricht, Netherlands, signed by the EC foreign and finance ministers on February 7, 1992, and entered into force November 1, 1993. (The ECSC terminated upon expiry of its founding treaty on July 23, 2002.)

Purpose: To strengthen economic and social cohesion; to establish an economic and monetary union, ultimately including a single currency; to implement a common foreign and security policy; to introduce a citizenship of the European Union; to develop close cooperation on justice and home affairs.

Headquarters: Brussels, Belgium. (Some bodies have headquarters elsewhere.)

Principal Organs: European Council (heads of state or government of all members), Council of the European Union (all members), Commission of the European Communities (referred to in all but legal and formal contexts as the European Commission—27 members), European Parliament (736 elected representatives), Court of Justice of the European Communities (informally, the European Court of Justice—27 judges and 8 advocates general), Court of Auditors (27 members, including its president plus a secretary general), European Central Bank.

Web site: http://europa.eu/index_en.htm

Presidency of the Council of the European Union: Rotates every six months among the member states (Czech Republic, from January 2009; Sweden, from July 1, 2009)

President of the European Council: Herman Van Rompuy (Belgium). (The European Council, which had been established in 1974 as an informal forum for discussions among the heads of state or government of the EU members and had been authorized by the 1992 Masstricht Treaty to provide political guidelines for EU development, became a formal EU institution on December 1, 2009, upon entry into force of the Lisbon Treaty.)

President of the European Commission: José Manuel Durão Barroso (Portugal).

President of the European Parliament: Jerzy Buzek (Poland).

President of the European Court of Justice: Vassilios Skouris (Greece).

President of the Court of Auditors: Vitor Manuel da Silva Caldeira (Portugal).

President of the European Central Bank: Jean-Claude Trichet (France).

Members (27): Austria, Belgium, Bulgaria, Cyprus, Czech Republic, Denmark, Estonia, Finland, France, Germany, Greece, Hungary, Ireland, Italy, Latvia, Lithuania, Luxembourg, Malta, Netherlands, Poland,

Portugal, Romania, Slovakia, Slovenia, Spain, Sweden, United Kingdom.

Official Languages (23): Bulgarian, Czech, Danish, Dutch, English, Estonian, Finnish, French, German, Greek, Hungarian, Irish, Italian, Latvian, Lithuanian, Maltese, Polish, Portuguese, Romanian, Slovak, Slovenian, Spanish, Swedish.

Note: The European Union (EU) is the most recent expansion of a process of European integration that was first formalized by the creation of the European Coal and Steel Community (ECSC) in 1952 and then expanded in 1958 by the launching of the European Economic Community (EEC, also known as the Common Market) and the European Atomic Energy Community (Euratom). Especially after entry into force in 1967 of the Merger Treaty, which established "Common Institutions" for the three European Communities, they were referred to as a singular European Community (EC). On November 1, 1993, the Treaty on European Union (also known as the Maastricht Treaty) added two new "pillars" of cooperation—foreign and security policy, and justice and home affairs—to the original pillar created by establishment of the EEC. At that time "EU" became the familiar designation for all three pillars. The Maastricht Treaty also amended the EEC's founding document to replace the term "European Economic Community" with the more encompassing "European Community," reflecting the first pillar's evolution beyond economic matters.

The ECSC was terminated when its treaty expired July 23, 2002, but the EC (that is, what was originally the EEC) continues to exist (as does Euratom) and in fact remains legally distinct from the EU despite sharing organs. Thus, references to EC activity are still correct (and even required) in some legal and other formal situations, but common practice has favored the use of "EU" as an umbrella, particularly given what EU officials themselves have described as "the difficulties of delineating what is strictly EC or EU business." The Treaty of Lisbon (Reform Treaty) signed in December 2007 would, upon ratification by all 27 EU members, bring the three pillars even closer together, as suggested by a provision that would rename the 1958 founding treaty of the EC as the Treaty on the Functioning of the European Union.

Origin and development. The formation of the European Communities was one of the most significant expressions of the movement toward European unity that grew out of the moral and material devastation of World War II. For many Europeans, the creation of a United States of Europe seemed to offer the best hope of avoiding a repetition of that catastrophe. Other influences included fear of aggression by the Union of Soviet Socialist Republics (USSR) and practical experience in economic cooperation gained by administering Marshall Plan aid through the Organization for European Economic Cooperation (OEEC).

These elements converged in a 1950 proposal by French foreign minister Robert Schuman that envisaged a common market for coal and steel that would, among other things, serve as a lasting guarantee of European peace by forging an organic link between France and Germany. Although the United Kingdom declined to participate in the project, the governments of France, the Federal Republic of Germany, Italy, Belgium, the Netherlands, and Luxembourg agreed to put the Schuman Plan into effect through the ECSC treaty, which they signed April 18, 1951, in Paris, France, and which entered into effect July 24, 1952. The original institutional structure of the ECSC, whose headquarters was established in Luxembourg, included a council of ministers, an executive high authority, a parliamentary assembly, and a court of justice.

The ECSC pioneered the concept of a European common market by abolishing price and transport discrimination and eliminating customs duties; quota restrictions; and other trade barriers on coal, steel, iron ore, and scrap. A common market for coal, iron ore, and scrap was established February 1, 1953; for steel May 1, 1953; and for specialty steels August 1, 1954. Concurrently, steps were taken to harmonize external tariffs on these products. In addition, community-wide industrial policy was facilitated through short- and long-term forecasts of supply and demand, investment guidance and coordination, joint research programs, and regional development assistance. These activities were financed by a direct levy on community coal and steel, the level being fixed by the commission in consultation with the European Parliament.

The next decisive stage in the development of the European Communities was reached with the signature on March 25, 1957, in Rome, Italy, of the Treaties of Rome, which established as separate organizations the EEC and Euratom, effective January 1, 1958. (By convention, "Treaty of Rome," in the singular, references just the EEC; for a detailed discussion of Euratom, see the end of the EU article.) Two types of national linkage to the EEC were detailed: full membership, under which an acceding state agreed to the basic principles of the Treaty of Rome, and associate membership, involving the establishment of agreed reciprocal rights and obligations in regard to such matters as commercial policy.

Although Euratom and the EEC from their inception shared the Assembly and Court of Justice already operating under the ECSC, they initially had separate, albeit similar, councils of ministers and commissions. Subsequently, a treaty establishing a single Council of Ministers (formally renamed as the Council of the European Union in 1993) and commission for all three communities was signed by the (then) six member governments (Belgium, France, Federal Republic of Germany, Italy, Luxembourg, Netherlands) on April 8, 1965, in Brussels, Belgium. However, application of the treaty's provisions was delayed by prolonged disagreement about selecting a president to head the newly merged commission. The choice of Jean Rey of Belgium was ultimately approved, and the new institutions were formally established as of July 1, 1967.

During this period the central issues of the communities—the sharing of authority by member governments and the communities' main administrative organs, and expansion through admission of additional European states—could be most clearly observed in the EEC, whose rapid development included a series of crises in which the French government, with its special concern for national sovereignty and its mistrust of supranational endeavors, frequently opposed the other members.

The crucial issue of national sovereignty versus community authority was initially posed in 1965. Ostensibly to protest EEC failure to reach timely agreement on agricultural policy, the French government instituted a boycott of all three communities that was maintained from July 1, 1965, to January 30, 1966, and was ended through an intergovernmental understanding that tended to restrict the independent authority of the commission to establish and execute community policy.

The membership issue had first been brought to the forefront by the decision of the United Kingdom in July 1961 to apply for admission to the EEC on condition that arrangements could be made to protect the interests of other Commonwealth states, the other members of the European Free Trade Association (EFTA), and British agriculture. Preliminary discussion of the British bid continued through 1962 but was cut short by France in early 1963 on the general ground that the United Kingdom was too close to the United States and not sufficiently European in outlook. A formal UK application for membership in the three communities was submitted in May 1967, with similar bids subsequently being advanced by Ireland, Denmark, and Norway. Action was again blocked by French opposition, despite support for British accession by the commission and the other five member states. Further negotiations for British, Irish, Danish, and Norwegian membership opened in June 1970, and on January 22, 1972, the treaty of accession and accompanying documents, which provided for expansion to a ten-state organization, were signed in Brussels. Accession was approved by referenda in Ireland (May 11) and Denmark (October 2). However, Norwegian voters, insufficiently placated by concessions offered for the benefit of their state's agricultural and fishing interests, rejected accession in a national referendum held September 24–25. In the case of the United Kingdom, legislation permitting entry was approved by parliament and entered into force October 17, the three accessions becoming effective January 1, 1973. (Greenland, after becoming internally independent of Danish rule in 1979, was permitted, on the basis of a 1982 referendum, to terminate its relationship effective February 1, 1985.) In February 1976 the EC foreign ministers stated that, in principle, they endorsed Greece's request for full membership (an agreement of association was approved in 1962), and a treaty of admission was signed May 28, 1979. Accordingly, Greece became the community's tenth member January 1, 1981.

Negotiations concerning Portuguese and Spanish membership began in October 1978 and February 1979, respectively, but were delayed due to apprehension about their ability to accelerate industrial diversification as well as the projected impact of their large agricultural sectors on the EC's Common Agricultural Policy (CAP; see below). Thus, Portugal and Spain were not formally admitted until January 1, 1986.

From the beginning, the EEC assumed the task of creating a community-wide customs union that would abolish all trade restrictions and establish freedom of movement for all goods, services, labor, and capital. A major part of this task was accomplished by July 1, 1968, a year and a half ahead of the schedule laid down in the Treaty of Rome. All customs duties on community internal trade had been gradually removed, and a common external tariff was ready to be applied in stages. At the end of the community's "transition period"—December 31, 1969—workers became legally free to seek employment in any member state, although in practice the freedom had already existed.

The Treaty of Rome provided steps toward a full economic union of the member states by stipulating common rules to ensure fair competition and coordinated policies governing agriculture, transport, and foreign trade. Consequently, CAP, centrally financed from a conjoint fund, was put into effect July 1, 1968. The product of extremely complex negotiations, it involved common marketing policies with free trade throughout the community, common price levels for major products, a uniform policy for external trade in agricultural products (including export subsidies), and a program to increase the efficiency of community farming. CAP became, however, a constant source of controversy, largely because of an inequitable burden of CAP financing and the escalating cost. The problem of finding a compromise package of agricultural and budgetary policy reforms—including budget rebates demanded by the United Kingdom—caused the breakup of both the December 1983 Athens and the March 1984 Brussels meetings of the ministerial council. The main division between members concerned the extent and speed of CAP reforms and the linking of members' contributions to the community budget to their individual wealth and EC benefits. European leaders meeting in June 1984 in Fontainebleau, France, finally reached accord on budgetary policy, which included for Britain a guaranteed rebate of two-thirds its net contribution to the community in future years, with EC revenues being enhanced by an increase from 1 percent to 1.4 percent of the value-added tax received from member states.

Agreement was reached in July 1978 for the establishment of a European currency association to include a joint reserve fund to prevent currency fluctuations between member states and a mechanism by which intracommunity accounts could be settled by use of European Currency Units (ECUs). The resultant European Monetary System (EMS), which included an Exchange Rate Mechanism (ERM) to limit currency fluctuations, came into effect March 13, 1979. In its first decade the ECU became an attractive medium for the issue of bonds by private and public financial institutions, placing it behind only the U.S. dollar and the German deutsch mark in popularity on the international bond market.

In 1985 the European Commission proposed almost three hundred regulations and directives to eliminate fiscal, physical, or technical barriers to trade. Late in the year the European Council approved a number of reforms, most of which were ultimately included in the Single European Act, which amended the Treaty of Rome in ways intended to streamline the decision-making process, open up more areas to EC jurisdiction, and reinvigorate the movement toward European economic and political cooperation. By 1985, tariff barriers to trade among members had been largely eliminated. Thus, it was primarily nontariff barriers that the Single European Act sought to eliminate when it went into effect on July 1, 1987, following ratification by each EC member state. With an overarching goal of establishing a single internal market by the end of 1992, the act's "1992 program" sought to remove most barriers to the free movement of goods, services, people, and capital within the community, resulting in a single market that would be larger, in terms of population and aggregate gross product, than that of the United States. The powers of the European Parliament also were expanded and a permanent secretariat, headquartered in Brussels, was established to assist the presidency of the Council of the European Communities in implementing a framework of European political cooperation.

Even as the community created a single market, EC summits in July and December 1987 broke up without resolution of a spending deficit that exceeded the members' total budgeted contributions of $35 billion by an additional $6 billion. Disagreement continued to center on the controversial CAP subsidies and large-scale storage of surplus food, which accounted for some 70 percent of EC spending. Britain refused to increase its EC contribution until "financial discipline" had been instituted.

In view of the problems involved, an emergency summit in February 1988 in Brussels, Belgium, achieved remarkable results. The participants established a budget ceiling of 1.3 percent of the EC's GNP, set a cap on future growth of agricultural subsidies, approved cuts in the intervention price for surplus farm commodities, and agreed to double aid to the EC's southern members over a five-year period.

With the agricultural and financial crises averted, the EC turned its attention to the single market plan. Subsequent rapid progress in that regard generated a surprisingly intense "Euro-enthusiasm." During an uncharacteristically harmonious June summit in Hannover, West Germany, EC leaders described the momentum toward the "1992 program" as "irreversible," particularly in view of an earlier agreement reached by EC finance ministers on a "crucial" plan to end all restrictions on the flow of capital within the community.

In London, the Margaret Thatcher government continued to serve as a brake on EC momentum, particularly in regard to the monetary union plan proposed in April 1989 by a committee headed by European Commission president Jacques Delors of France. The monetary union proposal, which was distinct from the "1992 program," called for EC members to endorse a three-stage program that would include, among other things, the creation of a regional central bank in the second stage and a common currency in the third stage. Despite strong support from most of the other EC countries, UK resistance necessitated a compromise at the summit held in June in Madrid, Spain. Consensus could be reached only on the first stage of the plan, under which EC members agreed to harmonize certain monetary and economic policies beginning in July 1990. Prime Minister Thatcher agreed to allow preparations to proceed for an EC conference on the much more controversial second and third stages of the plan but, on another matter, she opposed a draft EC charter of fundamental social rights that was supported by the 11 other national leaders, claiming it contained unacceptable "socialist" overtones.

In June 1989 the EC was asked to coordinate Western aid to Poland and Hungary from the Organization for Economic Cooperation and Development (OECD), a program (Poland/Hungary Aid for Restructuring of Economies—PHARE) that was later opened to other Eastern European states. In November, emphasizing the community's expanding political role, a special one-day EC summit in Paris expressed its "responsibility" to support the development of democracy throughout Eastern Europe. At a December summit in Strasbourg, France, EC leaders endorsed German unification provided it included recognition of Europe's postwar borders. In addition, the summit supported the proposed creation of the multibillion-dollar European Bank for Reconstruction and Development (EBRD; see separate article) to assist economic transformation throughout Eastern Europe. In 1991, as a further measure to promote economic and political reform in the countries that emerged from the collapse of the USSR, the EC introduced Technical Assistance to the Commonwealth of Independent States (TACIS), a program that was later expanded to include Mongolia and that subsequently worked closely with the EBRD.

The EC heads of state met for two-day summits in late April and June 1990 in Dublin, Ireland, to further delineate the community's future role in the "new architecture" of Europe. They declared that East Germany would be incorporated into the EC automatically after the creation of a single German state, gave "qualified" support to West German chancellor Helmut Kohl's call for up to $15 billion in economic assistance to the Soviet Union (seen as a means of reducing Soviet objections to unified Germany's membership in the North Atlantic Treaty Organization), and endorsed a sweeping environmental protection statement. In October 1990 the two Germanys formally unified.

During their December 1990 summit in Rome, the EC heads of state and government formally opened two parallel conferences: one to consider wide-ranging proposals for EC political union and the other to oversee negotiations on the more fully developed monetary union plan. Based on consensus proposals from both conferences, the heads of state and government initialed a Treaty on European Union and numerous related protocols and documents at a pivotal summit on December 9–11, 1991, in Maastricht, Netherlands. The Maastricht Treaty called for establishment of a single currency and regional central bank by 1999 and committed the signatories to the pursuit of "ever closer" political union by adding to the EC two new "pillars": common foreign and security policies, and justice and home affairs.

The plans for economic and monetary union were by far the most specific of the treaty's elements. The EU leaders agreed to launch a European Monetary Institute (EMI) on January 1, 1994, directing that the advisory powers of the EMI would eventually be transformed into the formal authority of a European Central Bank (ECB). It was initially envisaged that both the bank and the proposed single currency be operational as early as January 1, 1997, for those countries meeting certain economic criteria and wishing to proceed. However, if that timetable could not be achieved, the single currency was to be established January 1, 1999, and the ECB six months later for qualifying states. A separate "opt-out" protocol gave the United Kingdom the right to make a final decision later on adoption of the single currency, while Germany entered a similar stipulation in ratifying the treaty.

The articles on political union in the Maastricht Treaty were vaguer, although the treaty introduced the concept of EU "citizenship," designed to confer a variety of rights and responsibilities on all nationals of member states. However, in response to growing European concern about turning too much control over to Brussels, draft references to the union's "federal" nature were dropped from the final text of the treaty, which emphasized instead the notion of subsidiarity, under which all decisions would be "taken as closely as possible to the citizens." Regarding the proposed common foreign and security policies, the treaty, in one of its most widely discussed provisions, called for the strengthening of the Western European Union (WEU) to "elaborate and implement" defense decisions.

Included in the protocols affiliated with the treaty was a social policy charter that required all EU states (except the United Kingdom) to guarantee a variety of workers' rights. Those provisions were deleted from the treaty proper at the United Kingdom's insistence, Prime Minister John Major threatening to repudiate the accord otherwise. Negotiations were also required with Greece, Ireland, Portugal, and Spain to ensure their endorsement of the treaty through promises of a substantial expansion of development aid to the so-called poor four.

The EC foreign and finance ministers formally signed the Maastricht Treaty on February 7, 1992, the expectation being that it would proceed smoothly through the required national ratification process in time for its scheduled January 1, 1993, implementation. However, the optimism proved unjustified as Danish voters rejected the treaty by a narrow margin in its first electoral test June 2. Following a strong "yes" majority in the Irish referendum June 18, the treaty was approved without substantial opposition by Greece's and Luxembourg's parliaments in July; however, its future was once again clouded by the September 20 French referendum, which endorsed ratification by only 51 percent. The community was also severely shaken in September by a currency crisis that prompted the United Kingdom and Italy to drop out of the ERM.

Facing an apparent crisis of confidence, the EC leaders convened an emergency summit October 16, 1992, in Birmingham, England, to express their continued support for the Maastricht Treaty while reassuring opponents that some of its more ambitious goals were reduced in scope. Parliamentary approval of the treaty was subsequently achieved by the end of the year in Belgium, Italy, Germany, Netherlands, Portugal, and Spain. Germany's formal ratification was delayed pending the outcome of a constitutional challenge. In addition, the prospect for a reversal of the Danish position improved when the December 1992 EC summit in Edinburgh, Scotland, agreed to extend Denmark several "opt-out" concessions, most importantly regarding the monetary union plan. The EC leaders also agreed to postpone consideration of controversial proposals regarding the free movement of people within the community. Nevertheless, by the target date of January 1, 1993, it was estimated that approximately 80 percent of the provisions of the "1992 program" for establishing a single internal market had been implemented by the member states.

Danish voters accepted the Maastricht accord in a second referendum on May 18, 1993. With the treaty awaiting only UK ratification, the June 1993 EC summit focused on the community's economic woes, which were contributing as much as any of the other problems to a growing "Euro-pessimism." In particular, the summit proposed measures designed to reduce unemployment, which was above 10 percent in the community. Although French president Mitterrand attempted to portray the session as marking a "psychological recovery" for the EC, the community shortly thereafter experienced another currency crisis. Faced with a possible total breakdown of the ERM, the EC agreed in early August to let the franc and the six other non-German currencies still in the system float more freely against the mark.

UK ratification, albeit by a very narrow margin, occurred in July 1993, and a favorable ruling in the German court case in early October finally cleared the way for implementation of the treaty. The EC heads of state and government held a special summit October 29 in Brussels to celebrate the completion of the ratification process, and the EU was launched when the treaty officially went into force November 1.

The first EU summit was held December 11–12, 1993, in Brussels. The EU heads of state and government turned to the region's economic problems, particularly that of continued high unemployment. The summit adopted an economic recovery plan that appeared to represent a compromise between those advocating activist labor policies and those convinced that government influence was already too great in economic affairs. For the first camp, the summit approved a six-year public works program designed to create jobs in, among other areas, the transportation, energy, environmental, and telecommunications sectors. For those looking to the free market to resolve unemployment, the summit called for a reduction in "rigidities" in the European labor market, proposing that minimum wages be lowered and that labor costs supporting European social welfare programs be significantly reduced.

In other activity, the European Council endorsed negotiations toward a "stability pact" for Central and Eastern European nations seeking EU membership. The pact would attempt to establish agreement on the protection of minority rights in those countries and create mechanisms for the peaceful resolution of border disputes. Among other things, it was hoped that such an initiative would preclude a repetition of the breakdown that had occurred in the former Yugoslavia, the EU having been criticized for its seeming paralysis in dealing with that situation.

The European Council once again emphasized economic affairs during its June 24–25, 1994, summit in Corfu, Greece, one formal highlight of which was the signing of the Partnership and Cooperation Agreement with Russia. Nevertheless, media reports centered on the union's latest political difficulty—the failure of the council to agree on a successor to commission president Delors, who announced his retirement effective January 1, 1995. After the United Kingdom rejected the nomination of Belgian prime minister Jean-Luc Dehaene, who it deemed as too "federalist," a special summit was convened on July 15 in Brussels to approve a compromise nominee—Jacques Santer, the prime minister of Luxembourg. Nominees to the new commission subsequently faced intense confirmation hearings in the parliament, reflecting divisions between those in favor of rapid integration and an increasingly vocal group of "Euro-skeptics."

As members of the EFTA participating in the European Economic Area (EEA) with the EU, Austria, Finland, Norway, and Sweden had been formally invited in the spring of 1994 to join the EU at the beginning of 1995. Austria's membership was endorsed by a 66 percent "yes" vote June 12, 1994, while a positive vote also was obtained in the Finnish referendum October 16 and in Swedish balloting November 13. In contrast, Norway voted decisively against EU accession in its referendum during November 27–28. Switzerland's membership remained on file after Swiss voters rejected EEA membership in a 1992 referendum. More recently, in May 2001, Swiss voters decisively rejected applying for EU membership, although the country had entered into various economic agreements with the EU.

The focus of the December 9–10, 1994, summit in Essen, Germany, was on enlargement, with the heads of state of Austria, Finland, and Sweden participating in preparation for the accession of those countries January 1, 1995. The leaders of Bulgaria, Czech Republic, Hungary, Poland, Slovakia, and Romania also attended the summit to discuss in greater detail the criteria for eventual admission. However, despite the obvious external fervor for the EU, enthusiasm within the union subsequently appeared to wane, particularly in regard to the common currency proposal. Turbulence in the financial markets contributed to an acknowledgment by the European Council, which met June 26–27, in Cannes, France, that the proposed single currency would not be launched in 1997. The summit held December 15–16, 1995, in Madrid reaffirmed the EU's commitment to a 1999 final target date, although it was emphasized that the required economic standards would not be diluted for participation in the monetary union. The EU leaders also agreed that the new currency would be called the euro.

The December 1995 summit also gave formal approval for creation of an intergovernmental conference (IGC) that was authorized to propose revisions to the EC/EU founding treaties. Issues to be addressed included the possible elimination of the unanimity requirement for decisions involving the EU's two new pillars—foreign and security policy, and justice and home affairs. Potentially extensive structural changes were also to be considered in the hope that such bodies as the commission and the parliament could become less unwieldy, particularly given the anticipated admission of new members to the union. In addition, ardent integrationists hoped institutional reforms would convince a still largely skeptical European population that the EU was prepared to deal effectively with basic day-to-day concerns such as unemployment, environmental degradation, and internal security.

Although the IGC was launched in March 1996, little progress was apparent by the time of the June 21–22 summit in Florence, Italy. EU leaders reportedly hoped to provide a boost for the initiative at the summit, but the session was instead dominated by the conflict between the United Kingdom and its EU partners over the EU's March ban on exports of UK beef and beef products following the outbreak of bovine spongiform encephalopathy (BSE, the so-called mad-cow disease) in UK herds. A compromise was quickly reached. Much more problematic, however, was the strong UK response to the ban, the government of John Major having instituted a policy of "noncooperation" in May under which the UK veto was briefly used to block all EU action requiring unanimity.

Continued differences of opinion were still apparent at the summit regarding the social dimension of the EU, as Santer failed to gain approval of his proposed "confidence pact." The pact had called for unspent EU resources to be devoted to some 14 infrastructure projects in connection with an agreement among EU governments, unions, and employers to reduce employee benefits and otherwise make European labor markets more globally competitive.

Attention subsequently focused on negotiations regarding monetary union, German leaders indicating that the entire concept was in jeopardy unless other nations were willing to accept enforceable budgetary discipline as a means of keeping the euro "strong." Bonn's proposed "stability and growth pact" on the matter reportedly met with strong French resistance prior to the EU summit held December 13–14, 1996, in Dublin. However, a compromise favoring the German position was negotiated whereby participants in the monetary union would be subject to mandatory heavy financial penalties for breaching fiscal guidelines. (One goal of the accord was to prevent countries from attempting to "spend their way out" of future recessions by running up large budget deficits that would weaken the euro.) Agreement also was reached on the creation of a new exchange rate mechanism to determine the relationship of the euro to the currencies of the countries that postponed entry into the monetary union. In addition, the summit endorsed the Dublin Document on Employment, underscoring the continued problem of joblessness, which had somewhat deflated support for further integration among those concerned by how monetary union and devolution of trade authority to Brussels might disrupt local jobs.

Dissension continued within the EU ranks in early 1997 concerning the final IGC proposals on the extent of authority to be turned over by the national governments to EU control. Some members called for the elimination of the national veto completely, endorsing qualified majority voting (QMV—see the Structure section, below) in all areas and substantial restrictions on "selective cooperation," which permitted frequent "opt-out" decisions by national governments opposed to, or uncertain about, major EU plans. The Netherlands offered a compromise under which some 25 policy areas would be covered by majority voting while the national veto would be reserved for "sensitive" issues such as EU enlargement, direct taxation, and future treaty amendments. However, the UK government labeled the proposal "totally unacceptable."

A special heads of government summit May 23, 1997, in Noordwijk, Netherlands, was buoyed by the presence of the new UK prime minister, Tony Blair, whose Labour government was decidedly more enthusiastic regarding the EU than its Conservative Party predecessor. A meeting of the European Council on June 16–17, in Amsterdam, Netherlands, endorsed wide-ranging amendment of the various EC and EU treaties in the interest of broadening the purview of the EU and speeding up the decision-making process. Among other things, the proposed Amsterdam Treaty provided for formal inclusion in the EC/EU treaty structure of (1) the Social Charter (previously relegated to protocol status); (2) a new employment chapter; (3) the Schengen Accord regarding free movement of people and goods across internal EU borders (see article on Benelux Economic Union for further details); and (4) the stability and growth pact, designed to enforce budgetary discipline on those countries joining the Economic and Monetary Union (EMU). The treaty also removed several policy areas from national control in favor of "common" EU authority, while some additional areas already governed by the EU were moved into the category of requiring approval by QMV rather than unanimous national consent. Agreement also was reached, in principle, on giving the European Parliament additional authority and on limiting the size of the commission following expansion of EU membership.

Despite the perceived weakness of the Amsterdam Treaty, its completion did permit the EU to turn to its two other pressing issues: enlargement and monetary union. Regarding the former, a December 12–13 summit in Luxembourg invited five ex-communist states—Czech Republic, Estonia, Hungary, Poland, and Slovenia—and Cyprus to begin formal membership discussions in March 1998. The inclusion of Cyprus among the "first-wave" countries was controversial, particularly because Turkey was pointedly excluded. EU officials said they hoped that both the Cypriot and Turkish communities on Cyprus would participate in the membership negotiations, although the government of the Turkish Republic of Northern Cyprus declined the invitation.

Ireland approved the Amsterdam Treaty via national referendum in late May 1998, and Danish voters followed suit shortly thereafter with a 55 percent endorsement. The latter was considered an important test in light of the problems caused in 1993 by the initial Danish rejection of the Maastricht Treaty.

On March 26, 1998, Germany had officially endorsed the January 1999 EMU launching, despite the German Bundesbank's having questioned the "sustainability" of the financial status of several countries, with Belgium and Italy drawing particular attention because of their high level of official debt. In April the European Parliament called for treaty revisions to ensure the "accountability" of the incoming ECB, suggesting that a monitoring body (including several parliament members) be established to review ECB decisions and activity. An EU summit May 1–3 in Brussels formally agreed that the ECB would open June 1 and would assume responsibility at the start of 1999 for monitoring policy (including setting interest rates) for the countries adopting the euro.

Thus the currencies of the 11 participating countries—Austria, Belgium, Finland, France, Germany, Ireland, Italy, Luxembourg, Netherlands, Portugal, and Spain—were permanently linked with the initiation of the EMU on January 1, 1999, at which time the participants also began issuing debt in euros. The formal launch was marked by great fanfare, with supporters describing it as representing the "biggest leap forward" since the Treaty of Rome. Two years later, Greece, which had initially failed to qualify on the basis of economic performance, became the 12th EMU member. On January 1, 2002, euro banknotes and coins for public use were introduced in the 12 EMU members—plus Andorra, Monaco, Montenegro, San Marino, and the Vatican—and commercial use of old national currencies was discontinued by the end of February 2002. In 2003, Swedish voters rejected adoption of the euro. On January 1, 2007, Slovenia became the 13th EMU member. In 2007 the European Council noted that Cyprus and Malta had fulfilled the convergence criteria and legal requirements to adopt the euro and could do so on January 1, 2008. The eurozone broadened to 16 states with Slovakia's adoption of the euro on January 1, 2009.

Meanwhile, one of the EU's most serious crises to date had begun to develop over allegations of fraud and corruption in EU budgetary matters. In November 1998 the EU Court of Auditors had reported uncovering serious "mismanagement," and commission president Santer created an internal antifraud unit. In mid-January 1999 the European Parliament appeared poised to approve a censure motion that would have forced the resignation of the European Commission. The motion was ultimately defeated (293–232), but only after a "peace package" was negotiated under which the commission agreed to the establishment of an independent panel of experts to assess the situation. In March the panel reported that substantial fraud, mismanagement, and nepotism had "gone unnoticed" by the commissioners, many of whom had "lost control" over spending within their areas of responsibility. Consequently, the commission resigned en masse on March 16, and EU leaders convened in a special summit March 24–26 in Berlin to designate Romano Prodi, former prime minister of Italy, as the next president of the commission. Shortly after the summit, the French legislature ratified the Amsterdam Treaty, paving the way for its entry into force on May 1.

The elections to the European Parliament, held between June 10 and 13, 1999, in the differing venues, were notable in that they led to formation of a 233-seat, center-right bloc by the European People's Party and the European Democrats (EPP-ED), thereby unseating the Party of European Socialists (180 seats) as the plurality grouping. On September 15 the legislature confirmed Prodi as the head of a new European Commission scheduled to serve out the remainder of its predecessor's term and to start a new five-year term beginning in January 2000.

A special two-day session of the heads of government held October 15–16, 1999, in Tampere, Finland, focused on matters related to the EU's third pillar, justice and home affairs, including immigration, asylum, and organized crime. The summit also marked a change in strategy regarding enlargement, with leaders agreeing that negotiations on accession should be opened with six additional prospective members—Bulgaria, Latvia, Lithuania, Malta, Romania, and Slovakia—early in the new year. (Formal talks began February 15, 2000, in Brussels.) The decision received the assent of the European Council during its summit December 10–11 in Helsinki, putting the six countries on the same footing as the six that were regarded as "fast-track" entries: Cyprus, Czech Republic, Estonia, Hungary, Poland, and Slovenia. The council also formally approved Turkey as a candidate for admission, despite reservations regarding its human rights record.

During the same period the EU was moving steadily toward establishing its own military capability. On June 3–4, 1999, a European Council meeting in Cologne, Germany, selected (then) NATO secretary general Javier Solana Madariaga of Spain as the first EU high representative for foreign and security policy, a position authorized by the Treaty of Amsterdam, which also provided for the use of combat forces for "crisis management." Collaterally, the heads of state and government agreed to begin formalizing a much-debated joint security and defense policy, under which the EU would assume the WEU's defense role and its "Petersberg tasks" (named for the official German guesthouse near Bonn where, in 1992, the WEU defined its future military responsibilities): peacekeeping, humanitarian and rescue missions, and military crisis management.

An unprecedented joint meeting of EU foreign and defense ministers November 15, 1999, in Brussels confirmed Solana's WEU appointment and, drawing on the experiences of the conflicts in Bosnia and Kosovo, discussed how to handle future altercations. A central component of the EU strategy was formation of an EU rapid reaction force (RRF) that would be independent of NATO and the United States. A month later, at the Helsinki summit, the European Council authorized formation by 2003 of a 60,000-member RRF that could respond to crises that did not involve NATO as a whole. As the plan continued to evolve over the following year, the EU agreed to work closely with NATO, thereby mitigating U.S. objections. It also agreed to invite the participation in EU-led missions of non-EU states that were NATO members—most particularly, Turkey—as well as non-NATO European countries, such as Russia. Formation of the RRF was given a further go-ahead by the foreign and defense ministers' meeting November 20, 2000, in Brussels, although Denmark exercised its right to opt out. The ministers also agreed to assume the WEU's operational role. Earlier in the year, in April, the WEU/EU Eurocorps, which was inaugurated in November 1993, undertook its most significant mission to date, namely command of the NATO-led Kosovo Force (KFOR) in Yugoslavia.

During 2000 several important developments occurred in the economic sphere. A special heads of government summit March 23–24 in Lisbon introduced a ten-year program, dubbed the Lisbon Strategy, to develop the EU into "the world's most competitive and dynamic knowledge-driven economy," with attendant goals that included improving the employment rate from 61 percent to 70 percent and achieving an average annual growth rate of 3 percent. One of the core elements of the strategy was the creation of a European Research Area (ERA). In the ERA, researchers, technology, and knowledge would circulate as freely as possible—presumably without jeopardizing the EU's strong intellectual property protections. Research initiatives would also be implemented and funded at the European level.

Interim reports, the most recent a May 2007 "green paper," indicated that the EU was falling short of its ambitious goals of research integration. The slow pace of developing new pharmaceuticals, of which only a handful were commercialized in the EU in 2007, was a particular concern. Additionally, while the Lisbon goal was to match innovation in the United States by 2010, rising economic powers such as China and India were also becoming increasingly competitive. As a result, the "Ljubljana Process" was launched at a ministerial meeting on April 14–15, 2008, in Ljubljana, Slovenia, that set five new initiatives to be achieved by 2020 in the following areas: improving mobility of researchers, a legal framework to aid the development of pan-European research infrastructures, management of intellectual property rights, joint programming for research programs across the EU, and a common policy for international science and technology cooperation. Additionally, a consensus between member states on a new framework for governance of the ERA was commissioned for presentation by the end of 2009.

In July 2000 the EU finance ministers named a committee headed by former EMI president Alexandre Lamfalussy to examine the operation of EU securities markets and to propose changes in current practices and regulations. In September the Paris, Brussels, and Amsterdam stock exchanges merged as Euronext, and in 2002 Euronext acquired the London-based derivatives market LIFFE and merged with the Portuguese exchange. Already second only to London in terms of listings and market capitalization, Euronext anticipated becoming "the first fully integrated cross-border European market for equities, bonds, derivatives, and commodities." In April 2007, the New York Stock Exchange acquired Euronext and the merger of the two created the world's largest stock exchange.

In December 2000 the EU's comprehensive review of institutional reform, which included a special summit October 12–15 in Biarritz, France, drew to a close. Meeting on December 7–11, 2000, in Nice, the European Council agreed to significant restructuring of EU institutions, primarily to accommodate 12 new member countries. (The 13th potential member, Turkey, was excluded from the calculations, given that it had not yet begun formal accession negotiations.) Requiring ratification by the European Parliament and all 15 current member countries, the resultant Treaty of Nice bowed to German insistence that the expanded European Parliament and the QMV system give greater weight to the populations of the member states.

The Treaty of Nice, which was signed by the members' foreign ministers February 26, 2001, in Brussels, hit its first roadblock June 8 when some 54 percent of Ireland's voters rebuffed it. EU leaders insisted, however, that expansion plans would proceed and that efforts would be made to address the Irish public's concerns. These included the impact of expansion on Ireland's standing and the status of its military neutrality in the context of the EU's new military capabilities. Ultimately, the Irish voters were satisfied, and in an October 20, 2002, referendum, 62.9 percent endorsed the Treaty of Nice, permitting its entry into force February 1, 2003.

Meanwhile, the ECSC's founding treaty had expired on July 23, 2002, resulting in the closure of the European Coal and Steel Community. Perhaps its most significant accomplishment, apart from serving as a model for creation of the EEC, was a decades-long, painful reduction of overcapacity in the community's steel industry. The process introduced production quotas, banned state subsidies, closed obsolete facilities and modernized others, restructured the market, and expanded retraining funds and other support for former steelworkers. By 1999 the steel workforce had declined to 280,000 (from 870,000 in 1975), and some 63 million tons of capacity had been eliminated since 1980. In July 2002 all ECSC assets and liabilities were transferred to the EU. In the interim, ECSC net assets, which were valued at some $1.6 billion at that time, were to be managed by the European Commission and then, after completion of the community's liquidation, to be designated as Assets of the Research Fund for Coal and Steel. Matters related to the coal and steel industries are now addressed within the EU framework.

At a summit held December 12–13, 2002, in Copenhagen, Denmark, the EU formally approved the admission of ten new members: Czech Republic, Cyprus (excluding the Turkish Republic of Northern Cyprus), Estonia, Hungary, Latvia, Lithuania, Malta, Poland, Slovakia, and Slovenia. Accession treaties were signed at an informal European Council session on April, 16, 2003, with formal admission, following the necessary ratifications, then occurring on May 1, 2004. Macedonia was accepted as a candidate country in November 2005. Bulgaria and Romania, which signed accession treaties on April 25, 2005, were admitted on January 1, 2007. Formal membership negotiations with Croatia and Turkey began in October 2005, but Turkey's accession—a subject of continuing controversy within the EU—was not expected until the next decade.

The EU has relationships with special territories associated with its member states that vary based on their level and type of participation in EU policy areas and programs, spelled out in the European Community Treaty of 2002. Among them are the Spanish Canary Islands, which remain outside the European Value-Added Tax (VAT) areas but submit to EU policy in all other respects. The French islands of Guadeloupe and Martinique in the Caribbean, French Guiana on the northern coast of South America, and Reunion in the Indian Ocean are outside the Schengen and VAT areas, but carry the euro as legal tender and are part of the EU Customs Union.

The Overseas Countries and Territories (OTCs) are a grouping of 20 territories linked to Denmark, France, the Netherlands, and the United Kingdom whose nationals are in principle EU citizens, although they are not directly subject to EU law but rather benefit from association agreements, most of which pertain to trade. Bermuda is listed in the European Community Treaty, but the arrangements for association are not applied to it because of the wishes of the government. Development assistance from the EU for the OTCs amounts to $429 million in 2008–2013. In March 2009 the Indian Ocean island of Mayotte voted to become part of France, thereby reversing its status as an overseas collectivity and effectively joining the EU.

The Lisbon Treaty came into effect with new positions being filled from December 1, 2009. It amends existing EU and EC treaties, with the EC's 1958 founding treaty being renamed the Treaty on the Functioning of the European Union. Many of the new treaty's institutional reforms echo those originally proposed in the failed constitution: the president of the European Council is to be elected for a once-renewable term of two and a half years; the European Parliament will comprise a maximum of 750 seats, with no more than 96 and no fewer than 6 per country; the number of commissioners in the European Commission will be reduced, beginning in November 2014, to two-thirds the number of member states, filled by rotation; and, in the Council of the European Union a "double majority voting" (or DMV) system (55 percent of the members, representing at least 65 percent of the EU population) will apply to most policy areas, also beginning in 2014. In addition, the selection of a commission president will be linked to the results of parliamentary elections, and a new high representative for the union in foreign affairs and security policy will be named, with the officeholder also serving as commission vice president. For the first time, specific provisions have been included for the withdrawal of a member state from the union.

The Reform Treaty also stipulates that legal force be given to the Charter of Fundamental Rights, which was formally signed on December 12, 2007, by the presidents of the European Council, the European Commission, and the European Parliament. However, the charter is addressed to EU institutions, bodies, and agencies, not to national governments, legislatures, or courts when they enact, implement, or interpret national laws. Furthermore, specific provision was included limiting the justiciability of certain rights with regard to Poland and the United Kingdom, "except in so far as Poland or the United Kingdom has provided for such rights in its national law."

The treaty, if ratified, would give the European Parliament greater influence over legislation, the budget, and international agreements, thereby placing it on a more equal footing with the Council of the European Union. At the same time, under the principle of subsidiarity, national parliaments would be better able to monitor the union's institutions to ensure that they act only when the policy goals are best attained at the union level. In the realm of policy, the new treaty could enhance the union's ability to act in a number of key areas, including security and justice, energy, climate change, globalization, public health, research, space, and humanitarian assistance. The treaty also includes a provision for citizens' initiatives, whereby a proposal having the support of at least 1 million citizens from a number of states can be presented to the European Commission for discussion.

Irish approval of the Lisbon Treaty in an October 2, 2009, referendum removed a major barrier to its implementation, although at the time of passage Poland and the Czech Republic had still not officially signed the deal. The president of the Czech Republic, Václav Klaus, ratified the treaty on November 23 following the resolution of legal questions surrounding its compatibility with the Czech constitution. Poland's president, Lech Kaczyński, had signed the treaty on October 10.

Polish and Czech ratification allowed for implementation of the treaty, which began with the appointment of the Belgian prime minister, Herman Van Rompuy, as the permanent president of the European Council, for a term of two and a half years, and with the selection of Catherine Ashton, of the UK Labour Party, as the High Representative for Foreign Affairs.

Structure. The Treaty on European Union established two new pillars—a common foreign and security policy (CFSP), and justice and home affairs (JHA)—while also amending, but not superseding, EC treaties. Accordingly, the EC continues as the EU's first pillar—the "community domain" of common policies and laws decided by the "community method," involving the European Commission and two legislative organs, the Council of the European Union and the European Parliament. In reaching decisions involving the community domain, the Council of the European Union usually uses a qualified majority voting (QMV) system (see below). In contrast, decisions involving the second and third pillars are usually made by unanimous vote of the Council of the European Union, although the Treaty of Amsterdam provided for use of QMV in some areas not involving the military or defense. The Treaty of Amsterdam also renamed the JHA pillar as the Police and Judicial Cooperation in Criminal Matters (PJCC) and transferred some of that pillar's original tasks to the EC.

The EU founding treaty authorized the European Council (comprising the heads of state or government of the member states) to "provide the Union with the necessary impetus for its development" and to "define the general political guidelines" for the grouping. The council typically meets four times a year, chaired by the head of state or government of the member state holding its presidency. The remaining institutional framework of the EU has the same basic components as those originally allotted to the individual communities: the Council of the European Union (originally called the Council of Ministers) to provide overall direction and to legislate, the representative European Parliament with colegislative responsibilities, the executive and administrative European Commission charged with the initiation and implementation of EU policies, and the Court of Justice to adjudicate legal issues. A Court of Auditors was added in 1977.

Depending on the subject under discussion, EU states can be represented on the Council of the European Union by their foreign ministers, as is usually the case for major decisions, or by other ministers. As a result of the Luxembourg compromise in 1966, the principle of unanimity is retained for issues in which a member feels it has a "vital interest." However, changes approved in 1987 reduced the number of areas subject to such veto, the use of QMV in the council being increased to speed up integration efforts. The distribution of votes is as follows: France, Germany, Italy, and the United Kingdom, 29 each; Poland and Spain, 27 each; Romania, 14; Netherlands, 13; Belgium, Czech Republic, Greece, Hungary, and Portugal, 12 each; Austria, Bulgaria, and Sweden, 10 each; Denmark, Finland, Ireland, Lithuania, and Slovakia, 7 each; Cyprus, Estonia, Latvia, Luxembourg, and Slovenia, 4 each; and Malta, 3. Under QMV, passage of a proposal typically requires 255 of the 345 votes (73.9 percent), representing a majority of the member states. If challenged, however, those in the majority must demonstrate that they collectively represent at least 62 percent of the total EU population.

The Maastricht Treaty altered the required makeup of the European Commission and the method of its selection, eliminating country representation, per se, and stipulating only that the commission must include at least one and no more than two individuals from each EU state. However, the 20-member commission that took office in January 1995 preserved the established distribution of two members from each of the "big five" (France, Germany, Italy, Spain, and the United Kingdom) and one each from the smaller states. In November 2004, the commission was expanded to 25 members, one from each state, after a six-month period in which interim commissioners from the ten new states worked alongside those who were serving out their five-year terms. In a complicated selection process, the member states first nominate a commission president and then, in consultation with that person, nominate the full commission. The president and the rest of the commission are subject to confirmation (or possible rejection) by the European Parliament and final appointment "by common accord" of the member states. In general, the commission mediates among the member governments in community matters, exercises a broad range of executive powers, and initiates community action. Its members are completely independent and are forbidden by treaty to accept instructions from any national government. Decisions are made by majority vote, although in practice most are adopted by consensus.

In 2007 the commission was expanded to 27, one commission member from each of the member states. Below is a list of its members and the principal subject or subjects of their portfolios. The commissioners' terms expired in 2009 with appointments scheduled to be made following the October referendum in Ireland on the Lisbon Treaty (*see headnote*).

José Manuel Barroso (Portugal)	President
Jacques Barrot (France)	Vice President; justice, freedom, and security
Siim Kallas (Estonia)	Vice President; administrative affairs, audit, and antifraud
Antonio Tajani (Italy)	Vice President; transport
Günter Verheugen (Germany)	Vice President; enterprise and industry
Margot Wallström [f] (Sweden)	Vice President; institutional relations and communication strategy
Joaquín Almunia (Spain)	Economic and monetary affairs
Catherine Ashton [f] (United Kingdom)	Trade
Joe Borg (Malta)	Fisheries and maritime affairs
Karel De Gucht (Belgium)	Development and humanitarian aid
Stavros Dimas (Greece)	Environment

Benita Ferrero-Waldner [f] (Austria)	External relations and European Neighborhood Policy
Mariann Fischer Boel [f] (Denmark)	Agriculture and rural development
László Kovács (Hungary)	Taxation and customs union
Neelie Kroes [f] (Netherlands)	Competition
Meglena Kuneva [f] (Bulgaria)	Consumer protection
Charlie McCreevy (Ireland)	Internal market and services
Leonard Orban (Romania)	Multilingualism
Andris Piebalgs (Latvia)	Energy
Pawet Samecki (Poland)	Regional policy
Maroš Šefčovič (Slovakia)	Education, training, culture, and youth
Algirdas Ŝemeta (Lithuania)	Financial programming and budget
Vladimir Špidla (Czech Republic)	Employment, social affairs, and equal opportunities
Janez Potočnik (Slovenia)	Science and research
Viviane Reding [f] (Luxembourg)	Information society and media
Olli Rehn (Finland)	Enlargement of the EU
Androulla Vassiliou [f] (Cyprus)	Health

[f] = female

The European Parliament is an outgrowth of the consultative parliamentary assembly established for the ECSC and subsequently mandated to serve in the same capacity for the EEC and Euratom. The parliament's authority has gradually increased over its history, but as of 2007 remained quite limited relative to other EU organs. Many initiatives that would emanate from a national parliament instead emanate, in the case of the EU, from the European Commission and its professionals in the commission's directorates general in Brussels.

Under a 1975 treaty the parliament was empowered to participate in formulation of the annual EC budget and even reject it by a two-thirds vote—save for deference to the Council of Ministers regarding agricultural spending, the largest item in the community's budget. The Single European Act, the Treaty on European Union, and the Treaty of Amsterdam further extended parliament's budgetary powers and legislative purview. In addition, the parliament, previously only authorized to dismiss the entire commission (but not individual members) by a vote of censure, can now reject nominees for individual posts. The parliament, which meets annually (normally in Strasbourg, France) and has a five-year term, must also approve EU treaties, as well as the admission of new EU members. (The proposed Reform Treaty [see Recent activities, below] would further increase the parliament's powers.)

The move to direct elections in all member states in 1979 was followed by the Maastricht Treaty's direction that the parliament should draw up plans for future elections to take place under uniform voting procedures and constituency arrangements. Some progress was made in this regard for the 1994 elections, notably in that for the first time all EU citizens could vote in their EU country of residence.

Under the Treaty of Nice, as amended after the accession treaties with Bulgaria and Romania, the number of members of parliament reduced from 785 to 736 for the 2009–2014 parliamentary term.

Additionally, following the most recent parliamentary election in 2009, all political groups in the European Parliament must include members from at least seven member states with a minimum of 25 members. The statute of members, which was adopted in 2005, entered into force on the first day of the new term on July 14, 2009, and made the terms of conditions of a member's work more transparent and introduced a common salary for all members.

The most recent election was held June 4–7, 2009, and membership was allocated as follows: Austria, 17; Belgium, 22; Bulgaria, 17; Cyprus, 6; Czech Republic, 22; Denmark, 13; Estonia, 6; Finland, 13; France, 72; Germany, 99; Greece, 22; Hungary, 22; Ireland, 12; Italy, 72; Latvia, 8; Lithuania, 12; Luxembourg, 6; Malta, 5; Netherlands, 25; Poland, 50; Portugal, 22; Romania, 33; Slovakia, 13; Slovenia, 7; Spain, 50; Sweden, 18; United Kingdom, 72. Members sit not by nationality, but by political affiliation. As of July 2009, the makeup of the political groups was as follows:

European People's Party (EPP), 265

Austria	Austrian People's Party (ÖVP), 6
Belgium	Christian Democratic and Flemish (CD&V), 3
	Christian Social Party–*Europäische Volkspartei* (CSP-EVP), 1
	Democratic Humanist Center (CDH), 1
Bulgaria	Citizens for European Development of Bulgaria (GERB), 5
	Blue Coalition (SDS-DSB), 1
Cyprus	Democratic Rally (Disy), 2
Czech Republic	Christian and Democratic Union–Czech People's Party (KDU-ČSL), 2
Denmark	Conservative People's Party (C), 1
Estonia	Fatherland Union (IRL), 1
Finland	National Coalition Party (Kok), 3
	Christian Democrats-True Finn (KD-PS), 1
France	Union for a Popular Movement (UMP), 29
Germany	Christian Democratic Union (CDU), 34
	Christian Social Union (CSU), 8
Greece	New Democracy (ND), 8
Hungary	Federation of Young Democrats–Christian Democratic People's Party (FiDeSz-KDNP), 14
Ireland	*Fine Gael*, 4
Italy	People of Freedom (PdL), 29
	Union of Christian and Center Democrats (UDC), 5
	South Tyrol People's Party (SVP), 1
Latvia	Civil Union (PS), 2
	New Era (JL), 1
Lithuania	Homeland Union- Christian Democrats (TS-LKDP), 4
Luxembourg	Christian Social People's Party (CSV), 3
Malta	Nationalist Party (PN), 2
Netherlands	Christian Democratic Appeal (CDA), 5
Poland	Civic Platform (PO), 25
	Polish People's Party (PSL), 3
Portugal	Social Democratic Party (PSD), 8
	Popular Party (PP), 2
Romania	Democratic Liberal Party (DLP), 10
	Elena Băsescu (ind. candidate), 1
	Hungarian Democratic Union (UDMR), 3
Slovakia	Slovak Democratic and Christian Union (SDKÚ-DS), 2
	Christian Democratic Movement (KDH), 2
	Party of the Hungarian Coalition (SMK), 2
Slovenia	Slovenian Democratic Party (SDS), 2
	New Slovenia–Christian People's Party (NSi), 1
Spain	Popular Party (PP), 23
Sweden	Moderate Coalition Party (MSP), 4
	Christian Democratic Party (KD), 1

Progressive Alliance of Socialists and Democrats (S&D), 184

Austria	Austrian Social Democratic Party (SPÖ), 4
Belgium	Socialist Party (PS), 3
	Socialist Party–Differently (SP.A), 2
Bulgaria	Coalition for Bulgaria (BSP), 4
Czech Republic	Czech Social Democratic Party (ČSSD), 7
Denmark	Social Democratic Party (A), 4
Estonia	Social Democratic Party (SDE), 1
Finland	Finnish Social Democratic Party (SSDP), 2
France	Socialist Party (PS), 14
Germany	Social Democratic Party of Germany (SPD), 23
Greece	Panhellenic Socialist Movement (PA.SO.K), 8
Hungary	Hungarian Socialist Party (MSzP), 4
Ireland	The Labour Party, 3
Italy	Democratic Party (PD), 21
Lithuania	Lithuanian Social Democratic Party (LSDP), 3
Luxembourg	Socialist Workers' Party of Luxembourg (LSAP), 1

Malta	Malta Labour Party (MLP), 3
Netherlands	Labor Party (PvdA), 3
Poland	Democratic Left Alliance (SLD)/Union of Labor (UP), 7
Portugal	Portuguese Socialist Party (PSP), 7
Romania	Party of Social Democrats- Conservative Party (PSD-PS), 11
Slovakia	Direction (*Směr*), 5
Slovenia	Slovenian Democrats (SDS), 2
Spain	Spanish Socialist Workers' Party (PSOE), 21
Sweden	Social Democrats(s), 5
United Kingdom	Labour Party, 13

Alliance of Liberals and Democrats for Europe (ALDE), 84

Belgium	Flemish Liberals and Democrats (VLD), 3
	Reformist Movement (MR), 2
Bulgaria	Movement for Rights and Freedoms (DPS), 3
	National Movement for Stability and Progress (NDSV), 2
Denmark	Liberal Party (V), 3
Estonia	Estonian Center Party (KE), 2
	Estonian Reform Party (ER), 1
Finland	Finnish Center (*Kesk*), 3
	Swedish People's Party (RKP/SFP), 1
France	Democratic Movement (MoDem), 6
Germany	Free Democratic Party (FDP), 12
Ireland	Fianna Fáil (FF), 3
	Marian Harkan (ind. candidate), 1
Italy	Italy of Values-List Di Pietro (IdV), 7
Latvia	Latvia's First Party-Latvian Way (LPP-LC), 1
Lithuania	Darbo Party (DP), 1
	Lithuanian Republican Liberals (LRLS), 1
Luxembourg	Democratic Party (DP), 1
Netherlands	People's Party for Freedom and Democracy (VVD), 3
	Democrats 66 (D66), 3
Romania	National Liberal Party (PNL), 5
Slovakia	People's Party-Movement for a Democratic Slovakia (L'S-HZDS), 1
Slovenia	Liberal Democracy of Slovenia (LDS), 1
	For Real (*Zares*), 1
Spain	Coalition for Europe (CpE), 2
Sweden	Liberal People's Party (FP), 3
	Center Party (CP), 1
United Kingdom	Liberal Democrats (LD), 11

The Greens/European Free Alliance (Greens/EFA), 55

Austria	The Greens, 2
Belgium	Ecologists (ECOLO), 1
	Green!, 1
	New Flemish Alliance (N-VA), 1
Denmark	Socialist People's Party (SF), 2
Estonia	Indrek Tarand (ind. candidate), 1
Finland	Green League (*Vihr*), 2
France	Europe Écologie, 14
Germany	Alliance '90/The Greens, 14
Greece	Ecologist Greens (OP), 1
Latvia	For Human Rights in United Latvia (PCTVL), 1
Luxembourg	The Greens, 1
Netherlands	Green Left (GL), 3
	Independent, 1
Spain	United Left-Initiative for Catalonia–Greens-United and Alternative Left-Asturian Bloc (IU-ICV-EUIA-BA), 1
	People's Europe-The Greens (EdP-V), 1
Sweden	Green Ecology Party (MpG), 2
	Pirate Party, 1
United Kingdom	Green Party , 2
	Scottish National Party (SNP), 2
	Plaid Cymru, 1

European Conservatives and Reformists Group (ECR), 54

Belgium	Dedecker List (LDD), 1
Czech Republic	Civic Democratic Party (ODS), 9
Hungary	Hungarian Democratic Forum (MDF), 1
Latvia	For Fatherland and Freedom (TB-LNNK), 1
Lithuania	Lithuanian Poles' Electoral Action (LLRA), 1
Netherlands	Christian Union-Reformed Political Party, 1
Poland	Law and Justice (PiS), 15
United Kingdom	Conservative Party (Cons.), 24
	Ulster Conservatives and Unionists (UUP), 1

European United Left/Nordic Green Left (GUE/NGL), 35

Cyprus	Progressive Party of the Working People (AKEL), 2
Czech Republic	Communist Party of Bohemia and Moravia (KSČM), 4
Denmark	People's Movement against the European Union (N), 1
France	Left Front (FG), 4
	Alliance of the Overseas (AOM), 1
Germany	The Left, 8
Greece	Communist Party of Greece (KKE), 2
	Coalition of the Radical Left (SY.RIZ.A.), 1
Ireland	Socialist Party (SP), 1
Latvia	Harmony Center (SC), 1
Netherlands	Socialist Party (SP), 2
Portugal	Unified Democratic Coalition (CDU), 2
	Left Block (BE), 3
Spain	United Left-Initiative for Catalonia–Greens-United and Alternative Left-Asturian Bloc (IU-ICV-EUIA-BA), 1
Sweden	Left Party (Vp), 1
United Kingdom and Northern Ireland	*Sinn Féin,* 1

Europe of Freedom and Democracy (EFD), 32

Denmark	Danish People's Party (O), 2
Finland	Christian Democrats-True Finn (KD-PS), 1
France	Movement for France-Hunting,Fishing, Nature, Tradition (MPF – CPNT), 1
Greece	Popular Orthodox Rally (LA.O.S.), 2
Italy	Northern League (LN), 9
Lithuania	Order and Justice Party (TT), 2
Netherlands	Christian Union-Reformed Political Party, 1
Slovakia	Slovak Nationalist Party (SNS), 1
United Kingdom	United Kingdom Independence Party (UKIP), 13

Unattached, 27

Austria	List of Hans-Peter Martin "For Democracy, Control, Justice," 3
	Freedom Party of Austria (FPÖ), 2
Belgium	Flemish Interest, 2
Bulgaria	National Union Attack, 2
France	National Front (FN),3
Hungary	Jobbik, 3
Netherlands	Party for Freedom (PVV), 4
Romania	Greater Romania Party (PRM), 3
Spain	Union, Progress and Democracy (UPyD), 1
United Kingdom	Conservative Party (Cons.), 1
	British National Party (BNP), 1
	Democratic Unionist Party (DUP), 1

The Court of Justice of the European Communities (less formally, the European Court of Justice—ECJ), encompassing 27 judges and 8 advocates-general, sits in Luxembourg. In 1989 a Court of First Instance was established to help the ECJ deal with its increasingly large workload. The 27 members of each court are appointed for six years by agreement between the governments of the member states. The judges themselves appoint a president of their prospective court who serves a three-year term. Both courts can sit in plenary session or in chambers of three or five judges. Since the 2004 EU enlargement, instead of convening in a plenary session, 13 ECJ judges can sit as a Grand Chamber. The ECJ can sit in plenary session when a member state or an EU/EC institution that is party to the proceedings so requests or in particularly complex or important cases. A European Civil Service Tribunal, comprised of seven judges, is under the Court of First Instance.

The ECJ's principal role is to ensure EU/EC treaties are interpreted and applied properly. Accordingly, it can decide whether acts of the commission, the council, the member governments, and other bodies are compatible with the governing treaties. For example, it ruled in 1986 that the budget approved in December 1985 was invalid because of spending increases voted on by the parliament without the concurrence of the ministerial council. The ECJ can also rule in cases submitted by national courts regarding interpretation of the treaties and implementing legislation. In a seminal decision, the court ruled in October 1979 that the commission had the authority to represent the EC in global commodity agreement negotiations, with participation by individual member states dependent on such considerations as whether the EC as a whole or the separate states were to be responsible for financial arrangements. The ECJ can also decide if a community institution is in breach of the treaties for failing to act.

In addition, if the court finds that a member state has failed to fulfill an obligation under the treaties, it can impose financial penalties. In December 2001, for example, the ECJ ruled that France's continuing embargo against British beef imports was illegal; France, facing the prospect of heavy fines, finally relented in October 2002. In May 2002 the ECJ announced that henceforth individuals, businesses, and others would be given greater leeway to challenge EU legislation, regulations, and decisions in the ECJ and the Court of First Instance. On September 13, 2005, in what promised to be a landmark case, the ECJ ruled that a 2003 decision allowed the EC, with the support of the European Parliament, to require member states to enforce directives of the EU by means of national criminal law. Ten member states, most notably the United Kingdom, had vainly argued against the decision. On November 23 of the same year, the EC issued its first list of "EU crimes" that member countries would be required to prosecute. National laws would be used, but penalties would be the same EU-wide. An initial list of EU crimes included environmental crimes and marine pollution, corruption in the private sector, counterfeiting, financial fraud and money laundering, human trafficking, and improper and destructive use of computers.

The Court of Auditors, first established in 1977, was given institutional status on a par with the European Commission, the Council of the European Union, the ECJ, and European Parliament by the Treaty on European Union. The court, whose 27 members are appointed for six-year terms by the council in consultation with the parliament, is responsible for reviewing all EU expenditures and revenues and conducts external audits, sometimes unannounced, of EU and national institutions.

The European Monetary Institute (EMI), an interim advisory body that opened January 1, 1994, in Frankfurt, Germany, was transformed into the European Central Bank (ECB) as of June 1, 1998. The ECB's highest decision-making body, the Governing Council, comprises the governors of the central banks of the 12 euro-zone countries plus the six members of the ECB Executive Board. The board is appointed, by consensus, by the euro-zone countries' prime ministers or presidents. Among other things, the Governing Council determines monetary policy for the EMU members and sets ECB interest rates. An additional ECB governing body, the General Council, comprises the ECB president and vice president (who are chosen from among the members of the Executive Board) plus the central bank governors from all the EU countries.

Several other new institutions were approved in connection with the Treaty on European Union, including a European Environment Agency, located in Copenhagen, and Europol, a regional police agency. The latter, which opened its headquarters in February 1994 in The Hague, Netherlands, was mandated initially to assist the police forces of member states in collecting and analyzing information regarding drug trafficking and money laundering. However, under the Europol Convention, which was endorsed by the EU heads of state in July 1995 and entered into effect October 1, 1998, Europol can investigate a broader variety of illegalities, including trafficking in nuclear materials, pedophilia, and illegal immigration. Terrorism was added to its mandate in 1998.

Other organs include the 344-member advisory European Economic and Social Committee, which brings together a wide range of individuals representing civil society—for example, employers, trade unionists, consumers, and ecologists. The Committee of the Regions, also comprising 344 members (typically local or regional government leaders), advises on matters directly affecting education, employment, health, transport, and other sectors at the local or regional level.

Cooperation agreements with the African, Caribbean, and Pacific (ACP) countries and territories. A convention of association linking the EEC with 18 African states was signed July 20, 1963, in Yaoundé, Cameroon. A similar agreement was concluded with Kenya, Tanzania, and Uganda on July 26, 1968, in Arusha, Tanzania. Under the UK treaty of accession, all independent Commonwealth states became eligible for association with the community through the Yaoundé Convention, through aid and institutional ties or through special trade agreements. Both the Yaoundé and Arusha conventions were, however, superseded by the February 28, 1975, signing in Lomé, Togo, of a convention establishing a comprehensive trading and economic cooperation relationship between the EC and 46 (then becoming 78—see the list below) developing ACP countries and territories. Included in the Lomé Convention's provisions were: (1) the granting by the EC of duty-free access on a nonreciprocal basis to all industrial and to 96 percent of agricultural products exported from ACP members; (2) the setting up of a comprehensive export stabilization program (Stabex) guaranteeing income support to the ACP members for their primary products; (3) increased development assistance to the ACP members from EC sources; (4) industrial cooperation between the full members and the associated countries; and (5) the creation of the Council of Ministers, the Committee of Ambassadors, and the Consultative Assembly (superseded in 1985 by the Joint Parliamentary Assembly) to implement the agreement.

A second such convention (Lomé II), which entered into force January 1, 1981, increased community aid from 3.5 billion ECUs to 5.5 billion ECUs ($7.2 billion, at the prevailing rate of exchange) and included a plan to assist ACP producers of copper and tin. In addition, ACP workers in the community were guaranteed the same working conditions, social security benefits, and earning rights as the labor force of EC members. ACP members complained, however, that the new convention was little different from its predecessor, that inflation would consume most of the new aid, and that trade concessions were marginal. Indeed, the conclusion of a September 1980 conference in Luxembourg on the impact of Lomé II was that "trade relations had not dramatically improved and in fact had deteriorated for many ACP members, although those countries as a group had moved back into an overall [trade] surplus with the Community."

Following two years of decline, commodity prices stabilized somewhat during 1982 and 1983. Thus, the negotiations for Lomé III, which opened in October 1983, were less acrimonious than the earlier meetings between the EC and the ACP members. Under the new five-year pact, concluded December 8, 1984, the community agreed to expand the volume of financial resources to 8.5 billion ECUs ($6 billion), however, because of exchange rate slippage the expansion yielded an immediate net dollar value ($6 billion) less than that of the Lomé II endowment. The new funds were to be used largely to encourage "self-reliant and self-sustained development," with an emphasis on improving the living standards of the poorest people in the ACP countries and territories.

Negotiations on Lomé IV were launched in October 1988, with ACP leaders hoping to obtain an aid package of at least 15 billion ECUs ($23 billion) in view of debt problems in developing countries and difficulties associated with the structural adjustment programs recently implemented in many affected states. A compromise figure of 12 billion ECUs (about $14 billion) for five years (1991–1995) was agreed on in December 1989. Most of the other elements of previous conventions were maintained in Lomé IV, with additional emphasis being given to, among other things, environmental protection, human rights, and food security. Lomé IV was, however, to cover a ten-year period, twice that of its predecessors. Thus, further negotiations were required that yielded another compromise in mid-1995, under which an additional 14.6 billion ECUs (about $19.6 billion) were allocated for the ACP members to the end of the decade.

In April 1997 South Africa became the 71st ACP member to accede to the Lomé Convention. However, under a protocol approved by the commission a month earlier, South Africa was accorded only partial membership because of its comparatively advanced industrial economy. Its status was governed primarily by a separate Agreement on Trade, Development, and Cooperation among the European Community, its Member States, and South Africa (TDCA), which was signed October 11, 1999, in Pretoria, and which excluded South Africa from many of the aid and trade provisions applicable to the other ACP countries. With Lomé IV due to expire February 28, 2000, negotiations on a successor agreement opened at the end of September 1998 and continued until February 3, 2000, when they were completed in Brussels. Efforts at poverty reduction—the overarching goal of the new 20-year pact—were to be accompanied by political dialogue, additional developmental aid, and closer economic and trade cooperation. Formal signing of the Partnership Agreement to the Lomé Convention took place in Cotonou, Benin, where the signing of the accord, known as the Cotonou Agreement, occurred on June 23 before representatives of 92 countries. At the same time, six additional members joined the ACP grouping: Cook Islands, Marshall Islands, Micronesia, Nauru, Niue, and Palau. (South Africa's continuing participation was provided for in Protocol Three of the agreement.) The Cotonou Agreement identified a group of 39 least developed ACP states (excluding Cuba), which in certain cases benefited from special treatment. The Cotonou Agreement also called for ACP countries to take on the responsibilities of fostering democracy, upholding human rights, and maintaining good governance in order to participate and receive aid.

The 78 ACP members are Angola, Antigua and Barbuda, Bahamas, Barbados, Belize, Benin, Botswana, Burkina Faso, Burundi, Cameroon, Cape Verde Islands, Central African Republic, Chad, Comoro Islands, Democratic Republic of the Congo, Republic of the Congo, Cook Islands, Côte d'Ivoire, Djibouti, Dominica, Dominican Republic, Equatorial Guinea, Eritrea, Ethiopia, Fiji, Gabon, Gambia, Ghana, Grenada, Guinea, Guinea-Bissau, Guyana, Haiti, Jamaica, Kenya, Kiribati, Lesotho, Liberia, Madagascar, Malawi, Mali, Marshall Islands, Mauritania, Mauritius, Micronesia, Mozambique, Namibia, Nauru, Niger, Nigeria, Niue, Palau, Papua New Guinea, Rwanda, St. Kitts and Nevis, St. Lucia, St. Vincent, Samoa, Sao Tome and Principe, Senegal, Seychelles, Sierra Leone, Solomon Islands, Somalia, South Africa, Sudan, Suriname, Swaziland, Tanzania, Timor-Leste, Togo, Tonga, Trinidad and Tobago, Tuvalu, Uganda, Vanuatu, Zambia, Zimbabwe.

A December 2007 summit in Lisbon, Portugal, saw the adoption of the Joint EU-Africa Strategy, a set of policy goals for economic and political integration between EU and African nations. However, the summit was marked by discord. A number of African nations rejected new EU-backed EPAs on the grounds that they would lead to cheaper European goods flooding their markets. Some states reportedly delayed signing the agreements (including South Africa, Nigeria, and Ghana) to try to extend negotiations. As the Contonou Agreement's trade preferences expired in January 2008, they risked punitive tariffs on their exports to EU countries.

Tariffs were averted by interim agreements to allow ACP countries to retain access to EU markets while EPA negotiations continued, presumably complying with WTO rules in trade in goods. Cariforum, representing 15 Caribbean countries but excluding Haiti, signed the first comprehensive trade and investment agreement as a regional block with the EU on December 16, 2007, and began liberalizing tariffs that would, upon implementation in three years, cover nearly 90 percent of imports from the EU for a period of 25 years. However, Caribbean countries were expected to lose a major source of revenue in the form of import tariffs and there was a danger that local industries would be overwhelmed by products emerging from larger and more developed European countries. For these reasons and others, the EU faced substantial resistance by other ACP regional groups in signing EPAs in 2008 and 2009. Though countries initially negotiated with the EU as regional blocks, some countries advanced their interests as subgroups or individual units. Concerned that this approach would cede negotiating power, African Union heads of state met in Addis Ababa in February 2008 to call for joint action in blocking unfavorable trade arrangements. However, it appeared that the effort lacked a long-term strategy.

A final act was signed between the EU and Botswana, Lesotho, and Swaziland on June 4, 2009, and shortly after Mozambique added its signature. As of September 2009, most regions had not reached full EPAs with the EU, although the EU expected to finalize talks with the Eastern and Southern Africa regional group and the Pacific regional group by the end of the year. The Western Africa regional group was expected to begin end-phase negotiations in 2010. Notable exceptions to the proceedings were South Africa and the Eastern Africa regional group, which rejected giving the EU a "most favored nation" status because it would have hamstrung efforts to sign trade deals with China and other non-EU trading partners.

Other cooperation agreements. Over the years, the EC/EU has concluded cooperative agreements with many other countries and multilateral groups.

After nearly four years of effort by Prime Minister Pierre Trudeau's government to establish a "contractual relationship" between Canada and the EC, a Framework Agreement for Commercial and Economic Cooperation was signed July 6, 1976—the first such accord between the community and an industrialized country. In 1990 the original agreement was superseded by a Declaration of EC-Canada Relations. In the interim, many additional bilateral cooperation agreements were signed, including those with Algeria (1976), Bangladesh (1976), Brazil (1980), China (1978), Egypt (1977), India (1973 and 1981), Israel (1975), Japan (1980), Jordan (1977), Lebanon (1977), Mexico (1975), Morocco (1976), Pakistan (1976), Sri Lanka (1975), Syria (1977), Tunisia (1976), Uruguay (1974), and Yugoslavia (signed in 1980 but suspended following the breakup of Yugoslavia in 1991–1992). A joint cooperation agreement was signed with the five members of the Association of Southeast Asian Nations (ASEAN) in March 1980, with the Andean Group in December 1983, and with the members of the Central American Common Market in 1985. In addition, the then EFTA members (Austria, Finland, Iceland, Norway, Sweden, and Switzerland), after a longtime reliance on bilateral agreements with the EC, signed a multilateral accord in 1992 to create a European Economic Area (EEA) to promote the freedom of movement of people, goods, services, and capital among the 19 nations involved (see article on EFTA).

As a major consequence of the pace of change in Eastern Europe and attendant thaw in East-West relations, the EC in 1989 and 1990 concluded trade and cooperation pacts with Bulgaria, Czechoslovakia, the German Democratic Republic, Hungary, Poland, Romania, and the Soviet Union. Economic links with those nations were previously hindered by the desire of the now-defunct Council for Mutual Economic Assistance (CMEA) to negotiate trade agreements for the group as a whole. All but the Soviet Union soon expressed an interest in full EC membership.

Following the Soviet Union's collapse, the EC/EU began negotiating cooperative agreements with successor states that, by inclination or geographical location, were not at that time regarded as prospective candidates for admission. As authorized by the Council of the European Communities in October 1992, Partnership and Cooperation Agreements, which require the assent of the European Parliament and ratification by the member states, have been concluded with 12 countries: Armenia (signed April 1996), Azerbaijan (April 1996), Belarus (March 1995), Georgia (April 1996), Kazakhstan (January 1995), Kyrgyzstan (February 1995), Moldova (November 1994), Russia (June 1994), Tajikistan (October 2004), Turkmenistan (May 1998), Ukraine (June 1994), and Uzbekistan (June 1996). A distinctive Trade and Cooperation Agreement was concluded with Mongolia in March 1993. Unlike the European agreements, none of these pacts include free trade provisions. As of mid-2008, only the agreements with Belarus, Tajikistan, and Turkmenistan had not yet entered into force.

The EU also has varying cooperative arrangements with many other countries and regional groups, ranging from China to the Andean Group. A Euro-Mediterranean Partnership was initiated at a November 1995 conference in Barcelona, Spain, bringing together the EU and 12 (now 10) nonmembers: Algeria, Cyprus, Egypt, Israel, Jordan, Lebanon, Malta, Morocco, the Palestinian Authority, Syria, Tunisia, and Turkey. More recently, the EU initiated the European Neighborhood Policy, which encompasses countries to the east and along the southern and eastern shores of the Mediterranean—that is, Algeria, Armenia, Azerbaijan, Belarus, Egypt, Georgia, Israel, Jordan, Lebanon, Libya, Moldova, Morocco, Syria, Tunisia, and Ukraine—plus the Palestinian Authority. In October 2007 the EU and the six Central American states began negotiating an association agreement that is to have as its pillars political dialogue, cooperation, and trade. With regard to trade, the aim is to liberalize relations between the two regions even more than WTO rules have.

Also at the end of 2007, EU and Chinese officials held a series of high-level meetings to harmonize trade, although EU officials were said to have lobbed unusually direct criticism concerning China's undervalued currency, barriers to its domestic market, and weak protection of intellectual property rights. The main achievement of the talks was an agreement to create a high-level mechanism to improve economic ties, although the precise nature of this measure was not well defined.

Discussions regarding a free trade agreement with the Gulf Cooperation Council, which includes Saudi Arabia, United Arab Emirates, Qatar, Kuwait, Oman, and Bahrain, were suspended in December 2008 over EU efforts to include human rights clauses.

On June 17, 2009, the EU held its first summit with Pakistan in Brussels, which resulted in no immediate trade concessions but was seen as a first step toward a long-term agreement that could eventually eliminate duties on imports of Pakistani textile products. Additionally, in July the EU concluded a trade accord with South Korea that made 97 percent of trade between the two sides duty-free within five years, although the lifting of tariffs on automobiles was met with objections that Europe's ailing auto industry would be exposed to excessive competition.

Activities. The ratification process for the Treaty of Nice, which was signed on February 26, 2001, and which ultimately entered into force on February 1, 2003, coincided with a continuing debate over the EU's long-term purpose and structure. German leaders, on the one hand, called for even closer integration, including adoption of a federal structure. France, on the other hand, continued to oppose such a model, which it saw as threatening national constituencies. Another area of contention was the Charter of Fundamental Rights, which was drawn up in September 2000 and formally approved by the heads of government at the Nice summit. The charter's firmest opponent, the United Kingdom, argued that its incorporation into the EU treaty was unnecessary because all EU members had already acceded to the European Convention on Human Rights.

In a significant development for the EU's external relations, the first summit of Balkan states and the EU was held November 24, 2000, in Zagreb, Croatia. The EU pledged €4.7 billion ($3.9 billion) in aid during 2000–2006 to support "reconstruction, democratization, and stabilization" in Albania, Bosnia and Herzegovina, Croatia, Macedonia, and Yugoslavia. Most Balkan states had already expressed an interest in eventual EU membership.

During their February 25–26, 2001, meeting in Brussels, the EU foreign ministers agreed to abolish virtually all trade barriers for 48 of the least developed countries, including 39 members of the EC-affiliated ACP group. Dubbed the Everything But Arms Proposal, the initiative made trade in all manufactured and agricultural goods, except armaments, duty- and quota-free, although phase-in periods were established for bananas (to 2006), rice (2009), and sugar (2009)—three commodities that had caused major trade disputes in recent years.

Meeting in mid-June 2001, in Göteborg, Sweden, the EU heads of government established 2004 as the firm entry date for the next expansion, although it remained uncertain exactly how many of the eligible countries would be ready for admission at that time. The summit attendees also emphasized the importance of sustainable development in the EU's economic and social strategies, endorsed holding a new round of global trade negotiations, and reaffirmed their commitment to the Kyoto Protocol goals on global warming.

With regard to EU-U.S. trade, the summit participants agreed to reduce tensions, which in recent years had been particularly heated over bananas and beef, with the latter exacerbated by the earlier outbreak of "mad cow" disease. The most troublesome issue involved the U.S. Foreign Sales Corporations (FSC) Act. Shortly after the June summit, the WTO disputes panel ruled in favor of an EU complaint that the law violated world trade rules by allowing U.S. companies to shelter export income and other foreign sales from tax. The decision was upheld in 2002, thereby requiring a less-than-amiable U.S. Congress to reconsider the FSC law for the second time, an earlier EU complaint to the WTO having led to a 2000 revision.

In the immediate aftermath of the September 11, 2001, terrorist attacks on the United States, the EU heads of government held an emergency meeting September 21 in Brussels, where they extended full support to Washington. An informal summit, which convened October 19 in Ghent, Belgium, focused on the economic and political consequences of the attacks and of the recently launched U.S. "war on terrorism." Subsequent related actions included endorsement of a uniform arrest warrant and a May 2002 decision to freeze the assets of 11 suspected terrorist organizations. Developments at a June 21–22 summit in Seville, Spain, included acceptance of a plan to counter illegal immigration, adopt a common asylum policy, and introduce a common border force. Cooperation declined after the initiation of the Iraq War in 2003, typified by EU reluctance to accept cleared detainees from the U.S. military prison at Guantanamo Bay in 2009. In November that year, the EU also objected to an antiterrorism plan that would allow U.S. law enforcement to access EU citizen's financial data, but it ultimately signed a deal that limited the scope to terrorism inquiries.

Meeting on December 14–15, 2001, in Laeken, Belgium, the heads of government agreed to establish a constitutional convention, to be chaired by former French president Valéry Giscard d'Estaing, and to map out a more efficient and democratic structure for the union. On February 28, 2002, the convention began its task, which was expected to extend into 2003. A "skeleton draft" of the proposed constitution for a "union of European states" was published October 28, 2002, but the 46-article document deliberately avoided controversial issues that had yet to be resolved. It did, however, propose reserving powers not specifically conferred by the constitution on EU institutions to the member states. This was seen as an effort to restrain the growth and power of the European Commission in particular.

The January 1, 2002, launch of the euro as legal tender was preceded by the distribution throughout the 12 EMU members of new banknotes and coins worth €660 billion ($590 billion). The transition was accomplished without significant disruptions, and at the end of February the French franc, the German deutsch mark, the Italian lira, and the other national currencies were no longer in commercial use. During the next ten months the most significant problem facing a number of eurozone members was keeping fiscal deficits within targeted limits. In November France, Germany, and Portugal were all cited for failure to reduce deficits to 3 percent, as required by the EMU's stability and growth pact.

In the meantime, on March 23, 2002, responding to a U.S. decision to impose unilateral steel tariffs of between 8 and 30 percent, the EU announced retaliatory tariffs against up to 300 U.S. products. The steel products were manufactured by previously state-owned French, German, Italian, Spanish, Swedish, and UK companies that received subsidies before being privatized. The WTO proceeded to address the complex issue, while in December the EU and the United States, at a Paris meeting sponsored by the Organization for Economic Cooperation and Development (OECD), agreed to open negotiations on reducing or eliminating steel subsidies.

Proposed changes to CAP and a parallel Common Fisheries Policy (CFP) drew considerable attention in 2002. France and Spain, two principal beneficiaries of the existing CAP, voiced objections. Spain also expressed concern over efforts under the CFP to reduce fleet sizes and better manage fish stocks. A December 2002 decision to limit catches of Atlantic cod, haddock, and whiting also angered British fishermen.

Problems also persisted with regard to establishing the RRF as part of a comprehensive European Security and Defense Policy (ESDP). The first anticipated RRF mission, to assume control in October 2002 of peacekeepers in Macedonia, required the approval of NATO, but Turkey wanted assurances that the RRF would not undertake missions in the Aegean and locations near Turkey. The December 12–13, 2002, Copenhagen summit was highlighted not only by the decision to admit ten new members as of May 2004, but also by completion of a "comprehensive agreement" resolving the dispute with Turkey over the RRF. Under the pact, only EU members and candidates that also are members of NATO or participants in the NATO Partnership for Peace (PfP) program have access to NATO facilities. Accordingly, Malta and Cyprus are excluded.

The European Council met in emergency session February 17, 2003, to discuss the looming crisis regarding the United States and Iraq, but a deep divide separated France and Germany, which opposed threatened military action, from the United Kingdom, Spain, and Italy, the most vocal supporters of the Bush administration's stance against the Saddam Hussein regime. French president Chirac subsequently criticized statements supporting intervention made by the eight Eastern European prospective members, plus candidate countries Romania and Bulgaria. Iraq policy remained on the agenda at the regular council session March 20–21, which also addressed progress toward achieving the Lisbon Strategy goals for economic competitiveness.

On April 25, 2003, four opponents of the month-old invasion of Iraq met to discuss defense cooperation. At that time Belgium, France, Germany, and Luxembourg decided to establish a headquarters for planning joint military operations, although some critics, especially the United Kingdom, viewed the decision as contrary to a prior pledge not to compete with NATO's collective defense mission. A compromise was reached in November, with France and Germany withdrawing their headquarters plan and the United Kingdom agreeing to formation of a joint military planning unit independent of NATO. In addition, the EU foreign ministers agreed that common consent would be required to initiate any EU peacekeeping or humanitarian mission, and then only if NATO chose not to act. At the December 2003 council summit, the defense plan received the approval of the EU leaders. In February France, Germany, and the United Kingdom announced their support for forming joint battle groups, each with 1,500 personnel, within the RRF. The first such units (the total number was subsequently set at 13) were ready for deployment in January 2007. In June 2004 the EU foreign ministers approved establishment of the European Defense Agency (EDA), with responsibilities that included improving joint defense capabilities, promoting related research and development, and advancing development of a competitive defense market within the EU. In 2005 the EDA absorbed the functions of the Western European Armaments Group (WEAG), a subsidiary body of the WEU.

Meeting in regular session on June 19–20, 2003, in Salonika, Greece, the council received a draft constitution from the Convention on the Future of Europe and assigned preparation of a final text to an IGC, which was to begin its work in October. In other business, the council indicated its willingness to aid in Iraqi reconstruction and endorsed a statement by the EU foreign ministers on the possible use of military force to prevent the spread of weapons of mass destruction (WMD). Shortly thereafter, an EU-U.S. extradition treaty was signed. The EU members retained the right to refuse extradition in death penalty cases.

When the IGC on the constitution convened in October 2003, differences over many provisions still required resolution, principal among them the makeup of the European Commission and voting procedures in the proposed Council of Ministers. The draft text called for reducing the commission to 15 members beginning in 2009, but most of the smaller member countries argued that each should continue to be represented by at least one commissioner. With regard to the Council of Ministers, the constitutional text specified a "double majority" system under which passage of a measure would require support from a majority of ministers representing, collectively, at least 60 percent of the total EU population. An EU summit December 13 failed to resolve the issues, but the attendees managed to agree on the 2007 admission of Bulgaria and Romania to the union.

CAP was overhauled in 2003. The reform centered on a shift in emphasis from preventing food shortages to ensuring food safety, environmental standards, and animal welfare. At one time more than two-thirds of the EU budget was devoted to CAP. In 2004 it still accounted for almost half, but the aim is to reduce it to one-third by 2014.

In January 2004 the European Commission asked the ECJ to rule on the validity of a November 2003 decision by the EU finance ministers to suspend the stability and growth pact (SGP), thereby avoiding the imposition of penalties against France and Germany for failing to keep their budget deficits in check. In April 2004, with the ECJ not yet having ruled, the commission issued warnings to Greece, Italy, the Netherlands, and Portugal over their deficits. Three months later the ECJ determined that the finance ministers had exceeded their authority in suspending the SGP, but the judges also ruled they could not force the ministers to carry through on the commission's recommendations regarding sanctions. As a consequence, the issue of sanctions was thrown into the political arena, and reform of the SGP became an even more contentious issue.

The March 25–26, 2004, European Council summit was dominated by the March 11 terrorist bombings in Madrid and the subsequent election of a new Spanish government. In addition to appointing a new EU counterterrorism coordinator, the summit participants stated that they intended to act jointly, including with military force, in response to terrorist attacks, and they approved a 50-point plan of action.

In late April 2004, the justice and home affairs ministers sought consensus on another volatile issue: setting minimum standards for treating those seeking political asylum under a proposed Common European Asylum System (CEAS). The CEAS proposal was not, however, universally welcomed, with the UN's high commissioner for refugees, Ruud Lubbers, describing the plan as intended to reduce standards and to "deter or deny protection to as many people as possible."

As scheduled, the EU's enlargement from 15 to 25 members took place May 1, 2004, with the election of a new European Parliament following on June 10–13. As had been expected following the expansion, the voters returned the center-right European People's Party/European Democrats as the plurality grouping. Somewhat unexpectedly, however, the leading governing parties in 23 of the 25 member states won smaller vote shares than they had in the most recent national elections.

At a June 17–18, 2004, summit of EU leaders, a spirit of compromise resolved the remaining disputes over the text of the 350-article EU constitution, which required ratification by all 25 member countries. Predictably, the final draft was immediately attacked by both proponents of a unified Europe and those fearing the loss of national sovereignty and identity. Under the constitution, which was to supersede existing EU treaties, EU law would have primacy over national law in specified areas, when the objectives could best be achieved at the EU level. The European Council would elect an EU president for a once-renewable term of two and a half years and would also choose a minister for foreign affairs. The European Commission would retain the formula of one commissioner per state for one five-year term, after which the number of commissioners would be reduced to two-thirds the number of member states, filled by rotation. The Council of Ministers would meet in various configurations, depending on the sector involved (e.g., agriculture, transport). The European Parliament, comprising no more than 750 members (a maximum of 96 and a minimum of 6 per country), and the Council of Ministers would jointly "exercise legislative and budgetary functions." Unless otherwise specified in the constitution, European Council decisions would continue to be by consensus. In the Council of Ministers, unanimity would be required in such sensitive areas as foreign policy, defense, and tax law. Otherwise, a "double majority" QMV system would apply, generally requiring support from 55 percent of the ministers, representing at least 65 percent of the EU population.

Although the Charter of Fundamental Rights was incorporated into the constitution, its application was to be limited to matters of EU law, with the interpretation of guaranteed rights allowing for national differences based on, for example, tradition. The complete constitution also encompassed 36 protocols, including one amending the Euratom treaty, and 50 Declarations Concerning Provisions of the Constitution. Meeting October 29 in Rome, the EU heads of government and their foreign ministers signed a constitutional treaty to advance its ratification in all member countries, by referendum or legislative act, by November 2006.

Meanwhile, on July 22, 2004, the new parliament had approved the nomination of Portuguese prime minister José Manuel Barroso to serve as president of the European Commission for 2005–2010. Barroso soon encountered objections to his proposed list of commissioners, however, and on October 27, facing rejection by the parliament, he withdrew the list, even though the new commission was to have been installed November 1. On November 18 parliament approved the revised commission, which took office four days later.

A November 4–5, 2004, EU summit adopted a new five-year Hague Program on freedom, justice, and security that addressed terrorism and organized crime, basic rights and citizenship, and the CEAS. The Hague Program, a follow-up to a plan that was adopted at the 1999 Tampere summit, did not, however, resolve deep divisions over the proposed common asylum plan, especially the use of extraterritorial holding centers. There also were fundamental differences over whether asylum seekers who entered the EU would be deported to the centers or whether the centers would be used only to house those who had been intercepted while in transit to EU countries.

The EU summit of December 16–17, 2004, was highlighted by the announcement that accession talks with candidate country Croatia would begin March 17, 2005, provided that the Zagreb government fully cooperated with the International Criminal Tribunal for the former Yugoslavia (ICTY) in The Hague. The summit also confirmed that accession talks with Turkey would begin on October 3, 2005, but several EU members, including France and Italy, had already indicated their likely opposition to admitting the predominantly Asian and Islamic country. Questions also persisted regarding Turkey's stance toward Cyprus and its human rights record.

In 2005 President Bush visited institutions of the EU on February 22. U.S.-European relations had been strained considerably by the U.S.-led invasion of Iraq in 2003. Moreover, U.S. administration officials had made several statements that caused some in Europe to believe that the United States was no longer supportive of an integrated Europe, especially one that took stances counter to U.S. policy. Bush's trip was widely seen as an effort to allay such concerns.

In February 2005 President Barroso announced his commission's economic program, as well as its social and environmental agenda. The economic program recommended market liberalization, deregulation, and, most controversially, extension of the single market concept to services as well as goods. The goal was to meet Lisbon Strategy targets, which projected 3 percent annual growth and the creation of 6 million new jobs during the 2005–2010 term.

At a summit March 22–23, 2005, the EU leaders focused on reforming the stability and growth pact, which had largely been disregarded since the 2002 decision of the finance ministers not to impose economic penalties on France and Germany for noncompliance. At the summit the members retained the pact's principal benchmarks—keeping national budget deficits under 3 percent of GDP and public debt to less than 60 percent of GDP—but basically exempted countries experiencing low or negative growth. They excluded from the budget ceiling expenditures for education, defense, foreign aid, and research and extended the time limits for offending countries to make the necessary adjustments. France, Germany, Italy, and Spain, each of which failed to adhere to the original criteria, were among the countries backing the revisions, which critics described as rendering the pact worthless. The summit attendees also discussed President Barroso's economic agenda for 2005–2010 and requested that the commission reconsider the proposal for liberalizing the service sector.

On January 12, 2005, the European Parliament overwhelmingly endorsed the proposed EU constitution, although most UK, Polish, and Czech MEPs voted in opposition. On February 20 Spanish voters became the first to approve the constitution by referendum, but its prospects for unionwide ratification suffered a major blow in late May and early June when French and Dutch voters rejected the constitution by 54.7 percent and 61.5 percent, respectively. Analysts interpreted the French vote in large part as dissatisfaction with the current French government, while in the Netherlands it was a fear of a loss in national sovereignty and identity because of the rapid pace of enlargement and an influx of immigrants from the East. Despite the French and Dutch results, many supporters of the constitution urged that the ratification process continue, although the EU leaders, meeting June 16–17, instead called for a "period of reflection." As of August 2005 the following 15 countries had ratified the proposed constitution: Austria, Belgium, Cyprus, Estonia, Germany, Greece, Hungary, Italy, Latvia, Lithuania, Luxembourg, Malta, Slovakia, Slovenia, and Spain. The other eight EU members postponed consideration. If, in the end, five or fewer states failed to ratify the constitution, it could be reconsidered rather than scrapped. In mid-2006, European public opinion seemed to be turning more strongly against the constitution, but its supporters inside the EU structure were still enthusiastic about keeping it alive without substantial modification.

During the same period, a crisis erupted over the 2007–2013 EU budget when the United Kingdom refused to accept a reduction in its budget rebate (which was instituted in 1984 when the United Kingdom's economic position was much weaker) unless the reduction was accompanied by additional reforms, particularly with regard to CAP. In June 2003 the EU agricultural ministers approved further "decoupling" of CAP subsidies from productivity and redirected the program toward giving farmers flat payments related to rural development and environmental protection. Since then, the number of excluded or partially affected agricultural products has been reduced. Nevertheless, several EU members supported the UK argument that a continuing budgetary emphasis on agriculture was misdirected. France, the largest recipient of CAP support and a leading opponent of maintaining the UK budget rebate, disagreed. After protracted negotiations, a compromise was reached in December 2005 on the 2007–2013 EU budget. The United Kingdom agreed to give up approximately 20 percent of its rebate during the coming budget period, while the European Commission was asked to hold a "full and wide-ranging" review of all EU spending, including CAP and the UK rebate, and to draw up a report in 2008–2009. Additional substantial cuts in annual CAP subsidies are anticipated after 2013.

In February 2006 the European Parliament passed a bill authorizing an internal market for services, which, after subsequent revisions, resulted in the EU Services Directive that was adopted by the end of the year.

In 2006 and 2007 the EU also discussed the free movement of capital. In early 2006 the EU saw a spate of governments (in Spain, France, Poland, and Luxembourg) take action to oppose some foreign takeovers. The Takeover Bids Directive, passed in 2004 after 20 years of work, was intended to facilitate takeovers (within the parameters of EU competition policy), the premise being that they could advance corporate restructuring and consolidation, provide a means for companies to achieve optimal scale, and help disseminate good management practices and technology. The 2004 directive did, however, permit national governments to refrain from implementing two key provisions, thereby allowing some barriers to takeovers to remain in place. A revision to the directive is expected to take place in 2011.

In another move to extend the internal market, 22 EU governments in May 2006 agreed to an informal code of conduct to open competition to nonnational EU members in the €30 billion ($38 billion) defense market. Spain, Hungary, and Denmark chose not to participate, Spain and Hungary because they thought that their own firms would not be competitive, and Denmark because it has an opt-out from EU military cooperation.

On December 21, 2007, the Schengen area of the EU, where there are no internal border posts or passport checks for EU citizens (thereby promoting the free movement of people), was expanded to include 9 of the 10 countries that joined the EU in 2004. Zone membership thereby increased to 24 of the 27 EU member states, plus non-EU members Iceland and Norway (EU members Ireland and the United Kingdom do not participate).

The new countries included the Czech Republic, Estonia, Hungary, Latvia, Lithuania, Malta, Poland, Slovakia, and Slovenia. Cyprus, which joined the EU in 2004, had not met the technical requirements to join as expected in late 2009. Bulgaria and Romania were on track in 2009 to gain Schengen membership by 2011. On December 12, 2008, Switzerland became the 25th country to join the Schengen area with the lifting of land border controls, followed by the removal of airport controls for Schengen passport holders in March 2009.

On January 1, 2007, Russia interrupted its supply of gas to the EU after a conflict with Ukraine about gas prices. Although the EU has been attempting to diversify its sources, it currently gets a quarter of its gas from Russia. Gazprom, Russia's state-controlled gas monopoly, has been unwilling to open its pipeline network to independent companies and other gas-producing states such as Kazakhstan and Turkmenistan, arguing, among other things, that the network is already stretched to capacity to meet its commitments for the next 20 years. Regular energy talks between the EU and Russia have taken place since 2000. At the October 2007 annual summit, energy discussions centered on security of supply. EU officials were hoping to resume talks concerning Russian gas supplies and opening that country's energy sector to west European investors at a conference in June 2008, although there were concerns that member EU nations had no coordinated foreign policy platform on Russia. The EU has also called for Russian membership in the WTO, despite ongoing concerns about human rights in Russia.

In another foreign policy area, members of the EU have played a central role in negotiating with Iran regarding its production of weapons-grade uranium. In June 2006, as he had in 2003, Javier Solana delivered to Iran a proposal offering a package of incentives not to produce weapons-grade material. Iran rejected the overture. Thus, in 2007 Solana and the member states continued to pressure Iran through such measures as sanctions. In May 2008 Iran presented a counter package of proposals to EU officials outlining a different strategy to address security issues regarding the spread of nuclear powers but refused to suspend its own enrichment program. Relations with Iran deteriorated in 2009. Following Iran's detention of local staff from the British embassy in Tehran, the United Kingdom requested that EU members pull out their ambassadors. Iran maintained that the EU had disqualified itself from nuclear talks because it had interfered with Iran's disputed presidential election.

During 2007 the EU also directed its attention to the global economy, especially the safeguarding of the world's liberal multilateral trading system. The EU continued to call for progress to be made in the Doha Round of multilateral trade negotiations held under the auspices of the WTO. EU trade commissioner Peter Mandelson warned in February 2008 that the talks "faced a high risk of failure" if not completed that year because of the change in U.S. presidency, although his support within the EU was not concrete, with some member nations urging him to secure more concessions in the industrial sector while Ireland held firm on protecting agriculture. A principal difficulty facing the negotiators is Doha's focus on agricultural liberalization, given that aspects of CAP make global liberalization in this area difficult to achieve. The seventh year of WTO-led Doha talks at the end of July 2008 collapsed because of disagreements between India and the United States on farm import rules.

In 2007, following two years of reflection generated by the French and Dutch rejection of the proposed EU Constitution, the EU formally called a halt to plans for amending the document. The European Council session in Brussels in June 2006 had proposed reaching a decision on institutional reform by the end of 2008. Further impetus toward drawing up a framework for reform emerged from the informal Berlin summit held on March 25, 2007, to mark the 50th anniversary of the signing of the Treaty of Rome. On June 23 an IGC was given a detailed mandate to draw up a new reform treaty by the end of 2007. The European Parliament and the European Commission also participated in the deliberations, leading to council approval of a treaty text on October 19. It was later signed by the heads of state or government in Lisbon on December 13.

The Treaty of Lisbon, or the Reform Treaty, echoed many of the institutional changes proposed in the failed constitution and required ratification by all 27 EU members. On December 18, 2007, Hungary became the first member state to ratify the treaty. However, a number of setbacks delayed its passage. In March 2008 Poland's legislature postponed ratification as the main opposition party argued that the country might be forced to accept same-sex civil partnerships and that Germany might reclaim property lost after World War II. Finland, too, hesitated because of an internal legislative dispute over representation in the European Parliament. Additionally, the United Kingdom witnessed a legal challenge over whether ratification had to be put to a public referendum, which ultimately proved unsuccessful. Conservative Czech parliamentarians, meanwhile, asked for their supreme court to rule on whether multiple provisions within the treaty were compatible with the country's constitution. All four eventually accepted the treaty.

Of all the countries considering ratification, only Ireland was constitutionally required to put the Lisbon Treaty to a referendum, though critics in many other countries called for referenda, arguing that parliamentary approval was designed to avoid another rejection by voters. Irish activists campaigned hard against the treaty ahead of polling on June 12, 2008, when 53.4 percent of Irish voters rejected it, preventing its ratification. The Irish response rose out of concerns regarding tax hikes, changes to abortion law, distrust of the EU, and unease over an economic slowdown. EU leaders were thus thrust into a crisis over how to proceed. Calls for a second referendum in Ireland to be held before or on the European parliamentary elections June 4–7 2009, which could have allowed a new body to be elected under Lisbon Treaty stipulations, were ultimately rebuffed by Ireland as it attempted to secure changes to the treaty that would persuade hesitant voters. Meanwhile, the Polish and Czech presidents refused to ratify the treaty until an Irish approval, and Germany's ratification was slowed by a constitutional court case assessing the treaty's compatibility with domestic law.

Allegations of corruption and fraud in EU institutions have continued in recent years. For the 14th year in a row the European Court of Auditors found irregularities in EU budget spending. The most recent audit report in November 2008 on the 2007 $166 billion budget noted frequent errors in the inclusion of ineligible costs, billing overstatements, and violations of procurement rules. On a positive note, EU institutions had, for the first year ever, met auditing standards. However, spending irregularities were notably high for budgets handled by member governments, which comprise some 80 percent of EU funds. One particularly disorganized record concerned the EU's cohesion budget for regional policy, social affairs, and rural development, of which 11 percent of sampled spending was in error. Following a stinging audit report in 2007, the EC's antifraud office took a stricter stance on governments, nearly doubling the recovery of EU funds from error-strewn governments and in some cases freezing monies. Affected states included Bulgaria, Italy, Luxembourg, and the United Kingdom. Bulgaria, in particular, was experiencing epidemic levels of corruption, leading to a freeze on EU development funding in early 2008. Although Bulgaria had opened hundreds of fraud cases involving EU money, many having to do with agricultural subsidies, the EU's antifraud office in July 2009 said that not enough progress had been made in bringing them to trial. Critics of EU enlargement have pointed to corruption in Bulgaria in recent years as a reason to slow the pace of further expansion.

EU policy supports gradual and carefully managed enlargement. However, debate continues over how large the EU should become and whether prospective nations should reflect core European values. The classification of Turkey as a candidate country has been particularly controversial because of issues such as immigration, political Islam, human rights standards, and its shared border with Iraq and Syria. Although Turkey technically has territory in continental Europe, many argue that it belongs to Asia Minor.

Turkey first applied for membership in 1987 (at that time to the EEC). The European Council finally accepted its eligibility in 1997. Accession talks began in 2005, and as of late 2009 only 1 of the 35 chapters, or policy areas, had been provisionally closed, with Turkey meeting conditions concerning science and research. Another 7 chapters have been opened, but the process has been stymied by Turkey's refusal to open ports to Greek Cypriot ships and planes, as well as the continued objections of France.

Turkey's prospects have been dimmed by slow progress on political reforms and by the growing political influence of far-right and anti-immigrant parties in the European Parliament following the elections in June 2009. The country is not expected to satisfy all qualifications for membership within the decade. Given this outlook, there has been discussion about granting Turkey and other aspiring countries a special EU partnership that would be short of membership. Turkey has rebuffed alternatives to full integration.

In 2004 an EU "Neighborhood Policy" plan was launched with the aim of giving countries immediately bordering Europe by land or sea intermediary levels of EU benefits following bilateral agreements on "action plans" for political and economic reforms. Agreements were signed in 2005 with Israel, Jordan, Moldova, Morocco, the Palestinian Authority, Tunisia, and Ukraine; in 2006 with Armenia, Azerbaijan, and Georgia; and in 2007 with Egypt and Lebanon. Other countries reportedly on the list but without agreed upon action plans as of late 2009 included Algeria, Belarus, Libya, and Syria. A progress report filed by the Commission in April 2009 enunciated the difficulties of advancing the program because of the recent violent conflicts in Georgia and in Gaza, the slow pace of democratic reforms, and the global financial crisis, among other stated reasons.

Other partnerships with EU's satellite countries have also been advanced in recent years. The Union for the Mediterranean, formerly known as the Barcelona Process, was launched in July 2008 between the EU and 16 countries in the southern Mediterranean and Middle East and identified priority projects, including ridding pollution from the Mediterranean. Additionally, on May 8, 2009, in Prague, the EU launched an "Eastern Partnership" initiative with post-Soviet states to "accelerate political association and further economic integration" with the EU but without the prospect of eventual EU membership. Signatories included the EU along with Armenia, Azerbaijan, Belarus, Georgia, Moldova, and Ukraine. The initiative will establish free trade areas and offer EU economic aid, technical expertise, and security consultations in exchange for obligations by the six former Soviet states to commit to democracy, the rule of law, and human rights policies. Russia accused the EU of carving out a new sphere of influence.

In late 2007 Bosnia and Herzegovina signed stabilization and association agreements with the EU, a first step toward membership, while Serbia's stalled talks resumed after it agreed to arrest and extradite remaining fugitives wanted by the war crimes tribunal. Meanwhile, the EU council in February 2008 launched a crisis management mission to the newly declared country of Kosovo. The EU Rule of Law Mission in Kosovo is charged with assisting in the formation of "independent and multi-ethnic" law enforcement and judicial systems. Kosovo signed a pre-accession assistance agreement in May that provided $83 million for infrastructure and financial stabilization projects, although its future membership was considered uncertain given that four EU countries that would have to ratify its accession had not recognized Kosovo as an independent state. Additionally, in July 2009 the EC recommended visa-free access for Macedonians, although no date had been set for EU membership talks because of election violence and widespread corruption.

Croatia is expected to become the 28th country to join the EU in 2011. Negotiations were slowed in 2008 by Slovenia's veto of accession talks as a result of a longstanding border dispute. Talks resumed in September 2009 following Slovenia's agreement to handle the dispute separately. Montenegro submitted an application in December 2008, followed by Albania in April 2009.

At an EU summit in Brussels on March 13–14, 2008, an agreement was reached on greenhouse gas emissions and renewable energy to meet targets for a 20 percent reduction in emissions by 2020. The plan was approved by the European Parliament on December 17 despite objections by Eastern European countries that the measures would raise energy costs and be overly burdensome during an economic recession. Nevertheless, the plan gave each nation and sector mandated emission limits, while creating an auction system on emissions from industrial sources (currently free of charge) beginning in 2013, and set 20 percent targets for better energy efficiency and renewables in the EU's energy mix.

In one of the first concrete signs of defense cooperation between EU member states, the EU announced plans in November 2008 to build a pan-European military aircraft transport fleet. Expected to be operational within a decade, the European Air Transport Fleet would be housed by member nations and made available for humanitarian and peacekeeping missions.

In November 2008 the EU officially slipped into economic recession, its first since the creation of the eurozone in 1999. The downturn quickly became the single greatest challenge facing the union, with the Baltic states, Spain, and the United Kingdom especially exposed by inflated real estate markets. Countries with large current account deficits, notably Greece and Hungary, also suffered. Germany's economy also declined because of its heavy reliance on exports.

In response, EU institutions took unprecedented actions to salvage the block's financial industries. Initially injecting $270 billion into the EU banking system in August 2007, efforts were doubled a year later. Throughout the fall of 2008 and into 2009, the European Central Bank repeatedly cut interest rates in coordination with the central banks of member countries and the U.S. Federal Reserve. It was also announced that members that breached the budget deficit threshold of 3 percent of GDP would be given time to bring their spending in line before penalties would be imposed.

Meanwhile, in October and December 2008 the EU took directed action with the IMF and World Bank to assist Hungary and Latvia, whose currencies had dramatically depreciated. In November the EC outlined a $257 billion stimulus package for member states, equivalent to approximately 1.5 percent of the EU's GDP, to be drawn from member governments and from within EU budgets. The stimulus plan was passed in December and was viewed with skepticism, particularly by Germany, which resisted a return to large-scale deficit spending after having made painful strides in recent years to balance its own budget. Other analysts said the plan's combination of tax cuts and accelerated regional spending was not sufficiently targeted to provide immediate relief.

In March 2009 EU leaders, led by Germany, rejected a proposal for a special aid package to non-eurozone countries, although Hungary warned of a new "Iron Curtain" descending. However, soon after, at a leadership summit in Brussels, assistance available to non-eurozone countries was doubled to $68 billion and a $5 billion stimulus measure was directed toward green technology and digital communication projects. EU leaders rejected pressure from the United States to raise the size of their economic stimulus plans in favor of restraining budget deficits. Following the collapse of Iceland's banking industry, Iceland's parliament (*Althing*) narrowly voted in July 2009 to apply for EU membership in the hopes of achieving lasting economic stability. The decision was received warmly by EU leaders, although Iceland's entry was not assured because of likely differences over EU quotas that could affect its fish industry.

A cornerstone of the EU response to the recession has been to impose stricter regulation on financial markets. In February and March 2009 the EU announced new regulatory requirements for credit-rating agencies and additional oversight over hedge funds. Additionally, in September the EU called for limits on executive bonuses as part of G-20 discussions on an overhaul of the global financial system.

In May the IMF estimated for 2009 a decline of –4.2 percent across the eurozone countries and a –4.9 percent drop for emerging European economies. For 2010 it projected a more moderate decline of –0.4 percent while emerging economies return to growth at 0.7 percent.

The June 4–7, 2009, parliamentary election ushered in a smaller body dominated by center-right groups. The size of parliament decreased from a record of 785 members to 736, while center-left parties failed to articulate a socialist response to the ongoing economic recession. Populist parties and some environmental formations made some inroads, while in Hungary the far-right nationalist Jobbik party took third place. The election registered a new low in voter turnout at 43 percent, with Central and Eastern European countries displaying the most voter apathy. The resulting body split into a number of new formations. The largest remained the European People's Party, which dropped the suffix "European Democrats" after a 54-strong contingent led by the UK Conservatives dropped out and formed the European Conservatives and Reformists Group. The Party of European Socialists changed its name to Progressive Alliance of Socialists and Democrats to signify that it was not a rigidly socialist formation.

Following the election an EU summit in Brussels on June 18–19 resulted in a package of legal guarantees addressing policy areas important to Ireland to safeguard against a second Irish refusal of the Lisbon Treaty in a referendum to be held in October. Additionally, countries agreed to establish a "European system of financial supervisors" by 2010 that would consist of three new authorities with oversight powers of the banking, insurance, and securities sectors. The agreement represented a compromise solution between a contingent led by France that called for much stricter regulation over the financial industry and the United Kingdom, which worried that additional supervision would drive companies out of the country.

Meanwhile, in July 2009 four EU countries (Austria, Bulgaria, Romania, and Hungary) completed a deal with Turkey to cede territory for the construction of the Nabucco pipeline to bring stable gas supplies from the Caspian Sea to Europe, but the source of the supplies was not assured as Azerbaijan refused to commit its gas reserves to Europe, instead cooperating with Russia in building a rival pipeline. Repeated disruptions in winter deliveries of Russian gas to EU countries, the result of Russian disputes with Ukraine, have intensified the EU's efforts to find an alternative supplier to Russia, which currently provides one-quarter of the EU's gas supplies.

On September 16, 2009, Barroso was reelected to a second five-year term of office with the unanimous support of all members and no opposing candidate. However, he faced criticism for favoring large member states, such as Germany, France, and the United Kingdom.

At an earlier EU summit on June 18–19, 2009, the European Council approved a set of "legal guarantees" pertaining to the Lisbon Treaty that affirmed that Irish policies on taxation, abortion, education, family, workers' rights, and military neutrality would be addressed to "the mutual satisfaction of Ireland and the other member states." Upon the insistence of Ireland, the measures were to become protocol, meaning they would be incorporated into EU treaties, although several EU countries were uneasy about the designation because it would need to be ratified by all EU national parliaments. However, it was agreed this would be done as part of the next accession agreement, expected upon Croatian membership in 2011.

Irish voters approved the treaty by 67 percent in a referendum on October 2, 2009, thereby removing the last major hurdle to the treaty's implementation. Despite the strong margin of victory, analysts attributed the treaty's passage to Irish economic despair and fear over losing ties to the EU rather than genuine enthusiasm for the new constitution. Following Czech and Polish approval (see Origin and Development, above), the treaty came into force on December 1, 2009.

EUROPEAN ATOMIC ENERGY COMMUNITY

(Euratom)

Communauté Européenne de l'Energie Atomique

(CEEA)

Established: By Treaty of Rome (Italy), signed March 25, 1957, effective January 1, 1958.

Purpose: To develop research, to disseminate information, to enforce uniform safety standards, to facilitate investment, to ensure regular and equitable distribution of supplies of nuclear material, to guarantee that nuclear materials are not diverted from their designated uses and to exercise certain property rights in regard to such materials, to create a common market for the free movement of investment capital and personnel for nuclear industries, and to promote the peaceful uses of atomic energy.

Membership: (See European Union.)

Web site: http://euratom.org

Origin and development. Euratom was established in response to the assessment that atomic power on a large scale would be urgently needed to meet the growing energy requirements for economic expansion. The original six European Steel and Coal Community (ECSC) member states also sought to reduce the lead that Britain, the Soviet Union, and the United States had acquired in the field of peaceful uses of nuclear energy. To this end, the members decided to pool their efforts, as the area was too complex and expensive to be dealt with nationally. Structurally, the Treaty of Rome provided for a council, a commission, and the sharing of the assembly and court of justice already operating under the ECSC.

In December 1969 it was agreed to reshape Euratom so that it could conduct nuclear research under contract for community clients and extend its activities to other scientific research projects, especially those involving noncommunity states. The council also resolved to streamline the community's management, making its operations more flexible and ensuring more effective coordination of its nuclear activities. These reforms took effect in 1971.

Activities. In 1981 an agreement came into force between the community, France, and the International Atomic Energy Agency (IAEA) regarding safeguards on certain nuclear materials, and officials signed long-term agreements establishing conditions for the sale and security within the EC of nuclear materials supplied by Australia and Canada. In November 1995 Euratom and the United States completed negotiations on a controversial new agreement concerning "nuclear cooperation" to replace an accord set to expire at the end of the year. The most contentious element of the pact was a provision giving Euratom members greater latitude in selling plutonium originating from the United States. Previously, Washington had held a veto power over any such transactions; however, the new agreement permitted Euratom members to trade the plutonium within EU borders without U.S. approval. Some U.S. and international groups opposed the measure on the grounds that the plutonium could end up in the control of countries with looser standards, especially given anticipated EU expansion to the east.

Washington also reportedly lodged a protest with Euratom in 1996 concerning a uranium-powered research reactor planned for construction near Munich. The U.S. complaint apparently centered on reported Euratom contacts with Moscow regarding the possible purchase of uranium from Russia for the reactor. For their part, European officials reportedly objected to Washington's presenting itself as the "world policeman" on nuclear issues, noting that the United States had a multibillion-dollar economic stake in the trade of nuclear materials. Despite such strategic differences, in 2000 the United States and Euratom reached a cooperative agreement that covers fusion as well as fission research.

Given that approximately one-third of the EU's energy is nuclear, Euratom continues to be involved in efforts to prevent a disruption of nuclear fuel supplies. Since 1960 a Euratom Supply Agency operating under the commission has coordinated all of Euratom's contracts for the supply of fissionable material. Inspections of installations that use these supplies are conducted on a regular basis to ensure that nuclear materials are not diverted from peaceful uses and are otherwise maintained under appropriate safeguards.

Because of diminished popular support for nuclear energy, triggered in part by the 1986 Chernobyl disaster in the Soviet Union, the European Commission stopped approving new loans for construction of nuclear power plants within member countries. In June 2004, however, the commission approved a proposal for a Finnish plant, the first in the EU in over a decade and the world's first "third-generation" (post-2000) facility, which has new safety, reliability, and cost-saving features. Due to a revived interest in reducing dependence on hydrocarbon sources of energy, the commission also sought a significant increase in Euratom's loan fund. In June 2004 the commission approved a loan of €224 million ($275 million) for construction of a reactor in candidate country Romania. Bulgaria, which began decommissioning its Soviet-era first-generation nuclear power plants at the urging of the EU, was expected to request similar assistance for new construction. Loans for safety and modernization efforts were also extended to other Eastern European countries, including Russia and Ukraine, where the last Chernobyl reactor was permanently shut down in December 2000. Russia's disruption of natural gas supplies to the EU in the winter of 2005–2006 also led to an increased interest in nuclear power. As of January 2006, the Finnish plant was under construction; France and the Czech Republic had announced plans to build more nuclear plants; and Belgium, Italy, Germany, and Sweden had all begun reconsideration of the nuclear power moratorium.

Concurrently, scientists have intensified research on thermonuclear fusion, which many believe could provide power without most of the safety risks and environmental problems associated with fission reactors. The long-term goal of the EU Fusion Program is "the joint creation of prototype reactors which will lead to electric power plants that meet society's needs: operational safety, respect for the environment, economic viability." Since the first half of the 1980s, fusion research has been conducted at the Joint European Torus (JET), a research and development facility in Culham, United Kingdom. On January 1, 2000, the new European Fusion Development Agreement (EFDA) became operational to govern use of JET to coordinate fusion technology projects within the EU and to oversee EU participation in outside endeavors. These endeavors include the international thermonuclear experimental reactor (ITER) project initiated in 1988 by Japan, Russia, and the United States, for which a design was completed in 2001. China and South Korea also are participating in the $12 billion project. In June 2005 the partners announced that ITER would be built in Cadarache, France, with a target completion date of 2015.

Much of Euratom's current fusion research looks toward this "Next Step"—that is, construction and operation of an experimental reactor. At the same time, research on the physics of fusion continues, as does longer-range preparatory work for development of a demonstration reactor and, ultimately, a prototype reactor. The full process is expected to take at least another 20 years.

Meanwhile, research in the area of fission also continues, with principal focus on improving operational safety of existing and future reactors, as well as the fuel cycle and advancing understanding of radiation protection, including risk assessment, emergency management, severe accident phenomenology, waste management, decommissioning of reactors, and long-term management and restoration of contaminated sites. Past research projects, many stemming from the Chernobyl accident, have involved a wide range of activities, among them treating people exposed to radiation and setting permissible levels of contamination in foodstuffs. Euratom scientists and physicians also have participated in studies examining possible adverse health and environmental consequences associated with the use of depleted-uranium armaments in the Bosnian and Kosovo conflicts during the 1990s.

In December 2002 the European Court of Justice (ECJ), ruling in a dispute brought by the European Commission against the Council of the European Union, stated that Euratom, as well as the individual member countries, had competence with regard to broader nuclear safety concerns. In a declaration accompanying the Act of Accession to the 1994 global Convention on Nuclear Safety, the council had erred, according to the ECJ, by overly limiting Euratom's role to workplace-related protections and emergency planning, whereas the organization was also competent in safety matters related to siting facilities, design and construction, and operations. The court's decision came at a time when the EU, thanks to enlargement, was about to "inherit" outmoded Soviet-built nuclear plants, further complicating issues of safety and security, as well as transport of nuclear materials and disposal of nuclear waste. In May 2005, confirming a 2004 proposal by the commission, the council extended Euratom competence to two international conventions adopted in 1986, the Convention on Early Notification of a Nuclear Accident and the Convention on Assistance in the Case of a Nuclear Accident or Radiological Emergency.

Meanwhile, during the constitutional debates of the Convention on the Future of Europe, the question of Euratom's future role became a significant issue. Some opponents of nuclear power wanted the Euratom treaty to be abolished, which would cut off subsidies to the nuclear power industry, and its safety functions addressed by the proposed European Constitution. Other opponents argued that the Euratom treaty should be "unbundled" from other key EU documents and attached as a protocol to the constitution, thereby making it easier for countries to withdraw from the treaty without affecting their overall standing in the union. In the end, in 2003 the drafting convention left the treaty intact. Later, the European Parliament, which has long sought greater control over Euratom activities, urged the intergovernmental conference (IGC) on the constitution "to convene a Treaty revision conference in order to repeal the obsolete and outdated provisions of that Treaty, especially those relating to the promotion of nuclear energy and the lack of democratic decision-making procedures." The governments of Austria, Germany, Hungary, Ireland, and Sweden also called for convening a special IGC on Euratom and related nuclear matters, as they also did in a declaration attached to the proposed Treaty of Lisbon in 2007. That treaty, if ratified, would include Euratom's expenditures and revenues in the EU budget, excluding the Euratom Supply Agency and joint undertakings.

Euratom has its own "framework program" for nuclear research and training activities that is managed by common EC institutions. Euratom's Seventh Framework Program (FP7), which calls for spending €2.8 billion ($3.6 billion) during 2007–2011—more than double the €1.2 ($1.1 billion) budgeted for 2002–2006—encompasses two categories of research. "Indirect actions," which are managed by the commission's Directorate General for Research, involve fusion energy, nuclear fission, and radiation protection. "Direct actions," undertaken by the Joint Research Center (JRC), cover three themes: nuclear waste management; environmental impact; and basic knowledge, nuclear safety, and nuclear security. The JRC was established by Euratom and has become a leading European institute for nuclear research.

Pressure to expand nuclear power in EU borders, particularly in the East, has grown in recent years, although Euratom's role remains controversial. Despite safety concerns brought by activists, the EC in December 2007 approved construction of a new two-unit Russian-designed nuclear power plant in northern Bulgaria in Belene, paving the way for an application for a sizable Euratom loan, which would be the agency's first in 20 years. By late 2007 the Belene project was plagued with uncertainties, including corruption allegations and difficulties in attracting funding even as Euratom guaranteed a $780 million loan. Additionally, Lithuania and Estonia have plans to build nuclear reactors, the former acting in response to its EU accession agreement, which mandated the closure of a Soviet-era plant.

In February 2008 the European Council of Ministers updated Euratom statutes by shrinking its advisory committee from 75 to 56 members to improve the body's efficiency. The agency was also given approval to build a multinational nuclear fuel reserve to provide a backup supply of enriched uranium to be used if supplies from outside the EU were cut off for political reasons.

In March 2009 the EC announced its intent to advance a nuclear nonproliferation framework for bilateral agreements with nuclear countries seeking to have significant nuclear trade with EU countries or industries. Euratom would negotiate bilateral agreements and provide expertise in nuclear energy in exchange for commitments to use nuclear energy for entirely peaceful purposes.

Upon an EC directive in November 2008, Euratom drafted a Nuclear Safety Directive that established legally binding rules for safety standards on nuclear installations within EU member states and enhanced the powers of national regulatory bodies. The EC approved the directive on June 25, 2009.

Euratom's role in overseeing nuclear activities between EU members and other countries was expected to be debated as French companies were poised to grab a major share of India's nuclear energy market in late 2008. At issue was whether EU members could negotiate agreements without involving Euratom.

GROUP OF SEVEN/GROUP OF EIGHT

Established: As the Group of Seven (G-7) during the San Juan, Puerto Rico, summit of leading industrial democracies held on June 27–28, 1976; first met as the kindred Group of Eight (G-8) after the addition of Russia as a formal participant at the May 15–17, 1998, G-7 summit in Birmingham, United Kingdom.

Purpose: To discuss problems relating to the functioning and structure of the world economy, the international monetary and banking systems, international trade, and other economic and political concerns.

Principal Organs: The G-8 has no formal organs as such. There are annual summits (currently at the G-8 level), twice-a-year (and ad hoc) meetings of finance ministers and central bank governors (usually at the G-7 level), and other meetings of government ministers and officials.

Web site: None, but the University of Toronto maintains a very complete record of its activities at www.g7.utoronto.ca.

G-7 Membership (7): Canada, France, Germany, Italy, Japan, United Kingdom, United States.

G-8 Membership (8): G-7 plus Russia.

Origin and development. The origins of the G-7 and G-8 can be traced back to 1962 and the founding of the informal Group of Ten (G-10; see separate article) by Belgium, Canada, France, the Federal Republic of Germany, Italy, Japan, the Netherlands, Sweden, the United Kingdom, and the United States.

Later in the decade finance ministers and sometimes central bank governors from France, the Federal Republic of Germany, Japan, the United Kingdom, and the United States began to meet as an additional informal caucus that became known as the Group of Five (G-5). As a consequence of discussions at the July 30–August 1, 1975, Helsinki Conference on Security and Cooperation in Europe, the heads of state or government of the G-5 plus Italy convened in November 1975 in Rambouillet, France, to address various economic and financial concerns, including growth, inflation, exchange rates, monetary reform, oil prices, and unemployment. Canada joined as the seventh participant in the San Juan, Puerto Rico, summit in 1976, at which time the assembled leaders agreed on the utility of holding annual sessions. Thus the G-7 was born.

The agendas of the 1976 summit and then the May 7–8, 1977, summit in London, United Kingdom, were broadened to include such concerns as balance-of-payments problems and North-South relations. Also, beginning with the 1977 summit, the European Community (EC, subsequently the European Union—EU) was included in discussions, although not as a full participant. At the next summit, held July 16–17, 1978, in Bonn, West Germany, the G-7 issued an unprecedented statement denouncing aircraft hijacking that was widely recognized as the group's first political declaration. Developments at the 1979 summit in Paris included the establishment of the Financial Action Task Force (FATF), which was asked to identify and promote policies that would combat money laundering. (In 2001 the 33-member, independent FATF, which is headquartered at the Paris offices of the Organization for Economic Cooperation and Development [OECD], expanded its scope to combat terrorist financing—see the OECD article for additional details.) The agendas at succeeding summits expanded to arms control, the environment, political reform, and terrorism. During the second half of the 1980s the G-7 focused on such matters as rectifying trade imbalances, stabilizing exchange rates, combating protectionism, and relaxing debt repayment pressure on the world's poorest countries.

The issue of how best to encourage free-market reform in the Soviet Union and its former satellites in Eastern Europe dominated the G-7 summit July 15–17, 1991, in London, which was attended by Soviet leader Mikhail Gorbachev. Some observers predicted that the meeting might lead to creation of a Group of Eight, a possibility that U.S. president George H. W. Bush then broached at the 1992 summit in Munich, Germany, which Russian president Boris Yeltsin attended. By the 1994 summit in Naples, Italy, Russian participation in most nonfinancial discussions had become the norm, resulting in the designation Political-8 (P-8). Russia's formal inclusion at the May 15–17, 1998, summit in Birmingham, United Kingdom, marked the birth of the G-8, although the G-7 continued to issue separate statements and communiqués, primarily on financial and economic matters.

Structure. The G-7 and G-8 have no permanent secretariat or administrative bodies. Activities coalesce around annual summits of the members' heads of state or government, joined by the president of the European Commission. National delegations also include finance and foreign ministers and a personal representative of each president, prime minister, or chancellor. Summits typically include a day of private, informal bilateral and multilateral discussions among the leaders. Summits are hosted by the member countries in rotation.

Throughout the year high-level meetings can be held by the members' foreign ministers; by finance ministers and central bank governors (usually meeting as the G-7); or by ministers responsible for the environment, justice and interior, labor, development, and other areas. Ad hoc task forces and working groups also have been established.

Activities. In the first half of the 1990s, G-7 discussions often centered on how best to support the fledgling free-market systems in the former Communist world. The breakup of Yugoslavia and attendant crises in the Balkans, Russian actions in Chechnya, and the Mexico peso crisis of 1994–1995 also were among the most pressing topics during this period. Terrorism moved to the forefront of the agenda at the June 28–29, 1996, summit in Lyon, France, which took place only a week after the bombing of a U.S. military base in Saudi Arabia. At the urging of U.S. president Bill Clinton, the G-7 leaders approved a 40-point plan to combat crime and terrorism.

With the exception of a brief economic policy discussion, Russia participated fully in the June 20–21, 1997, summit in Denver, Colorado, in the United States. At that session, environmental policies were the focus of considerable debate as the United States and Japan resisted European pressure to set emission targets for greenhouse gases. The 1998 summit in Birmingham was dominated by the recent dramatic downturn in Asia's economic fortunes and by India's test of a nuclear weapon. In June the G-8 agreed to block all but humanitarian loans from international lenders to both India and Pakistan, which had exploded its own nuclear device in response to India's test.

Meeting in February 1999, the G-7 finance ministers and bank governors approved a plan to establish a Financial Stability Forum (FSF), its primary purpose being to prevent economic crises by improving oversight of, and information exchange within, the world's financial systems. The forum comprised representatives of the G-7 countries, the Netherlands, Australia, Hong Kong, Singapore, Switzerland, the European Central Bank, the Bank for International Settlements (BIS), the

International Monetary Fund (IMF), the OECD, the World Bank, the Basel Committee on Banking Supervision, the International Accounting Standards Board, the International Organization of Securities Commissions, the International Association of Insurance Supervisors, the Committee on the Global Financial System, and the Committee on Payment and Settlement Systems.

Steps were also taken to include developing countries in discussions related to reform of global financial systems. Largely at the instigation of President Clinton at the November 1997 Asia-Pacific Economic Cooperation (APEC) summit in Vancouver, Canada, a temporary Group of 22 (G-22) took shape. In addition to the G-7 countries, G-22 participants included Argentina, Australia, Brazil, China, Hong Kong, India, Indonesia, South Korea, Malaysia, Mexico, Poland, Russia, Singapore, South Africa, and Thailand. The grouping held its first meeting in April 1998. Less than a year later, on March 11, 1999, a successor Group of 33 (G-33) met for the first time in Bonn, Germany, with a second session convening April 25 in Washington, D.C. The 11 additions to the G-22 were Belgium, Chile, Côte d'Ivoire, Egypt, Morocco, Netherlands, Saudi Arabia, Spain, Sweden, Switzerland, and Turkey.

The G-33 was superseded September 26, 1999, by a new Group of 20 comprising representatives of the EU and the IMF/World Bank, as well as the G-7 members and the following 11 countries: Argentina, Australia, Brazil, China, India, Republic of Korea, Mexico, Russia, Saudi Arabia, South Africa, and Turkey. Intended to "broaden the dialogue on key economic and financial policy issues . . . and to achieve stable and sustainable world growth that benefits all," the G-20 met for the first time December 15–16 in Berlin, Germany.

The June 18–20, 1999, G-7/G-8 summit in Cologne, Germany, approved a debt relief package that increased the number of countries eligible for the IMF/World Bank's Heavily Indebted Poor Countries (HIPC) program by 7 to 36. Described as the largest debt-relief program in history, the initiative projected debt relief of up to $90 billion ($70 billion from the G-7 members) over the next several years, in part through IMF reinvestment of proceeds from gold sales. Eligible countries would have to provide assurances that the relief was being channeled into structural reforms and social policy concerns, such as health and education programs. At the summit the G-8 also worked on plans for peacekeeping in Kosovo and, more broadly, reconstruction and development throughout the Balkan states, principally in conjunction with the EU-sponsored Stability Pact for South-Eastern Europe.

At the annual G-7/G-8 summit July 21–23, 2000, in Nago, Okinawa, development funding and debt relief remained a focus of attention, one of the concerns being the slow pace of debt cancellation. Other matters under discussion included achieving gender equality, universal primary education by 2015, and improved health care. Rising world oil prices and recent action by G-7 central banks to prop up the euro dominated discussions at the G-7 ministerial session that immediately preceded the September annual meeting of the IMF and World Bank. At the latter, officials noted that slow progress on debt relief was linked to the failure of the G-7 countries to provide sufficient funding.

The G-7/G-8 summit July 20–22, 2001, in Genoa, Italy, took place amid disruptions caused by antiglobalization protests. In addition to the troubled state of the world economy, discussions centered on such topics as cutting emission of greenhouse gases, implementing a development plan for Africa, and overcoming the "digital divide." The session also approved a $1.3 billion fund to help combat AIDS, tuberculosis, and malaria. Meeting in Washington in October 2001, a month after the September terrorist attacks against the United States, the G-7 finance ministers and central bank governors stated their resolve to strengthen the faltering world economy, although they adopted no specific action plan.

Canada hosted the June 26–27, 2002, summit in Kananaskis, Alberta, sufficiently removed from the nearest large city, Calgary, to ease security concerns. Despite disagreements on particular issues—for example, U.S. tariffs directed against steel and softwood lumber imports and U.S. president George W. Bush's call for Palestinians to replace Yasir Arafat as leader of the Palestinian Authority—several initiatives were approved. The G-8 agreed to a ten-year aid package of $20 billion (half from the United States) to assist Russia and other countries of the former Soviet bloc in securing their remaining nuclear materials. The leaders also agreed to provide additional debt relief under the HIPC initiative, but the $1 billion commitment was far less than some advocates had sought. Similar criticism greeted the G-8 African Action Plan, which confirmed an earlier commitment of $6 billion per year, beginning in 2006, in support of the African Union's New Partnership for Africa's Development (NEPAD).

The June 2–3, 2003, summit in Evian-les-Bains, France, ended with fewer concrete results than its predecessor, in part because of President Bush's planned departure after only 24 hours, but more fundamentally because of lingering ill will attributable to the earlier U.S.-UK decision to invade Iraq and oust the Saddam Hussein regime. Canada, France, Germany, and Russia vocally opposed the March attack and resultant occupation, although the summit participants managed to voice a tepid collective commitment to establishing a sovereign, stable, and democratic Iraq. Unanimity was evident primarily in a condemnation of nuclear proliferation, the "pre-eminent threat to international security."

Earlier in2003, at a February meeting of G-7 finance ministers and central bankers, some participants had criticized the Bush administration for its large tax cuts and projected fiscal deficits. In February 2004 Japan and the European G-7 members expressed, with greater urgency, their concern about the consequences of a recent steep fall in the value of the U.S. dollar, which the Bush administration, facing a fall election, appeared willing to accept in the expectation that a weak dollar would spur export sales, encourage manufacturing, and create jobs.

Following President Bush's call in April 2004 for more engagement with China in the rich countries' economies, China was invited to participate for the first time in a meeting of the finance ministers and central bank governors at a G-7 meeting on October 1 in Washington. Meanwhile, some of the G-8 countries continued to be at odds with the United States and Britain over financing peacekeeping missions in Iraq, the topic dominating the June 8–10, 2004, summit in Sea Island, Georgia, with Iraqi interim president Sheikh Ghazi Ajil al-Yawar in attendance. Ultimately, the G-8 failed to agree to a full cancellation of the world's poorest countries' debt. Instead, they agreed to a two-year extension of their long-running effort to assist in debt reduction.

In 2005 G-7 ministers met often early in the year, struggling to come to terms with debt relief for Africa and many other of the poorest countries. On June 11, in what was described as a "landmark deal" brokered by Britain, the G-7 leaders, meeting in London, agreed to pay to relieve 18 of the poorest countries—most of them in Africa—of some $40 billion in debt. The agreement, the basis of which was hammered out by President Bush and British prime minister Tony Blair a week earlier, would also benefit another nine countries, bringing the total debt reduction tab to some $55 billion. On September 24, 2005, the G-7 pledged to uphold the agreement during its summit in Gleneagles, Scotland.

By the end of 2005, the developing world energy shortage was engaging G-7/G-8 attention, as were ways to combat international terrorism. These concerns were reflected in the report of the December 2–3 meeting of the G-7 finance ministers and central bank governors in London. The report remained generally positive about global growth, however, despite increased worries over inflation and a warning that the value of a country's currency (China was implied) must reflect economic reality. A similar message about the prospects for economic growth came from the April 21, 2006, meeting of the same group in Washington. The belief was that inflation was being contained, despite the run-up in oil prices, and growth in general was good. The group pledged to work for more transparency in oil markets, and it warned against global imbalances and a rise in protectionism.

The July 15-17, 2006, summit was the first to be hosted by Russia. The summit was supposed to deal primarily with energy security from the standpoint of both consumer and producer nations. The conference was dominated, however, by fighting in Lebanon between Israel and Hezbollah. The conference produced a statement which called for restraint but failed to mention all of the parties involved by name. In September 2006 the G-7 finance ministers met in Singapore, ahead of the annual meetings of the World Bank and IMF. The ministers called on China to adopt a more flexible attitude toward the value of its currency.

The value of the yuan and increasing concerns about the U.S. economy's health increasingly occupied G-7/G-8 attention during 2007. These concerns were in evidence at the June 6–8 summit in Heligendamm, Germany, but the main emphasis was on climate change. The meeting produced an agreement to "consider seriously" cutting carbon dioxide emissions by 50 percent by 2050, but no specifics were laid out. The conference also agreed to deliver on previous financial pledges to Africa and agreed to a new package of $60 billion to fight AIDS, malaria, and tuberculosis.

The July 7–8, 2008, summit in Hokkaido, Japan, was held amid sharply growing concerns about climate change. Tony Blair, now no longer the British prime minister, addressed the G-20 meeting in March 2008. He asked for revolutionary climate action by G-8 and other nations. In April Japanese prime minister Yasuo Fukuda met with EU representatives, promising to push for strong measures at the G-8 summit. By June, however, Fukuda was trying to lower expectations for results. He said the mission of the G-8 meeting was "to send out messages pointing to solutions," and the UN, rather than the G-8, should come up with medium-term goals for reducing emissions. Also in June Blair said the G-8 members were too far divided to set meaningful targets for 2050 or even 2020, and instead should focus on setting a course agreeable to all for the 2009 UN conference in Copenhagen, Denmark. The climate change discussions effectively ended in an impasse between the G-8 countries, particularly the U.S., India, and China. The summit agreed only to work towards halving greenhouse emissions by 2050, but without giving any specifics on how this could be achieved. To make matters worse, after the meeting U.S. president George W. Bush declared that the U.S would take no concrete steps towards reducing emissions during his presidency.

In other business, France proposed that China, India, Mexico, Brazil and South Africa, all large or developing industrial economies and attendees of the "outreach session" which preceded the summit proper, should become permanent members. This was opposed by the U.S. and Japan. The meeting pledged to take action on the 2005 summit promises of aid to Africa. Also, in a relatively mild statement, it took note of the political crisis in Zimbabwe.

The 2008 summit was generally not considered a success. At least one commentator suggested that if the G-8 was to be useful, it needed a permanent secretariat. Subsequently, the G-7 finance ministers met in Washington, D.C., October 10–11, 2008, in response to the worldwide financial crisis, producing a declaration of intent that each country would take steps to improve the situation. After this meeting the G-8 leaders agreed to hold a summit with other world leaders to discuss world financial reform. The statement said that changes had to be made to the "regulatory and institutional regimes for the world's financial sectors to remedy deficiencies exposed by the current crisis." The requested summit was a meeting of G-20 leaders, held in Washington on November 14–15.

The 2009 summit, scheduled for July 8–10 in Maddalena, on the Italian island of Sardinia, was moved to the town of L'Aquila, which had recently been badly damaged by an earthquake. The Italian government described the move as a gesture of solidarity with the stricken town, with an added benefit that security would be less expensive, and the savings could be diverted to earthquake relief. The conference was described as extremely disorganized, and its ability to deal with matters of pollution and climate change was reduced by Chinese president Hu Jintao's decision to leave early to deal with domestic unrest. The conference pledged, without offering specifics, that by 2050 average global temperatures should not rise more than two degrees Celsius above the year 1900 levels. The summit also pledged $20 billion for a three-year initiative to help poor countries develop their own agriculture. The sum was larger than many observers had expected, and the plan was felt likely to be more effective than if it had simply involved sending food.

GROUP OF TEN

Established: As the group of contributing countries to the General Arrangements to Borrow (GAB), negotiated in 1962 in Paris, France, by the Executive Board of the International Monetary Fund.

Purpose: To discuss problems relating to the function and structure of the international monetary system.

Principal Organs: None; communication within the group occurs at regular and ad hoc meetings of ministers, ministerial deputies, and governors or other representatives of the members' central banks.

Web site: www.g10.org (This is a very minimal collection of links to other institutions where related documents may be found. The collection on the OECD Web site is the most complete.)

Membership (11): Belgium, Canada, France, Germany, Italy, Japan, Netherlands, Sweden, Switzerland, United Kingdom, United States.

Nonstate Participants (4): International Monetary Fund (IMF), Organization for Economic Cooperation and Development (OECD), Bank for International Settlements (BIS), European Commission (EC).

Origin and development. The Group of Ten (G-10), also sometimes known as the Group of 11 since Switzerland's accession to membership in 1984, consists of those states that contribute to the General Arrangements to Borrow (GAB), a supplementary loan agreement negotiated to increase IMF lending resources. GAB was formally launched in October 1962, although prospective members had met earlier to examine the international monetary system.

Major decisions of the G-10 include a 1966 recommendation that led to the establishment of special drawing rights (SDRs) as a supplementary IMF liquidity resource and support for the IMF's 1983 expansion of GAB to deal with the potential default of heavily indebted countries. The G-10 also backed other changes allowing the use of some GAB resources by non-GAB participants and extended GAB association to certain borrowing arrangements between the IMF and non-GAB participants.

Over the years, G-10 activity became intertwined with, and even supplanted by, several subgroups. In 1967 finance ministers and central bank governors of five G-10 members (France, Federal Republic of, Germany, Japan, United Kingdom, United States) began to meet regularly as an additional informal caucus on international economic monetary developments. They became known as the Group of Five (G-5). In 1975 the G-5 promoted still another forum, comprising the heads of state or government of its members. With the addition of Italy and Canada, the group became known as the Group of Seven, subsequently with Russia, the Group of Eight (G-8; see separate G-8 article). In general, the G-5 continued to operate confidentially, whereas the G-8 summits generated wide publicity on a broad agenda that grew to include issues well beyond the G-10's purview, such as terrorism and arms control.

Structure. One of the least institutionalized intergovernmental organizations, the G-10 holds meetings at several levels. Ministerial sessions are attended by the finance ministers and central bank governors of member states, the president of the Swiss National Bank, the managing director of the IMF, the secretary general of the OECD, the general manager of BIS, and the president of the EC. Meetings are held in the spring and fall of each year immediately prior to meetings of the IMF's Interim Committee, with ad hoc sessions called as needed. In addition, the central bank governors typically meet monthly. Members also are represented at as-needed "deputy" meetings attended by high-level civil servants from finance ministries and central banks, senior staff members of the IMF, the OECD Secretariat, BIS, and the EC. In addition, there are various working and contact groups for particular concerns, such as legal and institutional aspects of the international financial system.

Activities. The G-10 addresses many problems relating to international liquidity, bank lending, monetary policy, trade balances, and other economic issues. Meetings are private, and detailed information on decisions often is not made public. However, broadly worded communiqués are sometimes issued prior to IMF meetings or at times of international economic unrest. The G-10 also produces studies on economic and financial topics and continues to be responsible for approving loan requests under GAB; such loans are financed only by those states that approve the particular requests, but G-10 members provide "multilateral surveillance" over loan recipients.

At its June 1995 summit in Halifax, Canada, the G-7 urged the G-10 and others to help prevent the kind of financial crisis that beset Mexico the previous winter. In response, the IMF Executive Board established the New Arrangements to Borrow (NAB), effective November 1998, in which 26 states and institutions participate: the 11 G-10 members plus Australia, Austria, Banco Central de Chile (since 2003), Denmark, Finland, Hong Kong Monetary Authority, Republic of Korea, Kuwait, Luxembourg, Malaysia, Norway, Saudi Arabia, Singapore, Spain, and Thailand. In effect, NAB doubled to SDR 34 billion the resources on which the IMF can draw in the event of a threat to the international monetary system. As of January 2004, GAB has been activated ten times, most recently in July 1998 to finance an IMF Extended Arrangement for Russia, while NAB has been activated just once, in December 1998 to provide a Stand-by Arrangement for Brazil. In line with a G-10 recommendation, GAB was renewed for the tenth time in November 2002, with effect from December 2003.

The G-10 met September 27, 2002, in Washington, D.C., and discussed procedures for resolving debt crises that would benefit both debtors and creditors, including the restructuring of sovereign bonds. The participants also discussed how regulatory, tax, and disclosure policies affect asset markets. A year later, convening September 21 in Dubai, United Arab Emirates, the G-10 noted positive developments in the international economic climate, particularly improvements in the

U.S. and Japanese economies and reforms taking place in Europe. The G-10's concluding communiqué also noted, however, that "significant internal and external imbalances" could undermine the ongoing recovery. In addition, the communiqué noted the need to address future fiscal pressures associated with an aging population.

On June 26, 2004, the G-10 central bank governors approved new rules on Banking Capital Adequacy to help stabilize the global financial system by allowing banks to hold more capital to cover risk. The rules were to be implemented in two phases at the ends of 2006 and 2007.

In September 2004, after meeting in Basel, G-10 governors reported an upswing in the global economy despite high oil prices, and by January 2005 they were predicting nothing short of robust growth. When the per-barrel price of oil topped $60 in June 2005, however, the G-10 governors gave a gloomier assessment, saying that spike would surely dampen economic growth in many areas of the world.

In their report dated September 2005, the group turned to the likely effects of the increasing population reaching retirement age in a period of worldwide deregulation. The report called for governments to encourage increased transparency and better risk management on the part of private pension schemes and for the promotion of financial literacy among the public in general. As the world's economic picture became more unsettled the G-10 governors and spokespeople issued statements in which optimism was increasingly mixed with concern. Warnings about inflation continued, and were joined in 2007 by concerns that the U.S. subprime mortgage crisis could affect the U.S. economy and beyond. The G-10 governors met in Singapore on September 17, 2006, and decided that, while the group's existence was important, the annual summit meetings served no useful purpose and should be discontinued.

As perhaps an indication of the G-10's continued importance, in September 2007 Barclay's Capital in the UK issued the world's first "synthetic currency." This was the European Borrowing Unit (EBU), based on a basket of G-10 currencies and designed to allow very large companies to borrow in foreign currencies with a minimum of exchange rate risk. Initial reactions to the idea were positive. At an October 20, 2007, meeting in Washington, D.C., the G-10 governors and finance ministers noted that misuse of hedge funds did not seem to be playing a large part in the world's economic difficulties, but they welcomed efforts to develop standards of best practices for these instruments. They also endorsed the proposed renewal of GAB for five years, from December 26, 2008.

As problems in the U.S. subprime mortgage market grew in 2008 into a general tightening of credit, inflation, caused by a steep rise in the price of food and petroleum, became a major concern. Statements from the European Central Bank's president, Jean-Claude Trichet, continued to speak of the world economy as growing, while warning with increasing seriousness about inflation. In September 2008 the G-10 announced coordinated action to inject liquidity into the short-term dollar money markets around the world to combat an unprecedented rise in interest rates in these markets. In January 2009 the group predicted that 2009 would be a very bad year for the world economy, but that there would be significant improvement in 2010. By May 2009, however, the forecast for the remainder of the year was somewhat less pessimistic.

GROUP OF TWENTY

Established: September 25, 1999, at a Washington, DC session of the G-7 finance ministers. The Group of Twenty (G-20) consists of 19 larger-economy countries and the European Union, in addition to representatives of the International Monetary Fund and the World Bank. The group's finance ministers and central bank governors began meeting in 1999, and since that time have met every fall. G-20 heads of state or government began meeting in November 2008 (see below) and this elevation of status seems to represent the G-20's future.

Purpose: "A new mechanism for informal dialogue in the framework of the Bretton Woods institutional system, to broaden the dialogue on key economic and financial policy issues among systemically significant economies and to promote cooperation to achieve stable and sustainable world growth that benefits all."

Principal Organs: The G-20 has no permanent organs. There is a meeting of its members' finance ministers and central bank governors each fall, with occasional meetings of deputies and seminars at other times. Recently the heads of state or government of G-20 countries have also met. Arrangements are principally in the hands of the country that chairs the group in any particular year. (See below under **Structure**.)

Web site: No permanent official site. The UK put up the site www.g20.org in connection with its chairing of the group in 2009. In spite of the site's name it concentrates on the UK's role in 2009, and is unlikely to be maintained afterward, although another host country might take the name. The University of Toronto maintains a very complete record of G-20 activities at www.g8.utoronto.ca/g20.

Membership (20): Argentina, Australia, Brazil, Canada, China, European Union, France, Germany, India, Indonesia, Italy, Japan, Mexico, Russia, Saudi Arabia, South Africa, South Korea, Turkey, United Kingdom, United States of America.

Origin and development. Reflection on the Asian economic crisis of the late 1990s caused the finance ministers of the G-7 countries (Canada, France, Germany, Italy, Japan, United Kingdom, and United States) to suggest establishing a larger group, inviting the participation of a wider range of countries whose economic importance was growing. The enlarged group held its inaugural meeting in Berlin, December 15–16, 1999.

The original routine of ministerial and other meetings, held each year in a different host country, continued essentially unaltered until the fall of 2008. In that year the annual ministerial meeting was held in São Paulo, Brazil, November 8–9. However, because of the global financial crisis, it was followed by a summit meeting of G-20 heads of state or government in Washington, D.C., held November 14–15. Further summit meetings of G-20 leaders were held in London, April 1–2, 2009, and in Pittsburgh, Pennsylvania, September 24–25, 2009, in addition to the regular ministerial meetings. With G-20 summit meetings planned into 2011, the group seems to have emerged as the leading forum for international economic cooperation.

Structure. The G-20 has no permanent staff. The G-20 chair rotates between members, and is selected from a different regional grouping of countries each year. The chair is part of a revolving three-member management Troika consisting of immediate past, present, and immediate future chairs. The Troika is intended to ensure continuity in the G-20's work and management through the years. The incumbent chair establishes a temporary secretariat for the duration of its term. This body coordinates the group's work and organizes its meetings. The latest Troika consists of Brazil (2008), Britain (2009), and South Korea (2010).

Activities. The meetings and documents of the G-20 reflect the change from the relatively quiet late 1990s through the period of turmoil that began with the September 11, 2001, terrorist attacks in the United States, to the boom of the mid-decade, and then to the huge global economic crisis which began to be felt in 2008, and the change in group's status which came in response to that crisis.

The communiqué from the group's kickoff meeting, held in Berlin on December 15–16, 1999, stated the G-20's intent, as a group of "systemically significant economies" to meet for informal dialogue within the framework of the Bretton Woods system (see the discussion of the International Bank for Reconstruction and Development in the article on United Nations Specialized Agencies). The G-20 expressed relief that economic conditions were improving, worldwide and particularly in Asia, and hoped it might be useful in guiding the world's economies into an era of humane globalization.

The second G-20 ministerial meeting, held October 24–25, 2000, in Montreal, Canada, maintained an almost equally placid and hopeful tone. It did however note that poor people, in whatever country, were being disproportionately hurt by unrestricted free trade. The euro was trading at a historic low against the U.S. dollar, but few observers expected the United States to do anything to change that a few weeks before its presidential election.

The third meeting, November 16–17, 2001, in Ottawa, Canada, was held in the shadow of the September 11, 2001, attacks. The G-20 condemned these attacks not only as acts of terrorism but as an assault on global economic confidence and security. It resolved to fight terrorism by attacking the sources of funds for terrorist organizations. Each member country was to implement the relevant UN Security Council resolutions if it had not already done so. G-20 states were also to freeze the assets of terrorists and their supporters, to close off their access to the international financial system, and, as far as each country's laws allowed, to publish the names of those so treated. The group promised to work intensively together to exchange information, to combat money laundering, and to provide technical assistance to other countries that might need it. The group also vowed to do all it could to maintain capital flows to poorer countries, which seemed particularly vulnerable to the downturn. It also promised to evaluate the recommendations of the Financial Action Task Force on Money Laundering (FATF, see Group of Eight article), with progress on all these matters to be reported at the next meeting.

The fourth G-20 ministerial meeting was held in New Delhi, India, November 22–23, 2002. The international financial outlook was far from unclouded, the group felt. They reaffirmed their determination to fight terrorism. The meeting's communiqué strongly mentioned the possible negative effects of unrestricted globalization, and—perhaps a sign of the future—it called for increased responsibility and accountability in the international capital markets. It also mentioned the consequences of "inappropriate domestic policies."

The October 26–27, 2003, meeting in Morelia, Mexico, took as its first topic the prevention and resolution of financial crises. The G-20 also discussed the continued promotion of responsibility in capital markets, and the fight against terrorism. The group showed an increased concern for social safety nets for those not benefiting from the new financial order, as well as the importance of institution building and financing for development. And for the first time it considered the consequences of living in a world where countries other than the United States were becoming significant engines of economic growth.

By 2004 the world economic outlook seemed brighter, and the tone of the November 19–21 meeting in Berlin reflected that. It set out some guidelines for the future in an Accord for Sustained Growth. It also announced a Reform Agenda, an account of what several member countries planned to do with their own economies. The United States, for example, was "determined to reduce its public budget deficit, to continue reforming health insurance and the pension system, and to raise private savings."

The 2005 meeting, held on October 15–16 in Xianghe, China, began to address some of the problems that would manifest themselves later in the decade. The group noted the problem of high and volatile world oil prices, and also the increased levels of poverty in some countries. It urged a speedy conclusion to the Doha round of tariff reduction talks (see article on World Trade Organization). And, it considered that it might be time to reform and revitalize the Bretton Woods institutions (the World Bank and the International Monetary Fund, IMF) themselves.

In 2006 the G-20 finance ministers met in Melbourne, Australia, November 18–19. The meeting chiefly reaffirmed the group's commitment to matters already enumerated, while warning of the danger that the present high levels of growth might lead to inflation. After "spirited discussion" the group agreed to remain in close touch with the ongoing process of reform within the World Bank and the IMF. The G-20 called for, among other things, more representation for smaller countries and a more transparent process for the selection of management in those bodies.

The 2007 meeting was held in Kleinmond, South Africa, November 17–18. The group expressed optimism for continued growth in the world economy, if at perhaps a slower rate than in the past. It warned against the bad consequences of fluctuating commodity prices, especially for oil, and called for "an orderly unwinding of global imbalances." Such imbalances would likely include too little individual saving in the United States, and saving at the expense of consumption in China. The final communiqué also noted that "recent events [troubles in the U.S. mortgage market] have emphasized the need for greater effectiveness of financial supervision and the management of financial risks." It called for a better understanding of the way in which financial shocks are transmitted around the world.

When the G-20 finance ministers met November 8–9, 2008, in São Paulo, Brazil, the difficulties in global credit markets had reached the point where lending had almost ceased, and a recession unparalleled since World War II was under way. The finance ministers blamed the crisis on excessive risk taking and faulty risk management practices in financial markets. They welcomed the fact that the problem was being elevated to a meeting of G-20 heads of state or government, to be held in Washington D.C. in a few days, and essentially deferred to that meeting. The emergency Washington summit took place on November 14–15. Never before had the heads of such a large group of emerging nations participated with the traditional financial powers in making economic policy for the world. Brazilian president Luiz Inacio "Lula" da Silva even declared that the G-8 was now irrelevant. The summit agreed that all member countries would take steps to stimulate their economies. The World Bank and the IMF were to do their part, as well as pushing ahead with reforming themselves, and the G-20 nations were to make sure that the IMF had sufficient funds for the purpose. Finance ministers were to produce a more specific plan by March 31, 2009. This plan was to allow for stricter standards for the valuation of securities, improved standards for disclosure of off-balance sheet instruments, strengthening of the international body responsible for setting financial standards, and an analysis of the best practices needed for the management of private hedge funds.

The G-20 leaders committed themselves to meeting again by April 30, 2009, to review progress. They actually met in London on April 1–2. This summit meeting declared that "prosperity is indivisible," that it must reflect the interest of all people, in all countries for present and future generations, in "an open world economy based on market principles, effective regulation, and strong global institutions." The G-20 agreed to treble the resources immediately available to the IMF to $750 billion, to support at least $100 billion in additional lending by the Multilateral Development Banks, and to authorize gold sales by the IMF. The group also agreed to abolish the Financial Stability Forum (FSF, see article on the Group of Eight) in favor of an expanded Financial Stability Board, to consist of all existing FSF members, all G-20 countries, Spain, and the European Commission. This new board was to work closely with the IMF to give early warning of macroeconomic and financial risks, and to offer ways to avoid them. The G-20 agreed to bring regulation to all "systemically important" financial institutions and markets, including hedge funds. The FSF's recent issuing of new principles on executive pay and compensation were to be endorsed and implemented. The G-20 also declared that "the era of banking secrecy is over." It promised to move aggressively in applying sanctions against countries that would not cooperate in making bank account information available when needed. It also promised to go after tax havens, of which the Organization for Economic Cooperation and Development (OECD, see separate article) had recently produced a list. Also, the G-20 proposed to bring registration and regulatory oversight to credit rating agencies, to ensure their practices did not involve conflicts of interest with the institutions whose products they were being asked to rate. Such conflicts of interest were widely believed to have played a part in the collapse of credit in the United States. Finally, the G-20 countries pledged to reach agreement at the December 2009 climate change conference, to be held in Copenhagen, Denmark.

The London summit was generally considered a success. It was marred by demonstrations, to which the London police reacted with a degree of violence that many considered unacceptable.

The G-20 leaders met again in Pittsburgh, U.S.A., September 24–25, 2009. Their judgment on what they did the previous April was that "it worked." Conditions were somewhat better, the leaders said, but there was no room for complacency. The general consensus was that the London goals had been at least partly met. The group of leaders agreed to meet again in Canada in June 2010, in South Korea in November 2010, and annually thereafter, beginning with a meeting in France in 2011. They also pledged to complete the Doha round of trade negotiations by the end of 2010. The Pittsburgh declaration thus completed the G-20's transformation from a relatively informal gathering of finance ministers into what is likely to be, for the foreseeable future, the most powerful public instrument for setting world financial policy.

GULF COOPERATION COUNCIL (GCC)

Formal Name: Cooperation Council for the Arab States of the Gulf.

Established: Initial agreement endorsed February 4–5, 1981, in Riyadh, Saudi Arabia; constitution formally adopted May 25–26, 1981, in Abu Dhabi, United Arab Emirates.

Purpose: "(i) To achieve coordination, integration, and cooperation among the member states in all fields in order to bring about their unity; (ii) to deepen and strengthen the bonds of cooperation existing among their peoples in all fields; (iii) to draw up similar systems in all fields . . . and (iv) to promote scientific and technical progress in the fields of industry, minerals, agriculture, sea wealth, and animal wealth . . . for the good of the peoples of the member states."

Headquarters: Riyadh, Saudi Arabia.

Principal Organs: Supreme Council; Ministerial Council; General Secretariat; various economic, social, industrial and trade, and political committees.

Web site: www.gcc-sg.org (In Arabic, with a considerable amount of material in English.)

Secretary General: Abdul Rahman bin Hamad al-Attiya (Qatar).

Membership (6): Bahrain, Kuwait, Oman, Qatar, Saudi Arabia, United Arab Emirates.

Official Language: Arabic.

Origin and development. The formal proposal for an organization designed to link the six Arabian Gulf states on the basis of their cultural and historical ties emerged from a set of plans formulated by the Kuwaiti government. At a meeting February 4–5, 1981, the Gulf foreign ministers codified the Kuwaiti proposals and issued the Riyadh Agreement, which proposed cooperative efforts in cultural, social, economic, and financial affairs. On March 10, after settling on legal and administrative provisions, the ministers initialed a constitution for the GCC in Muscat, Oman; the council came into formal existence with the signing of the constitution by the Gulf heads of state during the first Supreme Council meeting on May 25–26, 1981, in Abu Dhabi, United Arab Emirates (UAE). Two years later the Gulf Investment Corporation was established to finance joint venture projects.

Although members earlier denied that the GCC was intended as a military grouping, events in the Middle East prompted Gulf leaders to consider unified security measures, leading to the first GCC joint military exercises in late 1983 and the formation of a defense force called the Peninsula Shield. However, the GCC's failure to mount a coordinated diplomatic or military response to Iraq's occupation of Kuwait on August 2, 1990, threatened to erode the alliance's credibility. The organization was described as slow in condemning the invasion and then proved unable to deploy its defense force for three weeks (its troops then being absorbed into the U.S.-led international force assembled in Saudi Arabia).

Shortly after the initiation of military action to liberate Kuwait in early 1991, the GCC began to discuss the creation of a new regional defense organization with Egypt and Syria, the two other major Arab members of the anti-Iraq coalition. The so-called six plus two defense arrangement was further delineated by a declaration signed in early March in Damascus, Syria, in the wake of the successful conclusion of Operation Desert Storm, but initial enthusiasm for reliance on an Arab force to preserve Gulf security subsequently waned. An exclusively GCC military committee was established in 1994, and another step toward military coordination was taken in December 2001, when the Supreme Council authorized formation of the Supreme Defense Council of defense ministers to oversee a previously adopted joint defense pact.

Structure. The Supreme Council, comprised of the six members' heads of state, convenes annually and is the highest authority of the GCC, directing the general course and policies of the organization. Since 1998 a consultative session has been held between these summits. Extraordinary council sessions can also be convened when requested by two member states. Substantive decisions require consensus. On an ad hoc basis, the Supreme Council may establish a commission for the settlement of disputes. Advising the Supreme Council is the 30-member citizen's Consultative Commission, formation of which was authorized December 1997.

The foreign ministers of the member states, or other ministers representing them, comprise the Ministerial Council, which meets in regular session four times per year to formulate policy, make recommendations to the Supreme Council, initiate studies, and authorize projects. The General Secretariat, headquartered in Riyadh, Saudi Arabia, is the GCC's principal administrative body. The secretary general, who is chosen by the Supreme Council, serves a once-renewable, three-year term and is assisted by three assistant secretaries for economic, military, and political affairs. The office of secretary general rotates among the member countries. There are five assistant secretaries general who are responsible for political, economic, human and environmental, security, and military affairs. These officials, as well as the head of the GCC delegation to Brussels, are appointed by the Ministerial Council for renewable three-year terms upon nomination of the secretary general. The secretariat also encompasses a telecommunications bureau located in Bahrain, administrative development and internal auditing units, a patent bureau, and an information center.

Activities. In its early years the GCC emphasized economic integration, signing, for example, a Unified Economic Agreement in 1981 to provide coordination in commerce, industry, and finance and to prepare the way for an eventual common market. Further harmonization of investment and trade regulations was reached later the same year, while in 1983 the Gulf Investment Corporation opened.

During much of the 1980s, however, the protracted Iran-Iraq war generated concern over disruption of oil transport through the Gulf. With a cease-fire concluding in mid-1988, the December Supreme Council session called on GCC members for a renewed focus on regional economic integration and industrial diversification. The 1990 Iraqi invasion of Kuwait and its destructive consequences once again diverted attention from the GCC's economic mission.

At the conclusion of their 15th summit, held December 19–21, 1994, in Manama, Bahrain, the GCC heads of state called for a "redoubling" of efforts to resolve border disputes between members. (A dispute involving Qatar and Saudi Arabia had nearly sidetracked the December 1992 summit.) The summit's final declaration also noted concern over "extremism and excesses" associated with the Islamic fundamentalist movement in the region. Earlier in the year, a slump in oil prices put most members in the unfamiliar position of adopting austerity budgets, which might have influenced a subsequent decision by the GCC to end its boycott of foreign companies trading with Israel.

Despite the call for greater cohesion at the 1994 summit, tensions among members continued throughout 1995. At the 16th summit, held December 4–6, 1995, in Muscat, a reported coup attempt February 20, 1996, in Qatar exacerbated the tension. Qatar's new emir, Sheikh Hamad (who deposed his father in June), suggested possible involvement in the coup plot on the part of the UAE, Bahrain, and Saudi Arabia.

At the ministerial meeting held March 17, 1996, various issues continued to separate the GCC members. Bahrain, for instance, accused Qatar (and by extension, Iran, with whom Qatar's Hamad had sought expanded relations) of meddling in its internal affairs. As a consequence of these claims and its territorial dispute with Qatar, Bahrain boycotted the 17th GCC summit held December 1, 1996, in Doha, Qatar. Although the summit's official communiqué attempted to downplay the rift, observers suggested that "serious cracks" were apparent in the GCC structure.

In January 1997 the GCC initiated talks to try to mediate the Qatar-Bahrain dispute. Later in the year, the council took steps to improve relations with Iran. In contrast, Iraq was severely criticized at the GCC summit for its failure to comply with all United Nations (UN) Security Council resolutions. The council also declared the European Parliament's disapproval of the judicial systems in the Gulf to be unwanted "interference in internal affairs."

The November 27–29, 1999, Supreme Council session in Riyadh was highlighted by an agreement to establish a GCC customs union in March 2005 (four years later than initially proposed). The accord was achieved despite continuing political differences among members, particularly between Saudi Arabia and the United Arab Emirates. A recent warming of relations between the Saudi and Iranian governments was greeted with consternation by the UAE because of its long-standing insular dispute with Tehran over Persian Gulf islands (see separate article on the UAE).

The concluding communiqué of the 21st Supreme Council summit, held December 30–31, 2000, in Manama, included what had become routine criticism of Iraqi and Israeli policies. A more substantive development was the signing of a Joint Defense Treaty pledging mutual aid in the event of attack. Talks on economic and trade issues also moved forward. The heads of state urged continued work toward the anticipated customs union and toward coordinating financial, fiscal, and banking policies. Except for a few "reserved" areas, the summit participants also concurred that the nationals of all member states should be permitted to "engage in all economic activities and occupations" in any of the six GCC countries.

Meeting December 30–31, 2001, in Muscat, the Supreme Council called for an international summit on counterterrorism. Three months earlier, in the wake of the September 11 terrorist attacks against the United States, the GCC foreign ministers voiced support for U.S. efforts to form a coalition that would undertake a "war on terror," but at the same time they had reiterated their call for an end to Israeli actions against Palestinians. On the economic front, the December summit advanced the date for introducing the GCC customs union to January 2003 and also indicated that the GCC would seek a uniform currency by January 2010. Although the leaders had rejected council membership for Yemen in the mid-1990s, they now agreed to permit its ministerial-level participation in matters of health, education, and labor and social affairs. Also at the summit, Qatar saw its minister of energy, minerals, water, and electricity, Abdul Rahman al-Attiya, named as successor to Secretary General Jamil al-Hujaylan.

As scheduled, the customs union was introduced January 1, 2003. The union established a uniform 5 percent external tariff while permitting duty-free trade within the six GCC members. Introduction of the union had the added benefit of meeting a principal condition for achieving an anticipated free trade agreement with the European Union (EU).

In March 2003, responding to the U.S./UK-led invasion of Iraq, the GCC urged a return to negotiation but also noted Saddam Hussein's failure to meet all the terms of UN Security Council resolutions. At the 24th summit, held December 21–22, 2003, in Kuwait City, the participants voiced support for efforts to return power to the Iraqi people by mid-2004 and reaffirmed their own noninterference in Iraqi affairs—a somewhat disingenuous statement given that the land assault against Iraq was initiated and directed from GCC territory. They also broached the possibility of eventually allowing a new Iraqi government to join Yemen as an external participant in certain GCC functions. In other business, the summit passed resolutions on education, economic reform, and social affairs; agreed to take a joint stand on debt forgiveness for Iraq; and announced plans to draft an antiterrorism pact. On December 29, meeting in emergency session, the GCC finance and economy ministers authorized $400 million in aid to assist Iran in recovering from its recent devastating earthquake.

A rift surfaced in December 2004 after Bahrain signed a free trade agreement with the United States. Saudi leaders said the unilateral pact violated the GCC rules, but, perhaps more significantly, it was seen as undermining the economic power of Saudi Arabia in the region. The Saudi crown prince refused to attend a GCC meeting in December in Manama because of the breach and was replaced by the second deputy premier. Simmering below the surface was the reported "competition" between Saudi Arabia and the United States for greater control in the region.

Economic issues took a back seat to political and security issues, however, during the May 28, 2005, GCC summit in Riyadh. Council leaders focused on stability and security in Lebanon, calling for a united Lebanese front and the promotion of peace efforts in the Middle East in nonspecific ways. The conference covered environmental, humanitarian, and military matters as well.

In economic matters, China, India, New Zealand, and the EU entered into free trade talks with the GCC during 2006 and 2007. The May 6, 2006, GCC summit, also in Riyadh, was dominated by concern over Iran's nuclear ambitions. The group called for guarantees from Iran that its intentions were peaceful, citing environmental hazards for the region. The GCC members, all predominantly Sunni Muslim countries, also expressed concern about the prospect of a Shiite-dominated government in Iraq next to Shiite Iran, with its threat of increased Iranian influence in the region. In other business, the summit discussed ways of getting money to the newly elected Hamas government of Palestine, since the United States and the EU had withdrawn funding after the group's victory.

The year 2007 continued to be dominated by concerns over Iran's nuclear ambitions. Plans for the GCC's own peaceful nuclear program were circulated, and after the May 15, 2007, Riyadh summit the GCC made official contact with the International Atomic Energy Agency (IAEA) to ensure that the project met that organization's standards. In November 2007 Iran offered Bahrain technical assistance in establishing a civilian nuclear program. Bahrain declined, saying that such an agreement could only come under the GCC's auspices. Also in November there was talk of the GCC states offering to supply Iran with commercial-grade uranium as a way of forestalling any need for Iran to have its own nuclear development program. In December 2007 the GCC invited Iranian president Mahmoud Ahmadinejad to attend a group summit. At this meeting Ahmadinejad stated that Iran wanted economic and security treaties with the GCC states. The summit concluded with a renewed call for a peaceful resolution to the dispute about Iran's nuclear program. Iranian attendance at the meeting was generally well received; as a "charm offensive" it had certainly succeeded.

On January 1, 2008, the GCC member states formed a common market. This agreement gave all GCC citizens equality of status and freedom of movement throughout the group. It did not, however, apply to the millions of migrant workers, mostly from eastern and southern Asia, who live in the GCC area, and whose living and employment conditions are often harsh. In February 2008 these bad conditions caused demonstrations and strikes in Dubai and Bahrain. The people responsible were imprisoned and scheduled to be deported after serving a few months in jail.

The annual meeting of heads of GCC states, held in Damman, Saudi Arabia, in May 2008, commissioned a study about accepting Yemen into the group.

Ahmadinejad's "charm offensive" proved only a short-lived success. Through the rest of 2008 and into 2009 the GCC grew increasingly worried about Iranian expansionism. Not only did Iran's ongoing nuclear program make the GCC states nervous, but in February 2009 an adviser to Iran's supreme leader remarked that Bahrain was once a province of Iran. (Bahrain was actually ruled by Persia in the 18th century, and the late Shah of Iran formally renounced any claim to the territory in 1970.) Iran put out a strangely-worded nondenial of any designs on Bahrain, whose citizens were reminded of Saddam Hussein's behavior before invading Kuwait. Perhaps not coincidentally, a statement had come from a NATO source in October 2008, offering support in case GCC states were ever attacked.

Talks between the GCC and the EU about a free trade deal proceeded slowly, with a resolution expected some time in 2009. In other economic news, in June 2008 the GCC central banks reaffirmed their intention to form a single currency by 2010, and in September the organization decided to set up a Monetary Council to direct the endeavor. Linking the currency to the U.S. dollar was a matter of contention. By June 2009 all GCC states except Saudi Arabia, Kuwait, Qatar, and Bahrain had dropped out of the proposed monetary union. On June 7 these four countries signed an agreement to move forward with a currency pegged to the U.S. dollar, but they indicated that they might revisit the issue later.

INDIAN OCEAN COMMISSION (IOC)

Commission de l'Océean Indien

Established: Formation by Madagascar, Mauritius, and Seychelles announced July 17, 1982; General Agreement of Cooperation signed January 10, 1984, in Victoria, Seychelles.

Purpose: To organize and promote regional cooperation in all sectors, with particular emphasis on economic development; to affirm an Indian Ocean identity; and to represent the Indian Ocean islands regionally and internationally.

Headquarters: Quatre Bornes, Mauritius.

Principal Organs: Council of Ministers, Committee of Permanent Liaison Officers, Secretariat.

Web site: www.coi-ioc.org (under construction, in French only. A previous Web site with English-language content has been taken down.)

Secretary General: Callixte d'Offay (Seychelles).

Membership (5): Comoro Islands, France (representing the French Overseas Department of Réunion), Madagascar, Mauritius, Seychelles.

Origin and development. On July 17, 1982, Aneerood Jugnauth, the newly elected prime minister of Mauritius, announced at the conclusion of a state visit by President France Albert René of the Seychelles that an Indian Ocean Commission (IOC) had been formed by their two countries and Madagascar to examine possible regional cooperation. In December the three members' foreign affairs ministers agreed on an IOC constitution, which was submitted to their national parliaments for approval prior to the countries signing a general agreement of regional cooperation in January 1984 in Victoria, Seychelles.

In January 1985 an IOC ministerial session approved the membership request of the Comoro Islands and endorsed France's proposed accession to represent the island of Réunion. The Comoros and France were formally installed as members at the January 1986 ministerial session. At its 1989 session the IOC elected its first secretary general and settled on Mauritius as the site of its permanent headquarters.

Structure. The Council of Ministers is the highest IOC authority, meeting once per year; its presidency rotates among the membership annually. A Committee of Permanent Liaison Officers convenes three times per year to prepare proposals for council sessions, carry out council decisions, and promote cooperation between the council and national administrations. The Secretariat, headed by a secretary general, is responsible for the conduct of the organization's daily activities; the secretary general serves a four-year, nonrenewable term. Technical committees, made up of experts from each of the member countries, identify sectoral projects suited to regional cooperation. After approval of a particular project, the responsible committee assumes a managerial role.

At the second IOC Summit of Heads of State and Government, held December 1999 in St.-Denis, Réunion, the participants decided that henceforth informal summits would convene every four years.

Activities. IOC activities have greatly depended on external assistance, particularly from the European Union (EU). Areas addressed by IOC projects and programs have included tuna fishing research and development, exploration of new and renewable energy sources, promotion of tourism, environmental conservation, contingency planning for oil spills, coral reef monitoring, intraregional trade, investment regulations and capital transfers, regional meteorological cooperation, and technical cooperation.

Partly to try pushing integration beyond the "good intentions" state, the first IOC Summit of Heads of State and Government was held March 16, 1991, in Antananarivo, Madagascar. In June 1992 the IOC ministers endorsed a new integration plan and in October agreed to a review of the IOC organizational structure. Subsequently, a degree of discord was reported among IOC members who were apparently excluded from an initiative spearheaded by Mauritius to form a larger and more formidable Indian Ocean Rim Association. Officials from Australia, India, Kenya, Oman, Singapore, and South Africa attended preliminary meetings in Mauritius in early 1995 on the proposed organization, with discussions focusing on economic cooperation.

As a consequence, the IOC was shunted to the sidelines. France expressed deep concern for the lack of direction and progress of the IOC in the face of direct competition for resources and attention from the new "Anglo-Saxon" Indian Ocean Rim Association, which was officially inaugurated in March 1997 (see separate article on the IOR-ARC). One criticism leveled against the IOC by the French was that the organization collected no dues from its members and instead merely served as a channel for foreign development aid. Furthermore, Paris argued that "most IOC projects must be filed away as disappointing failures" because "results are unpredictable, coordination insufficient, and priorities little apparent."

The second IOC Summit of Heads of State and Government met December 3, 1999, in Réunion, although the government of the Comoro Islands, installed after an April coup, was not represented. (None of the other IOC members recognized its legitimacy.) The session was organized around four broad topics: economic and development issues, including regional cooperation and integration; political matters, including the IOC's relationship with other regional organizations; peacekeeping and security, including civil defense, drug trafficking, and money laundering; and culture, including matters of education and information technology.

Over the next several years IOC activities were restrained by domestic political difficulties. In February 2002 the African Union (AU) and the IOC dispatched a joint mediation mission to Madagascar to help resolve a postelection crisis. On October 30–31, 2003, an extraordinary meeting of foreign ministers in Moroni, Comoro Islands, discussed preparations for a quadrennial summit, which was scheduled to be held in Moroni, but continuing political instability in the Comoro Islands ultimately resulted in a decision to delay the gathering until 2004. (In late December 2003 the Comoran factions reached an accord, and a follow-up committee with IOC representation was organized under the auspices of the AU.)

The October meeting also focused on the fight against international terrorism and appointed a Committee of Sages to propose organizational reforms and to help define a future direction for the IOC.

In late 2003 the IOC's controversial secretary general, Wilfrid Bertile of Réunion, indicated his intention to resign to seek reelection to the Réunion legislature, the Regional Council. He came under criticism from some quarters for not having resigned his legislative seat after taking over as IOC secretary general in 2001.

The July 22, 2005, summit, held in Antananarivo, was attended by all member heads of state, including Jacques Chirac, the French president, who represented Réunion. France appeared to be interested in energizing the group, which was doing better as relations improved between Mauritius and the Seychelles. These countries, together with Réunion, are the richest IOC members. The meeting gave permission for Réunion to apply for membership in the Common Market for Eastern and Southern Africa (Comesa) (see separate article on Comesa). During 2005 the IOC also signed an agreement with the EU, which was to provide 30 million euros (US$50 million) to finance its programs.

In September 2006 the IOC announced an action plan to improve trade among member states during the period 2006–2010. Internal trade only accounted for 3 percent of the group's trade. Illegal fishing has become a problem in the area, and in November 2006 Comoro Islands was picked to host the new satellite-equipped Indian Ocean Center for Fishing Surveillance. In January 2007 the IOC signed an agreement with the EU to receive up to 7 million euros (US$9 million) over the following three years to combat illegal fishing. In June 2007 IOC representatives attended a conference sponsored by the UN Food and Agriculture Organization (FAO) on ways to improve inspection of fishing boats in area seaports. In September 2007 the EU announced an initiative, administered by the IOC, to foster the sustainability of marine and coastal resources in the area. This program, the Regional Program for the Sustainable Management of the Coastal Zones of the Indian Ocean (ReCoMap), also involved the non-IOC countries Kenya, Tanzania, and Somalia. Some wondered about the effect of including English-speaking Kenya and Tanzania, both influential countries in the region, in a project run by the determinedly Francophone IOC.

In September 2007 the Seychelles foreign minister, Patrick Pillay, met in Beijing with his Chinese counterpart, Yang Jiechi. The two discussed cooperation between the IOC and China. In October 2007 the new French president, Nicolas Sarkozy, met with his Seychelles counterpart, assuring him of France's continuing support for the organization and for the candidacy of Callixte d'Offay of the Seychelles as its next secretary general. D'Offay was confirmed at the IOC Council meeting in March 2008.

In February 2008 the IOC approved a project to link its member countries in a fiber-optic network, hopefully by 2010. In June 2008 an IOC delegation observed the presidential election on the Comoro Islands of Anjouan. The results were declared fair.

Food shortages, as well as the effects of the worldwide economic crisis and global warming, plagued the IOC's members throughout 2008 and into 2009. Delegates from IOC countries and other nations spoke at the UN General Assembly in September 2008, urging the most urgent action on climate change. Rising sea levels, they said, threatened to submerge many small island nations.

Political instability in Madagascar occupied the IOC for much of the first half of 2009. The country's president, Marc Ravalomanana, and his rival, Andry Rajoelina, the recently sacked mayor of Antananarivo, Madagascar's capital, held talks under IOC auspices in February. The parties came to a compromise, but on March 17 Rajoelina deposed Ravalomanana with help from the military. The IOC, along with other regional groups, continued engagement with Madagascar, and by April 30, 2009, the AU (see separate article) was able to announce that there would be elections by the end of the year.

INDIAN OCEAN RIM ASSOCIATION FOR REGIONAL COOPERATION (IOR-ARC)

Established: By charter signed at a meeting of 14 insular and littoral Indian Ocean countries March 6–7, 1997, in Port Louis, Mauritius.

Purpose: To "increase cooperation in trade, investment, infrastructure, tourism, science, technology, and human resource development."

Headquarters: Vacoas, Mauritius.

Principal Organs: Council of Ministers, Committee of Senior Officials, Indian Ocean Rim Business Forum, Indian Ocean Rim Academic Group, Coordinating Secretariat.

Web site: www.iornet.com (This is the site of the Indian Ocean Rim Business Facilitation Center and is endorsed by IOR-ARC. The IOR-ARC's own Web site is no longer in operation.)

Director of the Coordinating Secretariat: Devdasslall Dusoruth (Mauritius).

Membership (18): Australia, Bangladesh, India, Indonesia, Iran, Kenya, Madagascar, Malaysia, Mauritius, Mozambique, Oman, Singapore, South Africa, Sri Lanka, Tanzania, Thailand, United Arab Emirates, Yemen.

Observer (1): Indian Ocean Tourism Organization.

Official Language: English.

Origin and development. Responding to a proposal by the government of Mauritius, on March 29–31, 1995, representatives of Australia, India, Kenya, Oman, Singapore, and South Africa met in Mauritius to discuss economic cooperation, trade liberalization, and potential investment opportunities based on "principles of open regionalism and inclusivity." Subsequently, a working group of government officials, businesspersons, and academics developed a charter for a tripartite regional organization. At a ministerial-level meeting March 6–7, 1997, in Port Louis, Mauritius, representatives of the 14 founding states—Indonesia, Madagascar, Malaysia, Mozambique, Sri Lanka, Tanzania, and Yemen, plus the seven that met in 1995—signed the charter for the Indian Ocean Rim Association for Regional Cooperation (IOR-ARC).

At the second biennial meeting of the Council of Ministers, held in March 1999 in Maputo, Mozambique, the countries of Bangladesh, Iran, Seychelles, Thailand, and the United Arab Emirates were invited to join the IOR-ARC. They were welcomed into the organization at an extraordinary Council of Ministers session in Muscat, Oman, in January 2000, although Seychelles decided to withdraw in July 2003. Dialogue partners are China, Egypt, France, Japan, and the United Kingdom. Turkey also has requested dialogue status.

Structure. The Council of Ministers, comprising the foreign ministers of the member states, is the highest authority of the IOR-ARC, setting policy, reviewing progress toward the organization's goals, and creating new organizational bodies. It meets biennially in regular session, but ad hoc meetings also may be called. Convening as needed, a Committee of Senior Officials supervises implementation of council decisions, drafts work programs, and helps seek financing for projects. Working in cooperation with the senior officials are the Indian Ocean Rim Business Forum and the Indian Ocean Rim Academic Group. All organs reach decisions by consensus. The Coordinating Secretariat, headed by a director, is located in Vacoas, Mauritius.

Activities. Apart from providing a regional forum and conducting research in such areas as sectoral tariff levels, the IOR-ARC accomplished little in its first six years. During the March 1999 Council of Ministers session, participants agreed to promote trade facilitation and liberalization, as well as economic and technical cooperation. Accordingly, they set up a Working Group on Trade and Investment (WGTI), which met for the first time in conjunction with the extraordinary Council of Ministers session in Muscat in January 2000.

Meeting April 7–8, 2001, in Muscat, the Council of Ministers authorized formation of a High Level Task Force (HLTF) with a mandate that included proposing a future direction for the organization, devising a medium-term strategic plan, defining criteria for dialogue partners, raising the IOR-ARC's international profile, and examining the functioning and funding of the secretariat. On October 7–13, 2003, the various IOR-ARC organs held meetings in Colombo, Sri Lanka. At the culminating session, the Council of Ministers adopted the HLTF report, which offered recommendations on work programs and provided guidelines for organizing the secretariat.

One of the IOR-ARC's long-range organizational goals is the eventual elimination of internal tariffs, but some observers have noted that such a broad measure will be difficult to achieve. Wide economic disparities persist among the member states, which also participate in other intergovernmental organizations that frequently have competing goals. In addition, there have been reports of major differences between the IOR-ARC members with the largest economies, namely India and Australia.

Recent commentary suggests that the organization has not lived up to its promise. Beginning in July 2005, however, it agreed to allow projects to go ahead with the support of at least six members, rather than by full consensus, and this change in rules might help drive more action. The IOC-ARC has no Web site, and information about its activities must come from member governments and from general news reports.

Ministerial meetings were held August 26–27, 2004, in Colombo and February 21–22, 2006, in Tehran, Iran. In the 2006 meeting, Iran criticized supposed double standards on human rights by the European Union (EU) and the economic development plans of the "big powers" in smaller countries, holding the IOR-ARC up as a good example of small countries' response. At the seventh IOC-ARC forum, also in Tehran, held March 7–8, 2007, India offered its advice in responding to natural disasters. At the May 4–5, 2008, ministerial meeting, again held in Tehran, both the Indian and South African representatives expressed some dissatisfaction, calling for the organization to take a more positive stance in advancing the developmental agenda of "the South." India called for the IOR-ARC charter to be revised and for studies and proposals that had been in existence without translation into working projects to be scrapped. At the same meeting, Iran offered itself as a center for the promotion and exchange of technology among IOR-ARC members.

The June 24–25, 2009, ministerial meeting, held in Sana'a, Yemen, marked that country's assumption of the organization's chair for a three-year period. The meeting affirmed support for Yemen's efforts against maritime piracy, a problem of significance to all member states. The group announced plans to set up an anti-piracy center in Yemen. The Philippines put out feelers about joining the group, and was asked to submit a formal application. India was scheduled to take over the IOR-ARC's chair in 2012, and clearly had ambitious plans for the organization during its term. The Indian representative at the Sana'a meeting urged the group's members to think about projects that might usefully be done by the whole group, and then "implement them in a time-bound manner."

In August 2009 the Indian external affairs minister Shashi Tharoor announced that India would step up its cooperation with other IOR-ARC countries in the fight against piracy. He described it as a "tremendous opportunity" to increase cooperation with the group.

INTER-GOVERNMENTAL AUTHORITY ON DEVELOPMENT (IGAD)

Autorité Intergovernementale pour le Développement

Established: As the Inter-Governmental Authority on Drought and Development (IGADD) by six-nation summit meeting of heads of state and government January 15–16, 1986, in Djibouti; present name adopted March 21, 1996.

Purpose: To coordinate efforts to combat drought and desertification, to develop regional policies on short- and medium-term economic development, and, since March 1996, to assist in preventing and resolving conflicts in the region.

Headquarters: Djibouti, Djibouti.

Principal Organs: Assembly of Heads of State and Government, Council of Ministers, Committee of Ambassadors, Secretariat.

Web site: www.igad.org

Executive Secretary: Mahboub Maalim (Kenya

Membership (7)**:** Djibouti, Eritrea, Ethiopia, Kenya, Somalia, Sudan, Uganda. (In April 2007 Eritrea temporarily suspended its membership, but rejoined in 2008.)

Origin and development. In view of cyclical droughts, which brought widespread famine and death to the region, the leaders of Djibouti, Ethiopia, Kenya, Somalia, Sudan, and Uganda established IGADD during a January 15–16, 1986, conference in Djibouti. Eritrea was admitted in September 1993.

The name of the group was changed to the Inter-Governmental Authority on Development (IGAD) on March 21, 1996, in conjunction with an expansion of the organization's role to include regional conflict prevention and resolution, infrastructural development, food security, and environmental protection.

Structure. The policymaking IGAD body is the Assembly of Heads of State and Government, also called the IGAD annual summit; implementation of its decisions rests with the Council of Ministers, which meets at least twice per year, and the small Secretariat in Djibouti. The March 1996 restructuring increased the size of the Council of Ministers to 14 (2 from each member state) and directed that decisions would henceforth require the vote of two-thirds of the members. The executive secretary, who serves a four-year, once-renewable term, oversees three divisions of the Secretariat: economic cooperation, agriculture and the environment, and political/humanitarian affairs. Supporting the council and the Secretariat is the Committee of Ambassadors, which comprises the principal representatives of the member states to Djibouti.

Activities. The founders of the IGADD identified the new organization's first priority as the development of a regional "early warning system" to deal with the effects of drought. Other proposed projects emphasized agricultural research, human resources development, and creation of a regional plan for the storage of food and its distribution to needy areas in times of shortage. However, little effective action was achieved by 1990, in large part because of the civil wars in Ethiopia, Somalia, and Sudan and, to a lesser extent, continued sporadic rebel activity in Uganda. Consequently, by 1992 many Western donors had reportedly lost their enthusiasm for continued IGADD financing. In May the Council of Ministers announced its intention to restructure the IGADD Secretariat according to the wishes of donors. The council also endorsed France's proposal that IGADD cooperate with the Arab Maghreb Union (AMU) and the Permanent Inter-State Committee on Drought Control in the Sahel (CILSS) in creating an umbrella organization to monitor drought and desertification throughout much of North, East, and West Africa.

Western support for the IGADD subsequently regained strength, particularly as a result of the organization's growing role in Sudanese peace negotiations. Consequently, the IGADD Council of Ministers in January 1995 decided to establish the Friends of IGADD, a forum for informal consultation with current and potential development partners such as Canada, Netherlands, Norway, the United States, and the United Kingdom. In addition, in April a special one-day summit in Addis Ababa, Ethiopia, of six IGADD heads of state (the turmoil in Somalia still precluding that nation's participation) appointed a ministerial committee to review proposals for "revitalizing and expanding" the organization. Restructuring of the IGADD was approved at a second extraordinary summit March 21, 1996, in Nairobi, Kenya, at which time the organization became IGAD.

At the eighth IGAD summit, which met November 23, 2000, in Khartoum, Sudan, the closing declaration reflected a desire to move forward on many other concerns while continuing efforts to find resolutions for the conflicts in Somalia and Sudan. The declaration called for drafting a trade protocol; promoting infrastructural cooperation in transport, communications, and power; establishing a disaster preparedness mechanism; and devising national and regional food security programs. The summit also requested the Secretariat to prepare a draft protocol for the Conflict Early Warning and Response Mechanism (CEWARN). The completed protocol was then signed at the ninth summit January 10–11, 2002, in Khartoum. At the same time, IGAD was actively participating in preparations for the African Union's (AU) planned African Economic Community, serving as the "northern sector" representative within the Common Market for Eastern and Southern Africa (Comesa; see separate article).

The tenth ordinary summit, which met October 20–25, 2003, in Kampala, Uganda, convened in the context of renewed hope for resolution of the Sudanese and Somalian conflicts. In the preceding 15 months, as a consequence of ongoing IGAD-sponsored peace talks, a number of agreements were reached between the Sudanese factions. With regard to Somalia, the peace talks that were initiated under IGAD auspices in October 2002 eventually caused the Transitional Federal Government (TFG) for Somalia to be formed, temporarily based in Kenya until conditions in Somalia improved. IGAD received wide international praise and greatly increased visibility.

Despite its necessary focus on Sudan and Somalia, in 2002–2003 IGAD also addressed many other concerns. Recognizing the difficulty of financing development projects in the region, in 2002 the Assembly of Heads of State and Government directed the Secretariat to investigate establishing a special fund for that purpose. The Conference on the Prevention and Combating of Terrorism was held in June 2003 in Addis Ababa, while the first-ever Conference on Internal Displacement in the IGAD Subregion concluded in September.

Events in Somalia did not turn out as planned. The TFG moved to Somalia in 2005, but remained deeply split among the various warlords. IGAD offered peacekeeping troops to Somalia as early as January 2005, but elements of the TFG objected to receiving ethnic Somali peacekeepers from neighboring countries, and by June 2006 the whole picture changed when an Islamist militia drove warlord groups out of Mogadishu, the Somali capital. The situation altered yet again when Ethiopian troops entered Somalia in December 2006, rapidly dislodging the Islamists. This action was deplored by the African Union (AU) and IGAD. IGAD continued trying to organize a peacekeeping force, with little success, and in April 2007 Eritrea temporarily suspended its membership in the organization to protest Ethiopia's activities.

IGAD's 11th summit, held March 20, 2006, in Nairobi expressed more satisfaction over the outcome of the agreements regarding Sudan, though it called for all possible international help in returning refugees from the conflict. Implementation of the agreements dragged, however, and in August 2007 both sides of the dispute welcomed former Kenyan president Daniel Arap Moi as mediator.

The July 2006 AU summit decided to recognize no new Regional Economic Communities (RECs), such as IGAD. However, IGAD's recognition was grandfathered.

In a May 26, 2007, meeting IGAD agreed to create the IGAD Parliamentary Union. It began work in Addis Ababa in November 2007, with five parliamentarians representing each member state. Its executive committee met May 25–26 in Khartoum and approved a new structure for the IGAD Secretariat. Nominations for the new position of general secretary were said to be under consideration.

In other activities, in late 2007 and early 2008 IGAD urged Eritrea to return to full participation, praised Sudan for its efforts in addressing the Darfur crisis, and sent a delegation to help mediate the violent aftermath of Kenya's disputed presidential election. In what might be a sign that African regional organizations seek to merge, in February 2008 IGAD held a meeting on the sidelines of the AU summit in Addis Ababa. In May 2008 IGAD established a regional consulting group to address the problem of migration.

In August 2008 Eritrea rejoined the organization, if grudgingly. Eritrean president Isaias Afwerki met a delegation from IGAD, and declared that the organization, though not very effective, was worth his country's support. Afwerki recommended it be thoroughly restructured, perhaps even replaced with a more effective group. On October 29, 2008, IGAD called all Somali parliamentarians to attend an extraordinary summit meeting in Nairobi. This meeting spoke harshly of the Somali TFG, calling on it to take responsibility for its problems and stop blaming outsiders. For whatever reason, IGAD stopped covering the Somalis' hotel expenses, and did not immediately provide their transportation home after the meeting.

In November 2008 Secretary Mahboub Maalim declared that things were going well for IGAD. He noted the increasing disappearance of border controls between member states, as well as progress in the fight against desertification. He expected IGAD to become a free trade area in 2009. In December IGAD imposed sanctions on Somali president Abdullahi Yusuf, who had unconstitutionally removed his prime minister. Yusuf resigned. This all happened in the context of Ethiopia's impending pullout of its peacekeeping forces from Somalia. Ethiopian forces were gone by mid-January 2009, and IGAD called for an increased African Union (AU) presence to replace them. Islamist militias immediately took over the former Ethiopian bases, however.

On February 2, 2009, IGAD condemned the International Criminal Court (ICC) for issuing an arrest warrant for Sudanese president Al-Bashir. On May 29, 2009, IGAD called for a UN blockade of Somalia, to prevent weapons reaching Islamist forces. The group also called for sanctions against Eritrea, which the group claimed was supporting the Islamists and working for the overthrow of the TFG.

INTERNATIONAL CRIMINAL POLICE ORGANIZATION (ICPO/INTERPOL)

Organisation Internationale de Police Criminelle

Established: As the International Criminal Police Commission (ICPC) by the Second International Criminal Police Congress in 1923 in Vienna, Austria; present name and constitution adopted by the 25th Congress, with effect from June 13, 1956.

Purpose: "To ensure and promote the widest possible mutual assistance between all criminal police authorities within the limits of the law existing in the different countries and in the spirit of the Universal Declaration of Human Rights."

Headquarters: Lyon, France.

Principal Organs: General Assembly (all members), Executive Committee (13 members), General Secretariat.

Web site: www.interpol.int

Secretary General: Ronald K. Noble (United States).

Membership (187): Afghanistan, Albania, Algeria, Andorra, Angola, Antigua and Barbuda, Argentina, Armenia, Aruba, Australia, Austria, Azerbaijan, Bahamas, Bahrain, Bangladesh, Barbados, Belarus, Belgium, Belize, Benin, Bhutan, Bolivia, Bosnia and Herzegovina, Botswana, Brazil, Brunei, Bulgaria, Burkina Faso, Burundi, Cambodia, Cameroon, Canada, Cape Verde Islands, Central African Republic, Chad, Chile, China, Colombia, Comoro Islands, Democratic Republic of the Congo, Republic of the Congo, Costa Rica, Côte d'Ivoire, Croatia, Cuba, Cyprus, Czech Republic, Denmark, Djibouti, Dominica, Dominican Republic, Ecuador, Egypt, El Salvador, Equatorial Guinea, Eritrea, Estonia, Ethiopia, Fiji, Finland, France, Gabon, Gambia, Georgia, Germany, Ghana, Greece, Grenada, Guatemala, Guinea, Guinea-Bissau, Guyana, Haiti, Honduras, Hungary, Iceland, India, Indonesia, Iran, Iraq, Ireland, Israel, Italy, Jamaica, Japan, Jordan, Kazakhstan, Kenya, Republic of Korea, Kuwait, Kyrgyzstan, Laos, Latvia, Lebanon, Lesotho, Liberia, Libya, Liechtenstein, Lithuania, Luxembourg, Macedonia, Madagascar, Malawi, Malaysia, Maldives, Mali, Malta, Marshall Islands, Mauritania, Mauritius, Mexico, Moldova, Monaco, Mongolia, Montenegro, Morocco, Mozambique, Myanmar, Namibia, Nauru, Nepal, Netherlands, Netherlands Antilles, New Zealand, Nicaragua, Niger, Nigeria, Norway, Oman, Pakistan, Panama, Papua New Guinea, Paraguay, Peru, Philippines, Poland, Portugal, Qatar, Romania, Russia, Rwanda, St. Kitts-Nevis, St. Lucia, St. Vincent, San Marino, Sao Tome and Principe, Saudi Arabia, Senegal, Serbia, Seychelles, Sierra Leone, Singapore, Slovakia, Slovenia, Somalia, South Africa, Spain, Sri Lanka, Sudan, Suriname, Swaziland, Sweden, Switzerland, Syria, Tajikistan, Tanzania, Thailand, Timor-Leste, Togo, Tonga, Trinidad and Tobago, Tunisia, Turkey, Turkmenistan, Uganda, Ukraine, United Arab Emirates, United Kingdom, United States, Uruguay, Uzbekistan, Vatican City State, Venezuela, Vietnam, Yemen, Zambia, Zimbabwe. There also are national central sub-bureaus in Anguilla, American Samoa, Bermuda, British Virgin Islands, Cayman Islands, Gibraltar, Guam, Hong Kong, Macao, Montserrat, Northern Mariana Islands, Puerto Rico, Turks and Caicos Islands, and the U.S. Virgin Islands.

Official Languages: English, French, Spanish, Arabic.

Origin and development. Interpol's origins lie in the First International Criminal Police Congress, convened in 1914 in Monte Carlo, Monaco, by Prince Albert I, who felt that an international effort was required to combat crime. However, World War I intervened, and it was not until a second congress in 1923 in Vienna, Austria, that what was known as the International Criminal Police Commission (ICPC) was formally launched. It was agreed from the outset that the commission would not be a working police force but would serve as an information center with respect for each member's national sovereignty. In addition, the ICPC would focus entirely on ordinary criminal activity, avoiding involvement in political, military, racial, or religious matters. By 1930 a secretariat had been established in Vienna with a number of specialized departments covering such issues as criminal records, counterfeiting, fingerprinting, and passport forgery; an international police radio network was set up in 1935. Following the 1938 annexation of Austria by Germany, an Austrian Nazi was named Viennese police commissioner, and therefore president of the ICPC under its existing constitution. As a result, the 1938 Congress in Bucharest, Hungary, was the last to be convened prior to World War II, during which the ICPC, operating under Nazi control, was moved to Berlin.

Following the war the ICPC members agreed to establish permanent headquarters in Paris, France (relocation to the Paris suburb of Saint-Cloud occurring in 1967, and to Lyon in 1989). During the 25th congress in 1956 in Vienna, it was decided to change the name from "Commission" to "Organization," in accordance with prevailing multinational practice; concurrently the acronym "Interpol" was formally adopted, having previously been introduced as part of the body's on-the-air radio signature.

Under its 1956 constitution, Interpol was authorized to establish relations with the Customs Co-operation Council (CCC), now known as the World Customs Organization (WCO); the Economic and Social Council (ECOSOC) of the United Nations (UN); and other international bodies. However, it was not until 1971 that the organization was accorded recognized intergovernmental status through an agreement of cooperation with the Council of Europe and regularized linkage with ECOSOC.

Until the mid-1980s Interpol was reluctant to participate in measures to combat international terrorism because such acts are often politically motivated, and the organization's constitution prohibits investigation of political matters. However, members agreed at the 1984 assembly that it could become involved if the criminal element of a violent act, such as murder, kidnapping, or bombing, outweighed the political aspect. Subsequently, the 1985 assembly approved the creation of an International Terrorism Group (subsequently known as the Anti-Terrorism Branch), which commenced informational and analytical services in January 1986.

Structure. Interpol's governing body is its General Assembly, which meets in ordinary session at least once a year in different member countries. Extraordinary sessions, which may be called by the Executive Committee or a majority of the membership, are held in Lyon. The assembly decides general policy, rules on the work program submitted by the secretary general, approves the budget, elects the Executive Committee, and adopts resolutions on matters of international police concern. The 13-member Executive Committee, which meets three times a year, comprises a president (serving a four-year term), three vice presidents, and nine delegates (serving three-year terms). The secretary general, who is appointed for a five-year term by the assembly on recommendation of the Executive Committee, supervises a staff of about 400 persons. A large part of Interpol's work is coordinated, on a day-to-day basis, with National Central Bureaus or other police bodies designated by member states.

A major administrative reorganization took place in 2001. A new Executive Directorate for Police Services, which reports to the secretary general, oversees the core directorates for Regional and National Police Services, comprising subdirectorates for Africa, the Americas, Asia and the South Pacific, Europe, and the Middle East and North Africa; Operational Support Services; and Specialized Crimes, encompassing subdirectorates for Drugs and Criminal Organizations, Financial and High-Tech Crimes, Fugitive Investigative Support, Public Safety and Terrorism, and Trafficking in Human Beings. Also reporting to the secretary general are the Information Systems and Technology Directorate, the Administration and Finance Directorate, and various other offices concerned with, for example, management policy and planning, legal affairs, and protocol.

Interpol also maintains five subregional bureaus in Buenos Aires, Argentina; Abidjan, Côte d'Ivoire; San Salvador, El Salvador; Nairobi, Kenya; and Harare, Zimbabwe, plus a liaison office in Bangkok, Thailand. A Regional Coordination Office in Lyon supports the subregional and liaison centers.

Activities. Most of Interpol's activities deal with the exchange of information on counterfeiting, bank and other financial fraud, terrorism, drug trafficking, human trafficking, information technology crime, art theft, and related forms of criminal activity across national frontiers. In this endeavor, it maintains close relations with many intergovernmental bodies, including the Council of Europe, the European Commission, the International Atomic Energy Agency (IAEA), the International Maritime Organization (IMO), the International Narcotics Control Board (INCB), the Organization of American States (OAS), the UN Educational, Scientific, and Cultural Organization (UNESCO), the UN Office on Drugs and Crime, and the WCO.

In addition to issuing various "notices" regarding fugitives, missing persons, unidentified bodies, preventative alerts, and requests for information, Interpol provides training, sponsors meetings and conferences, offers regional services, and undertakes joint operations. In the area of criminal analysis, it makes regional and global threat assessments, provides weekly criminal intelligence briefings regarding terrorism, and offers forensic support related to counterfeiting, DNA identification, disaster victim identification, and fingerprint identification. It also offers analytical support for specific operations concerned with problems such as criminal organizations in Russia and Eastern Europe, illegal immigration, child pornography, and terrorism.

January 1999 saw the presentation of a Strategic Development Plan intended to define the future role and direction of Interpol in combating the increasing "globalization of crime" attributable, in large measure, to the sophisticated use of computer technology by criminals. Given the resultant need for increasing international cooperation, the plan proposed raising Interpol's profile and arguing its merits as the logical choice for coordinating international anti-crime activities.

At its 68th session, held October 3–November 3, 2000, in Rhodes, Greece, the General Assembly formally approved the appointment of Ronald K. Noble, a law professor and former U.S. Treasury undersecretary for enforcement, as secretary general. The nomination of Noble, one of eight candidates put forward more than a year earlier for consideration by the Executive Committee, marked the first time that the United States had proposed someone for the office. The move was generally regarded as an indication that Washington, which had long been criticized by some Interpol members for a "go-it-alone" attitude, had recognized the increasing necessity of international coordination.

The September 24–28, 2001, General Assembly in Budapest, Hungary, was dominated by discussion of the September 11 terrorist attacks on the United States. (On September 14 Secretary General Noble had established an "11 September Task Force" on terrorism, based at Interpol headquarters. A new round-the-clock Coordination and Command Center also was set up.) In addition, the assembly approved a cooperation agreement with the European Union's (EU's) Europol and called for the UN Civilian Police and the WCO to approve similar arrangements.

At the October 21–24, 2002, meeting of the General Assembly in Yaoundé, Cameroon, Interpol admitted Afghanistan and Timor-Leste as the 180th and 181st members. Principal topics of discussion included bioterrorism and cyberterrorism; small-arms proliferation; and trafficking in people, drugs, and vehicles. The session also adopted global standards for combating police corruption. In addition, 2002 marked the first full year of operation for the 24-hour-a-day, Internet-based Interpol Global Communications System (I-24/7), which replaced an outdated messaging system.

The 72nd General Assembly met September 29–October 2, 2003, in Benidorm, Spain. The assembly encouraged all members to utilize the I-24/7 and Interpol's extensive databases and to take advantage of interconnectivity with databases in other member countries. It also created an incident response team to advise senior officials during crises, including terrorist attacks. Earlier in the year, Interpol became directly involved in efforts to recover art and artifacts stolen from Iraqi museums following the fall of Baghdad to U.S.-led forces.

The 73rd General Assembly, which met October 5–8, 2004, in Cancun, Mexico, focused on international terrorism. It reinterpreted its constitution to allow for the issuance of wanted persons notices for people suspected of active involvement in a terrorist organization. The assembly also endorsed an agreement for expanded cooperation with the International Criminal Court, allowing the court access to Interpol's communications network and databases. Endorsement of a plan to combat bioterrorism followed the first Interpol conference on that subject, which representatives of 155 countries attended in March 2005.

The 74th General Assembly, which met September 19–22, 2005, in Berlin, welcomed Bhutan and Turkmenistan as new members. The 75th General Assembly, meeting September 18–21, 2006, in Rio de Janeiro, Brazil, admitted San Marino, as well as Montenegro, now independent of Serbia. Since that meeting, Interpol has concentrated on encouraging member countries to make the most use of its databases. In July 2007 the U.S. Department of Homeland Security announced plans to use Interpol's database of stolen travel documents (established after the September 11, 2001, attacks) in its watch on travelers to the United States.

During 2007, the last year for which figures are available, Interpol sent out more than 5,000 notices, the majority of them requests for arrest (Red Notices). Member countries used the Interpol communications system to transmit more than 14,000 messages regarding wanted persons (diffusions). There were 5,234 arrests in 2007 as a result of this message traffic. Prominent individuals for whom Red Notices have been issued include former Peruvian president Alberto Fujimori, who was sought by Peruvian authorities; former Liberian president Charles Taylor, who was sought by the UN-backed Special Court for Sierra Leone; the late Benazir Bhutto, formerly prime minister of Pakistan; and Raghad Saddam Hussein, daughter of the former president of Iraq. Interpol has also been active in searching for and arresting people wanted for genocide in Rwanda.

The 76th General Assembly, meeting November 5–8, 2007, in Marrakesh, Morocco, concentrated on ways to combat pedophilia and international sex tourism. This followed the arrest of a Canadian suspected pedophile in Thailand. Interpol had distributed his picture worldwide after German computer experts succeeded in restoring a digitally blurred image of it. At this meeting the secretary general said a large increase in the organization's budget was necessary, if it were to be effective in fighting international terrorism.

In January 2008 the organization suffered an embarrassment when its president, Jackie Selebie, National Commissioner of the South African Police, was forced to resign after being indicted for corruption in his own country. In May 2008 the organization became involved in a controversy about computers seized during a raid on a FARC rebel camp in Ecuador. Files on these computers seemed to implicate the Venezuelan government in FARC activities. Amid strong Venezuelan denials, Interpol certified that Venezuelan authorities had not tampered with the files on the captured computers. In May 2008 a second man was arrested, this time in the United States, for pedophilia, after Interpol distributed his photograph worldwide.

In October 2008, at the organization's 77th General Assembly, held in St. Petersburg, Russia, the Vatican City State was welcomed as the 187th member. The meeting also launched a Global Security Initiative, a framework for international police work in the 21st century. Interpol hoped for 1 billion euros to fund this effort. Also in October 2008 Interpol was embarrassed by the arrest of Mexico's senior liaison official with the organization, on charges involving drug cartels. The following month the Mexican government declared that Interpol's databases and communications had in no way been compromised. In November, 2008, also, the Georgian opposition leader Irakli Okruashvili was arrested in Germany on an Interpol warrant from Georgia, charged with corruption and money laundering.

Interpol volunteered to help following the December 2008, attacks in Mumbai, India. In March 2009, Pakistan agreed to provide DNA and other information pertaining to suspects.

On the technical front, in April, 2009, Interpol began an initiative with Microsoft Corp., to improve its capabilities in computer forensics. The previous General Assembly had approved the creation of a Computer Forensics Unit.

INTERNATIONAL ENERGY AGENCY (IEA)

Established: By the Agreement on an International Energy Program, which was signed by the Council of Ministers of the Organization for Economic Cooperation and Development (OECD) November 15, 1974, in Paris, France.

Purpose: To coordinate the responses of participating states to the world energy crisis and to develop an oil-sharing mechanism for use in times of supply difficulties; to coordinate national energy policies, share relevant information on energy supplies and markets, and establish closer relations between petroleum-producing countries and consumer states.

Headquarters: Paris, France.

Principal Organs: Governing Board, Standing Groups, Committee on Energy Research and Technology, Committee on Non-Member Countries, Secretariat.

Web site: www.iea.org

Executive Director: Nobuo Tanaka (Japan).

Membership (28, with year of entry)**:** Australia (1979), Austria (1974), Belgium (1974), Canada (1974), Czech Republic (2001), Denmark (1974), Finland (1992), France (1992), Germany (1974), Greece (1977), Hungary (1997), Ireland (1974), Italy (1978), Japan (1974), Republic of Korea (2002), Luxembourg (1974), Netherlands (1974), New Zealand (1977), Norway (participates under a special agreement), Poland (2008), Portugal (1981), Slovakia (2007), Spain (1974), Sweden (1974), Switzerland (1974), Turkey (1981), United Kingdom (1974), United States (1974).

Observers: All other OECD members, as well as the Commission of the European Communities, may participate as observers.

Origin and development. Created as a response by OECD member states to the energy crisis of 1973–1974, the IEA began provisional operation on November 18, 1974, with signatory governments given until May 1, 1975, to deposit instruments of ratification. Norway, one of the original sponsors, did not immediately participate as a full member because of fear that sovereignty over its own vast oil resources might be impaired. Spain, Austria, Sweden, and Switzerland applied for membership, although the last three reserved the right to withdraw if IEA operations interfered with their neutrality. New Zealand was admitted in 1975, and a later agreement with Norway gave it a special status close to full membership. Subsequently, Australia, Greece, and Portugal joined. France and Finland cooperated with the agency until becoming members in 1992. The Czech Republic joined in February 2001, as did South Korea the following year, and Poland in 2008.

Apart from the energy crisis of the 1970s, the most perilous events for the IEA have been the Iran-Iraq war of the 1980s and the Gulf crisis of 1990–1991. In 1984 IEA members discussed plans to be implemented should the Strait of Hormuz be closed because of the Iran-Iraq war. Members agreed to early use of government-owned or -controlled oil supplies to calm the market in cases of disruption. Prior to the U.S.-led invasion of Iraq in 2003, the IEA announced that it was considering the release of oil supplies if necessary.

A week after the Iraqi invasion of Kuwait on August 2, 1990, the IEA Governing Board met in emergency session, urging efforts to avert a possible oil crisis. Another IEA emergency session on January 11, 1991, unanimously approved a contingency plan to ensure "security of supply." Two days after the January 16 launching of Operation Desert Storm against Iraq, the plan was activated and IEA members were directed to make an additional 2.5 million barrels per day of oil available to the market. The IEA reported that 17 countries subsequently released oil from stockpiles during the war, helping to keep supplies and prices relatively stable.

Structure. The IEA's Governing Board is comprised of ministers of member governments. The board is assisted by three standing groups (Emergency Questions, Long-Term Cooperation, and the Oil Market) and two committees (Energy Research and Technology and Non-Member Countries). Decisions of the Governing Board are made by a weighted majority except in the case of procedural questions, when a simple majority suffices.

A Coal Industry Advisory Board reports to the Standing Group on Long-Term Cooperation. There also is an Industry Advisory Board on Oil. Working parties reporting to the Committee on Energy Research and Technology (CERT) focus on fossil fuels, renewable energy technologies, and end-use technologies; a Fusion Power Coordinating Committee also reports to the CERT. The Secretariat includes an Emergency Planning and Preparations Division, which helps carry out the work of the Standing Group on Emergency Questions.

Activities. In the event of an oil shortfall of 7 percent or more, the Governing Board can invoke oil-sharing contingency plans and order members to reduce demand and draw down oil reserves. Participating countries agree to maintain oil stocks equal to 90 days' worth of the previous year's net imports. A system of complementary Coordinated Emergency Response Measures (CERM), dating from 1984, may be invoked by the Governing Board under circumstances that do not necessarily constitute a full emergency.

Over the years, the IEA has broadened the scope of its activities to include analyses of various energy sectors as well as Country Reports that review energy policies, prices, and developments in key nonmembers as well as in member states. Ties with nonmembers have steadily increased, reflecting growing energy consumption. The IEA also has confronted nuclear energy issues, particularly as public and governmental support for nuclear power generation declined after the 1986 Chernobyl accident in what is now Ukraine.

Regular publications include the *World Energy Outlook* and annual statistical analyses of the oil, natural gas, electricity, and coal industries. Through Implementing Agreements the IEA also helps fund cooperative research efforts involving such areas as alternative energy sources (ocean power, wind, solar, battery, hydro, hydrogen, geothermal, biomass); clean coal technology; hybrid vehicles; energy efficiency; superconductivity; heat pump and heat exchange technology; and nuclear fusion.

The relationship of such environmental issues as rising carbon dioxide emissions—and the consequent greenhouse effect—to national and international energy goals also has been a major consideration for the IEA. The IEA's 1998 *World Energy Outlook* noted that carbon dioxide emissions were expected to exceed 1990 levels by 70 percent by 2020, with most of this growth occurring in the developing world, especially Asia, and with overall developing world emissions surpassing those of the developed countries by 2010. The 2000 *World Energy Outlook*, anticipating a rise in world energy use of 57 percent between 1997 and 2020, predicted that the emission targets set at the 1997 Kyoto, Japan, session of the Conference of the Parties to the United Nations Framework Convention on Climate Change could not be met.

The *World Energy Outlook* for 2002 predicted that by 2030 fossil fuels would continue to account for 90 percent of energy usage and that over the next three decades consumption of oil would increase at a faster rate than in the preceding 30 years, growing from 75 million barrels per day to 120 million. Consequently, emissions of carbon dioxide are expected to increase by 70 percent. China alone is expected to account for one-fifth of the growth in energy demand.

In 2003 the IEA issued its first *World Energy Investment Outlook*, which concluded that some $16 trillion was needed in energy-related investment by 2030, half of it for transportation and distribution systems. Among those contributing to the report were the Organization of the Petroleum Exporting Countries (OPEC), the World Bank, governmental institutions, and various corporations.

During the biennial International Energy Forum, held in September 2002 in Osaka, Japan, the IEA, OPEC ministers, and other key participants appeared increasingly comfortable about holding discussions in the open rather than behind closed doors. The IEA's contention that suppliers and consumers both benefit from collaborative planning was subsequently reinforced when a confluence of circumstances—the aftermath of a December general strike in Venezuela, Japan's decision to temporarily shut down nuclear plants because of security concerns, unrest in Nigeria, and the March 2003 invasion of Iraq—could have precipitated a major supply crisis. Instead, with the IEA, its members, oil corporations, and OPEC working in concert, no significant supply shortages or price spikes occurred.

By the 2005 Governing Board meeting, held on May 3 in Paris, the effect on the oil market of rapid economic growth in China and India had become increasingly evident. The final report warned against a business-as-usual approach to energy, stressing the need for more investment and more creative thinking to ensure adequate supplies and reduce the rise in greenhouse gases. The report concluded: "In order to bridge the gap between what is happening and what needs to be done, IEA will help to develop strategies aiming at a clean, clever and competitive energy future. This needs leadership and co-operation."

During 2005 and 2006, gasoline prices rose substantially throughout the developed world, with no promise of a return to previous levels. In addition to increased demand, real or perceived instability in major producer countries, notably in Iran and Nigeria, caused irregularity in energy markets. In mid-2006 the IEA revised upward its estimate of Chinese energy consumption, criticizing that country's use of energy as wasteful and unnecessarily polluting. In its November 2006 *World Energy Outlook,* the IEA declared that nuclear power must be an important part of any attempt to maintain the world's energy supply and to combat global warming. In June 2007 the IEA praised Germany for its environmental policies, but urged it to end plans to phase out nuclear energy. The following month it warned that pressure on oil supplies would continue for the foreseeable future.

On October 3, 2007, the IEA governing board approved Poland's application for membership. As of mid-2008, arrangements for Poland to join were not complete. On November 30, 2007, Slovakia joined the IEA, becoming its 27th member. As part of its qualification for membership, it set aside emergency stocks of oil, both in public and private hands, in excess of a 100-day supply.

In 2008 the IEA continued to warn about a long-term growth in demand for energy that would be difficult to manage. It urged OPEC to increase its production, even as oil prices rose dramatically, and worldwide consumption of petroleum products declined somewhat in response. The IEA noted that oil production from Russia had possibly peaked, and that Russian supplies to the world market might be problematic for some time to come.

In May 2008 the United States urged China and India to join the IEA, saying that membership would help them better manage their energy supplies. The United States' action was widely felt to be a recognition that the IEA would become much less effective without the participation of these two emerging industrial giants.

In September 2008 the IEA for the first time surveyed the energy policies of the entire European Union (EU) as opposed to only those countries that are IEA members. While praising the EU's approach to climate change, Executive Director Nobuo Tanaka called on the European Commission to support ownership unbundling as the best way to liberalize energy markets. "All other solutions are second best," he said. In September also the IEA called on India to abolish fuel subsidies, as a way to reduce demand. In the same month Poland was admitted to the IEA, fourteen years after it had first applied to join.

Historically, the IEA has been mostly concerned with the supply of oil and gas. In January 2009 the international group Energy Watch went so far as to claim that the IEA was obstructing the world's switch to renewable energy. The group claimed that the IEA had consistently underpredicted the growth of renewable energy. The Energy Watch report claimed that in 2007, net additions of wind power across the world were more than four times the average IEA estimate from its 1995–2004 predictions. The report declared that "the IEA numbers were neither empirically nor theoretically based."

The global economic crisis took the price of crude far down from its June 2008 peak of $124.52 per barrel to near $40 in early 2009. This period brought a variety of calls from the IEA about oil's future direction, though with an increasing sense that as the world economy seemed to stabilize late in 2009, the price of oil might rise again. A February 2009 IEA report predicted a worldwide oil shortage again in 2010, on the assumption that the global recession would be largely over by then.

INTERNATIONAL ORGANIZATION FOR MIGRATION (IOM/OIM)

Organisation Internationale pour les Migrations
Organización Internacional para las Migraciónes

Established: On December 5, 1951, in Brussels, Belgium, as a provisional movement to facilitate migration from Europe; formal constitution effective November 30, 1954; present name adopted in November 1989.

Purpose: To advance understanding of the causes and effects of migration; to collect, analyze, and disseminate information on migrant rights and welfare; to provide a forum for discussion of practical solutions to migration issues; to assist states in managing migration through resettlement, immigration, and the return and reintegration of migrants, refugees, displaced persons, and former combatants.

Headquarters: Geneva, Switzerland.

Principal Organs: Council (all members and observer states), Executive Committee (23 members), Director General's Office.

Web site: www.iom.int

Director General: William Lacey Swing (United States).

Membership (125): Afghanistan, Albania, Algeria, Angola, Argentina, Armenia, Australia, Austria, Azerbaijan, Bahamas, Bangladesh, Belarus, Belgium, Belize, Benin, Bolivia, Bosnia and Herzegovina, Brazil, Bulgaria, Burkina Faso, Burundi, Cambodia, Cameroon, Canada, Cape Verde, Chile, Colombia, Democratic Republic of the Congo, Republic of the Congo, Costa Rica, Côte d'Ivoire, Croatia, Cyprus, Czech Republic, Denmark, Dominican Republic, Ecuador, Egypt, El Salvador, Estonia, Finland, France, Gabon, Gambia, Georgia, Germany, Ghana, Greece, Guatemala, Guinea, Guinea-Bissau, Haiti, Honduras, Hungary, India, Iran, Ireland, Israel, Italy, Jamaica, Japan, Jordan, Kazakhstan, Kenya, Republic of Korea, Kyrgyzstan, Latvia, Liberia, Libya, Lithuania, Luxembourg, Madagascar, Mali, Malta, Mauritania, Mauritius, Mexico, Moldova, Mongolia, Montenegro, Morocco, Nepal, Netherlands, New Zealand, Nicaragua, Niger, Nigeria, Norway, Pakistan, Panama, Paraguay, Peru, Philippines, Poland, Portugal, Romania, Rwanda, Senegal, Serbia, Sierra Leone, Slovakia, Slovenia, Somalia, South Africa, Spain, Sri Lanka, Sudan, Sweden, Switzerland, Tajikistan, Tanzania, Thailand, Togo, Tunisia, Turkey, Uganda, Ukraine, United Kingdom, United States, Uruguay, Venezuela, Vietnam, Yemen, Zambia, Zimbabwe.

Observers (18): Bahrain, Bhutan, China, Cuba, Ethiopia, Guyana, Holy See, Indonesia, Macedonia, Mozambique, Namibia, Papua New Guinea, Qatar, Russian Federation, San Marino, Sao Tome and Principe, Saudi Arabia, Turkmenistan.

Official Languages: English, French, Spanish.

Origin and development. A Provisional Intergovernmental Committee for the Movement of Migrants from Europe was established by delegates to a 16-nation International Migration Conference in 1951 in Brussels, Belgium. The Intergovernmental Committee for European Migration (ICEM) was based on a constitution that came into force November 30, 1954. In November 1980 the group's name was changed to the Intergovernmental Committee for Migration (ICM), "European" being deleted from its name due to the broadened scope of the organization's activities. On May 20, 1987, a number of formal amendments to the ICM constitution, including another change of name to the International Organization for Migration (IOM), were approved to better reflect the worldwide nature and expanding mandate of ICM activity. The amendments came into effect on November 14, 1989, after being ratified by two-thirds of the member states.

Structure. The Council, which normally meets once a year, is comprised of representatives of all member and observer states. The 23-member Executive Committee, which meets twice a year, is elected by the Council for a two-year term. A Subcommittee on Budget and Finance assists the Council.

The Director General's Office oversees the daily operations of IOM headquarters, provides management coordination, and assists with policy formulation and program development. The director general is elected for a five-year term by the Council. Administrative divisions at IOM headquarters include External Relations; Administrative Support (Department of Budget and Finance, Department of Human Resources and Common Services Management); Information Technology and Communications; Migration Policy, Research, and Communication; Program Support, which includes the Donor Relations Division, the Emergency and Post-Crisis Division, and Project Tracking; Special Programs (Compensation Programs); and Migration Management Services (MMS). Also linked to the Director General's Office in Geneva are the Office of the Inspector General, Legal Services, Media and Public Information, and a Meetings Secretariat.

In the field, the IOM relies on its Manila and Panama Administrative Centers, which has additional responsibilities for information technology, security, and administration; 18 other Missions with Regional Functions scattered around the globe; some 225 Country Missions and suboffices; and short-term emergency Special-Purpose Missions. These centers interact with the IOM's field offices, providing project support and training in the core areas of movement (resettlement, repatriation, and transportation), assisted voluntary returns and integration, counter-trafficking, labor migration, mass information, migration health, and technical cooperation. Most of the organization's 6,690 staff work at the field level.

Activities. Since 1952, when ICEM operations began, more than 13 million migrants and refugees in more than 125 countries have been assisted with travel, placement, orientation, medical payments, vocational and language training, and other resettlement or repatriation services. Overall, the IOM has engaged in programs affecting every inhabited continent.

Beginning in 1965, for example, the organization carried out a Selective Migration Program to facilitate a transfer of technology from Europe to Latin America through the migration of highly qualified individuals. More than 27,000 European professionals, technicians, and skilled workers were relocated through the 1970s. Beginning in 1971 the organization also participated in the emigration of hundreds of thousands of Jews from the former Soviet Union, and it assisted in the resettlement of more than 1 million refugees from Indochina after 1975. In the second half of the 1990s, it began a counter-trafficking program in Cambodia and Thailand and also assisted in reintegrating demobilized soldiers in Angola and Guatemala. In 1996–1999 it undertook a Return of Qualified Nationals (RQN) program to assist Bosnia and Herzegovina in encouraging the return of professionals and other skilled emigrants. Similar efforts were subsequently undertaken in Timor-Leste (East Timor) and Afghanistan. The IOM also has participated in numerous efforts to address the problem of skilled workers leaving developing countries, most recently with a focus on Africa. An estimated 70,000 African professionals now emigrate to the West annually.

During 2001 the IOM drew on its earlier experiences in Bosnia and Herzegovina to organize, at the behest of the Organization for Security and Cooperation in Europe (OSCE), an Out-of-Kosovo Voting Program that registered more than 125,000 Kosovars living outside the province, either elsewhere in Yugoslavia or in some 35 other countries. About 80,000 of the total registrants voted in November's balloting for a Kosovo assembly. The IOM also has been directly involved in the German Forced Labor Compensation Program, which has sought to identify and compensate victims of slave and forced labor during the Nazi era, and in implementing the settlements won in the Holocaust Victim Assets Litigation against Swiss banks.

The number of IOM-assisted individuals fluctuates considerably from year to year, totaling 451,000 in 2000; dropping to 198,000 in 2001, as the level of aid to East Timorese, Kosovars, and Afghan refugees declined; and then jumping to 514,000 in 2002, swelled by 336,000 new Afghan refugees and internally displaced people (IDPs) as a consequence of the U.S.-led military campaign against the Taliban government and al-Qaida terrorist cells. In 2003, following the U.S.–led ouster of the Saddam Hussein government, the IOM introduced an Iraq Transition Initiative to help Iraqi refugees, IDPs, and former combatants. The IOM also responded to unrest in Côte d'Ivoire by helping repatriate individuals from neighboring states who were stranded in the region. The IOM has also been active in the response to the devastating earthquake of October 2005 in Pakistan; the Indian Ocean tsunami of December 26, 2005; the Indonesian government's efforts to build peace in the troubled province of Aceh; the May 2006 earthquake on the island of Java; and the disastrous cyclone of May 2008 in Myanmar.

At the June 2003 85th (Special) Session of the Council, Brunson McKinley of the United States, who had been director general since 1998, was reelected by acclamation to a second term, and the countries of Mauritania, Moldova, and New Zealand were admitted to membership. Malta joined the IOM at the 86th Session, held in November.

In the past decade IOM membership has more than doubled, and relations have been established or strengthened with dozens of other intergovernmental organizations. There has been a corresponding increase in the IOM budget, which leapt from $242 million in 1998 to more that $1 billion in 2008 (95 percent devoted to field operations). Some of the increase was attributable to payments under the German Forced Labor Compensation Program and the Holocaust Victim Assets Program, which both ended September 30, 2006. Until 2005 IOM's indirect costs were charged to all projects through an overhead charge of 12 percent on staff and office costs (approximately 5 percent on total costs). In 2006 the IOM administration started a phased conversion to an administrative support charge of 5 percent on total costs. IOM claims that its support costs are among the lowest of all international organizations.

According to the organization's *World Migration 2008* (the latest available as of June 2009), the number of migrants (legal and otherwise) grew from 76 million in 1965 to between 185 million and 192 million in early 2005, to an estimated 200 million at the present time. Migration now accounts for most of the population growth in the West. At present, only six countries encourage migration—Australia, Canada, Israel, New Zealand, the United Kingdom, and the United States. The 2008 report emphasizes the changing nature of migration; instead of being a movement chiefly from poor countries into a few rich ones, migration is now a phenomenon that encompasses most of the world, with people moving, for different reasons, in all directions.

The IOM continues to be active in virtually every country where there are refugees or in which migration is any kind of factor. In March 2007 it opened a liaison office in Beijing, China—a country greatly affected by migration from country to city. In its January 2007 report, the *Iraq Displacement 2006 Year in Review*, the IOM stated that as many as 1.5 million internally displaced Iraqis lacked the most basic services. Of particular concern in 2007 and 2008 was the rise of migration or attempted migration, often under desperate conditions, from Africa to Europe. The IOM worked in Africa to deter this migration through propaganda campaigns and programs to help stranded migrants go home. The problem of human trafficking continued to be a focus, with the IOM looking at trafficking to the Gulf States, and the Central Asian republics of the former Soviet Union. It also warned of fraudulent advertisements about immigration on the Internet, misusing the name and logo of the IOM, the UN, or other humanitarian organizations.

In May 2007 Director General Brunson McKinley announced that he would seek a third term as the head of the organization. This move was not universally welcomed, as many had criticized McKinley's tenure as one of poor and arbitrary management. The United States did not support McKinley's bid, instead nominating William Lacy Swing, a diplomat with U.S. and UN experience. Swing was elected at the June 2008 council meeting and assumed his post on October 1, 2008. At the same meeting India and Somalia were welcomed as full members, their status being upgraded from that of observers.

In a December 2008 report, the IOM estimated that by 2050 as many as 200 million people could be forced out of their homes by the various effects of climate change. But on the positive side, in the same month the IOM emphasized that, on balance, migration is a good thing. At its best, migration can take skills and labor where they are needed, improving the lives of all concerned. The organization warned against using migrants as scapegoats during the current economic downturn.

In May 2009 the IOM sent rapid response teams to assist Pakistanis displaced by fighting in that country's northwest region. Also in May the organization launched a Web site, funded by the European Commission (EC), which gives migrants in Europe "unbiased and up-to-date information on return and reintegration opportunities in their countries of origin."

INTERNATIONAL ORGANIZATION OF THE FRANCOPHONIE (OIF)

Organisation Internationale de la Francophonie

Established: As *La Francophonie* under a charter that was adopted on December 18, 1996, in Marrakesh, Morocco, by a Ministerial Conference of francophone states and then endorsed on November 15, 1997, by the Seventh Francophone Summit, held in Hanoi, Vietnam; present name adopted by the Ministerial Conference of the Francophonie on December 4–5, 1998, in Bucharest, Romania.

Purpose: To facilitate the exchange of cultural, educational, scientific, and technological information, particularly but not exclusively among countries with French in common usage; to promote cultural and linguistic diversity, including the teaching of French; to encourage democracy and respect for human rights; to advance the economic development of member states.

Headquarters: Paris, France.

Principal Organs: Conference of Heads of State and Government of Countries Using French as a Common Language (Francophone Summit), Ministerial Conference of the Francophonie, Permanent Council of the Francophonie, General Secretariat, Agency of the Francophonie (Intergovernmental Agency of the Francophonie), Parliamentary Assembly of the Francophonie.

Web site: www.francophonie.org

Secretary General: Abdou Diouf (Senegal).

Membership (53): Albania, Andorra, Belgium, French Community of Belgium, Benin, Bulgaria, Burkina Faso, Burundi, Cambodia, Cameroon, Canada, Canada–New Brunswick, Canada–Quebec, Cape Verde, Central African Republic, Chad, Comoro Islands, Democratic Republic of the Congo, Republic of the Congo, Côte d'Ivoire, Djibouti, Dominica, Egypt, Equatorial Guinea, France, Gabon, Greece, Guinea, Guinea-Bissau, Haiti, Laos, Lebanon, Luxembourg, Macedonia, Madagascar, Mali, Mauritania, Mauritius, Moldova, Monaco, Morocco, Niger, Romania, Rwanda, St. Lucia, Sao Tome and Principe, Senegal, Seychelles, Switzerland, Togo, Tunisia, Vanuatu, Vietnam.

Associate Members (2): Cyprus, Ghana.

Observers (14): Armenia, Austria, Croatia, Czech Republic, Georgia, Hungary, Latvia, Lithuania, Mozambique, Poland, Serbia, Slovakia, Slovenia, Ukraine.

Official Language: French.

Origin and development. Efforts to bring together the French-speaking countries of the world date back to the 1960s, some 80 years after the term "*francophonie*" was first used to identify those peoples and states speaking or otherwise using French. International cooperation initially centered on educational policy and institutions, followed in 1967 by creation of the International Association of French Language Parliamentarians (*Association Internationale des Parlementaires de Langue Français*—AIPLF). Near the end of the decade the francophone movement began to assume a somewhat more formal character as the First International Conference of Francophone Countries, meeting on February 17–20, 1969, in Niamey, Niger, proposed creation of a clearinghouse for members in the areas of culture, education, and technology. Spearheading the efforts were three African heads of state: Habib Bourguiba of Tunisia, Hamani Diori of Niger, and Léopold Sédar Senghor of Senegal. As a result, the Agency for Cultural and Technical Cooperation (*Agence de Coopération Culturelle et Technique*—ACCT) was established by a convention signed March 21, 1970, in Niamey, during the Second International Conference of Francophone Countries. ACCT subsequently grew to encompass all major French-speaking states except Algeria, as well as a number of countries in which French culture was deemed important, although not dominant.

In the 1980s and 1990s ACCT was involved in the proposed establishment of a full-fledged francophone "commonwealth." Although the idea was first suggested to ACCT members in 1980, disputes both within Canada and between Canada and France over the issue of Quebec separatism delayed the convening of a Francophone Summit to work on the proposal until February 17–19, 1986. The summit, held outside Paris, France, was attended by delegations from 42 countries and regions and adopted a 13-point program of action that called for, among other things, the formation of a francophone television network, the provision of linguistic data to the francophone world by means of videotext, and the strengthening of cooperation among francophone delegations at the United Nations (UN). Responsibility for a number of the summit's proposals was given to ACCT, whose ministerial-level General Conference met in an extraordinary session in December to consider structural and financial reforms that would permit it to assume greater francophone authority. Concurrently, Canada, already ACCT's leading financial contributor, announced it was doubling its level of support.

A second summit, attended by 43 delegations from 37 countries (including all ACCT members except Cameroon and Vanuatu), was held September 2–4, 1987, in Quebec, Canada. African economic issues, particularly the external debt crisis and falling world commodity prices, dominated the meeting, during which Canada announced that it was forgiving about $330 million in debts owed by seven African countries. Discussion also continued on the future role of ACCT in whatever francophone structure might emerge from the summits.

The Third Francophone Summit, held in May 1989 in Dakar, Senegal, maintained the emphasis on third world debt and development problems. French president François Mitterrand garnered the biggest headlines by announcing he intended to ask the French Parliament to forgive 40 percent (an estimated $2.3 billion) of the debt owed to France by the world's 35 poorest countries. The Fourth Francophone Summit was held November 19–21, 1991, in Chaillot, France, the venue having been changed from Zaire because of objections to Zairean president Mobutu Sese Seko's apparent antipathy toward political reform.

Continued friction between Canada and France over the role of ACCT was subsequently reported, Paris apparently charging the agency with promoting Canadian interests at the expense of broader francophone concerns. However, an understanding on the matter was reportedly reached at the Fifth Francophone Summit, held October 16–18, 1993, in Port Louis, Mauritius. France, acquiesced to a second term for ACCT secretary general Jean-Louis Roy, a Canadian, apparently in return for the summit's agreement to expand the authority of the Permanent Francophone Council (*Conseil Permanent de la Francophonie*—CPF), which had been established by the 1991 summit. The council was authorized to make political decisions on behalf of the francophone countries as well as to coordinate the institutional activities of the francophone community, including ACCT, between summits. Meanwhile, the summit also approved the renaming of the AIPLF (which in 1989 had changed from *Association* to *Assemblée*) to the Francophone Consultative Assembly (*Assemblée Consultative de la Francophonie*—ACF) and welcomed the grouping under the expanding francophone umbrella.

In anticipation of the next francophone summit, ACCT Secretary General Roy suggested that the group adopt a "more political" approach to enhance its effectiveness, observers taking this to mean, among other things, greater emphasis on such issues as democratization and human rights. However, as expected following the election of the conservative Jacques Chirac as the new president of France in May 1995, the sixth summit, held December 2–4, 1995, in Cotonou, Benin, concentrated on economic matters. Chirac indicated France would press other leading industrialized nations not to reduce their financial assistance to African nations. He also called for efforts to prevent English from becoming the default language of the Internet and the information superhighway.

Returning to the issue of a greater political emphasis, the Francophone Ministerial Conference (*Conférence Ministérielle de la Francophonie*—CMF) in 1996 proposed a new francophone charter, which was approved by the Seventh Francophone Summit, held November 14–16, 1997, in Hanoi, Vietnam. It was agreed that a permanent General Secretariat would be established for *La Francophonie* on January 1, 1998, under the leadership of former UN secretary general Boutros Boutros-Ghali of Egypt, whose selection as secretary general of the new body reportedly caused consternation among some French-speaking African countries. In addition, the new charter directed that the ACCT would subsequently be known as the Agency of the Francophonie (*Agence de la Francophonie*); the former ACCT thus became the lead agency of the newly formalized *La Francophonie*, with the summit leaders then selecting Roger Dehaybe of Belgium as the new general administrator of the agency. The summit also confirmed a shift in emphasis; all participants had indicated their desire to join forces with other countries attempting to ward off global domination by Anglo-Saxon (particularly American) culture and language.

The CMF, meeting in Bucharest, Romania, December 4–5, 1998, endorsed Boutros-Ghali's efforts to heighten the profile of the francophone community, henceforth to be known as the International Francophone Organization (*Organisation Internationale de la Francophonie*—OIF). In addition, the CMF endorsed renaming the ACF as the Parliamentary Assembly of the Francophonie (*Assemblée Parlementaire de la Francophonie*—APF) and asked it to play a wider role in helping to solidify legislative institutions in developing countries.

In 1999 the OIF decided that the Agency of the Francophonie would be commonly, although unofficially, referenced as the Intergovernmental Agency of the Francophonie (*Agence Intergouvernementale de la Francophonie*—AIF) to better reflect its character.

Structure. The Conference of Heads of State and Government of Countries Using French as a Common Language, better known as the Francophone Summit, usually meets every two years to set policy for the OIF. The Ministerial Conference of the Francophonie (CMF), consisting primarily of the members' foreign ministers, is responsible for seeing that summit decisions are carried out. Two additional permanent ministerial conferences address matters of education and of youth and sports; sectoral ministerial conferences also may be convened. The Permanent Council of the Francophonie (CPF), comprising the personal representatives of the members' heads of state and government, has among its responsibilities organizing summits and seeing that summit decisions are implemented.

The secretary general, who is elected by the summit for a four-year term, has multiple functions, including heading the General Secretariat, chairing the CPF, carrying out international policy, and serving as the OIF's principal international presence and spokesperson. In addition, the secretary general ranks as the senior official of the Agency of the Francophonie (unofficially, the Intergovernmental Agency of the Francophonie—AIF) and nominates that organ's general administrator. As the OIF's principal executing body, the AIF has as its main responsibility carrying out the cultural, scientific, technical, economic, and legal cooperative programs endorsed by the summit. The CMF also sits as the General Conference of the Agency, while the CPF periodically convenes as the agency's Administrative Council.

In January 2004 a new body, the High Council of the Francophonie (*Haut Conseil de la Francophonie*) convened for the first time. Encompassing between 30 and 40 individuals selected by the secretary general for once-renewable terms of four years, the High Council has as its mission reflection on matters concerning French language and cultural diversity. The 37 individuals named to the first High Council included politicians, artists, writers, media specialists, teachers, jurists, economists, and entrepreneurs from around the globe.

The OIF sponsors four specialized agencies: the Agency of Francophone Universities, the French-language TV5 international channel, the Senghor University of Alexandria, and the International Association of Francophone Mayors. Other affiliated bodies and offices include the Francophone Institute for Energy and the Environment in Quebec, Canada, and the Francophone Institute for New Information and Training Technologies in Bordeaux, France. A Parliamentary Assembly serves an advisory role.

Activities. The formal establishment of the OIF solidified efforts by the international francophone community to expand its membership and mission. Recent additions to the organization include numerous countries that have no significant French-speaking population; all, however, have been seeking wider international integration and access to economic and development assistance. Some commentators have suggested that these new or candidate members are diluting the French character of the group. In addition to advancing French cultural and linguistic programs, including sponsorship of more than 140 rural reading centers in a dozen African countries, the OIF promotes crisis prevention and resolution, strengthening of democratic practices and institutions, ratification of human rights conventions, and adoption of coordinated policies in multilateral trade negotiations. In furtherance of such goals it has established permanent missions to the UN, the European Union (EU), and the African Union (AU) and has opened regional AIF offices in Libreville, Gabon; Lomé, Togo; and Hanoi, Vietnam.

The Francophone Summit that convened September 3–5, 1999, in Moncton, New Brunswick, Canada, focused its attention once again on matters of cultural diversity. The meeting's final declaration noted that "cultural goods are in no way reducible to their economic dimension" and that the participating leaders "affirm the right of [their] states and governments to freely define their cultural policies and appropriate tools of intervention." The declaration cited the perceived threat posed by multilateral talks and globalization without, however, explicitly referencing an ongoing U.S.-Canadian dispute over Ottawa's efforts to protect Canadian publications, music, and other media from U.S. domination.

Having been postponed from October 2001 following the September 11 terrorist attacks on the United States, the ninth summit met October 18–20, 2002, in Beirut, Lebanon. The session was largely dominated by the looming crisis over Iraq's alleged weapons of mass destruction. A summit resolution noted the "essential role" of the UN in resolving the conflict, and the overall stance of the participants clearly supported President Chirac's opposition to preemptive military action in the absence of Security Council authorization. The ongoing political crisis in Côte d'Ivoire also drew the attention of the participants, who elected former Senegalese president Abdou Diouf as the new OIF secretary general. In a noteworthy development, the summit was attended by Algerian president Abdelaziz Bouteflika, who pointedly dismissed questions from the press about whether or not his country would seek admission to the OIF.

The OIF continues to promote the French language and the shared traditions of the francophone community. The secretary general frequently travels beyond the French-speaking world in support of this mission. The OIF has never failed to condemn antidemocratic moves in French-speaking Africa or to praise prodemocratic efforts, such as voters' approval of a new constitution in the Democratic Republic of the Congo in December 2005.

The 11th Francophone Summit was held September 28–29, 2006, in Bucharest, Romania. Summit resolutions are usually passed unanimously, so Canadian prime minister Stephen Harper caused concern when he vetoed a resolution that expressed sympathy for Lebanese civilians killed or displaced in the recent fighting, but which said nothing about Israeli civilians. The resolution was eventually modified to remove all mention of nationality. Shortly afterwards a Canadian senator asked in Parliament for the Canadian government to pursue Israel's inclusion in the OIF, saying that Israel had more French-speaking residents than several present members of the OIF.

On March 13, 2007, the OIF reported that the number of French speakers worldwide was a record 200 million, 72 million of whom also spoke a language other than French. The place of the French language outside metropolitan France, and by implication the OIF's promotion of France through the French language, came under attack in March 2007. The French newspaper *Le Monde* published a manifesto signed by 44 distinguished French writers. The memo attacked the concept of a "francophonie," centered on France and ultimately promoting French interests. Instead it advocated treating French literature—wherever written—as "world literature" that happened to be written in French. Foreign-born writers had recently won five of the country's seven major book awards; the coveted Prix Goncourt had gone to the New York–born bilingual writer Jonathan Littell for his novel *Les Bienveillantes*, or *The Kindly Ones*, set in Nazi-occupied Europe. The manifesto's signatories noted how much English literature had been enriched by writers from former British colonial territories, and suggested French literature should take a similar path.

Among the countries recently hosting OIF events were Zimbabwe (March 2008) and Bangladesh (March 2008). The government of Canada appeared ready to play an active part in OIF affairs in 2007 and 2008. In July 2008 Secretary General Diouf announced an agreement between the OIF and the International Olympic Committee reaffirming the status of French, along with English, as one of the official languages of the Olympics. In August 2009 a similar convention guaranteed the place of French at the 2010 Winter Olympic and Winter Paralympic Games, to be held in Vancouver, Canada.

The 2008 OIF summit took place October 17–19 in Quebec City, and as a gesture of support for bilingualism and biculturalism, the government pledged Can$57 million towards the event. As it happened, discussion of the French language at this meeting took a back seat to the world economic crisis. French president Nicholas Sarkozy called for a reform of capitalism, to make it more respectful of the future and not "obsessed by the frantic search for short-term profit." Sarkozy proposed that the United Nations should host multilateral talks to address the crisis, including as many countries as possible, and looking out for the interest of poor and vulnerable nations.

The conference pledged the Francophonie to do its part in reducing greenhouse gasses in half by 2050. It also welcomed Latvia as an Associate Member. In a less welcome development associated with the summit, the director of the Francophone Canadian branch of Amnesty International said that several members of the OIF had poor human rights records, and that such countries should be named and suspended from the organization.

In April 2009 Madagascar, currently in a state of violence and political turmoil, was suspended from full participation in the OIF. In July a delegation from the OIF joined other international organizations in observing presidential elections in Mauritania, as that country emerged from eleven months of military rule.

The next OIF summit was scheduled to be held in Madagascar in 2010.

LATIN AMERICAN AND CARIBBEAN ECONOMIC SYSTEM (LAES/SELA)

Systeme Economique Latinaméricain
Sistema Econômico Latino-Americano e do Caribe
Sistema Económico Latinoamericana y del Caribe

Established: By convention signed October 17, 1975, in Panama City, Panama.

Purpose: To promote intraregional cooperation to accelerate the economic and social development of its members; to provide a permanent system of consultation and coordination for the adoption of common positions and strategies on economic and social issues in international bodies and forums as well as before third countries and groups of countries.

Headquarters: Caracas, Venezuela.

Principal Organs: Latin American Council, Action Committees, Permanent Secretariat.

Web site: www.sela.org (A fairly complete English-language version is provided.)

Permanent Secretary: José Rivera Banuet (Mexico)

Membership (27): Argentina, Bahamas, Barbados, Belize, Bolivia, Brazil, Chile, Colombia, Costa Rica, Cuba, Dominican Republic, Ecuador, Grenada, Guatemala, Guyana, Haiti, Honduras, Jamaica, Mexico, Nicaragua, Panama, Paraguay, Peru, Suriname, Trinidad and Tobago, Uruguay, Venezuela.

Official Languages: English, French, Portuguese, Spanish.

Origin and development. Latin American and Caribbean Economic System (SELA) received its strongest impetus from discussions between Venezuelan president Carlos Andrés Pérez and Mexican president Luis Echeverría during the former's visit to Mexico in March 1975. It has been suggested that the two became convinced of the need for a purely Latin American economic organization after passage of the 1974 United States Trade Reform Act. The new agency, which was established under the October 17, 1975, Panama Convention, succeeded the Latin American Economic Coordination Commission (*Comisión Especial de Coordinación Latinoamericana*—CECLA), which had attempted to provide linkage between Latin American economic policies and those of more developed states. At the 30th ordinary meeting of SELA in 2004, the group's name was amended to include "and Caribbean," although at the 31st meeting in 2005 it was decided not to change the acronym.

Structure. SELA is one of numerous intergovernmental organizations in Latin America focused on trade integration. Its members include states that make up the Latin American Integration Association (ALADI), the Andean Community of Nations (CAN), the Southern Common Market (Mercosur), most of the members (all save El Salvador) of the Central American Common Market (CACM), and more than half the states of the Caribbean Community (Caricom). Like the rest of these groups, SELA is faced with the difficult political task of coordinating the needs of the member states in such a way as to foster trade and other cooperative enterprises. Unlike many of them (such as Mercosur), SELA is neither a customs union nor a free trade zone. It is simply a mechanism for consultation and coordination. The ongoing quest to achieve favorable trade within the community as well as with the United States and the European Union (EU) is a high priority.

The governing Latin American Council, comprised of ministers from each member state, convenes at least once a year. To facilitate its work the council may designate action committees; areas thus far covered include earthquake recovery, the production of high-protein foodstuffs, housing, and other social welfare endeavors. Each action committee is dissolved once it has achieved its objectives, unless a decision has been made to make it a permanent body, of which there are presently two: the Latin American Technological Information Network (*Red de Información Tecnológica Latinoamericana*—RITLA), based in Rio de Janeiro, Brazil, and the Latin American Fisheries Development Organization (*Organización Latinoamericana de Desarrollo Pesquero*—Oldepesca), based in Lima, Peru. The Permanent Secretariat is headed by a secretary whose term of office is four years.

Activities. While many observers believed that SELA had the potential at its inauguration to further regional integration in Latin America, progress was much slower than expected. Nevertheless, a number of cooperative agreements were signed in 1980, including accords to work with the United Nations Industrial Development Organization (UNIDO) and the UN Development Program (UNDP) on projects concerning energy and capital goods and the UN Economic Commission for Latin America and the Caribbean (ECLAC) to increase joint projects in finance and the exchange of technical information. In January 1982 SELA and the Economic Community of West African States (ECOWAS) concluded an agreement in Caracas, Venezuela, to promote trade among member countries of the two organizations.

One ongoing SELA concern has been debt relief. Although some SELA members, including Costa Rica, Mexico, and Venezuela, pursued individual debt reduction packages in the 1980s, SELA continued to push for a regional approach. Debt relief discussions, at least as far as official bilateral debt owed to the United States was concerned, were included in the Enterprise for the Americas Initiative proposed by U.S. president George H. W. Bush.

During the September 1992 Latin American Council meeting, SELA officials emphasized that external debt remained a "monumental" problem for the region, despite recent economic gains in many Latin American countries. SELA also continued to urge members to pursue favorable trade agreements as a bloc, a position that was seen by some as reflecting concern over Mexico's participation in the recently negotiated North American Free Trade Agreement (NAFTA).

At the July 1995 annual meeting, SELA consultants argued that the structural adjustment programs of the 1980s and early 1990s had produced "mixed results": economic growth had been stimulated and inflation brought under better control, but the region's external debt had grown and poverty had worsened. SELA urged members to refine their investment incentive polices to attract long-term capital, not speculation. Latin American countries also would be wise to attend to "social investment," SELA argued, to guard against political instability and conflicts that would undermine economic advancement.

In 1997 SELA reported that Latin American integration was continuing to move forward as trade within and between regional groups increased. Many obstacles, such as protectionist practices and political and economic instability, had been removed. The main topics at the Latin American Council meeting held on October 6–9, 1997, in Port of Spain, Trinidad, were growth and employment. The council also called on the United States to end its economic blockade of Cuba and criticized the U.S. Helms-Burton law, which threatened to impose sanctions on companies doing business with Cuba.

At an April 7–9, 2003, session, the Latin American Council, responding to a report entitled "The Role of SELA in the Future of the Region," prepared by its Reflections Group, concluded that it was necessary to refocus SELA's priorities, in part to ensure nonduplication of efforts being made by other organizations. The Permanent Secretariat was directed to propose an annual work program emphasizing integration, development, and technical cooperation. The next council session, held November 24–26, was highlighted by the election of a new permanent secretary, Roberto Guarnieri, a Venezuelan economist, as successor to Chile's Otto Boye Soto. The group commemorated its 30th anniversary at its 31st ordinary meeting held November 21–23, 2005. In Decision No. 471, it reaffirmed its commitment to the integration of the region.

An example of SELA's work that is linked to economic development rather than integration is the Ibero-American Institutional Development Program for the Development of Small and Medium Business (*El Programa Iberoamericano de Cooperación Institucional para el Desarrollo de la Pequeña y Mediana Empresa*—IBERPYME). The program was established at the Eighth Ibero-American Summit held in October of 1998 in Oporto, Portugal. It seeks to promote the development of public and private institutions that will aid the growth of small- and medium-sized businesses in the region.

While multilateral negotiations for the proposed Free Trade Area of the Americas (FTAA), which would encompass most members of SELA, remain on hold, the growth of free trade agreements within the group, particularly with the United Sates, continues. The largest such agreement is the Central American Free Trade Agreement (CAFTA-DR). SELA members Colombia, Ecuador, and Peru have signed free trade agreements with the United States, and Uruguay and the United States have started negotiations. The reconfiguration of regional trade organizations such as the Andean Community of Nations and Mercosur also has garnered the interest of SELA members. However, the prospect of a true regional trading bloc remains elusive.

SELA held a two-day meeting on the development of the Venezuelan tourist industry at its headquarters in May 2006. The organization's 32nd meeting, held in Caracas March 28–30, 2007, concluded on a note of caution, with the permanent secretary saying that while the organization's work program was to remain the same as in past years, lack of funds necessitated a severe austerity program and a hiring freeze. At the November 2007 meeting, the permanent secretary's report pointed out that contributions were still seriously in arrears and the annual work program much reduced. The organization was about $1.5 million in debt and was only operating at all due to a line of credit from the Banco Industrial de Venezuela.

Latin America's approach to the EU formed a large part of the agenda at meetings during 2007 and into 2008. These culminated in a summit of the EU and Latin American and Caribbean (EU-LAC) heads of state and government, held in Lima, Peru, on May 16–17, 2008. This meeting focused on poverty, social inclusion, and climate change. Microbusinesses were recognized as an important factor in future development. The world financial crisis continued to affect the region throughout 2008 and into 2009. SELA member states were affected by a run-up in food prices, a steep decline in tourism, trade, remittances, and, in 2008 at least, a weak U. S. dollar. In October 2008 SELA permanent secretary José Rivera Banuet declared that tough times were ahead for the group. However the current difficulties were a passing problem, Rivera added,, which pointed the direction for member countries in the future. The region must make stronger efforts to enter the knowledge economy.

In November 2008 a delegation of election monitors from SELA, along with other groups, arrived in Venezuela to observe the regional elections there. In November also, SELA welcomed Grenada back into the organization. Grenada had been a member previously, but in 2003 had denounced the Panama Convention and left.

Negotiations between SELA and the EU, as between other regional groupings and the EU, proceeded slowly. In February 2009 SELA members met in Caracas to evaluate the EU-LAC meeting of the previous May, and to prepare for the next such meeting, to be held in 2010 in Madrid, Spain. In a March 20, 2009, "Regional Seminar on the Economic Relations between the United States and Latin America and the Caribbean within the context of global crisis," SELA representatives criticized both private banks and the Inter-American Development Bank (IDB) for their parts in the financial crisis. In addition to the complaints against banks heard around the world, the IDB was criticized for policies that played against sustainable development and overcoming poverty. SELA warned that the crisis could push another six million Latin Americans into poverty. The same meeting called on the U.S. president Barack Obama's administration to avoid protectionism and end the blockade against Cuba.

In June 2009 SELA held a meeting to discuss the emigration of skilled workers from the region.

LATIN AMERICAN INTEGRATION ASSOCIATION (LAIA/ALADI)

Asociación Latinoamericana de Integración
Associaçao Latino-Americana de Integração

Established: By treaty signed August 12, 1980, in Montevideo, Uruguay, effective March 18, 1981, as successor to the Latin American Free Trade Association.

Purpose: To promote the expansion of regional integration, both economic and social, and ultimately to establish a Latin American common market.

Headquarters: Montevideo, Uruguay.

Principal Organs: Council of Ministers, Committee of Representatives, Evaluation and Convergence Conference, Secretariat.

Web site: www.aladi.org (The site offers an English-language option for its home page.)

Secretary General: Hugo Saguier Caballero (Paraguay).

Membership (13): Argentina, Bolivia, Brazil, Chile, Colombia, Cuba, Ecuador, Mexico, Panama, Paraguay, Peru, Uruguay, Venezuela.

Observers (27): Andean Development Corporation, China, Costa Rica, Dominican Republic, El Salvador, Commission of the European Communities, Guatemala, Honduras, Ibero-American Secretariat-General, Inter-American Development Bank, Inter-American Institute for Agricultural Cooperation, Italy, Japan, Republic of Korea, Latin American Economic System, Nicaragua, Organization of American States, Panama, Pan American Health Organization/World Health Organization, Portugal, Romania, Russia, Spain, Switzerland, United Nations Development Program, United Nations Economic Commission for Latin America and the Caribbean, Ukraine.

Official Languages: Spanish, Portuguese; Spanish is the working language.

Origin and development. The decision to establish Latin American Integration Association (ALADI) resulted from an 11-day meeting in June 1980 in Acapulco, Mexico, of the Latin American Free Trade Association—LAFTA (*Asociación Latinoamericana de Libre Comercio*—ALALC), an organization whose members all joined ALADI. At the Acapulco meeting it was argued that a new organization with more modest goals than those of LAFTA was needed, one without a specific timetable for the achievement of a free trade zone and one that would explicitly take into account the considerable national differences in economic development that made undesirable the reciprocal trade concessions on which LAFTA had focused. The opposition to ALADI was led by the Brazilian and Mexican foreign ministers, who claimed that all that was necessary was a new protocol to the LAFTA charter. The majority, however, followed the lead of the Andean Group (now the Andean Community; see separate entry) and agreed to establish the new grouping. The founding treaty was signed in Montevideo, Uruguay, in August and entered into effect on March 18, 1981.

A principal aim of ALADI is to decrease trade barriers among its member states, but flexibility is allowed for members to enter into bilateral tariff, trade, and technology agreements. Moreover, members are classified according to their levels of economic development, and all tariff concessions are to take into account these relative assessments: the less-developed members are Bolivia, Ecuador, and Paraguay; the medium-developed are Chile, Colombia, Cuba, Peru, Uruguay, and Venezuela; the more-developed are Argentina, Brazil, and Mexico.

Structure. The Council of Ministers, comprised of the foreign ministers of the member states, is ALADI's principal political organ. Its annual meetings provide a means for reviewing the work of the organization and determining policy. The Committee of Representatives, the association's permanent political body, meets regularly to ensure that the provisions of the treaty are being implemented. Assisting the Committee of Representatives are a number of auxiliary organs, including commissions and councils concerned with budget issues; customs valuation, nomenclature, and other customs matters; entrepreneurship; export financing; financial and monetary affairs; labor; technical support and cooperation; tourism; and transport. The Committee of Representatives also may create sectoral councils. The Evaluation and Convergence Conference, comprised of plenipotentiaries of the member states, has the broad task of reviewing integration efforts and promoting new endeavors. The General Secretariat, ALADI's "technical organ," is headed by a secretary general who serves a once-renewable three-year term.

Activities. During the first meeting of the Council of Ministers, held in November 1983 in Washington, D.C., work was completed on the Regional Tariff Preference (RTP) scheme. The RTP, subsequently approved during the April 1984 council meeting in Montevideo, Uruguay, established a system of tariff cuts from July 1, 1984, for all ALADI members on the basis of their level of development. The council also approved resolutions aimed at strengthening financial and monetary cooperation mechanisms; providing special aid measures for less-developed members; ending nontariff barriers to trade; and extending ALADI cooperative measures, including the RTP, to other Latin American and Caribbean states.

The Council of Ministers reaffirmed its "integrationist will" and dedication to the "reinvigoration" of ALADI in 1987. In support of that goal, the council approved expansion of the RTP, again endorsed the proposed elimination of nontariff barriers, established a plan of action to assist the region's less-developed countries, and announced an agreement designed to yield a 40 percent increase in intraregional trade by 1991.

In 1988 ALADI secretary general Norberto Bertaina called for concentration on six areas: construction, engineering, transportation, tourism, insurance, and information services. Reflecting an emphasis that had grown steadily in recent years, ALADI called on the private sector to play the leading role in regional cooperative ventures in these and other areas. In addition, it continued to stress the need to liberalize intraregional trade, observers noting that many members now appeared to exhibit the political will necessary to implement what had earlier been little more than a rhetorical commitment.

Despite the growing importance of subregional free trade zones such as the Southern Cone Common Market (Mercosur), in the mid-1990s ALADI was still perceived by some as playing a useful role in providing a negotiating framework and assisting in settling disputes within or between the fledgling groups. In addition, ALADI and the United Nations (UN) Economic Commission for Latin America and the Caribbean (ECLAC) were directed by a June 1994 meeting of the leaders of 19 Latin American nations to coordinate activity toward a proposed free trade zone for all of Latin America.

At the conclusion of the 1997 session of the Committee of Representatives, its president, Mario Lea Plaza, stated that the movement toward Latin American integration had taken on a "dynamic without precedence." ALADI's optimism regarding integration continued in 1998. By then, nearly 100 agreements had been concluded.

In addition to hearing trade disputes between member countries and reviewing members' trade agreements, ALADI continues to promote broader integration, assisting, for example, in efforts to coordinate transport systems and telecommunication. The General Secretariat also has set up an Information System on Foreign Trade that interconnects online databases on members' commerce, tariffs, trade laws and regulations, and preferences.

ALADI also continues to weigh in on questions affecting broader linkages. For example, on September 23, 2005, the organization's secretary general signed an agreement to create a technical cooperation plan with the Inter-American Development Bank to promote the development of a free trade zone in the region. Further, a technical meeting focusing on regional integration held May 4–5, 2006, in Montevideo reaffirmed Resolution 59 of the Council of Ministers (passed on October 18, 2004), which calls for a Free Trade Space (*Espacio de Libre Comercio*—ELC) among the ALADI members. The resolution specifically calls for free trade accords to be signed between Mercosur and non-Mercosur countries within ALADI.

Economic activity with the association has been growing rapidly in recent years. While the 2006–2007 period was one of tension between members within other regional trading blocs, ALADI avoided such troubles. In August 2007, however, the organization decided to give preferential tariff treatment to Bolivia, Ecuador, and Paraguay—its least developed members. Progress towards regional integration, however, has been limited. A November 15–16, 2007, meeting in Montevideo discussed the subject with few results. In 2008 there was still no consensus on establishing a free trade zone, and a mechanism to settle disputes was also lacking. Meanwhile, intrabloc trade grew by 19 percent in 2007 to $116 billion, with Brazil by far the predominant trading partner.

In July 2008 Chile and Uruguay signed a far-reaching agreement to remove duties on most trade products by the end of 2008—a deal that some said was in effect a free trade agreement reached on the sidelines of an ALADI meeting. At the same meeting Chilean president Michele Bachelet insisted that the agreement was not meant to detract either from ALADI or from MERCOSUR (see separate article), and she called for renewed efforts at regional integration with "diversity, without rigid patterns and seeking to attenuate asymmetries of the region." However, also in July the foreign-minister-designate of Paraguay, Fernando Lugo y Milda Rivarola, said ALADI and other regional organizations "are no big deal when you come right down to it. They do not help us show ourselves to the world and are very expensive."

The global economic crisis continued to affect the group's members through 2008 and 2009, at least temporarily pushing aside calls for regional integration and organizational reform. In March 2009 Nicaragua formalized its bid to join ALADI, and in April Panama became the group's thirteenth member.

MANO RIVER UNION

Union du Fleuve Mano

Established: By the Mano River Declaration issued by the presidents of Liberia and Sierra Leone on October 3, 1973, and accompanying protocols signed in 1974.

Purpose: To promote the economic development of member states by the elimination of tariff barriers and the creation of new productive capacity, with particular emphasis on the hydroelectric potential of the Mano River; also, in recent years, to further peace, security, and stability in the region.

Headquarters: Freetown, Sierra Leone.

Principal Organs: Ministerial Council, Secretariat.

Web site: www.manoriverunion.org

Secretary General: Aliou M. Diallo.

Membership (4): Côte d'Ivoire, Guinea, Liberia, Sierra Leone.

Working Languages: English, French.

Origin and development. The Mano River Union (MRU) was founded by Liberia and Sierra Leone in the hope that it might lead to the economic integration of a number of West African states. Guinea joined the group on October 3, 1980, and on May 28, 1981, a customs union was established, with tariff barriers eliminated between the original members and transitional arrangements established for Guinea. However, political conflicts between members, financial problems within the union, and political and economic turmoil within the member states have precluded the attainment of many of the organization's original objectives.

Meeting May 7–8, 2000, in Conakry, Guinea, the three countries' heads of state approved formation of a Joint Security Committee, a Technical Committee, and Border Security and Confidence-Building Units to resolve security issues and reinvigorate the union.

Structure. General policy, including approval of the union's budget, is normally established by the Ministerial Council, which was conceived to meet yearly. Day-to-day administration is the responsibility of the Secretariat, which maintains offices in Monrovia, Conakry, and Freetown; in 1980 an Industrial Development Unit was formed within the Secretariat.

Activities. From the mid-1980s, the MRU was increasingly beset not only by perennial financial problems but also by adverse political developments. In November 1985 Liberian president Samuel K. Doe accused Sierra Leone of involvement in an attempted coup by an opposition group. Guinea also was charged with complicity and, despite denials by both governments, borders with the two countries were closed. The tension caused virtually all activities to cease and left the organization without an approved budget.

Following mediation by Guinea president Lansana Conté in July 1986, President Joseph Saidu Momoh of Sierra Leone joined Doe and Conté in the first summit since 1983 in Conakry, Guinea, the three agreeing to end their differences "in the spirit of the Mano River Union." In November 1986 the three heads of state concluded a treaty of nonaggression and security cooperation that prohibited subversive activities by one member against another and called for the creation of a joint committee for settling disagreements within the framework of the Organization of African Unity (OAU). Existing bilateral defense cooperation agreements between Sierra Leone and Guinea and between Liberia and Guinea were incorporated into the agreement.

Ministerial sessions in 1989 and early 1990 authorized feasibility studies on a number of "harmonization" proposals, including the creation of a common currency and development of regional marketing and pricing policies. Subsequently, however, progress was severely compromised by the prolonged civil war in Liberia. Effective regional cooperation was further constrained by the military coup in Sierra Leone in late April 1992, with Guinea sending troops to assist forces remaining loyal to President Momoh before announcing that it would cooperate with the new Freetown government. The presidents of the union members, meeting for the first time in more than two years on July 21, 1994, in Conakry, Guinea, again called for the "revitalization" of the grouping. However, political affairs remained tumultuous in all three member states through 1997, yielding a virtual standstill in union activity and the abandonment of the Freetown headquarters by the secretary general.

In the context of continuing turmoil, the MRU's heads of state met U.S. presidential emissary Jesse Jackson in November 1998 in Conakry. The members pledged to abide by the union's nonaggression and security cooperation agreement and called for more international aid to the area. In March 1999 Felix Downes-Thomas, head of the United Nations (UN) office in Liberia, encouraged revival of the union, which he asserted might help resolve distrust between Sierra Leone and Liberia and provide a multilateral forum for addressing regional problems such as refugees, internally displaced persons, arms, and ex-combatants. Nevertheless, repeated efforts by individual countries, the OAU, and, especially, the Economic Community of West African States (ECOWAS) to mediate the multiple disputes proved unsuccessful until a foreign ministerial meeting of the three principals on March 18–19, 2000, in Monrovia announced that the union's Secretariat would be revived after a decade of inactivity. On May 7–8 Presidents Conté of Guinea, Charles Taylor of Liberia, and Ahmad Tejan Kabbah of Sierra Leone, joined by ECOWAS chair Alpha Ouma Konare of Mali, met in Conakry and approved proposals from the March ministerial meeting, one of which was the establishment of a Joint Security Committee. Through mid-2001, however, mutual hostility continued to characterize interactions between Liberia and its two neighbors, highlighted by ambassadorial expulsions and accusations of support for rebel and opposition groups.

A consultative meeting of foreign ministers held August 13–15, 2001, in Monrovia was followed by an August 22–23 meeting of the new Joint Security Committee, attended by ministers of foreign affairs, security, defense, internal security, and justice. After reviewing the regional security situation, the ministers agreed that restoration of peace and stability required measures to "rebuild the confidence of the three member states." One proposed step was the apprehension and return to the country of origin of dissidents, armed groups, and paramilitary forces responsible for destabilization. Another was enforcement of compliance with the Non-Aggression and Security Cooperation Treaty, which had been signed in Freetown on November 20, 1996, and with the 15th Protocol to the Declaration of the Mano River Union on Defense, Security, Internal, and Foreign Affairs, signed at the May 2000 Conakry summit. The participants also agreed to deploy Joint Border Security and Confidence-Building Units along their mutual borders, to encourage repatriation of refugees, and to seek international funds for reviving union organs and programs. Additional ministerial and joint security meetings were held in September, and another presidential summit was proposed for 2002.

Under the auspices of King Mohamed VI of Morocco, presidents Conté, Kabbah, and Taylor met in a one-day summit in Rabat, Morocco, on February 27, 2002, in what proved to be yet another abortive effort to resolve their countries' differences and reactivate the MRU. In late March the Joint Security Committee convened in Freetown, while in early April the three members' foreign ministers met in Rabat to discuss the peace process, including securing their borders and repatriating refugees, and to plan for another summit meeting. Thereafter, a renewed rebellion in Liberia halted progress and ultimately led, in 2003, to the forced resignation and exile of President Taylor. In August 2003 Liberia's interim chief executive, Moses Blah, paid visits to Guinea and Sierra Leone, as did the chair of a transitional government, Gyude Bryant, in November, in the expectation that 2004 could prove to be a better year for the region. These expectations were aided by a meeting in Conakry on May 20, 2004, among the heads of state of the member countries at which the Mano River Union was formally reactivated.

The MRU's fortunes began to improve with the return of stability to Liberia and the election in November 2005 of Ellen Johnson Sirleaf as its president. One week after her inauguration, a conference took place in Monrovia among delegates of all three MRU states, who discussed ways to build peace in the region. At the 16th Ministerial Council, meeting October 2006 in Monrovia, Secretary General Aliou M. Diallo appealed for all member countries to follow Liberia's example and pay their arrears of membership dues. At a meeting of MRU heads of state, held April 30–May 1, 2007, in Conakry, the Ivorian president Laurent Gbagbo attended, and Côte d'Ivoire was formally invited to join the union. On June 7, 2007, the Mano River Bridge, a major connection between Liberia and Sierra Leone long closed because of the disturbed times, was reopened. The MRU established a Youth Parliament, which met in July 2007 and deplored the continued closure of the cash-strapped University of Liberia. The MRU also established a Web site, still under construction in mid-2009.

The organization's 18th summit, held in Monrovia May 15–16, 2008, formally welcomed Côte d'Ivoire into the union. At this meeting President Sirleaf proposed that the MRU countries should not impose restrictions on the exportation of food between member countries, and that they should concentrate on growing rice. She offered these suggestions as a counter to the rising price of food worldwide. At an extraordinary meeting of member heads of state and government, held in Freetown on December 11, 2008, the members agreed to a closer cooperation in security matters and in mutual confidence-building. The members also agreed on arrangements for paying dues that had been in arrears and for the timely payment of salaries to MRU staff. President Sirleaf was authorized to request that the World Bank promote the MRU's newly created Rice Production Project.

In late December 2008 the president of Guinea, General Lansana Conte, died. Within hours a military coup occurred. The remaining MRU states stayed calm, and by February 2009 had joined a contact group of several international organizations. This group aimed to work with the new regime to bring about a return to democracy. Soon afterwards, the junta laid out such a timetable, with plans for legislative elections in October 2009 and a presidential election in December 2009.

In March 2009 the MRU secretariat conducted a workshop for senior civil servants from Liberia and Sierra Leone. The goal of the session was to train civil servants in "public sector policy formulation and management."

NONALIGNED MOVEMENT (NAM)

Established: In the course of an increasingly structured series of 11 nonaligned conferences, the first of which met September 1–6, 1961, in Belgrade, Yugoslavia, and the most recent February 24–25, 2003, in Kuala Lumpur, Malaysia.

Purpose: To promote a "transition from the old world order based on domination to a new order based on freedom, equality, and social justice and the well-being of all"; to pursue "peace, achievement of disarmament, and settlement of disputes by peaceful means"; to search for "effective and acceptable solutions" to world economic problems, particularly the disparities in the level of global development"; to support self-determination and independence "for all peoples living under colonial or alien domination and foreign occupation"; to seek "sustainable and environmentally sound development"; to promote "fundamental rights and freedom"; to contribute to strengthening "the role and effectiveness of the United Nations" (Final Declaration, Belgrade, 1989).

Headquarters: None.

Principal Organs: Conference of Heads of State, Meeting of Foreign Ministers, Coordinating Bureau (25 members).

Web site: None. Malaysia, which chaired the NAM from 2003–2006, now sponsors the NAM News Network www.namnewsnetwork.org as its "gift to NAM."

Chair: Hosni Mubarak (Egypt).

Membership (117): Afghanistan, Algeria, Angola, Antigua and Barbuda, Bahamas, Bahrain, Bangladesh, Barbados, Belarus, Belize, Benin, Bhutan, Bolivia, Botswana, Brunei, Burkina Faso, Burundi, Cambodia, Cameroon, Cape Verde Islands, Central African Republic, Chad, Chile, Colombia, Comoro Islands, Democratic Republic of the Congo, Republic of the Congo, Côte d'Ivoire, Cuba, Djibouti, Dominica, Dominican Republic, Ecuador, Egypt, Equatorial Guinea, Eritrea, Ethiopia, Gabon, Gambia, Ghana, Grenada, Guatemala, Guinea, Guinea-Bissau, Guyana, Honduras, India, Indonesia, Iran, Iraq, Jamaica, Jordan, Kenya, Democratic People's Republic of Korea, Kuwait, Laos, Lebanon, Lesotho, Liberia, Libya, Madagascar, Malawi, Malaysia, Maldives, Mali, Malta, Mauritania, Mauritius, Mongolia, Morocco, Mozambique, Myanmar, Namibia, Nepal, Nicaragua, Niger, Nigeria, Oman, Pakistan, Palestine (represented by the Palestinian Authority), Panama, Papua New Guinea, Peru, Philippines, Qatar, Rwanda, St. Lucia, St. Vincent and the Grenadines, Sao Tome and Principe, Saudi Arabia, Senegal, Seychelles, Sierra Leone, Singapore, Somalia, South Africa, Sri Lanka, Sudan, Suriname, Swaziland, Syria, Tanzania, Thailand, Timor-Leste, Togo, Trinidad and Tobago, Tunisia, Turkmenistan, Uganda, United Arab Emirates, Uzbekistan, Vanuatu, Venezuela, Vietnam, Yemen, Zambia, Zimbabwe. The 1979 conference refused to seat either delegation (representing the Khieu Samphan and Heng Samrin regimes) from Cambodia, that country being represented by an "empty seat" at subsequent NAM summits until the 1992 meeting. One of NAM's founding members, Burma (now Myanmar), withdrew in 1979 but was readmitted in 1992. Venezuela shifted from full member to observer because of a boundary dispute with Guyana and then back to full membership in 1989. In September 1991 Argentina's president, Carlos Menem, announced his nation's withdrawal on the grounds that NAM "no longer had any reason to exist." A June 1994 NAM meeting of foreign ministers refused to seat a delegation from the Federal Republic of Yugoslavia (the Serbian and Montenegrin constituent republics of the dissolved Socialist Federal Republic of Yugoslavia), which was attempting to claim the predecessor state's founding membership in NAM. Yugoslavia's membership remained suspended thereafter, and in July 2001 the Federal Republic applied for observer status, which was granted and retained upon the country's transformation to the State Union of Serbia and Montenegro. Cyprus and Malta became observer states in 2004 when they joined the European Union (EU). In May 2006 Antigua and Barbuda and Dominica, previously observers, became full members.

Observer States (16): Armenia, Azerbaijan, Brazil, China, Costa Rica, Croatia, Cyprus, El Salvador, Kazakhstan, Kyrgyzstan, Malta, Mexico, Paraguay, Serbia as the successor state after the June 2006 split of Serbia and Montenegro, Ukraine, Uruguay. In addition, the following organizations attended the 2003 summit as observers: the African Union, the Afro-Asian People's Solidarity Organization, the Arab League, the Kanaka Socialist National Liberation Front (New Caledonia), the Organization of the Islamic Conference, the New Independentist Movement of Puerto Rico, and the United Nations (UN).

Guests (32): Australia, Austria, Bosnia and Herzegovina, Bulgaria, Canada, Czech Republic, Finland, France, Germany, Greece, Hungary, Ireland, Italy, Japan, Republic of Korea, Macedonia, Netherlands, New Zealand, Norway, Poland, Portugal, Romania, Russia, San Marino, Slovakia, Slovenia, Spain, Sweden, Switzerland, United Kingdom, United States, Vatican. (In addition, many intergovernmental organizations had guest status at the most recent NAM summit in 2003.)

Origin and development. The first Conference of Nonaligned Heads of State, at which 25 countries were represented, was convened in September 1961 in Belgrade, largely through the initiative of Yugoslavian president Josip Tito, who had expressed concern that an accelerating arms race might result in war between the Soviet Union and the United States. Subsequent conferences, which attracted more and more third world countries, were convened in Cairo, Egypt, in 1964; Lusaka, Zambia, in 1970; Algiers, Algeria, in 1973; Colombo, Sri Lanka, in 1976; Havana, Cuba, in 1979; New Delhi, India, in 1983; Harare, Zimbabwe, in 1986; Belgrade, Serbia, in 1989; Jakarta, Indonesia, in 1992; Cartagena, Colombia, in 1995; and Durban, South Africa, in 1998. The most recent summit was held in July 2009 in Sharm-el-Sheikh, Egypt.

The 1964 conference in Cairo, with 47 countries represented, featured widespread condemnation of Western colonialism and of the retention of foreign military installations. Thereafter, the focus shifted away from essentially political issues, such as independence for dependent territories, to the advocacy of occasionally radical solutions to global economic and other problems. Thus, in 1973 in Algiers there was an appeal for concerted action by the "poor nations against the industrialized world"; this became a basis of debate within the UN for a New International Economic Order (NIEO) and led to the convening of an inconclusive Conference on International Economic Cooperation in late 1975 in Paris, France.

At the 1979 Havana meeting, political concerns resurfaced in the context of an intense debate between Cuban president Fidel Castro, who was charged with attempting to "bend" the movement in the direction of the "socialist camp," and President Tito of Yugoslavia, who urged that it remain true to its genuinely nonaligned origins. In search of a compromise, the Final Declaration of the Havana Conference referred to the movement's "non-bloc nature" and its opposition to both "hegemony" (a euphemism used in reference to presumed Soviet ambitions) and all forms of "imperialism, colonialism, and neocolonialism." In addition, the conference reiterated an earlier identification of "Zionism as a form of racism."

At the 1983 New Delhi conference, delegates focused on the precarious financial condition of third world countries. The conference's declaration stated, in part, that developed countries should meet with developing countries to discuss debt relief, reduced trade barriers, increased aid for development, and increased cash flow. Its economic proposals, already widely accepted by the world banking community, called for the rescheduling of third world debt and an increase in Special Drawing Rights by the International Monetary Fund (IMF).

The eighth NAM summit in Zimbabwe in 1986 marked the 25th anniversary of the movement. The site was chosen to underscore the group's main concern: the South African government's policy of forced racial segregation. A final declaration called on nonaligned nations to adopt selective, voluntary sanctions against South Africa pending the adoption of comprehensive, mandatory measures by the UN Security Council. The members demanded international pressure to eliminate apartheid, Pretoria's withdrawal from Namibia (Southwest Africa), and an end to aggression against neighboring states.

Some of NAM's most radical members (including Cuba, Iran, and Iraq) stayed away from the 1989 Belgrade summit after preparatory talks revealed that most members favored fewer polemics and a return to the group's original posture of neutrality. Consequently, the meeting's final declaration was markedly less anti-American and anti-Western than previous ones. Instead, the summit emphasized the need for the movement to "modernize" and develop a "realistic, far-sighted, and creative" approach to international issues in which concordance would be favored over confrontation. The declaration also praised Washington and Moscow for their rapprochement, which, by reducing tensions in many areas of the world, had created a "window of opportunity for the international community."

Structure. By convention, the chief executive of the country hosting the most recent Conference of Heads of State serves as NAM's chair. Foreign ministers' meetings are generally held annually between conferences, which are usually convened every three years. A Coordinating Bureau, established at the 1973 conference, currently numbers 25 (including the chair; a rapporteur-general; and, on an ex officio basis, the immediate past chair) with the following regional distribution: Africa, 10; Asia, 9; Latin America and the Caribbean, 4; Europe, 2. In addition to a Political Committee, an Economic and Social Committee, and a Committee on Palestine, NAM has created various working groups over the years.

Activities. NAM emerged somewhat revitalized from its tenth summit, held in 1992 in Jakarta, Indonesia. At the conclusion of the meeting NAM declared its intention to project itself as a "vibrant, constructive, and genuinely independent component of the mainstream of international relations." With anti-Western rhetoric kept to a minimum, NAM asked developed nations to give "urgent priority" to establishing "a more equitable global economy" and to assist developing nations in resolving the problems of low commodity prices and "crushing debt burdens." The summit agreed to establish a broad-based committee of experts to devise a debt reduction approach. For their part, reflecting the organization's increasingly pragmatic approach, NAM members committed themselves to a measure of "self-reliance" in such areas as population control and food self-sufficiency. The Jakarta Message also called for extended South/South trade and investment cooperation. In addition, NAM said it would press for a restructuring of the UN that would include the diminution or elimination of the veto power of the five permanent members of the Security Council and an expansion of council membership.

Yugoslavia remained unrepresented at the NAM Meeting of Foreign Ministers held in May–June 1994 in Cairo, Egypt, and action on politically sensitive membership applications from Macedonia and Russia was deferred indefinitely. However, in what was considered one of the high points of the movement's history (in view of its long-standing anti-apartheid stance), South Africa was welcomed to the NAM ranks following the installation of a multiracial government in Pretoria.

NAM continued to press for UN restructuring at its 11th summit, held October 18–20, 1995, in Cartagena de Indias, Colombia. It also argued that UN peacekeeping efforts should be cut so more resources could be used for combating poverty. The summit's communiqué strongly criticized the United States for continuing its heavy economic pressure against Cuba and urged the industrialized nations to adopt a more "just" system of world trade.

The 12th NAM summit, held September 2–3, 1998, in Durban, South Africa, was expected to concentrate on economic issues, but the ongoing fighting in the Democratic Republic of the Congo diverted attention. With regard to the May 1998 testing of nuclear weapons by India and Pakistan, NAM called on both members to settle their disputes peacefully and articulated its concern over the development of all weapons of mass destruction. The summit also condemned terrorism, insisting that it be countered in accordance with UN principles, not by unilateral initiatives, and expressed regret that the Middle East peace process remained at a standstill—a situation it attributed to Israeli intransigence.

On the economic front, the summit called for the IMF and the World Bank to expand funding to the developing world and for changes in international financial institutions to prevent the kind of economic crisis that was plaguing much of Asia. In more general terms, NAM criticized the direction of globalization, arguing that economic integration was leading many of the poorest countries toward greater poverty.

NAM was divided over the Kosovo crisis of 1999, with Muslim member states supporting intervention on behalf of the Kosovars and predominantly backing the U.S.-led NATO air war against Yugoslavia in March–June. The division came in the context of a more fundamental concern that the movement was being eclipsed by the then 133-member Group of 77, which had gained increasing recognition as an effective voice for the economic interests of developing countries.

The organization's 13th Meeting of Foreign Ministers convened April 8–9, 2000, in Cartagena, where the topics under discussion included barring participation by military regimes that had overthrown democratically elected governments. Championed by India, the proposal was generally viewed as an effort to establish democracy as the norm for all members, but observers also noted that New Delhi was clearly targeting Pakistan for exclusion.

The 13th summit was planned for October 2001 in Bangladesh, but the meeting was postponed because of preparations for that country's October 1 national election. The venue was subsequently changed to Amman, Jordan, but instability in the Middle East ultimately led the Coordinating Bureau, meeting in April 2002 in Durban, to designate Malaysia as the host. Thus the 13th summit convened on February 24–25, 2003, in Kuala Lumpur.

Attended by some 60 heads of state or government, the first day of the summit included an address by the outspoken, soon-to-retire Malaysian prime minister Mahathir bin Mohamad, who lambasted the West for using undemocratic means to force democracy on other countries, permitting international financial agencies to ignore the debt burden of developing countries, and leaving poorer countries "oppressed and terrorized." Among the specific issues debated at the summit were the threat of war against Iraq and the nuclear crisis in North Korea. In a "Statement Concerning Iraq," the movement warned against the dangers of preemptive action by the United States and its allies, but it also advised the Saddam Hussein regime to comply with UN Security Council resolutions. With regard to North Korea's nuclear program, the summit ultimately supported Pyongyang's contention that a solution would best be found if the U.S. George W. Bush administration would agree to negotiate directly instead of insisting on multilateral involvement. In addition, as at previous summits, the participants voiced support for the Palestinian people and condemned Israeli actions and alleged human rights abuses in the West Bank and Gaza.

In keeping with its overall theme of "Continuing the Revitalization of the Non-Aligned Movement," the 2003 summit approved the Kuala Lumpur Declaration, which broadly called for multilateral efforts to prevent the marginalization of poorer states but also focused on steps to be taken by the movement's members. Among other things, the declaration urged the wider international community to ensure that globalization led to the "prospering and empowering of the developing countries, not their continued impoverishment and dependence." In addition, the declaration called upon member states to improve the effectiveness and efficiency of the movement; to enhance unity and cohesion "by focusing on issues that unite rather than divide us"; to meet more frequently with the Group of 77 to improve South-South coordination and cooperation; to bring together states, civil society, and the private sector in a partnership that might bridge the "digital divide"; and to improve North-South understanding through "constructive dialog and interaction" with the Group of Eight and other development partners.

The 14th Conference of Heads of State took place from September 11–16, 2006, in Havana, Cuba. This meeting, coupled with Cuba's chairing of NAM in 2007 and statements of mutual encouragement between NAM members Venezuela and Iran, caused the United States to look on NAM with increasing disfavor. In June 2007 U.S. secretary of state Condoleezza Rice addressed the U.S. India Business Council and declared that NAM had "lost its meaning"—an opinion quickly contested by Indian foreign minister Pranab Mukherjee. In July 2007 David C. Mulford, the U.S. ambassador to India, put forth a different opinion, stating that "India has played a major role in Non-Aligned Movement over the years and still continues (to do so) in many cases."

Several commentaries, however, have suggested that while the ideal of nonalignment remains as important as ever, NAM might not be useful in its present form. Because NAM has no central headquarters, it has perhaps suffered in recent years from lack of an official, external face. During its period as chair of the group (2003–2006), Malaysia addressed this problem with a very comprehensive Web site, or E-Secretariat, which not only documented Malaysia's leadership of the organization, but also thoroughly recorded all aspects of the movement's work. While the E-Secretariat is now defunct, Malaysia has organized a NAM news site (see Web site section, above). This site declares that it can only succeed if member countries will contribute faithfully to it.

Iran hosted a meeting of NAM foreign ministers in September 2007. United Nations High Commissioner for Human Rights Louise Arbour participated in this meeting. Iranian foreign minister Manouchehr Mottaki was quoted as saying that discussions about human rights are a tool to put pressure on independent countries. He said that NAM's global manifesto should be modified, because no Islamic country had played a part in its preparation.

NAM involvement, now led by Cuba, in the UN continues. In November 2007 Cuba spoke for NAM against a resolution that condemned North Korea for its record on human rights, declaring that exploitation of this issue "for political purposes should be prohibited."

In February 2008 a NAM-sponsored resolution in the UN Security Council condemning Israel for the situation in the Gaza Strip failed to pass. This led to an unpleasant exchange between the Israeli and Cuban delegates. In February also, the NAM ambassadors voted unanimously in favor of a resolution at the IAEA, supporting Iran in its peaceful development of nuclear power. In May 2008 NAM condemned the Sudanese rebel Justice and Equality Movement and voiced its support for Sudan's territorial integrity, while calling on all parties to the Darfur conflict to reach a peaceful solution.

In July 2008 the NAM information ministers met in Venezuela, where they called for the use of advanced information technology to help the group cohere and change incorrect impressions about developing countries in the rest of the world. Also in July 2008 Iran hosted a NAM foreign ministerial meeting, at which Iran asked for NAM support in its bid for a seat on the UN Security Council. Sudan participated in this meeting, in which it expressed concern about the movement of the International Criminal Court (ICC) towards prosecuting the Sudanese president for crimes against humanity. Iran was chosen to host the organization's sixteenth summit, to be held in 2012.

At the July 2009 Sharm-el-Sheik summit Egypt took over the organization's presidency from Cuba. The meeting took place amid a general sense that the NAM needed a new role, possibly using the world financial crisis to address the distribution of global wealth. There was some feeling that, while the dangers of the Cold War era had passed, nonaligned nations needed to protect themselves from the bad effects of global capitalism. Russian president Dmitry Medvedev declared that Russia, a guest state, was ready to take a more active role in the NAM's business. The conference condemned the ICC, which had by now issued an arrest warrant for Sudanese president Al-Bashir, and reiterated its support for a peaceful nuclear program in Iran.

NORDIC COUNCIL

Established: By enabling legislation passed by the parliaments of the founding member states, following agreement at a foreign ministers' meeting on March 16, 1952, in Copenhagen, Denmark, with effect from February 12, 1953.

Purpose: To provide a forum for consultation among the legislatures and governments of the member states on matters of common interest and to promote cooperation on cultural, economic, legal, social, and other matters.

Headquarters: Copenhagen, Denmark.

Principal Organs: Plenary Assembly, Presidium, Secretariat.

Web site: www.norden.org

Secretary General: Halldór Ásgrímsson (Iceland).

Membership (5): Denmark (including Faroe Islands and Greenland), Finland (including Åland Islands), Iceland, Norway, Sweden.

Observers: The Sámi (Lapp) local parliaments of Finland, Norway, and Sweden.

Official Languages: Danish, Norwegian, Swedish.

Origin and development. First advocated by Denmark in 1938, the Nordic Council grew out of an unsuccessful attempt in 1948–1949 to negotiate a Scandinavian defense union. A drafting committee set up by the Nordic Interparliamentary Union in 1951 developed the legal basis of the organization, which was established not by treaty but by identical laws adopted by the parliaments of Denmark, Iceland, Norway, and Sweden with effect from February 1953. Finland joined in 1955. A supplementary Treaty of Cooperation (since subject to several amendments) was signed on March 23, 1962, in Helsinki, Finland, to further develop legal, cultural, social, economic, and communications cooperation. In 1970 the Faroe Islands and the Åland Islands were granted separate representation within the Danish and Finnish delegations, respectively. In 1971 a Council of Ministers was created as a separate forum for cooperation among the Nordic governments. In 1984 Greenland was granted separate representation within the Danish delegation.

Structure. The Nordic Council encompasses 87 members elected by national or territorial parliaments. The Swedish and Norwegian parliaments select 20 representatives each; Iceland's parliament selects 7. Of Denmark's 20 representatives, 16 are selected by the national parliament and 2 each by the parliaments of the Faroe Islands and Greenland. Of Finland's 20 representatives, 18 are selected by the national parliament and 2 by the parliament of the Åland Islands. In principle each delegation reflects the distribution of parties within its parent legislature. Since 1982 there also have been four main political groups (Social Democratic, Conservative, Center, and Socialist) within the council itself.

The elected council members join an unspecified number (usually about 80) of nonvoting government representatives to form the Plenary Assembly, the council's highest decision-making body, which meets once a year for a brief session. The Plenary Assembly's influence emanates primarily from recommendations and statements of opinion addressed to the Nordic Council of Ministers or one or more of the member governments. Under a 2002 restructuring, five committees were created: Business and Industry; Citizens' and Consumer Rights; Culture, Education, and Training; Environment and Natural Resources; and Welfare.

A Presidium, consisting of a president and 12 representatives, is appointed each spring by the Plenary Assembly from among its elected members. It presides over the assembly session and supervises the council's work between meetings, assisted by a Secretariat under the direction of a secretary general. The Secretariat also is responsible for day-to-day contact with the Nordic Council of Ministers and other international organizations.

The Nordic Council of Ministers, whose composition varies according to the subject under consideration, is a separate decision-making body, although it works closely with the Nordic Council and shares with it various administrative departments. In practice, the Nordic Council of Ministers consists of specialist ministerial councils for consumer affairs; construction and housing; culture; drug abuse; education and research; energy; the environment; equality; finance and economics; food, health, and social services; information technology; justice; labor; regional affairs; trade and industry; and transport. (Foreign affairs and defense are outside the organization's purview.) Decisions, which must be unanimous, are binding on the member states save in matters subject to ratification by the national parliaments. In 1996 the Nordic Council Secretariat was moved from Stockholm, Sweden, to Copenhagen so that it could cooperate more closely with the Secretariat of the Council of Ministers.

Activities. The Nordic Council has provided a forum for consultation among the Scandinavian parliaments on questions of economic, cultural, and legal cooperation. In some areas, the laws of the Nordic countries have been almost completely harmonized, while in others agreement has been reached on common principles or basic legal rules. Particularly impressive results have been obtained in civil and family law. In the commercial field, laws bearing on contracts, installment purchases, instruments of debt, commercial agents, insurance, bills of exchange, and checks are now almost identical, as are those governing copyrights, patents, trademarks, and industrial designs. In 1981 a Nordic Language Convention allowed citizens of one Nordic country to use their native language in court proceedings in another Nordic jurisdiction. An agreement on voting rights was concluded in October 1975, with subsequent revisions allowing all Nordic citizens reciprocal rights of voting and of contesting municipal elections in the country in which they are resident.

Cooperation in social and health policy was formalized in the 1955 Convention on Social Security, augmented in 1975 by an agreement on rights relating to sickness, pregnancy, and birth. A new Convention on Social Security, concluded in 1981, extended additional coverage to individuals temporarily resident in a Nordic country other than their own. In 1973 a Nordic Transport Agreement was enacted to increase efficiency in transportation and communications. Between 1979 and 1983, cooperation in the area of transport increased further with the construction of an interstate highway system, harmonization of road traffic rules, and establishment of a common Scandinavian Airline System. In the economic field, a Nordic Investment Bank (NIB) became operative June 1, 1976 (see section on Regional Development Banks). Additional conventions included a 1974 accord on protection of the environment, a 1981 treaty on Nordic cooperation in development assistance, and a 1982 common labor market agreement that guaranteed the right to seek work and residence within all member states.

The 1988 Plenary Assembly endorsed a number of proposals from the Council of Ministers to promote intraregional economic growth as well as heighten extraregional trade. They included the creation of a Nordic Industry Center in Oslo; a program of intensive research and development in biotechnology; extensive cooperation with the European Community (EC) in anticipation of the planned EC single market; expansion of the Nordic Project Fund, set up on a temporary basis in 1982 to help Nordic companies compete for export orders; and establishment of a Nordic Development Fund to provide concessionary loans to projects promoting social and economic development in developing countries. Environmental issues also continued to receive close attention; the assembly met in extraordinary session on November 16 in Helsingör, Denmark, to endorse a wide-ranging antipollution program.

Among the topics discussed at the 1990 Plenary Assembly were the Nordic region's growing contacts with the Soviet Union and other Eastern European nations and the evolving nature of continental relations in the wake of the East-West thaw. At the 1991 Plenary Assembly emphasis was given to cooperation with the Soviet Union's Baltic republics, which were characterized as "natural partners" of the Nordic countries.

During the March 1992 Plenary Assembly, the council proposed the short- and long-term reorganization of Nordic agreements and the incorporation of foreign policy and security issues within the cooperation sphere. In other activity, responding to continued economic and political liberalization in the Baltic states, the council approved funds to aid their private sector industrial development efforts.

In November 1992 a joint statement from the Nordic prime ministers endorsed a more prominent place for the council in budgetary affairs, a compromise position that was reluctantly endorsed by the March 1993 Plenary Assembly in Oslo, Norway. Otherwise, attention focused on the complicated negotiations on the European Economic Area (EEA) and on the applications of Finland, Norway, and Sweden to join the EC. The council also welcomed the region's expanding cooperation with Russia.

Relations with the rest of Europe continued to dominate Nordic debate over the next year, particularly as the EC transformed itself into the European Union (EU) with entry into force of the Maastricht Treaty on November 1, 1993. Apprehension was expressed during the March 1994 Plenary Assembly that Nordic cooperation would be pushed into the background as Finland, Norway, and Sweden contemplated joining the European Union (EU). The council also extended observer status to the Sámi (Lapp) parliaments of Finland, Norway, and Sweden, rejecting, for the time being at least, the request from Sámi representatives that they be accorded full membership privileges.

Attention in 1995 remained focused on interregional issues, such as the future role of the council in view of the admission of Finland and Sweden to the EU. (Norway's voters had rejected EU membership in a November 28, 1994, referendum.) At the Plenary Assembly held February 27–March 2 in Reykjavik, Iceland, the Nordic Council endorsed a recommendation from the Council of Ministers that both councils continue to operate, with priority given to culture, education, and research. In addition, the Nordic prime ministers in August agreed in principle to participate in the proposed Arctic Council, which would provide a forum for consultation among the Nordic countries, Canada, Russia, and the United States on environmental issues (see separate article on the Arctic Council).

As expected, restructuring of the Nordic Council began at the fall Plenary Assembly held in November 1995. In early 1996 many of the organization's institutions were eliminated or consolidated to streamline operations and enhance cooperation. In April the Nordic Council and the Baltic Assembly, encompassing the parliaments of Estonia, Latvia, and Lithuania, held their first joint conference in Vilnius, Lithuania.

International affairs dominated discussions at the November 9–12, 1998, Plenary Assembly—the Nordic Council's 50th such session—held in Oslo. Council members discussed ways of reducing crime in the "Adjacent Areas" (the Baltic states and Russia) and stressed the importance of including some of the Baltic republics in any EU expansion. The environment also was discussed at the assembly, with the Nordic Council receiving a report on pollution caused by nuclear waste and industry on Russia's Kola Peninsula.

In February 1999 a second joint Nordic-Baltic conference convened in Helsinki, the foci of attention being improved cooperation and Russia's economic and security status. In early April the council was joined by representatives of Russia's indigenous peoples and its northwest region in the first Barents parliamentary conference, which focused on welfare, health care, and other social concerns. The November 8–11, 1999, Nordic Council plenary session in Stockholm addressed such issues as the free movement of labor among the member countries and the impact of economic globalization on the Nordic welfare model. Relations with the EU were once again discussed, with Swedish prime minister Göran Persson, in particular, opposing formation of a formal Nordic bloc within the EU.

The 52nd Plenary Assembly session on November 6–8, 2000, in Reykjavik, Iceland, called for closer cooperation with Russia on military affairs but still insisted that Russia improve in the areas of human rights, democratization, and free press. Considerable interest greeted publication of a report entitled *Norden 2000—Open to the Winds of the World*, which proposed some 60 specific recommendations for restructuring Nordic cooperation. In addition to calling for a closer relationship between the national parliaments and the Nordic Council, the report proposed that "Adjacent Areas" be redefined to permit inclusion of Canada and Scotland, for example, in addition to the Baltic region and Russia.

Major events during the first half of 2001 included an April 2–3 meeting in Oslo to consider a proposal from the Nordic Council of Ministers on a 20-year strategy for sustainable development. A third joint session of the Baltic Assembly and the Nordic Council opened on May 31, in Riga, Latvia, with the council's president, Sven Erik Hovmand of Denmark, describing Baltic-Nordic cooperation as having achieved an equal partnership of eight countries, replacing a "five plus three" model.

Attention at the 53rd Plenary Assembly, held October 29–31, 2001, in Copenhagen was dominated by responses to the September terrorist attacks on the United States.

The Plenary Assembly session on October 29–31, 2002, in Helsinki marked a half-century for the Nordic Council. Delegates discussed free movement across open borders and sought greater EU support of the "Northern Dimension" initiative (see article on the European Union). Immediately before the October 28–30, 2003, Plenary Assembly session in Oslo, the Nordic prime ministers invited prospective EU members Estonia, Latvia, and Lithuania to join the NIB, which had financed projects in developing countries as well as in the Nordic area. (They joined at the beginning of 2005.) Although the new secretary general of the Nordic Council of Ministers, Per Unckel of Sweden, subsequently stated that he did not anticipate council membership for the three Baltic republics in the near future, he did expect regional cooperation to intensify. In 2003, for the first time, a representative from northwest Russia attended the assembly.

The 2004 session, held November 1–3 in Stockholm, again focused on cooperation with neighboring countries, including the indigenous peoples of northwest Russia. The assembly dealt with ways to resolve remaining cross-border issues and to ensure cooperation on research projects. The 2005 session, held October 25–27 in Reykjavik, discussed measures to counter illegal immigration from neighboring countries. Plans for a general reform of the organization's structure were also advanced. The 2006 session, held October 31–November 2 in Copenhagen, called for the group to increase its efforts to educate and impact world policy concerning global warming, while conservative elements called for this to be done with a smaller budget. The 2007 session, held in Oslo October 30–November 1, discussed a common Nordic response to climate change and to the challenges of economic globalization.

Mid-2007 saw an increase of interest in cooperation between the Nordic Council and the Baltic states. Estonia, Latvia, and Lithuania all had visits from the council's secretary general, amid a sense that a common approach might be needed to Russian regional interests. These concerns resulted, through 2007 and into 2008, in a series of meetings between representatives of the Nordic Council of Ministers and their opposite numbers in Northwest Russia. The meetings were held mostly in Saint Petersburg and Kaliningrad, where the Council of Ministers has offices. In September 2007 secretary general Halldór Ásgrímsson met Ilya Klebanov, the Russian presidential envoy for Northwest Russia. They agreed on the importance of the Nordic Council's Knowledge Building and Networking Program for the area, also on the need to maintain excellent relations between the countries of the region. In November the Council signed an agreement for cooperation between the Nordic parliaments and the regional assemblies in Northwest Russia. Some Russian parliamentarians expressed interest in having Russia joining the Nordic Council.

Observers came from the Nordic Council, as from several other foreign bodies, to monitor the December 2007 Russian parliamentary elections. Their report was less than favorable. Cooperation with Russia was not impaired, and in 2008 the Council of Ministers' Saint Petersburg office began several programs of social betterment in cooperation with the local city government, at a cost in excess of 1 million euros. In July 2008 Russian prime minister Vladimir Putin removed tax exemptions from all but 12 of the 101 foreign organizations working in Russia, effectively closing them down. The Nordic Council of Ministers was one of the groups allowed to keep its special tax status.

In financial matters, in October 2007 the Nordic Council concluded an agreement to improve the exchange of financial information with the tax-exile-friendly British territory, the Isle of Man.

In August 2008 a report commissioned by the Council of Ministers urged the EU to take a leading role in protecting the Arctic from exploitation during a period of climate change—this shortly after Canadian prime minister Stephen Harper had stated his government's position that the region was ripe for exploitation. The EU appeared sympathetic, but in September the European Commission stated that it would not consider the Arctic as a sanctuary from oil exploration. The Council's October 27–29, 2008, summit in Helsinki, spent time considering the world economic crisis; a matter of great local concern since Iceland's banking system had collapsed. The Faroe Islands offered Iceland a loan of approximately $60 million as a gesture of support. The summit called for the establishment of GMO-free zones within members' territory. These zones would have the competitive advantage of producing organic and GMO-free foodstuffs, but the Council members that also belonged to the EU would first require EU permission.

In December 2008 the Finnish government announced that one of the objectives of the recently begun Finnish presidency of the Nordic Council would be to strengthen defense cooperation among member states. In February 2009 a Council report recommended such cooperation, but pointed out the practical difficulties, such as cost, and the fact that some, but not all, member countries were also members of NATO. A prime ministers' meeting held in Iceland to discuss the worsening financial crisis recommended that all member countries join the EU and the eurozone.

In March 2009 the Council began working on a comprehensive assessment of the risks posed by and to shipping in a melting Arctic Ocean. The report would be a subject for debate at the group's October 2009 summit.

NORTH ATLANTIC TREATY ORGANIZATION (NATO/OTAN)

Organisation du Traité de l'Atlantique Nord

Established: September 17, 1949, by action of the North Atlantic Council pursuant to the North Atlantic Treaty signed on April 4, 1949, in Washington, D.C., and effective as of August 24, 1949.

Purpose: To provide a system of collective defense in the event of armed attack against any member by means of a policy based on the principles of credible deterrence and genuine détente; to work toward a constructive East-West relationship through dialogue and mutually advantageous cooperation, including efforts to reach agreement on militarily significant, equitable, and verifiable arms reduction; to cooperate within the alliance in economic, scientific, cultural, and other areas; and to promote human rights and international peace and stability.

Headquarters: Brussels, Belgium.

Principal Organs: North Atlantic Council (all members), Defense Planning Committee and Nuclear Planning Group (all members), Military Committee (all members).

Web site: www.nato.int

Chair of the North Atlantic Council and Secretary General: Anders Fogh Rasmussen (Denmark).

Membership (28): Albania, Belgium, Bulgaria, Canada, Croatia, Czech Republic, Denmark, Estonia, France, Germany, Greece, Hungary, Iceland, Italy, Latvia, Lithuania, Luxembourg, Netherlands, Norway, Poland, Portugal, Romania, Slovakia, Slovenia, Spain, Turkey, United Kingdom, United States.

Partnership for Peace Participants (22): Armenia, Austria, Azerbaijan, Belarus, Bosnia and Herzegovina, Finland, Georgia, Ireland, Kazakhstan, Kyrgyzstan, Macedonia, Malta, Moldova, Montenegro, Russia, Serbia, Sweden, Switzerland, Tajikistan, Turkmenistan, Ukraine, Uzbekistan.

Official Languages: English, French.

Origin and development. The postwar consolidation of Western defenses was undertaken in light of the perceived hostility of the Soviet Union as reflected in such actions as the creation of the Communist Information Bureau (Cominform) in October 1947, the February 1948 coup in Czechoslovakia, and the June 1948 blockade of West Berlin. U.S. willingness to join Western Europe in a common defense system was expressed in the Vandenberg Resolution adopted by the U.S. Senate on June 11, 1948, and subsequent negotiations culminated in the signing of the North Atlantic Treaty on April 4, 1949, by representatives of Belgium, Canada, Denmark, France, Iceland, Italy, Luxembourg, Netherlands, Norway, Portugal, the United Kingdom, and the United States.

The treaty did not prescribe the nature of the organization that was to carry out the obligations of the signatory states, stipulating only that the parties should establish a council that, in turn, would create a defense committee and any necessary subsidiary bodies. The outbreak of the Korean War on June 25, 1950, accelerated the growth of the alliance and led to the appointment in 1951 of Gen. Dwight D. Eisenhower as the first Supreme Allied Commander in Europe. Emphasis on strengthened military defense of a broad area, reflected in the accession of Greece and Turkey to the treaty in February 1952, reached a climax later that month at a meeting of the North Atlantic Council in Lisbon, Portugal, with the adoption of goals calling for a total of 50 divisions, 4,000 aircraft, and strengthened naval forces. Subsequent plans to strengthen the alliance by rearming the Federal Republic of Germany (FRG) as part of a separate European defense community collapsed, with the result that the FRG was permitted to establish its own armed forces and, in May 1955, to join NATO.

NATO's gravest problem during the mid-1960s was the estrangement of France over matters of defense. French resistance to military integration under NATO reached a climax in 1966 when President de Gaulle announced the removal of French forces from consolidated commands and gave notice that all allied troops not under French command had to be removed from French soil by early 1967. These stipulations necessitated the rerouting of supply lines for NATO forces in Germany; transfer of the alliance's European command from Paris, France, to Casteau, Belgium; and relocation of other allied commands and military facilities. Thereafter, France participated selectively in NATO's operations, although it rejoined the Military Committee in 1996.

During the 1970s NATO suffered from additional internal strains. Early in 1976 Iceland threatened to leave the organization because of a dispute with Britain over fishing rights off the Icelandic coast. Disputes between Greece and Turkey, initially over Cyprus and subsequently over offshore oil rights in the Aegean Sea, resulted in Greece's withdrawal from NATO's integrated military command and a refusal to participate in NATO military exercises. In October 1980, five months after Greece threatened to close down U.S. bases on its territory, negotiations yielded an agreement on its return as a full participant. However, relations between Greece and Turkey subsequently remained tenuous. For instance, in October 2000 Greece withdrew from a NATO exercise in Turkey when Ankara objected to the flight of Greek aircraft over disputed Aegean islands.

In June 1980 U.S. president Jimmy Carter reaffirmed his administration's conviction that Spanish membership in NATO would significantly enhance the organization's defensive capability. The Spanish government originally made its application contingent upon Britain's return of Gibraltar and the admission of Spain to the European Community, but Madrid later decided that it could negotiate both issues subsequent to entry. Therefore, following approval in late October by the Spanish courts, the government formally petitioned for NATO membership, with a protocol providing for Spanish accession being signed by the members in December 1981. A referendum in March 1986 ensured Spain's continued participation with three domestic stipulations: the maintenance of Spanish forces outside NATO's integrated command; a ban on the installation, storage, and introduction of nuclear weapons; and a progressive reduction in the U.S. military presence. In November 1996 the Spanish parliament endorsed Spain's full participation in NATO's military structure, which occurred in 1999.

The structure of East-West relations was irrevocably altered by the political whirlwind that swept through Eastern Europe during late 1989 and early 1990, with the demolition of the Berlin Wall (described by one reporter as the "ultimate symbol of NATO's reason for existence") dramatically underscoring the shifting security balance. With superpower rapprochement growing steadily, U.S. officials in early 1990 suggested that U.S. and Soviet troop levels could be sharply cut. NATO also endorsed Washington's decision not to modernize the short-range missiles in Europe and agreed to reduce the training and state of readiness of NATO forces.

A Warsaw Pact summit in Moscow in early June and a NATO summit in London in early July confirmed the end of the Cold War. Suggesting that "we are no longer adversaries," Western leaders proposed that a NATO–Warsaw Pact nonaggression agreement be negotiated. NATO's London Declaration also vowed a shift in military philosophy away from forward defense, involving heavy troop and weapon deployment at the East-West frontier, and toward the stationing of smaller, more mobile forces far away from the former front lines. The allies agreed that the Conference on (later Organization for) Security and Cooperation in Europe (CSCE/OSCE) should be strengthened as a forum for pan-European military and political dialogue and urged rapid conclusion of a conventional arms agreement so that talks could begin on reducing the continent's reliance on nuclear weapon systems. They also insisted that Germany remain a full NATO member upon unification, a condition initially resisted by Moscow but ultimately accepted as part of the German-Soviet treaty concluded in mid-July.

As the Warsaw Pact continued to disintegrate, NATO pursued its own military retrenchment and reorganization. In May 1991 the NATO defense ministers approved the most drastic overhaul in the alliance's history, agreeing to reduce total NATO troop strength over the next several years from 1.5 million to 750,000 (including a cutback of U.S. troops from the existing 320,000 to 160,000 or fewer). In addition, it was decided to redeploy most of the remaining troops into seven defense corps spread throughout Western and Central Europe. The new plan also called for the creation of an Allied Rapid Reaction Corps (ARRC) of 50,000–70,000 troops to deal quickly with relatively small-scale crises, such as those that might arise from the continent's myriad ethnic rivalries. At the same time, NATO nuclear weapons were retained in Europe as a hedge against a sudden shift in Soviet policy.

Other issues addressed by NATO in 1991 included a proposed charter change that would permit "out-of-area" military activity (the alliance's participation in the recent Gulf war having been constrained by the restriction against its forces being sent to a non-NATO country) and the security concerns of former Soviet satellites in Eastern Europe, several of which had inquired about admission to NATO. Although all such overtures were rejected as premature, the ministers called for the development of a "network of interlocking institutions and relationships with former communist-bloc nations." The impulse led to the establishment in December of the North Atlantic Cooperation Council (NACC) as a forum for dialogue among the past NATO–Warsaw Pact antagonists. Participating in the NACC were the 16 NATO countries plus Albania, Armenia, Azerbaijan, Belarus, Bulgaria, Czech Republic, Estonia, Georgia, Hungary, Kazakhstan, Kyrgyzstan, Latvia, Lithuania, Moldova, Poland, Romania, Russia, Slovakia, Tajikistan, Turkmenistan, Ukraine, and Uzbekistan. Austria, Finland, Malta, Slovenia, and Sweden had NACC observer status.

The NACC, which worked in liaison with various NATO bodies and met regularly in conjunction with the North Atlantic Council, played a growing role in implementing the new strategic concept endorsed at the November 1991 NATO summit. While reaffirming the essential military dimension of the alliance, the heads of state agreed that a political approach to security would become increasingly important in Europe. Consequently, the summit called for additional reductions in NATO's conventional and nuclear forces beyond those proposed in May.

The NATO leaders also endorsed a larger role for such organizations as the CSCE, the European Community (EC, later the European Union—EU), and the Western European Union (WEU) defensive and political alliance in dealing with the continent's security issues. Significantly, however, the 1991 summit continued to insist that proposed pan-European military forces would complement rather than supplant NATO. As further evidence of the alliance's intention to remain active in European affairs, the NATO foreign ministers in May 1992 agreed to make forces available on a case-by-case basis for future peacekeeping missions necessitated by ethnic disputes or interstate conflict on the continent.

In November 1992 NATO agreed to use its warships, in conjunction with WEU forces, to enforce the UN naval blockade against the truncated Federal Republic of Yugoslavia. In April 1993 the alliance authorized its jets to monitor the UN ban on flights over Bosnia and Herzegovina. Otherwise, NATO appeared to be locked in a somewhat paralyzing debate on how to deal with the fighting in that country. In May 1993 U.S. president Bill Clinton suggested that NATO forces be used to create "safe havens" for Bosnian Muslims, but agreement could not be reached within the alliance on the proposal. In midsummer Clinton, who had previously been criticized for not taking a more active role in the Bosnian controversy, suggested that U.S. planes might be used to bomb areas in Bosnia under Serbian control, if requested by the UN. Prodded by the new U.S. assertiveness, the NATO defense ministers endorsed the Clinton position and discussed plans for a 50,000-strong NATO peacekeeping force that could be used in the event of a permanent Bosnian cease-fire.

A NATO summit held January 10–11, 1994, in Brussels struck a compromise regarding expansion by launching a highly publicized Partnership for Peace (PfP) program, which extended military cooperation but not full-fledged defense pacts to the non-NATO countries. By mid-1996, 28 nations (including previous Warsaw Pact members, former Soviet republics, and several longtime "neutral" states) had signed the PfP Framework Document. Among other things, the PfP states pledged to share defense and security information with NATO and to ensure "democratic control" of their armed forces. In return NATO agreed to joint training and planning operations and the possible mingling of troops from PfP states with NATO forces in future UN or OSCE peacekeeping missions. NATO ambassadors in February 1994 agreed to conduct air strikes against certain Serbian targets if requested by the UN. Later in the month, in the first such direct military action in the alliance's history, NATO aircraft shot down four Serbian planes that were violating the "no-fly" zone in Bosnia and Herzegovina. In addition, NATO planes bombed several Serbian artillery locations around Sarajevo in April.

Two issues dominated NATO affairs over the next year—the continued conflict in Bosnia and planning for the expected accession of Eastern and Central European countries to the alliance. Regarding the former, NATO responded to growing aggressiveness on the part of Bosnian Serbs by launching a bombing campaign against Serbian positions on August 30, 1995, near Sarajevo. The Serbians subsequently agreed to withdraw their heavy guns from the area as demanded by NATO, the alliance's hard-line approach also apparently contributing to an intensification of peace talks among the combatants in Bosnia. Consequently, NATO tentatively approved the proposed deployment of some 60,000 troops (including 20,000 from the United States) to take over peacekeeping responsibilities from UN forces in Bosnia should a permanent cease-fire go into effect.

By that time a degree of progress had been achieved regarding the alliance's membership plans as well. Among other things, NATO said that applicants would have to display a commitment to democracy and human rights, foster development of a free-market economy, establish democratic control of the military, and not become mere "consumers of security." It also was agreed that new members would not have to accept the stationing of NATO forces or nuclear weapons in their territory.

In the autumn of 1995 NATO members were greatly concerned over a scandal involving Secretary General Willy Claes. Claes, who had succeeded the late Manfred Wörner of Germany in October 1994, was investigated in a corruption case involving a helicopter contract awarded while he was Belgium's economic affairs minister in 1988. He resigned from his NATO post on October 20, 1995. The subsequent selection process for a new candidate degenerated into a public dispute. The first candidate announced by the European NATO members, Ruud Lubbers (former prime minister of the Netherlands), was vetoed by the United States, apparently because of a lack of consultation beforehand. France then blocked Uffe Ellemann-Jensen from Denmark, whom the United States supported, reportedly due in part to the candidate's less-than-satisfactory mastery of French. (Many NATO observers also noted that Ellemann-Jensen had recently criticized French nuclear testing.) As a compromise, Javier Solana Madariaga, a prominent member of Spain's Socialist government since 1982, was appointed to the post on December 5. The new secretary general's announced priorities included the expansion of NATO and the promotion of a peace pact in Bosnia. Regarding the latter, the NATO foreign and defense ministers, meeting in joint session on December 5, formally approved the establishment of the peacekeeping force for Bosnia and Herzegovina (called the Implementation Force, or IFOR) to oversee the recently signed Dayton Accord. IFOR began its mission on December 20 (see article on Bosnia and Herzegovina for details).

The other major development at the December 1995 NATO session was an announcement from France that it planned to rejoin the NATO military structure after an absence of nearly three decades. However, it subsequently became apparent that the French decision was contingent on controversial restructuring that would provide greater European control of military affairs on the continent. A degree of progress on that question was perceived at the meeting of NATO foreign ministers on June 2–3, 1996, the United States agreeing that, under some circumstances, the European countries could conduct peacekeeping and/or humanitarian missions on their own under the command of an expanded WEU. However, even though the French defense minister was formally welcomed by his NATO counterparts at their session on June 13, Paris soon after threatened to reverse its recent decision unless Washington agreed to relinquish control of NATO's Southern Command to a European. The United States resisted that demand, primarily because of the prominence of the U.S. Sixth Fleet in the Southern Command.

The U.S.-French debate subsequently deteriorated into public insults prior to the meeting of NATO foreign ministers on December 10–11, 1996, at which Paris appeared to back away from its threat to block NATO expansion unless it got its way regarding the Southern Command. Meanwhile, on a more positive note, the NATO ministers endorsed the creation of a new mission for Bosnia and Herzegovina (the 31,000-strong Stabilization Force, or SFOR), scheduled to take over at the end of the month from IFOR. The Bosnian mission had been widely viewed as a major success for NATO, as had the PfP program, many of whose members had lent troops to IFOR. The streamlined

SFOR included troops from the United States, Russia, and some 23 other NATO and non-NATO countries, including, significantly, Germany, whose commitment of 2,000 soldiers marked the first time that combat-ready FRG ground troops had been deployed outside NATO borders since World War II.

It also was agreed at the December 1996 session that NATO would make its long-awaited announcement regarding the admission of new members at the summit scheduled for July 8–9, 1997, in Madrid, Spain. Russia immediately denounced any such plans as "completely inappropriate," and the topic dominated NATO affairs in early 1997. While describing expansion as "inevitable," U.S. representatives were reportedly hoping that a special relationship could still be established between the alliance and Russia that would make Moscow less "antagonistic" to the NATO decision. While Russia strongly preferred that Europe abandon NATO and instead focus on strengthening the OSCE, Moscow ultimately accepted NATO enlargement.

Following months of intense negotiations, NATO and Russia signed a Founding Act on Mutual Relations, Cooperation, and Security on May 27, 1997, in Paris, France. Both sides committed to stop viewing each other as "adversaries" and endorsed "a fundamentally new relationship." NATO also stated it had no intention of stationing nuclear weapons or "substantial combat forces" within the borders of new members. In addition, a NATO-Russia Permanent Joint Council (PJC) was established to discuss security issues, which appeared to satisfy Moscow's goal of having a say in NATO decision making, although NATO officials made it clear that Russia would not be able to veto any of the alliance's decisions. Collaterally, Western leaders promised Russia an expanded role in the Group of Seven and other major international forums.

Although Russia remained officially opposed to any expansion of NATO, the new accord permitted NATO to extend membership to the Czech Republic, Hungary, and Poland in 1999. A number of NATO leaders, led by French president Chirac, had supported the inclusion of Romania and Slovenia in the first round as well but deferred to the U.S.-UK position after a statement from NATO Secretary General Solana that Romania, Slovenia, and the three Baltic states were "strong candidates" for the second round of expansion.

Progress regarding the new members at the Madrid summit served to distract attention from the ongoing conflict between France and the United States. Washington once again refused Paris's demand that a European be put in charge of the Southern Command, and France therefore declined to return to the integrated military command. Meanwhile, at the conclusion of the summit, NATO signed an agreement with Ukraine that established a NATO-Ukraine Commission and provided for cooperation and consultation on a wide range of issues. In other activity in 1997 the alliance replaced the NACC with the Euro-Atlantic Partnership Council (EAPC), which was designed to enhance the PfP program and permit cultivation of broader political relationships among the "partners" and full NATO members. NATO also unveiled a new military command structure, scheduled to be in effect by April 1999. Subsequently, in early 1998, NATO announced it would keep its forces in Bosnia past June, with SFOR's mission now to include civil security. (At the 2004 Istanbul summit, NATO announced it would end the SFOR Mission at the end of that year.)

Events in 1998 were dominated by NATO's admonitions to Yugoslavia's Serbian leaders regarding their policies in the province of Kosovo, where actions against ethnic Albanian separatists had begun in late February. In June a newly authorized Euro-Atlantic Disaster Response Coordination Center (EDRCC) began operating, its first assignment being to assist Kosovar refugees. In June and August, with the cooperation of PfP members Albania and Macedonia, NATO held military exercises near Yugoslavia's borders, while in October continuing hostilities led NATO to warn Belgrade of imminent air strikes. In response, Yugoslavia agreed to admit OSCE observers and to begin military and security withdrawals from the province. To provide the 2,000-member observer force with air surveillance, NATO placed a coordination unit in Macedonia, where an additional command center was sited in November. Widespread hostilities in Kosovo nevertheless resumed in January 1999. In February peace talks opened in Rambouillet, France, cosponsored by France and the United States, but discussions came to an abrupt halt on March 19 when the Serbian delegation continued to reject one of the proposed peace plan's key provisions, namely the presence of NATO peacekeepers on Serbian soil. On March 24, 1999, NATO forces initiated Operation Allied Force—the first intensive bombing campaign in the organization's history—which in the following weeks extended throughout Yugoslavia (see article on Serbia and Montenegro for additional details).

The Kosovo situation dampened the alliance's 50th anniversary summit, which was held on April 23–25, 1999, in Washington. Highlights of the summit were the welcoming of the accession of the Czech Republic, Hungary, and Poland (which had been formally admitted at a ceremony at the Truman Library in Missouri on March 12) and the approval of a new Strategic Concept, including a European Security and Defense Identity (ESDI) within the alliance. The summit communiqué acknowledged that the WEU, using "separable but not separate NATO assets and capabilities," could conduct defensive operations without direct U.S. participation. It also noted "the resolve of the European Union to have the capacity for autonomous action" in military matters that did not involve the full alliance. Despite U.S. pressure for NATO to adopt a more global posture, the Strategic Concept continued to limit NATO's purview to the "Euro-Atlantic area," with the communiqué reiterating the primacy of the UN Security Council in international peace and security matters. The summit also saw issuance of a Membership Action Plan (MAP) for future enlargement and the launch of a Defense Capabilities Initiative (DCI), the latter of which emphasized the need for interoperability in command and control and information systems, particularly given the likelihood that future missions would require rapid deployment and sustained operations outside alliance territory. Finally, NATO agreed to build new headquarters in Belgium, at a cost of about $800 million. Construction began in 2008, with completion scheduled for 2012.

On August 5, 1999, NATO approved the appointment (effective the following October) of UK Secretary of State for Defense George Robertson (subsequently Lord Robertson of Port Ellen) as the successor to Secretary General Solana.

Meeting on November 20–22, 2002, in Prague, Czech Republic, the NATO heads of state extended membership invitations to Bulgaria, Estonia, Latvia, Lithuania, Romania, Slovakia, and Slovenia, with formal admission anticipated for 2004. At the same time, the summit approved establishment of a mobile, rapidly deployable NATO Response Force (NRF). Earlier in the year, on May 28, the NATO heads of state had signed the Rome Declaration, which institutionalized a closer working relationship with Moscow through creation of a NATO-Russia Council (NRC) as successor to the NATO-Russia PJC. The NRF was inaugurated on October 15, 2003. The force numbered 9,000 troops and was initially placed under the command of British Gen. Sir Jack Deverell. The NRF was designated fully operational with 25,000 available troops at the 2006 Riga summit. Since 2003, the NRF has undertaken five operations, including security missions to protect the 2004 Athens Olympics and elections in Iraq.

On September 22, 2003, NATO approved the appointment (effective January 5, 2004) of Dutch foreign minister Jaap de Hoop Scheffer as successor to Secretary General Lord Robertson. As was the case with many of his predecessors, de Hoop Scheffer's appointment was the result of compromises among the allies. Candidates such as Norway's defense minister Kristin Krohn and Portugal's António Vitorino (an EU commissioner) were rejected by France because of their countries' support of the U.S.-led invasion of Iraq, while the United States vetoed Canadian finance minister John Manley because of his country's opposition to the Iraq War.

Structure. NATO's complex structure encompasses a civilian component, a military component, and a number of partnership organizations. At the apex is the North Atlantic Council (NAC), the principal decision-making and policy organ. It normally meets twice a year at the ministerial level to consider major policy issues, with the participation of the member states' ministers of foreign affairs and/or defense. It also may meet as a summit of heads of state and government. Between ministerial sessions the NAC remains in permanent session at NATO headquarters, where permanent representatives, all of whom hold ambassadorial rank, convene. Decisions at all levels must be unanimous.

The civilian structure includes a Defense Planning Committee (DPC), which dates from 1963; it focuses on a range of matters related to collective defense planning and also offers guidance to military leaders. The DPC typically meets at the permanent representative level but also convenes twice a year as a meeting of defense ministers. The Nuclear Planning Group (NPG) consists of the defense ministers of the countries represented in the DPC. Its purview extends from nuclear safety and deployment to such related matters as proliferation and arms control. Like NAC, the DPC and NPG may call on a host of committees and other bodies, the most prominent of which are the Senior Political

Committee and the Defense Review Committee, to provide expert advice, to assist in preparing meetings, and to follow through on decisions.

The secretary general, who is designated by NAC, serves as chair of NAC, the DPC, the NPG, the EAPC, and the Mediterranean Cooperation Group (MCG), as well as joint chair of the NRC and the NATO-Ukraine Commission. As NATO's chief executive, the secretary general has an important political role in achieving consensus among member governments and also can offer his or her services in seeking solutions to bilateral disputes. Anders Fogh Rasmussen of Denmark succeeded de Hoop Scheffer as NATO secretary general on August 1, 2009. Rasmussen's appointment was initially blocked by Turkey because of the former Danish prime minister's defense in 2006 of the publication of newspaper cartoons depicting the Prophet Mohammed that many Muslims found offensive. Turkish officials reportedly opposed the nomination because of concerns that Rasmussen's appointment could serve as a focal point for Islamic extremists. The NATO deputy secretary general was Amb. Claudio Bisogniero of Italy, appointed in 2007. At the 2002 Prague summit, NAC approved a reorganization of NATO's civilian headquarters structure. The new system created a deputy secretary general post and six main divisions, each led by an assistant secretary general. The new divisions are Defense Investment, Defense Policy and Planning, Executive Management, Operations, Political Affairs and Security Policy, and Public Diplomacy. In addition to the six divisions, plans were made for a newly created NATO Office of Security to be headed by a director.

The highest military authority is the Military Committee, which operates under the overall authority of NAC, the DPC, and NPG. At its top level the Military Committee is attended by the members' chiefs of defense, although, as with the NAC, it is typically in continuous session attended by permanent military representatives from all members. The Military Committee is chaired by a non-U.S. officer of at least four-star rank. The current chair is Adm. Giampaolo Di Paola of Italy. The committee furnishes guidance on military questions, including the use of military force, both to NAC and to subordinate commands. It also meets with PfP partners on matters of military cooperation. The Military Committee is supported by the International Military Staff (IMS), which includes some 380 military personnel from the member states and 85 civilian personnel. The IMS is led by a three-star officer, currently Lt. Gen. P. J. M. Godderij of the Netherlands.

Until 1994 the NATO military structure embraced three main regional commands: Allied Command Europe (ACE), Allied Command Atlantic (ACLANT), and Allied Command Channel. However, in 1994 Allied Command Channel was disbanded, and its responsibilities were taken over by ACE. In addition, in 2002 NAC agreed to dissolve ACLANT as an operational command. It was replaced by Allied Command Transformation (ACT). Each command is responsible for developing defense plans for its area, for determining force requirements, and for the deployment and exercise of its forces. Except for certain air defense squads in Europe, however, the forces assigned to the various commands remain under national control in peacetime.

After it absorbed the Allied Command Channel responsibilities in 1994, ACE had three major subordinate commands: Northwest (led by a designee of the United Kingdom), Central (led by a designee of Germany), and Southern (led by a designee of the United States). In 1997 NATO defense ministers agreed to reduce the number of command headquarters from 65 to 20 by 1999. On September 1, 2003, ACE was transformed into Allied Command Operations (ACO). The reorganized ACO incorporated two major subordinate commands, Allied Forces North Europe and Allied Forces South Europe, which had a total of seven subregional commands between them, as well as separate air and naval component commands. No fewer than nine other commands and staffs fell under ACE, most of them encompassing rapid reaction forces established in the 1990s. Other major subordinate structures under ACO are regional headquarters for the West, East, and South Atlantic, plus a Standing Naval Force Atlantic, a Striking Fleet Atlantic, and a Submarine Allied Command Atlantic. There also is a separate Canada–United States Regional Planning Group, originally created in 1940 and incorporated into the NATO command structure in 1949. Its principal task is to recommend plans for the defense of the U.S.-Canada region.

ACO headquarters, known formally as Supreme Headquarters Allied Powers Europe (SHAPE), is located in Casteau, Belgium. The Supreme Allied Commander Europe (SACEUR) has traditionally been designated by the United States and serves concurrently as commander in chief of U.S. forces in Europe (CINCEUR). In May 2009 U.S. Adm. James G. Stavridis became the new SACEUR, replacing the previous commander, U.S. Gen. John "Bantz" Craddock. Stavridis was the first naval officer to be SACEUR.

ACT, with headquarters in Norfolk, Virginia, is headed by the Supreme Allied Commander Transformation (SACT), who is designated by the United States. In September 2009 French Gen Stéphane Abrial became the first non-U.S. SACT (see Recent activities, below). ACT includes the Joint Warfare Center in Stavanger, Norway; the Undersea Research Center in La Spezia, Italy; and the NATO School in Oberammergau, Germany. ACT's main mission is to transform NATO's military capabilities to respond more efficiently to new threats and operations.

The NATO Parliamentary Assembly is completely independent of NATO but constitutes an unofficial link between it and parliamentarians of the 28 member countries. It was founded in 1955 as the NATO Parliamentarians' Conference and was subsequently known, until 1998, as the North Atlantic Assembly. In October 2008 John Tenner of the United States was elected assembly president. PfP partners have associate delegation status in the assembly. By keeping alliance issues under constant review and by disseminating knowledge of NATO policies and activities, the assembly encourages political discussion of NATO matters. During the 1990s its mandate was broadened to include European security as a whole, plus economic, environmental, social, and cultural issues relevant to Central and Eastern Europe. The assembly meets twice a year in plenary session, with various committees and study groups convening throughout the year.

Political dialogue also takes place within the 50-member EAPC, which comprises the 28 NATO members plus the 22 PfP partners, the NRC, the NATO-Ukraine Commission, and the MCG. Established in 1997, the MCG grew out of a Mediterranean Dialogue proposed by NATO in 1994 and initiated in 1995, when Egypt, Israel, Jordan, Mauritania, Morocco, and Tunisia agreed to join. Algeria became the seventh non-NATO member in 2000. The MCG is intended to promote mutual understanding and to serve as a forum on security and stability in the Mediterranean region. At the Istanbul summit in June 2004, NAC decided to enhance the MCG. The seven MCG members were invited to join a new version of the grouping that would be modeled on the PfP through the Istanbul Cooperation Initiative (ICI). The ICI was designed to improve military and intelligence cooperation between NATO and the MCG states and standardize equipment and operational guidelines. In 2006 NATO ministers began searching for a host country in which to establish a joint NATO-MCG training center.

NATO has established more than three dozen subsidiary and related organizations, agencies, and groups that undertake studies, provide advice, formulate policies for referral to NAC or other NATO decision-making structures, manage specific programs and systems, and provide education and training. Many of these bodies are NATO Production and Logistics Organizations (NPLOs) concerned with technical aspects of design, production, cooperation, and management in communication and information systems; consumer logistics (pipelines, medical services); and production logistics (armaments, helicopters, other aircraft, missiles). Other bodies are concerned with standardization, civil-emergency planning, airborne early warning, air traffic management, electronic warfare, meteorology, and military oceanography. The Science for Peace and Security program was launched in 2006 to enhance scientific and technical cooperation between NATO and partner countries. The initiative provides funding and assistance for research and national projects ranging from environmental clean-up and protection to cybersecurity. In June 2007 NAC agreed to create a new agency to facilitate the alliance's Strategic Airlift Capability (SAC). Under SAC, 15 NATO members and two PfP states would have access to strategic airlift assets acquired by and managed by the alliance. In 2008 the SAC participants agreed to purchase three C-17 aircraft and to station the assets at Papa Airbase in Hungary.

Activities. The dramatic changes in the European political landscape that accompanied the fall of the Berlin Wall and the demise of the Soviet Union substantially altered NATO's perception of its role on the continent. At the same time, the EC was evolving what it initially called a Common Foreign and Security Policy as part of the Maastricht Treaty, which brought the EU into existence in November 1993. In response to these events NATO began developing a framework for Combined Joint Task Forces (CJTFs), which were envisaged as multinational, multiservice contingents that could be quickly deployed for humanitarian, peacekeeping, or defense purposes. In 1996 NATO reached agreement on a European Security and Defense Identity (ESDI), which derived from the EU's interest in being able to take autonomous military action in situations other than those involving NATO in its entirety. Building upon the existing WEU-NATO relationship, the ESDI would be permitted on a case-by-case basis to employ CJTFs, including "separable but not separate NATO assets," for WEU-led missions. Implementation of the CJTF concept began in 1999, and by 2004 three CJTF commands were established, two land-based and one naval. (In November 2000 the WEU transferred its operational role to the EU, in accordance with the EU's 1999 European Security and Defense Policy [ESDP]. Collaterally, the EU, minus Denmark, agreed to establish a Rapid Reaction Force, formation of which was delayed until December 2002, when differences with non-EU member Turkey over access to NATO facilities were resolved.)

During this same period NATO was negotiating cooperative military agreements with Russia, other former Soviet republics, and a number of Eastern and Central European nations under the PfP program. In May 2000 Croatia became a PfP partner and announced that it would ultimately seek full NATO membership. Also that month, the foreign ministers of nine Eastern and Central European PfP countries—Albania, Bulgaria, Estonia, Latvia, Lithuania, Macedonia, Romania, Slovakia, and Slovenia—agreed to apply collectively for NATO membership in 2002. At the same time, many PfP partners were pushing for greater participation in political decisions and military operations, citing the success of their continuing involvement in the SFOR and the Multinational Force in Kosovo (Kosovo Force, or KFOR).

Although NATO was criticized by United Nations (UN) Secretary General Kofi Annan, among others, for circumventing the UN in launching the air campaign against Yugoslavia in March 1999, the June 10 Security Council resolution that established the UN Interim Administration Mission in Kosovo (UNMIK) also included provision for the NATO-led KFOR. As of April 2001, KFOR encompassed some 50,000 troops, the bulk of them from NATO and PfP countries, although command had passed a year earlier to the WEU/EU's Eurocorps, consisting of German, French, Spanish, Belgian, and Luxembourgian units. (For additional information on KFOR, see the articles on Serbia and Montenegro and the Security Council.)

The NATO assault on Yugoslavia drew criticism for other reasons, too, and may have led to the early departure of U. S. Gen. Wesley Clark as SACEUR. Clark, who was succeeded by U.S. Gen. Joseph Ralston in April 2000, was believed to have strongly argued for sending ground forces into Kosovo during the conflict, but had been overruled. The unintentional bombing of the Chinese embassy on May 9, 1999, and the inadvertent bombing of ethnic Albanian refugees pointed out dangers inherent in air warfare, while some human rights organizations charged that NATO had dropped cluster bombs in populated areas, thereby inflicting avoidable civilian injuries. Furthermore, in March 2000 NATO admitted that it had used armor-piercing munitions that incorporated depleted uranium, raising concern in some quarters about environmental pollution. At a NAC meeting in January 2001, Germany, Greece, Italy, and Norway advocated a moratorium on use of depleted uranium shells pending scientific determination of any increased incidence of cancer, but the United States and United Kingdom objected.

Apart from its peacekeeping missions in the Balkans, NATO is currently engaged in numerous other efforts, including arms control. Having been involved since the height of the Cold War in attempts to reduce conventional as well as nuclear forces, NATO in April 1999 launched an Initiative on Weapons of Mass Destruction (WMD) and authorized creation of a WMD Center within the International Staff in Brussels.

In 2001 the U.S. George W. Bush administration unilaterally decided to proceed with development of a National Missile Defense (NMD), despite strong objections from most European allies, as well as Russia. Bush's plan was the major topic of discussion at a special one-day NATO summit held on June 13, 2001, in Brussels, the U.S. president declaring that the Anti-Ballistic Missile (ABM) Treaty, which prohibits the deployment of new missiles, was a "relic of the past" and needed to be scrapped. The summit, mostly given over to informal discussion among the NATO leaders, was seen as a success for Bush in that many of his European counterparts reportedly agreed to maintain an "open mind" on the NMD, although France and Germany remained explicitly opposed. Some allies also were reportedly reassured by Bush's pledge that Washington would unilaterally reduce the number of U.S. offensive nuclear weapons and would attempt to negotiate a new missile treaty with Russia. Further heartening the European leaders, Bush unequivocally endorsed the ESDP and the "new options" offered by "a capable European force, properly integrated with NATO." In other activity at the summit, the NATO leaders agreed to present a timetable for enlargement at the regular summit scheduled for 2002 in Prague, Czech Republic, and discussed a possible role for NATO in dealing with an intensifying crisis in Macedonia.

On August 22, 2001, responding to a request for assistance from the government of Macedonia, NATO began Operation Essential Harvest, a 30-day mission by approximately 3,500 troops to help disarm ethnic Albanian groups in that Balkan state. In September NATO authorized Operation Amber Fox, encompassing 700–1,000 personnel, primarily to protect international monitors overseeing implementation of the Macedonian peace plan. On December 16, 2002, Operation Amber Fox was in turn succeeded by a new mission, Operation Allied Harmony, to minimize any further risk of ethnic destabilization. This mission was to be of short duration, with NATO contingents being replaced in 2003 by elements of the EU's newly authorized Rapid Reaction Force.

The day after the September 11, 2001, terrorist attacks on the United States, NAC invoked the collective self-defense provisions of the founding treaty. The unprecedented decision was followed in October by authorization for specific steps requested by the United States in its efforts to confront international terrorism. These included access to military facilities and intelligence information and the deployment of NATO's airborne early-warning squadron to the United States. NATO also dispatched its Standing Naval Force Mediterranean to the Eastern Mediterranean to support the U.S.-led military operation in Afghanistan and to deter terrorism.

During the rest of 2001 and into early 2002, NATO continued to move toward a closer working relationship with Russia. Despite Moscow's assistance in the U.S. "war on terrorism," however, U.S. secretary of Defense Donald Rumsfeld and others expressed opposition to any arrangement that would significantly increase Russian involvement in military decisions. The negotiating process culminated in the May signing of the Rome Declaration, which not only established the NRC but also authorized the opening of a permanent Russian office at NATO headquarters. Four days earlier President Bush and Russian president Putin had signed in Moscow a Strategic Offensive Reduction Treaty (SORT) that committed both states to reducing their nuclear stockpiles from 6,000–7,000 warheads to 1,700–2,200 over the next decade.

In line with the 1997 Founding Act, the NRC focused on areas such as control of terrorism, crisis management, nonproliferation, arms control, and theater missile defenses. In addition, the negotiations leading up to the Rome Declaration had a more indirect consequence—namely, an easing of overt Russian opposition to NATO expansion into the Baltic. Meanwhile, Secretary Rumsfeld had begun advocating a redefined international role for NATO forces. Citing the danger that nuclear, biological, or chemical weapons might be obtained by terrorists, at a June 6–7, 2002, meeting of defense ministers in Brussels, Rumsfeld called upon NATO to consider preemptive strikes as an option. Lord Robertson, however, responded cautiously; although acknowledging a need for internal reform, he insisted that NATO "will remain a defensive alliance." On July 19 NATO announced that Gen. Ralston would be succeeded as SACEUR by Gen. James Jones, the first U.S. Marine to take command. The announcement was widely interpreted as presaging a strategic shift toward a more flexible military structure, and at an informal meeting of defense ministers on September 24–25 in Warsaw, Secretary Rumsfeld called for creation of a mobile strike force.

The November 20–22, 2002, summit in Prague was highlighted by the formal invitation to seven prospective Eastern European members and by an agreement to establish the NRF. In addition, the summit participants pledged their support for deployment of UN disarmament inspectors in Iraq, although some NATO states, particularly France and Germany, remained skeptical of U.S. assertions of Iraqi ties to the al-Qaida terrorist network.

In its first major military operation outside of the transatlantic region, in August 2003 NATO assumed command of the International Security Assistance Force (ISAF) authorized by the UN in Afghanistan. NATO oversaw 5,500 peacekeeping troops in the Kabul region. Efforts to expand the NATO-led mission to more remote regions of the country were constrained by the unwillingness of members and allies to contribute more troops to the ISAF. This inability of the alliance to deploy additional forces demonstrated the growing strain on European member states as the allies tried to maintain operations in areas such as the Balkans, Afghanistan, and Iraq. However, NATO agreed to provide 2,000 additional troops to provide security during the 2004 Afghan elections. In addition, at the 2004 Istanbul summit, NATO leaders agreed to provide troops for at least five provincial reconstruction teams in the Afghan countryside. At the June 2006 Brussels summit, NATO leaders announced that the alliance would increase its forces in Afghanistan to 17,000, allowing the United States to reduce its troop strength from 20,000 to 16,000. NATO also announced at the summit that the United States would succeed British command of the NATO-Afghan mission in 2007.

During the winter of 2002–2003, the United States asked individual NATO states to contribute forces to the anti-Iraq coalition. Belgium, France, Germany, and Luxembourg strongly resisted the U.S. initiative, which was supported by other members such as the United Kingdom, Netherlands, Italy, and Spain. The divide threatened the cohesiveness of the alliance in February 2003 after the antiwar allies blocked a request from Ankara for NATO to provide surveillance aircraft and antimissile batteries to protect Turkey in the event of armed conflict with Iraq. The deadlock was resolved on February 16 by having the Defense Planning Committee (of which France was not a member) resolve the dispute. NATO subsequently authorized the deployment of both early-warning aircraft and antimissile systems.

NATO did not formally participate in the March 2003 invasion of Iraq, but a number of individual NATO members, including the United Kingdom and Poland, contributed troops to the invasion force and to the postwar peacekeeping coalition that the UN authorized. At the June 2004 summit in Istanbul, interim Iraqi prime minister Iyad Allawi requested additional NATO aid. However, the prewar divide continued, and NATO leaders could only reach a compromise whereby alliance forces would train the Iraqi military and police forces. (NATO deployed 300 troops for the training mission, although Belgium, France, Germany, Greece, Luxembourg, and Spain declined to participate.) Nonetheless, the mission marked the second major nontransatlantic security operation by NATO. Also, in its June 28 communiqué following the summit, NAC affirmed support for Poland's command of the coalition's multinational division in Iraq.

On January 29, 2003, seven NATO aspirants (Bulgaria, Estonia, Latvia, Lithuania, Romania, Slovakia, and Slovenia) began formal accession negotiations with the alliance. On March 26, 2003, the protocols were signed and the ratification process began. On March 29, 2004, the seven nations became full members of NATO. The new members were expected to change the internal dynamics of NATO. All seven supported the U.S.-led invasion of Iraq and favored NATO as the cornerstone of European security, placing them at odds with other NATO members such as France and Germany, which sought a greater security role for the EU. In June 2006 Putin warned NATO against further expansion to states such as Ukraine; nonetheless, the alliance continued discussions with Ukraine and other states, including Croatia, Georgia, Armenia, and Azerbaijan. NATO also sought to strengthen ties with nonmembers, and in April 2006 the alliance announced plans for regular security forums with states such as Australia, Finland, Japan, New Zealand, South Korea, and Sweden. Proposals for a global version of PfP were also endorsed.

In line with NATO's broader antiterrorism campaign, the alliance in 2004 sought to bolster its relationship with Mediterranean states, an important topic at the December 2004 meeting of alliance foreign ministers. In June 2005 NATO agreed to provide air and other types of support to the African Union's (AU) proposed peacekeeping mission to the Darfur region of Sudan. NATO eventually provided transport for some 5,000 AU peacekeepers to Darfur and undertook two major humanitarian missions in the region in 2005. NATO also provided assistance and support for the United States in the aftermath of Hurricane Katrina and aid for Pakistan following a major earthquake on October 8, 2005.

At the NAC meeting in June 2006 in Brussels, the alliance's defense ministers decided to require all member states to devote 2 percent of their GDP to defense, replacing a longstanding "gentleman's agreement" regarding the 2 percent threshold that only 7 of the 26 NATO members reached in 2005. (The average expenditure per NATO country in 2005 was 1.8 percent.) At the same meeting, NAC agreed to reorient the alliance so that it could simultaneously conduct six medium-size operations (of up to 20,000 troops each) and two major missions (of up to 60,000 troops each). The change was designed to better reflect NATO's contemporary range of operations. Finally, NAC began examining other possible missions for the alliance, including expansion of counter-terrorist and antitrafficking activities, as well as a greater role in infrastructure security, such as guarding the oil and gas pipelines from Russia to the EU.

At the alliance's November summit in Riga, NATO invited Bosnia and Herzegovina, Montenegro, and Serbia to join PfP. A U.S. proposal to develop a new and enhanced partnership program for non-European allies such as Australia, Japan, and South Korea was rejected because of opposition from Belgium, France, Greece, and Poland on the grounds that the new arrangement would undermine the European character of NATO. By October 2006 NATO-led ISAF had completed its expansion so that it had a presence in the four main geographic regions of Afghanistan. NATO then initiated a countrywide stabilization program that included increased humanitarian projects and development initiatives, as well as new military operations against Taliban forces.

NAC extended the term of NATO Secretary General de Hoop Scheffer by two years in January 2007. De Hoop Scheffer would thus remain in office through 2009 and provide continuity when the alliance commemorated the 60th anniversary of its formation that year.

Alliance troops launched NATO's largest offensive in the southern provinces of Afghanistan, Operation Achilles, in March 2007. More than 4,500 NATO, and 1,000 Afghan, soldiers participated in the anti-Taliban strikes that began in March. At the alliance's June summit, NAC reaffirmed its commitment to Afghanistan and called on member states to increase their force contributions to ISAF. By the summer more than 33,000 soldiers from 37 NATO and allied countries were participating in ISAF. Nonetheless, Taliban attacks and other antigovernment activity continued to increase in remote areas of the country. In June NATO agreed to provide strategic airlift and other support for the AU Mission in Somalia (AMISOM) through 2007.

U.S. plans to deploy a missile defense system in Europe created strife within NATO and renewed tensions with Russia in 2007. Germany led the initial opposition to the missile shield, which was strongly supported by the Eastern European members of the alliance, led by the Czech Republic and Poland. At a defense ministers' meeting in Brussels in June, NATO agreed to continue efforts to develop an alliance-based theater missile defense system while launching a broad assessment of the U.S. initiative.

NATO and Russia reiterated their commitment to cooperation at a series of events that commemorated the fifth anniversary of the NATO-Russia Council in June 2007. However, Russia announced plans to unilaterally withdraw from the Conventional Forces in Europe Treaty (CFE) in July, and NAC responded by reaffirming its commitment to the CFE and urging the Russian government to reconsider and open a dialogue on the agreement. In December 2007 Russia stopped exchanging information with NATO about its troop movements, a development about which NATO expressed "deep regret" but no intention of retaliating. The second half of 2007 had seen conditions less and less conducive to good relations between Russia and NATO. Kosovo was a source of tension, with Russia strongly opposing it becoming an independent state, and the West tending to favor it. The former Soviet republics of Ukraine, Azerbaijan, and Georgia were all moving toward NATO membership, with Georgia's intentions a special irritant to Moscow. Georgia also planned to switch all its military purchases to Western equipment to ease future integration with NATO.

By everyone's admission the NATO operation in Afghanistan was having difficulties. At a December 2007 NATO foreign ministers' conference in Edinburgh, Scotland, both the U.S. and UK defense ministers declared that not enough NATO countries were deploying their troops where there was fighting. Germany was particularly mentioned in this context. Individual national force contributions to the Afghanistan mission dominated the February 2008 Vilnius meeting of NATO defense ministers, and Canada threatened to withdraw part of its forces unless other alliance members increased their presence. At the April 2008 Bucharest summit, French president Nicholas Sarkozy announced the deployment of an additional 1,000 troops, with other NATO states and partner countries dispatching smaller increases. NAC issued a new strategic vision for ISAF that reaffirmed NATO's commitment to Afghanistan and articulated a range of humanitarian and security goals through 2010. The April deployment of an additional 2,400-troop U.S. Marine expeditionary unit allowed ISAF to undertake Operation Azada Woza in the Helmand region of Southern Afghanistan to suppress Taliban forces and heroin production. By 2008 ISAF numbered 52,700, its highest level. Nonetheless, the Taliban continued a series of aggressive attacks. In June, for the first time, more coalition troops died in Afghanistan (45) than in Iraq (31).

Also at the 2008 Bucharest summit, the United States led an unsuccessful effort to invite Georgia and Ukraine to join NATO. Concerns over Russian reaction led France and Germany to oppose membership. Albania and Croatia were invited to begin accession discussions, and formal membership protocols were signed in July. Meanwhile, initial membership talks were launched with Bosnia and Herzegovina and Montenegro. In addition, Malta announced that it would rejoin PfP. At the summit, NATO heads of state endorsed a U.S. proposal for a missile defense system. In June NATO's Science for Peace and Security program completed the destruction of 1,300 tons of toxic, Soviet-era missile fuel in Azerbaijan. In August, in response to the Russian invasion of Georgia, NATO suspended meetings of the NATO-Russia Council. NATO also agreed to create the NATO-Georgia Commission to prepare Georgia for eventual membership in the alliance. Also in

August, the United States and Poland reached an agreement for the deployment of interceptor missiles as part of NATO's missile defense system.

In response to growing civilian casualties in Afghanistan, NATO issued a new tactical directive in January 2009 that implemented a number of new measures to minimize collateral damage during attacks. On April 3-4, NATO leaders met in Strasbourg, France. Rasmussen was formally designated the next NATO secretary general. France reentered NATO's integrated military structure following an agreement whereby the United States agreed that a non-U.S. military officer would be appointed SACT. French Adm. Abriel was subsequently appointed to the post (see Structure, above). On April 7 Albania and Croatia officially joined the alliance. The NATO-Russia Council resumed meetings on April 29 and the exchanges marked the formal resumption of interaction following the Georgian war. The following day two Russian diplomats were expelled for espionage. However, neither the incident, nor subsequent NATO-led military exercises in May and June, affected relations with Russia. In August a suicide bomber attacked ISAF headquarters in Kabul, killing seven and wounding more than 100, in a strike that was seen as part of a broader effort to disrupt the Afghan presidential and provincial elections that were held on August 20.

ORGANIZATION FOR ECONOMIC COOPERATION AND DEVELOPMENT (OECD/OCDE)

Organisation de Coopération et de Développement Economique

Established: By convention signed December 14, 1960, in Paris, France, effective September 30, 1961.

Purpose: "[T]o help member countries promote economic growth, employment, and improved standards of living through the coordination of policy [and] . . . to help promote the sound and harmonious development of the world economy and improve the lot of the developing countries, particularly the poorest."

Headquarters: Paris, France.

Principal Organs: Council (all full members plus the European Commission), Executive Committee (14 members), Economic Policy Committee, Development Assistance Committee, Secretariat.

Web site: www.oecd.org

Secretary General: Ángel Gurría (Mexico).

Membership (30): Australia, Austria, Belgium, Canada, Czech Republic, Denmark, Finland, France, Germany, Greece, Hungary, Iceland, Ireland, Italy, Japan, Republic of Korea, Luxembourg, Mexico, Netherlands, New Zealand, Norway, Poland, Portugal, Slovakia, Spain, Sweden, Switzerland, Turkey, United Kingdom, United States.

Limited Participant: European Commission.

Official Languages: English, French.

Origin and development. The OECD replaced the Organization for European Economic Cooperation (OEEC), whose original tasks—the administration of Marshall Plan aid and the cooperative effort for European recovery from World War II—had long been completed, although many of its activities had continued or had been adjusted to meet the needs of economic expansion. By the 1960s the once seemingly permanent postwar shortage of dollar reserves in Western European countries had disappeared, many quantitative restrictions on trade within Europe had been eliminated, and currency convertibility had been largely achieved. This increased economic interdependence suggested the need for an organization in which North American states could also participate on an equal footing. Thus, the OEEC, of which Canada and the United States had been only associate members, was transformed into the OECD. The new grouping also was viewed as a means of overseeing foreign aid contributions to less-developed states. It later expanded to include virtually all the economically advanced free-market states. Japan became a full member in 1964, followed by Finland in 1969, Australia in 1971, and New Zealand in 1973. The membership remained static until Mexico's accession in 1994. Subsequently, the Czech Republic (1995), Hungary (1996), Poland (1996), South Korea (1996), and Slovakia (2000) joined. There also has been discussion of future Russian membership, although there is still widespread disagreement on the matter among long-standing OECD members. Membership is limited to countries with market economies and pluralistic democracies and is granted by invitation only. New countries must be approved by each existing member, giving each country veto power. The 30 member states produce 60 percent of the world's goods and services, leading some detractors to label the organization a "rich man's club." The OECD Center for Cooperation with Non-Members promotes dialogue with 70 nonmember countries, which are invited to subscribe to OECD agreements and treaties and benefit from policy and economic recommendations.

Structure. The Council, the principal political organ, convenes at least once a year at the ministerial level, although regular meetings are held by permanent representatives. Generally, acts of the Council require unanimity, although different voting rules may be adopted in particular circumstances. Supervision of OECD activities is the responsibility of the 14-member Executive Committee, whose members are elected annually by the Council and usually meet once per week. The secretary general, who chairs the regular Council meetings, is responsible for implementing Council and Executive Committee decisions with the assistance of a Secretariat that employs some 2,000 people. The current annual budget is approximately $365 million, 25 percent of which is contributed by the United States. Japan is the next leading contributor.

Probably the best known of the OECD's subsidiary organs is the Development Assistance Committee (DAC), which evolved from the former Development Assistance Group and now includes most of the world's economically advanced states as well as the Commission of the European Communities. DAC oversees members' official resource transfers. The Economic Policy Committee, another major OECD organ, is responsible for reviewing economic activities in all member states. The OECD includes more than 200 committees that produce data, analyses, guidelines, or recommendations affecting policy in every major area of development. The number of committees continues to grow each year. The Committee on International Investment and Multinational Enterprises was responsible for formulating a voluntary code of conduct for multinational corporations, which was adopted by the OECD in 1976. In addition, high-level groups have been organized to investigate commodities, positive adjustment policies, employment of women, and many other issues.

To complement the work of DAC, an OECD Development Center was established in 1962. Its current priorities emphasize working to meet the basic needs of the world's poorest people, with a focus on rural development and appropriate technology in Africa, Asia, and Latin America. Twenty-six members and nonmembers (including Argentina, Brazil, Chile, and India) participate in the center's activities. The Center for Educational Research and Innovation (CERI), established in 1968, works toward similar goals.

The OECD Nuclear Energy Agency (NEA), established in December 1957, supplements national efforts toward peaceful nuclear development. All OECD members except New Zealand and Poland participate in the NEA. The secretary general attended the 1974 Washington Energy Conference, and representatives of the United States, Canada, and all of the members of the European Communities except France subsequently agreed to establish a new International Energy Agency (IEA; see separate entry) under OECD auspices.

Activities. The key to the OECD's major role in international economic cooperation has long been its continuous review of economic policies and trends in member states, each of which submits information annually on its economic status and policies and is required to answer questions prepared by the Secretariat and other members. This confrontational review procedure has led to very frank exchanges, often followed by recommendations for policy changes. OECD analyses, generated in part through the use of a highly sophisticated computerized model of the world economy, are widely respected for being free of the political concerns that often skew forecasts issued by individual countries. Furthermore, the OECD has been in the forefront of efforts to combat unstable currencies, massive trade imbalances, third world debt, and high unemployment in industrialized countries.

A degree of controversy developed during the 1989 Council meeting over a recent U.S. citation of Japan, Brazil, and India as "unfair traders" subject to possible penalties. Japan challenged the U.S. decision as a threat to the "open multilateral trading system" and asked for an OECD statement criticizing Washington. Thus, the final communiqué, while not specifically mentioning the United States, condemned any "tendency toward unilateralism." In other activity, the Council strongly urged expanded cooperation on environmental protection and endorsed recent initiatives to reduce third world debt.

On another controversial topic, the OECD, after having completed an extensive review of the cost of farm support, called for the elimination of all agricultural subsidies by wealthier producers. Attempts to overcome substantial differences among members regarding agricultural policy continued at the 1990 Council meeting, the ministers giving the "highest priority" to completing agreements on farm subsidies and other outstanding issues in the Uruguay Round of the General Agreement on Tariffs and Trade (GATT). Other activity during 1990 included the opening of the Center for Cooperation with European Economies in Transition, designed to advise and guide Central and Eastern European countries as they moved toward free-market economies.

In mid-1994 the OECD released the results of a two-year study on structural causes of unemployment among members. Noting the high rate of unemployment in Europe (about 12 percent) as opposed to the United States (about 6 percent), the report urged European governments to introduce a new flexibility in their labor markets. Some recommendations—such as the discouragement of minimum wages, promotion of early retirement, expansion of the part-time workforce, and reduction of unemployment benefits—were greeted cautiously by government officials who feared such measures would erode social benefits and the overall standard of living.

Mexico became the first new OECD member in 23 years when, with strong U.S. and Canadian backing, it acceded in May 1994. Argentina and Brazil also were reportedly pressing for inclusion, while the OECD announced it would begin negotiations with the Czech Republic, Hungary, Poland, and Slovakia. Perhaps most importantly, the OECD signed a cooperation agreement with Russia at the June 1994 ministerial session, pledging to assist Moscow with legal, structural, and statistical reforms to promote Russia's integration into the global economy, an effort that U.S. officials described as the "best investment we can make in our security."

At the 1996 ministerial meetings, a preliminary agreement was reached regarding corruption in the developing world. Negotiations subsequently continued on the proposed plan to make the bribing of foreign officials a criminal offense, and in November 1997 the treaty was finalized. (The treaty entered into force on February 15, 1999, following its ratification by 12 signatories.) In other activity, DAC was directed to use a new formula to monitor the effectiveness of OECD aid on overall development by focusing more on the impact on recipient societies and less on monetary values.

Topics discussed at the 1997 session included unemployment, the aging of OECD members' populations, and regulatory reform. Meanwhile, the OECD established a special liaison committee to assist Russia in developing a market economy and democratic institutions, as well as in qualifying to join the organization.

In January 1998 the OECD established the Center for Cooperation with Non-Members (CCNM) as its "focal point" for discussions on policy and to encourage dialogue with emerging market economies. At the April 1998 Council meeting, negotiations on the multilateral investment agreement, which had been seen as promising, were suspended. The negotiations came to an end later that year following France's withdrawal from them, reportedly because it would lose the ability to protect its domestic movie and television markets under the proposed agreement. Despite this setback, the Council did call for the continued liberalization of world trade and the adherence to World Trade Organization (WTO) rules.

In 1999 the OECD established guidelines for corporate governance, which were considered surprisingly progressive for their time. However, by late 2002 OECD officials urged that the guidelines be toughened in light of the recent years' corporate scandals. Among other things, the OECD argued that independent oversight bodies needed to be established because self-regulation had failed, particularly in the auditing sector. The OECD also called for development of guidelines for pension fund administrators.

Another major focus of OECD attention in recent years has been the harmful effect on international trade and investment of so-called tax havens around the globe, which provide foreign depositors with the opportunity to deposit large sums of money with little or no tax consequences. Additional momentum in pursuing reform in the havens developed following the terrorist attacks on the United States in September 2001, at which time the George W. Bush administration called on all banks to help identify and seize accounts that might be linked to terrorist organizations or activity. Many of the small countries on the tax haven blacklist initially proposed solidarity in resisting reform, arguing that financial services provided much of their income. However, OECD accords with several Caribbean countries in early 2002 appeared to stifle cohesive resistance, and by the end of the year only seven countries (Andorra, Liberia, Liechtenstein, Marshall Islands, Monaco, Nauru, and Vanuatu) were still considered uncooperative on the matter.

The OECD tax haven initiative has been conducted alongside efforts by the Financial Action Task Force (FATF) to combat money laundering through use of another "name-and-shame" blacklist. (The FATF, founded in 1989 by the Group of Seven, is an independent body, but it is housed at OECD headquarters and cooperates extensively with the OECD. Its membership comprises the OECD members [except Czech Republic, Hungary, Republic of Korea, Poland, and Slovakia] plus Argentina, Brazil, European Commission, Gulf Cooperation Council, Hong Kong, and Singapore.) By the end of 2001, 23 countries and territories were on the money laundering blacklist: Bahamas, Cayman Islands, Cook Islands, Dominica, Israel, Lebanon, Liechtenstein, Marshall Islands, Nauru, Niue, Panama, Philippines, Russia, St. Kitts-Nevis, and St. Vincent and the Grenadines as the initial group of mid-2000, with Egypt, Guatemala, Hungary, Indonesia, Myanmar, Nigeria, Grenada, and Ukraine added later. By October 2007 all countries had been delisted, with only Myanmar's practices still being monitored.

A major OECD tax initiative hit a wall in 2003 when some member states were reluctant to join in the establishment of a comprehensive exchange system of banking information to prevent money laundering by terrorist organizations and tax evasion by individuals and corporations. In September 2003 Switzerland and Luxembourg balked at the OECD's 2006 deadline for entrance into the system, seeking to preserve their nations' well-established practice of banking secrecy. The two nations blocked an agreement among the member countries, marking the first time member states had used a veto inside the governing Council.

According to a 2003 OECD report on agricultural reform, efforts to reduce agricultural subsidies had stagnated. The OECD also failed to achieve progress in its efforts to curb steel subsidies as talks with some 38 governments dissolved unceremoniously in 2004. On a more positive note, the organization developed guidelines for private pension fund administrators in its member states.

Pressure was placed on the organization in early 2003 to consider expanding its membership and scope. The OECD created a new working group, headed by Japanese diplomat Seiichiro Noboru, which was tasked with developing a strategy to dictate the organization's future structure and mission. Noboru recommended that relations be strengthened with the "Big Six" nonmember nations of Brazil, China, India, Indonesia, Russia, and South Africa. The working group was expected to create new criteria for membership, examine the current budgetary system, and assess the geopolitical ramifications of an expanded membership.

OECD Secretary General Donald J. Johnston announced in January 2005 that he would step down at the conclusion of his second term in May 2006. In November 2005 the organization elected Ángel Gurría of Mexico, who took office in June 2006.

The OECD continues to sponsor conferences and a large number of research papers on topics of interest to its members. Papers focus in particular on the economic circumstances of individual member states. Since 2005, the grouping's high-level conferences have dealt with such topics as aging in the developed world, the effect of rising fuel prices and possible shortages, balancing the effects of globalization, and restoring the trust of citizens in their governments.

In October 2006 the OECD was one of the organizations involved in trying to restart the stalled Doha Round of trade talks, but with little ultimate success. In its November 2006 Economic Outlook publication it predicted a drop in global economic growth to 2.7 percent from the previous year's 3.2 percent, chiefly because of weakness in the U.S. economy, though also predicting that strength in the Chinese and Indian economies would somewhat take up the slack. It criticized the Russian government for its tendency to reintroduce state control of the economy by taking majority positions in the directorate of many companies that had previously been privatized.

In May 2007 the organization invited five new countries to discuss membership: Russia, Estonia, Chile, Israel, and Slovenia. By December 2007 accession talks were beginning. The OECD also suggested that Brazil, China, India, Indonesia, and South Africa, all increasingly powerful economies, could be invited in the near future. In June 2007 South Africa became the first African country to sign the OECD's anti-bribery convention.

In December 2007 the organization warned of economic slowdowns, precipitated by turmoil in the housing markets in the most highly developed countries, particularly in the United States. By August 2008 the OECD was predicting continued weakness, along with higher inflation and unemployment, particularly in the United States and the eurozone, and revising downward its projections for 2009. But it said that growth in Brazil, China, and India should remain strong.

In other matters, Taiwan complained in March 2008 that China was trying to interfere with its participation in the OECD. Also in March the OECD rejected suggestions from U.S. and EU quarters that Sovereign Wealth Funds (SWFs)—funds that are controlled by a cash-rich nation-state, most often in Asia or the Middle—should be more transparent. Secretary General Gurría said he saw no problem as long as profit, rather than politics, drove the funds' strategies. In June 2008 Gurría declared that dealing with climate change was too important to be sidelined by an economic slowdown. He went so far as to praise high fuel prices as symptoms of a serious problem that must be urgently addressed and warned against using tax cuts and other fiscal measures to offset them. Gurría also warned against a return to protectionism in the current, relatively hard economic times.

In June 2008 the Estonian foreign minister said that his country should be ready to join the OECD by the end of 2009. Later in 2008 and through 2009 the OECD, like many other international organizations, was occupied by the global economic crisis. It went from forecasting an economic slowdown in August 2008, to a forecast of a protracted slowdown in November, to warnings about the U.S. economy in December, to a statement in June 2009 that the recession was "near bottom," and a declaration in August 2009 that the economies of rich countries were generally stabilized. The OECD also noted (in October 2008) that income inequality had risen sharply in rich countries where statistics were available. Since 2000, it reported, such inequality rose significantly in the United States and Germany, while it declined in the UK, Mexico, and Greece. In analyzing the world recession's effects, the OECD had a particularly gloomy view of Russia's prospects. The OECD saw a declining world demand for oil as stopping Russia's economic growth, while leaving it prey to the underlining problems of too much bureaucracy, and too much political interference in business. On June 24, 2009, Russia launched its formal bid for membership in the OECD.

The OECD continued to work against tax havens and other kinds of international malfeasance. In December 2008 Israel became the first Middle Eastern state to sign on to the OECD anti-bribery convention, thus putting it one step closer to membership in the organization. In April 2009 the OECD removed the last four countries— Costa Rica, Malaysia, the Philippines, and Uruguay—from its blacklist of tax havens. In August the organization reported that all OECD countries were in compliance with its convention on the exchange of bank data for tax purposes, and that Hong Kong and Macao had agreed to pass legislation to the same end.

ORGANIZATION FOR SECURITY AND COOPERATION IN EUROPE (OSCE)

Established: As the Conference on Security and Cooperation in Europe (CSCE) on July 3, 1973, by meeting of heads of states and other representatives of 35 nations in Helsinki, Finland; Helsinki Final Act adopted August 1, 1975; Charter of Paris for a New Europe adopted November 21, 1990; current name adopted at Heads of State or Government Summit on December 5–6, 1994, in Budapest, Hungary.

Purpose: "To consolidate respect for human rights, democracy, and the rule of law, to strengthen peace, and to promote unity in Europe."

Headquarters: Vienna, Austria.

Principal Organs: Heads of State or Government Meeting (Summit), Ministerial Council, Senior Council, Permanent Council, Conflict Prevention Center, Forum for Security Cooperation, Office for Democratic Institutions and Human Rights, High Commissioner on National Minorities, Office of the Representative on Freedom of the Media, Parliamentary Assembly, Secretariats.

Web site: www.osce.org

Secretary General: Marc Perrin de Brichambaut (France).

Membership (56): Albania, Andorra, Armenia, Austria, Azerbaijan, Belarus, Belgium, Bosnia and Herzegovina, Bulgaria, Canada, Croatia, Cyprus, Czech Republic, Denmark, Estonia, Finland, France, Georgia, Germany, Greece, Hungary, Iceland, Ireland, Italy, Kazakhstan, Kyrgyzstan, Latvia, Liechtenstein, Lithuania, Luxembourg, Macedonia, Malta, Moldova, Monaco, Montenegro, Netherlands, Norway, Poland, Portugal, Romania, Russia, San Marino, Serbia, Slovakia, Slovenia, Spain, Sweden, Switzerland, Tajikistan, Turkey, Turkmenistan, Ukraine, United Kingdom, United States, Uzbekistan, Vatican City State.

Origin and development. The creation of a forum for discussion of East-West security issues was first proposed in the late 1960s. The Soviet Union, in particular, supported the idea as a means of establishing dialogue between the North Atlantic Treaty Organization (NATO) and the Warsaw Treaty Organization (Warsaw Pact) and formalizing the post–World War II status quo in Europe. Preparatory talks in 1972 led to the establishment of the CSCE on July 3, 1973, in Helsinki, Finland, by the foreign ministers of Canada, the United States, and 33 European countries. After protracted negotiations, their heads of state and government held a summit July 30–August 1, 1975, at the conclusion of which they signed the Helsinki Final Act, which declared the inviolability of national frontiers in Europe and the right of each signatory "to choose and develop" its own "political, social, economic, and cultural systems."

The act called for ongoing discussion of three thematic "baskets"—security, economic cooperation, and human rights—and provided for periodic review of progress toward implementation of its objectives, although no provision was made for a permanent CSCE headquarters or staff. Consequently, the conference operated in relative obscurity and had little impact beyond the establishment of so-called Helsinki Groups in the Soviet Union and other Eastern European nations to monitor human rights.

The first two CSCE review conferences, held in Belgrade, Yugoslavia (1977–1978), and Madrid, Spain (1980–1983), produced little of substance, but the third, held in Vienna, Austria (1986–1989), was credited with laying the groundwork for subsequent negotiations that produced the Treaty on Conventional Armed Forces in Europe (CFE), through which NATO and Warsaw Pact members agreed to substantial arms reductions. The CFE treaty was formally signed at the second CSCE summit on November 19–21, 1990, in Paris. The NATO and Warsaw Pact members also signed a joint document declaring they were "no longer adversaries." In addition, the summit adopted the Charter of Paris, which significantly expanded the CSCE mandate and established a permanent institutional framework.

The November 1990 CSCE summit was viewed by many of the 34 national leaders in attendance as a landmark step toward the establishment of a pan-European security system, a long-standing goal that had seemed unattainable until the dramatic improvement in East-West relations. However, despite the formal opening of the CSCE Secretariat in Prague in February 1991 and a Conflict Prevention Center in Vienna in March, the euphoria over the CSCE's prospects faded somewhat by the time the Council of Foreign Ministers met in June. In light of the perceived potential for instability within the Soviet Union and ongoing ethnic confrontation elsewhere on the continent, Western leaders had recently reaffirmed NATO as the dominant body for addressing their defense and security concerns. In addition, some observers wondered if the CSCE would prove too unwieldy, as its decisions required unanimity and it lacked any enforcement powers.

Albania joined the CSCE in June 1991 and was followed in September by Estonia, Latvia, and Lithuania. Russia subsequently assumed the former USSR seat. The other ten members of the Commonwealth of Independent States (CIS) joined in early 1992, the CSCE having decided to include the five Central Asian republics because of their former inclusion in the Soviet Union. Croatia, Georgia, and Slovenia were admitted in March, followed shortly thereafter by Bosnia and Herzegovina. The Czech Republic and Slovakia were admitted in 1993 following the dissolution of Czechoslovakia, while Macedonia joined the renamed OSCE in October 1995, after Greece lifted its veto. Andorra's accession in 1996 brought the OSCE's active membership up to 54. Yugoslavia (subsequently Serbia and Montenegro) returned to active status in November 2000, Belgrade's membership having been suspended in July 1992. Montenegro joined in June 2006 following its split with Serbia, and the former Serbia and Montenegro membership now officially represents Serbia alone.

The fourth CSCE follow-up session, held from March to July 1992 in Helsinki, focused on reformulating the organization's aims and structures. Its recommendations were adopted as the Helsinki Document by the third CSCE summit, held in the Finnish capital July 9–10. The text specified that the CSCE's task was now "managing change"; that summit meetings should "set priorities and provide orientation"; that the Council of Foreign Ministers was "the central decision-making and governing body of the CSCE"; and that the Committee of Senior Officials (CSO) was responsible for ongoing "overview, management, and coordination" of CSCE activities. The summit also decided in principle that the CSCE should have its own peacekeeping capability, which should operate in conformity with United Nations (UN) resolutions and in concert with NATO, the CIS, the European Community, and the Western European Union.

Throughout 1994 Russia continued to press for a strengthening of the CSCE, hoping to position it rather than NATO as the preeminent security organization for the "new Europe." Although bluntly dismissive of the notion that it would supplant NATO, Western leaders did agree that the grouping needed, in the words of one participant, "more heft." Thus, the CSCE became the OSCE during the Heads of State or Government Summit on December 5–6 in Budapest, Hungary.

Structure. Prior to the signing of the Charter of Paris in November 1990, the CSCE had little formal structure, operating as what one correspondent described as a "floating set of occasional negotiations." The charter provided for Heads of State or Government Meetings (Summits) and established a Council of Foreign Ministers to meet at least once a year as the "central forum for political consultations within the CSCE process." A Committee of Senior Officials was empowered to carry out the decisions of the council. The charter also authorized the establishment of a Conflict Prevention Center in Vienna, for which a separate secretariat was created, and an Office for Free Elections in Warsaw. The latter body was subsequently renamed the Office for Democratic Institutions and Human Rights (ODIHR).

In 1992 the CSCE also established a Forum for Security Cooperation (for negotiations on further arms control, disarmament, and confidence-building measures) and a High Commissioner on National Minorities. It also adopted a Convention on Conciliation and Arbitration, which led to establishment of a Court of Conciliation and Arbitration to which signatories of the convention could submit disputes. Furthermore, the NATO and former Warsaw Pact members signed an Open Skies Treaty that permitted aerial reconnaissance. (The treaty entered into effect in January 2002.) In July 1992 the inaugural meeting of the CSCE Parliamentary Assembly took place in Budapest, Hungary.

In addition to adopting the OSCE designation, the December 1994 summit in Budapest enacted several structural changes designed to convey a greater sense of permanency. Thus, the Committee of Senior Officials was renamed the Senior Council and was mandated to meet at least three times a year (once as the Economic Forum). The Ministerial Council (formerly the Council of Foreign Ministers) was mandated to meet in non-summit years. While the Senior Council was given broad responsibility for the implementation of OSCE decisions, day-to-day operational oversight was assigned to a Permanent Council. OSCE members are generally represented on the Permanent Council by their ambassadors in Vienna, where the offices of the main Secretariat are located. (The Secretariat also maintains an office in Prague, Czech Republic.)

In 1997 OSCE members approved a plan to create within the Secretariat the post of coordinator of economic and environmental activities as part of an effort to "strengthen the ability of the Permanent Council and the OSCE institutions to address economic, social and environmental aspects of security." An Office of the Representative on Freedom of the Media was added in 1998. Although the 1994 summit called for upgrading the authority of the OSCE secretary general, the position subsequently remained to a large part subordinate to the organization's chairman-in-office (CiO), a post held by a foreign minister of a member country for a one-year term.

Activities. Although most prominently identified since 1990 with its field operations and with election-related activities in the Balkans, the states that succeeded the Soviet Union, and other Eastern European countries, the OSCE has seen its agenda expand to include a wide range of crucial issues facing its membership. Through various seminars, workshops, conferences, conventions, reports, and projects, it continues to address concerns in what it defines as three "dimensions": politico-military, human, and economic. More specifically, the OSCE has been involved in promoting human and minority rights; development of democratic institutions and procedures, including an independent judiciary and a free press; the participation of women in economic and political life; economic and environmental matters; and efforts to halt money laundering, organized crime, the financing of terrorism, human trafficking, and drugs.

Under the Charter of Paris and, later, the Helsinki Document, the CSCE took on an increasingly prominent role in conflict management; peacekeeping; the promotion of democratic standards; and the monitoring of political, legal, and other developments in Europe and Central Asia. In its first effort at mediation, in July 1991 the CSCE dispatched a mission to Yugoslavia that had no success in curtailing the violent ethnic conflicts resulting from that country's breakup, despite such CSCE actions as an arms embargo and the further authorization in August 1992 of the Missions of Long Duration in Kosovo, Sandjak, and Vojvodina. The latter missions, with never more than 20 international personnel, had as their mandate promoting dialogue between the Belgrade government and the ethnic communities in the three regions, but the rump Yugoslavia terminated the missions' memorandum of understanding in 1993. Technically, the regional missions remained in existence until 2001, when Yugoslavia welcomed a new undertaking—the OSCE Mission to Serbia and Montenegro—with a mandate to promote "democratization, tolerance, the rule of law, and conformity with OSCE principles, standards, and commitments." On June 29, 2006, following the separation of Serbia and Montenegro into independent countries, the mission was, in effect, divided into two: the OSCE Mission to Montenegro and the OSCE Mission to Serbia.

In September 1992 the CSCE established the Spillover Monitor Mission to Skopje, which was charged with preventing conflicts elsewhere in the former Yugoslavia from spilling over into newly independent Macedonia. In subsequent years the scope of what is now a joint civilian-military mission was expanded, and in 2001 the number of personnel was increased from fewer than 10 to more than 200. As of December 2003 the mission involved some 190 international personnel engaged not only in monitoring but also in police training and development and in implementing the 2001 Ohrid Accords, concluded between the minority Albanian population and the Macedonian majority.

A number of other OSCE missions became operational in 1992–1993. Missions to Estonia and Latvia, each comprising fewer than ten representatives, were concerned with institution-building; the inculcation of OSCE principles and, in the case of Estonia, promotion of integration and intercommunal understanding between ethnic Estonians and ethnic Russians. Both missions concluded at the end of 2001. In December 1992 a new civilian-military mission to Georgia was directed to promote negotiations with secessionists in South Ossetia and, secondarily, to assist the UN in its similar efforts with regard to Abkhazia. The Mission in Georgia later took on such additional tasks as building democratic institutions, promoting human rights, and encouraging development of a free press. In addition, a Border Monitoring Operation was directed to watch and report traffic crossing the Georgian border with the troubled Russian republics of Chechnya, Ingushetia, and Dagestan. These missions in the Caucasus came to an end in 2009 (see below). It is important to note that OSCE missions can be established only by consensus among the member countries.

Also in 1992, the Minsk Process was fashioned to convene a conference in Minsk, Belarus, that would resolve the Nagorno-Karabakh conflict between Armenia and Azerbaijan. Although the conference has yet to be held, an Initial Operation Planning Group (IOPG), dating from May 1993, was superseded in December 1994 by a High-Level Planning Group (HLPG) that continues to meet in Vienna. Also in 1992, the OSCE agreed to send what would have been its first multinational peacekeeping force to Nagorno-Karabakh if a cease-fire was achieved, but as of July 2008 the deployment had not taken place. The ongoing Minsk Process is cochaired by France, Russia, and the United States and includes eight other countries in addition to the principals. Separate from the Minsk Process, the OSCE launched a seven-person Office in

Yerevan (Armenia) in February 2000 and a six-person Office in Baku (Azerbaijan) in July 2000.

Two other OSCE missions date from 1993. The Mission to Moldova facilitated the formation of a peace plan that envisaged substantial autonomy for the Transdnestr region; the plan was accepted by the Moldovan government in 1994. The mission currently focuses on providing "advice and expertise" on such concerns as human and minority rights, democratic transformation, and the return of refugees. In December 1993 the council also established a Mission to Tajikistan because of the civil war. Deployed in February 1994, the handful of staff members helped secure a peace pact in 1997. In November 2002 the mission was redesignated the Center in Dushanbe (the Tajik capital) with a staff of 16 mandated to "promote the implementation of OSCE principles and commitments" with regard to such concerns as economic and environmental matters; security and stability; and the development of democratic institutions, legal frameworks, and human rights.

In 1995 the OSCE, with the goal of further integrating all five Central Asian members into the organization, established an OSCE liaison office in Central Asia in Tashkent, Uzbekistan. In July 1998 the OSCE decided to open individual offices in Almaty, Kazakhstan; Ashgabat, Turkmenistan; and Bishkek, Kyrgyzstan. Currently, the OSCE has separate offices in each of the Central Asian republics.

In March 1995 the OSCE was authorized by the concluding session of a yearlong Conference on Stability in Europe to monitor some 100 "good neighborliness" treaties signed by former Communist countries in Central and Eastern Europe. Thereafter, OSCE envoys were more actively involved in negotiations on various regional conflicts. The OSCE Assistance Group to Chechnya, for instance, helped arrange a series of cease-fires, leading to the conclusion in November 1996 of what appeared to be a definitive accord providing for the withdrawal of Russian forces. The accord failed to hold, however, and in subsequent years the handful of assistance group personnel was forced on several occasions to evacuate or otherwise relocate.

Under the November 1995 Dayton peace agreement for Bosnia and Herzegovina the OSCE was allotted a key role, notably in organizing elections. As of December 2003 the Mission to Bosnia and Herzegovina, numbering some 140 international personnel in more than two dozen field offices, continued to assist with regional stabilization, democracy building, human rights monitoring, and other related tasks.

In October 1998 the OSCE, with the approval of the United Nations, undertook its largest mission to date, the Kosovo Verification Mission (KVM). The KVM was authorized for one year and was supposed to verify that all sides of the conflict were in compliance with UN resolutions. It was also directed to monitor elections and help establish a police force and other institutions in Kosovo. Despite the presence of the KVM and several attempts at negotiating an end to the fighting, the violence in Kosovo continued, and the mission had to be withdrawn in March 1999 before NATO initiated its bombing campaign against Yugoslavia. The OSCE returned to Kosovo following the conclusion in June of a comprehensive peace plan that included establishment of a UN Interim Administration Mission for Kosovo (UNMIK), with the OSCE Mission in Kosovo to be responsible for implementing democratic reforms and building governmental institutions. As of July 2008 the mission comprised up to 262 international personnel, plus 664 local staff, with offices in all 30 municipalities.

A number of other field operations continue. The Mission to Croatia, established in 1996, had authorized a maximum of 280 personnel before the termination in 2000 of its Police Monitoring Group; it closed at the end of 2007 and was succeeded by the OSCE Office in Zagreb. The OSCE presence in Albania, dating from 1997, includes about 30 personnel based in Tirana and five field offices. The Project Coordinator in Ukraine was introduced in 1999 as the successor to the 1994–1999 OSCE Mission to Ukraine. The Office in Minsk was established in January 2003 as the successor to the Advisory and Monitoring Group in Belarus, which had been established in 1997 but had fallen into disfavor with the government; as of July 2008 there were only five international staff in the office. (Differences between the organization and Belarus arose in part from what were generally described as undemocratic legislative elections in 2001 and the resultant decision of the OSCE Parliamentary Assembly not to seat a Belarusan delegation.)

The ODIHR has reviewed electoral laws and observed elections in more than two-dozen member countries. Frequently, its reports have highlighted deficiencies in electoral processes, and, on occasion, the OSCE refuses to send monitoring teams.

In other field activities, the OSCE has been assisting since 1994 in implementing Russian-Latvian and Russian-Estonian agreements on military pensioners. The OSCE also provided a representative in 1995–1999 to another bilateral agreement between Russia and Latvia regarding the temporary operation and dismantling of the Skrunda Radar Station in Latvia.

The OSCE Heads of State or Government Meeting held on December 2–3, 1996, in Lisbon, Portugal, was also attended by representatives of the OSCE's Mediterranean "partners for cooperation" (Algeria, Egypt, Israel, Morocco, and Tunisia), Japan, and South Korea. The summit adopted a lengthy declaration on "a common and comprehensive security model for Europe in the twenty-first century" and resolved in favor of a negotiated revision of the 1990 CFE Treaty, as demanded by Russia in light of its perceived need to deploy additional forces in unstable border regions.

The major event of 1999 was a summit convened on November 18–19 in Istanbul, Turkey. Despite concerns over Russia's renewed offensive in Chechnya, criticism of which led to Russian president Boris Yeltsin's early departure from the meeting, the summit managed to conclude two major agreements. All 54 active member countries signed the new European Security Charter, which, in part, reinforced various agreements dealing with security and human rights and called for more rapid response to requests for assistance from member states, particularly with regard to conflict prevention and crisis management. In addition, the 30 states belonging to NATO or the defunct Warsaw Pact signed a revised CFE Treaty, in which all signatories accepted verifiable ceilings for such military equipment as tanks, artillery, and combat aircraft and agreed not to deploy forces outside their borders without approval by the affected country.

A heightened emphasis on opposing terrorism was well in evidence at the December 3–4, 2001, Ministerial Council session in Bucharest, Romania, and at the December 6–7, 2002, session held in Porto, Portugal. In the same vein, the 11th Ministerial Council meeting, held December 1–2, 2003, in Maastricht, Netherlands, voiced support for upgrading passports and other travel documentation to meet minimum security standards, as proposed by the International Civil Aviation Agency (ICAO), and concurred with recommendations by the Forum for Security Cooperation on keeping "man-portable air defense systems" from the hands of terrorists. As part of an OSCE Strategy to Address Threats to Security and Stability in the Twenty-first Century, the session also called for establishment of a Counter-Terrorism Network to coordinate counterterrorism measures; share information; and "strengthen the liaison" among OSCE delegations, government officials, and the new Action against Terrorism Unit (ATU) in the Secretariat.

A 2003 strategy document discussed other sources of instability, such as interstate and intrastate conflicts, organized crime, discrimination and intolerance, failure of social integration during a period of mobile migrant populations, environmental degradation, and economic factors (poverty, deepening income disparities, and unemployment). The 2003 ministerial session also endorsed an Action Plan to Combat Trafficking in Human Beings, which called for adding a related special unit in the Secretariat and the appointment by the CiO of a special representative. In addition, the session approved an Action Plan on Improving the Situation of Roma and Sinti (Gypsies) within the OSCE Area.

Extending its range, in 2004 the OSCE held a conference in Berlin on anti-Semitism, agreeing to collect and publish statistics on crimes against Jews in each member country. The conference's final declaration also included measures to fight racism on the Internet and bolster legal systems. Disagreement rather than consensus was widely reported as the outcome of the December 6–8, 2004, OSCE summit in Sofia, Bulgaria. The session ended with no political declaration.

Relations with Russia deteriorated in November 2004 when Moscow claimed the OSCE had taken an "intrusive" interest in the affairs of the former Soviet Union, particularly with regard to the monitoring of elections and borders. It was reported that U.S. and European Union (EU) diplomats believed the Kremlin was trying to separate Russia from the OSCE oversight. Concern over President Vladimir Putin's efforts to consolidate his authority prompted anxiety among U.S. officials and contributed to the postponement of a November summit between Russia and the EU. Meanwhile, Russia continued to refuse to uphold its commitment made to the OSCE in 1999 to remove its troops from Georgia and Moldova and prepared to contest the monitoring of the Georgian border. The U.S. ambassador to the OSCE intervened in January 2005 to help resolve the border issue, but nothing was finalized. When the disputed March 2005 Kyrgyz elections resulted in the ouster of the government, the OSCE called for harmony among the country's new leaders and declared that the ousted president, Askar

Akayev, should not attempt to return from Russia, whence he had fled. The OSCE's position prevailed, and an election to elect a new president was held in July. Also in 2005, an OSCE conference of justice ministers from Bosnia and Herzegovina, Croatia, and Serbia and Montenegro was held on June 8 in Croatia to discuss cooperation on war crimes trials.

The OSCE, best known for monitoring elections in countries where democracy is relatively new, broke new ground by announcing that it would monitor the 2005 British general election—not with the expectation of finding fraud but as a way to assess the issues around ballot security and postal voting in developed countries. In November 2004 it had conducted a "targeted observation" of legislative and presidential balloting in the United States, and in 2006 it sent teams to both Canada and Italy. During 2005 and the first half of 2006 the OSCE also monitored elections in Albania, Armenia, Azerbaijan, Belarus, Kazakhstan, Kyrgyzstan, Macedonia, Moldova, Tajikistan, and Ukraine, as well as the Montenegrin independence referendum of May 2006.

The OSCE was also concerned with the human rights records of Asian and European member countries. It called for an inquiry into the May 2005 shooting of demonstrators in Andijan, Uzbekistan, and warned against erosion of civil liberties in Western countries under pressure to combat terrorism.

At the October 2006 OSCE foreign ministers' meeting in Brussels, Russian rhetoric reminded some observers of Cold War days. Foreign minister Sergei Lavrov suggested divorcing humanitarian concerns from the OSCE, and perhaps establishing a special organization to deal such concerns exclusively. He said that each country could make its own decision about membership in such an organization.

In August 2007 the OSCE monitored parliamentary elections in Kazakhstan, considering them imperfect. In September 2007, when Georgia accused a Russian aircraft of entering its airspace and firing a missile, the OSCE played an important part in keeping channels of communication open between the two countries, perhaps preventing the crisis from worsening. But observers noted that the incident showed that the OSCE needed a faster procedure for reacting to such events.

Poll-watching during Russia's resurgence occupied the OSCE well into 2008. In September 2007 Poland, now a member of the EU and NATO, refused to admit OSCE observers to its October parliamentary elections, saying that it was now a democracy needing no such monitoring. A spokesperson for the ODIHR (based in Warsaw) called the decision "surprising." OSCE monitoring of the December 2, 2007, Russian parliamentary elections faced difficulties not encountered in the elections of 2003. At first Russia would allow only a much smaller number of observers than before, so ODIHR canceled the mission in mid-November, saying that it had been denied the necessary visas. In the end OSCE observers went to Russia, and OSCE branded the election—won decisively by president Vladimir Putin's party—as "not fair."

Differing U.S. and Russian agendas for the OSCE were apparent at the November 29–30 annual ministerial council meeting held in Madrid. Russia seemed to win the debate over allowing Kazakhstan, a close ally sometimes criticized for its record on human rights, to assume the OSCE presidency in 2010. However, Russia made no progress in its efforts to rein in the ODIHR. Russia continued to push, against the United States, for an OSCE charter. Such a charter, it said, would correct an imbalance among the OSCE's three concerns: human rights, political-military affairs, and economic and environmental issues.

The OSCE criticized the December 2007 parliamentary elections in Kyrgyzstan, in which the president's party won every seat. The OSCE likewise criticized the Uzbek presidential election in the same month, but a U.S. member of the mission called the criticism "nonsense," saying that ODIHR monitors often wrote their reports without leaving their hotels. ODIHR finally boycotted Russia's March 2008 presidential election after acrimonious disagreement with Russia about the size and duration of its mission. Russia called ODIHR's position a further reason for reforming the organization.

The seventeenth annual session of the Parliamentary Assembly met June 29–July 3, 2008 in Astana, Kazakhstan. It called for increased transparency in the OSCE and for the ODIHR and the Parliamentary Assembly to work more closely together to assure effective monitoring of elections. The Astana Declaration came close to seeking an OSCE charter.

The remainder of 2008, as well as 2009, were dominated by the threat of renewed fighting between Russia and Georgia after the August 2008 conflict was mediated to a close. In September 2008 talks about increasing the OSCE monitoring contingent came to a halt because Russia objected to the fact that monitors were also working in the breakaway Georgian regions of South Ossetia and Abkhazia. Russia regards these regions as independent states. On December 21, 2008, at the OSCE Permanent Council meeting in Vienna, Russia objected to any extension of the mission's mandate, unless the OSCE set up separate missions for South Ossetia and Abkhazia. Plans were put in place to end the Georgia mission by March 2009. On February 12, 2009, the OSCE extended the Georgia mission's mandate, by consensus, until June 30 of that year. Negotiations continued, but on May 21, 2009, the Greek chair of the OCSE suspended them indefinitely, citing lack of progress. The mission's mandate thus expired, though a EU mission remained in place. By the first anniversary of the August 2008 clash, tensions between Russia and Georgia seemed to be increasing.

On September 18, 2008, the Finnish foreign minister and chairman-in-office Alexander Stubb replaced Tim Guldimann (Switzerland) with Werner Almhofer (Austria) as head of the OSCE mission in Kosovo. Guldimann had been criticized by both sides in Kosovo, but Russia strongly objected to his replacement by Almhofer. Almhofer was also not acceptable to Belgrade.

In July 2009 the OSCE monitored presidential elections in Albania and Kyrgyzstan. It described the Albanian election as fair, but was less satisfied with the election in Kyrgyzstan.

ORGANIZATION OF AMERICAN STATES (OAS/OEA)

Organisation des Etats Américains
Organização dos Estados Americanos
Organización de los Estados Americanos

Established: By charter signed April 30, 1948, in Bogotá, Colombia, effective December 13, 1951.

Purpose: To achieve "an order of peace and justice, promoting solidarity among the American states; [to strengthen] their collaboration and [defend] their sovereignty, their territorial integrity, and their independence . . . as well as to establish . . . new objectives and standards for the promotion of the economic, social, and cultural development of the peoples of the Hemisphere, and to speed the process of economic integration."

Headquarters: Washington, D.C., United States.

Principal Organs: General Assembly, Meeting of Consultation of Ministers of Foreign Affairs, Permanent Council, Inter-American Council for Integral Development, Inter-American Juridical Committee (11 jurists from member states), Inter-American Commission on Human Rights (seven members), Inter-American Court of Human Rights (seven jurists from member states), Inter-American Drug Abuse Control Commission, Inter-American Telecommunications Commission, Inter-American Committee on Ports, General Secretariat.

Web site: www.oas.org

Secretary General: José Miguel Insulza (Chile).

Membership (35): Antigua and Barbuda, Argentina, Bahamas, Barbados, Belize, Bolivia, Brazil, Canada, Chile, Colombia, Costa Rica, Cuba (excluded from formal participation in OAS activities since 1962), Dominica, Dominican Republic, Ecuador, El Salvador, Grenada, Guatemala, Guyana, Haiti, Honduras, Jamaica, Mexico, Nicaragua, Panama, Paraguay, Peru, St. Kitts and Nevis, St. Lucia, St. Vincent and the Grenadines, Suriname, Trinidad and Tobago, United States, Uruguay, Venezuela.

Permanent Observers (63): Algeria, Angola, Armenia, Austria, Azerbaijan, Belgium, Benin, Bosnia and Herzegovina, Bulgaria, China, Croatia, Cyprus, Czech Republic, Denmark, Egypt, Equatorial Guinea, Estonia, European Union, Finland, France, Georgia, Germany, Ghana, Greece, Hungary, Iceland, India, Ireland, Israel, Italy, Japan,

Kazakhstan, Republic of Korea, Latvia, Lebanon, Luxembourg, Morocco, Netherlands, Nigeria, Norway, Pakistan, Philippines, Poland, Portugal, Qatar, Romania, Russia, Saudi Arabia, Serbia, Slovakia, Slovenia, Spain, Sri Lanka, Sweden, Switzerland, Thailand, Tunisia, Turkey, Ukraine, United Kingdom, Vatican City State, Yemen.

Official Languages: English, French, Portuguese, Spanish.

Origin and development. The foundations of the OAS were laid in 1890 at an International Conference of American States in Washington, D.C., where it was decided to form an International Union of American Republics to serve as a permanent secretariat. The name of the organization itself was changed in 1910 to Union of American Republics, and the secretariat was renamed the Pan American Union.

The experience of World War II encouraged further development of the still loosely organized "inter-American system." An Inter-American Conference on Problems of War and Peace, meeting in February–March 1945 in Mexico City, concluded that the American republics should consider adoption of a treaty for their mutual defense. Through the Inter-American Treaty of Reciprocal Assistance (Rio Treaty), which was opened for signature on September 2, 1947, in Rio de Janeiro, Brazil, they agreed an armed attack originating either within or outside the American system would be considered an attack against all members, and each would assist in meeting such an attack. (In September 2002 Mexico renounced the Rio Treaty, which it described as obsolete in the post–Cold War era.) Organizational streamlining was undertaken by the Ninth International Conference of American States, which met in March–May 1948 in Bogotá, Colombia, and established the 21-member OAS.

The adoption by Cuba of a Marxist-Leninist ideology generally was viewed by other American governments as incompatible with their fundamental principles, and the Eighth Meeting of Consultation of Ministers of Foreign Affairs, held January 23–31, 1962, in Punta del Este, Uruguay, determined that Cuba, in effect, had excluded itself from participation in the inter-American system because of its Rio Treaty provisions violation. Over time, however, several members began to question the value of continued ostracism of the Castro regime. The trade and diplomatic quarantine against Cuba was ultimately lifted at a special consultative meeting on July 29, 1975, in San José, Costa Rica, although the resolution did not lift Cuba's exclusion from formal participation in OAS activities.

Evidence of the organization's increasing economic and social concerns was manifested by the adoption of the Act of Bogotá, a program of social development, by a special OAS conference in September 1960. On August 17, 1961, an Inter-American Economic and Social Conference adopted the Charter of Punta de Este, a ten-year program designed to implement the provisions of the U.S.-sponsored Alliance for Progress, while a code of conduct for transnational corporations was approved in July 1978.

On July 18, 1978, the nine-year-old Convention on Human Rights entered into force. The agreement provided for an Inter-American Court of Human Rights, composed of seven judges elected by the OAS assembly, to serve in a private capacity. Most members ratified the convention with reservations, so the court's impact has been limited. The Inter-American Commission on Human Rights has been more active, devoting, for example, two weeks in September 1979 to an onsite investigation of alleged human rights violations in Argentina. The results of that investigation became the focus of the November 1980 General Assembly meeting, which concluded a compromise accord whereby the assembly deplored every form of human rights infringement without passing judgment on the specific cases enumerated in the commission report. Chile, following criticism of its human rights policy by the commission's president, suspended its participation in commission activities and accused the body of exceeding its powers.

The Falkland Islands crisis of 1982, which began with an Argentinean invasion on April 2, yielded an extended special session of the OAS during April and May. The participants passed a resolution that supported Argentina's claim to the Falklands (called Las Malvinas by Argentina), condemned the British effort to regain the island colony, and considered a possible U.S. breach of the 1947 Rio pact because of Washington's assistance to Britain.

The Falklands conflict pointed to a growing rift between, on the one hand, the United States and the English-speaking Caribbean members of the OAS and, on the other, most Latin American members. The United States and Nicaragua sparred over Central American issues within the OAS and at the United Nations (UN). Following the U.S. intervention in Grenada in October 1983, most OAS members attending a special session on October 26 condemned the U.S. action. Washington and its Caribbean allies countered that the United States had not violated the Rio Treaty, but instead had tried to bring order to Grenada.

A special foreign ministers' meeting convened on December 2, 1985, in Cartagena, Colombia, to consider proposed amendments to the OAS charter. The resulting Protocol of Cartagena, which entered into force in November 1988, modified admission rules to permit the entry of Belize and Guyana, previously ineligible because of territorial disputes with OAS members Guatemala and Venezuela, respectively. Under the new criteria, all American states that were members of the UN as of December 10, 1985, plus specified nonautonomous territories (Bermuda, French Guiana, Guadeloupe, Martinique, and Montserrat, but not the Falkland Islands) would be permitted to apply. The protocol also increased the authority of the secretary general, permitting him, on his own initiative, to bring to the attention of the assembly any matter that "could affect the peace and security of the continent and development of its member countries." At the same time, the Permanent Council was authorized to provide peacekeeping services to help ameliorate regional crises.

Despite initial opposition from the United States, the OAS played an active role in the Central American peace negotiations initiated in early 1987 by former Costa Rican president Oscar Arias, with efforts directed toward conflicts in El Salvador and Guatemala, as well as Nicaragua. In 1989 attention turned to Panama. The OAS foreign ministers met in emergency session on May 17 and established a four-member team to conduct negotiations with Panamanian leader Gen. Manuel Noriega in hopes of achieving a transition to democratic government. However, the OAS was unable to persuade Noriega to relinquish power and could only call for free elections "within the shortest possible time." Despite the diplomatic failure, 20 OAS members approved a resolution in December that "deeply deplored" the U.S. invasion of Panama and called for the immediate withdrawal of U.S. troops.

Canada, which had long avoided active participation in the OAS because of perceived U.S. dominance, finally joined as a full member in 1990. The complement of member states grew to 35 with the accession of Belize and Guyana in 1991. Meanwhile, Washington continued to insist that Cuban eligibility for reintegration into regional activity had to be preceded by democratic elections.

During its June 1991 General Assembly, the organization adopted Resolution 1080, which authorized an emergency meeting of the Permanent Council following a coup or other threat to democracy in any member country. The resolution reflected that, for the first time in OAS history, all active members had democratically elected governments. The first test of the resolution was the military overthrow of the Haitian government of Fr. Jean-Bertrand Aristide on September 30, 1991. Haiti remained a focus of attention throughout 1992 and into 1993 as OAS observers attempted to monitor the human rights situation in that nation during UN negotiations.

The OAS also met in special sessions to address the seizures of dictatorial power by democratically elected leaders in Peru in 1992 and in Guatemala in May 1993, condemning both events but rejecting any specific action. On December 14, 1992, 30 OAS members signed the Protocol of Washington, a proposed amendment to the OAS charter, which would upon ratification give the body the power to suspend a member state whose democratically elected government had been overthrown by force.

Still trying to counter criticism of OAS "inefficiency and passivity," the General Assembly adopted the Managua Declaration for the Promotion of Democracy and Development during its June 1993 session. The General Assembly also approved a charter amendment, the Protocol of Managua, to establish (subject to ratification by member states) an inter-American council to coordinate regional antipoverty and development programs. The resultant Inter-American Council for Integral Development (*Consejo Interamericano para el Desarrollo Integral*—CIDI) came into existence in 1996. Particular CIDI concerns are trade, social development, and sustainable development.

A major OAS concern in the first half of 1994 was Washington's preparation for a possible invasion of Haiti, as diplomatic measures and economic sanctions failed to sway the Haitian military leaders. The OAS General Assembly in June endorsed a tightening of sanctions but took no position on the use of military force, several leading members having argued against such intervention. Consequently, Washington looked to the UN for international approval of its Haitian policy, and in late July the UN Security Council authorized "all necessary action," including use of a U.S.-led multinational force, to return civilian government to Port-au-Prince.

Attesting to the surprisingly rapid restoration of the Aristide government in that nation, the next OAS summit was held June 5–9, 1995, in Montrouis, Haiti. Highlighting the session was the adoption of A New Vision for the OAS, a blueprint for the "rejuvenation" and strengthening of the organization. One priority was the new OAS Unit for the Promotion of Democracy, mandated to observe national elections, provide special training for the staffs of national legislatures, create mechanisms to expand the dissemination of information on governmental activities, and establish courses for the armed forces and police regarding human rights protection. Other areas specified for OAS emphasis were environmental preservation, cultural cooperation, and programs to combat corruption and drug trafficking.

In response to calls for reassessment and reform of the organization, including its structure and budget, a major reorganization occurred in 1996, with CIDI replacing the Inter-American Economic and Social Council and the Inter-American Council for Education, Science, and Culture. In 1997 the General Assembly eliminated the Inter-American Nuclear Energy Commission, which had not been funded since 1989, and in 1999 it authorized creation of the Inter-American Agency for Cooperation and Development (IACD) as a CIDI subsidiary. The IACD is the organization's principal development agency.

In September 1997 the 1992 Protocol of Washington came into effect following the deposit of Venezuela's instrument of ratification; thus, the OAS Charter was officially amended for the fourth time since 1948. In addition to shoring up the OAS's support for democratic government, the protocol established the eradication of extreme poverty as a basic goal.

Structure. As the principal political organ of the OAS, the General Assembly meets annually to set policy, discuss the budget, and supervise the work of the organization's specialized agencies. The Permanent Council meets throughout the year to oversee the organization's agenda and has the authority to form committees and working groups. In addition to a General Committee, current committees include Administrative and Budgetary Affairs, Hemispheric Security, Juridical and Political Affairs, Inter-American Summits Management, and Civil Society Participation in OAS Activities. Under the Rio Treaty, the Meeting of Consultation of Ministers of Foreign Affairs discharges the organization's security functions and is convened to consider urgent problems.

The General Secretariat, headed by a secretary general who serves a five-year term, encompasses more than two dozen offices, departments, units, and agencies. It also oversees two cultural institutions, the Art Museum of the Americas and the Columbus Memorial Library, both based in Washington.

Reporting to the General Assembly, the Inter-American Council for Integral Development (CIDI) comprises a ministerial-level representative from each member state; it meets annually on a regular basis but also may convene in special session or at a sectoral level at other times. In addition to a Permanent Executive Committee, it has an Executive Secretariat for Integral Development that operates within the overall OAS General Secretariat.

Affiliated in various ways with the OAS are many specialized agencies, bodies, and other organizations, many predating the establishment of the OAS itself. These include the Administrative Tribunal (established in 1971 in Washington), the Inter-American Children's Institute (1927, Montevideo, Uruguay); the Inter-American Commission of Women (1928, Washington); the Inter-American Commission on Human Rights (1959, Washington); the Inter-American Committee against Terrorism (*Comité Interamericano Contra el Terrorismo*—CICTE, 1999, Washington); the Inter-American Committee for Natural Disaster Reduction (1999, Washington); the Inter-American Committee on Ports (1998, Washington); the Inter-American Court of Human Rights (1978, San José); the Inter-American Defense Board (1942, Washington); the Inter-American Drug Abuse Control Commission (1986, Washington); the Inter-American Indigenous Institute (1940, Mexico City); the Inter-American Institute for Cooperation on Agriculture (1942 as the Inter-American Institute of Agricultural Sciences, San José); the Inter-American Juridical Committee (mandated by Article 68 of the OAS charter, Rio de Janeiro); the Inter-American Telecommunications Commission (1993, Washington); the Justice Studies Center of the Americas (1999, Santiago, Chile); the Pan American Development Foundation (1962, Washington); the Pan American Health Organization (1902, Washington); and the Pan American Institute of Geography and History (1928, Mexico City).

Activities. The 1996 creation of CIDI came about largely in response to a perception that the earlier donor-recipient model of technical assistance needed to be replaced by a structure entailing cooperation of equal partners on well-defined programs devoted to economic and social development. The addition of the IACD in 1999 continued the process of rationalizing the OAS's economic and development structures; in addition to serving as the principal agency responsible for promoting and organizing cooperative ventures, the IACD offers training programs and facilitates technical exchanges.

Although increasingly supplemented by economic and social considerations, political and security functions remain preeminent in OAS activities. For example, since its 1990 establishment, the Unit for the Promotion of Democracy has dispatched observer missions to monitor approximately 80 elections in 19 member countries. In 1998, through the Inter-American Drug Abuse Control Commission, the OAS instituted a Multilateral Evaluation Mechanism (MEM) for evaluating anti-drug programs and coordinating members' responses to the illicit trade in drugs. In recent years the OAS also has increasingly taken on the role of broker in bilateral disputes, including border issues involving El Salvador and Honduras, Honduras and Nicaragua, and Guatemala and Belize. To finance negotiations and such related activities as compliance monitoring, in 2000 the General Assembly authorized establishment of a Fund for Peace. Additional security-related efforts have included the adoption of the Inter-American Convention against the Illicit Manufacturing of and Trafficking in Firearms, Ammunition, Explosives, and Other Related Materials, which entered into force in 1998; and adoption and ratification of the Inter-American Convention on Conventional Arms Acquisitions in 1999.

Other recent OAS initiatives have included the following: formation under the General Secretariat of a Trade Unit, which has been an active participant in preparations for establishing the Free Trade Area of the Americas (FTAA); adoption in 1996 of the Inter-American Convention against Corruption—the world's first anti-corruption treaty—and approval in 1997 of the Inter-American Program for Cooperation in the Fight against Corruption; organization in 1996 of a Unit for Social Development and Education, also within the General Secretariat; approval in 1997 of an Inter-American Program to Combat Poverty; approval in 1998 of an Inter-American Program of Culture; and adoption in 2002 of a Strategic Plan for Partnership for Development 2002–2005. In 2003 the General Assembly instructed the Permanent Council to prepare in 2004 a Program for Democratic Governance in the Americas for consideration.

The FTAA negotiations were officially launched at the April 1998 Summit of the Americas in Santiago, Chile (see the discussion in the Latin American Economic System article), but have lagged since then.

At the 1998 Summit of the Americas, a gathering sponsored by the OAS, many participants again called for Cuba's reinstatement in the OAS and its inclusion in the next summit in 2002. Having earlier voiced opposition to the U.S. Helms-Burton Law, which tightened economic sanctions and penalized those conducting trade with Cuba, at the annual General Assembly in June, the OAS again addressed the proposed reinstatement of Cuba if the country adopted political reforms. Efforts were short-circuited later that month when the Castro government refused to accept any preconditions.

The June 6–8, 1999, General Assembly session in Guatemala City, Guatemala, saw considerable criticism of a U.S. proposal to establish a nonmilitary, consultative mechanism for intervention in cases of perceived threats to democracy. Given the U.S. history of unilateral intervention in Latin American affairs, Venezuela, Peru, Mexico, and a number of other OAS members immediately opposed the proposal, which Washington soon withdrew. Greater support greeted the signing by ten members of an Inter-American Convention on the Elimination of All Forms of Discrimination against Persons with Disabilities.

The 30th General Assembly met June 4–6, 2000, in Windsor, Canada, where the principal topic of discussion was the recent controversial reelection of Peruvian president Fujimori. A week before the May 31 runoff, OAS monitors had left the country, declaring the electoral process fundamentally flawed. In other business, Secretary General César Gaviria Trujillo specifically criticized the United States, Brazil, Argentina, and the Dominican Republic for payment arrears. At the time, Washington owed some $68 million, equivalent to more than three-fourths of the organization's budget for 2001.

The 2000 General Assembly also devoted considerable attention to the agenda of the Third Summit of the Americas, which was held April 20–22, 2001, in Quebec City, Canada. The summit assigned an increased workload to the OAS, which was recognized as playing a "central role" in implementing the Quebec Plan of Action. OAS areas of responsibility included not only trade, but also hemispheric security, drugs, indigenous rights, infrastructure, gender equity, natural disaster preparedness, sustainable development, and preparation of an Inter-American Democratic Charter. In addition, the OAS was assigned the role of technical secretariat for future summits.

At the General Assembly held June 3–6, 2001, in San José, anticipated approval of a draft Inter-American Democratic Charter was deferred because of objections from Venezuela, Chile, various Caribbean Community and Common Market (Caricom) states, and others. They argued that the fundamental definition of "representative democracy" leaned too heavily toward Washington's criteria. Meeting three months later on September 11–12 in special session in Lima, Peru, the OAS adopted the charter, which authorizes sanctions against a member state that experiences "an unconstitutional interruption of the democratic order or an unconstitutional alteration of the constitutional regime that seriously impairs the democratic order."

The special session coincided with the September 11, 2001, terrorist attacks on the United States, which led a September 19 emergency session of the Permanent Council to invoke the Rio Treaty and thereby authorize assistance to Washington in its "war on terrorism." Two days later, the 23rd Meeting of Consultation of Ministers of Foreign Affairs adopted the Resolution Strengthening Cooperation to Prevent, Combat, and Eliminate Terrorism. The events of September 11 also led to two special sessions of the Inter-American Committee against Terrorism (CICTE), which had been established in 1999 in furtherance of a commitment drafted in November 1998 at the Second Specialized Conference on Terrorism in Mar del Plata, Argentina. The CICTE met October 15 and again November 29 with a goal of drafting an action plan for 2002–2003 and, more immediately, identifying counterterrorism measures to be implemented by OAS member states.

An Intra-American Convention against Terrorism was opened for signature at the 2002 General Assembly session, which met June 2–4 in Bridgetown, Barbados. The meeting's closing declaration called for a "multidimensional" approach to hemispheric security, which "encompasses political, economic, social, health, and environmental factors." At the subsequent session, held June 9–10, 2003, in Santiago, the General Assembly issued the Declaration of Santiago on Democracy and Public Trust. In addition to characterizing the Inter-American Democratic Charter as the "principal hemispheric benchmark" for promoting and defending democratic principles and values, the summit identified "greater efficiency, probity, and transparency" as central to good governance. A month later, the Convention against Terrorism entered into force, 30 days after having obtained a sixth ratification.

In March 2004 the Inter-American Commission on Human Rights (IACHR) expressed concern about continuing "structural deficiencies" in American democracies and, in a separate statement, about adherence to the rule of law in Bolivia, Colombia, Cuba, Haiti, and Venezuela. All five countries had been the subject of numerous discussions, resolutions, or OAS missions in recent years, with international attention since the June 2003 General Assembly being particularly focused on the regimes of controversial presidents Hugo Chávez of Venezuela and Jean-Bertrand Aristide of Haiti. In response to the chaotic circumstances and violence surrounding the February 29, 2004, ouster and exile of Aristide, the commission called for the investigation, prosecution, and punishment of human rights violators.

In June 2003 the United States, for the first time in the IACHR's history, failed to retain one of the seven seats on the commission, whose membership through 2005 comprised Antigua and Barbuda, Brazil, Chile, El Salvador, Paraguay, Peru, and Venezuela. The vote that rejected the U.S. candidate was attributed by some observers to displeasure at a particularly stern assessment of the Cuban government by then U.S. secretary of state Colin Powell.

A Special Summit of the Americas met January 12–13, 2004, in Monterrey, Mexico, to focus attention on economic growth, social and human development, and democratic governance. The OAS also hosted a series of meetings on drafting an American Declaration on the Rights of Indigenous Peoples. As of mid-2009 the declaration had been drafted, but not yet signed by all member countries.

At the OAS General Assembly on June 7, 2004, in Quito, Ecuador, former Costa Rican president Miguel Angel Rodríguez was elected as the new secretary general. Rodríguez, who was favored by the United States, announced his resignation October 8, 2004, after allegations surfaced of financial corruption during his time in office in Costa Rica. Rodríguez was just two weeks into his five-year term in the OAS post, having been sworn in September 23.

Negotiations and debate over Rodríguez's successor occupied OAS leaders for the next six months, with the group deadlocking 17–17 through five rounds of voting on April 11, 2005. Chile's interior minister, José Miguel Insulza, and Mexico's foreign minister, Luis Derbez, were tied in the special election. Finally, on May 2, 2005, Insulza, a socialist, was elected in what was viewed as a setback for the United States. U.S. secretary of state Condoleezza Rice subsequently brokered a deal in which Insulza promised to hold governments accountable if they did not adhere to democratic principles, a pointed reference to Venezuelan president Chávez, whose arms buildup was of great concern to the United States. Insulza's election marked the first time in OAS history that a candidate opposed by the United States became secretary general.

At a three-day OAS meeting June 7–9, 2005, in Florida—the first to be held in the United States in 31 years—Venezuela accused the United States of seeking to impose a "global dictatorship" when Secretary of State Rice called for new ways to support "fragile" emerging democracies.

The 2006 meeting of the General Assembly, held on June 4–6 in Santo Domingo, was less contentious than the previous one. The U.S. delegate noted with satisfaction the June 5 election of Alan García as president of Peru. (Venezuelan president Chávez had denounced García as a tool of United States and had campaigned vigorously against him.) The secretary general said that although no member states were in arrears in their dues, inflation and the need to meet UN guidelines on staff compensation meant that many of the organization's programs would have to be funded privately. In July 2006 Brazil took over the chair of the Inter-American Defense Board—the responsibility leaving the United States for the first time in the organization's history. The OAS was active during 2006 in monitoring elections in Guyana, Nicaragua, and Venezuela. Insulza was able to report that 2006 had been a year in which many member countries held elections, all conducted well and with their results respected.

The year 2007 was marked by the actions of Venezuelan president Hugo Chávez and the organization's response. Amid widespread protests in Venezuela and beyond, the Chávez government refused to renew the license of a television station well known for criticizing the government. The United States condemned Venezuela and asked the OAS to intervene, but the only result was a general OAS call to respect media freedom. The OAS also complied when Venezuela demanded that it remove from its Web site a report from the Berlin-based organization Transparency International criticizing the amount of graft in Venezuela.

In February 2007 Insulza said that he was open to some form of renewed dialogue with Cuba. The OAS monitored elections in Jamaica and Guatemala, and in August 2007 Insulza stated that Latin America was experiencing a positive period in politics and economics. In the fall of 2007, OAS observers monitored elections in Jamaica, Guatemala, and Costa Rica, declaring all of them satisfactory. In October 2007 Insulza announced that he wanted the OAS to be have the right to monitor presidential and other general elections in *all* member countries, whether invited or not.

The March 1, 2008, raid by Colombia against a Revolutionary Armed Forces of Colombia (FARC) rebel camp inside Ecuador caused the OAS to set up a five-member commission to investigate. By March 18 the OAS had passed a resolution deploring the Colombian incursion and calling it "a clear violation of articles 19 and 21 of the OAS charter," but it noted that Colombia had already apologized and promised no more such incidents would occur. The resolution came after many hours of debate and was seen as a defeat for the U.S. position. The United States had wanted the resolution to recognize the raid as a legitimate act of self-defense, but the final resolution rejected this. The matter became more complicated when computer files, seized in the raid, seemed to suggest that Ecuador and Venezuela were actively supporting the rebels. Though under pressure from several U.S. legislators, the OAS did nothing further to investigate. In June 2008 Colombia and Ecuador restored diplomatic relations at a low level.

At the June 1–3, 2008, meeting of the General Assembly, of which the nominal theme was "Youth and Democratic Values," the representative from Antigua and Barbuda made a strong plea for the organization to work against greenhouse gas emissions, which he called a "clear and present danger" to the hemisphere.

In July 2008 an OAS team observed the general elections in Grenada. In September the OAS monitored negotiations between Bolivian president Evo Morales and several provincial governors who were bitterly opposed to his policies. The OAS was not invited to observe the November 8-9 local elections in Nicaragua, in which the left-leaning Sandinista party made large gains, and whose results were disputed. Secretary General Insulza said an OAS presence would have been helpful. An OAS mission also observed the February 2009 referendum in Venezuela. This referendum concerned a proposal to change the constitution to allow the president (Hugo Chávez) to be re-elected an unlimited number of times. Chávez won.

The election of Barack Obama as U.S. president in November 2008 caused the OAS to think once more about readmitting Cuba to full membership and ending the U.S. trade embargo against that country. In April 2009 former Cuban president Fidel Castro called for the forthcoming fifth Summit of the Americas to end Cuba's isolation. At this meeting, held April 17-19 in Port of Spain, Trinidad and Tobago, U.S. Secretary of State Hillary Clinton admitted that the U.S. policy towards Cuba had failed, and welcomed Cuban overtures for a new dialogue. President Obama attended the summit, to which Cuba had of course not been invited, and declared that the United States sought a "new beginning" with Cuba and an "equal partnership" with all states of the Americas. At the 39th regular session of the OAS General Assembly, meeting June 2–3, 2009, in San Pedro Sula, Honduras voted to rescind Cuba's 1962 banishment. On June 4 Ricardo Alarcon, the Speaker of the Cuban parliament, welcomed the decision, but said that Cuba might not necessarily want to rejoin the OAS immediately.

ORGANIZATION OF ARAB PETROLEUM EXPORTING COUNTRIES (OAPEC)

Established: By agreement concluded on January 9, 1968, in Beirut, Lebanon.

Purpose: To help coordinate members' petroleum policies, to adopt measures for harmonizing their legal systems to the extent needed for the group to fulfill its mission, to assist in the exchange of information and expertise, to provide training and employment opportunities for their citizens, and to utilize members' "resources and common potentialities" in establishing joint projects in the petroleum and petroleum-related industries.

Headquarters: Kuwait City, Kuwait.

Principal Organs: Ministerial Council, Executive Bureau, Judicial Tribunal, General Secretariat.

Web site: www.oapecorg.org

Secretary General: Abbas Ali Naqi (Kuwait).

Membership (10): Algeria, Bahrain, Egypt, Iraq, Kuwait, Libya, Qatar, Saudi Arabia, Syria, United Arab Emirates.

Official Language: Arabic.

Origin and development. Established by Kuwait, Libya, and Saudi Arabia in early 1968 in recognition of the need for further cooperation among Arab countries that relied on oil as their principal source of income, OAPEC was expanded in May 1970 by the accession of Algeria, Bahrain, Qatar, Abu Dhabi, and Dubai. In May 1972 the last two combined their membership as part of the United Arab Emirates. In December 1971 the founding agreement was liberalized to permit membership by any Arab country having oil as a significant—but not necessarily the major—source of income, with the result that Syria and Egypt joined in 1972 and 1973, respectively. Also in 1972, Iraq became a member. A Tunisian bid for membership failed at the December 1981 ministerial meeting because of Libyan opposition stemming from a dispute with Tunis over conflicting claims to offshore oil deposits. Tunisia was admitted in 1982 but four years later withdrew from active membership because it had become a net importer of energy and could not make its OAPEC contributions.

OAPEC joint ventures and projects include the Arab Maritime Petroleum Transport Company (AMPTC), founded in 1973 with headquarters in Kuwait; the Arab Shipbuilding and Repair Yard Company (ASRY), established in Bahrain in 1974; the Arab Petroleum Investments Corporation (APICORP), set up in 1975 in Damman, Saudi Arabia; and the Arab Petroleum Services Company (APSC), founded in 1977 and operating from Tripoli, Libya. The Arab Engineering Company (AREC), established in 1981 in Abu Dhabi, was dissolved in 1989. Shareholders in these ventures are typically either the member governments themselves or state-owned petroleum enterprises.

Subsidiary companies are the Arab Drilling and Workover Company (ADWOC), based in Tripoli since its formation in 1980; the Arab Well Logging Company (AWLCO), established in 1983 in Baghdad; and the Arab Geophysical Exploration Services Company (AGESCO), formed in 1984 in Tripoli. The APSC is the sole shareholder in AWLCO and the principal shareholder in the other two. The Arab Company for Detergent Chemicals (ARADET), founded in 1981 in Baghdad, is an APICORP subsidiary.

Structure. The Ministerial Council, OAPEC's supreme authority, is composed of the members' petroleum ministers, who convene at least twice a year to draw up policy guidelines and direct ongoing activities. An Executive Bureau, which meets at least three times a year, assists the council in management of the organization. A Judicial Tribunal, established in 1980, serves as an arbitration council between OAPEC members or between a member and a petroleum company operating in that country, with all decisions final and binding. The General Secretariat, headed by a secretary general and no more than three assistant secretaries general, encompasses the secretary's office and four departments: Finance and Administrative Affairs, Information and Library, Economics, and Technical Affairs. The last two comprise the Arab Center for Energy Studies. A largely ceremonial national presidency of the organization rotates annually among the member states.

Activities. Although OAPEC's activities are directly affected by the world oil market, it plays no institutional role in determining either output quotas or prices, deferring in both cases to the more encompassing Organization of Petroleum Exporting Countries (OPEC). Instead, OAPEC focuses on coordinating related policies within the Arab community. Over the years, it has also invested billions of dollars in its associated ventures and affiliates. APICORP, for example, has helped finance petroleum and petrochemical projects around the world, including gas liquefaction plants, refineries, pipelines and other means of transport, and facilities for making fertilizers and detergents. In addition to its administrative tasks, the OAPEC secretariat has compiled and continually updates a comprehensive database of information on oil and energy markets, reserves, production, refining, consumption, and downstream industries such as petrochemicals. OAPEC also conducts related research projects, sponsors seminars, and produces technical papers and studies.

The notable exception to OAPEC's lack of a stance about production quotas and prices came in October 1973, following the Arab-Israeli war in which Egypt and Syria attacked Israel. OAPEC initiated the oil embargo against the West that caused much economic dislocation and first established the power of oil production as a political tool.

The December 1990 Ministerial Council meeting was held in Cairo, Egypt, that city having been chosen as OAPEC's temporary headquarters following the Iraqi invasion of Kuwait the previous August. In mid-1992 a report coauthored by OAPEC estimated that the Gulf crisis had cost Arab countries as much as $620 billion and had contributed to rising inflation and a decline of 7 percent in the GNP of 21 Arab nations in 1991. The destruction of oil wells, pipelines, and other infrastructure alone cost Iraq an estimated $190 billion and Kuwait $160 billion, the report said.

Arab oil affairs remained turbulent into 1994 as several OAPEC members continued to quarrel over OPEC production quotas. There was ongoing disagreement over how and when Iraq would resume oil exports, while OAPEC officials described recent wide fluctuations in oil prices as making it difficult for member states to plan development programs effectively. The organization hoped, however, to return to a degree of normal activity following return to its permanent headquarters in Kuwait at midyear.

In recent years OAPEC has also been giving increasing attention to environmental concerns, in part to ensure that the economic standing of its members is not adversely affected by international initiatives intended to reduce greenhouse gases and other pollutants. The Eighth Coordinating Meeting of Environmental Experts was held in Cairo on September 29–30, 2001, its principal focus being coordination of member countries' positions regarding, for example, the United Nations (UN) Framework Convention on Climate Change and the associated Kyoto Protocol. At the same time, OAPEC was preparing for the Seventh Arab Energy Conference, held May 11–12, 2002, in Cairo, where again the focus was on "Energy and Arab Cooperation." Other organizations sponsoring the conference were the Arab Fund for Economic and Social Development (AFESD), the Arab League, and the Arab Industrial Development and Mining Organization (AIDMO).

During 2001–2003 oil prices and resultant income remained somewhat volatile despite improving communication between oil suppliers and consuming nations. At the same time OAPEC reported Arab petroleum-refining capacity was increasing, as was regional consumption of natural gas. Known Arab reserves of the latter commodity, about one-fourth of the world total, nevertheless continued to increase as new discoveries outpaced consumption. OAPEC also projected that global oil consumption would rise by about 1.6 percent annually, from 76 billion barrels per day in 2000 to nearly 90 billion barrels per day in 2010.

In March–May 2003 the invasion of Iraq by U.S.-led forces had a minimal impact on oil supplies. It was unclear, however, given the dilapidated state of Iraq's petroleum infrastructure, when or if Iraqi oil production would regain the levels that predated the 1991 Gulf War. A representative of the U.S.-sponsored interim Iraqi Governing Council was expected to attend the Ministerial Council session held in Cairo on December 13, 2003, but he withdrew because of an unspecified "emergency." In December 2005 the Ministerial Council canceled 70 percent of the debt owed the organization by Iraq.

A July 2005 report from OAPEC said that member countries planned to increase their share of world oil production from the then 32.2 percent to between 38 and 40 percent by 2010. The report noted that the increase would require substantial new investment by all member countries, but particularly by Egypt, Algeria, and Libya. In December 2005 OAPEC announced that the organization's presidency would go to Qatar in 2006, not, as in the normal rotation, to Iraq. OAPEC benefited from the worldwide rise in demand for and price of oil in 2006 and 2007. In May 2006 a meeting of OAPEC energy ministers called for increased reinvestment of oil revenues in exploration and research, but in the group's October bulletin it warned that rising construction costs were hampering this effort. OAPEC and OPEC coordinated their positions at the December 2007 climate conference in Bali, Indonesia. OAPEC issued a statement that it was important to cut greenhouse emissions, as long as the interests of the poorest nations were safeguarded. On November 29–30, 2008, Egypt hosted simultaneous meetings of OPEC and OAPEC ministers. The OAPEC representatives adopted the Egyptian suggestion to launch a joint study on cooperation and coordination among member states to respond to the global financial crisis and its effect on oil prices.

In March 2009 Secretary General Abbas Ali Naqi, addressing the 20th OAPEC forum, held in Kuwait, on the basics of oil and gas economics, declared that Arab oil producers must diversify their sources of income to meet future economic challenges. In June 2009 OAPEC published a study, which concludes that the oil reserves in Arab countries are significantly higher than previously thought, although not all of this oil can be extracted by presently known techniques. OAPEC expected that its members would constitute the world's largest bloc of petrochemical producers, as distinct from producers of crude oil, by 2010.

ORGANIZATION OF EASTERN CARIBBEAN STATES (OECS)

Established: By treaty signed June 18, 1981, in Basseterre, St. Kitts, effective July 4, 1981.

Purpose: To increase cooperation among members in foreign relations; to harmonize economic, trade, and financial policies; and to coordinate defense and security arrangements, ultimately leading to a deepening of subregional integration.

Headquarters: Castries, St. Lucia.

Principal Organs: Authority of Heads of Government of the Member States, Secretariat.

Web site: www.oecs.org

Director General: Len Ishmael (St. Lucia).

Membership (7): Antigua and Barbuda, Dominica, Grenada, Montserrat, St. Kitts and Nevis, St. Lucia, St. Vincent and the Grenadines.

Associate Members (2): Anguilla, British Virgin Islands.

Official Language: English.

Origin and development. The seven full participants in the OECS were formerly members of the West Indies Associated States, a preindependence grouping established in 1966 to serve various common economic, judicial, and diplomatic needs of British Caribbean territories. The attainment of independence by four of the members—Dominica, Grenada, St. Lucia, and St. Vincent—during 1974–1979 and the impending independence of Antigua on November 1, 1981, gave impetus to the formation of a subregional body.

Meeting in 1979 in Castries, St. Lucia, the prospective members called for establishment of the OECS as a means of strengthening relations between the seven least-developed members of the Caribbean Community and Common Market (Caricom; see separate entry). Following nearly a year and a half of negotiations, an OECS treaty (the Treaty of Basseterre) was concluded and came into force July 4, 1981. A dispute over location of the new organization's headquarters was settled by agreement that its central secretariat would be located in Castries (administrative center of the former associated states), while its economic affairs secretariat would be located in St. John's, Antigua, where the Secretariat of the Eastern Caribbean Common Market (ECCM) was sited.

To further cooperation and integration in the Caribbean, the OECS established the Eastern Caribbean Central Bank (ECCB) on October 1, 1983, in accordance with its decision in July 1982 to upgrade the Eastern Caribbean Currency Authority. The major functions of the ECCB are administering the EC dollar and exchange control, making currency rate adjustments, regulating credit policies, fixing interest rates, and establishing reserve requirements for members' commercial banks.

Following the U.S.-led invasion of Grenada in October 1983 to overthrow a pro-communist government, a Regional Security System (RSS) was established in cooperation with the United States to ensure the political stability of the OECS members.

In the mid-1980s, at the urging of Prime Minister John Compton of St. Lucia, the OECS considered forming a political union to counter nationalism and promote integration. When serious differences among the member states prevented significant progress, the four Windward countries (Dominica, Grenada, St. Lucia, and St. Vincent) indicated they might proceed toward their own political union, which would be open to accession by the Leeward states if they so wished. In 1990 the Windward group set up a widely representative Regional Constituent Assembly (RCA), which in January 1992 approved a draft constitution. By then, however, domestic political concerns had dampened enthusiasm for the project, and the RCA's final recommendations were never presented to the national legislatures and electorates.

More recently, the OECS was involved in establishing the independent Eastern Caribbean Telecommunication Authority (ECTEL) in Castries, with members Dominica, Grenada, St. Kitts and Nevis, St. Lucia, and St. Vincent and the Grenadines. ECTEL was described at its opening in October 2000 as the world's first regional telecommunications regulatory body. A year later the OECS launched in St. Kitts the Eastern Caribbean Securities Exchange, the first regional securities market in the hemisphere.

Structure. Normally meeting in biennial summits, the Authority of Heads of Government of the Member States is the highest OECS policymaking organ. It is supported by the OECS Secretariat, which is headed by a director general and encompasses four divisions: functional cooperation, external relations, corporate services, and economic affairs. The functional cooperation division oversees several specialized units, including the Environment and Sustainable Development Unit (ESDU), the OECS Education Reform Unit (OERU), the Pharmaceutical Procurement Service, the Export Development Unit (EDU), the Social Development Unit (SDU), the Directorate of Civil Aviation (DCA), and the Sports Desk. The External Relations Division maintains missions in Ottawa, Canada, and Brussels, Belgium. In general, the Secretariat prepares reports, extends administrative and legal expertise, and provides supervision for the organization.

Activities. The ongoing failure of the OECS to carry out many of its decisions was addressed, not for the first time, at the heads of government meeting held in January 1998 in Castries. Prime Minister Kenny Anthony of St. Lucia warned his colleagues that the OECS's lack of resolution was the biggest threat to integration efforts. As an example, he pointed to the environmental levy on tourist arrivals that was approved by the OECS in December but delayed in most member states because of objections from cruise companies.

Attention at the OECS meeting in January 1999 focused on the trade dispute between the United States and the European Union (EU) over the latter's preferential treatment of banana growers in the Caribbean. The OECS leaders strongly protested the stance of Washington (which called for the World Trade Organization to impose sanctions on the EU in the matter), arguing that Caribbean farmers could not compete with the low wages paid by U.S.-owned firms in Central and South America without severely undermining the standard of living in their countries.

A report from the Organization for Economic Cooperation and Development (OECD) in June 2000 labeled all of the OECS members except Montserrat as "tax havens" and threatened to impose sanctions if steps were not taken to tighten regulation of their offshore financial industries. At the same time the independent Financial Action Task Force on Money Laundering (FATF) included Dominica, St. Kitts and Nevis, and St. Vincent on its list of "noncooperative" jurisdictions, to which Grenada was subsequently added. The accusations drew heated denials from several OECS governments, some asserting that they had a sovereign right to establish their own banking and financial policies without external interference. Nevertheless, by 2003 all had taken sufficient action to be removed from both lists.

A special meeting of the heads of government in Grenada in April 2001 reviewed the organization's mission, structure, and financing. Despite previous restructuring and streamlining, budgetary problems continued to plague the group, with participants therefore naming the Technical Committee on the Functioning and Financing of the OECS Secretariat to develop a strategy for resolving financial arrears and also to consider additional reconfiguration. The 34th OECS summit, held July 25–26, 2001, in Dominica, received the report of the technical committee, which recommended maintaining the existing secretariat structure, writing off some arrears, and adopting a two-year strategy for member states to remit the balance of their outstanding commitments. Looking toward the future, the authority directed the Secretariat and the ECCB to formulate a "stabilisation and revitalisation programme" for the regional economies, all of which faced an economic slowdown and severe fiscal constraints.

At the same time, summit participants moved forward on two major initiatives. First, the authority set a January 2002 date for instituting the free movement of nationals, including elimination of restrictions on work and residency permits, throughout the member states. A task force was established to work out the details of the plan, which had been discussed for more than a decade, and also to address adoption of a common passport and ID (eventually abandoned). Member governments signed free movement legislation by the middle of 2002. Second, the heads of government authorized another task force to work toward establishing an OECS economic union modeled on the EU.

In what proved to be a controversial move that drew criticism from several other regional governments, including those of Barbados and Trinidad and Tobago, the July 2001 session authorized a mission to Libya that was led in late August by the prime ministers of Dominica, Grenada, and St. Vincent and the Grenadines. Shortly thereafter, Libya pledged assistance in establishing a new development bank for developing countries and offered the OECS states additional financial aid, mostly as grants and soft loans.

A special heads of government meeting convened September 28, 2001, to review the economic impact of the September 11 terrorist attacks against the United States. The region's tourism industry, for one, was already being adversely affected.

Meeting on January 31–February 1, 2002, in The Valley, Anguilla, the heads of government endorsed the economic union concept. (At least initially, associate members Anguilla and the British Virgin Islands were not expected to participate.) The authority cited the need for a "single economic space" to compete in the era of globalization and trade liberalization. The union was seen as a way to promote economic diversification and growth; increase export competitiveness; expand employment opportunities; further human resource development; and speed up free movement of people, goods, services, and capital. The six independent states and Montserrat also indicated that from March 2002 they would permit passport-free intracommunity travel and six-month stays.

On October 10, 2002, a special heads of government session on the economy convened in St. Kitts and Nevis to address such pressing concerns as declining tourism, a drop in investment inflows and aid, reduced export earnings, and higher oil prices, all of which combined to slow GDP growth and increase both fiscal deficits and debt burdens. Tax reform, public sector reform, and improved debt management were identified as necessary steps to improve conditions.

The 38th heads of government meeting, held January 22–23, 2004, in Castries reactivated the Technical Committee on Economic Union to work out principles of governance, the shape of union institutions, and possible arrangements for Montserrat and the OECS associate members. The heads of government also concluded that, rather than revising the Treaty of Basseterre, the economic union might best be accomplished through drafting a new treaty. In other decisions, the heads of government called for development of a plan to revitalize agriculture and directed the Secretariat to seek aid for reversing environmental damage caused by banana cultivation in the Windward Islands. Other matters still on the OECS agenda, and related to the proposed economic union, included a common passport, a proposal for common citizenship, a unified tourism policy, and a customs union.

With regard to the proposed Free Trade Area of the Americas (FTAA), a report prepared by the United Nations (UN) Economic Commission for Latin America and the Caribbean had concluded that the FTAA would be of little advantage to the OECS members. Half their exports to the United States already enter on a duty-free basis, and many other products have benefited from the U.S. Caribbean Basin Initiative (CBI). According to the report, an FTAA could, however, have a negative impact on trade within the 15-member Caricom, in which all the OECS members participate.

The anticipated inauguration of Caricom's Single Market and Economy (CSME) provided a focus for the 41st OECS heads of government meeting, which was held June 16–17, 2005, in Roseau, Dominica. Many OECS businesses opposed the CSME, fearing the subregion's relative disadvantages versus the larger Caricom economies. At the same time, the authority continued to advance subregional integration, including the final drafting of the OECS Economic Union Treaty. On June 23, 2006, the seven OECS heads of government signed a declaration of intent to place the Economic Union Treaty before their countries' legislatures. At the same event, an OECS flag was unveiled.

In May 2007 Cuba announced that it would build medical diagnostic centers in St. Vincent and the Grenadines, Dominica, and Antigua and Barbuda as well as an eye care facility in St. Lucia. This announcement came during the May 2007 summit of OECS leaders in Georgetown, Grenada. In September 2007 trade experts met in Dominica to attempt to harmonize tariffs prior to the December 31 deadline for completing an Economic Partnership Agreement (EPA) with the EU, in conjunction with the rest of Caricom. The agreement was completed as scheduled.

In January 2008 Dominica signed on to the Venezuela-sponsored Bolivarian Alternative for the Americas (ALBA), an agreement designed to counter U.S. influence in the region. Regional integration ran into further trouble in 2008, as the proposal for the economic union stalled. In January a conference of OECS heads of government agreed to shelve the issue until the will of the OECS citizens could be determined. A mechanism and timeframe for this determination was expected to come out of a second meeting, held in St. Lucia on May 21, 2008. This meeting proved inconclusive, however, as the nonindependent OECS members were unwilling, or in some cases needed the consent of the colonial power, to sign on to the treaty's main provisions. An important aspect of the treaty was that some decisions of the OECS Authority would now be binding on member states, where previously decisions were purely a matter of consensus.

In August 2008, Trinidad and Tobago, and three OECS Member States, Grenada, St. Lucia and St. Vincent and the Grenadines reached an accord to pursue an Economic Union by 2011 and deeper political integration by 2013. In September the OECS issued a statement supporting this move. A task force, chaired by former St Lucia prime minister Professor Vaughn Lewis, was set up to consider the proposal's merits. At the 48th Meeting of the OECS Authority, held in Brades, Montserrat, on November 19–21, 2008, there were rumors that Venezuela was seeking membership in the OECS—rumors which the organization officially denied.

OECS leaders originally welcomed the April 2009, decision of the G-20 countries to inject relief money into financial institutions as a response to the world financial crisis, but by May 2009 some in the group were having second thoughts. Caribbean countries were among the world's most heavily indebted, and it did not seem clear how the G-20's action would benefit them.

On June 2, 2009, the Trinidad and Tobago task force recommended that that country should be allowed to join the OECS. The Trinidadian opposition party was however opposed to joining without a referendum, and worried, as did many observers, about a negative effect on Caricom. In June OECS agreed to allow Libya to establish a commercial bank in the region.

ORGANIZATION OF THE BLACK SEA ECONOMIC COOPERATION (BSEC)

Established: As the Black Sea Economic Cooperation by political declaration signed by representatives of 11 states June 24–25, 1992, in Istanbul, Turkey; formalized as the Organization of the Black Sea Economic Cooperation by legally binding charter signed June 5, 1998, in Yalta, Ukraine, effective May 1, 1999, following requisite ratifications.

Purpose: To promote bilateral and multilateral cooperation, particularly in economic matters.

Headquarters: Istanbul, Turkey.

Principal Organs: Council of Foreign Ministers, Committee of Senior Officials, Parliamentary Assembly, Permanent International Secretariat.

Web site: www.bsec-organization.org

Secretary General: Leonidas Chrysanthopoulos (Greece).

Membership (12): Albania, Armenia, Azerbaijan, Bulgaria, Georgia, Greece, Moldova, Romania, Russia, Serbia, Turkey, Ukraine.

Observer States (14): Austria, Belarus, Croatia, Czech Republic, Egypt, European Union, France, Germany, Israel, Italy, Poland, Slovakia, Tunisia, United States.

Origin and development. The formation of an economic grouping of the nations in the Black Sea region was first proposed in the late 1980s by President Turgut Özal of Turkey. After a series of preliminary meetings in 1990 and 1991, the foreign ministers or deputy foreign ministers of Armenia, Azerbaijan, Bulgaria, Georgia, Moldova, Romania, Russia, Turkey, and Ukraine initialed a declaration outlining the group's objectives in February 1992. The Declaration on Black Sea Economic Cooperation was signed by the heads of state or government of those nine countries plus Greece, which was involved in the earlier negotiations, and Albania during a June 24–25 summit in Istanbul, Turkey.

The Socialist Federal Republic of Yugoslavia (SFRY) also participated in the preliminary talks; however, following the breakup of the SFRY in 1991, its truncated successor, the Federal Republic of Yugoslavia (FRY), was not invited to participate in the BSEC's formal launching because of the other members' concerns over the fighting in Bosnia and Herzegovina. At a Council of Foreign Ministers meeting April 18, 2003, Serbia and Montenegro (the reconfigured FRY) and Macedonia were invited to join the BSEC, with Serbia and Montenegro then becoming a member April 16, 2004. After Montenegro and Serbia separated in June 2006, Serbia took the seat of the former union.

The BSEC Charter, signed at a summit held in Yalta, Ukraine, in June 1998, with effect from May 1, 1999, raised the grouping to official regional status. Although redesignated as the Organization of the Black Sea Economic Cooperation, the association retained the BSEC acronym.

Structure. The Summit of Heads of State and Government is the highest BSEC policy forum, although the principal decision-making body is the Council of Foreign Ministers, which convenes at least once per year, its chair rotating among members. The council's work is supported by a Committee of Senior Officials and more than a dozen working groups in such areas as agribusiness, combating crime, communications, energy, health care, and transport. There is also an advisory Parliamentary Assembly of the BSEC (PABSEC), which was formed in 1993 and includes a bureau, a standing committee, and three specialized committees. These committees deal with economic, commercial, technological and environmental affairs; legal and political affairs; and cultural, educational, and social affairs. The Permanent International Secretariat, based in Istanbul and headed by a secretary general, began operations in 1994. A Black Sea Trade and Development Bank in Thessaloniki, Greece, opened in 1999 with a primary purpose of funding regional projects. Other organs include a BSEC Coordination Center for economic and statistical information, located in Ankara, Turkey, and an International Center for Black Sea Studies in Athens, Greece. The BSEC business council serves as a forum for private sector input.

Activities. The framers of the BSEC's founding declaration were careful to stress the new organization's complementarity with the Conference on Security and Cooperation in Europe (CSCE, subsequently the Organization for Security and Cooperation in Europe—OSCE); the European Community (EC, subsequently the European Union—EU); and other regional economic initiatives. Therefore, "institutional flexibility" was endorsed while various working groups assessed the arrangements necessary to promote cooperation in such areas as transportation, communications, energy, tourism, and agriculture without impinging on existing structures.

It was clear, however, that rivalries within the organization (such as those between Greece and Turkey, Russia and Ukraine, and Armenia and Azerbaijan) represented significant barriers to effective BSEC activity. Significant intrabloc conflict continued through 1996 as Russia and Ukraine failed to settle their long-standing dispute over the former Soviet Black Sea fleet and the conflict in Nagorno-Karabakh remained a point of contention for Armenia and Azerbaijan. Another topic of discussion at the third BSEC summit, held October 25, 1996, in Moscow, was Moldova's demand that all Russian troops be removed from eastern Moldova.

The possibility of creating a free trade zone was the main focus of attention at the February 7, 1997, meeting of foreign ministers held in Istanbul, Turkey, where the then Turkish foreign minister Tansu Çiller expressed her desire for BSEC "integration into Europe." Free trade was also a focus at the June 1998 summit held in Yalta, Ukraine. The Black Sea states expressed their commitment to harmonizing and liberalizing trade regulations in conformance with World Trade Organization (WTO) rules and practices. The BSEC also announced its intention to improve its relations with other international organizations, particularly the EU. Some of these ideas were expressed in the BSEC charter, which was signed at the summit. The charter, which incorporated most of the existing structure of the organization, was ratified by all member states effective May 1, 1999.

The 1999 BSEC summit was held November 19 in Istanbul, immediately before an OSCE summit. The BSEC summit declaration noted a desire to move forward from project development to cooperative project implementation. Meeting April 27, 2001, in Moscow, the Council of Foreign Ministers adopted a BSEC Economic Agenda for the Future: Toward a More Consolidated, Effective, and Viable BSEC Partnership.

In addition to celebrating the organization's tenth anniversary, the June 25, 2002, summit in Istanbul welcomed adoption of the economic agenda and the concomitant decision to establish a voluntary Project Development Fund. In other business, the participants noted a need for further security and stabilization efforts in the region, condemned all forms of terrorism, and called on all BSEC organs and national authorities to implement a BSEC Agreement on Cooperation in Combating Crime. The summit also emphasized the importance of establishing with the EU a "tangible relationship" focused on cooperation and coordination.

The eighth meeting of the Council of Foreign Ministers, held April 27, 2001, in Yerevan, Armenia, appointed Secretary General Valeri Chechelashvili to a second three-year term and commented favorably on recent progress toward setting up the Project Development Fund. On July 14–15, three months after receipt of the first contribution—$30,000 from Greece—the fund's steering committee convened for the first time.

In June 2004 Secretary General Chechelashvili was named Georgia's ambassador to Russia; accordingly, the Council of Foreign Ministers, meeting in October, named Georgia's Tedo Japaridze as his successor. Russia's renewed exertion of its influence, felt also in many other spheres, was demonstrated in increasingly active participation in BSEC. In late 2004 Russia and Greece (a North Atlantic Treaty Organization [NATO] member) agreed to enhance their political dialogue in the context of BSEC and of other organizations of joint interest. At the Council of Foreign Ministers meeting held on April 22–23, 2005, in Komontini, Greece, with the theme "Bringing BSEC Closer to the EU," the Russian delegate emphasized the need for all BSEC members to join the WTO. Turkey did not attend the conference, but Greece pledged to improve relations with its historical adversary.

The BSEC has continued to work on several mostly economic and environmental issues. A meeting of the group's environment ministers March 3, 2006, in Bucharest, Romania, produced a declaration calling for increased efforts against pollution and a harmonization of laws to protect marine resources. At the April 26, 2006, meeting of foreign ministers, held in Bucharest, Leonidas Chrysanthopoulos, a Greek career diplomat, was elected secretary general of the organization. One of his first acts in this position was to visit Turkey.

On June 7, 2006, the BSEC announced plans to develop "a practical mechanism of cooperation in emergency situations," with Russia hosting the effort. Russia assumed the six-month presidency of the organization in the latter half of 2006, with determination to energize it and focus anew on economic projects. The meeting closed with renewed enthusiasm for building a ring road around the Black Sea.

At the 15th anniversary summit, held June 25, 2007, in Istanbul, the EU was granted observer status in the organization. Russian president Vladimir Putin declared that the BSEC was working well as a regional organization, and that there was no need to enlarge it. Putin also mentioned Russia's return to Balkan and Black Sea energy markets.

The short military confrontation in August 2008 between Russia and Georgia (both members of BSEC) caused consternation in the group. Turkey, concerned with separatist tendencies in its Kurdish population, was unwilling to see Georgia lose territory to its own ethnic minorities. Turkey proposed setting up a Caucasus Stability and Cooperation Platform, and Russia supported this. At the October 23–25 BSEC foreign ministers' meeting, held in Tirana, Albania, secretary general Chrysanthopoulos declared the August conflict to have been a successful test of the organization. BSEC must focus on economic cooperation and development, leaving political disputes between members for settlement elsewhere. (Among such disputes was that between Turkey and Armenia, countries that have a long history of ethnic hatred. Armenia declared that it was ready to normalize relations with Turkey, but negotiations dragged on fruitlessly into 2009.) Chrysanthopoulos reaffirmed that the Black Sea ring road was BSEC's top priority. The meeting adopted guidelines for making the organization more efficient. The November meeting of the Parliamentary Assembly, held in Chisinau, Moldova, decided to appoint a third deputy secretary general, this person to work on integration between BSEC and the EU.

The 20th meeting of the Council of Ministers, held in Yerevan on April 16, 2009, reappointed Chrysanthopoulos as Secretary General. The meeting considered further measures for cooperation with the EU, though the Russian representative warned that BSEC must not allow the EU to deal with it from a position of superiority. At the same meeting the Armenian foreign minister reiterated that responsibility for settling the Nagorno-Karabakh conflict belonged to the OSCE Minsk Group (see separate article) and nowhere else.

ORGANIZATION OF THE ISLAMIC CONFERENCE (OIC)

Established: By agreement of participants at the Conference of the Kings and Heads of State and Government held September 22–25, 1969, in Rabat, Morocco; charter signed at the Third Islamic Conference of Foreign Ministers, held February 29–March 4, 1972, in Jiddah, Saudi Arabia.

Purpose: To promote Islamic solidarity and further cooperation among member states in the economic, social, cultural, scientific, and political fields.

Headquarters: Jiddah, Saudi Arabia.

Principal Organs: Conference of Kings and Heads of State and Government (Summit Conference), Conference of Foreign Ministers, General Secretariat.

Web site: www.oic-oci.org

Secretary General: Ekmeleddin İhsanoğlu (Turkey).

Membership (57): Afghanistan, Albania, Algeria, Azerbaijan, Bahrain, Bangladesh, Benin, Brunei, Burkina Faso, Cameroon, Chad, Comoro Islands, Côte d'Ivoire, Djibouti, Egypt, Gabon, Gambia, Guinea, Guinea-Bissau, Guyana, Indonesia, Iran, Iraq, Jordan, Kazakhstan, Kuwait, Kyrgyzstan, Lebanon, Libya, Malaysia, Maldives, Mali, Mauritania, Morocco, Mozambique, Niger, Nigeria, Oman, Pakistan, Palestine, Qatar, Saudi Arabia, Senegal, Sierra Leone, Somalia, Sudan, Suriname, Syria, Tajikistan, Togo, Tunisia, Turkey, Turkmenistan, Uganda, United Arab Emirates, Uzbekistan, Yemen. Afghanistan's membership was suspended in January 1980, following the Soviet invasion, but in March 1989 the seat was given to the government-in-exile announced by Afghan guerrillas and subsequently to the Afghan government formed after the guerrilla victory. The advent of the Taliban regime in September 1996 in Kabul yielded competition for OIC recognition between it and the overthrown government, with both being refused formal admittance to the OIC foreign ministers' conference in December in Jakarta, although Afghanistan as such continued to be regarded as a member. Egypt's membership, suspended in May 1979, was restored in April 1984. Nigeria's government approved that nation's admission into the OIC in 1986, but the membership was formally repudiated in 1991 in the wake of intense Christian opposition; the OIC has not recognized the latter decision. Uncertainty also surrounds the status of Zanzibar, whose membership request had been approved in December 1992; eight months later it was announced that Zanzibar's application, which precipitated contentious legislative debate in Tanzania, was withdrawn pending the possible forwarding of a Tanzanian membership request.

Observers (10): Bosnia and Herzegovina, Central African Republic, Economic Cooperation Organization, League of Arab States, Moro National Liberation Front, Nonaligned Movement, Organization of African Unity, Thailand, Turkish Republic of Northern Cyprus, United Nations.

Official Languages: Arabic, English, French.

Origin and development. Although the idea of an organization for coordinating and consolidating the interests of Islamic states originated in 1969 and meetings of the conference were held throughout the 1970s, the Organization of the Islamic Conference (OIC) only began to achieve worldwide attention in the early 1980s. From a base of 30 members in 1969, the grouping has doubled in size, with the most recent member, Côte d'Ivoire, being admitted in 2001.

Structure. The body's main institution is the Conference of Foreign Ministers, although a summit of members' heads of state and government is held every three years. Sectoral ministerial conferences have also convened in such areas as information, tourism, health, and youth and sports.

Over the years many committees and departments have evolved to provide input on policy decisions and to carry out the OIC's executive and administrative functions. The organization's secretary general, who serves a four-year, once-renewable term, heads the General Secretariat and is aided by four assistant secretaries general—for science and technology; cultural, social, and information affairs; political affairs; and economic affairs—and a director of the cabinet, who helps administer various departments. The secretariat also maintains permanent observer missions to the United Nations (UN) in New York City, United States, and Geneva, Switzerland, and an Office for Afghanistan was recently established in Islamabad, Pakistan. Other OIC organs include the al-Quds (Jerusalem) Committee, the Six-Member Committee on Palestine, the Standing Committee for Information and Cultural Affairs (COMIAC), the Standing Committee for Economic and Trade Cooperation (COMCEC), the Standing Committee for Scientific and Technological Cooperation (COMSTECH), and various additional permanent and specialized committees. Recent ad hoc committees and groups have included an Ad Hoc Committee on Afghanistan and contact groups for Jammu and Kashmir, Sierra Leone, and Bosnia and Herzegovina and Kosovo.

To date, the OIC has established four "specialized institutions and organs," including the International Islamic News Agency (IINA, founded in 1972); the Islamic Development Bank (IDB, 1974); the Islamic States Broadcasting Organization (ISBO, 1975); and the Islamic Educational, Scientific, and Cultural Organization (IESSCO, 1982). Of the organization's eight "subsidiary organs," one of the more prominent is the Islamic Solidarity Fund (ISF, 1977). The founding conference of the Parliamentary Union of the OIC Member States was held in June 1999.

Activities. During the 1980s three lengthy conflicts dominated the OIC's agenda: the Soviet occupation of Afghanistan, which began in December 1979 and concluded with the final withdrawal of Soviet troops in February 1989; the Iran-Iraq war, which began in September 1980 and ended with the cease-fire of August 1988; and the ongoing Arab-Israeli conflict. At their August 1990 meeting, the foreign ministers described the Palestinian problem as the primary concern for the Islamic world. However, much of the planned agenda was disrupted by emergency private sessions concerning Iraq's invasion of Kuwait on August 2. Most attending the meeting approved a resolution condemning the incursion and demanding the withdrawal of Iraqi troops. In addition to other ongoing conflicts among conference members, the Gulf crisis contributed to the postponement of the heads of state summit that normally would have been held in 1990.

When the sixth summit was finally held December 9–11, 1991, in Dakar, Senegal, more than half of members' heads of state failed to attend. Substantial lingering rancor concerning the Gulf crisis was reported at the meeting, while black African representatives asserted that Arab nations were giving insufficient attention to the problems of sub-Saharan Muslims. On the whole, the summit was perceived as unproductive, with *Middle East International* going so far as to wonder if the conference would "fade from the international political scene" because of its failure to generate genuine "Islamic solidarity."

In the following three years much of the conference's attention focused on the plight of the Muslim community in Bosnia and Herzegovina. The group's foreign ministers repeatedly called on the UN to use force, if necessary, to stop Serbian attacks against Bosnian Muslims, but the conference stopped well short of approving creation of an Islamic force to intervene on its own, as reportedly proposed by Iran and several other members.

OIC efforts to improve the international image of Islam continued in 1995, in conjunction with ceremonies marking the organization's 25th anniversary. U.S. vice president Al Gore held talks with OIC secretary general Hamid Algabid in March in Jiddah, Saudi Arabia, receiving assurances of the OIC's "unwavering" support for international stability and offering in return a U.S. commitment to dialogue with the Islamic world in the interests of peace and mutual understanding. The desire for a greater Islamic role in resolving international disputes, expressed in an anniversary declaration issued in September, was also apparent in enhanced OIC participation in UN and other mediatory frameworks.

The renewed Palestinian intifada and the Israeli response to it provided a principal focus for OIC meetings in 2000. These included the June 27–30 Conference of Foreign Ministers in Kuala Lumpur, Malaysia, and the ninth summit November 12–13 in Doha, Qatar, which devoted its first day to discussing "the serious situation prevailing in the Palestinian occupied territories following the savage actions perpetrated by the Israeli forces." Representatives of Iraq, Sudan, and Syria insisted that waging jihad against Israel was required, while others urged political and economic retaliation.

An eighth extraordinary session of the foreign ministers met May 26, 2001, in the context of the continuing hostilities. Meeting June 25–29 in Bamako, Mali, the regular 28th Conference of Foreign Ministers reiterated a call for member countries to halt political contacts with the Israeli government, sever economic relations, and end "all forms of normalization." The concluding declaration of the session also urged resolution of a familiar list of other conflicts involving, among others, Afghanistan, Armenia and Azerbaijan, Cyprus, Jammu and Kashmir, Iraq, Kosovo, and Somalia. In other areas, the conference urged member states to ratify the Statute of the International Islamic Court of Justice, called for formation of an expert group that would begin drafting an Islamic Convention on Human Rights, condemned international terrorism, noted the progress made toward instituting an Islamic Program for the Development of Information and Communication (PIDIC), and cautioned that care must be taken to ensure that the economic benefits of globalization were shared and the adverse effects minimized.

Immediately after the September 11, 2001, terrorist attacks against the United States, the OIC secretary general, Abdelouahed Belkeziz, condemned the terrorist acts, as did an extraordinary Conference of Foreign Ministers session in Doha. The Doha session did not directly oppose the ongoing U.S.-led military campaign against al-Qaida and the Taliban regime in Afghanistan, although it did argue that no state should be targeted under the pretext of attacking terrorism. The session also rejected as counter to Islamic teachings and values any attempt to justify terrorism on religious grounds. Four months later, as part of an effort to foster intercultural dialogue, the OIC foreign ministers met in Istanbul with counterparts from the European Union (EU).

On April 1–3, 2002, a special OIC session on terrorism convened in Kuala Lumpur. In addition to establishing a 13-member committee to implement a plan of action against terrorism, the session issued a declaration that, among other things, condemned efforts to link terrorism and Islam and called for a global conference to define terrorism and establish internationally accepted procedures for combating it. Notably, however, the conference did not voice consensual support for a speech by Malaysian prime minister Mahathir bin Mohamad in which he described all attacks on civilians, including those by Palestinians and Sri Lanka's Tamil Tigers, as terrorist acts. The call for a UN-sponsored conference on terrorism was repeated by the Council of Foreign Ministers at its June session in Khartoum.

The impending U.S.-led war against the Saddam Hussein regime in Iraq generated a second extraordinary session of the Islamic Summit Conference on March 5, 2003, in Doha. The meeting included an exchange of personal insults by the Iraqi and Kuwaiti representatives and a warning from the secretary general that a U.S. military campaign would lead to occupation and foreign rule. Concern was also expressed that the Israeli government was taking advantage of the world's preoccupation with the Iraqi crisis to intensify its campaign against Palestinians. The session concluded with a call for the elimination of all weapons of mass destruction (WMD) from the Middle East.

The tenth OIC Summit Conference, which met October 16–18, 2003, in Putrajaya, Malaysia, featured an address by Prime Minister Mahathir that many Western countries condemned as anti-Semitic because of its stereotypical description of Jewish and Israeli intentions and tactics. The comments came in the context of Mahathir's argument that the Islamic world should focus on winning "hearts and minds" by abjuring violence and adopting new political and economic strategies. The summit concluded with issuance of the Putrajaya Declaration, which noted the "need to restructure and strengthen the Organisation on the basis of an objective review and evaluation of its role, structure, methodology, and decision-making processes, as well as its global partnerships." Included in the closing declaration's plan of action were provisions that called for drafting strategies to strengthen unity, especially at international forums; engaging in further dialogue with the West and international organizations; completing a review of the structure, methods, and needs of the secretariat; promoting the advancement of science and technology (particularly information and communication technology) among member states; and taking steps to encourage the expansion of trade and investment.

In response to subsequent international developments, the secretary general praised improved cooperation between Iran and the International Atomic Energy Agency; condemned the November 2003 terrorist attacks against synagogues in Istanbul and a housing complex in Riyadh, Saudi Arabia; and welcomed Libya's decision to end the development of WMD. On February 25, 2004, the OIC argued before the International Court of Justice in The Hague, Netherlands, that the security wall being constructed by Israel on Palestinian land was illegal.

The OIC subsequently continued to condemn acts of terrorism around the world, including the March 2004 bombings in Madrid, Spain; the attacks against London's transit system in July 2005; and the explosions at the Egyptian resorts of Sharm El-Shiekh and Naama Bay later the same month. With regard to developments in Iraq, in August 2005 the OIC urged "prudence and consensus" during deliberations on the draft Iraqi constitution. In particular, the OIC advocated a policy of inclusion, cautioning that the exclusion of any component of the population (implicitly, the Sunni minority) would ill serve "the creation of commonly desired conditions of democracy, stability, peace, and welfare in this important member of the OIC."

A third extraordinary session took place December 7–8, 2005, in Jiddah to address the violent worldwide Islamic outrage following publication in a Danish newspaper of cartoons critical of the Prophet Mohammad. The conference condemned violence, saying that Islam was in a crisis, and offered an ambitious ten-year plan to "revamp Islamic mindsets." Symbolic of this decision was the intention to reorganize the OIC itself and to build a new headquarters in Saudi Arabia. By mid-2006 a design competition for the new facility was under way.

The 33rd meeting of OIC foreign ministers, held June 19–22, 2006, in Baku, Azerbaijan, reinforced the message of moderation in the Islamic world. Specifically, it warned the two rival factions in Palestine from dragging that territory into civil war. Later events may have pushed the OIC some distance away from its traditionally moderate stance. In early August 2006 the OIC held a crisis meeting in Kuala Lumpur on the fighting between Hezbollah and Israel. It condemned Israel's attacks on civilians in Lebanon, calling for an immediate cease-fire, which was to be supervised by a UN force. Malaysia promised troops.

In 2007 the OIC was one of several bodies involved with the UN in efforts to resolve the Darfur crisis, but it was noted that the UN Human Rights Council (UNHRC) had been thwarted in its efforts to pass any resolution against Sudan by the OIC and various African countries since its opening session in June 2006. In May 2007 UN secretary general Ban Ki-moon praised the relationship between the OIC and the UN and promised closer cooperation in the future. In March 2007 Ekmeleddin İhsanoğlu, secretary general of the OIC, suggested its name and charter might be changed, possibly removing the word "conference" in favor of a term that did not suggest a one-time meeting. In June 2007 U.S. president George W. Bush announced that he would appoint an envoy to the OIC as a gesture of the United States' wish for peaceful and constructive involvement with the Islamic world. This step was much criticized in circles unfriendly to Islam. Iran also criticized it, saying the United States had no business being involved in Islamic councils.

In July 2007 OIC secretary general İhsanoğlu issued a statement rejecting an election in the secessionist Nagorno-Karabakh region of Azerbaijan, declaring that, "the OIC fully recognizes the sovereignty and territorial integrity of Azerbaijan." Azerbaijan, not surprisingly, went on record in February 2008 as opposing any recognition of Kosovo's independence. In late 2007 and early 2008 the OIC was active in negotiations toward a peace settlement between the Philippines government and two Islamic rebel groups.

The March 13–14, 2008, OIC summit, held in Dakar, Senegal, adopted a revised charter. The new charter was intended to render decision making within the organization more effective and the OIC more productive in promoting humanitarian efforts around the world. İhsanoğlu went on record as favoring the European Union (EU) as a model for any large multinational organization. He stated that a joint effort between the OIC and the West could bridge the gap between the Muslim and Western worlds. The new charter may have signaled a more activist line on the part of an organization once renowned for its moderate tone. This new tone was most evident in a free-speech resolution introduced with the OIC's backing at the UN in November 2008, declaring defamation of religion to be a violation of international law. The resolution was discussed at the April 2009 UN "Durban II" conference on racism, held in Geneva. The declaration, while in no way binding, appears to have received the support of a UN majority. Some observers have regarded it, rightly or wrongly, as a charter for the reverse of religious freedom.

In other matters, in July 2008 the OIC opened an office in Iraq. In September Kosovo appealed to the OIC for support for its declaration of full independence from Serbia. Few OIC countries supported independence however, and Iran announced that it would block Kosovo from joining the OIC. At U.S. president Barack Obama's inauguration the OIC delivered a message of congratulation, declaring that Muslim nations have good reasons to cooperate with the West. Later, secretary general İhsanoğlu stated that the organization looked forward to the U.S. acting as an honest broker in Middle East negotiations for peace. The OIC also reached out to Russia. In March İhsanoğlu traveled to Moscow to meet President Medvedev; where the secretary general told a meeting of Russian Islamic leaders that Russia and the Islamic world should not be at odds.

In April 2009 an OIC official indicated that the organization wanted to establish a peacekeeping force; no further details were available. In June at the UN, OIC member states opposed the UN establishing a Special Rapporteur to monitor laws that discriminate against women.

ORGANIZATION OF THE PETROLEUM EXPORTING COUNTRIES (OPEC)

Established: By resolutions adopted September 14, 1960, in Baghdad, Iraq, and codified in a statute approved by the Eighth (Extraordinary) OPEC Conference, held April 5–10, 1965, in Geneva, Switzerland.

Purpose: To coordinate and unify petroleum policies of member countries; to devise ways to ensure stabilization of international oil prices to eliminate "harmful and unnecessary" price and supply fluctuations.

Headquarters: Vienna, Austria.

Principal Organs: Conference, Board of Governors, Economic Commission, Secretariat.

Web site: www.opec.org/home

Secretary General: Abdalla Salem El-Badri (Libya).

Membership (12, with years of entry)**:** Algeria (1969), Angola (2007), Iran (1960), Iraq (1960), Kuwait (1960), Libya (1962), Nigeria (1971), Qatar (1961), Saudi Arabia (1960), United Arab Emirates (Abu Dhabi in 1967, with the membership being transferred to the UAE in 1974), Venezuela (1960). Ecuador and Gabon, who joined OPEC in 1973, withdrew January 1, 1993, and January 1, 1997, respectively. Ecuador rejoined in October 2007. Indonesia, which joined in 1962, withdrew at the end of 2008. Iraq currently does not participate in OPEC production quotas.

Official Language: English.

Origin and development. A need for concerted action by petroleum exporters was first broached in 1946 by Dr. Juan Pablo Pérez Alfonso of Venezuela. His initiative led to a series of contacts in the late 1940s between oil-producing countries, but it was not until 1959 that the first Arab Petroleum Conference was held. At that meeting Dr. Pérez Alfonso convinced the Arabs, along with Iranian and Venezuelan observers, to form a union of producing states, with OPEC being formally created by Iran, Iraq, Kuwait, Saudi Arabia, and Venezuela on September 14, 1960, during a conference in Baghdad, Iraq.

The rapid growth of energy needs in the advanced industrialized states throughout the 1960s and early 1970s provided OPEC with the basis for extracting ever-increasing oil prices. However, OPEC demands were not limited to favorable prices; members also sought the establishment of an infrastructure for future industrialization, including petrochemical plants, steel mills, aluminum plants, and other high-energy industries as a hedge against the anticipated exhaustion of their oil reserves in the 21st century.

The addition of new members and negotiations with petroleum companies on prices, production levels, and tax revenues dominated OPEC's early years, with prices remaining low and relatively stable. However, largely because of OPEC-mandated increases, prices soared dramatically from approximately $3 for a 42-gallon barrel in the early 1970s to a peak of nearly $40 per barrel by the end of the decade. Thereafter, a world glut of petroleum, brought on by overproduction, global recession, and the implementation of at least rudimentary energy conservation programs by many industrialized nations subsequently reversed that trend. The influence of formal OPEC price setting waned as the organization began to increasingly depend on negotiated production quotas to stabilize prices (see Activities, below).

Structure. The OPEC Conference, which normally meets twice per year, is the supreme authority of the organization. Comprising the oil ministers of the member states, the conference formulates policy, considers recommendations from the Board of Governors, and approves the budget. The board consists of governors nominated by the various member states and approved by the conference for two-year terms. In addition to submitting the annual budget, various reports, and recommendations to the conference, the board directs the organization's management, while the Secretariat performs executive functions. Operating within the Secretariat are a research division and departments for administration and human resources, data services, energy studies, petroleum market analysis, and public relations and information. In addition, the Economic Commission, established as a specialized body in 1964, works within the Secretariat's framework to promote equitable and stable international oil prices. The Ministerial Monitoring Committee was established in 1982 to evaluate oil market conditions and to make recommendations to the conference.

The OPEC Fund for International Development has made significant contributions to developing countries, mostly Arabian and African, in the form of balance-of-payments support; direct financing of imports; and project loans in such areas as energy, transportation, and food production. All current OPEC members plus Gabon are members of the fund. As of 2002 more than $5 billion in loans were approved for nearly 1,000 operations in the public sector and about $200 million for private sector operations. In addition, grants totaling $300 million were approved for more than 600 operations.

Activities. In December 1985, as spot market prices dropped to $24 a barrel and production dipped to as low as 16 million barrels per day, OPEC abandoned its formal price structure to secure a larger share of the world's oil market. By mid-1986, however, oil prices had dropped by 50 percent or more to their lowest levels since 1978, generating intense concern among OPEC members with limited oil reserves, large populations, extensive international debts, and severe shortages of foreign exchange. As a result, Saudi Arabia increased its output by 2 million barrels per day in January 1986 to force non-OPEC producers to cooperate with the cartel in stabilizing the world oil market.

The acceptance of production ceilings in June 1986 appeared to signify a reduction of conflict within OPEC. Iran, which previously insisted that any increase in Iraq's quota be matched by an increase in its own allocation, reversed its position. Saudi Arabia, while maintaining that the ceilings did not preclude OPEC's attainment of a fair market share, relaxed its insistence that quotas be completely overhauled and appeared to have realigned itself with Algeria, Iran, and Libya, all of whom had long supported an end to the price war. In response to the renewed cohesiveness of the organization, oil prices increased slightly.

Relative calm prevailed within the organization during the first half of 1987, with prices ranging from $18 to $21 per barrel. By midyear, however, overproduction by most members and a weakening of world oil demand began to push prices downward. At the end of June, OPEC had adjusted its quota down to 16.6 million barrels per day, but individual quotas were largely ignored. Production subsequently approached 20 million barrels per day later in the year. Consequently, Saudi Arabia warned its partners that if the "cheating" continued, it would no longer serve as the oil market's stabilizer by reducing its own production to support higher prices.

During their December meeting in Vienna, OPEC oil ministers attempted to reimpose discipline, but the talks became embroiled in political considerations stemming from the Iran-Iraq war. Iraq again refused to accept quotas lower than those of Iran, while Tehran accused Gulf Arab states of conspiring with Baghdad against Iranian interests. For their part, non-Arab states protested that war issues were inhibiting the adoption of sound economic policies. The meeting concluded with 12 members endorsing the $18-per-barrel fixed-price concept and agreeing to a 15-million-barrels-per-day production quota, Iraq's nonparticipation leaving it free to produce at will. However, widespread discounting quickly forced prices down to about $15 per barrel. Subsequently, in the wake of a report that OPEC's share of the oil market (66 percent in 1979) had fallen below 30 percent, an appeal was issued to nonmember states to assume a greater role in stabilizing prices and production.

Disarray continued at the June 1988 OPEC meeting at which ministers, unable to reach a new accord, formally extended the December 1987 agreement despite the widespread assessment that it had become virtually meaningless. Led by the United Arab Emirates (UAE), quota-breaking countries subsequently pushed members' production to an estimated high of 22–23 million barrels per day, with prices dropping below $12 per barrel. In the wake of the Gulf cease-fire, however, OPEC cohesion seemed to return. In their first unanimous action in two years, the members agreed in late November to limit production to 18.5 million barrels per day as of January 1, 1989, while maintaining a "target price" of $18 per barrel. Responding to the organization's apparent renewal of self-control, oil prices rose to nearly $20 per barrel by March 1989. However, contention broke out again at the June OPEC session, with Saudi Arabia resisting demands for sizable quota increases. Although a compromise agreement was concluded, Kuwait and the UAE immediately declared they would continue to exceed their quotas.

In November 1989 OPEC raised its official production ceiling from 20.5 to 22 million barrels per day, allowing Kuwait a quota increase from 1.2 to 1.5 million barrels per day. However, the UAE, whose official quota remained at 1.1 million barrels per day, did not participate in the accord and continued, as did Kuwait, to produce close to 2 million barrels per day. Pledges for restraint were again issued at an emergency meeting in May 1990, but adherence proved negligible. Consequently, in July Iraq's president Saddam Hussein, in what was perceived as a challenge to Saudi leadership within OPEC and part of a campaign to achieve dominance in the Arab world, threatened to use military intervention to enforce the national quotas. While the pronouncement drew criticism from the West, several OPEC leaders quietly voiced support for Hussein's "enforcer" stance and, mollified by the Iraqi leader's promise not to use military force to settle a border dispute with Kuwait, agreed on July 27 to Iraqi-led demands for new quotas. However, on August 29, in a dramatic reversal prompted by Iraq's invasion of Kuwait on August 2 and the ensuing embargo on oil exports from the two countries, the organization authorized producers to disregard quotas to avert possible shortages. OPEC's action legitimized a 2-million-barrels-per-day increase already implemented by Saudi Arabia and dampened Iraq's hope that oil shortages and skyrocketing prices would weaken the resolve of the coalition embargo. In December production reached its highest level in a decade, while prices fluctuated between $25 and $40 in response to the continuing crisis.

In early March 1991, following Iraq's defeat in the Gulf War, OPEC agreed to cut production from 23.4 to 22.3 million barrels per day for the second quarter of the year. The decision to maintain production at a level that would keep prices below the July 1990 goal was opposed by Algeria and Iran, who called for larger cuts. Observers attributed the agreement to Saudi Arabia's desire to assert its postwar "muscle" and to continue producing 2.5 million barrels per day over its prewar quota. In June OPEC rejected Iraq's request to intercede with the United Nations (UN) to lift the Iraqi oil embargo.

In September 1991 OPEC agreed to raise its collective production ceiling to 23.6 million barrels per day in preparation for normal seasonal increases in demand. However, Iran and Saudi Arabia remained in what analysts described as a "trial of strength" for OPEC dominance, the former lobbying for lowered production ceilings and higher prices and the latter resisting production curbs or any challenge to its market share. Thereafter, between October and January 1992, prices fell to $16.50 per barrel, $4.50 below the new OPEC target, as production rose to more than 24 million barrels per day and projected demand levels failed to materialize. Consequently, on February 15, 1992, OPEC members agreed to their first individual production quotas since August 1990, with the Saudis grudgingly accepting a 7.8-million-barrels-per-day quota. In April and May the organization extended the February quotas despite reports of overproduction, citing the firm, albeit lower than desired, price of $17 per barrel.

Prices remained low for the rest of 1992 as the global recession undercut demand and overproduction continued to plague OPEC; meanwhile, Kuwait attempted to recover from the economic catastrophe inflicted by the Gulf crisis by pumping oil "at will." With a relatively mild winter in the Northern Hemisphere having further reduced demand, a February 1993 emergency OPEC meeting sought to reestablish some sense of constraint by endorsing a 23.5-million-barrels-per-day limit on its members.

Actual levels continued at more than 25 million barrels per day, however, and a more realistic quota of 24.5 million barrels per day was negotiated in September 1993. The new arrangement permitted Kuwait's quota to rise from 1.6 million to 2.0 million barrels per day while Iran's quota grew from 3.3 million to 3.6 million. Meanwhile, Saudi Arabia agreed to keep its production at 8 million.

With prices still depressed, some OPEC members, particularly Iran, argued for substantial quota cuts in 1994, but once again resistance from Saudi Arabia precluded such action. Those favoring current levels appeared to expect that increased demand, and therefore higher prices, would result from economic recovery in much of the industrialized world.

The November 1994 conference also agreed to maintain the current quota of 24.5 million barrels per day for at least one more year. However, pressure for change grew in 1995, particularly as non-OPEC production continued to expand. Secretary General Lukman and oil ministers from several OPEC countries argued that non-OPEC nations' failure to curb production could lead to serious problems for all oil producers. One of the options that at least some OPEC members were expected to pursue was the temporary lifting of quotas, which would permit the organization to use its vast oil reserves to recapture a greater market share. (It was estimated that OPEC countries controlled more than 75 percent of the world's reserves while being responsible for only 40 percent of total oil production at that time.)

The announcement of Gabon's impending withdrawal from OPEC was made at the ministerial meeting, held June 5–7, 1996. Among the reasons cited for the decision were the high membership fee and constraints imposed by OPEC production quotas.

In late 1997 OPEC decided to increase production by 10 percent to 27.5 million barrels per day for the first half of 1998. However, the organization reversed course sharply when the price fell to $12.80 per barrel, a nine-year low, in March 1998. Saudi Arabia and Venezuela (joined by nonmember Mexico) immediately announced a reduction of 2 million barrels per day in their output. When prices failed to rebound, OPEC announced a further reduction of 1.3 million barrels per day in July. Additional cuts were considered in November, but consensus on the issue could not be reached. Overall, OPEC's revenues in 1998 fell some 35 percent from the previous year, raising questions about the organization's ability to control prices on its own. Saudi Arabia proposed creating a larger, albeit less formal, group of oil-producing countries (comprising OPEC and non-OPEC members) to address price stability.

Oil prices fell to less than $10 per barrel in February 1999, prompting an agreement in March under which OPEC cut production by 1.7 million barrels per day while Mexico, Norway, Oman, and Russia accepted a collective reduction of 400,000 barrels per day. Prices subsequently rebounded to more than $26 per barrel late in the year and more than $30 per barrel in early 2000. Consequently, from March to October 2000, OPEC increased production four times by a total of 3.4 million barrels per day before prices, which reached a high of $37.80 per barrel in September, fell in December to $26 per barrel, safely within the OPEC target range of $25–$28 per barrel.

The heads of state of the OPEC countries met for only their second summit in history (the first was in 1975) in Venezuela in September 2000 amid intensified concern over the impact of high oil prices on the global economy. Among other things, OPEC leaders criticized several European countries for imposing high taxes on oil products, thereby driving up consumer energy costs. The summit also reportedly agreed to extend OPEC's political profile, and in November Ali Rodríguez Araque, the energy and mines minister from Venezuela (considered one of the more "activist" OPEC members), was elected to succeed Secretary General Lukman effective January 2001.

Declining economic conditions in the first eight months of 2001 sharply reduced the demand for oil, and OPEC responded with production cuts in February, April, and September totaling 3.5 million barrels per day. Prices for the most part remained within the target range for that period. However, the September 11, 2001, terrorist attacks in the United States severely undercut demand, in part because of plummeting air travel, and prices fell below $17 per barrel by November. OPEC demanded that non-OPEC producers again assist in reducing production, and Russia reluctantly agreed to cut its production by 150,000 barrels per day beginning in January 2002, in conjunction with an additional OPEC cut of 1.5 million barrels per day.

Prices rose to nearly $30 per barrel in fall 2002, despite evidence that many OPEC countries were producing above the quotas established in late 2001. OPEC leaders argued that prices were artificially inflated because of fears over a possible U.S. invasion of Iraq and concern emanating from other Middle East tensions. In December OPEC established a quota of 23 million barrels per day, formally an increase over 2001 levels, but in reality a decrease considering the year-long "cheating" by some members.

To address the potential for disturbances in the global oil market from the strikes by oil workers in Venezuela, OPEC agreed in January 2003 to raise the quota to 24.5 million barrels per day. However, by April discussion turned to what was viewed as an "unavoidable" production cut. Complicating factors included the potential for the full return of Iraqi oil to world markets following the toppling of the Saddam Hussein regime. In that regard, Iraq sent a delegation to OPEC's September session, at which quotas were cut by 900,000 barrels per day.

Despite rising prices, OPEC declined to increase production in January 2004 and, citing the upcoming seasonal dip in demand, reduced quotas again in February. Consequently, the United States warned OPEC that the cuts might harm an already fragile global economy. By March oil prices peaked at $37.45 per barrel, and some non-OPEC countries (such as Mexico) snubbed OPEC's request for production constraint.

Terror attacks on the oil infrastructures in Iraq and Saudi Arabia contributed to continued price increases in mid-2004, finally prompting OPEC to expand its production quotas. Nevertheless, "spare" oil capacity remained at its thinnest in decades. The Group of Eight issued a stern warning about the effects of rising oil prices, which reached a 21-year high in July of more than $43 per barrel. By October the price topped out at more than $55 per barrel; it then declined by 23 percent by the end of the year.

In December 2004 OPEC announced a production cut to stem the slide in oil prices. Meanwhile, it was estimated that OPEC members were enjoying their highest oil revenue ever in nominal terms. OPEC informally relaxed quota compliance in March 2005, and prices hovered at about $50 per barrel. However, the International Monetary Fund and the United States called for significant additional OPEC production increases to, among other things, provide a more substantial cushion against unforeseen oil shocks. OPEC agreed to that request in June, but the per-barrel price subsequently grew to almost $60.

In 2005 and 2006 the world's demand for oil seemed finally to be straining the producing countries' ability to supply, with some saying this was the long-predicted first sign that the world was running out of oil. Rapid economic growth in China, and to a lesser extent in India, was also said to be a factor. Tensions between the United States and Iran pushed prices to more than $75 per barrel for periods in May and June of 2006. In this environment Venezuela's president Hugo Chavez was able to call for the use of oil as a political lever against the developed world and to ask for Ecuador and Bolivia (both of which hold strong reserves) to be invited into the cartel. In December 2005 an OPEC delegation visited China, hoping to gain a better understanding of that country's energy needs.

In a meeting ending June 1, 2006, in Caracas, OPEC voted to keep its production level constant at 28 million barrels per day. Venezuela argued for a cut, while Saudi Arabia said high prices had begun to reduce demand, leaving oil markets "oversupplied and overpriced." Financial and political conditions remained disturbed through 2006 and 2007. The U.S. dollar, the currency in which OPEC trades, remained weak, with little sign of recovery, and China and India's appetite for oil and bilateral purchase arrangements increased. In March 2007 Angola joined OPEC—a move calculated to boost that country's international standing, but a disappointment to Western countries that had hoped to keep Angola's oil reserves outside the OPEC cartel. The phenomenon sometimes called resource nationalism—the use by poor countries of their natural resources to enhance their political standing in the world—increased, with Venezuela and Iran leading the way. Ecuador indicated that it wanted to rejoin OPEC, and did so in October 2007. In May 2007 Ecuador and Venezuela agreed to an exchange of Ecuadorian crude oil for Venezuelan refined product. As oil prices continued to rise and the use of biofuels and other alternative sources of energy became more economically feasible, OPEC's Secretary General Abdalla Salem El-Badri warned in June 2007 that serious investment in biofuels could "push oil prices through the roof." Such a development would cause OPEC members to consider cutting investment in new oil production, he said. At a meeting on September 11, 2007, OPEC agreed to raise production by 500,000 barrels a day. Later that month Canada, which is the world's seventh-largest oil producer and the subject of much discussion in the energy market, declared that it had no plans to join OPEC.

In May 2008 Indonesia announced that it would withdraw from OPEC by the end of the year because the country had become a net importer of oil.

OPEC held its third summit meeting November 17–18, 2007, in Riyadh, Saudi Arabia, with oil prices continuing to rise and a general expectation that the organization would not raise production quotas. At the meeting Iranian president Mahmoud Ahmadinejad suggested that the organization no longer trade in U.S. dollars, but Saudi Arabia opposed this option. In December 2007 Secretary General El-Badri said that trading in dollars should continue, despite the fall in the currency's value. At both its December 2007 and March 2008 extraordinary meetings, OPEC declined to raise production quotas. In January 2008 the price of crude oil reached $100 per barrel, and by June 2008 approached $140. This caused the price of gasoline to rise to more than $4 per gallon in the United States, with corresponding increases elsewhere in the world's developed economies. Many observers began to feel that OPEC was not in control of world oil prices, with commodity speculation and international instability overriding the basic considerations of supply and demand. In the United States, at least, it seemed that $4 per gallon was the point at which drivers began changing their habits, and demand for oil eased by 800,000 barrels per day in the first half of 2008. Crude oil prices declined, and were approaching $100 by September 2008. The worldwide economic crisis of late 2008 caused the price of crude oil to fall precipitously, reaching around $50 per barrel by early December. An October 24 OPEC production cut of 1.5 million barrels per day had no effect on the decline. A meeting in December 17, 2008, produced an agreement to cut production by 2.2 million barrels a day—the largest cut in OPEC history. The group encouraged non-OPEC oil producers to follow the group's lead. OPEC had been said to be aiming for a price near $75 per barrel; in the event the price stabilized around $40 per barrel, then gradually rose to around $70 per barrel by late 2009.

Late 2008 was also marked by Russia increasing its cooperation with OPEC, with that country speaking of joining the cartel in cutting production. There were rumors that Russia might actually join the organization. Russia attended OPEC's March 2009 meeting with a proposal for closer cooperation—in fact for setting up a Russian liaison office at OPEC headquarters—but declined, for the time being, an invitation to become a full member. In September Russia reiterated its desire to cooperate.

In April 2009 Brazil announced that it was again considering an invitation to join OPEC. Previously Brazil had concentrated on exporting refined, rather than crude, oil products. The September 9, 2009, OPEC meeting saw the group agreeing to maintain current production levels, with the price of oil slowly rising as the world economy appearing to come out of the worst of the recession.

PACIFIC COMMUNITY

Communauté du Pacifique

Established: As the South Pacific Commission by agreement signed February 6, 1947, in Canberra, Australia, effective July 29, 1948; structure modified by amending agreements signed on October 6, 1964, in London, United Kingdom, and in Nouméa, New Caledonia, on October 12, 1978; current name adopted effective February 8, 1998.

Purpose: "[T]o provide a common forum within which the Island peoples and their governments can express themselves on issues, problems, needs and ideas common to the region; . . . to assist in meeting the basic needs of the peoples of the region; . . . to serve as a catalyst for the development of regional resources . . . ; to act as a center for collection and dissemination of information on the needs of the region."

Headquarters: Nouméa, New Caledonia.

Principal Organs: Conference of the Pacific Community, Committee of Representatives of Governments and Administrations, Secretariat of the Pacific Community.

Web site: www.spc.int

Director General: Jimmie Rodgers (Solomon Islands).

Members (26): American Samoa, Australia, Cook Islands, Fiji, France, French Polynesia, Guam, Kiribati, Marshall Islands, Federated States of Micronesia, Nauru, New Caledonia, New Zealand, Niue, Northern Mariana Islands, Palau, Papua New Guinea, Pitcairn Islands, Samoa, Solomon Islands, Tokelau, Tonga, Tuvalu, United States, Vanuatu, Wallis and Futuna Islands. (The United Kingdom withdrew effective January 1, 1996, although it retained a minor affiliation with the South Pacific Commission via the membership of the Pitcairn Islands. It rejoined in 1998 and withdrew again in 2005.)

Official Languages: English, French.

Origin and development. The South Pacific Commission (SPC) was organized in 1947–1948 to coordinate the economic and social development policies of states administering dependent South Pacific territories. The original members were Australia, France, the Netherlands, New Zealand, the United Kingdom, and the United States. In 1951 the founding Canberra Agreement was amended to include within the organization's geographic scope U.S. dependency Guam and the U.S.-administered Trust Territory of the Pacific Islands, north of the equator. The Netherlands withdrew in 1962 when it ceased to administer the former colony of Dutch New Guinea, which was incorporated into Indonesia as Irian Jaya (West New Guinea).

In 1962 Western Samoa (now simply Samoa), a New Zealand dependency, became the first Pacific territory to achieve independence, and two years later the SPC approved an amending agreement that allowed the admission of newly independent states as full members. Accordingly, Western Samoa joined in 1965, followed by Nauru (1969), Fiji (1971), Papua New Guinea (1975), and Solomon Islands and Tuvalu (1978).

Collateral with this period of initial expansion, participants in the original South Pacific Conference, which was composed exclusively of dependent territories, called into question the SPC's retention of elements of its earlier tutelary character. Thus the conference members proposed in 1973 that joint sessions of the commission and conference be held. Under a 1974 memorandum of understanding, the commission and conference began meeting once per year in a joint session known as the South Pacific Conference. Two years later another memorandum of understanding revised SPC voting procedures. From 1964 each participating government was entitled to one vote for itself and one for each territory it administered. The 1976 change put all members on an equal footing, with one vote each in decision-making bodies.

In 1978 the SPC approved an additional amending agreement, which entered into force in 1980 and opened full membership to regional territories "in free association with a fully independent Government." Thus, the New Zealand dependencies Cook Islands and Niue joined in 1980. The 14 other current members (several of which were already independent) joined en masse in 1983.

Vanuatu, the Marshall Islands, and Papua New Guinea were absent from the 1987 commission session, with Papuan officials reportedly urging that the SPC be "scrapped" because of its "colonial" nature. Although the dissidents participated in the 1988 conference, they continued to press the SPC to accept merger overtures from the South Pacific Forum (SPF, now the Pacific Islands Forum), which was formed in 1971 to discuss areas outside the SPC mandate, especially political affairs. Collaterally, a decision on whether the SPC would join the South Pacific Organizations Coordinating Committee (SPOCC, now the Council of Regional Organizations in the Pacific—CROP), recently created by the SPF, was postponed. By the time of the October 1989 conference, however, it was apparent that agitation for abolition of the SPC in favor of an SPF-led single regional organization had largely disappeared.

Following the inclusion of Micronesian territories (all located north of the equator) to commission membership in the 1980s, it was suggested that the designations "South Pacific Commission" and "South Pacific Conference" were outdated, but the organization did not resolve to change its name until 1996. The October 1997 SPC session agreed to the designation "Pacific Community," after extended debate over several alternatives. The name change was formally adopted February 6, 1998.

Norfolk Island, a member of the original South Pacific Conference, has not been admitted to the Pacific Community because of Canberra's insistence that the territory is an integral part of Australia and therefore ineligible.

Structure. The Conference of the Pacific Community (successor to the South Pacific Conference) is the organization's governing body, with authority to appoint the director general, make broad policy decisions, and review the work of the Committee of Representatives of Governments and Administrations (CRGA). At its annual sessions the CRGA evaluates current programs, examines and approves the draft work program and budget for the coming year, selects topics for conference discussion, nominates the organization's principal officers, and reports to the conference on its work. The Secretariat of the Pacific Community (SPC, which deliberately retained the acronym of the South Pacific Commission) is based in Nouméa, New Caledonia, but also has a regional office in Suva, Fiji. Reporting to the secretariat's director general are the planning unit, corporate services, and three divisions: land resources (agriculture and forestry); marine resources;

and social resources (community education and training, cultural affairs, demography, energy, health, information and communication, statistics, women's resources, and youth resources).

Activities. At the 16th conference in 1976, members adopted a review committee recommendation that the SPC engage in the following specific activities: rural development; youth and community development; ad hoc expert consultancies; cultural exchanges in arts, sports, and education; training facilitation; and assessment and development of marine resources and research. In addition, special consideration was to be given to projects intended to meet pressing regional or subregional needs or the expressed needs of the smaller Pacific countries.

The environment dominated the 1990 conference, which endorsed expansion of the South Pacific Regional Environment Programme (SPREP) and agreed that it should evolve into an autonomous, financially independent organization. (Formed in 1982 by the SPC, the SPF, and several United Nations agencies, the SPREP became autonomous in 1995.) The 1990 conference also called for further strengthening of SPOCC in the hope of eliminating the duplication of services in the region.

At the 34th conference, held October 24–25, 1994, in Port Vila, Vanuatu, it was reported that Canada, Chile (because of its Easter Island territory), and South Korea were being considered as prospective new SPC members. In addition, broader cooperation links were proposed with other regional organizations, such as the Association of Southeast Asian Nations (ASEAN). However, progress on those fronts was impeded by subsequent SPC internal problems, most notably the United Kingdom's withdrawal as of January 1, 1996, and announced retrenchment on the part of other major donors who were frustrated by what they perceived as general inefficiency, waste, and lack of accountability within the SPC. At the 35th SPC conference, held in October 1995, in Nouméa, New Caledonia, Bob Dun of Australia was elected as the new SPC secretary general. At the fall 1996 conference, held in Saipan, Northern Marianas, the membership endorsed administrative staff cuts, procedural reforms, and consolidation of programs. It also gave the CRGA expanded authority for administrative and program budgets and for evaluating the performance of the director general (as the secretary general's post was to be renamed). In addition, the conference was to become a biennial rather than an annual event beginning in 1999, with the CRGA to convene annually instead of every six months.

At the May 1997 CRGA meeting a new structure for contributors was adopted and a Small Islands Fund was created to assist the 12 smallest Pacific states and territories. At the October 20–21, 1997, conference in Canberra, Australia, the SPC agreed to change its name to the Pacific Community effective February 6, 1998. The United Kingdom announced its decision to rejoin the organization.

Convening December 6–7, 1999, in Papeete, Tahiti, in its first biennial meeting, the Conference of the Pacific Community elected Lourdes Pangelinan of Guam as the organization's new director general. As the first woman to head a Pacific regional organization, Pangelinan indicated that among her priorities would be continued decentralization, including efforts to base new projects in locations other than Nouméa and Suva; gender equality throughout the organization; aquaculture research and development; and further steps toward rationalization of regional organizations. The session concluded by issuing the Declaration of Tahiti Nui, which updated the organization's guiding policies and procedures.

The second biennial Conference of the Pacific Community, held November 19–20, 2001, convened at the organization's Nouméa headquarters. The thematic focus of the conference was "Adapting to Global Changes," including globalization, trade issues, and the HIV/AIDS epidemic.

The spread of HIV and the potential dangers of severe acute respiratory syndrome (SARS) were among the topics addressed at the November 10–11, 2003, third biennial conference, held in Lami, Fiji, under the theme "The Pacific Response to Infectious Diseases." France and New Zealand announced they would sponsor a new program of regional disease surveillance and networking, while France and Australia committed additional funds to combat HIV and other sexually transmitted diseases. The SPC also joined the World Health Organization (WHO) in fighting such diseases as AIDS, malaria, and tuberculosis.

The fourth biennial conference was held November 18, 2005, in Koror, Palau. It discussed or adopted reports on several topics, including HIV/AIDS, response to a possible influenza pandemic, tuna fisheries, and deep-sea trawling. The meeting also took note of the Pacific Plan, developed under the auspices of the Pacific Islands Forum (see separate article). This comprehensive plan for integration of many aspects of Pacific nations' lives, while created outside the Pacific Community, seemed to be something in which the community might well want to be involved.

In July 2006 the secretariat announced a preliminary Pacific Youth Strategy 2010 for the region. This was amid a perception that issues associated with youth alienation and unemployment and the spread of HIV/AIDS were the region's chief long-term problems. In November 2006 the secretariat announced a Human Development Program that comprised a reorganization of many of the community's functions. In March 2007 the community established a task force to deal with avian and pandemic influenza, and in June 2007 the organization celebrated its 60th anniversary.

Globalization, deforestation, and the migration of marginalized people to the cities were the concerns of the Pacific Community in 2007 and 2008. In November 2007 a Samoan representative complained that the Pacific Community staff of 360 should consist of more than 45 percent Pacific islanders. At the 60th anniversary conference, held November 12–13 in Apia, Samoa, discussion ranged across a variety of topics, including the need to manage and preserve fish stocks as well as the dangers of deforestation and unmanaged urbanization on Pacific islands. In 2008 a large-scale program was established to tag and monitor tuna, with a view to better understanding their migration and life-cycle patterns. The community also set up, in November 2007, a course in forest management.

In July 2008 the Pacific Regional Rights Resource Team (RRRT), a hitherto independent body, joined the SPC. In August 2008 the One Laptop per Child program gave laptops to every schoolchild in Niue, the first Pacific Community country to receive them. The October 2008 CRGA presented the organization's efforts to streamline and improve its services. The Director General's report noted the failure to come to a complete understanding with the EU about funding as the reason for EU funding dropping from 19 percent to about 7.9 percent for 2009. The organization held talks with the representative of the Fiji regime about maintaining a tax exemption for Fiji nationals who work for the SPC in Suva. In October also the SPC and the World Health Organization (WHO) signed a four-year memorandum of understanding, designed to improve health outcomes in member countries.

In February 2009 the SPC promoted a campaign to encourage reliance on locally produced food. The rice shortage of 2008 was the impetus for this initiative. But in August 2009 the New Zealand foreign minister declared that the Pacific Community was generally achieving little progress on increasing local food production, especially considering the amount of money that donor countries and organizations were contributing.

PACIFIC ISLANDS FORUM

Established: As the South Pacific Forum by a subgroup of the South Pacific Commission meeting August 5, 1971, in Wellington, New Zealand; current name adopted October 3–5, 1999, effective October 2000.

Purpose: To facilitate cooperation among member states, to coordinate their views on political issues of concern to the subregion, and to accelerate member states' rates of economic development.

Headquarters: Suva, Fiji.

Principal Organs: Forum, Pacific Islands Forum Secretariat.

Web site: www.forumsec.org

Secretary General of Forum Secretariat: Tuiloma Neroni Slade (Samoa).

Membership (16): Australia, Cook Islands, Fiji, Kiribati, Marshall Islands, Federated States of Micronesia, Nauru, New Zealand, Niue, Palau, Papua New Guinea, Samoa, Solomon Islands, Tonga, Tuvalu, Vanuatu.

Observers (2): New Caledonia, Timor-Leste.

Official Language: English.

Origin and development. Since the South Pacific Commission (SPC, now the Pacific Community) was barred from concerning itself with political affairs, representatives of several South Pacific governments and territories decided in 1971 to set up a separate organization, the South Pacific Forum (SPF), in which they might speak with a common voice on a wider range of issues. At a meeting of the forum in April 1973, representatives of Australia, Cook Islands, Fiji, Nauru, New Zealand, Tonga, and Western Samoa signed the Apia Agreement, which established the South Pacific Bureau for Economic Cooperation as a technical subcommittee of the committee of the whole. The Gilbert Islands (now Kiribati), Niue, Papua New Guinea, Solomon Islands, Tuvalu, and Vanuatu subsequently acceded to the agreement. In 1975 the bureau was asked to serve as secretariat, although it was not reorganized and renamed the Forum Secretariat until 1988.

The Marshall Islands and the Federated States of Micronesia, formerly observers, were granted membership in 1987 after Washington, in late 1986, declared their compacts of free association with the United States to be in effect. Palau, formerly an SPF observer, became a full member in 1995 following resolution of its compact status.

The SPF-sponsored South Pacific Regional Trade and Cooperation Agreement (SPARTECA), providing for progressively less restricted access to the markets of Australia and New Zealand, came into effect in 1981. The process culminated in 1985 with approval by Canberra and Wellington of the elimination of all duties for most products from other SPF members.

Following a decision at the 15th annual SPF meeting, the delegates to the 16th annual meeting in 1985 concluded the Treaty of Rarotonga (Cook Islands), which established the South Pacific Nuclear-Free Zone (SPNFZ). The treaty forbids manufacturing, testing, storing, dumping, and using nuclear weapons and materials in the region. It does, however, allow each country to make its own defense arrangements, including deciding whether or not to host nuclear warships. The treaty became operative in December 1986 when Australia became the eighth SPF member to tender its ratification. Those countries known to possess nuclear weapons were asked to sign the treaty's three protocols, the SPF having added an "opt-out" provision that would permit adherents to withdraw if they believed their national interests were at stake. The Soviet Union and China both ratified the protocols in 1988. France, the United Kingdom, and the United States, after years of declining to support the treaty, signed the protocols March 25, 1996. France, the object of intense SPF criticism for its nuclear tests in the region in late 1995 and early 1996, ratified the SPNFZ on September 20, 1996, as did the United Kingdom on September 19, 1997. Washington has yet to ratify the treaty as of 2008.

To break a long-standing impasse on the proposed merger of the economic and technical functions of the SPF with the SPC, in 1988 the SPF created the South Pacific Organizations Coordinating Committee (SPOCC; renamed in 1999 as the Council of Regional Organizations in the Pacific—CROP). The SPF envisioned SPOCC as a loose-knit regional "umbrella" that would be able to reduce program duplication without the complications stemming from a single regional organization.

In January 1992 five of the smallest SPF members (Cook Islands, Kiribati, Nauru, Niue, and Tuvalu) formed the Small Island States (SIS) to address mutual concerns such as fishing rights, global warming, and airspace issues. The SIS members also began to explore the possible creation of their own development bank. The Marshall Islands became the sixth SIS member in 1997.

Meeting October 3–5, 1999, in Koror, Palau, the SPF decided to restyle itself as the Pacific Islands Forum, following a one-year transition period. At the 31st forum session, held October 27–30, 2000, in Tarawa, Kiribati, the renamed organization approved (with immediate effect) and opened for ratification the new Agreement Establishing the Pacific Island Forum Secretariat.

Structure. The Pacific Islands Forum has no constitution or codified rules of procedure. Decisions are reached at all levels by consensus.

The forum meets annually at the heads of government (summit) level but also convenes at other times on a ministerial basis to discuss particular concerns and prepare proposals for summit action. In recent years meetings have been held, for example, by the member states' ministers of foreign affairs, economy, education, trade, aviation, and communication. In addition, since 1989 forum summits have been followed by post-forum dialogue meetings, which constitute the organization's "highest level forum for multilateral consultations." As of mid-2008 there were 12 dialogue partners; Canada, China, the European Union (EU), France, Indonesia, Japan, Republic of Korea, Malaysia, Philippines, Thailand, United Kingdom, and United States. In 2008 Italy's application to become a dialogue partner was pending, but in the meantime it was planning a conference with forum countries for late that year. Taiwan applied for dialogue status in the early 1990s, but the forum sidestepped the issue by permitting individual members to establish the requested dialogue relationship without formal SPF involvement.

The Pacific Islands Forum Secretariat, headed by a secretary general, reports to the Forum Officials Committee, which includes representatives from all 16 member countries. The secretariat encompasses four divisions—corporate services; development and economic policy; political, international, and legal affairs; and trade and investment. Affiliated organizations include the Association of South Pacific Airlines (ASPA); the Pacific Forum Line, a shipping agency formed by ten SPF members in 1977; the Forum Fisheries Agency (FFA); the South Pacific Trade Commission, with offices in Auckland, New Zealand, and Sydney, Australia; the South Pacific Tourism Council; and the South Pacific Applied Geoscience Commission (SOPAC). In addition, the forum's secretary general chairs the eight-member Council of Regional Organizations in the Pacific (CROP), which includes the Secretariat of the Pacific Community and the South Pacific Regional Environment Programme (SPREP) among its participants.

Activities. During the first half of the 1990s, environmental concerns became an increasingly important focus for the forum. Among other things, it called for the abolition of drift-net fishing; argued that global warming could cause sea levels to rise and inundate such low-lying countries as Kiribati and Tuvalu; objected to the planned incineration of chemical weapons on Johnston Atoll, an unincorporated territory about 700 miles southwest of Hawaii controlled by the U.S. military since 1934; and announced in 1994 an attempt to negotiate regionwide logging and fishing agreements that would sharply curtail access and protect fragile ecosystems while providing for sustainable development.

The major concern for the SPF in 1995 was France's resumption of nuclear testing at Mururoa Atoll in French Polynesia. Soon after new French president Jacques Chirac announced in June that up to eight tests would be conducted, a special forum delegation was dispatched to Paris to protest the decision. Following the first detonation on September 5, the SPF, meeting September 10–11 in regular session in Madang, Papua New Guinea, expressed its "extreme outrage" at the situation, and on October 3 the SPF suspended France from its list of dialogue partners. In other activity at the 1995 summit, the SPF endorsed a draft logging code, although to the consternation of the measure's proponents, individual members were permitted to decide if they would implement the new regulations.

Partly in response to the intense international criticism France was receiving regarding the issue, President Chirac in January 1996 announced the "permanent end" of French nuclear testing, some three months and two explosions prior to completion of the schedule originally planned for the South Pacific series. Two months later France joined the United Kingdom and United States in signing the SPNFZ, and at the forum summit held September 3–5, in Majuro, Marshall Islands, France was readmitted as an active SPF dialogue partner.

The environment continued to be the dominant topic at the September 17–19, 1997, summit in Rarotonga, Cook Islands. Australia sparked intense debate when it insisted it would not support legally binding targets for the reduction of greenhouse gas emissions and proposed instead that reduction goals be pegged to the costs involved. Many of the other SPF members strongly criticized Australia's position, given the threat to small island states posed by global warming.

The tone was less confrontational at the August 24–25, 1998, summit, which was held in the Federated States of Micronesia. The SPF endorsed establishing a South Pacific whale sanctuary (a proposal that is repeatedly rejected by the International Whaling Commission), criticized India and Pakistan for testing nuclear devices, granted New Caledonia observer status for the next summit, and called on its members to ratify the Kyoto Protocol on climate change.

The 30th SPF summit was held October 3–5, 1999, in Koror and endorsed the concept of a Pacific free trade area (FTA) that, it was hoped might eventually include Australia and New Zealand. (In 1993 the Melanesian Spearhead Group of Papua New Guinea, Solomon Islands, and Vanuatu introduced their own FTA, which Fiji later joined.) As envisaged, free trade would be introduced in stages over the next decade, with the six SIS countries and other least-developed countries (LDCs) joining a bit later. In a related matter, the forum agreed to authorize a forum island trade officials group to work in conjunction with the World Trade Organization (WTO). The forum also called for continued work on a comprehensive "vulnerability index" for determining concessionary aid and trade status. Reiterating previous concerns, participants again called for action on global warming, condemned the shipment of radioactive waste and mixed oxide (MOX) fuels through the region, and noted that regional security had become "more fluid and uncertain" because of such factors as financial and cyber crime, people smuggling, civil unrest, and drug trafficking. The forum also decided to adopt the name Pacific Islands Forum, following a one-year transition period.

Meeting under its new name, the forum convened October 27–30, 2000, in Tarawa, Kiribati, and welcomed the Solomon Islands peace agreement of October 15 and efforts by Fiji's interim government to reestablish constitutional democracy. In a significant departure from previous decisions to maintain distance from the internal conflicts of member states, the leaders adopted the Biketawa Declaration, which outlined a series of steps to take in response to political instability related to ethnic tensions, socioeconomic disparities, land disputes, loss of cultural values, or lack of good governance. Despite its continuing commitment to noninterference in its members' internal affairs, the forum provided for the secretary general, after consultation with the forum chair and the members' foreign ministers, to undertake any of a number of actions, including conducting a fact-finding mission, creating a ministerial action group, seeking third-party mediation, and convening a special session of the Forum Regional Security Committee. Failing resolution of the crisis, a special meeting of forum leaders could consider additional steps, including "targeted measures."

Beginning in 1990 the forum expressed concern over possible sanctions against members that were classified as having harmful tax policies or regulations that allowed international money laundering. A "tax haven" list, first published in June 2000 by the Organization for Economic Cooperation and Development (OECD), singled out Cook Islands, Marshall Islands, Nauru, Niue, Samoa, Tonga, and Vanuatu among the 35 "noncompliant" international jurisdictions. At the same time, the independent Financial Action Task Force on Money Laundering (FATF) released its list of 15 Non-Cooperative Countries and Territories that included Cook Islands, Marshall Islands, Nauru, and Niue.

Hosted by Nauru, the August 16–18, 2001, forum session marked the organization's 30th anniversary with one of its most notable accomplishments: the opening for signature of the Pacific Island Countries Trade Agreement (PICTA) and the Pacific Agreement on Closer Economic Relations (PACER). PICTA was signed by all of the 12 Forum Island Countries (FICs) except the Marshall Islands, Micronesia, and Palau, which were given additional time to sign because of complexities related to their compact status with the United States. PICTA anticipates creation of an FTA by 2010, although the SIS members and LDCs do not have to eliminate their intracommunity tariffs until 2012. In addition, "excepted imports" are protected until 2016. PACER outlines a framework for future trade relations between PICTA states and the much larger economies of Australia and New Zealand. PACER contains provisions for "trade facilitation" and increased financial and technical assistance to the FICs, but it also offers assurances to Australia and New Zealand that they will not be disadvantaged by any external trade agreements negotiated by the PICTA group.

Following ratification by six signatories, PICTA entered into force in April 2003, at which time all nontariff barriers to trade were eliminated. PICTA signatories have as long-range goals creation of a single market to cover trade in services as well as goods and free movement of capital and labor. PACER, which entered into effect in October 2002, following ratification by seven signatories, provides for future trade negotiations but does not mandate a forum-wide FTA.

The 33rd forum meeting, held August 15–17, 2002, in Suva passed the Pacific Islands Regional Ocean Policy and the Nasonini Declaration on Regional Security, which addressed terrorism and transnational organized crime. Other topics discussed at the session included the regional impact of HIV/AIDS; climate change and other environmental concerns; and continuing negotiations related to disarmament, nonproliferation, and the transport of radioactive materials through the region. Later in the year, in line with the Biketawa Declaration, the first Forum Elections Observer Mission was sent to the Solomon Islands.

Meeting on August 14–16, 2003, in Auckland, the forum elected Australia's Greg Urwin as secretary general, a post that was traditionally awarded to an FIC national. The election came at a time of increasing regional involvement by Australia, whose prime minister, John Howard, emerged as a leading advocate for greater economic and political integration. The 2003 forum session also saw the adoption of the Forum Principles of Good Leadership, the first being respect for the rule of law and the system of government, including disclosure of fraud, corruption, and maladministration.

In another first, the year 2003 saw the forum countries fulfill a request from the government in Honiara, Solomon Islands, to deploy a policing mission. The Regional Assistance Mission to Solomon Islands (RAMSI) was asked to help restore law and order, strengthen the judicial system, and aid in the restoration of basic services. This mission was successful, and the Solomon Islands were able to hold peaceful general elections in April 2006.

The 2004 meeting of the Pacific Islands Forum was held August 3–10, 2004, in Apia, Samoa. The chief subject of the meeting was discussion and endorsement of the forum's emerging multiyear Pacific Plan, an instrument for encouraging the forum's vision of sustainable growth and integration in the Pacific region. The forum endorsed the plan as thus far developed and looked for more specifics in the future. The 36th Pacific Islands Forum summit was held October 25–27, 2005, in Papua New Guinea. It endorsed the Pacific Plan, noting the needs to expand access to markets for trade in goods under SPARTECA, PICTA, PACER, and with nonforum trading partners; to expand vocational education throughout the region; and to ensure the mutual recognition of technical qualifications and the free movement of labor. The plan paid particular attention to the interests of SIS, which endorsed it in a separate communiqué.

In 2006 and 2007 the Pacific Islands Forum was concerned with unrest among some of its members. In August 2006 Tonga asked to be excused from hosting the October summit because the king's health was deteriorating. He died in September 2006. Forum members had been warned in any case that a summit meeting in Tonga would be greeted with demonstrations against the king's authoritarian rule. The summit was eventually held in Suva and was notable for complaints about Australian heavy-handedness in its leadership of the peacekeeping force in the Solomon Islands. In February 2007 the Solomon Islands government asked the forum to discuss an "exit strategy."

In December 2006 there was a military coup in Fiji, followed by a partial return to civilian government in January 2007. The Fijian interim government first promised elections and a full democracy in 2010. The Pacific Islands Forum, in a March 2007 foreign ministers' meeting, demanded a swifter return to democracy, and the Fijian government advanced the likely date to 2009. The forum and Fiji established a working group to create a joint approach to restoring democracy, with the forum aiming for elections within two years. In July 2007 Samoa declared that Fiji should be allowed to attend the coming October summit, even if the coup leader came. However, in August 2007 Australian prime minister Alexander Downer declared that the leader of the Fiji coup and interim prime minister, Frank Bainimarama, would not be welcome at the forthcoming forum meeting in Tonga. Greg Urwin, the forum secretary general, defended Bainimarama, saying that the Forum Secretariat did not choose whom to invite or not. (Bainimarama had accused the Secretariat of working with the governments of Australia and New Zealand to keep him away.) In any event, Bainimarama attended the meeting, held October 16–17, 2007 in Vava'u, Tonga. He made a definite commitment to hold elections in early 2009 and to abide by their outcome. The meeting also declared that climate change, about which it had been issuing warnings since 1990, was now definitely under way and that palliative measures needed to be taken in the Pacific region.

Also in October 2007 Taiwan's six allies in the forum—Solomon Islands, Marshall Islands, Kiribati, Nauru, Palau, and Tuvalu—declared that Taiwan's status should be upgraded to that of a regular dialogue partner. On the sidelines of the annual forum meeting the EU announced a grant of 267 million euros ($178 million) for regional development in the period 2008–2013. In October 2007 China announced a grant of $650,000 to the forum as a gesture of friendship.

In March 2008 a meeting of forum foreign ministers in Auckland expressed concern that Fiji's interest in a so-called people's charter might get in the way of the promised early 2009 elections. In April the forum sent two representatives to observe elections in Nauru at the request of the Nauru government.

In May 2008 all French ambassadors and high commissioners in the Pacific region met in Canberra to coordinate and improve French relations with non-French Pacific states—particularly the members of the Pacific Islands Forum. Also that month Greg Urwin resigned as secretary general of the forum for health reasons. He was succeeded in an acting capacity by his deputy, Dr. Feleti Sevele of Vanuatu. In August 2008 Urwin died, and in that month Tuiloma Neroni Slade of Samoa was chosen as his permanent replacement.

Frank Bainimarama received heavy criticism for failing to attend the organization's August 2008 summit in Niue. The summit otherwise focused on economic issues, the world financial crisis weighing heavily on the economically weak Pacific islands. By this time Bainimarama was backing away from his promise of elections in 2009, and the forum issued a statement threatening to suspend Fiji. In late 2008 Fiji made some moves to re-engage with the forum. However by January 2009, with little progress made toward the restoration of democracy, the forum called on Bainimarama to set a date certain in 2009 for elections, and to do that by May 1. When Bainimarama failed to honor the deadline, Fiji was suspended from the forum. The group's headquarters in Fiji continue to function, however.

In other matters, in December 2008 the forum adopted a program for reorganizing its operations. In December China made a grant of $500,000 to the forum for several regional projects, including the Pacific Plan. In July 2009 Taiwan donated $57,000 for scholarships, and $406,000 for various CROP projects.

PERMANENT COURT OF ARBITRATION (PCA)

Cour Permanente d'Arbitrage

Established: By the First Hague Peace Conference, held in 1899 in The Hague, Netherlands. The Convention for the Pacific Settlement of International Disputes was signed July 29, 1899, and entered into force September 4, 1900. The convention was revised October 18, 1907, by the Second Hague Peace Conference and entered into force January 26, 1910.

Purpose: To facilitate international dispute resolution through arbitration, conciliation, and fact-finding and through assistance to other arbitration procedures.

Headquarters: The Hague, Netherlands.

Principal Organs: Administrative Council, International Bureau.

Web site: www.pca-cpa.org

Secretary General: Christiaan Kröner (Netherlands).

Membership (108): Argentina, Australia, Austria, Belarus, Belgium, Belize, Benin, Bolivia, Brazil, Bulgaria, Burkina Faso, Cambodia, Cameroon, Canada, Chile, China, Colombia, Democratic Republic of the Congo, Costa Rica, Croatia, Cuba, Cyprus, Czech Republic, Denmark, Dominican Republic, Ecuador, Egypt, El Salvador, Eritrea, Estonia, Ethiopia, Fiji, Finland, France, Germany, Greece, Guatemala, Guyana, Haiti, Honduras, Hungary, Iceland, India, Iran, Iraq, Ireland, Israel, Italy, Japan, Jordan, Kenya, Republic of Korea, Kuwait, Kyrgyzstan, Laos, Latvia, Lebanon, Libya, Liechtenstein, Lithuania, Luxembourg, Macedonia, Malaysia, Malta, Mauritius, Mexico, Montenegro, Morocco, Netherlands, New Zealand, Nicaragua, Nigeria, Norway, Pakistan, Panama, Paraguay, Peru, Poland, Portugal, Qatar, Romania, Russia, Saudi Arabia, Senegal, Serbia, Singapore, Slovakia, Slovenia, South Africa, Spain, Sri Lanka, Sudan, Suriname, Swaziland, Sweden, Switzerland, Thailand, Togo, Turkey, Uganda, Ukraine, United Kingdom, United Arab Emirates, United States, Uruguay, Venezuela, Zambia, Zimbabwe.

The People's Republic of China, which was first asked June 2, 1972, to clarify its position toward the Hague conventions, finally designated its four members of the court July 15, 1993. In 1991, following dissolution of the Soviet Union, Russia assumed the USSR's membership. The court subsequently announced that the three Baltic states (Estonia, Latvia, and Lithuania) and the members of the Commonwealth of Independent States not yet affiliated with the court would, as "successors" to the former Soviet Union, be considered contracting parties to the conventions if they filed a request for such status. However, only Kyrgyzstan and Latvia had done so by mid-2008. (The possible accession of the other Baltic states is complicated by their unwillingness to be designated as USSR successors.) The new republics that emerged following the breakup of the former Yugoslavia were also invited to declare their adherence to the conventions as successor states, and by 2008 all but Bosnia and Herzegovina had done so. The Czech Republic and Slovakia joined in 1993 as successors to the former Czechoslovakia. Following the May 2006 split between Serbia and Montenegro, Serbia became a member as the successor state, and Montenegro joined in its own right in April 2007.

Official Working Languages: English and French, although proceedings may be in any language on which the disputants agree.

Origin and development. A product of the First Hague Peace Conference in 1899, the Convention for the Pacific Settlement of International Disputes contained—in addition to provisions on good offices, mediation, and inquiry—several articles on international arbitration, the object of which was "the settlement of differences between States by judges of their own choice, and on the basis of respect of law." The convention did not impose any obligation to arbitrate but instead attempted to set up a structure that could be utilized when two or more states desired to submit a dispute. Detailed procedural rules were therefore set out in the convention, and the Permanent Court of Arbitration (PCA) was established. The 1907 revised convention included a method for selecting arbitrators.

Structure. Despite its name, the Permanent Court of Arbitration is in no sense a "permanent court"; instead, a court is selected from among a permanent panel of arbitrators. Each party to the convention is eligible to nominate a maximum of four people "of known competency in questions of international law, of the highest moral reputation, and disposed to accept the duties of Arbitrator." Arbitrators, currently totaling more than 300, are appointed for renewable six-year terms. Under procedures adopted in 1992, parties seeking arbitration may ask for a tribunal of one, three, or five persons.

The International Bureau is the administrative arm of the court and serves as its registry. It channels communications concerning court meetings, maintains archives, conducts administrative business, and receives from contracting parties reports on the results of arbitration proceedings. The Administrative Council of the bureau is composed of diplomatic representatives of contracting parties accredited to The Hague; the Netherlands's minister of foreign affairs acts as president of the council.

Activities. Historically, arbitration has been a relatively infrequent means of resolving international disputes. In 1976, however, the introduction under the United Nations Commission for International Trade Laws (UNCITRAL) of standard rules for commercial arbitration led to a renewal of interest in the court's services. Under the UNCITRAL regime, the PCA's secretary general may be requested to designate an appointing authority for an arbitration proceeding or to rule on challenges to appointment of particular arbitrators. In addition, under UNCITRAL rules as well as many private contracts and international bilateral or multilateral agreements, the secretary general is mentioned as an authority competent to designate arbitrators, a function he has performed frequently in recent years.

Since 1968 the court has had a working arrangement with the World Bank's International Center for Settlement of Investment Disputes, and it is also authorized to arbitrate cases issuing from the Multilateral Investment Guarantee Agency (MIGA), a World Bank affiliate inaugurated in 1988. The members of the International Court of Justice are elected by the United Nations (UN) General Assembly and the Security Council from a list of nominees chosen by the PCA members, who may also nominate candidates for the Nobel Peace Prize. More recently, the International Bureau has served as registry for a revived dispute resolution tribunal established by the Bank for International Settlements (BIS).

To provide greater flexibility and thereby promote greater use of its resources, the court adopted in 1992 a new set of optional rules for arbitrating disputes between two states. Based on proven successful UNCITRAL guidelines, the new procedures provided, among other things, for smaller (and presumably faster) tribunals. A model clause for inclusion in future bilateral and multilateral treaties was also devised whereby the court would be the designated arbitrator of disputes between their signatories. A similar set of new operating rules was adopted in 1993 for arbitrating disputes between a state and a nonstate party, and this was followed by adoption of optional rules for settling disputes between intergovernmental organizations and states or private parties. The PCA has also sought to identify other gaps in existing dispute resolution frameworks, including ground rules for procedures and statements of proof in mass claims cases.

Hopeful that the climate for the peaceful settlement of international disputes was continuing to improve, the PCA held its first Conference of Members in September 1993 in The Hague to discuss the court's future. Among other things, the conference called for intensified cooperation between the PCA and the UN, and the UN General Assembly subsequently accorded observer status to the court.

In 1994 the court's Administrative Council agreed to establish a Financial Assistance Fund to help developing nations meet the costs involved in bringing cases before the court. A group of experts also asked the International Bureau to appoint a working group to advise on whether special institutional arrangements should be made for settling environmental disputes. As a result, in June 2001 the Administrative Council adopted by consensus Optional Rules for Arbitration of Disputes Relating to Natural Resources and/or the Environment. In April 2002 the council adopted conciliation rules in the same area. Also in the environmental arena, the court has participated in conferences related to the UN Framework Convention on Climate Change, as well as the UN Convention on Biodiversity and the Intergovernmental Committee for the Biosafety Protocol.

In 1998–1999 the court announced a two-part settlement of land and marine boundary claims between Eritrea and Yemen. In a similar vein, the International Bureau has served as the registry for the Eritrea-Ethiopia Boundary Commission and for the Eritrea-Ethiopia Claims Commission. In November 2006, the commission declared that matters had dragged on long enough, and that the parties had a year to come to an agreement. Failing any agreement, the commission would issue a map showing boundaries, consider the dispute settled, and dissolve. The map was so issued, but tension remains high between the two sides. The PCA was also involved in a dispute in which Ireland, citing the UN Convention on the Law of the Sea and the Convention for the Protection of the Marine Environment of the North-East Atlantic (the OSPAR [Oslo/Paris] Convention), expressed concerns about operation of a mixed plutonium and uranium oxide processing plant in the United Kingdom (settled July 2, 2003). On September 19, 2003, a Tribunal Concerning BIS rendered a decision that determined compensation for privately held Bank for International Settlements(BIS) shares, all of which were recalled by the bank in 2001 (see BIS article). In February 2004 the court began hearing a dispute between Guyana and Suriname about their maritime boundary. The court rendered judgment in September 2007, generally favoring Guyana as to the boundary claim, but criticizing both parties for their behavior during the dispute.

In 1999 the court initiated a series of International Law Seminars that have addressed such diverse areas as mass claims procedures; dispute resolution with regard to international investments and environmental protection; air, space, and telecommunications law; relations with Arabic and Islamic countries in the context of e-commerce, foreign investment, and the World Trade Organization; labor law; and international water disputes.

In February 2007 the court ruled in favor of Eurotunnel, the company that operates the rail tunnel under the English Channel, in its claim against the UK and French governments for damages. The court decided that both countries were at fault in not ensuring orderly conditions around a refugee camp near the French entrance to the tunnel, thus facilitating the tunnel's use for illegal entry into the UK.

In early 2007 the court signed an agreement to establish its second regional facility in South Africa to deal with African disputes. The first, dating from December 2001, is based at the UN University for Peace in San José, Costa Rica. In late 2008 the court agreed to open a similar facility in New Delhi, India, for Asian cases.

On July 13, 2008, the leaders of the Northern and Southern sections of Sudan agreed to submit their dispute over the oil-rich region of Abyei to the court. As of mid-2009 arguments are still in progress.

On April 22, 2008, the then secretary general, Tjaco van den Hout, announced his intention to resign and return to diplomatic service. Christiaan Kröner, at that time the Netherlands' ambassador to the United States, was nominated to succeed him, effective September 2008. Also in April 2008, a claim by a shareholder of the government-expropriated Russian oil company Yukos was in its early stages.

In November 2008, the United Arab Emirates became the 108th member of the organization. On February 5, 2009, Secretary General Kröner visited Bangladesh and offered that country membership. In February 2009 also, it appeared that the boundary dispute between Croatia and Slovenia might end up before the court.

PERMANENT INTERSTATE COMMITTEE ON DROUGHT CONTROL IN THE SAHEL (CILSS)

Comité Inter-Etats de Lutte contre la Sécheresse dans le Sahel

Established: Following a March 1973 declaration of a drought-related disaster in the Sahel by Burkina Faso (then Upper Volta), Mali, Mauritania, Niger, and Senegal.

Purpose: To overcome drought, ensure food security, fight desertification, and promote sustainable cooperative development in the Sahel region.

Headquarters: Ouagadougou, Burkina Faso.

Principal Organs: Conference of Heads of State and Government, Council of Ministers, Regional Committee for Programming and Follow-up, Executive Council, Executive Secretariat.

Web site: www.cilss.bf (In French, but with an English section under development.)

Executive Secretary: Alhousseini Bretaudeau (Mali).

Membership (9): Burkina Faso, Cape Verde, Chad, Gambia, Guinea-Bissau, Mali, Mauritania, Niger, Senegal.

Working Languages: French and English. (The introduction of Portuguese and Arabic as working languages was approved in principle.)

Origin and development. CILSS was formed in 1973 by Burkina Faso (then Upper Volta), Mali, Mauritania, Niger, and Senegal in parallel with efforts by the new United Nations (UN) Special Sahelian Office to marshal aid for countries seriously affected by the 1968–1973 Sahel drought. Chad soon joined its neighbors in CILSS, as did Gambia in 1974 and Cape Verde in 1975. By then the Special Sahelian Office was superseded by the UN Sudano-Sahelian Office (UNSO), which closely coordinated its activities with CILSS. (In 1994 the UNSO was reorganized as the UN Development Programme's Office to Combat Desertification and Drought, which was replaced in 2002 by the Drylands Development Centre in Nairobi, Kenya.)

In its first year of existence, CILSS proposed some 300 projects directed toward its principal goals: preparing for future droughts and thereby mitigating their adverse effects, achieving regional security in cereals and other staple foods, and advancing development. The first Sahel UNSO/CILSS donor conference in July 1975 in Geneva, Switzerland, attracted considerable support for some 50 short-term projects expected to cost $150 million. Also in 1975 CILSS and various donor countries agreed to establish the Sahel Club, which was inaugurated in March 1976 as an informal forum for coordination and strategy formulation.

In 1984 CILSS approved the establishment of the Sahel Fund to finance and coordinate national food strategies. The most recent member, Guinea-Bissau, joined in 1986.

Structure. CILSS was initially a relatively unstructured organization that met in plenary session at least once per year to approve an annual budget and discuss major undertakings. At other times it held joint meetings with such bodies as the UN Food and Agriculture Organization (FAO) to address matters of common concern.

At present, the principal CILSS policymaking organs are the Conference of Heads of State and Government, which meets every three years to provide general direction and define major objectives, and a Council of Ministers, which is charged with realizing the organization's objectives. A Regional Committee for Programming and Follow-up reports to the ministers, while an Executive Council monitors overall operations, including budget preparation. An executive secretary serves a three-year term. The Executive Secretariat includes four councilors responsible for food security, natural resources management, planning, and communications. Affiliated specialized agencies are the Sahel Institute in Bamako, Mali, and the Agrometeorology and Operational Hydrology Center (AGRHYMET) in Niamey, Niger.

Activities. In the 1980s regional programs were created to develop an early warning system for food shortages, improve the quality and distribution of grain seeds, expand water supplies, protect plant life, educate the population on ways to counter the effects of drought and desertification in everyday life, and promote alternative energy sources. In addition, the Conference of the Heads of State and Government addressed several related problems, including the region's economic difficulties and its high population growth rate.

The 1992 CILSS summit endorsed a "renewed mandate" for the organization, which had experienced severe financial problems for several years because of arrears in members' payments. With the financial crisis continuing, the 11th summit, held in April 1994 in Praia, Cape Verde, approved a cutback in the CILSS staff from more than 100 employees to approximately 30. As a result of subsequent discussions about assuring adequate funding, the CILSS established the Foundation for Sustainable Development of the Sahel.

At the 12th heads of state and government summit, held in September 1997, in Banjul, Gambia, many outside donors praised CILSS for its progress. The European Union (EU), for one, called CILSS one of the continent's most credible institutions and announced it would be one of the three primary organizations in the region to play an important role in the implementation of the Convention for West Africa between the EU and affiliated African, Caribbean, and Pacific (ACP) countries. However, the donors stressed that their continued support was contingent on members meeting their financial obligations to CILSS. The financial situation of CILSS was described as "precarious," with the amount members owed to the committee totaling more than $1 million in 1996. To help raise money, the heads of state and government endorsed a Council of Ministers' proposal to set up an endowment.

In late 1998 CILSS ministers, meeting in Banjul, approved a program geared toward assisting women's organizations and improving the management of land and water resources in cooperation with the Islamic Development Bank (IDB) and Organization of the Islamic Conference (OIC). Since a June 1994 CILSS-sponsored Regional Conference on Land Tenure and Decentralization, held in Praia, CILSS has also placed particular emphasis on land tenure issues, and a Project on Local Development in the Sahel (*Projet d'Appui au Développement Local au Sahel*—PADLOS) was set up to study national land policies.

The 13th CILSS summit convened in Bamako November 25–26, 2000, immediately after sessions of the Regional Committee and the Council of Ministers. Leadership of the Conference of Heads of State and Government passed to Mali's Alpha Oumar Konaré, while Musa Mbenga of Kenya was elected executive secretary for a term that began in February 2001. At the council session ministers reported that, once again, the Sahel was experiencing a "large cereal deficit."

Convening January 25, 2004, in Nouakchott, Mauritania, the 14th conference reappointed Secretary General Mbenga for a second term and passed the leadership reins to the host country's president, Maaouya Ould Sid' Ahmed Taya. Most significantly, the conference resolved to reorient CILSS toward its original objectives of fighting desertification, addressing regional water needs, and establishing food security. In addition to redefining its focus, CILSS sought to eliminate duplication of efforts by other regional organizations and to emphasize funding for projects with concrete goals.

This refocusing of attention seems to have helped. Annual crop yields in 2004 and 2005, despite poor rains, were considerably better than forecast. With better food security, the organization had the opportunity to plan forward. In April 2006 it announced a grant of 79 million euros ($102 million) for a system of 500 solar-powered well pumps throughout its territory. This project was targeted for completion in 2008. In October 2006 the UN reported that Niger was actually reversing desertification by using such simple methods as planting trees and preserving natural vegetation, though it warned that these improvements would be short-lived unless Niger could control the increase in its population. CILSS estimated that West Africa's cereal production should reach 15 million tons for the 2006–2007 season, a 3 percent increase over the previous year's harvest. Small-scale village irrigation projects, combined with solar-generated electricity, continued to serve the area well. But by October 2007, Nigeria was predicting a bad harvest in its northern regions because of inadequate rains. Senegal likewise experienced bad harvests and hunger due to an abbreviated rainy season. Rains in 2008 were adequate, and were forecast to be good in 2009.

In mid-2008 CILSS, currently a completely French-speaking organization, was reported to be working toward an association with English-speaking Nigeria. Since that time Nigeria, while not formally joining the organization, has been working closely with it, especially on the proposed Great Green Wall (GGW), a project sponsored by CILSS of interest to all African countries at the same latitude. The GGW is envisaged as a belt of trees, together with new farms and mechanisms to collect water, that will stop the southward spread of the desert. The GGW would not cross the entire continent, but would at first be concentrated on areas most at risk from desertification. Nigeria is actively involved in the GGW project.

REGIONAL AND SUBREGIONAL DEVELOPMENT BANKS

Regional development banks are intended to accelerate economic and social development of member states by promoting public and private investment. The banks are not meant, however, to be mere financial institutions in the narrow sense of the term. Required by their charters to take an active interest in improving their members' capacities to make profitable use of local and external capital, they engage in such technical assistance activities as feasibility studies, evaluation and design of projects, and preparation of development programs. The banks also seek to coordinate their activities with the work of other national and international agencies engaged in financing international economic development. Subregional banks have historically concentrated more on integration projects than have regional development banks.

African Development Bank
(AfDB)
Banque Africaine de Développement
(BAD)

Web site: www.afdb.org

The Articles of Agreement of the AfDB were signed August 4, 1963, in Khartoum, Sudan, with formal establishment of the institution occurring in September 1964 after 20 signatories had deposited instruments of ratification. Lending operations commenced in July 1966 at the bank's headquarters in Abidjan, Côte d'Ivoire.

Until 1982 membership in the AfDB was limited to states within the region. At the 1979 Annual Meeting, the Board of Governors approved an amendment to the bank's statutes permitting nonregional membership as a means of augmenting the institution's capital resources; however, it was not until the 17th Annual Meeting, held in May 1982 in Lusaka, Zambia, that Nigeria announced withdrawal of its objection to the change. Non-African states became eligible for membership December 20, 1982, and by the end of 1983 more than 20 such states had joined the bank.

The bank's leading policymaking organ is its Board of Governors, encompassing the finance or economic ministers of the member states; the governors elect a bank president, who serves a five-year term and is chair of a Board of Directors. The governors are empowered to name 18 directors, each serving a three-year term, with 12 seats to be held by Africans. The bank's African members are the same as for the African Union (AU), save for the inclusion of Morocco (no longer a member of the AU) and the exclusion of Morocco's breakaway Sahrawi Arab Democratic Republic.

While limiting the bank's membership to African countries was initially viewed as a means of avoiding practical difficulties and undesirable political complications, it soon became evident that the major capital-exporting states were unwilling to lend funds without having a continuous voice in their use. In response to this problem, an African Development Fund (ADF) was established in November 1972 as a legally distinct intergovernmental institution in which contributing countries would have a shared managerial role. The ADF Board of Governors encompasses one representative from each state as well as the AfDB governors, ex officio; the 12-member Board of Directors includes six nonregional designees. Nonregional contributing countries—all of whom, except the United Arab Emirates, are now AfDB members—are Argentina, Austria, Belgium, Brazil, Canada, China, Denmark, Finland, France, Germany, India, Italy, Japan, the Republic of Korea, Kuwait, the Netherlands, Norway, Portugal, Saudi Arabia, Spain, Sweden, Switzerland, Turkey, the United Kingdom, and the United States. In addition, in February 1976 the bank and the government of Nigeria signed an agreement establishing a Nigeria Trust Fund (NTF) with an initial capitalization of 50 million Nigerian naira (about $80 million). Unlike the ADF, the NTF is directly administered by the AfDB. Together, the AfDB, the ADF, and the NTF constitute the African Development Bank Group.

Earlier, in November 1970, the AfDB participated in the founding of the International Financial Society for Investments and Development in Africa (*Société Internationale Financière pour les Investissements et le Développement en Afrique*—SIFIDA). Headquartered in Geneva, Switzerland, with the International Finance Corporation (IFC) and a large number of financial institutions from advanced industrial countries among its shareholders, SIFIDA is authorized to extend loans for the promotion and growth of productive enterprises in Africa. Another related agency, the Association of African Development Finance Institutions (AADFI), inaugurated in March 1975 in Abidjan, was established to aid and coordinate African development projects, while the African Reinsurance Corporation (Africa-Re), formally launched in March 1977 in Lagos, Nigeria, promotes the development of insurance and reinsurance activity throughout the continent. The AfDB holds 10 percent of Africa-Re's authorized capital of $50 million. Shelter-Afrique, established to facilitate lending that would improve Africa's housing situation, began operations in January 1984 in its Nairobi, Kenya, headquarters. The AfDB has also participated in the formation of the African Export-Import Bank (Afreximbank), which began operation in 1993.

At the bank's 1988 annual meeting, U.S. officials surprised observers by announcing that Washington was now willing to support concessional interest rate rescheduling for the "poorest of the poor" African countries. However, African representatives called for additional debt measures, such as extension of maturities and pegging repayment schedules to a country's debt-servicing "history" and "capacity." Following up on discussions initiated at the annual meeting on growing arrears in loan repayments and capital subscription payments, the bank announced late in the year that the countries involved faced suspension of existing loan disbursements and would not be eligible for new loans until the arrears were cleared.

During the 1989 annual meeting and 25th anniversary celebration, at which the bank was described as "probably the most successful of the African multinational institutions," the Board of Governors pledged that lending activity would continue to accelerate. On the topic of debt reduction, the bank praised the initiatives launched at the recent Group of Seven summit but called for further measures, including more debt cancellations by individual creditor nations.

A dispute between regional and nonregional members regarding the bank's future continued at the May 1993 AfDB annual meeting as Western nations continued to press for a stricter policy on arrears, better evaluation of project performance, and greater support for private sector activity. In addition, at the insistence of donor countries, an independent task force was established, chaired by former World Bank vice president David Knox to review all bank operations. The task force report, released shortly before the AfDB's May 1994 annual meeting, strongly criticized the bank for keeping poor records, maintaining a top-heavy bureaucracy, and emphasizing the quantity of lending at the expense of quality. The report also supported the contention of donor countries that the accumulation of arrears (more than $700 million) had become a threat to the bank's future. The nonregional members subsequently proposed that regular AfDB lending be limited to "solvent" nations, but African members rejected their advice.

Fractious debate continued at the May 1995 annual meeting. Outgoing AfDB president Babacar N'Diaye, blamed by some for the bank's deteriorating reputation, issued the counterclaim that responsibility rested with the Board of Directors, many of whose members, he charged, were concentrating on their own "finances and perquisites" at the expense of bank activity. Further tarnishing the bank's image, the governors were unable to elect a successor to N'Diaye, with regional and nonregional members backing different candidates. However, at a special meeting in Abidjan in late August, the Board of Governors, after nine rounds of balloting, finally chose Omar Kabbaj, one-time official of the International Monetary Fund (IMF) and a former member of the Moroccan cabinet, as the new AfDB president. Shortly thereafter, Kabbaj announced that an external committee would be established to evaluate the bank's operations, internal structures, and fiscal status. The new president also pledged that the AfDB would immediately begin to give greater emphasis to private sector loans, one issue on which regional and nonregional members appeared in agreement. Meanwhile, talks on the ADF replenishment remained suspended pending Kabbaj's restructuring proposals, expected by the end of the year.

Under the leadership of Kabbaj, the AfDB cut approximately 240 employees (20 percent of the staff) and otherwise restructured the bank's operations, paving the way for an infusion of new capital. At the annual meeting held May 21–22, 1996, the ADF was replenished with $2.6 billion, though this entailed a cut from prior levels. When ADF lending resumed shortly thereafter, the AfDB adopted guidelines recommended by the World Bank under which the number of states eligible for new loans was reduced from 53 to 12.

Although those changes were widely perceived as representing genuine progress, the AfDB governance report released in mid-1996 delineated several continuing problems. The report argued that further "stark" measures needed to be taken to prevent the bank from being relegated to the role of a minor player on the continent. Specific issues to be addressed included "incompetence" in some bank operations, low morale among the remaining employees, and a lack of "financial credibility" stemming from arrears of $800 million amassed by 25 out of 53 recipients. (About 75 percent of the late payments were owed by Angola, Cameroon, Congo, Liberia, Somalia, Sudan, and Zaire.)

In July 1996 a special summit was held in Libreville, Gabon, to discuss issues raised in the report and to plot the future of the bank, particularly in regard to the contentious issue of control. Led by Nigeria, some African countries opposed giving nonregional members additional decision-making power, despite the bank's weakened condition. The governance report outlined several alternatives, ranging from a 50–50 split of control between nonregional and African nations, to no change at all (which might have meant the cessation of Western contributions). Compromise alternatives called for a modest increase in nonregional decision-making power via a reduction in the total number of seats on the executive board as well a revision of AfDB voting procedures.

A compromise was reached in March 1998 when it was agreed that a capital increase of about 35 percent ($7.65 billion) would be implemented, with the nonregional share being set at 40 percent. Significantly, while the African members were allowed to retain control of 12 of the 18 seats on the Board of Directors, future discussions would require 70 percent (at least one nonregional vote) endorsement by that board on "crucial" issues.

Under President Kabbaj's leadership, significant structural reforms were implemented during the latter 1990s, contributing to improved international credibility for the bank. Collaterally, a vision statement approved by the Board of Governors in 1999 gave greater emphasis to reducing poverty and increasing productivity, with other concerns including good governance, regional cooperation and development, gender mainstreaming, and environmental sustainability. Operationally, the AfDB was rededicated to meeting client needs through strategic planning and compliance monitoring. An executive restructuring in early 2002 included the establishment of two additional vice presidencies, raising the total to five. Areas of vice presidential responsibility were defined as planning, policy, and research; operations in the Central and Western regions; operations in the Northern, Eastern, and Southern regions and the private sector; corporate management; and finance. The reorganization also involved establishing two operational complexes: sector departments, with responsibility for project management; and country departments, with responsibility for such broader areas as macroeconomic analyses, lending policy, and public sector management.

In February 2003 the AfDB temporarily moved its headquarters from Abidjan to Tunis, Tunisia, because of the outbreak of civil war in Côte d'Ivoire. International institutions (led by the Group of Eight) subsequently announced plans for the AfDB to manage a new fund slated to provide as much as $10 billion a year to improve infrastructure in Africa. However, some analysts suggested that the parameters of the new initiative might be reviewed in light of the long and often rancorous battle in mid-2005 to elect a successor to AfDB president Kabbaj, who was retiring after ten years in the position. After numerous ballots that weeded out several candidates, the Board of Governors elected Donald Kaberuka, the finance and economy minister from Rwanda, over Olabisi Ogunjobi, a Nigerian who had worked at the bank since 1978. It was widely reported that Kaberuka had enjoyed the support of most of the bank's Western members.

In May 2006 the organization was embarrassed that, for the first time, its external auditor was unable to approve its accounts without qualification. Effective in July 2006, a new organizational structure was introduced, principally affecting the operational complexes and the Office of the Chief Economist. In May 2007 the AfDB caused some controversy by holding its 47th annual meeting in Shanghai, China. At this meeting Chinese premier Wen Jiabao rejected criticism that China was only interested in Africa as a potential supplier of raw materials. In November 2007 the bank canceled Liberia's debt.

In December 2007 the bank won a new three-year replenishment for the ADF of $8.9 billion, a 57 percent increase over the previous three-year replenishment. Total bank group approvals reached $2.77 billion in 2002, $2.62 billion in 2003, $4.33 billion in 2004, $3.28 billion in 2005, $3.9 billion in 2006, $4.9 billion in 2007, and $5.4 billion in 2008. As of the end of 2008, cumulative disbursements reached $27.2 billion for 3481 loans and grants.

The bank's 2008 annual meeting, held May 14–15 in Maputo, Mozambique, welcomed Turkey as the 25th nonregional member. At this meeting the bank also pledged an extra $1 billion to combat the food crisis in Africa. The 2009 annual meeting, held May 14-15 in Dakar, Senegal, had as its theme "Africa and the Financial Crisis: An Agenda for Action." The AfDB had previously given input to the April 2009 G20 conference in London (see separate article). Kaberuka declared that, while six months had wiped out much of Africa's recent economic progress, the fact was that Africa's GDP was still growing, while that of the developed countries was generally declining. He said that Africa had not been part of the problem, but that it was determined to be part of the solution.

The 2010 AfDB annual meetings were scheduled for May 27–28,2010 in Abidjan, Côte d'Ivoire.

Arab Bank for Economic Development in Africa

Banque Arabe de Développement Economique en Afrique

(BADEA)

Web site: www.badea.org

The idea of an Arab bank to assist in the economic and social development of all non-Arab African states was first discussed by the Arab heads of state during the Sixth Arab Summit in Algiers, Algeria, in November 1973. BADEA, with headquarters in Khartoum, Sudan, began operations in March 1975. Its main functions include financing development projects, promoting and stimulating private Arab investment in Africa, and supplying technical assistance. BADEA financing, which cannot exceed $15 million, is limited to 80 percent of projects with total costs up to $12 million and 50 percent of those above that level. Technical assistance is provided in grant form. All member states of the African Union (AU), except Arab League participants, are eligible for funding. To date, the preponderance of aid has been devoted to infrastructural improvements, although the Board of Directors has also accorded additional priority to projects promoting increased food production. The bank has traditionally favored the least-developed countries in its disbursements.

The bank's highest authority is the Board of Governors (one governor for each member), with day-to-day administration assigned to a Board of Directors, one of whose 11 members serves as board chair. The Board of Governors appoints the bank's director general from among the countries not represented on the Board of Directors. The subscribing members of the bank are Algeria, Bahrain, Egypt, Iraq, Jordan, Kuwait, Lebanon, Libya, Mauritania, Morocco, Oman, Palestine, Qatar, Saudi Arabia, Sudan, Syria, Tunisia, and United Arab Emirates. Egypt's membership was suspended from 1979 to 1988.

In a review of its first 25 years of activity, BADEA reported that infrastructure received more than 50 percent of total commitments, followed by agriculture (30 percent), energy (8 percent), banking (4 percent), and industry (2 percent). In addition to maintaining support for "traditional fields of intervention," beginning with its 1990–1994 five-year plan, the bank has placed greater emphasis on projects with a "direct impact on the life of African citizens," such as water supply and food security projects. In December 2004 the Board of Directors approved the fifth five-year plan, which projected new lending of $900 million in 2005–2009.

At the end of 2008 the bank's subscribed and paid-up capital was $2.2 million, unchanged from 2005. BADEA approved $129 million in new loans in 2001, $134 million in 2002, $140 million in 2003, $139 million (for 21 projects) and $5.7 million in technical assistance (for 24 projects) in 2004, $160 million in 2005, for 23 projects and 28 technical assistance operations, in 2006, $170 million, with $164 million for 23 projects and $6 million for technical assistance operations, in 2007, $180 million, with $173.5 million for 25 projects and $6.5 million for technical assistance operations, and in 2008 $190 million, with $183.25 million for 23 projects and $6.75 million for technical assistance operations. Cumulative disbursements reached $1.97 billion at the end of 2008.

Arab Fund for Economic and Social Development

(AFESD)

Web site: www.arabfund.org

The Arab Fund for Economic and Social Development, which originated in an accord reached May 16, 1968, and began functioning in December 1971, is headquartered in Safat, Kuwait. Its aim is to assist in the financing of economic and social development projects in Arab states by offering loans on concessional terms to governments, particularly for joint ventures, and by providing technical expertise. The chief policymaking organ of the fund is the Board of Governors (one representative from each participating country), which elects an eight-member Board of Directors chaired by a director general. Members are Algeria, Bahrain, Djibouti, Egypt (suspended from 1979 to 1988), Iraq, Jordan, Kuwait, Lebanon, Libya, Mauritania, Morocco, Oman, Palestine, Qatar, Saudi Arabia, Somalia, Sudan, Syria, Tunisia, United Arab Emirates, and Yemen. (The memberships of Iraq and Somalia have been suspended since 1993 because of their failure to make loan repayments.)

The AFESD serves as the secretariat for the Coordination Group of the Arab and Regional Development Institutions, which also includes the Abu Dhabi Fund for Development, the Arab Bank for Economic Development in Africa (BADEA), the Islamic Development Bank (IDB), the Kuwait Fund for Arab Economic Development, the OPEC Fund for International Development, and the Saudi Fund for Development. The annual *Unified Arab Economic Report,* covering current economic issues and prospects, is prepared by the fund in cooperation with the Arab Monetary Fund (AMF), the Arab League, and the Organization of Arab Petroleum Exporting Countries (OAPEC).

The AFESD has been at the forefront of efforts to boost inter-Arab trade, which culminated in an early 1990 agreement to establish the $500 million Arab Trade Financing Program (see separate article on the AMF). The AFESD agreed to provide $100 million, making it the new program's second leading contributor after the AMF.

AFESD-backed projects continue to emphasize infrastructure, while technical assistance grants concentrate on improving government efficiency and manpower skills. Lending approvals in 2007 totaled 367 million Kuwaiti dinars (KD) ($1.3 billion) for 16 projects. Infrastructure projects accounted for all but two percent of that number. Cumulative loan disbursements since 1974 reached 6.2 billion Kuwaiti dinars ($21.6 billion).

The AFESD authorized capital remains at KD 800 million (80,000 shares). At the end of 2007, paid-up capital stood at KD 663 million, unchanged since 1989, although reserves grew over the same period from KD 513 million to KD 1.77 billion ($62 billion). In 2008 the Board of Governors authorized the transfer of KD 1336.96 million from the reserve, boosting the bank's paid-up capital to KD 2 billion. Total members' equity declined slightly in 2008 to KD 2.51 billion ($8.8 billion), as against KD 2.53 billion at the end of 2007.

Asian Development Bank

(ADB)

Web site: www.adb.org

Launched under the auspices of the United Nations (UN) Economic Commission for Asia and the Far East (ESCAFE), subsequently the Economic and Social Commission for Asia and the Pacific (ESCAP), the ADB began operations December 19, 1966, in its Manila, Philippines, headquarters as a means of aiding economic growth and cooperation among regional developing countries. Its original membership of

31 has since expanded to 63, including 45 regional members: Afghanistan, Australia, Azerbaijan, Bangladesh, Bhutan, Cambodia, China, Cook Islands, Fiji, "Hong Kong, China," India, Indonesia, Japan, Kazakhstan, Kiribati, the Republic of Korea, Kyrgyzstan, Laos, Malaysia, Maldives, Marshall Islands, Federated States of Micronesia, Mongolia, Myanmar, Nauru, Nepal, New Zealand, Pakistan, Palau, Papua New Guinea, Philippines, Samoa, Singapore, Solomon Islands, Sri Lanka, Tajikistan, "Taipei, China," Thailand, Timor-Leste, Tonga, Turkmenistan, Tuvalu, Uzbekistan, Vanuatu, and Vietnam; and 18 nonregional members: Austria, Belgium, Canada, Denmark, Finland, France, Germany, Italy, Luxembourg, Netherlands, Norway, Portugal, Spain, Sweden, Switzerland, Turkey, the United Kingdom, and the United States. The People's Republic of China acceded to membership March 10, 1986, after the ADB agreed to change Taiwan's membership title from "Republic of China" to "Taipei, China." Taiwan thereupon withdrew from participation in bank meetings for a year, although continuing its financial contributions, before returning "under protest." North Korea applied for membership in 1997, but the United States and Japan, in particular, remain opposed.

Each member state is represented on the Board of Governors, which selects a 12-member Board of Directors (eight from regional states) and a bank president who chairs the latter. Four vice presidents and a managing director general assist the president in managing the bank.

ADB resources are generated through subscriptions; borrowings on capital markets; and income from several sources, including interest on undisbursed assets. Most funds are in the form of country subscriptions. Leading shareholders as of 2007 were Japan (15.8 percent), the United States (15.8 percent), China (6.4 percent), India (6.4 percent), Australia (5.8 percent), Indonesia (5.4 percent), Canada (5.2 percent), the Republic of Korea (5.0 percent), and Germany (4.3 percent). In all, about 64 percent of subscribed capital is provided by regional members.

In June 1974 an Asian Development Fund (ADF) was established to consolidate the activities of two earlier facilities, the Multi-Purpose Special Fund (MPSF) and the Agricultural Special Fund (ASF), whose policies were criticized because of program linkages to procurement in donor countries. The ADF, which provides soft loans, receives most of its funding from voluntary contributions by the industrialized ADB members, who also support a Technical Assistance Special Fund (TASF). A Japan Special Fund for technical assistance grants was set up in 1988 to aid in economic restructuring and facilitating new investment; a Currency Crisis Support Facility was added in 1999. The ADB Institute Special Fund supports the ADB Institute, which was established in 1997 to examine development issues and to offer related training and assistance.

In the mid-1980s there was intense debate within the ADB regarding proposed changes in lending policies. Western contributors called on the bank, which in the past provided loans almost exclusively for specific development projects, to provide more "policy-based" funding, under which the recipient country would have spending discretion as long as certain economic reforms were implemented. A compromise agreement was reached in 1987 to allocate up to 15 percent of annual outlays to such loans. Also in partial response to Western demands, the ADB in 1986 established a private sector division to provide private enterprise loans that would not require government guarantees. During the same year, after potential loan recipients complained that ADB requirements were too stringent, the ADB adopted an adjustable lending rate system.

Extensive debate on the bank's direction and strategies for the next decade was generated by a report from an expert external panel submitted in early 1989. The report echoed many of the recommendations of an earlier internal task force that urged greater support for social programs. The report also called for expanded private sector activity, attention to the role of women in development, and additional environmental study in connection with all bank projects. In May the Board of Governors endorsed many of the proposed initiatives, especially those concerned with poverty alleviation and the environment.

As negotiations began in 1993 on a proposed doubling of the bank's authorized capital, an independent task force was established to review ADB operations in light of questions from several major subscribers over lending policies, internal operations, and loan failure rates. The task force recommended the bank shift from an "approval culture," in which quantity of lending was the major criteria, to a focus on "project quality." The bank also agreed to stricter guidelines regarding arrears.

Those proposed refinements notwithstanding, it was apparently widely agreed that the bank's past performance was satisfactory, and the Board of Governors in May 1994 approved an increase in ADB subscribed capital to $48 billion, with the replenishment expected to support lending for the next eight to ten years. Although members with combined 94 percent of the board's voting power supported the increase, some regional members, particularly China, reportedly voiced strong protest over the insistence of Western nations that future lending be tied to "good governance" and that additional emphasis be given to social and environmental development.

Some behind-the-scenes controversy attended a subsequent effort by the ADB to prepare a 2001–2015 Long-Term Strategic Framework, with recipient countries resisting pressure by donor countries for greater say in development plans and for making loan approvals partially dependent on such considerations as good governance.

Meanwhile, at the 2000 annual meeting, which was held May 6–8 in Chiang Mai, Thailand, the United States urged South Korea and other members to undertake early repayment of the loans borrowed during the 1997 economic crisis. A year later, at the 2001 annual ADB meeting, which opened May 10 in Honolulu, Hawaii, U.S. Treasury Secretary Paul O'Neill urged more rapid financial and corporate reform, while several countries, including Japan and South Korea, meeting on the sidelines of the session, announced swap arrangements designed to prevent the kind of currency speculation that led to the 1997 crisis.

In 2000 the Japanese government committed $90 million to establish a new Japan Fund for Poverty Reduction, and a year later it announced it would underwrite a Japan Fund for Information and Communication Technology that would have as a principal purpose narrowing the "digital divide" between rich and poor countries. Other special program funds authorized in 2001 included those by Canada, for managing climate change; the Netherlands, for promoting renewable energy and energy efficiency; and the United Kingdom, for poverty reduction in India. In addition, a multidonor Cooperative Fund for water management was established.

Under the leadership of bank president Tadao Chino, who was reelected to a second term in September 2001, the ADB undertook a partial administrative reorganization. As part of the 15-year strategic plan, greater emphasis was to be given to sustainable development, private sector participation (a Private Sector Operations Department was created), environmental considerations, and poverty reduction. Projects involving social infrastructure such as health facilities and programs, education, and water supplies were to receive greater support.

The ADB was criticized in the early 2000s for a perceived failure to allocate sufficient resources for poverty reduction. Perhaps as a consequence, the bank announced it would begin offering grants (as opposed to loans) to its poorer members. That decision was made after donors agreed to a $7 billion replenishment of the ADF for the four-year period through 2008. Bank officials estimated that about one-fifth of ADF assistance in the future would consist of grants.

Haruhiko Kuroda of Japan was installed as the ADB's new president in February 2005. A former special advisor to the Japanese prime minister, Kuroda was described as a proponent of greater financial integration among Asian countries. In early 2005 the ADB established a $600 million fund to assist victims of the recent devastating tsunami. At a donors' conference of November 19, 2005, the ADB pledged $1 billion to help Pakistan recover from a major earthquake and to provide winter support to its victims.

At its 2005 annual meeting, held May 4–5 in Kyoto, Japan, the ADB came under attack from environmental organizations for not doing more to abate environmental degradation. It was also criticized by some of its poorer member countries for doing little to prevent the growing disparity between rich and poor countries in the region. It was against this background that the ADB began considering a role change in an Asia no longer uniformly poor and a shift in its focus from the alleviation of poverty to promoting sustainable development.

ADB loan approvals in 2008 totaled $10.5 billion, compared to $10.1 billion in 2007, $7.4 billion in 2006 and 2005, $5.3 billion in 2004, $6.1 billion in 2003, and $5.6 billion in 2002. The leading recipient was India with $1.8 billion borrowed, followed by China with $1.5 billion, and Pakistan with $1.1 billion. The biggest share of loans went to transportation and communication, approximately 26 percent, followed by energy at 23 percent.

Criticism of the ADB's direction dominated the organization's 2007 annual meeting, held May 3–4 in Madrid, Spain. The U.S. representative alone voted against the bank's long-term strategy, protesting that China and India, now with huge cash reserves, should no longer be given huge loans to fight poverty. This protest was clearly not effective.

ADB's response to the world economic crisis has been to increase lending and to enhance its own liquidity. It expects its loan assistance to increase by approximately $10 billion over 2009 and 2010. It unanimously approved an initial capital infusion of $400 million for loans only to ADF member countries. At its annual meeting, held May 4, 2009, in Bali, Indonesia, the bank announced a $120 billion crisis fund to boost liquidity. The economic ministers at the forum denied that the fund was an attempt to circumvent IMF rules that would have forced member countries make unpopular economic reforms.

Caribbean Development Bank
(CDB)

Web site: www.caribank.org

The origins of the CDB can be traced to a July 1966 conference between Canada and the Anglophone Caribbean states in Ottawa, where it was decided to study the possibility of creating a development-oriented financial institution for the Commonwealth Caribbean territories. An agreement formally establishing the CDB was signed October 18, 1969, in Kingston, Jamaica. From the time it commenced operations in January 1970, the bank's activities have included offering aid in coordinating development among members, promoting trade, mobilizing public and private financing for developmental purposes, and providing technical assistance. The Commonwealth Caribbean members are Anguilla, Antigua and Barbuda, Bahamas, Barbados, Belize, the British Virgin Islands, the Cayman Islands, Dominica, Grenada, Guyana, Jamaica, Montserrat, St. Kitts and Nevis, St. Lucia, St. Vincent and the Grenadines, Trinidad and Tobago, and the Turks and Caicos Islands; Brazil, Colombia, Haiti, Mexico, and Venezuela also participate, as do five nonregional members—Canada, China, Germany, Italy, and the United Kingdom. France withdrew October 27, 2000.

The principal policymaking body is the Board of Governors, to which each CDB participant names a member, except for Anguilla, the British Virgin Islands, the Cayman Islands, Montserrat, and the Turks and Caicos Islands, which are collectively represented. A 17-member Board of Directors (including 5 nonregional directors) is elected by the Board of Governors, as is the bank president. Voting on both bodies is weighted on the basis of capital subscriptions, of which regional members must hold at least 60 percent. The president is assisted by two vice presidents, one for operations and the other for finance, planning, legal affairs, and administration. The bank is headquartered in St. Michael, Barbados.

In 1996 the CDB considered a membership request from China, which was a delicate matter because some members of the bank suggested that Taiwan be approached regarding possible CDB membership. The People's Republic of China was admitted as the sixth nonregional member during the May 1997 meeting of the CDB Board of Governors held in Toronto, Canada, having already paid an initial installment of capital. Despite China's admission, Eastern Caribbean members renewed their support for Taiwan's joining the bank. In October 2000, however, the bank suffered a significant setback when France withdrew its membership. In announcing its intention six months earlier, France attributed its decision to the CDB's inability to fulfill expectations and, more specifically, to its failure to extend lending to Cuba, the Dominican Republic, and Haiti. The decision was described by Denzil Douglas, prime minister of St. Kitts and Nevis, as "passing strange," given that of the three, only Haiti had even requested membership. (Haiti became a member in January 2007.) At the same time, the prime minister of Grenada and others again called for the CDB to admit Taiwan, although the CDB charter limits membership to countries in the United Nations. Grenadian prime minister Keith Mitchell noted that even associate membership status for Taiwan could make significant additional capital resources available for Caribbean development.

The CDB's strategic plan for the years 2005–2009 noted the problems of poverty, near-poverty, spreading crime and drug use, and the frequent incidence of natural disasters in the region. The plan concentrates on promoting broad-based economic growth, fostering inclusive social development, promoting good governance, and encouraging regional cooperation and integration—all with due consideration for environmental sustainability and the improvement of disaster risk management.

As of December 2006, the leading CDB subscribers were Jamaica and Trinidad and Tobago, each with 17.9 percent of capital stock, and Canada and the United Kingdom, each with 9.6 percent. The CDB's ordinary capital resources (OCR) stood at $1.8 billion, supplemented by $608 million in the Special Development Fund (SDF) and another $228 million in Other Special Funds, sources for which include the United States, Canada, Nigeria, the European Union (EU), the European Investment Bank (EIB), and the International Development Association (IDA).

Various managerial and organizational changes contributed to a 35 percent drop in approvals in 2001 to only $83.1 million for 28 projects. The bank subsequently intensified its efforts to reduce lag time between approvals and disbursement, a problem that has drawn frequent criticism. Gross approvals for loans, grants, and equity investments increased to $128 million in 2002 and $197 million in 2003, before declining to $124 million in 2004, and rebounding to $136 million in 2005, $146 million in 2006, and $179 million in 2007 (the latest year for which figures are available).

One important focus of the CDB's recent activity was raising $100 million for the new Caribbean Court of Justice (inaugurated in April 2005). Attention has also been given to improving disaster response and promoting regional air transportation and agriculture.

By 2008 the bank's main focus became the worldwide shortage of food, with the bank president, Compton Bourne, calling for increased local food production and decrying the region's excessive reliance on tourism. Brazil became a member of the bank in May 2008. Later in 2008, and well into 2009, the world economic crisis overshadowed all else. Bourne was warning governments and individuals to cut back where they could. He also warned of a region-wide decline in income from tourism and from the remittances of emigrants. In December 2008 the bank approved over $150 billion in loans to various member countries. Some of these loans were for development or infrastructure initiatives, but the major amount, $100 million, went to the government of Jamaica to assist in restructuring its finances.

In February 2008 the bank approved a $7.5 million loan to Guyana for education, infrastructure, and conservation projects. At the bank's 39th annual meeting, held May 26–27, 2009, discussion centered around ways in which the bank might lead the region out of the recession. Again, tourism came up as a potential source of greater income. In October 2009 the CDB adopted a complete suite of Oracle[tm] banking and general computer software, to modernize and improve its operations.

Central African States Development Bank
Banque de Développement des Etats de l'Afrique Centrale
(BDEAC)

Web site: www.bdeac.org

The Central African States Development Bank was established on December 3, 1975, as a joint venture of Cameroon, the Central African Republic, Chad, Republic of the Congo (Congo-Brazzaville), and Gabon, with Equatorial Guinea, previously an observer, joining as a sixth full member in 1986. The bank commenced operations January 2, 1977, as an affiliated organ of the Central African Customs and Economic Union (*Union Douanière et Economique de l'Afrique Centrale*—UDEAC), which was succeeded in 1994 by the Central African Economic and Monetary Community (*Communauté Economique et Monétaire d'Afrique Centrale*—CEMAC; see separate entry). Shareholders include the regional states, the African Development Bank, the Bank of Central African States (*Banque des Etats d'Afrique Central*—BEAC), and the governments of France and Kuwait, all of whom are represented on the Board of Directors. Germany had been a shareholder, but withdrew in 2005. The member states hold 51 percent of the bank's capital.

The bank's principal mission is to promote economic and social development through financing multinational and economic integration projects in the borrowing member countries. Particular attention is directed toward productive sectors, including efforts to modernize, convert, and privatize; rural infrastructure and development; and operations that contribute to economic integration and realization of the objectives of the CEMAC.

Throughout the 1990s the bank was under severe pressure as the result of growing arrears in loan repayments, unstable economic conditions in the region, and a series of political crises in various member countries. In the fiscal year 1991–1992, only two loans, totaling 3.9 billion CFA francs ($15 million at the time), were approved, bringing the number of cumulative loans to eighty-five. An external audit in 1992 recommended that the bank's operating costs be reduced, and in early 1993 the bank was temporarily closed and placed under military guard after it was announced that half the 80 staff positions would be eliminated. For the rest of the decade, the BDEAC failed to regain its momentum amid efforts to establish appropriate administrative structures and policies in the member states.

On January 9, 2001, Director General Emannuel Dokouna of the Central African Republic was suspended following allegations of mismanagement, which reportedly included spending more than 200 days abroad during the 1999–2000 fiscal year, using unauthorized funds to renovate his official residence, and consuming most of the bank's investment budget on personal missions. An audit was undertaken by the BEAC, the central facility for the CEMAC states. The post of director general remained vacant until August, when the CEMAC heads of state, meeting in Franceville, Gabon, named former Central African Republic prime minister Anicet Georges Dologuélé to the post. The heads of state had already indicated a desire to revitalize the BDEAC, and the new director general was expected to move rapidly toward addressing the perennial problem of arrears in loan repayments while also seeking renewed support from external partners.

By 2004 it appeared that Dologuélé had made progress in restoring the credibility of the BDEAC, with most outstanding repayments collected and the bank having paid off its own debts. It was also reported that technical experts replaced some "political" appointees on the bank's Board of Directors, while greater authority was given to external shareholders such as France and Kuwait. The BDEAC announced plans to focus new lending on small- and medium-sized businesses. At the end of 2007, the last year for which figures are available, BDEAC reported loans of 27.2 billion CFA francs (57.5 million), as against 2006's 23.1 billion CFA francs ($48.5 million), itself a large increase over 2005's 13.9 billion CFA francs ($26.7 million). A notable aspect of the bank's improved performance is the increased quality of its annual report. This report is considerably longer and more detailed than in the past. It is also bilingual, in French and English–a concession to the increasing importance of English in Francophone Africa.

Central American Bank for Economic Integration
Banco Centroamericano de Integración Económico
(BCIE/CABEI)

Web site: www.bcie.org/english/index.php

The BCIE was established December 13, 1960, as the result of an initiative originating in the Central American Economic Cooperation Committee of the (then) UN Economic Commission for Latin America (ECLA). In 1959 the committee called for the preparation, in conjunction with national and other international agencies, of a draft charter for a Central American institution dedicated to financing and promoting integrated economic development. The charter was drafted concurrently with the General Treaty on Central American Economic Integration, which established the Central American Common Market (CACM) of Costa Rica, El Salvador, Guatemala, Honduras, and Nicaragua. The latter four states signed the bank's constitutive agreement December 12, 1960, while Costa Rica became a signatory July 27, 1963. The BCIE document provides that only adherents to the general treaty are eligible for loans and guarantees. The Board of Governors constitutes the highest authority of the bank and consists of the finance minister and central bank president of each member country. The Board of Directors, responsible for BCIE's management, comprises one director from each member state.

Headquartered in Tegucigalpa, Honduras, the bank began operations May 31, 1961, and continued to function, with minimal structural changes, in the aftermath of the 1969 war between El Salvador and Honduras. The bank's mission is "promoting the progress and integration of the Isthmus, and furthering equitable economic growth and respect for the environment by supporting public and private programs that generate productive jobs and contribute to improving the region's productivity and competitiveness, as well as improving its human development indexes." It initially focused its lending on infrastructural projects (roads, water supplies, electrification, industrial development, housing, and technical education programs), but later expanded its scope to cover such additional sectors as nontraditional exports, tourism development, industrial development, agribusiness, telecommunications, and social development.

In 1985 the bank authorized the creation of a Fund for the Economic and Social Development of Central America (FESDCA) as a temporary mechanism to permit participation by extraregional countries independent of the bank's general resources. Mexico and the European Community (EC, subsequently the European Union—EU) registered as contributors to the fund in 1986, with Argentina, Colombia, and the Dominican Republic expressing interest in its operations. The FESDCA was absorbed into the bank's regular activity following the approval of BCIE charter changes in 1989 that extended full BCIE membership to extraregional countries. Argentina, Colombia, Mexico, and Taiwan have since become extraregional members, while Venezuela has contributed to the bank's subscribed capital without joining. In 1996 the EU and the BCIE created a Support Program for Small and Medium Enterprises in Central America (*Fondo Especial de Apoyo a la Micro y Pequeña Industria en América Central*—FAPIC), with donations that totaled $34.7 million as of mid-2001. Over the years, the BCIE has also utilized several other special funds, currently including the Special Fund for Honduran and Nicaraguan Export Promotion (*Fondo Especial de Promoción de Exportaciones de Honduras y Nicaragua*—FEPEX), the Fund for the Strengthening of Central American Exports (*Fondo para el Fortalecimiento de las Exportaciones Centroamericanas*—FOEXCA), and the Special Fund for the Social Transformation of Central America (*Fondo Especial para la Transformación Social de Centroamérica*—FETS). In addition, donations have been given by the U.S. Agency for International Development, the Inter-American Development Bank (IADB), Denmark, Germany, and Sweden. The bank also continues to be active in the World Bank–led initiative for Highly Indebted Poor Countries (HIPC).

Following the members' 1976 decision to undertake "special capital contributions," the bank's resources multiplied, with annual authorization peaking at $185 million in the 1980–1981 fiscal year and cumulative lending reaching $1.5 billion for 873 loans. Subsequently, bank activity plummeted because of economic, social, political, and military turmoil in the region, loan authorizations totaling only $11 million in 1983–1984, $34 million in 1984–1985, and $26 million in 1985–1986. Lending approval jumped to $117 million in 1986–1987 before falling again to $91 million in 1987–1988. Although hope for BCIE revitalization was expressed for several years in conjunction with the regional peace plan negotiated by Central American leaders, the bank was reported to be in serious difficulty in early 1991 because of the accumulation of $1.25 billion in repayment arrears. Rolando Ramírez, who directed the elimination of approximately 100 BCIE jobs and instituted other austerity measures after being named BCIE president in 1988, resigned in March 1991 because regional members "reneged" on a recently negotiated repayment plan. His successor, Frederico Alvarez, while careful to say the BCIE was not "bankrupt," called for an "urgent solution" to the problem of the bank's "low level of liquid reserves."

The bank reported some improvement in the arrears problem by mid-1992 while announcing loan authorizations for 1991–1992 of about $105 million. Thanks to the infusion of capital from its new extraregional members, the bank was generally perceived to be in a strengthened position, with BCIE officials indicating a desire to increase lending particularly in the energy and health sectors. In addition, the bank pledged to maintain its recent emphasis on the private sector, noting that more than 50 percent of the 1991–1992 loans went to private projects, compared to a previous average of only about 15 percent.

Disbursements rose to $178.5 million in 1992–1993, and bank officials announced in late 1993 that arrears were reduced from $260 million two years previously to about $53 million. The BCIE's return to sound fiscal footing was further underscored when disbursements in 1993–1994 grew to $275 million and then soared to $554 million for 118 loans in fiscal 1996–1997.

At the end of 2006, the last year for which figures are available, BCIE assets stood at $4.5 billion, including $1.5 billion in capital. Disbursements for 2008 amounted to $1.7 billion, as compared to $1.5 billion for 2007, $1.6 billion for 2006, $1.3 billion for 2005, and $1.1 billion for 2004, while new loan approvals totaled $1.4 billion, compared to $2.9 billion in 2007, $2.2 billion in 2006, $1.8 billion in 2005, and $763 million in 2004. The bank's 2004–2009 strategic plan called for emphasis on poverty reduction, regional integration, and globalization. During 2006 Panama, Belize, and the Dominican Republic joined the institution. Loans for new projects tended to lean markedly towards environmentally safe development, a trend that continued into 2009. These years were also marked by a struggle for influence in the organization between Taiwan and the People's Republic of China. Taiwan has long been active with the bank, but has recently felt increasing pressure from Beijing. The bank's president Harry Brautigan, however, attended the May 20, 2008, inauguration of Taiwanese president Ma Ying-jeou. On May 30, 2008, the bank suffered an unexpected loss when Brautigan died in an airplane crash in Honduras. Dr. Nick RISCHBIETH was named as a temporary successor and, at the end of 2008, was elected to the position in his own right. In June 2009 Rischbieth declared in an interview that, for good or ill, the world financial crisis had reinforced the relevance of development banks, such as the BCIE. Over the previous few years development banks had seemed less and less relevant as a source of funding, but now, in some of the poorest countries, they were the only institutions still making loans.

After the June 28, 2009, ouster of Honduran president Manuel Zelaya, the bank suspended all aid to that country. The new regime in Tegucigalpa (where the bank is headquartered) declared that it might end all cooperation with the bank, unless relations could be normalized.

East African Development Bank (EADB)

Web site: www.eadb.org

The charter of the East African Development Bank was contained in an annex to the December 1967 treaty establishing the East African Community (EAC), which collapsed in June 1977 because of tensions among the member countries of Kenya, Tanzania, and Uganda. Because the bank was not supported by EAC general funds, it remained formally in existence, with headquarters in Kampala, Uganda. Subsequently, a mediator responsible for dividing the community's assets among its former members was given the task of making recommendations concerning the bank's future, and in late 1979 a new tripartite treaty providing for a revival of EADB activity was drafted. The bank's revised charter, completed during the first half of 1980 and signed by the three members in July, sought to rechannel the thrust of bank lending toward agricultural, infrastructural, and technical assistance efforts.

The bank's principal organ is the Governing Council, which comprises the members' ministers of finance. A Board of Directors includes representatives of the African Development Bank (AfDB), the three member countries, and the private sector. The Danish International Development Agency (DANIDA) was also represented until it withdrew from the bank in 2000. An Advisory Panel of international financial experts also meets regularly.

In 1990 it was reported that 71 of the EADB's outstanding loans were in arrears, and officials in late 1991 indicated that the bank was experiencing severe operational problems. Much of the difficulty was attributed to currency devaluations arising from members' imposition of structural adjustment policies requested by the International Monetary Fund (IMF) as a condition for further support. (In 1984 the IMF gave the EADB permission to utilize its special drawing rights [SDR] as a unit of account.) Consequently, only two loans totaling SDR 1.53 million ($2.2 million) were approved in 1991, while the bank suffered the first operating loss in its history. The EADB subsequently announced that a "major restructuring" would be implemented.

In 1995 the bank announced it accepted the recommendations of an external panel of experts, who suggested that the EADB become more aggressive in collecting debts, give greater attention to the quality of its loans, and expand its financial advisory services. In addition, the EADB decided to emphasize export-oriented loans as well as those geared to promote tourism in the region. Lending approvals in 1998 totaled $42.1 million, compared to $30 million in 1996 and 1997.

In 2000 the Governing Council approved a long-term strategic plan for 2001–2005 that envisaged an expansion of assets to SDR 300 million ($391 million), partly in anticipation of strengthened international standing occasioned by the revival of the EAC (see separate entry on the EAC). The final ratification of the new EAC treaty was accomplished July 7, and the three-member community was formally relaunched January 15, 2001. In its annual report for 2006, still in late 2009 the latest available, the bank reported loan approvals for the year of $108 million, with disbursements of $89 million, a substantial increase over 2005's $52 million approvals and $41 million disbursements. The EADB also reported a threefold increase in profits during 2006, $4.6 million compared to $1.4 million for 2005. The bank attributed this increase to an increase in the volume and quality of lending activity.

The EADB and the China Development Bank signed an agreement in June 2006 to cooperate in mutually agreed development projects in East Africa. At the signing ceremony, the EADB's director general Godfrey Tumusiime described EADB as "poised to be transformed into the leading agency for facilitation of East African regional integration and development." Also in 2006 the EAC mandated a further reorganization of the EADB, designed to make it the leading economic development organ in the region. Plans were under way for a venture capital fund, the first in the region, to begin operation in 2008. A regional housing finance subsidiary, intended to help provide affordable housing, is also slated to open in 2008. During 2007 the EADB made overtures to Burundi and Rwanda, encouraging them to join. In December 2007 Rwanda pledged to do everything necessary to facilitate EADB's entry into the Rwanda market. In March 2008 Rwanda was accepted into membership of EADB, subject to it meeting the capital requirements for shareholder subscriptions. The arrangement was completed the following November. In June 2008 China opened a $30 million line of credit at EADB to finance projects in the region. The money was however only to be available to projects that had some Chinese involvement.

In November 2008 the bank announced that it anticipated a loss of $8.9 million for the year 2007. This loss, shocking after several years' slowly improving performance, was attributed to a large number of nonperforming loans that had been made to politically connected people and companies. The contract of director general Tumusiime, set to expire at the end of 2008, was not renewed. In March 2009 he was replaced by Vivienne Yega Apopo, of Zambia, with promises of further support by the bank's member states and financial institutions. To add to the bank's troubles, in July 2009 the Appeals Court of Zambia awarded an individual $100 million damages against the bank, in a lawsuit that had been in progress in different forms for some ten years. Observers described the award as "obscene," but it nonetheless threatened the bank's existence, if not overturned on further appeal. Member countries indicated that they would not intervene to pay a private person a sum greater than the bank's assets.

European Bank for Reconstruction and Development
Banque Européenne pour la Reconstruction et la Développement
(EBRD/BERD)

Web site: www.ebrd.com

The idea of a multibillion-dollar international lending effort to help revive the economies of Eastern European countries and assist their conversion to free-market activity was endorsed by the heads of the European Community (EC, subsequently the European Union—EU) in December 1989, based on a proposal from French president François Mitterrand. After several months of negotiation in which most other leading Western countries were brought into the project, a treaty to establish the EBRD with initial capitalization of $12.4 billion was signed by 40 nations, the EC, and the European Investment Bank (EIB) on May 29, 1990, in Paris, France. London was chosen as the headquarters for the bank, which proponents described as one of the most important international aid projects since World War II. Mitterrand's special adviser, Jacques Attali, who first suggested such an enterprise, was named to direct its operations. The bank officially opened April 15, 1991.

According to the bank's charter, its purpose is to "promote private and entrepreneurial initiative" in Eastern European countries "committed to applying the principles of multiparty democracy, pluralism, and market economics." Although the United Kingdom and the United States originally pressed for lending to be limited entirely to the private sector, a compromise was reached permitting up to 40 percent of the EBRD's resources to be used for public sector projects, such as roads and telecommunications. The bank operated using the basket of the currencies of EC member states known as the European Currency Unit (ECU) until January 1, 1999, when the euro came into existence, replacing the ECU at par.

Although Washington initially opposed its participation, the Soviet Union was permitted to become a member of the EBRD on the condition that it would not borrow more from the bank than it contributed in capital for at least three years, at which point the stipulation would be reviewed. The restriction was imposed because of fears that Soviet needs could draw down most of the EBRD resources and because of U.S. arguments that Moscow had yet to meet the criteria of democracy and market orientation. Despite the "net zero" limitation, Moscow was reportedly eager to join the organization because it would be its first capitalist-oriented membership in an international financial institution, and in March 1991 the Supreme Soviet endorsed participation by a vote of 380–1. The net zero condition was eliminated following the breakup of the Soviet Union, with the bank declaring the newly independent former Soviet republics to be eligible for up to 40 percent of total EBRD lending.

The United States is the largest shareholding member, with 10.1 percent of the capital, followed by Germany, France, Japan, Italy, and the United Kingdom, each with 8.6 percent as of December 31, 2007. At the launching of the EBRD, the Soviet Union held a 6 percent share, two-thirds of which was subsequently allocated to Russia and the remainder to the other 14 former Soviet republics, all of which (Armenia, Azerbaijan, Belarus, Estonia, Georgia, Kazakhstan, Kyrgyzstan, Latvia, Lithuania, Moldova, Tajikistan, Turkmenistan, Ukraine, and Uzbekistan) joined the bank in 1992. At the end of 2007, Russia held 4 percent of shares, while the EU itself and the EIB each held 3 percent. In addition to these 23 members, 40 other states are bank members: Albania, Australia, Austria, Belgium, Bosnia and Herzegovina, Bulgaria, Canada, Croatia, Cyprus, Czech Republic, Denmark, Egypt, Finland, Greece, Hungary, Iceland, Ireland, Israel, Republic of Korea, Liechtenstein, Luxembourg, Macedonia, Malta, Mexico, Mongolia, Montenegro, Morocco, Netherlands, New Zealand, Norway, Poland, Portugal, Romania, Serbia, Slovakia, Slovenia, Spain, Sweden, Switzerland, and Turkey.

Apart from ordinary resources, the EBRD also administers 11 special funds: the Baltic Investment Special Fund and the Baltic Technical Assistance Special Fund, to aid private sector development of small- and medium-sized enterprises (SMEs) in Estonia, Latvia, and Lithuania; the Russian Small Business Investment Special Fund and the Russian Small Business Technical Cooperation Special Fund; the Balkan Region Special Fund and the EBRD SME Special Fund, to assist, respectively, in reconstruction and in development of SMEs in Albania, Bosnia and Herzegovina, Bulgaria, Croatia, Macedonia, Romania, and Yugoslavia; the EBRD Technical Cooperation Fund, to aid in financing technical cooperation projects; the Financial Intermediary Investment Special Fund, to support financial intermediaries in all countries of operation; the Italian Investment Special Fund, to aid modernization, restructuring, expansion, and development of SMEs in selected countries; the Moldova Micro Business Investment Special Fund, to target SME development in Moldova; and the SME Finance Facility Special Fund, to aid SME financing in Bulgaria, Czech Republic, Estonia, Hungary, Latvia, Lithuania, Poland, Romania, Slovakia, and Slovenia. Some 16 countries—including non-EU members Canada, Iceland, Japan, Norway, Switzerland, "Taipei, China," and the United States—have pledged an aggregate of 311 million euros ($278 million) to the 11 funds. At the end of 2001 the eight special investment funds claimed 239 million euros ($213 million) in assets, while the three technical assistance/cooperation funds had a balance of 4.8 million euros ($4.3 million) in remaining available funds.

The first EBRD loans were approved in late 1991. At the first annual meeting of the Board of Governors in April 1992, bank officials reported that 20 loans totaling ECU 621 million (about $770 million) were thus far approved. However, the bank's impact was described as marginal by some East European leaders, and it was widely accepted that lending was restrained by problems in finding reliable borrowers for specific projects. EBRD President Attali reportedly suggested that the bank consider making loans in support of long-term economic restructuring, but the idea was quickly vetoed by the United States as beyond the EBRD mandate and a duplication of World Bank activities.

At the second Board of Governors' meeting in April 1993, it was announced that the bank approved 54 investment projects in 1992, involving a total EBRD contribution of ECU 1.2 billion (about $1.5 billion), although actual disbursements for the year totaled only ECU 126 million (about $156 million). The meeting was overshadowed by earlier press disclosures that EBRD disbursement up to the end of 1992 was only half the level of the bank's expenditure on its London offices, staff salaries, travel expenses, and administrative costs. Amid widespread criticism of his style of management, Attali announced his resignation as EBRD president June 25. In August, Jacques de Larosiére of France, a former managing director of the International Monetary Fund (IMF), was designated as Attali's successor, and in November the Board of Governors approved internal spending reforms he proposed.

At the March 1994 Board of Governors' meeting, it was announced that the EBRD earned an approximate $4.5 million profit in 1993, compared to a loss of $7.3 million the previous year. De Larosiére told the April 1995 annual meeting, however, that he expected the bank's capital base to be exhausted by the end of 1997 under the current rate of lending. Although it was widely conceded that the bank made significant improvement in its "budgetary discipline," Western donors reportedly were awaiting still further reform in bank operations before agreeing to launch replenishment talks.

At the EBRD's annual meeting held in mid-April 1996 in Sofia, Bulgaria, de Larosiére called on Eastern European nations to strengthen their banking regulations and supervision. The failure of private banks to follow "basic banking procedures" was contributing to economic difficulties in many Eastern European nations, he said. The shareholders also agreed to double the EBRD's authorized capital from ECU 10 billion to ECU 20 billion (about $25 billion at exchange rates then prevailing) to accommodate a proposed substantial lending increase. The increase went into effect in April 1997, with 48 of the 60 members depositing their instruments of subscription to the capital increase by the end of the year. President de Larosiére said the additional resources would ensure the EBRD would continue to operate "on the cutting edge" of the economic transition in Europe.

With the EBRD emerging in the post-Soviet era as the single largest source of private sector financing in Russia, that country's financial crisis in August 1998 resulted in a loss of 261 million ECUs ($283 million) for the year. At the end of 1998, Russia accounted for about 25 percent of the EBRD's disbursed outstanding loans, but despite the crisis and its profound impact throughout the region, only four Russian loans were classified as nonperforming. Overall financing for 1998 totaled 2.37 billion ECUs ($2.57 billion) for 96 projects, down from 108 in 1997. Only a year later, the EBRD had returned to profitability, earning 42.7 billion euros ($43.1 billion) as the region recovered more rapidly than expected.

EBRD President de Larosiére announced his retirement in January 1998, and was succeeded in July 1998 by Horst Köhler, president of the German Savings Bank Association. Köhler, who resigned after 20 months in office to become managing director of the IMF, was in turn succeeded in July 2000 by Jean Lemierre, a French financial official.

In recent years the bank has shifted attention from the more developed economies of Central Europe, which absorbed about half of EBRD investments in 1995, toward the east. In its November 2001 Transition Report, the EBRD, looking ahead to the eventual EU accession of ten bank members, urged that all 27 countries of operation continue to receive assistance. Otherwise, the bank feared a "Brussels lace curtain"—the financial and economic equivalent of the Iron Curtain—might divide the EU from the rest of the continent.

In April 2004 the EBRD announced plans for substantial expansion of lending to its seven poorest members (Armenia, Azerbaijan, Georgia, Kyrgyzstan, Moldova, Tajikistan, and Uzbekistan). In particular, the bank said it would direct support to the private sector in those countries.

Lending commitments in 2008 totaled 5.1 billion euros for 302projects. The 2008 commitments, affected by the world financial crisis, represented a 9 percent decrease from the 2007 level of 5.6 billion euros for 353 projects. The 2006 numbers were 4.9 billion euros for 301 projects, compared to 4.3 billion euros for 151 projects in 2005, 4.1 billion euros for 129 projects in 2004, 3.7 billion euros for 119 projects in 2003, and 3.9 billion euros for 102 projects in 2002. Of the 2008 commitments, 57 percent went to "early and intermediate transition countries," while 42 percent went to Russia, and only 1 percent went to "advanced transition countries."

The years 2005–2007 also marked a period of relative success in achieving the bank's aims. At the end of 2007, the Czech Republic was slated to be the first recipient country to "graduate" meaning that it had achieved "an advanced state of transition" and would receive no more EBRD investment. In March 2007 the bank announced that net profit had increased by 57 percent to a record 2.4 billion euros in 2006 from a year earlier, an increase largely caused by gains from stock investments. The bank entered into micro-lending projects in several less-developed countries of Eastern Europe and Asia. In September 2007 a project was announced (to be administered by the EBRD) to cover the site of the Chernobyl nuclear disaster in a giant steel protective casing.

In May 2008 the EBRD issued a $1 billion (711 million euro) global bond, its first benchmark issue since 2004. In May Thomas Mirow of Germany was named president, succeeding Lemierre at the end of his two four-year terms. Mirow's appointment was controversial, the process being condemned by some, especially Sweden, as not sufficiently transparent. He was also seen as Germany's candidate, with the German government known to be interested in merging the EBRD with the European Investment Bank. Berlin felt that with the economic maturation of much of the former Soviet bloc such a merger would be a good direction for the bank to take. Also in May 2008 Turkey applied for full membership in the bank, becoming a full country of operations as well as a shareholder in November of that year. In November 2008 the bank announced that it would boost investment in 2009, particularly in Central and Eastern Europe, to combat the growing international financial crisis. It also declared that, unlike many companies and institutions, it would not lay off staff. The year 2009 saw the bank making loans to many smaller enterprises in Eastern Europe and Western and Central Asia.

European Investment Bank
(EIB)

Web site: www.eib.org

The EIB is the European Union (EU) bank for long-term finance. It was created by the Treaty of Rome, which established the European Economic Community (EEC) on January 1, 1958. The bank, headquartered in Luxembourg, has as its basic function the balanced and steady development of EU member countries, with the greater part of its financing going to projects that favor the development of less-advanced regions and serve the common interests of several members or the whole community. Although industrial modernization remains important in the context of an expanded community and its transformation into the EU, emphasis has shifted more toward projects involving communications infrastructure, urban development, the environment, energy security, regional development, and cross-national industrial integration. Most recently, projects in health and education have taken on greater importance.

The EIB membership is identical to that of the EU: Austria, Belgium, Bulgaria, Cyprus, Czech Republic, Denmark, Estonia, Finland, France, Germany, Greece, Hungary, Ireland, Italy, Latvia, Lithuania, Luxembourg, Malta, Netherlands, Poland, Portugal, Romania, Slovakia, Slovenia, Spain, Sweden, and the United Kingdom. Each has subscribed part of the bank's capital of 164.8 billion euros, although most funds required to finance its operations are borrowed by the bank on international and national capital markets. Capital shares range from 0.4 percent of the total for Malta to 16.2 percent each for France, Germany, Italy, and the United Kingdom. Only 5 percent of capital is paid in. Outstanding loans are limited to 2.5 times the subscribed capital.

EIB activities were initially confined to the territory of member states but have gradually been extended to many other countries under terms of association or cooperation agreements. Current participants include 10 countries in the Mediterranean region (Algeria, Egypt, Israel, Jordan, Lebanon, Morocco, Serbia, Syria, Tunisia, and Turkey) and the 77 African, Caribbean, and Pacific (ACP) signatories of the Lomé IV Convention and its successor, the Cotonou Agreement of 2000.

The bank is administered by a 27-member Board of Governors (one representative—usually the finance or economy minister—from each EU state) and a 28-member Board of Directors (one from each member state and one representing the European Commission). The president of the bank, appointed by the Board of Governors, chairs the Board of Directors, heads a Management Committee that encompasses eight vice presidents, and oversees the 1,000-plus EIB staff. Other organs include a 9-member Management Committee, a 3-member Audit Committee, a General Secretariat, a General Administration Office, and five directorates (Lending Operations in Europe, Lending Operations Outside Europe, Finance, Projects, and Risk Management).

The EIB's lending rose rapidly in the 1990s in response to the "buoyant level of investment" in the member countries, financial requirements arising from the EU single market, and more flexible lending conditions. In addition, the bank began to approve its own loans in Eastern and Central Europe, Latin America, and Asia. Within the community itself, the EIB was directed by the European Council in December 1992 to assist in the development of the economic and monetary union envisioned by the Maastricht Treaty. In addition, in connection with the launching of the EU in November 1993, the EIB was asked to concentrate on trans-European projects (particularly those in the communications, energy, environmental, and transportation sectors) and small- and medium-sized enterprises (SMEs). Some of that activity was directed through a new European Investment Fund (EIF) launched in mid-1994 to provide loan guarantees to projects deemed valuable for "strengthening the internal market." The EIB also participated in the creation of the European Bank for Reconstruction and Development (EBRD, above) to assist in implementing economic reforms and support political democratization throughout Eastern Europe. Other initiatives include lending to assist in economic recovery programs in Northern Ireland and the Gaza Strip/West Bank territory administered by the Palestinian Authority. The EIB also began lending to South Africa. At the end of 2006 the EIB ended a freeze on loans to Israel.

In June 1997 the European Council asked the EIB to increase funding to infrastructure projects and SMEs to promote employment. The EIB, already one of the largest fund sources for such projects, responded by financing the Amsterdam Special Action Programme (ASAP) for three years. The ASAP channeled funding to the more "labor intensive" areas of health and education, "innovative, growth oriented" SMEs, and infrastructure projects.

In line with a March 2000 decision of the European Council to further increase support for SMEs, the EIB Board of Governors established an EIB Group comprising the EIB and the EIF. The EIB was directed to increase its shares in the latter from the original 40 percent to 60 percent, with the balance held by the European Commission (30 percent) and various European financial institutions (10 percent). The reorganization was intended to improve the group's ability to approve and administer loans, venture capital investments, and SME guarantees.

The EIB Group constituted a core component of the EIB's Innovation 2000 Initiative (i2i), which earmarked for the following three years 12–15 billion euros for loans involving SMEs and such sectors as health, education, research and development, and information and communications technology. Under its current president, former Belgian finance minister Philippe Maystadt, the bank has continued to shift its emphasis toward projects involving human resources and advanced technology.

The annual value of signed EIB financing contracts rose incrementally throughout the 1990s, reaching, in the last year of the decade, 31.8 billion euros. The total increased by 13 percent in 2000 to 36 billion euros and to 36.8 billion euros in 2001.

Although the impending expansion of the EU by ten members or more drew considerable attention to the EIB's preaccession assistance, its additional partners around the world also continued to avail themselves of EIB resources. For example, under the 2000 Cotonou pact, total EU aid to the ACP countries for 2002–2006 was set at 15.2 billion euros: 11.3 billion euros as grants from EU members, 2.2. billion euros to be managed by the EIB through an Investment Facility, and some 1.7 billion euros in loans from EIB resources.

In 2001 the EIB agreed to permit lending to Russia for environmental projects in regions that border EIB member states. Subsequently, the bank expanded its authorized capital in 2002–2003 to facilitate the inclusion of ten new members in 2004.

In March 2005 the bank announced plans to expand private sector lending in the southern Mediterranean and to resume lending in Palestinian areas. Lending approvals in 2008 totaled 59.3 billion euros, compared to 56.5 billion euros in 2007, 53 billion euros in 2006, 47.4 billion euros in 2005, 43.2 billion euros in 2004, 42.3 billion euros in 2003, and 39.6 billion euros in 2002. Of the 2008 total, 53.2 billion euros went to EU states and 6.1 billion to other countries.

Activity in 2007 concentrated on energy and climate-change matters. The EIB and the World Bank created a carbon-credit fund for Europe, and in June 2007 the EIB, long criticized for a lack of interest in such matters, formulated in its 2007–2009 operational plan a priority of "sustainable, competitive and secure energy." Likewise in March 2008 the bank declared that rail projects remained a top concern. In March also the EIB denied that it was interested in acquiring a majority stake in the EBRD (see previous article).

The bank's 2009 annual report rolled out an operational plan for the years 2009–2011. This plan called for a significant increase in lending, especially to SMEs, to counter the global recession. The bank's intention was to increase its total lending volume by approximately 30 percent in 2009 and 2010. To this end, in July 2009 the EIB's Board of Directors approved an increase in the bank's global long term borrowing authorization for the 2009 funding program from 70 billion euros to 80 billion euros.

Inter-American Development Bank
Banco Interamericano de Desarrollo
(IADB/BID)

Web site: www.iadb.org

Following a reversal of long-standing opposition by the United States, the IADB was launched in 1959 after acceptance of a charter drafted by a special commission to the Inter-American Economic and Social Council of the Organization of American States (OAS).

Operations began October 1, 1960, with permanent headquarters in Washington, D.C.

The current members of the IADB are Argentina, Austria, Bahamas, Barbados, Belgium, Belize, Bolivia, Brazil, Canada, Chile, China, Colombia, Costa Rica, Croatia, Denmark, the Dominican Republic, Ecuador, El Salvador, Finland, France, Germany, Guatemala, Guyana, Haiti, Honduras, Israel, Italy, Jamaica, Japan, the Republic of Korea, Mexico, the Netherlands, Nicaragua, Norway, Panama, Paraguay, Peru, Portugal, Slovenia, Spain, Suriname, Sweden, Switzerland, Trinidad and Tobago, the United Kingdom, the United States, Uruguay, and Venezuela.

The purpose of the IADB is to accelerate economic and social development in Latin America, in part by acting as a catalyst for public and private external capital. In addition to helping states in the region coordinate development efforts, the bank provides technical assistance; borrows on international capital markets; and participates in cofinancing with other multilateral agencies, national institutions, and commercial banks. Loans typically cover a maximum of 50–80 percent of project costs, depending on the level of development of the country in which the projects are located; poverty-reduction projects in the least-developed countries may be eligible for 90 percent financing. In the wake of criticism that the bank had not supported regional integration and had neglected the area's poorest nations, major contributors agreed in December 1978, after eight months of intense negotiations, to adopt a U.S.-sponsored policy that would allocate less assistance to wealthier developing nations—such as Argentina, Brazil, and Mexico—and, within such countries, would focus primarily on projects aimed at benefiting the neediest economic sectors.

Each IADB member is represented on the Board of Governors, the bank's policymaking body, by a governor and an alternate, who convene at least once a year. Administrative responsibilities are exercised by 14 executive directors. The Board of Executive Directors is responsible for day-to-day oversight of operations. The bank president, elected by the governors, presides over sessions of the Board of Executive Directors and, in conjunction with an executive vice president and a vice president for planning and administration, is responsible for the management of various offices as well as 13 departments. These departments cover such issues as regional operations, development effectiveness and strategic planning, the private sector, sustainable development, research, information technology and general services, human resources, budget and corporate procurement, integration and regional programs, finance, and legal. An Office of Evaluation and Oversight reports directly to the Board of Executive Directors. In addition, the IADB has established the Institute for Latin American and Caribbean Integration (*Instituto para la Integración de América Latina y el Caribe*—INTAL), founded in 1964 and headquartered in Buenos Aires, Argentina; and the Inter-American Institute for Social Development (*Instituto Interamericano para el Desarrollo Social*—INDES), which opened in 1995 in Washington, D.C.

IADB voting is on a weighted basis according to a country's capital subscription; leading subscribers as of December 31, 2007, were the United States (30.0 percent), Argentina and Brazil (10.8 percent), Mexico (6.9 percent), Venezuela (5.8 percent), Japan (5.0 percent), and Canada (4.0 percent). Non-American members held about 16 percent of the voting shares. Total subscribed capital at that time was $101 billion.

In November 1984 the Inter-American Investment Corporation (IIC) was established as an autonomous affiliate of the IADB to "encourage the establishment, expansion, and modernization of small- and medium-sized private enterprises" (SMEs) by extending long-term loans and otherwise assuming equity positions in such projects, helping to raise additional resources, and offering advisory services. The first joint meeting of the Boards of Governors of the IADB and the IIC was held in March 1987, with the IIC making its initial disbursements in late 1989.

In 1993 the IIC approved loans and equity investments totaling $124 million for 31 projects, but approvals fell to $42.7 million for 14 projects in 1994. The decline was attributed to a "period of consolidation" precipitated by calls for a review of the corporation's performance to date, including assessment of administrative costs. Based on the recommendation of an external committee of international experts, the IIC staff was halved to approximately 60 employees in 1994 and additional efficiency measures were instituted. Consequently, the IIC shareholders renewed their backing for the corporation at the April 1995 joint annual meeting with the IADB. Governors agreed to increase the IIC debt to equity ratio to 3:1, thereby permitting lending to increase to $600 million based on the corporation's subscribed capital of $200 million. The governors also agreed to open IIC membership to nonmembers of the IADB, a measure designed to permit the accession of Taiwan, which has strong economic ties with many Latin American countries. As of 2001, however, all nonregional members were IADB members. In 2000 the IADB Board of Governors approved a capital increase to $700 million for the IIC.

Another IADB affiliate, the Multilateral Investment Fund (MIF), was formally launched in January 1993. Together, the IADB, IIC, and MIF are identified as the IADB Group. Unlike the IIC, which supports individual projects directly, MIF attempts to improve the investment climate in the region in general by financing management training and developing local financial institutions designed to assist small-scale entrepreneurs. The fund also provides grants to help countries formulate policies designed to alleviate the "human and social costs" of structural adjustment. Like the IIC, MIF is an autonomous operation, although it uses IADB technical and administrative resources. About $1.3 billion was pledged (including $500 million each from Japan and the United States) for MIF's first five years. In 1994, MIF's first full year of operation, 29 projects totaling $64 million were approved.

The IADB also serves as administrator of more than 50 trust funds—for example, the U.S.-backed Social Progress Trust Fund, the Japan Special Fund, and the Venezuelan Trust Fund. Relations within the IADB between the United States and some Latin members have been tense on occasion. The bank called for a $25 billion replenishment in 1986, but a dispute ensued when the United States asked for greater influence, including virtual veto power over loans. Although willing to accept the U.S. proposal to link some loans to economic reforms, Latin American and Caribbean members objected strongly to the veto request. The conflict was seen as central to the February 1988 resignation of Antonio Ortiz Mena of Mexico after 17 years as IADB president. Uruguay's foreign minister, Enrique Iglesias, was named president effective April 1, and, shortly thereafter, a high-level review committee was established that in December called for wide-ranging reform of the bank's procedures and organization. Concurrently, the Board of Executive Directors adopted an austerity administrative budget for 1989 and endorsed plans to reduce the bank's staff by more than 10 percent.

In early 1989 the IADB reported that 32 loans were approved in 1988 totaling $1.7 billion, down significantly from $2.4 billion in 1987 and $3.0 billion in 1986, and the lowest total since 1976. The decline was attributed to the replenishment impasse as well as the difficulty many bank members faced in undertaking new projects because of the continued regional economic crisis. However, the bank's prospects improved significantly when an 11th-hour compromise was reached on the proposed replenishment at the March 1989 Board of Governors meeting. The agreement, considered a personal triumph for Iglesias, authorized a $26.5 billion capital increase (bringing total authorized capital to $61 billion), designed to permit aggregate lending of $22.5 billion in 1990–1993. Also, $200 million was approved for the Fund for Special Operations (FSO), the bank's concessional lending window. Although the United States was not given the blanket veto power it sought, a system of "staggered delays" was established under which challenges to specific loans would be reviewed before release of funds.

In conjunction with the replenishment, the Board of Governors for the first time directed that some bank resources be used to support national economic policy changes via so-called sector adjustment loans. The bank also agreed, as part of its "revival," to a thorough internal reorganization designed to enhance effectiveness and boost the IADB's capacity to transfer resources. As a result, several new divisions were created to reflect the bank's new priorities of regional economic integration, environmental protection, the financing of micro-enterprises, development of human resources, and additional channeling of nonregional funds (from Japan, in particular) to the region.

Stemming in part from resolution of the replenishment issue, lending approvals in 1989 grew to $2.6 billion for 36 loans involving 29 projects in 15 countries. Approvals in 1990 jumped to $3.9 billion for 45 loans; included were the first 6 sector adjustment loans (totaling $1.3 billion), the first 3 micro-enterprise loans, and 10 loans that were either directly designed to improve environmental conditions or that contained significant environmental components. Continuing its rapid expansion, the bank approved $5.3 billion in loans in 1991 and $6.0 billion in 1992 and 1993.

After 16 months of negotiations, agreement was reached in April 1994 on the bank's next and biggest replenishment, under which subscribed capital grew to $100 billion. Bank officials announced an expanded mandate for lending through the end of the century, consideration to be given for the first time to the "modernization of the state" through reform, for example, of legislative and judicial institutions. In addition, a projected 40 percent of the replenishment was to be earmarked for health services, education, poverty alleviation, and other "social commitments." More support in those areas was urged by a task force established in 1993, which otherwise described the bank's portfolio as "generally sound."

The IADB also made it clear it would continue to assist governments establish policies designed to encourage free-market activity, while at least five percent of the replenishment would be used for direct loans to the private sector. That emphasis was apparently underscored at the request of donor countries, particularly the United States, which were to have voting power virtually equal to that of borrowing countries. The bank was also given a lead role, in conjunction with the OAS, in following up on the recommendations of the Summit of the Americas, held in December 1994 in Miami, Florida. Among other things, the 34 nations represented at the summit agreed to work toward creation of a Free Trade Area of the Americas by 2005. To that end, the OAS and the IADB signed an agreement in mid-1995 to coordinate their policies and activities to promote regional economic integration. At the second Summit of the Americas, held in April 1998 in Santiago, Chile, IADB President Iglesias pledged that the bank would develop a training facility to improve its members' bargaining skills in matters of international trade and provide $40 billion in loans in the next five years, including $5 billion for education and $500 million for micro-enterprises.

IADB lending approvals dropped to $5.3 billion in 1994 before rebounding to a record level in 1995 of $7.3 billion for 82 projects in 22 countries. Mexico was the leading recipient of new loans, partly because of the economic crisis it suffered beginning in late 1994. The IADB credited the absence of a deeper economic crisis in Latin America to liberal economic reforms and regional integration. However, rising unemployment and social inequities within the region had begun to concern bank officials by 1996. Approvals totaled $6.8 billion in 1996 and $6.0 billion in 1997 before jumping to $10 billion in 1998. Lending in 1999 totaled $9.5 billion. In May that year the IADB and the World Bank committed a combined $5.3 billion toward a $9 billion reconstruction package for Central American countries devastated by Hurricane Mitch in October 1998. The funding concentrated on debt relief and concessional financing for infrastructure, with the IADB contribution of $3.5 billion combining soft loans and grants over a five-year period.

The annual IADB meeting in late March 2000 in Washington, D.C., served to refocus attention on the effectiveness of bank lending strategies. Addressing the meeting, U.S. Secretary of the Treasury Lawrence Summers proposed that the IADB reassess its programs, increase interest charged to the more affluent borrowing countries, and accelerate the move from large-scale projects—for example, power generation infrastructure—toward smaller ones designed to help alleviate poverty. His remarks, which were supported by Iglesias, came in the context of mounting evidence that despite rapid regional economic growth in the 1990s as a whole, the percent of the population in abject poverty had not changed over the decade. According to the United Nations (UN) Economic Commission for Latin America and the Caribbean (ECLAC), 15 percent of the population in borrowing countries remained in extreme poverty, with about 40 percent living on $2 a day or less. President Iglesias noted that various economic adjustment policies, although largely successful, had not adequately confronted social problems, and he warned that resultant discontent could ultimately erode democracy in the region.

In 2004 the IADB announced its support for the proposed Central American Free Trade Agreement (CAFTA) and began to allocate resources to projects designed to prepare for it. The bank also committed itself to providing greater assistance to small- and medium-sized businesses and to simplifying procedures for lending to businesses in general. The subject receiving the most attention in the first half of 2005 was China's request for membership. The United States continued to oppose China's application, officially because of Washington's belief that a country should not join a development bank as a donor if it owes money to another development bank (China has outstanding World Bank loans). Complicating the issue was the fact that ten IADB shareholders maintained diplomatic ties with Taiwan. Also in 2005, Luis Alberto Moreno of Colombia was elected to succeed Iglesias as IADB president.

On the sidelines of the bank's March 2007 annual meeting in Guatemala City, China signed a memorandum of understanding with the bank, laying down a framework for formal negotiations for membership. The United States withdrew its previous objections to China's membership. At this meeting the bank also announced that Bolivia, Guyana, Haiti, Honduras, and Nicaragua, five of the poorest countries in Latin America, were to have their debts to the bank, a sum of more than $4 billion, forgiven. Concurrently, it was announced that remittances from Latin American emigrants now exceeded all foreign investment and aid to the region.

Loan approvals and guarantees totaled $7.6 billion in 2008, compared to $7.1 billion in 2007, $6.5 billion in 2006, $6.7 billion in 2005, $5.5 billion in 2004, $6.2 billion in 2003, and $4.1 billion in 2002. Cumulative loans and guarantees reached $137 billion; cumulative disbursements reached $146.5 billion. It was noted that remittances from emigrants now far surpassed all other forms of aid to countries in the region, although the global economic downturn was putting some of this revenue stream at risk.

On January 12, 2009, China officially joined the bank as its 48th member. During 2009 the bank was discussing a significant capital increase, its first for fifteen years. In July 2009 the bank eliminated a rule known as the Policy-Based Lending Authority, in order to allow Canada to increase its callable (but not paid-in) capital available for lending. In August Canada temporarily increased its callable capital by $4 billion, the increase to last for between five and eight years.

Islamic Development Bank
(IDB)

Web site: www.isdb.org

The IDB originated in a Declaration of Intent issued by the Conference of Finance Ministers of Islamic Countries during their December 15, 1973, meeting in Jiddah, Saudi Arabia. The bank's Articles of Agreement were approved and adopted by the Second Conference of Finance Ministers on August 10, 1974, with the bank commencing activities in October 1975.

The purpose of the IDB, which is headquartered in Jiddah, is to "foster the economic development and social progress of member countries and Muslim communities individually as well as jointly," guided by the tenets of *sharia* (Islamic law). In addition to providing assistance for feasibility studies, infrastructural projects, development of industry and agriculture, import financing, and technology transfers, the IDB operates several special funds, including one to aid Muslim populations in nonmember countries. Because *sharia* proscriptions include the collection of interest, various alternative financing methods such as leasing and profit-sharing are pursued, with service charges for loans being based on the expected administrative costs of the loan operations. The IDB also attempts to promote cooperation with Islamic banks as well as with national development institutions and other international agencies.

The bank uses as its unit of account the Islamic Dinar (ID), which is on par with the special drawing rights (SDR) of the International Monetary Fund. In July 1992 the Board of Governors, acting on a recommendation of the Organization of the Islamic Conference (OIC), agreed to raise the authorized capital from ID 2 billion to ID 6 billion (about $8.5 billion) and subscribed capital to ID 4 billion (about $5.7 billion).

The bank's primary decision-making and administrative organs are a Board of Governors and a Board of Executive Directors, the former comprised of the member countries' ministers of finance or their designees. Of the 14 executive directors, 7 are appointed by the 7 largest subscribers to the bank's capital (Saudi Arabia, 24 percent; Kuwait, 12 percent; Libya, 10 percent; Iran, 9 percent; Egypt, 9 percent; Turkey, 8 percent; and the United Arab Emirates, 7 percent), while 7 are elected by the governors of the other member states.

A prerequisite to joining the bank is membership in the Organization of the Islamic Conference (OIC), 55 of whose members now belong to the IDB. The bank governors voted to suspend Afghanistan's membership at their 1981 annual meeting in conjunction with a similar suspension by the OIC. In early 1989 the OIC gave the vacant IDB seat to the government-in-exile announced by Afghan guerrilla groups, with the membership returning to normal status after the fall of the Najibullah government in April 1992.

In 1986 the Board of Governors approved the establishment of a Longer-term Trade Financing Scheme (LTTFS, subsequently renamed the Export Financing Scheme—EFS) as a strategy to increase member countries' exports; contributions for the scheme, in operation since 1988, are made to a trust fund within the IDB. An Import Trade Financing Operation (ITFO) also exists to help fund the import of capital, rather than consumer, goods.

The bank launched a $100 million IDB Unit Investment Fund (UIF) in 1990 to serve as a secondary market for mobilizing additional financial resources by pooling investors' savings and directing them to projects that would achieve a "reasonable level of investment return" while accelerating social and economic development. The fund's authorized resources were later increased to $500 million, although the full amount is not yet achieved.

In March 1987 the IDB was selected to manage the new Islamic Banks' Portfolio (IBP), a fund established by 21 Islamic banks primarily to finance private sector trade and investment between Islamic countries. The IDB also launched an Islamic Corporation for the Insurance of Investment and Export Credit (ICIEC) in mid-1995 to support trade and investment between Muslim states.

The UIF, the IBP, the ICIEC, and the IDB itself are core components of the IDB Group. Other participating institutions include the Islamic Research and Training Institute (IRTI), which began operations in 1983; the International Center for Biosaline Agriculture (ICBA), which the IDB, the Arab Fund for Economic and Social Development (AFESD, above), the OPEC Fund for International Development, and the United Arab Emirates founded in 1996 as a research and development facility; the $1.5 billion IDB Infrastructure Fund, which was formed in October 1998 to finance infrastructural projects; and the Islamic Corporation for the Development of the Private Sector, which was created by the Board of Governors in September 1999.

Recently the bank has given lending priority to projects designed to promote food security (particularly through increased agricultural productivity), improve health and educational services, alleviate poverty in rural areas, and modernize members' infrastructure. Special consideration has also been given to Muslim communities in the states that emerged from the breakup of the Soviet Union and former Yugoslavia.

Activity in 1994–1995 included the dedication of the bank's new headquarters building in Jiddah and the opening of regional offices in Rabat, Morocco, and Kuala Lumpur, Malaysia. In September 1998 bank chair Ahmad Mohammad Ali asserted that one of the IDB's goals was a 13 percent increase in trade among its members.

In October 2002 the IDB pledged $2 billion in loans to poor African countries. The aid was earmarked for, among other things, education, health services, and provision of safe drinking water. In 2004 the bank approved $500 million for reconstruction in Iraq. Other loans were approved for earthquake relief in Algeria and Iran and for reconstruction in southern Lebanon. At its annual meeting in March 2006, the bank announced an initiative to build the economic clout of Muslim nations by the year 2020.

Lending approvals for 2008 totaled $2.5 billion as against $2.2 billion for 2007, $1.7 billion for 2006, and $1.37 billion for 2005. In February 2007 a new member of the IDB Group was created—the International Islamic Trade Finance Corporation. This group was conceived to promote development and decrease economic burdens in the least-developed countries. In September 2007 the IDB began work on an internal reform, aligning its efforts more closely with the work of the OIC, whose work under Malaysia's chair the bank's president praised.

In February 2008, the bank held its annual meeting in Tehran, with mutual aid and ways of improving economic cooperation high on the agenda. In March 2008 the bank sought to relieve poverty among its African member countries with increased contributions to the newly-created Islamic Solidarity Fund. In June 2008, as the effects of the run-up in world food prices became ever more apparent, Egypt called for the bank to come up with new and creative ways of financing agricultural projects.

In October 2009 the bank announced plans to create an Islamic investment bank, with capital if $1 billion. The bank would be intended to promote the growth of international Islamic banking, according to *Sharia* principles.

Nordic Investment Bank
(NIB)

Web site: www.nib.int

A Nordic investment bank was first proposed in June 1957, but its creation was postponed by the founding of the European Free Trade Association. Though further discussed in 1962 and 1964, it was not until June 1, 1976, that an agreement establishing the bank came into force. It is headquartered in Helsinki, Finland.

Prior to 2005, the members of the NIB were the same as those of the Nordic Council: Denmark, Finland, Iceland, Norway, and Sweden. Each country appointed two members to the ten-member Board of Directors, which headed the bank under a rotating chairship. In addition, a ten-member Control Committee, on which all five countries were represented, oversaw bank audits and ensured that the bank was managed according to its statutes; the Nordic Council and the Nordic Council of Ministers each appointed five members.

On January 1, 2005, the NIB's membership expanded to include Estonia, Latvia, and Lithuania. In conjunction with the expansion, a new government structure was established for the bank. The most significant change was the creation of an eight-member (one from each member country) Board of Governors as the bank's supreme organ, assuming duties formerly exercised by the Nordic Council of Ministers such as amending bank statutes, deciding on increases in authorized capital stock, and determining membership issues. Decisions by the Board of Governors require unanimity. The Board of Directors, reduced from ten to eight members (again one from each member country) continues to oversee daily bank activity and policies in conjunction with the Control Committee, which now has one member from each member country and two members appointed by the Board of Governors to serve as the committee's chair and deputy chair. The bank is managed by a president (appointed by the Board of Directors for a five-year term) and seven vice presidents.

The main purpose of the bank is to provide financing "on normal banking terms, taking socioeconomic considerations into account," for projects that will expand Nordic production and exports and strengthen economic cooperation among member countries. Most NIB loans have gone to projects jointly undertaken by companies or institutions in two or more member countries. Such loans are always issued in conjunction with cofinancing from domestic banks and credit institutions, NIB participation being limited to no more than 50 percent of the total.

In the 1980s the NIB also became an international lender. In 1981 the first loans for joint Nordic projects outside the region were issued after Norway lifted its objection to them. Subsequently, in 1982, the Nordic Council of Ministers established a new Nordic Project Investment Loans (PIL) facility, administered by the NIB, to provide loans for projects "of Nordic interest" in credit-worthy developing countries and countries of Central and Eastern Europe. At the direction of the Nordic Council, the bank also helps to administer the Nordic Development Fund, established in 1989 to distribute long-term, interest-free loans to developing countries.

In a major new departure, the Nordic Council of Ministers decided at a March 1990 meeting to establish a Nordic Environmental Finance Company (NEFCO), administered by the NIB, to provide share capital or venture loans for joint projects by Nordic and Central and East European companies in the environmental sector. Formal NEFCO operations were initiated late in the year; in July 1993 NEFCO was reconstituted as a separate organization with its own president, although continued close cooperation with the NIB was expected. Approximately 30 projects were approved by that time, half of them in Poland. NEFCO also continued to participate with the NIB in a supranational task group established to chart the most severe pollution "hot spots" in the Baltic Sea region and facilitate clean-up projects.

In March 1991 the Nordic ministers of finance and economy agreed to provide expertise and hard currency in support of private sector development in the Baltic states. Through the Baltic Investment Program (BIP) launched in 1992, the NIB provided investment and technical assistance, including management and institutional support to the Baltic's national investment banks, as well as technical support for the preparation of investment projects and privatization. The BIP concluded its principal activities at the end of 1999, and a two-year phase-out followed.

Jannick Lindbaek, president of the NIB since 1986, left the bank at the end of 1993 to become head of the International Finance Corporation, the World Bank's affiliate for private investment. He was succeeded at the NIB in April by Jón Sigurn, the former governor of the central bank of Iceland. Among the issues facing the new NIB president was the future role of the bank, particularly in light of the accession of two more NIB members (Finland and Sweden) to the European Union (EU) in 1995. Increased cooperation between the NIB and the European Investment Bank (EIB, above) was seen as a consequence of the continent's changing political landscape. In addition, the NIB signed an agreement in 1995 with the European Bank for Reconstruction and Development (EBRD, above) to coordinate the activities of the two banks in the Baltic states as well as in Central and Eastern Europe.

In 1996 the Nordic Council of Ministers decided to establish a new environmental loan facility to extend loans to "neighboring areas"—Poland, the Baltic states, the Russian enclave of Kalingrad inside

Polish territory, and northwest Russia proper—for environmental projects. In 2001 the NIB joined with a number of partners—principally the EIB, the EBRD, the World Bank, and the EU Commission—to establish a forum, the Northern Dimension Environmental Partnership (NDEP), for addressing regional environmental problems.

The NIB has also adopted a new definition of what is in the "Nordic interest," expanding its pool of potential clients. A project can now be considered in the Nordic interest "if it has positive effects on employment and business conditions in the Nordic countries, and if it is carried out in one Nordic country by the combined efforts of that country and a non-Nordic one."

As of January 1, 2005, the bank's authorized capital was raised from 4 billion euros to 4.14 billion euros in conjunction with the addition of the three new members. The ordinary lending ceiling rose to 12.67 billion euros. PIL lending authorization, originally set at SDR 350 million, has risen in stages to the current 4.0 billion euros, while the newer environmental loan facility has a ceiling of 300 million euros (raised from 100 million euros in 2003). NIB subscriptions, based on the member countries' GNP, were led at the end of 2004 by Sweden (38 percent), followed by Denmark (22 percent), Norway (20 percent), Finland (19 percent), and Iceland (1 percent). The share amounts in 2005 for the new members were 1.6 percent for Lithuania, 1.1 percent for Latvia, and 0.7 percent for Estonia.

Disbursements in 2008 totaled 2.5 billion euros, compared to 2.4 billion euros in 2007, compared to 1.6 billion euros in 2006, compared to 2.1 billion euros in 2005, 1.3 billion euros in 2004, 1.8 billion euros in 2003, and 1.6 billion euros in 2002. About 1.9 billion euros of the 2008 disbursements remained within the member countries. The bank concentrated its lending activity into four targeted areas: the environment; energy; transport, logistics and communications; and innovation. Among non-member countries, loan activity was particularly high in Asia. The current president of the NIB is Johnny Åkerholm. In June 2009 his five-year term, due to expire in 2010, was extended for two years, after which he was to retire.

A period of intense and successful activity for the bank occurred in 2007 and the first part of 2008. Its AAA rating, acquired in September 2007, attracted business and allowed it to look beyond its home area for opportunities. In spite of the global economic downturn, the bank continued in 2009 to lend heavily to environmental and conservation projects.

West African Development Bank
Banque Ouest-Africaine de Développement
(BOAD)

Web site: www.boad.org (Contains little new material after 2005.)

An agreement to establish a West African Development Bank was initialed at a Paris, France, summit meeting of French-speaking African states on November 13–14, 1973. The bank formally commenced operations January 1, 1976, with headquarters in Lomé, Togo. The BOAD provides regional financing for the eight members (Benin, Burkina Faso, Côte d'Ivoire, Guinea-Bissau, Mali, Niger, Senegal, and Togo) of the West African Economic and Monetary Union (*Union Economique Monetaire Ouest-Africaine*—UEMOA; see separate entry), its goal being to promote equitable development and achieve economic integration through priority development projects. The other bank members are the African Development Bank, Belgium, the Central Bank of West African States (*Banque Centrale des Etats de l'Afrique de l'Ouest*—BCEAO), the European Investment Bank (EIB), France, and the German Development Company. The unit of account is the CFA franc, valued as of September 2007 at CFA 464 per U.S. dollar.

The organs of the bank include the Council of Ministers of the UEMOA and a Board of Directors comprising two directors from each UEMOA member, one director from the other six members, and the BOAD president, who serves as board chair.

A meeting of member ministers in October 1983 in Niamey, Niger, yielded approval of a bank proposal to implement regional integration projects, harmonize national development policies, and facilitate maximum utilization of internal and external resources. Later in the decade the BOAD, having considerably expanded its association with the international banking community, pledged to use the additional resources, in part, to assist member states in making the economic policy reforms requested by major international financial institutions. In 1989 the BOAD also agreed to seek regional projects for funding, as more than 80 percent of loans to that point had been for strictly national projects.

After undergoing internal restructuring to promote greater efficiency and better evaluation of loan performances, the BOAD announced in 1994 that upcoming lending would increase support for the private sector and efforts to strengthen the region's financial infrastructure. Much of that activity was expected to take place in conjunction with the new UEMOA, which was established in January 1994 as successor to the West African Economic Community (*Communauté Economique de l'Afrique de l'Ouest*—CEAO). Since then, the BOAD has been considered a "specialized institution" of the UEMOA.

Industry and agro-industry, rural development, transportation, telecommunications, energy, tourism, and other services have been among the sectors receiving support in recent years. In addition, the bank has supported feasibility studies, development of small- and medium-sized enterprises (SMEs), and partnerships with other financial institutions. Regional integration has focused particularly on agricultural processing and transport infrastructure.

In 2000 the bank approved some 24 projects—including its first to Guinea-Bissau, for a water and energy project—totaling CFA 72.4 billion ($104 million at the year-end exchange rate) in loans, an increase of about 4.7 percent from 1999. About 62 percent of lending went to the public sector, with greater emphasis on integration efforts and projects promoting poverty control. Lending to the private sector concentrated on privatization, industry, and refinancing for SMEs. BOAD cumulative lending reached CFA 555 billion ($796 million) for more than 300 operations, about two-thirds of them public. Leading recipients were Côte d'Ivoire (26 percent) and Benin (19 percent). The BOAD also participated in the multilateral Highly Indebted Poor Countries initiative, and in August 2001 BOAD President Yayi Boni indicated that the bank intended to move forward with a debt reduction program financed primarily by external sources and linked to reforms in individual countries.

In mid 2002 Boni announced BOAD would expand its support to the least-developed countries in the region, calling on national leaders to cooperate in formulating a new regional "vision" for reducing poverty. The bank, which celebrated its 30th anniversary in 2003, agreed to mobilize outside financial support to assist in integrating the region's financial markets and to protect private investors. Apparently in support of that initiative, the World Bank in 2004 approved a new financing package for BOAD totaling $409 million for the next five years. Late in 2004 attention focused on a membership application, eventually successful, from China. The latest financial report available is for 2007. It shows annual loan approvals at 84.2 billion CFA francs ($177 million) for 2004, 77.7 billion CFA francs ($163 million) for 2005, 106.7 billion CFA francs ($224 million) for 2006, and 102.5 billion CFA francs ($215million) for 2007.

Boni's position as bank president became vacant in April 2006 following his election and inauguration as president of Benin. He was replaced by Abdoulaye Bio-Tchané (Benin), who had previously been director of the African department of the IMF. In 2008 the bank participated in a multi-institution effort to finance transportation improvements in Mali, Burkina Faso, and Niger. It was also involved in a project to save the Niger River, a lifeline for these countries that was under pressure from drought and industrial waste. Among other development projects undertaken in 2009 was a joint effort with the EU to finance road construction in Guinea-Bissau.

SHANGHAI COOPERATION ORGANIZATION (SCO)

Established: By declaration of the heads of the member states, meeting in Shanghai, China, on June 15, 2001. The body's structure was formalized in a charter signed on June 7, 2002, in Moscow, Russia, and came into full effect September 19, 2003.

Purpose: To strengthen mutual trust, friendship, and good relations between the member states; to maintain peace, security, and stability in the region and to promote a new democratic, fair, and rational political and economic international order; to counteract terrorism, separatism, and extremism in all their manifestations; to fight against illicit narcotics and arms trafficking and other types of criminal activity of a transnational character, as well as illegal migration; to encourage efficient regional cooperation in such spheres as politics, trade and economy, defense, law enforcement, environment protection, culture, science and technology, education, energy, transportation, and credit and finance.

Headquarters: Beijing, China.

Principal Organs: Council of Heads of State, Council of Heads of Government, Council of Foreign Ministers, Council of National Coordinators, Secretariat.

Web site: www.sectsco.org

Secretary General: Bolat K. Nurgaliev (Kazakhstan).

Membership (6)**:** China, Kazakhstan, Kyrgyzstan, Russia, Tajikistan, and Uzbekistan.

Observers (4): Iran, India, Mongolia, and Pakistan.

Official Languages: Chinese, Russian.

Origin and development. The Shanghai Cooperation Organization (SCO) grew out of a less formal grouping, the so-called Shanghai Five, comprised of China, Kazakhstan, Kyrgyzstan, Russia, and Tajikistan, whose heads of state had been meeting annually since April 1996. This association was concerned with improving mutual trust in their border regions, as well as coordinating policy on other military and security topics. In July 2000 the president of Uzbekistan, Islam Karimov, attended a Shanghai Five meeting as an observer. When the SCO was founded in 2001, Uzbekistan joined as a full member.

Structure. The SCO exists as a forum for its heads of state to attempt to coordinate policy. The grouping initially concentrated on border, defense, and security policy, but more recently moved into wider economic, social, and geopolitical concerns. It maintains no kind of parliamentary representation, having instead a top-down structure in which the Heads of State Council (HSC) is the highest decision-making body. The HSC meets annually, as does the Heads of Government Council (HGC). Among other functions, the HGC adopts the SCO's annual budget. Among the representatives of the member countries who meet with their peers from time to time are speakers of parliament, secretaries of security councils, foreign ministers, and ministers of defense. There are also meetings of ministers of emergency relief, economy, transportation, culture, education, and healthcare, as well as heads of law enforcement agencies, supreme courts, courts of arbitration, and prosecutors general. The Council of National Coordinators (CNC) is in charge of coordinating SCO interaction among the member states. The SCO has two permanent bodies: the Secretariat in Beijing and the Regional Antiterrorism Structure in Tashkent, Uzbekistan. The secretary-general is appointed by the HSC for a period of three years. The office rotates among the member states, alphabetically by the Russian alphabet. A representative of Kazakhstan took the post beginning on January 1, 2007.

Activities. The SCO and its less structured predecessor, the Shanghai Five group, arose from an agreement "on deepening military trust in border regions" signed by the respective heads of state in Shanghai on April 26, 1996. A second meeting, held in Moscow on April 24, 1997, produced an agreement on mutual reductions of forces along the states' borders. The Shanghai Five held further summits on security and regional cooperation in Almaty, Kazakhstan, on July 3, 1998, and in Bishkek, Kyrgyzstan, on August 24–26, 1999. In November 1999 the group's first meeting of the heads of law enforcement bodies and security services was held, also in Bishkek. In March 2000 the Shanghai Five's defense ministers met for the first time, in Astana, Kazakhstan. On July 4–5, 2000, the foreign ministers and heads of state met in Dushanbe, Tajikistan, with the president of Uzbekistan in attendance as an observer. At a meeting of heads of state of all six countries in Shanghai, held June 14–15, 2001, the SCO was formally declared. The six participants issued a statement avowing the group's purpose of fighting terrorism, separatism, and Islamic militancy.

An aim of the SCO from its earliest days, unstated but recognized on all sides, was to counteract the influence of the United States in the region. The June 2001 meeting endorsed the Anti-Ballistic Missile (ABM) Treaty, which the U.S. government wanted to scrap. The anti-American tendency was initially most noticeable in China, and to a lesser extent in Russia. It was much less evident among the oil-rich Central Asian states, where the U.S. had large investments. In any event, the anti-American feeling was disrupted almost immediately after the SCO's formation by the September 11, 2001, terrorist attacks in New York and the Washington, D.C., area. The first meeting of SCO heads of government happened to take place in Almaty on September 13–14, 2001. It focused on determining the basic steps to be taken in regional economic cooperation and in mutual trade and investment matters. The meeting also condemned the September 11 attacks and declared that the SCO was ready to work with all countries to counter what it saw as the global threat of terrorism.

When the group's foreign ministers met in Beijing on January 2, 2002, U.S. forces were already in Afghanistan, and some Central Asian SCO members were giving them logistical support. This being the case, the meeting refrained from the indirect criticisms of U.S. hegemony that had characterized previous gatherings, instead failing to mention the United States and calling for the United Nations to take the lead in finding a solution to international terrorism and to the region's security problems. Throughout 2002, a series of meetings at the foreign minister and national coordinator levels pushed forward the establishment of the group's permanent organs, most urgently the Regional Antiterrorism Structure (RATS). At a June 7, 2002, summit in Moscow, the heads of state adopted the SCO Charter. This document formally established the SCO as an international organization with definite aims and a permanent secretariat.

In early October 2002, China and Kyrgyzstan held a joint antiterrorist exercise. Late in October the group's first meeting of public prosecutors took place in Shanghai. In November the transport ministers of the SCO held their first meeting, in Bishkek, to begin work on a common policy.

The 2003 SCO summit, held May 28–29 in Moscow, was taken up mainly with administrative matters, including the setting of regulations for the group's various councils and for its budget. From August 8–12, 2003, all SCO states except Uzbekistan held joint antiterrorism exercises. In September an SCO representative attended a meeting of the Organization for Security and Co-operation in Europe (OSCE) that was held in Lisbon, Portugal, and briefed the OSCE on what the SCO was doing. On October 31, 2003, the SCO RATS council held its first meeting, in Tashkent. RATS was designed as a structure (called by some a think tank) to exchange ideas and coordinate plans against terrorism.

The 2004 summit was held on June 17 in Tashkent under tight security, with demonstrations against the Uzbek president sternly repressed. Hamid Karzai, Afghanistan's president, attended the meeting as an observer. The SCO pledged itself to help in rebuilding Afghanistan. It also adopted agreements to combat narcotics trafficking. The meeting marked the formal opening of RATS—an event attended by representatives of the UN, the European Union (EU), the OSCE, and other international bodies.

The 2005 summit was held on July 5 in Astana. This was the first summit at which representatives of the observer states were officially present. The meeting attendees urged the United States to set a timetable for removing its bases from SCO member countries. They did this, they said, without in any way reducing SCO support for Afghanistan. In September 2005 an SCO delegation visited the UN General Assembly.

By 2006 the SCO was attracting increasing international attention, and debate began about whether it might turn into a military alliance—a Central Asian version of the North Atlantic Treaty Organization (NATO). Proponents of this idea pointed to the antiterrorism exercises already held and to plans announced in April 2006 for the entire group to hold war games in Russia in 2007. Giving a hint that these maneuvers might focus on more than defeating terrorists, the Russian defense minister, Sergei Ivanov, was quoted as saying that "the threat of SCO borders being crossed by armed groups is absolutely real," and that the armed forces of member states "should, if needed, help neighboring states block and possibly destroy large armed groups." Others maintained that the SCO had adequate economic reasons for existing and a military focus was unnecessary. China, they felt, needed the member states' raw materials and energy supplies, while the rest of the bloc needed to trade with China. And while Russia might be interested in the bloc as a military counterweight to the United States, China, not bordering any NATO countries, had little such concern.

The 2006 summit was held on June 15 in Shanghai. The meeting was notable for the fact that Mahmoud Ahmadinejad, president of Iran, attended as an observer. Subsequently, Iran began expressing interest in having full membership in the organization. The meeting approved establishment of the SCO Business Council and Interbank Consortium. Russian president Vladimir Putin advanced the idea that the SCO should not be a single economic space so much as a group that concentrated on specific economic and infrastructure projects. To this end he proposed setting up the SCO Energy Club to unite producers, transit carriers, and consumers of energy products. Later in the year, Russia offered to take the lead on developing new energy infrastructure projects in SCO countries. The summit also levied a two-year moratorium on admitting new full members to the group.

By March 2007 both India and Pakistan were seeking full membership in the SCO. By 2007 it was becoming clear that although Russia was very interested in promoting the military side of SCO, other member states were not. The chief of the Russian general staff complained of this lack of interest on the eve of the SCO war games that were held in Russia on August 17, 2007. The games took place at the same time as the 2007 summit, which was held in Bishkek. Again president Ahmadinejad was an honored guest, and he took the opportunity to attack the United States for its proposed antimissile shield in Eastern Europe. This project, he said, was not aimed just at Iran, but at all SCO countries.

In March 2008 Iran formally applied for full membership in the SCO. Russia seemed initially to favor the idea, but a meeting of SCO foreign ministers in Dushanbe, Tajikistan, on July 18, 2008, failed to address the matter or consider ending the moratorium on new full members. Reasons were not clear, but presumably Russia, China, or both, did not approve. Perhaps significantly, the meeting also decided to set up a "mechanism for dialog partnership to establish links with all countries and international organizations that are interested in the SCO." Some interpreted this to mean that the SCO might be edging towards a formal relationship with the United States. The 2008 summit was held August 28 in Dushanbe. It proved a diplomatic setback for Russia, as the meeting failed to endorse Russia's military action in Georgia (see separate article on Georgia). Observers noted that, beyond military cooperation and fighting terrorism, the SCO members had divergent interests. Russia was concerned to use the group as a counter to U.S. influence, while the central Asian members wanted good relations with the West, to sell oil undisturbed. Also Russia was nervous about China's growing economic power.

On November 4, 2008, SCO representatives, along with those of several other central Asian organizations, took part in a conference on ways to combat terrorism. The meeting was organized by the Kyrgyz security and foreign ministries, and held at the OSCE center in Bishkek. On March 27, 2009. the SCO also organized a conference on Afghanistan. The conference, which took place in Moscow, was also attended by UN secretary-general Ban Ki Moon and a delegation from the United States. There were speculations that U.S. and Iranian representatives might talk on the sidelines at the conference. The SCO members and observers expressed a desire to play a larger part in solving Afghanistan's problems. In mid-April 2009 SCO members conducted a military exercise in Tajikistan, simulating a response to a terrorist attack from Afghanistan.

The 2009 SCO summit was held in Yekaterinburg, Russia, from June 15-16. As a response to the global economic crisis, China promised a $10 billion loan to Kazakhstan, Uzbekistan, Kyrgyzstan, and Tajikistan. Russian president Dmitri Medvedev called for additional reserve currencies to supplement the U.S. dollar. And Mahmoud Ahmadinejad, recently declared the winner of a violently disputed presidential election in Iran, was warmly welcomed.

SOUTH ASIAN ASSOCIATION FOR REGIONAL COOPERATION (SAARC)

Established: By charter signed December 8, 1985, in Dhaka, Bangladesh.

Purpose: "[T]o promote the welfare of the peoples of South Asia and to improve their quality of life; . . . to promote and strengthen collective self-reliance among the countries of South Asia; . . . to promote active collaboration and mutual assistance in the economic, social, cultural, technical and scientific fields; . . . and to co-operate with international and regional organizations with similar aims and purposes."

Headquarters: Kathmandu, Nepal.

Principal Organs: Meeting of Heads of State or Government, Council of Ministers, Standing Committee, Programming Committee, Secretariat.

Web site: www.saarc-sec.org

Secretary General: Sheel Kant Sharma (India).

Membership (8): Afghanistan, Bangladesh, Bhutan, India, Maldives, Nepal, Pakistan, Sri Lanka.

Observers (9): Australia, Myanmar (Burma), China, European Union, Iran, Japan, Mauritius, South Korea, United States.

Origin and development. Prior to the formation of SAARC, South Asia was the only major world region without a formal venue for multigovernmental cooperation. The association was launched December 8, 1985, in Dhaka, Bangladesh, during the first high-level meeting of the political leaders of the participating governments. The summit was convened on recommendation of the ministerial South Asian Regional Cooperation Committee (SARC), formed August 1983 in New Delhi, India, with subsequent meetings in July 1984 in Malé, Maldives, and in May 1985 in Thimbu, Bhutan. At the conclusion of SAARC's founding session, the participants issued a charter setting forth the objectives of the new grouping and directed that decisions would be made by unanimous vote at annual summits, at which "bilateral and contentious" issues would be avoided.

Structure. General policies are formulated at the annual meeting of heads of state and, to a lesser extent, at the semiannual meetings of the Council of Ministers. Sectoral ministerial meetings may also convene. The Secretariat was established in January 1987 in Kathmandu. Seven technical committees address agriculture and rural development, communications and transport, energy, environment and meteorology, human resources development, science and technology, and social development. The committees report to the Standing Committee of foreign secretaries, which prepares recommendations for the Council of Ministers. The Programming Committee was established to assist the Standing Committee, which also oversees SAARC's regional centers: SAARC Agricultural Information Center (established in Dhaka in 1988); SAARC Documentation Center (New Delhi, 1994); SAARC Human Resources Development Center (Islamabad, Pakistan, 1999); SAARC Meteorological Research Center (Dhaka, 1995); and SAARC Tuberculosis Center (Kathmandu, 1992).

Activities. In light of SAARC's formal repudiation of involvement in purely bilateral concerns, the 1986 summit in Bangalore, India, did not officially address the major conflicts within the subcontinent, such as the Himalayan river waters dispute between India and Bangladesh, the confrontation between ethnically South Indian Tamil guerrillas and the Sri Lankan government, and the variety of problems affecting relations between India and Pakistan. Instead, the summit was devoted to discussion of proposed SAARC institutions that would serve to reduce regional tensions through cooperation in such areas as communication, transport, and rural development.

Little SAARC progress was achieved in 1989 and 1990, as national and international conflicts continued to hold center stage in the region. The 1989 summit, scheduled for November in Sri Lanka, was postponed as the result of widespread ethnic violence there, coupled with increased tension between Colombo and New Delhi over the presence of Indian troops. SAARC subsequently attempted to convene the meeting in March 1990, but intensified Indian-Pakistani friction over Kashmir necessitated another postponement. The summit was finally held in November in Malé, although substantive action was limited because India, Nepal, Pakistan, and Sri Lanka had recently installed new governments, and internal turmoil broke out in the other three countries that were members at the time.

The sixth summit eventually convened December 21, 1991, the heads of state agreeing to "suppress terrorism" while also committing themselves to support "civil and political rights" and to combat poverty in the region. In addition, an intergovernmental group was created to consider ways to dismantle long-standing barriers to trade between SAARC members. Meanwhile a SAARC development fund was discussed, with proponents arguing that "trade and business unity" would help reduce political cleavage in the region.

Unsettled conditions in the region continued to plague SAARC, and the summit scheduled for January 1993 was postponed at the request of Prime Minister Rao in the aftermath of severe communal disturbances in India. When the summit was finally held April 10–11 in Dhaka, Bangladesh, it was marred by mass demonstrations against Rao and his government's handling of the Hindu-Muslim conflict. The most significant development at the summit was the initialing of a plan to establish the South Asian Preferential Trade Agreement (SAPTA) for reducing or eliminating intraregional trade barriers.

No SAARC summit was held in 1994, primarily because of ongoing turmoil in India (where the meeting was scheduled to be held) and continued friction between SAARC members. By that time, many observers saw SAARC as having fallen significantly behind most counterparts elsewhere in terms of regional integration. When SAARC leaders finally met May 2–4, 1995, in New Delhi, they agreed to proceed with the SAPTA launching, with more than 200 products identified for lower tariff rates. Following ratification by all SAARC states, SAPTA formally went into effect December 8, concurrent with the commemoration of the grouping's tenth anniversary. However, it was widely agreed that SAPTA represented only a modest beginning, and SAARC established an "expert working group" to begin immediately on plans to expand it into the South Asian Free Trade Agreement (SAFTA).

Despite that apparent progress, at least "on paper," several SAARC members argued that genuine regional integration could not be achieved unless contentious political issues, such as the Indian-Pakistani dispute over Kashmir, were resolved. For its part, Pakistan formally called for a change in the section of the SAARC charter that precludes bilateral talks. India strongly resisted that concept, however, and at a symposium on SAARC in mid-1996 in Washington, D.C., U.S. officials also advised the grouping to avoid "the political realm." Although Pakistan was not swayed by that argument and several other members still appeared willing to expand the SAARC mandate, activity within the grouping for the rest of the year focused on economic matters.

The political question reemerged at the ninth SAARC summit, held May 12–14, 1997, in Malé. The seven heads of state or government agreed that a process of informal political consultations would help their efforts to foster better relations and faster economic integration. Although still officially opposed to a political component within SAARC, India nonetheless reached a bilateral agreement with Pakistan on May 12 within the "SAARC setting." SAARC leaders also agreed to move the formation of SAFTA forward to 2001 from 2005. At that time, approximately 20 percent of the world's population lived within SAARC's borders, but intraregional trade accounted for only 1 percent of the global total.

Following India's and Pakistan's tests of nuclear devices in May 1998, Pakistan again attempted to introduce a political element into SAARC at the tenth summit, held in late July 1998 in Colombo. Pakistani prime minister Nawaz Sharif offered changes to the SAARC charter that would allow for bilateral negotiations and establish a regional peace council, but the other members rejected the proposed changes. Although the prime ministers of India and Pakistan met during the summit for the first time since the nuclear tests, the talks were not considered successful since the dispute over Kashmir remained a stumbling block. Another focus of the summit was economic integration. SAARC reaffirmed its intention to complete and implement SAFTA in 2001 and decided to improve ties with other regional economic organizations, such as the Association of Southeastern Asian Nations (ASEAN). However, a group of eminent persons appointed by SAARC reported that 2008 was a more realistic date for launching SAFTA.

The 11th SAARC summit, scheduled for November 1999 in Kathmandu, was postponed at India's request following the October coup in Pakistan, and little progress on the organization's major concerns was accomplished in the following two years. A third special session of the Standing Committee met August 9–10, 2001, in Colombo, at which time the participating foreign secretaries agreed that the summit process should be resumed as quickly as possible. They also adopted a schedule for negotiating additional SAPTA concessions; drafting the SAFTA treaty; and holding meetings (some at the ministerial level) concerned with culture, the environment, health, information, media, telecommunications, and poverty alleviation.

As a further indication of the political differences impeding progress toward SAARC's regional goals, in October 2001 the organization abandoned its efforts to draft a unified statement condemning terrorism and the September 11 attacks against the United States. Once again, India and Pakistan strongly disagreed: India insisted the proposed statement condemn terrorism in Kashmir, whereas Pakistan rejected any such explicit reference to the disputed region.

The 11th SAARC summit was finally held January 5–6, 2002, in Kathmandu, Nepal, the attendees reaffirming their commitment to SAFTA and adopting a convention on preventing trafficking in women and children. However, renewed tension between India and Pakistan prompted postponement of the 12th summit scheduled for January 2003 until January 2004, at which time a new protocol was approved in regard to combating terrorism. SAARC leaders also endorsed tentative draft guidelines for SAFTA, which, fully established, would encompass approximately 20 percent of the world's population. (SAFTA came into force January 1, 2006.) Although the 2004 summit (which also adopted a new social charter) was deemed successful, political considerations again interrupted regional progress in early 2005 when the 13th summit was postponed because of turmoil in Nepal and Bangladesh.

The 13th summit was held November 8–13, 2005, in Dhaka. The participants declared the decade 2006–2015 the SAARC Decade of Poverty Alleviation, and decided to establish the SAARC Poverty Alleviation Fund (SPAF) with contributions both voluntary and assessed, as was to be agreed upon in future discussions. Some commentators felt that dealing with trade and economic concerns was SAARC's best way forward, given the intractable political differences between some of its members.

During 2006 and 2007, China, the European Union, Japan, South Korea, and the United States all applied for observer status with SAARC. All five entities were represented at the 14th summit, held April 3–4, 2007, in New Delhi. China's presence, as well many of its recent statements about SAARC, was described by some as a "charm offensive." This summit also welcomed Afghanistan as a member. The representatives of India and Pakistan declared that it was time to move beyond their historic antagonism, and, while not naming Pakistan, President Hamid Karzai of Afghanistan called for the lifting of barriers "that inhibit the movement of people and goods between our countries." The summit ended with a feeling of renewed energy in the group, and hopes for a future South Asian economic union and customs union. In June 2007 a SAARC delegation met in Jakarta, Indonesia, with ASEAN representatives to discuss cooperation in energy matters. SAARC committee meetings in November 2007 worked to speed the removal of customs barriers mandated by SAFTA.

In April 2008 it was announced that SAARC would be creating a database on terrorism and narcotics trafficking, modeled after the Interpol database. The services sector was also said to be ready for inclusion in SAFTA in the near future. In May 2008 Myanmar, formerly known as Burma, applied for full membership in SAARC, as Australia had recently done. Both applications were approved at the organization's fifteenth summit, held August 2–3 in Colombo. The meeting (for which the Tamil Tiger rebels had proclaimed a truce) also pledged several efforts to speed up regional economic growth. Some commentators criticized the meeting as producing little in the way of concrete results, particularly in contrast to ASEAN.

In October 2008 the Afghan representative announced that his country was interested in hosting some SAARC meetings in the near future. In February 2009 the Maldives, scheduled to host the 2009 summit, declared that it would not be able to do so before October, if at all. As a result no summit took place in 2009, but Bhutan would host a summit in spring 2010.

SOUTHERN AFRICAN DEVELOPMENT COMMUNITY (SADC)

Established: By the Treaty of Windhoek, signed August 17, 1992, in Windhoek, Namibia, by representatives from the ten members of the former Southern African Development Coordination Conference (SADCC); Agreement Amending the Treaty signed August 14, 2001, in Blantyre, Malawi.

Purpose: To achieve self-sustaining development and economic growth based on collective self-reliance and interdependence; to achieve sustainable use of natural resources while protecting the environment; to promote and defend regional peace and security; to enhance the standard of living through regional integration, including establishing a free trade area.

Headquarters: Gaborone, Botswana.

Principal Organs: Summit Meeting of Heads of State or Government; Council of Ministers; Organ on Politics, Defense, and Security; Executive Secretariat.

Web site: www.sadc.int

Executive Secretary: Tomaz Augusto Salomao (Mozambique).

Membership (15): Angola, Botswana, Democratic Republic of the Congo, Lesotho, Madagascar, Malawi, Mauritius, Mozambique, Namibia, Seychelles, South Africa, Swaziland, Tanzania, Zambia, Zimbabwe.

Working Languages: English, French, Portuguese.

Origin and development. The SADCC originated as the Southern African Development Coordination Conference that convened in July 1979, in Arusha, Tanzania, by Angola, Botswana, Mozambique, Tanzania, and Zambia (the "Front-Line States" opposed to white rule in southern Africa). A draft declaration entitled "Southern Africa: Towards Economic Liberation" was drawn up proposing a program of action to improve regional transportation, agriculture, industry, energy, and development planning, with a view toward reducing economic dependence on the Republic of South Africa. As a follow-up to the Arusha meeting, the SADCC was formally established during a summit of the heads of state or government of nine countries (the original five plus Lesotho, Malawi, Swaziland, and Zimbabwe) that convened April 1, 1980, in Lusaka, Zambia. Namibia joined the SADCC after achieving independence in 1990.

The SADCC was considered one of the most viable of the continent's regional groupings, although its actual accomplishments were modest compared to its members' development needs. During its first six years, the SADCC concentrated on the rehabilitation and expansion of transport corridors to permit the movement of goods from the interior of the region to ocean ports without the use of routes through South Africa. In 1986, however, SADCC leaders concluded that such infrastructure development would not reduce dependence on South Africa sufficiently unless accompanied by broad, long-term economic growth in the region. Consequently, the SADCC announced that additional emphasis would be given to programs and projects designed to increase production within the private sector and in enterprises with government involvement. It also sought to expand intraregional trade, support national economic reform, and encourage international investment. The program of action eventually encompassed some 500 projects, ranging from small feasibility studies to large port and railway construction projects.

Throughout the 1980s the conference called for the international community to impose comprehensive, mandatory sanctions against Pretoria, South Africa, to protest apartheid. However, consensus was not attained on regional action, such as the severance of air links with Pretoria, primarily because of objections from Lesotho and Swaziland, the SADCC members whose economies were most directly linked to South Africa.

At their tenth anniversary summit in August 1990, the SADCC leaders discussed proposals to expand the conference's mandate and influence, in part by enhancing the authority of the secretariat. The heads of state, concerned with the region's stagnant export revenue and mounting debt burden, emphasized the need to increase intraregional trade over the next decade. In addition, they endorsed automatic membership for South Africa once apartheid was dismantled.

While participants in the 1991 summit urged that sanctions be continued against Pretoria pending further democratic progress, they endorsed preliminary discussions with representatives of the liberation movements in South Africa regarding future coordination of economic policies. In addition to possible resolution of the South African issue, peace initiatives in Angola and Mozambique were cited by SADCC officials as cause for hope that after three decades of violence the region might be headed for a sustained period of peace. With this in mind, a treaty signed August 17, 1992, in Windhoek, Namibia, transformed the SADCC into the SADC, through which members were to seek development and integration in several areas, leading to a full-fledged common market. Although most details of the new organization were left to subsequent negotiations, the SADC members agreed to concentrate for the short term on joint infrastructure development, coordination of investment procedures, and establishment of regional production policies. Arrangements for the free movement of goods, capital, and labor among members were to be made at an undetermined date. The most ardent SADC integrationists also suggested the community might eventually pursue political union, perhaps through a regional parliament, and security coordination.

One immediate concern for the SADC was its relationship with the Preferential Trade Area for Eastern and Southern African States (PTA), established in 1981 with many of the same goals as those adopted by the SADC. In late 1992, with eight of the (then) ten SADC members also belonging to the PTA (with Botswana and Namibia as exceptions), the PTA called for a merger of the two organizations. Not surprisingly, the SADC Executive Secretariat opposed the proposal, and at a January 1993 meeting the SADC, reportedly concerned over the PTA's history of ineffectiveness, rejected the overture. However, the SADC indicated it would try to avoid duplicating PTA activities, suggesting that the PTA could assume full responsibility for economic cooperation among the 11 "northern," or non-SADC, countries, with the SADC doing the same for its members.

In one of a summer-long series of remarkable international events precipitated by the democratic transition in Pretoria, the SADC accepted South Africa as its 11th member at a summit held in late August 1994 in Gaborone, Botswana. Although they welcomed South Africa to their ranks, the other SADC members reportedly expressed concern they might be overwhelmed by its economic might. The summit also began to weigh greater security responsibilities, addressing such proposals as the creation of a mechanism for the peaceful resolution of conflicts among members and the establishment of regional peacekeeping and defense forces. Thus, the SADC defense ministers in November endorsed the concept of a regional deployment force, which would not be a permanent army but one available for quick mobilization from standing national armies.

Mauritius became the 12th SADC member in August 1995. The Seychelles and Democratic Republic of the Congo became the 13th and 14th members on September 8 and 9, 1997, respectively, although in 2003 the Seychelles, citing its inability to pay its annual membership fee, announced its intention to withdraw as of mid-2004. At the same time, Madagascar expressed its interest in joining, and the 2005 summit welcomed it as its 14th member.

Structure. Under the terms of the Lusaka Declaration issued in 1980, individual members of the SADCC were assigned coordinating roles over specified economic concerns. Thus, in July 1980 the conference's first operational body, the Southern African Transport and Communications Commission, was formed under Mozambique's leadership. Other states received the following assignments: Angola, energy; Botswana, livestock production, animal disease control, and crop production research; Lesotho, soil and water conservation, land utilization, and tourism; Malawi, fisheries, forestry, and wildlife; Swaziland, manpower development and training; Tanzania, industry and trade; Zambia, development funding and mining; and Zimbabwe, regional food security.

When the SADC was established to replace the SADCC in 1992, it was decided to keep the existing SADCC structure intact for the time being, with the following additional or reassigned sectoral responsibilities subsequently made: Mauritius, tourism; Mozambique, culture, information, and sports; Namibia, marine fisheries and resources; South Africa, finance and investment; and Zambia, employment and labor. Other changes were made in response to the community's post-apartheid regional security concerns, which led in mid-1996 to creation of the Organ on Politics, Defense, and Security. The objectives of the organ included fostering cooperation with regard to issues of law and order, defending against external aggression, and promoting democracy. The organ was also authorized to mediate domestic disputes and conflicts between members.

At an extraordinary summit held March 9, 2001, in Windhoek, the SADC approved a report on restructuring that called for phasing out within two years the nearly two dozen sector coordinating units and replacing them with four directorates: trade, finance, industry, and investment; infrastructure and services; food, agriculture, and natural resources; and social and human development and special programs. The structural reform was viewed as essential to advancing regional integration and strategic planning, efficient use of available resources, and equitable distribution of responsibilities.

Under the reorganization, the SADC's chief policymaking organ, the Summit Meeting of Heads of State or Government, convenes at least once per year, with the position of chair rotating annually. Between summit meetings, policy responsibility rests on a troika of the SADC chair, his predecessor, and his successor, with other national leaders co-opted as needed. The Organ on Politics, Defense, and Security was given a rotating chairship, with the organ's internal structure and functions detailed in a Protocol on Politics, Defense, and Security that was signed at the August 2001 summit. The Council of Ministers remains responsible for policy implementation and organizational oversight. The Standing Committee of Senior Officials, comprising a permanent secretary from each member country, serves as a technical advisory body to the council, with an emphasis on planning and finance.

In addition, the restructuring called for creation of the Integrated Committee of Ministers (ICM) to ensure "proper policy guidance, coordination and harmonization of cross-sectoral activities." The ICM, replacing the Sectoral Committee of Ministers, is primarily responsible for overseeing and guiding the work of the new directorates. It answers to the council and includes at least two ministers from each SADC state. To provide policy coordination, particularly with regard to interstate politics and international diplomacy, a new body, the Ministers of Foreign Affairs, Defense, and Security, was subsequently added to the SADC structure.

Duties of the Executive Secretariat, which is headed by an executive secretary, include strategic planning, management of the comprehensive SADC program of action, and general administration. Within the secretariat, the Department of Strategic Planning, Gender, and Development and Policy Harmonization was established. At the individual state level, representatives of government, the private sector, and civil society meet as SADC national committees to provide input to the central SADC organs and to oversee programs within each jurisdiction.

During the 2000 summit, SADC leaders signed a protocol establishing an SADC tribunal, as provided for in the founding treaty. The tribunal will have responsibility for interpreting the treaty and subsidiary documents and for adjudicating disputes between members.

Activities. The dominant concern for the SADC in 1995 remained the dual membership problem regarding the PTA, an issue further complicated by the recent signing of a treaty establishing the Common Market of Eastern and Southern Africa (Comesa). Although most SADC members signed the treaty, several postponed ratification, while South Africa and Botswana indicated their lack of interest in the alignment. Consequently, the SADC summit held August 28 in Johannesburg, South Africa, called for an immediate joint summit between the SADC and PTA/Comesa to resolve the matter. Meanwhile, SADC leaders endorsed the proposed elimination of trade barriers between SADC members and the establishment of a common SADC currency. The summit also signed a protocol for cooperation in water management and launched negotiations on similar protocols in the areas of tourism and energy.

During the summit held August 23–24, 1996, in Maseru, Lesotho, the SADC again declined to merge with Comesa and instead reemphasized its own goal of establishing a Southern Africa Free Trade Area within eight years. (Lesotho and Mozambique subsequently announced they did not intend to ratify the Comesa treaty, and Tanzania eventually dropped out in favor of continued membership in the SADC.) Other protocols were also signed at the SADC summit in the areas of energy, transportation and communications, and illicit narcotics, although an agreement could not be reached on the free movement of people among the SADC countries.

The Organ on Politics, Defense, and Security, launched at the 1996 summit, was at the center of controversy during the September 1997 summit, particularly because of its relative independence from the other SADC institutions. South African president Nelson Mandela, chair of the summit, insisted on bringing the organ under the direct control of the summit, while Zimbabwean president Robert Mugabe, chair of the organ, opposed such a move. Mandela also surprised the summit by proposing the SADC punish members via sanctions if they did not adopt the democratic values central to the organization. His proposal was particularly aimed at Swaziland's King Mswati III and Zambian president Frederick Chiluba, both of whom were unmoved, in Mandela's opinion, by attempts to encourage democracy in their countries.

An SADC summit in late July 1998 in Namibia attempted to refocus the community's attention on economic cooperation. Attendees pledged to eliminate tariffs and other restrictions on 90 percent of intra-community trade by 2005. However, security matters, particularly the recent outbreak of fighting in the Democratic Republic of the Congo (DRC), returned to the fore at the SADC summit September 13–15 in Mauritius. Several countries urged action in support of the government of DRC president Laurent Kabila; SADC members Angola, Namibia, and Zimbabwe reportedly had already sent troops to the DRC to oppose anti-Kabila rebels. The SADC summit, at Kabila's insistence, refused to meet with the representatives of Rwanda and Uganda (apparent supporters of the DRC rebels) who traveled to Mauritius to discuss the matter.

The SADC's role in domestic affairs became even more clouded shortly after the summit, when first South African and then Botswanan troops entered Lesotho to quell unrest generated by anger over the May election, which was followed by a mutiny within the Lesotho Defense Force (LDF). The initiative was described as an SADC intervention based on the community's established principles and procedures, but some SADC members reportedly objected to that classification. By May 1999 an advisory team mandated to help retrain and restructure the LDF replaced the troops.

The August 6–7, 2000, summit in Windhoek drew widespread international criticism for a decision to support the Mugabe government's expropriation of white-owned land in Zimbabwe. The summit's final communiqué also focused on such economic concerns as rising external debt, a regional cereal deficit, the HIV/AIDS crisis, and continuing poverty. The communiqué noted that GDP growth among member states had recently risen, but not at the projected 6.8 percent annual rate needed to achieve actual poverty reduction.

The March 9, 2001, summit in Windhoek, in addition to approving the organizational changes called for in a report on restructuring (see Structure, above), elected Mauritian Prega Ramsamy executive secretary as successor to Namibian Kaire Mbuende, who was dismissed in 2000. In addition, the summit continued to emphasize matters of defense and security. Considerable tension, particularly between South Africa and Zimbabwe, arose over Robert Mugabe's refusal to step aside as chair of the Organ on Politics, Defense, and Security. Some members clearly felt that Mugabe had misused his position in support of the Kabila regime in the DRC. Subsequently, however, it was agreed that the chairship would pass to Mozambique's President Chissano at the August 12–14 annual summit. Held in Blantyre, Malawi, the annual session again focused on regional security issues, but also formally approved a package of treaty amendments to accommodate the previously accepted structural reforms. The summit additionally authorized formation by Botswana, Mozambique, and South Africa of a task force to confer with Zimbabwe on domestic economic and political issues.

In September 2001 South Africa became the first SADC country to implement the free trade protocol signed in 1996 in Maseru. By then, however, the original free trade target date for the community as a whole was pushed back to 2008, when "substantially all" intra-SADC trade were to become tariff free. Exceptions will be permitted on a country-by-country temporary basis for "sensitive products." Looking further ahead, the SADC intends to introduce a customs union in 2010 and a full common market in 2012.

A January 14, 2002, extraordinary summit in Blantyre focused on conflicts and security matters in the DRC, Angola, and especially Zimbabwe. The SADC sent a ministerial delegation to Harare in December 2002 that received reassurances from the Mugabe regime about meeting democratic standards for the forthcoming presidential election, but the conduct of the balloting in March 2002 was nevertheless widely condemned internationally. At the October 2–3, 2002, summit in Luanda, Angola, the SADC took no substantive action with regard to Zimbabwe, the main issue under discussion being drought and a resultant food crisis that was severely affecting Lesotho, Malawi, Mozambique, Swaziland, Zambia, and Zimbabwe.

By the August 25–26, 2003, summit in Dar es Salaam, Tanzania, the food crisis had abated, and the SADC turned its focus to economic and social planning, adopting a blueprint called the Regional Indicative Strategic Development Plan (RISDP). The summit also adopted the SADC Charter on Fundamental Social Rights, the Strategic Indicative Plan for the Organ (SIPO), and a mutual defense pact. The defense pact provided for collective action against armed attack and denied support to groups seeking the destabilization of other members, but it continued to uphold the principle of nonintervention in members' internal affairs. Recent security-related measures have also addressed controlling trafficking in drugs, diamonds, and small arms and light weapons.

A meeting of the Council of Ministers on March 12–13, 2004, in Arusha, Tanzania, officially launched the RISDP, which included among its economic concerns food security, sustainable growth, trade promotion, regional integration, and development of transport and communications infrastructure. To further emphasize the importance given to combating food shortages and chronic malnutrition, the SADC scheduled an extraordinary summit on agriculture and food security for May 2004.

In the area of social and human development, concerns addressed by the RISDP included gender equality and the AIDS epidemic. In recent years the SADC has given a high priority to advancing gender equality, including the increased participation of women in government and economic development. With regard to HIV/AIDS, however, the SADC's record is less consistent. In July 2003 a special summit on HIV and AIDS convened in Maseru, but only 4 of the SADC's 14 heads of state or government participated in the effort to draft a comprehensive regional plan for confronting the epidemic.

In the past several years the relationship with Comesa has become less contentious, and a joint SADC/Comesa task force meets regularly. In addition, both have actively supported the African Union's New Partnership for Africa's Development (NEPAD). In the wider international sphere, the SADC and the European Union (EU) continue to hold biennial ministerial meetings. SADC/EU working groups have focused on political, security, and economic matters. Negotiations on an SADC/EU Economic Partnership Agreement opened in 2004 in Windhoek. These discussions took a different direction in March 2006 when the SADC, under South African leadership, asked the EU to negotiate a bilateral agreement with the SADC, as opposed to holding discussions about joining a larger agreement between the EU and less-developed countries.

At the August 2005 summit in Gabarone, Botswana, Tomaz Augusto Salomao of Mozambique was appointed as the new SADC executive secretary. Other activity included the appointment of the first five members of the SADC tribunal. Also in 2005 the SADC activated the first of five planned standby brigades of SADC peacekeeping forces. The force was planned to be full strength by 2010. In June 2006 South Africa proposed that the standby brigade be augmented by a military inspection and surveillance organization, to be called the African Defense Audit Association.

As negotiations with the EU and Africa's several economic blocs began to intensify in 2006, membership by some countries in multiple, competing blocs became a significant issue. The EU would not allow a country to be a part of more than one Economic Partnership Agreement (EPA), and membership in multiple customs unions could cause great difficulties. Tomaz Augusto Salomao declared that all members must decide to which bloc they would belong by 2010, when the SADC customs union comes into effect. In March 2007 the SADC signed a Memorandum of Understanding with the United States, paving the way for increased U.S. aid and consultancy to help the SADC implement a free trade area by 2008.

At the 27th summit of SADC heads of state, held in Lusaka, August 16–17, 2007, the Seychelles was readmitted to membership. But in September 2007, Rwanda, which had been negotiating for membership, announced that it was no longer interested in joining, preferring to work instead with Comesa.

A pressing problem facing the SADC in 2007 and 2008 was the deteriorating situation in Zimbabwe. In March 2007 SADC appointed South African president Thabo Mbeki to mediate between government and opposition parties in Zimbabwe. Mbeki met with Zimbabwean president Robert Mugabe numerous times in late 2007 and throughout the electoral crisis of 2008 (see separate article on Zimbabwe), but had little success in stopping the violence. He was widely criticized for his reticence, not least by Morgan Tsvangirai, Mugabe's rival. In July 2008 a "reference group" of senior diplomats was created to help Mbeki. Group members came from the SADC, the UN, and the African Union.

The SADC as an organization also received much criticism for its failure to confront Mugabe with more energy. Mugabe walked out of the August 2007 Lusaka summit after exchanging harsh words with Zambian president Levy Mwanawasa when the latter tried to put the situation in Zimbabwe on the meeting's agenda. The SADC surprised many people when the head of its observer mission to the March 2008 Zimbabwean elections initially ridiculed EU claims that the elections would not be free and fair. Mugabe did not attend a SADC meeting that Mwanawasa organized in April 2008, complaining that representatives of the Zimbabwean opposition parties had been invited. As chair of SADC, Mwanawasa rejected attempts to expel Zimbabwe, but in June 2008 described the SADC's failure to take a firmer line with Mugabe as "scandalous." (Mwanawasa died in August 2008 from the effects of a stroke suffered in June.) Negotiations at the August 16–17, 2008, summit in Sandton, South Africa, failed to move talks of power-sharing in Zimbabwe forward. At this meeting the chair of the organization passed to South Africa and Thabo Mbeki. Botswana president Ian Khama boycotted the meeting because Mugabe was present, calling Mugabe's presidency "illegitimate."

In economic matters, Salomao called in September 2007 for the SADC to pay less attention to the issue of overlapping trade blocs and to concentrate on long-term plans for Africa's economic integration. As of January 1, 2008, the SADC Free Trade Area (FTA) came into effect, and most goods were able to move between SADC countries without import duties. Some smaller SADC countries worried that the FTA would cause their economies to be swamped by the regional powerhouse South Africa. In March 2008 Levy Mwanawasa criticized the SADC secretariat as not sufficiently able to deal with financial aid. He warned that this might interfere with achievement of a complete FTA and customs union by 2010.

The SADC continued contacts with Mugabe. In September 2008 Mbeki and the SADC mediated a power-sharing agreement, with Mugabe to be president and Tsvangirai prime minister. This agreement only marked the start of many months of wrangling about the allocation of cabinet posts. A meeting on November 9 in South Africa between the rivals and the SADC produced a ruling that Tsvangirai's party must share control of the Home Affairs ministry, including the police, with Mugabe's party. Mugabe would remain in control of the army and security services. The SADC received widespread criticism for this ruling, which was felt to be a capitulation to Mugabe. The unity government was finally formed at the end of January 2009, but wrangling continued late into the year. At the end of the SADC summit, held September 2–9 in Kinshasa, DRC, the assembled leaders declared that sanctions against Zimbabwe should now end; the group was again accused of undue deference to Mugabe.

In other Zimbabwean affairs, Mugabe continued to seize white-owned farms during 2009. A group of 79 white farmers appealed to the SADC tribunal, which supported them. On September 2 Zimbabwe announced that it was resigning from the tribunal, and would not be bound by its decisions.

The SADC refused recognition to Andry Rajoelina, who seized power in Madagascar from President Marc Ravalomanana on March 18, 2009. It suspended Madagascar from full participation in SADC activities, but by early August had effected a power-sharing agreement between the two sides.

In economic news, the SADC came to an agreement on October 22, 2008, with the East African Community (EAC) and the Comesa to create a 26-nation free-trade zone, stretching uninterrupted from Egypt to South Africa.

SOUTHERN CONE COMMON MARKET (MERCOSUR/MERCOSUL)

Mercado Común do Cono Sur
Mercado Comum de Cone Sul

Established: By treaty signed March 26, 1991, in Asunción, Paraguay, by the presidents of Argentina, Brazil, Paraguay, and Uruguay.

Purpose: To establish a regional "common market of the southern cone" through the harmonization of policies in agriculture, industry, finance, transportation, and other sectors; to promote economic development through expanded extraregional trade and the pursuit of foreign investment.

Headquarters: Montevideo, Uruguay.

Principal Organs: Council of the Common Market, Common Market Group, Joint Parliamentary Commission, Secretariat.

Web site: www.mercosur.int (in Spanish and Portuguese only)

Director of the Secretariat: José Buttner (Paraguay).

Membership (4): Argentina, Brazil, Paraguay, Uruguay.

Associate Members (6): Bolivia, Chile, Colombia, Ecuador, Peru, Venezuela.

Observer (1): Mexico.

Official Languages: Guaraní, Portuguese, Spanish.

Origin and development. The idea of a regional common market was first advanced in the late 1980s by Argentina and Brazil, which had recently signed a series of bilateral agreements that they hoped could be extended to other countries. Supporters of the concept also argued that a regional bloc would be helpful in taking advantage of the Enterprise for the Americas Initiative recently announced by U.S. president George H. W. Bush. Paraguay and Uruguay responded positively to the integration overtures from their larger neighbors, but Chile, expressing concern about the volatility of Brazil's economy, declined to join the grouping at that point.

The Treaty of Asunción was signed March 26, 1991, with ratification by the members' legislatures completed by September. Membership discussions continued thereafter with Bolivia and Chile, one proposal being that they be given associate status pending expiration of a five-year moratorium on new memberships.

Meanwhile, Chilean officials continued to pursue duty-free trade with Mercosur countries that would not affect Chilean tariffs on products from other nations, and on October 1, 1996, Chile became an associate member of Mercosur, subject to intraregional free trade provisions but excluded from Mercosur's external tariff arrangements. Bolivia's eligibility was complicated by its participation in the Andean Group (subsequently the Andean Community of Nations—CAN) because the Treaty of Asunción forbids dual regional affiliations. Despite this, Bolivia was accorded observer status in 1994 and became an associate member in January 1997. Peru concluded an associate agreement in August 2003 and officially became the third associate member in December 2003.

In 2004, Colombia, Ecuador, and Venezuela were added as associate members, meaning that all CAN members were officially associated with Mercosur. In July 2005 all Mercosur members were similarly made associate members of CAN.

In 2005 Venezuela officially petitioned to become a full Mercosur member.

Structure. The Council of the Common Market (CMC), comprised of members' foreign and economic ministers, is responsible for policy decisions. Negotiations with third parties are carried out under the auspices of the Common Market Group (*Grupo Mercado Común*), comprised of four regular members and an equal number of deputy members from each country. Working under the direction of the ministers of foreign affairs, the group is assisted by the Mercosur Trade Commission, which also sees to the enforcement of "common trade policy instruments for the operation of the customs union." The Mercosur parliaments are represented in the Joint Parliamentary Commission, and there also is an Economic-Social Consultative Forum. The administrative Secretariat, assisted by several technical committees, was established in 1992 in Montevideo, Uruguay.

Activities. Although negotiations during Mercosur's first year of existence on a proposed common external tariff were unproductive, significant progress was achieved in reducing intraregional tariffs. By the end of 1992 annual intraregional trade had jumped by an estimated 50 percent, although a substantial portion of the increase resulted from a vast influx of Brazilian goods into Argentina. With the benefits of integration already accruing, the December Mercosur summit accepted further cuts in intraregional tariffs and endorsed study of the possible creation of a regional currency unit. Potential regional military cooperation was also discussed at a June 1993 summit, although that issue subsequently appeared to recede among Mercosur priorities.

At their fifth summit, held January 17, 1994, in Montevideo, Uruguay, the Mercosur heads of state again expressed their confidence in the common market's future. No immediate progress was reported on what became the major sticking point in Mercosur negotiations—the common external tariff. With Brazil apparently standing firm in its demand for substantial tariffs on such products as computers, telecommunications equipment, and petrochemicals, some negotiators predicted that external tariff arrangements could not be completed by the January 1, 1995, target date. However, intensive negotiations later in the year yielded sufficient agreement for the Mercosur presidents to sign the Protocol of Ouro Prêto on December 17 in Ouro Prêto, Brazil, providing for the launching of the intraregional free trade zone and common external tariff on January 1. Free trade within Mercosur was established for approximately 85 percent of the products under consideration. Intraregional tariffs on most of the others were scheduled to decline to zero within four to five years, although each Mercosur country was permitted to protect selected industries for a longer period. In regard to the common external tariff, duties of from 0 to 20 percent were applied to most imports from outside the region. Plans were also endorsed for further discussions toward monetary integration and the coordination of industrial and agricultural policies.

Although still far from a full common market, Mercosur, as one of the world's largest economic blocs (covering approximately 200 million people), subsequently attracted substantial interest from other regional groupings. Thus, the European Union (EU) signed a cooperation agreement in December 1995 with Mercosur, pledging to pursue a reduction in EU-Mercosur tariffs as well as broader economic, scientific, and social consultation.

In the period leading up to the 1997 Mercosur summit, held June 19 in Asunción, Brazilian import controls once again stirred controversy between Brazil and the other members. In response, on the day before the summit, Brazil extended the exemptions it made for Argentina, Paraguay, Uruguay, Bolivia, and Chile until October 1997. While that action temporarily mollified the other members, the controversy promised to resurface at a later date. Meanwhile, the current leaders agreed that the Mercosur members and associate members should enter as a group into trade negotiations with others, such as the EU, CAN, and Mexico. They adopted the same approach toward the proposed Free Trade Area of the Americas (FTAA).

Throughout 1997 Mercosur engaged in a series of meetings with Andean countries to create a free trade zone between the two groupings. In April 1998 Mercosur signed a framework agreement with CAN that envisaged the dismantling of trade barriers in 2000. Subsequently, a Mercosur summit in late July in Argentina reaffirmed its commitment to the proposed South American free trade zone. However, Mercosur was unable to resolve two issues for its own members: how to regulate the regional automobile market and how to settle Brazil's complaint over Argentina's tariffs on Brazilian sugar. On the political front, the presidents pledged to keep the region free of weapons of mass destruction and signed the Ushuaia Protocol on July 14, which committed the members to appropriate standards of democratic governance and threatened expulsion for noncompliance.

The June 30, 2000, summit in Buenos Aires was broadly viewed as an effort to revitalize Mercosur. Chile, despite reservations about what it regarded as the group's high external tariff, announced that it intended to seek full membership. Among other things, the presidents reiterated the importance of coordinating investment incentives and of presenting a unified front during trade negotiations. On September 1, at a meeting of South American presidents in Brasília, Brazil, participants agreed to relaunch the CAN-Mercosur talks on trade preferences and called for introduction of a South American free trade area in the "briefest term possible." The year concluded with a December 8 Mercosur summit in Florianópolis, Brazil, where the major news was a decision to suspend membership talks with Chile, given that country's decision to pursue a bilateral trade accord with the United States.

The tenth anniversary Mercosur summit convened June 20–21, 2001, in Asunción. Highlights included an agreement to cut the common external tariff by one point, to 12.5 percent, by January 1, 2002, and to establish a disputes tribunal. Also at the summit, Venezuelan president Hugo Chávez formally submitted his country's application for associate membership, and the Mercosur leaders voiced continuing support for lower trade barriers with the EU and the United States, despite slow progress in negotiations.

At the July 4–5, 2002, summit in Buenos Aires, Mercosur voiced firm support for Argentina's efforts to overcome its economic crisis, criticized the United States for a lack of attention to the needs of Latin America, and welcomed to the session Mexican president Vicente Fox, who argued for a Mexican-Mercosur tariff-free zone. Trade negotiations with the Andean Community continued to gain momentum. At the 23rd summit, held December 5–6 in Brasília, a framework agreement with CAN was signed, although some quarters expressed frustration that a detailed pact had yet to be concluded.

At the end of 2002, the Southern Cone was still laboring under the burden of adverse economic conditions, with national leaders being forced to abandon their collective commitment to holding inflation under 5 percent annually as one consequence. Mercosur was also unable to resolve internal differences relating to the organization's common external tariff and other matters that complicated trade negotiations involving the EU and the proposed FTAA. Nevertheless, Brazil's president-elect Luiz Inácio da Silva called for strengthening Mercosur through such measures as raising Bolivia and Chile to full membership and creating a directly elected Mercosur parliament. At the June 18–19, 2003, summit in Asunción, Mercosur set 2006 as the target date for establishing the parliament. The parliament actually opened in May 2007.

The 25th summit, held December 16–17, 2003, in Montevideo was highlighted by completion of a ten-year free trade agreement with CAN members Colombia, Venezuela, and Peru. The session also marked Peru's entry as an associate member of Mercosur, an agreement to that effect having been concluded August 25. A principal impetus for the Mercosur-CAN pact was to present a stronger front during FTAA negotiations, although prospects for a comprehensive hemispheric trade agreement had recently receded (see separate article on the Latin American Integration System for details). In early 2004 stalled trade discussions with the EU resumed, the union having signaled increased flexibility on the sticking points of its tariffs and agricultural subsidies. At the same time, Mercosur negotiators reportedly shifted their focus away from subsidies toward the issue of market access for exports from Mercosur members to the EU. Mercosur was also contemplating trade agreements in Africa and the Middle East as well as with China, India, and Japan. However, "fundamental differences" among the Mercosur members were still reportedly hamstringing progress as of the mid-2005 summit.

Conflict between Argentina and Uruguay over the construction on the Uruguayan side of the Uruguay River of two cellulose plants has been a central issue for Mercosur since 2005. The plants represent the largest foreign investment in Uruguay's history (approximately $1.7 billion) and are funded by European investors. The Argentines object to the plants on environmental grounds. Uruguay believes the matter should be settled via the conflict resolution mechanisms of Mercosur, while Argentina claims it is a bilateral matter that should be settled in The Hague. Argentina formally filed papers at The Hague in early May 2006.

Part of the conflict has manifested in a months-long blockade of bridges between the two countries by Argentine environmental groups. This blockade was suspended at the behest of the Argentina government when they filed with The Hague.

The conflict between Argentina and Uruguay has threatened the cohesion of Mercosur, which has been plagued by charges from Uruguay and Paraguay that the group disproportionately favors larger partners Argentina and Brazil. The rhetoric has been heated, including the statement by former Uruguayan president Jorge Battle that leaving Mercosur is "the best alternative" for his country. Another former president, Julio Maria Sanguinetti, claimed that Mercosur was a "wounded project" and that the paper mill conflict constitutes a "regional crisis."

In a clear political message to the other countries in the group, especially Argentina, President Tabare Vazquez of Uruguay used a visit to Washington to note his dissatisfaction with Mercosur "as it currently operates." Furthermore, his trip was focused on free trade negotiations with the United States, a point of contention among many Latin American states, including Mercosur members. In fact, Venezuela publicly stated it left CAN because its members signed free trade accords with the United States.

The prospect of Venezuela's accession, and that country's increased involvement with the organization, caused an immediate leftward turn in Mercosur politics. Cuban leader Fidel Castro made an appearance as a special guest at the July 20–21, 2006, summit in Cordoba, Argentina, although Cuba is not a member of Mercosur. By the time of the January 19, 2007, meeting in Rio de Janeiro, the bloc's new direction became more apparent, with Chávez proposing a shift in policy toward helping the region's poor and developing a "Socialism for the 21st century." Also at this time, Bolivia and Ecuador, both countries with suspicions about free trade, were said to be interested in joining Mercosur.

In April 2007 the first South American energy summit was held in Venezuela. At this meeting it was agreed that work should start on merging Mercosur and the Andean Community (see separate article) into a bloc to be known as the Union of South American Nations (UNASUR), with headquarters in Quito, Ecuador. Uruguay continued to criticize Mercosur's new political direction, even as a new Mercosur parliament opened in Montevideo in May 2007. In early July Chávez declared that Venezuela was not interested in full membership unless the organization was prepared to break with "U.S.-style capitalism." He also set a three-month deadline for Brazil and Paraguay's parliaments to support Venezuela. Brazil's president, Luiz Inacio Lula da Silva, said that such ratification by September 2007 was unlikely. He professed warm neighborly feelings for Chávez, but the matter rested there. In August Chávez blamed Washington for Venezuela's failure to gain full membership. In a possibly related matter, the June 28, 2007, summit, held in Asunción, declared that the participants were "willing to remain united." Chávez was not at the meeting, and there was some hope that the group's turn towards political rather than economic matters might be slowing. Mexico (an observer state) had expressed interest in closer association, but in July da Silva said that would be difficult as long as Mexico was a member of the North American Free Trade Association (NAFTA).

In August 2007 representatives of Mercosur and the Association of Southeast Asian Nations (ASEAN, see separate article) met in Brasilia and agreed that ties between the two groups should be strengthened. ASEAN representatives attended the December 2007 Mercosur summit in Montevideo. In September 2007 Mercosur and the EU resumed long-stalled discussions about a free trade agreement. During the December summit Mercosur asked the EU to relax its trading rules to encourage a better dialogue. At the same time the EU agreed to donate 50 million euros ($33 million) to the organization. The summit ended with a declaration committing the organization to speeding up Venezuela's accession to full membership. It was also notable for a call by da Silva to Argentina to work on eliminating "economic asymmetry," as the smaller members of Mercosur have long complained of being overshadowed by the economies of Brazil and Argentina. In December 2007 Mercosur and Israel signed an agreement liberalizing trade between them.

The year 2008 saw Mercosur's external dealings being as mostly with the EU. In May EU Commission president Manuel Barroso said that negotiations with Mercosur should be accelerated to achieve a free trade deal with both Mercosur and the Andean Community by 2009. Mercosur for its part demanded that the EU respect its "sensitivities" with regard to agricultural products. The July 2, 2008, summit, held in Tucumán, Argentina, focused on the rising prices of energy and food. At the summit Hugo Chávez offered to create an agricultural development fund for the region, donating one dollar for every barrel of oil that Venezuela sold at over $100 per barrel.

At the July 2008 summit, the group was united in indignation over a new EU law concerning illegal immigration. This law, due to come into effect in 2010, allows for illegal immigrants to be detained for up to 18 months and to be banned from re-entry on any terms for five years. The Mercosur heads of state issued a joint statement condemning "every effort to criminalize irregular migration and the adoption of restrictive immigration policies, in particular against the most vulnerable sectors of society, women and children." They also stressed "the necessity to fight against racism, discrimination, xenophobia and other forms of intolerance."

The December 16–17, 2008, summit, held in Costa do Sauipe, Brazil, addressed, but failed to resolve, one the group's most vexing problems, that of double taxation of goods that are imported from outside Mercosur, then passed from one member state to another. While all concerned recognized that charging customs duties inside the group violated the principle of a common market, it proved impossible to work out the modalities of distributing the cost of the external tariff around the member countries. At the meeting Mercosur's full members announced that they would absorb the exports of associate member Bolivia to the United States. These exports were about to be affected by the cancellation of trade preferences under the U.S.-Andean Trade Preferences and Drug Eradication Act (ATPDEA). To increase imports from Bolivia, Mercosur agreed to lower tariffs and increase the flexibility of rules of entry for Bolivian goods.

The July 2009 summit, held July 23–24 in Paraguay, came amidst general acknowledgement that on economic matters the group was making only very slow progress. Various bilateral disputes between members persisted. Matters moved faster on the political front, where the member states refused to recognize the regime that had ousted the president of Honduras, as well as promising not to recognize the results of any future potentially fraudulent elections in that country. Mercosur also recognized Guaraní, the indigenous language of Paraguay, as one of its three official languages. Venezuela's application for full membership made little progress.

UNITED NATIONS (UN)

Established: By charter signed June 26, 1945, in San Francisco, United States, effective October 24, 1945.

Purpose: To maintain international peace and security; to develop friendly relations among states based on respect for the principle of equal rights and self-determination of peoples; to achieve international cooperation in solving problems of an economic, social, cultural, or humanitarian character; and to harmonize the actions of states in the attainment of these common ends.

Headquarters: New York, United States.

Principal Organs: General Assembly (all members), Security Council (15 members), Economic and Social Council (54 members), Trusteeship Council (5 members), International Court of Justice (15 judges), Secretariat.

Web site: www.un.org

Secretary General: Ban Ki Moon (South Korea).

Membership (192): See Appendix C.

Official Languages: Arabic, Chinese, English, French, Russian, Spanish. All are also working languages.

Origin and development. The idea of creating a new intergovernmental organization to replace the League of Nations was born early in World War II and first found public expression in an Inter-Allied Declaration signed on June 12, 1941, in London, England, by representatives of five Commonwealth states and eight European governments-in-exile. Formal use of the term United Nations first occurred in the Declaration by United Nations, signed on January 1, 1942, in Washington, D.C., on behalf of 26 states that subscribed to the principles of the Atlantic Charter (August 14, 1941) and pledged their full cooperation for the defeat of the Axis powers. At the Moscow Conference on October 30, 1943, representatives of China, the Union of Soviet Socialist Republics (USSR), the United Kingdom, and the United States proclaimed that they "recognized the necessity of establishing at the earliest practicable date a general international organization, based on the principle of the sovereign equality of all peace-loving states, and open to membership by all such states, large and small, for the maintenance of international peace and security." In meetings in Dumbarton Oaks, Washington, D.C., between August 21 and October 7, 1944, the four powers reached agreement on preliminary proposals and determined to prepare more complete suggestions for discussion at a subsequent conference of all involved nations.

Meeting from April 25 to June 25, 1945, in San Francisco, California, representatives of 50 countries participated in drafting the United Nations Charter, which was formally signed June 26. Poland was not represented at the San Francisco Conference but later signed the charter and is counted among the 51 "original" UN members. Following ratification by the five permanent members of the Security Council and most other signatories, the charter entered into force October 24, 1945. The General Assembly, which convened in its first regular session January 10, 1946, accepted an invitation to establish the permanent home of the organization in the United States; privileges and immunities of the UN headquarters were defined in a Headquarters Agreement with the U.S. government signed June 26, 1947.

The membership of the UN, which increased from 51 to 60 during the period 1945–1950, remained frozen at that level for the next five years as a result of U.S.-Soviet disagreements over admission. The deadlock was broken in 1955 when the superpowers agreed on a "package" of 16 new members: four Soviet-bloc states, 4 Western states, and 8 "uncommitted" states. Since then, states have normally been admitted with little delay. The exceptions are worth noting. The admission of the two Germanys in 1973 led to proposals for admission of the two Koreas and of the two Vietnams. Neither occurred prior to the formal unification of Vietnam in 1976, and action in regard to the two Koreas was delayed for another 15 years. On November 16, 1976, the United States used its 18th veto in the Security Council to prevent the admission of the Socialist Republic of Vietnam, having earlier in the same session, on June 23, 1976, employed its 15th veto to prevent Angola from joining. Later in the session, however, the United States relented, and Angola gained admission. In July 1977 Washington dropped its objection to Vietnam's membership as well.

With the admission of Brunei, the total membership during the 39th session of the General Assembly in 1984 stood at 159. The figure rose to 160 with the admission of Namibia in April 1990, fell back to 159 after the merger of North and South Yemen in May, advanced again to 160 via the September admission of Liechtenstein, and returned to 159 when East and West Germany merged in October. Seven new members (Estonia, Democratic People's Republic of Korea, Republic of Korea, Latvia, Lithuania, Marshall Islands, and Federated States of Micronesia) were admitted September 17, 1991, at the opening of the 46th General Assembly. Eight of the new states resulting from the collapse of the Soviet Union (Armenia, Azerbaijan, Kazakhstan, Kyrgyzstan, Moldova, Tajikistan, Turkmenistan, and Uzbekistan) were admitted March 2, 1992, along with San Marino. Russia announced the previous December that it was assuming the former USSR seat. Three of the breakaway Yugoslavian republics (Bosnia and Herzegovina, Croatia, and Slovenia) were admitted May 22. Capping an unprecedented period of expansion, Georgia became the 179th member on July 31.

The total dropped back to 178 with the dissolution of Czechoslovakia on January 1, 1993, then moved up to 180 when the Czech Republic and Slovakia joined separately on January 19. On April 8 the General Assembly approved the admission of "the former Yugoslav Republic of Macedonia," the name being carefully fashioned because of the terminological dispute between the new nation and Greece (see separate article on Macedonia). Monaco and newly independent Eritrea were admitted May 28, followed by Andorra on July 28. Palau, which achieved independence following protracted difficulty in concluding its U.S. trusteeship status (see section on Trusteeship Council), became the 185th member December 15, 1994. Kiribati, Nauru, and Tonga were admitted September 14, 1999, and Tuvalu joined September 5, 2000.

A change of government in October 2000 led to the November 1, 2000, admission of the Federal Republic of Yugoslavia (FRY). On September 22, 1992, the General Assembly, acting on the recommendation of the Security Council, decided the FRY could not automatically assume the UN membership of the former Socialist Federal Republic of Yugoslavia. The assembly informed the FRY that it would have to apply on its own for UN membership, and such an application was submitted the following day. However, no action on the request was taken by the assembly because of concern over the Federal Republic's role in the conflict in Bosnia and Herzegovina and, later, its actions regarding the ethnic Albanian population in the Yugoslavian province of Kosovo. As a consequence, the FRY was excluded from participation in the work of the General Assembly and its subsidiary bodies. Throughout this period, however, the UN membership of the Socialist Federal Republic of Yugoslavia technically remained in effect. A certain ambiguity, apparently deliberate, surrounded the issue, permitting the FRY and others to claim that it was still a member, although excluded from active participation, while some nations argued that the membership referred only to the antecedent Yugoslavian state. In any event, the flag of the Socialist Federal Republic of Yugoslavia, which was also the flag of the FRY, continued to fly outside UN headquarters with the flags of all other UN members, and the old nameplate remained positioned in front of an empty chair during assembly proceedings. In October 2000 the Security Council, in a resolution recommending admission of the FRY, acknowledged "that the State formerly known as the Socialist Federal Republic of Yugoslavia has ceased to exist." A representative of the FRY took up the empty seat, and a new FRY flag replaced that of the former Yugoslavia.

On September 10, 2002, the UN admitted Switzerland, which had long maintained a permanent observer mission at UN headquarters and had actively participated as a full member of the various UN specialized and related agencies. The Swiss government, having concluded that UN membership in the post–Cold War era would not jeopardize its long-standing international neutrality, sought admission after winning majority support from Swiss voters at a March 2002 referendum. Timor-Leste became the 191st member on September 27.

In 2003 the FRY became the "state union" of Serbia and Montenegro, which dissolved in June 2006, following a successful independence referendum in Montenegro. Accordingly, on June 28 the world's newest independent state, Montenegro, was admitted as the UN's 192nd member. Serbia, as the successor state to the state union, retained the UN seat held to that point by the FRY.

The Holy See (Vatican City State) has formal observer status in the General Assembly and maintains a permanent observer mission at UN headquarters. In July 2004 the UN granted the Holy See the full range of membership privileges, with the exception of voting.

In July 2007 Taiwan formally applied for membership in the UN. The application marked the first effort by the island nation to gain membership as Taiwan and not the Republic of China. The bid was rejected by the UN legal affairs office on the grounds that General Assembly Resolution 2758 granted sole representation for China to the People's Republic of China. The General Assembly subsequently approved by consensus the recommendation of the legal affairs office in September.

Following its self-declared independence from Serbia in February 2008, Kosovo sought membership in the UN (see Security Council, below). However, in September Serbia, which considers the Kosovar declaration of independence to be illegal, asked the General Assembly to refer Kosovo's status to the International Court of Justice. In a vote on the Serbian motion on October 9, 77 members supported the proposal, 6 opposed it, and 74 abstained, thereby sending the matter to the court.

After 16 consecutive annual failures, in September 2009 Taiwan announced that it would not seek membership in the UN in response to improved relations with China.

Structure. The UN system can be viewed as comprising (1) the principal organs, (2) subsidiary organs established to deal with particular aspects of the organization's responsibilities, (3) a number of specialized and related agencies, and (4) a series of ad hoc global conferences to examine particularly pressing issues.

The institutional structure of the principal organs resulted from complex negotiations that attempted to balance both the conflicting claims of national sovereignty and international responsibility, and the rights of large and small states. The principle of sovereign equality of all member states is exemplified in the General Assembly; that of the special responsibility of the major powers, in the composition and procedure of the Security Council. The other principal organs included in the charter are the Economic and Social Council (ECOSOC), the Trusteeship Council (whose activity was suspended in 1994), the International Court of Justice (ICJ), and the Secretariat.

UN-related intergovernmental bodies constitute a network of Specialized Agencies established by intergovernmental agreement as legal and autonomous international entities with their own memberships and organs and which, for the purpose of "coordination," are brought "into relationship" with the UN. While sharing many of their characteristics, the International Atomic Energy Agency (IAEA) remains legally distinct from the Specialized Agencies; the World Trade Organization, which emerged from the UN-sponsored General Agreement on Tariffs and Trade (GATT), has no formal association with the UN.

The proliferation of subsidiary organs can be attributed to many complex factors, including new demands and needs as more states attained independence; the effects of the Cold War; a subsequent diminution of East-West bipolarity; a greater concern with promoting economic and social development through technical assistance programs (almost entirely financed by voluntary contributions); and a resistance to any radical change in international trade patterns. For many years, the largest and most politically significant of the subordinate organs were the United Nations Conference on Trade and Development (UNCTAD) and the United Nations Industrial Development Organization (UNIDO), which were initial venues for debates, for conducting studies and presenting reports, for convening conferences and specialized meetings, and for mobilizing the opinions of nongovernmental organizations. They also provided a way for less developed states to formulate positions in relation to the industrialized states. During the 1970s both became intimately involved in activities related to program implementation, and on January 1, 1986, UNIDO became the UN's 16th Specialized Agency.

One of the most important developments in the UN system has been the use of ad hoc conferences to deal with major international problems. (For a listing of such conferences and a brief description of their activities, see Appendix B. Some conferences are also discussed under General Assembly: Origin and Development, below, and within entries for various General Assembly Special Bodies or UN Specialized Agencies.)

GENERAL ASSEMBLY

Membership (192): All members of the United Nations (see Appendix C).

Observers (74): African, Caribbean, and Pacific Group of States; African Development Bank; African Union; Agency for the Prohibition of Nuclear Weapons in Latin America and the Caribbean; Andean Community of Nations; Asian-African Legal Consultative Organization; Asian Development Bank; Association of Caribbean States; Association of Southeast Asian Nations; Black Sea Economic Cooperation Organization; Caribbean Community; Central American Integration System; Collective Security Treaty Organization; Common Fund for Commodities; Commonwealth of Independent States; Commonwealth Secretariat; Community of Portuguese-Speaking Countries; Community of Sahelo-Saharan States; Conference on Interaction and Confidence Building Measures in Asia; Cooperation Council for the Arab States of the Gulf; Council of Europe; Customs Cooperation Council; East African Community; Economic Community of Central African States; Economic Community of West African States; Economic Cooperation Organization; Energy Charter Conference; Eurasian Development Bank; Eurasian Economic Community; European Union; GUUAM; Hague Conference on Private International Law; Holy See; Ibero-American Conference; Indian Ocean Commission; Inter-American Development Bank; Inter-Parliamentary Union; International Center for Migration Policy Development; International Committee of the Red Cross; International Criminal Court; International Criminal Police Organization; International Development Law Organization; International Federation of Red Cross and Red Crescent Societies; International Fund for Saving the Aral Sea; International Hydrographic Organization; International Institute for Democracy and Electoral Assistance; International Organization for Migration; International Organization of Francophones (*Organisation Internacionale de la Francophonie*); International Seabed Authority; International Tribunal for the Law of the Sea; International Union for the Conservation of Nature and Natural Resources; Islamic Development Bank; Italian-Latin American Institute; Latin American Economic System; Latin American Integration Association; Latin American Parliament; League of Arab States; Organization for Economic Cooperation and Development; Organization for Security and Cooperation in Europe; Organization of American States; Organization of Eastern Caribbean States; Organization of the Islamic Conference; Organization of Petroleum Exporting Countries Fund for International Development; Pacific Islands Forum; Palestine (formerly designated as the observer mission of the Palestine Liberation Organization); Partners in Population and Development; Permanent Court of Arbitration; Regional Center on Small Arms and Light Weapons in the Great Lakes Region, the Horn of Africa and Bordering States; Shanghai Cooperation Organization; South Asian Association for Regional Cooperation; South Center; Southern African Development Community; Sovereign Military Order of Malta; University for Peace. (On July 7, 1998, the General Assembly voted to upgrade the status of Palestine, granting it some of the rights usually reserved for members. Palestine can now cosponsor draft resolutions and raise points of order on issues concerning Palestine and the Middle East, has the right of reply, and can participate in debate within the General Assembly to a greater extent. Furthermore, the Palestinian delegation also now has six seats in the assembly [as opposed to the two usually given to observers], situated after the member states but before the other observers. The new seating arrangements reflect a unique standing, somewhere between member states and other observers; the term "super observer" has been coined by the media to reflect Palestine's status.)

Origin and development. Endowed with the broadest powers of discussion of any UN organ, the General Assembly can consider any matter within the scope of the charter or relating to the powers and functions of any organ provided for in the charter. It can also make corresponding recommendations to the members or to the Security Council, although it cannot make recommendations on any issue the Security Council has under consideration unless requested to do so by that body.

The General Assembly's prominence in the UN system cannot simply be traced to the charter but rather to the vigorous exercise of its clearly designated functions and to its assertion of additional authority in areas (most notably the maintenance of peace and security) in which its charter mandate is ambiguous. Since all members of the UN participate in the assembly on a one-country–one-vote basis, the kinds of resolutions passed in the organ have varied considerably as the membership has changed. Thus, while the assembly's early history was dominated by Cold War issues, the rapid expansion of the membership to include less developed and developing countries—which now comprise an overwhelming majority—led to a focus on issues of decolonization and, more recently, development. A Declaration on the Granting of Independence to Colonial Countries and Peoples, adopted December 14, 1960, proclaimed the "necessity of bringing to a speedy and unconditional end colonialism in all its forms and manifestations." A Special Committee on the Implementation of the Declaration on Decolonization, known informally as the Special Committee of 24, has maintained continuous pressure for its application to the remaining non-self-governing territories.

As the end of colonialism in the world at large approached, UN attention focused increasingly on problems of colonialism and racial discrimination in certain southern African territories, including the Portuguese dependencies of Angola, Mozambique, and Portuguese Guinea (subsequently Guinea-Bissau); Southern Rhodesia (Zimbabwe); and Namibia. During the 1960s the assembly moved from general assertions of moral and legal rights in this area to condemnations of specific governments, accompanied by requests for diplomatic and economic sanctions and threats of military sanctions. In 1972 the assembly "condemned," for the first time, violations by the United States of Security Council sanctions against importing chrome and nickel from Southern Rhodesia. In December 1976 the assembly took the unprecedented action of passing a resolution endorsing "armed struggle" by Namibians. Subsequently, a number of peace proposals were discussed, culminating in a 1978 UN plan for Namibian independence, which, however, would take another 12 years to achieve. In December 2000 the General Assembly marked the 40th anniversary of the 1960 decolonization declaration by declaring 2001–2010 to be the Second International Decade for the Eradication of Colonialism. The resolution passed by a vote of 125–2 (the United Kingdom and the United States in opposition), with 30 abstentions.

The assembly's work in development formally began with a proposal by U.S. President John F. Kennedy that the 1960s be officially designated as the UN Development Decade. The overall objective of the decade was the attainment in each less developed state of a minimum annual growth rate of 5 percent in aggregate national income. To this end, the developed states were asked to make available the equivalent of 1 percent of their income in the form of economic assistance and private investment. By 1967 it had become clear that not all objectives would be achieved by 1970, and a 55-member Preparatory Committee for the Second UN Development Decade was established by the General Assembly in 1968 to draft an international development strategy (IDS) for the 1970s. While the publicity surrounding the demand for a new international economic order (NIEO), particularly at the 1974, 1975, and 1980 special sessions of the General Assembly, tended to overshadow the IDS, the latter maintained its effectiveness, establishing quantitative targets for the Second Development Decade and on other issues such as human development, thus remaining the single most comprehensive program of action for less developed states. The Third Development Decade began January 1, 1981.

During the Second and Third Development Decades, the assembly increasingly concentrated on North-South relations, with an emphasis on economic links between advanced industrialized countries (often excluding those having centrally planned economies) and less developed countries. Major discussion topics, all of them integral to the NIEO, included international monetary reform and the transfer of real resources for financing development; transfer of technological and scientific advances, with specific emphasis on the reform of patent and licensing laws; restructuring of the economic and social sectors of the UN system; expansion of no-strings-attached aid; preferential and nonreciprocal treatment of less developed states' trade; recognition of the full permanent sovereignty of every state over its natural resources and the right of compensation for any expropriated foreign property; the regulation of foreign investment according to domestic law; supervision of the activities of transnational corporations; a "just and equitable relationship" between the prices of imports from and exports to less developed states ("indexation"); and enhancement of the role of commodity-producers' associations. Efforts were also made to conduct an all-encompassing discussion of development issues in the form of global negotiations. Although several UN special sessions have been held on this topic, advanced and developing countries have disagreed on the necessity, scope, and utility of such talks.

In 1990 the General Assembly acknowledged widespread failure in reaching many of its 1980 goals, blaming "adverse and unanticipated developments in the world economy," which had "wiped out the premises on which growth had been expected." In launching the Fourth UN Development Decade (effective January 1, 1991), the assembly warned that major international and national policy changes were needed to "reactivate" development and reduce the gap between rich and poor countries. The plan called for priority to be given to the development of human resources, entrepreneurship, and the transfer of technology to the developing countries. Because the targets set in 1980 had proven unrealistic, the new strategy established "flexible" objectives that could be revised as conditions warranted.

The charter entrusts both the General Assembly and the Security Council with responsibilities concerning disarmament and the regulation of armaments. Disarmament questions have been before the organization almost continuously since 1946, and a succession of specialized bodies was set up to deal with them. Among those currently in existence are the all-member Disarmament Commission, established in 1952 and reconstituted in 1978, and the 65-member Conference on Disarmament (known until 1984 as the Committee on Disarmament), which meets in Geneva, Switzerland. The UN played a role in drafting the Treaty Banning Nuclear Weapon Tests in the Atmosphere, in Outer Space, and Under Water (effective October 1963), as well as the Treaty on the Non-Proliferation of Nuclear Weapons (effective March 1970). The Second Special Session on Disarmament, held June–July 1982 at UN headquarters, had as its primary focus the adoption of a comprehensive disarmament program based on the draft program developed in 1980 by the Committee on Disarmament. Although the session heard messages from many of the world's leaders, two-thirds of the delegations, and almost 80 international organizations, no agreement was reached on the proposal.

The General Assembly also endorsed U.S.-Soviet bilateral agreements on the limitation of offensive and defensive strategic weapon systems; urged wide adherence to the Convention on the Prohibition of the Development, Production, and Stockpiling of Bacteriological (Biological) and Toxin Weapons and on Their Destruction (opened for signature in April 1972 and entered into force in March 1975); and in April 1981 opened for signature a Convention on Prohibition or Restrictions on the Use of Certain Conventional Weapons Which May Be Deemed to Be Excessively Injurious or to Have Indiscriminate Effects, the intention being to protect civilians from such weapons as napalm, land mines, and booby traps. The Convention on Conventional Weapons entered into force in December 1983.

The assembly met in special session May–June 1988 in another attempt to revise and update its disarmament aims and priorities. As in 1982, however, no consensus was reached on a final declaration. "Irreconcilable differences" were reported between Western countries and developing nations (usually supported by the Soviet bloc) on several issues, including conventional arms controls in said nations, proposed curbs on space weapons, nuclear-weapon-free zones, and nuclear arms questions pertaining to South Africa and Israel. However, negotiations were successfully completed in September 1992 during the Conference on Disarmament on a Convention on the Prohibition of the Development, Production, Stockpiling and Use of Chemical Weapons and on Their Destruction. The convention was endorsed by the General Assembly in November, was opened for signature in January 1993, and entered into effect April 29, 1997, six months after the 65th ratification. Accordingly, the Organization for the Prohibition of Chemical Weapons (OPCW), based in The Hague, Netherlands, began operations to oversee implementation of the convention. The highest OPCW organ, the Conference of States Parties, met for the first time in May 1997; responsibility for the organization's day-to-day activities has been delegated to a 41-member Executive Council. As of June 2009 instruments of ratification or accession had been deposited by 188 states.

Negotiations on a Comprehensive Nuclear-Test-Ban Treaty (CTBT) began in 1993 and concluded with its adoption on September 10, 1996, by the General Assembly. The CTBT was opened for signature September 24, and the 5 declared nuclear powers—China, France, Russia, the United Kingdom, and the United States—were among the initial signatories. A notable exception was India, which had exploded its first nuclear device in 1974 and whose August decision to reject the treaty was strongly condemned. As of July 2009, 181 countries had signed the CTBT, but its rejection by the U.S. Senate in October 1999 left the treaty in limbo: 155 countries have ratified it, including 35 of the 44 states having nuclear power or research reactors, but all 44 must ratify the treaty for it to enter into effect, at which time a Comprehensive Nuclear-Test-Ban Treaty Organization (CTBTO) would begin operations.

On December 3, 1997, in Ottawa, Canada, representatives of more than 120 states gathered to witness the signing of the Convention on the Prohibition of the Use, Stockpiling, Production, and Transfer of Anti-Personnel Mines and on Their Destruction (the Ottawa Convention). Although a protocol of the 1981 Conventional Weapons Convention had established limits on land mines, it had not called for an outright ban on their use. The Ottawa Convention entered into force March 1,

1999, sufficient signatory states having deposited their ratifications. As of August 2009 the United States was not one of the 154 countries to have ratified the document, in large part because of what it continued to see as the necessity of land mine use in the frontier between North and South Korea.

UN activity in regard to human rights also dates virtually from the organization's founding. The assembly's 1948 adoption of the Universal Declaration of Human Rights marked perhaps the high point of UN action in this field. Subsequently, the Commission on Human Rights directed efforts to embody key principles of the declaration in binding international agreements. These efforts culminated in two human rights covenants—one dealing with economic, social, and cultural rights, and the other with civil and political rights—both of which came into force in January 1976.

On October 3, 1975, concern for human rights was, for the first time, explicitly linked with nationalism in the form of a resolution contending that Zionism is a form of "racism and racial discrimination." After considerable parliamentary maneuvering, the resolution passed November 10 by a vote of 72–35, with 32 abstentions. Two days later, U.S. Ambassador to the UN Daniel P. Moynihan launched what appeared to be a counterattack. He presented a draft resolution appealing to "all governments to proclaim an unconditional amnesty by releasing . . . persons deprived of their liberty primarily because they have sought peaceful expression of beliefs at variance with those held by the governments." Although the U.S. proposal was quickly withdrawn in the face of hostile amendments, discussion of the two resolutions put the issue of human rights back on the UN's agenda after some years. Sixteen years later, in only the second such reversal in its history, the assembly voted 111–25, with 13 abstentions, to revoke the Zionism resolution.

The Commission on Human Rights sponsored a World Conference on Human Rights June 14–25, 1993, in Vienna, Austria. It was attended by a reported 5,000 delegates from 111 countries and numerous intergovernmental and nongovernmental organizations. The conference's final declaration affirmed the "universal nature" of UN human rights standards, although some activists in the field argued that the language in the document had been "watered down" because of the insistence of some nations that the standards should reflect varying cultural and religious traditions as well as levels of economic development. The declaration also encouraged the General Assembly to consider appointing a commissioner for human rights. The proposed creation of the Office of the UN High Commissioner for Human Rights (OHCHR) generated considerable controversy at the 1993 General Assembly session. China and several developing countries, many of which had been accused of human rights violations in the past, initially attempted to block the Western-led initiative. A compromise was eventually reached under which the assembly unanimously agreed to establish the office while leaving the extent of the new commissioner's authority "purposely vague." In February 1994 Secretary General Boutros Boutros-Ghali of Egypt appointed José Ayala Lasso of Ecuador as the first high commissioner, a choice criticized by some human rights advocates because Ayala Lasso had served as a foreign minister under the military regime in Ecuador in the late 1970s. He was succeeded in 1997 by Mary Robinson, former president of Ireland, who in May 2001 was reelected for an additional year, until September 2002. She had declined renomination for a second four-year term after complaining the office lacked the power needed to effectively advance human rights. On September 12, 2002, she was succeeded by Brazilian diplomat Sergio Vieira de Mello, who had most recently served as a special representative of the UN secretary general in Kosovo and then in East Timor. Vieira de Mello was killed in August 2003 while temporarily serving as a special representative of the secretary general in Iraq. His successor, Louise Arbour, had previously served as a justice of the Canadian Supreme Court. She assumed the office on July 1, 2004, and was replaced by Navanethem Pillay of South Africa on September 1, 2008.

Questions relating to outer space are the province of a 69-member Committee on the Peaceful Uses of Outer Space, established by the General Assembly in 1960 to deal with the scientific, technical, and legal aspects of the subject. In addition to promoting scientific and technical cooperation on many space endeavors, the committee was responsible for the adoption of the Treaty on Principles Governing the Activities of States in the Exploration and Use of Outer Space Including the Moon and Other Celestial Bodies (entered into force October 10, 1967), and the Agreement on the Rescue of Astronauts, the Return of Astronauts and the Return of Objects Launched into Outer Space (entered into force December 3, 1968). Three additional treaties have since been adopted. The General Assembly has also adopted five sets of "Legal Principles" based on the committee's work, which cover use of satellites for television broadcasting, nuclear power sources in outer space, remote sensing, and international cooperation in the exploration and use of outer space.

The Second Conference on the Exploration and Peaceful Uses of Outer Space was held August 9–21, 1982, in Vienna, where the first space conference had convened in 1968. In addition to reiterating a call for adherence to the 1967 treaty and for improved UN monitoring of compliance, the conference recommended that the General Assembly adopt measures designed to accelerate the transfer of peaceful space technology, to expand access to space and its resources for developing countries, and to establish a UN information service on the world's space programs. A third conference met on July 19–30, 1999, in Vienna.

Oceanic policy has also become a major UN concern. In 1968 the General Assembly established a 42-member Committee on the Peaceful Uses of the Seabed and the Ocean Floor. Detailed and controversial negotiations in this area ensued, most notably in conjunction with the Third UN Conference on the Law of the Sea (UNCLOS), which held 11 sessions during 1973–1982 devoted to the formulation of a highly complex UN Convention on the Law of the Sea. The convention addressed a wide range of issues, such as territorial rights in coastal waters, freedom of passage through strategic sea routes, and the exploitation of seabed resources. Delegates to the tenth session (August 1981) in Geneva reluctantly agreed to discuss several sensitive issues about which the U.S. Ronald Reagan administration had expressed reservations. Although the 440 articles of the proposed treaty had received consensual approval during previous UNCLOS sessions, the United States demanded that such items as the regulation of deep-sea mining and the distribution of members for a proposed International Seabed Authority (ISA) be reexamined before it would consider approving the document.

Following a year-long review of the proposed treaty, Washington ended its absence from the conference with the presentation of a list of demands and revisions to be discussed at the 11th session. Although compromises were reached in several disputed areas, other differences remained unresolved, including the rights of retention and the entry of private enterprises to seabed exploration and exploitation sites, mandatory technology transfers from private industry to the ISA, and amending procedures. On April 30, 1982, the treaty was approved by 130 conference members, with 17 abstentions and 4 voting against, including Israel, Turkey, the United States, and Venezuela. The treaty was opened for ratification and signed by 117 countries on December 10. On December 30 the Reagan administration informed the UN that it would not pay its 25 percent share of the costs for the Preparatory Commission established under the treaty. UN officials responded that the United States was obligated to meet its assessment because the commission was a subsidiary organ of the General Assembly, while Washington asserted that because the commission was established by treaty, only treaty signatories were legally bound to pay its expenses.

The Preparatory Commission was charged with establishing the two main organs of the convention—the ISA and the International Tribunal for the Law of the Sea. In addition, the General Assembly in 1983 created the Office of the Special Representative of the Secretary General for the Law of the Sea, whose functions included carrying out the central program on law of the sea affairs, assisting states in consistently and uniformly implementing the convention's provisions, and providing general information concerning the treaty.

China, France, India, Japan, the Republic of Korea, and Russia (as successor to the Soviet Union) were registered by the Preparatory Commission as the initial "pioneer investors" under a program established to recognize national investments already made in exploration, research, and development work related to seabed mining. Pioneer investors were entitled to explore allocated portions of the international seabed but had to wait until the convention entered into force to begin commercial exploitation.

Led by the United States, many states that had not signed the convention won a renegotiation in 1994 of the contentious section authorizing the proposed ISA to control seabed mining and allocate profits from it. Washington subsequently signed the agreement concerning seabed mining and indicated that it was prepared to sign the convention itself. (As of late 2008, however, the United States was the only major maritime country that was still a provisional member of the ISA and not a party to the convention.) The convention finally entered into effect November 16, 1994, one year after receiving the required 60th ratification from among its 159 signatories. On the same date the **International Seabed Authority** was formally launched at its headquarters in Kingston, Jamaica. It was agreed that an assembly comprising all authority members would be the supreme organ of the ISA. The assembly is authorized to select a 36-member council, which serves as an executive board; a secretary general; and the 21 judges of the **International Tribunal for the Law of the Sea**, designated to rule on disputes regarding provisions of the convention.

At its first session, held in August 1995, the assembly was unable to agree on the composition of the council, elections to that body subsequently being deferred until consensus was reached at an assembly session in March 1996. At that time the assembly also elected Satya N. Nandan of Fiji (theretofore the special representative of the secretary general for the law of the sea) as the first secretary general of the ISA. Elections for the 21 judges of the tribunal were held August 1, 1996, and they were sworn in the following October in Hamburg, Germany. On November 16, 1998, the ISA terminated the membership of all provisional members (then eight countries, including, notably, the United States, which had yet to become parties to the convention), thereby reducing the authority's membership to 130. The status of the former provisional members was downgraded to that of observer to the assembly. Both the ISA and the tribunal subsequently completed agreements with the UN whereby they became autonomous organizations with close ties to the UN. As of August 2009, the ISA had 159 members and 36 observer states.

The UN Convention on the Law of the Sea also established the **Commission on the Limits of the Continental Shelf** (CLCS) in New York, with 21 members elected by the parties to the convention. The first members were elected in March 1997 for five-year terms. The commission's purpose is to review members' plans to expand activities on the continental shelf beyond 200 miles off their shores.

Structure. All members of the UN, each with one vote, are represented in the General Assembly, which now meets for a full year in regular session, normally commencing the third Tuesday in September. Special sessions (convenable, contrary to earlier practice, without formal adjournment of a regular session) may be called at the request of the Security Council, of a majority of the member states, or of one member state with the concurrence of a majority. Twenty-eight such sessions have thus far been held: Palestine (1947 and 1948); Tunisia (1961); Financial and Budgetary Problems (1963); Review of Peace-Keeping Operations and Southwest Africa (1967); Raw Materials and Development (1974); Development and International Economic Cooperation (1975, 1980, and 1990); Disarmament (1978, 1982, and 1988); Financing for UN Forces in Lebanon (1978); Namibia (1978 and 1986); the Economic Crisis in Africa (1986); Apartheid in South Africa (1989); Illegal Drugs (1990 and 1998); Follow-up on the 1992 Earth Summit (1997); Population and Development (1999); Small Island Developing States (1999); Women: Gender Equality, Development, and Peace for the Twenty-First Century (2000); Social Development (2000); Implementation of the Habitat Agenda (2001); HIV/AIDS (2001); Children (2002); and Commemoration on the 60th Anniversary of the Liberation of the Nazi Concentration Camps (2005). The General Assembly may convene a follow-up to a special session. For instance, in 2007, a plenary meeting was held to follow-up on the 2002 session that created the "A World Fit for Children" action plan. The 2007 session issued a new declaration on the protection of children that was subsequently adopted by 140 countries.

Under the "Uniting for Peace" resolution of November 3, 1950, an emergency special session may be convened by nine members of the Security Council or by a majority of the UN members in the event that the Security Council is prevented, by lack of unanimity among its permanent members, from exercising its primary responsibility for the maintenance of international peace and security. The seventh, eighth, and ninth such sessions dealt, respectively, with the question of Palestine (July 22–29, 1980), negotiations for Namibian independence (September 3–14, 1981), and the occupied Arab territories (January 29–February 5, 1982). The tenth, on Israeli actions in the occupied territories, opened on April 24–25, 1997, and has reconvened 16 times, most recently in December 2006.

The General Assembly elects the ten nonpermanent members of the Security Council; the 54 members of ECOSOC; the elected members of the Trusteeship Council; and, together with the Security Council (but voting independently), the judges of the International Court of Justice. On recommendation of the Security Council, it appoints the secretary general and is empowered to admit new members. The assembly also approves the UN budget, apportions the expenses of the organization among the members, and receives and considers reports from the other UN organs.

At each session the General Assembly elects its own president and 21 vice presidents; approves its agenda; and distributes agenda items among its committees, which are grouped by its rules of procedure into three categories: Main, Procedural, and Standing.

All member states are represented on the six Main Committees: First Committee (Disarmament and International Security), Second Committee (Economic and Financial), Third Committee (Social, Humanitarian, and Cultural), Fourth Committee (Special Political and Decolonization), Fifth Committee (Administrative and Budgetary), and Sixth Committee (Legal). Each member has one vote; decisions are taken by a simple majority. Resolutions and recommendations approved by the Main Committees are returned for final action by a plenary session of the General Assembly, where each member again has one vote but where decisions on "important questions"—including recommendations on peace and security questions; election of members to UN organs; the admission, suspension, and expulsion of member states; and budget matters—require a two-thirds majority of the members present and voting. Agenda items not referred to a Main Committee are dealt with directly by the assembly in plenary session under the same voting rules.

There are two Procedural (Sessional) Committees. The General Committee, which is comprised of 28 members (the president of the General Assembly, the 21 vice presidents, and the chairs of the six Main Committees), draws up the agenda of the plenary meetings, determines agenda priorities, and coordinates the proceedings of the committees. The Credentials Committee, which consists of nine members, is appointed at the beginning of each assembly session and is responsible for examining and reporting on credentials of representatives.

The two Standing Committees deal with continuing problems during and between the regular sessions of the General Assembly. The Advisory Committee on Administrative and Budgetary Questions (16 members) handles the budget and accounts of the UN as well as the administrative budgets of the Specialized Agencies; the Committee on Contributions (18 members) makes recommendations on the scale of assessments to be used in apportioning expenses. The members of each Standing Committee are appointed on the basis of broad geographical representation, serve for terms of three years, retire by rotation, and are eligible for reappointment.

The General Assembly is also empowered to establish subsidiary organs and ad hoc committees. Apart from the Special Bodies (see below), dozens of such entities of varying size presently deal with political, legal, scientific, and administrative matters. Those of an essentially political character (with dates of establishment) include the UN Conciliation Commission for Palestine (1948), the Special Committee of 24 on Decolonization (1961), the Committee on the Elimination of Racial Discrimination (1965), the Special Committee on Peacekeeping Operations (1965), the Special Committee to Investigate Israeli Practices Affecting the Human Rights of the Palestinian People and Other Arabs of the Occupied Territories (1968), the Ad Hoc Committee on the Indian Ocean (1972), the Special Committee on the Charter of the United Nations and on the Strengthening of the Role of the Organization (1975), the Committee on the Exercise of the Inalienable Rights of the Palestinian People (1975), the Committee on Information (1978), the Advisory Board on Disarmament Matters (1978), the Disarmament Commission (1978), the Conference on Disarmament (1978), the Committee on the Elimination of Discrimination against Women (1982), the Committee against Torture (1984), the Trade and Development Board (1995), the UN Open-ended Informal Consultative Process on Oceans and the Law of the Sea (UNICPO, 1999), and the United Nations Peacebuilding Commission (2005). Subsidiary groups dealing with legal matters include the International Law Commission (1947); the Advisory Committee on the UN Program of Assistance in Teaching, Study, Dissemination, and Wider Appreciation of International Law (1965); the UN Commission on International Trade Law (1966); the Committee on the Rights of the Child (1989); the Ad Hoc Committee on Terrorism (1997); and the Ad Hoc Committee on a Comprehensive and Integral International Convention on Protection and Promotion of the Rights and Dignity of Persons with Disabilities (2002). Those dealing with scientific matters include the Committee on the Peaceful Uses of Outer Space (1959) and the UN Scientific Committee on the Effects of Atomic Radiation (1955). Subsidiary groups dealing with administrative and financial matters include the Board of Auditors (1946), the Investments Committee (1947), the International Civil Service Commission (1948), the UN Administrative Tribunal (1949), the UN Joint

Staff Pension Board (1948), the Panel of External Auditors (1959), the Joint Inspection Unit (1966), the Working Group on the Financing of the UN Relief and Works Agency for Palestinian Refugees in the Near East (UNRWA, 1970), the Committee on Relations with the Host Country (1971), and the Committee on Conferences (1974).

There are also a number of "open-ended" Working Groups considering the following: the Question of Equitable Representation and Increase in the Membership of the Security Council (1993), the Financial Situation of the United Nations (1994), the Causes of Conflict and the Promotion of Durable Peace and Sustainable Development in Africa (1999), and the Integrated and Coordinated Implementation and Follow-up to the Major UN Conferences and Summits in the Economic and Social Fields (2003).

In March 2006 the General Assembly established a Human Rights Council (UNHRC) as a subsidiary body of the General Assembly and made it directly accountable to and elected by the full membership of the UN. It replaced the controversial Commission on Human Rights, which had been one of ECOSOC's Functional Commissions. However, through 2007, the UNHCR had condemned only one country, Israel, for human rights abuses and remained unable to pass proposed resolutions on human rights violations in a number of other states. This led many critics to contend that the body was no more effective than its predecessor. Beginning in 2008, the UNHRC began conducting a periodic review of all 192 member states. The first round of reviews was scheduled to take four years. In March 2009 the United States announced it would be a candidate for election to the UNHRC, marking a reversal of the policy of the administration of President Geroge W. Bush. The United States was subsequently elected to the UNHRC for a three-year term in May.

Activities. In addition to two major international conferences—the World Summit for Social Development in Copenhagen, Denmark, in March, and the Fourth World Conference on Women in Beijing, China, in September—the agenda for 1995 included numerous special activities in honor of the UN's 50th anniversary, the most anticipated of which was the special assembly session on October 22–24. Billed as the largest gathering of world leaders in history, the anniversary session attracted 129 heads of state and government who adopted a declaration reaffirming the principals of the UN Charter while pledging to reform the organization's institutions in pursuit of more effective "service to humankind, especially to those who are suffering and are deeply deprived."

The inspirational mood of the anniversary ceremonies was tempered somewhat by the other major concern of the 50th General Assembly—the UN's debilitating financial crisis. UN officials reported that member states were $3.7 billion in arrears, led by the United States ($1.2 billion) and Russia ($590 million). Secretary General Boutros-Ghali, who suggested that the underlying problem might be that the countries of the world "simply do not regard the United Nations as a priority," called for a special assembly session to address the issue. For his part, Diogo Freitas de Amaral of Portugal, the president of the 50th assembly session, asked members to pursue reform of the organization. In other activity, the assembly adopted a "no-growth" $2.6 billion budget for the 1996–1997 biennium and established a preparatory commission to draft a convention for the creation of a proposed permanent international criminal court.

In February 1996 the assembly suspended the voting rights of 29 members (16 of them from Africa) for nonpayment. Brief hope for resolution of the UN's fiscal plight arose the following month when U.S. President Bill Clinton offered a plan whereby the United States would pay off its arrears in return for a reduction in U.S. dues from 25 to 20 percent of the UN budget. The Republican-controlled U.S. Congress voted against the proposal, however, and consequently the 51st assembly convened September 17, 1996, "without celebration," according to its president, Razali Ismail of Malaysia. On a more positive note, the assembly on September 24 witnessed the signing of the Comprehensive Nuclear-Test-Ban Treaty, which committed the five declared nuclear powers to a permanent cessation of nuclear weapons tests. Activity at the 51st assembly was overshadowed by the surprisingly contentious and public debate in the Security Council over a proposed second term for Secretary General Boutros-Ghali. Following the Security Council's recommendation on the matter, the assembly on December 17 appointed Kofi Annan of Ghana to succeed Boutros-Ghali, effective January 1, 1997.

Secretary General Annan called the 52nd General Assembly (which opened on September 16, 1997, under the presidency of Hennadiy Udovenko of Ukraine) the "reform Assembly" because it approved numerous changes to the UN's structure, one of the most important being the creation of the position of deputy secretary general. Also, a Department of Social and Economic Affairs was established to consolidate the Secretariat's operations in these two areas. Other reforms included the creation of a new department to "advance the disarmament agenda" and the consolidation of crime fighting and drug control programs based in Vienna into a single Office for Drug Control and Crime Prevention (ODCCP). In addition, the assembly passed an International Convention for the Suppression of Terrorist Bombings. The $2.5 billion 1998–1999 budget included a commitment to cut administrative costs by $200 million over the next four years.

In other business, the back dues owed to the UN by the United States remained unpaid. Also on the financial front, U.S. billionaire Ted Turner announced in September 1997 that he would donate $1 billion to the UN to support the organization's humanitarian efforts and urged similarly wealthy people to follow his example. In December 1999 the United States enacted the Helms-Biden Act, which linked payment of $612 million in arrears to specific reforms within the UN. (By 2006 the United States had paid the UN $100 million under the legislation.) The United States was also widely reproached for its positions regarding the formation of a permanent International Criminal Court (ICC), authorized by a mid-1998 UN conference in Rome. Citing fears that such a court could be used for politically motivated prosecutions of U.S. soldiers stationed abroad and infringe on its national sovereignty, the United States sought to limit the court's jurisdiction and give the Security Council veto power over what cases it could consider. Following five weeks of negotiations, the United States was 1 of only 7 conferees to vote against the establishment of the court; 120 voted in favor.

The United States was also unable to prevent the General Assembly from granting Palestine "super observer" status in the assembly in July 1998. By a vote of 124 to 4 (with 10 abstentions), Palestine was given many of the rights usually reserved for members, enabling the Palestinian representative to participate in a broader range of assembly activities. The United States and Israel had led the opposition to the measure, arguing that it would be harmful to the Middle East peace process. Despite this setback for Israel, the General Assembly labeled anti-Semitism a form of racism for the first time the following December.

At the 53rd session of the General Assembly, which convened September 21, 1998, support for the formation of the new criminal court was widespread, with many members calling for the assembly to take the necessary steps to bring it into existence. On another front, General Assembly President Didier Opertti Badan of Uruguay noted a rising frustration over the inability of the international community to develop effective conflict resolution mechanisms. There was also broad agreement in the assembly that the globalization of the economy, although positive, should emphasize improving the lives of those in the developing world, the majority of whom still lived in poverty. In a related vein, discussions focused on reforming the international financial system in such a fashion as to make it more stable and predictable.

The 54th session of the General Assembly, which opened September 20, 1999, began with Secretary General Annan advocating a redefinition of national sovereignty and arguing that the UN should be better prepared to intervene in defense of human rights and fundamental freedoms. At the same time, however, he criticized the North Atlantic Treaty Organization (NATO) for circumventing the UN in deciding to launch its March–June air campaign against Yugoslavia. Annan's call for intervention met strong objections from several countries, including China, whose foreign minister asserted before the assembly that national sovereignty and the principle of noninterference in countries' internal affairs were basic to international relations.

Chaired by Theo-Ben Gurirab of Namibia, the session's president, the general debate also touched on Security Council reform, sanctions, peace, sustainable development in Africa, and the HIV/AIDS pandemic. A special session was convened in the middle of the regular session to assess the progress on the action plan of the 1994 Global Conference on the Sustainable Development of Small Island Developing States. In other action the assembly approved an International Convention for the Suppression of the Financing of Terrorism; resolved to convene a 2001 conference on the illicit trade in light weapons and small arms; and decided to hold a special session, also in 2001, to reassess the goals of the 1990 World Summit for Children.

The 55th session, which opened on September 11, 2000, was preceded by the Millennium Summit, held September 6–8 and attended by some 150 heads of state and government in the largest such gathering in history. Described as a "working summit," the meeting provided an opportunity for bilateral talks between government leaders as well as for the signing of various treaties and conventions. The summit's final declaration, in addition to reaffirming the role of the United Nations and its charter as "indispensable foundations of a more peaceful, prosperous, and just world," committed the signatories to honor "fundamental" values: freedom, equality, solidarity, tolerance, respect for nature, and a shared responsibility for economic and social development.

Presided over by Harri Holkeri of Finland, the 55th regular session focused on globalization, authorized a June 2001 special session on HIV/AIDS, adopted resolutions on measures to eliminate international terrorism and on severing the link between illicit trade in diamonds and armed conflict, examined East Timor's ongoing transition to full independence, admitted Tuvalu as the 189th UN member, and accepted the Federal Republic of Yugoslavia as a full participant in the General Assembly. The long-standing issue of U.S. dues arrears and the scale of assessments for the regular budget ($2.54 billion for the 2000–2001 biennium) reached an apparent resolution in December. The U.S. share having been reduced from 25 percent to 22 percent of the budget (with the resultant 2001 shortfall to be offset by a voluntary contribution of some $34 million from Ted Turner), Washington agreed to begin paying its $1.3 billion in arrears. A new, complicated formula for funding peacekeeping operations was also accepted; the U.S. contribution would initially drop from 30 percent to 27 percent. (In May 2001, however, the U.S. Congress, angered that the Economic and Social Council had failed to reelect the United States to the UN Commission on Human Rights and the International Narcotics Control Board, threatened to withhold $582 million of its back dues.)

Major developments also occurred with regard to the ICC, the first permanent international tribunal with jurisdiction to try individuals for genocide, war crimes, and crimes against humanity. (For a discussion of existing nonpermanent courts, see Security Council: International Criminal Tribunals.) By the end of 2000, 139 states had signed the ICC Statute (also known as the Rome Statute), including the United States. Washington nevertheless remained concerned about removing its soldiers and officials from the court's jurisdiction, and the new George W. Bush administration was not expected to submit the treaty for Senate ratification. Indeed, on May 6, 2002, the Bush administration formally withdrew the U.S. signature from the Rome Statute. A month earlier, on April 11, the minimum 60 ratifications had been surpassed, and on July 1 the founding statute entered into effect and the **International Criminal Court** became a reality. Meeting on September 3–10, the Assembly of States Parties to the statute took a host of actions, including adopting rules of evidence and procedure; reviewing the specific genocidal crimes, crimes against humanity, and war crimes laid out in the Rome Statute; confirming procedures for the election of judges to the court; and approving an initial budget.

The court was inaugurated March 11, 2003. In February the 89 states that had ratified the founding treaty elected 18 judges to varying initial terms of three, six, and nine years. (Of the five permanent members of the Security Council, only France and the United Kingdom had completed ratifications.) The judges proceeded to elect a president, Philippe Kirsch of Canada, and two vice presidents, and on April 21 the Assembly of States Parties elected Luis Moreno-Ocampo of Argentina as chief prosecutor. On September 12 the ICC assembly established a Permanent Secretariat, with the UN Secretariat therefore concluding its services to the assembly at the end of the calendar year.

Meanwhile, the United States continued exerting financial pressure on signatory countries to exempt U.S. citizens from being turned over to the ICC. By July 2003 more than 40 ICC members had signed bilateral agreements to that effect with Washington, which threatened to suspend military aid to three dozen other countries, many in Latin America.

An agreement defining the court's continuing relationship with the UN was concluded by Judge Kirsch and Secretary General Annan on October 4, 2004. Among other things, it set forth the terms for cooperation between the UN and court prosecutors and provided for the Security Council to refer to the court matters within its purview. Accordingly, in March 2005 the Security Council referred the conflict in Darfur, Sudan, which led the prosecutor to open in June an investigation into allegations of genocide and crimes against humanity. Other referrals involved events in the Central African Republic, Democratic Republic of the Congo, and Uganda. As of November 2009, the court had 110 state parties. In March 2009 Song Sang-Hyun of South Korea was elected to replace Kirsch.

On July 9–20, 2001, a UN Conference on the Illicit Trade in Small Arms and Light Weapons in All Its Aspects convened in New York. The most contentious UN-sponsored gathering of the year, however, was the August 31–September 7, 2001, World Conference Against Racism, Racial Discrimination, Xenophobia, and Related Intolerance, held in Durban, South Africa. Among the topics drawing heated debate were the Middle East and slavery. On September 3 the United States, Canada, and Israel withdrew their delegations because of what U.S. Secretary of State Colin Powell labeled "censure and abuse" directed at Israel. In the end, the conference's lengthy closing declaration included a statement on Palestinian-Israeli matters that was less strident than Washington had feared. While expressing concern about "the plight of the Palestinian people under foreign occupation" and recognizing the right of Palestinians to self-determination and statehood, the document also recognized "the right to security for all States in the region, including Israel." On the matter of slavery and the slave trade, a number of European delegations had expressed concern the final declaration might, at least indirectly, call for reparations. A compromise was ultimately reached on the relevant passages, one of which asserted that "slavery and the slave trade are a crime against humanity and should always have been so."

The 56th General Assembly session began its work September 12, 2001, its opening having been delayed by a day because of the September 11 terrorist attacks in the United States. The start of the annual two-week general debate, presided over by Han Seung Soo of the Republic of Korea, was postponed from September 24 and reduced to a single week, November 10–16. A special General Assembly session on children (a follow-up to the 1990 World Summit for Children) was also postponed from September 19–21 until May 8–10, 2002. Not surprisingly, the 2001 general debate focused on terrorism, but such perennial issues as globalization, development, and poverty reduction also occupied the agenda. Among other actions, 118 states signed an International Convention for the Suppression of the Financing of Terrorism. On October 12 the UN in general and Kofi Annan in particular were awarded the Nobel Peace Prize in recognition of their work "for a better organized and more peaceful world." On June 29 the UN had unanimously elected Annan to a second term as secretary general.

On February 12, 2002, the Optional Protocol to the Convention on the Rights of the Child on the Involvement of Children in Armed Conflict, which had been passed by the General Assembly in May 2000, entered into effect, having been ratified by the specified minimum of 14 countries. On December 18 the General Assembly adopted another optional protocol, this one to the 1989 UN International Convention against Torture, by a 127–4 vote. Countries in opposition were the Marshall Islands, Nigeria, Palau, and the United States.

An International Conference on Financing for Development met May 18–22, 2002, in Monterrey, Mexico. Perhaps most notably, donor countries established as a goal 0.7 percent of GDP for Official Development Assistance, considerably more than either the United States or the European Union (EU), for example, were providing. At an International Conference on Sustainable Development, held in Johannesburg, South Africa, on August 26–September 4, long-standing North-South differences continued to be argued. The developed world urged adoption of a cautious approach favoring environmentally conscious sustainable development, while most of the developing country delegations placed greater emphasis on rapid expansion of trade and development opportunities.

The 57th General Assembly session, presided over by Jan Kavan of the Czech Republic, held its general debate September 12–20, 2002. Areas of focus included peace and security, terrorism, globalization, HIV/AIDS, sustainable development, and the mounting crisis in Iraq (see the Security Council, below). Specific measures included adoption of the New Partnership for Africa's Development (NEPAD), a broad, multilateral approach to African development (see the article on the African Union).

On August 19, 2003, a suicide truck bombing at UN headquarters in Baghdad, Iraq, killed 22, including Special Representative Sergio Vieira de Mello. Secretary General Annan later described the attack as "a direct challenge to the vision of global solidarity and collective security rooted in the United Nations Charter." An independent report published March 2004 faulted administrators for having failed to conduct a security review of the facility and for not taking other measures that might have mitigated the blast's effects.

The 58th General Assembly session held its general debate on September 23–October 2, 2003, under the presidency of Julian Hunte of St. Lucia. Secretary General Annan's opening address and annual report stressed the difficulty presented by the doctrine that individual states had the right to act preemptively and unilaterally against perceived threats. Annan warned that such a doctrine could result in a "proliferation of the unilateral and lawless use of force." He proposed instead a "common security agenda" that addressed the threats posed to international order not only by weapons of mass destruction and terrorism but also by poverty, deprivation, and civil war. Partly in response to a failure of diplomacy prior to the March 2003 U.S.-led invasion of Iraq, Annan later named a High-Level Panel on Threats, Challenges, and Change to review the role of the UN. The panel included among its 16 members former Chinese, Russian, and U.S. officials.

Continuing subjects of debate at the 2003 session included global warming, HIV/AIDS, and protectionist trade measures and debt as impediments to achieving the principal Millennium Development Goal of halving poverty by 2015. Delegates passed a resolution on "Revitalization of the Work of the General Assembly" with a view toward improving cooperation with the Security Council and the Economic and Social Council. Another resolution expressed "deep concern" over escalating threats to the safety and security of humanitarian and UN personnel. The General Assembly also endorsed a December 9–12 meeting in Merida, Mexico, that saw 95 countries sign a Convention against Corruption. It failed to reach agreement, however, on an even more controversial subject, namely a ban on human cloning, and in early November voted to postpone further action for two years.

With Jean Ping of Gabon having been named president, the general debate of the 59th session was held September 21–30, 2004, and was followed on October 4–5 by discussions related to strengthening the UN and revitalizing the General Assembly. In early December the High-Level Panel on Threats, Challenges, and Change submitted its report, which included 101 recommendations on matters as varied as Security Council reform, terrorism and nuclear proliferation, sustainable development, and use of force to protect human rights. On March 21, 2005, drawing on the panel's work, Secretary General Annan submitted to the General Assembly his own report on reform, which, among other things, called for expanding the Security Council to 24 members, streamlining the General Assembly agenda, and replacing the controversial UN Commission on Human Rights with a Human Rights Council elected by the General Assembly.

On April 13, 2005, the General Assembly adopted an International Convention for the Suppression of Acts of Nuclear Terrorism, which was opened for signature during the September 14–16 World Summit of national leaders, who gathered to mark the UN's 60th anniversary. The summit concluded with a final declaration covering UN reform and the Millennium Development Goals that had been adopted in 2000, but a number of proposals advocated by Secretary General Annan—most significantly those related to nuclear disarmament and nonproliferation—were dropped from the document or weakened in order to reach consensus. The declaration broke new ground primarily with regard to its assertion that the UN had the right to intervene if "national authorities manifestly [fail] to protect their populations from genocide, war crimes, ethnic cleansing and crimes against humanity." With Jan Eliasson of Sweden as president, the regular 2005 session was highlighted by the December approval of a resolution to create a Peacebuilding Commission. The 31-member advisory body, including national representatives from the Security Council, ECOSOC, and peacekeeping missions, was designed to focus on methods for stabilizing and rebuilding countries in the postconflict period. The General Assembly also voted to reconfigure the Central Emergency Revolving Fund as the Central Emergency Response Fund (CERF) for humanitarian disasters. Plans called for supplementing the preexisting $50 million revolving fund with a $450 million facility that could provide grants and loans.

On March 15, 2006, the General Assembly, by a vote of 170–4, approved creation of the Human Rights Council (UNHRC) to serve as the main UN forum for dialogue and cooperation on human rights. Israel, the Marshall Islands, Palau, and the United States voted against the resolution, and Belarus, Iran, and Venezuela abstained. The negative U.S. vote largely reflected concern that seats on the council, like those on the ECOSOC's Commission on Human Rights, would be filled on a regional basis. In the past, regional voting blocks had regularly elected to the commission acknowledged human rights violators. Election of the UNHRC's 47 members—a cohort considerably larger than had been envisaged by Secretary General Annan—took place on May 9, and its first session was held June 19. Through dialogue, capacity building, and technical assistance, the UNHRC assists UN members in meeting their human rights obligations. It is also expected to make recommendations to the General Assembly regarding international human rights law.

The General Assembly approved a series of reforms for UN management, procurement, and enhanced information technology efforts in July 2006. Annan was granted $20 million to implement the reform package. In August the sixteenth biennial AIDS Conference was held in Toronto. The gathering drew 20,000 participants. During the meeting, the UN's special envoy on HIV/AIDS to Africa, Stephen Lewis, accused the G-8 nations of failing to follow through on pledges made in 2005 to support enhanced access to drugs and treatment. (As of the Toronto conference, the UN had collected only $525 million to combat HIV/AIDS, tuberculosis, and malaria against a goal of $5.8 billion.) Partially in response to such criticism, the General Assembly launched the UNITAID, a multilateral program to purchase drugs to treat HIV/AIDS, tuberculosis, and malaria and redistribute them to 60 countries in Africa, Asia, Latin America, and the Caribbean. By 2007 UNITAID had 35 member states and an annual budget of $300 million.

Haya Rashed Al Khalifa of Bahrain was elected president of the 61st General Assembly session, becoming the third woman chosen for the post. The theme of the session was "Implementing a Partnership for Global Development." On September 13, 2006, the General Assembly approved the Declaration on the Rights of Indigenous Peoples. The nonbinding document articulated the rights of native peoples to unique cultures, languages, and traditions, and prohibited discrimination against them. Australia, Canada, New Zealand, and the United States were the only countries to vote against the declaration, which passed with 113 votes in favor and 11 abstentions.

The closing session of the 61st General Assembly was notable for anti-U.S. speeches by the presidents of Iran and Venezuela. At the time, Venezuela was campaigning for seat on the UN Security Council, and the harsh rhetoric used was reported to have undermined the effort and led to the selection of Panama as a compromise candidate for the seat.

During the assembly's meetings in September 2006, South Korean Foreign Minister Ban Ki Moon emerged as the leading candidate to succeed Annan after a series of informal polls of the Security Council. Ban's reputation for quiet diplomacy garnered him the support of the United States, China, and Russia, which collectively sought a less-activist secretary general than Annan. On October 13 the General Assembly appointed Ban as the eighth UN secretary general after the Security Council recommended his appointment in Resolution 1715. Annan announced in October that the UN Foundation, founded by Turner, had exceeded its $1 billion goal. Meanwhile, the High-Level Panel on UN Systems-Wide Coherence, formed in February 2006 to recommend internal reforms, released a report that contended duplication and inefficiency could be reduced by 20 percent by the creation of a single board or commission to coordinate the activities of the UN's agencies and bodies. On December 13 the General Assembly adopted the Convention on the Protection and Promotion of the Rights and Dignity of Persons with Disabilities, which opened for signatures on March 30, 2007, and was immediately signed by 81 countries and the EU, a record number for a UN convention.

The General Assembly adopted a resolution that condemned denial of the Holocaust on January 26, 2007. The resolution was in response to statements by the president of Iran that appeared to question the reality of the atrocities. The assembly also approved a reform proposal by Ban that included the division of the body's peacekeeping operations into two bodies: a department of peace operations and a department of field support.

In May 2007 the assembly elected Srgjan Kerim of Macedonia as the president of the 62nd session. Some delegations condemned Ban's decision to convene a September meeting of world leaders on climate change under the auspices of the Security Council, arguing that the General Assembly was the better forum for such an event. In June the General Assembly approved a proposed reform of UN peacekeeping operations that divided the current structure into two departments, Peacekeeping Operations and Field Support (see Secretariat, below). Meanwhile, in October the General Assembly held the High-Level Dialogue on Interreligious and Intercultural Understanding and Cooperation for Peace in an effort to promote interaction among diverse groups and cultures. In November the General Assembly designated September 15 of each year as International Democracy Day.

Miguel d'Escoto Brockmann was elected as president of the 63rd session of the General Assembly on June 4, 2008. The session's debate theme was "The Impact of the Global Food Crisis on Poverty and Hunger in the World as Well as the Need to Democraticize the United Nations." Brockmann called on the world body to enhance the power of the General Assembly by diluting the power of the Security Council and moving toward a system of "one country, one vote" in which all member states would be equal. In late October, Brockmann called on the international community to help reform the global financial system, in the wake of widespread economic turmoil. The General Assembly also declared 2008 the International Year of Sanitation and directed agencies to develop reports and recommendations to ensure that the 2015 Millennium Development Goals on sanitation were met.

On June 10, 2009, Ali Abdussalem Treki of Libya was elected as president of the 64th session of the General Assembly, which subsequently began on September 15. During the session, the assembly approved a draft resolution on the Alliance of Civilizations, an initiative that sought to promote a culture of peace throughout the world. The body also called on the secretary general to develop specific programs to support the Alliance of Civilizations. A resolution that pledged UN support for new, and newly restored, democracies was also approved. United States president Barack Obama, in his first speech before the General Assembly pledged a more cooperative foreign policy and called for a new international treaty to ban nuclear weapons. His remarks were seen as a foreshadowing of reduced tensions between the United States and the UN. On October 19 the assembly voted to grant observer status to the International Olympic Committee. For the 18th consecutive year, the assembly called on the United States to end its economic embargo on Cuba on a vote of 187 in support, 3 opposed (the United States, Israel, and Palau), and 2 abstentions (Micronenesia and the Marshall Islands). The assembly designated July 18 as Nelson Mandela International Day in honor of the accomplishments of the South African freedom fighter and leader.

GENERAL ASSEMBLY: SPECIAL BODIES

Over the years, the General Assembly has created a number of semiautonomous Special Bodies, two of which (UNCTAD, UNDP) deal with development problems, three (UNHCR, UNICEF, UNRWA) with relief and welfare problems, and two (UNEP, UNFPA) with demographic and environmental problems.

In addition to the United Nations University (UNU), which alone sponsors or cosponsors some dozen Research and Training Centers and Programs, a number of other specialized bodies for conducting research and providing training have been established. These include the UNITAR and the UNRISD (both discussed below); the UN Institute for Disarmament Research (UNIDIR), located in Geneva; the UN International Research and Training Institute for the Advancement of Women (INSTRAW), based in Santo Domingo, Dominican Republic; and the UN Interregional Crime and Justice Research Institute (UNICRI), based in Turin, Italy.

A former Special Body, the United Nations Industrial Development Organization (UNIDO), became a Specialized Agency on January 1, 1986. In 1992 the United Nations Disaster Relief Coordinator's Office (UNDRO), a Special Body since 1971, was incorporated into a new UN Department of Humanitarian Affairs. In May 1996 the World Food Council, a Special Body since 1974, was formally disbanded, its responsibilities being transferred to the Food and Agriculture Organization (FAO) and the World Food Program (WFP).

United Nations Children's Fund
(UNICEF)

Established: By General Assembly resolution of December 11, 1946, as the United Nations International Children's Emergency Fund. Initially a temporary body to provide emergency assistance to children in countries ravaged by war, the fund was made permanent by General Assembly resolution on October 6, 1953, the name being changed to United Nations Children's Fund while retaining the abbreviation UNICEF.

Purpose: To give assistance, particularly to less developed countries, in the establishment of permanent child health, educational, protective, and welfare services.

Headquarters: New York, United States.

Principal Organs: Executive Board (36 members), Program Committee (Committee of the Whole), National Committees, Secretariat. Membership on the Executive Board rotates on the following geographical basis: Africa, 8; Asia, 7; Latin America and the Caribbean, 5; Eastern Europe, 4; Western Europe and other, 12.

Web site: www.unicef.org

Executive Director: Ann M. Veneman (United States).

Activities. UNICEF has long been actively involved in programs dedicated to maternal and child health, nutrition, education, and social welfare. In keeping with the intent of the Child Survival and Development Revolution (CSDR), which was adopted in 1983 to provide "a creative and practical approach" to accelerating progress for children, UNICEF added emphasis on the problems of children affected by armed conflicts, exploitation, abandonment, abuse, and neglect. Increased attention was also given to the role of women in economic development, problems specific to female children, the need for family "spacing," and the provision of better water and sanitation facilities. In all the areas it covers, UNICEF's goal is to foster community-based services provided by workers selected by the community and supported by existing networks of government agencies and nongovernmental organizations.

UNICEF's activities are supported exclusively by voluntary contributions, approximately two-thirds of which are donated by governments and much of the remainder raised by its 37 National Committees, based primarily in more affluent countries. In addition to its New York headquarters, UNICEF maintains major offices in Tokyo, Japan, and Brussels, Belgium. Its crucial Supply Division operates out of Copenhagen, Denmark. In addition, its Innocenti Research Center, located in Florence, Italy, focuses on child development and advocacy. Eight regional offices around the globe help support 126 country offices. UNICEF reports indirectly to the General Assembly through the Economic and Social Council (ECOSOC).

The *State of the World's Children 1995* report announced that substantial gains had been achieved in the five years since the 1990 World Summit for Children, where 71 presidents and prime ministers—to that point, the largest gathering of heads of state and government in history—had signed a World Declaration on Survival, Protection and Development of Children. About 90 percent of the children in the developing world were living in countries that were likely to meet their summit goals, the report said. Over the preceding decade, however, more than 2 million children had died and 12 million had been rendered homeless in civil wars. The 1996 report continued the emphasis on the effects of war on children. UNICEF called for the elimination of land mines (of particular danger to civilians); the removal of children from war-torn areas; and better monitoring and reporting of those responsible for acts of torture, rape, and genocide.

Also in 1996, UNICEF cosponsored the World Congress against Commercial Sexual Exploitation of Children, held in August in Stockholm, Sweden. Representatives from more than 130 countries endorsed a "sweeping" final declaration, which called upon governments to allocate more resources to combat the problem, urged that tougher laws be enacted to protect children from exploitation, and asked for continued emphasis on policies geared to change the economic conditions that make so many children vulnerable to abuse. UNICEF also cosponsored the Second World Congress in December 2001 in Yokohama, Japan. UNICEF officials estimated in 2003 that 2 million children were forced into prostitution and/or the production of pornography each year, often under the influence of criminal organizations attracted by the multibillion dollar profits associated with such activity.

The *State of the World's Children 1997* report focused on the issue of child labor, UNICEF noting that most exploitive and hazardous child labor occurs in home, market, and agricultural settings (in the developing and developed world alike), not, as many people mistakenly believe, in "sweatshop" conditions. The "silent emergency," malnutrition, was the central focus of the 1998 *State of the World's Children* report, which stated that malnutrition contributes to the deaths of more than half of the 12 million children who die from preventable diseases in the developing world annually, while leaving hundreds of millions of others suffering from a variety of ailments, such as stunted growth and blindness. Furthermore, despite improvement in some areas, UNICEF reported an increase in the absolute number of malnourished children.

Education was the central focus of the *State of the World's Children 1999,* in which UNICEF predicted that almost one-sixth of the world's population would be unable to read or write in 2000. The report also emphasized the impact of the HIV/AIDS epidemic in eastern and southern Africa, where it had orphaned some 8 million children. By 2003 the total had risen to 11 million in Africa and 14 million orphans worldwide.

In mid-2000 UNICEF drew attention to a different kind of epidemic in a report entitled *Domestic Violence Against Women and Girls,* while the 2000 *State of the World's Children* report gave particular attention to brain development in the first three years of life and the importance of early childhood programs not only for children and caregivers but also for "the progress of nations as a whole." According to the report, every $1 invested in early care ultimately saved $7.

Recent UNICEF initiatives include participation in the Global Alliance for Vaccines and Immunization (GAVI), for which UNICEF's tasks include buying and distributing vaccines, disposable syringes, and related equipment. Other GAVI participants include the World Health Organization (WHO), the World Bank Group, pharmaceutical companies, and individual countries. Among the notable private foundations supporting GAVI is the Bill and Melinda Gates Foundation, established by the head of Microsoft and his wife. The foundation had already donated tens of millions of dollars to UNICEF for programs to immunize women and children against tetanus and to fight iodine deficiency, which inhibits brain development.

In 2000 UNICEF introduced a Global Movement for Children, which in 2001 launched a "Say Yes for Children" campaign with ten imperatives: ending discrimination against and exclusion of children; respecting the rights of children; caring for every child; fighting HIV/AIDS; ending violence against, and abuse of, children, as well as their sexual and economic exploitation; listening to children and facilitating their participation in decisions that affect them; educating every child; protecting them from war; safeguarding the environment; and fighting poverty by including children as a factor in debt relief programs, development assistance, government spending, and related activities.

On May 8–10, 2002, the General Assembly held a Special Session on Children as a follow-up to the 1990 World Summit for Children. (It had been postponed from 2001 because of the September 11 terrorist attack on New York City.) The session recommitted itself to the 1990 goals and adopted a corresponding plan of action under the theme "A World Fit for Children." UNICEF's 2002–2005 Medium-Term Strategic Plan identified five interlinked priorities: girls' education; integrated early childhood development; immunization and micronutrient supplementation (immunization "plus"); the fight against HIV/AIDS; and protection from violence, abuse, exploitation, and discrimination.

An October 2003 report commissioned by UNICEF, *Child Poverty in the Developing World,* reported that more than half the children in 46 of the poorest countries continued to live in absolute poverty (less than $1 a day per capita). The *State of the World's Children* annual reports for 2001 through 2003 focused on, respectively, early childhood; leadership, in the context of the 1990 goals and as a means to achieve peace, health, and integrity for children; and "Why Children Must Be Heard." The 2002 report, in addition to noting progress in some areas—for example, a reduction to 10 million in the number of children dying each year from preventable causes—identified armed conflict, HIV/AIDS, and poverty as the main obstacles to fulfillment of children's rights. The focus of the 2004 report was "Girls, Education, and Development." On the same theme, in 2002 UNICEF had introduced a "25 by 2005" program to seek gender parity in education in 25 mostly developing countries by 2005. Of the 211 million children who were victims of child labor abuses, 97 percent were in developing countries, according to a 2005 UNICEF report. UNICEF's 2006 *State of the World's Children, Excluded and Invisible* focused attention on children who fell outside the purview of traditional development programs and were, therefore, among the most vulnerable to exploitation. In September a UNICEF report found that 1.5 million children died each year due to a lack of clean water and access to proper sanitation.

In January 2007 UNICEF initiated an effort to raise $635 million to address 33 ongoing humanitarian crises around the world, with the largest share designated for the Darfur region of Sudan. In the previous year, the body raised $513 million for 53 emergencies through the year. UNICEF and the French government cosponsored a conference in February to eliminate the use of child soldiers. At the event, 58 nations agreed to take steps to disarm child soldiers and undertake steps to reintegrate the fighters into society. UNICEF director Ann Veneman noted that there were an estimated 250,000 underage soldiers then involved in conflicts around the world. UNICEF used June 16, the AU-sponsored Day of the African Child to launch an initiative to draw attention to the problem of child trafficking. Meanwhile, UNICEF offered support to expand the Measles Initiative, at that time focused on Africa, into India and Pakistan. The goal of the initiative was to reduce deaths from measles by 90 percent from 2000 levels by 2010. In its 2007 report, *State of the World's Children: Women and Children, the Double Dividend of Gender Equality*, UNICEF highlighted continuing discrimination against women and outlined steps through which repression could be alleviated to benefit both women and children. The report also asserted that improvements in gender equality would add to progress toward the UN's Millennium Development Goals. One offshoot of the report was a UNICEF partnership with the UN Fund for Population Activities (UNFPA) to launch a $44 million program to reduce female genital mutilation (see United Nations Fund for Population Activities, below).

UNICEF reported in September 2007 that the number of children who died annually dropped below 10 million in 2005 for the time since the organization began keeping records. On November 5, UNICEF called on governments to ban the use and stockpiling of cluster munitions through an international agreement. The body argued that such weaponry disproportionately affected women and children and specifically denounced their use in the 2006 conflict in Lebanon.

In 2008 UNICEF and the World Health Organization (see below) released the report of a Joint Monitoring Program that examined sanitation and access to safe drinking water around the world. The report found that the world was on track to meet the Millennium Development Goals on water and sanitation by 2015, but that 2.5 billion people, 38 percent of the world's population, still lacked access to safe water. UNICEF announced a range of programs to teach sanitation practices and improve access to safe water. UNICEF's *State of the World's Children 2008: Child Survival* called for increased measures to cut child mortality. It reported that 26,000 children under the age of five die every day, and that almost half of all child mortality occurred in sub-Saharan Africa.

In response to a global economic crisis, UNICEF and the Overseas Development Institute held a conference in November 2009 to highlight the impact of the worldwide recession on children. Throughout the year UNICEF undertook a leading role in disaster relief following tsunamis that affected areas such as Indonesia, the Philippines, and Samoa, and it launched a program with the WHO to better prepare countries for the H1N1 influenza through public education and preparedness campaigns. Its report, *State of the World's Children 2009: Maternal and Newborn Health,* noted that approxiamtley 1,500 expectant mothers died every day and called for global action to reduce maternal and neonatal mortality. It also reported that women in developing countries were 300 percent more likely to die during pregnancy or childbirth than women in developed states.

United Nations Conference on Trade and Development (UNCTAD)

Established: By General Assembly resolution of December 30, 1964.

Purpose: To promote international trade with a view to accelerating the economic growth of less developed countries, to formulate and implement policies related to trade and development, to review and facilitate the coordination of various institutions within the United Nations system in regard to international trade and development, to initiate action for the negotiation and adoption of multilateral legal instruments in the field of trade, and to harmonize trade and related development policies of governments and regional economic groups.

Headquarters: Geneva, Switzerland.

Principal Organs: Conference; Trade and Development Board (151 members); Commission on Trade in Goods and Services, and Commodities; Commission on Investment, Technology, and Related Financial Issues; Commission on Enterprise, Business Facilitation, and Development; Secretariat.

Web site: www.unctad.org

Secretary G eneral: Supachai Panitchpakdi (Thailand).

Membership (193)**:** All UN members, plus Holy See (Vatican City State). A number of intergovernmental and nongovernmental organizations have observer status.

Activities. The UNCTAD's quadrennial conference of governmental, intergovernmental, and nongovernmental representatives is considered the world's most comprehensive forum on North-South economic issues. Over the years it has addressed many of the economic and developmental difficulties faced by the developing world and the least developed countries (LDCs), although not always successfully. In the mid-1970s, for example, it established an Integrated Program for Commodities (IPC) to secure fair and stable prices for 18 commodities crucial to developing countries' foreign earnings, but relatively few agreements had been negotiated by producers through the IPC before commodity prices collapsed in the early 1980s. In 1980 the IPC's $750 million Common Fund for Commodity Stabilization was approved in an effort to combat extreme price fluctuations through buffer stocks, but it took eight years for the fund to secure ratification by the required number of UNCTAD members. It therefore didn't become operational (as an independent institution under its own Governing Council) until June 1989.

In April 1987 the Group of 77, which was organized in 1964 by 77 developing countries and which currently serves as a lobby for 131 developing countries within the UNCTAD, condemned "the current crisis in international economic relations and the state of disarray and disequilibrium which characterizes these relations." However, at UNCTAD VII the group adopted a less strident tone than at UNCTAD VI in 1983. The softening of rhetoric was deemed partially responsible for UNCTAD VII's adoption of a Final Act declaring consensus on debt, trade, development, and monetary issues. In general, the developing countries agreed to place more emphasis on private enterprise and free-market activity, while the West endorsed "flexibility" on debt repayments. Some observers suggested that the Final Act signaled a "new spirit" in North-South relations. In September 1988 the UNCTAD became one of the first major intergovernmental organizations to endorse extensive debt forgiveness by governments and commercial banks as "the only realistic way" of resolving the crisis.

Any remaining vestiges of disagreement over debt or other long-term development issues remained submerged at UNCTAD VIII, held February 8–25, 1992, in Cartagena de Indias, Colombia. The conference declared that a "new partnership for development" had been made possible by the disappearance of competing economic ideologies in the world. Priority was given to ensuring that national policies in developing countries would promote "efficient" free-market mechanisms, which UNCTAD VIII described as the cornerstone of accelerated growth and, by extension, social development.

UNCTAD subsequently continued an internal restructuring that had been requested by leading industrialized nations, and at UNCTAD IX, held April 27–May 11, 1996, in Midrand, South Africa, Secretary General Rubens Ricúpero asserted that UNCTAD had been granted "a new lease on life," particularly regarding the redefinition of its mandate so as not to appear to be in "competition" with the newly created World Trade Organization (WTO). In general, it was agreed that the UNCTAD would serve as an "advocate" for the developing countries by assessing the potential effect of policies in such areas as market access and the environment. Although some developing countries reportedly argued that a diminution of UNCTAD authority had taken place, the Group of Seven (G-7) industrialized nations praised the recent streamlining and endorsed the UNCTAD's new "focus" and decision to cooperate more extensively with the WTO. The UNCTAD subsequently continued to urge the LDCs to adopt free-market economic policies, which would help them develop "competitive" exports, while at the same time calling on the North to keep its markets open to products from the developing world.

The UNCTAD's primary concern in 1998 was the economic crisis afflicting much of the developing world. The UNCTAD board, meeting in October, called for revamping of the "international financial architecture" to help end this crisis and prevent others from occurring. It recommended greater supervision over the financial system and greater representation for developing countries in formulating economic reforms. The board also advocated more development assistance, debt relief, and continued special consideration in trade negotiations for LDCs.

The UNCTAD's annual *Trade and Development Report* for 1999 cautioned that many developing economies were overly dependent on capital inflows, foreign direct investment having surged by 39 percent in 1998. Concern was also expressed, on behalf of developing countries, about the impact of transnational corporations on environmental and labor conditions. The UNCTAD report again encouraged developed countries to remove import barriers that were costing developing countries an estimated $700 billion annually in lost earnings.

UNCTAD X, held February 12–19, 2000, in Bangkok, Thailand, followed closely on the heels of the contentious 1999 ministerial WTO meeting held in Seattle, Washington, in the United States. Although the Bangkok conference concluded with a statement calling for "consensual solutions" to problems of globalization, there was a clear emphasis on addressing the needs of the developing world. The resultant action plan focused particular attention on assisting LDCs and ensuring that the "development dimension" be considered in new trade negotiations.

The Third UN Conference on Least Developed Countries, held in Brussels, Belgium, on May 14–20, 2001, devoted sessions to such topics as governance, peace, and stability; human resources development and employment; infrastructure development; transport; financing growth and development; the roles of agriculture, health, and investment and enterprise development in enhancing productive capacities; energy; education; international trade in commodities and services; and intellectual property. It was also noted at the conference that less international aid was being targeted for LDCs, one apparent reason being "donor fatigue," attributable, at least in part, to corruption, fraud, and general administrative ineffectiveness on the part of recipient governments in carrying out sponsored programs. At the same time, only a handful of industrialized countries had ever approached the long-standing goal of donating 0.7 percent of GNP to the developing world.

In 2004 an UNCTAD study called for initiatives to help African countries break out of the "commodity trap"—that is, dependence on primary commodities that continue to experience international price volatility or long-term price declines. The report also noted, however, that agricultural subsidies paid by rich countries to their domestic producers had contributed to an oversupply of some commodities such as sugar, cotton, and groundnuts, and, thus, to depressed world prices.

According to the UNCTAD's *World Investment Report 2002,* foreign direct investment dropped by 50 percent in 2001, down from $1.4 trillion in 2000, as a consequence of the world economic downturn and, especially, the collapse of the mergers and acquisitions boom of the 1990s. Bucking the trend, however, a majority of developing countries, led by China and Mexico, saw gains. The downturn bottomed out in 2002, but 2003 saw no overall advance: a significant turnaround in the United States and continuing growth in China were offset by declines elsewhere, notably in the European Union (EU) countries and in Latin America. Africa showed a 30 percent gain, but from a low base of $11 billion in 2002.

The theme of UNCTAD XI, held June 13–18, 2004, in São Paolo, Brazil, was improving coherence between national development strategies and global economic processes. Additional discussion topics included corporate responsibility for development, creative industries and development, liberalization of trade in services, and trade and investment in biodiversity products and services.

In 2005 the UNCTAD released *Statistical Profiles of the Least Developed Countries,* which noted that developing countries accounted for 11 percent of the world's population but only 0.6 percent of world GDP. The report concluded that low per capita income, weak institutional capabilities, and high economic vulnerability were likely to continue this trend in the absence of specific support for improvement of human and physical infrastructure. In 2006 the UNCTAD reported that commodity prices, led by skyrocketing energy costs, rose by 12 percent in 2005, but it predicted that prices would stabilize over the next few years. The report noted that emerging markets, such as India and China, had become major players in the commodities market.

The UNCTAD's 2007 budget was $50 million, with an additional $25 million available for technical aid to individual countries. In an effort to standardize the manner in which information and communication technology statistics were reported by governments, the UNCTAD issued the *Manual for the Production of Statistics on the Information Economy* in February. The publication was designed to assist government and UN agencies in the collection of data and to serve as the basis for UN training and assistance courses on information technology. The UNCTAD reported in its 2007 annual trade and development index, which combines trade with economic and social standards, that the United States led developed countries for a second year in a row. The U.S. was followed by Germany and Denmark, while Singapore led developing countries, with South Korea in second place and China in third. In October the UNCTAD commenced an EU-funded program to increase Angola's international trade through training in sustainable development and intergovernmental cooperation in economic policy.

UNCTAD XII was held in April 2008 in Accra, Ghana, and resulted in the Accra Accords. Through the accords, UNCTAD pledged to assist developing countries narrow the gaps among nations in economic development, with a special focus on small island developing nations. UNCTAD also committed itself to developing methods to reduce rising food and commodity prices that disproportionately affected poorer countries. Finally, the accords noted the range of difficulties developing states faced and called for new development strategies, including increased aid and foreign investment and more technology transfers from developed nations. UNCTAD also launched a new database on global trade that provided governments with comparative statistics on more than 235 products in 130 countries. The UNCTAD's annual trade and development index noted that the global financial crisis was estimated to reduce economic growth to 3 percent in 2008, down 1 percent from the year before, but that the major impact would be on developing countries. The report also argued that official development assistance would have to be increased by $50 billion to $60 billion per year for the world to meet the 2015 Millennium Development Goals.

UNCTAD's 2009 trade and development report, *Responding to the Global Crisis, Climate Change Mitigation and Development,* focused on the responses of both developed and developing countries addressing the worldwide economic crisis. The report specifically highlighted the dangers of deregulation of financial markets and called for a range of government reforms. The publication also explored how efforts to mitigate global climate change would affect trade networks and development strategies. Other notable publications during the year were *Development and Globilization: Facts and Figures 2008* and the *UNCTAD Handbook of Statistics 2008.* UNCTAD also launched a new database to provide information on creative goods and services. The new source contains statistics for 130 countries and covers 1996–2006, with plans to update the database as information becomes available. In July Supachai Panitchpakdi of Thailand was reappointed for a second four-year term as UNCTAD's secretary general.

United Nations Development Program (UNDP)

Established: By General Assembly resolution of November 22, 1965, which combined the United Nations Expanded Program of Technical Assistance (UNEPTA) with the United Nations Special Fund (UNSF).

Purpose: To coordinate and administer technical assistance provided through the UN system, in order to assist less developed countries in their efforts to accelerate social and economic development.

Headquarters: New York, United States.

Principal Organs: Executive Board (36 members), Committee of the Whole, Regional Bureaus (Africa, Arab States, Asia and the Pacific, Europe and the Commonwealth of Independent States, Latin America and the Caribbean), Bureau for Resources and Strategic Partnerships, Bureau for Development Policy. Membership on the Executive Board rotates on the following geographical basis: Africa, 8; Asia, 7; Latin America and the Caribbean, 5; Eastern Europe, 4; Western Europe and other, 12.

Related Organs. The following special funds and programs are administered by the UNDP: the UN Capital Development Fund (UNCDF), established in 1960 but administered by the UNDP since 1972; the United Nations Volunteers (UNV), formed in 1971; the Program of Assistance to the Palestinian People (PAPP), authorized by the General Assembly in December 1978; the UN Development Fund for Women (UNIFEM), formerly the Voluntary Fund for the UN Decade for Women, established in 1976 and reconstituted in 1984; the Global Environment Facility (GEF), established in 1991 in conjunction with the UN Environment Program (see the UNEP entry) and the World Bank; the Drylands Development Center (DDC), established in 2002 in Nairobi, Kenya, as successor to the Office to Combat Desertification and Drought (UNSO, from the original UN Sudano-Sahelian Office); and the UN Office for Project Services (UNOPS), created in 1994 to assist other UN bodies and member states by providing management and support services for projects. In 2001 the Executive Board closed the UN Revolving Fund for Natural Resources Exploration (UNRFNRE), which had been established in 1974, and the UN Fund for Science and Technology for Development (UNFSTD), which had been set up in 1979, initially as an Interim Fund.

Web site: www.undp.org

Administrator: Helen Clark (New Zealand).

Activities. The UNDP works in partnership with 166 governments, dozens of intergovernmental agencies, and increasingly with civil society organizations and the private sector to promote "sustainable human development" throughout Africa, Asia, Latin America, the Middle East, and parts of Europe. In its early decades the organization focused its attention on five main areas: (1) surveying and assessing natural resources having industrial, commercial, or export potential; (2) stimulating capital investments; (3) training in a wide range of vocational and professional skills; (4) transferring appropriate technologies and stimulating the growth of local technological capabilities; and (5) aiding economic and social planning. In addition, in the 1980s the General Assembly assigned the UNDP three special mandates: the International Drinking Water Supply and Sanitation Decade (1981–1990), the Women in Development program, and implementation of the new international economic order (NIEO). During the 1990s priorities were redefined to encompass poverty elimination, good governance, environmental considerations, and women's development. For the first decade of the 21st century five "Communities of Practice" were identified: democratic governance, poverty reduction, energy and the environment, HIV/AIDS, and crisis prevention and recovery. Gender issues, information and communication technology, and capacity development cut across all five.

In mid-1999 Administrator James G. Speth, one of the highest-ranking UN officials from the United States, retired from his post. His replacement was Mark Malloch Brown of the United Kingdom, who had previously served with the World Bank. Malloch Brown immediately had to confront a loss of confidence in the agency's abilities and a collateral drop in donor funding. In an effort to reverse the trend, the UNDP introduced a 2000–2003 business plan that significantly restructured the organization's operations, adopted a Multi-Year Funding Framework (MYFF), and cut headquarters staff. Innovations included the establishment of nine subregional resource facilities (SURFs) for Arab states, the Caribbean, Central and Eastern Africa, Europe and the Commonwealth of Independent States countries, Latin America, the Pacific and North and Southeast Asia, Southern Africa, West and South Asia, and Western Africa. Each SURF supports the activities of country offices by making available policy specialists, expert referrals, technical support, and access to a global network of pertinent information. At the same time, the UNDP stepped up efforts to bring civil society organizations, foundations, and the private sector into partnership with donor countries, recipients, and intergovernmental organizations. To facilitate this process the UNDP created a Bureau for Research and Strategic Partnerships. In addition, "thematic trust funds" were established to utilize special donations for the UNDP's program emphases. Other changes included establishment of a Bureau for Crisis Prevention and Recovery as successor to the Emergency Response Division.

As a consequence, 2001 saw donors reverse a seven-year decline in committed resources, and in 2002 the UNDP received a record $2.83 billion in funding. Regular "core" resources rose to $670 million, while program country cost-sharing reached $1 billion and third-party cofinancing registered $935 million. Credited with the dramatic turnaround, Administrator Malloch Brown was appointed to a second term in April 2003.

The UNDP has been designated as the UN coordinating agency for achieving the Millennium Development Goals (MDGs) arising from the September 2000 Millennium Summit in New York. In addition to the broad goal of developing a global partnership for development, principal targets for 2015 include halving the billion-plus people living on less than $1 a day, guaranteeing completion of primary education by all children, eliminating gender disparities at all educational levels, reducing by two-thirds the mortality rate for children under five, cutting by three-fourths the number of women who die in childbirth, ensuring environmental sustainability, and reversing the spread of HIV/AIDS as well as reducing the incidence of malaria and other major diseases. To assist developing countries in meeting the MDGs, the UNDP launched Capacity 2015 at the World Summit for Sustainable Development, held August 26–September 4, 2002, in Johannesburg, South Africa. With its focus on capacity building, particularly through linking local sustainable development with national and international initiatives, Capacity 2015 expanded on the UNDP's earlier Capacity 21, which advanced the Agenda 21 goals set forth by the June 1992 UN

Conference on Environment and Development in Rio de Janeiro, Brazil.

Since 1990 the UNDP has issued an annual *Human Development Report,* containing an index that incorporates data on infant mortality, life expectancy, literacy, education expenditure, and individual purchasing power. Using what has been described as "unusually direct language," various reports have called for a drastic reduction in military spending, the promotion of human rights and gender equality as an integral component of economic development, curtailment of government corruption, and steps to overcome a growing global income disparity. The *Human Development Report 2002: Deepening Democracy in a Fragmented World* exemplified the UNDP's recent shift in focus toward good governance as a prerequisite for development. The 2002 report cautioned that in many countries the recent worldwide economic downturn had fed the perception that democracy cannot improve lives—a perception reinforced, according to the report, by authoritarian leaders who subvert electoral processes.

In the 2003 *Human Development Report* the UNDP focused on achieving the MDGs. The report noted that the goal of halving by 2015 the number of people living in absolute poverty was still attainable, largely because of successful governmental efforts in key populous countries—China, India, Brazil, and Mexico—toward "moving people out of poverty." Development aid nevertheless remained a crucial component for small, isolated countries, many of which were falling behind. According to the report, 54 countries were poorer than they had been in 1990. In sub-Saharan Africa, for example, half the population remained in extreme poverty and one-third regularly went hungry. Also, in much of Central and Eastern Europe and the Commonwealth of Independent States poverty had increased and life expectancy had declined in the preceding decade.

The *Human Development Report 2005: International Cooperation at a Crossroads* examined the extreme inequality between different countries and highlighted the human toll of failed aid programs. Latin America and sub-Saharan Africa were identified as the regions with the greatest inequalities, and the developed states and South Asia were identified as having the least. UNDP found that over the last 20 years, 53 countries with 80 percent of the world's population had seen inequality rise, whereas 9 states, with only 4 percent of the population, had seen it decrease. The report concluded that inequality was one of the main barriers to meeting the MDGs.

Kemal Dervis, former minister for economic affairs in Turkey, was appointed as the new UNDP administrator in mid-2005 after Malloch Brown was named chief of Secretary General Kofi Annan's cabinet. The UNDP budget for 2005 was $4.4 billion.

In 2006 UNDP halted its disarmament program in Uganda in response to reported human rights violations by government and rebel forces. The *Human Development Report 2006: Focus on Water* concentrated on sanitation, resource scarcity, and transborder water management. The report, developed with WHO, detailed a variety of strategies for dealing with water crises and shortages.

In August 2007 a UN ethics investigation reported that UNDP officials retaliated against an employee who reported corruption in the program's operations in North Korea, but the UNDP refused to accept the results of the investigation. In October the UNDP agreed to oversee the disbursement of $150 million in loans from the Japan Bank for International Cooperation to the Iraqi government to aid in reconstruction of electricity networks. The funds were the first disbursement in a $3.5 billion pledge made by Japan in 2005. The agreement was touted by the UNDP as a model for future aid arrangements. The following month, the UNDP and the Mohammed bin Rashid Al Maktoum Foundation, the largest private Arab charity, launched a $20 million program to promote education in the Middle East and Persian Gulf. Progress would be measured by an annual UNDP report, the *Arab Knowledge Report.*

The 2008 *Human Development Report—Fighting Climate Change: Human Solidarity in a Divided World* analyzes the nexus of development and climate change and provides recommendations for countries on how to pursue economic growth in a sustainable manner. The report also includes various visual and interactive materials on carbon emissions in an effort to make the document more accessible to a broader audience. In September the UNDP sponsored a weeklong series of meetings on the Millennium Development Goals to support the meeting on these goals convened by the secretary general for heads of state. The UNDP brought together business leaders, private groups, and government officials to discuss progress and to devise new strategies to achieve the UN's objectives. Norway, Spain, and the United Kingdom subsequently pledged $275 million in additional funding to help meet the Millennium Development Goals. In November an internal review was highly critical of the way the UN handled the aftermath of the death of Joe Comerford, a British engineer working for the UNDP in the DRC. The incident prompted a series of reforms (see Secretariat, activities, below).

On March 31, 2009, the UN General Assembly unanimously approved former New Zealand prime minister Helen Clark as the new administrator for UNDP. For the 2008–2009 biennium the UNDP projected its budget to be $10.7 billion, of which $8.67 billion would be spent on programs and activities, with the remainder devoted to operational and support costs. The global economic crisis prompted the UNDP to announce in 2009 that finalization of the 2010–2011 biennium budget would be postponed until January 2010, instead of the planned May 2009. The 2009 *Annual Report: Living Up to Commitments* highlighted the need for governments, nongovernmental organizations and private volunteer groups to continue to support programs to aid the needy and disadvantaged during the international recession.

United Nations Environment Program (UNEP)

Established: By General Assembly resolution of December 15, 1972, as the outgrowth of a United Nations Conference on the Human Environment held June 6–16, 1972, in Stockholm, Sweden.

Purpose: To facilitate international cooperation in all matters affecting the human environment; to ensure that environmental problems of wide international significance receive appropriate governmental consideration; and to promote the acquisition, assessment, and exchange of environmental knowledge.

Principal Organs: Governing Council (58 members), Committee of Permanent Representatives, High-Level Committee of Ministers and Officials, Secretariat. Membership on the Governing Council rotates on the following geographical basis: Africa, 16 seats; Asia, 13; Latin America and the Caribbean, 10; Eastern Europe, 6; Western Europe and other, 13.

Web site: www.unep.org

Headquarters: Nairobi, Kenya.

Executive Director: Achim Steiner (Germany).

Activities. In addition to distributing both technical and general information, notably through its "state of the environment" reports, UNEP acts as a catalyst within the UN system on environmental matters. Recent priorities have included climate change (particularly global warming), freshwater resources, deforestation and desertification, protection of wildlife and flora, handling of hazardous wastes and toxic chemicals, preservation of oceans and coastal areas, the effect of environmental degradation on human health, and biotechnology. UNEP also supports a broad range of public education programs designed to combat the mismanagement of natural resources and to build environmental considerations into development planning. Regional offices are located in Bangkok, Thailand; Geneva, Switzerland; Manama, Bahrain; Mexico City, Mexico; Nairobi, Kenya; and Washington, D.C., United States.

UNEP has been at the forefront of efforts to negotiate international agreements on environmental issues and has provided an institutional framework for administering various conventions. The Ozone Secretariat, which services the 1985 Vienna Convention for the Protection of the Ozone Layer, is headquartered in Nairobi, while the allied Multilateral Fund Secretariat for the Implementation of the (1987) Montreal Protocol on Substances That Deplete the Ozone Layer is based in Montreal. Other secretariats are responsible for administering the 1973 Convention on International Trade in Endangered Species of Wild Fauna and Flora (CITES); the 1979 Bonn Convention on the Conservation of Migratory Species of Wild Animals; the 1989 Basel Convention on the Control of Transboundary Movements of Hazardous Wastes and Their Disposal; the 1992 UN Framework Convention on Climate Change, which the UNEP drafted in conjunction with the World Meteorological Organization (WMO); the Convention on Biological Diversity, which came into force in December 1993; the Convention to

Combat Desertification in Countries Experiencing Serious Drought and/or Desertification, Especially in Africa, adopted in June 1994; the Regional Seas program, including the Global Program of Action for the Protection of the Marine Environment from Land-Based Activities, adopted in November 1995; the Rotterdam Convention on the Prior Informed Consent (PIC) Procedure for Certain Hazardous Chemicals and Pesticides in International Trade, adopted in September 1998; and the Stockholm Convention on Persistent Organic Pollutants, which entered into effect in May 2004.

UNEP provides the secretariat for the Scientific and Technical Advisory Panel (STAP) of the Global Environment Facility (GEF), which UNEP administers in conjunction with the UNDP and the World Bank. It also maintains a Global Resource Information Database (GRID), a Global Environment Information Exchange Network (Infoterra), and an International Register of Potentially Toxic Chemicals. In 1993 it launched an International Environmental Technology Center in Osaka, Japan. In partnership with the UN Office for the Coordination of Humanitarian Affairs (OCHA), it maintains a Joint UNEP/OCHA Environment Unit to respond to environmental emergencies. In 2000 the previously independent World Conservation Monitoring Center, which had been organized in 1988 with UNEP support, was reorganized as a UNEP "collaborating center" in Cambridge, England. Other recent partnerships include the UNEP Risø Center on Energy, Climate, and Sustainable Development (URC) in Roskilde, Denmark, and the UNEP Collaborating Center on Water and the Environment (UCC Water) in Hørsholm, Denmark. In 2001 the UNEP Post-Conflict Assessment Unit was established in Geneva on the strength of work performed in the Balkans (primarily Kosovo) since 1999. In 2003 a secretariat for the UN's multiagency Environmental Management Group became fully operational, also in Geneva.

A highlight of UNEP activities during the 1990s was the UN Conference on Environment and Development (UNCED, also informally referred to as the Earth Summit), held June 3–14, 1992, in Rio de Janeiro, Brazil. The conference was viewed as a "mixed success" by most environmentalists, although the sheer number of prominent attendees—at the time, the largest-ever gathering of world leaders—highlighted the extent to which environmental issues had risen on the world's political agenda. Formal action taken at UNCED included issuance of the Rio Declaration, a nonbinding statement of broad principles for environmentally sound development, and the signing (by 153 nations) of the legally binding Biological Diversity Convention and the Framework Convention on Climate Change. The United States, however, refused to sign the former, and the latter was approved only after specific targets for reducing carbon dioxide emissions had been deleted at Washington's insistence.

By consensus, the summit also endorsed a statement on Forest Principles, designed to reduce deforestation; however, resistance from timber-exporting nations precluded its adoption as a binding convention. In addition, UNCED issued an 800-page document titled *Agenda 21*, which outlined plans for a global environmental cleanup and proposed measures to assure that third world nations pursue development policies compatible with environmental protection. *Agenda 21* also called for enhancement of UNEP's role in the areas of environmental monitoring, research, education, and the creation of international environmental law. It endorsed the creation of a new UN Commission on Sustainable Development to assess compliance with the summit conventions and proposed a doubling of GEF resources to help developing nations meet environmental targets.

After being designated to oversee many of the Earth Summit decisions, UNEP hoped that donors would substantially increase its budget. However, one year later the UNEP budget stood at only about $65 million annually, essentially the same as before. There was also continued debate as to how the organization should spend its money, developed nations urging continued priority for protection of the atmosphere and developing countries calling for a shift toward specific development projects in such areas as freshwater resources.

Some progress in the North-South environmental debate was achieved in March 1994 when the United States and other donors pledged $2 billion toward a "new and restructured GEF." A 32-member GEF Council, with equal participation by developed and developing states, was established to oversee the GEF, while day-to-day activities remained the responsibility of a GEF secretariat comprising representatives from UNEP, the UNDP, the World Bank, and other UN affiliates. The UNEP also welcomed the entry into force of the Biological Diversity Convention (effective December 1993) and in May 1994 sponsored a Global Conference on the Sustainable Development of Small Island Developing States, which adopted an action program for monitoring climate change, particularly in regard to the threat posed by rising sea levels.

Global warming was also a major focus of the First Conference of Parties to the UN Framework Convention on Climate Change, held March 25–April 7, 1995, in Berlin, Germany. To the consternation of environmental groups and the small island states, the conference was unable to reach a decision on specific targets for reductions in carbon dioxide emissions, agreeing instead to continue negotiations for up to two more years on the matter, under the direction of the Intergovernmental Panel on Climate Change (IPCC).

Attention in 1996 focused primarily on the ongoing debate on climate change, spurred by an IPCC report that, for the first time, concluded that human behavior was having a "discernible influence" on climate. The IPCC estimated that the earth could experience an increase of 2°–6° Celsius in average temperature by 2100 if the emissions of greenhouse gases were not curtailed. Although acknowledging that such predictions were still surrounded by uncertainty, the IPCC argued that it would be foolhardy for the world to adopt a "wait-and-see" approach toward global warming.

Representatives from 159 countries attended the Third Conference of Parties to the UN Framework Convention on Climate Change, held December 1–11, 1997, in Kyoto, Japan, in an effort to establish specific, legally binding targets for reductions in greenhouse gas emissions. After sustained rancorous debate and behind-the-scenes negotiations, the conference finally adopted the Kyoto Protocol, under which 38 industrialized nations would by 2012 reduce such emissions to an average 5.2 percent below the 1990 levels. At best, however, the accord could be considered only a first step in dealing with global warming since no targets were established for developing nations and since implementation on the part of the developed world depended on country-by-country ratification. In addition, many environmental organizations criticized the protocol as a "sellout" for failing to require much deeper cuts, and some business representatives attacked the accord as "economically unsound." The protocol was opened for signature on March 16, 1998, and was scheduled to enter into force following ratification by countries responsible for at least 55 percent of the 1990 carbon dioxide emissions. Negotiations continued in late 1998 in Buenos Aires, Argentina, and in October–November 1999 in Bonn, Germany, in an effort to work out the details of how to implement the 1997 agreement.

The UN World Conference on Climate Change, which met November 13–25, 2000, in The Hague, Netherlands, ended in failure because of a disagreement between the United States and members of the European Union (EU) over greenhouse gas reductions. The conference had been expected to conclude a treaty that would meet the requirements of the Kyoto Protocol, but many EU member states objected to U.S. efforts to achieve the target not by an absolute reduction in emissions from fossil fuels, but by "supplementary, flexible" measures that would include transferring cleaner-burning technology to the developing world and earning credits "calculated for carbon sinks"—forests capable of absorbing carbon dioxide from the atmosphere. Talks were scheduled to resume in Berlin, Germany, in mid-2001, but in March the new U.S. president, George W. Bush, announced that the United States would insist on renegotiating the Kyoto Protocol, in part because it did not include standards for developing countries.

Meeting under UNEP auspices December 4–11, 2000, in Johannesburg, South Africa, delegates from 122 countries agreed to ban 12 toxic chemicals known as persistent organic pollutants (POPs). POPs break down slowly, travel easily, are readily absorbed by animals, and have been linked to birth defects and other abnormalities in humans. The targeted "dirty dozen" included dioxins, polychlorinated biphenyls (PCBs), and various pesticides, although 25 developing countries would be permitted to continue use of DDT in their fight against malaria. The new convention was signed in May 2001 in Stockholm, Sweden, and entered into force in May 2004, three months after deposit of a 50th ratification.

From October 29–November 10, 2001, representatives from 164 countries met in Marrakesh, Morocco, to complete the legal text for the 1997 Kyoto Protocol. Because protocol approval requires the ratification of countries accounting for at least 55 percent of global greenhouse gas emissions, the Kyoto standards suffered a potentially fatal blow in September 2003 when Russia, during a World Conference on Climate Change in Moscow, indicated that it would not commit to ratification. Without support by either the United States or Russia, the 55 percent goal could not be achieved. Three months later Russian President

Vladimir Putin reportedly described ratification as contrary to his country's national interests.

During the 2001 Marrakesh meeting, UNEP released a report warning that global warming could reduce the output of rice, maize, and wheat by one-third during the next half-century. Earlier in the year, UNEP's second *Global Environment Outlook* report had focused on problems related to the world's supply of fresh water, including pollution and scarcity, and emphasized the need to embrace environmental considerations in economic planning, particularly given the accelerating pace of globalization. The report also noted that some 3 million people die annually from diarrhea attributable to contaminated water, that each year polluted water contributes to the deaths of millions of children under five years of age, and that poor management of water systems is a significant factor in the spread of malaria and other insect-borne diseases. The UNEP also reported in 2001 significantly greater loss of coral reefs and forests than had previously been estimated. The third *Global Environment Outlook* cautioned that as of 2002 half of all rivers were polluted or seriously depleted and that by 2032 over half of the world's population could be living in "water-stressed" areas.

With the 1999 General Assembly session having endorsed creation of an annual, high-level environmental gathering, the UNEP responded by converting what had been biennial Governing Council sessions into annual meetings of the Governing Council/Global Ministerial Environment Forum (GMEF), which met for the first time May 29–31, 2000, in Malmö, Sweden. (In odd-numbered years the Governing Council/GMEF convenes in regular session; meetings in alternate years are designated as special sessions.) At the Seventh Special Session of the Governing Council/GMEF, held February 13–15, 2002, the board adopted a report on International Environmental Governance that called for an expanded UNEP role in coordinating environmental aspects of sustainable development and in assisting countries with capacity building and training. The session, held in Cartagena, Colombia, also devoted attention to preparations for the August 26–September 4 World Summit on Sustainable Development, held in Johannesburg.

The 22nd Regular Session of the Governing Council/GMEF met at UNEP headquarters on February 3–7, 2003. One focus of attention was mercury pollution, although the U.S. George W. Bush administration effectively blocked efforts to begin drafting a global protocol that would define mandatory restrictions.

The Eighth Special Session of the Governing Council/GMEF met March 29–31, 2004, in Jeju, South Korea, where issues related to water and sanitation were preeminent. A total of 158 countries sent representatives to the meeting, which considered such topics as water shortages, overfishing, and the recent increase in the number and severity of dust storms in Northeast Asia. Collaterally, UNEP released the *Global Environment Year Book 2003,* which called attention to the growing problem of "dead zones"—oxygen-depleted ocean areas caused by the runoff from nitrogen fertilizers, sewage, and industrial pollution. Also coming under scrutiny was solid waste and sewage disposal for small island countries, which often have neither the space nor the money for proper disposal. According to UNEP, some 90–98 percent of sewage from Pacific and Caribbean islands enters coastal waters untreated. Perhaps the most controversial proposal discussed at the March session involved conducting research on how environmental problems and pressures contribute to international conflict.

On November 18, 2004, reversing its previous stance, Russia completed formal ratification of the Kyoto Protocol, which went into effect on February 16, 2005. As of July 2006, a total of 163 countries and dependent territories plus the EU had ratified the protocol, the notable exception, apart from the United States, being Australia.

In March 2005 UNEP published the *Millennium Ecosystem Assessment,* the result of work by 1,300 authors and scientists from 95 countries. The report focused on the consequences, both positive and negative, of changes in ecosystems in preceding decades and on the requirements for preventing further degradation. While acknowledging the human benefits in terms of economic development and general well-being that have accrued from some ecosystem changes, the report found that 60 percent of the areas examined had been substantially degraded or overused—a rate of deterioration that could result in dire consequences for future generations if sustained. Suggested corrective actions included education, changes in consumption patterns, technological advances, and factoring into production costs environmental considerations. Follow-up reports were scheduled to be released every five years.

In 2006 UNEP released *Marine and Coastal Ecosystems & Human Well-being: Synthesis,* which examined the loss of coastal marine resources and tied those degradations to human activities, such as overfishing, habitat loss, climate change, pollution, and poor land use. For example, the report found that 75 percent of the fish stocks studied were in need of management programs to reverse declines and stabilize populations. UNEP's budget for the year was $105 million.

UNEP proclaimed 2007 as the Year of the Dolphin and launched a global effort to increase awareness of the threats facing different species. The IPCC issued its fourth assessment report on climate change in February 2007. The study was composed of four main reports and found that "global warming was unequivocal" and caused mainly by human activities and the production of greenhouse gases. It warned that temperatures would continue to rise for centuries even if current production of pollutants was curtailed.

In February 2007 at a conference in Paris, French President Jacques Chirac called for UNEP to be absorbed into a new, strengthened body to be titled the United Nations Environment Organization (UNEO). Chirac's proposal was endorsed by 46 countries, but opposed by the United States, Russia, and China. No action was taken on the plan. In October UNEP published the *Global Environment Outlook: Environment for Development* (GEO-4). GEO-4 was described as the most comprehensive review of the changes in the global ecosystem since 1987 and was the work of more than 300 scientists. It identified climate change, loss of biodiversity, and degradation of the world's oceans as the main environmental threats facing the world. UNEP also announced that it had met its goal of hiring women for half of its professional staff in 2007.

For its work on climate change, the IPCC was awarded the 2007 Nobel Peace Prize, along with former U.S. vice president Albert Gore Jr., a leading advocate for action against global warming. In November UNEP chartered the International Panel for Sustainable Resource Management. The new body was charged to examine the impact of biofuels and recycling on the environment.

In 2008 UNEP announced that it had fallen short of its 2007 target of $72 million in contributions to the Environment Fund by $2.8 million. Building on GEO-4, the UNEP developed a series of intermediate objectives, highlighted in the 2008 publication *UNEP Medium-Term Strategy 2010–2013: Environment for Development.* The report named six areas of focus: "climate change; disasters and conflicts; ecosystem management; environmental governance; harmful substances and hazardous waste; and resource efficiency—sustainable consumption and production." The publication also set measurable goals for each area and emphasized the transition of UNEP into a results-oriented organization with a goal of becoming the world's foremost environmental body. UNEP created a new strategic partnership with the Democratic Republic of the Congo to assist the country in developing its resources in an environmentally friendly manner. The arrangement was seen as a prototype for future relationships with individual states. UNEP also created the Poverty and Environment Facility to oversee the disbursement of aid under the joint UNEP-UNDP Poverty and Environment Initiative.

UNEP's staff increased to 597 in 2009, mainly in response to the need to oversee and coordinate new environmental programs across the globe. UNEP budgeted $171 million in expenditures for the Environment Fund that year. Through 2009, UNEP prepared for the Seal the Deal summit in Copenhagen in December 2009. The meeting was designed to bring together heads of state and other leaders to finalize strategies to address climate change and develop a successor agreement to the Kyoto Protocols. Meanwhile, UNEP *Global Trends in Sustainable Energy Investment 2009* was produced in an effort to influence the Copenhagen meeting by providing information on best energy practices and encouraging the use of renewable resources.

United Nations Institute for Training and Research (UNITAR)

Established: By General Assembly resolution of December 11, 1963. The inaugural meeting of the Board of Trustees was held March 24, 1965, and the institute became operational the following year.

Purpose: "To enhance the effectiveness of the United Nations through training and research in the maintenance of peace and security and in the promotion of economic and social development."

Headquarters: Geneva, Switzerland.

Principal Organ: Board of Trustees (up to 30 members appointed by the UN secretary general), of whom one or more may be officials of the UN Secretariat and the others governmental representatives. The UN secretary general, the president of the General Assembly, the president of the Economic and Social Council, and the institute's executive director are ex-officio members.

Web site: www.unitar.org

Executive Director: Carlos Lopes (Guinea-Bissau).

Activities. UNITAR provides practical assistance to the UN system, with particular emphasis on the problems of less developed countries. The institute is also concerned with the professional enrichment of national officials and diplomats dealing with UN-related issues and provides training for officials within the UN system. Seminars, courses, and symposia have dealt with multilateral diplomacy, economic development, international law, and UN documentation.

Despite years of declining pledge contributions and a decision in the late 1980s to reorient its programs toward training and away from research, UNITAR ended the decade with the General Assembly having reaffirmed the "validity and relevance" of UNITAR's mandate. In 1991 a high-level report on the future role of UNITAR was presented to the General Assembly, which endorsed a strengthening of UNITAR's training mandate, provided the institute avoided duplicating the work of other UN bodies. As a result, the Board of Trustees in mid-1992 approved a proposal from Secretary General Boutros-Ghali that UNITAR focus on these training areas: multilateral diplomacy; negotiations training for conflict resolution; economic and social development on selected matters in which UNITAR has a "competitive advantage" over other UN agencies; environmental and natural resource management training; peacekeeping, peacemaking, and peacebuilding; and the application of information systems. Training programs would be open to UN and non-UN diplomats, representatives from intergovernmental and nongovernmental organizations, national officials, and even the private sector.

In April 1993 the General Assembly approved a resolution providing for the shift of UNITAR's headquarters from New York City, New York, in the United States, to Geneva, Switzerland, and directed that the institute's future activities would have to be financed completely by voluntary contributions or special purpose grants. New York and Hiroshima, Japan, continue to host UNITAR offices.

As of 2006 there were about 60 UNITAR staff members, the majority engaged in training and capacity-building programs in various programs. UNITAR's 2006–2007 biennial report emphasized the body's increasing diversity in programs and its ability to offer specialized training as requested by individual governments. In March 2007 Carlos LOPES of Guinea-Bissau was appointed UNITAR's executive director. Lopes announced in November that UNITAR was undergoing a major transition to focus its efforts on standardizing methodologies between governments as the main goal of its training programs. The new director also noted that UNITAR had developed relationships with Columbia University, New York, United States; the University of Cape Town, Cape Town, South Africa; and the Ecole Libre des Sciences Politiques (Sciences Po), Paris, France, and that these academic partners would certify future training and educational initiatives.

As of 2008 the number of UNITAR staff members engaged in training and capacity-building programs had increased to about 80. The majority were engaged in the following areas: decentralized cooperation (local action) for development, chemicals and waste management, climate change, environmental law, foreign economic relations, HIV/AIDS, international affairs management, international migration policy, legal aspects of debt and financial management, needs of women and children in conflict and postconflict zones, peacekeeping operations instruction, peacemaking and preventive diplomacy, and technology and information systems for sustainable development. In April UN secretary general Ban initiated a new UNITAR lecture series in Geneva on global challenges. The series was designed to engage the public and increase awareness of the major issues facing the UN and the global community. UNITAR announced that it would reconfigure its peacekeeping training to better address challenges and to make better use of new training technologies, including web-based programs.

UNITAR reinitiated its global migration program in 2009 and became the chair of the interagency body, the Global Migration Group. UNITAR saw a 57 percent increase in its biennial operating budget in 2009, mainly due to a rise in funding from donor states. Through the year, UNITAR increased the activities of the UN Operational Satellite Applications Program (UNOSAT). The program used satellite imagery to produce maps and data to support UN activities and research. UNOSAT launched discussions with the European Space Agency over cooperative ventures and was involved in disaster mapping of 34 incidents in 2009, including the Samoan tsunami and flooding in the Philippines and Vietnam. UNOSAT's increased activities were made possible by a rise in funding from Denmark, Norway, and Sweden.

United Nations Office of High Commissioner for Refugees (UNHCR)

Established: By General Assembly resolution of December 3, 1949, with operations commencing January 1, 1951, for a three-year period; five-year extensions subsequently approved through December 31, 2008.

Purpose: To provide protection, emergency relief, and resettlement assistance to refugees, and to promote permanent solutions to refugee problems.

Headquarters: Geneva, Switzerland.

Principal Organs: Executive Committee, Standing Committee.

Web site: www.unhcr.org

High Commissioner: António Guterres (Portugal).

Membership of Executive Committee (76): Algeria, Argentina, Australia, Austria, Bangladesh, Belgium, Benin, Brazil, Canada, Chile, China, Colombia, Côte d'Ivoire, Democratic Republic of the Congo, Costa Rica, Cyprus, Denmark, Ecuador, Egypt, Estonia, Ethiopia, Finland, France, Germany, Ghana, Greece, Guinea, Holy See (Vatican City State), Hungary, India, Iran, Ireland, Israel, Italy, Japan, Jordan, Kenya, Republic of Korea, Lebanon, Lesotho, Luxembourg, Macedonia, Madagascar, Mexico, Montenegro, Morocco, Mozambique, Namibia, Netherlands, New Zealand, Nicaragua, Nigeria, Norway, Pakistan, Philippines, Poland, Portugal, Romania, Russia, Serbia, Somalia, South Africa, Spain, Sudan, Sweden, Switzerland, Tanzania, Thailand, Tunisia, Turkey, Uganda, United Kingdom, United States, Venezuela, Yemen, Zambia. Membership on the Executive Committee is permanent following approval by the Economic and Social Council and the General Assembly.

Activities. The UNHCR, financed partly by a limited UN subsidy for administration but primarily by contributions from governments, nongovernmental organizations, and individuals, attempts to ensure the treatment of refugees according to internationally accepted standards. In all, the UNHCR maintains 259 offices in 118 countries, with a total staff of 6,650.

The UNHCR promoted the adoption of the UN Convention on the Status of Refugees in 1951 and an additional protocol in 1967 that together provide a widely applicable definition of the term "refugee," establish minimum standards for treatment of refugees, grant favorable legal status to refugees, and accord refugees certain economic and social rights. (As of October 2008 there were 147 parties to either the convention or protocol, 141 being party to both.) In addition, the UNHCR conducts material assistance programs that provide emergency relief (food, medicine) and supplementary aid while work proceeds on the durable solutions of (in order of priority) the voluntary repatriation of refugees, their integration into the country where asylum was first sought, or their resettlement to a third country. Activities are often conducted in cooperation with other UN agencies, national governments, regional bodies, and private relief organizations.

The growth in the number and magnitude of refugee problems has resulted in a corresponding increase in the responsibilities entrusted to the UNHCR. In 1991, as refugee problems associated with the Gulf crisis multiplied, the UNHCR raised its estimate of the world's external refugee population to more than 15 million, higher than at any time since the end of World War II. By July 1992 the figure had risen to over 17 million, with the dislocation of 2.3 million people arising from fighting and "ethnic cleansing" campaigns in former Yugoslavia. Having experienced several years of "one crisis after another," the UNHCR projected an outlay of over $1 billion in 1992, more than twice previous budgets.

During the second half of 1992 and first half of 1993, the UNHCR remained highly visible in Bosnia and Herzegovina, where more than 2 million people were relying on its assistance in the wake of "the failure of all parties" to the conflict to respect humanitarian principles. The problems in the former Yugoslavia highlighted what had become a growing and complicated role for the UNHCR—assisting internally displaced persons (IDPs). Dealing with refugees in their own countries often raises the issue of human rights abuses and, therefore, requires extensive coordination with other UN bodies with expertise and authority in that area.

In 1994 the UNHCR reported that many nations were becoming less and less inclined to serve as permanent, or even temporary, hosts to refugees. Consequently, High Commissioner Sadako Ogata called for additional emphasis on the prevention of mass refugee movements. To that end, she proposed increased cooperation among the UNHCR, the World Bank, the International Monetary Fund, and other governmental and nongovernmental bodies to attack the causes of displacement.

In 1995 the UNHCR launched one of its biggest operations to date: providing assistance to more than 2 million refugees who had fled to Zaire and Tanzania from Rwanda. In addition, refugee problems intensified in the former Yugoslavia while UNHCR missions continued in a number of former Soviet republics, including Armenia, Azerbaijan, Georgia, and Tajikistan. On a more positive note, it was estimated that in the preceding five years some 9 million people had been repatriated with UNHCR assistance to countries such as Afghanistan, Cambodia, El Salvador, Ethiopia, Iraq, and Mozambique.

The UNHCR estimated it was trying to assist nearly 28 million people in early 1996, including 15 million external refugees, 5 million internal refugees, 4 million returnees requiring help in reintegrating into communities in their countries of origin, and 3.4 million "people of humanitarian concern." Activity later in the year included the termination of UNHCR support for Vietnamese refugees. Some 40,000 "boat people" in camps in several Asian countries and Hong Kong subsequently were forcibly repatriated to Vietnam on the grounds that they were economic, not political, refugees.

The March–June 1999 NATO-led air assault against Yugoslavia and the attendant "ethnic cleansing" of Kosovo by Serbian forces generated what the UNHCR would later characterize as "probably the most complex emergency in UNHCR's history." In a mere 11 weeks nearly 1 million people fled the province and then, following Yugoslavia's capitulation, returned. Neighboring states, particularly Macedonia and Albania, shouldered much of the burden and required emergency assistance from the UNHCR and other sources.

On the opposite side of the globe, in August 1999 an independence referendum in East Timor easily passed, but the outcome quickly led to a wave of violence by anti-independence militias, resulting in a massive flight to the Indonesian province of West Timor. In September Jakarta agreed to place East Timor under UN supervision, with the UNHCR then participating in efforts that helped more than 150,000 refugees return home by mid-2000. By the time East Timor achieved independence in May 2002 as the Democratic Republic of Timor-Leste, the number had risen to 200,000, with about 60,000 refugees still encamped in Indonesia's West Timor province.

Also in 2000 the UNHCR joined UN criticism of a number of European governments that had forcibly repatriated thousands of refugees to Kosovo. While many of the Kosovar Albanians had been accepted on a temporary basis during the conflict, some countries, particularly Germany and Switzerland, had forcibly returned thousands of additional refugees, allegedly including criminals, whose arrival had preceded the UN's Humanitarian Evacuation Program. As a further indication of Western Europe's increasing reluctance to accept refugees and asylum seekers, in March UK Home Secretary Jack Straw called for a "thorough overhaul" of the 1951 convention. He was responding in part to a February plane hijacking in which many of the passengers on the Afghan airliner had requested asylum in the United Kingdom. The incident, he said, had revealed "serious weaknesses in the way in which international conventions relating to refugees, terrorism and human rights operate." In October 2000 former Dutch prime minister Ruud Lubbers was unexpectedly named to succeed Sadako Ogata as high commissioner, effective January 1, 2001.

Among the agency's more immediate concerns was a crisis in Guinea, where some 500,000 people, fleeing from the prolonged civil conflicts in Sierra Leone and Liberia, had sought refuge. In the Horn of Africa renewed fighting between Ethiopia and Eritrea in 2000 had not only delayed efforts to repatriate more than 150,000 Eritreans from Sudan but had also caused an additional increase in the displaced population. Other African "hot spots" continued to be Burundi, the Democratic Republic of the Congo, and Angola. In Asia, the UNHCR signed agreements with Iran, Pakistan, and Afghanistan in 2000 for the voluntary return of 200,000 Afghan refugees, but well over 2 million remained in Pakistan and Iran. Also in Asia, the UNHCR continued to aid some 600,000 Sri Lankans displaced by the civil conflict between the government and Tamil separatists. (By October 2002, eight months after conclusion of a cease-fire, more than 210,000 IDPs had returned to their homes.) In the Americas, a principal focus of the organization's efforts was Colombia, where up to 2 million people had been displaced since 1985 by conflicts involving Marxist rebels, the military, drug cartels, and right-wing paramilitary forces.

In February 2001 newly installed High Commissioner Lubbers cautioned the European Union (EU) not to create a "fortress Europe" against asylum-seekers, although he supported the EU's effort to formulate a common asylum policy. Referring to UK Home Secretary Straw's proposal that the 1951 UN convention be reexamined, Lubbers commented that the solution to contemporary concerns was "to practice the convention in a modern way," not to rewrite it. On December 12–13, 2001, in the first meeting of its kind, the states that were party to the 1951 convention convened in Geneva, where they reaffirmed the "enduring importance" and "continuing relevance" of the convention and the 1967 protocol. They also called on the UNHCR to draft an Agenda for Protection. In 2000 the UNHCR had initiated a series of Global Consultations on International Protection. The results of those consultations led to publication in 2002 of the agenda in which High Commissioner Lubbers advocated "convention plus": the "development of special agreements or multilateral arrangements to ensure improved burden sharing, with countries in the North and South working together to find durable solutions for refugees." The basic goals set forth in the agenda were strengthening implementation of the convention and protocol, protecting refugees within wide migration movements, sharing burdens and responsibilities more equitably, finding more effective ways to deal with security-related issues, impelling the search for "durable solutions," and improving protection for women and children refugees.

In 2002 the UNHCR's largest repatriation and assistance effort focused on Afghanistan. The U.S.-led invasion of Afghanistan in October 2001 to oust the Taliban from power and uproot al-Qaida's terrorist bases once again led to outflows and internal displacements, but in 2002, with the Taliban having been driven from power and with hostilities having diminished, many Afghans began returning home. The UNHCR assisted in the voluntary return of some 1.8 million Afghans during the year but also reported that those who were yet to be repatriated numbered some 2.5 million, 95 percent of whom had received UNHCR assistance. The Iranian and Pakistani governments, however, estimated the number of refugees to be much higher.

A crisis of a different sort erupted early in 2002 when a report prepared by the UNHCR and UK-based Save the Children alleged that aid workers in Guinea, Liberia, and Sierra Leone had sexually exploited and abused women and children in return for humanitarian aid and services. High Commissioner Lubbers responded with a pledge of "zero tolerance" for such actions.

At the end of 2002 Southwest Asia ranked as the region with the highest number of refugees (7.2 million), followed by Western Europe (1.8 million), Eastern Europe (1.6 million), the Great Lakes and Central African region (1.4 million), Southeast Europe (1.3 million), West Africa (1.1 million), the Horn of Africa (1 million), and South Asia (1 million). Altogether, the UNHCR estimated that some 20.8 million "people of concern" fell within its purview, including 10.4 million refugees, 5.8 million IDPs, 2.4 million returnees, 1 million stateless or other persons, and 1 million asylum seekers.

During 2003 the U.S.-led invasion of Iraq did not generate a major refugee exodus, as had been feared, but caused considerable internal displacement. As of May 2004 the UNHCR was preparing to help in the "phased return" of some 500,000 Iraqis to their homes, beginning as soon as the security situation stabilized. At the same time, the organization was facing renewed difficulties in Sudan's Darfur region, where increased hostilities in late 2003 had led some 120,000 refugees to scatter just across the remote border with Chad.

In 2004 the UNHCR reported that the number of asylum applications in 36 developed countries dropped by 20 percent in 2003 to 471,000, down from 587,000 the previous year and the lowest number in six years. While the UNHCR attributed the improvement to more stable situations in Afghanistan, the Balkans, and Iraq, an additional factor was the rise of intolerance and anti-asylum measures in Europe and elsewhere. However, the UNHCR reported that the number of "people of concern" rose to 19.2 million in 2005 after declining to 17 million in 2004. In 2005 there was a worldwide decrease in the number of refugees, from 9.54 million to 8.39 million. This capped a five-year decrease of 31 percent and brought the overall number of refugees to its lowest level since 1980. Among refugee populations, the largest was some 1.1 million Afghans living in Pakistani camps, although the UNHCR projected that an additional 1.5 million Afghans were probably residing outside camps where there were no UNHCR services. The largest IDP population was 2 million in Colombia. In Iraq, the number of IDPs increased to 1.2 million. Sudan accounted for 840,000 IDPs and 150,000 refugees.

High Commissioner Lubbers resigned in February 2005 after he was accused of sexual harassment by women employees. He was succeeded by former Portuguese prime minister António Guterres, who initiated a series of reforms in budgeting and crisis management.

By January 2007 the UNHCR estimated that there were 32.86 million asylum seekers, refugees, or IDPs worldwide. The largest number was in Asia, 14.91 million, followed by Africa with 9.72 million, and Europe with 3.43 million. In April Estonia and Costa Rica were elected to the UNHCR executive committee. Also during the year the UNHCR announced a partnership with the Clinton Global Initiative in an effort to raise $220 million to provide educational programs for 9 million refugee children. Among the UNHCR's major operations in 2007 were the resettlement of Roma refugees in Hungary, Kosovo, and Montenegro, and the closure of the last major temporary refugee camp in Kosovo. The body also undertook a major initiative to provide supplies for 160,000 refugees in Kenya who were displaced by flooding. In cooperation with the Afghan government, the UNHCR oversaw the return of 200,000 Afghan refugees who had been in Pakistan and undertook major missions to support displaced persons in Somalia and Sudan. In July the UNHCR doubled its aid to $123 million annually to support the estimated 2.2 million externally displaced Iraqis in neighboring states and the 2 million internal refugees. The UNHCR also called on the United States to increase the number of Iraqi asylum seekers admitted from the 8,000 granted refuge in 2006. During 2007, the UNHCR signed an agreement with Morocco to enhance its presence in the country and an accord with Kazakhstan to facilitate operations in that country.

On April 29, 2008, the UN General Assembly voted to increase the membership of the executive committee from 72 to 76 states. In June the UNHCR report *2007 Global Trends: Refugees, Asylum-Seekers, Returnees, Internally Displaced and Stateless Persons* noted that by the end of 2007, the number of IDPs was 51 million, including 26 million displaced by conflict and 25 million displaced as the result of natural disasters. Of the two categories, at least 31.7 million were in the UNHCR's areas of operations, a decline of 3 percent from the previous year. The report also found that 80 percent of refugees remained in the region of their origin and that more than half resided in urban areas. In the publication the UNHCR changed the way it counted refugees and IDPs. Those who had been resettled through host country programs for periods of five to ten years, depending on the country, were no longer classified as refugees. The report found that the number of refugees and IDPs rose for the second consecutive year, after annual declines from 2001–2005.

Between October 2007 and 2008 the UNHCR assisted more than 250,000 Afghans in their return, mainly from Iran and Pakistan. In addition, the UNHCR aided the government of Tanzania in beginning the return of an estimated 110,000 Burundians to their homes and in consolidating Tanzania's 11 refugee camps into 5. The initiative was part of a cooperative program with other UN agencies to provide training and resources so that refugees and IDPs were able to transition back into their local economies. In another example, as part of an effort to return Hutu refugees to Rwanda, the UNHCR launched a construction program to build new housing for the returnees. The UNHCR built 98 homes and gave each returning family a half-acre in a pilot program that was expected to be replicated in other areas.

The UNHCR's 2009 budget was a record $2 billion. Completed in 2008, UNHCR's global service center in Budapest became the organization's second largest office in 2009, with a staff of 180 (behind only its headquarters in Geneva with 740). The center was created to consolidate a number of smaller regional offices and centralize functions as part of a broader reform effort to reduce costs and increase efficiency. In May the UNHCR responded when fighting between the Taliban and Pakistani government forces created more than 200,000 refugees in northwestern Pakistan. The agency's annual report noted that there were approximately 15.2 million refugees (including 4.7 million in UN-administered camps in the Middle East), which represented an 8 percent reduction from the previous year. The agency also noted that there were about 26 million internally displaced persons, including 14.4 million under the care of the UN. This figure was stable from the previous year but included new displaced populations in Colombia, Pakistan, the Philippines, Somalia, Sri Lanka, and Sudan. Colombia, Iraq, and Sudan remained the countries with the largest numbers of internally displaced persons.

United Nations Population Fund
(UNFPA)

Established: By the secretary general in July 1967 as the Trust Fund for Population Activities; name changed in May 1969 to United Nations Fund for Population Activities (UNFPA), with administration assigned to United Nations Development Program (UNDP); became operational in October 1969; placed under authority of the General Assembly in December 1972; became a subsidiary organ of the assembly in December 1979; name changed to United Nations Population Fund in December 1987, with the UNFPA designation being retained.

Purpose: To enhance the capacity to respond to needs in population and family planning, promote awareness of population problems in both developed and developing countries and possible strategies to deal with them, assist developing countries in dealing with their population problems in the forms and means best suited to their needs, and play a leading role in the UN system in promoting population programs and reproductive health.

Principal Organ: Executive Board (same membership as the UNDP Executive Board).

Web site: www.unfpa.org

Headquarters: New York, United States.

Executive Director: Thoraya Ahmed Obaid (Saudi Arabia).

Activities. The UNFPA continues to be the largest source of multilateral population assistance to less developed areas. It sponsored the United Nations Second International Conference on Population, held in August 1984, with an agenda that included revision of the World Population Plan of Action adopted in August 1974 in Bucharest, Romania. After much controversy and debate the final declaration, entitled the Mexico City Declaration on Population and Development, was adopted by consensus. Its numerous proposals recommended that population and development policies should strive for community backing to achieve the best results; that the complete equality of women in social, economic, and political life should be hastened, by government action if necessary; that universal access to family planning information should be provided; and that special attention should be given to maternal and child health services within primary health care systems, as well as to the implications for public health policy of increasingly youthful populations in developing countries and increasingly elderly populations in developed countries.

Beginning in 1985 and continuing into the 1990s, a powerful antiabortion coalition in Washington gained sufficient influence to cause the United States, previously the UNFPA's largest donor, to withhold parts of its annual pledges. The U.S. Agency for International Development (USAID) said the action was taken because of the UNFPA's continued activity in China, despite allegations that Beijing's population policies resulted in coerced abortions and sterilizations. The UNFPA strongly denied that it supported abortion anywhere "in policy or practice," pointing out that its programs in China involved census assistance, training for family planning experts, and the production and importation of contraceptives.

As the UNFPA prepared to celebrate its 20th anniversary in 1989, Executive Director Dr. Nafis Sadik said the fund deserved credit for having helped to desensitize the population issue, now recognized as an "acceptable" concern by most developing countries. However, she reported that 50 percent of the world's women still did not have access to family planning services and called for "firm action" by governments and international organizations in the 1990s to ameliorate the "grave threats" still posed by unbalanced population growth.

The 1991 *State of World Population* report announced that fertility rates were falling in all regions of the developing world, in some countries very rapidly. However, those rates were still "much higher" than desired. The population explosion was also straining the world's ecosystems, exacerbating the steady decline in the ability of developing countries to feed their populations, and contributing to "monumental urban growth" for which most countries were not prepared.

In its 1994 *State of World Population* report, the UNFPA again argued that empowerment of women was the key to solving the world's population problems. That theme was also emphasized at the UN's International Conference on Population and Development (ICPD), held September 5–13, 1994, in Cairo, Egypt. Although the Vatican, a number of Muslim countries, and several Latin American nations objected to references to legal abortions, contraception, and other sexual matters, the ICPD adopted a 20-year Program of Action.

On July 2, 1999, despite additional opposition from some predominantly Roman Catholic and Muslim countries, 170 General Assembly participants reached agreement on nonbinding guidelines for population control. UNFPA head Sadik cautioned, however, that the biggest obstacle to implementing the program would be raising the required $5.7 billion in funding. Many of the pledges made at the 1994 ICPD for education, health care, and family planning had not been honored. Symbolically, October 12, 1999, was designated by the UN as the day upon which the world population reached 6 billion. After more than 13 years of service, Dr. Sadik retired at the end of 2000. Thoraya Obaid of Saudi Arabia succeeded her.

The 2000 *State of World Population* report, entitled "Lives Together, Worlds Apart: Men and Women in a Time of Change," argued that women's needs often remained "invisible" to men. Partly as a consequence, women experienced much higher levels of illiteracy and sexually transmitted diseases, and many continued to die from the complications of pregnancy (at the rate of one a minute). The 2001–2003 annual reports focused on, respectively, population and environmental change, people and poverty, and the health and rights of the world's 1.2 billion adolescents.

For 2002 the UNFPA reported total income of $373 million, some 83 percent from voluntary contributions and most of the rest from trust funds and cost-sharing program arrangements. Expenditures reached $411 million, producing a deficit of $38 million. Leading donors were the Netherlands, Japan, the United Kingdom, Norway, and Denmark.

A major recent issue for the UNFPA has been hostility from the United States, which has not committed funds to the organization since mid-2002. The George W. Bush administration has continued to cite abortion and sterilization policies in China as justification, although a report by its own investigators showed no link between such policies and the UNFPA. Critics have asserted that the withdrawal of U.S. funds represents an effort to appease religious conservatives among the U.S. electorate.

Despite the U.S. failure to contribute funds, in 2005 the UNFPA had a record year in funding, with 172 countries and a range of nongovernmental and private organizations contributing $565 million, compared with $506 million in 2004. Expenditures, including programs in 148 developing countries, were $523 million.

In 2007 UNFPA initiated a joint program with the UN Children's Fund (UNICEF) to reduce female genital mutilation by 40 percent in 16 countries by 2015. The ultimate goal of the program was to end the practice entirely within 20 years through increased education and government action.

In the *State of World Population 2007: Unleashing the Potential of Urban Growth*, UNFPA noted that in 2008, for the first time in history, more than half of the world's population, or 3.3 billion people, lived in urban areas, marking the first time in history that city-dwellers outnumber their rural counterparts. By 2030, a projected 60 percent of the world's population would be urban. The report stated that the benefits of urbanization outweighed the negative consequences, especially in regard to reproductive healthcare and infant mortality rates. Nonetheless, the study also found that the population living in slums in urban areas doubled to 200 million, or 72 percent of the urban population, by 2005 in sub-Saharan Africa, compared with 56 percent of the urban population in South Asia.

In 2008 the UNFPA had programs in 158 countries and offices in 112 nations with 1,031 staff members, 44 percent of whom were women. In order to increase efficiency, the UNFPA developed and implemented a new strategic plan to guide the organization through 2011. The plan identified three main areas at the core of the UNFPA's mission: "population and development, reproductive health and rights, and gender equality." The agency also carried out a reorganization that established new regional offices in Bangkok, Bratislava, Cairo, Johannesburg, and Panama City, with six additional, new sub-regional offices. The UNFPA also reorganized its technical division and created a new program division to develop and oversee individual projects. The *State of World Population 2008: Reaching Common Ground; Culture, Gender and Human Rights* asserted the universality of human rights and the need to ensure the application of global frameworks to all countries. It presented an overview of strategies to implement culturally sensitive development plans that both promoted human rights and respected local traditions and mores. The UNFPA also launched the Maternal Health Trust Fund to provide assistance to mothers and newborns in 2008. Through 2009, the program was active in 61 countries.

United Nations Relief and Works Agency for Palestine Refugees in the Near East (UNRWA)

Established: By General Assembly resolution of December 8, 1949; mandate most recently extended through June 30, 2011.

Purpose: To provide relief, education, and health and social services to Palestinian refugees (i.e., people [and later the descendants of people] who resided in Palestine for a minimum of two years preceding the Arab-Israeli conflict in 1948 and who, as a result of that conflict, lost both their homes and their means of livelihood).

Headquarters: Gaza and Amman, Jordan. (Most of the operations, previously in Vienna, Austria, were moved to Gaza in July 1996. The remainder were relocated to the agency's other longstanding headquarters in Amman.)

Web site: www.un.org/unrwa

Commissioner General: Karen Koning Abu Zayd (United States).

Advisory Commission: Comprised of representatives of the governments of Australia, Belgium, Canada, Denmark, Egypt, France, Germany, Italy, Japan, Jordan, Lebanon, the Netherlands, Norway, Saudi Arabia, Spain, Sweden, Switzerland, Syria, Turkey, the United Kingdom, and the United States. The Palestine Liberation Organization (PLO), the European Union and the League of Arab States are observers.

Activities. As of October 2009, approximately 4.7 million people who met the established definition of Palestinian refugee were registered with the UNRWA. About 1.31 million of that number lived in 58 refugee camps, many of which had in effect become permanent towns; the remainder lived in previously established towns and villages in the areas served by UNRWA—Jordan, Lebanon, Syria, the West Bank, and Gaza. The UNRWA's original priority was to provide direct humanitarian relief to refugees uprooted by the fighting that followed the creation of Israel. In the absence of a peaceful settlement to the Palestinian question, the UNRWA's attention shifted to education (it runs about 660 schools attended by approximately 485,000 students) and the provision of public health services (it operates 127 health centers) to a basically self-supporting population. The UNRWA employs some 27,000 people, including 19,600 educators and 4,100 medical personnel.

In the late 1980s the UNRWA's budget came under severe pressure. The number of people who qualified as refugees in need of "special hardship" assistance increased because of economic decline in the Middle East and the effects on the population of the first intifada (uprising) in the occupied territories. A separate Project Fund for specific projects and a Capital Construction Fund for UNRWA facilities were constricted.

In 1988 the UNRWA found itself "back in the relief business" in three of the five geographic areas it served. In Lebanon, where 33 UNRWA employees had been killed since 1982, deteriorating conditions in and around Beirut prompted the agency to offer its services to the non-Palestinian population. In the West Bank and Gaza, the UNRWA was forced to divert some of its resources to emergency medical treatment, food relief, and physical rehabilitation services; many schools were closed for much of the year because of the intifada. Several special emergency funds were established for the occupied territories, where an estimated 55 percent of the population consisted of Palestinian refugees.

In mid-1990 UNRWA officials reported that Palestinian "frustration" was increasing as peace prospects appeared to recede and emergency conditions persisted in Lebanon, the West Bank, and Gaza. The agency's difficulties intensified still further during the subsequent Gulf crisis as hundreds of thousands of Palestinians fled the conflict (many returning to UNRWA camps) or lost their sources of income and thereby their ability to remit funds to family members in UNRWA's service area.

After the war, several hundred thousand Palestinians were expelled from Kuwait. In early 1992 improved security in Lebanon permitted some stabilization of UNRWA activity.

Shortly after the September 1993 accord between Israel and the Palestine Liberation Organization (PLO), the UNRWA established an internal task force to determine how best to support the peace process. Its first action was to develop a Peace Implementation Program (PIP) designed to rehabilitate long-neglected infrastructure and create jobs for Palestinians. Donors pledged more than $100 million for the first phase of the operation (PIP 1); most of the projects were located in Gaza and the West Bank in cities and towns that were the first to fall under Palestinian self-rule. PIP 2 envisioned additional projects worth $250 million throughout the area served by the UNRWA; the largest proposed project was the construction of a hospital in Gaza, which the European Union planned to finance. As negotiations between Israel and the PLO proceeded, Commissioner General Türkmen called upon donors to underwrite a five-year plan for the agency to lead to a possible reduction of refugee services if there was a final peace accord. However, Türkmen cautioned that refugees, particularly those outside the West Bank and Gaza, felt "a great sense of concern and apprehension about their future."

In December 1995 the General Assembly extended the UNRWA's mandate to June 30, 1999, the hope being that Palestinians would, at that point, be fully responsible for their own affairs under a final agreement with Israel. The following month Türkmen retired from the post of UNRWA commissioner general and was succeeded by Peter Hansen of Denmark, theretofore UN undersecretary general for humanitarian affairs.

The outlook for the agency was relatively bright as 1996 began; the September 1995 Interim Agreement between Israel and the PLO had prompted a further withdrawal of Israeli troops from the West Bank. In addition, the UNRWA welcomed the January 1996 Palestinian elections as an important step toward permanent Israeli-Palestinian peace. However, it lamented the lack of further Israeli withdrawals and Israel's failure to extend responsibility to the new Palestinian (National) Authority, with which, as directed by the General Assembly, the UNRWA had recently established a full working relationship. Commissioner General Hansen also reported that the agency was in the midst of a financial crisis that threatened its ability to fulfill its mandate. In the face of an $8.4 million deficit for 1995, the UNRWA imposed austerity measures and called for a special meeting of the agency's donors to resolve ongoing financial difficulties.

Continuing financial straits brought the agency to near breakdown in 1998, and the Palestinian staff held a one-day strike on September 15 to protest poor pay and work conditions. In October–November 1998 *Middle East International* reported that serious allegations of corruption and misuse of funds had been leveled at several agency staff and that UN Secretary General Kofi Annan had sent a team to the region to look into the allegations and check the agency's accounts.

Beginning in September 2000, the UNRWA's efforts to contain expenditures without jeopardizing its programs were set back as open hostilities between Israel and the Palestinians resumed. In October a second intifada led the UNRWA to launch a flash appeal for additional funds. This was followed in November by an emergency appeal to underwrite job creation and help offset unemployment caused by Israel's closure of its border. From November 2000 through the first half of 2004, the UNRWA issued seven emergency appeals for sums totaling over $650 million to cover basic food and medical supplies, repair local infrastructure, provide temporary shelter for those whose homes had been damaged or destroyed during Israeli incursions into the West Bank and Gaza, and find employment for Palestinians whose movements had been restricted. According to Commissioner General Hansen, two-thirds of Palestinians were unemployed, and half were living in absolute poverty. A study conducted by Johns Hopkins University indicated that one-third of Palestinian children were either chronically or acutely malnourished.

Some Israelis and members of the U.S. Congress, among others, accused the UNRWA of allowing refugee camps to be used for terrorist training and activities. The UNRWA responded that it had "no police force, no intelligence service and no mandate to report on political and military activities" in the camps. Instead, its role was to provide health, education, and humanitarian services. Security was the responsibility of host countries or the Palestinian Authority. A recent audit by the U.S. General Accounting Office concluded that no money provided by the United States—the source of some 30 percent of UNRWA funds—could be linked to terrorist activities in the refugee camps.

The UNRWA had a budget of $339 million in 2005, with expenditures of $345 million. The estimated 2006 budget was $470.9 million, but renewed fighting in Gaza and southern Lebanon substantially increased expenditures. In response, the agency issued a flash appeal for $7.2 million in emergency aid for food, shelter, water, health care, staff security, and associated expenses. Strife created an additional 200,000 permanent refugees and led the agency to issue another flash appeal in 2007 for $11.5 million in emergency funding.

In 2007 the UNRWA's budget was $487.1 million. The United States, the European Commission, Sweden, Norway, and the United Kingdom were the agency's largest donors for the year. In February the EU announced that it would increase support for the UNRWA by 7 percent between 2008 and 2010 with total funding during that period at €264 million ($379.1 million). Fighting in the Nahr al-Bared refugee camp in Lebanon between security forces and Islamic militants forced most of the 31,000 inhabitants of the settlement to flee. The UNRWA estimated that it would take three years to rebuild the camp. Meanwhile, fighting between Hamas and Fatah in June created a new refugee crisis and led the UNRWA to issue an appeal for $246.15 million in emergency funding to support an estimated 1.7 million Palestinians in Gaza and the West Bank. Through November, the UNRWA had collected $111 million in emergency relief.

The UNRWA's 2008 budget was $541.8 million, and the agency's main donors were, in order of contributions, the United States, the European Commission, Sweden, the United Kingdom, Norway, and the Netherlands. The continuing refugee crisis in Gaza and the West Bank led the UNRWA to again request emergency donations. For 2008, the UNRWA sought $263.4 million. However, by October 2008 the agency had received only about 60 percent of that amount. At the same time, the UNRWA's appeal for emergency funding for refugees in Lebanon exceeded its goal of $54.8 million as the organization had secured $57.2 million by October. In June the UNRWA and the UAE Red Crescent launched a major initiative to rebuild and refurbish some of the oldest refugee camps that had facilities dating back 60 years. The first phase of the project was the construction of a new health clinic and 140 housing units in the Neirab Camp, the largest of the UNRWA's facilities in Syria. Also in June the UNRWA began reconstruction of the Nahr al-Bared camp in Lebanon. In September the UNRWA issued a flash appeal for $43 million to cover temporary operations in the camp while the rebuilding work continued.

For 2009 the UNRWA's budget remained flat at $541 million, but by May it was estimated that falling donations would result in an operating deficit of $125 million for the year. Efforts to reduce expenditures at some camps led to protests by refugees through the summer. The UNRWA launched the Gaza quick response program in 2009 as an effort to coordinate all of the emergency funding appeals into a single initiative for the region. The UNRWA sought $371.3 million but had raised only $192.6 million through August. A similar effort for the West Bank performed even more poorly, securing only $31 million of the requested $90 million. In October the UNRWA began the da'am (support) program, which was designed to better identify the needs of the most disadvantaged groups and provide assistance more efficiently. Eight communities were initially involved in the project, which was expected to be expanded throughout the system in late 2010.

United Nations Research Institute for Social Development
(UNRISD)

Established: July 1, 1964, by means of an initial grant from the government of the Netherlands, in furtherance of a General Assembly resolution of December 5, 1963, on social targets and social planning.

Purpose: To conduct research into the "problems and policies of social development and relationships between various types of social and economic development during different phases of economic growth."

Headquarters: Geneva, Switzerland.

Principal Organ: Board of Advisors, consisting of a chair appointed by the UN secretary general and ten individual members nominated by the Commission for Social Development and confirmed by the Economic and Social Council. There are also seven ex-officio members—a representative of the UN Secretariat; two representatives (in rotation) from the FAO, ILO, UNDP, UNESCO, UNHCR, UNU, and WHO; the executive secretary of the Economic Commission for Western Asia; the directors of the Latin American Institute for Economic and Social Planning and the African Institute for Economic Development and Planning; and the institute director.

Web site: www.unrisd.org

Director: Sarah Cook (United Kingdom).

Activities. The focus of UNRISD activities has shifted over the years to reflect current concerns in social development and public policy. Thus, in 1988 the board approved redefinitions of priority research areas to include food policy in the world recession, refugees and returnees, and the social impact of the economic crisis. Subsequent areas of research interest included participation and changes in property relations in communist and post-communist societies; integrating gender into development policy; and the environment, sustainable development, and social change. The institute currently considers eradicating poverty, promoting democracy and human rights, establishing gender equity, examining the effects of globalization, and ensuring environmental sustainability as "overarching concerns" in all UNRISD efforts.

Current research emphases include civil society and social movements; democracy, governance, and human rights; identities, conflict, and cohesion; social policy and development; and technology, business, and society. Ongoing projects include, for example, examination of grassroots movements and land reform initiatives, public sector reform in crisis-ridden countries, HIV/AIDS and development, the interaction of information technologies and social development, and social policy and "late industrializers" in Africa, Latin America, and the Middle East.

In addition, the UNRISD frequently prepares papers and reports for international conferences and forums. As a follow-up to the 1996 Second UN Conference on Human Settlements (Habitat II), which met in Istanbul, Turkey, the UNRISD participated in a June 2001 Special Session of the General Assembly (Istanbul + 5), which reviewed progress toward implementing the conference's Habitat Agenda. Also in 2001, the UNRISD prepared a Racism and Public Policy forum as a contribution to the World Conference against Racism, Racial Discrimination, Xenophobia, and Related Intolerance, held August–September in Durban, South Africa. In 2002 it presented a report on environmental issues for the August–September World Summit on Sustainable Development, held in Johannesburg, South Africa. For the March 2005 session of the UN Commission on the Status of Women, which assessed progress since the 1995 Beijing Fourth World Conference on Women, the UNRISD prepared a report on gender and development titled *Gender Equality: Striving for Justice in an Unequal World.* Among the report's findings were that progress had been made in increasing women's roles in public life, including increases in the number of women holding office, but that economic inequalities had increased in some regions and across certain occupations.

In 2007 the UNRISD launched a major research project on poverty reduction, scheduled to be completed and published in 2009. To facilitate the research, the UNRISD sponsored a series of conferences around the world to bring together scholars and policymakers. The agency announced that its other research programs for the next two years would be organized into five broad areas: social policy and development; markets, business and regulation; civil society and social movements; identities, conflict and cohesion; and gender development. Through 2008 the UNRISD supported 118 researchers in 40 countries examining social policy and economic development. In 2008 the UNRISD reported that it had produced 34 publications and conducted 20 research seminars, meetings, or other events in the past year. Its core funding was \$3.3 million, an increase from \$2.8 million in the prior year, and its project funding was \$859,479 versus \$1.2 million in the previous year.

The UNRISD's operating budget for 2009 increased to approximately \$4 million. In September 2009 UNRISD sponsored a major conference in Seoul, South Korea, on poverty reduction programs. Meanwhile, Sarah Cook of the United Kingdom was appointed the director of UNRISD in November, following the resignation of Thandika Mkandawire of Sweden in April. From 2006 through 2009, UNRISD commissioned more than 40 research papers to support the publication of the *Flagship Report on Poverty,* due to be published in 2010.

United Nations University
(UNU)

Established: By General Assembly resolution of December 11, 1972; charter adopted December 6, 1973; began operations September 1, 1975.

Purpose: To conduct action-oriented research in fields related to development, welfare, and human survival, and to train young scholars and research workers.

Headquarters: Tokyo, Japan.

Principal Organs: University Council (comprising 24 educators, each from a different country, in addition to the UN secretary general, the director general of UNESCO, the executive director of UNITAR, and the university rector, ex officio); Boards and Advisory Committees overseeing Research and Training Centers and Programs (RTC/Ps).

Web site: www.unu.edu

Rector: Konrad Osterwalder (Switzerland).

Activities. In July 1997 UN Secretary General Kofi Annan addressed the role of the UNU and other research bodies in his plan for overall UN reform. Annan argued that research institutes sometimes appeared to be living "in a world of their own, largely removed from the work and concerns of the United Nations." Furthermore, he wrote, these institutes rarely communicated among themselves and sometimes duplicated each other's work. In September new UNU Rector Hans van Ginkel of the Netherlands urged the UNU to tie its own proposed reforms to those of the UN in general and to increase cooperation with other UN entities, such as the UNDP, UNESCO, UNEP, UNICEF, and WHO. He also suggested that new UNU research concentrate on two program areas—peace and governance, and environment and sustainable development.

A mission statement adopted in 1999 defines the UNU's purpose as contributing "through research and capacity building, to efforts to resolve the pressing global problems that are the concern of the United Nations, its peoples and its Member States." Accordingly, the university considers as its principal functions fostering an international community of scholars; providing a bridge between the UN and the academic community; serving as a think tank for the UN; and aiding capacity building, especially in the developing world. Scholars affiliated with and contracted by the UNU conduct research and address needs in five general thematic areas: peace and security (international relations, the UN system, human security, armed conflicts); good governance (democracy and civil society, leadership, human rights, and ethics); development and poverty reduction (globalization and development, growth and employment, poverty and basic needs, urbanization); science, technology, and society (innovation, information technology and biotechnology, software technology, food and nutrition); and the environment and sustainability (resource management, sustainable industry and cities, water, global climate, and governance).

Much of the UNU's work is conducted through 13 Reserved and Training Center (RTC/Ps) located around the world. In 1985 the university established its first RTC, the World Institute for Development Economics Research (UNU-WIDER) in Helsinki, Finland. UNU-WIDER currently directs its programs toward conducting multidisciplinary research and analysis on how structural changes affect the world's poorest populations, training scholars and government officials in economic and social policy, and providing a forum on issues related to equitable and environmentally sustainable growth. In 1987 the council approved the creation of the Institute for Natural Resources in Africa (UNU-INRA) with the goal of strengthening scientific and technological capacities in such areas as land use, water management, energy resources, and minerals development. After being temporarily housed in Nairobi, Kenya, the UNU-INRA moved into permanent headquarters in Accra, Ghana, in 1993.

In mid-1990 an Institute for New Technologies (UNU-INTECH) was inaugurated in Maastricht, the Netherlands, and an International Institute for Software Technology (UNU-IIST) was opened in Macao, China, in 1992. In addition, there is a UNU International Leadership Academy (UNU-ILA) in Amman, Jordan, which was inaugurated in 1995, and an Institute for Advanced Studies (UNU-IAS), which was based in Tokyo from 1996 until it moved to Yokohama, Japan, in April 2004. The Institute for Environment and Human Security (UNU-EHS) in Bonn, Germany, began operations in 2004. In January 2006 the UNU-INTECH merged with the Maastricht Economic Research Institute on Innovation and Technology (MERIT) to form UNU-MERIT. Four months later, the UNU and the Malaysian Ministry of Higher Education signed an agreement to establish the International Institute for Global Health (UNU-IIGH) in Kuala Lumpur. A number of specialized programs are currently in operation. The initial venture, the Geothermal Training Program (UNU-GTP), was established in 1979 in cooperation with the National Energy Authority of Iceland. Another program based in Reykjavík, the Fisheries Training Program (UNU-FTP) for postgraduate research and fisheries development, began in 1998. A Program for Biotechnology in Latin America and the Caribbean (UNU-BIOLAC), based in Caracas, Venezuela, was founded in 1988. In 1993 a cooperative agreement was signed with Cornell University for establishment of a Food and Nutrition Program for Human and Social Development (UNU-FNP), which would be coordinated by Cornell at its campus in Ithaca, New York. The International Network on Water, Environment, and Health (UNU-INWEH) was established in 1996 in Hamilton, Ontario, Canada, and the Program for Comparative Regional Integration Studies (UNU-CRIS) was founded in Bruges, Belgium.

An Initiative on Conflict Resolution and Ethnicity (INCORE) was established in conjunction with the University of Ulster in Northern Ireland in 1993 to examine and assist in resolution of ethnic, political, and religious conflicts. In 2001 the UNU joined with South Korea's Kwangju Institute of Science and Technology to initiate a pilot program on Science and Technology for Sustainability.

Voluntary contributions fund all UNU programs and projects. In 2005 about 140 projects were ongoing, and some 375 fellows and interns received support. The 2004–2005 budget totaled approximately $76 million.

In August 2007 Konrad Osterwalder of Switzerland became rector of the UNU, replacing van Ginkel. The European Commission asked the UNU to examine the issue of recycling electronic waste (e-waste) and develop a report, published in November, on how best to increase recycling of e-waste such as cellular phones, old computing equipment, and household appliances. The UNU also produced *Accountability and the United Nations System* (Policy Brief Number 8, 2007) in an effort to guide UN reforms and enhance financial and managerial accountability in the world body.

The UNU and the University of Tokyo created a joint initiative in July 2008 to facilitate research in the science of sustainability. The UNU and the government of Japan launched a pilot program through the Hiroshima Peacebuilders' Center to train people in conflict mediation and prevention. The training program also involved other UN bodies, including the UNHCR, UNDP, and UNICEF. The UNU documentary film *Voices of the Chichinautzin*, about the challenges faced by indigenous people of the Chichinautzin region of Mexico, won the best feature award at the Moondance International Film Festival.

The UNU staff numbers more than 210 individuals from more than 30 countries. In 2008 there were 237 research fellows and 125 interns. The system produced 806 publications, ranging from books to policy and technical briefs, and it sponsored 378 public events, including conferences, seminars, lectures, and presentations. The UNU articulated a new vision through the publication of the *United Nations University Strategic Plan, 2009–2012,* which called for the university to become a globally recognized research institution by reorganizing and reinvigorating its core functions and engaging in a sustained outreach program.

SECURITY COUNCIL

Permanent Membership (5): China, France, Russia, United Kingdom, United States. (The other permanent members in late December 1991 accepted Russia's assumption of the seat previously filled by the Union of Soviet Socialist Republics.)

Nonpermanent Membership (10): Terms ending December 31, 2009: Burkina Faso, Costa Rica, Croatia, Libya, and Vietnam. Terms ending December 31, 2010: Austria, Japan, Mexico, Turkey, and Uganda.

Web site: www.un.org/Docs/sc

Origin and development. In declaring the primary purpose of the UN to be the maintenance of international peace and security, the charter established a system for collective enforcement of the peace based on unity among the five permanent members of the Security Council. Peace efforts of the council are effective only to the degree that political accord is possible in relation to specific international disputes and only when the parties to such conflicts are willing to allow the UN to play its intended role.

The only instance of an actual military operation undertaken under UN auspices in response to an act of aggression was the Korean involvement of 1950–1953. The action was possible because the Soviet Union was boycotting the Security Council at the time and was thus unable to exercise a veto. The United States, which had military forces readily available in the area, was in a position to assume direction of a UN-established Unified Command, to which military forces were ultimately supplied by 16 member states. As of December 2002 the UN command remained in South Korea, with troops from the United States constituting the only foreign contingent. In 1975 the U.S. representative to the UN proposed, in a letter to the president of the Security Council, that the command be dissolved, with U.S. and South Korean officers as "successors in command," if North Korea and China would first agree to continue the armistice. However, no such agreement was subsequently concluded.

In certain other instances, as in the India-Pakistan War of 1965 and the Arab-Israeli War of 1967, the positions of the major powers have been close enough to lend weight to Security Council resolutions calling for cease-fires. The Security Council endorsed the use of "all necessary means" to liberate Kuwait from occupying Iraqi forces in early 1991; however, unlike the 1950 Korean deployment, the Desert Storm campaign was not a formal UN operation, the United States preferring to maintain military control rather than defer to an overall UN command.

The NATO-led air campaign against Yugoslavia's repression of the ethnic Albanian population in Kosovo during March–June 1999 was, again, initiated without direct Security Council backing, the United States and its NATO allies knowing full well that Russia and probably China would have vetoed a call for direct military action. On May 14 the Security Council did, however, pass a resolution urging support for humanitarian relief efforts to aid Kosovar refugees and internally displaced persons. The resolution also called for a political solution in line with principles put forward on May 6 by Canada, France, Germany, Italy, Japan, Russia, the United Kingdom, and the United States. A June 10 resolution authorized a United Nations Interim Administration Mission in Kosovo (UNMIK) and a NATO-led Multinational Force in Kosovo (KFOR), the latter to maintain security pending a handover to an UNMIK-established civilian police corps.

The Kosovo mission was the most comprehensive ever undertaken under Security Council auspices, going well beyond peacekeeping, and was followed only four months later by a similarly all-encompassing effort, the United Nations Transitional Administration in East Timor (UNTAET), which had as its task nation-building in preparation for East Timor's full independence. On May 17, 2002, with that goal accomplished, the Security Council authorized formation of a United Nations Mission of Support in East Timor (UNMISET) as a successor to the UNTAET. The new mission was mandated to ensure East Timor's domestic and international security and to offer support to the government of the new state. On May 21, 2005, UNMISET was succeeded by the United Nations Office in Timor-Leste (UNOTIL), which had been established by Security Council resolution as a special political mission to be directed by the UN Department of Peacekeeping Operations. In view of civil disorder in Timor-Leste, UNOTIL's one-year mandate was extended to August 20, 2006. There was general acknowledgement, however, that UNMISET had been withdrawn too hastily and that a comparable new mission would be required to assist the new state (see the article on Timor-Leste).

The 1990s also saw the Security Council assume a leading role in establishing venues for prosecuting and trying alleged war crimes. It authorized creation of an International Criminal Tribunal for the former Yugoslavia in 1993 and an International Criminal Tribunal for Rwanda in 1994, as well as the special court for Sierra Leone in 2002, and the special tribunals for Cambodia in 2003 and Lebanon in 2005.

Structure. Originally comprising 5 permanent and 6 nonpermanent members, the council was expanded as of January 1, 1966, to a membership of 15, including ten nonpermanent members elected by the General Assembly for two-year terms. The charter stipulates that in the election of the nonpermanent members due regard must be paid to the contribution of members to the maintenance of international peace and security and to the other purposes of the organization, and also to equitable geographic distribution. The presidency of the Security Council rotates monthly.

Council decisions on procedural matters are made by an affirmative vote of any nine members. Decisions on all other matters, however, require a nine-member affirmative vote that must include the concurring votes of the permanent members; the one exception is that in matters involving pacific settlement of disputes, a party to a dispute must abstain from voting. It is the requirement for the concurring votes of the permanent members on all but procedural questions that enables any one of the five to exercise a veto, no matter how large the affirmative majority.

In discharging its responsibilities the Security Council may investigate the existence of any threat to peace, breach of the peace, or act of aggression, and in the event of such a finding, may make recommendations for resolution or decide to take enforcement measures to maintain or restore international peace and security. Enforcement action may include a call on members to apply economic sanctions and other measures short of the use of armed force. Should these steps prove inadequate, the Security Council may then take such military action as is deemed necessary.

The charter established a Military Staff Committee, composed of the permanent members' chiefs of staff (or their representatives), to advise and assist the Security Council on such questions as the council's military requirements for the maintenance of peace, the regulation of armaments, and possible disarmament. In the absence of agreements to place armed forces at the council's disposal, as envisaged by the charter, the committee has not assumed an important operational role.

In addition to the Military Staff Committee, the Security Council currently has three Standing Committees—the Committee on the Admission of New Members, the Committee of Experts on Rules of Procedure, and the Committee on Council Meetings away from Headquarters—each composed of representatives of all council members. There is also a UN Compensation Commission, which was established in 1991 to pay damages to governments, individuals, and businesses injured by the Gulf War. On September 28, 2001, responding to the September 11 terrorist attacks on the United States, the Security Council authorized creation of a new ad hoc Counter-Terrorism Committee. On April 28, 2004, Resolution 1540 authorized creation of another ad hoc committee concerned with preventing the proliferation of weapons of mass destruction (WMD) and their delivery. Resolution 1673, passed unanimously on April 27, 2006, authorized the 1540 Committee to also focus on preventing "non-state actors" from acquiring WMD.

The Security Council is also empowered to establish so-called sanctions committees, 11 of which were functioning as of 2009. Most were established to oversee arms embargoes—against, for instance, Somalia (since 1992), Rwanda (since 1994), and Sudan (since 2004)—and/or to freeze assets or impose travel restrictions on government officials or other individuals. In some cases, the original mandate of a sanctions committee has been expanded or redefined. In December 2000, for example, the Security Council expanded the mission of the Afghanistan committee, which it had created in 1999 primarily in response to Afghanistan's failure to extradite suspects in the 1998 bombings of U.S. embassies in Kenya and Tanzania. Initially assigned to monitor air travel restrictions and a freeze on the Afghan Taliban regime's financial assets, the committee's mandate was extended to include monitoring an air and arms embargo and the freezing of funds of Osama bin Laden and associates. In 2002, following the demise of the Taliban regime, several additional resolutions further modified the terms of the sanctions.

The council has created a number of working groups to address peacekeeping operations, conflict prevention and resolution in Africa, and improving the effectiveness of sanctions. In February 2001 the Working Group on General Issues on Sanctions issued dozens of recommendations for more effective use of sanctions, including monitoring their impact, providing incentives to lift them, and setting time limits for them. The committee also proposed that the Security Council consider imposing secondary sanctions on countries that fail to adhere to direct sanctions. The committee's final report was issued in 2006.

Activities. Peacekeeping activities include observation, fact-finding, mediation, conciliation, and assistance in maintaining internal order. UN observer groups to supervise cease-fire lines, truce arrangements, and the like have functioned in Africa, the Balkans, Indonesia, the Middle East, Kashmir, and former Soviet republics. On a larger scale, the UN Operation in the Congo (UNOC) was initiated in 1960 and continued until 1964 in an attempt to stabilize the chaotic situation in that state (subsequently Zaire and, since mid-1997, the Democratic Republic of the Congo). Since 1964 the UN Force in Cyprus (UNFICYP) has attempted to alleviate conflict between the Greek and Turkish elements in the Cypriot population under a mandate subject to semiannual renewal.

There have been several peacekeeping operations in the Middle East. A UN Emergency Force (UNEF) was interposed between the military forces of Egypt and Israel in the Sinai and Gaza areas from early 1957 until its withdrawal at the insistence of Egypt in 1967. The UNEF was reconstituted in October 1973 to supervise a cease-fire along the Suez Canal and to ensure a return of Israeli and Egyptian forces to the positions that they held on October 22, 1973. Soon after the signing of the Egyptian-Israeli peace treaty in March 1979, it became clear that the Soviet Union—on behalf of its Arab friends—would veto an extension of the force when its mandate expired on July 25. Faced with this prospect, the United States concluded an agreement with the Soviet Union to allow monitoring of the treaty arrangements by the UN Truce Supervision Organization (UNTSO), established in 1948 to oversee the Arab-Israeli cease-fire. Other forces currently serving in the Middle East are the UN Interim Forces in Lebanon (UNIFIL), established in 1978, and the UN Disengagement Observer Force (UNDOF), deployed in Syria's Golan Heights since 1974. (For organizational details on existing peacekeeping forces, see the next section.)

As a body that meets year-round and is frequently called upon to respond to world crises, the Security Council is often the most visible of the UN organs. Given its composition and the nature of its duties, political considerations typically dominate its deliberations. In the 1980s the council tended to focus on problems in the Middle East, Central America, and southern Africa. During 1986 it debated resolutions condemning Israel for continued military activity in southern Lebanon, the alleged violation of the sanctity of a Jerusalem mosque, and the interception of a Libyan airliner in the search for suspected terrorists. The resolutions failed as the result of vetoes by the United States, itself the subject of condemnation resolutions later in the year. Other Western-bloc council members joined the United States in defeating a measure denouncing the U.S. bombing of Libya in April, while the United States cast the only vote against a resolution seeking to ban military and financial aid to contra rebels fighting the government of Nicaragua.

The major topics of debate in 1987 were the proposed imposition of mandatory sanctions against South Africa for its apartheid and Namibian policies, Israeli actions in Gaza and the West Bank, and the Iran-Iraq war. U.S. and UK vetoes continued to block the imposition of sanctions against South Africa, although the council late in 1987 unanimously condemned the "illegal entry" of South African troops into Angola. In December the council approved (with the United States abstaining) a resolution "deploring Israeli practices and policies" during recent outbreaks of violence in the occupied territories. The council also urged a reactivation of UN leadership in Middle East peace negotiations.

In September 1987 the council approved a peace plan that provided the framework for termination of the Iran-Iraq war in August 1988. In conjunction with that agreement, the council established the UN Iran-Iraq Military Observer Group (UNIIMOG) to supervise the cease-fire and monitor the withdrawal of troops to internationally recognized boundaries. (UNIIMOG's mandate was terminated in early 1990 following the successful completion of its mission.) Other UN groups mobilized in 1988 and 1989 were the UN Good Offices Mission in Afghanistan and Pakistan (UNGOMAP—terminated in March 1990 after monitoring the withdrawal of Soviet troops from Afghanistan); the UN Angola Verification Mission (UNAVEM); the UN Transition Assistance Group (UNTAG), established to supervise the withdrawal of South African troops from Namibia and the transition to Namibian independence; the United Nations Observer Group in Central America (*Grupo de Observadores de las Naciones Unidas en Centroamérica*—ONUCA); and the UN Observation Mission for the Verification of Elections in Nicaragua (*Observadores de Naciones Unidas para la Verificación de las Elecciones en Nicaragua*—ONUVEN).

The Security Council's prominent role in conflict resolution was widely perceived as having significantly enhanced the global reputation of the peacekeeping forces (which were awarded the 1988 Nobel Peace Prize), the Secretariat, and the United Nations as a whole. Improved relations within the council were attributed to the reduction in East-West tension, UN Secretary General Javier Pérez de Cuéllar praising Washington and Moscow for permitting the body to become "more responsive [and] collegial." Building upon the unqualified successes of UNTAG and ONUVEN (the first UN force to supervise an election in an established nation), the permanent members of the council in early 1990 endorsed an Australian proposal that a peacekeeping force be deployed to help resolve the long-standing conflict in Cambodia and supervise the election of a new national government. In addition, the council in late April approved a peace plan for the Western Sahara under which a UN group would oversee a referendum in the territory. The council also considered creating a small UN observer force to monitor the treatment of Palestinians in the occupied territories, but the United States vetoed the measure in May.

The Security Council moved even further to the forefront of the global stage by assuming a major role in an international response to Iraq's invasion of Kuwait on August 2, 1990. Launching what would eventually be perceived as a historic series of resolutions (most adopted unanimously) through which "the teeth" of the UN Charter were bared with rare decisiveness and speed, the council condemned the takeover within hours of its occurrence and demanded the withdrawal of Iraqi troops. Several days later the council also imposed comprehensive economic sanctions on Iraq and established a special committee to monitor the sanctions process. In addition, the council endorsed a naval blockade of Iraq and approved UN aid for "innocent victims" of the crisis as well as countries adversely affected by the trade embargo. Finally, in its most dramatic decision, the council on November 28 authorized U.S.-led coalition forces to use "all necessary means" to implement previous resolutions and "to restore international peace and security in the area" if Iraq did not withdraw from Kuwait by January 15, 1991, thereby providing the basis for launching Operation Desert Storm on January 16, 1991.

Following the liberation of Kuwait and the announcement of a suspension of military operations by allied forces in late February 1991, the council adopted a permanent cease-fire plan on April 3 demanding that Iraq return all Kuwaiti property, accept liability for the damage it caused during the war, and destroy all its chemical and biological weapons, as well as its long-range ballistic missiles. After Iraqi acceptance of the conditions on April 6, the council established the UN Iraq-Kuwait Observation Mission (UNIKOM) to monitor a demilitarized zone between the two countries. The council also remained deeply involved in efforts to resolve refugee problems associated with the conflict, especially in regard to Iraq's Kurdish population.

Tension between the council and Iraq continued throughout the ensuing year, particularly over what were perceived as attempts by Baghdad to undermine UN supervision of the destruction of plants and equipment related to nuclear, chemical, and biological weapons. With some Western nations reportedly considering a resumption of military action, the Security Council in the spring of 1992 warned that "grave consequences" would ensue if Iraq interfered any further with UN oversight activity.

Even without the extraordinary burden of the Gulf crisis, the council would have encountered a busier schedule than usual in 1990–1991. Following extended debate prompted by the death of a number of Palestinians in the occupied territories in October 1990, the council approved a carefully worded resolution rebuking Israel and asking the UN secretary general to monitor the status of Palestinian civilians "under Israeli occupation." In addition, the council reaffirmed its support for a UN-sponsored Middle East Peace Conference. Other activity in late 1990 included negotiations on the final framework for a comprehensive settlement of the Cambodian situation and the creation of a UN observer group to help monitor elections in Haiti.

Discussions also continued toward finalization of the Western Saharan peace plan, with the council in April 1991 authorizing a UN Mission for the Referendum in Western Sahara (*Mission des Nations Unies le Référendum dans le Sahara Ouest*—MINURSO). A month later the council approved a United Nations Observer Mission in El Salvador (*Observadores de las Naciones Unidas en El Salvador*—ONUSAL) as part of a continuing effort to foster a peace settlement in that country's long-standing civil war. Initially, ONUSAL's mandate was limited to verifying adherence to a human rights agreement signed by the government and the rebels in 1990, but the council expanded the mission's mandate in January 1992 to include monitoring the permanent cease-fire.

In February 1992 the council authorized two of its largest operations to date, the UN Protection Force (UNPROFOR) to help implement and monitor a cease-fire in eastern Croatia, and the UN Transitional Authority in Cambodia (UNTAC). Two months later the council also established the UN Operation in Somalia (UNOSOM) in an effort to mediate an end to the civil war in that country and permit the delivery of much-needed food relief. Other April activity included the declaration of an air and arms embargo against Libya because of Tripoli's refusal to permit the extradition of two of its nationals suspected of complicity in the 1988 airplane bombing over Lockerbie, Scotland.

In June 1992 UN Secretary General Boutros Boutros-Ghali proposed a number of changes to improve the peacemaking and peacekeeping abilities of the Security Council. The most striking recommendation was for "as many countries as are willing" to make 1,000 of their troops available for immediate council deployment, thereby establishing, in essence at least, the long-debated UN standing army. Boutros-Ghali said such forces would be instrumental in implementing the "preventative diplomacy" strategy endorsed at a Security Council summit in New York in January. The meeting, the first ever of the heads of state of the permanent and nonpermanent council members, had agreed that greater effort should be made to identify trouble spots in advance so intervention could be ordered before the outbreak of violence.

Throughout 1992 and the first half of 1993, the Security Council became more and more caught up in the maelstrom of the former Yugoslavia, particularly after authorizing UNPROFOR troops to enter Bosnia and Herzegovina for humanitarian purposes. Some 40 resolutions were approved in response to conflicts in the region. Included were the imposition of sanctions against the Federal Republic of Yugoslavia, condemnation of "ethnic cleansing" and myriad human rights violations in Bosnia, approval of an International Criminal Tribunal for the former Yugoslavia, and a number of generally unsuccessful or unimplemented peacemaking efforts, such as the imposition of no-fly zones and the establishment of "safe areas" for Bosnian Muslims. Following the collapse of talks launched by the European Community, the council also found itself responsible, virtually by default, for efforts to negotiate an end to the complex Bosnian conflict.

Concurrently, the council fell into a quagmire in Somalia, its UNOSOM II resolution of March having introduced a controversial "nation-building" element to UN intervention. Although credited with having brought food relief to the starving population and having pacified most of the country, UNOSOM troops, acting in conjunction with a U.S. rapid deployment force, found themselves locked in deadly combat with the supporters of clan leader Gen. Mohamed Farah Aidid in Mogadishu. As losses mounted within the UNOSOM and U.S. contingents, council members began to consider a more "realistic" attitude toward what it could accomplish in such situations.

In other activity during 1992–1993, the council fought in what was described as a "war of nerves" with Baghdad concerning UN monitoring of Iraqi weapon sites. The council also expressed its concern over the renewal of fighting in Afghanistan, condemned the Israeli deportation of about 400 Palestinians from the occupied territories in December 1992, and demanded the withdrawal of Armenian forces from Azerbaijan in August 1993.

Peacekeeping operations over the next year continued the recent pattern of occasional successes mixed with inconclusive or seemingly failed missions. UNTAC was disbanded in November 1993 following elections and installation of a coalition government in Cambodia, while ONUSAL was widely praised for its contribution to the completion of elections in El Salvador in early 1994. In addition, Mozambique conducted its first multiparty elections in October 1994 with the assistance of the UN Operation in Mozambique (*Opération des Nations Unies au Mozambique*—ONUMOZ). However, positive results were scarce in the former Yugoslavia, Somalia, Angola, and Liberia, while the council was embarrassed by the refusal of the military regime in Port-au-Prince to permit the deployment of the UN Mission in Haiti (UNMIH). Consequently, the council's permanent members continued to reassess the limits of peacekeeping endeavors, and in early May 1994 new guidelines were established. Future missions would require a "clear political goal" reflected in a "precise mandate," a cease-fire among combatants, and the integration, if possible, of forces from regional peacekeeping organizations.

The council's new caution was reflected in its response to the violence and mass dislocations in Rwanda. The United States initially resisted the call for large-scale reinforcement of the UN Assistance

Mission for Rwanda (UNAMIR) in April 1994 (see article on Rwanda for details.) Although 5,500 additional troops were eventually authorized, the council was strongly criticized in many quarters for the delay. Late in the year, amid mounting evidence of widespread atrocities, the Security Council authorized creation of an International Criminal Tribunal for Rwanda.

The Rwandan situation also underscored the ongoing need for the council to develop rapid deployment capability. UN Secretary General Boutros-Ghali announced in early 1994 that some 15 countries had pledged troops and/or equipment to the proposed standby force. Nevertheless, he argued that rhetorical backing for peacekeeping operations, which cost an estimated $3.2 billion in 1993, was still not matched by sufficient tangible support.

In February 1995 UNOSOM withdrew from Somalia, having failed in its goal of fostering political stability there, although being credited with having provided significant humanitarian assistance. Success also remained elusive in former Yugoslavia, where it appeared that beleaguered UNPROFOR forces would be replaced by U.S.-led NATO troops in Bosnia and Herzegovina if a permanent cease-fire were to be negotiated by the combatants. (UNPROFOR's responsibilities in Croatia and Macedonia had been delegated in March to two new missions—the UN Confidence Restoration Operation in Croatia [UNCRO] and the UN Preventive Deployment Force [UNPREDEP].) On the positive side, ONUMOZ and ONUSAL were disbanded after successfully completing their missions in Mozambique and El Salvador, respectively. In addition, the UNMIH was finally able to deploy its forces in Haiti following the return of the civilian government to Port-au-Prince. Hope also grew for a resolution of the protracted conflict in Angola, some 7,000 UNAVEM III troops being authorized to help implement the most recent cease-fire.

In contrast to the large scale of several recent deployments, the new UN Mission of Observers in Tajikistan (UNMOT) was very limited in scope as the Security Council deferred to a large peacekeeping force provided by Russia under the aegis of the Commonwealth of Independent States. This arrangement was considered significant in regard to future peacekeeping efforts, particularly given that UN resources were, in the words of Secretary General Boutros-Ghali, "overstretched and underfinanced."

The Security Council's reassessment of its peacekeeping limitations continued throughout 1995, particularly in view of developments in Bosnia and Herzegovina, where, in the face of UNPROFOR ineffectiveness, NATO launched a bombing campaign in late summer designed to constrain aggressiveness on the part of the Bosnian Serbs. Its military assertiveness having contributed to the conclusion of a U.S.-brokered comprehensive peace agreement in November, NATO for all practical purposes assumed full responsibility in December for overseeing the cease-fire through, among other things, the deployment of some 60,000 troops (see articles on Bosnia and Herzegovina and NATO for details). Concurrently, UNPROFOR was disbanded (effective January 31, 1996), having been deemed a failure for the most part, at least in Bosnia. The counterpoint between NATO action and the UN's previous impotence came into even sharper focus as the cease-fire held throughout 1996 and the complicated new electoral process was completed successfully in Bosnia under NATO supervision.

Concluding another star-crossed endeavor, the Security Council also closed down UNAMIR in August 1996, the mission having had no impact on the raging Hutu-Tutsi ethnic conflict in Rwanda. Significantly, when related violence intensified in Zaire in the fall, the proposed international responses focused on regional or Western-led intervention forces, not on a UN operation. A growing "go-it-alone" attitude had also been apparent in the unilateral action taken by the United States in Iraq in September, Washington ordering the launch of cruise missiles against Iraqi positions without seeking Security Council endorsement (see article on Iraq).

Attention in the council during the second half of 1996 was focused to a large extent on the acrimonious selection of the next UN secretary general. Washington's implacable opposition to a second term for Boutros-Ghali eventually resulted in council endorsement of Kofi Annan. In other activity, the council's long-delayed "oil-for-food" proposal to Iraq was implemented in mid-December, thereby permitting Baghdad to sell Iraqi oil for purposes of funding importation of materials and supplies crucial for meeting civilian needs. Later in the month a permanent cease-fire was concluded in Guatemala. UN negotiators had played a significant part in the attainment of the final settlement, while the UN Human Rights Verification Mission in Guatemala, deployed in 1994, was credited with having defused numerous potential threats to the cease-fire. (That verification mission was augmented for several months in the first half of 1997 by some 155 military observers, although the deployment had been delayed temporarily at the insistence of China, which objected to Guatemala's having extended diplomatic recognition to Taiwan.)

No major new peacekeeping missions were launched in 1997, although small successor operations were authorized for Angola, Haiti, and Croatia. Meanwhile, the limited UN Observer Mission in Liberia (UNOMIL) closed down following the installation of an elected civilian government in Monrovia, the Security Council having left most of the peacemaking and peacekeeping activity there in the hands of regional forces directed by the Economic Community of West African States (ECOWAS). The council also deferred to ECOWAS regarding the turmoil in Sierra Leone, although it formally condemned the May 1997 military coup and endorsed the forced reinstallation of the civilian government in Freetown in March 1998.

Meanwhile, discussion continued on proposed enlargement of the council. A special panel that had been studying the issue for three years called in 1997 for the council to be expanded to 24 members, including 5 new permanent members who, however, would not have veto power. The panel suggested that two new permanent members come from the industrialized countries (probably Germany and Japan) and one each from Africa, Asia, and Latin America. However, the proposed expansion was initially viewed with little enthusiasm by the current permanent council members, who expressed concern that the body might become unwieldy.

The council's agenda in 1997 and early 1998 was dominated by its efforts to compel Iraq to cooperate fully with the weapons inspection program instituted earlier in the decade but still subject to a "cat-and-mouse" approach by Baghdad. Following up on a negative report from the UN Special Commission (UNSCOM), which was responsible for oversight of the inspections, the Security Council in mid-1997 formally rebuked Iraq for noncompliance and interference with UNSCOM's work and threatened to impose additional sanctions. Baghdad responded provocatively, ordering all U.S. members of UNSCOM out of the country on the grounds that they were involved in intelligence-gathering activity beyond the purview of UNSCOM. Although the United States and United Kingdom adopted a hard line and urged consideration of the use of force against Iraq, the other Security Council members declined to endorse such action. Consequently, when Iraq declared in early 1998 that certain sites were off limits to inspectors (who by then had reincorporated the U.S. personnel), Washington, backed by London, announced it would proceed independently against Baghdad and ordered a significant buildup of troops, planes, and ships in the region. With some Security Council members, including the three other permanent members, remaining steadfastly opposed to an attack, the council authorized Secretary General Kofi Annan to discuss a negotiated settlement with Iraqi President Saddam Hussein. Following the last-minute success of Annan's mission in late February, the Security Council threatened Iraq with the "severest consequences" if further violations of the inspection protocols ensued.

The Annan agreement of early 1998 provided only a temporary break in the conflict between the Iraqi government and the Security Council, as Baghdad continued to impede the work of UNSCOM throughout the rest of the year. Tensions came to a head in December following another unfavorable review of Iraqi compliance by UNSCOM. Arguing that previous council resolutions gave them the authority to do so, the United States and United Kingdom bombed Iraq for four days in an effort to force the Iraqi government to resume cooperating with the weapons inspectors. The attack seemed to have backfired, however, when Baghdad refused to allow UNSCOM personnel, who had been withdrawn from the country prior to the attack, to reenter Iraq unless sanctions were lifted. The commission's position was further weakened by reports in the U.S. media that the U.S. Central Intelligence Agency had spied on Iraq under cover of UNSCOM surveillance activities, apparently without the knowledge of successive UNSCOM chairs.

In April 1999 the Security Council opened discussions on reforming UNSCOM, in part to counter the appearance of domination by the United States and the United Kingdom, and on December 17, after months of negotiations, the Security Council approved—with China, France, Malaysia, and Russia abstaining—UNSCOM's replacement by a UN Monitoring, Verification and Inspection Commission (UNMOVIC). The resolution also provided for the possible suspension of sanctions, but Iraq immediately rejected the attendant conditions as "impossible to fulfill." Although the International Atomic Energy

Agency (IAEA) was permitted to renew limited inspections beginning in January 2000, Iraq refused entry to UNMOVIC personnel.

Meanwhile, much of the Security Council's attention had been diverted, once again, to the Balkans. In 1998 it had passed resolutions calling for an end to arms sales to Yugoslavia and for a cease-fire in that country's province of Kosovo. In October the council had also endorsed the establishment of an Organization for Security and Cooperation in Europe (OSCE) mission for the purpose of verifying that the Yugoslav federal government was abiding by these resolutions, but the mission ended in failure with the withdrawal of the OSCE monitors and the subsequent bombing of Yugoslavia by NATO in March–June 1999. Formation of the UNMIK was authorized upon suspension of the air campaign on June 10. As of 2007 the UNMIK, supported by KFOR troops under NATO/EU command, continued to function in Kosovo.

In February 1999 the UNPREDEP mission in Macedonia and a UN Observer Mission in Angola (*Mission d'Observation des Nations Unies en Angola*—MONUA) both came to an end, the former successfully and the latter as a failure. The Security Council had authorized the MONUA in June 1997 to assist in national reconciliation and demobilization, but the peace between the Angolan government and the National Union for the Total Independence of Angola (UNITA) never took hold. With the government making gains on the battlefield, Luanda concurred in the decision to terminate the MONUA. On October 15, however, the Security Council authorized establishment of a United Nations Office in Angola (UNOA), its mandate being to pursue opportunities for peace and to assist with humanitarian efforts, capacity building, and human rights.

The protracted conflict in the neighboring Democratic Republic of the Congo (DRC) led the council in late November 1999 to authorize a United Nations Organization Mission in the Democratic Republic of the Congo (*Mission de l'Organisation des Nations Unies en République Démocratique du Congo*—MONUC) in the hope that a July cease-fire signed by Angola, Namibia, Rwanda, Uganda, and Zimbabwe, as well as the DRC and rebel forces, would hold. Also in Africa, a small UN Observer Mission in Sierra Leone (UNOMSIL), which the council had authorized in June 1998 primarily to monitor security and human rights conditions, gave way in October 1999 to a much larger UN Mission in Sierra Leone (UNAMSIL).

The last of several follow-up efforts in Haiti—the UN Civilian Police Mission in Haiti (*Mission de Police Civile des Nations Unies en Haïti*—MIPONUH)—concluded in March 2000, and the UNMOT effort in Tajikistan drew to a close two months later. A UN Mission in the Central African Republic (*Mission des Nations Unies en République Centrafricaine*—MINURCA), which had been authorized by a Security Council resolution in March 1997 to facilitate stability and security in the wake of a mutiny within the country's armed forces, was succeeded in February 2000 by a UN Peacebuilding Support Office under the UN secretary general. Another Security Council peacekeeping effort, the UN Mission in Ethiopia and Eritrea (UNMEE), came into existence in June 2000, in cooperation with the Organization for African Unity (OAU), following a cease-fire in the Horn of Africa.

A Panel on United Nations Peace Operations, chaired by Algerian Lakhda Brahimi, issued its report in August 2000, with the Security Council then establishing a working group in October to consider the recommendations in Brahimi's report. In a resolution passed unanimously on November 13, the council endorsed the report's conclusion that peacekeeping missions needed clear, credible, and achievable mandates, as well as the capacity to present a believable deterrent in hostile circumstances. The report also called for expansion and restructuring of the Secretariat's Department of Peacekeeping Operations, a greater reliance on intelligence gathering, adoption of means for responding more rapidly to potential crises, and allocation of additional resources.

During the Millennium Summit at UN headquarters in New York, the heads of state and government of the Security Council members convened for only the second time in UN history, with nine presidents, five prime ministers, and one foreign minister in attendance. The council unanimously adopted a September 7 resolution endorsing the body's continuing role in maintaining peace even while recognizing that poverty, infectious disease, and illegal trade in diamonds and other natural resources were among the social and economic pressures most linked to peace and stability.

Another issue addressed during 2000 was the HIV/AIDS crisis; the Security Council called in a July resolution for UN member states to consider voluntary HIV testing and counseling for their troops undertaking peacekeeping missions. January was labeled the "month of Africa" as the council considered a host of Africa-related concerns, while an October meeting examined the role of women in peace and security. With regard to the resumption of the Palestinian intifada (uprising) in September, an October 7 unanimous resolution (the United States abstaining) "deplored the provocation" caused by the visit of future Israeli prime minister Ariel Sharon to the Temple Mount (Haram al-Sharif) in September. In mid-December the council considered an additional resolution that would have authorized creation of an observer force of police and military for the occupied Palestinian territories, but the measure fell a single vote short of the nine needed for approval when seven council members abstained. A renewed effort to approve an observer force met with a U.S. veto on March 28, 2001.

Against a backdrop of the September 11, 2001, al-Qaida assault on the United States, on September 12 and 28 the Security Council unanimously condemned the attacks and requested all states to deny terrorists access to bases and financing, and to aid in bringing the perpetrators to justice. Resolution 1373, passed on September 28, also authorized formation of the ad hoc committee on counterterrorism.

Despite such firm support for U.S.-led efforts to forge an international coalition to combat terrorism, protracted debate slowed a subsequent U.S. push against the Saddam Hussein regime and its alleged WMD. On September 16, 2002, UN Secretary General Kofi Annan announced that Iraq had unconditionally offered entry to UNMOVIC teams, which, Baghdad claimed, would confirm that it harbored no biological, chemical, or other sanctioned weapons. The United States and its chief ally on the Security Council, the United Kingdom, quickly dismissed the offer as a probable ruse. Washington also asserted that Iraq had ties to the al-Qaida terrorist network, but most members of the Security Council found the evidence less than compelling. Meanwhile, U.S. and UK aircraft continued their latest in a series of air assaults against military targets within Iraq's southern no-fly zone.

On November 8, 2002, the Security Council unanimously approved Resolution 1441, which threatened "serious consequences" if Iraq failed to disarm. Although the compromise resolution stopped short of the broad imprimatur that Washington and London had sought, it was interpreted by the United States as not requiring further Security Council approval before launching military action—a prospect that seemed increasingly likely as the year drew to a close. Responding to Iraq's December 8 delivery to the UNMOVIC of a 12,000-page Iraqi weapons declaration, U.S. Secretary of State Colin Powell asserted that it "totally fail[ed]" to meet the Security Council's demands for a comprehensive, accurate accounting of WMD. At the end of the year inspectors from both the UNMOVIC and the IAEA were continuing their work despite only marginal Iraqi compliance.

Also during 2002 the United States, having withdrawn its signature in May from the treaty establishing the International Criminal Court (ICC), insisted that its troops on council-sponsored peacekeeping missions be exempted from the ICC's jurisdiction. In June the Security Council rejected a U.S. resolution that would have exempted all UN peacekeepers. Washington then attempted, again unsuccessfully, to exempt peacekeepers in Bosnia and Herzegovina, where the NATO-led Stabilization Force (SFOR) included some 4,000 U.S. military personnel. A compromise resolution on July 12 specified that the troops of states that had not joined the ICC would be granted a one-year exemption, renewable upon request. With regard to the UN Mission in Bosnia and Herzegovina (UNMIBH), the decision was made largely moot when the council decided to terminate the mission at the close of 2002. December 2002 also saw the completion of a much smaller operation, the United Nations Mission of Observers in Prevlaka (UNMOP), which had been established in 1996 to monitor demilitarization of the Prevlaka peninsula based on a 1992 agreement between Croatia and Montenegro.

In January 2003 UNMOVIC Executive Chair Hans Blix reported that Iraq might have misinformed the UN about Iraqi weapons' programs and called for greater cooperation from the Saddam Hussein regime. Soon afterward, Blix indicated that Iraq had indeed become more forthcoming, and he asked the Security Council to allow the UNMOVIC a number of additional months to verify Iraq's compliance with Resolution 1441's provisions regarding chemical and biological weapons. In addition, Director General Mohamed El Baradei of the IAEA asked for more time for his inspectors to assess the possible presence of nuclear weapons in Iraq. However, in late February the United States, the United Kingdom, and Spain introduced a resolution calling for Security Council authorization of military action against Iraq unless immediate steps were taken by the Hussein regime to prove its submission to Resolution 1441. After some of the bitterest debate in the council since the end of the Cold War, Russia joined France and Germany in blocking the resolution, adamantly insisting that the UNMOVIC needed more time to complete its inspections. The UNMOVIC inspectors left Iraq in mid-March, however, when it became clear that a U.S.-led invasion of Iraq was imminent.

Despite the rancor of the prewar debate, the antiwar members of the council in May 2003 joined the rest of the members in authorizing the allied forces to occupy Iraq and to proceed with planned reconstruction. To assist in the rebuilding, the council agreed to discontinue its sanctions against Iraq and to phase out the "oil-for-food" program, with a view toward ramping up oil production. (In 2004 the council welcomed Secretary General Annan's appointment of a high-level committee to investigate charges of corruption in regard to the "oil-for-food" program. See the discussion of the Secretariat, below, for further details.) Given the radically changed circumstances in Iraq, the UNIKOM mandate concluded on October 6. The council also endorsed the interim government established in Iraq in 2004 and approved the allies' schedule for the transition to an elected government.

In other activity in 2003–2004, the council endorsed the "road map for peace" regarding the Israeli-Palestinian conflict, declared any acts of violence against civilians to be "unjustifiable," voted to discontinue sanctions against Libya after Tripoli renounced its controversial weapons programs, and passed a resolution (at the request of the United States) requiring all UN members to adopt legislation designed to prevent terrorists from gaining possession of WMD. The council also faced a significantly increased demand for peacekeeping forces, particularly in Africa, where extensive missions were approved for Burundi, Côte d'Ivoire, Liberia, and Sudan (see below). In 2003 the Security Council imposed an arms embargo and other restrictions on various foreign and Congolese groups and militias operating in the Democratic Republic of the Congo. These sanctions were followed by establishment of a sanctions committee, expansion of the embargo in 2004, and implementation of an associated travel ban in 2005. Also in 2004, the Security Council imposed an arms embargo on Côte d'Ivoire; froze assets of, and instituted a travel ban on, various Ivorian officials; and authorized creation of a corresponding sanctions committee. Resolution 1556 imposed an arms embargo on "all non-governmental entities and individuals" operating in North, South, and West Darfur, Sudan. The Darfur embargo was expanded in March 2005, when asset and travel restrictions were also imposed and a sanctions committee was created. (In April 2006 the travel ban and assets freeze were expanded to additional individuals.)

The issue of possible expansion of the council returned to the forefront in early 2005 when Secretary General Annan proposed increasing the membership from 15 to 25 as part of his recommendations for broad UN reform and restructuring. Brazil, Germany, India, and Japan, known as the G-4, intensified their campaign to gain permanent council membership. The G-4 proposal called for six new permanent seats, including two seats for African countries, as well as for the addition of four new nonpermanent members. Although the case for expansion appeared to gain momentum when the G-4 dropped their demand for veto power, in August 2005 the African Union voted to reject the proposal primarily because the new permanent members would not have the veto. The expansion question was discussed at the September General Assembly session, although support among the current permanent members of the Security Council was reportedly lukewarm at best.

In May 2005 UNOTIL began operations in Timor-Leste as the second currently functioning "political or peacebuilding" mission. The first was the United Nations Assistance Mission in Afghanistan (UNAMA), which had been established in March 2002 to advise on the peace process, promote human rights, provide technical assistance, and manage UN relief and development aid. Although authorized by Security Council resolutions, both missions function under the Department of Peacekeeping Operations within the Secretariat. A third such operation, the United Nations Integrated Office in Sierra Leone (UNIOSIL), succeeded the UNAMSIL when that mission's mandate expired on December 31, 2005. Two months earlier, the Security Council had established its most recent sanctions committee in connection with the February assassination of former Lebanese prime minister Rafiq Hariri. Resolution 1636 authorized the imposition of travel restrictions and financial measures directed against Syrians and Lebanese suspected of involvement in the assassination.

The increasing burden of peacekeeping operations was highlighted in February 2006 by New York University's annual review of global operations. The review, which gave additional support to the idea of creating emergency standby arrangements, noted that in the previous six years the number of UN peacekeeping personnel had grown from under 13,000 to more than 60,000. Also in February, Under Secretary General for Peacekeeping Operations Jean-Marie Guéhenno reported that the number of sexual abuse complaints directed against peacekeeping personnel had fallen since introduction of a new reporting system in 2005, although he characterized the number, 295, as still unacceptable.

In response to fighting in Southern Lebanon between Israel and Hezbollah forces in July 2006, the Security Council adopted Resolution 1701, which called for an end to combat and the withdrawal of combatants from the region. The resolution also authorized an increase of the United Nations Interim Force in Lebanon (UNIFIL) to 15,000 troops and expanded the mandate of the mission (see United Nations Interim Force in Lebanon, below).

The Security Council launched an effort to reform its working methods in 2006. It reconvened the ad hoc Working Group on Documentation and Other Procedural Questions and tasked the body to examine practices and recommend changes to improve transparency and efficiency. The group's recommendations were approved in July and included a range of minor reforms including increased communication between the Security Council and the General Assembly, more documentation from the council, and enhanced open meetings. The success of the group led the Security Council to authorize it for another year.

Ban Ki-Moon of the Republic of Korea was unanimously recommended by the Security Council in October 2006 to replace Annan as the new UN secretary general. Also in October, the Security Council adopted Resolution 1718, which placed economic sanctions on North Korea following that country's nuclear tests. The sanctions helped prompt renewed diplomacy, which led to an agreement whereby North Korea agreed to dismantle its nuclear weapons program. Meanwhile, the success of the United Nations Operation in Burundi (*Opération des Nations Unies au Burundi*—ONUB, see below) in facilitating a peace accord between rebels and the government led the Security Council to replace the mission with the smaller United Nations Integrated Office in Burundi (*Bureau Intégré des Nations Unies au Burundi*—BINUB).

In 2006 the United States vetoed two resolutions, both calling for the Israeli withdrawal from Gaza, while in 2007 China vetoed a draft resolution calling on Myanmar's government to release political prisoners and stop repressive measures enacted in response to a prodemocracy movement. Also in 2007 Venezuela sought to gain a nonpermanent seat on the Security Council but was opposed by the United States, which instead supported Guatemala. The result was a deadlock that lasted through 47 votes before a compromise was reached through which Venezuela and the United States agreed to support Panama, which was subsequently elected to the body. Concern over Iran's noncompliance with UN nuclear inspectors and the possibility that the country had undertaken a nuclear weapons program prompted the Security Council to adopt Resolution 1737 in December 2006 in an effort to prompt a peaceful settlement of the growing crisis. The resolution imposed limited sanctions on Iran. Divisions between the United States, France, and the United Kingdom, all of which endorsed more stringent measures, and China and Russia, which opposed tougher action, prevented substantive further action through 2007.

In February 2007 UN representative Martti Ahtisaari recommended to the Security Council that the Serbian province of Kosovo be granted eventual independence under the supervision of the UN. However, independence was opposed by both Serbia and Russia. Negotiators from Russia, the United States, and the EU launched a new round of talks with Serb and Kosovar leaders with the goal of developing a new proposal for the Security Council in December 2007. Meanwhile, efforts to forge a common policy on Sudan were stymied by Chinese opposition. While a joint peacekeeping force between the AU and the United Nations Mission in Sudan (UNMIS) had been approved (see below), Sudanese opposition to the deployment of non-African troops limited the size and scope of the operation. In May the United States imposed new economic sanctions on Sudan and developed a draft resolution that would increase pressure on the Sudanese government to end interference with the UNMIS. Subsequently, however, the United States agreed to delay its resolution to allow Ban time to negotiate a new agreement. The secretary general held a ministerial meeting in September which brought together representatives from 20 countries, but the meeting failed to break the impasse over the expanded UN mission in Sudan. The Security Council extended the mandate of the UNMIS through 2007.

The Security Council conducted its first open debate on climate change in April 2007. The session was initiated by the United Kingdom, which, along with other members of the council, asserted that global warming had significant security implications, including increased competition for resources. However, countries such as China and Pakistan criticized the forum and argued that there were other agencies within the UN that were better suited to discuss climate change. Meanwhile, in June, the council voted in Resolution 1762 to end the UNMOVIC mission in Iraq.

To protect the growing number of refugees in the region, estimated at 230,000, and to deter attacks by Sudanese rebel groups in the area, the Security Council authorized the creation of the United Nations Mission in the Central African Republic and Chad (*Mission des Nations Unies en République Centrafricaine et au Tchad*—MINURCAT) in September 2007.

A report delivered to the Security Council by the Stockholm International Peace Research Institute (SIPRI), published in November 2007, questioned the efficiency of UN arms embargoes. The report found that since 1990 only one-fourth of the 27 arms embargoes had been effective. The study did conclude that the presence of UN peacekeepers, however, dramatically increased the likelihood that the sanctions would be successful. SIPRI recommended that the Security Council increase the frequency of reviews of embargo regimes. It also advocated that the council work to have more countries criminalize violations of UN sanctions and prosecute nationals who contravene the embargoes.

In February 2008, following Kosovo's unilateral declaration of independence, the Security Council conducted an emergency session at the request of Serbia and Russia, both of which sought to block the Kosovar bid. No resolution was reached and Russia then circulated a draft resolution to the Security Council in March that would have preserved the territorial integrity of Serbia. However, Russia gained the support of only 6 of the council's 15 members. Serbia then requested that the issue of Kosovar independence be adjudicated through the ICC. The General Assembly voted in favor of the Serbian initiative in October 2008 (see General Assembly).

On June 19, 2008, the Security Council adopted Resolution 1820, which called on the world body to take greater steps to protect women and children in zones of conflict and specifically requested that the secretary general adopt stronger rules to ensure "zero tolerance of sexual exploitation and abuse in UN peacekeeping operations." On June 24 the undersecretary general for security and safety, Sir David Veness, resigned in the aftermath of a car bomb attack that killed 17 UN personnel at the world body's main office in Algiers. Partially in response to the attack, the Security Council adopted Resolution 1822, which called on all nations to work together to cut funding for such terrorist organizations as al-Qaida. In August Ban named Andrew Hughes of Australia as the new chief of UN police missions to replace Mark Kroeker of the United States, who resigned in April.

The Security Council was briefed by the special prosecutor for Sudan of the International Criminal Court (ICC) in June 2008 on allegations that the government was not cooperating with the court. The ICC later charged Sudanese president Omar al-Bashir with genocide for his role in the humanitarian crisis (see article on Sudan). Pressure by the United States for the Security Council to take stronger action regarding the conflict in Darfur was repeatedly blocked through 2008, though the council did extend the mandate of UNMIL through 2009.

In May 2008 China and Russia vetoed a Security Council resolution condemning the government of Zimbabwe for violence against its opposition groups and leaders in the aftermath of elections in that country. In response to demands by Eritrea that the UN Mission in Ethiopia and Eritrea (UNMEE) reduce its staff and limit helicopter flights, along with fuel blockages, the Security Council ended the operation on July 31.

Following an October 2008 report by the International Atomic Energy Agency that Iran continued to block inspectors' access to its nuclear facilities, the Security Council unanimously adopted Resolution 1835, which reaffirmed existing sanctions on Iran and called on the government to immediately suspend its uranium-enrichment program. Meanwhile, in response to increased piracy off of the coast of Somalia, the Security Council adopted Resolution 1838 in October, calling on states to work with Somalia's interim Transitional Federal Government to use air and naval resources to end the attacks on merchant and humanitarian shipping. Also in October, former UN envoy Martti Ahtisaari won the Nobel Peace Prize for his work with the world body, including his efforts to resolve the status of Kosovo.

On January 14, 2009, the Security Council extended the mandate of MINURCAT and authorized an increase in the number of peacekeeping forces, up to 5,200 troops. The council subsequently extended a number of other UN operations, including those in Burundi, Liberia, and the Western Sahara. In January the Security Council also passed a resolution calling on Eritrea and Ethiopia to peacefully settle an ongoing border dispute between the two nations. The Security Council unanimously adopted Resolution 1874 on June 12. The measure increased sanctions on Noth Korea, following that country's second nuclear weapons test. On June 15 Russia vetoed a Security Council resolution to extent the UN observer mission in Georgia and Abkhazia.

SECURITY COUNCIL: PEACEKEEPING FORCES AND MISSIONS

In addition to the forces and missions listed below, the United Nations Command in Korea (established on June 25, 1950) remains technically in existence. The only UN member now contributing to the command is the United States, which proposed in June 1975 that it be dissolved. As of 2008 no formal action had been taken on the proposal (see Security Council: Origin and development).

United Nations Disengagement Observer Force (UNDOF)

Established: By Security Council resolution of May 31, 1974.

Purpose: To observe the cease-fire between Israel and Syria following the 1973 Arab-Israeli War.

Headquarters: Camp Faouar (Syrian Golan Heights). (A UNDOF office is located in Damascus, Syria.)

Force Commander: Maj. Gen. Wolfgang Jilke (Austria).

Composition: As of October 1, 2009, 1,038 troops from the Austrian, Canadian, Croatian, Indian, Japanese, and Polish armed forces.

United Nations Force in Cyprus (UNFICYP)

Established: By Security Council resolution of March 4, 1964, after consultation with the governments of Cyprus, Greece, Turkey, and the United Kingdom.

Purpose: To serve as a peacekeeping force between Greek and Turkish Cypriots.

Headquarters: Nicosia, Cyprus.

Force Commander: Rear Adm. Mario Sánchez Debernardi (Peru).

Composition: As of October 1, 2009, 872 troops and 66 civilian police from Argentina (including soldiers from Brazil, Paraguay, and Peru), Australia, Austria, Bosnia-Herzegovina, Canada, Croatia, El Salvador, Hungary, India, Ireland, Italy, the Netherlands, Slovakia (including soldiers from Croatia), and the United Kingdom.

United Nations Integrated Mission in Timor-Leste (UNMIT)

Established: By Security Council resolution of August 25, 2006; and augmented by a subsequent Security Council resolution on February 25, 2008.

Purpose: To promote political and economic stability in Timor-Leste and aid in national reconciliation.

Headquarters: Dili, Timor-Leste.

Head: Atul Khare (India).

Composition: As of October 1, 2009, 1,578 police officers and 33 military observers from Australia, Bangladesh, Brazil, Canada, China, Croatia, Ecuador, Egypt, El Salvador, Fiji, Gambia, India, Jamaica, Jordan, Kyrgyzstan, Malaysia, Namibia, Nepal, New Zealand, Nigeria,

Pakistan, Philippines, Portugal, Republic of Korea, Romania, Russia, Samoa, Senegal, Sierra Leone, Singapore, Spain, Sri Lanka, Sweden, Thailand, Turkey, Uganda, Ukraine, Uruguay, Vanuatu, Yemen, Zambia, and Zimbabwe.

United Nations Interim Administration Mission in Kosovo
(UNMIK)

Established: By Security Council resolution of June 10, 1999, which also authorized formation of a Multinational Force in Kosovo (Kosovo Force—KFOR).

Purpose: To promote significant autonomy and self-government in Kosovo; to provide civilian administrative functions, including holding elections; to maintain law and order while promoting human rights and ensuring the safe and voluntary return of Kosovar refugees and displaced persons; and to ultimately oversee a transfer of authority to civilian institutions established under a political settlement. KFOR was authorized to establish and maintain a secure environment in Kosovo until such time as the UNMIK Civilian Police could assume this task on a region-by-region basis. In December 2008 the EU Rule of Law Mission in Kosovo (EULEX) took over most of UNMIK's duties in terms of civilian police and security, allowing a substantial reduction in UN personnel.

Headquarters: Priština, Kosovo, Serbia.

Head: Lamberto Zannier (Italy).

Operational Framework: Four "pillars"—peace and justice, civil administration, democratization and institution-building under the direction of the Organization for Security and Cooperation in Europe; reconstruction and economic development under the European Union. KFOR is now under NATO/EU command.

Composition: As of October 1, 2009, 22 police officers and 8 military liaisons from Germany, Ghana, Italy, Pakistan, Russia, Slovenia, Turkey, and Ukraine, in addition to the NATO-led peacekeeping and monitoring force.

United Nations Interim Force in Lebanon
(UNIFIL)

Established: By Security Council resolution of March 19, 1978, and augmented by subsequent resolution on August 11, 2006.

Purpose: To confirm the withdrawal of Israeli troops from Lebanon, to restore peace and help ensure the return of Lebanese authority to southern Lebanon, to extend access to humanitarian support for the civilian population, to facilitate the return of displaced persons, to establish a zone free of weapons and armed personnel other than those of the Lebanese security forces and UNIFIL, and to aid the government of Lebanon in securing its borders.

Headquarters: Naqoura, Lebanon.

Force Commander: Maj. Gen. Claudio Graziano (Italy).

Composition: As of October 1, 2009, 12,235 troops from Belgium, Brunei, China, Croatia, Cyprus, El Salvador, France, FYR of Macedonia, Germany, Ghana, Greece, Guatemala, Hungary, India, Indonesia, Ireland, Italy, Luxemburg, Malaysia, Nepal, New Zealand, Norway, Poland, Portugal, Qatar, Republic of Korea, Sierra Leone, Spain, Slovenia, Tanzania, and Turkey.

United Nations Military Observer Group in India and Pakistan
(UNMOGIP)

Established: By resolutions adopted by the United Nations Commission for India and Pakistan on August 13, 1948, and January 5, 1949; augmented and brought under the jurisdiction of the Security Council by resolution of September 6, 1965, in view of a worsening situation in Kashmir.

Purpose: To assist in implementing the cease-fire agreement of January 1, 1949.

Headquarters: Rawalpindi, Pakistan (November–April); Srinagar, India (May–October).

Chief Military Observer: Maj. Gen. Kim Moon Hwa (Republic of Korea).

Composition: As of October 1, 2009, 45 military observers from Chile, Croatia, Denmark, Finland, Italy, Philippines, Republic of Korea, Sweden, and Uruguay.

United Nations Mission for the Referendum in Western Sahara
Mission des Nations Unies pour le Référendum dans le Sahara Ouest
(MINURSO)

Established: By Security Council resolution of April 29, 1991.

Purpose: To enforce a cease-fire in the Western Sahara between Morocco and the Polisario Front, to identify those eligible to vote in the proposed self-determination referendum in the region, and to supervise the referendum and settlement plan.

Headquarters: Laayoune, Western Sahara.

Force Commander: Maj. Gen. Zhao Jingman (China).

Composition: As of October 1, 2009, 216 military observers, 20 troops, and 6 civilian police from Egypt and El Salvador; the military personnel are from Argentina, Austria, Bangladesh, Brazil, China, Croatia, Djibouti, Egypt, El Salvador, France, Ghana, Greece, Guinea, Honduras, Hungary, Ireland, Italy, Jordan, Malaysia, Mongolia, Nigeria, Pakistan, Paraguay, Poland, Republic of Korea, Russia, Sri Lanka, Uruguay, and Yemen. An additional 2,200 troops and observers were authorized but not deployed because of the lack of progress in referendum negotiations.

United Nations Mission in the Central African Republic and Chad
Mission des Nations Unies en République Centrafricaine et au Tchad
(MINURCAT)

Established: By Security Council resolution of September 25, 2007; and augmented by Security Council Resolution of January 14, 2009.

Purpose: To promote peace and stability in the region and to facilitate the voluntary return of refugees and displaced persons to both Chad and the Central African Republic.

Headquarters: N'Djamena, Chad, with a liaison office in Bangui, the Central African Republic.

Head: Victor de Silva Angelo (Portugal).

Composition: As of October 1, 2009, 2,368 troops and 21 military observers from Albania, Austria, Bangladesh, Brazil, Croatia, Democratic Republic of the Congo, Egypt, Ethiopia, Finland, France, Gabon, Gambia, Ghana, Ireland, Kenya, Malawi, Mali, Mongolia, Namibia, Nepal, Nigeria, Norway, Pakistan, Poland, Russia, Rwanda, Senegal, Togo, Tunisia, United States, and Yemen; 248 civilian police from Benin, Burkina Faso, Burundi, Cameroon, Côte d'Ivoire, Egypt, France, Guinea, Jordan, Libya, Madagascar, Mali, Niger, Portugal, Rwanda, Senegal, Sweden, Togo, Turkey, and Yemen.

United Nations Mission in Ethiopia and Eritrea
(UNMEE)

Established: By Security Council resolution of July 31, 2000; unit strength reduced by Security Council resolutions of May 31, 2006, and January 30, 2007. On July 30, 2008, the Security Council terminated the mission in response to restrictions placed on UNMEE by Eritrea.

Purpose: To monitor the cessation of hostilities, the redeployment of Ethiopian and Eritrean forces, and the temporary security zone (TSZ); to chair the Military Coordination Commission formed by the UN and the Organization of African Unity; to coordinate and provide technical assistance for humanitarian mine-action activities in and around the TSZ; and to coordinate mission activities with other humanitarian and human rights activities.

Headquarters: Asmara, Eritrea, and Addis Ababa, Ethiopia.

Force Commander: Maj. Gen. Mohammad Taisar Masadeh (Jordan) (through July 31, 2008).

Composition: As of October 1, 2009, 0 personnel.

United Nations Mission in Liberia
(UNMIL)

Established: By Security Council resolution of September 19, 2003.

Purpose: To support implementation of the recent cease-fire agreement in Liberia, to support humanitarian and human rights activities, and to assist in training national police and the proposed restructured military.

Headquarters: Monrovia, Liberia.

Force Commander: Lt. Gen. Sikander Afzal (Pakistan).

Composition: As of October 1, 2009, 10,046 troops, 139 military observers, and 1,331 civilian police from Argentina, Bangladesh, Benin, Bolivia, Bosnia and Herzegovina, Brazil, Bulgaria, China, Croatia, Czech Republic, Denmark, Ecuador, Egypt, El Salvador, Ethiopia, Fiji, Finland, France, Gambia, Germany, Ghana, Iceland, India, Indonesia, Jamaica, Jordan, Kenya, Republic of Korea, Kyrgyzstan, Malaysia, Malawi, Mali, Moldova, Mongolia, Montenegro, Namibia, Nepal, Niger, Nigeria, Norway, Pakistan, Paraguay, Peru, Philippines, Poland, Romania, Russia, Rwanda, Senegal, Serbia, Sri Lanka, Sweden, Togo, Turkey, Uganda, Ukraine, United States, Uruguay, Yemen, Zambia, and Zimbabwe.

United Nations Mission in the Sudan
(UNMIS)

Established: By Security Council resolution of March 24, 2005.

Purpose: To support implementation of the peace agreement signed by the government of Sudan and the Sudanese People's Liberation Movement in January 2005, to provide humanitarian assistance, and to protect and promote human rights in Sudan.

Headquarters: Khartoum, Sudan.

Force Commander: Maj. Gen. Paban Jung Thapa (Nepal).

Composition: As of October 1, 2009, 8,545 troops, 485 military observers, and 693 civilian police from Australia, Bangladesh, Belgium, Benin, Bolivia, Bosnia and Herzegovina, Brazil, Burkina Fuso, Cambodia, Canada, China, Croatia, Denmark, Ecuador, Egypt, El Salvador, Fiji, Finland, France, Gabon, Gambia, Germany, Ghana, Greece, Guatemala, Guinea, India, Indonesia, Iran, Jamaica, Japan, Jordan, Kenya, Kyrgyzstan, Malaysia, Mali, Moldova, Mongolia, Namibia, Nepal, Netherlands, Nigeria, Norway, Pakistan, Paraguay, Peru, Philippines, Poland, Republic of Korea, Romania, Russia, Rwanda, Samoa, Sierra Leone, Sri Lanka, Sweden, Tanzania, Thailand, Turkey, Uganda, Ukraine, United Kingdom, United States, Uruguay, Yemen, Zambia, and Zimbabwe.

United Nations Observer Mission in Georgia
(UNOMIG)

Established: By Security Council resolution of August 24, 1993; and expanded by Security Council Resolution on July 30, 2003.

Purpose: To monitor the cease-fire approved on July 27, 1993, by the Republic of Georgia and Abkhazian secessionists. The UNOMIG mandate was subsequently expanded to monitor and verify (in conjunction with peacekeeping forces from the Commonwealth of Independent States) a second cease-fire signed on May 14, 1994.

Headquarters: Sukhumi, Georgia.

Chief Military Observer: Maj. Gen. Anwar Hussain (Bangladesh).

Composition: As of October 1, 2009, 129 military observers and 16 civilian police from Albania, Austria, Bangladesh, Croatia, Czech Republic, Denmark, Egypt, France, Germany, Ghana, Greece, Hungary, Indonesia, Israel, Jordan, Republic of Korea, Lithuania, Moldova, Mongolia, Pakistan, Poland, Republic of Korea, Romania, Russia, Sweden, Switzerland, Turkey, Ukraine, United Kingdom, United States, Uruguay, and Yemen.

United Nations Operation in Burundi
Opération des Nations Unies au Burundi
(ONUB)

Established: By Security Council resolution of May 21, 2004; mandate completed on December 31, 2006, and transitioned to the United Nations Integrated Operation in Burundi (*Bureau Intégré des Nations Unies au Burundi*—BINUB), established by Security Council resolution of October 25, 2006.

Purpose: To help implement the Arusha Agreement negotiated by the parties to the conflict in Burundi.

Headquarters: Bujumbura, Burundi.

Executive Representative: Youssef Mahmoud (Tunisia).

Composition: As of October 1, 2009, 15 civilian police from Turkey.

United Nations Operation in Côte d'Ivoire
Opération des Nations Unies en Côte d'Ivoire
(ONUCI)

Established: By Security Council resolution of February 27, 2004.

Purpose: To facilitate implementation of the peace agreement signed by the parties to the conflict in Côte d'Ivoire. (The ONUCI was a successor to the United Nations Mission in Côte d'Ivoire [*Mission des Nations Unies en Côte d'Ivoire*—MINUCI], a political mission that had been established by the Security Council in May 2003.)

Headquarters: Abidjan, Côte d'Ivoire.

Force Commander: Maj. Gen. Fernand Marcel Amoussou (Benin).

Composition: As of October 1, 2009, 7,027 troops, 192 military observers, and 1,166 civilian police from Argentina, Bangladesh, Benin, Bolivia, Brazil, Burundi, Cameroon, Canada, Central African Republic, Chad, Chile, Democratic Republic of the Congo, Djibouti, Ecuador, El Salvador, Ethiopia, Finland, France, Gambia, Ghana, Guatemala, Guinea, Hungary, India, Ireland, Jordan, Libya, Moldova, Morocco, Namibia, Nepal, Niger, Nigeria, Pakistan, Paraguay, Peru, Philippines, Poland, Romania, Russia, Rwanda, Senegal, Serbia, Sweden, Switzerland, Tanzania, Togo, Tunisia, Turkey, Uganda, Uruguay, Yemen, Zambia, and Zimbabwe.

United Nations Organization Mission in the Democratic Republic of the Congo
Mission de l'Organisation des Nations Unies en République Démocratique du Congo
(MONUC)

Established: By Security Council resolution of November 30, 1999, which specified that the MONUC would comprise the military liaison personnel authorized by a resolution of August 6, 1999. The MONUC's authorized strength was increased in October 2004; its mission was expanded on January 10, 2007.

Purpose: In cooperation with the Joint Military Commission (JMC) of the states that signed the July 1999 cease-fire accord, to implement, monitor, and investigate violations of the cease-fire; to assist in the disengagement, redeployment, disarmament, demobilization, resettlement, and reintegration of combatants; to assist in planning and conducting mine-action activities; to assist in the release of prisoners of war, military captives, and remains; to facilitate humanitarian assistance and human rights monitoring in cooperation with various organizations; and to cooperate with and provide assistance to the Facilitator of the National Dialogue.

Headquarters: Kinshasa, Democratic Republic of the Congo. Liaison offices are maintained in Addis Ababa, Ethiopia; Bujumbura, Burundi; Harare, Zimbabwe; Kampala, Uganda; Kigali, Rwanda; Lusaka, Zambia; and Windhoek, Namibia.

Force Commander: Lt. Gen. Babacar Gaye (Senegal).

Composition: As of October 1, 2009, 16,844 troops, 705 military observers, and 1,089 civilian police from Algeria, Bangladesh, Belgium, Benin, Bolivia, Bosnia and Herzegovina, Burkina Faso, Cameroon, Canada, Central African Republic, Chad, China, Côte d'Ivoire, Czech Republic, Denmark, Egypt, France, Ghana, Guatemala, Guinea, India, Indonesia, Ireland, Jordan, Kenya, Madagascar, Malawi, Malaysia, Mali, Morocco, Mozambique, Nepal, Niger, Nigeria, Norway, Pakistan, Paraguay, Peru, Poland, Romania, Russia, Senegal, Serbia, South Africa, Spain, Sri Lanka, Sweden, Switzerland, Togo, Tunisia, Turkey, Ukraine, United Kingdom, Uruguay, Yemen, and Zambia.

United Nations Stabilization Mission in Haiti
Mission des Nations Unies pour la Stabilisation en Haïti
(MINUSTAH)

Established: By Security Council resolution of April 30, 2004. (MINUSTAH assumed the authority previously exercised by the Multinational Interim Force [MIF] that had been authorized by the Security Council in February 2004.)

Purpose: To support the constitutional and political process underway in Haiti; to help maintain security and stability; to assist with the restoration and maintenance of the rule of law, public safety, and public order; to assist the transitional government in Haiti in reforming the Haitian national police; to assist in the disarmament and demobilization of armed groups; and to provide support for the holding of free and fair elections.

Headquarters: Port-au-Prince, Haiti.

Force Commander: Maj. Gen. Floriano Peixoto Viera Neta (Brazil).

Composition: As of October 1, 2009, 7,057 troops and 2,066 civilian police from Argentina, Benin, Bolivia, Brazil, Burkina Faso, Cameroon, Canada, Central African Republic, Chad, Chile, China, Colombia, Côte d'Ivoire, Croatia, Democratic Republic of the Congo, Ecuador, Egypt, El Salvador, France, Guatemala, Guinea, India, Jamaica, Jordan, Madagascar, Mali, Nepal, Niger, Nigeria, Pakistan, Paraguay, Peru, Philippines, Romania, Russia, Rwanda, Senegal, Serbia, Spain, Sri Lanka, Switzerland, Togo, Turkey, United States, Uruguay, and Yemen.

United Nations Truce Supervision Organization
(UNTSO)

Established: By Security Council resolution of May 29, 1948.

Purpose: To supervise the cease-fire arranged by the Security Council following the 1948 Arab-Israeli War. Its mandate was subsequently extended to embrace the armistice agreements concluded in 1949; the Egyptian-Israeli peace treaty of 1979; and assistance to other UN forces in the Middle East, specifically the UNDOF and UNIFIL.

Headquarters: Jerusalem, Israel.

Chief of Staff: Maj. Gen. Robert Mood (Norway).

Composition: As of October 1, 2009, 151 military observers from Argentina, Australia, Austria, Belgium, Canada, Chile, China, Denmark, Estonia, Finland, France, Ireland, Italy, Nepal, Netherlands, New Zealand, Norway, Russia, Slovakia, Slovenia, Sweden, Switzerland, and the United States.

SECURITY COUNCIL: INTERNATIONAL CRIMINAL TRIBUNALS

Lacking a permanent international court with jurisdiction to prosecute and try cases involving accusations of war crimes, genocide, and crimes against humanity, the Security Council established the International Criminal Tribunal for the former Yugoslavia (ICTY) in 1993 and the International Criminal Tribunal for Rwanda (ICTR) in 1994. Meeting in Rome, Italy, in 1998, a UN conference approved formation of a permanent International Criminal Court (ICC), which by April 2002 had obtained sufficient ratifications for its establishment in July (see the General Assembly section). In September 2007 Fausto Pocar of Italy was reelected president of the court and Kevin Parker of Australia was reelected vice president.

As of October 2009 the ICTY had brought public indictments against 161 individuals, including those who had been acquitted and those whose cases had been withdrawn. Proceedings had been brought against 120 persons and there were 22 individuals serving sentences, while 18 had completed their sentences; 33 cases were still proceeding, including appeals, 9 individuals were on provisional release, 5 were acquitted, and 6 indicted individuals remained at large, including two high-profile figures, Ratko Mladić and Goran Hadžić.

On November 2, 2002, Biljana Plavšić, former president of the Serb Republic of Bosnia and Herzegovina, pleaded guilty to one count of a crime against humanity for political, racial, and religious persecution, and on February 27, 2003, she was sentenced to 11 years in prison. By far the most prominent figure turned over to the court by national forces was former Yugoslav president Slobodan Milošević, who died on March 11, 2006, during his trial. The former president of the Republic of Srpska, Radovan Karadžić, was arrested on July 18, 2008, and turned over to the ICTY on July 30. Karadžić refused to recognize the authority of the ITCY and avoided entering a plea as of October. In 2009 the ICTY announced that it planned to have all remaining trials completed by 2012.

As of May 2009 the ICTR had brought public indictments against some 86 individuals and had arrested more than 50 people, while 13 individuals remained at large; 35 trials had reached their conclusion (with 29 convictions), 5 trials were in progress, and 6 persons were in detention awaiting adjudication. Thirty cases had been passed to Rwandan national courts for adjudication. The highest-ranking defendant, former Rwandan prime minister Jean Kambanda, pleaded guilty to genocide in 1998 and was sentenced to life in prison. In 2008 three of the remaining high-level indictees were arrested, including Callixte Nsabonimana, Dominique Ntawukulilyayo, and Augustin Ngirabatware. In June the ICTR requested a one-year extension from the Security Council to complete its trial work, partially as a result of the three arrests. In 2009 the ICTR again requested an additional year to complete all trials.

In August 2000 the Security Council unanimously indicated its support for forming a third war crimes tribunal, for Sierra Leone, which began its proceedings in 2003, although not as a subsidiary body of the Security Council. Former Liberian president Charles Taylor was the highest-ranking defendant tried by the court. His case was ongoing as of October 2009, but the court had completed trials against 8 of 12 other indictees. A similar joint criminal tribunal in Lebanon began in 2005, and in 2007 a tribunal began in Cambodia to prosecute and try former Khmer Rouge regime members.

International Criminal Tribunal for the Former Yugoslavia
(ICTY)

Formal Name: International Tribunal for the Prosecution of Persons Responsible for Serious Violations of International Humanitarian Law Committed in the Territory of the Former Yugoslavia since 1991.

Established: By Security Council resolution of May 25, 1993.

Purpose: To prosecute and try persons who allegedly committed serious violations of international humanitarian law on the territory of the former Yugoslavia since 1991, the subject offenses being genocide, crimes against humanity, and violations of the 1949 Geneva Conventions and the laws or customs of war.

Headquarters: The Hague, Netherlands.

Chief Prosecutor: Serge Brammertz (Belgium).

Permanent Judges: Patrick Lipton Robinson (Jamaica, President), O-gon Kwon (Republic of Korea, Vice President), Carmel A. Agius (Malta), Jean-Claude Antonetti (France), Christoph Flügge (Germany), Liu Daqun (China), Guy Delvoie (Belgium), Mehmet Güney (Turkey), Burton Hall (Bahamas), Theodor Meron (United States), Bakone Justice Moloto (South Africa), Howard Morrison (United Kingdom), Alphonsus Martinus Maria Orie (Netherlands), Kevin Parker (Australia), Fausto Pocar (Italy), and Andrésia Vaz (Senegal). There are also 16 *ad litem* judges.

Registrar: John Hocking (Australia).

Web site: www.un.org/icty

International Criminal Tribunal for Rwanda
(ICTR)
Tribunal Pénal International pour le Rwanda (French)
Urukiko Nshinjabyaha Mpuzamahanga Rwagenewe u Rwanda (Kinyarwanda)

Formal Name: International Criminal Tribunal for the Prosecution of Persons Responsible for Genocide and Other Serious Violations of International Humanitarian Law Committed in the Territory of Rwanda and Rwandan Citizens Responsible for Genocide and Other Such Violations Committed in the Territory of Neighboring States, between 1 January 1994 and 31 December 1994.

Established: By Security Council resolution of November 8, 1994.

Purpose: To prosecute crimes allegedly committed by Rwandans and others in Rwanda, and by Rwandans in neighboring states, between January 1, 1994, and December 31, 1994, the subject offenses being violations of the 1949 Geneva Conventions, genocide, and crimes against humanity.

Headquarters: Arusha, Tanzania. The office of the prosecutor is located in Kigali, Rwanda.

Chief Prosecutor: Hassan Bubacar Jallow (Gambia).

Permanent Judges: Charles Michael Dennis Byron (St. Kitts and Nevis, President), Khalida Rachid Khan (Pakistan, Vice President), Erik Møse (Norway), Arlette Ramarosen (Madagascar), Patrick Robinson (Jamaica), Carmel Agius (Malta), Sergei Alekseevich Egorov (Russia), Mehmet Güney (Turkey), Liu Daqun (China), Theodor Meron (United States), Fausto Pocar (Italy), William Sekule (Tanzania), Joseph Asoka Nihal De Silva (Sri Lanka), Bakhtiyar Tuzmukhamedov (Russia), and Andrésia Vaz (Senegal). There are also nine *ad litem* judges.

Registrar: Adama Dieng (Senegal).

Web site: www.un.org/ictr

ECONOMIC AND SOCIAL COUNCIL
(ECOSOC)

Membership (54): Algeria, Barbados, Belarus, Bolivia, Brazil, Cameroon, Canada, Cape Verde, China, Democratic Republic of the Congo, Côte d'Ivoire, El Salvador, Estonia, France, Germany, Greece, Guatemala, Guinea-Bissau, India, Indonesia, Iraq, Japan, Kazakhstan, Liechtenstein, Luxembourg, Malawi, Malaysia, Mauritius, Moldova, Morocco, Mozambique, Namibia, Netherlands, New Zealand, Niger, Norway, Pakistan, Peru, Philippines, Poland, Portugal, Republic of Korea, Romania, Russia, St. Kitts and Nevis, St. Lucia, Saudi Arabia, Somalia, Sudan, Sweden, United Kingdom, United States, Uruguay, and Venezuela. One-third of the members rotate annually on the following geographical basis: Africa, 14 seats; Asia, 11; Latin America and the Caribbean, 10; Eastern Europe, 6; Western Europe and others, 13.

Web site: www.un.org/ecosoc

President of the 2009 Session: Sylvie Lucas (Luxembourg).

Origin and development. Initially, the activities of ECOSOC were directed primarily to the twin problems of relief and reconstruction in war-torn Europe, Asia, and, after 1948, Israel. By the mid-1950s, however, the problems of less developed states of Africa, Asia, and Latin America began to claim primary attention.

Substantially increased activity has occurred under the auspices of ECOSOC subsidiary organs as UN operations have proliferated in the economic and social fields. At the direction of the General Assembly, ECOSOC in 1987 established a special commission to identify ways to simplify UN structures and functions in those areas. In May 1988, however, the commission announced that it was unable to reach a consensus, its chair citing "political concerns" within the international community and "vested interests" within the UN as hindering effective reorganization. Nevertheless, ECOSOC continued to attempt to streamline and "revitalize" its own operations. As part of that effort, the council in mid-1991 agreed to discontinue its practice of holding two or more sessions each year in various locations in favor of a single four- to five-week substantive session annually (alternating between New York and Geneva), preceded by a number of organizational sessions.

In mid-1992 ECOSOC once again found itself immersed in debate on the proposed restructuring of UN bodies dealing with economic and social issues, pressure having grown to eliminate overlapping mandates and provide "more efficient and cost-effective" services. Secretary General Boutros Boutros-Ghali, a major force behind the streamlining efforts, said he hoped ECOSOC would achieve the same "relevance" to economic and social development in the world that the Security Council had recently achieved regarding peacemaking and peacekeeping. Under Boutros-Ghali and his successor, Kofi Annan, ECOSOC underwent considerable reorganization, including a reduction in the number of Standing Committees and Commissions.

Structure. By a charter amendment that entered into force in 1965, the membership of ECOSOC was increased from 18 to 27 in order to provide wider representation to new states in Africa and Asia. Similarly, membership was raised to 54 as of September 1973. One-third of the members are elected each year for three-year terms, and all voting is by simple majority; each member has one vote.

Much of ECOSOC's activity is carried out through its eight Functional and five Regional Commissions (described in separate sections, below) and a number of Standing Committees and Commissions that currently include the Commission on Human Settlements (established in 1977), the Committee on Negotiations with Intergovernmental Agencies (1946), the Committee on Non-Governmental Organizations (1946), and the Committee for Program and Coordination (1962). In 2000 ECOSOC established the United Nations Forestry Forum (UNFF) to promote conservation and sustainable development. Membership in the UNFF is open to all UN member states. In addition, there are assorted ECOSOC Expert Bodies, such as the Ad Hoc Group of Experts on International Cooperation in Tax Matters; the Committee for Development Policy; the Committee of Experts on Public Administration; the Committee of Experts on the Transport of Dangerous Goods and on the Globally Harmonized System of Classification and Labeling of Chemicals; the Committee on Economic, Social, and Cultural Rights; the Permanent Forum on Indigenous Issues; and the United Nations Group of Experts on Geographical Names. In 2001 ECOSOC created two Ad Hoc Advisory Groups On African Countries Emerging From Conflict, one for Burundi and the other for Guinea-Bissau. These were followed in 2004 by the reactivation of the Ad Hoc Advisory Group on Haiti, which had been active in 1999. In 2006 the advisory group on Burundi was terminated, as was the group on Guinea-Bissau the following year, when the newly created Peace Building Commission was tasked to oversee the countries.

Because of the scope of its responsibilities, ECOSOC also has complex relationships with a number of UN subsidiary and related organs. It participates in the Chief Executives Board (CEB, formerly the

Administrative Committee on Coordination [ACC]), which comprises the secretary general and the heads of the Specialized Agencies and the International Atomic Energy Agency (IAEA), and elects the members of the independent International Narcotics Control Board (INCB), three from nominees proposed by the World Health Organization and ten from other nominees offered by UN members and parties to the 1961 Single Convention on Narcotic Drugs. It also elects the executive boards of the United Nations Development Program/United Nations Population Fund and the United Nations Children's Fund, the Executive Committee of the United Nations Office of High Commissioner for Refugees, half of the members of the UN/FAO Intergovernmental Committee of the World Food Program, 10 board members of the United Nations Research Institute for Social Development, and the 22 members of the Program Coordination Board for the Joint UN Program on HIV/AIDS (UNAIDS).

Activities. ECOSOC produces or initiates studies, reports, and recommendations on international economic, /social, cultural, educational, health, and related matters; promotes respect for, and observance of, human rights and fundamental freedoms; negotiates agreements with the UN Specialized Agencies to define their relations with the UN; and coordinates the activities of the Specialized Agencies through consultations and recommendations.

In recent years ECOSOC has called for increased consultation and cooperation among UN bodies, other intergovernmental and nongovernmental organizations, governments, and the private sector to deal with the world's growing economic and social turmoil. Among the problems the commission considers of most pressing concern are the flow of resources for sustainable development, the external indebtedness of developing countries, rising crime rates, widespread hunger and malnutrition, insufficient economic integration of women, human rights violations, housing shortages, population growth, drug abuse, the spread of AIDS, the dumping of nuclear and other toxic waste, environmental degradation, and the abuse of children's rights.

At its 1997 substantive session, ECOSOC noted that democracy is an important part of social and sustainable development. The representatives of some members complained about the reduced level of funding the council has received and called on the developed countries to provide more money for the UN and developmental assistance.

At its mid-1998 substantive session, the council met with representatives of the International Monetary Fund (IMF), World Bank, UN Conference on Trade and Development (UNCTAD), and World Trade Organization (WTO) to discuss the movement toward global free trade. Some participants noted that progress toward liberalizing trade had occurred, but that the least developed countries (LDCs) were being left out of the process. To address what it saw as such shortcomings, the council called on the WTO to provide assistance to developing countries and to take their special needs into consideration during future negotiations. The council also called for continued efforts in support of women's rights and discussed ways in which the UN could respond more quickly to humanitarian crises.

Discussions on sustainable development and globalization continued in 1999, with employment-oriented growth being one focus of attention at the 2000 Geneva substantive session. In addition, ECOSOC continued to stress the importance of full gender equality, good governance, and participation by all sectors of society. Also during 2000 ECOSOC agreed to establish a permanent forum for indigenous peoples, and considerable attention has recently been given to the importance of extending access to information and communication technology. ECOSOC also created the UN Forum on Forests, with membership open to all UN members, to promote sustainable development and conservation.

ECOSOC drew international notice at its early May 2001 organizing session when, in secret balloting, the United States lost its seat on the Commission on Human Rights and on the International Narcotics Control Board, effective January 1 and March 1, 2002, respectively. The United States had been represented on both the commission and the board continuously since their formation. The outcome of the votes drew predictable ire from members of the U.S. Congress, who threatened to retaliate, in part by withholding $582 million in back UN dues. Many observers described the slight as an indication of dissatisfaction within the UN over recent stances taken by the George W. Bush administration, particularly its opposition to formation of the International Criminal Court and its withdrawal from the Kyoto Protocol, which was aimed at reducing emissions of greenhouse gases (see the article on the UN Environment Program). Further controversy broke out in July 2002 when ECOSOC endorsed a plan for a system of regular inspections of prisons and detention centers throughout the world to combat the abuse of prisoners. Washington opposed that measure, apparently unwilling to permit such scrutiny of U.S. facilities in the United States and elsewhere. Nevertheless, the United States was returned to the Commission on Human Rights in 2003.

In early 2003 ECOSOC announced plans to coordinate its activities more closely with the IMF, World Bank, and the WTO in order to implement the goals set at the 2002 International Conference on Financing for Development. The council also subsequently indicated a desire to become more involved with "practical activities on the ground" as directed by the Security Council. Among other things, ECOSOC cited "expanded investment in health and education as a critical component in the UN's recently enhanced peacebuilding role." Collaterally, the council reported that the plight of poor countries as of 2005 had improved very little despite much attention given to the issue during the first half of the decade. ECOSOC pledged to intensify its oversight of the many commissions and agencies under its purview as part of proposed overall UN reform geared toward enhancing efficiency and effectiveness.

In accordance with the March 2006 General Assembly resolution creating the UN Human Rights Council, ECOSOC abolished the Commission on Human Rights on June 16. In addition, the ECOSOC voted to increase the membership of its Commission on Science and Technology for Development from 33 to 43 members beginning in February 2007 in order to broaden participation in the body.

In accordance with a proposal accepted at the 2005 World Summit, ECOSOC conducted its first Annual Ministerial Review (AMR) in July 2007 in Geneva. The AMR brought together national delegations and representatives from the UN and private sector to assess goals related to sustainable development in line with the theme of the meeting, "Strengthening Efforts to Eradicate Poverty and Hunger, Including through the Global Partnership for Development." In July the ECOSOC launched the Development Cooperation Forum (DCF), a biennial meeting to facilitate progress on the Millennium Development Goals. The DCF was designed to draw together participants from individual countries and representatives from various UN bodies, as well as the World Bank, IMF, and business sector. The initial meeting of the group was held in New York in June 2008.

The 2008 AMR, conducted in July in New York, focused on "Implementing the Internationally Agreed Goals and Commitments in Regard to Sustainable Development." The AMR included sessions on the UN's development agenda, implementing global development goals on a national basis, and the integration of the Millennium Development Goals with other initiatives. In addition, Belgium, Finland, Luxembourg, and the United Kingdom reported on national efforts to promote development. At ECOSOC's 2008 substantive session, the council passed 9 resolutions and 3 decisions, the most ever at one of its annual meetings. The resolutions included a condemnation of sexual violence against humanitarian and aid workers, an expression of concern over the growing number of people affected by natural disasters, and a call for joint action to lessen the impact of rising food and commodity prices.

ECOSOC's third AMR was conducted in July 2009 in Geneva. The event was centered on three goals: reviewing the UN's development initiatives, analyzing the main global challenges and opportunities surrounding public health, and examining potential new ECOSOC programs. Bolivia, China, Jamaica, Japan, Mali, Sri Lanka, and Sudan each gave national presentations on development issues. Among the resolutions adopted at ECOSOC's substantive session in Geneva in July was a call for the UN development programs to try to achieve gender balance in their personnel. The second DCF was scheduled for 2010, and preparations for the meeting proceeded throughout 2009.

ECONOMIC AND SOCIAL COUNCIL: FUNCTIONAL COMMISSIONS

ECOSOC's Functional Commissions prepare reports, evaluate services, and make recommendations to the council on matters of economic and social concern to member states. Participants are elected for terms of three or four years, depending on the particular commission. Selection is made with due regard for geographical distribution; in the case of the Commission on Narcotic Drugs, emphasis is also given to countries producing or manufacturing narcotic materials. The Commission on Narcotic Drugs has a Subcommission on Illicit Drug Traffic and Related Matters in the Near and Middle East, and four regional Heads of National Drug Law Enforcement Agencies (HONLEA).

Commission on Crime Prevention and Criminal Justice

Established: February 6, 1992.

Purpose: To provide policy guidance on crime prevention and criminal justice, including the treatment of offenders, and to facilitate the activities of UN and other international programs in those areas. (Commission mandates are implemented by the Center for International Crime Prevention [CICP] of the Office for Drug Control and Crime Prevention [ODCCP].)

Membership (40): Algeria, Argentina, Austria, Belgium, Brazil, Cameroon, Canada, China, Columbia, Comoro Islands, Cuba, Democratic Republic of the Congo, El Salvador, Germany, Ghana, Guatemala, India, Indonesia, Iran, Jamaica, Japan, Kenya, Republic of Korea, Lesotho, Libya, Moldova, Nigeria, Romania, Russia, Saudi Arabia, Sierra Leone, South Africa, Sudan, Thailand, Turkey, Ukraine, United Arab Emirates, United Kingdom, United States, and Uruguay.

Commission on Narcotic Drugs

Established: February 16, 1946.

Purpose: To serve as the UN's principal policymaking body on drugs and to advise the council on matters related to the abuse and control of narcotic drugs. (Commission mandates may be implemented through the UN International Drug Control Program [UNDCP] within the Office for Drug Control and Crime Prevention [ODCCP].)

Membership (53): Argentina, Australia, Austria, Belgium, Bolivia, Botswana, Cameroon, Canada, China, Colombia, Cuba, Czech Republic, Democratic Republic of the Congo, El Salvador, Ethiopia, Finland, Germany, Iran, Israel, Italy, Jamaica, Japan, Kazakhstan, Lithuania, Mexico, Moldova, Morocco, Namibia, the Netherlands, Niger, Nigeria, Pakistan, Peru, Poland, Republic of Korea, Russia, Saudi Arabia, Senegal, Spain, Sudan, Switzerland, Tajikistan, Thailand, Trinidad and Tobago, Turkey, Uganda, Ukraine, United Arab Emirates, United Kingdom, United States, Uruguay, Venezuela, and Yemen.

Commission on Population and Development

Established: October 3, 1946, as the Population Commission. Current name adopted in 1994.

Purpose: To study and advise the council on population issues and on integrating population and development strategies. As of 1996 the commission has also been charged with monitoring, reviewing, and implementing the International Conference on Population and Development Program of Action (1994) at the national, regional, and international levels.

Membership (47): Bangladesh, Belgium, Benin, Brazil, Bulgaria, Canada, Cameroon, China, Colombia, Comoro Islands, Croatia, Equatorial Guinea, Finland, Gambia, Germany, Grenada, Guyana, Honduras, India, Indonesia, Iran, Jamaica, Japan, Kazakhstan, Kenya, Lebanon, Malaysia, Mexico, Morocco, Netherlands, Oman, Peru, Poland, Russia, Sierra Leone, South Africa, Spain, Sri Lanka, Sweden, Switzerland, Tunisia, Uganda, Ukraine, United Kingdom, United States, Uruguay, and Zambia.

Commission on Science and Technology for Development

Established: April 30, 1992.

Purpose: To promote international cooperation in the field of science and technology for development; to formulate guidelines for the harmonization of UN scientific and technological activities and to monitor those activities.

Membership (43): Argentina, Austria, Belarus, Belgium, Brazil, Burkina Faso, Chile, China, Costa Rica, Democratic Republic of the Congo, Cuba, Dominican Republic, El Salvador, Eritrea, Equatorial Guinea, Finland, France, Germany, Ghana, India, Iran, Israel, Jamaica, Jordan, Latvia, Lesotho, Malaysia, Mali, Oman, Pakistan, Philippines, Portugal, Russia, Slovakia, South Africa, Sri Lanka, Sudan, Switzerland, Tunisia, Turkey, Uganda, and the United States (one vacancy).

Commission for Social Development

Established: June 21, 1946, as the Social Commission; renamed the Commission for Social Development on July 29, 1966.

Purpose: To advise the council on all aspects of social development policies, including, recently, an increased emphasis on policies aimed at increasing the equitable distribution of national income.

Membership (46): Andorra, Angola, Argentina, Armenia, Bangladesh, Benin, Bolivia, Cameroon, China, Cuba, Czech Republic, Democratic People's Republic of Korea, Democratic Republic of the Congo, El Salvador, Egypt, Finland, France, Germany, Ghana, Guatemala, India, Italy, Jamaica, Japan, Republic of Korea, Mexico, Monaco, Myanmar, Namibia, Nepal, Netherlands, Nigeria, Pakistan, Paraguay, Russia, Senegal, Slovakia, South Africa, Spain, Sudan, Tanzania, Turkey, Ukraine, United Arab Emirates, United States, and Venezuela.

Commission on the Status of Women

Established: June 21, 1946.

Purpose: To report to the council on methods to promote women's rights; to develop proposals giving effect to the principle that men and women should have equal rights.

Membership (45): Armenia, Azerbaijan, Belarus, Belgium, Brazil, Cambodia, Cameroon, China, Colombia, Cuba, Djibouti, Dominican Republic, Ecuador, Eritrea, Gabon, Germany, Guinea, Haiti, India, Indonesia, Iran, Iraq, Israel, Italy, Japan, Republic of Korea, Lesotho, Malaysia, Mauritania, Mexico, Namibia, Nicaragua, Niger, Pakistan, Paraguay, Russia, Rwanda, Senegal, Spain, Sweden, Togo, Turkey, United Arab Emirates, United States, and Zambia.

Commission on Sustainable Development

Established: February 12, 1993.

Purpose: To monitor implementation of agreements reached at the 1992 UN Conference on Environment and Development; to oversee the integration of those two areas throughout the UN system.

Membership (53): Antigua and Barbuda, Argentina, Australia, Bahrain, Bangladesh, Belgium, Brazil, Canada, Cape Verde, Chile, China, Costa Rica, Democratic Republic of the Congo, Croatia, Czech Republic, Djibouti, Estonia, France, Gabon, Gambia, Germany, Guatemala, Guinea, Haiti, India, Indonesia, Iran, Israel, Japan, Republic of Korea, Kuwait, Libya, Malawi, Monaco, Namibia, Netherlands, Pakistan, Peru, Poland, Romania, Russia, Saudi Arabia, Senegal, South Africa, Spain, Sudan, Sweden, Switzerland, Tanzania, United Arab Emirates, United Kingdom, United States, Uruguay, and Venezuela.

Statistical Commission

Established: June 21, 1946.

Purpose: To develop international statistical services, to promote the development of national statistics and to make them more readily comparable, and to assist the UN Secretariat and Specialized Agencies in their statistical work.

Membership (24): Armenia, Australia, Belarus, Botswana, Cameroon, China, Colombia, Germany, Honduras, Italy, Japan, Lebanon, Lithuania, Mexico, Morocco, Netherlands, Norway, Oman, Russia, Sudan, Suriname, Togo, United Kingdom, and the United States.

ECONOMIC AND SOCIAL COUNCIL: REGIONAL COMMISSIONS

The primary aim of the five Regional Commissions, which report annually to ECOSOC, is to assist in raising the level of economic activity in their respective regions and to maintain and strengthen the economic relations of the states in each region, both among themselves and with others. The commissions adopt their own procedural rules, including how they select officers. Each commission is headed by an executive secretary, who holds the rank of under secretary of the UN, while their Secretariats are integral parts of the overall United Nations Secretariat.

The commissions are empowered to make recommendations directly to member governments and to Specialized Agencies of the United Nations, but no action can be taken in respect to any state without the agreement of that state.

Economic Commission for Africa (ECA)

Established: April 29, 1958.

Purpose: To "initiate and participate in measures for facilitating concerted action for the economic development of Africa, including its social aspects, with a view to raising the level of economic activity and levels of living in Africa, and for maintaining and strengthening the economic relations of countries and territories of Africa, both among themselves and with other countries of the world."

Headquarters: Addis Ababa, Ethiopia. Subregional Development Centers are located in Tangier, Morocco, for Northern Africa; Kigali, Rwanda, for Eastern Africa; Yaoundé, Cameroon, for Central Africa; Niamey, Niger, for Western Africa; and Lusaka, Zambia, for Southern Africa.

Principal Subsidiary Organs: Conference of African Ministers of Finance, Planning and Economic Development; Sectoral Ministerial Conferences; Technical Preparatory Committee of the Whole; Follow-up Committee on the Conference of Ministers; seven expert-level committees (Women in Development, Development Information, Sustainable Development, Human Development and Civil Society, Industry and Private Sector Development, Natural Resources and Science and Technology, Regional Cooperation and Integration); Secretariat. The Secretariat includes an Office of Policy Planning and Resource Management and six substantive divisions: African Center for Gender and Development, Development Information Services, Development Policy Management, Economic and Social Policy, Sustainable Development, and Trade and Regional Integration.

Executive Secretary: Abdoulie Janneh (Gambia).

Membership (53): Algeria, Angola, Benin, Botswana, Burkina Faso, Burundi, Cameroon, Cape Verde Islands, Central African Republic, Chad, Comoro Islands, Democratic Republic of the Congo, Republic of the Congo, Côte d'Ivoire, Djibouti, Egypt, Equatorial Guinea, Eritrea, Ethiopia, Gabon, Gambia, Ghana, Guinea, Guinea-Bissau, Kenya, Lesotho, Liberia, Libya, Madagascar, Malawi, Mali, Mauritania, Mauritius, Morocco, Mozambique, Namibia, Niger, Nigeria, Rwanda, Sao Tome and Principe, Senegal, Seychelles, Sierra Leone, Somalia, South Africa, Sudan, Swaziland, Tanzania, Togo, Tunisia, Uganda, Zambia, and Zimbabwe. (Switzerland also participates in a consultative capacity.)

Web site: www.uneca.org

Activities. In early 1993 ECA Executive Director Layashi Yaker, a former Algerian trade minister, joined the heads of the Organization of African Unity (OAU) and the African Development Bank in criticizing the industrialized world's handling of the African debt problem, arguing that many of the continent's countries had made "bold efforts to reform and adjust their economies" but were still facing negative resource flows. At the same time, the trio reproached national leaders in Africa for not having pursued regional economic integration with sufficient vigor. In 1994 Yaker told African finance ministers that the role of government in certain economic areas needed to be strengthened rather than weakened, as external donors had insisted. In particular, "public investment" was required in infrastructure and the development of agricultural technology, Yaker argued, while a "close partnership" was needed between governments and other major institutions in defining national economic strategies. Furthermore, in his end-of-the-year analysis of the continent's economic affairs, Yaker renewed his criticism of Western donors for failing to completely honor their commitments under the UN's New Agenda for Development of Africa in the 1990s.

In 1995 Yaker was succeeded as ECA executive secretary by K.Y. Amoako of Ghana, who stressed the need for national governments to provide "a sound and secure environment for private enterprise" in order to attract additional foreign aid. Amoako, a longtime employee of the World Bank, also launched a wide-ranging evaluation and, ultimately, a reorganization of ECA operations to improve efficiency and sharpen the commission's focus. Subsequently, in the spring of 1996, the ECA was given a number of responsibilities in the new $25 billion UN System-wide Special Initiative on Africa, launched by the World Bank, a number of other UN-related agencies, and the OAU. Among other things, the initiative was designed to expand basic education and health care on the continent, promote "better governance," and improve water and food security. The reforms sought to reduce the number of meetings and reports, to provide greater cooperation with other important actors in Africa, to encourage more technical support for members as well as greater interaction with them, to stimulate the formation of strategic partnerships, and to refocus the ECA from nine subprograms covering 21 areas to five core programs and two cross-cutting themes. The five core programs were facilitating economic and social policy analysis, ensuring food security and sustainable development, harnessing information for development, promoting regional cooperation and integration, and strengthening development management. The two themes, permeating all five core programs, were fostering the leadership and empowerment of women and strengthening the ECA's capacities. In 1997 the ECA's five Multinational Programming and Operational Centers (MULPOCs) were reorganized as Subregional Development Centers (SRDCs) with an expanded mission and a planned increase in their share of the organization's personnel and budget. The SRDCs were established to facilitate planning, integration, development, cooperation, and information gathering and dissemination at national and regional levels.

Recent ECA initiatives have included sponsorship of African Development Forums, the first of which convened in Addis Ababa in October 1999. Looking toward the 2001 Third UN Conference on Least Developed Countries (LDCs), in November 2000 Executive Director Amoako proposed a New Global Compact with Africa as a contribution to the ongoing debate over how best to effect debt relief and expand aid to the developing world. In return for increased development assistance, debt relief under a reformed international financial system, and improved market access, "Africa should be able to put in place the necessary political and economic reforms to ensure that their economies take off," Amoako said. He has also advocated, with increasing urgency, a coordinated, expanded program to fight the HIV/AIDS epidemic, noting during a speech to the April 2001 OAU Special Summit on HIV/AIDS and Related Infectious Diseases, held in Abuja, Nigeria, that health is a prerequisite for development and that "without a healthy population, economic growth is going to remain a mirage."

In 2002 the ECA reported that growth in Africa was falling short of expectations, and the commission endorsed the recently proposed New Partnership for Africa's Development (NEPAD). The ECA proposed a "ground up" approach for that initiative, whereby attention would first focus on development at the national level before progressing to the subregional, regional, and continental levels. ECA activity in 2003–2005 included criticism of increased U.S. subsidies for U.S. agricultural products. The commission called for revitalization of negotiations in the World Trade Organization that would provide better access to global markets for African commodities. The ECA also noted that the much-publicized debt relief initiative of recent years had to date helped only a handful of African countries. Meanwhile, in mid-2005 the ECA urged its members to deregulate and otherwise reform their communication sectors in order to participate in the "information economy."

In its publication *Economic Report on Africa 2007: Accelerating Africa's Development through Diversification,* the ECA noted that African countries had an average GDP growth rate of 5.7 percent in 2006. The report also asserted that diversification was the most important factor in sustained economic growth. In June 2007 the ECA, the African Development Bank, and the AU cosponsored a conference that approved the African Charter on Statistics, which aimed to standardize the collection and dissemination of data. The ECA also cooperated with the Central Bank of Nigeria to launch the Africa Finance Cooperation (AFC) in March. The AFC provided funding for projects to support NEPAD and had an initial capitalization of $2 billion.

In March 2008 the ECA conducted a symposium in New York on the commission's support for NEPAD. The symposium called for the ECA to better coordinate UN efforts on behalf of NEPAD. A follow-up meeting was held in September in Addis Ababa. In the *Economic Report on Africa 2008: Africa and the Monterrey Consensus, Tracking Performance and Progress*, the ECA noted that Africa's economic growth rate was 5.7 percent in 2007 and that inflation remained generally low, though some countries, most notably Zimbabwe, had unsustainable levels of inflation. While income growth exceeded 3 percent between 2001 and 2006, the publication noted that growth would have to increase dramatically to close the gap between Africa and the developed countries of the North. The report also highlighted the changing nature of direct foreign investment in Africa, as Asia, and particularly China, had significantly increased investment in the continent over the past five years.

At the second ECA-sponsored annual joint meeting of the African ministers of economy, finance, and planning, held in Addis Ababa in June 2009, the ministers issued a call for swift and innovative action on the part of member states to address the global economic crisis. The *Economic Report on Africa 2009: Developing African Agriculture Through Regional Value Chains* was divided into two main parts. The first section examined recent global economic patterns and trends, while the second part explored methods to enhance regional agricultural markets and supply chains. The report noted that GDP expansion in Africa contracted from 5.7 percent in 2007 to 5.1 percent in 2008 and was expected to fall to 2 percent in 2009. In addition, the ECA identified rising fuel and energy prices as the greatest threats to economic stability on the continent.

Economic Commission for Europe (ECE)

Established: March 28, 1947.

Purpose: To promote economic cooperation, integration, and sustainable development among member countries.

Headquarters: Geneva, Switzerland.

Principal Subsidiary Organs: Committee on Economic Cooperation and Integration; Committee on Sustainable Energy; Committee on Environmental Policy; Committee on Housing and Land Management; Committee on Trade, Industry and Enterprise Development; Conference of European Statisticians; Inland Transport Committee; Timber Committee; Secretariat.

Web site: www.unece.org

Executive Secretary: Ján Kubiš (Slovakia).

Membership (56): Albania, Andorra, Armenia, Austria, Azerbaijan, Belarus, Belgium, Bosnia and Herzegovina, Bulgaria, Canada, Croatia, Cyprus, Czech Republic, Denmark, Estonia, Finland, France, Georgia, Germany, Greece, Hungary, Iceland, Ireland, Israel, Italy, Kazakhstan, Kyrgyzstan, Latvia, Liechtenstein, Lithuania, Luxembourg, Macedonia, Malta, Moldova, Monaco, Montenegro, Netherlands, Norway, Poland, Portugal, Romania, Russia, San Marino, Serbia, Slovakia, Slovenia, Spain, Sweden, Switzerland, Tajikistan, Turkey, Turkmenistan, Ukraine, United Kingdom, United States and Uzbekistan. (Israel's long-standing application for membership, based on its "fundamental economic relations" with the European Community and the United States, was approved by ECOSOC in July 1991. The Holy See also participates in the work of the commission in a consultative capacity.)

Activities. In 1987 the commission created an ad hoc committee to review ECE structures and functions as part of the UN streamlining campaign. At a special session (the first of its kind) held November 9–10, in Geneva, the commission adopted the committee's recommendations for substantial cuts in the number of ECE subsidiary bodies, reduction in documentation levels, and consolidation or elimination of lower priority programs. The major fields of ECE activity were listed as agriculture and timber, economic projections, energy, environment, human settlements, industry, inland transport, science and technology, statistics, and trade.

In 1988 the ECE resisted further cutbacks as it focused on fast-moving political and economic developments in Europe, including the European Community's drive toward a single internal market and reforms in the centrally planned economies of the Eastern bloc. In fact, describing the commission as uniquely organized to serve as a framework for "all-European integration," ECE officials urged that its role be augmented to take advantage of the continuing reduction in East-West political tensions and economic barriers.

Subsequently, the ECE identified assistance to the Central and Eastern European nations undergoing economic transformation as its top priority, specific areas of concentration including trade facilitation, transport, the environment, statistics, and economic analysis. The commission was also formally delegated by the Conference on Security and Cooperation in Europe (subsequently the Organization for Security and Cooperation in Europe—OSCE) to coordinate economic cooperation agreements emanating from that body. The ECE called on Western donors to increase their aid to the Eastern European countries and the new republics from the former Soviet Union, warning that the "shattered economies" in many might require decades to complete a successful shift to free-market activity.

In 1993 ECOSOC ruled that all the former Soviet republics were eligible to join the ECE, the Asian countries in that group also being entitled to dual membership in the Economic and Social Commission for Asia and the Pacific (ESCAP). Subsequently, Armenia, Azerbaijan, Georgia, Kazakhstan, Kyrgyzstan, Tajikistan, Turkmenistan, and Uzbekistan joined the ECE, bringing total membership, which had been 34 three years before, to 55 by mid-1995. The ECE asked for additional UN resources to deal with the increase, noting that nearly half its members belonged to the "transitional" category and that many of them had experienced a deep economic depression following their reorientation.

ECE attention in 1996 continued to focus on the economies of the Central and Eastern European countries, most of which had become "very open" and heavily influenced by trade with Western European countries. Among other things, the commission offered to help those countries seeking membership in the European Union in developing and implementing a "preaccession strategy." The commission also took part in the inception of the Southeast European Cooperative Initiative (SECI), along with other UN agencies and international organizations. The SECI was designed to help southeastern European countries, from Croatia and Moldova to Turkey, cooperate on economic and environmental matters and become part of "European structures." The initiative's first meeting was held in early December 1996. At the same time, in consonance with overall UN reform efforts, the ECE cut back on the size of its staff, redeployed senior officials to the field so they could better understand the needs of the ECE members, and discontinued a number of "obsolete" annual meetings.

The push for reform continued in 1997. At the commission's 50th anniversary session held in late April, the ECE decided to eliminate 60 percent of all programs and 7 of its 14 subsidiary bodies in order to free resources to concentrate on the core areas of economic analysis, the environment, human settlements, development of industry and enterprises, population analysis, sustainable energy, agricultural standards, statistics, timber, trade, and transportation. In a continuation of the reform process, the ECE subsequently decided to bolster its cooperation with other UN entities, such as the UN Conference on Trade and Development (UNCTAD).

In March 1998, in conjunction with ESCAP, the ECE inaugurated a Special Program for the Economies of Central Asia (SPECA), specifically the former Soviet republics of Kazakhstan, Kyrgyzstan, Tajikistan, Turkmenistan, and Uzbekistan. SPECA has focused its attention on such concerns as attracting foreign investment to the region; fostering regional development in transport, including the movement of natural gas and oil; and sustainable use of energy and water.

In May 2000 UN Secretary General Kofi Annan appointed Danuta Hübner of Poland to succeed France's Yves Berthelot as ECE executive secretary, with effect from June. Berthelot was succeeded in 2002 by Brigita Schmögnerová, a former foreign minister and deputy prime minister from Slovakia.

In 2003 the ECE launched a new energy security forum to help prevent insecurity and instability in global energy markets. Other recent activity included expansion of the ECE's convention on environmental matters, considered one of the world's most far-reaching treaties with regard to public access to environmental information; establishment of an external commission to evaluate the ECE's future "role, mandate, and functions in light of the changed European institutional landscape"; and agreement to cooperate more closely with the OSCE. In 2005 the ECE, noting that European output and productivity continued to fall behind the levels achieved by the United States, called for intensified regional cooperation to improve the business climate in Europe. In December the ECE established the Economic Cooperation and Integrated Division (ECID). ECID was tasked to develop strategies to enhance competitiveness through increased innovation.

At its February 2006 meeting the member states proposed a series of initiatives to increase economic cooperation and integration. In response to rising fuel costs, the ECE tasked one of its expert groups to explore energy efficiency, costs, and resources. It also decided to include the issue of energy security in its annual meetings. In November the Committee on Sustainable Energy voted to undertake an intergovernmental dialogue on energy. Meanwhile, the Committee on Trade adopted a new mandate to develop joint programs with other UN bodies and agencies. The ECE also initiated a project to identify and remove nontariff trade barriers between Europe and the countries of Central Asia, in cooperation with SPECA. The joint ECE-SPECA program endorsed 28 projects through 2007. It also conducted two high-level conferences, the first, Focus on Asia, in May in Almaty, Kazakhstan, and the second, Focus on Europe, in November in Berlin, Germany. In addition, in 2007 the ECE signed a memorandum of understanding with the Inter-Parliamentary Assembly of the Eurasian Economic Community to promote deeper integration of the regions.

The ECE's ministerial conference in Belgrade, Serbia, in October 2007 was titled "Environment for Europe" and concentrated on issues such as energy efficiency and sustainability. In February 2008 the ECE launched an initiative to help transitioning economies develop public-private partnerships. A pilot program was scheduled to begin in Moscow in October to better train officials and members of the private sector on issues related to public-private ventures. In August, in response to continuing problems in the United States and European housing markets, the ECE created a new advisory body, the Real Estate Market Advisory Group. The new group was formed to work with the existing Working Party on Land Administration to develop new guidelines for the regulation of real estate markets and financing, as well as develop programs with individual countries to increase housing capacity in an environmentally friendly manner.

Through 2008 the ECE undertook 60 technical cooperation programs with 18 countries in Central and Eastern Europe and Central Asia. These initiatives were designed to enhance economic and technical knowledge and increase the competitiveness of countries in transition. The ECE undertook environmental performance reviews of the legal and official policy frameworks of Kazakhstan, Kyrgyzstan, and Ukraine. In response to recommendations developed in 2006, the ECE finalized a series of internal reforms that were designed to streamline the governing structure of the organization and increase transparency. A central goal of the reforms was to bolster the relationship between the secretariat and the individual member states. Meanwhile, former Slovak foreign minister and former secretary general of the OSCE Ján Kubiš was appointed executive secretary of the ECE in December.

Economic Commission for Latin America and the Caribbean (ECLAC)
Comisión Económica para America Latina y el Caribe (CEPAL)

Established: February 25, 1948, as the Economic Commission for Latin America; current name adopted in 1984.

Purpose: To "initiate and participate in measures for facilitating concerted actions for . . . raising the level of economic activity in Latin America and the Caribbean and for maintaining and strengthening the economic relations of the Latin American and Caribbean countries, both among themselves and with other countries of the world."

Headquarters: Santiago, Chile. Subregional headquarters are located in Mexico City, Mexico, and Port of Spain, Trinidad and Tobago, with offices in Bogota, Columbia, Buenos Aries, Argentina, Brasilia, Brazil, Montevideo, Uruguay, and Washington, D.C., United States.

Principal Subsidiary Organs: Caribbean Development and Cooperation Committee, Central American Economic Cooperation Committee, Committee of High-Level Government Experts from Developing Member Countries for Analysis of the Achievement of the International Development Strategy in the Latin American Region, Conference on the Integration of Women into the Economic and Social Development of Latin America and the Caribbean, Latin American and Caribbean Institute for Economic and Social Planning (*Instituto Latinoamericano y del Caribe de Planificación Económica y Social*—ILPES), Latin American Demographic Center (*Centro Latinoamericano y Caribeño de Demografía*—CELADE), Statistical Conference of the Americas of ECLAC, Secretariat. The Secretariat includes ten divisions: Economic Development, Economic and Social Planning, Gender Development; Sustainable Development and Human Settlements, International Trade and Integration, Natural Resources and Infrastructure, Population and Development, Productive Development and Management, Social Development, and Statistics and Economic Projections.

Web site: www.eclac.org

Executive Secretary: Alicia Bárcena (Chile).

Membership (44): Antigua and Barbuda, Argentina, Bahamas, Barbados, Belize, Bolivia, Brazil, Canada, Chile, Colombia, Costa Rica, Cuba, Dominica, Dominican Republic, Ecuador, El Salvador, France, Germany, Grenada, Guatemala, Guyana, Haiti, Honduras, Italy, Jamaica, Japan, Mexico, Netherlands, Nicaragua, Panama, Paraguay, Peru, Portugal, Republic of Korea, St. Kitts and Nevis, St. Lucia, St. Vincent, Spain, Suriname, Trinidad and Tobago, United Kingdom, United States, Uruguay, and Venezuela.

Associate Members (9): Anguilla, Aruba, British Virgin Islands, Cayman Islands, Montserrat, Netherlands Antilles, Puerto Rico, Turks and Caicos, and United States Virgin Islands.

Activities. Following a decade of political instability and economic crisis, in early 1992 ECLAC Executive Secretary Gert Rosenthal said that the region had reached an economic turning point as reduced inflation, growth in per capita output, and a return of foreign and domestic investment justified a sense of optimism concerning the future. However, he added that high debt remained a severe drain, while the "black mark" of widespread poverty underscored the fact that national economic advances did not always translate into a better standard of living for the poor.

In early 1995 ECLAC reported that the region had just completed its fourth consecutive year of strong economic growth, GDP having risen an estimated 3.7 percent in 1994. However, the commission noted that a greater percentage of the region's population lived in poverty than had in 1980. That trend continued into 1996, commission officials describing the prospects for the elimination of poverty as poor during the April ECLAC session held in San José, Costa Rica. Among other things, ECLAC called upon its members to emphasize privatization of former state-run enterprises in order to attract greater foreign investment. The commission also pledged to conduct regular consultations with national governments to ensure the relevance of ECLAC operations and agreed to undertake a thorough review of its organization and programs in the context of the ongoing reform process being conducted throughout the UN.

At the 27th ECLAC session in Oranjestad, Aruba, in May 1999, the commission approved a work program for 2000–2001 with a dozen subprograms focusing on, for example, competitiveness, production specialization, and the global economy; integration, regionalism, and cooperation; productive, technological, and entrepreneurial development; social development and social equity; environmental and land resource sustainability; and population and development.

The 2002 ECLAC review of economic performance in the region described the past five years as "a lost half-decade" marked by recession, rising inflation, increased poverty, and higher unemployment. Although recovery started in 2003 and the regional economy grew by 5.5 percent in 2004, ECLAC leaders argued that poverty and unemployment "had not budged" and that the wealthy segment of the population was the primary beneficiary of the recent expansion. In 2005 ECLAC and the Caribbean Community (CARICOM) announced a new program of cooperation on economic and social development in the region. Specifically, ECLAC began providing training to officials on issues such as trade negotiations, disaster assessment, and tourism management.

In July 2006 ECLAC predicted that economic growth in the region would exceed 5 percent for the year but urged member states to implement economic safeguards against rising energy prices. ECLAC conferred membership on Japan and associate membership on the Turks and Caicos in 2006 and full membership on the Republic of Korea in 2007. For 2007 ECLAC and Germany launched the program Toward a More Just and Equitable Globalization to cooperate on tax reform, government technology, and renewable energy. The accord covered a three-year period and was designed to support projects in individual countries. The program was undertaken in tandem with ECLAC's 2007–2008 cooperation program with the Swedish International Development Cooperation Agency (SIDA) titled "Enhancing Economic and Social Conditions and Opportunities of Vulnerable Groups in Latin America."

ECLAC estimated that the region's economic growth would be 4.7 percent in 2008, despite rising food and energy prices. Notably, ECLAC found that direct foreign investment in Latin America and the Caribbean exceeded $100 billion for the first time in 2007 and was likely to continue to grow through 2008. In the report *Economic Survey of Latin America and the Caribbean, 2007–2008*, ECLAC urged the nations of the region to consolidate their economic development and take steps to prevent wide fluctuations in economic performance. In cooperation with UNDP and 12 other UN agencies, ECLAC produced *Millennium Development Goals: Progression Toward the Right to Health in Latin America and the Caribbean* in 2008. The report highlighted the accomplishments and challenges of the region as it worked toward the health-related goals of the UN in areas such as malnutrition, access to health care, and poverty reduction programs.

In the publication *Preliminary Overview of the Economies of Latin America and the Caribbean 2008,* ECLAC noted that 2008 was the sixth year of overall GDP growth in the region, with expansion averaging 5 percent between 2003 and 2008. However, the report also warned that growth would fall to less than 2 percent in 2009, with unemployment increasing from a regional average of 7.5 percent to more than 8 percent, although inflation was expected to fall from 8.5 percent to 6 percent. Through 2009 ECLAC produced a regular series of reports on the policies that governments in the region undertook in response to the global economic crisis. Separate research predicted that regional trade would decline by 13 percent through the year. In September 2009 ECLAC hosted the Second Latin American and Caribbean for Negotiations on Climate Change. Held in Santiago, Chile, the session was designed to promote common positions on climate change issues within the region ahead of the December UN climate change conference in Copenhagen.

Economic and Social Commission for Asia and the Pacific (ESCAP)

Established: March 28, 1947, as the Economic Commission for Asia and the Far East; current name adopted in 1974.

Purpose: To facilitate cooperation in economic and social development within the region, to provide technical assistance and serve as an executing agency for operational projects, to conduct research and related activities, to offer advisory services as requested by governments, and to serve as the principal forum for the region within the UN system.

Headquarters: Bangkok, Thailand. A Pacific Operations Center opened in Port Vila, Vanuatu, in 1984, and then relocated to Suva, Fiji in 2005.

Principal Subsidiary Organs: Advisory Committee of Permanent Representatives and Other Representatives Designated by ESCAP Members; Asian and Pacific Center for Agricultural Engineering and Machinery (Beijing, China); Asian and Pacific Training Center for Information and Communication Technology for Development (Incheon, Republic of Korea); Asian and Pacific Center for Transfer of Technology (New Delhi, India); Committee on Emerging Social Issues; Committee on Managing Globalization; Committee on Poverty Reduction; Regional Coordination Center for Research and Development of Coarse Grains, Pulses, Roots, and Tuber Crops in the Humid Tropics of Asia and the Pacific (Bogor, Indonesia); Special Body on Least Developed and Landlocked Developing Countries; Special Body on Pacific Island Developing Countries; Statistical Institute for Asia and the Pacific (Chiba, Japan); Secretariat. The Secretariat includes an Office of the Executive Secretary, an Office of the Deputy Executive Secretary, the United Nations Information Services, the Pacific Operations Center, and nine divisions, two of them largely administrative (Program Management and Administration) and the other seven substantive: Emerging Social Issues; Environment and Sustainable Development; Information, Communication, and Space Technology; Poverty and Development; Statistics; Trade and Investment; and Transport and Tourism.

Executive Secretary: Noeleen Heyzer (Singapore).

Web site: www.unescap.org

Membership (53): Afghanistan, Armenia, Australia, Azerbaijan, Bangladesh, Bhutan, Brunei, Cambodia, China, Fiji, France, Georgia, India, Indonesia, Iran, Japan, Kazakhstan, Kiribati, Republic of Korea, Democratic People's Republic of Korea, Kyrgyzstan, Laos, Malaysia, Maldives, Marshall Islands, Federated States of Micronesia, Mongolia, Myanmar, Nauru, Nepal, Netherlands, New Zealand, Pakistan, Palau, Papua New Guinea, Philippines, Russia, Samoa, Singapore, Solomon Islands, Sri Lanka, Tajikistan, Thailand, Timor-Leste, Tonga, Turkey, Turkmenistan, Tuvalu, United Kingdom, United States, Uzbekistan, Vanuatu, and Vietnam.

Associate Members (9): American Samoa, Commonwealth of the Northern Mariana Islands, Cook Islands, French Polynesia, Guam, Hong Kong, Macao, New Caledonia, and Niue. Switzerland participates in a consultative capacity.

Activities. ESCAP is the largest of the five ECOSOC Regional Commissions, with its member countries encompassing about 60 percent of the world's population. It operates with a general staff of nearly 400, as well as 200 professionals, advisers, and project personnel. The various divisions of the Secretariat (see Principal Subsidiary Organs) carry out the projects and programs formulated by the organization's policymaking committees. To strengthen its role in helping South Pacific island nations and territories, ESCAP inaugurated a Pacific Operations Center in Vanuatu in 1984. In 1993 ESCAP signed an agreement with the Asian Development Bank (ADB) that delineates 11 areas of common interest in which closer cooperation will be pursued. The two organizations agreed to prepare joint studies, develop and carry out projects together, and conduct ESCAP/ADB workshops and conferences. In addition, ESCAP remains a source of highly respected economic analyses, including its annual *Economic and Social Survey of Asia and the Pacific.*

A continuing area of concern for ESCAP in 1994 was the "wide gap" between economic progress in the region and social development. Although many members were to be congratulated for fostering dynamic economic growth, ESCAP officials said, governments needed to give greater emphasis to the integration of "social concerns" in development policies. In addition, staff members in 1995 reported that many South Pacific countries were experiencing a reduction in growth rates. The ESCAP officials criticized governments in that region for not using their resources wisely and for making poor investments with aid from donor countries and international organizations. ESCAP activity in 1996 included administration of a new program, financed by Australia, to encourage cooperation between the region's island nations and the expanding Asian economies. The commission also cautioned the island states that they would face declining living standards unless population growth was reduced. In October 1996 various international agencies, including ESCAP, inaugurated more than 45 initiatives aimed at building cooperation between the private and public sectors. Two of the most prominent initiatives concerned developing Asian infrastructure—the New Delhi Action Plan on Infrastructure (1997–2006) and the Asian Infrastructure Development Alliance.

ESCAP celebrated its 50th anniversary on March 28, 1997, by holding a three-day symposium at which participants praised the achievements of the region but also noted that some 700–800 million inhabitants continued to live in poverty. At the 53rd commission session, held at the end of April, the delegates agreed to organization reforms, particularly with regard to the committee and divisional structure.

The central topic of the 1998 commission session was the financial crisis impacting several of its members. ESCAP called for greater regional economic integration to prevent future crises and to help foster economic development. The continuing economic turbulence was also discussed at the commission's 1999 session, participants calling for greater social spending on the part of national governments.

ESCAP held its 2001 session under the leadership of Executive Secretary Kim Hak-Su of South Korea, who had succeeded Adrianus Mooy of Indonesia in July 2000. The main topic of the meeting concerned balanced development for urban and rural areas and regions. Subsequent sessions focused on the role of health (particularly the impact of HIV/AIDS) in development, the need to foster "secondary crops" for poor farmers in the region, and the pervasive negative effect of corruption and poor governance on the economies of Pacific island nations. In 2005 ESCAP proposed the establishment of an Asian Investment Bank to, among other things, improve regional financial services. The commission also called for the provision of soft loans for infrastructure projects in Southeast Asia. In addition, in December 2005 ESCAP announced the creation of a $12.5 million regional trust fund to develop early warning systems for tsunamis. ESCAP also sponsored the Intergovernmental Agreement on the Asian Highway Network, which called for the creation of a highway system to link more than 140,000 kilometers of existing roadways in 32 countries.

For the first time in its history, in 2006 ESCAP initiated a work program that concentrated solely on Pacific issues, including efforts to integrate urban and regional planning based on the recommendations of the 2004 Pacific Urban Agenda. The agenda called for the reduction of urban poor by half by 2015 and improvements in housing and land development.

In conjunction with humanitarian and labor organizations, in September 2008 ESCAP held a series of training sessions to promote better data collection as one means to reduce child labor. Also in 2008 ESCAP created a Transportation Committee to facilitate multinational cooperation on transport networks and capabilities. Following huge earthquakes in China, ESCAP announced a joint program to help China and other East Asian states reduce vulnerabilities to natural disasters. In October ESCAP and the Republic of Korea announced a joint $200-million, five-year initiative to promote low-carbon and environmentally friendly economic growth as part of the broader East Asia Climate Partnership created by the Republic of Korea.

In 2009 ESCAP began efforts to create three more regional offices, one each for East and Northeast Asia, North and Central Asia, and South and Southwest Asia. ESCAP's publication, *Economic and Social Survey of Asia and the Pacific 2009: Addressing Triple Threats to Development*, identified the global economic recession, volatility in commodities markets, and climate change as the three main obstacles to continued growth and stability. The report also highlighted the continuing disparity in economic growth rates among developed and developing states. For instance, GDP growth among developing states was 5.8 percent, while GDP among developed countries was –0.4 percent. In November ESCAP held the first Asia-Pacific Trade and Investment Week, which included conferences, summits, and workshops designed to promote balanced trade.

Economic and Social Commission for Western Asia (ESCWA)

Established: August 9, 1973, as the Economic Commission for Western Asia; current name adopted in 1985.

Purpose: To "initiate and participate in measures for facilitating concerted action for the economic reconstruction and development of Western Asia, for raising the level of economic activity in Western Asia, and for maintaining and strengthening the economic relations of the countries of that area, both among themselves and with other countries of the world."

Headquarters: Beirut, Lebanon.

Principal Subsidiary Organs: Preparatory Committee; Advisory Committee; seven specialized committees (Energy, Liberalization of Foreign Trade and Economic Globalization, Social Development, Statistics, Transport, Water Resources, Women); Secretariat. The Secretariat includes seven divisions: Administrative Services; Program Planning and Technical Cooperation; Economic Analysis, Information and Communication Technology; Globalization and Regional Integration; Social Development; and Sustainable Development and Productivity. There are also a Statistics Coordination Unit and an ESCWA Center for Women.

Web site: www.escwa.un.org

Executive Secretary: Bader Al-Dafa (Qatar).

Membership (14): Bahrain, Egypt, Iraq, Jordan, Kuwait, Lebanon, Oman, Palestine, Qatar, Saudi Arabia, Sudan, Syria, United Arab Emirates, and Yemen.

Activities. The most important procedural event in the commission's history was the 1977 decision to grant full membership to the Palestine Liberation Organization (PLO)—the first nonstate organization to achieve such standing in a UN agency—despite a fear on the part of some UN members that the PLO would use its membership to gain full membership in the General Assembly. Israeli-Palestinian agreements, beginning with the 1993 Declaration of Principles, led to the redesignation of the PLO membership as, simply, Palestine, even though no de jure Palestinian state existed.

In view of growing regional economic cooperation throughout the world, the commission at the 1992 Ministerial Session urged members to adopt policies designed to promote inter-Arab trade and the eventual creation of an Arab common market. A decision was postponed on the designation of a new permanent headquarters for the commission, which had moved to Amman, Jordan, from Baghdad, Iraq, during the Gulf crisis. It was subsequently decided to move the headquarters to Beirut, Lebanon; the relocation was completed in early 1998.

During the mid-1990s the ESCWA reorganized its work agenda, reducing the number of operational programs from 15 to 5: Natural Resources and Environmental Management, Improvement of the Quality of Life, Economic Development and Global Changes, Coordination of Policies and Harmonization of Norms and Regulations for Sectoral Development, and Coordination and Harmonization of Statistics and Information Development.

In 1997 ECOSOC established a Technical Committee on Liberalization of Foreign Trade and Globalization in Countries of the ESCWA Region in order to observe movement toward free trade in other parts of the world and advise members on its benefits.

At its 19th session, held in Beirut May 5–8, 1997, the ESCWA discussed a proposed 1998–2001 medium-term plan that stressed sustainable development and cooperation within the region, reported on the development of databases on population and gender issues, and followed up on actions taken at the previous session regarding new committees on energy and water resources. The 1999 biennial session coincided with the commission's 25th anniversary. The May 8–11, 2000, ministerial meeting focused on the topic of Regional Integration and Globalization. In November 2000 Mervat M. Tallawy of Egypt succeeded Hazem El Beblawi, also of Egypt, as executive secretary.

In 2003 Tallawy lamented the fact that UN negotiations had failed to prevent the U.S./UK-led invasion of Iraq and called for the UN to take a greater role than initially envisioned in the reconstruction of Iraq following the war. For its part, the ESCWA pledged to concentrate on reviving civil society in Iraq, noting that "turmoil and anxiety" in the region had diverted resources away from development. The 2005 ESCWA session further addressed the question of "peace and security" and determined that too much money had been spent on armaments at the expense of employment and other social programs. The ESCWA also announced plans for its own restructuring to emphasize local community development and cooperation with the private sector. The commission continued to express deep concern over the repercussions of Israeli "occupation" on the living conditions of Palestinians. The ESCWA released a report in June 2005, *Social and Economic Situation of Palestinian Women, 1990–2004,* that specifically criticized Israel for the erosion of living standards among women in the Palestinian territories. In July 2006 the ESCWA protested the Israeli incursion into Lebanon, including attacks on UN facilities. The ESCWA's Sustainable Management of the Environment Team increased its efforts to support sustainable development through 2007. The team worked with a number of ESCWA members to create national sustainable development strategies and to harmonize environmental regulations across borders. ESCWA reported that foreign direct investment in the region exceeded $62 billion, the highest figure in the area's history. For 2007, ESCWA estimated that economic growth for Western Asia would be 5.4 percent.

On January 16, 2008, ESCWA held the first meetings of its newly formed technical committee, a body created to bolster integration and coordination among the national representatives of ESCWA. In July ESCWA, Germany and the government of Iraq sponsored a series of meetings and training seminars for Iraqi officials on water-dispute resolution tactics and strategies. As part of its ongoing effort to enhance foreign trade and direct investment, ESCWA conducted the "Third Forum on Arab Business Community and the WTO Agreements," in Beirut, Lebanon. The forum provided a means for ESCWA to discuss the Doha round of trade negotiations with senior political and business leaders. Sudan joined ESCWA on August 15, becoming the 14th member of the group.

ECSWA convened a conference on land management and sustainable development in March 2009 as a means to identify and promote best practices for rural development. In addition to regional leaders and ministers, the event brought together experts from organizations such as the UN University, the UN Development Program, and the Food and Agriculture Organization. In July ECSWA launched a year-long celebration of the 35th anniversary of the creation of the organization. Meanwhile, research by ECSWA found that foreign direct investment into the region had declined by 6.3 percent in 2008, mainly as the result of the global economic crisis and falling energy prices. Saudi Arabia, the United Arab Emirates, and Egypt were the main recipients of foreign investment and accounted for 76 percent of the total flows into the region.

TRUSTEESHIP COUNCIL

Web site: www.un.org/en/mainbodies/trusteeship/

Membership (5): *Permanent Members of the Security Council:* China, France, Russia, United Kingdom, and United States. China, theretofore not an active participant in Trusteeship affairs, assumed its seat at the May 1989 session.

Structure. Under the UN Charter the membership of the Trusteeship Council includes (1) those UN member states administering Trust Territories, (2) those permanent members of the Security Council that do not administer Trust Territories, and (3) enough other members elected by the General Assembly for three-year terms to ensure that the membership of the council is equally divided between administering and nonadministering members. These specifications became increasingly difficult to meet as the number of Trust Territories dwindled. In consequence, no members have been elected to the council since 1965. (The Trusteeship Council formally suspended its operations on November 1, 1994. See below for details.)

Activities. The Trusteeship Council is the organ principally responsible for the supervision of territories placed under the International Trusteeship System. Originally embracing 11 territories that had been either League of Nations mandates or possessions of states defeated in World War II, the system was explicitly designed to promote advancement toward self-government or political independence. By 1976 ten of the former Trust Territories (British Togoland, French Togoland, British Cameroons, French Cameroons, Ruanda-Urundi, Somaliland, Tanganyika, Nauru, northern New Guinea, and Western Samoa) had become independent, either as sovereign states or through division or merger with neighboring states in accordance with the wishes of the inhabitants.

The last Trust Territory was the U.S.-administered Trust Territory of the Pacific Islands, which had undergone several administrative reorganizations, the most recent yielding four groupings: the Northern Mariana Islands, the Federated States of Micronesia, the Marshall Islands, and Palau. In 1975 the Northern Mariana Islands voted for commonwealth status in political union with the United States. In 1983 the Federated States of Micronesia and the Marshall Islands approved "compacts of free association" providing for internal sovereignty combined with continued U.S. economic aid and control of defense. A similar compact was endorsed by majorities in several plebiscites in Palau, but the Palauan Supreme Court ruled in 1986 that a collateral revision of the Palauan constitution to permit facilities for nuclear-armed U.S. forces had to first secure 75 percent approval.

In addition to the Palauan question, termination of the territory's trust status remained clouded until the late 1980s by opposition from the former Soviet Union, then a permanent member of both the Trusteeship and Security Council. Since the Trust Territory of the Pacific Islands, unlike other trust territories, was designated a "strategic area" at its inception, a supervisory role, according to the UN Charter, was "exercised" by the Security Council, implying that its approval was required for termination of the trusteeship.

At its 53rd session, held May 12–June 30, 1986, the Trusteeship Council endorsed by a three-to-one vote the position that the United States had satisfactorily discharged its obligations and that it was appropriate to terminate the trusteeship. The majority argued that UN missions sent to observe the plebiscites had concluded that the results constituted a free and fair expression of the wishes of the people. In casting its negative vote, the Soviet Union was highly critical of U.S. policy regarding economic development and potential military use of the territory. Subsequently, Washington declared the compacts with the Marshall Islands and the Federated States to be in effect from October 21 and November 3, 1986, respectively, with inhabitants of the Commonwealth of the Northern Mariana Islands acquiring U.S. citizenship on the latter date. Thus, Palau remained—under U.S. law—the one remaining component of the Trust Territory.

Amid growing violence and political turmoil, referendums were held in Palau in August 1987 that led the Palauan government to declare the constitutional issue resolved and the compact approved. However, in April 1988 the Supreme Court of Palau declared the voting invalid. Subsequently, at its May meeting the Trusteeship Council recommended by a vote of three to one that the compact be approved as soon as possible, with disagreements of interpretation to be left to bilateral Palau-U.S. negotiations. The dissenting vote was cast by the Soviet Union, which continued to charge the United States with "anticharter" activity in the handling of the Trust Territory.

Similar sentiments were expressed at the May 1989 council meeting, which was most noteworthy for the return of Chinese representatives. China joined France, the United Kingdom, and the United States in endorsing the compact as the appropriate vehicle for resolution of Palau's political status. The council's report to the Security Council noted that a recent mission to Palau had concluded that "an overwhelming majority" of its citizens endorsed the compact and that criticism of U.S. spending on economic and social development by some islanders "reflected tactical considerations" aimed at "obtaining additional concessions." The United States subsequently pledged further aid to Palau, but a seventh vote on the compact, held in February 1990, again failed to achieve 75 percent approval.

In light of the continuing diminution of East-West tension, the Soviet Union in late 1990 withdrew its objection to the formal termination of UN involvement in those trusteeship areas whose permanent political status had been resolved. Consequently, upon the recommendation of all five Trusteeship Council members, the Security Council on December 22 voted to terminate the Trusteeship Agreements for the Marshall Islands, the Federated States of Micronesia, and the Northern Mariana Islands. The vote was reportedly facilitated by a U.S. pledge not to expand its military presence in the region.

The Trusteeship Council met in May 1991 to discuss the Palauan situation, which remained unresolved despite hopes that changes in U.S. policy in the region would break the long-standing "logjam." During the May 1992 meeting (at which Russia assumed the former USSR seat) U.S. officials said that Palau was facing its last chance to approve the proposed compact of free association. In November a national referendum approved an amendment to the Palauan constitution to permit ratification of the compact by a simple majority. Consequently, the eighth (and final) vote on the issue was held November 9, 1993, with the compact receiving a 68 percent endorsement.

Palauan and U.S. officials subsequently announced the implementation of the compact effective October 1, 1994, after all possible legal challenges to the final vote had been exhausted. Therefore, on November 1 the Trusteeship Council formally suspended its operations, and on November 10 the Security Council declared that the applicability of the Trusteeship Agreement regarding Palau had been terminated. However, the Trusteeship Council was not dissolved, an action that would have required a change in the UN Charter. Instead, the council remained in existence with the proviso that it would henceforth meet "only on an extraordinary basis, as the need arises." Also in 1994, a proposal was submitted for the Trusteeship Council to have oversight of the areas of the world outside of national boundaries, including the majority of the world's oceans. However, no action was taken.

In 1997 Secretary General Kofi Annan proposed that the UN consider reconstituting the council as a forum for UN members to "exercise their collective trusteeship for the integrity of the global environment and common areas such as oceans, atmosphere and outer space." Later, in 2005, he proposed the abolition of the council. Neither proposal was acted upon. Options continue to be discussed as part of an overall review of the UN Charter.

INTERNATIONAL COURT OF JUSTICE (ICJ)

Established: By statute signed as an integral part of the United Nations Charter in San Francisco, United States, June 26, 1945, effective October 24, 1945.

Purpose: To adjudicate disputes referred by member states and to serve as the principal judicial organ of the United Nations; to provide advisory opinions on any legal question requested of it by the General Assembly, Security Council, or other organs of the United Nations and Specialized Agencies that have been authorized by the General Assembly to make such requests.

Headquarters: The Hague, Netherlands.

Web site: www.icj-cij.org

Composition: 15 judges, elected by the UN General Assembly and Security Council for terms ending on February 5 of the years indicated:

Hishashi Owada (President)	Japan	2012
Peter Tomka (Vice President)	Slovakia	2012
Awn Shawkat al-Khasawneh	Jordan	2018
Ronny Abraham	France	2018
Mohamed Bennouna	Morocco	2015
Thomas Buergenthal	United States	2015
Christopher Greenwood	United Kingdom	2018
Kenneth Keith	New Zealand	2015
Abdul G. Koroma	Sierra Leone	2012
Bernado Sepúlveda Amor	Mexico	2015
Shi Jiuyong	China	2012
Bruno Simma	Germany	2012
Leonid Skotnikov	Russia	2015
Antonio Augusto Cançado Trindade	Brazil	2018
Abdulqawi Yusuf	Somalia	2018

Parties to the Statute (192): All members of the United Nations (see Appendix C).

Official Languages: English, French.

Origin and development. The International Court of Justice (ICJ), often called the World Court, is the direct descendant of the Permanent Court of International Justice (PCIJ). Created in 1920 under the Covenant of the League of Nations, the PCIJ, which between 1922 and 1938 had 79 cases referred to it by states and 28 by the League Council, was dissolved on April 19, 1946, along with the other organs of the league.

The Statute of the International Court of Justice was adopted at the San Francisco Conference in June 1945 as an integral part of the UN Charter and, as such, entered into force with the charter on October 24, 1945. Except for a few essentially formal changes, the statute is identical to that of the PCIJ. All members of the UN are automatically parties to the statute. States that are not UN members are entitled to become parties to the statute (under conditions to be determined in each case by the General Assembly upon the recommendation of the Security Council) or to appear before the court without being a party to the statute (under conditions to be laid down by the Security Council). Only states may be parties to cases before the court, whose jurisdiction extends to all cases that the parties refer to it and all matters specifically provided for in the UN Charter or other existing treaties. In the event of a dispute as to whether the court has jurisdiction, the matter is settled by a decision of the court itself. The General Assembly or the Security Council may request the ICJ to give an advisory opinion on any legal question; other UN organs or Specialized Agencies, if authorized by the General Assembly, may request advisory opinions on legal questions arising within the scope of their activities.

States adhering to the statute are not required to submit disputes to the court, whose jurisdiction in a contentious case depends upon the consent of the disputing states. In accordance with Article 36 of the statute, states may declare that they recognize as compulsory, in relation to any other country accepting the same obligation, the jurisdiction of the court in all legal disputes concerning (1) the interpretation of a treaty; (2) any question of international law; (3) the existence of any fact which, if established, would constitute a breach of an international obligation; and (4) the nature or extent of the reparation to be made for the breach of such an obligation. However, declarations under Article 36 have often been qualified by conditions relating, for example, to reciprocity, the duration of the obligation, or the nature of the dispute. The United States, in accepting the court's compulsory jurisdiction in 1946, excluded matters of domestic jurisdiction "as determined by the United States of America." This exception, often called the Connally Amendment, has been something of a model for other states.

Structure. The ICJ consists of 15 judges elected for renewable nine-year terms by separate majority votes of the UN General Assembly and the Security Council, one-third of the judges being elected every three years. Candidates are nominated by national groups in the Permanent Court of Arbitration (PCA) and national groups appointed by non-PCA UN members, with the General Assembly and Security Council assessing the nominees according to the qualifications required for appointment to the highest judicial offices of their respective states. Due consideration is also given to ensuring that the principal legal systems of the world are represented. No two judges may be nationals of the same state, and no judge may exercise any political or administrative function or engage in any other occupation of a professional nature while serving on the ICJ. As a protection against political pressure, no judge can be dismissed unless, in the unanimous opinion of the other judges, he or she has ceased to fulfill the required conditions for service. If there are no judges of their nationality on the court, the parties to a case are entitled to choose ad hoc or national judges to sit for that particular case. Such judges take part in the decision on terms of complete equality with the other judges.

The procedural rules of the ICJ have been adopted without substantial change from those of the PCIJ, the court itself electing a president and a vice president from among its members for three-year terms. In accordance with Article 38 of the statute, the court in deciding cases applies (1) international treaties and conventions; (2) international custom; (3) the general principles of law "recognized by civilized nations"; and (4) judicial decisions and the teachings of the most highly qualified publicists, as a subsidiary means of determining the rules of law. All questions are decided by a majority of the judges present, with nine judges constituting a quorum. In the event of a tie vote, the president of the court may cast a second, deciding vote.

The Registry of the Court is headed by a registrar (currently Philippe Couvreur of Belgium, reelected for another seven-year term on February 8, 2007), who maintains the list of cases submitted to the court and is the normal channel to and from the court.

Activities. From 1946 through 2009 the ICJ heard 144 cases, issued 94 judgments, and rendered 40 advisory opinions. Among the most celebrated of the advisory opinions was its determination in July 1962 that the expenses of the UN Operation in the Congo and the UN Emergency Force in the Middle East were "expenses of the Organization" within the meaning of Article 17 of the UN Charter, which stipulates that such expenses "shall be borne by the members as apportioned by the General Assembly."

Of special importance were court actions with respect to South Africa's administration of the former League of Nations mandate of South West Africa (Namibia) and the extension of apartheid to that territory. In an advisory opinion rendered in 1950, the court held that South Africa's administration was subject to supervision and control by the UN General Assembly; in 1962 it declared itself competent to adjudicate a formal complaint against South Africa that had been instituted by Ethiopia and Liberia. In July 1966, however, the court by an 8–7 vote dismissed the Ethiopian and Liberian complaints on the ground that those two states had not established "any legal right or interest appertaining to them in the subject matter of their claims." Because of this decision, confidence in the ICJ decreased, especially among African states.

In 1970 the ICJ again rendered an advisory opinion concerning Namibia. This opinion stated that South Africa was obligated to withdraw its administration from the territory immediately, that members of the UN were under an obligation to recognize the illegality of the South African presence and the invalidity of any actions taken by South Africa on behalf of Namibia, and that members were to refrain from any dealings with South Africa that might imply recognition of the legality of its presence there. States not belonging to the UN were also requested to follow these recommendations.

In November 1979 the United States, claiming violation of several international treaties and conventions, asked the court to order Iran to release the 53 U.S. hostages who were being held in the U.S. Embassy in Tehran; in December the court unanimously upheld the U.S. complaint. In May 1980 the court issued its formal holdings in the case, which ordered Iran to release all of the hostages immediately and warned its government not to put them on trial; the court also held that Iran was liable to pay reparations for its actions. However, in April 1981, following the release of the hostages, the United States requested that the court dismiss its claim against Iran for payment of damages and a special Iran-United States Claims Tribunal was set up to attempt to resolve approximately 3,000 cases from U.S. companies and individuals filing for damages from Iran's government (see article on Permanent Court of Arbitration). In May 1992 the tribunal ruled that Iran was entitled to compensation for nonmilitary assets frozen in the United States following the embassy seizure, although the amount of reimbursement was yet to be determined.

In November 1992 Iran initiated another suit against the United States for damages caused by the U.S. Navy when it attacked Iranian oil platforms in the Persian Gulf during 1987–1988. Iran claimed that such action violated the 1955 Iran-United States Treaty of Amity, Economic Relations, and Consular Rights. Despite U.S. objections, the court ruled that it had jurisdiction over the matter. In 1997 the United States submitted a counterclaim stating that Iran, by attacking shipping in the Persian Gulf during its war with Iraq, had "breached its obligations to the United States" under the treaty in question. The United States asked the court to grant it restitution for the resultant damages. On November 6, 2003, the court ruled that the U.S. action had not been justified but that both countries' requests for reparations were invalid because the treaty was inapplicable.

In October 1984 the court ruled on a dispute between the United States and Canada over possession of some 30,000 square nautical miles of the Gulf of Maine southeast of New England and Newfoundland. The ruling awarded about two-thirds of the area in question to the United States and the remainder to Canada. The court also settled a long-standing border dispute between Mali and Burkina Faso with a decision in December 1986 that divided the contested area into roughly equal parts.

One of the court's most publicized cases in the 1980s involved a suit brought by Nicaragua challenging U.S. involvement in the mining of its harbors. During preliminary hearings, begun in April 1984, Nicaragua charged that the action was a violation of international law and asked for reparations. The United States sought, unsuccessfully, to have the case dismissed on the ground that Nicaragua's failure to submit an instrument of ratification of the court's statutes prevented it from appearing before the court. In May the ICJ rendered an interim decision that directed the defendant to cease and refrain from mining operations and to respect Nicaraguan sovereignty. In November the court ruled that it had a right to hear the case, but in early 1985 Washington, anticipating an adverse ruling, stated it would not participate in further proceedings on the ground that it was a political issue, over which the court lacked jurisdiction. In June 1986, citing numerous military and paramilitary activities, the court ruled the United States had breached international law by using force to violate Nicaragua's sovereignty. In a series of 16 rulings, each approved by a substantial majority, the court directed the United States to cease the activities cited and to pay reparations to Nicaragua. The judgment was nonenforceable, however, as the United States had previously informed the court that it would not submit to ICJ jurisdiction regarding conflicts in Central America.

In 1986 Nicaragua also filed suit against Honduras and Costa Rica for frontier incidents and attacks allegedly organized by anti-Sandinista forces. Honduras announced it did not consent to the court's jurisdiction in the matter, although in February 1987 it agreed to refer to the ICJ a dispute with El Salvador involving both land border demarcation and maritime jurisdiction. Later in the year, as negotiations on a proposed Central American peace plan proceeded, Nicaragua dropped the suit against Costa Rica and "postponed" its action against Honduras. Deliberations in the latter suit resumed in late 1988 but were again suspended as part of the peace plan negotiated by the presidents of five Central American nations in late 1989.

In April 1988, at the request of the General Assembly, the court was brought into the dispute between the UN and the United States over U.S. attempts to close the UN observer mission of the Palestine Liberation Organization (PLO). The United States had ordered the closing because recent legislation classified the PLO as a "terrorist" organization, but the General Assembly strongly denounced the U.S. action as a violation of the 1947 "host country" treaty. The court ruled that the United States must submit the issue to binding international arbitration, although it was unclear whether the United States would accept the decision. However, the issue became moot later in the year when a U.S. district court declared that the government had no authority to close the mission and the U.S. Justice Department announced it would not appeal that decision.

The likelihood of an expansion in the court's calendar grew in early 1989 when the Soviet Union announced its recognition of ICJ jurisdiction over "interpretation and application" of five international human rights agreements. Washington also appeared to be supporting a broader mandate for the court after several years of aloofness triggered by the 1986 ruling on the Nicaraguan suit. Thus, in August the two superpowers agreed to give the ICJ jurisdiction in resolving disputes stemming from the interpretation of seven treaties on the extradition and prosecution of terrorists and drug traffickers.

Washington underscored its new attitude in 1989 by permitting the ICJ to rule on a long-standing investment dispute with Italy and by agreeing to defend itself in a suit filed by Iran for financial compensation for those killed when an Iranian jetliner was shot down by the USS *Vincennes* over the Persian Gulf in July 1988 (see article on the International Civil Aviation Organization). UN Secretary General Pérez de Cuéllar strongly welcomed the heightened respect being accorded to the ICJ, describing the court as a "crucial component of the UN's recent attempt to prove its ability to function as the guardian of world security." To further the ICJ's role in the peaceful settlement of bilateral disputes, Pérez de Cuéllar announced late in the year that a trust fund would be established to help pay the legal expenses of poorer nations appearing before the court.

The most publicized ICJ case in the first half of 1992 involved Libya's request for the court to block the U.S.-UK attempt to force the extradition of two Libyans for trial in connection with the 1988 bombing of a Pan Am airliner over Scotland. Libya asked the court to declare sanctions imposed by the Security Council in the matter to be illegal, but the court ruled 11 to 5 that it did not have the authority to block compliance with the council's decision. Libya ultimately agreed to have the accused tried under Scottish law at a court in the Netherlands, but the ICJ still had before it jurisdictional questions relating to the 1971 Montreal Convention for the Suppression of Unlawful Acts against the Safety of Civil Aviation. In September 2003, however, improved relations led the three parties to request that the proceedings be discontinued, and the ICJ obliged.

In April 1993, acting on a request from Bosnia and Herzegovina, the court ordered the Federal Republic of Yugoslavia to "take all measures within its power to prevent the commission of genocide" against the Bosnian Muslim community. The court was brought further into the Balkan dispute in August when Bosnia and Herzegovina asked it to overturn the Security Council arms embargo and to declare that any partitioning of Bosnia would be illegal. Although the court rejected both requests in September, it demanded the "immediate and effective" implementation of its April genocide order, the decision being described as an "implicit rebuke" to Yugoslavia and a political boost to the Bosnian cause.

In February 1994 the ICJ ruled in favor of Chad in its long-standing dispute over the border territory known as the Aozou Strip (see articles on Chad and Libya). Other subsequent ICJ activity included the formation of a seven-member Chamber of Environmental Matters to assist in what was expected to be a growing caseload in that area. The court also urged that greater use be made of its ability to offer "advisory opinions" as part of the UN's overall preventative diplomacy strategy.

Cases related to nuclear weapons dominated the ICJ calendar in late 1995, beginning with a request from New Zealand (supported by a number of smaller island states) for a court injunction against the resumption of French nuclear testing in the South Pacific. The ICJ declined the request, ruling that its authority from a 1973 case extended only to above-ground nuclear tests. The court also heard about three weeks of widely publicized testimony in November 1995 regarding an advisory opinion sought by the General Assembly on whether the threat or use of nuclear weapons was a violation of international law. In July 1996 the ICJ ruled by an 8–7 vote that "generally" the use of such weapons would be contrary to international law, although the court equivocated on their use in self-defense. In the face of "legal uncertainty" the ICJ urged the international community to resolve the question permanently through disarmament negotiations.

On September 25, 1997, the court issued its ruling on a dispute between Hungary and Slovakia over the construction of two dams on the Danube River, finding that both were guilty of breaching a treaty originally signed in 1977, Hungary for failing to build one dam and Slovakia for diverting flow of the Danube through another it built in

1992. In early 1998 Hungary and Slovakia reached agreement on where a new dam on the Danube was to be built in accordance with the decision, but Budapest subsequently backed away from the agreement, stating that an assessment of the project's impact on the environment had to be completed before the Hungarian legislature could consider the accord. Consequently, in September 1998 Slovakia filed a request for an additional judgment. Bilateral negotiations subsequently resumed, and the court has therefore not ruled on the case.

In the first, although indirect, death penalty case before the ICJ, in 1999 Germany accused the United States of violating international legal obligations when it failed to inform two German citizens, Walter and Karl LaGrand, of their right to contact the German consulate following their U.S. arrest. Both defendants were ultimately convicted of murder and executed without the United States having provided, according to Germany, "effective review of and remedies for criminal convictions impaired by a violation of the rights under Article 36" of the Vienna Convention on Consular Relations. The United States acknowledged the failure of "competent authorities" to adhere to the convention, and in June 2001 the court ruled for Germany. In a similar case, *Mexico v. United States,* in 2004 the court ruled in favor of Mexico, which in 2003 had charged the United States with a failure to avail some 50 Mexican nationals of their consular rights. The court proposed as a remedy that the United States undertake a "review and reconsideration" of the convictions and sentences.

In October 1999 the Democratic Republic of the Congo (DRC) filed a case against Uganda for invasion, human rights violations, and the plunder of natural resources. In a July 2000 interim ruling, the court urged Uganda to withdraw its troops in accordance with a June UN resolution that had called for the removal of all foreign troops from the country. A final ruling had not been made as of mid-2007. In 1998 Guinea had filed a case against the DRC on behalf of an expatriate businessman who had been imprisoned, stripped of his assets, and expelled; that case also remained open. Earlier in the year, the court ruled that it did not have jurisdiction in a case brought by the DRC against Rwanda in 2002.

Many of the court's most recent judgments have concerned territorial disputes. In December 1999 the court ruled in Botswana's favor and against Namibia in a case involving competing claims to Kasikili (Sedudu) Island in the Chobe River. A boundary dispute between Bahrain and Qatar was concluded in March 2001, when the judges awarded the Huwar Islands and adjacent shoals to Bahrain and the contested Zubarah strip to Qatar. In October 2002 the court addressed issues of land and maritime boundaries between Cameroon and Nigeria; although neither disputant won a complete victory, the complex decision largely favored Cameroon, which was awarded oil-rich Bakassi Peninsula. Two months later the court ruled that Malaysia, not Indonesia, held sovereignty over Pulau Ligitan and Pulau Sipadan in the Celebes Sea. In July 2005 the court settled a frontier dispute between Benin and Niger.

In its first advisory ruling in five years, the court announced on July 9, 2004, its opinion that the construction of a wall by Israel in the occupied Palestinian territory was "contrary to international law." In addition to ruling that affected Palestinians should receive reparations from Israel and that part of the security barrier should be torn down, the court referred the matter to the General Assembly and Security Council for further action. The lone dissenting vote in the 14–1 nonbinding ruling was cast by Judge Thomas Buergenthal of the United States.

On December 15, 2004, the court unanimously dismissed eight cases that had been brought by the Federal Republic of Yugoslavia (now the separate states of Serbia and Montenegro) against individual NATO countries (Belgium, Canada, France, Germany, Italy, Netherlands, Portugal, and the United Kingdom) in connection with the legality of the 1999 NATO air campaign during the Kosovo conflict. The cases, filed under the 1948 UN Convention on the Prevention and Punishment of the Crime of Genocide, initially numbered ten, but the court had immediately dismissed those against Spain and the United States because Madrid and Washington had signed the 1948 convention with the proviso that they could refuse court jurisdiction. In 2004 the eight outstanding cases were rejected by a majority of the judges on the grounds that at the time the Federal Republic of Yugoslavia filed its complaints it had not yet formally been admitted to the United Nations (and was therefore not a party to the ICJ Statute), following the breakup of the former Socialist Federal Republic of Yugoslavia in the early 1990s. As of July 2006 Serbia and Montenegro remained party to separate Genocide Convention cases brought against Yugoslavia by Bosnia and Herzegovina in 1993 and by Croatia in 1999.

In February 2005 the court ruled that it could not settle a dispute between Liechtenstein and Germany over property that had been confiscated during World War II by Czechoslovakia but that had subsequently come into German possession. The court ruled that it did not have jurisdiction because the conflict dated to 1945, and the applicable convention on the peaceful settlement of disputes had not entered into force between Germany and Liechtenstein until 1980.

As of August 2006, 12 cases remained before the court, including the Hungary-Slovakia case, 2 involving the DRC, and 2 involving Serbia and Montenegro. Four of the remaining 7 were territorial disputes. Nicaragua filed in 1999 against Honduras over a shared maritime border and in 2001 against Colombia "concerning title to territory and maritime delimitation" in the western Caribbean. Cases filed in 2003 concerned rival claims by Malaysia and Singapore to Pedra Branca/Pulau Batu Puteh, Middle Rocks, and South Ledge, and a Congolese-French dispute over the latter's judicial actions against Congolese officials charged with torture and crimes against humanity. In 2004 Romania submitted a claim against Ukraine over their shared maritime boundary in the Black Sea.

In May 2006 Argentina filed suit against Uruguay to stop the construction of two pulp mills on the Uruguay River, asserting that the mills would do irreparable environmental damage. (In July, the ICJ declined to order construction stopped until the case was tried.) In August France consented to the court's jurisdiction in a case brought by Djibouti, which had charged France with violating a bilateral treaty and a bilateral convention.

On January 23, 2007, on a vote of 14 to 1, the court declined Uruguay's request to issue an order for Argentina to end blockades of roads and bridges to the construction sites in the pulp mills case. In February the ICJ reaffirmed in *Bosnia and Herzegovina vs. Serbia and Montenegro* that the court had jurisdiction under Article IX of the Convention on the Prevention and Punishment of the Crime of Genocide when one country alleged genocide by another. In May the court ruled on an issue of diplomatic protection for Ahmadou Sadio Diallo related to his role in two private companies in a dispute with the Democratic Republic of the Congo.

In January 2008 Peru initiated a suit against Chile over the maritime boundary between the two countries. The countries were given until 2010 to enter their initial briefs. Ecuador filed suit against Colombia in April over the use of aerial herbicides to destroy illicit drugs near the two countries' border. In June Mexico asked for clarification in the 2004 case *Mexico v. United States.* Mexico argued that the United States was required to reexamine past cases in which Mexican nationals were convicted by U.S. courts. After collecting evidence and briefs from both sides, the court was still deliberating over the case as of October 1, 2009. On October 10 the UN General Assembly asked the ICJ to rule on Kosovo's unilateral declaration of independence. In December the ICJ heard oral arguments in an advisory case on Kosovar independence.

In February 2009 in *Belgium v. Senegal,* the ICJ was asked to rule on whether or not Senegal was obligated to either prosecute or extradite former Chadian president Hissène Habré. Habré had been in exile in Senegal since 1990 and had been arrested for crimes against humanity in 2000. However, a Senegalese court dismissed the charges since the country did not at the time have statutes expressly prohibiting crimes against humanity. Senegal did amend its legal code to include genocide and crimes against humanity in 2007. Meanwhile, a Belgian national filed charges in Belgium against Habré in 2005, and the country issued an international arrest warrant for the former president. In its 2009 motion Belgium asked the court to determine if Senegal should prosecute Habré under its new laws or turn him over to Brussels.

SECRETARIAT

Secretary General	Ban Ki-Moon (Republic of Korea)
Deputy Secretary General	Asha-Rose Migiro (Tanzania)

Executive Office of the Secretary General

Chief of Protocol	Alice Hecht (Belgium)
Chief of Cabinet	Vijay Nambiar (India)
Assistant Secretary General and Deputy Chief of Cabinet	Kim Wan-soo (Republic of Korea)
Political Affairs	Nicholas Haysom (South Africa)

Assistant Secretary General for Policy Planning and Strategic Coordination	Robert Orr (United States)
Spokesperson	Michele Montas (Haiti)

Under Secretaries General

Department of Management	Angela Kane (Germany)
Department of Economic and Social Affairs	Sha Zukang (China)
Department of Field Support	Susana Malcorra (Argentina)
Department for General Assembly Affairs and Conference Management	Franz Baumann (Germany)
Department of Peacekeeping Operations	Alain Le Roy (France)
Department of Public Information	Kiyotaka Akasaka (Japan)
Department of Political Affairs	B. Lynn Pascoe (United States)
Department for Disarmament Affairs	Sergio de Queiroz Duarte (Brazil)
Department for Safety and Security	Gregory B. Starr (United States)
Office for the Coordination of Humanitarian Affairs, Emergency Relief Coordinator	John Holmes (United Kingdom)
Office of the High Representative for the Least Developed Countries, Landlocked and Small Island Developing States	Cheick Sidi Diarra (Mali)
Office of Legal Affairs	Patricia O'Brien (Ireland)
Office of Internal Oversight Services	Inga-Britt Ahlenius (Sweden)
UN Office in Geneva (Director General)	Sergei Ordzhonikidze (Russia)
UN Office in Nairobi (Director General)	Achim Steiner (Germany)
UN Office in Vienna (Director General) and Office of Drugs and Crime (Executive Director)	Antonio Mario Costa (Italy)

Note: The executive secretaries of the ECOSOC Regional Commissions are also under secretaries general, as are the heads and associate administrators of some UN Special Bodies.

Assistant Secretaries General

Chief Information Technology Officer	Choi Soon-hong (Republic of Korea)
Department of Economic and Social Affairs	Jomo Kwame Sundaram (Malaysia)
Special Adviser on Gender Issues and Advancement of Women	Rachel Mayanja (Uganda)
Department for General Assembly Affairs and Conference Management	Yohannes Mengesha (Ethiopia)
Department of Management	Warren Sach (United Kingdom)
Department of Peacebuilding Support	Judy Cheng-Hopkins (Malaysia)
Department of Political Affairs	Haile Menkerios (Eritrea)
Office for the Coordination of Humanitarian Affairs, Deputy Emergency Relief Coordinator	Margareta Wahlström (Sweden)
Office of Capital Master Plan	Michael Alderstein (United States)
Office of Legal Affairs	Peter Taksøe-Jensen (Denmark)
Policy Coordination and Inter-Agency Affairs	Thomas Stelzer (Austria)

Note: Some of the military and civilian heads of UN peacekeeping operations are also assistant secretaries general, as are the deputies of some UN Special Bodies.

Other Senior Officers

UN Special Coordinator for the Middle East Peace Process	Michael Williams (United Kingdom)
Executive Director, Counter-Terrorism	Mike Smith (Australia)
UN Ombudsman	Johnston Barkat (United States)

Special/Personal Representatives or Envoys of or Advisers to the Secretary General

Afghanistan	Kai Eide (Norway)
Africa	Cheikh Sidi Diarra (Mali)
Alliance of Civilizations	Jorge Sampaio (Portugal)
Avian and Human Influenza	(Vacant)
Burundi	Youssef Mahmoud (Tunisia)
Cambodia	Yash Ghai (Kenya)
Central African Republic	Sahle-Work Zewde (Ethiopia)
Central African Republic and Chad	Victor da Silva Angelo (Portugal)
Central Asia	Miroslav Jenča (Slovakia)
Children and Armed Conflict	Radhika Coomaraswamy (Sri Lanka)
Climate Change	Gro Harlem Brundtland (Norway)
	Srgjan Kerim (Macedonia)
	Festus Mogae (Botswana)
	Ricardo Lagos Escobar (Chile)
Conference on Disarmament	Sergei Ordzhonikidze (Russia)
Côte d'Ivoire	Choi Young-Jin (Republic of Korea)
Cyprus	Taye-Brook Zerihoun (Ethiopia)
Democratic Republic of the Congo	Alan Doss (United Kingdom)
Equatorial Guinea and Gabon	Nicholas Michel (Switzerland)
Eritrea/Ethiopia	Azouz Ennifar (Tunisia) (Acting)
Financing for Development	Philippe Douste-Blazy (France)
Food Security and Nutrition	David Nabarro (United Kingdom)
Georgia	Johann Verbeke (Belgium)
Gender Issues and Advancement of Women	Rachel N. Mayanja (Uganda)
Great Lakes Region	Olusegun Obasanjo (Nigeria)
Greece and the former Yugoslav Republic of Macedonia	Matthew Nimetz (United States)
Guatemala	Carlos Castresana Fernandez (Spain)
Guinea-Bissau	Joseph Mutaboba (Rwanda)
Haiti	Hédi Annabi (Tunisia)
HIV/AIDS in Africa	Elizabeth Mataka (Botswana)
HIV/AIDS in Asia	Nafis Sadik (Pakistan)
HIV/AIDS in the Caribbean	George Alleyne (Barbados)
HIV/AIDS in Eastern Europe	(Vacant)
Horn of Africa	Kjell Magne Bondevik (Norway)
Human Rights	Margaret Sekaggya (Uganda)
Human Rights and the Business Community	John Ruggie (United States)
Human Rights and Internally Displaced Persons	Walter Kälin (Switzerland)
Human Rights in Cambodia	Yash Gai (Kenya)
Humanitarian Activities in the Palestinian Territories	Max Gaylord (Australia)
Humanitarian Aid	Abdulaziz bin Mohamed Arrukban (Saudi Arabia)

Iraq	Ad Melkert (Netherlands)
Iraq/International Compact	Ibrahim Gambari (Nigeria)
Iraq/Kuwait	Gennady P. Tarasov (Russia)
Kosovo	Lamberto Zannier (Italy)
Lebanon	Michael C. Williams (United Kingdom)
Least Developed Countries, Landlocked Developing Countries, and Small Developing Island States	Cheikh Sidi Diarra (Mali)
Liberia	Ellen Margrethe Løj (Norway)
Malaria	Ray Chambers (United States)
Middle East	Robert Serry (Netherlands)
Migration	Peter Sutherland (Ireland)
Millennium Development Goals	Jeffrey Sachs (United States)
Myanmar	Ibrahim Gambari (Nigeria)
Nepal	Karin Landgren (Sweden)
Pakistan	Jean-Maurice Ripert (France)
Palestine Liberation Organization and Palestinian Authority	Michael Williams (United Kingdom)
Prevention of Genocide	Francis Deng (Sudan)
Sierra Leone	Michael von der Schulenburg (Germany)
Somalia	Ahmedou Ould Abdallah (Mauritania)
Sport for Development and Peace	Wifried Lemke (Germany)
Sudan	Ashraf Jehangir Qazi (Pakistan)
Sudan/Darfur	Djibril Yipéné Bassolé (Burkina Faso)
Timor-Leste	Atul Khare (India)
Tuberculosis	Jorge Sampaio (Portugal)
Uganda	Joaquim Chissano (Mozambique)
United Nations International School	Silvia Fuhrman (United States)
Violence Against Children	Marta Santos Pais (Portugal)
West Africa	Said Djinnit (Algeria)
Western Sahara	Hany Abdel-Aziz (Egypt)
	Christopher Ross (United States)
World Summit on Information Society	Nitin Desai (India)

Web site: www.un.org/sg

Structure. The Secretariat consists of the secretary general and the UN staff, which, since early 1998, includes a deputy secretary general. The secretary general, who is appointed for a five-year term by the General Assembly on recommendation of the Security Council, is designated chief administrative officer by the charter, which directs him to report annually to the General Assembly on the work of the UN, to appoint the staff, and to perform such other functions as are entrusted to him by the various UN organs. Under Article 99 of the charter, the secretary general may bring to the attention of the Security Council any matter that in his opinion may threaten international peace and security. Other functions of the secretary general include acting in that capacity at all meetings of the General Assembly, the Security Council, the Economic and Social Council, and the Trusteeship Council, and presenting any supplementary reports on the work of the UN that are necessary to the General Assembly.

The charter defines the "paramount consideration" in employing staff as the necessity of securing the highest standards of efficiency, competency, and integrity, with due regard to the importance of recruiting on as wide a geographical basis as possible. In the performance of their duties, the secretary general and the staff are forbidden to seek or receive any instructions from any government or any other authority external to the UN. Each member of the UN, in turn, is bound to respect the exclusively international character of the Secretariat's responsibilities and not to seek to influence it in the discharge of its duties.

In addition to its New York headquarters, the UN maintains offices in Geneva, Switzerland; Nairobi, Kenya; and Vienna, Austria. Personnel of various specialized and subsidiary organs are also headquartered in New York or other UN sites around the globe.

The regular budget of the organization is financed primarily by obligatory contributions from the member states, as determined by a scale of assessments that is based on capacity to pay and currently varies from 0.001 percent of the total for the poorest members to 22 percent for the United States. Collectively, eight Western industrialized countries (Canada, France, Germany, Italy, Japan, Spain, United Kingdom, and the United States) contribute approximately 72 percent of the budget. China is the largest contributor among developing states and provides 2.67 percent of the budget. Activities outside the regular budget, including most peacekeeping activities and technical cooperation programs, are separately financed, partly through voluntary contributions.

Activities. The level of international political activity undertaken by various secretaries general has depended as much on the political environment and their own personalities as on charter provisions. Prior to the breakup of the Soviet Union in the early 1990s, the most important factor was often the acquiescence of the superpowers. This was vividly demonstrated by the Soviet challenge to the Secretariat during the Belgian Congo crisis of 1960. UN intervention in the Congo, initiated on the authority of the Security Council in the summer of 1960, led to sharp Soviet criticism of Secretary General Dag Hammarskjöld and a proposal by Soviet Chair Nikita Khrushchev in September 1960 to abolish the Secretariat and substitute a tripartite executive body made up of Western, communist, and neutral representatives. Although the proposal was not adopted, the USSR maintained a virtual boycott of the Secretariat up to the time of Hammarskjöld's death in September 1961 and imposed a number of conditions before agreeing to U Thant of Burma as his successor. U Thant was in turn succeeded in 1971 by Kurt Waldheim of Austria.

In December 1981, in the wake of decisions by Waldheim and Salim A. Salim of Tanzania to withdraw from consideration, Javier Pérez de Cuéllar, a relatively obscure Peruvian diplomat, was selected by a closed session of the UN Security Council as the recommended candidate for UN secretary general. The full UN General Assembly unanimously elected Pérez de Cuéllar on December 15, and his five-year term as the fifth secretary general began January 1, 1982. Despite earlier hints that he might not seek a second term because of budget problems, Pérez de Cuéllar, upon the unanimous recommendation of the Security Council, was reelected by the General Assembly in October 1986 for an additional five years beginning January 1, 1987.

In September 1987 Pérez de Cuéllar launched an intensive campaign to win support from Iran and Iraq for a Security Council plan to settle the war between them. Further underscoring his heightened visibility in international diplomacy, the secretary general in October was selected to serve on the committee charged with verifying compliance with the recently negotiated Central American peace plan. The Secretariat's peacemaking role continued to grow throughout 1988 as ceasefires were negotiated in the Iran-Iraq and Western Saharan conflicts in August and agreements were signed by Angola, Cuba, and South Africa in December that permitted implementation of the long-delayed UN plan for the independence of Namibia.

To take advantage of the "extraordinary improvement in the world political climate," Pérez de Cuéllar in 1989 suggested further extension of the UN's peacekeeping role, calling upon countries to designate standby troops for that purpose out of their national armies. He also urged the United Nations to assemble a more sophisticated information gathering system so that it could monitor "incipient conflicts" and possibly prevent them from erupting. The Secretariat, hoping to build upon its role in the highly successful Namibian settlement, pursued negotiations in Cambodia, Cyprus, El Salvador, and the Western Sahara, while also sending a delegation in June 1990 to review progress toward the dismantling of apartheid in South Africa.

Other topics addressed by Pérez de Cuéllar as his second term neared completion included the "old, stubborn problems, unrelated to the cold war," such as "grave" global economic disparity, third world debt, and environmental degradation. The secretary general was also highly visible in international efforts to negotiate a withdrawal of Iraqi forces from Kuwait in late 1990 and early 1991, prior to the launching of the U.S.-led Desert Storm campaign.

As expected, the widely respected Pérez de Cuéllar declined to stand for a third term, and in the fall of 1991 the General Assembly, acting upon the recommendation of the Security Council, unanimously elected Boutros Boutros-Ghali, the Egyptian deputy prime minister for foreign affairs, as the UN's sixth secretary general, effective January 1, 1992. Boutros-Ghali, the first Arab and the first African to hold the post, rose to prominence initially as part of the Egyptian team that negotiated the Camp David peace treaty with Israel.

Because he was well known in UN circles and familiar with the organization's bureaucracy, the new secretary general was able to institute a significant restructuring of the Secretariat in February 1992 as part of ongoing streamlining throughout the UN system. Most operations were consolidated into four major new departments, permitting a reduction in the number of under secretaries general and assistant secretaries general while also providing a more direct and, it was hoped, a more efficient chain of command. One of the new departments was devoted to peacekeeping, an area in which Boutros-Ghali suggested UN influence could be expanded even further.

In June 1992 Boutros-Ghali outlined an Agenda for Peace, which called upon UN members to make armed forces available to the Security Council on a permanent on-call basis. The secretary general also suggested that the council's long-dormant Military Staff Committee be reactivated to assume authority over what would essentially become the UN's standby army. A wider role in "preventative diplomacy" was also urged, Boutros-Ghali asking regional organizations to seek UN intervention before disputes escalated into warfare.

Boutros-Ghali's recommendations were initially endorsed in many quarters. However, a degree of disillusionment was apparent a year later, stemming from the failure of UN efforts in Bosnia and Herzegovina, ongoing difficulties in Somalia and Angola, and the inability of fact-finding missions in Azerbaijan, Georgia, and Tajikistan to prevent bloodshed. For his part, Boutros-Ghali argued that the United Nations was being asked to take on more than it could handle, especially considering the "chasm" that existed between its assignments and the money member states were willing to provide. The secretary general was also facing resistance both from member states and from UN employees in his efforts to further revamp the Secretariat and other UN bureaucracies, despite general agreement that the organization remained highly inefficient in many areas. However, a new Office for Inspections and Investigations (OII) was established in 1993 to combat waste and mismanagement and to address allegations of corruption within the UN system. A year later, the office was replaced by an Office of Internal Oversight Services, which is headed by an assistant secretary general who has operational independence.

As a counterpoint to his 1992 Agenda for Peace, Boutros-Ghali unveiled an Agenda for Development in May 1994. Despite the "distorted perception" throughout the world that peacekeeping was being emphasized at the expense of other areas, the secretary general stressed that "development is still the major activity of the UN." However, Boutros-Ghali argued that new levels of coordination were required within the UN and between the UN and other international organizations to combat donor fatigue and to mobilize public opinion in support of development assistance. Progress also depended on the ability of developing nations to find "the right blend" of governmental influence and private initiative for maximum economic growth.

In late 1994 and during the first nine months of 1995, Boutros-Ghali consistently criticized UN members for failing to meet their financial obligations, especially those for peacekeeping operations. The secretary general reported that arrears had reached $3.24 billion as of September 1995, making it "impossible for us to do our job." Boutros-Ghali also argued, however, that the United Nations retained a "moral obligation" to go into crisis areas, whatever the financial and/or political limitations might be. In a related vein, the secretary general was reported to be somewhat at odds with the Security Council, which he described as being too involved with the conflict in Bosnia and Herzegovina at the expense of problems in other sections of the world. Underscoring his determination to focus attention on "underdog conflicts," Boutros-Ghali made a week-long trip across Central Africa in mid-1995. The secretary general's concern for his home continent was further highlighted in March 1996 when he launched the ten-year, $25 billion UN System-wide Special Initiative on Africa, described as one of the largest cooperative operations ever attempted by UN agencies and other regional organizations.

In June 1996 the United States issued a surprisingly strong statement pledging to veto a second term for Boutros-Ghali, arguing that he was ill-suited to implementing the reforms Washington was demanding in return for payment of some of its $1.3 billion in arrears. Representatives from many countries rushed to the defense of the secretary general, pointing out that he had reduced UN staffing by some 10 percent and had attempted to restructure the UN's bureaucratic maze of agencies. Nevertheless, at the first round of balloting in the Security Council on November 19, the United States cast the lone dissenting vote against Boutros-Ghali's reelection. Thus, his supporters were reluctantly forced to consider other candidates.

The four primary contenders to emerge were Kofi Annan of Ghana, then the under secretary general for peacekeeping operations; Amara Essy, the foreign minister of Côte d'Ivoire; Hamid Algabid of Niger, then the secretary general of the Organization of the Islamic Conference; and Mauritanian diplomat Ahmedou Ould Abdallah. Several straw votes in the Security Council in early December effectively reduced the choices to Annan (backed by the United States) and Essy. Although France, an ardent supporter of Boutros-Ghali, reportedly threatened to veto Annan to protest Washington's heavy-handedness in the selection process, Annan was finally approved on December 13, with the General Assembly making the appointment official four days later.

Upon taking office on January 1, 1997, Annan, the first black African to hold the job, called for "a time for healing" and pledged to pursue UN reform. Among the most important reforms approved by the General Assembly late in the year was the creation of the position of the deputy secretary general, Louise Fréchette of Canada becoming in January 1998 the first person to hold the position. Other changes included the formation of a cabinet-like Senior Management Group, the creation of the Department of Disarmament Affairs, the merger of three departments into the newly created Department of Economic and Social Affairs, the reorganization of the UN Drug Control Program (UNDCP) and the Center for International Crime Prevention (CICP) under the new Office for Drug Control and Crime Prevention (ODCCP) in Vienna, the consolidation of the Geneva-based Center for Human Rights under the Office of the High Commissioner for Human Rights (UNHCHR), and a proposed reduction in administrative costs of at least $200 million over four years.

In April 1998 Annan issued a wide-ranging report on African issues, particularly the wars being fought across the continent and the lack of economic development. Exhibiting a growing willingness to address such issues bluntly, he criticized African leaders for relying on military rather than political approaches to problems and for their failure to attend to good governance. In September 1998 Annan questioned the U.S. bomb attacks on suspected terrorist sites in Afghanistan and Sudan, arguing that "individual action by member states" was not the solution to the "global menace" of terrorism.

In subsequent speeches and reports, the secretary general staked out a clear position in support of UN intervention to prevent a recurrence of the genocidal events in Rwanda and Kosovo during the 1990s. In addition to urging the Security Council to respond faster to the outbreak of civil wars, Annan countered ardent advocates for the primacy of national sovereignty by arguing that "nothing in the Charter precludes a recognition that there are rights beyond borders," particularly when a state was violating human rights within those borders. He also strongly supported establishment of a permanent International Criminal Court (ICC; see General Assembly) and chastised the United States for its objections to such a court, as well as for its unwillingness to provide more than transport and logistical support to peacekeeping ventures in Africa.

The April 2000 secretary general's report focused on development issues. Annan called for efforts to reduce youth unemployment and to "bridge the digital divide" between technologically advanced and developing states. He also urged the developed world to provide debt relief and to drop tariffs on commodities from developing countries, thereby helping them increase the export earnings needed to finance development. In addition, Annan advocated greater involvement by private sector partners in humanitarian relief efforts. In December 2000 he named a high-level panel of financial experts, chaired by former Mexican president Ernesto Zedillo, to propose steps to help speed development in poor countries. With a special UN session on HIV/AIDS approaching in June 2001, Annan subsequently called for creation of a Global AIDS and Health Fund.

In April 2001 China indicated that it would back Secretary General Annan's bid for a second term, making it virtually certain that he would not be confronted by a veto from any of the Security Council's permanent members. On June 29 the General Assembly unanimously elected him to a second term, which began January 1, 2002. On October 12 Annan and the UN were awarded the Nobel Peace Prize.

In late 2002 not only the Security Council but also the General Assembly and Secretariat became increasingly tied up in the debate over weapons inspections in Iraq and a threatened U.S. invasion of that country. From then until the actual launch of hostilities in March 2003, Secretary General Annan argued for adherence to the international rule of law and the need to address matters of peace and security in the context of "the unique legitimacy provided by the UN Security Council." He subsequently incurred Washington's wrath, not to mention that of right-wing U.S. media outlets, by branding the war "illegal" and by asserting that going to war had not made the world safer. He also opposed the George W. Bush administration's efforts to keep U.S. peacekeeping troops exempt from prosecution by the new ICC.

A major shake-up in the UN's security structure followed a suicide truck bombing at UN headquarters in Baghdad, Iraq, on August 19, 2003. Twenty-two people died in the blast, including Annan's special representative to Iraq, Sergio Vieira de Mello of Brazil, and the former UN chief of protocol, Nadia Younes of Egypt. An independent report published in March 2004 faulted administrators for having failed to conduct a security review of the facility, in the mistaken assumption that UN personnel would not be targeted by insurgents. As a consequence, Secretary General Annan fired his security coordinator, Tun Myat of Myanmar, and demoted other personnel. Annan refused, however, to accept the resignation of Deputy Secretary General Fréchette, who had headed a committee that recommended a UN return to Iraq. On January 13, 2005, Annan named David Veness, an assistant commissioner of London's Metropolitan Police Service and an antiterrorism expert, to head a newly created Department of Safety and Security.

Meanwhile, the secretary general was drawing increasing criticism in connection with the $64 billion "oil-for-food" program, which had permitted Iraq to sell oil and use the income to meet humanitarian needs. An investigation initiated by the secretary general in April 2004 into bribery and illicit payments led to the revelation that Annan's son, Kojo Annan, had been paid by a Swiss contractor, Cotecna Inspection Services, which had been responsible for monitoring Iraqi compliance with the program. February and March 2005 interim reports by the Independent Inquiry Committee, headed by former chair of the U.S. Federal Reserve Paul Volcker, exonerated Kofi Annan of involvement in awarding the contract to Cotecna but found procedural errors and procurement violations dating back to Boutros-Ghali's term as secretary general. The committee also criticized Annan's former chief of cabinet, Syed Iqbal Riza of Pakistan, for having shredded documents relevant to the case. The first UN staffer held criminally culpable in the "oil-for-food" scandal was Aleksandr Yakovlev of Russia, who in August 2005 pleaded guilty to taking some $1.3 million in bribes while heading a procurement department.

The Volcker committee report issued on September 7, 2005, indicted the UN for "illicit, unethical and corrupt behavior" as well as inadequate auditing and overall bureaucratic inefficiency. During the 1996–2003 "oil-for-food" program, the Saddam Hussein regime illicitly pocketed billions of dollars while paying bribes to some 270 politicians and journalists. Although Annan accepted responsibility for the "deeply embarrassing" shortcomings documented in the report, he rejected calls for his resignation and vowed to press ahead with his reform agenda.

On March 21, 2005, drawing on the work of a High-Level Panel on Threats, Challenges, and Change that he had named in November 2003, Secretary General Annan submitted to the General Assembly his long-awaited report on reform, "In Larger Freedom: Toward Development, Security, and Human Rights for All." Among other things, the secretary general called for expanding the Security Council to better reflect a geopolitical balance; streamlining the General Assembly agenda; making the Secretariat more flexible, transparent, and accountable; and replacing the controversial UN Commission on Human Rights with a Human Rights Council elected by the General Assembly. He asked all developing countries to improve governance, target corruption, and uphold the rule of law while striving to meet the Millennium Development Goals set forth in 2000. At the same time, he urged developed countries to significantly increase their amount of development assistance and debt relief and to permit duty-free and quota-free imports from the least developed countries. He cautioned, however, that sustainable development required due attention to environmental factors and concerns about the depletion of natural resources. In the area of security he emphasized the importance of working in concert to control terrorism, end weapons proliferation, and stop civil wars. He also urged collective action against genocide, ethnic cleansing, and crimes against humanity if individual countries were unable or unwilling to act.

In January 2006 eight UN officials, including Andrew Toh, the assistant secretary general for central support services, were suspended in connection with more than 200 alleged instances of fraud in the purchase of equipment for peacekeeping missions. The allegations resulted from an inquiry into procurement practices that led Chief of Staff Mark Malloch Brown, speaking to the Security Council in February, to confirm the need for reform, particularly in the awarding of contracts. Also in February, Secretary General Annan announced the formation of a senior 15-member panel to propose methods to enhance collaboration and cooperation between agencies. The panel was one of the recommendations from the UN 60th anniversary summit. It suggested changes as part of Annan's broader reform program and focused on the UN's role in environmental, humanitarian, and development policies. In March, in addition to naming Malloch Brown as successor to Deputy Secretary General Fréchette, Annan announced additional specific reforms, including increased training for UN staff and improvements in technology, communications, and records. Annan also called for relocating some UN agencies from New York and Geneva to less expensive locations as a means of reducing expenditures.

A report on sexual misconduct by UN peacekeeping forces released in August 2006 detailed 313 investigations and noted that the inquiries had resulted in the dismissal of 17 UN peacekeepers and the forced repatriation of 161 others. In September the UN's first all-female peacekeeping unit was deployed to UNMIL. The force consisted of 125 woman officers from India. Women comprised less than 4 percent of the personnel of all UN peacekeeping missions as of 2008.

In informal polling in September and October 2006 among Security Council members to determine the next secretary general, Foreign Minister Ban Ki-Moon of the Republic of Korea emerged as the leading candidate among seven contenders mostly from Asia. Ban was the favored candidate of the United States and China, but France and the United Kingdom initially sought a more activist candidate. However, after Ban won the fourth informal poll on October 2, all of the other candidates withdrew. He was unanimously recommended by the Security Council and appointed by the General Assembly on October 13.

Once in office, Ban replaced two-thirds of the body's senior management team. He named Asha-Rose Migiro of Tanzania as the new deputy secretary general. She was the third person to hold the post and the first non-Westerner. Throughout the senior management, the new secretary general increased the number of appointments from the developing world. Ban also detailed five priorities for his term in office. First, he called for the UN to strengthen its traditional core pillars of security, development, and human rights. Second, he declared his intent to restore confidence in the office of the secretary general. Third, Ban wanted to improve the efficiency of the UN management system, particularly its human resource system. Fourth, the new secretary general sought to set higher ethical and professional standards for all UN employees and agencies, including the adoption of annual performance reviews. Fifth and finally, Ban declared his intent to revolutionize the relationship between the Secretariat and UN member states. In order to demonstrate his earnestness about ethical reform, Ban released his personal financial disclosure form for external review and promised to continue to do so each year. His deputy secretary general has also adopted this practice. In June 2007 the UN's peacekeeping structure was divided into two departments, peacekeeping operations and field support, as part of a broader reform effort proposed by Ban in January to increase efficiency through greater specialization. Each of the new departments was headed by an undersecretary general.

In November Ban became the first UN secretary general to make an official visit to Antarctica. While touring the region, Ban called for greater action to slow global warming. He also announced the launch of a system-wide UN campaign to combat violence against women. Ban's initiative was scheduled to last through 2015 and mandate that the General Assembly include at least one agenda item per year to address gender violence. The secretary general also pledged to reform UN agencies to better address violence against women, particularly during peacekeeping operations. In 2008 Ban released a report that showed attacks on UN staff had increased dramatically in the preceding year, and that deaths of UN workers due to attacks had increased by 38 percent.

Following attacks on UN workers, including the bombing of UN offices in Algiers in December 2007, Ban pledged to better protect UN staffers, and in 2008 convened the Independent Panel on Safety and Security to develop recommendations on how to better secure UN facilities and personnel. Meanwhile, throughout 2008, Ban continued to undertake a series of reforms at the world body. He appointed a chief information officer to oversee the UN's information technology systems, and he altered the UN's procurement system to ensure greater transparency and efficiency. He also shortened the hiring process for new UN staffers.

In response to rising food prices, in April 2008 Ban established the High Level Task Force on the Global Food Security Crisis to identify problems and develop strategies, as well as to coordinate the UN response. Ban brought together more than 100 world leaders at the High Level Event on the Millennium Development Goals in New York in September and was able to secure pledges of more than $16 billion in additional funding for poverty reduction efforts and an additional $3 billion to combat malaria and other diseases. In October Ban reported that an independent review of the $500-million Central Emergency Response Fund (CERF) found the reserve had been largely successful in its mission of providing assistance for natural disasters, and he urged members to annually contribute to CERF. Also in October, Ban conducted a high-level meeting of the heads of 17 major pharmaceutical and medical companies and received pledges that the firms would expand research and increase access to drugs and medicines in developing countries. In November Ban issued an urgent appeal for all member states to pay their dues. At the time, member states owed $756 million to the regular budget and $2.9 to the peacekeeping budget.

An investigation into the UN's handling of an inquiry into the death in 2000 of a British contractor working for UNDP led to the creation of the five-member Internal Justice Council (IJC). After Joe Comerford died, the UN refused his widow compensation until 2008 when she was awarded £143,000. The world body engaged in behavior that was later described by investigators as "reckless and callous" toward the widow. The IJC was formed to be an independent, judicial body for arbitration within the UN.

In 2008 Ban initiated the program UNiTE to End Violence Against Women. The program sought by 2015 to have nations adopt national legislation that mirrored international conventions and to institute plans to curb gender violence. UNiTE also promoted the development of global data collection and analysis of violence against women. The initiative was developed in response to a 2006 report that highlighted trends in gender violence and was in response to a 2007 General Assembly resolution that called for greater progress in the elimination of violence against women.

On Janaury 31, 2009, Ban's special representative to Myanmar, Ibrahim Gambari, visited the country for a series of meetings in an effort to persuade the military government to restore democracy. The sessions were unsuccessful, although Gambari was able to meet with opposition leader Aung San Suu Kyi, who remained under house arrest. Ban launched the We Must Disarm (WMD) campaign on June 13. The WMD initiative was a multimedia effort to promote nuclear disarmament and increase awareness of the dangers of weapons proliferation. The secretary general worked with actor Michael Douglas, a UN messenger of peace, in the campaign, which culminated in the International Day of Peace on September 21. The secretary general convened the UN Climate Change Summit in September. The event brought together more than 100 world leaders and was a precursor to the Copenhagen conference on climate change later that year. United States president Obama pledged that the country would recommit itself to involvement in global efforts to reduce greenhouse gases and address climate change.

In September 2009 Ban removed Peter Galbraith as a UN deputy special representative to Afghanistan. Galbraith had a public dispute with the senior UN figure in Afghanistan, Kai Eide, over the management of run-off balloting following a disputed presidential election in August.

UNITED NATIONS: SPECIALIZED AGENCIES

FOOD AND AGRICULTURE ORGANIZATION OF THE UNITED NATIONS (FAO)

Established: By constitution signed in Quebec, Canada, October 16, 1945. The FAO became a UN Specialized Agency by agreement with the Economic and Social Council (approved by the General Assembly on December 14, 1946).

Purpose: "To promote the common welfare by furthering separate and collective action . . . for the purpose of: raising levels of nutrition and standards of living . . . securing improvements in the efficiency of the production and distribution of all food and agricultural products; bettering the condition of rural populations; and thus contributing toward an expanding world economy."

Headquarters: Rome, Italy.

Principal Organs: General Conference (all members), Council (49 members), Secretariat.

Web site: www.fao.org

Director General: Jacques Diouf (Senegal).

Membership (192, plus 1 Associate Member): See Appendix C.

Official Languages: Arabic, Chinese, English, French, German, Spanish.

Working Languages: Arabic, Chinese, English, French, Spanish.

Origin and development. The 34 governments represented at the UN Conference on Food and Agriculture held May 18–June 3, 1943, in Hot Springs, Virginia, agreed that a permanent international body should be established to deal with problems of food and agriculture. The Interim Commission on Food and Agriculture submitted a draft constitution that was signed October 15, 1945, in Quebec, Canada, by the 30 governments attending the first session of the FAO General Conference. The organization, which inherited the functions and assets of the former International Institute of Agriculture in Rome, Italy, was made a Specialized Agency of the United Nations effective December 14, 1946.

In November 1991 the conference admitted the European Community (subsequently the European Union—EU) as a regular FAO member, marking the first time such an organization had joined a UN Specialized Agency. The EU's rights are somewhat circumscribed, however, in that it cannot vote in elections or hold office, and it may otherwise participate as an alternative to, not in addition to, its individual member states. The November 1993 General Conference readmitted South Africa, which had withdrawn in 1964. FAO membership rose to 188 in December 2003 with the admission of Micronesia, Timor-Leste, Tuvalu, and Ukraine, and to 189 members in 2006 with the addition of the Russian Federation.

FAO responsibilities were significantly broadened in 1963 when, following a suggestion by the United States, the UN/FAO World Food Program (WFP) began operations to provide food aid in furtherance of economic and social development, to offer relief services in the event of natural and man-made disasters, and to promote world food security. Subsequently, as part of its effort to avoid overlapping mandates, the General Assembly in 1995 authorized the FAO and the WFP to absorb the responsibilities of the World Food Council (WFC), a special body of the assembly that was disbanded in May 1996. The vast majority of the FAO's 10,600 employees serve in the field.

Structure. The General Conference, which normally meets at Rome once every two years, is the organization's major policymaking organ; each member has one vote. Its responsibilities include approving the FAO budget and program of work, adopting procedural rules and financial regulations, formulating recommendations on food and agricultural questions, and reviewing the decisions of the FAO Council and subsidiary bodies.

The FAO Council's 49 members are elected for three-year rotating terms by the conference from seven regional groupings (Africa, 12 seats; Asia, 9; Europe, 10; Latin America and the Caribbean, 9; Near East, 6; North America, 2; Southwest Pacific, 1). The council meets between sessions of the conference and acts on its behalf as an executive organ responsible for monitoring the world food and agriculture situation and recommending any appropriate action. Assisting the council are 3 elected managerial committees that deal with program, finance, and constitutional and legal matters. Committees on commodity problems, fisheries, agriculture, forestry, and world food security address specialized issues and are open to all members.

Responsibility for implementing the FAO program rests with its Secretariat, which is headed by a director general serving a six-year term of office. Its headquarters staff embraces some 1,800 individuals, while 1,300 are assigned to regional and subregional offices and field projects. There were 1,440 field program projects in 2006, of which 444 were emergency operations. The regional offices are located in Accra, Ghana (Africa); Bangkok, Thailand (Asia and the Pacific); Cairo, Egypt (Near East); Rome, Italy (Europe); and Santiago, Chile (Latin America and the Caribbean). Liaison offices are maintained at UN headquarters in New York and Geneva; in Yokohama, Japan; in Brussels, Belgium (for the EU); and in Washington, D.C.

The FAO's work programs are divided among eight departments, which typically encompass a varying number of divisions, each with its own mandate and programs. The Agriculture and Consumer Protection Department includes the Animal Production and Health Division, FAO/International Atomic Energy Agency (IAEA) Joint Division for Nuclear Techniques in Food and Agriculture, the Land and Water Development Division, the Plant Production and Protection Division, the Rural Agriculture and Agro-Industries Division, and the Nutrition and Consumer Protection Division. The Economic and Social Development Department has three divisions: Agricultural and Development Economics, Commodities and Trade, and Statistics. The Fisheries and Aquaculture Department includes three divisions: Economics and Policy, Management, and Fish Products and Industry; and the Forestry Department has divisions titled Forestry Economics and Policy, Forest Management, and Forest Products and Industries. The Natural Resources Management and Environment Department includes four divisions: Environment, Climate Change and Bioenergy, the Land and Water Division, and the Research and Extension Division. The Technical Cooperation Department encompasses the Policy Assistance Division, the Investment Center, the Field Operations Division, and the Emergency Operations and Rehabilitation Division. Two other FAO departments are Human, Financial and Physical Resources, and Knowledge and Communication. The latter is responsible for issuing the FAO's numerous publications, which include the annual *State of Food and Agriculture* and, since 1999, the annual *State of Food Insecurity in the World*. It also maintains a number of databases, most prominently the International Information System for the Agricultural Sciences and Technology (AGRIS) and the Current Agricultural Research Information System (CARIS). The FAO is also giving increasing attention to providing electronic data access.

Other FAO services are offered through the administrative Office of Program, Budget, and Evaluations. An FAO legal office is responsible for providing in-house legal services, advising member states, and assisting in preparation of relevant treaties.

The FAO sponsors some 30, mostly regional, commissions concerned with, for example, agricultural statistics, forestry, fisheries, plant protection, and pests and diseases (including desert locusts, African animal sleeping sickness, and foot-and-mouth disease). The joint FAO/World Health Organization (WHO) Codex Alimentarius Commission, established in 1962 and now numbering 170 member countries, assists in the preparation, publication, and updating of international food standards; to date, over 300 standards and over 40 codes of practice have been adopted. Other bodies include the Commission on Fertilizers, the Commission on Plant Genetic Resources, and the International Rice Commission.

The WFP is supervised by a 36-member executive board (half elected by the Economic and Social Council of the United Nations and half by the FAO Council), which succeeded the Committee on Food Aid Policies and Programs in January 1996. Its executive director, currently Josette Sheeran of the United States, is jointly named by the UN secretary general and the FAO director general. Sheeran, an influential 20-year member of the Unification Church (known as the "Moonies"), was appointed in November 2006.

Activities. To fulfill its stated purposes of raising living standards and securing improvement in the availability of agricultural products, the FAO collects, analyzes, interprets, and disseminates information relating to nutrition, food, and agriculture. It recommends national and international action in these fields, furnishes such technical assistance as governments may request, and cooperates with governments in organizing missions needed to help them meet their obligations.

The FAO's work is supported through the Regular Program budget and through the separate Field Program of technical assistance. The Regular Program, with mandatory contributions from member states, covers the costs of Secretariat operations but also includes as one component the Technical Cooperation Program (TCP). The TCP constitutes the portion of the regular budget contributed to field projects, which are primarily funded through trust funds established by donor countries. Other international institutions also participate. For 2002–2003 the Regular Program budget stood at about $650 million, as it had for the preceding two bienniums. The falling value of the U.S. dollar (especially against the euro) and an adjustment for inflation were the primary factors necessitating a nominally higher 2004–2005 budget of $749 million. For 2006–2007 the budget had increased slightly to $766 million and the council was reporting serious concerns regarding the organization's worsening financial situation, including large unbudgeted costs, external borrowing, a General Fund deficit and cash flow problems due to delayed payments from member contributions. The 2008–2009 budget was aimed at restoring the organization's financial health and long-term sustainability.

In 1994 the FAO established the Special Program for Food Security (SPFS), which focuses on helping low-income food-deficit countries (LIFDCs) improve agricultural productivity and output on an environmentally sound, economically sustainable basis. As of 2007, more than 100 countries had started SPFS projects, which are primarily funded through extrabudgetary means. Other special programs include the Global Information and Early Warning System (GIEWS), which began operations in 1975, and the Emergency Prevention System (EMPRES) for Transboundary Animal and Plant Pests and Diseases, founded in 1994. The GIEWS attempts to gauge future food supplies in order to forestall food emergencies, while the EMPRES focuses on the control and eradication of targeted diseases and pests (desert locusts, rinderpest, and animal sleeping sickness).

The WFS convened November 13–17, 1996, in Rome. In an apparent effort to avoid public contention, much of the content of the summit's declaration was approved in advance, including a call for the nations of the world to ensure access to safe and nutritious food. The document also asserted the "fundamental right of everyone to be free from hunger," a provision that proved troublesome, however, as the United States expressed reservations about its possible legal implications and argued that this goal should not suggest any "international obligations" nor reduce the "responsibility of national governments toward their citizens." At the same time, some developing countries and international aid organizations objected to the declaration's emphasis on "free-market principles" regarding the distribution of food, noting that agricultural subsidies in the developed nations were unfairly skewing the international market. In any event, the summit attendees pledged to try to halve the number of people suffering from hunger by 2015.

At the November 12–23, 1999, General Conference, the FAO reelected Director General Jacques Diouf to a second term despite opposition from the United Kingdom and some other industrialized countries. It also approved a strategic framework for 2000–2015 that established three overarching goals: "access of all people at all times to sufficient nutritionally adequate and safe food"; the "continued contribution of sustainable agricultural and rural development, including fisheries and forestry, to economic and social progress and the well-being of all"; and the conservation, improvement, and sustainable use of national resources, "including land, water, forests, fisheries and genetic resources." The framework goals also repeated the WFS target of halving the number of undernourished by 2015.

The World Food Summit: Five Years Later, which was postponed from November 2001 because of security concerns following the September 11, 2001, attacks on the United States, convened June 10–13, 2002, in Rome. Although the summit was attended by 74 heads of state or government, few leaders of industrialized countries participated; of the 30 members of the Organization for Economic Cooperation and Development, only Spain and Italy were represented at the highest level, prompting Director General Diouf to comment that the absence of so many Western leaders was "a good indication of the political priority that is given to the tragedy of hunger."

A year later, the 2003 *State of Food Insecurity in the World* made it clear that without a significant acceleration in food production and distribution, the goal of halving the undernourished population by 2015 remained unattainable. Although hunger decreased in the first half of the 1990s, the overall trend was reversed in the second half of the decade, according to the report, leaving 840 million people undernourished in 1999–2001. Reasons for the lack of progress included insufficient resources for distributing food, conflicts in central and western Africa, a severe drought in southern Africa, and the spread of HIV/AIDS.

In response to this setback, the FAO called for wide adoption of an anti-hunger program that combines increased agricultural productivity in rural communities with immediate access to food for the hungry. The FAO emphases include improving rural infrastructure and market access; using available water resources and irrigation more effectively; utilizing both chemical and organic fertilizers; and adopting integrated biological controls to help combat pests, insects, and plant diseases. The FAO has also emphasized, despite continuing criticism from some quarters, greater use of biotechnology as one component of a multi-pronged approach toward crop diversity that also includes conventional plant breeding techniques.

On June 29, 2004, the FAO-sponsored International Treaty on Plant Genetic Resources for Food and Agriculture entered into effect. Among other things, the treaty provides for the Multilateral System for Access and Benefit Sharing to streamline procedures and reduce transaction costs for plant breeders, farmers, and researchers seeking access to the genetic resources of over 60 of the world's most important food and forage crops. In addition, some 600,000 genetic samples held by the 16 research centers of the Consultative Group on International Agricultural Research (CGIAR) come under the terms of the treaty, and the Global Crop Diversity Trust was established to support gene conservation and assist developing countries. Since 2003 the FAO has spent $35 million in agency and donor aid to combat and track the spread of avian influenza. It has also been involved in tracking Creutzfeldt-Jakob disease, otherwise known as "mad cow disease," in cattle and served an advisory role in rehabilitating areas impacted by the December 2004 tsunami in Southeast Asia.

In October 2006, the agency issued a warning that in the ten years following the World Food Summit pledge to halve world hunger, little to no progress had been made. A 2007 FAO brief, *The State of Food and Agriculture,* reported widespread waste in the processing and shipping of food aid by donor countries.

The FAO commissioned the first-ever independent evaluation of itself, and in July 2007 a draft form was released. "FAO: The Challenge of Renewal" gave a harsh review of the 60-year-old organization, calling for a three-to-four year immediate action plan to address longstanding management and budget failings. The report, finalized later in the year, called the FAO's governance "weak" and noted a lack of clear priorities, insufficient trust and mutual understanding between member states and the Secretariat, declining budget resources, and needed re-appraisal of the FAO's development efforts. The report urged the FAO to shift its focus from food production to employment as a means of income generation and food access and warned that failure to do so would cause the FAO to fade into insignificance. Director General Diouf declared that he "welcomed" the report as "a significant and historic effort to improve the organization's work," adding that the report "recognizes that change is a shared responsibility of the (FAO) secretariat and the member countries." The FAO conference of November 2007 established an elaborately structured committee, or set of working groups, to address the report's recommendations. These working groups were scheduled to report back late in 2008 (see below).

Meanwhile the FAO was forced to respond to the steep rise in food prices in 2008. In advance of a June 4, 2008, FAO conference on world food security, to be held in Rome, President Abdoulaye Wade of Senegal lashed out at the FAO and his fellow countryman Jacques Diouf. Wade called the FAO an "inefficient money-gobbler" that should be abolished. He also threatened to sue the FAO for deducting, as he claimed, 20 percent of all funds collected to alleviate the food crisis.

In September 2008 Diouf said that the number of hungry people worldwide had risen from 850 million to 925 million in 2007, and that he could see the number reaching one billion by the end of 2008. He called for an annual investment of $30 billion to double world food production. On November 20, 2008, the FAO adopted a plan of reform. The plan involved spending $42.6 million over three years, roughly half of it in 2009, to effect "reform with growth." Among other things, the plan would reduce the agency's 120 directorships by one third, freeing up $17.4 million to be spent on technical assistance programs. Director-General Diouf said, "We must build a new FAO," promising a "sweeping overhaul of the way FAO works."

The year 2009 saw a reduction in world food prices from their peaks of the previous year, but prices still remained a concern, particularly in poor countries. The FAO remained critical of biofuels because they compete with food production. UN aid to Colombia's extensive biofuel program was suspended. By June 2009 the FAO stated that the number of people worldwide without enough food had reached 1 billion—a number driven by the global economic crisis. At a seminar held in October 2009, Diouf warned that world food production must increase by 70 percent if the world's growing population was to be fed.

INTERNATIONAL BANK FOR RECONSTRUCTION AND DEVELOPMENT (IBRD)

Established: By Articles of Agreement signed in Bretton Woods, New Hampshire, July 22, 1944, effective December 27, 1945; began operation June 25, 1946. The IBRD became a UN Specialized Agency by agreement with the Economic and Social Council (approved by the General Assembly on November 15, 1947).

Purpose: To promote the international flow of capital for productive purposes, initially the rebuilding of nations devastated by World War II. The main objective of the bank at present is to offer loans at reasonable terms to member developing countries willing to engage in projects that will ultimately increase their productive capacities and reduce poverty.

Headquarters: Washington, D.C., United States.

Principal Organs: Board of Governors (all members), Executive Directors (24).

Web site: www.worldbank.org/ibrd

President: Robert Zoellick (United States).

Membership (186)**:** See Appendix C.

Working Language: English.

Origin and development. The International Bank for Reconstruction and Development was one of the two main products of the United Nations Monetary and Financial Conference held July 1–22, 1944, in Bretton Woods, New Hampshire. The bank was conceived as a center for mobilizing and allocating capital resources for the reconstruction of war-torn states and for the expansion of world production and trade; its sister institution, the International Monetary Fund (IMF), was created to maintain order in the field of currencies and exchange rates and thus to prevent a repetition of the financial chaos of the 1930s. The Articles of Agreement of the two institutions were annexed to the Final Act of the Bretton Woods Conference and went into effect December 27, 1945, following ratification by the required 28 states.

With the commencement of the U.S.-sponsored European Recovery Program in 1948 and the enunciation in 1949 of the U.S. "Point Four" program of technical assistance to less developed areas, the focus of IBRD activities began to shift toward economic development. Accordingly, two affiliated institutions—the International Finance Corporation (IFC) and the International Development Association (IDA), created in 1956 and 1960, respectively (see separate entries)—were established within the IBRD's framework to undertake developmental responsibilities for which the IBRD itself was not qualified under its Articles of Agreement. In 1985 the IBRD approved a charter for another affiliate, the Multilateral Investment Guarantee Agency (MIGA), to provide borrowers with protection against noncommercial risks such as war, uncompensated expropriations, or repudiation of contracts by host governments without adequate legal redress for affected parties. The MIGA, operating as a distinct legal and financial entity, came into being on April 12, 1988, with about 54 percent of its initial $1.1 billion in authorized capital having been subscribed. As of 2007 there were 171 MIGA members.

The IBRD and IDA have long been referred to as the World Bank, or as the World Bank Group when considered in conjunction with affiliate organizations the IFC, the MIGA, and the International Center for Settlement of Investment Disputes (ICSID). The IBRD is responsible for lending to middle-income and creditworthy poor countries, while IDA extends grants and interest-free loans to the world's poorest countries. Loan statistics for both the IBRD and the IDA are given in this article.

In 1959 the bank authorized its first general capital increase, from $10 billion to $21 billion. Several special capital increases followed, and in January 1980 the Board of Governors authorized a second general capital increase of $40 billion—a virtual doubling of resources. A third general increase was approved in 1988 (see Activities, below).

Structure. All of the IBRD's powers are formally vested in the Board of Governors, which consists of a governor and an alternate appointed by each member state. The IBRD governors, who are usually finance ministers or equivalent national authorities, serve concurrently as governors of the IMF, as well as of the IFC, the IDA, and the MIGA, assuming that a given country's affiliations extend beyond the parent organization. The board meets each fall to review the operations of these institutions within the framework of a general examination of the world financial and economic situation. One meeting in three is held away from Washington, D.C.

Most powers of the Board of Governors are delegated to the IBRD's 24 executive directors, who meet at least once a month at the bank's headquarters and are responsible for the general conduct of its operations. Five of the directors are separately appointed by those members holding the largest number of shares of capital stock (France, Germany, Japan, the United Kingdom, and the United States). The others are individually elected for two-year terms by the remaining IBRD members, who are divided into 19 essentially geographical groupings, each of which selects one director. (Since Saudi Arabia by itself constitutes one of the geographical entities, its "election" of a director amounts, in practical terms, to an appointment. Similarly, China and the Russian Federation have single directors.) Each director is entitled to cast as a unit the votes of those members who elected him.

The bank operates on a weighted voting system that is largely based on individual country subscriptions (themselves based on IMF quotas), but with poorer states being accorded a slightly disproportionate share. As of 2008, the leading subscribers were the United States, with 16.84 percent (16.38 percent of voting power); Japan, 8.07 (7.86); Germany, 4.60 (4.49); France and the United Kingdom, 4.41 (4.30); Canada, China, India, Italy, the Russian Federation, and Saudi Arabia, 2.85 (2.78) each; Netherlands, 2.26 (2.21); Brazil, 2.12 (2.07); Belgium, 1.84 (1.81); Spain, 1.78 (1.74); Switzerland, 1.69 (1.66); and Australia, 1.55 (1.53).

The president of the IBRD is elected to a renewable five-year term by the executive directors, serves as their chair, and is responsible for conducting the business of the bank as well as that of the IDA and the IFC. In accordance with the wishes of the U.S. government, Robert McNamara was replaced upon his retirement in June 1981 by Alden W. Clausen, a former president of the Bank of America, who restructured the bank's upper echelon to reflect his preference for collegial management and delegation of authority. On June 30, 1986, Clausen was succeeded by Barber B. Conable Jr., who had served on a number of financial committees in the course of ten consecutive terms in the U.S. House of Representatives. In May 1987 Conable announced a major reorganization within the bank to clarify and strengthen the roles of the president and senior management. Another change was the creation of country departments to oversee all aspects of individual lending projects; Conable also ordered a controversial review of all bank positions, which ultimately yielded about 350 redundancies.

Following the announcement of Conable's retirement, the executive directors in April 1991 approved the appointment of Lewis T. Preston, former chair of the board of J. P. Morgan and Morgan Guaranty Trust Company, as the next president, effective August 31. Preston's selection was seen as reflecting the insistence of the United States on additional private sector involvement by the bank and greater commercial bank influence in debt reduction negotiations. Like his predecessor, Preston instituted a number of structural changes early in his term that appeared to further concentrate power in the president's hands. Three senior vice presidents were eliminated and the remaining sixteen vice presidents were ordered to report directly to the president. Preston died on May 4, 1995, and was succeeded on June 1 by James D. Wolfensohn, a prominent New York investment banker (see below). Administrative reforms continued under Wolfensohn, who in December 1996 appointed two new managing directors. Wolfensohn was succeeded in June 2005 by Paul Wolfowitz, previously the U.S. deputy secretary of defense. After implementing a string of controversial anticorruption measures, Wolfowitz resigned after two years in office under conflict-of-interest charges. He was replaced in July 2007 by former U.S. deputy secretary of state Robert Zoellick, then a vice chair of leading New York investment house Goldman Sachs.

Activities. The IBRD describes itself as structured like a cooperative. It is the organ of the World Bank that "works with middle-income and creditworthy poorer countries to promote sustainable, equitable and job-creating growth, reduce poverty and address issues of regional and global importance." Most funds available for lending are obtained by direct borrowing on world financial markets. Only a small percentage of the capital subscription of the member states represents paid-in capital in dollars, other currencies, or demand notes; the balance is "callable capital" that is subject to call by the bank only when needed to meet obligations incurred through borrowing or through guaranteeing loans. Most of the bank's operating funds are obtained by issuing interest-bearing bonds and notes to public and private investors.

The Articles of Agreement state that the IBRD can make loans only for productive purposes for which funds are not obtainable in the private market on reasonable terms. Loans are long-term (generally repayable over as much as 20 years, with a 5-year grace period) and are available only to member states, their political subdivisions, and enterprises located in the territories of member states (in which case, the states involved must guarantee the projects).

In order to maintain the bank's financial strength and integrity as a borrower in the world capital markets, the executive directors agreed on July 2, 1982, to switch from the bank's traditional fixed-interest policy to a variable-interest policy. This action, taken in conjunction with the bank's borrowing operations in short-term capital markets, was intended to enable the bank to charge interest rates that more accurately reflect the institution's current capital costs. Under the revised system, interest rates are adjusted each January 1 and July 1 to reflect the cost of funds in a pool of bank borrowings from the preceding six-month period, plus a 0.5 percent surcharge. The bank has also initiated currency swap arrangements as an additional method of reducing its overall borrowing costs.

In the field of aid coordination, the bank has taken the lead in promoting a multilateral approach to the development problems of particular states by organizing groups of potential donors to work out long-range comprehensive plans for assistance. In addition, the bank has worked on projects with a large number of multilateral financial agencies, including the African Development Bank, the Asian Development Bank, the Inter-American Development Bank, the European Development Fund, and the Arab Fund for Economic and Social Development.

IBRD technical-assistance activities are directed toward overcoming the shortage of skills that tends to hamper economic growth in less developed states. The bank finances and organizes numerous pre-investment studies, ranging from those aimed at determining the feasibility of particular projects to sector studies directed toward formulating investment programs in such major fields as power and transport. It also sends expert missions to assist members in designing development programs and adopting policies conducive to economic growth, while the Economic Development Institute, the IBRD staff college, helps train senior officials of less developed states in development techniques.

In 1984, a time of review and reappraisal, which some critics described as a "mid-life crisis," the IBRD implemented new mechanisms to boost central bank borrowing as well as borrowing in floating rate notes. However, despite pressures arising from recession and indebtedness in the third world, donor members—especially the United States—opposed any increase in the bank's general resources. A year later, in a significant policy shift, the United States reversed itself, and in 1986 negotiations on an increase intensified as the global debt burden placed pressure on the bank for new and expanded strategies for helping developing countries.

In May 1987 the bank entered an unusually turbulent period when President Conable launched a structural reorganization and staff retrenchment (see Structure, above). However, response was widely favorable to policy statements by Conable "rededicating" the bank to the alleviation of poverty in the developing world while expanding emphasis on environmental protection, debt-front action, and the integration of women in development. During its annual meeting in the fall, the Board of Governors broadly endorsed Conable's initiatives, and a capital increase of $74.8 billion (payable within three years) was approved in early 1988, bringing total authorized capital to $171 billion.

Prior to the joint World Bank–IMF meetings in West Berlin in September, the IBRD reported that in fiscal 1987–1988 it had received $1.9 billion more in repayments on previous loans from developing countries than it had disbursed in new loans, a continuation of the "negative transfer of resources" that had elicited criticism of both the bank and the IMF in recent years. Subsequently, in April 1989 the two organizations adopted a significantly revised approach to the debt crisis, including use of their resources to encourage commercial banks to reduce obligations of countries who had implemented policy reforms. As the new debt strategy evolved, the IBRD and the IMF agreed to permit approved countries to use up to 40 percent of their allocated credits to eliminate some commercial bank debt and to help make payments on new or rescheduled loans.

The environment was the primary focus of the 1992 *World Development Report*, which was issued shortly before the June 1992 Earth Summit in Rio de Janeiro, Brazil. The IBRD argued that environmental protection in developing nations depended to a large extent on the ability of the governments of those nations to generate "the political will" to insist on pollution control and the wise management of natural resources. Ironically, the bank itself had been coming under growing attack for the negative effects some of its projects were having on the environment. Consequently, the bank announced in its annual report published later in the year that it would reassess the environmental impact of many current projects and insist that all future projects address any "well founded" environmental concerns.

In April 1993 it was reported that an internal review had acknowledged a "significant failure rate" within the bank's operations, with about 20 percent of the loans active in 1991 having "major problems." Although the design of some projects and the bank's follow-up procedures were criticized, the failures were primarily attributed to poor economic conditions during the 1980s in Africa, Latin America, and parts of Asia.

In July 1993 the leaders of the world's seven leading industrialized nations agreed during a summit in Tokyo to offer Moscow an aid package that included up to $1 billion in World Bank lending. Initial approvals were constrained by Moscow's difficulty in controlling government spending and inflation, coupled with economic and political turmoil within many of its newly independent neighbors. However, an improved situation led to what was expected to be at least $2 billion in additional lending.

In mid-1994 the bank embarked on another major project: the coordination of $2.4 billion in pledges from international donors for the Gaza Strip and Jericho, where the new Palestinian National Authority had recently been installed. Much of the Palestinian aid was earmarked for infrastructure development, a focus of the 1994 *World Development Report*.

For the fiscal year July 1, 1993, through June 30, 1994, the IBRD reported loan approvals of $14.2 billion for 124 operations in 60 countries, significantly less than the previous fiscal year, when approvals totaled $17 billion. Bank officials said that progress had been made in monitoring loan performance and in integrating environmental concerns into IBRD activity. In addition, the bank established the three-member Independent Inspection Panel to investigate complaints about specific loans. However, the changes did not placate many of the bank's critics, environmentalists in particular continuing to assail the IBRD's "obsolete" industrial development policies. Questions also continued over the bank's role in the external debt problems facing many developing countries, highlighted by the fact that the IBRD in 1993–1994 took in $731 million more in repayments than it disbursed in new funds.

Lending approvals increased in fiscal year July 1, 1994, through June 30, 1995, totaling $16.9 billion for 134 projects. However, a decline in lending was expected under new bank president Wolfensohn, who proposed significant changes for the IBRD, including a shift away from "megaprojects" that often had proven difficult for developing countries to manage after they had been completed. In their stead, Wolfensohn said the bank should concentrate on small, environmentally sound projects that offered direct benefits to the poor. He also urged the bank to devote much more of its energy and resources to the promotion of private investment in developing countries and spearheaded the establishment of a new debt relief program, the Heavily Indebted Poor Countries (HIPC) debt-reduction initiative, for the poorest developing nations, most of which are African.

In March 1997 the Executive Board approved a Strategic Compact with the goal of increasing the World Bank's efficiency and effectiveness through "fundamental reform." Among the substantive goals of the 30-month program were the reduction of overhead and administrative costs, decentralization of the bank's operation, and the development and improvement of relationships with other organizations.

In the 1997 *World Development Report*, the IBRD asserted that "effective" governments, i.e., those that are relatively free of corruption and limited in scope, are a necessary precondition for social and economic development. Furthermore, both the IBRD and IMF began to insist on effective governance as a condition for their assistance. The bank subsequently emphasized the role of local governments in fostering development, arguing that corruption at the municipal level often undermined the best intentions of national policies. In 1998 President Wolfensohn also challenged the international financial community to develop a new long-term strategy to provide relief to the poor, and asserted, among other things, that the IMF was paying insufficient attention to the human costs of its financial stabilization activities. Debate on the subject continued into the preparation of the 2000 *World Development Report*, at which time several authors objected to the overdependence on "pro-market orthodoxy." The final report appeared to favor the "reformist" camp by calling for "empowerment" of the poor and protection of "vulnerable groups." Along those same lines, Wolfensohn subsequently called for dialogue with anti-globalization protesters who had recently conducted highly publicized demonstrations against the World Bank, IMF, and World Trade Organization (WTO). At the same time, the United States continued to press the IBRD to reduce its lending to certain middle-income countries (particularly in Latin America) which, according to the United States, needed to be weaned away from World Bank lending in favor of loans from the private sector.

In 2001–2002 the IBRD called on the wealthy nations of the world to increase their assistance to developing countries substantially, particularly in view of the global economic slowdown, which had exacerbated debt problems. The bank acknowledged that the HIPC Initiative had so far come up very short in reaching the goal of "sustainable" debt for the 34 countries considered eligible for assistance. Nevertheless, bank officials maintained their hope that more than $50 billion in debt would ultimately be canceled through the program.

IBRD lending approvals increased dramatically to $21.1 billion for 151 projects in 1997–1998 and $22.2 billion for 131 projects in 1998–1999, primarily due to the financial crises in Asia and Latin America. However, after conditions improved and the private sector resumed lending to emerging market economies, IBRD approvals declined to $10.9 billion for 97 projects in 1999–2000, $10.5 billion for 91 projects in 2000–2001, and $11.5 billion for 96 projects in 2000–2002. The reduced lending also underscored the bank's increased emphasis on "quality rather than quantity" in its lending. Special assistance was provided in 2002 for countries that had suffered particularly strong "economic shocks" in the wake of the September 11, 2001, attacks in the United States and the economic downturn that had begun even prior to those events. As of mid-2002, cumulative IBRD lending had reached over $370 billion for more than 4,600 projects.

In 2003 the bank announced that it would resume lending for large-scale infrastructure projects in developing countries after a hiatus of years. In other activity in 2003, the bank urged governments in the Middle East and North Africa to institute economic reform to combat high unemployment among the young, which the IBRD characterized as the "driving force" behind Islamic radicalism.

In May 2004 the Group of Eight (G-8) pledged to continue the HPIC Debt Initiative, then scheduled to expire at the end of the year. It was estimated that some 25 countries had qualified for debt relief to date. Meanwhile, President Wolfensohn blamed the industrialized countries for the collapse of WTO negotiations in 2003, arguing that developing countries deserved a stronger voice in the global economy. Wolfensohn also said it was "unacceptable" that unprecedented military spending around the world was impeding efforts to help the poor.

In March 2005 the U.S. George W. Bush administration announced that Wolfensohn's successor would be Paul Wolfowitz, the U.S. deputy secretary of defense who had recently attracted attention as one of the main architects of the U.S.-led overthrow of the Saddam Hussein regime in Iraq. Considering the global antipathy to the war, the appointment was viewed as controversial. However, Wolfowitz pledged that he would not direct the World Bank as a vehicle for promoting U.S. policy and would maintain his predecessor's emphasis on reducing poverty.

In July 2005 the IBRD announced it would provide $500 million in loans for "priority sectors" in Iraq. It was the first bank lending to Iraq in three decades. In its *World Development Report* for 2006, issued September 2005, the bank declared that reducing inequality by liberal economic actions was the key to reducing poverty, while admitting that such inequality had risen. It suggested that the world's richest countries should abandon subsidies and encourage freer migration of skilled workers from developing countries. The report endorsed a decision by the G-8 countries at their July 2005 summit in Scotland to cancel some $55 billion in debt from the world's poorest countries.

Meanwhile, controversy surrounding Wolfowitz mounted as staff began resenting his heavy use of outside advisers. The anticorruption measures he imposed in developing countries, one of his major pledges coming into office, came under increasing criticism. Also, a December 2006 report by the bank's Independent Evaluation Group (IEG) noted that many of the anticorruption policies were failing because they lacked broad-based political consensus and were often implemented at the expense of poverty reduction and job creation goals. In March 2007 the World Bank executive board adopted a new policy that reined in the president's ability to cut funding without first consulting the board and allowed the bank to deal with independent groups in a country when it cut off loans to that country's government.

Two months later, Wolfowitz came under personal scrutiny over his role in engineering the promotion and salary raise of his companion, a female bank employee. He resigned in June 2007 amid calls for better internal controls and a more open and transparent hiring process for the bank president. Less influential member nations also renewed calls for more voting and decision-making powers. In July 2007 the bank appointed as president U.S. nominee Robert Zoellick, a former U.S. deputy secretary of state and U.S. trade representative. Zoellick announced a major policy shift in the bank's lending strategy that would boost funding for agricultural projects as a more effective means towards poverty reduction.

In advance of the World Bank and IMF annual meeting in October 2007, Zoellick called on wealthy nations to significantly increase their financial support for poor nations as part of a plan to more than double the bank's funding in grants and credits for poor countries under the IDA. He directed the IBRD and the IFC to increase contributions to the IDA as well.

In September, the bank's executive board simplified and reduced loan charges by a quarter percentage point for the 79 creditworthy countries funded by the IBRD. The change was part of an effort to increase the relevancy and attractiveness of the IBRD, which has faced competition from private sector lending sources.

As the price of food increased dramatically, causing distress in many countries of the world, the World Bank took a new interest in farming. The 2007 edition of the *World Development Report* stressed the importance of agriculture as the fastest way of improving a poor nation's economy, and the 2008 food crisis drove the point home. In April 2008 Zoellick announced, and the World Bank endorsed, a "new deal" action plan to pump more money into agricultural economies. On April 29 the UN set up an emergency task force to deal with the food situation, the members drawn from interested UN agencies and the World Bank. In July Zoellick called on the United States and the EU to use less biofuels and to concentrate instead on growing food products for human consumption.

The World Bank reported providing $47 billion in loans during the 2008–2009 fiscal year, with $33 billion coming from the IBRD and $14 billion from the IDA. It provided $25 billion for 2007–2008 (IBRD $14 billion and IDA $11 billion) and $25 billion for 2006–2007 (IBRD $13 billion and IDA $12 billion).

During 2009 the World Bank issued various statements about the global financial crisis. On April 24 it published a report declaring that the United States and the EU were leading the world in a new round of protectionism. Also in April Zoellick warned of a "human catastrophe" unless more was done to combat the economic crisis. By September 2009 the organization warned that, while things might be going better for the world's rich, the poor were in no way recovering.

In March 2009 the World Bank launched a commission to investigate its own operations and suggest ways in which it might improve. The commission, headed by former Mexican president Ernesto ZEDILLO, released its report in October 2009. Among other suggestions, the Zedillo commission recommended restructuring the bank's governing bodies, strengthening management accountability, and making the selection of a president "merit-based, transparent, and open."

INTERNATIONAL CIVIL AVIATION ORGANIZATION (ICAO)

Established: By Convention signed in Chicago, Illinois, United States, December 7, 1944, effective April 4, 1947. The ICAO became a UN Specialized Agency by agreement with the Economic and Social Council (approved by the General Assembly on December 14, 1946, effective May 13, 1947).

Purpose: To promote international cooperation in the development of principles and techniques of air navigation and air transport.

Headquarters: Montreal, Canada.

Principal Organs: Assembly (all members), Council (36 members), Air Navigation Commission, Secretariat.

Web site: www.icao.int

Secretary General: Raymond Benjamin (France).

Membership (190): See Appendix C.

Official Languages: Arabic, Chinese, English, French, Russian, Spanish.

Origin and development. The accelerated development of aviation during World War II provided the impetus for expanding international cooperation, beginning in 1919 with the establishment of the International Commission for Air Navigation (ICAN) under the so-called Paris Convention drafted at the Versailles Peace Conference. The main result of the International Civil Aviation Conference held November–December 1944 in Chicago, Illinois, was the adoption of a 96-article convention providing, among other things, for a new international organization that would supersede both ICAN and the Pan-American Convention on Commercial Aviation (concluded in 1928). Responsibilities assigned to the new organization included developing international air navigation; fostering the planning and orderly growth of safe international air transport; encouraging the development of airways, airports, and air navigation facilities; preventing economic waste caused by unreasonable competition; and promoting the development of all aspects of international civil aeronautics.

An interim agreement, signed December 7, 1944, in Chicago, established the Provisional International Civil Aviation Organization (PICAO), which functioned from June 1945 until the deposit of ratifications brought the ICAO itself into existence in April 1947. Its status as a UN Specialized Agency was defined by an agreement approved during the first session of the ICAO Assembly.

Structure. The ICAO Assembly, in which each member state has one vote, is convened at least once every three years to determine general policy, establish a budget, elect the members of the Council, and act on any matter referred to it by the Council.

Continuous supervision of the ICAO's operation is the responsibility of the Council, which is composed of 36 states elected by the ICAO Assembly for three-year terms on the basis of their importance in air transport, their contribution of facilities for air navigation, and their geographical distribution. Meeting frequently in Montreal, the Council implements assembly decisions; appoints the secretary general; administers ICAO finances; collects, analyzes, and disseminates information concerning air navigation; and adopts international standards and recommended practices with respect to civil aviation. The Council is assisted by, and appoints the members of, the Air Navigation Commission and the various standing committees. Regional offices are maintained in Cairo, Egypt (Middle East); Bangkok, Thailand (Asia and the Pacific); Neuilly-sur-Seine Cedex, France (Europe and the North Atlantic); Mexico City, Mexico (North America, Central America, and the Caribbean) Lima, Peru (South America); Dakar, Senegal (Western and Central Africa); and Nairobi, Kenya (Eastern and Southern Africa).

The Secretariat, headed by the secretary general, is assisted by five subsidiary bureaus: Air Navigation, Air Transport, Technical Cooperation, Legal, and Administration and Services.

Activities. The ICAO has been instrumental in generating international action in such areas as meteorological services, air traffic control, communications, and navigation facilities. It also has an impressive record of advancing uniform standards and practices to ensure safety and efficiency. Any member unable to implement an established civil aviation standard must notify the ICAO, which in turn notifies all other members. Standards and practices are constantly reviewed and, when necessary, amended by the Council. Other areas of involvement have ranged from the leasing and chartering of aircraft to minimizing the effects of aircraft noise and engine emissions on the environment.

The ICAO also provides technical assistance to most of the world's developing countries. Among its most important activities have been analyses of long-term civil aviation requirements and the preparation of national civil aviation plans as well as the development and updating of aviation skills and the harmonization of air transport regulations.

The ICAO's intensified efforts to devise effective deterrents to hijacking and air piracy resulted in a series of international conventions developed under its auspices: Tokyo, Japan (1963); The Hague, Netherlands (1970); and Montreal (1971). The ICAO also considered the issue of the interception of civil aircraft following the 1983 destruction by Soviet fighters of a Korean Air Lines (KAL) Boeing 747 carrying 269 civilians. As a result of the ICAO investigation, which concluded that the plane had deviated from its course as a result of a navigational error probably caused by an improperly programmed flight computer, an amendment to the Chicago Convention was adopted that recognized the duty to refrain from the use of weapons against civil aircraft in flight. The amendment, approved in May 1984 at a special assembly session at Montreal, came into force on October 1, 1998. In the interim, an extraordinary Council session in 1988 had addressed the downing of Iran Air Flight 655 in the Persian Gulf by the USS *Vincennes* in July, which resulted in 290 fatalities. An ICAO team of experts attributed the incident to poor planning by the U.S. Navy, which resulted in inadequate monitoring of civilian air traffic control frequencies and "the absence of a clear method of addressing challenged civil aircraft."

Another special Council session was held in February 1989 at U.S.-UK request to discuss the December 1988 bombing over Scotland of Pan American World Airways Flight 103, in which 270 people died. In December 1985 the ICAO Council had required all contracting states to apply more stringent security measures for international flights, including tighter controls on baggage and cargo, the denial of access to aircraft by unauthorized personnel, and a ban on contact between screened and unscreened passengers. Following the Pan Am incident, the Council unanimously adopted a resolution calling for further aviation security measures, particularly regarding electronic devices, while urging further study of proposals to set higher training standards for security personnel, restrict access to planes by airport workers, and increase the ICAO's role in enforcing security.

In 1991 the ICAO's tenth annual Air Navigation Conference endorsed plans for the implementation of a satellite-based communications, navigation, surveillance, and air traffic management system (CNS/ATM). The decision to speed the switch from a ground-based system was facilitated in large part by U.S. and USSR offers of free access to their navigation satellite networks.

In 1996 the ICAO issued a statement deploring the downing of two American civilian aircraft by the Cuban air force over international waters on February 26. The UN General Assembly subsequently endorsed a resolution, originating from the ICAO, calling on all nations to reaffirm their pledge to take precautions against such actions.

In 1997 the organization initiated the first ICAO Strategic Action Plan, Guiding Civil Aviation into the 21st Century, a comprehensive reevaluation of the ICAO's mission. It set eight major objectives for the organization: promote the use of ICAO standards and recommended practices (SARPs) throughout the world; update the standards and practices as circumstances dictate; bolster civilian aviation's legal framework; update, coordinate, and set in motion regional air navigation plans; facilitate "timely" response to difficulties facing civilian aviation; update ICAO "guidance and information" regarding the economic regulations placed on international air travel; help mobilize resources for civil aviation; and make the operation of the ICAO as efficient and effective as possible.

Safety was the main focus at the meeting of the ICAO Assembly in September–October 1998. In addition to authorizing creation of the Universal Safety Oversight Audit Program (USOAP), which entered into effect at the beginning of 1999, the assembly approved the Charter on the Rights and Obligations of States Relating to Global Navigation Satellite Systems (GNSS), preparatory to eventual drafting of a GNSS convention.

The 33rd ICAO Assembly opened September 25, 2001, in Montreal, two weeks after al-Qaida operatives hijacked four commercial airlines and caused nearly 3,000 deaths in the United States. Accordingly, security issues dominated the ten-day session. In addition to recommending a review of current aviation security conventions and the development of a security oversight audit program, the session called for convening a conference on civil aviation and the threat of terrorism.

Attended by delegates from 154 countries, the resultant High-Level Ministerial Conference on Aviation Security met February 19–20, 2002, in Montreal and endorsed creation of an Aviation Security Plan of Action that would include "regular, mandatory, systematic and harmonized audits" of security procedures and controls. The plan is, in effect, in process as a living document, but is currently being implemented. The conference's concluding declaration, in addition to condemning "the use of civil aircraft as weapons of destruction," specified that the action plan be developed within four months for adoption by the ICAO Council. On July 1, 2002, an amendment to the security provisions of the Chicago Convention entered into effect, making the convention applicable to domestic as well as international flights, requiring measures to prevent unauthorized entry to the flight deck, limiting preflight access to aircraft, and aiming for screening of all checked baggage by 2006.

The Fifth Worldwide Air Transport Conference met March 24–28, 2003, in Montreal and concluded with near unanimity on the need to liberalize rules governing market access and ownership in the airline industry. Although the ICAO itself has no authority over questions of pricing, capacity, and market entry and access, all of which are regulated by individual countries and some 3,000 bilateral agreements, the session participants endorsed the Conference Declaration of Global Principles for the Liberalization of International Air Transport to spur regulatory reform. Immediately after the conference, the ICAO held an extraordinary assembly session that focused on security and safety issues, including the creation of the International Financial Facility for Aviation Safety.

In November 2003 the Montreal Convention of 1999 entered into force, superseding provisions of the 1929 Warsaw Convention and updating rules on liability for death, injury, or other losses involving civil aircraft.

In quick response to the August 2006 alleged terrorist plot in the United Kingdom that involved the potential use of liquids as explosives, the ICAO set a March 2007 deadline to restrict liquids, gels, and aerosol products that might be used as improvised explosive devices on aircraft. It also approved the Global Air Navigation Plan in November 2006 to increase efficiency of air transport operations through changes to global air traffic management systems.

European Commission (EC) efforts to apply a cap and trade system on carbon dioxide emissions for foreign airlines flying into Europe failed in a controversial vote during the 36th ICAO Assembly meeting on September 18–29, 2007. Facing stiff resistance from the United States, Brazil, Japan, and China, who argued the emissions restrictions would unduly burden companies, the ICAO instead created the Group on International Aviation and Climate Change, composed of senior government officials, to recommend an action plan by 2009 on reducing global warming emissions in the airline industry. Some observers reported significant EU discontent with the ICAO as it presently operates. Complaints have been made that the organization should produce fewer, but clearer, regulations and that it should concentrate less on bilateral agreements and more on dealings with regional groups of countries, such as the EU itself. In December 2007 the EU began negotiations with the ICAO to ease some of the security restrictions that had been imposed after the September 11, 2001, terrorist attacks in the United States. An agreement was announced in September 2008.

In March 2008 the ICAO revealed that only 39 member states had met the organization's March 5 deadline for testing the English-language skills of pilots and air traffic controllers. The ICAO extended a grace period to March 5, 2011, and asked member nations not to exclude aircraft from non-compliant countries. In July 2008 the organization announced that all countries being monitored under USOAP had authorized it to post audit results on its public website. As of late 2009 these reports were available and up to date.

A December 2008 preliminary ICAO report reflected the impact of the world economic crisis on civil aviation. It noted "a significant drop in growth with only a 1.8 percent increase over 2007 in terms of Passenger Kilometers Performed (PKP)." The report predicted a modest recovery by 2010. An ICAO message for International Civil Aviation Day, December 7, 2008, was titled "Tomorrow's Aviation—a world of opportunity for skilled aviation personnel." It stated that many skilled aviation staff would be retiring in the next few years and would need to be replaced.

In April 2009 the ICAO, in cooperation with many business and world governmental partners, rolled out a new air navigation concept called "Performance-based Navigation (PBN)," with the aim of promoting "safer, shorter, and greener flights."

INTERNATIONAL DEVELOPMENT ASSOCIATION (IDA)

Established: By Articles of Agreement concluded in Washington, D.C., January 26, 1960, effective September 24, 1960. The IDA became a UN Specialized Agency by agreement with the Economic and Social Council (approved by the General Assembly on March 27, 1961).

Purpose: To assist in financing economic development in less developed member states by providing development credits on special terms, with particular emphasis on projects not attractive to private investors.

Headquarters: Washington, D.C., United States.

Web site: www.worldbank.org/ida

Membership (169): See Appendix C.

Working Language: English.

Origin and development. The IDA was established in response to an increasing awareness during the latter 1950s that the needs of less developed states for additional capital resources could not be fully satisfied through existing lending institutions and procedures. This was particularly true of the very poor states, which urgently needed finance on terms more concessionary than those of the International Bank for Reconstruction and Development (IBRD). Thus, in 1958 the United States proposed the creation of an institution with authority to provide credits on special terms in support of approved development projects for which normal financing was not available. Following approval by the Board of Governors of the IBRD, the IDA was established as an affiliate of that institution and was given a mandate to provide development financing, within the limits of its resources, on terms more flexible than those of conventional loans and less burdensome to the balance of payments of recipient states. Today, the IBRD and the IDA together are generally known as the World Bank.

The authorized capital of the IDA was initially fixed at $1 billion, of which the United States contributed $320 million. Members of the institution were divided by the IDA Articles of Agreement into two groups in accordance with their economic status and the nature of their contributions to the institution's resources. Part I (high-income) states pay their entire subscription in convertible currencies, all of which may be used for IDA credits; Part II (low-income) states pay only 10 percent of their subscriptions in convertible currencies and the remainder in their own currencies. Part I countries account for about 97 percent of total subscriptions and supplementary resources (special voluntary contributions and transfers from IBRD net earnings). As of 2007, leading Part I contributors were the United States, $38.9 billion in subscriptions and contributions (12.94 percent of voting power under the IDA's weighted system); Japan, $28.9 billion (10.05); Germany, $19.7 billion (6.45); United Kingdom, $18.3 billion (5.14); France, $12.6 billion (4.12); Italy, $6.8 billion (2.59); and Canada, $6.3 billion (2.77). Leading Part II contributors are Saudi Arabia, $2.3 billion (3.34); Republic of Korea, $1.1 billion (0.64); Brazil, $584 million (1.69); Turkey, $142 million (0.64); Mexico, $138 million (0.62); and Argentina, $69.8 million (0.81). The weighted voting system has sometimes been criticized as unfair to smaller, poorer countries.

Member countries agreed to significant increases in the IDA's lending capital in 1964, 1968, 1972, 1977, and 1979. The sixth replenishment (IDA-VI), agreed to in January 1980, was to provide for legal commitments of $12 billion for the three-year period beginning July 1, 1981. However, with formal approval requiring adherence by members representing 80 percent of the new subscriptions, the replenishment was delayed because of inaction by the United States, which was to provide 27 percent of the increase. Although the replenishment was finally authorized in August, a decision of the U.S. Congress to divide the U.S. share into four contributions during 1981–1983 caused deep concern at the annual meeting of the World Bank Group in September, because it threatened loan credits already approved by the IDA in advance of the increase. The seventh replenishment (for 1984–1987) was also adversely affected by U.S. action, with only $9 billion of a target of $16 billion becoming available after the United States decided to cut its annual contributions by 20 percent (see Activities, below, for subsequent replenishments).

Structure. As an affiliate of the IBRD, the IDA has no separate institutions; its directors, officers, and staff are those of the IBRD.

Activities. The IDA is the single largest multilateral source of concessional assistance for low-income countries. Countries that had a 2006 annual per capita income of less than $1,065, had limited or no ability to borrow from the IBRD, and had good performance in implementation of IDA economic and social policies could qualify for IDA funds. (Thus 80 countries comprising 2.5 billion people, many living on less than $2 per day, were eligible.) IDA also provides grants to countries at risk of debt distress. To date, IDA credits and grants have totaled $182 billion, with the largest share directed to Africa.

Under conditions revised as part of the IDA's eighth replenishment, credits are extended for terms as long as 40 years for the least developed countries and 20 and 35 years for other countries. Credits are free of interest but there is a 0.75 percent annual service charge on disbursed credits (a 0.50 percent "commitment fee" on undisbursed credits was eliminated July 1, 1988). All credits carry a ten-year grace period, with complete repayment of principal due over the remaining 20 or 35 years of the loans.

Most IDA credits have been provided for projects to improve physical infrastructure such as road and rail systems, electrical generation and transmission facilities, irrigation and flood-control installations, educational facilities, telephone exchanges and transmission lines, and industrial plants. Loans have also been extended for rural development projects designed specifically to raise the productivity of the rural-dwelling poor. These credits often cut across sector lines.

After lengthy negotiations in 1986, an agreement (formally approved by the Board of Governors in June 1987) was reached on an eighth replenishment for 1988–1990: a basic replenishment of $11.5 billion, with an additional $0.9 billion promised in supplemental contributions from a number of countries, led by Japan ($450 million) and the Netherlands ($126 million). About 45–50 percent of the additional resources were to be allocated to countries in Sub-Saharan Africa, 30 percent to China and India, and the rest to other third world recipients. Donors earmarked $3–3.5 billion for support of structural adjustment policies, particularly in Africa. In addition, the governors shortened repayment schedules somewhat to promote earlier and more extensive reflow of credits back through the association.

Negotiations on a ninth replenishment were initiated in early 1989, IDA officials hoping its total would exceed that of the eighth replenishment and thereby permit "sizable expansion" of concessional assistance to low-income countries in Latin America and South and East Asia, while maintaining appropriate levels of assistance in Africa. In December the IDA announced that agreement had been reached for a $15.5 billion replenishment to cover the three-year period beginning July 1, 1990. Additional priority was urged for antipoverty initiatives, environmental protection, structural adjustment, and programs in Sub-Saharan Africa.

The tenth replenishment, agreed on in December 1992 (covering July 1, 1993, to June 30, 1996), was for $18 billion, of which the United States pledged $3.75 billion. For the fiscal year July 1, 1994, through June 30, 1995, the IDA approved $5.7 billion in credits (down from $6.59 billion in the previous fiscal year) for 108 projects and adjustment programs in 51 countries. Despite deep concern that action by the U.S. Congress would severely curtail IDA lending in fiscal year 1995–1996, the United States, in the end, contributed $934 million, thereby clearing its arrears from the tenth replenishment. In return, the IDA agreed that the United States would be able to skip the first year's contribution to the 11th replenishment.

The negotiations for the 11th replenishment were buoyed by the renewed U.S. commitment, and pledges for July 1996 to June 1999 amounted to $22 billion, including $11 billion from donor countries. The remainder of the fund was to be financed through repaid credits, past donations, and other World Bank resources.

Negotiations for the 12th replenishment, covering the period from July 1999 to June 2002, were concluded in November 1998 when, during a meeting in Copenhagen, Denmark, donor countries agreed to a $20.5 billion infusion of funds to the IDA, $11.6 billion from the donors themselves. The apparent reduction in funding from the 11th replenishment was explained by changes in exchange rates and became a 13 percent increase when the funds were measured in special drawing rights (SDRs).

Borrowing countries and representatives of nongovernmental organizations were invited for the first time to participate in discussions regarding the 13th replenishment. The IDA also invited public comment on the negotiations, which culminated in a three-year (July 2002 to June 2005) replenishment of $23 billion. It was agreed that about 20 percent of overall IDA resources would henceforth be allocated in the form of grants rather than loans. (The United States had called for a 50 percent grant level on the theory that lending to date had done little to combat poverty while piling debt on developing countries.) Donors also insisted that future IDA assistance be tied to measurable progress on the part of recipient countries in areas such as education and health. Similar linkage was also endorsed to reward countries that encouraged good governance, free trade, and environmental protection.

Negotiations for the 14th replenishment (for July 2006–June 2009) concluded in April 2005 in Athens, Greece. Under this agreement, $34 billion was made available to the world's 81 poorest countries, which includes $18 billion in new contributions from 40 donor countries. At almost a 25 percent increase, it was the largest expansion of IDA resources in 20 years. Additionally, the countries facing the most difficult debt problems, mostly in Sub-Saharan Africa, are receiving all of their financial support in grants. Less debt-burdened countries are receiving mostly highly concessional long-term loans, or a mixture of grants and loans. Since the replenishment the IDA has approved loans that include funding for a mining project in Mauritania, electrical power generation projects in Ghana and Benin, and for educational projects in Albania.

In 2005 the IDA revised and enhanced a system to manage the success of its projects and review progress of recipient nations. Indicators such as growth and poverty reduction, governance and investment climate, infrastructure development, and human development criteria such as health and education were considered. In the 15th replenishment, completed in December 2007, to cover years 2009–2011, the IDA was to receive more than $41 billion as part of a stepped-up effort to meet 2015 Millennium Development Goals. The vast majority of funding increases were to go to Africa and South Asia, the regions farthest away from attaining poverty reduction goals. Additionally, World Bank president Robert Zoellick offered a new proposal to raise funding for the IDA from private sector businesses and foundations and pledged to focus on agricultural initiatives as a means to battle poverty. On June 26, 2008, U.S. senator Joseph R. Biden introduced the IDA Replenishment Act, authorizing U.S. funds for that purpose, in the U.S. Senate. The bill not having reached a vote in 2008 was reintroduced on May 15, 2009, by U.S. senator John Kerry (D-Mass) as the World Bank International Development Association Replenishment Act. As of late 2009 the bill had not yet become law.

INTERNATIONAL FINANCE CORPORATION (IFC)

Established: By Articles of Agreement concluded in Washington, D.C., May 25, 1955, effective July 20, 1956. The IFC became a UN Specialized Agency by agreement with the Economic and Social Council (approved by the General Assembly on February 20, 1957).

Purpose: To further economic development by encouraging the growth of productive private enterprise in member states, particularly the less developed areas. Its investment is usually in private or partially governmental enterprises.

Headquarters: Washington, D.C., United States.

Web site: www.ifc.org

Membership (182)**:** See Appendix C.

Working Language: English.

Origin and development. A suggestion that an international agency be formed to extend loans to private enterprises without government guarantees and to undertake equity investments in participation with other investors was made in 1951 by the U.S. International Development Advisory Board. That summer the UN Economic and Social Council requested that the International Bank for Reconstruction and Development (IBRD) investigate the possibility of creating such an agency, and a staff report was submitted to the UN secretary general in April 1952. The General Assembly in late 1954 requested the IBRD to draw up a charter, and the following April the bank formally submitted a draft for consideration. The IFC came into being on July 20, 1956, when 31 governments representing a sufficient percentage of total capital subscriptions accepted the Articles of Agreement.

Structure. As an affiliate of the IBRD, and thus a member of the World Bank Group, the IFC shares the same institutional structure. The president of the IBRD is also president of the IFC, and those governors and executive directors of the IBRD whose states belong to the IFC hold identical positions in the latter institution. The corporation has its own operating and legal staff but draws on the bank for administrative and other services. An executive vice president directs daily operations. As is true of the IBRD and the IDA, the IFC employs a weighted voting system based on country subscriptions, but with less developed states holding a disproportionate share of voting power.

IFC investments are handled through sectors, or industry departments, that process transactions and provide regional departments with expertise. They include Agribusiness; Global Financial Markets; Global Manufacturing and Services; Health and Education; Information and Communication Technologies; Infrastructure; Oil, Gas, Mining, and Chemicals; Private Equity and Investment Funds; and Subnational Finance. The corporation divides its 3,100-employees roughly in half between field offices and agency headquarters.

Activities. The IFC concentrates its efforts in three principal areas: project finance; resource mobilization; and financial, technical, and other advisory services. It conducts its own investment program, investigates the soundness of proposed projects to furnish expert advice to potential investors, and generally seeks to promote conditions conducive to the flow of private investment into development tasks. Investments, in the form of share subscriptions and long-term loans, are made in projects of economic priority to less developed member states where sufficient private capital is not available on reasonable terms and when the projects offer acceptable prospects for adequate returns. The IFC also carries out standby and underwriting arrangements and, under a policy adopted in July 1968, may give support in the pre-investment stage of potential projects by helping to pay for feasibility studies and for coordinating industrial, technical, and financial components, including the search for business sponsors. In addition, the IFC may join other investment groups interested in backing pilot or promotional companies, which then carry out the necessary studies and negotiations needed to implement the projects. The corporation neither seeks nor accepts government guarantees in its operations.

In June 1984 the IBRD Board of Directors approved a resolution to increase the IFC's authorized capital from $650 million to $1.3 billion to support total project investments of $8.1 billion for developing countries in the corporation's new five-year program. The program included responses to high-priority private sector development needs, assistance in corporate restructuring, creation of a bonding facility for construction firms operating internationally, and establishment of a secondary mortgage-market institution.

In late 1985 the IFC announced the creation of a special mutual fund, the Emerging Markets Growth Fund, to invest in securities of companies listed on third world stock exchanges, with the intention of accelerating capital investment. The fund commenced operations in early 1986 with a capital base of $50 million for investment in developing countries with relatively open securities markets.

The IFC reported that disbursements, which had lagged the previous year, rose sharply in 1987–1988 as clients took advantage of recently introduced flexibility in financing arrangements and the streamlining of approval procedures. Activity continued to increase during the following fiscal year as the IFC approved $1.7 billion in gross investments (up from $1.3 billion the previous year) for 90 projects. However, approvals dropped to $1.5 billion for 122 projects the following year. In view of the lending slowdown, a $1 billion increase in authorized capital was approved by the Board of Directors in June 1991, albeit only after a reportedly rancorous debate in which some directors charged the United States with pushing private sector aid too aggressively within the World Bank Group. Critics of the stance of the United States were concerned that well-connected businessmen from emerging markets would profit from the private sector aid at the expense of the group's overall goal of poverty alleviation. The capital increase (approved by the Board of Governors in May 1992) was intended, in part, to accelerate IFC lending in Eastern and Central Europe and Central Asia.

On January 1, 1994, Jannik Landbaek of Norway, previously vice president of the Nordic Investment Bank (NIB), took over as IFC executive vice president. Peter Woicke of Germany, a former investment banker for J. P. Morgan for 29 years, succeeded him on January 1, 1999. During his five-year tenure, Woicke was credited for making the IFC "operate less like an international bureaucracy and more like a private-sector financial institution." Under a massive reorganization, Woicke shifted the IFC's resources away from large corporations in developed countries to smaller local companies that became increasingly involved in the global market. In 2004 the corporation had a record $982 million in operation profits, nearly 90 percent more than in 2003, with 80 percent of business involving small companies. Woicke also made strides in tightening corporate governance. Following his retirement in January 2005, Woicke was succeeded by Assad Jabre of Lebanon, who served as acting executive vice president until the permanent appointment of Lars H. Thunnel of Sweden, effective January 1, 2006.

In early 1998 the IFC announced several potential reforms in regard to, among other things, the environment, the social impact of lending, and the disclosure of information. Public comment in those and other areas was solicited as the IFC sought to promote a better understanding of the projects it financed and their effects on communities. In 1999 the IFC announced that it had created the post of ombudsman to improve accountability within local communities, particularly in regard to the environmental and social impact of IFC-affiliated projects.

The IFC has also continued to emphasize good corporate governance and greater loan transparency, due in part to the corporate scandals that erupted in the United States and elsewhere in the early 2000s. In November 2002, the IFC created three new environmental funds to encourage private sector investors to be aware of environmental and social issues in emerging markets. They include the Environmental Opportunities Facility to provide funding for innovative projects addressing local environmental concerns, the Sustainable Financial Markets Facility to address environmentally and socially responsible lending and investments, and the Corporate Citizenship Facility to work more closely with project sponsors. In November 2003, the IFC also established guidelines, known as the Equator Principles, to ensure banks invest in projects that are both environmentally and socially sound. In 2006 the IFC began programs to improve labor standards in global supply chains in partnership with the International Labour Organization. Under World Bank Group president Robert Zoellick's direction in 2007, the IFC began integrating financing with the bank's public sector arms. In late 2007, the IFC contributed $1.75 billion to the International Development Association (IDA) for private-sector development in the poorest nations; the program was slated to run through 2010.

The IFC also doubled the size of its global trade financing program to $1 billion in 2007 in order to boost trade among small- and medium-sized import and export businesses. In recent years the program has focused increasingly on investment projects in the poorest nations and post-conflict areas, such as the Democratic Republic of the Congo, Liberia, Lebanon, and Sierra Leone. In October 2007, the IFC announced the launch of the new $5 billion Global Emergency Markets Local Currency Bond Fund to help countries develop local currency bond markets to attract more private investment and allow poor nations to borrow using their own currencies. In an innovative development, in May 2008 the IFC announced a partnership with Standard Chartered Bank to issue notes backed by loans to microfinance institutions in Africa and Asia. These notes establish a new product to provide investors with access to microfinance as an asset class, and it will enable Standard Chartered to expand its lending to the microfinance sector.

The IFC reported investments of $11.4 billion for the 2008 fiscal year, with an additional $4.7 billion raised from outside sources for 372 projects in 85 countries. It also reported that it provided advisory services in 97 countries. The 2009 fiscal year saw some contraction in light of the global financial crisis. IFC financing for private sector development totaled $14.5 billion, including $4.0 billion obtained through syndications, structured finance, and crisis-related initiatives, down from the record $19 billion high of the previous year. IFC invested in 447 projects during the year, of which half were in IDA countries.

As part of its response to the crisis, in May 2009 IFC took an unprecedented step in launching a subsidiary to act as a fund manager for third-party capital. The new unit, called IFC Asset Management Company, LLC, initially was to manage a $3 billion IFC Recapitalization Fund, which was designed to protect emerging-markets banks from the effects of the global downturn. Now, it will also manage a new $1 billion private equity fund that will allow national pension funds, sovereign funds, and other sovereign investors from IFC's shareholder countries to support investments in IFC transactions in Africa, Latin America, and the Caribbean.

INTERNATIONAL FUND FOR AGRICULTURAL DEVELOPMENT
(IFAD)

Established: By the World Food Conference held November 1974 in Rome, Italy. IFAD became a UN Specialized Agency by an April 1977 decision of the Committee on Negotiations with Intergovernmental Agencies of the Economic and Social Council (approved by the General Assembly on December 29, 1977).

Purpose: To channel investment funds to developing countries to help increase their financial commitments to food production, storage, and distribution, and to nutritional and agricultural research.

Headquarters: Rome, Italy.

Principal Organs: Governing Council (all members), Executive Board (18 members), Secretariat.

Web site: www.ifad.org

President: Kanayo F. Nwanze (Nigeria).

Membership (165): See Appendix C.

Official Languages: Arabic, English, French, Spanish.

Origin and development. The creation of the International Fund for Agricultural Development is regarded as one of the most significant recommendations approved by the November 1974 World Food Conference, which set a 1980 target for agricultural development of $5 billion to be disbursed either directly or indirectly through the fund. At the Seventh Special Session of the General Assembly, held in September 1975, it was agreed that the fund should have an initial target of 1 billion special drawing rights (SDRs), or about $1.25 billion. Until that sum was pledged and the IFAD agreement was ratified by 36 states—including 6 developed, 6 oil-producing, and 24 developing states—the fund took the form of a preparatory commission. The Governing Council first convened December 13, 1977, and IFAD approved its first projects in April 1978.

In 1981 the fund approved its first replenishment in the amount of $1.07 billion, $620 million from members of the Organization for Economic Cooperation and Development (OECD) and $450 million from members of the Organization of Petroleum Exporting Countries (OPEC). However, falling oil prices, the general slowdown in the world economy, and the issue of OECD/OPEC "burden sharing" within the fund led to contentious negotiations on a second replenishment. Agreement was finally reached on a 1985–1987 replenishment of nearly $485 million, $273 million from OECD members, $184 million from OPEC countries, and $28 million from non-oil-producing developing countries.

A review of the fund's first decade of activity noted that the IFAD had moved away from costly infrastructure, large-scale irrigation, and massive resettlement schemes to smaller and simpler projects emphasizing low-cost technologies. Additional emphasis was to be given to the fund's highly successful program of small loans to poor persons in rural areas. The report concluded that priorities for the next decade should include the greater involvement of women in loans, attention to environmental protection, the development of livestock and fisheries projects, the extension of applied research and training, and provision of services to nomadic pastoralists and indigenous and remote populations.

At its 12th annual session in January 1989, the Governing Council experienced difficulty in agreeing on a proposed third replenishment, with OPEC countries arguing that the five-year decline in oil prices had curtailed their ability to contribute. After extensive negotiations, the council reconvened in early June and approved a third replenishment of $532.9 million, well below the $750 million sought. Non-oil-producing developing countries pledged $52.9 million, OPEC countries $124.4 million, and OECD countries $345.6 million to the replenishment, which extended through June 30, 1992. The replenishment was expected to permit the fund to maintain annual lending levels of about $250 million. To address the growing threat of widespread famine in Africa, the Executive Board in January 1991 endorsed a second phase of the Special Program for Sub-Saharan African Countries Affected by Drought and Desertification, which had been initiated in 1986.

Negotiations on a fourth replenishment initially stalled because of ongoing differences between the OECD and OPEC countries regarding their relative contributions, mounting uncertainty as to the fund's role among overlapping UN bodies, and Western concern that IFAD administrative costs were too high. Consequently, the 17th Governing Council, held January 26–28, 1994, in Rome, established a 36-member special committee to "scrutinize" current arrangements and propose "substantive changes" to the council. The committee's recommendations for a significant IFAD restructuring were subsequently approved by the January 1995 council. The council agreed that the voting power of members would be tied in the future to the size of their contributions. The council scheduled implementation of the new structure upon completion of the $460 million fourth replenishment, which was approved in February 1997.

Structure. The Governing Council, which normally meets annually but can convene special sessions, is the fund's policymaking organ, with each member state having one representative. The council may delegate certain of its powers to the 18-member Executive Board, comprised of delegates from eight developed (List A), four oil-producing (List B), and six non-oil-producing developing (List C) states (two each from sublists C1, Africa; C2, Europe, Asia, and the Pacific; and C3, Latin America and the Caribbean). Decisions of the council are made on the basis of a complex weighted voting system under which a member's voting power is partly determined by their past and present contributions.

IFAD administers most of its programs through three departments: External Affairs, Program Management, and Finance and Administration. The Program Management Department, which runs the fund's overall lending program, encompasses five regional divisions: Near East and North Africa, Asia and the Pacific, Latin America and the Caribbean, Western and Central Africa (Africa I), and Eastern and Southern Africa (Africa II). It also includes the Technical Advisory Division, which offers expertise in, and manages technical assistance grants for, agronomy, livestock, rural infrastructure, rural finance, institutions, natural resource management, the environment, gender issues, public health and nutrition, household food security, irrigation, livestock, rural finance, household food security, and sustainable livelihoods. IFAD has a total staff of about 440.

IFAD also serves as the "housing institution" for the Global Mechanism, which was established in October 1997 by the First Conference of Parties to the Convention to Combat Desertification. The Global Mechanism serves primarily as a coordinating program for financing antipoverty and antidesertification efforts in Africa. IFAD also houses the International Land Coalition, a global consortium of multilateral, bilateral, and civil society organizations that emerged from the IFAD-sponsored Conference on Hunger and Poverty in November 1995. Called the Popular Coalition to Eradicate Hunger and Poverty until its present name was assumed in February 2003, the International Land Coalition reflects the view that the rural poor can best achieve empowerment through land reform and increased access to productive assets, especially "common-property resources," and through active involvement in decision making at all levels of governance. Other participating organizations include the Food and Agriculture Organization (FAO), the World Food Program (WFP), the Inter-American Development Bank (IADB), the World Bank, and the European Commission. In 2001 IFAD was also designated as an executing agency for the Global Environment Facility (GEF), which is administered by the UN Development Program (UNDP), the UN Environment Program (UNEP), and the World Bank. In 2006 the Farmer's Forum was started as a way to feed information from small farmer and rural producers' organizations into IFAD. It meets biannually in conjunction with IFAD Governing Council meetings.

Activities. The fund was the first international institution established exclusively to provide multilateral resources for agricultural development of rural populations. IFAD-supported projects have often combined three interrelated objectives: raising food production, particularly on small farms; providing employment and additional income for poor and landless farmers; and reducing malnutrition by improving food distribution systems and enhancing cultivation of the kinds of crops the poorest populations normally consume. In its first quarter-century, specific emphases included access to land, water, and other productive resources; sustainable rural production; water management and irrigation; rural financing; rural microenterprises; storage and processing of agricultural output; access to markets; small-scale rural infrastructure; capacity-building for small producer groups and organizations; and research, extension, and training.

The bulk of the fund's resources are made available in the form of highly concessional loans. Outright grants are limited to 7.5 percent of each year's budget. Low-income countries are eligible for loans repayable over 40 years (including a ten-year grace period) with no interest and only a 0.75 percent annual service charge. Those countries with moderately higher per capita GNPs are extended loans on intermediate terms, while the rest may borrow on ordinary terms. Many projects receiving IFAD assistance have been cofinanced with the Asian Development Bank, the African Development Bank, the IADB, the World Bank, UNDP, the OPEC Fund, the Islamic Development Bank, the Arab Fund for Economic and Social Development, and other international funding sources. Activity during the February 1998 meeting of the Governing Council included the establishment of an IFAD Trust Fund to aid the poorest countries in taking advantage of the World Bank–led Heavily Indebted Poor Countries (HIPC) debt-reduction initiative. The countries in which IFAD projects are located also often contribute financially.

Given previous difficulties in replenishing its resources, IFAD recorded a major accomplishment in July 2000 with the completion of negotiations on its fifth replenishment, totaling $460 million. The sixth replenishment, covering 2004–2006, was targeted at $560 million; negotiations in 2005 on a seventh, covering 2007–2009, produced a replenishment target of $800 million. This replenishment assumed an annual project growth of 10 percent.

Apart from replenishments, IFAD supports programs and projects through a number of other means. During 2002, supplementary funds were used, for example, to enhance the role of women in various projects, to provide short-term technical assistance, to mitigate the impact of HIV/AIDS in eastern and southern Africa, and to assist with irrigation in northern Africa. Donors to these and other projects included Canada, Germany, Italy, Japan, Netherlands, Portugal, Switzerland, and the United Kingdom.

In early February 2001 IFAD released its *Rural Poverty Report 2001*, which noted that poverty reduction was proceeding at less than one-third the rate needed to reduce by half the number of people in poverty by 2015, the target set by the World Food Summit in 1996 and repeated at the September 2000 Millennium Summit at UN headquarters. Under present conditions, the effort was doomed to fail, according to the report, in part because the real value of agricultural aid had dropped by two-thirds between 1987 and 1998, even though three-fourths of the world's poor continue to live off the land.

IFAD's Strategic Framework for 2002–2006, which focused on how the organization could best contribute to achieving the Millennial Development Goals (MDGs) set forth at the Millennium Summit, restated IFAD's overall mission in simple terms: "enabling the rural poor to overcome their poverty." Emphasis was placed on strengthening the capacity of the poor and their organizations, improving equitable access to resources and technology, and increasing access to financial assets and markets. During 2002 IFAD joined various other UN organs and specialized agencies as a leading participant in the International Conference on Financing for Development, held in Monterrey, Mexico, in March; the World Food Summit: Five Years Later, held in Rome in June; and the World Summit on Sustainable Development, held August–September in Johannesburg, South Africa.

In June 2006 it was announced that IFAD would launch a microfinance strategy targeting some remote and mountainous areas of China. In partnership with other international donor agencies in 2007, IFAD also created the African Enterprise Challenge Fund to support rural businesses and entrepreneurship beginning in 2008 and the $10 million Financing Facility for Remittances to assist foreign workers in transferring money back to rural families. IFAD's 2007–2010 Strategic Framework defined its focus as working exclusively with the rural poor, particularly women and indigenous peoples, through financing social service projects in places where other financing sources are unavailable. Projects are to involve local water supplies, health, and educational facilities as well as building collective organizations formed by, and for, poor people.

As of the end of 2006, IFAD had invested more than $9 billion in 738 projects and programs and assisted more than 300 million rural poor. It had cofinanced another $16.2 billion with partner organizations.

Effective July 31, 2007, Australia withdrew from the IFAD. In introducing related legislation in the Federal Parliament in June 2004, the Australian government had cited IFAD's "limited relevance" to the country's overall aid program and its focus on Southeast Asia and the Pacific. The government also noted the failure of the IFAD senior managers to address Australia's concerns.

In 2007 and 2008 IFAD was active in projects to bring the economic benefits of mobile telephone service to poor rural areas in the developing world. Creative uses of mobile phones range from a greater ability for farmers to negotiate prices to safe and inexpensive ways to move money. In October 2007 IFAD reported that in 2006 remittances from migrants sent to family members in their home countries amounted to more than all international aid given to developing countries, approximately $300 billion as against approximately $270 billion.

In April 2008, in response to the worldwide rise in food prices, IFAD made up to $200 million available to help poor farmers plant more crops in the forthcoming season. In June UN secretary general Ban Ki-Moon praised IFAD as having one of the UN's most successful development programs. Consultations on IFAD's eighth replenishment ended in December 2008, with an agreement on a target of $3 billion for the period 2010–2012.

With food prices down from their peak in 2008, but still high; the world in a serious economic recession; and agricultural production continuing to fall, there was what amounted to competition between developing and developed countries to provide IFAD's next president. Many representatives of developing countries said that the agency's presidents had always come from developed countries and that, no disrespect to past presidents, it was time for a change. When IFAD's Governing Council met in Rome February 18–19, 2009, it elected Kanayo Nwanze of Nigeria to replace Sweden's Lennart Båge. Nwanze was vice president of IFAD.

Among the loans made by IFAD in 2009 was a $31 million loan to China to help reduce rural poverty in a remote tea-growing area. IFAD publications continued to stress the importance of remittances. An October 2009 report, "Sending Money Home to Africa," emphasized the point and called on African countries to make the process easier and less costly for their expatriates.

INTERNATIONAL LABOUR ORGANIZATION (ILO)

Established: By constitution adopted April 11, 1919; instrument of amendment signed in Montreal, Canada, October 9, 1946, effective April 20, 1948. The ILO became a UN Specialized Agency by agreement with the Economic and Social Council (approved by the General Assembly on December 14, 1946).

Purpose: To promote international action aimed at achieving full employment, higher living standards, and improvement in the conditions of labor.

Headquarters: Geneva, Switzerland.

Principal Organs: International Labour Conference (all members); Governing Body (28 governmental, 14 employer, and 14 employee representatives); International Labour Office.

Web site: www.ilo.org

Director General: Juan Somavía (Chile).

Membership (183): See Appendix C.

Official Languages: English, French, Spanish.

Origin and development. The International Labour Organization's original constitution, drafted by a commission representing employers, employees, and governments, formed an integral part of the 1919 post–World War I peace treaties and established the organization as an autonomous intergovernmental agency associated with the League of Nations. The ILO's tasks were significantly expanded by the 1944 International Labour Conference in Philadelphia, which declared the right of all human beings to pursue their "material well-being and their spiritual development in conditions of dignity, of economic security and equal opportunity." The Declaration of Philadelphia was subsequently appended to the ILO's revised constitution, which took effect June 28, 1948.

In 1946 the ILO became the first Specialized Agency associated with the United Nations. Since then, the organization's considerable growth has been accompanied by numerous changes in policy and geographical representation. While improved working and living conditions and the promotion of full employment remain central aims, the ILO also deals with such matters as migrant workers, child labor, the working environment, and the social consequences of globalization.

In 1970 one of the first official acts of Director General Wilfred Jenks of the United Kingdom was to appoint a Soviet assistant director general. The hostile reaction of the American Federation of Labor–Congress of Industrial Organizations (AFL-CIO) led the U.S. Congress to temporarily suspend payment of U.S. contributions to the organization. The ire of Congress and the AFL-CIO was again aroused in 1975 when the ILO granted observer status to the Palestine Liberation Organization (PLO). Finally, on November 5, 1975, the United States filed its intention to withdraw from the ILO, objecting to a growing governmental domination of workers' and employers' groups and what it considered the ILO's "appallingly selective concern" for human rights as well as other philosophical differences. On November 1, 1977, U.S. president Jimmy Carter formally announced his country's withdrawal, effective November 5. Shortly thereafter, however, U.S. secretary of labor F. Ray Marshall strongly hinted that the United States might reconsider. Thus, the Carter administration carefully watched events at subsequent annual conferences, and in February 1980 Carter announced that the United States would return to the organization.

In early 1988 the United States, after a 35-year hiatus, ratified two ILO conventions. One of the documents, relating to mandatory consultation on ILO standards, was also the first non-maritime convention it had ever endorsed. The improvement in the U.S.-ILO relationship was further underscored at the 1988 annual session of the conference when the United States expressed its "common views and interests" with the ILO.

At the 1998 ILO conference the organization adopted the Declaration on Fundamental Principles and Rights at Work, which called on members to respect the principles embodied in the ILO constitution, the Declaration of Philadelphia, and conventions on fundamental rights, even if the countries had not ratified particular conventions. Those fundamental rights encompass the abolition of forced labor, child labor, and employment discrimination, plus the right to collective bargaining and freedom of association.

Structure. The ILO is unique among international organizations in that it is based on a tripartite system of representation that includes not only governments, but also employer and employee groups.

The International Labour Conference, which meets annually, is the ILO's principal political organ; all member states are represented. Each national delegation to the conference consists of two governmental delegates, one employer delegate, and one employee delegate. Each delegate has one vote, and split votes within a delegation are common. Conference duties include approving the ILO budget, electing the Governing Body, and setting labor standards through the adoption of conventions. Most important items require a two-thirds affirmative vote.

The Governing Body normally meets three times per year. Of the 28 governmental delegates, 10 represent the "states of chief industrial importance"; the other 18 are elected for three-year terms by the governmental representatives in the conference. The 14 employer and 14 employee representatives are similarly elected by their respective caucuses. The Governing Body reviews the budget before its submission to the conference, supervises the work of the International Labour Office, appoints and reviews the work of the various industrial committees, and appoints the director general.

The International Labour Office, headed by the director general, is the secretariat of the ILO. Its responsibilities include preparing documentation for the numerous meetings of ILO bodies, compiling and publishing information on social and economic questions, conducting special studies ordered by the conference or the Governing Body, and providing requested advice and assistance to governments and to employer and employee groups.

ILO subdivisions include the following, each headed by an executive director: Standards and Fundamental Principles and Rights at Work, Employment, Social Protection, Social Dialog, Management and Administration, and Regions and Technical Cooperation (with regional offices for Africa, the Americas, Arab states, Asia and the Pacific, and Europe and Central Asia). Additional offices, programs, and institutes report directly to the director general. These include the International Institute for Labour Studies, which was founded in 1960 in Geneva. The International Training Center of the ILO, which was established in 1964 in Turin, Italy, as the International Centre for Advanced Technical and Vocational Training, initially provided residential training programs to those in charge of technical and vocational institutions, although it now offers postgraduate work and high-level in-service programs.

Activities. The ILO is charged by its constitution with advancing programs to achieve the following: full employment and higher standards of living; the employment of workers in occupations in which they can use the fullest measure of their skills and make the greatest contribution to the common well-being; the establishment of facilities for training and the transfer of labor; policies (in regard to wages, hours, and other conditions of work) calculated to ensure a just share of the fruits of progress to all; the effective recognition of the right of collective bargaining; the extension of social security benefits to all in need of such protection; the availability of comprehensive medical care; the provision of adequate nutrition, housing, and facilities for recreation and culture; and the assurance of equality of educational and vocational opportunity. In addition, the ILO has established an International Program for the Improvement of Working Conditions and Environment (*Programme International pour l'Amélioration des Conditions et du Milieu de Travail*—PIACT). PIACT activities include studies, tripartite meetings, clearing-house and operational functions, and the setting of standards.

The ILO's chief instruments for achieving its constitutional mandates are conventions and recommendations. Conventions are legal instruments open for ratification by governments; while not bound to ratify a convention adopted by the conference, member states are obligated to bring it to the attention of their national legislators and also to report periodically to the ILO on relevant aspects of their own labor law and practices. Typical ILO conventions include Hours of Work, Industry (1919); Underground Work, Women (1935); Shipowners' Liability, Sick and Injured Seamen (1936); and Abolition of Forced Labor (1957). Recommendations only suggest guidelines and therefore do not require ratification by the member states. In both instances, however, governments are subject to a supervisory procedure—the establishment of a commission of inquiry—that involves an objective evaluation by independent experts and an examination of cases by the ILO's tripartite bodies to ensure the conventions and recommendations are being applied. There is also a widely used special procedure whereby the Governing Body investigates alleged governmental violations of trade unionists' right to "freedom of association."

At the June 3–19, 2003, International Labour Conference the ILO adopted its 185th convention. A year earlier it had approved its 193rd and 194th recommendations. While many of these standards pertain to specific industries and occupations—for example, seafaring, agriculture, and mining—others address broader concerns and rights. In 1999 the conference adopted Convention 182 on the Worst Forms of Child Labour, which prohibits child slavery; the selling of, and trafficking in, children; debt bondage; serfdom; forced or compulsory child labor; child prostitution; the use of children for pornography and such illegal activities as drug production and trafficking; and employment of children in jobs apt to harm their health, safety, or morals. Convention 182, supported by the ILO's International Program for the Elimination of Child Labour (IPEC), achieved the quickest ratification rate in ILO history.

Convention 183 addresses Maternity Protection (a subject initially addressed by Convention 3, dating from 1919, and previously revisited in Convention 103 of 1952) and calls in part for maternity leave of at least 14 weeks at, basically, two-thirds pay. Other recently adopted conventions address such subjects as working conditions in the hotel and restaurant industry (1991), protection of workers' claims in the event of employer insolvency (1992), prevention of major industrial accidents (1993), part-time work (1994), safety and health in mines (1995), home work (1996), private employment agencies (1997), safety and health of agricultural workers (2001), and seafarers' identity documents (2003).

Quite apart from the child labor and maternity conventions, a number of recent ILO reports and actions have been more controversial. A 2000 report on labor rights listed Oman, Saudi Arabia, and the United Arab Emirates as states barring labor unions, and cited Bahrain and Qatar for imposing severe restrictions. The report also discussed the cases of murdered trade unionists in Colombia, the Dominican Republic, Ecuador, Guatemala, and Indonesia, and noted that arrests and detentions had recently occurred in more than 20 other countries.

On November 16, 2000, in an unprecedented action, the ILO Governing Body urged member states and fellow UN agencies to apply sanctions against Myanmar (Burma) for its continued use of forced labor and threatened to send its dossiers to the International Criminal Court to prosecute members of the ruling junta. The 1999 conference had already barred Myanmar from participating in ILO sessions and programs. Estimates suggested 800,000 or more Myanmar workers might have been forced to work in agriculture and construction by the country's military regime. The ILO's demands for basic labor rights in Myanmar continued in 2007 when the ILO won a concession from the government to allow victims of forced labor to bring complaints to the agency without retaliatory action. The 12-month trial agreement postponed legal sanctions even as the Commission on Inquiry noted at the June 2007 ILO conference that none of its recommendations to Myanmar on stemming forced labor had been implemented.

The *World Employment Report 2001*, published in January 2001, examined "Life at Work in the Information Economy." It saw "hopeful signs" that new information technology would have a positive effect on employment despite a "digital divide" not only between developed and developing countries, but within even the most technologically sophisticated societies. The report also projected that 500 million additional jobs would be needed during the next decade to reduce by half global unemployment while keeping up with the flow of new workers into the labor force. In 2004 the ILO began investigating Belarus for impeding workers' rights to establish independent trade union organizations and formed 12 recommendations with a June 2005 compliance deadline. After continued violations of workers' freedom of association, the European Union (EU) in June 2007 withdrew Belarus from the union's generalized system of trade preferences—thereby forcing certain manufacturers to pay higher export tariffs to EU countries—in an effort to force ILO compliance. This situation still existed in late 2008.

In February 2004, two years after being launched by the ILO, the World Commission on the Social Dimension of Globalization released its final report. Having been established to consider how economic, social, and environmental objectives could be combined while spreading the benefits of globalization to all, the commission warned of "deep-seated and persistent imbalances in the current workings of the global economy, which are ethically unacceptable and politically unsustainable." It claimed "wealth is being created, but too many countries and people are not sharing in its benefits." As a consequence, the world risked "a slide into further spirals of insecurity, political turbulence, conflicts and wars." Chaired by the presidents of Finland and Tanzania, the commission echoed the ILO's call for "decent work" as a global goal.

The report led to the ILO adopting the Decent Work Agenda, which serves as a framework within the agency and in its international policy goals to discuss and define adequate working conditions, rights, and opportunities. Since 2005 the agenda has included decent work programs in many member states to support initiatives and laws that better working conditions, and international forums have been hosted on a number of related topics, such as globalization and working conditions in African and Asian states. The agenda has also served as a basis for declarations of support by such international bodies as the Group of Eight, which promised in June 2007 to use "decent work" and ILO labor standards in bilateral trade agreements. Earlier in the year, the ILO and the United Nations Development Program signed an agreement to coordinate development efforts toward decent work policy goals.

Delegates to the 92nd International Labour Conference, held June 1–19, 2004, continued to debate the social and economic consequences of globalization. They also maintained the ILO's recent emphasis on children by focusing on child domestic labor. In addition, the conference adopted an action plan for assisting migrant workers and discussed creation of a new standard for safety and work conditions in the fishing industry. The new fishing industry standard was realized at the 94th International Labor Conference (Maritime) held February 7–23, 2006, in Geneva, which set forth a Maritime Labor Convention designed to guarantee merchant sailors' rights in a globalized economy. The 95th conference, held May 31–June 16, 2006, focused on occupational health and safety, violence in the workplace, and, again, on the changes wrought by globalization. The 96th conference, held May 30–June 15, 2007, was named the Work in Fishing Convention and ended with the adoption of standards promoting medical care at sea and social security protection for fishing industry workers. Speaking at the 97th conference, held June 9–13, 2008, Director General Somavía called for urgent measures to address "globalization without social justice." In September 2008 the ILO issued a more hopeful report entitled "Green Jobs: Towards Decent Work in a Sustainable, Low-Carbon World." This report said that the emerging green economy could create "tens of millions of new green jobs."

The organization celebrated its 90th anniversary in April 2009 against what Director General Somavía called "the frightening backdrop of the crisis with rising unemployment and underemployment, business closures, deteriorating conditions of work, growing inequality, poverty and insecurity, and the undermining of respect for rights at work." The ILO warned against a crippling worldwide rise in the rate of unemployment, also stating that the crisis was partly responsible for a global rise in human trafficking and forced labor. An ILO report stated that forced labor was present, from some part of the world, in the supply chain of virtually every country, advanced or not.

The 98th conference, held June 3–19, 2009, adopted a Global Jobs Pact, which called on all concerned to respond to the crisis, and promote recovery from it, in a way that would advance decent and humane working conditions. The G8 group (see separate article) supported this position at its summit meeting, held July 8–10, 2009, in L'Aquila, Italy. The G20 group (see separate article) at its meeting in Pittsburgh, Pennsylvania, on September 25, 2009, likewise made a commitment to putting high-quality jobs at the heart of the economic recovery. In October 2009 the ILO and the World Trade Organization (WTO, see separate article) jointly issued a report titled "Globalisation and Informal Jobs in Developing Countries." This report pointed out an increase in the informal workforce as a result of unfettered free trade and marked a step toward the ILO and WTO cooperating in new ways. Previously, the ILO dealt exclusively with workforce issues and the WTO with matters of trade. The ILO's position in late 2009 was that, for the majority of the world's workers at least, the crisis was far from over.

INTERNATIONAL MARITIME ORGANIZATION (IMO)

Established: March 17, 1958, as the Inter-Governmental Maritime Consultative Organization (IMCO) on the basis of a convention opened for signature on March 6, 1948. IMCO became a UN Specialized Agency as authorized by a General Assembly resolution of November 18, 1948, with the present designation being assumed on May 22, 1982, upon entry into force of amendments to the IMCO convention.

Purpose: To facilitate cooperation among governments "in the field of governmental regulation and practices relating to technical matters of all kinds affecting shipping engaged in international trade; to encourage the general adoption of the highest practicable standards in matters concerning maritime safety, efficiency of navigation and the prevention and control of marine pollution from ships; and to deal with legal matters" related to its purposes.

Headquarters: London, United Kingdom.

Principal Organs: Assembly, Council (40 members), Legal Committee, Maritime Safety Committee, Marine Environment Protection Committee, Technical Cooperation Committee, Secretariat.

Web site: www.imo.org

Secretary General: Efthimios Mitropoulos (Greece).

Membership (169, plus 3 Associate Members): See Appendix C.

Official Languages: Arabic, Chinese, English, French, Russian, Spanish.

Working Languages: English, French, Spanish.

Origin and development. Preparations for the establishment of the Inter-Governmental Maritime Consultative Organization were initiated shortly after World War II but were not completed for well over a decade. Meeting in Washington, D.C., in 1946 at the request of the UN Economic and Social Council, representatives of a group of maritime states prepared a draft convention that was further elaborated at the UN Maritime Conference held in early 1948 in Geneva, Switzerland. Despite the strictly limited objectives set forth in the convention, the pace of ratification was slow, primarily because some signatory states were apprehensive about possible international interference in their shipping policies. Canada accepted the convention in 1948 and the U.S. Senate approved it in 1950, but the necessary 21 ratifications were not completed until Japan deposited its ratification on March 17, 1958. Additional difficulties developed at the first IMCO Assembly, held January 1959 in London, England, due to claims by Panama and Liberia that, as "major shipowning nations," they were eligible for election to the Maritime Safety Committee. Panama and Liberia were widely regarded as "flags of convenience" for shipowners wishing to avoid less permissive regulation elsewhere. An affirmative ruling by the International Court of Justice paved the way for a resolution of the issue at the second IMCO Assembly, held in 1961.

The thrust of IMCO activities during its first decade involved maritime safety, particularly in regard to routing schemes. Adherence was voluntary until 1977, when the Convention on the International Regulations for Preventing Collisions at Sea (1972) went into force. In 1979 the (1974) International Convention on the Safety of Life at Sea (SOLAS), specifying minimum safety standards for ship construction, equipment, and operation, received the final ratification needed to bring it into force, effective May 1980. In terms of individual safety, the first International Convention on Maritime Search and Rescue was adopted in 1979, although it did not come into effect until 1985.

Problems of maritime pollution were the subject of a November 1968 special session of the assembly, which led to the establishment of the Legal Committee and the scheduling of the first of several major conferences on marine pollution. In 1978 sufficient ratifications were finally received for the 1969 amendments to the International Convention for the Prevention of Pollution of the Sea by Oil (1954) to come into force, while the International Convention on Civil Liability for Oil Pollution Damage (1969) and the International Convention on the Establishment of an International Fund for Compensation for Oil Pollution Damage (1971) entered into force in 1975 and 1978, respectively. In January 1986 amendments formulated in 1984 to the International Convention for the Prevention of Pollution from Ships (1973), as modified by a 1978 protocol, became binding. This treaty is regarded as the most important in the area of maritime pollution as it is concerned with both accidents and spills resulting from normal tanker operations. Other pollution-related conventions concern the dumping of wastes at sea (including low-level nuclear waste); preparedness, response, and cooperation regarding oil spills; and high seas intervention in cases of oil pollution casualties.

By 1974 the tasks of the organization had so expanded beyond those originally envisioned that the assembly proposed a number of amendments to the original IMCO convention, including a new statement of purpose and a new name, the International Maritime Organization (IMO).

Of importance in the area of maritime travel and transport was the entry into force in 1979 of a convention establishing the International Maritime Satellite Organization (Inmarsat). Inmarsat faced increasing competition from the private sector for satellite communication services, and became private itself in 1999. It was later renamed the International Mobile Satellite Organization (IMSO); the IMO retains oversight and enforcement powers over the IMSO. The IMSO has signed agreements with the IMO, the International Civil Aviation Organization (ICAO), and the International Telecommunication Union (ITU) to implement policies and standards.

A new procedure was introduced in 1986 to facilitate the adoption of most amendments to conventions. Originally, positive action by two-thirds of the contracting parties to a convention was required. Under the new "tacit acceptance" procedure, amendments are deemed to be accepted if less than one-third take negative action for a period generally set at two years (in no case less than one), assuming that rejections are not forthcoming from parties whose combined fleets represent 50 percent of the world's gross tonnage of merchant ships.

In 1988 the IMO approved the Convention for the Suppression of Unlawful Acts against the Safety of Maritime Navigation, promoted by several countries directly or indirectly affected by the hijacking of the Italian cruise ship *Achille Lauro* in 1985. It came into effect in 1992.

Structure. The IMO Assembly, in which all member states are represented and have an equal vote, is the principal policymaking body of the organization. Meeting in regular session every two years (occasional extraordinary sessions are also held), the assembly decides upon the work program of the IMO, approves the budget, elects the members of the Council, and approves the appointment of the secretary general. The IMO Council normally meets twice a year and is responsible, between sessions of the assembly, for performing all IMO functions except those under the purview of the Maritime Safety Committee (MSC) and the Marine Environment Protection Committee (MEPC). The Facilitation Committee, which is primarily concerned with reducing documentation requirements for port entry and departure, became a formally institutionalized Committee of the Organization only in January 2009, although its origins go back to 1972 as a subsidiary committee of the council.

There are currently 40 members on the IMO Council, comprising three groups: 10 members representing "states with the largest interest in providing international shipping services," 10 having "the largest interest in providing international seaborne trade," and 20 elected from other countries with "a special interest in maritime transport and navigation and whose election . . . will ensure the representation of all major geographic areas of the world."

The organization's technical work is largely carried out by the following nine subcommittees of the MSC and the MEPC: Safety of Navigation; Radiocommunications and Search and Rescue; Ship Design and Equipment; Fire Protection; Stability and Load Lines and Fishing Vessels Safety; Bulk Liquids and Gases; Standards of Training and Watchkeeping; Flag State Implementation; and Carriage of Dangerous Goods, Solid Cargoes, and Containers.

The IMO's Technical Cooperation Committee provides training and advisory services to help developing countries establish and operate their maritime programs in conformity with international standards. Such activities are often linked to UN Development Program (UNDP) projects and to the World Maritime University, established by the IMO in Malmö, Sweden, in 1983 to train high-level administrative and technical personnel. In 1988 the IMO inaugurated the International Maritime Law Institute at the University of Malta.

Activities. The IMO's programs fall under five major rubrics: maritime safety, technical training and assistance, marine pollution, facilitation of maritime travel and transport, and legal efforts to establish an international framework of maritime cooperation. In most of these areas, IMO activity is primarily devoted to extensive negotiation, review, and revision of highly technical conventions, recommendations, and guidelines. The IMO also regulates unique and permanent identification numbers on commercial ships, although the identification and assigning of numbers is maintained by the company Lloyd's Register-Fairplay in the United Kingdom. An IMO regulation scheduled to take effect in 2009 mandates unique identification numbers for shipping companies and registered owners.

On February 1, 1992, the Global Maritime Distress and Safety System (GMDSS), adopted in 1988 as an amendment to the 1974 SOLAS Convention, entered into force. Hailed by the IMO as the "biggest change to communications at sea since the introduction of the radio," the GMDSS requires the use of satellite communications during international voyages undertaken by ocean-going ships of 300 gross tons or more. Fully implemented as of February 1999, the GMDSS was intended to eliminate outdated radiotelegraphy or radiotelephony technology for transmitting location and distress information.

In mid-1993 an amendment to the 1973 convention on pollution from ships went into effect that requires new oil tankers to be fitted with double hulls or some other equally secure method of protecting the cargo. Under an amendment approved by the MEPC in December 2003, in part because of the sinking of the oil tanker *Prestige* off the coast of Spain in November 2002, virtually all single-hull tankers are to be phased out by 2010.

Concern was expressed at the 18th IMO Assembly meeting, held October–November 1993 in London, that some shipowners were neglecting appropriate repairs and maintenance for economic reasons. Secretary General William A. O'Neil of Canada, who was reelected at the meeting for a second four-year term, urged governments, particularly those that provided "flags of convenience" to ships from other nations, to enforce IMO regulations vigorously so that international standards would not be jeopardized. In what appeared to be a related matter, Liberia, which registers more ship tonnage than any other nation, was rebuffed in its attempt to win a seat on the IMO Council.

In 1995 significant new design requirements were proposed for "roll-on, roll-off" ferries (ships where vehicles enter through large doors at one end and leave through similar doors at the other) by an expert panel appointed to investigate the September 1994 capsizing of the ferry *Estonia*, in which 859 people died. In November 1995 the IMO approved a somewhat diluted version of the new "roll-on, roll-off" safety standards, concurrently asking national governments to adopt even stricter controls on a voluntary basis.

In 1996 the International Convention on Salvage (1989) entered into force, and the IMO adopted the International Convention on Liability and Compensation for Damage in Connection with the Carriage of Hazardous and Noxious Substances (HNS) by Sea. The allied HNS Protocol on Preparedness, Response, and Cooperation to Pollution Incidents was approved in 2000. In 2001 the International Convention on the Control of Harmful Anti-fouling Systems on Ships was opened for ratification, as was the International Convention on Civil Liability for Bunker Oil Pollution Damage. In February 2004 the IMO adopted the International Convention for the Control and Management of Ships' Ballast Water and Sediments, while the Convention on the Removal of Wrecks in May 2007 resulted in a set of uniform international rules to ensure the prompt and effective removal of shipwrecks beyond and within territorial waters, including making shipowners financially liable for wreck removal by requiring they post a form of financial security.

The IMO's 21st assembly meeting, held November 15–26, 1999, passed resolutions defining the IMO's objectives for the 2000s. Goals include implementing a more proactive policy toward the safety of ships, passengers, crews, and the environment; ensuring uniform implementation of existing standards and regulations; strengthening the Integrated Technical Cooperation Program (ITCP), particularly with regard to "capacity-building for safer shipping and cleaner oceans"; and promoting efforts to stop such unlawful acts as terrorism at sea, piracy, drug trafficking, and illegal migration.

The November 19–30, 2001, assembly session was dominated by a renewed emphasis on security occasioned by the September 11, 2001, al-Qaida assaults on the United States. During the next year the MSC and its inter-sessional working group rapidly prepared measures designed to tighten ship and port security, and at the December 9–13, 2002, Conference of Contracting Governments to the 1974 SOLAS Convention the delegates, meeting at IMO headquarters, approved a series of major amendments. These included adoption of the new International Ship and Port Facility Security Code (ISPS Code) specifying mandatory security requirements for governments, port authorities, and shipping companies, and various nonmandatory guidelines for meeting those requirements. Earlier in the month the MSC had adopted additional SOLAS amendments to improve the safety of bulk carriers.

The 23rd session of the assembly, which met November 24–December 5, 2003, endorsed establishment of a voluntary audit scheme intended to promote safety and environmental protection by determining member state compliance with convention standards. The assembly also adopted new guidelines on refuge for ships needing assistance when lives were not at risk, approved guidelines on ship recycling, and confirmed the appointment of Efthimios Mitropoulos of Greece as successor to Secretary General William O'Neill, who had served in that capacity for 14 years.

The 24th session of the assembly, meeting November 21–December 2, 2005, called on member states to use naval and air forces to combat piracy off the coast of Somalia. It endorsed continuation and expansion of the long-term antipiracy effort which had begun in 1998. To that end the IMO contributed towards the May 2006 opening of an antipiracy center in Mombasa, Kenya. As the Somali piracy problem continued into 2007, the IMO and the World Food Program issued a joint call for the UN Security Council to arrange for foreign naval ships to patrol the coastline.

On July 1, 2006, a new convention came into force regarding treatment of people rescued at sea. This convention was partly inspired by the increasing number of people attempting to migrate in overcrowded, unseaworthy boats, and, among other things, it spells out a ship captain's absolute responsibility to rescue people whose lives are in danger, irrespective of the wishes of the ship's owner.

In recent years, the IMO has also shown increased concern for the shipping industry's impact on global climate change. In May 2000 the IMO prohibited the use of perfluoro carbons on board ships. Also in 2000 the IMO published a study on the contribution of ships to global warming emissions that identified options for ship design changes to reduce those emissions. Interim guidelines on carbon dioxide indexing were approved by the MEPC in 2005. In October 2006 the MEPC officially recognized that the threat from global warming was severe enough to require action. However, in July 2007 the MEPC postponed immediate action in favor of further study even as political pressure from the European Union (EU) was building. The EU proposed applying a carbon dioxide cap and trade system on the shipping industry and threatened to impose restrictions on ships visiting EU ports by the end of the year if the IMO did not act.

In November 2007 the IMO participated in a UN Security Council committee meeting on boosting border security and detecting illegal arms shipments to better deal with terrorist threats. The meeting resulted in plans to streamline information sharing and coordination between member organizations on border control and security matters.

The IMO has also changed shipping routes in recent years in an effort to preserve ocean wildlife, including labeling a basin off the coast of Nova Scotia as an "area to be avoided" seasonally by commercial shipping in order to protect the endangered right whale.

In 2008 the IMO began to implement a satellite tracking system, the Long Range Information and Tracking (LRIT) of Vessels, to reduce collisions and serve as a rescue tool. All ships constructed after December 31, 2008, are mandated to include the system, and it is being phased in for earlier vessels.

The most serious matter before the IMO, and the shipping community as a whole, in 2008 was piracy. This menace has re-emerged in the waters off Southeast Asia and Indonesia, and particularly off the coasts of Nigeria and East Africa. Lives are being lost, and shipping has become more expensive. Most attacks are being launched from Somalia, and according to the IMO roughly 80 percent of world food assistance to that country arrives by sea. Because of pirate attacks, the number of ships willing to deliver food to Somalia had declined by half in 2007.

In April 2008 the IMO states of East Africa began working on a regional agreement for patrol of their seas. In the meantime Western naval forces continue to guard the region. In June the IMO welcomed a Security Council resolution allowing foreign ships to enter Somali waters at will in pursuit of pirates. In September Yemen announced plans to build a regional antipiracy center to assist ships attacked by pirates, but some observers complained that the world's navies were not doing enough about the problem. Another problem facing the world's shippers in 2008 was a lack of crew, particularly of officers. In November 2008 the IMO announced a "Go to Sea" campaign, in cooperation with the ILO and private industry groups, to encourage recruitment into the merchant marine and to improve the industry's image.

On February 24, 2009, the organization held the first meeting of a contact group on piracy. This group was authorized by a UN Security Council resolution of December 2008. On March 2, 2009, the IMO launched a partnership between itself, the UN Development Programme (UNDP), and several large shipping companies to tackle the problem of marine bio-invasions caused by the transfer of alien plants and animals in ships' ballast tanks.

The Hong Kong International Convention for the Safe and Environmentally Sound Recycling of Ships, 2009, was adopted at a conference held there in May 2009. The convention was felt to be of added importance because the worldwide recession was causing more ships to be retired and broken up. On July 27, 2009, the MPEC produced a package of energy efficiency measures for ships but could not come to a decision about raising the cost of ships' fuel and using the money to help poor nations tackle climate change.

INTERNATIONAL MONETARY FUND (IMF)

Established: By Articles of Agreement signed at Bretton Woods, New Hampshire, United States, July 22, 1944, effective December 27, 1945; formal operations began March 1, 1947. The IMF became a UN Specialized Agency by agreement with the Economic and Social Council (approved by the General Assembly on November 15, 1947).

Purpose: "To promote international monetary cooperation through a permanent institution which provides the machinery for consultation and collaboration on international monetary problems. To facilitate the expansion and balanced growth of international trade, and to contribute thereby to the promotion and maintenance of high levels of employment and real income and to the development of the productive resources of all members as primary objectives of economic policy. To promote exchange stability, to maintain orderly exchange arrangements among members, and to avoid competitive depreciation. To assist in the establishment of a multilateral system of payments in respect of current transactions between members and in the elimination of foreign exchange restrictions which hamper the growth of world trade. To give confidence to members by making the Fund's resources temporarily available to them under adequate safeguards, thus providing them with the opportunity to correct maladjustments in their balance of payments without resorting to measures destructive of national or international prosperity . . . [and] to shorten the duration and lessen the degree of disequilibrium in the international balance of payments of members."

Headquarters: Washington, D.C., United States.

Principal Organs: Board of Governors (all members), Board of Executive Directors (25 members [24 elected by member countries or groups of countries plus the IMF managing director, who serves as chair of the board]), International Monetary and Financial Committee (24 members), Managing Director and Staff.

Web site: www.imf.org

Managing Director: Dominique Strauss-Kahn (France).

Membership (186): See Appendix C.

Origin and development. The International Monetary Fund is one of the two key institutions that emerged from the July 1–22, 1944, UN Monetary and Financial Conference in Bretton Woods, New Hampshire: the International Bank for Reconstruction and Development (IBRD) was established to mobilize and invest available capital resources for the reconstruction of war-damaged areas and for the promotion of general economic development where private capital was lacking; the IMF was created with the complementary objectives of safeguarding international financial and monetary stability and of providing financial backing for the revival and expansion of international trade.

Following ratification by the required 28 states, the Articles of Agreement of the bank and fund went into effect December 27, 1945, and formal IMF operations commenced March 1, 1947, under the guidance of Managing Director Camille Gutt (Belgium). While the membership of the IMF expanded rapidly over the next three decades, most communist countries, including the Soviet Union, remained nonmembers. However, the pressures of external debt to the West mounted rapidly for some participants in the Soviet-bloc Council for Mutual Economic Assistance (CMEA) in the late 1970s, and in 1981 Hungary and Poland, both CMEA members, applied for IMF membership (Romania was previously the only Eastern European participant). Hungary became a member in 1982, but Poland's admission was deferred pending resolution of questions regarding its existing debt and international payment obligations. In December 1984 the United States, with the largest proportion of voting power, lifted all objections concerning Poland, thus opening the way for its entry in June 1986. Angola joined in 1989, while Bulgaria, Czechoslovakia, and Namibia joined in 1990. Mongolia joined in 1991.

In a move that surprised many observers, the Soviet Union formally applied for IMF membership in July 1991. In conjunction with the World Bank, the IMF in October approved a special associate status for the USSR, but the action proved of little practical consequence as the country's dissolution occurred shortly thereafter. In 1992 the IMF offered regular membership to the former Soviet republics, all of which were admitted by September 1993. In December 1992 the IMF's Board of Executive Directors decided that, in view of the breakup of the former Socialist Federal Republic of Yugoslavia, Yugoslavia's membership in the IMF had ceased to exist. At the same time, the board declared Bosnia and Herzegovina, Croatia, Macedonia, Slovenia, and the new Federal Republic of Yugoslavia to be successors to the assets and liabilities of the former Yugoslavia and established their respective shares. In January 1993 the board made a similar ruling regarding the former Czechoslovakia. Membership was quickly approved for Croatia, Czech Republic, Macedonia, Slovakia, and Slovenia, but unsettled conditions in Bosnia and Herzegovina postponed its membership until December 1995. In addition, it took until December 2000 for the board to conclude that the Federal Republic of Yugoslavia had fulfilled the necessary requirements to become a member. Montenegro became the 185th member in 2007.

The development of the IMF has occurred in four phases, the first spanning from Bretton Woods until about 1957. Under the managing directorships of Camille Gutt and Ivor Rooth (Sweden), the fund was seldom in the news, and its activity, in the form of "drawings" or borrowings, was light. During much of this period, the U.S. Marshall Plan was providing the needed balance-of-payments support to the states of Europe because the IMF lacked the capital to perform such a massive task.

At the end of 1956, when Per Jacobsson (Sweden) was named managing director, the fund entered a more active phase, the outstanding example being large drawings by the United Kingdom, partly as a result of the 1956–1957 Suez crisis. While Jacobsson was a major participant in discussions concerning reform of the international monetary system, the IMF was not the primary institutional venue for those talks.

The third phase of development can be dated from Jacobsson's death in 1963. His successor, Pierre-Paul Schweitzer (France), managed the IMF during a period in which its activities were directed increasingly toward the needs of developing states. Also, by the mid-1960s the need for reform of the international monetary system had become more evident. Thus, beginning in 1965, the IMF became increasingly involved in talks regarding the creation of additional "international liquidity" to supplement existing resources for financing trade. Discussion between the Group of Ten (see separate entry) and the fund's executive directors led in 1967 to the development of a plan for creating new international reserves through the establishment of special drawing rights (SDRs) over and above the drawing rights already available to fund members. Following approval in principle by the IMF Board of Governors in September 1967, an amendment to the Articles of Agreement was submitted by the Board of Executive Directors and approved by the Board of Governors in May 1968, preparatory to consideration by the member governments. On July 28, 1969, with three-fifths of the IMF members (controlling four-fifths of the voting power) having accepted it, the amendment was added to the Articles of Agreement. In general, SDRs may be allocated to IMF members proportionate to their IMF quotas, subject to restrictions relating to the allocation and use of such rights.

The U.S. suspension of the convertibility of the dollar into gold in August 1971 compounded the previous need for reform. By 1972 many states were "floating" their currencies and thus fundamentally violating the rules of the fund, which were based on a system of fixed exchange rates normally pegged to the U.S. gold price. That year, the United States decided not to support Schweitzer's reelection bid, largely because of his outspoken criticism of the U.S. failure to "set its own economic house in order" and control its balance-of-payments deficits.

When H. Johannes Witteveen (Netherlands) took over as managing director in 1973, his chief task was to continue reform of the international monetary system while enhancing the role of the IMF. Consequently, Witteveen proposed creation of an IMF oil facility that was established in June 1974 and served, in effect, as a separate borrowing window through which members could cover that portion of their balance-of-payments deficits attributable to higher imported oil prices. This facility provided 55 members with SDR 802 million until its termination in 1976. Three months later the fund set up an "extended facility" to aid those members with payments problems attributable to structural difficulties in their economies. In addition, as part of the accords reached at the January 1976 session of the Interim Committee, one-sixth of the fund's gold was auctioned for the benefit of less developed countries. The sales, which began in June 1976, continued until April 1980, with profits of $1.3 billion transferred directly to 104 countries and with another $3.3 billion placed in a trust fund to assist poorer countries. The final loan disbursement from the fund upon the latter's discontinuance in March 1981 yielded a cumulative total of SDR 2.9 billion committed to 55 members. Trust fund repayments have subsequently been used to support other IMF assistance programs.

Another plateau was reached when, at the end of April 1976, the Board of Governors approved its most comprehensive package of monetary reforms since the IMF's establishment. Taking the form of a second amendment to the Articles of Agreement, the reforms entered into force April 1, 1978. Their effect was to legalize the system of "floating" exchange arrangements, end the existing system of par values based on gold, and impose upon members an obligation to collaborate with the fund and with each other in order to promote better surveillance of international liquidity. In addition, the requirement that gold be paid into the fund was lifted, and the fund's governors were given the authority to decide, by an 85 percent majority, to create a new council that would be composed of governors, finance ministers, and persons of comparable rank, and which would concern itself with the adjustment process and global liquidity.

The fourth phase of development was initiated with the entrance into office on June 17, 1978, of Jacques de Larosière (France). Aided by a massive increase in IMF funds, Larosière addressed the major problems of the fund's members: burdensome debts for non-oil-producing developing countries, inflation and stagnant economic growth among the developed members, and balance-of-payments disequilibria for virtually all. In order to assist the non-oil-producing third world countries, the fund further liberalized its "compensatory facility" (established in 1963) for financing temporary export shortfalls, extended standby arrangements through the creation in 1979 of a "supplementary financing facility," and expanded the activities of the trust fund to provide additional credits on concessional terms.

To support the drain on its resources, the IMF has relied on periodic quota increases; the Eighth General Review of Quotas came into effect in January 1984 and raised the fund's capital from SDR 61.1 billion to SDR 90 billion. Increases were also approved in 1990 and 1997 (see Activities, below).

Structure. The IMF operates through the IMF Board of Governors, the IMF Board of Executive Directors, the International Monetary and Financial Committee (known until September 1999 as the Interim Committee on the International Monetary System), and a managing director and staff of some 2,600 persons. Upon joining the fund, each country is assigned a quota that determines both the amount of foreign exchange a member may borrow under the rules of the fund (its "drawing rights") and its approximate voting power on IMF policy matters. As of 2007 the largest contributor, the United States, had 16.79 percent of the voting power, while the smallest contributors held considerably less than 1 percent each.

The Board of Governors, in which all powers of the fund are theoretically vested, consists of one governor and one alternate appointed by each member state. In practice, its membership is virtually identical to that of the Board of Governors of the IBRD, and its annual meetings are actually joint sessions (which similarly include the governing boards of the International Development Association and the International Finance Corporation). One meeting in three is held away from Washington, D.C.

The Board of Executive Directors, which has 25 members (including the managing director as chair) generally meets at least once a week and is responsible for day-to-day operations; its powers are delegated to it by the Board of Governors. Each of the five members having the largest quotas (currently the United States, the United Kingdom, Germany, France, and Japan) appoints a director. Appointment privilege is also extended to each of the two largest lenders to the fund, providing they are not among the countries with the five largest quotas. Consequently, Saudi Arabia, the largest lender, has appointed a director since 1978. The other directors are elected biennially by the remaining IMF members, who are divided into 18 geographic groupings, each of which selects one director. (The People's Republic of China and Russia constitute geographic entities by themselves and therefore the "election" by each of a director, in practical terms, amounts to an appointment.) Each elected director casts as a unit all the votes of the states that elected him.

Pending the proposed establishment of a new council at the ministerial level, the Interim Committee on the International Monetary System was established by a resolution adopted at the 1974 annual meetings. In September 1999, the committee was renamed the International Monetary and Financial Committee to reflect its de facto permanent status. The committee's 24 members represent the same countries or groups of countries as represented on the Board of Executive Directors. The committee advises the Board of Governors as to the management and adaptation of the international monetary system and makes recommendations to the board on how to deal with sudden disturbances that threaten the system.

The managing director, who is appointed by the Board of Executive Directors and serves as its chair, conducts the ordinary business of the fund and supervises the staff. In the first major management restructuring since 1949, the number of deputy managing directors was increased from one to three in 1994.

There are several other ministerial-level committees and groups that routinely interact with the fund, usually in conjunction with joint IMF-World Bank sessions. One is the Development Committee, which was established in 1974 by the IMF and the World Bank to report on the global development process and to make recommendations to promote the transfer of real resources to developing countries. The committee, whose structure mirrors that of the Interim Committee, generally issues extensive communiqués prior to IMF–World Bank meetings.

Regular statements are similarly issued by the Group of Ten, the Group of Seven (for details on both see article on the Group of Ten), and the Group of 24. The latter group, which receives secretariat support from the fund, represents the interests of the developing countries in negotiations on international monetary matters.

Activities. The IMF's central activity is to assist members in overcoming short-term balance-of-payments difficulties by permitting them to draw temporarily upon the fund's reserves, subject to established limits and conditions with respect to the amount of drawing rights, terms of repayment, etc. Assistance may take the form of standby credits (credits approved in advance), which may or may not be fully utilized. A member can also arrange to buy the currency of another member from the fund in exchange for its own.

A second major IMF responsibility has been to supervise the operation of the international exchange-rate system in order to maintain stability among the world currencies and prevent competitive devaluations. In part because stable exchange-rate patterns depend on economic stability, particularly the containment of inflationary pressures, the fund since 1952 has regularly consulted with member states about their economic problems, the formulation and implementation of economic stabilization programs, and the preparation of requests for standby IMF assistance.

In the area of assistance to less developed states, the fund participates in many of the consultative groups and consortia organized by the IBRD. It also conducts a separate program of technical assistance—largely with reference to banking and fiscal problems—utilizing its own staff and outside experts through a training program organized by the IMF Institute at Washington, D.C.

Beginning in the early 1980s, the fund encountered growing demands from the developing world for reform in its procedures. In particular, a number of states objected to the imposition of the IMF's so-called standard package of conditionality, which often required, for example, that a country reduce consumer imports, devalue its currency, and tighten domestic money supplies in return for standby credit. Subsequently, the issue continued to be a constant center of controversy for the IMF. Non-oil-producing developing countries struggling under massive balance-of-payments deficits called for greater fund access but with fewer domestically unpopular restrictive conditions attached. At the same time, industrialized countries, adversely affected by high unemployment, inflation, and economic stagnation, demanded stricter structural adjustment clauses and called for increased reliance on the private sector as a source of aid and development capital for all but the poorest of the developing countries.

With the third world's debt crisis worsening, the Board of Governors in October 1985 approved the creation of the Structural Adjustment Facility (SAF) to provide low-income countries with concessional loans in support of national policy changes designed to resolve persistent balance of payments problems. The SAF, funded by SDR 2.7 billion in reflows from the discontinued trust fund, was formally established in March 1986, offering ten-year loans with a 0.5 percent interest charge and a five-and-one-half-year grace period.

Pressure for further IMF initiatives continued throughout 1986 and 1987 in light of what many observers described as a "wrong-way" flow of resources that yielded pay-back obligations to the IMF in excess of funds received in new loans. In addition, many national leaders, particularly in Africa, intensified their challenge to the "rigidity and austerity" of IMF lending conditions which, in the words of one critic, had driven governments "far beyond the limit of social tolerance."

Soon after his appointment as IMF managing director in January 1987, Michel Camdessus called for a complete review of IMF conditionality and a tripling of SAF funding. Following endorsement of the latter at the October 1987 joint IMF-World Bank annual meeting, the fund announced the establishment of an Enhanced Structural Adjustment Facility (ESAF) funded by SDR 6 billion from 20 countries, led by Japan (SDR 2.8 billion) and West Germany (SDR 1 billion), but not including the United States. The new facility generally offered the same terms and followed the same procedures as the SAF. (In February 1994 the IMF launched an enlarged and extended ESAF; in late 1999 the ESAF was renamed the Poverty Reduction and Growth Facility [PRGF] and given an expanded mandate to include poverty reduction and promotion of sustainable development.)

The April 1988 interim committee meeting approved additional changes, including the launching of an external contingency mechanism to assist borrowers in case of external "shocks" such as collapsing commodity prices or higher interest rates in world markets. However, borrowers facing unforeseen sharp drops in export earnings were required to engage in rigorous domestic action to qualify for the new relief program. The influence of the fund's most conservative members, led by the United States, could also be seen in the managing director's assessment that, while study would continue on additional debt initiatives, the basic elements of the fund's debt strategy remained "valid."

By the time of the joint annual meeting with the World Bank held September 1988 in West Berlin, a consensus was emerging that debt reduction, not simply more restructuring, was required. The issue was brought into sharper focus in April 1989 when the Interim Committee, while praising recent announcements by several large creditor nations that they would forgive portions of government-to-government debts, called for "urgent considerations" of proposals for reducing the much larger debt owed by developing nations to commercial banks. The IMF and the World Bank subsequently approved the use of their resources to support debt reduction, especially by providing incentives to commercial banks.

In line with the Brady Plan proposed by the United States (see article on the Group of Ten), the new strategy was designed to produce partial write-offs of debts, additional rescheduling of remaining debts for longer terms and/or lower interest rates, and an infusion of new loans from the banks. Countries "with a strong element of structural reform" were permitted to apply up to 25 percent of their access to fund resources to support principal reduction and an additional 15 percent for interest support. Moreover, in another major policy change, the IMF agreed that its funds could be released prior to conclusion of a commercial bank financing arrangement.

Although packages for Mexico and Venezuela were finally completed in early 1990, the commercial banks generally remained unenthusiastic about the plan, particularly in regard to new loan approvals; in addition, many developing countries appeared to consider the new approach as insufficient for their needs. However, by the conclusion of agreements with Brazil and Poland in 1994, the assessment of the "Brady bonds" program had turned more favorable. At that point, about 80 percent of the commercial bank debt had been restructured, leading some observers to declare the debt crisis, as far as commercial banks were concerned, to be over.

A major IMF issue appeared resolved when a 50 percent quota increase was approved in the first half of 1990 to raise the quota total from SDR 90 billion to SDR 135 billion (nearly $180 billion). A logjam in negotiations was broken when the United States endorsed the action after other IMF members had accepted the U.S. demand that a stricter policy be adopted regarding countries in arrears on payments.

The quota increase was made contingent on the approval of an amendment to the IMF Articles of Agreement that would permit the Board of Executive Directors to suspend the voting rights and certain related rights of members that failed to fulfill their IMF obligations. The amendment had been accepted by the required number of IMF members by November 1992, at which time the new quotas, now totaling SDR 146 billion (about $217 billion) because of the addition of new members, took effect.

As negotiations on a tenth quota increase were being conducted, some members called for a substantial enlargement in anticipation of a heavy draw on IMF resources from the former Soviet republics and former Soviet satellites as they switched from centrally planned to free-market economies. In April 1993 the IMF established a temporary systemic transformation facility (STF) to assist such transitional nations in their balance of payment problems and help them pay for much-needed imports such as spare parts to modernize their industries. About $5 billion had been allocated from the STF by the end of 1994, the date initially established for terminating the facility; however, the IMF agreed to extend STF operations.

In June 1993 the IMF approved what was expected to be the most important STF arrangement—a $3 billion credit to Russia. However, in September, with almost half of the loan disbursed, the IMF halted the flow because of Russia's failure to limit inflation and implement other economic reforms prescribed by the fund. Such problems also restricted Moscow's access to other IMF resources, despite estimates that Russia needed up to $30 billion in fund assistance over the next five years to complete its economic conversion.

The Russian issue was a major topic of discussion at the September 1993 IMF-IBRD annual meeting, with supporters of Russian president Boris Yeltsin arguing that he needed backing in his battle with the Russian parliament, which had resisted many of the IMF reforms. With criticism of its "rigidity" in the matter having intensified, the IMF finally released the remaining $1.5 billion to Russia in April 1994, fund officials crediting Moscow's economic reforms with, among other things, having brought previously runaway inflation down to a manageable level. A $6.8 billion standby loan was approved for Russia in 1995 and another $10.2 billion loan in 1996. In return, the Russian government pledged to reduce its budget deficit and cut tariffs on imports, but in October the IMF briefly suspended disbursements of the loan because of slow progress in revenue collection. The lending resumed in December when a new Russian tax commission agreed, among other things, to close loopholes in its collection system.

In February 1995 the IMF approved a $17.8 billion standby loan to assist in the U.S.-led "bailout" of Mexico, whose financial markets had recently experienced severe turmoil. The fund subsequently announced it would require borrowers to provide better financial data on a monthly basis to help prevent such "meltdowns" in the future. Among other things, stricter economic surveillance was expected to preclude national governments from "hiding" negative developments in their infancy, a practice that often sabotages the market's corrective mechanisms until it is too late. Managing Director Camdessus also endorsed a proposal from the Group of Seven that the IMF establish a

$50 billion emergency fund to assist countries caught in circumstances such as Mexico's.

The other primary focus of attention for the IMF in the second half of 1996 was approval (in cooperation with the World Bank and the Group of Seven) of a new debt relief program, the Heavily Indebted Poor Countries (HIPC) Initiative, which was expected to lead to the eventual forgiveness of some $5.6–$7.7 billion of the debt owed by 20 of the world's poorest countries. The plan, formally endorsed at the joint IMF–World Bank meeting in September, was to permit forgiveness of up to 100 percent of debt owed to the IMF and World Bank by the eligible countries, provided they met certain criteria regarding free-market influence, the encouragement of foreign investment, and attention to basic social needs. Concurrently, the Paris Club of creditor nations agreed to forgive up to 25 percent of the debt owed to them by the countries concerned.

In February 1997 the IMF Executive Board approved the creation of a trust fund to serve as a conduit for dispersal of resources to the new debt relief fund. Subsequently, 41 countries were identified as eligible for aid, with Uganda, Bolivia, Burkina Faso, and Guyana receiving quick approval for assistance. Thereafter, IMF concerns quickly turned to the financial crisis gripping Southeast Asia. In August the IMF announced that it would extend a $3.9 million loan to Thailand as part of a $16 billion rescue package, which also included pledges from leading regional economic powers, the United States, and the World Bank. In November a $10 billion loan was offered to Indonesia, and in December South Korea received a $21 billion standby credit from the IMF, the largest ever approved for an IMF member at that time. According to the IMF's director, the economic reform requirements attached to the loan packages were markedly different from their predecessors in their insistence that the recipients enact structural reforms in their finance sectors with the aim of increasing transparency and reducing corruption.

Meanwhile, at the IMF–World Bank summit on September 20–25, 1997, delegates proposed a 45 percent increase in the IMF quotas, from SDR 146 billion (approximately $199 billion) to SDR 212 billion ($288 billion). In addition, the fund was urged to adopt the necessary measures to allow it to expand its role in ensuring the maintenance of an "open and liberal" international monetary system through which its members could freely exchange capital.

Despite the rhetorical emphasis on good governance, the IMF in early 1998 decided to continue lending to Russia even though Moscow had failed to meet fund-mandated tax collection targets. An additional $11.2 billion in support for Russia was approved at midyear in connection with renewed pledges from Russian leaders that significant reform was in the offing. Meanwhile, extensive crisis lending proceeded smoothly for South Korea and Thailand, although disbursements for Indonesia were compromised by political developments in that country. In addition, in December the IMF agreed to $18 billion in emergency support as part of a $41.5 billion rescue package endorsed by the international financial community for Brazil. The fund also in late 1998 resumed lending to Pakistan, whose testing of a nuclear device earlier in the year had led to a suspension of IMF support.

In late 1998 the U.S. House of Representatives agreed, after substantial initial reluctance, to provide U.S. funding for the IMF quota increase that had been proposed in 1997. Consequently, the 45 percent quota increase went into effect in January 1999, the fund having accepted U.S. insistence on greater transparency in the IMF decision-making process. Subsequently, in November, Managing Director Camdessus, who had been appointed to a third five-year term in 1997, announced his intention to resign, effective February 2000. However, the selection of his successor proved surprisingly difficult as the United States pushed for a conservative candidate who would return the IMF to its initial limited mission, Japan suggested its own candidate, and developing nations demanded a role in the selection process. A compromise was finally reached on Horst Köhler of Germany, the president of the European Bank for Reconstruction and Development best known for his role in the reunification of East and West Germany while a member of the German cabinet. Following Köhler's appointment, the IMF and World Bank agreed to reduce the overlap in their objectives, with the fund concentrating on the promotion of global economic stability while letting the bank attend to the "institutional, structural, and social dimensions" of development.

Managing Director Köhler also indicated a desire to establish a more "consultative" relationship with recipient countries in order to ease domestic political pressure often felt by national governments forced to implement IMF-mandated reforms. At the same time, the IMF addressed recent conservative criticism of its policies by agreeing to reduce the length of its loans and charge higher interest rates. In the eyes of many observers the fund turned a significant psychological corner in December 2001 when it refused additional support for Argentina, thereby permitting that country to slide into default. The IMF in 2002 continued to resist pressure to assist the Argentinian government on the grounds that it had failed to adopt necessary reforms, especially in its banking sector. However, as part of an effort to combat the "contagion" affect of the Argentinian crisis on neighboring countries, the IMF in September 2002 approved substantial new credits for Brazil.

In January 2004 the IMF issued a surprisingly harsh critique of U.S. fiscal policy, describing the U.S. foreign debt as reaching record-breaking proportions that could threaten the stability of the global economy. The fund called upon the George W. Bush administration to reverse its recent tax cuts in order to reduce the U.S. budget deficit.

In March 2004 Köhler resigned as managing director in order to run for president of Germany. He was succeeded by Rodrigo de Rato y Figaredo, who, while serving as Spain's finance minister, had been credited with balancing the Spanish budget and halving unemployment. A year later de Rato announced that he favored selling some $7 billion of the IMF's gold reserves to assist in the global effort to reduce the debt burdens of developing nations.

The communiqué following the IMF's September 24, 2005, annual meeting warned against an increasing gap between rich and poor nations, while it commended many poor countries on the economic progress they had made. It also warned against increasing oil prices as a potential cause of inflation, which it felt was otherwise under control, and it encouraged oil-producing and oil-consuming nations to work together to combat this problem.

In answer to widening concerns about the U.S. trade deficit with China, the IMF was given a greater role in leading multilateral consultations with relevant member nations to correct major trade imbalances. The decision at the April 2006 IMF–World Bank meeting also included the establishment of a surveillance unit to monitor trade deficits, surpluses, and currency exchange rates. It was agreed that the IMF would be able to force groups of countries to the table to discuss their economic policies and reach agreement on changes as problems surfaced. The first multilateral consultation on global trade imbalances took place later that year between China, Saudi Arabia, the United States, Japan, and Eurozone countries. However, little progress was made amid criticisms that the countries involved showed little interest in concrete policy adjustments.

By the IMF–World Bank meeting in September 2006, demands for giving growing economies greater contributory quotas (and thereby greater voting shares) in IMF decision making were answered. Member states increased the voting shares of China, South Korea, Mexico, and Turkey and agreed to devise a new quota formula for other IMF members, including African nations, in 2008. The process was expected to be contentious because of Western countries' reluctance to concede influence in the body.

In late 2007, as fallout from the U.S. mortgage crisis and a global credit crunch roiled international financial markets, the IMF faced increasing pressure to shore up global economic stability. Developing countries publicly railed against the IMF for failing to rein in speculative lending practices in advanced economies, while the United States and other Western countries leaned on the IMF to correct major trade imbalances with China by forcing an appreciation of the renminbi. When pressed at the spring 2007 meeting, China agreed to make its exchange rate more flexible "in a gradual and controlled manner" and cut tax rebates on its exports. In June, the IMF announced the first overhaul of its surveillance policy in 30 years, largely seen as directed towards China. The agency set up a more rigorous system to scrutinize and expose exchange rate policies in individual countries. Regardless of the intentions of a government, if its economic policy resulted in "fundamental exchange-rate misalignment" or "large and prolonged current account deficits or surpluses," it could be labeled as an exchange rate manipulator.

The IMF took an increasingly hardened stance towards China that year, labeling its currency as "considerably undervalued" and its double-digit economic growth unsustainable. The agency also monitored the danger posed to international markets by the dollar's devaluation, urging the United States to balance its budget in the next five years and consider higher energy taxes.

Growing criticism about the IMF's relevance and effectiveness was a backdrop to much of its activities in 2007. With indebted countries paying back IMF loans ahead of schedule and emerging economies relying on their own foreign exchange reserves rather than IMF funds for financial security, the agency ended its fiscal year 2007 in tight financial straits.

An expert panel of outside economists recommended it sell some of its gold reserves to shore up its financial profile. In May, the Independent Evaluation Office (IEO) said the IMF's advice on foreign exchange rate policy was ineffective and inadequate, blaming the agency management for failing to provide clear direction and incentives to countries.

Further discussions about internal IMF reform continued as de Rato announced his resignation in June 2007. The managing director's vacancy came amidst calls for a non-European to fill the post, but former French finance minister and economics professor Dominique Strauss-Kahn was appointed in November, pledging to make IMF financing a priority by adopting a new income model. The aims of the model were to make the fund less dependent on lending, increase representation of large developing countries in the body, and continue aiding low-income countries despite calls that such work should be left to its sister organization, the World Bank.

Strauss-Kahn also agreed to press ahead with agency goals to scrutinize sovereign wealth funds, which have become increasingly influential in world markets despite a lack of transparency. The government-held funds, many developed by oil-rich nations, have come to control as much as $2.5 trillion in investments, often by targeting the strategic assets of developed nations. However, the funds do not routinely disclose their size or asset allocations. Under pressure from the United States, Strauss-Kahn said the IMF would develop a set of best-practices guidelines for sovereign wealth funds, which would include restrictions on fund holders' interference in a host country's politics. During 2008 the IMF negotiated a voluntary code of conduct with 26 countries that have sovereign wealth funds. The deal was up for approval at the October 2008 World Bank–IMF meeting.

The IMF's record as an economic prognosticator in 2008 was mixed. Early in the year, while warning of the risks of inflation and a global economic slowdown, the IMF paid relatively little attention to problems in the world's credit markets. By April it revised its estimate of world economic growth downwards and admitted it had not warned about the credit situation insistently enough or early enough. Yet by mid-May the IMF saw the worst of the economic crisis as past. On July 17 it raised its world economic forecast again, but by July 28 was saying that the credit crisis was getting much worse and was likely to spread from developed to less developed economies. On September 28, 2008, Strauss-Kahn suggested that the IMF could act as a kind of watchdog and "honest broker" for world financial markets during difficult times. During the late fall of 2008 the IMF issued increasingly dire statements about the world economy, culminating in an October 12 warning that it stood at "the brink of systemic meltdown." The IMF activated special rules for emergency lending to countries whose economies were in danger of collapse, rules last used in the Asian financial crisis of 1997. In late 2008 and into 2009 several countries applied for, and were granted, emergency loans, including Iceland, whose banks had collapsed from exposure to international subprime mortgage securities.

On October 26, 2009, the IMF board "admonished" Strauss-Kahn for unprofessional behavior and bad judgement, although clearing him of charges of abuse and sexual harassment and allowing him to keep his job. Many female IMF staffers had been uncomfortable with Strauss-Kahn's behavior. He apologized to the staff in general and specifically for a brief affair with an IMF senior economist, who had since left the organization.

The G-20 meeting held in London in early April 2009 (see separate article) enhanced the IMF's role in responding to the crisis. The group agreed that the IMF should triple the amount it borrows to ensure that it has enough funds to lend to countries in need. This new money was to be guaranteed by the financially stronger member countries. The IMF was also to issue $250 billion of its own new currency. The intention was that an IMF member could seek IMF assistance when it saw trouble on the horizon, rather than when disaster was imminent. Such IMF help would become a regularly accepted part of the world financial scene and would have less chance of causing panic in the affected country than a last-minute IMF intervention. The London meeting also gave the IMF and the World Bank much increased authority to carry out G-20 policies, developing an early-warning system against the kind of crisis that the world was presently suffering and perhaps ultimately acting as a world financial regulator. The IMF was charged with reporting progress by late 2009.

INTERNATIONAL TELECOMMUNICATION UNION

(ITU)

Established: By the International Telecommunication Convention signed in Madrid, Spain, December 9, 1932, effective January 1, 1934. The ITU became a UN Specialized Agency by agreement with the Economic and Social Council (approved by the General Assembly on November 15, 1947).

Purpose: To foster international cooperation for the improvement and rational use of telecommunications.

Headquarters: Geneva, Switzerland.

Principal Organs: Plenipotentiary Conference (all members), World and Regional Conferences on International Telecommunications, Council (46 members), General Secretariat.

Web site: www.itu.int

Secretary General: Hamadoun Touré (Mali).

Membership (191): See Appendix C.

Official Languages: English, French, Spanish.

Working Languages: Arabic, Chinese, English, French, Russian, Spanish.

Origin and development. The beginnings of the ITU can be traced to the International Telegraph Union founded May 17, 1865, in Paris, France. The International Telegraph Convention concluded at that time, together with the International Radiotelegraph Convention concluded in Berlin in 1906, was revised and incorporated into the International Telecommunication Convention signed in 1932 in Madrid, Spain. Entering into force in 1934, the Madrid convention established the ITU as the successor to previous agencies in the telecommunications field. A new convention adopted in 1947 took account of subsequent advances in telecommunications and also of the new position acquired by the ITU as a UN Specialized Agency. Conventions have since been periodically revised to address changing standards and needs as radio communication and telecommunication continue to evolve.

Structure. The ITU's complicated structure is a reflection of its long history and growth. As international telecommunications expanded, new organs and functions were typically grafted onto the preexisting ITU structure, producing a plethora of conferences, assemblies, organs, and secretariats, and necessitating a major reorganization in the early 1990s. At an extraordinary Plenipotentiary Conference in Geneva, Switzerland, in December 1992, the ITU adopted its current constitution, which rationalized the organization's structure, effective March 1993.

The Plenipotentiary Conference remains the principal political organ of the ITU. Regular sessions are held every four years to make any necessary revisions in the conventions, determine general policy, establish the organization's budget, and set a limit on expenditures until the next conference. Each member has one vote on the conference, which elects the Council, as well as the secretary general and the deputy secretary general. The Council, comprised of 46 members from six administrative regions (Africa, Americas, Asia, Australasia, Eastern Europe, and Western Europe), supervises the ITU between sessions of the parent body. Meeting annually at the organization's headquarters, it reviews and approves the annual budget and coordinates the work of the ITU with other international organizations.

Under the 1993 restructuring, the Plenipotentiary Conference can approve the convening of World and Regional Conferences on International Telecommunication. There are three types of global conferences, corresponding to the ITU's three program sectors: Radiocommunication Conferences, generally held every two to three years in conjunction with technically oriented Radiocommunication Assemblies; Telecommunication Standardization Assemblies, typically held every four years; and Telecommunication Development Conferences, also held at four-year intervals.

The General Secretariat, headed by the elected secretary general, administers the budget, directs the ITU's sizable research and publishing program, and otherwise provides administrative support. Each of the three sectors—Radiocommunication, Telecommunication Standardization, and Telecommunication Development—has its own administrative bureau headed by a director.

Activities. The general aims of the ITU are to maintain and extend international cooperation for the improvement and rational use of radiocommunication and telecommunication and to aid developing countries in obtaining appropriate technologies and establishing needed services. In addition, the ITU undertakes studies, issues recommendations and opinions, and collects and publishes information for the benefit of its members.

The Radiocommunication Sector (ITU-R) was established by consolidation of the International Radio Consultative Committee (founded in 1927) and the International Frequency Registration Board (IFRB), the latter of which had been responsible since 1947 for allocating and recording frequency assignments and for handling interference disputes. These tasks currently fall under the purview of the ITU-R's 12-member Radio Regulations Board, which maintains the Master International Frequency Register (MIFR) for radio services—everything from ham radio to high-definition television. The Radiocommunication Sector's basic mission is to ensure "rational, equitable, efficient and economical use of the radiofrequency spectrum by all radiocommunication services, including those using satellite orbit."

The Telecommunication Standardization Sector (ITU-T) has as its mission ensuring "an efficient and on-time production of high quality standards covering all fields of telecommunications except radio." It relies on more than a dozen study groups to formulate recommendations, which are nonbinding standards covering, for example, network interconnectivity and electromagnetic compatibility.

The purpose of the Telecommunication Development Sector (ITU-D) is to "facilitate and enhance telecommunication development worldwide by offering, organizing, and coordinating technical cooperation and assistance activities." The ITU recognized this need even before the 1993 reorganization, having authorized creation of the Telecommunication Development Bureau in 1989. In 1987 ITU secretary general Richard E. Butler called for measures that would ensure the accessibility of basic telecommunication facilities to "every inhabitant of our planet" by 2000. Subsequently, in 2003 ITU secretary general Yoshio Utsumi called for a heightened global policy perspective to increase access to information and communication technology (ICT) to the developing world, asking for a "concerted global effort" to "eliminate the gap between rich and poor when it comes to access to information."

The ITU's first World Telecommunication Development Conference (WTDC) was held in March 1993 in Buenos Aires, Argentina, amid widespread concern the "telecommunications gap" was still widening between rich and poor countries. U.S. vice president Al Gore called for creation of a "planetary information network," built primarily by the private sector, to foster economic growth and political liberalization. The second WTDC took place in Valletta, Malta, in March 1998 and adopted an action plan that paid particular attention to the telecommunication needs of the world's least developed countries (LDCs). That theme was bolstered at the third WTDC held in 2002 in Istanbul, Turkey, at which delegates adopted an action plan to close the "digital divide" between rich and poor countries and to aid in the transition to the modern telecommunication and ICT environment. The action plan included six programs: regulatory reform; expanding access to developing countries; applying Internet networks to government, health, and education sectors; enhancing private sector investment; human resources development; and a special program to assist LDCs. The most recent WTDC was held in March 2006 in Doha, Qatar.

The first World Radiocommunication Conference (WRC) convened October 23–November 17, 1995, in Geneva, Switzerland. The primary purpose of the WRC is to review and revise the Radio Regulations, the international treaty governing the use of the radio-frequency spectrum and the geostationary-satellite and non-geostationary-satellite orbits. The conference also discussed the ever-increasing problem of allocation of the radio-frequency spectrum, pressure in that area having grown particularly intense in regard to mobile satellite communications. The ITU-R administers the organization's International Mobile Telecommunications-2000 (IMP-2000) program, which establishes standards governing third-generation (3G) wireless communications via satellite and wireless terrestrial links. At a WRC meeting June 9–July 4, 2003, in Geneva, delegates placed a heavy emphasis on the further allocation of spectrum in regard to wireless access services, broadband wireless services aboard airplanes and ships, and satellite data services.

In 1998 the ITU approved an Internet-related standard to foster faster two-way data transfers over cable. At the 15th Plenipotentiary Conference, held in Minneapolis, Minnesota, delegates discussed the role the ITU should play in the development of the Internet, sought to strengthen the ITU's ties to the business community, and elected Yoshio Utsumi of Japan as ITU secretary general.

The 2000 World Telecommunication Standardization Assembly (WTSA) in Montreal, Quebec, Canada, adopted many varied resolutions emphasizing collaboration among ITU sectors and also established ground rules for associate membership and accounting rate principles for international telephone services. The October 5–14, 2004, meeting in Florianopolis, Brazil, adopted a four-year plan focused on setting global standards for network security, compatibility of old and new network systems, and transitions to new technologies. Internet governance and next-generation networks (NGNs) were prominent issues, prompting the ITU to create a new study group on NGNs. The WTSA also adopted a series of Internet resolutions to counter spam and to increase ITU involvement in the debate over internationalized domain names.

World Telecommunication Policy Forums (WTPF) have been held in 1996, 1998, and most recently March 2001 in Geneva. The 2001 WTPF focused on Internet Protocol (IP) telephony. However, because of ongoing ITU budget constraints, there are no scheduled forums for 2004–2007.

Additionally, the ITU took a lead role, along with the UN secretary general, in organizing the two-phase World Summit on the Information Society. The first phase took place in Geneva in December 2003 and adopted a declaration of principles and a plan of action to expand universal access to the Information Society. The second phase took place November 16–18, 2005, in Tunisia. Discussions about freedom of use and universal access to the Internet dominated the second phase, with China in particular arguing for a state's right to place some restrictions in the name of national security.

The two summits led to the adoption of the Doha Action Plan in March 2006 at the ITU's World Telecommunication Development Conference. The Doha plan spelled out a strategy to develop telecommunications infrastructure for use in underserved areas and with marginalized populations. In response to a series of natural disasters, including the 2004 tsunami in Southeast Asia, the Doha plan also targeted poor countries and small island nations for emergency telecommunications development.

Governance of the Internet again became a topic at the first ever Internet Governance Forum in November 2006, during which Secretary General Utsumi pressed for greater worldwide influence in overseeing Internet functions. The U.S. government refused to cede control of computers directing Internet traffic but later announced it would relax oversight over the Internet Corporation for Assigned Names and Numbers (ICANN), the private agency that controls domain names and other key functions.

The 17th Plenipotentiary Conference in Antalya, Turkey, held November 6–24, 2006, saw renewed commitments to the implementation of the World Summit on the Information Society (WSIS) and Doha Action Plan goals for universal access as well as discussions on internationalized Internet domain names, Internet interoperability, and convergence. The conference also appointed a new secretary general, Mali-born Hamadoun Touré, then director of the ITU's Telecommunications Development Sector.

Touré caused a stir in early 2007 when he seemed to back away from the union's previously stated position on global Internet governance, stating he did not see the ITU becoming the governing body. He said his priorities instead were to bridge the so-called information divide between rich and poor countries and curb Internet-related crime. In May that year, the ITU announced the two-year Global Cybersecurity Agenda to address issues of network security, financial fraud, identity theft, virus attacks, spam, and child pornography.

In June 2006 the ITU helped negotiate an agreement between 101 nations in Europe, Africa, and the Middle East to introduce a standardized digital system for radio and TV broadcasts. In October 2007 the ITU and the African Development Bank cohosted the Connect Africa Summit and raised investment commitments of $55 billion from private industry and government sources (to be completed by 2012) to provide widespread access to broadband communication technology in Africa. Also in October 2007 the Radiocommunication Assembly endorsed WiMAX, a wireless phone signal standard used heavily in emerging markets.

In December 2007 the ITU made a presentation at the UN Conference on Climate Change in Bali, Indonesia. It pointed out that improved telecommunications could be part of the solution to climate change, but that, as they produced high-tech garbage, they were also part of the problem. In July 2008 the ITU created the new Focus Group on Information and Communication Technologies (ICTs) and Climate Change. The group had an aggressive work plan to be completed by April 2009.

In March 2008 the ITU deployed 25 satellite terminals to parts of Zambia that had been cut off by flooding. In May it deployed 100 such terminals to China after the disastrous earthquake there. In June it called on all countries to adopt a single standardized telephone number, 116.111, for children to use if they needed any kind of help. In September the organization predicted that there would be four billion mobile phones in use by the end of the year. In October 2008 the ITU held its first ever Global Standards Symposium, in Johannesburg, South Africa. This meeting called for the "bewildering" array of global telecommunication standards and protocols to be simplified. At this meeting and elsewhere concern was voiced that the EU was trying to develop its own set of standards, usurping the ITU's traditional role in this regard.

In March 2009 the ITU opened headquarters for its Global Cybersecurity Agenda on the outskirts of Kuala Lumpur, Malaysia. In October the organization approved a new, and energy-efficient, universal charger that would work with any mobile telephone. The ITU estimated that currently 51,000 tonnes of obsolete chargers added to the world's pollution each year. On November 3, 2009, the ITU introduced a "standards conformity and interoperability program," designed to give potential buyers of communications equipment a better idea of how their purchase might (or might not) work with the rest of the world.

UNITED NATIONS EDUCATIONAL, SCIENTIFIC, AND CULTURAL ORGANIZATION (UNESCO)

Established: By constitution adopted in London, England, November 16, 1945, effective November 4, 1946. UNESCO became a UN Specialized Agency by agreement concluded with the Economic and Social Council (approved by the General Assembly on December 14, 1946).

Purpose: To contribute to peace and security by promoting collaboration among states in education, the natural and social sciences, communications, and culture.

Headquarters: Paris, France.

Principal Organs: General Conference (all members), Executive Board (58 members), Secretariat.

Web site: www.unesco.org

Director General: Irina Bokova (Bulgaria).

Membership (193, plus seven Associate Members)**:** See Appendix C.

Official Languages: Arabic, Chinese, English, French, Russian, Spanish. French and English are working languages.

Origin and development. UNESCO resulted from the concern of European governments-in-exile over the problem of restoring the educational systems of Nazi-occupied territories after World War II. Meetings of the Allied Ministers of Education began in London, England, in 1942, and proposals for a postwar agency for educational and cultural reconstruction were drafted in April 1944; the constitution of UNESCO, adopted at a special conference in London, November 1–16, 1945, came into force a year later, following ratification by 20 states.

The 1974 General Conference voted to exclude Israel from the European regional groups of UNESCO, thus making that country the only member to belong to no regional groups. At the same session a motion was passed to withhold UNESCO aid from Israel on the ground that it had persisted "in altering the historical features" of Jerusalem during archaeological excavations. At the 1976 General Conference, Israel was restored to full membership in the organization; however, the conference voted to condemn Israeli educational and cultural policies in occupied Arab territories, charging that the latter amounted to "cultural assimilation." The adoption of this resolution was reported to be part of the price demanded by Arab and Soviet-bloc member countries for agreeing to Israel's return to the regional group. In November 1978 the organization again voted to condemn and cut off funds to Israel, charging that Arab monuments in Jerusalem had been destroyed in the course of further archaeological activity.

Debate at the 21st General Conference in 1980 raged over a resolution calling for the establishment of the New World Information and Communication Order (NWICO). Western delegates objected to the proposal, which called for an international code of journalistic ethics, on the ground that it might restrict freedom of the press. The 1980 conference did, however, approve resolutions creating the International Program for the Development of Communications (IPDC). At the fourth extraordinary session of the General Conference, held in Paris in late 1982, the NWICO was included as a major component of the proposed medium-term UNESCO work plan for 1985–1989. The conference finally adopted a compromise plan for the NWICO that entailed the deletion of passages unacceptable to the industrialized countries, the rejection of a proposed study of Western news agencies, and the addition of material calling for freedom of the press and referencing its role as a watchdog against abuses of power.

Debate over the NWICO continued in 1983. Despite the compromise seemingly accepted at the 1982 Paris meeting, the document presented at a symposium on the news media and disarmament in Nairobi, Kenya, in April called for "national news agencies" and "codes of conduct" for journalists, with no mention of the right of news organs to operate freely. It also called for a study of the obstacles to circulation in industrialized countries of information produced in developing countries. In response, a number of industrial nations, including the United States, indicated that they would withhold funds from the organization, forcing it to appeal to external sources to meet its projected 1984–1985 budget of $328.8 million.

Subsequently, the organization came under even greater attack from members alleging unnecessary politicization of UNESCO activities and mismanagement by Director General Amadou Mahtar M'Bow of Senegal. The United States, at the forefront of the critics, called for major reforms in 1984. Rebuffed in the effort, it withdrew from membership, with the United Kingdom and Singapore following suit in 1985.

The controversial director general announced in late 1986 that he would not seek reelection upon expiration of his second term in November 1987, but, at the urging of the Organization of African Unity, subsequently reversed his position. Several additional Western nations threatened to withdraw from UNESCO in the event of M'Bow's reelection, and acrimony dominated efforts by the October meeting of the Executive Board to determine its nominee for the post. After four ballots, M'Bow withdrew, it having become apparent that the Soviet bloc planned to cast its decisive votes for his opponent, Federico Mayor Zaragoza of Spain. The board thereupon nominated Mayor, although 20 (mostly African) members voted against him.

The General Conference in November formally elected Mayor, who promised to restructure and reinvigorate the organization in hopes of bringing the United States and the United Kingdom back into its fold. In March 1988 Mayor reported extensive budget austerity measures had been introduced and a month later urged UNESCO to "talk less and less about political issues and more and more about education, culture, and science." The 1989 General Conference also attempted to mollify the United States by calling for a "free, independent, pluralistic press" throughout the world and by deferring a membership request from the Palestine Liberation Organization. Acting against the recommendations of a panel of distinguished Americans, who reported that UNESCO was making "clear and undeniable progress," the United States announced in April 1990 that it would not rejoin the organization.

The 1991 General Conference continued to urge the United States and the United Kingdom to reconsider their positions regarding UNESCO. Mayor intensified the lobbying campaign to get the former members to rejoin in the spring of 1992, noting that sharp cutbacks in contributions from the former Soviet Union and its successor states in 1991 had created financial distress for UNESCO. The director general presented a report from an independent commission appointed to evaluate UNESCO, which described the organization as having made progress in ending waste and inefficiency. Later in the year, in what was seen as an additional image-building effort, UNESCO established a high-level group of experts from around the world to make recommendations on the organization's activities over the next ten years.

The 27th General Conference, held October 1993 in Paris, unanimously reelected Mayor to a second term, as recommended by the Executive Board. The conference also approved a $455 million biennial budget for 1994–1995, with priorities to include literacy, special educational programs for women and children, environmental and antidrug projects, and journalist training courses. Not coincidentally, much of the UNESCO emphasis reflected well-known interests of the U.S. Bill Clinton administration, which was described as adopting a more positive attitude toward the organization. Consequently, in early 1994, U.S. State Department officials said they had suggested the United States rejoin UNESCO, although not until 1997 because of budget considerations. A highlight of UNESCO activity later in the year was the readmission in December of South Africa, which had withdrawn from the organization in 1956 because of criticism of its apartheid policies. The United Kingdom rejoined on July 1, 1997.

In a secret ballot on October 20, 1999, Japan's Koichiro Matsuura defeated ten candidates for the Executive Board's endorsement to succeed Director General Mayor for a six-year term. His nomination coincided with release of an independent audit of UNESCO that uncovered mismanagement, corruption, and financial irregularities, including millions of dollars in payments to consultants and advisers who were deemed unqualified. Matsuura quickly vowed to undertake reforms. Matsuura achieved another important goal September 12, 2002, when U.S. president George W. Bush announced to the UN General Assembly that the United States would rejoin UNESCO following an 18-year estrangement, stating, "This organization has been reformed and America will participate fully in its mission." Bush later pledged a $60 million reentry fee, returning the United States as the largest contributor to UNESCO. In October 2003 the United States was elected to serve on the 58-member Executive Board. In 2007 Montenegro joined and Singapore rejoined after walking out 22 years previously in protest of agency mismanagement.

Structure. The General Conference, which usually meets every odd-dated year, has final responsibility for approving the budget, electing the director general, and deciding overall policy. Each member state has one vote; decisions are usually made by a simple majority, although some questions, such as amendments to UNESCO's constitution, require a two-thirds majority.

The Executive Board is charged with general oversight of the UNESCO program and the budget; the board examines drafts of both covering the ensuing two-year period and submits them, with its own recommendations, to the General Conference. Previously elected by, and from, General Conference participants, the members of the board under a 1991 constitutional revision are now the representatives of 58 governments selected by the conference to control board seats.

The Secretariat, which is headed by a director general selected for a six-year term by the General Conference (on recommendation of the Executive Board), is responsible for executing the program and applying the decisions of those two bodies. A distinctive feature of UNESCO's constitutional structure is the role of the national commissions. Comprising representatives of governments and nongovernmental organizations in the member states, the commissions were initially intended to act as advisory bodies for UNESCO's program. However, they have also come to serve as liaison agents between the Secretariat and the diverse educational, scientific, and cultural activities in the participant states.

Activities. UNESCO's program of activities derives from its broad mandate to "maintain, increase and diffuse knowledge," to "give fresh impulse to popular education and to the spread of knowledge," and to "collaborate in the work of advancing the mutual knowledge and understanding of peoples." Within this mandate it (1) holds international conferences, conducts expert studies, and disseminates factual information concerning education, the natural and social sciences, cultural activities, and mass communication; (2) promotes the free flow of ideas by word and image; (3) encourages the exchange of persons and of publications and other informational materials; (4) attempts to ensure conservation and protection of books, works of art, and monuments of historical and scientific significance; and (5) collaborates with member states in developing educational, scientific, and cultural programs.

To promote intellectual cooperation, UNESCO has granted financial assistance to many international nongovernmental organizations engaged in the transfer of knowledge. It has also attempted to encourage the exchange of ideas by convening major conferences on such topics as life-long education, oceanographic research, problems of youth, eradication of illiteracy, and cultural and scientific policy. To further cooperation in science and technology, UNESCO was instrumental in the establishment of the European Organization for Nuclear Research (see separate entry) in 1954, the International Brain Research Organization (IBRO) in 1960, the International Cell Research Organization in 1962, the program on Man and the Biosphere (MAB) that currently involves more than 140 countries, the International Geological Correlation Program, the International Hydrological Program (IHP), and a Coastal Regions and Small Islands (CSI) endeavor. In addition, UNESCO provides the secretariat for the Intergovernmental Oceanographic Commission (ICO).

UNESCO has paid particular attention to the human genome, establishing in 1993 a bioethics program that led to the adoption of the Universal Declaration on the Human Genome and Human Rights in 1997, which banned human reproductive cloning. At the 32nd General Conference, held September 29–October 17, 2003, in Paris, UNESCO adopted the International Declaration on Human Genetic Data that laid down ethical principles governing genome research. UNESCO's International Bioethics Committee (IBC) and Intergovernmental Bioethics Committee (IGBC) played a large role in the declaration. In November 2002 UNESCO announced a cooperative research program in conjunction with its MAB program to study more than 100 mountain regions to evaluate the impact of global warming.

UNESCO's developmental efforts also focus on modernizing educational facilities, training teachers, combating illiteracy, improving science and social science teaching, and training scientists and engineers. The International Bureau of Education (IBE) in Geneva, which dates from 1925, became part of UNESCO in 1969, while the International Institute for Educational Planning (IIEP) and the Intergovernmental Committee for Physical Education and Sport (ICPES), both located in Paris, France, were established by the organization in 1963 and 1978, respectively. Other educational units include the Caribbean Network of Educational Innovation for Development, located in Kingston, Jamaica; the European Center for Higher Education in Bucharest, Romania; the International Institute for Higher Education in Latin America and the Caribbean in Caracas, Venezuela; the Institute for Education in Hamburg, Germany; and the Institute for Information Technologies in Education in Moscow, Russia.

The 2000 UN World Education Forum held on April 25–28 in Dakar, Senegal, proved somewhat contentious, with various nongovernmental participants accusing governments and multilateral institutions, including the World Bank, of indifference toward the educational needs of developing countries. The Dakar session also saw 160 countries adopt the current six-part program under the Education for All (EFA) initiative, which set ambitious goals to provide developing countries with basic education standards by 2015. However, the 2002 *EFA Global Monitoring Report* said more than 70 countries would fail to meet these goals, due in part to underfunding and teacher shortages.

The UN adopted a resolution in December 2001 declaring the UNESCO-monitored Literacy Decade from 2003 to 2012, with the goal of cutting illiteracy rates in half. The action plan is comprised of five two-year periods, the first of which focuses on women's education, with later focuses on ethnic minorities, indigenous populations, migrants and refugees, and disabled persons.

In social sciences, UNESCO focuses its attention on diverse issues such as human rights, ethics in science and technology, peace and disarmament, environment and population issues, and socioeconomic conditions. The 1978 General Conference adopted the Declaration on Race and Racial Prejudice that rejected the concept that any racial or ethnic group was inherently inferior or superior. UNESCO's *Medium-Term Report* for 2002–2007 reinforced the 2001 Universal Declaration on Cultural Diversity that tasks UNESCO with a three-part, six-year strategy to implement standards to protect cultural diversity, promote cross-cultural dialogue, and enhance links between culture and development. Since 1946, UNESCO has worked to preserve cultural heritage. Most recently, Director General Matsuura decried the Taliban's willful destruction in March 2001 of the stone Buddhas of Bamiyan in Afghanistan as a "crime against culture." Additionally, UNESCO has taken steps to prevent the illicit traffic of artifacts following extensive looting in Baghdad, Iraq, after the fall of Saddam Hussein's regime in 2003 and has also worked to preserve dying languages. The February 2009 edition of UNESCO's *Atlas of the World's Languages in Danger of Disappearing* caused some comment. It listed the Manx Gaelic and Cornish languages as extinct. This brought letters of protest from schoolchildren on the Isle of Man, written in the supposedly dead language, as well as complaints from Cornish speakers. Both languages were reclassified as "critically endangered."

In communications, UNESCO has attempted to advance the free flow of information and book development, expand the use of media, assist countries in developing the media they need, and disseminate UN ideals. Since 1976 the General Information Program (PGI) has concentrated on improving the organization and dissemination of scientific and technical information. The Intergovernmental Informatics Program (IIP) has directed its attention to policy considerations and training in computer-based knowledge dissemination. Also under the communications arm of UNESCO is the ICO, which built an early-warning system for tsunamis in the Indian Ocean following the December 2004 tsunami that killed more than 200,000 people in the region.

The 33rd General Conference was held on October 17–20, 2005, in Paris. It adopted a budget of $610 million, with an additional $25 million in extra-budgetary voluntary funding. It also adopted the Convention on the Protection and Promotion of the Diversity of Cultural Expressions, the International Convention against Doping in Sport, and the Universal Declaration on Bioethics and Human Rights. The convention on cultural diversity was intended, among other things, to support national movie industries, and was opposed by the United States. The director general agreed that the organization should, for the time being, concentrate on implementing standards that had been recently promulgated, rather than on creating new ones.

With enough countries ratifying support, the Convention for the Safeguarding of the Intangible Heritage entered into force in 2006. The convention requires member nations to take steps to protect oral and cultural traditions, traditional craft-making, and performing arts and includes funding for preservation efforts and two official registry lists.

Additionally, another report entitled *Case Studies on Climate Change and World Heritage* that year found that world heritage sites, including coral reefs and archaeological sites sensitive to changes in humidity and precipitation, can be threatened by the effects of climate change.

At the 34th General Conference on October 16 to November 2, 2007 in Paris, Matsuura recommended recruiting a financial comptroller to strengthen internal agency monitoring. The conference also adopted a strategy for 2008–2013 of "attaining lifelong quality education for all"; furthering sustainable development through science and technology; and creating activities directed towards youth, least developed nations, and small island states. A 2008–2009 budget of $631 million was adopted, with educational programs receiving the largest share, followed by the natural and social science sectors, and then culture.

The conference also approved a resolution directing the director general to explore the role UNESCO could play in preserving the memory of the Holocaust and preventing all forms of its denial in reaction to Iranian president Mahmoud Ahmadinejad's calling the Holocaust "a myth" earlier in the year. In other measures in 2007, UNESCO called for Israel to end archaeological excavation work near the al-Aqsa mosque in Jerusalem out of concern Islam's third holiest site could be damaged, and listed the Galapagos Islands in the Pacific Ocean as an endangered world heritage site because of the growing pressure of tourism. It also renamed the Nazi concentration camp Auschwitz Birkenau as the German Nazi Concentration and Extermination Camp to clearly identify Germany's responsibility after a lobbying effort by Poland. UNESCO designated the Iraqi city of Samarra as an endangered world cultural treasure after insurgent attacks destroyed a number of the city's holy sites.

The state of education was summarized in a 2007 UNESCO report called *Corrupt Schools, Corrupt Universities: What Can Be Done.* The report found that illegal registration fees, academic fraud (including fake university degrees available on the Internet), embezzlement, and other corrupt practices were seriously undermining educational systems around the world.

The creation of World Heritage sites and institutions was productive in 2008, but some efforts were controversial. Cambodia attempted to register the temple of Prey Vihear as a World Heritage site, but the temple stands on ground that is disputed between Thailand and Cambodia. The ground is recognized as Cambodian, but the only access is through Thai territory. Thailand did not object to Cambodia's action, but wanted to manage the area jointly with Cambodia. UNESCO's position was that the two countries must resolve their differences before the site could be registered. Occasional violent clashes continued at the site through 2008 and into late 2009, but both sides declared they would not allow the conflict to escalate.

Also in 2008 Egypt's culture minister, Farouk HOSNY, a potential candidate to be UNESCO's next director general, was attacked with the allegation that he had made statements against Israel. He denied the accusation and said he "dreamed" of visiting Israel after ties with the Palestinians were normalized. Also controversial was UNESCO's decision to recognize Jerusalem as "the capital of Arab culture" in 2009. The celebration was to include all Jerusalem, not just the present Arab part of the city. Eventually, Hosny was beaten out by Irina Bokova, the former external affairs minister of Bulgaria. Hosny declared that he had lost because of "Zionist pressures." Bokova was elected and sworn in at the 35th General Conference, held October 6–23, 2009, in Paris. She was the first woman and the first person from Eastern Europe to become director general. The conference adopted a budget only nominally larger than that of the previous biennium, with education as its priority, and it welcomed the Faroe Islands as a new associate member.

In other action, UNESCO declared, in a November 2008 report, that the world was likely to miss the goal of providing elementary education for all children by 2015. In June 2009 it deleted Dresden, Germany, from the list of World Heritage Sites, to which it had been added in 2004, because of a new bridge that UNESCO deemed unsuitable.

UNITED NATIONS INDUSTRIAL DEVELOPMENT ORGANIZATION (UNIDO)

Established: By General Assembly resolution of November 17, 1966, effective January 1, 1967. UNIDO became a UN Specialized Agency January 1, 1986, as authorized by a resolution of the Seventh Special Session of the General Assembly on September 16, 1975, based on a revised constitution adopted April 8, 1979.

Purpose: To review and promote the coordination of UN activities in the area of industrial development, with particular emphasis on industrialization in less developed countries, including both agro-based or agro-related industries and basic industries.

Headquarters: Vienna, Austria.

Principal Organs: General Conference (all members), Industrial Development Board (53 members), Program and Budget Committee (27 members), Secretariat.

Web site: www.unido.org

Director General: Kandeh Yumkella (Sierra Leone).

Membership: (173): See Appendix C. (The United States withdrew as of December 31, 1996, and Australia withdrew as of December 31, 1997. The United Kingdom, which in 1996 had announced its intention to withdraw, reversed its decision in 1997 and remained a member.)

Origin and development. The creation of a comprehensive organization responsible for UN efforts in the field of industrial development was proposed to the General Assembly in 1964 by the first UN Conference on Trade and Development (UNCTAD). The General Assembly endorsed the proposal in 1965 and, through a 1966 resolution effective January 1, 1967, established UNIDO as a semi-autonomous Special Body of the General Assembly with budgetary and programmatic ties to other special bodies, such as UNCTAD and the UN Development Program (UNDP).

During its first General Conference in Vienna in 1971, UNIDO appealed for greater independence, particularly in light of the UNDP's extensive budgetary control. The plea was reiterated at the second General Conference, held in 1975 in Lima, Peru, and later that year the General Assembly, in an unprecedented move, authorized the change in status from a Special Body to a Specialized Agency, subject to the development and ratification of a UNIDO constitution. After extensive negotiations, representatives from 82 countries participating in a conference of plenipotentiaries held on March 19–April 8, 1979 in Vienna adopted such a document, and the ratification process, which was to take six years, began.

The 1980 conference proved to be highly confrontational, with the industrialized countries objecting not only to the call for the establishment of a 20-year, $300 billion global development fund, but to what they considered political provisions—including statements condemning colonialism and racism—in the New Delhi Declaration drafted by the developing countries' Group of 77. The disagreement between rich and poor continued at the 1984 conference, little being achieved apart from a renewed call for capital mobilization in support of industrial progress in the third world.

Although 120 governments ratified the UNIDO constitution by March 1985, it was not until June 21 that the minimum of 80 formal notifications of such action had been tendered, in part because of an insistence by Eastern European countries that they be guaranteed a deputy director generalship. Subsequently, a General Conference met in Vienna on August 12–17 and December 9–13 to pave the way for launching the organization as the United Nations's 16th Specialized Agency.

In the early 1990s observers described the organization as facing "a leadership and identity crisis," underscored by its failure to approve either of two proposed restructuring plans. Members' arrears also continued to be a major concern, with dozens of countries losing voting rights for nonpayment of dues. On March 30, 1993, a special session of the General Conference appointed Mauricio de María y Campos of Mexico as UNIDO director general, the former director general, Domingo L. Siazon Jr., having resigned to take a position in the Philippine government. The new director general called for an "urgent restructuring," with emphasis placed on helping companies in developing countries to become internationally competitive via an expanded private sector and global cooperation in the transfer of technology. Many of the recommendations were endorsed in the Yaoundé Declaration issued following the fifth General Conference, held December 6–9 in Yaoundé, Cameroon.

Despite its restructuring, UNIDO's future remained in jeopardy as a review of overlapping UN bodies proceeded. It was reported in early 1995 that a UN report had recommended the dismantling of UNIDO, a proposal endorsed by the world's leading industrialized countries during their midyear summit. Consequently, the United States announced at UNIDO's sixth General Conference in December that it would withdraw from the organization at the end of 1996. UNIDO subsequently continued to restructure its operations, cutting a number of senior managers, reducing its overall workforce by more than one-third from its 1993 total, and slashing its budget.

The 1997 General Conference endorsed the Business Plan for the Future Role and Functions of UNIDO, under which the organization's overall goals in meeting the needs of developing countries and economies in transition were defined as "the three Es": competitive economy, productive employment, and sound environment. The conference approved the nomination of a new director general, Carlos Magariños of Argentina, making him the youngest director general in UN history. Magariños was widely credited for revamping the organization's structure and was reelected to a second four-year term at the December 2001 conference.

At the 11th session of the UNIDO General Conference, held on November 28–December 2, 2005, in Vienna, Magariños was succeeded by Kandeh Yumkella of Sierra Leone.

Structure. The General Conference, which meets every two years, establishes UNIDO policy and is responsible for final approval of its biennial budgets. The Industrial Development Board (IDB), which meets annually, exercises wide-ranging "policy review" authority, and its recommendations exert significant influence on the decisions of the conference. The Program and Budget Committee also meets annually to conduct extensive preliminary budget preparations.

The Secretariat, comprising some 630 staff members in Vienna and 123 in the field, is headed by a director general appointed by the General Conference upon the recommendation of the IDB. The 1985 General Conference decided to name five deputy directors general, thus permitting greater regional/bloc representation. However, the 1993 General Conference approved a streamlined staff structure that eliminated the deputy directors general and instead named eight managing directors. In late 1997 UNIDO decided to reduce the number of divisions to three. In February 2002 the Secretariat instituted a new organizational structure with three divisions: Program Development and Technical Cooperation, Program Coordination and Field Operations, and Administration. Staff was also streamlined (143 posts abolished), and there was a significant reduction in the number of committees.

UNIDO activity in most developing countries is coordinated by a resident senior industrial development field adviser or a resident junior professional officer. In addition, expert advisers or consultants, numbering more than 2,000 in recent years, are hired from throughout the world to work temporarily on many of the development projects administered by UNIDO. As of 2004, 29 countries had regional offices.

Activities. UNIDO serves both as a technical cooperation agency and as a global forum. Its research, analysis, statistical compilation, dissemination of information, and training provide general support for industrial development throughout the world. In addition, the organization operates (usually in conjunction with other UN affiliates and national governments) hundreds of field projects per year in such areas as planning, feasibility study, research and development for specific proposals, and installation of pilot industrial plants.

UNIDO facilities include 17 Investment and Technology Promotion Offices, which encourage contacts between businessmen and governments in developing or transitional countries and industrial and financial leaders in developed countries; 10 closely associated International Technology Centers; 5 Investment Promotion Units in Africa and the Near East; 35 National Cleaner Production Centers under a program jointly organized with the UN Environment Program (UNEP); and 59 Subcontracting and Partnership Exchanges in more than 30 countries to link local manufacturers with the global market. UNIDO was also instrumental in the creation of the International Center for Genetic Engineering and Biotechnology, with bases in Trieste, Italy, and New Delhi, India; the International Center for Science and High Technology in Trieste; the Center for the Application of Solar Energy in Perth, Australia; the International Center for Small Hydro Power in Hangzhou, China; the International Center for Materials Evaluation Technology in Taejon, South Korea; and the International Center for Hydrogen Energy Technology in Istanbul, Turkey. Special UNIDO funds include the Industrial Development Fund (IDF), established in 1978 to provide financing for innovative development projects outside the criteria of existing financial services, and the Working Capital Fund, established in 1986.

Since the mid-1990s, UNIDO's programs have undergone a shift of emphasis, in part as an adjustment to tighter budgets. The 1995 General Conference directed the organization to emphasize African development as part of the UN's overall special African initiative; particular attention has since been given to exploitation of natural resources, development of the continent's labor potential, and aiding government efforts to reach global markets. In November 2001 the organization launched the Africa Investment Promotion Agency Network that focused on spurring domestic and foreign investment in 14 countries in Sub-Saharan Africa. However, in July 2004 UNIDO released a report stating that the poorest African nations were "seriously off-track" for meeting the 2015 poverty reduction deadline set by the UN. Environmental sustainability has also emerged as a major theme of UNIDO's efforts. In addition to establishing the National Cleaner Production Centers Program in conjunction with the UNEP, it continues to serve as one of the UN's four implementing agencies for the Montreal Protocol on ozone-depleting chemicals and has been active in the Kyoto Protocol, which was implemented in February 2005 in an effort to combat greenhouse gases and global warming (see the discussion of both protocols in the UNEP article).

In late 1999 UNIDO held the first UNIDO Forum on Sustainable Industrial Development in Vienna, Austria, in tandem with the eighth General Conference to address the effects of economic integration in developing economies; the impact of globalization; environmental challenges to sustainable development; and the status of the recently initiated UNIDO Partnership Program, which is an effort to coordinate local and intergovernmental entities, both public and private, in assisting small- and medium-sized enterprises (SMEs).

The tenth General Conference was held in December 2003 in Vienna, where the main objective was to discuss the organization's role in fulfilling the Millennium Development Goals (MDGs) set by the UN in the environmental and developmental areas. No trade agreements, global declarations, or major funds were under negotiation.

At the 2005 11th General Conference, UNIDO adopted a strategic long-term vision statement and a medium-term program framework to cover the years 2006–2009. The 2007 General Conference took place on December 3–7 in Vienna. The Secretariat noted that member countries continued to be in arrears for payment of membership dues.

So-called south-south cooperation has become a key policy focus in recent years in an effort to promote trade and increased production capacities between advanced developing countries and poorer nations with emerging economies. To that end, UNIDO planned on opening industrial cooperation centers in China, Egypt, Brazil, and South Africa to enhance business networks. The first center opened in New Delhi, India, in February 2007, and a second in Beijing in July 2008.

In 2007 UNIDO hosted the International Conference on Biofuels in Kuala Lumpur, Malaysia, the first in a three-year series of conferences aimed at developing industrial conversion processes and uses of biofuels. UNIDO signed several agreements with India to promote SMEs in 2007 and 2008. However India was warned about its overreliance on fossil fuels and was encouraged to generate one-fifth of its electricity from renewable sources in the current UNIDO-India plan period, 2007–2012.

In April 2008 Director General Yumkella urged Africa to industrialize as a way to combat poverty and urged Nigeria to take the lead in this effort. In June UNIDO and Microsoft announced plans to set up a computer refurbishment operation in Uganda, with the twin aims of reducing pollution from discarded computers and of putting more and cheaper computers in African hands. In September UNIDO told India that it should aim to generate one fifth of the capacity expansion in its current economic plan (that covers 2007–2012) from renewable energy, thus alleviating its effect on climate change. In November UNIDO signed a Memorandum of Understanding (MOU) with China for cooperation in clean industrial development. On December 12, 2008, Samoa joined UNIDO as its 173rd member.

In January 2009 UNIDO signed an MOU for increased cooperation with the Eurasian Economic Community, an offshoot of the Commonwealth of Independent States (CIS, see separate article). In UNIDO's Industrial Development Report 2009, released February 24, 2009, it argued against using the world economic crisis as an excuse for returning to protectionism. Poor countries needed to move beyond trading raw materials and into manufacturing, it said. In June 2009 UNIDO announced the expansion of a joint program with the technology company Hewlett-Packard. This program would build additional IT training centers in Africa and the Middle East

UNIVERSAL POSTAL UNION

Union Postale Universelle

(UPU)

Established: By treaty signed on October 9, 1874, in Berne, Switzerland; present name adopted in 1878. The UPU became a UN Specialized Agency by agreement with the Economic and Social Council (approved by the General Assembly on November 15, 1947, with effect from July 1, 1948).

Purpose: To organize and improve world postal services and to promote the development of international postal collaboration.

Headquarters: Berne, Switzerland.

Principal Organs: Universal Postal Congress (all members), Council of Administration (40 members), Postal Operations Council (40 members), International Bureau, Consultative Committee.

Web site: www.upu.int

Director General: Edouard Dayan (France).

Membership (191)**:** See Appendix C.

Official Language: French. (English was approved as a working language by the 1994 Universal Postal Congress.)

Origin and development. The second oldest of the UN Specialized Agencies, the Universal Postal Union traces its origins to a 15-state international conference held in 1863 in Paris, France, in recognition of the growing need to establish principles governing international postal exchange. The first International Postal Congress was convened in 1874 in Berne, Switzerland, and yielded the Treaty Concerning the Establishment of a General Postal Union, commonly known as the Berne Treaty. This was the forerunner of a multilateral convention that governed international postal service as of July 1, 1875; three years later, at the Second International Postal Congress, held in Paris, the name of the organization was changed to the Universal Postal Union (UPU). By an agreement signed in Paris in 1947 and effective July 1, 1948, the UPU was recognized as the UN Specialized Agency responsible for international postal activity. A revision of the basic acts of the UPU to make them more compatible with the structure of other UN Specialized Agencies was carried out by the 15th Universal Postal Congress in Vienna, Austria, in 1964. The revised constitution, general regulations, and convention (dated July 10, 1964) entered into force January 1, 1966.

Despite the union's nonpolitical tradition and the absence in the UPU constitution of any provision for expulsion, South Africa was expelled from the UPU by majority vote of the 1979 congress for its apartheid policies. Taking advantage of an apparent oversight in the language of that resolution, however, South Africa attained readmission under an article of the UPU constitution providing that "any member of the United Nations may accede to the Union." However, the 1984 congress again excluded South Africa by a majority vote "until a future congress of the UPU decides otherwise." Although the legality of the expulsion remained highly questionable, South Africa did not take any action to challenge it, apparently because there was no discernible impact on postal service to and from the country. In the wake of the installation of a nonracial government in Pretoria, South Africa was readmitted to the UPU at the 1994 congress.

Structure. The Universal Postal Congress, composed of all UPU members and usually meeting at five-year intervals, is the principal organ of the union. It establishes the UPU's work program and budget, reviews its acts and subsidiary agreements, and elects the director general and deputy director general. Until recently, the Executive Council, consisting of 40 members elected by the congress, provided continuity between congresses, maintained relations with the rest of the UN system and other international organizations, and prepared technical postal studies as a basis for recommendations to the congress. In addition, the Consultative Council for Postal Studies, consisting of 35 members elected by the congress, was established in 1957 to conduct studies; organize symposiums on technical postal topics; and give advice on technical, operational, and economic questions affecting international postal services. However, the 1994 congress voted to replace the Executive Council and the Consultative Council with, respectively, the Council of Administration to be responsible primarily for regulatory matters and the Postal Operations Council.

The Council of Administration is composed of 41 members elected by the congress, plus a chair from the host country of the last congress. It provides continuity between congresses, prepares technical postal studies as a basis for recommendations to the congress, and is charged with approving the union's budget and accounts. The council can also adopt regulations that it "considers necessary to resolve urgent matters" as well as Postal Operations Council proposals that are subject to approval by the next congress. The Postal Operations Council, encompassing 40 elected members and a chair elected by the council itself, is concerned with "the operational, economic and commercial aspects of international postal services," especially the modernization of postal products.

The International Bureau, the permanent secretariat of the UPU, is headed by a director general. In addition to serving as a liaison for the membership, the bureau acts as a clearinghouse for the settlement of charges incurred in the exchange of postal services among the member countries.

In September 2004 the 23rd congress approved the creation of the Consultative Committee to give a voice in deliberations and future decisions to a new union body of external postal stakeholders, the representatives of nongovernmental organizations that represent consumers, delivery service providers, and workers' organizations. The committee replaced the Advisory Group established in 2000, and members of that group automatically became committee members and full observers in the Universal Postal Congress. The committee meets twice yearly and consists of 19 international organizations and 6 member countries (in 2008 Barbados, Benin, Great Britain, Japan, Korea, Spain).

Activities. The basic aims of the UPU are the improvement of the world's postal services and the maintenance of "a single territory for the reciprocal exchange of correspondence." This single-territory principle contained in the 1874 UPU treaty suggests the ideas of standardization and close cooperation. The concept remains essentially figurative and does not preclude separate agreements between countries on postal matters; however, all member countries have pledged to expedite mail originating in other member states by the best means used to expedite their own mail. All members must also agree to certain common rules regarding regular letter mail, while special agreements—binding only on those UPU members that accede to them—cover such areas as insured letters, postal parcels, postal money orders, newspapers and periodicals, and cash-on-delivery items. In addition to its routine functions, the UPU participates in UN technical cooperation programs for developing states, while related activities have included recruiting and supplying experts, awarding fellowships for vocational training, and furnishing minor equipment and training and demonstration materials.

During the late 1980s UPU operated under net annual budgets of 22 million Swiss francs (an estimated U.S. $33 million at that time). However, the 20th congress, held in Washington, D.C., in 1989, agreed to raise budget ceilings, and the 1991 budget was subsequently set at 26.2 million Swiss francs (approximately $16.9 million at the January 1, 1990, exchange rate). The increase was earmarked, in part, for a campaign to enhance the quality of international postal services, apparently in response to growing competition from private companies. The budget included plans to identify and correct causes of delivery delays, improve the "security and integrity" of international mail, and provide customers with a wider range of services and price options. Since 1992 the union budget increases have not exceeded the rate of inflation, the most recently approved budget in fiscal year 2008–2009 being 36 million Swiss francs (an estimated U.S. $43 million).

To keep pace with the increasingly rapid changes in postal services, the 21st congress, held August 22–September 14, 1994, in Seoul, South Korea, discussed many UPU restructuring and reorientation proposals. Decisions included the revamping of the union's principal organs (see Structure, above) to accommodate the growing European and UN preference for distinct governing bodies for regulators and operators.

Participants at the 22nd congress, held August 23–September 15, 1999, in Beijing, China, were warned that opening postal services to competition from the private sector should not mean a reduction in, or elimination of, traditional services needed to meet "every citizen's right to communicate." Instead, members were encouraged to upgrade their services, in part by adopting new technologies such as e-mail and electronic tracking and tracing. Also discussed was the need for major investments to narrow a widening gap between the capabilities of developed and developing countries. The congress concluded by adopting the Beijing Postal Strategy for action over the next five years. In addition, the congress formed a 25-member high-level group to propose changes to the union and an advisory group open to regional unions, nongovernmental organizations, and the private sector. The World Postal Policy Forum was also authorized to meet between congresses.

The UPU also seeks to support human development by restoring postal networks where they have been destroyed by human conflict and natural disasters. In 2003 the UPU developed an assistance plan for Afghanistan to restore its network after the fall of the Taliban and created a special fund to restore postal networks in Indian Ocean countries devastated by the 2004 tsunami. The Quality of Service Fund, created in 2001 through membership contributions, funds projects to improve postal service in developing countries. By March 2006 the fund reported financing 279 projects at a cost of $40 million.

The 23rd Universal Postal Congress was held September 15–October 5, 2004, in Bucharest, Romania. Among its major decisions were approval of an additional UPU body (see Structure, above) and the adoption of the Bucharest World Postal Strategy, a four-year roadmap to modernize union operations in light of the increasing global use of e-mail. While the postal services make up the world's largest network, with 650,000 outlets and 5 million employees, 1 person in every 20 has no access to postal services; consequently, the conference agreed to make universal service a top priority. The congress also adopted a worldwide quality of service standard for international mail services, approved several resolutions on the need to improve security to combat terrorism and money laundering through the postal service, and adopted a proposal to amend the UPU convention formally to recognize the Electronic Postmark (EPM) as a new optional postal service. The EPM is a service to encrypt e-mail—validating who sends it, who receives it, and when it is received—in order to give the transmission better legal standing. Other major activity included the creation of a new terminal dues system to balance delivery costs between countries and the election of Edouard Dayan, the French post's director of European and international affairs, as director general. Dayan defeated Carlos Silva of Portugal by a 102–63 vote. Dayan is the first French citizen to take the post in the history of the UPU.

On April 17, 2006, the UPU approved international standards for digital postmarks to assist worldwide adoption of the technology. Some commentators, however, felt that the future of digital postmarks—designed to facilitate electronic postal activity—was still in doubt, and indeed progress over the next two years was slow. In October 2007 the UPU proposed a top-level internet domain "post," which would be used only for postally secure transmissions.

Of necessity, the UPU has been making the case for the continued relevance of postal services in an electronic age. As national postal systems struggled to revamp their services to adjust to current conditions, the organization held the UPU Strategy Conference November 14–16, 2006, in Dubai. Additionally, discussions were held concerning the development of a worldwide electronic payment network to provide affordable and secure means of money transfer for migrant workers to use as an alternative to private carriers. These and other issues formed the basis for the 2008–2012 World Postal Strategy to be adopted at the 24th UPU Congress, which was scheduled to be held in Nairobi, Kenya, in 2008. The conference was moved to Geneva because of the disturbed conditions in Kenya at the beginning of 2008 and was held from July 23 to August 12.

In August 2009 UPU began a test of its state-of-the-art global monitoring system (GMS), in which test letters containing radio frequency identification tags were sent through the world postal system. GMS is designed to monitor the speed and efficiency with which a piece of mail travels. An October 20, 2009, UPU report indicated that worldwide, mail volumes were holding up surprisingly well at a time when steep declines had been predicted. A rise in parcel traffic from online orders of merchandise generally offset a decline in first-class mail, and overall mail volumes were increasing modestly. In the same month UPU announced that it was close to securing the top-level Internet domain ". post" for its activities, to take its place along such familiar domains as ".com" and ".org."

WORLD HEALTH ORGANIZATION (WHO)

Established: By constitution signed in New York, United States, July 22, 1946, effective April 7, 1948. WHO became a UN Specialized Agency by agreement with the Economic and Social Council (approved by the General Assembly on November 15, 1947, with effect from September 1, 1948).

Purpose: To aid in "the attainment by all peoples of the highest possible levels of health."

Headquarters: Geneva, Switzerland.

Principal Organs: World Health Assembly (all members), Executive Board (32 experts), Regional Committees (all regional members), Secretariat.

Web site: www.who.int/en/

Director General: Margaret Chan (Hong Kong SAR).

Membership (193, plus two Associate Members and two Observers)**:** See Appendix C.

Official Languages: Arabic, Chinese, English, French, Russian, Spanish.

Origin and development. Attempts to institutionalize international cooperation in health matters originated as early as 1851 but reached full fruition only with establishment of WHO. The need for a single international health agency was emphasized in a special declaration of the UN Conference on International Organization held in 1945 in San Francisco, California, and the constitution of WHO was adopted at the specially convened International Health Conference held in June–July 1946 in New York. Formally established on April 8, 1948, WHO also took over the functions of the International Office of Public Health, established in 1907; those of the League of Nations Health Organization; and the health activities of the UN Relief and Rehabilitation Administration (UNRRA).

A turning point in WHO's evolution occurred in 1976. As a result of decisions reached during that year's World Health Assembly, it began to reorient its work so that by 1980 a full 60 percent of its regular budget would be allocated for technical cooperation and for the provision of services to member states. In addition, all nonessential expenditures were to be eliminated, resulting in a reduction of several hundred administrative positions. A further step in this process was taken in May 1979 when the 32nd World Health Assembly adopted a report and declaration on primary health care and its relationship to socioeconomic development. Members were asked to submit collective, regional, and individual health care strategies to be used as the basis for the Global Strategy for Health for All, targeting objectives for the year 2000. The global strategy was adopted by the 34th assembly in 1981, and a plan of action for its implementation followed in 1982.

Controversy at the 32nd World Health Assembly was generated by an abortive attempt by Arab representatives to suspend Israeli membership. The United States, objecting to politicization of the organization, warned that it would probably withdraw from WHO if the proposal were adopted. At the 33rd assembly in May 1980, Arab members succeeded in gaining approval of a resolution that declared "the establishment of Israeli settlements in the occupied Arab territories, including Palestine, a source of "serious damage" to the inhabitants' health. Moreover, the conferees condemned the "inhuman practices to which Arab prisoners and detainees are subject in Israeli prisons." A clause that would have denied Israel's membership rights was deleted from a resolution before the 35th assembly in May 1982, after the United States had again threatened withdrawal.

In 1989 a proposal to grant membership to the Palestine Liberation Organization (PLO) received strong backing from Arab states and many developing countries but was condemned by the United States, which threatened to withhold its WHO contribution. The assembly deferred the question and in 1990 postponed action "indefinitely," although it increased direct assistance to Palestinians. Currently, Palestine has observer status in the WHO.

Taiwan has been denied membership eight times, most recently in 2004, because China claims sovereignty and has successfully blocked its bids.

The 1994 assembly received a director general's report outlining recent budgetary and accounting reforms, with even stricter controls subsequently being recommended by some WHO members. At the same session the assembly reinstated South Africa, under suspension since 1964, to full membership privileges.

Controversy broke out over Director General Nakajima at the 1995 assembly. WHO's external auditor told the assembly that the WHO Secretariat failed to cooperate with his inquiry into alleged fraud, waste, and financial impropriety. Consequently, the assembly rejected Nakajima's request for a 16 percent increase in the WHO regular budget, approving instead a total of $842.7 million for the 1996–1997 biennium, an increase of only 2.5 percent. At the 1998 World Health Assembly, Dr. Gro Harlem Brundtland, former prime minister of Norway, was elected director general, effective in July. In August 2002 Brundtland announced she would not run for reelection, adding that she was content with the progress WHO had made during her tenure (Brundtland is widely credited for coining the term "sustainable development.") Lee Jong-Wook, a South Korean doctor with expertise on vaccines and diseases associated with poverty, was selected as director general in January 2003. In May 2006 Dr. Lee died suddenly, and was replaced in an acting capacity by his deputy, Dr. Anders Nordström of Sweden. In November 2006 the assembly appointed Margaret Chan as director general. Chan was the former health director of Hong Kong during the severe acute respiratory syndrome (SARS) outbreak and had worked for three years at WHO in various high level posts.

Structure. The World Health Assembly, in which all members are represented, is the principal political organ of WHO. At its annual sessions, usually held at WHO headquarters in May, the assembly approves the organization's long-range work program as well as its annual program and budget. International health conventions may be approved and recommended to governments by a two-thirds majority vote. The assembly similarly adopts technical health regulations that come into force immediately for those governments that do not specifically reject them.

The Executive Board is composed of 32 members who, although designated by governments selected by the assembly, serve in an individual expert capacity rather than as governmental representatives. Meeting at least twice a year, the board prepares the assembly agenda and oversees implementation of assembly decisions. The Secretariat is headed by a director general designated by the assembly on recommendation of the board.

WHO is the least centralized of the UN Specialized Agencies, much of its program centering on six regional organizations: Southeast Asia (headquartered in New Delhi, India); the Eastern Mediterranean (Cairo, Egypt); the Western Pacific (Manila, Philippines); the Americas (Washington, D.C.); Africa (Brazzaville, Congo); and Europe (Copenhagen, Denmark). Each of the six has a regional committee of all members in the area and an office headed by a regional director.

Activities. Generally considered one of the more successful UN agencies, WHO acts as a guiding authority on international health work, actively promotes cooperation in health matters, sets global health standards, and works toward development and transfer of health-related technology and information. Since the early 1980s WHO has accepted as a leading principle "Health for All," which in its most recent incarnation entails the equitable distribution of health resources coupled with universal access to essential health services. In addition, WHO has increasingly emphasized that the public itself needs to make wiser choices, including adherence to healthier lifestyles, to escape "the avoidable burden of disease." WHO identified ten major avoidable health risks in its October 2002 annual report that are responsible for 56 million deaths each year, including hunger, unprotected sex, high blood pressure, smoking, alcohol, contaminated water or poor sanitation, high cholesterol, nutritional deficiencies, and obesity. As part of a landmark strategy to combat obesity, the organization encouraged governments to increase taxes on foods with high sugar, salt, and saturated fat content, which prompted strong opposition from the sugar industry in 2004. However, the nonbinding strategy was ultimately adopted in May 2004 and endorses a series of policy guidelines.

The organization is perhaps best known for its highly successful immunization programs, beginning with its coordination of the worldwide smallpox vaccination campaign that by 1980 had eradicated the disease. WHO announced in January 2002 that the destruction of the remaining smallpox stocks would be postponed for up to three years to give researchers more time to develop new treatments and vaccines for the disease after terrorist attacks sparked fears that the virus could be used as a weapon. Following the September 11, 2001, terrorist attacks in the United States, U.S. president George W. Bush's administration stockpiled the vaccine. In 1974 WHO also embarked, in conjunction with the UN Children's Fund (UNICEF), on a worldwide campaign to immunize children against measles, poliomyelitis, diphtheria, pertussis (whooping cough), tetanus, and tuberculosis (TB); hepatitis B was added in 1992, as was yellow fever in relevant geographical areas. In June 2002 WHO declared Europe free of polio, marking it as the third region worldwide to be certifiably free of the disease.

Soon after taking office, Director General Brundtland set about reorganizing WHO, reducing its programs from 50 to 35 and placing them in nine clusters. Subsequent restructuring brought the number of clusters down to eight and then to six in a further realignment in October 2007 under Director General Chan.

WHO organizes its clusters into broad areas of disease management. The Health Security and Environment cluster, formerly named the Communicable Disease cluster, includes the Department of Epidemic and Pandemic Alert and Response; the Department of Protection of the Human Environment; and the Department of Food Safety, Zoonoses [diseases transmitted through contact with animals], and Food-borne Diseases. The changes reflect an expansion in the agency's scope to encompass environmental hazards and foodborne diseases as a result of implementation in 2007 of the International Health Regulations (IHR) of 2005 (see below).

The Noncommunicable Diseases and Mental Health cluster, which retained its name under the realignment, has a broad mandate that includes issues regarding aging, psychiatric and other mental disorders, substance abuse, tobacco use, violence and injury prevention, and oral health as well as such "lifestyle" diseases as diabetes, avoidable blindness, cardiovascular disease, and cancer. The 1999 World Health Assembly opened negotiations on the Framework Convention on Tobacco Control (FCTC), and tumultuous negotiations continued until May 2003 when all of the 192 member countries ultimately adopted the landmark treaty. The United States, a reluctant supporter, was the last country to sign on because of contentious language on advertising that the United States said could violate constitutional rights to free speech. The treaty regulates that health warnings must be no less than 30 percent the size of a cigarette pack, bans terms such as "light" and "low tar," encourages higher taxes on tobacco products, and condemns certain marketing efforts. The treaty went into force in February 2005 and has been ratified by 146 countries. A second FCTC meeting of signatory countries in July 2007 in Bangkok, Thailand, reviewed further changes to the tobacco treaty, including the development of protocols to curb illicit trade in tobacco products and exposure to second-hand smoke.

The HIV/AIDS, TB, Malaria, and Neglected Tropical Diseases cluster includes the Department of Neglected Tropical Diseases. Longstanding WHO efforts to eradicate polio and control maladies such as "river blindness" (onchocerciasis), lymphatic filariasis, "Chagas disease" (American trypanosomiasis), guinea-worm disease (dracunculiasis), leprosy, and Buruli ulcer fall under this cluster. In October 2006 the agency announced new guidelines to tackle "neglected" tropical diseases, which would include the use of inexpensive, preventative drugs in both healthy and infected people.

Additionally, the cluster handles the Department of HIV/AIDS, a major focus of WHO attention since the 1993 World Health Assembly called for a coordinated attack against the condition. In early 1996 WHO became one of the original cosponsoring agencies of the resultant Joint UN Program on HIV/AIDS (UNAIDS), which later set a millennium development goal of reversing the spread of the disease by 2015. Since then, a number of coordinated efforts to track the spread of the disease and provide treatment to ailing populations have been formed. The "3 by 5" program launched in 2003 by UNAIDS had a target of providing 3 million people with antiretroviral treatment by the end of 2005. In July 2004 WHO officials said they would meet that target, but by 2005 it became clear that the agency would far fall short. High drug prices and delivery problems were blamed for the agency's delivery of drugs to only 1 million people.

In September 2003 WHO announced it would organize a drug-buying facility for AIDS treatments to make it easier for developing countries to access treatments. Additionally, in 2005 the Global Price Reporting Mechanism for Antiretroviral Drugs was created to screen and share drug prices with procurement agencies to allow price comparisons for optimal purchasing.

Subsequent efforts on handling HIV/AIDS have moved toward the goal of providing universal access to prevention and treatment programs. The June 2006 General Assembly set a new goal of achieving such access by 2010. However, the release later that year of the *UNAIDS/WHO 2006 AIDS Epidemic Update* suggested the task would be more difficult than anticipated, reporting a resurgence in new HIV infection rates in some countries that were previously stable or in decline. Though the largest number of infection rates continued to be in sub-Saharan Africa, the report stated that Eastern Europe and Central Asia had HIV growth rates of more than 50 percent in some areas. In 2006, 2.9 million people died of AIDS-related illnesses globally, and 4.3 million were newly infected, according to the report. Though there was "a positive trend in young people's sexual behaviors," the report noted that many HIV prevention programs were not reaching people most at risk.

However, an April 2007 progress report on universal access found some encouraging trends. Nearly one-third of those living with HIV/AIDS in low- and middle-income countries were receiving treatment. Antiretroviral drug prices in those same countries had reduced from one-third to one-half between the years 2003–2006. The signs of progress were offset by a warning that treatment needed to be greatly expanded to account for a steep increase in future need. It also outlined the emergence of an alarming growth in drug-resistant tuberculosis in settings of high HIV prevalence.

In other areas, WHO's Information, Evidence, and Research cluster focuses on epidemiology, statistics, quality assurance, access to care, cost-effectiveness, health system reform, and regulatory and legislative matters. It also publishes the *Bulletin of the World Health Organization* and the annual *World Health Report.* The cluster includes the Special Program for Research and Training in Tropical Diseases and the newly created Department on Ethics, Equity, Trade, and Human Rights. The latter handles information on bioethics and ethical aspects of health care delivery and research.

Additionally, WHO publishes the *International Pharmacopoeia* and the *WHO Model List of Essential Drugs* (more than 330 in the 2007 edition), establishes drug standards, and assists in the formulation of national drug policies.

The 1998 *World Health Report* noted that there had been impressive advances in global health, with average life expectancy increasing from 48 in 1950 to 66. Despite these gains, the report also estimated that 40 percent of all deaths were premature. The 1999 *World Health Report,* acknowledging financial and other constraints in delivery of health care, recommended that priority be given to helping poorer countries combat infectious disease and malnutrition. The report also proposed that developed countries set clear health service priorities and attempt to provide universal coverage for the selected conditions. This new "universalism" has as a founding principle that "if services are to be provided for all, then not all services can be provided."

In June 2000 WHO published a report, *Overcoming Microbial Resistance*, which focused on the growing problem of multidrug-resistant tuberculosis, pneumonia, typhoid, AIDS, and sexually transmitted diseases. In October WHO joined governments, private firms, and charitable organizations in establishing a research program, budgeted at $150 million for the first five years, to develop a new drug against TB, which continues to claim some 2 million lives annually.

In May 2002 WHO announced it was taking the first steps to becoming the global watchdog over unconventional medicine, or non-Western treatments, as at least 80 percent of the world's poorest countries use them. The organization seeks to catalog all folk remedies.

WHO played a significant role during the SARS outbreak in 2003, which centered in China and caused the deaths of at least 78 people worldwide. To stem the outbreak, WHO urged airports in affected cities to screen ill passengers and connected a network of 11 laboratories in nine countries to identify the agent causing the illness and devise treatments—a rapid response strategy considered unprecedented for the organization. However, research efforts were temporarily hindered when Chinese officials repeatedly denied WHO experts access to the Guangdong Province, where the disease was believed to have originated. China eventually relented and provided data, although not full access, to WHO. By June 2003 the organization announced that the SARS outbreak was over in Vietnam and in Hong Kong.

The following month WHO approved sweeping new powers to respond to international health threats such as SARS. The resolution established round-the-clock communication between countries, allows WHO to use nonofficial sources of information such as reports from nongovernmental organizations or the news media to respond to threats, authorizes the organization to issue global alerts, and authorizes the director general to send teams to conduct on-the-spot studies to ensure countries take adequate measures to stop diseases from spreading.

In recent years WHO has been active in coordinating tsunami relief, has continued its efforts against the spread of avian influenza, and has seen the world's first global health treaty, the Framework Convention on Tobacco Control, come into force (February 2005). The organization subsequently decided to hire only nonsmokers.

In an external development that could have a significant impact on WHO's future activities, American financier Warren Buffet announced in July 2006 that he was giving $31 billion of his fortune to the Bill and Melinda Gates Foundation, a philanthropy dedicated to "bringing innovations in health and learning to the global community." Some commentators suggested that this gift would create a private health-related charity with a larger budget than WHO.

The 2007 *World Health Report* focused on public health in a time of environmental changes and diseases that spread rapidly around the world. It called for complete implementation of the IHR as well as increased global cooperation and surveillance in public health matters. In a related effort, in October 2007 WHO announced support for a campaign to register every birth in the world, pointing out the dangers to which unregistered children are subject.

The 61st World Health Assembly, held May 19–24, 2008, in Geneva, was attended by a record number of participants. It endorsed a six-year plan to deal with noncommunicable diseases, which are considered the leading threats to human health in the early twenty-first century. It also called for a draft strategy by 2010 to deal with the harmful use of alcohol and requested more information about the health aspects of migrant environments. Assembly participants asked member states to work decisively against the effects of climate change and to utilize education and legislation to eliminate female genital mutilation.

The year 2008 was notable for the increasing danger from diseases that had been thought completely or nearly extinct, coupled with a decline in childhood immunization rates in advanced countries. WHO warned about the spread of drug-resistant tuberculosis, which had grown to account for 20 percent of all cases. But it noted that a cheap, rapid test for the condition was had become available. WHO sent vaccine to Paraguay to combat a yellow fever outbreak and to the Sahel when polio emerged in the region, but it was able to declare Somalia free of tuberculosis and Zimbabwe of polio. A June 2008 report declared that there was no longer the threat of an AIDS pandemic among heterosexuals, except in Africa. In September 2008 WHO criticized China for initially not doing more to stop the sale of melamine-tainted milk products; the organization then issued guidelines to help affected countries assess and deal with the problem.

In a sign that some stability was returning to Iraq, in July 2008 the WHO office in Baghdad reopened. In October 2008 WHO scientific experts agreed to a research agenda to develop an evidence-based framework for action on human health in a time of climate change.

The 2008 World Health Report, published in October of that year, noted inequities in health care around the world, even between areas of the same country a few miles apart, and recommended a renewed emphasis on primary medicine. A December 2008 report pointed out that essential medicines were out many people's reach. The May 2009 World Health Assembly was dominated by concerns about the H1N1 strain of influenza, which threatened to become a pandemic. It also noted efforts to fight new strains of drug-resistent tuberculosis. On June 12, 2009, Director General Chan declared H1N1 influenza to be pandemic.

In September 2009 a WHO-sponsored study found the leading causes of death among children and young adults to be road accidents, suicide, and complications from childbirth. By October 2009, with a vaccine against H1N1 influenza becoming available, the WHO advised that in most cases people over ten years of age need only receive a single dose in order to be protected.

WORLD INTELLECTUAL PROPERTY ORGANIZATION
(WIPO)

Established: By a convention signed in Stockholm, Sweden, July 14, 1967, entering into force April 26, 1970. WIPO became a UN Specialized Agency by a General Assembly resolution on December 17, 1974.

Purpose: To ensure administrative cooperation among numerous intellectual property "unions" and to promote, by means of cooperation among states and international organizations, the protection of "intellectual property," including literary, artistic, and scientific works; the contents of broadcasts, films, and photographs; and all types of inventions, industrial designs, and trademarks.

Headquarters: Geneva, Switzerland.

Principal Organs: General Assembly (172 members), Conference (all members), Coordination Committee (80 members), Program and Budget Committee (41 members), Permanent Committee on Cooperation for Development Related to Intellectual Property (all members), Standing Committee on Information Technologies (all state members plus seven nonvoting organizations), International Bureau.

Web site: www.wipo.int/portal/index.html.en

Director General: Dr. Francis Gurry (Australia).

Membership (184): See Appendix C.

Working Languages: Arabic, Chinese, English, French, Portuguese, Russian, Spanish.

Origin and development. The origins of WIPO can be traced to the establishment of the Paris Convention on the Protection of Industrial Property in 1883 and the Berne Convention for the Protection of Literary and Artistic Works in 1886. Both conventions provided for separate international bureaus, or secretariats, which were united in 1893 and functioned under various names, the last being the United International Bureau for the Protection of Intellectual Property (BIRPI). The BIRPI still has a legal existence, but for practical purposes is indistinguishable from WIPO. WIPO also assumed responsibility for administering a number of smaller unions based on other multilateral agreements and for coordinating subsequent negotiations on additional agreements. In December 1974 WIPO became the UN's 14th Specialized Agency.

In September 1977 the Coordination Committee agreed to ban South Africa from future meetings because of its apartheid policy, but a move to exclude it from the organization was narrowly defeated in 1979. South Africa's full membership privileges were restored in 1994 in concert with similar steps throughout the UN system.

Structure. The General Assembly, comprising states that are parties to the WIPO Convention and are also members of the Paris and/or Berne conventions, is the organization's highest authority. In addition, the WIPO Conference, comprising all parties to WIPO's convention, serves as a forum for discussion of all matters relating to intellectual property and has authority over WIPO's activities and budget.

The International Bureau is the WIPO secretariat, which also services the Paris Convention, the Berne Convention, and other such unions. With regard to WIPO, the International Bureau is controlled by the General Assembly and the WIPO Conference, while in regard to the unions it is governed by the separate assemblies and conferences of representatives of each. The Paris and Berne unions elect executive committees, whose joint membership constitutes the Coordination Committee of WIPO, which meets annually. The General Assembly, the WIPO Conference, and the Coordination Committee meet in September and October once every two years and in an extraordinary session in alternate years.

A September 1998 extraordinary WIPO Conference session approved formation of the Permanent Committee on Cooperation for Development Related to Intellectual Property (PCIPD), which combined the functions and programs of the Permanent Committee for Development Cooperation Related to Industrial Property (PC/IP) and the Permanent Committee for Development Cooperation Related to Copyright and Neighboring Rights (PC/CR), both of which had been established in the 1970s. The former had as its mandate aiding in the transfer of technology from highly industrialized to developing countries; the latter had been responsible for promoting and facilitating the dissemination of literary, scientific, and artistic works protected under the rights of authors and of performing artists, producers, and broadcast organizations. All WIPO states may participate in the PCIPD, which held its first session in May–June 1999, and in the Standing Committee on Information Technologies (SCIT), which was created in 1998 as successor to the Permanent Committee on Industrial Property Information (PCIPI). The SCIT, in part, serves as a forum for, and provides technical advice on, WIPO's overall information strategy. In January 2001 the SCIT established two working groups to aid its mission, one responsible for information technology and the other for standards and documentation.

The Arbitration and Mediation Center was created in 1994 to help resolve intellectual property disputes, and in 1998 the WIPO Worldwide Academy was formed, with many training courses now available through electronic media. The March 1998 assemblies of the member states of WIPO decided to form two new independent advisory boards: the Policy Advisory Commission (PAC), which identifies issues of interest to WIPO and provides policy recommendations, and the Industrial Advisory Commission, mandated to improve WIPO's relationships with its industrial and market sector constituents.

Unlike most UN agencies, which are supported by levies on members, WIPO is mostly self-financed through charges for its services.

Activities. WIPO administers 24 international treaties dealing with the two main categories of intellectual property: copyright (involving written material, film, recording, and other works of art) and industrial property (covering inventions, patents, trademarks, and industrial designs). The most important treaty in the copyright field is the 156-member Berne Convention, most recently amended in 1979. It requires signatories to give copyright protection to works originating in other member states and establishes minimum standards for such protection.

The principal treaty affecting industrial property is the 167-member Paris Convention, under which a member state must give the same protection to nationals of other contracting states as it gives to its own. The convention contains numerous additional regulations, some of which were the subject of contentious revision conferences during the 1980s. Discord most frequently involved attempts by developing countries to shorten protection periods in order to facilitate the transfer of technology and speed up the development of product manufacturing.

In addition to its administrative function, WIPO spearheads the review and revision of treaties already under its jurisdiction, while encouraging the negotiation of new accords where needed. Among the issues under study during the past decade were piracy and counterfeiting of sound and audiovisual recordings; standards for regulating the cable television industry; expansion of copyright protection for dramatic, choreographic, and musical works; and protection in new fields such as biotechnology. WIPO has also promoted expanded activity under the Patent Cooperation Treaty (PCT), established in 1970 to help inventors and industries obtain patent protection in foreign countries by filing single international applications rather than separate applications for each country. As of July 2007, 138 countries had acceded to the treaty. Following four years of increased application levels, the PCT hit a major milestone in January 2005 when its millionth application was filed, prompting a ceremony and celebration at its Geneva headquarters. On June 1, 2000, WIPO adopted the new Patent Law Treaty (PLT) at the conclusion of a three-week diplomatic conference. The PLT simplified and harmonized patent filings by applying many PCT procedures at the national level. As of July 2007, the treaty had been signed by 16 countries.

Faced with myriad new issues arising from the rapid growth in popular use of personal computers, CD-ROM players, advanced video machines, and other systems based on digital technology, representatives of some 160 nations met in Geneva in December 1996 to update WIPO copyright guidelines. After three weeks of often difficult negotiations, the conference adopted two new treaties designed to protect intellectual property while guaranteeing fair access to information on the part of consumers. One accord (the WIPO Copyright Treaty) provides specific new regulations regarding literary and artistic works that can be reproduced in seconds on personal computers. The second agreement (the WIPO Performances and Phonograms Treaty—WPPT) extended copyright protection to recording artists and producers, except in regard to audiovisual products, about which consensus could not be reached and further negotiations were planned. As of July 2005, 51 countries had signed the WPPT. The two treaties went into effect in 2002, despite disagreements in the United States and Europe over whether they stimulated or stifled creativity on the Internet.

In April 1999 WIPO published a report titled *The Management of Internet Names and Addresses* as part of an effort to confront issues related to trademarks and domain names. Particular attention was given to "cybersquatting," the practice of purchasing the rights to Internet addresses that resemble company trademarks or the names of celebrities and then reselling the addresses to the companies or individuals for large profits. The Internet Corporation for Assigned Names and Numbers (ICANN), the international domain name regulator, subsequently adopted many of the report's recommendations, which has led to a significant decrease in instances of cybersquatting. In October 1999 WIPO adopted ICANN's Uniform Domain Name Dispute Resolution Policy (UDRP) and since December 1999 its Arbitration and Mediation Center has been in operation, tasked with arbitrating disputes over registration and use of Internet domain names. More than 70 countries have made officials available to the center to resolve disputes. Resolution is largely conducted online to expedite decisions, which are usually made within two months. (The arbitration process, as well as WIPO's operation in general, has sometimes been described as heavy-handed and tending to favor large financial interests.) In October 2009 WIPO held a conference to celebrate the tenth anniversary of the UDRP, bringing together over 200 "stakeholders" from around the world.

In July 2000 the SCIT passed an implementation plan for WIPOnet, which facilitates the secure online exchange of information by the global intellectual property community. Access to various WIPO programs and activities, including the recently established Intellectual Property Digital Library (IPDL) system, are incorporated into WIPOnet, which permits online filing of applications under the PTC. Establishment of WIPOnet was a key element in a nine-point "digital agenda" drawn up at the First International Conference on Electronic Commerce and Intellectual Property in September 1999.

In 2003 U.S.-led opposition scrapped a WIPO convention for talks on information sharing to promote innovation. Major U.S. lobbying interests, including Microsoft and the Business Software Alliance, reportedly prompted the United States to pull the plug on the convention despite the urging of more than 60 international academics and researchers, who called on WIPO to convene the meeting in 2004. The group contends that the United States' proliferation of patents (accounting for about one-third registered with the PCT) hinder scientific advances and innovations.

In November 2004 WIPO announced some progress during three-day negotiations on a treaty to protect broadcasters' rights for digital technologies. Negotiators failed to reach consensus over whether protection should extend to webcasts, the scope of the treaty, and whether protection rights should be 50 years or fewer. The proposed broadcast treaty, an update to the 1961 Rome Convention on the Protection of Performers, Producers of Phonograms, and Broadcasting Organizations, was the subject of a June 2006 WIPO meeting held in Barcelona, Spain. Criticized for being held on short notice with little publicity, the meeting produced no agreements on matters of copyright protection for the broadcasters of television simulcasts and material on the Internet, including podcasts. The broadcast treaty was addressed again at WIPO's September 2006 General Assembly meeting, but a lack of agreement on how to proceed continued.

The Singapore Treaty on the Law of Trademarks was adopted in March 2006 at a special diplomatic conference. The treaty, an update to the 1994 Trademark Law Treaty, widened the scope of trademark law to include nontraditional marks such as holograms; three-dimensional marks; and nonvisible marks of sound, smell, taste, and feel. The treaty also simplified and standardized administrative rules for trademark applications.

The needs of the developing world have become a growing part of WIPO. In 2004 Argentina and Brazil advocated a proposal to reform WIPO's practices to stimulate innovation in developing countries and reorient the agency towards development goals rather than protecting property rights. The proposal, cosponsored by 12 member states, called for more transparency, participation, and accountability in the organization. However, WIPO negotiations the following year on the creation of a development agenda for the agency stalled and were not resolved until late 2007 at the WIPO General Assembly meeting held in Geneva September 27–October 3. The assembly agreed on a 45-point development agenda to address the needs of the developing world in the agency's technical assistance and capacity-building programs; it also established a framework for treaty-making that takes development issues into account and created the Committee on Development and Intellectual Property to implement the agenda. A less happy development at this meeting was the attempt by the United States and some European countries to remove the director general, Kamil Idris, of Sudan. The countries that objected to Idris blocked approval of the organization's 2008–2008 budget. Idris had been accused of financial and other irregularities, and his management was said to have damaged WIPO's credibility. He eventually agreed to step down a year early, the budget was finally adopted on March 31, 2008, and on September 24, 2008, Dr. Francis Gurry of Australia was elected director general for a six-year term. On October 1, 2008, the United States ratified the Singapore Treaty.

Further meetings during 2008 refined WIPO's new development agenda. Some observers wondered whether the plan would change the organization's focus to favor the interests of small nations as much as had been anticipated. In other matters, the organization received requests from Indonesia and from the European Union to develop intellectual property (IP) standards for the protection of folklore. The issue was discussed at the 13th session of its Intergovernmental Committee on Intellectual Property and Genetic Resources, Traditional Knowledge and Folklore, held in October 2008. Gurry declared that in this, as in all WIPO efforts, he expected to see results. On December 12, 2008, WIPO announced a program of strategic change, to concentrate on nine goals relating to improving respect for IP and for WIPO. The organization committed itself to working from a balanced budget henceforward. The organization also began a comprehensive review of the international patent system.

In July 2009 WIPO announced that it would open an arbitration and mediation center in Singapore early in 2010. In October 2009 Nigeria began working with WIPO to have a similar office opened in Abuja, its capital.

WORLD METEOROLOGICAL ORGANIZATION (WMO)

Established: April 4, 1951, under authority of the World Meteorological Convention signed October 11, 1947, in Washington, D.C. The WMO became a UN Specialized Agency by agreement with the Economic and Social Council (approved by the General Assembly on December 20, 1951).

Purpose: To consider the need for sustainable development; to work towards the reduction of loss of life and property caused by natural disasters and other catastrophic events related to weather, climate, and water; and to safeguard the environment and the global climate for present and future generations of humankind.

Headquarters: Geneva, Switzerland.

Principal Organs: World Meteorological Congress (all members), Executive Council (37 members), Regional Associations (all regional members), Technical Commissions, Secretariat.

Web site: www.wmo.ch/pages/index_en.html

Secretary General: Michel Jarraud (France).

Membership (189)**:** See Appendix C.

Official Languages: Arabic, English, French, Russian, Spanish.

Origin and development. The World Meteorological Organization is the successor to the International Meteorological Organization (IMO), which was established in 1878 in a pioneering attempt to organize cooperation in meteorology. Technically, the IMO was not an intergovernmental organization, its members being the directors of various national meteorological services rather than the states themselves. Upon establishment of the UN, the IMO decided to restructure itself as an intergovernmental body. The World Meteorological Convention, drafted in 1947, entered into force March 23, 1950; formal establishment of the WMO took place April 4, 1951, at its first World Meteorological Congress. A Specialized Agency of the UN under an agreement approved in 1951, the WMO includes in its membership most UN members as well as several territories.

Structure. The World Meteorological Congress, in which all WMO members have one vote, is the organization's main political organ. It meets at least once every four years to elect its officers and the members of the Executive Council, to adopt technical regulations on meteorological practices and procedures, and to determine general policies. Decisions are made by a two-thirds majority except for the election of officers, which requires only a simple majority.

The Executive Council, comprising 37 directors of national meteorological services, meets at least once per year to prepare studies and recommendations for the congress, supervise the implementation of the congress's decisions, assist members on technical matters, and approve the annual financial appropriation within the overall budget set by the congress. The WMO has 350 employees and an annual budget of approximately $75 million.

Six regional associations have been established by the congress, for Africa, Asia, Europe, North America, Central America, and the Caribbean. Composed of those member states whose meteorological networks lie in, or extend into, the given area, each association meets once every four years and is responsible for coordinating regional meteorological activities and for examining, from a regional point of view, questions referred by the Executive Council. The congress has also established eight technical commissions to provide expert advice in aeronautical meteorology, agricultural meteorology, atmospheric sciences, basic systems, climatology, hydrology, instruments and methods of observation, and marine meteorology. All members may be represented on the commissions, which meet every four years.

The WMO Secretariat is headed by a secretary general, who is appointed by the congress and is responsible for conducting technical studies, preparing and publishing the results of the WMO's activities, and generally supervising organization activities.

Activities. The WMO facilitates worldwide cooperation in the establishment of meteorological observation stations; promotes the establishment and maintenance of systems for the rapid exchange of weather information; fosters standardization of meteorological observations and ensures the uniform publication of observations and statistics; furthers the application of meteorology to aviation, shipping, agriculture, and other activities; and encourages research and training in meteorology.

An expanded program of global weather observation and reporting involving the use of earth-orbiting satellites, high-speed telecommunications, and computers was approved in April 1967 by the Fifth World Meteorological Congress. In addition, a suggestion advanced by U.S. president John F. Kennedy in 1961 and subsequently elaborated upon by the UN and the WMO resulted in creation of the World Weather Watch (WWW). Closely coordinated with the World Climate Research Program (WCRP) developed by the International Council of Scientific Unions (ICSU), the WWW keeps the global atmosphere under continuous surveillance with the aid of some 10,000 ground observation stations, 7,000 merchant ships, 750 buoys, climatological stations in all parts of the world, and meteorological satellites operated by several members.

The Eighth World Meteorological Congress, held in Geneva in 1979, adopted a World Climate Program (WCO) that, in cooperation with a number of other UN-related agencies, encompassed projects in data gathering, practical application of climatic information to economic and social activities, and basic research. Other major WMO efforts include the Applications of Meteorology Program (AMP), the Atmospheric Research and Environment Program (AREP), the Education and Training Program (ETRP), the Global Climate Observing System (GCOS), the Hydrology and Water Resources Program (HWRP), and the Technical Cooperation Program (TCOP).

In keeping with growing international concern, the WMO has become involved in assessing global climate change. In late 1988, in conjunction with the UN Environmental Program (UNEP), the WMO organized the Intergovernmental Panel on Climate Change (IPCC) to make recommendations on the problem of global warming to the upcoming Second World Climate Conference. In addition, in 1990 the WMO established the Global Atmosphere Watch (GAW), which comprises several hundred observatories for monitoring atmospheric changes caused by human activity. However, negotiations on measures to reduce global warming proved difficult at the Climate Conference, held in November 1990 in Geneva. In particular, the United States and the Soviet Union were criticized by environmental groups and many developing nations for refusing to set specific targets to curtail emissions of carbon dioxide, considered the major contributor to the greenhouse effect. In its annual climate report, the WMO reported in 2002 that it would be the second-hottest year on record and that the rate of global temperatures appeared to be continually increasing. The 2003 annual report said it would be the third-hottest year in nearly 150 years.

The WMO has also been tracking record extremes in weather patterns linked to global warming. Its 2002 and 2003 annual climate reports stated those years were among the hottest on record. In 2007 the IPCC released the Fourth Assessment on Climate Change, its strongest statement to date on the issue, in a series of installment reports spread throughout the year. Widely publicized, the reports claimed that the physical evidence of global warming was "unequivocal" and that it was 90 percent probable that human activity was responsible. The reports went on to say that global warming was already causing serious environmental damage, particularly in the Southern Hemisphere and at the poles, though it was still possible to rein in global warming if governments acted decisively to bring greenhouse gas emissions under control.

Additionally, the WMO has issued warnings about the links between the rise in global temperatures and desertification. It stated that decreases and variability in precipitation will hit Africa, Asia, and Latin America the worst and threaten world food security. In 2006 it reported in its *Greenhouse Gas Bulletin* that globally averaged concentrations of carbon dioxide had reached their highest levels ever the previous year.

The WMO considers as part of its development goals assisting poor nations in bettering their meteorological and disaster warning systems. In May 1994 a new storm warning system established by Bangladesh with WMO assistance was credited with saving many lives when a cyclone hit that nation's low-lying areas. Following the December 26, 2004, Indian Ocean earthquake and subsequent tsunami that resulted in the deaths of more than 200,000 people in Southeast Asia, organizations including the WMO and the Intergovernmental Oceanographic Commission (IOC) announced in July 2005 that initial work had begun in several countries on an all-hazards early warning system in the Indian Ocean.

In September 1995 the WMO reported that its observations had revealed the biggest hole ever discovered in the earth's ozone layer above Antarctica. WMO officials said the study underscored the need for further reductions in the use of chemicals that deplete the ozone layer, which serves as a barrier to cancer-causing ultraviolet rays from the sun. By 2000, as industrialized countries met targets set by the Montreal Protocol for reducing ozone-depleting emissions, the amount of chlorine compounds in the atmosphere had stabilized. In 2007 the WMO stated that the amount of ozone-depleting gases in the Antarctic stratosphere was declining at a rate of 1 percent per year from record levels in 2000, although enough still exists to cause severe ozone holes for another one to two decades. The WMO estimated the current ozone hole will take 15 years longer than previously expected, until 2065, to close.

In May 2003 the 14th congress adopted the sixth long-term plan (LTP) covering the years 2004 to 2011. Major elements of the plan include enhancing environmental observation capabilities on the WMO's real-time network, improving weather forecasting, ensuring nations' safety against natural hazards, applying scientific advances to WMO studies, and partnering developing with developed nations for capacity building. The congress also adopted a global communication strategy to improve dialogue to and from the organization.

Following his election in January 2004, Secretary General Michel Jarraud of France imposed a series of internal reforms at the WMO following a money laundering scandal that rocked the organization starting in 2003. The investigation occurred around the same time as other scandals and questions of mismanagement erupted at the UN.

The 15th congress passed significant changes to the preamble of the convention under which the WMO operates. The new preamble broadened the agency's mandate from a largely technical and analytical role to name it as a principal actor in saving and protecting lives and property. To that end, the congress endorsed disaster risk reduction as its highest priority and directed the agency to develop a disaster risk reduction action plan to modernize national meteorological systems and early warning systems in developing countries and better their cooperation with agencies providing disaster relief. The congress also decided to hold a third World Climate Conference in 2009, the subject being helping countries come to terms with the impacts of climate change through better observations, research, and guidance. In June 2007 the WMO called on the Group of Eight (G-8) countries (see separate article) to support the program Climate Development for Africa. This program was to improve climate monitoring and risk management and help African countries achieve sustainable development in a time of climate change.

Earlier, in February 2007, the WMO partnered with the International Council for Science (ICSU) to launch a two-year research and publicity program on the polar regions, calling it the largest internationally coordinated science research program in 50 years.

In October 2007 former U.S. vice president Al Gore, known for his work in combating climate change, shared the Nobel Peace Prize with the IPCC. At the UN Climate Summit, held in Bali, Indonesia, in November 2007, the WMO presented evidence that the previous decade had been the warmest since reliable records had been kept.

The 2008 Executive Council session, held in Geneva June 18–27, concentrated on measures to get more and better information to national weather services. It also focused on the standardization and improvement of methods for early warning and risk reduction in the case of weather disasters. The meeting placed high expectations on the World Climate Conference, to be held in Geneva in the fall of 2009. In August 2008 the members of WMO coordinated their efforts to provide weather data for the Beijing summer Olympic games. New Chinese weather satellites were used. In September 2009 the WMO announced a system for cooperation between it and the Secretariats of the Vienna-based Preparatory Commission for the Comprehensive Nuclear-Test-Ban Treaty Organization (CTBTO). This enhanced cooperation was intended to ease the CTBTO's mission of detecting nuclear accidents and clandestine nuclear tests.

The WMO announced in December that 2008 had been the tenth warmest year on record, with Arctic ice levels declining faster than predicted and a record level of greenhouse gases observed. It was also a very bad year for weather-related natural disasters. On December 10, 2008, Secretary General Jarraud announced a new initiative, led by the WMO, to give governments and other institutions short- and long-term information about climate change to help them plan to mitigate its effects. This effort culminated in the World Climate Conference-3, held August 31–December 4, 2009, in Geneva. High-level policy makers from more than 150 countries attended, and the conference established a Global Framework for Climate Services "to strengthen production, availability, delivery and application of science-based climate prediction and services." The Global Framework was also intended to feature in international negotiations about reducing atmospheric pollution.

UNITED NATIONS: RELATED ORGANIZATION

INTERNATIONAL ATOMIC ENERGY AGENCY (IAEA)

Established: By statute signed in New York, United States, October 26, 1956, effective July 29, 1957. A working relationship with the United Nations was approved by the General Assembly on November 14, 1957.

Purpose: To "seek to accelerate and enlarge the contribution of atomic energy to peace, health and prosperity throughout the world" and to ensure that such assistance "is not used in such a way as to further any military purposes."

Headquarters: Vienna, Austria.

Principal Organs: General Conference (all members), Board of Governors (35 members), Secretariat.

Web site: www.iaea.org

Director General: Yukiya Amano (Japan).

Membership (151): See Appendix C.

Official Languages: Arabic, Chinese, English, French, Russian, Spanish. All are also working languages.

Origin and development. In a 1953 address before the UN General Assembly, U.S. president Dwight Eisenhower urged the establishment of an international organization devoted exclusively to the peaceful uses of atomic energy. The General Assembly endorsed the essentials of the U.S. proposal on December 4, 1954, and 70 governments signed the Statute of the IAEA on October 26, 1956. Following ratification by 26 governments, the statute entered into force July 29, 1957.

Although the statute makes no provision for expelling member states, a two-thirds majority may vote for suspension upon recommendation of the Executive Board. This procedure was followed in 1972, when the membership of the Republic of China was suspended and the People's Republic of China took its place. (International safeguards on the Republic of China's subsequent extensive atomic development have been possible only because that government still allows agency controls.)

A decision at the 26th General Conference in September 1982 to reject the Israeli delegation's credentials led to a walkout by the United States and 15 other countries. The conference charged that Israel had violated IAEA principles and undermined the agency's safeguards with its preemptive attack on Iraq's Osirak nuclear facility in June 1981. The United States, which supplies 25 percent of the agency's regular budget, announced that it would suspend its payments and contributions while reassessing its membership. Following Director General Hans Blix's certification of Israel's continued membership in March 1983, Washington paid $8.5 million in back dues and resumed full participation in the agency.

South Africa signed the Treaty on the Non-Proliferation of Nuclear Weapons (NPT) in July 1991, agreeing to open plants for IAEA inspection and forgo the development of nuclear weapons. In March 1993 South African president F. W. de Klerk acknowledged that his country had developed nuclear weapons in the late 1970s but said they had all been dismantled after his inauguration in 1989. Pretoria subsequently invited the IAEA to verify the claim, and in late 1993 the agency's inspectors concluded that South Africa was indeed the first country ever to abandon nuclear weapon capability.

Following conclusion of the 1990–1991 Persian Gulf conflict, the UN Security Council asked the IAEA to investigate Iraq's nuclear weapons capability, which led to an unprecedented determination that Baghdad had violated its safeguards agreement with the IAEA by concealing a weapons-related program. After the removal from Iraq of all declared weapons-grade nuclear materials, the IAEA, in cooperation with the UN Security Council's Special Commission (UNSCOM), attempted to maintain a monitoring and verification program that frequently put it in conflict with the Iraqi government (see Activities, below, and the article on Iraq).

Structure. The General Conference is the highest policymaking body at which all members are entitled to be represented. It meets annually at the organization's headquarters, usually in the latter part of September. Conference responsibilities include final approval of the agency's budget and program, approval of the appointment of the director general, and election of 22 members of the Board of Governors. Decisions on financial questions, amendments to the statute, and suspension from membership require a two-thirds majority; other matters are decided by a simple majority.

The Board of Governors, which normally meets five times a year, is vested with general authority for carrying out the functions of the IAEA. Of its 35 members, 22 are elected by the General Conference with due regard to equitable representation by geographic areas, while 13 are designated by the outgoing Board of Governors as the leaders in nuclear technology and production of atomic source material. Decisions are usually by simple majority, although budget approval and a few other matters require a two-thirds majority.

The IAEA Secretariat is headed by a director general appointed for a four-year term by the Board of Governors with the approval of the General Conference. The director general is responsible for the appointment, organization, and functioning of the staff, under the authority and subject to the control of the board. He also prepares the initial annual budget estimates for submission by the board to the General Conference. The Secretariat includes six departments: Technical Cooperation, Nuclear Energy, Nuclear Safety and Security, Management, Nuclear Sciences and Applications, and Safeguards. The Office of External Relations and Policy Coordination and the Office of Internal Audit also report to the director general.

The IAEA had a 2008 budget of €291 million ($396 million) with a staff of 2,307 stationed in more than 90 countries.

Activities. The IAEA differs from President Eisenhower's original concept in that it has not become a major center for distributing fissionable material. Its activities in promoting the peaceful uses of atomic energy fall into four main areas: (1) nuclear research and development, (2) health and safety standards, (3) technical assistance, and (4) administration of a safeguards program to ensure that atomic materials are not diverted from peaceful to military uses.

Included in IAEA operations are the IAEA Marine Environment Laboratory in Monaco; the International Centre for Theoretical Physics in Trieste, Italy (administered jointly with the UN Educational, Scientific and Cultural Organization); the International Nuclear Information System, which provides a comprehensive bibliographic database on peaceful applications of nuclear science and technology; the IAEA/World Health Organization Network of Secondary Standard Dosimetry Laboratories; and a large multidisciplinary nuclear research laboratory in Seibersdorf, Austria. The IAEA also coordinates the work of physicists from the European Union, Japan, Russia, and the United States on a planned thermonuclear fusion reactor. (France was chosen in 2005 as the site of the new reactor, which is scheduled to begin operation in 2016.) In addition, the IAEA administers a number of multilateral conventions on nuclear matters, including civil liability for nuclear damage and the protection of nuclear material from theft, sabotage, and other hazards, such as those posed during international transport.

In the wake of the world's worst-ever nuclear accident at the Chernobyl Nuclear Power Plant in the USSR in April 1986, nuclear safety drew increased attention. Special IAEA sessions evaluated the immediate implications of the accident and laid the groundwork for full assessment of its long-term radiological consequences. A new convention establishing an early warning system for such accidents went into force in October 1986, while a convention for the provision of assistance in the case of nuclear or radiological emergency went into force in February 1987.

In addition to nuclear power plant safety, IAEA symposia have addressed such topics as the management of spent fuel and radioactive waste, a proposed global radiation monitoring system, issues specific to "aging" nuclear plants, food irradiation, and new uranium mining techniques. The IAEA has also continued its extensive involvement in research and development projects in such areas as nuclear medicine, radiation-induced plant mutation to increase crop yield and resistance to disease, and insect control through large-scale release of radioactively sterilized male insects. In 2009 the IAEA announced that its scientists were working on such a technique with mosquitoes to combat malaria.

IAEA technical assistance to developing countries involves not only offering training programs and fellowships, but also bringing together customers and suppliers of such specialized services as plant maintenance and oversight safety. More than one-half of the funds for such activities come in the form of voluntary contributions, despite complaints from poorer states, who believe that such funding should come from the IAEA's regular budget. In 2008 more than 4,000 experts and lecturers carried out project assignments, and nearly 2,500 individuals participated in IAEA training courses.

The IAEA is probably most closely associated with its role as administrator of the safeguards system for containing the proliferation of nuclear weapons, although critics have often argued that manpower deficiencies, a lack of reliable monitoring equipment, and political influence, particularly in imposing effective sanctions, have undermined its credibility. The Treaty on the Non-Proliferation of Nuclear Weapons (NPT), signed July 1, 1968, and effective March 5, 1970, obligates signatory states (189, the exceptions being India, Israel, and Pakistan) that possess no nuclear weapons to accept safeguards as set forth in agreements concluded with the agency. After the May 1974 surprise nuclear explosion by India, the IAEA initiated a major effort to tighten controls. Specifically, the director general called upon the governments of states possessing nuclear weapons to accept outside inspection when they conducted nuclear tests for peaceful purposes. Subsequently, the United Kingdom (1978), the United States (1980), France (1981), the Soviet Union (1985), and China (1985) concluded agreements with the IAEA regarding application of safeguards and inspection of certain civilian nuclear facilities.

The agency also provides safeguard regimes for the Treaty for the Prohibition of Nuclear Weapons in Latin America and the Caribbean (Tlatelolco Treaty), which dates from 1967; the South Pacific Nuclear-Free Zone Treaty (Rarotonga Treaty), concluded in 1985; the African Nuclear-Weapon-Free Zone Treaty (Pelindaba Treaty), concluded in 1996; and the Treaty on the Southeast Asia Nuclear Weapon-Free Zone (Treaty of Bangkok), which entered into force in 1997.

In May 1995 NPT signatories convened in New York to determine if the treaty was to be extended indefinitely or for a fixed period of time. Although the United States and other nuclear powers strongly supported the indefinite option, a number of developing countries initially announced their preference for a fixed extension in order to gain leverage on several nuclear issues. The indefinite extension was finally approved after contentious discussions. Declared nuclear powers also pledged to complete a ban on nuclear testing by the end of 1996, and stronger IAEA safeguards were endorsed to monitor clandestine production or shipment of nuclear arms.

Consequently, in June 1995 the IAEA Board of Governors adopted new guidelines to permit broader inspections with little or even no advance notice. Two years later, under U.S. pressure for even stricter controls, the Board of Governors at its May 15–16, 1997, meeting adopted a model protocol granting IAEA inspectors greater access to members' nuclear facilities and sites. As of November 2009, 136 countries had signed the resultant Protocols Additional to Safeguards Agreements.

At the 1997 IAEA General Conference, held in late September and early October, Dr. Mohamed ElBaradei's appointment as successor to Director General Blix was approved.

The May 1998 nuclear weapons tests conducted by India and Pakistan drew immediate criticism from the IAEA. The agency also noted that Israel remained on the probable threshold of weapons production. Although Argentina, Brazil, and Iran were believed to have the necessary technology to make weapons, an agency spokesman stated that, like the current regime in South Africa, none had shown any inclination to do so.

The September 1998 General Conference, in addition to calling for North Korea's compliance, focused its attention on Iraq, which had suspended its cooperation the preceding August after having engaged in a series of disputes with weapons inspectors. In November it was announced that the inspectors would be withdrawn in view of pending air strikes by the United States and the United Kingdom. Although the IAEA declared late in 1998 that it had found no evidence of Iraqi nuclear weapons production, it warned that Baghdad's failure to cooperate made drawing any conclusion difficult.

The April–May 2000 Third Review Conference on the NPT confirmed the importance of IAEA safeguards as a "fundamental pillar of the non-proliferation regime." During the 44th annual IAEA General Conference on September 18–22, 2000, a number of Arab states repeated a proposal for a nuclear-weapon-free zone in the Middle East, knowing full well that Israel was not ready to accept such a proposal. Israel indicated that it was firmly committed to the concept "in the proper context and time," but an obvious concern of the Israeli government was the projection that Iran might have nuclear weapons capacity by 2005 and a missile delivery system capable of hitting Israel within a decade.

The General Conference also called on North Korea and Iraq to come into full compliance with their obligations under the NPT and, in the case of Iraq, to permit renewed inspections under Security Council resolutions. Although Iraq permitted the IAEA in January 2000 to resume inspections of its declared nuclear material stocks in Tuwaitha, in accordance with its NPT safeguards agreement, from December 1998 Baghdad had not allowed verification and monitoring inspections ordered by the Security Council.

In December 2002 IAEA director general ElBaradei accused North Korea of "nuclear brinkmanship" after Korean technicians reopened a reactor that had been shut down in 1994. Pyongyang subsequently demanded a "nonaggression" agreement from the United States and several of North Korea's neighbors in exchange for closing the reactor. In early 2003 the IAEA board condemned North Korea for expelling the IAEA's weapons inspectors and dismantling IAEA monitoring cameras. (North Korea withdrew from the NPT in April 2003.) Regarding its other major focus of attention, the IAEA in early 2003 reported that it did not believe that Iraq had resumed its nuclear weapons program, as suspected by the United States.

Pressure mounted in 2003 for the IAEA to take a greater supervisory role regarding Iran's alleged "non-disclosed" nuclear program. ElBaradei urged Iran to "demonstrate full transparency," and in October Iran agreed to expanded inspections, although angrily insisting that all its nuclear activities were for civilian purposes only. In November 2004 the IAEA board noted Iran had made "good progress" on the issue, although Washington continued to insist on a harder line regarding inspections.

In November 2003 the IAEA called upon the UN to develop a system of multinational control over the production of nuclear material that could be used to make weapons. ElBaradei also subsequently proposed that significant additional resources be allocated to guard uranium stockpiles. (The agency estimated that more than 40 countries had the necessary knowledge to produce nuclear weapons.)

Early in 2005 the U.S. George W. Bush administration signaled its opposition to a third term for ElBaradei. However, the director general otherwise received strong international support and was reelected at the September General Conference. This conference, held September 26–30 in Vienna, focused on the dangers of nuclear proliferation, essentially acknowledging that it would be impossible to prevent states from developing nuclear weapons if they really wanted to do so. Attendees noted a revived interest in nuclear power for electricity generation—a development that was not foreseen even a year or so previously—spurred by the run-up in oil prices and increased concern about global warning. The conference also welcomed development of a new generation of inherently safer nuclear power plants. In November 2005 the IAEA and ElBaradei jointly won the Nobel Peace Prize.

Since that time world attention has been focused on the nuclear ambitions of North Korea and Iran. In 2006 and 2007 the IAEA inspected nuclear sites in both countries, served as a primary source of information to international bodies on the evidence behind their nuclear ambitions, and engaged in high-level talks concerning the suspension of nuclear programs. Significant developments over that time period included North Korea's first nuclear test in October 2006, reportedly an underground nuclear explosion, and Iran's further attempts at uranium enrichment. However, UN Security Council sanctions against both countries and the high-level talks resulted in some acquiescence on the part of North Korea and Iran to IAEA inspections. In the summer of 2007, IAEA inspectors gained access to North Korea's nuclear facilities at Yongbyon for the first time since 2002 and entered a heavy water research reactor in Arak, Iran, which the agency had previously been banned from viewing. By late 2007, North Korea had reportedly shut down its nuclear reactor in exchange for shipments of heavy fuel oil and access to an overseas bank account that had been frozen. However, the situation with Iran steadily deteriorated into late 2007 with the IAEA unable to negotiate full access to information on Iran's nuclear program. The IAEA announced in May that Iran could develop a nuclear weapon in three to eight years, and by October the United States imposed the toughest sanctions against Iran in 30 years.

Against the backdrop of growing concern over Iran, the IAEA's 51st General Conference on September 17–21, 2007, saw a confrontation between Arab and Western states over a resolution to create a nuclear-free zone in the Middle East, aimed at Israel. The nonbinding resolution, in the past typically introduced by Arab states but later withdrawn under U.S. pressure, passed this time in a vote of 53 to 2 (the United States and Israel voting against) with 43 abstentions (many of them European states). The move was seen as a sign of growing international tension over the Middle East and an effort by Arab nations to deflect pressure from Iran by pointing the finger at Israel, which has not signed the NPT and is widely believed to have nuclear weapons.

In other measures, the IAEA launched the International Decommissioning Network (IDN), an initiative aimed at sharing information and resources for use in shutting down the more than 350 nuclear installations that are approaching the end of their operational lifespans.

Also in 2007, Director General ElBaradei highlighted the agency's finances as cause for concern, noting at a July Board of Governors meeting and later at the General Conference that the 2008–2009 budget of €291 million ($396 million) put the agency in a state of "financial vulnerability." He also said the IAEA lacked essential equipment to verify covert nuclear activities and would not be able to respond to another disaster on the scale of the 1986 Chernobyl accident.

In mid-2007, ElBaradei drew the ire of the United States, France, and the United Kingdom for engaging in so-called freelance diplomacy after he agreed on a "work plan" with Iran under which key questions about its nuclear program would be answered. The states' position was to demand immediate compliance from Iran on the suspension of uranium enrichment or face tougher sanctions. A November report on Iran's compliance was less unfavorable to Iran than had been anticipated. It concluded that, although Iran was not completely forthcoming about its nuclear program and continued to enrich uranium in defiance of the UN, there was no positive evidence that the country was working on a nuclear weapon. Western states' rejoinder to this was that it was cheaper to buy, rather than make, commercial-grade uranium, and the only reason for Iran to enrich its own was to build a bomb. The picture was further clouded by a U.S. intelligence estimate, released in December 2007, stating that Iran had halted its nuclear weapons program in 2003. ElBaradei said that Iran was "somewhat vindicated."

In a February 22, 2008, report to the UN Security Council, ElBaradei said that although Iran had recently been more open about its activities, it was not possible to say with complete confidence that it was not working on a bomb. The IAEA had confronted Iran with documents from the United States suggesting that it was working on matters peripheral to nuclear bomb-making (such as developing long-range missiles), but Iran dismissed these as forgeries or irrelevant. The United States and France said the report bolstered the case for further sanctions against Iran. On March 4, 2008, the Security Council approved a relatively mild new round of sanctions against Iran, the strongest that Russia and China would support. At the end of April Iran promised to clarify matters within a month, but at the end of May the IAEA reported that Iran was still withholding material information. Iran branded the IAEA report "deceitful" and the result of Western pressure. In late June an Iranian spokesman declared "the matter is over." At the same time Elbaradei warned that any preemptive strikes on Iran could turn the whole Middle East into a "ball of fire." A September 15, 2008, report by the IAEA said that it had made no more progress in discovering Iran's nuclear intentions, as that country was being uncooperative. At the beginning of October, sources within the Iranian government began issuing conflicting statements, some saying that Iran would continue its cooperation with the IAEA, and others stating it would limit or end its cooperation.

A February 2009 IAEA report stated that Iran had built up a stockpile of fissile material. On June 17, 2009, ElBaradei said he felt that Iran was interested in having a bomb, mainly to increase its importance on the international stage. In August 2009 Iran's position appeared to soften, with IAEA inspectors given access to two nuclear facilities after several months of requests. By early September the IAEA itself seemed uncertain about Iran's intentions, but on September 25 Iran informed the IAEA that it had built a second nuclear enrichment plant, previously secret, and promised to open it to IAEA inspection. In early October 2009 Iran began a new round of negotiations and seemed more willing to be cooperative. On October 21, 2009, a draft agreement was announced whereby Iran would send nuclear material abroad for enrichment. Iran seemed to react positively, but on November 2 it asked the IAEA to establish a committee to review its details. Proof of Iran's ultimate intentions remained elusive.

The IAEA also tried to determine Syria's nuclear position. In September 2007 Israel had attacked Al-Kibar, a Syrian site which it claimed was being used to develop nuclear weapons. In April 2008 the United States released material which, it claimed, showed that Syria was indeed engaging in nuclear development at the site and that it had received help from North Korea. The IAEA asked to investigate, and Syria agreed to let it inspect Al-Kibar, but no other sites. On September 22 the IAEA said it had found no radioactivity at Al-Kibar, but it was still waiting for permission to investigate other sites. Matters were delayed further by the September 25, 2008, assassination of the IAEA's chief liaison in the Syrian government. In November 2008 and again in February 2009 the IAEA announced that it had found radioactive traces at Al-Kibar. The Syrian government said the radioactive material could have come from IAEA inspectors' clothing, or from the 2007 Israeli attack—something that the IAEA said was very unlikely.

On July 18, 2008, the IAEA confirmed that North Korea had shut down its nuclear reactor at Yongbyon, along with certain other facilities, thus beginning to fulfill its part of an international agreement. But through the late summer and early fall, North Korea complained that the United States was not keeping its end of the agreement. On September 24 North Korea said it was removing the seals from the Yongbyon plant, and that the IAEA would have no further access there. In April

2009 North Korea tested a long-range missile. Following general international condemnation of this test, North Korea announced that it was withdrawing from all nuclear negotiations and ordered all IAEA personnel out of the country.

From late 2007 through most of 2008, India was trying to gain IAEA approval for a deal with the United States allowing India to receive commercial nuclear technology. India already has nuclear weapons, and has not signed the NPT. France in particular was pressing for nuclear commerce with India, while Pakistan and the Indian political left were opposed. On July 10, 2008, the Indian government gave the IAEA its detailed plans for safeguarding nuclear technology. On July 22 the Indian government survived a no-confidence vote on the issue, and on August 1 the IAEA board approved the deal.

In other matters, the IAEA had difficulty electing a successor to ElBaradei, whose term in office was to end in November 2009. A March 2009 meeting of the board failed to elect either Yukiya Amano, a Japanese diplomat generally considered favorable to U.S. positions, and Abdul Samad Minty of South Africa, an arms control specialist who was felt to be more sympathetic to the interests of poorer countries. The matter was deferred to a board meeting on July 2, 2009, where Amano was elected.

WEST AFRICAN ECONOMIC AND MONETARY UNION (UEMOA)

Union Economique et Monétaire Ouest-Africaine

Established: By treaty signed in Dakar, Senegal, on January 10, 1994, by the seven West African countries in the CFA franc monetary zone, with effect from August 1.

Purpose: To coordinate the economic policies of the member states, particularly with regard to human resources, territorial management, agriculture, energy, industry, mines, transportation, infrastructure, and telecommunications; to promote regional monetary and economic integration, coordinated trade policies, and a common external tariff; to create a common market based on the free circulation of people, goods, services, and capital.

Headquarters: Ouagadougou, Burkina Faso.

Principal Organs: Conference of Heads of State and Government, Council of Ministers, Commission, Court of Justice, Court of Accounts, Interparliamentary Committee.

Web site: www.uemoa.int (In French only.)

President of the Commission: Soumaäla Cissé (Mali).

Membership (8): Benin, Burkina Faso, Côte d'Ivoire, Guinea-Bissau, Mali, Niger, Senegal, and Togo.

Official Language: French.

Origin and development. The UEMOA was established in 1994 as successor to the West African Economic Community (*Communauté Economique de l'Afrique de l'Ouest*—CEAO). The CEAO, which traced its origins to an earlier West African Customs and Economic Union (*Union Douanière et Economique de l'Afrique de l'Ouest*—UDEAO), had been established under a treaty adopted June 3, 1972, in Bamako, Mali, and related protocols signed April 16–17, 1973, in Abidjan, Côte d'Ivoire. CEAO signatory states included Benin (then Dahomey), Burkina Faso (then Upper Volta), Côte d'Ivoire, Mali, Mauritania, Niger, and Senegal; the organization came into formal existence on January 1, 1974, although it did not become fully operational until later that year. In addition to advancing cooperation in such sectors as agriculture, animal husbandry, fishing, industry, transport, communications, and tourism, the CEAO was envisaged as a step toward establishing a regional common market.

Constrained by such factors as income disparities among its members, rising trade barriers enacted by national legislatures, and huge payment arrears, by 1993 the union was described as "virtually moribund." It had also been damaged in the 1980s by a financial scandal involving misappropriations from its Solidarity and Intervention Fund (Fosidec), which had been created in 1977 to aid development in poorer member states.

By the early 1990s the larger Economic Community of West African States (ECOWAS), to which all the CEAO members also belonged, was pushing for establishment of a single West African economic community that would absorb other subregional groupings. Chafing at ECOWAS's presumption of regional preeminence, the francophone CEAO instead moved toward creation of an economic and monetary authority that would function more effectively than its current incarnation. Accordingly, at a CEAO summit in January 1994, the participating states signed the treaty establishing the West African Economic and Monetary Union (UEMOA), which superseded the CEAO on August 1, following completion of the requisite ratifications. Guinea-Bissau became the eighth UEMOA member on May 2, 1997.

Structure. The UEMOA's principal policy-making organ is the Conference of Heads of State and Government, which meets annually. Supporting organs include the Council of Ministers; the Court of Justice; the administrative Commission, which is headed by a president elected for a four-year term; and the Interparliamentary Committee. Also included within the UEMOA structure is the preexisting West African Monetary Union (*Union Monétaire Ouest-Africaine*—UMOA), which was established by a treaty in November 1973 to oversee financial institutions in the West African CFA franc zone. Affiliated with the UEMOA as specialized autonomous institutions are the Central Bank of West African States (*Banque Centrale des Etats de l'Afrique de l'Ouest*—BCEAO) and the West African Development Bank (*Banque Ouest-Africaine de Développement*—BOAD; see separate entry under Regional Development Banks).

Activities. At its first meeting, held May 1996 in Ouagadougou, Burkina Faso, the Conference of Heads of State and Government called for establishment of a customs union, initially with a target date of January 1998. Although that target was not achieved, the UEMOA moved progressively toward the twin goals of reducing internal tariffs and establishing a common external tariff. In July 1996 the union initiated a transitional preferential tariff scheme that eliminated internal levies on locally produced agricultural goods and crafts while reducing by 30 percent import duties on industrial products originating within the union. The second UEMOA summit, held June 1997 in Lomé, Togo, was quickly followed by a further cut of 30 percent on industrial levies. The summit also agreed to reorganize the Abidjan stock exchange as a regional exchange, the *Bourse Régionale des Valeurs Mobilières* (BRVM).

Meeting in Lomé, the Conference of Heads of State and Government convened twice in 1999, in January and December. In January a principal focus was regional indebtedness and external debt servicing. In December the attendees adopted a common industrial policy and the Convergence, Stability, Growth, and Solidarity Pact. Shortly thereafter, on January 1, 2000, the member states, with the exception of politically troubled Guinea-Bissau, eliminated tariffs on all internally produced goods and instituted a common external tariff (CET) capped at 22 percent. In the following two years it also adopted a code governing transparency of public financing and common policies with regard to energy and agriculture. At the same time, it moved toward accommodation with ECOWAS in anticipation of the formation of a second regional monetary union by English-speaking, non-UEMOA ECOWAS members.

A growing convergence of views between the UEMOA and ECOWAS has also been evident in other arenas. (As with the predecessor CAEO, all UEMOA members are also members of ECOWAS.) For example, following conclusion in June 2000 of the Cotonou Agreement between the European Union (EU) and the associated African, Caribbean, and Pacific (ACP) countries, the members' trade and finance ministers collaborated on preparations for negotiating an Economic Partnership Agreement with the EU. A similar strategy was adopted toward World Trade Organization discussions. Concurrently, the UEMOA reached agreement with the United States on improving trade and investment relations and pursued similar arrangements with several Northern African countries. In addition, the UEMOA actively sought to improve world market conditions for a leading regional commodity, cotton, and took steps to prevent use of the CFA franc, with its direct link to the euro, in money laundering and the financing of terrorism.

At the January 29, 2003, Conference of Heads of State and Government in Dakar, Senegal, discussions were dominated by the political crisis that had erupted in Côte d'Ivoire in 2002. The conference called for accelerating structural and institutional reforms as well as measures that would permit freedom of movement, liberalize trade in services as well as goods, and establish community-wide rights of residence and entrepreneurship. In other business, the conference decided to move forward with creation of the Union Parliament.

In the following year, Ivorian instability continued to have a significant impact on the other UEMOA states, not only because Côte d'Ivoire's economy had previously accounted for 40–50 percent of the union's collective GDP, but also because the hostilities had deprived land-locked Burkino Faso, Mali, and Niger of access to their principal seaport, Abidjan.

At its January 10, 2004, session in Niamey, the conference reaffirmed regional integration as the cornerstone of development and reiterated its commitment to creation of a customs union and common market. To accelerate growth and promote sustainable development, the attendees adopted a Regional Economic Program with an emphasis on modernizing infrastructure and reducing cost factors in production.

In its annual report for 2005, UEMOA noted an improved rate of economic growth among its members: 3.6 percent in 2005 as against 3.2 percent in 2004. The report gave credit chiefly to improved agricultural practices. Growth was uneven, however, ranging from 7.5 percent for Burkina Faso to 1 percent for Côte d'Ivoire and Togo.

In November 2006 China signed an agreement to provide 70 million euros ($90.7 million) in credits to regional banks in the UEMOA group. This agreement was hailed as marking a new phase of cooperation between China and the UEMOA. Otherwise, the region's economic prospects for 2007 were considered poor, with cotton exports declining and the still-disturbed state of Côte d'Ivoire depressing the entire region.

In May 2007 a meeting of ECOWAS financial experts began work on creating a common currency for all ECOWAS countries, and thus all UEMOA countries, an act that could signal a move away from the CFA franc. A generally bleak outlook was relieved by the arrival of peace in Côte d'Ivoire in July, and the UEMOA's interparliamentary committee was able to meet there in August. Côte d'Ivoire, the only member state not to have ratified the treaty that would create the UEMOA Parliament, was urged to do so. The problem of migration was also addressed at this and other meetings during the year.

In October 2007 the UEMOA signed a cooperative agreement in the biofuels sector with Brazil, a world leader in that area. The agreement involved an exchange of experts.

At the January 19, 2008, summit, held in Ouagadougou, the group agreed to set up an ad hoc working group to find solutions to the area's continuing problems with the energy supply and to suggest additional ways of boosting the region's economy. In May UEMOA president Soumaila Cissé met with EU representatives in Brussels to discuss a greater degree of cooperation and assistance between the two organizations, and with ECOWAS, particularly in the area of food security. In June 2008 plans were announced to create an electronic link between about 80 banks in UEMOA countries, for credit card and ATM transactions.

By October 2008 economic matters consumed the group. The July 2009 deadline for conclusion of an Economic Partnership Agreement (EPA) with the EU was approaching, and UEMOA was holding to a much lower CET than the rest of ECOWAS. In October also the governor of the Central Bank of West African States (BCEAO) stated that UEMOA was somewhat protected from the global financial crisis, thanks its sound banking practices and lack of exposure to risky loans. At the December 22, 2008, 35th summit of ECOWAS, the leaders of ECOWAS and UEMOA announced a joint plan to ward off the crisis, chiefly through new infrastructure projects and the development of renewable energy. The 12th UEMOA summit, held in Oagadougou, Burkina Faso, on January 17, 2009, ran along similar lines. In March 2009 UEMOA announced that measures to deal with food shortages had cost the community the equivalent of €475 million. But an April 17, 2009, meeting of UEMOA finance ministers, considering the outcome of the G20 meeting earlier that month, stressed the benefits of the CFA franc being pegged to the euro, which was felt to be in sounder condition than the U.S. dollar.

WESTERN EUROPEAN UNION (WEU)

Established: By protocols signed in Paris, France, October 23, 1954, effective May 6, 1955.

Purpose: Collective self-defense and political collaboration in support of European unity.

Headquarters: Brussels, Belgium.

Principal Organs: Council of Ministers, Permanent Council, Inter-Parliamentary European Security and Defense Assembly, Secretariat.

Web site: www.weu.int

Secretary General: Javier Solana Madariaga (Spain).

Membership (10): Belgium, France, Germany, Greece, Italy, Luxembourg, Netherlands, Portugal, Spain, United Kingdom.

Associate Members (6): Czech Republic, Hungary, Iceland, Norway, Poland, and Turkey.

Associate Partners (8): Bulgaria, Croatia, Estonia, Latvia, Lithuania, Romania, Slovakia, and Slovenia.

Observers (5): Austria, Denmark, Finland, Ireland, and Sweden.

Official Languages: English, French.

Origin and development. The Western European Union (WEU) is the direct successor of the five-power Brussels Treaty Organization, which was established by the United Kingdom, France, and the Benelux states through the Treaty of Economic, Social, and Cultural Collaboration and Collective Self-Defense, signed March 17, 1948, in Brussels, Belgium. The Brussels pact had included provisions for automatic mutual defense assistance and envisioned coordination of military activity. However, de facto responsibilities in those areas were transferred to the 12-power North Atlantic Treaty Organization (NATO) following its creation in 1949. Shortly thereafter, the call for West German rearmament to permit participation in NATO by the Federal Republic of Germany (FRG) led to a revival of interest in a European army. In 1952 the six countries that had recently established the European Coal and Steel Community (ECSC; see the European Union (EU) article)—France, West Germany, Italy, and the Benelux countries—signed a treaty to institute a European Defense Community (EDC) that would have placed their military forces under a single authority. Following rejection of the EDC by the French parliament in 1954, the United Kingdom invited the ECSC countries to revive the 1948 treaty, which was modified and expanded to provide a framework for the rearming of West Germany and its admission to NATO. Under a series of protocols effective May 6, 1955, the Brussels organization was enlarged to include Italy and West Germany and was renamed the WEU.

The protocols redefined the purposes of the organization by including a reference to the unity and progressive integration of Europe. They also remodeled its institutional structure; established norms for member states' contributions to NATO military forces; provided for limitation of the strength and armaments of forces maintained under national command; took note of the United Kingdom's pledge to maintain forces on the mainland of Europe; acknowledged West Germany's intention to refrain from manufacturing atomic, chemical, biological, and certain other types of weapons; and established the Agency for the Control of Armaments to police restrictions on the armaments of all WEU members. The binding defense alliance between WEU members remained in force, but the exercise of military responsibilities remained subordinate to NATO.

The concern over duplication of efforts caused the WEU to transfer many of its social and cultural activities in 1960 to the Council of Europe. However, the union remained active in economic affairs, serving as a link between the European Community (EC) and the United Kingdom after French president Charles de Gaulle's first veto of British entry into the EC in 1963. Activity in that area effectively ceased in the wake of UK admission to the EC in 1973; likewise WEU activity in the political field diminished in proportion to the growth of political consultation within the EC.

In 1984, after a lengthy period of relative inactivity, members called for a "reactivation" and restructuring of the WEU to foster the harmonization of views on defense, security, and other military issues precluded from EC debate. At its Council of Ministers meeting held October 26–27 in Rome, Italy, the WEU issued a statement that detailed the tasks of the revived union to be assessment of the Soviet threat, increased European arms collaboration, and the formulating of European views on arms control and East-West dialogue. The perceived advantages of a revived WEU were the assurance of military aid in case of attack, security cooperation between France and West Germany, and an enhanced capacity to respond to public opinion on European defense issues.

In early 1987 the United Kingdom, which had long relied primarily on security links with the United States, called for strengthening the WEU. In August Britain and France persuaded Belgium, Italy, and the Netherlands to join them in sending naval forces to the Persian Gulf to assist in the U.S.-led escort of oil tankers. Adding to the WEU's heightened visibility, a Council of Ministers meeting held October 1987 in The Hague, Netherlands, approved a strongly worded Platform on European Security Interests that stressed the need for the retention of some nuclear forces and an increase in conventional forces in Western Europe to maintain deterrence vis-à-vis the forces of the Soviet-led Warsaw Treaty Organization (WTO). During 1988, European concern over a possible reduction in the U.S. military commitment on the continent contributed to increased interest in the expansion of WEU membership, with Portugal and Spain signing accession protocols in November.

The post-1989 collapse of European communism and the disintegration of the Soviet Union supplied additional impetus to the WEU regeneration process. Following a November 1991 NATO meeting in Rome that endorsed "specific arrangements for the defense of Europe," the EC's Maastricht summit in December 1991 adopted a Declaration on the Role of the WEU and Its Relations with the European Union (EU) and with the Atlantic Alliance, envisaging that the WEU would be responsible for EU defense coordination. Consequently, in the Petersberg (Germany) Declaration of June 1992, the WEU Council of Ministers endorsed the eventual establishment of a permanent WEU military force that could be deployed for peacekeeping, humanitarian and rescue missions, and crisis management—collectively, known as the "Petersberg tasks."

Following Maastricht, the WEU transferred its headquarters from London to Brussels (the seat of the EU) and invited the EC and NATO states that were not already WEU members to become participants. As a result, Greece signed a WEU membership agreement on November 20, 1992; however, that nation's accession was not formally completed until March 5, 1995, following ratification by the individual WEU states. Also in November 1992, EC members Denmark and Ireland became observers, while Iceland, Norway, and Turkey (non-EC NATO members) became WEU associates. New EU members Austria and Sweden were granted observer status on January 1, 1995, followed by Finland on February 3.

In May 1994 the new status of "associate partner" was established for Eastern European states, and they were authorized to participate in WEU deliberations as well as future peacekeeping and humanitarian missions. However, the partners were given no vote in any union decisions, nor were they covered by the security guarantee of the 1948 Brussels Treaty. In December 2004 Croatia became the eighth associate partner.

The November 1994 WEU ministerial session adopted "preliminary conclusions" on the formulation of a common European defense policy. Additional progress was reported at the May 1995 meeting of the Council of Ministers, which established a politico-military support group to advise on future crises and help formulate possible WEU interventions. The council also approved the creation of a WEU Satellite Center in Torrejón, Spain, to develop satellite imaging capabilities that could be required in upcoming military operations.

With France spearheading the push for better delineation of an independent European military capability, NATO foreign ministers in June 1996 endorsed a compromise proposal to create the European Security and Defense Identity (ESDI) within the alliance, which, in certain circumstances, could operate under WEU command. The plan centered on the establishment of combined joint task forces (CJTFs) for specific peacekeeping and/or humanitarian missions in Europe. It was anticipated that non-NATO countries, such as those involved in NATO's Partnership for Peace (PfP) program, would be invited to participate in the new task forces; the deployment of any NATO forces for such missions would still require unanimous support of the alliance's members.

Although the United States, the United Kingdom, and non-EU member Turkey, in particular, continued to favor leaving military decisions to NATO, the ESDI and subsequent EU decisions were clearly leading toward absorption of the WEU by the EU. In May 1999 the 10 full WEU members agreed to a merger in principle with the EU, and the Cologne, Germany, EU summit in June ratified the decision and set the end of 2000 as a target for assumption of what had been the WEU's military role. On November 13, 2000, at a meeting in Marseilles, France, the 28 WEU countries formally decided that the organization's operational capacity for defense and for carrying out the Petersberg tasks would be transferred to the EU, which would also take over the WEU Institute for Security Studies at Paris and the Torrejón satellite facility. At least for the time being, the WEU would maintain a formal existence and some WEU bodies would continue to meet, including the assembly, which had restyled itself as the Inter-Parliamentary European Security and Defense Assembly in June.

Structure. The WEU's decision-making body, the Council, traditionally operated through two distinct groupings—the Council of Ministers and the Permanent Council. The Council of Ministers, composed of foreign and defense ministers of WEU countries, normally met twice a year. The Permanent Council was mandated "to discuss in greater detail the views expressed by the Ministers and to follow up their decisions." Comprising ambassadors or other senior officials of member countries, the Permanent Council usually met weekly, its composition alternating between 28 members (all full and associate members, associate partners, and observers) and 21 (all full and associate members and observers).

Although the ministerial-level council continues to exist, it has not met since November 2000; the Permanent Council met most recently in May 2002. Of the WEU's various committees and standing groups, only the Budget and Organization Committee remains active. The EU has assumed the functions of other WEU organs, including the Military Committee, which had been established in 1998 as the WEU's senior military authority.

The WEU's other main organ is the Inter-Parliamentary European Security and Defense Assembly, which is still frequently referenced as the WEU Assembly, as it was originally called. It encompasses the 115 representatives of the WEU member countries to the Parliamentary Assembly of the Council of Europe. There are also 115 substitutes appointed to the WEU Assembly from members' national parliaments in general proportion to the strength of government and opposition parties. Representatives and substitutes may form political groups within the assembly.

The assembly's regularly scheduled annual meeting, held in Paris, is divided into two sessions, the first in June and the second in December. The assembly, which draws up its own agenda, has functioned as an independent consultative body, making recommendations to the WEU Council of Ministers and to other intergovernmental organizations, sending resolutions to governments and national parliaments, and rendering its opinion on the annual reports of the council. Its subordinate organs have included a Committee on Defense Questions and Armaments, the reports of which have been considered among the most authoritative and incisive published analyses of Western European security needs and developments.

The Western European Armaments Group (WEAG), a subsidiary body of the WEU, originated in NATO's Independent European Program Group (IEPG), which had been formed in 1976 as a forum for improving cooperation in armaments. In December 1992 the IEPG members decided to transfer its functions to the WEU, and in 1993 the group became the WEAG, which had as its principal mission harmonizing and integrating development, production, and procurement of armaments among its members. Meeting in Brussels in November 2004, the defense ministers of the 19 WEAG members (all full WEU states, all associate members except Iceland, and all observers except Ireland) directed their national armaments directors (NADs) to bring the WEAG to a close, given that its functions were to be assumed by the EU's new European Defense Agency (EDA). Thus the WEAG came to an end on May 23, 2005. The related Western European Armaments Organization (WEAO), established in November 1996 as a transitional step toward formation of a long-discussed European Armaments Agency, continues to function in the form of the WEAO Research Cell (WRC), which offers services in defense-related research and technology to members. Provision for establishment of an armaments agency was made in the proposed European Constitution, but in the meantime the WEU continues to provide administrative support for the WRC.

Activities. Throughout most of its history, the WEU served as a forum for European security issues, conducting research, issuing reports, and providing advice. Although the WEU helped coordinate the military participation of member states during the 1990–1991 Persian Gulf crisis, the organization did not assume an overt operational role until after the 1992 Maastricht Treaty identified the WEU as the proposed EU's security arm. Collaterally, the WEU Council of Ministers outlined the Petersberg tasks of peacekeeping, humanitarian aid and rescue missions, and military crisis management.

Meanwhile, France and Germany had in October 1990 initiated a joint European Corps (Eurocorps), consisting initially of a combined brigade of some 4,000 French and German troops. The two governments agreed in May 1992 that the Strasbourg-based force would eventually be enlarged to at least 35,000, while a Franco-German memorandum of November 1992 described Eurocorps as "forces answerable to the WEU." Seen by its proponents as "the embryo of a European" army in the context of the Maastricht decisions, the Eurocorps concept aroused disquiet in other governments, notably those of the UK and United States, who feared it could undermine NATO cohesiveness in Europe. However, these problems appeared to be resolved by a January 1993 agreement under which Eurocorps would come under NATO command in an emergency. In October 1993 Belgium agreed to join Eurocorps, which was formally inaugurated on November 5 under the command of a German general. Spain announced its intended participation the same month and Luxembourg followed suit in May 1994. Eurocorps was officially declared operational on November 30, 1995, by which time France, Italy, Portugal, and Spain had organized two additional forces, one of ground troops (Eurofor) and the other with maritime capabilities (Euromarfor). These and other multinational contingents were all considered Forces Answerable to WEU (FAWEU).

In July 1992 warships and aircraft of WEU member states, in coordination with NATO, began an operation in the Adriatic code named Sharp Guard to monitor compliance with UN sanctions against rump Yugoslavia (i.e., Serbia and Montenegro). In June 1993 a joint session of the WEU and NATO councils agreed upon a single command and control system for the operation, which continued until June 1996. Beginning in May 1997, the WEU offered Albania assistance through a Multinational Advisory Police Element (MAPE), with a mandate to help in reorganizing and training the Albanian police. In April 1999 the WEU agreed to aid Croatia through a WEU De-mining Assistance Mission (WEUDAM), in support of the Croatia Mine Action Center. Its most significant operational assignment began in April 2000, when Eurocorps assumed command of the peacekeeping Multinational Force in Kosovo (Kosovo Force, or KFOR).

In October 1999 Javier Solana Madariaga, the departing NATO secretary general, became secretary general of the Council of the European Union and its first high representative for foreign and security policy. A month later he was also named WEU secretary general in anticipation of the EU's assumption of the WEU's mandate. Thus the November 2000 decision to transfer WEU operational capability to the EU was anticlimactic, leaving as the principal unresolved question the ultimate status of the WEU's assembly and other remaining WEU organs.

An additional issue was the status of the WEU's associate members. In May 1999 the three new NATO members (the Czech Republic, Hungary, and Poland) officially rose from WEU associate partners to associate members. At that time, however, none of the six associate members belonged to the EU, thereby complicating the EU/WEU/NATO relationship. (Turkey was particularly vocal in its objections to the use of its NATO contingents by the EU unless Ankara was given a voice in ESDI decisions.) In June 2001 Secretary General Solana announced that, in view of the WEU's diminished role, no further changes would be made in the status of associate members.

Since the most recent meeting of the WEU's Permanent Council in May 2002, the WEU has performed only "residual functions," chiefly administrative matters, although the Inter-Parliamentary European Security and Defense Assembly continues to meet semi-annually. The 51st meeting was held June 2005 in Paris, at which time the assembly adopted a recommendation on defending against terrorism that called for "a more proactive, not merely reactive, defense strategy, without this signifying a justification for preventive military action." At the 52nd meeting in December 2005 and the 53rd meeting in June 2006, there were calls for greater public awareness and understanding of the EU's European Security and Defense Policy (ESDP).

Although a March 2007 BBC feature article described the WEU as "now defunct," an increase of tension between Western Europe and Russia may have somewhat revived it. In the 54th meeting, held June 2007 in Paris, the WEU Assembly called for the development of a European "anti-missile concept." The WEU said the new program should be "driven by European interests" and that it should be "interoperable with the United States Ballistic Missile Defense System (BMDS) and amenable to Russian proposals for cooperation" within the framework of the WEU and NATO. As of 2009 the Assembly continues to meet. It regularly sends delegations to the conferences of other international organizations in which it has an interest. Its delegations are also active in visiting former Soviet territories in Western Asia.

WORLD CUSTOMS ORGANIZATION (WCO)/CUSTOMS CO-OPERATION COUNCIL (CCC)

Conseil de Coopération Douanière/
Organisation Mondiale des Douanes

Established: By convention signed by the 13 governments comprising the Committee for European Economic Cooperation on December 15, 1950.

Purpose: To study questions relating to cooperation in customs matters among members; to examine political and economic aspects of customs systems with the hope of achieving harmony and uniformity; to promote international cooperation in customs matters.

Headquarters: Brussels, Belgium.

Principal Organs: Council, Subordinate Committees (Technical Committee on Customs Valuation, Technical Committee on Rules of Origin, Enforcement Committee, Finance Committee, Harmonized System Committee, Permanent Technical Committee), Policy Commission (24 members), Secretariat.

Web site: www.wcoomd.org

Secretary General: Kunio Mikuriya (Japan).

Membership (174): Afghanistan, Albania, Algeria, Andorra, Angola, Argentina, Armenia, Australia, Austria, Azerbaijan, Bahamas, Bahrain, Bangladesh, Barbados, Belarus, Belgium, Belize, Benin, Bermuda, Bhutan, Bolivia, Bosnia and Herzegovina, Botswana, Brazil, Brunei, Bulgaria, Burkina Faso, Burundi, Cambodia, Cameroon, Canada, Cape Verde, Central African Republic, Chad, Chile, China, Colombia, Comoro Islands, Congo (Republic of the), Costa Rica, Côte d'Ivoire, Croatia, Cuba, Cyprus, Czech Republic, Democratic Republic of the Congo, Denmark, Djibouti, Dominican Republic, Ecuador, Egypt, El Salvador, Eritrea, Estonia, Ethiopia, European Community, Fiji, Finland, France, Gabon, Gambia, Georgia, Germany, Ghana, Greece, Guatemala, Guinea, Guyana, Haiti, Honduras (Republic of), Hong Kong, Hungary, Iceland, India, Indonesia, Iran (Islamic Republic of), Iraq, Ireland, Israel, Italy, Jamaica, Japan, Jordan, Kazakhstan, Kenya, Korea (Republic of), Kuwait, Kyrgyzstan, Lao People's Democratic Republic, Latvia, Lebanon, Lesotho, Liberia, Libya, Lithuania, Luxembourg, Macau, Macedonia, Madagascar, Malawi, Malaysia, Maldives, Mali, Malta, Mauritania, Mauritius, Mexico, Moldova, Mongolia, Montenegro, Morocco, Mozambique, Myanmar, Namibia, Nepal, Netherlands, Netherlands Antilles, New Zealand, Nicaragua, Niger, Nigeria, Norway, Oman, Pakistan, Panama, Papua New Guinea, Paraguay, Peru, Philippines, Poland, Portugal, Qatar, Romania, Russian Federation, Rwanda, Saint Lucia, Samoa, Saudi Arabia, Senegal, Serbia, Seychelles, Sierra Leone, Singapore, Slovakia, Slovenia, South Africa, Spain, Sri Lanka, Sudan, Swaziland, Sweden, Switzerland, Syrian Arab Republic, Tajikistan, Tanzania, Thailand, Timor-Leste, Togo, Tonga,

Trinidad and Tobago, Tunisia, Turkey, Turkmenistan, Uganda, Ukraine, United Arab Emirates, United Kingdom, United States, Uruguay, Uzbekistan, Venezuela, Vietnam, Yemen, Zambia, and Zimbabwe.

Official Languages: English, French. Spanish is also used at certain technical meetings.

Origin and development. In an effort to facilitate the movement of goods within Western Europe and thereby aid in post–World War II reconstruction, the 13 governments comprising the Committee for European Economic Cooperation issued a joint declaration in September 1947 establishing a study group to consider the feasibility of a European customs union. A year later the group created an Economic Committee (disbanded following the formation of the Organisation for European Economic Co-operation, predecessor of the Organization for Economic Cooperation and Development [OECD]) and a Customs Committee, the latter to be assisted by a Permanent Tariff Bureau. In 1949, however, the study group abandoned the concept of a customs union as an immediate priority, choosing instead to standardize customs definitions and procedures. As a result, three conventions were signed on December 15, 1950, establishing the Customs Co-operation Council (CCC) and adopting the Brussels Definition of Value and the Brussels Nomenclature. The council held its inaugural session on January 16, 1953. Participation in the council does not oblige members to adopt regulations and recommendations incompatible with their existing policies.

In June 1994 the CCC adopted World Customs Organization (WCO) as its informal working name in order to indicate the "nature and worldwide status" of the organization more clearly. The CCC convention was not amended, and the official name remains Customs Co-operation Council, though that name is no longer in use.

Structure. The WCO Council meets annually to set policy, hear reports, and approve conventions and recommendations. Since 1979 a Policy Commission, comprising a "representative group" of 24 Council members, has served as a steering committee within the WCO. Administrative functions are directed by the Secretariat.

A Customs Co-operation Fund was established in 1984 to assist in the training of national customs officers. As of early 2008, the WCO was reorganizing its training program to operate online.

Activities. In the interest of liberalizing international trade, the WCO promotes practical means for harmonizing and standardizing customs systems. One of the organization's principal means of doing so is the adoption of conventions, including those covering such areas as nomenclature; international transit of goods; temporary importation of professional or scientific equipment and of pedagogic materials; and the prevention, investigation, and repression of customs offenses. The council also disseminates information on customs procedures and advises members on matters of nomenclature and valuation. Over the years, various services and technical assistance have been extended to nonmember developing countries, many of which subsequently joined the WCO.

In a major step forward in the achievement of the organization's goals, the Harmonized Commodity Description and Coding System, providing universal customs nomenclature, went into force on January 1, 1988. One year later, in an event of particular significance to the organization, the United States adopted the system, which is now used by more than 180 nations and customs unions.

Much of the organization's attention during the early 1990s focused on developments in Central and Eastern Europe, where economic liberalization was spurring interest in more sophisticated customs policies. The Soviet Union joined the council in July 1991; its seat was subsequently filled by the Russian Federation after the dissolution of the USSR. A number of the other former Soviet republics joined the council in 1992, and Croatia, Macedonia, Slovenia, and the rump Federal Republic of Yugoslavia (subsequently known as Serbia and Montenegro) also become members. After the separation of Serbia and Montenegro in June 2006, Serbia retained its membership as the successor state, Montenegro joining in its own right in November 2006. Laos joined in January 2007 and Djibouti and Belize in April 2008. In July 2007 the European Community, the economic organ of the European Union (EU), was admitted and became the first supranational organization to be associated with the WCO.

In April 1993 the WCO conducted the first in an ongoing series of seminars devoted to the question of "integrity" in customs administration, an issue that had previously been avoided in international forums despite evidence of widespread corruption at many borders. In addition, the organization adopted a plan to combat commercial fraud; discussed measures to protect intellectual property rights through customs procedures; and assumed additional responsibilities as the result of its close cooperation with the World Trade Organization (WTO), which was launched in 1995. In 1996 The World Customs Organization, at the behest of the Group of Seven (G-7) finance ministers, created a model to revise and expand nomenclature and coding and to harmonize and clarify the "rules of origin" for international goods and services. The model is under continuous revision.

In 1998, with the cooperation of Interpol, the WCO helped organize Operation Roadrunner, a two-week multinational European effort aimed at stopping the flow of drugs through the Balkans, and signed an agreement with the International Atomic Energy Agency in May enhancing the cooperation between the two agencies in combating the illegal trade in nuclear materials.

On June 26, 1999, the WCO Council adopted a revised International Convention on the Simplification and Harmonization of Customs Procedures (Kyoto Convention), the original convention having served since 1974. The updated convention entered into force on February 3, 2006, when it was ratified by Azerbaijan, the 40th member state to do so. By January 2008 it had been ratified by 56 member states. At the Council session held June 28–30, 2001, the WCO agreed to assume the G-7's Customs Data Harmonization Initiative, the goal being to establish a global standard for customs data. Attention has also recently focused on solidifying a cooperative relationship with the WTO and the United Nations Conference on Trade and Development (UNCTAD) to create a program for standardizing risk management and to address issues related to electronic commerce.

Responding to concerns expressed by the Group of Eight and the International Maritime Organization (IMO) regarding the potential threat posed by concealment of weapons of mass destruction in shipping containers, in 2002 the WCO established a Task Force on Supply Chain Security and Facilitation of International Trade. A year later, at the June 2003 Council session, the WCO approved the resultant International Convention on Mutual Administrative Assistance in Customs Matters.

The WCO has continued to focus on international crime and terrorism. For example, in 2003 it joined with the United Nations Environment Program (UNEP) and Interpol, among others, in a UNEP-initiated Green Customs project to assist customs officers in stemming environmental crime, including illegal trade in chemicals, waste, and endangered species. Efforts to stop the smuggling of tobacco and drugs also continued. In addition, the WCO assisted Interpol; the UN Educational, Scientific and Cultural Organization (UNESCO); and other agencies in efforts to prevent the international distribution of Iraqi artifacts that had been pillaged from museums following the fall of Iraq to U.S.–led forces. Most importantly for 2003, the WCO promulgated the so-called SAFE Framework of Standards for shippers in an age of terrorism. Among other things, the standards introduce the concept of Authorized Economic Operators (AEOs). This is basically an accreditation program, whose graduates can expect faster and less intrusive customs service. The SAFE scheme has been widely adopted in subsequent years.

On January 22–23, 2004, the WCO held a conference in Baku, Azerbaijan, on efforts to combat "drug trafficking by the Silk Route." On May 25–26, 2004, it held a Global Congress on Combating Counterfeiting. On January 26, 2005, it held a convention on facilitating trade through customs regulations in the age of the WTO, and during 2006 and 2007 it sponsored a series of events concerning such matters as information technology, biometrics, and counterfeiting as they relate to trade and customs. Its June 2007 Council meeting concentrated on these problems, as well as the increasing danger from counterfeit medicines.

In 2008 India led many Asia-Pacific countries in opposition to a U.S. law which requires that all material to be imported into the U.S. be scanned at the port of origin, asking the WCO to address the matter. Various countries, including the EU, subsequently objected, and in October 2008 the WCO put out a report criticizing the law as an impediment to global trade. The law will take effect in 2012, and in the meantime the WCO plans to lobby Congress and the executive branch vigorously against it. Some observers felt that the Obama administration might be more receptive to changes than its predecessor.

World Customs day, celebrated January 26, 2009, took as its theme the role of customs agencies in protecting the environment. Customs organizations were encouraged to focus on the smuggling of toxic materials, including the dumping of such materials on poor countries by rich countries, as well as the illegal movement of protected flora and fauna.

In April 20009, the WCO released a memorandum to the participants in the London G-20 conference (see separate article), outlining the rôle that customs should play in addressing the world economic crisis. It noted the decline in customs revenues, of particular concern to poor countries, it recommended that the actions of customs and related organizations be harmonized, and it looked to public-private partnerships, especially with well-trusted shippers, to help relieve the financial burden.

WORLD TRADE ORGANIZATION (WTO)

Established: By the Marrakesh Agreement signed in Marrakesh, Morocco, on April 15, 1994, effective January 1, 1995.

Purpose: To administer the agreements contained in the Final Act of the Uruguay Round of the General Agreement on Tariffs and Trade (GATT); to provide conciliation mechanisms to resolve trade conflicts between members and, if necessary, adjudicate disputes; to provide a forum for ongoing negotiations in pursuit of further lowering and/or elimination of tariffs and other trade barriers.

Headquarters: Geneva, Switzerland.

Principal Organs: Ministerial Conference (all members), General Council (all members), Trade Policy Review Body, Dispute Settlement Body, Appellate Body, Council on Trade in Goods, Council on Trade in Services, Council on the Trade-Related Aspects of Intellectual Property Rights, Secretariat.

Web site: www.wto.org

Director General: Pascal Lamy (France).

Membership (153): Albania, Angola, Antigua and Barbuda, Argentina, Armenia, Australia, Austria, Bahrain, Bangladesh, Barbados, Belgium, Belize, Benin, Bolivia, Botswana, Brazil, Brunei, Bulgaria, Burkina Faso, Burundi, Cambodia, Cameroon, Canada, Cape Verde, Central African Republic, Chad, Chile, China, China: Hong Kong, China: Macao, Colombia, Democratic Republic of the Congo, Republic of the Congo, Costa Rica, Côte d'Ivoire, Croatia, Cuba, Cyprus, Czech Republic, Denmark, Djibouti, Dominica, Dominican Republic, Ecuador, Egypt, El Salvador, Estonia, European Communities, Fiji, Finland, France, Gabon, Gambia, Georgia, Germany, Ghana, Greece, Grenada, Guatemala, Guinea, Guinea Bissau, Guyana, Haiti, Honduras, Hungary, Iceland, India, Indonesia, Ireland, Israel, Italy, Jamaica, Japan, Jordan, Kenya, Republic of Korea, Kuwait, Kyrgyzstan, Latvia, Lesotho, Liechtenstein, Lithuania, Luxembourg, Macedonia, Madagascar, Malawi, Malaysia, Maldives, Mali, Malta, Mauritania, Mauritius, Mexico, Moldova, Mongolia, Morocco, Mozambique, Myanmar, Namibia, Nepal, Netherlands, New Zealand, Nicaragua, Niger, Nigeria, Norway, Oman, Pakistan, Panama, Papua New Guinea, Paraguay, Peru, Philippines, Poland, Portugal, Qatar, Romania, Rwanda, St. Kitts and Nevis, St. Lucia, St. Vincent and the Grenadines, Saudi Arabia, Senegal, Sierra Leone, Singapore, Slovakia, Slovenia, Solomon Islands, South Africa, Spain, Sri Lanka, Suriname, Swaziland, Sweden, Switzerland, Taiwan (Separate Customs Territory of Taiwan, Penghu, Kinmen, and Matsu), Tanzania, Thailand, Togo, Tonga, Trinidad and Tobago, Tunisia, Turkey, Uganda, Ukraine, United Arab Emirates, United Kingdom, United States, Uruguay, Venezuela, Vietnam, Zambia, Zimbabwe.

Observers (38): Afghanistan, Algeria, Andorra, Azerbaijan, Bahamas, Belarus, Bhutan, Bosnia and Herzegovina, Comoro Islands, Equatorial Guinea, Ethiopia, Food and Agriculture Organization, Holy See, International Monetary Fund, International Trade Center, Iran, Iraq, Kazakhstan, Laos, Lebanon, Liberia, Libya, Montenegro, Organization for Economic Cooperation and Development, Russia, Samoa, Sao Tomé and Principe, Serbia, Seychelles, Sudan, Tajikistan, United Nations, United Nations Conference on Trade and Development, Uzbekistan, Vanuatu, World Bank, World Intellectual Property Organization, Yemen.

Official Languages: English, French, Spanish.

Origin and development. The General Agreement on Tariffs and Trade (GATT), signed in 1947, was not designed to set up a permanent international organization but merely to provide a temporary framework for tariff negotiations pending the establishment of a full-fledged International Trade Organization (ITO) under United Nations (UN) auspices. A charter establishing an ITO in the form of a UN Specialized Agency responsible for developing and administering a comprehensive international commercial policy was drafted at the UN Conference on Trade and Employment, which met November 1947–March 1948 in Havana, Cuba. However, the so-called Havana Charter never went into effect, principally because opposition within the United States blocked the required approval by the U.S. Senate. Delay in creating the ITO left GATT as the only available instrument for seeking agreement on rules for the conduct of international trade. (Since the general agreement was not cast as a treaty, it did not require formal ratification by the United States and could be implemented solely by executive action.) As of 1950, when it became apparent that the launching of a Specialized Agency would be indefinitely postponed, GATT attempted to fill part of the resultant vacuum through a series of ad hoc arrangements.

The broad objective of GATT was to contribute to general economic progress through the acceptance of agreed rights and obligations governing the conduct of trade relations. Four main principles, from which detailed rules emerged, underlay the General Agreement: (1) since trade should be conducted on a nondiscriminatory basis, all contracting parties were bound to deal with each other on the most favorable terms that they offered to any nation in the application of import and export duties; (2) protection of domestic industries was to be achieved through customs tariffs and not through other commercial measures (thus protective import quotas were prohibited); (3) consultations were to be undertaken to avoid damage to the trading interests of other contracting parties; and (4) GATT was to provide a framework for negotiating the reduction of tariffs and other barriers to trade, as well as a structure for embodying the results of such negotiations in a legal instrument. In addition, GATT assisted in activities in the area of conciliation and settlement of disputes.

Reducing tariffs through multilateral negotiations and agreements was one of the principal techniques employed by GATT. Eight major tariff-negotiating conferences were completed under GATT auspices: Geneva in 1947; Annecy, France, in 1949; Torquay, England, in 1951–1952; Geneva in 1955–1956, 1961–1962 (the Dillon Round, named for U.S. secretary of the treasury Douglas Dillon), and 1963–1967 (the Kennedy Round, named for U.S. president John F. Kennedy); and Tokyo and Geneva in 1973–1979 (the Tokyo Round). The eighth round commenced in September 1986 and, despite an original deadline of 1990, was not completed until December 1993, at which time agreement was reached upon the formation (effective January 1, 1995) of the World Trade Organization (WTO). The Kennedy Round far outdistanced its predecessors in magnitude and scope. For the first time, tariff reductions averaging about 33 percent were negotiated on an "across-the-board" basis, involving whole categories of products rather than single items. Efforts to reduce trade barriers for agricultural products and with regard to less developed states were not as successful, although an antidumping code designed to prevent companies from selling goods cheaper abroad than in their home markets was approved.

GATT subsequently devoted particular attention to two matters left over from the Kennedy Round negotiations: the trade needs of less developed states and the problem of nontariff barriers to trade (NTBs), especially among industrialized states. Efforts to assist less developed states in increasing their exports dated back at least to 1964, when GATT established the International Trade Center for this purpose in Geneva. In 1965 the contracting parties formally added the new Part IV on Trade and Development to the general agreement, thereby providing a formal basis for augmenting the participation of less developed states in international trade and promoting the sustained growth of their export earnings. Continuous review of the implementation of these provisions was entrusted to GATT's Committee on Trade and Development.

The 1972 Session of the GATT Contracting Parties adopted a timetable for new multilateral trade negotiations of even wider scope than the Kennedy Round. The aim of the new negotiations was nothing less than a broad restructuring of international trade to complement the reconstruction of the international monetary system as undertaken through the International Monetary Fund (IMF). The result, the Tokyo Round of negotiations, produced the most comprehensive agreement to date under GATT auspices. Some of the Tokyo accords that provided for an improved framework for the conduct of world trade took effect in November 1979. Most of the other agreements took effect on January 1, 1980. These covered tariff reductions (averaging 35–38 percent in a series of eight annual rounds), subsidies and countervailing duties, technical barriers to trade, import licensing procedures, a revised GATT antidumping code, bovine meat, dairy products, and civil aircraft. Agreements covering government procurement and customs valuation entered into effect January 1, 1981.

The September 1986 meeting of the contracting parties in Punta del Este, Uruguay, launched GATT's eighth round of negotiations, known as the Uruguay Round. Pending its formal completion, members agreed not to raise current levels of protection, with GATT serving as a "surveillance body" to address breaches of discipline.

The objectives of the new negotiations were by far the most ambitious ever attempted by GATT. The Uruguay Round sought extensive liberalization and proposed negotiations in important new areas such as agricultural subsidies, investment, and intellectual property rights. In addition, the Uruguay Round advanced more effective GATT procedures to resolve disputes and monitor compliance. The Punta del Este Declaration also proposed negotiations for the first time on trade in services (such as banking, data processing, insurance, tourism, construction, and transportation), described as the fastest-growing segment of international trade. The negotiating pace accelerated in 1988, and by the end of the year tentative agreements were reported on 11 of the 15 official categories. Of the unresolved areas—agriculture, textiles, intellectual property rights, and reform on the safeguards system—agriculture was most contentious, the European Community (EC) firmly opposing a U.S. proposal to eliminate all trade-restricting farm subsidies within ten years. However, in early 1989 Washington indicated it would accept a "ratcheting down" of subsidies over a longer period of time, a position that was expected to be more acceptable to the EC.

With Washington exhibiting a growing enthusiasm for the GATT process, promising negotiations took place on many of the service areas during the remainder of 1989 and early 1990. Nevertheless, GATT officials warned that extensive compromise was still required by all participants if a final package was to be adopted in Brussels in December 1990, as scheduled. Specifically, talks on agricultural subsidies, described as the "underpinning of the whole round," reached a critical stage in July. As the December deadline approached, many observers predicted that a last-minute compromise would be reached; however, a deadlock was declared in Brussels on December 7, and negotiations were suspended indefinitely.

Discussions between U.S. and EC officials in May 1992 again raised hopes for a settlement, but the Group of Seven summit in Munich in July failed to produce a breakthrough. Moreover, interest in the Uruguay Round appeared to be waning among the leaders of many of the industrialized nations, who seemed to be concentrating on the creation or extension of regional free trade agreements.

In late 1992 the United States and the EC encouraged GATT supporters by again appearing to reach an agreement on farm subsidies. However, it was quickly apparent that Paris's support for the accord was lukewarm at best, and the new French government installed in May—described as being in the midst of an "acute protectionist surge"— subsequently demanded that new negotiations be launched. As of September 1993 the dispute remained as contentious as ever, threatening completion of the Uruguay Round by what many observers considered its "final" deadline on December 15. This was the date on which U.S. president Bill Clinton would lose his so-called fast track authority to secure rapid ratification of a GATT agreement in the U.S. Senate (action limited to a simple yes or no vote with no opportunity to offer amendments).

Although the outcome remained in doubt until the very end, the Uruguay Round Final Act was approved by GATT's Trade Negotiations Committee on December 15, 1993, after a series of last-minute compromises, primarily between the United States and the European Union (EU), which watered down or eliminated some of the most contentious areas. Although an intellectual property component was approved, the EU (led by France on this point) succeeded in having television shows and films exempted. At the same time, however, the long-standing impasse on agricultural subsidies eased when the EU and the United States agreed to reduce subsidies substantially over the next six years. In addition, the signatories accepted what was expected eventually to amount to tariff reductions of about 40 percent on a wide range of goods, including agricultural products. Just as significantly, by providing for creation of the WTO, the GATT members committed themselves to a much more authoritative dispute settlement procedure.

On April 15, 1994, in Marrakesh, Morocco, ministers from more than 100 countries formally endorsed the Uruguay Round agreements and called for the establishment of the WTO by January 1, 1995. In July a preliminary committee, which had been established to oversee the transition to the WTO, voted to keep the new trade organization in Geneva, despite German efforts to have the headquarters moved to Bonn.

Although ratification by signatories proceeded more slowly than anticipated, a surge late in 1994 led to the convening on December 6 in Geneva of the Implementation Conference, which authorized the official launching of the WTO on January 1, 1995. The WTO was launched with 76 members, GATT countries being eligible for automatic membership upon their acceptance of the Uruguay Round Agreement and completion of other ratification procedures. As of late 2008 the WTO had 153 members, while working parties had been established to address WTO membership requests from 27 other countries. The United States has continued to block membership requests from Iran, Libya, and Syria, claiming that those countries retain connections with terrorist organizations. Russia, though it has made adjustments in a number of economic sectors in order to facilitate accession, remains an observer.

Structure. The WTO's supreme organ is the Ministerial Conference, in which each member state has one vote. It is mandated to meet at least every two years. Between ministerial sessions, oversight is the responsibility of the General Council, also composed of delegates from all member states. The General Council additionally acts as the Dispute Settlement Body, which establishes panels to adjudicate disputes brought before the WTO. Decisions of the panels can be appealed by either party in a dispute to the WTO Appellate Body, whose seven members are appointed by the Dispute Settlement Body. In addition, the General Council also acts as the Trade Policy Review Body, which conducts regular evaluations of the trade practices of all WTO members. Subcouncils have been established on trade in goods, trade in services, and the trade-related aspects of intellectual property rights. Permanent committees reporting directly to the General Council include Trade and Environment; Trade and Development; Regional Trade Agreements; Balance of Payments Restrictions; and Budget, Finance, and Administration. The Trade Negotiations Committee, which also reports directly to the General Council, was established in connection with the launching of the Doha Development Round of negotiations in 2001. The WTO governing bodies are assisted by the 650-employee Secretariat, which is headed by a director general selected for a four-year term by consensus of the WTO members at the ministerial level.

Although its founding treaty stipulated that the WTO would be accorded privileges and immunities similar to those of the Specialized Agencies affiliated with the United Nations, the organization was not officially designated as a Specialized Agency. However, the organization cooperates extensively with a number of UN-affiliated bodies as well as other non-UN organizations. For example, the WTO works with the United Nations Conference on Trade and Development (UNCTAD) in running the International Trade Center (ITC), originally set up by UNCTAD and GATT. Also, the ITC, UNCTAD, and the WTO administer a common trust fund to assist African countries in integrating themselves into the wider world economy. In addition, the WTO signed a cooperation agreement with the IMF in April 1997.

Activities. To the consternation of the WTO's most ardent supporters, the first few months of the grouping's existence were marked by an "unseemly" struggle among leading members over the director general's post, GATT's Peter Sutherland having agreed to serve only temporarily once the WTO was launched. Three major candidates emerged to succeed Sutherland: Carlos Salinas de Gortari, the former president of Mexico who was strongly supported by the United States; Renato Ruggiero, an Italian diplomat favored by the EU; and South Korea's Kim Chul Su, backed by Japan and other Asian countries. No inclination toward compromise was apparent in any of the three camps until Salinas was essentially forced to withdraw in the wake of growing criticism over his government's handling of Mexico's recent currency crisis. Washington subsequently threw its support to Ruggiero, although only after an agreement had been reached that he would serve only one four-year term (to April 30, 1999) and that the next director general would be a non-European.

One of Ruggiero's first stated priorities was to promote conclusion of a WTO agreement covering financial services, which was one of the three major areas (along with telecommunications and maritime transportation) left unresolved by GATT's Uruguay Round. In July 1995 more than 30 countries signed an accord governing trade in financial services; however, the United States, the world leader in the area, refused to sign on the ground that access to foreign markets would still be too restricted. Consequently, the agreement was implemented only until November 1997, pending further efforts to achieve U.S. endorsement of a permanent pact of broader scope. A permanent pact was finally accepted by the Committee on Trade in Financial Services on December 12, 1997. Seventy members submitted new or revised plans liberalizing their financial markets, joining the 32 who already had turned in their proposals. The agreement came into effect in 1999, the United States being one of 67 countries to have signed and ratified the document.

Attention subsequently focused on activity within the initial WTO arbitration panels. In early 1996 a WTO panel (and ultimately the Appellate Body) ruled in favor of Venezuela and Brazil in their contention that U.S. environmental regulations on gasoline were being unfairly applied to their exports, while U.S. refiners had been given an extension of time to conform to the new standards. Washington announced its intention to comply with the WTO verdict in June. A second successful case was brought by Canada, the European Community, and the United States against Japan, regarding Japan's taxes on imported alcoholic beverages.

By October 1996 more than 50 other disputes presented to the WTO were either settled during the consultation process or still under review by arbitration panels. Although the high rate of "out-of-court" settlements generally pleased WTO proponents, some member states argued that the trend reflected ongoing "capitulation" on behalf of the developing countries to the demands of industrialized nations. Their contention that the organization remained a "rich man's club" reportedly received informal attention during the first biennial meeting of the WTO's Ministerial Conference in December 1996, particularly when the developed countries rejected a proposal from Director General Ruggiero that they consider eliminating the tariffs on all imports from the 40 poorest nations in the world. Officially, however, the council presented a positive public image, lauding WTO efforts to date and expressing confidence that broader cooperation was on the horizon in regard to a number of trade issues. The most significant practical development at the 1996 session appeared to be the approval of the U.S.-sponsored Information Technology Agreement (ITA) for the gradual elimination of tariffs on computers and other high-tech products by January 1, 2000. The agreement took effect on July 1, 1997, by which time some 40 states, representing more than 92 percent of the market, had signed on.

Proposed membership expansion also remained a focus of WTO attention in late 1996. Membership is open to any state or customs territory with autonomy in the conduct of its trade policies, but all WTO members must agree on the terms of its accession. This is done by usually protracted negotiations. Of the nearly 30 accession requests under consideration in 1996, the most significant were those from Russia and China. The United States and other Western nations had announced they would support China's entry (possibly in 2000), provided Beijing reduced its tariffs and dismantled other trade barriers.

In September 1997 the Appellate Body ruled on a dispute initiated by Ecuador, Guatemala, Honduras, Mexico, and the United States against the EU's banana importation regime, which gave preferential market access to African, Caribbean, and Pacific (ACP) countries under the Lomé Convention. The Appellate Body upheld the findings of a panel in agreeing that these preferences were "inconsistent with the WTO rules." The EU said it would accept the Appellate Body's verdict but expressed concern over the potential effects it could have on ACP countries. The dispute nevertheless continued into 1998, with the United States claiming late in the year that a modified regime was still inadequate and announcing it would seek WTO approval for levying sanctions on EU goods. In early 1999 both sides agreed to allow the dispute panel that had heard the original case to arbitrate the matter. In April the panel again ruled in favor of the United States, but it approved sanctions valued at only $191.4 million, not the $520 million requested by Washington.

In February 1998, an agreement opening up the telecommunications market entered into force. Also during the year, the WTO held its second Ministerial Conference in Geneva in May, at which time a number of poor countries claimed they were not benefiting from liberalized trade.

A contentious search for a successor to Director General Ruggiero dragged into 1999, and when his term expired on April 30, the office fell vacant. Principal candidates were Michael Moore, a former prime minister of New Zealand, and Supachai Panitchpakdi, a deputy prime minister of Thailand. A compromise agreement provided for Moore to serve a special three-year term (effective July 22) with Panitchpakdi to succeed Moore for a three-year term in 2002. Substantial controversy also surrounded the third meeting of the WTO's Ministerial Conference on November 30–December 3, 1999, in Seattle, Washington, which, among other things, prompted massive demonstrations by "antiglobalizationists" and others who objected to the perceived negative effect of WTO activity to date on the poor and on environmental and labor standards in the developing world. Internal disputes (such as disagreements among the EU, the United States, and others over agricultural subsidies) also marred the session, which ended without a final communiqué. No agreement was reached again in 2001 in regard to a timetable and agenda for a proposed ninth round of trade negotiations. In particular, the developed and developing countries remained at loggerheads regarding how much power the latter should have within the WTO. One UN report described the WTO as a "nightmare" for developing countries and urged that the WTO be placed under a degree of formal UN jurisdiction.

After several years of disastrous public relations and growing concern over its future effectiveness, the WTO attempted to chart a positive course by launching the Doha Development Round at the fourth meeting of the Ministerial Conference in Doha, Qatar, in November 2001. The new trade negotiations were originally scheduled for completion by 2005, although vague language about agricultural subsidies in the Doha document concerned many analysts. Other major developments at Doha included the acceptance of China as a WTO member (effective December 11), a decision that facilitated Taiwan's admission (as the Separate Customs Territory of Taiwan, Penghu, Kinmen, and Matsu) on January 1, 2002.

In January 2002 the WTO Appellate Body endorsed a 2001 dispute tribunal's ruling that the United States was in violation of WTO agreements by providing tax breaks for U.S. companies in regard to income earned in foreign countries. The EU, which had pursued the complaint, was authorized to impose a staggering $4 billion in retaliatory tariffs, although no such action was taken while the United States and EU attempted to reach a negotiated settlement. That dispute, coupled with severe criticism from the EU, Japan, and China over Washington's decision in March to apply substantial tariffs on imported steel, contributed to a continued sense of malaise within the WTO as Director General Panitchpakdi took office in September 2002.

In March 2003 a WTO dispute panel ruled against the United States regarding its steel tariffs, and Washington lifted the tariffs in November after a WTO appeals panel upheld the original decision. The WTO also ruled against the United States in 2004 on the issues of U.S. subsidies to cotton farmers (followed by a second ruling against the United States in 2007) and the so-called Byrd Amendment that paid out antidumping duties collected by the United States directly to private firms. In October 2004 a WTO panel began its assessment of one of the WTO's largest and most complex cases to date—the disputes over U.S. and EU aid to their largest aircraft manufacturers (Boeing and Airbus, respectively). A dispute involving U.S. tax breaks for U.S. companies in regard to income earned abroad subsequently came to a conclusion when the U.S. Congress, after two years of foot-dragging, finally approved legislation to comply with the WTO findings. Meanwhile, progress was also reported at the August 2004 WTO summit on the issue of agricultural subsidies, which had prompted the walkout of some 90 newly assertive developing countries from the 2003 summit.

In January 2005 Director General Panitchpakdi announced that he did not intend to seek a second term. In May EU trade commissioner Pascal Lamy was named to the post, effective September of that year.

There were hopes that a significant agreement on the Doha Round might come at the sixth Ministerial Conference, held December 13–18, 2005, in Hong Kong, but that did not happen. Instead there was a modest agreement that the EU would end farm export subsidies by 2013 and the United States would reduce subsidies for cotton exports. It was generally recognized, however, that the conference produced only marginal benefit for poorer countries. In June 2006 Director General Lamy organized what amounted to an emergency meeting of any WTO members who cared to attend in an attempt to broker a broader resolution of the disputes over cutting tariffs and subsidies in agriculture and opening markets for industrial goods. The meeting aimed to produce template agreements known as "modalities" for this purpose. The meeting, held in Geneva beginning June 28, effectively collapsed by July 1, with no agreements reached and many delegations going home early. As a consequence, there was considerable speculation that the WTO would have to rethink some of its aims and principals. Some commentators predicted a flurry of more and angrier disputes coming before an increasingly ineffective WTO. Others mentioned the possibility that many trading countries, perhaps led by the United States, would turn to bilateral agreements with trading partners, thus producing a complicated and inefficient bureaucratic web and impeding global trade.

Indeed, a series of trade complaints was filed with the WTO in 2006 and 2007, in some cases to gain leverage in the continuing Doha talks. Canada took the lead, backed by more than a half dozen countries, in challenging the United States on farm subsidies in early 2007, saying Washington's aid to farmers exceeds WTO limits. Ongoing cases involving the EU's banana import regime and U.S. cotton subsidies were still before the WTO as contentious negotiations on a trade deal stretched through 2007 and into 2008. (Both cases were subsequently decided against the EU and the United States.)

With the faltering of talks again in the fall of 2006, observers cautioned that the WTO risked losing credibility. After months of small group consultations into the spring of 2007, four key trade powers (the United States, the EU, India, and Brazil) attempted to hammer out a deal in Potsdam, Germany, on June 19–21. The talks again collapsed with India and Brazil complaining that the United States and the EU were demanding too much access to industrial goods markets in exchange for too little cutting of tariffs and subsidies on their agricultural goods. When talks resumed among key WTO trade members in 2008, the issues were no different: agricultural subsidies in the most developed countries versus protection for industries and services in the rest. In any event the talks collapsed in late July 2008 for much the same reasons as the previous year. This time India and Brazil were joined by South Africa in speaking for a coalition of more than 100 smaller and less developed countries.

Growing frustration with China's progress in implementing trade accords has been reflected in a series of complaints filed with the WTO in recent years. China's fifth anniversary in the WTO in 2006 was marked by U.S. calls to open its banking and financial sectors further. Subsequently, the United States, faced with discontent over its growing trade imbalance with China, led complaints against China concerning inadequate efforts in fighting piracy and counterfeiting; restrictions on the sale of U.S. films, books, and software; and allegations that China was giving tax breaks to exporters in a wide range of industries. In July 2008 China lost its first case before the WTO, a complaint over discrimination against foreign-made auto parts.

In other matters, as public concern over environmental issues has grown, the WTO has made a concerted effort to express support for an environmental agenda. Director General Lamy attended the UN Environment Program (UNEP) Global Ministerial Environment Forum in Nairobi, Kenya, in February 2007 and said that the "WTO stands ready to do its part" in achieving sustainable development. The organization has no specific agreement dealing with environmental issues, though the 2001 Doha Ministerial Conference for the first time allowed members to take into account multilateral environmental agreements that contain "specific trade obligations" during trade negotiations (the scope of any trade deal would be limited to those members party to the environmental agreement). The WTO has also faced calls to play a part in implementing the Kyoto Protocol on global warming, or its successor agreement.

Also in 2007, Lamy expressed interest in the WTO playing a stronger role in international energy trade, due to the growing number of large oil-producing states joining and seeking membership.

A number of issues regarding WTO membership have occurred in recent years. Vietnam's communist-run legislature cleared up remaining hurdles, notably the removal of quotas on garment exports, and joined the WTO in November 2007. Ukraine's 14-year effort at accession continued to progress, and it became a full member at the end of 2008. Russia, whose economy is the largest outside the WTO, worked throughout 2006 and 2007 on deals to lift remaining trade restrictions, though there was some concern it lacked a sense of urgency in fulfilling commitments. By the end of 2007, the possibility of Russia's accession narrowed to two remaining issues with the EU, namely export duties on timber and a reform of railway fees that have favored Russian ports. In 2008, however, Russia's prospects deteriorated sharply. Georgia declared in May of that year that it would block Russia's admission until Russia ceased supporting the breakaway Georgian provinces of Abkhazia and South Ossetia. The fighting between Russia and Georgia in August 2008 only worsened the situation, and by then Russia appeared to be losing interest in the WTO. There was no more formal movement on Russia's accession through late 2009.

On November 4, 2008, Director General Lamy announced that he would be a candidate for a second term in office, when his first term expired in 2010. On November 15, 2008, the Group of Twenty (G-20, see separate article), meeting in Washington, D.C., to discuss the world financial crisis, committed its members not to take any actions for twelve months that might raise new trade barriers, or otherwise interfere with the WTO's work against protectionism. The G-20 also agreed to "strive to reach agreement this year on modalities that leads to a successful conclusion to the WTO's Doha Development Agenda with an ambitious and balanced outcome." On December 12, 2008, Lamy declared, after consultation with the United States, India, China, Brazil, and the EU, that there was insufficient basis to restart talks on the Doha Round.

In January 2009 the WTO issued a statement, bearing on a U.S. complaint against China's allegedly lax attitude toward pirated DVDs and other intellectual property, that was highly critical of China's position. The WTO recommended that China bring its copyright law "into conformity with its obligations." On August 12, 2009, the WTO ruled definitively in favor of the United States on the bulk of the complaint. Shortly thereafter China announced an appeal. On December 4, 2009, the organization handed down a decision in the Boeing-Airbus case. The decision was given sealed to the parties involved, and not expected to be made public for several months thereafter. It was widely reported, however, to be marginally favorable to the U.S. position. On November 6, 2009, the WTO announced that it had received its 400th request for settlement of a dispute.

APPENDIXES

APPENDIX A CHRONOLOGY OF MAJOR INTERNATIONAL EVENTS: 1945–2009

1945, **May 8.** Proclamation of end of the war in Europe.
June 26. United Nations Charter signed in San Francisco.
August 6. United States drops atomic bomb on Hiroshima, Japan.
September 2. Surrender of Japan.

1946, **July 29–October 15.** Peace Conference meets in Paris, France.
December 30. UN Atomic Energy Commission approves U.S. proposal for world control of atomic weapons.

1947, **February 10.** Peace treaties signed with Bulgaria, Finland, Hungary, Italy, Romania.
June 5. Marshall Plan inaugurated.
October 30. General Agreement on Tariffs and Trade (GATT) negotiated in Geneva, Switzerland.

1948, **March 17.** Brussels Treaty signed by Belgium, France, Luxembourg, Netherlands, United Kingdom.
March 20. Soviet representatives walk out of Allied Control Council for Germany.
April 16. Organization for European Economic Cooperation (OEEC) established in Paris, France.
April 30. Organization of American States (OAS) Charter signed in Bogotá, Colombia.
May 14. State of Israel proclaimed.
May 12, July 24–1949. Berlin blockade.
December 10. UN General Assembly adopts Universal Declaration of Human Rights.

1949, **January 25.** Council for Mutual Economic Assistance (CMEA) established in Moscow, USSR.
April 4. Treaty establishing North Atlantic Treaty Organization (NATO) signed in Washington.
May 4. Statute establishing Council of Europe signed in London, United Kingdom.

1950, **January 31.** U.S. president Harry S. Truman orders construction of hydrogen bomb.
June 27. United States intervenes in Korean War.

1951, **April 18.** Treaty establishing European Coal and Steel Community signed by Belgium, France, Federal Republic of Germany, Italy, Luxembourg, Netherlands.
September 1. Anzus Pact signed in San Francisco, by Australia, New Zealand, United States.
September 8. Peace Treaty signed by Japan and non-Communist Allied powers in San Francisco.

1952, **May 27.** European Defense Community (EDC) Charter signed by Belgium, France, Federal Republic of Germany, Italy, Luxembourg, Netherlands.
November 1. United States explodes hydrogen bomb in Eniwetok Atoll.

1953, **March 5.** Death of Joseph Stalin.
December 8. U.S. president Dwight D. Eisenhower proposes international control of atomic energy.

1954, **September 8.** Treaty establishing Southeast Asia Treaty Organization (SEATO) signed in Manila, Philippines.
October 23. Allied occupation of West Germany ends.

1955, **May 6.** Western European Union (WEU) inaugurated by admission of Italy and Federal Republic of Germany to Brussels Treaty.
May 9. Federal Republic of Germany admitted to NATO.
May 14. Warsaw Pact signed by East European communist governments.

1956, **July 26.** Egypt nationalizes Suez Canal.
October 23–November 22. Anticommunist rebellion in Hungary suppressed by Soviet troops.
October 29–November 6. Suez crisis.

1957, **March 25.** Rome Treaty establishing European Economic Community (EEC) and European Atomic Energy Community (Euratom) signed.

1960, **May 1.** U-2 incident.
May 3. European Free Trade Association (EFTA) of "Outer Seven" (Austria, Denmark, Norway, Sweden, Switzerland, Portugal, United Kingdom) established.
May 14. Beginning of Sino-Soviet dispute.
December 14. Charter of Organization for Economic Cooperation and Development (OECD) to replace OEEC signed in Paris, France.

1961, **April 17–20.** Bay of Pigs invasion of Cuba.
August 15. Start of construction of Berlin Wall between East and West Germany.
September 1–6. First conference of Nonaligned Nations in Belgrade, Yugoslavia.

1962, **October 22–28.** Cuban missile crisis.

1963, **January 29.** France vetoes British bid for admission to EEC.
May 25. Organization of African Unity (OAU) Charter adopted in Addis Ababa, Ethiopia.
August 5. Limited Nuclear Test-Ban Treaty signed in Moscow, USSR.

1964, **May 28.** Palestine Liberation Organization (PLO) established.

1965, **February 21.** Decision to merge European Economic Community (EEC), European Coal and Steel Community (ECSC), and European Atomic Energy Community (Euratom).

1966, **March 11.** France withdraws troops from NATO.

1967, **January 27.** Treaty governing exploration and use of outer space signed by the United States, USSR, and 60 other nations.
June 5. Beginning of Arab-Israeli War.
June 17. China explodes its first hydrogen bomb.

1968, **January 16.** Britain announces withdrawal of forces from Persian Gulf and Far East.
May 13. Beginning of Vietnam peace talks in Paris, France.
June 4. Nuclear Nonproliferation Treaty approved by UN General Assembly.
August 20–21. Warsaw Pact forces occupy Czechoslovakia.
August 25. France explodes its first hydrogen bomb.
September 12. Albania withdraws from Warsaw Pact.
October 5. Outbreak of civil rights violence in Londonderry, Northern Ireland.

1969, **April 28.** Charles de Gaulle resigns as French president.
July 21. United States lands first men on moon.
November 17–December 22. Initiation of Strategic Arms Limitation Talks (SALT) between the United States and USSR.

1970, **March 2.** Rhodesia issues unilateral declaration of independence from Britain.

1971, **November 12.** U.S. president Richard Nixon announces end of U.S. offensive action in Vietnam.

1972, **February 21–28.** U.S. president Richard Nixon visits China.
May 22–29. U.S. president Richard Nixon visits Soviet Union.

1973, **January 1.** Denmark, Ireland, and the United Kingdom enter European Communities.
February 12. Last U.S. ground troops leave Vietnam.
October 6–22. Fourth Arab-Israeli war.
October 17. Arab embargo launched on oil shipments to United States and other Western nations (embargo ends March 18, 1974).

1974, **January 18.** Egypt and Israel sign agreement on disengagement of forces along Suez Canal.

1975, **February 28.** First Lomé (Togo) Convention signed between EEC and developing African, Caribbean, and Pacific (ACP) states.
May 28. Treaty establishing Economic Community of West African States (ECOWAS) signed in Lagos, Nigeria.
June 5. Suez Canal reopened to international shipping.
July 30–August 1. Conference on Security and Cooperation in Europe (CSCE) concludes in Helsinki, Finland.
September 4. Agreement between Egypt and Israel provides for Israeli withdrawal in Sinai and establishment of UN buffer zone.
November 20. Death of Spain's Gen. Francisco Franco.

1976, **June 17.** Outbreak of racial violence in Soweto, South Africa.
July 3–4. Israeli raid on Entebbe Airport, Uganda.
September 9. Death of China's Mao Zedong.

1977, **June 30.** Southeast Asia Treaty Organization (SEATO) dissolved.
November 19–21. Egyptian president Anwar Sadat visits Israel.

1978, **September 9–17.** President Anwar Sadat and Prime Minister Menachem Begin meet with U.S. President Jimmy Carter at Camp David.

1979, **January 1.** People's Republic of China and United States establish diplomatic relations.
January 16. Shah of Iran goes into exile.
March 26. Egyptian-Israeli peace treaty signed in Washington.
November 4. Iranian students seize U.S. embassy in Tehran.
December 27. Soviet military forces support coup in Afghanistan.

1980, **April 18.** Zimbabwe (formerly Rhodesia) declared legally independent.
May 4. Death of Yugoslavian president Josip Broz Tito.
September 22. Iraqi invasion of Iran initiates Iran-Iraq war.
October 24. Independent trade union (Solidarity) officially registered in Poland.

1981, **January 1.** Greece enters European Communities.
January 20. Iran frees remaining U.S. hostages.

October 6. Egyptian president Anwar Sadat assassinated.
December 13. Martial law declared in Poland.
December 14. Occupied Golan Heights placed under Israeli law.

1982, April 2–July 15. Falkland Islands (*Islas Malvinas*) war between Argentina and the United Kingdom.
June 6. Israeli invasion of Lebanon.
August 21–September 1. PLO forces evacuate Beirut, Lebanon.
November 10. Soviet leader Leonid Brezhnev dies.

1983, September 1. USSR shoots down Korean Air Lines Boeing 747 passenger plane.
October 25. United States, in concert with six Caribbean states, invades Grenada (last troops withdrawn December 12).

1984, October 31. Indian prime minister Indira Gandhi assassinated.

1985, March 11. Mikhail S. Gorbachev named general secretary of Soviet Communist Party.
October 7. Palestinian terrorists seize Italian cruise ship Achille Lauro.
November 15. Ireland and the United Kingdom sign accord granting Irish Republic consultative role in governance of Northern Ireland.
November 19–21. U.S. president Ronald Reagan and Soviet leader Gorbachev hold summit meeting in Geneva.

1986, January 1. Spain and Portugal enter European Communities.
January 28. U.S. space shuttle *Challenger*, on 25th shuttle mission, breaks apart after lift-off.
February 7. Jean-Claude Duvalier flees from Haiti to France, ending nearly three decades of his family's rule.
February 25. General Secretary Mikhail Gorbachev calls for sweeping reforms in Soviet economic system.
February 25. Corazon Aquino inaugurated as Philippines president following disputed election February 7; after holding rival inauguration, Ferdinand Marcos flies to Hawaii.
April 15. U.S. aircraft bomb Tripoli and Benghazi in response to alleged Libyan-backed terrorist activity in Europe.
April 26. Explosion in Chernobyl, USSR, power plant results in worst nuclear accident in history.
November 25. Attorney General Edwin Meese says $10–$30 million paid by Iran for U.S. arms was diverted by Lt. Col. Oliver North to Nicaraguan insurgents.

1987, June 11. Margaret Thatcher becomes first prime minister in modern British history to lead her party to a third consecutive electoral victory.
August 7. Five Central American presidents sign regional peace plan proposed by Oscar Arias of Costa Rica.
September 1. Erich Honecker becomes first East German head of state to visit West Germany.
October 19. U.S. stock market crashes, with Dow Jones Industrial Average falling 508.32 points in one session; foreign markets plummet the next day.
December 8. U.S. president Ronald Reagan and Soviet general secretary Mikhail Gorbachev sign INF treaty calling for elimination of entire class of nuclear weapons.
December 9. Intifada begins among Palestinians in the Gaza Strip, spreading to the West Bank the following day.

1988, April 14. Afghanistan, Pakistan, Soviet Union, United States conclude agreement on Soviet withdrawal from Afghanistan (withdrawal completed February 15, 1989).
June 28. Soviet general secretary Mikhail Gorbachev proposes wide-ranging changes in Soviet political system.
August 17. Pakistan's president Zia ul-Haq dies in plane crash.
August 20. Cease-fire begins in Iran-Iraq war.
November 15. Yasir Arafat issues PLO statement declaring an independent state of Palestine.
December 22. Angola, Cuba, South Africa sign agreements providing for Cuban withdrawal from Angola and transition to independence for Namibia.

1989, January 7. Japanese emperor Hirohito dies.
January 19. Conference on Security and Cooperation in Europe concludes 26-month meeting in Vienna, Austria, with expansion of 1975 Helsinki Final Act to emphasize freedom of religion, information, travel, and privacy.
March 10. U.S. treasury secretary Nicholas Brady announces "Brady Plan" for commercial banks to make voluntary reductions in outstanding Third World debts and for the IMF and World Bank to provide debt-reduction assistance to debtor nations that adopt market-oriented reforms.
March 26. Soviet Union holds nationwide contested elections.
April 17. Solidarity relegalized by court action 12 days after reaching agreement with Polish government on political reforms.
May 13. Students demanding meeting with Chinese leaders begin hunger strike after occupying Beijing's Tiananmen Square.
May 15–18. Soviet leader Mikhail Gorbachev goes to China for the first Sino-Soviet summit in 20 years; antigovernment protests break out in more than 20 Chinese cities, including a demonstration by an estimated 1 million people in Tiananmen Square.
June 4. Many deaths reported as troops clear Tiananmen Square.
June 4–18. Solidarity sweeps two-stage, partially open election in Poland.
June 6. Iranian Ayatollah Khomeini dies.
November 9. East German government permits citizens to leave without special permits, thus effectively opening the country's borders, including the Berlin Wall.
December 20. U.S. forces invade Panama.
December 25. Romanian president Nicolae Ceauşescu and his wife executed.

1990, March 11. Lithuania becomes first Soviet republic to issue declaration of independence.
March 13. Soviet Congress of People's Deputies revokes monopoly status of Communist Party.
March 15. Soviet Congress of People's Deputies elects Mikhail Gorbachev to new office of executive president.
March 21. Namibia becomes independent.
June 7. Warsaw Pact leaders meeting in Moscow declare the West is no longer an "ideological enemy."
August 2. Iraq invades Kuwait.
August 6. UN Security Council votes to impose mandatory economic sanctions on Iraq. United States deploys troops to Gulf in defense of Saudi Arabia ("Operation Desert Shield").
September 7. Liberian president Samuel Doe killed by rebels.
October 3. East and West Germany unite as the Federal Republic of Germany.
November 19. NATO and Warsaw Pact leaders sign Conventional Forces in Europe (CFE) treaty.
November 21. CSCE summit participants sign Charter of Paris for a New Europe devoid of East-West division and committed to democracy and human rights.
November 29. UN Security Council authorizes U.S.-led forces "to use all means necessary" to secure Iraq's unconditional withdrawal from Kuwait.

1991, January 16. "Operation Desert Storm" air attacks initiated against Iraq.
February 27. U.S. president George H. W. Bush announces liberation of Kuwait; Iraq agrees to cease-fire.
March 26. Presidents of Argentina, Brazil, Paraguay, Uruguay sign treaty in Asunción, Paraguay, creating Southern Cone Common Market (Mercosur).
April 11. UN Security Council officially declares end of Gulf war after receiving Iraq's acceptance of permanent cease-fire terms.
May 26. Zviad Gamsakhurdia of Georgia becomes first freely elected leader of a Soviet republic.
May 28. Ethiopian civil war ends as rebel forces occupy Addis Ababa.
June 12. Boris Yeltsin elected president of the Russian Soviet Federative Socialist Republic.
June 25. Croatia and Slovenia declare independence from Yugoslavia.
June 28. Communist Council for Mutual Economic Assistance (Comecon) agrees to disband. The Warsaw Treaty Organization (WTO) follows suit July 1.
July 17. U.S. president George H. W. Bush and Soviet president Mikhail Gorbachev reach agreement on Strategic Arms Reduction Treaty (START), signed July 31.
August 19–21. Hard-line Soviet leaders are defeated in coup attempt.
August 20. Estonia declares independence; other Soviet republics follow with similar declarations.
August 24. Mikhail Gorbachev resigns as general secretary of the Soviet Communist Party.
August 29. Supreme Soviet bans Communist Party activities.
September 7. Croatia and Slovenia formally secede from Yugoslavia; Macedonia declares independence September 8.
December 8. Leaders of Russia, Ukraine, and Belarus announce dissolution of the Soviet Union.
December 9–11. EC leaders agree on treaty for political and monetary union during meeting in Maastricht, Netherlands.
December 21. Eleven former Soviet republics launch Commonwealth of Independent States (CIS).
December 25. Mikhail Gorbachev resigns as Soviet president.

1992, February 7. EC's Maastricht Treaty formally signed.
March 2. Eight former Soviet republics admitted to UN.
April 27. Serbia and Montenegro proclaim new Federal Republic of Yugoslavia.
April 28. Islamic Jihad Council assumes power in Afghanistan following fall of Kabul to mujahidin rebels.
May 30. UN Security Council imposes sweeping sanctions against Serbia and Montenegro in response to aggression against Bosnia and Herzegovina.

August 1. First Lebanese parliamentary election in 20 years.
November 3. Arkansas governor Bill Clinton defeats incumbent U.S. president George H. W. Bush.
December 18. Kim Young Sam becomes first genuinely civilian president of South Korea after three decades of military leadership.

1993, **January 1.** Czech and Slovak Republics become separate states one day after the dissolution ("velvet divorce") of the 74-year-old Czech and Slovak Federative Republic.
January 1. Single European market established, paving the way for free movement of goods, services, capital, and people throughout all 12 EC countries.
January 3. U.S. and Russian presidents Bill Clinton and Boris Yeltsin sign second Strategic Arms Reduction Treaty (START II) under which the two nations will dismantle approximately two-thirds of their strategic nuclear warheads.
February 26. New York World Trade Center bombed by individuals linked to Islamic militants.
April 23–25. Eritrean people vote for independence (effective May 24) from Ethiopia, ending 30-year independence struggle.
April 27–28. China and Taiwan hold "unofficial" talks in Singapore, representing highest level of contact since Communists' 1949 seizure of the mainland.
May 23–28. Cambodia holds Constituent Assembly elections, first balloting since 1981.
July 18. Japanese Liberal Democratic Party loses its overall majority in the House of Representatives for first time since 1955 and is ousted from government by seven-party coalition on August 6.
September 13. Israeli-PLO peace accord signed in Washington.
October 3–4. Forces loyal to Russian President Boris Yeltsin battle with rebels opposed to his suspension of the parliament, ultimately ousting them from the parliament building.
October 8. UN General Assembly lifts economic sanctions against South Africa.
November 1. Maastricht Treaty on European Union formally enters into effect following the completion of the ratification process in October.
November 18. Interim constitution endorsed by South African multiparty negotiators.
December 15. Uruguay Round of the General Agreement on Tariffs and Trade (GATT) concludes.
December 15. Prime ministers of Ireland and United Kingdom sign "Downing Street Declaration," a 12-point document delineating principles for holding peace talks on Northern Ireland.

1994, **January 1.** European Economic Area (EEA), joining the EU and EFTA in a free market trading zone, comes into effect.
January 1. North American Free Trade Agreement (NAFTA), the first such agreement to link two industrialized countries (Canada and the United States) with a developing country (Mexico), becomes effective.
January 10. Announcement of Partnership for Peace (PfP), which affords military cooperation with, but not full-fledged defense guarantees by, NATO to nonmember countries.
February 28. In first offensive action by NATO, its fighters shoot down four Serbian warplanes for defying no-fly zone over Bosnia-Herzegovina.
March 27. Right-wing Freedom Alliance headed by Silvio Berlusconi wins Italian general election.
April 6. Presidents Juvénal Habyarimana of Rwanda and Cyprien Ntaryamire of Burundi die in downing of plane over Kilgali, Rwanda.
April 27. Multiracial constitution for South Africa comes into effect.
May 4. Israel and PLO sign accord in Cairo, Egypt, ending Israeli military rule in the Gaza Strip and Jericho.
May 6. Channel tunnel linking Britain and France formally opened by Queen Elizabeth II and President François Mitterrand.
May 10. Nelson Mandela sworn in as first black president of South Africa.
July 8. North Korean leader Kim Il Sung dies.
July 15. Over 500,000 Rwandan refugees arrive in Zaire, the initial wave of an exodus that would eventually involve more than 2 million people.
July 25. Israeli prime minister Yitzhak Rabin and Jordanian King Hussein sign declaration in Washington, ending 46-year state of war between their countries.
November 8. Republicans gain control of both houses of U.S. Congress for the first time in four decades.
December 11. Russian forces invade secessionist republic of Chechnya.

1995, **January 1.** Austria, Finland, and Sweden accede to EU.
January 1. World Trade Organization (WTO) inaugurated as successor to GATT.
April 19. Bombing of U.S. federal government building kills 168 in Oklahoma City.
May 7. Jacques Chirac (Gaullist) elected president of France in succession to François Mitterrand (Socialist).
September 5. France begins new series of underground nuclear tests in South Pacific, attracting worldwide protests.
September 28. Second accord in Israeli-PLO peace process signed in Washington, providing for extensive additional withdrawal of Israeli troops from West Bank and expansion of Palestinian self-rule.
November 4. Prime Minister Yitzhak Rabin of Israel assassinated by right-wing Jewish extremist in Tel Aviv.
November 21. U.S.-brokered peace agreement for Bosnia and Herzegovina initialed by contending parties in Dayton, Ohio (formally signed in Paris December 14).

1996, **January 20.** Yasir Arafat elected president of self-governing Palestinian Authority.
January 29. France announces permanent end to nuclear testing.
May 7. The first war crimes trial of the UN International Tribunal for the former Yugoslavia opens in The Hague.
May 18. Romano Prodi sworn in to head Italy's first left-dominated government, the 55th since World War II.
June 18. Conservative Benjamin Netanyahu becomes prime minister of Israel following election May 29.
June 28. Necmettin Erbakan appointed first avowedly Islamist prime minister of modern Turkey.
September 14. Post-Dayton elections in Bosnia and Herzegovina confirm entrenched ethnic loyalties.
September 24. China, France, Russia, the United Kingdom, and the United States sign Comprehensive Test Ban Treaty (CTBT) in UN headquarters, New York.
September 27. Afghanistan's Taliban militia seizes power in Kabul, immediately hanging ex-president Mohammad Najibullah.
December 10. Iraqi president Saddam Hussein reopens Iraqi oil pipelines under UN "oil-for-food" program.
December 17. Kofi Annan (Ghana) appointed (effective January 1, 1997) to succeed Boutros Boutros-Ghali (Egypt) as UN secretary general.
December 29. Guatemalan peace agreement ends 36-year-old guerrilla insurgency.

1997, **January 15.** Israeli prime minister Benjamin Netanyahu and Palestinian leader Yasir Arafat sign accord whereby Israel agrees to partial withdrawal from Hebron.
February 19. Deng Xiaoping, China's "paramount leader," dies.
April 22. Peruvian commandos raid the Japanese embassy in Lima, ending 126-day hostage crisis by Túpac Amaru Revolutionary Movement guerrillas.
May 1. Led by Tony Blair, Britain's Labour Party overwhelms the Conservative Party in legislative balloting and assumes power for first time in 18 years.
May 16–17. Mobutu Sese Seko, Zaire's leader for 32 years, flees the country and rebel leader Laurent Kabila pronounces the establishment of the Democratic Republic of the Congo.
May 25. Ahmad Tejan Kabbah, Sierra Leone's first democratically elected president, flees country following military coup.
July 1. China takes control of Hong Kong after Britain's 99-year lease expires.
July 2. The Bank of Thailand abandons fixed exchange rate after months of attacks on its currency (baht) by speculators, thus sparking East Asian financial crisis.
October 23. Former president of the Republic of the Congo Denis Sassou-Nguesso overthrows the nation's first democratically elected president, Pascal Lissouba.
December 9. North Korea, South Korea, China, and the United States open talks on creation of a permanent Korean peace treaty.

1998, **March 19.** Nationalist Hindu leader Atal Bihari Vajpayee sworn in as prime minister of India.
April 10. Northern Ireland pow[er-]sharing agreement reached.
May 6. Border dispute breaks ... [E]ritrea and Ethiopia.
May 11. India conducts unde...
May 21. President Haji Moh... [a]nd is succeeded by Vice Presiden...
May 28. Pakistan conducts ...
August 2. Rebellion laun... Congo against the Kabila ...
August 7. Terrorist bomb... Dar es Salaam, Tanzania ...
September 27. German... bid by Social Democrat...
October 23. Wye acc... Netanyahu and PLO l...
October 31. Iraq ann... from UNSCOM.

1999, **January 1.** Eleven ... tary Union (EMU...

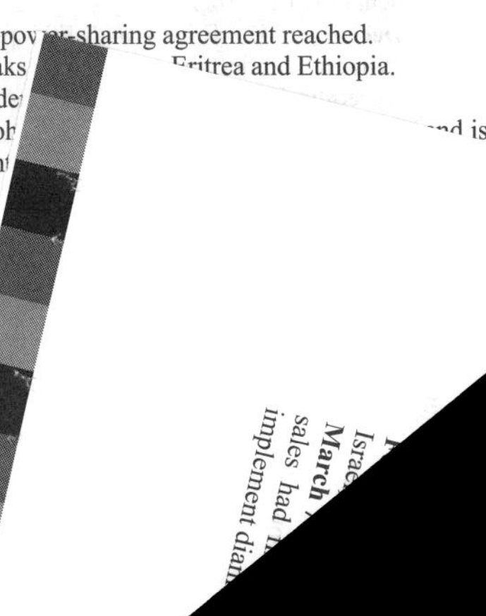

toward replacement of national currencies by euro notes and coins in 2002.
February 6. King Hussein of Jordan dies.
February 12. Impeached U.S. president Bill Clinton acquitted by Senate on charges of perjury before a grand jury and obstruction of justice.
February 27. Gen. Olusegun Obasanjo, former military ruler in 1970s, elected civilian president of Nigeria (inaugurated May 29, ending most recent period of military rule).
March 12. Czech Republic, Hungary, and Poland join NATO.
March 24. Responding to Serbian "ethnic cleansing" of Kosovo's Albanian population, NATO launches a campaign against Yugoslavia that is the biggest military operation in Europe since World War II.
June 7. Indonesia concludes first free national election in 45 years.
June 10. NATO officially terminates Operation Allied Force against Yugoslavia; UN Security Council authorizes deployment of peacekeeping forces to Kosovo.
July 27. King Hassan II of Morocco dies.
August 30. East Timorese voters overwhelmingly vote for independence from Indonesia, leading to UN intervention following massive violence by anti-independence militias.
October 12. Gen. Pervez Musharraf declares himself chief executive of Pakistan, following military coup against elected government of Prime Minister Mohammad Nawaz Sharif.
October 14. U.S. Senate rejects Comprehensive Test Ban Treaty (CTBT) by 51–48 vote.
October 20. Abdurrahman Wahid elected president of Indonesia by People's Consultative Assembly.
December 19. Portugal returns Macao to China, ending 442 years of rule.
December 19. Center-right groups wrest control of State Duma from plurality Communist Party in Russian parliamentary elections.
December 31. U.S. officially returns Panama Canal to Panama, ending 89 years of Canal Zone control.
December 31. Boris Yeltsin resigns Russian presidency and is succeeded in an acting capacity by Prime Minister Vladimir Putin.

2000, **March 18.** Chen Shui-bian elected as first non-Kuomintang president of Taiwan.
March 26. Vladimir Putin elected president of Russia.
April 6. Zimbabwe's Parliament passes controversial Land Acquisition Act, permitting uncompensated appropriation of white-owned farms and redistribution of farmland to blacks.
April 14. 1993's START II enters into effect after Russian ratification.
April 21. Russian State Duma ratifies Comprehensive Test Ban Treaty.
May 19. Armed coup launched against multiethnic government of Fiji.
May 24. Israel withdraws final troops from "security zone" in Lebanon, ending 22 years of occupation.
June 10. President Hafiz al-Assad of Syria dies.
June 13. Chairman Kim Jong Il of North Korea and President Kim Dae Jung of South Korea begin historic three-day summit in Pyongyang, North Korea.
July 2. Vicente Fox of National Action Party wins Mexican presidential election, ending 71 years of rule by Institutional Revolutionary Party.
September 28. Visit by Israeli opposition leader Ariel Sharon to Temple Mount (Haram al-Sharif) triggers new Palestinian intifada.
October 7. Vojislav Koštunica sworn in as president of Yugoslavia following capitulation of President Slobodan Milošević, who lost September 24 election.
October 12. Seventeen U.S. sailors die in suicide attack on USS *Cole* off the coast of Aden, Yemen.
November 17. Alberto Fujimori, having fled to Japan, resigns as president of Peru.
December 12. Eritrea and Ethiopia sign peace agreement, ending 19-month border war.
December 13. U.S. Vice President Al Gore, despite plurality of popular votes, concedes November 7 presidential election to George W. Bush, one day after Supreme Court decision effectively ended vote recounting in electorally decisive Florida.

2001, **January 7.** Nineteen years after coming to power by coup, Ghana's Jerry Rawlings hands over presidency to newly elected John Kufuor.
January 16. President Laurent Kabila of Democratic Republic of Congo assassinated.
January 20. Philippine vice president Gloria Macapagal Arroyo assumes presidency, protests having forced her predecessor, Joseph Estrada, from office.
[illegible]ebruary 6. Ariel Sharon wins special prime ministerial election in [illegible], defeating Prime Minister Ehud Barak by wide margin.
[illegible]7. Responding to increasing evidence that international diamond [illegible] financed African conflicts, UN Security Council votes to [illegible]ond embargo against Liberia (effective May 7).

March 28. The administration of U.S. president George W. Bush announces its intention to renounce 1997 Kyoto Protocol on reducing emissions of greenhouse gases.
April 26. Junichiro Koizumi, after unexpected victory in intraparty presidential balloting, sworn in as Japan's prime minister.
May 1. U.S. president George W. Bush announces decision to unilaterally deploy antimissile defense shield.
May 13. Former prime minister Silvio Berlusconi leads center-right alliance to victory in Italian general election.
June 28. Former Yugoslav president Slobodan Milošević indicted for crimes against humanity and other offenses and handed over to International Criminal Tribunal for the former Yugoslavia.
July 1. Crown Prince Dipendra of Nepal kills King Birendra and other members of royal family before committing suicide.
July 16. Russia and China conclude 20-year treaty of friendship and cooperation.
July 23. Peace agreement signed in Arusha, Tanzania, in latest effort to end eight-year civil war in Burundi.
July 23. Indonesia's People's Consultative Assembly unanimously removes President Abdurrahman Wahid from office and elects Vice President Megawati Sukarnoputri as his successor.
August 30. Bougainville secessionists sign peace agreement with Papua New Guinea government, ending 12-year conflict.
September 11. In the worst terrorist attacks in U.S. history, militants fly two hijacked commercial airliners into New York's World Trade Center twin towers, precipitating their collapse and causing more than 2,500 deaths. A third hijacked jet damages Department of Defense headquarters (the Pentagon) in Washington, D.C., and a fourth crashes in rural Pennsylvania.
September 23. Irish Republican Army (IRA) announces first confirmed "decommissioning" of weaponry, thereby preventing collapse of Northern Ireland power-sharing government.
October 5. First of five victims dies from exposure to anthrax spores mailed to U.S. government offices in Washington and to media outlets in Florida and New York.
October 7. U.S.-led air assault begins against al-Qaida bases and Taliban regime in Afghanistan in response to September 11 attacks in the United States.
October 29–November 10. Meeting in Marrakesh, Morocco, 164 countries negotiate final text of Kyoto Protocol to 1992 Framework Convention on Climate Change.
December 5. Hamid Karzai appointed head of interim Afghan government by factions meeting in Bonn, Germany; two days later Taliban surrenders Kandahar, its final stronghold.
December 12. China accedes to WTO.
December 20. Argentine president Fernando de la Rúa resigns in response to civil disturbances precipitated by government efforts aimed at controlling mounting financial crisis.

2002, **January 1.** The euro becomes legal tender in 12 European states.
February 22. Jonas Savimbi, leader of National Union for the Total Independence of Angola (UNITA), is killed.
April 4. UNITA and Angolan government sign cease-fire agreement ending civil war that dates from Angola's independence from Portugal in 1975.
April 11. International Criminal Court wins ratification by 60th UN member state, triggering its entry into force in sixty days, or July 1. United States does not ratify treaty, citing jeopardy to American citizens overseas.
April 14. Former guerilla leader José Gusmão elected first president of Timor-Leste (East Timor).
May 13. U.S. president George W. Bush and Russian president Vladimir Putin announce pact to cut nuclear arsenals by up to two-thirds over ten years.
May 20. International community recognizes Timor-Leste's independence from Indonesia.
June 13. Thirty-year-old Anti-Ballistic Missile Treaty lapses six months after President George W. Bush announced U.S. withdrawal.
June 13. Hamid Karzai elected interim president of Afghanistan.
June 16. Israel begins construction of 217-mile barrier in West Bank to thwart attacks.
July 1. International Criminal Court convenes in The Hague.
July 8. More than 30 African leaders meet in Durban to establish the African Union (AU) as the successor to the OAU.
July 30. President Paul Kagame of Rwanda and President Joseph Kabila of the Democratic Republic of the Congo sign peace agreement.
October 14. UK's secretary of state for Northern Ireland assumes powers of the suspended Northern Ireland Executive after Ulster Unionist Party withdraws its support from the Assembly.
November 21. Bulgaria, Estonia, Latvia, Lithuania, Romania, and Slovenia join NATO.

November 27. After a nearly four year hiatus, UN weapons inspectors return to Iraq to search for weapons of mass destruction.

December 4. Israeli prime minister Ariel Sharon endorses U.S. proposal for a Palestinian state in parts of the West Bank and Gaza Strip.

2003, January 9. North Korea withdraws from nuclear nonproliferation treaty.

January 27. Chief UN weapons inspector Hans Blix cites Iraq for noncooperation while Mohamed El-Baradei, the head of the International Atomic Energy Agency (IAEA) reports no evidence found of Iraqi nuclear weapons production.

February 4. Parliament of Federal Republic of Yugoslavia adopts new constitution renaming the country Serbia and Montenegro.

March 7. In the a report of the UN Monitoring, Verification and Inspection Commission (UNMOVIC), Hans Blix reports improved Iraqi cooperation but lack of Iraqi documentation.

March 14. U.S. Centers for Disease Control and Prevention activates emergency operations center after travelers from Asia arrive in North America with an atypical pneumonia dubbed by the World Health Organization "severe acute respiratory syndrome" (SARS).

March 17. Facing certain veto by France, the United States, Britain, and Spain withdraw proposed Security Council resolution authorizing war against Iraq.

March 19. United States and allies attack Iraq.

April 9. Baghdad falls to U.S. forces.

May 22. Security Council Resolution 1483 ends economic sanctions on Iraq and recognizes United States and United Kingdom as occupying powers.

June 5. Israeli prime minister Ariel Sharon and Palestinian prime minister Mahmoud Abbas commit during summit in Aqaba, Jordan, to "roadmap" peace plan proposed by the United States.

June 6. French peacekeepers deploy in the Democratic Republic of the Congo to quell tribal warfare.

August 4. Peacekeepers from West African states arrive in Liberia to quell fighting between government and antigovernment forces.

August 7. Liberian president Charles Taylor resigns.

August 11. NATO takes command of peacekeeping operations in Afghanistan in first such mission outside Europe in alliance history.

September 14. Sweden's voters buck government to reject euro—56.1 percent to 41.8 percent—thereby retaining krona as national currency.

December 13. U.S. military captures Saddam Hussein.

December 19. Libyan leader Muammar Abu Minyar al-Qadhafi pledges to abandon pursuit of weapons of mass destruction.

2004, January 4. Afghan *loya jirga* approves constitution of Islamic Republic of Afghanistan.

February 29. Haitian president Jean Bertrand Aristide resigns and goes into exile.

March 11. Al-Qaida bombers target Madrid commuter trains.

March 12. South Korean National Assembly impeaches President Roh Moo Hyun for election law violations.

April 24. UN-sponsored referendums on Cyprus end in split vote: 75 percent of Greek Cypriots reject reunification plan while 65 percent of Turkish Cypriots approve.

April 28. U.S. news program *60 Minutes II* broadcasts photos of U.S. troops abusing prisoners in Iraq's Abu Ghraib prison, publicizing an investigation under way in the military.

May 1. Ten countries—Cyprus, Czech Republic, Estonia, Hungary, Latvia, Lithuania, Malta, Poland, Slovak Republic, and Slovenia—join European Union, bringing the number of member states to 25.

May 9. Chechen president Akhmad Kadyrov assassinated in Grozny.

May 26. Conflict between Arabs and blacks continues in Darfur region of Sudan despite accord between Islamic government and Sudan People's Liberation Army.

June 18. IAEA censures but does not impose sanctions on Iran for covering up its nuclear activity.

June 28. U.S. administrator in Iraq L. Paul Bremer III transfers sovereignty to Iraqi Prime Minister Iyad Allawi.

November 3. Interim president Hamid Karzai declared official winner of Afghan presidential election.

November 11. Long-time Palestinian leader and Palestinian Authority president Yasir Arafat dies.

November 27. Ukrainian parliament nullifies results of November 21 election runoff, citing election fraud; Prime Minister Viktor Yanukovich claims a narrow 3 percent margin over challenger Viktor Yushchenko.

December 26. Yushchenko defeats Yanukovich in Ukrainian presidential runoff.

December 26. Tsunami hits Southeast Asia, killing an estimated 225,000 people and affecting a dozen states in Asia and Africa.

2005, January 30. Iraqis vote for representatives to national and provincial assemblies in first democratic elections since 1953.

February 1. King Gyanendra Bir Bikram Shah Dev of Nepal declares a state of emergency, dissolves coalition government, and arrests leading politicians, citing his constitutional authority and the lack of progress toward holding elections.

February 14. Former prime minister of Lebanon Rafik al-Hariri and others die in a car bomb explosion, leading to anti-Syria demonstrations and international pressure on Syria to withdraw its troops from the country.

February 16. Kyoto Protocol to UN Framework Convention on Climate Change takes effect. United States is not a party to the agreement.

March 16. Israel turns over control of Jericho to Palestinians.

April 2. Pope John Paul II dies.

April 19. Conclave of cardinals elects Cardinal Joseph Ratzinger of Germany as pope. Ratzinger takes the name Benedict XVI.

April 26. Last Syrian troops leave Lebanon, ending 29-year stay.

May 29. French voters reject proposed European constitution by margin of 55 percent to 45 percent in nationwide referendum.

June 16. After European constitution is voted down in nationwide referendums in Netherlands and France, leaders of EU halt efforts to ratify the draft constitution.

July 7. Suicide bombers in London kill 52 people, including themselves, and wound hundreds.

August 1. King Fahd ibn Abd al-Aziz Al Saud of Saudi Arabia dies; Prince Abdullah assumes the throne.

August 10. Iran removes UN seals it voluntarily accepted at nuclear production sites eight months previously and begins converting raw uranium into gas for enrichment.

August 15. Indonesia and the Free Aceh Movement sign a peace accord ending 30 years of civil war.

August 15. Israel begins withdrawing more than 8,700 Jewish settlers from the Gaza Strip, enabling Palestinians to assume control of the area.

August 29. Hurricane Katrina lashes U.S. city of New Orleans, flooding the city and coastal areas, and killing over 1,500; federal emergency response is widely criticized.

September 18. Afghanistan holds its first democratic parliamentary elections in more than 25 years.

October 10. German legislative parties agree to resolve their September parliamentary election disputes by creating a Grand Coalition that includes Angela Merkel as Germany's first woman chancellor.

October 15. Iraqis endorse new constitution with 79 percent "yes" vote.

November 21. Voters defeat proposed new constitution in Kenya.

December 15. Iraq elects its first permanent parliament since the removal of President Saddam Hussein.

December 18. Bolivia holds its presidential election after the resignation of President Carlos Mesa in June because of widespread unrest; Evo Morales, the candidate of the Movement to Socialism, wins with 51.1 percent of the vote.

December 23. Lech Kaczyński sworn in as president of Poland after winning the election on the second runoff.

2006, January 4. Israeli leader Ariel Sharon suffers a second, catastrophic stroke and slips into a coma. Ehud Olmert named acting prime minister.

January 15. Ellen Johnson-Sirleaf sworn in as president of Liberia, thereby becoming Africa's first female president.

January 15. In a runoff election, center-left candidate Michelle Bachelet wins 53 percent of the vote to become Chile's first female president.

January 25. Hamas wins a majority in elections to the Palestinian Legislative Council, ending Fatah's dominance.

February 7. René Préval of the *Lespwa* coalition elected president of Haiti.

February 14. Iran announces it has successfully begun small-scale nuclear enrichment.

February 28. Former opposition leader Milorad Dodik confirmed as prime minister of the Serb Republic of Bosnia and Herzegovina.

April 19. The South Korean parliament approves Han Myeong Sook as prime minister following the resignation of Lee Hae Chan on March 14.

April 23. Prime Minister Ferenc Gyurcsány's coalition, led by the Hungarian Socialist Party, wins runoff parliamentary elections, making it the first administration to win reelection in Hungary since the fall of communism.

April 27. Following weeks of demonstrations in Nepal in opposition to King Gyanendra's continued absolute power, consensus candidate Girija Prasad Koirala appointed prime minister by the king, who earlier had announced his intention to step down as chair of the council of ministers.

May 4. Ehud Olmert, leader of the recently launched Kadima party, forms a coalition government in Israel following the *Knesset* balloting on March 28 in which Kadima secured a plurality of seats.

May 5. The Sudanese government and the leader of Darfur's main rebel group agree to a cease-fire after three years of hostilities and the displacement of an estimated 2 million people.

May 17. Romano Prodi, leader of the new Union coalition, returns to the premiership of Italy after the Union secured a majority of the seats in the legislative poll of April 9–10.

May 20. Nurad Jawad al-Maliki forms national unity government in Iraq.
May 26. Nepal's prime minister Girija Prasad Koirala and rebel Maoist leader Prachanda sign a cease-fire code of conduct, bringing a degree of political stability to the country.
June 3. Former Yugoslav republic of Montenegro declares independence from Serbia, following a May 21 independence referendum passed by a vote of 55.5 percent to 44.5 percent.
June 4. Alan García wins Peru's runoff presidential election, regaining control 16 years after his first presidential term ended in economic distress and rebel violence.
June 5. Islamic forces seize control of the Somali capital from a U.S.-backed, warlord-led coalition.
June 7. U.S. air strike kills Abu Musab al-Zarqawi, the leader of al-Qaida in Iraq.
June 27. Economic reformer and Communist Party chief Nguyen Minh Triet elected president of Vietnam after the country's top three leaders officially retire.
July 11. Bombs attributed to Islamic militants explode on rush hour commuter trains in Mumbai, India, killing 182 people and injuring more than 800.
July 12. The Lebanese Shiite Muslim group Hezbollah kills three Israeli soldiers and captures two others during a raid into Israel; Israel subsequently responds with air-strike bombing of Lebanon to which Hezbollah retaliates by launching rockets and missiles into Israel.
July 31. Cuban president Fidel Castro temporarily transfers power to his brother while recuperating from abdominal surgery, marking the first time he has relinquished power in 47 years.
July 31. The UN Security Council passes a resolution giving Iran until August 31 to suspend its nuclear enrichment program or face the threat of economic and diplomatic sanctions.
August 3. Viktor Yanukovych of the pro-Russian Party of Regions named prime minister of Ukraine following protracted negotiations with the Orange Revolution parties.
August 10. British officials arrest 24 British citizens believed to be party to a terrorist plot to use liquid explosives to blow up airplanes flying from Britain to the United States.
August 14. Israel and Hezbollah declare a cease-fire.
September 12. In a speech at Regensburg University in his native Germany, Pope Benedict XVI quotes a Byzantine emperor who linked Islam with coerced and violent conversions, prompting outrage in Islamic communities around the world.
September 19. A military coup led by Gen. Sonthi Boonyaratkalin, with the support of the royal family and numerous citizens, overthrows Prime Minister Thaksin Shinawatra of Thailand, who is out of the country to attend the UN General Assembly in New York.
October 8. North Korea announces its first successful underground nuclear weapons test, prompting widespread international condemnation.
October 14. In a unanimous vote, the UN Security Council approves trade and travel sanctions against North Korea in response to the alleged nuclear test six days earlier.
October 27. After failed talks with the West, Iran restarts its nuclear program, claiming its reactors are for peaceful purposes, despite concerns expressed by the UN and Western nations.
November 7. In U.S. midterm elections, Democrats gain control of the House of Representatives and the Senate, giving the party control of Congress for the first time in 12 years.
November 21. The Nepalese government signs a Comprehensive Peace Agreement with former Maoist insurgents.
November 27. Leftist Rafael Correa defeats Alvaro Noboa in Ecuadorian presidential elections.
December 1. Conservative Felipe Calderón inaugurated as president of Mexico amid controversy over his victory against leftist Andrés Manuel López Obrador in balloting on July 6.
December 3. Venezuelan president Hugo Chávez wins reelection with 61 percent of the vote.
December 5. The Fijian military, led by Commander Frank Bainimarama, takes over the government of Prime Minister Laisenia Qarase in the fourth coup in 20 years.
December 6. Joseph Kabila sworn in as president of the Democratic Republic of the Congo, making him the nation's first elected president in forty years.
December 14. King of Bhutan Jigme Singye Wangchuk abdicates the throne in favor of his son, Crown Prince Jigme Khesar Namgyal Wangchuk.
December 21. Turkmen president Saparmurad Niyazov, the country's leader since 1985, dies.
December 23. Resolution 1737 is unanimously approved by the UN Security Council, imposing sanctions on Iran for failing to comply with resolution 1696, which prohibited it from enrichment activities.
December 24–28. As it authorizes aerial bombings in Somalia, Ethiopia formally admits to having troops engaged in battle within the borders of Somalia. Somali government forces, backed by Ethiopian troops, retake the capital, Mogadishu, from the Islamic Courts Union.
December 30. Former Iraqi president Saddam Hussein hanged, having been found guilty of crimes against humanity by an Iraqi tribunal on November 5.
December 30. Spanish Basque separatist group ETA detonates a bomb at Madrid's Barajas Airport, killing 2 people and injuring 26, thereby ending its cease-fire and prompting Spanish prime minister Jose Luis Rodriguez Zapatero to suspend peace talks.

2007, **January 1.** Romania and Bulgaria become members of the EU.
January 1. Ban Ki Moon, theretofore the foreign minister of South Korea, succeeds Kofi Annan as secretary general of the UN.
January 10. Sandinista leader Daniel Ortega returns to the presidency of Nicaragua.
January 11. President Iajuddin Ahmed of Bangladesh, with the backing of the military, postpones legislative elections indefinitely following demonstrations, strikes, and other disruptions against the caretaker administration charged with conducting the elections.
February 11. Gurbanguly Berdymukhammedov, acting president of Turkmenistan, secures 89.2 percent of the vote in presidential elections.
February 13. North Korea agrees to nuclear disarmament steps in exchange for energy assistance.
February 14. U.S. and Iraqi forces launch a new security sweep in Iraq as the beginning of the George W. Bush administration's "surge," under which some 30,000 additional U.S. troops are slated for deployment in Iraq.
March 4. Peace agreement signed in Côte d'Ivoire, preparing the groundwork for formation of a new national unity government.
March 17. The Palestinian Legislative Council approves a Fatah/Hamas unity government led by Ismail Haniyeh of Hamas.
April 1. Former Maoist insurgents join the cabinet in Nepal.
April 11. Al-Qaida claims responsibility for two suicide car bombings in Algeria, one targeting the prime minister (uninjured), that resulted in 33 deaths in the capital of Algiers.
May 6. Conservative Nicolas Sarkozy wins the French presidential runoff election with 53.1 percent of the vote over Socialist Ségolène Royal.
May 8. Limited self-rule returns to Northern Ireland based on the St. Andrews Agreement of October 2006 and subsequent agreements between unionist and republican/nationalist parties.
May 12. Su Tseng-Chang resigns as the premier of the Republic of China (Taiwan) following a loss in a presidential primary election; President Chen Shui-bian replaces him with Chang Chun-hsiung on May 14.
June 14. Palestinian president Mahmoud Abbas dissolves the Palestinian government and installs emergency rule in the wake of Hamas's recent takeover of the Gaza Strip.
June 17. The Union for a Popular Movement, led by President Nicolas Sarkozy, secures a comfortable majority following the second round of legislative elections in France.
June 18. The United States and EU restore foreign aid to the Palestinian Authority, excluding the Hamas-controlled Gaza Strip.
July 18. IAEA inspectors confirm the closure of all five nuclear reactors in North Korea as six-party talks resume in Beijing.
June 27. Gordon Brown succeeds Tony Blair as prime minister of the United Kingdom.
August 28. Despite military opposition, Abdullah Gul of the Justice and Development Party is elected as the first Islamist president of Turkey.
September 2. Talks begin between the United States and North Korea, leading North Korea to agree to dismantle its nuclear weapons program in exchange for economic and diplomatic overtures.
September 19. Buddhist monks march in Myanmar as part of an historic prodemocracy standoff with the nation's junta dictatorship, prompting a government crackdown several days later.
September 25. Yasuo Fukuda elected prime minister of Japan in succession to Shinzo Abe, who resigned on September 12.
October 3. North Korea agrees to release details of its nuclear production and to close all of its nuclear facilities by the end of the year.
October 17. Former Pakistani prime minister Benazir Bhutto returns to the country after eight years of self-imposed exile.
October 22. Poland's opposition parties win the parliamentary election, ending two years of rule by the nationalistic Law and Justice Party.
October 28. Argentine first lady Cristina Kirchner elected to succeed her husband, *peronista* Nestor Kirchner, as president.
November 3. Pakistani president Pervez Musharraf declares a state of emergency in Pakistan.
November 4. Center-left candidate Alvaro Colom Caballeros wins the runoff presidential election in Guatemala.
November 7. Georgian president Mikhail Saakashvili declares a state of emergency amid protests calling for his resignation.

November 24. Lebanese prime minister Fouad Siniroa becomes leader of a caretaker government after President Émile Lahoud's term expires and presidential elections are delayed.

November 27. U.S.-sponsored peace talks begin in Annapolis, Maryland, to negotiate a peace agreement between Israeli and Palestinian leaders.

November 29. Pervez Musharraf sworn in for another five-year term as Pakistan's president after relinquishing his military posts.

December 2. Russian president Vladimir Putin's party secures 70 percent of the vote in Russian parliamentary elections.

December 2. National referendum in Venezuela defeats constitutional revision proposed by President Hugo Chávez that would have permitted him to run for an unlimited number of terms.

December 3. Kevin Rudd of the Australian Labor Party, which won a majority in lower house elections on November 24, becomes prime minister in succession to John Howard of the Liberal Party of Australia, who served as prime minister for 11 years.

December 13. Leaders of the member states of the EU sign the Lisbon Treaty, which, if ratified by all member states, will reform and reorganize EU institutions.

December 18. The ruling African National Congress (ANC) rejects the candidacy of South African president Thabo Mbeki and instead elects Jacob Zuma as ANC president, thereby making Zuma the presumptive ANC candidate for the 2009 national presidential election.

December 18. Yulia Tymoshenko returns as prime minister of Ukraine to head a coalition government dominated by the Orange Revolution parties, who secured a slim majority in the legislative poll of September 30 that was prompted by intense conflict between President Viktor Yushchenko and Prime Minister Viktor Yanukovych.

December 23. Thailand's People Power Party (supportive of ousted prime minister Thaksin Shinawatra) wins the Thai parliamentary elections.

December 27. Former Pakistani prime minister Benazir Bhutto assassinated at a campaign rally.

December 30. Kenya's election commission declares incumbent Mwai Kibaki the winner of the December 27 national election, sparking violent protests from opposition party supporters, who charge that the election was rigged.

2008, January 5. Mikhail Saakashvili reelected president of Georgia in snap elections; 77 percent of voters endorse proposed NATO membership for Georgia.

January 8. Joint U.S./Iraqi forces launch campaign against militias in Iraq.

January 12. Opposition Nationalist Party (Kuomintang) defeats ruling Democratic Progressive Party in legislative elections in Taiwan.

January 13. Croatian Assembly approves new coalition government led by Ivo Sanader of the Croatian Democratic Union, a conservative, nationalist party.

January 15. Ukraine formally requests a Membership Action Plan from NATO.

January 22. The military's Council for National Security in Thailand announces its dissolution and acceptance of the December legislative election results.

January 24. Italian prime minister Romano Prodi offers his resignation following no-confidence vote in the Senate.

January 28. Samak Sundaravej, considered a "proxy" for former prime minister Thaksin Shinawatra, elected prime minister by Thailand's House of Representatives. (Samak forms a coalition government on February 6.)

February 3. Pro-Western president Boris Tadić reelected in Serbia over nationalist rival Tomislav Nikolić, who had led in the first round of balloting.

February 7. Ten years of rule in Belize by the People's United Party ends when the United Democratic Party (UDP) wins legislative elections; the UDP's Dean Barrow subsequently becomes independent Belize's first black prime minister.

February 11. Timor-Leste's president José Ramos-Horta barely survives assassination attempt by rebel soldiers, prompting the deployment of additional Australian peacekeeping forces.

February 13. Australian prime minister Kevin Rudd formally apologizes for the past mistreatment of indigenous Aborigines by "white Australia."

February 15. Václav Klaus, an opponent of additional European integration, narrowly reelected president of the Czech Republic by a joint session of parliament.

February 17. Prime Minister Hashim Thaçi declares Kosovo independent, prompting fierce criticism from Serbia and Russia but quick recognition from the United States, the United Kingdom, France, Germany, Japan, and others.

February 18. Opposition parties dominate legislative elections in Pakistan in what is generally perceived as a referendum on the rule of President Musharraf.

February 24. Raúl Castro confirmed by the National Assembly of People's Power as president of Cuba's Council of State and Council of Ministers after Fidel Castro had announced earlier that he would not accept reelection to those posts.

February 27. Israel launches air and ground offensive in Gaza Strip.

February 28. Dimitrios Christofias, leader of the Progressive Party of the Working People, inaugurated as the first communist president of Cyprus following his second-round election victory on February 24.

March 1. Colombian military initiates anti-FARC campaign in Ecuador, prompting a regional crisis (later diffused by Colombia's apology for violating Ecuador's territory).

March 2. Dmitri Medvedev, a first deputy prime minister, elected president of Russia as Vladimir Putin's handpicked successor.

March 5. Separatist legislature in South Ossetia appeals for the international community's recognition of independence in view of recent developments regarding Kosovo.

March 8. Coalition government collapses in Serbia.

March 9. Ruling Spanish Socialist Workers' Party wins legislative elections.

March 19. Prime Minister Vasile Tarlev resigns in Moldova, paving the way for Zinaida Grecianîi, a deputy prime minister, to become the country's first female prime minister.

March 20. New coalition government, headed by former opposition leader Yves Leterme, installed in Belgium after nine months of negotiations following the June 2007 legislative elections.

March 21. The presidents of Cyprus and the Turkish Republic of Northern Cyprus agree to new reunification talks.

March 22. Ma Ying-jeou of the Nationalist Party (Kuomintang) elected president of Taiwan.

March 24. The lower house in Pakistan elects Yusuf Raza Gilani, an ally of the late Benazir Bhutto, as prime minister of Pakistan.

March 24. Bhutan Peace and Prosperity Party wins landslide victory in two-party elections to the National Assembly in Bhutan.

March 29. Opposition claims victory for Morgan Tsvangirai in first round of troubled presidential balloting in Zimbabwe.

April 2–4. NATO summit approves Membership Action Plans for Albania and Croatia but not for Macedonia (due to Greece's objection) or Georgia and Ukraine (despite support from the United States); however, the summit appears to endorse eventual membership for Georgia and Ukraine, angering Russia.

April 8. President Ahmadinejad of Iran announces plans for additional uranium enrichment.

April 9. New constitution, providing for a multiparty system headed by a president and a bicameral legislature, proposed by Myanmar's military junta.

April 9. The conservative Grand National Party wins legislative balloting in South Korea.

April 9. Jigme Yoser Thinley of the Bhutan Peace and Prosperity Party installed as prime minister of Bhutan.

April 10. Maoists secure legislative victory in Nepal.

April 13. Power-sharing cabinet announced in Kenya; Mwai Kibaki remains as president and opposition leader Raila Odinga named prime minister.

April 14. Peter Robinson elected unopposed to succeed Rev. Ian Paisley as leader of the Democratic Unionist Party in Northern Ireland.

April 15. The Iraqi Accord Front, a Sunni coalition, returns to the Shiite-dominated Iraqi cabinet.

April 20. Fernando Lugo, a leftist former Catholic bishop, elected president of Paraguay with the support of numerous opposition parties, thereby ending more than 60 years of rule by the Colorado Party.

April 27. Coalition government collapses in Hungary.

May 2. Election commission in Zimbabwe declares that opposition candidate Tsvangirai won only 48 percent of the vote in the March 29 balloting, thereby necessitating a runoff between him and President Mugabe, who finished second in the first round.

May 7. Brian Cowen of Fianna Fáil elected prime minister by the lower house of the legislature in Ireland, following Bertie Ahern's resignation from the post (effective May 6) amidst corruption investigations.

May 8. Silvio Berlusconi becomes prime minister for the third time in Italy following legislative elections on April 13–14.

May 8. Former president Vladimir Putin confirmed as prime minister by the Russian State Duma.

May 16. United States resumes food aid to North Korea after receiving information from that country on the history of its nuclear program.

May 21. Resumption confirmed of indirect talks (the first since 2000) between Israel and Syria.

May 21. Supporters of Georgian president Mikhail Saakashvili dominate legislative balloting.
May 25. Gen. Michel Suleiman elected president of Lebanon by the National Assembly as part of the May 21 agreement designed to stem strife between Hezbollah (and other Shiite groups) and progovernment forces. Prime Minister Fouad Siniroa subsequently forms a new cabinet that includes members of Hezbollah.
May 26. Cease-fire announced between the government of Burundi and the last active rebel group.
May 28. Nepal's Constituent Assembly agrees to abolish the monarchy (with the king's cooperation) and establish a federal republic.
June 2. Bhutan's National Assembly approves draft constitution transferring power from the king to a government formed by the leading legislative party.
June 5. Northern Ireland's National Assembly elects Peter Robinson of the Democratic Unionist Party as first minister.
June 11. Upper house of Japan's legislature passes censure motion against Prime Minister Yasuo Fukuda.
June 12. Irish voters reject the EU's proposed reform treaty, jeopardizing the pact's implementation.
June 18. Israel and Hamas initiate a cease-fire.
June 26. The interim prime minister of Nepal announces his resignation as efforts to establish a transitional government falter.
June 27. Pro-European coalition government announced in Serbia.
June 27. Zimbabwean president Robert Mugabe wins highly controversial second-round presidential balloting after first-round leader Morgan Tsvangirai withdraws to protest violence against his supporters in the run-up to the election.
June 29. Ruling Mongolian People's Revolutionary Party wins legislative balloting, prompting massive antigovernment demonstrations by protesters alleging electoral fraud.
July 14. Prosecutors in the International Criminal Court charge President al-Bashir of Sudan with genocide in connection with events in Darfur.
July 23. EU Commission suspends $800 million in aid to Bulgaria because of corruption concerns.
July 27. Ruling Cambodian People's Party wins two-thirds majority in legislative elections.
July 30. Israeli prime minister Ehud Olmert announces his intention to resign.
August 6. Military coup overthrows the government in Mauritania.
August 7. Georgian forces enter South Ossetia, triggering massive response by Russia in which Russian forces move deeply into Georgia proper. Russia subsequently recognizes the independence of South Ossetia and Abkhazia.
August 11. Bolivian president Evo Morales survives recall referendum.
August 15. Maoist Pushpa Kamal Dahal elected prime minister of Nepal.
August 17. Coalition government in Pakistan vows to initiate impeachment proceedings against President Musharraf.
August 18. Pakistani president Musharraf resigns.
August 19. Zambian president Levy Mwanawasa dies.
September 1. Japanese prime minister Fukuda resigns; Taro Aso elected leader of the Liberal Democratic Party on September 22 and installed as prime minister on September 24.
September 1. Massive crowds demonstrate in Thailand against Prime Minister Samak, prompting him to impose a state of emergency.
September 5. Senate in Haiti approves government of new prime minister Michèle Pierre-Louis.
September 5–6. The Popular Movement for the Liberation of Angola dominates the first legislative balloting since 1992.
September 7. U.S. government approves takeover of two privately owned (albeit government-sponsored) mortgage companies as an unprecedented financial intervention develops, in which Congress ultimately authorizes a $700 billion bailout of banking system in the midst of a global "credit crisis" and steep declines in the stock market.
September 8. Asif Ali Zardari, the widower of Benazir Bhutto, elected president of Pakistan in a vote by the federal legislature and provincial assemblies.
September 9. Thai prime minister Samak forced to resign; succeeded on September 17 by Somchai Wongsawat, the brother-in-law of former prime minister Thaksin.
September 11. Power-sharing agreement announced in Zimbabwe, although implementation proves contentious.
September 16. Coalition government collapses in Ukraine.
September 17. Tzipi Livni elected new leader of Kadima in Israel and announces effort to form new coalition government.
September 20. South African President Mbeki agrees to resign under pressure from the African National Congress (ANC); Kgalema Motlanthe, deputy leader of the ANC, elected as Mbeki's successor by the National Assembly on September 25.
September 21. Opposition Social Democrats win narrow plurality in lower-house balloting in Slovenia; party leader forms coalition government on November 11 with support of other leftist parties.
September 28. Far-right parties gain ground in early legislative elections in Austria but ruling centrist parties form new coalition government on December 2.
September 28. Supporters of President Lukashenka win all seats in lower-house balloting in Belarus.
September 28. New constitution (proposed by the leftist government) endorsed in national referendum in Ecuador.
September 29. Government in Iceland forced to nationalize the country's third largest bank as value of the krona plummets in midst of global financial crisis.
October 5. German government announces guarantee of all personal bank deposits to protect against banking meltdown; subsequently announces $760 billion support package for banks.
October 7. Occupation of government offices by protesters in Thailand intensifies.
October 8. Malaysian prime minister Abdullah announces he will resign in March 2009 in the wake of his party's poor performance in the March 2008 legislative elections.
October 8. UK government announces the partial nationalization of several banks and other bailout initiatives in extension of measures first initiated in September to combat the global financial crisis.
October 11. North Korea removed from U.S. list of state sponsors of terrorism after agreeing to resume dismantling of controversial nuclear reactor.
October 12 and 26. Conservative opposition party wins plurality in legislative balloting in Lithuania and heads four-party center-right coalition government appointed on December 9 under the leadership of Andrius Kubilius..
October 13. French government authorizes $480 billion support package for banks.
October 26. Tzipi Livni declares her efforts to form a new coalition government in Israel unsuccessful, setting the stage for new legislative elections in early 2009.
October 26. Fighting intensifies in eastern Democratic Republic of the Congo, ultimately displacing 250,000 people.
October 28. Mohamed Nasheed, a journalist and former political prisoner, elected president of Maldives, defeating incumbent Maumoon Gayoom, who had held the post since 1978.
October 30. Rupiah Banda of the ruling Movement for Multiparty Democracy narrowly elected president of Zambia.
October 30. Canadian prime minister Stephen Harper forms another minority government following snap legislative elections on October 14.
November 2. Pirates hijack oil tanker off the coast of Somalia.
November 4. Barack Obama elected president of the United States, and his Democratic Party extends its legislative control.
November 7. Mass demonstrations in Georgia demand resignation of President Mikhail Saakashvili.
November 8. Opposition National Party wins legislative balloting in New Zealand, permitting party leader John Key to form a coalition government on November 17.
November 9. China unveils $586 billion economic stimulus plan for the next two years.
November 10. More than 100 dissidents sentenced to jail terms in Myanmar.
November 25. Referendum in Greenland approves extension of self-rule in anticipation of eventual independence.
November 26. Terrorists kill more than 170 people in Mumbai, India.
November 27. Another state of emergency declared in Thailand as protests expand.
December 2. Thailand's Constitutional Court prompts expulsion of Prime Minister Somchai via ruling that his People Power Party committed fraud in the 2007 elections; opposition leader Abhisit Vejjajiva elected prime minister by the legislature on December 15.
December 9. Ukrainian prime minister Yulia Tymoshenko announces agreement on new majority coalition, thereby precluding the need for immediate early lections.
December 11–12. EU summit endorses fiscal stimulus and recovery plan estimated at 200 billion euros.
December 14. Somali president Yussuf unsuccessfully attempts to dismiss the prime minister; Yusuf himself resigns on December 29.
December 22. President Lansana Conté of Guinea dies; military leaders assume power in a bloodless coup the following day and install Capt. Moussa Dadis Camara as president of a ruling National Council for Democracy and Development.
December 28. Israel launches air strikes on Gaza following resumption of Hamas rocket attacks.
December 28. Herman Van Rompuy named prime minister of Belgium.

December 28. Opposition leader John Atta Mills elected president of Ghana.

December 29. The Awami League, a former opposition party led by former prime minister Sheikh Hasina Wajed, wins an overwhelming victory in legislative elections in Bangladesh.

2009, January 3. Ground offensive into Gaza launched by Israel, which announces unilateral cease-fire January 17.

January 13. German chancellor Angela Merkel announces additional stimulus package totaling 49 billion euros.

January 19. Left-wing opposition gains legislative victory in El Salvador.

January 26. Iceland's government collapses; minority interim government formed February 1 under the country's first female prime minister..

January 26. Violent antigovernment protests begin in Madagascar as supporters of Andry Rajoelina, the mayor of Antananarivo, demand the resignation of President Marc Ravalomanana; both sides subsequently claim to be in control of the country.

January 27. Canada announces C$40 billion stimulus package.

January 30. Leader of the moderate wing of the Islamist opposition elected president of Somalia; new cabinet and prime minister installed on February 13..

January 31. Provincial elections held in Iraq.

February 11. Morgan Tsvangirai sworn in as prime minister to head national unity government in Zimbabwe.

February 13. U.S. Congress approves $789 billion stimulus package.

February 15. Voters in Venezuela approve constitutional revision eliminating presidential term limits.

February 20. Declining economic conditions trigger collapse of Latvian government.

February 27. U.S. president Barack Obama announces "exit plan" for Iraq that calls for two-thirds of U.S. troops to be removed from Iraq by August 2010.

March 2. President João Bernardo Vieira assassinated by "rogue" army troops in Guinea-Bissau; the army denies a coup has occurred.

March 4. International Criminal Court issues arrest warrant for President Bashir of Sudan.

March 15. Opposition leader Mauricio Funes elected president of El Salvador.

March 17. Marc Ravalomanana steps down as president of Madagascar after army supports Andry Rajoelina in power struggle.

March 18. New center-right government coalition approved in Latvia.

March 18. Voters in Azerbaijan approve constitutional amendment abolishing presidential term limits.

March 27. Center-right government falls in Czech Republic after losing confidence motion over its handling of economic affairs.

March 21. Hungarian prime minister Ferenc Gyurcsány resigns.

March 26–30. Antigovernment protests strengthen throughout Thailand.

March 29. Ruling pro-European coalition wins early legislative elections in Montenegro.

March 31. Likud's Benjamin Netanyahu sworn in as leader of center-right government in Israel.

April 2. G-20 summit pledges $1.1 trillion for economic stimulus in developing countries.

April 3. Najib Razak inaugurated as prime minister of Malaysia following the resignation of Abdullah Badawi, whose government had been under year-long pressure.

April 4. Ivan Gašparovič, supported by two parties in the current government coalition, elected president of Slovakia.

April 5. Lars Rasmussen named prime minister of Denmark in succession to Anders Rasmussen, who had resigned to become the new secretary general of NATO.

April 5. Official results of legislative elections in Moldova give majority to the ruling Communist Party of Moldova, prompting massive protests, charges of fraud, and, ultimately, new elections.

April 5. Gjorgje Ivanov, candidate of the ruling party, elected president of Macedonia.

April 10. Fiji's president Ratu Iloilo abrogates 1997 constitution in wake of earlier Court of Appeals ruling that called for new elections; Iloilo revokes all judicial appointments, declares himself head of state, and says elections will not be held until 2014.

April 12. Prime minister of Thailand declares state of emergency in Bangkok in wake of large-scale antigovernment demonstrations.

April 22. African National Congress wins another solid legislative majority in South Africa; ANC leader Jacob Zuma elected president of South Africa by the legislature on May 6.

April 25. Left-wing parties win legislative majority in Iceland; Prime Minister Sigurðardóttir calls for EU accession.

April 26. Rafael Correa reelected as president of Ecuador, and his left-wing Country Alliance secures legislative plurality.

May 3. Conservative business leader Ricardo Martinelli Berrocal elected president of Panama; his four-party coalition secures legislative majority.

May 7. Inaugural meeting held of EU's Eastern Partnership, which pledged deeper relations, but not EU membership, to Armenia, Azerbaijan, Belarus, Georgia, Moldova, and Ukraine.

May 15. Curaçao voters approve proposal for the island to become a separate autonomous member of Netherlands, thereby preparing the way for the break-up of the Netherlands Antilles in 2010.

May 17. Ruling Cambodian People's Party dominates nation's first local elections.

May 17. Independent Dalia Grybauskaitė elected president of Lithuania.

May 18. Sri Lankan military announces final victory over the separatist Liberation Tigers of Tamil Eelam after 26 years of conflict.

May 22. Manmohan Singh in India becomes the first Indian prime minister since Jawaharlal Nehru (1946–1964) to continue in office following completion of a full first term.

May 23. Madhave Kumar Nepal elected prime minister of Nepal following resignation of Pushpa Kamal Dahal, who had been embroiled in a dispute with the military.

May 25. North Korea announces its second underground test of a nuclear weapon.

June 2. Greenland's legislative elections won by leftist, proindependence opposition.

June 4–7. Center-right parties retain dominance in elections to the European Parliament.

June 7. Anti-Syrian, pro-Western alliance wins legislative majority in Lebanon.

June 8. President Omar Bongo, Gabon's president since 1967, dies of natural causes.

June 11. World Health Organization declares swine flu pandemic, the first pandemic declaration in more than 40 years.

June 12. Incumbent Mahmoud Ahmadinejad declared winner of presidential election in Iran, prompting massive protests alleging fraud, followed by a violent government crackdown on dissidents.

June 28. President Mel Zelaya ousted in Honduras, prompting widespread international condemnation of his opponents.

June 30. U.S. combat forces complete their withdrawal from Baghdad and other Iraqi cities.

July 5. Center-right opposition gains plurality in legislative balloting in Bulgaria; Boiko Borisov, theretofore mayor of Sofia, named prime minister on July 27.

July 5. Opposition Institutional Revolutionary Party and allies win majority in elections to the Mexican Chamber of Deputies.

July 6. Jadranka Kosor becomes Croatia's first female prime minister.

July 6. Racial violence breaks out in Urumqi, China, between Muslim Uygurs (Uighurs) and Han Chinese, ultimately leaving more than 150 dead and prompting the sentencing of many Uygurs later in the year.

July 6–8. United States pledges to "press the reset button" in relations with Russia at Moscow summit.

July 10. Peruvian prime minister Yehude Simon resigns following antigovernment protests.

July 18. Mohamed Ould Abdelaziz, who led the 2008 coup in Mauritania, elected president in first-round balloting disputed as fraudulent by his opponents.

July 29. The ruling Communist Party of Moldova loses its majority in rerun of legislative elections (originally held in April); Vladimir Filat sworn in as head of a four-party, pro-EU coalition government on September 25.

August 4. In a referendum boycotted by the opposition, voters in Niger approve allowing President Mamadou Tandja to seek a third term

August 5. Pakistani Taliban leader Baitullah Mehsud killed by missile fired from U.S. drone.

August 20. Presidential elections held in Afghanistan; incumbent Hamid Karzai is later credited with a first-round victory, prompting widespread accusations of fraud.

August 30. Opposition Democratic Party of Japan wins legislative elections in Japan, ending longtime dominance of Liberal Democratic party.

September 1. Fiji suspended from the Commonwealth for government's refusal to negotiate a new election schedule with the opposition.

September 3. Ali-Ben Bongo Ondimba, son of the late president Bongo, declared winner of the August 30 presidential election in Gabon.

September 7. Premier Liu Chao-shiuan resignes as Taiwan's premier following criticism of his government's response to a recent typhoon.

September 15. UN factfinding report is particularly critical of Israeli military actions against civilians in the Gaza offensive of late December 2008–mid-January 2009.

September 25. Western leaders accuse Iran of operating a secret uranium enrichment facilty.

September 28. More than 150 people killed when soldiers fire on opposition supporters in Conakry, Guinea, protesting the recent announcement that Capt. Moussa Camara, leader of the military junta, would be a candidate in the presidential election scheduled for January 2010.

October 2. National referendum in Ireland handily approves EU's Lisbon Treaty.

October 4. Opposition Panhellenic Socialist Movement (PASOK) scores landslide victory in legislative elections in Greece; PASOK leader Georgios Papandreou forms new government October 7.

October 9. U.S. president Barack Obama awarded Nobel Peace Prize.

October 10. Turkey and Armenia agree to establish normal diplomatic relations and reopen border.

October 17. Pakistani military initiates offensive against the Taliban in South Waziristan.

October 20. Supporters of President Mamadou Tandja, benefiting from opposition boycott, gain all seats in early legislative balloting in Niger; Niger suspended from ECOWAS on October 21.

October 25. Suicide bombers kill more than 150 people in Baghdad.

November 1. Abdullah Abdullah, who finished second to incumbent Hamid Karzai in the disputed presidential balloting in Afghanistan in August, withdraws from run-off; Karzai is inaugurated for another term on November 20.

November 6–7. Saudi military continues raids and bombing of Houthi rebels in Yemen.

November 9. Prime Minister Saad Hariri forms unity government (which includes Hezbollah) in Lebanon after months of wrangling.

November 15. Ruling Democratic Party of Kosovo claims victory in nation's first local elections.

November 29. Central bank of United Arab Emirates bails out Dubai, which had earlier roiled world financial markets by asking for a moratorium on $59 billion in debt.

November 29. Iran approves construction of new uranium enrichment plants, prompting U.S. threats of additional sanctions.

November 29. Porfirio Lobo Sosa elected president of Honduras.

December 1. U.S. president Barack Obama announces that 30,000 additional troops will be sent to Afghanistan.

December 1. EU's Lisbon Treaty enters into force; Herman Van Rompuy, former prime minister of Belgium, to become the first permanent president of the European Council under the EU's revamped and expanded institutional structure.

December 3. Guinea's president Moussa Camara seriously wounded in assassination attempt by an aide.

December 6. President Evo Morales handily reelected in Bolivia.

December 8. Japan announces new $80 billion stimulus package.

December 7–8. Antigovernment protests continue in Iran; more than 200 people arrested.

December 18. Power-sharing plan abandoned in Madagascar.

APPENDIX B CHRONOLOGY OF MAJOR INTERNATIONAL CONFERENCES SPONSORED BY THE UNITED NATIONS: 1946–2009

1946, June 19–July 22 (New York, New York). International Health Conference. Adopted constitution of the World Health Organization.

1947–1948, November 21–March 24 (Havana, Cuba). Conference on Trade and Employment. Drafted a charter that would have established an International Trade Organization under UN auspices but that never went into effect because of U.S. opposition.

1948, February 19–March 6 (Geneva, Switzerland). Maritime Conference. Drafted and approved a convention leading to establishment of the Inter-Governmental Maritime Consultative Organization, later the International Maritime Organization.

March 23–April 21 (Geneva, Switzerland). Conference on Freedom of Information. Adopted conventions on the gathering and international transmission of news, the institution of an international right of correction, and freedom of information.

August 23–September 19 (Geneva, Switzerland). Conference on Road and Motor Transport. Drafted and adopted the Convention on Road Traffic and a Protocol on Road Signs and Signals superseding obsolete 1926 and 1931 conventions.

1949, August 17–September 6 (Lake Success, New York). Scientific Conference on the Conservation and Utilization of Resources. Discussed the costs and benefits of practical application of technical knowledge.

1950, March 15–April 6 (Lake Success, New York). Conference on Declaration of Death of Missing Persons. Adopted a convention calling for international cooperation in alleviating the legal problems burdening individuals whose families disappeared in World War II but whose deaths could not be established with certainty.

1953, May 11–June 18 (New York, New York). Opium Conference. Adopted a protocol to control the production, trade, and use of opium.

1954, May 11–June 4 (New York, New York). Conference on Customs Formalities for the Temporary Importation of Road Motor Vehicles and for Tourism. Adopted a convention establishing custom facilities for touring and a convention establishing import regulations for road motor vehicles.

August 31–September 10 (Rome, Italy). World Population Conference. Provided a forum for an exchange of views and experiences among experts on a wide variety of questions connected with population.

September 13–23 (New York, New York). Conference of Plenipotentiaries Relating to the Status of Stateless Persons. Drafted and approved a convention putting stateless people on equal footing with nationals of a contracting state in some matters and giving them the same privileges as those generally granted to aliens in others.

1955, April 18–May 10 (Rome, Italy). International Technical Conference on the Conservation of the Living Resources of the Sea. Discussed the conservation of fish and other marine resources.

August 8–20 (Geneva, Switzerland). First International Conference on the Peaceful Uses of Atomic Energy. Surveyed all major aspects of the topic.

1958, February 24–April 27 (Geneva, Switzerland). First UN Conference on the Law of the Sea. Failed to agree on the issue of the width of the territorial sea.

September 1–12 (Geneva, Switzerland). Second International Conference on the Peaceful Uses of Atomic Energy. Addressed, among other things, the issues of nuclear power reactors, fusion power, application of radioactive isotopes, nuclear power station accidents, and risks involved with exposure to radiation in industrial settings.

1960, March 17–April 26 (Geneva, Switzerland). Second UN Conference on the Law of the Sea. Failed to adopt any substantive measures regarding the questions of the breadth of territorial seas and fishery limits.

1961, January 24–March 25 (New York, New York). Plenipotentiary Conference for the Adoption of a Single Convention on Narcotic Drugs. Adopted the convention, which replaced international control instruments with one treaty and extended the control system to the cultivation of plants that are grown for the raw materials of natural drugs.

August 21–31 (Rome, Italy). Conference on New Sources of Energy. Discussed the recent breakthrough in knowledge of geothermal energy, the need for more intensive wind surveys, and applications of solar energy.

1962, August 6–22 (Bonn, Federal Republic of Germany). Technical Conference on the International Map of the World on Millionth Scale. Reviewed and revised the International Map of the World.

1963, February 4–20 (Geneva, Switzerland). Conference on the Application of Science and Technology for the Benefit of Less Developed Areas. Discussed relevant proposals for accelerating development.

1964, March 23–June 16 (Geneva, Switzerland). UN Conference on Trade and Development (UNCTAD). Subsequently established as a Special Body of the General Assembly convening quadrennially (see under UN General Assembly: Special Bodies).

August 31–September 9 (Geneva, Switzerland). Third International Conference on the Peaceful Uses of Atomic Energy. Focused exclusively on nuclear power as a commercially competitive energy source.

1965, August 30–September 10 (Belgrade, Yugoslavia). Second World Population Conference. Gathered international experts to discuss population problems, especially as they related to development.

1967, September 4–22 (Geneva, Switzerland). Conference on the Standardization of Geographical Names. Subsequent conferences have been held every five years.

1968, March 26–May 24; reconvened April 9–May 22, 1969 (Vienna, Austria). Conference on Law of Treaties. Adopted the Vienna Convention on the Law of Treaties.

April 22–May 13 (Tehran, Iran). International Conference on Human Rights. Adopted the Proclamation of Tehran and 29 resolutions reviewing and evaluating progress since the adoption of the Universal Declaration of Human Rights in 1948 and formulating further measures to be taken.

August 14–27 (Vienna, Austria). First Conference on the Exploration and Peaceful Uses of Outer Space. Examined the practical benefits to be derived from space research and exploration as well as how the United Nations might help make those benefits widely available and enable nonspace powers to cooperate in international space activities.

1971, January 11–February 21 (Vienna, Austria). Conference for the Adoption of a Protocol on Psychotropic Substances. Adopted the instrument after renaming it a convention.

September 6–16 (Geneva, Switzerland). Fourth International Conference on the Peaceful Uses of Atomic Energy. Discussed the ramifications of the rapid increase in nuclear power generation.

1972, June 5–16 (Stockholm, Sweden). Conference on the Human Environment. Resulted in establishment of the United Nations Environment Program (UNEP).

1973, December 3–15 (New York, New York). Third UN Conference on the Law of the Sea; reconvened for ten additional sessions, the last in three parts in **1982, March 8–April 30** and **September 22–24** (New York) and **December 6–10** (Montego Bay, Jamaica). Drafted and adopted the UN Convention on the Law of the Sea (UNCLOS).

1974, May 20–June 14 (New York, New York). Conference on Proscription (Limitation) in the International Sale of Goods. Adopted Convention on the Limitation Period in the International Sale of Goods.

August 19–30 (Bucharest, Romania). World Population Conference. Adopted, as the first international governmental meeting on population (previous World Population Conferences were for scientific discussion only), the World Population Plan of Action, including guidelines for national population policies.

November 5–16 (Rome, Italy). World Food Conference. Adopted the Universal Declaration on the Eradication of Hunger and Malnutrition and called on the General Assembly to create the World Food Council to coordinate programs to give the world (particularly less developed states) more and better food.

1975, February 4–March 14 (Vienna, Austria). Conference on the Representation of States in their Relations with International Organizations (of a Universal Character). Adopted convention of the same name.

May 5–30 (Geneva, Switzerland). Review Conference of the Parties to the Treaty on the Nonproliferation of Nuclear Weapons. Reaffirmed support for the treaty and called for more effective implementation of its provisions.

June 19–July 1, 1975 (Mexico City, Mexico). World Conference of the International Women's Year. Adopted the Declaration of Mexico on the Equality of Women and Their Contribution to Development and Peace, 1975, and the World Plan of Action for the Implementation of the Objectives of the International Women's Year.

1976, January 5–8 (Dakar, Senegal). International Conference on Namibia and Human Rights. Condemned South Africa's occupation of Namibia.

May 31–June 11 (Vancouver, British Columbia). Conference on Human Settlements. Issued recommendations for assuring the basic requirements of human habitation (shelter, clean water, sanitation, and a decent physical environment), plus the opportunity for cultural and personal growth.

June 14–17 (Geneva, Switzerland). World Employment Conference. Adopted, subject to reservations by some countries, a Declaration of Principles and a Program of Action regarding employment and related issues.

1977, January 10–February 4 (Geneva, Switzerland). Conference of Plenipotentiaries on Territorial Asylum. Failed to adopt a convention defining groups of people to be covered by a proposed convention within this category or on the allowable activities of refugees in the country of asylum.

March 14–25 (Mar del Plata, Argentina). Water Conference. Approved resolutions dealing with water use, health, and pollution control as well as training and research in water management.

April 4–May 6; reconvened **July 31–August 23, 1978** (Vienna, Austria). Conference on the Succession of States in Respect to Treaties. Adopted a convention elaborating uniform principles for such succession.

May 16–21 (Maputo, Mozambique). International Conference in Support of the Peoples of Zimbabwe and Namibia. Drafted a Declaration and Program of Action to mobilize international support for the right to self-determination by the people of the two territories.

June 20–July 1 (Geneva, Switzerland). Review Conference of the Parties to the Treaty on the Prohibition of the Emplacement of Nuclear Weapons and Other Weapons of Mass Destruction on the Seabed and the Ocean Floor and in the Subsoil Thereof. Reaffirmed interest in avoiding an arms race on the seabed and concluded that signatory states had faithfully observed the conditions of the treaty, which was concluded by a non-UN conference in 1970 and entered into force in 1972. (Similar conclusions were reached by review conferences in Geneva on **September 12–23, 1983,** and on **September 19–28, 1989.**)

August 22–26 (Lagos, Nigeria). World Conference for Action against Apartheid (cosponsored by the Organization of African Unity). Called for international support for efforts to eliminate apartheid and enable the South African people to attain their "inalienable right" to self-determination.

August 29–September 9 (Nairobi, Kenya). Conference on Desertification. Adopted a plan of action addressing desertification, improvement of land management, antidrought measures, and related science and technology.

1978, February 12–March 11; reconvened **March 19–April 8, 1979** (Vienna, Austria). Conference on the Establishment of the United Nations Industrial Development Organization (UNIDO) as a Specialized Agency. Recommended such establishment and adopted a constitution for UNIDO.

March 6–31 (Hamburg, Federal Republic of Germany). Conference on an International Convention on the Carriage of Goods by Sea. Adopted a convention designed to balance the risks of carriers and cargo owners.

August 14–25 (Geneva, Switzerland). First World Conference to Combat Racism and Racial Discrimination. Adopted a declaration and program of action recommending comprehensive and mandatory sanctions against South Africa, as well as measures to prevent multinational corporations from investing in territories "subject to racism, colonialism, and foreign domination."

August 30–September 12 (Buenos Aires, Argentina). Conference on Technical Cooperation among Developing Countries. Discussed, but did not endorse, the proposed creation of an independent, but UN-funded, body to foster technical cooperation among developing countries.

October 16–November 11; reconvened six times through 1985 (Geneva, Switzerland). Conference on an International Code of Conduct on the Transfer of Technology.

1979, July 12–20 (Rome, Italy). World Conference on Agrarian Reform and Rural Development. Adopted a declaration of principles and a program of action to abolish poverty and hunger.

August 20–31 (Vienna, Austria). Conference on Science and Technology for Development. Endorsed recommendations to promote financial and institutional arrangements for freer technology flow to developing nations.

September 10–28; reconvened **September 15–October 10, 1980** (Geneva, Switzerland). Convention on Prohibitions or Restrictions on the Use of Certain Conventional Weapons Which May Be Deemed to Be Excessively Injurious or to Have Indiscriminate Effects. Adopted a convention banning such weapons.

November 12–30; reconvened **May 24, 1980** (Geneva, Switzerland). Conference on International Multimodal Transportation. Adopted a convention on the legal obligations of multimodal transport operators.

November 19–December 8; reconvened **April 8–22, 1980** (Geneva, Switzerland). Conference on Restrictive Business Practices. Adopted the Set of Multilaterally Agreed Equitable Principles and Rules for the Control of Restrictive Business Practices.

1980, March 3–21 (Geneva, Switzerland). First Review Conference of States Parties to the Convention on the Prohibition of the Development, Production and Stockpiling of Bacteriological (Biological) and Toxin Weapons and on Their Destruction. Reaffirmed commitment to the convention (signed in 1972 and entered into force in 1975) and declared a "determination to exclude the possibility of bacteriological agents and toxins being used as weapons."

March 10–April 11 (Vienna, Austria). Conference on Contracts for International Sale of Goods. Adopted a convention to govern the sale of goods between parties in different countries, replacing the two Hague conventions of 1964.

July 14–30 (Copenhagen, Denmark). World Conference of the UN Decade for Women: Equality, Development, and Peace. Adopted a program of action for the second half of the decade.

August 11–September 7 (Geneva, Switzerland). Second Review Conference of the Parties to the Treaty on the Nonproliferation of Nuclear Weapons. Failed to agree on a final document.

1981, April 9–10 (Geneva, Switzerland). First International Conference on Assistance to African Refugees. Urged that international priority be given to the African refugee problem and received $560 million in pledges to assist the estimated 5 million people in that category.

May 20–27 (Paris, France). International Conference on Sanctions against Racist South Africa. Proposed sanctions against South Africa and discussed the situation in Namibia.

June 13–17 (New York, New York). International Conference on Kampuchea. Approved a plan, unimplementable at the time because of the absence of the Soviet Union and Vietnam from the conference, for the withdrawal of Vietnamese forces and the holding of UN-supervised elections.

August 10–21 (Nairobi, Kenya). Conference on New and Renewable Sources of Energy. Promoted the development and utilization of nonconventional energy sources, particularly by developing countries.

September 1–14 (Paris, France). Conference on the Least Developed Countries. Adopted a substantial new program of action to assist the economies of the world's 31 poorest states.

1982, July 26–August 6 (Vienna, Austria). World Assembly on Aging. Adopted an international plan of action aimed at providing the growing number of older people with economic and social security.

August 9–21 (Vienna, Austria). Second Conference on the Exploration and Peaceful Uses of Outer Space. Recommended that the General Assembly adopt measures to accelerate the transfer of peaceful space technology, to expand access to space and its resources for developing countries, and to establish a UN information service on the world's space programs.

1983, March 1–April 8 (Vienna, Austria). Conference on the Succession of States in Respect of State Property, Archives, and Debts. Adopted a convention on the subject.

April 25–29 (Paris, France). International Conference in Support of Namibian People for Independence. Reaffirmed Namibia's right to independence.

June 27–29 (London, United Kingdom). International Conference for Sanctions against Apartheid in Sports. Reviewed progress in the campaign for a sports boycott of South Africa.

August 1–12 (Geneva, Switzerland). Second World Conference to Combat Racism and Racial Discrimination. Adopted a program of action against racism, racial discrimination, and apartheid.

August 29–September 7 (Geneva, Switzerland). International Conference on the Question of Palestine. Adopted the Geneva Declaration on Palestine and a Program of Action for the Achievement of Palestinian Rights.

1984, July 9–11 (Geneva, Switzerland). Second International Conference on Assistance to African Refugees. Declared that caring for African refugees was a global responsibility and proposed long-term solutions to the problem.

July 16–August 3 (Geneva, Switzerland); reconvened **January 28–February 15,** and **July 8–9, 1985** (Geneva), and **January 20–February 8, 1986** (New York). Conference on Conditions for the Registration of Ships. Adopted a convention designed to assure "genuine links" between ships and their flags of state.

August 6–14 (Mexico City, Mexico). International Conference on Population. Adopted Mexico City Declaration on Population and Development covering a wide range of population policy proposals, including further implementation of the 1974 World Population Plan of Action.

September 10–21 (Geneva, Switzerland). Review Conference of the Parties to the Convention on the Prohibition of Military or Any Other Hostile Use of Environmental Modification Techniques. Noted the effectiveness of the convention, which went into effect in 1978.

1985, March 11–12 (Geneva, Switzerland). International Conference on the Emergency Situation in Africa. Mobilized international aid to drought-stricken states in Africa.

May 7–9 (Arusha, Tanzania). International Conference on Women and Children Under Apartheid. Condemned South Africa for the effects of its policies on black women and children.

May 15–18 (Paris, France). Second International Conference on the Sports Boycott against South Africa. Supported the position that South Africa should not be readmitted to the Olympic games until apartheid ends.

July 15–27 (Nairobi, Kenya). World Conference to Review and Appraise the Achievement of the UN Decade for Women. Assessed steps taken over the past decade to improve the situation of women and drafted the Nairobi Forward Looking Strategies for the Achievement of Women.

August 27–September 21 (Geneva, Switzerland). Third Review Conference of the Parties to the Treaty on the Nonproliferation of Nuclear Weapons. Called for resumption of talks toward a comprehensive multilateral nuclear test ban treaty.

September 11–13 (New York, New York). Conference on the Intensification of International Action for the Independence of Namibia. Rejected U.S. policy of "constructive engagement" with South Africa and urged boycott of Namibian and South African products.

November 4–15 (Geneva, Switzerland). Conference to Review All Aspects of the Set of Multilaterally Agreed Equitable Principles and Rules for the Control of Restrictive Business Practices. Failed to agree on proposals to improve and further develop the principles.

November 13–18 (New York, New York). World Conference on the International Youth Year, 1985. Endorsed guidelines for youth and asked member states and other interested organizations to ensure that the year's activities be reinforced and maintained.

1986, **February 18–March 21** (Vienna, Austria). Conference on the Law of Treaties between States and International Organizations or between International Organizations. Adopted a convention delineating the manner in which international organizations should conclude, adopt, enforce, and observe treaties.

June 16–20 (Paris, France). World Conference on Sanctions against Racist South Africa. Called for comprehensive economic sanctions against South Africa.

July 7–11 (Vienna, Austria). International Conference for the Immediate Independence of Namibia. Called for the adoption and imposition of sanctions against South Africa and the implementation of the UN plan for the independence of Namibia.

September 8–16 (Geneva, Switzerland). Second Review Conference of States Parties to the Convention on the Prohibition of the Development, Production and Stockpiling of Bacteriological (Biological) and Toxin Weapons and on Their Destruction. Adopted a final act designed to strengthen confidence in the convention, to reduce "the occurrence of ambiguities, doubts, or suspicion" involving bacteriological activities, and to enhance international cooperation in peaceful microbiology use.

1987, **February 10–13** (Nairobi, Kenya). Safe Motherhood Conference (cosponsored by the World Bank, World Health Organization, and UN Fund for Population Activities).

March 23–April 10 (Geneva, Switzerland). Conference for Promotion of International Cooperation in the Peaceful Uses of Nuclear Energy. Failed to reach consensus.

June 17–26 (Vienna, Austria). International Conference on Drug Abuse and Illicit Trafficking. Adopted a declaration committing all participants to "vigorous action" to reduce drug supply and demand and approved a handbook of guidelines to assist governments and organizations in reaching a total of 35 "action targets."

August 24–September 11 (New York, New York). International Conference on the Relationship between Disarmament and Development. Recommended that a portion of resources released by disarmament be allocated to social and economic development.

1988, **August 22–24** (Oslo, Norway). International Conference on the Plight of Refugees, Returnees, and Displaced Persons in Southern Africa. Adopted a plan of action to improve the economic and social conditions of the populations under consideration.

November 25–December 20 (Geneva, Switzerland). Plenipotentiary Conference to Adopt the New Convention Against Illicit Traffic in Narcotic Drugs and Psychotropic Substances. Adopted the Convention.

1989, **January 7–11** (Paris, France). Conference of States Parties to the 1925 Geneva Protocol and Other Interested States on the Prohibition of Chemical Weapons. Called for early conclusion of a convention that would prohibit the development, production, stockpiling, and use of all chemical weapons and provide for the destruction of all such existing weapons.

May 29–31 (Guatemala City, Guatemala). International Conference on Central American Refugees. Adopted a three-year, $380 million program to aid an estimated two million refugees, displaced persons, and returnees in seven countries.

June 13–14 (Geneva, Switzerland). International Conference on Indochinese Refugees. Adopted a plan of action designed to promote a "lasting multilateral solution" to the problem of refugees and asylum-seekers from Laos and Vietnam.

1990, **March 5–9** (Jomtien, Thailand). World Conference on Education for All: Meeting Basic Learning Needs. Adopted Declaration on Education for All.

April 9–11 (London, United Kingdom). World Ministerial Summit to Reduce the Demand for Drugs and to Combat the Cocaine Threat (organized in association with the United Kingdom). Adopted a declaration by which 124 nations pledged to give higher priority to curtailing illicit drug demand.

August 20–September 15 (Geneva, Switzerland). Fourth Review Conference of Parties to the Treaty on the Nonproliferation of Nuclear Weapons. Failed to reach agreement on a final declaration.

September 3–14 (Paris, France). Second Conference on the Least Developed Countries. Adopted a new program of action stressing bilateral assistance in the form of grants or highly concessional loans from developed nations.

September 29–30 (New York, New York). World Summit for Children. Adopted a ten-point program to promote the well-being of children through political action "at the highest level."

October 29–November 7 (Geneva, Switzerland). World Climate Conference. Urged developed nations to establish targets for the reduction in the emission of "greenhouse" gases, such as carbon dioxide, to curtail a possible warming of the global atmosphere.

November 26–December 7 (Geneva, Switzerland). Second Conference to Review All Aspects of the Set of Multilaterally Agreed Equitable Principles and Rules for the Control of Restrictive Business Practices. Urged developing countries to adopt national legislation on restrictive business practices.

1991, **January 7–18** (New York, New York). Amendment Conference of the States Parties to the 1963 Treaty Banning Nuclear Weapon Tests in the Atmosphere, in Outer Space, and Under Water. Decided further work was needed before a proposed amendment could be adopted that would convert the treaty into a comprehensive test ban treaty.

September 9–17 (Geneva, Switzerland). Third Review Conference of the States Parties to the Convention on the Prohibition of the Development, Production and Stockpiling of Bacteriological (Biological) and Toxin Weapons and on Their Destruction. Called for full implementation of the convention without the placement of constraints on economic and technological development and international cooperation in peaceful biological activities.

1992, **June 3–14** (Rio de Janeiro, Brazil). UN Conference on Environment and Development. Adopted Rio Declaration on Environment and Development and several other documents designed to promote global environmental cleanup and "sustainable" development.

October 15–16 (New York, New York). International Conference on Aging. Reviewed progress on the 1982 International Plan of Action on Aging.

1993, **June 14–25** (Vienna, Austria). World Conference on Human Rights. Adopted nonbinding Declaration and Program of Action affirming the "universal nature" of human rights and recommending, among other things, that the General Assembly appoint a UN High Commissioner for Human Rights.

July 12–30; reconvened **March 14–31** and **August 15–26, 1994,** and **March 27–April 12** and **July 24–August 4, 1995** (New York, New York). UN Conference on Straddling Fish Stocks and Highly Migratory Fish Stocks. Adopted global treaty (opened for signature December 4, 1995) binding signatories to adopt measures to conserve and otherwise manage high-seas fisheries and to settle fishing disputes peacefully.

October 5–6 (Tokyo, Japan). International Conference on African Development (sponsored in conjunction with Japan and the U.S.-based Global Coalition of Africa). Adopted a declaration intended to "refocus" attention on African problems, such as heavy debt burden, rapid population growth, drought, hunger, and political instability.

1994, **April 25–May 6** (Bridgetown, Barbados). Global Conference on the Sustainable Development of Small Island Developing States. Adopted a program of action to guide the environmental and development policies of small island states and issued the "Barbados Declaration" calling on the international community to support those states in combating rising sea levels, the loss of reefs and rain forests, shortages of fresh water, and import dependency.

May 23–27 (Yokohama, Japan). World Conference on Natural Disaster Reduction. Adopted the Yokohama Strategy for a Safer World: Guidelines for Natural Disaster Prevention, Preparedness, and Mitigation, designed to put recent technological advances at the service of disaster-prone regions of the world.

September 5–13 (Cairo, Egypt). International Conference on Population and Development. Adopted a program of action aimed at stabilizing the world's population at about 7.27 billion in 2015.

October 18 (New York, New York). International Conference on Families. Convened by the UN General Assembly to discuss activities in regard to the International Year of the Family, 1994.

November 21–23 (Naples, Italy). World Ministerial Conference on Organized Transnational Crime. Adopted the Naples Political Declaration and Global Action Plan, proposing, among other things, the establishment of an international convention on transnational crime, greater cooperation among national law enforcement agencies, and greater "transparency" of banks and other financial enterprises that can be used to "launder" money.

1995, March 6–13 (Copenhagen, Denmark). World Summit for Social Development. Adopted the Copenhagen Declaration and Program of Action recommending measures to be taken by national governments, the United Nations, and other international organizations in pursuit of "social development and social justice."

April 7–May 12 (New York, New York). Review and Extension Conference of the Parties to the Treaty on the Nonproliferation of Nuclear Weapons. Agreed to extend treaty "indefinitely" and strengthen its review process.

September 4–15 (Beijing, China). Fourth World Conference on Women. Adopted the Beijing Declaration and Platform for Action delineating nonbinding guidelines for national policies designed to enhance the status of women and to promote international cooperation in the same regard.

September 25–October 13 (Vienna, Austria); reconvened **April 22–May 3, 1996** (Geneva, Switzerland). Review Conference of States Parties to the 1980 Convention on Prohibitions or Restrictions on the Use of Certain Conventional Weapons Which May Be Deemed to Be Excessively Injurious or to Have Indiscriminate Effects. Failed to reach agreement on a proposed complete ban on land mines but adopted stricter controls on their use and export and agreed to extend the provisions of the convention to domestic conflicts; banned the use of blinding laser weapons.

1996, June 3–14 (Istanbul, Turkey). Second UN Conference on Human Settlements. Adopted a declaration urging national governments to implement policies designed to meet their citizens' "right to adequate housing" and to establish comprehensive plans to manage urban development.

November 13–17 (Rome, Italy). World Food Summit. Adopted a declaration asserting the "fundamental right of everyone to be free from hunger" and recommending national policies that will guarantee "access to safe and nutritious food."

November 25–December 6 (Geneva, Switzerland). Fourth Review Conference of States Parties to the Convention on the Prohibition of the Development, Production and Stockpiling of Bacteriological (Biological) and Toxin Weapons and on Their Destruction. Supported continuing work by an ad hoc group designing a verification protocol for the convention.

1997, June 23–27 (New York, New York). Second UN Conference on Environment and Development. Reviewed implementation (or lack thereof) of commitments made at the 1992 conference.

December 1–11 (Kyoto, Japan). Third Conference of the Parties to the UN Framework Convention on Climate Change. Issued Kyoto Protocol in which 38 industrialized countries agreed to cut the emission of greenhouse gases to combat global warming.

1998, June 15–July 18 (Rome, Italy). UN Conference of Plenipotentiaries on the Establishment of an International Criminal Court. Voted to establish an International Criminal Court under UN auspices.

August 8–12 (Lisbon, Portugal). World Conference of Ministers Responsible for Youth. Adopted the Lisbon Declaration on Youth Policies and Programs, pledging to act on youth participation, development, peace, education, employment, health, and drug and substance abuse.

1999, July 19–30 (Vienna, Austria). Third Conference on the Exploration and Peaceful Uses of Outer Space. Adopted the Vienna Declaration on Space and Human Development.

2000, April 24–May 19 (New York, New York). Review Conference of the Treaty on the Nonproliferation of Nuclear Weapons. Concluded with a commitment by China, France, Russia, the United Kingdom, and the United States to the "total elimination" of their nuclear arsenals.

September 6–8 (New York, New York). Millennium Summit. Adopted the Millennium Declaration, which reaffirmed the role of the United Nations and its charter as "indispensable foundations of a more peaceful, prosperous, and just world."

November 13–25 (The Hague, Netherlands). World Conference on Climate Change. Failed to conclude a treaty to meet the greenhouse gas emissions requirements called for by the 1997 Kyoto Protocol.

December 12–15 (Palermo, Italy). High-Level Political Signing Conference for the UN Convention against Transnational Organized Crime. Opened for signature the first legally binding UN convention on crime.

2001, May 14–20 (Brussels, Belgium). Third Conference on the Least Developed Countries. Adopted a plan of action for 2001–2010 that emphasized good governance, capacity-building, the role of trade in development, environmental protection, and the mobilization of financial resources.

May 21–23 (Stockholm, Sweden). Diplomatic Conference for an Internationally Legally Binding Instrument for Implementing International Action on Certain Persistent Organic Pollutants (POPs). Opened for signature a convention banning 12 toxic chemicals, including dioxins, polychlorinated biphenyls (PCBs), and various pesticides.

July 9–20 (New York, New York). UN Conference on the Illicit Trade in Small Arms and Light Weapons in All Its Aspects. Adopted a program of action to prevent, combat, and eradicate illicit trade in small arms and light weapons (SALW) at national, regional, and global levels.

August 31–September 7 (Durban, South Africa). World Conference against Racism, Racial Discrimination, Xenophobia, and Related Intolerance. Adopted the Durban Declaration and Program of Action, in which states were urged to end enslavement and slavery-like practices, to promote and protect human rights, and to prosecute perpetrators of racist and other discriminatory acts against Africans, indigenous peoples, migrants, refugees, and other victims.

November 19–December 7; reconvened **November 11–22, 2002** (Geneva, Switzerland). Fifth Review Conference of States Parties to the Convention on the Prohibition of the Development, Production and Stockpiling of Bacteriological (Biological) and Toxin Weapons and on Their Destruction. Adopted a three-year work plan focusing on national measures to implement prohibitions; enhancement of international capabilities in responding to, investigating, and mitigating the effects of biological attacks and suspicious disease outbreaks; and adoption of a code of conduct for scientists.

December 11–21 (Geneva, Switzerland). Second Review Conference of the States Parties to the Convention on Prohibitions or Restrictions on the Use of Certain Conventional Weapons Which May Be Deemed to Be Excessively Injurious or to Have Indiscriminate Effects. Addressed various proposals to strengthen the convention, including extending its application to domestic as well as international conflicts and exploring how to deal with such explosive remnants of war as cluster bombs, shells, and munitions.

2002, March 18–22 (Monterrey, Mexico). International Conference on Financing for Development. Adopted the Monterrey Consensus on promoting development through such means as increasing foreign direct investment and official development assistance, improving market access, fighting corruption, and reducing debt.

April 8–12 (Madrid, Spain). Second World Assembly on Aging. Adopted the International Plan of Action on Aging 2002, which identified three priority areas: older persons and development, the extension of health and well-being into old age, and enhancement of enabling and supportive environments for the aged.

June 10–13 (Rome, Italy). World Food Summit: Five Years Later. Reviewed the "disappointingly slow" progress since the 1996 summit and called for an international alliance against hunger.

August 26–September 4 (Johannesburg, South Africa). World Summit on Sustainable Development. Set new targets for sustainable development in a variety of areas.

2003, August 28–29 (Almaty, Kazakhstan). International Ministerial Conference of Landlocked and Transit Developing Countries and Donor Countries and International Financial and Development Institutions on Transit Transport Cooperation. Adopted the Almaty Program of Action, addressing rail, road, and air transportation, as well as communications, pipelines, and means of facilitating international trade.

December 9–11. (Merida, Mexico). High-Level Political Conference for the Signature of the United Nations Convention Against Corruption. Ninety-four countries signed the Convention Against Corruption (previously approved by the General Assembly) requiring signatories (upon ratification) to criminalize a range of corrupt activities and to cooperate with other signatories in combating corruption.

December 10–12 (Geneva, Switzerland). World Summit on the Information Society (Phase One). Adopted the Geneva Declaration of Principles and Geneva Plan of Action in support of the creation of a "people-centered, inclusive, and development-oriented information society," with a particular emphasis on reducing the "information gap" between developed and developing countries.

2004, February 9–20 (Kuala Lumpur, Malaysia). Conference of the Parties to the Convention on Biological Diversity. Addressed the biological diversity of mountain ecosystems, technology transfer and cooperation, and the proposed reduction of the rate of loss of biodiversity.

June 24 (New York, New York). Global Compact Leaders Summit. Participants (including more than 1,200 corporations as well as representatives from labor and civil society) recommitted themselves to the Global Compact (introduced by UN Secretary General Kofi Annan in 1999 to promote responsible "corporate citizenship") and agreed to add anticorruption efforts (particularly aimed at extortion and bribery) to the compact's guiding principles.

November 29–December 3 (Nairobi, Kenya). First Review Conference of the State Parties to the Convention on the Prohibition of the Use, Stockpiling, Production, and Transfer of Anti-personnel Mines and on their Destruction. Adopted a 70-point action plan for the coming five-year period.

2005, January 18–22 (Kobe, Japan). World Conference on Disaster Reduction. Addressed the issues of investing in disaster preparedness and enhancing risk assessment, particularly in view of the devastating tsunami in the Indian Ocean.

April 18–25 (Bangkok, Thailand). Eleventh UN Conference on Crime Prevention and Criminal Justice. Addressed organized crime, terrorism, human trafficking, money-laundering, corruption, cyber-crime, and "restorative" justice.

May 2–27. (New York, New York). Review Conference of the Parties to the Treaty on the Nonproliferation of Nuclear Weapons. Failed to reach consensus on proposed steps for strengthening the treaty despite the recent increase in the spread of nuclear weapons.

September 14–16. (New York, New York). World Summit. Adopted a compromise declaration regarding proposed UN reform and steps to be taken in pursuit of a broad range of security and development goals.

September 21–23 (New York, New York). Conference on Facilitating the Entry into Force of the Comprehensive Nuclear Test-Ban Treaty. Reiterated that cessation of all nuclear weapon tests remains necessary in the pursuit of nuclear disarmament, despite the lack of progress toward the treaty entering into force (ratification from 11 countries still required).

November 16–18. (Tunis, Tunisia). World Summit on the Information Society (Phase Two). Monitored progress regarding the action plan approved in 2003 and endorsed the creation of an advisory body (comprised of representatives from government, business, and civil society) to review issues surrounding the Internet.

2006, March 20–31 (Curitiba, Brazil). Conference of the Parties to the Convention on Biological Diversity. Addressed threats posed by genetically-modified trees and urged caution in applying that technology.

June 26–July 7 (New York, New York). United Nations Conference to Review Progress Made in the Implementation of the Program of Action to Prevent, Combat, and Eradicate the Illicit Trade in Small Arms and Light Weapons in All Its Aspects. Discussed proposed guidelines for control of small arms transfers and small arms development but was unable to conclude a final document.

November 7–17 (Geneva, Switzerland). Third Review Conference of the States Parties to the Convention on Prohibitions or Restrictions on the Use of Certain Conventional Weapons Which May Be Deemed to Be Excessively Injurious or to Have Indiscriminate Effects. Welcomed the entry into force of a protocol requiring signatories to mark and clear mines and other "explosive remnants of war."

November 20–December 8 (Geneva, Switzerland). Sixth Review Conference of the States Parties to the Convention on the Prohibition of the Development, Production and Stockpiling of Bacteriological (Biological) and Toxin Weapons and on Their Destruction. Approved a general framework for future discussions and negotiations regarding the effective implementation and strengthening of the Convention.

December 10–14 (Amman, Jordan). Conference of the Parties to the United Nations Convention against Corruption, first session. Adopted a self-assessment plan (in view of criticism regarding a perceived lack of implementation of the Convention) and pledged additional aid to developing countries to combat corruption.

2007, July 5–6 (Geneva, Switzerland). Second Global Compact Leaders Summit. Adopted a 21-point declaration designed to enhance implementation of the Global Compact regarding corporate citizenship.

October 1–3 (Davos, Switzerland). Second International Conference on Climate Change and Tourism. Agreed that the tourism industry must "respond rapidly" to climate change by curbing greenhouse gas emissions and urged tourists to assess the environmental impact of their travels.

December 3–14 (Bali, Indonesia). United Nations Climate Change Conference. Launched negotiations on a successor to the Kyoto Protocol.

2008, January 28–February 1 (Bali, Indonesia). Conference of the Parties to the United Nations Convention against Corruption, second session. Reviewed implementation of the convention and discussed asset recovery procedures, the need for mutual legal assistance mechanisms, various ways to strengthen coordination and enhance technical assistance, and the issue of bribery as it relates to officials of public international organizations.

June 3–6 (Rome, Italy). High-Level Conference on World Food Security: the Challenges of Climate Change and Bioenergy. Called upon the international community to increase food assistance, particularly to the least developed countries and those adversely affected by escalating food prices.

November 29–December 2 (Doha, Qatar). Follow-up International Conference on Financing for Development to Review the Implementation of the Monterrey Consensus. Adopted the Doha Declaration on Financing for Development, which affirmed the Monterrey Consensus and called on the UN to examine how the ongoing world financial and economic crisis is affecting development.

2009, April 20–24 (Geneva, Switzerland). Durban Review Conference. Evaluated progress towards goals set by the 2001 World Conference against Racism, Racial Discrimination, Xenophobia, and Related Intolerance and called for greater "political will" to combat racism. (Canada, Israel, the United States, and five other countries boycotted the conference out of concern over possible anti-Israeli and/or anti-Western "polemics", while additional countries walked out of the conference during a controversial speech by Iranian President Mahmoud Ahmadinejad.)

June 24–30 (New York, New York). Conference on the World Financial and Economic Crisis and Its Impact on Development. Called for reform of "deficiencies" in the regulation and supervision of the international financial system.

September 24–25 (New York, New York). Conference on Facilitating the Entry into Force of the Comprehensive Nuclear Test-Ban Treaty. Called upon China, Egypt, Indonesia, Iran, Israel, and the United States (who have signed but not ratified the treaty) and North Korea, India, and Pakistan (who have not signed the treaty) to complete accession to the treaty, which cannot enter into force without their ratification. (The delegation from the United States, attending such conferences for the first time in a decade, announced plans for the Obama administration to seek Senate ratification of the treaty.)

November 16–18 (Rome, Italy). World Food Summit on Food Security. Adopted declaration pledging to promote greater domestic and international funding for agriculture in an effort to combat hunger, estimated to affect 1 billion people; few leaders from the world's wealthy nations attend.

December 1–3. (Nairobi, Kenya). High-Level Conference on South-South Cooperation. Reviewed progress toward the goals established by the 1978 Conference on Technical Cooperation among Developing Countries and called for, among other things, additional resources to be allocated to south-south technology transfer.

December 7–18 (Copenhagen, Denmark). Climate Change Conference (Conference of the Parties to the United Nations Framework Convention on Climate Change and the Parties to the 1997 Kyoto Protocol). Adopted the Copenhagen Document, which called for cooperation in reducing greenhouse gases and for greater assistance to developing countries to pursue clean energy but which did not include specific, legally binding targets.

APPENDIX C
MEMBERSHIP OF THE UNITED NATIONS AND ITS SPECIALIZED AND RELATED AGENCIES

ORGANIZATION[a]	UN	FAO	IAEA	IBRD	ICAO	IDA	IFAD	IFC	ILO	IMF	IMO	ITU	UNESCO	UNIDO	UPU	WHO	WIPO	WMO
Members[b]	192	192[c]	151[d]	186[e]	190[f]	169[g]	165[h]	182[i]	183	186[j]	169[k]	191[l]	193[m]	173	191[n]	193[o]	184[p]	189[q]
COUNTRIES																		
Afghanistan	1946	x	x	x	x	x	C	x	x	x		x	x	x	x	x	x	x
Albania	1955	x	x	x	x	x	C	x	x	x	x	x	x	x	x	x	x	x
Algeria	1962	x	x	x	x	x	B	x	x	x	x	x	x	x	x	x	x	x
Andorra	1993	x			x							x	x			x	x	
Angola	1976	x	x	x	x	x	C	x	x	x	x	x	x	x	x	x	x	x
Antigua and Barbuda	1981	x		x	x		C	x	x	x	x	x	x		x	x	x	x
Argentina	1945	x	x	x	x	x	C	x	x	x	x	x	x	x	x	x	x	x
Armenia	1992	x	x	x	x	x	C	x	x	x		x	x	x	x	x	x	x
Australia	1945	x	x	x	x	x		x	x	x	x	x	x		x	x	x	x
Austria	1955	x	x	x	x	x	A	x	x	x	x	x	x	x	x	x	x	x
Azerbaijan	1992	x	x	x	x	x	C	x	x	x	x	x	x	x	x	x	x	x
Bahamas	1973	x		x	x	x	C	x	x	x	x	x	x	x	x	x	x	x
Bahrain	1971	x	x	x	x			x	x	x	x	x	x	x	x	x	x	x
Bangladesh	1974	x	x	x	x	x	C	x	x	x	x	x	x	x	x	x	x	x
Barbados	1966	x		x	x	x	C	x	x	x	x	x	x	x	x	x	x	x
Belarus	1945	x	x	x	x			x	x	x		x	x	x	x	x	x	x
Belgium	1945	x	x	x	x	x	A	x	x	x	x	x	x	x	x	x	x	x
Belize	1981	x	x	x	x	x	C	x	x	x	x	x	x	x	x	x	x	x
Benin	1960	x	x	x	x	x	C	x	x	x	x	x	x	x	x	x	x	x
Bhutan	1971	x		x	x	x	C	x		x		x	x	x	x	x	x	x

[a] The following abbreviations are used: UN—United Nations; FAO—Food and Agriculture Organization; IAEA—International Atomic Energy Agency; IBRD—International Bank for Reconstruction and Development; ICAO—International Civil Aviation Organization; IDA—International Development Association; IFAD—International Fund for Agricultural Development; IFC—International Finance Corporation; ILO—International Labour Organisation; IMF—International Monetary Fund; IMO—International Maritime Organization; ITU—International Telecommunication Union; UNESCO—United Nations Educational, Scientific and Cultural Organization; UNIDO—United Nations Industrial Development Organization; UPU—Universal Postal Union; WHO—World Health Organization; WIPO—World Intellectual Property Organization; WMO—World Meterological Organization. Dates are those of each member's admission to the United Nations.

[b] Totals for all columns beginning with FAO include non-UN members.

[c] The 192 members of FAO include the following not listed in the table: Cook Islands, European Union, and Niue. Faroe Islands is an associate member.

[d] The 151 members of IAEA include the following not listed in the table: Holy See (Vatican City State). As of December 2009, Cape Verde, Papua New Guinea, Rwanda, and Togo had been approved for membership but had not yet deposited the necessary legal instruments with the IAEA.

[e] The 186 members of IBRD include the following not listed in the table: Kosovo.

[f] The 190 members of ICAO include the following not listed in the table: Cook Islands.

[g] The 169 members of IDA include the following not listed in the table: Kosovo.

[h] The 165 members of IFAD are divided into three categories: (A) developed states, (B) most members of the Organization of Petroleum Exporting Countries, and (C) developing states. Members include the following not listed in the table: Cook Islands (C) and Niue (C).

[i] The 182 members of IFC include the following not listed in the table: Kosovo.

[j] The 186 members of IMF include the following not listed in the table: Kosovo.

[k] The 169 members of the IMO include the following not listed in the table: Cook Islands. The IMO also has three associate members: Faroe Islands, Hong Kong, and Macao.

[l] The 191 members of ITU include the following not listed in the table: Holy See (Vatican City State).

[m] The 193 members of UNESCO include the following not listed in the table: Cook Islands and Niue. UNESCO also has seven associate members: Aruba, British Virgin Islands, Cayman Islands, Faroe Islands, Macao, Netherlands Antilles, and Tokelau.

[n] The 191 members of UPU include the following not listed in the table: Holy See (Vatican City State), Netherlands Antilles and Aruba, and Overseas Territories of the United Kingdom.

[o] The 193 members of WHO include the following not listed in the table: Cook Islands and Niue. WHO also has two associate members: Puerto Rico and Tokelau.

[p] The 184 members of WIPO include the following not listed in the table: Holy See (Vatican City State).

[q] The 189 members of WMO include the following (not listed in the table), which maintain their own meteorological services: British Caribbean Territories, Cook Islands, French Polynesia, Hong Kong, Macao, Netherlands Antilles and Aruba, New Caledonia, and Niue.

[r] Czechoslovakia was a member from the founding of the UN in 1945 until that nation's dissolution on January 1, 1993. The Czech Republic and Slovakia were admitted separately on January 19.

[s] German Democratic Republic and Federal Republic of Germany admitted separately to the UN in 1973; merged as Federal Republic of Germany in 1990.

[t] The status of the Yugoslavian seat was in question from September 1992 until the admission of the Federal Republic of Yugoslavia in October 2000 (see article on UN: General Assembly for further information). During that period Yugoslavian participation was not permitted in some specialized and related agencies of the United Nations. Serbia and Montenegro (the successor to the Federal Republic of Yugoslavia) participated in all such UN agencies except the IFAD until it split in mid-2006. Serbia kept membership status in the UN and its specialized and related agencies; Montenegro was required to reapply for memberships.

[u] Russia assumed the seat formerly held by the Union of Soviet Socialist Republics following the USSR's dissolution on December 8, 1991.

[v] Merger of the two Yemens; the former Yemen Arab Republic joined the UN in 1947 and the former People's Democratic Republic of Yemen in 1967.

ORGANIZATION[a]	UN	FAO	IAEA	IBRD	ICAO	IDA	IFAD	IFC	ILO	IMF	IMO	ITU	UNESCO	UNIDO	UPU	WHO	WIPO	WMO
COUNTRIES (Cont.)																		
Bolivia	1945	x	x	x	x	x	C	x	x	x	x	x	x	x	x	x	x	x
Bosnia and Herzegovina	1992	x	x	x	x	x	C	x	x	x	x	x	x	x	x	x	x	x
Botswana	1966	x	x	x	x	x	C	x	x	x		x	x	x	x	x	x	x
Brazil	1945	x	x	x	x	x	C	x	x	x	x	x	x	x	x	x	x	x
Brunei	1984			x	x				x	x	x	x	x		x	x	x	x
Bulgaria	1955	x	x	x	x			x	x	x	x	x	x	x	x	x	x	x
Burkina Faso	1960	x	x	x	x	x	C	x	x	x		x	x	x	x	x	x	x
Burundi	1962	x	x	x	x	x	C	x	x	x		x	x	x	x	x	x	x
Cambodia	1955	x	x	x	x	x	C	x	x	x	x	x	x	x	x	x	x	x
Cameroon	1960	x	x	x	x	x	C	x	x	x	x	x	x	x	x	x	x	x
Canada	1945	x	x	x	x	x	A	x	x	x	x	x	x		x	x	x	x
Cape Verde	1975	x		x	x	x	C	x	x	x	x	x	x	x	x	x	x	x
Central African Republic	1960	x	x	x	x	x	C	x	x	x		x	x	x	x	x	x	x
Chad	1960	x	x	x	x	x	C	x	x	x		x	x	x	x	x	x	x
Chile	1945	x	x	x	x	x	C	x	x	x	x	x	x	x	x	x	x	x
China	1945	x	x	x	x	x	C	x	x	x	x	x	x	x	x	x	x	x
Colombia	1945	x	x	x	x	x	C	x	x	x	x	x	x	x	x	x	x	x
Comoro Islands	1975	x		x	x	x	C	x	x	x	x	x	x	x	x	x	x	x
Democratic Republic of the Congo	1960	x	x	x	x	x	C	x	x	x	x	x	x	x	x	x	x	x
Republic of the Congo	1960	x	x	x	x	x	C	x	x	x	x	x	x	x	x	x	x	x
Costa Rica	1945	x	x	x	x	x	C	x	x	x	x	x	x	x	x	x	x	x
Côte d'Ivoire	1960	x	x	x	x	x	C	x	x	x	x	x	x	x	x	x	x	x
Croatia	1992	x	x	x	x	x	C	x	x	x	x	x	x	x	x	x	x	x
Cuba	1945	x	x		x		C		x		x	x	x	x	x	x	x	x
Cyprus	1960	x	x	x	x	x	C	x	x	x	x	x	x	x	x	x	x	x
Czech Republic[r]	1993	x	x	x	x	x		x	x	x	x	x	x	x	x	x	x	x
Denmark	1945	x	x	x	x	x	A	x	x	x	x	x	x	x	x	x	x	x
Djibouti	1977	x		x	x	x	C	x	x	x	x	x	x	x	x	x	x	x
Dominica	1978	x		x		x	C	x	x	x	x	x	x	x	x	x	x	x
Dominican Republic	1945	x	x	x	x	x	C	x	x	x	x	x	x	x	x	x	x	x
Ecuador	1945	x	x	x	x	x	C	x	x	x	x	x	x	x	x	x	x	x
Egypt	1945	x	x	x	x	x	C	x	x	x	x	x	x	x	x	x	x	x
El Salvador	1945	x	x	x	x	x	C	x	x	x	x	x	x	x	x	x	x	x
Equatorial Guinea	1968	x		x	x	x	C	x	x	x	x	x	x	x	x	x	x	
Eritrea	1993	x	x	x	x	x	C	x	x	x	x	x	x	x	x	x	x	x
Estonia	1991	x	x	x	x			x	x	x	x	x	x		x	x	x	x
Ethiopia	1945	x	x	x	x	x	C	x	x	x	x	x	x	x	x	x	x	x
Fiji	1970	x		x	x	x	C	x	x	x	x	x	x	x	x	x	x	x
Finland	1955	x	x	x	x	x	A	x	x	x	x	x	x	x	x	x	x	x
France	1945	x	x	x	x	x	A	x	x	x	x	x	x	x	x	x	x	x
Gabon	1960	x	x	x	x	x	B	x	x	x	x	x	x	x	x	x	x	x
Gambia	1965	x		x	x	x	C	x	x	x	x	x	x	x	x	x	x	x
Georgia	1992	x	x	x	x	x	C	x	x	x	x	x	x	x	x	x	x	x
Germany[s]	1973	x	x	x	x	x	A	x	x	x	x	x	x	x	x	x	x	x
Ghana	1957	x	x	x	x	x	C	x	x	x	x	x	x	x	x	x	x	x
Greece	1945	x	x	x	x	x	A	x	x	x	x	x	x	x	x	x	x	x
Grenada	1974	x		x	x	x	C	x	x	x	x	x	x	x	x	x	x	
Guatemala	1945	x	x	x	x	x	C	x	x	x	x	x	x	x	x	x	x	x
Guinea	1958	x		x	x	x	C	x	x	x	x	x	x	x	x	x	x	x
Guinea-Bissau	1974	x		x	x	x	C	x	x	x	x	x	x	x	x	x	x	x
Guyana	1966	x		x	x	x	C	x	x	x	x	x	x	x	x	x	x	x
Haiti	1945	x	x	x	x	x	C	x	x	x	x	x	x	x	x	x	x	x
Honduras	1945	x	x	x	x	x	C	x	x	x	x	x	x	x	x	x	x	x
Hungary	1955	x	x	x	x	x		x	x	x	x	x	x	x	x	x	x	x
Iceland	1946	x	x	x	x	x	A	x	x	x	x	x	x		x	x	x	x
India	1945	x	x	x	x	x	C	x	x	x	x	x	x	x	x	x	x	x
Indonesia	1950	x	x	x	x	x	B	x	x	x	x	x	x	x	x	x	x	x
Iran	1945	x	x	x	x	x	B	x	x	x	x	x	x	x	x	x	x	x
Iraq	1945	x	x	x	x	x	B	x	x	x	x	x	x	x	x	x	x	x
Ireland	1955	x	x	x	x	x	A	x	x	x	x	x	x	x	x	x	x	x

ORGANIZATION[a]	UN	FAO	IAEA	IBRD	ICAO	IDA	IFAD	IFC	ILO	IMF	IMO	ITU	UNESCO	UNIDO	UPU	WHO	WIPO	WMO
COUNTRIES (Cont.)																		
Israel	1949	x	x	x	x	x	C	x	x	x	x	x	x	x	x	x	x	x
Italy	1955	x	x	x	x	x	A	x	x	x	x	x	x	x	x	x	x	x
Jamaica	1962	x	x	x	x		C	x	x	x	x	x	x	x	x	x	x	x
Japan	1956	x	x	x	x	x	A	x	x	x	x	x	x	x	x	x	x	x
Jordan	1955	x	x	x	x	x	C	x	x	x	x	x	x	x	x	x	x	x
Kazakhstan	1992	x	x	x	x	x	C	x	x	x	x	x	x	x	x	x	x	x
Kenya	1963	x	x	x	x	x	C	x	x	x	x	x	x	x	x	x	x	x
Kiribati	1999	x		x	x	x	C	x	x	x	x	x	x		x	x		x
Democratic People's Republic of Korea	1991	x			x		C				x	x	x	x	x	x	x	x
Republic of Korea	1991	x	x	x	x	x	C	x	x	x	x	x	x	x	x	x	x	x
Kuwait	1963	x	x	x	x	x	B	x	x	x	x	x	x	x	x	x	x	x
Kyrgyzstan	1992	x	x	x	x	x	C	x	x	x		x	x	x	x	x	x	x
Laos	1955	x		x	x	x	C	x	x	x		x	x	x	x	x	x	x
Latvia	1991	x	x	x	x	x		x	x	x	x	x	x		x	x	x	x
Lebanon	1945	x	x	x	x	x	C	x	x	x	x	x	x	x	x	x	x	x
Lesotho	1966	x	x	x	x	x	C	x	x	x		x	x	x	x	x	x	x
Liberia	1945	x	x	x	x	x	C	x	x	x	x	x	x	x	x	x	x	x
Libya	1955	x	x	x	x	x	B	x	x	x	x	x	x	x	x	x	x	x
Liechtenstein	1990		x									x			x		x	
Lithuania	1991	x	x	x	x			x	x	x	x	x	x	x	x	x	x	x
Luxembourg	1945	x	x	x	x	x	A	x	x	x	x	x	x	x	x	x	x	x
The former Yugoslav Republic of Macedonia	1993	x	x	x	x	x	C	x	x	x	x	x	x	x	x	x	x	x
Madagascar	1960	x	x	x	x	x	C	x	x	x	x	x	x	x	x	x	x	x
Malawi	1964	x	x	x	x	x	C	x	x	x	x	x	x	x	x	x	x	x
Malaysia	1957	x	x	x	x	x	C	x	x	x	x	x	x	x	x	x	x	x
Maldives	1965	x		x	x	x	C	x	x	x	x	x	x	x	x	x	x	x
Mali	1960	x	x	x	x	x	C	x	x	x		x	x	x	x	x	x	x
Malta	1964	x	x	x	x		C	x	x	x	x	x	x	x	x	x	x	x
Marshall Islands	1991	x	x	x	x	x	C	x	x	x	x	x	x			x		
Mauritania	1961	x	x	x	x	x	C	x	x	x	x	x	x	x	x	x	x	x
Mauritius	1968	x	x	x	x	x	C	x	x	x	x	x	x	x	x	x	x	x
Mexico	1945	x	x	x	x	x	C	x	x	x	x	x	x	x	x	x	x	x
Federated States of Micronesia	1991	x		x	x	x		x		x		x	x			x		x
Moldova	1992	x	x	x	x	x	C	x	x	x	x	x	x	x	x	x	x	x
Monaco	1993	x	x		x						x	x	x	x	x	x	x	x
Mongolia	1961	x	x	x	x	x	C	x	x	x	x	x	x	x	x	x	x	x
Montenegro[t]	2006	x	x	x	x	x		x	x	x	x	x	x	x	x	x	x	x
Morocco	1956	x	x	x	x	x	C	x	x	x	x	x	x	x	x	x	x	x
Mozambique	1975	x	x	x	x	x	C	x	x	x	x	x	x	x	x	x	x	x
Myanmar (Burma)	1948	x	x	x	x	x	C	x	x	x	x	x	x	x	x	x	x	x
Namibia	1990	x	x	x	x		C	x	x	x	x	x	x	x	x	x	x	x
Nauru	1999	x			x							x	x		x	x		
Nepal	1955	x	x	x	x	x	C	x	x	x	x	x	x	x	x	x	x	x
Netherlands	1945	x	x	x	x	x	A	x	x	x	x	x	x	x	x	x	x	x
New Zealand	1945	x	x	x	x	x	A	x	x	x	x	x	x	x	x	x	x	x
Nicaragua	1945	x	x	x	x	x	C	x	x	x	x	x	x	x	x	x	x	x
Niger	1960	x	x	x	x	x	C	x	x	x		x	x	x	x	x	x	x
Nigeria	1960	x	x	x	x	x	B	x	x	x	x	x	x	x	x	x	x	x
Norway	1945	x	x	x	x	x	A	x	x	x	x	x	x	x	x	x	x	x
Oman	1971	x	x	x	x	x	C	x	x	x	x	x	x	x	x	x	x	x
Pakistan	1947	x	x	x	x	x	C	x	x	x	x	x	x	x	x	x	x	x
Palau	1994	x	x	x	x	x		x		x			x			x		
Panama	1945	x	x	x	x	x	C	x	x	x	x	x	x	x	x	x	x	x
Papua New Guinea	1975	x		x	x	x	C	x	x	x	x	x	x	x	x	x	x	x
Paraguay	1945	x	x	x	x	x	C	x	x	x	x	x	x	x	x	x	x	x
Peru	1945	x	x	x	x	x	C	x	x	x	x	x	x	x	x	x	x	x
Philippines	1945	x	x	x	x	x	C	x	x	x	x	x	x	x	x	x	x	x
Poland	1945	x	x	x	x	x		x	x	x	x	x	x	x	x	x	x	x
Portugal	1955	x	x	x	x	x	A	x	x	x	x	x	x	x	x	x	x	x
Qatar	1971	x	x	x	x		B	x	x	x	x	x	x	x	x	x	x	x

ORGANIZATION[a]	UN	FAO	IAEA	IBRD	ICAO	IDA	IFAD	IFC	ILO	IMF	IMO	ITU	UNESCO	UNIDO	UPU	WHO	WIPO	WMO
COUNTRIES (Cont.)																		
Romania	1955	x	x	x	x		C	x	x	x	x	x	x	x	x	x	x	x
Russia[u]	1945	x	x	x	x	x		x	x	x	x	x	x	x	x	x	x	x
Rwanda	1962	x		x	x	x	C	x	x	x		x	x	x	x	x	x	x
St. Kitts and Nevis	1983	x		x	x	x	C	x	x	x	x	x	x	x	x	x	x	
St. Lucia	1979	x		x	x	x	C	x	x	x	x	x	x	x	x	x	x	x
St. Vincent	1980	x		x	x	x	C		x	x	x	x	x	x	x	x	x	
Samoa	1976	x		x	x	x	C	x	x	x	x	x	x	x	x	x	x	x
San Marino	1992	x		x	x				x	x	x	x	x		x	x	x	
Sao Tome and Principe	1975	x		x	x	x	C	x	x	x	x	x	x	x	x	x	x	x
Saudi Arabia	1945	x	x	x	x	x	B	x	x	x	x	x	x	x	x	x	x	x
Senegal	1960	x	x	x	x	x	C	x	x	x	x	x	x	x	x	x	x	x
Serbia[t]	1945	x	x	x	x	x		x	x	x	x	x	x	x	x	x	x	x
Seychelles	1976	x	x	x	x		C	x	x	x	x	x	x	x	x	x	x	x
Sierra Leone	1961	x	x	x	x	x	C	x	x	x	x	x	x	x	x	x	x	x
Singapore	1965		x	x	x	x		x	x	x	x	x	x		x	x	x	x
Slovakia[r]	1993	x	x	x	x	x		x	x	x	x	x	x	x	x	x	x	x
Slovenia	1992	x	x	x	x	x		x	x	x	x	x	x	x	x	x	x	x
Solomon Islands	1978	x		x	x	x	C	x	x	x	x	x	x		x	x		x
Somalia	1960	x		x	x	x	C	x	x	x	x	x	x	x	x	x	x	x
South Africa	1945	x	x	x	x	x	C	x	x	x	x	x	x	x	x	x	x	x
Spain	1955	x	x	x	x	x	A	x	x	x	x	x	x	x	x	x	x	x
Sri Lanka	1955	x	x	x	x	x	C	x	x	x	x	x	x	x	x	x	x	x
Sudan	1956	x	x	x	x	x	C	x	x	x	x	x	x	x	x	x	x	x
Suriname	1975	x		x	x		C		x	x	x	x	x	x	x	x	x	x
Swaziland	1968	x		x	x	x	C	x	x	x		x	x	x	x	x	x	x
Sweden	1946	x	x	x	x	x	A	x	x	x	x	x	x	x	x	x	x	x
Switzerland	2002	x	x	x	x	x	A	x	x	x	x	x	x	x	x	x	x	x
Syria	1945	x	x	x	x	x	C	x	x	x	x	x	x	x	x	x	x	x
Tajikistan	1992	x	x	x	x	x	C	x	x	x		x	x	x	x	x	x	x
Tanzania	1961	x	x	x	x	x	C	x	x	x	x	x	x	x	x	x	x	x
Thailand	1946	x	x	x	x	x	C	x	x	x	x	x	x	x	x	x	x	x
Timor-Leste (East Timor)	2002	x		x	x	x	C	x	x	x	x		x	x	x	x		x
Togo	1960	x		x	x	x	C	x	x	x	x	x	x	x	x	x	x	x
Tonga	1999	x		x	x	x	C	x		x	x	x	x	x	x	x	x	x
Trinidad and Tobago	1962	x		x	x	x	C	x	x	x	x	x	x	x	x	x	x	x
Tunisia	1956	x	x	x	x	x	C	x	x	x	x	x	x	x	x	x	x	x
Turkey	1945	x	x	x	x	x	C	x	x	x	x	x	x	x	x	x	x	x
Turkmenistan	1992	x		x	x			x	x	x	x	x	x	x	x	x	x	x
Tuvalu	2000	x							x		x	x	x		x	x		
Uganda	1962	x	x	x	x	x	C	x	x	x	x	x	x	x	x	x	x	x
Ukraine	1945	x	x	x	x	x		x	x	x	x	x	x	x	x	x	x	x
United Arab Emirates	1971	x	x	x	x	x	B	x	x	x	x	x	x	x	x	x	x	x
United Kingdom	1945	x	x	x	x	x	A	x	x	x	x	x	x	x	x	x	x	x
United States	1945	x	x	x	x	x	A	x	x	x	x	x	x		x	x	x	x
Uruguay	1945	x	x	x	x		C	x	x	x	x	x	x	x	x	x	x	x
Uzbekistan	1992	x	x	x	x	x		x	x	x		x	x	x	x	x	x	x
Vanuatu	1981	x		x	x	x		x	x	x	x	x	x	x	x	x		x
Venezuela	1945	x	x	x	x		B	x	x	x	x	x	x	x	x	x	x	x
Vietnam	1977	x	x	x	x	x	C	x	x	x	x	x	x	x	x	x	x	x
Yemen[v]	1990	x	x	x	x	x	C	x	x	x	x	x	x	x	x	x	x	x
Zambia	1964	x	x	x	x	x	C	x	x	x		x	x	x	x	x	x	x
Zimbabwe	1980	x	x	x	x	x	C	x	x	x	x	x	x	x	x	x	x	x

APPENDIX D
SERIALS LIST

Africa Confidential
Africa Research Bulletin (Economic Series)
Africa Research Bulletin (Political Series)
The Annual Register
Asian News Digest
The Boston Globe
Caribbean Insight
CARICOM Reports
Central America Report
The Christian Science Monitor
Constitutions of the Countries of the World
The Economist
Editor & Publisher International
The Europa World Year Book
Facts on File
Financial Times
IAEA Bulletin
IMF Article IV Reports
IMF Balance of Payments Statistics
IMF Direction of Trade Statistics
IMF Government Finance Statistics
IMF International Financial Statistics
IMF Survey
IMF World Economic Outlook
Indian Ocean Newsletter
International Herald Tribune
Keesing's Record of World Events
Latin America Regional Reports
Latin America Weekly Report
Le Monde (Paris)
NATO Review
The New York Times
People in Power
Permanent Missions to the United Nations
Radio Free Europe/Radio Liberty
Reporters Without Borders Annual Report
Der Spiegel
Statistical Abstract of the United States
UN Chronicle
UN Handbook
UN Population and Vital Statistics Report
UN Statistical Yearbook
UNESCO Statistical Yearbook
US CIA Heads of State and Cabinet Members
US Department of State, Diplomatic List
The Washington Post
Willings Press Guide
World Bank Atlas
World Bank Country Reports
World Development Report

PUBLISHING HISTORY OF THE *Political Handbook*

A Political Handbook of Europe: 1927, ed. Malcolm W. Davis. Council on Foreign Relations.

A Political Handbook of the World: 1928, ed. Malcolm W. Davis and Walter H. Mallory. Harvard University Press and Yale University Press.

Political Handbook of the World: 1929, ed. Malcolm W. Davis and Walter H. Mallory. Yale University Press.

Political Handbook of the World: 1930–1931, ed. Walter H. Mallory. Yale University Press.

Political Handbook of the World: 1932–1962, ed. Walter H. Mallory. Harper & Brothers.

Political Handbook and Atlas of the World: 1963–1967, ed. Walter H. Mallory. Harper & Row.

Political Handbook and Atlas of the World: 1968, ed. Walter H. Mallory. Simon and Schuster.

Political Handbook and Atlas of the World: 1970, ed. Richard P. Stebbins and Alba Amoia. Simon and Schuster.

The World This Year: 1971–1973 (supplements to the *Political Handbook and Atlas of the World: 1970*), ed. Richard P. Stebbins and Alba Amoia. Simon and Schuster.

Political Handbook of the World: 1975, ed. Arthur S. Banks and Robert S. Jordan. McGraw-Hill.

Political Handbook of the World: 1976–1979, ed. Arthur S. Banks. McGraw-Hill.

Political Handbook of the World: 1980–1983, ed. Arthur S. Banks and William R. Overstreet. McGraw-Hill.

Political Handbook of the World: 1984–1995, ed. Arthur S. Banks. CSA Publications.

Political Handbook of the World: 1995–1997, ed. Arthur S. Banks, Alan J. Day, and Thomas C. Muller. CSA Publications.

Political Handbook of the World: 1998–1999, ed. Arthur S. Banks and Thomas C. Muller. CSA Publications.

Political Handbook of the World: 2000–2002, ed. Arthur S. Banks, Thomas C. Muller, and William R. Overstreet. CSA Publications.

Political Handbook of the World: 2005–2006, ed. Arthur S. Banks, Thomas C. Muller, and William R. Overstreet. CQ Press.

Political Handbook of the World: 2007, ed. Arthur S. Banks, Thomas C. Muller, and William R. Overstreet. CQ Press.

Political Handbook of the World: 2008, ed. Arthur S. Banks, Thomas C. Muller, and William R. Overstreet. CQ Press.

Political Handbook of the World: 2009, ed. Arthur S. Banks, Thomas C. Muller, William R. Overstreet, and Judith F. Isacoff. CQ Press.

(All editions published before 2007 were annual, except for 1982–1983 and 1984–1985, which were biennial, and 2000–2002 and 2005–2006, which were triennial.)